INTERNATIONAL AUTHORS AND WRITERS WHO'S WHO

INTERNATIONAL AUTHORS AND WRITERS
WHO'S WHO

Publisher:
Nicholas S Law

Consultant Editor:
Dennis K McIntire

Production Manager:
Jocelyn Timothy

Editor in Chief:
Jon Gifford

Senior Editor:
Barbara Cooper

Editorial Assistants:
Ann Dewison
Gillian George

All communications to: International Biographical Centre,
Cambridge CB2 3QP, England

INTERNATIONAL AUTHORS AND WRITERS WHO'S WHO

(WITH A BIOGRAPHICAL COMPENDIUM OF LITERARY FIGURES OF THE PAST)

SIXTEENTH EDITION

1999-2000

Consultant Editor:
Dennis K McIntire

Routledge
Taylor & Francis Group

LONDON AND NEW YORK

This edition published 2014 by Routledge
2 Park Square, Milton Park, Abingdon, Oxon, OX14 4RN
711 Third Avenue, New York, NY 10017

Routledge is an imprint of the Taylor & Francis Group, an informa business

First published	1934
Second Edition	1935
Third Edition	1948
Fourth Edition	1960
Fifth Edition	1963
Sixth Edition	1972
Reprinted	1972
Seventh Edition	1976
Eighth Edition	1977
Ninth Edition	1982
Tenth Edition	1986
Eleventh Edition	1989
Twelfth Edition	1991
Thirteenth Edition	1993
Fourteenth Edition	1995
Fifteenth Edition	1997
Sixteenth Edition	1999

ISBN 978-0-948-87518-2 (hbk)

FOREWORD

This Sixteenth Edition of the *International Authors and Writers Who's Who* marks a significant milestone in the publishing history of what has now become a standard work of reference. This year we celebrate the 65th anniversary of its first appearance in 1934.

When this volume was first published, the role of the author was thought to be so well defined that little thought was given to the matter. All the same, the Great War of 1914-18, the Bolshevik Revolution of 1917, the rise of Fascism and unchecked militarism and the worldwide economic depression led the literary world to question its relevancy. Indeed, the year before this volume first reached the public, Germany had renounced its humanistic ideals to embrace a totalitarian ideology which would plunge the world into the greatest military conflict in history in just seven brief years. That war, the concomitant genocide of the Holocaust and the dawning of the Atomic Age compelled the author to reassess his role in delineating the human condition.

As we approach the close of this tumultuous century and look warily to the beginning of a new millennium, the literary art is being questioned as never before. Television, the computer, and mass culture have so altered man's conception of himself and his world that the author is compelled to reach out for a literate and caring audience in the face of a benumbing ennui.

It is well to note that in the face of such challenges, the emergence of new authors and the production of countless new books continues to astonish the harried chronicler of the contemporary literary scene. Works of genuine merit and lasting value continue to be published. Particularly noteworthy are the many important tomes of non-fiction, ranging from history and biography to theology and philosophy.

This anniversary edition attempts to reflect the state of the literary world in 1999 with the inclusion of more than 1000 new authors. The scope of the volume has been expanded to include many of the authors outside the English-speaking world, especially those whose writings are now being made available in English.

In addition to the new authors, an exhaustive revision has been carried out on the remaining 7000 entries carried over from the last edition. A policy of continuous revision is now in place, and it is hoped that future editions will be more up-to-date than ever before.

I would like to thank all the authors who took time to correspond with me during the past two years. Their willingness to do so has made my arduous task so much easier and more rewarding. While the art of the personal letter appears to be another casualty of our impersonal and electronic age, it is heartwarming to be the recipient of so many kind letters from all over the globe. Perhaps the epistolary art can be rescued as a worthwhile tradition after all.

Although the biographical section of this volume has received our undivided attention, the appendices have not been neglected. They have undergone a thorough revision and expansion. A substantive addition has been made with the new Appendix E, "A Biographical Compendium of Literary Figures of the Past". Every effort has been expended on this appendix to make it the most comprehensive survey possible. Authors from all eras and representatives of every genre have been included. It is intended for use by both the scholar and the general reader as a ready-reference guide to over 8000 literary figures of the past.

Since the last edition of this volume, the world of letters has sustained the loss of many authors of prominence. Among those who died in 1997 were Jürek Becker, Sir Isaiah Berlin, Barry S Brook, William S Burroughs, James Dickey, Leon Edel, Allen Ginsberg, Bohumil Hrabil, David Ignatow, Denise Levertov, James Michener, Sir V S Pritchett, A L Rowse, Andrei Sinyavsky, Amos Tutuola and Dame Veronica Wedgwood. In 1998 death took from us Eric Ambler, Alain Bosquet, Raymond E Brown, Henry Steele Commager, Dame Catherine Cookson, William Gaddis, Sir Anthony Glyn, Rumer Godden, Julien Green, John Hawkes, Miroslav Holub, Ted Hughes, Ernst Jünger, Alfred Kazin, Halldór Laxness, Arthur S Link, Jean-François Lyotard, Octavio Paz, Nino Pirrotta, Anatoly Rybakov and Martin Seymour-Smith. All of these authors have been accorded a place of honour in the new Appendix E.

It is with sincere thanks that I now acknowledge the confidence placed in me by Nicholas S Law, publisher of Melrose Press. It has been an honour to serve as Consultant Editor of this special anniversary edition. A volume of so vast a scope requires the assistance of many individuals and I have been blessed to have the help of the editors in Cambridge. They have worked closely with me to ensure that this edition reflects the highest editorial standards. They have proved themselves more than up to the task. I also pay homage to the many unnamed members of staff of Melrose Press for their diligence in preparing the proofs and the final drafts for publication. Such a daunting task can only be appreciated by one who has attempted it oneself.

Several other individuals have given me cause to thank them at this time for their generous assistance. I extend grateful thanks to the esteemed heads and staff members of the Arts, Social Sciences, and Newspapers and Periodicals divisions of the Central Library of the Indianapolis-Marion County Public Library; Stephen W Ellis of Glenview, Illinois; India Amos of the Academy of American Poets; Birgitta Fogelvik of the Royal Library and National Library of Sweden in Stockholm, and Judith Brookner of the National Library of Australia in Canberra.

With our labours concluded, we now offer this new edition to the reference user with hope that it will serve as a comprehensive, accurate and up-to-date guide to the world of letters, both past and present.

Dennis K McIntire - Consultant Editor

Indianapolis
May 1999

INTERNATIONAL BIOGRAPHICAL CENTRE
RANGE OF REFERENCE TITLES

From one of the widest ranges of contemporary biographical reference works published under any one imprint, some IBC titles date back to the 1930's. Each edition is compiled from information supplied by those listed, who include leading personalities of particular countries or professions. Information offered usually includes date and place of birth; family details; qualifications; career histories; awards and honours received; books published or other creative works; other relevant information including postal address. Naturally there is no charge or fee for inclusion.

New editions are freshly compiled and contain on average 80-90% new information. New titles are regularly added to the IBC reference library.

Titles include:

Dictionary of International Biography

Who's Who in Asia and the Pacific Nations

International Authors and Writers Who's Who

International Who's Who in Community Service

International Who's Who in Education

International Who's Who in Medicine

International Who's Who in Music and Musicians' Directory, Volume One, Classical and Light Classical

International Who's Who in Music, Volume Two, Popular Music

Men of Achievement

The World Who's Who of Women

International Who's Who in Poetry and Poets' Encyclopaedia

Outstanding People of the 20th Century

2000 Outstanding Scientists of the 20th Century

2000 Outstanding Religious Personalities of the 20th Century

2000 Outstanding Artists and Designers of the 20th Century

2000 Outstanding Scholars of the 20th Century

Enquiries to:
International Biographical Centre
Cambridge CB2 3QP
England

CONTENTS

CONTENTS

Biographies

Biographies

A

AARDEMA Verna Geneva, b. 6 June 1911, New Era, Michigan, USA. Elementary Teacher; Journalist. m. (1) Albert Aardema, 30 May 1936, dec 1974, 1 son, 1 daughter, (2) Dr Joel Vugteveen, 3 Aug 1975. Education: BA, Michigan State College (now University), 1934. Appointments: Publicity Chairman, Juvenile Writers' Workshop, 1955-69; Staff Correspondent, Muskegon Chronicle. Publications: Tales for the Third Ear, 1969; Behind the Back of the Mountain, 1975; Why Mosquitoes Buzz in People's Ears, 1975; Who's in Rabbit's House?, 1977; Riddle of the Drum, 1978; Bringing the Rain to Kapiti Plain, 1981; What's So Funny, Ketu?, 1982; The Vingananee & the Tree Toad, 1983; Oh, Kojo! How Could You!, 1984; Bimwili & the Zimwi, 1985; Princess Gorilla and a New Kind of Water, 1988; Anansi Finds a Fool, 1992; A Bookworm Who Hatched, 1993; Sebgugu the Glutton, 1993; Misoso: Tales from Africa, 1993. Honours: Caldecott Award, 1976; Lewis Carroll Shelf Award, 1978; Parents' Choice Awards, 1984, 1985, 1989, 1991; Junior Library Guild Selection, 1991; Redbook Award, 1991; American Library Association Notable Book, 1991. Memberships: Juvenile Writers' Workshop; Childrens' Reading Round Table, Chicago; National and Michigan Education Associations; Womens' National Book Association. Literary Agent: Curtis Brown Ltd. Address: 784 Via Del Sol, North Fort Myers, Florida, USA.

AARON Hugh, (Max Barnet), b. 30 Nov 1924, Worcester, USA. Writer. m. Ann Stein, 29 Apr 1989, 1 son, 2 daughters. Education: AB, University of Chicago, 1951. Publications: Business Not As Usual, 1993; Driven, 1995; When Wars Were Won, 1995; It's All Chaos, 1996; Go West Old Man, 1996; Letters From the Good War, 1997; Films in Review, 1998; Suzy, Fair Suzy, 1998. Contributions to: Sail Magazine; Wall Street Journal. Membership: National Writers Union. Literary Agent: Charles Doors. Address: 71 Congress Street, Belfast, ME 04915, USA.

AAZIM Muzaffar, b. 29 Apr 1934, Kashmir, India. Poet; Writer; Dramatist; Translator; Educator; Administrator. m. Padshah Jan, 14 Oct 1956, 2 sons. Education: BSc, University of Kashmir, 1954; Various administrative courses. Appointment: Examiner in Kashmiri, University of Kashmir. Publications: Poetry: Zolana, 1964; Man-i-Kaman, 1974. Other: Plays and translations. Contributions to: Radio, television, magazines, and periodicals. Honours: Best Book of the Year Awards, Jammu and Kashmir Academy of Art, Culture, and Languages, 1965, 1975. Memberships: Brontë Society, England; Kashmir Academy of Art, Culture, and Languages; National Authors Registry, USA; Sahitya Akademi (National Academy of Letters), India. Address: 1733 Gosnell Road, No 202, Vienna, VA 22182, USA.

ABALUTA Constantin, b. 8 Oct 1938, Bucharest, Romania. Poet; Writer. m. Gabriela, 1989. Education: Master of Architecture, 1961. Publications: The Rock, poems, 1968; Objects of Silence, poems, 1979; Air: Directions for Use, poems, 1982; To Stay Upright, proses, 1986; The Cyclops' Solitude, selected poems, 1995. Contributions to: Contemporanul magazine; poems, essays, translations in Romanian and foreign magazines and journals. Honours: Prize of Breve revue, Napoli, 1970; Prix des Poètes Francophones, 1973. Memberships: Romanian Writers Union, Council Member; Constantza Haiku Society, Romania. Address: Str Arh D Hirjeu 76, Sect 2, 73281 Bucharest, Romania.

ABBENSETTS Michael, b. 8 June 1938, British Guiana (British citizen, 1974). Writer. Education: Queen's College, Guyana, 1952-56; Stanstead College, Quebec; Sir George Williams University, Montreal, 1960-61. Appointments: Security Attendant, Tower of London, 1963-67; Staff Member, Sir John Soane Museum, London, 1968-71; Resident playwright, Royal Court Theatre, London, 1974; Visiting Professor of Drama, Carnegie Mellon University, Pittsburgh, 1981. Publications: Plays: Sweet Talk (produced London, 1973, New York, 1974); Alterations (produced London and New York, 1978; revised version produced London, 1985); Samba (produced London, 1980); In the Mood (produced London, 1981); Outlaw (produced Leicester and London, 1983); El Dorado (produced London, 1984); Writer for radio and television. Novel: Empire Road (novelization of television series), 1979. Honours: George Devine Award, 1973; Arts Council Bursary, 1977; Afro-Caribbean Award, 1979. Address: Sheil Associates, 43 Doughty Street, London WC1N 2LF, England.

ABBOTT John B Jr, b. 25 Feb 1956, Plainfield, New Jersey, USA. Mystery Writer. m. Maria G Di Tommaso, 3 Oct 1992. Education: BA, English, 1985, MEd, 1995, Rutgers University; Attending EdD Program, Graduate School of Education, Rutgers University. Appointments: Writing Tutor, English Department, 1988-94, Part-time Lecturer, 1989-, Rutgers University; Adjunct Instructor, Mercer County Community College, Trenton, New Jersey, 1993-94; Writing Tutor, Middlesex County College, Edison, New Jersey, 1994-95. Publications: Knight Moves, 1990; Interactive Murder Mystery Scripts: All in the Game; Two for the Money; The Botsford Inn Mystery; The Kris Kringle Kaper; How the West was Fun and Birthdays Can Be Murder; Smithsonian's Knight, 1992. Memberships: Mystery Writers of America; New Jersey College English Association; National Council of Teachers of English; New Jersey Institute for Collegiate Learning and Teaching; New Jersey Association for Developemental Education. Address: 22 Church Street, PO Box 439, Kingston, NJ 08528-0439, USA.

ABBS Peter Francis, b. 22 Feb 1942, Cromer, Norfolk, England. Author; Lecturer. m. Barbara Beazeley, 10 June 1963, 1 son, 2 daughters. Education: BA, University of Bristol, England; DPhil, University of Sussex, England. Appointments: Lecturer, Senior Lecturer, Reader, University of Sussex, England. Publications: Poetry For Man and Islands; Songs of a New Taliesin; Icons of Time; Personae; Non-Fiction: English for Diversity; Root and Blossom - The Philosophy, Practice and Politics of English Teaching; English Within the Arts; The Forms of Poetry; The Forms of Narrative; Autobiography in Education; Proposal for a New College (with Graham Carey); Reclamations - Essays on Culture, Mass-Culture and the Curriculum; A is for Aesthetic - Essays on Creative and Aesthetic Education; The Educational Imperative; The Polemics of Education; Editor, The Black Rainbow - Essays on the Present Breakdown of Culture; Living Powers - The Arts in Education; The Symbolic Order - A Contemporary Reader on the Arts Debate; The Polemics of Imagination: Essays on Art, Culture and Society. Contributions to: Times Higher Education Supplement Times; Agenda; Independent; Acumen; Stand. Membership: Founding Member, New Metaphysical Art. Address: Institute of Education, University of Sussex, Falmer, Brighton BN1 9RG, England.

ABISH Walter, b. 24 Dec 1931, Vienna, Austria. Writer. m. Cecile Abish. Publications: Duel Site, 1970; Alphabetical Africa, 1974; Minds Meet, 1975; In the Future Perfect, 1977; How German Is It?, 1980; 99: The New Meaning, 1990; Eclipse Fever, 1993. Contributions to: Antaeus; Conjunctions; Granta; Manuskripte; New Directions Annual; Paris Review; Partisan Review; Tri-Quarterly; Salmagundi. Honours: Ingram Merrill Foundation Grant, 1977; National Endowment for the Arts Fellowships, 1979, 1985; PEN-Faulkner Award, 1981; Guggenheim Fellowship, 1981; Deutscher Akademischer Austauschdienst Residency, Berlin, 1987; John D and Catharine T MacArthur Foundation Fellowship, 1987-92; Medal of Merit, American Academy of Arts and Letters, 1991; Lila Wallace-Reader's Digest Fellowship, 1992-95; Honorary Doctor of Letters, State University of New York College at Oneonta, 1996. Membership: PEN, American Centre, Executive Board, 1982-88; New York Foundation for the Arts, Board of Governors, 1990-93; Fellow, American Academy of Arts and Sciences, 1998- . Address: PO Box 485, Cooper Square, NY 10276, USA.

ABLEMAN Paul, b. 13 June 1927, Leeds, Yorkshire, England. Writer. Education: King's College, London. Publications: Even His Enemy (with Gertrude Macauley), 1948; I Hear Voices, 1958; As Near As I Can Get, 1962; Green Julia (play), 1966; Tests (playlets), 1966; Vac, 1968; Blue Comedy: Madly in Love, Hawk's Night, 1968; The Twilight of the Vilp, 1969; Bits: Some Prose Poems, 1969; Tornado Pratt, 1977; Shoestring (novelization of television play), 1979; Porridge (novelization of screenplay), 1979; Shoestring's Finest House, 1980; County Hall (novelization of television series), 1981; The Anatomy of Nakedness, 1982; The Doomed Rebellion, 1983. Address: Flat 37, Duncan House, Fellows Road, London NW3, England.

ABRAHAM Claude (Kurt), b. 13 Dec 1931, Lorsch, Germany. Professor of French; Writer; Editor; Translator. m. Marcia Phillips, 3 June 1956, 1 son, 3 daughters. Education: BA, 1953, MA, 1956, University of Cincinnati; PhD, Indiana University, 1959. Appointments: Instructor, 1959-61, Assistant Professor, 1961-64, University of Illinois; Associate Professor, 1964-70, Professor of French, 1970-75, University of Florida at Gainesville; Professor of French, University of California at Davis, 1975-; Guest Lecturer, University of Paris, 1992. Publications: Gaston d'Orléans et sa cour, 1963, revised edition, 1975; The Strangers: The Tragic World of Tristan L'Hermite, 1966; Enfin Malherbe: The Influence of Malherbe on French Lyric Prosody, 1605-1674, 1971; Pierre Cornielle, 1972; Théâtre de Tristan L'Hermite (editor with J Schweitzer and J V Baelen), 1975; Le Théâtre Complet de Tristan L'Hermite, 1975; Jean Racine, 1977; Tristan L'Hermite, 1980; Norman Satirists of the Age of Louis XIII, 1983; On the Structure of Molière's Comedies-Ballets, 1984; Actes de Davis (editor), 1988. Contributions to: Scholarly journals. Honours: National Endowment for the Humanities Grant, 1969; Guggenheim Fellowship, 1982-83; Humboldt Prize, 1982; Knight, French Academie de Plames, 1984; Phi Beta Kappa Teaching Award, 1988. Address: 1604 Westshore Street, Davis, CA 95616, USA.

ABRAHAM Henry J(ulian), b. 25 Aug 1921, Offenbach am Main, Germany. Political Scientist. m. Mildred Kosches, 13 Apr 1954, 2 sons. Education: AB, Kenyon College, 1948; AM, Columbia University, 1949; PhD, University of Pennsylvania, 1952. Appointments: Instructor, 1949-53, Assistant Professor, 1953-57, Associate Professor, 1957-62, Professor, 1962-72, of Political Science, University of Pennsylvania; Henry L and Grace Doherty Memorial Foundation Professor in Government and Foreign Affairs, 1972-78, James Hart Professor in Government and Foreign Affairs, 1978-, University of Virginia; Visiting Lecturer and Visiting Professor at many universities and colleges in the US and abroad. Publications: Compulsory Voting, 1955; Government as Entrepeneur and Social Servant, 1956; Elements of Democratic Government (with J A Corry), 3rd edition, 1958, 4th edition, 1964; Courts and Judges: An Introduction to the Judicial Process, 1959; The Judicial Process: An Introductory Analysis of the Courts of the United States, England, and France, 1962, 7th edition, 1998; The Judiciary: The Supreme Court in the Governmental Process, 1965, 10th edition, 1996; Essentials of American National Government (with J C Phillips), 2nd edition, 1966, 3rd edition, 1971; Freedom and the Court: Civil Rights and Liberties in the United States, 1967, 6th edition (with B A Perry), 1994; 7th edition, 1998; Justices and Presidents: A Political History of Appointments to the Supreme Court, 1974, 4th edition, 1999; American Democracy, 1983, 3rd edition (with W J Keefe et al), 1989. Contributions to: Numerous chapters in books, articles, monographs and essays. Honours: Fulbright Lecturer, 1959-60; American Philosophical Society Fellow, 1960-61, 1970-71, 1979; Rockefeller Foundation Resident Scholar, Bellagio, Italy, 1978; Thomas Jefferson Award, University of Virginia, 1983; First Lifetime Achievement Award, Organized Section on Law and Courts, American Political Science Association, 1996; Phi Beta Kappa; Pi Gamma Mu; Pi Sigma Alpha. Memberships: American Judicature Society; American Political Science Association, vice-president, 1980-82; American Society for Legal History; International Political Science Association; National Association of Scholars; Southern Political Science Association; Many editorial boards; Phi Beta Kappa; Pi Gamma Mu; Pi Sigma Alpha. Address: 906 Fendall Terrace, Charlottesville, VA 22903, USA.

ABRAHAMS Peter (Henry), b. 19 Mar 1919, Vrededorp, Johannesburg, South Africa. Novelist. m. Daphne Elizabeth Miller, 3 children. Education: Church of England mission schools and colleges. Appointments: Controller, West Indian News, Jamaica, 1955-64; Chairman, Radio Jamaica, Kingston, 1977-80. Publications: Song of the City, 1945; Mine Boy, 1946; The Path of Thunder, 1948; Wild Conquest, 1950; A Wreath for Udomo, 1956; A Night of Their Own, 1965; This Island Now, 1966; The View from Coyaba, 1985. Short stories: Dark Testament, 1942. Verse: A Black Man Speaks of Freedom, 1938. Address: Red Hills, PO Box 20, St Andrew, Jamaica.

ABRAHAMS Roger (David), b. 12 June 1933, Philadelphia, Pennsylvania, USA. Professor of Folklore and Folklife; Writer. Education: BA, Swarthmore College, 1955; MA, Columbia University, 1958; PhD, University of Pennsylvania, 1961. Appointments: Instructor, 1960-63, Assistant Professor, 1963-66, Associate Professor, 1966-69, Professor of English and Anthropology, 1969-79, Chairman, English Department, 1974-79, University of Texas at Austin; Alexander H Kenan Professor of Humanities and Anthropology, Pitzer College and Scripps College, Claremont, California, 1979-85; Professor of Folklore and Folklife, University of Pennsylvania, 1985-; Various visiting professorships. Publications: Deep Down in the Jungle: Negro Narrative Folklore from the Streets of Philadelphia, 1964, revised edition, 1970; Anglo-American Folksong Style (with George W Foss, Jr), 1968; Positively Black, 1970; Deep the Water, Shallow the Shore: Three Essays on Shantying in the West Indies, 1974; Talking Black, 1976; Afro-American Folk Culture: An Annotated Bibliography, 1977; Between the Living and the Dead: Riddles Which Tell Stories, 1980; The Man-of-Words in the West Indies, 1983; Singing the Master: The Emergence of African-American Culture in the Plantation South, 1992. Honours: Guggenheim Fellowship, 1965-66; American Folklore Society Fellow, 1970; National Humanities Institute Fellow, 1976-77; Lifetime Achievement Award, American Folklore Society, 1989. Memberships: American Folklore Society, president, 1978-79; International Society for Folk Narrative Research; Phi Beta Kappa. Address: University of Pennsylvania, Philadelphia, PA 19104, USA.

ABRAMS M(eyer) H(oward), b. 23 July 1912, Long Branch, New Jersey, USA. Writer; Professor of English Emeritus. m. Ruth Gaynes, 1 Sept 1937, 2 daughters. Education: AB, 1934, MA, 1937, PhD, 1940, Harvard University; Graduate Studies, Cambridge University, 1934-35. Appointments: Instructor in English, 1938-42, Research Associate, Psycho-Acoustic Laboratory, 1942-45, Harvard University; Assistant Professor, 1945-47, Associate Professor, 1947-53, Professor of English, 1953-61, Frederic J Whiton Professor, 1961-73, Class of 1916 Professor, 1973-83, Professor Emeritus, 1983-, Cornell University; Visiting Lecturer at several institutions of higher learning. Publications: The Milk of Paradise: The Effects of Opium Visions on the Works of De Quincey, Crabbe, Francis Thompson and Coleridge, 1934, 2nd edition, 1970; The Mirror and the Lamp: Romantic Theory and the Critical Tradition, 1953; A Glossary of Literary Terms, 1957, 6th edition, 1993; Natural Supernaturalism: Tradition and Revolution in Romantic Literature, 1971. The Correspondent Breeze: Essays in English Romanticism, 1984; Doing Things With Texts: Essays in Criticism and Critical Theory, 1989. Editor: The Poetry of Pope, 1954; Literature and Belief, 1958; English Romantic Poets: Modern Essays in Criticism, 1960, 2nd edition, revised, 1975; The Norton Anthology of English Literature, 1962, 6th edition, 1993; Wordsworth: A Collection of Critical Essays, 1972; William Wordsworth: Prelude, 1979. Contributions to: Several volumes. Honours: Rockefeller Foundation Fellowship, 1946-47; Ford Foundation Fellowship, 1953; Fulbright Scholarship, 1954; Guggenheim Fellowships, 1958, 1960; Fellow, Center for Advanced Study in the Behavioral Sciences, 1967; James Russell Lowell Prize, Modern Language Association of America, 1971; Visiting Fellow, All Soul's Colllege, Oxford, 1977; Award in Humanistic Studies, American Academy of Arts and Sciences, 1984; Distinguished Scholar Award, Keats-Shelley Association, 1987; American Academy and Institute of Arts and Letters Award, 1990. Memberships: American Academy of Arts and Sciences; American Association of University Professors; American Philosophical Society; British Academy, corresponding fellow; Modern Language Association of America; Founders' Group, National Humanities Center. Address: 378 Savage Farm Drive, Ithaca, NY 14850, USA.

ABSE Dannie, b. 22 Sept 1923, Cardiff, Glamorgan, Wales. Physician; Poet; Writer; Dramatist. m. Joan Mercer, 4 Aug 1951, 1 son, 2 daughters. Education: St Illtyd's College, Cardiff; University of South Wales and Monmouthshire, Cardiff; King's College, London; MD, Westminster Hospital, London, 1950. Appointments: Manager, Chest Clinic, Central Medical Establishment, London, 1954-82; Senior Fellow in Humanities, Princeton University, New Jersey, 1973-74. Publications: Poetry: Funland and Other Poems, 1973; Lunchtime, 1974; Way Out in the Centre, 1981; White Coat, Purple Coat: Collected Poems, 1948-88, 1989; Remembrance of Crimes Past, 1990; On the Evening Road, 1994. Editor: The Music Lover's Literary Companion, 1988; The Hutchinson Book of Post-War British Poets, 1989. Fiction: Ash on a Young Man's Sleeve, 1954; Some Corner of an English Field, 1956; O Jones, O Jones, 1970; Voices in the Gallery, 1986. Contributions to: BBC and various publications in UK and USA. Honours: Foyle Award, 1960; Welsh Arts Council Literature Prizes, 1971, 1987. Cholmondeley Award, 1985. Memberships: Poetry Society, president, 1979-92; Royal Society of Literature, fellow, 1983; Welsh Academy, fellow, 1990, president, 1995. Address: c/o Shiel Land Associates Ltd, 43 Doughty Street, London WC1N 2LF, England.

ACCAD Evelyne, b. 6 Oct 1943, Beirut, Lebanon. Professor; Writer. Education: Beirut College for Women; BA, English Literature, Anderson College, 1967; MA, French, Ball State University, 1968; PhD, Comparative Literature, Indiana University, 1973. Appointments: Professor, University of Illinois, Champaign-Urbana, 1974-; Teacher, Beirut University College, 1978-84, Northwestern University, 1991. Publications: Blessures des Mois, 1993; Wounding Words: A Woman's Journal in Tunisia, 1996; Des femmes, des hommes et la guerre: Fiction et Réalité au Prache-Orient, 1993, 1994; Sexuality and War: Literary Masks of the Middle East, 1990; Coquelicot du Massacre, 1988; L'Excisée, 1982, 1992; Montjoie Palestine! or Last Year in Jerusalem, 1980; Veil of Shame: The Role of Women in the Modern Fiction of North Africa and the Arab World, 1978. Honour: France Lebanon Literary Award, 1993. Address: 306 West Michigan, Urbana, Illinois, IL 61801, USA.

ACHEBE (Albert) Chinua(lumogu), b. 16 Nov 1930, Ogidi, Nigeria. Writer; Poet; Editor; Professor. m. Christie Chinwe Okoli, 10 Sept 1961, 2 sons, 2 daughters. Education: University College, Ibadan, 1948-53; BA, London University, 1953; Received training in broadcasting, BBC, London, 1956. Appointments: Producer, 1954-58, Controller, Eastern Region, Enugu, Nigeria, 1958-61, Founder-Director, Voice of Nigeria, 1961-66, Nigerian Broadcasting Corp, Lagos; Senior Research Fellow, 1967-72, Professor of English, 1976-81, Professor Emeritus, 1985-, University of Nigeria, Nsukka; Editor, Okike: A Nigerian Journal of New Writing, 1971-; Professor of English, University of Massachusetts, 1972-75; Director, Okike Arts Centre, Nsukka, 1984-; Founder-Publisher, Uwa Ndi Igbo: A Bilingual Journal of Igbo Life and Arts, 1984-; Pro-Chancellor and Chairman of the Council, Anambra State University of Technology, Enugu, 1986-88; Charles P Stevenson Professor, Bard College, New York, 1990-; Visiting Professor and Lecturer at universities in Canada and the US. Publications: Novels: Things Fall Apart, 1958; No Longer at Ease, 1960; Arrow of God, 1964; A Man of the People, 1966; Anthills of the Savannah, 1987. Other Fiction: The Sacrificial Egg and Other Stories, 1962; Girls at War (short stories), 1973. Juvenile Fiction: Chike and the River, 1966; How the Leopard Got His Claws (with John Iroaganachi), 1972; The Flute, 1978; The Drum, 1978. Poetry: Beware, Soul-Brother and Other Poems, 1971; Christmas in Biafra and Other Poems, 1973. Essays: Morning Yet on Creation Day, 1975; The Trouble With Nigeria, 1983; Hopes and Impediments, 1988. Editor: Don't Let Him Die: An Anthology of Memorial Poems for Christopher Okigbo (with Dubem Okafor), 1978; Aka Weta: An Anthology of Igbo Poetry (with Obiora Udechukwu), 1982; African Short Stories (with C L Innes), 1984; The Heinemann Book of Contemporary African Short Stories (with C L Innes), 1992. Contributions to: New York Review of Books; Transition; Callaloo. Honours: Margaret Wrong Memorial Prize, 1959; Nigerian National Trophy, 1961; Jock Campbell/New Statesman Award, 1965; Commonwealth Poetry Prize, 1972; Neil Gunn International Fellow, Scottish Arts Council, 1975; Lotus Award for Afro-Asian Writers, 1975; Nigerian National Order of Merit 1979; Order of the Federal Republic of Nigeria, 1979; Commonwealth Foundation Senior Visiting Practitioner Award, 1984; Booker Prize Nomination, 1987; Campion Medal, New York, 1996; 26 honorary doctorates, 1972-96. Memberships: American Academy of Arts and Letters, honorary member; Association of Nigerian Authors, founder and president, 1981-86; Commonwealth Arts Organization; Modern Language Association of America, honorary fellow; Royal Society of Literature, fellow, London, 1981; Writers and Scholars International, London. Literary Agent: David Bolt and Associates. Address: Bard College, Annandale on Hudson, NY 12504, USA.

ACKERMAN Diane, b. 7 Oct 1948, Waukegan, Illinois, USA. Poet; Writer. Education: Boston University, 1966-67; BA, English, Pennsylvania State University, 1970; MFA, Creative Writing, 1973, MA, English, 1976, PhD, English, 1978, Cornell University. Appointments: Teaching Assistant, 1971-78, Lecturer, 1978, Visiting Writer, 1987, Visiting Professor, 1998-99, Cornell University; Assistant Professor, University of Pittsburgh, 1980-83; Writer-in-Residence, College of William and Mary, 1982-83, Ohio University, 1983, New York University, 1986, Columbia University, 1986-87; Writer-in-Residence, 1983-86, Director, Writers' Program, 1984-86, Washington University; Staff Writer, New Yorker magazine, 1988-94. Publications: Poetry: The Planets: A Cosmic Pastoral, 1976; Wife of Light, 1978; Lady Faustus, 1983; Reverse Thunder, 1988; Jaguar of Sweet Laughter: New and Selected Poems, 1991, revised edition, 1992; I Praise My Destroyer, 1998. Non-Fiction: Twilight of the Tenderfoot, 1980; On Extended Wings, 1985; A Natural History of the Senses, 1990; The Moon by Whale Light, and Other Adventures Among Bats, Crocodilians, Penguins and Whales, 1991; A Natural History of Love, 1994; The Rarest of the Rare, 1995; Monk Seal Hideaway (for children), 1995; A Slender Thread, 1997; Bats: Shadows in the Night (for children), 1997; The Norton Book of Love (editor with Jeanne Mackin), 1998. Contributions to: Numerous anthologies, books, newspapers, journals, and magazines. Honours: Abbie Copps Poetry Prize, 1974; National Endowment for the Creative Writing Fellowships, 1976, 1986; Black Warrior Review Poetry Prize, 1981; Pushcart Prize, 1984; Peter I B Lavan Award, Academy of American Poets, 1985; Lowell Thomas Award, 1990; New York Times Book Review Notable Book of the Year, 1991, 1992, and New and Noteworthy Book of the Year, 1993, 1997; Wordsmith Award, 1992; Literary Lion, New York Public Library, 1994; John Burroughts Nature Award, 1997. Address: c/o Cullen Stanley, Janklow and Nesbit Associates, 598 Madison Avenue, New York, NY 10022, USA.

ACKERMAN Forrest J, (Weaver Wright, Spencer Strong, Laurajean Ermayne, Fisher Trentworth, Jack Erman, Cameron Silverscreen), b. 24 Nov 1916, Los Angeles, California, USA. Author. m. Wendayne Mondelle, 19 Feb 1951. Education: University of California at Berkeley, 1934-35. Publications: The Frankenscience Monster; Science Fiction Worlds of Forrest J Ackerman and Friends; Best Science Fiction of

1974; Mr Monster's Movie Gold; Lon of 1000 Faces!; The Greatest Horror Stories, Spain; Sense of Wonder Science Fiction, limited edition; Reel Future; Future Eves; I, Vampire; Ackermanthology; Forrest J Ackerman's World of Science Fiction, British, French, German and Spanish editions; Amazing Movies, Germany; Classic Science Fiction That Morphed into Movies. Contributions to: Famous Monsters of Filmland; Sex and Censorship; Scarlet Street; Cult Movies; CIAK, Italy; Off Beat; Spacemen; Spacewomen; Monster World Wonderama; After Hours; Vice Versa, Lesbian; V, France; Utopia, Germany; Voice of the Imagi-nation; Heroldo de Esperanto; San Francisco Chronicle. Honours: 6 Science Fiction Hugos; 2 Golden Saturn Awards; 1st TV Grimmy. Membership: Director, Los Angeles Science Fantasy Society, 1940. Address: 2495 Glendower Avenue, Hollywood, CA 90027-1110, USA.

ACKLIN Jurg, b. 20 Feb 1945, Zurich, Switzerland. Psychoanalyst; Writer. m. Claudia Acklin-Gaiser, 1984, 2 daughters. Education: Social Sciences, Universities of Zurich and Bremen; Doctoral Thesis, 1974. Appointment: Leader, Literturclub, Swiss Television. Publications: Novels: Michael Häuptli, 1969; Alias, 1971; Das Uberhandnehmen, 1973; Der Aufstieg des Fessel-ballons, 1980; Der Känguruhmann, 1992; Das Tangopaat, 1994; Froschgesang, 1996; Der Vater, 1998. Honours: C F Meyer Prize, 1971; Bremer Literature Prize, 1972; Zurcher Buch Prize, 1997. Address: Flühgasse 1g, 8008 Zurich, Switzerland.

ACKROYD Peter, b. 5 Oct 1949, London, England. Writer. Education: MA, Cambridge University, 1971; Mellon Fellowship, Yale University, 1971-73. Appointments: Literary Editor, Spectator, 1973-77; Lead Reviewer, Times, 1976-. Publications: Dressing Up: Transvestism and Drag: The History of an Obsession, 1979; Ezra Pound and His World, 1981; The Great Fire of London, 1982; The Last Testament of Oscar Wilde, 1983; Hawksmoor, 1985; Chatterton, 1987; Dickens, 1990; Introduction to Dickens, 1991; English Music, 1992; The House of Doctor Dee, 1993; Dan Leno and the Limehouse Golem, 1994; Blake, 1995; Milton in America, 1996; The Life of Thomas More, 1998; The Plato Papers, 1999. Honours: Somerset Maugham Award, 1984; Whitbread Prize for Biography, 1985 and for Fiction, 1986; Royal Society of Literatures WE Heinemann Award, 1985; Guardian Fiction Award, 1986; Honorary DLitt, Exeter University, 1992. Membership: Royal Society of Literature. Address: c/o Anthony Sheil Ltd, 43 Doughty Street, London WC1N 2LF, England.

ACLAND Alice. See: WIGNALL Anne.

ACOSTA Devashish Donald, b. 9 Nov 1956, New York, New York, USA. Writer. Education: MFA, Fiction, San Diego State University. Publications: Felicitavia: A Spiritual Journey, 1997; When the Time Comes, 1998. Address: c/o Innerworld Publications: PO Box 1613, San German, Puerto Rico 00683, USA.

ADAIR Christy, b. 20 June 1949, Reading, Berks, England. 2 d. Education: MA; Dip Educ, Laran Centre, London, England; Cert Ed, Leicester, England. Appointments: Lecturer in Dance Studies, Northern School of Contemporary Dance; Visiting Lectr, collges in England and abroad, 1992-98. Publication: Women and Dance: Sylphs and Sirens, 1992. Contributions to: Dance Theatre Journal; New Dance Magazine. Address: 17 Levisham Street, York YO10 4BL, England.

ADAIR Ian (Hugh), b. 20 Dec 1942, Scotland. Writer. Appointments: Writer; Partner, Supreme Magic Company, Devon, England; President, Ideas Associated; Former Television Announcer and Presenter, STV, Westward Television. Publications: Adair's Ideas, 1958; Magic with Doves, 1958; Dove Magic, Parts 1 and 2, 1959; Dove Magic Finale, 1960; Ideen, 1960; Television Dove Magic, 1961; Television Card Manipulations, 1962; Television Puppet Magic, 1963; Doves in Magic, 1964; Doves from Silks, 1964; New Doves from Silks, 1964; Dove Classics, 1964; More Modern Dove Classics, 1964; Further Dove Classics, 1964; Classical Dove Secrets, 1964; Diary of a

Dove Worker, 1964; Magic on the Wing, 1965; Balloon-o-Dove, 1965; Spotlite on Doves, 1965; Watch the Birdie, 1965; Dove Dexterity, 1965; Rainbow Dove Routines, 1965; Heads Off!, 1965; Tricks and Stunts with a Rubber Dove, 1965; Television Dove Steals, 1965; A La Zombie, 1966; Pot Pourri, 1966; Magical Menu, 3 volumes, 1967; Encyclopedia of Dove Magic, 5 volumes, 1968-80; Magic with Latex Budgies, 1969; Paddle Antics, 1969; Conjuring as a Craft, 1970; Magic Step by Step, 1970; Party Planning and Entertainment, 1972; Oceans of Notions, 1973; Papercraft-Step by Step, 1975; Card Tricks, 1975; Glove Puppetry, 1975; The Know How Book of Jokes and Tricks, 1977; Complete Party Planner, 1978; Complete Guide to Conjuring, 1978; Magic, 1979; Complete Guide to Card Conjuring, 1980; Swindles: The Cheating Game, 1980. Address: 20 Ashley Terrace, Bideford, Devon, England.

ADAIR Jack. See: PAVEY Don.

ADAIR James Radford, b. 2 Feb 1923, Asheville, North Carolina, USA. Writer; Editor. Appointments: Editor, Power for Living, Free Way, Teen Power, and Counselor, weekly churchpapers, 1949-77; Senior Editor, Victor Books Division, Scripture Press Publications Inc, Wheaton, Illinois, 1970-96. Publications: Saints Alive, 1951; God's Power Within (editor), 1961; We Found Our Way (editor with Ted Miller), 1965; The Old Lighthouse, 1966; The Man from Steamhouse, 1967; Tom Skinner: Top Man of the Lord's and Other Stories (editor), 1967; M R DeHaan: The Man and His Ministry, 1969; Hooked on Jesus (editor), 1971; A Greater Strength (with Jerry Jenkins), 1975; Surgeon on Safari, 1976; Escape from Darkness (editor with Ted Miller), 1982; 101 Days in the Gospels with Oswald Chambers (editor with Harry Verploegh), 1992; 101 Days in the the Epistles with Oswald Chambers (editor with Harry Verploegh), 1994; A New Testament Walk with Oswald Chambers (with Henry Verploegh), 1998; The Story of Scripture Press: The Whole Word for the Whole World, 1998; Through the Year with Warren W Wiersbe, 1999. Address: 703 Webster Avenue, Wheaton, IL 60187, USA.

ADAM SMITH Patricia (Patsy) Jean, b. 31 May 1926, Gippsland, Victoria, Australia. Author. Appointments: Adult Education Officer, Hobart, Tasmania, 1960-66; Manuscripts Field Officer, State Library of Victoria, 1970-82; President, Federal Fellowship of Australian Writers, 1973-75. Publications: Hear the Train Blow, 1963; Moon Bird People, 1964; There Was a Ship, 1965; Tiger Country, 1966; The Rails Go Westward, 1967; Folklore of Australian Railmen, 1969; No Tribesmen, 1970; Tasmania Sketchbook, 1972; Launceston Sketchbook, 1972; Port Arthur Sketchbook, 1973; Carcoo Salute, 1973; The Desert Railway, 1974; Romance of Australian Railways, 1974; The Anzacs, 1978; Outback Heroes, 1981; The Shearers, 1982; Australian Women at War, 1984; Heart of Exile, 1986; Prisoner of War from Gallipoli to Korea, 1992; Goodbye Girlie, 1994. Honours: Officer of the Order of the British Empire, 1980; Triennial Award; Order of Australia. Address: 47 Hawksburn Road, South Yarra, Victoria 3141, Australia.

ADAMS Alice, b. 14 Aug 1926, Fredericksburg, Virginia, USA. Author. m. 1946, div 1958, 1 son. Education: BA, Radcliffe College, 1945. Publications: Careless Love (in UK as The Fall of Daisy Duke), 1966; Families and Survivors, 1975; Listening to Billie, 1978; Beautiful Girl (short stories), 1979; Tich Rewards, 1980; Superior Women, 1984; Return Trips, 1985; Second Chances, 1988; After You're Gone, 1989; Caroline's Daughters, 1991; Mexico, 1991; Almost Perfect, 1993. Contributions to: New Yorker; Atlantic Monthly; Redbook; McCalls; Paris Review. Honour: American Academy of Arts and Letters Award, 1992. Address: 2661 Clay Street, San Francisco, CA 94115, USA.

ADAMS Chuck. See: TUBB E(dwin) C(harles).

ADAMS Clifton, (Jonathon Gant, Matt Kinkaid, Clay Randall), b. 1 Dec 1919, Commanche, Oklahoma, USA. Author; Musician; Freelance Writer. Publications: Western Novels: The Desperado, 1950; A Noose for the

Desperado, 1951; Six Gun Boss (as Clay Randall), 1952; The Colonel's Lady, 1952; When Oil Ran Red (as Clay Randall), 1953; Two Gun Law, 1954; Gambling Man, 1955; Law of the Trigger, 1956; Outlaw's Son, 1957; Boomer (as Clay Randall), 1957; Killer in Town, 1959; Stranger in Town, 1960; The Legend of Lonnie Hall, 1960; Day of the Gun, 1962; Reckless Men, 1962; The Moonlight War, 1963; The Dangerous Days of Kiowa Jones, 1963; The Oceola Kid (as Clay Randall), 1963; Hardcase for Hire (as Clay Randall), 1963; Amos Flagg Series, 6 volumes (as Clay Randall), 1963-69; Doomsday Creek, 1964; The Hottest Fourth of July in the History of Hangtree County, 1964 (in UK as The Hottest Fourth of July, 1965); The Grabhorn Bounty, 1965; Shorty, 1966; A Partnership with Death, 1967; The Most Dangerous Profession, 1967; Dude Sheriff, 1969; Tragg's Choice, 1969; The Last Days of Wolf Garnett, 1970 (in UK as Outlaw Destiny, 1972); Biscuit-Shooter, 1971; Rogue Cowboy, 1971; The Badge and Harry Cole, 1972 (in UK as Lawman's Badge, 1973); Concannon, 1972; Hard Times and Arnie Smith, 1972; Once an Outlaw, 1973; The Hard Time Bunch, 1973; Hasle and the Medicine Man, 1973. Crime Novels: Whom Gods Destroy, 1953; Hardcase (as Matt Kinkaid), 1953; Death's Sweet Song, 1955; The Race of Giants (as Matt Kinkaid), 1956; Never Say No to a Killer (as Jonathon Gant), 1956; The Very Wicked, 1960; The Long Vendetta (as Jonathon Gant), 1963. Address: c/o Ace Books, Berkeley Publishing Group, 200 Madison Avenue, New York, NY 10016, USA.

ADAMS Daniel. See: NICOLE Christopher Robin.

ADAMS Deborah, b. 22 Jan 1956, Tennessee, USA. Writer; Poet. m. 3 children. Education: University of Tennessee at Martin; Austin Peay University. Appointment: Adjunct Faculty, Nashville State Technical Institute. Publications: Fiction: All the Great Pretenders, 1992; All the Crazy Winters, 1992; All the Dark Disguises, 1993; All the Hungry Mothers, 1994; All the Deadly Beloved, 1995; All the Blood Relatives, 1997. Poetry: Propriety, 1976; Looking for Heroes, 1984. Memberships: Appalachian Writers' Association; Mystery Writers of America; Sisters in Crime. Address: Route 4, Box 664, Waverly, TN 37185, USA.

ADAMS Douglas (Noel), b. 11 Mar 1952, Writer; Producer. Education: BA, MA, St John's College, Cambridge. Appointments: Radio Producer, BBC, London, 1978; Script Editor, Doctor Who, BBC TV, 1978-80. Publications: The Hitch Hiker's Guide to the Galaxy, 1978; The Restaurant at the End of the Universe, 1980; The Meaning of Life, 1984; So Long, And Thanks for All the Fish, 1984; The Utterly Utterly Merry Comic Relief Christmas Book, 1986; The Long Dark Tea Time of the Soul, 1988; Last Chance to See, 1990; Mostly Harmless, 1991. Address: c/o The Digital Village Ltd, 11 Maiden Lane, London WC2E 7NA, England.

ADAMS Harold, b. 20 Feb 1923, Clark, South Dakota, USA. Executive. m. Betty E Skogsberg, 17 Sept 1959, div Apr 1965, 1 daughter. Education: BA, University of Minnesota, 1950. Publications: Murder, 1981; Paint the Town Red, 1982; The Missing Moon, 1983; The Naked Liar, 1985; The Fourth Widow, 1986; When Rich Men Die, 1987; The Barbed Wire Noose, 1987; The Man Who Met the Train, 1988; The Man Who Missed the Party, 1989; The Man Who Was Taller Than God, 1992; A Perfectly Proper Murder, 1993; A Way with Widows, 1994; The Ditched Blonde, 1995; The Hatchet Job, 1996; The Ice Pick Artist, 1997; No Badge, No Gun, 1998. Honours: Shamus Award, Best Private Eye Novel, 1992; Minnesota Book Award, Mystery and Detective, 1993. Memberships: Author's Guild; Mystery Writers of America. Literary Agent: Ivy Fischer Stone. Address: 12916 Greenwood Road, Minnetonka, MN 55343, USA.

ADAMS Hazard (Simeon), b. 15 Feb 1926, Cleveland, Ohio, USA. Professor of Humanities Emeritus; Writer; Poet; Editor. m. Diana White, 17 Sept 1949, 2 sons. Education: BA, Princeton University, 1948; MA, 1949, PhD, 1953, University of Washington. Appointments: Instructor, Cornell University, 1952-56; Assistant Professor, University of Texas, 1956-59; Associate

Professor to Professor, Michigan State University, 1959-64; Fulbright Lecturer, Trinity College, Dublin, 1961-62; Professor, University of California at Irvine, 1964-77, 1990-94; Byron W and Alice L Lockwood Professor of Humanities, 1977-90, Professor Emeritus, 1990-, University of Washington. Publications: Blake and Yeats: The Contrary Vision, 1955, 2nd edition, 1968; William Blake: A Reading of the Shorter Poems, 1963; The Contexts of Poetry, 1963; The Horses of Instruction: A Novel, 1968; The Interests of Criticism, 1969; The Truth About Dragons: An Anti-Romance, 1971; Lady Gregory, 1973; The Academic Tribes, 1976, 2nd edition, 1987; Philosophy of the Literary Symbolic, 1983; Joyce Cary's Trilogies: Pursuit of the Particular Real, 1983; Antithetical Essays in Literary Criticism and Liberal Education, 1990; The Book of Yeats's Poems, 1990; The Book of Yeat's Vision, 1995; The Farm at Richwood and Other Poems, 1997; Many Pretty Toys: A Novel, 1998. Editor: Poems by Robert Simeon Adams, 1952; Poetry: An Introductory Anthology, 1968; Fiction as Process (with Carl Hartman), 1968; William Blake: Jerusalem, Selected Poems and Prose, 1970; Critical Theory Since Plato, 1971, revised edition, 1992; Critical Theory Since 1965 (with Leroy Searle), 1986; Critical Essays on William Blake, 1991. Contributions to: Numerous poetry, scholarly, and critical journals. Honour: Guggenheim Fellowship, 1974. Address: 3930 North East 157th Place, Seattle, WA 98155, USA.

ADAMS James MacGregor David, b. 22 Apr 1951, Newcastle, England. Journalist; Author. m. Rene Thatcher Riley, 1 July 1990, 1 daughter. Education: Harrow, 1964-69; Neuchâtel University, 1979-71. Publications: The Unnatural Alliance, 1984; The Financing of Terror, 1986; Secret Armies, 1988; Ambush (the War Between the SAS and the IRA) with Robin, Morgan and Anthony Bambridge, 1988; Merchants of Death, 1990; The Final Terror, 1991; Bull's Eye, 1992; Taking the Tunnel, 1993. Contributions to: Sunday Times; Washington Post; Los Angeles Times; Atlantic. Literary Agent: Janklow Nesbit. Address: c/o The Sunday Times, 1 Pennington Street, London E1 9XW, England.

ADAMS Joanna Z. See: KOCH Joanne Barbara.

ADAMS Perseus, b. 11 Mar 1933, Cape Town, South Africa. Writer; Journalist; Poet; Teacher (Retired). m. 1958. Education: BA, University of Cape Town, 1952; Cert Ed, 1961. Appointments: Journalist; English Teacher. Publications: The Land at My Door, 1965; Grass for the Unicorn, 1975; Cries and Silences: Selected Poems, 1996. Contributions to: Numerous, mostly to Contrast, Cape Town. Honours: South Africa State Poetry Prize, 1963; Festival of Rhodesia Prize, 1970; Keats Memorial International Prize, 1971; Bridport Arts Festival Prize, 1984; Co-Winner, Writing Section, Bard of the Year, 1993; Nominated for the Forward Prize for the Outstanding Poem in the UK, 1994-95. Address: 21 Mapesbury Road, Kilburn, London NW2, England.

ADAMS Richard (George), b. 9 May 1920, Newbury, Berkshire, England. Author; Poet. m. Barbara Elizabeth Acland, 26 Sept 1949, 2 daughters. Education: MA in Modern University, Worcester College, Oxford, 1948. Appointment: Civil Servant, 1948-74. Publications: Watership Down, 1972; Shardik, 1974; Nature Through the Seasons (with Max Hooper), 1975; The Tyger Voyage, 1976; The Plague Dogs, 1977; The Ship's Cat, 1977; Nature Day and Night, 1978; The Iron Wolf, 1980; The Girl in a Swing, 1980; Voyage Through the Antarctic (with Ronald Lockley), 1982; Maia, 1984; The Bureaucats, 1985; A Nature Diary, 1985; Occasional Poets (anthology), 1986; The Legend of Te Tuna, 1986; Traveller, 1988; The Day Gone By (autobiography), 1990; Tales from Watership Down, 1996. Contributions to: Numerous journals and magazines. Honours: Carnegie Medal, 1972; Guardian Award for Children's Literature, 1972; Medal, CA Young Reader's Association, 1977. Memberships: John Clare Society; Royal Society of Arts, fellow; Royal Society of Literature, fellow. Address: 26 Church Street, Whitchurch, Hampshire RG28 7AR, England.

ADAMS Susan Steves, b. 17 Apr 1943, Chicago, Illinois, USA. Professor of English. m. Michael C C Adams, 11 July 1985, 2 sons. Education: BA, 1964, BS Educ, 1965, MA, 1967, PhD, 1975, University of Cincinnati, Ohio, USA. Appointments: Instructor in English, University of Cincinnati, 1967-69; Adjunct Instructor in English, University of Cincinnati, 1975-78; Lecturer in English, Evening College, University of Cincinnati, 1977-82; Assistant Professor, 1978-83, Associate Professor, 1984-92, Professor of English, 1993-, Northern Kentucky University. Publications: The Story of the Pewter Basin and Other Occasional Writings: Collected in Southern Ohio and Northern Kentucky, co-edited with Margery Rouse, 1981; In Common Cause: The "Conservative" Frances Trollope and The "Radical" Frances Wright, 1993; Moving On: The Heroines of Shirley Anne Grau, Anne Tyler, and Gail Godwin, 1996. Contributions to: Cyclopedia of World Authors; Masterplots; The Midwest Quarterly; Studies in the Novel; Children's Literature in Education; Kentucky Philological Review; Frontiers; The Southern Quarterly; Studies in Short Fiction; The Southern Literary Journal. Honours: Alumni Association Strongest Influence Teaching Award, Northern Kentucky University, 1998; Kentucky Humanities Scholar, 1989-93; Phi Beta Kappa; Sigma Tau Delta; Mortar Board, Kentucky Philological Association. Memberships: North Central Women's Studies Association, Regional Coordinator, 1982-84, Conference Coordinator, 1983; Popular Culture and American Culture Associations; South Atlantic Modern Languages Association. Address: Literature & Language Department, Northern Kentucky University, Higland Heights, KY 41099, USA.

ADAMS Wilfried, b. 23 Nov 1947, Flanders, Belgium. Author; Critic; Translator; Teacher. 1 son. Education: Candidate in Law, 1967, Licentiate in Germanic Philosophy, 1972, Catholic University of Louvain. Publications: Graafschap, 1970; Dagwaarts Eeen Woord, 1972; Geen Vogelkreet de Roos, 1975; Ontginning, 1976; Aanspraak, 1981; Lettre de Cachet, 1982; Uw Afwezigheid, 1986; Dicta Dura, 1988; Zayin, 1992; VII Sirventes, 1993. Contributions to: Flemish and Dutch periodicals. Honours: Prys Vlaamse Poeziedagen, 1971; Knokke-Heist, 1976; Provincie Antwerpen, 1988. Memberships: Several. Address: c/o Dirk Adams, Bovenbosstraat 78A, B-3052 Haasrode, Belgium.

ADAMSON Donald, b. 30 Mar 1939, Culcheth, Cheshire, England. Critic; Biographer; Historian. m. Helen Freda Griffiths, 24 Sept 1966, 2 sons. Education: Magdalen College, Oxford, England, 1956-59; University of Paris, France, 1960-61; MA, MLitt, DPhil (Oxon). Appointment: Visiting Fellow, Wolfson College, Cambridge. Publications: T S Eliot: A Memoir, 1971; The House of Nell Gwyn, jointly, 1974; Les Romantiques Français Devant La Peinture Espagnole, 1989; Blaise Pascal: Mathematician, Physicist, And Thinker About God, 1995; Rides Round Britain, The Travel Journals of John Byng, 5th Viscount Torrington, 1996; various translations of Balzac and Maupassant. Honour: JP, Cornwall, England, 1993. Membership: FRSL, 1983. Address: Topple Cottage, Polperro, Cornwall, PL13 2RS, England.

ADAMSON Robert (Harry), b. 17 May 1943, Sydney, New South Wales, Australia; Poet; Writer; Editor; Publisher. m. (1) Cheryl Adamson, 1973, (2) Juno Adamson, 19 Feb 1989, 1 son. Appointments: Associate Editor, 1968-70, Editor, 1970-75, Assistant Editor, 1975-77, New Poetry magazine, Sydney; Editor and Director, Prism Books, Sydney, 1970-77; Founding Editor and Director (with Dorothy Hewett), Big Smoke Books, Sydney, 1979-; Founder (with Michael Wilding), Paper Bark Press, 1988-. Publications: Poetry: Canticles on the Skin, 1970; The Rumour, 1971; Swamp Riddles, 1974; Theatre I-XIX, 1976; Cross the Border, 1977; Selected Poems, 1977; Where I Come From, 1979; The Law at Heart's Desire, 1982; The Clean Dark, 1989; Robert Adamson Selected Poems, 1970-1989, 1990; Waving to Hart Crane, 1994. Fiction: Zimmer's Essay (with Bruce Hanford), 1974; Wards of the State: An Autobiographical Novella, 1992. Editor: Australian Writing Now (with

Manfred Jurgensen), 1988. Contributions to: Periodicals. Honours: Australia Council Fellowships, 1976, 1977; Grace Leven Prize for Poetry, 1977; Kenneth Slessor Award, 1990; Turnbull-Fox Philips Poetry Prize, 1990; C J Dennis Prize for Poetry, 1990. Memberships: Australian Society of Authors; Poetry Society of Australia, president, 1970-80. Address: PO Box 59, Brooklyn, New South Wales, 2083, Australia.

ADCOCK Fleur, b. 10 Feb 1934, Papakura, New Zealand. Poet. Education: MA Victoria University of Wellington, 1955. Publications: The Eye of the Hurricane, 1964; Tigers, 1967; High Tide in the Garden, 1971; The Scenic Route, 1974; The Inner Harbour, 1979; Below Loughrigg, 1979; Selected Poems, 1983; The Virgin and the Nightingale, 1983; The Incident Book, 1986; Time Zones, 1991; Looking Back, 1997. Editor: The Oxford Book of Contemporary New Zealand Poetry, 1982; The Faber Book of 20th Century Women's Poetry, 1987; Translator and Editor: Hugh Primas and the Archpoet, 1994. Honour: Order of the British Empire, 1996. Membership: Fellow, Royal Society of Literature. Address: 14 Lincoln Road, London N2 9DL, England.

ADDINGTON Larry H(olbrook), b. 16 Nov 1932, Charlotte, North Carolina, USA. Professor of History Emeritus; Writer. Education: BA, 1955, MA, 1956, University of North Carolina at Chapel Hill; PhD, Duke University, 1962. Appointments: Assistant Professor, San Jose State College, 1962-64; Assistant Professor, 1964-66, Associate Professor, 1966-70, Professor, 1970-94, Professor Emeritus, 1994-, of History, The Citadel; Visiting Professor, Duke University, 1976-77. Publications: From Moltke to Hitler: The Evolution of German Military Doctrine, 1865-1939, 1966; Firepower and Manuever: The European Inheritance in the Two World Wars, 1967; Firepower and Manuever: Historical Case Studies, 1969; The Blitzkrieg Era and the German General Staff, 1865-1941, 1971; The Patterns of War Since the Eighteenth Century, 1984, revised edition, 1994; The Patterns of War Through the Eighteenth Century, 1990. Contributions to: Encyclopedias, books and scholarly journals. Honour: AMI Award for Best Seminal Work, 1984. Memberships: American Historical Association; Society for Military History; Phi Beta Kappa. Address: 1341 New Castle Street, Charleston, SC 29407, USA.

ADDLETON Jonathan S, b. 27 June 1957, Murree, Pakistan. USAID Official; Writer. m. Fiona Riach, 17 Aug 1985, 2 sons, 1 daughter. Education: BS, Northwestern University; MA, PhD, Tufts University. Appointment: Programme Officer, US Agency for International Development, Jordan, Kazakstan, South Africa, Yemen, Pakistan, 1984-. Publications: Undermining the Center, political economy, 1992; Some Far and Distant Place, memoir, 1997. Contributions to: Washington Post; Asian Survey; Asian Affairs; Muslim World; International Migration. Honour: Fellow, Bread Loaf Writing Conference, 1977. Address: c/o USAID/Amman, Unit 70206, Box 6, APO AE 09892-0206, USA.

ADELBERG Doris. See: ORGEL Doris.

ADELI Hojjat, b. 3 June 1950, Southern Shore of Caspian Sea, Iran. Engineering Educator; Author. m. Nahid Dadmehr, Feb 1979, 2 sons, 2 daughters. Education: BS, MS, University of Tehran, 1973; PhD, Stanford University, USA, 1976. Appointments: Founder, Editor-in-Chief, International Journal of Microcomputers in Civil Engineering, 1986-; Editor-in-Chief, Heuristics, The Journal of Knowledge Engineering, 1991-93; Founder, Editor-in-Chief, Integrated Computer-Aided Engineering, 1993-; Plenary Lecturer, international conferences in Italy, Mexico, Japan, China, USA, Canada, Portugal, Germany, Morocco, Singapore. Publications: Interactive Microcomputer-Aided Structural Design, 1988; Expert Systems for Structural Design (with K V Balasubramanyam), 1988; Parallel Processing in Structural Engineering (with O Kamal), 1993; Machine Learning - Neural Networks, Genetic Algorithms, and Fuzzy Systems (with S L Hung), 1995; Editor, 10 books. Contributions to: Over 250 articles to 40 research journals. Honours: Numerous awards including: Lichtenstein Award for Faculty Excellence, 1990; Lumely Research Award, Ohio State University, 1994. Memberships: Fellow, World Literary Academy; Editorial Board, 22 journals. Address: 1540 Picardae Court, Powell, OH 43065, USA.

ADENEY (Howard) Martin, b. 7 Sept 1942, Jerusalem. Public Relations Manager. m. Ann Corcoran, 18 Dec 1971, 3 sons. Education: BA (Cantab), Queens College, Cambridge, England. Appointments: Reporter, Guardian, 1965-77 (Labour Correspondent, 1972-77); Feature Writer, Colombo Plan Bureau, 1968-69; Industrial Correspondent, Sunday Telegraph, 1977-78; BBC TV News Labour Correspondent, 1978-82; Industrial Editor, 1982-89; International Media Relations Manager, ICI, 1989-93; PR Manager, 1993-97; Vice President, Public Relations, 1997-. Publications: Books: The Miners' Strike (with John Lloyd), 1986; The Motormakers: The Turbulent History of Britain's Car Industry, 1988; Nuffield: A Biography, 1993; Pamphlets: Community Action: Four Examples, 1971. Contributions to: Numerous contributions to various newspapers including Listener, New Society. Address: ICI, 9 Millbank, London SW1P 3JF, England.

ADHIKARI Santosh Kumar, b. 24 Nov 1923, West Bengal, India. College Administrator (Retired); Writer; Poet. m. Mar 1948, 1 son, 2 daughters. Education: Graduated, University of Calcutta, 1943; Diploma in Industrial Finance, Indian Institute of Bankers, Bombay; Diploma in Management, Indian Institute of Management. Appointments: Principal, Staff College, United Bank of India, Calcutta, retired 1983; Vidyasagar Lecturer, University of Calcutta, 1979; Speaker, Bengal Studies Conference, University of Chicago, 1990. Publications: Over 25 books, including novels, short stories, biographies, poetry collections, and anthologies, 1948-95. Contributions to: All India Radio and major journals. Honours: Prasad Puraskar for Poetry, 1986; Honorary title of Bharat Bhasa Bhusan, 1991. Memberships: Asiatic Society; Akhil Bharat, Bhasa Sahitya Sammelan; Vidyasagar Research Centre. Address: c/o Vidyasagar Research Centre, 81 Raja Basanta Roy Road, Calcutta, 700 029, India.

ADICKES Sandra, b. 14 July 1933, New York, New York, USA. Professor of English; Writer. 3 daughters. Education: BA in English, Douglass College, 1954; MA in English Education, Hunter College of the City University of New York, 1964; PhD in English and American Literature, New York University, 1977. Appointment: Professor of English, Winona State University, 1988-. Publications: The Social Quest, 1991; Legends of Good Women (novel), 1992; To Be Young Was Very Heaven: Women in New York Before the First World War, 1997. Contributions to: Reference books and journals. Address: 579 West 7th Street, Winona, MN 55987, USA.

ADISA Opal Palmer, b. 6 Nov 1954, Kingston, Jamaica. Teacher. 1 son, 2 daughters. Education: BA, Hunter College, City University of New York, 1975; MA, English, San Francisco State University, 1981; MA, Drama, 1986; PhD, University of California, 1992. Appointments: Head Teacher, Booker T Washington Child Development Center, San Francisco, 1978-79; Teacher, Counselor, Lucinda Weeks Center, San Francisco, 1979-81; Instructor, City College of San Francisco, 1980-84; Lecturer, San Francisco State University, 1981-87; Writer, Development Studies Center, San Ramon, California, 1991; Lecturer, University of California, Berkeley, 1992; Associate Professor and Chair of Ethnic Studies, California College of Arts and Crafts, 1993-; Writer-in-Residence, Headlands Centre for the Arts, Sansaulito, California, 1996. Publications: Tamarind and Other Mango Women; Traveling Women; Bake Face and Other Guava Stories; Pina: The Many Eyed Fruit; It Begins With Tears, 1997. Contributions to: Frontiers; Berkeley Poetry Review; The Caribbean Writer; Zyzzzva. Honours: Master Folk Artist; Pushcart Prize; Affirmative Action Dissertation Year Fellowship; Feminist Institute and Gender Study Research Grant; PEN Oakland/Josephine Miles Award; Creative Work Fund Grant, San Francisco, California, 1998-99. Memberships: Society for the Study of Multi Ethnic Literature of the US; National Writers Union; Local 3; California Poets in the Schools; Caribbean Association of Feminist Research and Action. Address: PO Box 10625, Oakland, CA 94610, USA.

ADLARD David Boyd, b. 13 June 1944, Norwich, England. Chef; Patron. m. Mary Ellen Healy, 31 Aug 1984, 1 son, 1 daughter. Education: BSc, Chemistry, Upper Second, University of Sussex, England, 1963-66. Appointments: Journalist, Eastern Daily Press, Norwich, England; Writing columns on food/wine and associated subjects. Contributions to: Gardener on Line Magazine. Address: Adlards Restaurant, 79 Upper St Giles Street, Norwich, Norfolk, NR2 1AB, England.

ADLER C(arole) S(chwerdtfeger), b. 23 Feb 1932, Long Island, New York, USA. Children's Book Author. m. Arnold R Adler, 22 June 1952, 3 sons. Education: BA, Hunter College, 1952; MS, Russell Sage College, 1964. Publications: The Magic of the Glits, 1979; The Silver Coach, 1979; In Our House Scott is My Brother, 1980; The Cat That Was Left Behind, 1981; Down By the River, 1981; Shelter on Blue Barns Road, 1981; Footsteps on the Stairs, 1982; The Evidence That Wasn't There, 1982; The Once in a While Hero, 1982; Some Other Summer, 1982; The Shell Lady's Daughter, 1983; Get Lost Little Brother, 1983; Roadside Valentine, 1983; Shadows on Little Reef Bay, 1984; Fly Free, 1984; Binding Ties, 1985; With Westie and the Tin Man, 1985; Good-Bye Pink Pig, 1985; Split Sisters, 1986; Kiss the Clown, 1986; Carly's Buck, 1987; Always and Forever Friends, 1988; If You Need Me, 1988; Eddie's Blue Winged Dragon, 1988; One Sister Too Many, 1989; The Lump in the Middle, 1989; Help Pink Pig!, 1990; Ghost Brother, 1990; Mismatched Summer, 1991; A Tribe for Lexi, 1991; Tuna Fish Thanksgiving, 1992; Daddy's Climbing Tree, 1993; Willie, the Frog Prince, 1994; That Horse Whiskey, 1994; Youn Hee and Me, 1995; Court Yard Cat, 1995; What's to be Scared of, Suki?, 1996; More Than a Horse, 1997; Her Blue Straw Hat, 1997; Not Just A Summer Crush, 1998; Winning, 1999. Honours: William Allen White Award, 1980; Golden Kite Award, 1980; American Library Association Best Young Adult Book, 1984; Children's Book Award, Child Study Committee, 1986; IRA Children's Selections, 1987, 1991. Memberships: Society of Children's Book Writers; Authors Guild. Address: 7041 North Cathedral Rock Place, Tucson, AZ 85718, USA.

ADLER Margot Susanna, b. 16 Apr 1946, Little Rock, Arkansas, USA. Journalist; Radio Producer; Talk Show Host. Education: BA, University of California, Berkeley, 1968; MS, Columbia School of Journalism, 1970; Nieman Fellow, Harvard University, 1982. Publications: Drawing Down the Moon: Witches, Druids, Goddess-Worshippers and Other Pagans in America Today, 1979, revised edition, 1986; Heretic's Heart: A Journey Through Spirit and Revolution, 1997. Memberships: Authors Guild; American Federation of Radio and Television Artists. Literary Agent: Jane Rotrosen. Address: 333 Central Park West, New York, NY 10025, USA.

ADLER Mortimer J(erome), b. 28 Dec 1902, New York, New York, USA. Philosopher; Author. m. (1) Helen Leavenworth Boynton, 2 May 1927, div 1961, 2 sons, (2) Caroline Sage Pring, 22 Feb 1963, 2 sons. Education: PhD, Columbia University, 1928; BA, Columbia College, 1983. Appointments: Instructor, Columbia University, 1923-30; Assistant Director, People's Institute, New York City, 1927-29; Associate Professor of the Philosophy of Law, 1930-42, Professor, 1942-52, University of Chicago; Visiting Lecturer, 1937-85, Visting Lecturer Emeritus, 1985-, St John's College, Maryland; Director, Institute for Philosophical Research, Chicago, 1952-95; President, San Francisco Productions Inc, 1954-94; Chairman, Board of Editors, 1974-95, Chairman Emeritus, 1995-, Encyclopaedia Britannica; Co-Founder and Honorary Chairman, Center for the Study of Great Ideas, 1990-. Publications: Dialectic, 1927; Crime, Law and Social Science (with Jerome Michael), 1933; Diagrammatics (with Maude Phelps Hutchins), 1932; Art and Prudence: A Study in Practical Philosophy, 1937, revised edition as Poetry and Politics, 1965; What Man Has Made of Man, 1938; How to Read a Book: The Art of Getting a Liberal Education (with Charles Van Doren), 1940, revised edition, 1972; Problems for Thomists: The Problem of Species, 1940; A Dialectic of Morals, 1941; The Capitalist Manifesto (with Louis Kelso), 1958; The New Capitalists, 1961; The Revolution in Education (with Milton Mayer), 1958; The Idea of Freedom, 2 volumes, 1958, 1961; Great Ideas from the Great Books, 1961; The Conditions of Philosophy, 1965; The Difference of Man and the Difference It Makes, 1967; The Time of Our Lives, 1970; The Common Sense of Politics, 1971; The American Testament (with William Gorman), 1975; Some Questions About Language: A Theory of Human Discourse, 1976; Philosopher at Large: An Intellectual Autobiography, 1977; Reforming Education, 1977; Aristotle for Everybody, 1978; How to Think About God, 1980; Six Great Ideas, 1981; The Angels and Us, 1982; The Paideia Proposal, 1982; Paideia Problems and Possibilitites, 1983; How to Speak/How to Listen, 1983; The Paidia Program, 1984; A Vision of the Future, 1984; Ten Philosophical Mistakes, 1985; A Guidebook to Learning: For the Lifelong Pursuit of Wisdom, 1986; We Hold These Truths: Understanding the Ideas and Ideals of the Constitution, 1987; Reforming Education: The Opening of the American Mind, 1989; Intellect: Mind Over Matter, 1990; Truth in Religion, 1990; Haves Without Have-Nots, 1991; Desires Right and Wrong, 1991; A Second Look at the Rearview Mirror, 1992; The Great Ideas: A Lexicon of Western Thought, 1992; The Four Dimensions of Philosophy, 1993; Art, the Arts and the Great Ideas, 1994; Adler's Philosophical Dictionary, 1995. Editor-in-Chief: Great Books of the Western World, 2nd edition, 1990 et seq. Memberships; American Catholic Philosophers Association; American Maritain Association; International Listening Association. Address: Institute for Philosophical Research, 310 South Michigan Avenue, 7th Floor, Chicago, IL 60604, USA.

ADLER Renata, b. 19 Oct 1938, Milan, Italy. Writer. Education: AB, Bryn Mawr College, 1959; Dd'ES, Sorbonne University, Paris, 1961; MA, Harvard University, 1962; Law Degree, Yale University. Appointments: Writer-Reporter, New Yorker magazine, 1962-68, 1970-82; Fellow, Trubull College, Yale University, 1969-72; Associate Professor of Theatre and Cinema, Hunter College of the City University of New York, 1972-73. Publications: Toward a Radical Middle: Fourteen Pieces of Reporting and Criticism, 1969; A Year in the Dark: Journal of a Film Critic, 1968-69, 1970; Speedboat (novel), 1976; Pitch Dark (novel), 1983; Reckless Disregard: Westmoreland v. CBS et al: Sharon v. Time, 1986. Contributions to: Many periodicals. Honours: Guggenheim Fellowship, 1973-74; 1st Prize, O Henry Short Story Awards, 1974; American Academy and Institute of Arts and Letters Award, 1976; Ernest Hemingway Prize, 1976. Memberships: American Academy and Institute of Arts and Letters; PEN. Address: 178 East 64th Street, New York, NY 10021, USA.

ADLER Warren, b. 16 Dec 1927, New York, New York, USA. Author. m. Sonia Kline, 5 May 1951, 3 sons. Education: BA, New York University, 1947; New School for Social Research, New York City. Appointments: Editor, Queens Post, Forest Hills, New York; President, advertising and public relations agency, Washington, DC, 1959-78. Publications: Options, 1974; Banquet Before Dawn, 1976; The Henderson Equation, 1976; Trans-Siberian Express, 1977; The Sunset Gang, 1978; The Casanova Embrace, 1978; Blood Ties, 1979; Natural Enemies, 1980; The War of the Roses, 1981; American Quartet, 1982; American Sextet, 1983; Random Hearts, 1984; Twilight Child, 1989; Immaculate Deception, 1991; Senator Love, 1991; Private Lies, 1992; The Witch of Watergate, 1992; The Ties That Bind, 1994. Memberships: Authors Guild; Authors League of America; Mystery Writers of America. Address: 45 Hucklberry Drive, Jackson Hole, WY 83001, USA.

ADNAN Etel, b. 24 Feb 1925, Beirut, Lebanon. Poet; Writer; Painter; Tapestry Designer. Education: Sorbonne, University of Paris; University of California, Berkeley; Harvard University. Appointments: Teacher, Philosophy of Art and Humanities, Dominican College, San Rafael, California, 1958-72; Cultural Editor, Al-Safa newspaper, Lebanon, 1972-79; Paintings exhibited around the world. Publications: Poetry: Moonshots, 1966; Five Senses for One Death, 1971; From A to Z, 1982; The Indian Never Had a Horse and Other Poems, 1985; The Arab Apocalypse, 1989; The Spring Flowers Own and the Manifestations of the Voyage, 1990. Novel: Sitt Marie-Rose, 1982. Other: Journey to Mount Tamalpais, 1986; Of Cities and Women, 1993; Paris, When It's Naked, 1993. Contributions to: Poems and short stories in many publications. Honour: France-Pays-Arabes Prize, 1978. Membership: Poetry Center, San Francisco. Address: 35 Marie Street, Sausalito, CA 94965, USA.

ADOFF Arnold, b. 16 July 1935, New York, New York, USA. Poet; Writer; Literary Agent. m. Virginia Hamilton, 19 Mar 1960, 2 children. Education: BA, City College of New York, 1956; Columbia University, 1956-58; New School for Social Research Poetry Workshops, New York City, 1965-67. Appointments: Teacher, New York City Public Schools, 1957-69; Literary Agent, Yellow Springs, Ohio, 1977-; Distinguished Visiting Professor, Queens College, 1986-87; Guest Lecturer in many US venues. Publications: Poetry: Black Is Brown Is Tan, 1973; Make a Circle Keep Us In: Poems for a Good Day, 1975; Big Sister Tells Me That I'm Black, 1976; Tornado!: Poems, 1977; Under the Early Morning Trees, 1978; Where Wild Willie, 1978; Eats: Poems, 1979; I Am the Running Girl, 1979; Friend Dog, 1980; OUTside INside Poems, 1981; Today We Are Brother and Sister, 1981; Birds, 1982; All the Colors of the Race, 1982; The Cabbages Are Chasing the Rabbits, 1985; Sports Pages, 1986; Flamboyan, 1988; Greens, 1988; Chocolate Dreams, 1989; Hard to Be Six, 1990; In for Winter, Out for Spring, 1991. Other: Malcolm X (biography), 1970; MA nDA LA, (picture book), 1971. Editor: I Am the Darker Brother: An Anthology of Modern Poems by Negro Americans, 1968; Black on Black: Commentaries by Negro Americans, 1968; City in All Directions: An Anthology of Modern Poems by Black Americans, 1970; Brothers and Sisters: Modern Stories by Black Americans, 1970; It Is the Poem Singing into Your Eyes: An Anthology of New Young Poets, 1971; The Poetry of Black America: An Anthology of the 20th Century, 1973; My Black Me: A Beginning Book of Black Poetry, 1974; Celebrations: A New Anthology of Black American Poetry, 1978. Contributions to: Articles and reviews in periodicals. Honours: Children's Book of the Year Citations, Child Study Association of America, 1968, 1969, 1986; American Library Association Notable Book Awards, 1968, 1970, 1971, 1972, 1979; Best Children's Book Citations, School Library Journal, 1971, 1973; Notable Children's Trade Book Citation, Children's Book Council-National Council for Social Studies, 1974; Jane Addams Peace Association Special Certificate, 1983; Children's Choice Citation, International Reading Association-Children's Book Council, 1985; National Council of Teachers of English Poetry Award, 1988. Address: Arnold Adoff Agency, PO Box 293, Yellow Springs, OH 45387, USA.

ADONIS. See: **ESBER Ali Ahmad Said.**

ADORJAN Carol (Madden), (Kate Kenyon), b. 17 Aug 1934, Chicago, Illinois, USA. Writer; Teacher. m. William W Adorjan, 17 Aug 1957, 2 sons, 2 daughters. Education: BA, English Literature, Magna Cum Laude, Mundelein College, 1956. Appointments: Fellow, Midwest Playwrights Lab, 1977; Writer-in-Residence, Illinois Arts Council, 1981-; National Radio Theatre, 1980-81. Publications: Someone I Know, 1968; The Cat Sitter Mystery, 1972; Eighth Grade to the Rescue (as Kate Kenyon), 1987; A Little Princess (abridgment), 1987; Those Crazy Eighth Grade Pictures (as Kate Kenyon), 1987; WKID: Easy Radio Plays (with Yuri Rasovsky), 1988; The Copy Cat Mystery, 1990; That's What Friends Are For, 1990. Radio and Stage Plays: Julian Theater, BBC, National Radio Theatre, etc. Contributions to: Redbook; Woman's Day; North American Review; Denver Quarterly; Four Quarters; Yankee. Honours: Josephine Lusk Fiction Award, Munderlein College, 1955; Earplay, 1972; Illinois Arts Council Completion Grant, 1977-78; Dubuque Fine Arts Society National One-Act Playwriting

Competition, 1978; Ohio State Award, 1980. Memberships: Dramatists Guild; Society of Midland Authors; Poets and Writers; Children's Reading Roundtable. Address: 1667 Winnetka Road, Glenview, IL 60025, USA.

ADRIAN Frances. See: **POLLAND Madelaine Angela.**

AESCHBACHER-SINECKA Helena, b. 11 May 1945, Kozly, Czechoslovakia. Poet; Photographer; Painter. div. Education: Russian, History, 1962-66, Library Science, 1968-73, Charles University, Prague. Appointments: Librarian, Zurich, Switzerland, 1973-85; Artist, 1985-. Publications: Poetry books: Mlhavé dny, 1981; Am Rande der tiefsten Schlucht, 1986; Hab' keine Angst vor dem Winter, 1989; Herbstzeit-Podzimní cas, 1991. Membership: Schweizerischer Schriftsteller-Verband. Address: Haus der Stille, 8926 Kappel a.A., Switzerland.

AFRICANO Lillian, (Nora Ashby, Lila Cook, Jessica March), b. 7 June 1935, Paterson, New Jersey, USA. Author; Columnist. Div. 2 sons, 1 daughter. Education: BA, summa cum laude, Barnard College, 1957; Columbia University Graduate School, 1958. Appointments: Arts Editor, The Villager, 1971; News Editor, Penthouse/Forum, 1973; Columnist, New York Times Syndicate, 1977, Woman's World, 1980. Publications: Businessman's Guide to the Middle East, 1977; Doctor's Walking Book (co-author), 1980; Something Old, Something New, 1983; Passions, 1985; Gone From Breezy Hill (as Nora Ashby), 1985; Illusions (as Jessica March), 1988; Consenting Adults (as Lila Cook), 1988; Temptations (as Jessica March), 1989; Obsessions, 1990. Contributions to: New York Times; New York News; Reader's Digest; Harper's Bazaar; Woman's Day; Woman's World; National Review; Nation. Honour: Phi Beta Kappa, 1956. Memberships: Drama Desk, Vice President, Secretary; Outer Critics' Circle; American Society of Journalists and Authors; Authors Guild. Address: 95 West RiverRoad, Rumson, NJ 07760, USA.

AGARWAL Sarla, b. 12 July 1933, Bulandshahr. Writer; Vaastu Consultant. m. Mr Harikrishna Agarwala, 4 Dec 1954, 3 daughters. Education: BA, Agra University, 1953; Vidushi Exam, Prayag Mahila Vidyapeeth, 1950. Publications: Mujhe Bela Se Pyar Hai, short stories; Mutthi Bhur Ujaas, short stories; Vyauhar Aapka, essays; Vaastu Darshan; Bhartiya Vaastu Vigyan; Anumeha; Manzil Kiore; Tivra Jal Gayil; Sanjha Pyar; Tai Tai Phiss. Contributions to: 600 articles, stories, essays, poems in Hindi Magazines of national repute. Honours: Shaitya Samman, 1995; Vaastu Martand, 1996. Memberships: Vice President & Regional Vice President, Akhil Bhartiya Sahitya Parishad, 1991-93, 1993-95, 1995-97; Bhartendu Samiti Kota; Association of Writers for Children, Delhi; Executive Member in International Vaastu Association, Jodhpur. Address: Aastha 5-13-20 Talwandi Kota, Rejasthan, India.

AGATE W. See: **WILLIAMS Michael Arnold.**

AGEE Jonis, b. 31 May 1943, Omaha, Nebraska, USA. Writer; Poet; Professor. m. Paul McDonough, 1 daughter. Education: BA, University of Iowa, 1966; MA, 1969, PhD, 1976, State University of New York at Binghampton. Appointments: Teacher, College of St Catherine, St Paul, Minnesota, 1975-95; Literary Consultant, Walker Arts Center, Minneapolis, 1978-84; Adjunct Teacher, Macalester College, St Paul, Minnesota, 1980-88; Teacher and Editor, Literary Post Program for Senior Citizen Writers, 1986-89; Professor, University of Michigan, 1995-; Many poetry readings. Publications: Houses (poem), 1976; Mercury (poems), 1981; Two Poems, 1982; Border Crossings (editor), 1984; Stiller's Pond (editor), 1988, expanded edition, 1991; Bend This Heart (stories), 1989; Pretend We've Never Met (stories), 1989; Sweet Eyes (novel), 1991; Strange Angels (novel), 1993; A .38 Special and a Broken Heart (stories), 1995; South of Resurrection (novel), forthcoming. Contributions to: Anthologies and periodicals. Honours: Minnesota State Arts Board Award, 1977; National Endowment for the Arts Fellowship, 1978;

Loft-McKnight Awards, 1987, 1991. Memberships: Literary Guild. Address: 503 South First Street, Ann Arbor, MI 48103, USA.

AGUIRRE Eugenio, b. 31 July 1944, Mexico City, Mexico. Writer. m. 6 Aug 1971, 1 son, 1 daughter. Education: BA, Law, MA, Literature, Universidad Nacional Autonoma de Mexico. Appointments: Lecturer, University of Lawrence, Kansas, USA; Wabash College, USA; Writers Association of Panama; Several bank and government offices, Mexico. Publications: Novels: Jesucristo Perez, 1973; Pajar de Imaginacion, 1975; El caballero de las espadas, 1978; Gonzalo Guerrero, 1980; El testamento del diablo, 1981; En el campo, 1982; Cadaver exquisito, 1984; El rumor que llego del mar, 1985; Pajaros de fuego, 1986; Un mundo de nino lleno de mar, 1986; Pasos de sangre, 1988; Amor de mis amores, 1988; De cuerpo entero, 1991; El guerrero del sur, 1991; Cosas de angeles y otros cuentos, 1992; Los ninos de colores, 1993;Elena o el laberinto de la lujuria, 1994; El demonio me visita, 1994; La fascinacion de la bestia, 1994; Desierto ardiente, 1995; Ruiz Massieu: el mejor enemigo, 1995. Contributions to: Mexican and foreign publications. Honours: Great Silver Medal, International Academy of Lutece, Paris, 1981; Finalist. 1st crime novel, Plaza de Janes, 1985; Finalist, Fuentes Mares Prize for Literature, 1986; Finalist, 1st International Award, Diana Publishers, 1986. Memberships: Past president, Asociacion de Escritores de Mexico; Board, Sociedad General de Escritores de Mexico; International PEN Club. Address: Buhos no 32, Fracc Loma de Guadalupe, Mexico DF 01720, Mexico.

AHERNE Owen. See: **CASSILL R(onald) V(erlin).**

AHLSEN Leopold, b. 12 Jan 1927, Munich, Germany. Author. m. Ruth Gehwald, 1964, 1 son, 1 daughter. Publications: 13 Plays, 23 radio plays, 42 television plays, 5 novels. Honours: Gerhart Hauptmann Prize; Schiller-Forderungspreis; Golden Bildschirm; Horspielpreis der Kriegsblinden; Silver Nymph of Monaco. Address: Waldschulstrasse 58, 81827 Munich, Germany.

AHRENS Bridget, b. 9 Jan 1958, Buffalo, New York, USA. Writer. m. 1 Aug 1981, 1 son, 1 daughter. Education: BA, Medical Technology, State University of New York, 1980; MPH, University of California, 1981; MFA, Writing, Vermont College, 1990. Appointments: Instructor, Fiction and Non-Fiction Writing, Lebanon College, 1990-; Associate Editor, AIDS and Society: An International Research and Policy Bulletin. Publications: Our Lady of the Keyboard, 1989; The Problems and Pitfalls of Writing about Sex, 1989; A Woman's Place is Intuition, 1990; The Art of Baking, The Politics of Love, 1991; The Eye of the Needle, 1991; Atlas's Revenge, 1992. Honour: Fellowship, Vermont Council on the Arts, 1992. Membership: Poets and Writers. Address: 78 Brigham Hill Road, Norwich, VT 05055, USA.

AICHINGER Ilse, b. 1 Nov 1921, Vienna, Austria. Novelist; Playwright. Education: University of Vienna, 1945-48. Appointments: Member of Grupe 47, 1951-. Publications: Die Grössere Hoffnung, 1948; Rede Unter dem Galgen, 1953; Eliza, Eliza, 1965; Selected Short Stories and Dialogue, 1966; Nachricht und Tag: Erzählungen, 1970; Schlechte Worter, 1976; Meine Sprache und Ich Erzählungen, 1978; Spiegelesichte: Erzählungen und Dialoge, 1979. Plays, Zu Keiner Stunde, 1957, 1980; Besuch im Pfarrhaus, 1961; Auckland: 4 Horspiele, 1969; Knopfe, 1978; Weisse Chrysanthemum, 1979; Radio Plays, Selected Poetry and Prose of Ilse Aichinger, 1983; Collected Works, 8 volumes, 1991. Honours: Belgian Europe Festival Prize, 1987; Town of Solothurn Prize, 1991. Address: c/o Fischer Verlag, Postfach 700480, 6000 Frankfurt, Germany.

AIDOO (Christina) Ama Ata, b. 1942, Abeadzi Kyiakor, Ghana. Writer. 1 daughter. Appointments: Lecturer, University of Cape Coast, Ghana, 1970-83; Minister of Education, Ghana, 1982-83; Chair, Africa Regional Panel of Commonwealth Writers Prize,

1990-91. Publications: Changes, A Love Story; The Dilemma of a Ghost; Anowa; No Sweetness Here; Our Sister Killjoy; Someone Talking to Sometime; The Eagle and the Chickens; Birds and Other Poems; Short Stories. Contributions to: BBC African Service; MS Magazine; South Magazine; Kumapipi; Rapport; Chapman Review. Address: PO Box 4930, Harare, Zimbabwe.

AIKEN Joan Delano, b. 4 Sept 1924, Rye, Sussex, England. Writer. m. (1)Ronald George Brown, Dec 1955, 1 son, 1 daughter, (2)Julius Goldstein, 2 Sept 1976. Appointments: Librarian, United Nations London Information Centre, 1945-49; Features Editor, Argosy Magazine, 1955-60; Freelance Writer, Full Time, 1961-. Publications: The Fortune Hunters, 1965; Died on a Rainy Sunday, 1972; A Harp of Fishbones, 1972; The Mooncusser's Daughter, 1973; The Skin Spinners (poems), 1976; The Teeth of the Gale, 1988; Give Yourself a Fright, 1989; Mortimer and Arabel, 1992; A Creepy Company, 1993; Eliza's Daughter, 1994; The Winter Sleepwalker, 1994; Cold Shoulder Road, 1995; Emma Watson, 1996; The Cockatrice Boys, 1996; The Jewel Seed, 1997; Moon Cake, 1998; The Youngest Miss Ward, 1998; Limbo Lodge, forthcoming. Contributions to: New Statesman; Washington Post; Good Housekeeping; Womans Journal; Childrens Literature in Education. Honours: Guardian Award, 1969; Lewis Carroll Award, 1970. Memberships: Society of Authors; Writers Guild; Mystery Writers of America; Crime Writers Association. Literary Agent: A M Heath Ltd. Address: The Hermitage, East Street, Petworth, West Sussex GU28 0AB, England.

AITCHISON Winifred. See: ROBINSON Bina Aitchison

AITMATOV Chingiz (Torekulovich), b. 12 Dec 1928, Sheker, Kirghizstan. Novelist. Education: Gorky Literary Institute, Moscow, 1956-58. Appointments: Deputy, Supreme Soviet, 1966-89; Ambassador, Luxembourg, 1990. Publications: Melody, 1959; Milky Way, 1963; The First Master, 1963; Short Novels, 1964; The Son of a Soldier, 1970; The White Ship, 1972; The Lament of a Migrating Bird, 1973; The Soldier, 1974; Night Dew, 1975; Collected Works, 2 volumes, 1978; The Legend of the Horned Mother Deer, 1979; Short Stories, 1982; Collected Works, 3 volumes, 1982-84; Echo of the World, 1985; The Place of the Skull, 1989; Mother Earth and Other Stories, 1989. Honours: Lenin Prize, 1963; Hero of Socialist Labour, 1978; Membership: World Academy of Art and Science, 1987. Address: Russian Writers Union, Moscow, Russia.

AJIBADE (Ade)Yemi (Olanrewaju), b. 28 July 1939, Nigeria. Actor; Dramatist; Director. m. Gwendoline Augusta Ebonywhite, May 1973, 2 daughters. Education: Diplomas in dramatic arts films technique; Diploma in Theatre Production, British Drama League; Associate, Drama board; MA, London University, 1985. Appointments: Visiting Director, Actors Workshop, London; Artistic Director, Pan-African Players, Keskidee Centre, London; Senior Arts Fellow and Artistic Director, Unibadan Masques, Ibadan University, Nigeria; Artist-in-Residence, Colby College, Waterville, Maine, USA, 1987. Contributions to: Plays produced in Nigeria, London, and Paris. Honours: British Arts Council Bursaries for Drama. Memberships: Black Writers Association; British Kinematographic Society; Royal Society of Arts, fellow; Theatre Writers Union. Address: 29 Seymour House, Churchway, London NW1, England.

AKAEKE Osonye Tess. See: ONWUEME Tess Osonye.

AKAVIA Miriam, b. 20 Nov 1927, Krakow, Poland. Novelist; Translator. m. 3 Dec 1946, 2 daughters. Appointments: Co-editor of some bulletins. Publications: Adolescence of Autumn, 1975; Ha mechir (The Price), 1978; Galia & Miklosh, 1982; Karmi Sheli (My Own Vineyard), 1984; Adventure on a Bus, 1986; Ma Vigne A Moi, 1992; The Other Way: The Story of a Group (in Hebrew), 1992; An End To Childhood (in English), 1995, (in Polish), 1996. Contributions to: Various literary magazines. Honours: Dvorsecki Prize; Korczak Prize,

SEK Prize (Société Européen de Culture); Amicus Polonie; Cracovians Prize; Golden Medal, President Wolesa, Poland, 1991; Prime Minister Prize, I Rabin, 1993; Prize Wizo, Creative Woman in Literature, Tel-Aviv, 1998. Address: PO 53050, 61530 Tel-Aviv, Israel.

AKEN Paul Van, b. 20 Nov 1948, Reet, Belgium. Teacher; Literary Critic. Education: Free University, Brussels, 1966-70. Publications: Features of the Essay; Lettermarker, A History of Dutch Literature; Paul De Wispelaer; About Sugar by Hugo Claus; About Lucifer by Vondel; About the Wall by Jos Vandeloo. Contributions to: Nieuw Vlaams Tydschrift; De Vlaamse Gids; Yang; Kunst & Cultuur; Kruispunt; Ons Erfdeel; Creare; Septentrion. Memberships: PEN; FLANDERS. Address: Dirk Martensstraat 60, 9300 Aalst, Belgium.

AKERS Alan Burt. See: BULMER Henry Kenneth.

AKHMADULINA Bella Akhatovna, b. 10 Apr 1937, Moscow, Russia. Poet. m. Boris Messerer, 1974. Education: Gorky Literary Institute, Moscow, 1960. Appointments: Secretary, Union of Soviet, (later Russian) Writers, 1986-. Publications: Fire Tree, 1958; String, 1962; Tale of the Rain, 1963; My Genealogy, 1963; Adventure in an Antique Store, 1967; Fever and Other Poems, 1968; Snowstorm, 1968; Music Lessons, 1969; Candle, 1977; Three Russian Poets, 1979; The Garden, 1987; Seashore, 1991. Screenplay: Clear Ponds, 1965. Honours: American Academy of Arts and Letters, 1977. Address: Cherniachovskoho Street 4, Apt 37, 125319 Moscow, Russia.

AKMAKJIAN Alan Paul, b. 18 July 1948, Highland Park, Michigan, USA. University Teacher; Poet; Writer. Education: BA, 1973, MA, 1974, Eastern Michigan University; PhD, University of Texas at Dallas, St John's University, New York City, Wayne State University, Detroit, 1979; MA, California State University, San Francisco, 1991. Appointments: Teacher, California State University, San Francisco, 1985, St John's University, New York City, 1994-95, University of Texas at Dallas, 1995-; Instructor, Poets in the Schools, California, 1986-91. Publications: Treading Pages of Water, 1992; Let the Sun Go, 1992; California Picnic, 1992; Grounded Angels, 1993; Breaking the Silence, 1994; California Picnic and Other Poems, 1997. Contributions to: Anthologies, journals, reviews and magazines. Honours: National Endowment for the Arts Grant, 1984; California Arts Council Grant, 1984; St John's University Fellowship, 1994-95; University of Texas Fellowships, 1994-95, 1995-96, 1996-97; Texas Public Educational Grant, 1996-97. Memberships: Academy of American Poets; Associated Writing Programs; Modern Language Association; PEN; Poetry Society of America. Address: 2200 Waterview Parkway, Apt 2134, Richardson, TX 75080, USA.

AKSENOV Vasilii (Pavlovich), b. 20 Aug 1932, Kazan, Russia. Novelist; Dramatist. m. Maia Karmen, 1979. Education: Povlov Medical Institute, 1956. Appointments: Exiled to USA, 1980; Writer-in-Residence, University of Michigan, University of Southern California and George Washington University; Returned to Russia, 1992. Publications: Colleagues, 1961; Oranges from Morocco, 1963; Catapult, 1964; Its Time My Friend Its Time, 1969; Surplussed Barrelware, 1972; Samson and Samsoness, 1972; Around the Clock Non-Stop, 1976; In Search of a Genre, 1977; The Steel Bird and Other Stories, 1979; Our Golden Ironburg, 1980; The Island of Crimea, 1983; The Paperscape, 1983; The Burn, 1984; The Day of the First Snowfall, 1990; Capital Displacement, 1990; The Yolk of an Egg, 1990; Moscow Saga, 1991; Rendezvous, 1991. Plays: Kollegi, 1962; Always on Sale, 1965; Your Murderer, 1977; The Four Temperaments, 1979; Aristophaniana and the Frogs, 1981; The Heron, 1984. Screenplays: The Blues with a Russian Accent, 1987; In Search of Melancholy Baby, 1987. Address: Krasnoirmeskaia Str 21, Apt 20, 125319 Moscow, Russia.

AL NASAYYIR Yassin Nazzall, b. 1 July 1941, Basra, Iraq. Poetry Critic. m. 18 May 1961, 3 sons, 4 daughters.

Education: Graduated, Very Good, Baghdad University, 1975. Appointments: Primary School Teacher; Journalist. Publications: Romans and Places, parts 1 and 2; The Beginnings; The Beauties of Space in Al Sayap's Poetry; The Problems in Literary Texts; Point Light, Point Shadow; The Hidden Text. Contributions to: Al-Thakafa Al Jadida; Finon; Al Torath Al Sha'abi; Tarik Alshab; Al-Jumharia. Memberships: Iraqi University Literary Society, 7 years; Iraqi Theatre. Address: Schildersgaarde 11, 2542 EA Den Haag, Netherlands.

AL'HAQQ Fakhroddin. See: LOIDL Peter Christian.

AL-AZM Sadik J, b. 7 Nov 1934, Damascus, Syria. University Professor. m. Fawz Touqan, 2 July 1957, 2 sons. Education: American University, Beirut, 1953-57; Yale University, 1957-61. Appointments: Visiting Professor, Princeton University, 1988-90, 1991-92; Visiting Fellow, Woodrow Wilson International Centre for Scholars, 1992-93; Chairman, Department of Philosophy and Sociology, Damascus University, 1993-98; Visiting Professor, University of Oldenburg, Germany, 1995; Visiting Professor, Hamburg University, Germany, 1998. Publications: Kant's Theory of Time: The Origins of Kant's Arguments in the Antinonnies; Critique of Religious Thought; Studies in Modern Western Philosophy; Of Love and Arabic Courtly Love; Materialism and History: A Defense; The Tabooing Mentality: Salman Rushdie and the Truth of Literature, 1992, 3rd edition, 1997; Unbehagen in Der Moderne: Auklarung im Islam, 1993; Sadik Al-Azm: Mot Hevdvunne Sannheter, 1995; Reading the Satanic Verses, 1998. Contributions to: Orientalism and Orientalism in Reverse; Sionisme Une Entreprise de Colonisation; Der Palastinensiche Widerstand neu Durchdacht; Palestinian Zionism; The Importance of Being Earnest About Salman Rushdie; South Asia Bulletin; European Academy of Sciences and Arts, member.Address: Department of Philosophy, Faculty of Letters, Damascus University, Damascus, Syria.

AL-KHARRAT Edwar, b. 16 Mar 1926, Alexandria, Egypt. Writer; Poet. 2 sons. Education: LLB, Alexandria University, 1946. Appointments: Editor, Gallery 68 Magazine, 1968, Afro Asian Writings Magazine, 1968, Special Issue, Egyptian Literature of AL Karmal Magazine, 1984. Publications: High Walls, 1959; Hours of Pride, 1972; Ramah and the Dragon, 1980; Suffocations of Love and Mornings, 1983; The Other Time, 1985; City of Saffron, 1986; Girls of Alexandria, 1990; Waves of Nights, 1991; Bobello's Ruins, 1992; Penetrations of Love and Perdition, 1993; My Alexandria, 1993; The New Sensibility, 1994; From Silence to Rebellion, 1994; Transgeneric Writing, 1994; Ripples of Salt Dreams, 1994; Fire of Phantasies, 1995; Hymn to Density, 1995; 7 Interpretations, 1996; Wings of Your Bird Struck Me, 1996; Why?: Extracts of a Love Poem, 1996; Soaring Edifices, 1997; The Certitude of Thirst, 1998; Cry of the Unicorn, 1998; Throes of Facts and Madness, 1998; Beyond Reality, 1998. Contributions to: Many Arab literary magazines. Honours: Arts and Letters Medal, 1972; State Prize for Short Story, 1972; Franco Arab Friendship Award, 1989; UWAIS Award for Fiction, 1995. Memberships: Egyptian Writers Union; Gezira Sporting Club; Egyptian PEN Club; Committee on Fiction, High Council of Culture. Address: 45 Ahmed Hishmat Street, Zamalak 11211, Cairo, Egypt.

AL-KHATIB Burhan, (Fanus), b. 10 Oct 1944, Mosaib, Babel, Iraq. m. (1) 8 Feb 1978 - 9 Feb 1982, (2) 30 July 1988 - 27 Apr 1994, 2 sons, 1 daughter. Education: Engineering practice in Egypt, 1965; Degree in Engineering, BSME, Engineering College, Baghdad University, 1967; MA, The Gorky Literary Institute, 1975. Appointments: Engineer, 1968-69; Journalist, 1970-80; Stylist and Translator, 1975-86; Publisher, 1990-94. Publications: Khutwat ila Alufq Albaid (Steps Toward a Distant Horizon), 1967; Dabab fi Addahira (Mist at Midday), 1968; Shiqqatun fi Shari' Abi Nuwas (An Apartment on Abi Nuwas Street), 1972; Ajusur Azujajiyya (Bridges of Glass), 1975; Ashari 'aljadid (A New Street), 1980; Nujum Oldhuhr (Under the Heat of Midday), 1986; Suqut Sparta (The Fall of Sparta), 1992; Layla Baghdadia (A Baghdad Night), 1993; Babel alfaiha (The Aromatic

Babylon), 1995; Thalik assaif fi Iskendria (That Summer in Alexandria), 1998. Contributions to: Translated 13 books, wrote number of essays and stories in Arab magazines and journals, between 1975-85. Membership: Sveriges författar förbund (The Writers Union of Sweden), 1989-. Address: Berg V 22 tr 3, 19631 Kungsangen, Sweden.

AL-SHAROUNI Youssef, b. 14 Oct 1924, Menuf, Egypt. Retired Educator and Government Official; Writer. m. Nargis S Basta, 2 Oct 1952, 1 son, 1 daughter. Education: BA, Cairo University. Appointments: Under-Secretary, High Council of Arts, Ministry of Culture, 1978-83; Professor for Postgraduate Courses, Faculty of Information, Cairo University, 1979-81; Ministry of Information, Oman, 1985-92. Publications: The Five Lovers: A Message to a Woman; The Last Eve; Studies on Love and Friendship in Arabic Tradition; Complete Short Stories, volume 1, 1992, volume 2, 1993. Contributions to: Al Adib; Al Adab; Al Arabi; Al Muntada; Al Ahram; Al Quissa. Honours: Egyptian State Prizes in Short Story, 1970, and Literary studies, 1978; First Grade Order of Science and Arts, Arab Republic of Egypt, 1970; Order of the Republic, 1978; Fellow, German Academic Exchange Service, Free University of Berlin, 1976, Netherlands Organisation for Advancement of Pure Research, 1981-82. Memberships: Story Club, Cairo, board, 1970-; Writers' Union, Cairo; Pen Club; Fiction Committee at High Council of Culture, 1963-83. Address: 12 El-Sad El Aali Street, El-Maadi, PC 11431, Cairo, Egypt.

ALBADA JELGERSMA Jill Elizabeth, b. 23 Jan 1939, Leicester, England. Independent Scholar. m. Frits Albada Jelgersma, 8 Feb 1969, 2 sons. Education: BA, 1981, MPhil, 1988, University of the West Indies, Trinidad and Tobago; PhD, Spanish, University of California at Davis, 1995. Appointments: Principal, Hilos Cadena School, Pereira, Colombia; Lecturer, University of the West Indies, Trinidad and Tobago; Lecturer, University of California, Davis, USA; Currently Independent Scholar of Spanish-American Literature. Publications: Articles on Spanish American literature, in Antilia, Trinidad, 1984, Revista de Crítica Literaria Latinoamericana, 1996, Chasqui, 1996, Bulletin of Hispanic Studies, 1997, Revista Canadiense de Estudios Hispánicos, 1997, Hispanic Journal, 1998, Anclajes, 1998, Confluencia, 1999. Contributions to: Encyclopaedias, 1998; Book reviews to Bulletin of Hispanic Studies and Asocíación de Lit Fem Hisp, 1998. Memberships: Modern Language Association; National Coalition of Independent Scholars. Address: 1221 Lexington Court, El Dorado Hills, CA 95762, USA.

ALBANY James. See: **RAE Hugh Crauford.**

ALBEE Edward (Franklin III), b. 12 Mar 1928, Virginia, USA. Playwright. Education: Trinity College, Hartford, Connecticut, 1946-47. Appointments: Lecturer at various US colleges and universities. Publications: Plays: The Zoo Story, 1958; The Death of Bessie Smith, 1959; The Sandbox, 1959; The American Dream, 1960; Who's Afraid of Virginia Woolf?, 1962; Tiny Alice, 1963; A Delicate Balance, 1966; Box, 1970; Quotations from Chairman Mao, 1970; All Over, 1971; Seascape, 1975; Counting the Ways, 1976; Listening, 1977; The Lady from Dubuque, 1979; Finding the Sun, 1982; The Man Who Had Three Arms, 1983; Walking, 1984; Marriage Play, 1987; Three Tall Women, 1991; Fragments, 1993; The Play about the Baby, 1996. Adaptions of: Carson McCuller's The Ballad of the Sad Café, 1963; James Purdy's Malcolm, 1965; Giles Cooper's Everything in the Garden, 1967; Vladimir Nabokov's Lolita, 1980. Honours; Pulitzer Prizes in Drama, 1967, 1975, 1994; American Academy and Institute of Arts and Letters Gold Medal, 1980; Theater Hall of Fame, 1985. Memberships: Dramatists Guild Council; Edward F Albee Foundation, president; International Theatre Institute, president. Address: 14 Harrison Street, New York, NY 10013, USA.

ALBERT Gábor, b. 30 Oct 1929, Hungary. Writer; Essayist. m. Zsuzsanna Marek, 30 Oct 1954, 1 son, 1 daughter. Education: Eötvös Lorand University, 1955. Appointments: Editor-in-Chief, Uj Magyarország, 1991-92, Magyarok Világlapja, 1992-96; Editor, The Pointer, 1994. Publications: Dragon and Octahedron: After Scattering, Essays; Where Are Those Columns; In a Shell; Book of Kings; Heroes of the Failures; Atheist; Final Settlement of a Wedding; Stephen King's Tart Wine, 1993; ...We Have Survived Him, 1996; The Stone Don't Feel It (essays), 1998. Memberships: Association of Hungarian Writers; Association of D Berzsenyi. Address: Erdő u 150, H 2092 Budakeszi, Hungary.

ALBEVERIO MANZONI Solvejg, b. 6 Nov 1939, Arogno, Switzerland. Painter; Writer; Poet. m. Sergio Albeverio, 7 Feb 1970, 1 daughter. Education: Textile Designer, Diploma, Como, Italy, 1960; Art Courses, Zürich, 1969; Drawing and Etching Statens - Kunsthåndverkskole, Oslo, 1972-77. Publications: Da stanze chiuse; Il pensatore con il mantello come meteora; Illustrations to Controcanto al chiuso and All'ombra delle farfalle in fiore; Il fiore, il frutto, triandro donna; Frange di solitudine; Spiagge confinanti. Contributions to: Poems and drawings in literary journals and reviews; Exhibitions, many countries. Honours: Premio Ascona, 1987; Pro Helvetia Prize, 1995. Memberships: Swiss Society of Painters, Sculptors and Architects; Swiss Society of Writers; PEN; Associazione Scrittori della Svizzera Italiana. Address: Auf dem Aspei 55, D-44801 Bochum, Germany.

ALBRIGHT Daniel, b. 29 Oct 1945, Chicago, Illinois, USA. Professor of English; Writer. m. Karin Larson, 18 June 1977, 1 daughter. Education: BA, Rice University, 1967; MPhil, 1969, PhD, 1970, Yale University. Appointments: Assistant Professor, 1970-75, Associate Professor, 1975-81, Professor, 1981-87, University of Virginia; Visiting Professor, University of Munich, 1986-87; Professor, 1987-, Richard L Turner Professor in the Humanities, 1995-, University of Rochester. Publications: The Myth against Myth: A Study of Yeats' Imagination in Old Age, 1972; Personality and Impersonality: Lawrence, Woolf, Mann, 1978; Representation and the Imagination: Beckett, Kafka, Nabokov and Schoenberg, 1981; Lyricality in English Literature, 1985; Tennyson: The Muses' Tug-of-War, 1986; Stravinsky: The Music-Box and the Nightingale, 1989; W B Yeats: The Poems (editor), 1990, 3rd printing, revised, 1994; Quantum Poetics: Yeats, Pound, Eliot, and the Science of Modernism, 1997. Contributions to: Various periodicals. Honours: Phi Beta Kappa, 1966; National Endowment for the Arts Fellowship, 1973-74; Guggenheim Fellowship, 1976-77. Address: 121 Van Voorhis Road, Pittsford, NY 14534, USA.

ALCOCK (Garfield) Vivien, b. 23 Sept 1924, Worthing, England. Author. m. Leon Garfield, 23 Oct 1948, 1 daughter. Education: Oxford School of Art. Publications: The Haunting of Cassie Palmer, 1980; The Stonewalker, 1981; The Sylvia Game, 1982; Travellers by Night, 1983; Ghostly Companions, 1984; The Cuckoo Sister, 1985; The Mysterious Mr Ross, 1987; The Monster Garden, 1988; The Trial of Anna Cotman, 1989; A Kind of Thief, 1991. Membership: Authors Society. Literary Agent: John Johnson. Address: 59 Wood Lane, London N6 5UD, England.

ALDEN Peter Charles, b. 8 July 1944, Concord, Massachusetts, USA. Author; Safari Leader; Cruise Lecturer. Education: BA, Geography, University of Arizona, Tucson. Publications: Finding Birds in Western Mexico, 1969; Finding Birds Around the World, 1982; Peterson First Guide to Mammals (of North America), 1987; National Audubon Society Field Guide to African Wildlife, 1995; Collins Guide to African Wildlife, 1996; National Audubon Society Field Guides to New England, Florida, California, Pacific Northwest, 1998; National Audubon Society Field Guides to Mid-Atlantic, Southeast, Southwest, Rocky Mountains, 1999. Address: 11 Riverside Avenue, Concord, MA 01742, USA.

ALDERSEY-WILLIAMS Hugh Arthur, b. 17 June 1959, London, England. Journalist; Author. m. Moira Morrissey, 2 Sept 1989. Education: BA, 1980, MA, 1984, St John's College, Cambridge. Publications: New American Design, 1988; World Design: Nationalism and Globalism in Design, 1992; The Most Beautiful Molecule: The Discovery of the Buckyball, 1995; Monographs on leading designers and various book chapters. Contributions to: The Independent; Independent on Sunday. Memberships: Society of Authors; Royal Society of Arts. Literary Agent: The Caroline Davidson Literary Agency, 5 Queen Anne's Gardens, London W4 1TU, England.

ALDISS Brian, b. 18 Aug 1925, East Dereham, England. Literary Editor; Writer; Critic. m. (2) Margaret Manson, 11 Dec 1965, 2 sons, 2 daughters. Appointments: President, British Science Fiction Association, 1960-64; Guest of Honour at World Science Fiction Convention, London, 1965, World Science Fiction Convention Brighton, 1979; Chairman, Committee of Management, Society of Authors, 1977-78; Arts Council Literature Panel, 1978-80; Booker McConnell Prize Judge, 1981; Fellow, Royal Society of Literature, 1990. Publications: Novels include: Frankenstein Unbound, 1973; The Malacia Tapestry, 1976; Life in the West, 1980; The Helliconia Trilogy, 1982, 1983, 1985, 1996; Forgotten Life, 1988; Dracula Unbound, 1991; Remembrance Day, 1993; Somewhere East of Life, 1994; Story collections include: Seasons in Flight, 1984; Best SF Stories of Brian W Aldiss, 1988; A Romance of the Equator, Best Fantasy Stories, 1989; A Tupolev Too Far, 1993; The Secret of This book, 1995. Non-Fiction includes: Cities and Stones: A Traveller's Yugoslavia, 1966; Bury My Heart Heart at W H Smith's: A Writing Life, 1990; The Detached Retina (essays), 1995; At the Caligula Hotel (collected poems), 1995; Songs From the Steppes of Central Asia, 1996; The Twinkling of an Eye, 1998; My Life as a Englishman, 1998. Honours: Hugo Awards, 1962, 1987; Nebula Award, 1965; various British Science Fiction Association awards; Ferara Cometa d'Argento, 1977; Prix Jules Verne, Sweden, 1977; Science Fiction Research Association Pilgrim Awards, 1978; First International Association of the Fantastic in the Arts Distinguished Scholarship Award, 1986; J Lloyd Eaton Award, 1988; World Science Fiction President's Award, 1988. Hugo Nomination, 1991. Membership: Royal Society of Literature, fellow. Address: Hambleden, 39 St Andrews Road, Old Headington, Oxford OX3 9DL, England.

ALDRIDGE (Harold Edward) James, b. 10 July 1918, White Hills, Victoria, Australia. Writer. m. Dina Mitchnik, 1942, 2 sons. Appointments: Staff, Herald and Sun, Melbourne, 1937-38, Daily Sketch, and Sunday Dispatch, London, 1939, Australian Newspaper Service and North American Newspaper Alliance, 1939-45, Time and Life, 1944. Publications: Signed with Their Honour, 1942; The Sea Eagle, 1944; Of Many Men, 1946; The Diplomat, 1950; The Hunter, 1951; Heroes of the Empty View, 1954; Underwater Hunting for Inexperienced Englishmen, 1955; I Wish He Would Not Die, 1958; Gold and Sand (short stories), 1960; The Last Exile, 1961; A Captive in the Land, 1962; The Statesman's Game, 1966; My Brother Tom, 1966; The Flying 19, 1966; Living Egypt (with Paul Strand), 1969; Cairo: Biography of a City, 1970; A Sporting Proposition, 1973; The Marvellous Mongolian, 1974; Mockery in Arms, 1974; The Untouchable Juli, 1975; One Last Glimpse, 1977; Goodbye Un-America, 1974; The Broken Saddle, 1983; The True Story of Lola Mackellar, 1993. Honours: Rhys Memorial Award, 1945; Lenin Peace Prize, 1972; Australian Children's Book of the Year Award, 1985; Guardian Children's Fiction Prize, 1986; New South Wales Premier's Literary Award, 1986. Address: c/o Curtis Brown, 28-29 Haymarket, London SW1Y 4SP, England.

ALDRIDGE John Watson, b. 26 Sept 1922, Sioux City, Iowa, USA. Literary Critic; Educator. m. (2) Patricia McGuire Eby, 16 July 1983, 5 sons, previous marriage. Education: BA, University of California, Berkeley, 1947. Appointments: Lecturer, Christian Gauss seminars in criticism, Princeton University, 1953-54, Breadloaf Writers Conference, 1966-69; Special Advisor on American Studies, The American Embassy, Bonn, Germany, 1972-73; Rockefeller Humanities Fellowship, 1976; Book

Critic, MacNeil/Lehrer TV News, 1983-84. Publications: After the Lost Generation, 1951; In Search of Heresy, 1956; The Party at Cranton (novel) 1960; Time to Murder and Create, 1966; In the Country of the Young, 1970; The Devil in the Fire, 1972; The American Novel and the Way We Live Now, 1983; Talents and Technicians, 1992; Classics and Contemporaries, criticism, 1992. Literary Agent: Gerard F McCauley. Address: 1050 Wall Street, No 4C, Ann Arbor, MI 48105, USA.

ALDRIDGE Sarah. See: **MARCHANT Anyda.**

ALDYNE Nathan. See: **McDOWELL Michael.**

ALEGRIA Claribel, b. 12 May 1924, Esteli, Nicaragua. Writer; Poet. m. Darwin J Flakoll, 29 Dec 1947, dec 1995, 1 son, 3 daughters. Education: BA, George Washington University, Washington, DC, USA. Publications: Anillo de Silencio, 1948; Suite, 1950; Vigilias, 1953; Acuario, 1955; Huesped de mi Tiempo, 1961; Via Unica, 1965; Aprendizenje, 1972; Pagare a Cobrar y Otros Poemas, 1973; Sobevivo, 1978; Suma y Sigue, 1981; Y este Poema Rio, 1989; Luisa en El Pais de la Realidad, 1989; Fugues, 1993; Thresholds, 1996. Contributions to: Many periodicals. Honours: Premio Casa de las Americas, Havana, Cuba, 1978; Doctor Honoris Causa, University of Eastern Connecticut, 1998. Address: Apartado Postal A-36, Managua, Nicaragua.

ALEMANY-VALDEZ Herminia M, b. 16 June 1961, Chicago, Illinois, USA. Spanish and Literature Instructor. m. Juan Irizarry-Rivera, 22 Mar 1986. Education: BA, 1986, MA, 1991, Universidad de Puerto Rico, Mayaguez; PhD, Universidad Nacional Autónoma de México. Appointment: Board of Editors, El Cuervo, Universidad de Puerto Rico, Aguadilla, 1996. Publications: Galería de mujeres: La mujer en Album de familia y Papeles de Pandora, 1994; Abriendo la caja de Pandora: La obra de Rosario Castellanos y Rosario Ferré; El proceso de la creación en la recreación: lo mítico indígena en la obra de Rosario Castellanos. Contributions to: Periodicals and journals. Memberships: Instituto Literario y Cultural Hispánico; International Society for Luso-Hispanic Humor Studies; Modern Languages Association; Asociación de Literatura Femenina Hispánica; Instituto Internacional de Literatura Iberoamericana. Address: PO Box 5640, Mayaguez, Puerto Rico 00681, USA.

ALEX Peter. See: **HAINING Peter Alexander.**

ALEXANDER Caroline Elizabeth, b. 13 Mar 1956, Florida, USA. Writer. Education: BA, Florida State University, 1977; BA, Oxford University, 1980; PhD, Columbia University, 1991. Publications: One Dry Season: In the Footsteps of Mary Kingsley, 1990; The Way to Xanadu, 1994; Battle's End; Mrs Chippy's Last Expedition, 1997; The Endurance, 1998. Contributions to: New Yorker; Smithsonian; Independent; Sunday Telegraph Weekend Magazine; Others. Honours: Mellon Fellowship; Rhodes Scholarship. Memberships: American Philological Society; Royal Geographical Society. Address: c/o Anthony Sheil, 43 Doughty Street, London WC1 N2LF, England.

ALEXANDER Christine Anne, b. 9 July 1949, Hastings, New Zealand. Associate Professor; Writer. m. Peter Fraser Alexander, 18 June 1977, 1 son, 1 daughter. Education: BA, 1970, MA, 1971, University of Canterbury; PhD, University of Cambridge, 1978. Appointments: Assistant Lectureship, University of Canterbury, 1972; Tutor, 1978-83, Lecturer, 1986-88, Senior Lecturer, 1988-92, Associate Professor, 1993-, University of New South Wales, Australia. Publications: Bibliography of the Manuscripts of Charlotte Brontë, 1982; The Early Writings of Charlotte Brontë, 1983; An Edition of the Early Writings of Charlotte Brontë, 3 volumes, 1987-; The Art of the Brontës, 1994. Contributions to: Books and journals. Honours: New Zealand Postgraduate Scholarships; New Zealand University Womens Fellowship; Travel Grants; Special Research Grants; British Academy Rose Mary Crawshay Prize, 1984; Australian Research Council Senior Research Fellowship; Fellow, Australian Academy of the Humanities, 1995. Memberships: Brontë Society;

Australasian Language and Literature Association; Australian Victorian Studies Association; Australian and South Pacific Association for Comparative Literary Studies; Cambridge Society; Jane Austen Society; Association for the Study of Australian Literature; Bibliographical Society of Australia and New Zealand; Society for Textual Scholarship; Society for the History of Authorship, Reading and Publishing. Address: School of English, University of New South Wales, Sydney, New South Wales 2052, Australia.

ALEXANDER Doris Muriel, b. 14 Dec 1922, Newark, New Jersey, USA. Professor; Writer. Education: BA, University of Missouri, 1944; MA, University of Pennsylvania, 1946; PhD, New York University, 1952. Appointments: Instructor, Rutgers University, 1950-56; Associate Professor, then Department Chairman, City University of New York, 1956-62. Publications: The Tempering of Eugene O'Neill, 1962; Creating Characters with Charles Dickens, 1991; Eugene O'Neill's Creative Struggle, 1992; Creating Literature Out of Life, 1996. Contributions to: Many journals. Honours: Penfield Fellowship, New York University, 1946; Fulbright Professor, University of Athens, 1966-67. Memberships: Trustee, Dickens Society; Association of Literary Scholars and Critics; Eugene O'Neill Society. Literary Agent: Gunther Stuhlmann. Address: San Trovaso 1116, Dorsoduro, 30123 Venice, Italy.

ALEXANDER Francis. See: **HEATH-STUBBS John.**

ALEXANDER Gary (Roy), b. 18 Jan 1941, Bremerton, Washington, USA. Writer. m. Shari, 9 Aug 1969, 3 daughters. Education: Olympic Community College; University of Washington. Publications: Pigeon Blood, 1988; Unfunny Money, 1989; Kiet and the Golden Peacock, 1989; Kiet and the Opium War, 1990; Deadly Drought, 1991; Dead Dinosaurs, 1994. Contributions to: Many stories in magazines. Membership: Mystery Writers of America. Address: 6709 South 238th Place, H-102, Kent, WA 98032, USA.

ALEXANDER Lloyd (Chudley), b. 30 Jan 1924, Philadelphia, Pennsylvania, USA. Writer. m. Janine Denni, 8 Jan 1946, 1 daughter. Education: West Chester State Teachers College, 1942; Lafayette College, 1943; Sorbonne, University of Paris, 1946. Appointment: Author-in-Residence, Temple University, 1970-74. Publications: And Let the Credit Go, 1955; My Five Tigers, 1956; Janine is French, 1958; My Love Affair with Music, 1960; Park Avenue Vet (with Louis Camuti), 1962; Fifty Years in the Doghouse, 1963; My Cats and Me: The Story of an Understanding, 1989; Juvenile Books: Border Hawk: August Bondi, 1959; Aaron Lopez and the Flagship Hope, 1960; Time Cat: The Remarkable Journeys of Jason and Gareth, 1963; Coll and His White Pig, 1965; The Truthful Harp, 1967; The Marvelous Misadventures of Sebastian, 1970; The King's Fountain, 1971; The Four Donkeys, 1972; The Foundling and Other Tales of Prydain, 1973; The Cat Who Wished to Be a Man, 1973; The Wizard in the Tree, 1975; The Town Cats and Other Tales, 1977; The First Two Lives of Lukas-Kasha, 1978; The Remarkable Journey of Prince Jen, 1991; The Fortune-Tellers, 1992; The House Gobbaleen, 1995; The Arkadians, 1995; The Iron Ring, 1997; Gypsy Rizka, 1999. Honours: Newbery Honor Book, 1965; Newbery Medal, 1969; National Book Award, 1971; Drexel Awards, 1972, 1976; American Book Award, 1982; Austrian Children's Book Award, 1984; Regina Medal, Catholic Library Association, 1986; Church and Synagogue Library Association Award, 1987; Lifetime Achievement Award, Pennsylvania Center for the Book in Philadelphia, 1991; Horn Book Award, 1993. Memberships: Amnesty International; Authors Guild; Authors League of America; PEN. Address: 1005 Drexel Avenue, Drexel Hill, PA 19026, USA.

ALEXANDER Louis George, b. 1932. Writer. Publications: Sixty Steps, 1962; Poetry and Prose Appreciation, 1963; A First Book in Comprehension, 1965; Essays and Letter Writing, 1965; The Carters of Greenwood, 1966; Detectives from Scotland Yard, 1966; April Fools Day, 1966; New Concept English (4 volumes),

1967; Worth a Fortune, 1967; Question and Answer, 1967; For and Against, 1968; Look, Listen and Learn, Sets 1-4, 1968-71; Reading and Writing English, 1969; Car Thieves, 1969; K's First Case, 1975; Good Morning, Mexico!, 1975; Operation Janus, 1976; Clint Magee, 1976; Dangerous Game, 1977; Some Methodological Implications of Waystage and Threshold Level, Council of Europe, 1977; Follow Me, 1979; Survive in French/Spanish/German/Italian, 1980; Conversational French/Spanish/German/Italian, 1981; Excel, 1985-87; Plain English, 1987-88; Longman English Grammar, 1988-89; Longman English Grammar Practice, 1990; Step by Step 1-3, 1991; Longman Advanced Grammar, 1993; The Essential English Grammar, 1993; Right Word, Wrong Word, 1994; Direct English, 1994-97. Address: Flat 6, 23 Down Street, London W1Y 7DN, England.

ALEXANDER Meena, b. 17 Feb 1951, Allahabad, India. Writer; Poet; Professor. m. David Lelyveld, 1 May 1979, 1 son, 1 daughter. Education: BA, Khartoum University, 1969; PhD, Nottingham University, 1973. Appointments: Lecturer, Miranda House, Delhi University, 1974, Jawaharlal Nehru University, 1975, Central Institute of English and Foreign Languages, Hyderabad, 1975-77; Lecturer, 1977-79, Reader, 1979, University of Hyderabad; Assistant Professor, Fordham University, 1980-87, Hunter College, 1987-89; Associate Professor, Member, Graduate Faculty, City University of New York, 1989-92; Lecturer in Poetry, Columbia University, 1991-; Professor of English and Women's Studies, Hunter College and the Graduate Center, City University of New York, 1992-. Publications: The Bird's Bright Ring (poem), 1976; In the Middle Earth (play), 1977; Without Place, 1977; I Root My Name, 1977; The Poetic Self: Towards a Phenomenology of Romanticism, 1979; Stone Roots, 1980; House of a Thousand Doors (poetry and prose), 1988; Women in Romanticism: Mary Wollstonecraft, Dorothy Wordsworth and Mary Shelley, 1989; The Storm: A Poem in Five Parts, 1989; Nampally Road (novel) 1991; Night-Scene: The Garden (poem), 1992; Fault Lines (memoir), 1993; River and Bridge (poems), 1995, expanded edition, 1996; The Shock of Arrival: Reflections on Postcolonial Experience (poetry and prose), 1996; Manhattan Music (novel), 1997. Contributions to: Poetry and prose in various publications. Honours: Altrusa International Award, 1973; MacDowell Fellow, 1993; International Writer-in-Residence, Arts Council of England, 1995; Lila Wallace Writer-in-Residence, Asian American Renaissance, Minneapolis, 1995; Various grants. Memberships: Modern Language Association; PEN American Centre. Literary Agent: Ellen Levine. Address: English Department, Hunter College, CUNY, 695 Park Avenue, New York, NY 10025, USA.

ALEXANDER Sue, b. 20 Aug 1933, Tucson, Arizona, USA. Writer. m., 2 sons, 1 daughter. Education: Drake University, 1950-52; Northwestern University, 1952-53. Publications: Small Plays for You and a Friend, 1973; Nadir of the Streets, 1975; Peacocks Are Very Special, 1976; Witch, Goblin and Sometimes Ghost, 1976; Smalls Plays for Special Days, 1977; Marc the Magnificent, 1978; More Witch, Goblin and Ghost Stories, 1978; Seymour the Prince, 1979; Finding Your First Job, 1980; Whatever Happened to Uncle Albert? and Other Plays, 1980; Witch, Goblin and Ghost in the Haunted Woods, 1981; Witch, Goblin and Ghost's Book of Things to Do, 1982; Nadia the Willful, 1983; Dear Phoebe, 1984; World Famous Muriel, 1984; Witch, Goblin and Ghost Are Back, 1985; World Famous Muriel and the Scary Dragon, 1985; America's Own Holidays, 1986; Lila on the Landing, 1987; There's More - Much More, 1987; World Famous Muriel and the Magic Mystery, 1990; Who Goes Out on Halloween?, 1990; Sara's City, 1995; What's Wrong Now, Millicent, 1996. Literary Agent: Marilyn E Marlow/Curtis Brown Ltd. Address: 6846 McLaren, Canoga Park, CA 91307, USA.

ALFEROVA Lubov, b. 7 Apr 1946, Riga, Latvia. Journalist; Writer. m. Grigorev Igor, 30 Oct 1982, 1 daughter. Education: Degree, University of Leningrad, St Petersburg, 1969. Appointments: Correspondent Journalist, Sovetskaja Molodej, 1969, Rabochee Slovo, 1971, Sovetskaja Molodej, 1973, Energostoroitel, 1974,

Latinform Agency News, 1975, PH Liesma, 1980, PH Avots, 1981, Jelernodorgnik Pribaltic, 1983-87. Publications: The Way Through Sunlight and Rain, 1973; Wonder of Nicola Burikin, 1977; The Old yard, 1979; The Blue Gobelin, 1980; The Summerly Cold Weather, 1981; The Platinum Hoop, 1982; The Night into Different Dimension, 1982; The Crystal Medusa, 1985. Membership: Union of Latvian Writers. Address: Salaspili Rigas iela 2 dz 11, Riga, LV-2121, Latvia.

ALFRED William, b. 16 Aug 1922, New York, New York, USA. Dramatist; Professor of English. Education: BA, Brooklyn College, 1948; MA, 1949, PhD, 1954, Harvard University. Appointments: Associate Editor, American Poet magazine, Brooklyn, 1942-44; Instructor, 1954-57, Assistant Professor, 1957-59, Associate Professor, 1959-63, Professor of English, 1963-, Harvard University. Publications: Plays: The Annunciation Rosary, 1948; Agamemnon, 1953; Hogan's Goat, 1965, revised as Cry for Us All, 1970; The Curse of an Aching Heart, 1979; Holy Saturday, 1980. Editor: Complete Prose Works of John Milton, Vol I (with others), 1953. Translator: Beowulf, 1963. Honours: Brooklyn College Literary Association Award, 1953; Amy Lowell Traveling Poetry Scholarship, 1956; Brandeis University Creative Arts Award, 1960; American Academy and Institute of Arts and Letters Grant, 1965. Address: 31 Athens Street, Cambridge, MA 02138, USA.

ALIOTH Gabrielle, b. 21 Apr 1955, Basel, Switzerland. Writer. m. Martin Alioth, 7 Sept 1979. Education: Master of Economics, Universities of Basel and Salzburg. Appointments: Economist, Prognos AG, Basel; Arbeitsgruppe für Konjunkturforschung, BAK; Assistant Lecturer, Operations Research, University of Basel. Publications: Novels: Der Narr, 1990; Wie ein kostbarer Stein, 1994; Die Arche der Frauen, 1996; Die stumme Reiterin, 1998; Short stories and essays in various anthologies. Contributions to: Arts sections of Swiss and Austrian daily newspapers and periodicals; Features for German radio. Honour: Hamburger Literaturpreis for Der Narr, 1991. Memberships: PEN Centre for German-Speaking Writers Abroad; Gruppe Olten. Address: Rosemount, Julianstown, Co Meath, Ireland.

ALLABY John Michael, b. 18 Sept 1933, Belper, Derbyshire, England. Author; Editor. m. Ailsa Marthe McGregor, 3 Jan 1957, 1 son, 1 daughter. Publications: Inventing Tomorrow, 1976; Dictionary of the Environment, 1977, 4th edition, 1994; The Oxford Dictionary of Natural History, 1980; A Year in the Life of a Field, 1981; Animal Artisans, 1982; The Greening of Mars, 1984; The Concise Oxford Dictionary of Earth Sciences, 1986, 2nd edition, 1998; All the National Trails in England and Wales, 1987; Conservation at Home, 1988; Guide to Gaia, 1989; Concise Oxford Dictionary of Zoology, 1991, 2nd edition, 1998; Concise Oxford Dictionary of Botany, 1992, 2nd edition, 1998; Elements: Air, 1992; Elements: Water, 1992; Elements: Fire, 1993; Elements: Earth, 1993; The Concise Oxford Dictionary of Ecology, 1994, 2nd edition, 1998; Facing the Future, 1995; Basic Environmental Science, 1996; Dangerous Weather, 6 vols, 1998; Temperate Forests, 1998. Contributions to: Newspapers and magazines. Memberships: Association of British Science Writers; New York Academy of Sciences; Society of Authors. Address: Penquite, Fernleigh Road, Wadebridge, Cornwall Pl27 7BB, England.

ALLAN Elkan. b. 8 Dec 1922, London, England. Journalist. Appointments: Writer, Odhams Press, 1950-55; Writer, Producer, Executive and Head of Entertainment, Rediffusion Television, 1955-66; Television Columnist, Sunday Times, 1966-82; Editor, Video Viewer, 1982-83; Columnist, Video Week, 1983-; Listings Editor, 1986-88, Senior Editor, 1988-, The Independent. Publications: Quiz Team, 1945; Living Opinion (editor), 1946; Good Listening: A Survey of Broadcasting, (with D M Robinson), 1948; The Sunday Times Guide to Movies on Television, (with A Allan), 1973, 2nd edition, 1980; Video Year Book (editor), 1984, 1985; 10 monographs on Silent Films Makers, 1990-. Contributions to: Senior Editor, The Independent. Honours: Triple Berlin TV Awards, 1965; British Press Awards, 1988. Address: The Independent, 40 City Road, London EC1Y 2DB, England.

ALLAN Keith, b. 27 Mar 1943, London, England. Linguist; Writer. m. Wendy F Allen, 1 Jan 1993, 2 daughters. Education: BA Hons, Leeds University, 1964; MLitt 1970, PhD 1977, Edinburgh University. Publications: Linguistic Meaning, 2 volumes, 1986; Euphemism and Dysphemism: Language Used as Shield and Weapon (with Kate Burridge), 1991. Contributions to: Many articles in professional journals on various topics in linguistics. Honour: Fellow, Australian Academy of Humanities, 1995-. Address: Linguistics Department, Monash University, Clayton, 3168, Australia.

ALLAN Mabel Esther, (Jean Estoril, Priscilla Hagon, Anne Pilgrim), b. 11 Feb 1915, Wallasey, Cheshire, England. Author. Publications: A Dream of Hunger Moss, 1983; The Pride of Pine Street, 1985; The Rod to Huntingland, 1986; The Crumble Lane Mystery, 1987; Up the Victorian Staircse, 1987; First Term at Ash Grove, 1988; Drina Ballerina, 1991; Over 150 other books. Contributions to: Over 320 Short Stories; Articles; Poetry. Honours: Various Honours and Awards. Literary Agent: Curtis Brown Ltd. Address: 11 Oldfield Way, Heswall, Wirral L60 6RQ, England.

ALLASON Rupert William Simon, b. 8 Nov 1951, London, England. Author. m. Nicole Van Moppes, 15 June 1979, diss 1996, 1 son, 1 daughter. Education: Downside School, Bath, England; University of Grenoble, France; University of London, England. Appointments: Member of Parliament (Con) for Torbay, 1987-97; Editor, World Intelligence Review, 1985-. Publications: SPY!, with Richard Deacon, 1980; British Security Service Operations 1909-45, Bodley Head, 1981; A Matter of Trust: MI5 1945-72, 1982; MI6: British Secret Intelligence Service Operations 1909-45, 1983; The Branch: A History of the Metropolitan Police Special Branch, 1983; Unreliable Witness: Espionage Myths of the Second World War, 1984; GARBO, co-authored with Juan Pjujol, 1985; GCHQ: The Secret Wireless War, 1986; Molehunt, 1987; The Friends: Britain's Postwar Secret Intelligence Operations, 1988; Games of Intelligence, 1989; Seven Spies Who Changed the World, 1991; Secret War: The Story of SOE, 1992; The Faber Book of Espionage, 1993; The Illegals, 1993; The Faber Book of Treachery, 1995; The Secret War for the Falklands, 1997; Counterfeit Spies, 1998; Crown Jewels, 1998. Literary Agent: Peters, Frasser and Dunlop. Address: 503/4 The Chambers, Chelsea Harbour, London SW10 0XF, England.

ALLBEURY Theodore Edward le Bouthillier, (Ted Allbeury, Richard Butler, Patrick Kelly), b. 20 Oct 1917. Author. Publications: A Choice of Enemies, 1973; Snowball, 1974; The Special Collection, 1975; Palomino Blonde, 1975; The Only Good German, 1976; Moscow Quadrille, 1976; The Man with the President's Mind, 1977; The Lantern Network, 1978; Consequence of Fear, 1979; The Alpha List, 1979; The Twentieth Day of January, 1980; The Reaper, 1980; The Other Side of Silence, 1981; The Secret Whispers, 1981; All Our Tomorrows, 1982; Shadow of Shadows, 1982; Pay Any Price, 1983; The Judas Factor, 1984; No Place To Hide, 1984; The Girl from Addis, 1984; Children of Tender Years, 1985; The Choice, 1986; The Seeds of Treason, 1986; The Crossing, 1987; A Wilderness of Mirrors, 1988; Deep Purple, 1989; A Time Without Shadows, 1990; Other Kinds of Treason, 1990; Dangerous Edge, 1991; Show Me a Hero, 1992; The Line Crosser, 1993; As Time Goes By, 1994; Beyond the Silence, 1995; The Long Run, 1996; Aid and Comfort, 1997; Shadow of a Doubt, 1998. As Patrick Kelly: Codeword Cromwell, 1980; The Lonely Margins, 1981. As Richard Butler: Where All the Girls are Sweeter, 1975; Italian Assets, 1976. Membership: Society of Authors. Literary Agent: Blake Friedmann Literary Agency. Address: Cheriton House, Furnace Lane, Lamberhurst, Kent, England.

ALLCOT Guy. See: **POCOCK Tom.**

ALLDRITT Keith, b. 10 Dec 1935, Wolverhampton, England. Professor of English; Writer. m. Joan Hardwick, 10 Apr 1980, 1 son, 1 daughter. Education: BA, MA, St Catherine's College, Cambridge. Publications: The Making of George Orwell, 1969; The Visual Imagination of D H Lawrence, 1970; The Good Pit Man, 1975; The Lover Next Door, 1977; Elgar on the Journey to Hanley, 1978; Poetry as Chamber Music, 1978; Modernism in the Second World War, 1989; Churchill the Writer: His Life as a Man of Letters, 1992; The Greatest of Friends: Franklin Roosevelt and Winston Churchill 1939-45, 1995. Honour: Fellow, Royal Society of Literature. Memberships: Arnold Bennett Society; Society of Authors; D H Lawrence Society; International Churchill Society; Modern Language Association. Literary Agent: Murray Pollinger Agency. Address: 48 Church Street, Lichfield, Staffordshire WS13 6ED, England.

ALLEN Blair H, b. 2 July 1933, Los Angeles, California, USA. Writer; Poet; Editor; Artist. m. Juanita Aguilar Raya, 27 Jan 1968, 1 son, 1 daughter. Education: AA, San Diego City College, 1964; University of Washington, 1965-66; BA, San Diego State University, 1970. Appointments: Book Reviewer, Los Angeles Times, 1977-78; Special Feature Editor, Cerulean Press and Kent Publications, 1982-. Publications: Televisual Poems for Bloodshot Eyeballs, 1973; Malice in Blunderland, 1974; N/Z, 1979; The Atlantis Trilogy, 1982; Dreamwish of the Magician, 1983; Right Through the Silver Lined 1984 Looking Glass, 1984; The Magical World of David Cole (editor), 1984; Snow Summits in the Sun (editor), 1988; Trapped in a Cold War Travelogue, 1991; May Burning into August, 1992; The Subway Poems, 1993; Bonfire on the Beach, by John Brander (editor), 1993; The Cerulean Anthology of Sci-Fi/Outer Space/Fantasy/Poetry and Prose Poems (editor), 1995; When the Ghost of Cassandra Whispers in My Ears, 1996; Ashes Ashes All Fall Down, 1997; Around the World in 56 Days, 1998. Contributions to: Numerous periodicals. Honours: 1st Prize for Poetry, Pacificus Foundation Competition, 1992; Various other honours and awards. Memberships: Association for Applied Poetry; Beyond Baroque Foundation; California State Poetry Society; Medina Foundation. Address: 9651 Estacia Court, Cucamonga, CA 91730, USA.

ALLEN Carol, b. 8 Aug 1941, Hatfield, England. Writer; Broadcaster; Producer. m. 15 June 1973, div Aug 1978. Education: Central School of Speech & Drama, University of London; Diploma (Drama) and Teaching Diploma. Appointments: Production Assistant, BBC TV, 1963-65; Producer, COI (Radio), 1966-70; Freelance Writer, Broadcaster, 1970-79; Presenter/Newsreader/Cinema Specialist, LBC Radio, 1980-87; Freelance Writer/Broadcaster, 1987-. Publications: The Virgin Encyclopaedia of the Movies, part author, 1995; As Cat's Whiskers: Producer/Script Development Various Series BBC Radio, including The Man Who Put the Rainbow Into Oz (with Ned Sherrin); Screenplays in Development (co-author Peter Thornton) include The Escape of Charles II; If Winter Comes' (Three Lions). Contributions to: Arts Features/Profiles and Reviews: The Times, The Independent, New Woman, Cosmopolitan. Honours: Radio Times Drama Award, 1990. Membership: Critics Circle, 1989-. Literary Agent: Gilly Schuster, Cecily Ware Agents, 19C John Spencer Square, N1 2CX, England. Address: Cat's Whiskers Productions, 132 Dawes Road, London SW6 7EF, England.

ALLEN Diogenes, b. 17 Oct 1932, Lexington, Kentucky, USA. Professor of Philosophy; Writer. m. Jane Mary Billing, 8 Sept 1958, 3 sons, 1 daughter. Education: BA, University of Kentucky, 1954; Princeton University, 1954-55; BA with Honours, 1957, MA, 1961, Oxford University; BD, 1959, MA, 1962, PhD, 1965, Yale University. Appointments: Ordained, Presbyterian Church, 1959; Pastor, Windham Presbyterian Church, New Hampshire, 1958-61; Assistant Professor, 1964-66, Associate Professor, 1966-67, York University, Toronto; Associate Professor, 1967-74, Professor of Philosophy, 1974-81, Chairman, Department of Theology, 1977-79, 1988-91, Stuart Professor of Philosophy, 1981-,

Princeton Theological Seminary. Publications: Leibniz' Theodicy (editor), 1966; The Reasonableness of Faith, 1968; Finding Our Father, 1974, 2nd edition as The Path of Perfect Love, 1992; Between Two Worlds, 1977, 2nd edition as Temptation, 1986; Traces of God in a Frequently Hostile World, 1981; Three Outsiders: Pascal, Kierkegaard and Simone Weil, 1983; Mechanical Explanations and the Ultimate Origin of the Universe According to Leibniz, 1983; Philosophy for Understanding Theology, 1985; Love: Christian Romance, Marriage and Friendship, 1987; Christian Relief in a Postmodern World: The Full Wealth of Conviction, 1989; Quest: The Search for Meaning Through Christ, 1990; Primary Reading in Philosophy for Understanding Theology (editor with Eric O Sprinsted), 1992; Nature, Spirit, and Community: Issues in the Thought of Yesterday for Help Today, (with Eric Springsted 1997. Contributions to: Scholarly books and journals. Honours: Rhodes Scholar, 1955-57, 1963-64; Rockefeller Doctoral Fellow, 1962-64; Canada Council Fellowship, 1966; Outstanding Educator of America, 1974; Research Fellowships, Association of Theological Schools, 1975-76, Center of Theological Inquiry, 1985-86, 1994-95; Pew Evangelical Scholarship, 1991-92; John Templeton Awards in Science and Theology, 1992, 1993, and Prize for Best Courses in Science and Religion, 1995. Memberships: American Philosophical Association; American Theological Society; American Weil Society, co-founder and executive board member; Association étude pensées S Weil; Canadian Philosophical Association; Leibniz Gesellschaft; Society of Christian Philosophers. Address: 133 Cedar Lane, Princeton, NJ 08540, USA.

ALLEN John. See: **PERRY Ritchie.**

ALLEN Malcolm Dennis, b. 20 Oct 1951, Wakefield, England. Associate Professor of English; Writer. m. Susan Beatrice Anne Whitehead, 24 Nov 1979, 2 sons, 2 daughters. Education: BA with Honours in English and French Studies, University of Lancaster, 1974; MA in English, Louisiana State University, 1975; PhD in English, Pennsylvania State Univesrity, 1983. Appointments: Instructor, University of London, 1982-83; Tutor-Counsellor, The Open University, London Region, 1982-83; Lecturer, 1983-84, Assistant Professor of English, 1984-89, University of Jordan; Visiting Assistant Professor of English, Pennsylvania State University, Wilkes-Barre Campus, 1989-90; Assistant Professor of English, 1990-94; Associate Professor of English, 1994-, University of Wisconsin, Fox Valley. Publication: The Medievalism of Lawrence of Arabia, 1991. Contributions to: Reference works, scholarly books and journals. Memberships: Association of Literary Scholars and Critics; National Association of Scholars; T E Lawrence Society; Wisconsin Association of Scholars. Address: c/o University of Wisconsin, Fox Valley, 1478 Midway Road, Menasha, WI 54952, USA.

ALLEN Oliver E, b. 29 June 1922, Cambridge, Massachusetts, USA. Writer. m. Deborah Hutchison, 8 May 1948, 3 sons, 2 daughters. Education: AB, Harvard University, 1943. Publications: New York, New York; Gardening with the New Small Plants; Wildflower Gardening; Decorating With Plants; Pruning & Grafting; Shade Gardens; Winter Gardens; The Windjammers; The Airline Builders; The Pacific Navigators; Building Sound Bones & Muscles; The Atmosphere; Secrets of a Good Digestion; The Vegetable Gardener's Journal; The Tiger, 1993. Contributions to: Horticulture Magazine; American Heritage; Smithsonian. Literary Agent: Curtis Brown Ltd. Address: 42 Hudson Street, New York, NY 10013, USA.

ALLEN Paula Gunn, b. 1939, Cubero, New Mexico, USA. Writer; Poet; University Lecturer. Education: BA; MFA; PhD. Appointments: Lecturer, San Francisco State University, University of New Mexico, Fort Lewis College, University of California at Berkeley. Publications: The Blind Lion, 1974; Sipapu: A Cultural Perspective, 1975; Coyote's Daylight Trip, 1978; A Cannon Between My Knees, 1981; From the Center: A Folio of Native American Art and Poetry (editor), 1981; Shadow Country, 1982; Studies of American Indian Literature: Critical Essays and Course Designs (editor), 1983; The Woman Who Owned the Shadows, 1983; The Sacred Hoop: Recovering the Feminine in American Indian Traditions (essays), 1986, new edition, 1992; Skins and Bones, 1988; Spider Woman's Granddaughters: Traditional Tales and Contemporary Writing by Native American Women (editor), 1989; Grandmothers of the Light: A Medicine Woman's Sourcebook, 1991; Columbus and Beyond, 1992; Voice of the Turtle, 1994. Honours: American Book Award, 1990; Ford Foundation Grant; National Endowment for the Arts Award. Address: c/o Diane Cleaver Inc, 55 Fifth Avenue, 15th Floor, New York, NY 10003, USA.

ALLEN Roberta, b. 6 Oct 1945, New York, New York, USA. Writer. Appointments: Creative Writing Instructor, Parsons School of Design, 1986; Guest Lecturer, Murdoch University, Perth, Australia, 1989; Instructor, The Writer's Voice, 1992-97, 1996, The New School, 1993-97, 1998, New York University, 1998, Continuing Education, 1993-95. Publications: The Traveling Woman, 1986; The Daughter, 1992; Amazon Dream, 1993; Certain People, 1996; Fast Fiction, 1997. Contributions to: Various anthologies, journals and periodicals. Honours: LINE grant, 1985; Yaddo Fellowships, 1987, 1993; VCCA, 1994. Membership: PEN. Literary Agent: Georges Borchadt Inc. Address: 5 West 16th Street, New York, NY 10011, USA.

ALLEN Steve, (Stephen Valentine Patrick Allen), b. 26 Dec 1921, New York, New York, USA. Entertainer; Author; Songwriter. m. (1) Dorothy Goodman, 23 Aug 1943, 3 sons, (2) Jayne Meadows, 31 July 1954, 1 son. Education: Drake University, 1941; State Teachers College, Arizona, 1942. Appointments: Comedian, Mutual Broadcasting System, 1945; Entertainer, CBS, 1948-50; Creator-Host, The Tonight Show, NBC-TV, 1953-57; Host, The Steve Allen Show, NBC-TV, 1956-60, WBC Syndicate, 1961-64, I've Got a Secret, 1964-67; Laughback, 1976-77; Creator-Host, Meeting of Minds, PBS-TV, 1977-81. Publications: Some 45 books, including: The Funny Men, 1956; The Question Man, 1959; Not All of Your Laughter, Not All of Your Tears, 1962; Letter to a Conservative, 1965; Bigger Than a Breadbox, 1967; Funny People, 1981; The Talk Show Murders, 1982; More Funny People, 1982; Beloved Son: A Story of the Jesus Cults, 1982; How to Be Funny, 1987; Murder on the Glitter Box, 1989; Dumbth: And 81 Ways to Make Americans Smarter, 1989; The Public Hating, 1990; Steve Allen on the Bible, Religion and Morality, 1990; Hi-Ho, Steverino: My Adventures in the Wonderful Wacky World of TV, 1992; More Steve Allen on the Bible, Religion and Morality, 1993; Reflections, 1994; Murder on the Atlantic, 1995; The Man Who Turned Back the Clock and Other Short Stories, 1995. Other: Over 7,000 songs. Honours: Grammy Award, 1964; TV Hall of Fame, 1986; Gala 75th Birthday Tribute, PBS-TV, 1997. Address: c/o Meadowlane Entertainment Inc, 15201 Burbank Boulevard, Suite B, Van Nuys, CA 91411, USA.

ALLENDE Isabel, b. 2 Aug 1942, Lima, Peru. Writer. m. William C Gordon, 17 July 1988, 1 son, 1 daughter. Publications: The House of the Spirits, 1982; Of Love and Shadows, 1984; Eva Luna, 1986; The Stories of Eva Luna, 1988; The Infinite Plan, 1991; Paula, 1994; Aphrodite, 1997. Address: c/o Carmen Balcells, Diagonal 580, Barcelona 21, Spain.

ALLISON Michael John, b. 30 June 1940. Consultant; Writer. m. Janette Eaves Morse, 10 Mar 1967, 2 sons. Education: Ordinary Certificate in Mechanical Engineering, Ipswich Civic College, England, 1956-58; HND in Mechanical Engineering, North East Essex Technical College, England, 1958-61; Fellowship Diploma in Mechanical Engineering, 1974-76; Graduate Diploma in Quality Technology, AOQ Prize, 1976-79, RMIT; Cert Quality Engineer, American Society for Quality Control. Appointments: Project Engineer, Product Engineering, Ford Motor Company, Geelong, 1964-67; Manufacturing Research Engineer, Boeing Co, Seattle, USA, 1967-70; Manager of Product Engineering and Quality Control, Flexdrive Inds Pty Ltd, Melbourne, 1971-78; Class 2 through to Principal Engineer, 1978-88; Supervising Engineer, TQM Dev, TNE Metro, 1988-90; Australian Telecomms Corp, Melbourne; Consultant for various industries, Stockdales Pty Ltd, Melbourne, 1990-; Visiting Lecturer, Auckland Institute of Technology. Publications: Counting Out Random Numbers, in Your Computer, 1989; Quality Systems (audio tape), 1992; Productivity Improvement Through Quality Management, 1993; The Conversion Kit: The Guide to Problem Busting, 1994; Service Quality Systems (audio tape), 1995. Honours: Managing Director's Prize, Ransomes & Rapier Ltd; Shilkin Prize for Literature in the Field of Quality, 1994. Memberships: Chairman of Certification Committee, Council, Australian Organization for Quality, Victoria Division; Australian Society of Authors; American Society for Quality Control. Address: 8 Brixton Avenue, Eltham, Vic 3095, Australia.

ALLOTT Miriam, b. 16 June 1920, London, England. Professor of English Emeritus; Writer. m. Kenneth Allott, 2 June 1951, dec 1973. Education: MA, 1946, PhD, 1949, University of Liverpool. Appointments: Lecturer to Reader in English Literature, 1948-73, Andrew Cecil Bradley Professor of Modern English Literature, 1973-81, University of Liverpool; Professor of English, 1981-85, Professor Emeritus, 1985-, Birkbeck College, University of London. Publications: The Art of Graham Greene (with Kenneth Allott), 1951; Novelists on the Novel, 1959; The Complete Poems of Matthew Arnold (editor with Kenneth Allott), 1965, 2nd edition, 1979; The Complete Poems of John Keats (editor), 1970; Matthew Arnold (with R H Super), 1986. Contributions to: Scholarly books and journals. Honours: William Noble Fellowship in English Literature, 1946-48; Honorary Senior Fellow, University of Liverpool. Membership: English Association, executive committee. Address: 21 Mersey Avenue, Liverpool L19 3QU, England.

ALLSOPP (Harold) Bruce, b. 4 July 1912, Oxford, England. Author; Artist. m. Florence Cyrilla Woodruffe, 29 Dec 1936, dec 1991, 2 sons. Education: BArch, 1933, Dip CD, 1935, Liverpool University. Appointments: Senior Lecturer, 1969-73, Reader, 1973-77, University of Newcastle-upon-Tyne. Publications: Art and the Nature of Architecture, 1952; General History of Architecture, 1955; Civilization, The Next Stage, 1969; A Modern Theory of Architecture, 1970; The Country Life Companion to British and European Architecture, 1977; Social Responsibility and the Responsible Society, 1985; Spirit of Europe, A Subliminal History, 1997. Contributions to: Various journals. Memberships: Athenaeum; Art Workers Guild Master, 1970; MRTPI; Society of Architecture, fellow; Society of Architectural Historians. Address: Ferndale, Mount View, Stocksfield, Northumberland NE43 7HL, England.

ALLWOOD Martin Samuel, b. 13 Apr 1916, Jönköping, Sweden. Author; Poet; Dramatist; Professor. m. Enelia Paz Gomez, 20 Dec 1976, 2 sons, 3 daughters. Education: MA, Cantab; MA, Columbia University, 1949; Dr Rer Pol Technische Hochschule Darmstadt, 1953. Appointments: President, Anglo-American Centre, Sweden; Professor, Nordic College of Journalism. Publications: The Cemetery of the Cathedrals, 1945; The Swedish Crime, play, 1976; New English Poems, 1981; Valda Svenska Dikter, 1982; Meet Will Shakespeare, 1985; Essays on Contemporary Civilization, 1988; The Roots of Western Civilization, 1990; The Empress and Her Lover, 1993; Verona Bratesch, 1993; The Big Book of Humo(u)r From Britain and America, 1993; The Empress and Her Lover, plays, 1994. Contributions to: Numerous articles. Honour: Kaj Munk Society Award, 1992. Memberships: Gothenburg Society of Authors; Swedish Society of Immigrant Authors. Address: Anglo-American Centre, 56532 Mullsjo, Sweden.

ALMOND Brenda Margaret, b. 19 Sept 1937, Liverpool, England. University Professor; Professor of Philosophy. m. Charles Desmond Cohen, 9 Jan 1960, 1 son, 3 daughters. Education: BA, London University, University College, 1956-59; MPhil, London University, 1976. Appointments: Lecturer, Philosophy, University of Ghana, 1959-60; Keele, England, 1960-62; Brighton, England, 1967-74; Surrey, England, 1974-86; Professor of Moral and Social Philosophy, Hull, 1986-. Publications:

Education and the Individual, 1981; Moral Concerns, 1987; AIDS: A Moral Issue (ed), 1990, 2nd ed, 1996; The Philosophical Quest, 1990; Exploring Philosophy, 1995; Exploring Ethics: Traveller's Tale, 1998. Contributions to: Editor, Journal of Applied Philosophy. Honour: Honorary Doctorate, University of Utrecht, Netherlands, 1998. Membership: Fellow, The Royal Society of Arts. Address: Deptartment of Philosophy, University of Hull, Hull HU6 7RX, England.

ALMQUIST Gregg Andrew, b. 1 Dec 1948, Minneapolis, Minnesota, USA. Actor; Novelist; Playwright. Education: BA, University of Minnesota, 1971. Publications: Beast Rising, 1988 (published in France under the title L'eveil de la bete); Wolf Kill, 1990. Plays (produced): The Duke; The Eve of Saint Venus (adapted from Burgess); The Winter That Ended in June; Pavan for a Dead Princess. Address: c/o International Creative Management, 40 West 57th Street, New York, NY 10019, USA.

ALONGI Constance Veronica, b. 18 Aug 1933, New York, New York, USA. Retired Educator; Freelance Writer. m. Carlo J Alongi, 24 June 1956, 1 son, 2 daughters. Education: BA, Montclair State University, 1955; MA, Rutgers University, 1967. Appointments: Editor, Council Newsletter I-R-ADLIBS, 1972-74, Programme Chairman and President-Elect, 1973-74, President, 1974, Middlesex Council International Reading Association; Garden State Arts Center Cultural Commission, 1979; Associate Editor and Columnist, 1978-82, Editor-in-Chief, 1982-86, Reading Instruction Journal, New Jersey Reading Association; Middlesex County Board of Mental Health, 1984; Middlesex County Commission on the Status of Women, 1986. Publications: Tyrone and Moby Dick, story, 1968; Cassette tape on changing role of parents in public education, from early 20th Century to the presemt, 1975; Developing Active Readers: Ideas for Parents, Teachers, Librarians (contributing author), 1979: Helping Children Read (contributing author), anthology of articles, 1980. Contributions to: The PTA Magazine, NJEA Review, The Reading Teacher, Reading Instruction Journal, Graduate Woman-AAUW journal, Focus-New Jersey Association for Supervision and Curriculum Development journal, Jersey Woman magazine, School Leader magazine, The School Administrator and Phi Delta Kappa's Backtalk. Memberships: New Jersey Reading Association, Chairperson, Teacher Literacy Committee, 1974-75, Chairman, Nominating Committee, 1976-79, President, 1985-86; International Reading Association, National Chairman, Parents and Reading Committee, 1972-76, Reading and Library Services Committee, 1976-77, Literature for Adolescents Committee, 1982, re-appointed, 1984, several Convention positions; Education Writers Association, 1984-. Address: 302 Schoolhouse Road, Monroe Township, NJ 08831, USA.

ALONSO ALVAREZ Emilio, (Andrenio), b. 2 July 1940, Minera de Luna, León, Spain. Naval Architect; Poet; Dramatist. m. Mercedes Pueyo, 29 July 1966, 1 son. Education: Naval Architecture, Escuela Técnica Superior de Ingenieros Navales, 1965. Publications: Coplas de la Transicion, De Franco a Tejero (poems), 1986; Octavas Reales Callejeras sin Ton ni Son (poems), 1987; An Anonymous Livel Against the Gulf War-El Amor Petrolero es Signo de Mal Agüro (theater), 1991. Contributions to: Various publications. Honour: Casa Villas Poetry Award, Madrid, 1983. Address: Juan Ramón Jiménez 24, 28036 Madrid, Spain.

ALONZO Anne-Marie, b. 13 Dec 1951, Alexandria, Egypt. Author; Poet; Dramatist; Journalist; Publisher. Education: BA, 1976, MA, 1978, PhD, 1986, University of Montreal. Appointments: Co-Founder and Vice President, Auto/Graphe theatre and production co, 1981-87; Co-Founder, Les Editions Trois, 1985; Co-Founder and Director, Trois review, 1985-; Founder and Coordinator, Festival de Trois, 1989-. Publications: Une Lettre rouge orange et ocre, 1984; Bleus de mine, 1985; Ecoute, Sultane, 1987; Seul le désir, 1987; Esmai, 1987; Le Livre des ruptures, 1988; Lead Blues, 1990; L'Immobile, 1990; Linked Alive (co-author), 1990; Galia qu'elle nommait Amour, 1992; Margie Gillis, La Danse des marches, 1993; Lettres a Cassandre (with Denise Desautels), 1994; Tout au loin la lumière, 1994. Contributions to: Various publications. Honours: Prix Emile-Nelligan, 1985; Prix Lizette-Gervais, 1990; Grand Prix d'excellence artistique en creation littéraire, 1992; Member of the Order of Canada, 1997. Memberships: Amnesty International; Artistes pour la paix; Greenpeace Foundation; Société littéraire de Laval; Society of Composers, Authors and Music Publishers of Canada; Union de écrivaines et écrivains québécois. Address: 2033 Jessop, Laval, Quebec H7S 1X3, Canada.

ALPERIN Richard Junius, b. 16 Feb 1941, Philadelphia, USA. Biomedical Scientist; College Professor. Education: AB, 1963, MS, 1965, PhD, 1969, University of Pennsylvania; 5 Yr Postdoctoral Training, 1974; MS, PhD, Columbia State University, 1996. Appointments: Fellow, University of Pennsylvania, 1963-69; Postdoctoral Fellow, Veterinary School, 1969-74; Professor of Biology, Community College, 1969-. Publications: Studies on Chicken Hypoblast Function, 1969; Rimmonim Bells, 1980; Art's Anglo-American Paper Lion: John McLure Hamilton's Untold Story, 1993. Contributions to: American Zoologist; Welcomat; FFCCP Newsletter. Honour: Grand Golden Academic Collar, Pontzen Academy, Naples, Italy. Literary Agent: Junius Inc. Address: 842 Lombard Street, Philadelphia, PA 19147, USA.

ALPERT Cathryn, b. 1 Apr 1952, Santa Monica, California, USA. Writer. m. Marco Alpert, 8 Feb 1982, 2 sons, 2 daughters. Education: BA, 1973, MA, 1974, PhD, 1979, University of California at Los Angeles. Appointments: Assistant Professor, Centre College, 1980-84; Writer, 1984-. Publications: Rocket City - MacMurray and Beck, 1995; Rocket City - Vintage Contemporaries, 1996. Contributions to: Puerto Del Sol; Thema; Wittenberg Review. Honours: 2nd Place, O Henry Festival Short Story Contest, 1989; Finalist, Poets and Writers Exchange Program, 1989; Honorable Mention, Raymond Carver Short Story Contest, 1989; Finalist, Gamut Tenth Anniversary Short Story Contest, 1990; 1st Place, Amaranth Review Short Fiction Contest, 1991; Finalist, The Chris O'Malley Award, 1990; Finalist, O Henry Festival Short Story Contest, 1991; 3rd Place, CPU Short Story Contest, 1991; Finalist, Barnes and Noble Discover Great New Writers Award, 1996. Membership: San Francisco Literary Society, board director. Literary Agent: Felicia Eth. Address: 555 Bryant Street, Suite 350, Palo Alto, CA 94301, USA.

ALPHONSO-KARKALA John B, b. 30 May 1923, South Kanara, Mysore State, India. Writer; Poet; Professor of Literature. m. Leena Anneli Hakalehto, 20 Dec 1964, 3 children. Education: BA, 1950, MA, 1953, Bombay University; University of London, 1954-55; PhD, Columbia University, 1964. Appointments: Visiting Lecturer, City College of the City University of New York, 1963; Assistant Professor, 1964-65, Associate Professor, 1965-68, Professor of Literature, 1969-, State University of New York at New Paltz; Visiting Professor, Columbia University, 1969-70. Publications: Indo-English Literature in the Nineteenth Century, 1970; Anthology of Indian Literature (editor), 1971, revised edition as Ages of Rishis, Buddha, Acharyas, Bhaktas and Mahatma, 1987; Bibliography of Indo-English Literature, 1800-1966 (editor with Leena Karkala), 1974; Comparative World Literature: Seven Essays, 1974; Passions of the Nightless Night (novel), 1974; Jawaharlal Nehru: A Literary Portrait, 1975; When Night Falls (poems), 1980; Vedic Vision (editor), 1980; Joys of Jayanagara (novel), 1981; Indo-English Literature: Essays (with Leena A Karkala), 1994 . Memberships: American Oriental Society; Association for Asian Studies; International Congress of Comparative Literature; International Congress of Orientalists; Modern Language Association of America. Address: 20 Millrock Road, New Paltz, NY 12561, USA.

ALSTON William (Payne), b. 29 Nov 1921, Shreveport, Louisiana, USA. Professor of Philosophy; Writer. m. (1) Mary Frances Collins, 15 Aug 1943, div, 1 daughter, (2) Valerie Tibbetts Barnes, 3 July 1963. Education: BM, Centenary College, 1942; PhD, University of Chicago, 1951. Appointments: Instructor, 1949-52, Assistant Professor, 1952-56, Associate Professor, 1956-61, Professor, 1961-71, Acting Chairman, 1961-64, Director of Graduate Studies, 1966-71, Department of Philosophy, University of Michigan; Visiting Lecturer, Harvard University, 1955-56; Fellow, Centre for Advanced Studies in Behavioural Sciences, 1965-66; Professor of Philosophy, Douglass College, Rutgers University, 1971-76, University of Illinois at Urbana-Champaign, 1976-80, Syracuse University, 1980-99; Austin Fagothey Visiting Professor of Philosophy, Santa Clara University, 1991. Publications: Religious Belief and Philosophical Thought, 1963; Readings in Twentieth Century Philosophy (with G Nakhnikian), 1963; The Philosophy of Language, 1964; The Problems of Philosophy: Introductory Readings (with R B Brandt), 1967, 3rd edition, 1978; Divine Nature and Human Language, 1989; Epistemic Justification, 1989; Perceiving God, 1991; The Reliability of Sense Perception, 1993; A Realist Conception of Truth, 1996. Editor: Philosophical Research Archives, 1974-77; Faith and Philosophy, 1982-90; Cornell Studies in the Philosophy of Religion, 1987-. Contributions to: Scholarly books and journals. Honours: Doc. Hum. Litt. (Honoris Causae), Church Divinity School of the Pacific, 1988; Chancellor's Exceptional Academic Achievement Award, Syracuse University, 1990. Memberships: American Academy of Arts and Sciences; Society for Philosophy and Psychology, president, 1976-77; American Philosophical Association, president of Central Division, 1978-79; President, Society of Christian Philosophers, 1978-81. Address: c/o Department of Philosophy, Syracuse University, Syracuse, NY 13244, USA.

ALTER Robert B(ernard), b. 2 Apr 1935, New York, New York, USA. Professor; Literary Critic. m. Carol Cosman, 17 June 1974, 3 sons, 1 daughter. Education: BA, Columbia College, 1957; MA, 1958, PhD, 1962, Harvard University. Appointments: Instructor, Assistant Professor of English, Columbia University, 1962-66; Associate Professor of Hebrew and Comparative Literature, 1967-69, Professor of Hebrew and Comparative Literature, 1969-89, Class of 1937 Professor, 1989-, University of California, Berkeley. Publications: Partial Magic, 1975; Defenses of the Imagination, 1978; Stendhal: A Biography, 1979; The Art of Biblical Narrative, 1981; Motives for Fiction, 1984; The Art of Biblical Poetry, 1985; The Pleasures of Reading in an Ideological Age, 1989; Necessary Angels, 1991; The World of Biblical Literature, 1992; Hebrew and Modernity, 1994; Genesis: Translation and Commentary, 1996. Contributions to: Commentary; New Republic; New York Times Book Review; London Review of Books; Times Literary Supplement. Honours: English Institute Essay Prize, 1965; National Jewish Book Award for Jewish Thought, 1982; Present Tense Award for Religious Thought, 1986; Award for Scholarship, National Foundation for Jewish Culture, 1995. Memberships: American Comparative Literature Association; Association of Literary Scholars and Critics; Council of Scholars of the Library of Congress; American Academy of Arts and Sciences. Literary Agent: Georges Borchardt. Address: 1475 Le Roy Avenue, Berkeley, CA 94708, USA.

ALTHER Lisa, b. 23 July 1944, Tennessee, USA. Author. m. Richard Alther, 26 Aug 1966, 1 daughter. Education: BA, Wellesley College, 1966. Appointments: Staff Member, Atheneum Publishers, New York City; Lecturer, St Michael's College, Burlington, 1980. Publications: Kinflicks, 1976; Original Sins, 1981; Other Women, 1984; Bedrock, 1990; Five Minutes in Heaven, 1995. Contributions to: New York Times Magazine; New York Times Book Review; Natural History; New Society; Arts and Antiques; Boston Globe; Washington Post; Los Angeles Times; San Francisco Chronicle; Southern Living. Memberships: Authors Guild; National Writers Union. Address: 1086 Silver Street, Hinesburg, VT 05461, USA.

ALTICK Richard Daniel, b. 19 Sept 1915, Lancaster, Pennsylvania, USA. Regent's Professor Emeritus of

English; Writer. m. Helen W Keller, 15 Aug 1942, 2 daughters. Education: AB, Franklin and Marshall College, 1936; PhD, University of Pennsylvania, 1941. Appointments: Faculty, 1945, Regent's Professor of English, 1968-82, Regent's Professor Emeritus of English, 1982-, Ohio State University, Columbus. Publications: Preface to Critical Reading, 1946, 6th revised edition, 1984; The Cowden Clarkes, 1948; The Scholar Adventurers, 1950; The English Common Reader: A Social History of the Mass Reading Public, 1800-1900, 1957; The Art of Literary Research, 1963, 4th revised edition, 1992; Lives and Letters: A History of Literary Biography in England and America, 1965; Carlyle: Past and Present (editor), 1965; Browning's Roman Murder Story (with J F Loucks), 1968; To Be in England, 1969; Victorian Studies in Scarlet, 1970; Browning: The Ring and the Book (editor), 1971; Victorian People and Ideas: A Companion for the Modern Reader of Victorian Literature, 1973; The Shows of London, 1978; Paintings from Books: Art and Literature in Britain 1760-1900, 1985; Deadly Encounters: Two Victorian Sensations (in UK as Evil Encounters), 1986; Writers, Readers and Occasions, 1989; The Presence of the Present: Topics of the Day in the Victorian Novel, 1991; Punch: The Lively Youth of a British Institution 1841-51, 1997. Honours: Guggenheim Fellowship, 1975; Phi Beta Kappa's Christian Gauss Award, 1991. Address: 276 West Southington Avenue, Worthington, OH 43085, USA.

ALTMAN Philip, b. 6 Jan 1924, Kansas City, Missouri, USA. Editor; Administrator. m. Lillian Berlinsky, 1 Sept 1946, 1 son, 1 daughter. Education: BA, University of Southern California, 1948; MSc, Western Reserve University, 1949. Appointments: Director, Editor, Office of Biological Handbooks, 1959-79; Executive Director, Council of Biology Editors, 1981-; Executive Editor, Biology Databook Series, 1983-86. Publications: Handbook of Respiration, 1958; Handbook of Circulation, 1959; Blood and Other Body Fluids, 1961; Growth, 1962; Biology Data Book, 1964, 2nd edition, 3 volumes, 1972-74; Environmental Biology, 1966; Metabolism, 1968; Respiration & Circulation, 1971; Cell Biology, 1976; Human Health and Disease, 1977; Inbred and Genetically Defined Strains of Laboratory Animals, 1979; Pathology of Laboratory Mice and Rats, 1985. Contributions to: Scientific journals and other publications. Address: Council of Biology Editors, 9650 Rockville Pike, Bethesda, MD 20814, USA.

ALUIT Alfonso J, b. 18 Apr 1930, Philippines. Journalist; Historian; Travel Writer. Education: BA, Far Eastern University, Manila, Philippines; Diploma, Stanford University, California, USA. Appointments: Director of Public Relations and Fund Raising, Philippines National Red Cross; Deputy Executive Director, Philippine Tourist and Travel Association; Deputy Secretary General, Philippine Chamber of Tourism; Editor and Publisher, Galleon Publications, publishers of travel literature. Publications: The Conscience of the Nation: A History of the Red Cross in the Philippines, 1963, 1972, 1998; By Sword & Fire: The Destruction of Manila in World War II, Feb 3 - Mar 3 1945, 1994; The Pigafetta Legacy; Travel and Tourism in the Philippines from Pre-Spanish to Contemporary Times, 1999; Guidebooks to the Philippines; Manila; Manila By Night; Philippine Festivals; Corregidor, under imprint; Portrait of a Filipino Patriot - Biography of the First Woman Senator in the Philippines, 1998. Contributions to: Editor and Publisher, Philippines Travelogue Magazine, Fortnightly Travel Magazine for Trade and Consumer. Honour: Philippine Republic Civic Award for Historical Writing, 1995. Memberships: Society of American Travel Writers, 1976-; International Federation of Tourism Journalists, 1977-. Address: Suite 309, NFWC Bldng, 962 Josefa L Escoda St, Ermita, Manila, Philippines.

ALUKO Timothy Mofolorunso, b. 14 June 1918, Ilesha, Nigeria. Novelist. m. Janet Adebisi Fajemisin, 1948, 6 children. Education: BSc, University of London, 1950; PhD in Public Health Engineering, University of Lagos, 1976. Appointments: Senior Lecturer, University of Ibadan, 1966; Commissioner of Finance, Government

of Western Nigeria, 1971-73. Publications: One Man, One Wife, 1959; One Man, One Matchet, 1964; Kinsman and Foreman, 1966; Chief the Honourable Minister, 1970; His Worshipful Majesty, 1973; Wrong Ones in the Dock, 1982; A State of Our Own, 1986; Conduct Unbecoming, 1993; Uncollected short story: The New Engineer, 1968. Honours: Officer of the Order of the British Empire, 1963; OON, 1964. Address: 53 Ladipo Oluwote Road, Apapa, Lagos, Nigeria.

ALVAREZ Alfred, b. 5 Aug 1929, London, England. Poet; Author. m. 7 Apr 1966, 2 sons, 1 daughter. Education: BA, 1952, MA, 1956, Corpus Christi College, Oxford. Appointments: Poetry Critic and Editor, Observer, 1956-66; Advisory Editor, Penguin Modern European Poets, 1964-76. Publications: The Shaping Spirit, 1958; The School of Donne, 1961; The New Poetry, 1962; Under Pressure, 1965; Beyond All the Fiddle, 1968; Penguin Modern Poets No 18, 1970; Apparition, 1971; The Savage God, 1971; Beckett, 1973; Hers, 1974; Autumn to Autumn and Selected Poems, 1978; Hunt, 1978; Life After Marriage, 1982; The Bigger Game in Town, 1983; Offshore, 1986; Feeding the Rat, 1988; Rain Forest, 1988; Day of Atonement, 1991; Faber Book of Modern European Poetry, 1992; Night, 1995. Contributions to: Numerous magazines and journals. Honours: Vachel Lindsay Prize for Poetry, 1961; Hon DLitt, University of East London, 1998. Memberships: Climbers; Alpine; Beefsteak. Address: c/o Aitken & Stone, 29 Fernshaw Road, London SW10 0TG, England.

ALVAREZ FERRERAS Felix, (Nines, Vyday Akrasiap Paratodos), b. 8 June 1921, Velaux, Bouches du Rhône, France. Educator. m. Hélène Slawinska, 1 Dec 1947, 3 sons, 1 daughter. Education: Universities, Spain, France and Canada. Appointments: Educator, Sociology, Geography, Letters; Poet, Translator. Publications: Vicisitudes de la Lucha - Epistolas de Libertarios Ilustres atraves del Mundo; Las Maravillas de los Paises Socialistas Autoritarios. Contributions to: Cenit; Tierra y Libertad; L'Homme Libre; Orto; Siembra. Membership: Accademia di Pontzen. Address: 7 Rue des Chênes Verts, Saint Estève 66240, France.

ALVES Ivia Iracema, b. 22 Sept 1939. University Teacher; Researcher; Critic. Education: Graduate in Letters, University Federal of Bahia, 1964; Master in Brazilian Literature, University of Sao Paulo, 1976; PhD in Brazilian Literature, USP, 1996. Appointments: Associate Researcher of NEIM, Center of Interdisciplinary Studies of Women Condition, University Federal of Bahia (UFBA), 1994; Associate Professor of Brazilian Literature Graduate Program Letters, UFBA, 1994-; Assistance and Supervision: Brazilian Literature Teaching at State College System, 1973-76; Consultant Curricula for Elementary Teacher's, 1981-82; Member of the Publishing Committee Revista Estudos, 1983-87; Member of the Assessment Board of FAPEX Prize, 1994. Publications: Arco & Flexa: Contribuicao para o estudo do modernismo, 1978; Herberto Sales, 1979; Textos de Autores Brasileiros, 1976; O Lobisomem e Outros Contos Folcloricos, 1975. Contributions include: La Narrativa de Herberto Sales, 1976; Uma Breve Noticia Sobre Samba, 1987; Roteiro de um tema, 1988; Um Olhar critico entre Brasil e a Inglaterra, 1994. Honours: Premio Eugenio Gomes, essays, 1991. Memberships: Brazilian Association of Comparative Literature; Brazilian Studies Association. Address: R Aloisio de Carvalho, 14/apto 1203, Salvador-Bahia, Brazil.

AMABILE George, b. 29 May 1936, Jersey City, New Jersey, USA. Professor of English; Poet; Writer. Education: AB, Amherst College, 1957; MA, University of Minnesota, 1961; PhD, University of Connecticut, 1969. Appointments: Lecturer, 1963, Assistant Professor, 1966-68, 1969-71, Associate Professor, 1972-86, Professor of English, 1987-, University of Manitoba; Visiting Writer-in-Residence, University of British Columbia, 1968-69; Various readings, Manitoba Theatre Centre, radio, and television. Publications: Blood Ties, 1972; Open Country, 1976; Flower and Song, 1977; Ideas of Shelter, 1981; The Presence of Fire, 1982; Four of a Kind, 1994; Rumours of Paradise/Rumours of War,

1995. Contributions to: Many anthologies, journals, and periodicals. Honours: Canada Council Grants, 1968, 1969, 1981, 1982, 1995, 1996; Canadian Authors Association National Prize for Poetry, 1983; 3rd Prize, CBC National Literary Competition, 1992. Memberships: League of Canadian Poets; Western Canadian Publishers Association. Address: c/o Department of English, University of Manitoba, Winnipeg, Manitoba R3T 2N2, Canada.

AMADI Elechi, b. 12 May 1934, Aluu, Nigeria. Novelist; Dramatist. m. Doah Ohlae, 1957, 8 children. Education: BSc in Mathematics and Physics, University College, Ibadan, 1959. Appointments: Writer-in-Residence and Dean of the Faculty of Arts, College of Education, Port Harcourt, 1984-87; Commissioner of Education, 1987-89, and Commissioner of Lands and Housing, 1989-90, Rivers State. Publications: The Concubine, 1966; The Great Ponds, 1969; The Slave, 1978; Estrangement, 1986. Plays: Isiburu, 1969; Peppersoup, and The Road to Ibadan, 1977; Dancer of Johannesburg, 1979. Other: Hymn and Prayer books. Honour: International Writers Program Grant, University of Iowa, 1973. Membership: Chairman, Association of Nigerian Authors, 1994-. Address: Box 331, Port Harcourt, Nigeria.

AMANN Jürg, b. 2 July 1947, Winterthur, Switzerland. Writer. Education: Doctor phil I, University of Zürich. Appointments: Critic of Literature; Dramaturg at the Schauspielhaus of Zürich, 1974-76; Literary Winner, Playwright, 1976-. Publications: Drs Symbol Kafka, 1974; Hardenberg, 1978; Verirren oder das plötzliche Sckweigen des Robert Walser, 1978; Die Kunst des wirkungsvelleu Abgangs, 1979; Die Baumschule, 1982; Frauz Kafka, 1983; Nachgerufen, 1983; Ach,diese Wegesind sehr dunkel, 1985; Patagonien, 1985; Robert Walser, 1985; Fort, 1987; Aus dem Hoken Lied, 1987; Nach dem Fest, 1988; Tod Weidigs, 1989; Der Rücktritt, 1989; Der Vater der Mutter und der Vater des Vaters, 1990; Der Aufang der Augst, 1991; Der Lauf der Zeit, 1993; Zwei oder drei Diuge, 1993; Uber die Jahre, 1994; Und über die Liebe wäre wieder zu sprechen, 1994; Robert Walser, 1995; Rondo, 1996; Schöne Aussicht, 1997; Iphigenie oder Operation Meereswind, 1998; Ikarus, 1998. Honours: Ingeborg Bachmann Prize, 1982; Conrad Ferdinand Meyer Prize, 1983; Schiller-Foundation Award, 1989; Art Prize of Winterthur, 1989; International Award of Radio Play, 1998. Membership: Group of Olten; PEN. Literary Agent: Piper Verlag, Arche Verlag, Haymon Verlag, Eremiten-Presse, Sessler Verlag. Address: Rindermarkt 8, CH-8001 Zürich, Switzerland.

AMANSHAUSER Gerhard, b. 2 Jan 1928, Salzburg, Austria. Writer. Education: Technical University of Graz; Universities of Vienna, Austria and Marburg. Publications: Aus der Leben der Quaden, 1968; Der Deserteur, 1970; Ärgernisse eines Zauberers, 1973; Schloss mit späten Gäten, 1975; Grenzen Essays, 1977; Aufzeichnungen einer Sonde, 1979; List der Illusionen, 1985; Gedichte, 1986; Fahrt zur verbotenen Stadt, 1987; Der Ohne Namen See, Chinese Impressions, 1988; Moloch Horridus, 1989; Lektüre, 1991; Gegensätze, 1993; Das Erschlagen von Stechmücken, 1993; Tische, Stühle and Bierseidel, Vorträge, 1997. Contributions to: Literatur und Kritik; Neues Forum; Protokolle; Neue Rundschau. Honours: Georg Trakl Promotion Prize, 1952; Theodor Körner Prize, 1970; Rauriser Literaturpreis, 1973; Förderungspreis der Stadt Salzburg, 1975; Preis der Salzburger Wirtschaft, 1985; Alma Johanna Koenig Preis, 1987; Doctor honoris causa, 1993; Würdigungspreis für Literatur, Bundesministeriums für Unterricht und Kunst, 1994. Address: Brunnhausgasse 10, 5020 Salzburg, Austria.

AMB Daniel. See: ANDERSEN Baltser.

AMBAT Gladys, b. 31 Aug 1920; Administrative Assistant, Central Government New Delhi; Retired General Secretary. Education: BA, Madras University, India; Certificates for several courses attended in India and abroad. Appointments: Laboratory Assistant, Meeret

India; Administrative Assistant, Central Government Office, New Delhi & YWCA; Secretary, Lucknow, New Delhi; General Secretary, Fiji; Observer Staff, Australia, USA, Canada & UK and YWCA of Madras, General Secretary, 30 years; Leader of Cluster Groups. Publications: More Grasps to Reach (A 100 Years History of the YWCA of Madras), 1992; Brain Teasers, 1994, 1998; Bible Quiz - Your Word a Lamp and Alight, 1998. Contributions to: Hindu-Christian Studies, Calgary Institute for YWCA, national & local magazines. Literary Agent: Rupa & Co, New Delhi and Ispek, New Delhi. Address: Gambat 84B AE154, IV Ave, Annanagar, Chennai 600040, India.

AMBERT Alba, b. 10 Oct 1946, San Juan, Puerto Rico, USA. Author Fiction and Poetry. m. Walter McCann, 11 Feb 1984, 1 daughter. Education: BA, Universidad de Puerto Rico, 1974; MEd, Harvard University, 1975; EdD, Harvard University, 1980. Appointments: Bilingual Teacher, Boston Public Schools, 1975-80; Assistant Professor and Director, Bilingual Special Education Teacher Training Program, University of Hartford, 1980-84; Visiting Scientist, Massachusetts Institute of Technology, Department of Philosophy and Linguistics, Cambridge, MA, USA, 1984-85; Senior Research Scholar, Athens College, Athens, Greece, 1985-93; Writer in Residence, Richmond, The American International University in London, 1993-. Publications: Fiction: Porque hay silencio, novel, 1989; A Perfect Silence, novel, 1995; The Eighth Continent and Other Stories, 1997; An Inclination of Mirrors, 1997; Poetry: Gotas sobre el columpio, 1980; The Fifth Sun, 1989; The Mirror Is Always There; Habito tu nombre, 1994; At Dawn We Start Again, 1997; Children's Books: Thunder from the Earth, 1997; Why the Wild Winds Blow, 1997; Face to Sky, 1998. Honours: Ford Foundation, National Research Council Postdoctoral Fellowship, 1984; Literature Award, Institute of Puerto Rican Literature for the novel Porque hay silencio, 1989; Carey McWilliams Award, 1996; President's Award of the Massachusetts Association for Bilingual Education, 1997. Memberships: PEN International, London Centre; Authors' Guild, New York; The Writer's Union, New York. Address: Richmond University, Queens Road, Richmond, Surrey TW10 6JP, England.

AMBROSE David Edwin, b. 21 Feb 1943, Chorley, Lancashire, England. Playwright; Screenwriter; Novelist. m. Laurence Huguette Hammerli, 13 Sept 1979. Education: Degree in Law, University of Oxford, Merton College, 1965. Publications: Novels: The Man Who Turned Into Himself, 1993; Mother of God, 1995; Hollywood Lies; Superstition, 1997. Other: Many TV Plays and Screenplays in Hollywood and Worldwide; also Seige, Cambridge Theatre, London, 1972. Honour: 1st Prize Screenplay, Sitges Film Festival, 1980. Membership: Dramatists' Club, London. Literary Agent: William Morris Agency. Address: c/o 1 Stratton Street, London W1X 6HB, England.

AMBROSE John. See: **CALVOCORESSI Peter.**

AMBROSE Stephen E(dward), b. 10 Jan 1936, Decatur, Illinois, USA. Historian; Writer; Professor. m. (1) Judith Dorlester, 6 June 1957, dec Oct 1966, 1 son, 1 daughter, (2) Moira Buckley, 30 Sept 1967. Education: BS, University of Wisconsin, 1957; MA, Louisiana State University, 1958; PhD, University of Wisconsin, 1963. Appointments: Assistant Professor, Louisiana State University, 1960-64; Associate Professor, Johns Hopkins University, 1964-69; Ernest J King Professor, Naval War College, Newport, Rhode Island, 1969-70; Dwight D Eisenhower Professor of War and Peace, Kansas State University, 1970-71; Professor, 1971-, Alumni Distinguished Professor, 1982-, University of New Orleans; Mary Ball Washington Professor, University College, Dublin, 1981-82; Visiting Professor, University of California at Berkeley, 1986, US Army War College, Carlisle, Pennsylvania, 1990. Publications: Halleck: Lincoln's Chief of Staff, 1962; Upton and the Army, 1964; Duty, Honor, Country: A History of West Point, 1966; Eisenhower and Berlin, 1945; The Decision to Halt at the Elbe, 1967; Institutions in Modern America: Innovation in

Structure and Process (editor), 1967; The Papers of Dwight D Eisenhower: The War Years (assistant editor), 5 volumes, 1970; The Supreme Commander: The War Years of General Dwight D Eisenhower, 1970; Rise to Globalism: American Foreign Policy since 1938, 1971, 6th edition, revised, 1991; The Military and American Society (with James Barber), 1972; Crazy Horse and Custer: The Parallel Lives of Two American Warriors, 1975; Ike's Spies: Eisenhower and the Espionage Establishment (with Richard Immerman), 1981; Eisenhower: Soldier, General of the Army, President-Elect, 1890-1952, 1983; Milton S Eisenhower: Educational Statesman (with Richard Immerman), 1983; Eisenhower: The President, 1984; Pegasus Bridge: 6 June 1944, 1985; Nixon: The Education of a Politician, 1913-1962, 1987; Nixon: The Triumph of a Politician, 1962-1972, 1989; The Wisdom of Dwight D Eisenhower: Quotations from Ike's Speeches and Writings, 1939-1969 (editor), 1990; Nixon: Ruin and Recovery, 1973-1990, 1991; Band of Brothers: E Company, 506th Regiment, 101st Airborne, from Normandy to Hitler's Eagle's Nest, 1992; Eisenhower and the German POWs: Fact against Falsehood, editor, 1992; Undaunted Courage: Meriwether Lewis, Thomas Jefferson, and the Opening of the American West, 1996; American Heritage New History of World War II (editor), 1997; Citizen Soldier, 1997; Americans at war, 1997; The Victors: Eisenhower and His Boys, 1998. Contributions to: Books, journals and television documentaries. Honours: National Book Award, Freedom, Foundation, 1984; National Humanities Medal, 1998. Memberships: American Committee on World War II; American Historical Association; American Military Institute; Southern Historical Association. Address: c/o Ambrose Tubbs Inc, 1606 Hauser Boulevard, Helena, MT 59601, USA.

AMERY Carl, b. 9 Apr 1922, Munich, Germany. Writer. m. Marijane Gerth, 10 Apr 1950, 3 sons, 2 daughters. Education: Humanistisches Gymnasium, 1940; Literary and Language Studies, Munich and Washington, DC, 1946-50. Appointments: Editor, Bavarian Radio, 1950, 1962; Director, Munich Library System, 1967-71. Publications: Novels: Die Grosse Deutsche Tour, 1959; Das Koenigsprojekt, 1974; Die Wallfahrer, 1986; Das Geheimnis der Krypta, 1990. Essays: Die Kapitulation, 1963; Das Ende der Vorsehung, 1972. Honour: Cross of Merit, Germany, 1988. Memberships: German Writer's Association; PEN Center, Germany. Address: Draechslstrasse 7, D-8 Munich 90, Germany.

AMES Leslie. See: **RIGONI Orlando Joseph.**

AMICHAI Yehuda, b. 1924, Würzburg, Germany (Israeli citizen). Poet. m. Chang Sokolov. Education: Hebrew University, Jerusalem. Appointments: Visiting Poet, University of California, Berkeley, 1976, New York University, 1987. Publications: Now and in Other Days, 1955; Two Hopes Away, 1958; In The Park, 1959; Now in the Turmoil, 1968; And Not in Order to Remember, 1971; Songs of Jerusalem and Myself, 1973; Behind All This Lies Great Happiness, 1974; Amen, 1978; On New Years Day, Next to a House Being Built, 1979; Time, 1979; Love Poems, 1981; Hour of Charity, 1982; Great Tranquility: Questions and Answers, 1983; From Man You Came, and to Men You Will Return, 1985; The Selected Poetry of Yehuda Amichai, 1986; Poems of Jerusalem, 1987; Even a Fist was Once an Open Palm with Fingers, 1991. Honour: Honorary Doctorate, Hebrew University, 1990. Address: 26 Malki Street, Yemin Moshe, Jerusalem, Israel.

AMICOLA José, b. 15 Feb 1942, Buenos Aires, Argentina. Professor; Writer. Education: Licenciado en Letras, Universidad de Buenos Aires, Argentina; Dr Philosophiae, Universität Göttingen, Germany, 1982. Publications: Sobre Cortazar, 1969; Astrologia y Fascismo en la Obra de Arlt, 1984; Manuel Puig y La Tela Que Atrapa Al Lector, 1992; Dostoievski, 1994; De La Forma a La Informacion, 1997. Honour: Premio Banco Mercantil, 1992. Memberships: Instituto Intern Literatura Iberoamericana, Pittsburgh. Address: Las Heras, 3794 - 11A, 1425 Buenos Aires, Argentina.

AMIN Sayed-Hassan, b. 25 Nov 1948, Persia. University Professor Emeritus; Author; Advocate. m. 2 sons, 2 daughters. Education: LLB, 1970; LLM, 1975; PhD, 1979; Scottish Bar Exams, 1980-82; Mufti-at-large in Islamic Law. Appointments: Lecturer, 1979, Senior Lecturer, 1981, Reader, 1984, Professor, 1991, Glasgow Caledonian University; President, Islamic Institute of International and Comparative Law, 1994-. Publications: 36 Books including: Philosophy of Mulla Sadra; International and Legal Problems of the Gulf; Middle East Legal Systems; Law and Justice in Contemporary Yemen; Islamic Law and its Implications for the Modern World; Legal System of Iraq; Legal System of Kuwait; Law of Intellectual Property in Developing Countries. Contributions to: International and Comparative Law Quarterly; Oil and Gas Law and Taxation Review; Kayhan-e Andisheh. Memberships: Society of Authors; Royal Institute of International Affairs; Faculty of Advocates; Council for National Academic Awards; World Development Movement; Fellow, Islamic Academy. Address: Faculty of Advocates. Parliament House. Edinburgh EH1 1RF, Scotland.

AMIS Martin Louis, b. 25 Aug 1949, Oxford, England. Author. Education: BA, Exeter College, Oxford. Appointments: Fiction and Poetry Editor, Times Literary Supplement, 1974; Literary Editor, New Statesman, 1977-79; Special Writer, The Observer Newspaper, 1980-. Publications: The Rachel Papers, 1973; Dead Babies, 1975; Success, 1978; Other People: A Mystery Story, 1981; Invasion of the Space Invaders, 1982; Money, 1984; Einstein's Monsters: Five Stories, 1987; London Fields, 1989; Night Train, 1997; The Information, 1995. Honour: Somerset Maugham Award, 1974. Address: c/o Peters Fraser & Dunlop, 5th Floor, The Chambers, Chelsea Harbour, Lots Road, London SW10 0XP, England.

AMMONS A(rchie) R(andolph), b. 18 Feb 1926, Whiteville, North Carolina, USA. Poet; Professor of English. m. Phyllis Plumbo, 26 Nov 1949, 1 son. Education: BS, Wake Forest College, 1949; University of California at Berkeley, 1950-52. Appointments: Principal, Elementary School, Hatteras, North Carolina, 1949-50; Executive Vice President, Friedrich and Dimmock Inc, Millville, New Jersey, 1952-62; Poetry Editor, Nation, New York City, 1963; Assistant Professor, 1964-68, Associate Professor, 1968-71, Professor of English, 1971-73, Goldwin Smith Professor of English, 1973-, Cornell University; Visiting Professor, Wake Forest University, 1974-75. Publications: Ommateum, with Doxology, 1955; Expressions of Sea Level, 1964; Corsons Inlet, 1965; Tape for the Turn of the Year, 1965; Northfield Poems, 1966; Selected Poems, 1968; Uplands, 1970; Briefings, 1971; Collected Poems, 1951-1971, 1972; Sphere: The Form of a Motion, 1973; Diversifications, 1975; For Doyle Fosso, 1977; Highgate Road, 1977; The Snow Poems, 1977; The Selected Poems, 1951-1977, 1977, expanded edition, 1987; Breaking Out, 1978; Six-Piece Suite, 1978; Selected Longer Poems, 1980; Changing Things, 1981; A Coast of Trees, 1981; Worldly Hopes, 1982; Lake Effect Country, 1982; Sumerian Vistas, 1987; The Really Short Poems of A R Ammons, 1991; Garbage, 1993; Brink Road, 1996; Glare, 1997. Contributions to: Periodicals. Honours: Guggenheim Fellowship, 1966; Levinson Prize, 1970; National Book Awards for Poetry, 1973, 1993; Bollingen Prize for Poetry, 1974-75; John D and Catharine T MacArthur Foundation Prize, 1981-86; National Book Critics Circle Award, 1982; North Carolina Award for Literature, 1986; Robert Frost Silver Medal, Poetry Society of America, 1993; Rebekah Johnson Bobbitt National Prize for Poetry, 1994; Tanning Prize, Academy of American Poets, 1998. Address: Department of English, Cornell University, Ithaca, NY 14853, USA.

AMOR Anne Clark, (Anne Clark), b. 4 Feb 1933. Author. m. 23 Feb 1982, 1 son, 1 daughter. Education: BA Honours, English, Birkbeck College, London University. Publications: Books: Beasts and Bawdy, 1975; The Real Alice, 1981; Mrs Oscar Wilde: A Woman of Some Importance, 1983; William Holman Hunt: The True Pre-Raphaelite, 1989; Mr Dodgson: Nine Lewis Carroll Studies, contributor, 1994; Lewis Carroll: Child of the

North, 1995; Editor: The Genius of Lewis Carroll, 1999; Letters to Skeffington Dodgson from His Father; The Carrollian. Contributions to: The New Book of Knowledge; The Washington Post; Los Angeles Times; The Lady; The Literary Review. Memberships: Chairman, Trustee, Founder Member, The Lewis Carroll Society, 1969; The Pre-Raphaelite Society; Committee Member, The Oscar Wilde Society, 1993-. Address: 16 Parkfields Avenue, Kingsbury, London NW9 7PE, England.

AMOROSO Bruno, b. 11 Dec 1936, Rome, Italy. Associate Professor in Economic Policy. Education: MD, University La Sapienza, Rome, 1966. Publications: Lo Stato Imprenditore, 1978; Rapporto Dalla Scandinavia, 1980; European Industrial Relations, 1990; Scandinavian Perspectives on European Integration, 1990; Macroeconomic Theories and Policies for the 1990's, 1992. Contributions to: Comparative Labour Law Journal; International Journal of Human Resource Management; Economia Pubblica. Memberships: European Inter-University Association on Society, Science and Technology, vice president, Brussels; European Culture Association, Venice. Address: Webersgade 28, Copenhagen DK-2100, Denmark.

AMORY Ian Mark Heathcoat, b. 1 May 1941, Washington, DC, USA. Journalist. m. Charlotte Joll, 18 Oct 1982, 3 daughters. Education: Christ Church College, Oxford, 1959-62. Appointments: Tutor to the Son of Kabaka of Buganda; Sunday Telegraph; Evening Standard; Observer; Publisher: Rainbird; Weidenfeld & Nicolson; Journalist, Sunday Times; Literary Editor, Spectator, 1986-. Publications: Lord Dunsany; Editor, Letters of Evelyn Waugh; Editor, Letters of Ann Fleming; Editor, Marc; Lord Berners, The Last Eccentric. Contributions to: Theatre and film writing for: Spectator; Observer. Membership: FRSL Council, 1996-. Literary Agent: Curtis Brown. Address: Hele Manor, Aulverton, Somerset TA22 9RN, England.

AN Tai Sung, b. 3 Feb 1931, Seoul, Korea. College Professor; Author. m. Sihn Ja Lee, 23 Aug 1969, 2 daughters. Education: BA, Indiana University, 1956; MA, Yale University, 1957; PhD, University of Pennsylvania, USA, 1963. Appointments: Professor of Political Science, 1963-73, Everett E Nuttle Professor of Political Science, 1973-, Washington College, Chestertown, Maryland. Publications: Mao Tse Tung's Cultural Revolution; The Sino Soviet Territorial Dispute; The Lin Piao Affair; North Korea in Transition: From Dictatorship to Dynasty; North Korea: A Political Handbook: The Vietnam War; About 80 articles. Honours: Lindback Award for Distinguished Teaching; Sears Roebuck Foundation Teaching Excellence and Campus Leadership Award. Memberships: American Political Science Association; Association for Asian Studies; Asia Society; Korean Association of Oriental History and Civilization; American Association of University Professors. Address: Department of Political Science and International Studies, Washington College, 300 Washington Avenue, Chestertown, MD 21620, USA.

ANAND Mulk Raj, b. 12 Dec 1905, Peshawar, India. Novelist; University Teacher. m. (2) Shirin Vajifdar, 1950, 1 daughter. Education: BA (Hons), Punjab University, 1924; PhD, University College, University of London, 1929; Cambridge University, 1929-30. Appointments: Director, Kutub publishers, Bombay, 1946-; Teacher, Universities of Punjab, Benares, and Rajasthan, Jaipur, 1948-66. Publications: Untouchable, 1935; The Coolie, 1936; Two Leaves and a Bud, 1937; The Village, 1939; Lament on the Death of a Master of Arts, 1939; Across the Black Waters, 1940; The Sword and the Sickle, 1942; The Big Heart, 1945; Seven Summers: The Story of an Indian Childhood, 1951; Private Life of an Indian Prince, 1953; The Old Woman and the Cow, 1960; The Road, 1961; Morning Face, 1968; Confession of a Lover, 1976; The Bubble, 1984; Death of a Hero, 1995; Also: Various short stories and other works. Honours: Sahitya Academy Award, 1974. Address: 25 Cuffe Parade, Bombay 400 005, India.

ANAND Valerie May Florence, (Fiona Buckley), b. 6 July 1937, North London, England. Novelist. m. Dalip Singh Anand, 26 Mar 1970. Education: A Level English with Honours. Appointments: Secretary, Odhams Press, 1956-60; Sub-Editor, Guarry Managers Journal, 1960-62; Tech Journalist, Accountancy Journal, 1963-66; Tech Journalist, Index to Office Equipment, 1966-68; PR Assistant, E J Poole, 1968-71; Editor, House Magazine, Heals, 1971-75; Editor, House Newspapers, Matthew Hall Engineering Group, 1975-89; Part time Novelist, 1973-89; Full Time Novelist, 1989-. Publications: Historical Novels: Gildenford, The Norman Pretender; The Disputed Crown; Crown of Roses; King of the Wood; Bridges Over Time Series (SAGA; Pre-Conquest to 1960s; The Proud Villeins; The Ruthless Yeomen; Women of Ashdon; The Faithful Lovers; The Cherished Wives; The Dowerless Sisters); Contemporary Novels: To a Native Shore; West of Sunset; As Fiona Buckley: Elizabethan Thrillers: The Robsart Mystery: The Doublet Affair. Contributions to: Short stories; Evening News, 1950s and 1960s; Freelance Technical Articles; Accountancy, 1970s. Memberships: Society of Authors; Romantic Novelists; Crime Writers Association, Exmoor Society. Literary Agent: David Grossman, 118B Holland Park Avenue, London W11 4UA, England. Address: 53 Melrose Avenue, Mitcham, Surrey CR4 2EH, England.

ANDELSON Robert V, b. 19 Feb 1931, Los Angeles, California, USA. Professor of Philosophy Emeritus; Writer; Editor. m. Bonny Orange Johnson, 7 June 1964. Education: AB equivalent, University of Chicago, 1952; AM, 1954, PhD, 1960, University of Southern California, Los Angeles. Appointments: Assistant Professor to Professor of Philosophy Emeritus, Auburn University, 1965-92; Distinguished Research Fellow, American Institute for Economic Research, 1993-. Publications: Imputed Rights: An Essay in Christian Social Theory, 1971; Critics of Henry George (editor and co-author), 1979; Commons Without Tragedy (editor and co-author), 1991; From Wasteland to Promised Land (with J M Dawsey), 1992; Land-Value Taxation Around the World (editor and co-author), 1997. Contributions to: Scholarly journals. Honours: Foundation for Social Research Award, 1959; Relm Foundation Award, 1967; George Washington Honor Medals, Freedoms Foundation, 1970, 1972; International Union for Land-Value Taxation and Free Trade, president, 1997-; Robert Schalkenbach Foundation, vice-president, 1998-. Address: 534 Cary Drive, Auburn, AL 36830, USA.

ANDERS Isabel, b. 16 Dec 1946. Writer. 2 daughters. Education: BA English, Wheaton College, Illinois, 1969; Northwestern University, Medill School of Journalism; MA, Mundelein College, Loyola University, Chicago, 1980. Appointments: Editor, David C Cook Communications, Elgin, Illinois, 1969-76; Book Editor, Tyndale House Publishers, Wheaton, Illinois, 1976-83; Managing Editor, Synthesis Publications, 1990-. Publications: Books: Awaiting the Child, 1987; Letter to Kristi, 1989; The Lord's Prayer, 1991; The Faces of Friendship, 1992; The Lord's Blessings, 1992; Walking with the Shepherd, 1994; Standing on High Places, 1994; A Book of Blessings for Working Mothers, 1994; The Wisdom of Little Women, 1995; Sand and Shells, Carousels and Silver Bells, 1996; Simple Blessings for Sacred Moments, 1998; The REAL Night Before Christmas, 1999. Honour: Ohio Arts Council Individual Artist in Creative Writing Award, 1988-89. Address: PO Box 277, Winchester, TN 37398, USA.

ANDERSEN Baltser, (Daniel Amb), b. 3 Jan 1956, Ribe, Denmark. Schoolteacher; Author; Poet. m. Magdaline Mattak, 26 Dec 1984, 2 daughters. Education: Tonder, 1975; Århus, 1976, 1986-88. Appointments: Teacher, Tonder, 1981, Greenland, 1982-87; Leader, Greenlandic Peace Movement, Sorsunnata, 1984-87. Publications: Poetry: Interlocking Hands, 1973; To Be Awake, 1974; Grey Asphalt, 1979; Travelling Spaceship, 1992; Angantyr and the Black Sword, 1993. Essay: In the Name of Democracy. Contributions to: Many leftwing Danish newspapers. Memberships: Norse Mythological Circle, Alfheim; Danish Writers' Union; Red-Green Alliance, 1993-. Address: Krusaavej 33 Alslevb, 6240 Logumkloster, Denmark.

ANDERSEN Benny Allan, b. 7 Nov 1929, Copenhagen, Denmark. Author. m. Cynthia La Touche Andersen, 28 Dec 1981. Publications: Den Musikalske al, 1960; Den Indre Bowlerhat, 1964; Portraetgaller, 1966; Tykke Olsen M Fl, 1968; Her i Reservatet, 1971; Himmelspraet, 1979; Tiden og Storken, 1985; Chagall & Skorpiondans, 1991; Denne Kommen og Gaen, 1993. Contributions to: Anthologies; Poetry Now; Prism International; West Coast Review; Literary Review; Scandinavian Review; Liberte; Svetova Literature. Address: Kaerparken 11, 2800 Lyngby, Denmark.

ANDERSEN Jolanta Buch, b. 9 Apr 1939, Miejsce Piastowe, Poland. President; Chief Executive Officer. m. Erling Buch Andersen, 6 Oct 1962. Education: BBA, 1974, 1982. Publications: Samfundsfjende, 1986; Samfundsven, 1987; Business Plan, Alex to Proste, 1994; How Easy. Contributions to: Various books and journals. Honour: Merkonomprisen, 1987. Membership: Danske Forfattforening. Address: Vejlesoparken 31, DK-2840 Holte, Denmark.

ANDERSON Barbara, b. 4 Apr 1926, New Zealand. Writer; Novelist. m. Neil Anderson, 2 sons. Education: BA, University of Otago, 1946; BA, Victoria University, Wellington. Publications: The Peacocks; Uncollected Short Stories, 1985; I Think We Should Go Into the Jungle (short stories), 1989; Girls High, 1990; We Could Celebrate, 1991; Portrait of the Artist's Wife, 1992; All the Nice Girls, 1993; The House Guest, 1995; Proud Garments, 1996; The Peacocks and Other Stories, 1997; Beginnings (essay), 1998; Several radio plays; Many short stories. Honours: John Cowie Reid Memorial Award (play), 1986; Ansett/Sunday Star Short Story Award, 1988; Timaru Herald/Aorak Short Story Award, 1990; Victoria University Fellowship, 1991; Goodman Fielder Wattie Award, 1992; Scholarship of Letters, 1994. Membership; PEN (New Zealand) committee member, 1992-94. Literary Agent: Caroline Dawnay, Peters Fraser & Dunlop, The Chambers, Chelsea Harbour, Lots Road, London SW10 0XF, England. Address: Victoria University Press, Victoria University, PO Box 600, Wellington, New Zealand.

ANDERSON David D(aniel), b. 8 June 1924, Lorain, Ohio, USA. Professor; Writer. m. Patricia Ann Rittenhour, 1 Feb 1953. Education: BS, 1951, MA, 1952, Bowling Green State University; PhD, Michigan State University, 1960. Appointments: Distinguished University Professor, Department of American Thought and Language, Michigan State University, East Lansing, 1957-; Editor, Midwestern Miscellany Annual; Executive Secretary, Society for the Study of Midwestern Literature, 1971-73. Publications: Louis Bromfield, 1964; Critical Studies in American Literature, 1964; Sherwood Anderson, 1967; Sherwood Anderson's Winesburg, Ohio, 1967; Brand Whitlock, 1968; The Black Experience (editor-in-chief), 1969; Abraham Lincoln, 1970; The Literary Works of Abraham Lincoln, 1970; The Dark and Tangled Path (with R Wright), 1971; Sunshine and Smoke, 1971; Robert Ingersoll, 1972; Mid-America I-XIV, 1974-87; Sherwood Anderson: Dimensions of His Literary Art (essays), 1976; Woodrow Wilson, 1978; Sherwood Anderson: The Writer at his Craft, 1979; Ignatius Donnelly, 1980; William Jennings Bryan, 1981; Critical Essays on Sherwood Anderson, 1981; Michigan: A State Anthology, 1982; Route Two, Titus, Ohio, 1993. Address: Department of American Thought and Language, Michigan State University, East Lansing, MI 48821, USA.

ANDERSON Eric George, b. 22 Apr 1932, Crieff, Perthshire, Scotland. Writer. m. Margaret Innes Hunter, 14 Sept 1955, 1 son, 2 daughters. Education: MB, ChB (Edin), 1958. Publications: Lightplane Vacationing, 1975; Plane Safety and Survival, 1978; The Pilot's Health, 1984. Contributions to: American Medical News; Geriatrics; Physician's Money Digest; Postgraduate Medicine; Medical Tribune. Memberships: American Society of Journalists and Authors; Motor Press Guild; Society of American Travel Writers. Address: 10205 Rue Touraine, San Diego, CA 92131-2230, USA.

ANDERSON Kenneth Lynn, b. 18 Sept 1945, Pineville, Louisiana, USA. Professor of English. 2 daughters. Education: Master Degree, Twentieth Century American & British Literature, Indiana University, 1969. Appointment: Professor, English, Floyd College. Publications: Someone Bought the House on the Island: A Novel; The Intense Lover: A Suite of Poems; Mattie Cushman: A Psychodrama. Contributions to: Chattahoochee Review; Lullwater Review; James White Review; Connecticut Poetry Review; Poem; International Poetry Review. Honours: Louisiana State University's Medal. Memberships: Poets & Writers; Associated Writing Programs. Address: 55 Pharr Road NW, A-108, Atlanta GA 30305, USA.

ANDERSON Kenneth Norman, b. 10 July 1921, Omaha, Nebraska, USA. Writer; Editor. Education: University of Omaha, 1939-41; BS, Oregon State College, 1944; Stanford University, 1944-45; Northwestern University, 1945-46. Appointments: Executive Editor, Publishers Editorial Services; President, Editorial Guild; Editor, Holt, Rinehart and Winston Inc, New York, 1965-70; Executive Director, Coffee Information Institute, New York, 1970-. Publications: Lawyer's Medical Cyclopedia (co-author), 1962; The Family Physician (with Robert Addison), 1963; Today's Health Guide (with William Baver), 1965; Pictorial Medical Guide (with Robert Addison), 1967; Field and Stream Guide to Physical Fitness, 1969; Home Medical Encyclopedia (with Paul Kuhn), 1973; Sterno Guide to the Outdoors, 1977; Eagle Claw Fish Cookbook, 1977; The Newsweek Encyclopedia of Family Health and Fitness, 1980; Banham Medical Dictionary (with Walter Glanze), 1980; How Long Will You Live, 1981; Dictionary of Dangerous Pollutants, Ecology and Environment (with David Tver), 1981; The Pocket Guide to Coffees and Teas, 1982; Orphan Drugs, 1983; Longman Dictionary of Psychology and Psychiatry (with Walter Glanze and Robert Goldenson), 1984; History of the US Marines (with Jack Murphy), 1984; Prentice-Hall Dictionary of Nutrition and Health (with Lois Harmon Anderson), 1985; Mosby Medical Encyclopedia (with Lois Harman Anderson and Walter Glanze), 1985; The International Dictionary of Food and Nutrition (with Lois Anderson), 1993; International Menu Speller (with Lois Anderson), 1993. Address: Coffee Information Institute, 60 East 42nd Street, New York, NY 10017, USA.

ANDERSON Leone Castell, b. 12 Aug 1923, Los Angeles, California, USA. Writer; Bookstore Proprietor. m. J Eric Anderson, 17 Aug 1946, 3 sons. Education: Austin Academy of Music, 1942-43. Appointments: Member of library staff, Elmhurst Public Library, Illinois, 1969-74; Owner and Operator, Lee's Booklover's, 1979-. Publications: Children's Books: The Good-By Day, 1984, reprinted as Moving Day, 1987; My Friend Next Door, 1984; Surprise at Muddy Creek, 1984; How Come You're So Shy?, 1987; My Own Grandpa, 1987; Other: Reader's theater pieces. Contributions to: Books, newspapers and magazines. Memberships: Society of Children's Book Writers (Midwest representative, 1981-87); Children's Reading Round Table; Authors Guild; Off-Campus Writer's Workshop. Address: Lee's Booklover's, 127 South Main, Stockton, IL 61085, USA.

ANDERSON Matthew Smith, b. 23 May 1922, Perth, Scotland. Historian; Retired Professor. m. Olive Ruth Gee, 10 July 1954, 2 daughters. Education: MA, 1947, PhD, 1952, University of Edinburgh. Appointments: Assistant Lecturer in History, University of Edinburgh, 1947-49; Assistant Lecturer, 1949-53, Lecturer, 1953-61, Reader, 1961-72, Professor of International History, 1972, now retired, London School of Economics and Political Science, University of London. Publications: Britain's Discovery of Russia, 1553-1815, 1958; Europe in the Eighteenth Century, 1713-1783, 1961, 3rd edition, 1987; The Eastern Question, 1966; Eighteenth Century Europe, 1966; The Great Powers and the Near East, 1774-1923, 1970; The Ascendancy of Europe, 1815-1914, 1972, 2nd edition, 1985; British Parliamentary Papers Relating to Russia, 1800-1900: A Critical Commentary, 1973; Peter the Great, 1978; Historians and Eighteenth-Century Europe, 1979; War and Society in Europe of the Old Regime, 1618-1789, 1988; The Rise of Modern Diplomacy, 1450-1919, 1993; The War of the Austrian Succession, 1740-1748, 1995; The Origins of the Modern European State System 1494-1618, 1998. Contributions to: Numerous historical periodicals. Memberships: Royal Historical Society; Past and Present Society. Address: 45 Cholmeley Crescent, Highgate, London N6 5EX, England.

ANDERSON Michael Falconer, b. 16 Jan 1947, Aberdeen, Scotland. Author; Journalist. m. Hildegarde Becze, 16 Apr 1970, 2 sons. Appointments: Newspaper and Magazine Editor; Chief Sub-Editor of a national weekly; Sub-Editor of a daily newspaper; Showbusiness Writer; Reporter; Correspondent in newspapers, television and radio. Publications: The Woodsmen, 1986; The Unholy, 1987; God of a Thousand Faces, 1987; The Covenant, 1988; Black Trinity, 1989; The Clan of Golgotha Scalp, 1990; Numerous short stories and plays for radio and television. Contributions to: Feature articles on everything from travel to history, the environment to books, in newspapers and magazines around the world. Memberships: Society of Authors; National Union of Journalists. Address: Portlehen, Aberdeen, Scotland.

ANDERSON Poul William, b. 25 Nov 1926, Bristol, Pennsylvania, USA. Writer. m. Karen Kruse, 12 Dec 1953, 1 daughter. Education: BS, University of Minnesota, 1948. Publications: Brain Wave, 1954; The High Crusade, 1960; Guardians of Time, 1961; Three Hearts and Three Lions, 1961; Tau Zero, 1971; The Broken Sword (revised edition), 1971; Hrolf Kraki's Saga, 1973; A Midsummer's Tempest, 1974; The Atavar, 1978; The Merman's Children, 1979; Orion Shall Rise, 1983; The Boat of a Million Years, 1989; Harvest of Stars, 1993; The Stars Are Also Fire, 1994; The Fleet of Stars, 1997; War of the Gods, 1997; Starfarers, 1998. Contributions to: Analog; Magazine of Fantasy and Science Fiction; Destinies; National Review; Boy's Life and others. Honours: Hugo Awards, 1961, 1964, 1968, 1971, 1973, 1978, 1982; Nebula Awards, 1971, 1972, 1981; Knight of Mark Twain, 1971; Mythopoeic Award, 1975; J R R Tolkien Memorial Award, 1978; Grand Master Award, Science Fiction Writers of America, 1998. Memberships: Science Fiction Writers of America, president, 1972-73; Baker Street Irregulars. Literary Agent: Chichak Inc, New York. Address: 3 Las Palomas, Orinda, CA 94563, USA.

ANDERSON Quentin, b. 21 July 1912, Minnewaukan, North Dakota, USA. Writer; Retired University Lecturer. Education: AB, 1937, PhD, 1953, Columbia University; MA, Harvard University, 1945. Appointments: Columbia University, 1939-82; University of Sussex, 1966-67; University of Barcelona, 1985. Publications: Selected Short Stories by Henry James, 1950; The American Henry James, 1957; The Proper Study: Essays on Western Classics (with Joseph A Mazzeo), 1962; The Imperial Self: An Essay in American Literary and Cultural History, 1971; Art, Politics and Will: Essays in Honor of Lionel Trilling (with others), 1977; Making Americans: An Essay on Individualism and Money, 1992. Honours: National Endowment for the Humanities, Senior Fellow, 1973; Fellow, National Humanities Center, 1979-80, New York Institute for the Humanities, 1981-95; Paley Lecturer, Hebrew University of Jerusalem, 1982. Address: 29 Claremont Avenue, New York, NY 10027, USA.

ANDERSON Rachel, b. 18 Mar 1943, Hampton Court, Surrey, England. Writer; Dramatist. m. David Bradby, 4 children. Publications: Books for adults: Pineapple, 1965; The Purple Heart Throbs: A Survey of Popular Romantic Fiction, 1850-1972, 1974; Dream Lovers, 1978; For the Love of Sang, 1990. Books for small children: Tim Walks, 1985; The Cat's Tale, 1985; Wild Goose Chase, 1986; Jessy Runs Away, 1988; Best Friends, 1991; Jessy and the Long-Short Dress, 1992; Tough as Old Boots, 1991; Little Lost Fox, 1992. For older children: Moffatt's Road, 1978; The Poacher's Son, 1982; The War Orphan, 1984; Little Angel Comes to Stay, 1985; Renard the Fox (with David Bradby), 1986; Little Angel, Bonjour, 1988; French Lessons, 1988; The Boy Who Laughed, 1989; The Bus People, 1989; Paper Faces, 1991; When Mum Went to Work, 1992; The Working Class, 1993. Honours: Medical Journalists Association Award 1990; 25th Anniversary Guardian Children's Fiction Award, 1992. Address: c/o Oxford University Press, Oxford OX2 6DP, England.

ANDERSON Robert David, b. 20 Aug 1927, Shillong, Assam, India. Lecturer; Writer. Education: MA, Gonville and Caius College, Cambridge, England, 1957. Appointments: Director, Music, Gordonstoun School, 1958-62; Extra-Mural Lecturer, University of London, 1966-77; Associate Editor, The Musical Times, 1967-85; Visiting Lectr, City University, 1983-92. Publications: Egyptian Antiquities in the British Museum III: Musical Instruments, 1976; Wagner, 1980; Egypt In 1800, joint editor, 1988; Elgar in Manuscript, 1990; Elgar, 1993. Contributions to: Many contributions to The Musical Times. Honour: Honorary DMus, City Univ, 1985. Memberships: Egypt Exploration Society, Honorary Secretary, 1971-82. Address: 54 Hornton Street, London W8 4NT, England.

ANDERSON Robert Woodruff, b. 28 Apr 1917, New York, New York, USA. Playwright; Screenwriter; Novelist. Education: AB, Magna Cum Laude, 1939, MA, 1940, Harvard University. Publications: Plays: Tea and Sympathy, 1953; All Summer Long, 1954; Silent Night Lonely Night, 1959; The Days Between, 1965; You Know I Can't Hear When the Water's Running, 1967; I Never Sang for My Father, 1968; Solitaire/Double Solitaire, 1971; Free and Clear, 1983. Co-Author: Elements of Literature, 1988; Novels: After, 1973; Getting Up and Going Home, 1978. Screenplays: Tea and Sympathy, 1956; Until They Sail, 1957; The Nun's Story, 1959; The Sand Pebbles, 1966; I Never Sang For My Father, 1970; The Last Act is a Solo, 1991; Absolute Strangers, 1991. Honours: Writer's Guild Award, 1970; Ace Award, 1991. Memberships: Dramatists Guild, president, 1971-73; Authors League Council; Writers Guild of America West; American Playwrights Theatre, board of trustees; Theatre Hall of Fame, 1981; PEN. Address: 14 Sutton Place South, New York, NY 10022, USA.

ANDERSONE Maija, b. 7 Nov 1930, Latvia. Translator. 1 daughter. Education: Riga Pedagogical Institute, Foreign Language Faculty, 1953. Appointments: Editor, Latvian Publishing House of Newspapers and Magazines, 1953-56; Teacher of English Philology, Foreign Language Faculty, Latvia State University, 1956-87. Publications: Translations: Collection of English and American Stories, 1965; J Cusack, Heatware in Berlin, 1966; Black Lightning, 1980; R Bradbury, The Martian Chronicles, 1967; Sillitoe, The Loneliness of the Longdistance Runner, 1968; E Hemingway, To Have and Have Not, 1972; Across the River and Into the Trees, 1973; J Murdoch, Under the Net, 1978; J Fowles, The Ebony Tower, 1982; N Price, Sleeping with the Enemy, 1994; D Simpson, Close Her Eyes, 1995; P Scott, The Jewel in the Crown, 1998. Memberships: Latvian Writers Union, 1976. Address: Ligatnes 1-1, Riga, LV-1014, Latvia.

ANDRÉE Alice. See: CLUYSENAAR Anne.

ANDRENIO. See: ALONSO ALVAREZ Emilio.

ANDRESKI Stanislav Leonard, b. 18 May 1919, Czestochowa, Poland. Writer; Professor Emeritus. 2 sons, 2 daughters. Education: BSc, 1st Class Honours, 1943, MSc, 1947, Economics, PhD, 1953. Appointments: Professor Emeritus, University of Reading and Polish University in London; Editorial Board, Journal of Strategic Studies. Publications: Military Organisation & Society, 1954, 2nd edition, 1968; Elements of Comparative Sociology, 1964; Parasitism & Subversion: The Case of Latin America, 1966, 2nd edition, 1969; The African Predicament: A Study in Pathology of Modernisation, 1968; Social Sciences as Sorcery, 1972; The Prospects of a Revolution in the USA, 1973; Max Weber's Insights & Errors, 1984; Syphilis, Puritanism and Witch Hunts: Historical Explanations in the Light of Medicine and Psychoanalysis with a Forecast About Aids, 1989; Wars, Revolutions, Dictatorships, 1992. Editor: Herbert Spencer: Principles of Sociology, 1968; Herbert Spencer: Structure, Function and Evolution, 1971; The Essential

Comte, 1974; Reflections on Inequality, 1975; Max Weber on Capitalism, Bureaucracy and Religion, 1984. Contributions to: Approximately 90 articles in learned journals. Memberships: Writers' Guild; Institute of Patentees and Inventors. Address: Farriers, Village Green, Upper Basildon, Berkshire RG8 8LS, England.

ANDREW Prudence (Hastings), b. 23 May 1924, London, England. Author. Education: Honours degree in history, St Anne's College, Oxford, 1946. Publications: The Hooded Falcon, 1960; Ordeal by Silence, 1961; Ginger Over the Wall, 1962; A Question of Choice, 1963; Ginger and Batty Billy, 1963; The Earthworms, 1964; Ginger and No 10, 1964; The Constant Star, 1964; A Sparkle from the Coal, 1964; Christmas Card, 1966; Mr Morgan's Marrow, 1967; Mister O'Brien, 1972; Rodge, Sylvie and Munch, 1973; Una and Grubstreet, 1973; Goodbye to the Rat, 1974; The Heroic Deeds of Jason Jones, 1975; Where Are You Going To, My Pretty Maid?, 1977; Robinson Daniel Crusoe, 1978 (in USA as Close Within My Own Circle, 1980); The Other Side of the Park, 1984. Address: c/o W Heinemann Ltd, 10 Upper Grosvenor Street, London W1X 9PA, England.

ANDREWS Elmer (Elmer Kennedy-Andrews), b. 26 Jan 1948, Northern Ireland. Senior Lecturer in English. m.(1) 20 June 1976, 2 daughters, (2) 16 Mar 1998. Education: BA, 1970, MA, 1973, PhD, 1976, Queen's University, Belfast. Appointments: Thessaloniki University, Greece, 1972-74; Mohammed V University, Rabat, Morocco, 1976-80; Queen's University, Belfast, 1980-81; University of Ulster, 1981-. Publications: The Poetry of Seamus Heaney; All the Realms of Whisper; Seamus Heaney: A Collection of Critical Essays; Contemporary Irish Poetry; The Art of Brian Frièl: Neither Reality nor Dreams; National Hawlkorne: The Scarlet Letters. Contributions to: Many journals and magazines on Irish and American literature and culture. Honours: Porter Scholarship; Foundation Scholarship. Address: Department of English, University of Ulster, Coleraine, Northern Ireland.

ANDREWS Graham, b. 3 Feb 1948, Belfast, Northern Ireland. Writer. m. Agnes Helena Ferguson, 10 Apr 1982. Education: BA, History and Psychology, Open University, Milton Keynes, England, 1979-86. Appointments: Associate Editor, Extro Science Fiction Magazine, 1980-81; Staff Writer, World Association for Orphans and Abandoned Children, 1990-91. Publications: The Fragile Future, 1990; The Wao Vocational Training Programme, 1990; Darkness Audible (science fiction novel), 1991; St Jame's Guide to Fantasy Writers (contributor), 1996; Two Just Men: Richard S Prather and Shell Scott (forthcoming). Contributions to: Belfast Telegraph; Brussels Bulletin; The Guardian; Interzone; Million Vector Foundation Book and Magazine. Honour: Aisling Gheal (Bright Vision) Award, Irish Science Fiction Association, 1980. Memberships: Society of Authors; Royal Society of Literature; British Science Fiction Association. Address: Avenue Du Merle 37, 1640 Rhode-Saint-Genese, Belgium.

ANDREWS Lucilla Matthew, (Diana Gordon, Joanna Marcus), Writer. Publications: The Print Petticoat, 1954; The Secret Armour, 1955; The Quiet Wards, 1956; The First Year, 1957; A Hospital Summer, 1958; My Friend the Professor, 1960; Nurse Errant, 1961; The Young Doctors Downstairs, 1963; Flowers for the Doctor, 1963; The New Sister Theatre, 1964; The Light in the Ward, 1965; A House for Sister Mary, 1966; Hospital Circles, 1967; A Few Days in Endel (as Diana Gordon), 1968; Highland Interlude, 1968; The Healing Time, 1969; Edinburgh Excursion, 1970; Ring o' Roses, 1972; Silent Song, 1973; In Storm and in Calm, 1975; No Time for Romance: An Autobiographical Account of a Few Moments in British and Personal History (non-fiction), 1977; The Crystal Gull, 1978; One Night in London, 1979; Marsh Blood (as Joanna Marcus), 1980; A Weekend in the Garden, 1981; In an Edinburgh Drawing Room, 1983; After a Famous Victory, 1984; The Lights of London, 1985. Address: c/o W Heinemann Ltd, 81 Fulham Road, London SW3 6RB, England.

ANDREWS Lyman, b. 2 Apr 1938, Denver, Colorado, USA. Poet. Education: BA, Brandeis University, 1960. Appointments: Lecturer, American Literature, University of Leicester, 1965-88; Visiting Professor of English, Indiana University, Bloomington, 1978-79; Poetry Critic, The Sunday Times, London, 1968-79. Publications: Ash Flowers, 1958; Fugitive Visions, 1962; The Death of Mayakovsky and Other Poems, 1968; Kaleidoscope: New and Selected Poems, 1973. Address: Flat 4-32, Victoria Centre, Nottingham NG1 3PA, England.

ANGEL Leonard Jay, b. 20 Sept 1945. Writer; Dramatist; Lecturer. m. Susan, 1 son, 1 daughter, 1 stepdaughter. Education: BA, Philosophy, McGill University, 1966; MA, Philosophy, 1968, MA, Creative Writing and Theatre, 1970, PhD, Philosophy, 1974, University of British Columbia. Appointments: Department of Creative Writing, University of British Columbia, 1981-82; University of Victoria, 1984-86. Publications: Antietam, 1975; Isadora and G B, 1976; The Unveiling, 1981; The Silence of the Mystic, 1983; Eleanor Marx, 1985; How to Build a Conscious Machine, 1989; Englightenment East and West, 1994; The Book of Miriam, 1997. Contributions to: Dialogue and Dialectic, Dialogue, 1991; Six of One: Capilano Review, 1985. Honours: 1st Prize, Short Fiction, McGill Daily, 1963; 1st Prize (joint), Playhouse Theatre Award, 1971; Canada Council Artist B Grants, 1979, 1982; Nominee, Jessie Award, Best New Play, 1982. Memberships: Playwrights Canada, 1976-88; Guild of Canadian Playwrights, chairman, British Columbia region, 1978-79; Regional Representative, 1980-81. Address: 865 Durward Avenue, Vancouver, British Columbia V5V 2Z1, Canada.

ANGELOU Maya, b. 4 Apr 1928, St Louis, Missouri, USA. Poet; Writer; Professor. m. (1) Tosh Angelou, div, (2) Paul Du Feu, 1973, div, 1 son. Education: Studied music; Received training in modern dance from Martha Graham, Pearl Primus, and Ann Halprin, in drama from Frank Silvera and Gene Frankel. Appointments: Taught modern dance, Rome Opera and Hambina Theater, Tel Aviv, 1955; Appeared in Off-Broadway plays; Northern Coordinator, Southern Christian Leadership Conference, 1959-60; Assistant Administrator, School of Music and Drama, Institute of African Studies, University of Ghana, 1963-66; Lecturer, University of California at Los Angeles, 1966; Writer-in-Residence, University of Kansas, 1970; Distinguished Visiting Professor, Wake Forest University, 1974, Wichita State University, 1974, California State University at Sacramento, 1974; 1st Reynolds Professor of American Studies, Wake Forest University (lifetime appointment), 1981-; Many television appearances in various capacities. Publications: Poetry: Just Give Me a Cool Drink of Water 'fore I Diie, 1971; Oh Pray My Wings Are Gonna Fit Me Well, 1975; And Still I Rise, 1978; Shaker, Why Don't You Sing?, 1983; Poems: Maya Angelou, 1986; I Shall Not Be Moved, 1990; On the Pulse of Morning, for the inauguration of President Bill Clinton, 1993; The Complete Poems of Maya Angelou, 1994; Phenomenal Woman: Four Poems Celebrating Women, 1995. Fiction: Mrs. Flowers: A Moment of Friendship, 1986; Short stories; stage, film and television plays. Non-Fiction: I Know Why the Caged Bird Sings, 1970; Gather Together In My Name, 1974; Singin' and Swingin' and Gettin' Merry Like Christmas, 1976; The Heart of a Woman, 1981; All God's Children Need Traveling Shoes, 1986; Even the Stars Look Lonesome, 1998. Contributions to: Many publications. Honours: Yale University Fellowship, 1970; Rockefeller Foundation Scholarship for Italy, 1975; Member, American Revolution Bicentennial Comission, 1975-76; Woman of the Year in Communications, 1976; Matrix Award, 1983; North Carolina Award in Literature, 1987; Distinguished Woman of North Carolina, 1992; Horatio Alger Award, 1992; Grammy Award for On the Pulse of Morning, 1994; National Women's Hall of Fame, 1998. Memberships: Directors Guild; Harlem Writers Guild; Women's Prison Association, advisory board. Address: c/o Dave La Camera, Lordly and Dame Inc, 51 Church Street, Boston, MA 02116, USA.

ANGHELAKI-ROOKE Katerina, b. 22 Feb 1939, Athens, Greece. Poet; Translator. Education: Universities of Nice, Athens, Geneva, 1957-63. Appointments: Freelance Translator, 1962-; Visiting Professor (Fulbright), Harvard University, 1980; Visiting Fellow, Princeton University, 1987. Publications: Wolves and Clouds, 1963; Poems, 1963-69, 1971; The Body is the Victory and the Defeat of Dreams, 1975; The Scattered Papers of Penelope, 1977; The Triumph of Constant Loss, 1978; Counter Love, 1982; The Suitors, 1984; Beings and Things on Their Own, 1986; When the Body, 1988; Wind Epilogue, 1990; Empty Nature, 1993; Translations of Works by Shakespeare, Albee, Dylan Thomas, Beckett and Nikos Kazantzakis. Honour: Greek National Poetry Prize, 1985. Address: Synesiou Kyrenes 4, 114 71 Athens, Greece.

ANGLUND Joan Walsh, b. 3 Jan 1926, Hinsdale, Illinois, USA. Children's Writer. Education: Chicago Art Institute, 1944. Publications: A Friend is Someone Who Likes You, 1958; Look Out the Window, 1959; The Brave Cowboy, 1959; Love is a Special Way of Feeling, 1960; In a Pumpkin Shell: A Mother Goose ABC, 1960; Christmas Is a Time of Giving, 1961; Cowboy and His Friend, 1961; Nibble Nible Mousekin: A Tale of Hansel and Gretel, 1962; Cowboy's Secret Life, 1963; Spring is a New Beginning, 1963; Childhood Is a Time of Innocence, 1964; A Pocketful of Proverbs (verse), 1964; A Book of Good Tidings from the Bible, 1965; What Color is Love?, 1966; A Year is Round, 1966; A Cup of Sun: A Book of Poems, 1967; A Is for Always: An ABC Book, 1968; Morning Is a Little Child (verse), 1969; A Slice of Snow: A Book of Poems, 1970; Do You Love Someone?, 1971; The Cowboy's Christmas, 1972; A Child's Book of Old Nursery Rhymes, 1973; Goodbye, Yesterday: A Book of Poems, 1974; Storybook, 1978; Emily and Adam, 1979; Almost a Rainbow, 1980; A Gift of Love, 5 volumes, 1980; A Christmas Cookie Book, 1982; Rainbow Love, 1982; Christmas Candy Book, 1983; A Christmas Book, 1983; See the Year, 1984; Coloring Book, 1984; Memories of the Heart, 1984; Teddy Bear Tales, 1985; Baby Brother, 1985; All About Me!, 1986; Christmas is Here!, 1986; Tubtime for Thaddeus, 1986; A Mother Goose Book, 1991; A Child's Year, 1992; Love is a Baby, 1992; The Way of Love, 1992; Bedtime Book, 1993; The Friend We Have Not Met, 1993; Peace is a Circle of Love, 1993. Address: c/o Random House, 201 East 50th Street, New York, NY 10022, USA.

ANGREMY Jean-Pierre, (Pierre-Jean Remy), b. 21 Mar 1937, Angouleme, France. Diplomat; Author. m.(1) Odile Cail, 1963, div 1979, 1 son, 1 daughter, (2) Sophie Schmit, 1986, 1 son. Education: Institut d'Études Politiques, 1955-60; Brandeis University, 1958-59; École Nationale d'Administration, 1960-63. Appointments: Diplomatic Service, Hong Kong, 1963; Second Secretary, Beijing, 1964, London, 1966; First Secretary, London, 1968; Counsellor, Ministry of Foreign Affairs, 1971; Director and Programme Coordinator, ORTF, 1972; Cultural Counsellor, French Embassy, London, 1975-79, French Ministry of Culture, 1979-81; Consul General de France, Florence, 1985-87; Director General, Cultural Exchanges, Ministry of Foreign Affairs, 1987-90; French Ambassador to UNESCO, 1990-93; Director, French Academy, Rome, 1994-97; President, French National Library, 1997. Publications: Et Gulliver mourut de sommeil, 1961; Midi ou l'attentat, 1962; Gaugins a gogo, 1971; La sac du palais d'ete, 1971; Urbanisme, 1972; Une mort sale, 1973; La vie d'Adrian Putney, 1973; Ava, La mort de Floria Tosca, memoires secrets pour servir a l'histoire de ce siècle, 1974; Rever la vie, 1975; La figure dans la pierre, 1976; Chine: Un itineraire, 1977; Les Enfans du parc, 1977; Si j'etais romancier, 1977; Callas: Une vie, 1978; Les nouvelles aventures du Chevalier de la Barre, 1978; Orient Express, 1979; Cordelia ou l'Angleterre, 1979; Don Giovanni, 1979; Pandora, 1980; Slaue pour moir le monde, 1980; Un voyage d'hiver, 1981; Don Juan, 1982; Le dernier été, 1983; Mata Hari, 1983; La vie d'un hero, 1985; Une ville immortelle, 1986; Des Chatevoux Allamagne, 1987; Toscanes, 1989; Algerie bords-de-Seine, 1990; Un cimitière rouge en Nouvelle Angleterre, 1991; Desir d'Europe, 1995; Le Rose et le Blanc, 1997. Honours: Officier, Légion d'Honneur; Officier, Ordre National du Merité; Commandeur des Arts et des Lettres. Membership:

Academie Française, member, 1987. Address: Bibliotheque Nationale de France, 58 Rue de Richelieu, 75002, Paris, France.

ANGUS Ian. See: **MACKAY James Alexander.**

ANGUS Tom. See: **POWELL Geoffrey Stewart.**

ANMAR Frank. See: **NOLAN William F(rancis).**

ANNOTATOR. See: **PEK Pal.**

ANNWN David, (David James Jones), b. 9 May 1953, Congleton, Cheshire, England. Poet; Critic; Lecturer. m. 26 Apr 1994. Education: Wigan Technical College, 1970-72; BA, Honours, English, 1975, PhD, Modern Poetry, 1978, University College of Wales, Aberystwyth; PGCE, Bath University, 1979. Appointments: Postgraduate Tutor, Aberystwyth University, 1975-78; Lecturer, 1981-88, Head of English Degree Work, 1988-95, Wakefield College; Lecturer, Tutor, and Examiner, Open University, 1995-96; Lecturer in Creative Writing, Leeds University, 1996. Publications: Poetry: Foster the Ghost, 1984; King Saturn's Book, 1986; The Other, 1988; Primavera Violin, 1990; The Spirit/That Kiss, 1993; Dantean Designs, 1995; Danse Macabre, Death and the Printers (with Kelvin Corcoran, Alan Halsey, and Gavin Selerie), 1997. Other: Inhabited Voices: Myth and History in the Poetry of Seamus Heaney, Geoffrey Hill and George Mackay Brown, 1984; Catgut and Blossom: Jonathon Williams in England (editor), 1989; A Different Can of Words (editor), 1992; Presence, Spacing Sign: The Graphic Art of Peterjon Skelt, 1993; Hear the Voice of the Bard!: The Early Bards, William Blake and Robert Duncan, 1995; Poetry in the British Isles: Non-Metropolitan Perspectives, 1995; Inner Celtia (with Alan Richardson), 1996; A Breton Herbal: Translations of Poems by Eugene Guillevic, 1998. Contributions to: Anthologies: Anglo-Welsh Review; Poetry Wales; Ambit; Iron; Scintilla; David Jones Society Journal. Honours: Winner, International Collegiate Eisteddfod, 1975; Prize, Ilkley Arts Festival, 1982; Bursary Award, Yorkshire Arts, 1985; 1st Prize, Cardiff International Poetry Competition, 1996. Memberships: H.A.N. Humanities and Arts Higher Education Network; Northern Associatioin of Writers in Education; Welsh Academy. Address: 3 Westfield Park, College Grove, Wakefield, West Yorkshire WF1 3RP, England.

ANSCOMBE Isabelle Mary, b. 4 Oct 1954, London, England. Author; Journalist; Scriptwriter; Broadcaster. m. Howard Grey, 17 Dec 1981, 1 daughter. Education: BA, 1976, MA, 1978, Newnham College, Cambridge. Publications: Not Another Punk Book, 1978; Arts & Crafts in Britain and America, 1978; Omega and After, 1981; A Woman's Touch, 1860 to the Present Day, 1984; Arts and Crafts Style, 1991. Contributions to: Sunday Times; Independent; Daily Telegraph; Cosmopolitan. Memberships: Writers' Guild; Romantic Novelists Association. Address: c/o AM Heath Ltd, 79 St Martins Lane, London WC2N 4AA, England.

ANSELL Jonathan. See: **WOLFF Tobias.**

ANTHONY Barbara, (Antonia Barber), b. Aug 1956, London, England. Writer. m. Kenneth Charles Anthony, 2 sons, 1 daughter. Education: BA Hons, English Language Literature, University College, London, England. Publications: The Ghosts (filmed as The Amazing Mr Blunden); The Ring in the Rough Stuff; The Enchanters Daughter; The Mousehole Cat; Catkin; Taken from the Ballet; Noah and the Ark; The Monkey and the Panda; Tales From Grimm; Apollo and Daphne; Dancing Shoes (series). Membership: Society of Authors. Literary Agent: David Higham, 5-8 Lower John Street, Golden Square, London W1R 4HA, England. Address: David Higham, 5-8 Lower John Street, Golden Square, London W1R 4HA, England.

ANTHONY Evelyn, b. 3 July 1928, England. m. Michael Ward-Thomas, 1955. Education: Convent of Sacred Heart, Roehampton. Publications: Imperial Highness, 1953; Curse Not the King, 1954; Far Flies the Eagle, 1955; Anne Boleyn, 1957; Victoria and Albert, 1958; Elizabeth, 1960; Charles the King, 1961; The Heiress, 1964; The Rendezvous, 1967; Anne of Austria, 1968; The Legend, 1969; The Assassin, 1970; The Tamarind Seed, 1971; The Occupying Power, 1973; The Malaspiga Exit, 1974; The Persian Ransom, 1975; The Silver Falcon, 1977; The Return, 1978; The Grave of Truth, 1979; The Defector, 1980; The Avenue of the Dead, 1981; Albatross, 1982; The Company of Saints, 1983; Voices on the Wind, 1985; No Enemy but Time, 1987; The House of Vandekar, 1988; The Scarlet Thread, 1989; The Relic, 1991; The Doll's House, 1992; Exposure, 1993; Bloodstones, 1994; The Legacy, 1996. Honours: US Literary Guild Award, 1958; Yorkshire Post Fiction Prize, 1974; High Sheriff of Essex, 1994; Deputy Lieutenant of Essex, 1995. Address: Horham Hall, Thaxted, Essex, England.

ANTHONY James R(aymond), b. 18 Feb 1922, Providence, Rhode Island, USA. Professor; Musicologist. m. Louise MacNair, 24 May 1952, 1 son, 2 daughters. Education: BS, 1946, MA, 1948, Columbia University; Diploma, Sorbonne, University of Paris, 1951; PhD, University of Southern California at Los Angeles, 1964. Appointments: Faculty, University of Montana, 1948-50; University of Arizona, 1952-. Publications: French Baroque Music from Beaujoyeul to Rameau, 1973, revised edition, 1978; revised and enlarged edition, 1997; translated into French as La musique en France a L'epoque baroque, 1981; Edited music by Baroque composers. Contributions to: Church Music in France, 1661-1750, New Oxford History of Music (with N Dufourcq), 1975; More than 40 articles in The New Grove Dictionary of Music and Musicians, 1980; Many journals, including Acta Musicologia; Early Music; Journal of the American Musicological Society; Notes. Honours: Research Grants; J Heyer, editor, Jean-Baptist Lully and the Music of the French Baroque: Essays in Honour of James Anthony, 1988. Memberships: American Musicological Society, council member, 1975-77, 1983-85; American Association of University Professors; Société Française de Musicologie. Address: 800 North Wilson Avenue, Tucson, AZ 85719, USA.

ANTHONY Michael, b. 10 Feb 1930, Mayaro, Trinidad and Tobago. Writer. m. Yvette Francesca, 8 Feb 1958, 2 sons, 2 daughters. Education: Mayaro Roman Catholic School; Junior Technical College, San Fernando, Trinidad. Appointments: Sub Editor, Reuters News Agency, London, 1964-68; Assistant Editor, Texas Star, Texaco Trinidad, Pointe-a-Pierre, Trinidad and Tobago, 1972-88; Teacher of Creative Writing, University of Richmond, Virginia, USA, 1992. Publications: Novels: The Games Were Coming, 1963; The Year in San Fernando, 1965; Green Days by the River, 1967; Streets of Conflict, 1976; All That Glitters, 1981; Bright Road to Eldorado, 1982. Stories: Cricket in the Road and Other Stories, 1973; Sandra Street and Other Stories, 1973; Folk Tales and Fantasies, 1976; The Chieftain's Carnival and Other Stories, 1993. Other: Glimpses of Trinidad and Tobago, with a Glance at the West Indies, 1974; King of the Masquerade, 1974; Profile Trinidad: A Historical Survey from the Discovery to 1900, 1975; The Making of Port-of-Spain, 1757-1939, 1978; Port-of-Spain in a World War, 1939-1945, 1984; First in Trinidad, 1985; Heroes of the People of Trinidad and Tobago, 1986; A Brighter and Better day, 1987; Towns and Villages of Trinidad and Tobago, 1988; Parade of the Carnivals of Trinidad, 1839-1989, 1989; The Golden Quest: The Four Voyages of Christopher Columbus, 1992. Editor: The History of Aviation in Trinidad and Tobago, 1913-1962, 1987. Contributions to: Various periodicals. Address: 99 Long Circular Road, St James, Port-of-Spain, Trinidad and Tobago.

ANTIN David, b. 1 Feb 1932, New York, New York, USA. Professor of Visual Arts; Poet. m. Eleanor Fineman, 1960, 1 son. Education: BA, City College, New York City, 1955; MA in Linguistics, New York University, 1966. Appointments: Chief Editor and Scientific Director, Research Information Service, 1958-60; Curator, Institute of Contemporary Art, Boston, 1967; Director, University Art Gallery, 1968-72, Assistant Professor, 1968-72, Professor of Visual Arts, 1972-, University of California at San Diego. Publications: Definitions, 1967; Autobiography, 1967; Code of Flag Behavior, 1968; Meditiations, 1971; Talking, 1972; After the War, 1973; Talking at the Boundaries, 1976; Who's Listening Out There?, 1980; Tuning, 1984; Poèmes Parlés, 1984; Selected Poems 1963-73, 1991; What it Means to be Avant Garde, 1993. Contributions to: Periodicals. Honours: Longview Award, 1960; University of California Creative Arts Award, 1972; Guggenheim Fellowship, 1976; National Endowment for the Humanities Fellowship, 1983; PEN Award for Poetry, 1984. Address: PO Box 1147, Del Mar, CA 92014, USA.

ANTOINE Yves, b. 12 Dec 1941, Port-au-Prince, Haiti. Professor; Writer; Poet. 1 daughter. Education: MEd, 1972, LittD, 1988, University of Ottawa. Publications: La Veillée, 1964; Témoin Oculaire, 1970; Au gré des heures, 1972; Les sabots de la nuit, 1974; Alliage, 1979; Libations pour le soleil, 1985; Sémiologie et personnage romanesque chez Jacques S Alexis, 1993; Polyphonie (poetry and prose), 1996. Contributions to: Une affligeante réalité, Le Droit, Ottawa, 1987; L'indélébile, Symbiosis, Ottawa, 1992; Inventeurs et savants noirs, 1998. Honour: Guest, Harambee Foundation Society, 1988. Memberships: Union of Writers, Quebec; Ligue des Droits et Liberté; Association des auteurs de l'Outaouais québécois. Address: 200 boul Cité des Jeunes, app 403, Hull, Quebec J8Y 6M1, Canada.

ANTROBUS John, b. 2 July 1933, London, England. Dramatist; Author; Screenwriter. m. Margaret McCormick, 1958, div 1980, 2 sons, 1 daughter. Education: King Edward VII Nautical College; Royal Military Academy, Sandhurst. Publications: Plays: The Bed-Sitting Room (with Spike Milligan), 1963; Captain Oate's Left Sock, 1969; Walton on Thames, 1970, revised version as The Bed-Sitting Room 2, 1983; Crete and Sergeant Pepper, 1972; Jonah, 1979; Hitler in Liverpool, 1980; One Orange for the Baby, 1980; Up in the Hide, 1980; When Did You Last See Your Trousers? (with Ray Galton), 1986. Screenplays: Carry on Sergeant (with Norman Hudis), 1958; Idol on Parade, 1959; The Wrong Arm of the Law (with others), 1962; The Big Job (with Talbot Rothwell), 1965; The Bed-Sitting Room (with Charles Wood), 1969. Children's Books: The Boy with Illuminating Measles, 1978; Help! I'm a Prisoner in a Toothpaste Factory, 1978; Ronnie and the Haunted Rolls Royce, 1982; Ronnie and the Great Knitted Robbery, 1982; Ronnie and the High Rise, 1992; Ronnie and the Flying Carpet, 1992. Contributions to: Radio and television. Honours: George Devine Award, 1970; Writers Guild Award, 1971; Arts Council Bursaries, 1973, 1976, 1980, 1982; Banff Television Festival Award for Best Comedy, 1987; Finalist, International Emmy Awards, 1987. Memberships: Writers Guild of America West; Writers Guild of Great Britain. Address: 20 Powis Mews, London W11 1JN, England.

ANVIL Christopher. See: **CROSBY Harry Clifton.**

ANYWAR Ojera Frank, b. 3 Mar 1953, Gulu, Uganda. Consultant. m. Olivia Anywar, 4 sons, 2 daughters. Education: Certificate, Animal Disease, Husbandry and Industry, Entebbe, Uganda, 1975-77; Diploma, Dairy Technology, Egerton, Kenya, 1978-81; MSc, Business Management, Marlborough, USA, 1997-99. Appointments: Production Supervisor, Dairy Corporation, Uganda, 1982-89; Regional Dairy Officer, Southwest Uganda, 1989-91, Northeast Uganda, 1991-96; Sales Representative, APV East Africa, 1996-98; Managing Director, Lacto-Talents Ltd, 1999-. Publications: Voices of the Dead (poetry), 1989; The Storm of Succession (satire), 1990; Wars No More (poetry), 1991; The False Success (fiction), 1998; The Cursed Generation, 1999; Warrior Without Choice. Honours: Literary Award, National Library of Poetry, USA, 1991. Membership: International Society of Poets, distinguished member; Uganda Writers Association, chairman. Address: c/o Panywar Foundation Ltd, PO Box 4070, Kampala, Uganda.

APFEL Necia H(alpern), b. 31 July 1930, Mt Vernon, New York, USA. Science Writer. m. Donald A Apfel, 7 Sept 1952, dec, 1 son, 1 daughter. Education: BA magna cum laude, Tufts University, 1952; Radcliffe College Graduate School, 1952-53; Northwestern University Graduate School, 1962-69. Publications: Astronomy One (with J Allen Hynek), 1972; Architecture of the Universe (with J Allen Hynek), 1979; It's All Relative: Einstein's Theory of Relativity, 1981; The Moon and Its Exploration, 1982; Stars and Galaxies, 1982; Astronomy and Planetology, 1983, soft-cover edition as Astronomy Projects for Young Scientists, 1984; Calendars, 1985; It's All Elementary From Atoms to the Quantum World of Quarks, Leptons, and Gluons, 1985; Space Station, 1987; Space Law, 1988; Nebulae: The Birth and Death of Stars, 1988; Voyager to the Planets, 1991; Orion the Hunter, 1995. Contributions to: Various articles to Odyssey magazine; Ask Ulysses, and I/O Port monthly columns. Honours: Phi Beta Kappa, 1952; Nebulae chosen as 1 of 100 Best Children's Books, 1988. Memberships: Society of Midland Authors; Society of Children's Book Writers; Astronomical Society of the Pacific; American Association for the Advancement of Science; Planetary Society. Address: 3461 University Avenue, Highland Park, IL 60035, USA.

APOSTOLOU John L, b. 4 Jan 1930, Brooklyn, New York, USA. Writer. Education: City College, New York, 1948-50; Columbia University, 1950-51; BA, University of Southern California, 1956. Publications: Murder in Japan, 1987; The Best Japanese Science Fiction Stories, 1989. Contributions to: Detective and Mystery Fiction, 1985; Twentieth Century Crime and Mystery Writers, 1991; Armchair Detective; Extrapolation. Address: 532 North Rossmore Avenue, No 114, Los Angeles, CA 90004, USA.

APPELFELD Aharon, b. 1932, Czernowitz, Poland (Israeli citizen). Novelist. Education: Hebrew University, Jerusalem. Appointments: Lecturer, Be'er Shev'a University, 1984. Publications: In the Wilderness, 1965; Frost in the Land, 1965; At Ground Level, 1968; Five Stories, 1970; The Skin and the Gown, 1971; My Master the River, 1971; Like the Pupil of an Eye, 1972; Years and Hours, 1975; Lika a Hundred Witnesses: A Selection, 1975; The Age of Wonders, 1978; Essays in the First Person, 1979; Badenheim, 1939, 1980; Tzili: The Story of a Life, 1983; The Shirt and the Stripes, 1983; The Retreat, 1985; At One and the Same Time, 1985; To the Land of the Cattails, 1986; The Immortal Bartfuss, 1988; Tongues of Fire, 1988; Writing and the Holocaust, 1988; For Every Sin, 1989; The Railway, 1991; Katerina, 1992. Honours: H H Wingate Literary Award, 1989. Address: c/o Keter Publishing House, PO Box 7145, Jerusalem 91071, Israel.

APPIAH Peggy, b. 21 May 1921, England. Children's Writer. Publications: Ananse the Spider, 1966; Tales of an Ashanti Father, 1967; The Pineapple Child and Other Tales from Ashanti, 1969; Children of Ananse, 1969; A Smell of Onions, 1971; Why Are There So Many Roads?, 1972; Gift of the Mmoatia, 1973; Ring of Gold, 1976; A Dirge Too Soon, 1976; Why the Hyena Does Not Care for Fish and Other Tales, 1977; Poems of Three Generations, 1978; Young Readers Afua and The Mouse, Alena and the Python, Kofi and the Crow, The Twins, 1991. Literary Agent: David Higham Associates. Address: PO Box 829, Kumasi, Ashanti, Ghana.

APPLE Jacki, b. 11 Dec 1941, New York, New York, USA. Writer; Artist; Producer. Education: Syracuse University; Parsons School of Design. Appointments: Contributing Editor, 1984-95, Media Arts Editor, High Performance Magazine, 1993-95; Faculty Member, Art Center College of Design, Pasadena, California, 1993-; Instructor, Screenwriting, University of California, San Diego, 1995, 1996, 1997. Publications: Trunk Pieces; Doing it Right in LA; The Mexican Tapes; Swan Lake; Voices in the Dark; The Culture of Disappearance; The Garden Planet Revisited; The Amazon, The Mekong, The Missouri and The Nile; One Word at a Time; Thank You for Flying American, CD, 1995; Ghost Dances/on the event horizon, CD, 1996. Contributions to: High

Performance; Artweek; LA Weekly; Media Arts; Visions; Public Art Review; Drama Review; Performing Arts Journal; Art Journal. Honour: VESTA Award. Memberships: International Association of Art Critics; National Writers Union; College Art Association. Address: 3827 Mentone Avenue, No 3, Culver City, CA 90232, USA.

APPLE Max (Isaac), b. 22 Oct 1941, Grand Rapids, Michigan, USA. Professor of English; Writer. 1 son, 1 daughter. Education: AB, 1963, PhD, 1970, University of Michigan; Graduate Studies, Stanford University, 1964. Appointments: Assistant Professor, Reed College, Portland, Oregon, 1970-71; Assistant Professor, 1972-76, Associate Professor, 1976-80, Professor of English, 1980-, Rice University. Publications: Studies in English (with others), 1975; The Oranging of America and Other Stories, 1976; Zip: A Novel of the Left and the Right, 1978; Southwest Fiction (editor), 1980; Three Stories, 1983; Free Agents, 1984; The Propheteers: A Novel, 1987; Roomates: My Grandfather's Story (memoir), 1994. Contributions to: Many publications. Honours: National Endowment for the Humanities Fellowship, 1971; Jesse Jones Awards, Texas Institute of Letters, 1976, 1985; Ribalous Award, Hadassah Magazine, 1985. Memberships: Modern Language Association; PEN; Texas Institute of Letters. Address: c/o Department of English, Rice University, Houston, TX 77001, USA.

APPLEMAN M(arjorie) H(aberkorn), b. Fort Wayne, Indiana, USA. Dramatist; Poet. m. Philip Appleman, 19 Aug 1950. Education: BA, Northwestern University; MA, Indiana University; Degré Supérieur, Sorbonne, University of Paris. Appointments: Professor of English and Playwriting, New York University, Columbia University; International Honors Program, Indiana University. Publications: Plays: Seduction Duet, 1982; The Commuter, 1985. Other: Over 25 plays given in full productions or staged readings, 1971-97. Poetry: Against Time, 1994. Opera libretto: Let's Not Talk About Lenny Anymore, 1989. Contributions to: Numerous anthologies and journals. Honours: Several playwriting awards. Memberships: Academy of American Poets; Authors League of America; Circle Repertory Company Playwrights Unit; Dramatists Guild; League of Professional Theatre; PEN American Center; Poets and Writers. Address: PO Box 39, Sagaponack, NY 11962, USA.

APPLEMAN Philip (Dean), b. 8 Feb 1926, Kendallville, Indiana, USA. Writer; Poet; Distinguished Professor of English Emeritus. m. Marjorie Ann Haberkorn, 19 Aug 1950. Education BS, 1950, PhD, 1955, Northwestern University; AM, University of Michigan, 1951. Appointments: Fulbright Scholar, University of Lyon, 1951-52; Instructor to Professor, 1955-67, Professor, 1967-84, Distinguished Professor of English, 1984-86, Professor Emeritus, 1986-, Indiana University; Director and Instructor, International School of America, 1960-61, 1962-63; Visiting Professor, State University of New York College at Purchase, 1973, Columbia University, 1974; Visiting Scholar, New York University, University of Southern California at Los Angeles; John Steinbeck Visiting Writer, Long Island University at Southampton, 1992. Publications: Novels: In the Twelfth Year of the War, 1970; Shame the Devil, 1981; Apes and Angels, 1989. Poetry: Kites on a Windy Day, 1967; Summer Love and Surf, 1968; Open Doorways, 1976; Darwin's Ark, 1984; Darwin's Bestiary, 1986; Let There Be Light, 1991; New and Selected Poems, 1956-1996, 1996. Non-Fiction: The Silent Explosion, 1965. Editor: 1859: Entering an Age of Crisis, 1959; Darwin, 1970, 2nd edition, revised, 1979; The Origin of Species, 1975; An Essay on the Principle of Population, 1976. Contributions to: Numerous publications. Honours: Ferguson Memorial Award, Friends of Literature Society, 1969; Christopher Morley Awards, Poetry Society of America, 1970, 1975; Castanola Award, Poetry Society of America, 1975; National Endowment for the Arts Fellowship, 1975; Pushcart Prize, 1985; Humanist Arts Award, American Humanist Association, 1994. Memberships: Academy of American Poets; American Association of University

Professors; Authors Guild of America; Modern Language Association; National Council of Teachers of English; PEN American Center; Poetry Society of America; Poets and Writers. Address: PO Box 39, Sagaponack, NY 11962, USA.

ARCHER Fred, b. 30 Apr 1915, Ashton Underhill, England. Publications: The Distant Scene, 1967; Under the Parish Lantern, 1969; Hawthorn Hedge Country, 1970; The Secrets of Bredon Hill, 1971; A Lad of Evesham Vale, 1972; Muddy Boots and Sunday Suits, 1973; Golden Sheaves and Black Horses, 1974; The Countryman Cottage Life Book, 1974; When Village Bells were Silent, 1975; Poachers Pie, 1976; By Hook and By Crook, 1978; When Adam was a Boy, 1979; A Hill Called Bredon, 1983; Fred Archer: Farmer's Son, 1984; The Village Doctor, 1986; Evesham to Bredon in Old Photographs, 1988; The Village of My Childhood, 1989; Country Sayings, 1990. Address: 54 Stanchester Way, Curry Rivel, Langport, Somerset TA10 0PU, Gloucestershire, England.

ARCHER Geoffrey Wilson, b. 21 May 1944, London, England. Author. m. Eva Janson, 1 son, 1 daughter. Appointments: Researcher, Southern TV, 1964; Reporter, Anglia TV, Norwich, 1965-69; Tyne-Tees TV, Newcastle, 1969; Reporter, ITN, 1969-95; Defence Correspondent, 1980-95. Publications: Novels: Skydancer, 1987; Shadow Hunter, 1989; Eagle Trap, 1992; Scorpion Trail, 1995; Java Spider, 1997; Fire Hawk, 1998. Memberships: Society of Authors; Crime Writers Association. Literary Agent: Peters, Fraser and Dunlop. Address: c/o Century/Arrow Books, 20 Vauxhall Bridge Road, London SW1V 2SA, England.

ARCHER Jeffrey Howard, (Lord Archer of Weston Super Mare), b. 15 Apr 1940, Mark, Somerset, England. Author; Politician. m. Mary Weeden, 2 sons. Education: Brasenose College, Oxford. Publications: Not a Penny More, Not a Penny Less, 1975; Shall We Tell the President?, 1977; Kane & Abel, 1979; A Quiver Full of Arrows, 1980; The Prodigal Daughter, 1982; First Among Equals, 1984; A Matter of Honour, 1986; A Twist in the Tale, 1988; As The Crow Flies, 1991; Honour Among Thieves, 1993; Twelve Red Herrings, 1994; A Woman's Place, 1996; The Fourth Estate, 1997; The Eleventh Commandment, 1998; Plays: Beyond Reasonable Doubt, 1987; Exclusive, 1989. Contributions to: Numerous journals and magazines. Honours: Queen's Birthday Honours, 1992; Lord Archer of Weston Super Mare. Address: Peninsula Heights, 93 Albert Embankment, London SE1 7TY, England.

ARCHERY Helen. See: ARGERS Helen.

ARCHIBALD Rupert Douglas, b. 25 Apr 1919, Port of Spain, Trinidad. Author; Playwright. Education: BA, McGill University, 1946. Appointments: Editor, Progress Magazine, 1952; Member, Editorial Board, Clarion Newspaper, 1954-56. Publications: Junction Village, 1954; Anne Marie, 1958; The Bamboo Clump, 1962; The Rose Slip, 1962; Old Maid's Tale, 1965; Island Tide, 1972; Defeat with Honour, 1973; Isidore and the Turtle (novel), 1973. Address: 7 Stephens Road, Maraval, Trinidad and Tobago, West Indies.

ARDAI Charles, b. 25 Oct 1969, New York, New York, USA. Author; Editor. Education: BA, English, summa cum laude, Columbia University, 1991. Appointments: Contributing Editor, Computer Entertainment and K-Power, 1985; Editor, Davis Publications, 1990-91. Publications: Great Tales of Madness and the Macabre, 1990; Kingpins, 1992; Futurecrime, 1992. Contributions to: Alfred Hitchcock's Mystery Magazine; Ellery Queen's Mystery Magazine; Twilight Zone; The Year's Best Horror Stories; Computer Gaming World; and others. Honour: Pearlman Prize for Fiction, Columbia University, 1991. Membership: Active Member, Mystery Writers of America. Address: 350 East 52nd Street, New York, NY 10022, USA.

ARDEN John, b. 26 Oct 1930, Barnsley, Yorkshire, England. Playwright. m. Margaretta Ruth D'Arcy, 4 sons,

1 dec. Education: King's College, Cambridge; Edinburgh College of Art. Publications include: Novels: Silence Among the Weapons, 1982; Books of Bale, 1988; Cogs Tyrannic, 1991; Jack Juggler and the Emperor's Whore, 1995. Essays: To Present the Pretence, 1977; Awkward Corners (with M D'Arcy), 1988. Plays produced include: All Fall Down, 1955; The Life of Man, 1956; The Waters of Babylon, 1957; Live Like Pigs, 1958; Serjeant Musgrave's Dance, 1959; Soldier Soldier, 1960; Wet Fish, 1961; The Workhouse Donkey, 1963; Ironhand, 1963; Armstrong's Last Goodnight, 1964; Left-Handed Liberty, 1965; Squire Jonathan, 1968; The Bagman, 1970; Pearl, 1978; Don Quixote, 1980; Garland for a Hoar Head, 1982; The Old Man Sleeps Alone, 1982; The Little Novels of Wilkie Collins, 1998. With M D'Arcy: The Happy Haven, 1960; The Business of Good Government, 1960; Ars Longa Vita Brevis, 1964; The Royal Pardon, 1966; Friday's Hiding, 1966; Harold Muggins is a Martyr, 1968; The Hero Rises Up, 1968; The Ballygombeen Bequest, 1972; The Island of the Mighty, 1972; The Non-Stop Connolly Show, 1975; Vandaleur's Folly, 1978; The Manchester Enthusiasts, 1984; Whose is the Kingdom?, 1988; A Suburban Suicide, 1994. Address: c/o Casarotto Ramsay Ltd, National House, 60-66 Wardour Street, London W1V 3HP, England.

ARDEN William. See: **LYNDS Dennis.**

ARDLEY Neil Richard, b. 26 May 1937, Wallington, Surrey, England. Writer. m. Bridget Mary Gantley, 3 Sept 1960, 1 daughter. Education: BSc, Bristol University, 1959. Publications: Man on the Moon (with John Clark), 1969; Birds of Towns, 1975; Birds of the Country, 1975; Birds of Coasts, Lakes and Rivers, 1976; Birdwatching, 1978; Birds, 1978; Birds of Britain and Europe, 1978; Birds and Birdwatching, 1980; 1001 Questions and Answers (with Bridget Ardley), 1981; The World of Tomorrow Series, 1981-82; Fact or Fantasy?, 1982; Action Science Series, 1983-84; Discovering Electricity, 1984; Air and Flight, 1984; Sound and Music, 1984; Simple Chemistry, 1984; My Favourite Science Encyclopedia, 1984; Just Look At...Flight, 1984; Just Look At...The Universe, 1985; The Science of Energy, 1985; Music-An Illustrated Encyclopedia, 1986; My Own Science Encyclopedia, 1987; The Universe - Exploring the Universe, 1987; The Inner Planets, 1988; The Outer Planets, 1988; The Way Things Work, (with David Macaulay), 1988; The World of the Atom, 1989; Music, 1989; India, 1989; Greece, 1989; Twentieth Century Science, 1989; The Giant Book of the Human Body, 1989; Language and Communications, 1989; Sound Waves to Music, 1990; Wings and Things, 1990; Snap Happy, 1990; Tune In, 1991; Bits and Chips, 1991; How It Works, 1991; The Way It Works, Light, 1991; The Way It Works, Electricity, 1991; My Science a series of 15 science books, 1991-92; 101 Great Science Experiments, 1993; Dictionary of Science, 1994; How Things Work, 1995; A Young Person's Guide to Music (with Poul Ruders), 1995; The Oxford Childrens' A-Z of the Human Body (with Bridget Ardley), 1996; The New Way Things Work (with David Macaulay), 1998. Contributions to: Reference books. Honours: Fellow, Royal Society of Arts, 1982; Science Book Prize (under 16), 1989; Times Educational Supplement Senior Information Book Award, 1989. Address: Lathkill House, Youlgrave, Derbyshire DE45 1WL, England.

ARENDT Erica Elisabeth. See: **HARVOR Elisabeth.**

ARGERS Helen, (Helen Archery), b. New Jersey, USA. Novelist; Dramatist. Education: BA; Graduate Studies. Publications: A Lady of Independence, 1982; A Scandalous Lady, 1991; A Captain's Lady, 1991; An Unlikely Lady, 1992; A Season of Loving, 1992; The Age of Elegance, 1992; Lady Adventures, 1994; Duel of Hearts, 1994; Noblesse Oblige, 1994; The Gilded Lily, 1998. Honours: Writer's Digest Short Story Award, 1987; Resolution of Honour, State of New Jersey, 1994. Address: c/o Creatorwrites Literary Agency, 78 Woodbine Avenue, Newark, NJ 07106, USA.

ARGIRIDIS Michalis, b. 1952, Larissa, Greece. Teacher; Writer. Education: Pedagogical Academy,

Larissa. Appointment: Primary Schoolteacher, Larissa. Publications: Books for children and young people. Honour: Panhellenic Prize. Memberships: Circle of Greek Children's Book Writers; Union of Children's Book Writers. Address: 68-70 Ipsilantou Street, Larissa 41223, Greece.

ARGUETA Manilo, b. 24 Nov 1935, San Miguel, El Salvador. Poet; Novelist. Education: Universidad Nacional, San Salvador. Publications: Fiction: El Valle des Hamacas, 1970; Caperucita en la Zona Rosa, 1977; One Day of Life, 1980; Cuzcatalan, Where the Southern Sea Beats, 1987. Verse: Poemas, 1967; En el Costado de la Luz, 1979; El Salvador, 1990. Editor: Poesia de El Salvador, 1983. Honour: University of Central America Prize, 1980. Address: c/o Chatto and Windus, 20 Vauxhall Bridge Road, London SW1N 2SA, England.

ARIDJIS Homero, b. 6 Apr 1940, Mexico. Poet; Novelist. m. Betty Ferber, 1965, 2 daughters. Education: Autonomous University of Mexico, 1961. Appointment: Director, Festival Internacional de Poesia, 1981-87. Publications: Verse: Los Ojos Desdoblados, 1960; Antes del Reino, 1963; La Dificil Ceremonia, 1963; Quemar Las Naves, 1975; Antologa, 1976; Vivir Para Ver, 1977; Construir la Muerte, 1982; Republica de Poetas, 1985; Obra Poetica, 1960-86, 1987; Imagenes Para el Fin del Milenio, 1990. Fiction: Mirandola Dormir, 1964; Persefone, 1967-86; El Encantador Solitario, 1972; Playa Nudista; El Ultimo Adan, 1982; Memorias del Nuevo Mundo, 1988. Honour: Novela Novedades Prize, 1988. Address: Sirra Jiutepec 1558, Lomas Barrilaco, Mexico City 11010, Mexico.

ARLEN Leslie. See: **NICOLE Christopher Robin.**

ARLEN Michael (John), b. 9 Dec 1930, London, England. Author. m. Alice Albright, 1972, 4 daughters. Education: BA, Harvard University, 1952. Publications: Living-Room War, 1969; Exiles, 1970; An American Verdist, 1972; Passage to Ararat, 1974; The View From Highway One, 1975; Thirty Seconds, 1980; The Camera Age, 1982; Say Goodbye to Sam, 1984. Contributions to: New Yorker magazine. Honours: National Book Award, 1975; Le Prix Bremond, 1976; Honorary DLitt, 1984. Memberships: Authors Guild; PEN. Address: 1120 Fifth Avenue, New York, NY 10128, USA.

ARMAH Ayi Kwei, b. 1938, Takoradi, Ghana. Novelist. Education: AB in Social Studies, Harvard University, Massachusetts; Columbia University, New York. Appointments: Scriptwriter, Ghana Television; Teacher, Teacher's College, Dar-es-Salaam, and Universities of Massachusetts, Amherst, Lesotho, and Wisconsin, Madison. Publications: The Beautiful Ones Are Not Yet Born, 1968; Fragments, 1970; Why Are We So Blest?, 1972; Two Thousand Seasons, 1973; The Heales, 1978. Uncollected short stories: A Short Story, 1965; Yaw Manu's Charm, 1968; The Offal Kind, 1969; Doctor Kamikaze, 1989. Address: c/o Heinemann Educational, Ighorado Road, Jericho PMB 5205, Ibadan, Oyo State, Nigeria.

ARMES Roy (Philip), b. 16 Mar 1937, Norwich, England. Author; Lecturer. m. Margaret Anne Johnson, 12 Aug 1960, 1 son, 2 daughters. Education: BA, University of Bristol, 1959; Teacher's Certificate, University of Exeter, 1960; PhD, University of London, 1978. Appointments: Teacher, Royal Liberty School, Romford, 1960-69; Associate Lecturer in Film, University of Surrey, 1969-72; Research Fellow, 1969-72, Lecturer, 1972-73, Hornsey College of Art; Senior Lecturer, 1973-78, Reader in Film and Television, 1978-, Middlesex Polytechnic; Visiting Lecturer at many colleges and universities. Publications: French Cinema since 1946, 2 volumes, 1966, 2nd edition, 1970; The Cinema of Alain Resnais, 1968; French Film, 1970; Patterns of Realism, 1972; Film and Reality: An Historical Survey, 1974; The Ambiguous Image, 1976; A Critical History of British Cinema, 1978; The Films of Alain Robbe-Grillet, 1981; French Cinema, 1984; Third World Film Making and the West, 1987; Action and Image: Dramatic Structure in Cinema, 1994. Contributions to: Many books

and periodicals. Address: 19 New End, Hampstead, London NW3, England.

ARMITAGE G(ary) E(dric), (Robert Edric), b. 14 Apr 1956, Sheffield, England. Writer. m. Sara Jones, 12 Aug 1978. Education: BA, 1977, PhD, 1980, Hull University. Publications: Winter Garden, 1985; A Season of Peace, 1985; A New Ice Age, 1986; Across the Autumn Grass, 1986. As Robert Edric: A Lunar Eclipse, 1989; In the Days of the American Museum, 1990; The Broken Lands, 1992; Hallowed Ground, 1993; The Earth Made of Glass, 1994; Elysium, 1995; In Desolate Heaven, 1997; Gathering the Water, 1998. Contributions to: Various periodicals. Honours: James Tait Black Memorial Award, 1985; Trask Award, 1985; Society of Authors Award, 1994; Arts Council Bursary, 1995. Address: The Lindens, Atwick Road, Hornsea, North Humberside, England.

ARMITAGE Ronda (Jacqueline), b. 11 Mar 1943, Kaikoura, New Zealand. Author; Teacher; Family Therapist. m. David Armitage, 1966, 2 children. Education: Teacher's Certificate, 1962, Teacher's Diploma, 1969, Hamilton Teacher's College. Appointments: Schoolteacher, Duvauchelle, New Zealand, 1964-66, London, England, 1966, Auckland, New Zealand, 1968-69; Advisor on Children's Books, Dorothy Butler Ltd, Auckland, 1970-71; Assistant Librarian, Lewes Priory Comprehensive School, Sussex, England, 1976-77; Teacher, East Sussex County Council, England, 1978-; Family Therapist. Publications: Let's Talk About Drinking, 1982; New Zealand, 1983. Juvenile Fiction: The Lighthouse Keeper's Lunch, 1977; The Trouble With Mr Harris, 1978; Don't Forget, Matilda!, 1978; The Bossing of Josie, 1980, in the USA as The Birthday Spell, 1981; Ice Creams for Rosie, 1981; One Moonlit Night, 1983; Grandma Goes Shopping, 1984; The Lighthouse Keeper's Catastrophe, 1986; The Lighthouse Keeper's Rescue, 1989; When Dad Did the Washing, 1990; Watch the Baby, Daisy, 1991; Looking After Chocolates, 1992; A Quarrel of Koalas, 1992; The Lighthouse Keeper's Picnic, 1993; The Lighthouse Keeper's Cat, 1996; Flora and the Strawberry Red Birthday Party, 1997. Honour: Esther Glen Award, New Zealand Library Association, 1978. Membership: Society of Authors. Address: Old Tiles Cottage, Church Lane, Hellingly, East Sussex BN27 4HA, England.

ARMOUR Peter (James), b. 19 Nov 1940, Fleetwood, England. University Lecturer; Writer; Translator. Education: PhL, English College and Gregorian University, Rome, 1961; BA with Honours, Victoria University of Manchester, 1966; PhD, University of Leicester, 1980. Appointments: Lecturer in Italian, University of Sheffield, 1966-72, University of Leicester, 1972-79, University of London, 1979-. Publications: The Door of Purgatory: A Study of Multiple Symbolism in Dante's "Purgatorio", 1983; Dante's Griffin and the History of the World: A Study of the Earthly Paradise ("Purgatorio", Cantos XXIX-XXXIII), 1989. Contributions to: Many scholarly books and journals. Memberships: Dante Society of America; London Medieval Society; Modern Humanities Research Association; Societa Dantescà Italiana; Society for Italian Studies. Address: c/o Department of Italian, Royal Holloway, University of London, Egham, Surrey TW20 0EX, England.

ARMSTRONG Alice Catt, b. Fort Scott, Kansas, USA. Author; Editor; Publisher. 1 son. Education: LittD, St Andrews University, England, 1969; St Paul's College and Seminary, Italy, 1970. Publications: 17 books including: California Biographical and Historical Series, 1950-; Dining & Lodging on the North American Continent, 1958; And They Called It Society, 1961-62; Editor, special issue, 200th Anniversary of California, 1968; Also radio skits, travel guides abd children's stories. Honours: National Travel Guide Award, National Writers Club, 1958; Dame Grand Cross, Order of St Jaurent; Outstanding Citizen. Memberships: National Society of Magna Charta Dames; Los Angeles World Affairs Council; National Writers Club; Historical Los Angeles Association; Art Patrons Association of America. Address: 1331 Cordell Views, Cordell Place, Los Angeles, CA 90069, USA.

ARMSTRONG Jeannette Christine, b. 5 Feb 1948, Canada. Educator; Writer; Poet. 1 son, 1 daughter. Education: Diploma in Fine Arts, Okanagan College, 1975; BFA, University of Victoria, British Columbia, 1978. Appointment: Adjunct Professor, Enbwkin School of Writing, University of Victoria, British Columbia, 1989-. Publications: Enwhisteetkwa, 1982; Neekna and Chemai, 1984; Slash, 1985; Native Creative Process, 1991; Breath Tracks, 1991; Looking at the Words of Our People, 1993. Honour: Children's Book Centre Choice Award, 1983. Memberships: PEN International; Writers Union of Canada. Address: c/o Theytus Books, Green Mountain Road, Lot 45, RR#2, Site 50, Comp 8, Penticton, BC V2A 6J7, Canada.

ARMSTRONG John Alexander, b. 4 May 1922, Saint Augustine, Florida, USA. Professor Emeritus of Political Science; Author; Consultant. m. Annette Taylor, 14 June 1952, 3 daughters. Education: PhB 1948, University of Frankfurt am Main; MA, 1949, University of Chicago; 1949-50; PhD, Public Law and Government, 1953, Certificate of Russian Institute, 1954, Columbia University. Appointments: Research Analyst, War Documentation Project, Alexandria, Virginia, 1951, 1953-54; Assistant Professor, University of Denver, 1952; Visiting Assistant Professor, Russian Institute, Columbia University, 1957; Assistant Professor to Philippe de Commynes Professor of Political Science (presently Emeritus), University of Wisconsin, Madison, 1954-86. Publications: Ukrainian Nationalism, 1955, 3rd edition, 1990; The Soviet Bureaucratic Elite, 1959; The Politics of Totalitarianism, 1961; Ideology, Politics and Government in the Soviet Union, 1962, 4th edition, 1978; Soviet Partisans in World War II (editor), 1964; The European Administrative Elite, 1973; Nations Before Nationalism, 1982. Address: 40 Water Street, Saint Augustine, FL 32084, USA.

ARMSTRONG Karen Andersen, b. 14 Nov 1944, Stourbridge, England. Writer. Education: Convent of the Holy Child Jesus, Edgbaston, 1950-62; St Anne's College, Oxford University, 1967-74; MA; MLitt. Appointments: Junior Research Fellow, Bedford College, London University, 1973-76; Head of English, James Allen's Girls' School, Dulwich, England, 1976-82; Lecturer, Leo Baeck College, 1993-. Publications: Through the Narrow Gate, 1981; The Gospel According to Women, 1986; Holy War, 1988; Muhammaed, A Biography of the Prophet, 1991; A History of God, 1993; A History of Jerusalem, 1996; In the Beginning, A New Reading of Genesis, 1996. Contributions to: The Times; The Sunday Times; London Illustrated News; The Economist; The Independent; The Guardian; The Daily Telegraph; European Judaism; The Tablet. Literary Agent: Felicity Bryan. Address: 2A North Parade, Banbury Road, Oxford OX2 6PE, England.

ARMSTRONG Patrick Hamilton, b. 10 Oct 1941, Leeds, Yorkshire, England. University Lecturer. m. Moyra E J Irvine, 8 Aug 1964, 2 sons. Education: BSc, 1963, Dip Ed, 1964, MA, 1966, University of Durham; PhD, 1970. Appointment: Faculty, Department of Geography, University of Western Australia. Publications: Discovering Ecology, 1973; Discovering Geology, 1974; The Changing Landscape, 1975; A Series of Children's Book for Ladybird Books, 1976-79; Ecology, 1977; Reading and Interpretation of Australian and New Zealand Maps, 1981; Living in the Environment, 1982; The Earth: Home of Humanity, 1984; Charles Darwin in Western Australia, 1985; A Sketch Map Geography of Australia, 1988; A Sketch Map Physical Geography for Australia, 1989; Darwin's Desolate Islands, 1992. Contributions to: New Scientist; Geographical Magazine; East Anglian Magazine; Geography; Cambridgeshire Life; Eastern Daily Press; Work and Travel Abroad; West Australian Newspaper; Weekly Telegraph. Literary Agent: Curtis Brown Pty Ltd, PO Box 19, Paddington, NSW 2021, Australia. Address: Department of Geography, University of Western Australia, Nedlands, Western Australia 6907, Australia.

ARMSTRONG Richard B, b. 29 Nov 1956, Winston-Salem, North Carolina, USA. Writer; Training Developer. m. Mary Willems Armstrong, 23 May 1981. Education: BA, Telecommunications, 1979, MSc, Instructional Systems Technology, 1981, Doctorate of Education in Instructional Systems Technology, 1993, Indiana University. Publication: The Movie List Book: A Reference Guide to Film Themes, Settings and Series (with Mary Willems Armstrong), 1990, 2nd edition, 1994. Contributions to: Reviews published in Film Quarterly and Film Fax; Training Development articles published in Performance Improvement Quarterly, and Armor magazine. Honour: Article of the Year Award, Performance Improvement Quarterly, 1993. Address: c/o McFarland and Co Inc, Publishers, Box 611, Jefferson, NC 28640, USA.

ARNOLD Arnold, b. 6 Feb 1928, Germany. m. (1) Eve Arnold, 1942, (2) Alison Pilpel, 1982. Education: St Martins School of Art, London, 1937-38; Pratt Institute, New York, 1938-39; New York University, Columbia University, 1939-42. Appointments: Graphic and Industrial Designer, 1946; Director, Workshop School, New York, 1949-52; President, Arnold Arnold Design Inc, 1960-66, Manuscript Press Inc, 1963-66; Consultant Editor, Rutledge Books, New York, 1962-65; Cyberneticist, Writer, Consultant, Systems Analysis and Operational Research, London, 1980-. Publications: How To Play with Your Child; Your Child's Play; Your Child and You; The World Book of Children's Games; The World Book of Arts and Crafts for Children; The Corrupted Sciences; The I Ching and the Theory of Everything; Career Guidance for the 70's; Teaching Your Child To Learn; Winner and Other Losers. Contributions to: Newspapers, journals and reviews. Honours: Fellow, Boston University; Leverhulme Fellow. Address: 29 Borough Hill, Petersfield, Hants GU32 3LQ, England.

ARNOLD Eleanor Parsons, b. 4 May 1929, Indiana, USA. Farm homemaker; Editor. m. Clarence E Arnold, 26 Dec 1948, 1 son, 2 daughters. Education: Clayton High School, valedictorian Indiana University, 1946; BA, English, Honours, 1950. Publications: Voices of American Homemakers, 1985; Series: Memories of Hoosier Homemakers, including books as follows: Feeding Our Families, 1983; Party Lines, Pumps and Privies, 1984; Budgies and Bad Times, 1985; Girlhood Days, 1987; Going to Club, 1988; Living Rich Lives, 1990. Contributions to: Interpreting Women's Culture; American Association of State and Local History; Hoosier Hoemakers; National Oral History; Voices of American Homemakers; National Extension Homemakers. Honours: Sagamore of the Wabash (Indiana award), Commendation: AASLH. Memberships: American Association of State and Local Hiistory; National Oral History Association; Indiana Oral History Roundtable; Indianapolis Press Club. Address: 1744 North 450 East, Rushville, IN 46173, USA.

ARNOLD Emily. See: McCULLY Emily Arnold.

ARNOLD Heinz Ludwig, b. 29 Mar 1940, Essen, Ruhr, Germany. Writer; Critic; Editor. Education: University of Göttingen. Appointments: Editor, Text und Kritik, 1963, Kritisches Lexikon zur Deutschsprachigen Gegenwartsliteratur, 1978, Kritisches Lexikon zur Fremdsprachigen Gegenwartsliteratur, 1983. Publications: Brauchen wir noch die Literatur? 1972; Gespräche mit Schriftstellern, 1975; Gespräch mit F Dürrenmatt, 1976; Handbuch der Deutschen Arbeiterliteratur, 1977; Als Schriftsteller leben, 1979; Vom Verlust der Scham und Dem Allmaehlichen Verschwinden der Demokratie, 1988; Krieger Waldgaenger, Anarch Versuch über E Jünger, 1990; Querfahrt mit Dürrenmatt, 1990; Die Drei Sprunge der Westdeutschen Gegenwartsliteratur, 1993; Die Deutsche Literatur 1945-1960, 4 volumes, 1995; Grundzüge der Literaturwissenschaft, 1996; F Dürrenmatt, Gespräche, 1996; Einigkeit und in Ruinen, 1999. Contributions to: Die Zeit; Deutsches Allgemeines Sonntagblatt; Frankfurter Allgemeine Zeitung; Various radio stations. Honour: Honorary Professor, University of Göttingen. Memberships: Association of German Writers; PEN; OH Tulip Order. Address: Tuckermannweg 10, 37085 Göttingen, Germany.

ARNOLD Margot. See: COOK Petronelle Marguerite Mary.

ARNOLD Susan Hilary, b. 9 Aug 1944, India. Journalist. m. (1) 3 Oct 1969, (2) Ian Hutchinson, 4 Nov 1985, 3 sons, 3 daughters. Education: MA Hons, Trinity College, Dublin, 1962-66. Appointments: London Evening Standard, 1966; Daily Sketch, 1967; Teheran Journal, 1968; Observer, 1969-98. Publications: Little Princes, 1981; Curiouser and Curiouser, 1984; A Burmese Legacy, 1996. Honours: Runner Up, IPC Magazine Writer, 1983; Winner, IPC Magazine Writer, 1984. Literary Agent: Jacqueline Korn, David Higham Associates. Address: 4 Honiton Mansions, Flood Street, London SW3 5TU, England.

ARONSON Theo, b. 13 Nov 1930, South Africa. Writer. Education: BA, University of Cape Town, 1950. Publications: The Golden Bees, 1965; Royal Vendetta, 1967; The Coburgs of Belgium, 1968; The Fall of the Third Napoleon, 1970; The Kaisers, 1971; Queen Victoria and the Bonapartes, 1972; Grandmama of Europe, 1973; A Family of Kings, 1975; Victoria and Disraeli, 1977; Kings Over the Water, 1979; Princess Alice, 1981; Royal Family, 1983; Crowns in Conflict, 1986; The King in Love, 1988; Napoleon and Josephine, 1990; Heart of a Queen, 1991; The Royal Family at War, 1993; Prince Eddy, 1994; Princess Margaret, 1997. Contributions to: Various journals and magazines. Literary Agent: Andrew Lownie. Address: North Knoll Cottage, 15 Bridge Street, Frome, Somerset BA11 1BB, England.

ARRABAL Fernando, b. 11 Aug 1932, Melilla, Morocco. Writer; Poet; Dramatist. m. Luce Moreau, 1958, 1 son, 1 daughter. Education: University of Madrid. Appointments: Political prisoner in Spain, 1967; Co-Founder, Panique Movement. Publications: Novels: Baal Babylone, 1959; L'Enterrement de la Sardine, 1961; Fêtes et Rites de la Confusion, 1965; La Torre Herida por el Rayo, 1983. Poetry: Le Pierre de la Folie, 1963; 100 Sonnets, 1966; Les Evêques se Noient, 1969; Poèmes, 1982; Lanzarote, 1988; Arrabalesques, 1994; J-L Borges (Una Vida de Poesia), 1998. Plays: Numerous, both published and unpublished. Honours: Ford Foundation Fellowship, 1960; Société des Auteurs Prize, 1966; Grand Prix du Théâtre, 1967; Grand Prix Humour Noir, 1968; Obie Award, Village Voice newspaper, New York City, 1976; Premio Nadal (novel), 1983; World's Theatre Prize, 1984; Prix du Théâtre, Académie Française, 1993; Prix International Nabokov, 1994; Premio Espasa de Ensayo, 1994. Address: 22 Rue Jouffroy d'Abbans, Paris 75017, France.

ARREOLA Juan José, b. 12 Sept 1918, Ciudad Guzman, Jalisco, Mexico. Novelist. Education: Paris, 1945. Appointment: Founding Member, Actor, Poesia en Voz Alta Group. Publications: Gunther Stapenhorst: Vinetas de Isidoro Ocampo, 1946; Varia Invencion, 1949; Cinco Cuentes, 1951; Confabulario and Other Inventions, 1952-64; Besitario, 1958; Punta de Plata, 1958; Le Feria, 1963; Cuentos, 1969; Antologia de Juan José Arreola, 1969; Palindroma, 1971; Mi Confabulario, 1979; Confabulario Personal, 1980; Imagen Obra Escogida, 1984; Estas Paginas Mias, 1985. Address: Editorial Joaquin Mortiz, Avenue Insurgentes Sur 1162-3, Col del Valle, 03100 Mexico City, Mexico.

ARRINGTON Stephen, b. 27 Sept 1948, Pasadena, CA, USA. Motivational Speaker; Writer. m. Cynthia Hamren, 1 Apr 1989, 1 son, 2 daughters. Appointments: Chief Diver and Expedition Leader for The Cousteau Society. Publications: Journey Into Darkness; High on Adventure I, II and III; Expedition and Diving Operations Handbook. Honours: Certificate of Merit Sign by President Ronald Reagan. Address: Stephen Arrington, PO Box 3234, Paradise, CA 95967, USA.

ARROW Kenneth (Joseph), b. 23 Aug 1921, New York, New York, USA. Professor of Economics Emeritus; Writer. m. Selma Schweitzer, 31 Aug 1947, 2 sons. Education: BS, City College of New York, 1940; MA, 1941, PhD, 1951, Columbia University. Appointments: Assistant Professor, University of Chicago, 1948-49;

Acting Assistant Professor, 1949-50, Associate Professor, 1950-53, Professor of Economics, 1953-68, Joan Kenney Professor of Economics, 1979-91, Professor Emeritus, 1991-, Stanford University; Professor of Economics, 1968-74, James Bryant Conant University Professor, 1974-79, Harvard University. Publications: Social Choice and Individual Values, 1951; Mathematical Studies in Inventory and Production (co-author), 1958; Studies in Linear and Nonlinear Programming (co-author), 1958; Time Series Analysis of Inter-industry Demands (co-author), 1959; Essays in the Theory of Risk Bearing, 1971; Public Investment, the Rate of Return and Optimal Fiscal Policy (co-author), 1971; General Competitive Analysis (co-author), 1971; The Limits of Organization, 1974; Studies in Resource Allocation Processes (co-author), 1977; Collected Papers, 6 volumes, 1983-85; Social Choice and Multicriterion Decision Making (co-author), 1985. Contributions to: Professional journals. Honours: John Bates Clark Medal, American Economic Association, 1957; Nobel Memorial Prize in Economic Science, 1972; Guggenheim Fellowship, 1972-73; 18 honorary doctorates. Memberships: American Academy of Arts and Sciences, vice president, 1979-81, 1991-93; American Economic Association, president, 1973; American Philosophical Society; British Academy, corresponding member; International Economic Association, president, 1983-86. Address: c/o Department of Economics, Stanford University, Stanford, CA 94305, USA.

ARTHUR Elizabeth Ann, b. 15 Nov 1953, New York, New York, USA. Writer. m. Steven Bauer, 19 June 1982. Education: BA, English, University of Victoria, 1978; Diploma, Education, 1979. Appointments: Visiting Instructor, Creative Writing, University of Cincinnati, 1983-84; Visiting Assistant Professor, English, Miami University, 1984-85; Assistant Professor, English, 1985-92, Associate Professor, 1992-96, Indiana University-Purdue University at Indianapolis; Visiting Associate Professor, English, Miami University, 1996. Publications: Island Sojourn (memoir), 1980; Beyond the Mountain (novel), 1983; Bad Guys (novel), 1986; Binding Spell (novel), 1988; Looking for the Klondike Stone (memoir), 1993; Antarctic Navigation, (novel), 1995. Contributions to: New York Times; Outside; Backpacker; Ski-XC; Shenandoah. Honours: William Sloane Fellowship, Bread Loaf Writers' Conference, 1980; Writing Fellowship, Ossabaw Island Project, 1981; Grant in Aid, Vermont Council on the Arts, 1982; Fellowship in Prose, National Endowment for the Arts, 1982-83; Master Artist Fellowship, Indiana Arts Commission, Indianapolis, 1988; Fellowship in Fiction, National Endowment for the Arts, 1989-90; Antarctic Artists and Writers Grant, National Science Foundation, 1990; Critics Choice Award for Antarctic Navigation, 1995; Notable Book, New York Times Book Review, 1995. Membership: Poets and Writers. Literary Agent: Peter Matson, Sterling Lord Literistic. Address: Bath, IN 47010, USA.

ARTMANN H(ans) C(arl), b. 12 June 1921, St Achatz am Walde, Austria. Poet; Author; Translator. Publications: kein pfeffer für czermak, 1954; reime verse formeln, 1954; die missglückte luftreise, 1955; XXV epigrammata, in teuschen alexandrinern gesetzt, 1956; bei überreichung seines herzens, 1958; hosn rosn baa (with F Achleitner and G Rügm), 1959; Verbarium, 1966; allerleirausch, 1967; Grünverschlossene Botschaft, 1967; tök ph' rong süleng, 1967; Die Anfangsbuchstaben der Flagge, 1968; ein lilienweisser brief aus lincolnshire: gedichte aus 21 jahren, 1969; Frankenstein in Sussex, 1969; Die Wanderer, 1978; Grammatik der Rosen: Gesammelte Prosa, 3 volumes, 1979; Die Sonne war ein grünes Ei, 1982; Von der Erschaffung der Welt und ihren Dingen, 1982; wer dichten kann ist dichtersmann, 1986; dedichte von der wollust des dichtens in worte gefasst, 1989; Der zerbrochne Krug (adaptation of work by Kleist), 1992. Honours: Austrian State Prize, 1974; Literature Prize of the City of Vienna, 1977; Literature Prize of Salzburg, 1981; Büchner Prize, 1997. Memberships: Akademie der Künste, Berlin. Address: c/o Residenz-Verlag, Salzburg, Austria.

ARZILLE Juliette (d'), b. 23 Nov 1932, La Neuveille, Switzerland. Writer. m. Walter Friedemann, 26 Sept 1955, 1 son, 1 daughter. Education: Studies of music and autodidactical literary education. Appointment: Member, Literature Committee, Canton of Neuchâtel, 1993-. Publications: Le Deuxieme Soleil, 1973; Identite suivi de les Embellies, 1976; Une Innocence Verte, 1982; Nocturne, 1984; Esquisses et Propos, 1986; D'Ici et d'Ailleurs, 1989; Hommage pluriel, 1998; Alentour, 1998; Acqua serena, 1998. Contributions to: Newspapers and magazines. Honour: French Literature Award, Canton of Bern, 1982. Memberships: PEN International; Swiss Society of Writers; AENJ. Address:En Arzille, CH-1788 Praz, Switzerland.

ASANTE Molefi Kete, b. 14 Aug 1942, Vaidosta, California, USA. Professor; Professor; Poet. m. Kariamu Welsh, 1981, 2 sons, 1 daughter. Education: BA, Oklahoma Christian University, 1964; MA, Pepperdine University, 1965; PhD, University of California at Los Angeles, 1968. Appointments: Professor, University of California at Los Angeles, 1969-73, State University of New York at Buffalo, 1973-84, Temple University, 1984-. Publications: Break of Dawn, 1964; Epic in Search of African Kings, 1979; Afrocentricity, 1980; The Afrocentric Idea, 1987; Kemet, Afrocentricity and Knowledge, 1992; Classical Africa, 1992; African American History, 1995; African Intellectual Heritage, 1996; Love Dance, 1997; African American Atlas, 1998. Contributions to: Journals. Honours: Honorary degress, citations, and awards. Membership: African Writers Union, vice president, 1994-. Literary Agent: Marie Brown Associates, New York, USA. Address: Temple University, Philadelphia, PA 19122, USA.

ASCH Frank, b. 6 Aug 1946, Somerville, New Jersey, USA. Education: BA, Cooper Union. Publications: George's Store, 1969; Elvira Everything, 1970; The Blue Balloon, 1971; I Met a Penguin, 1972; In the Eye of the Teddy, 1973; Gia and the $100 Worth of Bubblegum, 1974; Good Lemonade, 1975; The Inside Kid, 1977; Macgoose's Grocery, 1978; Country Pie, 1979; The Last Puppy, 1980; Just Like Daddy, 1981; Happy Birthday Moon, 1982; Mooncake, 1983; Moongame, 1984; Baby in the Box, 1990; Journey to Terezor, 1991; Here Comes the Cat, 1991; Little Fish, Big Fish, 1992; Short Train, Long Train, 1992; Dear Brother, 1992; The Flower Faerie, 1993; Moonbear's Books, 1993; Moonbear's Canoe, 1993; Moonbear's Friend, 1993; The Earth & I, 1994. Address: Holiday House, 40 E 49th Street, New York, NY 10017, USA.

ASCHER Sheila, (Ascher/Straus), b. New York, USA. Writer. Education: MA, Columbia University. Publications: ABC Street; Letter to an Unknown Woman; The Other Planet; The Menaced Assassin; Red Moon/Red Lake. Contributions to: Chicago Review; Paris Review; Epoch; Top Stories; Chelsea; Exile; Calyx; Zone; Confrontation; Central Park; New American Writing; Asylum Annual; Top Top Stories (anthology); 15 Years in Exile (anthology); Likely Stories (anthology); The Pushcart Prize Anthology III. Honours: Panache Experimental Fiction Prize; Pushcart Prize; New York State Caps Fellowship. Address: PO Box 176, Rockaway Park, NY 11694, USA.

ASCHERSON (Charles) Neal, b. 5 Oct 1932, Edinburgh, Scotland. Journalist; Editor; Writer. m. (1) Corinna Adam, 20 Nov 1958, div 1982, 2 daughters, (2) Isabel Hilton, Aug 1984, 1 son, 1 daughter. Education: Eton College; MA, King's College, Cambridge, 1955. Appointment: Reporter and Leader Writer, Manchester Guardian, 1956-58; Commonwealth Correspondent, 1959-60, Scottish Politics Correspondent, 1975-79, Scotsman; Reporter, 1960-63, Central Europe Correspondent, 1963-68, Eastern Europe Correspondent, 1968-75, Correspondent The Scotsman, 1975-79, Foreign Writer, 1979-85, Associate Editor, 1985-89, Columnist, 1985-90, The Observer; Columnist, The Independent on Sunday, 1990-98. Publications: The King Incorporated, 1963; The Polish August: The Self-Limiting Revolution, 1981; The Struggles for Poland, 1987; Games with Shadows, 1988; Black Sea, 1995. Honours: Reporter of the Year, 1982, Journalist of the Year, 1987,

Granada Awards; James Cameron Award, 1989; David Watt Memorial Prize, 1991; Golden Insignia, Order of Merit, Poland, 1992; Honorary Fellow, King's College, Cambridge, 1993; George Orwell Award, Political Quarterly, 1993; Saltire Award for Literature, 1995; Honorary doctorates. Address: 27 Corsica Street, London N5 1JT, England.

ASH John, b. 29 June 1948, Manchester, England. Writer; Poet; Teacher. Education: BA, University of Birmingham, 1969. Publications: The Golden Hordes: International Tourism and the Pleasure Periphery (with Louis Turner), 1975; Casino: A Poem in Three Parts, 1978; The Bed and Other Poems, 1981; The Goodbyes, 1982; The Branching Stairs, 1984; Disbelief, 1987; The Burnt Pages, 1991. Contributions to: Periodicals. Honours: Ingram Merrill Foundation Grant, 1985; Writing Foundation Award, 1986. Address: c/o Carcanet Press Ltd, 208-212 Corn Exchange Buildings, Manchester M4 3BQ, England.

ASHANTI Baron James, b. 5 Sept 1950, New York, New York, USA. Poet;Writer; Editor; Critic; Lecturer. m. Brenda Cummings, 11 Sept 1979, 1 son, 1 daughter. Appointments: Literary Editor, Impressions Magazine, 1972-75; City and Third World Editor, Liberation News Service, 1974-79; Contributing Editor, The Paper, 1978; Lecturer; Director, Arts-in-Education Program, Frederick Douglass Creative Arts Center, New York City, 1988-. Publications: Nubiana, 1977; Nova, 1990. Contributions to: Many periodicals. Honours: Killen Prize for Poetry, St Peter's College, 1982; PEN Fellowships, 1985, 1987; Pulitzer Prize in Poetry Nomination, 1991. Address: 274 West 140th Street, Apt No 45, New York, NY 10030, USA.

ASHBERY John Lawrence, b. 28 July 1927, Rochester, New York, USA. Professor of Languages and Literature; Poet; Dramatist; Critic. Education: BA, Harvard University, 1949; MA, Columbia University, 1951; Postgraduate Studies, New York University, 1957-58. Appointments: Editor, Locus Solus, Lans-en-Vercors, France, 1960-62; Art and Literature, Paris, 1963-66; Art Critic, New York Herald Tribune, Paris, 1960-65, Art International, Lugano, Switzerland, 1961-64, New York Magazine, 1978-80, Newsweek, 1980-85; Executive Editor, Art News, New York City, 1966-72; Professor of English, 1974-90, Distinguished Professor, 1980-90, Distinguished Professor Emeritus, 1990-, Brooklyn College; Poetry Editor, Partisan Review, 1976-80; Charles Eliot Norton Professor of Poetry, Harvard University, 1989-90; Charles P Stevenson Professor of Languages and Literature, Bard College, 1990-. Publications: Poetry: Turandot and Other Poems, 1953; Some Trees, 1956, 3rd edition, 1978; The Poems, 1960; The Tennis Court Oath, 1962; Rivers and Mountains, 1966, 2nd edition, 1977; Selected Poems, 1967; Three Madrigals, 1968; Sunrise in Suburbia, 1968; Fragment, 1969; The Double Dream of Spring, 1970, 2nd edition, 1976; The New Spirit, 1970; Three Poems, 1972, 3rd edition, 1989; The Vermont Notebook, 1975; Self-Portrait in a Convex Mirror, 1975, 3rd edition, 1977; Houseboat Days, 1976; As We Know, 1979; Shadow Train, 1981; A Wave, 1984; Selected Poems, 1985, 3rd edition, 1987; April Galleons, 1987, 4th edition, 1990; Flow Chart, 1991; Hotel Lautreamont, 1992; And the Stars Were Shining, 1994; Can You Hear, Bird, 1995. Plays: The Heroes, 1952; The Compromise, 1956; The Philosopher, 1963. Novel: A Nest of Ninnies (with James Schuyler), 1969, 3rd edition, 1987. Contributions to: Many anthologies, journals, and periodicals. Honours: Fulbright Scholarships, 1955-56, 1956-57; Yale Series of Younger Poets Prize, 1956; Poets Foundatioin Grants, 1960, 1964; Ingram Merrill Foundation Grants, 1962, 1972; Harriet Monroe Poetry Awards, 1963, 1975; Guggenheim Fellowships, 1967, 1973; National Institute of Arts and Letters Award, 1969; Pulitzer Prize in Poetry, 1976; National Book Award, 1976; National Book Critics Circle Award, 1976; English-Speaking Union Poetry Award, 1979; Rockefeller Foundation Grant, 1979-80; Mayor's Award, New York City, 1983; Charles Flint Kellogg Award, Bard College, 1983; Bollingen Prize in Poetry, Yale University Library, 1985; Lenore Marshall Poetry

Prize, 1985; Wallace Stevens Fellow, Yale University, 1985; John D and Catharine T McArthur Foundation Fellowship, 1985-90; Creative Arts Award, Brandeis University, 1989; Ruth Lilly Poetry Prize, 1992; Robert Frost Medal, 1995. Memberships: Academy of American Poets, fellow; American Academy and Institute of Arts and Letters; American Academy of Arts and Sciences. Address: c/o Department of Languages and Literature, Bard College, Annandale-on-Hudson, NY 12504, USA.

ASHBY Nora. See: **AFRICANO Lillian.**

ASHDOWN Dulcie Margaret, b. 24 Feb 1946, London, England. Writer; Editor. Education: BA, Bristol University, 1967. Publications: Christmas Past, 1976; Ladies in Waiting, 1976; Princess of Wales, 1976; Royal Children, 1980; Royal Weddings, 1981; Victoria and the Coburgs, 1981; 4 Other books. Contributions to: Majesty; Heritage; Writers' Monthly; The Lady. Address: c/o National Westminster Bank, 1302 High Road, Whetstone, London N20, England.

ASHE Geoffrey Thomas, b. 29 Mar 1923, London, England. Writer; Lecturer. m. (1) Dorothy Irene Train, 3 May 1946, dec, 4 sons, 1 daughter, (2) Maxine Lefever, 8 Dec 1992, div, (3) Patricia Chandler, 3 Apr 1998. Education: BA, University of British Columbia, Canada, 1943; BA, Trinity College, Cambridge University, 1948. Appointment: Associate Editor, Arthurian Encyclopaedia, 1986. Publications: King Arthur's Avalon, 1957; From Caesar to Arthur, 1960; Land to the West, 1962; The Land and the Book, 1965; Gandhi, 1968; The Quest for Arthur's Britain, 1968; Camelot and the Vision of Albion, 1971; The Art of Writing Made Simple, 1972; The Finger and the Moon, 1973; The Virgin, 1976; The Ancient Wisdom, 1977; Miracles, 1978; Guidebook to Arthurian Britain, 1980; Kings and Queens of Early Britain, 1982; Avalonian Quest, 1982; The Discovery of King Arthur, 1985; Landscape of King Arthur, 1987; Mythology of the British Isles, 1990; King Arthur: The Dream of a Golden Age, 1990; Dawn Behind the Dawn, 1992; Atlantis, 1992; The Traveller's Guide to Arthurian Britain, 1997. Contributions to: Numerous magazines and journals. Honour: Fellow, Royal Society of Literature, 1963. Memberships: Medieval Academy of America; Camelot Research Committee, secretary. Literary Agent: Rogers, Coleridge and White Ltd, 20 Powis Mews, London W11 1JN, England. Address: Chalice Orchard, Well House Lane, Glastonbury, Somerset BA6 8BJ, England.

ASHER Neal Lewis, b. 4 Feb 1961, Billericay, Essex, England. Education: Mechanical and Production Engineering ONC. Publications: Another England, 1989; Out of the Leaflight, 1991; Mason's Rats, 1992; The Thrake, 1993; Woodsmith, 1993; Dragon in the Flower, 1993; Blue Holes & Bloody Waters, 1994; Mason's Rats II, 1994; Stinging Things, 1994; Adaptogenic, 1994; Blue Holes and Bloody Waters, 1994; The Flame, 1994; Great African Vampire, 1994; Stones of Straw, 1994; Oceana Foods, 1994; Jable Sharks, 1994; Cavefish, 1995; Spatterjay, 1995; Jack O'Gravestones, 1995; Snairls, 1995; The Bacon, 1996; Page Dow, 1996; Out of the Leaf-Light, 1996; The Devil You Know, 1996; The Berserker Captain, 1996; Alternative Hospital, 1996; Floundering, 1996; Plastipak, 1996; Dragon in the Flower, 1996; The Gurnard, 1997; Snow in the Desert, 1997; Conversations, 1998; The Beserker Captain, 1998; The Gurnard, 1998; Dragon in the Flower, 1999. Address: 22 Snoreham Gardens, Latchingdon, Chelmsford, Essex CM3 6UN, England.

ASHLEY Bernard, b. 2 Apr 1935, London, England. Writer. Education: Teachers Certificate; Advanced Diploma, Cambridge Institute of Education. Publications: The Trouble with Donovan Croft, 1974; Terry on the Fence, 1975; All My Men, 1977; A Kind of Wild Justice, 1978; Break in the Sun, 1980; Dinner Ladies Don't Count, 1981; Dodgem, 1982; High Pavement Blues, 1983; Janey, 1985; Running Scared, 1986; Bad Blood, 1988; The Country Boy, 1989; The Secret of Theodore Brown, 1989; Clipper Street, 1990; Seeing off Uncle Jack, 1992; Cleversticks, 1993; Three Seven Eleven, 1993; Johnnie's Blitz, 1995; I Forgot, Said Troy, 1996; A Present for Paul, 1996; City Limits, 1997; Tiger Without Teeth, 1998; Growing Good, 1999. Contributions to: Books for Your Children; Junior Education; Books for Keeps; Times Educational Supplement; School Librarian. Honours: The Other Award, 1976; Runner Up, Carnegie Medal, 1979, 1986; Royal TV Society Best Children's Entertainment Programme, 1993. Membership: Writers Guild. Address: 128 Heathwood Gardens, London SE7 8ER, England.

ASHLEY Leonard (Raymond Nelligan), b. 5 Dec 1928, Miami, Florida, USA. Professor Emeritus of English; Author; Editor. Education: BA, 1949, MA, 1950, McGill University; AM, 1953, PhD, 1956, Princeton University. Appointments: Instructor, University of Utah, 1953-56; Assistant to the Air Historian, Royal Canadian Airforce, 1956-58; Instructor, University of Rochester, 1958-61; Faculty, New School for Social Research (part-time), 1962-72; Faculty, Brooklyn College of the City University, New York, 1961-95. Publications: What's in a Name?; Elizabethan Popular Culture; Colley Cibber; Nineteenth-Century British Drama; Authorship and Evidence in Renaissance Drama; Mirrors for Man; Other People's Lives; The Complete Book of Superstition, Prophecy and Luck; The Complete Book of Magic and Witchcraft; The Complete Book of Devils and Demons; The Complete Book of the Devil's Disciples; The Complete Book of Spells, Curses and Magical Recipes; The Complete Book of Vampires; The Complete Book of Ghosts and Poltergeists; Ripley's Believe It Or Not Book of the Military; The Air Defence of North America; George Alfred Henty and the Victorian Mind; Turkey: Names and Naming Practices; A Military History of Modern China (collaborator); Shakespeare's Jest Book; George Peele: The Man and His Work; Language in Contemporary Society (co-editor); Geolinguistic Perspectives (co-editor); Phantasms of the Living (editor). Contributions to: Books. Honours: Shakespeare Gold Medal; LHD (Columbia Theological) honoris causa, 1987, 1998. American Name Society Best Article Award; Fellowships and grants. Memberships: American Name Society, president 1979, 1987, member editorial board, executive board; International Linguistics Association; American Association of University Professors, Brooklyn College Chapter; American Society of Geolinguistics, president 1991-; Princeton Club of New York; Modern Language Association; American Dialect Society. Address: Department of English, Brooklyn College of the City University of New York, Brooklyn, NY 11230, USA.

ASHTON Christina Julia Allen, b. 16 Sept 1934, Brooklyn, New York, USA. Writer; Teacher. m. 21 Aug 1954, 1 daughter. Education: BA, English, 1957, Washington State University; MS, Special Education, 1975, Dominican College. Publications: Words Can Tell: A Book About Our Language, 1988; Codes and Ciphers, 1993. Contributions to: Calliope Magazine. Honours: English Honours, University of Oregon, 1954; Second Prize, California Writers Club, short story, 1991; 2nd Prize, National Writers Club, short story, 1991; Honorable Mention, National Writers Club, non-fiction book, 1992. Memberships: National Writers Club; California Writers Club, secretary, Peninsular Branch. Literary Agent: Norma Lewis Agency, New York. Address: 4009 Kingridge Drive, San Mateo, CA 94403, USA.

ASHTON Dore, b. 21 May 1928, Newark, New Jersey, USA. Professor of Art History; Writer. m. (1) Adja Yunkers, 8 July 1952, dec 1983, 2 daughters, (2) Matti Megged. Education: BA, University of Wisconsin, 1949; MA, Harvard University, 1950. Appointments: Associate Editor, Art Digest, 1951-54; Art Critic, New York Times, 1955-60; Lecturer, Pratt Institute, 1962-63; Head, Department of Humanities, School of Visual Arts, 1965-68; Professor of Art History, Cooper Union, 1969-; Adjunct Professor of Art History, City University of New York, 1973, Columbia University, 1975, New School for Social Research, 1986-; Associate Editor, Arts, 1974-92. Publications: Abstract Art Before Columbus, 1957; Poets and the Past, 1959; Philip Guston, 1960; Redon, Moreau, Bresden (co-author), 1961; The Unknown Shore, 1962; Rauschenberg's Dante, 1964; A Reading of Modern Art; Richard Lindoner, 1969; Modern American Sculpture; Pol Bury, 1971; Picasso on Art, 1972; Cultural Guide New York, 1972; The New York School: A Cultural Reckoning, 1973; A Joseph Cornell Album, 1974; Yes, But: A Critical Biography of Philip Guston, 1976; A Fable of Modern Art, 1980; Rosa Bonheur: A Life and Legend (with Denise Browne Hare), 1981; American Art Since 1945, 1982; About Rothko, 1983; 20th Century Artists on Art, 1985; Out of the Whirlwind, 1987; Fragonard in the Universe of Painting, 1988; Noguchi East and West, 1992; The Delicate Thread: Hiroshi Teshigahana, 1997. Contributions to: Journals and magazines. Honours: Ford Foundation Fellow, 1960; Graham Fellow, 1963; Mather Award for Art Criticism, College Art Association, 1963; Guggenheim Fellowship, 1964; National Endowment for the Humanities Grant, 1980; Art Criticism Prize, St Louis Art Museum, 1988. Memberships: International Association of Art Critics; Phi Beta Kappa. Address: 217 East 11th Street, New York, NY 10003, USA.

ASHTON Robert, b. 21 July 1924, Chester, England. Retired University Professor. m. Margaret Alice Sedgwick, 30 Aug 1946, 2 daughters. Education: Magdalen College School, Oxford, 1938-40; University College, Southampton, 1946-49; BA, First Class Honours, London, 1949; PhD, London School of Economics, 1953. Appointments: Assistant Lecturer, Lecturer, Senior Lecturer, Nottingham University, 1952-63; Visiting Associate Professor, University of California, Berkeley, 1962-63; Professor, 1963-89, Emeritus Professor, 1989-, University of East Anglia; Visiting Fellow, All Souls College, Oxford, 1974-75, 1987. Publications: The English Civil War: Conservatism and Revolution 1603-49, 1978, 2nd edition, 1989; The Crown and the Money Market 1603-40, 1960; James I by his Contemporaries, 1969; The City and the Court 1603-1643, 1979; Reformation and Revolution, 1558-1660, 1984; Counter Revolution: The Second Civil War and its Origins 1646-1648, 1994. Contributions to: Economic History Review; Bulletin of Institute of Historical Research; Past and Present; Historical journals. Membership: Royal Historical Society, fellow 1961-, vice-president, 1983-84. Address: The Manor House, Brundall, Norwich NR13 5JY, England.

ASIMOV Janet O Jeppson, b. 6 Aug 1926, Ashland, Pennsylvania, USA. Physician; Writer. m. Isaac Asimov, 30 Nov 1973. Education: BA, Stanford University, 1948; MD, New York University College of Medicine, 1952; Diploma, Psychoanalysis, William Alanson White Institute, 1960. Publications: The Second Experiment, 1974; The Last Immortal, 1980; The Mysterious Cure, 1985; The Package in Hyperspace, 1988; Mind Transfer, 1988; Murder at the Galactic Writers Society, 1995; Norby and the Terrified Taxi, 1997. With Isaac Asimov: How to Enjoy Writing; Laughing Space, 1982; Norby, the Mixed-Up Robot, 1983; Norby's Other Secret, 1984; Norby and the Lost Princess, 1985; Norby and the Invaders, 1985; Norby and the Queen's Necklace, 1986; Norby Finds a Villain, 1987; Norby and Yobo's Great Adventure, 1989; Norby and the Oldest Dragon, 1990; Norby Down to Earth, 1991; Norby and the Court Jester, 1991; Frontiers II. Contributions to: Several journals; Science column in various newspapers. Honour: Phi Beta Kappa, 1948. Memberships: Science Fiction Writers of America; William Alanson White Society; American Academy of Psychoanalysis; American Psychiatric Association. Address: 10 West 66th Street, New York, NY 10023, USA.

ASMUNDSDOTTIR Gudrun Gerdur, b. 19 Nov 1935, Reykjavik, Iceland. Actress. m. Birgir Matthiasson, 2 sons, 1 daughter. Education: Gagnyraedaskoli Austurbuar, 1951; Leiklistaskli Larlisa Palssonar, 1951-53; Leiklistarsk National Theatre, 1954-56; Central School of Drama, London, 1957-58. Appointments: Actress, City Theatre, Reykjavik, 1962-. Publications: Loma, childrens play; Kajmunk, church play about Danish priest killed by The Nazis, 1944; Up with the Carpet, play; Holy Sinners, play; Not Again into the Pool, childrens play; Don't Cry Granny, film script for children; Kormakur, childrens story. Honour: Kajmunk Prize in Kopenhagen, 1986. Membership: Writer's Association in Iceland. Address: Gudrun Asmundsdottir, Grandaveg 36 107, Reykjavik, Iceland.

ASMUNDSDOTTIR Steinunn, b. 1 Mar 1966, Reykjavík, Iceland. Environmental Educator; Writer; Editor; Poet. Education: General studies. Appointment: Editor, Andblaer (Breeze) magazine, 1995-. Publications: Solo on the Rainbow, 1989; Words of the Muses, 1993; A House on the Moor, 1996. Contributions to: Various publications. Membership: Icelandic Writers Union, 1994-. Address: Egilsstadir IV, 700 Egilsstadir, Iceland.

ASMUSSEN Jesper, (Torkel F Daneskjald), b. 13 Nov 1954, Copenhagen North, Denmark. Teacher. m. Merete Hojgaard Hansen, 15 Feb 1986, div May 1999, 1 daughter. Education: Teachers College, University of Copenhagen, 1982; Berkeley College of Music, USA, 1985. Publications: Alle Tiders Soldatersange, 1988; Soemandens Sange - Og Fantastiske Historier, 1994; De Danskes Sange - Og Hyggelige Historier, 1997; Soldaternes Sange: Og Tapre Historier, 1999. Honour: Dansk Forfatterforening, Autorkontoen. Membership: Dansk Forfatterforening. Address: Skjoldagervej 74, 2 Sal th, Jaegersborg, 2820 Gentofte, Denmark.

ASPENSTROM Werner, b. 13 Nov 1918, Norrbarke, Sweden. Poet; Playwright; Writer. m. Signe Lund, 1946. Education: BA, University of Stockholm, 1945. Publications: Verse: The Scream and the Silence, 1946; Snow Legend, 1949; Litany, 1952; The Dogs, 1954; Poems Under the Trees, 1956; The Stairs, 1964; Within, 1969; Meanwhile, 1972; Earth Cradle Sky Ceiling, 1973; Dictionary, 1976; Early One Morning Late on Earth, 1976-80; You and I and the World, 1980; Murmur, 1983; Beings, 1988. Plays: A Clown Must Have Lost His Way, 1949; The Snare, 1959. Television Plays: Theatre I, 1959; Theatre II, 1963; The Carpet, 1964; The Spiders and a Short Play, 1966; With One's Own Eyes, 1967; Poor Job, 1969; The Nose, 1971; Not So Young Anymore, 1972; Those Who Wait, 1976. Other: Sidelights: A Selection of Prose, 1989. Honour: Honorary Doctorate, University of Stockholm, 1976. Address: c/o Bonniers Forlag, Box 3159, 103 63 Stockholm, Sweden.

ASPLER Tony, b. 12 May 1939, London, England. Writer. 1 son, 1 daughter. Education: BA, McGill University, Canada, 1959. Publications: Streets of Askelon, 1972; One of My Marionettes, 1973; Chain Reaction (with Gordon Page), 1978; The Scorpion Sanction (with Gordon Page), 1980; Vintage Canada, 1983, updated edition, 1992; The Music Wars (with Gordon Page), 1983; Titanic (novel), 1989; Blood is Thicker than Beaujolais (novel), 1993; Cellar and Silver (with Rose Murray), 1993; Aligoté to Zinfandel, 1994; The Beast of Barbaresco (novel), 1996; Death on the Douro (novel); Travels With My Corkscrew (non-fiction). Contributions to: Periodicals. Membership: Crime Writers of Canada, founding chairman, 1982-84. Literary Agent: Livingston Cooke. Address: 27B Claxton Boulevard, Toronto, Ontario M6C 1L7, Canada.

ASPREY Robert B, b. 16 Feb 1923, Sioux City, Iowa, USA. Writer. Education: University of Iowa; New College, Oxford; University of Vienna; University of Nice. Publications: The Panther's Feast; The First Battle of the Marne; Once a Marine; At Belleau Wood; Semper Fidelis; War in the Shadows; Operation Prophet; Frederick the Great - the Magnificent Enigma; The German High Command at War. Contributions to: Marine Corps Gazette; New Yorker; Naval Institute Proceedings; Brassey's Annual; Army Quarterly; New York Times; Army (magazine). Honour: Fulbright Scholarship. Memberships: Authors Guild; Oxford University Society; New College Society; Army and Navy Club, Washington, DC; Special Forces Club, London. Address: Robert Gottlieb, William Morris Agency, 1350 Avenue of the Americas, New York, NY 10019, USA.

ASSAAD Fawzia, b. 17 July 1929, Cairo, Egypt. Author. m. Dr Fakhry Assaad, 17 Dec 1959, 1 son, 2 daughters. Education: French Baccalaureate, Cairo, 1946; BA, 1949, PhD, 1956, Sorbonne, University of Paris; Arabic Baccalaureate, Cairo, 1957. Appointments: Lecturer in Philosophy, University of Ain Shams, Cairo, 1957, 1964, University of Taipei, Taiwan, 1964-65. Publications: Fiction (in French): L'Egyptienne, 1975; Des Enfants et des Chats, 1987; La Grande Maison de Louxor, 1992. Non-Fiction: Soren Kierkegaard (in Arabic), 1960; Les Préfigurations Egyptiennes de la Pensée de Nietzsche (French), 1986. Contributions to: Journals. Honours: Prix de l'association des Ecrivains de Genève, 1985, 1991. Memberships: Association des Critiques Litteraires; PEN International. Address: 2 ch. de Sous-Cherre, 1245 Collonge-Bellerive, Geneva, Switzerland.

ASSELINEAU Roger Maurice, (Maurice Herra), b. 24 Mar 1915, Orleans, France. Emeritus Professor, American Literature. Education: Licence es Lettres, Agregation, English, 1938, Docteur es Lettres, 1953, Sorbonne, Paris. Publications: L'Evolution de Walt Whitman, 1954; The Literary Reputation of Mark Twain, 1954; Poèsies incomplètes, 1959; E A Poe, 1970; Transcendentalist Constant in American Literature, 1980; St John de Crevecoeur: The Life of an American Farmer (with Gay Wilson Allen), 1987; Poésies incomplètes (II), 1989; Poètes anglais de la Grande Guerre, 1991; As Maurice Herra, Poèmes de Guerre 1939-1944, 1991. Contributions to: Etudes Anglaises; Revue de Litterature Comparee; Forum; Dialogue; Calamus; Walt Whitman Quarterly Review. Honours: Walt Whitman Prize, Poetry Society of America; Honorary Doctorate, University of Poznan. Memberships: Former President, French Association for American Studies; Modern Language Association of America, honorary member; Hemingway Society; International Association of University Professors of English; Societé des Gens de Lettres. Address: 114 Avenue Leon Blum, 92160 Antony, France.

ASTLEY Thea, (Beatrice May), b. 25 Aug 1925, Brisbane, Queensland, Australia. Novelist. m. Edmund John Gregson, 1948, 1 son. Education: BA, University of Brisbane, 1947. Appointments: Senior Tutor, then Fellow in English, Macquarie University, Sydney, New South Wales, 1968-85. Publications: Girl With a Monkey, 1958; A Descant for Gossips, 1960; The Well-Dressed Explorer, 1962; The Slow Natives, 1965; A Boat Load of Home Folk, 1968; The Acolyte, 1972; A Kindness Cup, 1974; An Item from the Late News, 1982; Beachmasters, 1985; It's Raining in Mango, 1987; Reach Tin River, 1990; Reaching in River, 1990; Vanishing Points, 1992; Coda, 1994; Short stories: Hunting the Wild Pineapple, 1979; Uncollected short stories. Honours: Age Book of the Year Award, 1975, 1996; Patrick White Award, 1989; Miles Franklin Awards, 1962, 1965, 1972. Literary Agent: Hickson Associates, Sydney, Australia. Address: c/o Elise Goodman, Goodman Associates, 500 West End Avenue, New York, NY 10024, USA.

ASTOR Gerald (Morton), b. 3 Aug 1926, New Haven, Connecticut, USA. Writer. m. Sonia Sacoder, 23 Nov 1949, 3 sons. Education: AB, Princeton University, 1949; Columbia University, 1949-51. Publications: The New York Cops: An Informed History, 1971; "...And a Credit to His Race": The Hard Life and Times of Joseph Louis Barrow, a.k.a. Joe Louis, 1974; The Charge is Rape, 1974; A Question of Rape, 1974; Hot Paper, 1975; Photographing Sports: John Zimmerman, Mark Kauffman and Neil Leifer (with Sean Callahan), 1975; Brick Agent: Inside the Mafia for the FBI (with Anthony Villano), 1977; The Disease Detectives: Deadly Medical Mysteries and the People Who Solved Them, 1983; The "Last" Nazi: The Life and Times of Dr. Joseph Mengele, 1985; The Baseball Hall of Fame Anniversary Book, 1988; The PGA World Golf Hall of Fame Book, 1991; Hostage: My Nightmare in Beirut (with David Jacobsen), 1991; A Blood-Dimmed Tide: The Battle of the Bulge by the Men Who Fought It, 1992; Battling Buzzards: The Odyssey of the 517th Regimental Parachute Combat Team, 1943-1945, 1993; June 6, 1944: The Voices of D-Day, 1994; Operation Iceberg: The Invasion and Conquest of Okinawa in World War II: An Oral History, 1995; Crisis in the Pacific: The Battles for the Philippines, 1996; The Mighty Eighth: The Air War in Europe by the Men Who Fought It, forthcoming. Contributions to: Periodicals. Memberships: Authors Guild; Authors League of America. Address: 50 Sprain Valley Road, Scarsdale, NY 10583, USA.

ATHANASSIADIS Tassos, b. 1 Nov 1913, Salichli of Asia Minor, Turkey. Author; Novelist; Essayist; Biographer. m. Maria Dimitropoulou, 1979. Education: Law and Foreign Languages, Law School, Athens University, 1931-36. Publications: The Panthei Saga, 1948-61; The Guards of Achaia, 1974; The Last Grandchildren, 1981-84; Niobe's Children, 1985-88. Essays: Recognitions, 1965; Certainites and Doubts, 1980; From Ourself to Others, 1992; Holy Youth, 1993. Honours: State Literary Awards, 1955, 1961, 1963; Athens Academy Award, 1961; Ipeski Prize of Greek-Turkish Friendship, 1989; Doctor Honoris Causa, Athens University, 1994. Memberships: Athens Academy; PEN; Greek Lyric Opera; Greek National Theatre. Address: 83 Drossopoulou Street, Athens 112 57, Greece.

ATKINS Stephen E, b. 29 Jan 1941, Columbia, Missouri, USA. Librarian; Professor. m. Susan Starr Jordan, 9 June 1966, 1 son, 1 daughter. Education: BA (Honours), European History, 1963, MA (Honours), French History, 1964, University of Missouri-Columbia; PhD, French History, 1976, MA, Library Science, 1983, University of Iowa. Appointments: Political Science Specialist, Education and Social Science Library, Associate Professor, University of Illinois, Urbana-Champaign, 1983-89; Head of Collection Development, Sterling C Evans Library, 1989-, Professor, 1994-, Texas A&M University, College Station. Publications: Arms Control and Disarmament, Defense and Military, International Security and Peace: An Annotated Guide to Success, 1980-1987, 1989; The Academic Library in the American University, 1991; Terrorism: A Reference Handbook, 1992. Contributions to: National Forum, 1986; Library Trends, 1988; Proceedings of the Western Society for French History; Several others. Honour: Peace Award, American Library Association, 1992. Memberships: Western Society for French History, executive board, 1984-87; American Library Association; ACCESS: A Security Information Service; Association of College and Research Libraries; Social Science History Association; Library Administration and Management Association. Address: 2724 Normand Circle, College Station, TX 77845, USA.

ATKINSON James, b. 27 Apr 1914, Tynemouth, Northumberland, England. Retired Professor of Theology; Writer. m. Laura Jean Nutley, dec 1967, 1 son, 1 daughter. Education: BA, 1936, MA, 1938, M Litt, 1950, University of Durham; DTh, University of Münster, Germany, 1955; Hon DD, University of Hull, 1997. Publications: Library of Christian Classics, 1962; Rome and Reformation, 1966; Luther's Works, Vol 44, 1967; Luther and the Birth of Protestantism, 1968; The Reformation, 1968; The Trial of Luther, 1971; Martin Luther, 1983; The Darkness of Faith, 1987. Contributions to: Books and learned journals. Memberships: President of the Society for the Study of Theology; Society of the Study of Ecclesiastical History; L'Academie Internationale des Sciences Religieuses. Address: Leach House, Hathersage, Hope Valley, S32 1BA, England.

ATKINSON Mary. See: **HARDWICK Mollie.**

ATLAN Liliane, b. 14 Jan 1932, Montpellier, France. Writer; Dramatist; Poet. m. June 1952, div 1976, 1 son, 1 daughter. Education: Diploma in Philosophy; Studies in Modern Literature. Publications: Poetry: Lapsus, 1971; Bonheur mais sur quel ton le dire, 1996. Videotexts: Meme les oiseaux ne peuvent pas toujours planer, 1979; The Passerby, 1989; An Opera for Terezin, 1989; Quelques pages arrachées au grand livre des reves, 1994. Plays: The Passerby, 1997; An Opera for Terezin, 1997; Un Opéra pour Terezin, L'Avant-Scène, 1007/1008, 1997; Je m'appelle Non (play for children), Collection Théatre, 1998; Corridor Paradise Concert Brisé, Récit/Poème, 1998; Les mers rouges: Un conte à plusieurs Voix, 1998; Le mère des animaux norgeurs (Poème-Recit), 1998; Les passants, suivi du Corridor Paradise Concert (un recit en deux temps), 1998. Contributions to: Radio; magazines. Honours: Prix Habimah, 1972; Prix Wizo, 1989; Chevalier de l'Ordre des Arts et des Lettres, 1984; Villa Medicis Prize for

Outside the Walls, 1992. Membership: Writers Union of France. Address: 70 Rue du Javelot, 75645 Paris, Cedex 13, France.

ATODA Takashi, b. 13 Jan 1935, Tokyo, Japan. Author. m. 1965, 2 sons, 1 daughter. Education: Graduate, Literary Department, Waseda University, 1961. Publications: Napoleon Crazy, 1979; Do You Know Greek Mythology?, 1981; You Resemble Somebody, 1984; The New Illiad, 1994; The Fantasy of Azuchi Castle, 1996. Honours: Mystery Writers of Japan Award, 1979; Naoki Award, 1979; Yoshikawa Eiji Award, 1994. Memberships: Japan Writers Association; Japan Pen Club; Mystery Writers of Japan; Mystery Writers of America. Literary Agent: Woodbell Co Ltd. Address: 3-1-18 Takaido-Higashi, Suginami-ku, Tokyo, Japan.

ATTENBOROUGH David Frederick, b. 8 May 1926, London, England. Broadcaster; Naturalist. m. Jane Elizabeth Ebsworth Oriel, 11 Feb 1950, 1 son, 1 daughter. Education: Wyggeston Grammar School, Leicester; Clare College, Cambridge. Publications: Zoo Quest to Guiana, 1956; Zoo Quest for a Dragon, 1957; Zoo Quest in Paraguay, 1959; Quest in Paradise, 1960; Zoo Quest to Madagascar, 1961; Quest Under Capricorn, 1963; The Tribal Eye, 1976; Life on Earth, 1979; The Living Planet, 1984; The First Eden, 1987; Atlas of Living World, 1989; The Trials of Life, 1990. Honours: Silver Medal, Zoological Society of London, 1966; Gold Medal, Royal Geographical Society; Kalinga Prize, UNESCO; Honorary Degrees: Leicester, London, Birmingham, Liverpool, Heriot-Watt, Sussex, Bath, Ulster, Durham, Bristol, Glasgow, Essex, Cambridge, Oxford. Memberships: Fellow, Royal Society; Honorary Fellow, British Academy of Film and Television Arts. Address: 5 Park Road, Richmond, Surrey, England.

ATWOOD Margaret (Eleanor), b. 18 Nov 1939, Ottawa, Ontario, Canada. Poet; Author; Critic. m. Graeme Gibson, 1 daughter. Education: BA, Victoria College, University of Toronto, 1961; AM, Radcliffe College, Cambridge, Massachusetts, 1962; Harvard University, 1962-63, 1965-67. Appointments: Teacher, University of British Columbia, 1964-65, Sir George Williams University, Montreal, 1967-68, University of Alberta, 1969-70, York University, 1971-72; Writer-in-Residence, University of Toronto, 1972-73, University of Alabama, Tuscaloosa, 1985, Macquarie University, Australia, 1987; Berg Chair, New York University, 1986. Publications: Poetry: Double Persephone, 1961; The Circle Game, 1964; Kaleidoscopes Baroque, 1965; Talismans for Children, 1965; Speeches for Doctor Frankenstein, 1966; The Animals in That Country, 1968; The Journals of Susanna Moodie, 1970; Procedures for Underground, 1970; Oratorio for Sasquatch, Man and Two Androids, 1970; Power Politics, 1971; You Are Happy, 1974; Selected Poems, 1976; Marsh Hawk, 1977; Two-Headed Poems, 1978; True Stories, 1981; Notes Towards a Poem That Can Never Be Written, 1981; Snake Poems, 1983; Interlunar, 1984; Selected Poems II: Poems Selected and New, 1976-1986, 1986; Selected Poems 1966-1984, 1990; Margaret Atwood Poems 1965-1975, 1991; Morning in the Burned House, 1995. Fiction: The Edible Woman, 1969; Surfacing, 1972; Lady Oracle, 1976; Dancing Girls, 1977; Life Before Man, 1979; Bodily Harm, 1981; Encounters With the Element Man, 1982; Murder in the Dark, 1983; Bluebeard's Egg, 1983; Unearthing Suite, 1983; The Handmaid's Tale, 1985; Cat's Eye, 1988; Wilderness Tips, 1991; Good Bones, 1992; The Robber Bride, 1993; Alias Grace, 1996. Non-Fiction: Survival: A Thematic Guide to Canadian Literature, 1972; Days of The Rebels 1815-1840, 1977; Second Words: Selected Critical Prose, 1982; The Oxford Book of Canadian Verse in English (editor), 1982; The Best American Short Stories (editor with Shannon Ravenel), 1989; Strange Things: The Malevolent North in Canadian Literature, 1995. Contributions to: Books in Canada; Canadian Literature; Globe and Mail; Harvard Educational Review; The Nation; New York Times Book Review; Washington Post. Honours: Guggenheim Fellowship, 1981; Companion of the Order of Canada, 1981; Fellow, Royal Society of Canada; Foreign Honorary Member, American Academy of Arts and Sciences, 1988; Order of Ontario, 1990; Centennial Medal, Harvard University, 1990; Commemorative Medal, 125th Anniversary of Canadian Confederation, 1992; Giller Prize, 1996; Author of the Year, Canadian Book Industry Award, 1997; Marian McFadden Memorial Lecturer, Indianapolis-Marion County Public Libraru Foundation, 1998; Honorary degrees. Memberships: Writers Union of Canada, president, 1981-82; PEN International, president, 1985-86. Address: c/o Oxford University Press, 70 Wynford Drive, Don Mills, Ontario M3C 1J9, Canada.

AUBERT Alvin (Bernard), b. 12 Mar 1930, Lutcher, Louisiana, USA. Professor of English Emeritus; Poet. m. (1) Olga Alexis, 1948, div, 1 daughter, (2) Bernardine Tenant, 1960, 2 daughters. Education: BA, Southern University, Baton Rouge, 1959; AM, University of Michigan, 1960; University of Illinois at Urbana-Champaign, 1963-64, 1966-67. Appointments: Instructor, 1960-62, Assistant Professor, 1962-65, Associate Professor of English, 1965-70, Southern University; Visiting Professor of English, University of Oregon at Eugene, 1970; Associate Professor, 1970-74, Professor of English, 1974-79, State University of New York at Fredonia; Founder-Editor, Obsidian magazine, 1975-85; Professor of English, 1980-92, Professor Emeritus, 1992-, Wayne State University, Detroit. Publications: Against the Blues, 1972; Feeling Through, 1975; South Louisiana: New and Selected Poems, 1985; If Winter Come: Collected Poems, 1994; Harlem Wrestler, 1995. Honours: Bread Loaf Writers Conference Scholarship, 1968; National Endowment for the Arts Grants, 1973, 1981; Coordinating Council of Literary Magazines Grant, 1979; Annual Callaloo Award, 1989. Address: 18234 Parkside Avenue, Detroit, MI 48221, USA.

AUBURN Hugues. See: **BLACKBURN Gaston.**

AUCHINLOSS Louis Stanton, b. 27 Sept 1917, Lawrence, New York, USA. Lawyer; Author. m. Adele Lawrence, 1957, 3 sons. Education: Yale University; University of Virginia; Admitted, New York Bar, 1941. Publications: The Indifferent Children, 1947; The Injustice Collectors, 1950; Sybil, 1952; A Law for the Lion, 1953; The Romantic Egoists, 1954; The Great World and Timothy Colt, 1956; Venus in Sparta, 1958; Pursuit of the Prodigal, 1959; House of Five Talents, 1960; Reflections of a Jacobite, 1961; Portrait in Brownstone, 1962; Powers of Attorney, 1963; The Rector of Justin, 1964; Pioneers and Caretakers, 1965; The Embezzler, 1966; Tales of Manhattan, 1967; A World of Profit, 1969; Motiveless Malignity, 1969; Edith Wharton: A Woman in her Time, 1971; I Come as a Thief, 1972; Richelieu, 1972; The Partners, 1974; A Winter's Capital, 1974; Reading Henry James, 1975; The Winthrop Convenant, 1976; The Dark Lady, 1977; The Country Cousin, 1978; Persons of Consequence, 1979; Life, Law and Letters, 1979; The House of the Prophet, 1980; The Cat and the King, 1981; Watchfires, 1982; Exit Lady Masham, 1983; The Book Clan, 1984; Honorable Men, 1985; Diary of a Yuppie, 1987; The Golden Calves, 1989; Fellow Passengers, 1990; J P Morgan, 1990; False Gods, 1992; Family Fortunes: 3 Collected Novels, 1993; Three Lives, 1993; The Style's the Man, 1994. Contributions to: New York Review of Books; New Criterion. Membership: American Academy of Arts and Letters, president, 1997-2000. Address: 1111 Park Avenue, New York, NY 10028, USA.

AUEL Jean Marie, b. 18 Feb 1936, Chicago, Illinois, USA. Writer. m. Ray Bernard Auel, 19 Mar 1954, 2 sons, 3 daughters. Education: MBA, University of Portland, 1976. Publications: The Clan of the Cave Bear, 1980; The Valley of Horses, 1982; The Mammoth Hunters, 1985; The Plains of Passage, 1990. Honours: Excellence in Writing Award, Pacific North West Booksellers Association, 1980; Scandinavian Kaleidoscope of Art and Life Award, 1982; LittD, University of Portland, 1984; HHD, University of Maine, 1986; LHD, Mount Vernon College, 1986; Centennial Medal, Smithsonian Institution, 1990; HHD, Pacific University, 1995. Memberships: Authors Guild; International Women's Forum, board of directors, 1985-93; Mensa, Honorary Vice President, 1990-; Oregon Museum of Science and Industry, board of directors, 1993-; Oregon Writers Colony; PEN. Address: c/o Jean V Naggar Literary Agency, 217 East 75th Street, New York, NY 10021, USA.

AUERBACH Nina (Joan), b. 24 May 1943, New York, New York, USA. Professor of English; Writer. Education: BA, University of Wisconsin at Madison, 1964; MA, 1967, PhD, 1970, Columbia University. Appointments: Adjunct Professor, Hunter College of the City University of New York, 1969-70; Assistant Professor of English, California State University at Los Angeles, 1970-72; Assistant Professor, 1972-77, Associate Professor, 1977-83, Professor, 1983-, of English, University of Pennsylvania. Publications: Communities of Women: An Idea in Fiction, 1978; Woman and the Demon: The Life of a Victorian Myth, 1982; Romantic Imprisonment: Women and Other Glorified Outcasts, 1985; Ellen Terry: Player in Her Time, 1987; Private Theatrical: The Lives of the Victorians, 1990; Forbidden Journeys: Fairy Tales and Fantasies by Victorian Women Writers (editor with U C Knoepflmacher), 1992; Our Vampires, Ourselves, 1995. Contributions to: Books and periodicals. Honours: Ford Foundation Fellowship, 1975-76; Radcliffe Institute Fellowship, 1975-76; Guggenheim Fellowship, 1979-80; National Book Critics Circle Nomination for Criticism, 1982; Phi Beta Kappa; Phi Beta Phi. Memberships: Modern Language Association of America; Victorian Society of America. Address: Department of English, University of Pennsylvania, Philadelphia, PA 19104, USA.

AUGUST Marcus. See: **BANTOCK Gavin.**

AUMBRY Alan. See: **BAYLEY Barrington (John).**

AUSTER Paul, b. 3 Feb 1947, Newark, New Jersey, USA. Writer; Poet. m. (1) Lydia Davis, 6 Oct 1974, div 1979, 1 son, (2) Siri Hustvedt, 16 June 1981, 1 daughter. Education: BA, 1969, MA, 1970, Columbia University. Appointment: Lecturer, Princeton University, 1986-90. Publications: Novels: City of Glass, 1985; Ghosts, 1986; The Locked Room, 1986; In the Country of Last Things, 1987; Moon Palace, 1989; The Music of Chance, 1990; Leviathan, 1992; Mr Vertigo, 1994. Poetry: Unearth, 1974; Wall Writing, 1976; Fragments from Cold, 1977; Facing the Music, 1980; Disappearances: Selected Poems, 1988; Why Write?, 1996; Translations, 1996; Hand to Mouth, 1997; Non-Fiction: White Spaces, 1980; The Invention of Solitude, 1982; The Art of Hunger, 1982, augmented edition, 1992; Hand to Mouth (autobiography), 1997. Editor: The Random House Book of Twentieth-Century French Poetry, 1982. Films: Smoke, 1995; Blue in the Face, 1995. Contributions to: Numerous periodicals. Honours: National Endowment for the Arts Fellowships, 1979, 1985; Chevalier, l'Ordre des Arts et des Lettres, France; Prix Medicis Étranger, 1993. Membership: PEN. Address: c/o Carol Mann Agency, 55 Fifth Avenue, New York, NY 10003, USA.

AUSTIN Brett. See: **FLOREN Lee.**

AUSTIN William W(eaver), b. 18 Jan 1920, Lawton, Oklahoma, USA. Musicologist. Education: BA, 1939, MA, 1940, PhD, 1951, Harvard University. Appointments: Assistant Professor, 1947-50, Associate Professor, 1950-60, Professor, 1960-69, Goldwin Smith Professor of Musicology, 1969-80, Given Foundation Professor of Musicology, 1980-90, Professor Emeritus, 1990-, Cornell University. Publications: Music in the 20th Century from Debussy Through Stravinsky, 1966; "Susanna", "Jeanie", and "The Old Folks At Home": Meanings and Contexts of the Songs of Stephen C Foster from His Time to Ours, 1975, 2nd edition, 1987. Editor: New Looks at Italian Opera: Essays in Honor of Donald J Grout, 1968. Translator: Carl Dahlhaus's Musikästhetik as Esthetics of Music, 1982. Honours: Guggenheim Fellowship, 1961-62; Fellow, American Academy of Arts and Sciences. Membership: American Musicological Society. Address: 205 White Park Road, Ithaca, NY 14850, USA.

AVERILL Gage, b. 16 May 1954, Greenwich, CT, USA. Professor of Ethnomusicology. m. Giovanna Maria Perot-Averill, 25 July 1992. Education: University of Wisconsin, 1972-74; BA, University of Washington, 1984;

PhD, University of Washington, 1989. Appointments: Visiting Assistant Professor, Columbia University, 1989-90; Assistant Professor, Wesleyan University, 1990-96; Associate Professor, Wesleyan University, 1996-97; Assoc Prof, New York Univ, 1997-. Publications: Making & Selling Culture, co-edited with Prin Ed Richard Ohmann, 1996; A Day for the Hunter, A Day for the Prey: Popular Music & Power in Haiti, 1997; Four Parts No Waiting: A Social History of American Barbershop Harmony, forthcoming. Contributions to: Beat Magazine Columns, 1988-97; Ethnomusicology; Diaspora; Latin America Music Review; Book Review Editor for the Yearbook for Traditional Music. Honours: Best Research in Field of Recorded Folk or Ethnic Music, Association of Recorded Sound Collections, 1997; Mellon Fellowship, 1989. Address: Music Department, New York University, 24 Waverly Pl #268, New York, NY 10003-6789, USA.

AVERY Gillian (Elise), b. 30 Sept 1926, England. Writer; Editor. Appointments: Junior Reporter, Surrey Mirror, Redhill, Surrey, 1944-47; Staff, Chambers Encyclopaedia, London, 1947-50; Assistant Illustrations Editor, Clarendon Press, Oxford, 1950-54. Publications: Victorian People in Life and Literature, 1970; A Likely Lad, 1971; Ellen's Birthday, 1971; Jemima and the Welsh Rabbit, 1972; The Echoing Green: Memories of Victorian and Regency Youth, 1974; Ellen and the Queen, 1974; Book of Strange and Odd, 1975; Childhood's Pattern: A Study of the Heroes and Heroines of Children's Fiction, 1770-1850, 1975; Freddie's Feet, 1976; Huck and Her Time Machine, 1977; Mouldy's Orphan, 1978; Sixpence, 1979; The Lost Railway, 1980; Onlookers, 1983; The Best Type of Girl, 1991. Editor: Many books. Address: 32 Charlbury Road, Oxford OX2 6UU, England.

AVGERINOS Cecily T Grazio, b. 16 Apr 1945, New York, New York, USA. Poet; Novelist. m. Robert T Avgerinos, 24 May 1969, 2 sons, 1 daughter. Education: BA, New York University, 1966. Publications: Poems: My Tatterdemalion, 1985; Sunrises, 1985; Eternity, 1986; Summer Fantasy, 1986; My Prayer, 1986; Lunch in the Park, 1986; Circle of Gold, 1986; Lord, I Wonder, 1986; The Fig Tree, 1987; Fishing, 1987; Septecential, 1987; Loss, 1987; Bridge Across Tomorrow, 1987; To My Children, 1987; The Stringless Guitar, 1988; Pink Socks, 1988; My Dogwood-Love's Analogy, 1989; Merry-Go-Round, 1989; Strawsticks, 1989. Contributions to: Numerous anthologies. Honours: 25 Awards of Merit, World of Poetry, 1985-; 4 Golden Poet Awards, 1985-. Address: 173 Momar Drive, Ramsey, NJ 07446, USA.

AVI. See: **WORTIS Avi.**

AVICE Claude (Pierre Marie), (Pierre Barbet, David Maine, Oliver Sprigel), b. 16 May 1925, Le Mans, France. Science Fiction Writer. m. Marianne Brunswick, 23 July 1952, 2 sons, 1 daughter. Education: Diplomas in Bacteriology, Serology and Parasitology, 1954, PhD, Summa cum laude, in Pharmacy, 1955, Institut Pasteur, University of Paris. Appointments: Pharmacist, Paris, 1952-81; Science Fiction Writer, 1962-. Publications: Over 70 books including: Les Grognards d'Eridan, 1970, English translation as The Napoleons of Eridanus, 1976; A quoi songent les psyborgs?, 1971, English translation as Games Psyborgs Play, 1973; L'Empire du Baphomet, 1972, English translation as Baphomet's Meteor, 1972; La Planete enchantée, 1973, English translation as Enchanted Planet, 1975; Liane de Noldaz, 1973, English translation as The Joan-of-Arc Replay, 1978; L'Empereur d'Eridan, 1982, English translation as The Emperor of Eridanus, 1983. Contributions to: Many publications both fiction and non-fiction. Honour: Gold Medal, International Institute of Science Fiction, Poznań, Poland. Memberships: Association Internationale des Critiques litteraires; European Academy of Arts, Letters and Science; European Society of Science Fiction; Science Fiction Writers of America; Society of Doctors in Pharmacy; Société francophone de Science-Fiction; World Science Fiction. Address: 4 Square de l'Avenue du Bois, 75116 Paris, France.

AVISON Margaret (Kirkland), b. 23 Apr 1918, Galt, Ontario, Canada. Poet. Education: BA, English, Victoria College, University of Toronto, 1940; Indiana University; University of Chicago; Graduate Studies, University of Toronto, 1963-66. Appointments: Teacher, Scarborough College, University of Toronto, 1966-68; Writer-in-Residence, University of Western Ontario, 1972-73; Staff, Mustard Seed Mission, Toronto, 1978-. Publications: Poetry: Winter Sun, 1960; The Dumbfounding, 1966; Sunblue, 1978; No Time, 1989; Margaret Avison: Selected Poems, 1991. Other: A Kind of Perseverance (lectures), 1993. Honours: Guggenheim Fellowship, 1956; Governor-General's Awards for Poetry, 1960, 1990. Address: c/o Mustard Seed Mission, Toronto, Ontario, Canada.

AVRAMESCU Lucian, b. 14 Aug 1948, Sângeru-Prahova, Romania. Journalist. m. Maria Croitoru, 17 Oct 1971, 1 son, 1 daughter. Education: Degree in Garden Architecture, Faculty of Horticulture Specialisation, University of Craiova; Degree in Journalism, Faculty of Journalism. Appointments: Journalist, Horizon newspaper, Râmnicu Vâlcea, 1971-78; Journalist, The Youth's Spark, 1978-89; Leader, Youth Celebrations, cultural show, 1981-85; Editor-in-Chief, Consecventa, youth film festival review, 1985-88; Editor-in-Chief, SLAST, young writers review, 1985-89; Founder, Editor-in-Chief, Free Youth newspaper, 1989; Founder, Owner, General Manager, A M Press, independent press agency, 1991-; Weekly Poetry Programme, in The 5 O'Clock Tea, National Romanian Television, 1993-98. Publications: Poems, 1975; Stars on the hills, poems, 1976; The transplant of blue, travel notes, 1976; A free albatross, poems, 1978; So what! was saying the poet, poems, 1979; I don't ask for forgiveness, Part 1, 1981, Part 2, 1983, Part 3, 1985; This generation, poems, 1985; Good evening, my love!, 1986, 2nd edition, 1987; Translated poems in anthologies and literary reviews, Poland, Bulgaria, Russia, Israel, China, England, USA, Germany, France, Netherlands, Turkey, Yugoslavia, Iraq. Contributions to: The Evening Star; Amphitheatre; Literary Romania; Branches; Arges; Horizon; The Hearth; The Family; SLAST; The Romanian Life; The Contemporary; Permanent column, Free Romania; Radio and television. Honours: Debut Prize, Albatross Publishing House, 1975; Prize for Best Book of Poems by a Young Writer, 1979. Membership: Union of Writers, Romania, 1979-. Address: Sfintii Voievozi Str, No 9, Sector 1, ap 1, Bucharest, Romania.

AWALGAONKAR Avinash, b. 1 July 1958, Kati, Amraoti, Maharashtra, India. m. 13 Mar 1989, 1 son, 1 daughter. Education: BA, Nagpur University, 1978; MA, 1980, MPhil, 1982, PhD, 1990, Marathwada University, Aurangabad. Appointments: MSG College, Malegaon Camp, Nashik, 1982; Ahmednagar College, Ahmednagar, 1991; Marathi Department, University of Pune, Pune, 1995. Publications: Kilbil, poem, 1983; Sanjbavari, poem, 1995; A Critical Study of Mahanubhav Literature with Special Reference to Shri Govindprabhu, 1996; A Poetry of V S Khandekar, 1999. Contributions to: 35 research articles published in magazines and journals. Honours: Maharashtra State Government Award, 1985-; Vishvabharati Award, 1997. Membership: Life Member, Maharashtra Sahity Parishad. Address: Department of Marathi, Pune University, Pune 411007, Maharashtra, India.

AWOONOR Kofi, b, 13 Mar 1935, Wheta, Ghana. Educator; Diplomat; Poet; Writer. 4 sons, 1 daughter. Education: BA, University of Ghana, 1960; MA, University of London, 1968; PhD in Comparative Literature, State University of New York at Stony Brook, 1973. Appointments: Research Fellow, Institute of American Studies, 1960-64; Director, Ghana Ministry of Information Film Corp, 1964-67; Poet-in-Residence, 1968, Assistant Professor, 1968-72, Associate Professor, 1973-74, Chair, Department of Comparative Literature, 1974-75, State University of New York; Senior Lecturer, Professor of Literature, and Dean of the Faculty of Arts, University of Cape Coast, 1977-82; Ghana Ambassador to Brazil, 1984-88, Cuba, 1988-90, United Nations, 1990-. Publications: Rediscovery and Other Poems, 1964; Night of My Blood, 1971; This Earth, My Brother, 1972; Ride Me, Memory, 1973; Guardian of the Sacred Word, 1974; Breast of the Earth (essays), 1974; The House by the Sea, 1978; Until the Morning After: Collected Poems 1963-1985, 1987; Ghana: A Political History, 1990; Comes the Voyage at Last, 1992; Latin American and Caribbean Notebook, 1993. Honours: Translation Award, Columbia University, 1972; Ghana Book Award, 1978; Commonwealth Poetry Prize, 1989; Distinguished Authors Award, Ghana Association of Writers, 1992. Address: c/o Permanent Mission of Ghana to the United Nations, 19 East 47th Street, New York, NY 10017, USA.

AXTON David. See: **KOONTZ Dean R(ay).**

AYCKBOURN Alan, b. 12 Apr 1939, London, England. Theatre Director; Playwright; Artistic Director. Plays: Mr Whatnot, 1963; Relatively Speaking, 1965; How the Other Half Loves, 1969; Time and Time Again, 1971; Absurd Person Singular, 1972; The Norman Conquests, 1973; Absent Friends, 1974; Confusions, 1975; Bedroom Farce, 1975; Just Between Ourselves, 1976; Ten Times Table, 1977; Joking Apart, 1978; Sisterly Feelings, 1979; Taking Steps, 1979; Season's Greetings, 1980; Way Upstream, 1981; Intimate Exchanges, 1982; A Chorus of Disapproval, 1984; Woman in Mind, 1985; A Small Family Business, 1986; Henceforward, 1987; Man of the Moment, 1988; The Revengers' Comedies, 1989; Time of My Life, 1992; Dreams From a Summer House, 1992; Communicating Doors, 1994; Hunting Julia, 1994; The Musical Jigsaw Play, 1994; A Word From Our Sponsor, 1995; By Jeeves (with Andrew Lloyd Webber), 1996; The Champion of Paribanou, 1996; Things We Do For Love, 1997; Comic Potential, 1998; The Boy Who Fell into a Book, 1998; Gizmo, 1998. Honours: Hon DLitt, Hull, 1981, Keele, 1987, Leeds, 1987, York, 1992, Bradford, 1994, Cardiff University of Wales, 1996, Open University, 1998; Commander of the Order of the British Empire, 1987; Cameron Mackintosh Professor of Contemporary Theatre, 1992; Knighthood, 1997. Memberships: Garrick Club; Royal Society of Arts. Address: c/o Casarotto Ramsay Ltd, National House, 60-66 Wardour Street, London W1V 4ND, England.

AYDY Catherine. See: **TENNANT Emma Christina.**

AYERST David (George Ogilvy), b. 24 July 1904, London, England. Appointments: Editorial Staff Member, 1929-34, Historian, 1964-73, The Guardian, Manchester and London; H M Inspector of Schools, 1947-64. Publications: Europe in the 19th Century, 1940; Understanding Schools, 1967; Records of Christianity (editor with A S T Fisher), 1970, 1977; Guardian: Biography of a Newspaper (in US as The Manchester Guardian), 1971; The Guardian Omnibus (editor), 1973; Garvin of the Observer, 1985. Address: Littlecote, Burford, Oxford OX18 4SE, England.

AYIM May. See: **OPITZ May.**

AYLEN Leo (William), b. Vryheid, South Africa. Writer; Poet. m. Annette Battam. Education: MA, New College, Oxford, 1959; PhD, University of Bristol, 1962. Appointments: Producer, BBC-TV, London, 1965-70; Poet-in-Residence, Fairleigh Dickinson University, USA, 1972-74; Hooker Distinguished Visiting Professor, McMaster University, Canada, 1982; Numerous appearances as a poet on radio and TV in the UK, USA and South Africa. Publications: Greek Tragedy in the Modern World, 1964; Greece for Everyone, 1976; The Greek Theater, 1985. Poetry: Discontinued Design, 1969; I, Odysseus, 1971; Sunflower, 1976; Return to Zululand, 1980; Jumping-Shoes, 1983; Rhymoceros, 1989; Feast of the Bones: New and Selected Poems, 1996; Dancing the Impossible: Selected Poems, 1997; Play: Red Alert: This is a God Warning, 1981. Children's Opera: The Apples of Youth, 1980. Contributions to: Many anthologies. Honours: C Day-Lewis Fellowship, 1979-80; Runner-up Prizewinner, Arvon International Competition, 1992. Memberships: Poetry Society of Great Britain; Poetry Society of America; Writers Guild of Great Britain; Writers Guild of America. Address: 13 St Saviour's Road, London SW2 5HP, England.

AYLING Stanley (Edward), b. 15 Mar 1909, London, England. Retired History Teacher; Writer. m. Gwendoline Hawkins, 17 Dec 1936, 2 sons. Education: BA, 1931, MA, 1934, Emmanuel College, Cambridge. Appointments: Grammar school teacher, Exeter and London, 1932-45; Senior history master, Sandown Grammar School, Isle of Wight, England, 1945-69. Publications: Twelve Portraits of Power: An Introduction to Twentieth Century History, 1961, 5th edition, 1971; Georgian Century, 1971; Nineteenth Century Gallery: Portraits of Power and Rebellion, 1970; George the Third, 1972; The Elder Pitt, Earl of Chatham, 1976; John Wesley, 1979; A Portrait of Sheridan, 1985; Edmund Burke: His Life and Opinions, 1988; Fox: The Life of Charles James Fox, 1991. Membership: Fellow, Royal Society of Literature, 1980-. Address: The Beeches, Middle Winterslow, Salisbury, Wiltshire, England.

AYLMER Gerald Edward, b. 30 Apr 1926, England. Historian. Education: BA, 1950, MA, 1951, PhD, 1955, Oxford University. Appointments: J E Proctor Visiting Fellow, Princeton University, New Jersey, 1950-51; Junior Research Fellow, Balliol College, Oxford, 1951-54; Assistant Lecturer, 1954-57, Lecturer, 1957-62, University of Manchester; Professor and Head of Department, University of York, 1963-78; Master, St Peter's College, Oxford, 1978-91, Honorary Fellow, 1991; Editorial Board, 1968-, Chairman, 1989, History of Parliament; Member, 1978-, Chairman, 1989-94, Royal Commission on Historical Manuscripts. Publications: The King's Servants, 1625-1642, 1961; The Diary of William Lawrence, 1961; The Struggle for the Constitution 1603-1689, 1963; The Interregnum 1646-1660, 1972; The State's Servants, 1649-1660, 1973; The Levellers in the English Revolution, 1975; A History of York Minster, 1977; Rebellion or Revolution 1640-1660, 1986. Honour: Fellow, British Academy, 1976; Honorary Degrees, Exeter University, Manchester University, 1991. Memberships: Royal Historical Society, vice president, 1973-77, president, 1984-88, honorary vice president, 1988; Historical Association, honorary vice president, 1992-. Address: 18 Albert Street, Jericho, Oxford OX2 6AZ, England.

AYRES Philip (James), b. 28 July 1944, South Australia. Writer; Lecturer. m. (1) Maruta Sudrabs, 11 Dec 1965, div 1981, (2) Patricia San Martin, 28 Nov 1981, 1 son. Education: BA, 1965, PhD, 1971, University of Adelaide. Appointments: Lecturer, 1972-79, Senior Lecturer, 1979-, Monash University; Associate Professor, 1993-; Visiting Professor, Vassar College, New York, 1993. Publications: The Revenger's Tragedy, 1977; The English Roman Life, 1980; Malcolm Fraser: A Biography, 1987. Editor: Ben Jonson: Sejanus His Fall, 1990; Classical Culture and the Idea of Rome in Eighteenth Century England, 1997; Douglas Mawson, 1999; Editor, Shaftesbury 3rd Earl, Characteristics, 1999. Contributions to: English Literary Renaissance; Modern Philiology; Studies in Bibliography; Studies in English Literature; Studies in Philology. Honour: Fellow, Royal Historical Society. Address: 13 Harris Avenue, Glen Iris, Victoria 3146, Australia.

AZIZ Meena Zebun Nahar, b. 1 Jan 1942, Dhaka, Bangladesh. Writer; Housewife. m. Dr M A Aziz, 24 Sept 1954, 2 sons, 2 daughters. Education: MA, Begali Literature, Dhaka University, Bangladesh. Publications: Saudi Arab Ke Jemon Dekhechi; Chetaner Digante; Nil Nayaner Deshe; Parir Deshe Ekmas; Samajo Jiban; Himalaya Tanay Nepal; Ajo Bahe Jamuna; Ravi Nadir Tirey; Mohomoee California; Shawapner Basati. Contributions to: Regular writing in various newspapers and weekly and monthly magazines. Honours: Award for Literature, 1988, 1992, 1998. Memberships: Life Member, Bangla Academi; Secretary, Dhan Mondi Shahitya Chakra; Treasurer, Bangladesh Lekhika Songha. Address: Mousumi, 55 Central Road, Dhanmondi, Dhaka 1205, Bangladesh.

B

B Dick. See: BURNS Richard Gordon.

BAAL Voldemar, (V Nemchin, V Murma), b. 17 July 1936, Saratov Region, Russia. Engineer; Mechanic; Writer. m. Violeta Semyonova, 10 Feb 1977, 1 daughter. Education: Kzasnoyazsk Agricultural Institute, 1960; Literature Institute, Moscow, 1968. Appointments: Engineer, Designer, Riga Radiofactory, 1964-69; Journalist, Latvian Radio and Newspapers, 1969-74; Literary Consultant, Writers' Union of Latvia, 1974-83. Publications: The Voices, 1969; Stories, 1972; Bakhzov's Stories, 1974; A Magician's Stories, 1978; The Day and the Night (novel), 1980; From the Point A (novel), 1983; Golden (novel), 1984; A Source of Oblivion (novel), 1985; Selected Novels and Collective Magazines, 1986. Contributions to: Youth; Aurora; Daugava; Journals in Bulgaria and Germany. Honours: Liesma Award, 1983; Writers' Union Award, 1994, 1996. Membership: Writers' Union of Latvia, 1969. Address: Dzelzavas str 11, Flat 46, Riga, LV1084, Latvia.

BAANTJER Albert Cornelis, b. 16 Sept 1923, Urk, Holland. Retired Police Officer; Writer. m. Marretje van der Vaart, 3 Dec 1952. Education: Police High School, 1945. Publications: Dr Kok and the Sorrowing Tomcat; Dr Kok and the Brothers of the Easy Death; Dr Kok and the Mask of Death; Murder in Amsterdam. Contributions to: Nieuws van de Dag; Margriet; Libelle. Honours: Winner, Short Story Competition, 1961; Silver Medal, 1979; Television Book Award, 1985. Literary Agent: John Bakkenhoven. Address: Poortweydt 4, 1671RC Medemblik, Holland.

BABB Sanora, b. 21 Apr 1907, Leavenworth, Kansas, USA. Writer. m. James Wong Howe, 12 Sept 1949, dec 1976. Education: Kansas University. Publications: The Lost Traveler, 1958; An Owl on Every Post, 1970; The Dark Earth, (stories), 1987; Cry of the Tinamou, 1997; Told in the Seed, 1998. Contributions to: Periodicals. Honour: Barestone Mountain Poetry Award, 1967. Membership: Authors Guild. Literary Agent: McIntosh and Otis, 310 Madison Avenue, New York, NY 10017, USA. Address: 1562 Queen's Road, West Hollywood, CA 90069, USA.

BABINEAU Jean Joseph, b. 10 Aug 1952, Moncton, New Brunswick, Canada. Teacher; Writer. m. Gisèle Ouellette, 27 Aug 1993, 1 son. Education: BA, 1977; BA, French, 1981; BEd, 1985. Publication: Bloupe, 1993; Gîte, 1998. Contributions to: Éloizes; Mots en Volet; Littéréalité; Satellite;ouvelles d'Amerique; Virages. Honour: Canada Council Exploration Grant, 1989; New Brunswick Arts Branch Creation Grant, 1998. Membership: AAAPNB. Address: Boîte 1516, Robichaud, New Brunswick E0A 2S0, Canada.

BABINGTON Anthony Patrick, b. 4 Apr 1920, Cork, Ireland. Retired Judge; Writer. Education: Inns of Court Law School. Appointments: Called to Bar, 1948; Circuit Judge, London, 1972-90. Publications: For the Sake of Example; No Memorial; Military Intervention in Britain; A House in Bow Street; The Rule of Law in Britain; The Devil to Pay; The Power to Silence; The English Bastille; Shell-Shock. Memberships: PEN; Society of Authors; Special Forces Club; Garrick. Address: Thydon Cottage, Chilham, Canterbury, Kent CT4 8BX, England.

BABSON Marian, b. USA. Writer. Appointment: Secretary, Crime Writers Association, London, 1976-86. Publications: Cover-up Story, 1971; Murder on Show, 1972; Pretty Lady, 1973; The Stalking Lamb, 1974; Unfair Exchange, 1974; Murder Sails at Midnight, 1975; There Must Be Some Mistake, 1975; Untimely Guest, 1976; The Lord Mayor's Death, 1977; Murder Murder Little Star, 1977; Tightrope for Three, 1978; So Soon Done For, 1979; The Twelve Deaths of Christmas, 1979; Dangerous to Know, 1980; Queue Here for Murder, 1980; Bejewelled Death, 1981; Death Warmed Up, 1982; Death Beside the Seaside, 1982; A Fool for Murder, 1983; The Cruise of a Deathtime, 1984; A Trail of Ashes, 1984; Death Swap, 1984; Death in Fashion, 1985; Weekend for Murder, 1985; Reel Murder, 1986; Fatal Fortune, 1987; Guilty Party, 1989; Encore Murder, 1989; Past Regret, 1990. Address: c/o William Collins Sons & Co Ltd, 8 Grafton Street, London W1X 3LA, England.

BACHMAN Richard. See: KING Stephen (Edwin).

BOCOCK Robert James, b. 29 Sept 1940, England. Senior Lecturer in Social Science. Publications: Freud and Modern Society, 1976; Sigmund Freud, 1983; Ritual in Industrial Society, 1974; Hegemony, 1986; Consumption, 1993. Contributor to: British Journal of Sociology; Sociology. *Membership:* British Sociological Association. Literary Agent: A D Peters, London. Address: Department of Sociology, Faculty of Social Sciences, Crowther Building, The Open University, Walton Hall, Milton Keynes, Buckinghamshire, England.

BADAWI Mohamed Mustafa, b. 10 June 1925, Alexandria, Egypt. Lecturer; Writer. Education: BA, Alexandria University, 1946; BA, 1950, PhD, 1954, London University. Appointments: Research Fellow, 1947-54, Lecturer, 1954-60, Assistant Professor, 1960-64, Alexandria University, Egypt; Lecturer, Oxford University, and Brasenose College, 1964-92; Fellow, St Antony's College, Oxford, 1967-; Editor, Journal of Arabic Literature, Leiden, 1970; Advisory Board Member, Cambridge History of Arabic Literature. Publications: An Anthology of Modern Arabic Verse, 1970; Coleridge as Critic of Shakespeare, 1973; A Critical Introduction to Modern Arabic Poetry, 1975; Background to Shakespeare, 1981; Modern Arabic Literature and the West, 1985; Modern Arabic Drama in Egypt, 1987; Early Arabic Drama, 1988; Modern Arabic Literature: Cambridge History of Arabic literature (editor), 1992; A Short History of Modern Arabic Literature, 1993. Honour: King Faisal International Prize for Arabic Literature. Memberships: Ministry of Culture, Egypt; Unesco Expert on Modern Arabic Culture. Address: St Antony's College, Oxford, England.

BADCOCK Gary David, b. 13 Jan 1961, Bay Roberts, Canada. Lecturer. m. Susan Dorothy Greig, 21 Dec 1988, 2 daughters. Education: BA, 1981, MA, 1984, Memorial University of Newfoundland; BD, 1987, PhD, 1991, University of Edinburgh, Scotland. Appointments: Teaching Fellow, University of Aberdeen, 1991-92; Meldrum Lecturer in Dogmatic Theology, University of Edinburgh, 1993-. Publications: Edited with D F Wright, Disruption to Diversity: Edinburgh Divinity, 1846-1996; Edinburgh, 1996; Theology After the Storm, by John McIntyre (editor), 1995; Light of Truth and Fire of Love, 1997; The Way of Life, 1998. Contributions to: Co-author, books and scholarly journals. Honour: Leslie Tarr Award, 1998. Address: New College, Mound Place, Edinburgh EH1 2LX, Scotland.

BADER-MOLNAR Katarina Elisabeth, b. Berlin, Germany. Retired Teacher, Professor; Writer; Poet. m. Imre Molnar, div. Education: Diploma, Librarian, Berlin, 1934; English Literature Studies, Liverpool, England; MA, French Philology, Kopernikus University, 1950; English Philosophy Diploma, 1950; DLitt, Albert Einstein International Academy Foundation, 1965. Appointments: Professor and Librarian, Torun, Grudziadz, Danzig, Zürich; Freelance Writer. Publications: L'idée d'humanité dans l'oeuvre de Voltaire jusqu'en y, 1750, 1950; Lyriden (poems), 1976; Romantisches Gefuege (poems and stories), 1978; Teufelskreis und Lethequelle (novel), 1979; Karola contra Isegrim und Reineke (story), 1980; Da waren Träume noch süss (novel), 1988; Vom Leuchten der Liebe (novel), 1990; Gehn und Sein (selected poems), 1991; Bruderkriegy Neue Gedichte (poems), 1994. Contributions to: Anthologies and journals. Honours: Several medals and diplomas. Memberships: Schweizerischer Schriftsteller-Verband, Zürich; PEN Zentrum, Bern; Schriftsteller-Verband, Zürich; Literarischer Club, Zürich; Mozart Gesellschaft; Académie Internationale de Lutèce et Paris, life fellow. Address: Tobelhofstrasse 6, CH-8044, Zurich, Switzerland.

BADMAN May Edith, (May Ivimy), b. 10 Nov 1912, Greenwich, London, England. Retired Local Government Officer; Poet. m. Raymond Frank Badman, 19 Oct 1968, 1 son, 1 daughter. Appointments: Former Council Member and Honorary Treasurer, The Poetry Society; Founder-Organiser, Ver Poets, 1966-. Publications: Night is Another World, 1964; Midway This Path, 1966; Late Swings, 1980; Prayer Sticks, 1980; Parting the Leaves, 1984; Strawberries in the Salad, 1992; The Best Part of the Day, 1992. Contributions to: Many anthologies, magazines, and radio. Honours: Dorothy Tutin Award, 1983; Howard Sergeant Memorial Award, 1990. Memberships: Poetry Society; Royal Society of Literature; St Albans Art Society; Society of Women Writers and Journalists. Address: Haycroft, 61/63 Chiswell Green Lane, St Albans, Hertfordshire, AL2 3AL, England.

BAERWALD Hans H(erman), b. 18 June 1927, Tokyo, Japan. Professor Emeritus of Political Science; Writer. Education: BA, 1950, MA, 1952, PhD, 1956, University of California at Berkeley. Appointments: Assistant Professor, 1956-61, Associate Professor, 1961-62, of Government, Miami University, Oxford, Ohio; Lecturer, 1962-65, Associate Professor, 1965-69, Professor, 1969-91, of Political Science, University of California at Los Angeles. Publications: The Purge of Japanese Leaders Under the Occupation, 1959; American Government: Structure, Problems, Policies (with Peter H Odegard), 1962; Chinese Communism: Selected Documents (with Dan N Jacobs), 1963; The American Republic, Its Government and Politics (with Peter H Odegard), 1964, revised edition (with William Harvard), 1969; Japan's Parliament: An Introduction, 1974; Party Politics in Japan, 1986. Contributions to: Asian Survey. Honour: Order of the Sacred Treasure with Gold and Silver Star, Japan, 1989. Address: 2221 Barnett Road, St Helens, CA 94574, USA.

BAHN Paul Gerard, b. 29 July 1953, Hull, England. Archaeologist. Education: BA, 1974, MA, 1978, PhD, 1979, Archaeology, University of Cambridge, 1971-79, Gonville and Caius College. Appointments: Research Fellow, Dept of Prehistoric Archaeology, University of Liverpool, 1979-82; Canada Blanch Senior Research Fellow, Univ of London, 1982-83; J Paul Getty Postdoctoral Fellow, History of Art and the Humanities, 1985-86; Freelance Writer, 1986-. Publications include: Easter Island, Earth island, 1992; Mammoths, 1994; The Story of Archaeology, 1995; The Cambridge Illustrated History of Archaeology, 1996; Archaeology: Theories, Methods and Practice, 2nd ed, revised and expanded, 1996; Archaeology: A Very Short Introduction, 1996; Tombs, Graves and Mummies, 1996; Journey Through the Ice Age, 1997; The Cambridge Illustrated History of Prehistoric Art, 1998. Contributions to: Contributing Editor, Archaeology Magazine, New York. Literary Agent: Watson Little Ltd, London. Address: 428 Anlaby Road, Hull, HU3 6QP, England.

BAI Hua, b. 20 Nov 1930, He Nan, China. Writer; Poet. m. Wang Pei, 30 Dec 1956, 1 son. Education: Hsin Yang College of Education. Appointments: Various assignments with the People's Liberation Army, 1947-58, 1964-85; Editor, Shanghai Film Production Co, 1962-64. Publications: Several volumes in Chinese. Contributions to: Many magazines and journals. Honours: National Best Poem Award, 1981; Golden Tripod Award, Taiwan, 1993. Memberships: Chinese Film Artists Association; Chinese Writers Association; PEN Centre, Beijing; Shanghai Writers Association. Address: Jiangning Road, Lane 83, No 4, Room 706, Shanghai, China.

BAIGELL Matthew, b. 27 Apr 1933, New York, New York, USA. Professor of Art History; Writer. m. Renee Moses, 1 Feb 1959, 2 daughters. Education: BA, University of Vermont, 1954; MA, Columbia University, 1955; PhD, University of Pennsylvania, 1965. Appointments: Instructor, 1961-65, Assistant Professor, 1965-67, Associate Professor of Art, 1967-68, Ohio State University; Associate Professor, 1968-72, Professor, 1972-78, Professor II, 1978-, Rutgers, the State University of New Jersey at New Brunswick. Publications: A History of American Painting, 1971; A Thomas Hart

Benton Miscellany (editor), 1971; The American Scene: American Painting in the 1930's, 1974; Thomas Hart Benton, 1974; Charles Burchfield, 1976; The Western Art of Frederic Remington, 1976; Dictionary of American Art, 1979; Albert Bierstadt, 1981; Thomas Cole, 1981; A Concise History of American Painting and Sculpture, 1984; The Papers of the American Artists' Congress (1936), 1985; Artists Against War and Fascism (editor with J Williams), 1986; Soviet Dissident Artists: Interviews After Perestroika (with Renee Baigell), 1995; Jewish-American Artists and the Holocaust, 1997 Address: c/o Department of Art History, Rutgers, the State University of New Jersey at New Brunswick, New Brunswick, NJ 08903, USA.

BAIGENT Beryl, b. 16 Dec 1937, Llay, Wrexham, North Wales. Teacher; Writer; Poet. m. Alan H Baigent, 19 Jan 1963, 3 daughters. Education: BA in Physical Education, MA in English Literature, University of Western Ontario, London, Canada. Publications: The Quiet Village, 1972; Pause, 1974; In Counterpoint, 1976; Ancestral Dreams, 1981; The Sacred Beech, 1985; Mystic Animals, 1988; Absorbing the Dark, 1990; Hiraeth: In Search of Celtic Origins, 1994; Triptych: Virgins, Victims, Votives, 1996; The Celtic Tree Calendar, forthcoming. Contributions to: Various anthologies and periodicals. Honours: Ontario Weekly Newspaper Award, 1979; Fritch Memorial, Canadian Authors Association, 1982; Ontario Arts Council Awards, 1983, 1985, 1987; Kent Writers Award, 1986; Black Mountain Award, 1986; Canada Council Touring Awards, 1990, 1992, 1993, 1994; Forest City Poetry Award, 1991; International Affairs Touring Award, 1991; North Wales Arts Association Awards, 1993, 1994, 1996, 1998; Muse Journal Award, 1994. Memberships: Celtic Arts Association; Canadian Poetry Association; League of Canadian Poets, Ontario Representative, 1994-96. Address: 137 Byron Avenue, Thamesford, Ontario N0M 2M0, Canada.

BAIL Murray, b. 22 Sept 1941, Adelaide, South Australia, Australia. Writer. m. Margaret Wordsworth, 1965. Education: Norwood Technical High School, Adelaide. Publications: Contemporary Portraits and Other Stories, 1976; Homesickness, 1980; Holden's Performance, 1987; The Faber Book of Contemporary Australian Short Stories (editor), 1988. Honours: The Age Book of the Year Award, 1980; Victoria Premier's Award, 1988. Address: 39/75 Buckland Street, Chippendale, New South Wales, 2008, Australia.

BAILEY Anthony (Cowper), b. 5 Jan 1933, Portsmouth, England. Author; Journalist. Education: BA, 1955, MA, 1956, Merton College, Oxford. Appointment: Staff Writer, New Yorker magazine, 1956-92. Publications: Making Progress, 1959; The Mother Tongue, 1961; The Inside Passage, 1965; Through the Great City, 1967; The Thousand Dollar Yacht, 1968; The Light in Holland, 1970; In the Village, 1971; A Concise History of the Low Countries, 1972; Rembrandt's House, 1978; Acts of Union: Reports on Ireland, 1973-79, 1980; America, Lost and Found, 1981; Along the Edge of the Forest: An Iron Curtain Journey, 1983; England, First and Last, 1985; Spring Jaunts: Some Walks, Excursions, and Personal Explorations of City, Country and Seashore, 1986; Major André, 1987; The Outer Banks, 1989; A Walk Through Wales, 1992; Responses to Rembrandt, 1994; A Coast of Summer: Sailing New England Waters from Shelter Island to Cape Cod, 1994. Honour: Overeas Press Club Award, 1974. Memberships: Authors Guild; International PEN; Society of Authors. Address: c/o Donadio and Ashworth Inc, 231 West 22nd Street, New York, NY 10011, USA.

BAILEY D(avid) R(oy) Shackleton, b. 10 Dec 1917, Lancaster, England. Professor Emeritus of Latin Language and Literature; Writer; Editor; Translator. m. (1) Hilary Ann Bardwell, 1967, diss 1974, (2) Kristine Zvirbulis, 1994. Education: BA, 1939, MA, 1943, LittD, 1957, Cambridge University. Appointments: Fellow, 1944-55, Praelector, 1954-55, Fellow and Deputy Bursar, 1964, Senior Bursar, 1965-68, Gonville and Gaius College, Cambridge; University Lecturer in Tibetan, Cambridge University, 1948-68; Fellow and Director of Studies in Classics, Jesus College, Cambridge, 1955-64; Visiting Lecturer in Classics, Harvard College, 1963; Professor of Latin, 1968-74, Adjunct Professor, 1989-, University of Michigan; Andrew V Raymond Visiting Professor, State University of New York at Buffalo, 1973-74; Professor of Greek and Latin, 1975-82, Pope Professor of Latin Language and Literature, 1982-88, Professor Emeritus, 1988-, Harvard University; Editor, Harvard Studies in Classical Philology, 1978-84; Visiting Professor, Peterhouse, Cambridge, 1980-81. Publications: The Sátapañcasátka of Matrceta, 1951; Propertiana, 1956; Towards a Text of Cicero ad Atticum, 1960; Ciceronis Epistulae ad Atticum IX-XVI, 1961; Cicero's Letters to Atticus, vols I and II, 1965, vol V, 1966, vol VI, 1967, vols III and IV, 1968, vol VII, 1970; Cicero, 1971; Two Studies in Roman Nomenclature, 1976; Cicero: Epistulae ad Familiares, 2 volumes, 1977; Cicero's Letters to Atticus, 1978; Cicero's Letters to His Friends, 2 volumes, 1978; Towards a Text of Anthologia Latina, 1979; Selected Letters of Cicero, 1980; Cicero: Epistulae ad Q Fratrem et M Brutum, 1981; Profile of Horace, 1982; Anthologia Latina I.I, 1982; Horatius, 1985; Cicero: Philippics, 1986; Ciceronis Epistulae, 4 volumes, 1987-88; Lucanus, 1988; Onomasticon to Cicero's Speeches, 1988; Quintilianus: Declamationes minores, 1989; Martialis, 1990; Back from Exile, 1991; Martial, 3 volumes, 1993; Homoeoteleuton in Latin Dactylic Verse, 1994; Onomasticon to Cicero's Letters, 1995; Onomasticon to Cicero's Treatises, 1996; Selected Classical Papers, 1997; Cicero: Letters to Atticus, forthcoming. Contributions to: Scholarly periodicals. Honours: Charles Goodwin Prize, American Philological Association, 1978; National Endowment for the Humanities Fellowship, 1980-81; Hon LittD, University of Dublin, 1984; Kenyon Medal, British Academy, 1985. Memberships: American Academy of Arts and Science, fellow, 1979-; American Philosophical Society; British Academy, fellow. Address: 303 North Division, Ann Arbor, MI 48104, USA.

BAILEY Martin, b. 26 Oct 1947, London, England. Journalist. Education: PhD, London School of Economics, 1974. Appointment: The Observer, 1983-. Publications: Freedom Railway, 1976; Oilgate: The Sanctions Scandal, 1979; A Green Part of the World, 1984; Young Vincent: Van Gogh's Years in England, 1990; Van Gogh: Letters from Provence, 1990; Van Gogh in England: Portrait of the Artist as a Young Man, 1992. Honour: Journalist of the Year, 1979. Literary Agent: A D Peters. Address: The Observer, Chelsea Bridge House, Queenstown Road, London SW8 4NN, England.

BAILEY Paul, b. 16 Feb 1937, London, England. Writer. *Education:* Central School of Speech and Drama, 1953-56. *Appointment:* Actor, 1953-63. *Publications:* At the Jerusalem, 1967; Trespasses, 1971; A Worthy Guest, A Distant Likeness, 1973; Peter Smart's Confessions, 1977; Old Soldiers, 1980; An English Madam: The Life and Work of Cynthia Payne, 1982; Gabriel's Lament, 1986; An Immaculate Mistake, 1990; Hearth and Home, 1990. *Honours:* Maugham Award, 1968; Arts Council Award, 1968; E M Forster Award, 1974; Orwell Memorial Prize, 1978; Fellow, Royal Society of Literature, 1982. *Address:* 79 Davisville Road, London W12 9SH, England.

BAILYN Bernard, b. 10 Sept 1922, Hartford, Connecticut, USA. Professor Emeritus of History; Writer. m. Lotte Lazarsfeld, 18 June 1952, 2 sons. Education: AB, Williams College, 1945; MA, 1947, PhD, 1953, Harvard University. Appointments: Instructor, 1953-54, Assistant Professor, 1954-58, Associate Professor, 1958-61, Professor of History, 1961-66, Winthrop Professor of History, 1966-81, Adams University Professor, 1981-93, Director, Charles Warren Center for Studies in American History, 1983-94, James Duncan Phillips Professor of Early American History, 1991-93, Professor Emeritus, 1993-, Harvard University; Colver Lecturer, Brown University, 1965; Phelps Lecturer, New York University, 1969; Trevelyan Lecturer, 1971, Pitt Professor of American History, 1986-87, Cambridge University; Becker Lecturer, Cornell University, 1975; Walker-Ames Lecturer, University of Washington, 1983; Curti Lecturer, University of Wisconsin, 1984; Lewin Visiting Professor, Washington University, St Louis, 1985; Thompson Lecturer, Pomona College, 1991; Fellow, British Academy, and Christ's College, Cambridge, 1991; Montgomery Fellow, Dartmouth College, 1991. Publications: The New England Merchants in the Seventeenth Century, 1955; Massachusetts Shipping, 1697-1714: A Statistical Study (with Lotte Bailyn), 1959; Education in the Forming of American Society: Needs and Opportunities for Study, 1960; Pamphlets of the American Revolution, 1750-1776, Vol 1 (editor), 1965; The Apologia of Robert Keayne: The Self-Portrait of a Puritan Merchant (editor), 1965; The Ideological Origins of the American Revolution, 1967, new edition, 1992; The Origins of American Politics, 1968; The Intellectual Migration: Europe and America, 1930-1960 (editor with Donald Fleming), 1969; Religion and Revolution: Three Biographical Studies, 1970; Law in American History (editor with Donald Fleming), 1972; The Ordeal of Thomas Hutchinson, 1974; The Great Republic: A History of the American People (with others), 1977, 4th edition, 1992; The Press and the American Revolution (editor with John B Hench), 1980; The Peopling of British North America: An Introduction, 1986; Voyagers to the West: A Passage in the Peopling of America on the Eve of the Revolution, 1986; Faces of Revolution: Personalities and Themes in the Struggle for American Independence, 1990; Strangers within the Realm: Cultural Margins of the First British Empire (editor with Philip B Morgan), 1991; The Debate on the Constitution: Federalist and Antifederalist Speeches, Articles and Letters during the Struggle over Ratification, 2 volumes, 1993. Contributions to: Scholarly journals. Honours: Robert H Lord Award, Emmanuel College, 1967; Bancroft Prize, 1968; Pulitzer Prizes in History, 1968, 1987; National Book Award in History, 1975; Saloutos Award, Immigration History Society, 1986; Triennial Book Award, 1986; Thomas Jefferson Medal, American Philosophical Society, 1993; Henry Allen Moe Prize, 1994; Honorary doctorates. Memberships: American Academy of Arts and Sciences; American Historical Association, president, 1981; American Philosophical Society; National Academy of Education; Royal Historical Society. Address: 170 Clifton Street, Belmont, MA 02178, USA.

BAINBRIDGE Beryl Margaret, b. 21 Nov 1934, Liverpool, England. Appointments: Actress, Repertory Theatres in UK, 1949-60; Clerk, Gerald Duckworth & Co Ltd, London, 1971-73. Publications: A Weekend with Claude, 1967; Another Part of the Wood, 1968; Harriet Said, 1972; The Dressmaker, 1973; The Bottle Factory Outing, 1974; Sweet William, 1975; A Quiet Life, Injury Time, 1976; Young Adolf, 1978; Winter Garden, 1980; English Journey or the Road to Milton Keynes, 1984; Watson's Apology, 1984; Mum & Mr Amitage, 1985; Forever England, 1986; Fifthy Lucra, 1986; An Awfully Big Adventure, 1989; The Birthday Boys, 1991; Every Man For Himself, 1996; Master Georgie, 1998. Honours: Guardian Fiction Award, 1974; Whitbread Award, 1977; Fellow, Royal Society of Literature, 1978; DLitt, University of Liverpool, 1986; Whitbread Award, 1997. Address: 42 Albert Street, London NW1 7NU, England.

BAINBRIDGE Cyril, b. 15 Nov 1928, Bradford, West Yorkshire, England. Author; Journalist. m. Barbara Hannah Crook, 20 Jan 1953, 1 son, 2 daughters. Education: Negus College, Bradford. Appointments: Reporter, Bingley Guardian, 1944-45, Yorkshire Observer & Bradford Telegraph, 1945-54, Press Association, 1954-63; Assistant News Editor, 1963-67, Deputy News Editor, 1967-69, Regional News Editor, 1969-77, Managing News Editor, 1977-82, Assistant Managing Editor, 1982-88, The Times. Publications: Pavilions on the Sea; Brass Triumphant; The Brontës and Their Country; North Yorkshire and North Humberside; One Hundred Years of Journalism; The News of the World Story, 1993. Contributions to: Newspapers, magazines and periodicals. Memberships: Brontë Society; Chartered Institute of Journalists; Society of Authors. Literary Agent: Laurence Pollinger. Address: 6 Lea Road, Hemingford Grey, Huntingdon, Cambs PE18 9ED, England.

BAINES John, (Dario Salas Sommer), b. 4 Mar 1935, Santiago, Chile. Writer; Lecturer; Philosopher. Education: Dario Salas College, Santiago de Chile, 1954-59; BA, Humanities and Arts, University of Santiago, 1959. Publications: In Spanish: Hypsoconciencia, 1965; Los Brujos Hablan, 1968; El Hombre Estelar, 1979; La Ciencia del Amor, 1982; Existe la Mujer?, 1983; El Desarrollo del Mundo Interno, 1984; Moral para el Siglo XXI, 1998; In English: The Secret Science, 1980; The Stellar Man, 1985; The Science of Love, 1993; Hypsoconsciousness, 1995; Some titles published in German, Russian, Bulgarian, Italian, Portuguese and Latvian. Membership: Authors Guild of America, 1988-. Address: PO Box # 8556, FDR Station, New York, NY 10150, USA.

BAINS Sunny R E, b. 14 Nov 1967, Port Chester, New York, USA. Scientist; Writer. Education: Imperial College of Science, Technoloyg and Medicine, London, 1985-87; BSc, Physics, Queen Mary and Westfield College, London, 1990; MS, Journalism, Boston University, USA, 1994; PhD, Open University, in progress, UK, 1997-. Appointments: Editor, Publisher, Holographics International, magazine, 1987-90; Technical Consultant, Editor, SPIE, full-time, 1991-92, contract, 1992-; Associate Editor, Technology, Laser Focus World, magazine, 1992-93; Freelance, 1994-. Publication: Building HAL, in progress. Contributions to: The Economist; New Scientist; Electronic Engineering Times; Laser Focus World; OE Reports. Memberships: Association of British Science Writers; National Union of Journalists; National Association of Science Writers. Address: c/o SPIE, PO Box 10, Bellingham, WA 98227-0010, USA.

BAITZ Jon Robin, b. 1961, Los Angeles, California, USA. Playwright. Plays: The Film Society, 1987; Dutch Landscape, 1989; The Substance of Fire, 1991; Three Hotels, 1993; The End of the Day, 1993. Contributions to: Anthologies. Honour: Fellow, American Academy and Institute of Arts and Letters, 1994. Address: c/o William Morris Agency Inc, 1350 Avenue of the Americas, New York, NY 10019, USA.

BAKER David (Anthony), b. 27 Dec 1954, Bangor, Maine, USA. Associate Professor of English; Poet; Editor. m. Ann Townsend, 19 July 1987. Education: BSE, 1976, MA, 1977, Central Missouri State University; PhD, University of Utah, 1983. Appointments: Poetry Editor, 1980-81, Editor-in-Chief, 1981-83, Quarterly West; Visiting Assistant Professor, Kenyon College, 1983-84; Assistant Editor, 1983-89, Poetry Editor/Consulting Poetry Editor, 1989-94, Poetry Editor, 1994-, Kenyon Review; Assistant Professor of English, 1984-90, Associate Professor of English, 1990-, Denison University; Visiting Telluride Professor, Cornell University, 1985; Contributing Editor, The Pushcart Prize, 1992-; Visiting Associate Professor, University of Michigan, 1996; Many poetry readings. Publications: Poetry: Looking Ahead, 1975; Rivers in the Sea, 1977; Laws of the Land, 1981; Summer Sleep, 1984; Haunts, 1985; Sweet Home, Saturday Night, 1991; Echo for an Anniversary, 1992; After the Reunion, 1994; Holding Katherine, 1997. Editor: The Soil is Suited to the Seed: A Miscellany in Honor of Paul Bennett, 1986; Meter in English: A Critical Engagement, 1996. Contributions to: Anthologies and periodicals. Honours: Margaret Bridgman Scholar of Poetry, Bread Loaf, 1982; Outstanding Writer, Pushcart Press, 1982, 1984, 1985, 1986, 1990, 1991, 1994, 1995; James Wright Prize for Poetry, Mid-American Review, 1983; National Endowment for the Arts Fellowship, 1985-86; Bread Loaf Poetry Fellow, 1989; Pushcart Prize, 1992; Mary Carolyn Davies Award, Poetry Society of America, 1995; Thomas B Fordham Endowed Chair in Creative Writing, Denison University, 1996. Memberships: Associated Writing Programs; Modern Languages Association; National Book Critics Circle; Poetry Society of America; Poets and Writers. Address: 135 Granview Road, Granville, OH 43023, USA.

BAKER Houston A(lfred Jr), b. 22 Mar 1943, Louisville, Kentucky, USA. Professor of English and of Human Relations; Writer; Editor; Poet. m. Charlotte Pierce-Baker, 10 Sept 1966, 1 son. Education: BA, magna cum laude, Howard University, 1965; MA, 1966, PhD, 1968, University of California at Los Angeles; PhD Studies, University of Edinburgh, 1967-68. Appointments: Instructor, Howard University, 1966; Instructor, 1968-69, Assistant Professor of English, 1969-70, Yale University; Associate Professor and Member, Center for Advanced Studies, 1970-73, Professor of English, 1973-74, University of Virginia; Professor of English, 1974-, Director, Afro-American Studies Program, 1974-77, Albert M Greenfield Professor of Human Relations, 1982-, Director, Center for the Study of Black Literature and Culture, 1987-, University of Pennsylvania; Fellow, Center for Advanced Study in the Behavioral Sciences, 1977-78, National Humanities Center, 1982-83; Bucknell Distinguished Scholar, University of Vermont, 1992; Berg Visiting Professor of English, New York University, 1994; Fulbright 50th Anniversary Distinguished Fellow, Brazil, 1996; Senior Fellow, School of Criticism and Theory, Cornell University, 1996-2002. Publications: Long Black Song: Essays in Black American Literature and Culture, 1972; Singers of Daybreak: Studies in Black American Literature, 1974; A Many-Colored Coat of Dreams: The Poetry of Countee Cullen, 1974; The Journey Back: Issues in Black Literature and Criticism, 1980; Blues, Ideology, and Afro-American Literature: A Vernacular Theory, 1984; Modernism and Harlem Renaissance, 1987; Afro-American Poetics: Revisions of Harlem and the Black Aesthetic, 1988; Workings of the Spirit: A Poetics of Afro-American Women's Writing, 1991; Black Studies, Rap, and the Academy, 1993. Poetry: No Matter Where You Travel, You Still Be Black, 1979; Spirit Run, 1982; Blues Journeys Home, 1985. Editor: Black Literature in America, 1971; Twentieth-Century Interpretations of Native Son, 1972; Reading Black: Essays in the Criticism of African, Caribbean, and Black American Literature, 1976; Renewal: A Volume of Black Poems (with Charlotte Pierce-Baker), 1977; A Dark and Sudden Beauty: Two Essays in Black American Poetry by George Kent and Stephen Henderson, 1977; English Literature: Opening Up the Canon (with Leslie Fiedler), 1981; Three American Literatures: Essays in Chicano, Native American, and Asian American Literature for Teachers of American Literature, 1982; Narrative of the Life of Frederick Douglass, An American Slave, 1982; Afro-American Literary Study of Frederick Douglass, An American Slave, 1982; Afro-American Literary Study in the 1990s (with Patricia Redmond), 1989; Black British Cultural Studies: A Reader (with Manthia Diawara and Ruth Lindeborg), 1996. Contributions to: Scholarly books and journals. Honours: Legion of Honor, Chapel of the Four Chaplains, Philadelphia, 1981; Christian R and Mary F Lindback Foundation Award for Distinguished Teaching, University of Pennsylvania, 1984; Alumni Award for Distinguished Achievement in Literature and the Humanities, Howard University, 1985; Distinguished Writer of the Year Award, Middle Atlantic Writers Association, 1986; Creative Scholarship Award, College Language Association of America, 1988; Pennsylvania Governor's Award for Excellence in the Humanities, 1990; Pennbook/Philadelphia Award, 1990; Special issue of Chung Wai literary journal, Taiwan, 1993; Several honorary doctorates. Memberships: College Language Association; English Institute, board of supervisors, 1989-91; Modern Language Association, president, 1992. Address: c/o Center for the Study of Black Literature and Culture, University of Pennsylvania, Philadelphia, PA 19104, USA.

BAKER Kenneth (Wilfred), b. 3 Nov 1934, England. Politician; Writer. m. Mary Elizabeth Muir, 1963, 1 son, 2 daughters. Education: Magdalen College, Oxford. Appointments: MP for Acton, 1968-70, St Marylebone, 1970-83, Mole Valley, 1983-97; Secretary of State for Education and Science, 1986-89; Home Secretary, 1990-92. Publications include: I Have No Gun But I Can Spit (editor), 1980; London Lines (editor), 1982; The Faber Book of English History in Verse (editor), 1988; Unauthorized Versions: Poems and Their Parodies (editor), 1990; The Faber Anthology of Conservatism (editor), 1993; The Turbulent Years, My Life in Politics, 1993; The Prime Ministers - An Irreverent Political History in Cartoons, 1995. Honour: Companion of Honour, 1992. Address: c/o House of Commons, London SW1A 0AA, England.

BAKER Margaret Joyce, b. 21 May 1918, Reading, Berkshire, England. Education: King's College, London, 1936-37. Publications: The Fighting Cocks, 1949; Four Farthings and a Thimble, 1950; A Castle and Sixpence, 1951; The Family That Grew and Grew, 1952; Lions in the Potting Shed, 1954; The Wonderful Wellington Boots, 1955; Anna Sewell and Black Beauty, 1956; The Birds of Thimblepins, 1960; Homer in Orbit, 1961; The Cats of Honeytown, 1962; Castaway Christmas, 1963; Cut off from Crumpets, 1964; The Shoe Shop Bears, 1964; Home from the Hill, 1968; Snail's Place, 1970; The Last Straw, 1971; Boots and the Ginger Bears, 1972; The Sand Bird, 1973; Lock, Stock and Barrel, 1974; Sand in Our Shoes, 1976; The Gift Horse, 1982; Catch as Catch Can, 1983; Beware of the Gnomes, 1985; The Waiting Room Doll, 1986; Fresh Fields for Daisy, 1987. Address: Prickets, Old Cleeve, Nr Minehead, Somerset TA24 6HW, England.

BAKER Michael John, b. 5 Nov 1935, England. Professor of Marketing. m. Sheila Bell, 19 Sept 1959, 1 son, 2 daughters. Education: BA, Dunelm, 1959; BSc, Econ, London, 1962; Cert ITP, DBA, Harvard, 1971; DipM, 1964. Appointments: 2nd Lt, Royal Artillery, 1956-57; Salesman, Richard Thomas & Baldwins, 1958-64; Assistant Lecturer, Medway College, 1964-66; Lecturer, Hull College, 1966-68; FME Fellow, Research Associate, Harvard Business School, 1968-71; Professor of Marketing, Strathclyde Univesrsity, 1971-. Publications: Marketing, 6th edition, 1996; Marketing New Industrial Products, 1975; Innovation - Technology, Policy and Diffusion, 1979; Marketing - Theory and Practice, 3rd edition, 1995; Market Development, 1983; Marketing: Management & Strategy, 2nd edition, 1992; Organizational Buying Behaviour, 1986; Role of Design in International Competitiveness, 1989; Marketing and Competitive Success, 1989; Dictionary of Marketing & Advertising, 3rd edition, 1998; Marketing Manual, 1998; Product Strategy & Management, 1998; Marketing Book, 4th edition, 1999; Foundations of Marketing, 1998. Address: Westburn, Helensburgh, G84 9NH, Argyll, Scotland.

BAKER Paul Raymond, b. 28 Sept 1927, Everett, Washington, USA. Professor. m. Elizabeth Kemp, 1 child. Education: AB, Stanford University, 1949; MA, Columbia University, 1951; PhD, Harvard University, 1960. Appointments: Professor of History, 1965-; Director of American Civilization Program, 1972-92, New York University. Publications: Views of Society and Manners in America, by Frances Wright D'Arusmont, 1963; The Fortunate Pilgrims: Americans in Italy 1800-1860, 1964; The Atomic Bomb: The Great Decision, 1968; The American Experience, 5 volumes, 1976-79; Richard Morris Hunt, 1980; Stanny: The Gilded Life of Stanford White, 1989. Contributions to: Around the Square, 1982; Master Builders, 1985; The Architecture of Richard Morris Hunt, 1986. Honour: The Turpic Award in American Studies, 1994. Address: c/o Department of History, New York University, 19 University Place, Room 523, New York, NY 10003, USA.

BAKER Peter Gorton, b. 28 Mar 1924, Eastbourne, Sussex, England. Writer. Appointments: Reporter, Sussex Daily News, 1944-45; Chief Reporter, Kinematograph Weekly, 1945-53; Editor, films and filming magazine, British Representative on Film Festival Juries at Cannes, Venice, Moscow, Berlin, 1953-70. Publications: Plays for television including: The Offence; Little Girl Blue; Contributor, many TV drama series; Novels: To Win a Prize on Sunday; Casino; Cruise; Clinic; The Bedroom Sailors; Babel Beach; Jesus. Screenplay, Jesus, forthcoming. Literary Agent: Peter Mills. Address: Calle Don Juan de Málaga 6, Málaga 29015, Espana.

BAKER Russell (Wayne), b. 14 Aug 1925, Loudoun County, Virginia, USA. Columnist; Writer. m. Miriam Emily Nash, 11 Mar 1950, 2 sons, 1 daughter. Education: BA,

Johns Hopkins University, 1947. Appointments: Staff, Baltimore Sun, 1947-54; Washington Bureau, 1954-62; Columnist, Editorial Page, 1962-, New York Times. Publications: City on the Potomac, 1958; American in Washington, 1961; No Cause for Panic, 1964; All Things Considered, 1965; Our Next President, 1968; Poor Russell's Almanac, 1972; The Upside Down Man, 1977; Home Again, Home Again (with others), 1979; So This is Depravity, 1980; Growing Up, 1982; The Rescue of Miss Yaskell and Other Pipe Dreams, 1983; The Norton Book of Light Verse (editor), 1986; The Good Times, 1989; There's a Country in My Cellar: The Best of Russell Baker, 1990; Russell Baker's Book of American Humor, 1993. Honours: Frank Sullivan Memorial Award, 1976; George Polk Award for Commentary, 1979; Pulitzer Prizes for Distinguished Commentary, 1979, and for Biography, 1983; Elmer Holmes Bobst Prize for Non-Fiction, 1983; Howland Memorial Prize, Yale University, 1989; Fourth Estate Award, National Press Club, 1989; Various honorary doctorates. Memberships: American Academy and Institute of Arts and Letters; American Academy of Arts and Sciences, fellow. Address: c/o New York Times, 229 West 43rd Street, New York, NY 10036, USA.

BAKER William, b. 6 July 1944, Shipston, Warwicks, England. Professor. m. 16 Nov 1969, 2 daughters. Education: BA Hons, Sussex University, England, 1963-66; MPhil, London University, 1966-69; PhD, 1974; MLS, Loughborough, 1986. Appointments: Lecturer, City Literature, 1966-69; Thurrock Technical College, 1969-71; Ben-Gurion University, 1971-77; University of Kent, 1977-78; West Midlands College, 1978-85; Professor, Pitzer College, Claremont, CA, USA, 1981-82; Housemaster, Clifton College, 1986-89; Professor, Northern Illinois University, 1989-. Publications: Harold Pinter, 1973; George Eliot and Judaism, 1975; The George Eliot-G H Lewes Library, 1977; The Libraries of George Eliot and G H Lewes, 1981; Shakespeare, The Merchant of Venice, 1985; Shakespeare, Antony and Cleopatra, New edition, 1985; F R Leavis and Q D Leavis, An Annotated Bibliography, 1989; Some George Eliot Notebooks, 1976-1985; The Early History of the London Library, 1992; The Letters of George Henry Lewes, 1995; Recent Work in Critical Theory, 1989-1995: An Annotated Bibliography, 1996; Literary Theories: A Case Study in Critical Performance, 1996; Sir Walter Scott: Tales of a Grandfather The History of France, second series, 1996; Nineteenth Century British Bibliographers and Book Collectors: Dictionary of Literary Biography, 2 volumes 1984, 1999. Honours: British Academy Thank-Offering to Britain Research Fellowship, 1978-79; British Academy Research Award, 1981; NIU Libraries, Illinois Cooperative Collection Acquisition Grants, 1990-92; NIU Library Directors Research Award, 1990-91; NIU Graduate School, Summer Research Grant, 1991-95; Ball Brothers Foundation Fellowship, Lilly Library, Indiana University, 1993; Bibliographical Society of America, Fellowship, 1994-95; Illinois Cooperative Collection Grant, Post-Colonial Literature, 1997; American Philosophical Society Grant, 1997. Memberships: Bibliographical Society of America; AIA; British Library Association; MLA; Society for Textual Scholarship; Editor, George Eliot- G H Lewes Studies. Address: Department of English, Northern Illinois University, DeKalb, Illinois, USA.

BAKER Winona Louise, b. 18 Mar 1924, Saskatchewan, British Columbia, Canada. Retired Educator; Poet. m. Arthur Baker, 9 May 1945, 3 sons, 1 daughter. Education: Teaching degree. Publications: Clouds Empty Themselves, 1987; Not So Scarlet a Woman, 1987; Moss-hung Trees, 1992; Beyond the Lighthouse, 1992. Contributions to: Numerous anthologies and other publications. Honours: Shikishi for Haiku in English, 1986; Expo Japan Book Award for Haiku, 1986; Foreign Minister's Prize, World Haiku Contest, 1989; Fundatia Nipponica Societatea Romana de Haiku Commemorative Medal, 1994. Memberships: Canadian, American, European, and Japanese Haiku Associations; Federation of British Columbia Writers; League of Canadian Poets. Address: 606 First Street, Nanaimo, British Columbia, V9R 1Y9, Canada.

BAKOLAS Nikos, b. 26 July 1927, Thessaloniki, Greece. Retired Journalist; Artistic Manager; Writer. m. Helene Issidorou, 6 Sept 1957, 2 sons. Education: University of Thessaloniki; University of Michigan. Appointment: Artistic Manager, National Theatre of Northern Greece, 1980-81, 1990-. Publications: The Big Square; Mythology; The Prince's Garden; Trepass; Don't Cry Darling; Marches; Death Sleep. Contributions to: Numerous publications. Honours: Plotin Literary Award; National Book Award. Memberships: Greek Literary Society; Journalists Union of Macedonia. Address: 16 Papadiamandi Street, 546 45 Thessaloniki, Greece.

BAKR Salwa, b. June 1949, Cairo, Egypt. Novelist. Education: BA, 1972, BA, 1976, Ayn Shams University, Cairo. Appointment: Founder, Hagar journal, 1993. Publications: Zinat at the President's Funeral, 1986; Atiyyah's Shrine, 1986; About the Soul that was Spirited Away, 1989; The Wiles of Men and Other Stories, 1992; Monkey Business, 1992; Depicting the Nightingale, 1993; The Golden Chariot Does Not Ascend to Heaven, 1994. Address: c/o Atelier of Writers, Karim al-Dawla Street, Talat Harb Square, Cairo, Eygpt.

BALABAN John, b. 2 Dec 1943, Philadelphia, Pennsylvania, USA. Professor of English; Writer; Poet; Translator. m. 28 Nov 1970, 1 daughter. Education: BA, Pennsylvania State University, 1966; AM, Harvard University, 1967. Appointments: Instructor in Linguistics, University of Can Tho, South Vietnam, 1967-68; Instructor, 1970-73, Assistant Professor, 1973-76, Associate Professor, 1976-82, Professor, 1982-92, of English, Pennsylvania State University; Professor of English, Director of Creative Writing, University of Miami, 1992-97. Publications: Vietnam Poems, 1970; Vietnamese Folk Poetry (editor and translator), 1974; After Our War (poems), 1974; Letters From Across the Sea (poems), 1978; Ca Dao Vietnam: A Bilingual Anthology of Vietnamese Folk Poetry (editor and translator), 1980; Blue Mountain (poems), 1982; Coming Down Again (novel), 1985, revised edition, 1989; The Hawk's Tale (children's fiction), 1988; Three Poems, 1989; Vietnam: The Land We Never Knew, 1989; Words for My Daughter (poems), 1991; Remembering Heaven's Face (memoir), 1991; Vietnam: A Traveler's Literary Companion (editor with Nguyen Qui Duc), 1996; Locusts at the Edge of Summer: New and Selected Poems and Translations, 1997. Contributions to: Anthologies, books, scholarly journals and periodicals. Honours: National Endowment for the Humanities Younger Humanist Fellow, 1971-72; Lamont Selection, Academy of American Poets, 1974; Finalist, National Book Award, 1975, 1997; Fulbright-Hays Senior Lectureship in Romania, 1976-77; Steaua Prize, Romanian Writers Union, 1978; National Endowment for the Arts Fellowships, 1978, 1985; Fulbright Distinguished Visiting Lectureship in Romania, 1979; Vaptsarov Medal, Union of Bulgarian Writers, 1980; National Poetry Series Book Selection, 1990; Pushcart Prize XV, 1990; William Carlos Williams Award, 1997. Memberships: American Literary Translators Association, president, 1994-97; National Endowment for the Arts Translation Panel, chair, 1993-94. Address: Department of English, University of Miami, PO Box 248145, Coral Gables, FL 33124, USA.

BALACI Alexandru, b. 12 June 1916, Aurora Village, Romania. Writer; University Teacher. m. Anca-Magdalena Udisteanu, 25 Jan 1964, 2 daughters. Education: Philology and Philosophy Faculty, University of Bucharest, 1939; Doctorate, 1943. Appointments: Curator, Library, 1938-41, Teacher, 1947-86, University of Bucharest; Vice-President, State Committee for Culture and Art, 1965-69; Manager, Romanian Academy, Rome, 1969-73; Vice-President, World Federation of UN Organizations, 1974-90; Vice-President, Writers Society, Romania, 1980-90. Publications: Dolores, poems, 1941; Monographs: Giovanni Pascolo, 1944; Giosue Carducci, 1947; Michelangelo, 1964; Dante, 1966, 1995; Francesco Petrarca, 1968; Nicolo Machiavelli, 1969; Nicolae Balcescu, 1969; Giacomo Leopardi, 1972; Alessandro Manzoni, 1974; Ludovico Ariosto, 1974; Giovanni Boccaccio, 1976; Ugo Foscolo, 1978; Mantegna, 1980; Torquato Tasso, 1982; Tiepolo, 1983; Vittorio Alfieri, 1989; Many books on Italian literature and culture including: Italian Studies, 1958, new volume, 1960, vol 3, 1964, vol 4, 1968; Storia della Letteratura Italiana, 1962; Antologia della Letteratura Italiana, 1973; Italian Diary, 1973; Romeo Romeno a Roma, 1979; History of Italian Literature, 1985-87; Venetian Paintings of the XVIIth Century, 1988; 8 Italian dictionaries, 1964-98; Other books: The University of Bucharest, 1964; Literary Studies and Notes, 1979; Parallel Routes, 1981; Humanist Synthesis, 1984; Over 30 translations from Italian including: Manzoni's I Promessi Sposi; The Short Stories of Luigi Pirandello. Contributions to: Il Dramma; Incontri; Il Veltro; Gândirea; România Literara; Viata Româneasca. Honours: Tormagana Award, Italy, 1971; Etna Taormina Award, Italy, 1978; Circe Sabaudia Award, Italy, 1983; Special Award, Writers Society of Romania, 1986. Memberships: Romanaian Academy; Arcadia Literary Academy, Italy; Accademia Tiberina d'Italia; Società Europea di Cultura, Venice; International PEN Club. Address: Intrarea Visinilor Nr 9, Sector 2, 73109 Bucharest, Romania.

BALCOMB Mary Nelson, b. 29 Apr 1928, Ontonagon, Michigan, USA. Painter-Etcher; Writer. m. Robert S Balcomb, 3 July 1948, 1 son, 1 daughter. Education: AA, American Academy of Art, 1948; BFA cum laude, University of New Mexico, 1961; MFA, University of Washington, 1971. Publications: Nicolai Fechin: Russian and American Artist, 1975; Les Perhacs Sculptor, 1978; William F Reese: American Artist, 1984; Robin-Robin: A Journal, 1995. Contributions to: Periodicals. Memberships: Authors Guild; Phi Kappa Phi. Address: PO Box 1922, Silverdale, WA 98383, USA.

BALDWIN Mark, b. 29 July 1944, Simla, India. Publisher; Author. m. Myfanwy Dundas, 2 July 1977, 3 sons. Education: BA, MA, St Catharine's College, Cambridge, 1962-65; MSc, DIC, PhD, Imperial College, 1970-86. Appointments: Engineer with Mott Hay & Anderson, 1965-70; Lecturer, Imperial College, London, England, 1971-86; Publisher & Bookseller, 1986-. Publications: British Freight Waterways Today and Tomorrow, 1980; Canals - A New Look, 1984; Canal Books, 1984; Simon Evans - His Life and Later Work, 1992. Contributions to: Proc Institution Civil Engineers; Waterways World; Canal and Riverboat, Antiquarian Book Monthly Review, Book and Magazine Collector. Address: 24 High Street, Cleobury Mortimer, Kidderminster DY14 8BY, England.

BALL B(rian) N(eville), b. 19 June 1932, Cheshire, England. Writer. Education: BA, University of London, 1960; MA, University of Sheffield, 1968. Appointments: Staff Member to Senior Lecturer in English, Doncaster College of Education, 1965-81. Publications: Over 50 books, including: Basic Linguistics for Secondary Schools, 3 volumes, 1966-67; Lay Down Your Wife for Another, 1971; Night of the Robots (in the US as The Regiments of Night), 1972; The Venomous Serpent (in the US as The Night Creature), 1974; Witchfinder: The Mark of the Beast, 1976; Witchfinder: The Evil at Monteine, 1977; The Witch in Our Attic, 1979; The Baker Street Boys, 1983; Frog Island Summer, 1987; Magic on the Tide, 1995. Contributions to: Anthologies, newspapers, radio, and television. Address: c/o Hamish Hamilton Ltd, 27 Wrights Lane, London W8 5TZ, England.

BALLA Vladimir, b. 1967, Nove Zamky, Slovakia. Clerk. Education: Economist, University of Economy, Bratislava. Appointment: Employment Office, Nove Zamky, 1990-. Publications: Leptokaria, 1995; Outsideria, 1997. Contributions to: Dotyky; Kalligram; Rombold; Rak; Pulz. Honours: Best First Book Award, 1996; Best Story of the Year Award, 1997. Membership: Society of Slovak Writers. Address: Soltesovej 17, 94059 Nove Zamky, Slovakia.

BALLANTYNE Sheila, b. 26 July 1936, Seattle, Washington, USA. Writer; Teacher. m. Philip Speilman, 22 Dec 1963, 1 son, 1 daughter. Education: BA, Mills College. Appointments: Dominican College, 1983; Mills College, 1984-97; Bay Area Writers Workshop, 1988,

1989. Publications: Norma Jean the Termite Queen, 1975; Imaginary Crimes, 1982; Life on Earth, 1988. Contributions to: New Yorker; American Review; Prize Stories: O Henry Awards; Short Story International; Aphra. Honours: O Henry Award; MacDowell Colony Fellowship; Guggenheim Fellowship; National Women's Political Caucus Distinguished Achievement Award. Memberships: Authors Guild; National Writers Union; PEN. Literary Agent: Owen Laster, William Morris Agency, New York, New York. Address: 2 Encina Place, Berkeley, California, 94705, USA.

BALLARD James Graham, b. 15 Nov 1930, Shanghai, China. Novelist; Short Story Writer. m. Helen Mary Mathews, 1954, dec 1964, 1 son, 2 daughters. *Education:* King's College, Cambridge. Publications: The Drowned World, 1963; The Terminal Beach, 1964; The Drought, 1965; The Crystal World, 1966; The Disaster Area, 1967; Crash, 1973; Vermilion Sands, 1973; Concrete Island, 1974; High Rise, 1975; Low Flying Aircraft, 1976; The Unlimited Dream Company, 1979; Myths of the Near Future, 1982; Empire of the Sun, 1984; The Day of Creation, 1987; Running Wild, 1988; War Forever, 1990; The Kindness of Women, 1991. *Honours:* Guardian Fiction Prize, 1984; James Tait Black Prize, 1984. *Address:* 36 Old Charlton Road, Shepperton, Middlesex, England.

BALLARD Terry Lee, b. 24 Aug 1946, Phoenix, Arizona, USA. Librarian. m. Donna Gael Weiss, 23 Jan 1972, 1 son. Education: AA, Phoenix College, 1966; BA, Arizona State University, 1968; MEd, Arizona State University, 1980; MLS, University of Arizona, 1989. Appointments: Assistant Professor and Systems Librarian, Adelphi University, 1990; Library Automation Coordinator, NYU Law, 1995; Automation Librarian, Quinnipiac College, 1997-. Publication: Innopac: A Reference Guide to the System, 1995. Contributions to: Columnist, Information Today, 1995-; Wrote for American Libraries and Wilson Library Bulletin. Honour: Computers in Libraries Article of Year, 1992. Address: 1230 Ott Lane, N Merrick, NY 11566, USA.

BALLAURI Robert, (Bec), b. 20 June 1925, Korça, Albania. m. Zoika Katro, 27 Jan 1957, 2 daughters. Education: Painter-Graphist; Architect, Tirana University; Historian of Cultural Monuments. Career: Painter-Graphist, 1949; Architect, 1965; Museolog, 1971-. Historian and Restorer of 19th-century Cultural Monuments, 1975-; Creator, about 20 major artworks, mainly placards; Planned and organised about 34 museums including 15 national historical museums, and more than 25 national and general thematic exhibitions in Albania and abroad; Currently: Organiser, Albanian Federation of Collectors; Chief Editor, The Collector magazine; Participant, various world philatelics exhibitions. Contributions to: Philatelic magazines including Collectio (Greece), Qui Filatelia, Notiziaro AIM and Fiscali (Italy), Belgica and Bulletin AIJP. Honours: Various diplomas. Memberships: 6 philately and journalists societies, Albania and abroad, including Association Internationale des Journalistes Philatéliques, 1966-. Address: Rue 1 Mai 15/4. Tirana, Albania.

BALLE Solvej, b. 16 Aug 1962, Denmark. Writer; Editor. m. Ole Kiehn, 9 Sept 1990. Education: Studies in Philosophy, Literature, University of Copenhagen, 1984-; The Writers' School, Copenhagen, 1987-89. Appointment: Co-Editor, Den Bla Port, Literary Magazine, 1994-. Publications: Lyrefugl, 1986; Prose Poetry, 1990; According to the Law, (short stories), 1993. Membership: Danish PEN. Literary Agent: L & R, Kristianiagade 14, 2100 Copenhagen, Denmark. Address: Bakkehuset, Rahbeks Allé 23, 1801 Frederiksberg C, Denmark.

BALLEM John Bishop, b. 2 Feb 1925, New Glasgow, Nova Scotia, Canada. Lawyer; Writer; Poet. m. Grace Louise Flavelle, 31 Aug 1951, 2 sons, 1 daughter. Education: BA, 1946, MA, 1948, LLB, 1949, Dalhousie University; LLM, Harvard University, 1950. Publications: The Devil's Lighter, 1973; Dirty Scenario, 1974; Judas Conspiracy, 1976; The Moon Pool, 1978; Sacrifice Play, 1981; Marigot Run, 1983; Oilpatch Empire, 1985; The Oil

and Gas Lease in Canada, 2nd edition, 1985; Death Spiral, 1989; The Barons, 1991; The Oil and Gas Lease in Canada, 3rd Edition, 1999. Other: Short stories and poems. Contributions to: Legal journals. Honours: Queen's Counsel, 1966; Honorary Doctor of Laws Degree, University of Calgary, 1993. Memberships: Calgary Writers Association; Crime Writers of Canada; International Bar Association; Law Society of Alberta; Phi Delta Theta; Writers Guild of Alberta; Writers Union of Canada. Address: High Trees, Box 20, Site 32, RR No 12, Calgary, Alberta T3E 6W3, Canada.

BALLINA Osvaldo Enrique, b. 7 Feb 1942, La Plata, Argentina. m. Curvaichaga Maria Rosa, 30 Apr 1991, 1 son. Education: Colegio Nacional Universidad de la Plata, General Certificate of Education, University of London; Higher Studies in Languages at private schools. Publications: El dia mayor, 1971; Esta unica esperanza contra todo, 1973; Es temprano, 1973; Aun tengo la vida, 1975; En tierra de uno, 1977; Caminante en Italia, 1979; Diario veneciano, 1982; Ceremonia diurna, 1984; La poesia no es necesaria, 1986; La vida, la mas bella, 1988; Sol que ocupa el corazón, 1991; Sondas, 1992; Estamos vivos y vamos a vivir (Poemas 1971-1992), 1993; final del estante, 1994; Verano del incurable, 1996. Honour: Faja de Honor Sociedad Argentina de Escritores, 1975; Consagracion Pcia Bs As, Argentina, 1996. Address: Calle 45 No 561, 1900 La Plata, Argentina.

BALY Elaine Vivienne. See: BROWNING Vivenne.

BAMBER Juliette Madeleine, b. 21 Aug 1930, Tidworth, England. Occupational Therapist; Counsellor. m. Donald Liddle, 1957, div 1995, 2 sons. Education: Psychology, Honours, Birkbeck College, 1957-60. Publications: Breathy Space, 1991; On the Edge, 1993; Altered States, 1996; Touch Paper, 1996; The Ring of Words, 1996; The Wasting Game, 1997; The Long Pale Corridor, 1998. Honours: 1st Prize, London Writers; 1st Prize, National Poetry Foundation. Address: 9 Western Road, East Finchley, London N2 9JB, England.

BANCROFT Anne, b. 17 Apr 1923, London, England. Author. 2 sons, 2 daughters. Education: Sidney Webb Teacher's Training College, 1961-63. Publications: Religions of the East, 1974; Twentieth Century Mystics and Sages, 1976, republished 1989; Zen: Direct Pointing to Reality, 1980; The Luminous Vision, 1980, republished 1989; Six Medieval Mystics, 1981; Chinse New Year, 1984; Festivals of the Buddha, 1984; The Buddhist World, 1984; The New Religious World, 1985; Origins of the Sacred: The Spiritual Way in Western Tradition, 1987; Weavers of Wisdom, 1989. Contributions to: The Middle Way; Everyman's Encyclopedia; Women in the World's Religions. Memberships: Society of Authors; Society of Women Writers and Journalists. Address: 1 Grange Villas, The Street, Charmouth, Bridport, Dorset DT6 6QQ, England.

BANCROFT Iris (May Nelson), (Julia Barnright, Iris Brent, Andrea Layton), b. 26 May 1922, King Chow, China. Writer. m. (1) Robert Koenig, 1945, div 1962, (2) Keith O Bancroft, 1 son. Education: BEd, Chicago Teachers College, 1945; MEd, Northwestern University, 1962. Appointments: Public School Teacher, Elmhurst, Illinois, 1957-61, Chicago, 1961-62; Writer, Photographer, Editor, Elysium Publications and American Art, Los Angeles, 1962-77. Publications: Novels: Love's Gentle Fugitive, 1978; So Wild a Rapture, 1978; Midnight Fires, 1979; Love's Burning Flame, 1979; Rapture's Rebel, 1980; Rebel's Passion, 1981; Dawn of Desire, 1981. Other: The Sexually Exciting Female, 1971; The Sexually Superior Male, 1971; Swinger's Diary, 1973; My Love Is Free, 1975; Whispering Hope, 1981; The Five-Minute Phobia Cure (with Roger Callahan), 1984; Any Man Can (with William Hartman and Marilyn Fithian), 1984; Sex and the Single Parent (with Mary Mattis), 1986; Reaching Intimacy (with Jerry DeHaan), 1986. Memberships: Mensa; PEN. Address: c/o Teal and Watt Literary Agency, 8033 Sunset Boulevard, Los Angeles, CA 90046, USA.

BANDELE THOMAS Biyi, b. 13 Oct 1967, Kafanchan, Nigeria. Author; Dramatist. Education: Dramatic Arts, Obafemi Awolowo University, Ife, 1987-90. Publications: The Man Who Came in From the Back of Beyond: The Sympathetic Undertaker and Other Dreams; Incantations on the Eve of an Execution. Plays: Rain; Marching for Fausa; Death Catches the Hunter. Contributions to: Films, radio, and journals. Honours: Arts Council Writers Bursary. Memberships: PEN; Society of Authors; Writers Guild. Address: 45 Fitzroy Street, London W1P 5HR, England.

BANFIELD Stephen David, b. 15 July 1951, Dulwich, London, England. University Professor. Education: BA, 1st Class Hons, Clare College, Cambridge, England, 1969-72; DPhil, St John's College, Oxford, England, 1972-75; Harvard University, 1975-76. Appointments: Lecturer in Music, University of Keele, 1978, Senior Lecturer, 1988-92; Elgar Professor of Music, 1992-, Head of School of Performance Studies, 1992-97, Head of Department of Music, 1996-98, University of Birmingham. Publications: Sensibility and English Song, 1985; Sondheim's Broadway Musicals, 1993; The Blackwell History of Music in Britain, vol VI: The Twentieth Century, 1995; Gerald Finzi, 1997. Honours: First Kurt Weill Prize, USA; Irving Lowens Award, USA, 1995. Address: 6 King's Court, 108 Livery St, Birmingham B3 1RR, England.

BANKS Brian (Robert), b. 4 Oct 1956, Carshalton, Surrey, England. Antiquarian Bookseller; Writer; Poet. m. Catherine Walton, 28 Sept 1987, 1 son, 2 daughters. Education: Westminister College; Middlesex Polytechnic. Publications: The Image of J-K Huysmans, 1990; Phantoms of the Belle Epoque, 1993; Atmosphere and Attitudes, 1993. Contributions to: Books and journals. Memberships: Société de J-K Huysmans, Paris; 1890's Society. Address: c/o 4 Meretune Court, Martin Way, Morden, Surrey SM4 4AN, England.

BANKS Iain Menzies, b. 16 Feb 1954, Fife, Scotland. Writer. Education: BA, University of Stirling, 1975. Publications: The Wasp Factory, 1984; Walking on Glass, 1985; The Bridge, 1986; Consider Phlebas, 1987; Espedair Street, 1987; The Player of Games, 1988; Canal Dreams, 1989; The Use of Weapons, 1990; The State of the Art, 1991; The Crow Road, 1992; Against a Dark Background, 1993; Complicity, 1993; Feersum Endjinn, 1994; Whit, 1995; Excession, 1996. Address: c/o Little Brown, Brettenham House, Lancaster Place, London WC2E 7EN, England.

BANKS Lynne Reid, b. 31 July 1929, London, England. Writer; Journalist; Playwright. m. Chaim Stephenson, 1965, 3 sons. Education: Italia Conti Stage School, 1946; Royal Academy of Dramatic Art, 1947-49. Appointments: Actress, 1949-54; Reporter and Scriptwriter, Independent Television News, London, 1955-62; English Teacher, Western Galilee, Israel, 1963-71; Writer, Lecturer, Journalist, 1971-. Publications: The L-Shaped Room, 1960; An End to Running, 1962; Children at the Gate, 1968; The Backward Shadow, 1970; Two is Lonely, 1974; Dark Quartet: The Story of the Brontës, 1976; Path to the Silent Country: Charlotte Brontë's Years of Fame, 1977; Defy the Wilderness, 1981; Torn Country: An Oral History of the Israeli War of Independence, 1982; The Warning Bell, 1984; Casualities, 1986; Fair Exchange, 1998. Juvenile: One More River, 1973, revised edition, 1993; Sarah and After: The Matriarchs, 1975; The Adventures of King Midas, 1976, revised edition, 1994; The Farthest-Away Mountain, 1977; My Darling Villain, 1977; I, Houdini: The Autobiography of a Self-Educated Hamster, 1978; Letters to My Israeli Sons: The Story of Jewish Survival, 1979; The Indian in the Cupboard, 1980; The Writing on the Wall, 1981; Maura's Angel, 1984; The Fairy Rebel, 1985; Return of the Indian, 1985; Melusine: A Mystery, 1988; The Secret of the Indian, 1988; The Magic Hare, 1992; The Mystery of the Cupboard, 1993; Broken Bridge, 1994; Harry the Poisonous Centipede, 1996; Angela and Diabola; Moses in Egypt, 1998; The Key to the Indian, 1999. Plays: It Never Rains, 1954; All in a Row, 1956; The Killer Dies Twice, 1956; Already, It's Tomorrow, 1962; The Wednesday Caller (television), 1963; The Last

Word on Julie (television), 1964; The Gift, 1965; The Stowaway (radio), 1967; The Eye of the Beholder (television), 1977; The Real Thing, 1977; Lame Duck (radio), 1978; Purely from Principal (radio), 1985; The Travels of Yoshi and the Tea-Kettle (children), 1993. Anthologies: Is Anyone There?, 1978; Women Writing 3, 1980; A Treasury of Jewish Stories, 1996; Ballet Stories, forthcoming. Contributions to: Short stories and articles in various publications. Honours: Best Books for Young Adults Award, American Library Association, 1977; Outstanding Books of the Year Award, 1981, Notable Books Award, 1986, New York Times; Children's Books of the Year Award, 1987; Rebecca Caudill Young Reader's Books Award, Illinois Association for Media in Education, 1988; Several children's Choice Awards. Memberships: Society of Authors; PEN. Literary Agent: Sheila Watson, Capo di Monte, Windmill Hill, London NW3 6RJ. Address: c/o Watson, Little Ltd, Capo di Monte, Windmill Hill, Hampstead, London NW3 6RJ, England.

BANKS Russell, b. 28 Mar 1940, Newton, Massachusetts, USA. Novelist. 4 daughters. Education: BA, highest honours, English, University of North Carolina. Publications: Searching for Survivors, 1975; Family Life, 1975; Hamilton Stark, 1978; The New World, 1978; The Book of Jamaica, 1980; Trailerpark, 1982; The Relation of My Imprisonment, 1984; Continental Drift, 1985; Success Stories, 1986; Affliction, 1989; Sweet Hereafter, 1992; Rule of the Bone, 1995; Cloudsplitter, 1998. Contributions to: New York Times Book Review; Washington Post; American Review; Vanity Fair; Antaeus; Partisan Review; New England Review; Fiction International; Boston Globe Magazine. Honours: Best American Short Stories, 1971, 1985; Fels Award, fiction, 1974; Prize story, O Henry Awards, 1975; St Lawrence Award, fiction, 1976; Guggenheim Fellowship, 1976; National Endowment for the Arts Fellowships, 1977, 1983; John dos Passos Award, 1986; Pulitzer Prize nominee, 1986; Award, American Academy of Arts and Letters, 1986. Memberships: American Academy of Arts and Letters; PEN American Centre; Coordinating Council of Literary Magazines. Address: c/o Ellen Levine Literary Agency Inc., 15 East 26th Street, Suite 1801, New York, NY 10010, USA.

BANNERMAN Mark. See: **LEWING Anthony Charles,**

BANNON Paul. See: **DURST Paul.**

BANTOCK Gavin (Marcus August), b. 4 July 1939, Barnt Green, Worcestershire, England. Retired Educator; Poet; Writer. Education: BA, 1963, Diploma of Education, 1964, MA, 1968, Oxford University. Appointments: Educator in UK schools, 1964-69; Faculty, Department of English, Reitaku University, Chiba-ken, Japan, 1969-94. Publications: Christ: A Poem in Twenty-Six Parts, 1965; Juggernaut: Selected Poems, 1968; A New Thing Breathing, 1969; Anhaga, 1970; Gleeman, 1972; Eirenikon, 1973; Isles, 1974; Dragons, 1979. Other: Essay collections. Contributions to: Anthologies. Honours: Richard Hillary Memorial Prize, 1964; Alice-Hunt-Bartlett Prize, 1966; Eric Gregory Award, 1969. Address: c/o Peter Jay, 69 King George Street, London SE10 8PX, England.

BANTOCK Nick, b. 1950, Worcestershire, England. Writer; Book Jacket Illustrator. m. Kim Kasasian, 4 children. Publications: There Was an Old Lady, 1990; Wings: A Pop-Up Book of Things That Fly, 1990; Griffin and Sabine: An Extraordinary Correspondence, 1991; Sabine's Notebook: In Which the Extraordinary Correspondence of Griffin and Sabine Continues, 1992; Runners, Sliders, Bouncers, Climbers: A Pop-Up Look at Animals in Motion (with Stacie Strong), 1992; The Walrus and the Carpenter, 1992; The Golden Mean: In Which the Extraordinary Correspondence of Griffin and Sabine Concludes, 1993; The Egyptian Jukebox: A Conundrum, 1993; Robin Hood: A Pop-Up Rhyme Book, 1993; Averse to Beasts: Twenty-Three Reasonless Rhymes, 1994. Address: c/o Chronicle Books, Chronicle Publishing Co, 275 Fifth Street, San Francisco, CA 94103, USA.

BANVILLE John, b. 8 Dec 1945, Wexford, Ireland. Author. m. Janet Dunham, 2 sons. Education: St Peter's College, Wexford. Appointment: Literary Editor, Irish Times, Dublin, 1988. Publications: Nightspawn, 1971; Birchwood, 1973; Doctor Copernicus, 1976; Kepler, 1983; The Newton Letter: An Interlude, 1985; Mefisto, 1987; The Book of Evidence, 1989; Ghosts, 1993; Athena, 1995. Contributions to: Observer; New York Review of Books; Irish Times. Address c/o Sheil Land Associates Ltd., 43 Doughty Street, London WC1N 2LF, England.

BARAKA Amiri. See **JONES (Everett) LeRoi.**

BARANCZAK Stanisław, b. 13 Nov 1946, Poznań, Poland. Professor of Polish Language and Literature; Poet; Writer; Editor; Translator. m. 2 children. Education: MA 1969, PhD 1973, Adam Mickiewicz University, Poznań. Appointments: Assistant Professor, Institute of Polish Philology, Adam Mickiewicz University, 1969-77, 1980; Co-Founder and Member, KOR, human rights group, 1976-81; Blacklisted for political reasons, 1977-80; Associate Professor of Slavic Languages and Literatures, 1981-84, Alfred Jurzykowski Professor of Polish Language and Literature, 1984-, Harvard University; Co-Editor, Zeszyty Literackie, 1982-; Associate Editor, 1986-87, Editor-in-Chief, 1987-90, The Polish Review. Publications: Poetry: Selected Poems: The Weight of the Body, 1989; 18 other books in Polish, 1968-96. Criticism and essays: Breathing Under Water, and Other East European Essays, 1990; 14 other books in Polish, 1971-96. Other: 43 books translated from English into Polish, 1974-96. Contributions to: Many scholarly journals and periodicals. Honours: Alfred Jurzykowski Foundation Literary Award, 1980; Guggenheim Fellowship, 1989; Terrence Des Pres Poetry Prize, 1989; Chivalric Cross of the Order of Polonia Restituta, 1991; Special Diploma for Lifetime Achievement in Promoting Polish Culture Abroad, Polish Minister of Foreign Affairs, 1993; PEN and Book-of-the-Month Club Award for the Best Literary Translation (with Clare Cavanagh), 1996. Memberships: American Association for Advancement of Slavic Studies; American Association for Polish-Jewish Studies; PEN Polish Centre; Polish Institute of Arts and Sciences in America; Polish Writers' Association; Union of Polish Writers Abroad; ZAIKS (Union of Polish Authors). Address: c/o Department of Slavic Languages and Literatures, Harvard University, 301 Boylston Hall, Cambridge, MA 02138, USA.

BARBALET Margaret , b. 19 Dec 1949, Adelaide, South Australia, Australia. Writer. m. Jack Barbalet, 12 May 1970, div 10 Jan 1989, 3 sons. Education: MA, Adelaide University, 1973. Appointments: Historian, Adelaide Children's Hospital, 1973-74; Research Officer, Adelaide City Council, 1973-75; Research Consultant, Commonwealth Schools Commission, 1984-88; Staff, Department of Foreign Affairs and Trade, Australia, 1990-. Publications: Far From a Low Gutter Girl: The Forgotten World of State Wards, 1983; Blood in the Rain (novel), 1986; Steel Beach (novel), 1988; The Wolf (children's book), 1991; Lady, Baby, Gypsy, Queen (novel), 1992. Honours: Literature Grant, 1985; New Writers Fellowship, 1986; Vogel Award Shortlist, 1988; Children's Book of the Year Award Shortlist, 1992. Memberships: Amnesty International; Australian Society of Authors. Address: c/o Penguin Books, PO Box 257, Ringwood, Victoria 3134, Australia.

BARBER Antonia. See: **ANTHONY Barbara.**

BARBER Charles Laurence, b. 20 Apr 1915, Harold Wood, Essex, England. Retired University Teacher; Writer. m. Barbara Best, 27 July 1943, 2 sons, 2 daughters. Education: BA, 1937, MA, 1941, St Catharine's College, Cambridge; Teacher's Diploma, London University, 1938; PhD, University of Goteborg, Sweden, 1957. Appointments: Lecturer, University of Goteborg, 1947-56, Queen's University of Belfast, 1956-59, University of Leeds, 1959-80. Publications: The Idea of Honour in the English Drama, 1957; The Story of Language, 1964; Linguistic Change in Present Day English, 1964; Early Modern English, 1976; Poetry in English: An Introduction, 1983; The Theme of Honour's

Tongue, 1985; The English Language: A Historical Introduction, 1993. Other: Editor of plays by Thomas Middleton and Shakespeare. Contributions to: Numerous learned journals. Address: 7 North Parade, Leeds, West Yorkshire LS16 5AY, England.

BARBER Elizabeth Jane, b. 2 Dec 1940, Pasadena, California, USA. College Professor. m. Paul Thomas Barber, 14 June 1965. Education: BA, Bryn Mawr College, 1962; PhD, Yale University, 1968. Appointments: Research Associate, Princeton University, 1968-69; Assistant Professor, Associate Professor, Full Professor of Linguistics and Archaeology, Occidental College, 1970-. Publications: Books: Archaeological Decipherment, 1974; Prehistoric Textiles, 1991; Women's Work - The First 20,000 Years, 1994; The Mummies of Ürümchi, 1998; 30 articles printed in edited books and encyclopaedias. Contributions to: 15 articles in professional journals. Honours: Costume Society of America's Davenport Book Prize; American Historical Association's Breasted Prize in Ancient History. Address: Language Department, Occidental College, Los Angeles, CA 90041, USA.

BARBER Lynn, b. 22 May 1944, England. Journalist. m. David Cloudesley Cardiff, 1 Sept 1971, 2 daughters. Education: BA Honours, English, Oxford University. Appointments: Assistant Editor, Penthouse Magazine, 1968-73; Staff Feature Writer, Sunday Express Magazine, 1984-89; Feature Writer, Independent on Sunday, 1990-. Publications: How to Improve Your Man in Bed, 1970; The Penthouse Sexindex, 1973; The Single Women's Sexbook, 1975; The Heyday of Natural History, 1980. Honours: British Press Awards as Magazine Writer of the Year, 1986, 1987. Address: Independent on Sunday, 40 City Road, London EC1Y 2DH, England.

BARBER Richard William, b. 30 Oct 1941, Dunmow, Essex, England. Publisher; Author. m. Helen Tolson, 7 May 1970, 1 son, 1 daughter. Education: BA, MA, 1967, PhD, 1982, Corpus Christi College, Cambridge. Publications: Arthur of Albion, 1961; The Knight and Chivalry, 1972; Edward Prince of Wales and Aquitaine, 1976; Companion Guide to South West France, 1977; Tournaments, 1978; The Arthurian Legends, 1979; The Penguin Guide to Medieval Europe, 1984; Fuller's Worthies, 1987; The Worlds of John Aubrey, 1988; Pilgrimages, 1991; British Myths and Legends, 1998; Contributions to: Arthurian Literature. Honours: Somerset Maugham Award, 1972; Times Higher Educational Supplement Book Award, 1978. Memberships: Royal Society of Literature; Royal Historical Society; Society of Antiquaries. Address: Stangrove Hall, Alderton, Nr Woodbridge, Suffolk IP12 3BL, England.

BARBET Pierre. See: **AVICE Claude.**

BARBOSA Miguel, b. 22 Nov 1925, Lisbon, Portugal. Writer; Dramatist; Poet; Painter. Education: Economics and Finance, University of Lisbon. Appointments: Moulin de l'Ecluse - Le Mur de la Poesie, Carnac, France, 1993; Poesia Pace, Milan, Italy, 1994; Jeux Floreaux d'Aquitaine, Bordeaux, France, 1995. Publications: Short Stories: Retalhos de Vida, 1955; Manta de Trapos, 1962. Plays: O Palheiro, 1963; Os Carnivoros, 1964; O Piquenique, 1964; O Insecticida, 1965; A Mulher que Paris a France, 1971; Los profetas de la Paja, 1973; How New York was Destroyed by Rats, 1977; The Materialisation of Love, 1978. Novels: Trineu do Morro, 1972; Mulher Macumba, 1973; A Pileca no Poleiro, 1976; As Confissoes de Um Cacador de Dinossauros, 1981; Esta Louca Profissao de Escritor, 1983; Cartas a Um Fogo-Fatuo, 1985. Poetry: Dans un Cri de Couleurs, 1991; Um Gesto no Rosto da Utopia, 1994; Prima del Verbo, 1995; Mare di Illusioni Naufragate, 1995; Prelúdio Poético de um Vagabundo da Madrugada, 1996; Mouthfuls of Red Confetti and the Hunt for God's Skull, 1996; O Teu Corpo na Minha Alma, 1996. Contributions to: Various publications. Honours: Prix Nu, Jubile Mondial d'arts Plastiques, Nice, France, 1984; Honourable Mention, Le Quadriennale Mondiale des Beaux Arts, Lyon, France, 1985; Medaille D'Argent, Academie de Lutece, Paris, 1987; Prix de La Revue D'Art, La Cote des

Arts, Cannes, 1990. Memberships: Society of Portuguese Authors; Instituto de Sintra, Portugal; Accademia Italiana Gli Etruschi, Italy; Accademia Internazionale Greci-Marino di Lettere, Arti e Scienze. Address: Avenue Joao Crisostomo 91-2, Lisbon 1050, Portugal.

BARBOUR Douglas (Fleming), b. 21 Mar 1940, Winnipeg, Manitoba, Canada. Professor of English; Poet; Writer. m. M Sharon Nicoll, 21 May 1966. Education: BA, Acadia University, 1962; MA, Dalhousie University, 1964; PhD, Queen's University, Kingston, Ontario, 1976. Appointments: Teacher, Alderwood Collegiate Institute, 1968-69; Assistant Professor, 1969-77, Associate Professor, 1977-82, Professor of English, 1982-, University of Alberta. Publications: Poetry: Land Fall, 1971; A Poem as Long as the Highway, 1971; White, 1972; Song Book, 1973; He and She and, 1974; Visions of My Grandfather, 1977; Shore Lines, 1979; Vision/Sounding, 1980; The Pirates of Pen's Chance (with Stephen Scobie), 1981; The Harbingers, 1984; Visible Visions: Selected Poems, 1984; Canadian Poetry Chronicle, 1985. Other: Worlds Out of Words: The Science Fiction Novels of Samuel R Delany, 1978; The Maple Laugh Forever: An Anthology of Canadian Comic Poetry (editor with Stephen Scobie), 1981; Writing Right: New Poetry by Canadian Women (editor with Marni Stanley), 1982; Tesseracts 2 (editor with Phyllis Gollieb), 1987; B P Nichol and His Works, 1992; Daphne Marlatt and Her Works, 1992; John Newlove and His Works, 1992; Michael Ondaatje, 1993. Memberships: Association of Canadian University Teachers; League of Canadian Poets, co-chairman, 1972-74. Address: c/o Department of English, University of Alberta, Edmonton, Alberta T6G 2E5, Canada.

BARCLAY Patrick, b. 15 Aug 1947, London, England. Journalist. 1 son, 1 daughter. Appointments: Football Writer, The Guardian, 1976-86; Today, 1986; The Independent, 1986-91; The Observer, 1991-96; The Sunday Telegraph, 1996-. Honour: Sports Journalist of the Year, 1993. Address: c/o The Sunday Telegraph, Canary Wharf, London E14 5DT, England.

BARCLAY Robert Leslie, b. 17 July 1946, London, England. Conservator; Trumpet-maker. m. Janet Mair Fenwick, 21 Jan 1971, 2 sons, 2 daughters. Education: City and Guilds of London, Science Laboratory Technology, 1969; BA, Honours, University of Toronto, 1975. Publications: The Care of Musical Instruments in Canadian Collections, 1982; Anatomy of an Exhibition: The Look of Music, 1983; The Art of the Trumpet-maker, 1992; Recommendations for the Conservation of Musical Instruments, 1993. Contributions to: Museum International, Studies in Conservation; Historic Brass Society Journal; Galpin Society Journal. Honour: Nicholas Bessaraboff Prize, American Musical Instrument Society, 1995. Address: Canadian Conservation Institute, 1030 Innes Road, Ottawa, Ontario K1A 0M5, Canada.

BARDILL Linard, b. 16 Oct 1956, Chur, Switzerland. Author; Singer; Songwriter. div, 3 sons. Education: Master of Theology Degree. Publications: Lieder Verbrannter Dichter, 1988; Aufs Leben Los, 1990; Tanz auf den Feldern, 1993; Nachttiere, 1994; Tamangur, 1996; Luege, was des Mond so macht, 1997; Lieder und Gschichte u s em Rudesack vom Andri, 1998; Fortunat Kauer (novel), 1998; Das geheimnisvolle Buch (stories for children), 1998. Contributions to: Weltwoche; Literatura. Honours: Deutsche Kleinkunstpreis, Salzburger Stier. Address: Cresta, CH-7412, Scharans, Switzerland.

BAREHAM Terence, b. 17 Oct 1937, Clacton-on-Sea, Essex, England. University Professor. Education: Open Scholar and State Scholar, 1959-62, BA (Hons), 1962, MA, 1969, Lincoln College, Oxford; DPhil, Ulster University, Northern Ireland, 1977. Publications: George Crabbe: A Critical Study, 1977; George Crabbe: A Bibliography (joint author), 1978; The Art of Anthony Trollope, 1980; Anthony Trollope (Casebook Series), 1982; Tom Stoppard (Casebook Series), 1989; Malcolm Lowry, 1989; Charles Lever: New Evaluations (editor), 1991; York Notes, Monographs on Robert Bolt, T S Eliot, Shakespeare. Contributions to: Numerous on literature of 17th - 20th Century. Address: c/o Department of English, University of Ulster, Coleraine, County Derry, Northern Ireland.

BARER Burl, b. 8 Aug 1947, Walla Walla, Washington, USA. Writer. m. Britt Johnsen, 2 Mar 1974, 1 son, 1 daughter. Education: Communications, University of Washington. Publications: Selections from the Holy Quran, 1987; The Saint: A Complete History in Print, Radio, Film and Television, 1993; Maverick: The Making of the Movie/The Official Guide to the Television Series, 1994; Man Overbaord: The Counterfeit Resurrection of Phil Champagne, 1994; The Saint, (novel from screenplay), 1997; Capture the Saint (novel), 1998. Contributions to: The Epistle; Oxford Companion to Mystery and Detective Fiction. Honour: Edgar Award, 1994. Membership: Mystery Writers of America. Literary Agent: Gelfman/Schnieder. Address: 1839 Crestline Drive, Walla Walla, WA 99362, USA.

BARGER Timothy Knox, b. 4 Jan 1958, Edwards AFB, California, USA. Writer; Editor. Education: BA, Humanities, Hendrix College, 1978; BJ, Magazine Journalism, Texas, Austin, 1987; MLIS, Library Science, Texas, Austin, 1994; Doctoral Studies, Mass Communication, Syracuse University, 1994-. Appointments: Associate Editor, The Austin Light, Austin, Texas, 1987-88; Coordinating Editor, Butterworth Legal Publishers, Austin, Texas, 1989-92; Writer and Researcher, The Reference Press, Austin, Texas, 1992-94. Publications: Co-author: Hoover's Handbook of American Business, 1993, 1994, 1995; Hoover's Handbook of World Business, 1993; Hoover's Guide to the Book Business, 1993; Hoover's Handbook of Emerging Companies, 1993-94; Hoover's Guide to Private Companies, 1994-95; The Bay Area 500, 1994; The Texas 500, 1994. Contributions to: Austin American-Statesman; Austin Chronicle; Austin Light. Honours: Phi Kappa Phi, 1993; Beta Phi Mu, 1996; Syracuse University Graduate Fellow, 1994-97. Memberships: Austin Writers' League; Society of Professional Journalists; Association for Education in Journalism and Mass Communications; American Library Association. Address: 256 Thurber Street, Apt 8, Syracuse, NY 13210-3655, USA.

BARICH Bill, b. 23 Aug 1943, Winona, Minnesota, USA. Writer. Education: BA, Colgate University, 1965. Appointments: Staff Writer, The New Yorker, 1981-94; Adjunct Professor, Creative Writing, 1988-89, Graduate School of Journalism, 1999- University of California, Berkeley, USA. Publications: Laughing in the Hills, 1980; Traveling Light, 1984; Hard to Be Good, 1987; Big Dreams, 1994; Carson Valley, 1997; Crazy For Rivers, 1999; The Sporting Life, 1999. Contributions to: The New Yorker; Esquire; American Poetry Review; Outside. Honours: Best American Short Stories, 1982; Guggenheim Fellow in Fiction, 1985; Marin County Arts Council Fellow, 1995; Literary Laureate, San Francisco Public Library, 1998. Membership: PEN. Literary Agent: Amanda Urban. Address: c/o ICM, 40 W 57th St, New York, 10019, USA.

BARING Louise Olivia, b. 28 July 1957, London, England. Journalist; Magazine Writer. m. Eric Franck, 5 Feb 1997, 1 son. Appointments: The Economist, 1983-89; Mail on Sunday, 1989-90; Assistant Features Editor, The Independent on Sunday, 1990-93; Feature Writer, Conoé Nast Publications, 1994-, Contributor Editor, 1997-. Address: 7 Victoria Square, London SW1W 0QY, England.

BARKER Audrey Lilian, b. 13 Apr 1918, St Paul's Cray, Kent, England. Author. Appointments: Staff, Amalgamated Press, 1936; Reader, Cresset Press, 1947; Secretary, Sub Editor, BBC, London, 1948-78. Publications: Innocents, 1947; The Middling, 1967; John Brown's Body, 1969; Life Stories, 1981; No Word of Love, 1985; The Gooseboy, 1987; The Woman Who Talked to Herself, 1989; Any Excuse for a Party: Selected Stories, 1991; Zeph, 1991. Contributions to: Anthologies and magazines. Honours: Atlantic Award in Literature, 1946; Somerset Maugham Award, 1947; Cheltenham Festival Award, 1963; Arts Council Award, 1970; SE Arts Creative Book Award, 1981. Memberships: Fellow, Royal Society of Literature; English PEN. Literary Agent: Jennifer Kavanagh. Address: 103 Harrow Road, Carshalton, Surrey, England.

BARKER Clive, b. 1952, Liverpool, England. Writer; Dramatist; Artist. Education: University of Liverpool. Publications: Novels: The Damnation Game, 1985; Weaveworld, 1987; Cabal, 1988; The Great and Secret Show, 1989; Imajica, 1991; The Thief of Always, 1992; Emerville, 1994; Sacrament, 1996; Galilee, 1998. Other: Plays, screenplays, and short stories. Address: c/o HarperCollins, 10 East 53rd Street, New York, NY 10022, USA.

BARKER Dennis (Malcolm), b. 21 June 1929, Lowestoft, England. Journalist; Novelist. m. Sarah Katherine Alwyn, 1 daughter. Education: National Diploma in Journalism, 1959. Appointments: Reporter and Sub-Editor, Suffolk Chronicle & Mercury, Ipswich, 1947-48; Reporter, Feature Writer, Theatre and Film Critic, 1948-58, East Anglian Daily Times; Estates and Property Columnist, 1958-63, Express & Star, Wolverhampton; Midlands Correspondent, 1963-67, Reporter, Feature Writer, Columnist, The Guardian, 1967-91 (contributor). Publications: Novels: Candidate of Promise, 1969; The Scandalisers, 1974; Winston Three Three Three, 1987; Non-fiction: The People of the Forces Trilogy (Soldiering On, 1981, Ruling the Waves, 1986, Guarding the Skies, 1989); One Man's Estate, 1983; Parian Ware, 1985; Fresh Start, 1990; The Craft of the Media Interview, 1998. Contributions to: BBC; Punch; East Anglian Architecture & Building Review (editor and editorial director, 1956-58); The Guardian, 1991-. Memberships: National Union of Journalists, secretary, Suffolk Branch, 1953-58, Chairman 1958; Chairman, Home Counties District Council, 1956-57; Life Member, 1991; Life Member, Newspaper Press Fund; Writers Guild of Great Britain; Broadcasting Press Guild; Society of Authors. Address: 67 Speldhurst Road, London W4 1BY, England.

BARKER Elspeth, b. 16 Nov 1940, Edinburgh, Scotland. Writer. m. George Granville Barker, 29 July 1989, 3 sons, 2 daughters. Education: St Leonards School, Scotland, 1953-57; Oxford University, England, 1958-61. Publications: O Caledonia, 1991; Anthology of Loss, 1997. Contributions to: Independent on Sunday; Guardian; Harpers & Queen; TLS; Vogue; Big Issue; Sunday Times; Observer; Daily Mail. Honours: David Higham Award, Scottish Arts Council; Angel Literary Award; Royal Society of Literature Winifred Holtby Award. Address: Bintry House, Ittenigham, Aylsham, Norfolk NR11 7AT, England.

BARKER Howard, b. 28 June 1946, London, England. Dramatist; Poet. Education: MA, University of Sussex, 1968. Appointment: Resident Dramatist, Open Space Theatre, London, 1974-75. Publications: Over 30 plays, including Collected Plays, Volume I, 1990; Poetry. Address: c/o Judy Daish Associates, 83 Eastbourne Mews, Brighton, Sussex, England.

BARKER Nicola, b. 30 Mar 1966, Ely, Cambridgeshire, England. Writer. Education: Read Philosophy and English, Cambridge University, 1988. Appointments: Regular Reviewer, The Observer. Publications: Love Your Enemies (short stories), 1992; Reversed Forecast (novel), 1994; mall Holdings (novel), 1995; Heading Inland (short stories), 1996; Wide Open (novel), 1998. Contributions to: The Time Out Book of London Short Stories; Food With Feeling, story adapted for BBC Radio 4. Honours: David Higham Prize for Fiction; Joint Winner, Macmillan Silver PEN Award for Fiction; Mail on Sunday/John Llewellyn Rhys Award, 1997. Address: c/o Rogers, Coleridge and White Ltd, 20 Powis Mews, London W11 1JN, England.

BARKER Patricia Margaret, b. 8 May 1943, Thornaby on Tees, England. Writer. m. 27 Jan 1978, 1 son, 1 daughter. Education: BSc, London School of Economics, 1965. Appointment: Patron, New Writing North.

Publications: Union Street, 1982; Blow Your House Down, 1984; The Century's Daughter, 1986; The Man Who Wasn't There, 1989; Regeneration, 1991; The Eye in the Door, 1993; The Ghost Road, 1995; The Century's Daughter, retitled Liza's England, 1996; Another World, 1998. Honours: One of Best of Young British Novelists, 1982; Joint Winner, Fawcett Prize, 1982; Honorary M Litt University of Teesside, 1993; Guardian Fiction Prize, 1994; Northern Electric Special Arts Award, 1994; Booker Prize, 1995; Honorary DLitt, Napier University, 1996; Honorary Doctorate, Open University, 1997; Honorary Fellow, London School of Economics, 1997; Honorary DLitt, Durham University, 1998; Honorary DLitt, University of Hertfordshire, 1998. Memberships: Society of Authors; PEN; Fellow of the Royal Society of Literature. Address: c/o Gillon Aitken Associates, 29 Fernshaw Road, London SW10 0TG, England.

BARKER Paul, b. 24 Aug 1935, Halifax, Yorkshire, England. Journalist; Editor; Writer; Broadcaster. m. Sally Huddleston, 3 sons, 1 daughter. Education: MA, University of Oxford. Appointments: Editor, New Society, 1968-86; Director, Advisory Editor, Fiction Magazine, 1982-87; Social Policy Editor, Sunday Telegraph, 1986-88; Visiting Fellow, University of Bath, 1986-; Columnist, 1987-92, Social Policy Commentator, 1992-, London Evening Standard; Associate Editor, The Independent Magazine, 1988-90. Publications: A Sociological Portrait, 1972; One for Sorrow, Two for Joy, 1972; The Social Sciences Today, 1975; Arts in Society, 1977; The Other Britain, 1982; Founders of the Welfare State, 1985; Britain in the Eighties, 1989; Towards a New Landscape, 1993; Young at Eighty, 1995; Gulliver and Beyond, 1996; Living as Equals, 1996; A Critic Writes, 1997; Town and Country, 1998; Plan/Non-Plan, 1999. Honour: Leverhulme Research Fellow, 1993-95. Memberships: Institute of Community Studies, fellow, senior fellow; Royal Society of Arts, fellow. Address: 15 Dartmouth Park Avenue, London NW5 1JL, England.

BARLOW Frank, b. 19 Apr 1911, Wolstanton, England. Historian; Emeritus Professor. m. Moira Stella Brigid Garvey, 1 July 1936, 2 sons. Education: BA, 1933, BLitt, 1934, MA, DPhil, 1937, St John's College, Oxford. Appointments: Assistant Lecturer, University College, London, 1936-40; Lecturer, 1946-49, Reader, 1949-53, Professor of History and Head of the Department of History, 1953-76, Emeritus Professor, 1976-, Deputy Vice-Chancellor, 1961-63, Public Orator, 1974-76, University of Exeter. Publications: The Letters of Arnulf of Lisieux, 1939; Durham Annals and Documents of the Thirteenth Century, 1945; Durham Jurisdictional Peculiars, 1950; The Feudal Kingdom of England, 1955; The Life of King Edward the Confessor (editor and Translator), 1962; The English Church, 1000-1066, 1963; William I and the Norman Conquest, 1965; Edward the Confessor, 1970; Winchester in the Early Middle Ages (with Martin Biddle, Olof von Feilitzen, and D J Keene), 1976; the English Church, 1066-1154, 1979; The Norman Conquest and Beyond, 1983; William Rufus, 1983; Thomas Becket, 1986; Introduction to Devonshire Domesday Book, 1991; English Episcopal Acta, XI-XII (Exeter 1046-1257), 1995. Contributions to: Various professional journals. Honours: Fereday Fellow, St John's College, Oxford, 1935-38; Honorary DLitt, Exon, 1981; Commander of the Order of the British Empire, 1989. Memberships: British Academy, fellow; Royal Society of Literature, fellow. Address: Middle Court Hall, Kenton, Exeter, EX6 8NA, England.

BARLTROP Robert (Arthur Horace), b. 6 Nov 1922, Walthamstow, England. Journalist; Writer. m. Mary Gleeson, 18 July 1947, 3 sons. Education: Teacher's Certificate, Forest Training College, 1950. Appointments: Editor, Socialist Standard, 1972-78, Cockney Ancestor, 1983-86. Publications: The Monument, 1974; Jack London: The Man, the Writer, the Rebel, 1977; The Bar Tree, 1979; The Muvver Tongue, 1980; Revolution: Stories and Essays by Jack London (editor), 1981; My Mother's Calling Me, 1984; A Funny Age, 1985; Bright Summer, Dark Autumn, 1986. Contributions to: Guardian Newspapers; Recorder Newspapers. Membership:

Institute of Journalists. Address: 77 Idmiston Road, London E15 1RG, England.

BARNABY (Charles) Frank, b. 27 Sept 1927, Andover, Hampshire, England. Author. m. 12 Dec 1972, 1 son, 1 daughter. Education: BSc, 1951, MSc, 1954, PhD, 1960, London University. Publications: Man and the Atom, 1970; Nuclear Energy, 1975; Prospects for Peace, 1981; Future Warfare, 1983; The Automated Battlefield, 1986; Star Wars Brought Down to Earth, 1986; The Invisible Bomb, 1989; The Gaia Peace Atlas, 1989; The Role and Control of Arms in the 1990's, 1993; How Nuclear Weapons Spread, 1993; Instruments of Terror, 1997. Contributions to: Ambio; New Scientist; Technology Review. Honour: Honorary Doctorates, Free University, Amsterdam, University of Southampton, 1996. Address: Brandreth, Station Road, Chilbolton, Stockbridge, Hampshire SO20 6HW, England.

BARNARD Christiaan (Neethling), b. 8 Nov 1922, Beaufort West, Cape Province, South Africa. Physician; Professor of Surgical Science Emeritus; Senior Consultant and Scientist-in-Residence; Writer. m. (1) Aletta Gertruida Louw, 6 Nov 1948, diss 1970, 1 son dec, 1 daughter, (2) Barbara Maria Zoellner, 1970, diss 1980, 2 sons, (3) Karin Setzkon, 1988, 1 son. Education: MB, ChB, 1946, MD, 1953, MMed, 1953, University of Cape Town; MS, PhD, 1958, University of Minnesota. Appointments: Private Practice, Ceres, South Africa, 1948-51; Senior Resident Medical Officer, City Fever Hospital, Cape Town, 1951-53; Registrar, Groote Schuur Hospital, 1953-55; Research Fellow in Surgery, University of Cape Town, 1953-55; Charles Adams Memorial Scholar and Dazian Foundation for Medical Research Scholar, University of Minnesota, 1956-58; Lecturer, 1958-63, Associate Professor, 1963-68, Professor of Surgical Science, 1968-83, Professor Emeritus, 1983-, University of Cape Town; Senior Cardiothoracic Surgeon, Groote Schuur Hospital, 1958-83; Senior Consultant and Scientist-in-Residence, Oklahoma Heart Center, Baptist Medical Center, 1985-; Performed first human heart transplant operation, 1967, and first human double-heart transplant operation, 1974. Publications: The Surgery of the Common Congenital Cardiac Malformation (with Velva Schrire), 1968; Christiaan Barnard: One Life (with Curtis Bill Pepper), 1970; Heart Attack: You Don't Have to Die, 1971; The Unwanted (with Siegfried Stander), novel, 1974; South Africa: Sharp Dissection, 1977; In the Night Season (with Siegfried Stander), novel, 1977; The Best Medicine, 1979; Good Life, Good Death: A Doctor's Case for Euthanasia and Suicide, 1980; The Arthritis Handbook, 1984. Contributions to: Many medical journals. Honours: Numerous. Address: 18 Silwood Road, Rondebosch 7700, South Africa.

BARNARD Michael, b. 4 May 1944, Ipswich, Suffolk, England. Publisher. m. Jayne Jenkinson, 1 Mar 1996, 1 son. Appointments: Journalist, Kent Web Offset Group, 1962-66; Journalist, Thomson Newspapers, 1966-72; Production Manager, Macmillan Publishers, 1972-79; Director, Macmillan Ltd, 1979-; Editor, Publishing Technology Review, 1995-. Publications include: Desktop Publishing (with Wilson-Davies and St John Bate), 1988; Inside Magazines, 1989; Making Electronic Manuscripts, 1989; Introduction to Print Buying, 3rd edition, 1989; Magazine and Journal Production, 3rd edition, 1990; Publisher's Guide to Desktop Publishing (with Wilson-Davies and St John Bate), 1991; Dictionary of Printing and Publishing (with Peacock), 1991; Introduction to Printing Processes, 1991; Glossary of Advertising Terms, 1991, French edition, 1992; Glossary of Printing, Binding and Paper Terms, 1991, French edition, 1992; Handbook of Print and Production (with Berrill and Peacock), 1994; Visual Guide to Printing Processes, 1994; Pindar Pocket Print Production Guide, 1995; Visual Guide to Offset Litho, 1995; Print Buyer's Bible (with Shobbrook), 1996; Book Distribution Handbook (with Webb), 1996; The Print and Production Manual, 8th edition, 1998. Contributions to: Many articles in newspapers and magazines. Honour: Visiting Professor, London Institute, 1998. Membership: Fellow of Royal Society of Arts, 1993. Address: Macmillan Ltd,

Brunel Road, Basingstoke, Hampshire RG21 6XS, England.

BARNARD Robert, b. 23 Nov 1936, Burnham on Crouch, Essex, England. Crime Writer. m. Mary Louise Tabor, 7 Feb 1963. Education: Balliol College, Oxford, 1956-59; Dr Phil, University of Bergen, Norway, 1972. Publications: Death of an Old Goat, 1974; Sheer Torture, 1981; A Corpse in a Gilded Cage, 1984; Out of the Blackout, 1985; Skeleton in the Grass, 1987; At Death's Door, 1988; Death and the Chaste Apprentice, 1989; Masters of the House, 1994. As Bernard Bastable: Dead, Mr Mozart, 1995; Too Many Notes, Mr Mozart, 1995. Honours: Seven Times Nominated for Edgar Awards. Memberships: Crime Writers Association; Chairman, Brontë Society, 1996-; Society of Authors. Literary Agent: Gregory & Radice. Address: Hazeldene, Houghley Lane, Leeds LS13 2DT, England.

BARNES Christopher J(ohn), b. 10 Mar 1942, Sheffield, England. Professor of Slavic Languages and Literatures; Writer. m. Svetlana Tzapina, 20 Apr 1994, 2 daughters. Education: BA, 1963, MA, 1967, PhD, 1970, Corpus Christi College, Cambridge. Appointments: Lecturer in Russian Language and Literature, University of St Andrews, Scotland, 1967-89; Professor and Chairman of the Department of Slavic Languages and Literatures, University of Toronto, 1989-. Publications: Studies in Twentieth-Century Russian Literature (editor), 1976; Boris Pasternak: Collected Short Prose (editor and translator), 1977; Boris Pasternak: The Voice of Prose (editor and translator) 2 volumes, 1986, 1990; Boris Pasternak: A Literary Biography, Vol 1, 1890-1928, 1989, Vol 2, 1928-1960, 1998; Boris Pasternak and European Literature (editor), 1990. Contributions to: Scholarly journals. Memberships: American Association for the Advancement of Slavic Studies; American Association of Teachers of Slavic and East European Languages; British Royal Musical Association; British Universities Association of Slavists; Canadian Association of Slavists; Modern Language Association of America. Address: c/o Department of Slavic Languages and Literatures, University of Toronto, Toronto, Ontario M5S 1A1, Canada.

BARNES Clive (Alexander), b. 13 May 1927, London, England. Journalist; Dance and Theatre Critic. m. (2) Patricia Amy Evelyn Winckley, 26 June 1958, 1 son, 1 daughter. Education: King's College, London; BA, St Catherine's College, Oxford, 1951. Appointments: Co-Editor, Arabesque, 1950; Assistant Editor, 1950-58, Associate Editor, 1958-61, Executive Editor, 1961-65, Dance and Dancers; Administrative Officer in Town Planning, London County Council, 1952-61; Chief Dance Critic, 1961-65, New York Correspondent, 1970-, The Times, London; Dance Critic, 1965-78, Drama Critic, 1967-78, New York Times; Associate Editor and Chief Dance and Drama Critic, New York Post, 1978-. Publications: Ballet in Britain Since the War, 1953; Frederick Ashton and His Ballets, 1961; Ballet Here and Now (with A V Coton and Frank Jackson), 1961; Ballett, 1965: Chronik und Bilanz des Ballettjahres (editor with Horst Koegler), 1965; Ballett 1966: Chronik und Bilanz des Ballettjahres (editor with Horst Koegler), 1966; Fifty Best Plays of the American Theatre from 1787 to the Present (editor), 4 volumes, 1969; Best American Plays: Sixth Series, 1963-1967 (editor with John Gassner), 1971; Best American Plays: Seventh Series (editor), 1975; Inside American Ballet Theatre, 1977; Nureyev, 1982; Best American Plays: Eighth Series, 1974-1982 (editor), 1983; Best American Plays: Ninth Series, 1983-1992 (editor), 1993. Contributions to: Many periodicals. Honours: Knight of the Order of Dannebrog, Denmark, 1972; Commander of the Order of the British Empire, 1975. Address: 241 West 23rd Street, Apt 4A, New York, NY 10011, USA.

BARNES Jonathan, b. 26 Dec 1942, England. Professor of Ancient Philosophy. m. Jennifer Postgate, 2 daughters. Education: Balliol College, Oxford. Appointments: Fellow, Oriel College, 1968-78, Balliol College, 1978-94, Oxford; Visiting positions, Institute for Advanced Study, Princeton, New Jersey, 1972, University of Texas, 1981, Wissenschaftskolleg zu Berlin, 1985, University of Alberta, 1986, University of Zürich, 1987, Istituto Italiano per gli studi filosofici, 1988; Professor of Ancient Philosophy, Oxford University, 1989-94, University of Geneva, 1994-. Publications: The Ontological Argument, 1972; Aristotle's Posterior Analytics, 1975; The Presocratic Philosphers, 1979; Aristotle, 1982; Early Greek Philosophy, 1987; The Toils of Scepticism, 1991; A Companion to Aristotle, 1995; Logic and the Imperial Stoa, 1997. Address: 1, place de la Taconnerie, 1204 Geneva, Switzerland.

BARNES Julian Patrick, (Dan Kavanagh, Basil Seal), b. 19 Jan 1946, Leicester, England. Writer. Education: Magdalen College, Oxford, 1964-68. Appointments: Lexicographer, Oxford English Dictionary Supplement, 1969-72; TV Critic, 1977-81, Assistant Literary Editor, 1977-79, New Statesman; Contributing Editor, New Review, 1977-78; Deputy Literary Editor, Sunday Times, 1979-81; TV Critic, The Observer, 1982-86. Publications: Metroland Duffy, 1980; Before She Met Me, 1982; Fiddle City, 1983; Flaubert's Parrot, 1984; Putting the Boot In, 1985; Staring at the Sun, 1986; History of the World in Ten and a Half Chapters, 1989; Talking it Over, 1991; The Porcupine, 1992; Cross Channel, 1996. Address: The Chambers, Chelsea Harbour, Lots Road, London SW10 0XF, England.

BARNES Michael, b. 1934. Author. Education: BA; MEd. Appointments: Teacher. Publications: Over 35 books. Contributions to: Periodicals, journals, reviews, magazines, quarterlies and newspapers. Honours: Canada 125 Medal, 1992; Leaf Award for Best Promotion of a Community, 1994; Order of Canada, 1995; Kirkland Lake Celebrity Hall of Fame, 1998; Canadian Honour Roll, 1998. Address: 126 First Street, Kirkland Lake, Ontario P2N 3H7m, Canada.

BARNES Patience Rogers Plummer, b. 28 Sept 1932, Mt Vernon, NY, USA. Writer; Editor. m. James John Barnes, 1 son, 1 daughter. Education: BA, Smith College, 1954. Appointments: J Walter Thompson Co, NYC, NY, 1950-55; Freelance Writer & Editor, 1955-; Research Associate, Wabash College, 1988-. Publications: Free Trade in Books: A Study of the London Book Trade Since 1800, 1964; Authors, Publishers and Politicians: The Quest for an Anglo-American Copyright Agreement, 1815-54, 1974; Hitler's Mein Kampf in Britain and America, co-auth w James J Barnes, 1930-39; James Vincent Murphy, Translator and Interpreter of Fascist Europe, 1880-1946, co-auth w James J Barnes, 1987; Nazis in London 1930-39, co-auth w James J Barnes, in progress; Nazi Refugee Turned Spy: the Career of Hans Wesemann 1895-1971, co-auth w James J Barnes, in progress. Memberships: Alumnae Association of Smith College; Friends of the Crawfordsville Public Library; League of Women Voters; Montgomery County Historical Society; The London Goodenough Trust for Overseas Grads, Eng; Metropolitan Opera Guild. Address: 7 Locust Hill, Crawfordsville, IN 47933, USA.

BARNES Peter, b. 10 Jan 1931, London, England. Writer; Dramatist. m. 28 Aug 1963. Publications: The Ruling Class, 1969; Red Noses, 1985; Collected Plays, 3 volumes, 1989-96; Nobody Here But Us Chickens, 1990; The Spirit of Man, 1990; Sunsets and Glories, 1990. Honours: John Whiting Award, 1969; Evening Standard Award, 1969; Giles Cooper Award, 1981; Olivier Award, 1985; Royal Television Award, 1989. Literary Agent: Casarotto Ramsay. Address: 7 Archery Close, Connaught Street, London W2, England.

BARNES Dick, (Richard Gordon Barnes), b. 5 Nov 1932, San Bernardino, California, USA. Professor of English; Poet; Writer; Dramatist; Rubboardist. m. Patricia Casey, 30 July 1982, 5 sons, 4 daughters. Education: BA, Pomona College, 1954; AM, Harvard University, 1955; PhD, Claremont Graduate School, 1959. Appointments: Part-time Instructor, 1956-58, Instructor, 1961-62, Assistant Professor, 1962-67, Associate Professor, 1967-72, Professor, 1972-, Director of Creative Writing, 1978-, Fanny M Dole and Arthur M Dole Professor of

English, 1980-, Emeritus, Department of English, 1993-96, Pomona College; Numerous poetry readings. Publications: Poetry: A Lake on the Earth, 1982; The Real Time Jazz Band, 1990; Few and Far Between, 1994. Chapbooks: The Complete Poems of R G Barnes, 1972; Thirty-One Views of San Bernardino, 1975; Hungry Again the Next Day, 1978; Lyrical Ballads, 1979; All Kinds of Tremendous Things Can Happen, 1982; A Pentecostal, 1985. Plays: Nacho, 1964; A Lulu for the Lively Arts, 1965; San Antonio Noh, 1966; The Cucamonga Wrapdown, 1967; The Eighth Avatar, 1970; The Death of Buster Quinine, 1972; Purple, 1973; The Detestable Life of Alfred Furkeisar, 1975; The Bradford and Barnes Poverty Circus, 1977; Tenebrae, 1979; Come Sunday, 1982; A New Death of Buster Quinine, 1994; The Sand Mirror, 1998. Other: Translations, films, and recordings. Contributions to: Many anthologies and magazines. Address: 434 West 7th Street, Claremont, CA 91711, USA.

BARNES Richard John Black, b. 13 Aug 1950, Nyasaland, Malawi. Editor. m. Lucette Aylmer, 21 June 1975, 1 son, 1 daughter. Education: Stonyhurst College, 1959-68; Royal College of Agriculture, 1970-72; Polytechnic of Central London, 1972-75. Publications: The Sun in the East, 1983; Eye on the Hill - Horse Travels in Britain, 1987; John Bell, Sculptor, 1999. Address: c/o Frontier Publishing, Windetts Farm, Long Lane, Kirstead, Norwich NR15 1EG, England.

BARNES-SVARNEY Patricia, b. 10 May 1953, Binghamton, New York, USA. Writer. m. Thomas E Svarney, 8 Jan 1977. Education: Bachelor Degree, Catawba College, 1975; Master Degree, Binghamton University, 1983. Publications: Secret World of Alex Mack: Computer Crunch!; How The New Technology Works; Secret World of Alex Mack: Junkyard Jitters/High Flyer; Star Trek Voyager; Starfleet Academy: Quarantine; Create a Space Shuttle; Asteroid: Earth Destroyer or New Frontier?; Star Trek: The Next Generation; Starfleet Academy: Loyalties; The New York Public Library Science Desk Reference; Comparing Planets; Traveler's Guide to the Solar System. Contributions to: Popular Science; Omni; Technology Review; Astronomy; Popular Astronomy; Air and Space; Smithsonian; US Air; Writer. Memberships: National Association of Science Writers; American Society of Journalists and Authors; Science Fiction and Fantasy Writers of America. Literary Agent: Agnes Birnbaum, Bleecker Street Associates. Address: 840 Hooper Road, Ste 305, Endwell, NY 13760, USA.

BARNET Max. See: **AARON Hugh.**

BARNETT Anthony (Peter John), b. 10 Sept 1941, London, England. Author; Publisher. Education: MA, University of Essex. Appointment: Editorial Director, Allardyce, Barnett, Publishers. Publications: Poetry: Blood Flow, 1975; Fear and Misadventure, 1977; The Resting Bell, Collected Poems, 1987. Prose and Poetry: Carp and Rubato, 1995; Anti-Beauty, 1999. Critical and Biographical: The Poetry of Anthony Barnett, 1993. Music Biography: Desert Sands, The Recordings and Performances of Stuff Smith, 1995; Black Gypsy, The Recordings of Eddie South, 1999. Contributions to: Anthologies, journals and periodicals. Address: c/o Allardyce, Barnett, Publishers, 14 Mount Street, Lewes, East Sussex BN7 1HL, England.

BARNETT Correlli (Douglas), b. 28 June 1927, Norbury, Surrey, England. Author. m. Ruth Murby, 28 Dec 1950, 2 daughters. Education: BA, 1951, MA, 1955, Exeter College, Oxford. Appointments: Keeper of the Churchill Archives Centre and Fellow, Churchill College, 1977-95; Defence Lecturer, Cambridge University, 1980-84; Development Fellow, Churchill College, 1997-. Publications: The Hump Organisation, 1957; The Channel Tunnel (co-author), 1958; The Desert Generals, 1960, new enlarged edition 1984; The Swordbearers, 1963; The Great War (co-author), 1964; The Lost Peace (co-author), 1966; Britain and Her Army, 1970; The Collapse of British Power, 1972; The Commanders, 1973; Marlborough, 1974; Strategy and Society, 1975; Bonaparte, 1978; The Great War, 1979; The Audit of

War, 1986; Engage the Enemy More Closely: The Royal Navy in the Second World War, 1991; The Lost Victory: British Dreams, British Realities 1945-1950, 1995. Honours: Royal Society of Literature Award, 1970; Best Television Documentary Script Award, Screenwriter's Guild, 1979; Chesney Gold Medal, Royal United Services Institute for Defence Studies, 1991; Yorkshire Post Book of the Year Award, 1991; DSc Honoris Causa, Cranfield University, 1993; CBE, 1997. Literary Agent: Bruce Hunter, David Higham Associates, 5-8 Lower John Street, Golden Square, London W1R 4HA, England. Address: Catbridge House, East Carleton, Norwich NR14 8JX, England.

BARNETT Paul (le Page), (Dennis Brezhnev, Eve Devereux, Freddie Duff-Ware, John Grant, Armytage Ware), b. 22 Nov 1949, Aberdeen, Scotland. Writer; Freelance Editor. m. Catherine Stewart, 7 July 1974, 1 daughter, plus 1 other daughter. Education: King's and University Colleges, London (no degree), 1967-68. Publications: As John Grant: Book of Time (with Colin Wilson), 1979; Aries 1, 1979; Directory of Discarded Ideas, 1981; Directory of Possibilities, with Colin Wilson, 1981; A Book of Numbers, 1982; Dreamers, 1983; The Truth About the Flaming Ghoulies, 1983; Sex Secrets of Ancient Atlantis, 1985; The Depths of Cricket, 1986; Encyclopedia of Walt Disney's Animated Characters, 1987, 2nd edition, 1997; Earthdoom (with David Langford), 1987; The Advanced Trivia Quizbook, 1987; Great Mysteries, 1988; Introduction to Viking Mythology, 1989; Great Unsolved Mysteries of Science, 1989; Eclipse of the Kai (with Joe Dever), 1989; The Dark Door Opens (with Joe Dever), 1989; Sword of the Sun (with Joe Dever), 1989; Hunting Wolf (with Joe Dever), 1990; Albion, 1991; Unexplained Mysteries of the World, 1991; The Claws of Helgedad (with Joe Dever), 1991; The Sacrifice of Ruanon (with Joe Dever), 1991; The World, 1992; Monsters, 1992; The Birthplace (with Joe Dever), 1992; The Book of the Magnakai (with Joe Dever), 1992; Legends of Lone Wolf Omnibus (with Joe Dever), 1992; The Tellings (with Joe Dever), 1993; The Lorestone of Varetta (with Joe Dever), 1993; Technical Encyclopedia of Science Fiction, by John Clute and Peter Nicholls (editor), 1993; A Thog the Mighty Text (history book), 1994; The Secret of Kazan-Oud (with Joe Dever), 1994; The Rotting Land (with Joe Dever), 1994; The Hundredfold Problem, 1994; Dr Jekyll and Mr Hyde, 1995; Encyclopedia of Fantasy Art Techniques (with Ron Tiner), 1996; Frankenstein, 1997; Encyclopedia of Fantasy (editor, with John Clute), 1997. As Paul Barnett: Translation and Expansion, Electric Children: Roots and Branches of Modern Folk-Rock, 1976; Planet Earth: An Encyclopedia of Geology (editor, with A Hallam and Peter Hutchinson); Phaidon Concise Encyclopedia of Science and Technology (contributing editor), 1978; Strider's Galaxy, 1997. As Eve Devereux: Book of World Flags, 1992; Ultimate Card Trick Book, 1994; Pamper Your Pooch, 1996; Cosset Your Cat, 1996. As Armytage Ware (joint pseudonym with Ron Tiner): Parlour Games, 1992; Conjuring Tricks, 1992; Juggling and Feats of Dexterity, 1992; Card Games, 1992. As Freddie Duff-Ware (joint pseudonym with Ron Tiner): Practical Jokes, 1993. Membership: West Country Writers' Association. Address: 17 Polsloe Road, Exter, Devon EX1 2HL, England.

BARNHARDT Wilton, b. 25 July 1960, Winston-Salem, North Carolina, USA. Writer. Education: BA, Michigan State University, 1982; MPhil, University of Oxford, 1989. Publications: Emma Who Saved My Life, 1989; Gospel, 1993. Contributions to: Magazines. Membership: Phi Beta Kappa. Address: c/o St Martin's Press Inc, 175 Fifth Avenue, New York, NY 10010, USA.

BARNRIGHT Julia. See: **BANCROFT Iris.**

BARR Densil Neve. See: **BUTTREY Douglas N.**

BARR Patricia Miriam, b. 25 Apr 1934, Norwich, Norfolk, England. Writer. Education: BA, University of Birmingham; MA, University College, London. Publications: The Coming of the Barbarians, 1967; The Deer Cry Pavilion, 1968; A Curious Life for a Lady, 1970;

To China with Love, 1972; The Memsahibs, 1976; Taming the Jungle, 1978; Chinese Alice, 1981; Uncut Jade, 1983; Kenjiro, 1985; Coromandel, 1988; The Dust in the Balance, 1989. Honour: Winston Churchill Fellowship for Historical Biography, 1972. Membership: Society of Authors. Address: 6 Mount Pleasant, Norwich NR2 2DG, England.

BARRATT Michael Fieldhouse, b. 3 Jan 1928, Leeds, England. Writer; TV Commentator. m. (1) Joan Warner, dec, 3 sons, 3 daughters, (2) Dilys Jane Morgan, 21 July 1977, 2 sons, 1 daughter. Education: LLD Hons, Aberdeen. Appointments: Editor, Nigerian Citizen; Assistant Editor, Wolverhampton Chronicle; Contract BBC, Panorama. Publications: Michael Barratt, 1973; Michael Barratt's Down-to-Earth Gardening Book, 1974; Michael Barratt's Complete Gardening Guide, 1977; Golf With Tony Jacklin, 1978; Making the Most of the Media, 1996. Address: Field House, Ascot Road, Berkshire SL6 3LD, England.

BARRERA Carlos, b. 11 Aug 1962, Burgos, Spain. University Professor; Journalist. Education: PhD, Public Communication, University of Navarra, Spain, 1991. Publications: La Informacion como Relato (co-editor), 1991; Historia del Periodismo Espanol (co-author), 1992; Periodismo y Franquismo, 1995; Sin Mordaza Veinte Años de Prensa en Democracia, 1995; El Diario Madrid: Realidad y Simbolo de Una Epoca, 1995. Contributions to: Scientific reviews. Memberships: Asociacion de Historiadores de la Comunicacion; AIERI-IAMCR (History Section); AEJMC (History Section). Address: Department of Public Communication, University of Navarra, 31080 Pamplona, Spain.

BARRETT Andrea, b. 16 Nov 1954, Boston, Massachusetts, USA. Writer. Education: BS in Biology, Union College, Schenectady, New York, 1974. Publications: Lucid Stars, 1988; Secret Harmonies, 1989; The Middle Kingdom, 1991; The Forms of Water, 1993; Ship Fever & Other Stories, 1996; The Voyage of the Narwhal, 1998. Contributions to: Anthologies and magazines. Honours: National Endowment for the Arts Fellowship in Fiction, 1992; Peden Prize, Missouri Review, 1995; Honorary Doctor of Letters, Union College, 1996; Southern Review Fiction Prize, 1996; Finalist, Los Angeles Times Book Prize, 1996; National Book Award in Fiction, 1996; Pushcart Prize, 1997; Guggenheim Fellowship, 1997. Address: c/o Wendy Weil Literary Agency, 232 Madison Avenue, Suite 1300, New York, NY 10016, USA.

BARRETT Cathlene Gillespie, b. 14 Aug 1962, Utah, USA. Poet; Publisher; Editor. m. Kevin Barrett, 29 Aug 1981, 1 son, 1 daughter. Education: College. Appointment: Publisher, Editor, Midge Literary Magazine, 1991-. Contributions to: Anthologies and periodicals. Honours: Golden Poet Award; Honorable Mention, Poet of the Year, Utah State Poetry Society. Membership: Utah State Poetry Society. Address: 2330 Tierra Rose Drive, West Jordan, UT 84084, USA.

BARRETT Charles Kingsley, b. 4 May 1917, Salford, England. Retired University Professor. m. Margaret E Heap, 16 Aug 1944, 1 son, 1 daughter. Education: BA, 1938, MA, 1942, BD, 1948, DD, 1956, Cambridge University, England. Appointments: Lecturer, 1945-58, Professor, 1958-82, University of Durham. Publications: The Holy Spirit and the Gospel Tradition, 1947; The Epistle to the Romans, 1957, new edition, 1991; From First Adam to Last, 1962; The First Epistle to the Corinthians, 1968; The Signs of an Apostle, 1970; The Second Epistle to the Corinthians, 1973; The Gospel According to St John, 1955, new edition, 1978; Freedom and Obligation, 1985; Paul: An Introduction to His Thought, 1994; The Acts of the Apostles, Volume 1, 1994, Volume 2, 1998; Jesus and the Word, 1996. Contributions to: Many learned journals. Honours: Fellow, British Academy, 1961; Burkitt Medal for Biblical Studies, 1966; Honorary DD, Hull University, 1970; Aberdeen University, 1972; DTheol, Hamburg University, 1981. Memberships: Studiorum Novi Testamenti Societas, president, 1973-74; Society for Old Testament Study;

Royal Norwegian Society of Sciences and Letters, 1991; Honorary Member, Society of Biblical Literature (USA). Address: 22 Rosemount, Pity Me, Durham DH1 5GA, England.

BARRETT Edwin Radford, (Ted Barrett), b. 26 Mar 1929, Southampton, England. Sports Writer. m. Patricia Shuttleworth, 28 Sept 1957, 1 son, 1 daughter. Education: BSc, Econ, Lond, 1950. Appointments: Reporter, Northern Daily Telegraph, 1952-56; Sub Editor, Press Association, 1956-59; Sub Editor, Reporter, Daily Telegraph, 1959-90; Sports Editor, 1979-88. Publications: Golf Chronicle/Daily Telegraph, 1994; The Ultimate Encyclopaedia of Golf, with Michael Hobbs, 1995, revised edition as Complete Book of Golf, 1998. Contributions to: Golf Weekly; Amateur Golf; the Lady Magazine. Address: 12 Oak Avenue, Upminster, Essex RM14 2LB, England.

BARRETT Jalma. See: **BOERSMA June Elaine.**

BARRETT Susan (Mary), b. 24 June 1938, Plymouth, England. Writer. m. Peter Barrett, 18 June 1960, 1 son, 1 daughter. Publications: Louisa, 1969; Moses, 1970; The Circle Sarah Drew (with Peter Barrett), 1970; The Square Ben Drew (with Peter Barrett), 1970; Noah's Ark, 1971; Private View, 1972; Rubbish, 1974; The Beacon, 1981; Travels with a Wildlife Artist: Greek Landscape and Wildlife (with Peter Barrett), 1986; Stephen and Violet, 1988; A Day in the Life of a Baby Deer: The Fawn's First Snowfall (with Peter Barrett), 1996. Address: c/o Toby Eady Associates Ltd, Orme Court, 3rd Floor, London W2 4RL England.

BARRINGTON Judith Mary, b. 7 July 1944, Brighton, England. Poet; Critic. Education: BA, 1978; MA, 1980. Appointments: West Coast Editor, Motheroot Journal, 1985-86; Poet in the Schools, Oregon, 1986-87. Publications: Deviation, 1975; Why Children (co-author), 1980; Trying to Be an Honest Woman, 1985; History and Geography, 1989; An Intimate Wilderness (editor), 1991; Contributions to: Anthologies, journals, and magazines. Honours: Fairlie Place Essay Prize, 1963; Jeanette Rankin Award for Feminist Journalism, 1983; Oregon Institute of Literary Arts Fellowships, 1989, 1992; Andre's Berger Award in Creative Non-Fiction, 1996; Stuart H Holbrook Award from Literary Arts Inc, 1997. Memberships: National Book Critics Circle; National Writers Union; Poetry Society of America. Address: 622 South East 29th Avenue, Portland, OR 97214, USA.

BARRON Judith (Welch), b. 3 Aug 1939, Youngstown, Ohio, USA. Lyricist; Author. m. John Ronald Barron, 12 Sept 1959, 1 son, 1 daughter. Education: Grove City College; BEd, Youngstown State University, 1969. Publication: There's a Boy in Here, 1992. Honour: Christopher Award, 1993. Membership: American Society of Composers, Authors and Publishers. Literary Agent: Jed Mattes. Address: 529 West 42nd Street, No 7F, New York, NY 10036, USA.

BARROS Joseph De, b. 22 July 1921, Goa. Educator; History Researcher; Writer. Education: MA, PhD, DLitt. Appointments: Professor, Principal, National Lyceum, Goa; Doctoral Research Teacher, Goa University; General Secretary, Institute Menezes, Braganza. Publications: Geography of Goa; History of Goa; Buddhism and World Peace; Francisco Luis Gomes - The Historian. Contributions to: Navhind Times; Herald; Institute Menezea Braganza; Bulletin; R C Acau; Gomantak Times. Memberships: Indian Academy of Science; Academia Portuguesa da Historia; Academia Canadense de Historia; Geographic Society, Lisbon; Royal Asiatic Society of London; Indian History Congress, New Delhi; World Academy of Arts and Culture; Institute Menezes Braganza. Address: PO Box 221, Institute Menezes Braganza, Panaji Gao, India.

BARROW Iris (Lena), b. 8 Oct 1933, Auckland, New Zealand. Psychological Counsellor; Human Resources Consultant; Author. m. Robert Barrow, 1 son, 4 daughters. Education: ATCL, Speech and Communications, 1952. Appointment: Head, Seminar/Counselling Agency; Human Resources

Consultant. Publications: Your Marriage Can Work, 1979; Relax and Come Alive (with Helen Place), 1981; Know Your Strengths and Be Confident, 1982; You Can Communicate, 1983; 15 Steps to Overcome Anxiety and Depression, 1985; From Strength to Strength, 1988; Make Peace with Yourself, 1990; You Can Do It, 1993; How to Lead and Motivate Others, 1995. Other: Radio plays; 8 self-help personal and interpersonal skills-training tapes, 1981-89; Video training tape: Celebrating Life with Iris Barrow, 1990. Contributions to: Various periodicals. Membership: New Zealand PEN. Address: 334 Onemana Drive, Onemana Beach, Whangamata, New Zealand.

BARROW Jedediah. See: **BENSON Gerard John.**

BARROW Robin St Clair, b. 18 Nov 1944, Oxford, England. Professor of Education; Author. Education: BA, MA, 1967, Oxford University; Postgraduate Certificate in Education, Institute of Education, London, 1968; PhD, University of London, 1972. Appointments: Lecturer in Philosophy of Education, 1972-80, Personal Readership in Education, 1980-82, University of Leicester; Visiting Professor of Philosophy of Education, University of Western Ontario, 1977-78; Professor of Education, 1982-, Dean of Education, 1992-, Simon Fraser University. Burnaby, British Columbia. Publications: Athenian Democracy, 1973, 2nd edition, 1976; An Introduction to the Philosophy of Education, 1974, 3rd edition, 1987; Sparta, 1975; Plato, Utilitarianism and Education, 1975; Moral Philosophy for Education, 1975; Greek and Roman Education, 1976; Plato and Education, 1976; Common Sense and the Curriculum, 1976; Plato's Apology, 1978; The Canadian Curriculum: A Personal View, 1978; Radical Education, 1978; Happiness, 1979; The Philosophy of Schooling, 1981, 2nd edition, 1983; Injustice, Inequality and Ethics, 1982; Language and Thought: Rethinking Language Across the Curriculum, 1982; Giving Teaching Back to Teachers: A Critical Introduction to Curriculum Theory, 1984; A Critical Dictionary of Educational Concepts: An Appraisal of Selected Ideas and Issues in Educational Theory and Practice, 1986, 2nd edition, 1990; Understanding Skills: Thinking, Feeling and Caring, 1990; Utilitarianism: A Contemporary Statement, 1991; Beyond Liberal Education (editor with Patricia White), 1993; Language, Intelligence and Thought, 1993. Contributions to: Books and scholarly journals. Memberships: Philosophy of Education Society of Great Britain, vice chairman, 1980-83; Northwestern Philosophy of Education Society of North America, president, 1984-85; Canadian Philosophy of Education Society, president, 1990-91; Royal Society of Canada, fellow, 1996-. Address: Faculty of Education, Simon Fraser University, Burnaby, British Columbia V5A 1S6, Canada.

BARRY James P, b. 23 Oct 1918, Alton, Illinois, USA. Writer; Editor. m. Anne Elizabeth Jackson, 16 Apr 1966. Education: BA cum laude, Ohio State University. Appointments: Director, Ohioana Library Association, 1977-88; Editor, Ohioana Quarterly, 1977-88. Publications: Georgian Bay: The Sixth Great Lake, 1968, 3rd edition, 1995; The Battle of Lake Erie, 1970; Bloody Kansas, 1972; The Noble Experiment, 1972; The Fate of the Lakes, 1972; The Louisiana Purchase, 1973; Ships of the Great Lakes: 300 Years of Navigation, 1973, revised edition, 1996; Wrecks and Rescues of the Great Lakes, 1981; Georgian Bay: An Illustrated History, 1992; Old Forts of the Great Lakes, 1994. Honours: American Society of State and Local History Award, 1974; Great Lakes Historian of the Year, Marine History Society of Detroit, 1995. Membership: Ohioana Library Association. Address: 353 Fairway Boulevard, Columbus, OH 43213, USA.

BARRY Mike. See: **MALZBERG Barry.**

BARRY Sebastian, b. 5 July 1955, Dublin, Ireland. Writer; Dramatist; Poet. Education: LCC, Newend, London; Catholic University School, Dublin; BA, Trinity College, Dublin, 1977. Appointments: Iowa International Writing Fellowship, 1984; Writer in Association, Abbey Theatre, Dublin, 1989-90; Director of Board, Abbey

Theatre, 1989-90. Publications: The Engine of Owl-Light, 1987; Boss Grady's Boys, play, 1989; Fanny Hawke Goes to the Mainland Forever, verse, 1989. Contributions to: Antaeus; London Review of Books; Stand; Observer. Honours: Arts Council Bursary, 1982; Hawthornden International Fellowships, 1985, 1988; BBC/Stewart Parker Award, 1989. Memberships: Irish Writers' Union; Aosdana; Half Moon Swimming Club. Literary Agent: Curtis Brown Ltd, 162-168 Regent Street, London, England. Address: c/o The Abbey Theatre, Abbey Street, Dublin 1, Ireland.

BARSTOW Stan(ley), b. 28 June 1928, Horbury, Yorkshire, England. Author; Playwright; Scriptwriter. m. Constance Mary Kershaw, 8 Sept 1951, 1 son, 1 daughter. Publications: Novels: A Kind of Loving, 1960; Ask Me Tomorrow, 1962; Joby, 1964; The Watchers on the Shore, 1966; A Raging Calm, 1968; The Right True End, 1976; A Brother's Tale, 1980; Just You Wait and See, 1986; B-Movie, 1987; Give Us This Day, 1989; Next of Kin, 1991. Short Stories: The Desperados, 1961; A Season with Eros, 1971; The Glad Eye and Other Stories, 1984. Plays: Listen for the Trains, Love, 1970; Stringer's Last Stand (with Alfred Bradley), 1971. Other: Television plays and scripts. Honours: Best British Dramatization Award, Writers Guild of Great Britain, 1974; Best Drama Series Award, British Broadcasting Press Guild, 1974; Writer's Award, Royal Television Society, 1975; Honorary MA, Open University, 1982; Honorary Fellow, Bretton College, 1985. Address: c/o The Agency, 24 Pottery Lane, London W11 4LZ, England.

BARTH John (Simmons), b. 27 May 1930, Cambridge, Maryland, USA. Professor Emeritus; Author. m. (1) Harriette Anne Strickland, 11 Jan 1950, div 1969, 2 sons, 1 daughter, (2) Shelly Rosenberg, 27 Dec 1970. Education: Juilliard School of Music; AB, 1951, MA, 1952, Johns Hopkins University. Appointments: Instructor, 1953-56, Assistant Professor, 1957-60, Associate Professor, 1960-65, of English, Pennsylvania State University; Professor of English, 1965-71, Edward H Butler Professor of English, 1971-73, State University of New York at Buffalo; Alumni Centennial Professor of English and Creative Writing, 1973-90, Professor Emeritus, 1990-, Johns Hopkins University. Publications: Fiction: The Floating Opera, 1956, revised edition, 1967; The End of the Road, 1958, revised edition, 1967; The Sot-Weed Factor, 1960, revised edition, 1967; Giles, Goat-Boy: or, the Revised New Syllabus, 1966; Lost in the Funhouse: Fiction for Print, Tape, Live Voice, 1964; Chimera, 1972; LETTERS, 1979; Sabbatical: A Romance, 1982; Tidewater Tales: A Novel, 1987; The Last Voyage of Somebody the Sailor, 1991; Once Upon a Time: A Floating Opera, 1994; On with the Story (short stories), 1996. Non-Fiction: The Literature of Exhaustion, and the Literature of Replenishment, 1982; The Friday Book: Essays and Other Nonfiction, 1984; Don't Count on It: A Note on the Number of 1001 Nights, 1984; Further Fridays: Essays, Lectures, and Other Nonfiction, 1984-1994, 1995. Contributions to: Books and many periodicals. Honours: Brandeis University Creative Arts Award, 1965; Rockefeller Foundation Grant, 1965-66; National Institute of Arts and Letters Grant, 1966; National Book Award, 1973; F Scott Fitzgerald Award, 1997; Lannan Foundation Award, 1998; PEN/Malamud Award, 1998. Memberships: American Academy and Institute of Arts and Letters; American Academy of Arts and Sciences. Address: Writing Seminars, John Hopkins University, Baltimore, MD 21218, USA.

BARTH J(ohn) Robert, b. 23 Feb 1931, Buffalo, New York, USA. College Dean; Writer. Education: AB, 1954, MA, 1956, Fordham University; PhL, Bellarmine College, 1955; STB, 1961, STL, 1962, Woodstock College; PhD in English, Harvard University, 1967. Appointments: Society of Jesus; Assistant Professor of English, Canisius College, Buffalo, 1967-70; Assistant Professor of English, Harvard University, 1970-74; Associate Professor of English, 1974-77, Professor of English, 1977-88, Chairman, Department of English, 1980-83, University of Missouri-Columbia; Thomas I Gasson Professor of English, 1985-86, Dean, College of Arts and Sciences, 1988-, Boston College. Publications: Coleridge and Christian Doctrine, 1969; Religious Perspectives in Faulkner's Fiction: Yoknapatawpha and Beyond (editor), 1972; The Symbolic Imagination: Coleridge and the Romantic Tradition, 1977; Marginalia: The Collected Works of Samuel Taylor Coleridge (editor with George Whalley), 1984-; Coleridge and the Power of Love, 1988; Coleridge, Keats and the Imagination: Romanticism and Adam's Dream-Essays in Honor of Walter Jackson Bate (editor with John L Mahoney), 1990. Contributions to: Books and journals. Honour: Book of the Year Award, Conference on Christianity and Literature, 1977. Memberships: American Association of University Professors; Conference on Christianity and Literature; Friends of Coleridge; Keats-Shelley Association; Modern Language Association; Wordsworth-Coleridge Association, president, 1979. Address: Office of the Dean, College of Arts and Sciences, Boston College, Chestnut Hill, MA 02167, USA.

BARTHELME Frederick, b. 10 Oct 1943, Houston, Texas, USA. Professor of English; Writer; Editor. Education: Tulane University, 1961-62; University of Houston, 1962-65, 1966-67; Museum of Fine Art, Houston, 1965-66; MA, Johns Hopkins University, 1977. Appointments: Assistant Director, Kornblee Gallery, New York, 1967-68; Creative Director, BMA Advertising, Houston, 1971-73; Senior Writer, GDL&W Advertising, Houston, 1973-76; Teaching Fellow, Johns Hopkins University, 1976-77; Professor of English, Director, Center for Writers, Editor, Mississippi Review, University of Southern Mississippi, Hattiesburg, 1977-. Publications: Rangoon (stories), 1970; War & War, 1971; Moon Deluxe (stories), 1983; Second Marriage, 1984; Tracer, 1985; Chroma (stories), 1987; Two Against One, 1988; Natural Selection, 1990; The Brothers, 1993; Painted Desert, 1995; Bob the Gambler, 1997. Screenplays: Second Marriage, 1985; Tracer, 1986-87. Contributions to: Periodicals. Honour: National Endowment for the Arts Grant, 1980. Memberships: Associated Writing Programs; Author's Guild; Coordinating Council of Literary Magazines; PEN; Writers Guild. Address: 203 Sherwood Drive, Hattiesburg, MS 39402, USA.

BARTHELMESS Klaus, b. 4 Sept 1955, Cologne, Germany. Historian; Whaling Expert. m. Helga Kietzmann, 1992, 2 sons. Education: MA, University of Cologne, 1989 (PhD pending). Appointments: Kendall Whaling Museum, Sharon, Massachusetts, 1987; German Maritime Museum, Bremerhaven, 1991; Cologne Historic Museum, 1996. Publications: Das Bild des Wals, 1982; Monstrum Horrendum (with Joachim Münzing), 1991; Whaling - Con and Pro, 1994; Zoologische Einblattdrucke und Flugschriften vor 1800 (with Ingrid Faust and Klaus Stopp), 5 vols, 1998. Dozens of scholarly articles on whaling, sealing and the history of cetology. Memberships: Editorial Board of Historisch-Meereskundliches Jahrbuch, Berlin and Hamburg; International Network for Whaling Digest, Edmonton, Alberta. Address: PO Box 620255, 50695 Cologne, Germany.

BARTLETT Christopher John, b. 12 Oct 1931, Bournemouth, England. Emeritus and Honorary Professor of International History; Writer. m. Shirley Maureen Briggs, 7 Aug 1958, 3 sons. Education: BA, 1st Class Honours, History, University College, Exeter, 1953; PhD, International History, London School of Economics, 1956. Appointments: Assistant Lecturer, University of Edinburgh, 1957-59; Lecturer in Modern History, University of the West Indies, Jamaica, 1959-62, Queen's College, Dundee, 1962-68; Reader in International History, 1968-78, Professor of International History, 1978-96, Head, Department of History, 1983-88, Emeritus and Honorary Professor of International History, 1996-, University of Dundee. Publications: Great Britain and Sea Power, 1815-53, 1963; Castlereagh, 1966; Britain Pre-eminent: Studies of British World Influence in the Nineteenth Century (editor), 1969; The Long Retreat: A Short History of British Defence Policy, 1945-70, 1972; The Rise and Fall of the Pax Americana: American Foreign Policy in the Twentieth Century, 1974; A History of Postwar Britain, 1945-74, 1977; The Global Conflict, 1880-1970: The International Rivalry of the Great Powers, 1984, 2nd edition, revised, 1994; British Foreign Policy in the Twentieth Century, 1989; 'The Special Relationship': A Political History or Anglo-American Relations Since 1945, 1992; Defence and Diplomacy: Britain and the Great Powers, 1815-1914, 1993; Peace, War and the European Great Powers, 1814-1914, 1996. Contributions to: UK Chapters, Annual Register, 1987-97; Scholarly books and journals. Honours: Royal Historical Society, fellow; Royal Society of Edinburgh, fellow. Address: c/o Department of History, University of Dundee DD1 4HN, Scotland.

BARTLETT Elizabeth, b. 28 Apr 1924, Deal, Kent, England. Poet. Education: Dover County School for Girls, 1935-39. Appointment: Lecturer, Workers Education Association, Burgess Hill, 1960-63. Publications: A Lifetime of Dying, 1979; Strange Territory, 1983; The Czar is Dead, 1986; Look, No Face, 1991; Instead of a Mass, 1991; Two Women Dancing, 1994. Honours: Cheltenham Poetry Competition Prize, 1982; Arts Council Bursary, 1985; Cholmendeley Award, Society of Authors, 1996. Address: 17 St John's Avenue, Burgess Hill, West Sussex RH15 8HJ, England.

BARTOSZEWSKI Wladyslaw, b. 19 Feb 1922, Warsaw, Poland. Writer; Historian; Diplomat. Education: Doctor honoris causa, Polish University in exile, London, 1981; Baltimore Hebrew College, USA, 1984. Appointments: Vice President, Institute for Polish Jewish Studies, Oxford, England; Visiting Professor, Munich, Eichstaett, Augsburg, 1983-90; Voted Chairman, International Council of the Museum, Auschwitz, 1990; Polish Ambassador in Vienna, 1990-95; Polish Foreign Minister, 1995; Senator, 1997-. Publications: Warsaw Death Ring, 1939-44, 2nd edition, 1970; The Samaritans, Heroes of the Holocaust (with Z Lewin), 1970; 1859 Days of Warsaw, 1974; The Warsaw Ghetto As It Really Was, 1983; Days of the Fighting Capital: A Chronicle of the Warsaw Uprising, 1984; On the Road to Independence, 1987; Experiences of My Life, 1989. Contributions to: Various Catholic Magazines and Papers. Honours: Polish Military Cross, 1944; Medal and Title of the Righteous Among the Nations, the Martyrs and Heroes Remembrance Yad Vashem, Jerusalem, 1963; Prize, Alfred Jurzykowski Foundation, New York, 1967; Prize, Polish Pen, Warsaw, 1975; Herder Prize, Vienna, 1983; Peace Prize, German Publishers' and Booksellers Association, 1986; Commander, Polonia Restituta (with Star), London, 1986; Honorary Citizen of the State of Israel, 1991; Distinguished Service Cross, Order of Merit of Germany, 1991; Austrian Cross of Honour for Science and Art, 1st Class, 1992; R Guardini Prize, Munich, 1995; Mitteleuropa Prize, Vienna, 1995; Brücken Prize, Regensburg, 1995; St Vincent de Paul Award, Chicago, 1995; Order of the White Eagle, Warsaw, 1995; Grand Decoration of Honour in Gold with Sash for Services to the Republic of Austria, Vienna, 1995; Heinrich Heine Prize, Düsseldorf, 1996; Honorary Doctorate, University of Wroclaw, Poland, 1996. Memberships: Polish PEN, secretary general, 1972-83, board member, 1988-90, vice president, 1995-; French PEN, associate member. Address: ul Karolinki 12, 02 635 Warsaw, Poland.

BARTSCH William Henry, b. 18 Jan 1933, Washington, District of Columbia, USA. Military Historian; Development Economist. m. Lila Sepehri, 5 Aug 1965, 1 son, 1 daughter. Education: BA, Washington and Lee University, 1955; Fulbright Fellow to Sweden, 1956-57; MA, University of Virginia, 1959; PhD, University of London, 1970. Publications: Problems of Employment Creation in Iran, 1970; Draft Chapters of Human Resources for Development Plans of Fiji, Marshall Islands and Federated States of Micronsia, 1975, 1986-90; Employment and Technology Choice in Asian Agriculture, 1977; Doomed at the Start, 1992. Contributions to: Articles on employment problems and planning in developing countries, 1971-90, also articles in Air Power Histoy and Marine Corps Gazette. Honour: Phi Beta Kappa, 1955; Robert D Heinl Award for Best Article published in Marine Corps History, 1998. Memberships: American Economic Association; Society for Military

History. Address: 2434 Brussels Court, Reston, VA 22091, USA.

BARZUN Jacques (Martin), b. 30 Nov 1907, Créteil, France (US citizen, 1933). Historian; Educator. m. (1) Mariana Lowell, Aug 1936, dec 1979, 2 sons, 1 daughter, (2) Marguerite Davenport, June 1980. Education: AB, 1927, MA, 1928, PhD, 1932, Columbia University. Appointments: Lecturer, 1927-29, Assistant Professor, 1938-42, Associate Professor, 1942-45, Professor, 1945-67, Dean, Graduate Faculties, 1955-58, Dean, Faculties and Provost, 1958-67, Professor Emeritus, 1967-, Columbia University; Literary Advisor, Charles Scribner's Sons, publishers, New York City, 1975-93. Publications: The French Race: Theories of Its Origins and Their Social and Political Implications Prior to the Revolution, 1932; Race: A Study in Modern Superstition, 1937, revised edition as Race: A Study in Superstition, 1956; Of Human Freedom, 1939, revised edition, 1964; Darwin, Marx, Wagner: Critique of a Heritage, 1941, revised edition, 1958; Romanticism and the Modern Ego, 1943, 2nd edition, revised, as Classic, Romantic, and Modern, 1961; Introduction to Naval History (with Paul H Beik, George Crothers and E O Golob), 1944; Teacher in America, 1945; Berlioz and the Romantic Century, 1950, 3rd edition, revised, 1969; God's Country and Mine: A Declaration of Love Spiced with a Few Harsh Words, 1954; Music in American Life, 1956; The Energies of Art: Studies of Authors, Classic and Modern, 1956; The Modern Researcher (with Henry F Graff), 1957, 5th edition, 1993; Lincoln the Literary Genius, 1959; The House of Intellect, 1959, 2nd edition, 1975; Science: The Glorious Entertainment, 1964; The American University: How It Runs, Where It Is Going, 1968; On Writing, Editing and Publishing: Essays Explicative and Horatory, 1971; A Catalogue of Crime (with Wendell Hertig Taylor), 1971; The Use and Abuse of Art, 1974; Clio and the Doctors: Psycho-History, Quanto-History and History, 1974; Simple and Direct: A Rhetoric for Writers, 1975; A Stroll with William James, 1983; A Word or Two Before You Go..., 1986; The Culture We Deserve, 1989; Begin Here: On Teaching and Learning, 1990; An Essay on French Verse, 1991. Other: Editor and translator of several books. Contributions to: Scholarly and non-scholarly periodicals. Honours: Chevalier de la Légion d'Honneur, France; George Polk Memorial Award, 1967. Memberships: American Academy of Arts and Letters, president, 1972-75, 1977-78; American Academy of Arts and Sciences; American Philosophical Society; Phi Beta Kappa; Royal Society of Arts, fellow; Royal Society of Literature; Society of American Historians. Address: 18 Wolfeton Way, San Antonio, TX 78218-6045, USA.

BASINGER Jeanine (Deyling), b. 3 Feb 1936, Ravenden, Arkansas, USA. Professor of Film Studies; Curator; Writer. m. John Peter Basinger, 22 Sept 1967, 1 daughter. Education: BS, 1957, MS, 1959, South Dakota State University. Appointments: Instructor, South Dakota State University, 1958-59; Teaching Associate, 1971-72, Adjunct Lecturer, 1972-76, Adjunct Associate Professor, 1976-80, Associate Professor, 1980-84, Professor, 1984-88, Corwin-Fuller Professor of Film Studies, 1988-, Wesleyan University; Founder-Curator, Wesleyan Cinema Archives, 1985-. Publications: Working with Kazan (editor with John Frazer and Joseph W Reed), 1973; Shirley Temple, 1975; Gene Kelly, 1976; Lana Turner, 1977; Anthony Mann: A Critical Analysis, 1979; Anatomy of a Genre: World War II Combat Films, 1986; The It's A Wonderful Life Book, 1986; A Woman's View: How Hollywood Saw Women, 1930-1960, 1993; American Cinema: 100 Years of Filmmaking, 1994. Contributions to: Books and periodicals. Honours: Best Film Book of the Year Nomination, National Film Society, 1976; Distinguished Alumni Award, 1994 and Honorary PhD, 1996, South Dakota State University; Outstanding Teaching Award, Wesleyan University, 1996. Memberships: American Film Institute, trustee; Phi Kappa Phi. Address: 133 Lincoln Street, Middletown, CT 06457, USA.

BASS Jack, b. 24 June 1934, Columbia, South Carolina, USA. Writer. m. Carolyn McClung, 3 Mar 1957, div 1984, (2) Alice Calsaniss, 22 June 1984, 2 sons, 1 daughter. Education: AB, 1956, MA, 1976, Harvard University. Appointments: Bureau Chief, Knight Newspapers, Columbia, South Carolina, 1966-73; Visiting Research Fellow, Institute of Policy Sciences and Public Affairs, Duke University, 1973-75; Writer-in-Residence, South Carolina State College, 1975-78; Research Fellow, Director of American South Special Projects, University of South Carolina, 1979-85. Publications: The Orangeburg Massacre (with Jack Nelson), 1970; You Can't Eat Magnolias (co-author), 1972; Porgy Comes Home, 1972; The Transformation of Southern Politics (with Walter DeVires), 1978; Unlikely Heroes, 1981; The American South Comes of Age, 1985; Taming the Storm, 1993. Address: 2327 Terrace Way, Columbia, SC 29205, USA.

BASS Rick, b. 7 Mar 1958, Fort Worth, Texas, USA. Writer. Education: BS, Utah State University, 1979. Publications: The Deer Pasture, 1985; Wild to the Heart, 1987; Oil Notes, 1989; The Watch: Stories, 1989; Platte River, 1994; The Lost Grizzlies, 1995; In the Loyal Mountains: Stories, 1995; The Book of YAAK, 1996; Where the Sea Used to Be, 1998. Contributions to: Anthologies and periodicals. Honours: Pushcart Prize; O Henry Award; PEN-Nelson Award, 1988. Address: 3801 Vinal Lake Road, Troy, MT 59935, USA.

BASS Thomas (Alden), b. 9 Mar 1951, Chagrin Falls, Ohio, USA. Writer. Education: AB, University of Chicago, 1973; PhD, University of California, 1980. Publications: The Eudaemonic Pie, 1985; Camping with the Prince and Other Tales of Science in Africa, 1990; Reinventing the Future: Conversations with the World's Leading Scientists, 1993; Vietnamerica: The War Comes Home, 1996. Contributions to: Audubon; New York Times; Smithonian; Wired. Memberships: Authors Guild; PEN. Address: 31 Rue Saint Placide, Paris 75006, France.

BASSETT Ronald Leslie, (William Clive), b. 10 Apr 1924, London, England. Writer. Appointments: Served with King's Royal Rifle Corps, 1938-39, Royal Navy, 1940-54; Full-time Author, Documentary and Medical Film Scriptwriter, 1958-. Publications: The Carthaginian, 1963; The Pompeians, 1965; Witchfinder General, 1966; Amorous Trooper, 1968; Rebecca's Brat, 1969; Kill the Stuart, 1970; Dando on Delhi Ridge (as W Clive), 1971; Dando and the Summer Palace (as W Clive), 1972; Dando and the Mad Emperor (as W Clive), 1973; The Tune That They Play (as W Clive), 1974; Blood of an Englishman (as W Clive), 1975; Fighting Mac (as W Clive), 1976; Tinfish Run, 1977; Pierhead Jump, 1978; Neptune Landing, 1979; Guns of Evening, 1980; Battle-Cruisers, 1982. Address: 19 Binstead Drive, Blackwater, Camberley, Surrey, England.

BASSIL Andrea, b. 16 Sept 1948, Manchester, England. Children's Book Author/Illustrator. Education: Dip AD, Edinburgh College of Art, 1967-72; SCSE, Moray House College of Education, 1972-73. Appointments: Full Time Assistant Teacher of Art, Mussleburgh Grammar School, 1973-74, St Margaret's School Edinburgh, 1974-85; ND and HND Course Director, Natural History Illustration, Bournemouth, 1985-90; Head of Graphic Arts and Illustration, Anglia Polytechnic University, 1990-94; Children's Author/Illustrator, 1994-. Publications include: Terrormazia, 1995; Percy the Park Keeper Activity Book, 1996; Fairy Tales, 1996; Where is Percy's Dinner?, 1996; Ble Mae Cinio Bonso?, 1996; Follow the Kite, 1997; In the Jungle, 1998; On the Farm, 1998; People in My Neighborhood, 1998; Follow the Kite, 1998; I Can Spell Three Letter Words, 1998; Let's all Dig and Burrow, 1998; Lets all Hang and Dangle, 1998; Lets all Swim and Dive, 1999; Lets all Leap and Jump, 1999. Honour: Goldsmith's Hall, Travelling Scholarship, 1981. Membership: Society of Authors. Literary Agent: Rosemary Canter, Peters Fraser and Dunlop. Address: 503/504 The Chambers, Chelsea Harbour, London S10 0XF, England.

BATARDE Eduarde. See: **THOMPSON Tom.**

BATCHELOR John Barham, b. 15 Mar 1942, Farnborough, England. Professor of English Literature; Writer; Editor. m. Henrietta Jane Letts, 14 Sept 1968, 2 sons, 1 daughter. Education: MA, 1964, PhD, 1969, Magdalene College, Cambridge; MA, University of New Brunswick, 1965. Appointments: Lecturer in English, Birmingham University, 1968-76; Fellow and Tutor, New College, Oxford, 1976-90; Joseph Cowen Professor of English Literature, University of Newcastle upon Tyne, 1990-. Publications: Mervyn Peake, 1974; Breathless Hush (novel), 1974; The Edwardian Novelists, 1982; H G Wells, 1985; Virginia Woolf, 1991; The Life of Joseph Conrad: A Critical Biography, 1994; The Art of Literary Biography (editor), 1995; Shakespearean Continuities (joint editor), 1997.Contributions to: Times Literary Supplement; Observer; Economist; Articles in English, Yearbook of English Studies; Review of English Studies. Membership: International Association of Professors of English. Literary Agent: Felicity Bryan, 2a North Parade, Oxford. Address: Department of English, University of Newcastle, Newcastle upon Tyne NE1 7RU, England.

BATE (Andrew) Jonathan, b. 26 June 1958, Sevenoaks, Kent, England. Professor of English Literature; Critic; Novelist. m. (1) Hilary Gaskin, 1984, div 1995, (2) Paula Byrne, 1996, 1 son. Education: MA, 1980, PhD, 1984, St Catharine's College, Cambridge. Appointments: Harkness Fellow, Harvard University, 1980-81; Research Fellow, St Catharine's College, Cambridge, 1983-85; Fellow, Trinity Hall, and Lecturer, Trinity Hall and Girton College, Cambridge, 1985-90; Visiting Associate Professor, University of California at Los Angeles, 1989; King Alfred Professor of English Literature, University of Liverpool, 1991-; Research Reader, British Academy, 1994-96. Publications: Shakespeare and the English Romantic Imagination, 1986; Charles Lamb: Essays of Elia (editor), 1987; Shakespearean Constitutions: Politics, Theatre, Criticism 1730-1830, 1989; Romantic Ecology: Wordsworth and the Environmental Tradition, 1991; The Romantics on Shakespeare (editor), 1992; Shakespeare and Ovid, 1993; The Arden Shakespeare: Titus Andronicus (editor), 1995; Shakespeare: An Illustrated Stage History (editor), 1996; The Genius of Shakespeare, 1997; The Cure for Love, 1998. Contributions to: Scholarly publications. Honour: Calvin & Rose Hoffman Prize, 1996. Address: c/o Department of English, University of Liverpool, PO Box 147, Liverpool L69 3BX, England.

BATE Walter Jackson, b. 23 May 1918, Mankato, Minnesota, USA. Professor of English; Writer. Education: AB, 1939, MA, 1940, PhD, 1942, Harvard University. Appointments: Faculty, 1946-56, Professor of English, 1956-, Chairman, Department of English, 1956-63, 1966-68, Abbott Lawrence Lowell Professor of the Humanities, 1962-79, Kingsley Porter University Professor, 1979-, Harvard University; Various guest professorships. Publications: Negative Capability, 1939; The Stylistic Development of Keats, 1945; From Classic to Romantic, 1946; Criticism: The Major Texts, 1952; The Achievement of Samuel Johnson, 1955; Prefaces to Criticism, 1959; The Writings of Edmund Burke, 1960; John Keats, 1963; The Yale Edition of the Works of Samuel Johnson (co-editor), Vol II, 1963, Vols III-V, 1969; Coleridge, 1968; The Burden of the Past and the English Poet, 1970; Samuel Johnson, 1977; The Collected Works of Samuel Taylor Coleridge: Biographia Literaria (co-editor), 1982; British and American Poets, 1985; Harvard Scholars in English, 1991. Contributions to: Books and professional journals. Honours: Guggenheim Fellowships, 1956, 1965; Christian Gauss Awards, 1956, 1964, 1970; Pulitzer Prizes in Biography, 1964, 1978; Notable Book Award, 1978; National Book Critics Circle Award, 1978; Various honorary doctorates. Memberships: American Academy of Arts and Sciences; American Philosophical Society; British Academy; Phi Beta Kappa. Address: c/o Warren House, Harvard University, Cambridge, MA 02138, USA.

BATEMAN Philip Christiaan, b. 5 Jan 1945, Cape Town, South Africa. World Champion: Creative Thinking; Journalist; Copywriter; Author; Researcher; Lecturer/Tutor; Director of Companies; Trustee; Creative Director. Education: St Andrew's, Cape College for Advanced Technical Education, British Association of Industrial Editors; MCB (Dip), Eng; F Inst C; MSAAIE;

APR; Cert Com Art; MCIJ. Appointments: Artist/Writer, The Cape Argus, 1967-68; Creative Manager, one of three founder editors, South African edition of Reader's Digest (SARD), 1968-74; Consultant, 1974-79; Collaborated w Pulitzer author James Michener on world bestseller The Covenant, 1978-79; Creative Director, South African Historical Mint (Pty) Ltd; Edited Connoisseur, 1980-81, Financial Columnist for Woman's Value, Nov 1993-97; Offshoots and Medical Contributor, Wine magazine, 1997-; Numerous Directorships including: Automobile Association The Motorist Publications (Pty) Ltd., Reader's Digest Investments (Pty) Ltd., Reader's Digest Association South Africa (Pty) Ltd., Ritz Trade 102 (Pty) Ltd., Heritage Collection Holdings Ltd., The Heritage Collection (Pty) Ltd., Heritage Properties (Pty) Ltd., South African Historical Mint (Pty) Ltd., Lamburn International Ltd., Balph Trading (Pty) Ltd., Anchor International Exports CC, Sureflo CC, Four University Street (Pty) Ltd., S A Home and Leisure (Pty) Ltd. Publications: Author, numerous articles in magazines inclng: The Reader's Digest; Personality, Farmer's Weekly; Contributor to MENSA In-News, Telicom (USA), Mensa International (Canada); Contributor to newspapers, originator of brochures, booklets and mailings; Author, bibliographies and books including: Generals of the Anglo-Boer War, 1977; Pioneers of Southern Africa, 1978; Talk to Syfrets(ms), 1983. Honours: Guest Speaker, Marketing Conference, Cannes, France, 1971; Diploma Winner, Agfa Photo Comp, Germany, 1972; Fair Lady Writing Prize, 1974; Top in South Africa in Public Relations Institute of South Africa (PRISA); Won for SARD State President's Award for Combatting Inflation, Top in South Africa in final PRISA Exam, 1978; Harry Klein Award Winner; Everton Offset Trophy, 1980; Designed Queen Mother's 80th Birthday Medallion, 1980; Honoured by official Vote of Thanks from Most Venerable Order of the Hospital of St John of Jerusalem, 1983; Place Winner, BBC Poetry Competition, 1997; equalled several IQ sub-test world records, various dates; achieved highest marks in world in Test of Poetic Ingenuity, 1998; Citation for Meritorious Achievement, 1998; Fourth in World in MSO Creative Thinking Champs, Hammersmith, 1998; Distinguished Leadership Award, Decree of Merit 1998, 20th Century Award; Outstanding Achievement Diploma and more. One of only three South African MENSA members to have qualified for Fellowship of US ultra-high IQ (genius) Society, International Society for Philosophical Enquiry; Achieved World Championship, Creative Thinking; Gold Medal, First Mind Sports Olympiad in London, 1989; one of three winners in 'Wine' Writer of the Year Competition, 1996; Honoured by biographical articles in, inter alia, Style, YOU, Outstanding People of the 20th Century, 500 Leaders of Influence, Telicom, USA, 1997; CTM qualification, Toastmasters, 1998. Memberships: Kelvin Grove, Friends of SA Library, English Assoc, PEN, DMA, LIAP, IBT, MENSA, National Association for Gifted and Talented Children in South Africa, History Society, Toastmasters, Shakespeare Oxford Society, Chartered Institute of Journalists; Charter Member, Library of International Academy of Philosophy, 1997; On Cape Executive, DMA Chairman, Direct Mail Special Interest group, DMA, 1997; Council Member Free Market Foundation, 1998. Life Member: Classical Association, British Association of Communicators in Business, ISPE. Hobbies: History; Psychology; Books; Research; People. Address: Windsor House, 2 Maclear Road, Bishopscourt 7700, South Africa.

BATES Harry. See: **HOME Stewart Ramsay.**

BATES Milton J(ames), b. 4 June 1945, Warrensburg, Missouri, USA. Professor of English; Writer. m. 6 May 1972, 1 son, 1 daughter. Education: BA, St Louis University, 1968; MA, 1972, PhD, 1977, University of California at Berkeley. Appointments: Assistant Professor of English, Williams College, 1975-81; Assistant Professor, 1981-86, Associate Professor, 1986-91, Professor, 1991-, of English, Marquette University. Publications: Wallace Stevens: A Mythology of Self, 1985; Sur Plusieurs Beaux Sujects: Wallace Stevens' Commonplace Book, 1989; Wallace Stevens: Opus Posthumous, revised edition, 1989; The Wars We Took to Vietnam: Cultural Conflict and Storytelling, 1996. Contributions to: Articles and book reviews in journals and periodicals. Honours: Notable Book of the Year, New York Times Book Review, 1985; Outstanding Achievement in Literature, Wisconsin Library Association, 1985; National Book Critics Circle Award Nomination, 1985; Guggenheim Fellowship, 1989-90; Kenneth Kingery Scholarly Book Award, 1996; Council for Wisconsin Writers Scholarly Book Award, 1996. Membership: Wallace Stevens Society, secretary, 1990-. Address: Department of English, Marquette University, PO Box 1881, Milwaukee, WI 53201, USA.

BATTESTIN Martin C(arey), b. 25 Mar 1930, New York, New York, USA. Professor of English; Author. m. Ruthe Rootes, 14 June 1963, 1 son, 1 daughter. Education: BA, 1952, PhD, 1958, Princeton University. Appointments: Instructor, 1956-58, Assistant Professor, 1958-61, Wesleyan University; Assistant Professor, 1961-63, Associate Professor, 1963-67, Professor, 1967-75, William R Kenan, Jr, Professor of English, 1975-98, Emeritus, 1998-; Chairman, Department of English, 1983-86, University of Virginia; Visiting Professor, Rice University, 1967-68; Associate, Clare Hall, Cambridge, England, 1972. Publications: The Moral Basis of Fielding's Art: A Study of "Joseph Andrews", 1959; The Providence of Wit: Aspects of Form in Augustan Literature and the Arts, 1974; New Essays by Fielding: His Contributions to "The Craftsman" (1734-39) and Other Early Journalism, 1989; Henry Fielding: A Life (with Ruthe R Battestin), 1989-90, corrected edition, 1993. Editor: Henry Fielding: "Joseph Andrews" and "Shamela", 1961; Henry Fielding: The History of the Adventures of Joseph Andrews, 1967; Tom Jones: A Collection of Critical Essays, 1968; Henry Fielding: The History of Tom Jones, a Foundling (with Fredson Bowers), 2 volumes, 1974, corrected edition, 1975; Henry Fielding: Amelia, 1983; British Novelists, 1660-1800, 1985; The Correspondence of Henry and Sarah Fielding (with Clive T Probyn), 1993. Contributions to: Books and scholarly journals. Honours: American Council of Learned Societies Fellowships, 1960-61, 1972; Guggenheim Fellowship, 1964-65; Council of the Humanities Senior Fellow, Princeton University, 1971-; Center for Advanced Studies, University of Virginia, 1974-75; National Endowment for the Humanities Bicentennial Research Fellow, 1975-76; Festschrift, 1997. Memberships: Association of Literary Critics and Scholars; American Society of 18th Century Studies; International Association of University Professors of English; The Johnsonians; Modern Language Association. Address: 1832 Westview Road, Charlottesville, VA 22903, USA.

BATTIN B W (S W Bradford, Alexander Brinton, Warner Lee, Casey McAllister), b. 15 Nov 1941, Ridgewood, New Jersey, USA. Writer. m. Sandra McCraw, 14 Feb 1976. Education: BA, University of New Mexico, 1969. Publications: As B W Battin: Angel of the Night, 1983; The Boogeyman, 1984; Satan's Servant, 1984; Mary, Mary, 1985; Programmed for Terror, 1985; The Attraction, 1985; The Creep, 1987; Smithereens, 1987; Demented 1988; As Warner Lee: Into the Pit, 1989; It's Loose, 1990; Night Sounds, 1992; As S W Bradford: Tender Prey, 1990; Fair Game, 1992; As Alexander Brinton: Serial Blood, 1992; As Casey McAllister: Catch Me if You Can, 1993. Literary Agent: Dominick Abel, New York. Address: 711 North Mesa Road, Belen, NM 87002, USA.

BATTISCOMBE (Esther) Georgina (Harwood), b. 21 Nov 1905, London, England. Biographer. m. Lt Col C F Battiscombe, 1 Oct 1932, 1 daughter. Education: St Michael's School, Oxford; BA Honours, History, Lady Margaret Hall, Oxford. Publications: Charlotte Mary Yonge, 1943; Mrs Gladstone, 1956; John Keble, 1963; Queen Alexandra, 1970; Lord Shaftesbury, 1974; Reluctant Pioneer, Life of Elizabeth Wordsworth, 1978; Christina Rossetti, 1981; The Spencers of Althorp, 1984; Winter Song, 1992. Contributions to: Times; Sunday Telegraph; Times Literary Supplement; Spectator; Country Life; Books & Bookmen; History Today. Honour: James Tait Black Prize, 1963. Memberships: Fellow, Royal Society of Literature; Society of Authors. Literary Agent: A M Heath & Company. Address: Thamesfield, Wargrave Road, Henley-on-Thames RG9 2LX, England.

BATTLES Roxy (Edith Baker), b. 29 Mar 1921, Spokane, Washington, USA. Writer; Poet; Children's Author; Teacher. m. Willis Ralph Battles, 2 May 1941, 1 son, 2 daughters. Education: AA, Bakersfield Junior College, 1940; BA, California State University, 1959; MA, Pepperdine University, 1976. Appointments: Elementary Teacher, Torrance Unified Schools, 1959-85; Instructor, Torrance Adult School, 1968-88, Pepperdine University, 1976-79; Instructor, Creative Writing, Los Angeles Harbor College, 1995. Publications: Over the Rickety Fence, 1967; The Terrible Trick or Treat, 1970; 501 Balloons Sail East, 1971; The Terrible Terrier, 1972; One to Teeter Totter, 1973; Eddie Couldn't Find the Elephants, 1974; What Does the Rooster Say, Yoshio?, 1978; The Secret of Castle Drai, 1980; The Witch in Room 6, 1987; The Chemistry of Whispering Caves, 1989; The Lavender Castle (stage play), 1996. Contributions to: Numerous periodicals. Honours: National Science Award, 1971; United Nations Award, 1978; Author-in-Residence, American School of Madrid, Spain, 1991. Membership: Southwest Manuscripters. Address: 560 South Helberta Avenue, Redondo Beach, CA 90277, USA.

BAUER Caroline Feller, b. 12 May 1935, Washington, District of Columbia, USA. Author; Lecturer. m. 21 Dec 1969, 1 daughter. Education: BA, Sarah Lawrence College, 1956; MLS, Columbia University, 1958; PhD, University of Oregon, 1971. Publications: My Mom Travels a Lot, 1981; This Way to Books, 1983; Too Many Books, 1984; Celebrations, 1985; Rainy Day, 1986; Snowy Day, 1986; Midnight Snowman, 1987; Presenting Reader's Theater, 1987; Windy Day, 1988; Halloween, 1989; Read for the Fun of It, 1992; New Handbook for Storytellers, 1993; Putting on a Play, 1993; Valentine's Day, 1993; Thanksgiving Day, 1994; The Poetry Break, 1995; Leading Kids to Books Through Magic, 1996. Honours: ERSTED Award for Distinguished Teaching; Christopher Award; Dorothy McKenzie Award for Distinguished Contribution to Children's Literature. Memberships: American Library Association; Society of Children's Book Writers. Address: 10155 Collins Avenue, No 402, Miami Beach, FL 33154, USA.

BAUER Christoph, b. 30 Mar 1956, Lucerne, Switzerland. Writer; Bookseller. Education: Unfinished course of German Studies and History of Art. Publications: Ecstasy, novel, 1981; Freaks, novel, 1982; Harakiri, stories, 1983; European Book of Death, 1984; Paranormal, novel, 1985; Close Combat, novel, 1987; Popular Encyclopedia of Everyday Repulsiveness, 1990; Amoral Fables, 1993; Micromelodra Mas, 1994; Monkey Mind, 1996. Contributions to: Essays on F Pessoa, U Johnson, Y Mishima, P Weiss, H H Jahnn, R D Brinkmann, 7 Dürrenmatt. Membership: Groupe of Olten. Literary Agent: Literarische Agentur, Susanne Sigrist. Address: De Castellaweg 21, CH-3280, Greng, Switzerland.

BAUER Steven (Albert), b. 10 Sept 1948, Newark, New Jersey, USA. Professor of English; Writer; Poet. m. Elizabeth Arthur, 19 June 1982. Education: BA, Trinity College, Hartford, Connecticut, 1970; MFA, University of Massachusetts, Amherst, 1975. Appointments: Instructor, 1979-81, Assistant Professor, 1981-82, Colby College, Waterville, Maine; Assistant Professor, 1982-86, Associate Professor, 1986-96, Professor, 1996-, of English, Director of Creative Writing, 1986-96, Internal Director of Creative Writing, 1996-, Miami University, Oxford, Ohio. Publications: Satyrday (novel), 1980; The River (novel), 1985; Steven Spielberg's Amazing Stories, 2 volumes, 1986; Daylight Savings (poems), 1989; The Strange and Wonderful Tale of Robert McDoodle (Who Wanted to be a Dog), children's book, 1999. Contributions to: Essays, stories and poems in many periodicals. Honours: Strouse Award for Poetry, Prairie Schooner, 1982; Master Artist Fellowship Award, Indiana Arts Council, 1988; Peregrine Smith Poetry Prize, 1988. Address: 14100 Harmony Road, Bath, IN 47010, USA.

BAUER Yehuda, b. 6 Apr 1926, Prague, Czechoslovakia. Historian; Professor. 2 daughters. Education: BA, 1949, MA, 1950, University of Wales; PhD, Hebrew University, Jerusalem, 1960. Appointments: Served in Palmach Forces of the Haganah (Jewish Underground), 1944-45, and in Israel's War of Independence, 1948-49; Lecturer, 1961-73, Head of Division of Holocaust Studies, 1968-95, Associate Professor, 1973-77, Head, 1973-75, 1977-79, Professor, 1977-95, Institute of Contemporary Jewry, Hebrew University; Founder-Chairman, Vidal Sassoon International Center for the Study of Antisemitism, Hebrew University, 1982-95; Editor, Journal of Holocaust and Genocide Studies, 1986-95; Visiting Professor, University of Honolulu at Manoa, 1992, Yale University, 1993; Distinguished Visiting Professor, Ida E King Chair of Holocaust Studies, Richard Stockton College, New Jersey, 1995-96; Director, International Center for Holocaust Studies, Yad Vashem, Jerusalem, 1996-. Publications: (in English): From Diplomacy to Resistance: A History of Jewish Palestine, 1939-1945, 1970; My Brother's Keeper, 1974; Flight and Rescue, 1975; The Holocaust in Historical Perspective, 1978; The Jewish Emergence From Powerlessness, 1979; The Holocaust as Historical Experience (editor), 1981; American Jewry and the Holocaust, 1982; History of the Holocaust, 1984; Jewish Reactions to the Holocaust, 1988; Out of the Ashes, 1989; Jews for Sale?: Nazi-Jewish Negotiations, 1939-1945, 1994. Contributions to: Scholarly books, yearbooks and journals. Address: c/o International Center for Holocaust Studies, Yad Vashem, PO Box 3477, Jerusalem 91034, Israel.

BAUMAN Janina, b. 18 Aug 1926, Warsaw, Poland. Writer. m. Zygmunt Bauman, 18 Aug 1948, 3 daughters. Education: Academy of Social Sciences, 1951; University of Warsaw, 1959. Appointments: Script Editor, Polish Film, 1948-68. Publications: Winter in the Morning: A Dream of Belonging; Various other books and short stories published in Poland since 1990. Contributions to: Jewish Quarterly; Oral History; Polin; British Journal of Holocaust Education. Honour: Award by Polityka Weekly, Poland, 1991. Address: 1 Lawnswood Gardens, Leeds, Yorkshire LS16 6HF, England.

BAUMAN M Garrett, b. 7 Aug 1948, Paterson, New Jersey, USA. Essayist; Professor. m. Carol Nobles, 6 Mar 1978, 1 son, 3 daughters. Education: BA, Upsala College, 1969; MA, SUNY-Binghamton, 1971. Appointment: Monroe Community College, 1971-. Publications: Ideas and Details, 1992; The Shape of Ideas, 1995. Contributions to: New York Times; Sierra; National Forum; Yankee. Honours: Leavey Award, Saltonstall Award, Roberts Foundation; New York State Council on the Arts Award. Address: c/o Department of English, Monroe Community College, Rochester, NY 14623, USA.

BAUMAN Zygmunt, b. 19 Nov 1925, Poznań, Poland. Sociologist. m. Janina Bauman, 18 Aug 1948, 3 daughters. Education: MA, 1954; PhD, 1956. Appointments: Warsaw University, 1953-68; Tel Aviv University, 1968-75; University of Leeds, 1971-91. Publications: Modernity and the Holocaust; Legislators and Interpreters; Intimations of Postinedermity; Thinking Sociologically; Modernity and Ambivalence; Freedom; Memories of Class; Culture as Praxis; Between Class and Elite; Mortality, Immortality and Other Life Strategies; Postmodernity and its Discontents, 1997; In Search of Politics, 1999. Contributions to: Times Literary Supplement; New Statesman; Professional Periodicals. Honour: Amalfi European Prize for Sociology; Theodor Adorno Prize, 1998. Memberships: British Sociological Association; Polish Sociological Association. Address: 1 Lawnswood Gardens, Leeds LS16 6HF, England.

BAUMBACH Jonathan, b. 5 July 1933, New York, USA. Writer; Professor. 3 sons, 1 daughter. Education: AB, Brooklyn College, 1955; MFA, Columbia University, 1956; PhD, Stanford University, 1961. Appointments: Instructor, Stanford University, 1958-60; Assistant Professor, Ohio State University, 1961-64; Director of Writing, New York University, 1964-66; Professor, English, Brooklyn College, 1966-; Visiting Professorships,

Tufts University, 1970, University of Washington, 1978, 1983. Publications: The Landscape of Nightmare, 1965; A Man to Conjure With,1965; What Comes Next, 1968; Reruns, 1974; Babble, 1976; Chez, Charlotte and Emily, 1979; Return of Service, 1979; My Father More or Less, 1984; The Life and Times of Major Fiction, 1987; Separate Hours, 1990; Seven Wives, 1994. Contributions to: Movie Critic, Partisan Review, 1973-82; Articles, Fiction in Esquire; New American Review; Tri Quarterly; Iowa Review; North American Review; Fiction. Honours: National Endowment for the Arts Fellowship, 1978; Guggenheim Fellowship, 1980; O Henry Prize Stories, 1980, 1984, 1988. Memberships: Teachers and Writers Collaborative, board of directors; National Society of Film Critics, chairman, 1982-84. Literary Agent: Robert Cornfield. Address: 320 Stratford Road, Brooklyn, NY 11218, USA.

BAUMM Stefanie Paulina, b. 14 Nov 1963, Germany. Freelance Journalist; Author. m. 22 May 1987, 3 sons. Appointments: Freelance Journalist, 1995-. Publication: Der Gesang Der Bäume, 1997. Contributions to: Schleswig Holsteinischer Zeitungskerlag. Address: Hohenlockstedt, Ridders, D-25551, Germany.

BAUSCH Richard (Carl), b. 18 Apr 1945, Fort Benning, Georgia, USA. Author; Professor of English. m. Karen Miller, 3 May 1969, 2 sons, 1 daughter. Education: BA, George Mason University, 1974; MFA, University of Iowa, 1975. Appointment: Professor of English, George Mason University, 1980-. Publications: Real Presence, 1980; Take Me Back, 1981; The Last Good Time, 1984; Spirits and Other Stories, 1987; Mr Field's Daughter, 1989; The Fireman's Wife and Other Stories, 1990; Violence, 1992; Rebel Powers, 1993; Rare and Endangered Species: A Novella and Stories, 1994; The Selected Stories of Richard Bausch, 1996; Good Evening Mr and Mrs America, and All the Ships at Sea, 1996. Honours: PEN-Faulkner Award Nominations, 1982, 1988; Guggenheim Fellowship, 1984. Membership: Associated Writing Programs. Address: Department of English, George Mason University, 4400 University Drive, Fairfax, VA 22030, USA.

BAWDEN Nina Mary, b. 19 Jan 1924, London, England. Novelist. m. (1) Henry Walton Bawden, Oct 1946, (2) Austen Kark, Aug 1954, 2 sons, 1 daughter. Education: Somerville College, Oxford, England. Publications include: Devil By the Sea, 1958; Just Like a Lady, 1960; Tortoise By Candlelight, 1963; A Woman of My Age, 1967; The Grain of Truth, 1969; The Birds on the Trees, 1970; Anna Apparent, 1972; George Beneath A Paper Moon, 1974; Family Money, 1991; In My Own Time, autobiography, 1994; Children's Books: Carrie's War; The Peppermint Pig; The Finding; Keeping Henry; Granny the Pig. Contributions to: Various. Honour: Guardian Children's Book Award, 1975; Yorkshire Post Novel of the Year, 1976. Memberships: PEN; Society of Authors, council; Royal Society of Literature; Society of Women Writers and Journalists, president. Literary Agent: Curtis Brown. Address: 22 Noel Road, London N1 8HA, England.

BAXT George, b. 11 June 1923, Brooklyn, New York, USA. Writer. Education: City College, New York City; Brooklyn College. Publications: A Queer Kind of Death, 1966; A Parade of Cockeyed Creatures, 1967; I! Said the Demon, 1968; Burning Sappho, 1972; The Dorothy Parker Murder Case, 1984; The Alfred Hitchcock Murder Case: An Unauthorized Novel, 1986; The Tallulah Bankhead Murder Case, 1987; The Talking Picture Murder Case, 1990; The Mae West Murder Case, 1993; The Marlene Dietrich Murder Case, 1993; The Bette Davis Murder Case, 1994; The Clark Gable and Carole Lombard Murder Case, 1997. Contributions to: Ellery Queen Mystery Magazine. Address: c/o St Martin's Press, 175 Fifth Avenue, New York, NY 10010, USA.

BAXTER Charles, b. 13 May 1947, Minneapolis, Minnesota, USA. Professor of English; Author; Poet. m. Martha Hauser, 1 son. Education: BA, Macalester College, 1969; PhD, State University of New York at Buffalo, 1974. Appointments: Assistant Professor,

1974-79, Associate Professor, 1979-85, Professor of English, 1985-89, Wayne State University; Faculty, Warren Wilson College, 1986; Visiting Faculty, 1987, Professor of English, 1989-, University of Michigan. Publications: Fiction: Harmony of the World, 1984; Through the Safety Net, 1985; First Light, 1987; A Relative Stranger, 1990; Shadow Play, 1993; Believers, 1997. Non-Fiction: Burning Down the House, 1997. Poetry: Chameleon, 1970; The South Dakota Guidebook, 1974; Imaginary Paintings and Other Poems, 1990. Contributions to: Numerous anthologies, journals, reviews, and newspapers. Honours: National Endowment for the Arts Grant, 1983; Guggenheim Fellowship, 1985-86; Arts Foundation of Michigan Award, 1991; Lila Wallace-Reader's Digest Foundation Fellowship, 1992-95; Michigan Author of the Year Award, 1993; American Academy of Arts and Letters Award in Literature, 1997. Address: 1585 Woodland Drive, Ann Arbor, MN 48103, USA.

BAXTER Craig, b. 16 Feb 1929, Elizabeth, New Jersey, USA. Professor of Politics and History; Author; Consultant. m. Barbara T Stevens, 28 May 1984, 1 son, 1 daughter. Education: BA, 1951, AM, 1954, PhD, 1967, University of Pennsylvania. Appointments: Vice Consul, Bombay, 1958-60, Political Officer, New Delhi, 1961-64, Deputy Principal Officer and Political Officer, Lahore, 1965-68, Analyst for India, 1968-69, Senior Political Officer for Pakistan and Afghanistan, 1969-71, Visiting Associate Professor in Social Sciences, United State Military Academy, 1971-74, Political Counselor, Accra, 1974-76, and Dhaka, 1976-78, Officer-in-Charge, International Scientific Relations for the Near East, South Asia, and Africa, 1978-80, US Foreign Service; Adjunct Lecturer, University of Virginia, Falls Church, 1969-71; Lecturer, Mount Vernon College, Washington, DC, 1981; Visiting Professor of Political Science and Diplomat-in-Residence, 1981-82, Professor of Politics and History, 1982-, Chairman, Department of Political Science, 1991-94, Juniata College, Huntingdon, Pennsylvania; Consultant to various organizations. Publications: The Jana Sangh: A Biography of an Indian Political Party, 1969; District Voting Trends in India: A Research Tool, 1969; Bangladesh: A New Nation in an Old Setting, 1984, 2nd edition, 1996; Zia's Pakistan: Politics and Stability in a Frontline State (editor and contributor), 1985; Government and Politics in South Asia (with Yogendra K Malik, Charles H Kennedy, and Robert C Oberst), 1987, 4th edition, 1998; Historical Dictionary of Bangladesh (with Syedur Rahman), 1989, 2nd edition, 1996; Pakistan Under the Military: Eleven Years of Zia ul-Haq (with Shahid Javed Burki), 1990; Pakistan: Authoritarianism in the 1980s (editor with Syed Razi Wasti and contributor), 1992; Bangladesh: From a Nation to a State, 1996; Pakistan, 1997, with Charles H. Kennedy, 1998. Contributions to: Books, encyclopedias, and scholarly journals. Memberships: American Foreign Service Association; Association for Asian Studies; American Institute of Pakistan Studies, President, 1984-; American Institute of Bangladesh Studies, President, 1989-98. Address: RR No 4, Box 103, Huntingdon, PA 16652, USA.

BAXTER John, b. 14 Dec 1939, Sydney, New South Wales, Australia. Writer. Education: Waverly College, Sydney, 1944-54. Appointments: Director of Publicity, Australian Commonwealth Film Unit, Sydney, 1968-70; Lecturer in Film and Theatre, Hollins College, 1974-78; Freelance TV Producer and Screenwriter, 1978-87; Visiting Lecturer, Mitchell College, 1987. Publications: The Off Worlders, 1966, in Australia as The God Killers: Hollywood in the Thirties, 1968; The Pacific Book of Australian Science Fiction, 1970; The Australian Cinema, 1970; Science Fiction in the Cinema, 1970; The Gangster Film, 1970; The Cinema of Josef von Sternburg, 1971; The Cinema of John Ford, 1971; The Second Pacific Book of Australian Science Fiction, 1971; Hollywood in the Sixties, 1972; Sixty Years of Hollywood, 1973; An Appalling Talent: Kent Russell, 1973; Stunt: The Story of the Great Movie Stunt Men, 1974; The Hollywood Exiles, 1976; The Fire Came By (with Thomas R Atkins), 1976; King Vidor, 1976; The Hermes Fall, 1978; The Bidders (in UK as Bidding), 1979; The Kid, 1981; The Video

Handbook (with Brian Norris), 1982; The Black Yacht, 1982; Who Burned Australia? The Ash Wednesday Fires, 1984; Filmstruck, 1987; Bondi Blues, 1993; Fellini, 1993; Buñuel, 1994; Steven Spielberg: The Unauthorised Biography, 1996. Feature Film Scripts: The Time Guardian, 1988. TV Series: The Cutting Room, 1986; First Take, 1986; Filmstruck, 1986. Address: c/o Curtis Brown Literary Agents, Haymarket House, 28-29 Haymarket, London SW1Y 4SP, England.

BAYATI Abed Al-Wahab, b. 1926, Baghdad, Iraq. Poet. Education: Baghdad Teachers Training College. Appointments: Cultural Adviser, Ministry of Culture and Fine Arts, Baghdad. Publications: Angels and Devils, 1950; Broken Pitchers, 1954; Glory Be to Children and the Olive, 1956; Poems in Exile, 1957; 15 Poems from Vienna, 1958; 20 Poems from Berlin, 1959; Words that Never Die, 1960; Fire and Words, 1964; The Book of Poverty and Revolution, 1965; That Which Comes and Does Not Come, 1966; Death in Life, 1968; Dead Dogs' Eyes, 1969; The Writing on Clay, 1970; Love Poems on the Seven Gates of the World, 1971; Collected Poems, 1971; Lilies and Death, 1972; The Moon of Shiraz, 1975; The Singer and the Moon, 1976; Eye of the Sun, 1978; Kingdom of the Spike, 1979; Love in the Rain, 1985; Love, Death and Exile, 1990; Book of Elegies, 1995. Play: Trial in Nishapur, 1963. Works have been translated into many languages including English, French, German, Russian and Spanish. Honour: Sultan Al-Owais Poetry Award, United Arab Emirates, 1995. Address: PO Box 927293, Amman, Jordan.

BAYBARS Taner, (Timothy Bayliss), b. 18 June 1936, Cyprus (British citizen). Writer; Painter. 1 daughter. Education: Private, Turkish Lycée. Publications: To Catch a Falling Man, 1963; A Trap for the Burglar, 1965; Plucked in a Far-Off Land, 1970, (translated into Turkish as Uzak Ulke, 1997); Susila in the Autumn Woods, 1974; Narcissus in a Dry Pool, 1978; Pregnant Shadows, 1981; A Sad State of Freedom, 1990; Selected Poems (in Turkish translation), 1997; Fox and the Cradle Makers, forthcoming. Contributions to: Critical Quarterly; Ambit; Orte; Détours d'Ecritures; Hudson Review; Dalhousie Review; M25; Others. Memberships: Club de Vin d'Angoulême; Poetry Society of London. Literary Agent: MBA Literary Agents. Address: 2 rue de L'Evêque, 34360 Saint-Chinian, France.

BAYLEY Barrington (John), (Alan Aumbry, P F Woods), b. 9 Apr 1937, Birmingham, England. Author. m. Joan Lucy Clarke, 31 Oct 1969, 1 son, 1 daughter. Publications: Star Virus, 1970; Annihilation Factor, 1972; Empire of Two Worlds, 1972; Collision with Chronos, 1973; The Fall of Chronopolis, 1974; The Soul of the Robot, 1974; The Garments of Caean, 1976; The Grand Wheel, 1977; The Knights of the Limits, 1978; Star Winds, 1978; The Seed of Evil, 1979; The Pillars of Eternity, 1982; The Zen Gun, 1984; The Forest of Peldain, 1985; The Rod of Light, 1985. Honour: Seiun Award for Best Foreign Science Fiction Novel Published in Japan, 1984-85. Address: 48 Turreff Avenue, Donnington, Telford, Shropshire TF2 8HE, England.

BAYLEY John (Oliver), b. 27 Mar 1925, Lahore, India. Professor of English Literature (Retired); Writer. m. Dame Jean Irish Murdoch, 1956. Education: Eton College, 1938-43; 1st Class Hons in English, New College, Oxford, 1950. Appointments: Member, St Antony's College and Magdalen College, Oxford, 1951-55; Fellow and Tutor in English, New College, Oxford, 1955-74; Warton Professor of English Literature and Fellow, St Catherine's College, Oxford, 1974-92. Publications: In Another Country (novel), 1954; The Romantic Survival: A Study in Poetic Evolution, 1956; The Characters of Love, 1961; Tolstoy and the Novel, 1966; Pushkin: A Comparative Commentary, 1971; The Uses of Division: Unity and Disharmony in Literature, 1976; An Essay on Hardy, 1978; Shakespeare and Tragedy, 1981; The Order of Battle at Trafalgar, 1987; The Short Story: Henry James and Elizabeth Bowen, 1988; Housman's Poems, 1992; Alice (novel), 1994; The Queer Captain (novel), 1995; George's Liar (novel), 1996. Membership: British

Academy, fellow. Address: c/o St Catherine's College, Oxford, England.

BAYLEY Peter (Charles), b. 25 Jan 1921, Gloucester, England. Professor Emeritus; Writer. Education: MA, Oxford University, 1947. Appointments: Fellow, University College, 1947-72; Praelector in English, 1949-72, University Lecturer, 1952-72, Oxford University; Master, Collingwood College, University of Durham, 1972-78; Berry Professor and Head of English Department, 1978-85, Berry Professor Emeritus, 1985-, University of St Andrews, Fife. Publications: Edmund Spenser, Prince of Poets, 1971; Poems of Milton, 1982; An ABC of Shakespeare, 1985; Editor: The Faerie Queene, by Spenser, Book II, 1965, Book 1, 1966, 1970; Loves and Deaths, 1972; A Casebook on Spenser's Faerie Queene, 1977. Contributions to: Patterns of Love and Courtesy, 1966; Oxford Biographical Guides, 1971; C S Lewis at the Breakfast Table, 1979; The Encyclopedia of Oxford, 1988; Sir William Jones 1746-94, 1998. Address: 63 Oxford Street, Woodstock, Oxford OX20 1TJ, England.

BAYLISS Timothy. See: BAYBARS Taner.

BEACHCROFT Ellinor Nina, b. 10 Nov 1931, London, England. Writer. m. Dr Richard Gardner, 7 Aug 1954, 2 daughters. Education: Wimbledon High School, 1942-49; 2nd Class Hons Degree in English Literature, St Hilda's College, Oxford, 1953. Publications: Well Met by Witchlight, 1972; Under the Enchanter, 1974; Cold Christmas, 1974; A Spell of Sleep, 1975; A Visit to Folly Castle, 1976; A Farthing for the Fair, 1977; The Wishing People, 1978; The Genie and Her Bottle, 1983; Beyond World's End, 1985. Memberships: Society of Authors; Children's Writers' Group, twice a Committee Member. Literary Agent: David Highams. Address: 9 Raffin Green Lane, Datchworth, Hertfordshire SG3 6RJ, England.

BEAGLE Peter S(oyer), b. 20 Apr 1939, New York, New York, USA. Writer; Musician; Singer; Songwriter. m. 1) Enid Nordeen, 8 May 1964, div 1980, 1 son, 2 daughters, 2) Padma Hejmadi, 21 Sept 1988. Education: BA, University of Pittsburgh, 1959. Appointments: Many readings, lectures, and concerts; Visiting Assistant Professor, University of Washington, 1988. Publications: Novels: A Fine and Private Place, 1960; The Last Unicorn, 1968; The Folk of the Air, 1986; The Innkeeper's Song, 1993; The Unicorn Sonata, 1996. Fiction Collections: The Fantasy Worlds of Peter S Beagle, 1978; Giant Bones, 1997; The Rhinoceros Who Quoted Nietzsche, and Other Odd Acquaintances, 1997. Editor: Peter Beagle's Immortal Unicorn (with Janet Berliner), 1995. Opera Libretto: The Midnight Angel, 1993. Non-Fiction: I See By My Outfit, 1965; The California Feeling, 1969; American Denim: A New Folk Art, 1975; The Lady and Her Tiger (with Pat Derby), 1976; The Garden of Earthly Delights, 1982; In the Presence of Elephants (with Pat Derby), 1995. Contributions to: Anthologies, periodicals, films, and television. Address: 2135 Humboldt Avenue, Davis, CA 95616, USA.

BEALES Derek (Edward Dawson), . b. 12 June 1931, Felixstowe, England. Professor of Modern History; Writer. Education: BA, 1953, MA, PhD, 1957, Cambridge University. Appointments: Research Fellow, 1955-58, Fellow, 1958-, Tutor, 1961-70, Vice Master, 1973-75, Sidney Sussex College; Assistant Lecturer, 1962-65, Lecturer, 1965-80, Chairman, Faculty Board of History, 1979-81, Professor of Modern History, 1980-97, Emeritus Professor, 1997-, Cambridge University; Editor, Historical Journal, 1971-75; Member of Council, Royal Historical Society, 1984-87; Editor, Historical Journal, 1971-75; British Academy Representative, Standing Committee for Humanities, European Science Foundation, 1993-; Recurring Visiting Professor, Central European University, Budapest, 1995-. Publications: England and Italy 1859-60, 1961; From Castlereagh to Gladstone, 1969; The Risorgimento and the Unification of Italy, 1971; History and Biography, 1981; History, Society and the Churches (editor with G F A Best), 1985; Joseph II: In the Shadow of Maria Theresa 1741-80, 1987; Mozart and the Habsburgs, 1993; Sidney Sussex College Quatercentenary Essays, (editor with H B Nisbet), 1996.

Honours: Doctor of Letters, 1988; Fellow, British Academy, 1989; Stenton Lecturer, University of Reading, 1992; Birkbeck Lecturer, Trinity College, Cambridge, 1993. Address: Sidney Sussex College, Cambridge CB2 3HU, England.

BEAR Carolyn Ann, (Chlöe Rayban), b. 10 Apr 1944, Exeter, England. Author. m. Peter Julian Bear, 2 daughters. Education: University of Western Australia (1 year); University of Newcastle upon Tyne; BA Hons, Philosophy. Publications: Under Different Stars, 1988; Wild Child, 1991; Virtual Sexual Reality, 1994; Love in Cyberia, 1996; Screen Kiss, 1997; Clash on the Catwalk, 1997; Havana to Hollywood, 1997; Street to Stardom, 1997; Models Move On, 1998. Honours: Shortlisted for Guardian Children's Fiction Prize, 1995; Shortlisted for Guardian Children's Fiction Prize, 1996; Shortlisted for Carnegie Medal Fiction Prize, 1996. Literary Agent: Laura Cecil. Address: 17 Alwyne Villas, London N1 2HG, England.

BEAR Greg(ory Dale), b. 20 Aug 1951, San Diego, California, USA. Writer. m. (1) Christina Nielsen, 12 Jan 1975, div Aug 1981, (2) Astrid Anderson, 18 June 1983, 1 son, 1 daughter. Education: AB, San Diego State College, 1969. Publications: Hegira, 1979; Psychlone, 1979; Beyond Heaven's River, 1980; Strength of Stones, 1981; The Wind From a Burning Woman, 1983; Corona, 1984; The Infinity Concerto, 1984; Eon, 1985; Blood Music, 1985; The Serpent Mage, 1986; The Forge of God, 1987; Sleepside Story, 1987; Eternity, 1988; Hardfought, 1988; Early Harvest, 1988; Tangents, 1989; Queen of Angels, 1990; Heads, 1990; Anvil of Stars, 1992; Moving Mars, 1993; Legacy, 1995; Dinosaur Summer, 1998. Honours: Awards from Science Fiction Writers of America. Membership: Science Fiction Writers of America, president, 1988-90. Address: 506 Lakeview Road, Alderwood Manor, WA 98036, USA.

BEARDSLEY J(ohn) Douglas, b. 27 Apr 1941, Montreal, Quebec, Canada. Writer; Poet; Editor; Reviewer; Teacher. Education: BA, University of Victoria, British Columbia, 1976; MA, York University, Toronto, Ontario, 1978. Appointments: Chief Editor, Gregson Graham Ltd, 1980-82; Senior Instructor, Department of English, University of Victoria, 1981-; Writer, Editor and Graphic Designer, Osborne, Beardsley and Associates, Victoria, 1982-85; Writer, Editor and Proofreader, Beardsley and Associates, Victoria, 1985-. Publications: Going Down into History, 1976; The Only Country in the World Called Canada, 1976; Six Saanich Poems, 1977; Play on the Water: The Paul Klee Poems, 1978; Premonitions and Gifts (with Theresa Kishkan), 1979; Poems (with Charles Lillard), 1979; Pacific Sands, 1980; Kissing the Body of My Lord: The Marie Poems, 1982; Country on Ice, 1987; A Dancing Star, 1988; The Rocket, the Flower, the Hammer and Me (anthology of Canadian hockey fiction) (editor), 1988; Free to Talk, 1992; Inside Passage, 1994; Wrestling with Angels (Selected Poems, 1960-1995), 1996; My Friends the Strangers, 1996; Our Game (editor), 1998; No One Else is Lawrence! (with Al Purdy), 1998. Contributions to: Anthologies, newspapers, magazines, and periodicals. Honours: Canada Council Arts Award, 1978; British Columbia Book Prize for Poetry Nomination, 1989. Address: 1074 Lodge Avenue, Victoria, British Columbia V8X 3A8, Canada.

BEASLEY John David, (David Sellers), b. 26 Oct 1944, Hornsea, Yorkshire, England. Social Worker. m. Marian Ruth Orford, 15 Mar 1969, 1 son, 2 daughters. Education: London University Diploma in Sociology; Certificate of Qualification in Social Work, Polytechnic of North London, England. Appointments: United Kingdom Band of Hope Union, 1960-70; Social Worker, London Borough of Tower Hamlets, 1970-94. Publications: Who Was Who in Peckham, 1985; The Bitter Cry Heard and Heeded, 1989; 500 Quotes and Anecdotes, 1992; Origin of Names in Peckham and Nunhead, 1993; Peckham and Nunhead Churches, 1995; Peckham Rye Park Centenary, 1995; Peckham and Nunhead, 1995; Another 500 quotes and anecdotes, 1996; Transport in Peckham and Nunhead, 1997; East Dulwich, 1998. Contributions to: Challenge; Memory Lane in Southwark Local. Honour:

Southwark Civic Award, 1997. Membership: Society of Authors. Address: 6 Everthorpe Road, London SE15 4DA, England.

BEASLEY W(illiam) G(erald), b. 22 Dec 1919, England. Professor Emeritus; Writer. Education: BA, 1940, PhD, 1950, University of London. Appointment: Professor of History of the Far East, School of Oriental and African Studies, 1954-83, Professor Emeritus, 1983-, University of London. Publications: Great Britain and the Opening of Japan 1833-1858, 1951; Select Documents on Japanese Foreign Policy 1853-1868 (editor and translator), 1955; Historians of China and Japan (editor with E G Pulleyblank), 1961; The Modern History of Japan, 1963, 3rd edition, 1981; The Meiji Restoration, 1972; Modern Japan: Aspects of History, Literature and Society (editor), 1975; Japanese Imperialism 1894-1945, 1987; The Rise of Modern Japan, 1990; Japan Encounters the Barbarian: Japanese Travellers in America and Europe, 1995; The Japanese Experience: A Short History of Japan, 1999. Address: 172 Hampton Road, Twickenham TW2 5NJ, England.

BEASLEY-MURRAY George Raymond, b. 10 Oct 1916, London, England. Retired Professor; Writer. m. Ruth Weston, 4 Apr 1942, 3 sons, 1 daughter. Education: BD, 1941, MTh, 1945, PhD, 1952, King's College; MA, 1954; DD, London University, 1963; DD, Cambridge University, 1989. Appointments: Lecturer, 1950-56, Principal, 1958-73, Spurgeon's College, London; Professor of Greek New Testament, Ruschlikon, Zürich, 1956-58; Professor, 1973-80, Senior Professor, 1980-92, Southern Baptist Seminary, Louisville, Kentucky. Publications: Jesus and the Future, 1954; A Commentary on Mark Thirteen, 1957; Baptism in the New Testament, 1962; Baptism Today and Tomorrow, 1966; Commentary on Gospel of John, Word Biblical Commentary, 1987; Gospel of Life: Theology in the Fourth Gospel, 1991; Jesus and the Last Days, 1993; Preaching the Gospel from the Gospels, 1996. Contributions to: Books and scholarly journals. Memberships: Catholic Biblical Association of America; Society of Biblical Literature; Studiorum Novi Testamenti Societas; Tyndale Fellowship for Biblical and Theological Research. Address: 4 Holland Road, Hove, East Sussex BN3 1JJ, England.

BEATTIE Ann, b. 7 Sept 1947, Washington, District of Columbia, USA. Writer; Poet. Education: BA, American University, Washington, DC, 1969; MA, University of Connecticut, 1970. Publications: Secrets and Surprises, 1978; Where You'll Find the Other Stories, 1986; What Was Mine and Other Stories, 1991; With This Ring, 1997; My Life, Starring Dara Falcon, 1998; Park City: New and Selected Storiese, 1998; New and Selected Poems, 1999. Contributions to: Various publications. Address: c/o Janklow and Nesbit, 598 Madison Avenue, New York, NY 10022, USA.

BEATY (Arthur) David, b. 28 Mar 1919, Hatton, Ceylon. Author. m. Betty Joan Campbell Smith, 29 Apr 1948, 3 daughters. Education: MA, History, Merton College, Oxford University, England, 1940; MPhil, Psychology, University College, 1965; Airline Transport Pilot's Licence; Navigation and Radio Licences. Appointments: RAF, 1940-46; Squadron Leader, British Overseas Airways Corporation, Senior Captain, Principal Atlantic Routes, 1946-53; Foreign Office, 1966-74. Publications: The Take Off, 1948; The Heart of the Storm, 1954; The Proving Flight, 1956; Cone of Silence, 1958; Call Me Captain, 1959; Village of Stars, 1960; The Wind off the Sea, 1962; The Siren Song, 1964; Milk and Honey, 1964; Sword of Honour, 1965; The Human Factor in Aircraft Accidents, 1969; The Temple Tree, 1971; Electric Train, 1974; The Water Jumper: History of North Atlantic Flight, 1976; Excellency, 1977; The Complete Sky Traveller, 1978; The White Sea Bird, 1979; Wings of the Morning, with Betty Beaty, 1982; Strange Encounters, 1982; The Stick, 1984; The Blood Brothers, 1987; Eagles, 1990; The Naked Pilot, 1991; Light Perpetual, Airmen's Memorial Windows, 1995; The Ghosts of the Eighth Attack, 1998. Honour: Member of the Order of the British Empire. Membership: Royal Aeronautical Society. Address: Manchester House, Church Hill, Slindon, Near Arundel, West Sussex BN18 0RD, England.

BEATY Betty Joan Campbell Smith, (Karen Campbell, Catherine Ross). British. m. (Arthur) David Beaty, 29 Apr 1943, 3 daughters. Appointments: WAAF Officer; Airline Hostess; Medical Social Worker, London. Publications: Maiden Flight, 1956; South to the Sea, 1956; Amber Five, 1958; The Butternut Tree, 1958; From This Day Forward, 1959; The Colours of the Night, 1962; The Path of the Moonfish, 1964; The Trysting Tower, 1964; Miss Miranda's Walk, 1967; Suddenly in the Air, 1969; Thunder on Sunday, 1971; The Swallows of San Fedora, 1973; Love and the Kentish Maid, 1973; Head of Chancery, 1974; Master at Arms, 1975; Fly Away Love, 1976; Death Descending, 1976; Exchange of Hearts, 1977; The Bells of St Martin, 1979; Battle Dress, 1979; Wings of the Morning (with David Beaty), 1982; The Missionary's Daughter, 1983; Matchmaker Nurse, 1983. Address: Manchester House, Church Hill, Slindon, Near Arundel, West Sussex BN18 0RD, England.

BEAUCHEMIN Yves, b. 26 June 1941, Noranda, Quebec, Canada. Author. m. Viviane St Onge, 26 May 1973, 2 children. Education: BA, Collège de Joliette, 1962; Licence ès lettres, University of Montreal, 1965. Publications: L'enfirouapé, 1974; Le matou, 1981, English translation as The Alley Cat, 1986; Du sommet d'un arbre, 1986; Juliette Pomerleau, 1989; Finalement ... les enfants, 1991; Une histoire a faire japper, 1991; Antoine et Alfred, 1992; Le second violon, 1996. Contributions to: Newspapers, magazines, and radio. Honours: Prix France-Quèbec, 1975; Prix de la communauté urbaine, Montreal, 1982; Prix des jeunes romanciers, Journal de Montréal, 1982; Prix du roman de l'ete, Cannes, France, 1982. Memberships: Amnesty International; International PEN; Union des écrivains québecois, president, 1986-87. Address: 247 Saint-Jacques Street, Longueil, Quebec J4H 3B8, Canada.

BEAUD Roger Raymond, b. 5 Nov 1951, Zürich, Switzerland. Teacher; Freelance Writer. Education: Swiss Matura, Modern Languages, Feusi Schule, Bern, 1977; Diploma as Engineer in Tropical Agriculture, Swiss Tropical Institute, Basel, 1979; Studied Linguistics, English and German, School of Applied Linguistics, Zürich, 1986. Appointments: Practical work as agricultural engineer in animal husbandry and wine-making, Swiss Polytechnic, Zong/Zurich, 1980; Teacher, English and American Literature and English Writing, Foreign Languages Normal School, Guangzhou, School, 1994; English Teacher Adult Training Section, 1995; Tutor of German at Island School, Hong Kong, 1998. Publication: A Jobhunter's Guide to China, 1998. Contributions to: Neue Zürichsee-Zeitung: Momentaufnahme Hong Kong, 1989; Das Museum für Frieden, Samarkand, Uzbekistan, 1993. Membership: Swiss Writers' Association. Literary Agent: Barbara Bauer Inc, USA. Address: c/o GPO, PR, Connaught Road, Hong Kong.

BEAULIEU Victor-Lévy, b. 2 Sept 1945, Saint-Paul-de-la-Croix, Quebec, Canada. Author; Dramatist. m. Francine Cantin, 2 daughters. Education: University of Rallonge. Publications: Jos Connaissant, 1970, revised edition, 1978, English translation, 1982; Pour saluer Victor Hugo, 1971; Les Grands-Pères, 1972, revised edition, 1979, English translation as The Grandfathers: A Novel, 1975; Jack Kerouac: Essai-poulet, 1972, English translation as Don Quixote in Nighttown, 1978; Manuel de la petite littérature de Québec, 1974; Blanche forcée, 1975; Ma Corriveau, suivi de La sorcellerie en finale sexuée, 1976; N'évoque plus que le désenchantement de ta ténèbre, mon si pauvre Abel, 1976; Sagamo Job J, 1977; Monsieur Melville, 3 volumes, 1978, English translation, 1984; Una, 1980; Satan Belhumeur, 1981, English translation, 1983; Moi Pierre Leroy, prophète, martyr et un peu felé du chaudron, 1982; Entre la sainteté et le terrorisme, 1984; Docteur Ferron, 1991. Other: Television Series: Race de Monde, 1978-81; L'héritage, 1987-89; Montréal PQ, 1991-94; Bouscotte, 1997-2001. Contributions to: Various publications. Honours: Grand Prix de la Ville de Montreal, 1972; Governor-General's Award for Fiction, 1974; Beraud-Molson Prize, 1981; Prix Canada-Belgique, 1981. Address: c/o Union des écrivaines et écrivains québécois, La Maison des écrivains, 3492 Avenue Laval, Montreal, Quebec H2X 3C8, Canada.

BEAUMAN Sally Vanessa, b. 25 July 1944, Torquay, Devon, England. Writer; Journalist. 1 son. Education: MA, Honours, English Literature, Girton College, Cambridge, 1963-66. Appointments: Associate Editor, New York magazine, 1968-72; Features Editor, Harper's Bazaar, 1969-71; Contributing and Arts Editor, Telegraph magazine, 1971-79. Publictions: The Royal Shakespeare Company: A History of Ten Decades, 1983; Destiny, 1986; Dark Angel, 1988; Lovers and Liars, 1992; Danger Zones, 1994; Sextet, 1997. Contributions to: Newspapers and periodicals. Membership: Society of Authors. Literary Agent: Peters, Fraser and Dunlop, London. Address: c/o Peters, Fraser and Dunlop, The Chambers, 5th Floor Chelsea Harbour, Lots Road, London SW10 0XF, England.

BEAUMONT Roger A(lban), b. 2 Oct 1935, Milwaukee, Wisconsin, USA. Professor of History; Writer. m. Jean Beaumont, 8 Dec 1974, 1 son, 2 daughters. Education: BS, History, 1957, MS, History, 1960, University of Wisconsin, Madison; PhD, History, Kansas State University, 1973. Appointments: Part-Time Lecturer, 1965-67, 1969-73, Associate Director, Center for Advanced Study in Organization Science, 1970-73, Associate Professor of Organization Science, 1972-74, University of Wisconsin, Milwaukee; Instructor, University of Wisconsin, Oshkosh, 1968-69; Fellow, Inter-University Seminar on the Armed Forces and Society, 1969-; Part-time Lecturer, Marquette University, 1970-73; Associate Professor, 1974-79, Professor of History, 1979-, Texas A & M University; Co-Founder and North American Editor, Defense Analysis, 1983-90. Publications: War in the Next Decade (editor with Martin Edmonds), 1974; Military Elites: Special Fighting Units in the Modern World, 1974; Sword of the Raj: The British Army in India, 1747-1947, 1977; Special Operations and Elite Units, 1939-1988: A Reference Guide, 1988; Joint Military Operations: A Short History, 1993; War, Chaos and History, 1994. Other: 5 monographs; 19 book chapters. Contributions to: Reference works and many scholarly journals. Honours: Department of the Army Patriotic Civilian Service Award, 1987; Secretary of the Navy Fellow, History Department, US Naval Academy, 1989-90; Faculty Teaching Award, Delta Delta Delta Sorority, 1994; Research Award, College of Liberal Arts, 1997. Memberships: American Military Institute, trustee, 1978-81, chairman, editorial advisory board, 1984-85; Department of the Army Historical Advisory Committee, 1983-87; International Institute for Strategic Studies, 1974-92; Phi Alpha Theta. Address: 308 East Brookside Drive, Bryan, TX 77801, USA.

BEAUSOLEIL Claude, b. 1948, Montreal, Quebec, Canada. Poet; Writer; Translator; Editor; Professor. Education: BA, Collège Sainte-Marie, University of Montreal; Bac Specialisé, MA, Université du Québec a Montréal; PhD, Sherbrooke University. Appointments: Professor of Quebec Literature, College Edouard-Montpetit, Longueuil, 1973-; Editor, Livrès urbaines. Publications: Intrusion ralentie, 1972; Journal mobile, 1974; Promenade modern style, 1975; Sens interdit, 1976; La surface du paysage, 1979; Au milieu du corps l'attraction s'insinue, 1980; Dans la matière revant comme une émeute, 1982; Le livre du voyage, 1983; Concrete City: Selected Poems 1972-82, 1983; Une certaine fin de siècle, 2 volumes, 1983, 1991; Les livres parlent, 1984; Il y a des nuits que nous habitons tous, 1986; Extase et déchirure, 1987; Grand hotel des étrangers, 1988; Fureur de Mexico, 1992; Montréal est une vill de poèmes vous savez, 1992; L'USage du temps, 1994. Honours: Prix Emile-Nelligan, 1980; Ordre des francophones d'Amérique, 1989. Address: c/o Union des écrivaines et écrivains québécois, La Maison des écrivains, 3492 Avenue Laval, Montreal, H2X 3C8, Canada.

BEAVER Bruce (Victor), b. 14 Feb 1928, Sydney, New South Wales, Australia. Journalist; Writer; Poet. m. Brenda Bellam, 30 Sept 1963. Publications: Under the

Bridge, 1961; Seawall and Shoreline, 1964; The Hot Spring, 1965; You Can't Come Back, 1966; Open at Random, 1967; Letters to Live Poets, 1969; Lauds and Plaints, 1968-72, 1974; Odes and Days, 1975; Death's Directives, 1978; As It Was: Selected Poems, 1979; Prose Sketches, 1986; Charmed Lives, 1988; New and Selected Poems, 1960-90, 1991. Contributions to: Periodicals. Honours: Poetry Society of Australia Awards, 1983; Christopher Brennan Award, Fellowship of Australian Writers, 1983; New South Wales State Literary Awards Special Citation, 1990; AM Award, 1991. Membership: Australian Society of Authors. Address: 14 Malvern Avenue, Manly, New South Wales 2095, Australia.

BEAVER Paul Eli, b. 3 Apr 1953, Winchester, England. Journalist; Author; Broadcaster. m. Ann Middleton, 20 May 1978, div June 1993. Education: Sheffield City Polytechnic; Henley Management College. Appointments: Editor, IPMS Magazine, 1976-80, Helicopter World, 1981-86, Defence Helicopter World, 1982-86, Jane's Videotape, 1986-87; Assistant Compiler, Jane's Fighting Ships, 1987-88; Managing Editor, Jane's Defence Yearbooks, 1988-89; Publisher, Jane's Defence Weekly, 1989-93; Senior Publisher, Jane's SENTINEL, 1993-94; Group Spokesman for Jane's, 1994-; Defence and Aerospace Correspondent, CNBC - Europe; Research Fellow, Centre for Defence and International Security Studies, Lancaster University, 1997-. Publications: Ark Royal - A Pictorial History, 1979; U-Boats in the Atlantic, 1979; German Capital Ships, 1980; German Destroyers and Escorts, 1981; Fleet Command, 1984; Invincible Class, 1984; Encyclopaedia of Aviation, 1986; Encyclopaedia of the Fleet Air Arm Since 1945, 1987; The Gulf States Regional Security Assessment, 1993; The Balkans Regional Security Assessment, 1994; D-DAY: Private Lines, 1994; The South China Sea Regional Security Assessment, 1994; The CIS Regional Security Assessment, 1994; The North Africa Regional Security Assessment, 1994; The China and North East Asia Regional Security Assessment, 1995; Baltics and Central Europe Regional Security Assessment, 1996; The Modern Royal Navy, 1996. Contributions to: Many journals. Address: Avenir House, Barton Stacey, Winchester, Hampshire, SO21 3RL, England.

BEBB Prudence, b. 20 Mar 1939, Catterick, England. Writer. Education: BA; Dip Ed. Publications: The Eleventh Emerald; The Ridgeway Ruby; The White Swan; The Nabob's Nephew; Life in Regency York; Butcher, Baker, Candlestick Maker; Life in Regency Harrogate, 1995; Life in Regency Scarborough, 1997. Membership: English Centre of International PEN. Address: 12 Brackenhills, Upper Poppleton, York YO26 6DH, England.

BEC. See: **BALLAURI Robert.**

BECHMANN Roland (Philippe), b. 1 Apr 1919, Paris, France. Architect; Historian; Writer. m. Martine Cohen, 18 July 1942, 6 daughters. Education: Licencié és Lettres, 1938; Government Architect Diploma, 1944; Doctor (3C) in Geography, 1978. Appointments: Architect; Chief Editor, Amenagement et Nature, 1966-. Publications: Les Racines des Cathedrales, L'architecture gothique, expression des conditions du milieu, 1981, 4th edition, 1996; Des Arbres et des Hommes: La foret au Moyen Age, 1984, English translation as Trees and Man: The Forest in the Middle Ages, 1990; Carnet de Villard de Honnecourt XIII e siècle (joint author), 1986; Villard de Honnecourt Disegni (joint author), 1987; Villard de Honnecourt: La pensée technique au XIIIe siècle et sa communication, 1991, 2nd edition, 1993; L'Arbre au Ciel (novel), 1997. Contributions to: Journals. Honours: Chevalier de la Légion d'Honneur, 1952; Croix de guerre, 1994. Membership: Association des Journalistes de l'Environnement. Address: 21-23 rue du Conseiller Collignon, 75116 Paris, France.

BECK Tatyana, b. 21 Apr 1949, Moscow, Russia. Poet; Writer. m. div. Education: Diploma of a Literary Editor, Moscow State University, 1972. Publications: Skvoreshniky, 1974; Snegir, 1980; Zamysel, 1987.

Poetry: Mixed Forest, 1993. Contributions to: Poems and Articles in: Novymir; Znamya; Oktyabr; Voprosy; Literatury; Literatyrnoe Obozrenie; Ogoniek; others. Memberships: Writers Union (former USSR); Russian PEN Centre, secretary. Address: Krasnoarmeiskaya Street, House No 23, Apartment 91, Moscow 125319, Russia.

BECKER Gary Stanley, b. 2 Dec 1930, Pottsville, Pennsylvania, USA. Professor of Economics and Sociology. m. (1) Doria Slote, 19 Sept 1954, 2 daughters, dec, (2) Guity Nashat, 31 Oct 1979, 2 sons. Education: AB summa cum laude, Princeton University, 1951; AM, 1953, PhD, 1955, University of Chicago. Appointments: Assistant and Associate Prof essor, Economics, Columbia University 1957-60; Professor, Economics, Columbia University, 1960-69; Professor Economics, University of Chicago 1969-83; University Professor, Economics, Sociology, 1983-, Chairman, Department of Economics, 1984-85, University of Chicago; Columnist, Business Week, 1985-. Publications: The Economics of Discrimination, 1957, 2nd edition, 1971; Human Capital, 1964, 3rd edition, 1993; Human Capital and the Personal Distribution of Income: An Analytical Approach, 1967; Economic Theory, 1971; Essays in the Economics of Crime and Punishment (editor with William M Landes), 1974; The Allocation of Time and Goods Over the Life Cycle (with Gilbert Ghez), 1975; Essays in Labor Economics in Honor of H Gregg Lewis (editor), 1976; The Economic Approach to Human Behavior, 1976; A Treatise on the Family, 1981, expanded edition, 1991; Accounting for Tastes, 1996; The Economics of Life (with Guity Nashat Becker), 1996; Several translated into other languages. Contributions to: American Economic Review; Journal of Political Economy; Quarterly Journal of Economics; Journal of Law and Economics; Journal of Population Economics; Econometrica; Business Economics; Several books. Honours: Nobel Prize for Economic Science, 1992; 7 honorary doctorates. Memberships: Phi Beta Kappa, 1950; Economic History Association; National Academy of Sciences; Distinguished Fellow, Past President, American Economic Association; Fellow: American Statistical Association; Econometric Society; American Academy of Arts and Sciences; National Association of Business Econometrics. Address: Department of Economics, University of Chicago, 1126 East 59th Street, Chicago, IL 60637, USA.

BECKER Jürgen, b. 10 July 1932, Cologne, Germany. Poet; Writer; Dramatist. m. 1) Marie, 1954, div 1965, 1 son, 2) Rango Bohne, 1965, 1 stepson, 1 stepdaughter. Education: University of Cologne, 1953-54. Appointments: Writer, Westdeutscher Rundfunk, Cologne, 1959-64; Reader, Rowohlt Verlag, 1964-66; Head, Department of Drama, Deutsche Welle, Cologne, 1974-93. Publications: Felder, 1964; Ränder, 1968; Umgebungen, 1970; Schnee, 1971; Das Ende der Landschaftsmalerei, 1974; Erzahl mir nichts vom Krieg, 1977; In der verbleibenden Zeit, 1979; Erzählen bis Ostende, 1981; Gedichte 1965-1980, 1981; Odenthals Küste, 1986; Das Gedicht von der wiedervereinigten Landschaft, 1988; Das englische Fenster, 1990; Foxtrott im Erfurter Stadio, 1993; Korrespondenzen mit Landschaft (with Rango Bohne), 1996; Das heilende Rest, 1997. Other: Various radio plays. Honours: Literature Prize, Cologne, 1968; Literature Prize, Bavarian Academy of Fine Arts, Munich, 1980; Critics' Prize, 1981; Literature Prize, Bremen, 1986; Peter Huchel Prize, 1994; Literature Prize, Berlin, 1994; Heinrich Böll Prize, 1995. Memberships: Akademie der Künste, Berlin-Brandenburg; Deutsche Akademie für Sprache und Dichtung e.v., Darmstadt; PEN Centre, Federal Republic of Germany. Address: Am Klausenberg 84, D-51109 Cologne, Germany.

BECKER Lucille (F(rackman), b. 4 Feb 1929, USA. Professor of French Emerita; Writer. Education: University of Mexico, 1948; BA, Barnard College, 1949; Teachers College, Columbia University, 1949; Fulbright Scholar Diplôme d'études francaises, Université d'Aix-Marseille, 1950; MA, 1954, PhD, 1958, Columbia University. Appointments: Part Time Instructor, Columbia

University, 1954-58, University College, Rutgers University, 1958-68; Associate Professor of French, 1968-77, Chair, Department of French, 1976-81, Professor of French, 1977-93, Professor of French Emerita, 1993-; Drew University. Publications: Le Maitre de Santiago, by Henry de Montherlant (co-editor), 1965; Henry de Montherlant, 1970; Louis Aragon, 1971; Georges Simenon, 1977; Francoise Mallet-Joris, 1985; Twentieth-Century French Women Novelists, 1989; Pierre Boulle, 1996. Contributions to: Scholarly books and journals. Memberships: American Association of Teachers of French; American Association of University Professors; French Institute/Alliance Francaise; Modern Language Association; South Atlantic Modern Language Association. Address: 82 Harding Drive, South Orange, NJ 07079, USA.

BECKER Stephen David, b. 31 Mar 1927, Mt Vernon, New York, USA. Novelist; Translator. m. Mary Elizabeth Freeburg, 24 Dec 1947, 2 sons, 1 daughter. Education: AB, Harvard College, 1947; Yenching University, Beijing, 1947-48. Appointments: Occasional teaching and lecturing at several universities. Publications: Novels: The Season of the Stranger, 1951; Shanghai Incident, 1955; Juice, 1959; A Covenant with Death, 1965; The Outcasts, 1967; When the War is Over, 1970; Dog Tags, 1973, new edition, 1987; The Chinese Bandit, 1975; The Last Mandarin, 1979; The Blue-Eyed Shan, 1982; A Rendezvous in Haiti, 1987. Non-fiction: Comic Art in America, 1959; Marshall Field III, 1964. Translations: The Colours of the Day, 1953; Mountains in the Desert, 1954; The Sacred Forest, 1954; Faraway, 1957; Someone Will Die Tonight in the Caribbean, 1958; The Last of the Just, 1961; The Town Beyond the Wall, 1964; The Conquerors, 1976; Diary of My Travels in America, 1977; Ana No, 1980; The Aristotle System, 1985; Cruel April, 1990; Between Tides, 1991; The Forgotten, 1992. Contributions to: Dozens of short stories, essays, reviews, columns, introductions. Honours: Rotary Fellowship to Peking, 1947; Guggenheim Fellowship, 1954; National Endowment for the Arts grant in translation, 1984; Judge, Hopwood Awards, fiction, University of Michigan, 1989. Literary Agent: Russell & Volkening, New York. Address: 1281 North East 85th Street, Miami, FL 33138, USA.

BECKET Henry S A. See. **GOULDEN Joseph C.**

BECKET Michael Ivan H, b. 11 Sept 1938, Budapest, Hungary. Publications: Computer By the Jail; Economic Alphabet; Bluff Your Way in Finance; Office Warfare; A-Z of Finance. Address: 9 Kensington Park Gardens, London W11 3HB, England.

BECKETT Kenneth Albert, b. 12 Jan 1929, Brighton, Sussex, England. Horticulturalist; Technical Advisor; Editor. m. Gillian Tuck, 1 Aug 1973, 1 son. Education: Diploma, Horticulture, Royal Horticulture Society. Appointments: Technical Editor, Gardener's Chronicle, Reader's Digest; Retired. Publications: The Love of Trees, 1975; Illustrated Dictionary of Botany, 1977; Concise Encyclopaedia of Garden Plants, 1978; Amateur Greenhouse Gardening, 1979; Growing Under Glass, 1981; Complete Book of Evergreens, 1981; Growing Hardy Perennials, 1981; Climbing Plants, 1983; The Garden Library, 4 volumes: Flowering House Plants, Annuals and Biennials, Roses, Herbs, 1984; The RHS Encyclopaedia of House Plants, 1987; Evergreens, 1990; Alpine Garden Society Encyclopaedia of Alpines, 2 volumes, 1993-94. Contributions to: The Garden; The Plantsman. Honours: Veitch Memorial Medal, Royal Horticultural Society, 1987; Lyttel Trophy, 1995 and Clarence Elliott Memorial Award, 1995, Alpine garden Society. Memberships: The Wild Plant conservation Charity; Friends of the Royal Botanic Gardens, Kiev; Australasian Plant Society; Botanical Society of the British Isles; Plantsman; International Dendrology Society; Butterfly Conservation; Alpine Garden Society. Address: Bramley Cottage, Stanhoe, King's Lynn, Norfolk PE31 8QF, England.

BECKLES WILLSON Robina Elizabeth, b. 26 Sept 1930, London, England. Writer. m. Anthony Beckles

Willson, 1 son, 1 daughter, Education: BA, 1948, MA, 1952, University of Liverpool. Appointments: Teacher, Liverpool School of Art, 1952-56; Ballet Rambert Educational School, London, 1956-58. Publications: Leopards on the Loire, 1961; A Time to Dance, 1962; Musical Instruments, 1964; A Reflection of Rachel, 1967; The Leader of the Band, 1967; Roundabout Ride, 1968; Dancing Day, 1971; The Last Harper, 1972; The Shell on Your Back, 1972; What a Noise, 1974; The Voice of Music, 1975; Musical Merry-go-Round, 1977; The Beaver Book of Ballet, 1979; Eyes Wide Open, 1981; Anna Pavlova: A Legend Among Dancers, 1981; Pocket Book of Ballet, 1982; Secret Witch, 1982; Square Bear, 1 983; Merry Christmas, 1983; Holiday Witch, 1983; Sophie and Nicky series, 2 volumes, Hungry Witch, 1984; Music Maker, 1986; Sporty Witch, 1986; The Haunting Music, 1987; Mozart's Story, 1991; Just Imagine, 1993; Harry Stories in Animal World, 1996; Ambulance!, 1996. Address: 44 Popes Avenue, Twickenham, Middlesex TW2 5TL, England.

BECKWITH Lillian, b. 25 Apr 1916, Ellesmere Port, England. Author. m. Edward Thornthwaite Comber, 3 June 1937, 1 son, 1 daughter. Education: Ornum College, Birkenhead. Publications: The Hebridean Stories: The Hill is Lonely, 1959; The Sea for Breakfast, 1961; The Loud Halo, 1964; Green Hand, 1967; A Rope in Case, 1968; About My Father's Business, 1971; Lightly Poached, 1973; The Spuddy, 1974; Beautiful Just, 1975; The Lillian Beckwith Hebridean Cookbook, 1976; Bruach Blend, 1978; A Shine of Rainbows, 1984; A Proper Woman, 1986; The Bay of Strangers, 1989 The Small Party, 1989; An Island Apart, 1992. Contributions to: Countryman; Woman's Own and various other magazines for women. Memberships: Society of Authors; Mark Twain Society; Women of the Year Association, Consultative Committee. Address: c/o Curtis Brown Ltd, 4th Floor Haymarket House, 28/29 Haymarket, London SW1Y 4SP.

BEDAU Hugo Adam, b. 23 Sept 1926, Portland, Oregon, USA. Professor of Philosophy; Author. m. (1) Jan Mastin, 1952, div 1988, 3 sons, 1 daughter, (2) Constance Putnam, 1990. Education: BA, University of Redlands, 1949; MA, Boston University, 1951; MA, 1953, PhD, 1961, Harvard University. Appointments: Instructor, Dartmouth College, 1953-54; Lecturer, Princeton University, 1954-57, 1958-61; Associate Professor, Reed College, 1962-66; Professor of Philosophy, Tufts University, 1966-. Publications: Victimless Crimes: Two Views (with Edwin M Schur), 1974; The Courts, the Constitution, and Capital Punishment, 1977; Current Issues and Enduring Questions (with Sylvan Barnet), 1987, 5th edition, 1999; Death is Different: Studies in the Morality, Law, and Politics of Capital Punishment, 1987; In Spite of Innocence (with Michael Radelet and Constance Putnam), 1992; Critical Thinking, Reading, and Writing (with Sylvan Barnet), 1993, 3rd edition, 1999; Thinking and Writing About Philosophy, 1996; Making Mortal Choices, 1996. Editor: The Death Penalty in America, 1964, 4th edition, 1997; Civil Disobedience: Theory and Practice, 1969; Justice and Equality, 1971; Capital Punishment in the United States (with Chester M Pierce), 1976; Civil Disobedience in Focus, 1991. Contributions to: Many books, journals, and magazines. Honours: Visiting Life Fellow, Clare Hall/Cambridge University, 1980, 1988, Max Planck Institutes, Heidelberg and Freiburg im Breisgau, 1988, Wolfson College, Oxford, 1989; Romanell-Phi Beta Kappa Professor of Philosophy, 1995. Memberships: American Association of University Professors; American Philosophical Association; American Society for Political and Legal Philosophy. Address: Department of Philosophy, Tufts University, Medford, MA 02155, USA.

BEDE. See: JOHNSON Paul

BEDFORD Martyn Corby, b. 10 Oct 1959, Croydon, Surrey, England. Writer. m. Damaris Croxall, 8 Jan 1994. Education: MA, Creative Writing, University of East Anglia, Norwich, England, 1994. Appointments: Bank Clerk, London, 1978-79; Reporter, South London Press, 1980-83, 1985; English Teacher, Hong Kong, 1984; Sports Reporter, South Wales Echo, Cardiff, 1985-87;

Reporter, Gloucester Citizen, 1988; Reporter, Sub-Editor, Features Writer, Oxford Mail/Times, 1988-93; Sub-Editor, Bradford Telegraph & Argus, 1994-95. Publications: Acts of Revision, novel, 1996; Yorkshire Post Best First Work Award; Exit, Orange & Red, novel, 1997; The Houdini Girl (novel), 1999. Honour: Yorkshire Post Best First Work Award. Membership: Ilkley Literary Festival Management Committee, 1996-. Literary Agent: Jonny Geller, Curtis Brown. Address: c/o Curtis Brown, Haymarket House, 28-29 Haymarket, London SW1Y 4SP, England.

BEDFORD Sybille, b. 16 Mar 1911, Charlottenburg, Germany (British citizen). Writer. m. Walter Bedford, 1935. Education: Private studies in Italy, England, and France. Publications: A Legacy, 1956; A Favorite of the Gods, 1963; A Compass Error, 1968; Aldous Huxley, 2 volumese, 1973-74; Jigsaw: An Unsentimental Education, 1989. Contributions to: Magazines. Honours: Officer of the Order of the British Empire, 1981; Society of Authors Travelling Scholarship, 1989; Companion of Literature, 1994. Memberships: English PEN, vice president; Royal Society of Literature, fellow, 1964-. Address: c/o Lutyens and Rubenstein, 231 Westbourne Park Road, London W11 1EB, England.

BEECHING Jack, b. 8 May 1922, Hastings, Sussex, England. Writer; Poet. Publications: Fiction: Let Me See Your Face, 1958; The Dakota Project, 1967; Death of a Terrorist, 1982; Tides of Fortune, 1988. Non-Fiction: The Chinese Opium Wars, 1975; An Open Path: Christian Missionaries 1515-1914, 1979; The Galleys at Lepanto, 1982. Poetry: Aspects of Love, 1950; The Polythene Maidenhead, in Penguin Modern Poets, 1969; Twenty-Five Short Poems, 1982; The View From the Balloon, 1990; The Invention of Love, 1996. Address: c/o Tessa Sayle Agency, 11 Jubilee Place, London SW3 3CE, England.

BEER Gillian Patricia Kempster, b. 27 Jan 1935, Bookham, Surrey, England. University Professor. m. John Bernard Beer, 7 July 1962, 3 sons. Education: BA 1st class, English, BLitt, St Anne's College, Oxford, 1954-59; LittD, University of Cambridge, 1989. Appointments: Bedford College, University of London, 1959-62; University of Liverpool, 1962-64; Currently: King Edward VII Professor, University of Cambridge; President, Clare Hall, University of Cambridge. Publications: Meredith: A Change of Masks, 1970; The Romance, 1970; Darwin's Plots, 1983; George Eliot, 1986; Arguing with the Past, 1989; Open Fields: Science in Cultural Encounter, 1996; Virginia Woolf: the Common Ground, 1996. Contributions to: Numerous. Honours: Rose Mary Crawshay Prize, 1983; Fellow, British Academy, 1991-; Dame Commander, 1998. Membership: PEN. Address: Clare Hall, Cambridge CB3 9AL, England.

BEER Patricia, b.4 Nov 1924, Exmouth, Devon, England. Writer; Poet. m. (2) John Damien Parsons, 1964. Education: BA, University of London; BLitt, St Hugh's College, Oxford. Appointments: Lecturer in English, University of Padua, 1946-48, Ministero Aeronautica, Rome, 1950-53; Senior Lecturer in English, Goldsmiths' College, University of London, 1962-68. Publications: Loss of the Magyar and Other Poems, 1959; New Poems (editor with Ted Hughes and Vernon Scannell), 1962; The Survivors, 1963; Just Like the Resurrection, 1967; Mrs Beer's House (autobiography), 1968; The Estuary, 1971; An Introduction to the Metaphysical Poets, 1972; Spanish Balcony, 1973; Reader, I Married Him, 1974; Driving West, 1975; Moon's Ottery, 1978; Poems 1967-79, Selected Poems, 1979; The Lie of the Land, 1983; Wessex, 1985; Collected Poems, 1988. Contributions to: Listener; London Review of Books. Address: Tiphayes, Up Ottery, Near Honiton, Devon, England.

BEERS Burton F(loyd), b. 13 Sept 1927, Chemung, New York, USA. Professor of History; Writer. m. Pauline Cone Beers, 6 Sept 1952, 1 son, 1 daughter. Education: AB, Hobart College, 1950; MA, 1952, PhD, 1956, Duke University. Appointments: Instructor, 1955-57, Assistant Professor, 1957-61, Associate Professor, 1961-66, Professor, 1966-96, North Carolina State University.

Publications: Vain Endeavor: Robert Lansing's Attempts to End the American-Japanese Rivalry, 1962; The Far East: A History of Western Impacts and Eastern Responses, 1830-1875 (with Paul H Clyde), 4th to 6th editions, 1966-75; China in Old Photographs, 1981; North Carolina's China Connection 1840-1949 (with Lawrence Kessler and Charles LaMonica), 1981; North Carolina State University: A Pictorial History (with Murray S Downs), 1986; The Vietnam War: An Historical Case Study (with Rose Ann Mulford), 1997; Living in our World (chief executive editor), 1998. Contributions to: Textbooks, books, scholarly journals, and periodicals. Honours: Alexander Quarles Holladay Medal for Excellence, North Carolina State University Board of Trustees, 1992; Medal for Excellence, Hobart and William Smith Colleges, 1994; Watauga Medal, North Carolina State University, 1998. Memberships: American Historical Association; Association for Asian Studies; Association of Historians in North Carolina; Historical Society of North Carolina; Phi Alpha Theta; Phi Beta Kappa; Phi Kappa Phi; North Carolina Literary and Historical Society; Sigma Iota Rho; Society for Historians of American Foreign Relations; Southern Historical Association. Address: 629 South Lakeside Drive, Raleigh, NC 27606, USA.

BEESON Diane Kay, b. 3 Sept 1949, Boulder, Colorado, USA. Teacher; Writer; Poet; Translator. Education: BA, Lindenwood College, 1972; MA, Middlebury College, 1974; TOEFL Certificate, Fundación Ponce de Leon, Madrid, 1981; Diploma, Translation, Institute of Linguists, England, 1987. Appointments: Director, English Classes, Grupo Anaya, 1983-92; Staff, Linguacentre Academy, 1984-89; Faculty, British Institute for Young Learners, British Council, 1994-98; Faculty, University of Delaware at University of Madrid, 1988-89; Professor, University of Cluny of Paris in Madrid, 1992-93. Publications: 8 books (co-author); Translator, 4 books. Contributions to: Anthologies, journals, and periodicals. Honours: Outstanding Woman of America, 1975; Joyce Kilmer Contest, Colorado, 1982; Honourable citations. Memberships: American Association of University Women; Association of Teachers of Spanish and Portuguese; Institute of Linguists; Modern Language Association; National League of American Pen Women; Teachers of English to Speakers of Other Languages, Spain. Address: 685 5 La Posada Circle, Green Valley, AZ 85614, USA.

BEEVOR Antony, b. 14 Dec 1946, London, England. Historian; Novelist. m. Artemis Cooper, 2 Feb 1986, 1 son, 1 daughter. Education: Winchester College; Grenoble University; Royal Military Academy, Sandhurst. Appointment: Executive Council French Theatre Season, 1997. Publications: The Spanish Civil War, 1982; The Enchantment of Christina Von Retzen (novel), 1988; Inside the British Army, 1990; Crete: The Battle and the Resistance, 1991; Paris After the Liberation 1944-49, 1994; Stalingrad, 1998. Contributions to: Times Literary Supplement; Times; Telegraph; Independent, Spectator. Honours: Runciman Award, 1992; Chevalier de l'Ordre des Arts et Lettres, (French Government), 1997. Memberships: Society of Authors; Royal Geographical Society; Anglo Hellenic League; Friends of the British Libraries. Literary Agent: Andrew Nurnberg. Address: 54 Saint Maur Road, London SW6 4DP, England.

BEGLEY Louis, b. 6 Oct 1933, Stryj, Poland. Lawyer; Writer. m. (1) Sally Higginson, 11 Feb 1956, div May 1970, 2 sons, 1 daughter, (2) Anne Muhlstein Dujarric dela Riviere, 30 Mar 1974. Education: AB, 1954, LLB, 1959, Harvard University. Appointments: Specialist in international corporate law; writer; lecturer. Publications: Novels: Wartime Lies, 1991; The Man Who Was Late, 1993; As Max Saw It, 1994; About Schmidt, 1996. Contributions to: Periodicals. Honours: Irish Times-Aer Lingus International Fiction Prize, 1991; PEN/Ernest Hemingway First Fiction Award, 1992; Prix Medicis Étranger, 1992; Jeanette-Schocken Preis, Bremerhaven Bürgerpreis für Literatur, 1995; American Academy of Letters Award in Literature, 1995. Memberships: Bar Association of the City of New York; Council on Foreign Relations; Union Internationale des Avocats. Address: c/o

Georges Borchardt, 136 East 57th Street, New York, NY 10022, USA.

BEGUIN Louis-Paul, b. 31 Mar 1923, Amiens, France. Writer; Poet. Education: BA, Sorbonne, University of Paris. Publicatioins: Miroir de Janus, 1966; Impromptu de Québec, 1974; Un Homme et son langage, 1977; Problèmes de langage, 1978; Idoles et Paraboles, 1982; Yourcenar, 1982; Poèmes et pastiches, 1985; Parcours paralleles, 1988; 'Ange Pleureur, 1991; Poèmes depuis la tendre enfance, 1995; The Weeping Angel, 1996. Contributions to: Newspapers and magazines. Honours: Poetry Award, 1967; Prix Montcalm, 1974. Memberships: PEN, Quebec; Quebec Writers Union. Address: 1800 rue Bercy, Apartment 1218, Montreal, Quebec H2K 4K5, Canada.

BEHLEN Charles (William), b. 29 Jan 1949, Slaton, Texas, USA. Poet. 1 daughter. Education: New Mexico Junior College, 1968-70. Publications: Perdition's Keepsake; Three Texas Poets; Dreaming at the Wheel; Uirsche's First Three Decades; The Voices Under the Floor. Contributions to: Bloomsbury Review; Cedar Rock; New Mexico Humanities Review; Poetry Now; Puerto del Sol; The Smith; Texas Observer; Borderlands; New Texas '91; New Texas '95. Honours: Pushcart Prize (nominee); Ruth Stephan Reader; Manuscripts Displayed and Placed in Time Capsule by San Antonio Museum of Art; Guest Poet, Tenth Annual Houston Poetry Fest; Dobie-Paisano Fellowship in Poetry (1995-96). Address: 501 West Industrial Drive, Apartment 503-B, Sulphur Springs, TX 75482, USA.

BEHR Edward (Samuel), b. 7 May 1926, Paris, France. Journalist; Editor; Writer. m. Christiane Wagrez, 1 Apr 1967. Education: BA, 1951, MA, 1953, Magdalene College, Cambridge. Appointments: Correspondent, Reuters, 1950-54; Time Inc, 1957-63; Contributing Editor, Saturday Evening Post, 1963-65; Reporter-Director, Cinq Colonnes a la Une TV Programme, 1963-65; Paris Correspondent, 1965-66, Hong Kong Bureau Chief, 1966-68, Paris Bureau Chief, 1968-72, European Editor, Paris, 1973-83, Cultural Editor, 1984-87, Contributing Editor, 1987-, Newsweek Magazine. Publications: The Algerian Problem, 1961; Lai Ying: The Thirty-Sixth Way: A Personal Account of Imprisonment and Escape from Red Chine (translator and editor with Sydney Liu), 1969; Bearings: A Foreign Correspondent's Life Behind the Lines, 1978 (in the UK as Anyone Here Been Raped and Speaks English?, 1981); Getting Even (novel), 1980; The Last Emperor (novel based on the film), 1987; Hirohito: Behind the Myth, 1989; The Complete Book of Les Miserables, 1990; Indonesia: A Voyage Through the Archipelago, 1990; The Story of Miss Saigon (with Mark Steyn), 1991; Kiss the Hand You Cannot Bite: The Rise and Fall of the Ceausescus, 1991; The Good Frenchman: The True Story of the Life and Times of Maurice Chevalier, 1993. Honour: Gutenberg Prize, 1988. Address: c/o Newsweek, 162 Faubour St Honore, Paris 75008, France.

BEILBY Alexander John, (Alec Beilby), b. 4 Jan 1938, London, England. Journalist; Writer. Appointments: Daily Mail, 1966-71; Financial Times, 1971-80; Sunday Express/Daily Express, 1980-89. Publications: To Beat the Clipper, 1976; Rough Passage, 1986; Survival at Sea, 1989; Heroes All!, 1992. Contributions to: Country Life; Field; Yachtsman; Sunday Express Magazine; Australian Life. Membership: Yachting Journalists Association. Address: Bow Cottage, Ermington, Ivybridge, Devon PL1 2LP, England.

BEIM Norman, b. 2 Oct 1923, Newark, New Jersey, USA. Dramatist; Director; Actor. Education: Ohio State University; Hedgerow Theatre School, Philadelphia; Institute of Contemporary Art, Washington, DC. Appointments: Many theatre productions, 1950-. Publications: Six Award Winning Plays, 1994; Plays at Home and Abroad, 1996; My Family, The Jewish Immigrants, 1997. Honours: Various theatre awards. Memberships: Actors Equity Association; Dramatists Guild; Federation of Television and Radio Artists; Literary Managers and Dramatists; Screen Actors Guild. Address: 425 West 57th Street, Apt 2J, New York, NY 10019, USA.

BEISSEL Henry (Eric), b. 12 Apr 1929, Cologne, Germany. Poet; Dramatist; Writer; Translator; Editor; Teacher. m. (1) 2 daughters, (2) Arlette Francière, 3 Apr 1981, 1 daughter. Education: University of London, 1949; BA, 1958, MA, 1960, University of Toronto, Canada. Appointments: Teacher, University of Edmonton, 1962-64; University of Trinidad, 1964-66, Concordia University, Montreal, 1966-96; Founder-Editor, Edge Journal, 1963-69. Publications: Poetry: Witness the Heart, 1963; New Wings for Icarus, 1966; The World is a Rainbow, 1968; Face on the Dark, 1970; The Salt I Taste, 1975; Cantos North, 1980; Season of Blood, 1984; Poems New and Selected, 1987; Ammonite, 1987; Stones to Harvest, 1987; Dying I Was Born, 1992. Plays: Inook and the Sun, 1974; Goya, 1978; Under Coyote's Eye, 1980; The Noose, 1989; Improvisations for Mr X, 1989. Other: Kanada: Romantik und Wirklichkeit, 1981; Raging Like a Fire: A Celebration of Irving Layton (editor with Joy Bennett), 1993; Translations of poetry and plays. Contributions to: Journals. Honours: Epstein Award, 1958; Davidson Award, 1959; Deutscher Akademischer Austauschdienst Fellowship, 1977; Walter-Bauer Literaturpreis, Germany, 1994. Memberships: International Academy of Poets; League of Canadian Poets, president, 1980-81; PEN; Playwrights Canada. Address: Box 339, Alexandria, Ontario K0C 1A0, Canada.

BEKEDEREMO J P Clark. See: **CLARK John Pepper.**

BEKRI Tahar, b. 7 July 1951, Gabes, Tunisia. Writer; Poet. m. Annick Letheor, 16 Jan 1987. Education: Licence in French Literature, University of Tunisia, 1975; PhD in French Literature, Sorbonne, University of Paris, 1981. Publications: Le Laboureur du soleil, 1983; Le Chant du roi errant, 1985; Malek Haddad, 1986; Le coeur rompu aux oceans, 1988; Les Chapelets d'attaché, 1994; Litteratures de Tunisie et du Maghreb, 1994; Poèmes a Selma, 1996. Contributions to: Various publications. Honour: Officier Mérite Cultural, Tunisia, 1993. Address: 32 Rue Pierre Nicole, 75005 Paris, France.

BELCZYNSKA Barbara, b. 3 Sept 1947, Mlynary, Poland. Writer. Education: Coll in Bydgoszcz, 1970; Econ. Appointments: Econ, 1971-90; Writer, 1990-. Publications: The Silver Wind, 1990; Nobody's Pearls, 1991; The Tear Among Stars, 1992; The Diogenesis Lantern, 1993; The Conjure, 1995; The Matrimonial Announcement, 1997; Meditations, 1999. Contributions to: Metafora Literary Magazine. Membership: Lit Soc, Klin. Literary Agent: Wydawnictwo Ksiazkowe, Festinus, Lodz, Poland. Address: Broniewskiego 111 m 31, 93-253 Lodz, Poland.

BELIC Oldrich, b. 9 June 1920, Nasedlovice, Czech Republic. Professor. m. Zdenka Neubauerova, 1996, 1 son, 1 daughter. Education: Masaryk University Brno, Romance and Slavonic Philology, 1947, Dr of Philology, 1947, Dr of Philological Sciences, 1963. Appointments: Assistant, University of Olomuc, 1947; Assistant Professor, Olomouc, 1954, Prague, 1958; Professor of Spanish and Spanish-American Literature, University of Prague, 1963. Publications: The Spanish Picaresque Novel and the Realism, 1963; Spanish Literature, 1968; Structural Analysis of Hispanic Texts, 1969, 1977; The Essence of the Spanish Verse, 1975; Introduction to the Theory of Literature, with J Hrabak, 1983, 1988. Contributions to: Numerous essays on Spanish and Spanish-American Literature, in Spanish published mostly in: Philologica Pragensia, Romanistica Pragensia; Ibero-Americana Pragensia. Honour: Commander of the Order of Elisabeth the Catholic, 1991. Address: Vranovska 108, 614 00, Brno, Czech Republic.

BELITT Ben, b. 2 May 1911, New York, New York, USA. Professor of Literature and Languages; Poet; Writer. Education: BA, 1932, MA, 1934, Postgraduate Studies, 1934-36, University of Virginia. Appointments: Assistant Literary Editor, The Nation, 1936-37; Faculty Member to Professor of Literature and Languages, Bennington College, Vermont, 1938-. Publications: Poetry: Wilderness Stair, 1955; The Enemy Joy: New and Selected Poems, 1964; Nowhere But Light: Poems, 1964-1969, 1970; The Double Witness: Poems, 1970-1976, 1977; Possessions: New and Selected Poems, 1938-1985, 1986; Graffiti, 1990. Other: School of the Soldier, 1949; Adam's Dream: A Preface to Translation, 1978; The Forged Feature: Toward a Poetics of Uncertainty, 1994. Editor and translator of several volumes. Contributions to: Books. Honours: Shelley Memorial Award in Poetry, 1936; Guggenheim Fellowship, 1947; Brandeis University Creative Arts Award, 1962; National Institute of Arts and Letters Award, 1965; National Endowment for the Arts Grant, 1967-68; Ben Belitt Lectureship Endowment, Bennington College, 1977; Russell Loines Award for Poetry, American Academy and Institute of Arts and Letters, 1981; Rockefeller Foundation Residency, Bellagio, Italy, 1984; Williams/Derwood Award for Poetry, 1986. Memberships: Authors Guild; Phi Beta Kappa; PEN; Vermont Academy of Arts and Sciences, fellow. Address: PO Box 88, North Bennington, VT 05257, USA.

BELL Charles Greenleaf, b. 31 Oct 1916, Greenville, Mississippi, USA. Retired Teacher; Writer; Poet. Education: BS, University of Virginia, 1936; BA, 1938, LittB, 1939, MA, 1966, University of Oxford, England. Publications: Fiction: The Married Land, 1962; The Half Gods, 1968. Poetry: Songs for a New America, 1953, revised edition, 1966; Delta Return, 1955, revised edition 1969; Five Chambered Heart, 1985. Other: The Spirit of Rome (film), 1965; Symbolic History: Through Sight and Sound (40 slide tape/video dramas). Contributions to: Magazines. Honours: Ford Foundation Fellowship; Rhodes Scholarship; Rockefeller Foundation Grant. Address: 1260 Canyon Road, Santa Fe, NM 87501, USA.

BELL James Edward, b. 12 May 1941, Chicago, Illinois, USA. Psychologist; Professor; Writer. m. Ruth Wilder Bell, 5 Sept 1964, 1 son, 1 daughter. Education: BA, Psychology, 1963; PhD, Psychology, 1967, University of Minnesota. Appointments: Assistant Professor, Hanover College, Indiana, 1966-68, Elmira College, New York, 1968-71; Assistant Professor, 1971-74, Associate Professor, 1974-82, Professor, 1982-, Howard Community College, Columbia, Maryland. Publications: A Guide to Library Research in Psychology, 1971; Ideas and Issues in Psychology (editor), 7th edition, 1993; Evaluating Psychological Information: A Guide to Critical Thinking in Psychology, 3rd edition, 1998. Contributions to: Professional books and journals. Honours: Fellowships and grants. Memberships: American Psychological Association; Council of Teachers of Undergraduate Psychology. Address: 5411 Storm Drift, Columbia, MD 21045, USA.

BELL Madison Smartt, b. 1 Aug 1957, Nashville, Tennessee, USA. Author; College Teacher. m. Elizabeth Spires, 15 June 1985. Education: AB, Princeton University, 1979; MA, Hollins College, 1981. Appointments: Lecturer, Poetry Center of the 92nd Street YMHA, New York City, 1984-86; Writer-in-Residence, Director of the Creative Writing Program, Goucher College, 1984-86, 1988-; Visiting Lecturer, University of Iowa, 1987-88; Visiting Associate Professor, Johns Hopkins University, 1989-95. Publications: Fiction: The Washington Square Ensemble, 1983; Waiting for the End of the World, 1985; Straight Cut, 1986; Zero db, 1987; The Year of Silence, 1987; Soldier's Joy, 1989; Barking Man, 1990; Doctor Sleep, 1991; Save Me, Joe Louis, 1993; All Souls' Rising, 1995; Ten Indians, 1996. Non-Fiction: Readers' guides on various authors, 1979-83; The History of the Owen Graduate School of Management, 1988. Contributions to: Fiction in many anthologies and periodicals; Essays, book reviews, etc. Honours: Lillian Smith Award, 1989; Guggenheim Fellowship, 1991; George A and Eliza Gardner Howard Foundation Award, 1991-92; National Endowment for the Arts Fellowship, 1992; National Book Award Finalist, 1995; PEN/Faulkner Award Finalist, 1996. Address: 6208 Pinehurst Road, Baltimore, MD 21212, USA.

BELL Marvin (Hartley), b. 3 Aug 1937, New York, New York, USA. Flannery O'Connor Professor of Letters; Poet; Writer. m. Dorothy Murphy, 2 sons. Education: BA, Alfred University, 1958; MA in Literature, University of Chicago, 1961; MFA in Literature, University of Iowa, 1963. Appointments: Faculty, Writers Workshop, 1965-, Flannery O'Connor Professor of Letters, 1986-, University of Iowa; Visiting Lecturer, Goddard College, 1970; Columnist, American Poetry Review, 1975-78, 1990-92; Distinguished Visiting Professor, University of Hawaii, 1981; Visiting Professor, University of Washington, 1982; Lila Wallace-Reader's Digest Writing Fellow, University of Redlands, 1991-93; Woodrow Wilson Visiting Fellow, Saint Mary's College of California, 1994-95, Pacific University, 1996-97, Nebraska-Wesleyan University, 1996-97; Series Poetry Editor, Pushcart Prize, 1997-. Publications: Poetry: Things We Dreamt We Died For, 1966; A Probable Volume of Dreams, 1969; The Escape Into You, 1971; Residue of Song, 1974; Stars Which See, Stars Which Do Not See, 1977; These Green-Going-to-Yellow, 1981; Segues: A Correspondence in Poetry (with William Stafford), 1983; Drawn by Stones, by Earth, by Things That Have Been in the Fire, 1984; New and Selected Poems, 1987; Iris of Creation, 1990; The Book of the Dead Man, 1994; Ardor: The Book of the Dead Man, Vol 2, 1997; Poetry for a Midsummer's Night, 1998; Wednesday: Selected Poems 1966-1997, 1998. Other: Old Snow Just Melting: Essays and Interviews, 1983; A Marvin Bell Reader: Selected Prose and Poetry, 1994. Contributions to: Many anthologies and periodicals. Honours: Lamont Award, Academy of American Poets, 1969; Bess Hokin Award, Poetry magazine, 1969; Emily Clark Balch Prize, Virginia Quarterly Review, 1970; National Book Award Finalist, 1977; Guggenheim Fellowship, 1977; National Endowment for the Arts Fellowships, 1978, 1984; American Poetry Review Prize, 1982; Senior Fulbright Scholar to Yugoslavia, 1983, and to Australia, 1986; Honorary Doctorate of Letters, Alfred University, 1986; American Academy of Arts and Letters Award in Literature, 1994. Address: 1416 East College Street, Iowa City, IA 52245, USA.

BELL Robin, b. 4 Jan 1945, Dundee, Scotland. Writer. 2 daughters. Education: MA, St Andrews University, Scotland; MS, Columbia University, New York, USA. Appointments: Various appointments in publishing & university teaching in New York, London and Edinburgh, 1968-82. Publications: Sawing Logs, 1980; Strathinver: A Portrait Album, 1984; Radio Poems, 1989; Scanning the Forth Bridge, 1994; Editor: The Best of Scottish Poetry, 1989; Collected poems of the Marquis of Montrose, 1990; Bittersweet Within My Heart, The Collected Poems of Mary, Queen of Scots, 1992. Honours: Best Documentary Television and Radio Industries of Scotland Award, 1994; Sony Award for Best British Radio Feature, 1995. Memberships: General Secretary, Poetry Association of Scotland, 1983-. Address: The Orchard Muirton, Auchterarder, Perthshire, PH3 1ND, Scotland.

BELLAMY David James, b. 18 Jan 1933, England. Botanist; Writer. m. Rosemary Froy, 1959, 2 sons, 3 daughters. Education: Chelsea College of Science and Technology; PhD, Bedford College, London University. Appointments: Lecturer, Botany, 1960-68, Senior Lecturer, Botany, 1968-82, Honorary Professor, Adult Education, 1982-, University of Durham; Television and radio presenter, scriptwriter of series including: Bellamy's New World, 1983; Seaside Safari, 1985; The End of the Rainbow Show, 1986; Bellamy on Top of the World, 1987; Turning the Tide, 1987; Bellamy's Bulge, 1987-88; Bellamy's Birds Eye View, 1988; Moa's Ark, 1989-90; Special Professor of Botany, University of Nottingham, 1987-; Visiting Professor, Natural Heritage Studies, Massey University, New Zealand, 1989-91; Director, Botanical Enterprises, David Bellamy Associates, National Heritage Conservation Fund, New Zealand, Conservation Foundation, London. Publications: The Great Seasons, 1981; Discovering the Countryside with David Bellamy, 4 volumes, 1982-83; The Mouse Book, 1983; The Queen's Hidden Garden, 1984; Bellamy's Ireland, 1986; Bellamy's Changing World, 4 volumes, 1988; England's Last Wilderness, 1989; How Green are

You?, 1991; Tomorrow's Earth, 1991; World Medicine, 1992; Various books connected with Television series. Honours: Officer of the Order of the British Empire; Dutch Order of the Golden Ark; UNEP Global 500 Award; Duke of Edinburgh's Award for Underwater Research; British Academy of Film and Television Arts; BSAC Diver of the Year; Richard Dimbleby Award; Chartered Institute of Water and Environmental Management, fellow. Memberships: Fellow, Linnaean Society; Founder-Director, Conservation Foundation; President, WATCH, 1982-83; President, Youth Hostels Association, 1983; President, Population Concern; President, National Association of Environmental Education. Address: Mill House, Bedburn, Bishop Auckland, County Durham DL13 3NW, England.

BELLAMY Joe David, b. 29 Dec 1941, Cincinnati, Ohio, USA. Professor of English; Writer; Poet; Writer. m. Connie Sue Arendsee, 16 Sept 1964, 1 son, 1 daughter. Education: Duke University, 1959-61; BA in Literature, Antioch College, 1964; MFA in English and Creative Writing, University of Iowa, 1969. Appointments: Instructor, 1969-70, Assistant Professor, 1970-72, Mansfield State College, Pennsylvania; Publisher and Editor, Fiction International magazine and press, 1972-84; Assistant Professor, 1972-74, Associate Professor, 1974-80, Professor of English, 1980-, St Lawrence University, Canton, New York; Program Consultant in American Literature, Divisions of Public Programs and Research Programs, National Endowment for the Humanities, 1976-90; President and Chair, Board of Directors, Coordinating Council of Literary Magazines, 1979-81, and Associated Writing Programs, 1990; Distinguished Visiting Professor, George Mason University, 1987-88; Director, Literature Program, National Endowment for the Arts, 1990-92; Whichard Distinguished Professor in the Humanities, East Carolina University, 1994-96. Publications: Apocalypse: Dominant Contemporary Forms, 1972; The New Fiction: Interviews with Innovative Writers, 1974; Superfiction, or the American Story Transformed, 1975; Olympic Gold Medallist (poems), 1978; Moral Fiction: An Anthology, 1980; New Writers for the Eighties: An Anthology, 1981; Love Stories/Love Poems: An Anthology (with Roger Weingarten), 1982; American Poetry Observed: Poets on Their Work, 1984; The Frozen Sea (poems), 1988; Suzi Sinzinnati (novel), 1989; Atomic Love (stories), 1993; Literary Luxuries: American Writing at the End of the Millennium, 1995. Contributions to: Books, anthologies, journals, and magazines. Honours: Bread Loaf Scholar-Bridgman Award, 1973; National Endowment for the Humanities Fellowship, 1974; Fels Award, 1976; Coordinating Council of Literary Magazine Award for Fiction, 1977; Kansas Quarterly-Kansas Arts Commission Fiction Prize, 1982; Pushcart Prize Nominations and Listings, 1983 et seq.; New York State Council on the Arts Grant in Fiction, 1984; National Endowment for the Arts Fellowship for Creative Writers, 1985; Editors' Book Award, 1989. Membership: National Book Critics Circle. Address: 1145 Lawson Cove, Virginia Beach, VA 23455, USA.

BELLE Pamela Dorothy Alice, b. 16 June 1952, Ipswich, England. Author. m. Steve Thomas, 6 Aug 1990, 2 sons. Education: BA Hons, History, University of Sussex, England, 1972-75; Postgraduate Teaching Certificate, Coventry College of Education, 1975-76. Appointments: Teacher, Northchurch First School, Berkhamsted, Herts, 1978-85; Full time Author, 1985-. Publications: The Moon in the Water, 1983; The Chains of Fate, 1984; Alathea, 1985; The Lodestar, 1987; Wintercombe, 1988; Herald of Joy, 1989; A Falling Star, 1990; Treason's Gift, 1992; The Silver City, 1994; The Wolf Within, 1995; Blood Imperial, 1996; Mermaid's Ground, 1998; No Love Lost, 1999. Contributions to: Occasional articles including Wiltshire Life; Solander (Journal of the Historical Novel Society). Memberships: Society of Authors; Historical Novel Society. Literary Agent: Vivienne Schuster of Curtis Brown. Address: 61 New Road, Bromham, Chippenham, Wilts SN1S 2JB, England.

BELLI Gioconda, b. 9 Dec 1949, Managua, Nicaragua. Poet; Author. m. (2) Charles Castaldi, 10 Apr 1987, 4 children. Education: Advertising and Journalism, Charles Morris Price School, Philadelphia; Advertising Management, INCAE (Harvard University School of Business Administration in Central America); Philosophy and Literature, Georgetown University, Washington, DC. Appointments: Member, Political-Diplomatic Commission, 1978-79, International Press Liaison, 1982-83, Executive Secretary and Spokesperson for the Electoral Campaign, 1983-84, Sandinista National Liberation Front; Director of Communications and Public Relations, Ministry of Economic Planning, 1979-82; Foreign Affairs Secretary, Nicaragua Writer's Union, 1983-88; Managing Director, Sistema Nacional de Publicidad, 1984-86. Publications: Poetry: Sobre la Grama, 1972, English translation as On the Grass; Línea de Fuego, 1978, English translation as Line of Fire; Truenos y Arco Iris, 1982; Amor Insurrecto (anthology), 1985; De la Costilla de Eva, 1987, English translation as From Eve's Rib; El Ojo de la Mujer, 1991; Sortilegio contral el Frío (erotic collection), 1992; Apogeo, 1997. Novels: La mujer Habitada, 1988, English translation as The Inhabited Woman, 1994; Sofía de los Presagios, 1990; Waslala, 1996. Other: The Workshop of the Butterflies (children's story), 1994. Contributions to: Anthologies and periodicals. Honours: National University Poetry Prize, Nicaragua, 1972; Casa de las Americas Poetry Prize, Cuba, 1978; Friedrich Ebhert Foundation Booksellers, Editors and Publishers Literary Prize, Germany, 1989; Anna Seghers Literary Fellowship, Germany, 1989. Address: 1842 Union Street, San Francisco, CA 94123, USA.

BELLOW Saul, b. 10 June 1915, Lachine, Quebec, Canada. Writer. m. (1) Anita Goshkin, div, 1 son, (2) Alexandra Tschacbasov, 1956, div, 1 son, (3) Susan Glassman, 1961, div, 1 son, (4) Alexandra Ionesco Tuleca, 1974, div, (5) Janis Freedman, 1989. Education: University of Chicago, 1933-35; BS, Northwestern University, 1937. Appointments: Instructor, Pestalozzi-Froebel Teachers College, Chicago, 1938-42; Editorial Department, Great Books of the Western World, Encyclopaedia Britannica, Chicago, 1943-46; Instructor, 1946, Assistant Professor, 1948-49, Associate Professor, 1954-59, University of Minnesota; Visiting Lecturer, New York University, 1950-52; Creative Writing Fellow, Princeton University, 1952-53; Teacher, Bard College, 1953-54; Grunier Distinguished Services Professor, University of Chicago, 1962-; Lecturer, Oxford University, 1990. Publications: Fiction: Dangling Man, 1944; The Victim, 1947; The Adventures of Augie March, 1953; Seize the Day, 1956; Henderson the Rain King, 1959; Herzog, 1964; Mr Sammler's Planet, 1970; Humboldt's Gift, 1975; The Dean's December, 1982; More Die of Heartbreak, 1986; A Theft, 1989; The Bellarosa Connection, 1989; The Actual, 1997. Stories: Mosby's Memoirs and Other Stories, 1968; Him With His Foot in His Mouth and Other Stories, 1984; Something to Remeber Me By: Three Tales, 1991; Occasional Pieces, 1993. Plays: The Wrecker, 1954; The Last Analysis, 1964; Under the Weather, 1966. Non-Fiction: To Jerusalem and Back: A Personal Account, 1976; It All Adds Up: From the Dim Past to the Uncertain Future, 1994. Contributions to: Many periodicals. Honours: Guggenheim Fellowship, 1948; National Book Awards, 1954, 1964, 1970; Nobel Prize for Literature, 1976; Pulitzer Prize in Fiction, 1976; American Academy of Arts and Letters Gold Medal, 1977; Brandeis University Creative Arts Award, 1978; Commander, Legion of Honour, 1983, Order of Arts and Letters, 1985, France; National Medal of Arts, 1988; National Book Award Lifetime Achievement Award, 1990. Membership: American Academy of Arts and Letters. Address: 1126 East 59th Street, Chicago, IL 60637, USA.

BELOFF Baron, (Max Beloff), b. 2 July 1913, London, England. Historian; Professor Emeritus. m. Helen Dobrin, 20 Mar 1938, 2 sons. Education: Corpus Christi College, Oxford; 1st Class Honours, School of Modern History, 1935; Senior Demy, Magdalen College, Oxford, 1935. Appointments: Junior Research Fellow, Corpus Christi College, 1937; Assistant Lecturer in History, University of Manchester; University of Oxford, 1939-46; Nuffield

Reader in the Comparative Study of Institutions, 1946-56, Gladstone Professor of Government and Public Administration, 1957-74, later Professor Emeritus, University of Oxford; Fellow, Nuffield College, 1947-57; Fellow, 1957-74, Emeritus Fellow, 1980-, All Souls College, Oxford; Principal, University College, Buckingham, 1974-79; Supernumerary Fellow, St Antony's College, Oxford, 1975-84; Honorary Professor, St Andrews University, 1993-98. Publications: Public Order and Popular Disturbances, 1660-1714, 1938; The Foreign Policy of Soviet Russia, 2 volumees, 1947, 1949; Thomas Jefferson and American Democracy, 1948; Soviet Policy in the Far East, 1944-1951, 1953; The Age of Absolutism, 1660-1815, 1954; Foreign Policy and the Democratic Process, 1955; Europe and the Europeans, 1957; The Great Powers, 1959; The American Federal Government, 1959; New Dimensions in Foreign Policy, 1961; The United States and the Unity of Europe, 1963; The Balance of Power, 1967; The Future of British Foreign Policy, 1969; Imperial Sunset, Vol I, Britain's Liberal Empire, 1969, 2nd edition, 1988, Vol II, Dream of Commonwealth, 1921-1942, 1989; The Intellectual in Politics, 1970; The Government of the United Kingdom (with G R Peele), 1980, 2nd edition, 1985; Wars and Welfare, 1914-1945, 1984; An Historian in the Twentieth Century, 1992; Britain and European Union: Dialogue of the Deaf, 1996. Editor: The Federalist, 1948, 2nd edition, 1987; Mankind and His Story, 1948; The Debate on the American Revolution, 1949, 2nd edition, 1989; On the Track of Tyranny, 1959; L'Europe du XIXe et XXe siècle (joint editor), 1960-67; American Political Institutions in the 1970's, 1975. Contributions to: Many scholarly journals, both domestic and foreign. Honours: Knighted, 1980; Life Peer, 1981; Honorary Fellow, Corpus Christi College, 1993; Honorary doctorates. Memberships: British Academy, fellow; Royal Historical Society, fellow; Royal Society of Arts, fellow. Address: c/o House of Lords, London SW1A 0PW, England.

BEN JELLOUN Tahar, b. 1 Dec 1944, Fes, Morocco. Writer; Poet; Dramatist. m. Aicha Ben Jelloun, 8 Aug 1986, 2 sons, 2 daughters. Education: University of Rabat, 1963-68; PhD, University of Paris, 1975. Publications: Fiction: Harrouda, 1973; La Réclusion solitaire, 1976, English translation as Solitaire, 1988; Moha le fou, Moha le sage, 1978; La Prière de l'absent, 1981; Muha al-ma'twah, Muha al-hakim, 1982; L'Écrivain public, 1983; L'Enfant de sable, 1985, English translation as The Sand Child, 1987; La Nuit sacreé, 1987, English translation as The Sacred Night, 1989; Jour de silence à Tanger, 1990, English translation as Silent Day in Tangier, 1991; Les Yeux baissés, 1991; Corruption, 1995; Le Premier Amour et Toujours le Dernier, 1995; La Nuit de l'erreur, 1997. Poetry: Hommes sous linceul de silence, 1970; Cicatrices du soleil, 1972; Le Discours du chameau, 1974; La Memoire future: Anthologie de la nouvelle poésie du Maroc, 1976; Les Amandiers sont morts de leurs blessures, 1976; A l'insu du souvenir, 1980; Sahara, 1987; La Remontée des cendres, 1991; Poésie Complète (1966-1995). Plays: Chronique d'une solitude, 1976; Entretien avec Monsieur Said Hammadi, ouvrier algerien, 1982; La Fiancée de l'eau, 1984. Non-Fiction: La Plus Haute des solitudes: Misere sexuelle d'emigres nord-africains, 1977; Haut Atlas: L'Exil de pierres, 1982; Hospitalité française: Racisme et immigration maghrebine, 1984; Marseille, comme un matin d'insomnie, 1986; Giacometti, 1991; Le racisme expliqué à ma fille, 1998. Honours: Prix de l'Amitie Franco-Arabe, 1976; Chevalier des Arts et des Lettres, 1983; Prix Goncourt, 1987; Chevalier de la Légion d'Honneur, 1988; Prix des Hemispheres, 1991. Address: 27 Rue Jacob, 75 Paris 6, France.

BEN-RAFAEL Eliezer, b. 3 Oct 1938, Brussels, Belgium. Professor of Sociology. m. Miriam Neufeld, 3 Aug 1960, 2 daughters. Education: BA, 1966, MA, 1970, PhD, 1973, Hebrew University, Jerusalem. Appointments: Research Fellow, Harvard University, 1974-75; Professor of Sociology, Tel-Aviv University, 1980-; Directeur d'Études Associé, École des Hautes Études en Sciences Sociales, 1984-85; Visiting Scholar, Oxford Centre for Postgraduate Hebrew Studies, 1989-90; Co-Editor, Israel Social Sciences Review, 1992-; Jima and Zalman

Weinberg Chair of Political Sociology, 1997-. Publications: The Emergence of Ethnicity: Cultural Groups and Social Conflict in Israel, 1982; Le kibboutz, 1983; Status, Power and Conflict in the Kibbutz, 1988; Ethnicity, Religion and Class in Israeli Society, 1991; Language, Identity and Social Division: The Case of Israel, 1994; Crisis and Transformation: The Kibbutz at Century's End, 1997. Contributions to: International Sociology; Ethnics Racial Relations; European Journal of Sociology; British Journal of Sociology; International Journal of Comparative Sociology. Membership: Israel Society of Sociology, president, 1994-; Vice-President, International Institute of Sociology. Address: Department of Sociology, Tel-Aviv University, Tel-Aviv 69978, Israel.

BENCE-JONES Mark, b. 29 May 1930, London, England. Writer. m. Gillian Pretyman, 2 Feb 1965, 1 son, 2 daughters. Education: BA, 1952, MA, 1958, Pembroke College, Cambridge; MRAC, Royal Agricultural College, Cirencester, 1954. Publications: All a Nonsense, 1957; Paradise Escaped, 1958; Nothing in the City, 1965; The Remarkable Irish, 1966; Palaces of the Raj, 1973; Clive of India, 1974; The Cavaliers, 1976; Burke's Guide to Irish Country Houses, 1978; The British Aristocracy (co-author), 1979; The Viceroys of India, 1982; Ancestral Houses, 1984; Twilight of the Ascendancy, 1987; A Guide to Irish Country Houses, 1989; The Catholic Families, 1992; Life in an Irish Country House, 1996. Contributions to: Books and periodicals. Address: Glenville Park, Glenville, County Cork, Ireland.

BENCHLEY Peter (Bradford), b. 8 May 1940, New York, New York, USA. Writer. m. Winifred B Wesson, 19 Sept 1964, 2 sons, 1 daughter. Education: BA, Harvard University, 1961. Appointments: Reporter, Washington Post, 1963; Associate Editor, Newsweek magazine, New York City, 1963-67; Staff Assistant, Office of the President of the US, Washington, DC, 1967-69; Writer, Narrator, and Host, The American Sportsman television programme, 1974-83, Galapagos television special, 1987; Host and Narrator, Sharks television special, 1989, Expedition Earth television series, 1990-96; Co-Creator, Dolphin Cove television series, 1989; Executive Producer, Beast television miniseries, 1996. Publications: Time and a Ticket, 1964; Jaws, 1974; The Deep, 1976; The Island, 1978; The Girl of the Sea of Cortez, 1982; Q Clearance, 1986; Rummies, 1989; Beast, 1991; White Shark, 1994. Other: Various screenplays. Contributions to: Newspapers and magazines. Address: c/o International Creative Management, 40 West 57th Street, New York, NY 10019, USA.

BENEDICTUS David (Henry), b. 16 Sept 1938, London, England. Writer; Dramatist; Reviewer; Director. m. Yvonne Daphne Antrobus, 1971, 1 son, 1 daughter. Education: BA, English, Balliol College, Oxford, 1959. Appointments: BBC News and Current Affairs, 1961, Editor, Readings, 1989-91, and Radio 3 Drama, 1992, Senior Producer, Serial Readings, 1992-95, BBC Radio; Drama Director, 1962, Story Editor, 1965, BBC-TV; Assistant Director, Royal Shakespeare Co, 1970; Writer-in-Residence, Sutton Library, Surrey, 1975; Kibbutz Gezer, Israel, 1978, Bitterne Library, Southampton, 1983-84; Antiques Correspondent, Evening Standard, 1977-80; Judith E Wilson Visiting Fellow, Cambridge, and Fellow Commoner, Churchill College, Cambridge, 1981-82; Commissioning Editor, Drama Series, Channel 4 TV, 1984-86. Publications: The Fourth of June, 1962; You're a Big Boy Now, 1963; This Animal is Mischievous, 1965; Hump, or Bone by Bone Alive, 1967; The Guru and the Golf Club, 1969; A World of Windows, 1971; The Rabbi's Wife, 1976; Junk: How and Where to Buy Beautiful Things at Next to Nothing Prices, 1976; A Twentieth Century Man, 1978; The Antique Collector's Guide, 1980; Lloyd George (after Elaine Morgan's screenplay), 1981; Whose Life is it Anyway? (after Brian Clarke's screenplay), 1981; Who Killed the Prince Consort?, 1982; Local Hero (after Bill Forsyth's screenplay), 1983; The Essential London Guide, 1984; Floating Down to Camelot, 1985; The Streets of London, 1986; The Absolutely Essential London Guide, 1986; Little Sir Nicholas, 1990; Odyssey of a Scientist (with Hans Kalmus), 1991; Sunny Intervals

and Showers, 1992; The Stamp Collector, 1994; How to Cope When the Money Runs Out, 1998. Plays: Betjemania, 1976; The Golden Key, 1982; What a Way to Run a Revolution!, 1985; You Say Potato, 1992. Contributions to: Newspapers and magazines. Address: The Old Rectory, Wetheringsett-cum-Brockford, Stowmarket, Suffolk IP14 5PP, England.

BENEDIKT Michael, b. 26 May 1935, New York, New York, USA. Writer; Poet; Critic; Editor. Education: BA, New York University, 1956; MA, Columbia University, 1961. Appointments: Professorships in Literature and Poetry, Bennington College, 1968-69, Sarah Lawrence College, 1969-73, Hampshire College, 1973-75, Vassar College, 1976-77, Boston University, 1977-79; Contributing Editor, American Poetry Review, 1973-; Poetry Editor, Paris Review, 1974-78. Publications: The Body (verse), 1968; Sky (verse), 1970; Mole Notes (prose poems), 1971; Night Cries (prose poems), 1976; The Badminton at Great Barrington or Gustav Mahler and the Chattanooga Choo-Choo (poems), 1980. Anthologies: Modern French Theatre: The Avant-Garde, Dada and Surrealism (with George E Wellwarth), 1964, in UK as Modern French Plays: An Anthology from Jarry to Ionesco, 1965; Post-War German Theatre (with George E Wellwarth), 1967; Modern Spanish Theatre (with George E Wellwarth), 1968; Theatre Experiment, 1968; The Poetry of Surrealism, 1975; The Prose Poem: An International Anthology, 1976. Contributions to: Agni Review; Ambit; Art International; Art News; London Magazine; Massachusetts Review; New York Quarterly; Paris Review; Partisan Review; Poetry. Honours: Guggenheim Fellowship, 1968-69; Bess Hokin Prize, 1969; National Endowment for the Arts Prize, 1970; Benedikt: A Profile (critical monograph/Festschrift), 1978; National Endowment for the Arts Fellowship, 1979-80; Retrospective, Library of Congress, videotape, 1986. Memberships: PEN Club of America; Poetry Society of America. Address: 315 West 98th Street, No 6 A, New York, NY 10025, USA.

BENFIELD Derek, b. 11 Mar 1926, Bradford, Yorkshire, England. Playwright; Actor. m. Susan Elspeth Lyall Grant, 17 July 1953, 1 son, 1 daughter. Education: Bingley Grammar School; Royal Academy of Dramatic Art. Publications: Plays: Wild Goose Chase, 1956; Running Riot, 1958; Post Horn Gallop, 1965; Murder for the Asking, 1967; Off the Hook, 1970; Bird in the Hand, 1973; Panic Stations, 1975; Caught on the Hop, 1979; Beyond a Joke, 1980; In for the Kill, 1981; Look Who's Talking, 1984; Touch & Go, 1985; Fish Out of Water, 1986; Flying Feathers, 1987; Bedside Manners, 1988; A Toe in the Water, 1991; Don't Lose the Place, 1992; Anyone for Breakfast?, 1994; Up and Running, 1995; A Fly in the Ointment, 1996; Two and Two Together, 1998. Membership: Society of Authors. Literary Agent: Lemon Unna & Durbridge Ltd, 24 Pottery Lane, Holland Park, London W11 4LZ, England.

BENFORD Gregory (Albert), b. 30 Jan 1941, Mobile, Alabama, USA. Physicist; Science Fiction Author. m. Joan Abbe, 26 Aug 1967, 1 son, 1 daughter. Education: BA, University of Oklahoma, 1963; MS, 1965, PhD, 1967, University of California at San Diego. Appointments: Fellow, 1967-69, Research Physicist, 1969-71, Lawrence Radiation Laboratory, Livermore, California; Assistant Professor, 1971-73, Associate Professor, 1973-79, Professor of Physics, 1979-, University of California at Irvine. Publications: Deeper Than the Darkness, 1970, revised edition as The Stars in the Shroud, 1979; If the Stars Are Gods (with Gordon Eklund), 1977; In the Ocean of Night, 1977; Find the Changeling (with Gordon Eklund), 1980; Shiva Descending (with William Rotsler), 1980; Timescape, 1980; Against Infinity, 1983; Across the Sea of Suns, 1984; Artifact, 1985; Of Space-Time and the River, 1985; In Alien Flesh, 1986; Heart of the Comet (with David Brin), 1986; Great Sky River, 1987; Under the Wheel (with others), 1987; Hitler Victorious: Eleven Stories of the German Victory in World War II (editor with Martin H Greenberg), 1987; We Could Do Worse, 1988; Tides of Light, 1989; Beyond the Fall of Night (with Arthur C Clarke), 1990; Centigrade 233, 1990; Matter's End (editor), 1991; Chiller, 1993; Furious Gulf, 1994; Far

Futures, 1995; Sailing Bright Eternity, 1995; Foundation's Fear, 1997. Honours: Woodrow Wilson Fellowship, 1963-64; Nebula Awards, Science Fiction Writers of America, 1975, 1981; British Science Fiction Association Award, 1981; John W Campbell Award, World Science Fiction Convention, 1981; Ditmar Award, Australia, 1981; Various grants. Memberships: American Physical Society; Phi Beta Kappa; Royal Astronomical Society; Science Fiction Writers of America; Social Science Exploration. Address: 1105 Skyline Drive, Lagune Beach, CA 92651, USA.

BENITEZ Sandra, b. 26 Mar 1941, Washington, District of Columbia, USA. Writer. m. James F Kondrick, 25 May 1980, 2 sons. Education: BS in Education, 1963, MA in Comparative Literature, 1974, Northeast Missouri State University. Appointment: Distinguished Edelstein-Keller Writer-in-Residence, University of Minnesota, 1997. Publications: A Place Where the Sea Remembers, 1993; Bitter Grounds, 1997. Honours: Minnesota Book Award for Fiction, 1993; Barnes and Noble Fiction Award, 1994. Memberships: Authors Guild; Poets and Writers. Address: c/o Ellen Levine Literary Agency, 15 East 26th Street, No 1801, New York, NY 10010, USA.

BENJAMIN David. See: **SLAVITT David Rytman.**

BENN Tony, (Anthony Neil Wedgwood Benn), b. 3 Apr 1925, London, England. Member of Parliament; Writer. m. Caroline Middleton De Camp, 1949, 3 sons, 1 daughter. Education: MA, New College, Oxford, 1948. Appointments: Member of Parliament, Bristol South East, 1950-60, 1963-83, Chesterfield, 1984-, Member, 1959-60, 1962-93, Chairman, 1971-72, National Executive Committee, Labour Party; Postmaster-General, 1964-66; Privy Counsellor, 1964-; Minister of Technology, 1966-70; Secretary of State for Industry and Minister for Posts and Telecommunications, 1974-75; Secretary of State fof Energy, 1975-79; President, European Economic Community Council of Energy Ministers, 1977, Socialist Campaign Group of labour MPs, 1987-. Publications: The Privy Council as a Second Chamber, 1957; The Regeneration of Britain, 1964; The New Politics, 1970; Speeches, 1974; Arguments for Socialism, 1979; Arguments for Democracy, 1981; Parliament, People and Power, 1982; Writings on the Wall: A Radical and Socialist Anthology 1215-1984 (editor), 1984; Out of the Wilderness: Diaries 1963-1967, 1987; Office Without Power: Diaries 1968-1972, 1988; Fighting Back: Speaking Out for Socialism in the Eighties, 1988; Against the Tide: Diaries 1973-1976, 1989; Conflicts of Interest: Diaries 1977-1980, 1990; A Future for Socialism, 1991; The End of an Era: Diaries 1980-1990, 1992; Common Sense: A New Constitution for Britain (co-author), 1993; Years of Hope: Diaries, Letters and Papers 1940-1962, 1994; The Benn Diaries 1940-1990, 1995. Contributions to: Various journals in the UK and abroad; Broadcaster: Various current affairs programmes. Membership: National Union of Journalists. Address: House of Commons, London SW1A 0AA, England.

BENNASSAR Bartolomé, b. 8 Apr 1929, Nîmes, France. Professor of History; Historian; Novelist. m. 20 Apr 1954, 1 son, 2 daughter. Education: University of Montpellier; University of Toulouse. Appointments: Professor of History, High Schools of Rodez, Agen and Marseille; Assistant Professor, Professor, then President, University of Toulouse Le Mirail. Publications: Valladolid au siècle d'or, 1967; Recherches sur les grandes épidémies dans le Nord de l'Espagne, 1969; L'Homme espagnol, 1975, US translation as The Spanish Character; L'Inquisition espagnole XV-XIX, 1979; Un siècle d'or espagnol, 1982; Histoire d'Espagnols, 1985; Les Chrétiens d'Allah, 1989; 1492: Un monde nouveau?, 1991; Histoire de la tauromachie, 1993; Franco, 1995; Le Voyage en Espagne, 1998; Numerous Italian and Spanish translations; Novels: Le baptême du Mort, 1962; Picture: le dernier saut, 1970; Les tribulations de Mustafa des Six-Fours, 1995. Contributions to: Annales ESC; L'Histoire; Historia. Honours: Bronze Medal, Centre National de la Recherche Scientifique; Doctor Honoris Causa, University of Valladolid, Spain. Address: 11 allée de Val d'Aran, 31240 Saint-Jean, France.

BENNETT Alan, b. 9 May 1934, Leeds, England. Dramatist. Education: BA, Modern History, Oxford, 1957. Publications: Forty Years On, 1968; Getting On, 1971; Habeas Corpus, 1973; The Old Country, 1977; Enjoy, 1980; Objects of Affection, 1983; Writer in Disguise, 1984;Kafka's Dick, 1986; Talking Heads, 1988; Single Spies, 1989; The Lady in the Van, 1990; Poetry in Motion, 1990; The Wind in the Willows (adaptation), 1991; The Madness of George III, 1992; Writing Home (autobiography), 1994; Diaries, 1997; The Clothes They Stood Up In, 1998, Talking Heads II, 1998; The Complete Talking Heads, 1998. Screenplays: A Private Function, 1984; Prick Up Your Ears, 1987; The Madness of King George, 1995. Contributions to: London Review of Books. Address: Peter, Fraser and Dunlop, The Chambers, Chelsea Harbour, London, SW10 0XF, England.

BENNETT Bruce (Harry), b. 23 Mar 1941, Perth, Western Australia, Australia. Professor of English; Editor; Writer. m. Patricia Ann Bennett, 8 July 1967, 1 son, 1 daughter. Education: BA, DipEd, University of Western Australia, 1963; BA, 1967, MA, 1972, Oxford University; MA, Ed, London University, 1974. Appointments: Lecturer, 1968-75, Senior Lecturer, 1975-85, Associate Professor, 1985-92, University of Western Australia; Co-Editor, 1975-92, Eastern States Editor, 1983-, Westerly: A Quarterly Review; Professor of English and Head of the School of English, University College, University of New South Wales, Australian Defence Force Academy. Publications: Place, Region and Community, 1985; An Australian Compass: Essays on Place and Direction in Australian Literature, 1991; Spirit in Exile: Peter Porter and his Poetry, 1991. Other: Editor, co-editor, etc. of various volumes, including: The Literature of Western Australia, 1979; The Writer's Sense of the Contemporary: Papers in Southeast Asian and Australian Literature (with Ee Tiang Hong and Ron Shepherd), 1987; The Oxford Literary Guide to Australia, 1987; The Penguin New Literary History of Australia, 1988; Peter Cowan: New Critical Essays (with Susan Miller), 1992; Myths, Heroes and Anti-Heroes: Essays on Literature and Culture of the Asia-Pacific Region (with Dennis Hasskell), 1992; "Westerly" Looks to Asia (with Peter Cowan, Dennis Haskell and Susan Miller), 1992; Crossing Cultures: Essays on Literature and Culture of the Asia-Pacific (with Jeff Doyle and Satendra Nandan), 1996; Oxford Literary History of Australia (with Jennifer Strauss), 1998. Contributions to: Many books and journals. Honours: Rhodes Scholar, Pembroke College, Oxford, 1964-67; Officer of the Order of Australia, 1993. Memberships: Academy of Humanities of Australia, fellow; Association for the Study of Australian Literature, president, 1983-85; Australian College of Education, fellow; European and South Pacific Associations of Commonwealth Literature and Language Societies; Modern Language Association, USA; PEN International. Address: c/o School of English, University College, University of New South Wales, Australian Defence Force Academy, Canberra, Australian Capital Territory 2600, Australia.

BENNETT John J, b. 8 Aug 1938, Brooklyn, New York, USA. Writer. Education: George Washington University; University of Munich. Publications: Tripping in America, 1984; Crime of the Century, 1986; The New World Order, 1991; Bodo (novel), 1995; Karmic Four-Star Buckaroo, 1997; Others: The Adventures of Achilles Jones; The Night of the Great Butcher. Contributions to: Chicago Review; Exquisite Corpse; Northwest Review; Transatlantic Review; New York Quarterly; Seattle Weekly. Honours: Iron Country, 1st prize fiction, 1978; William Wantling Award, 1987; Darrell Bob Houston Award, 1988; Finalist, Drue Heing Literary Prize, 1991. Address: PO Box 1634, Ellensburg, WA 98926, USA.

BENNETT Paul (Lewis), b. 10 Jan 1921, Gnadenhutten, Ohio, USA. Professor of English (Retired); Poet; Writer; Gardener; Orchardist. m. Martha Jeanne Leonhart, 31 Dec 1941, dec 1995, 2 sons. Education: BA, Ohio University, 1942; AM, Harvard University, 1947. Appointments: Instructor, Samuel Adams School of Social Studies, Boston, 1945-46; Teaching Assistant, Harvard University, 1945-46; Instructor in English, University of Maine, Orono, 1946-47; Instructor to Professor of English, 1947-86, Poet-in-Residence, 1986-, Denison University; Gardener and Orchardist, 1948-; Consultant, Aerospace Laboratories, Owens-Corning Fiberglass Corp, 1964-67, Ohio Arts Council, 1978-81, Ohio Board of Regents, 1985-86. Publications: Poetry: A Strange Affinity, 1975; The Eye of Reason, 1976; Building a House, 1986; The Sun and What It Says Endlessly, 1995; Appalachian Mettle, 1997. Novels: Robbery on the Highway, 1961; The Living Things, 1975; Follow the River, 1987. Contributions to: Many periodicals. Honours: National Endowment for the Arts Fellowship, 1973-74; Phi Beta Kappa; Pi Delta Epsilon; Significant Achievement Award, Ohio University, 1992. Address: 1281 Burg Street, Granville, OH 43023, USA.

BENNETT Louise (Simone), b. 7 Sept 1919, Kingston, Jamaica. Lecturer; Poet. m. Eric Coverley. Education: Royal Academy of Dramatic Art, London. Appointments: Resident Artist with the BBC West Indies section, 1950-53; Lecturer and Radio and Television Commentator in Jamaica. Publications: Dialect Verses, 1940; Jamaican Dialect Verses, 1942; Jamaican Humour in Dialect, 1943; Miss Lulu Sez, 1948; Anancy Stories and Dialect Verses, 1950; Laugh with Louise, 1960; Jamaica Labrish, 1966; Anancy and Miss Lou, 1979; Selected Poems, 1982; Aunt Roachy Seh, 1993. Other: Various recordings of Jamaican songs and poems. Honours: Norman Manley Award of Excellence; DLitt, University of the West Indies, 1982; Member of the Order of the British Empire; Order of Jamaica. Address: Enfield House, Gordon Town, St Andrew, Jamaica.

BENNETT William J(ohn), b. 31 July 1943, New York, New York, USA. Lawyer; Educator; Writer. m. Mary Elaine Glover, 1982, 2 sona. Education: BA, Williams College, 1965; PhD, University of Texas, 1970; JD, Harvard University Law School, 1972. Appointments: Assistant Professor, University of Southern Mississippi, 1967-68, University of Texas, 1970, University of Wisconsin, 1973; Resident Advisor and Tutor, Harvard University, 1969-71; Assistant Professor and Assistant to the President, Boston University, 1971-76; Executive Director, 1976-79, President and Director, 1979-81, National Humanities Center, Triangle Park, North Carolina; Adjunct Associate Professor, University of North Carolina and North Carolina State University, 1979-81; Chairman, National Endowment for the Humanities, Washington, DC, 1981-85; Secretary of Education, US Department of Education, Washington, DC, 1985-88; Partner, Dunnels, Duvall, Bennett and Porter, Washington, DC, 1988-; Director, National Drug Policy, Executive Office of the President of the US, Washington, DC, 1989-90; Co-Director, Empower America, Washington, DC, 1993. Publications: Counting by Race: Equality from the Founding Fathers to Bakke and Weber (with Terry Eastland), 1979; Our Children and Our Country: Improving America's Schools and Affirming the Common Culture, 1988; The De-Valuing of America: The Fight for Our Culture and Our Children, 1992; The Book of Virtues: A Treasury of Great Moral Stories, 1993; The Index of Leading Cultural Indicators: Facts and Figures of the State of American Society, 1994; The Moral Compass: Stories for a Life's Journey, 1995; Our Sacred Honor, 1997; The Death of Outrage: Bill Clinton and the Assault on American Ideals, 1998. Contributions to: Various publications. Honours: Many honorary doctorates. Memberships; American Society for Political and Legal Philosophy; National Academy of Education; National Humanities Faculty; Society for Values in Higher Education; Southern Education Communications Association. Address: 862 Venable Place North West, Washington, DC 20012, USA.

BENNION Francis Alan Roscoe, b. 2 Jan 1923, Wallasey, Cheshire, England. m. (1) Barbara Elisabeth Braendle, 28 July 1951, div 1975, 3 daughters, (2) Mary Anne Field, 2 Nov 1977. Education: John Lyon's School, Harrow, England, 1934-39; St Andrews University, Scotland, 1941; Balliol College, Oxford, 1946-48; BA,

Law, 1949, MA, 1951, University of Oxford, England; Called to the Bar by Middle Temple, Jan 1951. Appointments: Royal Air Force Volunteer Reserve, Commissioned Pilot, 1941-46; Editor, Halsbury's Statutes with Butterworths, 1948; Lecturer and Tutor in Law, St Edmund Hall, University of Oxford, 1951-53; Practice at the Bar of England and Wales, 1951-94; Parliamentary Counsel, 1953-68, 1973-75; Chief Executive, Royal Institution of Chartered Surveyors, Governor of College of Estate Management, 1965-68; Research Associate, University of Oxford Centre for Socio-Legal Studies, Member of Law Faculty, University of Oxford, 1984-; Chairman, Oxford City Football Club, 1988-89. Publications: The Constitutional Law of Ghana, 1962; Professional Ethics: The Consultant Professions and Their Code, 1969; Tangling with the Law: Reforms in Legal Process, 1970; Consumer Credit Control, 1976-; The Consumer Credit Act Manual 1978, 3rd edition, 1986; Statute Law, 1980, 3rd edition, 1990; Statutory Interpretation, 1984, 3rd edition, 1997; Victorian Railway Days, 1989; The Sex Code: Morals for Moderns, 1991. Contributions to: Annual Volumes of All England Law Reports Annual Review, 1985-98; Information Sources in Law, editor R G Logan, 1986; The Law Commission and Law Reform, editor G Zellick, 1988; Reviewing Legal Education, editor P Birks, 1994; Halsbury's Laws of England, 1995. Honours: Gibbs Law Scholar, Oxford University; Jenkyns Law Prize, Younger Prize, Paton Memorial Studentship, Balliol College, Oxford; Harmsworth Scholarship, Middle Temple. Memberships: Society of Authors, 1971-; Defence of Literature and the Arts Society, 1971-91; International Committee for the Defence of Salman Rushdie and his Publishers, 1988-90. Literary Agent: Jeffrey Simmons. Address: 5 Old Nursery View, Kennington, Oxford OX1 5NT, England.

BENOIST Alain de, b. 11 Dec 1943, Saint-Symphorien, France. Journalist; Essayist; Lecturer. m. Doris M Christians, 21 June 1972, 2 sons. Education: Diploma, Lycées Montaigne et Louis-le-Grand, Paris. Appointments: Editor-in-Chief, L'Observateur européen, 1964-68, Nouvelle Ecole, 1969-, Midi-France, 1970-71; Journalist, L'Echo de la presse et de la publicité, 1968, Courrier de Paul Dehème, 1969-76; Critic, Valeurs actuelles and Spectacle du monde, 1970-82, Figaro-Magazine, 1977-92; Director, Krisis, 1988-. Publications: Les Indo-Européens, 1966; L'Empirisme logique et la Philosophie du Cercle de Vienne, 1970; Avec ou sans Dieu, 1970; Morale et Politique de Nietzsche, 1974; Vu de droite: Anthologie critique des idées contemporaines, 1977; Les Idées a l'endroit, 1979; Guide pratique des prénoms, 1980, new edition, 1990; Comment peut-on etre paien?, 1981; Feter Noël, 1982; Orientations pour des années décisives, 1982; Traditions d'Europe, 1983; Démocratie: Le problème, 1985; Europe, Tiers monde, meme combat, 1986; Le Grain de sable, 1994; La Ligne de mire, 1995; L'Empire intérieur, 1995; Céline et l'Allemagne, 1996; Famille et société, 1996; Ernst Jünger, 1997. Contributions to: Various publications. Honour: Grand prix de l'essai de l'Académie francaise, 1978. Memberships: Several societies, research groups, etc. Address: 41 rue Barrault, 75013 Paris, France.

BENOIT William Lyon, b. 17 Mar 1953, New Castle, IN, USA. Professor of Communication. m. Pamela Jean Gay, 18 May 1974, 1 daughter. Education: BS, Ball State University, 1975; MA, Central Michigan University, 1976; PhD, Wayne State University, 1979. Appointments: Miami University, 1979-80; Bowling Green State University, 1980-84; University of Missouri, 1984-. Publications: Accounts, Excuses, Apologies, 1995; Candidates in Conflict, with William Wells, 1995; Campaign '96, with J Blaney and P M Pier, 1998. Contributions to: over 80 articles. Honour: Choice, Outstanding Academic Book of 1995. Address: 115 Switzler, University of Missouri, Columbia, MO 65211, USA.

BENSLEY Connie, b. 28 July 1929, London, England. Poet; Writer. m. J A Bensley, 2 Aug 1952, 2 sons. Education: Diploma, Social Sciences, University of London, 1962. Appointment: Poetry Editor, PEN Magazine, 1984-85. Publications: Progress Report, 1981;

Moving In, 1984; Central Reservations, 1990; Choosing to be a Swan, 1994. Contributions to: Observer; Poetry Review; Spectator; Times Literary Supplement. Honours: 1st Place, Times Literary Supplement Poetry Competition, 1986; 2nd Place, Leek Poetry Competition, 1988; Prizewinner, Arvon/Observer Poetry Competition, 1994; 2nd Place, Tate Gallery Poetry Competition, 1995. Memberships: Poetry Society. Address: 49 Westfields Avenue, Barnes, London SW13 0AT, England.

BENSON Daniel. See: **COOPER Colin Symons.**

BENSON Eugene, b. 6 July 1928, Larne, Northern Ireland. Professor Emeritus; Writer. m. Renate Niklaus, 30 Apr 1968, 2 sons. Education: BA, National University of Ireland, 1950; MA, University of Western Ontario, 1958; PhD, University of Toronto, 1966. Appointments: Lecturer, Royal Military College, Kingston, Ontario, 1960-61; Assistant Professor of English, Laurentian University, 1961-64; Assistant Professor, 1965-67, Associate Professor, 1967-71, Professor of English, 1971-93, University Professor Emeritus, 1994-, University of Guelph. Publications: Encounter: Canadian Drama in Four Media, anthology (editor), 1973; The Bulls of Ronda (novel), 1976; Power Game, or the Making of a Prime Minister (novel), 1980; J M Synge, 1982; English-Canadian Theatre (co-author), 1987; Oxford Companion to Canadian Theatre (co-editor), 1989; Encyclopedia of Post-Colonial Literatures in English (co-editor), 1994; The Oxford Companian to Canadian Literature (co-editor), 1997. Memberships: Association of Canadian Theatre Historians; Canadian Association of Irish Studies; Writers' Union of Canada, chair, 1983-84; PEN Canada, co-president 1984-85. Address: 55 Palmer Street, Guelph, Ontario N1E 2P9, Canada.

BENSON Gerard John, (Jedediah Barrow), b. 9 Apr 1931, London, England. Poet; Writer; Editor. m. 2) 1 son, 1 daughter, 3). Education: Rendcomb College; Exeter University; Diplomas, Distinction, Drama and Education, Central School of Speech and Drama, University of London; IPA 1st Class. Appointments: Resident Tutor, Arvon Foundation and Taliesen Centre; Senior Lecturer, Central School of Speech and Drama; Arts Council Poet-in-Residence, Dove Cottage, Wordsworth Trust, 1994-; British Council Writer in Residence, Stavanger and Kristionsand, 1998. Publications: Name Game, 1971; Gorgon, 1983; This Poem Doesn't Rhyme (editor), 1990; 100 Poems on the Underground (editor), 1991; Poems on the Underground, illustrated edition (editor), 1992, 5th edition, 1995; The Magnificent Callisto, 1993; Does W Trouble You? (editor), 1994; Evidence of Elephants, 1995; In Wordsworth's Chair, 1995; Love Poems on the Underground, 1996; Bradford and Beyond, 1997. Contributions to: Newspapers, journals, reviews, and the Internet. Honours: Signal Award for Poetry, 1991; Carnegie Medal Nominee, 1996. Memberships: Barrow Poets; National Association of Writers in Education, past chairman; Poems on the Underground; Poetry Society, education advisory panel; Writers Guild. Address: 46 Ashwell Road, Manningham, Bradford, West Yorkshire BD8 9DU, England.

BENSON Mary, b. 9 Dec 1919, Pretoria, South Africa. Writer. Publications: Tshekedi Khama, 1960; The African Patriots, 1963; At the Still Point, 1969; South Africa: The Struggle for a Birthright, 1969; Nelson Mandela: The Man and the Movement, 1986, updated, 1994; A Far Cry (autobiography), 1989, updated, 1995; Athol Fugard Notebooks (editor), 1983; Athol Fugard and Barney Simon: Bare Stage, a Few Props, Great Theatre, 1997. Contributions to: London Magazine; Observer; Yale Theatre; Granta; Botswana Notes & Records; BBC Radio Drama and Documentaries. Address: 34 Langford Court, London NW8 9DN, England.

BENSON Richard, b. 13 Feb 1966, Doncaster, England. Journalism. Education: BA, AKC, Kings College, London, 1985-88; Dip.J. City University of London, 1989-90. Appointments: Features Editor, The Way, 1990; Associate Editor, 1992, Editor, 1995, The Face; Group Editor, Wagadon Publishing, 1998. Publications: Night Fever: Club Writing in The Face 1980-1997, 1997.

Contributions to: Newspapers and magazines. Address: c/o Wagadon, Exmouth House, Pine Street, London EC1R 0JL, England.

BENTLEY Eric (Russell), b. 14 Sept 1916, Bolton, Lancashire, England (US citizen, 1948). Dramatist. m. (1) Maja Tschemjakow, diss, (2) Joanne Davis, 1953, twin sons. Education: BA, 1938, BLitt, 1939, Oxford University; PhD, Yale University, 1941. Appointments: Drama Critic, New Republic, 1952-56; Charles Eliot Norton Professor of Poetry, Harvard University, 1960-61; Fulbright Professor, Belgrade, 1980; Professor of Comparative Literature, University of Maryland, College Park, 1982-89. Publications: Larry Park's Day in Court, 1979; Lord Alfred's Lover, 1979; The Kleist Variations, 1982; Monstrous Martyrdoms, 1985; The Pirandello Commentaries, 1985; The Brecht Memoir, 1986; German Requiem, 1990; Round 2, 1991. Honours: Festschrift: The Critic and the Play, 1986; Florida Theatre Festival named in his honour, 1992; Honorary Doctorate, New School for Social Research, 1992; Robert Lewis Award for Life Achievement in the Theatre, 1992. Memberships: American Academy of Arts and Sciences, 1969-; American Academy of Arts and Letters, 1990-. Address: 194 Riverdale Drive, Apt 4 E, New York, NY 10025, USA.

BERCH Bettina, b. 25 May 1950, Washington District of Columbia, USA. Writer. 1 daughter. Education: BA, Barnard College, 1971; MA, 1973, PhD, 1976, University of Wisconsin. Publications: The Endless Day: The Political Economy of Women and Work, 1982; Radical by Design: The Life and Style of Elizabeth Hawes, 1988; The Woman Behind the Lens: The Life and Work of Frances Benjamin Johnston, forthcoming. Contributions to: Early Feminist Fashion; The Resurrection of Out Work; Belles Lettres; Paradise of a Kind. Address: 878 West End, New York, NY 10025, USA.

BERENBAUM Michael, b. 31 July 1945, Newark, New Jersey, USA. Professor; Museum and Foundation Executive. m. Melissa Patack, 25 June 1995, 1 son, 1 daughter. Education: AB, Philosophy, 1967, Queens College, 1963-67; Jewish Theological Seminary, 1963-67; Hebrew University, 1965-66; Boston University, 1967-69; PhD, Florida State University, 1971-75. Appointments: Executive Director, Jewish Community Council of Greater Washington, 1980-83; Opinion Page Editor, Washington Jewish Week, 1983-86, Acting Ed, 1985; Adjunct Professor of Judaic Studies, American University, 1987; Senior Scholar, Religious Action Center, 1986-89; Hymen Goldman Professor of Theology, Georgetown University, 1983-97; Project Director, US Holocaust Memorial Museum, 1988-93, Research Fellow, 1987-88; Director, United States Holocaust Research Institute, US Holocaust Memorial Museum, 1993-97; Professor of Theology, University of Judaism, 1998-; President and Chief Executive Officer, Survivors of Shoah Visual History Foundation, 1997-. Publications include: The World Must Know: A History of the Holocaust, 1993; Anatomy of the Auschwitz Death Camp, co-ed with Israel Gutman, 1994; What Kind of God?, co-ed with Betty Rogers Rubenstein, 1995; Witness to the Holocaust: An Illustrated Documentary History of the Holocaust in the Words of Its Victims, Perpetrators and Bystanders, 1997; The Holocaust and History: The Known, The Unknown, the Disputed and the Reexamined, 1998. Honours include: Silver Angel Award, 1981; Simon Rockower Memorial Award, 1986 x 2, 1987. Literary Agent: Ronald Goldfarb. Address: 2101 Hillsboro Avenue, Los Angeles, CA 90035, USA.

BERESFORD Anne. See: **HAMBURGER Anne (Ellen).**

BERESFORD Elisabeth, b. Paris, France. Writer. 1 son, 1 daughter. Appointments: Founder, Alderney Youth Trust. Publications: The Television Mystery, 1957; Trouble at Tullington Castle, 1958; Gappy Goes West, 1959; Two Gold Dolphins, 1961; Paradise Island, 1963; Escape to Happiness, 1964; Game, Set and Match, 1965; The Hidden Mill, 1965; The Black Mountain Mystery, 1967; Sea-Green Magic, 1968; Stephen and the Shaggy Dog, 1970; The Wandering Wombles, 1970; Dangerous

Magic, 1972; The Secret Railway, 1973; The Wombles at Work, 1973; The Wombles Annual, yearly, 1975-78; Snuffle to the Rescue, 1975; Orinoco Runs Away, 1975; Bungo Knows Best, 1976; Tobermory's Big Surprise, 1976; Wombling Free, 1978; The Happy Ghost, 1979; Curious Magic, 1980; The Four of Us, 1982; The Animals Nobody Wanted, 1982; The Tovers, 1982; The Adventures of Poon, 1984; One of the Family, 1985; The Ghosts of Lupus Street School, 1986; The Secret Room, 1987; Emily and the Haunted Castle, 1987; The Oscar Puffin Book, 1987; Once Upon a Time Stories, 1988; The Island Railway Armada Adventure, 1989; Rose, 1992; Charlie's Ark, 1992; The Wooden Gun, 1992; Tim the Trumpet, 1992; Jamie and the Rola Polar Bear, 1993; Lizzy's War, 1993; Rola Polar Bear and the Heatwave, 1995; Lizzy's War, Part II, 1996; The Smallest Whale, 1996; Chris the Climber, 1997; Island Treasure, 1998; Shansi's Surprise, 1998; Ghost of Wimbledon Common, 1998; Orinoco the Magnificent, 1998; Tomsk to the Rescue, 1998; Beautiful Boating Weather, 1998; Camping and Cloudberries, 1998; 6 Womble Picture Books, 1998. Honour: MBE, 1998. Literary Agent: Juvenilia, Avington, Winchester, Hampshire SO21 1DB, England; Stephen Durbridge, 24 Pottery Lane, Holland Park, London W11 4LZ, England. Address: Little Street, Alderney, Channel Islands.

BERESFORD-HOWE Constance, b. 10 Nov 1922, Montreal, Quebec, Canada. Professor of English; Novelist. m. 31 Dec 1960, 1 son. Education: BA, 1945, MA, 1946, McGill University; PhD, Brown University, 1950. Publications: The Book of Eve, 1973; A Population of One, 1976; The Marriage Bed, 1980; Night Studies, 1984; Prospero's Daughter, 1989; A Serious Widow, 1990. Honours: Dodd Mead Intercollegiate Literary Fellowship, 1948; Canadian Booksellers Award, 1974. Memberships:International PEN; International PEN, Writers in Prison Committee. Address: c/o McClelland and Stewart, 481 University Avenue, Toronto, Ontario M4V 1E2, Canada.

BERG Leila, b. 12 Nov 1917, Salford, Lancashire, England. Writer; Children's Author. 1 son, 1 daughter. Education: University of London. Publications: Risinghill: Death of a Comprehensive School, 1968; Look at Kids, 1972; Reading and Loving, 1977; Many books and stories for children, including: The Hidden Road, 1958; Folk Tales, 1966; The Nippers Stories, 1968-76; The Snap series, 1977; The Chatterbooks series, 1981; The Small World series, 1983; The Steep Street Stories, 1987; Backwards and Forwards. 1994. Contributions to: Anarchy; Guardian; Times Educational Supplement; Times Literary Supplement. Honour: Eleanor Farjeon Award for Services to Children's Literature, 1973. Address: Alice's Cottage, Brook Street, Wivenhoe, Near Colchester CO7 9DS, England.

BERG Stephen (Walter), b. 2 Aug 1934, Philadelphia, Pennsylvania, USA. Poet; Writer; Editor. m. Millie Lane, 1959, 2 daughters. Education: University of Pennsylvania; Boston University; BA, University of Iowa, 1959; Indiana University. Appointments: Teacher, Temple University, Philadelphia, Princeton University, Haverford College, Pennsylvania; Professor, Philadelphia College of Art; Poetry Editor, Saturday Evening Post, 1961-62; Founding Editor (with Stephen Parker and Rhoda Schwartz), American Poetry Review, 1972-. Publications: Poetry: Berg Goodman Mezey, 1957; Bearing Weapons, 1963; The Queen's Triangle: A Romance, 1970; The Daughters, 1971; Nothing in the Word: Versions of Aztec Poetry, 1972; Grief: Poems and Versions of Poems, 1975; With Akmatova at the Black Gates: Variations, 1981; In It, 1986; First Song, Bankei, 1653, 1989; Homage to the Afterlife, 1991; New and Selected Poems, 1992; Oblivion: Poems, 1995. Editor: Naked Poetry: Recent American Poetry in Open Forms (with Robert Mezey), 1969; Between People (with S J Marks), 1972; About Women (with S J Marks), 1973; The New Naked Poetry (with Robert Mezey), 1976; In Praise of What Persists, 1983; Singular Voices: American Poetry Today, 1985. Other: Sea Ice: Versions of Eskimo Songs, 1988. Contributions to: Periodicals. Honours: Rockefeller-Centro Mexicano de Escritores Grant, 1959-61; National Translation Center Grant, 1969; Frank O'Hara Prize, Poetry magazine, 1970; Guggenheim Fellowship, 1974; National Endowment for the Arts Grant, 1976; Columbia University Translation Center Award, 1976. Address: 2005 Mt Vernon Street, Philadelphia, PA 19130, USA.

BERG Y L. See: **ELBERG Yehuda.**

BERGÉ Carol, b. 4 Oct 1928, New York, New York, USA. Fiction Writer; Poet; Editor; Publisher; Antiques Dealer. m. Jack Henry Berge, June 1955, 1 son. Education: New York University; New School for Social Research, New York City. Appointments: Editor 1970-84, Publisher 1991-, CENTER Magazine and Press; Distinguished Professor of Literature, Thomas Jefferson College, Allendale, Michigan, 1975-76; Instructor, Goddard College, 1976; Teacher, University of California Extension Program, Berkeley, 1976-77; Associate Professor, University of Southern Mississippi, 1977-78; Editor, Mississippi Review, 1977-78; Visiting Professor, University of New Mexico, 1978-79, 1987; Visiting Lecturer, Wright State University, Dayton, Ohio, 1979, State University of New York at Albany 1980-81; Proprietor, Blue Gate Gallery of Art and Antiques, 1988-; Editor-Publisher, Center Press, 1991-93. Publications: Fiction: The Unfolding, 1969; A Couple Called Moebius, 1972; Acts of Love: An American Novel, 1973; Timepieces, 1977; The Doppler Effect, 1979; Fierce Metronome, 1981; Secrets, Gossip and Slander, 1984; Zebras, or, Contour Lines, 1991. Poetry: The Vulnerable Island, 1964; Lumina, 1965; Poems Made of Skin, 1968; The Chambers, 1969; Circles, as in the Eye, 1969; An American Romance, 1969; From a Soft Angle: Poems About Women, 1972; The Unexpected, 1976; Rituals and Gargoyles, 1976; A Song, A Chant, 1978; Alba Genesis, 1979; Alba Nemesis, 1979. Editor: Light Years: The New York City Coffeehouse Poets of the 1960's, 1997. Reportage: The Vancouver Report, 1965. Contributions to: Literary periodicals, Anthologies, Art and Antiques magazines. Honours: New York State Council on the Arts CAPS Award, 1974; National Endowment for the Arts Fellowship, 1979-80. Memberships: Authors League; MacDowell Fellows Association; National Press Women; Poets & Writers. Address: 2070 Calle Contento, Santa Fe, NM 87505, USA.

BERGE Hans (Cornelis Ten), b. 24 Dec 1938, Netherlands. Poet; Writer; Editor. Appointments: Lecturer, Art Academy, Arnhem; Writer-in-Residence, University of Texas; Editor, Raster, Grid, literary journals. Publications: Poetry: Gedichten, 3 volumes, 1969; White Shaman, 1973; Poetry of the Aztecs, 1972; Va-banque, 1977; Semblance of Reality, 1981; Texas Elegies, 1983; Songs of Anxiety and Despair, 1988; Materia Prima, Poems, 1963-93. Novels: Zelfportret met witte muts, 1985; Het geheim van een oppewekt humeur, 1986; The Home Loving Traveller, 1995; Women, Jealousy and Other Discomforts, 1996. Other: The Defence of Poetry, essays, 1988; Prose books; Books of myths and fables of Arctic peoples; Numerous poetry translations. Contributions to: Periodicals. Honours: Van der Hoogt Prize, 1968; Prose Prize, City of Amsterdam, 1971; Multatuli Prize, 1987; Contantijn Huÿgens Prize, 1996. Memberships: PEN; Society of Dutch Literature. Address: c/o Meulenhoff Publishers, PO Box 100, 1000 AC Amsterdam, Netherlands.

BERGEL Hans, b. 26 July 1925, Kronstadt, Romania. Author. Education: History of Arts, University of Cluj-Napoca. Publications: Rumanien, Portrait einer Nation, 1969; Ten Southern European Short Stories, 1972; Die Sachsen in Siebenburgen nach dreissig Jahren Kommunismus, 1976; Der Tanz in Ketten, 1977; Siebenburgen, 1980; Gestalten und Gewalten, 1982; Hermann Oberth oder Der mythische Traum vom Fliegen, 1984; Der Tod des Hirten, 1985; Literaturgeschichte der Deutschen in Siebenburgen, 1987; Das Venusherz (short novel), 1987; Weihnacht ist uberall (eleven short stories), 1988. Contributions to: Periodicals. Honours: Short Story Prize, Bucharest, 1957, Bonn, 1972; Georg Dehio Prize, Esslingen, 1972; Goethe Foundation Prize, Basel, 1972; Medien Prizes, Bavarian Broadcasting Company, 1983, 1989; Bundesverdienstkreuz, 1987; Saxon of Transylvania Culture Prize, 1988; Geyphius-Prize, 1990. Memberships: Kunstlergilde e V Esslingen; PEN International. Address: Rabensteinstrasse 28, D 8000 Munich 60, Germany.

BERGER Arthur Asa, b. 3 Jan 1933, Boston, Massachusetts, USA. Professor; Writer. m. Phyllis Wolfson Berger, 1961, 2 children. Education: BA, University of Massachusetts; MA, University of Iowa; PhD, University of Minnesota. Appointments: Instructor, University of Minnesota, 1960-65; Fulbright Lecturer, University of Milan, 1963-64; Instructor to Professor, Broadcast and Electronic Communication Arts Department, San Francisco State University, 1965-; Visiting Professor, University of California, Los Angeles, 1984-85. Publications: Li'l Abner, 1970; Pop Culture, 1973; About Man, 1974; The Comic Stripped American, 1974; The TV-Guided American, 1975; Language in Thought and Action, 1975; Film in Society, 1978; Television as an Instrument of Terror, 1978; Media Analysis Techniques, 1982; Signs in Contemporary Culture, 1984; Television in Society, 1986; Semiotics of Advertising, 1987; Media, USA, 1988, 2nd edition, 1991; Seeing is Believing: An Introduction to Visual Communication, 1989; Political Culture and Public Opinion, 1989; Agitpop: Political Culture and Communication Theory, 1989; Scripts: Writing for Radio and Television, 1990; Media Research Techniques, 1991; Reading Matter, 1992; Popular Culture Genres, 1992; An Anatomy of Humor, 1993; Improving Writing Skills, 1993; Blindmen and Elephants: Perspectives on Humor, 1995; Narratives in Media: Modern Culture and Everyday Life, 1996; Bloom's Morning, 1997; The Genius of the Jewish Joke, 1997; The Art of Comedy Writing, 1997. Address: c/o Broadcast and Electronic Communication Arts Department, CA34, San Francisco State University, San Francisco, CA 94132, USA.

BERGER François, b. 16 May 1950, Neuchâtel, Switzerland. Barrister; Poet; Writer. Education: Licence Degree in Law, Neuchâtel University, 1977; Barrister, Neuchâtel. Publications: Poetry: Mémoire d'anges, 1981; Gestes du veilleur, 1984; Le Pré, 1986, Italian translation, 1996; Les Indiennes, 1988; Le Repos d'Ariane, 1990. Novel: Le Jour avant, 1995. Contributions to: L'Express Feuille d'Avis de Neuchâtel. Honours: Louise Labé Prize, Paris, 1982; Citation of Distinction, Schiller Foundation, Zürich, 1985; Auguste Bachelin Prize, Neuchâtel, 1988. Memberships: Association des écrivains de langue française; Association des écrivains neuchâtelois et jurassiens; Literature Committee, Canton of Neuchâtel, president; Société suisse des écrivains. Address: 28, Rebatte, CH-2068 Hauterive (Neuchâtel), Switzerland.

BERGER John (Peter), b. 5 Nov 1926, Stoke Newington, London, England. Novelist; Dramatist. m. twice, 3 children. Education: Central School of Art and the Chelsea School of Art, London. Appointments: Television Narrator, About Time, 1985, and Another Way of Telling, 1989; Artist, exhibitions at Wildenstein, Redfern, and Leicester galleries, London. Publications: A Painter of Our Time, 1958; The Foot of Clive, 1962; Corker's Freedom, 1964; G., 1972; Into Their Labours: Pig Earth, 1979; Once in Europa, 1987; Lilac and Flag: An Old Wives' Tale of a City, 1990. Plays: A Question of Geography, 1984; Boris, 1985; Goya's Last Portrait: The Painter Played Today, 1989. Contributions to: Tribune and New Statesman, both London, 1951-60. Honours: Booker Prize, 1972; Guardian Fiction Prize, 1973; New York's Critics Prize, for screenplay, 1976; George Orwell Memorial Prize, 1977; Barcelona Film Festival Europa Award, 1989. Address: Quincy, Mieussy, 74440 Taninges, France.

BERGER Terry, b. 11 Aug 1933, New York, New York, USA. Writer; Children's Author. Education: BA, Brooklyn College, 1954; Teacher's Degree, Hunter College, 1962. Publications: Black Fairy Tales (adaptation), 1969; I Have Feelings (psychology), 1971; Lucky, 1974; Being Alone, Being Together, 1974; Big Sister, Little Brother, 1974; A Friend Can Help, 1974; A New Baby, 1974; Not Everything Changes, 1975; The Turtles' Picnic, 1977;

How Does it Feel When Your Parents Get Divorced?, 1977; Special Friends, 1979; Stepchild, 1980; Friends, 1981; The Haunted Dollhouse (co-author), 1982; Ben's ABC Day, 1982; Country Inns: The Rocky Mountains, 1983. Address: 130 Hill Park Avenue, Great Neck, NY 11021, USA.

BERGER Thomas (Louis), b. 20 July 1924, Cincinnati, Ohio, USA. Author. m. Jeanne Redpath, 12 June 1950. Education: BA, University of Cincinnati, 1948; Postgraduate Studies, Columbia University, 1950-51. Appointments: Librarian, Rand School of Social Science, New York City, 1948-51; Staff, New York Times Index, 1951-52; Associate Editor, Popular Science Monthly, 1952-53; Distinguished Visiting Professor, Southampton College, 1975-76; Visiting Lecturer, Yale University, 1981, 1982; Regent's Lecturer, University of California at Davis, 1982. Publications: Crazy in Berlin, 1958; Reinhart in Love, 1962; Little Big Man, 1964; Killing Time, 1967; Vital Parts, 1970; Regiment of Women, 1973; Sneaky People, 1975; Who is Teddy Villanova?, 1977; Arthur Rex, 1978; Neighbors, 1980; Reinhart's Women, 1981; The Freud, 1983; Nowhere, 1985; Being Invisible, 1987; The Houseguest, 1988; Changing the Past, 1989; Orrie's Story, 1990; Meeting Evil, 1992; Robert Crews, 1994. Other: Plays and screenplays. Honours: Dial Fellow, 1962; Rosenthal Award, National Institute of Arts and Letters, 1965; Western Heritage Award, 1965; Ohiona Book Award, 1982; LittD, Long Island University, 1986. Address: PO Box 11, Palisades, NY 10964, USA.

BERGMAN (Ernst) Ingmar, b. 14 July 1918, Uppsala, Sweden. Film Director; Script Writer. m. Ingrid von Rosen, 1971. Education: University of Stockholm, 1938-40. Publications: Plays and Screenplays: The Day Ends Early, 1947; Moralities, 1948; Summer with Monica, 1953; Sawdust and Tinsel, 1953; Journey into Autumn, 1955; Smiles of a Summer Night, 1955; The Seventh Seal, 1957; Wild Strawberries, 1957; So Close to Life, 1958; The Virgin Spring, 1960; Through a Glass Darkly, 1961; Winter Light, 1963; The Silence, 1963; Persona, 1966; Hour of the Wolf, 1968; The Rite, 1969; The Passion, 1969; The Touch, 1971; Cries and Whispers, 1973; Scenes from a Marriage, 1973; Face to Face, 1973; Autumn Sonata, 1978; From the Life of the Marionettes, 1980; Fanny and Alexander, 1982; Best Intentions, 1992; Sunday's Children, 1992. Other: The Magic Lantern: An Autobiography, 1988. Honours: Academy Awards, 1961, 1962, 1984; Goethe Prize, 1976; Honorary Professor, Stockholm University, 1985. Address: c/o Norstedts Forlag, Box 2052, 103 12 Stockholm, Sweden.

BERGON Frank, b. 24 Feb 1943, Ely, Nevada, USA. Novelist; Professor. m. Holly St John Bergon, 28 July 1979. Education: BA, English, summa cum laude, Boston College, 1965; Postgraduate, Stanford University, 1965-66; PhD, English, Harvard University, 1973. Appointments: Teaching Fellow, Harvard University, 1968-70; Lecturer, Newton College, 1971-72; Visiting Associate Professor, University of Washington, 1980-81; Professor of English, Vassar College, 1972-; Director, American Culture Program, Vassar College, 1982-85. Publications: Stephen Crane's Artistry, 1975; Looking Far West: The Search for the American West in History, Myth and Literature (co-editor), 1978; The Western Writing of Stephen Crane (editor), 1979; The Wilderness Reader (editor), 1980; Shoshone Mike (novel), 1987; A Sharp Lookout: Selected Nature Essays of John Burroughs (editor), 1987; The Journals of Lewis & Clark (editor), 1989; The Temptations of St Ed & Brother S (novel), 1993; Wild Game (novel), 1995. Contributions to: American Literary History; Terra Nova; Journal of Nature and Culture. Honours: Wallace Stegner Fellowship, 1965-66; Best Novel of West Finalist, Western Writers of America, 1993; Nevada Writers Hall of Fame, 1998. Memberships: MLA; Western Literature Association; Association of the Study of Literature and the Environment. Literary Agent: Peter Matson. Address: 136 Chapel Hill Road, Highland, NY 12528, USA.

BERGONZI Bernard, b. 13 Apr 1929, London, England. Author; Poet; Professor of English Emeritus. Education: BLitt, 1961, MA, 1962, Wadham College, Oxford. Appointments: Senior Lecturer, 1966-71, Professor of English, 1971-92, Professor Emeritus, 1992-, University of Warwick, Coventry. Publications: The Early H G Wells, 1961; Heroes' Twilight, 1965, 3rd edition, 1996; Innovations: Essays on Art and Ideas, 1968; T S Eliot: Four Quartets: A Casebook, 1969; The Situation of the Novel, 1970, 2nd edition, 1979; T S Eliot, 1972, 2nd edition, 1978; The Turn of a Century, 1973; H G Wells: A Collection of Critical Essays, 1975; Gerard Manley Hopkins, 1977; Reading the Thirties, 1978; Years: Sixteen Poems, 1979; Poetry 1870-1914, 1980; The Roman Persuasion (novel), 1981; The Myth of Modernism and Twentieth Century Literature, 1986; Exploding English, 1990; Wartime and Aftermath, 1993; David Lodge, 1995. Address: 19 St Mary's Crescent, Leamington Spa CV31 1JL, England.

BERGSON Leo. See: **STEBEL Sidney Leo.**

BERKELEY Humphry John, b. 1 Feb 1926, Marlow, England. Writer; Author; Former Member of Parliament. Education: (Exhibitioner),BA, 1947, MA, 1963, Pembroke College, Cambridge. Appointments: Member of Parliament (Conservative) for Lancaster, 1959-66, joined Labour Party 1970; Chairman, United Nations Association of Great Britain and Northern Ireland, 1966-70. Publications: The Power of the Prime Minister, 1968; Crossing the Floor, 1972; The Life and Death of Rochester Sneath, 1974; The Odyssey of Enoch: A Political Memoir, 1977; The Myth That Will Not Die: The Formation of the National Government, 1978; Faces of the Eighties (with Jeffrey Archer), 1987. Contributions to: Times; Sunday Times; Daily Telegraph; Financial Times; Spectator; New Statesman. Membership: Savile Club. Literary Agent: Mark Hamilton, A M Heath, 79 St Martin's Lane, London WC2, England. Address: 3 Pages Yard, Church Street, Chiswick, London W4 2PA, England.

BERKOFF Steven, b. 3 Aug 1937, London, England. Writer; Director; Actor. m. Shelley Lee, 1976, div. Education: Webber-Douglas Academy of Dramatic Art, London, 1958-59; École Jacques Lecoq, Paris, 1965. Appointments: Director of plays and actor in many plays, films and television; Founding Director, London Theatre Group, 1973. Publications: Plays: In the Penal Colony, 1968; Metamorphosis, 1969; The Trial, 1970; East, 1975; Agamemnon, 1977; The Fall of the House of Usher, 1977; Greek, 1980; Decadence, 1981; West, 1983; Harry's Christmas, 1985; Kvetch and Acapulco, 1986; Sink the Belgrano!, 1986; Massage, 1987; Lunch, Dog, Actor, 1994; Brighton Beach Scumbags, 1994; Dahling you were Marvellous, 1994. Other: Gross Intrusion and Other Stories, 1979, reprinted, 1993; Steven Berkoff's America, 1988; The Theatre of Steven Berkoff: Photographic Record, 1992; Overview, 1994; Free Association, autobiography, 1996. Honours: Los Angeles Drama Critics Circle Award for Directing, 1983; Comedy of the Year Award, Evening Standard, 1991. Address: c/o Joanna Marston, Rosica Colin Ltd, 1 Clareville Grove Mews, London SW7 5AH, England.

BERKSON William Craig, (William Graig), b. 30 Aug 1939, New York, New York, USA. Poet; Critic; Editor; Teacher. m. Lynn O'Hare, 17 July 1975, 1 son, 1 daughter. Education: Brown University, 1957-59; Columbia University, 1959-60; New School for Social Research, New York City, 1959-61; New York University Institute of Fine Arts, 1960-61. Appointments: Instructor, New School for Social Research, 1964-69; Editor and Publisher, Big Sky magazine and books, 1971-78; Adjunct Professor, Southampton College, Long Island University, 1980; Associate Professor, California College of Arts and Crafts, 1983-84; Instructor, Marin Community College, 1983-84; Professor and Coordinator of Public Lectures Program, 1984-, Director, Letters and Science, 1994-, San Francisco Art Institute; Poetry Editor, Video and the Arts, 1985-86; Contributing Editor, Zyzzyva, 1987-92; Corresponding Editor, Art in America, 1988-; Visiting Artist/Scholar, American Academy in Rome, 1991. Publications: Poetry: Saturday Night: Poems 1960-1961, 1961; Shining Leaves, 1969; Two Serious Poems and One Other (with Larry Fagin), 1972; Recent Visitors, 1973; Hymns of St Bridget (with Frank O'Hara), 1975; Enigma Variations, 1975; Ants, 1975; 100 Women, 1975; The World of Leon (with Ron Padgett, Larry Fagin and Michael Brownstein), 1976; Blue is the Hero, 1976; Red Devil, 1983; Lush Life, 1983; Start Over, 1984. Criticism: Ronald Bladen: Early and Late, 1991. Editor: Frank O'Hara: In Memory of My Feelings, 1967; Best & Company, 1969; Alex Katz (with Irving Sandler), 1971; Homage to Frank O'Hara (with Joe LeSueur), 1978; Special De Kooning Issue, Art Journal (with Rackstraw Downes), 1989. Contributions to: Anthologies and periodicals. Honours: Poets Foundation Grant, 1968; Yaddo Fellowship, 1968; National Endowment for the Arts Fellowship, 1980; Briarcombe Fellowship, 1983; Artspace Award for New Writing in Art Criticism, 1990; Fund for Poetry Award, 1994. Memberships: International Art Critics Association; PEN West. Address: 787B Castro Street, San Francisco, CA 94114, USA.

BERMAN Claire, b. 4 July 1936, New York, New York, USA. Author; Journalist. Education: AB, Barnard College, 1957. Appointments: Senior Editor, Cosmopolitan, 1958-63; Contributing Editor, New York Magazine, 1972-78; Former Director of Public Education, Permanent Families for Children, Child Welfare League of America. Publications: A Great City for Kids: A Parent's Guide to a Child's New York, 1969; We Take This Child: A Candid Look at Modern Adoption, 1974; Making It as a Stepparent, 1980; "What Am I Doing in a Stepfamily?", 1982; A Hole in My Heart: Adult Children of Divorce Speak Out, 1991; Golden Cradle: How the Adoption Establishment Works, 1991; Caring for Yourself while Caring for Your Aging Parents, 1996. Memberships: Past Secretary, American Society of Journalists and Authors; Authors Guild. Literary Agent: James Levine. Address: 52 Riverside Drive, New York, NY 10024, USA.

BERMAN David,b. 20 Nov 1942, New York, New York, USA. Associate Professor of Philosophy; Writer. m. Aileen Jill Mitchell, 25 Dec 1970, 2 sons, 2 daughters. Education: BA, New School for Social Research, New York City, 1965; MA, University of Denver, 1966; PhD, Trinity College, Dublin, 1972; Diploma in Psychoanalytic Psychotherapy, St Vincent's Hospital, Dublin, 1992. Appointments: Senior Lecturer in Philosophy, 1981-94, Fellow, 1984, Associate Professor of Philosophy, 1994-97, Head of Philosophy Department, 1997-, Trinity College, Dublin. Publications: A History of Atheism in Britain: From Hobbes to Russell, 1988; George Berkeley: Eighteenth Century Responses (editor), 2 volumes, 1989; George Berkeley's Alciphron or the Minute Philosopher in Focus (editor), 1993; George Berkeley: Idealism and the Man, 1994; Arthur Schopenauer's World as Will and Idea (editor), 1995; Berkeley: Experimental Philosophy, 1997. Contributions to: Reference works, books, and numerous scholarly journals. Address: c/o Department of Philosophy, Trinity College, University of Dublin, Dublin 2, Ireland.

BERMAN Philip Averill, b. 30 May 1932, New York City, New York, USA. Editorial Consultant. m. Evelyn Haber, 12 July 1986, div 1988. Education: BA, Stanford University, 1955. Appointments: Assistant Editor and Writer, San Francisco Chronicle, San Francisco, California, 1955-62; Assistant Writer and Editor, TV Guide Magazine, New York, 1963-64; Senior Editor, Women's Wear Daily and W Magazine, New York, 1965-91. Publications: Numerous newspaper articles for United Press and Associated Press, 1951-62. Contributions to: Look Magazine; Byline Bulletin; Stanford Magazine; Deadliner Newsletter; Raiders Magazine;. Honour: Lamston Medal, Dwight School, New York, 1950. Memberships: Society of Professional Journalists; Deadline Club, New York; New York Press Club. Address: 177 East 75th Street, Apartment 9D, New York, NY 10021. USA.

BERMAN Raeann, (Abbey Fields), b. 1 Mar 1932, Chicago, Illinois, USA. Journalist; Novelist. m. Sidney M Berman, 15 Dec 1956, 2 daughters. Education: BA, Roosevelt University, Chicago, 1953; University of Michigan, 1950-52. Appointments: Picture Editor, Encyclopedia Britanica, 1954-56; Associate Editor, Health

Magazine, 1956-59; Freelance Writer and Editor, 1959-68; Public Relations Specialist, Manpower Inc, 1968-70; Director of Public Relations, Barat College, Lake Forest, Illinois, 1970-72; Copywriter, American Hospital Supply Corporation, 1975-79; Director of Public Relations, Mundelein College, Chicago, 1983-85; Director of Media Relations, Northeastern Illinois University, 1990-92; Public Relations Consultant, US Committee for UNICEF, Chicago, 1994-; Freelance Writer. Publications: How To Survive Your Aging Parents, 1988. Contributions to: Chicago Tribune; US Racquetball; University of Chicago Better Health Letter; University of Kansas Parenting Program. Honours: Fellow, Knight Center for Specialized Journalism, University of Maryland, 1994; 1st Place, Arthritis Foundation, 1995; 1st Place for Television Video for UNICEF, 1996. Membership: American Society of Journalists and Authors. Address: 3145 Applewood Court, Highland Park, IL 60035, USA.

BERNARD David Kane, b. 20 Nov 1956, Baton Rouge, USA. Pastor; Author; Editor. m. Connie Sharpe Bernard, 6 June 1981, 2 sons, 1 daughter. Education: BA, Rice University; Greek, Wesley Biblical Seminary; JD, University of Texas. Appointments: Instructor, Administrator, Jackson College of Ministries, 1981-86; Associate Editor, United Pentecostal Church International, 1986-; Pastor, New Life United Pentecostal Church, Austin, Texas, 1992-. Publications: In Search of Holiness, 1981; The Oneness of God, 1983; The New Birth, 1984; Practical Holiness, 1985; A History of Christian Doctrine, 3 volumes, 1995-99; Spiritual Gifts, 1997. Contributions to: Pentecostal Herald; Forward. Honour: Word Aflame Press Writer of the Year, 1987. Membership: Society for Pentecostal Studies. Address: 4405 Andalusia Drive, Austin, TX 78759, USA.

BERNARD Oliver (Owen), b. 6 Dec 1925, Chalfont St Peter, Buckinghamshire, England. Retired Teacher; Poet; Translator. 2 sons, 2 daughters. Education: BA, Goldsmiths College, 1953; ACSD, Central School of Speech and Drama, 1971. Appointments: Teacher of English, Suffolk and Norfolk, 1964-74; Advisory Teacher of Drama, Norfolk Education Committee, 1974-81. Publications: Country Matters, 1960; Rimbaud: Collected Poems (translating editor), 1961; Apollinaire: Selected Poems (translator), 1965, new expanded edition, 1983; Moons and Tides, 1978; Poems, 1983; Five Peace Poems, 1985; The Finger Points at the Moon (translator), 1989; Salvador Espriu: Forms and Words, 1990; Getting Over It (autobiography), 1992; Quia Amore Langueo (translator), 1995. Contributions to: Various publications. Honour: Gold Medal for Verse Speaking, Poetry Society, 1982. Memberships: British Actors' Equity Association; Speak-a-Poem, committee member; William Morris Society. Address: 1 East Church Street, Kenninghall, Norwich NR16 2EP, England.

BERNARD Robert. See: **MARTIN Robert Bernard.**

BERNAUW Patrick, b. 15 Apr 1962, Alost, Belgium. Writer. m. Elke Van der Elst, 24 Mar 1984, 1 daughter. Appointments: Scenarist Comic Books, Gucky, 1983-84; Producer and Director of Radio Plays, 1988-; Editor, Historische Verhalen (Historical Studies), 1991-97. Publications: Mijn Lieve Spooklidmaat, 1983; De Stillevens Van De Dood, 1985; Mysteries Van Het Lam Gods, 1991; Dromen Van Een Farao, 1991; Landru Bestaat Niet, 1992; De Moord op Albert I, (with Guy Didelez), 1993; In Het Teken Van De Ram, (with Guy Didelez), 1996; Spookrÿders, 1997. Several plays and radio plays. Contributions to: Vlaamse Filmpjes; Kreatief; Bres; Plot; Crime; Ganymedes; short stories and essays. Honours: John Flanders Awards, 1987, 1991; Paul de Mont Prÿs, 1994; Prÿs Knokke-Heist Voor de Beste Jeugdroman, 1996; Eule des Monats, 1997, Wim Verbeke Prÿs, 1997. Membership: Bestuurslid Vereniging Van Vlaamse Toneelauteurs en Scenaristen. Address: Brusselbaan 296, 9320 Erembodegem, Belgium.

BERNAYS Anne Fleischman, b. 14 Sept 1930, New York, New York, USA. Writer; Teacher. m. Justin Kaplan, 29 July 1954, 3 daughters. Education: BA, Barnard College, 1952. Publications: Growing Up Rich (novel); Professor Romeo (novel); The Language of Names (non-fiction, with Justin Kaplan). Contributions to: New York Times Book Review; Nation; Sports Illustrated; Travel and Leisure; Sophisticated Traveller. Honour: Edward Lewis Wallant Award. Membership: PEN New England. Literary Agent: Zachary Shuster. Address: 16 Francis Avenue, Cambridge, MA 02138, USA.

BERNE Stanley, b. 8 June 1923, Port Richmond, Staten Island, New York, USA. Research Professor; Writer. m. Arlene Zekowski, July 1952. Education: BS, Rutgers University, 1947; MA, New York University, 1950; Graduate Fellow, Louisiana State University, Baton Rouge, 1954-59. Appointments: Associate Professor, English, 1960-80, Research Professor, English, 1980-, Eastern New Mexico University, Portales; Host, Co-Producer, TV series, Future Writing Today, KENW-TV, PBS, 1984-85. Publications: A First Book of the Neo-Narrative, 1954; Cardinals and Saints: On the aims and purposes of the arts in our time, 1958; The Dialogues, 1962; The Multiple Modern Gods and Other Stories, 1969; The New Rubaiyat of Stanley Berne (poetry), 1973; Future Language, 1976; The Great American Empire, 1981; Every Person's Little Book of P-L-U-T-O-N-I-U-M (with Arlene Zekowski), 1992; Alphabet Soup: A Dictionary of Ideas, 1993. Contributions to: Anthologies and other publications. Honours: Literary research awards, Eastern New Mexico University, 1966-76. Memberships: PEN; New England Small Press Association; Rio Grande Writers Association; Santa Fe Writers. Address: Box 4595, Santa Fe, NM 87502, USA.

BERNER Urs, b. 17 Apr 1944, Schafisheim, Switzerland. Writer. Div. Education: Teacher's Training; Studies in History, University of Zürich. Appointments: Editor, then Freelance Journalist. Publications: Friedrichs einsame Träume in der Stadt am Fluss (novel), 1977; Fluchtrouten (novel), 1980; Wunschzeiten (novel), 1985; Das Wunder von Dublin (stories), 1987; Die Lottokönige (novel), 1989. Address: Scharerstrasse 9, CH-3014 Bern, Switzerland.

BERNIK France, b. 13 May 1927, Ljubljana, Slovenia. Literary Historian. m. Marija Kanc, 14 July 1956, 1 daughter. Education: Graduated, Slavic Philology, 1951, PhD, Literary Sciences, 1960, University of Ljubljana. Appointments: Teaching Assistant, University of Ljubljana, 1951-57; Editor, Secretary, Slovenska matica, 1961-72; Scientific Collaborator, 1972; Scientific Advisor, Institute of Slovene Literature and Literary Science, Scientific Research Centre, Slovenian Academy of Sciences and Arts, 1977-; Elected Associate Member, 1983, Member 1987, President, 1992-, Slovenian Academy of Sciences and Arts. Publications: The Lyrics of Simon Jenko, 1962; Cankar's Early Prose, 1976; Simon Jenko, 1979; Problems of Slovene Literature, 1980; Typology of Cankar's Prose, 1983; Ivan Cankar: A Monograph, 1987; Slovene War Prose 1841-80, 1988; Studies on Slovene Poetry, 1993; Slowenische Literatur im europäischen Kontext, 1993; Ivan Cankar: Ein slowenischer Schriftsteller des europäischen Symbolismus, 1997. Honours: Ambassador of Republic of Slovenia in Science, 1994; Commandeur, Ordre de Saint Fortunat, 1996; International Cultural Diploma of Honour, 1996; Eques Commendator Ordinis Sancti Gregorii Magni, 1997; Golden Honorary Decoration of Freedom, Republic of Slovenia, 1997. Memberships: Honorary Member, Society for Slovene Studies, 1991; Member, Senator, Academia Scientiarum et Artium Europaea, 1993; Croatian Academy of Sciences and Arts, 1994; Editorial boards of numerous scholarly journals. Address: Novi trg 3, 1000 Ljubljana, Slovenia.

BERNSTEIN Carl, b. 14 Feb 1944, Washington, District of Columbia, USA. Journalist; Writer. m. Nora Ephron, 14 Apr 1976, div, 2 sons. Education: University of Maryland, 1961-64. Appointments: Copyboy to Reporter, Washington Star, 1960-65; Reporter, Elizabeth Journal, New Jersey, 1965-66, Washington Post, 1966-76; Washington Bureau Chief, 1979-81, Correspondent, 1981-84, ABC-TV; Correspondent, Contributor, Time magazine, 1990-91; Visiting Professor, New York University, 1992-. Publications: All the President's Men (with Bob Woodward), 1973; The Final Days (with Bob Woodward), 1976; Loyalties: A Son's Memoir, 1989. Honours: Drew Pearson Prize for Investigative Reporting, 1972; Pulitzer Prize Citation, 1972; Honorary LLD, Boston University, 1975. Address: c/o Janklow and Nesbit Associates, 598 Madison Avenue, New York, NY 10022, USA.

BERNSTEIN Charles, b. 4 Apr 1950, New York, New York, USA. Professor of Poetry and Poetics; Poet; Writer; Editor. m. Susan Bee Laufer, 1977, 1 son, 1 daughter. Education: AB, Harvard College, 1972. Appointments: Freelance writer in the medical field, 1976-89; Visiting Lecturer in Literature, University of California at San Diego, 1987; Lecturer in Creative Writing, Princeton University, 1989, 1990; David Gray Professor of Poetry and Letters, State University of New York at Buffalo, 1990-. Publications: Poetry: Asylums, 1975; Parsing, 1976; Shade, 1978; Poetic Justice, 1979; Senses of Responsibility, 1979; Legend (with others), 1980; Controlling Interests, 1980; Disfrutes, 1981; The Occurrence of Tune, 1981; Stigma, 1981; Islets/Irritations, 1983; Resistance, 1983; Veil, 1987; The Sophist, 1987; Four Poems, 1988; The Nude Formalism, 1989; The Absent Father in Dumbo, 1990; Fool's Gold (with Susan Bee), 1991; Rough Trades, 1991; Dark City, 1994; The Subject, 1995; Republics of Reality: Poems 1975-1995, 1999. Essays: Content's Dream: Essays 1975-1984, 1986; A Poetics, 1992; My Way: Speeches and poems, 1999. Editor: L=A=N=G=U=A=G=E Book (with Bruce Andrews), 4 volumes, 1978-81; The L=A=N=G=U=A=G=E Book (with Bruce Andrews), 1984; The Politics of Poetic Form: Poetry and Public Policy, 1990; Close Listening: Poetry and the Performed Word, 1998. Contributions to: Numerous anthologies, collections, and periodicals. Honours: Phi Beta Kappa, 1972; William Lyon Mackenzie King Fellow, Simon Fraser University, 1973; National Endowment for the Arts Fellowship, 1980; Guggenheim Fellowship, 1985; University of Auckland Foundation Fellowship, 1986; New York Foundation for the Arts Fellowships, 1990, 1995; American Society of Composers, Authors and Publishers Standard Award, 1993-95. Address: Poetics Program, Department of English, 438 Clemens Hall, State University of New York at Buffalo, Buffalo, NY 14260, USA.

BERNSTEIN Marcelle. See: **CLARK Marcelle Ruth.**

BERRIDGE Elizabeth, b. 3 Dec 1919, London, England. Author; Critic. m. Reginald Moore, 1940, 1 son, 1 daughter. Appointments: Critic, BBC, Spectator, Books and Bookmen, Tribune, Country Life, 1952-74; Fiction Reviewer, Daily Telegraph, 1967-88; Evening Standard; Judge: David Higham First Novel Award, 1989-97 Publications: House of Defence, 1945; Story of Stanley Brent, 1945; Be Clean, Be Tidy, 1949; Upon Several Occasions, 1953; Across the Common, 1964; Rose Under Glass, 1967; Sing Me Who You Are, 1972; That Surprising Summer, 1973; The Barretts at Hope End (editor), 1974; Run for Home, 1981; Family Matters, 1981; People at Play, 1982; Touch and Go, 1995. Contributions to: New Writing; London Magazine; Folio; Contemporary Writers; T.L.S; Virago Book of Women's War Poetry. Honour: Novel of the Year, Yorkshire Post, 1964. Memberships: Chase Charity, Trustee; Fellow, PEN; Fellow, Royal Society of Literature, 1998. Address: c/o David Higham Associates, 5-8 Lower John Street, London W1R 4HA, England.

BERRY Adrian M(ichael), b. 15 June 1937, London, England. Writer; Journalist. Education: Christ Church, Oxford, 1959. Appointments: Correspondent, Time Magazine, New York City, 1965-67; Science Correspondent, Daily Telegraph, London, 1977-. Publications: The Next Ten Thousand Years: A Vision of Man's Future in the Universe, 1974; The Iron Sun: Crossing the Universe Through Black Holes, 1977; From Apes to Astronauts, 1981; The Super Intelligent Machine, 1983; High Skies and Yellow Rain, 1983; Koyama's Diamond (fiction), 1984; Labryinth of Lies (fiction), 1985; Ice With Your Evolution, 1986; Computer Software: The Kings and Queens of England, 1985; Harrap's Book of

Scientific Anecdotes, 1989; The Next 500 Years, 1995; Galileo and the Dolphins, 1996. Honour: Royal Geographic Society, fellow, 1984-. Memberships: Royal Astronomical Society, London, fellow, 1973-; British Interplanetary Society, fellow, 1986-. Address: 11 Cottesmore Gardens, Kensington, London W8, England.

BERRY Anthony Scyld Ivens, b. 28 Apr 1954, Sheffield, England. Cricket Correspondent. m. Sunita, 2 Apr 1984, 3 children. Education: MA, Cantab. Appointments: Cricket Correspondent: The Observer, 1978, 1989; The Sunday Correspondent, 1989-90; Independent on Sunday, 1991-93; Sunday Telegraph, 1993-. Publications: Cricket Wallah; Train to Julia Creek; Cricket Odyssey; The Observer on Cricket (edited). Contributions to: Wisden Cricket Monthly. Address: c/o Sunday Telegraph, 1 Canada Square, Canary Wharf, London E14 5DT, England.

BERRY Francis, b. 23 Mar 1915, Ipoh, Malaysia. Poet; Writer; Professor Emeritus. m. (1) Nancy Melloney Graham, 4 Sept 1947, 1 son, 1 daughter, (2) Eileen Marjorie Lear, 9 Apr 1970. Education: University College of the South West, 1937-39, 1946-47; BA, University of London, 1947; MA, University of Exeter, 1949. Appointments: Professor of English Literature, University of Sheffield, 1967-70; Professor of English, Royal Holloway, University of London, 1970-80. Publications: Gospel of Fire, 1933; Snake in the Moon, 1936; The Iron Christ, 1938; Fall of a Tower, 1943; The Galloping Centaur, 1952; Murdock and Other Poems, 1955; Poets' Grammar, 1958; Morant Bay and Other Poems, 1961; Poetry and the Physical Voice, 1962; Ghosts of Greenland, 1966; The Shakespeare Inset, 1966; I Tell of Greenland, 1977; From the Red Fort, 1984; Collected Poems, 1994. Contributions to: Periodicals; BBC. Membership: Fellow, Royal Society of Literature. Address: 4 Eastgate Street, Winchester, Hampshire SO23 8EB, England.

BERRY Ila, b. 9 June 1922, USA. Poet; Writer. Education: AA, Fullerton College, California; BA, John F Kennedy University, Orinda, California; MA, English and Creative Writing, San Francisco State University, 1985. Publications: Poetry: Come Walk With Me, 1979; Rearranging the Landscape, 1986; Rowing in Eden, 1987; Behold the Bright Demons, 1993. Contributions to: Periodicals. Honours: Jessamyn West Creative Award, 1969; Woman of Distinction, Fullerton College, 1969. Memberships: California Federation of Chaparral Poets, Robert Frost Chapter; California State Poetry Society; California Writers Club; Ina Coolbrith Circle, president, 1977-79; National League of American Pen Women. Address: 761 Sequoia Woods Place, Concord, CA 94518, USA.

BERRY James, b. 1925, Fair Prospect, Jamaica. Poet; Writer; Editor. Publications: Bluefoot Traveller: An Anthology of West Indian Poets in Britain (editor), 1976; Fractured Circles, 1979; News for Babylon: The Chatto Book of West Indian-British Poetry (editor), 1984; Chain of Days, 1985; The Girls and Yanga Marshall (stories), 1987; A Thief in the Village and Other Stories, 1988; Don't Leave an Elephant to Go and Chase a Bird, 1990; When I Dance (poems), 1991; Ajeema and His Son, 1992. Honours: C Day-Lewis Fellowship; Poetry Society Prize, 1981; Boston Globe/Horn Book Award, 1993. Address: c/o Hamish Hamilton Ltd, 27 Wrights Lane, London W8 5TZ, England.

BERRY Paul, b. 25 Dec 1919, Weston-by-Welland, England. Writer; Lecturer. Publications: Daughters of Cain (with Renee Huggett), 1956; By Royal Appointment: A Biography of Mary Ann Clarke, Mistress of the Duke of York 1803-07, 1970; The Selected Journalism of Winifred Holtby and Vera Brittain (joint editor), 1985; Vera Brittain: A Life (with Mark Bostridge), 1995; Winifred Holtby: Selected Short Stories (with Marion Shaw), forthcoming. Address: 1 Bridgefoot Cottages, Stedham, Midhurst, Sussex, England.

BERRY Wendell (Erdman), b. 5 Aug 1934, Henry County, Kentucky, USA. Writer; Poet; Professor. m. Tanya Amyx Berry, 29 May 1957, 1 son, 1 daughter. Education: BA, 1956, MA, 1957, University of Kentucky. Appointments: Instructor, Georgetown College, 1957-58; E H Jones Lecturer in Creative Writing, 1959-60, Visiting Professor of Creative Writing, 1968-69, Stanford University; Assistant Professor, New York University, 1962-64; Faculty Member, 1964-77, Professor, 1987-93, University of Kentucky; Elliston Poet, University of Cincinnati, 1974; Writer-in-Residence, Centre College, 1977, Bucknell University, 1987. Publications: Fiction: Nathan Coulter, 1960, revised edition, 1985; A Place on North, 1967, revised edition, 1985; The Memory of Old Jack, 1974; The Wild Birds, 1986; Remembering, 1988; The Discovery of Kentucky, 1991; Fidelity, 1992; A Consent, 1993; Watch With Me, 1994; A World Lost, 1996. Poetry: The Broken Ground, 1964; Openings, 1968; Findings, 1969; Farming: A Handbook, 1970; The Country of Marriage, 1973; Sayings and Doings, 1975; Clearing, 1977; A Part, 1980; The Wheel, 1982; Collected Peoms, 1985; Sabbaths, 1987; Sayings and Doings and an Eastward Look, 1990; Entries, 1994; The Farm, 1995. Non-Fiction: The Long-Legged House, 1969; The Hidden Wound, 1970, revised edition, 1989; The Unforseen Wilderness, 1971, revised edition, 1991; A Continuous Harmony, 1972; The Unsettling of America, 1977; Recollected Essays 1965-1980, 1981; The Gift of Good Land, 1981; Standing by Words, 1983; Home Economics, 1987; What Are People For?, 1990; Harlan Hubbard: Life and Work, 1990; Standing on Earth, 1991; Sex, Economy, Freedom and Community, 1993; Another Turn of the Crank, 1995. Honours: Guggenheim Fellowship, 1962; Rockefeller Fellowship, 1965; National Institute of Arts and Letters Award, 1971; Jean Stein Award, American Academy of Arts and Letters, 1987; Lannan Foundation Award for Non-Fiction, 1989; T S Eliot Award, Ingersoll Foundation, 1994; Award for Excellence in Poetry, The Christian Century, 1994; Harry M Caudill Conservationist Award, Cumberland Chapter, Sierra Club, 1996. Address: Lanes Landing Farm, Port Royal, KY 40058, USA.

BERTHA Zoltan, b. 4 June 1955, Szentes, Hungary. Writer; Professor. m. Hajdu Csilla, 5 July 1985, 1 son. Education: MA, 1978, Doctor's Degree, 1982, PhD, 1994, University of Debrecen. Appointments: Scholar, University of Debrecen, 1978-90; Editorial Board, Holnap, 1990-93, Magyar Elet, 1993-95, Alföld, 1991-93; Member of Parliament, 1990-94; Professor, Protestant University, Budapest, 1994-. Publications: Hungarian Literature in Romania and Transylvania in the 1970s (with A Görömbei), 1983, second edition, 1985; A Szellem Jelzöfenyei, 1988; Balint Tibor, 1990; Gond es Mu, 1994; Arcvonalban, 1994; Sütö Andras, 1995, second edition, 1998. Contributions to: Many journals. Honours: Young Critics Scholarship, 1983; Moricz Zsigmond Literary Scholarship, 1989; Kölcsey Prize, 1996. Memberships: Association of Hungarian Writers; International Association of Hungarian Studies; Protestant Cultural Society; Society of Hungarian Literary History; Union of Hungarian Artists; Community of Hungarian Journalists; World Association of Hungarians. Address: Böszörmenyi ut 69, IV 15, H-4032 Debrecen, Hungary.

BERTOLINO James, b. 4 Oct 1942, Hurley, Wisconsin, USA. Poet; Writer; University Teacher. m. Lois Behling, 29 Nov 1966. Education: BS, University of Wisconsin, 1970; MFA, Cornell University, 1973. Appointments: Teacher, Washington State University, 1970-71, Cornell University, 1971-74, University of Cincinnati, 1974-84, Washington Community Colleges, 1984-91, Chapman University, 1989-96, Western Washington University, 1991-96. Publications: Poetry: Employed, 1972; Soft Rock, 1973; The Gestures, 1975; Making Space for Our Living, 1975; The Alleged Conception, 1976; New & Selected Poems, 1978; Precint Kali, 1982; First Credo, 1986; Snail River, 1995. Chapbooks: Drool, 1968; Day of Change, 1968; Stone Marrow, 1969; Becoming Human, 1970; Edging Through, 1972; Terminal Placebos, 1975; Are You Tough Enough for the Eighties?, 1979; Like a Planet, 1993. Contributions to: Poetry in 27 anthologies; Prose in 3 anthologies; Poetry, stories, essays, and reviews in periodicals. Honours: Hart Crane Poetry Award, 1969; Discovery Award, 1972; National Endowment for the Arts Fellowship, 1974; Quarterly Review of Literature International Book Awards, 1986, 1995; Djerassi Foundation Residency, 1987; Bumbershoot Big Book Award, 1994. Address: 533 Section Avenue, Anacortes, WA 98221, USA.

BERZINS Uldis E, b. 17 May 1944, Riga, Latvia. Poet; Translator. m. Yelena Staburova, 17 Dec 1974, 1 son, 1 daughter. Education: BPh, Leningrad University, 1971. Appointment: Writer, 1974-. Publications: Poetry: Piemineklis kazai, English translation as Monument to a Nanny-Goat, 1980; Poetisms baltkrievs (Poetico Bielorussian), 1984; Nenotikusie atentati, English translation as Assasinations Not Carried Out, 1990; Parasts akmens, English translation as An Ordinary Stone, 1992; Laiks, English translation as Time, 1994; Kukainu soli, English translation as Stepsounds of Insects, 1994. Honour: The Baltic Assembly Prize for Literature Memberships include: PEN; Latvian Writers Union. Address: Maskavas iela 54 dz 3, Riga, LV-1003, Latvia.

BESS Clayton. See: **LOCKE Robert Howard.**

BETTS Peter J, b. 8 Apr 1941, Livingston, Northern Rhodesia (British Citizen). Writer; Head, Berne, Department of Cultural Affairs. m. Christine Tschannen, 4 Apr 1981, 1 daughter. Education: Linguistics, University of Berne; Teachers Diploma. Appointments: Writer, 1960-; Teacher, Secondary School and Grammar School, 1962-77; Journalist, 1962-77; Head, Office for Cultural Affairs, 1977-. Publications: Die Pendler, 1975; Anpassungsversuche, 1978; Der Spiegel des Kadschiwe, 1983; Natter-ein Imperium, 1989; Die Schwarze Kiste, 1998. Several theatre plays. Contributions to: Magazines. Honours: Award for Drama, 1974; Book Awards, Berne, 1975, 1976; Schillerstifung, 1985. Memberships: PEN International;; Gruppe Olten. Address: Schlossmatt 2, Hinterkappelen, CH-3032, Switzerland.

BETTS Raymond F(rederick), b. 23 Dec 1925, Bloomfield, New Jersey, USA. Professor of History; Author. m. Irene Donahue, 25 June 1956, 2 sons, 1 daughter. Education: BA, Rutgers University, 1949; MA, 1950, PhD, 1958, Columbia University; Doctorat d'Université, University of Grenoble, 1955; Certificat d'Études africaines, Institut d'Études Politiques, University of Paris, 1955. Appointments: Instructor to Assistant Professor, Bryn Mawr College, 1956-61; Assistant Professor to Professor, Grinnell College, 1961-71; Professor of History, 1971-98, Director, Gaines Center for the Humanities, 1983-98, University of Kentucky; Contributing Editor, Britannia Com, 1999-. Publications: Assimilation and Association in French Colonial Theory, 1890-1914, 1961; The Scramble for Africa (editor), 1966, 2nd edition, revised, 1972; Europe Overseas: Phases of Imperialism, 1968; The Ideology of Blackness (editor), 1971; The False Dawn: European Imperialism in the Nineteenth Century, 1975; Tricouleur: A Brief History of Modern French Colonial Empire, 1978; Europe in Retrospect: A Brief History of the Last Two Hundred Years, 1979; Uncertain Dimensions: Western Overseas Empires in the Twentieth Century, 1985; France and Decolonisation, 1991; Decolonization, 1998. Contributions to: Books and scholarly journals. Honours: Hallam Book Awards, University of Kentucky, 1976, 1986; Outstanding Kentucky Humanist Award, Kentucky Humanities Council, 1989; Great Teacher Award, University of Kentucky, 1979, 1998; Fellowships; Grants. Memberships: African Studies Association; American Historical Association; French Colonial Historical Society; Society for French Historical Studies. Address: 311 Mariemont Drive, Lexington, KY 40505, USA.

BEVAN Alistair. See: **ROBERTS Keith (John Kingston).**

BEWES Richard Thomas, b. 1 Dec 1934, Nairobi, Kenya. Anglican Rector; Writer. m. Elisabeth Ingrid Jaques, 18 Apr 1964, 2 sons, 1 daughter. Education: Marlborough School, 1948-53; MA, Emmanuel College, Cambridge, 1954-57; Ridley Hall Theological College,

Cambridge, 1957-59. Publications: Talking About Prayer, 1979; The Pocket Handbook of Christian Truth, 1981; The Church Reaches Out, 1981; John Wesley's England, 1981; The Church Overcomes, 1983; On the Way, 1984; Quest for Life, 1985; The Church Marches On, 1986; When God Suprises, 1986; A New Beginning, 1989; The Resurrection, 1989; Does God Reign?, 1995; Speaking in Public - Effectively, 1998. Contributions to: The Church of England Newspaper. Membership: Guild of British Songwriters. Address: 2 All Souls Place, London W1N 3DB, England.

BEYFUS Drusilla, b. London, England. Editor; Columnist; Writer. Appointments: Women's Editor, Sunday Express, London, 1952-53; Columnist, Daily Express, London, 1953-56, You Magazine, Mail on Sunday, 1994-; Associate Editor, Queen Magazine, London, 1959-63, Weekend Telegraph Magazine, London, 1963-71, Vogue Magazine, London, 1980-87; Home Editor, The Observer, London, 1962-64; Editor, Brides and Setting Up Home Magazine, London, 1971-79; Visiting Tutor, Central St Martin's College of Art, 1989-; Contributing Editor, Telegraph Magazine, 1991-. Publications: Lady Behave (with Anne Edwards), 1956, new edition, 1969; The English Marriage, 1968; The Bride's Book, 1981; The Art of Giving, 1987; Modern Manners, 1992; The Done Thing: Courtship, Parties, 1992; Business, Sex, 1993. Contributions to: Many periodicals. Address: 51g Eaton Square, London SW1, England.

BHARTI Dharmvir, b. 1926, India. Novelist; Poet; Editor. Education: MA, University of Allahabad, 1947. Appointments: Founder-Editor, Charmayug magazine; Editor, Alocha quarterly. Publications: Fiction: The Village of the Dead, 1946; The God of Sins, 1949; The Seventh House of the Sun God, 1952; Immortal Son, 1952; The Moon and Broken People, 1965. Poetry: Cold Iron, 1952; The Beloved of Krishna, 1959; Seven Years of Lyrics, 1959. Address: c/o Dharmayug, Bennett, Coleman & Co, Times Building, Dr D B Road, Bombay 400001, India.

BHATNAGAR Om Prakash, b. 30 May 1932, Agra, India. University Teacher of English; Writer; Poet. m. Parvati Bhatnagar, 21 Oct 1959, 1 son, 1 daughter. Education: MA, 1954; MA, 1956; DLitt, 1959; PhD, 1991. Appointments: University Teacher of English; Editorial Board, Indian Journal of English Studies, 1979-86. Publications: Thought Poems: Angles of Retreat; Oneiric Visions; Shadows in Floodlights; Audible Landscape; Perspectives on Indian Poetry in English; Studies in Indian Drama in English. Contributions to: Many literary and research publications. Honours: Plaque of Honour for Excellence in Poetry; G Ramachandran Award for International Understanding Through Literature. Memberships: Indian Association for English Studies; University English Teachers Association. Address: Rituraj Camp, Amravati 444 602, India.

BHATNAGAR Raghuvir Prasad, b. 8 Nov 1927, Kota, India. Retired University Professor. m. Rama Bhatnagar, 5 May 1955, 1 son, 1 daughter. Education: BA, Herbert College, Kota; MA, English, Agra University; MA, Linguistics, Lancaster, England; PG. Dip. T.E. (CIEFL), Hyderabad. Appointments: Assistant Professor, Nadiad, 1950, Surat, 1951, Meerut, 1952, Pilani, 1959; Assistant Professor, Associate Professor, Professor, University of Rajasthan, Jaipur, 1964-84. Publications: Textbook of Logic, 1952; Speak Better, Write Better English, 1952; English for India, 1969; Introduction to Modern Linguistics (in Hindi), 1977; Communication in English, 1980; Living English, 1982; A University Level Grammar of English, 1983; Law and Language, 1985; English for Competitive Examinations, 1989; English Grammar, Composition and Reference Skills, 1991; Anuvrat: A Shield Against Immortality, 1993; Nonviolence and its Many Facets, 1995. Honours: British Council T & T Award, 1973-74; Fulbright Hays Postdoctoral Senior Research Fellowship, 1976-77; DLitt, Honoris Causa, Netherlands. Memberships: IAES, general secretary; RETA, president. Address: C 177 Gyan Marg, Tilak Nagar, Jaipur 302 004, India.

BHATTACHARYA Anadi Charan, (Abola Kanto Brahmachari), b. 14 Mar 1936, South Tripura, India. Writer. 1 son. Education: BA, Calcutta University, 1965; PhD. Appointments: Teacher, Secondary School, 1960-87; Lecturer, Basic Training College, Kakrabon, South Tripura, 1987-97. Publications: Tripura O tripuri (Bengali), 1987; Bindute Sindhur Swad (Bengali), 1989; Tatkshinik, 1990; Itihaser Aloke Puran (Bengali), 1991; Kok Boroker Padanka, 1993; A Few Words About Our State Gaddess, Tripureshori, 1996; Tripurar Upajatider Bhasha O Sanskriti (Bengali), 1996. Contributions to: Magazines. Honours: All India Radio Award, 1994; Dainik Sambad Award, 1995. Membership: Gramin Sahity Sammelon, Calcutta. Address: PO Radhakishorepur, South Tripura 799120, India.

BHATTACHARYA Parnendu Prasad, b. 10 Oct 1920, Gouripur, Mymensing (now in Bangla Desh). m. Kabita Bhattacharya, 10 July 1954, 2 sons, 1 daughter. Education: MA, Calcutta University, 1957. Appointments: Teacher, Mrityunjay High School; Sub Editor, Daily Loksevak; Inspector, National Sample Survey, Indian Statistical Institute, Calcutta, 1951-; Section Officer, Linguistic Research Unit; Section Officer, Personnel Unit, Next Professor in Value-Oriented Teachers' Training Centre, Bangavani, Nabadwip, under Human Resources Development, Government of India, until 1985. Publications: Book of Poems: Pran Basanta, 1946; Tritiya Nayan, 1956; Swayambar, 1960; Mancher Janya, 1965; Pitari Pritimapanne, 1967; Krisna Amar Satyaban Radhai Sabitri, 1981; Selection of Poems: Purnendu Prasad Bhattacharya-R Bachhai Cabita, 1985; Short Stories: Jayanta-R Dinalipi, 1980; Poems on Spot Visits: Dinalipi Thee, 1996; Mythology Revalued in Epic: Swarga Martya Puran, 1996; Research From Sivaji to Ahalyabai: Sivaji-R Dharapat, 1997; Research From Jaydev to Ramprasad: Jaydeverdharapat, 1997. Contributions to: Many journals including Sahitya Mela. Honours: Copper Inscription, Government of India as Freedom Fighter; Certificate, Bharat Bhasa Bhusan, Akhil Bharatiya Bhasa Sahitya Sammelan. Memberships: Executive Member, Bangiya Sahitya Parisad; Nikhil Bharat Banga Sahitya Sammelan, New Delhi. Address: 28/1 Manna Para Road, Calcutta 700090, India.

BHYRAPPA Santeshivara Lingannaiah, b. 26 July 1934, Santeshivara, Karnataka, India. Writer; Critic. m. Saraswati Bhyrappa, 13 Dec 1958, 2 sons. Education: BA, Honours, 1957; MA, Philosophy, 1958; PhD, Aesthetics, 1963. Publications: Novels: Vamsha Vriksha, 1966; Grihabhanga, 1970; Dattu, 1974; Parva, 1979; Nele, 1983; Sakshi, 1986. Non-Fictioin: Truth and Beauty, 1964; Story and Its Substance, 1969; Why Do I Write and Other Essays, 1982; Tantu, 1993; Bhitti (Canvas, autobiography), 1996. Contributions to: Numerous journals. Honours: Best Book of the Year Awards, 1967, 1975; Central Sahihya Akademi Award, 1975. Memberships: Bharatiya Jnaanapeeth Foundation; Central Sahitya Akademi; Indian Philosophical Congress; Karnataka State Sahitya Akademi. Address: 1007 Kuvempunagar, Mysore 570023, India.

BIBBY Peter Leonard, b. 21 Dec 1940, London, England. Poet; Writer; Dramatist; Screenwriter; Editor. m. 15 Apr 1967, 2 sons, 2 daughters. Education: BA, University of Western Australia; DipEd, Murdoch University. Appointments: Editor, Fellowship of Australian Writers, and Bagabala Books. Publication: Island Weekend, 1960. Contributions to: Various anthologies and journals. Honours: Tom Collins Literary Awards, 1978, 1982; Lyndall Hadow National Short Story Award, 1983; Donald Stuart National Short Story Award, 1985. Memberships: Australian Film Institute; Australian Writers Guild; Computer Graphics Association; Fellowship of Australian Writers. Address: c/o PO Box 668, Broome, Western Australia, Australia.

BIBERGER Eric Ludwig, b. 20 July 1927, Passau, Bavaria, Germany. Editor; Writer. Education: Examination Stadt; Wirtschafsaubauschule Passau, 1944; Volkhochschule Passau. Publications include: Dreiklang der Stille (poems), 1955; Rundgang über dem Nordlicht (philosophy, fairy tales of atomic age), 1958; Die Traumwelle (novel), 1962; Denn im Allsein der Welt (poems), 1966; Duadu oder der Mann im Mond (radio plays), 1967; Gar mancher (satirical verses), 1967; Anthology Quer, 1974; Anthology 3 (in 47 languages), 1979; Andere Wege bis Zitterluft (poems), 1982; Was ist hier Schilf, was Reiher (haiku), 1984; Nichts als das Meer (poems), 1984; Zwei Pfund Morgenduft (feuilletons), 1987; Drei Millimeter Erd-Kugel, Trei Milimetristerapamanteasca (poems), 1997; Fantasieschutzgebeit, Imaginationis hortulus (haiku), 1998. Honours: Recipient of several honours. Memberships include: Chairman, Regensburger Schriftslellergruppe International, Joint Association of Authors in 25 countries of the world, 1960-, Honorary President, 1995-; Founder, Director, Internationale Regensbürger Literaturtage, 1967-94; Internationale Jungautoren-Wettbewerbe, 1972-94; Founder, Editor, Publication series RSG Studio International, 1973-, RSG-Forum 15/25, 1977-; Humboldt-Gesllschaft für Wissenschaft und Kunst, 1993-. Address: Altmühlstrasse 12, D 93059 Regensburg, Germany.

BICHSEL Peter, b. 24 Mar 1935, b. 24 Mar 1935, Lucerne, Switzerland. Author. m. Therese Spörri, 1956, 1 son, 1 daughter. Education: Graduate, Teacher's College, Solothurn, 1955. Appointments: Writer-in-Residence, Oberlin College, Ohio, 1971-72; Visiting Lecturer, University of Essen, 1980, Univeristy of Frankfurt am Main, 1982; Dartmouth College, Hanover, New Hampshire, 1987, Middlebury College, Vermont, 1989, City University of New York, 1992. Publications: Eigentlich möchte Frau Blum den Milchmann kennenlernen, 1964; Das Gästehaus, 1965; Die Jahreszeiten, 1967; Kindergeschichten, 1969; Des Schweizers Schweiz, 1969; Geschichten zur falschen Zeit, 1979; Der Leser: Das Erzählen, 1982; Der Busant: Von Trinkern, Polizisten und der schönen Magelone, 1985; Schulmeistereien, 1985; Irgendwo anderswo, 1986; Im Gegenteil, 1990; Zur Stadt Paris, 1993; Die Totaldemokraten, 1998; Cherubin Hammer und Cherubin Hammer, 1999. Honours: Gruppe 47 Prize, 1965; Lessing Prize, Hamburg, 1965; Arts Prize, Solothurn, 1979; Literature Prize, Bern, 1979; Johann Peter Hebel Prize, 1986; Culture Prize, Lucerne, 1989. Memberships: Akademie der Künste; American Association of Teachers of German, honorary member; Deutsche Akademie für Sprache und Dichtung, Darmstadt, corresponding member. Address: Nelkenweg 24, CH-4512 Bellach, Switzerland.

BIDDISS Michael Denis, b. 15 Apr 1942, Farnborough, Kent, England. Professor of History; Writer. m. Ruth Margaret Cartwright, 8 Apr 1967, 4 daughters. Education: MA, PhD, Queens' College, Cambridge, 1961-66; Centre des Hautes Etudes Européennes, University of Strasbourg, 1965-66. Appointments: Fellow in History, Downing College, Cambridge, 1966-73; Lecturer/Reader in History, University of Leicester, 1973-79; Professor of History, University of Reading, 1979-. Publications: Father of Racist Ideology, 1970; Gobineau: Selected Political Writings (editor), 1970; Disease and History (co-author), 1972; The Age of the Masses, 1977; Images of Race (editor), 1979; Thatchersim: Personality and Politics (co-editor), 1987; The Nuremberg Trial and the Third Reich, 1992; The Uses and Abuses of Antiquity (co-editor), 1999. Memberships: Historical Association, president, 1991-94; Faculty, History and Philosophy of Medicine, Society of Apothecaries, London, president, 1994-98; Royal Historical Society, joint vice president, 1995-. Address: Department of History, University of Reading, Whiteknights, Reading RG6 6AA, England.

BIEBER Konrad, b. 24 Mar 1916, Berlin, Germany (US citizen, 1955). Professor of French and Comparative Literature Emeritus; Writer; Translator. m. Tamara Siew, 29 Aug 1939, dec 1995, 1 son. Education: Licence de Lettres, Sorbonne, University of Paris, 1938; PhD, Comparative Literature, Yale University, 1953. Appointments: Instructor, French, Yale University, 1948-53; Visiting Lecturer in French and Comparative Literature, University of Colorado at Boulder, 1952; Assistant Professor, 1953-57, Associate Professor,

1957-60, Professor of French and Chairman, Department of French, 1960-68, Connecticut College, New London; Professor of French and Comparative Literature, 1968-86, Professor Emeritus, 1986-, State University of New York. Publications: L'Allemagne vue par les Ecrivains de la Résistance Française, 1954; Simone de Beauvoir, 1979; Outwitting the Gestapo (translation of Lucie Aubrac's Ils partiront dans l'Ivresse), 1993. Contributions to: Encyclopedias, dictionaries, books, and journals including Historical Dictionary of World War II - France, 1998. Honours: Guggenheim Fellowship, 1957-58; Chevalier des Palmes Académiques, 1970; Book-of-the-Month and History Club selections, 1993. Address: 1211 Foulkeways, Gwynedd, PA 19436, USA.

BIEGEL Paul Johannes, b. 25 Mar 1925, Bussum, Netherlands. Author. Education: University of Amsterdam. Publications: The King of the Copper Mountains, 1969; The Seven Times Search, 1971; The Little Captain, 1971; The Twelve Robbers, 1974; The Gardens of Dorr, 1975; Far Beyond & Back Again, 1977; The Elephant Party, 1977; Letters from the General, 1979; The Looking-Glass Castle, 1979; The Dwarfs of Nosegay, 1978; Robber Hopsika, 1978; The Fattest Dwarf of Nosegay, 1980; The Tin Can Beast, 1980; The Curse of the Werewolf, 1981; Virgil Nosegay and the Cake Hunt, 1981; Crocodile Man, 1982; Virgil Nosegay and the Wellington Boots, 1984. Honours: Best Children's Book of the Year, 1965; Golden Pencil Prizes, 1972, 1993; Silver Pencil Awards, 1972, 1974, 1981, 1988; Nienke van Hichtum Prize for Children's Literature, 1973; State Prize, 1974; Woutertje Pieterse Prize, 1991. Memberships: Vereninging van Letterkudigen; Maatschappij van Letterkunde. Address: Keizersgracht 227, Amsterdam, Netherlands.

BIELSKI Alison Joy Prosser, b. 24 Nov 1925, Newport, Gwent, Wales. Poet; Writer; Lecturer. m. (1) Dennis Ford Treverton Jones, 19 June 1948, (2) Anthony Edward Bielski, 30 Nov 1955, 1 son, 1 daughter. Appointment: Lecturer, Writers on Tour, Welsh Arts Council. Publications: The Story of the Welsh Dragon, 1969; Across the Burning Sand, 1970; Eve, 1973; Flower Legends of the Wye Valley, 1974; Shapes and Colours, 1974; The Lovetree, 1974; Mermaid Poems, 1974; Seth, 1980; Night Sequence, 1981; Eagles, 1983; The Story of St Mellons, 1985; That Crimson Flame, 1996; The Green-Eyed Pool (poems), 1997. Contributions to: Anthologies and journals. Honours: Premium Prize, Poetry Society, 1964; Anglo-Welsh Review Poetry Prize, 1970; Arnold Vincent Bowen Poetry Prize, 1971; 3rd Place, Alice Gregory Memorial Competition, 1979; Orbis Poetry Prize, 1984; 2nd Prize, Julia Cairns Trophy, Society of Women Writers and Journalists, 1984, 1992. Memberships: Gwent Poetry Society; Society of Women Writers and Journalists; Welsh Academy; Welsh Union of Writers. Address: 64 Glendower Court, Velindre Road, Whitchurch, Cardiff CF4 7JJ, Wales.

BIENEN Leigh Buchanan, b. 24 Apr 1938, Berkeley, California, USA. Lawyer; Writer; University Educator. m. Henry Bienon, 1861. Education: BA, Cornell University; MA, University of Iowa Writers Workshop; JD, Rutgers School of Law. Appointment: Senior Lecturer, Northwestern University School of Law, Chicago, Illinois. Publications: Jurors and Rape, with H Feild, 1980; O'Henry Prize Stories, 1983; Tri-Quarterly, 1997, 1999; Crimes of the Century, with G Geis, 1998. Contributions to: Journal of Criminology and Criminal Law; African Law Journal; Journal of Modern African Studies. Address: 639 Central Street, Evanston, IL 60201, USA.

BIERMANN Pieke, b. 22 Mar 1950, Stolzenau, Germany. Writer; Translator. m. Dr Thomas Woertche, 15 Oct 1993. Education: MA, German Literature and Political Sciences, University of Hanover, 1976. Appointments: Editor for Foreign Literature, Rowohlt Publishers, 1980-81; Freelance, 1982-. Publications: Author and translator of numerous books, including Novels: Potsdamer Ableben, 1987; Violetta, 1990; Herzrasen, 1993; Vier, Fuenf, Sechs, 1997; Berlin, Kabbala (short-stories), 1997. Contributions to: Magazines and periodicals. Honours: Grant, Ingeborg Bachmann Wettbewerb, Austria, 1990; Best German Crime Novel Awards, 1991, 1994. Membership: IG Medien. Literary Agent: M Meller, PO Box 400323, 80703 Munich, Germany. Address: PO Box 15 14 10, 10676 Berlin, Germany.

BIERMANN Wolf, b. 15 Nov 1936, Hamburg, Germany. Poet; Songwriter; Musician. m. Christine Bark, 2 sons. Education: Humboldt University, Berlin, 1959-63. Appointments: Assistant Director, Berliner Ensemble, 1957-59; Song and guitar performances throughout Germany. Publications: Die Drahtharfe: Balladen, Gedichte, Lieder, 1965; Mit Marx-und Engelszungen, 1968; Der Dra-Dra (play), 1970; Für meine Genossen, 1972; Deutschland: Ein Wintermärchen, 1972; Nachlass I, 1977; Wolf Biermann; Poems and Ballads, 1977; Preussicher Ikarus, 1978; Verdrehte welt das seh'ich gerne, 1982; Und als ich von Deutschland nach Deutschland: Three Contemporary German Poets, 1985; Affenels und Barrikade, 1986; Alle Lieder, 1991; Ich hatte viele Bekümmernis: Meditation on Cantata No 21 by J S Bach, 1991; Vier Neue Lieder, 1992. Honours: Büchner Prize, 1991; Mörlcke Prize, 1991; Heine Prize, 1993. Address: c/o Verlag Kiepenheuer und Witsch, Rondorferstrasse 5, 5000 Colonge-Marienurg, Germany.

BIGGLE Lloyd Jr, b. 17 Apr 1923, Waterloo, Iowa, USA. Author. m. Hedwig T Janiszewski, 1947, 1 son, 1 daughter. Education: AB, with High Distiction, Wayne University, 1947; MM in Music Literature, 1948, PhD in Musicology, 1953, University of Michigan. Publications: The Angry Espers, 1961; All the Colors of Darkness, 1963; The Fury Out of Time, 1965; Watchers of the Dark, 1966; The Rule of the Door and Other Fanciful Regulations (short stories), 1967 (in UK as The Silent Sky), 1979; The Still Small Voice of Trumpets, 1968; The World Menders, 1971; The Light That Never Was, 1972; Nebula Award Stories 7 (editor), 1972; The Metallic Muse (short stories), 1972; Monument, 1974; This Darkening Universe, 1975; A Galaxy of Strangers (short stories), 1976; Silence is Deadly, 1977; The Whirligig of Time, 1979; Alien Main (with T L Sherred), 1985; The Quallsford Inheritance: A Memoir of Sherlock Holmes, 1986; Interface for Murder, 1987; The Glendower Conspiracy: A Memoir of Sherlock Holmes, 1990; A Hazard of Losers, 1991; Where Dead Soldiers Walk (novel), 1994. Membership: Science Fiction Oral History Association, founder, 1977, president, 1994-. Address: 569 Dubie Avenue, Ypsilanti, MI 48198, USA.

BIGGS Margaret Annette, (Margaret Key Biggs), b. 26 Oct 1933, Pike County, Alabama, USA. Writer; Poet. m. 1 Mar 1956. Education: BS, Troy State University, 1954; MA, California State University, 1979. Publications: Swampfire, 1980; Sister to the Sun, 1981; Magnolias and Such, 1982; Petals from the Womanflower, 1983; Plumage of the Sun, 1986. Contributions to: Anthologies, journals and reviews. Address: PO Box 551, Port St Joseph, FL 32456, USA.

BIGSBY Christopher William Edgar, b. 27 June 1941, Dundee, Scotland. University Professor; Broadcaster; Novelist. Education: BA, MA, Sheffield University; PhD, Nottingham University. Publications: Confrontation and Commitment: A Study of Contemporary American Drama, 1967; Edward Albee, 1969; The Black American Writer (editor), 1969; Three Negro Plays, 1969; Dada and Surrealism, 1972; Approaches to Popular Culture, 1975; Tom Stoppard, 1976; Superculture, 1976; Edward Albee, 1976; The Second Black Renaissance, 1980; Contemporary English Drama, 1981; Joe Orton, 1982; A Critical Introduction to 20th Century American Drama, 3 volumes, 1982, 1984, 1985; The Radical Imagination and the Liberal Tradition, 1982; David Mamet, 1985; Cultural Change in the United States since World War II, 1986; Plays by Susan Glaspell, 1987; File on Miller, 1988; American Drama: 1945-1990, 1992; Hester (novel), 1994; Pearl (novel), 1995; 19th Century American Short Stories (editor), 1995; Portable Arthur Miller (editor), 1995; Still Lives (novel), 1996; Cambridge Companion to Arthur Miller (editor), 1998; Cambridge History of American Theatre (joint editor), 1998. Contributions to: Radio; Television; Times Literary Supplement; Times Higher Education Supplement; Sunday Independent; American Quarterly; Modern Drama; Theatre Quarterly; Guardian; Sunday Telegraph. Address: 3 Church Farm, Colney, Norwich, England.

BIKE William S, b. 9 Apr 1957, Chicago, Illinois, USA. Writer. m. Anne M Nordhaus, 11 May 1986. Education: BA, Political Science, DePaul University, 1979. Appointments: Publication-Production Assistant, Business Insurance Magazine, Crain Communications, Chicago, 1979-81; Editor-in-Chief, Oak Park News, Berwyn-Cicero News, Sanford Publishing Co, Oak Park, Illinois, 1981; Assistant Editor, 1982, Associate Editor, 1982-84, Dental Products Report, Dental Products Report International, Dental Lab Products, Irving-Cloud Publications, Skokie, Illinois; Associate Editor, Near West Gazette, Near West Gazette Publishing Co, Chicago, 1983-; Writer, Editor, Manager, Director, Loyola University publications, 1984-93; Publications Director, University of Chicago Graduate School of Business, 1993-95; Editor-in-Chief, Alumni Report, Chicago College of Dentistry, University of Illinois, 1996. Publications: Streets of the Near West Side, 1996; Winning Political Campaigns, 1998. Contributions to: The Bur, 1992, Quayle Quarterly, 1992; Delta Epsilon Sigma Journal, 1992, 1995; Nine: A Journal of Baseball History and Social Policy Perspectives, 1993; DePaul Law, 1995; Illinois Quarterly, 1995-96; P-O-P Times, 1995-; Others. Honours: 1st Place, DePaul University Annual Newswriting Award, 1977, 1978, 1979; Communication Concepts' National Apex Award of Excellence, Most Improved Magazine, 1990, Total Publications Programme, 1990, Feature Writing, 1991; W Daniel Conroyd Employee Award, Loyola University, 1993; Peter Lisagor Exemplary Journalism Award, 1993, 1995, Chicago Headline. Membership: Society of Professional Journalists. Literary Agent: Jeanine Mielecki. Address: 3632 N Central Park Avenue, Chicago, IL 60618, USA.

BILGRAMI Akeel, b. 28 Feb 1950, Hyderabad, India. Professor. m. Carol Rovane, 25 Aug 1990, 1 daughter. Education: BA, Bombay University, 1970; BA, University of Oxford, 1974; PhD, University of Chicago, 1983. Appointments: Professor of Philosophy, Chairman of Philosophy Department, Columbia University. Publications: Belief and Meaning, 1992; Self-Knowledge and Intentionality, 1996; Internal Dialectics: The Moral Psychology of Identity. Contributions to: Journal of Philosophy; Philosophical Quarterly; Philosophical Topics. Honours: Rhodes Scholarship, 1971; Whitney Humanities Fellow, 1992. Membership: American Philosophical Society. Address: 110 Morningside Drive, No 58, New York,NY 10027, USA.

BILLING Graham John, b. 12 Jan 1936, Dunedin, New Zealand. Author. Dramatist; Poet. m. Rowan Innes Cunningham, 29 Aug 1978, 1 son, 1 daughter by previous marriage. Education: Otago University, 1955-58. Appointments: Staff, Dunedin Evening Star, 1958-62; Antarctic Division, DSIR, 1962-64; New Zealand Broadcasting Corporation News Service and TV Service, 1964-67; Staff, Dominion Sunday Times, 1967-69; Lecturer, writing, Mitchell College Advanced Education, Bathurst, Australia, 1974-75. Publications: Forbush and the Penguins, 1965; The Alpha Trip, 1969; Statues, 1971; The Slipway, 1973; The Primal Therapy of Tom Purslane, 1980; Changing Countries (poetry), 1980. Non-Fiction: South: Man and Nature in Antarctica, 1965; New Zealand, the Sunlit Land, 1966; The New Zealanders, 1974. Radio Plays: Forbush and the Penguins, 1965; Mervyn Gridfern versus the Babsons, 1965; The Slipway, 1976; The Prince of Therapy of Tom Purslane, 1980. Address: 89 Mersey Street, St Albans, Christchurch 1, New Zealand.

BILLINGTON Michael, b. 16 Nov 1939, Leamington Spa, England. Drama Critic; Writer. m. Jeanine Bradlaugh, 1978. Education: BA, St Catherine's College, Oxford. Appointments: Journalist Trainee, Liverpool Daily Post and Echo, 1961-62; Public Liaison Officer, Director, Lincoln Theatre Co, 1962-64; Reviewer, The Times, 1965-71; Film Critic, Birmingham Post, 1968-78,

Illustrated London News, 1968-81; Drama Critic, The Guardian, 1971-, Country Life, 1987-; London Arts Correspondent, New York Times, 1978-. Publications: The Modern Actor, 1974; How Tickled I Am, 1977; The Performing Arts, 1980; The Guiness Book of Theatre Facts and Feats, 1982; Alan Ayckbourn, 1983; Stoppard: The Playwright, 1987; Peggy Ashcroft, 1989; Twelfth Night, 1990; One Night Stands, 1993; Harold Pinter, 1996. Address: 15 Hearne Road, London W4 3NJ, England.

BILLINGTON Rachel (Mary), b. 11 May 1942, Oxford, England. Writer. m. 16 Dec 1967, 2 sons, 2 daughters. Education: BA, English, London University. Publications: Over 20 books, including: Loving Attitudes, 1988; Theo and Matilda, 1990; The First Miracles, 1990; Bodily Harm, 1992; The Family Year, 1992; The Great Umbilical, 1994; Magic and Fate, 1996; The Life of Jesus (for children), 1996; Perfect Happiness, 1996; The Tiger Sky, 1998; The Life of St. Francs (for children), 1999. Contributions to: Reviewer, Columnist and short story writer for various publications; 2 plays for BBC TV; 4 plays for Radio. Memberships: Society of Authors; President, PEN, 1997-. Address: The Court House, Poyntington, Near Sherborne, Dorset DT9 4LF, England.

BINCHY Maeve, b. 28 May 1940, Dublin, Ireland. Writer. m. Gordon Thomas Snell, 29 Jan 1977. Education: BA, University College, Dublin, 1960. Appointments: Columnist, Irish Times, London, 1968-; Writer. Publications: My First Book, 1976; The Central Line: Stories of Big City Life, 1978; Maeve's Diary, 1979; Victoria Line, 1980; Light a Penny Candle, 1982; Maeve Binchy's Dublin Four, 1982; The Lilac Bus, 1984; Echoes, 1985; Firefly Summer, 1987; Silver Wedding, 1988; Circle of Friends, 1991; The Copper Beech, 1992; The Glass Lake, 1995. Other: Plays; Television screenplays. Honours: International Television Festival Golden Prague Award, Czech TV, 1979; Jacobs Award, 1979. Address: c/o Irish Times, 85 Fleet Street, London EC4, England.

BINDER Elisabeth, b. 19 May 1956, Dortmund, Germany. Writer; Reporter. Education: PhD, University of Münster, 1983. Publications: Die Entstehung Unternehmerischer Public Relations, dissertation, 1983; Restaurants in Berlin, 1991; Von Tisch zu Tisch, 1994; Berlin zu Tisch, 1996. Contributions to: Many to Der Tagesspiegel, also to Die Zeit, Der Feinschmecker; Merian. Address: c/o Der Tagesspiegel, Potsdamer Strasse 87, 10785 Berlin, Germany.

BINDRA Pritpal Singh, b. 11 Sept 1929, India. Retired. m. Surjit Kaur Bindra, 14 Feb 1954, 1 son, 1 daughter. Education: BA, 1952, Bachelor of Teaching, 1957, Punjab University. Appointments: Teacher, Government Middle and High Schools, Punjab, 1953-60; Teacher, Secondary Technical School, Dudden Hil, London, England, 1961-63; Insurance Business, England, 1964-83; Retired, 1984; Writing, Canada, 1984-. Publications: Thus Sayeth Gurban, reference book on Guru Granth Sahib, Holy Scripture of Sikh Religion; Muklawa and Other Stories, 16 short stories and novellas in English. Contributions to: Regular columnist and contributor, India Journal, Toronto, Indo-Canadian Voice, Toronto, and Spokesman Monthly, Chandigarh, India. Address: 3292 Bathune Road, Mississauga, Ontario L5R 4R1, Canada.

BINGHAM Charlotte Marie-Therese, b. 29 June 1942, Sussex, England. Playwright; Novelist. m. 15 Jan 1964, 1 son, 1 daughter. Education: Educated in England and France. Publications: Coronet Among the Weeds; Lucinda; Coronet Among the Grass; Belgravia; Country Life; At Home; Television series (with Terence Brady): Upstairs, Downstairs; Nanny; No Honestly; Yes Honestly; Play for Today; Pig in the Middle; Father Matthew's Daughter; Thomas and Sarah. Novels: To Hear a Nightingale; The Business; In Sunshine or In Shadow; Stardust; Change of Heart. Contributions to: Vogue; Tatler; Woman's Journal; Town and Country. Honour: Romantic Novelists Best Novel Award, 1996. Membership: Society of Authors. Literary Agent: Murray Pollinger, c/o 222 Old Brompton Road, London SW5 0BZ,

England. Address: c/o 10 Buckingham Street, London WC1, England.

BINHAM Philip Frank, b. 19 July 1924, England. Retired Teacher; Writer; Translator. m. Marja Sola, 21 June 1952, 1 son, 1 daughter. Education: Magdalen College, Oxford, 1935-41; Wadham College, Oxford, 1946-49; BA (Oxon), 1949; MA (Oxon), 1954. Publications: How To Say It, 1965; UK edition, 1968; Executive English I-III, 1968-70; Speak Up, 1975; Snow in May: An Anthology of Finnish Literature 1945-72, 1978; Service with a Smile: Hotel English, Restaurant English, 1979, UK edition, 1982; Team 7, 8, 9, 1983-85. Translations: Tamara (Eeva Kilpi) (novel), 1972; The Horseman (Paavo Haavikko); Compass Rose (Eka Laine), 1985; In Search of Helsinki (Paavo Haavikko), 1986; Five Decades of Social Security (Paavo Haavikko), 1989; The Northeast Passage from the Vikings to Nordenskiöld, 1992; Mare Balticum: The Baltic - Two Thousand Years, 1996; Ah, The Savoy, 1997; Taidekoti Kirpilä, 1998; Havis Amanda, Mermaid's Delicacies, 1998. Contributions to: World Literature Today (formerly Books Abroad), 1972-. Honours: Order of the Finnish Lion, 1972; Finnish State Prize for Foreign Translators, 1990. Memberships: Society of Authors; Finnish Society of Scientific Writers; Finnish Literature Society, honorary member. Address: Seunalantie 34A, 04200 Kerava, Finland.

BIRCH Carol, b. 3 Jan 1951, Manchester, England. Writer. m. Martin Lucas Butler, 26 Oct 1990, 2 sons. Education: University of Keele, 1968-72. Publications: Life in the Palace, 1988; The Fog Line, 1989; The Unmaking, 1992; Songs of the West, 1994; Little Sister, 1998. Contributions to: Times Literary Supplement; Independent; New Statesman. Honours: David Higham Prize; Geoffrey Faber Memorial Award. Membership: Society of Authors. Literary Agent: Mic Cheetham Agency. Address: c/o Mic Cheetham Agency, 11-12 Dover Street, London W1X 3PH, England.

BIRD Charles. See: **WITTICH John Charles Bird.**

BIRD Kai, b. 2 Sept 1951, Eugene, Oregon, USA. Author. m. Susan Gloria Goldmark, 7 June 1975, 1 son. Education: MS, Journalism, Northwestern University, 1975; BA, History, Carleton College, 1973. Publications: The Chairman: John J McCloy, The Making of the American Establishment, 1992; Hiroshima's Shadow: Writings on the Denial of History and the Smithsonian Controversy, (editor with Lawrence Lifeshultz), 1997. Contributions to: New York Times; Los Angeles Times; Washington Post; Boston Globe; Christian Science Monitor; Foreign Policy; Journal of Diplomatic History; Washington Monthly; Foreign Service Journal. Honours: John D and Catherine T MacArthur Foundation Fellow; German Marshall Fund Fellow; Alicia Patterson Journalism Fellowship; Guggenheim Fellowship. Address: 1914 Biltmore Street, North West Washington, DC 20009, USA.

BIRDSELL Sandra (Louise), b. 22 Apr 1942, Hamiota, Manitoba, Canada. Writer. m. Stanley Vivian Birdsell, 1 July 1959, 1 son, 2 daughters. Appointments: Several writer-in-residencies; Instructor in English, Capilano College, North Vancouver. Publications: Night Travellers, 1982; Ladies of the House, 1984; The Missing Child, 1989; The Chrome Suite, 1992; The Two-Headed Calf, 1997; The Town That Floated Away, 1997. Contributions to: Various publications. Honours: Gerald Lampert Memorial Award, 1982; W H Smith-Books in Canada First Novel Award, 1989; McNally Robinson Award for Manitoba Book of the Year, 1992. Memberships: Manitoba Writers Guild; PEN International; Writers Guild of Canada; Writers Union of Canada. Address: 755 Westminster Avenue, Winnipeg, Manitoba R3G 1A5, Canada.

BIRLEY Julia (Davies), b. 13 May 1928, London, England. Writer. m. 12 Sept 1954, 1 son, 3 daughters. Education: BA, Classics, Oxn. Publications: Novels: The Children on the Shore; The Time of the Cuckoo; When You Were There; A Serpent's Egg; Dr Spicer; Short

Stories. Contributions to: Guardian. Memberships: PEN; Charlotte Yonge Society. Address: Upper Bryn, Longtown, Hereford HR2 0NA, England.

BIRMINGHAM Stephen, b. 28 May 1931, Hartford, Connecticut, USA. Writer. m. Janet Tillson, 5 Jan 1951, div, 1 son, 2 daughters. Education: BA, Williams College, 1950; Postgraduate Studies, University of Oxford, 1951. Appointment: Advertising Copywriter, Needham, Harper & Steers Inc, 1953-67. Publications: Young Mr Keefe, 1958; Baraba Greer, 1959; The Towers of Love, 1961; Those Harper Women, 1963; Fast Start, Fast Finish, 1966; Our Crowd: The Great Jewish Families of New York, 1967; The Right People, 1968; Heart Troubles, 1968; The Grandees, 1971; The Late John Marquand, 1972; The Right Places, 1973; Real Lace, 1973; Certain People: America's Black Elite, 1977; The Golden Dream: Suburbia in the 1970's, 1978; Jacqueline Bouvier Kennedy Onassis, 1978; Life at the Dakota, 1979; California Rich, 1980; Duchess, 1981; The Grandes Dames, 1982; The Auerbach Will, 1983; The Rest of Us, 1984; The LeBaron Secret, 1986; America's Secret Aristocracy, 1987; Shades of Fortune, 1989; The Rothman Scandal, 1991; Carriage Trade, 1993. Contributions to: Periodicals. Memberships: New England Society of the City of New York; Phi Beta Kappa. Address: 1247 Ida Street, Cincinnati, OH 45202, USA.

BIRO József, b. 19 May 1951, Budapest, Hungary. Poet; Performing Artist. m. Antal Edith Katalin, 20 March 1976, 1 daughter. Publications: 18 anthologies and solo books: Fieling the Space, 1986; Fly-Flap of Venus, 1989; Trismus. Honours: Omoroka Prize, Novezamky, Slovakia, 1990; Dip, Bienal Intl De Poesia Visual, Mexico, 1995. Memberships: Hungarian Alliance of Writers; Art Foundation Hungarian's Republic. Literary Agent: Hungarian Alliance of Writers. Address: Deakferenc utca 73 1/4, 1041, Budapest, Hungary.

BIRO Val, b. 6 Oct 1921, Budapest, Hungary. Author; Illustrator. m. (2) Marie Louise Ellaway, 25 Sept 1970, 1 stepson, 1 daughter, 1 stepdaughter. Education: Cistercian School, Budapest; Central School of Art, London, Graduated 1942. Appointments: Designer, Sylvan Press; Production Manager, C&J Temple, Art Director; John Lehmann; Freelance, 1953-. Publications: The Gumdrop (series of children's picture books): Gumdrop, 1965; Gumdrop and the Martians, 37th title, 1998; The Magic Doctor, 1982, 1998; My Oxford Picture Word Book, 1994; Over 360 titles written and/or illustrated, 1945-. Contributions to: Occasionally, various. Membership: Society of Authors, London. Literary Agent: Jennifer Luithlen, Leicester. Address: Bridge Cottage, Brook Avenue, Bosham, W Sussex PO18 8LQ, England.

BISCHOFF David F(rederick), b. 15 Dec 1951, Washington, District of Columbia, USA. Writer. Appointments: Staff member, NBC-TV, Washington, DC, 1974-; Associate Editor, Amazing Magazine. Publications: The Seeker (with Christopher Lampton), 1976; Quest (juvenile), 1977; Strange Encounters (juvenile), 1977; The Phantom of the Opera (juvenile), 1977; The Woodman (with Dennis R Bailey), 1979; Nightworld, 1979; Star Fall, 1980; The Vampires of the Nightworld, 1981; Tin Woodman (with Dennis Bailey), 1982; Star Spring, 1982; War Games, 1983; Mandala, 1983; Day of the Dragonstar (with Thomas F Monteleone), 1983; The Crunch Bunch, 1985; Destiny Dice, 1985; Galactic Warriors, 1985; The Infinite Battle, 1985; The Macrocosmic Conflict, 1986; Manhattan Project, 1986; The Unicorn Gambit, 1986; Abduction: The UFO Conspiracy, 1990; Revelation: The UFO Conspiracy, 1991; Deception: The UFO Conspiracy, 1991; Aliens Versus Predator: Hunter's Planet, 1994. Address: c/o Henry Morrison Inc, 320 Mclain Street, Bedford Hill, NY 10705, USA.

BISHOP Ian Benjamin, b. 18 Apr 1927, Gillingham, Kent, England. University Teacher. m. Pamela Rosemary Haddacks, 14 Dec 1968, 2 daughters. Education: MA, MLitt, Queen's College, Oxford, 1945-51. Appointment: Reader in English, University of Bristol, 1982. Publications: Pearl in Its Setting, 1968; Chaucer's Troilus and Criseyde: A Critical Study, 1981; The Narrative Art of the Canterbury Tales, 1988. Contributions to: Review of English Studies; Medium Aevum; Times Higher Education Supplement; Notes and Queries. Address: 8 Benville Avenue, Coombe Dingle, Bristol BS9 2RX, England.

BISHOP James Drew, b. 18 June 1929, London, England. Journalist. m. 5 June 1959, 2 sons. Education: BA, History, Corpus Christi College, Cambridge, 1953. Appointments: Foreign Correspondent, 1957-64, Foreign News Editor, 1964-66, Features Editor, 1966-70, The Times; Editor, 1971-87, Editor-in-Chief, 1987-94, The Illustrated London News. Publications: Social History of Edwardian Britain, 1977; Social History of the First World War, 1982; The Story of The Times (with Oliver Woods), 1983; Illustrated Counties of England, editor, 1985; The Sedgwick story, 1998. Contributions to: Books, newspapers and magazines. Membership: Association of British Editors, chairman. Address: 11 Willow Road, London NW3 1TJ, England.

BISHOP Jan, See: MCCONCHIE Lyn.

BISHOP Michael (Lawson), b. 12 Nov 1945, Lincoln, Nebraska, USA. Writer. m. Jeri Whitaker, 7 June 1969, 1 son, 1 daughter. Education: BA, 1967, MA, 1968, University of Georgia. Appointments: Writer-in-residence, LaGrange College, 1997-. Publications: Novels: A Funeral for the Eyes of Fire, 1975, revised edition as Eyes of Fire, 1980; And Strange at Ecbatan the Trees, 1976; Stolen Faces, 1977; A Little Knowledge, 1977; Transfigurations, 1979; Under Heaven's Bridge (with Ian Watson), 1981; No Enemy but Time, 1982; Who Made Steve Cry?, 1984; Ancient of Days, 1985; The Secret Ascension, or, Philip K Dick Is Dead, Alas, 1987; Unicorn Mountain, 1988; Apartheid, Superstrings and Mordecai Thubana, 1989; Count Geiger's Blues, 1992; Brittle Innings, 1994; Would it kill you to Smile? (with Paul Di Filippo), 1998. Stories: Catacomb Years, 1979; Blooded on Arachne, 1982; One Winter in Eden, 1984; Close Encounters with the Deity, 1986; Emphatically Not SF, Almost, 1990; At the City Limits of Fate, 1996. Poetry: Windows and Mirrors, 1977; Time Pieces, 1998. Editor: Changes (with Ian Watson), anthology, 1982; Light Years and Dark, anthology, 1984; Nebula Awards: Science Fiction Writers of America's Choices for the Best Science Fiction and Fantasy, volumes 23-25, 1989-91. Contributions to: Anthologies and many periodicals. Honours: Phoenix Award, 1977; Clark Ashton Smith Award, 1978; Rhysling Award, Science Fiction Poetry Association, 1979; Nebula Awards, Science Fiction Writers of America, 1981, 1982; Mythopoetic Fantasy Award, 1988; Locus Award, best fantasy novel, 1994. Memberships: Science Fiction Poetry Association; Science Fiction Fantasy Writers of America. Address: Box 646, Pine Mountain, GA 31822, USA.

BISHOP Pike. See: OBSTFELD Raymond.

BISHOP Wendy, b. 13 Jan 1953, Japan. Professor of English; Writer; Poet. m. Marvin E Pollard Jr, 1 son, 1 daughter. Education: BA, English, 1975, BA, Studio Art, 1975, MA, English, Creative Writing, 1976; MA, English, Teaching Writing, 1979, University of California at Davis; PhD, English, Rhetoric and Linguistics, Indiana University of Pennsylvania, 1988. Appointments: Bayero University, Kano, Nigeria, 1980-81; Northern Arizona University, 1981-82; Chair, Communications, Humanities, and Fine Arts, Navajo Community College, Tsaile, Arizona, 1984-85; Assistant Professor of English, University of Alaska, Fairbanks, 1985-89; Professor of English, Florida State University, Tallahassee, 1989-. Publications: Released into Language: Options for Teaching Creative Writing, 1990; Something Old, Something New: College Writing Teachers and Classroom Change, 1990; Working Words: The Process of Creative Writing, 1992; The Subject in Writing: Essays by Teachers and Students in Writing, 1993; Colors of a Different Horse (editor with Hans Ostrom), 1994; Water's Night (poems with Hans Ostrom), 1994; Genres of Writing: Mapping the Territories of Discourse (editor with Hans Ostrom), 1997. Contributions to: Poems, fiction, and essays in various

reviews and journals. Honours: Joseph Henry Jackson Award, 1980; Several fellowships; Many literary awards. Memberships: Associated Writing Programs; Modern Language Association; National Council of Teachers of English; National Writing Centres Association; Poetry Society of America. Address: c/o Department of English, Florida State University, Tallahassee, FL 32306, USA.

BISK Anatole. See: BOSQUET Alain.

BISSELL Frances Mary, b. 19 Aug 1946, Harrogate, Yorkshire, England. Food and Cookery Writer. m. Thomas E Bissell, 12 Dec 1970. Education: BA Hons, University of Leeds, England, 1970. Appointment: The British Council, 1970-87. Publications: A Cooks Calendar, 1985; The Pleasures of Cookery, 1986; Ten Dinner Parties for Two, 1988; Oriental Flavours, 1989; The Book of Food, 1990; The Real Meat Cookbook, 1992; The Times Cookbook, 1994; The Times Book of Vegetarian Cookery, 1995; Frances Bissell's Westcountry Kitchen, 1996. Contributions to: The Times Cook, 1987-; many others in Britain & abroad. Honour: Glenfiddich Award, 1994; James Beard Award, 1995. Membership: Founder Member, Guild of Food Writers, 1985; Academy of Culinary Arts, academician. Literary Agent: Peters Fraser and Dunlop. Address: 5th Floor, The Chambers, Chelsea Harbour, Lots Road, London SW10 0XF, England.

BISSETT Bill, b. 23 Nov 1939, Halifax, Nova Scotia, Canada. Poet; Artist. Education: Dalhousie University, 1956-57; University of British Columbia, 1963-65. Appointment: Editor, Printer, Blewointmentpress, Vancouver, 1962-83. Publications: The Jinx Ship and other Trips: Poems-drawings-collage, 1966; We Sleep Inside Each Other All, 1966; Fires in the Temple, 1967; Where Is Miss Florence Riddle, 1967; What Poetiks, 1967; Gossamer Bed Pan, 1967; Lebanon Voices, 1967; Of the Land/Divine Service Poems, 1968; Awake in the Red Desert, 1968; Killer Whale, 1969; Sunday Work?, 1969; Liberating Skies, 1969; The Lost Angel Mining Company, 1969; The Outlaw, 1970; Blew Trewz, 1970; Nobody Owns the Earth, 1971; Air 6, 1971; Dragon Fly, 1971; Four Parts Sand: Concrete Poems, 1972; The Ice Bag, 1972; Poems for Yoshi, 1972; Drifting into War, 1972; Air 10-11-12, 1973; Pass the Food, Release the Spirit Book, 1973; The First Sufi Line, 1973; Vancouver Mainland Ice and Cold Storage, 1973; Living with the Vishyan, 1974; What, 1974; Drawings, 1974; Medicine My Mouths on Fire, 1974; Space Travel, 1974; You Can Eat it at the Opening, 1974; The Fifth Sun, 1975; The Wind up Tongue, 1975; Stardust, 1975; An Allusyun to Macbeth, 1976; Plutonium Missing, 1976; Sailor, 1978; Beyond Even Faithful Legends, 1979; Soul Arrow, 1980; Northern Birds in Color, 1981; Parlant, 1982; Seagull on Yonge Street, 1983; Canada Gees Mate for Life, 1985; Animal Uproar, 1987; What we Have, 1989; Hard 2 Beleev, 1990; Incorrect Thoughts, 1992; Vocalist with the Luddites, Dreaming of the Night, 1992; The Last Photo of the Human Soul, 1993; th Influenza uv Logik, 1995-; loving without being vulnrabul, 1997; Offthroad (cassette), 1998; Skars onth seehors, 1999. Address: Box 272, Str F, Toronto, Ontario M4K 2L7, Canada.

BISSOONDATH Neil (Devindra), b. 19 Apr 1955, Arima, Trinidad, West Indies. Author. Education: BA, French, York University, Toronto, 1977. Publications: Digging Up the Mountains (short stories), 1985; A Casual Brutality (novel), 1988; On the Eve of Uncertain Tomorrows (short stories), 1990; The Innocence of Age (novel), 1992; In Selling Illusions: The Cult of Multiculturalism in Canada, 1994. Contributions to: Periodicals. Honour: Canadian Authors Association Literary Award, 1993. Address: c/o Random House Inc, 201 East 50th Street, New York, NY 10022, USA.

BISWAS Anil Ranjan (Oneil), b. 1 Feb 1916, Bangladesh. Writer; Former Civil Servant and Teacher. m. Lily Mullick, 15 May 1941, 1 son. Education: BA (Hons), 1937; MA, 1942; LLM, 1968; PhD, 1976. Appointments: Editor, Eastern Law Reports, 1982; Laikhi (writing), 1985; Poetimetrics, 1996. Publications: Footsteps, 1951; Twentieth Century Bengali Literature, 1952; Curly Waters, 1961; Shakespeare's Sonnets, 1966;

Asutosh's Thoughts on Education, 1968; At Whose Bid the Bell Rings, 1972; Continuum becomes Calcutta, 1973; On the Shores of Anxiety, 1980; Squaring the Circle, 1985; From Justice to Welfare 1985; History of India's Freedom Movement, 1990; Variegated Days, 1991; Bengali Prosody, 1992; Calcutta and Calcuttans, 1992; Democracy for All, 1996; Bengal and Bengalees, 1996. Contributions to: Purvasa; Ananda Bazar Patrika; Desh; Calcutta Review; Journal of the Indian Law Institute. Honours: Onauth Nauth Deb Gold Medal, 1971; Anandaram Barooah Medal, 1977; Griffith Memorial Prize, 1977; D. Litt. (Hon), 1997; Adwaita Malla Burman Memorial Award, 1997. Memberships: Life Member, Asiatic Society; Life Member, Bangia Sahitya Parishad; Laikhi Sahitya Academy; Indian Bar Association (West Bengal Branch); Life Member, Indian Law Institute. Address: Gairick, 18 Cooperative Road, Calcutta 700070, India.

BJERG Anne Marie, b. 17 Dec 1937, Copenhagen, Denmark. Literary Translator; Writer. m. Chrenn Bjerg, 29 Dec 1962, div, 1 daughter. Education: BA, University of Copenhagen, 1970. Appointments: Regular Reader, Gyldendal's Publishing House, 1971-86. Publications: Love from Signe, novel, 1979; Surviving, short stories, 1985; 68 literary translations including 8 novels by Anita Brookner, Dubliners by James Joyce, The Waves by Virginia Woolf, from English; Live or Die, poems by Anne Sexton, Fear of Flying by Erica Jong, Two Serious Ladies by Jane Bowles, from American English; Numerous novels by Selma Lagerlöf, Kerstin Ekman, Göran Tunström, Per Wästberg, from Swedish. Contributions to: Bonniers Litterära Magasin, Stockholm. Honours: Translators' Award, Danish Academy, 1989; Honorary Award, Danish Translators Association, 1991; Award, Danish/Swedish Friendship and Cultural Foundation, 1998; Lifelong Grant, Danish State Art Foundation. Memberships: Danish Language Council, University of Copenhagen; Danish Writers Association; Danish PEN; James Joyce Society. Address: Lærdalsgade 6A, 1tv, DK-2300 Copenhagen. Denmark.

BJORGMOSE Rasmus Johannes, b. 25 Mar 1933, Denmark. 1 son, 1 daughter. Education: Teaching Certificate, 1954; Journalism Degree, 1955; Degr Greenlandik, 1963. Appointments: Teacher, 1955-65, Headmaster, 1955-58, 1962-65, schools in Greenland; Journalist, Sub-Editor, Odense, 1968-79. Publications: Den blinde Storm (nvoel), 1975; Stop for Roat (nvoel), 1983; 4 collections of poems; 6 childrens books. Contributions to: Journals, periodicals, reviews, magazines and newspapers in Danmark, Norway, Greenland and Germany. Address: Kirkebakken 41, 5250 Odense SV, Denmark.

BJORKSKOG Doris Margareta, b. 19 Mar 1929, Nykarleby, Finland. Writer; Poet. m. 15 July 1956. Publications: Minnesgrönskan, poems, 1978; Draken och kärleken, 1982; Lunke och Lina, for children, 1984; På vindens villkor, 1987; Den mörka fågeln, 1989; Sommarens spegel, 1993; Stenharen, 1994. Honour: Karleby Culture Prize, 1994. Membership: Finlands Svenska Författareförening. Address: Björkskog 40, 67410 Karleby, Finland.

BJORNSSON Oddur, b. 25 Oct 1932, W-Skaft, Iceland. Playwright; Director. m. Borghildur Thors, 1954, div 1976, partner Bergljot Gunnarsdottir, 1983-, 1 son, 1 daughter. Education: Theaterwissenschaft, Wienna University, 1954-56. Appointment: Director, Akureyri Theatre Company, 1978-80. Publications: Yolk-Life, 1965; Ten Variations, 1968; A Grand Ball, 1974; The Master, 1977; After the Concert, 1983; The 13th Crusade, 1993. Contributions to: Morgunbladid newspaper. Honour: Culture Award, DV newspaper, 1980. Membership: Union of Icelandic Writers; Association of Icelandic Playwrights. Address: Njardargata 9, 101 Reykjavik, Iceland.

BLACK David, b. 21 Apr 1945, Boston, Massachusetts, USA. Writer; Producer. m. Deborah Hughes Keehn, 22 June 1968, 1 son, 1 daughter. Education: BA Magna cum Laude, Amherst College,

1967; MFA, Columbia University, 1971. Appointments: Contributing Writer, New Times, 1975-76; Writer-in-Residence, Mt Holyoke College, 1982-86; Contributing Editor, Rolling Stone, 1986-89. Publications: Mirrors, 1968; Ekstasy, 1975; Like Father, 1978; The King of Fifth Avenue, 1981; Minds, 1982; Murder at the Met, 1984; Medicine Man, 1985; Peep Show, 1986; The Plague Years, 1986. Feature Scripts: Murder at the Met, 1982; Falling Angel, 1984; Catching It, 1988; Passion, 1990; The Man in the Slouch Hat, 1992; Detectives of the Heart, 1992. Various television scripts. Contributions to: Over 150 stories and articles to numerous national and international magazines. Honours: National Magazine Award; National Association of Science Writers Award; Best Article of the Year Award, Playboy; National Endowment for the Arts Grant in Fiction; Firsts Award, short story, Atlantic Monthly; Notable Book of the Year, New York Times (2); Writers Foundation of America Gold Medal for Excellence in Writing, 1992. Memberships: PEN; Writers Guild-East; Mystery Writers of America; International Association of Crime Writers; Century Association; Williams Club. Address: c/o Mystery Writers of America Inc., 17 East 47th Street, 6th Floor, New York, NY 10017, USA.

BLACK David Macleod, b. 8 Nov 1941, Cape Town, South Africa (British citizen). Lecturer; Poet. m. Jeanne Magagna, 28 Jan 1984. Education: MA, University of Edinburgh, 1966; MA in Religious Studies, University of Lancaster, 1971. Appointments: Teacher, Chelsea Art School, London, 1966-70; Lecturer and Supervisor, Westminster Pastoral Foundation, London. Publications: Rocklestrakes, 1960; From the Mountain, 1963; Theory of Diet, 1966; With Decorum, 1967; A Dozen Short Poems, 1968; Penguin Modern Poets 11, 1968; The Educators, 1969; The Old Hag, 1972; The Happy Crow, 1974; Gravitations, 1979; Collected Poems 1964-1987, 1991; A Place for Exploration, 1991. Honours: Scottish Arts Council Prize, 1968 and Publication Award, 1991; Arts Council of Great Britain Bursary, 1968. Address: 30 Cholmley Gardens, Aldred Road, London NW6 1AG, England.

BLACK Jim. See: **HAINING Peter Alexander.**

BLACKBURN Alexander Lambert, b. 6 Sept 1929, Durham, North Carolina, USA. Novelist; Editor. m. Ine's Dōlz, 14 Oct 1975, 2 sons, 1 daughter. Education: BA, Yale University, 1947-51; MA, English, University of North Carolina, 1954-55; PhD, English, Cambridge University, England, 1959-60, 1961-63. Appointments: Instructor, Hampden-Sydney College, 1960-61, University of Pennsylvania, 1963-65; Lecturer, University of Maryland Euro Division, 1967-72; Professor of English, University of Colorado at Colorado Springs, 1973-95; Emeritus Professor English, 1996-. Publications: The Myth of the Picaro, 1979; The Cold War of Kitty Pentecost, novel, 1979; Ed, The Interior Country: Stories of the Modern West, 1987; A Sunrise Brighter Still: The Visionary Novels of Frank Waters, 1991; Ed, Higher Elevations: Stories from the West, 1993; Suddenly a Mortal Splendor, novel, 1995. Contributions to: Founder and Ed-in-Chief; Writers Forum, 1974-95. Honours: Faculty Book Award, Colorado University, 1993; Runnerup, Colorado Book Award, 1996. Memberships: Authors Guild; PEN West; Colorado Authors League. Address: 6030 Twin Rock Court, Colorado Springs, CO 80918, USA.

BLACKBURN Gaston, (Hugues Auburn), b. 4 Mar 1927, Kenogami, Canada. Pastor; Writer; Poet. Education: BA, 1949; Bacc. pédagogie, 1963; Licençe ès lettres, 1964; Bacc. théologie, 1965; Diploma, École Normale supérieure, 1965; Brevet enseignement spécialisé, 1965; Bacc. bibliothéconomie, 1966. Appointments: Ministère paroissial and ministère en milieu hospitalier, 1953-94; Professor, French and Latin, 1960-62, Literature, 1966-67. Publications: La Tourmente, 1965; Sous la tente, 1970; Essai de toponymie saguenéenne, 1970; Petits poèmes des Rocheuses, 1974; Promenades septiliennes, 1979; Rocaille, 1981; Promenades hospitalières, 1987. Honours: Chevalier Ordre de la Croix du Sud Guyane française, 1982; Médaille de bronze du Club Muse de Karukera, 1982. Memberships: Équipiers de St Michel, 1946; Société historique du Saguenay, 1959; Société d'archéologie Saguenay, 1964; Corp bibliothécaires, 1970; Union des écrivains, Québec, 1981. Address: 7640, Chemin Coopérative, Alma, Québec G8B 5V3, Canada.

BLACKBURN Julia Karen Eugenie, b. 12 Aug 1948, London, England. Writer. m. May 1978, div 1995, 1 son, 1 daughter. Education: BA Hons, English Literature, York University. Publications: The White Men, 1978; Charles Waterton, 1989; The Emperor's Last Island, 1991; Daisy Bates in the Desert, 1994; The Book of Colour, 1995; The Leper's Companions, 1999; For a Child: A Selection of the Poems of Thomas Blackburn, 1999. Memberships: Society of Authors; PEN. Literary Agent: Toby Eady, London, England. Address: c/o Toby Eady, Third Floor, 9 Orme Court, London W2 4RL, England.

BLACKIN Malcolm. See: **CHAMBERS Aidan.**

BLAGROVE David Richard, b. 22 Sept 1937, Oxford, England. Schoolmaster (retired). m. Jean Hazel King, 15 Apr 1964, 2 daughters. Education: Law Society's Intermediate, 1958; Teaching Diploma, Reading University, England, 1966. Publications: The Canal at Stoke Bruerne, 1969; Bread Upon the Waters, 1984; Northamptonshire's Waterways, 1990; At the Heart of the Waterways, 1996; The Quiet Waters By, 1998. Contributions to: Regular Contributor to Waterways World, 1972-; Regular Monthly Column, 1996-. Honour: Best Work of Local History, 1990. Address: Wharf Cottage, Stoke Bruerne, Towcester, Northants NN12 7SE, England.

BLAINEY Geoffrey Norman, b. 11 Mar 1930, Melbourne, Victoria, Australia. Writer. Education: Wesley College, Melbourne; Queen's College, University of Melbourne. Publications: The Peaks of Lyell, 1954; A Centenary History of the University of Melbourne, 1957; Gold and Paper, 1958; Mines in the Spinifex, 1960; The Rush That Never Ended, 1963; A History of Camberwell, 1965; If I Remember Rightly: The Memoirs of W S Robinson, 1966; Wesley College: The First Hundred Years (co-author and editor), 1967; The Tyranny of Distance, 1966; Across a Red World, 1968; The Rise of Broken Hill, 1968; The Steel Master, 1971; The Causes of War, 1973; Triumph of the Nomads, 1975; A Land Half Won, 1980; The Blainey View, 1982; Our Side of the Country, 1984; All for Australia, 1984; The Great Seesaw, 1988; A Game of our Own: The Origins of Australian Football, 1990; Odd Fellows, 1991; Eye on Australia, 1991; Jumping Over the Wheel, 1993; The Golden Mile, 1993; A Shorter History of Australia, 1994; White Gold, 1997. Honours: Gold Medal, Australian Literature Society, 1963; Encyclopaedia Britannica Gold Award, New York, 1988. Memberships: Australia Council, chairman, 1977-81; Commonwealth Literary Fund, chairman, 1971-73; Inaugural Chancellor of University of Ballarat, 1994-98. Address: PO Box 257, East Melbourne, Victoria 3002, Australia.

BLAIR Anna Dempster, b. 12 Feb 1927, Glasgow, Scotland. Author. m. Matthew Blair, 13 June 1952, 1 son, 1 daughter. Education: Dunfermline College, Graduated 1947. Appointment: Teacher, Glasgow Education Authority, 1947-52, 1965-75. Publications: A Tree in the West; The Rowan on the Ridge, 1980; Historical Novels: Tales of Ayrshire (Traditional Tales Retold), 1993; Tea at Miss Cranston's Reminiscences/Social History, 1985; Croft and Creel, 1987; Scottish Tales, 1987; The Goose-Girl of Eriska, 1989; Traditional Tales: More Tea at Miss Cranston's, 1991; Seed Corn, 1989. Contributions to: Various. Literary Agent: David Bolt. Address: 20 Barrland Drive, Giffnock, Glasgow G46 7QD, Scotland.

BLAIR Claude, b. 22 Nov 1922, Manchester, England. Antiquarian; Art Historian. Education: BA, 1950, MA, 1963, University of Manchester. Appointments: Assistant, Tower of London Armouries, 1951-56; Honorary Editor, Journal of Arms and Armour Society, 1953-77; Assistant Keeper, 1966-72, Deputy Keeper, 1966-72, Keeper, 1972-82, Metalwork, Victoria and Albert Museum, London; Consultant, Christie's, London, 1982-. Publications: European Armour, 1958; European and American Arms, 1962; Pistols of the World, 1968; Three Presentation Swords in the Victoria and Albert Museum, 1972; The James A de Rothschild Collection at Waddesdon Manor: Arms, Armour and Base-Metalwork, 1974; Pollard's History of Firearms, 1983; A History of Silver, 1987; General Editor, The Crown Jewels, 1998. Honours: FSA, 1956; OBE, 1994; Gold Medal of the Society of Antiquaries, 1998. Literary Agent: MBA Literary Agents, Lts, 12 Grafton Way, London W1P 5LD. Address: 90 Links Road, Ashtead, Surrey KT21 2HW, England.

BLAIR David Chalmers Leslie Jr, b. 8 Apr 1951. Long Beach, California, USA. Composer; Writer. Education: BA, California State University at Long Beach, 1979; Postgraduate, University de Provence, Aix-en-Provence, France, 1979-80. Publications: Novels: Death of an Artist, 1982; Vive la France, 1993; Death of America, 1994. Albums: Her Garden of Earthly Delights; Sir Blair of Rothes; Europe; St Luke; Passion. Address: 19331 105th Avenue, Cadott, WI 54727, USA.

BLAIR Iain John, (Emma Blair), b. 12 Aug 1942, Glasgow, Scotland. Novelist. m. 26 Apr 1975, 2 sons. Education: Royal Scottish Academy of Music and Dramatic Art. Publications: Where No Man Cries, 1982; Nellie Wildchild, 1983; Hester Dark, 1984; This Side of Heaven, 1985; Jessie Gray, 1985; The Princess of Poor Street, 1986; Street Song, 1986; When Dreams Come True, 1987; A Most Determined Woman, 1988; The Blackbird's Tale, 1989; Maggie Jordan, 1990; Scarlet Ribbons, 1991; The Water Meadows, 1992. Memberships: Romantic Novelists Association; British Actors Equity. Literary Agent: Rogers, Coleridge and White, 20 Powis Mews, London W11 1JN, England. Address: The Old Vicarage, Stoke Canon, Near Exeter, Devon EX5 4AS, England.

BLAIR Jessica. See: **SPENCE William (John Duncan).**

BLAIS Marie-Claire, b. 5 Oct 1939, Quebec, Quebec, Canada. Writer; Dramatist; Poet. Education: Courses in literature and philosophy, Laval University. Publications: Fiction: La Belle Bete, 1959, English translation as Mad Shadows, 1960; Tete blanche, 1960, English Translation, 1961; Le Jour est noir, 1962, English translation as The Day is Dark, 1966; Une saison dans la vie d'Emmanuel, 1965, English translation as A Season in the Life of Emmanuel, 1966; L'imsoumise, 1966, English translation as The Fugitive, 1991; David Sterne, 1967, English translation, 1972; Manuscrits de Pauline Archange, 1968, and Vivre! Vivre!, 1969, both in English translations as Manuscripts of Pauline Archange, 1970; Les Apparences, 1971, English translation as Durer's Angel, 1976; Le Loup, 1972, English translation as The Wolf, 1974; Un Joualonais, sa Joualonie, 1973, English translation as St Lawrence Blues, 1975; Une liaison parisienne, 1975, English translation as A Literary Affair, 1979; Les Nuits de l'Underground, 1978, English translation as Nights in the Underground, 1979; Le Sourd dans la ville, 1980, English translation as Deaf to the City, 1980; Visions d'Anna, 1982, English translation as Anna's World, 1984; Pierre ou La Guerre du printemps 81, 1984; L'Ange de la solitude, 1989, English translation as Angel of Solitude, 1993; Pierre, 1991, English translation, 1993; Soifs, 1995, English translation as The Execution, 1976; Fièvre et autres textes dramatiques, 1974; L'Océan suivi de Murmures, 1977; La Nef des sorcières, 1977; Sommeil d'hiver, 1986; L'Ile, 1988. Poetry: Pays voiles, 1964; Existences, 1964. Autobiography: Parcours d'un écrivain notes américaines, 1993. Honours: Prix de la Langue francaise, 1961; Guggenheim Fellowship, 1963; Prix France-Québec, Paris, 1966; Prix Médicis, Paris, 1966; Governor-General of Canada Prizes, 1969, 1979, 1996; Order of Canada, 1975; Prix Belgique-Canada, Brussels, 1976; Prix Athanase-David, Quebec, 1982; Prix de l'Académie Francaise, Paris, 1983; Commemorative Medal for the 125th Anniversary of the Confederation of Canada, 1982; Ordre National du Québec, 1995. Membership: Académie Royale de langue et de littérature francaises de Belgique, Brussels. Address: 4411 Rue St Denis, Apt 401, Montreal, Quebec H2J 2L2, Canada.

BLAISE Clark (Lee), b. 10 Apr 1940, Fargo, North Dakota, USA. Writer; Teacher. m. Bharati Mukherjee, 19 Sept 1963, 2 sons. Education: AB, Denison University, 1961; MFA, University of Iowa, 1964. Appointments: Professor, Concordia University, 1966-78, York University, 1978-80, Skidmore College, 1980-81, 1982-83; Visiting Professor, 1981-82, Director, International Writing Program, 1990-, University of Iowa; Writer-in-Residence, David Thompson University Center, 1983, Emory University, 1985; Adjunct Professor, Columbia University, 1986. Publications: A North American Education, 1973; Tribal Justice, 1974; Days and Nights in Calcutta (with B Mukherjee), 1977; Here and Now (co-editor), 1977; Lunar Attractions, 1978; Lusts, 1983; Resident Alien, 1986; The Sorrow and the Terror: The Haunting Legacy of the Air India Tragedy, 1987; Man and His World, 1992; I Had a Father; A Post-Modern Autobiography, 1993. Contributions to: Various publications. Honours: Guggenheim Fellowship; Canada Council Grants; Honorary PhD, Denison University, 1979. Membership: PEN. Address: c/o The Porcupine's Quill Inc, 68 Main Street, Erin, Ontario, Canada N0B 1T0.

BLAKE Jennifer. See: **MAXWELL Patricia Anne.**

BLAKE Norman (Francis), b. 19 Apr 1934, Ceara, Brazil. Professor; Writer; Editor; Translator. Education: BA, 1956, BLitt, 1959, MA, 1960, Oxford University. Appointments: Lecturer, 1959-68, Senior Lecturer, 1968-73, Professor, 1973-, University of Sheffield. Publications: The Saga of the Jomsvikings, 1962; The Phoenix, 1964, 2nd edition, 1990; Caxton and His World, 1969; William Caxton's Reynard the Fox, 1970; Middle English Religious Prose, 1972; Selections from William Caxton, 1973; Caxton's Own Prose, 1975; Caxton's Quattuor Sermiones, 1973; Caxton: England's First Publisher, 1976; The English Language in Medieval Literature, 1977; Non-Standard Language in English Literature, 1981; Shakespeare's Language, 1983; Textual Tradition of the Canterbury Tales, 1985; William Caxton: A Bibliographical Guide, 1985; Traditional English Grammar and Beyond, 1988; Index of Printed Middle English Prose, 1985; The Language of Shakespeare (with R E Lewis and A S G Edwards), 1989, 2nd edition, 1994; An Introduction to the Languages of Literature, 1990; William Caxton and English Literary Culture, 1991; The Cambridge History of the English Language, Vol II: 1066-1476, 1992; Introduction to English Language (with J Moorhead), 1993; William Caxton, 1996; Essays in Shakespeare's Language, 1996; History of the English Language, 1996. Address: Department of English Language and Linguistics, University of Sheffield, Sheffield, S10 2TN, England.

BLAKE Patrick. See: **EGLETON Clive Frederick William.**

BLAKE Robert (Norman William), (Lord Blake of Braydeston, Norfolk), b. 23 Dec 1916, Norfolk, England. Historian. m. Patricia Mary Waters, 22 Aug 1953, 4 daughters. Education: MA, Magdalen College, 1938. Appointments: Lecturer, 1946-47, Tutor in Politics, 1947-68, Censor, 1950-55, University Lecturer and Senior Proctor, 1959-60, Ford Lecturer in English History, 1967-68, Christ Church, Oxford; Conservative Member,Oxford City Council, 1957-64; Provost, 1968-76, Pro-Vice Chancellor of the University, 1971-87, Queen's College, Oxford University; Member, Royal Commission on Historical Manuscripts, 1975-; Trustee, British Museum, 1978-88. Publications: The Private Papers of Diouglas Haig, editor, 1952; The Unknown Prime Minister: The Life and Times of Andrew Bonar Law, 1858-1923, 1955; Esto Perpetua: The Norwich Union Life Insurance Society, 1958; Disraeli, 1966; Conservatism Today: Four Personal Points of View (with others), 1966; Disraeli and Gladstone, 1970; The Conservative Party from Peel to Churchill: Based on the Ford Lectures, Delivered before the University of Oxford in the Hilary Term of 1968, 1970, revised edition as The Conservative Party from Peel to Thatcher, 1977; Dictionary of National Biography (joint editor), 1980-90; Disraeli's Grand Tour: Benjamin Disraeli and the Holy Land, 1830-31, 1982; The English World: History, Character and People (editor), 1982; The Decline of Power, 1915-1964, 1985; An Incongrous Partnership, Lloyd George and Bonar Law, 1992; Gladstone, Disraeli and Queen Victoria, 1993; Churchill: A Major New Assessment of His Life in Peace and War (editor with Roger Louis), 1993. Contributions to: Periodicals. Honours: Life Peer, 1971; DLitt, Glasgow University, 1972, East Anglia University, 1983, Westminster College, Fulton, Missouri, 1987, Buckingham University, 1988; Fellow, Queen's College, Oxford, 1987, Pembroke College, Cambridge. Memberships: Authors Society; British Academy, fellow; Literary Society, president. Address: Riverview House, Brundall, Norwich, Norfolk NR13 5LA, England.

BLAKE-HANNAH Barbara Makeda, (Makeda Levi), b. 5 June 1941, Kingston, Jamaica. Writer; Filmmaker; Lecturer. m. Deeb Roy Hanna, 12 Feb 1984, 1 son. Education: Institute of Public Relations, London, 1964. Appointments: Independent Senator, Jamaican Parliament, 1984-87; Producer, Writer, Director, films: Race, Rhetoric, Rastafari, 1983; By The Land We Live, 1986; Kids Paradise, 1993; Kids Paradise II, 1995. Publications: Rastafari - The New Creation, thesis on Jamaican religion, 1981, 4th edition, 1997; Joseph - A Rasta Reggae Fable, novel, 1992. Contributions to: Daily Gleaner; Daily Observer, Sunday Herald, Jamaica; Columnist, Jamaican Daily Star; Columnist, Sunday Herald. Honours: UN Peace Medal, 1975; Gold Ethiopia Adowa Medal, 1997. Literary Agent: Jamaica Media Productions Ltd. Address: 17 Lords Road, Kingston 5, Jamaica.

BLAMIRES Harry, b. 6 Nov 1916, Bradford, England. Lecturer in Higher Education; Author. m. Nancy Bowles, 26 Dec 1940, 5 sons. Education: BA, 1938, MA, 1945, University College, Oxford. Appointments: Head, English Department, 1948-72, Dean, Arts and Sciences, 1972-76, King Alfred's College, Winchester; Clyde Kilby Visiting Professor of English, Wheaton College, Wheaton, Illinois, 1987. Publications: The Christian Mind, 1963; The Bloomsday Book: Guide to Joyce's Ulysses, 1966, revised edition, 1988; Word Unheard: Guide Through Eliot's Four Quartets, 1969; Milton's Creation, 1971; A Short History of English Literature, 1974, revised edition, 1984; Where Do We Stand?, 1980; Twentieth-Century English Literature, 1982, revised edition, 1986; Guide to 20th Century Literature in English, 1983; On Christian Truth, 1983; Words Made Flesh, 1985 (UK edition as The Marks of the Maker, 1987); The Victorian Age of Literature, 1988; Meat Not Milk, 1988; The Age of Romantic Literature, 1989; A History of Literary Criticism, 1991; The Queen's English, 1994; The Cassell Guide to Common Errors in English, 1997. Honour: Hon DLitt, Southampton University, 1993. Membership: Society of Authors. Address: Pinfold, 3 Glebe Close, Keswick, Cumbria CA12 5QQ, England.

BLAND Peter, b. 12 May 1934, Scarborough, Yorkshire, England. Poet; Reviewer; Actor; Dramatist. m. Beryl Matilda Connolly, 27 Apr 1956, 1 son, 2 daughters. Education: English, Victoria University of Wellington, New Zealand. Appointments: Journalist and Talks Producer, New Zealand Broadcasting Corp, 1960-64; Co-Founder, Director, Actor, and Dramatist, Downstage Theatre, Wellington, 1964-68; Actor, West End plays and numerous television productions, London; Leading role, Came a Hot Friday (New Zealand film), 1985. Publications: Poetry: My Side of the Story, 1964; The Man with the Carpet Bag, 1972; Mr Maui, 1976; Stone Tents, 1981; The Crusoe Factor, 1985; Selected Poems, 1987; Paper Boats, 1991; Selected Poems, 1998. Plays: Father's Day, 1967; George the Mad Ad Man, 1967. Contributions to: Anthologies; Landfall; London Magazine; P.N. Review; Sport; Times Literary Supplement. Honours: Macmillan-Brown Prize for Creative Writing, Victoria University of Wellington, 1958; Melbourne Arts Festival Literary Award, 1960; Queen Elizabeth II Arts Council Drama Fellowship, 1968; Poetry Book Society Recommendation, 1987; Cholmondeley

Award for Poetry, 1977; Best Film Actor Award, Guild of Film and Television Arts, New Zealand, 1985. Address: 20 Oxford Road, Worthing, West Sussex BN11 1XQ, England.

BLANDIANA Ana, (Otila Valeria Rusan), b. 25 Mar 1942, Timisoara, Romania. Poet; Writer. m. Romulus Rusan. Education: Graduated, University of Cluj, 1967. Appointments: Columnist, Romania literara magazine, 1974-88; Librarian, Institute of Fine Arts, Bucharest, 1975-77. Publications: Poetry: 50 Poems, 1972; The Hour of Sand: Selected Poems, 1969-89, 1989; The Architecture of the Waves, 1990; 100 Poems, 1991; The Morning After the Death, 1996. Fiction: The Drawer with Applause (novel), 1992; Imitation of a Nightmare (short stories), 1995. Other: Several essays. Honours: Romanian Writers Union Poetry Prize, 1969; Romanian Academy Poetry Prize, 1980; Herder Prize, Austria, 1982. Address: Academia Civica, Piata Amzei 13 et 2, CP 22-216, Bucharest, Romania.

BLASER Robin (Francis), b. 18 May 1925, Denver, Colorado, USA. Professor of English; Poet. Education: MA, 1954, MLS, 1955, University of California at Berkeley. Appointments: Professor of English, Centre for the Arts, Simon Fraser University, Burnaby, British Columbia, Canada, 1972-86. Publications: The Moth Poem, 1964; Les Chimères, 1965; Cups, 1968; The Holy Forest Section, 1970; Image-nations 1-12 and The Stadium of the Mirror, 1974; Image-nations 13-14, 1975; Suddenly, 1976; Syntax, 1983; The Faerie Queene and the Park, 1987; Pell Mell, 1988; The Holy Forest, 1993. Honours: Poetry Society Award, 1965; Canada Council Grant, 1989-90; Fund for Poetry Award, New York, 1995. Address: 1636 Trafalgar Street, Vancouver, British Columbia V6K 3R7, Canada.

BLASHFORD-SNELL John Nicholas, b. 22 Oct 1936, Hereford, England. Soldier; Colonel; Explorer; Writer. Education: Victoria College, Jersey, Channel Islands; Royal Military Academy, Sandhurst. Publications: A Taste for Adventure, 1978; Operation Drake, 1981; In the Wake of Drake (with M Cable), 1982; Mysteries: Encounters with the Unexplained, 1983; Operation Raleigh: The Start of an Adventure, 1985; Operation Raleigh: Adventure Challenge (with Ann Tweedy), 1988; Operation Raleigh: Adventure Unlimited (with Ann Tweedy), 1990; Something Lost Behind the Ranges, 1994; Mammoth Hunt (with Rula Lenska), 1996. Contributions to: Expedition: The Field; Explorers Journal; British Army Review; Gun Digest; Spectator; Yorkshire Post; Scotsman; Traveller; Guardian; You Magazine; Daily Telegraph; Sunday Telegraph; Country Life. Address: c/o The Scientific Exploration Society, Expedition Base, Motcombe, Dorset SP7 9PB, England.

BLATNIK Andrej, b. 22 May 1963, Ljubljana, Slovenia. Writer. Publictions: Novels: Plamenice in solze, 1987; Tao ljubezni, 1996. Short stories: Sopki za Adama venijo, 1983; Biografije brezimenih, 1989; Menjave koz, 1990. Essays: Labirinti iz papirja, 1994. Criticism: Gledanje cez ramo, 1996. Honours: Award of the City of Ljubljana and Zlata ptica. Membership: Jury, Vilenica Central European Literary Awards. Address: Gornji trg 7, 1000 Ljubljana, Slovenia.

BLAYNE Diana. See: **KYLE Susan (Eloise Spaeth).**

BLEAKLEY David (Wylie), b. 11 Jan 1925, Belfast, Northern Ireland. Educator; President, Church Mission Society; Writer. m. Winifred Wason, 5 Aug 1949, 3 sons. Education: Diploma in Economics and Political Science, Ruskin College, Oxford, 1949; BA, 1951, MA, 1955, Queen's University, Belfast. Appointments: Principal, Belfast Further Education Centre, 1955-58; MP, Labour Party, Victoria, Parliament of Northern Ireland, Belfast, 1958-65; Lecturer in Industrial Relations, Kivukoni College, Dar-es-Salaam, 1967-69; Head, Department of Economics and Political Studies, Methodist College, Belfast, 1969-79; Minister of Community Relations, Government of Northern Ireland, 1971; Member, Northern Ireland Labour Party, East Belfast, Northern Ireland Assembly, 1973-75; Visiting Senior Lecturer in Peace

Studies, University of Bradford, 1974-; Chief Executive, Irish Council of Churches, 1980-92; President, Church Mission Society, 1983-. Publications: Ulster Since 1800: Regional History Symposium, 1958; Young Ulster and Religion in the Sixties, 1964; Peace in Ulster, 1972; Faulkner: A Biography, 1974; Saidie Patterson: Irish Peacemaker, 1980; In Place of Work, 1981; The Shadow and Substance, 1983; Beyond Work: Free to Be, 1985; Will the Future Work?, 1986; Europe: A Christian Vision, 1992; Ageing and Ageism in a Technological Society, 1994; Peace in Ireland: Two States, One People, 1995; C S Lewis: At Home in Ireland, 1998. Contributions to: BBC and periodicals. Honours: Appointed PC, 1971; Honorary MA, Open University, 1975; Commander of the Order of the British Empire, 1984. Address: 8 Thornhill, Bangor, County Down BT19 1RD, Northern Ireland.

BLEASDALE Alan, b. 23 Mar 1946. Playwright; Novelist. m. Julia Moses, 1970, 2 sons, 1 daughter. Education: Teachers Certificate, Padgate Teachers Training College. Publications: Scully, 1975; Who's Been Sleeping in My Bed, 1977; No More Sitting on the Old School Bench, 1979; Boys From the Blackstuff (televised), 1982; Are You Lonesome Tonight?, 1985; No Surrender, 1986; Having a Ball, 1986; It's a Madhouse, 1986; The Monocled Mutineer (televised), 1986; GBH (television series), 1992. Honours: BAFTA Writer's Award, 1982; RTS Writer's Award, 1982; Broadcasting Press Guild TV Award for Best Series, 1982; Best Musical, London Standard Drama Awards, 1985. Address: c/o Harvey Unna and Stephen Durbridge Ltd, 24 Pottery Lane, Holland Park, London W11 4LZ, England.

BLEDSOE Lucy Jane, b. 1 Feb 1957, Portland, Oregon, USA. Writer; Editor. Companion: Patricia E Mullan. Education: Williams College, 1975-77; BA, University of California at Berkeley, 1979. Appointments: Instructor, University of California Graduate Program of Creative Writing; Instructor, Creative Writing workshops in adult literacy programmes. Publications: Sweat: Stories and a Novella, 1995; The Big Bike Race, 1995; Working Parts, 1997; Tracks in the Snow, 1997; Editor: Gay Travels, 1998; Lesbian Travels, 1998. Contributions to: Books and magazines. Honours: National Endowment for the Humanities Youthgrant, 1982; PEN Syndicated Fiction Award, 1985; Creative Writing Fellowship, Money for Women/Barbara Deming Memorial Fund, 1989; Gay/Lesbian/Bisexual Award for Literture, 1998. Memberships: Media Alliance; National Writers Union; PEN. Address: 1226 Cedar Street, Berkeley, CA 94702, USA.

BLICKER Seymour, b. 12 Feb 1940, Montreal, Quebec, Canada. Writer. m. Susan Wanda Colman, 13 June 1963, 3 sons, 1 daughter. Education: BA, Loyola College, 1962. Appointments: Special Lecturer, Creative Writing, Concordia University, 1978-90. Publications: Novels: Blues Chased a Rabbit, 1969; Shmucks, 1972; The Last Collection, 1976. Stage Plays: Up Your Alley, 1987; Never Judge a Book By Its Cover, 1987; Pals, 1995; Home Free, 1998. Honours: Canada Council Senior Arts Fellowship, 1974; British Councils International New Playwriting Award for the Americas Region, 1997. Memberships: Writers Union of Canada; Playwrights Union of Canada; Academy of Canadian Cinema and Television; Writers Guild of America West. Address: 7460 Kingsley Road #804, Montreal, Quebec H4W 1P3, Canada.

BLIVEN Bruce, b. 31 Jan 1916, Los Angeles, California, USA. Writer. m. Naomi Horowitz, 26 May 1950, 1 son. Education: AB, Harvard College, 1937. Publications: The Wonderful Writing Machine, 1954; Battle for Manhattan, 1956; The Story of D-Day, 1956, 50th anniversary edition, 1994; The American Revolution, 1958; From Pearl Harbor to Okinawa, 1960; From Casablanca to Berlin, 1965; New York (with Naomi Bliven), 1969; Under the Guns, 1972; Book Traveller, 1975; Volunteers, One and All, 1976; The Finishing Touch, 1978; New York: A History, 1981. Contributions to: New Yorker; Many other national magazines. Memberships: Authors Guild, council, 1970-; Society of American Historians, board, 1975-; PEN American Centre; American Society of Journalists and Authors. Address: New Yorker, 20 West 43rd Street, New York, NY 10036, USA.

BLIX Jacqueline, b. 15 June 1949, Glendale, California, USA. Writer. m. David Heitmiller, 19 July 1986, 1 son, 1 daughter. Education: BA, History, California State University at San Jose, 1974; BA, Communications, 1989, MA, Communications, 1991, PhD, Communications, 1995, University of Washington. Publication: Getting a Life: Real Lives Transformed By "Your Money or Your Life". Contributions to: Journal of Communication Inquiry, 1992. Literary Agent: Beth Vesél, Greenberger and Associates, New York, USA. Address: c/o Greenberger and Associates, 55 5th Avenue, New York, NY 10003, USA.

BLOCH Andrew Danby, b. 19 Dec 1945, England. Publisher; Independent Financial Advisor. m. Sandra Wilkinson, 29 July 1968, 1 son, 1 daughter. Education: MA Hons, Philosophy Politics Economics, Wadham College, Oxford, England; Member, Society of Financial Advisers. Appointments: Researcher, Oxford Centre for Management Studies (now Templeton College), 1968-70; Dir, Grosvenor Advisory Services Ltd, 1971-74; Raymond Godrey & Partners Ltd, 1974-; Taxbriefs Ltd, 1975-; Governor, Oxford Brookes University, formerly Oxford Poly, 1990-; Chair of Governors, 1998-; Council, Museum of Modern Art, 1990-. Publications: Planning for School & College Fees, co-author, 1988; Providing Financial Advice, 1995, 1996, 1997, 1998; Financial Advice, 1996; Editor of Textbooks for The Chartered Insurance Institutes Advanced Financial Planning Certificate - Annually from 1995; Taxation and Trusts, Personal Investment Planning, Business Financial Planning, Pensions, Holistic Financial Planning, Investing Portfolio Management. Contributions to: Regular contributor to The Times, Daily Telegraph, Sunday Times and Investors Chronicle, 1979-92. Address: 17 Norham Road, Oxford OX2 6SF, England.

BLOCH Chana (Florence), b. 15 Mar 1940, New York, New York, USA. Professor of English; Poet; Translator; Critic; Essayist. m. Ariel Bloch, 26 Oct 1969, div, 2 sons. Education: BA, Cornell University, 1961; MA, 1963, MA, 1965, Brandeis University; PhD, University of California at Berkeley, 1975. Appointments: Instructor of English, Hebrew University, Jerusalem, 1964-67; Associate in Near Eastern Studies, University of California at Berkeley, 1967-69; Instructor, 1973-75, Assistant Professor, 1975-81, Associate Professor, 1981-87, Chairman, Department of English, 1986-89, Professor of English, 1987-, Director, Creative Writing Program, 1993-, Mills College, Oakland, California. Publications: Poetry: The Secrets of the Tribe, 1981; The Past Keeps Changing, 1992; Mrs Dumpty, 1998. Literary Critisim: Spelling the Word: George Herbert and the Bible, 1985. Translator: Dahlia Ravikovitch: A Dress of Fire, 1978; Yehuda Amichai: The Selected Poetry (with Stephen Mitchell), 1986, revised and expanded edition, 1996; Dahlia Ravikovitch: The Window: New and Selected Poems (with Ariel Bloch), 1989; The Song of Songs: A New Translation, Introduction and Commentary (with Ariel Bloch), 1995; A Dress of Fire by Dahlia Ravikovitch. Contributions to: Poetry, translations, criticism, and essays in various anthologies and periodicals. Honours: Discovery Award, Poetry Centre, New York, 1974; Translation Award, Columbia University, 1978; National Endowment for the Humanities Fellowship, 1980; Book of the Year Award, Conference on Christianity and Literature, 1986; Writers Exchange Award, Poets and Writers, 1988; Yaddo Residencies, 1988, 1990, 1993, 1994, 1995, 1996; 1997; MacDowell Colony Residencies, 1988, 1992, 1993; Djerassi Foundation Residencies, 1989, 1991; National Endowment for the Arts Fellowship, 1989-90; Felix Pollak Prize, 1997. Memberships: PEN; Poetry Society of America; Modern Language Association. Literary Agent: Geoarges Borchardt. Address: c/o Department of English, Mills College, Oakland, CA 94613, USA.

BLOCK Francesca Lia, b. 3 Dec 1962, Hollywood, California, USA. Author; Screenwriter. Education: BA, English Literature, University of California at Berkeley. Publications: Weetzie Bat, 1989; Witch Baby, 1991; Cherokee Bat and the GoatGuys, 1992; Missing Angel Juan, 1993; Baby Be Bop, 1995; Girl Goddess #9, 1996; Dangerous Angels - The Weetzie Bat Books, 1998; I Was a Teenage Fairy, 1998. Contributions to: Newspapers. Honours: Phi Beta Kappa; American Library Association Best Books, 1989, 1992, 1993, 1995; School Library Journal Best Book, 1991, 1993. Publishers Weekly Best Books, 1992, 1995. Address: Artist's Agency, 230 West 55th Street, 29D, New York, NY 10019, USA.

BLOCK DE BEHAR Lisa, b. 12 Mar 1937, Montevideo, Uruguay. Professor; Writer. m. Isaac Behar, 25 June 1957, 2 sons. Education: BA, 1961, MS, 1973, Institute de Profesors, Montevideo; PhD, École de Haute Études en Sciences Sociales, Paris, 1983. Appointments: Professor of Literary Theory, Montevideo, 1976; Professor of Semiotics, Montevideo, 1985. Publications: El Lenguajede la Publicidad, 1974, 1976-92; Una retórica del silencio, 1984-94; Al Margen de Borges, 1987; Jules Laforgue, 1987; Dos medios entre dos medios, 1990; Una palabra propiamente dicha, 1994; Al Marginedi Borges Bari, 1997; Borges ou les Gestes D'un Voyant Avenugle Champion Paris, 1998. Contributions to: Periodicals. Honour: Prize Xavier Villurrutia, 1984. Address: Avenida Rivera 6195, Montevideo, Uruguay.

BLOND Anthony, b. 20 Mar 1928, Sale, England. Author. m. Laura Hesketh, 1 Mar 1981, 1 son. Education: MA, New College, Oxford, 1951. Appointments: Active with Anthony Blond Ltd, 1957-71; Director, Blond and Brigg Ltd, publishers, London, 1971-90. Publications: The Publishing Game, 1971; Family Business, 1978; The Lord My Light, 1982; A Book on Books, 1983; Blond's Roman Emperors, 1994; Carnets d'un Promeneur Anglais en France, 1997.Contributions to: Literary Review; Spectator. Literary Agent: Gillon Aitken. Address: 9 Rue Thiers, 87300 Bellac, France.

BLONDEL Jean Fernand Pierre, b. 26 Oct 1929, Toulon, France. University Professor; Writer. m. (1) Michele Hadet, 1954, div, (2) Teresa Ashton, 1982, 2 daughters. Education: Diploma, Institut Études Politiques, Paris, 1953; BLitt, Oxford, England, 1955. Publications: Voters, Parties and Leaders, 1963; An Introduction to Conservative Government, 1969; Comparative Legislatures, 1973; Political Parties, 1978; World Leaders, 1980; The Discipline of Politics, 1982; The Organisation of Governments, 1982; Government Ministers in the Contemporary World, 1985; Political Leadership, 1987; Governing Together, co-editor, 1993; Comparative Government, 1995; Party and Government (co-editor), 1996. Contributions to: European Journal of Political Research. Honours; Honorary Doctorates, University of Salford, 1990, University of Essex, 1992, Catholic University of Louvain, 1992, University of Turku, 1995. Memberships: Royal Swedish Academy of Sciences; American Political Science Association; British Political Studies Association; Association Française de Science Politique. Address: 15 Marloes Road, London W8 6LQ, England.

BLOOM Harold, b. 11 July 1930, New York, New York, USA. Professor of Humanities; Writer. m. Jeanne Gould, 8 May 1958, 2 sons. Education: BA, Cornell University, 1951; PhD, Yale University, 1955. Appointments: Faculty, 1955-65, Professor of English, 1965-77, DeVane Professor of Humanities, 1974-77, Professor of Humanities, 1977-83, Sterling Professor of Humanities, 1983-, Yale University; Visiting Professor, Hebrew University, Jerusalem, 1959, Breadloaf Summer School, 1965-66, Cornell University, 1968-69; Visiting University Professor, New School for Social Research, New York City, 1982-84; Charles Eliot Norton Professor of Poetry, Harvard University, 1987-88; Berg Professor of English, New York University, 1988-. Publications: Shelley's Mythmaking, 1959; The Visionary Company, 1961; Blake's Apocalypse, 1963; Commentary to Blake, 1965; Yeats, 1970; The Ringers in the Tower, 1971; The Anxiety of Influence, 1973; A Map of Misreading, 1975;

Kabbalah and Criticism, 1975; Poetry and Repression, 1976; Figures of Capable Imagination, 1976; Wallace Stevens: The Poems of Our Climate, 1977; The Flight to Lucifer: A Gnostic Fantasy, 1979; Agon: Towards a Theory of Revisionism, 1981; The Breaking of the Vessels, 1981; The Strong Light of the Canonical, 1987; Freud: Transference and Authority, 1988; Poetics of Influence: New and Selected Criticism, 1988; Ruin the Sacred Truths, 1988; The Book of J, 1989; The American Religion, 1990; The Western Canon, 1994; Omens of Millennium: The Gnosis of Angels, Dreams and Resurrection, 1996; Shakespeare: The Invention of the Human, 1998. Contributions to: Scholarly books and journals. Honours: Fulbright Fellowship, 1955; Guggenheim Fellowship, 1962; Newton Arvin Award, 1967; Melville Caine Award, 1970; Zabel Prize, 1982; John D and Catharine T MacArthur Foundation Fellowship, 1985; Christian Gauss Prize, 1989; Honorary Doctorates: University of Bologna, 1997, St Michael College, 1998. Membership: American Academy of Arts and Letters. Literary Agent: Glen Hartley and Lynn Chu, Writers Representatives, Inc, New York City. Address: 179 Linden Street, New Haven, CT 06511, USA.

BLOOMFIELD Louis Aub, b. 11 Oct 1956, Boston, Massachusetts, USA. Professor of Physics. m. Karen Shatkin, 28 Aug 1983, 1 son, 1 daughter. Education: BA, Physics, Amherst College, 1979; PhD, Physics, Stanford University. Appointments: Postdoctoral Member, Technical Staff, AT&T Bell Labs, 1983-85; Assistant Professor of Physics, 1985-91, Associate Professor of Physics, 1991-96, Professor of Physics, 1996-, University of Virginia. Publication: How Things Work: The Physics of Everyday Life, 1997. Address: Department of Physics, University of Virginia, Charlottesville, VA 22903, USA.

BLOUNT Roy (Alton) Jr, (Noah Sanders, C R Ways), b. 4 Oct 1941, Indianapolis, Indiana, USA. Writer; Poet; Dramatist; Artist. m. 1) Ellen Pearson, 6 Sept 1964, div Mar 1973, 2 sons, 2) Joan Ackerman, 1976, div 1990. Education: BA, magna cum laude, Vanderbilt University, 1963; MA, Harvard University, 1964. Appointments: Staff, Decatur-DeKalb News, Georgia, 1958-59, Morning Telegraph, New York City, 1961, New Orleans Times-Picayune, 1963; Reporter, Editorial Writer, Columnist, Atlanta Journal, 1966-68; Staff Writer, 1968-74, Associate Editor, 1974-75, Sports Illustrated; Contributing Editor, Atlantic Monthly, 1983-. Publications: About Three Bricks Shy of a Load, 1974, revised edition as About Three Bricks Shy--and the Load Filled Up: The Story of the Greatest Football Team Ever, 1989; Crackers: This Whole Many-Sided Thing of Jimmy, More Carters, Ominous Little Animals, Sad-Singing Women, My Daddy and Me, 1980; One Fell Soup, or, I'm Just a Bug on the Windshield of Life, 1982; What Men Don't Tell Women, 1984; Not Exactly What I Had in Mind, 1985; It Grows on You: A Hair-Raising Survey of Human Plumage, 1986; Soupsongs/Webster's Ark, 1987; Now, Where Were We?, 1989; First Hubby, 1990; Camels Are Easy, Comedy's Hard, 1991; Roy Blount's Book of Southern Humor, 1994; Be Sweet: A Conditional Love Story, 1998; If Only You Knew How Much I Smell You, 1998. Contributions to: Many anthologies and periodicals. Membership: Phi Beta Kappa. Address: c/o Atlantic Monthly, 77 North Washington Street, Suite 5, Boston, MA 02114, USA.

BLUME Judy (Sussman), b. 12 Feb 1938, Elizabeth, New Jersey, USA. Writer. 1 son, 1 daughter. Education: BS, New York University, 1961. Publications: Are You There, God?; It's Me Margaret; Blubber; Deenie; Freckle Juice; Iggie's House; It's Not the End of the World; The One in the Middle is the Green Kangaroo; Otherwise Known as Sheila the Great; Starring Sally J Freedman as Herself; Superfudge; Tales of a Fourth Grade Nothing; Then Again, Maybe I Won't; Tiger Eyes; The Pain and the Great One; The Judy Blume Diary; Forever; Wifey; Smart Women; Letters to Judy; What Kids Wish They Could Tell You; Just as Long As We're Together; Here's To You, Rachel Robinson. Honours: Numerous. Memberships: Authors Guild Council; PEN; Board, Society of Children's Book Writers. Address: c/o Owen Lster, William Morris

Agency, 1325 Avenue of the Americas, 43rd Street, New York, NY 10022, USA.

BLUNDELL Sue, b. 4 Aug 1947, Manchester, England. Lecturer. Education: BA, 1968, PhD, 1975, Westfield College, University of London; Dip Cont Ed, Goldsmiths College, University of London, 1989. Appointments: Part time Lecturer, Birkbeck College, University of London, 1979-; Assistant Lecturer, Classical Civilisation, Open University, 1986-. Publications: The Origins of Civilisation in Greek and Roman Thought, 1986; Women in Ancient Greece, 1995; The Sacred and the Feminine in Ancient Greece (co-editor with Margaret Williamson), 1998; Women in Classical Athens, 1998. Address: 59b Goodge Street, London W1P 1FA, England.

BLY Robert (Elwood), b. 23 Dec 1926, Madison, Minnesota, USA. Poet; Translator; Editor; Publisher. m. (1) Carolyn McLean, 1955, div 1979, (2) Ruth Counsell, 1980, 2 sons, 2 daughters. Education: St Olaf College, 1946-47; AB, Harvard University, 1950; MA, University of Iowa, 1956. Appointments: Publisher and Editor, 1958-; Various writing workshops. Publications: Poetry: The Lion's Tail and Eyes: Poems Written Out of Laziness and Silence (with William Duffy and James Wright), 1962; Silence in the Snowy Fields, 1962; The Light Around the Body, 1967; Chrysanthemums, 1967; Ducks, 1968; The Morning Glory: Another Thing That Will Never Be My Friend, 1969, revised edition, 1970; The Teeth Mother Naked at Last, 1971; Poems for Tennessee (with William Stafford and William Matthews), 1971; Christmas Eve Service at Midnight at St Michael's, 1972; Water Under the Earth, 1972; The Dead Seal Near McClure's Beach, 1973; Sleepers Joining Hands, 1973; Jumping Out of Bed, 1973; The Hockey Poem, 1974; Point Reyes Poems, 1974; Old Man Rubbing His Eyes, 1975; The Loon, 1977; This Body is Made of Camphor and Gopherwood, 1977; Visiting Emily Dickinson's Grave and Other Poems, 1979; This Tree Will Be Here for a Thousand Years, 1979; The Man in the Black Coat Turns, 1981; Finding an Old Ant Mansion, 1981; Four Ramages, 1983; The Whole Moisty Night, 1983; Out of the Rolling Ocean, 1984; Mirabai Versions, 1984; In the Month of May, 1985; A Love of Minute Particulars, 1985; Selected Poems, 1986; Loving a Woman in Two Worlds, 1987; The Moon on a Fencepost, 1988; The Apple Found in the Plowing, 1989; What Have I Ever Lost By Dying?: Collected Prose Poems, 1993; Gratitude to Old Teachers, 1993; Meditations on the Insatiable Soul, 1994; Morning Poems, 1997. Editor: The Sea and the Honeycomb, 1966; A Poetry Reading Against the Vietnam War (with David Ray), 1967; Forty Poems Touching Upon Recent History, 1970; News of the Universe: Poems of Twofold Consciousness, 1980; Ten Love Poems, 1981; The Fifties and the Sixties, 10 volumes, 1982; The Winged Life: The Poetic Voice of Henry David Thoreau, 1986; The Rag and Bone Shop of the Heart: Poems for Men, 1992; The Soul Is Here for Its Own Joy, 1995. Translator: Over 35 books. Other: A Broadsheet Against the New York Times Book Review, 1961; Talking All Morning: Collected Conversations and Interviews, 1980; The Eight Stages of Translation, 1983, 2nd edition, 1986; The Pillow and the Key: Commentary on the Fairy Tale Iron John, 1987; A Little Book on the Human Shadow (edited by William Booth), 1988; American Poetry: Wildness and Domesticity, 1990; Iron John: A Book About Men, 1990; Remembering James Wright, 1991; The Sibling Society, 1996. Honours: Fulbright Grant, 1956-57; Lowell Travelling Fellowship, 1964; Guggenheim Fellowships, 1964, 1972; American Academy of Arts and Letters Grant, 1965; Rockefeller Foundation Fellowship, 1967; National Book Award, 1968. Memberships: American Academy and Institute of Arts and Letters; Association of Literary Magazines of America, executive committee. Address: 1904 Girard Avenue South, Minneapolis, MN 54403, USA.

BLYTH Alan, b. 27 July 1929, London, England. Music Critic; Editor. m. Ursula Zumloh. Education: MA, Oxford University. Appointments: Contributor as Critic, The Times, 1963-76; Associate Editor, Opera, 1967-84; Music Editor, Encyclopaedia Britannica, 1971-76; Critic, Daily

Telegraph, 1976-89. Publications: The Enjoyment of Opera, 1969; Colin Davis, A Short Biography, 1972; Opera on Record (editor), 1979; Remembering Britten, 1980; Wagner's Ring: An Introduction, 1980; Opera on Record 2 (editor), 1983; Opera on Record 3 (editor), 1984; Song on Record (editor), Volume 1, 1986, Volume 2, 1988; Choral Music on Record, 1990; Opera on CD, 1992; Opera on Video, 1995. Contributions to: Gramophone; BBC. Memberships: Critics' Circle; Garrick Club. Address: 22 Shilling Street, Lavenham, Suffolk CO10 9RH, England.

BLYTHE Julia. See: BOGLE Joanna Margaret.

BLYTHE Ronald George, b. 6 Nov 1922, Acton, Suffolk, England. Author. Appointments: Associate Editor, New Wessex Edition of the Works of Thomas Hardy, 1978. Publications: A Treasonable Growth, 1960; Immediate Possession, 1961; The Age of Illusion, 1963; Akenfield, 1969; William Hazlett: Selected Writings, editor, 1970; The View in Winter, 1979; From the Headlands, 1982; The Stories of Ronald Blythe, 1985; Divine Landscapes, 1986; Each Returning Day, 1989; Private Words, 1991; Word from Wormingford, 1997; First Friends, 1998; Going to the George, 1998; The Papers of the Late Lieutenant, 1998. Critical Studies of Jane Austen, Thomas Hardy, Leo Tolstoy, Literature of the Second World War. Contributions to: Observer; Sunday Times; New York Times; Listener; Atlantic Monthly; London Magazine; Tablet; New Statesman; Bottegue Oscure; Guardian. Honours: Heinemann Award, 1969; Society of Authors Travel Scholarship, 1970; Angel Prize for Literature, 1986; Honorary MA, University of East Anglia, 1991. Memberships: Royal Society of Literature, fellow; Society of Authors; The John Clare Society, president; Fabian Society. Literary Agent: Deborah Rogers, London. Address: Bottengoms Farm, Wormingford, Colchester, Essex, England.

BOARDMAN Sir John, b. 20 Aug 1927, Ilford, Essex, England. Professor Emeritus of Classical Art and Archaeology. Education: BA, 1948, MA, 1951, Magdalene College. Appointments: Assistant Keeper, Ashmolean Museum, 1955-59; Reader in Classical Archaeology, 1959-78, Lincoln Professor of Classical Art and Archaeology, 1978-94, University of Oxford; Editor, Journal of Hellenic Studies, 1958-65; Co-Editor, Oxford Monographs in Classical Archaeology; Delegate, OUP, 1979-89. Publications: S Marinatos and M Hirmer: Crete and Mycenae (translator), 1960; The Cretan Collection in Oxford, 1961; Island Gems, 1963; The Date of the Knossos Tablets, 1963; The Greek Overseas, 1964, 3rd edition, 1980; Greek Art, 1964, 4th edition, 1996; Excavations at Tocra (with J Dorig, W Fuchs and M Hirmer), 1966; Architecture of Ancient Greece (with J Dorig); Greek Emporio, 1967; Pre-Classical Style and Civilisation, 1967; Engraved Gems: The Ionides Collection, 1968; Archaic Greek Gems, 1968; Eros in Greece (with E la Rocca), 1978; Greek Sculpture: Archaic Period, 1978; Catalogue of Gems and Finger Rings (with M L Vollenweider), vol I, 1978; Castle Ashby Corpus Vasorum (with M Robertson), 1979; Greek Sculpture: Classical Period, 1985; The Parthenon and its Sculptures, 1985; Athenian Red Figure Vases: Classical Period, 1989; The Diffusion of Classical Art in Antiquity, 1994; Greek Sculpture: The Late Classical Period, 1995; The Great God Pan, 1998; Early Greek Vase Painting. Honours: Knighted, 1989; Professor of Ancient History, Royal Academy, 1989-; Honorary Doctorate, University of Athens, 1990, University of Paris, 1994. Membership: British Academy, fellow, 1969-. Address: 11 Park Street, Woodstock, Oxford OX20 1SJ, England.

BOAST Philip (James), b. 30 Apr 1952, London, England. Writer. m. Rosalind Thorpe, 20 June 1981, 2 sons, 1 daughter. Education: Mill Hill School, 1965-69. Publications: The Assassinators, 1976; London's Child, 1987; The Millionaire, 1989; Watersmeet, 1990; Pride, 1991; The Londons of London, 1992; Gloria, 1993; London's Daughter, 1994; City, 1994; The Foundling, 1995; Resurrection, 1996; Deus, 1997; Sion, 1998. Contributions to: Science Fiction Monthly. Literary Agent:

Carol Smith. Address: Rhydda Bank Cottage, Trentishoe, Barnstaple, North Devon EX31 4PL, England.

BOBER Natalie Susan, b. 27 Dec 1930, New York, New York, USA. Author; Biographer; Historian. m. Lawrence H Bober, 27 Aug 1950, 2 sons, 1 daughter. Education: BA, English, 1951; MS, Reading, Education, 1966; Permanent Certification, Teacher of Reading, 1977. Appointment: Consultant to Ken Burns, Television Documentary, 1995. Publications: William Wordsworth: The Wandering Poet, 1975; A Restless Spirit: The Story of Robert Frost, 1981, new edition, 1991; Breaking Tradition: The Story of Louise Nevelson, 1984; Let's Pretend: Poems of Flight and Fancy, 1986, 2nd edition, 1990; Thomas Jefferson: Man on a Mountain, 1988, 3rd edition, 1997; Marc Chagall: Painter of Dreams, 1991; Abigail Adams: Witness to a Revolution, 1995, new edition 1998. Contributions to: Lion and the Unicorn; Horn Book. Honours: Boston Globe-Horn Book Award for Best Non-Fiction, 1995; Boston Globe Best Books of 1995; School Library Journal Best Books of 1995; Booklist, Editor's Choices, 1995; Hungry Minds Review, Best Non-Fiction, Children's Books of Distinction, 1996; Society of Children's Book Writers Award, 1996; American Library Association Best Books for Young Adults, 1996; Washington Irving Children's Choice Honor Book, 1998. Membership: Society of Children's Bookwriters and Illustrators. Address: 7 Westfield Lane, White Plains, NY 10605, USA.

BOCEK Alois. See: **VANICEK Zdenek.**

BOCOCK Robert James, b. 29 Sept 1940, Lincoln, Lincolnshire, England. Sociologist; Writer; Lecturer. Education: Diploma, University of London, 1963; PhD, Brunel University, 1973. Appointments: Lecturer in Sociology, Brunel University, 1966-79, Open University, Buckinghamshire, 1979-. Publications: Ritual in Industrial Society, 1974; Freud and Modern Society, 1976; An Introduction to Sociology, 1980; Sigmund Freud, 1983; Religion and Ideology (editor), 1985; Hegemony, 1986; Consumption, 1993. Contributions to: Journals. Memberships: Association of University Teachers; British Sociological Association. Address: Department of Sociology, Faculty of Social Sciences, Crowther Building, The Open University, Walton Hall, Milton Keynes, Buckinghamshire, England.

BODELSEN Anders, b. 11 Feb 1937, Copenhagen, Denmark. Novelist; Dramatist. m. Eva Sindahl-Pedersen, 1975. Education: University of Copenhagen, 1956-60. Appointment: Staff, Politiken, 1967-. Publications: Villa Sunset, 1964; The Greenhouse, 1965; Rama Sama, 1967; The Silent Partner, 1968; Hit and Run, Run, Run, 1968; Freezing Point, 1969; Holiday, 1970; Straus, 1971; Help: Seven Stories, 1971; The Girls on the Bridge, 1972; Opposite Number, 1972; Outside Number, 1972; Consider the Verdict, 1973; Law and Order, 1973; Everything You Wish, 1974; The Wind in the Alley, 1974; Operation Cobra, 1975; Money and the Life, 1976; The Good Times, 1977; Year by Year, 1978; Over the Rainbow, 1982; Domino, 1984; The Shelter, 1984; Revision, 1985; I Must Run, 1987; The Blue Hour, 1987; Blackout, 1988; The Town Without Fires, 1989; Red September, 1991. Other: Radio and Television plays. Honour: Swedish Crime Writers Academy Prize, 1990. Address: Christiansholms Parkvej 12, 2930 Klampenborg, Denmark.

BODIE (Elizabeth) Idella (Fallaw), b. 2 Dec 1925, Ridge Spring, South Carolina, USA. Teacher; Author. m. James E Bodie Sr, 15 Aug 1947, 2 sons, 2 daughters. Education: Associate Degree, Mars Hill Junior College, 1942-44; BA, Columbia College, 1946; Graduate Study, University of South Carolina, 1950-51. Publications: Young readers books: The Secret of Telfair Inn, 1971; Mystery of the Pirates Treasure, 1973; Ghost in the Capitol, 1976; Stranded, 1984, Whopper, 1989; Trouble at Star Fort, 1992; Mystery of Edisto Island, 1994; Ghost Tales for Retelling, 1994. Other: South Carolina Women, 1978; Archibald Rutledge, 1980; The Man Who Loved the Flag, 1997; Carolina Girl: A Writer's Beginning, 1998; The Secret Message, 1998. Contributions to: Guideposts; Mature Living; Sandlapper; Instruction; Christian Home. Honours: Business and Professional Woman of the Year, 1980; Toastmasters International Communication Achievement Award, 1985; Idella Bodie Creative Writing Award, 1985; Willou Gray Educator Award, 1988; Youth Prison Volunteer of Year, 1990; 3 books nominated for South Carolina Children's Book Award. Membership: Society of Children's Book Writers and Illustrators. Address: 1113 Evans Road, Aiken, SC 29803, USA.

BODNER Alvin, b. 15 Apr 1950, Manchester, England. Medical Practitioner. m. Bernice Elizabeth Simon, 15 July 1973, 1 daughter. Education: University of Manchester Medical School, 1968-73; MBChB, 1973; MRCGP, 1978. Appointments include: Clinical Medical Officer, Child Health, Rochdale Area Health Authority, 1976-84; Insurance Medical Panel work for various companies, 1989-; Company Medical Officer, Local Transport/Distribution Co, 1992-; Medical Professional Adviser to Lay Conciliation Service, Bury/Rochdale Health Authority Complaints Procedure, 1997-; Fellowship, Royal College of General Practitioners, 1998; GP Principal, 1977-. Publications: On Attempting to Educate One's GP Colleagues, 1986; On Introducing a 4 Week Introductory Period to General Practice - A Personal Experience, 1994; Avoiding Complaints, 1994; Practice Questioned, 1995; Health Care in Sri Lanka - A Personal Experience, 1995; Practice Questioned, 1996; Lessons From Experience, 1997; Child Abuse; Hodgkins Disease; The Precarious Relationship Between a Doctor and Patient, 1997; Life at the Co-op, 1997; Teaching Exchange - Palliative Care - A Pilot Study in Self Directed Learning, 1998. Membership: GP Writers Association. Address: Castleton Health Centre, 2 Elizabeth Street, Rochdale, Lancashire OL11 3HY, England.

BOECKMAN Charles, b. 9 Nov 1920, San Antonio, Texas, USA. Author. m. Patricia Kennelly, 25 July 1965, 1 daughter. Publications: Maverick Brand, 1961; Unsolved Riddles of the Ages, 1965; Our Regional Industries, 1966; Cool, Hot and Blue, 1968; And the Beat Goes On, 1972; Surviving Your Parent's Divorce, 1980; Remember Our Yesterdays, 1991; House of Secrets, 1992. Contributions to: Many anthologies and periodicals. Membership: American Society of Journalists and Authors. Address: 322 Del Mar Boulevard, Corpus Christi, TX 78404, USA.

BOERSMA June Elaine, (Jalma Barrett), b. 27 Apr 1926, New York, USA. Writer; Photographer. m. (1) Kenneth Thomas McKim, 8 June 1946, div 1957, 2 sons, (2) Lawrence Allan Boersma, 22 Nov 1962, 1 s, 1 d. Co-Owner, Photographer, Allan/The Animal Photographers, San Diego, 1980-; VP, Board of Directors, The Photographic Institute International, 1982-86. Publications: H-book Series: Wildcats of North America - Bobcat, Cougar, Feral Cat, and Lynx, 1998; The Dove Family Tale, A True Story, 1998. Contributions to: Ladies' Home Journal; Dog Fancy; Cat Fancy; Dog World; Horse Illustrated; Popular Photography; Petersen's Photographic; Studio Photography; MotoFocus. Address: 3503 Argonne Street, San Diego, CA 92117, USA. 9.

BOESCH Hans, b. 13 Mar 1926, Frumsen, Sennwald, Switzerland. Traffic Engineer; Writer; Poet. m. Mathilde Kerler, 1 July 1950, 3 daughters. Education: HTL Winterthur, 1941-46. Appointments: Head, Transport Planning, Baudirektion, Canton of Aargau; Scientific Collaborator, Dozent, ORL-Institut, ETH Zürich. Publications: Der junge Os (novel), 1957; Das Gerust (novel), 1960; Die Fliegenfalle (novel), 1968; Menschen im Bau (stories), 1970; Der Kiosk (novel), 1978; Ein David (poems), 1978; Unternehmen Normkopf (satire), 1985; Der Sog (novel), 1988; Der Bann (novel), 1996; Der Kreis (novel), 1998. Contributions to: Weltwoch, Zürich; Neue Züricher Zeitung, Zürich; Tagesanzeigen, Zürich. Honours: C F Meyer Prize, 1954; Medal of Honour, City of Zürich, 1970, 1978; Prize for Literature, Canton of Aargau, 1983; Prize, Schillerstiftung, 1988; International Bodensee Prize for Literature, 1989; Prize, Jaeckle-Treadwell-Stiftung, Zürich, 1996. Address: Eichstr 10a, 8712 Stafa, Switzerland.

BOGARDE Dirk (Sir), (Derek Jules Gaspard Ulric Niven Van den Bogard), b. 28 Mar 1921, London, England. Actor; Writer. Education: University College School; Allan Glen's, Scotland. Appointment: Actor, 1939-. Publications: A Postillion Struck by Lightning (autobiography), 1977; Snakes and Ladders, 1978; An Orderely Man, 1983; Backcloth, 1986; A Particular Friendship, 1989; The Great Meadow, 1992; A Short Walk from Harrods, 1993; Cleared for Take Off, 1995. Novels: A Gentle Occupation, 1980; Voices in the Garden, 1981; Nest of Sunset, 1984; Jericho, 1992; A Period of Adjustment, 1994. Honour: Knighted, 1992. Address: c/o JAA, 2 Goodwins Court, London WC2N 4LL, England.

BOGDAN Dan, b. 2 Dec 1948, Bilciuresti, Romania. Writer. Education: Diploma, Faculty of Law, Bucharest, 1972. Publications: Relaxation, humourous sketches, in Litera, 1979; The Wandering Master, novel, in Albatros, 1982; Going After Alexandru Ioan Cuza, essay, in Sport-Tourism, 1985; The Characters in Crystalline, short story, in Albatros, 1987; Going After Ion Ghica, essay, in Sport-Tourism, 1988; Scorpion of Durango, novel, in Militara, 1991; The Sewer, novel, in Sylvi, 1992; Staing On Que For Mortadella, novel, in Scripta, 1993; Waiting To Get Up, interview, in Scripta, 1994; Crepuscule To Heidelberg, essay, in Viitorul romanesc, 1995; Landscape With Butterfly and Scorpions, novel, in Eminescu, 1996. Honours: Prize, Albatros publishing house, 1983; Prize, Salon Books, Cluj, 1996. Membership: Writers Union of Romania, 1990. Address: Str Mitropolit Andrei Saguna, nr 114, Sector 1, Bucharest, Romania.

BOGDANOVICH Peter, b. 30 July 1939, Kingston, New York, USA. Film Director; Writer; Producer; Actor. m. (1) Polly Platt, 1962, div 1970, 2 daughters, (2) L B Straten, 1988. Appointments: Film Feature-Writer, Esquire, New York Times, Village Voice, Cahiers du Cinema, Los Angeles Times, New York Magazine, Vogue, Variety and others, 1961-. *Publications:* The Cinema of Orson Welles, 1961; The Cinema of Howard Hawks, 1962; The Cinema of Alfred Hitchcock, 1963; John Ford, 1968; Fritz Lang in America, 1969; Allan Dwan: The Last Pioneer, 1971; Pieces of Time: Peter Bogdanovich on the Movies (in UK as Picture Shows), 1961, enlarged edition, 1985; The Killing of the Unicorn: Dorothy Stratten (1960-1980), 1984; A Year and a Day Calendar (editor), 1991; This is Orson Welles, 1992. Films: The Wild Angels, 1966; Targets, 1968; The Last Picture Show, 1971; What's Up Doc?, 1972; Paper Moon, 1973; Daisy Miller, 1974; At Long Last Love, 1975; Nickelodeon, 1976; Saint Jack, 1979; They All Laughed, 1981; Mask, 1985; Illegally Yours, 1988; Texasville, 1990; Noises Off, 1992; The Thing Called Love, 1993. *Honours:* New York Film Critics' Award for Best Screenplay, British Academy Award for Best Screenplay, 1971; Writer's Guild of America Award for Best Screenplay, 1972; Silver Shell, Mar del Plata, Spain, 1973; Best Director, Brussels Festival, 1974; Pasinetti Award, Critics Prize, Venice Festival, 1979. *Memberships:* Directors Guild of America; Writer's Guild of America; Academy of Motion Picture Arts and Sciences. *Address:* c/o William Peiffer, 2040 Avenue of the Stars, Century City, CA 90067, USA.

BOGLE Joanna Margaret, (Julia Blythe), b. 7 Sept 1952, Carshalton, Surrey, England. Author; Journalist. m. James Stewart Lockhart Bogle, 20 Sept 1980. Appointments: Local Borough Councillor, London Borough of Sutton, 1974-81; Governor, London Oratory School, 1976-86. Publications: A Book of Feasts and Seasons, 1986; When the Summer Ended (with Cecylia Wolkowinska), 1991; A Heart for Europe (with James Bogle), 1992; Caroline Chisholm, 1993; Come On In - It's Awful!, editor, 1994; We Didn't Mean to Start a School, 1998. Contributions to: local newspapers, 1970-74; South London News, 1984-86; Catholic Times, 1994-; various national newspapers, 1980-. Memberships: Vice Chairman, Catholic Writers Guild, 1992-. Address: c/o 58 Hanover Gardens, London SE11 5TN, England.

BOHJALIAN Chris, b. 12 Aug 1960, White Plains, New York, USA. Novelist; Journalist. m. Victoria Blewer, 12 Oct 1984. Appointments: Book Critic and Columnist,

Burlington Free Press, Vermont, 1987-; Book Critic, Vermont Life magazine, Montpelier, 1991-. Publications: A Killing in the Real World, 1988; Hangman, 1991; Past the Bleachers, 1992; Water Witches, 1995. Contributions to: Many magazines. Memberships: League of Vermont Writers; Phi Beta Kappa. Address: c/o Ellen Levine Literary Agency, 15 East 26th Street, Suite 1801, New York, NY 10010, USA.

BOHM-DUCHEN Monica Teresa, b. 10 May 1957, London, England. Art Historian; Critic. m. Michael Duchen, 25 June 1978, 1 son, 1 daughter. Education: BA, Joint Hons, English Literature, History of Art, University College, London, 1976-79; MA, History of Art, Courtauld Institute of Art, London, 1979-80. Appointment: Freelance. Publications: Arnold Daghani, 1987; Thomas Lowinsky, 1990; Understanding Modern Art, 1992; The Nude, 1992; After Auschwitz: Responses to the Holocaust in Contemporary Art (contributing editor), 1995; Rubies and Rebels: Jewish Female Identity (contributing editor); Chagall (contributing editor), 1998. Honour: Understanding Modern Art shortlisted for TES Senior Information Book Award. Membership: Society of Authors. Address: 14 Gayton Road, London NW3 1TX, England.

BÖHME Gernot, b. 3 Jan 1937, Dessau, Germany. University Professor. m. (2) Dr Farideh Akashe, 15 Apr 1983, 5 daughters. Education: Degree, University of Göttingen, 1958; PhD, University of Hamburg, 1964;Habilitation for Philosophy, University of Munich, 1972. Career: Assistant Professor, University of Hamburg and University of Heidelberg, 1965-69; Research Fellow, Max-Planck-Institute, Starnberg, 1969-77; Professor of Philosophy, Technical University of Darmstadt, 1977-. Publications: Über die Zeitmodi, 1966; Zeit und Zahl, 1974; Protophysik, 1976; Experimentelle Philosophie (with W v.d.Daele and W Krohn), 1977; Starnberger Studien I, 1978; Entfremdete Wissenschaft (with M V.Engelhardt), 1979; Alternativen der Wissenschaft, 1980; Finalization in Science: The Social Orientation of Scientific Progress (edited by W Schaefer), 1983; Das Andere der Vernunft (with H Böhme), 1983; Anthropologie in pragmatischer Hinsicht, 1985; Soziale Naturwissenschaft (with E Schramm), 1985; The Knowledge Society (eidotr with N Stehr), 1986; Philosophieren mit Kant, 1986; Natur, Leib, Sprache, 1986; Der Typ Sokrates, 1988; Isaac Newton: Über die Gravitation, 1988; Klassiker der Naturphilosophie, 1989; Für eine ökologische Naturaisthetik, 1989; Natürlische Natur, 1992; Coping with Science, 1992; Am Ende des Baconschen Zeitalters, 1993; Atmosphäre, 1995; Briefe an meine Töchter, 1995; Idee und Kosmos, 1996; Feuw-Wasser-Erde-Luft, 1996. Memberships: Association for Philosophy in Germany; Oeko Institute, Freiburg. Address: Institute for Philosophy, TH Darmstadt, Schloss, D-64283 Darmstadt, Germany.

BOISDEFFRE Pierre Jules Marie Raoul (Néraud Le Mouton de), b. 11 July 1926, Paris, France. Writer; Diplomatist; Broadcasting Official. m. Beatrice Wiedemann-Goiran, 1957, 3 sons. Education: École Libre des Sciences Politiques; Ecole Nationale d'Administration; Harvard University, USA. Appointments: Director of Sound Broadcasting, Office de Radiodiffusion et Television Française (ORTF), 1963-68; Cultural Counsellor, French Embassy, London, 1968-71, Brussels, 1972-77; Ministry of Foreign Affairs, 1977-78; Minister Plenipotentiary, 1979; Ambassador to Uruguay, 1981-84, Colombia, 1984-88, Council of Europe, Strasbourg, 1988-91. Publications: Metamorphose de la litterature, 2 volumes, 1950; Ou va le Roman?, 1962; Les ecrivains français d'aujourd'hui, 1963; Lettre ouverte aux hommes de gauche, 1969; La foi des anciens jours, 1977; Le roman francais depuis 1900, 1979; Les nuits, l'Ile aux livres, Paroles de vie, La Belgique, 1980; Histoire de la litterature, 2 volumes, 1985; Souvenirs: Contre le Vent Majeur, 1994. Honours: Numerous national awards, including Prix de la Critique, 1950; Doctor honoris causa, Universities of Hull (Great Britian) and Bogota (Colombia); Officer de la Legion d'honneur; Commandeur de l'ordre national du Merite. Address: 5 Cité Vaneau, 75007 Paris, France.

BOISVERT France, (Marguerite de Nevers), b. 10 June 1959, Sherbrooke, Quebec, Canada. French Teacher; Writer; Poet. 1 son. Education: Baccalaureat, 1983; Master in Literature, 1986. Appointments: Salon, 1991; York University, Canada, 1991; Speeches, Montreal, Public Lectures, 1991-93. Publications: Les Samourailles, 1987; Li Tsing-tao ou Le grand avoir (prose), 1989; Massawippi (poem), 1992; Comme un vol de gerfauts (poem), 1993; Les Herities de Lord Durham, 1995. Contributions to: Liberté; La Presse. Honours: Bursary, Minister of Culture, Quebec, 1989, 1990, 1991. Memberships: Union des Ecrivains du Québec; Administration éLue au Conseil d'administration de L'UNEQ. Address: A/S UNEQ Maison des Ecrivains, 3492 Avenue Laval, Montreal H2X 3C8, Canada.

BOK Sissela (Ann), b. 2 Dec 1934, Stockholm, Sweden. Philosopher; Distinguished Fellow; Writer. m. Derek Bok, 7 May 1955, 1 son, 2 daughters. Education: BA, 1957, MA, 1958, George Washington University; PhD, Harvard University, 1970. Appointments: Lecturer, Simmons College, Boston, 1971-72, Harvard-Massachusetts Institute of Technology Division of Health Sciences and Technology, Cambridge, 1975-82, Harvard University, 1982-84; Associate Professor, 1985-89, Professor of Philosophy, 1989-92, Brandeis University; Fellow, Center for Advanced Study, Stanford, California, 1991-92; Distinguished Fellow, Harvard Center for Population and Development Studies, 1993-. Publications: Lying: Moral Choice in Public and Private Life, 1978; Secrets: On the Ethics of Concealment and Revelation, 1982; Alva: Ett kvinnoliv, 1987; A Strategy for Peace, 1989; Alva Myrdal: A Daughter's Memoir, 1991; Common Values, 1996; Mayhem: Violence as Public Entertainment, 1998. Contributions to: Scholarly publications. Honours: George Orwell Award, 1978; Melcher Awards, 1978, 1991; Abram L Sacher Silver Medallion, Brandeis University, 1985; Honorary doctorates, Mt Holyoke College, 1985, George Washington University, 1986, Clark University, 1988, University of Massachusetts, 1991, Georgetown University, 1992; Radcliffe College Graduate Society Medal, 1993; Barnard College Medal of Distinction, 1995. Memberships: American Philosophical Association; Hasting Center, fellow, director, 1976-84, 1994-97; Pulitzer Prize Board, 1988-97, chairman, 1996-97. Address: c/o Harvard Center for Population and Development Studies, Cambridge, MA 02138, USA.

BOLAND Michael (John), b. 14 Nov 1950, Kingston, Surrey, England. Poet; Civil Servant. Appointment: Editor, The Arcadian, poetry magazine. Publication: The Midnight Circus; The Trout... Minus One (co-author), 1993. Contributions to: Envoi; Purple Patch; Weyfarers; Firing Squad; Various anthologies. Honours: Patricia Chown Sonnet Award. Memberships: PEN; Society of Civil Service Authors; Keats-Shelley Memorial Association; Wordsworth Trust; Friends of Coleridge; MIAP. Address: 11 Boxtree Lane, Harrow Weald, Middlesex HA3 6JU, England.

BOLGER Dermot, b. 6 Feb 1959, Finglas, Ireland. Novelist; Dramatist; Poet; Editor. m. Bernadette Bolger, 1988, 2 children. Education: Beneavin College Secondary School. Appointments: Founder-Editor, Raven Arts Press, 1979-92; Executive Editor, New Island Books, 1992-. Publications: Novels: Night Shift, 1985; The Woman's Daughter, 1987, augmented edition, 1991; The Journey Home, 1990; Emily's Shoes, 1992; A Second Life, 1994; Father's Music, 1997; Finbar's Hotel (collaborative novel), 1997. Plays: The Lament for Arthur Cleary, 1989; Blinded by the Light, 1990; In High Germany, 1990; The Holy Ground, 1990; One Last White Horse, 1991; The Dublin Bloom, 1994; April Bright, 1995; The Passion of Jerome, 1999. Poetry: The Habit of Flesh, 1979; Finglas Lilies, 1980; No Waiting America, 1981; Internal Exiles, 1986; Leinster Street Ghosts, 1989; Taking My Letters Back: New and Selected Poems, 1998. Editor: The Dolmen Book of Irish Christmas Stories, 1986; The Bright Wave: Poetry in Irish Now, 1986; 16 on 16: Irish Writers on the Easter Rising, 1988; Invisible Cities: The New Dubliners: A Journey through Unofficial Dublin, 1988; Invisible Dublin: A Journey through Its Writers, 1992; The Picador Book of Contemporary Irish Fiction, 1993; 12 Bar Blues (with Aidan Murphy), 1993. Contributions to: Anthologies. Honours: A E Memorial Prize, 1986; Macauley Fellowship, 1987; A Z Whitehead Prize, 1987; Samuel Beckett Award, 1991; Edinburgh Fringe First Award, 1991, 1995; Stewart Parker BBC Award, 1991. Address: c/o A P Watt, 20 John Street, London WC1N 2DR, England.

BOLITHO Elaine Elizabeth, b. 12 Dec 1940, Christchurch, New Zealand. Researcher; Writer. m. Ian James Bolitho, 14 Dec 1963, 2 sons, 2 daughters. Education: BA, 1988, BA, Hons, 1989, PhD, World Religions, 1993, Victoria University of Wellington, New Zealand. Publications: Meet the Baptists - Postwar Personalities and Perspectives, 1993; Meet the Methodists - Postwar Personalities and Perspectives, 1994; New Vision New Zealand, Vol II (2 chapters), 1997. Contributions to: Stimulus; Wesley Historical Society Journal; Affirm; Baptist Research Journal; Evening Post; Apostolic News. Honours: Eileen Duggan Prize for New Zealand Literature, 1986; Epworth Book of the Month, 1993. Memberships: Christian Writers Guild; Christian Research Association of Aotearoa, New Zealand; New Zealand Society of Authors (PEN NZ Inc). Address: 33 Kandy Crescent, Ngaio, Wellington 6004, New Zealand.

BOLMIN Jerzy. See: **BRAUN Kazimierz.**

BOND Edward, b. 18 July 1934, London, England. Playwright; Poet; Director. Publications: Saved, 1966; Three Sisters (Chekov), translator, 1967; Narrow Road to the Deep North, 1968; Early Morning, 1968; The Pope's Wedding and Other Plays, 1971; Lear, 1972; The Sea, 1973; Bingo: Scenes of Money and Death, 1974; Spring's Awakening (translator), 1974; The Fool, 1975; We Come to the River, libretto for Henze, 1976; A-A-America - The Swing and Grandma Faust, 1976; A-A-America, and Stone, 1976; Plays, 4 volumes, 1977-92; Theatre Poems and Songs, 1978; The Woman, 1978; The Bundle, 1980; The Cat, libretto, 1980; The Restoration, 1981; Summer, 1982; Human Cannon, 1985; War Plays (Red, Black and Ignorant; The Tin Can Riots; Great Peace), 1985; Collected Poems, 1978-85, 1985; Jackets, 1988; In the Company of Men, 1988; Notes on Post-Modernism, 1988; September, 1988; Olly's Prison (3 TV plays), 1992; Tuesday (TV Play), 1993; Selected Letters, 4 volumes, 1994-95; Coffee, 1995; Lulu: A Monster Tragedy (by Frank Wedekind - Translated). Honour: Honorary D Litt, Yale University, 1977. Membership: Theatre Writers Union. Address: c/o Margaret Ramsay Ltd, 14A Goodwin's Court, London WC2N 4LL, England.

BOND Gillian. See: **McEVOY Marjorie.**

BOND (Thomas) Michael, b. 13 Jan 1926, Newbury, Berkshire, England. Author. m. (1) Brenda May Johnson, 29 June 1950, div 1981, 1 son, 1 daughter, (2) Susan Marfrey Rogers, 1981. Education: Presentation College, 1934-40. Publications: Children's Books: A Bear Called Paddington, 1958; More About Paddington, 1959; Paddington Helps Out, 1960; Paddington Abroad, 1961; Paddington at Large, 1962; Paddington Marches On, 1964; Paddington at Work, 1966; Here Comes Thursday, 1966; Thursday Rides Again, 1968; Paddington Goes to Town, 1968; Thursday Ahoy, 1969; Parsley's Tail, 1969; Parsley's Good Deed, 1969; Parsley's Problem Present, 1970; Parsley's Last Stand, 1970; Paddington Takes the Air, 1970; Thursday in Paris, 1970; Michael Bond's Book of Bears, 1971; Michael Bond's Book of Mice, 1971; The Day the Animals Went on Strike, 1972; Paddington Bear, 1972; Paddington's Garden, 1972; Parsley Parade, 1972; The Tales of Olga de Polga, 1972; Olga Meets Her Match, 1973; Paddington's Blue Peter Story Book, 1973; Paddington at the Circus, 1973; Paddington Goes Shopping, 1973; Paddington at the Seaside, 1974; Paddington at the Tower, 1974; Paddington on Top, 1974; Windmill, 1975; How to Make Flying Things, 1975; Eight Olga Readers, 1975; Paddington's Cartoon Book, 1979; J D Polson and the Dillogate Affair, 1981; Paddington on Screen, 1981; Olga Takes Charge, 1982; The Caravan Puppets, 1983; Paddington at the Zoo, 1984; Paddington's Painting Exhibition, 1985; Elephant,

1985; Paddington Minds the House, 1986; Paddington at the Palace, 1986; Paddington's Busy Day, 1987; Paddington and the Magical Maze, 1987; Paddington and the Christmas Surprise, 1997; Paddington at the Carnival, 1998; Paddington Bear, 1998. Adult Books: Monsieur Pamplemousse, 1983; Monsieur Pamplemousse and the Secret Mission, 1984; Monsieur Pamplemousse Takes the Cure, 1987; The Pleasures of Paris, Guide Book, 1987; Monsieur Pamplemousse Aloft, 1989; Monsieur Pamplemousse Investigates, 1990; Monsieur Pamplemousse Rests His Case, 1991; Monsieur Pamplemousse Stands Firm, 1992; Monsieur Pamplemousse on Location, 1992; Monsieur Pamplemousse Takes the Train, 1993; Bears and Forebears (autobiography), 1996; Monsieur Pamplemousse Afloat, 1998. Honour: Officer of the Order of the British Empire, 1997. Address: The Agency, 24 Pottery Lane, Holland Park, London W11 4LZ, England.

BOND Nancy Barbara, b. 8 Jan 1945, Bethesda, Maryland, USA. Librarian; Writer. Education: BA, Mount Holyoke College, 1966; Dip Lib Wales, College of Librarianship, Wales, 1972. Appointment: Instructor, part-time, Simmons College, Centre for the Study of Children's Literature, 1979-. Publications: A String in the Harp, 1976; The Best of Enemies, 1978; Country of Broken Stone, 1980; The Voyage Begun, 1981; A Place to Come Back To, 1984; Another Shore, 1988; Truth to Tell, 1994; The Love of Friends, 1997. Honours: International Reading Association Award, 1976; Newbery Honour, 1976; Welsh Arts Council Tir na n'Og Award, 1976. Address: 109 The Valley Road, Concord, MA 01742, USA.

BOND Ruskin, b. 19 May 1934, Kasauli, India. Author; Journalist; Children's Writer. Education: Bishop Cotton School, Simla, India, 1943-50. Appointment: Managing Editor, Imprint, Bombay, 1975-79. Publications: The Room on the Roof, 1956; Grandfather's Private Zoo, 1967; The Last Tiger, 1971; Angry River, 1972; The Blue Umbrella, 1974; Once Upon a Monsoon Time, memoirs, 1974; Man of Destiny: A Biography of Jawaharlal Nehru, 1976; Night of the Leopard, 1979; Big Business, 1979; The Cherry Tree, 1980; The Road to the Bazaar, 1980; A Flight of Pigeons, 1980; The Young Vagrants, 1981; Flames in the Forest, 1981; The Adventures of Rusty, 1981; Tales and Legends of India, 1982; A Garland of Memories, 1982; To Live in Magic, 1982; Tigers Forever, 1983; Earthquakes, 1984; Getting Granny's Glasses, 1985; The Eyes of the Eagle, 1987; The Night Train at Deoli, short stories, 1988; Times Stops at Shamli, short stories, 1989; Ghost Trouble, 1989; Snake Trouble, 1990; Dust on the Mountain, 1990; Our Trees Still Grow in Dehra, 1992; Rain in the Mountains, 1994. Contributions to: Christian Science Monitor (Boston); Books for Keeps (UK); Cricket (USA); School (Australia); Telegraph (Calcutta);Khaleej Times (Dubai); Weekly Sun (New Delhi). Honours: John Hewellyn Rhys Prize, 1957; Sahitya Akademi Award for English Writing in India, 1992. Address: Ivy Cottage, Landour, Mussouri, UP 248179, India.

BONE Jesse F, b. 15 June 1916, Tacoma, Washington, USA. Professor of Veterinary Medicine (Retired); Writer. m. (1) Jayne M Clark, 20 Jan 1942, div 1946, 1 daughter, (2) Felizitas Margarete Endter, 15 June 1950, 2 sons, 1 daughter. Education: BA, 1937, BS, 1949, DVM, 1950, Washington State University; MS, Oregon State University, 1953. Appointments: Instructor to Professor of Veterinary Medicine, Oregon State University, Corvallis, 1950-79, now retired Professor Emeritus. Publications: Observations of the Ovaries of Infertile and Reportedly Infertile Dairy Cattle, 1954; Animal Anatomy, 1958, revised edition as Animal Anatomy and Physiology, 1975, 3rd edition, revised, 1988; Canine Medicine (editor), 1959, 2nd edition, 1962; Equine Medicine and Surgery (co-editor), 1963, 2nd edition, 1972. Fiction: The Lani People, 1962; Legacy, 1976; The Meddlers, 1976; Gift of the Manti (with R Myers), 1977; Confederation Matador, 1978. Honours: Fulbright Lecturer in Egypt, 1965-66 and in Kenya 1980-82; Postdoctoral Award, US Department of Health, Education and Welfare, 1969-70. Memberships: American Veterinary Medical Association; Phi Kappa Phi; Sigma Xi; Science Fiction Writers of America. Address: 3017 Brae Burn Street, Sierra Vista, AZ 85635, USA.

BONHAM-CARTER Victor, b. 13 Dec 1913, Bearsted, Kent, England. Author. m. (1) Audrey Stogdon, 22 July 1938, 2 sons, (2) Cynthia Clare Sanford, 9 Feb, 1979. Education: MA, Magdalene College, 1935. Appointments: Historian, Records Officer, Dartington Hall Estate, 1951-65; Secretary, Royal Literary Fund, 1966-82; Joint Secretary, Society of Authors, London, 1971-78. Publications: The English Village, 1952; Dartington Hall (with W B Curry), 1958; Exploring Parish Churches, 1959; Farming the Land, 1959; In a Liberal Tradition, 1960; Soldier True, US edition as The Strategy of Victory, 1965; Surgeon in the Crimea (editor), 1968; The Survival of the English Countryside, US edition as Land and Environment, 1971; Authors by Profession, 2 volumes, 1978-84; The Essence of Exmoor, 1991; What Countryman, Sir? (autobiography), 1996; A Filthy Barren Ground (editor), 1998. Memberships: Royal Society of Literature, fellow; Exmoor Society, president, 1975-. Literary Agent: Curtis Brown. Address: The Mount, Milverton House, Taunton, Somerset TA4 1QZ, England.

BONNEFOY Yves Jean, b. 24 June 1923, Tours, France. Professor; Writer; Poet. m. Lucille Vine, 1968, 1 daughter. Education: Faculté des Sciences, Poitiers, Faculté des Lettres, Paris. Appointments: Professor, Collège de France, Paris, 1981-. Publications: Poetry: Du mouvement et de l'immobilitè de Douve, 1953; Pierre écrite, 1964; Selected Poems, 1968; Dans le leurre de seuill, 1975; Poems, 1947-75, 1978. Non-Fiction: Peintures murales de la France Gothique, 1954; L'Improbable, 1959; Arthur Rimbaud, 1961; Miró, 1963; Un reve fait a Mantoue, 1967; Rome 1630, 1970 L'Arrière-Pays, 1972; Le nuage rouge, 1977; Rue traversière, 1977; Entretiens sur la poèsie, 1981; La Prèsence et l'Image, 1983; Ce qui fut sans lumière, 1987; Récits en reve, 1987. Contributions to: Journals. Honours: Prix Montaigne, 1980; Grand Prix de Poésie, Académie Francaise, 1981; Grand Prix, Société des gens de Lettres, 1987; Prix Balzac, 1995. Address: c/o Collège de France, 11 France Marcelin-Berthelot, 75005 Paris, France.

BONNER James. See: **FLANAGAN Thomas.**

BONNER Terry Nelson. See: **KRAUZER Steven M.**

BONTLY Thomas J(ohn), b. 25 Aug 1939, Madison, Wisconsin, USA. Professor; Author. m. Marilyn R Mackie, 25 Aug 1962, 1 son. Education: BA, University of Wisconsin at Madison, 1961; Research Student, Corpus Christi College, Cambridge University, 1961-62; PhD, Stanford University, 1966. Appointments: Assistant Professor, 1966-71, Associate Professor, 1971-76, Coordinator of Creative Writing, 1975-77, 1987-90, 1995-97, and Chairman, 1979-82, Department of English, Professor, 1976-, University of Wisconsin-Milwaukee; Fulbright Senior Lectureship, West Germany, 1984. Publications: Novels: The Competitor, 1966; The Adventures of a Young Outlaw, 1974; Celestial Chess, 1979; The Giant's Shadow, 1989. Other: Short stories in anthologies and many periodicals; Essays and reviews. Honours: Wallace Stegner Creative Writing Fellowship, 1965-66; Maxwell Perkins Commemorative Award, 1966; 1st Prizes for Short Fiction, Council for Wisconsin Writers, 1975, 1989, 1997; Wisconsin Arts Board New Work Award, 1990. Membership: Council for Wisconsin Writers, board of directors, 1991-. Literary Agent: Curtis Brown Ltd. Address: Department of English, University of Wisconsin-Milwaukee, Milwaukee, WI 53201.

BOOKER Christopher (John Penrice), b. 7 Oct 1937, Eastbourne, Sussex, England. Journalist; Writer. m. Valerie Booker, 1979, 2 sons. Education: Corpus Christi College, Cambridge. Appointments: Contributor, 1959-97, Way of the World column, 1987-90, Daily Telegraph; Liberal News, 1960; Jazz Critic, 1961, Columnist, 1990-, Sunday Telegraph; Editor, 1961-63, Regular Contributor, 1965-, Private Eye; Resident Scriptwriter, That Was the Week That Was, 1962-63; Contributor, Spectator, 1962-87; Editor, Global Britain, 1998-. Publications: The Neophiliacs: A Study of the Revolution in English Life in the 50's and 60's, 1969; Goodbye London (with Candida Lycett-Green), 1973; The Booker Quiz, 1976; The Seventies, 1980; The Games War: A Moscow Journal, 1981; The Repatriations from Austria in 1945, 1990; The Mad Officials: How the Bureaucrats Are Strangling Britain (with Richard North), 1994; The Castle of Lies: Why Britain Must Get Out of Europe (with Richard North), 1996; A Looking Glass Tragedy: The Controversy Over The Repatriations from Austria in 1945, 1997; Scared to Death, An Anatomy of Food Scare pheonomen (with Richard North), 1999. Honours: Co-Winner, Campaigning Journalist of the Year, 1973; Aims of Industry Free Enterprise Award, 1992. Address: The Old Rectory, Litton, Bath BA3 4PW, England.

BOONE Danyel, b. 11 Nov 1979, Rochester, New York, USA. Student. Education: Writing Course, Long Ridge Writers Group. Publications: Poems: I Love You; From the Heart. Anthology: A Quiet Place. Address: 7 Marburger Street, Rochester, NY 14621, USA.

BOORSTIN Daniel J(oseph), b. 1 Oct 1914, Atlanta, Georgia, USA. Historian; Librarian of Congress Emeritus. m. Ruth Carolyn Frankel, 9 Apr 1941, 3 sons. Education: AB, summa cum laude, Harvard University, 1934; BA, 1st class honours, Rhodes Scholar, 1936, BCL, 1st class honours, 1937, Balliol College, Oxford, 1937; Postgraduate Studies, Inner Temple, London, 1934-37; JSD, Sterling Fellow, Yale University, 1940. Appointments: Instructor, Tutor in History and Literature, Harvard University and Radcliffe College, 1938-42; Lecturer in Legal History, Harvard Law School, 1939-42; Assistant Professor of History, Swarthmore College, 1942-44; Assistant Professor, 1944-49, Professor, 1949-56, Professor of American History, 1956-64, Preston and Sterling Morton Distinguished Service Professor, 1964-69, University of Chicago; Fulbright Visiting Lecturer in American History, University of Rome, 1950-51, Kyoto University, 1957; 1st Incumbent of the Chair in American History, University of Paris, 1961-62; Pitt Professor of American History and Institutions, Cambridge University, 1964-65; Director, 1969-73, Senior Historian, 1973-75, National Museum of History and Technology, Smithsonian Institution, Washington, DC; Shelby and Kathryn Cullom Davis Lecturer, Graduate Institute of International Studies, Geneva, 1973-74; Librarian of Congress, 1975-87, Librarian of Congress Emeritus, 1987-, Washington, DC. Publications: The Mysterious Science of the Law, 1941; Delaware Cases, 1792-1830, 1943; The Lost World of Thomas Jefferson, 1948; The Genius of American Politics, 1953; The Americans: The Colonial Experience, 1958; America and the Image of Europe, 1960; The Image or What Happened to the American Dream, 1962; The Americans: The National Experience, 1965; The Landmark History of the American People, 1968, new edition, 1987; The Decline of Radicalism, 1969; The Sociology of the Absurd, 1970; The Americans: The Democratic Experience, 1973; Democracy and Its Discontents, 1974; The Exploring Spirit, 1976; The Republic of Technology, 1978; A History of the United States (with Brooks M Kelley), 1980, new edition, 1991; The Discoverers, 1983; Hidden History, 1987; The Creators, 1992; Cleopatra's Nose: Essays on the Unexpected, 1994; The Daniel J Boorstin Reader, 1995; The Seekers, 1998. Honours: Bancroft Award, 1959; Francis Parkman Prize, 1966; Pulitzer Prize in History, 1974; Dexter Prize, 1974; Watson-Davis Prize, 1986; Charles Frankel Prize, 1989; National Book Award, 1989; Many other honours, including numerous honorary doctorates. Memberships: American Academy of Arts and Sciences; American Antiquarian Society; American Philosophical Society; American Studies Association, president, 1969-71; Organization of American Historians; Royal Historical Society, corresponding member. Address: 3541 Ordway Street North West, Washington, DC 20016, USA.

BOOTH Geoffrey Thornton, (Edward Booth O P), b. 16 Aug 1928, Evesham, Worcestershire, England. Roman Catholic Dominican Priest; Teacher; Writer. Education: BA, 1952, MA, 1970, PhD, 1975, Cambridge

University. Appointments: Entered English province, Order of Dominicans, 1952; Ordained, Roman Catholic Priest, 1958; Lecturer, Pontifical Beda College, 1978-80, Pontifical University of St Thomas, 1980-88, Rome. Publications: Aristotelian Aporetic Ontology in Islamic and Christian Thinkers, 1983; Saint Augustine and the Western Tradition of Self Knowing: The Saint Augustine Lecture 1986, 1989. Contributions to: The New Grove Dictionary of Music and Musicians, 1980; La Production du livre universitaire au moyen age: Exemplar et Pecia, 1988; Kategorie und Kategorialität, Historisch-Systematische Untersuchungen zum Begriff der Kategorie im philosophischen Denken, Festschrift für Klaus Hartmann, 1990; Also many articles and book reviews in journals. Address: Dominikanerinnen: Maria Viktoria, Vellarsweg 2, Wetten, D-47625 Kevelaer, Germany.

BOOTH Martin, b. 7 Sept 1944, Lancashire, England. Writer. m. 1 son, 1 daughter. Publications: Fiction: The Carrier, 1978; The Bad Track, 1980; Hiroshima Joe, 1985; The Jade Pavilion, 1987; Black Chameleon, 1988; Dreaming of Samarkand, 1989; A Very Private Gentleman, 1991; The Humble Disciple, 1992; The Iron Tree, 1993; Toys of Glass, 1995; Adrift in the Oceans of Mercy, 1996; The Industry of Souls, 1998; Fiction for Children: War Dog, 1996; Music on the Bamboo Radio, 1997; Panther, 1999; Non-fiction: Carpet Sahib: A Life of Jim Corbett, 1986; The Triads, 1990; Rhino Road: the Natural History and Conservation of the African Rhinos, 1992; The Dragon and the Pearl: A Hong Kong Notebook, 1994; Opium: A History, 1996-; The Doctor, The Detective and Arthur Conan Doyle: A Biography of Sir Arthur Conan Doyle, 1997; The Dragon Syndicates, 1999; Also verse, criticism and screenplays. Honour: Fellow, Royal Society of Literature, 1980. Address: Gillon Aitken Associates, 29 Fernshaw Road, London SW10 0TG, England.

BOOTH Philip, b. 8 Oct 1925, Hanover, New Hampshire, USA. Professor of English (Retired); Poet. m. Margaret Tillman, 1946, 3 daughters. Education: AB, Dartmouth College, 1948; MA, Columbia University, 1949. Appointments: Assistant Professor, Wellesley College, 1954-61; Associate Professor, 1961-65, Professor of English and Poet-in-Residence, 1965-85, Syracuse University. Publications: Letter from a Distant Land, 1957; The Islanders, 1961; North by East, 1966; Weathers and Edges, 1966; Margins: A Sequence of New and Selected Poems, 1970; Available Light, 1976; Before Sleep, 1980; Relations: Selected Poems, 1950-85, 1986; Selves, 1990; Pairs: New Poems, 1994; Trying to Say It: Outlooks and Insights on How Poems Happen, 1996; Lifelines: New and Selected poems 1950-1999, fothcomming. Honours: Guggenheim Fellowships, 1958, 1965; Theodore Roethke Prize, 1970; National Endowment for the Arts Fellowship, 1980; Academy of American Poets Fellowship, 1983; Rockefeller Fellowship, 1986; Maurice English Poetry Award, 1987. Address: PO Box 330, Castine, ME 04421, USA.

BOOTH Rosemary, (Frances Murray), b. 10 Feb 1928, Glasgow, Scotland. History Teacher; Author. m. Robert Edward Booth, 28 Aug 1950, 3 daughters. Education: University of Glasgow, 1945-47; MA, 1965, Ed Diploma, 1966, University of St Andrews; Teacher's Certificate, Dundee College of Education, 1966. Appointments: History Teacher; Author. Publications: Ponies on the Heather, 1966, revised edition, 1973; The Dear Colleague, 1972; The Burning Lamp, 1973; The Heroine's Sister, 1975; Ponies and Parachutes, 1975; Red Rowan Berry, 1976; Castaway, 1978; White Hope, 1978; Payment for the Piper, 1983, US edition as Brave Kingdom; The Belchamber Scandal, 1985; Shadow Over the Islands, 1986. Address: c/o David Higham Associates, 5-8 Lower John Street, London W1R 4HA, England.

BORBON Carlos Estuardo de. See: **MCCLAIN Michael H.**

BORCH-JACOBSEN Mikkel, b. 30 Sept 1951, Strasbourg, France. Professor of Comparative Literature. m. Charlotte Laufbaum, 16 Nov 1984, 2 daughters. Education: PhD, Philosophy, University of Strasbourg, France, 1981. Appointments: Professor of French, 1986-, and Comparative Literature, 1993-, University of Washington, USA. Publications: The Freudian Subject, 1988, original French edition, 1982; Hypnoses, 1984; Psychanalyse et Hypnose, 1987; Lacan, The Absolute Master, 1991, French edition, 1990; The Emotional Tie Psychoanalysis, Mimesis and Affect, 1993, original French edition, 1991; Remembering Anna O. A Century of Mystification, 1996, French edition, 1995. Contributions to: Representations; October; Critical Inquiry; Critique; New York Review of Books; Le Monde; La Quinzaine Littéraire. Honours: Prix de la Psyché, 1987; Gradiva Award, 1997. Address: Department of Comparative Literature, University of Washington, Seattle, WA 98195, USA.

BØRDAHL Vibeke, (Yi Debo), b. 1 Mar 1945, Taastrup, Denmark. Research Fellow. m. Per Børdahl, 15 July 1967, 3 sons. Education: Mag Art, University of Copenhagen, 1972; PhD, University of Copenhagen, 1991; Dr Phil, University of Copenhagen, 1996. Appointments: Associate Professor, University of Aarhus, Denmark, 1972; Associate Professor, University of Oslo, 1979; Research Fellow, University of Copenhagen, 1992; Research Fellow, University of Oslo, 1994. Publications include: Strateger i Kinas litteratur (Strategists in Chinese Literature), 1978; Kapitler af et flygtigt liv (translator) Shen Fu= Fu sheng liu ji (Chapters of a Floating Life), 1986; Tigerdroeberen Wu Song og andre fortoellinger fra De Store Kinesiske Roamner (The Tiger-killer Wu Song and Other Stories From The Great Chinese Novels), 1989. Contibutions to: A Selective Guide to Chinese Literature 1900-1949, 1988-89; Along the Broad Road of Realism, Qin Zhaoyang's World of Fiction, 1990; The Oral Tradition of Yangzhou Storytelling, 1996; The Eternal Storyteller, Oral Literature in Modern China, 1998. Address: Ramstadasveien 19, 1322 Hovik, Norway.

BORDEN Louise Walker, b. 30 Oct 1949, Cincinnati, Ohio, USA. Writer. m. Peter A Borden, 4 Sept 1971, 1 son, 2 daughters. Education: BA, Denison University, 1971. Publications: Caps, Hats, Socks and Mittens, 1989; The Neighborhood Trucker, 1990; The Watching Game, 1991; Albie the Lifeguard, 1993; Just in Time for Christmas, 1994; Paperboy, 1996; The Little Ships, 1997; Thanksgiving Is..., 1997; Good-bye, Charles Lindbergh, 1998; Good Luck Mrs K!, 1999. Honour: The Silver Gertie Award, 1998; Parents' choice Award, 1997. Memberships: Society of Children's Book Writers; Authors Guild. Address: 628 Myrtle Avenue, Terrace Park, OH 45174, USA.

BORDEN William (Vickers), b. 27 Jan 1938, Indianapolis, Indiana, USA. Chester Fritz Distinguished Professor of English, Emeritus; Writer; Poet; Dramatist; Novelist; Editor. m. Nancy Lee Johnson, 17 Dec 1960, 1 son, 2 daughters. Education: AB, Columbia University, 1960; MA, University of California at Berkeley, 1962. Appointments: Instructor, 1962-64, Assistant Professor, 1966-70, Associate Professor, 1970-82, Professor of English, 1982-, University of North Dakota; Fiction Editor, North Dakota Quarterly. Publications: Fiction: Superstoe (novel), 1967, new edition, 1996; Many short stories. Poetry: Slow Step and Dance (chapbook), 1991; Eurydice's song, 1999. Other: Numerous plays, including the full-length plays: The Last Prostitute, 1980; Tap Dancing Across the Universe, 1981; Loon Dance, 1982; The Only Woman Awake is the Woman Who Has Heard the Flute, 1983; Makin' It, 1984; The Consolation of Philosophy, 1986; When the Meadowlark Sings, 1988; Meet Again, 1990; Turtle Island Blues, 1991; Don't Dance Me Outside, 1993. Musical Drama: Sakakawea, 1987. Also Screenplays, radio plays, and video scripts. Contributions to: Many anthologies and periodicals. Honours: North Dakota Centennial Drama Prize, 1989; American Society of Composers, Authors and Pyblishers Awards, 1990, 1991, 1992; Burlington Northern Award, University of North Dakota, 1990; Minnesota Distinguished Artist Award, 1992; Minnesota State Arts Board Career Opportunity Grant, 1996. Memberships: American Society of Composers, Authors and Publishers; Associated Writing Programs; Authors League of America; Dramatists Guild; PEN. Address: Route 6, Box 284, Bemidji, MN 56601, USA.

BORENSTEIN Audrey F, b. 7 Oct 1930, Chicago, Illinois, USA. Freelance Writer. m. Walter Borenstein, 5 Sept 1953, 1 son, 1 daughter. Education: AB, 1953, MA, 1954 University of Illinois; PhD, Louisiana State University, 1958. Appointments: Instructor, Assistant Professor, Louisiana State University, 1958-60; Adjunct Professor, Cornell College, Mount Vernon, Iowa, 1965-69; Adjunct Professor, SUNY College at New Paltz, New York, 1970-86. Publications: Custom, 1961; Redeeming the Sin: Social Science and Literature, 1978; Older Women in 20th Century America, 1982; Chimes of Change and Hours, 1983; Through the Years: A Chronicle of Congregation Ahavath Achim, 1989; Simurgh: A Novel-in-the-Pound, 1991. Contributions to: Journals, magazines and anthologies. Honours: NEA Fellowship, 1976; Rockefeller Humanities Fellowship, 1978. Membership: Poets and Writers. Address: Four Henry Court, New Paltz, NY 12561, USA.

BORIS Martin, b. 7 Aug 1930, New York, New York, USA. Writer. m. Gloria Shanf, 13 June 1952, 1 son, 2 daughters. Education: BA, New York University, University Heights, 1951; MA, New York University, Washington Square, 1953; BA, Lond Island University, Brooklyn College of Pharmacy, 1957. Publications: Two and Two, 1979; Woodridge 1946, 1980; Brief Candle, 1990. Literary Agent: Arthur Pine Literary Agency. Address: 1019 Northfield Road, Woodmere, NY 11598, USA.

BORN Anne, b. 9 July 1930, Cooden Beach, Sussex, England. Poet; Reviewer; Translator. m. Povl Born, 1 June 1950, 3 sons, 1 daughter. Education: MA, Copenhagen, 1955; MLitt, Oxford, 1976. Appointments: Writer-in-Residence: Barnstaple, 1983-85; Kingsbridge, 1985-87; Buckinghamshire, January-February, 1996. Publications: 10 Collections of Poetry; 4 History books; 35 translated books. Contributions to: Poems in: Times Literary Supplement; Ambit; Rialto; Green Book; Scratch; Cimarron Review; many published articles and reviews. Honours: Over 20 prizes and commendations. Memberships: Society of Authors; Translators Association, Chair, 1987, 1993-95. Address: Oversteps, Froude Road, Salcombe, South Devon TQ8 8LH, England.

BOROWS Lu. See: **KEBL Anna-Luise.**

BORSON Roo, b. 20 Jan 1952, Berkeley, California, USA. Poet; Writer. Education: BA, Goddard College, Vermont, 1973; MFA, University of British Columbia, 1977. Appointments: Teacher, many writing workshops; Writer-in-Residence, University of Western Ontario, 1987-88, Concordia University, 1993. Publications: Landfall, 1977; In the Smoky Light of the Fields, 1980; Rain, 1980; A Sad Device, 1981; The Whole Night, Coming Home, 1984; The Transparence of November/Snow (with Kim Maltman), 1985; Intent, or the Weight of the World, 1989; Night Walk: Selected Poems, 1994; Water Memory, 1996. Contributions to: Many anthologies and journals. Honours: Various grants; MacMillan Prize for Poetry, 1977; 1st Prize, 1982, 3rd Prize, 1989, for Poetry, and 3rd Prize for Personal Essay, 1990, CBC Literary Competition; Governor-General's Award Nominations for Poetry, 1984, 1994. Memberships: International PEN; League of Canadian Poets; Pain Not Bread (writer's group); Writer's Union of Canada. Address: c/o Writer's Union of Canada, 24 Ryerson Avenue, Toronto, Ontario M5T 2P3, Canada.

BOSLEY Keith Anthony, b. 16 Sept 1937, Bourne End, Buckinghamshire, England. Poet; Translator. m. Satu Salo, 27 Aug 1982, 3 sons. Education: Universities of Reading, Paris, and Caen, 1956-60; BA, Honours, French. Appointments: Staff, BBC, 1961-93; Visiting Lecturer, BBC and British Council, Middle East, 1981. Publications: The Possibility of Angels, 1969; And I

Dance, 1972; Dark Summer, 1976; Mallarmé: The Poems (translator), 1977; Eino Leino: Whitsongs (translator), 1978; Stations, 1979; The Elek Book of Oriental Verse, 1979; From the Theorems of Master Jean de la Ceppède (translator), 1983; A Chiltern Hundred, 1987; The Kalevala (translator), 1989; I Will Sing of What I Know (translator), 1990; Luis de Camoes: Epic and Lyric (translator), 1990; The Kanteletar (translator), 1992; The Great Bear (translator), 1993; Aleksis Kivi: Odes (translator), 1994; André Frénaud: Rome the Sorceress (translator), 1996; Eve Blossom has Wheels: German Love Poetry, 1997; Skating on the Sea: Poetry from Finland, 1997. Contributions to: Many newspapers, reviews, magazines and journals. Honours: Finnish State Prize for Translators, 1978; 1st Prize, British Comparative Literature Association Translation Competition, 1980; 1st Prize, Goethe Society Translation Competition, 1982; Knight, 1st Class, Order of the White Rose of Finland, 1991. Membership: Finnish Literature Society, Helsinki, corresponding member. Address: 108 Upton Road, Upton-cum-Chalvey, Slough SL1 2AW, England.

BOSQUET Alain, (Anatole Bisk), b. 28 Mar 1919, Odessa, Russia. Poet; Writer; Critic. m. Norma E Caplan, 9 Jan 1954. Education: Free University of Brussels, 1938-40; Belgian and French Armies, 1940; University of Montpellier, 1940; US Army, 1942-45; MA, Sorbonne, University of Paris, 1951. Appointments: Literary Critic, Combat, 1953-74; Professor of French Literature, Brandeis University, 1958-59; Professor of American Literature, University of Lyons, 1959-60. Publications: Poetry: A la mémoire de ma planète, 1948; Langue morte, 1951; Quel royaume oublié, 1955; Premier Testament, 1957; Deuxième Testament, 1959; Maitre objet, 1962; 100 notes pour une solitude, 1970; Notes pour un Amour, 1972; Notes pour un pluriel, 1974; Le livre du doute et de la grace, 1977; Sonnets pour une fin de siècle, 1981; Un jour apés la vie, 1984; Le tourment de Dieu, 1987; Borreaux et acrobates, 1990; Demain sans moi, 1994; Je ne suis pas un poète d'eau douce (collected poems, 1945-94), 1996. Novels: La grande éclipse, 1952; Le mécréant, 1960; Un besoin de malheur, 1963; La confession mexicaine, 1965; Les tigres de papier, 1968; Chicago oignon sauvage, 1971; Monsieur Vaudeville, 1973; Les bonnes intentions, 1975; Une mère russe, 1978; Jean-Louis Trabart, Médecin, 1981; L'enfant que tu étais, 1982; Ni guerre ni paix, 1983; Les fêtes cruelles, 1984; Lettre a mon pére qui aurait eu cent ans, 1987; Claudette comme tout le monde, 1991; Les solitudes, 1992; Georges et Arnold, Arnold et Georges, 1995; Portrait d'un milliardaire malheureux, 1997; Un parc, une femme, quelques mensonges, 1997.Stories: Un homme pour un autre, 1985; Comme un refus de la planete, 1989; Le métier d'otage, 1989. Non-Fiction: Saint-John Perse, Emily Dickinson, Walt Whitman: Anthologie de la poésie américaine, 1956; 35 jeunes poétes américaines, 1961; Verbe et vertige, 1961; La mémoire ou l'oubli, 1990; Le gardien des rosées, 1991; Marlene Dietrich: Un amour par téléphone, 1992; La Fable et le Fouet, 1995; Les fruits de l'an dernier, 1996. Contributions to: Periodicals. Honours: Prix Guillaume Apollinaire, 1952; Prix Sainte-Beuve, 1957; Prix Max Jacob, 1959; Prix Fémina-Vacaresco, 1962; Prix interallié, 1965; Grand Prix de Poésie, 1967; Grand Prix du Roman of l'Académie Francaise, 1978; Prix Marcel Proust, 1982; Prix Chateaubriand, 1987; Grand Prix de la langue, 1992; Officer of the Order of the Crown of Belgium, 1993; Officier Légion d'Honneur, 1995; Grand Prix de Poésie, Société des gens de lettres, 1996. Memberships: Académie des lettres du Québec, honorary member; Académie Mallarmé, honorary president; Académie Royale de langue et de litterature francaises, Belgium; European Academy of Poetry, founding president. Address: 32 rue de Laborde, 75008 Paris, France.

BOTT George, b. 21 Sept 1920, Ashbourne, England. Retired Educator; Writer. m. Elizabeth Belshaw, 5 Feb 1944, 2 sons. Education: BA, 1942, Diploma in Education, 1947, Leeds University. Appointments: Senior English Master and Librarian, Cockermouth Grammar School, 1949-79; Editor, Scholastic Publications, 1960-68. Publications: George Orwell: Selected Writings (editor), 1958; Read and Relate (editor), 1960; Shakespeare: Man and Boy (editor), 1961; Sponsored Talk, 1971; Read and Respond, 1984; Read, Relate, Communicate, 1984; The Mary Hewetson Cottage Hospital, Keswick: Brief History, 1892-1992, 1992; Keswick: The Story of a Lake District Town, 1994; Call-out: The First Fifty Years, Keswick Mountain Rescue Team, 1997. Address: 16 Penrith Road, Keswick, Cumbria CA12 4HF, England.

BOTTING Douglas (Scott), b. 22 Feb 1934, London, England. Author. m. 27 Aug 1964, 2 daughters. Education: MA, St Edmund Hall, Oxford, 1958. Publications: Island of the Dragon's Blood, 1958; The Knights of Bornu, 1961; One Chilly Siberian Morning, 1965; Wilderness Europe, 1976; Humboldt and the Cosmos, 1973; Rio de Janeiro, 1977; The Pirates, 1978; The Second Front, 1978; The U-Boats, 1979; The Giant Airships, 1980; The Aftermath in Europe, 1945, 1983; Nazi Gold, 1984; In the Ruins of the Reich, 1985; Wild Britain, 1988; Hitler's Last General: The Case Against Wilhelm Mohnke, 1989; America's Secret Army, 1989; Gavin Maxwell: A Life, 1993; Sex Appeal: The Art and Science of Sexual Attraction (with Kate Botting), 1995; Nazi Gold (revised edition), 1998; Gerald Durrell: The Authorised Biography, 1999. Contributions to: BBC TV and Radio; Various periodicals. Memberships: Royal Geographical Society; Royal Institute of International Affairs; Society of Authors; NCICA. Literary Agent: John Johnson Ltd, London. Address: 2 Dinton House, 1 Dinton Road, Kingston upon Thames, Surrey, KT2 5JT, England.

BOUCHER David (Ewart George), b. 15 Oct 1951, Ebbw Vale, Monmouthshire, Wales. Professor of Political Theory and Government; Writer; Editor. m. Clare Mary ffrench Mullen, 8 Sept 1979, 2 daughters. Education: University College, Swansea, 1973-76; BA, London School of Economics and Political Science, 1976; MSc, 1977, PhD, 1983, University of Liverpool. Appointments: Tutorial Fellow, 1980-83; Temporary Lecturer in Politics, 1983-84, University College, Cardiff; Lecturer, 1985-88, Senior Lecturer in Politics, 1988-89, La Trobe University, Melbourne, Australia; Research Fellow, 1989-90, Lecturer, 1990, Senior Lecturer in Politics, 1991, Australian National University, Canberra; Reader, 1995-98, Professor of Political Theory and Government, 1998-, University of Wales, Swansea. Publications: Texts in Context: Revisionist Methods for Studying the History of Ideas, 1985; The Social and Political Thought of R G Collingwood, 1989; A Radical Hegelian: The Political Thought of Henry Jones (with Andrew Vincent), 1994; Political Theories of International Relations: From Thucydides to the Present, 1998. Editor: Essays in Political Philosophy, by R G Collingwood, 1989; The New Leviathan, revised edition, by R G Collingwood, 1992; The Social Contract from Hobbes to Rawls (with Paul Kelly), 1994; Philosophy, Politics and Civilizatioin (with T Modood and J Connelly), 1995; The British Idealists, 1997; Social Justice: From Hume to Walzer (with Paul Kelly), 1998. Contributions to: Scholarly journals. Honour: Royal Historical Society, fellow, 1992. Memberships: Professional organisations. Address: c/o Department of Political Theory and Government, University of Wales, Singleton Park, Swansea SA2 8PP, Wales.

BOULTON David, b. 3 Oct 1935, Richmond, Surrey, England. Author; Television Producer. m. Anthea Ingham, 14 Feb 1969, 2 daughters. Education: Hampton Grammar School, 1947-52. Publications: Jazz in Britain, 1958; Objection Overruled, 1968; The UVF: Protestant Paramilitary Organizations in Ireland, 1973; The Making of Tania Hearst, 1975; The Lockheed Papers (in USA, The Greae Machine), 1980; Early Friends in Dent, 1986. Contributions to: Tribune; New Statesman; The Listener; Guardian. Honour: Cyril Bennet Awards, Royal Television Society, 1981. Address: Hobsons Farm, Dent, Cumbria LA10 5RF, England.

BOULTON James Thompson, b. 17 Feb 1924, Pickering, Yorkshire, England. Emeritus Professor of English Studies. m. Margaret Helen Leary, 6 Aug 1949, 1 son, 1 daughter. Education: BA, University College, University of Durham, 1948; BLitt, Lincoln College, University of Oxford, 1952; PhD, University of Nottingham, 1960. Appointments: Lecturer, Senior Lecturer, Reader in English Literature, 1951-63, Professor, 1964-75, Dean of Faculty of Arts, 1970-73, University of Nottingham; Professor of English Studies and Head of Department, 1975-88, Dean of Faculty of Arts, 1981-84, Public Orator, 1984-88, Emeritus Professor, 1989-, University of Birmingham. Publications: Edmund Burke: Sublime and Beautiful (editor), 1958, 3rd edition, 1987; The Language of Politics in the Age of Wilkes and Burke, 1963; Samuel Johnson: The Critical Heritage, 1971; Defoe: Memoirs of a Cavalier (editor), 1972; The Letters of D H Lawrence (editor), 7 volumes, 1979-93; Selected letters of D H Lawrence (editor), 1997. Honours: Hon DLitt, Durham University, 1991, Nottingham University, 1993; Fellow, British Academy, 1994. Address: Institute for Advanced Research in the Arts and Social Sciences, University of Birmingham, Edgbaston, Birmingham B15 2TT, England.

BOUMELHA Penelope (Ann), (Penny Boumelha), b. 10 May 1950, London, England. University Professor. 1 daughter. *Education:* BA, 1972, MA, 1981, DPhil, 1981. Appointments: Researcher, Compiler, Mansell Publishing, 1981-84; Lecturer, University of Western Australia, 1985-90; Jury Professor, 1990-, Head, Division of Humanities and Social Sciences, 1996, University of Adelaide. Publications: Thomas Hardy and Women: Sexual Ideology and Narrative Form; Charlotte Brontë; Index of English Literary Manuscripts, Vol 3. Contributions to: Women Reading Women's Writing; Grafts: Feminist Cultural Criticism; Feminist Criticism: Theory & Practice; The Sense of Sex: Feminist Perspectives on Hardy; Realism, 1992; Constructing Gender, 1994; Southern Review; Times Literary Supplement English; Australian Victorian Studies Association Conference Papers; Review of English Studies; English Australian Feminist Studies; London Review of Books; English Literature in Transition. Honour: Fellow of the Academy of the Humanities of Australia, 1997. Address: Faculty of Arts, University of Adelaide, South Australia 5005, Australia.

BOUMIL Marcia Anne Mobilia, b. 7 Apr 1958, Boston, Massachusetts, USA. Attorney; Professor. m. S James Boumil Jr, 10 Aug 1986, 2 sons. Education: BS cum laude, 1979, MS, Public Health, 1982, Tufts University; JD, University of Connecticut School of Law, 1983; LLM, Health Law and Policy, Columbia University School of Law, 1984; MA, Clinical Psychology, Boston College, 1992. Appointments: Associate, Herrick & Smith, 1984-85; Associate, Parker, Coulter, Daley & White, Massachusetts, 1985-88; Associate Clinical Professor of Family Medicine and Community Health, Tufts University School of Medicine, 1986-; Visiting Assistant Professor of Law, Boston College Law School, 1987-89; Instructor, Psychology, Graduate School of Arts and Sciences, Boston College, 1992-96; Adjunct Professor, Graduate Program in Health Care Administration, Simmons College, 1993-; Guardian Ad Litem and Independent Court Investigator, Commonwealth of Massachusetts, 1993-; Senior Mediator, Commonwealth Mediation and Conciliation Inc, 1995-; Adjunct Professor of Psychology, University of Massachusetts at Lowell, 1996-. Publications: Medical Liability: Cases and Materials, (co-author), 1990; Medical Liability: Teachers Manual (co-author), 1990; Women and the Law (co-author), 1992; Sexual Harassment (co-author), 1992; Date Rape: The Silent Epidemic (co-author), 1993; Law and Gender Bias (co-author), 1994; Law, Ethics and Reproductive Choice, 1994; Medical Liability in a Nutshell (co-author), 1995; Betrayal of Trust: Sex and Power in Professional Relationships (co-author), 1995; Dead-Beat Dads: A National Child Support Scandal (co-author), 1996. Contributions to: Articles in professional journals, chapters in textbooks. Memberships: Admitted, Supreme Judicial Court of Massachusetts, 1983, States District Court for the District of Massachusetts, 1985, United States Court of Appeals, First Circuit, 1987; Massachusetts Bar Association; Massachusetts Association of Guardians Ad Litem; Juvenile Bar Association. Address: 243 River Road, Andover, MA 01810, USA.

BOUNDY Donna, b. 4 Dec 1949, Framingham, Connecticut, USA. Journalist; Author. Education: BA, University of Connecticut, 1971; MSW, Hunter College, City University of New York, 1981. Publications: Straight Talk About Cocaine and Crack, 1988; Willpower's Not Enough, 1989; When Money is the Drug, 1993. Other: Many video scripts. Contributions to: Periodicals. Address: PO Box 1208, Woodstock, NY 12498, USA.

BOURJAILY Vance (Nye), b. 17 Sept 1922, Cleveland, Ohio, USA. Author; Professor. m. (1) Bettina Yensen, 1946, 2 children, (2) Yasmin Mobul, 1985, 1 child. Education: AB, Bowdoin College, 1947. Appointments: Co-Founder, Editor, Discovery, 1951-53; Faculty, University of Iowa Writers Workshops, 1958-80; Distinguished Visiting Professor, Oregon State University, 1968; Visiting Professor, University of Arizona, 1977-78; Boyd Professor, Louisiana State University, 1985-. Publications: The End of My Life, 1947; The Hound of the Earth, 1953; The Violated, 1958; Confessions of a Spent Youth, 1960; The Unnatural Enemy, 1963; The Man Who Knew Kennedy, 1967; Brill Among the Ruins, 1970; Country Matters, 1973; Now Playing at Canterbury, 1976; A Game Men Play, 1980; The Great Fake Book, 1987; Old Soldier, 1990; Fishing By Mail: The Outdoor Life of a Father and Son, 1993. Honour: American Academy of Arts and Letters Award, 1993. Address: c/o Department of English, Louisiana State University, Baton Rouge, LA 70803, USA.

BOURNE (Rowland) Richard. Journalist; Author. m. Juliet Mary Attenborough, 1966, 2 sons, 1 daughter. Education: BA, Brasenose College, Oxford. Appointments: Journalist, The Guardian, 1962-72; Assistant Editor, New Society, 1972-77; Deputy Editor, 1977-78, London Columnist, 1978-79, Evening Standard; Founder, Editor, Learn Magazine, 1979; Consultant, International Broadcasting Trust, 1980-81; Advisor, Council for Adult and Continuing Education, 1982; Deputy Director, Commonwealth Institute, 1983-89; Director, Commonwealth Human Rights Institute, 1990-92, Commonwealth Non-Governmental Office for South Africa and Mozanbique, 1995-. Publications: Political Leaders of Latin America, 1969; The Struggle for Education (with Brian MacArthur), 1970; Getulio Vargas of Brazil, 1974; Assault on the Amazon, 1978; Londoners, 1981; Self-Sufficiency, 16-25 (with Jessica Gould), 1983; Lords of Fleet Street, 1990; News on a Knife-Edge, 1995. Literary Agent: Curtis Brown. Address: 36 Burney Street, London SE10 8EX, England.

BOURNE-JONES Derek, b. 4 Sept 1928, St Leonards-on-Sea, Sussex, England. Poet; Writer; Linguist. m. Hilary Clare Marsh, 2 Aug 1975. Education: BA, Honours, Modern Languages, 1954, MA, 1958, Oxon. Appointment: Director of Studies, B J Tutorials. Publications: Senlac, 1978; Floating Reefs, 1981; The Singing Days, 1986; Merrilly to Meet, 1988; Behold the Man, 1990; Brief Candle, 1991. Contributions to: Various journals. Memberships: Downland Poets Society of Sussex, founder-member, 1975-90; Oxford Society. Address: 88 Oxendean Gardens, Lower Willingdon, East Sussex BN22 0RS, England.

BOURQUIN Irène Hélène Marthe, b. 28 Aug 1950, Zürich, Switzerland. Editor; Writer. 1 son. Education: Matura Typus A, 1969; Dr Phil, University of Zürich, 1976. Publications: Atlasblau, 1991; Im Auge des Taifuns, 1992; Das Meer im Dachstock, 1995; Insektenbrevier, 1995; Literaquarium, 1996. Contributions to: Neue Zürcher Zeitung; Entwürfe. Membership: Literarische Vereinigung, Winterhur. Address: Am Bach 25, 8352 Räterschen, Switzerland.

BOURRET Annie, b. 22 Jan 1961, Val-d'Or, Québec, Canada. Linguist; Freelance Writer and Copy Editor. Education: BA, French Studies and Linguistics, 1986, MA, French Linguistics, 1989, Laval University. Publications: Regards sur la guerre et la paix (with E Poole), 1989; Guerre, paix et désarmement (with E Poole), 1989; Pour l'amour du français, 1999. Contributions to: Journals and magazines. Membership: Association des auteures et des auteurs franco-ontariens. Address: 7205 Hewitt Street, Burnaby, British Columbia V5A 3M1, Canada.

BOUVERIE William. See: **CARPENTER Humphrey.**

BOVA Ben(jamin William), b. 8 Nov 1932, Philadelphia, Pennsylvania, USA. Author; Editor; Lecturer. Education: BA, Temple University, 1954; MA, State University of New York at Albany, 1987. Appointments: Editorial Director, Omni Magazine; Editor, Analog Magazine; Lecturer. Publications: Gremlins, Go Home!, 1974; Notes to a Science Fiction Writer, 1975; Science: Who Needs It?, 1975; Viewpoint, 1977; The Exiles Trilogy, 1980; Vision of Tomorrow, 1982; The Astral Mirror, 1985; Voyager Two: The Alien Within, 1986; As on a Darkling Plain, 1991; Empire Builders, 1993; Orion and the Conqueror, 1994; Orion Among the Stars, 1995; Moonwar, 1998. Contributions to: Numerous books and periodicals. Honours: Distinguished Alumnus, 1981, Alumni Fellow, 1982, Temple University. Memberships: British Interplanetary Society, fellow; National Space Society, president emeritus; PEN; Science Fiction Writers of America. Address: 32 Gramercy Park South, New York, NY 10003, USA.

BOWDEN Jim. See: **SPENCE William (John Duncan).**

BOWDEN Roland Heywood, b. 19 Dec 1916, Lincoln, England. Retired Teacher; Poet; Dramatist. m. 2 Jan 1946, 1 son, 1 daughter. Education: School of Architecture, Liverpool University, 1934-39. Publications: Poems From Italy, 1970; Every Season is Another, 1986. Plays: Death of Paolini, 1980; After Neruda, 1984; The Fence, 1985. Contributions to: Arts Review: London Magazine; Panurge; Words International. Honours: Arts Council Drama Bursary, 1978; Cheltenham Festival Poetry Prize, 1982; 1st Prize, All-Sussex Poets, 1983. Membership: National Poetry Secretariat. Address: 2 Roughmere Cottage, Lavant, Chichester, West Sussex PO18 0BG, England.

BOWEN John Griffith, b. 5 Nov 1924, Calcutta, India. Writer; Dramatist. Education: MA, Oxford University. Publications: The Truth Will Not Help Us; After the Rain; The Centre of the Green; Storyboard; The Birdcage; A World Elsewhere; Squeak; The McGuffin; The Girls; Fighting Back; The Precious Gift; No Retreat. Plays: I Love You Mrs Patterson; After the Rain; Little Boxes; The Disorderly Women; The Corsican Brothers; Hail Caesar; The Waiting Room; Singles; The Inconstant Couple; Which Way Are You Facing?; The Geordie Gentlemen; The Oak Tree Tea-Room Siege; Uncle Jeremy. Contributions to: London Magazine; Times Literary Supplement; Spectator; Gambit; Oldie Journal of Royal Asiatic Society; Times Educational Supplement; Listener. Honour: Tokyo Prize, 1974. Memberships: PEN; Society of Authors; Writers Guild of Great Britain, executive committee; Address: Old Lodge Farm, Sugarswell Lane, Edgehill, Banbury, Oxon OX15 6HP, England.

BOWEN Lynne, b. 22 Aug 1940, Indian Head, Saskatchewan, Canada. Author. Education: BSc, University of Alberta, 1963; MA, University of Victoria, 1980. Appointment: Maclean Hunter Co-Chair of Creative Non-Fiction Writing, University of British Columbia, 1992-. Publications: Boss Whistle: The Coal Miners of Vancouver Island Remember, 1982; Three Dollar Dreams, 1987; Muddling Through: The Remarkable Story of the Barr Colonists, 1992; Those Lake People: Stories of Cowichan Lake, 1995. Honours: Canadian Historical Association Regional Certificates of Merit, 1984, 1993; Lieutenant Governor's Medal, 1987; Hubert Evans Non-Fiction Prize, 1993. Memberships: Writers' Union of Canada; PEN International. Address: 4982 Fillinger Crescent, Nanaimo, British Columbia V9V 1J1, Canada.

BOWERING George (Harry), b. 1 Dec 1936, Penticton, British Columbia, Canada. Author; Poet; Dramatist; University Teacher. m. Angela Luoma, 14 Dec 1963, 1 daughter. Education: Victoria College; MA, University of British Columbia, 1963; University of Western Ontario. Appointments: Teacher, University of Calgary, 1963-66, Simon Fraser University, 1972-; Writer-in-Residence, 1967-68, Teacher, 1968-71, Sir George Williams University. Publications: Novels: Mirror on the Floor, 1967; A Short Sad Book, 1977; Burning Water, 1980; En eaux troubles, 1982; Caprice, 1987; Harry's Fragments, 1990; Shoot!, 1994; Parents From Space, 1994; Piccolo Mondo, 1998. Stories: Flycatcher & Other Stories, 1974; Concentric Circles, 1977; Protective Footwear, 1978; A Place to Die, 1983; The Rain Barrel, 1994; Diamond back Dog, 1998. Poetry Collections: Sticks & Stones, 1963; Points on the Grid, 1964; The Man in Yellow Boots/El hombre de las botas amarillas, 1965; The Silver Wire, 1966; Rocky Mountain Foot, 1969; The Gangs of Kosmos, 1969; Touch: Selected Poems 1960-1969, 1971; In the Flesh, 1974; The Catch, 1976; Poem & Other Baseballs, 1976; The Concrete Island, 1977; Another Mouth, 1979; Particular Accidents: Selected Poems, 1981; West Window: Selected Poetry, 1982; Smoking Poetry, 1982; Smoking Mirrow, 1982; Seventy-One Poems for People, 1985; Delayed Mercy & Other Poems, 1986; Urban Snow, 1992; George Bowering Selected: Poems 1961-1992, 1993; Blonds on Bikes, 1997. Non-Fiction: Al Purdy, 1970; Three Vancouver Writers, 1979; A Way with Words, 1982; The Mask in Place, 1983; Craft Slices, 1985; Errata, 1988; Imaginary Hand, 1988; The Moustache: Remembering Greg Curnoe, 1993; Bowering's B.C., 1996. Other: Chapbooks, plays, and editions of works by other authors. Honours: Governor-General's Award for Poetry, 1969, and for Fiction, 1980; bp Nichol Chapbook Awards for Poetry, 1991, 1992; Canadian Authors' Association Award for Poetry, 1993; Honorary DLitt, University of British Columbia, 1994. Address: 2499 West 37th Avenue, Vancouver, British Columbia V6M 1P4, Canada.

BOWERING Marilyn (Ruthe), b. 13 Apr 1949, Winnipeg, Ontario, Canada. Poet; Writer. m. Michael S Elcock, 3 Sept 1982, 1 daughter. Education: University of British Columbia, 1968-69; BA, 1971, MA, 1973, University of Victoria; University of New Brunswick, 1975-78. Appointments: Writer-in-Residence, Aegean School of Fine Arts, Paris, 1973-74; Visiting Lecturer, 1978-82, Lecturer in Creative Writing, 1982-86, 1989, Visiting Associate Professor of Creative Writing, 1993-96, University of Victoria, British Columbia; Faculty, 1992, Writer-in-Residence, 1993-94, Banff Centre, Alberta; Writer in Residence, Memorial University of Newfoundland, 1995. Publications: Poetry: The Liberation of Newfoundland, 1973; One Who Became Lost, 1976; The Killing Room, 1977; Third/Child Zian, 1978; The Book of Glass, 1978; Sleeping with Lambs, 1980; Giving Back Diamonds, 1982; The Sunday Before Winter, 1984; Anyone Can See I Love You, 1987; Grandfather was a Soldier, 1987; Calling All the World, 1989; Love As It Is, 1993. Autobiography, 1996. Novels: The Visitors Have All Returned, 1979; To All Appearances a Lady, 1990. Editor: Many Voices: An Anthology of Contemporary Canadian Indian Poetry (with David A Day), 1977; Guide to the Labor Code of British Columbia, 1980. Contributions to: Anthologies and journals. Honours: Many Canada Council Awards for Poetry; Du Maurier Award for Poetry, 1978; National Magazine Award for Poetry, 1989; Long Poem prize, Malahat Review, 1994. Memberships: League of Canadian Poets; Writers Union of Canada. Address: 3777 Jennifer Road, Victoria, British Columbia V8P 3X1, Canada.

BOWERS Edgar, b. 2 Mar 1924, Rome, Georgia, USA. Poet; Professor of English Emeritus. Education: Erskine College, 1941-42; Princeton University, 1943-44; BA, University of North Carolina, 1947; PhD, Stanford University, 1953. Appointments: Instructor in English, Duke University, 1952-55; Assistant Professor of English, Harpur College, State University of New York at Endicott, 1955-58; Assistant Professor, 1958-61, Associate Professor, 1961-67, Professor of English, 1967-91, Professor Emeritus, 1991-, University of California at Santa Barbara. Publications: The Form of Loss, 1956; The Astronomers, 1965; Living Together, 1973; Witnesses, 1981; Chaco Canyon, 1987; Thirteen Views of Santa Barabra, 1989; For Louis Pasteur, 1990; How We Came from Paris to Blois, 1991. Contributions to: Anthologies and periodicals. Honours: Fulbright

Fellowship, 1950-51; Guggenheim Fellowships, 1959, 1969; University of California Creative Arts Award, 1963; Ingram Merrill Award, 1976; Brandeis University Creative Arts Award, 1978; Bollingen Prize, 1989; Harriet Monroe Prize, 1989; American Institute of Arts and Letters Award, 1991. Address: 1201 Greenwich Street, Apt 601, San Francisco, CA 94109, USA.

BOWKER John Westerdale, b. 30 July 1935, London, England. Professor; Writer. Education: BA, Oxford, 1958. Appointments: Fellow, Corpus Christi College, Cambridge, 1962-74; Lecturer, University of Cambridge, 1965-74; Professor of Religious Studies, University of Lancaster, 1974-85; Fellow, Dean, Trinity College, Cambridge, 1984-93; Honorary Cannon, Canterbury Cathedral, 1985-; Gresham Professor, Gresham College, London, 1992-97; Fellow, Gresham College, 1997-. Publications: The Targums and Rabbinic Literature, 1969; Problems of Suffering in Religions of the World, 1970; Jesus and the Pharisees, 1973; The Sense of God: Sociological, Anthropological and Psychological Approaches to the Origin of the Sense of God, 1973; Uncle Bolpenny Tries Things Out, 1973; The Religious Imagination and the Sense of God, 1978; Worlds of Faith, 1983; Violence and Aggression (editor), 1984; The Meanings of Death, 1991; A Year to Live, 1991; Hallowed Ground, 1993; Is God a Virus? Genes, Culture and Religion, 1995; The Oxford Dictionery of World Religions, 1997; World Religions, 1997; The Complete Bible Handbook, 1998. Honour: Harper Collins Biennial Prize, 1993. Address: 14 Bowers Croft, Cambridge CB1 4RP, England.

BOWLER Peter John, b. 8 Oct 1944, Leicester, England. Professor of History and Philosophy of Science; Author. m. Sheila Mary Holt, 24 Sept 1966, 1 son, 1 daughter. Education: BA, University of Cambridge, 1966; MSc, University of Sussex, 1967; PhD, University of Toronto, 1971. Appointments: Assistant Professor, University of Toronto, 1971-72; Lecturer, Science University of Malaysia, Penang, 1972-75; Assistant Professor, University of Winnipeg, 1975-79; Lecturer, 1979-87, Reader, 1987-92, Professor of History and Philosophy of Science, 1992-, Queen's University, Belfast. Publications: Fossils and Progress: Paleontology and the Idea of Progressive Evolution in the Nineteenth Century, 1976; The Eclipse of Darwinism: Anti-Darwinian Evolution Theories in the Decades Around 1900, 1983, new edition, 1992; Evolution: The History of an Idea, 1984, revised edition, 1989; Theories of Human Evolution: A Century of Debate, 1844-1944, 1986; The Non-Darwinian Revolution: Reinterpreting a Historical Myth, 1988; The Mendelian Revolution: The Emergence of Hereditarian Concepts in Modern Science and Society, 1989; The Invention of Progress: The Victorians and the Past, 1990; Darwin: L'origine delle specie, 1990; Charles Darwin: The Man and his Influence, 1990, new edition, 1996; The Fontana History of the Environmental Sciences, 1992, US edition as The Norton History of the Environmental Sciences, 1993; Biology and Social Thought, 1850-1914, 5 lectures, 1993; Darwinism, 1993; E Ray Lankester and the Making of Modern British Biology (editor and co-author with J Lester), 1995; Life's Splendid Drama: Evolutionary Biology and the Reconstruction of Life's Ancestry, 1860-1940, 1996. Contributions to: Journals. Memberships: British Society for the History of Science; History of Science Society. Address: c/o School of Anthropological Studies, Queen's University of Belfast, Belfast BT7 1NN, Northern Ireland.

BOWLES Paul (Frederic), b. 30 Dec 1910, New York, New York, USA. Author; Poet; Composer. m. Jane Sydney Auer, Feb 1938, dec 1973. Education: Studied music with Aaron Copland and Nadia Boulanger. Publications: Novels: The Sheltering Sky, 1949; Let It Come Down, 1952; The Spider's House, 1955; Up Above the World, 1966. Stories: A Little Stone, 1950; Collected Stories, 1979; A Delicate Episode, 1988; Unwelcome Words, 1989. Poetry: The Thicket of Spring, 1972; Next to Nothing, 1981. Other: Their Heads are Green and Their Hands are Blue, 1963; Without Stopping (autobiography), 1972; Points in Time, 1982; In Touch: The Letters of Paul Bowles, 1994; Paul Bowles: Music (essays, interviews, reviews), 1995. Honours: Guggenheim Fellowship, 1941; Rockefeller Grant, 1959. Address: c/o Ecco Press, 100 West Broad Street, Hopewell, NJ 08525, USA.

BOWLING Harry, b. 30 Sept 1931, Bermondsey, London, England. m. Shirley Burgess, 27 July 1957, 1 son, 2 daughters. Publications: Conner Street's War, 1988; Tuppence to Tooley Street, 1989; Ironmonger's Daughter, 1989; Paragon Place, 1990; Gaslight in Page Street, 1991; The Girl From Cotton Lane, 1992; Backstreet Girl, 1993. Literary Agent: Jennifer Kavanagh. Address: Headline Book Publishing plc, Headline House, 79 Great Tichfield Street, London W1P 7FN, England.

BOWLT John Ellis, b. 6 Dec 1943, London, England (US citizen). Professor; Writer. m. Nicoletta Misler, 25 Dec 1981. Education: BA,Russian, 1965, MA, Russian Literature, 1966, University of Birmingham; PhD, Russian Literature and Art, University of St Andrews, Scotland, 1971. Appointments: Lecturer, University of St Andrews, 1968-79, University of Birmingham, 1970; Assistant Professor, University of Kansas at Lawrence, 1970-71; Assistant to Associate Professor, 1971-81, Associate Professor to Professor, 1981-88, University of Texas, Austin; Visiting Professor, University of Otago, New Zealand, 1982, Hebrew University, Jerusalem, 1985; Professor, University of Southern California, Los Angeles, 1988-. Publications: Russian Formalism (editor with Stephen Bann), 1973; The Russian Avant-Garde: Theory and Criticism 1902-1934, 1976, revised edition, 1988; The Silver Age: Russian Art of the Early Twentieth Century, 1979; The Life of Vasilii Kandinsky in Russian Art (with Rose Carol Washton-Long), 1980; Pavel Filonov: A Hero and His Fate (with Nicoletta Misler), 1984; Mikalojus Konstantinas Ciurlionis: Music of the Spheres (with Alfred Senn and Danute Staskevicius), 1986; Russian Samizdat Art (co-author), 1986; Gustav Kluzis, 1988; Aus Vollem Halse: Russische Buchillustration und Typographie 1900-1930 (with B Hernad), 1993; Russian and East European Paintings in the Thyssen-Bornemisza Collection (with Nicoletta Misler), 1993; The Salon Album of Vera Sudeikin-Stravinsky, 1995. Contributions to: Books, scholarly journals, periodicals and exhibition catalogues. Honours: British Council Scholarship, 1966-68; Woodrow Wilson National Fellowship, 1971; National Humanities Institute Fellow, Yale University, 1977-78; Fulbright-Hays Award, Paris, 1981; American Council of Learned Societies Award, Italy, 1984; Senior Fellow, Wolfsonian Foundation, Miami, 1995. Memberships: American Association for the Advancement of Slavic Studies; College Art Association, New York. Address: c/o Department of Slavic Languages and Literatures, University of Southern California at Los Angeles, Los Angeles, CA 90089, USA.

BOX Edgar. See: **VIDAL Gore.**

BOYCOTT Geoffrey, b. 21 Oct 1940, Fitzwilliam, Yorkshire, England. Cricketer; Broadcaster; Writer. Appointments: First class Cricketer for Yorkshire, 1962-86; Test Cricketer for England, 1964-82; Scored 100th first class 100 vs Australia at Headingley, 1977; Commentator for BBC and Channel 9 Television. Publications: Geoff Boycott's Book for Young Cricketers, 1976; Put to the Test: England in Australia 1978-79, 1979; Geoff Boycott's Cricket Quiz, 1979; On Batting, 1980; Opening Up, 1980; In the Fast Lane, 1981; Master Class, 1982; Boycott, The Autobiography, 1987; Boycott on Cricket, 1990. Honour: Officer of the Order of the British Empire. Address: c/o Yorkshire County Cricket Club, Headingley Cricket Ground, Leeds, Yorkshire LS6 3BY, England.

BOYD Brian David, b. 30 July 1952, Belfast, Northern Ireland. University Teacher; Writer. m. (1) Janet Bower Eden, 1974, div 1980, (2) Bronwen Mary Nicholson, 1983, 3 stepdaughters. Education: BA, 1972, MA, Hons, 1974, University of Canterbury, Christchurch, New Zealand; PhD, University of Toronto, Canada, 1979; Postdoctoral Fellow, University of Auckland, 1979. Appointments: Lecturer, 1980-85, Senior Lecturer, 1985-92, Associate Professor, 1992-98, Professor 1998-, University of Auckland, New Zealand; Editorial Board, Nabokov Studies; Visiting Professor, University of Nice-Sophia Antipolis, 1994-95. Publications: Nabokov's Ada: The Place of Consciousness, 1985; Vladimir Nabokov: The Russian Years, 1990; Vladimir Nabokov: The American Years, 1991; Nabokov's Pale Fire: The Magic of Artistic Discovery, forthcoming. Editor: Nabokov: Novels and Memoirs 1941-1951, 1996; Nabokov: Novels 1955-1962, 1996; Nabokov: Novels 1969-1974, 1996; Presents of the Past: Literature in English Before 1900, 1998; Co-editor: Nabokov's Butterflies, forthcoming. Honours: Claude McCarthy Fellowship, 1982; Goodman Fielder Wattie Prize (Third), 1991; Goodman Fielder Wattie Prize (Second), 1992; James Cook Research Fellowship, 1997-99. Literary Agent: Georges Borchardt. Address: Department of English, University of Auckland, Private Bag 92019, Auckland, New Zealand.

BOYD (Charles) Malcolm, b. 24 May 1932, Newcastle upon Tyne, England. Lecturer in Music (Retired); Author. m. Beryl Gowen, 3 Apr 1956, 2 sons. Education: BA, 1953, MA, 1962, Durham University. Appointment: Lecturer, University College, Cardiff, retired, 1992. Publications: Harmonizing Bach Chorales, 1967; Bach's Instrumental Counterpoint, 1967; Palestrina Style, 1973; William Mathias, 1978; Grace Williams, 1980; Bach, 1983; Domenico Scarlatti: Master of Music, 1986; Bach: The Brandenburg Concertos, 1993. Contributions to: Dictionaries, encyclopaedias, periodicals. Honour: Yorkshire Post Literary Award for Music. Membership: Royal Musical Association. Address: 211 Fidlas Road, Llanishen, Cardiff CF4 5NA, Wales.

BOYD William, b. 7 Mar 1952, Ghana. Writer. Education: Jesus College, Oxford, 1975-80. Appointments: Lecturer in English Literature, St Hilda's College, Oxford, 1980-83; Television Critic, New Statesman, London, 1982-83. Publications: A Good Man in Africa (novel), 1981; On the Yankee Station (short stories), 1981; An Ice-Cream War (novel), 1982; Stars and Bars (novel), 1984; School Ties (screenplay), 1985; The New Confessions (novel), 1987; Brazzaville Beach, 1990; The Blue Afternoon (novel), 1993. Television Plays: Good and Bad at Games, 1985; Dutch Girls, 1985; Scoop, 1987. Honours: Whitbread Prize, 1981; Somerset Maugham Award, 1982; James Tait Black Memorial Prize, 1990; McVitie's Prize, 1991. Address: c/o Harvey Unna and Stephen Durbridge Ltd, 24 Pottery Lane, London W11 4LZ, England.

BOYLAN Clare Catherine, b. 21 Apr 1948, Dublin, Ireland. Novelist; Writer. m. Alan Wilkes, 18 Sept 1970. Appointments: Editor, Young Woman Magazine, 1968; Feature Writer, Evening Press, 1972; Editor, Image Magazine, 1980-83. Publications: Novels: Holy Pictures, 1983; Last Resorts, 1984; Black Baby, 1988; Home Rule, 1992; Room for a Single Lady, 1997. Short Story Collections: A Nail on the Head, 1983; Concerning Virgins, 1989; The Bad Woman, 1996; Another Family Christmas, 1997. Non Fiction: The Agony and the Ego. Literary Essay: The Literary Companion to Cats, 1994. Contributions to: New York Times; Sunday Times; Irish Times; Guardian; Independent; Telegraph. Honours: Journalist of the Year, 1974; Spirit of Life Arts Award, 1997. Memberships: Irish PEN; Aosdana. Literary Agent: Gill Coleridge. Address: c/o Rogers Coleridge and White, 20 Powis Mews, London W11 1JN, England.

BOYLE T(homas) Coraghessan, b. 2 Dec 1948, Peekskill, New York, USA. Professor of English; Author. m. Karen Kvashay, 25 May 1974, 2 sons, 1 daughter. Education: BA, State University of New York at Potsdam, 1968; MFA, 1974, PhD, 1977, University of Iowa. Appointments: Founder-Director, Creative Writing Program, 1978-86, Assistant Professor, 1978-82, Associate Professor, 1982-86, Professor, 1986-, of English, University of Southern California at Los Angeles. Publications: Descent of Man, 1979; Water Music, 1982; Budding Prospects, 1984; Greasy Lake, 1985; World's End, 1987; If the River Was Whiskey, 1989; East is East, 1990; The Road to Wellville, 1993; Without a Hero, 1994; The Tortilla Curtain, 1995; Riven Rock, 1998; T.C. Boyle

Stories, 1998. Contributions to: Numerous anthologies and periodicals. Honours: National Endowment for the Arts Grants, 1977, 1983; Guggenheim Fellowship, 1988; PEN/Faulkner Award, 1988; Commonwealth Club of California Gold Medal for Literature, 1988; O Henry Short Story Awards, 1988, 1989; Prix Passion Publishers' Prize, France, 1989; Editors' Choice, New York Times Book Review, 1989; Honorary Doctor of Humane Letters, State University of New York, 1991; Howard D Vursell Memorial Award, National Academy of Arts and Letters, 1993; Prix Médicis Étranger, France, 1997. Membership: National Endowment of the Arts Literature Panel, 1986-87. Literary Agent: Georges Borchandt, 136E 57th St. NY 10022. Address: c/o Department of English, University of Southern California, Los Angeles, CA 90089, USA.

BOZEMAN Adda B(ruemmer), b. 17 Dec 1908, Geistershof, Latvia. Retired Teacher; Author. m. (1) Virgil Bozeman, 28 Mar 1937, div, 1 daughter, (2) Arne Barkhaus, 8 Feb 1951. Education: École Libre des Sciences Politiques, 1934; Middle Temple, 1936; JD, Southern Methodist University, Dallas, 1937; Hoover Institution, Stanford University, 1938-40. Publications: Regional Conflicts Around Geneva, 1948; The Future of Law in a Multicultural World, 1971; How to Think About Human Rights, 1978; Politics and Culture in International History, 1994. Contributions to: Various publications. Memberships: American Political Science Association; Consortium for the Study of Civilization; International Studies Association. Address: 24 Beale Circle, Bronxville, NY 10708, USA.

BRACEGIRDLE Brian, b. 31 May 1933, Macclesfield, England. Museum Curator; Writer. Education: BSc, 1957, PhD, 1975, University of London. Appointments: Research Consultant in Microscopy, Science Museum. Publications: An Atlas of Embryology (with W H Freeman), 1963; An Atlas of Histology (with W H Freeman), 1966; Photography for Books and Reports, 1970; An Atlas of Invertebrate Structure (with W H Freeman), 1971; An Atlas of Plant Structure (with P H Miles), 2 volumes, 1971, 1973; The Archaeology of the Industrial Revolution, 1973; Thomas Telford (with P H Miles), 1973; The Darbys and the Ironbridge Gorge (with P H Miles), 1974; An Advanced Atlas of Histology (with W H Freeman), 1976; An Atlas of Chordate Structure (with P H Miles), 1977; The Evolution of Microtechnique, 1978; Beads of Glass: Leeuwenhoek and the Early Microscope (editor), 1983; The Microscopic Photographs of J S Dancer (with J B McCormick), 1993; Scientific Photomicrography (with S Bradbury), 1995; Modern Microscope Manufacturers, 1996. Address: Cold Aston Lodge, Cold Aston, Cheltenham, Glos GL54 3BN, England.

BRACKENBURY Alison, b. 20 May 1953, Gainsborough, Lincolnshire, England. Poet. Education: BA, English, St Hugh's College, Oxford, 1975. Publications: Journey to a Cornish Wedding, 1977; Two Poems, 1979; Dreams of Power and Other Poems, 1981; Breaking Ground and Other Poems, 1984; Christmas Roses and Other Poems, 1988; Selected Poems, 1991; 1982, 1985. Radio play: The Country of Afternoon, 1985. Honours: Eric Gregory Award, 1982; Cholmondeley Award, 1997. Address: Carcanet Press, 208-212 Corn Exchange Buildings, Manchester M4 3BQ, England.

BRADBURY Edward P. See: **MOORCOCK Michael (John)**.

BRADBURY Malcolm Stanley, b. 7 Sept 1932, Sheffield, England. Author; Writer; Emeritus Professor of American Studies. Education: Queen Mary College, University of London, 1953-55; Indiana University, 1955-56. Appointment: Professor of American Studies, University of East Anglia. Publications: Eating People is Wrong, 1959; All Dressed Up and Nowhere To Go, 1962; Evelyn Waugh, 1964; Two Poets (with A Rodway), 1966; The Social Context of Modern English Literature, 1971; Penguin Companion to Literature: American, 1972; Possibilities: Essays on the State of the Novel, 1973; The History Man, 1975; Who Do You Think You Are?: Stories and Parodies, 1976; The Novel Today, 1977; Introduction to American Studies, 1981; Saul Bellow, 1982; The After Dinner Game: Three Television Plays, 1982; Rates of Exchange, 1983; Cuts, 1987; The Modern American Novel, 1984; Doctor Criminale, 1992; The Modern British Novel, 1993; Dangerous Pilgrimages: Transatlantic Mythologies and the Novel, 1995; Atlas of Literature, 1996. Honour: Commander of the Order of the British Empire, 1991. Address: University of East Anglia, Norwich NR4 7TJ, England.

BRADBURY Ray (Douglas), b. 22 Aug 1920, Waukegan, Illinois, USA. Writer; Poet; Dramatist. m. Marguerite Susan McClure, 27 Sept 1947, 4 daughters. Education: Public Schools. Publications: Novels: The Martian Chronicles, 1950; Dandelion Wine, 1957; Something Wicked This Way Comes, 1962; Death is a Lonely Business, 1985; A Graveyard for Lunatics, 1990; Green Shadows, White Whale, 1992. Short Story Collections: Dark Carnival, 1947; The Illustrated Man, 1951; The Golden Apples of the Sun, 1953; Fahrenheit 451, 1953; The October Country, 1955; A Medicine for Melancholy, 1959; The Ghoul Keepers, 1961; The Small Assassin, 1962; The Machineries of Joy, 1964; The Vintage Bradbury, 1965; The Autumn People, 1965; Tomorrow Midnight, 1966; Twice Twenty-Two, 1966; I Sing the Body Electric!, 1969; Bloch and Bradbury: Ten Masterpieces of Science Fiction (with Robert Bloch), 1969; Whispers From Beyond (with Robert Bloch), 1972; Harrap, 1975; Long After Midnight, 1976; To Sing Strange Songs, 1979; Dinosaur Tales, 1983; A Memory of Murder, 1984; The Toynbee Convector, 1988; Kaleidoscope, 1994; Quicker Than the Eye, 1996; Driving Blind, 1997. Poetry: Old Ahab's Friend, and Friend to Noah, Speaks His Piece: A Celebration, 1971; When Elephants Last in the Dooryard Bloomed: Celebrations for Almost Any Day in the Year, 1973; That Son of Richard III: A Birth Announcement, 1974; Where Robot Mice and Robot Men Run Round in Robot Towns, 1977; Twin Hieroglyphs That Swim the River Dust, 1978; The Bike Repairman, 1978; The Author Considers His Resources, 1979; The Aqueduct, 1979; The Attic Where the Meadow Greens, 1979; The Last Circus, 1980; The Ghosts of Forever, 1980; The Haunted Computer and the Android Pope, 1981; The Complete Poems of Ray Bradbury, 1982; The Love Affair, 1983; Forever and the Earth, 1984; Death Has Lost Its Charm for Me, 1987. Plays: The Meadow, 1960; Way in the Middle of the Air, 1962; The Anthem Sprinters and Other Antics, 1963; The World of Ray Bradbury, 1964; Leviathan 99, 1966; The Day it Rained Forever, 1966; The Pedestrian, 1966; Dandelion Wine, 1967; Christus Apollo, 1969; The Wonderful Ice-Cream Suit and Other Plays, 1972; Madrigals for the Space Age, 1972; Pillars of Fire and Other Plays for Today, Tomorrow, and Beyond Tomorrow, 1975; That Ghost, That Bride of Time: Excerpts from a Play-in-Progress, 1976; The Martian Chronicles, 1977; Farenheit 451, 1979; A Device Out of Time, 1986; Falling Upward, 1988. Non-Fiction: Teacher's Guide: Science Fiction, 1968; Zen and the Art of Writing, 1973; Mars and the Mind of Man, 1973; The Mummies of Guanajuato, 1978; Beyond, 1984; Remembrance of Things Future, 1979; Los Angeles, 1984; Orange County, 1985; The Art of Playboy, 1985; Yestermorrow: Obvious Answers to Impossible Futures, 1991; Ray Bradbury on Stage: A Chrestomathy of His Plays, 1991; Journey to Far Metaphor: Further Essays on Creativity, Writing, Literature, and the Arts, 1994; The First Book of Dichotomy, The Second Book of Symbiosis, 1995. Other: Television and film scripts. Honours: O Henry Prizes, 1947, 1948; National Institute of Arts and Letters Award, 1954; Writers Club Award, 1974; Balrog Award for Best Poet, 1979; PEN Body of Work Award, 1985. Memberships: Science Fantasy Writers of America; Screen Writers Guild of America; Writers Guild of America. Address: 10265 Cheviot Drive, Los Angeles, CA 90064, USA.

BRADFORD Barbara Taylor, b. 10 May 1933, Leeds, Yorkshire, England. Journalist; Novelist. m. Robert Bradford, 1963. Appointments: Editor, Columnist, UK and US periodicals. Publications: Complete Encyclopedia of Homemaking Ideas, 1968; How to Be the Perfect Wife, 1969; Easy Steps to Successful Decorating, 1971; Making Space Grow, 1979; A Woman of Substance, 1979; Voice of the Heart, 1983; Hold the Dream, 1985; Act of Will, 1986; To Be the Best, 1988; The Women in His Life, 1990; Remember, 1991; Angel, 1993; Everything to Gain, 1994; Dangerous to Know, 1995; Love in Another Town, 1995; Her Own Rules, 1996; A Secret Affair, 1996; Power of a Woman, 1997; A Sudden Change of Heart, 1998. Literary Agent: Morton L Janklow, 598 Madison Avenue, New York 10022. Address: c/o Bradford Enterprises, 450 Park Avenue, Suite 1903, New York, NY 10022, USA.

BRADFORD Karleen, b. 16 Dec 1936, Toronto, Ontario, Canada. Writer. m. James Creighton Bradford, 22 Aug 1959, 2 sons, 1 daughter. Education: BA, University of Toronto, 1959. Appointment: Vice-Chair, The Writers' Union of Canada, 1997-98; Chair, Public Lending Right Commission of Canada, 1998-2000. Publications: A Year for Growing, 1977; The Other Elizabeth, 1982; Wrong Again, Robbie, 1983; I Wish There Were Unicorns, 1983; The Stone in the Meadow, 1984; The Haunting at Cliff House, 1985; The Nine Days Queen, 1986; Write Now!, 1988; Windward Island, 1989; There Will be Wolves, 1992; Thirteenth Child, 1994; Animal Heroes, 1995; Shadows on a Sword, 1996; More Animal Heroes, 1996; Dragonfire, 1997; A Different Kind of Champion; Lionhearts Scribe, 1999, The Canadian Library Association Young Adult Novel Award, 1993. Memberships: PEN; IBBY; Writers' Union of Canada. Address: RR #2, Owen Sound, Ontario, Canada, N4K 5N4.

BRADFORD S W. See: **BATTIN B W.**

BRADFORD Sarah Mary Malet, b. 3 Sept 1938, Bournemouth, England. Author; Journalist; Critic. m. (1) Anthony John Bradford, 31 Apr 1959, 1 son, 1 daughter (2) Viscount Bangor, 1 Oct 1976. Education: Lady Margaret Hall, Oxford, England, 1956-59. Appointment: Manuscript Expert, Christie's, 1975-78. Publications: The Story of Port, 1978, 1983; Portugal and Madeira, 1969; Portugal, 1973; Cesare Borgia, 1976; Disraeli, 1982; Princess Grace, 1984; King George VI, 1989; Elizabeth: A Biography of Her Majesty The Queen, 1996. Contributions to: Reviews in Daily Telegraph, Sunday Telegraph, The Times, Sunday Times, Times Literary Supplement, Literary Review; Mail on Sunday; Daily Mail; Highlife. Literary Agent: Gillon Aitken Associates. Address: 29 Fernshaw Road, London SW10 0TG, England.

BRADLEY George, b. 22 Jan 1953, Roslyn, New York, USA. Writer; Poet. m. Spencer Boyd, 8 Sept 1984. Education: BA, Yale University, 1975; University of Virginia, 1977-78. Publications: Terms to Be Met, 1986; Of the Knowledge of Good and Evil, 1991; The Fire Fetched Down, 1996; Editor: The Yale Younger Poets Anthology, 1998 Other: Criticism. Contributions to: The New Yorker; The Paris Review; The New Republic. Honours: Academy of American Poets Prize, 1978; Yale Younger Poets Prize, 1985; Lavan Younger Poets Award, 1990; The Witter Bynner Prize, 1992. Address: 82 West Main Street, Chester, CT 06412, USA.

BRADLEY John, b. 26 Sept 1950, Brooklyn, New York, USA. Teacher; Writer. m. Jana Brubaker, 27 May 1988, 1 son. Education: BA, History, 1973, BA, English, 1977, University of Minnesota; MA, English, Colorado State University, 1981; MFA, Bowling Green State University, 1989. Appointments: Instructor in English, Bowling Green State University, 1989-91, Northern Illinois University, 1992-. Publications: Love in Idleness: The Poetry of Roberto Zingarelle, 1989; Atomic Ghost: Poets Respond to the Nuclear Age, 1995; Learning to Glow: On Living in a Radioactive World, 1999. Contributions to: Iron Wood; Rolling Stone; Poetry East. Honour: National Endowment in the Arts Fellowship. Address: 504 Sycamore Road, DeKalb, IL 60115, USA.

BRADLEY John (Lewis), b. 5 Aug 1917, London, England. Professor (Retired); Writer. m. Elizabeth Hilton Pettingell, 4 Nov 1943, 1 daughter. Education: BA, 1940,

PhD, 1950, Yale University; MA, Harvard University, 1946. Publications: Ruskin's Letters from Venice, 1851-52, 1955; Ruskin's Letters to Lord and Lady Mount Temple, 1964; Selections from Mayhew's London Labour and The London Poor, 1965; Ruskin's Unto This Last and Traffic, 1967; An Introduction to Ruskin, 1971; Ruskin: The Critical Heritage, 1984; Lady Curzon's India: Letters of a Vicereine, 1985; Correspondence of John Ruskin and Charles Eliot Norton (with Ian Ousby), 1987; Contributor, The Cambridge Guide to Literature in English, 1988; A Shelley Chronology, 1993; A Ruskin Chronology, 1997. Contributions to: Essays in Criticism; Journal of English and Germanic Philology; Modern Language Review; Notes and Queries; Times Literary Supplement; Victorian Studies. Honours: Fellow and Grantee, American Philosophical Society; Guggenheim Fellowship, 1961-62. Address: Church Cottage, Hinton St George, Somerset TA17 8SA, England.

BRADLEY Vee (Vi), b. 17 Sept 1915, Harrogate, Yorkshire, England. Retired Civil Servant. m. Charles Bradley, 18 Sept 1948, dec 1976. Education: Art, Painting, Continuing Adult Courses. Appointment: Exhibitor, paintings. Contributions to: Poetry in: Veins of Gold, book; Magazines and journals including Ore, Orbis, First Time, Poetry One, Poetry Two, Focus, Arcadian, Poetic License. Honour: English, Royal Society of Arts. Address: 161 More Close, St Paul's Court, London W14 9BW, England.

BRADWELL James. See: **KENT Arthur (William Charles)**.

BRADY Anne M (Cannon), b. 23 May 1926, Dublin, Ireland. Writer. m. 2 Feb 1957, 2 sons, 2 daughters. Education: BA, English Literature and Language, University College, Dublin; Diploma in Hospital Administration, College of Commerce. Appointments: University Library Assistant, Dublin and Ottawa; Farm Secretary, County Meath. Publications: The Winds of God, 1985; The Biographical Dictionary of Irish writers (with Brian Cleeve), 1985; Honey Off Thorns, 1988. Memberships: University College Dublin Graduates Association; Royal Dublin Society. Address: Rosbeg, 12 Ard Mhuire Park, Dalkey, County Dublin, Ireland.

BRADY James Winston, b. 15 Nov 1928, Brooklyn, New York, USA. Writer; Broadcaster. m. Florence Kelly, 12 Apr 1958, 2 daughters. Education: AB, Manhattan College, 1950; New York University. Publications: Novels: Paris One, 1977; Nielsen's Children, 1979; Press Lord, 1981; Holy Wars, 1983; Designs, 1986. Non Fiction: The Coldest War, 1990; Fashion Show, 1992. Contributions to: Parade; Esquire; Advertising Age; TV Guide; People; Harper's Bazaar. Honour: Emmy Award, 1973-74. Address: PO Box 1584, East Hampton, NY 11937, USA.

BRADY Joan, b. 4 Dec 1939, San Francisco, CA, USA. Writer. m. Dexter Masters, 23 Sept 1963, 1 son. Education: BS, Columbia University, 1965; Open University, 1992-. Publications: The Imposter, novel, 1979; The Unmaking of a Dancer, autobiography, 1982; US Theory of War, novel, 1992, UK, US, The Netherlands, Germany, France, Spain, Sweden, Denmark, Norway, Korea, Poland. Prologue, autobiography, 1994, UK, The Netherlands, France; Death Comes for Peter Pan, novel, 1996, UK, France, The Netherlands; The Emigré (novel), 1999. Contributions to: Harpers, London Times; Sunday Times, Telegraph, Independent. Honours: NEA Grantee, 1986; Whitbread Novel, 1992; Whitbread Book of the Year, 1993; Prix du Meilleur Livre Étranger, 1995. Literary Agent: Laura Morris, 21 Highshore Road, London SE15 5AA, England.

BRADY John Mary, b. 10 July 1955, Dublin, Ireland. Teacher; Writer. m. Johanna Wagner, 1 Aug 1981, 1 son, 1 daughter. Education: BA, Trinity College, 1980; BEd, 1981, MEd, 1985, University of Toronto. Publications: Kaddish in Dublin; Unholy Ground; A Stone of the Heart; All Souls, 1993; The Good Life, 1995. Honours: Arthur Ellis Award; Best First Novel. Address: c/o MGA Agency, 10 St Mary Street, Suite 510, Toronto, Ontario, Canada.

BRADY Nicholas. See: **LEVINSON Leonard**.

BRADY Patricia, b. 20 Jan 1943, Danville, Illinois, USA. Historian. 1 son, 1 daughter. Education: BA cum laude, with honours, Newcomb College, 1965; MA, History, 1966; PhD, History, 1977, Tulane University. Publications: Nelly Custis Lewis's Housekeeping Book, 1982; Encyclopaedia of New Orleans Artists, 1718-1918, 1987; George Washington's Beautiful Nelly, 1991; Mollie Moore Davis: A Literary Life, 1992; The Cities of the Dead: Free Men of Color as Tomb Builders, 1993. Contributions to: Journals. Honours: Phi Beta Kappa, 1965; Honorary Woodrow Wilson Fellow, 1965; National Defense Foreign Language Fellow, 1965-68; Fulbright-Hays Fellow, 1974. Memberships: Tennessee Williams-New Orleans Literary Festival; Association for Documentary Editing; Southern Historical Association. Address: 1205 Valence Street, New Orleans, LA 70115, USA.

BRADY Terence Joseph, b. 13 Mar 1939, London, England. Dramatist; Writer; Actor. m. Charlotte Mary Therese Bingham, 1 son, 1 daughter. Education: BA Moderatorship, History and Political Science, Trinity College, Dublin, 1961. Appointments: Actor in films, radio, and television. Publications: Rehearsal, 1972; Victoria (with Charlotte Bingham), 1972; Rose's Story (with Charlotte Bingham), 1973; Victoria and Company (with Charlotte Bingham), 1974; The Fight Against Slavery, 1976; Yes--Honestly, 1977; Point-to-Point (with Michael Felton), 1990. Other: Television Films: Losing Control, 1987; The Seventh Raven, 1987; This Magic Moment, 1988; Riders, 1990; Polo, 1993. Contributions to: Stage, radio, television series, and periodicals. Honour: BBC Radio Writers' Guild Award, 1972. Memberships: Point-to-Point Owners Association; Society of Authors. Address: c/o Hurley Lowe Management, 3a Imperial Studios, Imperial Road, London SW6 2AG, England.

BRAGG Melvyn, b. 6 Oct 1939, Carlisle, Cumberland, England. Writer; Dramatist; Broadcaster. m. (1) Marie-Elizabeth Roche, 1961, dec, 1 daughter, (2) Catherine Mary Haste, 1973, 1 son, 1 daughter. Education: MA, Wadham College, Oxford. Appointments: Producer, BBC Radio and TV, 1961-67; Presenter, 2nd House, 1973-77, Read All About It, 1976-77, BBC TV, Start the Week, Radio 4, 1988-98; Presenter and Editor, The South Bank Show, ITV, 1978-; Head of Arts, 1982-90; Controller of Arts, 1990-, London Weekend Television; Deputy Chairman, 1985-90, Chairman, 1990-95, Border Television. Publications: Fiction: For Want of a Nail, 1965; The Second Inheritance, 1966; Without a City Wall, 1968; The Hired Man, 1969; A Place in England, 1970; The Nerve, 1971; Josh Lawton, 1972; The Silken Net, 1974; A Christmas Child, 1976; Autumn Manoeuvres, 1978; Kingdom Come, 1980; Love and Glory, 1983; The Maid of Buttermere, 1987; A Time to Dance, 1990; Crystal Rooms, 1992; Credo, 1996; The Sword and the Miracle, 1997; On Giants' Shoulders, 1998. Other: Speak for England, 1976; Land of the Lakes, 1983; Laurence Olivier, 1984; Rich: The Life of Richard Burton, 1988; The Seventh Seal: A Study on Ingmar Bergman, 1993. Also works for the stage, films, and television. Contributions to: Periodicals. Honours: John Llewellyn-Rhys Memorial Award; PEN Award for Fiction; Richard Dimbleby Award for Outstanding Contribution to Television, 1987; 3 Prix Italia's for South Bank Show; Honorary Fellow, Lancashire Polytechnic, 1987; Wadham College, Oxford, 1995; Domus Fellow, St Catherine's College, Oxford, 1990; Honorary doctorates; Life Peerage, 1998. Memberships: Council for National Academic Awards; Royal Society of Literature, fellow; Royal Television Society, fellow; National Campaign for the Arts, president. Address: 12 Hampstead Hill Gardens, London NW3 2PL, England.

BRAHMACHARI Abola Kanto. See: **BHATTACHARYA Anadi Charan**.

BRAINARD Cecilia Manguerra, b. 1947, Cebu, Philippines. Writer. 3 sons. Education: Graduate Studies, UCLA; BA, Maryknoll College. Publications: Woman with Horns and Other Stories, 1988; Philippine Woman in America, 1991; Fiction by Filipinos in America, editor, 1993; When the Rainbow Goddess Wept, 1994; Acapulco At Sunset and Other Stories, 1995; Contemporary Fiction by Filipinos in America, editor, 1998. Honours: Fortner Prize, 1985; NAMFREL Recognition Award, 1987; PALM Honorable Mention Award, 1989; California Arts Council Artists' Fellowship in Fiction, 1989-90; City of Los Angeles Cultural Grant, 1990-91; LA Board of Education Special Recognition Award, 1991; Brody Arts Fund Fellowship, 1991; Literature Award, Filipino Women's Network, 1992; Outstanding Individual Award, City of Cebu, 1998. Membership: PEN American Center; Founding Member, Philippine American Women Writers and Artists. Address: PO Box 5099, SM, CA 90409, USA.

BRAM Christopher, b. 22 Feb 1952, Buffalo, New York, USA. Novelist. Education: BA, College of William & Mary, Williamsburg, Virginia, 1974. Publications: Surprising Myself, 1987; Hold Tight, 1988; In Memory of Angel Clare, 1989; Almost History, 1992; Father of Frankenstein, 1995. Screenplays: George and Al, 1987; Lost Language of Cranes, 1989. Contributions to: New York Times Book Review; Newsday; Lambda Book Report; Christopher Street. Membership: Publishing Triangle. Literary Agent: Donadio & Ashworth Associates. Address: 231 West 22nd Street, New York, NY 10011, USA.

BRANCH Edgar Marquess, b. 21 Mar 1913, Chicago, Illinois, USA. University Professor; Educator; Editor; Author. m. Mary Josephine Emerson, 29 Apr 1939, 1 son, 2 daughters. Education: University College, University of London, England, 1932-33; BA, Beloit College,1934; Brown University, 1934-35; MA, University of Chicago, 1938; PhD, University of Iowa, 1941. Appointments: Instructor, 1941-43, Assistant Professor, 1943-49, Associate Professor, 1949-57, Professor, 1957-64, Chairman, Department of English, 1959-64, Research Professor, 1964-78, Miami University, Oxford, Ohio; Visiting Associate Professor, University of Missouri, 1950; Independent Author and Editor, Mark Twain Project, University of California, Berkeley, 1978-. Publications: The Literary Apprenticeship of Mark Twain, 1950; A Bibliography of the Writings of James T Farrell, 1921-1957, 1959; James T Farrell, 1963; Clemens of the Call, 1969; James T Farrell, 1971; The Great Landslide Case, 1972; The Grangerford-Shepherdson Feud: Life and Death at Compromse (with Robert H Hirst), 1985; Men Call Me Lucky, 1985; Mark Twain and the Starky Boys, 1992; Mark Twain Roughing It (editor with Harriet Smith), 1993; Studs Lonigan's Neighborhood and the Making of James T Farrell, 1996; A Paris Year: Dorothy and James Farrell in Paris 1931-32, 1998. Contributions to: Anthologies, magazines, and journals. Honours: National Endowment for the Humanities Fellowships, 1971-72, 1976-77; Benjamin Harrison Medallion, Miami University, 1978; Guggenheim Fellowship, 1978-79; Distinguished Service Citation, Beloit College, 1979; First Modern Language Association Prize for Distinguished Scholarly Edition, 1995; Pegasus Award, Ohioana Library Association, 1996. Memberships: Phi Beta Kappa; Phi Kappa Psi; Modern Language Association of America; National Council of Teachers of English; Beta Theta Pi. Address: 4810 Bonham Road, Oxford, OH 45056, USA.

BRANCH Taylor, b. 14 Jan 1947, Atlanta, Georgia, USA. Writer. m. Christina Macy, 1 son, 1 daughter. Education: AB, University of North Carolina, 1968; Postgraduate Studies, Princeton University, 1968-70. Appointments: Staff, Washington (DC) Monthly magazine, 1970-73, Harper's magazine, New York City, 1973-75, Esquire magazine, New York City, 1975-76. Publications: Blowing the Whistle: Dissent in the Public Interest (with Charles Peters), 1972; Second Wind: The Memoirs of an Opinionated Man (with Bill Russell), 1979; The Empire Blues, 1981; Labyrinth (with Eugene M Propper), 1982; Parting the Waters: America in the King Years, 1954-63, 1988. Honours: Christopher Award, 1988; Pulitzer Prize in History, 1989. Address: c/o Diskant and Associates, 1033 Gayley Avenue, Suite 202, Los Angeles, CA 90024, USA.

BRAND Oscar, b. 7 Feb 1920, Winnipeg, Manitoba, Canada. Folk Singer; Folklorist; Writer. Education: BA, Brooklyn College, 1942. Appointments: President, Harlequin Productions, Gypsy Hill Music; Lecturer on Dramatic Writing, Hofstra University; Coordinator of Folk Music, WNYC; Host, numerous TV folk-songs programmes; Curator, Songwriters Hall of Fame, New York City. Publications: Courting Songs, 1952; Folksongs for Fun, 1957; The Ballad Mongers, authobiography, 1957; Bawdy Songs, 1958; The Gold Rush (writer, composer), ballet, 1961; In White America (composer), play 1962; A Joyful Noise (co-writer, composer), musical play, 1966; The Education of Hyman Kaplan (co-writer, composer), musical play, 1967; Celebrate (writer-composer), religious songs, 1968; How to Steal an Election (co-writer, composer), musical play, 1969; Songs of '76, music history, 1973; Thunder Rock (writer, composer), musical play, 1974; Party Songs, 1985. Honours: Laureate, Fairfield University, 1972; Peabody Awards, 1982, 1996; PhD, University of Winnipeg, 1989; Radio Pioneers of America, 1991; Friends of Old Time Radio, 1991. Memberships: American Federation of Television and Radio Artists; Screen Actors Guild; American Federation of Musicians; Dramatists Guild. Address: 141 Baker Hill, Great Neck, NY 11023, USA.

BRANDEWYNE (Mary) Rebecca (Wadsworth), b. 4 Mar 1955, Knoxville, Kentucky, USA. Writer. Education: BA, 1975, MA, 1979, Wichita State University. Publications: No Gentle Love, 1980; Forever My Love, 1982; Love, Cherish Me, 1983; Rose of Rapture, 1984; And Gold Was Ours, 1984; The Outlaw Hearts, 1986; Desire in Disguise, 1987; Passion Moon Rising, 1988; Upon a Moon-Dark Moor, 1988; Heatland, 1990; Across a Starlit Sea, 1991; Rainbow's End, 1991; Desperado, 1992; Swan Road, 1994; The Jacarancta Tree, 1995. Memberships: Mensa; National Writers Club; Romance Writers of America; Society of Professional Journalists. Address: PO Box 780036, Wichita, KS 67206, USA.

BRANDIS Marianne, (Marianne Brender a Brandis), b. 5 Oct 1938, Netherlands. Writer. Education: BA, 1960, MA, 1964, McMaster University. Publications: This Spring's Sowing, 1970; A Sense of Dust, 1972; The Tinderbox, 1982; The Quarter Pie Window, 1985; Elizabeth, Duchess of Somerset, 1989; The Sign of the Scales, 1990; Special Nests, 1990; Fire Ship, 1992. Honours: Young Adult Canadian Book Award, 1986; National Chapter IODE Book Award, 1986; Bilson Award, 1991. Membership: Writer's Union of Canada.

BRANDON Joe. See:**DAVIS Robert Prunier.**

BRANDON Sheila. See: **RAYNER Claire Berenice.**

BRANDT Di(ana Ruth), b. 31 Jan 1952, Winkler, Manitoba, Canada. Poet; Writer. m. Les Brandt, 1971, div 1990, 2 daughters. Education: BTh, Canadian Mennonite Bible College, 1972; BA, Honours, 1975, PhD, 1993, University of Manitoba; MA, English, University of Toronto, 1976. Appointments: Faculty, University of Winnipeg, 1986-95; Writer-in-Residence, University of Alberta, 1995-96; Research Fellow, University of Alberta, 1996-97; Associate Professor of English and Creative Writing, University of Windsor, 1997-. Publications: Poetry: questions i asked my mother, 1987; Agnes in the sky, 1990; mother, not mother, 1992; Jerusalem, beloved, 1995. Other: Wild Mother Dancing: Maternal Narrative in Canadian Literature, 1993; Dancing Naked: Narrative Strategies for Writing Across Centuries, 1996. Contributions to: Various publications. Honours: Gerald Lampert Award for Best First Book of Poetry in Canada, 1987; McNally Robinson Award for Manitoba Book of the Year, 1990; Silver National Magazine Award, 1995; Canadian Authors' Association National Poetry Award, 1996. Memberships: Canadian PEN; League of Canadian Poets; Manitoba Writers Guild; Writers' Union of Canada. Address: c/o The Writers Union of Canada, 24 Ryerson Avenue, Toronto, Ontario M5T 2P3, Canada.

BRANDT Richard B(ooker), b. 17 Oct 1910, Wilmington, Ohio, USA. Professor of Philosophy (retired); Writer. m. Mary Elizabeth Harris, 19 June 1937, div 1968, 1 son, 1 daughter. Education: AB, Denison University, 1930; BA, Cambridge University, 1933; Trinity College, Cambridge, 1933-35; University of Tübingen, 1934-35; PhD, Yale University, 1936. Appointments: Instructor to Associate Professor, 1937-52, Professor, 1952-64, Chairman, Department of Philosophy and Religion, 1957-64, Swarthmore College; Professor of Philosophy and Chairman, Department of Philosophy, 1964-77, Sellars Collegiate Professor, 1978-81, Associate, Center for Philosophy and Public Affairs, 1980-81, University of Maryland; Fellow, Center for Advanced Study in the Behavioral Sciences, 1969-70; John Locke Lecturer, Oxford University, 1973-74; Visiting Professor, Florida State University, 1982, Georgetown University, 1982-83, University of California, Irvine, 1990. Publications: The Philosophy of Schleiermacher, 1941; Hopi Ethics: A Theoretical Analysis, 1954; Ethical Theory, 1959; Value and Obligation, 1961; A Theory of the Good and the Right, 1979; Morality, Utilitarianism and Rights, 1992. Contributions to: Scholarly journals. Honours: Guggenheim Fellowship, 1944-45; Senior Fellow, National Endowment for the Humanities, 1971-72; Honorary LDH, Denison University, 1977. Memberships: American Academy of Arts and Sciences; American Association of University Professors; American Philosophical Association; American Society for Political and Legal Philosophy, president, 1965-66; Phi Beta Kappa; Society for Philosophy and Psychology, president, 1979. Address: c/o Department of Philosophy, University of Michigan, Ann Arbor, MI 48109, USA.

BRANFIELD John Charles, b. 19 Jan 1931, Burrow Bridge, Somerset, England. Writer; Teacher. m. Kathleen Elizabeth Peplow, 2 sons, 2 daughters. Education: MA, Queens' College, Cambridge University; MEd, University of Exeter. Publications: Nancekuke,1972; Sugar Mouse, 1973; The Fox in Winter, 1980; Thin Ice, 1983; The Falklands Summer, 1987; The Day I Shot My Dad, 1989; Lanhydrock Days, 1991. Literary Agent: A P Watt Ltd, 20 John Street, London WC1N 2DR, England. Address: Mingoose Villa, Mingoose, Mount Hawke, Truro, Cornwall TR4 8BX, England.

BRANFORD Henrietta, b. 12 Jan 1946, India. Writer. m. Paul Carter, 30 May 1979, 1 son, 2 daughters. Education: Certificate in Community and Youth Work, Goldsmiths College, London, England, 1970-72. Publications: Royal Blunder; Clare's Summer; Somewhere Somewhere; Dimanche Diller; Royal Blunder and the Haunted House; Dimanche Diller in Danger; Birdo; Nightmare Neighbours; The Theft of Thor's Hammer; Dimanche Diller at Sea; Spacebaby; The Fated Sky; Chance of Safety; Ruby Red; Fire Bed and Bone; Hansel and Gretel; White Wolf. Honour: Smarties Prize, 1994, 1998; Guardian Children's Fiction Prize, 1998. Literary Agent: David Higham Associates. Address: 5-8 Lower John St, Golden Square, London W1R 4HA, England.

BRANIGAN Keith, b. 15 Apr 1940, Buckinghamshire, England. Professor of Prehistory and Archaeology; Writer. m. Kuabrat Sivadith, 20 June 1965, 1 son, 2 daughters. Education: BA, 1963, PhD, 1966, University of Birmingham. Appointments: Research Fellow, University of Birmingham, 1965-66; Lecturer, University of Bristol, 1966-67; Professor of Prehistory and Archaeology, University of Sheffield, 1976-. Publications: Copper and Bronzeworking in Early Bronze Age Crete, 1968; The Foundations of Palatial Crete: A Survey of Crete in the Early Bronze Age, 1970; The Tombs of Mesara: A Study of Funerary Architecture and Ritual in Southern Crete, 2800-1700 B.C., 1970; Latimer: Belgic, Roman, Dark Age, and Early Modern Farm, 1971; Town and Country: The Archaeology of Verulamium and the Roman Chilterns, 1973; Reconstructing the Past: A Basic Introduction to Archaeology, 1974; Aegean Metalwork of the Early and Middle Bronze Ages, 1974; Atlas of Ancient Civilizations, 1976; Prehistoric Britain: An Illustrated Survey, 1976; The Roman West Country: Classical Culture and Celtic Society (editor with P J Fowler), 1976; The Roman Villa in Southwest England, 1977; Gatcombe: The Excavation and Study of a Romano-British Villa Estate, 1967-1976, 1978; Rome and the Brigantes: The Impact of Rome on Northern England (editor), 1980; Roman Britain: Life in an Imperial Province, 1980; Hellas: The Civilizations of Ancient Greece (with Michael Vickers), 1980; Atlas of Archaeology, 1982; Prehistory, 1984; The Catuvellauni, 1986; Archaeology Explained, 1988; Romano-British Cavemen (with M J Dearne), 1992; Dancing with Death: Life and Death in Southern Crete c.3000-2000 B.C., 1993; Lexicon of the Greek & Roman Cities & Place Names in Antiquity, c.1500 B.C.-A.D. 500 (editor with others), 1993; The Archaeology of the Chilterns (editor), 1994; Barra: Archaeological Research on Ben Tangaval (with P Foster), 1995; Cemetery and Society in the Aegean Bronze Age (editor), 1998. Contributions to: Professional journals. Honour: Society of Antiquaries, fellow, 1970-. Memberships: Prehistory Society, vice president, 1984-86; Society for the Promotion of Roman Studies. Address: c/o Department of Prehistory and Archaeology, University of Sheffield, Sheffield S10 2TN, England.

BRANTENBERG Gerd, b. 27 Oct 1941, Oslo, Norway. Novelist. Education: Graduated, University of Oslo, 1970. Appointments: Teacher until 1982; Founder of Literary Women's Forum, Norway. Publications: What Comes Naturally, 1973; The Daughters of Egalia, 1977; Stop Smoking, 1978; The Song of St Croix, 1978; Embraces, 1983; At the Ferry Crossing, 1985; The Four Winds, 1989; Hermit and Entertainer (essay), 1991; The Ompadora Place, 1992; Augusta and Bjormstjirni, 1997 (novel). Play: Egalia, 1982. Honours: Sarpsborg Prize, 1989. Address: Medo gård, Medovn 72, 3145 Tjome, Norway.

BRANTLINGER Patrick Morgan, b. 20 Mar 1941, Indianapolis, IN, USA. Professor of English. m. Ellen Anderson, 21 June 1963, 2 s, 1 d. Education: BA, Antioch College, 1964; MA, 1965; PhD, Harvard University, 1968. Appointments: Assistant Professor, Department of English, Indiana University, Bloomington, IN, 1968; Associate Professor, 1974; Full Professsor, 1979-; Editor, Victorian Studies, 1980-90; Chair, Department of English, Indiana University, 1990-94. Publications: The Spirit of Reform: British Literature and Politics, 1832-1867, 1977; Bread and Circuses: Theories of Mass Culture and Social Decay, 1983; Rule of Darkness: British Literature of Imperialism, 1830-1914, 1986; Crusoe's Footprints: Cultural Studies in Britain and America, 1990; Fictions of State: Culture and Credit in Britain, 1694-1994, 1996; The Reading Lesson: Mass Literacy and Threat in British Fiction, 1998. Honours: John Simon Guggenheim Fellowships, 1978; NEH Fellowship, 1983. Memberships: Modern Language Association; Midwest Victorian Studies Association. Address: Department of English, Indiana University, Bloomington, IN 47405, USA.

BRASHER Christopher William, b. 21 Aug 1928, Guyana. Journalist. m. Shirley Bloomer, 28 Apr 1959, 1 son, 2 daughters. Education: MA, St John's College, Cambridge. Appointments: Columnist, The Observer, 1961-92; Chairman, Berghaus Ltd, 1993-98; Chairman, The Brasher Boot Co Ltd; President, The London Marathon Ltd. Publications: The Red Snows with Sir John Hunt, 1960; Sportsman of Our Time, 1962; A Diary of the XVIIIth Olympiad, 1964; Mexico, 1968; Munich, 1972; The London Marathon: The First Ten Years (editor), 1991. Contributions to: Times, Sunday Times and numerous professional journals and magazines. Honours: Sportswriter of the Year, 1968, 1976; National Medal of Honour, Finland, 1975; Commander of Order of the British Empire, 1996. Address: The Navigator's House, River Lane, Richmond, Surrey TW10 7AG, England.

BRATA Sasthi (Sasthibrata Chakravarti), b. 16 July 1939, Calcutta, India (British). Novelist. m. Pamela Joyce Radcliffe, div. Education: Calcutta University. Appointment: London Columnist, Statesman, 1977-80. Publications: Confessions of an Indian Woman Eater, 1971; She and He, 1973; The Sensuous Guru: The Making of a Mystic President, 1980. Short stories: Encounter, 1978. Verse: Eleven Poems, 1960. Address: 33 Savernake Road, London NW3 2JU, England.

BRATCHER Juanita, (Nita), b. 23 Sept 1939, Columbus, Georgia, USA. Journalist; Publisher; Poet; Songwriter. m. Neal A Bratcher Sr, 1 son, 3 daughters. Education: AA, Liberal Arts, Olive Harvey College, Alabama State University; Bachelor's degree in Journalism, Columbia. Appointments: News Reporter, Roseland Review; News Reporter, Chicago Daily Defender; Publisher, CopyLine Magazine. Publications: Harold: The Making of a Big City Mayor; I Cry For a People: In Their Struggle For Justice and Equality; Recordings: Too Many Memories, Everything But Love, 1996; I'm Here For You, You've Been Gone Too Long, 1997; 2 songs: I'm Here For You, You've Been Gone Too Long, included in songbook Hilltop Country. Contributions to: Chicago Defender; CopyLine Magazine. Honours: Kizzy Award, Kizzy Foundation, 1983; Portraits of Achievers, Probation Challenge, 1983, 1987, 1991; Outstanding Support of Human Rights, Illinois Department of Human Rights, 1985; Par Excellence Journalism, Coalition for United Community Action, 1987; Dedicated Service to Community, Firefighters for United Community Action, 1987; Humanitarian Award, Dorcas Care Center, 1988; Community Service Award, Ada Park Advisory Council, 1990; Everyday Hero Award, Illinois Secretary of State, 1993; Black Businesswoman of the Year, Parkway Community House, 1993; International Poet of Merit, International Society of Poets, 1996; 6 Editor's Choice Awards for Outstanding Achievement in Poetry, National Library of Poetry, 1996-98; Included in Best Poems of 1997, Best Poets of 1998, Best Poems of 1998, National Library of Poetry. Membership: International Society of Poets. Address: 9026 S Cregier Ave, Chicago, IL 60617, USA.

BRATHWAITE Edward Kamau, b. 11 May 1930, Bridgetown, Barbados. Professor of Social and Cultural History; Poet; Writer; Editor. m. Doris Monica Welcome, 1960, 1 son. Education: Harrison College, Barbados; BA, Honours, History, 1953, CertEd, 1954, Pembroke College, Cambridge; DPhil, University of Sussex, 1968. Appointments: Education Officer, Ministry of Education, Ghana, 1955-62; Tutor, Extra Mural Department, University of the West Indies, St Lucia, 1962-63; Lecturer, 1963-76, Reader, 1976-82, Professor of Social and Cultural History, 1982-, University of the West Indies, Kingston; Founding Secretary, Caribbean Artists Movement, 1966; Editor, Savacou magazine, 1970-; Visiting Fellow, Harvard University, 1987; Several visiting professorships. Publications: Poetry: Rights of Passage, 1967; Masks, 1968; Islands, 1969; Penguin Modern Poets 15 (with Alan Bold and Edwin Morgan), 1969; Panda No 349, 1969; The Arrivants: A New World Trilogy, 1973; Days and Nights, 1975; Other Exiles, 1975; Poetry '75 International, 1975; Black + Blues, 1976; Mother Poem, 1977; Soweto, 1979; Word Making Man: A Poem for Nicolas Guillen, 1979; Sun Poem, 1982; Third World Poems, 1983; X-Self, 1987; Sappho Sakyi's Meditations, 1989; Shar, 1990. Other: Folk Culture of the Slaves in Jamaica, 1970, revised edition, 1981; The Development of Creole Society in Jamaica, 1770-1820, 1971; Caribbean Man in Space and Time, 1974; Contradictory Omens: Cultural Diversity and Integration in the Caribbean, 1974; Our Ancestral Heritage: A Bibliography of the Roots of Culture in the English-Speaking Caribbean, 1976; Wars of Respect: Nanny, Sam Sharpe, and the Struggle for People's Liberation, 1977; Jamaica Poetry: A Checklist 1686-1978, 1979; Barbados Poetry: A Checklist, Slavery to the Present, 1979; Kumina, 1982; Gods of the Middle East, 1982; National Language Poetry, 1982; The Colonial Encounter: Language, 1984; History of the Voice: The Development of a National Language in Anglophone Caribbean Poetry, 1984; Jah Music, 1986; Roots, 1986. Editor: Iouanaloa: Recent Writing from St Lucia, 1963; New Poets from Jamaica, 1979; Dream Rock, 1987. Honours: Arts Council of Great Britain Bursary, 1967; Camden Arts Festival Prize, 1967; Cholmondeley Award, 1970; Guggenheim Fellowship, 1972; Bussa Award, 1973; Casa de las Américas Prize, 1976; Fulbright Fellowships, 1982-83, 1987-88; Musgrave Medal, Institute of Jamaica, 1983. Address: c/o Department of History, University of the West Indies, Mona, Kingston 7, Jamaica.

BRAUN Kazimierz, (Jerzy Tymicki, Jerzy Bolmin), b. 29 June 1936, Poland. Director; Writer; Scholar. m. Zofia Reklewska, 15 July 1962, 1 son, 2 daughters. Education: MLett, Poznan University, 1958; MFA, Directing, School of Drama, Warsaw, 1962; PhD, Philosophy, Posnan University, 1971; PhD, Humanities, Wroclaw University, 1975. Appointments: Head of Acting Program, 1987-, Professor, 1989-, SUNY. Publications: Teofil Trzcinski (co-author), 1967; The New Theater in the World, 1975; The Great Reform of Theater in Europe, 1984; A History of Polish Theater 1939-1989, 1996. Contributions to: Anthologies, periodicals, journals, quarterlies and reviews. Membership: Polish Writers Association. Address: c/o State University of New York at Buffalo, 278 Alumni Arena, Amherst, NY 14260-5030, USA.

BRAUN Volker, b. 7 May 1939, Dresden, Germany. Author; Poet; Dramatist. Education: Philosophy, University of Leipzig, 1960-64. Appointments: Assistant Director, Deutschen Theater, Berlin, 1972-77, Berlin Ensemble, 1979-90. Publications: Prose: Unvollendete Geschichte, 1977; Hinze-Kunze-Roman, 1985; Bodenloser Satz, 1990; Der Wendehals: Eine Enterhaltung, 1995. Essays: Verheerende Folgen magnelnden Anscheins innerbetrieblicher Demokratie, 1988. Poetry: Gegen die symmetrische Welt, 1974; Training des aufrechten Gangs, 1979; Langsamer knirschender Morgen, 1987; Der Sotff zum Leben, 1990; Lustgarten Preussen, 1996. Plays: Grosser Frieden, 1979; Dmitri, 1982; Die Ubergangsgesellschaft, 1987; Lenins Tod, 1988; Transit Europa: Der Ausflug der Toten, 1988; Böhmen am Meer, 1992. Honours: Heinrich Mann Prize, 1980; Bremen Literature Prize, 1986; National Prize, 1st Class, 1988; Berlin Prize, 1989; Schiller Commemorative Prize, 1992. Membership: Akademie der Künste, Berlin. Address: Wolfshagenerstrasse 68, D-13187, Berlin, Germany.

BRAXTON Joanne M(argaret), b. 25 May 1950, Washington, District of Columbia, USA. Poet; Critic; Professor. 1 daughter. Education: BA, Sarah Lawrence College, 1972; MA, 1974, PhD, 1984, Yale University. Appointments: Lecturer, University of Michigan, 1979; Assistant Professor, 1980-86, Associate Professor, 1986-89, Professor of English, 1989-, College of William and Mary. Publications: Sometimes I Think of Maryland (poems), 1977; Black Women Writing Autobiography: A Tradition Within a Tradition, 1989; Wild Women in the Whirlwind: The Renaissance in Contemporary Afra-American Writing (editor with Andree N McLaughlin), 1990; The Collected Poems of Paul Laurence Dunbar (editor), 1993. Contributions to: Books, anthologies, journals and periodicals. Honours: Outstanding Faculty Award, State Council for Higher Education for Virginia, 1992; Fellowships; grants. Memberships: American Studies Association; College Language Association; Modern Language Association. Address: c/o Department of English, St George Tucker Hall, College of William and Mary, Williamsburg, VA 23185, USA.

BRAY J(ohn) J(efferson), b. 16 Sept 1912, Adelaide, South Australia, Australia. Barrister; Retired Chief Justice; Poet. Education: LLB, 1932, LLB, Honours, 1933, LLD, 1937, University of Adelaide. Appointments: Admitted to South Australian Bar, 1933; Chief Justice of South Australia, 1967-78; Chancellor, University of Adelaide, 1968-83. Publications: Poems, 1962; Poems 1961-71, 1972; Poems 1972-79, 1979; The Bay of Salamis and Other Poems, 1986; Satura: Selected Poetry and Prose, 1988; The Emperor's Doorkeeper (occasional addresses), 1988; Seventy Seven (poems), 1990. Contributions to: Periodicals. Honour: South Australian Non-Fiction Award, Adelaide Festival of the Arts, 1990. Memberships: Australian Society of Authors; Friendly Street Poets, Adelaide. Address: 39 Hurtle Square, Adelaide, South Australia 5000, Australia.

BRAYBROOKE Neville Patrick Bellairs, b. 30 May 1923, London, England. Writer. m. June Guesddon Jolliffe, 5 Dec 1953, 1 stepdaughter. Publications: London Green: The Story of Kensington Gardens, Hyde Park, Green Park and St James' Park, 1959; London, 1961; The Delicate Investigation, play for BBC, 1969; Four Poems for Christians, 1986; Dialogue with Judas, poem, 1989; Two Birthdays, poem, 1996; Life of Olivia Manning, with Isobel English, 1999. Contributions to: Independent; The Guardian; The Times; The Times Literary Supplement; New Yorker; Sunday Times; Sunday Telegraph. Address: 29 Castle Road, Cowes, Isle of Wight, PO31 7QZ.

BRAYFIELD Celia Frances, b. 21 Aug 1945, Ealing, England. Writer. 1 daughter. Education: Universitaire de Grenoble. Appointments: TV Critic, The Evening Standard, 1974-82, The Times, 1984-89, London Daily News, 1987, The Sunday Telegraph, 1989. Publications: The Body Show Book, 1981; Glitter: The Truth About Fame, 1985; Pearls, 1987; The Prince, 1990; White Ice, 1993; Harvest, 1995; Bestseller, 1996; Getting Home, Little, Brown, 1998. Contributions to: Various journals, magazines and newspapers. Memberships: Society of Authors; National Council for One Parent Families, committee of management, 1989-. Address: c/o Curtis Brown, Haymarket House, 28/9 Haymanrket, London, SW1Y 4SP, England.

BREARS Peter C(harles) D(avid), b. 30 Aug 1944, Wakefield, Yorkshire, England. Writer; Museum Consultant. Education: Dip AD, Leeds College of Art, 1968. Publications: English Country Pottery, 1971; Yorkshire Probate Inventories, 1972; Collector's Book of English Country Pottery, 1974; Horse Brasses, 1980; Traditional Food in Yorkshire, 1987; North Country Folk Art, 1989; Of Curiosities and Rare Things, 1989; Treasures for the People, 1989; Images of Leeds, 1993; Leeds Desrib'd, 1993; Leeds Waterfront Heritage Trail, 1993; The Country House Kitchen, 1996; The Old Devon Farmhouse, 1998; Ryedale Recipes, 1998; A Taste of Leeds, 1998. Contributions to: Connoisseur; Folk Life; Post Medieval Archaeology. Memberships: Museums Association, fellow; Society of Antiquities, fellow; Society for Folk Life Studies, president, 1995. Address: 4 Woodbine Terrace, Headingley, Leeds LS6 4AF, England.

BRECHER Michael, b. 14 Mar 1925, Montreal, Quebec, Canada. Political Science Educator. m. Eva Danon, 7 Dec 1950, 3 children. Education: BA, McGill University, 1946; MA, 1948, PhD, 1953, Yale University. Appointments: Faculty, 1952-63, Professor, 1963-93, R B Angus Professor, 1993-, McGill University; Visiting Professor, University of Chicago, Hebrew University of Jerusalem, University of California at Berkeley, Stanford University. Publications: The Struggle for Kashmir, 1953; Nehru: A Political Biography , 1959; The New States of Asia, 1963; Succession in India, 1966; India and World Politics, 1968; Political Leadership in India, 1969; The Foreign Policy System of Israel, 1972; Decisions in Israel's Foreign Policy, 1975; Studies in Crisis Behavior, 1979; Decisions in Crisis, 1980; Crises in the Twentieth Century, 2 volumes, 1988; Crises, Conflict and Instability, 1989; Crises in World Politics, 1993; A Study of Crisis, 1997. Contributions to: 80 articles in professional journals. Honours: Canada Council and Social Sciences and Humanities Research Council of Canada, Research Grantee; Killam Awards; Watamull Prize, American Historical Association; Woodrow Wilson Foundation Award, American Political Science Association; Fieldhouse Teaching Award, McGill University; Distinguished Scholar Award, International Studies Association. Memberships: Shastri Indo-Canadian Institute, founder, 1969, president, 1970; International Studies Association, president, 1998-99. Address: McGill University, 855 Sherbrooke Street West, Montreal, Quebec H3A 2T7, Canada.

BREE Marlin, b. 16 May 1933, Norfolk, Nebraska, USA. Author; Publisher. m. Loris Gutzmer, 5 Oct 1962, 1 son. Education: BA and Certificate in Journalism, University of Nebraska, Lincoln, 1955. Appointments: Editor's Reporter, Stars and Stripes Newspaper, 1956; Editor, Sunday Magazine, Minneapolis Star-Tribune, 1968-72; Columnist, Corporate Report Magazine, 1973-77; Editorial Director, Marlor Press, 1983-. Publications: In the Teeth of the Northeaster: Alone

Against the Atlantic (co-author), 1981; A Solo Voyage on Lake Superior, 1988; Call of the North Wind, 1996. Memberships: Minnesota Press Club, president, 1963; Midwest Book Awards, chair, 1992. Address: 4304 Brigadoon Drive, St Paul, MN 55126, USA.

BRENCHLEY Chaz, b. 4 Jan 1959, Oxford, England. Writer. Education: St Andrews University, 1976-77. Appointment: Crimewriter-in-Residence, St Peter's Riverside Sculpture Project, Sunderland, 1993-94. Publications: The Samaritan; The Refuge; The Garden; Mall Time; Paradise: Dead of Light; Dispossession; Light Errant; Tower of the King's Daughter; Blood Waters. Contributions to: More than 500 short stories in various publications. Honour: August Derleth Fantasy Award, 1998; Memberships: Society of Authors; Crime Writers' Association, Committee 1995-98. Literary Agent: Carol Smith. Address: Fenham View, 6 Studley Terrace, Newcastle-upon-Tyne NE4 5AH, England.

BRENDER A BRANDIS Marianne. See: **BRANDIS Marianne.**

BRENDON Piers George Rundle, b. 21 Dec 1940, Stratton, Cornwall, England. Writer. m. Vyvyen Davis, 1968, 2 sons. Education: MA, PhD, Magdelene College, Cambridge. Publications: Hurrell Froude and the Oxford Movement, 1974; Hawker of Morwenstow, 1975; Eminent Edwardians, 1979; The Life and Death of the Press Barons, 1982; Winston Churchill: A Brief Life, 1984; Our Own Dear Queen, 1985; Ike: The Life and Times of Dwight D Eisenhower, 1986; Thomas Cook: 150 Years of Popular Tourism, 1991; The Windsors (with Phillip Whitehead), 1994; The Motoring Century: The Story of the Royal Automobile Club, 1997. Contributions to: Times; Observer; The Mail on Sunday; New York Times; New Statesman. Literary Agent: Curtis Brown Ltd. Address: 4B Millington Road, Cambridge CB3 9HP, England.

BRENNAN Patricia Winifred, (Patricia Daly, Anne Rodway), b. Shaftesbury, Dorset, England. Writer. m. (1) Denis William Reed, 31 Dec 1947, dec, (2) Peter Brennan, 19 Sept 1960, dec. Education: Bristol University; University of London, 1967. Appointments: Production Editor, Pitman Publishing, 1946-48; British Council, 1956-78. Publications: Penguin Parade; Writing Today; Albion; Poems: PEN; The Iron Dominion; Arts Council New Poetry; Women Writing. Contributions to: Kimber Anthologies of Ghost Stories; After Midnight Stories; In My Father's House; The Day Trip; Hesperios; Narcissus; Night Driver; Institute of Jewish Affairs; Patterns of Prejudice; Art and Sexual Taboo; Encounter; Our Family Doctors; Swedish Veekojournalen. Memberships: Society of Authors; PEN; Royal Society of Arts; British Federation of Graduate Women; Richmond & Hampton Association; Bath Association. Address: Iford House, 30 Newbridge Road, Bath BA1 3JZ, England.

BRENNER Rachael Feldhay, b. 2 July 1946, Poland. Professor. 1 son, 1 daughter. Education: BA, Hebrew University; MA, Tel Aviv University; PhD, York University. Appointment: Associate Professor, University of Wisconsin-Madison. Publications: Assimilation and Assertion: The Response to the Holocaust in Mardecai Richeler's Writings, 1989; A M Klein, The Father of Canadian Turkish Literature, 1990; Writing as Resistance: Four Women Confronting the Holocaust: Edith Stein, Simone Weil, Anne Frank and Etty Hillesum, 1997. Honours: Canada Research Fellowship; Literary Scholarship Award. Address: 1220 Linden Drive, Room 1346, Madison, WI 53706, USA.

BRENT Iris. See: **BANCROFT Iris.**

BRENT Madeleine. See: **O'DONNELL Peter.**

BRENTON Howard, b. 13 Dec 1942, Portsmouth, England. Playwright; Poet. Education: BA, St Catherine's College, Cambridge, 1965. Appointments: Resident Dramatist, Royal Court Theatre, London, 1972-73; Resident Writer, University of Warwick, 1978-79; Granada Artist in Residence, University of California,

Davis, 1997. Publications: Adaptation of Goethe's Faust, 1966; Notes from a Psychotic Journal and Other Poems, 1969; Revenge, 1969; Scott of the Antartic (or what God didn't see), 1970; Christie in Love and Other Plays, 1970; Lay By (co-author), 1972; Plays for Public Places, 1972; Hitler Diaries, 1972; Brassneck (with David Hare), 1973; Magnificence, 1973; Weapons of Happiness, 1976; The Paradise Run (television play), 1976; Epsom Downs, 1977; Sore Throats, with Sonnets of Love and Opposition, 1979; The Life of Galileo (adaptor), 1980; The Romans in Britain, 1980; Plays for the Poor Theatre,1980; Thirteenth Night and A Short Sharp Shock, 1981; Danton's Death (adaptor), 1982; The Genius, 1983; Desert of Lies (television play), 1983; Sleeping Policemen (with Tunde Ikoli), 1984; Bloody Poetry, 1984; Pravda (with David Hare),1985; Dead Head (television series), 1987; Greenland, 1988; H.I.D. (Hess is Dead), 1989; Iranian Night (with Tariq Ali), 1989; Diving for Pearls (novel), 1989; Moscow Gold (with Tariq Ali), 1990; Berlin Bertie, 1992; Playing Away (opera libretto), 1994; Hot Irons (essays and diaries), 1995. Honour: Honorary Doctorate University of North London, 1996. Address: c/o Casarotto Ramsay Ltd, National House, 60-66 Wardour Street, London W1V 3HP, England.

BRETNOR Reginald, (Grendel Briarton), b. 30 July 1911, Vladivostock, Russia. Writer; Editor. m. (1) Helen Harding, dec 1967, (2) Rosalie Leveille, 1969. Publications: Fiction: A Killing in Swords, 1978; The Schimmelhorn File, 1979; Schimmelhorn's Gold, 1986; Gilpin's Space, 1986. Non-Fiction: Decisive Warfare: A Study on Military Theory, 1969, 2nd edition, 1986. Editor: Modern Science Fiction: Its Meaning and Its Future, 1953, 2nd edition, 1979; Science Fiction, Today and Tomorrow, 1974; The Craft of Science Fiction, 1976; The Future of War, 3 volumes, 1978-80; Of Force and Violence and Other Imponderables, 1992; One Man's BEM: Thoughts on Science Fiction, 1993. Contributions to: Periodicals. Memberships: Military Conflict Institute; National Rifle Association; Science Fiction Writers of America; Writers Guild of America. Address: PO Box 1481, Medford, OR 97501, USA.

BRETT Jan (Churchill), b. 1 Dec 1949, Bryn Mawr, Pennsylvania, USA. Illustrator and Writer of Children's Books. m. Joseph Heame, 18 Aug 1980, 1 daughter. Education: Colby Junior College, 1968-69; Boston Museum School, 1970. Publications: Illustrator and/or Writer of more than 25 children's books. Honours: Outstanding Science Trade Book for Children, National Science Teachers Association, 1984; Children's Book Award, University of Nebraska, 1984; Top Ten Children's Book Award of the Year, Redbook Magazine, 1985; Booklist Magazine Editor's Choice, American Library Association, 1986. Membership: Society of Children's Book Writers. Address: 132 Pleasant Street, Norwell, MA 02061, USA.

BRETT John Michael. See: **TRIPP Miles Barton.**

BRETT Simon Anthony Lee, b. 28 Oct 1945, Surrey, England. Writer. m. Lucy Victoria McLaren, 27 Nov 1971, 2 sons, 1 daughter. Education: BA, Honours, 1st Class, English, Wadham College, Oxford, 1967. Publications: 17 Charles Paris crime novels, 1975-97; A Shock to the System, 1984; Dead Romantic, 1985; 5 Mrs Pargeter crime novels, 1986-96; The Booker Book, 1989; How to be a Little Sod, 1992; Singled Out, 1995; Editor, several Faber books. Other: After Henry (radio and television series), 1985-92. Honours: Best Radio Feature, Writers' Guild, 1973; Outstanding Radio Programme, Broadcasting Press Guild, 1987. Memberships: Crime Writers' Association, chairman, 1986-87; Detection Club; PEN; Society of Authors, chairman, 1995-97; Writers' Guild. Literary Agent: Michael Motley. Address: Frith House, Burpham, Arundel, West Sussex BN18 9RR, England.

BREW (Osborne Henry) Kwesi, b. 27 May 1928, Cape Coast, Ghana. Retired Ambassador; Poet. Education: BA, University College of the Gold Coast, Legon, 1953. Appointments: Former Ghanian Ambassador to Britain, India, France, USSR, Germany

and Mexico. Publicationis: The Shadows of Laughter, 1968; African Panorama and Other Poems, 1981. Contributions to: Anthologies and periodicals. Honour: British Council Prize. Address: c/o Greenfield Review Press, PO Box 80, Greenfield Center, NY 12833, USA.

BREWER Derek Stanley, b. 13 July 1923, Cardiff, Wales. Writer; Editor; Emeritus Professor. m. Lucie Elisabeth Hoole, 17 Aug 1951, 3 sons, 2 daughters. Education: Magdalen College, Oxford, 1941-42, 1945-48; BA, MA (Oxon), 1948; PhD, Birmingham University, 1956; LittD, Cambridge University, 1980. Appointments: Master, Emmanuel College, Cambridge, 1977-90; Editor, The Cambridge Review, 1981-86. Publications: Chaucer, 1953; Proteus, 1958; The Parlement of Foulys, (editor), 1960; Chaucer: The Critical Heritage, 1978; Chaucer and his World, 1978, reprinted, 1992; Symbolic Stories, 1980, reprinted, 1988; English Gothic Literature, 1983; Chaucer: An Introduction, 1984; Medieval Comic Tales (editor), 1996; A Companion to the Gawain-Poet, 1996, (editor); A New Introduction to Chaucer, 1998. Contributions to: Scholarly books and journals. Address: Emmanuel College, Cambridge, England.

BREWSTER Elizabeth (Winifred), b. 26 Aug 1922, Chipman, New Brunswick, Canada. Professor Emeritus of English; Poet; Novelist. Education: BA, University of New Brunswick, 1946; MA, Radcliffe College, Cambridge, Massachusetts, 1947; BLS, University of Toronto, 1953; PhD, Indiana University, 1962. Appointments: Faculty, Department of English, University of Victoria, 1960-61; Reference Librarian, Mt Allison University, 1961-65; Visiting Assistant Professor of English, University of Alberta, 1970-71; Assistant Professor, 1972-75, Associate Professor, 1975-80, Professor, 1980-90, Professor Emeritus, 1990-, of English, University of Saskatchewan. Publications: East Coast, 1951; Lillooet, 1954; Roads, 1957; Passage of Summer: Selected Poems, 1969; Sunrise North, 1972; In Search of Eros, 1974; The Sisters, 1974; It's Easy to Fall on the Ice, 1977; Sometimes I Think of Moving, 1977; Digging In, 1982; Junction, 1982; The Way Home, 1982; A House Full of Women, 1983; Selected Poems of Elizabeth Brewster, 1944-1984, 1985; Entertaining Angels, 1988; Spring Again, 1990; The Invention of Truth, 1991; Wheel of Change, 1993; Footnotes to the Book of Job, 1995; Away from Home (autobiography), 1995; Garden of Sculpture, 1998. Honours: E J Pratt Award for Poetry, University of Toronto, 1953; President's Medal for Poetry, University of Western Ontario, 1980; Honorary LittD, University of New Brunswick, 1982; Canada Council Award, 1985; Lifetime Award for Excellence in the Arts, Saskatchewan Arts Board, 1995; Shortlisted, Governor General's Award for Poetry, 1996. Memberships: League of Canadian Poets; Writers' Union of Canada; Saskatchewan Writers' Guild; PEN. Address: 206, 910-9th Street East, Saskatoon, Saskatchewan S7H 0N1, Canada.

BREWSTER Robin. See: **STAPLES Reginald Thomas.**

BREYTENBACH Breyten, b. 16 Sept 1939, Bonnievale, South Africa. Poet; Writer. Education: Graduated, University of Cape Town, 1959. Publications: And Death White as Words: Anthology, 1978; In Africa Even the Flies Are Happy: Selected Poems, 1964-77, 1978; Mouroir: Mirrornotes of a Novel, 1984; End Papers, 1986; All One Horse, 1990; The Memory of Birds in Times of Revolution (essays), 1996. Honour: Rapport Prize, 1986. Address: c/o Faber Ltd, 3 Queen Square, London WC1N 3AU, England.

BREZHNEV Dennis. See: **BARNETT Paul le Page.**

BRIARTON Grendel. See: **BRETNOR Reginald.**

BRICKNER Richard P(ilpel), b. 14 May 1933, New York, New York, USA. Writer; Teacher. Education: Middlebury College, 1951-53; BA, Columbia College, 1957. Appointments: Adjunct in Writing, City College of the City University of New York, 1967-70; Faculty, Writing Program, New School for Social Research, New York

City, 1970-. Publications: Novels: The Broken Year, 1962; Bringing Down the House, 1972; Tickets, 1981; After She Left, 1988. Non-Fiction: My Second Twenty Years, 1976. Contributions to: American Review; Life; New Leader; New York Times Book Review; Time. Honours: National Endowment for the Arts Grant, 1974; Guggenheim Fellowship, 1983. Address: 245 East 72nd Street, New York, NY 10021, USA.

BRIDGEMAN Harriet (Victoria Lucy) (Viscountess), b. 30 Mar 1942, Durham, England. Library Director; Writer. Education: MA, Trinity College, Dublin, 1964. Appointment: Director, Bridgeman Art Library, London and New York. Publications: The British Eccentric, 1974; An Encyclopaedia of Victoriana, 1975; Society Scandals, 1976; Beside the Seaside, 1976; Needlework: An Illustrated History, 1978; A Guide to Gardens of Europe, 1979; The Last Word, 1983. Honour: FRSA. Address: 19 Chepstow Road, London W2 5BP, England.

BRIDWELL Norman (Ray), b. 15 Feb 1928, Kokomo, Indiana, USA. Children's Writer; Artist. Education: John Herron Art Institute, Indianapolis, 1945-49; Cooper Union Art School, New York, 1953-54. Publications: Clifford the Big Red Dog, 1962; Bird in the Hat, 1964; The Witch Next Door, 1965; The Country Cat, 1969; What Do They Do When It Rains, 1969; The Witch's Christmas, 1970; Clifford the Small Red Puppy, 1972; Monster Holidays, 1974; Clifford's Good Deeds, 1974; Clifford at the Circus, 1977; The Witch Grows Up, 1979; Clifford Goes to Hollywood, 1980; Clifford's Kitten, 1984; Clifford's Birthday Party, 1988; Clifford We Love You, 1991; Clifford's Animal Noises, 1991; Clifford's Thanksgiving Visit, 1993; Clifford's Happy Easter, 1994; Clifford the Firehouse Dog, 1994; Clifford the Puppy's First Christmas, 1994. Honours: Jeremiah Ludington Memorial Award, 1991; Honorary Doctor of Humane Letters, Indiana University, 1994. Address: Box 869, Edgartown, MA 02539, USA.

BRIEN Alan, b. 12 Mar 1925, Sunderland, England. Novelist; Journalist. m. (1) Pamela Mary Jones, 1947, 3 daughters, (2)Nancy Newbold Ryan, 1 son, 1 daughter, 1961, (3)Jill Sheila Tweedie, 1973. Education: BA, English Literature, Jesus College, Oxford. Appointments: Associate Editor, Mini-Cinema, 1950-52, Courier, 1952-53; Film Critic, Columnist, Truth, 1953-54; TV Critic, Observer, 1954-55; Film Critic, 1954-56, New York Correspondent, 1956-58, Evening Standard; Drama Critic, Features Editor, 1958-61, Columnist, 1963-65, Spectator; Columnist, Sunday Daily Mail, 1958-62, Sunday Dispatch, 1962-63; Political Columnist, Sunday Pictorial, 1963-64; Drama Critic, Sunday Telegraph, 1964-67; Columnist New Statesman, 1966-72, Punch, 1972-84; Diarist, 1967-75, Film Critic, 1976-84, Sunday Times. Publications: Domes of Fortune, 1979; Lenin: The Novel, 1986; Heaven's Will (novel), 1989; And When Rome Falls (novel), 1991. Contributions to: Various professional journals. Address: 14 Falkland Road, London NW5, England.

BRIERLEY David, b. 30 July 1936, Durban, South Africa. Author. Separated, 1 daughter. Education; BA, Honours, Oxon. Publications: Cold War, 1979; Blood Group O, 1980; Big Bear, Little Bear, 1981; Shooting Star, 1983; Czechmate, 1984; Skorpion's Death, 1985; Snowline, 1986; One Lives, One Dies, 1987; On Leaving a Prague Window, 1995; The Horizontal Woman, 1996; The Cloak-and-Dagger Girl, 1998. Literary Agent: James Hale. Address: 27 St Lucien's Lane, Wallingford, Oxon OX10 9ER, England.

BRIGGS Asa (Baron), b. 7 May 1921, Keighley, Yorkshire, England. Writer. m. Susan Anne Banwell, 1955, 2 sons, 2 daughters. Education: 1st Class History Tripos, Parts I and II, Sidney Sussex College, Cambridge, 1941; BSc, 1st Class (Economics), London, 1941. Publications: Victorian People, 1954; The Age of Improvement, 1959; History of Broadcasting in the United Kingdom, 5 volumes, 1961-95; Victorian Cities, 1963; A Social History of England, 1983, new edition, 1994; Victorian Things, 1988. Honours: Marconi Medal for Communications History, 1975; Life Peerage, 1976; Medaille de Vermeil de la Formation, Foundation de l'Académie d'Architecture, 1979; 20 honorary degrees. Memberships: British Academy, fellow; American Academy of Arts and Sciences; Social History Society, president. Address: The Caprons, Keere Street, Lewes BN7 1TY, England.

BRIGGS Raymond Redvers, b. 18 Jan 1934, Wimbledon, London, England. Illustrator; Writer; Cartoonist. m. Jean T Clark, 1963, dec 1973. Education: Wimbledon School of Art; Slade School of Fine Art, London, NDD; DFA; FSIAD. Appointments: Freelance illustrator, 1957-; Children's author, 1961-. Publications: Midnight Adventure, 1961;Ring-a-Ring o'Roses, 1962; The Strange House, 1963; Sledges to the Rescue, 1963; The White Land, 1963; Fee Fi Fo Fum, 1964; The Mother Goose Treasury, 1966; Jim and the Beanstalk, 1970; The Fairy Tale Treasury, 1975; Fungus the Bogeyman, 1977; The Snowman, 1978; Gentleman Jim, 1980; When the Wind Blows, 1982, stage and radio versions, 1983; The Tinpot Foreign General & the Old Iron Woman, 1984; Unlucky Wally, 1987; Unlucky Wally, Twenty Years On, 1989; The Man, 1992; The Bear 1994; Ethel and Ernest, 1998. Honours: Kate Greenaway Medals, 1966, 1973; British Academy of Film and Television Arts Award; Francis Williams Illustration Awards, V & A Museum, 1982; Broadcasting Press Guild Radio Award, 1983. Memberships: Royal Society of Literature; Society of Authors. Literary Agent: The Agency. Address: Weston, Underhill Lane, Westmeston, Near Hassocks, Sussex BN6 8XG, England.

BRIN David, b. 6 Oct 1950, Glendale, California, USA. Author; Book Reviewer; Science Editor. Education: BS, California Institute of Technology, 1972; MS, 1979, PhD, 1981, University of California at San Diego; Post-doctoral Research Fellow, California Space Institute, La Jolla, 1982-84. Appointment: Book Reviewer and Science Editor, Heritage Press, Los Angeles, 1980-. Publications: Sundiver, 1980; Startide Rising, 1983; The Practice Effect, 1984; The Postman, 1985; Heart of the Comet (with Gregory Benford), 1986; The River of Time (short stories), 1986; The Uplift War, 1987; Earth, 1990; The Glory Season, 1993. Contributions to: Scientific journals and popular periodicals. Honours: Locus Awards, 1984, 1986; Nebula Award, 1984; Hugo Awards, 1984, 1985; John W Campbell Memorial Award, 1986. Address: 5081 Baxter Street, San Diego, CA 92117, USA.

BRINGHURST Robert, b. 16 Oct 1946, Los Angeles, California, USA. Poet; Writer. 1 daughter. Education: Massachusetts Institute of Technology, 1963-64, 1970-71; University of Utah, 1964-65; Defense Language Institute, 1966-67; BA, Comparative Literature, Indiana University, 1973; MFA, University of British Columbia, 1975. Appointments: General Editor, Kanchenjunga Poetry Series, 1973-79; Reviews Editor, Canadian Fiction Magazine, 1974-75; Visiting Lecturer, 1975-77, Lecturer, 1979-80, University of British Columbia; Poet-in-Residence, Banff School of Fine Arts, 1983, Ojibway and Cree Cultural Centre Writers' Workshops, 1985; Adjunct Lecturer, Simon Fraser University, 1983-84; Lecturer, 1984, Ashley Fellow, 1994, Trent University; Contributing Editor, Fine Print: A Review for the Arts of the Book, 1985-90; Writer-in-Residence, University of Edinburgh, 1989-90; Poet-in-Residence, University of Western Ontario, 1998-99. Publications: The Shipwright's Log, 1972; Cadastre, 1973; Bergschrund, 1975; The Stonecutter's Horses, 1979; Tzuhalem's Mountain, 1982; The Beauty of the Weapons: Selected Poems 1972-82, 1982; Visions: Contemporary Art in Canada, 1983; The Raven Steals the Light, 1984, 2nd edition, 1988; Ocean, Paper, Stone, 1984; Tending the Fire, 1985; The Blue Roofs of Japan, 1986; Pieces of Map, Pieces of Music, 1986; Conversations with Toad, 1987; The Black Canoe, 1991, 2nd edition, 1992; The Elements of Typrographic Style, 1992, 2nd edition, 1996; The Calling: Selected Poems, 1970-95, 1995; Elements, 1995; Native American Oral Literatures and the Unity of the Humanities, 1998; New World Suite No 3, forthcoming; A Story as Sharp as a Knife: An Introduction to Classical Haida Literature, forthcoming. Contributions to: Many anthologies. Honours: Macmillan Prize, 1975; Alcuin Society Design Awards, 1984, 1985; Canadian Broadcasting Corporation Poetry Prize, 1985; Guggenheim Fellowship, 1987-88. Address: Box 357, 1917 West 4th Avenue, Vancouver, British Columbia, V6J 1M7, Canada.

BRINK André Philippus, b. 29 May 1935, Vrede, South Africa. Professorof English; Writer. Education: DLitt, Rhodes University; Appointment: Professor of English, University of Cape Town. Publications: Lobola vir die Lewe, 1962; File on a diplomat, 1966; Mapmakers (essays), 1973; Looking on Darkness, 1974; An Instant in The Wind, 1976; Rumours of Rain, 1978; A Dry White Season, 1979; A Chain of Voices, 1982; The Wall of the Plague, 1984; The Ambassador, 1985; A Land Apart, 1986; States of Emergency, 1988; An Act of Terror, 1991; The First Life of Adamastor, 1993; On the Contrary, 1993; Imaginings of Sand, 1996; Reinventing a Continent (essays), 1996; The Novel: Language and Narrative from Cervantes to Calvino, 1998; Devil's Valley, 1998. Contributions to: World Literature Today; Theatre Quartely; Standpunte. Honours: Reina Prinsen Geerlings Prize, 1964; CNA Awards, Twentieth Century Literature, 1965, 1978, 1982; Academy Prize for Prose Translation, 1970; Martin Luther King Memorial Prize, 1980; Prix Medics Etranger, 1980; Chevalier de la Legion d'Honneur, 1982; Commandeur de l'Ordre des Arts et des Lettres, 1992; Premio Mondello, Italy, 1997. Literary Agent: Liepman Agency Maienburgweg 23, CH-8044, Zürich. Address: Department of English, University of Cape Town, Rondebosch 7700, South Africa.

BRINKLEY Alan, b. 2 June 1949, Washington, District of Columbia, USA. Historian; Professor. m. Evangeline Morphos, 3 June 1989. Education: AB, Public and International Affairs, Princeton University, 1971; AM, 1975, PhD, 1979, History, Harvard University. Appointments: Assistant Professor of History, Massachusetts Institute of Technology, 1978-82; Visiting position, 1980, Dunwalke Associate Professor of American History, 1982-88, Harvard University; Visiting positions, Princeton University, 1991, University of Turin, 1992, New York University, 1993, Ecole des Hautes Etudes en Sciences Sociales, Paris, 1996; Professor of History, Graduate School, City University of New York, 1988-91; Professor of History, 1991-98; Allan Nevins Professor of History, 1998-, Columbia University; Harmsworth Professor of American History, University of Oxford, 1998-99. Publications: Voices of Protesst: Huey Long, Father Coughlin, and the Great Depression, 1982; American History: A Survey (with others), 1983, 10th edition, revised, 1998; The Unfinished Nation: A Concise History of the American People, 1993, revised edition, 1997; The End of Reform: New Deal Liberalism in Recession and War, 1995; Eyes of the Nation: A Visual History of the United States (with others), 1997; New Federalist Papers (with Kathleen Sullivan and Nelson Polsby), 1997; Liberalism and Its Discontents, 1998. Contributions to: Scholarly books and journals. Honours: National Endowment for the Humanities Fellowship, 1972-73; American Council of Learned Societies Fellowship, 1981; Robert L Brown Prize, Louisiana Historical Association, 1982; National Book Award for History, 1983; Guggenheim Fellowship, 1984-85; Woodrow Wilson Center for International Scholars Fellowship, 1985; Joseph R Levenson Memorial Teaching Prize, Harvard University, 1987; National Humanities Center Fellowship, 1988-89; Media Studies Center Fellowship, 1993-94; Russell Sage Foundation Fellowship, 1996-97. Memberships: American Historical Association; Organization of American Historians, executive board member, 1990-93; Society of Americah Historians, fellow, 1984-, executive board member, 1989-; Twentieth Century Fund, trustee, 1995-. Address: c/o Department of History, Columbia University, New York, NY 10027, USA.

BRINKLEY Douglas (Gregg), b. 14 Dec 1960, Atlanta, Georgia, USA. Professor of History; Author. Education: BA, Ohio State University, 1982; MA, 1983, PhD, 1989, Georgetown University. Appointments: Instructor, US Naval Academy, 1987; Visiting Research Fellow, Woodrow Wilson School of Public Policy and

International Affairs, 1987-88; Lecturer, Princeton University, 1988; Assistant Professor of History, Hofstra University, 1989-93; Visiting Associate Director, 1993-94, Director, 1994-, Eisenhower Center for American Studies, Associate Professor of History, 1993-96, Distinguished Professor of History, 1997-, University of New Orleans. Publications: Jean Monnet: The Path of European Unity (editor with Clifford Hackett), 1991; The Atlantic Charter (editor with D Facey-Crowther), 1992; Dean Acheson: The Cold War Years, 1953-1971, 1992; Driven Patriot: The Life and Times of James Forrestal (with Townsend Hoopes), 1992; Dean Acheson and the Making of US Foreign Policy (editor), 1993; Theodore Roosevelt: The Many-Sided American (editor with Gable and Naylor), 1993; The Majic Bus: An American Odyssey, 1993; Franklin Roosevelt and the Creation of the United Nations (with Townsend Hoopes), 1997; John F Kennedy and Europe (editor), 1998; Strategies of Enlargement: The Clinton Doctrine and US Foreign Policy, 1997; Hunter S Thompson: The Proud Highway: Saga of a Desperate Southern Gentleman 1955-1967 (editor), 1997; American Heritage: History of the United States, 1998; The Unfinished Presidency: Jimmy Carter's Journey Beyond The White House, 1998. Contributions to: Books and scholarly journals. Honours: New York Times Notable Book of the Year, 1993, 1993, 1998; Stessin Award for Distinguished Scholarship, Hofstra University, 1993; Theodore and Franklin Roosevelt Naval History Prize, 1993; Bernath Lecture Prize 1996; Honorary Doctorate in Humanities, Trinity College, Connecticut, 1997. Memberships: Theodore Roosevelt Association; Franklin and Eleanor Roosevelt Institute; Century Association; National D-Day Museum. Literary Agent: International Creative Management. Address: c/o Eisenhower Center, University of New Orleans, 923 Magazine Street, New Orleans, LA 70130, USA.

BRINTON Alexander. See: **BATTIN B W.**

BRISCO Patty. See: **MATTHEWS Patricia Anne.**

BRISKIN Jacqueline, b. 18 Dec 1927, London, England. Novelist; Short Story Writer. m. Bert Briskin, 2 sons, 1 daughter. Education: University of California at Los Angeles, 1946-47. Publications: California Generation, 1970; Afterlove, 1974; Rich Friends, 1976; Paloverde, 1978; The Onyx, 1982; Everything and More, 1983; Too Much Too Soon, 1985; Dreams Are Not Enough, 1987; The Naked Heart, 1989; The Other Side of Love, 1991. Memberships: PEN; Author's Guild. Address: Los Angeles, California, USA.

BRISKIN Mae, b. 20 Oct 1924, Brooklyn, New York, USA. Freelance Writer. m. Herbert B Briskin, 1 Dec 1946, 2 sons, 1 daughter. Education: BA, Brooklyn College; MA, Columbia University. Publications: A Boy Like Astrid's Mother, 1988; The Tree Still Stands, 1991. Contributions to: Western Humanities Review; American Review; Ascent; Chicago Tribune Magazine; San Francisco Chronicle Magazine. Honours: PEN International; USA West Award for Fiction, 1989; PEN Syndicated Fiction, 4 years.

BRISTOW Robert O'Neil, b. 17 Nov 1926, St Louis, Missouri, USA. Author. m. Gaylon Walker, 23 Dec 1950, 2 sons, 2 daughters. Education: BA, 1951, MA, 1965, University of Oklahoma. Appointments: Writer-in-Residence, Winthrop College, South Carolina, 1961-87. Publications: Time for Glory, 1968; Night Season, 1970; A Faraway Drummer, 1973; Laughter in Darkness, 1974. Contributions to: Approximately 200 Short Stories to magazines and journals. Honours: Award for Literary Excellence, 1969; Friends of American Writer's Award, 1974. Address: 613 1/2 Charlotte Avenue, Rock Hill, SC 29730, USA.

BRITTAN Sir Samuel, b. 29 Dec 1933, London, England. Journalist; Writer. Education: 1st Class, Economics, Jesus College, Cambridge, 1955; MA, Cantab. Appointments: Various posts, 1955-61, Principal Economic Commentator, 1966-, Assistant Editor, 1978-, Financial Times; Economics Editor, Observer, 1961-64; Fellow, 1973-74, Visiting Fellow, 1974-82, Nuffield College, Oxford; Visiting Professor of Economics, Chicago Law School, 1978; Honorary Professor of Politics, Warwick University, 1987-92. Publications: The Treasury Under the Tories, 1964, revised edition as Steering the Economy, 1969, new edition, 1971; Left or Right: The Bogus Dilemma, 1968; The Price of Economic Freedom: A Guide to Flexible Rates, 1970; Capitalism and the Permissive Society, 1973, revised edition as A Restatement of Economic Liberalism, 1988; Is There an Economic Consensus?, 1973; The Delusion of Incomes Policy (with P Lilley), 1977; The Economic Consequences of Democracy, 1977; How to End the "Monetarist" Controversy, 1981; The Role and Limits of Government: Essays in Political Economy, 1983; Capitalism with a Human Face, 1995; Essays, Moral, Political and Economic, 1998. Contributions to: Many journals. Honours: Financial Journalist of the Year Award, 1971; George Orwell Prize for Political Journalism, 1980; Honorary doctorates, Heriot-Watt University, 1988; Honorary Fellow, Jesus College, Cambridge, 1988; Chevalier de la Légion d'Honneur, 1993; Knighted, 1993; Ludwig Erhard Prize for Economic Writing, 1998. Address: c/o Financial Times, Number One Southwark Bridge, London SE1 9HL, England.

BRITTON David, b. 18 Feb 1945, Manchester, England. Writer; Publisher. Education: Mount Carmel, Corpus Christie, 1950-66. Appointment: Editor, Savoy Books, 1975-. Publications: Lord Horror, 1990; Motherfuckers, 1996; The Adventures of Meng and Ecker, 1996. Contributions to: New Worlds; The Independent; The Times. Honour: Frank Randel Literary Award, 1991. Literary Agent: Giles Gordon. Address: 615b Wilbraham Road, Chorlton, Manchester M16 8EW, England.

BROBST Richard Alan, b. 13 May 1958, Sarasota, Florida, USA. Teacher, High School English. m. Pamela Millace, 27 Dec 1986, 2 sons, 1 daughter. Education: BA, University of Florida, 1988. Appointment: Resident Poet, Charlotte County Schools, 1989-. Publication: Inherited Roles (poetry), 1992. Contributions to: Florida In Poetry: An Anthology; Southern Poetry Review; Kentucky Poetry Review; California Quarterly. Honour: Winner, Duane Locke Chapbook Series, 1997. Membership: Co-editor, Albatross Poetry Journal. Address: PO Box 7787, North Port, FL 34287, USA.

BROCK Rose. See: **HANSEN Joseph.**

BROCK William Ranulf, b. 16 May 1916, Farnham, Surrey, England. Retired Professor of Modern History. m. Constance Helen Brown, 8 July 1950, 1 son, 1 daughter. Education: BA, 1937, MA, 1945, PhD, 1941, Trinity College, Cambridge; Hon D Litt, 1998. Appointments: Fellow, Selwyn College, Cambridge; Professor of Modern History, University of Glasgow, 1967-81. Publications: Lord Liverpool and Liberal Toryism, 1941; Character of American History, 1960; An American Crisis, 1963; Conflict and Transformation: USA 1944-77, 1973, USA 1739-1870 (Sources of History), 1975; Parties and Political Conscience (USA 1840-52), 1979; Evolution of American Democracy, 1979; Welfare, Democracy and the New Deal, 1988; Selwyn College: A History (with P H M Cooper), 1994. Memberships: British Academy, fellow; British Association of American Studies, founding member; Royal Historical society, fellow. Address: 49 Barton Road, Cambridge CB3 9LG, England.

BROCKHOFF Stefan. See: **PLANT Richard.**

BRODA-CONNOLLY Beatrice, b. 28 Feb, Winnipeg, Canada. Television Producer; Writer; Host. m. Robert Connolly, 23 Nov 1988. Education: BA, Psychology, University of Manitoba; Theatrical Performance, Seneca College. Publications: Passport to Adventure (tv series); The Search for Ancient Wisdom (cd rom); Timeless Places (tv series, documentary, cd rom, interactive web site). Memberships: Society of American Travel Writers. Address: 245 Britannia Road East, Mississauga, Ontario L4Z 2Y7, Canada.

BRODER David (Salzer), b. 11 Sept 1929, Chicago Heights, Illinois, USA. Reporter; Associate Editor; Columnist; Writer. m. Ann Creighton Collar, 8 June 1951, 4 sons. Education: BA, 1947, MA, 1951, University of Chicago. Appointments: Reporter, Pantagraph, Bloomington, Illinois, 1953-55, Congressional Quarterly, Washington, DC, 1955-60, Washington Star, 1960-65, New York Times, 1965-66; Reporter, 1966-75, Associate Editor, 1975-, Washington Post; Syndicated Columnist. Publications: The Republican Establishment (with Stephen Hess), 1967; The Party's Over: The Failure of Politics in America, 1972; Changing of the Guard: Power and Leadership in America, 1980; Behind the Front Page: A Candid Look at How the News is Made, 1987; The Man Who Would be President: Dan Quayle (with Bob Woodward), 1992. Contributions to: Books, newspapers and magazines. Honours: Fellow, John F Kennedy School of Government, Harvard University, 1969-70; Pulitzer Prize in Journalism, 1973; Poynter Fellow, Yale University and Indiana University, 1973; Carey McWilliams Award, 1983; 4th Estate Award, National Press Club, 1988; Elijah Parrish Lovejoy Award, 1990. Memberships: American Academy of Arts and Sciences, fellow; American Political Science Association; American Society of Public Administration; Gridiron Club; National Press Club; Sigma Delta Chi. Address: c/o Washington Post, 1150 15th Street North West, Washington, DC 20071, USA.

BRODERICK Damien (Francis), b. 22 Apr 1944, Melbourne, Victoria, Australia. Writer. Education: BA, Monash University, 1966; PhD, Deakin University, 1990. Appointment: Writer-in-Residence, Deakin University, 1986. Publications: A Man Returned (stories), 1965; The Zeitgeist Machine (editor), 1977; The Dreaming Dragons, 1980; The Judas Mandala, 1982, revised edition, 1990; Valencies (with Rory Barnes), 1983; Transmitters, 1984; Strange Attractors (editor), 1985; The Black Grail, 1986; Striped Holes, 1988; Matilda at the Speed of Light (editor), 1988; The Dark Between the Stars (stories), 1991; The Lotto Effect, 1992; The Sea's Furthest End, 1993; The Architecture of Babel: Discourses of Literature and Science, 1994; Reading by Starlight: Postmodern Science Fiction, 1995; The White Abacus, 1997; Zones (with Rory Barnes), 1997; Theory and its Discontents, 1997; The Spike, 1997. Contributions to: Periodicals. Honours: Australian Science Fiction Achievement Awards, 1981, 1985, 1989. Address: 23 Huchinson Street, Brunswick East, Victoria 3057, Australia.

BRODEUR Hélène, b. 13 July 1923, Val Racine, Quebec, Canada. Civil Servant retired; Writer. m. Robert L Nantais, 26 Aug 1947, 3 sons, 2 daughters. Education: 1st Class Teacher's Certificate, Ottawa University Normal School, 1940; BA, Ottawa University, 1946; Diploma in Senior Management, Canadian Government College, 1974. Appointments: Writer-in-Residence, Visiting Professor, French Creative Writing, Ottawa University. Publications: Chroniques du Nouvel-Ontario, Vol 1, La quête d'Alexandre, 1981, Vol 2, Entre l'aube et le jour, 1983, Vol 3, Les routes incertaines, 1986, Vol 4 L'Ermitage, 1996; Alexander, 1983; Rose-Delima, 1987; The Honourable Donald, 1990. Miniseries for Television: Les Ontariens, 1983. Contributions to: Extension Magazine, 1968; A serial, Murder in the Monastery. Honours: Champlain Award, 1981; Le Droit Award, 1983; Prix du Nouvel-Ontario, 1984. Memberships: Ontario Authors Association; Union des écrivains; PEN International; Press Club. Address: 1506 160 George Street, Ottawa, Ontario K1N 9M2, Canada.

BRODEUR Paul (Adrian, Jr), b. 16 May 1931, Boston, Massachusetts, USA. Writer. Div, 1 son, 1 daughter. Education: BA, Harvard College, 1953. Appointments: Staff Writer, The New Yorker magazine, 1958-96; Lecturer, Columbia University Graduate School of Journalism, 1969-80, Boston University School of Public Communications, 1978-79, University of California at San Diego, 1989. Publications: The Sick Fox, 1963; The Stunt Man, 1970; Downstream, 1972; Expendable Americans, 1974; The Zapping of America, 1977; Outrageous Misconduct, 1985; Restitution, 1985; Currents of Death, 1989; The Great Power-Line Coverup, 1993; Secrets,

1997. Contributions to: The New Yorker magazine. Honours: Sidney Hillman Prize, 1973; Columbia University National Magazine Award, 1973; American Association for the Advancement of Science Award, 1976; Guggenheim Fellowship, 1976-77; Alicia Patterson Foundation Fellowship, 1978; American Bar Association Certificate of Merit, 1983;United Nations Environment Program Global 500 Honor Roll, 1989; Public Service Award American Society of Professional Journalists, 1990. Address: c/o The New Yorker, 20 West 43rd Street, New York, NY 10036, USA.

BROGGER Suzanne, b. 18 Nov 1944, Copenhagen, Denmark. Writer; Poet; Dramatist. m. Keld Zeruneith, 1991. Education: University of Copenhagen. Publications: 4 novels; 8 poetry books; 1 play. Honour: Gabor Prize, 1987. Address: Knudstrup Gl Skole, 4270 Hong, Denmark.

BROMBERT Victor Henri, b. 11 Nov 1923, France (US citizen, 1943). Professor of Romance and Comparative Literatures; Writer. m. Beth Anne Archer, 18 June 1950, 1 son, 1 daughter. Education: BA, 1948, MA, 1949, PhD, 1953, Yale University; Postgraduate Studies, University of Rome, 1950-51. Appointments: Faculty, 1951-58, Associate Professor, 1958-61, Professor, 1961-75, Benjamin F Barge Professor of Romance Literatures, Yale University, 1969-75; Henry Putnam University Professor of Romance and Comparative Literatures, 1975-, Princeton University; Many visiting lectureships and professorships. Publications: The Criticism of T S Eliot, 1949; Stendhal et la Voie Oblique, 1954; The Intellectual Hero, 1961; Stendhal: A Collection of Critical Essays (editor), 1962; The Novels of Flaubert, 1966; Stendhal: Fiction and the Themes of Freedom, 1968; Flaubert par lui-même, 1971; La Prison romantique, 1976; The Romantic Prison: The French Tradition, 1978; Victor Hugo and the Visionary Novel, 1984; The Hidden Reader, 1988; In Praise of Antiheroes, forthcoming. Contributions to: Many books, journals, and periodicals. Honours: Fulbright Fellowship, 1950-51; Guggenheim Fellowships, 1954-55, 1970; National Endowment for the Humanities Senior Fellow, 1973-74; Honorary Degrees, University of Chicago, 1981, University of Toronto, 1997; Rockefeller Foundation Resident Feloow, Bellagio, Italy, 1975, 1990; Médaille Vermeil de la Ville de Paris, 1985; Officier des Palmes Académiques. Memberships: American Academy of Arts and Sciences, fellow; American Comparative Literature Association; American Association of Teachers of French; American Philosophical Society; Modern Language Association, president, 1989; Société des Etudes Françaises; Société des Etudes Romantiques. Address: 187 Library Place, Princeton, NJ 08540, USA.

BROME Vincent, b. 14 July 1910, London, England. Author. Education: Streatham, England, schools. Publications: Clement Attlee, 1949; H G Wells, 1951; The Way Back: The Story of Lieutenant Commander Pat O'Leary, 1953; Aneurin Bevan: A Biography, 1953; Acquaintance with Grief, 1954; The Last Surrender, 1954; Six Studies in Quarrelling, 1958; Sometimes at Night, 1959; Frank Harris, 1959, new edition as Frank Harris: The Life and Loves of a Scoundrel, 1960; We Have Come a Long Way, 1962; The Problem of Progress, 1963; Love in Our Time, 1964; Four Realist Novelists: Arthur Morrison, Edwin Pugh, Richard Whiting, and William Pett Ridge, 1965; The International Brigades: Spain, 1936-39, 1965; The World of Luke Simpson, 1966; The Embassy, 1967, new edition as The Ambassador and the Spy, 1973; Freud and His Early Circle: The Struggle of Psychoanalysis, 1967, new edition as Freud and His Disciples, 1984; The Surgeon, 1967, new edition as The Operating Theatre, 1968; The Imaginary Crime, 1969; Te Revolution, 1969; Confessions of a Writer, 1970; The Brain Operators, 1971; Reverse Your Verdict: A Collection of Private Prosecutions, 1971; London Consequences, 1972; The Day of Destruction, 1974; The Happy Hostage, 1976; Diary of a Revolution, 1978; Jung: Man and Myth, 1978; Havelock Ellis: Philosopher of Sex, 1979; Ernest Jones: Freud's Alter Ego, 1982, new edition as Ernest Jones: A Biography, 1983; The Day of the Fifth Moon, 1984; J B Priestley, 1988; The Other Pepys, 1992. Other: Six plays produced, one at Edinburgh. Contributions to: Various periodicals. Address: 45 Great Ormond Street, London WC1, England.

BROMIGE David (Mansfield), b. 22 Oct 1933, London, England(Canadian citizen, 1961). Poet; Writer; Professor of English. m. 1 son, 1 daughter. Education: BA, University of British Columbia, 1962; MA, 1964, ABD, 1969, University of California at Berkeley. Appointments: Poetry Editor, Northwest Review, 1962-64; Instructor, University of California at Berkeley, 1965-69; Lecturer, California College of Arts and Crafts, 1969; Professor of English, Sonoma State University, California, 1970-93; Contributing editor, Avec, Penngrove, 1986-, Kaimana, Honolulu, 1989-. Publications: The Gathering, 1965; Please, Like Me, 1968; The Ends of the Earth, 1968; The Quivering Roadway, 1969; Threads, 1970; Ten Years in the Making, 1973; Three Stories, 1973; Birds of the West, 1974; Out of My Hands, 1974; Spells and Blessings, 1974; Tight Corners and What's Around Them, 1974; Credences of Winter, 1976; Living in Advance, 1976; My Poetry, 1980; P-E-A-C-E, 1981; In the Uneven Steps of Hung Chow, 1982; It's the Same Only Different, 1984; The Melancholy Owed Categories, 1984; You See, 1985; Red Hats, 1986; Desire, 1988; Men, Women and Vehicles, 1990; Tiny Courts in a World Without Scales, 1991; They Ate, 1992; The Harbormaster of Hong Kong, 1993; A Cast of Tens, 1994; Romantic Traceries, 1994; From the First Century, 1995. Contributions to Anthologies and periodicals. Honours: Macmillan Poetry Prize, 1957-59; Poet Laureate, University of California (all campuses), 1965; Discovery Award, 1969, Poetry Fellowship, 1980, National Endowment for the Arts; Canada Council Grant in Poetry, 1976-77; Pushcart Prize in Poetry, 1980; Western States Arts Federation Prize in Poetry, 1988; Gertrude Stein Award in Innovative Writing, 1994; Award from the Fund for Living Treasure Award, Sonoma County, 1994; Poetry, 1998. Address: 461 High Street, Sebastopol, CA 95472, USA.

BRONNUM Jakob, b. 16 Apr 1959, Copenhagen, Denmark. Writer; Poet; m. Anette Bronnum, 12 Aug 1995. Education: MA, Theology, 1992. Publications: Skyggedage (prose), 1989; Europadigte (poetry), 1991, 2nd edition, 1996; Den Lange Sondag (novel), 1994; Morke (novel), 1996; Sjaelen og Landskaberne (poetry), 1997 Contributions to: Literaturnaja Gazetta; Parnasso. Memberships: Danish Writers Association. Address: Draabydalen 30, DK-8400 Ebeltoft, Denmark.

BROOKE. See: **JACKMAN Stuart.**

BROOKE Michael Zachary, b. 5 Nov 1921, Cambridge, England. Author; Consultant. m. Hilda Gilatt, 25 July 1953, 2 sons, 1 daughter. Education: BA, History, 1st Class Honours, 1943, MA, 1945, Cambridge University; MA, 1964, PhD, 1969, University of Manchester. Publications: Frederic Le Play: Engineer and Social Scientist, 1970; The Strategy of Multinational Enterprise (co-author), 1970, 2nd edition, 1978; The Multinational Company in Europe (co-author), 1972; A Bibliogrpahy of International Business (co-author), 1977; The International Firm (co-author), 1977; International Corporate Planning (co-author), 1979; International Financial Management Handbook (co-author), 2 volumes, 1983; Centralization and Autonomy, 1984; Selling Mangement Service Contracts in International Business, 1985; International Travel and Tourism Forecasts (co-author), 1985; International Management, 1986, 2nd edition, 1995; Financial Management Handbook, 1987; Handbook of International Trade (co-author), 1988; Profits from Abroad (co-author), 1988; International Business Studies (co-author), 1991; Licensing (co-author), 1995; Easy Cycling in Britain (co-author), 1995; The Visionary Executive (co-author), 1998. Contributions to: Numerous professional journals. Honour: Fellow, Academy of International Business. Memberships: Authors North, chairman, 1978-80; Independent Publishers' Guild, chairman, North West Region, 1989-91. Address: 21 Barnfield, Urmston, Manchester M41 9EW, England.

BROOKE Tal, (Robert Taliaferro Brooke), b. 21 Jan 1945, Washington, District of Columbia, USA. Think-Tank President and Chairman; Author; Lecturer. Education: BA, University of Virginia, 1969; MDiv, Princeton University, 1986. Appointments: Vice President of Public Relations, Telecom Inc, 1982-83; President and Chairman, SCP Inc, Conservative Think-Tank, Berkeley, California, 1988-; Lecturer on Eastern Thought and the Occult at colleges, universities, conventions and seminars in the US and abroad; Many radio and television appearances. Publications: Lord of the Air, 1976, new edition, 1990; The Other Side of Death, 1979; Avatar of Night, 1979, new edition, 1984; Riders of the Cosmic Circut, 1986; Harvest (with Chuck Smith), 1988; When the World Will Be As One, 1989; Virtual Gods, Designer Universes, 1997. Honours: Spring Arbor National Bestseller, 1989; 1st Place, Critical Review Category, National EPA Awards, 1991. Membership: Society of the Cincinnati. Address: SCP Inc, Box 4308, Berkeley, CA 94704, USA.

BROOKE-ROSE Christine, b. 1923, England. Novelist; Critic. Education: MA, Oxford University, 1953; PhD, London University, 1954. Appointments: Lecturer, 1969-75, Professor of English Language and Literature, 1975-88, University of Paris. Publications: Novels: The Languages of Love, 1957; The Sycamore Tree, 1958; The Dear Deceit, 1960; The Middlemen, 1961; Out, 1964; Such, 1965; Between, 1968; Thru, 1975; Amalgamemnon, 1984; Xorandor, 1986; Verbivore, 1990; Textermination, 1991; Remake, 1996; Next, 1998. Criticism: A Grammar of Metaphor, 1958; A ZBC of Ezra Pound, 1971; A Rhetoric of the Unreal, 1981; Stories, Theories and Things, 1991. Other: Short Stories and essays. Contributions to: Newspapers, journals, radio, and television. Honours: Travelling Prize, Society of Authors, 1964; James Tait Black Memorial Prize, 1966; Translation Prize, Arts Council of Great Britain, 1969; Honorary LittD, University of East Anglia, 1988. Address: c/o Cambridge University Press, PO Box 110, Cambridge CB2 3RL, England.

BROOKES John Andrew, b. 11 Oct 1933, Durham, England. Education: Commercial Horticulture Durham County School of Horticulture; 3 Year Apprenticeship with Nottingham Corp Parks Department; 1 Year Assistant to Brenda Colvin PPILA; Diploma, Landscape Design, University College, London; 3 Years Assistant to Dame Sylvia Crowe PPILA; 3 Years Assistant Editorial Architectural Design; Private Practice, 1964-; Fellow, Society of Garden Designers. Appointments: Lecturer in Landscape Design, Institute of Park Administration; Assistant Lecturer, Landscape Design, Regent Street Polytechnic; Lecturer, Landscape Design, Royal Botanical Gardens, Kew; Director, Inchbald School of Garden Design; Set up Inchbald School of Interior Design, Teheran, Iran, 1978; Founded Clock House School of Garden Design, 1980; Faculty Lecturer, Henry Clews Foundation, La Napoule, S France, 1986-95; Principal Lecturer, Guarden Design School, Royal Botanic Gardens, Kew, 1990-95; Chairman, Society of Garden Designers, 1996. Publications include: Gardens of Paradise, 1987; The Country Garden, 1987; The Small Garden Book, 1989; John Brookes' Garden Design Book, 1991; Planting the Country Way, 1994; John Brookes' Garden Design Workbook, 1994; Home and Garden Style, 1996; John Brookes' The New Garden, 1998. Membership: External Review Group, National Botanical Institute, Kirstenbosch, South Africa, 1995. Literary Agent: Felicity Bryan. Address: 2A North Parade, Banbury Road, Oxford OX2 6PE, England.

BROOKNER Anita, b. 16 July 1928, London, England. Novelist; Art Historian. Education: BA, King's College, London; PhD, Courtauld Institute of Art, London. Appointments: Visiting Lecturer in Art History, University of Reading, 1959-64; Lecturer, 1964-77, Reader in Art History, 1977-88, Courtauld Institute of Art; Slade Professor of Art, Cambridge University, 1967-68. Publications: Fiction: A Start in Life, 1981; Providence, 1982; Look at Me, 1983; Hotel du Lac, 1984; Family and Friends, 1985; A Misalliance, 1986; A Friend from England, 1987; Latecomers, 1988; Lewis Percy, 1989;

Brief Lives, 1990; A Closed Eye, 1991; Fraud, 1992; A Family Romance, 1993; A Private View, 1994; Incidents in the Rue Laugier, 1995; Visitors, 1998. Non-Fiction: An Iconography of Cecil Rhodes, 1956; J A Dominique Ingres, 1965; Watteau, 1968; The Genius of the Future: Studies in French Art Criticism, 1971; Greuze: The Rise and Fall of an Eighteenth-Century Phenomenon, 1972; Jacques-Louis David, a Personal Interpretation: Lecture on Aspects of Art, 1974; Jacques-Louis David, 1980, revised edition, 1987. Editor: The Stories of Edith Wharton, 2 volumes, 1988, 1989. Contributions to: Books and periodicals. Honours: Fellow, Royal Society of Literature, 1983; Booker McConnell Prize, National Book League, 1984; Commander of the Order of the British Empire, 1990. Address: 68 Elm Park Gardens, London SW10 9PB, England.

BROOKS Amanda. See: **MCCRACKEN Amanda Jane.**

BROOKS Andree Nicole Aelion, b. 2 Feb 1937, London, England. Journalist; Author; Lecturer; Columnist; Educator. m. Ronald J Brooks, div 19 Aug 1959, 1 son, 1 daughter. Education: Queens College, London, 1952; Journalism Certificate, 1958. Appointments: Adjunct Professor, Fairfield University, 1982-87; Associate Fellow, Yale University, 1989-; President, Founder, Womens Campaign School, Yale University; Director, Seraphim History Curriculum Project, 1998. Publication: Dona Gracia Nasi: A Jewish Woman Leader (biography), forthcoming. Contributions to: Over 3000 Articles; Contributing Columnist, New York Times. Honours: Best Non Fiction Book of Year, National Association of Press Women, USA, 1990; Over 30 other Journalism Awards. Address: 15 Hitchcock Road, Westport, CT 06880, USA.

BROOKS George E(dward), b. 20 Apr 1933, Lynn, Massachusetts, USA. Professor; Historian; Writer. m. Elaine Claire Rivron, 16 Aug 1985, 2 daughters. Education: AB, Dartmouth College, 1957; MA, 1958, PhD, 1962, Boston University. Appointments: Instructor, Boston University, 1960, 1962; Assistant Professor, 1962-68, Associate Professor, 1968-75, Professor, 1975-, Indiana University; Visiting Associate Professor, Tufts University, 1969; Visiting Fulbright Professor, University of Zimbabwe, 1984; Visiting Professor, Shandong University, China, 1985. Publications: New England Merchants in Africa: A History Through Documents, 1802-1865 (editor with Norman R Bennett), 1965; Yankee Traders, Old Coasters and African Middlemen: History of American Legitimate Trade with West Africa in the Nineteenth Century, 1970; The Kru Mariner in the Nineteenth Century: An Historical Compendium, 1972; Themes in African and World History, 1973, revised edition, 1983; Perspectives on Luso-African Commerce and Settlement in The Gambia and Guinea-Bissau Region, 16th-19th Centuries, 1980; Kola Trade and State-Building: Upper Guinea Coast and Senegambia, 15th-17th Centuries, 1980; Western Africa to c.1860 A.D.: A Provisional Historical Scheme Based on Climate Periods, 1985; Landlords and Strangers: Ecology, Society, and Trade in Western Africa, 1000-1630, 1993; The Aspen World History Handbook: An Organizational Framework, Lessons, and Book Reviews for Non-Centric World History (editor with Dik A Daso, Marilyn Hitchens, and Heidi Roupp), 1994. Contributions to: Many scholarly books and journals. Honours: Ford Foundation Training Fellowship, 1960-62; Social Science Research Council Grant, 1971-72; National Endowment for the Humanities Grant, 1976-77; Indiana University President's Council on International Programs Award, 1978; American Council of Learned Societies Grant, 1990; Visiting Fellowship, Africa, Precolonial Achievement Conference, Humanities Research Centre, Australian National University, 1995. Memberships: African Studies Association, fellow; American Historical Association; Liberian Studies Association; MANSA/Mande Studies Association; World History Association, executive council, 1990-93. Address: 1615 E University Street, Bloomington, IN 47401, USA.

BROOKS Gwendolyn, b. 7 June 1917, Topeka, Kansas, USA. Poet; Writer. m. Henry L Blakely, 17 Sept 1939, 1 son, 1 daughter. Education: Graduated, Wilson Junior College, Chicago, 1936. Appointments: Teacher, Northeastern Illinois State College, Chicago, Columbia College, Chicago, Elmhurst College, Illinois; Rennebohm Professor of English, University of Wisconsin at Madison; Distinguished Professor of the Arts, City College of the City University of New York, 1971; Consultant in Poetry, Library of Congress, Washington, DC, 1985-86; Jefferson Lecturer, 1994. Publications: Poetry: A Street in Bronzeville, 1945; Annie Allen, 1949; Bronzeville Boys and Girls, 1956; The Bean Eaters, 1960; Selected Poems, 1963; We Real Cool, 1966; The Wall, 1967; In the Mecca, 1968; Riot, 1969; Family Pictures, 1970; Black Steel: Joe Frazier and Muhammad Ali, 1971; Aloneness, 1971; Aurora, 1972; Beckonings, 1975; To Disembark, 1981; Black Love, 1982; Mayor Harold Washington, and Chicago, The I Will City, 1983; The Near-Johannesburg Boy and Other Poems, 1986; Blacks, 1987; Winnie, 1988; Gottschalk and the Grande Tarantelle, 1988; Children Coming Home, 1991. Other: Maud Martha, 1953; A Portion of That Field (with others), 1967; The World of Gwedolyn Brooks, 1971; A Broadside Treasury (editor), 1971; Jump Bed: A New Chicago Anthology (editor), 1971; Report from Part One, 1972; The Tiger Who Wore White Gloves, or, What You Are You Are, 1974; A Capsule Course in Black Poetry Writing (with Don L Lee, Keorapetse Kgositsile and Dudley Randall), 1975; Primer for Blacks, 1980; Young Poets' Primer, 1981; Very Young Poets, 1983; Report from Part Two, 1995. Contributions to: Various publications. Honours: American Academy of Arts and Letters Grant, 1946; Guggenheim Fellowship, 1946-47; Pulitzer Prize in Poetry, 1950; Thormod Monsen Award, 1964; Ferguson Memorial Award, 1964; Poet Laureate of Illinois, 1968; Anisfield-Wolf Award, 1968; Black Academy Award, 1971; Shelley Memorial Award, 1976; Frost Medal, Poetry Society of America, 1988; National Endowment for the Arts Lifetime Achievement Award, 1989; Aiken-Taylor Awardm, 1992; National Book Foundation Medal, 1994. Memberships: National Women's Hall of Fame; Society of Midland Authors. Address: 5530 South Shore Drive, Apt 2A, Chicago, IL 60637, USA.

BROSS Irwin D, b. 13 Nov 1921, Halloway, Ohio, USA. Biostatistician. m. Rida S Singer, 7 Aug 1949, 2 sons, 1 daughter. Education: BA, University of California at Los Angeles, 1942; MA, North Carolina State University, 1949; PhD, University of North Carolina, 1949. Publications: Design for Decision, 1953; Scientific Strategies in Human Affairs: To Tell the Truth Exposition, 1975; Scientific Strategies to Save Your Life, 1981; Crimes of Official Science, 1988; Others: A History of US Science and Medicine in the Cold War, 1996. Contributions to: Author, Co-Author of more than 350 publications; Biostatistics, Cancer Research and Public Health. Address: 109 Maynard Drive, Eggertsville, NY 14226, USA.

BROSSARD Nicole, b. 27 Nov 1943, Montreal, Quebec, Canada. Poet; Novelist. Education: Licence ès Lettres, 1968, Scolarité de maîtrise en lettres, 1972, Université de Montréal; Bacc. spécialisé en pédagogie, Université du Québec à Montréal, 1971. Publications: Poetry: Mécanique jongleuse, 1973, English translation as Daydream Mechanics, 1980; Le centre blanc, 1978; Amantes, 1980, English translation as Lovers, 1986; Double Impression, 1984; Mauve, 1984; Character/Jeu de lettres, 1986; Sous la langue/Under Tongue, bilingual edition, 1987; A tout regard, 1989; Installations, 1989; Langues obscures, 1991; La Nuit verte du parc labyrinthe, trilingual edition, 1992; Ventige de l'awant-scene, 1997; Muscé de l'os et de l'eau, 1999. Fiction: Un livre, 1970, English translation as A Book, 1976; Sold-Out, 1973, English translation as Turn of a Pang, 1976; French Kiss, 1974, English translation, 1986; L'amèr, 1977, English translation as These Our Mothers, or, the Disintegrating Chapter, 1983; Le Sens apparent, 1980, English translation as Surfaces of Sense, 1989; Picture Theory, 1982, English translation, 1991; Le Désert mauve, 1987, English translation as Mauve Desert, 1990; Baroque d'aube, 1995, English translation as Baroque at Dawn, 1997. Essays: La Lettre aèrienne, 1985, English translation as The Aerial Letter, 1988. Contributions to: Numerous anthologies. Honours: Governor-General Prizes, 1974, 1984; Chapbook Award, Therafields Foundation, 1986; Grand Prix de Poésie, Foundation Les Forges, 1989; Honorary Doctorate, University of Western Ontario, 1991; Prix Athanase-David, 1991; Honarary doctorate, Universitof Shelbrooke, 1997. Membership: l'Académie des Lettres du Québec, 1993-. Address: 34 Avenue Robert, Outrement, Quebec H3S 2P2, Canada.

BROSSET Georges, b. 21 January 1910, Geneva, Switzerland. m. Simone Jaccottet, 18 July 1935, 2 sons, 3 daughters. Education: Docteur en Droit, 1946; Université de Genéve. Appointments: Avocat au Barreau de Genève, 1930-1990; Chargé de Cours a la Faculté de Droit de l'Université de Genève, 1950-1980. Publications: Le procès des Fleurs du Mal ou l'affaire Charles Baudelaire, 1947; Le temps de la Gravière, 1987; Le précepteur d'été, 1994; Quai des Bergues, 1996; Dames de Venise, 1998. Honour: Lauréat de la Sté Genevoise des écrivains, 1995. Memberships: Sté suisse des écrivains; Sté genevoise des écrivains. Address: 5 avenue Théodore=Flournoy, CH 1207 Genéve, Switzerland.

BROUGHTON John Renata, b. 19 Mar 1947, Hastings, New Zealand. University Lecturer in Maori Health; Dramatist; Writer. Education: BSc, Massey University, 1971; Bachelor of Dental Surgery, Otago University, 1977. Publications: A Time Journal for Halley's Comet, children's book, 1985; Te Hokinga Mai (The Return Home), stage play, 1990; Te Hara (The Sin), stage play, 1990; Nga Puke (The Hills), stage play, 1990; Nga Mahi Ora, TV documentary on health career for young Maori people, 1990; Michael James Manaia, stage play, 1991; Maraq, stage play, 1992. Contributions to: Te Hau Ora Sports Journal. Honour: Dominion Sunday Times Bruce Mason Playwright Award, 1990. Memberships: PEN New Zealand; Araiteura Marae Council, chairman; New Zealand Dental Association. Literary Agent: Playmarket, PO Box 9767, Wellington New Zealand. Address: Te Maraeunui, 176 Queen Street, Dunedin, New Zealand.

BROUMAS Olga, b. 6 May 1949, Hermoupolis, Greece. Poet. m. Stephen Edward Bangs, 1973, div 1979. Education: BA, University of Pennsylvania, 1970; MFA, University of Oregon at Eugene, 1973. Appointments: Instructor, University of Oregon, 1972-76; Visiting Associate Professor, University of Idaho, 1978; Poet-in-Residence, Goddard College, Plainfield, Vermont, 1979-81, Women Writers Center, Cazenovia, New York, 1981-82; Founder-Associate Faculty, Freehand Women Writers and Photographers Community, Provincetown, Massachusetts, 1982-87; Visiting Associate Professor, Boston University, 1988-90; Fanny Hurst Poet-in-Residence, Brandeis University, 1990. Publications: Restlessness, 1967; Caritas, 1976; Beginning with O, 1977; Soie Sauvage, 1980; Pastoral Jazz, 1983; Black Holes, Black Stockings, 1985; Perpetua, 1989; Sappho's Gymnasium, 1994. Honours: Yale Younger Poets Award, 1977; National Endowment for the Arts Grant, 1978; Guggenheim Fellowship, 1981-82. Address: 162 Mill Pond Drive, Brewster, MA 02631, USA.

BROWN A(lfred) Peter, b. 30 Apr 1943, Chicago, Illinois, USA. Professor of Music; Musicologist; Writer; Editor. m. Carol Vanderbilt, 23 Mar 1968, 1 daughter. Education: BME, 1965, MM, 1966, PhD, 1970, Northwestern University; Domaine School for Conductors, Hancock, Maine, 1965; Postdoctoral Studies, New York University, 1970. Appointments: Lecturer, Indiana University Northwest, 1967-69; Assistant Professor, University of Hawaii, 1969-74; Assistant Professor, 1974-77, Associate Professor, 1977-81, Professor of Music, 1981-, Chair, Department of Musicology, 1997-, Indiana University; Visiting Scholar, University of Missouri, Columbia, 1981; Faculty, Aston Magna Academy, 1989; Ida Beam Distinguished Visiting Professor, University of Iowa, 1991; Distinguished Alumnae Lecturer, Northwestern University School of Music, 1993. Publications: Joseph Haydn in Literature: A bibliography (with J T Berkenstock and C V Brown),

1974; Carlo d'Ordonez (1734-1786): A Thematic Catalog, 1978; The String Quartets Opus 1 of Carlo d'Ordonez: A Critical Edition, 1980; Performing Haydn's The Creation: Reconstructing the Earliest Renditions, 1985; Haydn's Keyboard Music: Sources and Style, 1986; The French Music Publisher Guera of Lyon: A Dated List (with Richard Griscom), 1987; Haydn's The Creation: A New Performing Edition, vocal score (with Julie Schnepel), 1991, full score, 1995; The Symphony from Sammartini to Lutoslawski, 5 volumes, 1998-. Contributions to: Seven Symphonies of Carlo d'Ordonez: An Edition (with Peter Alexander), in The Symphony, 1720-1840 (Barry S Brook editor), 1979; Scholarly books and journals. Honours: American Council of Learned Societies Fellow, 1972-73; Guggenheim Fellowship, 1978-79; Malin Memorial Award, American Choral Directors' Association and Music Publishers' Association, 1992; Clowes Foundation Publication Grant, 1997. Memberships: American Musicological Society; Music Library Association. Address: c/o School of Music, Indiana University, Bloomington, IN 47405, USA.

BROWN Archibald Haworth, b. 10 May 1938, Annan, Scotland. Professor of Politics; Writer. m. Patricia Susan Cornwell, 22 Mar 1963, 1 son, 1 daughter. Education: City of Westminster College, 1958-59; BSc in Economics, 1st Class Honours, London School of Economics and Political Science, 1962; MA, Oxford University, 1972. Appointments: Lecturer in Politics, Glasgow University, 1964-71; British Council Exchange Scholar, Moscow University, 1967-68; Lecturer in Soviet Institutions, 1971-89, Professor of Politics, 1989-, Oxford University; Visiting Professor and Henry L Stimson Lecturer, Yale University, 1980; Visiting Professor, University of Connecticut, 1980, Columbia University, 1985, University of Texas at Austin, 1990-91; Distinguished Residential Fellow, Kellogg Institute for International Studies, University of Notre Dame, 1998. Publications: Soviet Politics and Political Science, 1974; The Soviet Union Since the Fall of Khrushchev (editor with Michael Kaser), 1975, 2nd edition, 1978; Political Culture and Political Change in Communist States (editor with Jack Gray), 1977, 2nd edition, 1979; Authority, Power, and Policy in the USSR: Essays Dedicated to Leonard Schapiro (editor with T H Rigby and Peter Reddaway), 1980; The Cambridge Encyclopedia of Russia and the Soviet Union (editor with John Fennell, Michael Kaser, and Harry T Willetts), 1982; Soviet Union Policy for the 1980s (editor), 1984; Political Leadership in the Soviet Union (editor), 1989; The Soviet Union: A Biographical Dictionary (editor), 1990; New Thinking in Soviet Politics (editor), 1992; The Cambridge Encyclopedia of Russia and the Former Soviet Union (editor with Michael Kaser and Gerald S Smith), 1994; The Gorbachev Factor, 1996. Contributions to: Scholarly journals and symposia. Memberships: American Association for the Advancement of Slavic Studies; American Political Science Association; British Academy, fellow; British National Association for Russian and East European Studies; International Political Science Association; Political Studies Association of the United Kingdom. Address: St Antony's College, Oxford University, Oxford OX2 6JF, England.

BROWN Craig (Edward Moncrieff), b. 23 May 1967, England. Journalist; Author. m. Frances Welch, 1987, 1 son, 1 daughter. Education: University of Bristol. Appointments: Columnist (as Wallace Arnold), The Spectator, 1987-, The Times, 1988, Private Eye, 1989-, Independent on Sunday, 1991, The Evening Standard, 1993-, The Guardian (as Bel Littlejohn), 1995-; Restaurant Columnist, Sunday Times, 1988-93. Publications: The Marsh Marlowe Letters, 1983; A Year Inside, 1988; The Agreeable World of Wallace Arnold, 1990; Rear Columns, 1992; Welcome to My Worlds, 1993; Craig Brown's Greatest Hits, 1993; The Hounding of John Thenos, 1994; The Private Eye Book of Craig Brown Parodies, 1995. Address: c/o The Evening Standard, Northcliffe House, 2 Derry Street, London, W8 5EE, England.

BROWN Diana, b. 8 Aug 1928, Twickenham, England. Research Librarian; Author. m. Ralph Herman Brown, 31

Dec 1964, dec, 2 daughters. Education: AA, San Jose City College, 1974; BA, 1975, MLS, 1976, MA, 1977, San Jose State University. Appointments: Librarian, Signetics Corp, Sunnyvale, California, 1978-79, NASA/Ames Research Center, Moffett Field, 1979-80; Academic Information Specialist, University of Phoenix, San Jose Division, 1984-86; Research Librarian, San Jose Public Library, 1988-. Publications: The Emerald Necklace, 1980; Come Be My Love, 1981; A Debt of Honour, 1981; St Martin's Summer, 1981; The Sandalwood Fan, 1983; The Hand of a Woman, 1984; The Blue Dragon, 1988. Honour: American Library Association Booklist Outstanding Adult Novel, 1984. Memberships: Authors Guild; Jane Austen Society; Special Libraries Association; Phi Kappa Phi. Address: Gate Tree Cottage, PO Box 2846, Carmel by the Sea, CA 93921, USA.

BROWN Hamish Macmillan, (James MacMillan), b. 13 Aug 1934, Colombo, Sri Lanka. Author; Mountaineer; Photographer. Appointments include: Pioneered outdoor education, Braehead School; Founder Member, Training Boards; County Adviser on Outdoor Education; Led groups in Atlas mountains, Morocco, 3-4 months annually; Freelance Writer, Photographer, 1962-. Publications: Hamish's Mountain Walk, 1978; Hamish's Groats End Walk, 1981; Poems of the Scottish Hills, editor, 1982; The Gentlemen, selected poems, 1983; Speak to the Hills, editor, 1985; Climbing the Corbetts, 1988; The Great Walking Adventure; Hamish Brown's Scotland, 1988; The Bothy Brew, short stories, 1993; The Fife Coast, 1994; The Last Hundred, 1994; Exploring the Edinburgh to Glasgow Canals, 1997. Contributions to: Over 100 publications worldwide. Honours: SAC Award for Hamish's Mountain Walk; Honorary DLitt, St Andrew's University, 1997. Membership: Outdoor Writers Guild. Address: 26 Kirkcaldy Road, Burntisland, Fife KY3 9HQ, Scotland.

BROWN Iain Duncan, b. 3 Sept 1967, Sydney, New South Wales, Australia. Publisher. Education: BA, English Literature, Macquarie University, Sydney, 1994; MA, History of the Book, School of Advanced Study, University of London, England, 1996. Publications: The Young Publishers' Handbook, 1991; EDline (E-Mail Editorial Discussion List), 1996; How Americans Publish Commercial Fiction, (1997). Contributions to: The Tony Godwin Legacy, in The Bookseller, 1995. Memberships: Royal Society of Literature; The Paternosters; Society of Young Publishers; Society of Freelance Editors and Proof Readers; The Electric Editors. Address: 67a Prince of Wales Mansions, Prince of Wales Drive, London, SW11 4BJ, England.

BROWN Ian James Morris, b. 28 Feb 1945, Barnet, England. m. (1) Judith Sidaway, 8 June 1969, div, 1997, (2) Nicola Axford, 7 June 1997, 1 son, 1 daughter. Education: Dollar Academy, University of Edinburgh and Crewe and Alsager College; MA; DipEd; MLitt; PhD. Appointments: Playwright, 1967-; School Teacher, 1967-69, 1970-71; Lecturer in Drama: Dunfermline College Edinburgh, 1971-76; Br Council Edinburgh and Istanbul, 1976-78; Principal Lecturer, Crewe and Alsager College, 1978-86 (seconded as sec Cork Enq into Professional Theatre, 1985-86); Drama Director, Arts Council of GB, 1986-94; Professor and Head Drama Department, Queen Margaret College, Edinburgh, 1995- (Reader in Drama, 1994-95); Director, Scottish Centre for Cultural Management and Policy, 1996-; Programme Director, Alsager Arts Centre, 1980-86; Chairman, Scot Soc of Playwrights, 1973-75, 1984-87 and 1997-; Convenor NW Playwrights' Workshop, 1982-85; Chairman, British Theatre Institute, 1985-87 (Vice Chairman 1983-85), Dionysia Chianti World Festival of Theatre, 1991-93; FRSA, 1991; Plays include: Mother Earth, 1970; The Bacchae, 1972; Positively the Last Final Farewell Performance (ballet scenario), 1972; Carnegie, 1973; Rune (choral work), 1973; The Knife, 1973; Rabelais, 1973; The Fork, 1976; New Reekie, 1977; Mary, 1977; Runners, 1978; Mary Queen and the Loch Tower, 1979; Pottersville, 1982; Joker in the Pack, 1983; Beatrice, 1989; First Strike, 1990; The Scotch Play, 1991; Bacchai, 1991; Wasting Reality, 1992. Recreations: Theatre; Cooking; Sport; Travel. Address: Queen

Margaret College, Clerwood Terrace, Edinburgh EH12 8TS, Scotland.

BROWN James Willie Jr. See: **KOMUNYAKAA Yusef.**

BROWN John Russell, b. 15 Sept 1923, Bristol, England. Professor of Theatre; Theatre Director; Writer. m. Hilary Sue Baker, 5 Apr 1961, 1 son, 2 daughters. Education: BA, 1949, BLitt, 1951, Oxford University; PhD, University of Birmingham, 1960. Appointments: Fellow, Shakespeare Institute, Stratford-upon-Avon, 1951-53; Faculty, 1955-63, Head, Department of Drama and Theatre Arts, 1964-71, University of Birmingham; Professor of English, Sussex University, 1971-82; Professor of Theatre Arts, State University of New York at Stony Brook, 1982-85; Artistic Director, Project Theatre, 1985-89, Professor of Theatre, 1985-97, University of Michigan; Consultant, Middlesex University,1994-; Director of various theatre productions in Europe and North America; Visiting Lecturer or Professor in Europe, North America and New Zealand. Publications: Shakespeare and his Comedies, 1957; Shakespeare: The Tragedy of Macbeth, 1963; Shakespeare's Plays in Performance, 1966; Effective Theatre, 1969; Shakespeare's The Tempest, 1969; Shakespeare's Dramatic Style, 1970; Theatre Language, 1972; Free Shakespeare, 1974; Discovering Shakespeare, 1981; Shakespeare and His Theatre, 1982; A Short Guide to Modern British Drama, 1983; Shakescenes, 1993; William Shakespeare: Writing for Performance, 1996; What is Theatre?: An Introduction and Exploration, 1997; New Sites for Shakespeare, forthcoming. Contributions to: General Editor: Stratford-upon-Avon Studies, 1960-67; Stratford-upon-Avon Library, 1964-69; Theatre Production Studies, 1981-; Theatre Concepts, 1992-; Oxford Illustrated History of Theatre, 1995. Editor: Various plays of Shakespeare. Contributions to: Scholarly journals. Memberships: Advisory Council, Theatre Museum, 1974-83, chairman, 1979-83; Arts Council of Great Britain, drama panel chairman, 1980-83. Address: 318 The Circle, Queen Elizabeth Street, London SE1.

BROWN Kevin, b. 3 Sept 1960, Kansas City, Missouri, USA. Essayist; Biographer; Journalist. Education: BA, Columbia University, 1988. Publications: Romare Bearden, 1994; Malcom X: His Life & Legacy, 1995; Countée Cullen, 1996. Contributions to: London Times Literary Supplement; Washington Post Bookworld; Threepenny Review; Kirkus Reviews. Honours: General Studies Scholar, Columbia University; New York Public Library Book Awards, 1995, 1996. Membership: PEN International. Literary Agent: Scott Meredith Literary Agency, c/o Lisa Edwards, 845 Third Avenue, New York, NY 10022, USA. Address: 166 West 75th Street, Apt 920, New York, NY 10023, USA.

BROWN Malcolm Carey, b. 7 May 1930, Bradford, West Yorkshire, England. Freelance Historian. m. Beatrice Elsie Rose Light, 19 Dec 1953, 2 sons, 1 daughter. Education: BA, Honours 1st Class, English, 1952, MA, 1957, St John's College, Oxford. Appointments: General Trainee, BBC, 1955; Production Assistant, BBC TV, 1958-60; Television Documentary Producer, BBC, 1960-86; Freelance Historian, Imerial War Museum, 1989-. Publications: Scapa Flow (co-author), 1968; Tommy Goes to War, 1978; Christmas Truce (co-author), 1984; A Touch of Genius (co-author), 1988; The Letters of T E Lawrence (editor), 1988; The Imperial War Museum Book of the First World War, 1991; The Imperial War Museum Book of the Western Front, 1993; The Imperial War Museum Book of the Somme, 1996; The Imperial War Museum Book of 1918 Year of Victory, 1998. Honour: Nominated for Non-Fiction Award, 1989. Address: 4 Northbury Avenue, Ruscombe, Reading RG10 9LF, England.

BROWN Marc (Tolon), b. 25 Nov 1946, Erie, Pennsylvania, USA. Author and Illustrator of Children's Books. m. (1) Stephanie Marini, 1 Sept 1968, diss 1977, 2 sons, (2) Laurene Krasny, 11 Sept 1983, 1 daughter. Education: BFA, Cleveland Institute of Art, 1969.

Appointments: Assistant Professor, Garland Junior College, Boston, 1969-76; Author and Illustrator of children's books, 1976-. Publications: Author of over 40 children's books including: Arthur's Nose, 1976, Arthur's Family Vacation, 1993, Kiss Hello, Kiss Goodbye, 1997; Arthur Makes the Team, 1998. Illustrator of other children's books. Honours: Many citations and awards incluyding: Library of Congress Book of the Year Citation, 1985; Weekly Reader Children's Book Club Award, 1992; Gold Medal Award, Best Children's Software, Bologna, Italy, 1997. Memberships: Author's Guild; Author's League of America; National Braille Press; Advisory Council for the Harvard Centre for Children's Health, 1997. Address: Hinham, MA, and Martha's Vineyard, MA, USA.

BROWN Marion Marsh, b. 22 July 1908, Brownsville, Nebraska, USA. Professor; Author. m. Gilbert S Brown, 11 June 1937, 1 son. Education: BA, Peru (Nebraska) State College; MA, University of Nebraska. Appointments: Assistant Professor, Department of English, Peru State College; Professor of English, Omaha Public Schools, Adult Eduction, University of Nebraska. Publications: Young Nathan; The Swamp Fox; Broad Stripes and Bright Stars; Frontier Beacon; Stuarts landing; Marnie; The Silent Storm; Homeward The Arrows Flight; Dream Catcher; Prairie Teacher; A Norse Abroad; Portrait of a Phoenix; Learning Words in Contexxt I; Learning Words in Context II; Sacagawea; Singapore; Susette la Flesche. Honours: Several. Address: Apt 133, Silvercrest, 11909 Miracle Hills Drive, Omaha, NE 68154, USA.

BROWN Matthew Kemp, b, 21 Sept 1964, Leicester, England. Journalist. Education: BSc Honours, 1st Class, Physical Education, Sports Science, Loughborough University, 1986; MA, Sociology of Contemporary Culture, York University, 1989; PTC Certificate in Periodical Journalism, PMA Training, London, 1990. Appointments: Editor, IAAF Magazine, 1991-93; Editor, Agenda magazine, Liberty, 1994; Press and Publications Officer, British Olympic Association, 1994; Editor, Writer, Commission for Racial Equality, 1995. Publications include: Editor: Lillehammer '94, 1994; Kick It Again, 1995; Kick It Out, 1996; Connections, 1997; 365, 1997; Citizen, 1997-98; Arkive, 1997-98. Contributor to: The Guardian; The Observer; New Statesman; Times Educational Supplement; The Big Issue; Time Out; When Saturday Comes; Red Pepper. Honour: PTC Certificate in Periodical Journalism. Membership: National Union of Journalists. Address: 51 Graham Mansions, Sylvester Road, London E8 1EU, England.

BROWN Patricia Ann Fortini, b. 16 Nov 1936, Oakland, California, USA. University Professor; Art Historian. m. (1) Peter Claus Meyer, May 1957, div 1978, 2 sons, (2) Peter Robert Lamont Brown, Aug 1980, div 1989. Education: AB, 1959, MA, 1978, PhD, 1983, University of California at Berkeley. Appointments: Assistant Professor, 1983-89, Associate Professor, 1989-91, Andrew W Mellon Professor, 1991-95, Professor, 1997-, Princeton University. Publications: Venetian Narrative Painting in the Age of Carpaccio, 1988; Venice and Antiquity: The Venetian Sense of the Past, 1996; The Renaissance in Venice: A World Apart, 1997. Contributions to: Art History; Christian Science Monitor; Monitor Book Review; Burlington Magazine; Renaissance Quarterly; Biography. Honours: Premio Salotto Veneto, Italy; Phyllis Goodhart Gordon Book Prize, 1998. Memberships: Renaissance Society of America; American Academy in Rome; College Art Association. Address: Department of Art and Archaeology, Princeton University, Princeton, NJ 08544, USA.

BROWN Rita Mae, b. 28 Nov 1944, Hanover, Pennsylvania, USA. Author; Poet. Education: AA, Broward Junior College, 1965; BA, New York University, 1968; Cinematography Degree, School of the Visual Arts, 1968; PhD, Institute for Policy Studies, 1976. Appointments: Writer-in-Residence, Women's Writing Center, Cazenovia College, New York, 1977-78; President, American Artists Inc, 1981-; Visiting Instructor,

University of Virginia, 1992. Publications: Hrotsvitha: Six Medieval Latin Plays, 1961; The Hand that Cradles the Rock (poem), 1971; Rubyfruit Jungle (novel), 1973; Songs to a Handsome Woman (poems), 1973; In Her Day (novel), 1976; The Plain Brown Rapper (political articles), 1976; Six of One (novel), 1978; Southern Discomfort (novel), 1982; Sudden Death (novel), 1983; High Hearts (novel), 1986; Bingo (novel), 1988; Starting from Scratch: A Different Kind of Writer's Manual, 1988; Wish You Were Here (novel), 1990; Rest in Pieces (novel), 1992; Venus Envy (novel), 1993; Murder at Monticello (novel), 1994; Pay Dirt, or Adventures at Ash Lawn (novel), 1995; Riding Shotgun (novel), 1996; Murder, She Meowed (novel), 1996; Stars and Bars (novel), 1997; Murder on the Prowl (novel), 1998. Other: Screenplays; teleplays. Contributions to: Anthologies. Honours: National Endowment for the Arts Grant, 1978; New York Public Library Literary Lion, 1987; Honorary Doctorate, Wilson College, 1992. Memberships: International Academy of Poets; PEN International; Poets and Writers. Address: c/o American Artists Inc, PO Box 4671, Charlottesville, VA 22905, USA.

BROWN Robert Douglas, b. 17 Aug 1919, Trealaw, Wales. Journalist; Publisher. m. Elsie Mary Warner, 17 Aug 1940, dec 1997, 1 son, 2 daughters. Education: BA, Open University, 1986. Appointments: Political Staff, News Chronicle, 1951-60; Managing Director, Anglia Echo Newspapers, 1964-80. Publications: The Battle of Crichel Down; The Survival of the Printed Word; The Port of London; East Anglia-The War Years, 7 volumes. Membership: Fellow, PEN. Address: 15 Westbourne Gardens, Glasgow, G12 9XD, Scotland.

BROWN Rosellen, b. 12 May 1939, Philadelphia, Pennsylvania, USA. Writer; Poet; Associate Professor. m. Marvin Hoffman, 16 Mar 1963, 2 daughters. Education: BA, Barnard College, 1960; MA, Brandeis University, 1962. Appointments: Instructor, Tougaloo College, Mississippi, 1965-67; Staff, Bread Loaf Writer's Conference, Middlebury, Vermont, 1974, 1991, 1992; Instructor, Goddard College, Plainfield, Vermont, 1976; Visiting Professor of Creative Writing, Boston University, 1977-78; Associate Professor in Creative Writing, University of Houston, 1982-85, 1989-. Publications: Some Deaths in the Delta and Other Poems, 1970; The Whole World Catalog: Creative Writing Ideas for Elementary and Secondary Schools (with others), 1972; Street Games: A Neighborhood (stories), 1974; The Autobiography of My Mother (novel), 1976; Cora Fry (poems), 1977; Banquet: Five Short Stories, 1978; Tender Mercies (novel), 1978; Civil Wars: A Novel, 1984; A Rosellen Brown Reader: Selected Poetry and Prose, 1992; Before and After (novel), 1992; Cora Fry's Pillow Book (poems), 1994. Contributions to: Books, anthologies, and periodicals. Honours: Woodrow Wilson Fellow, 1960; Howard Foundation Grant, 1971-72; National Endowment for the Humanities Grants, 1973-74, 1981-82; Radcliffe Institute Fellow, 1973-75; Great Lakes Colleges New Writers Award, 1976; Guggenheim Fellowship, 1976-77; American Academy and Institute of Arts and Letters Award, 1988; Ingram Merrill Grant, 1989-90. Address: c/o Creative Writing Program, University of Houston, Houston, TX 77204, USA.

BROWN Sheila, b. 1 Apr 1947, England. Housewife. m. Raymond Brown, 24 Dec 1983. Education: Hull University, 1965-66; Fielden Park College RSA Typing & Shorthand, Oldham Technical College; City & Guilds Catering. Publication: Dream Don't Dream. Contributions to: Church Magazine; Bolton Evening News. Address: 53 Crosby Road, Bolton BL1 4EL, England.

BROWN Stewart, b. 14 Mar 1951, Lymington, Hampshire, England. University Lecturer in African and Caribbean Literature; Writer; Poet; Editor. m. Priscilla Margaret Brant, 1976, 1 son, 1 daughter. Education: BA, Falmouth School of Art, 1978; MA, University of Sussex, 1979; PhD, University of Wales, 1987. Appointments: Lecturer in English, Bayero University, Kano, Nigeria, 1980-83; Lecturer in African and Caribbean Literature, University of Birmingham, 1988-. Publications: Mekin Foolishness (poems), 1981; Caribbean Poetry Now,

1984, new edition, 1992; Zinder (poems), 1986; Lugard's Bridge (poems), 1989; Voiceprint: An Anthology of Oral and Related Poetry from the Caribbean (editor with Mervyn Morris and Gordon Rohler), 1989; Writers from Africa: A Readers' Guide, 1989; New Wave: The Contemporary Caribbean Short Story, 1990; The Art of Derek Walcott: A Collection of Critical Essays, 1991; The Art of Edward Kamau Brathwaite: A Collection of Critical Essays, 1992; The Heinemann Book of Caribbean Poetry (with Ian McDonald), 1992; The Pressures of the Text: Orality, Texts and the Telling of Tales, 1995; Caribbean New Voices I, 1996; African New Voices, 1997; The Oxford Book of Carribbean Short-stories (with John Wilkham), 1998; Elsewhere: New and Selected poems, 1998. Contributions to: Anthologies and periodicals. Honours: Eric Gregory Award, 1976; Southwest Arts Literature Award, 1978; Honorary Fellow, Centre for Caribbean Studies, University of Warwick, 1990. Memberships: Welsh Academy; Welsh Union of Writers. Address: Centre of West African Studies, University of Birmingham, Edgbaston, Birmingham B15 2TT, England.

BROWN Terence, b. 17 Jan 1944, Loping, China. Professor of Anglo-Irish Literature; Writer; Editor. m. Suzanne Marie Krochalis, 1969, 1 son, 1 daughter. Education: BA, 1966, PhD, 1970, Trinity College, Dublin. Appointments: Lecturer, 1968-82, Director of Modern English, 1976-83, Fellow, 1976-86, Registrar, 1980-81, Associate Professor of English, 1982-93, Professor of Anglo-Irish Literature, 1993-, Trinity College, Dublin. Publications: Time Was Away: The World of Louis MacNeice (editor with Alec Reid), 1974; Louis MacNeice: Sceptical Vision, 1975; Northern Voices: Poets from Northern Ulster, 1975; The Irish Short Story (editor with Patrick Rafroidi), 1979; Ireland: A Social and Cultural History, 1922-1979, 1981, new edition as Ireland: A Social and Cultural History, 1922 to the Present, 1985; The Whole Protestant Community: The Making of a Historical Myth, 1985; Hermathena (editor with N Grene), 1986; Samuel Ferguson: A Centenary Tribute (editor with B Hayley), 1987; Ireland's Literature: Selected Essays, 1988; Traditions and Influence in Anglo-Irish Literature (editor with N Grene), 1989; The Field Day Anthology of Irish Writing (contributing editor), 1991; James Joyce: Dubliners (editor), 1992; Celticism (editor), 1996; Journalism: Derek Mahon, Selected Prose (editor), 1996. Memberships: International Association for the Study of Anglo-Irish Literature; Royal Irish Academy; European Society for the Study of English, board member; Academia Europaea; International Association of Professors of English. Address: Department of English, Trinity College, Dublin 2, Ireland.

BROWNE Michael Dennis, b. 28 May 1940, Walton-on-Thames, England (US citizen, 1978). Professor; Writer; Poet. m. Lisa Furlong McLean, 18 July 1981, 1 son, 2 daughters. Education: BA, Hull University, 1962; Oxford University, 1962-63; Ministry of Education Teacher's Certificate, 1963; MA, University of Iowa, 1967. Appointments: Visiting Lecturer, University of Iowa, 1967-68; Instructor, 1967, 1968, Visiting Adjunct Assistant Professor, 1968, Columbia University; Faculty, Bennington College, Vermont, 1969-71; Visiting Assistant Professor, 1971-72, Assistant Professor, 1972-75, Associate Professor, 1975-83, Professor, 1983-, University of Minnesota. Publications: The Wife of Winter, 1970; Sun Exercises, 1976; The Sun Fetcher, 1978; Smoke From the Fires, 1985; You Won't Remember This, 1992; Selected Poems 1965-1995, 1997. Contributions to: Numerous anthologies and journals. Other: Texts for various musical compositions. Honours: Fulbright Scholarship, 1965-67; Borestone Poetry Prize, 1974; National Endowment for the Arts Fellowships, 1977, 1978; Bush Fellowship, 1981; Loft-McKnight Writers' Award, 1986; Minnesota Book Award for Poetry, 1993, 1998. Memberships: The Loft; Poetry Society of America. Address: 2111 East 22nd Street, Minneapolis, MN 55404, USA.

BROWNING Vivenne, (Elaine Vivenne Browning Baly), b. 1 Dec 1922, Sydney, New South Wales, Australia. Writer; Lecturer; Broadcaster. m. W F Baly, 21 Aug 1954, 1 son, 3 daughter. Education: Mary Datchelor,

London, 1942; Hazelhurst College, Melbourne. Appointments: Staff Sergeant, Intelligence Corps ATS, 1942-46; Civil Resettlement of Repatriated Prisioners of War, 1945-46; Metropolitan Police, CID, London, 1946-50; Board of Directors, International Browning Society, Baylor University. Publications: My Browning Family Album; The Uncommon Medium; From Store Detective to Private Eye; Living in Addis Ababa; Lord Haw Haw; St Ives Summer; The Leach Pottery. Contributions to: Magazines. Memberships: Browning Society; New Barnet Literary and Debating Society; Boston Browning Society; Arthur Machen Society; Intelligence Corps Comrades Association; Metropolitan Police Association; Friend of the Royal Academy of Arts; Australian Film Society; Keats Shelley Association; Royal Society of Literature; Society of Authors; PEN; Metropolitan Women Police Association. Address: c/o SKOOB Pub, 25 Lowman Road, North London, England.

BROWNJOHN Alan (Charles), b. 28 July 1931, London, England. Poet; Novelist; Critic. Education: BA, 1953, MA, 1961, Merton College, Oxford. Appointments: Lecturer, Battersea College of Education, 1965-76, Polytechnic of the South Bank, 1976-79; Poetry Critic, New Statesman, 1968-76, Encounter, 1978-82, Sunday Times, 1990-. Publications: Poetry: Travellers Alone, 1954; The Railings, 1961; The Lions' Mouths, 1967; Sandgrains on a Tray, 1969; Penguin Modern Poets 14, 1969; First I Say This: A Selection of Poems for Reading Aloud, 1969; Brownjohn's Beasts, 1970; Warrior's Career, 1972; A Song of Good Life, 1975; The Old Flea-Pit, 1987; The Observation Car, 1990; In the Cruel Arcade, 1994. Fiction: To Clear the River, 1964; The Way You Tell Them, 1990; The Long Shadows, 1997. Other: Philip Larkin, 1975; Meet and Write, 1985-87; The Gregory Anthology, 1990. Translations: Torquato Tasso (play), Goethe, 1985; Horace (play), Corneille, 1996. Memberships: Arts Council of Great Britain Literature Panel, 1968-72; Poetry Society, chairman. 1982-88, London; Writers' Guild of Great Britain; Society of Authors. Literary Agent: Rosica Colin Ltd, London, SW7 5AH. Address: 2 Belsize Park, London NW3, England.

BROWNJOHN J(ohn Nevil) Maxwell, b. Rickmansworth, Hertfordshire, England. Literary Translator; Screenwriter. Education: MA, Lincoln College, Oxford. Publications: Night of the Generals, 1962; Memories of Teilhard de Chardin, 1964; Klemperer Recollections, 1964; Brothers in Arms, 1965; Goya, 1965; Rodin, 1967; The Interpreter, 1967; Alexander the Great, 1968; The Poisoned Stream, 1969; The Human Animal, 1971; Hero in the Tower, 1972; Strength Through Joy, 1973; Madam Kitty, 1973; A Time for Truth, 1974; The Boat, 1974; A Direct Flight to Allah, 1975; The Manipulation Game, 1976; The Hittites, 1977; Willy Brandt Memoirs, 1978; Canaris, 1979; Life with the Enemy, 1979; A German Love Story, 1980; Richard Wagner, 1983; The Middle Kingdom, 1983; Solo Run, 1984; Momo, 1985; The Last Spring in Paris, 1985; Invisible Walls, 1986; Mirror in the Mirror, 1986; The Battle of Wagram, 1987; Asassin, 1987; Daddy, 1989; The Marquis of Bolibar, 1989; Eunuchs for Heaven, 1990; Little Apple, 1990; Jaguar, 1990; Siberian Transfer, 1992; The Swedish Cavalier, 1992; Infanta, 1992; The Survivor, 1994; Acts, 1994; Love Letters From Cell 92, 1994; Turlupin, 1995; Nostradamus, 1995; The Karnau Tapes, 1997; Heroes Like Us, 1998; The Photograpger's Wife, forthcoming. Screen Credits: Tess (with Roman Polanski), 1979; The Boat, 1981; Pirates, 1986; The Name of the Rose, 1986; The Bear, 1989; Bitter Moon (with Roman Polanski), 1992; The Ninth Gate (with Roman Polanski), forthcoming. Honours: Schlegel Tieck Special Award, 1979; US Pen Prize, 1981; Schlegel Tieck Prize, 1993; US Christopher Award, 1995; Helen and Kurt Wolff Award, US, 1998. Memberships: Translators Association; Society of Authors. Address: The Vine House, Nether Compton, Sherborne, Dorset DT9 4QA, England.

BROWNLOW Kevin, b. 2 June 1938, Crowborough, Sussex, England. Author; Film Director; Former Film Editor. Publications: The Parade's Gone By, 1968; How It Happened Here, 1968; Adventures with D W Griffith, (editor), 1973; Hollywood: The Pioneers, 1979; The War, the West, and the Wilderness, 1979; Napoleon: Abel Gance's Classic Film, 1983; Behind the Mask of Innocence, 1990; David Lean - A Biography, 1996. Address: c/o Photoplay, 21 Princess Road, London NW1 8JR, England.

BROXHOLME John Franklin, (Duncan Kyle, James Meldrum), b. 11 June 1930, Bradford, England. Former Journalist; Author. m. Alison Millar Hair, 22 Sept 1956, 3 children. Education: Bradford, England. Publications: As Duncan Kyle: A Cage of Ice, 1970; Flight into Fear, 1972; A Raft of Swords, 1973; The Suvarov Adventure, 1974; Terror's Cradle, 1975; White-Out, 1976; In Deep, 1976; Black Camelot, 1978; Green River High, 1979; Stalking Point, 1981; The King's Commissar, 1984; The Dancing Men, 1985; The Honey Ant, 1988. As James Meldrum: The Semonov Impulse, 1975. Address: Oak Lodge, Valley Farm Road, Newton, Sudbury, Suffolk, England.

BRUCE George, b. 10 Mar 1909, Fraserburgh, Aberdeenshire, Scotland. Poet; Writer; Broadcaster; Lecturer. m. Elizabeth Duncan, 25 July 1935, 1 son, 1 daughter. Education: MA, Aberdeen University, 1932. Appointments: English Master, Dundee High School, 1934-46; Producer, BBC, Aberdeen, 1946-56, Edinburgh, 1956-70; First Fellow in Creative Writing, Glasgow University, 1971-73; Lecturer in Scotland and abroad. Publications: Sea Talk, 1944; Landscapes and Figures, 1967; Collected Poems, 1940-1970, 1970; Perspectives: Selected Poems, 1970-1986, 1986; The Land Out There, 1991; Pursuit: Poems 1986-1998, forthcoming. Other: Anne Redpath: A Monograph of the Scottish Painter, 1975; Some Practical Good: The Cockburn Association, 1875-1975, 1975; Festival in the North, 1947-1975, 1975. Contributions to: Anthologies, books, and periodicals. Honours: Scottish Arts Council Awards, 1967, 1971; Honorary DLitt, College of Wooster, Ohio, USA, 1977; Officer of the Order of the British Empire, 1984. Memberships: Honorary Member of the Saltire Society, 1992-; Honorary President, Scottish Poetry Library; Poetry Society, 1992-. Address: 25 Warriston Crescent, Edinburgh EH3 5LB, Scotland.

BRUCE Lennart, b. 21 Feb 1919, Stockholm, Sweden. Writer; Poet. m. Sonja Wiegandt, 22 July 1960, 1 son, 1 daughter. Education: College and university studies. Appointment: International financier, 1945-64. Publications: In English: Making the Rounds, 1967; Observations, 1968; Moments of Doubt, 1969; Mullioned Windows, 1970; The Robot Failure, 1971; Exposure, 1972; Letter of Credit, 1973; Subpoemas, 1974; The Broker, 1984. In Swedish: En Sannsaga, 1982; Utan Synbar Anledning, 1988; Forskingringen, 1990; En Nasares Gang, 1993; Kafferepet, 1995. Translations: Instructioins for Undressing the Human Race (with Matthew Zion), 1968; Agenda, 1976; The Second Light, 1986; Speak to Me, 1989; The Ways of a Carpetbagger, 1993. Contributions to: Many US and Swedish literary magazines. Honour: Royal Swedish Academy of Letters Awards, 1978, 1988. Memberships: PEN American Centre; Poetry Society of America; Swedish Writers Union. Address: 31 Los Cerros Place, Walnut Creek, CA 94598, USA.

BRUCE Robert V(ance), b. 19 Dec 1923, Malden, Massachusetts, USA. Historian; Professor Emeritus. Education: Massachusetts Institute of Technology, 1941-43; BS, University of New Hampshire, 1945; AM, 1947, PhD, 1953, Boston University. Appointments: Instructor, University of Bridgeport, 1947-48; History Master, Lawrence Academy, Groton, Massachusetts, 1948-51; Research Assistant to Benjamin P Thomas, 1953-54; Instructor to Professor of History, 1955-84, Professor Emeritus, 1984-, Boston University; Visiting Professor, University of Wisconsin at Madison, 1962-63. Publications: Lincoln and the Tools of War, 1956; 1877: Year of Violence, 1959; Bell: Alexander Graham Bell and the Conquest of Solitude, 1973; The Launching of Modern American Science, 1846-1876, 1987. Contributions to: Various publications. Honours: Guggenheim Fellowship, 1957-58; Huntington Library Fellow, 1966; Pulitzer Prize in History, 1988; Distinguished Alumni Award, Boston University, 1991. Memberships: Fellow, American Association for the Advancement of Science; Phi Beta Kappa, honorary; Society of American Historians, fellow. Address: 28 Evans Road, Madbury, NH 03820, USA.

BRUCE (William) Harry, b. 8 July 1934, Toronto, Ontario, Canada. Journalist; Editor; Writer. m. Penny Meadows, 10 Sept 1955, 2 sons, 1 daughter. Education: BA, Mount Allison University, 1955; London School of Economics and Political Science, 1956-57; Massey College, University of Toronto, 1969-70. Appointments: Reporter, Ottawa Journal, 1955-59, Globe and Mail, 1959-61; Assistant Editor, 1961-64, Columnist, 1970-71, Maclean's; Managing Editor, Saturday Night, 1964-65, Canadian Magazine, 1965-66; Associate Editor and Columnist, Star Weekly, 1967-68; Columnist, Toronto Daily Star, 1968-69; Talk-show Host, CBC-TV, Halifax, Nova Scotia, 1972; Editor, 1979-80, Executive Editor, 1981, Atlantic Insight; Editor, Atlantic Salmon Journal, 1991-. Publications: The Short Happy Walks of Max MacPherson, 1968; Nova Scotia, 1975; Lifeline, 1977; R A: The Story of R A Jodrey, Entrepreneur, 1979; A Basket of Apples: Recollections of Historic Nova Scotia, 1982; The Gulf of St Lawrence, 1984; Each Moment as it Flies, 1984; Movin' East: The Further Writings of Harry Bruce, 1985; The Man and the Empire: Frank Sobey, 1985; Down Home: Notes of a Maritime Son, 1988; Maud: The Life of L M Montgomery, 1992; Corporate Navigator, 1995. Contributions to: Various anthologies and periodicals. Honours: Evelyn Richardson Memorial Literary Award, 1978; Brascan Award for Culture, National Magazine Awards, 1981; Top Prize for Magazine Writing, Atlantic Journalism Awards, 1983, 1984, 1986, 1993; City of Dartmouth Book Award, 1989; Booksellers' Choice Award, Atlantic Provinces Booksellers' Association, 1989. Address: General Delivery, St Andrews, New Brunswick E0G 2X0, Canada.

BRUCE-LOCKHART Robin, b. 13 Apr 1920, London, England. Author. m. (1) Margaret Crookdake, 14 Dec 1941, div 1953, 1 daughter, (2) Eila McLean, 1987. Education: Royal Naval College, Dartmouth; Cambridge University, Economics. Appointments: Foreign Manager, Financial Times, 1946-53; General Manager, Beaverbrook Newspapers, Daily Express, Sunday Express, Evening Standard, 1953-60; Member, London Stock Exchange, 1960. Publications: Reilly Ace of Spies, 1967; Half Way to Heaven; The Secret Life of the Carthusians, 1965, 1985, Reilly - The First Man, 1987; Listening to Silence, 1997. Contributions to: Various, in various countries. Membership: Chairman, Sussex Author Assocation, 1970-78. Address: c/o Campbell, Thomson & McLaughlan Ltd, 1 Kings Mews, London WC1N 2JA, England.

BRUCHAC Joseph, b. 16 Oct 1942, Saratoga Springs, New York, USA. Author; Poet; Storyteller; Publisher; Editor. m. Carol Worthen, 12 June 1964, 2 sons. Education: AB, Cornell University, 1965; MA, Syracuse University, 1966; Graduate Studies, State University of New York at Albany, 1971-73; PhD, Union Institute, Ohio, 1975. Appointments: Co-Founder, Director, Greenfield Review Press, 1969-; Editor, Greenfield Review literary magazine, 1971-90; Visiting Scholar and Writer-in-Residence at various institutions; Member, Dawnland Singers, 1993-. Publications: Fiction and Poetry: Indian Mountain and Other Poems, 1971; Turkey Brother and Other Iroquois Folk Tales, 1976; The Dreams of Jesse Brown (novel), 1977; Stone Giants and Flying Heads: More Iroquois Folk Tales, 1978; The Wind Eagle and Other Abenaki Stories, 1984; Iroquois Stories, 1985; Walking With My Sons and Other Poems, 1986; Near the Mountains: New and Selected Poems, 1987; Keepers of the Earth (stories), 1988; The Faithful Hunter: Abenaki Stories, 1988; Long Memory and Other Poems, 1989; Return of the Sun: Native American Tales from the Northeast Woodlands, 1989; Hoop Snakes, Hide-Behinds and Side-Hill Winders: Tall Tales from the Adirondacks, 1991; Keepers of the Animals (with Michael Caduto) (stories), 1991; Thirteen Moons on Turtle's Back (with Jonathan London) (poems and stories), 1992; Dawn Land (novel), 1993; The First Strawberries, 1993; Flying With the Eagle, Racing the Great Bear (stories), 1993; The Girl Who Married the Moon (with Gayle Ross) (stories), 1994; A Boy Called Slow, 1995; The Boy Who Lived With Bears (stories), 1995; Dog People (stories), 1995; Long River (novel), 1995; The Story of the Milky Way (with Gayle Ross), 1995; Beneath Earth and Sky, 1996; Children of the Long House (novel), 1996; Four Ancestors: Stories, Songs and Poems from Native North America, 1996. Other: Survival This Way: Interviews with Native American Poets, 1987; The Native American Sweat Lodge: History and Legends, 1993; Roots of Survival: Native American Storytelling and the Sacred, 1996. Editor: Words from the House of the Dead: An Anthology of Prison Writings from Soledad (with William Witherup), 1971; The Last Stop: Writings from Comstock Prison, 1974; Aftermath: An Anthology of Poems in English from Africa, Asia and the Caribbean, 1977; The Next World: Poems by Thirty-Two Third-World Americans, 1978; Songs from This Earth on Turtle's Back: Contemporary American Indian Poetry, 1983; The Light from Another Country: Poetry from American Prisons, 1984; Breaking Silence: An Anthology of Asian American Poetry, 1984; North Country: An Anthology of Contemporary Writing from the Adirondacks and the Upper Hudson Valley (with others), 1985; New Voices from the Longhouse: An Anthology of Contemporary Iroquois Writing, 1989; Returning the Gift: Poetry and Prose from the First North American Native Writers Festival, 1994; Smoke Rising: The Native North American Literary Companion (with others), 1995; When the Chenoo Howls (with James Bruchac, 1998; Lasting Echoes, 1998; Arrow Over the Door, 1998; Heart of a Chief, 1998; The Waters Between, 1998. Contributions to: Many anthologies, books and periodicals. Honours: National Endowment for the Arts Fellowship, 1974; Rockefeller Foundation Humanities Fellowship, 1982-83; American Book Award, 1985; Notable Children's Book in the Language Arts Award, 1993; Scientific American Young Readers Book Award, 1995; Parents Choice Award, 1995; American Library Association Notable Book Award, 1996; Knickerbocker Award for Juvenile Literature, New York Library Association, 1996. Memberships: National Association for the Preservation and Perpetuation of Storytelling; PEN; Poetry Society of America. Address: PO Box 308, Greenfield Center, NY 12833, USA.

BRUIN John. See: **BRUTUS Dennis (Vincent).**

BRULOTTE Gaëtan, b. Apr 1945, Lévis, Quebec, Canada. Professor; Writer. Education: BA, 1966, 1969, MA, 1972, Laval University; PhD, École des Hautes Études en Sciences Sociales, Paris, 1977. Appointments: Instructor, Laval University, 1969; Professor of French, Trois-Rivières College, 1970-83; Visiting Professor, Université du Québec á Trois-Rivières, 1973, 1980, 1981, 1989, 1990, University of New Mexico, 1981, 1982, 1983, 1984, 1993-94, University of California at Santa Barbara, 1982, Brevard Community College, 1983-84, Université Stendahl, 1993, Sorbonne, Paris, 1994; Distinguished Visiting Professor, New Mexico State University, 1988; Visiting Professor, 1984-88, Professor, 1988-, University of South Florida. Publications: L'Imaginaire et l'écriture: Ghelderode, 1972; Aspects du texte érotique, 1977, revised edition as Oeuvres de chair: Figures du discours érotique, 1998; L'Emprise (novel), 1979, revised edition, 1988, English translation as Double Exposure, 1988; Ecrivains de la Mauricie (editor), 1981; Le Surveillant (short stories), 1982, 3rd edition, revised, 1995, English translation as The Secret Voice, 1990; Le Client (play), 1983; Ce qui nous tient, 1988; L'Univers du peintre Jean Paul Lemieux (critical essay), 1996; Les cahiers de Limentinus: Lectures fin de Siècle (essays), 1998. Contributions to: Books, anthologies, textbooks, scholarly journals, and periodicals. Honours: Adrienne-Choquette Award, 1981; France-Quebec Award, 1983; 1st Prize, XI CBC Radio Drama Contest, 1983; Literary Grand Prize, Trois-Rivières, 1989; John-Glassco Translation Award, 1990. Memberships: International Comparative Literature Association; International Council on Francophone Studies; Modern Language Association. Address: c/o Division of Modern Language, University of South Florida, Tampa, FL 33620, USA.

BRUMMER Alexander, b. 25 May 1949, Hove, England. Journalist. m. Tricia Brummer, 2 sons. Education: BSc, Economics, University of Southampton; MBA, University of Bradford Management Center. Publications: American Destiny, 1986; Hanson - A Biography, 1994; Weinstock - A Biography, 1998. Contributions to: Guardian. Address: 119 Farringdon Road, London EC1 3ER, England.

BRUNNER Eva, b. 26 Nov 1952, Lucerne, Switzerland. Writer; Playwright; Translator. Education: Communications, American College of Rome, c/o University of Charleston, West Virginia, 1979-82. Publications: Plays: Kalt, 1984; Granit, 1985; Alles Wird Gut, 1994; Frieda Flachmann, 1997; Sutters Salut, 1998. Radio: Geist trug die Steine, 1988; Herrscher und Herrscherin, 1989; Der Schweiz den Rückenkehren, 1991. Honours: Various scholarships. Membership: Swiss Writers' Association. Address: Kuglerstrasse 22, 10439 Berlin, Germany.

BRUNSE Niels (Henning), b. 24 Aug 1949, Silkeborg, Denmark. Editor; Writer; Translator. m. Galina Ivashkina, 18 Mar 1977, div. Education: University of Copenhagen; University of Moscow. Appointments: Co-Editor, Hug magazine, 1974-76, Politisk Revy, bi-weekly, 1978-82; Reviewer, Information newspaper, 1982-94; Editor, Danish Writers Association Journal, 1983-85; Writer, Politiken, 1994-. Publications: Several books; Numerous translations. Contributions to: Many periodicals. Honours: Danish State Art Foundation Lifetime Grant; Danish Translators Association Honorary Award; Thornton Niven Wilder Award, Columbia University. Memberships: Danish Dramatists Association; Danish PEN; Danish Writers Association. Address: Aalandsgade 26, DK-2300 Copenhagen, Denmark.

BRUNSKILL Ronald William, b. 3 Jan 1929, Lowton, England. Retired Architect; Professor; Writer. m. Miriam Allsopp, 1960, 2 daughters. Education: BA, 1951, MA, 1952, PhD, 1963, University of Manchester. Appointments: Commonwealth Fund Fellow in Architecture and Town Planning, Massachusetts Institute of Technology, 1956-57; Architect, Williams Deacon's Bank, 1957-60; Lecturer, 1960-73, Senior Lecturer, 1973-84, Reader in Architecture, 1984-89, Honorary Fellow, School of Architecture, 1989-95, University of Manchester; Partner, 1966-69, Consultant, 1969-73, Carter, Brunskill & Associates, architects; Visiting Professor, University of Florida at Gainesville, 1969-70; President, Vernacular Architect Group, 1974-77; Honorary Visiting Professor, 1994-95, Professor, School of the Built Environment, 1995-, De Montfort University. Publications: Illustrated Handbook of Vernacular Architecture, 1971, 3rd edition, enlarged, 1987; Vernacular Architecture of the Lake Counties, 1974; English Brickwork (with Alec Clifton-Taylor), 1977; Traditional Buildings of Britain, 1981, 2nd edition, enlarged, 1992; Traditional Farm Buildings of Britain, 1982, 2nd edition, enlarged, 1987, 3rd edition, enlarged, 1999; Timber Building in Britain, 1985, 2nd edition, enlarged, 1994; Brick Building in Britain, 1990; Houses and Cottages of Britain, 1997;Traditional Farm Building of Britain and their conservation, 1999; Vernacular Architecture: An Illustrated Handbook, forthcoming. Contributions to: Scholarly journals. Honours: Fellow, Society of Antiquaries, 1975-; President's Award, Manchester Society of Architects, 1977; Officer of the Order of the British Empire, 1990. Memberships: Cumberland and Westmorland Antiquarian and Archaeological Society, vice president, 1975-90, president, 1990-93; Historic Buildings Council for England, 1978-84; Cathedrals Advisory Committee for England, 1981-91; Cathedrals Fabric Commission, 1991-96; Ancient Monuments Society, honorary architect, 1983-88, vice chairman, 1988-90, chairman, 1990-; Royal Commission on the Ancient and Historical Monuments for Wales, 1983-97, vice chairman 1993-97; British Historic Buildings Trust, trustee, 1985-92; Historic Buildings and Monuments Commission, 1989-95; Address: De Montfort University, Centre for Conservation Studies, School of Architecture, 12 Castle View, Leicester LE1 5WH, England.

BRUSEWITZ Gunnar (Kurt), b. 7 Oct 1924, Stockholm, Sweden. Author; Artist. m. Ingrid Andersson, 21 Oct 1946, 2 daughter. Education: Royal Academy of Art. Publications: Hunting - A Cultural History Chronicle of Hunting in Europe, 1967; Bjornjagare och Fjarilsmalare, 1968; Skissbok, 1970; Nature in Gambia, 1971; Skog, 1974; Strandspegling, 1979; Wings and Seasons, 1980; Sveriges Natur, 1984; Memoirs I-III, 1994-98; The Amazing Miss Brooke, 1998. Contributions to: Stockholms Tidningen; Svenska Dagbladet; Various Other Swedish Magazines and Publications. Honours: Stockholm City Presentation Prize, 1970; Dag Hammarskjold Medal, 1975; Honorary PhD, 1982; Die Goldene Blume Von Rheydt Düsseldorf, 1989; Memberships: PEN; World Wildlife Fund; Royal Society of Science in Uppsala. Literary Agent: Wahlstrom & Windstrand Forlag, Stockholm, Sweden. Address: Lisinge, 762 93 Rimbo, Sweden.

BRUTON Eric, (Eric Moore), b. 1915, London, England. Author; Company Director. Appointments: Managing Director, NAG Press Ltd, Colchester, 1963-93, Diamond Boutique Ltd, 1965-80; Chairman, Things & Ideas Ltd, 1970-78. Publications: True Book about Clocks, 1957; Death in Ten Point Bold, 1957; Die Darling Die, 1959; Violent Brothers, 1960; True Book about Diamonds, 1961; The Hold Out, 1961; King Diamond, 1961; The Devil's Pawn, 1962; Automation, 1962; Dictionary of Clocks and Watches, 1962; The Laughing Policeman, 1963; The Longcase Clock, 1964, 2nd edition, 1978; The Finsbury Mob, 1964; The Smithfield Slayer, 1964; The Wicked Saint, 1965; The Fire Bug, 1967; Clocks and Watches 1400-1900, 1967; Clocks and Watches, 1968; Diamonds, 1970, 2nd edition, 1977; Antique Clocks and Clock Collecting, 1974; The History of Clocks, 1978; The Wetherby Collection of Clocks, 1980; Legendary Gems, 1984; Collector's Dictionary of Clocks and Watches, 1999. Honour: Eric Bruton Medal created for awarding to outstanding student in annual international diamond exams, 1996. Memberships: British Horological Institute, 1955-62; Crime Writers Association, 1959-62; Gemmological Association of Great Britain, council member, 1972-91, president, 1994-95; National Association of Goldsmiths, president, 1983-85. Address: Pond House, Great Bentley, Colchester CO7 8QG, England.

BRUTUS Dennis (Vincent), (John Bruin), b. 28 Nov 1924, Salisbury, Rhodesia. Professor; Poet; Writer. m. May Jaggers, 14 May 1950, 4 sons, 4 daughters. Education: BA, University of the Witwatersrand, Johannesburg, South Africa, 1947. Appointments: Professor at universities in Pittsburgh, Austin, Dartmouth, and Boston. Publications: Sirens, Knuckles, Boots, 1963; Letters to Martha and Other Poems from a South African Prison, 1968; Poems from Algiers, 1970; Thoughts Abroad, 1970; A Simple Lust: Selected Poems, 1973; China Poems, 1975; Stubborn Hope, 1978; Strains, 1982; Salutes and Censures, 1984; Airs and Tributes, 1988; Still the Sirens, 1993. Contributions to: Periodicals. Honours: Paul Robeson Award; Langston Hughes Award. Memberships: African Literature Association; American Civil Liberties Union; Amnesty International; PEN; Union of Writers of African Peoples. Address: 3812 Bates Street, Pittsburgh, PA 15213, USA.

BRUYN Günter de, b. 1 Nov 1926, Berlin, Germany. Author. 1 son. Education: Library Science, Berlin. Publications: Der Hohlweg, 1963; Buridans Esel, 1968; Preisverleihung, 1972; Das Leben des Jean Paul Richter, 1975; Tristan und Isolde, 1975; Märkische Forschungen: Erzahlung fur Freunde der Literaturgeschichte, 1978; Im Querschnitt, 1979; Babylon, 1980; Neue Herlichkeit, 1984; Rahels erste Liebe: Rahel Levin und Karl Graf von Finckenstein in ihren Briefen, 1985; Frauendienst, 1986; Lesefreuden: Uber Bücher und Menschen, 1986; Jubelschreie, Trauergesänge: Deutsche Befindlichkeiten, 1991; Zwischenbilanz: Eine Jugen in Berlin, 1992; Vierzig Jahre: Ein Lebensbericht, 1996. Honours: Heinrich Mann Prize, 1992; Vierzig Jahre: Ein Lebensbericht, 1996. Honours: Heinrich Mann Prize, 1965; Lion Feuchtwanger Prize, 1980; Thomas Mann Prize, 1990; Heinrich Böll Prize, 1990; Grant Cross of Merit, Federal Republic of

Germany, 1994; Konrad Adenauer Foundation Prize for Literature, 1996. Memberships: Akademie der Künste, Berlin; Deutsche Akademie für Sprache und Dichtung e. v., Darmstadt. Address: Blabber 1, D-1548 Görsdorf Bei Beeskow. Germany.

BRYAN Lynne, b. 10 May 1961, Leicester, England. Writer. Education: BA, Humanities, Wolverhampton Polytechnic, 1980-83; MA, Creative Writing, University of East Anglia, 1984-85. Publications: Envy at the Cheese Handout, 1995; Gorgeous, 1999. Contributions to: Anthologies and magazines. Honours: Eastern Arts Grant, 1996; BBC Arts Council Award, 1996. Address: c/o Curtis Brown, Haymarket House, 28-29 Haymarket, London SW1Y 4SP, England.

BRYANS Robin. See: **HARBINSON-BRYANS Robert.**

BRYANT Dorothy (Mae), b. 8 Feb 1930, San Francisco, California, USA. Writer; Dramatist; Teacher; Publisher. m. (1) 1949-64, 1 son, 1 daughter, (2) Robert Bryant, 18 Oct 1968, 1 stepson, 1 stepdaughter. Education: BA, 1950, MA, 1964, San Francisco State University. Appointments: Teacher, High School, 1953-64, San Francisco State University, San Francisco Mission Adult School, Golden Gate College, 1961-64, Contra Costa College, 1964-76; Publisher, Ata Books, 1978-. Publications: Fiction: Ella Price's Journal, 1972; The Kin of Ata Are Waiting for You, 1976; Miss Giardino, 1978; The Garden of Eros, 1979; Prisoners, 1980; Killing Wonder, 1981; A Day in San Francisco, 1983; Confessions of Madame Psyche, 1986; The Test, 1991; Anita, Anita, 1993. Plays: Dear Master, 1991; Tea With Mrs Hardy, 1992; The Panel, 1996; The Trial of Cornelia Connelly, 1996; Posing for Gauguiro, 1998. Non-Fiction: Writing a Novel, 1979; Myths to Lie By: Essays and Stories, 1984. Honour: American Book Award, 1987. Address: 1928 Stuart Street, Berkeley, CA 94703, USA.

BRYANT J(oseph) A(llen) Jr, b. 26 Nov 1919, Glasgow, Kentucky, USA. Professor (retired); Writer. m. (1) Mary Virginia Woodruff, 28 Dec 1946, 2 sons, (2) Sara C Bryant, 9 Mar 1993. Education: AB, Western Kentucky University, 1940; MA, Vanderbilt University, 1941; PhD, Yale University, 1948. Appointments: Instructor to Associate Professor, Vanderbilt University, 1945-56; Associate Professor, University of the South at Sewanee, 1956-59, Duke University, 1959-61; Professor, University of North Carolina, Greensboro, 1961-68, Syracuse University, 1968-71, University of Kentucky, 1973-90. Publications: Hippolyta's View: Some Christian Aspects of Shakespeare's Plays, 1961; The Compassionate Satirist: Ben Jonson and His Imperfect World, 1972; Understanding Randall Jarrell, 1986; Shakespeare and the Uses of Comedy, 1986; Twentieth Century Southern Literature, 1997. Honour: DLitt, University of the South, 1993. Memberships: MLA, SAMLA, ALSC. Address: 713 Old Dobbin Road, Lexington, KY 40502, USA.

BRYDEN John Herbert, b. 15 July 1943, Dundas, Ontario, Canada. Politician; Writer. m. Catherine Armstrong, 26 Aug 1967, 1 son, 2 daughters. Education: BA, Honours, McMaster University, 1966; MPhil, University of Leeds, 1968. Appointments: Staff, Hamilton Spectator, 1969-77, Globe and Mail, 1977-79, Toronto Star, 1979-89; Liberal Member of Parliament, Hamilton-Wentworth, 1993-. Publications: Deadly Allies: Canada's Secret War, 1937-1947, 1989; Best-Kept Secret: Canadian Secret Intelligence in the Second World War, 1993. Address: 83 Lynden Road, Lynden, Ontario L04 1TO, Canada.

BRYNJULFSDOTTIR Anna Kristin, b. 23 Dec 1938, Reykjavik, Iceland. Teacher of Latin and Mathematics. m. Elias Sneland Jónsson, 24 June 1967, 3 sons. Education: MR, 1958; Teacher, University, 1960; BA Latin, Greek University of Iceland, 1987. Publications: Four Little Teddybears, 1964; Four Little Teddybears in Caveland, 1965; Tiny Miny (Matti Patti), 1976; Trilli, Being from Outer Space, 1977; Gliding Down the Rainbow, 1978; Julia and Snorri, 1979; Klappadu Kongulo (Cuddle a Spider), 1996; Poems in: Six in Poems 1998.

Memberships: Association of Icelandic Writers; Icelandic Teachers Association. Address: Brekkutun 18, Kopavogur 200, Box 24, Iceland.

BRYSON Norman, b. 4 Sept 1949, Glasgow, Scotland. University Teacher. m. Margaret Pinder, 1 d. Education: BA, Cambridge University, 1970; MA, Cambridge, 1971; Special Student, University of California, Berkeley, 1970-72; PhD, Cambridge, 1977. Appointments: Professor, Visual abd Cultural Studies, University of Rochester, New York, 1988-90; Professor of Art History, Harvard University, 1990-. Publications: Word and Image: French Paintings of the Ancien Regime; Vision and Painting: The Logic of the Gaze; Tradition and Desire: From David to Delacroix; Looking at the Overlooked: Four Essays on Still Life Painting. Contributions to: Regular Contributor to The Times Literary Supplement, Parkett, Art and Text. Honour: Cinoa Prize, Brussels. Address: Department of Art History and Architecture, Harvard University, 485 Broadway, Cambridge, MA 02138, USA.

BRZEZINSKI Zbigniew (Kazimierz), b. 28 Mar 1928, Warsaw, Poland (US citizen, 1958). Professor of American Foreign Policy; Author. m. Emilie Anna Benes, 3 children. Education: BA, 1949, MA, 1950, McGill University; PhD, Harvard University, 1953. Appointments: Instructor and Research Fellow, 1953-56, Assistant Professor of Government and Research Associate, 1956-60, Harvard University; Associate Professor, 1960-62, Professor of Public Law and Government and Director of the Research Institute on International Change, 1962-77, 1981-89, Columbia University; Director, Trilateral Commission, 1973-76; Special Assistant to President Jimmy Carter for National Security Affairs, and member of the National Security Council, 1977-81; Counselor, Center for Strategic and International Studies, 1981-; Robert E Osgood Professor of American Foreign Policy, Paul Nitze School of Advanced International Studies, Johns Hopkins University, 1989-; Guest Lecturer and Advisor to governmental and private institutions in the US and abroad; Public Speaker; Television Commentator. Publications: Political Controls in the Soviet Army (editor), 1954; The Permanent Purge: Politics in Soviet Totalitarianism, 1956; Ideology and Foreign Affairs (with others), 1959; The Soviet Bloc: Unity and Conflict, 1960, revised edition, 1967; Totalitarian Dictatorship and Autocracy (with Carl Joachim Friedrich), 1961, 2nd edition, 1965; Ideology and Power in Soviet Politics, 1962, revised edition, 1967; Africa and the Communist World (editor), 1963; Political Power: USA/USSR (with Samuel P Huntington), 1964, 2nd edition, 1977; Alternative to Partition: For a Broader Conception of America's Role in Europe, 1965; Dilemmas of Change in Soviet Politics (editor), 1969; The Fragile Blossom: Crisis and Change in Japan, 1972; Between Two Ages: America's Role in the Technetronic Era, 1972; The relevance of Liberalism, 1977; Power and Principle: Memoirs of the National Security Advisor, 1977-1981, 1983; Democracy Must Work: A Trilateral Agenda for the Decade: A Task Force Report of the Trilateral Commission (with others), 1984; Game Plan: A Geostrategic Framework for the Conduct of the US-Soviet Contest, 1986; Promise or Peril, the Strategic Defense Initiative: Thirty-Five Essays by Statesmen, Scholars, and Strategic Analysts (with Richard Sincere, Marin Strmecki, and Peter Wehner), 1986; American Security in an Interdependent World: A Collection of Papers Presented at the Atlantic Council's 1987 Annual Conference (with others), 1988; In Quest of National Security, 1988; The Grand Failure: The Birth and Death of Communism in the Twentieth Century, 1989; Out of Control: Global Turmoil on the Eve of the Twenty-First Century, 1993; The Grand Chessboard: American Primacy and its Geostrategic Imperatives, 1996. Contributions to: Many publications, journals, and periodicals. Honours: Guggenheim Fellowship, 1960; Presidential Medal of Freedom, 1981; U Thant Award, 1995; Order of the White Eagle, Poland, 1995; Ukraine's Order of Merit, 1st Class, 1996; Czech Republi's Masaryk Order, 1st Class, 1998; Lithuania's Gediminas Order, 1st Class, 1998. Memberships: American Academy of Arts

and Sciences, fellow; Amnesty International; Atlantic Council; Council on Foreign Relations; Freedom House; National Endowment for Democracy; Trilateral Commission. Address: Center for Strategic and International Studies, 1800 K Street North West, Washington DC 20006, USA.

BUCH JENSEN Poul, b. 4 Jan 1937, Copenhagen, Denmark. Mechanical Engineer. m. Anna-Lise, 28 July 1962, 1 son, 1 daughter. Education: Bachelor, Engineering; Bachelor, Economics and Marketing. Publications: ISO 9000: A Guide and Commentary, 1991; ISO 9000: Internal Quality Audits, 1992; Service, 1994; Environmental Management and Environmental Certifications, 1994. Contributions to: Numerous magazines and journals. Memberships: Danish Authors Society; American Society for Quality Control; Rotary Club. Address: Alfarvejen 30 - Osted, DK-4000 Roskilde, Denmark.

BUCHANAN Colin Ogilvie, b. 9 Aug 1934, Croydon, Surrey, England. Church of England Clerk in Holy Orders. Education: BA, 1959, MA, 1962, Lincoln College, Oxford; Tyndale Hall, Bristol, 1959-61; DD, 1993. Appointments: Editor, News of Liturgy Monthly, 1975-; Bishop of Woolwich, Diocese of Southark, 1996-. Publications: Modern Anglican Liturgies, 1958-68, 1968; Further Anglican Liturgies, 1968-75, 1975; Latest Anglican Liturgies, 1976-84, 1985; Modern Anglican Ordination Rites, 1987; The Bishop in Liturgy, 1988; Open to Others, 1992; Joint Author: Growing into Union, 1970; Anglican Worship Today, 1980; Reforming Infant Baptism, 1990; Infant Baptism and the Gospel, 1993; Cut the Connection: Disestablishment and the Church of England, 1994; Is the Church of England Biblical?, 1998. Membership: House of Bishops of General Synod of the Church of England; Executive Committee of the Church of England General Synod Council for Christian Unity; Vice President, Electoral Reform Society. Address: 37 South Road, London, SE23 2UJ.

BUCHANAN Pat(rick Joseph), b. 2 Nov 1938, Washington, District of Columbia, USA. Journalist; Columnist; Broadcaster; Writer. m. Shelley Ann Scarney, 8 May 1971. Education: AB, English, cum laude, Georgetown University, 1961; MS, Journalism, Columbia University, 1962. Appointments: Editorial Writer, 1962-64, Assistant Editorial Editor, 1964-66, St Louis Globe Democrat; Executive Assistant to Richard M Nixon, 1966-69; Special Assistant to President Richard M Nixon, 1969-73; Consultant to Presidents Richard M Nixon and Gerald R Ford, 1973-74; Syndicated Columnist, 1975-; Various radio and television broadcasts as commentator, panelist, moderator, etc, 1978-; Assistant to President Ronald Reagan and Director of Communications, White House, Washington DC, 1985-87; Candidate for the Republican Party Nomination for President of the US, 1992, 1996; Chairman, The American Cause, 1993-95, 1997-. Publications: The New Majority, 1973; Conservative Votes, Liberal Victories, 1975; Right from the Beginning, 1988; The Great Betrayal: How American Sovereignty and Social Justice Are Being Sacrificed to the Gods of the Global Economy, 1998. Contributions to: Newspapers and periodicals. Honour: Knight of Malta, 1987. Memberships: Republican Party; Roman Catholic Church. Address: c/o Creators Syndicate, 5777 West Century Boulevard, Suite 700, Los Angeles, CA 90045, USA.

BUCHER Werner, b. 19 Aug 1938, Zürich, Switzerland. Poet; Writer; Journalist; Editor. m. Josiane Fidanza, 2 May 1968. Publications: Nicht Solche Aengste, du ... (poems), 1974; Zeitzünder 3: Dank an den Engel, 1987; Was ist mit Lazarus?, 1989; Einst & Jetzt & Morgen (poems), 1989; Mouchette (poems), 1995; Wegschleudern die Brillen, die Lügen (poems), 1995; Unruhen, 1998. Contributions to: Entwürfe. Memberships: PEN; Swiss Writers Union. Address: Rest, Kreuz, 9427 Zelg-Wolfhalden, Switzerland.

BUCHWALD Art, b. 20 Oct 1925, Mt Vernon, New York, USA. Columnist; Author. m. Ann McGarry, 11 Oct 1952, 1 son, 2 daughters. Education: University of

Southern California, Los Angeles, 1945-48. Appointments: Syndicated columnist for newspapers around the world. Publications: Paris After Dark, 1950; Art Buchwald's Paris, 1954; The Brave Coward, 1957; More Caviar, 1958; Un Cadeau Pour le Patron, 1958; A Gift From the Boys, 1959; Don't Forget to Write, 1960; How Much is That in Dollars?, 1961; Is it Safe to Drink the Water?, 1962; Art Buchwald's Secret List to Paris, 1963; I Chose Capitol Punishment, 1963; And Then I Told the President, 1965; Son of the Great Society, 1966; Have I Ever Lied to You?, 1968; The Establishment is Alive and Well in Washington, 1969; Counting Sheep, 1970; Getting High in Government Circles, 1971; I Never Danced at the White House, 1973; The Bollo Caper, 1974; I Am Not a Crook, 1974; Irving's Delight, 1975; Washington is Leaking, 1976; Down the Seine and Up the Potomac, 1977; The Buchwald Stops Here, 1978; Laid Back in Washington, 1981; While Reagan Slept, 1983; You CAN Fool All of the People All of the Time, 1985; I Think I Don't Remember, 1987; Whose Rose Garden is it Anyway?, 1989; Lighten Up, George, 1991; Leaving Home: A Memoir, 1994; I'll Always Have Paris, 1996. Honours: Priz de la Bonne Humeur, 1958; Pulitzer Prize in Commentary, 1982. Memberships: American Academy of Arts and Sciences; American Academy of Humor Columnists. Address: 2000 Pennsylvania Avenue North West, Washington DC 20006, USA.

BUCK Lilli Lee, b. 25 Feb 1950, Butler, Pennsylvania, USA. Teacher; Professional Astrologer. Education: BA, Anthropology, 1972, MEd, Special Education, 1984, College of William and Mary. Publications: Poems in following books: A Vagabond's Sketchbook, 1980; A Lyrical Fiesta, 1985; Poetic Symphony, 1987; Golden Voices, Past and Present, 1989; Voices on the Wind, 1989; Special Poets' Series, 1990; The Poet's Domain, Vol III, 1991, Vol V, 1992; A Treasury of Verse, 1997; Tenth Anniversary Issue, 1998; More Terrible than Thirst, 1998. Contribution to: Fate magazine, 1984. Honours: 3rd Place, World of Poetry Contest, 1983; Excellence in Poetry Award, Fine Arts Press, 1985; Editors Choice Award, National Library of Poetry, 1994. Memberships: Poetry Society of Virginia; Association for Research and Enlightenment; Kappa Delta Pi. Address: 7000 Reedy Creek Rd, Bristol, VA 24202, USA.

BUCKERIDGE Anthony Malcolm, b. 20 June 1912, London, England. Writer. m (1) Sylvia Brown, 1936, (2) Eileen Norah Selby, 25 Feb 1972, 2 sons, 1 daughter. Education: University College, London, 1932-35. Publications: Jennings Series of Children's Books, 25 Titles, 1950-91; Rex Milligan Series, 4 Titles, 1953-56; A Funny Thing Happened, 1953; Jennings Abounding, 1979; Musicals: It Happened in Hamelin, 1980;The Cardboard Conspiracy, 1985. Memberships: Society of Authors; Writers Guild of Great Britain; British Actors Equity. Address: East Crink, Barcombe Mills, Lewes, Sussex BN8 5BL, England.

BUCKLE (Christopher) Richard (Sandford), b. 6 Aug 1916, England. Writer; Ballet Critic. Education: Balliol College, Oxford. Appointments: Ballet Critic, Observer newspaper, 1948-55, The Sunday Times, 1959-75. Publications: John Innocent at Oxford (novel), 1939; The Adventures of a Ballet Critic, 1953; In Search of Diaghilev, 1955; Modern Ballet Design, 1955; The Prettiest Girl in England, 1958; Jacob Epstein, Sculptor, 1963; Nijinsky, 1969; Diaghilev, 1979; Buckle at the Ballet, 1980. Autobiographies: The Most Upsetting Woman, 1981; In the Wake of Diaghilev, 1982; George Balanchine: Ballet Master (with John Taras), 1988. Honour: Commander of the Order of the British Empire, 1979. Address: Roman Road, Gutch Common, Semley, Shaftesbury, Dorset, England.

BUCKLEY Fiona. See: **ANAND Valerie May Florence.**

BUCKLEY William K, b. 14 Nov 1946, San Diego, California, USA. Professor; Writer; Poet. m. Mary Patricia, 25 Nov 1969, 1 son. Education: BA, University of San Diego, 1969; MA, 1972, MA, 1975, California State University at San Diego; PhD, Miami University, Oxford, Ohio, 1980. Appointments: Instructor, San Diego Community Colleges, 1972-74; Co-Founder and Co-Editor, Recovering Literature, 1972-; Director, Learning Skills Center, California State University at San Diego, 1974-75; Teaching Fellow, Miami University, Oxford, Ohio, 1975-79; Visiting Assistant Professor, Hanover College, 1979-82; Visiting Assistant Professor, 1982-85, Professor, 1989-, Indiana University Northwest, Gary, Indiana. Publications: A Half-Century of Celine (co-author), 1983; Critical Essays on Louis-Ferdinand Celine (editor), 1989; Senses' Tender: Recovering the Novel for the Reader, 1989; New Perspectives on the Closing of the American Mind (co-editor), 1992; Lady Chatterley's Lover: Loss and Hope, 1993. Poetry: Meditation on the Grid, 1995; By the Horses Before the Rains, 1996; Heart Maps, 1997; Images Entitled to Their Recoil From Utopia, 1998; 81 Mygrations, 1998; Athena in Steeltown, forthcoming. Contributions to: Best Chapbook of the Year, Modern Poetry, 1997; Grants. Memberships: Academy of American Poets; Modern Language Association. Address: c/o Department of English, Indiana University Northwest, 3400 Broadway, Gary, IN 46408, USA.

BUCKLEY William F(rank), Jr, b. 24 Nov 1925, New York, New York, USA. Editor; Author. m. Patricia Taylor, 6 July 1950, 1 son. Education: University of Mexico, 1943; BA, Yale University, 1950. Appointments: Associate Editor, American Mercury magazine, 1952; Founder, President, Editor-in-Chief, 1955-90, Editor-at-Large, 1991-, National Review magazine; Syndicated columnist, 1962-; Host, Firing Line TV programme, 1966-; Lecturer, New School for Social Research, 1967-68; Froman Distinguished Professor, Russell Sage College, 1973; US Delegate, 28th General Assembly, United Nations, 1973. Publications: God and Man at Yale, 1951; McCarthy and His Enemies (with L Brent Bozell), 1954; Up from Liberalism, 1959; Rumbles Left and Right, 1963; The Unmaking of a Mayor, 1966; The Jeweler's Eye, 1968; The Governor Listeth, 1970; Cruising Speed, 1971; Inveighing We Will Go, 1972; Four Reforms, 1973; United Nations Journal, 1974; Execution Eve, 1975; Saving the Queen, 1976; Airborne, 1976; Stained Glass, 1978; A Hymnal, 1978; Who's On First, 1980; Marco Polo, If You Can, 1982; Atlantic High, 1982; Overdrive, 1983; The Story of Henri Tod, 1984; The Temptation of Wilfred Malachey, 1985; See You Later Alligator, 1985; Right Reason, 1985; High Jinx, 1986; Racing Through Paradise, 1987; Mongoose, R.I.P., 1988; On the Firing Line, 1989; Gratitude, 1990; Tucker's Last Stand, 1991; Windfall, 1992; In Search of Anti-Semitism, 1992; Happy Days Were Here Again: Reflections of a Libertarian Journalist, 1993; A Very Private Plot, 1994; The Blackford Oakes Reader, 1995; Brothers No More, 1995; Buckley: The Right Word, 1996; Nearer My God: An Autobiography of Faith, 1997; The Lexicon, 1998. Editor: The Committee and Its Critics, 1962; Odyssey of a Friend: Whittaker Chamber's Letters to William F. Buckley, Jr., 1954-61, 1970; American Conservative Thought in the Twentieth Century, 1970; Keeping the Tablets (with Charles Kesler), 1988.Contributions to: Books and periodicals. Honours: Best Columnist of the Year Award, 1967; Distinguished Achievement Award in Journalism, 1968, Julius Award for Outstanding Public Service, 1990, University of Southern California; Emmy Award for Outstanding Program Achievement, National Academy of Television Arts and Sciences, 1969; Bellarime Medal, 1977; Shelby Cullom Davis Award, 1986; Presidential Medal of Freedom, 1991; Gold Medal, National Institute of Social Sciences, 1992. Memberships: Council on Foreign Relations; Fellow, Society of Professional Journalists, Sigma Delta Chi. Address: c/o National Review, 150 East 35th Street, New York, NY 10016, USA.

BUCZACKI Stefan Tadeusz, b. 16 Oct 1945, Derby, England. Writer; Broadcaster. m. Beverley Ann Charman, 8 Aug 1970, 2 sons. Education: BSc, Southampton University; DPhil, Oxford University. Publications: Collins Guide to Pests, Diseases and Disorders of Garden Plants, 1981, 2nd edition, 1998; Collins Gem Guide to Mushrooms and Toadstools, 1982; Zoosporic Plant Pathogens, 1983; Beat Garden Pests and Diseases, 1985; Gardener's Questions Answered, 1985; Garden Warfare, 1988; Understanding Your Garden, 1990; The Essential Gardener, 1991; The Plant Care Manual, 1992; Collins Guide to Mushrooms and Toadstools of Britain and Europe, 1993; The Gardener's Handbook, 1993; Stefan Buczacki's Best Gardening Series, 1994-99; Stefan Buczacki's Gardening Dictionery, 1998. Contributions to: Numerous journals and magazines. Memberships: Royal Photographic Society, associate; Fellowships: Institute of Biology; Institute of Horticulture; Linnean Society; British Mycological Society, president. Address: c/o Knight Ayton Management, 10 Argyll St, London W1V 1AB.

BUDDEE Paul (Edgar), b. 12 Mar 1913, Western Australia. Retired School Principal; Author; Poet. m. Elizabeth Vere Bremner, 1944, 1 son, 1 daughter. Education: Claremont Teachers College. Appointments: School Principal, 1935-72. Publications: Stand to and Other War Poems, 1943; The Oscar and Olga Trilogy, 1943-47; The Unwilling Adventurers, 1967; The Mystery of Moma Island, 1969; The Air Patrol Series, 1972; The Ann Rankin Series, 1972; The Escape of the Fenians, 1972; The Peter Devlin Series, 1972; The Escape of John O'Reilly, 1973; The Call of the Sky, 1978; The Fate of the Artful Dodger, 1984; Poems of the Second World War, 1986. Contributions to: Many periodicals. Honours: Australia Citizen of the Year, 1979; Australia Commonwealth Literary Board Grants, 1977, 1978, 1984; OAM, 1989. Memberships: Australian Society of Authors; Fellowship of Writers; PEN International. Address: 2 Butson Road, Leeming, Western Australia 6149, Australia.

BUDRYS Algis, (Algirdas Jonas Budrys), b. 9 Jan 1931, Königsberg, Germany (Lithuanian citizen from birth, US citizen, 1996). Writer; Editor; Publisher. m. Edna F Duna, 24 July 1954, 4 sons. Education: University of Miami, 1947-49; Columbia University, 1951-52. Appointments: Editor-in-Chief, Regency Books, 1962-63, Playboy Press, 1963-65; Operations Manager, Woodall Publishing Co, 1974-75; President, Unifont Co, 1975-; Editor and Publisher, Tomorrow Speculative Fiction magazine, 1992-. Publications: Novels: False Night, 1954, revised edition as Some Will Not Die, 1962; Man of Earth, 1955; Who?, 1958; The Falling Torch, 1959, revised edition, 1991; Rogue Moon, 1960; The Iron Thorn, 1967; Michaelmas, 1977; Hard Landing, 1993. Collections: The Unexpected Dimension, 1960; The Furious Future, 1963; Blood and Burning, 1979. Non-Fiction: Truman and the Pendergasts, 1963; Bicycles: How They Work and How to Fix Them, 1976; Writing to the Point, 1994. Contributions to: Numerous magazines. Honours: Many awards. Membership: Science Fiction Hall of Fame. Address: 824 Seward Street, Evanston, IL 60202, USA.

BUECHNER (Carl) Frederick, b. 11 July 1926, New York, New York, USA. Author; Minister. m. Judith Friedrike Merck, 7 Apr 1956, 3 children. Education: AB, Princeton University, 1947; BD, Union Theological Seminary, 1958. Appointments: Teacher of Creative Writing, New York University, summers, 1954, 1955; Ordained Minister, United Presbyterian Church, 1958; Chairman, Department of Religion, 1958-67, Minister, 1960-67, Phillips Exeter Academy; William Belden Noble Lecturer, Harvard University, 1969; Russell Lecturer, Tufts University, 1971; Lyman Beecher Lecturer, Yale University, 1977; Harris Lector, Bangor Seminary, 1979; Smyth Lecturer, Columbia Seminary, 1981; Lecturer, Trinity Institute, 1990. Publications: A Long Day's Dying, 1950; The Season's Difference, 1952; The Return of Ansel Gibbs, 1958; The Final Beast, 1965; The Magnificent Defeat, 1966; The Hungering Dark, 1969; The Alphabet of Grace, 1970; The Entrance to Porlock, 1970; Lion Country, 1971; Open Heart, 1972; Wishful Thinking, 1973; The Faces of Jesus, 1974; Love Feast, 1974; Telling the Truth, 1977; Treasure Hunt, 1977; The Book of Bebb, 1979; Peculiar Treasures, 1979; Godric, 1980; The Sacred Journey, 1982; Now and Then, 1983; A Room Called Remember, 1984; Brendan, 1987; Whistling in the Dark, 1988; The Wizard's Tide, 1990; Telling Secrets, 1991; The Clown in the Belfry, 1992;

Listening to Your Life, 1992; The Son of Laughter, 1993; The Longing for Home, 1996; On the Road with the Archangel, 1997; The Storm, 1998. Honours: O'Henry Prize, 1955; Richard and Hinda Rosenthal Award, 1958; National Book Award Nomination, 1971; Pulitzer Prize Nomination, 1980. Memberships: Council on Religion in Independent Schools, regional chairman, 1958-63; National Council of Churches, committee on literature, 1954-57; Presbytery of Northern New England. Address: RR1, Box 1145, Pawlet, VT 05761, USA.

BUERO VALLEJO Antonio, b. 29 Sept 1916, Guadalajara, Spain. Dramatist. m. Victoria Rodriguez, 5 Mar 1959, 2 sons. Education: BA, 1932; San Fernando School of Fine Arts, Madrid, 1934-36. Publications: Plays in English Translation: En la ardiente oscuridad, 1951, In the Burning Darkness, 1975; La tejedora de suenos, 1952, The Dreamweaver, 1967; Un sonador para un pueblo, 1959, A Dreamer for the People, 1994; Las meninas: Fantasia velazquena, 1961, Las meninas: A Fantasy, 1987; El concierto de San Ovidio, 1963, The Concert at Saint Ovide, 1967; El tragaluz, 1968, The Skylight, 1992; La doble historia del doctor Valmy, 1967, The Double Case History of Doctor Valmy, 1967; El sueno de la razon, 1970, The Sleep of Reason, 1971; La fundacion, 1974, The Foundation, 1985; La detonacion, 1977, The Shot, 1989; Jueces en la noche, 1979, Judges in the Night, 1989; Lazaro en el laberinto, 1986, Lazarus in the Labyrinth, 1992; Musica cercana, 1989, The Music Window, 1994; Many other plays in Spanish only. Honours: Premio Lope de Vega, 1949; Premio Nacional de Teatro, 1957, 1958, 1959, 1980; Medalla de Oro del Espectador y la critica, 1967, 1970, 1974, 1976, 1977, 1981, 1984, 1986; Officier des Palmes Académiques de France, 1980; Premio Pablo Iglesias, 1986; Premio Miguel de Cervantes, 1986; Medalla de Oro al Merite en las Bellas Artes, 1994; Medalla de Oro de la Sociedad General de Autores de España, 1994; National Letters Prize, 1996. Memberships: Ateneo de Madrid, honorary fellow; Circulo de Bellas Artes de Madrid, honorary fellow; Deutscher Hispanistenverband, honorary fellow; International Committee of the Theatre of the Nations; Modern Language Association of America, honorary fellow; Real Academia Española; Sociedad General de Autores de España. Address: Calle General Diaz Porlier 36, Madrid 28001, Spain.

BUFFTON Barbara, b. 4 June 1953, Cheltenham, Gloucester, England. Writer; Trainer. m. Barry Mortimer, 27 June 1981. Education: BA, Hons, French & Linguistics, Essex University, 1980; Diploma in Careers Guidance, University of East London, England, 1986. Appointments: Careers Advisor, 1986-87; Careers Information Officer, 1988-90; Freelance Writer & Trainer, 1990-. Publications: The Which? Guide to Choosing a Career, 1998; Working for the Environment, 1999; Taking Control of Your Own Career, How to Books Ltd, 1999. Contributions to: Working In; Series of Booklets; COIC; Careerscope; Springboard. Memberships: Careers Writers Association, Membership Secretary, 1997-. Address: 71 Wimborne Road, Colehill, Wimborne, Dorset BH21 7RP, England.

BUHLER Jean Charles Alexis, b. 3 July 1919, La Chaux-de-Fonds. Writer. m. Nelly Turban, 13 Nov 1947, 2 sons, 1 daughter. Education: Universities Neuchâtel and Geneva. Appointments: Editor, L'Impartial (La Chaux-de-Fonds, 1941-43); Press Officer, 1947-83 (part time); UNESCO Adviser, Togo, 1963-64; Editor, Fao in Rome, 1972-73. Publications: Sur Les Routes D'Europe; Prends Ma Vie Camarade; Sur Les Routes d'Afrique; Blaise Cendrars; Tuez-Les Tous; L'Homme Des Iles. Contributions to: About 5000 articles and features. Membership: Société des Ecrivains Suisses. Address: 8 Edmond-De-Reynier, 2000 Neuchâtel, Switzerland.

BUISSERET David (Joseph), b. 18 Dec 1934, Totland Bay, Isle of Wight, England; Historian; Professor. m. Patricia Connolly, 9 Sept 1961, 3 sons, 2 daughters. Education: History Tripos, Part I, Class II.1, Part II, Class I, 1955-58, PhD, 1961, Corpus Christi College, Cambridge. Appointments: Research Fellow, Corpus Christi College, Cambridge, 1961-64; Lecturer to Senior Lecturer, 1964-72, Reader, 1972-75, Professor of History, 1975-80, University of the West Indies; Editor, The Jamaican Historial Review, 1968-80, Terrae Incognitae, 1982-; Director, Hermon Dunlap Smith Center for the History of Cartography, Newberry Library, Chicago, 1980-95; Jenkins and Virginia Garrett Professor in Southwestern Studies and the History of Cartography, University of Texas at Arlington, 1995-. Publications: Sully and the Growth of Centralized Government in France, 1598-1610, 1969; The Wars of Religion, Vol 10 of the Hamlyn History of the World, 1969; Historic Jamaica from the Air (with J S Tyndale-Biscoe), 1969, 2nd edition, 1997; Les Oeconomies Royales de Sully (editor with Bernard Barbiche), Vol I, 1970, Vol II, 1988; The Fortifications of Kingston, 1660-1900, 1971; Huguenots and Papists, 1972; A Popular History of the Port of Kingston, 1973, revised and enlarged edition, 1976; Port Royal, Jamaica (with Michael Pawson), 1975; Historic Architecture of the Caribbean, 1980; Henry IV, 1984; Histoire de l'Architecture dans la Caraibe, 1984; Skokie: A Community History using Old Maps (with Gerald Danzer), 1985; From Sea Charts to Satellite Images: Interpreting North American History through Maps (editor), 1990; Historic Illinois from the Air, 1990; A Guidebook to Resources for Teachers of the Columbian Encounter (editor with Tina Reithmaier), 1992; Monarchs, Ministers and Maps: The Emergence of Cartography as a Tool of Government in Early Modern Europe (editor), 1992; Elk Grove: A Community History in Maps (with James Issel), 1996; Rural Images: The Estate Map in the Old and New Worlds (editor), 1996; Envisioning the City, 1998. Contributions to: Scholarly books and journals. Honours: Centennial Medal, Institute of Jamaica, 1979; Chevalier dans l'Ordre des Palmes Académiques, France, 1993; Various grants. Memberships: Royal Historical Society, fellow; Texas Map Society, secretary-treasurer, 1996-. Address: 2901 Norwood Lane, Arlington, TX 76013, USA.

BULLA Clyde Robert, b. 9 Jan 1914, King City, Missouri, USA. Author. Publications: A Tree is a Plant, 1960; Three-Dollar Mule, 1960; The Sugar Pear Tree, 1961; Benito, 1961; What Makes a Shadow?, 1962; The Ring and the Fire: Stories from Wagner's Niebelung Operas, 1962; Viking Adventure, 1963; Indian Hill, 1963; St Valentine's Day, 1965; More Stories of Favorite Operas, 1965; White Bird, 1966; Lincoln's Birthday, 1967; Washington's Bithday, 1967; Flowerpot Gardens, 1967; Stories of Gilbert and Sullivan Operas, 1968; The Ghost of Windy Hill, 1968; Mika's Apple Tree: A Story of Finland, 1968; The Moon Singer, 1969; New Boy in Dublin: A Story of Ireland, 1969; Jonah and the Great Fish, 1970; Joseph the Dreamer, 1971; Pocahontas and the Strangers, 1971; Open the Door and See All the People, 1972; Dexter, 1973; The Wish at the Top, 1974; Shoeshine Girl, 1975; Marco Moonlight, 1976; The Beast of Lor, 1977; Conquista! (with Michael Syson), 1978; Last Look, 1979; The Stubborn Old Woman, 1980; My Friend the Monster, 1980; Daniel's Duck, 1980; A Lion to Guard Us, 1981; Almost a Hero, 1981; Dandelion Hill, 1982; Poor Boy, Rich Boy, 1982; Charlie's House, 1983; The Cardboard Crown, 1984; A Grain of Wheat, 1985; The Chalk Box Kid, 1987; Singing Sam, 1989; The Christmas Coat, 1989; A Place for Angels, 1995. Memberships: Authors Guild; Society of Children's Book Writers and Illustrators. Literary Agent: Curtis Brown Ltd, 10 Astor Place, New York, NY 10003, USA. Address: 1230 Las Flores Drive, Los Angeles, CA 90041, USA.

BULLINS Ed, b. 2 July 1935, Philadelphia, Pennsylvania, USA. Dramatist; Author; Teacher. Education: BA, Antioch University, 1989; MFA, San Francisco State University, 1994. Appointments: Instructor, City College of San Francisco, 1984-88, Contra Costa College, 1989-; Lecturer, Sonoma State University, 1987-88, San Francisco State University, 1993. Publications: Over 40 published plays, many others unpublished. Other: The Hungered One (stories), 1971; The Reluctant Rapist (novel), 1973. Honours: National Endowment for the Arts Grants; Rockefeller Foundation Grants; Guggenheim Fellowships, 1971, 1976; Obie Award, 1975; New York Drama Critics Circle Award, 1975; Honorary LittD, Columbia College, Chicago, 1975. Address: 3617 San Pablo Avenue, No 118, Emeryville, CA 94608, USA.

BULLOCK John Angel, b. 15 Apr 1928, Penarth, England. Journalist. m. Jill Brown, 2 sons, 2 daughters. Education: HMS Conway. Appointments: Reporter PA, Africa Correspondent, Daily Telegraph; Correspondent, Daily Telegraph, Diplomatic Correspondent, The Independent; Diplomatic Correspondent, Independent on Sunday. Publications: Spy Ring, 1961; Akin to Treason, 1966; MI5, 1963; Death of a Country, 1977; Final Conflict, 1983; The Gulf, 1986; The Gulf War (with H Morris); The Making of a War, 1975; No Friends But the Mountains (with H Morris); Saddam's War (with H Morris); Water Wars (with A Darwish). Contributions to: Frequent contributor to Middle East journals. Address: 71 Bainton Road, Oxford OX2 7AG, England.

BULLOCK Kenneth K(en), b. 26 July 1929, Liverpool, England (Canadian citizen, 1951-66, Australian citizen, 1966-). Writing Consultant; Writer. Partner, Shirley Asser, 2 sons, 2 daughters. Education: Dip Comm, 1961, Royal Canadian Naval College, HMCS, Victoria. Appointments: British Merchant Navy, 1946-49; Service aircrew, RCN, RAN, 1950-72; Papua New Guinea Prime Minister's Department, Office of Information, 1980-83; Writer, Editor, Teacher, Journalist Counsellor/External Tutor, James Cook University, 1984-98. Publications: Emergency, 1979; Family Guide to Beach and Water Safety, 1980; Silly Billy Learns a Lesson, 1981; Papua New Guinea, 1981; Water Proofing Your Child, 1982; Pelandok, 1986; Port Pirie the Friendly City, 1988; Chopstik, 1993; Beyond Peril, 1996. Contributions to: Papua New Guinea; Post Courier; National Times; Australia; Adelaide Advertiser; Sunshine Coast Daily. Honours: CD, Canadian Military Service Decoration, 1963; Citizen of the Year, 1984; Port Pirie, 1984-88; Canadian Special Service Medal (Contribution to NATO), 1997; Australian Active Service Medal (Vietnam), 1998. Memberships: Fellowship of Australian Writers; Australian Society of Authors. Address: 8 Park Street, Buderim, Queensland 4556, Australia.

BULLOCK Michael, b. 19 Apr 1918, London, England. Professor Emeritus; Poet; Dramatist; Writer; Translator. Education: Hornsey College of Art. Appointments: Commonwealth Fellow, 1968, Professor of Creative Writing, 1969-83, Professor Emeritus, 1983-, University of British Columbia, Vancouver, Canada; McGuffey Visiting Professor of English, Ohio University, Athens, Ohio, 1969; New Asia Ming Yu Visiting Scholar, 1989, Writer-in-Residence, 1996, New Asia College, Chinese University of Hong Kong; Adviser, New Poetry Society of China, 1995-. Publications: Poetry: Transmutations, 1938; Sunday is a Day of Incest, 1961; World Without Beginning Amen, 1963, 2nd edition, 1973; Two Voices in My Mouth/Zwei Stimmen in meinem Mund, bilingual edition, 1967; A Savage Darkness, 1969; Black Wings White Dead, 1978; Lines in the Dark Wood, 1981; Quadriga for Judy, 1982; Prisoner of the Rain, poems in prose, 1983; Brambled Heart, 1985; Dark Water, 1987; Poems on Green Paper, 1988; The Secret Garden, 1990; Avatars of the Moon, 1990; Labyrinths, 1992; The Walled Garden, 1992; The Sorcerer with Deadly Nightshade Eyes, 1993; The Inflowing River, 1993; Moons and Mirrors, 1994; Dark Roses, 1994; Stone and Shadow, 1996. Fiction: Sixteen Stories as They Happened, 1969; Green Beginning Black Ending, 1971; Randolph Cranstone and the Pursuing River, 1975; Randolph Cranstone and the Glass Thimble, 1977; The Man with Flowers Through His Hands, 1985; The Double Ego, 1985; Randolph Cranstone and the Veil of Maya, 1986; The Story of Noire, 1987; Randolph Cranstone Takes the Inward Path, 1988; The Burning Chapel, 1991; The Invulnerable Ovoid Aura, Stories and Poems, 1995; Voices of the River, 1995; Der Grüne Mond, 1997; Sonnet in Black and Other Poems, 1998. Other: Selected Works, 1936-1996, (co-editors Peter Loeffler and Jack Stewart), 1998. Contributions to: Many anthologies. Honours: Schlegel-Tieck German Translation Prize, 1966; British New Fiction Society Book of the Month, 1977; Canada Council French Translation Award, 1979; San Francisco Review of Books Best Book List, 1982;

San Jose Mercury News Best Booklist, 1984; Okanagan Short Fiction Award, 1986. Address: 103-3626 West 28th Avenue, Vancouver, British Columbia V6S 1S4, Canada.

BULMER Henry Kenneth, (Alan Burt Akers, Ken Blake, Ernest Corley, Arthur Frazier, Adam Hardy, Kenneth Johns, Philip Kent, Bruno Krauss, Neil Langholm, Karl Maras, Charles R Pike, Andrew Quiller, Richard Silver, Tully Zetford), b. 14 Jan 1921, London, England. Author. m. Pamela Buckmaster, 7 Mar 1953, 1 son, 2 daughters. Publications: City Under the Sea, 1957; The Ulcer Culture, 1969; Dray Prescot Saga, 1972; Roller Coaster World, 1972; Fox Series, 1972-77; Sea Wolf Series, 1978-82; Strike Force Falklands, 1984-86; Fox and Falklands. Contributions to: Periodicals. Address: 5 Holly Mansions, 20 Frant Road, Tunbridge Wells, Kent TN2 5SN, England.

BULO Jorgo, b. 27 Apr 1939, Gjirokaster, Albania. Historian of Literature. m. Kristina Pasko, 5 Aug 1962, 1 daughter. Education: Graduated, Albanian Language and Literature, Philology Faculty, University of Tirana, 1960; Doctor of Philological Sciences, 1982; University Reader, 1983; Professor, 1994. Appointments: Scientific Researcher, 1966, Head, Department of History of Old and Contemporary Albanian Literature, 1972, Vice-Director, 1987, Director, 1997, Head, Scientific Council, 1998, Institute of Linguistics and Literature, Academy of Sciences of Albania; Scientific Secretary, Social Sciences Section, 1974, Member, Leading Council, 1997, Academy of Sciences of Albania; Chief Editor, Studime filologjike journal, 1998. Publications: The History of the Albanian Literature of the Socialist Realism (co-author), 1978; The Albanian novel on the National Liberation War, 1982; Literary traditions and innovations, 1983; The History of Albanian Literature (co-author), 1983; The Albanian Encyclopedia (co-author), 1985. Contributions to: Studia albanica; Studime filologjike; Cahiers Balkaniques, Paris; Albanistica, Naples; Balkanistic Forum, Bulgaria; Quaderni del Dipartimento di Linguistica, Kosenza, Italy; Balkan Review, Thessaloniki. Honour: 1st Class Order of Naim Frasheri. Memberships: League of Writers and Artists of Albania, 1972; National Albanian Committee of Balkan Studies, 1976. Address: Instituti i Gjuhësisë dhe i Letërsisë, Tirana, Albania.

BULPIN Thomas Victor, b. 31 Mar 1918, Umkomaas, South Africa. Writer; Publisher. Education: St John's College, Johannesburg. Appointments: Writer and Publisher, Books of South Africa (Pty) Ltd and TV Bulpin Ltd, Cape Town, 1946-. Publications: Lost Trails on the Low Veld, 1950; Shaka's Country, 1952; To the Shores of Natal, 1953; The Golden Republic, 1953; The Ivory Trail, 1954; Storm Over the Transvaal, 1955; Lost Trails of the Transvaal, 1956; Islands in a Forgotten Sea, 1958; Trail of the Copper King, 1959; The White Whirlwind, 1961; The Hunter is Death, 1962; To the Banks of the Zambexi, 1965; Natal and the Zulu Country, 1966; Low Veld Trails, 1968; The Great Trek, 1969; Discovering South Africa, 1970; Treasury of Travel Series, 1973-74; Southern Africa: Land of Beauty and Splendour, 1976; Illustrated Guide to Southern Africa, 1978; Scenic Wonders of Southern Africa, 1985. Address: PO Box 1516, Cape Town, South Africa.

BUNCH Charlotte (Anne), b. 13 Oct 1944, West Jefferson, North Carolina, USA. Feminist Author and Organizer; Professor in Urban Studies. m. James L Weeks, 25 Mar 1967, div 1971. Education: University of California at Berkeley, 1965; BA in History and Political Science, Duke University, 1966; Graduate Research, Institute for Policy Studies, Washington, DC, 1967-68. Appointments: Visiting President and Tenured Fellow, Institute for Policy Studies, 1969-77; Adjunct Professor, George Washington University, Washington, DC, 1975-76, University of Maryland, College Park, 1978-79; Founding Director, Public Resource Center, Washington, DC, 1977-79; Director, Interfem Consultants, New York, 1979-87; Visiting Professor, 1987-89, Executive Director, Center for Women's Global Leadership, 1989-, Douglass College, Rutgers University; Professor in Urban Studies, Bloustein School of Planning and Public Policy, Rutgers,

The State University of New Jersey, 1991-; Speaker at many universities, conferences, seminars, and rallies. Publications: The New Women: A Motive Anthology on Women's Liberation (editor with Joanne Cooke), 1970; Women Remembered: Short Biographies of Women in History (editor with Nancy Myron), 1974; Class and Feminism (editor with Nancy Myron), 1974; Lesbianism and the Woman's Movement (editor with Nancy Myron), 1975; Building Feminist Theory: Essays from Quest (editor with others), 1981; Learning Our Way: Essays in Feminist Education (editor with Sandra Pollack), 1983; International Feminism: Networking Against Female Sexual Slavery (editor with Barry and Castley), 1984; Passionate Politics: Feminist Theory in Action, 1987; Demanding Accountability: The Global Campaign and Vienna Tribunal for Women's Human Righs (with Niamh Reilly), 1994. Contributions to: Many books, journals and periodicals. Memberships: National Women's Political Caucus, advisory board, 1982-; Ms Foundation, board of directors, 1991-; National Council for Research on Women, board of directors, 1991-; Center for Women's Policy Studies, board of directors, 1992-95; Independent Commission on Human Rights Education, 1994-. Address: 19 Bond Street, No 5A, New York, NY 10012, USA.

BUNCH Richard Alan, b. 1 June 1945, Honolulu, Hawaii. Educator; Poet; Writer. m. Rita Anne Glazar, 11 Aug 1990, 1 son, 1 daughter. Education: AA, Napa Valley College, 1965; BA, Stanford University, 1967; MA, University of Arizona, 1969; MDiv, 1970, DD, 1971, Graduate Studies in Philosophy, 1972-75, Vanderbilt University; Graduate Studies in Asian Religions, Temple University, 1975-76; JD, University of Memphis, 1980; Teaching Credential, Sonoma State University, 1988. Appointments: Teaching Assistant, Philosophy, Vanderbilt University, 1973-74; Instructor, Philosophy, Belmont University, 1973-74; Instructor, Law, University of Memphis, 1982-83; Instructor, Philosophy, Chapman University, 1986-87; Instructor, Law, Sonoma State University, 1986-87, 1990-91. Publications: Poetry: Summer Hawk, 1991; Wading the Russian River, 1993; A Foggy Morning, 1996; Santa Rosa Plums, 1996; South by Southwest, 1997; Rivers of the Sea, 1998; Sacred Space, 1998. Prose: Night Blooms, 1992. Contributions to: Many reviews. Honours: Grand Prize, Ina Coolbrith National Poetry Day Contest, 1989; Jessamyn West Prize, 1990; Pushcart Prize nominations, 1988, 1997. Memberships: Academy of American Poets; Ina Coolbrith Poetry Circle; Russian River Writers Guild. Address: 248 Sandpiper Drive, Davis, CA 95616, USA.

BUNGAY Stephen (Francis), b. 2 Sept 1954, Kent, England. Management Consultant. m. Atalanta Armstrong Beaumont, 31 Oct 1987, 2 sons. Education: MA, 1976, PhD, 1981, Oxford University. Publications: Beauty and Truth, 1984; Der Entwurf einer Kategorialen Asthetik bei Hegel, in Kategorie und Kategorialität, 1990. Contributions to: Kategorie und Kategorialität, 1990; Hegel Reconsidered, 1994. Address: The Boston Consulting Group Ltd, London W1X 5FH, England.

BUNSHICHI Niyauchi, b. 1 Dec 1908, Kagoshima, Japan. Professor Emeritus of English Language and Literature; Writer. m. 1 Apr 1935, 3 sons, 2 daughters. Education: Department of English Language and Literature, Hiroshima Normal College, 1930; Litterarum Doctor. Appointments: Professor of English Language and Literature, 1955-74, Professor Emeritus, 1974-, Kagoshima University. Publications: Shakespeare's First Step Abroad, 1972; Immortal Longings: The Structure of Shakespeare's Antony and Cleopatra, 1978; Shakespeare's Structural Poetics, 1979; In and Out of Old Sites, 1985. Contributions to: Tragicality of Dialogue, 1950; Whether an Artificer or Not: APlea for Shakespeare, 1951; Shakespeare's Drifting Soliloquy, 1953; Desire Named Utopia, 1984. Honour: Decorated, Third Order of Merit with the Sacred Treasure, 1993. Memberships: Iternational John Steinbeck Society; Renaissance Institute of Japan; Japan Society of Shakespeare. Address: 201 Cosmo Kamifukuoka, 57-910 Fujma Kawagoe Shi, Saitama Ken 356, Japan.

BURACK Sylvia Kamerman, b. 16 Dec 1916, Hartford, Connecticut, USA. Editor; Publisher. m. Abraham S Burack, 28 Nov 1940, dec, 3 daughters. Education: BA, Smith College, 1938. Appointments: Editor, Publisher, magazines, 1978-. Publications: Editor: Little Plays for Little Players, 1952; Blue Ribbon Plays for Girls, 1955; Blue Ribbon Plays for Graduation, 1957; Fifty Plays for Junior Actors, 1966; Fifty Plays for Holidays, 1969; On Stage for Christmas, 1978; Holiday Plays Round the Year, 1983; Plays of Black Americans, 1987; Patriotic and Historical Plays for Young People, 1987; Plays from Favorite Folk Tales, 1987; The Big Book of Comedies, 1989; The Big Book of Holiday Plays, 1990; The Big Book of Folktale Plays, 1991; Plays of Great Achievers, 1992; The Big Book of Dramatized Classics, 1993; The Big Book of Large-Cast Plays, 1995; The Big Book of Skits, 1996. Adult Books: Writing the Short Short Story, 1942; Book Reviewing, 1978; Writing and Selling Fillers, Light Verse, and Short Humor, 1982; Writing and Selling Romance Novels, 1983; Writing Mystery and Crime Fiction, 1985; How to Write and Sell Mystery Fiction, 1990; The Writers Handbook, (annual), 1989-96. Honours: Distinguished Service Award, 1973; Honorary Doctor of Letters, Boston University, 1985; Brookline High School Library Named in Honour; Freedoms Foundation Award, 1988; Smith College Medal, 1995; Raven Award, Mystery Writers of America, 1998. Memberships: National Book Critics Circle; Friends of the Libraries of Boston University; Phi Beta Kappa; PEN; English Speaking Union, American Branch, director, 1994-98. Address: 72 Penniman Road, Brookline, MA 02146, USA.

BURCH Claire, b. 19 Feb 1925, New York, New York, USA. Writer; Poet; Filmmaker. m. Bradley Bunch, 14 Apr 1944,dec, 1 son, dec, 2 daughters. Education: BA, Washington Square College, 1947. Publications: Stranger in the Family, 1972; Notes of a Survivor, 1972; Shredded Millions, 1980; Goodbye My Coney Island Baby, 1989; Homeless in the Eighties, 1989; Solid Gold Illusion, 1991; You Be the Mother Follies, 1994; Homeless in the Nineties, 1994; Stranger on the Planet: The Small Book of Laurie, 1996. Contributions to: Periodicals. Honours: Carnegie Awards, 1978, 1979; California Arts Council Grants, 1991, 1992, 1993, 1994; Seva Foundation Award, 1996. Membership: Writer's Guild. Address: c/o Regent Press, 6020A Adeline, Oakland, CA 94808, USA.

BURCHFIELD Robert William, b. 27 Jan 1923, Wanganui, New Zealand. Lexicographer; Grammarian. m. (1) Ethel May Yates, 2 July 1949, 1 son, 2 daughters, div, (2) Elizabeth Austen Knight, 5 Nov, 1976. Education: MA, Victoria University of Wellington, 1948; BA, 1951, MA, 1955, Magdalen College, Oxford. Appointments: Lecturer, Christ Church, Oxford, 1953-57; Lecturer, Tutorial Fellow, Still Emeritus Fellow, St Peter's College, Oxford, 1955-. Publications: A Supplement to the Oxford English Dictionary, 4 volumes, 1972-86; The Spoken Word, 1981; The English Language, 1985; The New Zealand Pocket Oxford Dictionary, 1986; Studies in Lexicography, 1987; Unlocking the English Language, 1989; Points of View, 1992; The Cambridge History of the English Language, Vol 5, 1994; The New Fowler's Modern English Usage, 1996. Contributions to: Sunday Times; Encounter; Transactions of the Philological Society. Honours: Commander of the Order of the British Empire, 1975; Hon DLitt, Liverpool, 1978, Victoria University of Wellington, 1983; Freedom of City of Wanganui, 1986; Shakespeare Prize, 1994. Memberships: Early English Text Society; American Academy of Arts and Sciences. Address: 14 The Green, Sutton Courtenay, Oxon OX14 4AE, England.

BURCHILL Julie, b. 3 July 1959, England. Journalist; Writer. m. (1) Tony Parsons, div, (2) Cosmo Landesman. Education: Brislington Comprehensive, Bristol. Appointments: Journalist and Writer, New Musical Express, 1976-79, The Face, 1979-84, The Mail on Sunday, 1984-93, The Sunday Times, 1993-94, The Guardian, 1998-. Publications: The Boy Looked at Johnny, 1979; Love It or Shove It, 1983; Girls on Film, 1986; Damaged Goods, 1987; Ambition, 1989; No Exit, 1991; Sex and Sensibility, 1992; I Knew I Was Right,

1998; Diana, 1998; Married Alive (novel), 1998. Address: c/o Simpson Fox, 52 Shaftesbury Avenue, London W1.

BURFIELD Eva. See: **EBBETT Frances Eva.**

BURGESS Michael (Roy), b. 11 Feb 1948, Fukuoka, Japan. Librarian; Publisher; Writer; Editor. m. Mary Alice Wickizer Rogers, 15 Oct 1976, 1 stepson, 1 stepdaughter. Education: AB, Gonzaga University, 1969; MLS, University of Southern California at Los Angeles, 1970. Appointments: Periodicals Librarian, 1970-75, Assistant Librarian, 1975-78, Senior Assistant Librarian, 1978-81, Associate Librarian, 1981-84, Librarian with rank of Professor, 1984-, California State University at San Bernardino; Editor, Newcastle Publishing Co Inc, North Hollywood, California, 1971-92; Co-Founder, Publisher, Editor, Borgo Press, San Bernardino, California, 1975-. Publications: Author or editor of some 40 fiction or non-fiction books, many under various pseudonyms, 1970-98. Honours: Many awards and citations. Memberships: American Association of University Professors; American Civil Liberties Union; American Library Association; Horror Writers of America; International PEN; Science Fiction and Fantasy Writers of America; Science Fiction Research Association; World Science Fiction Society. Address: c/o California State University at San Bernardino, 5500 University Parkway, San Bernardino, CA 92407, USA.

BURGIN Richard (Weston), b. 30 June 1947, Boston, Massachusetts, USA. Associate Professor of Communications and English; Writer; Editor. m. Linda K Harris, 7 Sept 1991, 1 stepdaughter. Education: BA, Brandeis University, 1968; MA, 1969, MPhil, 1981, Columbia University. Appointments: Instructor, Tufts University, 1970-74; Critic-at-Large, Globe Magazine, 1973-74; Founding Editor and Director, New Arts Journal, 1976-83; Visiting Lecturer, University of California at Santa Barbara, 1981-84; Associate Professor of Humanities, Drexel University, 1984-96; Founder-Editor, Boulevard, literary journal, 1985-; Associate Professor of Communications and English, St Louis University, 1996-. Publications: Conservations with Jorge Luis Borges, 1969; The Man with Missing Parts (novella), 1974; Conversations with Isaac Bashevis Singer, 1985; Man Without Memory (short stories), 1989; Private Fame (short stories), 1991. Contributions to: Many anthologies and periodicals. Honours: Pushcart Prizes, 1983, 1986; Various honorable mentions and listings. Membership: National Book Critics Circle, 1988-. Address: Montclair on the Park, 18 South Kingshighway, Apt 10JK, St Louis, MO 63108, USA.

BURKE Colleen Zeita, b. Sydney, New South Wales, Australia. Poet; Author; Tutor. m. Declan Affley, 11 Dec 1967, dec 1985, 1 son, 1 daughter. Education: BA, Sydney University, 1974. Appointments: Tutor creative writing and poetry, 1981-; Writer-in-Community, 1985-93. Publications: Go Down Singing, 1974; Hags, Rags & Scriptures, 1977; The Incurable Romantic, 1979; She Moves Mountains, 1984; Doherty's Corner, 1985; The Edge of It, 1992; Wildlife in Newtown, 1994; Home Brewed and Lethal - New and Selected Poems, 1997. Contributions to: Sydney Morning Herald; Southerly; Westerly; Hecate; Imago; Overland; Blast; New South Wales School Magazine; Linq; Ukitarra; The Bridge. Honours: Shortlisted New South Wales Literary Awards, 1993; 3 Australia Council. Literary Agent, Tim Curnow, Curtis Brown. Address: 126 Lennox Street, Newtown, NSW 2042, Australia.

BURKE James, b. 22 Dec 1936, Londonderry, Northern Ireland. Writer; Broadcaster. m. Madeline Hamilton, 27 Jan 1967. Education: MA, English Literature, Jesus College, Oxford, 1961. Publications: Tomorrow's World I, 1971; Tomorrow's World II, 1972; Connections, UK, 1978, USA, 1979; Foreign, 1980; The Day the Universe Changed, UK, 1985, USA, 1986; Foreign, 1987. Editor: Weidenfeld and Nicholason Encyclopaedia of World Art, 1964; Zanichelli Italian-English Dictionary, 1965. Contriutions to: Daily Mail; Listener; Vogue; Vanity Fair; Punch; TV Times; Radio Times. Honours: Gold Medal, 1971, Silver Medal,

1972, Royal Televison Society; Edgar Dale Award for Screenwriting, USA, 1986. Memberships: Royal Institution; Savile Club. Address: c/o Jonathan Clowes Ltd, 22 Prince Albert Road, London NW1 7ST, England.

BURKE James Lee, b. 5 Dec 1936, Houston, Texas, USA. Author. m. Pearl Pai, 22 Jan 1960, 1 son, 3 daughters. Education: University of Southwest Louisiana, 1955-57; BA, 1959, MA, 1960, University of Missouri. Publications: Half of Paradise, 1965; To the Bright and Shining Sun, 1970; Lay Down My Sword and Shield, 1971; Two for Texas, 1983; The Convict and Other Stories, 1985; The Lost Get-Back Boogie, 1986; The Neon Rain, 1987; Heaven's Prisoners, 1988; Black Cherry Blues, 1989; A Morning for Flamingos, 1990; Ohio's Heritage (with Kenneth E Dawson), 1989. A Stained White Radiance, 1992; Texas City, Nineteen Forty-Seven, 1992; In the Electric Mist with Confederate Dead, 1993; Dixie City Jam, 1994; Burning Angel, 1995. Contributions to: Periodicals. Honours: Breadloaf Fellow, 1970; Southern Federation of State Arts Agencies Grant, 1977; Guggenheim Fellowship, 1989; Edgar Allan Poe Award, Mystery Writers of America, 1989. Membership: Amnesty International. Address: 11100 Grant Creek, Missoula, MT 59802, USA.

BURKE John Frederick, (Owen Burke, Harriet Esmond, Jonathan George, Joanna Jones, Robert Miall, Sara Morris, Martin Sands), b. 8 Mar 1922, Rye, England. Author. m. (1) Joan Morris, 13 Sept 1940, 5 daughters, (2) Jean Williams, 29 June 1963, 2 sons. Appointments: Production Manager, Museum Press; Editorial Manager, Paul Hamlyn Books for Pleasure Group: European Story Editor, 20th Century Fox Productions. Publications: Swift Summer, 1949; An Illustrated History of England, 1974; Dr Caspian Trilogy, 1976-78; Musical Landscapes, 1983; Illustrated Dictionary of Music, 1988; A Travellers History of Scotland, 1990; Bareback, 1998. Film and TV Novelisations. Contributions to: The Bookseller; Country Life; Denmark. Honour: Atlantic Award in Literature, 1948-49. Memberships: Society of Authors; Danish Club. Literary Agent: David Higham Associates. Address: 5 Castle Gardens, Kirkcudbright, Dumfries & Galloway DG6 4JE, Scotland.

BURKE Owen. See: **BURKE John Frederick.**

BURKHOLZ Herbert Laurence, b. 9 Dec 1932, New York, New York, USA. Author. m. Susan Blaine, 1 Nov 1961, 2 sons. Education: BA, New York University, 1951. Appointment: Writer-in-Residence, College of William and Mary, 1975. Publications: Sister Bear, 1969; Spy, 1969; The Spanish Soldier, 1973; Mulligan's Seed, 1975; The Death Freak, 1978; The Sleeping Spy, 1983; The Snow Gods, 1985; The Sensitives, 1987; Strange Bedfellows, 1988; Brain Damage, 1992; Writer in Residence, 1992; The FDA Follies, 1994. Contributions to: New York Times; Town & Country; Playboy; Penthouse; Longevity. Honours: Distinguished Scholar, 1976. Address: c/o Georges Borchardt Inc, 136 East 57th Street, New York, NY 10022, USA.

BURLEY William John, b. 1 Aug 1914, Falmouth, Cornwall, England. Retired Teacher; Writer. m. Muriel Wolsey, 10 Apr 1938, 2 sons. Education: Balliol College, Oxford, 1950-53. Publications: A Taste of Power, 1966; Three Toed Pussey, 1968; Death in Willow Pattern, 1969; Guilt Edged, 1971; Death in a Salubrious Place, 1973; Wycliffe and the Schoolgirls, 1976; The Schoolmaster, 1977; Charles and Elizabeth, 1979; Wycliffe and the Beales, 1983; Wycliffe and the Four Jacks, 1985; Wycliffe and the Quiet Virgin, 1986; Wycliffe and the Windsor Blue, 1987; Wycliffe and the Tangled Web, 1988; Wycliffe and the Cycle of Death, 1989; Wycliffe and a Dead Flautist, 1991; Wycliffe and the Last Rites, 1992; Wycliffe and the Dunes Mystery, 1993; Wycliffe and the House of Fear, 1995; Wycliffe and the Redhead, 1997. Novels successfully adapted for television, 4th series in preparation. Memberships: Authors Copyright and Lending Society; Crime Writers Association; South West Writers. Address: St Patricks, Holywell, Newquay, Cornwall TR8 5PT, England.

BURN Gordon, b. 16 Jan 1948, Newcastle upon Tyne, England. Writer. Education: BA, University of London, 1969. Publications: Somebody's Husband, Somebody's Son: The Story of Peter Sutcliffe, 1984; Pocket Money, 1986; Alma Cogan: A Novel, 1991; Fullalove (novel), 1995; Happy like Murderers, 1998. Contributions to: Sunday Times Magazine; Telegraph; Face; Independent. Honours: Whitbread First Novel Award, 1991; Honorary DLitt, University of Plymouth, 1992 Address: c/o Gillon Aitken & Stone, 29 Fernshaw Road, London SW10 0TG, England.

BURN Michael Clive, b. 11 Dec 1912, London, England. Writer; Poet. m. Mary Walter, 27 Mar 1947. Education: Winchester, 1926-31; Open Scholar, New College, Oxford, 1931; POW, Colditz, 1944. Appointments: Staff, The Times, 1938-39; Correspondent, Vienna, Budapest, Belgrade, 1947-49. Publications: Yes Farewell, 1946; The Modern Everyman, 1947; Childhood at Oriol, 1951; The Midnight Diary, 1952; The Flying Castle, 1954; Mr Lyward's Answer, 1956; The Trouble with Jake, 1967; The Debatable Land, 1970; Out on a Limb, 1973; Open Day and Night, 1978; Mary and Richard, 1988. Contributions to: Articles and Poems to Encounter; Guardian; Times Literary Supplement. Honour: Keats Poetry First Prize, 1973. Membership: Society of Authors. Address: Beudy Gwyn, Minffordd, Gwynedd, North Wales.

BURNET Sir James (William Alexander), (Sir Alastair Burnet), b. 12 July 1928, Sheffield, Yorkshire, England. Journalist. m. Maureen Campbell Sinclair, 1958. Education: Worcester College, Oxford. Appointments: Sub-Editor, Leader Writer, Glasgow Herald, 1951-58; Leader Writer, 1958-62, Editor, 1965-74, The Economist; Political Editor, 1963-64, Broadcaster, 1976-91; Associate Editor, 1982-91, Independent Television News; Editor, Daily Express, 1974-76; Director, Times Newspapers Holdings Ltd, 1982-, United Racecourses Holdings Ltd, 1985-94. Publications: The Time of Our Lives (with Willie Landels), 1981; The Queen Mother, 1985. Contributions to: Television programmes. Honours: Richard Dimbleby Awards, BAFTA, 1966, 1970, 1979; Judges' Award, Royal Television Society, 1981; Knighted, 1984. Membership: Institute of Journalists, honorary vice president, 1990-. Address: 33 Westbourne Gardens, Glasgow G12 9PF, Scotland.

BURNETT Al. See: **BURNETT LEYS Alan Arbuthnott.**

BURNETT John, b. 20 Dec 1925, Nottingham, England. Professor of Social History Emeritus; Author. m. Denise Brayshaw, 2 Aug 1951, 1 son. Education: BA, 1946, MA, 1950, LLB, 1951, Cambridge University; PhD, London University, 1958. Appointments: Lecturer, Guildford Technical College, London, 1948-59; Head, Liberal Studies, South Bank Polytechnic, London, 1959-63; General Studies, Brunel College of Technology, 1963-66; Reader, 1966-73, Professor, 1973-90, in Social History, Pro-Vice Chancellor, 1980-85, Professor Emeritus, 1990-, Brunel University. Publications: Plenty and Want: A Social History of Food in England, 1966; A History of the Cost of Living, 1969; Useful Toil, 1974; A Social History of Housing, 1978; Destiny Obscure, 1982; The Autobiography of the Working Class (editor with David Vincent and David Mayall), 3 volumes, 1984-89; Idle Hands, 1994; The Origins and Development of Food Policies in Europe (editor with D J Oddy), 1994. Contributions to: Scholarly journals. Membership: Chairman, Social History Society of the U.K. 1985-90. Address: Castle Dene, Burgess Wood Road, Beaconsfield, Bucks HP9 1EQ, England.

BURNETT LEYS Alan Arbuthnott, (Al Burnett), b. 10 Jan 1921, Natal, South Africa. Author; Screenwriter. Education: BSc, Glasgow University, 1952; DLitt, University of California, 1969. Appointments: Scenario Writer, MGM, 1954-59; Fox, 1960-63; Freelance Scenario Writer, USA, Australia, 1964-80; Editor, Sphere International, 1981-84; Freelance Screenwriter; Freelance Musical Playwright, 1998-. Publications: Water Wings, 1953; 8 Feature Films; Over 180 Telefilm Series

Episodes. Contributions to: Flight International; Rotor and Wing; Yatching Monthly; Motor Boat; Various Travel and Technical Publications. Honour: Croix de Guerre. Memberships: Aviation, Space Writers Association; Australian Writers Guild; Writers Guild of Great Britain; RNVR Officers Association. Agent: Hollywood Writers Association, 5423 Sunset Boulevard Los Angeles, CA 60046. Address: 8 Seaview Place, Cullen, Banffshire AB56 4WA, Scotland.

BURNHAM Sophy, b. 12 Dec 1936, Baltimore, Maryland, USA. Writer; Dramatist. m. David Bright Burnham, 12 Mar 1960, div 1984, 2 daughters. Education: BA, cum laude, Smith College, 1958. Appointments: Acquisitions Editor, David McKay Inc, 1971-73; Contributing Editor, Town & Country, 1975-80, New Art Examiner, 1985-86; Independent Consultant to various organizations, 1975-88; Adjunct Lecturer, George Mason University, 1982-83; Staff Writer, New Woman magazine, 1984-92; Staff Writer and Columnist, Museum & Arts/Washington, 1987-96; Manager, Fund for New American Plays, John F Kennedy Center for the Performing Arts, Washington, DC, 1992-. Publications: The Exhibits Speak, 1964; The Art Crowd, 1973; The Threat to Licensed Nuclear Facilities (editor), 1975; Buccaneer (novel), 1977; The Landed Gentry, 1978; The Dogwalker (novel), 1979; A Book of Angels, 1990; Angel Letters, 1991; Revelations (novel), 1992; The President's Angel (novel), 1993; For Writers Only, 1994; Mystical Ecstasies: Running Toward God, 1997. Plays: Penelope, 1976; The Witch's Tale, 1978; The Study, 1979, revised as Snowstorms, 1993; Beauty and the Beast, 1979; The Nightingale, 1980; The Warrior, 1988. Contributions to: Essays and articles in many periodicals. Honours: Daughter of Mark Twain, Mark Twain Society, 1974; 1st Prize, Women's Theatre Award, Seattle, 1981; Helene Wurlitzer Foundation Grants, 1981, 1983, 1991; Virginia Duvall Mann Award, 1993. Memberships: Authors Guild; Authors League of America; Cosmos Club. Address: 1405 31st Street North West, Washington, DC 20007, USA.

BURNINGHAM John Mackingtosh, b. 27 Apr 1936, Farnham, Surrey, England. Author; Designer. m. Helen Gilliam Oxenbury, 15 Aug 1964, 1 son, 2 daughters. Education: National Diploma in Design, Central School of Art, London, 1959. Publications: Borka: The Adventures of a Goose with No Feathers, 1963; Chitty Chitty Bang Bang, 1964; Humbert, Mister Firkin and the Lord Mayor of London, 1965; Cannonball Simp, 1966; Storyland: Wall Frieze, 1966; Harquin: The Fox Who Went Down to the Valley, 1967; Jungleland: Wall Frieze, 1968; Mr Gumpy's Outing, 1970; Around the World: Two Wall Friezes, 1972; Mr Gumpy's Motor Car, 1974; Little Book Series: The Blanket, The Cupboard, The Dog, The Friend, 1975; Come Away From the Water, Shirley, 1977; Would You Rather, 1978; Avocado Baby, 1982; The Wind in the Willows (illustrator), 1983; Granpa, 1984; First Words, 1984; Play and Learn Book, 1985; Where's Julius, 1986; John Patrick Norman McHennessy - The Boy Who is Always Late, 1987; Rhymetime: A Good Job, 1988; Rhyme, 1989; Oi Get Off Our Train, 1989; Aldo, 1991; England, 1992; Harvey Slumfenburger's Christmas Present, 1993; Courtney, 1994; Cloudland, 1996. Films: Cannonball Simp, 1967; Granpa, 1989. Honours: Kate Greenaway Medals, 1963, 1972; W H Smith Award for Harvey Slumfenburgers, 1994. Address: c/o Jonathan Cape Ltd, 20 Vauxhall Bridge Road, London SW1V 2FA, England.

BURNS Alan, b. 29 Dec 1929, London, England. Author; Dramatist; Professor. m. (1) Carol Lynn, 1954, (2) Jean Illien, 1980, 1 son, 2 daughters. Education: Merchant Taylors' School, London. Appointments: C Day-Lewis Writing Fellow, Woodberry Down School, 1973; Professor of English, University of Minnesota, 1977-90; Writer-in-Residence, Associated Colleges of the Twin Cities, Minneapolis-St Paul, 1980; Writing Fellow, Bush Foundation of Minnesota, 1984-85; Lecturer, Lancaster University, 1993-96. Publications: Buster, 1961; Europe After the Rain, 1965; Celebrations, 1967; Babel, 1969; Dreamerika, 1972; The Angry Brigade, 1973; The Day Daddy Died, 1981; Revolutions of the Night, 1986; Art by Accident, 1997. Plays: Palach, 1970; To Deprave and Corrupt, 1972; The Imagination on Trial, 1981. Contributions to: Journals and periodicals. Honours: Arts Council Maintenance Grant, 1967, and Bursaries, 1969, 1973. Address: Creative Writing Department, Lancaster University, Lancaster LA1 4YN, England.

BURNS James MacGregor, b. 3 Aug 1918, Melrose, Massachusetts, USA. Political Scientist; Historian; Professor Emeritus; Writer. m. (1) Janet Rose Dismorr Thompson, 23 May 1942, div 1968, 2 sons, 2 daughters, (2) Joan Simpson Meyers, 7 Sept 1969, div 1991. Education: BA, Williams College, 1939; Postgraduate Studies, National Institute of Public Affairs, 1939-40; MA, 1947, PhD, 1947, Harvard University; Postdoctoral Studies, London School of Economics, 1949. Appointments: Faculty, 1941-47, Assistant Professor, 1947-50, Associate Professor, 1950-53, Professor of Political Science, 1953-88, Professor Emeritus, 1988-, Williams College; Faculty, Salzburg Seminar in American Studies, 1954, 1961; Co-Chairman, Project 87, Interdisciplinary Study of the Constitution during the Bicentennial Era, 1976-87; Senior Scholar, Jepson School of Leadership, University of Richmond, 1990-93; Scholar-in-Residence, Center for Political Leadership and Participation, University of Maryland at College Park, 1993-. Publications: Guam: Operations of the 77th Infantry Division, 1944; Okinawa: The Last Battle (co-author), 1947; Congress on Trial: The Legislative Process and the Administrative State, 1949; Government by the People: The Dynamics of American National Government and Local Government (with Jack Walter Peltason and Thomas E Cronin), 1952, 12th edition, 1985; Roosevelt: The Lion and the Fox, 1956; Functions and Policies of American Government (with Jack Walter Peltason), 1958, 3rd edition, 1967; John Kennedy: A Political Profile, 1960; The Deadlock of Democracy: Four-Party Politics in America, 1963; Presidential Government: The Crucible of Leadership, 1966; Roosevelt: The Soldier of Freedom, 1970; Uncommon Sense, 1972; Edward Kennedy and the Camelot Legacy, 1976; State and Local Politics: Government by the People, 1976; Leadership, 1978; The American Constitutional System Under Strong and Weak Parties (with others), 1981; The American Experiment: Vol I, The Vineyard of Liberty, 1982, Vol II, The Workshop of Democracy, 1985, Vol III, The Crosswinds of Freedom, 1989; The Power to Lead: The Crisis of the American Presidency, 1984; Cobblestone Leadership: Majority Rule, Minority Power (with L Marvin Overby), 1990; A People's Charter: The Pursuit of Rights in America (with Stewart Burns), 1991; The Democrats Must Lead (with others), 1992. Honours: Tamiment Institute Award for Best Biography, 1956; Woodrow Wilson Prize, 1957; Pulitzer Prize in History, 1971; National Book Award, 1971; Francis Parkman Prize, Society of American Historians, 1971; Sarah Josepha Hale Award, 1979; Christopher Awards, 1983, 1990; Harold D Lassell Award, 1984; Robert F Kennedy Book Award, 1990; Rollo May Award in Humanistic Services, 1994. Memberships: American Civil Liberties Union; American Historical Association; American Legion; American Philosophical Association; American Political Science Association, president, 1975-76; Delta Sigma Rho; International Society of Political Psychology, president, 1982-83; New England Political Science Association, president, 1960-61; Phi Beta Kappa. Address: Highgate Barn, High Mowing, Bee Hill Road, Williamstown, MA 01267, USA.

BURNS Jim, b. 19 Feb 1936, Preston, Lancashire, England. Writer; Part-time Teacher. Education: BA Honours, Bolton Institute of Tcchnology, 1980. Appointments: Editor, Move, 1964-68; Editor, Palantir, 1976-83; Jazz Editor, Beat Scene, 1990-. Publications: A Single Flower, 1972; The Goldfish Speaks from beyond the Grave, 1976; Fred Engels bei Woolworth, 1977; Internal Memorandum, 1982; Out of the Past: Selected Poems 1961-1986, 1987; Confessions of an Old Believer, 1996; The Five Senses, 1999; As Good a Reason As Any, 1999; Beats, Bohemians and Intellectuals, 1999. Contributions to: London Magazine; Stand; Ambit; Jazz Journal; Critical Survey; The Guardian; New Statesman; Tribune; New Society; Penniless Press; Prop; Verse; Others. Address: 11 Gatley Green, Gatley, Cheadle, Cheshire SK8 4NF, England.

BURNS Rex (Sehler), b. 13 June 1935, San Diego, California, USA. Professor of English; Writer. m. Terry Fostvedt, 10 Apr 1987, div 17 June, 1996, 3 sons, 1 daughter. Education: AB, Stanford University, 1958; MA, 1963, PhD, 1965, University of Minnesota. Appointments: Assistant Professor, Central Missouri State College, 1965-68; Associate Professor, 1968-75, Professor of English, 1975-, Chairman, Department of English, 1996-99, University of Colorado at Denver; Fulbright Lecturer, Aristotle University, Thessaloniki, 1969-70, Universidad Catolico, Buenos Aires, 1974; Book Reviewer, Rocky Mountain News, 1982-92; Senior Lecturer, University of Kent, Canterbury, 1992-93. Publications: Novels: The Alvarez Journal, 1975; The Farnsworth Score, 1977; Speak for the Dead, 1978; Angle of Attack, 1979; The Avenging Angel, 1983; Strip Search, 1984; Ground Money, 1986; Suicide Season, 1987; The Killing Zone, 1988; Parts Unkown, 1990; When Reason Sleeps, 1991; Body Guard, 1991; Endangered Species, 1993; Blood Line, 1995; The Leaning Land, 1997. Editor: Crime Classics: The Mystery Story from Poe to the Present (with Mary Rose Sullivan), 1990. Non-Fiction: Success in America: The Yeoman Dream and the Industrial Revolution, 1976. Contributions to: Periodicals and anthologies. Honours: Edgar Allan Poe Award, Mystery Writers of America, 1976; Colorado Authors League Awards, 1978, 1979, 1980; President's Teaching Scholar (Lifetime Title), University of Colorado System, 1990. Memberships: International Association of Crime Writers; Mystery Writers of America. Address: c/o Department of English, University of Colorado at Denver, Campus Box 175, PO Box 173364, Denver, CO 80217, USA.

BURNS Richard Gordon, b. 15 May 1925, Stockton, California, USA. Author; Retired Attorney. m. Eloise Beil, 23 June 1951, 2 sons. Education: AA with honours, University of California, Berkeley, 1946; AB, Stanford University, 1949; JD, Stanford University Law School, 1951. Publications: New Light on Alcoholism: The AA Legacy from Sam Shoemaker, 1994; Courage to Change (with Bill Pittman), 1994; That Amazing Grace: The Role of Clarence and Grace S in Early AA, 1996; Turning Point: A History of Early AA's Spiritual Roots and Successes, 1997; Good Book and the Big Book: AA's Roots in the Bible, 1997; Anne Smith's Journal, 1998; The Books Early AAs Read for Spiritual Growth, 1998; The Akron Genesis of Alcoholics Anonymous, 1998; Good Morning: Quiet Time, the Morning Watch, Meditation, and Early AA, 1998; Hope!: The Story of Geraldine D Alina Lodge and Recovery, 1998; The Oxford Group and Alcoholics Anonymous, 1998; Dr Bob and His Library, 1998; Utilizing AA's Spiritual Roots Today, 1998. Memberships: American Historical Association; Maui Writers Guild; Author's Guild; Phi Beta Kappa. Address: PO Box 837, Kihei, HI 96753-0959, USA.

BURNSHAW Stanley, b. 20 June 1906, New York, New York, USA. Publisher; Poet; Writer. m. Lydia Powsner, 2 Sept 1942, dec, 1 daughter. Education: BA, University of Pittsburgh, 1925; University of Poitiers, France, 1927; University of Paris, 1927; MA, Cornell University, 1933. Appointments: President and Editor-in-Chief, The Dryden Press, 1937-58; Program Director, Graduate Institute of Book Publishing, New York University, 1958-62; Vice President, Holt, Rinehart and Winston, publishers, 1958-67; Regents Visiting Lecturer, University of California, 1980; Visiting Distinguished Professor, Miami University, 1989.Publications: Poems, 1927; The Great Dark Love, 1932; Andre Spire and His Poetry, 1933; The Iron Land, 1936; The Bridge, 1945; The Revolt of the Cats in Paradise, 1945; Early and Late Testament, 1952; Caged in an Animal's Mind, 1963; The Hero of Silence, 1965; In the Terrified Radiance, 1972; Mirages: Travel Notes in the Promised Land, 1977; Robert Frost Himself, 1986; A Stanley Burnshaw Reader, 1990; The Seamless Web, 1991. Contributions to: Many periodicals. Honours: National Institute of Arts and Letters

Award, 1971; Honorary Doctorate of Humane Letters, Hebrew Union College, 1983; Honorary Doctorate of Letters, City University of New York, 1996. Address: 250 West 89th Street, No PH2G, New York, NY 10024, USA.

BURNSIDE John, b. 19 Mar 1955, Dunfermline, Fife, Scotland. Poet. Publications: The Hoop, 1988; Common Knowledge, 1991; Feast Days, 1992; The Myth of the Twin, 1994; Swimming in the Flood, 1995. Contributions to: Newspapers, journals, and periodicals. Honours: Scottish Arts Council Book Awards, 1988, 1991; Geoffrey Faber Memorial Prize, 1994. Address: c/o Jonathon Cape, 20 Vauxhall Bridge Road, London SW1V 2SA, England.

BURROW John Anthony, b. 1932, Loughton, England. Professor; Writer. Education: BA, 1953, MA, 1955, Christ Church, Oxford. Appointments: Fellow, Jesus College, Oxford University, 1961-75; Winterstoke Professor, University of Bristol, 1976-98. Publications: A Reading of Sir Gawain and the Green Knight, 1965; Geoffrey Chaucer: A Critical Anthology, 1969; Ricardian Poetry: Chaucer, Gower Langland and the Gawain Poet, 1971; Sir Gawain and the Green Knight, 1972; English Verse 1300-1500, 1977; Medieval Writers and Their Work, 1982; Essays on Medieval Literature, 1984; The Ages of Man, 1986; A Book of Middle English, 1992; Langlands Fictions, 1993; Thomas Hoccleve, 1994. Address: 9 The Polygon, Clifton, Bristol, England.

BURROWAY Janet (Gay), b. 21 Sept 1936, Tucson, Arizona, USA. Professor; Writer; Poet. m. (1) Walter Eysselinck, 1961, div 1973, 2 sons, (2) William Dean Humphries, 1978, div 1981, (3) Peter Ruppert, 1993, 1 stepdaughter. Education: University of Arizona, 1954-55; AB, Barnard College, 1958; BA, 1960, MA, 1965, Cambridge University; Yale School of Drama, 1960-61. Appointments: Instructor, Harpur College, Binghamton, New York, 1961-62; Lecturer, University of Sussex, 1965-70; Associate Professor, 1972-77, Professor, 1977-, MacKenzie Professor of English, 1989-95, Robert O Lawson Distinguished Professor, 1995-, Florida State University; Fiction Reviewer, Philadelphia Enquirer, 1986-90; Review, New York Times Book Review, 1991-; Essay-Columnist, New Letters: A Magazine of Writing and Art, 1994-. Publications: Fiction: Descend Again, 1960; The Dancer From the Dance, 1965; Eyes, 1966; The Buzzards, 1969; The Truck on the Track, children's book, 1970; The Giant Jam Sandwich, children's book, 1972; Raw Silk, 1977; Opening Nights, 1985; Cutting Stone, 1992. Poetry: But to the Season, 1961; Material Goods, 1980. Other: Writing Fiction: A Guide to Narrative Craft, 1982, 4th edition, 1995. Contributions to: Numerous journals and periodicals. Honours: National Endowment for the Arts Fellowship, 1976; Yaddo Residency Fellowships, 1985, 1987; Lila Wallace-Reader's Digest Fellow, 1993-94; Carolyn Benton Cockefaire Distinguished Writer-in-Residence, University of Missouri, 1995; Woodrow Wilson Visiting Fellow, Furman University, Greenville, South Carolina, 1995; Erskine College, Due West, South Carolina, 1997; Drury College, Springfield, Illinois, 1999. Memberships: Associated Writing Programs, vice president, 1988-89; Authors Guild. Literary Agent: Gail Hochman, Brandt & Brandt, 1501 Broadway, New York 10036. Address: 240 De Soto Street, Tallahassee, FL 32303, USA.

BURTON Anthony George Graham, b. 24 Dec 1934, Thornaby, England. Writer; Broadcaster. m. 28 Mar 1959, 2 sons, 1 daughter. Education: St James Grammar School. Publications: A Programmed Guide to Office Warfare, 1969; The Jones Report, 1970; The Canal Builders, 1972, 3rd edition, 1993; The Reluctant Musketeer, 1973; Canals in Colour, 1974; Remains of a Revolution, 1975; The Master Idol, 1975; The Miners, 1976; The Navigators, 1976; Josiah Wedgewood, 1976; Canal, 1976; Back Door Britain, 1977; A Place to Stand, 1977; Industrial Archaeological Sites of Great Britain, 1977; The Green Bag Travellers, 1978; The Past At Work, 1980; The Rainhill Story, 1980; The Past Afloat, 1982; The Changing River, 1982; The Shell Book of Curious Britain, 1982; The National Trust Guide to Our Industrial Past, 1983; The Waterways of Britain, 1983;

The Rise and Fall of King Cotton, 1984; Walking the Line, 1985; Wilderness Britain, 1985; Britain's Light Railways, 1985; The Shell Book of Undiscovered Britain and Ireland, 1986; Britain Revisited, 1986; Landscape Detective, 1986; Opening Time, 1987; Steaming Through Britain, 1987; Walk the South Downs, 1988; Walking Through History, 1988; The Great Days and the Canals, 1989; Cityscapes, 1990; Astonishing Britain, 1990; Slow Roads, 1991; The Railway Builders, 1992; Canal Mania, 1993; The Grand Union Canal Walk, 1993; The Railway Empire, 1994; The Rise and Fall of British Shipbuilding, 1994; The Cotswold Way, 1995; The Dales Way, 1995; The West Highland Way, 1996; The Southern Upland Way, 1997; William Cobbett: Englishman, 1997; The Wye Valley Walk, 1998; The Caledonian Canal, 1998; Best Foot Forward, 1998; The Cumbria Way, 1999; The Wessex Ridgeway, 1999. Literary Agent: David Higham Associates Ltd. Address: 31 Lansdown, Stroud, Gloucestershire, Gl5 1BE, England.

BURTON Gabrielle, b. 21 Feb 1939, Lansing, Michigan, USA. Writer; Poet. m. Roger V Burton, 18 August 1962, 5 daughters. Education: BA, Marygrove College, Michigan, 1960; MFA, American Film Institute, Los Angeles, 1997; Appointments: Teacher, Fiction in the Schools, Writers in Education Project, New York, 1985; Various prose readings and workshops. Publications: I'm Running Away From Home But I'm Not Allowed to Cross the Street (non-fiction), 1972; Heartbreak Hotel (novel), 1986, reprint, forthcoming. Contributions to: Articles, essays, poems, and reviews in numerous publications. Honours; MacDowell Colony Fellow, 1982, 1987, 1989; Yaddo Fellow, 1983; Maxwell Perkins Prize, 1986; Great Lakes Colleges Association Award, 1987; Bernard De Voto Fellow in Non-Fiction, Breadloaf Writer's Conference, 1994; Mary Pickford Foundation Award for 1st Year Screenwriter, 1996. Address: 211 LeBrun Road, Eggertsville, NY 14226, USA.

BURTON Gregory Keith, b. 12 Feb 1956, Sydney, New South Wales, Australia. Barrister-at-Law; Arbitrator; Mediator; Author. m. Suzanne Brandstater, 1 son, 1 daughter. Education: BA Honours, University of Sydney, 1978; LLB Honours, 1980; Bursary to Oxford University; BCL, 1984. Appointments: Editorial Committee, Sydney Law Review, 1978-79; Foundation Editor, Journal of Banking and Finance Law and Practice, 1990-; Co-editor, Weaver and Craigie's Banker and Customer in Australia; Australia/New Zealand Editor, Commercial Law Practitioner, 1993-; Banking and Finance Editor, Australasian Dispute Resolution, 1995-. Title Editor, Finance, Banking and Securities, The Laws of Australia, 1998. Publications: Directions in Finance Law, 1990; Australian Financial Transactions Law, 1991; Trusts, 1992; Australian Commentary to Halsbury's Laws of England, 1992; Bills of Exchange and Other Negotiable Instruments, 1992; Halsbury's Laws of Australia, 1992, 1998; Set-Off, The Laws of Australia, 1993; Arbitration in Australia, 1994. Contributions to: Journal of Banking and Finance Law and Practice; Australian Law Journal; Sydney Law Review; Banking Law Association conference publications; Australian Legal Dictionaries. Honours: University Medal in History, 1978. Memberships: New South Wales Bar Association; Business Law Section, Law Council of Australia; Banking Law Association; Commercial Law Association; Australian Institute of Administrative Law; Associate, Institute Arbitrators and Mediators Australia. Address: 5th Floor, Wentworth Chambers, 180 Phillip Street, Sydney, New South Wales 2000, Australia.

BURTON John Andrew, b. 2 Apr 1944, London, England. Writer; Wildlife Consultant. m. Vivien Gledhill, 1 Nov 1980. Publications: The Naturalist in London, 1975; Nature in the City, 1976; Owls of the World (editor), 1976; Field Guide to Amphibians and Reptiles of Europe, 1978; Gem Guide to Animals, 1980; Gem Guide to Zoo Animals, 1984; Collins Guide to Rare Mammals of the World, 1987. Contributions to: New Scientist; Vole; Oryx. Memberships: Linnean Society of London, fellow; Fauna and Flora Preservation Scoiety, executive secretary, 1975-87; Royal Geographical Society; British Ornithologists Union. Address: 222 Old Brompton Road,

London SW5 0BZ, England.

BUSBEE Shirlee, b. 9 Aug 1941, San Jose, California, USA. Author. m. Howard Leon Busbee, 22 June 1963. Eductation: Burbank Business College. Publications: Gypsy Lady, 1977; Lady Vixen, 1980; White Passion Sleeps,1983; Deceive Not My Heart, 1984; The Tiger Lily, 1985; Spanish Rose, 1986; Midnight Masquerade,1988; Whisper to Me of Love, 1991; Each Time We Love, 1993; Love a Dark Rider, 1994. Address: c/o Avon Books, 105 Madison Avenue, New York, NY 10016, USA.

BUSBY F M, b. 11 Mar 1921, Indianapolis, Indiana, USA. Author. m. Elinor Doub, 28 Apr 1954, 1 daughter. Education: BSc, 1946, BScEE, 1947, Washington State University. Appointments: Trick Chief and Project Supervisor, 1947-53, Telegraph Engineer, 1953-70, Alaska Communication System; Writer, 1970-. Publications: Cage a Man, 1974; The Proud Enemy, 1975; Rissa Kerguelen, 1976; The Long View, 1976; All These Earths, 1978; Zelde M'tana, 1980; The Demu Trilogy, 1980; Star Rebel, 1984; The Alien Debt, 1984; Rebel's Quest, 1985; Rebel's Seed, 1986; Getting Home, 1987; The Breeds of Man, 1988; Slow Freight, 1991; The Singularity Project, 1993; Islands of Tomorrow, 1994; Arrow from Earth, 1995; The Triad Worlds, 1996. Contributions to: Approximately 45 anthologies and magazines. Memberships: Science Fiction Writers of America, vice president, 1974-76; Spectator Amateur Press Society. Address: 2852 14th Avenue West, Seattle, WA 98119, USA.

BUSBY Roger C(harles), b. 24 July 1941, Leicester, England. Writer; Public Relations Officer. Education: Certificate in Journalism, University of Aston, Birmingham. Appointments: Journalist, Caters News Agency, Birmingham, 1959-66; Journalist, Birmingham Evening Mail, 1966-73; Head of Public Relations, Devon & Cornwall Police, 1973-. Publications: Main Line Kill, 1968; Robbery Blue, 1969; The Frighteners, 1970; Deadlock, 1971; A Reasonable Man, 1972; Pattern of Violence, 1973; New Face in Hell, 1976; Garvey's Code, 1978; Fading Blue, 1984; The Hunter, 1986; Snow Man, 1987; Crackhot, 1990; High Jump, 1992. Memberships: Crime Writers Association; Institute of Public Relations; National Union of Journalists. Address: Sunnymoor, Bridford, Nr Exeter, Devon, England.

BUSCH Frederick (Matthew), b. 1 Aug 1941, New York, New York, USA. Professor of Literature; Writer. m. Judith Burroughs, 29 Nov 1963, 2 sons. Education: BA, Muhlenberg College, 1962; MA, Columbia University, 1967. Appointments: Magazine Writer; Instructor to Professor, 1966-87, Fairchild Professor of Literature, 1987-, Colgate University; Acting Director, Program in Creative Writing, University of Iowa, 1978-79; Visiting Lecturer, Creative Writing Program, Columbia University, 1979. Publications: I Wanted a Year Without Fall, 1971; Breathing Trouble, 1973; Hawkes, 1973; Manual Labor, 1974; Domestic Particulars, 1976; The Mutual Friend, 1978; Hardwater Country, 1979; A Dangerous Profession, 1980; Invisible Mending, 1984; Sometimes I Live in the Country, 1986; Absent Friends, 1989; Harry and Catherine, 1990; Closing Arguments, 1991; Long Way From Home, 1993; The Children in the Woods: New and Selected Stories, 1994; Girls, 1997; A Dangerous Profession (essays), 1998. Contributions to: Various periodicals. Honours: National Endowment for the Arts Fellowship, 1976; Guggenheim Fellowship, 1981-82; Ingram Merrill Foundation Fellowship, 1981-82; National Jewish Book Award for Fiction, Jewish Book Council, 1985; PEN/Malamud Award, 1991; PEN/Faulkner Award Nomination, 1995. Memberships: Authors Guild of America; PEN; Writers Guild of America. Literary Agent: Elaine Markson, USA; Rachel Calder, UK. Address: 839 Turnpike Road, Sherburne, NY 13460, USA.

BUSH Duncan (Eric), b. 6 Apr 1946, Cardiff, Wales. Poet; Writer; Teacher. m. Annette Jane Weaver, 4 June 1981, 2 sons. Education: BA, 1st Class Honours, in English and European Literature, Warwick University, 1978; Exchange Scholarship, Duke University, USA, 1976-77; DPhil, Research in English Literature, Wadham

College, Oxford, 1978-81. Appointments: European editor, The Kansas Quarterly and Arkansas Review; Writing Tutor with various institutions. Publications: Aquarium, 1983; Salt, 1985; Black Faces, Red Mouths, 1986; The Genre of Silence, 1987; Glass Shot, 1991; Masks, 1994; The Hook, 1997; Midway, 1998. Editor: On Censorship, 1985. Contributions to: BBC and periodicals. Honours: Eric Gregory Award for Poetry, 1978; Barbara Campion Memorial Award for Poetry, 1982; Welsh Arts Council Prizes for Poetry; Arts Council of Wales Book of the Year, 1995. Memberships: Welsh Academy; Society of Authors. Literary Agent; Peters, Fraser & Dunlop, London. Address: Godre Waun Oleu, Brecon Road, Ynyswen, Penycae, Powys SA9 1YY, Wales.

BUSH Ronald, b. 16 June 1946, Philadelphia, Pennsylvania, USA. Professor of American Literature; Writer. m. Marilyn Wolin, 14 Dec 1969, 1 son. Education: BA, University of Pennsylvania, 1968; BA, Cambridge University, 1970; PhD, Princeton University, 1974. Appointments: Assistant to Associate Professor, Harvard University, 1974-82; Associate Professor, 1982-85, Professor, 1985-97, California Institute of Technology; Visiting Fellow, Exeter College, Oxford, 1994-95; Drue Heinz Professor of American Literature, Oxford University, 1997-. Publications: The Genesis of Ezra Pound's Cantos, 1976; T S Eliot: A Study in Character and Style, 1983; T S Eliot: The Modernist in History (editor), 1991; Prehistories of the Future: The Primitivist Project and the Culture of Modernism (editor with Elazar Barkan), 1995. Contributions to: Scholarly books and journals. Honours: National Endowment for the Humanities fellowships, 1977-78, 1992-93. Address: St John's College, Oxford, England.

BUSKIN Richard, b. 30 Mar 1959, London, England. Author; Journalist. Partner, Dorothy-Jean Lloyd, 1 daughter. Publications: John Lennon: His Life and Legend, 1992; The Films of Marilyn Monroe, 1992; Princess Diana: The Real Story, 1992; The Beatles: Memories and Memorabilia, 1994; Elvi Memories and Memorabilia, 1995 Princess Diana: Her Life Story, 1997; The Complete Idiot's Guide to the Beatles, 1997; The Complete Idiot's Guide to British Royalty, 1998; Inside Tracks, 1999. Contributions to: Magazines and newspapers. Literary Agent: Linda Konner, USA. Address: 2615 Deodar Circle, Pasadena, California, USA.

BUTALA Sharon Annette, b. 24 Aug 1940, Nipawin, Saskatchewan, Canada. Writer. m. Peter Butala, 21 May 1976, 1 son. Education: BEd, 1962, BA, 1963, Postgraduate Diploma in Special Education, 1973, University of Saskatchewan. Appointment: Writer. Publications: Country of the Heart, novel, 1984; Queen of the Headaches, novel, 1985; The Gates of the Sun, 1986; Luna, novel, 1988; Upstream, novel, 1991; FEVER, fiction, 1990; The Fourth Archangel, novel, 1992; The Perfection of the Morning, non-fiction, 1994; The Garden of Eden, novel, 1998; Coyote's Morning Cry, non-fiction, 1995. Contributions to: MacLeans; Story; Canadian Fiction Magazine; Saturday Night; Flare; Books in Canada; Prairie Schooner; Great Plains Quarterly; Canadian Forum. Honours: Saskatechewan Book Awards: Non-Fiction and Spirit of Saskatchewan, 1994; Marian Engel Award, 1998. Memberships: The Writer's Union of Canada; PEN Canada; Saskatchewan Writers' Guild. Literary Agent: Westwood Creative Artists. Address: 94 Harbord Street, Toronto, Ontario M5S 1G6, Canada.

BUTLER (Frederick) Guy, b. 21 Jan 1918, Cradock, Cape Province, South Africa. Retired Professor of English Literature; Poet; Writer; Dramatist. m. Jean Murray Satchwell, 7 Dec 1940, 4 children. Education: BA, 1938, MA, 1939, Rhodes University; BA, 1947, MA, 1951, Brasenose College, Oxford. Appointments: Schoolmaster, St John's College, Johannesbury, 1940; Lecturer, University of Witwatersrand, 1948-50; Senior Lecturer, 1951, Professor of English Literature, 1952-86, Rhodes University. Publications: Stranger to Europe 1939-49, 1952, with additional poems, 1960; A Book of South African Verse (editor), 1959; South of the Zambezi: Poems from South Africa, London and New York, 1966; On First Seeing Florence, 1968; Selected Poems, 1975, with additional poems, 1989; Songs and Ballads, 1978; Pilgrimage to Dias Cross, 1987; Out of the African Ark: Animal Poems (editor with David Butler), 1988; A Rackety Colt (novel), 1989; The Magic Tree: South African Stories in Verse (editor with Jeff Opland), 1989; Guy Butler: Essays and Lectures (edited by Stephen Watson), 1994. Contributions to: Various publications. Honours: 1st Prize, 1949, 2nd Prize, 1953, for Poetry, South African Broadcasting Corporation; Honorary DLitt, University of Natal, 1970, University of Witwatersrand, 1984, Rhodes University, 1994; Central News Agency Award, 1976; Literary Award, Cape Tercentenary Foundation, 1981; Honorary DLitt et Phil, University of South Africa, 1989; Gold Medal, English Academy of South Africa, 1989; Lady Usher Prize for Literature, 1992; Freedom of the City of Grahamstown, 1994. Memberships: English Academy of South Africa, honorary life member; Shakespeare Society of South Africa, national president, 1985. Address: High Corner, 122 High Street, Grahamstown, Cape Province 0461, South Africa.

BUTLER Gwendoline (Williams), (Jennie Melville), b. 19 Aug 1922, London, England. Author. Education: MA, Lady Margaret Hall, Oxford, 1948. Publications: Receipt for Murder, 1956; Dead in a Row, 1957; The Dull Dead, 1958; The Murdering Kind, 1958; The Interloper, 1959; Death Lives Next Door, US edition as Dine and Be Dead, 1960; Make Me a Murderer, 1961; Coffin on the Water, 1962; Coffin in Oxford, 1962; Coffin for Baby, 1963; Coffin Waiting, 1963; Coffin in Malta, 1964; A Nameless Coffin, 1966; Coffin Following, 1968; Coffin's Dark Number, 1969; A Coffin form the Past, 1970; A Coffin for Pandora, 1973, US edition as Olivia, 1974; A Coffin for the Canary, US edition as Sarsen Place, 1974; The Vesey Inheritance, 1975; Brides of Friedberg, US edition as Meadowsweet, 1977; The Red Staircase, 1979; Albion Walk, 1982. As Jennie Melville: Come Home and Be Killed, 1962; Burning Is a Substitute for Loving, 1963; Murderers' Houses, 1964; There Lies Your Love, 1965; Nell Alone, 1966; A Different Kind of Summer, 1967; The Hunter in the Shadows, 1969; A New Kind of Killer, An Old Kind of Death, 1970, US edition as A New Kind of Killer, 1971; Ironwood, 1972; Nun's Castle, 1973; Raven's Forge, 1975; Dragon's Eye, 1976; Axwater, US edition as Tarot's Tower, 1978; Murder Has a Pretty Face, 1981; The Painted Castle, 1982; The Hand of Glass, 1983; A Series of Charmian Daniels' novels begining with Windsor Red, 1985. Address: c/o Vanessa Holt Ltd, 59 Crescent Road, Leigh-on-Sea, Essex SS9 2PF, England.

BUTLER Joseph T(homas), b. 25 Jan 1932, Winchester, Virginia, USA. Museum Operations Director Emeritus; Adjunct Assistant Professor. Education: BS, University of Maryland, 1954; MA, Ohio University, 1955; MA, University of Delaware, 1957. Appointments: Director, Museum Operations, Sleepy Hollow Restorations, later Historic Hudson Valley, Tarrytown, New York, 1957-93; American Editor, The Connoisseur, 1967-77; Adjunct Associate Professor of Architecture, Columbia University, 1970-80; Editorial Board, Art & Antiques, 1978-83; Adjunct Assistant Professor, Graduate Division, Fashion Institute of Technology, New York, 1986-. Publications: Washington Irving's Sunnyside, 1962, 3rd edition, revised, 1974; American Antiques 1800-1900: A Collector's History and Guide, 1965; World Furniture, co-author, 1965; Candleholders in America 1650-1900, 1967; The Family Collections at Van Cortlandt Manor, 1967; The Arts in America: The 19th Century (co-author), 1973; The Story of Boscobel and its Builder: States Morris Dyckman, 1974; Warner House: A Compendium, 1975; Van Cortlandt Manor, 1978; Sleepy Hollow Restorations: A Cross Section of the Collection, 1983; A Field Guide to American Antique Furniture, 1985; Treasures of State (co-author), 1991. Contributions to: Encyclopedias and periodicals. Honour: Winterthur Fellow, University of Delaware, 1957. Address: 222 Martling Avenue, Tarrytown, NY 10591, USA.

BUTLER Marilyn, (Speers), b. 11 Feb 1937, Kingston on Thames, England. Rector; Professor; Author. Education: BA, 1958, PhD, 1966, Oxford University. Appointments: Current Affairs Producer, BBC, 1960-63; Research Fellow, St Hilda's College, Oxford, 1970-73; Fellow, Tutor, St Hugh's College, Lecturer, Oxford University, 1973-86; King Edward VII Professor, Cambridge University, 1986-93; Professorial Fellow, King's College, Cambridge, 1988-93; Rector, Exeter College, Oxford, 1993-. Publications: Maria Edgeworth: A Literary Biography, 1972; Jane Austen and the War of Ideas, 1975; Peacock Displayed: A Satirist in His Context, 1979; Romantics, Rebels and Reactionaries, 1760-1830, 1981; Burke, Paine, Godwin and the Revolution Controversy, 1984; Collected Works of Mary Wollstonecraft, 1989; Maria Edgeworth, Castle Rackrent and Ennui, editor, 1992; Frankenstein, the 1818 Edition, editor, 1993; Northanger Abbey, editor, 1995. Address: Exeter College, Oxford, England.

BUTLER (Muriel) Dorothy, b. 24 Apr 1925, Auckland, New Zealand. Teacher; Bookseller; Author. m. Roy Edward Butler, 11 Jan 1947, 2 sons, 6 daughters. Education: BA, University of Auckland, 1940; Diploma in Education, 1976. Publications: Gushla And Her Books; Babies Need books; Five to Eight; Come Back Ginger; A Bundle of Birds; My Brown Bear Barney; Higgledy Piddledy Hobbledy Hoy; Good Morning Mrs Martin; Reading Begins at Home; I Will Build You A House. Honours: Eleanor Farjeon Award; May Hill Arbuthnot Honour Lectureshop, American Library Citation; Childrens Literature Association of New Zealand Honour Award; Margaret Mahy Lecture Award; Officer of the Order of the British Empire, 1993. Memberships: PEN; Childrens Literature Association; Reading Association, Childrens Book Foundation. Literary Agent: Richards Literary Agency. Address: The Old House, Karekare, Auckland West, New Zealand.

BUTLER Octavia E(stelle), b. 22 June 1947, Pasadena, California, USA. Writer. Education: AA, Pasadena City College, 1968; California State University at Los Angeles; University of California at Los Angeles. Publications: Pattermaster, 1976; Mind of My Mind, 1977; Survivor, 1978; Kindred, 1979; Wild Seed, 1980; Clay's Ark, 1984; Dawn: Xenogenesis, 1987; Adulthood Rites, 1988; Imago, 1989; Parable of the Sower, 1993. Address: PO Box 6604, Los Angeles, CA 90055, USA.

BUTLER Richard. See: **ALLBEURY Theodore Edward le Bouthillier.**

BUTLER Robert Olen, b. 20 Jan 1945, Granite City, Illinois, USA. Author; Screenwriter; Professor of Creative Writing. m. 1) Carol Supplee, 10 Aug 1968, div Jan 1972, 2) Marylin Geller, 1 July 1972, div July 1987, 2 son, 3) Maureen Donlan, 21 July 1987, div Mar 1995, 4) Elizabeth Dewberry, 23 Apr 1995. Education: BS, Northwestern University, 1967; MA, University of Iowa, 1969; Postgraduate Studies, New School for Social Research, New York City, 1979-81. Appointments: Editor-in-Chief, Energy User News, 1975-85; Professor, Master of Fine Arts in Creative Writing Program, McNeese State University, 1985-; Faculty, various summer writing conferences. Publications: The Alleys of Eden, 1981; Sun Dogs, 1982; Countrymen of Bones, 1983; On Distant Ground, 1985; Wabash, 1987; The Deuce, 1989; A Good Scent from a Strange Mountain, 1992; They Whisper, 1994; Coffee, Cigarettes, and a Run in the Park, 1996; Tabloid Dreams, 1996; The Deep Green Sea, 1998. Other: Several screenplays. Contributions to: Anthologies, newspapers, and journals. Honours: Charter Recipient, Tu Do Chinh Kien Award, Vietnam Veterans of America, 1987; Emily Clark Balch Award, Virginia Quarterly Review, 1991; Southern Review/Louisiana State University Prize for Short Fiction, 1992; Honorary Doctor of Humane Letters, McNeese State University, 1993; Notable Book Citation, American Library Association, 1993; Finalist, PEN/Faulkner Award for Fiction, 1993; Richard and Hinda Rosenthal Foundation Award, American Academy of Arts and Letters, 1993; Guggenheim Fellowship, 1993; Pulitzer Prize for Fiction, 1993; National Endowment for the Arts Fellowship, 1994; Lotos Club Award of Merit, 1996; William Peden Prize, Missouri Review, 1997; Author of the Year Award, Illinois Association of Teachers of

English, 1997. Membership: Writers Guild of America West. Address: 665 Sixth Street, Lake Charles, LA 70601, USA.

BUTLIN Martin (Richard Fletcher), b. 7 June 1929, Birmingham, England. Art Consultant; Writer. m. Frances Caroline Chodzko, 1969. Education: BA, 1952, MA, 1957, Trinity College, Cambridge; BA, Courtauld Institute of Art, 1955, D Lit, 1984. Appointments: Assistant Keeper, 1955-67, Keeper of Historic British Collection, 1967-89, Tate Gallery, London; Art Consultant, Christie's, London, 1989-. Publications: A Catalogue of the Works of William Blake in the Tate Gallery, 1957, 3rd edition, 1990; Samuel Palmer's Sketchbook of 1824, 1962; Turner Watercolours, 1962; Turner (with Sir John Rothenstein), 1964; Tate Gallery Catalogues: The Modern British Paintings, Drawings and Sculpture (with Mary Chamot and Dennis Farr), 1964; The Later Works of J M W Turner, 1965; William Blake, 1966; The Blake-Varley Sketchbook of 1819, 1969; The Paintings of J M W Turner (with E Joll), 1977, 2nd edition, 1984; The Paintings and Drawings of William Blake, 1981; Aspects of British Painting 1550-1800, from the Collection of the Sarah Campbell Blaffer Foundation, 1988; Turner at Petworth (with Mollie Luther and Ian Warrell), 1989; William Blake in the Collection of the National Gallery of Victoria (with Ted Gott and Irena Zdanowicz), 1989. Contributions to: Periodicals. Honours: Mitchell Prize for the History of Art, 1978; Commander of the Order of the British Empire, 1990. Membership: British Academy, fellow, 1984-. Address: 74c Eccleston Square, London SW1V 1PJ, England.

BUTLIN Ron, b. 17 Nov 1949, Edinburgh, Scotland; Poet. Writer. m. Regula Staub (the writer Regi Claire), 18 June 1993. Education: MA, Dip CDAE, Edinburgh University. Appointments: Writer-in-Residence, Edinburgh University, 1983, 1985, Midlothian Region, 1990-91, Stirling University, 1993; Writer-in-Residence, The Craigmillar Literacy Trust, 1997-98; Examiner in Creative Writing, Stirling University, 1997-; Writer in Residence, St Andrews University, 1998-. Publications: Creatures Tamed by Cruelty, 1979; The Exquisite Instrument, 1982; The Tilting Room, 1984; Ragtime in Unfamiliar Bars, 1985; The Sound of My Voice, 1987; Histories of Desire, 1995; Night Visits, 1997; When We Jump We Jump High! (editor), 1998; Faber Book of Twentieth Century Scottish Poetry. Contributions to: Scotsman; Edinburgh Review; Poetry Review; Times Literary Supplement. Honours: Writing Bursaries, 1977, 1987, 1990, 1994; Scottish Arts Council Book Awards, 1982, 1984, 1985; Scottish Canadian Writing Fellow, 1984; Poetry Book Society Recommendation, 1985. Membership: Scottish Arts Council, literature committee, 1995-96. Literary Agent: Giles Gordon, Curtis Brown, Haymarket House, 28/29 Haymarket, London SW1Y 4SP. Address: 7W Newington Place, Edinburgh EH9 1QT, Scotland.

BUTOR Michel (Marie François), b. 14 Sept 1926, Mons-en-Baroeul, Nord, France. Author; Poet; Professor. m. Marie-Josephe Mas, 22 Aug 1958, 4 daughters. Education: Licence en philosophie, 1946, Diplôme d'études superieures de philosophie, 1947, Sorbonne, University of Paris; Docteur es Lettres, Université of Tours, 1972. Appointments: Associate Professor, University of Vincennes, 1969, University of Nice, 1970-73; Professor of Modern French Language and Literature, University of Geneva, 1973-91; Visiting Professorships in the U.S. Publications: Passage de Milan, 1954; L'Emploi du temps, 1956, English translation as Passing Time, 1960; La Modification, 1957, English translation as Change of Heart, 1959; La Génie du lieu, 5 volumes, 1958, 1971, 1978, 1988, 1995; Degrés, 1960, English translation as Degrees, 1961; Répertoire, 5 volumes, 1960, 1964, 1968, 1974, 1982; Histoire extraordinaire: Essai sur un rêve de Baudelaire, 1961, English translation as Histoire extraordinaire: Essay on a Dream of Baudelaire's, 1969; Mobile: Étude pour une representation des Etats-Unis, 1962, English translation as Mobile: Study for a Representation of the United States, 1963; Description de San Marco, 1963, English translation as Description of San Marco, 1983; Illustrations, 4 volumes, 1964, 1969, 1973, 1976;

6,810,00 litres d'eau par seconde: Étude stéréophonique, 1965, English translation as Niagara, 1969; Essai sur "Les Essais", 1968; La Rose des vents: 32 rhumbs pour Charles Fourier, 1970; Matière de rêves, 5 volumes, 1975, 1976, 1977, 1981, 1985; Improvisations sur Flaubert, 1984; Improvisations sur Henri Michaux, 1985; Improvisations sur Rimbaud, 1989; Improvisations sur Michel Butor, 1994; Dozens of other volumes of fiction, poetry, essays, etc. Honours: Chevalier de l'Ordre National du Mérite; Chevalier des Arts et des Lettres; Several literary prizes. Address: à l'Ecart, Lucinges, 74380 Bonne, France.

BUTORA Martin, b. 7 Oct 1944, Bratislava, Czechoslovakia. Sociologist; Writer. m. Zora Butorova, 18 Aug 1978, 3 sons, 1 daughter. Education: Graduated in Philosophy, 1976, PhD, 1980, Comenius University, Bratislava. Appointment: Senior Lecturer in Sociology, Charles University, Prague, 1992. Publications: Non-Fiction: Sociological Chapters on Alcoholism, 1989; Self-help Groups in Health Care, 1991; From the Velvet Revolution to the Velvet Divorce?, 1993. Fiction: Several books. Contributions to: Periodicals. Honour: Slovak Literary Fund Prize, 1991. Memberships: International Sociological Association; PEN Club, Bratislava. Address: Lubinska 6, 811 03 Bratislava, Slovakia.

BUTTER Peter Herbert, b. 7 Apr 1921, Coldstream, Scotland. University Professor; Writer; Editor. m. Bridget Younger, 30 Aug 1958, 1 son, 2 daughters. Education: MA, Balliol College, Oxford 1948. Publications: Shelley's Idols of the Cave, 1954; Francis Thompson, 1961; Edwin Muir, 1962; Edwin Muir: Man & Poet, 1966; Shelley's Alastor, Prometheus Unbound and Other Poems (editor), 1971; Selected Letters of Edwin Muir (editor), 1974; Selected Poems of William Blake (editor), 1982; The Truth of Imagination: Some Uncollected Essays and Reviews of Edwin Muir (editor), 1988; Complete Poems of Edwin Muir (editor), 1992; William Blake (editor), 1996. Contributions to: Akros; Lines Review; Modern Language Review; North Wind; Review of English Literature; Review of English Studies; Scottish Literary Journal. Membership: International Association of University Professors of English. Address: Ashfield, Prieston Road, Bridge of Weir, Renfrewshire PA11 3AW, Scotland.

BUTTERS Dorothy Gilman. See: GILMAN Dorothy.

BUTTERWORTH (David) Neil, b. 4 Sept 1934, London, England. Composer; Conductor; Writer; Broadcaster. m. Anne Mary Barnes, 23 Apr 1960, 3 daughters. Education: BA, Honours, English, 1957, BA, Honours, Music, 1958, London University; Guildhall School of Music, London, 1960-62; MA, Nottingham University, 1965. Appointments: Lecturer, Kingston College of Technology, 1960-68; Conductor, Edinburgh Schools Choir, 1968-72, Glasgow Orchestral Society, 1975-83, 1989-, Edinburgh Chamber Orchestra, 1983-85; Head of Music Department, Napier College, Edinburgh, 1968-87. Publications: 400 Aural Training Exercises, 1970; A Musical Quiz Book, 1974; Haydn, 1976; Dvorák, 1980; A Dictionary of American Composers, 1983; Aaron Copland, 1984; Sight-singing Exercises from the Masters, 1984; 20th Century Sight-singing Exercises, 1984; Vaughan Williams, 1989; Neglected Music, 1991; Samuel Barber, 1996; The American Symphony, 1998. Contributions to: Periodicals. Honours: Conducting Prize; Fellow, London College of Music; Winston Churchill Travelling Fellowship. Memberships: Incorporated Society of Musicians; Performing Rights Society; Scottish Society of Composers. Address: 1 Roderick Place, West Linton, Peeblesshire EH46 7ES, Scotland.

BUTTREY Douglas N(orton), (Densil Neve Barr), b. Harrogate, Yorkshire, England. Playwright; Author. Education: MSc, University of London. Publications: Radio Plays: The Clapham Lamp-Post Saga, 1967; Gladys on the Wardrobe, 1970; But Petrovsky Goes on Forever, 1971; The Last Tramp, 1972; The Square at Bastogne, 1973; The Battle of Brighton Beach, 1975; With Puffins for Pawns, 1978; Anatomy of an Alibi, 1978; The Speech, 1979; Two Gaps in the Curtain, 1979; Klemp's Diary, 1980; Who Was Karl Raeder?, 1980; The

Boy in the Cellar, 1981; The Glory Hallelujah Microchip, 1981; The Dog That Was Only a Prophet, 1982; St Paul Transferred, 1983; The Mythical Isles, 1983. Novels: The Man with Only One Head, 1955; Death of Four Presidents, 1991. Contributions to: Periodicals. Membership: Fellow, PEN. Address: 15 Churchfields, Broxbourne, Hertfordshire EN10 7JU, England.

BUZAN Barry, b. 28 April 1946, London, England. Professor of International Studies. m. Deborah Skinner, 10 Mar 1973. Education: BA, First Class Honours, Political Science & International Relations, University of British Columbia, Canada, 1964-69; PhD, London School of Economics, 1970-73. Appointments: Research Fellow, Institute of International Relations, University of British Columbia, 1973-75; Lecturer, Department of International Studies, University of Warwick, 1976-95, promoted to Senior Lecturer, 1983, Reader, 1988, Professor, 1990, Department of Politics and International Studies; Visiting Professor, autumn term, Graduate School of International Relations, International University of Japan, 1993; Professor, International Studies, University of Westminster, 1995-; Olof Palme Visiting Professor in Sweden, 1997-98. Publications: Seabed Politics, 1976; Change and the Study of International Relations: the Evaded Dimension, 1981; People, States, and Fear: the National Security Problem in International Relations, 1983; South Asian Insecurity and the Great Powers, 1986; An Introduction to Strategic Studies: Military Technology and International Relations, 1987; The European Security Order Recast: Scenarios for the Post-Cold War Era, 1990; The Logic of Anarchy: Neorealism to Structural Realism, 1993; Identity, Migration and the New Security Agenda in Europe, 1993; The Mind Map Book, 1993; Security: A New Framework for Analysis, 1998; Anticipating the Future: Twenty Millennia for Analysis, 1998; Anticipating the Future: Twenty Millennia of Human Progress, 1998; The Arms Dynamic in World Politics, 1998. Contributions to: Peace, Power and Security: Contending Concepts in the Study of International Relations, Journal of Peace Reseasrch, 1984; Key Concepts in International Political Economy, forthcoming; The Southeast Asia Security Complex, Contemporary Southeast Asia, 1988; Japan's Future: Old History versus New Roles', International Affairs, 1988. Honours: Francis Deak Prize, American Journal of International Law, 1982; Olof Palme Visiting Professorship in Sweden, 1997-98; Elected Fellow of British Academy, 1998. Address: Garden Flat, 17 Lambolle Road, London NW3 4HS, England.

BUZO Alexander John, b. 23 July 1944, Sydney, New South Wales, Australia. Playwright. Author. m. Merelyn Johnson, 21 Dec 1968. Education: BA, University of New South Wales, 1966. Appointments: Resident Dramatist, Melbourne Theatre Company, 1972-73; Writer-in-Residence, James Cook University, 1985, University of Wollongong, 1989, University of Central Queensland, 1991, University of Indonesia, 1995. Publications: Tautology, 1980; Meet the New Class, 1981; The Search for Harry Allway, 1985; Glancing Blows, 1987; The Young Person's Guide to the Theatre and Almost Everything Else, 1988. Plays: Rooted, 1968; The Front Room Boys, 1969; The Roy Murphy Show, 1970; Coralie Landsdowns Says No, 1974; Martello Towers, 1976; Big River, 1980; Shellcove Road, 1989; The Longest Game, 1990; Prue Flies North, 1991; Kiwese, 1994; Pacific Union, 1995. Contributions to: Australian Way; Independent Monthly; Reader's Digest; Playboy; Sydney Morning Herald; Pacific Islands Monthly; New Straits Times; Australian; Bulletin; Discovery; Heritage. Honour: Gold Medal, Australian Literature Society, 1972. Memberships: Centre for Australian Language and Literature Studies; Australian Writers Guild. Address: 14 Rawson Avenue, Bondi Junction, Sydney, New South Wales 2022, Australia.

BYARS Betsy (Cromer), b. 7 Aug 1928, Charlotte, North Carolina, USA. Children's Author. m. Edward Ford Byars, 24 June 1950, 1 son, 3 daughters. Education: Furman University, 1946-48; BA, Queen's College, Charlotte, 1950. Publications: Clementine, 1962; The Dancing Camel, 1965; Rama, The Gypsy Cat, 1966; The

Groober, 1967; The Midnight Fox, 1968; Trouble River, 1969; The Summer of the Swans,1970; Go and Hush the Baby, 1971; The House of Wings, 1972; The 18th Emergency, 1973; The Winged Colt of Casa Mia, 1973; After the Goat Man, 1974; The Lace Snail, 1975; The TV Kid, 1976; The Pinballs, 1977; The Cartoonist, 1978; Goodbye, Chicken Little, 1979; Night Swimmers, 1980; The Animal, the Vegetable and John D Jones, 1981; The Two Thousand Pound Goldfish, 1981; The Cybil War, 1982; The Glory Girl, 1983; The Computer Nut, 1984; Cracker Jackson, 1985; Sugar and Other Stories, 1987; McMummy, 1993; Wanted...Mud Blossom, 1993; The Golly Sisters Ride Again, 1994. Address: 4 Riverpoint, Clemson, SC 29631, USA.

BYATT A(ntonia) S(usan), b. 24 Aug 1936, Sheffield, Yorkshire, England. Author. m. (1) Ian Charles Rayner Byatt, 1959, div. 1969, 1 son, dec, 1 daughter, (2) Peter John Duffy, 1969, 2 daughters. Education: BA, Newnham College, Cambridge; Bryn Mawr College, Pennsylvania; Somerville College, Oxford. Appointments: Extra-Mural Lecturer, University of London, 1962-71; Lecturer in Literature, Central School of Art and Design, 1965-69; Lecturer in English, 1972-81, Senior Lecturer, 1981-83, University College, London; Associate, Newnham College, Cambridge, 1977-82. Publications: Fiction: Shadow of the Sun, 1964; Degrees of Freedom, 1965; The Game, 1967; The Virgin in the Garden, 1978; Still Life, 1985; Sugar and Other Stories, 1987; Possession: A Romance, 1990; Angels and Insects, 1992; The Matisse Stories, 1994; The Djinn in the Nightingale's Eye: Five Fairy Stories, 1995; Babel Tower, 1996; Elementals, 1998. Non-Fiction: Wordsworth and Coleridge in their Time, 1970, reprinted as Unruly Times: Wordsworth and Coleridge, Poetry and Life, 1989; Iris Murdoch, 1976; George Eliot: The Mill on the Floss, (editor), 1985; George Eliot: Selected Essays, (editor), 1990; Passions of the Mind, 1991; Imagining Characters, (with Ignes Sodre), 1995; The Oxford Book of English Short Stories, (editor), 1998. Honours: Fellow, Royal Society of Literature, 1983; Honorary DLitt, Universities of Bradford, 1987, Durham, 1991, York, 1991, Nottingham, 1992, Liverpool, 1993, Portsmouth, 1994, London 1995; Commander of the Order of the British Empire, 1990; Booker Prize, 1990; Irish Times/Aer Lingus International Fiction Prize, 1990; Eurasian Section, Best Book in the Commonwealth Prize, 1991. Address: 37 Rusholme Road, London SW15 3LF, England.

BYRNE John, b. 6 Jan 1940, Paisley, Renfrewshire, Scotland. Dramatist; Theatre Designer. m. Alice Simpson, 1964, 1 son, 1 daughter. Education: St Mirin's Academy and Glasgow School of Art, 1958-63. Appointments: Graphic Designer, Scottish TV, Glasgow, 1964-69; Writer-in-Residence, Borderline Theatre, Irvine, Ayrshire, 1978-79, Duncan of Jordanstone College, Dundee, 1981; Associate Director, Haymarket Theatre, Leicester, 1984-85. Publications: Several plays for the stage, radio, and television. Honour: Evening Standard Award, 1978. Address: 3 Castle Brae, Newport-on-Tay, Fife, Scotland.

BYRNE John Keyes. See: LEONARD Hugh (John, Jr).

C

CABRERA INFANTE G(uillermo), b. 22 Apr 1929, Gibara, Cuba (British citizen). Novelist. m. Miriam Gomez, 1961. Education: University of Havana, 1949-54. Appointments: Former Chargé d'Affaires in Brussels, Scriptwriter and Professor. Publications: Asi en la paz como en la guerra: cuentos, 1960; Three Trapped Tigers, 1965; A View of Dawn in the Tropics, 1974; Infante's Inferno, 1979. Screenplays: Vanishing Point, 1970; Holy Smoke, 1985; A Twentieth-Century Job, 1991. Honour: Guggenheim Fellowship, 1970. Address: 53 Gloucester Road, London SW7 4QN, England.

CADAVAL Rudy de. See: **CAMPEDELLI Giancarlo.**

CADDEL Richard Ivo, b. 13 July 1949, Bedford, England. Librarian; Poet; Writer; Critic. m. Ann Barker, 31 Aug 1971, 1 son, dec, 1 daughter. Education: BA, Newcastle University, 1971; Newcastle Polytechnic, 1971-72; ALA, 1974. Appointments: Staff, Durham University Library, 1972-; Director, Pig Press, 1973-, Basil Bunting Poetry Centre, 1989-. Publications: Sweet Cicely, 1983; Uncertain Time, 1990; Ground, 1994; Larksong Signal, 1997; Basil Bunting: A Northern Life (with Anthony Flowers), 1997; 26 New British Poets (editor), 1991; Basil Bunting: Uncollected Poems (editor), 1991; Basil Bunting: Three Essays, 1994; Basil Bunting: Complete Poems (editor), 1994; Sharp, Sturdy and Long Toil (editor) 1995; Other: British and Irish Poetry since 1970 (editor with Peter Quartermain), 1998. Contributions to: Poems and criticism in numerous magazines and periodicals. Honours: Northern Arts Writers Awards, 1985, 1988, 1990; Fund for Poetry Award, 1992. Address: 7 Cross View Terrace, Nevilles Cross, Durham, DH1 4JY, England.

CADE Robin. See: **NICOLE Christopher Robin.**

CADET Maurice, b. Jacmel, Haiti. Professor of Literature. Div, 2 sons, 3 daughters. Education: Diplomas in Letters and Modern Languages, Audio-Visual and BS Law. Publications: Turbulences (poetry), 1989; Chalè Pimen (creole poems), 1990; Haute Dissidence (poetry), 1991; Itinéraires d'un enchantment (poetry), 1992; Réjouissances (poetry), 1994. Contributions to: Text published in a number of Quebec Magazines, including: Focus; Résistances; Estuaire; Brèves Littéraires; Ruptures. Honours: Haute dissidence Finalist, Literary Prize, BCP, 1991; Itinéraires d'un enchantment Finalist; Literary Prize Journal of Montreal, 1994; Réjouissances Finalist Price Gala du Livre de Jonquière, Quebec, Canada. Memberships: National Authors Union of Quebec; Language Plus Arts Gallery, Alma, Quebec. Address: 630 Robert Jean Apartment 2, Alma, Quebec G8B 7H1, Canada.

CADOGAN Mary (Rose), b. 30 May 1928, London, England. Writer. m. Alexander Cadogan, 27 May 1950, 1 daughter. Education: Teaching and Performance Diplomas, Margaret Morris School of Dance and Movement, 1954. Appointments: Secretary, Krishnamurti Writing Inc, London, 1958-68; Krishnamurti Foundation, Beckenham, Kent, 1968-; Governor, Brockwood Park Education Centre, Bramdean, Hants, 1968-; Editor, The Collectors Digest, 1987-. Publications: The Greyfriars Characters (with John Wernham), 1976; You're a Brick, Angela: A New Look at Girls' Fiction from 1839 to 1975 (with Patricia Craig), 1976; Women and Children First: The Fiction of Two World Wars (with Patricia Craig), 1978; Charles Hamilton Schoolgirls' Album (with John Wernham), 1978; The Lady Investigates: Women Detectives and Spies in Fiction (with Patricia Craig), 1981; The Morcove Companion (with Tommy Keen), 1981; From Wharton Lodge to Linton Hall; The Charles Hamilton Christmas Companion (with Tommy Keen), 1984; Richmal Crompton: The Woman Behind William, 1986. Address: 46 Overbury Avenue, Beckenham, Kent BR3 2PY, England.

CADY Jack (Andrew), b. 20 Mar 1932, Columbus, Ohio, USA. Writer; Teacher. Education: BS, University of Louisville, 1961. Appointments: Assistant Professor, 1968-73, Associate, Continuing Education, 1981-, University of Washington; Visiting Writer, Knox College, Galesburg, Illinois, 1973-74, Clarion College, Pennsylvania, 1974, Olympic College, Bremerton, Washington, 1984, 1985; Senior Faculty, University of Alaska Southeast, 1977-78; Visiting Writer, 1984, Assistant Professor, 1986, Senior Lecturer, 1986-87, Adjunct Professor, 1987-94, Writer-in-Residence, 1994-, Pacific Lutheran University, Tacoma, Washington, Retired Professor Emeritus. Publications: The Burning and Other Stories, 1972; Tattoo and Other Stories, 1978; The Well, 1981; Singleton, 1981; The Jonah Watch, 1982; McDowell's Ghost, 1982; The Man Who Could Make Things Vanish, 1983; The Sons of Noah, and Other Stories, 1992; Inagehi, 1993; Street, 1994; The Off Season, 1995; Kilroy was Here, 1996; The Night We Buried Road Dog, 1998. Contributions to: Many anthologies and periodicals. Honours: Atlantic Monthly First Award, 1965; National Literary Anthology Award, 1970; Iowa Prize for Short Fiction, 1972; Washington State Governor's Award, 1972; National Endowment for the Arts Fellowship, 1972; Nebula Award, 1993; Bram Stoker Award; Phillip K Dick Award, 1993; World Fantasy Award, 1993; Distinguished Teaching Award, Pacific Lutheran University, 1994. Membership: Science Fiction and Fantasy Writers of America. Address: 315 Logan Street, PO Box 872, Port Townsend, WA 98368, USA.

CAFFREY Idris, b. 16 Nov 1949, Rhayader, Powys. Education: Swansea College of Education, 1968-71. Publications: Pacing Backwards, 1996; Pathways, 1997; Other Places, 1998. Address: 5 Lyndale, Wilnecote, Tamworth, B77 5DX, England.

CAFOPOULOS Catherine Constance Delyannis, b. 22 May 1947, Johannesburg, South Africa. Art Critic; Freelance Curator. m. Panayiotes-Akis Cafopoulos, 1 son, 1 daughter. Education: BA, University of Witwatersrand, Johannesburg; BA Honours, MPhil, University of South Africa; CEP, Ecole de Sciences Politiques. Appointments: Art Editor, The Athenian, 1976-83; Correspondent, Art Forum, New York, 1986-; Commissioner for Greece, Alexandria Biennial, 1991. Publications: Legend, History and Modern Heroes, 1990; Akrithakis imitates Akrithakis: Fragments and Blow-ups, 1991; Assault on the Senses, 1991; The Artist Appropriated, 1991; Timeworn Monuments, Modern Perceptions, 1992; Aphrodite Littis: Recent Works, 1994; Words Unsaid, Songs Unsung, 1994. Contributions to: De Arte, Pretoria, 1971-75; Zygos, 1975-80; To Trito Mati, 1977-79; Eikastika, 1981-84; Arti, 1990-. Memberships: Greek Art Critics Society, 1980-, Board Member 1992-94; Full Member, International Art Critics Society, 1981-. Address: 10 Vas Pyrrhou Street, Politeia, Athens 14671, Greece.

CAHILL Mike. See: **NOLAN William F(rancis).**

CAIRNCROSS Alexander Kirkland, b. 11 Feb 1911, Lesmahagow, Scotland. Economist. m. Mary Frances Glynn, 29 May 1943, 3 sons, 2 daughters. Education: MA, University of Glasgow, 1933; PhD, University of Cambridge, 1936. Publications: Introduction to Economics, 1944, 6th edition, 1982; Home and Foreign Investment, 1870-1913, 1953; Factors in Economic Development, 1962; Essays in Economic Management, 1971; Control of Long-Term International Capital Movements, 1973; Inflation, Growth and International Finance, 1975; Snatches, 1980; Sterling in Decline (with Barry Eichengreen), 1983; Years of Recovery, 1985; Economics and Economic Policy, 1986; The Price of War, 1986; A Country to Play With, 1987; The Economic Section (with Nita Watts), 1989; Planning in Wartime, 1991; Goodbye Great Britain (with Kathleen Burk), 1992; The Legacy of the Golden Age (with Frances Cairncross), 1992; Austin Robinson: The Life of an Economic Adviser, 1993; The British Economy Since 1945, 1992, 2nd edition, 1995; Economic Ideas and Government Policy, 1995; Managing the British Economy in the 1960s, 1996; The Wilson Years 1964-69, 1997; Living with the Century (Autobiography), 1998; The Diaries of Robert Hall, 2 volumes (editor). Contributions to: Numerous journals. Honour: Fellow, British Academy. Memberships: British Association for Advancement of Science and Technology; Royal Economic Society; Scottish Economic Society. Address: 14 Staverton Road, Oxford OX2 6XJ, England.

CAIRNCROSS Frances Anne, b. 30 Aug 1944, Otley, Yorkshire, England. Journalist. m. Hamish McRae, 10 Sept 1971, 2 daughters. Education: Honours Degree in Modern History, Oxford University, 1962-65; MA, Economics, Brown University, Providence, Rhode Island, USA, 1965-66. Appointments: Staff, The Times, 1967-69, The Banker, 1969, The Observer, 1969-71; Economics Correspondent, 1971-81, Women's Editor, 1981-84, The Guardian; Britain Editor, The Economist, 1984-89, Public Policy Editor, 1997-. Publications: Capital City (with Hamish McRae), 1971; The Second Great Crash, 1973; The Guardian Guide to the Economy, 1981; Changing Perceptions of Economic Policy, 1981; Second Guardian Guide to the Economy, 1983; Guide to the Economy, 1987; Costing the Earth, 1991; Green, Inc, 1995; The Death of Distance, 1997. Address: 6 Canonbury Lane, London N1 2AP, England.

CAIRNS. See: **DOWLING Basil.**

CAIRNS David (Adam), b. 8 June 1926, Loughton, Essex, England. Music Critic; Writer. m. Rosemary Goodwin, 19 Dec 1959, 3 sons. Education: Trinity College, Oxford. Appointments: Music Critic, Evening Standard, and Spectator, 1958-62, Financial Times, 1963-67, New Statesman, 1967-70, Sunday Times, 1985-; Classical Programme Coordination, Philips Records, 1967-73; Distinguished Visiting Scholar, Getty Center for the History of Art and Humanities, 1992; Visiting Resident Fellow, Merton College, Oxford, 1993. Publications: The Memoirs of Hector Berlioz (editor and translator), 1969, 4th edition, 1990; Responses: Musical Essays and Reviews, 1973; The Magic Flute, 1980; Falstaff, 1982; Berlioz, Volume I: The Making of an Artist 1803-1832, 1989. Honours: Chevalier, 1975, Officier, 1991, de l'Ordre des Arts des Lettres, France; Derek Allen Memorial Prize, British Academy, 1990; Royal Philharmonic Society Award, 1990; Yorkshire Post Prize, 1990; Commander of the Order of the British Empire, 1997. Address: 49 Amerland Road, London SW18 1QA, England.

CAIRO Luiz Roberto Velloso, b. 26 Nov 1944, Salvador, Brazil. Professor. Education: Master in Literary Theory and Comparative Literature, Universidade de São Paulo, 1978; PhDr in Literary Theory and Comparative Literature, Universidade de São Paulo, 1989. Appointment: Professor of Brazilian Literature, Universidade Estadual Paulista. Publications: O Salto por cima da propria sombra, 1996; Literatura Comparada: Ensaios, 1996. Contributions to: Revista do Instituto de Estudos Brasileiros; Revista de Letras da UNESP; Revista de Estudos Literarios da FALE/UFMG; Anuario Brasileño de Estudios Hispanicos. Address: Rua da Assembleia,226 19800-000 Assis-SP Brazil.

CALCAGNO Anne, b. 14 Nov 1957, San Diego, California, USA. Fiction Writer. m. Leo, 1986, 1 son, 1 daughter. Education: MFA, University of Montana. Appointment: Assistant Professor of English, DePaul University, 1993-. Publications: Pray for Yourself and Other Stories, 1993; Travelers Tales: Italy, 1998. Contributions to: North American Review; Epoch; TriQuarterly; Denver Quarterly; Fiction Monthly; Rhino. Honours: National Endowment for the Arts Fellowship Award, 1989; Illinois Arts Council Fellowship, 1991. Memberships: Associated Writing Programs; Poets and Writers; Modern Language Association. Literary Agent: Jean Naggar, New York. Address: c/o Department of English, DePaul University, 802 West Belden Avenue, Chicago, IL 60614-3214, USA.

CALDECOTT Moyra, b. 1 June 1927, Pretoria, South Africa (British citizen). Author. m. Oliver Zerffi Stratford Caldecott, 5 Apr 1951, 2 sons, 1 daughter. Education: BA, 1949, MA, 1950, University of Natal. Publications:

The Weapons of the Wolfhound, 1976; The Sacred Stones, Vol I, The Tall Stones, 1977, Vol II, The Temple of the Sun, 1977, Vol III, Shadow on the Stones, 1978; Adventures by Leaf Light, 1978; The Lily and the Bull, 1979; Child of the Dark Star, 1980; The King of Shadows: A Glastonbury Story, 1981; The Twins of the Tylwyth Teg, 1983; Taliesin and Avagddu, 1983; Bran, Son of Llyr, 1985; The Tower and the Emerald, 1985; Guardians of the Tall Stones, 1986; The Son of the Sun, 1986; The Silver Vortex, 1987; Etheldreda, 1987; Women in Celtic Myth, 1988; Daughter of Amun, 1989; The Green Lady and the King of Shadows, 1989; The Daughter of Ra, 1990; The Crystal Legends, 1990; Myths of the Sacred Tree, 1993; The Winged Man, 1994; Mythical Journeys: Legendary Quests, 1996; The Waters of Sul, 1998. Contributions to: Anthologies and periodicals. Address: 52 Southdown Road, Southdown. Bath BA2 1JQ, England.

CALDER Angus Lindsay Ritchie, b. 5 Feb 1942, Sutton, Surrey, England. (1) Jenni Daiches, (2) Kate Kyle, 2 sons, 2 daughters. Education: MA, King's College, Cambridge, 1960-63; DPhil, University of Sussex, 1963-68. Appointments: Lecturer in Literature, University of Nairobi, 1968-71; Staff Tutor in Arts, Open University in Scotland, 1979-93; Visiting Professor of English, University of Zimbabwe, 1992; Editor, Journal of Commonwealth Literature. Publications: The People's War: Britain, 1939-1945, 1969; Russia Discovered: Nineteenth Century Fiction, 1976; Revolutionary Empire: The Rise of the English - Speaking Empires, 1981; The Myth of the Blitz, 1991; Revolving Culture: Notes From the Scottish Republic, 1994; Waking in Waikato (poems), 1997. Contributions to: Cencrastus, Chapman, Herald, London Review of Books, New Statesman, Scotland on Sunday. Honours: Eric Gregory Award, 1967; John Llewellyn Rhys Memorial Prize, 1970; Scottish Arts Council Book Awards, 1981, 1994. Membership: Scottish PEN. Literary Agent: Giles Gordon, Curtis Brown. Address: 15 Spittal Street, Edinburgh EH3 9DY, Scotland.

CALDER Nigel (David Ritchie), b. 2 Dec 1931, London, England. Writer. m. Elisabeth Palmer, 22 May 1954, 2 sons, 3 daughters. Education: BA, 1954, MA, 1957, Sidney Sussex College, Cambridge. Appointments: Research Physicist, Mullard Research Laboratories, Redhill, Surrey, 1954-56; Staff Writer, 1956-60, Science Editor, 1960-62, Editor, 1962-66, New Scientist; Science Correspondent, New Statesman, 1959-62, 1966-71. Publications: The Environment Game, 1967, US edition as Eden Was No Garden: An Inquiry Into the Environment of Man, 1967; Technopolis: Social Control of the Uses of Science, 1969; Violent Universe: An Eyewitness Account of the New Astronomy, 1970; The Mind of Man: An Investigation into Current Research on the Brain and Human Nature, 1970; Restless Earth: A Report on the New Geology, 1972; The Life Game: Evolution and the New Biology, 1974; The Weather Machine: How Our Weather Works and Why It Is Changing, 1975; The Human Conspiracy, 1976; The Key to the Universe: A Report on the New Physics, 1977; Spaceships of the Mind, 1978; Einstein's Universe, 1979; Nuclear Nightmares: An Investigation into Possible Wars, 1980; The Comet is Coming!: The Feverish Legacy of Mr Halley, 1981; Timescale: An Atlas of the Fourth Dimension, 1984; 1984 and Beyond: Nigel Calder Talks to His Computer About the Future, 1984; The English Channel, 1986; The Green Machines, 1986; Future Earth: Exploring the Frontiers of Science (editor with John Newell), 1989; Scientific Europe, 1990; Spaceship Earth, 1991; Giotto to the Comets, 1992; Beyondthis World, 1995; The Manic Sun, 1997. Contributions to: Television documentaries; Numerous periodicals. Honours: UNESCO Kalinga Prize, 1972; AAAS, honorary fellow, 1986. Memberships: Association of British Science Writers; Cruising Association; Royal Astronomical Society; Royal Geographical Society. Address: 26 Boundary Road, Northgate, Crawley, West Sussex RH10 2BT, England.

CALDERWOOD James L(ee), b. 7 Apr 1930, Corvallis, Oregon, USA. Professor Emeritus; Writer. m.

Cleo Xeniades Calderwood, 15 Aug 1955, 2 sons. Education: BA, University of Oregon, 1953; PhD, University of Washington, 1963. Appointments: Instructor, Michigan State University, 1961-63; Assistant Professor, University of California at Irvine, 1963-66; Assistant Professor, 1966-68, Associate Professor, 1968-71, Professor, 1971-94, Associate Dean of Humanities, 1974-94, Professor Emeritus, 1994-, University of California at Irvine; Editorial Board, Studies in English Literature, 1978-, Shakespeare Criticism, 1989-; Evaluator, National Endowment for the Humanities, 1979-. Publications: Shakespearean Metadrama, 1971; Metadrama in Shakespeare's Henriad, 1979; To Be and Not to Be: Negation and Metadrama in Hamlet, 1983; If It Were Done: Tragic Action in Macbeth, 1986; Shakespeare and the Denial of Death, 1987; The Properties of Othello, 1989; A Midsummer Night's Dream, 1992. Editor: Shakespeare's Love's Labour's Lost, 1970. Editor with H E Toliver: Forms of Poetry, 1968; Perspectives on Drama, 1968; Perspectives on Poetry, 1968; Perspectives on Fiction, 1968; Forms of Drama, 1969; Essays in Shakespearean Criticism, 1969; Forms of Prose Fiction, 1972; Forms of Tragedy, 1972. Contributions to: Scholarly journals. Honour: Alumni Achievement Award, University of Oregon, 1991. Address: 1323 Terrace Way, Laguna Beach, CA 92651, USA.

CALHOUN Craig Jackson, b. 16 June 1952, Watseka, Illinois, USA. Professor of Sociology; Writer; Editor. m. Pamela F DeLargy, 2 children. Education: BA in Anthropology, University of Southern California, 1972; MA in Anthropology, Columbia University, 1974; MA in Social Anthropology, Manchester University, 1975; PhD in Sociology and History, St Antony's College, Oxford, 1980. Appointments: Instructor, 1977-80, Assistant Professor, 1980-85, Associate Professor, 1985-89, Professor of Sociology and History, 1989-96, Director, University Center for International Studies, 1993-96, University of North Carolina at Chapel Hill; Editor, Comparative Social Research, 1988-93, Sociological Theory, 1994-; Visiting Lecturer, 1991, Professor, part-time, 1993-, Unviersity of Oslo; Professor of Sociology, Chair, Department of Sociology, New York University, 1996-; Visiting Lecturer, 1991, Professor, part-time, 1993-, University of Oslo. Publications: The Anthropological Study of Education (editor with F A J Ianni), 1976; The Question of Class Struggle: Social Foundations of Popular Radicalism During the Industrial Revolution, 1982; Sociology (with Donald Light and Suzanne Keller), 1989, 4th edition, 1997; Structures of Power and Constraint: Essays in Honor of Peter M Blau (editor with W R Scott and M Meyer), 1990; Habermas and the Public Sphere (editor), 1992; Bourdieu: Critical Perspectives (editor with E LiPuma and M Postone), 1993; Social Theory and the Politics of Identity (editor), 1994; Neither Gods Nor Emperors: Students and the Struggle for Democracy in China, 1995; Critical Social Theory: Culture, History and the Challenge of Difference, 1995. Contributions to: Numerous books and scholarly journals. Honours: W K Kellogg National Fellowship, 1982-85; Distinguished Contribution to Scholarship Award, Section on Political Sociology, American Sociological Association, 1995. Memberships: American Anthropological Association; American Historical Association; American Sociological Association; International Sociological Association; International Studies Association; Royal Anthropological Institute; Social Science History Association; Society for the Study of Social Problems; Sociological Research Association. Address: Department of Sociology, New York University, 269 Mercer Street, New York, NY 10003, USA.

CALIFANO Joseph A(nthony) Jr, b. 15 May 1931, Brooklyn, New York, USA. Lawyer; Professor of Public Health Policy; Writer. m. (1), 2 sons, 1 daughter, (2) Hilary Paley Byers, 1983, 2 stepchildren. Education: AB, Holy Cross College, 1952; LLB, Harvard University, 1955. Appointments: Admitted to the Bar, New York, 1955; Lawyer, Dewey Ballantine firm, New York City, 1958-61; Special Assistant to the General Counsel, US Department of Defense, 1961-62, the Secretary of the Army, 1962-63; General Counsel, Department of the

Army, 1963-64; Special Assistant to the Secretary and Deputy Secreatry of Defense, 1964-65, to President Lyndon B Johnson, 1965-69; Partner, Arnold & Porter, Washington, DC, 1969-71, Williams, Connolly & Califano, Washington, DC, 1971-77; Secretary, US Department of Health, Education, and Welfare, 1977-79; Partner, Califano, Ross & Heineman, Washington, DC, 1980-82; Senior Partner, Dewey, Ballantine, Bushby, Palmer, & Wood, Washington, DC, 1983-92; Professor of Public Health Policy, Columbia University, 1992-; Chairman, President, National Center on Addiction and Substance Abuse, Columbia University, 1992-. Publications: The Student Revolution: A Global Confrontation, 1969; A Presidential Nation, 1975; The Media and the Law (with Howard Simons), 1976; The Media and Business (with Howard Simons), 1978; Governing America: An Insider's Report (from the White House and the Cabinet), 1981; The 1982 Report on Drug Abuse and Alcoholism: America's Health Care Revolution, 1985; The Triumph and Tragedy of Lyndon Johnson, 1991; Radical Surgery: What's Next for America's Health Care, 1994. Honours: Distinguished Public Service Medal, US Department of Defense, 1965; Man of the Year Award, Justinian Society of Lawyers, 1966. Address: c/o National Center on Addiction and Substance Abuse at Columbia University, 152 West 57th Street, New York, NY 10019, USA.

CALISHER Hortense, (Jack Fenno), b. 20 Dec 1911, New York, New York, USA. Writer. m. (1) 2 sons, (2) Curtis Harnack, 23 Mar 1959. Education: AB, Barnard College, 1932. Appointments: Adjunct Professor, Barnard College, 1956-57, Columbia University, 1968-70, City College of the City University of New York, 1969; Various visiting professorships and lectureships. Publications: Novels: False Entry, 1961; Textures of Life, 1962; Journal from Ellipsis, 1965; The New Yorkers, 1969; Queenie, 1971; Standard Dreaming, 1972; Eagle Eye, 1973; On Keeping Women, 1977; Mysteries of Motion, 1984; The Bobby-Soxer, 1986; Age, 1987; The Small Bang, 1992; In the Palace of the Movie King, 1994. Other: Collected Stories, 1975; The Novellas of Hortense Calisher, 1998. Non-Fiction: Herself (autobiography), 1972; Kissing Cousins (memoir), 1988. Contributions to: Periodicals. Honours: Guggenheim Fellowships, 1952, 1955; American Academy of Arts and Letters Award, 1967; Kafka Prize, University of Rochester, 1987; National Endowment for the Arts Lifetime Achievement Award, 1989. Memberships: American Academy of Arts and Letters, president, 1987-90; PEN, president, 1986-87. Address: c/o Donadio & Associates, 121 West 27th Street, Suite 704, New York, NY 10001, USA.

CALLAGHAN Barry, b. 5 July 1937, Toronto, Ontario, Canada. Writer; Poet; Editor; Publisher; Translator; College Teacher. 1 son. Education: BA, 1960, MA, 1962, St Michael's College, University of Toronto. Appointments: Teacher, Atkinson College, York University, Toronto, 1965-; Writer-in-Residence, University of Rome, 1987; Literary Editor, Telegram, Toronto, 1966-71; Host and Documentary Producer, Weekend, CBC-TV, 1969-72; Founder-Publisher, Exile, 1972-, Exile Editions, 1976-. Publications: Poetry: The Hogg Poems and Drawings, 1978; Seven Last Words, 1983; Stone Blind Love, 1987; Hogg: The Poems and Drawings, 1997. Fiction: The Black Queen Stories, 1982; The Way the Angel Spreads Her Wings, 1989; When Things Get Worst, 1993; A Kiss is Still a Kiss, 1995. Non-Fiction: Barrel-house Kings, 1998. Editor: Various anthologies and books. Honours: Many National Magazine Awards; Gold Medal, University of Western Ontario, 1979; Co-Winner, International Authors Festival Award, Harbourfront, Toronto, 1986; Toronto Arts Award, 1993; Honorary Doctor of Letters, State University of New York, 1999. Address: 20 Dale Avenue, Toronto, Ontario M4W 1K4, Canada.

CALLAHAN Steven (Patrick), b. 6 Feb 1952, Needham, Massachusetts, USA. Author; Illustrator. Education: BA, Syracuse University, 1974. Appointments: Contributing Editor, Sail Magazine, 1982-84; Sailor Magazine, 1984-85; Associate Editor, Cruising World Magazine, 1994-. Publications: Adrift, 76 Days Lost at Sea, 1986; Capsized, 1993. Contributions to: Sail; Sailor;

Cruising World; Sailing; Multihull; NE Offshore; Yankee; New York Times; Ultrasport; International Wildlife; Yachting World; Yachts and Yachting. Honours: Salon Du Libre Maritime, 1986; Best Books for Young Adults, 1986. Address: 804 Newport Green, Newport, RI 02840, USA.

CALLAWAY C Wayne, b. 28 May 1941, Easton, Maryland, USA. Physician. m. Jackie Chalkley, 7 Sept 1996. Education: BA, University of Delaware, 1963; MD, Northwestern University, 1967. Publications: The Callaway Diet: Successful Permanent Weight Loss for Starvers, Stuffers and Skippers, 1990; Surviving with AIDS: A Comprehensive Program of Nutritional Co-Therapy, 1991; Clinical Nutrition for the House Officer, 1992; American Medical Association Family Healty Cookbook (medical editor), 1997. Contributions to: Periodicals. Honour: Finalist, James Beard Award. Literary Agent: Jane Dystel. Address: 2311 M Street North West, No 301, Washington, DC 20037, USA.

CALLICOTT J(ohn) Baird, b. 9 May 1941, Memphis, Tennessee, USA. Professor of Philosophy and Natural Resources; Writer. m. (1) Ann Nelson Archer, 7 June 1963, div 15 May 1985, 1 son, (2) Frances Moore Lappe, 25 Nov 1985, div 15 July 1990. Education: BA, Rhodes College, 1963; MA, 1966, PhD, 1971, Syracuse University. Appointments: Lecturer, Syracuse University, 1965-66; Instructor, University of Memphis, 1966-69; Assistant Professor, 1969-74, Associate Professor, 1974-82, Professor of Philosophy, 1982-, Professor of Natural Resources, 1984-, University of Wisconsin at Stevens Point; Visiting Professor of Philosophy, University of Florida, 1983; Visiting Professor of Environmental Studies, University of California at Santa Barbara, 1988; Visiting Professor, Philosophy and Geography, University of Hawaii, 1988; Rose Morgan Visiting Professor, University of Kansas, 1993; Knight Visiting Scholar, Presbyterian College, 1995; Visting Professorial Fellow, James Cook University of North Queensland, Australia, 1995; Associate Professor of Philosophy, University of North Texas, 1995-. Publications: Plato's Aesthetics: An Introduction to the Theory of Forms, 1971; Clothed-in-Fur and Other Tales: An Introduction to An Ojibwa World View, 1982; In Defense of the Land Ethic: Essays in Environmental Philosophy, 1989; Earth's Insights: A Survey of Ecological Ethics from the Mediterranean Basin to the Australian Outback, 1994; Beyond the Land Ethic: More Essays in Environmental Philosophy, 1999; Editor: Companion to a Sand County Almanac: Interpretive and Critical Essays, 1987; Nature in Asian Traditions of Thought: Essays in Environmental Philosophy (with Roger T Ames), 1989; The River of the Mother of God and Other Essays by Aldo Leopold (with Susan L Flader), 1991; Environmental Philosophy: From Animal Rights to Social Ecology (with Michael Zimmerman, George Sessions, Karen Warren, and John Clark), 1993, 2nd edition, 1997; Earth Summit Ethics: Toward a Reconstructive Postmodern Environmental Philosophy on the Atlantic Rim (with Fernando J R da Rocha), 1996; The Great New Wilderness Debate (with Michael P Nelson), 1998. Contributions to: Many books and numerous journals. Honours: Woodrow Wilson Fellow, 1963-64; Wisconsin Library Association Outstanding Achievement Awards, 1988, 1992; University Scholar Award, University of Wisconsin at Stevens Point, 1995. Memberships: American Philosophical Association; American Society for Environmental History; International Development Ethics Association; International Society for Environmental Ethics, President, 1997-2000; Society for Asian and Comparative Philosophy; Society for Conservation Biology. Address: c/o Department of Philosophy and Religion, University of North Texas, Denton, TX 76203, USA.

CALLISON Brian (Richard), b. 13 July 1934, Manchester, England. Writer. m. Phyllis Joyce Jobson, 12 May 1958, 2 sons. Education: Dundee College of Art, 1954-56. Publications: A Flock of Ships, 1970; A Plague of Sailors, 1971; Dawn Attack, 1972; A Web of Salvage, 1973; Trapp's War, 1974; A Ship is Dying, 1976; A Frenzy of Merchantmen, 1977; The Judas Ship, 1978; Trapp's Peace, 1979; The Auriga Madness, 1980; The

Sextant, 1981; Spearfish, 1982; Bone Collectors, 1984; Thunder of Crude, 1986; Trapp and World War Three, 1988; The Trojan Hearse, 1990; Crocodile Trapp, 1993. Memberships: Royal Institute of Nagivation (M.R.I.N); Society of Authors. Address: c/o Harper Collins Publishers, 77-85 Fulham Palace Road, Hammersmith, London W6 8JB, England.

CALLOW Philip (Kenneth), b. 26 Oct 1924, Birmingham, England. Writer; Poet. Education: St Luke's College, Exeter, 1968-70. Appointment: Creative Writing Fellow, Open University, 1979. Publications: The Hosanna Man, 1956; Common People, 1958; Native Ground, 1959; Pledge for the Earth, 1960; The Honeymooners, 1960; Turning Point, 1961; Clipped Wings, 1963; The Real Life, 1964; In My Own Land, 1965; Going to the Moon, 1968; The Bliss Body, 1969; Flesh of Morning, 1971; The Lamb, 1971; Bare Wires, 1972; Yours, 1972; Son and Lover: The Young D H Lawrence, 1975; The Story of My Desire, 1976; Janine, 1977; The Subway to New York, 1979; Cave Light, 1981; Woman with a Poet, 1983; New York Insomnia, 1984; Poetry: Icons, 1987; Soliloquires of an Eye, 1990; Some Love, 1991. Address: Little Thatch, Haselbury, Nr Crewkerne, Somerset, England.

CALLWOOD June, b. 2 June 1924, Chatham, Ontario, Canada. Writer. m. Trent Frayne, 13 May 1944, 2 sons, 1 dec, 2 daughters. Appointments: Reporter, Brantford Expositor, 1941, Toronto Globe and Mail, 1942; Freelance Journalist, 1945-; Columnist, Globe and Mail, 1983-89. Publications: Emma, 1984; Twelve Weeks in Spring, 1986; Emotions, 1986; Jim: A Life with AIDS, 1988; The Sleepwalker, 1990; Trial Without End, 1995. Honours: City of Toronto Award of Merit, 1974; Order of Canada, 1978, 1986; Canadian News Hall of Fame, 1984; Windsor Press Club Quill Award, 1987; Order of Ontario, 1989; Udo Award, 1989; Lifetime Achievement Award, 1991; 16 Honorary Degrees; Margaret Lawrence Lecture, 1993. Memberships: Writers Union of Canada, Chair; Canadian Centre PEN, President; Toronto Arts Council; Chair Literary Awards; Book and Periodical Council Chair; Beaver Valley Soaring Club. Address: 21 Hillcroft Drive, Toronto, Ontario M9B 4X4, Canada.

CALMENSON Stephanie Lyn, b. 28 Nov 1952, New York, New York, USA. Children's Writer. Education: BA, Brooklyn College, 1973; MA, New York University, 1976. Publications include: Never Take a Pig to Lunch (anthology), 1982; One Little Monkey, 1982, 4th edition, 1983; My Book of the Seasons, 1982; Where Will the Animals Stay?, 1983; That's Not Fair!, 1983; Where is Grandma Potamus?, 1983; The Birthday Hat: A Grandma Potamus Story, 1983; The Kindergarten Book, 1983; Barney's Sand Castle, 1983; Bambi and the Butterfly, 1983; Ten Furry Monsters, 1984; The Afterschool Book, 1984; All Aboard the Goodnight Train, 1984; Waggleby of Fraggle Rock, 1985; Ten Items or Less, 1985; Happy Birthday Buddy Blue, 1985; The Laugh Book, anthology (with Joanna Cole), 1986; Gobo and the Prize from Outer Space, 1986; The Sesame Street ABC Book, 1986; The Sesame Street Book of First Times, 1986; Little Duck's Moving Day, 1986; Who Said Moo?, 1987; Beginning Sounds Workbook, 1987; The Read-Aloud Treasury, anthology (with Joanna Cole), 1987; Tiger's Bedtime, 1987; One Red Shoe (The Other One's Blue!), 1987; Spaghetti Manners, 1987; The Giggle Book, 1987; Fido, 1987; Where's Rufus?, 1988; Little Duck and the New Baby, 1988; The Children's Aesop, 1988; The Read-Aloud Treasury (with Joanna Cole), 1988; No Stage Fright for Me, 1988; Where is Grandma Rabbit?, 1988; 101 Turkey Jokes, 1988; Ho! Ho! Ho!: Christmas Jokes and Riddles, 1988; What Am I! Very First Riddles, 1989; The Principal's New Clothes, 1989; Zip, Whiz, Zoom, 1992; The Little Witch Sisters, 1993; Engine, Engine, Number 1, 1996; My Dog's The Best, 1997; The Gator Girls: Rockin' Reptiles (with Joanna Cole). 1997; Shaggy Waggy Dogs and Others, 1998. Contributions to: Periodicals. Memberships: PEN American Centre; Society of Children's Book Writers; Authors Guild. Address: c/o Scholastic Press Inc, 555 Broadway, New York, NY 10012, USA.

CALVERT Patricia Joyce, b. 22 July 1931, Great Falls, Montana, USA. Writer; Editor; Proofreader. m. George J Calvert, 27 Jan 1951, 2 daughters. Education: BS, Summa Cum Laude, Winona State University, 1976. Publications: The Snowbird, 1980; The Stone Pony, 1982; The Hour of the Wolf, 1983; Hadder MacColl, 1985; Yesterday's Daughter, 1986; Stranger, You and I, 1987; When Morning Comes, 1989; Picking Up the Pieces, 1993. Contributions to: Highlights for Children; Junior Life; Adventurer; American Farmer; Friend; Capper's Weeky; Grit; Writer Magazine; Farmland News; War Cry. Honours: Society of Children's Book Writers, Work-in-Progress Award, 1978; American Library Society, Best Book Award, 1980; Woman in the Arts Award, YWCA, 1981; Friends of American Writers Award, 1981; Society of Midland Authors, 1981. Memberships: Society of Children's Book Writers; Children's Reading Round Table; Minnesota Reading Association; International Reading Association. Literary Agent: Wendy Schmalz, Harold Ober Agency, 426 Madison Avenue, New York, NY 10017, USA. Address: Foxwood Farm, 6130 County Road, No 7 South East, Chatfield, MN 55923, USA.

CALVERT Peter Anthony Richard, b. 19 Nov 1936, Islandmagee, County Antrim, Northern Ireland. Professor of Politics; Writer. m. Susan Ann Milbank, 1987. Education: Campbell College, Belfast; Queens' College, Cambridge; University of Michigan. Appointments: Lecturer, 1964-71, Senior Lecturer, 1971-74, Reader, 1974-83, Professor, 1984-, University of Southampton. Publications: The Mexican Revolution 1910-1914, 1968; A Study of Revolution, 1970; The Falklands Crisis, 1982; Guatemala, 1985; The Foreign Policy of New States, 1986; Argentina: Political Culture and Instability (with Susan Calvert) 1989; Revolution and Counter Revolution, 1990; Latin America in the 20th Century (with Susan Calvert) 1993; An Introduction to Comparative Politics, 1993; International Politics of Latin America, 1994; Politics and Society in the Third World (with Susan Calvert), 1996; Revolution and International Politics, 1984, 1996. Editor: The Process of Political Succession, 1987; The Central American Security System, 1988; Political and Economic Encyclopedia of South America and the Caribbean, 1991; Democratization, 1996-. Contributions to: International Affairs' Political Studies; World Today. Membership: Royal Historical Society, fellow; Royal Institute of International Affairs. Address: Department of Politics, University of Southampton, Southampton SO17 1BJ, England.

CALVIN Henry. See: **HANLEY Clifford.**

CALVOCORESSI Peter (John Ambrose), b. 17 Nov 1912, England. Author; Publisher. m. Barbara Dorothy Eden, 1938, 2 sons. Education: King's Scholar, Eton; Balliol College, Oxford. Appointments: Called to the Bar, 1935; Wing Commander, Trial of Major War Criminals, Nuremburg, 1945-46; Staff, 1949-54, Council, 1955-70, Royal Institute of International Affairs; Director, Chatto & Windus Ltd and The Hogarth Press Ltd, 1954-65; Chairman, The Africa Bureau, 1963-71; The London Library, 1970-73, Chairman, Open University Educational Enterprises, 1979-88; Part-Time Reader in International Relations, University of Sussex, 1965-71; Editorial Director, 1972-76, Publisher and Chief Executive, 1973-76, Penguin Books. Publications: Nuremburg: The Facts, the Law and the Consequences, 1947; Survey of International Affairs, Vol I, 1947-48, 1959, Vol II, 1949-50, 1951, Vol III, 1951, 1952, Vol IV, 1952, 1953, Vol V, 1953, 1954; Middle East Crisis (with Guy Wint), 1957; South Africa and World Opinion, 1961; World Order and New States, 1962; World Politics Since 1945, 1968, 7th edition, 1996; Total War (with Guy Wint), 1972, 2nd edition, 1989; The British Experience, 1945-75, 1978; Top Secret Ultra, 1980; Independent Africa and the World, 1985; A Time for Peace, 1987; Who's Who in the Bible, 1987; Resilient Europe, 1870-2000, 1991; Threading My Way (memoirs), 1994; Fall Out: World War II and the Shaping of Europe, 1997. Honour: Doctor of the University, Open University, 1986. Memberships: Institute for Strategic Studies, council, 1961-71; Amnesty

International, international executive, 1969-71. Address: 1 Queen's Parade, Bath BA1 2NJ, England.

CAMELO Mario, b. 19 Jan 1952, Colombia. Traducteur. m. Verena Wieland, 1981, 3 daughters. Publications: Las Victorias del Miedo, 1978; Cronica del Reino, 1997; Proposicion de Lamparas, 1998. Membership: Société Suisse des Ecrivains. Literary Agent: Amelia Romero, Ap 220, St Cuigat, Barcelona, Espagne.

CAMERON D Y. See: **COOK Dorothy Mary.**

CAMERON Deborah, b. 10 Nov 1958, Glasgow, Scotland. Lecturer; Writer. Education: BA, Honours, University of Newcastle upon Tyne, 1980; MLitt, Oxford University, 1985. Appointments: Lecturer, Roehampton Institute of Higher Education, Digby Stuart College, London, 1983-; Visiting Professor, College of William and Mary, 1988-90. Publications: Feminism and Linguistic Theory, 1985; Analysing Conversation (with T J Taylor), 1987; The Lust to Kill (with Elizabeth Frazer), 1987; Women in Their Speech Communities (editor with Jennifer Coates), 1989; The Feminist Critique of Language (editor), 1990. Contributions to: Articles and reviews to magazines and newspapers, including Language and Communicaiton, City Limits and Cosmopolitan. Address: Digby Stuart College, Roehampton Lane, London SW25 5PH, England.

CAMERON Donald (Allan), (Silver Donald Cameron), b. 21 June 1937, Toronto, Ontario, Canada. Author. m. (1) Catherine Ann Cahoon, 21 Aug 1959, 3 sons, 1 daughter. (2) Lulu Terrio, 17 May 1980, dec 6 Apr 1996, 1 son, (3) Marjorie L Simmins, 14 Mar 1998. Education: BA, University of British Columbia, 1959; MA, University of California, 1962; PhD, University of London, 1967. Appointments: Associate Professor of English, University of New Brunswick, 1968-71; Writer-in-Residence, 1978-80, Dean, School of Community Studies, 1994-96, Special Assistant to the President, 1997-, University College of Cape Breton, Nova Scotia; Writer-in-Residence, University of Prince Edward Island, 1985-86, Nova Scotia College of Art and Design, 1987-88. Publications: Faces of Leacock, 1967; Conversations with Canadian Novelists, 1973; The Education of Everett Richardson, 1977; Seasons in the Rain (essays), 1978; Dragon Lady, 1980; The Baitchopper (children's novel), 1982; Schooner: Bluenose and Bluenose II, 1984; Outhouses of the West, 1988; Wind, Whales and Whisky: A Cape Breton Voyage, 1991; Lifetime: A Treasury of Uncommon Wisdoms (co-author), 1992; Once Upon a Schooner: An Offshore Voyage In Bluenose II, 1992; Iceboats to Superferries: An Illustrated History of Marine Atlantic Superferries (co-author); Sniffing the Coast: An Acadian Voyage, 1993; Sterling Silver: Rants, Raves and Revelations, 1994; The Living Beach, 1998; Other: Numerous articles, radio dramas, short stories, television scripts and stage plays. Honours: 4 National Magazine Awards; Best Short Film, Canadian Film Celebration; Nominated, Prix Italia for Radio Drama, 1980; City of Dartmouth Book Award, 1992; Atlantic Provinces Booksellers Choice Award, 1992. Memberships: Writers Union, Canada; ACTRA; Writers Federation, Nova Scotia. Address: D'Escousse, Nova Scotia B0E 1K0, Canada.

CAMERON Ian. See: **PAYNE Donald Gordon.**

CAMERON WATT Donald, b. 17 May 1928, Rugby, England. Professor Emeritus; Writer. Education: BA, 1951, MA, 1954, Oriel College, Oxford. Appointments: Assistant Lecturer, 1954-56, Lecturer, 1956-61, Senior Lecturer, 1962-66, Reader, 1966-72, Titular Professor, 1971-82, Stevenson Professor of International History, 1982-93, Professor Emeritus, 1993-, London School of Economics and Political Science, University of London; Editor, Survey of International Affairs, 1962-71; Chairman, Greenwich Forum, 1974-84; Official Historian, Cabinet Office Historical Section, 1976-95. Publications: Britain and the Suez Canal, 1956; Documents on the Suez Crisis, 1957; Britain Looks to Germany, 1965; Personalities and Policies. Studies in the Formulation of

British Foreign Policy in the 10th Century, 1965; A History of the World in the 20th Century, 1967; Contemporary History in Europe, 1969; Current British Foreign Policy, 1970-72; Documents on British Foreign Affairs, 1867-1939, 1985-97; Succeeeding John Bull, America in Britain's Place 1900-1975, 1983; How War Came, 1989; Argentina Between the Great Powers, 1990. Honours: Fellow, British Academy, DLitt, Oxon; Polish Academy of Arts and Science, fellow; Wolfson Prize, 1990. Literary Agent: Michael Sissons, A D Peters and Co, 5th Floor, The Chambers, Chelsea Harbour, Lots Road, London SW10 0XF, England. Address: c/o London School of Economics and Political Science, Houghton Street, London WC2A 2AE, England.

CAMPBELL Alistair Te Ariki, b. 25 June 1925, Rarotonga, New Zealand. Writer; Poet; Dramatist. m. (1) Fleur Adcock, 1952, (2) Meg Andersen, 1958, 3 sons, 2 daughters. Education: BA, Victoria University of Wellington, 1953; Diploma of Teaching, Wellington Teachers College, 1954. Appointments: Senior Editor, New Zealand Council for Educational Research, 1972-87; Writer's Fellow, Victoria University of Wellington, 1992. Publications: Poetry: Mine Eyes Dazzle, 1950; Sanctuary of Spirits, 1963; Wild Honey, 1964; Blue Rain, 1967; Kapiti: Selected Poems, 1972; Dreams, Yellow Lions, 1975; The Dark Lord of Savaiki, 1980; Collected Poems, 1981; Soul Traps, 1985; Stone Rain: The Polynesian Strain, 1992; Death and the Tagua, 1995; Pocket Collected Poems, 1996. Novels: The Frigate Bird, 1989; Sidewinder, 1991; Tia, 1993; Fantasy with Witches, 1998; Autobiography: Island to Island, 1984. Plays: The Suicide, 1965; When the Bough Breaks, 1970. Contributions to: Anthologies and periodicals. Honours: Gold Medal for TV documentary, La Spezia International Film Festival, 1974; New Zealand Book Award for Poetry, 1982;Pacific Islands Artist Award, 1998. Membership: PEN International, New Zealand Centre. Address: 4B Rawhiti Road, Pukerua Bay, Wellington, New Zealand.

CAMPBELL Donald, b. 25 Feb 1940, Caithness, Scotland. Poet; Dramatist. m. Jean Fairgrieve, 1966, 1 son. Appointments: Writer-in-Residence, Edinburgh Education Department, 1974-77, Royal Lyceum Theatre, 1981-82. Publications: Poetry: Poems, 1971; Rhymes 'n Reasons, 1972; Murals: Poems in Scots, 1975; Blether: A Collection of Poems, 1979; A Brighter Sunshine, 1983; An Audience for McGonagall, 1987; Selected Poems 1870-90, 1990. Other: Plays for stage, radio and television. Address: 85 Spottiswood Street, Edinburgh EH9 1BZ, Scotland.

CAMPBELL Ewing, b. 26 Dec 1940, Alice, Texas, USA. Author; Associate Professor. Education: BBA, North Texas State University, 1968; MA, University of Southern Mississippi, 1972; PhD, Oklahoma State University, 1980. Appointments: Lecturer, University of Texas at Austin, 1981-82, Oklahoma State University, 1982-83, Wharton Community College, 1983-84; Assistant Professor 1984-90, Associate Professor, 1990-, Texas A & M University. Publications: Novels: Weave It Like Nightfall, 1977; The Way of Sequestered Places, 1982; The Rincón Triptych, 1984; The Tex-Mex Express, 1993; Madonna, Maleva, 1995. Short Fiction: Piranesi's Dream, 1986. Criticism: Raymond Carver: A Study of the Short Fiction, 1992. Contributions to: Stories and articles to many periodicals. Honours: Fulbright Scholar, Argentina, 1989, Spain, 1997; National Endowments for the Arts Fellowship, 1990; Dobie-Paisano Ralph A Johnston Award, 1992; Chris O'Malley Fiction Prize, 1998. Address: 1003 Magnolia, Hearne, TX 77859, USA.

CAMPBELL Ian, b. 25 Aug 1942, Lausanne, Switzerland. Reader in English. Education: MA, University of Aberdeen, 1964; PhD, University of Edinburgh, 1970; Appointments: Reader in English, University of Edinburgh, 1967-; British Council Appointments, France, Germany. Publications: Thomas Carlyle Letters, 15 volumes, 1970-87; Carlyle, 1974, 1975, 1978; Nineteenth Century Scottish Ficton: Critical Esays, 1978; Thomas and Jane, 1980; Kailyard, 1981; Lewis Grassic Gibbon, 1986; Spartacus, 1987. Contributions to: Numerous papers to learned journals.

Honour: British Academy Research Fellowship, 1980. Memberships: Carlyle Society, president; Scottish Association for the Speaking of Verse; council member, Association for Scottish Literary Studies. Address: Department of English, University of Edinburgh, David Hume Tower, George Square, Edinburgh EH8 9JX, Scotland.

CAMPBELL John Malcolm, b. 2 Sept 1947, London, England. Writer. m. Alison McCracken, 5 Aug 1972, 1 son, 1 daughter. Education: Charterhouse, 1960-65; MA, 1970, PhD, 1975, University of Edinburgh. Publications: Lloyd George: The Goat in the Wilderness, 1977; F E Smith, First Earl of Birkenhead, 1983; Roy Jenkins: A Biography, 1983; Nye Bevan and the Mirage of British Socialism, 1987; The Experience of World War II, editor, 1989; Makers of the Twentieth Century, editor, 1990-92; Edward Heath, 1993. Contributions to: Regular Book Reviews, The Times; Times Literary Supplement; The Independent; Sunday Telegraph. Honours: Yorkshire Post, Best First Book Award; NCR Book Award for non-fiction, 1994. Memberships: Society of Authors; Royal Historical Society. Literary Agent: Bruce Hunter, David Higham Associates. Address: 35 Ladbroke Square, London W11 3NB, England.

CAMPBELL Judith. See: **PARES Marion.**

CAMPBELL Karen. See: **BEATY Betty Joan Campbell Smith.**

CAMPBELL Martin Crafts, (Marty Campbell), b. 24 June 1946, Oakland, California, USA. Writer; Poet. Education: BS, University of Chicago, 1968; MA, Northwestern University, 1972. Appointments: Featured Performer, Poetry, USA and St Croix, 1976-; Publisher, Mar Crafts, 1981-; Editor, SENYA and Companion of Senya, 1989; Collage Two, 1991; Poetry Corner, 1991-. Publications: Chapters of Poems, Mesh Up, 1981; Croix These Tears, 1982; Dreem, 1982; Church, 1985; Saint Sea, 1986; Companion to Senya, 1989; Seed, 1994. Contributions to: Hammers; Collage 1, 2 & 3; Caribbean Writer; Verve. Honours: 1st Place, Caribbean Poetry Contest, London, 1981; Black History Monthly Poetry Contest, 1987. Memberships: Performance Poet and Writer; Poets and Writers; Finmen Ocean Swimmers; St Croix Basket Ball Association; Courtyard Players; Island Center for the Performing Arts. Address: 5016 Est Boetzberg, C'sted, VI 00820-451641, USA.

CAMPBELL (John) Ramsey, b. 4 Jan 1946, Liverpool, England. Writer; Film Reviewer. m. Jenny Chandler, 1 Jan 1971, 1 son, 1 daughter. Appointments: Film Reviewer, BBC Radio Merseyside, 1969-; Full-time Writer, 1973-. Publications: Novels: The Doll Who Ate His Mother, 1976; The Face That Must Die, 1979; The Parasite, 1980; The Nameless, 1981; Incarnate, 1983; The Claw, 1983, US edition as Night of the Claw; Obsession, 1985; The Hungry Moon, 1986; The Influence, 1988; Ancient Images, 1989; Midnight Sun, 1990; The Count of Eleven, 1991; The Long Lost, 1993; The One Safe Place, 1995; The House on Nazareth Hill, 1996; The Last Voice They Hear, 1998; Silent Children, 1999. Short stories: The Inhabitant of the Lake and Less Welcome Tenants, 1964; Demons by Daylight, 1973; The Height of the Scream, 1976; Dark Companions, 1982; Cold Print, 1985; Black Wine (with Charles L Grant), 1986; Night Visions 3 (with Clive Barker and Lisa Tuttle), 1986; Scared Stiff, 1987; Dark Feasts: The World of Ramsey Campbell, 1987; Waking Nightmares, 1991; Alone With The Horrors, 1993; Strange Things and Stranger Places, 1993; Ghosts and Grisly Things (short stories), 1998; Novella: Needing Ghosts, 1990. Honours: Liverpool Daily Post and Echo Award for Literature, 1993; World Fantasy Award, Bram Stoker Award, Best Collection, 1994; Best Novel, International Horror Guild, 1998. Memberships: British Fantasy Society, president; Society of Fantastic Films. Literary Agents: Carol Smith, UK; Pimlico Agency, USA; Ralph Vicinanza, foreign. Address: 31 Penkett Road, Wallasey L45 7QE, Merseyside, England.

CAMPEDELLI Giancarlo, (Rudy de Cadaval), b. 1 Jan 1933, Verona, Italy. Writer; Poet. m. Grazia Corsini, 31 Mar 1962, 1 son, 1 daughter. Appointments: Director, Grolier International Inc, 1972-83; Vice President, Kronos Europea SPA and IBI Inc, New York. Publications: Cocktail di poesie, 1959; 23 Poemas Contemporaines, 1968; L'ultime clarte du soir, 1976; Dove senza di loro, 1978; Schiavo, 1933, 1979; Et Apres, 1983; Colloquio con la pietra, 1985; L'Albero del silenzio, 1988; Viaggio nello specchio della vita, 1994; Il muro del tempo (poetry), 1998; Muta pietra (poems), 1999. Contributions to: Various publications in Europe and the USA. Honours: 10 National Poetry Prize, 1959-90; 4 International Poetry Prizes, 1959-94; Lupa Capitalina Prize, City Hall, Rome, 1979; Knight, Grand Officer of the Order of Merit of the Italian Republic, 1989; Knight Commander, Sovereign Order of St John of Jerusalem, 1990; Honorary Doctorates, Pro Dea University, Albany, New York, 1993, World Academy of Arts and Culture, California, 1995, University of St Petersburg, Russia, 1995; Knight, Sovereign Military Teutonic Order of Levante, 1994. Memberships: Several Italian and foreign literary organisations. Address: G Gioacchino Belli 2, 37124 Verona, Italy.

CAMPS-OLIVÉ Assumpta, b. 30 July 1960, Barcelona, Spain. Professor. m. José Pértegas, 14 Apr 1988. Education: Degree in Romance Philology, Universidad de Barcelona, 1984; Doctorate, Universidad Autónoma de Barcelona, 1991. Appointments: Professor of Italian, 1986-90, Professor of Italian Literature and Translation Studies, 1990-99, Universidad de Barcelona. Publications: La Recepció de G D'Annunzio a Catalunya, 2 volumes, 1996, 1999; Lecciones de Literatura Italiana Contemporánea, 1997; Estudis Literaris I. La traducció, 1998; Many translations of D'Annunzio, V Consolo, A Busi, Vladimir Nabokov, Patricia Highsmith, S Tammaro, L Sciascia and G Leopardi. Contributions to: Revista de Catalunya; Serra D'Or; Galleria; Rassegna Iberistica; Catalan Review; Esperienze Letterarie; Revue Canadienne de Littérature Comparée; La Ricerca; Others. Honour: Premio Critica Serra D'or de Traducción Memberships include: NACS; AISLLI; ICLA; SELGYC. Address: Viaducte de Vallcarca, 5 bis, E-08023 Barcelona, Spain.

CAMPTON David, b. 5 June 1924, Leicester, England. Playwright; Children's Fiction Writer. Publications: On Stage: Containing 17 Sketches and 1 Monologue, 1964; Resting Place, 1964; The Manipulator, 1964; Split Down the Middle, 1965; Little Brother, Little Sister and Out of the Flying Pan, 1966; Two Leaves and a Stalk, 1967; Angel Unwilling, 1967; Ladies Night: 4 Plays for Women, 1967; More Sketches, 1967; Laughter and Fear, 9 One-Act Plays, 1969; The Right Place, 1969; On Stage Again: Containing 14 Sketches and 2 Monologues, 1969; Now and Then, 1970; The Life and Death of Almost Everybody, 1970; Timesneeze, 1970; Gulliver in Lilliput (reader), 1970; Gulliver in The Land of Giants (reader), 1970; The Wooden Horse of Troy (reader), 1970; Jonah, 1971; The Cagebirds, 1971; Us and Them, 1972; Carmilla, 1972; In Committee, 1972; Come Back Tomorrow, 1972; Three Gothic Plays, 1973; Modern Aesop (reader), 1976; One Possessed, 1977; What Are You Doing Here?, 1978; The Do-It-Yourself Frankenstein Outfit, 1978; Zodiac, 1978; After Midnight: Before Dawn, 1978; Pieces of Campton, 1979; Parcel, 1979; Everybody's Friend, 1979; Who Calls?, 1980; Attitudes, 1980; Freedom Log, 1980; Dark Wings, 1981; Look-Sea, 1981; Great Whales, 1981; Who's a Hero, Then?, 1981; Dead and Alive, 1983; But Not Here, 1984; Singing in the Wilderness, 1986; Mrs Meadowsweet, 1986; The Vampyre (children's book), 1986; Our Branch in Brussels, 1986; Cards, Cups and Crystal Ball, 1986; Can You Hear the Music?, 1988; The Winter of 1917, 1989; Smile, 1990; Becoming a Playwright, 1992; The Evergreens, 1994; Permission to Cry, 1996. Contributions to: Amateur Stage; Writers News; Drama; Whispers. Memberships: Writers Guild of Great Britain; Society of Authors. Address: 35 Liberty Road, Glenfield, Leicester LE3 8JF, England.

CANDIA Jane, (Jane Candia Coleman), b. 1 Sept 1939, Pittsburgh, Pennsylvania, USA. m. Bernard Coleman, 27 Mar 1965, div 1989, 2 sons. Education: BA, Creative Writing, University of Pittsburgh. Publications: No Roof But Sky (poetry), 1990; Stories From Mesa Country, 1991; Discovering Eve (short fiction), 1993; Shadows in My Hands (memoir), 1993; The Red Drum (poetry), 1994; Doc Holliday's Woman (historical novel), 1995; Moving On (short fiction), 1997; I, Pearl Hart (historical novel), 1998; The O'Keefe Empire (historical novel), 1999. Contributions to: Christian Science Monitor; Border Beat; Puerto del Sol; South Dakota Review. Honours: Western Heritage Award, 1991, 1992, 1994. Memberships: Authors Guild; Women Writing the West. Literary Agent: Jon Tuska. Address: PO Box 40, Rodeo, NM 88056, USA.

CANNON Curt. See: **LOMBINO Salvatore A.**

CANNON Frank. See: **MAYHAR Ardath.**

CANNON Geoffrey John, b. 12 Apr 1940, Witham, Essex, England.Writer; Administrator. m. (1) Antonia Mole, 1961, div, (2) Caroline Walker, 1987, dec, 2 sons, 1 daughter. Education: MA, Philosophy and Psychology, Balliol College, Oxford, 1961. Publications: Dieting Makes You Fat (co-author), 1983; The Food Scandal (co-author), 1984; Fat To Fit, 1986; The Politics of Food, 1987; The Good Fight, 1989; Food and Health: The Experts Agree, 1992; Superbug, 1995; Food, Nutrition and the Prevention of Cancer: A Global Perspective (editor), 1997. Contributions to: Most leading British newspapers. Honour: Cantor Lecturer, Royal Society of Arts, 1988. Memberships: Guild of Food Writers, secretary, 1988-91; Caroline Walker Trust, secretary, 1988-97; National Food Alliance, chairman, 1991-. Literary Agent: Deborah Rogers. Address: 6 Aldridge Road Villas, London W11 1BP, England.

CANNON Steve, b. 10 Apr 1935, New Orleans, Louisiana, USA. Writer; Dramatist; Educator; Publisher. 1 son, dec. Education: BA, History, University of Nebraska, 1954. Appointment: Professor of Humanities, Medgar Evers College, 1971-92. Publications: Groove, Bang and Jive Around, 1969; Introduction to Rouzing the Rubble, 1991; Reminicin' in C, 1995. Plays: The Set Up, 1991; Chump Change, 1992; Nothing to Lose, 1993; Now What, What Now?, 1994; En Vogue, 1994; Top of the World, 1995; Marvellous, 1996. Contributions to: Excerpts from novel Looney Tunes under Deep Blue Moon, to Gathering of the Tribes, 1991, Pean Sensible, 1992. Membership: PEN, New York Chapter. Address: 285 East Third Street, New York, NY 10009, USA.

CANTALUPO Charles, b. 17 Oct 1951, Orange, New Jersey, USA. Professor of English; Poet; Writer. m. (1) Catherine Musello, 21 Aug 1976, dec 1983, 1 son, dec, (2) Barbara Dorosh, 29 Oct 1988, 1 son, 3 daughters. Education: University of Kent at Canterbury, 1972; BA, Washington University, St Louis, 1973; MA, 1978, PhD, 1980, Rutgers University. Appointments: Teaching Assistant, 1973-76, Instructor, 1977-79, Rutgers University; Instructor, 1980-81, Assistant Professor, 1981-89, Associate Professor, 1989-96, Professor of English, 1996-, Pennsylvania State University, Schuylkill Haven. Publications: The Art of Hope (poems), 1983; A Literary Leviathan: Thomas Hobbe's Masterpiece of Language, 1991; The World of Ngugi wa Thiong'o (editor), 1995; Poetry, Mysticism, and Feminism: From th' Nave to the Chops, 1995; Ngugi wa Thiong'o: Text and Contexts (editor), 1995; Anima/I Wo/man and Other Spirits (poems), 1996. Contributions to: Books, anthologies, scholarly journals, and periodicals. Honour: American Academy of Poets Prize, 1976. Address: c/o Department of English, Pennsylvania State University, 200 University Drive, Schuylkill Haven, PA 17972, USA.

CANTOR Norman F(rank), b. 1929, Winnipeg, Manitoba, Canada (US citizen, 1968). Professor; Writer. m. Mindy M Cantor, 1 son, 1 daughter. Education: BA, University of Manitoba, 1951; MA, 1953, PhD, 1957, Princeton University; Rhodes Scholar, Oxford University, 1954-55. Appointments: Instructor to Assistant Professor of History, Princeton University, 1955-60; Visiting Professor, Johns Hopkins University, 1960, Yeshiva University, 1960-61, 1963-64, Brooklyn College, 1972-74; Associate Professor to Professor, Columbia University, 1960-66; Professor, Brandeis University, 1966-70; Distinguished Professor of History, State University of New York at Binghamton, 1970-76; Professor of History, University of Illinois at Chicago Circle, 1976-78; Professor of History, 1978-80, Professor of History and Sociology, 1980-85, Affiliated Professor of Legal History, 1982-88, Professor of History, Sociology, and Comparative Literature, 1983-, New York University; Fulbright Visiting Professor, University of Tel Aviv, 1987-88; University Distinguished Visiting Scholar, Adelphi University, 1988-89; Lecturer in Jewish History, Institute of Secular Jewish Humanism, Detroit, 1996-. Publications: Church, Kingship and Lay Investiture, 1958; Medieval History: The Life and Death of a Civilization, 1963, revised edition as The Civilization of the Middle Ages, 1993; How to Study History (with R Schneider), 1967; The English, 1968; The Age of Protest, 1969; Western Civilization, 2 volumes, 1969-70; Perspectives on the European Past, 1971; The Meaning of the Middle Ages, 1973; Twentieth Century Culture, 1988; Inventing the Middle Ages, 1991; The Civilization of the Middle Ages, 1993; Medieval Lives, 1994; The Medieval Reader, 1994; The Sacred Chain, 1994; The Jewish Experience, 1996; The American Century, 1997; Imagining the Law, 1997. Contributions to: Books and scholarly journals. Honours include: Natinal Book Critics Circle Award, 1991; New York Public Library Award, 1998. Membership: Fellow, Royal Historical Society. Literary Agent: Alexander Hoyt, New York, USA. Address: 42 Bayview Avenue, Sag Harbour, New York, NY 11963, USA.

CANTSIN Monty. See: **HOME Stewart Ramsay.**

CAPIE Forrest H(unter), b. 1 Dec 1940, Glasgow, Scotland. Professor of Economic History. m. Dianna Dix, 11 Feb 1967. Education: BA, University of Auckland, New Zealand, 1967; MSc, 1969, PhD, 1973, University of London. Appointments: Lecturer, University of Warwick, 1972-74, University of Leeds, 1974-79; Visiting Lecturer, 1978-79, Lecturer, 1979-82, Senior Lecturer, 1982-83, Reader, 1983-86, Professor of Economic History, 1986-, City University, London; Various guest lectureships; Editor, Economic History Review, 1993-. Publications: The British Economy Between the Wars (with M Collins), 1983; Depression and Protectionism: Britain Between the Wars, 1983; A Monetary History of the United Kingdom, 1870-1982: Data Sources and Methods (with A Webber), 1985; Financial Crises and the World Banking System (editor with G E Wood), 1986; Monetary Economics in the 1980s: Some Themes from Henry Thornton (editor with G E Wood), 1989; A Directory of Economic Institutions (editor), 1990; Unregulated Banking: Chaos or Order? (editor with G E Wood), 1991; Major Inflations in History (editor), 1991; Protectionism in the World Economy (editor), 1992; Did the Banks Fail British Industry? (with M Collins), 1992; Monetary Regimes in Transition (editor with M Bordo), 1993; A History of Banking (editor), 10 volumes, 1993; Tariffs and Growth, 1994; The Future of Central Banking (with Charles Goodhart, Stanley Fischer and Norbert Schnadt), 1994; Monetary Economics in the 1990s (editor with G E Wood), 1996; Asset Prices and the Real Economy (editor with G E Wood), 1997. Contributions to: Scholarly books and journals. Honours: Several grants and fellowships. Memberships: Association of Business Historians; Cliometrics Society; Economic History Association; Economic History Society; Royal Economic Society; Royal Society of Arts, fellow; Western Economics Association. Address: 2 Fitzroy Road, Primrose Hill, London NW1 8TX, England.

CAPUS Alex, b. 23 July 1967, Mortagne, France. Author. m. Nadja, 5 Dec 1998, 1 son. Education: Studied history and philosophy of University of Basel, 1981-85. Publications: Diese verfluchte Schwerkraft; Munzinger Pascha, 1997; Eigermonchundjungfran, 1998. Honour: Forderpreis der deutschen, Wirtschaft, 1998. Address: Hübelistrasse 23, Postfach 1023, CH-4603, Olten, Switzerland.

CAPUTO Philip (Joseph), b. 10 June 1941, Chicago, Illinois, USA. Author; Screenwriter. m. (1) Jill Esther Ongemach, 21 June 1969, div 1982, 2 sons, (2) Marcelle Lynn Besse, 30 Oct 1982, div 1985, (3) Leslie Blanchard Ware, 4 June 1988. Education: Purdue University; BA, Loyola University, 1964. Appointments: Staff, 1969-72, Foreign Correspondent, 1972-77, Chicago Tribune; Freelance Writer, 1977-; Screenwriter, Mercury-Douglas Productions, Paramount Pictures, 1987-. Publications: A Rumor of War (memoir), 1977; Horn of Africa (novel), 1980; Del Corso's Gallery (novel), 1983; Indian Country: A Novel, 1987; Means of Escape (memoir), 1991; Equation for Evil (novel), 1996. Contributions to: Various periodicals. Honours: Pulitzer Prize for Reporting (with George Bliss), 1973; George Polk Award, 1973; Overseas Press Club Award; Sidney Hillman Award. Memberships: Authors Guild; National Writers Union. Address: c/o Aaron Priest Literary Agency, 708 Third Avenue, New York, NY 10017, USA.

CARAS Roger (Andrew), (Roger Sarac), b. 24 May 1928, Methuen, Massachusetts, USA. Author; Radio and Television Broadcaster. m. Jill Langdon Barclay, 5 Sept 1954, 1 son, 1 daughter. Education: Northeastern University, 1948-49; Western Reserve University, 1949-50; AB, University of Southern California at Los Angeles, 1954. Appointments: Vice-President, Polaris Productions Inc, New York City, and Hawk Films Ltd, London, 1965-68; Producer, Ivan Tors Productions, Los Angeles, 1968-69; Author and Radio and Television Broadcaster, 1969-; President, American Society for the Prevention of Cruelty to Animals, 1991-; Adjunct Professor of English, Southampton College, New York; Adjunct Professor of Animal Ecology and Member of the Board of Overseers, School of Veterinary Medicine, University of Pennsylvania. Publications: Antarctica: Lord of Frozen Time, 1962; The Custer Wolf, 1965; Dangerous to Man: Wild Animals: A Definitive Study of Their Reputed Dangers to Man, 1964, revised edition, 1976; Last Chance on Earth: A Requiem for Wildlife, 1966; North American Mammals: Fur-Bearing Animals of the United States and Canada, 1967; Death as a Way of Life, 1971; Venomous Animals of the World, 1974; The Private Lives of Animals, 1974; The Roger Caras Pet Book, 1976; Dog Owner's Bible (editor), 1978; The Forest: A Dramatic Portrait of Life in the American Wild, 1979; The Roger Caras Dog Book, 1980, revised edition, 1992; The Endless Migrations, 1985; Harper's Illustrated Handbook of Cats (editor), 1985; Harper's Illustrated Handbook of Dogs (editor), 1985; Roger Caras' Treasury of Great Cat Stories (editor), 1987; Roger Caras' Treasury of Great Dog Stories (editor), 1987; Animals in Their Places: Tales from the Natural World, 1987; A Cat Is Watching: A Look at the Way Cats See Us, 1989; That Our Children May Know: Vanishing Wildlife in Zoo Portraits (with Sue Pressman), 1990; Roger Caras' Treasury of Great Horse Stories (editor), 1990; Roger Caras' Treasury of Classic Nature Tales (editor), 1992; A Dog Is Listening: The Way Some of Our Closest Friends View Us, 1992; The Cats of Thistle Hill Farm, 1994; Most Dangerous Journey, 1995; A Perfect Harmony, 1996; The Bond: People and their Animals, 1997. Contributions to: Numerous journals. Honours: Joseph Wood Krutch Medal, 1977; Oryx Award, Israel, 1984; Humane Award of the Year, American Veterinary Medical Association, 1985; James Herriot Award, 1988; Emmy Award, 1990. Memberships: Authors Guild; Delta Kappa Alpha; Holy Land Conservation Fund; Humane Society of the United States; Outdoor Writers Association of America; Royal Society of Arts, fellow; Wilderness Society; Wildlife Society; Writers Guild of America; Zero Population Growth. Address: Thistle Hill Farm, 21108 Slab Bridge Road, Freeland, MD 21053, USA.

CARD Orson Scott, (Brian Green, Byron Walley), b. 24 Aug 1951, Richland, Washington, USA. Writer; Dramatist; Editor. m. Kristine Allen, 17 May 1977, 2 sons, 2 daughters. Education: BA, Brigham Young University, 1975; MA, University of Utah, 1981. Appointments: Director, Repertory Theatre, Provo, Utah, 1974-75; Editor, Brigham Young University Press, 1974-76; Assistant Editor, Ensign, Salt Lake City, 1976-78; Freelance Writer and Editor, 1978-; Senior Editor, Compute! Books, Greensboro, North Carolina, 1983; Teacher at universities and workshops. Publications: A Planet Called Treason, 1979; Songmaster, 1980; Hart's Hope, 1983; The Worthing Chronicle, 1983; Ender's Game, 1985; Speaker for the Dead, 1986; Seventh Son, 1987; Red Prophet, 1988; Prentice Alvin, 1989; Xenocide, 1991; Lost Boys, 1992; The Memory of Earth, 1992; The Call of Earth, 1993; The Ships of Earth, 1993; Lovelock (with Kathryn H Kidd), 1994; Earthfall, 1994. Contributions to: Periodicals. Honours: Nebula Awards, 1985, 1986; Hugo Awards, 1986, 1987, 1991; Locus Awards, 1988, 1989. Membership: Science Fiction Writers of America. Address: 546 Lindley Road, Greensboro, NC 27410, USA.

CARDENAL (Martinez) Ernesto, b. 20 Jan 1925, Granada, Nicaragua. Roman Catholic Priest; Poet. Education: University of Mexico, 1944-48; Columbia University, New York, 1948-49. Appointments: Roman Catholic Priest, 1965-; Minister of Culture, 1979-90. Publications: Proclama del conquistador, 1947; Gethsemani, Ky., 1960; La hora O, 1960; Epigramas: poemas, 1961; Oracion por Marilyn Monroe and Other Poems, 1965; El estrecho dudoso, 1966; Poemas, 1967; Psalms of Struggle and Liberation, 1967; Mayapan, 1968; Poemas reunidos 1949-69, 1969; Homage to the American Indians, 1969; Zero Hour and Other Documentary Poems, 1971; Poemas, 1971; Canto nacional, 1973; Oraculo sobre Managua, 1973; Poesia escogida, 1975; Apocalypse and Other Poems, 1977; Canto a un pais que nace, 1978; Nueva antologia poetica, 1979; Waslala, 1983; Poesia dela nueva Nicaragua, 1983; Flights of Victory, 1984; With Walker in Nicaragua and Other Early Poems 1949-54, 1985; From Nicaragua with Love: Poems 1976-1986, 1986; Golden UFOS: The Indian Poems, 1992; Cosmic Canticle, 1993. Honour: Premio de la Paz Grant, 1980. Address: Apartado Postal A-252, Managua, Nicaragua.

CARDINAL Marie, b. 9 Mar 1929, Algiers, Algeria. Novelist. m. Jean-Pierre Ronfard, 1953, 1 son, 2 daughters. Education: University of Algiers; Sorbonne, University of Paris. Appointments: Teacher of French and Philosophy in Greece, Portugal, Austria. Publications: Ecoutez la mer, 1962; La Mule de Corbillard, 1963; La Souricière, 1965; Mao (co-author), 1970; La Clé sur la porte, 1972; The Words To Say It, 1975; Une Vie pour Deux, 1978; Le Passé empiété, 1983; Devotion and Disorder, 1987; Commesi de rien n'était, 1990. Other: Translations of works by Euripides and Ibsen. Honour: Prix Littre, 1976. Address: 831 Viger Est, Montreal, Quebec H2L 2P5, Canada.

CARDOSO PIRES José (Augusto Neves), b. 2 Oct 1925, Peso, Castelo, Branco, Portugal. Novelist; Dramatist. Education: University of Lisbon. Appointments: Literary Director of various publishing houses in Lisbon. Publications: Historuas de amor, 1952; Estrada 43, 1955; A ancorado, 1958; Jogos de azar, 1963; O hospede de Job, 1963; O delfin, 1968; Dinossauro excelentissimo, 1972; O burro-em-pe, 1978; Ballad of Dogs' Beach: dossier of a crime, 1982; Alexandra Alpha, 1987; A Republica dos Corvos, 1988. Plays: O render dos herois, 1960; Corpo-delito na sala de espelhos, 1980. Honour: Grande Premio do Romance e da Novela, 1983. Address: Rua Sao Joao de Brito 7-1, 1700 Lisbon, Portugal.

CAREW Jan (Rynveld), b. 24 Sept 1925, Agricola, Guyana. Professor Emeritus. Appointments: Lecturer in Race Relations, University of London Extra-Mural Department, 1953-57; Writer and Editor, BBC Overseas Service, London, 1954-65; Editor, African Review, Ghana, 1965-66; CBC Broadcaster, Toronto, 1966-69; Senior Fellow, Council of Humanities and Lecturer, Department of Afro-American Studies, Princeton University, 1969-72; Professor, Department of African-American Studies, Northwestern University, 1972-87; Visiting Clarence J Robinson Professor of Caribbean Literature and History, George Mason University, 1989-91; Visiting Professor of International Studies, Illinois Wesleyan University, 1992-93. Publications: Streets of Eternity, 1952; Black Midas, 1958, US edition as A Touch of Midas; 1958; The Last Barbarian, 1961; Green Winter, 1964; University of Hunger, 1966; The Third Gift, 1975; The Origins of Racism and Resistance in the Americas, 1976; Rape of the Sun-people, 1976; Children of the Sun, 1980; Sea Drums in My Blood, 1981; Grenada: The Hour Will Strike Again, 1985; Fulcrums of Change, 1987. Memberships: Africa Network, co-chairman, 1981-; Caribbean Society for Culture and Science, chairman, 1979-. Address: Department of African-American Studies, Northwestern University, Evanston, IL 60208, USA.

CAREY Duncan. See: **GARNETT Richard.**

CAREY John, b. 5 Apr 1934, London, England. University Professor. m. Gillian Booth, 13 Aug 1960, 2 sons. Education: Lambe Open Scholar, 1954-57; BA, 1957; D Phil, 1960, St John's College, Oxford. Publications: Milton, 1969; The Violent Effigy: A Study of Dickens' Imagination, 1973; Thackeray, Prodigal Genius, 1977; John Donne: Life, Mind and Art, 1981; Original Copy: Selected Reviews and Journalism, 1987; The Faber Book of Reportage, 1987; Donne, 1990; The Intellectuals and the Masses, 1992; The Faber Book of Science, 1995; The Faber Book of Utopias, 1999. Contributions to: Principal Book Reviewer, Sunday Times. Honours: Royal Society of Literature, fellow; British Academy, fellow; Honorary Fellow, St John's College, 1991, Balliol College, 1992. Literary Agent: Toby Eady, London. Address: Merton College, Oxford OX1 4SD, England.

CAREY Peter Philip, b. 7 May 1943, Bacchus Marsh, Australia. Novelist. m. Alison Summers, 16 Mar 1985, 2 sons. Education: Dr of Letters, University of Queensland, 1989. Appointment: Writer in Residence, New York University, 1990. Publications: The Fat Man in History, 1974; War Crimes, 1979, 1981; Illywhacker, 1985; Oscar and Lucinda, 1989; Until the End of the World, 1990; The Tax Inspector, 1991; The Unusual Life of Tristan Smith, 1994; Collected Stories, 1995; Jack Maggs, 1997. Honours: New South Wales Premier's Literary Award; Miles Franklin Award; National Book Council Award; The Age Book of Year Award; Victorian Premier's Literary Award; Booker Prize. Membership: Royal Society of Literature. Address: c/o Deborah Rogers, Rogers, Coleridge & White Ltd, 20 Powis Mews, London W11 1JN, England.

CARFAX Catherine. See: **FAIRBURN Eleanor M.**

CARKEET David (Corydon), b. 15 Nov 1946, Sonora, California, USA. Professor; Author. m. Barbara Lubin, 16 Aug 1975, 3 daughters. Education: AB, University of California at Davis, 1968; MA, University of Wisconsin, 1970; PhD, Indiana University, 1973. Appointments: Assistant Professor, 1973-79, Associate Professor, 1979-87, Professor, 1987-, University of Missouri. Publications: Novels: Double Negative, 1980; The Greatest Slump of All Time, 1984; I Been There Before, 1985; The Full Catastrophe, 1990; The Error of Our Ways, 1997. Young Adult Novels: The Silent Treatment, 1988; Quiver River, 1991. Contributions to: Scholarly journals; Short stories and popular essays in periodicals. Honours: James D Phelan Award in Literature, San Francisco Foundation, 1976; Notable Books of the Year, New York Times Book Review, 1981, 1990, 1997; O Henry Award, 1982; National Endowment for the Arts Fellowship, 1983. Address: 9307 Old Bonhomme Road, St Louis, MO 63132, USA.

CARLILE Henry (David), b. 6 May 1934, San Francisco, California, USA. Professor of English; Poet; Writer. 1 daughter. Education: AA, Grays Harbor College, 1958; BA, 1962, MA, 1967, University of Washington. Appointments: Instructor, 1967-69, Assistant Professor, 1969-72, Associate Professor, 1972-78, Professor of English, 1980-, Portland State University; Visiting Lecturer, Writers Workshop, University of Iowa, 1978-80. Publications: The Rought-Hewn Table, 1971; Running Lights, 1981; Rain, 1994. Contributions to: Many anthologies, reviews, and journals. Honours: National Endowment for the Arts Discovery Grant, 1970, and

Fellowship in Poetry, 1976; Devins Award, 1971; PEN Syndicated Fiction Awards, 1983, 1986; Ingram Merrill Poetry Fellowship, 1985; Felen Foundation Award, 1986; Pushcart Prizes, 1986, 1992; Poetry Award, Crazyhorse, 1988; Oregon Arts Commission Literary Fellowship, 1994. Address: c/o Department of English, Portland State University, PO Box 751, Portland, OR 97207, USA.

CARLISLE D M. See: **COOK Dorothy Mary.**

CARLS Stephen Douglas, b. 15 Feb 1944, Minneapolis, Minnesota, USA. Professor of History. m. Alice-Catherine Maire, 25 June 1977, 2 sons, 1 daughter. Education: BA, Wheaton College, Illinois, 1966; MA, History, 1968, PhD, History, 1982, University of Minnesota. Appointments: Assistant Professor, 1971-81, Associate Professor, 1981-83, Sterling College, Kansas; Associate Professor, 1983-90, Professor, 1990-, Chair, Department of History and Political Science, 1990-, Union University, Jackson, Tennessee. Publication: Louis Loucheur and the Shaping of Modern France, 1916-1931, 1993. Contributions to: Scholarly journals. Honours: American Historical Association First Books Program Recommendation for Publication, 1983; Faculty Recognition Award, Lambda Chi Alpha Fraternity, Union University, 1987; Scholarships and grants. Memberships: American Historical Association; Council for European Studies; Economic and Business Historical Society; Society for French Historical Studies; West Tennessee Historical Society; Western Society for French History. Address: c/o Department of History and Political Science, Union University, Jackson, TN 38305, USA.

CARLSON Dale, b. 24 May 1935, New York City, New York, USA. Writer. 1 son, 1 daughter. Education: BA, Wellesley Coll, 1957; Licenced Wildlife Rehabilitator, 1991. Appointments: Founder, President, Bick Publishing House, 1993-. Publications: Author: Children's books, adult books, 1961-, including: Perkins the Brain, 1964; The House of Perkins, 1965; Miss Maloo, 1966; The Brainstormers, 1966; Frankenstein, Dracula, 1968; Counting is Easy, 1969; Your Country, 1969; Arithmetic 1, 2, 3, 1969; The Electronic Teabow, 1969; Warlord of the Genji, 1970; The Beggar King of China, 1971; The Mountain of Truth (Spring Fest Hon Book, named Amn Lib Assn Notable Book), 1972; Good Morning Danny, 1972; Good Morning, Hannah, 1972; Girls are Equal Too, 1973; The Human Apes, 1973; Baby Needs Shoes, 1974; Triple Boy, 1976; Where's Your Head?, 1977; The Plant People, 1977; The Wild Heart, 1977; The Shining Pool, 1979; Lovingsex for Both Sexes, 1979; Boys Have Feelings Too, 1980; Call Me Amanda, 1981; Manners That Matter, 1982; The Frog People, 1982; Charlie the Hero, 1983, 1984-85; The James Budd Mysteries (6 vols), 1984-85; The Jenny Dean Science Fiction Mysteries, The Mystery of the Shining Children, The Mystery of the Hidden Trap, The Secret of the Third Eye, The James Budd Mysteries, The Mystery of Galaxy Games, The Mystery of Operation Brain, 1985; Miss Mary's Husbands, 1988; Basic Manuals in Wildlife Rehabilitation Series, 7 vols, 1993-94; Basic Manuals for Friends of the Disabled Series, 6 vols, 1995-96, Living with Disabilities, 1997; Wildlife Care for Birds and Mammals, 1997; Stop the Pain: Meditations for Teenagers, 1998, Confessions of a Brain-Impaired Writer: A Memoir, 1998. Membership: Authors League of America; Authors Guild. Address: 307 Neck Road, Madison, CT 06443-2755, USA.

CARMI T. See: **CHARNY Carmi.**

CARMICHAEL Jack B(lake), b. 31 Jan 1938, Ravenswood, West Virginia, USA. Writer; Poet; Editor. m. Julie Ann Carmichael, 2 Oct 1981, 4 daughters. Education: BA, Ohio Wesleyan University, 1959; PhD, Michigan State University, 1964; Postdoctoral Studies, University of Oregon, 1966-67. Appointment: Editor and Publisher, Dynamics Press, 1990-. Publications: Novels: A New Slain Knight, 1991; Black Knight, 1991; Tales of the Cousin, 1992; Memoirs of the Great Gorgeous, 1992; The Humpty Boys in Michigan, 1996. Contributions to: Poems in anthologies and journals. Honour: Outstanding Achievement Award, American Poetry Association, 1990.

Membership: Academy of American Poets. Address: c/o Dynamic Press, 519 South Rogers Street, Mason, MI 48854, USA.

CARMICHAEL Joel, b. 31 Dec 1915, New York, New York, USA. Author; Editor; Translator. Education: BA, MA, Oxford University, 1940; Sorbonne, University of Paris; École Nationale des Langues Orientales Vivantes. Appointments: European Correspondent, The Nation magazine, 1946-47; Editor, Midstream magazine, 1975-87, 1990-. Publications: An Illustrated History of Russia, 1960; The Death of Jesus, 1962; A Short History of the Russian Revolution, 1964; The Shaping of the Arabs: A Study in Ethnic Identity, 1967; Karl Marx: The Passionate Logician, 1967; An Open Letter to Moses and Muhammed, 1968; A Cultural History of Russia, 1968; Arabs and Jews, 1969; Trotsky: An Appreciation of His Life, 1976; Stalin's Masterpiece, 1977; Arabs Today, 1977; St Paul and the Jews, 1980; The Birth of Christianity: Reality and Myth, 1989; The Satanizing of the Jews: Origin and Development of Mystical Anti-Semitism, 1992; The Unriddling of Christian Origins: A Secular Account, 1995. Translations from Russian: The Russian Revolution 1917, N N Sukhanov, 1955; Anna Karenina, Leo Tolstoy, 1975. Contributions to: Journals and periodicals. Honour: Fulbright Fellowship, 1949-51. Address: 302 West 86th Street, New York, NY 10024, USA.

CARNOVALE Maria Eugenia, b. 15 Dec 1944, San Pietro di Carida, Italy. Teacher. m. Paola, 14 Aug 1969, 2 sons, 2 daughters. Education: Various diplomas. Publications: Primi Piani; Poesia Contemporinea; Nuova Dimenzione; Mezzaggero del Sud; La Conca. Honours: Premio Internazionale di Poesia; Parola Immagine; Il Silenzio del Pesco; Stelle di Europa; Premio Nord-Sud. Address: Via San Giorgio 5, Verderio Inferior (LS), Italy.

CARON Louis, b. 1942, Sorel, Quebec, Canada. Author; Poet; Dramatist. Publications: L'illusionniste suivi de Le guetteur, 1973; L'emmitouflé, 1977, English translation as The Draft-Dodger, 1980; Bonhomme sept-heures, 1978; Le canard de bois, 1981; La corne de brume, 1982; Le coup de poing, 1990; La tuque et le béret, 1992; Le bouleau et l'epinette, 1993. Other: Many radio and television plays. Honours: Prix Hermes, France, 1977; Prix France-Canada, 1977; Prix Ludger-Duvernay, Société Saint-Jean-Baptiste, Montreal, 1984. Membership: Académie des lettres de Québec, 1995-. Address: c/o Union des écrivaines et écrivains québécois, La Maison des écrivains, 3492 Avenue Laval, Montreal, Quebec H2X 3C8, Canada.

CARPENTER (John) Allan, b. 11 May 1917, Waterloo, Iowa, USA. Author; Editor; Publisher. Education: BA, Iowa State Teachers College, 1938. Appointments: Founder, Publisher, Teacher's Digest, Chicago, 1940-48; Public Relations Director, Popular Mechanics, Chicago, 1943-62; Founder, Editor, Publisher, Carpenter Publishing House, Chicago, 1962-; Founder, Chairman of the Board of Directors, Infordata International Inc, 1974-90. Publications: Home Handyman Encyclopedia and Guide, 16 volumes, 1961, supplement, 1963; Enchantment of America, 52 volumes, 1963-68; Enchantment of South America, 13 volumes, 1968-70; Enchantment of Central America, 7 volumes, 1971; Enchantment of Central Africa, 38 volumes, 1972-78; The Encyclopedia of the Midwest, 1989; The Encyclopedia of the Central West, 1990; The Encyclopedia of the Far West, 1990; Facts About the Cities, 1992. Contributions to: Many magazines. Honour: Achievement Award, University of Northern Iowa, 1988. Address: 175 East Delaware Place, Suite 4602, Chicago, IL 60611, USA.

CARPENTER Bogdana (Maria Magdalene), b. 2 June 1941, Czestochowa, Poland (US citizen, 1969). Professor of Slavic Languages and Literatures; Writer; Translator. m. John Randell Carpenter, 15 Apr 1963, 1 son, 1 daughter. Education: MA, University of Warsaw, 1963; PhD, University of California at Berkeley, 1974. Appointments: Acting Assistant Professor, 1971-73, Lecturer, 1973-74, University of California at Berkeley;

Assistant Professor, University of Washington, Seattle, 1974-83; Staff Reviewer, World Literature Today, 1977-; Assistant Professor, 1983-85, Associate Professor, 1985-91, Professor of Slavic Langauges and Literatures, 1991-, Chair, Department of Slavic Languages and Literatures, 1991-95, University of Michigan, Ann Arbor. Publications: The Poetic Avant-Garde in Poland, 1918-1939, 1983; Cross Currents: A Yearbook of Central European Culture (associate editor), 1987-93; Monumenta Polonica: The First Four Centuries of Polish Poetry, 1989. Translator: Works by Zbigniew Herbert (with John Carpenter): Selected Poems of Zbigniew Herbert, 1977; Report from the Besieged City and Other Poems, 1987; Still Life with a Bridle, 1991; Mr Cogito, 1993; Elegy for Departure and Other Poems, 1999; The King of Ants, 1999. Contributions to: Books, scholarly journals, and general periodicals. Honours: Witter Bynner Poetry Translation Prize, Poetry Society of America, 1979; National Endowment for the Humanities Translation Grant, 1987-88; American Council of Learned Societies Fellowship, 1990-91; 1st Prize, American Council for Polish Culture Clubs, 1991; Columbia University Translation Center Merit Award, 1992. Membership: The Polish Review, advisory boarad, 1993-. Address: 1606 Granger, Ann Arbor, MI 48104, USA.

CARPENTER Humphrey (William Bouverie), b. 29 Apr 1946, Oxford, England. Writer; Dramatist; Broadcaster; Musician. m. Mari Christina Prichard, 1973, 2 daughters. Education: Marlborough College; MA, DipEd, Keble College, Oxford. Appointments: Staff Producer, BBC Radio, Oxford, 1970-74; Freelance Writer and Broadcaster, 1975-; Founder, Vile Bodies band, 1983, Mushy Pea Theatre Co for children, 1984; Programme Director, Cheltenham Festival of Literature, 1994-96. Publications: A Thames Companion (with Mari Prichard), 1975; J R R Tolkien: A Biography, 1977; The Inklings, 1978; Jesus, 1980; The Letters of J R R Tolkien (editor with Christopher Tolkien), 1981; W H Auden: A Biography, 1981; The Oxford Companion to Children's Literature (editor with Mari Prichard), 1984; OUDS: A Centenary History of the Oxford University Dramatic Society, 1985; Secret Gardens: The Golden Age of Children's Literature, 1985; Geniuses Together: American Writers in Paris, 1987; A Serious Character: The Life of Ezra Pound, 1988; The Brideshead Generation: Evelyn Waugh and his Friends, 1989; Benjamin Britten: A Biography, 1992; The Envy of the World: Fifty Years of the BBC Third Programme and Radio 3, 1996. Children's Books: The Joshers, 1977; The Captain Hook Affair, 1979; Mr Majeika, 1984; Mr Majeika and the Music Teacher, 1986; Mr Majeika and the Haunted Hotel, 1987; The Television Adventures of Mr Majeika, 1987; More Television Adventures of Mr Majeika, 1990; Mr Majeika and the School Play, 1991; Mr Majeika and the School Book Week, 1992; Wellington and Boot (with Jenny McDade), 1991; What Did You Do At School Today?, 1992; Charlie Crazee's Teevee, 1993; Mr Majeika and the School Inspector, 1993; Mr Majeika and the Ghost Train, 1994; Shakespeare Without the Boring Bits, 1994; Mr Majeika and the School Caretaker, 1996; The Puffin Book of Classic Children's Stories (editor), 1996. Other: Several plays for stage and radio. Honours: Somerset Maugham Award, 1978; E M Forster Award, American Academy of Arts and Letters, 1984; Duff Cooper Memorial Prize, 1988; Royal Philharmonic Society Award, 1992. Membership: Royal Society of Literature, fellow, 1983-. Address: 6 Farndon Road, Oxford OX2 6RS, England.

CARPENTER Lucas, b. 23 Apr 1947, Elberton, Georgia, USA. Professor of English; Writer; Poet; Editor. m. Judith Leidner, 2 Sept 1972, 1 daughter. Education: BS, College of Charleston, 1968; MA, University of North Carolina at Chapel Hill, 1973; PhD, State University of New York at Stony Brook, 1982. Appointments: Instructor, State University of New York at Stony Brook, 1973-78; Instructor, 1978-80, Associate Professor of English, 1980-85, Suffolk Community College; Editorial Consultant, Prentice-Hall Inc, 1981-; Associate Professor of English, 1985-94, Professor of English, 1994-, Oxford College of Emory University. Publications: A Year for the Spider (poems), 1972; The Selected Poems of John

Gould Fletcher (editor with E Leighton Rudolph), 1988; The Selected Essays of John Gould Fletcher (editor), 1989; John Gould Fletcher and Southern Modernism, 1990; The Selected Correspondence of John Gould Fletcher (editor with E Leighton Rudolph), 1996. Contributions to: Anthologies, scholarly journals, and periodicals. Honours: Resident Fellow in Poetry and Fiction Writing, Hambidge Center for the Creative Arts, 1991; Oxford College Professor of the Year Awards, 1994, 1996. Memberships: National Council of Teachers of English; Poetry Atlanta; Poetry Society of America; Southeast Modern Language Association. Address: c/o Department of English, Oxford College of Emory University, Oxford, GA 30267, USA.

CARR Alison Victoria, b. 23 Feb 1969. Performer; Singer; Writer. Education: London Academy of Music and Dramatic Arts, Certificate, Speaking of Verse and Prose, Grade 1, 1981, Certificate, Speaking of Verse and Prose, 1982, Certificate, Speaking of Verse and Prose, Grade 2, 1983. Honour: Linkway 2nd Place Award, 1994. Memberships: Society of Authors, 1997; New Writing North, 1997; Poetry Society, 1998; Performing Rights Society, 1999; Diamond Studios, Bristol, 1999. Address: 1 Lambton Drive, Bishop Auckland, Co Durham, DL14 6LG, England.

CARR Caleb, b. 2 Aug 1955, New York, New York, USA. Author; Historian. Education: Kenyon College, 1973-75; BA, New York University, 1977. Publications: Casing the Promised Land, 1980; America Invulnerable: The Quest for Absolute Security, from 1812 to Star Wars (with James Chace), 1988; The Devil Soldier: The Story of Frederick Townsend Ward, 1991; The Alienist, 1994; The Angel of Darkness, 1997. Contributions to: Professional journals, newspapers and periodicals. Address: c/o International Creative Management, 40 West 57th Street, New York, NY 10019, USA.

CARR Glyn. See: STYLES Frank Showell.

CARR Margaret, (Martin Carroll, Carole Kerr), b. 25 Nov 1935, Salford, England. Writer. Publications: Begotten Murder, 1967; Spring into Love, 1967; Blood Vengeance, 1968; Goodbye is Forever, 1968; Too Beautiful to Die, 1969; Hear No Evil, 1971; Tread Warily at Midnight, 1971; Sitting Duck, 1972; Who's the Target, 1974; Not for Sale, 1975; Shadow of the Hunter, 1975; A Time to Surrender, 1975; Out of the Past, 1976; Twin Tragedy, 1977; Lamb to the Slaughter, 1978; The Witch of Wykham, 1978; Daggers Drawn, 1980; Stolen Heart, 1981; Deadly Pursuit, 1991; Dark Intruder, 1991. Address: Waverly, Wavering Lane, Gillingham, Dorset SD8 4NR, England.

CARR Pat (Moore), b. 13 Mar 1932, Grass Creek, Wyoming, USA. Writer; University Teacher. m. (1) Jack Esslinger, 4 June 1955, div 1970, (2) Duane Carr, 26 Mar 1971, 1 son, 3 daughters. Education: BA, MA, Rice University; PhD, Tulane University. Appointments: Teacher, Texas Southern University, 1956-58, University of New Orleans, 1961, 1965-69, 1987-88, University of Texas at El Paso, 1969-79, University of Arkansas at Little Rock, 1983, 1986-87, Western Kentucky University, 1988-96. Publications: Novels: The Grass Creek Chronicle, 1976, 3rd edition, 1996; Bluebirds, 1993. Short Story Collections: Beneath the Hill of the Three Crosses, 1969; The Women in the Mirror, 1977; Night of the Luminarias, 1986; Sonahchi, 1988, 2nd edition, 1994; Our Brothers' War, 1993. Criticism: Bernard Shaw, 1976; Mimbres Mythology, 1979; In Fine Spirits, 1986. Contributions to: Articles and short stories in numerous publications, including: The Southern Review and Best American Short Stories. Honours: South and West Fiction Award, 1969; Library of Congress Marc IV Award for Short Fiction, 1970; National Endowment for the Humanities Award, 1973; IOWA Fiction Award, 1977; Texas Institute of Letters Short Story Award, 1978; Arkansas Endowment for the Humanities Award, 1985; Green Mountain Short Fiction Award, 1986; First Stage Drama Award, 1990; Al Smith Fellowship in Fiction, 1995. Memberships: Board Member, International Women's

Writing Guild, 1996-; Texas Institute of Letters. Address: 10695 Venice Road, Elkins, AR 72727, USA.

CARR Roberta. See: ROBERTS Irene.

CARR Terry (Gene), (Norman Edwards), b. 19 Feb 1937, Grants Pass, Oregon, USA. Writer; Editor; Lecturer. Education: AA, City College of San Francisco, 1957; University of California at Berkeley, 1957-59. Appointments: Editor, Ace Books, 1964-71, SFWA Bulletin, 1967-68; Founder, Science Fiction Writers of America Forum, 1967-68. Publications: Warlord of Kor (with Ted White), 1963; World's Best Science Fiction (editor), 7 volumes, 1965-71; Universe (editor), 13 volumes, 1971-83; The Best Science Fiction of the Year (editor), 13 volumes, 1972-84; The Light at the End of the Universe (stories), 1976; Cirque, 1977; Classic Science Fiction: The First Golden Age (editor), 1978; The Year's Finest Fantasy (editor), 1978-84; Between Two Worlds, 1986; Spill! The Story of the Exxon Valdez, 1991. Address: c/o Watts Publishing Company, PO Box 4039, Culver City, CA 90231, USA.

CARRIER Roch, b. 13 May 1937, Sainte-Justine-de-Dorchester, Quebec, Canada. Author; Dramatist; Poet. m. Diane Gosselin, 1959, 2 daughters. Education: Collège Saint-Louis; BA, MA, University of Montreal; Doctoral Studies, Sorbonne, University of Paris. Appointments: Secretary-General, Théatre du Nouveau Monde, Montreal; Teacher, Collège Militaire, St-Jean; Director, Canada Council, until 1997. Publications: Fiction: Jolis deuils, 1964; La guerre, yes sir!, 1968, English translation, 1970; Floralie, ou es-tu?, 1969, English translation as Floralie, Where Are You?, 1971; Il est par la le soleil, 1970, English translation as Is it the Sun, Philibert?, 1972; Le deux-millième é'tage, 1973, English translation as They Won't Demolish Me!, 1974; Le jardin des délices, 1975, English translation as The Garden of Delights, 1978; Les enfants du bonhomme dans la lune, 1979, English translation as The Hockey Sweater and Other Stories, 1979; Il n'y a pas de pays sans grand-père, 1979, English translation as No Country Without Grandfathers, 1981; Les fleurs vivent-elles ailleurs que sur la terre, 1980; La dame qui avait des chaines aux cheville, 1981; De l'amour dans la feraille, 1984, English translation as Heartbreaks Along the Road, 1987; La fleur et autres personnages, 1985; Prières d'un enfant très très sage, 1988; L'homme dans le placard, 1991; Fin, 1992; The Longest Home Run, 1993; Petit homme tornade, 1996. Plays: La celeste bicyclette, 1980, English translation as The Celestial Bycycle, 1982; Le cirque noir, 1982; L'ours et le kangourou, 1986. Other: Various poems. Honours: Prix Littéraire de la Province de Québec, 1965; Grand Prix Littéraire de la Ville de Montréal, 1980; Quebec Writer of the Year, 1981. Address: c/o The Canada Council, 350 Albert Street, PO Box 1047, Ottawa, Ontario, K1P 5V8, Canada.

CARRIER Warren (Pendleton), b. 3 July 1918, Cheviot, Ohio, USA. University Chancellor (retired); Writer; Poet. m. (1) Marjorie Jane Regan, 3 Apr 1947, dec, 1 son, (2) Judy Lynn Hall, 14 June 1973, 1 son. Education: Wabash College, 1938-40; AB, Miami University, Oxford, Ohio, 1942; MA, Harvard University, 1948; PhD, Occidental College, 1962. Appointments: Founder-Editor, Quarterly Review of Literature, 1943-44; Associate Editor, Western Review, 1949-51; Assistant Professor, University of Iowa, 1949-52; Associate Professor, Bard College, 1953-57; Faculty, Bennington College, 1955-58; Visiting Professor, Sweet Briar College, 1958-60; Professor, Deep Springs College, California, 1960-62; Portland State University, Oregon, 1962-64; Professor, Chairman, Department of English, University of Montana, 1964-68; Associate Dean, Professor of English and Comparative Literature, Chairman, Department of Comparative Literature, Livingston College, Rutgers University, 1968-69; Dean, College of Arts and Letters, San Diego State University, 1969-72; Vice-President, Academic Affairs, University of Bridgeport, Connecticut, 1972-75; Chancellor, University of Wisconsin at Platteville, 1975-82. Publications: City Stopped in Time, 1949; The Hunt, 1952; The Cost of Love, 1953; Reading Modern Poetry (co-editor), 1955,

2nd edition, 1968; Bay of the Damned, 1957; Toward Montebello, 1966; Leave Your Sugar for the Cold Morning, 1977; Guide to World Literature (editor), 1980; Literature from the World (co-editor), 1981; The Diver, 1986; Death of a Chancellor, 1986; An Honorable Spy, 1992; Murder at the Strawberry Festival, 1993; An Ordinary Man, 1997. Contributions to: Periodicals. Honours: Phi Beta Kappa, 1942; Award for Poetry, National Foundation for the Arts, 1971; Collady Prize for Poetry, 1986. Address: 69 Colony Park Circle, Galveston, TX 77551, USA.

CARROLL Martin. See: CARR Margaret.

CARROLL Paul (Donnelly Michael), b. 15 July 1927, Chicago, Illinois, USA. Professor of English; Poet; Writer. m. Maryrose Carroll, June 1979, 1 son. Education: MA, University of Chicago, 1952. Appointments: Poetry Editor, Chicago Review, 1957-59; Editor, Big Table Magazine, 1959-61, Big Table Books, Follett Publishing Company, 1966-71; Visiting Poet and Professor, University of Iowa, 1966-67; Professor of English, University of Illinois, 1968-. Publications: Edward Dahlberg Reader (editor), 1966; The Young American Poets, 1968; The Luke Poets, 1971; New and Selected Poems, 1978; The Garden of Earthly Delights, 1986; Poems, 1950-1990, 1990. Contributions to: Periodicals. Address: 1682 North Ada Street, Chicago, IL 60622, USA.

CARRUTH Hayden, b. 3 Aug 1921, Waterbury, Connecticut, USA. Poet; Writer; Professor Emeritus. m. (1) Sara Anderson, 14 Mar 1943, 1 daughter, (2) Eleanor Ray, 29 Nov 1952, (3) Rose Marie Dorn, 28 Oct 1961, 1 son, (4) Joe-Anne McLaughlin, 29 Dec 1989. Education: AB, University of North Carolina, 1943; MA, University of Chicago, 1948. Appointments: Editor-in-Chief, Poetry magazine, 1949-50; Associate Editor, University of Chicago Press, 1950-51; Project Administrator, Intercultural Publications Inc, New York City, 1952-53; Poet-in-Residence, Johnson State College, Vermont, 1972-74; Adjunct Professor, University of Vermont, 1975-78; Poetry Editor, Harper's magazine, 1977-83; Professor, Syracuse University, 1979-85, Bucknell University, 1985-86; Professor, 1986-91, Professor Emeritus, 1991-, Syracuse University. Publications: Poetry: The Crow and the Heart, 1946-1959, 1959; In Memoriam: G V C, 1960; Journey to a Known Place, 1961; The Norfolk Poems: 1 June to 1 September 1961, 1962; North Winter, 1964; Nothing for Tigers: Poems, 1959-1964, 1965; Contra Mortem, 1967; For You, 1970; The Clay Hill Anthology, 1970; From Snow and Rock, From Chaos: Poems, 1965-1972, 1973; Dark World, 1974; The Bloomingdale Papers, 1975; Loneliness: An Outburst of Hexasyllables, 1976; Aura, 1977; Brothers, I Loved You All, 1978; Almanach du Printemps Vivarois, 1979; The Mythology of Dark and Light, 1982; The Sleeping Beauty, 1983, revised edition, 1990; If You Call This Cry a Song, 1983; Asphalt Georgics, 1985; Lighter Than Air Craft, 1985; The Oldest Killed Lake in North America, 1985; Mother, 1985; The Selected Poetry of Hayden Carruth, 1986; Sonnets, 1989; Tell Me Again How the White Heron Rises and Flies Across the Nacreous River at Twilight Toward the Distant Islands, 1989; Collected Shorter Poems, 1946-1991, 1992; Collected Longer Poems, 1994; Scrambled Eggs and Whiskey: Poems, 1991-1995, 1995. Other: Appendix A (novel), 1963; After "The Stranger": Imaginary Dialogues with Camus, 1964; Working Papers: Selected Essays and Reviews, 1981; Effluences from the Sacred Caves: More Selected Essays and Reviews, 1984; Sitting In: Selected Writings on Jazz, Blues, and Related Topics, 1986. Editor: A New Directions Reader (with James Laughlin), 1964; The Voice That is Great Within Us: American Poetry of the Twentieth Century, 1970; The Bird/Poem Book: Poems on the Wild Birds of North America, 1970. Contributions to: Various periodicals. Honours: Bess Hokin Prize, 1954; Vachel Lindsay Prize, 1956; Levinson Prize, 1958; Harriet Monroe Poetry Prize, 1960; Bollingen Foundation Fellowship, 1962; Helen Bullis Award, 1962; Carl Sandburg Award, 1963; Emily Clark Balch Prize, 1964; Eunice Tietjens Memorial Prize, 1964; Guggenheim Fellowships, 1965, 1979; Morton Dauwen Zabel Prize, 1967; National Endowment for the

Humanities Fellowship, 1967; Governor's Medal, Vermont, 1974; Sheele Memorial Award, 1978; Lenore Marshall Poetry Prize, 1978; Whiting Writers Award, 1986; National Endowment for the Arts Senior Fellowship, 1988; Ruth Lilly Poetry Prize, 1990; National Book Critics Circle Award in Poetry, 1993; National Book Award for Poetry, 1996. Address: RR 1, Box 128, Munnsville, NY 13409, USA.

CARRUTHERS Peter (Michael), b. 16 June 1952, Manila, Philippines. Philosopher; Professor; Writer. m. Susan Levi, 21 Oct 1978, 2 sons. Education: University of Leeds, 1971-77; Balliol College, Oxford, 1977-79. Appointments: Lecturer, University of St Andrews, 1979-81, Queens University of Belfast, 1981-83, University of Essex, 1985-91; Visiting Professor, University of Michigan, 1989-90; Senior Lecturer, 1991-92, Professor, 1992-, University of Sheffield. Publications: The Metaphysics of the Tractatus, 1990; Introducing Persons: Theories and Arguments in the Philosophy of Mind, 1991; Human Knowledge and Human Nature: A New Introduction to the Ancient Debate, 1992; The Animals Issue: Moral Theory in Practice, 1992. Contributions to: Journals. Membership: Aristotelian Society. Address: Department of Philosophy, University of Sheffield, Sheffield S10 2TN, England.

CARSON Anne, b. 21 June 1950, Toronto, Ontario, Canada. Professor of Classics; Poet; Writer. Education: BA, 1974, MA, 1975, PhD, 1980, University of Toronto. Appointments: Professor of Classics, University of Calgary, 1979-80, Princeton University, 1980-87, Emory University, 1987-88, McGill University, 1988-; Writer and Co-Host, The Nobel Legacy, PBS TV, 1994. Publications: Eros the Bittersweet: An Essay, 1986; Short Talks, 1992; Plainwater, 1995; Glass, Irony and God, 1995; Simonides: Greed, 1997. Contributions to: Anthologies and journals. Honour: Lannan Literary Award, 1996. Address: 5900 Esplanade Avenue, Montreal, Quebec H2T 3A3, Canada.

CARTANO Tony, b. 27 July 1944, Bayonne, France. Author; Editor. m. Françoise Perrin, 10 Nov 1966, 1 son, 1 daughter. Education: Licence es Lettres, 1964, Diploma d'Études Superieurers, 1965, University of Paris. Appointment: Director, Foreign Department, Editions Albin Michel, Paris. Publications: Le Single Hurteur, 1978; Malcolm Lowry (essay), 1979; Blackbird, 1980; La Sourde Oreille, 1982; Schmutz, 1987; Le Bel Arturo, 1989; Le soufflé de Satan, 1991; American Boulevard (travel book), 1992. Honour: Chevalier, l'ordre des Arts et Lettres. Address: 157 Boulevard Davout, 75020 Paris, France.

CARTENS Jan, b. 25 May 1929, Roosendaal, Netherlands. Writer. Publications: Dat meisje uit Munchen, 1975; De thuiskomst, 1976; Vroege herfst, 1978; Een Roomsche Jeugd, 1980; De verleiding, 1983; Maagdenbruiloft, 1987; Het verraad van Nausikaa, 1989; Een indringer, 1990; De bekentenis, 1993; De roze bisschop, 1994; Oorlogsbruid, 1995. Address: Markenland 15, 4871 AM, Etten-Leur, Netherlands.

CARTER Bruce. See: **HOUGH Richard Alexander.**

CARTER Francis W(illiam), B. 4 July 1938, Wednesfireld, Staffordshire, England. University Reader in Geography. m. Krystyna Stephania Tomaszewska, 3 June 1977. Education: BA, Honours, Sheffield University, 1960; DipEduc, Cambridge University, 1961; MA, 1967, PhD, 1979, London University; DNatSc, University of Prague, 1974; DPhil, University of Krakow, 1990. Appointments: Joint Hayter Lecturer in the Geography of Eastern Europe, University College, London, and School of Slavonic and East European Studies, London University, 1966-90; Head, Department of Social Sciences, School of Slavonic and East European Studies, 1990-, Reader in Geography, 1997-, London University; Various guest lectureships. Publications: Dubrovnik (Ragusa): A Classic City-State, 1972; An Historical Geography of the Balkans (editor), 1977; Environmental Problems in Eastern Europe (editor with D Turnock), 1993, revised edition, 1996; Trade and Urban

Development in Poland: An Economic Geography of Cracow, from its origins to 1795, 1994; Proces Przekształceń Społeczno-Gospodarczych w Europie Środkowej i Wschodniej po roku 1989 (editor with W Maik), 1995; The Changing Shape of the Balkans (editor with H T Norris), 1996; Central Europe after the Fall of the Iron Curtain: Geographical Perspectives, Spatial Patterns and Trends (editor with P Jordan and V Rey), 1996, 2nd edition, 1998. Contributions to: Scholarly publications. Honours: Diploma, Geographical Institute, Romanian Academy of Sciences, 1994; Honorary Member Diploma, Croatian Geographical Society, 1995; Rockefeller Foundation Scholarship, Bellagio, Italy, 1995; Edward Heath Award, Royal Geographical Society, 1997. Memberships: Institute of British Geographers; PEN Club; Royal Asiatic Society, fellow; Royal Geographical Society, fellow. Address: c/o Department of Social Sciences, School of Slavonic and East European Studies, London University, London WC1E 7HU, England.

CARTER Harold Burnell, b. 3 Jan 1910, Mosman, Sydney, New South Wales, Australia. Scientific Civil Servant. m. Dr Mary Brandon Jones, 21 Sep 1940, 3 sons. Education: University of Sydney, BVSC, 1933. Appointments: Veterinary Officer, Australian Estates Co Ltd. 1933-36; Walter and Eliza Hall Fellow, University of Sydney, 1936-39; Research Scientist, CSIRO, Australia, 1939-54; Senior Principal Scientific Officer, ARC, UK, 1954-70; Honorary Fellow, University of Leeds, 1962-70; Director, Banks Archive Project, British Museum Natural History, 1989-96. Publications: His Majesty's Spanish Flock; The Sheep and Wool Correspondence of Sir Joseph Banks; Sir Joseph Banks: A Guide to Biographical and Bibliographical Sources; Sir Joseph Banks 1743-1820. Contributions to: Australian and British Scientific Journals; Bulletin; British Museum; Historical Series. Honours: American Philosophical Society History of Science Grants; Royal Society History of Science Grants; British Academy Major Awards; Honorary DVSc, University of Sydney, 1996. Memberships: Royal Society of Edinburgh; FLS; FIBiol. Address: Yeo Bank, Congresbury, Nr Bristol, Avon BS19 5JA, England.

CARTER Jared, b. 10 Jan 1939, Elwood, Indiana, USA. Poet. m. Diane Haston, 21 June 1979, 1 daughter by previous marriage. Education: Yale University; AB, Goddard College, 1969. Publications: Early Warning, 1979; Work, for the Night is Coming, 1981; Fugue State, 1984; Pincushion's Strawberry, 1984; Millennial Harbinger, 1986; The Shriving, 1990; Situation Normal, 1991; Blues Project, 1991; After the Rain, 1993; Les Barricades Mystérieuses, 1999. Contributions to: Many anthologies and periodicals. Honours: Walt Whitman Award, 1980; Bridgman Fellowship, Bread Loaf Writers Conference, 1981; National Endowment for the Arts Fellowships, 1981, 1991; Great Lakes Colleges Association New Writers Award, 1982; Guggenheim Fellowship, 1983; Governor's Arts Award, Indiana, 1985; New Letters Literary Award for Poetry, 1992; The Poets' Prize, 1995. Membership: PEN American Center. Address: 1220 North State Avenue, Indianapolis, IN 46201-1162, USA.

CARTER Nick. See: **LYNDS Dennis.**

CARTER Peter, b. 13 Aug 1929, England. Writer. m. Gudrun Willege, 17 Feb 1974. Education: MA, Wadham College, Oxford, 1962. Publications: Novels: The Gates of Paradise, 1974; Madatan, 1974. Books for Young People: The Black Lamp, 1973; Mao, biography, 1976; Under Goliath, 1977; The Sentinels, 1980; Children of the Book, 1984; Bury the Dead, 1986; Borderlands, 1990. Translator: Grimms' Fairy Tales, 1982. Honours: Children's Book of the Year, Child Study Association of America, 1975; Carnegie Medal Commendation, British Library Association, 1978; Guardian Award, 1981; Book for the Teen Age, New York Public Library, 1982; Young Observer/Rank Teenage Fiction Award, 1984. Address: c/o Oxford University Press, Walton Street, Oxford OX2 6DP, England.

CARTER Robert Ayres, b. 16 Sept 1923, Omaha, Nebraska, USA. Writer; Lecturer. m. 17 Dec 1983, 2

sons. Education: AB, New School for Social Research, New York City. Publications: Manhattan Primitive, 1972; Written in Blood, US edition as Casual Slaughters, 1992; Final Edit, 1994; Three Textbooks. Contributions to: Publishers Weekly; International Journal of Book Publishing. Honour: Fulbright Scholar, 1949. Memberships: Poets and Writers; Mystery Writers of America; International Crime Writers Association; The Players, life member. Literary Agent: Regula Noetzli, c/o Charlotte Sheedy Agency. Address: 510 North Meadow Street, Richmond, VA 23220, USA.

CARTER Stephen L(isle), b. 1954, USA. Professor of Law; Writer. Education: BA, Stanford University, 1976; JD, Yale University Law School, 1979. Appointments: Admitted to the Bar, Washington, DC, 1981; Law Clerk, US Court of Appeals, District of Columbia Circuit, 1979-80, and to Justice Thurgood Marshall, US Supreme Court, Washington, DC, 1980-81; Associate, Shea & Garner, law firm, Washington, DC, 1981-82; Assistant Professor, 1982-84, Associate Professor, 1984-85, Professor of Law, 1985-, Yale University Law School. Publications: Reflections of an Affirmative Action Baby, 1991; The Culture of Disbelief: How American Law and Politics Trivialize Religious Devotion, 1993; The Confirmation Mess, 1994; Integrity, 1996. Address: c/o Yale University Law School, PO Box 1303a, New Haven, CT 06520, USA.

CARTER Walter Horace, b. 20 Jan 1921, North Carolina, USA. Writer. m. (1)Lucille Miller Carter, dec, (2)Brenda C Strickland, 29 Oct 1983, 1 son, 2 daughters. Education: AB, University of North California. Publications: Land That I love, 1978; Creatures and Chronicles from Cross Creek, 1980; Wild and Wonderful Santee Cooper Country, 1982; Nature's Masterpiece, 1984; Return to Cross Creek, 1985; Virus of Fear, 1991; Nature Coast Tales & Truths, 1993; Headstart Fishing Handbook, 1994; Tremblin Earth, 1995; Coastal Carolina's Tales and Truths, 1996. Contributions to: Various magazines. Honours: Pulitzer Prize, 1953; Sidney Hillman award, 1954. Memberships: Outdoor Writers Association of America; Florida Outdoor Writers Association; Southwestern Outdoor Press Association. Address: Rt3 Box 139A, Hawthorne, FL 32640, USA.

CARTLAND Dame Barbara (Hamilton), b. 9 July 1901, England. Author; Dramatist; Poet. m. (1) Alexander George McCorquodale, 1927, div, 1933, 1 daughter, (2) Hugh McCorquodale, 1936, dec 1963, 2 sons. Publications: About 690 novels, 1923-95; Over 60 other books, including non-fiction titles of general interest, history, biography, and autobiography. Other: Poetry and plays. Honours: Médaille de Vermeil de la Ville de Paris, 1988; Dame Commander of the Order of the British Empire, 1991; Certified bestselling author of the world, Guinness Book of Records. Memberships: National Association for Health, founder-president, 1964-; Royal Society of Arts, fellow. Address: Camfield Place, Hatfield, Herts AL9 6JE, England.

CARTWRIGHT Justin, (Suzy Crispin, Penny Sutton), b. 1933, South Africa. Writer. Education: University of Oxford. Publications: Fighting Men, 1977; The Revenge, 1978; The Horse of Darius, 1980; Freedom for the Wolves, 1983; Interior, 1988; Look at It This Way, 1990; Masai Dreaming, 1993; In Every Face I Meet, 1995. Address: c/o Peters, Fraser & Dunlop Group Ltd, 503/4 The Chambers, Chelsea Harbour, Lots Road, London SW10 0XF, England.

CARVALHO Mario Costa Martins de, b. 25 Sept 1944, Lisbon, Portugal. Lawyer; Writer. m. Maria Helena Taborda Duarte, 3 Aug 1968, 2 daughters. Education: Graduated Law, School of Lisbon, 1970. Publications: Contos Da Setima Esfera, 1981; A Paixao Do Conde De Frois, 1986; Os Alferes, 1990; Quatrocentos Mil Sestercios... Um Deus Passendo Pela Brisa Da Tarde, 1994 (A God Strolling in the Cool of The Evening); Era Bom Que Trocassemos Umas Ideias Sobre o Assunto, 1995. Contributions to: Columnist in jornal de Letras, and Publico; Nouvelle Revue Francaise. Honours:Premio Cidade de Lisboa; Grande Premio APE. Membership:

Portuguese Writers Association. Literary Agent: Ray - Güde Meritiu, Germany. Address: R Antonio Pereira Carrilho, 27 R/C 1000 Lisboa, Portugal.

CARWARDINE Richard John, b. 12 Jan 1947, Cardiff, Wales. University Professor. m. Linda Margaret Kirk, 17 May 1975. Education: BA, Oxford University, 1968; MA, 1972; DPhil, 1975. Appointments: Lecturer, Senior Lecturer, Reader, Professor, University of Sheffield, 1971-; Visiting Professor, Syracuse University, New York, 1974-75; Visiting Fellow, University of North Carolina, Chapel Hill, 1989. Publications: Transatlantic Revivalism: Popular Evangelicalism in Britain and America 1790-1865, 1978; Evangelicals and Politics in Antebellum America, 1993. Address: c/o Department of History, University of Sheffield, Sheffield S10 2TN, England.

CARY Emily Marshall Pritchard, b. 6 Sept 1931, Pittsburgh, Pennsylvania, USA. Educator; Writer. m. Boyd Balford Cary Jr, 28 Sept 1953, 2 sons. Education: BA, University of Pennsylvania, 1952; MA, Kean College, New Jersey, 1975; Graduate work in Communications; University of Maryland; Archaeological Fellowship, University of Arizona; Environment and Ecology Fellowship, Rutgers University. Appointments: Teacher; Music Writer, Teacher Magazine, 1972-81; Music Columnist, Journal Newspapers, syndicated, 1981-. Publications: My High Love Calling, 1977; The Ghost of Whitaker Mountain, 1979; Duet: Melodrama in Three-Quarter Time, 1991; In progress: The Pohick Priest; Denyce Graves, a biography of a diva; The Pritchard Family History, from Jamestown, Virginia to the present. Contributions to: More than 500 articles on music, education and Americana in The New York Times, The Los Angeles Times, The Washington Post, The Washington Times, Philadelphia Inquirer, Phi Delta Kappan, others. Honours: 1 of 5 Virginia Finalists, NASA Teacher in Space Project, 1985; Outstanding Teacher of Gifted and Talented, Virginia, 1995. Memberships: Phi Delta Kappa; Alpha Delta Kappa, Representative to WCOTP, Stockholm, 1993. Literary Agent: Singer Communications, San Clemente, California, USA. Address: 27653 North 72nd Way, Scottsdale, AZ 85255-1105, USA.

CARY Jud. See: **TUBB E(dwin) C(harles).**

CARY Lorene (Emily), b. 29 Nov 1956, Philadelphia, Pennsylvania, USA. Writer. m. R C Smith, 27 Aug 1983, 2 daughters, 1 stepson. Education: BA, MA, 1978, University of Pennsylvania; MA, University of Sussex, 1979. Appointments: Associate Editor, TV Guide, 1980-82; Contributing Editor, Newsweek Magazine, 1991; Lecturer, University of Pennsylvania, 1995-. Publications: Black Ice, 1991; The Price of a Child, 1995; Pride, 1998. Honour: Honorary Doctorate of Letters. Memberships: PEN; Authors Guild. Address: Department of English, University of Pennsylvania, 34th and Walnut Street, Philadelphia, PA 19104, USA.

CASEY John (Dudley), b. 18 Jan 1939, Worcester, Massachusetts, USA. Writer; Professor. m. Rosamond Pinchot Pittman, 26 June 1982, 4 daughters. Education: BA, Harvard College, 1962; LLB, Harvard Law School, 1965; MFA, University of Iowa, 1967. Appointments: Professor, University of Virginia, 1972-92, 1999-; Guggenheim Fellow, 1979-80; Residency, American Academy in Rome, 1990-91; Residency, American Academy of Arts and Letters, 1992-97. Publications: An American Romance, 1977; Testimony and Demeanor, 1979; Spartina, 1989; Supper at the Black Pearl, 1996; The Half-Life of Happiness, 1998. Contributions to: Stories, articles and reviews in newspapers and magazines. Honours: Runner Up, Ernest Hemingway Award, 1978; Guggenheim Fellowship, 1979-80; Friends of American Writers Award, 1980; National Endowment for the Arts Fellowship, 1983; National Book Award, 1989; O Henry Award, 1989; Ingram Merril Fellowship, 1990. Membership: PEN. Literary Agent: Michael Carlisle. Address: c/o Michael Carlisle, 24 E 64th Street, New York, NY 10021, USA.

CASS Zoe. See: **LOW Lois Dorothea.**

CASSELET Countesse de. See: **COTTINGHAM Valery Jean.**

CASSELLS Cyrus Curtis, b. 16 May 1957, Dover, Delaware, USA. Poet; Teacher; Translator. Education: BA, Stanford University, 1979. Publications: The Mud Actor, 1982; Soul Make a Path Through Shouting, 1994; Beautiful Signor, 1997. Contributions to: Southern Review; Callaloo; Translation; Seneca Review; Quilt; Sequoia. Honours: Academy of American Poets Prize, 1979; National Poetry Series Winner, 1982; Bay Area Book Reviewers Association Award Nominee, 1983; Callaloo Creative Writing Award, 1983; Massachusetts Artists Foundation Fellowship, 1985; National Endowment for the Arts Fellowship, 1986; Lavan Younger Poets Award, 1992; Lannan Award, 1993; William Carlos Williams Award, 1994; Finalist, Lenore Marshall Prize, 1995. Memberships: PEN; Poetry Society of America. Address: c/o Mary Cassells, 2190 Belden Place, Escondido, CA 92029, USA.

CASSIAN Nina, b. 27 Nov 1924, Galati, Romania. Poet; Dramatist; Composer; Translator. Education: University of Bucharest and Conservatory of Music. Appointment: Visiting Professor, New York University, 1985-86. Publications: Verses: 50 books including: At the Scale 1/1, 1947; Ages of the Year, 1957; The Dialogue of Wind and Sea, 1957; Outdoor Performance, 1961; Everyday Holidays, 1961; Gift Giving, 1963; The Discipline of the Harp, 1965; Blood, 1966; Parallel Destinies, 1967; Ambitus, 1968; Chronophagy 1944-69, 1969; The Big Conjugation, 1971; Requiem, 1971; Lotto Poems, 1974; 100 Poems, 1974; Suave, 1977; Mercy, 1981; Lady of Miracles, 1982; Countdown, 1983; Call Yourself Alive?, 1988; Life Sentence: Selected Poems, 1990; Cheer Leader for a Funeral, 1993; Arguing with Chaos, 1994. Other: Prose; children's plays and poetry. Honours: Writers Union of Romania Awards, 1967, 1984; Writers Association of Bucharest Award, 1981; Fulbright Grant. 1986. Address: 555 Main Street, No 502, Roosevelt Island, New York, NY 10044, USA.

CASSILL R(onald) V(erlin), (Owen Aherne, Jesse Webster), b. 17 May 1919, Cedar Falls, Iowa, USA. Author; Professor Emeritus. m. (1) Kathleen Rosecrans, 4 June 1941, div 1952, (2) Karilyn Kay Adams, 23 Nov 1956, 2 sons, 1 daughter. Education: BA, 1939, MA, 1949, University of Iowa. Appointments: Instructor, Monticello College, Godfrey, Illinois, 1946-48; Instructor in Writing Workshop, University of Iowa, 1948-52, 1960-66; Editor, Western Review, Iowa City, 1951-52; Collier's Encyclopedia, New York City, 1953-54, Dude and Gent magazines, New York City, 1958; Lecturer, Columbia University and New School for Social Research, New York City, 1957-59; Writer-in-Residence, Purdue University, 1965-66; Associate Professor, 1966-71, Professor of English, 1972-83, Professor Emeritus, 1983-, Brown University. Publications: Novels: The Eagle on the Coin, 1950; Dormitory Women, 1954; The General Said "Nuts", 1955; The Left Bank of Desire (with Eric Potter), 1955; The Wound of Love, 1956; A Taste of Sin, 1956; The Hungering Shame, 1956; Naked Morning, 1957; Lustful Summer, 1958; Nurses Quarters, 1958; The Wife Next Door, 1959; My Sister's Keeper, 1961; Night School, 1961; Clem Anderson, 1961; Pretty Leslie, 1963; The President, 1964; La Vie Passionnee of Rodney Buckthorne: A Tale of the Great American's Last Rally and Curious Death, 1968; Doctor Cobb's Game, 1970; The Goss Women, 1974; Hoyt's Child, 1976; Labors of Love, 1980; Flame, 1980; After Goliath, 1985; Two Short Novels (with James White), 1990. Stories: Fifteen by Three: R V Cassill, Herbert Gold, and James B Hall, 1957; The Father and Other Stories, 1965; The Happy Marriage and Other Stories, 1966; Three Stories, 1982; Collected Stories, 1989; Late Stories, 1993. Poetry: Patrimonies, 1988. Other: Writing Fiction, 1962, 2nd edition, 1975; In an Iron Time: Statements and Reiterations, 1969; The Norton Anthology of Short Fiction, 1978, 5th edition, 1994; The Norton Anthology of Contemporary Fiction, 1988. Contributions to: Many anthologies and periodicals. Honours: Atlantic "Firsts"

Award, 1947; Fulbright Grant, 1952; Rockefeller Foundation Grant, 1954; Blackhawk Award, 1965; Guggenheim Fellowship, 1968-69. Membership: Phi Beta Kappa. Address: 22 Boylston Avenue, Providence, RI 02906, USA.

CASTANEDA Omar, b. 6 Sept 1954, Guatemala City, Guatemala. Professor; Writer. m. (1) 11 Aug 1984, (2) 26 Feb 1992, 1 son, 1 daughter. Education: BA, 1980, MFA, 1983, Indiana University. Appointment: Professor, University of Washington. Publications: Remembering to Say Mouth or Face, 1993; Imagining Isabel, 1994. Contributions to: Many periodicals. Honours: Various awards. Memberships: Modern Language Association; PEN. Address: Department of English, Western Washington University, Bellingham, WA 98225, USA.

CASTEDO Elena, b. 1 Sept 1937, Barcelona, Spain. Writer. m. A Denny Elleman, 15 Apr 1973, 2 sons, 1 daughter. Education: University of Chile, 1966; University of California, 1968; Harvard University, 1976. Appointments: Teacher; Teaching Fellow, Harvard University, 1969-72; Lecturer, American University, 1976-77; Editor, Inter American Review, 1987-80; Visiting Writer at Universities of California, Cornell, Chicago, Illinois, Miami, Washington, Wisconsin and Yale, 1990-94. Publications: El Praiso; Paradise; Iquana Dreams; The Sound of Writing; El Teato Chileno de Mediados de Sigioxx; El Teatro Chileuo de mediadis siglo XX, 1982; El paraiso, 1990; Paradise, 1990. Contributions to: Anthologies and periodicals. Honours: University of California at Los Angeles Masters Award; Simon Bolivar Medal; Several Fellowships; Phoebe Award; Nominated, National Book Award; El Mercurio Book of the Year. Memberships: PEN; Authors Guild; Modern Language Association; Poets and Writers. Address: c/o Accent Media, 36 Lancaster Street, Cambridge, MA 02140, USA.

CASTEL Albert (Edward), b. 11 Nov 1928, Wichita, Kansas, USA. Historian; Professor (Retired). m. GeorgeAnn Bennett, 25 June 1959, 1 son, 1 daughter. Education: BA, 1950, MA, 1951, Wichita State University; PhD, University of Chicago, 1955. Appointments: Instructor, University of California at Los Angeles, 1957-58; Assistant Professor, Waynesburg College, Pennsylvania, 1958-60; Assistant Professor, 1960-63, Associate Professor, 1963-67, Professor, 1967-91, Western Michigan University. Publications: A Frontier State of War, 1958; William Clarke Quantrill, 1962; Sterling Price and the Civil War in the West, 1968; The Guerrilla War, 1974; Fort Sumter: 1861, 1976; The Presidency of Andrew Johnson, 1979; Decision in the West: The Atlanta Campaign of 1864, 1992; Winning and Losing in the Civil War: Essays and Stories, 1996. Contributions to: Many scholarly journals. Honours: Albert J Beveridge Award, American Historical Association, 1957; Best Author Award, Civil War Times Illustrated, 1979; Peterson Award, Eastern National Park and Monument Association, 1989; Harwell Award, Atlanta Civil War Round Table, 1993; Lincoln Prize, Gettysburg College, 1993; Truman Award, Civil War Round Table of Kansas City, 1994. Address: 66 Westwood Drive, Hillsdale, MI 49242, USA.

CASTELL Megan. See: **WILLIAMS Jeanne.**

CASTELLIN Philippe, b. 26 June 1948, Isle sur Sorgnes, Vaucluse, France. Writer; Poet; Fisherman; Publisher. 3 sons. Education: Arege de Philosophie, ENS; Docteur de Lettres, Sorbonne, University of Paris. Publications: René Char, Traces, 1988; Paesine, 1989; Livre, 1990; Vers la Poesie Totale, 1992; HPS, 1992. Contributions to: Periodicals. Honour: Charge de Mission, 1990. Memberships: Société des Gens de Lettres. Address: c/o Akenaton Docks, 20 rue Bonaparte, F-20000 Ajaccio, France.

CASTELLO BRANCO Lucia, b. 4 July 1955, Rio De Janeiro, Brazil. Teacher. m. Paulinho Assuncao, 3 Oct 1983, 1 son, 1 daughter. Education: Master Degree in Brazilian Literature, Indiana University, USA, 1981; PhD, Comparative Literature, Brazil, 1989. Appointment: De

Minas Gerais, 1984-. Publications: Theory of Literature: O que i erotism, 1984; A Traicao de Penelope, 1995; Literaterras, 1996; Literature: Julia-Toda-Azul, 1993; O Fazedor de Palairas, 1996; Desiderare, 1997; A Falla, 1997. Contributions to: Revista Presenca Pedagogica. Address: Arenida Antonio Carlos, 6627 Faculdade de Letras, BH-MG. Address: 81/12 Fuxemburgo-BH-MG, 30380-540 Brazil.

CASTLE Barbara Anne, (Baroness Castle of Blackburn), b. 6 Oct 1910, Chesterfield, England. Journalist; Author. m. Edward Cyril Castle, 1944. Education: St Hugh's College, Oxford. Appointments: Editor, Town and County Councillor, 1936-40; Housing Correspondent and Affairs Advisor, Daily Mirror, 1940-45; Labour Member, Blackburn, 1945-79; Member, National Executive Committee, 1950-79, Vice-Chairman, 1957-58, Chairman, 1958-59, Labour Party; Minister of Overseas Development, 1964-65; Privy Counsellor, 1964; Minister of Transport, 1965-68; First Secretary of State for Employment and Productivity, 1968-70; Secretary of State for Social Services, 1974-76; Member, European Parliament, Greater Manchester North, 1979-84, Greater Manchester West, 1984-89; Leader, British Labour Party, European Parliament, 1979-85; Vice-Chairman, Socialist Group, European Parliament, 1979-86. Publications: Castle Diaries 1964-70, 1984; Sylvia & Christabel Pankhurst, 1987; Castle Diaries 1964-76, 1990; Fighting All the Way, 1993. Honours: Honorary Fellow, St Hugh's College, Oxford, 1966, Bradford & Ilkley Community College, 1985, UMIST, 1991, Humberside Polytechnic, 1991, York University, 1992; Honorary doctorates, Bradford University, 1968, Loughborough, 1969, Lancaster, 1991, Manchester University, 1993, Cambridge University, 1998, De Montfort University, 1998; Cross of Order of Merit, Germany, 1990; Created Life Peer, 1990. Literary Agent: David Higham Associates Ltd. Address: House of Lords, London SW1A 0PW, England.

CASTLEDEN Rodney, b. 23 Mar 1945, Worthing, Sussex, England. Geomorphologist; Writer. m. Sarah Dee, 29 July 1987. Education: BA, Geography, Hertford College, 1967, Dip Ed, 1968, MA, 1972, MSc, Geomorphology, 1980, Oxford University. Publications: Classic Landforms of the Sussex Coast, 1982; The Wilmington Giant: The Quest for a Lost Myth, 1983; The Stonehenge People: An Exploration of Life in Neolithic Britain, 1987; The Knossos Labyrinth, 1989; Minoans: Life in Bronze Age Crete, 1990; Book of British Dates, 1991; Neolithic Britain, 1992; The Making of Stonehenge, 1993; World History: a Chronological Dictionary of Dates, 1994; British History: A Chronological Dictionary of Dates, 1994; The Cerne Giant, 1996; Knossos, Temple of the Goddess, 1996; Classic Landforms Series, editor; Atlantis Destroyed, 1998; Out in the Cold, 1998; History of Roedean, 1998; The English Lake District, 1998; The Search for King Arthur, 1999. Contributions to: The Origin of Chalk Dry Valleys; A General Theory of Fluvial Valley Development. Memberships: Geomorphological Society, fellow; Geographical Society, fellow; Quaternary Research Association; Society of Authors. Address: 15 Knepp Close, Brighton, Sussex, BN2 4LD, England.

CASTLES Alexander Cuthbert, b. 7 Mar 1933, Australia. Emeritus Professor of Law; Author. m. Florence Amelia Ross, 15 Mar 1958, 1 son, 3 daughters. Education: LLB (Hons), University of Melbourne, 1955; JD, Chicago, 1957. Publications: Introduction to Australian Legal History, 1971; Australia and the United Nations, 1973; Chronology of Australia, 1978; Source Book of Legal History (with J M Bennett), 1979; An Australian Legal History, 1982; Law Makers and Wayward Whigs, with M C Harris, 1987; Annotated Bibliography of Australian Law, 1994; Shark Arm Murders, 1995. Contributions to: Australian and foreign journals. Address: 2/112 Beulah Road, Norwood, South Australia 5067, Australia.

CASTRO-KLAREN Sara, b. 9 June 1940, Arequipa, Peru. Professor. m. Peter F Klarén, 1963, 1 daughter. Education: BA, UCLA, 1962; MA, UCLA, 1965; PhD, UCLA, 1968. Appointments: Assistant Professor, Idaho University, 1968; Assistant Professor, Dartmouth College, 1970; Professor, Johns Hopkins University, 1987. Publications include: El Mundo Mágico de José Maria Arguedas, 1973; Mario Vargas Llosa, 1988; Escritura, transgresión y sujeto en la literatura latino americana, 1989. Contributions to: Many contributions to books on Vargas Llosa, 1981; Cortázar, 1978, 1990; Jean de Lery, 1992, 1997; Guaman Poma, 1979, 1993, 1996; Diamela Eltit, 1993; Rosario Ferre, 1993; Cultural studies and colonial topics. Address: Department of Romance Languages, The Johns Hopkins University, Baltimore, MD 21218, USA.

CAULDWELL Frank. See: **KING Francis Henry.**

CAUSLEY Charles (Stanley), b. 24 Aug 1917, Launceton, Cornwall, England. Poet; Dramatist; Editor. Education: Launceston College. Appointment: Teacher, Cornwall, 1947-76. Publications: Survivors Leave, 1953; Union Street, 1957; Johnny Alleluia, 1961; Penguin Modern Poets 3, 1962; Underneath the Water, 1968; Pergamon Poets 10, 1970; Timothy Winters, 1970; Six Women, 1974; Ward 14, 1974; St Martha and the Dragon, 1978; Collected Poems, 1951-75, 1975; Secret Destinations, 1984; 21 Poems, 1986; The Young Man of Cury, 1991; Bring in the Holly, 1992; Collected Poems for Children, 1996; Penguin Modern Poets 6, 1996; Collected Poems, 1951-97, 1997. Other: Several plays: Libretto for William Mathias's opera Jonah, 1990. Contributions to: Various publications. Honours: Queen's Gold Medal for Poetry, 1967; Honorary DLitt, University of Exeter, 1977; Honorary MA, Open University, 1982; Commander of the Order of the British Empire, 1986; T S Eliot Award, Ingersoll Foundation, USA, 1990. Address: 2 Cyprus Well, Launceston, Cornwall, PL15 8BT, England.

CAUTE (John) David, (John Salisbury), b. 16 Dec 1936 Alexandria, Egypt. Writer. Education: DPhil, Wadham College, Oxford, 1962. Appointments: Fellow, All Soul's College, Oxford, 1959-65; Visiting Professor, New York and Columbia Universities, 1966-67; Reader in Social and Political Theory, Brunel University, 1967-70; Regent's Lecturer, University of California, 1974; Literary and Arts Editor, New Statesman, London, 1979-80; Co-Chairman, Writers Guild of Great Britain, 1981-82. Publications: At Fever Pitch, 1959; Comrade Jacob, 1961; Communism and the French Intellectuals 1914-1960, 1964; The Decline of the West, 1966; The Left in Europe Since 1789, 1966; Essential Writings of Karl Marx (editor), 1967; The Fanon, 1970; Demonstration, 1971; The Occupation, 1971; The Illusion, 1971; The Fellow-Travellers, 1973, revised edition, 1988; Collisions: Essays and Reviews, 1974; Cuba Yes?, 1974; The Great Fear: The Anti-Communist Purge Under Truman and Eisenhower, 1978; The K-Factor, 1983; Under the Skin: The Death of White Rhodesia, 1983; The Espionage of The Saints, 1986; News From Nowhere, 1986; Sixty-Eight: The Year of the Barricades, 1988; Veronica of the Two Nations, 1989; The Women's Hour, 1991; Joseph Losey: A Revenge on Life, 1994; Orwell and Mr Blair, 1994; Fatima's Scarf, 1998. Radio Plays: The Demonstration, 1971; Fallout, 1972; The Zimbabwe Tapes, 1983; Henry and the Dogs, 1986; Sanctions, 1988; Animal Fun Park, 1995. Address: 41 Westcroft Square, London W6 0TA, England.

CAVAZOS-GAITHER Alma Elisa, b. 6 Jan 1955, San Juan, Texas, USA. Freelance Writer. m. Carl Clifford Gaither, 14 Dec 1995, 3 sons, 3 daughters. Education: AA, Central Texas College, 1988. Appointments: US Navy, 1974-77; Recpetionist, 1978-79; Bookkeeper, 1980-82; Material Control Clerk, 1983-85; Recreational Aide, 1989-93; Bilingual Data Collector, 1994; Test Data Collector, 1995; Freelance Writer, 1995-; US Navy Reserves, 1995-. Publications: Statistically Speaking: A Dictionary of Quotations, 1996; Physically Speaking: A Dictionary of Quotations in Physics and Astronomy, 1997; Mathematically Speaking: A Dictionary of Quotations, 1998; Practically Speaking: A Dictionary of Quotations on Engineering, Technology and Architecture, 1999; Medically Speaking: A Dictionary of Quotations on Dentistry, Medicine and Nursing, 1999; Scientifically Speaking: A Dictionary of Quotations, 1999. Literary

Agent: Institute of Physics Publishing. Address: Dirac House, Temple Back, Bristol BS1 6BE, England.

CAVE Hugh Barnett, b. 11 July 1910, Chester, England. Writer. m. Margaret Long, 11 July 1935, 2 sons. Education: Boston University. Publications include: Fishermen Four, 1942; The Cross on the Drum, 1959; The Mission, 1960; Larks Will Sing, 1969; Murgunstrumm and Others, 1977; The Evil, 1981; The Voyage, 1988; Disciples of Dread, 1988; The Corpse Maker, 1988; Conquering Kilmarnie, 1989; The Lower Deep, 1990; Lucifer's Eye, 1991; Death Stalks the Night, 1995; The Door Below (stories). Non-fiction: Long Were The Nights: The Saga of PT Squadron X in the Solomons, 1943; Wings Across the World: The Story of the Air Transport Command, 1945; Four Paths to Paradise: A Book About Jamaica, 1961; Collections: The Witching Lands: Tales of the West Indies, 1962; The Corpse Maker, 1988; The Dagger of Tsiang, 1997; The Door Below, 1997; Escapades of the Eel, 1997; The dawning, 1999. Contributions to: Over 800 stories in 100 magazines in 1930s and 1940s; 350 fiction pieces in magazines, including 43 in Saturday Evening Post, 36 in Good Housekeeping; Short stories in over 30 countries. Honours: World Fantasy Award; Phoenix Award; Horror Writers Association's Lifetime Achievement; International Horror Guild'a Lifetime Achievement Award, 1998. Literary Agent: Dorian Literary Agency, England. Address: 437 Thomas Street, Sebastian, FL 32958, USA.

CAWS Ian, b. 19 Mar 1945, Bramshott, Hants, England. Local Government Officer. m. Hilary Walsh, 20 June 1970, 3 sons, 2 daughters. Education: Certificate in Social Work, 1970; Certificate for Social Workers with the Deaf, 1973. Appointments: Senior Social Worker with the Deaf, 1974; County Team Leader of Deaf Services, 1986; Arts Development Officer, 1991. Publications: Looking for Bonfires, 1975; Bruised Madonna, 1979; Boy with a Kite, 1981; The Ragman Totts, 1990; Chamomile, 1994; The Feast of Fools, 1994; The Playing of the Easter Music (with Martin C Caseley and B L Pearce), 1996; Herrick's Women, 1996. Contributions to: Acumen Magazine; London Magazine; New Welsh Review; Observer; Poetry Review; Scotsman; Spectator; Stand Magazine; Swansea Review. Honours: Eric Gregory Award, 1973; Poetry Book Society Recommendation, 1990. Membership: Poetry Society. Address: 9 Tennyson Avenue, Rustington, West Sussex BN16 2PB, England.

CAWS Mary Ann, b. 10 Sept 1933, Wilmington, North Carolina, USA. Professor of English, French, and Comparative Literature; Writer; Editor; Translator. m. Peter Caws, 2 June 1956, div 1987, 1 son, 1 daughter. Education: BA, Bryn Mawr College, 1954; MA, Yale University, 1956; PhD, University of Kansas, 1962. Appointments: Lecturer, Barnard College, 1962-63; Visiting Faculty, Sarah Lawrence College, 1965-66; Assistant Professor, 1966-68, Associate Professor, 1968-70, Professor, 1970-83, Distinguished Professor, 1983-86, Hunter College of the City University of New York; Distinguished Professor of English, French, and Comparative Literature, Graduate School, City University of New York, 1986-; Faculty, Dartmouth School of Theory and Criticism, 1988; Professeur associé, University of Paris VII, 1993-94; School of Visualists, 1993-94. Publications: Surrealism and the Literary Imagination, 1966; The Poetry of Dada and Surrealism, 1971; The Inner Theatre of Recent French Poetry, 1972; André Breton, 1974; The Presence of René Char, 1976; René Char, 1976; The Surrealist Voice of Robert Desnos, 1977; La Main de Pierre Reverdy, 1979; The Eye in the Text: Essays on Perception, Mannerist to Modern, 1981; A Metapoetics of the Passage: Architextures Surrealist and After, 1981; L'Oeuvre Filante de René Char, 1981; Yves Bonnefoy, 1984; Reading Frames in Modern Fiction, 1986; Edmond Jabès, 1988; The Art of Interference: Stressed Readings in Visual and Verbal Texts, 1988; Women of Bloomsbury: Virginia, Vanessa, and Carrington, 1990; Robert Motherwell: What Art Holds, 1995; Carrington and Lytton/Alone Together, 1996; André Breton, Revisited, 1996; The Surrealist Look: An Erotics of Encounter, 1997; Bloomsbury and France (with Sarah Bird Wright), 1997; Editor: About

French Poetry from Dada to Tel Quel: Theory and Text, 1984; Writing in a Modern Temper, 1984; The Prose Poem in France (with Hermine Riffaterre), 1985; Textual Analysis: Some Readers Reading, 1986; Perspectives on Perception: Philosophy, Art, and Literature, 1988; Edmond Jabès (with Richard Stamelman), 1989; Reading Proust Now (with Eugene Nicole), 1991; City Images, 1991; Women and Surrealism; Selected Poems of René Char (with Tina Jolas), 1992; Contre-Courants: Les femmes s'écrivent à travers les siècles (with Nancy K Miller, Elizabeth Houlding, and Cheryl Morgan), 1994; HarperCollins World Reader, 1994, expanded edition, 1996; Joseph Cornell's Theater of the Mind: Selected Journals, Letters, and Files, 1994; Carto-graphies (with Mary Jean Green, Marianne Hirsch, and Ronnie Scharfman), 1995; The Surrealist Painters and Poets, forthcoming; Modernist Manifestos (editor), forthcoming. Contributions to: Books, scholarly journals, and periodicals. Honours: Guggenheim Fellowship, 1972; Fulbright Fellowship, 1972; National Endowment for the Humanities Senior Fellowship, 1979-80; Doctor of Humane Letters, 1983; Getty Scholar, 1989-90; Rockefeller Foundation Residency, Bellagio, Italy, 1994. Memberships: Academy of Literary Studies, president, 1989-; Association for the Study of Dada and Surrealism, president, 1982-86; Authors' Guild; International Association for Philosophy and Literature; Modern Language Association, president, 1983-84; Phi Beta Kappa; PEN. Literary Agent: Gloria Loomis. Address: 140 East 81st Street, New York, NY 10028, USA.

CEBRIAN ECHARRI Juan Luis, b. 30 Oct 1944, Madrid, Spain. Chief Executive Officer. m. Teresa Aranda, 8 Sept 1988, 3 sons, 3 daughters. Education: BA, Journalism School, Spain. Appointments: Editor-in-Chief, El Pais, 1976; Chief Executive Officer, PRISA, 1988; Publisher, El Pais, 1988; Vice Chairman, SER, 1989; Chief Executive, CANAL, 1989. Publications: La Prensa y la Calle; La Espana que bosteza; Qué pasa en el Mundo; Cronicas de mi Pais; La Rusa; El Tamano del Elefante; La Isla del Viento; El Siglo de las Sombras; Cartas a un Joven Periodista. Contributions to: El Pais; Cinco Dias; Economist. Honours: International Editor of the Year, 1980; Spanish National Journalism Prize, 1983. Membership: Spanish Academy. Literary Agent: Antonia Kerrigan. Address: PRISA Group, Gran Via 32, 28013 Madrid, Spain.

CEDERING Siv, b. 5 Feb 1939, Sweden. Writer; Poet; Artist. 1 son, 2 daughters. Publications: Mother Is, 1975; The Juggler, 1977; The Blue Horse, 1979; Oxen, 1981; Letters from the Floating Worlds, 1984. Contributions to: Harper's; Ms; New Republic; Paris Review; Partisan Review; New York Times; Goergia Review; Fiction Interntional Shenandoah; Confrontation; Over 80 anthologies and textbooks. Honours: New York Foundation Fellowship, 1985, 1992. Memberships: Coordinating Council of Literary Magazines; PEN; Poetry Society of America; Poets and Writers. Address: PO Box 800, Amagansett, NY 11930, USA.

CELA Camilo José, b. 11 May 1916, Iria Flavia, La Coruña, Spain. Writer; Poet. m. (1) María del Rosario Conde Picavea, 12 Mar 1944, 1 son, (2) Marina Castano, 1991. Education: University of Madrid, 1933-36, 1939-43. Publications: Fiction: La Familia de Pascual Duarte, 1942, English translation as Pascual Duarte's Family, 1946; Pabellón de reposo, 1943, English translation as Rest Home, 1961; Nuevas andanzas y desventuras de Lazarillo de Tormes, 1944; Caminos inciertos: La colmena, 1951, English translation as The Hive, 1953; Santa Balbina 37: Gas en cada piso, 1952; Timoteo, el incomprendido, 1952; Mrs Caldwell habla con su hijo, 1953, English translation as Mrs Caldwell Speaks to Her Son, 1968; Café de artistas, 1955; Historias de Venezuela: La catira, 1955; Tobogán de hambrientos, 1962; Visperas, festividad y octava de San Camilo del año 1936 en Madrid, 1969; Oficio de tinieblas 5, o, Novela de tesis escrita para ser cantada por un de enfermos, 1973; Mazurca para doe muertos, 1983; Cristo versus Arizona, 1988; Also many volumes of stories. Poetry: Pisando la dudosa luz del día, 1945; Reloj de Sangre, 1989. Non-Fiction: Diccionario Secreto, 2 volumes, 1968, 1971; Enciclopedia del Erotismo, 1976-77; Memorias, entendimientos y voluntades (memoirs), 1993. Other: Volumes of essays, travel books. Honours: Premio de la crítica, 1955; Spanish National Prize for Literature, 1984; Nobel Prize for Literature, 1989; Planeta Prize, 1994. Membership: Real Academia Espanola, 1957. Address: c/o Agencia Literaria Carmen Balcells, Diagonal 580, 08021 Barcelona, Spain.

CELATI Gianni, b. 1937, Sondrio, Ferrara, Italy. Novelist. Appointments: Lecturer in Anglo-American Literature, University of Bologna. Publications: Comiche, 1971; Le avventure di Guizzardi, 1971; Il chiodo in testa, 1975; Finzioni occidentali, 1975; La banda dei sospiri, 1976; La bottega dei mimi, 1977; Lunario del paradiso, 1978; Narratori delle pianure, 1985; Quattro novelle sulle apparenze, 1987; Verso la foce, 1989. Other: Parlamenti buffi, 1989; Profili delle nuvole, 1989. Editions and translations. Honours: Mondello Prize, 1990. Address: c/o Feltrinelli, Via Andegari 6, 20121 Milan, Italy.

CEREDIG. See: **REES David Benjamin.**

CESAIRE Aimé (Fernand), b. 25 June 1913, Basse-Pointe, Martinique, West Indies. Poet; Playwright. Education: École Normale Supérieure, Paris, 1935-39. Appointments: Mayor of Forte-de-France, 1945-84; President, Conseil Régional Martinique, 1983-86. Publications: Les Armes miraculeuses, 1946; Notebook of a Return to the Native Land, 1947; Soloeil cou-coupe, 1948; Lost Body, 1960; Ferrements, 1960; Cadastre, 1961; State of the Union, 1966; Aimé Cesaire: The Collected Poetry, 1983; Non-Viscious Circle: Twenty Poems, 1984; Lyric and Dramatic Poetry 1946-83, 1990. Plays: Et les Chiens se taisaient, 1956; The Tragedy of King Christophe, 1964; A Season in the Congo, 1966; A Tempest, adaptation of Shakespeare, 1969. Other: Toussaint L'ouverture: la révolution française et le problème colonial, 1960. Honour: National Grand Prize for Poetry, 1982. Address: La Mairie, 97200 Fort-de-France, Martinique, West Indies.

CEZ. See: **RUDZINSKI Cezary Aleksander.**

CEZAR, Aleksander Rzepecki. See: **RUDZINSKI Cezary Aleksander.**

CHADWICK (William) Owen, b. 20 May 1916, Bromley, Kent, England. Historian. m. Ruth Hallward, 28 Dec 1949, 2 sons, 2 daughters. Education: BA, 1939, St John's College, Cambridge. Appointments: Dean, Trinity Hall, 1949-56, Master, Selwyn College, 1956-83, Dixie Professor of Ecclesiastical History, 1958-68, Regius Professor of Modern History, 1968-83, Cambridge University. Publications: John Cassian, 1950, revised edition, 1968; The Founding of Cuddesdon, 1954; From Bossuet to Newman, 1957, 2nd edition, 1987; Western Asceticism, 1958; Creighton on Luther, 1959; Mackenzie's Grave, 1959; Victorian Miniature, 1960, 2nd edition, 1991; The Mind of the Oxford Movement, 1960; From Uniformity to Unity 1662-1962 (with G Nuttall), 1962; Westcott and the University, 1962; The Reformation, 1964; The Victorian Church, Vol 1, 1966, 3rd edition, 1972; Vol II, 1970, 2nd edition, 1972; Acton and Gladstone, 1976; The Oxford History of the Christian Church (editor with Henry Chadwick, brother), 1976-; The Secularization of the European Mind, 1977; Catholicism and History, 1978; The Popes and European Revolution, 1981; Newman, 1983; Hensley Henson: A Study in the Friction Between Church and State, 1983; Britain and the Vatican in the Second World War, 1986; Michael Ramsey, 1990, 2nd edition, 1991; The Spirit of the Oxford Movement: Tractarian Essays, 1990; The Christian Church in the Cold War, 1992; A History of Christianity, 1995; A History of the Popes 1830-1914, 1998; Aston and History, 1998. Contributions to: Times (London); New Statesman; Spectator; Guardian; Sunday Times; Observer; History journals. Honours: Wolfson Prize for History, 1981; Knighted, 1982; Order of Merit, 1983. Memberships: Fellow, British Academy; Royal Historical Society, fellow. Address: 67 Grantchester Street, Cambridge CB3 9HZ, England.

CHADWICK Geoffrey. See: **WALL Geoffrey.**

CHADWICK Whitney, b. 28 July 1943, Niagara Falls, New York, USA. Professor of Art; Writer. m. Robert A Bechtle, 6 Nov 1982. Education: BA, Middlebury College, 1965; MA, 1968, PhD, 1975, Pennsylvania State University. Appointments: Lecturer, 1972, Assistant Professor, 1973-77, Associate Professor, 1978, Massachusetts Institute of Technology; Visiting Assistant Professor of Art History, University of California at Berkeley, 1977; Associate Professor, 1978-82, Professor of Art, 1982-, San Francisco State University; Visting Professor, Massachusetts College of Art, 1996; Visiting Scholar, Institute for Research on Women and Gender, Stanford University, 1997-98. Publications: Myth and Surrealist Painting, 1929-1939, 1980; Women Artists and the Surrealist Movement, 1985; Women, Art, and Society, 1990; Significant Others: Creativity and Intimate Partnership, 1993; Leonora Carrington: La Realidad de la Imaginacion, 1995; Framed, 1998; Mirror Images: Women, Surrealism and Self-Representaion (editor), 1998. Contributions to: Books, scholarly journals, and exhibition catalogues; Oxford Art Journal. Honours: National Endowment for the Humanities Fellowship, 1981-82; Senior Scholar, American Council of Learned Societies Fellowship; British Council Travel Grant, 1994; Eleanor Tufts Distinguished Visiting Lecturer, Southern Methodist University, 1995. Address: 871 De Haro Street, San Francisco, CA 94107, USA.

CHADZINIKOLAU Nikos, b. 1935, Trifilli, Greece. Education: Philological Studies; School of Music. Appointments: Educator, primary, secondary and tertiary education. Publications: 60 books including, 25 volumes of poetry, 2 novels: The History of Freek Literature; Translated into Polish; Sappho's Songs, Aesop's Fables, Sophocles' Dramas Antigone, Electra, King Oedipus; The Aphorism of Greeks; Zorba the Greek of Nikos Kazantzakis; Polish Fairy Tales. Honour: Polish Nobel Prize Winner, 1996. Memberships: Polish Forum of Young Writers and Poets. Address: ul L Staffa 61, 60-194 Poznan, Poland.

CHAGALL David, b. 22 Nov 1930, Philadelphia, Pennsylvania, USA. Author; Journalist. m. Juneau Joan Alsin, 15 Nov 1957. Education: Swarthmore College, 1948-49; BA, Pennsylvania State University, 1952; Sorbonne, University of Paris. Appointments: Associate Editor, IEE, 1960-61; Investigative Reporter, Nation Magazine, 1975-; Editor, Publisher, Inside Campaigning, 1984; Contributing Editor, Los Angeles Magazine, 1986-89; Host, TV Series, The Last Hour, 1994-. Publications: The Century God Slept, 1963; Diary of a Deaf Mute, 1971; The Spieler for the Holy Spirit, 1972; The New Kingmakers, 1981; Television Today, 1981; The Sunshine Road, 1988; The World's Greatest Comebacks, 1989; Surviving the Media Jungle, 1996; Media and Morality, 1999. Contributions to: Periodicals. Honours: Carnegie Award, 1964; National Book Award, 1972; Health Journalism Award, 1980; Presidential Achievement Award, 1982. Memberships: Authors Guild; American Academy of Political Science. Address: PO Box 85, Agoura Hills, CA 91376, USA.

CHAKRAVARTI Sasthibrata. See: **BRATA Sasthi.**

CHALFONT Baron, (Alun Arthur Gwynne Jones), b. 5 Dec 1919, Llantarnam, Wales. Member, House of Lords; Writer. m. Mona Mitchell, 6 Nov 1948, 1 daughter dec. Education: West Monmouth, Wales. Appointments: Regular Officer, British Army, 1940-61; Broadcaster and Consultant on Foreign Affairs, BBC, 1961-64; Minister of State, Foreign and Commonwealth Office, 1964-70; Permanent Representative, Western European Union, 1969-70; Foreign Editor, New Statesman, 1970-71; Chairman, Industrial Cleaning Papers, 1979-86, All Party Defence Group of the House of Lords, 1980-, Peter Hamilton Security Consultants Ltd, 1984-86, VSEL Consortium, later VSEL plc, 1987-95, Radio Authority, 1991-94, Marlborough Stirling Group, 1994-; Director, W S Atkins International, 1979-83, IBM UK Ltd, 1973-90, Lazard Brothers & Company Ltd, 1983-90, Shandwick plc, 1985-95, Triangle Holdings, 1986-90; President,

Abington Corporation Ltd, 1981-, Nottingham Building Society, 1983-90. Publications: The Sword and the Spirit, 1963; The Great Commanders (editor), 1973; Montgomery of Alamein, 1976; Waterloo: Battle of Three Armies (editor), 1979; Star Wars: Suicide or Survival, 1985; Defence of the Realm, 1987; By God's Will: A Portrait of the Sultan of Brunei, 1989. Contributions to: Periodicals and journals. Honours: Officer of the Order of the British Empire, 1961; Created a Life Peer, 1964; Honorary Fellow, University College of Wales, 1974; Liveryman, Worshipful Company of Paviors; Freeman of the City of London. Memberships: International Institute for Strategic Studies; Royal Institute of International Affairs; Royal Society of the Arts, fellow; United Nations Association, chairman, 1972-73. Address: House of Lords, London SW1A 0PW, England.

CHALKER Jack L(aurence), b. 17 Dec 1944, Norfolk, Virginia, USA. Editor; Writer. m. Eva C Whitley, 1978. Education: BA, Towson State College, 1966; MLA, Johns Hopkins University, 1969. Appointments: Founder-Editor, 1960-72, Editorial and Marketing Director, 1961-, Mirage Press Ltd, Baltimore. Publications: Numerous science fiction and fantasy novels, including: A Jungle of Stars, 1976; Dancers in the Afterglow, 1978; The Web of the Chosen, 1978; A War of Shadows, 1979; And the Devil Will Drag You Under, 1979; The Devil's Voyage, 1981; The Identity Matrix, 1982; The Messiah Choice, 1985; Downtiming the Night Side, 1985; The Armlet of the Gods, 1986; The Red Tape War (with Mike Resnick and George Alec Effinger), 1991; Various series. Short Stories: Dance Band on the Titanic, 1988. Other: In Memoriam: Clark Ashton Smith (editor), 1963; Mirage on Lovecraft (editor), 1964; The Necronomicon: A Study (with Mark Owings), 1968; An Informal Biography of Scrooge McDuck, 1974; Jack Chalker (autobiography), 1985. Memberships: Science Fiction Writers of America; World Science Fiction Society. Address: c/o Ace Books, 200 Madison Avenue, New York, NY 10016, USA.

CHALMERS Mary Eilleen, b. 16 Mar 1927, Camden, New Jersey, USA. Author; Artist. Education: Diploma, College of Art, 1945-48; Barnes Foundation, 1948-49. Publications: A Christmas Story, 1956; Throw a Kiss, Harry, 1958; Take a Nap, Harry, 1964; Come to the Doctor, Harry, 1981; 6 Dogs, 23 Cats, 45 Mice and 116 Spiders, 1986; Easter Parade, 1988. Address: 4Q Laurel Hill Road, Greenbelt, MD 20770, USA.

CHALON Jon. See: CHALONER John.

CHALONER John (Seymour), (Jon Chalon), b. 1924, London, England. Writer. Education: Royal Military College, Sandhurst. Publications: Three for the Road, 1954; Eager Beaver, 1965; The Flying Steamroller, 1966; The House Next Door, 1967; Sir Lance A Little and the Knights of the Kitchen Table, 1971; The Green Bus, 1973; Family Hold Back, 1975; The Dustman's Holiday, 1976; To the Manor Born, 1978; The Great Balloon Adventure; Will O the Wheels and Speedy Sue, 1990; Occupational Hazard, 1991. Honour: Bundesverdienstkreuz 1st Class for Services to Anglo-German Relations, 1990. Address: 4 Warwick Square, London SW1, England.

CHAMBERS Aidan, b. 27 Dec 1934, Chester-le-Street, County Durham, England. Author; Publisher. m. Nancy Harris Lockwood, 30 Mar 1968. Education: Borough Road College, Isleworth, London University. Publications: The Reluctant Reader, 1969; Introducing Books to Children, 1973; Breaktime, 1978; Seal Secret, 1980; The Dream Cage, 1981; Dance on My Grave, 1982; The Present Takers, 1983; Booktalk, 1985; Now I Know, 1987; The Reading Environment, 1991; The Toll Bridge, 1992; Tell Me: Children, Reading and Talk, 1993; Only Once, 1998; Postcards From No Man's Land, 1999; Contributions to: Numerous magazines and journals. Honours: Children's Literature Award for Outstanding Criticism, 1978; Eleanor Farjeon Award, 1982; Silver Pencil Awards, 1985, 1986, 1994. Membership: Society of Authors. Address: Lockwood, Station Road, Woodchester, Stroud, Gloucs GL5 5EQ, England.

CHAMBERS Marjorie (Elizabeth), b. 15 May 1938, Dromore, County Tyrone, Northern Ireland. University Teacher; Translator. m. Cyril Weir Chambers, 30 June 1969, 1 son. Education: BA, 1962, MA, 1968, Trinity College, Dublin; Sorbonne, University of Paris, 1961-62; PGCE, Goldsmiths College, London, 1964; University of Thessalonika, 1981. Appointments: Teacher, Institute of Continuing Education, 1980-98, School of Greek, Roman, and Semitic Studies, 1985-90, School of Modern Languages, 1990-98, Queen's University, Belfast. Contributions to: Translations of poems and short stories in journals and magazines, 1987-96. Memberships: Association of University Teachers; Greek Institute, Northern Ireland Representative, 1976-94, Northern Ireland Examiner, 1980-98; Standing Committee on Modern Greek in the Universities, 1985-98; Society of Authors Translators' Association. Address: 3 The Esplanade, Holywood, County Down BT18 9JG, Northern Ireland.

CHAMBERS Raymond J(ohn), b. 16 Nov 1917, Newcastle, New South Wales, Australia. Professor Emeritus of Accounting. m. Margaret Scott Brown, 9 Sept 1939, 1 son, 2 daughters. Education: DSc, Economics, 1939; BEc, University of Sydney, 1973. Appointments: Senior Lecturer, 1953-55, Associate Professor, 1955-59, Professor of Accounting, 1960-82, Professor Emeritus, University of Sydney; Member, Inaugural Editorial Committee, Journal of Accounting Research, 1962-64; Founder and Editor, Abacus, 1964-75. Publications: Financial Management, 1947; Function and Design of Company Annual Reports, 1955; Accounting and Action, 1957; The Accounting Frontier, 1965; Accounting, Evaluation and Economic Behavior, 1966; Accounting Finance and Management, 1969; Securities and Obscurities, 1973; Price Variation and Inflation Accounting, 1980; Foundations of Accounting, 1991; An Accounting Thesaurus, 1995. Contributions to: Chambers on Accounting, 1986; Professional journals. Honours include: Erskine Fellowship, University of Canterbury, 1971; Officer of the Order of Australia, 1978; Life Member, Australian Society of Accountants, 1979; Gordon Fellowship, Deakin University, 1989; R J Chambers PhD Scholarship established by the Accounting and Finance Foundation, University of Sydney, 1991; Inaugural AAANZ Award, for Outstanding Contribution to accounting research literature, 1996; Three Honorary Doctorates from universities. Address: 18 Amy Street, Blakehurst, NSW 2221, Australia.

CHAMPAGNE Maurice (Joseph Pierre), b. 7 May 1936, Montreal, Quebec, Canada. Philosopher; Human Rights Consultant. m. 1 son, 1 daughter. Education: MA, Montreal, 1956; DES, 1967, DLitt, 1968, Nice. Appointment: Literature Teaching Coordinator, Quebec Education Department, 1968-69. Publications: La Vlolewce Au Powvoir, 1971; Lettres D'Amour, 1972; La Famille et L'Homme A Délivrer du Pouvoir, 1980; Batir ou Détruire le Quebec, 1983; L'Homme-Tetard, 1991. Contributions to: Le Devoir and Lapresse. Honour: Governor-General of Canada Award, 1980. Memberships: Quebec Writers Union; Quebec Criminology Association; Quebec Human Rights Commission; Civil Liberties Union. Literary Agent: Louise Myette. Address: 3741 Saint Andre, Montreal, Quebec, H2L 3V6, Canada.

CHAMPION Larry Stephen, b. 27 Apr 1932, Shelby, North Carolina, USA. Professor Emeritus of English; Writer. m. Nancy Ann Blanchard, 22 Dec 1956, 1 son, 2 daughters. Education: BA, Davidson College, 1954; MA, University of Virginia, 1955; PhD, University of North Carolina, 1961. Appointments: Instructor, Davidson College, 1955-56; University of North Carolina, Chapel Hill, 1959-60; Instructor, 1960-61, Assistant Professor, 1961-65, Associate Professor, 1965-68, Professor of English, 1968-94, North Carolina State University. Publications: Ben Jonson's "Dotages": A Reconsideration of the Late Plays, 1967; The Evolution of Shakespeare's Comedy: A Study in Dramatic Perspective, 1970; Quick Springs of Sense: Studies in the Eighteenth Century (editor), 1974; Shakespeare's Tragic Perspective: The Development of His Dramatic Technique, 1976; Tragic

Patterns in Jacobean and Caroline Drama: A Study in Perspective, 1977; Perspective in Shakespeare's English Histories, 1980; King Lear: An Annotated Bibliography Since 1940, 2 volumes, 1981; Thomas Dekker and the Traditions of English Drama, 1985, 2nd edition, 1987; The Essential Shakespeare: An Annotated Bibliography of Major Modern Studies, 1986, 2nd edition, revised, 1993; The Noise of Threatening Drum: Dramatic Strategy and Political Ideology in Shakespeare and the English Chronicle Plays, 1990. Contributions to: Books and scholarly journals. Honours: Academy of Outstanding Teachers Award, 1966; Alumni Distinguished Professor, 1987. Memberships: Modern Language Association; National Council of Teachers of English; Phi Beta Kappa; Phi Kappa Phi; Renaissance English Text Society; Renaissance Society of America. Address: 5320 Sendero Drive, Raleigh, NC 27612, USA.

CHAMPOUX Pierrette, b. 26 Jan 1930, Montréal, Quebec, Canada. Journalist; Radio Reporter; Singer; Composer. Education: Dramatic School. Appointments: Daily News Reporter, Radio Station CKVL-Verdun; Writer for several newspapers and magazines; Composer, Songs, Music; Numerous public appearances on TV Shows, Radio Programs; Fashion Commentator. Publications: Parle-Moi Du Canada, 1992; Raconte-Moi-Montreal, 1992; Les Pionnieres, 1992; Quebec, en Ballades, 1994; Sur Les Bords Du St-Laurent, 1966, Un Enfant, 1979. Contributions to: Canada Nouveau; Radio-Monde. Honours: Grand Prix, Women's International Year's Contest, 1975; Honorable Mention, Canadian Committee for the International Year of the Handicapped, 1981; 1st Prize, Le Concours International des Arts et Lettres, France, 1993. Memberships: Women's Press Club; United Nations Canadian Association, Montreal Branch; La Société des Ecrivains Canadiens; L'Union des Artistes, Socan. Address: 1770 rue Perrot, Ile Perrot, Quebec J7V 7P2, Canada.

CHAN Stephen, b. 11 May 1949, Auckland, New Zealand. Professor in International Relations and Ethics; Writer; Poet. Education: BA, 1972, MA, 1975, University of Auckland; MA, King's College, London, 1977; PhD, University of Kent, Canterbury, 1992. Appointments: International Civil Servant, Commonwealth Secretariat, 1977-83; Lecturer in International Relations, University of Zambia, 1983-85; Visiting Lecturer in International Relations, Victoria University of Wellington, 1986; Faculty, University of Kent, 1987-96; Visiting Professor, Graduate Institute of International Studies, Geneva, 1991; University of Tampere, 1994-95; Visiting Lecturer, University of Natal, 1992; Professor in International Relations and Ethics, Head of International Studies, Dean of Humanities, Nottingham Trent University, 1996-. Publications: Scholarly: The Commonwealth Observer Group in Zimbabwe: A Personal Memoir, 1985; Issues in International Relations: A View from Africa, 1987; The Commonwealth in World Politics: A Study of International Action, 1965-85, 1988; Exporting Apartheid: Foreign Policies in Southern Africa, 1978-1988, 1990; Social Development in Africa Today: Some Radical Proposals, 1991; Kaunda and Southern Africa: Image and Reality in Foreign Policy, 1991; Twelve Years of Commonwealth Diplomatic History: Commonwealth Summit Meetings, 1979-1991, 1992; Mediation in South Africa (editor with Vivienne Jabri), 1993; Renegade States: The Foreign Policies of Revolutionary States (editor with Andrew Williams), 1994; Towards a Multicultural Roshamon Paradigm in International Relations, 1996; Portuguese Foreign Policy in Southern Africa (with Moises Venancio), 1996; Theorists and Theorising in International Relations (editor with Jarrold Wiener), 1997; War and Peace in Mozambique (with Moses Vanancio), 1998; Giving Thought: Currents in International Relations (editor, with Jarrold Wiener), 1998; Twentieth Century International History (Editor with Jarrold Wiener), 1998; The Rise and Fall of Kenneth Kaunda, forthcoming; Poetry: Postcards from Paradise (with Rupert Glover and Merlene Young), 1971; A Charlatan's Mosaic: New Zealand Universities Literary Yearbook (editor), 1972; Arden's Summer, 1975; Songs of the Maori King, 1986; Crimson Rain, 1991. Honours: Visiting fellowships; Honorary LittD, WAAC,

Istanbul; Honorary Professor, University of Zambia, 1993-95. Address: c/o Department of International Studies, Nottingham Trent University, Clifton Lane, Nottingham NG11 8NS, England.

CHANCE Jane, b. 26 Oct 1945, Neosho, Missouri, USA. Professor of English; Writer; Poet; Editor. m. (1) Dennis Carl Nitzsche, June 1966, div 1967, 1 daughter, (2) Paolo Passaro, 30 Apr 1981, 2 sons. Education: BA, English, Purdue University, 1967; AM, English, 1968, PhD, English, 1971, University of Illinois. Appointments: Lecturer, 1971-72, Assistant Professor of English, 1972-73, University of Saskatchewan; Assistant Professor, 1973-77, Associate Professor, 1977-80, Professor of English, 1980-, Rice University; Member, Institute for Advanced Study, Princeton, New Jersey, 1988-89; General Editor, Library of Medieval Women, 1988-; Visiting Research Fellow, Institute for Advanced Studies in the Humanities, University of Edinburgh, 1994; Eccles Research Fellow, University of Utah, 1994-95; Various guest lectureships. Publications: The Genius Figure in Antiquity and the Middle Ages, 1975; Tolkien's Art: A 'Mythology for England', 1979; Woman as Hero in Old English Literature, 1986; Christine de Pizan, The Letter of Othea to Hector, Translated with Introduction and Interpretative Essay, 1990; Tolkien's Lord of the Rings: The Mythology of Power, 1992; Medieval Mythology: From Roman North Africa to the School of Chartres, AD 433 to 1177, 1994; The Mythographic Chaucer: The Fabulation of Sexual Politics, 1995. Editor: Mapping the Cosmos (with R O Wells Jr), 1985; Approaches to Teaching Sir Gawain and the Green Knight (with Miriam Youngerman Miller), 1986; The Mythographic Art: Classical Fable and the Rise of the Vernacular in Early France and England, 1990; Medievalism in the Twentieth Century, 1991; Inklings and Others, 1991; Gender and Text in the Later Middle Ages, 1996; Assembly of Gods, 1999. Contributions to: Scholarly books and journals. Honours: Honorary Research Fellow, University College, London, 1977-78; National Endowment for the Humanities Fellowship, 1977-78; Guggenheim Fellowship, 1980-81; Rockefeller Foundation Residency, Bellagio, Italy, 1988; South Central Modern Language Association Best Book Award, 1994. Memberships: American Association of University Professors; Authors Guild; Christine de Pizan Society; Gower Society; International Association of Neo-Latin Studies; International Society in Classical Studies; Medieval Academy of America; Modern Language Association; New Chaucer Society; South Central Modern Language Association; Texas Faculty Association. Address: 2306 Wroxton Road, Houston, TX 77005, USA.

CHANCE Stephen. See: **TURNER Philip William.**

CHANCELLOR Alexander Surtees, b. 4 Jan 1940, Ware, Hertfordshire, England. Journalist. m. Susanna Elisabeth Debenham, 1964, 2 daughters. Education: Eton; Trinity Hall, Cambridge. Appointments: Staff, Reuters News Agency, 1964-74, Independent Television News, 1974-75; Editor, The Spectator, 1975-84, Time and Tide, 1984-86, The Independent, 1986-88, The Independent Magazine, 1989-92; Associate Editor, The Sunday Telegraph, 1994-. Address: 1 Souldern Road, London W14 0JE, England.

CHANDLER David (Geoffrey), b. 15 Jan 1934, England. Military Historian. Education: DLitt, Oxford, 1991. Appointments: British Army Officer, 1957-60; Lecturer, 1960-64, Senior Lecturer, 1964-69, Deputy Head, 1969-80, Head, 1980-94, Royal Military Academy, Sandhurst; President, 1967-86, President Emeritus, 1986-, British Military History Commission; Vice President, International Commission of Military History, 1975-94; Editor, David Chandler's Newsletter on the Age of Napoleon, 1987-89; Military Affairs Visiting Professor, Quantico, 1991; Trustee, Royal Armouries, Tower of London, later Leeds, 6 years. Publications: A Traveller's Guide to Battlefields of Europe, 1965; The Campaigns of Napoleon, 1966; Marlborough as Military Commander, 1973; The Art of Warfare on Land, 1975; The Art of Warfare in the Age of Marlborough, 1976; Atlas of Military Strategy, 1980, 2nd edition, 1996; A Journal of Marlborough's Wars, 1984; Napoleon's Military Maxims, 1987; On the Napoleonic Wars, 1994; The Oxford Illustrated History of the British Army, 1994. Contributions to: History Today. Honours: Literary Award, Napoleonic Society of America, 1994; Literary Award, International Napoleonic Society of Canada, 1995. Memberships: European Union of Re-enactment Societies; Napoleonic Society of Great Britain; Royal Historical Society, fellow. Address: Hindford, Monteagle Lane, Yateley, Hampshire, England.

CHANDLER Frank. See: **HARKNETT Terry.**

CHANEY Edward P(aul) de G(ruyter), b. 11 Apr 1951, Hayes, Middlesex, England. Professor. m. Lisa Maria Jacka, 15 Sept 1973, 2 daughters. Education: BA, University of Reading, 1975; MPhil, 1977, PhD, 1982, Warburg Institute, University of London; Researcher, European University Institute, Florence, 1978-81. Appointments: Lecturer, University of Pisa, 1979-85; Adjunct Assistant Professor, Charles A Strong Center, Georgetown University Florence Program, Villa Le Balze, Florence, 1982, 1983; Associate, Harvard University Center for Italian Renaissance Studies, Florence, 1984-85; Shuffrey Research Fellow in Architectural History, Lincoln College, Oxford, 1985-90; Part-time Lecturer, Oxford Polytechnic, 1991, Oxford Brookes University, 1993-; Historian, London Division, English Heritage, 1991-93. Publications: Oxford, China and Italy: Writings in Honour of Sir Harold Acton on his Eightieth Birthday (editor with N Ritchie), 1984; The Grand Tour and the Great Rebellion: Richard Lassels and 'The Voyage of Italy' in the Seventeenth Century, 1985; Florence: A Travellers' Companion (with Harold Acton), 1986; England and the Continental Renaissance: Essays in Honour of J B Trapp (editor with Peter Mack), 1990; English Architecture: Public and Private: Essays for Kerry Downes (editor with John Bold), 1993; The Evolution of the Grand Tour, 1998; Inigo Jones's 'Roman Sketchbook', forthcomng. Contributions to: Reference works, books, scholarly journals, periodicals, etc. Honours: Laurea di Dottore in Lingue e Letterature Straniere, University of Pisa, 1983; Honorary Life Member, British Institute of Florence, 1984; Elected Fellow, Society of Antiquaries, 1993. Memberships: Beckford Society; British-Italian Society; Catholic Record Society; Georgian Group; International Berkeley Society; Leonardo da Vinci Society; Renaissance Society; Royal Stuart Society; Society of Architectural Historians; Wyndham Lewis Society. Address: Southampton Institute, East Park Terrace, Southampton SO14 0YN, England.

CHANG Lee. See: **LEVINSON Leonard.**

CHANTLER Ashley, b. 14 Feb 1974, Ashford, Kent. Student. Education: BA, MA, University of Leicester. Publications: Essay, William Burroughs: In My Kind of Angel, 1999; Lateral Moves, 1999. Contributions to: Poetry and Prosse in: Vigil, 1997, 1998; Peace and Freedom, 1998; Poetry Now, 1997; Poetry Today, 1997, 1998. Address: 4 Westbury Road, Leicester, LE2 6AG, England.

CHAPLIN Jenny, (Tracie Telfer, Wendy Wentworth), b. 22 Dec 1928, Glasgow, Scotland. Head Mistress; Editor; Publisher; Writer. m. J McDonald Chaplin, 21 Apr 1951, 1 daughter. Education; Jordanhill College of Education, 1946-49. Appointments: Editor, Founder, Publisher, International, The Writers Rostrum, 1984-93; Organiser, Lecturer, Writers Workshop, Raring to Go, 1991. Publications: Tales of a Glasgow Childhood, 1994; Happy Days in Rothesay, 1995; From Scotland's Past, 1996; Childhood Days in Glasgow, 1996; An Emigrant's Farewell, in A Scottish Childhood, Vol II, anthology of memoirs from famous Scottish people, 1998. Contributions to: The Scots Magazine; The Highlander Magazine; Scottish Memories. Address: Tigh na Mara Cottage, 14 Ardbeg Road, Rothesay, Bute PA20 0NJ, Scotland.

CHAPMAN (Constance) Elizabeth, b. 5 Jan 1919. Writer. m. Frank Chapman, 22 Nov 1941, 3 sons. Education: College of Technology, Barnsley, 1938-39. Publictions: Marmaduke the Lorry, 1953; Marmaduke and Joe, 1954; Riding with Marmaduke, 1955; Merry Marmaduke, 1957; Marmaduke and His Friends, 1958; Marmaduke and the Elephant, 1959; Marmaduke and the Lambs, 1960; Marmaduke Goes to France, 1961; Marmaduke Goes to Holland, 1963; Marmaduke Goes to America, 1965; Marmaduke Goes to Italy, 1970; Marmaduke Goes to Switzerland, 1977; Marmaduke Goes to Spain, 1978; Marmaduke Goes to Morocco, 1979; Marmaduke Goes to Wales, 1982; Marmaduke Goes to Scotland 1986; Marmaduke Goes to Ireland, 1987. Contributions to: Sunny Stories; Radio Short Stories, Listen With Mother; TV Short Stories, Rainbow. Address: 88 Grange Gardens, Pinner, Middlesex HA5 5QF, England.

CHAPMAN Ivan Douglas, b. 14 Feb 1919, Werris Creek, New South Wales, Australia. Journalist; Military Historian. m. Moria Helen Menzies, 12 Sept 1953, 3 daughters. Education: Sydney Technical College, 1946-47. Appointments: Journalist, ABC News Radio, 1947-52, TV, 1956-76, BBC News, Radio, 1952-54, TV, 1954-56, 1973-74, SBS News Radio, 1979-80. Publications: Details Enclosed; Iven G Mackay; Private Eddie Leonski; Toyko Calling. Contributions to: Australian Dictionary of Biography; Australian Encylopaedia; Weekend Australian; The Bulletin; British History Illustrated; Time Life Books. Memberships: Australian Society of Authors; National Press Club, Canberra; Journalists Club Sydney; Ex PoW Association of Australia. Address: c/o Australian Society of Authors, PO Box 1566, Strawberry Hills, New South Wales 2012, Australia.

CHAPMAN Jean, b. 30 Oct 1939, England. Writer. m. Lionel Alan Chapman, 24 Mar 1951, 1 son, 2 daughters. Education: BA (Hons), Open University, 1989. Appointments: Creative Writing Tutor for East Midlands Arts and Community Colleges. Publications: The Unreasoning Earth, 1981; Tangled Dynasty, 1984; Forbidden Path, 1986; Savage Legacy, 1987; The Bell Makers, 1990; Fortune's Woman, 1992; A World Apart, 1993; The Red Pavilion, 1995; The Soldier's Girl, 1997; This Time Last Year, 1999. Other: Many short stories. Honours: Shortlisted, Romantic Novel of Year, 1982, 1996, and Kathleen Fidler Award, 1990. Memberships: Society of Authors; Romantic Novelists Association. Literary Agent: Jane Judd. Address: 3 Arnesby Lane, Peatling Magna, Leicester LE8 5UN, England.

CHAPMAN Stanley D(avid), b. 31 Jan 1935, Nottingham, England. Professor; Writer. Education: BSc, London School of Economics and Political Science, 1956; MA, University of Nottingham, 1960; PhD, University of London, 1966. Appointments: Lecturer, 1968-73, Pasold Reader in Business History, 1973-, Professor, 1993-, University of Nottingham; Editor, Textile History Bi Annual. Publications: The Early Factory Masters, 1967; The Beginnings of Industrial Britain, 1970; The History of Working Class Housing, 1971; The Cotton Industry in the Industrial Revolution, 1972; Jesse Boot of Boots the Chemists, 1974; The Devon Cloth Industry in the 18th Century, 1978; Stanton and Staveley, 1981; The Rise of Merchant Banking, 1984; Merchant Enterprise in Britain from the Industrial Revolution to World War I, 1992. Address: Birchlea, Beetham Close, Bingham, Nottinghamshire NG13 8EQ, England.

CHAPPELL Fred (Davis), b. 28 May 1936, Canton, North Carolina, USA. University Teacher; Poet; Writer. m. Susan Nicholls, 2 Aug 1959, 1 son. Education: BA, 1961, MA, 1964, Duke University. Appointment: Teacher, University of North Carolina at Greensboro, 1964-; Poet Laureate, North Carolina, 1997. Publications: Poetry: The World Between the Eyes, 1971; River, 1975; The Man Twiced Married to Fire, 1977; Bloodfire, 1978; Awakening to Music, 1979; Wind Mountain, 1979; Earthsleep, 1980; Driftlake: A Lieder Cycle, 1981; Midquest, 1981; Castle Tzingal, 1984; Source, 1985; First and Last Words, 1989; C: 100 Poems, 1993; Spring Garden: New and Selected Poems, 1995. Novels: It is Time, Lord, 1963; The Inkling, 1965; Dagon, 1968; The Gaudy Place, 1972; I Am One of

You Forever, 1985; Brighten the Corner Where You Are, 1989; Farewell, I'm Bound to Leave You, 1996. Short Fiction: Moments of Light, 1980; More Shapes Than One, 1991. Collection: The Fred Chappell Reader, 1987. Other: Plow Naked: Selected Writings on Poetry, 1993; A Way of Happening: Observation of Contemporary Poetry, 1998. Honours: Rockefeller Grant, 1967-68; National Institute of Arts and Letters Award, 1968; Prix de Meilleur des Livres Étrangers, Académie Française, 1972; Sir Walter Raleigh Prize, 1972; Roanoke-Chowan Poetry Prizes, 1972, 1975, 1979, 1980, 1985, 1989; North Carolina Award in Literature, 1980; Bollingen Prize in Poetry, 1985; World Fantasy Awards, 1992, 1994; T S Eliot Prize, Ingersoll Foundation, 1993; Aiken Taylor Award in Poetry, 1996. Address: 305 Kensington Road, Greensboro, NC 27403, USA.

CHAPPLE J(ohn) A(lfred) V(ictor), b. 25 Apr 1928, Barnstaple, Devonshire, England. Professor Emeritus; Writer. Education: BA, 1953, MA, 1955, University College, London. Appointments: Assistant, University College, 1953-55; Research Assistant, Yale University, 1955-58; Assistant Lecturer, Aberdeen University, 1958-59; Assistant Lecturer, 1959-61, Lecturer, 1961-67, Senior Lecturer, 1967-71, Manchester University; Professor, 1971-92, Professor Emeritus, 1992-, Hull University; Visiting Fellow, Corpus Christi College, Cambridge, 1991-92. Publications: The Letters of Mrs Gaskell, 1966; Documentary and Imaginative Literature 1880-1920, 1970; Elizabeth Gaskell: A Portrait in Letters, 1980; Science and Literature in the 19th Century, 1986; Private Voices: The Diaries of Elizabeth Gaskell and Sophia Holland, 1996; Elizabeth Gaskell: The Early Years, 1998. Memberships: Brontë Society; Gaskell Society, chairman, 1992-; International Association of University Professors of English; Larkin Society. Address: 173 Newland Park, Hull, Yorkshire HU5 2DX, England.

CHARD Dorothy Doreen, (Judy Chard), b. 8 May 1916, Tuffley, Gloucester, England. Writer. m. Maurice Noel Chard, 26 July 1941. Education: Elstree Junior School, Eastbourne, England, 1927-29; St Winifred's School, Eastbourne, 1929-33; Matriculated, 1932. Publications: 1973-94: Through the Green Woods; The Weeping and the Laughter; Encounter in Berlin; The Uncertain Heart; The Other Side of Sorrow; In the Heart of Love; Out of the Shadows; All Passion Spent; Seven Lonely Years; The Darkening Skies; When the Journey's Over; Haunted by the Past; Sweet Love Remembered; Where the Dream Begins; Rendezvous with Love; Hold Me in Your Heart; To Live With Fear; Wings of the Morning; A Time to Love; Wild Justice; Person Unknown; For Love's Sake Only; To Be So Loved; Enchantment; Appointment with Danger; Betrayed; Encounter in Spain, 1994. Contributions to: 300 short stories; 12 local books on Devon. Address: Morley Farm, Highweek, Newton Abbot, Devon TQ12 6NA, England.

CHARLES Francis. See: **DE BONO Edward.**

CHARLES Gerda, b. 1930, Liverpool, England. Novelist. Education: Liverpool schools. Appointments: Journalist and Reviewer for New Statesman, Daily Telegraph, New York Times, Jewish Chronicle, and other periodicals; Television Critic, Jewish Observer, London, 1978-79. Publications: The True Voice, 1959; The Crossing Point, 1960; A Slanting Light, 1963; A Logical Girl, 1967; The Destiny Waltz, 1971; Several short stories. Honours: James Tait Black Memorial Prize, 1964; Whitbread Award, 1971. Address: 22 Cunningham Court, London W9 1AE, England.

CHARLES Nicholas. See: **KUSKIN Karla.**

CHARLIER Roger H(enri), (Henri Rochard), b. 10 Nov 1924, Antwerp, Belgium (Belgian and US citizen). Geologist; Geographer; Oceanographer; Professor Emeritus; Writer. m. Patricia Mary Simonet, 17 June 1958, 1 son, 1 daughter. Education: Lic Pol and Ec Sc, 1941, Lic Sc, 1945, Free University of Brussels; PhD, Friedrich Alexander University, Erlangen, 1947; Diploma, Industrial College of the Armed Forces, Washington, DC, 1952; Postdoctoral Diploma, Graduate School of Geography, McGill University, 1953; LittD, 1957, ScD, 1958, University of Paris. Appointments: Professor of Geology, Geography and Oceanography, 1961-87, Professor Emeritus, 1988-, Northeastern IL University; Visiting Professor, 1970-74, 1983, 1984, Honorary Professor en Associé, 1986-, University of Bordeaux I; Professor Extraordinary, 1971-87, Professor Emeritus, 1988-, Free University of Brussels; Executive Director, Institute for the Development of Riverine and Estuarine Systems, 1974-76; Adjunct Professor, Union Graduate School, 1980-90; Member, European Community, XII General Directorate, Commission on Bioconversion, 1985-92; Scientific Advisor, SOPEX NV, Antwerp, 1988-89, HAECON IV, Ghent, 1984-88, 1989-. Publications: Ocean Resources: An Introduction to Economic Oceanography, 1976; Marine Science and Technology, 1981; Tidal Energy, 1982; Ocean Energies: Environmental, Economic and Social Significance, 1993; Coastal Erosion: Response and Management, 1998. Contributions to: Numerous books, scholarly journals, and periodicals. Honours: Great Medal, University of Bordeaux, 1973; Fulbright Scholar, 1975, 1976; Paul-Henri Spaak Memorial Lecture Award, 1992; Various grants and awards. Memberships: Association of American University Professors; Geological Society of America; International Association for the History of Oceanography; Marine Technology Society; National Academy of Sciences, Letters and Arts, France; New Jersey Academy of Science; Royal Belgian Society for Geographical Studies. Address: 4055 North Keystone Avenue, Chicago, IL 60641, USA.

CHARLIP Remy, b. 10 Jan 1929, New York, New York, USA. Actor; Dancer; Choreographer; Director; Writer; Illustrator. Education: BFA, Cooper Union, 1949. Appointments: Choreographer, London Contemporary Dance Theatre, 1972-76, Scottish Theatre Ballet, 1973, Welsh Dance Theatre, 1974; Director, Remy Charlip Dance Co; Guest lecturer at colleges and universities. Publications: The Dead Bird, 1958, 1986; I Love You, 1967, 1999; Arm in Arm, 1973, 1997; Hooray for Me! (with Lilian Moore), 1975; Thirteen, 1975; First Remy Charlip Reader, 1986; Sleeptime Rhyme, 1999, Peanut Butter Party, 1999; Various self-illustrated children's books. Other: Amaterasu (performance piece), 1988; Young Omelet (play), 1991; Halequin (musical), 1997. Honours: Ingram Merrill Awards, 1961, 1963; Obie Awards, 1965, 1966; 1st Prize, Bologna Book Fair, 1971; 2 Gulbenkian Awards, 1972; Boston Globe/Horn Book Award, 1976; Award for Professional Achievement, Cooper Union of Fine Arts, 1988. Address: 521 Precita Avenue, San Francisco, CA 94110, USA.

CHARNAS Suzy McKee, b. 22 Oct 1939, New York, New York, USA. Writer. m. Stephen Charnas, 4 Oct 1968, 1 stepson, 1 stepdaughter. Education: BA, Barnard College, 1961; MA, New York University, 1965. Publications: Walk to the End of the World, 1974; Motherlines, 1979; The Vampire Tapestry, 1980; The Bronze King, 1985; Dorothea Dreams, 1986; The Silver Glove, 1988; The Golden Thread, 1989; The Kingdom of Kevin Malone, 1993; Vampire Dreams (play), 1990; The Furies, 1994; The Ruby Tear, 1997. Contributions to: Womens Review of Books. Honours: Nebula Award, 1980; Hugo Award, 1989. Memberships: Authors Guild; Science Fictiopn Writers of America; Dramatists Guild. Address: 212 High Street North East, Albuquerque, NM 87102, USA.

CHARNY Carmi, (T Carmi), b. 31 Dec 1925, New York, New York, USA (Israeli citizen). Poet; Editor; Teacher. m. Lilach Peled, 3 sons. Education: BA, Yeshiva University, 1946; Graduate Studies, Columbia University, 1946, Sorbonne, University of Paris, 1946-47, Hebrew University, 1947, 1949-51. Appointments: Co-Editor, Massa, bi-weekly, Tel Aviv, 1951-54; Editor, Orot, quarterly, Jerusalem, 1955; Sifriat Hapoalim Publishers, Tel Aviv, 1957-62; Am Oved Publishers, Tel Aviv, 1963-70; Ziskind Visiting Professor of Humanities, Brandeis University, 1969-70; Adjunct Associate Professor, University of Tel Aviv, 1971-73; Editor-in-Chief, Ariel, quarterly, Jerusalem, 1971-74; Visiting Fellow, Oxford Centre for Postgraduate Hebrew Studies, 1974-76; Visiting Professor, Hebrew Union College, Jerusalem, 1978-, Stanford University, 1979, Yale University, 1986, New York University, 1986, University of Texas at Austin, 1987. Publications: Poetry: As T Carmi: Mum Vahalom, 1951; Eyn Prahim Shehorim, 1953; Sheleg Birushalayim, 1955; Hayam Ha'aharon, 1958; Nehash Hanehoshet, 1961, English translation as The Brass Serpent, 1964; Ha'unicorn Mistakel Bamar'ah, 1967; Tevi'ah, 1967; Davar Aher/Selected Poems, 1951-1969, 1970; Somebody Likes You, 1971; Hitnatslut Hamehaber, 1974; T Carmi and Dan Pagis: Selected Poems (with Dan Pagis), 1976; El Erets Aheret, 1977; Leyad Even Hato'im, 1981, English translation as At the Stone of Losses, 1983; Hatsi Ta'avati, 1984; Ahat Hi Li, 1985; Shirim Min Ha'azuva, 1989; Emet Vehova, 1993. Editor: As T Carmi: The Modern Hebrew Poem Itself (with Stanley Burnshaw and Ezra Spicehandler), 1965; The Penguin Book of Hebrew Verse, 1981. Other: Translations of plays into Hebrew. Contributions to: Periodicals. Honours: Brenner Prize for Literature, 1972; Prime Minister's Awards for Creative Writing, 1973, 1994; Jewish Memorial Foundation Grants, 1975, 1990; Kovner Award for Poetry, Jewish Book Council, 1978; Guggenheim Fellowship, 1987-88; Tel Aviv Foundation for Literature and Art Grant, 1988; Bialik Prize, 1990; Honorary Doctor of Humane Letters, Hebrew Union College, Jewish Institute of Religion, 1993. Memberships: Academy for the Hebrew Language; Writers Assocaition of Israel. Address: Hebrew Union College, Jewish Institute of Religion, 13 King David Street, Jerusalem 94101, Israel.

CHARYN Jerome, b. 13 May 1937, New York, New York, USA. Author; Educator. Education: BA, Columbia College, 1959. Appointments: English Teacher, High School of Music and Art, School of Performing Arts, New York City, 1962-64; Assistant Professor, Stanford University, 1965-68; Professor, Herbert Lehman College, City University of New York, 1968-80; Founding Editor, The Dutton Review, 1970; Lecturer, Princeton University, 1980-86; Professor of Film Studies, American University of Paris, 1995-. Publications: Once Upon a Droshky, 1964; On the Darkening Green, 1965; Going to Jersualem, 1967; American Scrapbook, 1969; The Single Voice: An Anthology of Contemporary Fiction, 1969; The Troubled Vision, 1970; The Tar Baby, 1973; Blue Eyes, 1975; Marilyn the Wild, 1976; The Franklin Scare, 1977; Secret Isaac, 1978; The Seventh Babe, 1979; Darlin' Bill, 1980; Panna Maria, 1982; Pinocchio's Nose, 1983; The Isaac Quartet, 1984; Metropolis, 1986; Paradise Man, 1987; Movieland, 1989; The Good Policeman, 1990; Maria's Girls, 1992; Montezuma's Man, 1993; Little Angel Street, 1994; El Bronx, 1997; The Dark Lady from Bulornsie, 1997; Death of a Tango King, 1998; Citizen Sidul, 1999; Captain Kidd, 1999. Memberships: PEN; Mystery Writers of America; International Association of Crime Writers. Literary Agent: George Borchardt. Address: 302 West 12th Street, Apt 10c, New York, NY 10014, USA.

CHASE Elaine Raco, b. 31 Aug 1949, Schenectady, New York, USA. Author. m. Gary Dale Chase, 26 Oct 1969, 1 son, 1 daughter. Education: AA, Albany Business College, 1968; Union College, 1968; State University of New York, 1977. Publications: Rules of the Game, 1980; Tender Yearnings, 1981; A Dream Come True, 1982; Double Occupancy, 1982; Designing Woman, 1982; No Easy Way Out, 1983; Video Vixen, 1983; Best Laid Plans, 1983; Special Delivery, 1984; Lady Be Bad, 1984; Dare the Devil, 1987; Dark Corners, 1988; Partners in Crime, 1994; Amateur Detective (non-fiction), 1996; Rough Edges, forthcoming. Contributions to: Loves Leading Ladies and How to Write a Romance; Lovelines; So You Want a TV Career; Fine Art of Murder; Sex and The Mystery Novel; Who Are All These Sister's in Crime. Honours: Walden Book Award, 1985; Top Romantic Supsense Series Award, 1987-88; Agatha Christie Award nomination for best non-fiction, 1997. Memberships: Romance Writers of America; Sisters in Crime, national president, 1995-96. Address: 4333 Majestic Lane, Fairfax, VA 22033, USA.

CHASE Glen. See: **LEVINSON Leonard.**

CHASE Isobel. See: **DE GUISE Elizabeth (Mary Teresa).**

CHATTERTON-NEWMAN Roger, b. 17 Mar 1949, Haslemere, Surrey, England. Author. Appointment: Editorial Staff, Haymarket Publishing, 1970-89; Deputy Editor, PQ International. Publications: A Hampshire Parish, 1976; Brian Boru, King of Ireland, 1983; Murtagh and the Vikings, 1986; Betwixt Petersfield and Midhurst, 1991; Edward Bruce: A Medieval Tragedy, 1992; Polo at Cowdray, 1992; Murtagh the Warrior, 1996. Contributions to: Hampshire Magazine; Horse and Hound; Polo Quarterly International; West Sussex History; Downs Country; International Polo Review; The Ring Fort Annual. Honour: Commendation, Reading Association of Ireland Awards, 1987. Address: Rose Cottage, Rake, West Sussex GU33 7JA, England.

CHATTOPADHYAY Ashoke, (Haranath Thakur), b. 25 Nov 1957, Basudevpur, Daspur, Midnapore District, West Bengal, India. Journalist; Poet; Story Writer; Essayist; Archaeologist. m. Anima Chattopadhyay, 13 Aug 1987, 1 son. Education: HS, WBBSE, 1977; BA, 1981, MA, Journalism, 1988, Calcutta University; Certificate in Museum Studies, Indian Museum, Calcutta. Appointments: Honorary Curator, Paribrazak Panchanan Roy Museum and Culture Centre, 1983-; Trainee, Indian Museum, Calcutta, 1986; West Bengal Government Accredited Press Reporter, 1987-. Publications: Uro-Megh, poetry book, 1989; The Ghatal Year Book, co-author, 1989; Ghatal Barsa Panji, co-author, 1990-91; Professor Dr Pranab Roy's Jeeban Panji, life history, 1990; Sei-Nadi-Et-Jal, poetry, 1990; Editor, poetry: Hunttey-Hunttey-Eto-Door, 1991; Kabi-O-Kabita-Daspur, 1991; Editor, periodicals: Chetua Sambad, 1985; Purnima, 1986; Eai-Purnima, 1989; Sisti, 1996; Bharati, 1997. Contributions to: Desh; Jugantar; Dainik Basumati; Ganasakti; Aagikal; Bartaman; Bharatkatha; Kalantar; Many small magazines. Honours: Best Editor, 1987, Best Poet, 1988, Chandrakona Sahitya Sansad; Daspur thana Nikhil varat Samabay Saptaha Award, 1988; Aalor Joyar Sahitya Garbete Medal, 1988, 1993; Srinagar Mallick Academy Literary Medal, 1991; Hare Krishnapur Sandipan Sahitya and Sanskriti Award, 1992; Sonali Rod Sahitya Award, 1994; Sukanta Award, 1995; Harirampur Cultural Centre Award, 1997; Midnapore Sahitya Sansad Kabyashree Award, 1997. Memberships: Paribrazak Panchanan Roy Museum and Culture Centre, Founder, Executive Member, 1980-; Chetua Sahitya Sangstha, Founder, Secretary, 1985; Nikhil Banga Kabi Parisad, 1985-; Bangiya Sahitya, 1985-; Ghatal Sub-Division Press Club, 1985-, former International Secretary; Chetua Daspur Sahitya Sanskriti Sansad, Founder, General Secretary, 1986-; All-India Rural Newspaper Association, 1987-; District Journalists Association, Founder, Executive Member, Vice-President, 1997-; Several others. Address: Vill Basudevpur, PO Sankarpur, PS Daspur, Dist Midnapore, West Bengal, PIN 721211, India.

CHAUDHURI Amit, b. 15 May 1962, Calcutta, India. Author. m. Rinka Khastgir, 12 Dec 1991. Education: BA, University College, London, 1986; DPhil, Balliol College, Oxford, 1993. Appointment: Creative Arts Fellow, Wolfson College, Oxford, 1992-95. Publications: A Strange and Sublime Address, 1991; Afternoon Raag, 1993. Contributions to: Numerous publications. Honours: Betty Trask Award, 1991; Commonwealth Writers Prize, 1992; Southern Arts Literature Prize, 1993; Arts Council of Great Britain Writers Award, 1993-94; Encore Prize, Society of Authors, 1994. Address: 6 Sunny Park, Flat 10, 8th Floor, Calcutta 700019, India.

CHEDID Andrée, b. 20 Mar 1920, Cairo, Egypt. Poet; Novelist; Dramatist. m. Louis A Chedid, 23 Aug 1942, 1 son, 1 daughter. Education: Graduated, American University of Cairo, 1942. Publications: Poetry Collections: Textes pour un poème (1949-1970), 1987; Poèmes pour un texte (1970-91), 1991. Novels: Le Sommeil délivré, 1952, English translation as From Sleep Unbound, 1983; Jonathon, 1955; Le Sixième Jour, 1960, English translation as The Sixth Day, 1988; L'Autre, 1969; La Cité fertile, 1972; Nefertiti et le reve d'Akhnaton, 1974; Les Marches de sable, 1981; La Maison sans racines, 1985, English translation as The Return to Beirut, 1989; L'Enfant multiple, 1989. Play: Bérénice d'Egypte, 1981. Other: The Prose and Poetry of Andrée Chedid: Selected Poems, Short Stories, and Essays (Renée Linkhorn, translator), 1990. Honours: Prix Louise Labe, 1966; Grand Prix des Lettres Francaise, l'Académie Royale de Belgique, 1975; Prix de l'Académie Mallarmé, 1976; Prix Goncourt, 1979; Prix de Poèsie, Société des Gens de Lettres, 1991; Prix de PEN Club International, 1992. Membership: PEN Club International. Address: c/o Flammarion, 26 rue Racine, Paris 75006, France.

CHELEKIS George C, b. 21 Sept 1951, Ithaca, New York, USA. Author; Journalist. m. Gwen Content, 7 July 1979, 1 daughter. Education: BA, summa cum laude, English Language and Literature, Ohio University, 1973. Publications: The Complete Guide to US Government Real Estate, 1989; The Action Guide to Government Auctions, 1989; Distress Sale!, 1990; The Magic of Credit, 1991; The Official Government Auction Guide, 1992; The Action Guide to Government Grants, Loans and Give-Aways, 1993. Contributions to: Nation's Business; Sky Magazine; Boardroom Reports; Consumer's Digest; Entrepreneur; Business; Bull and Bear. Honour: Gold Charlie, 1993. Memberships: American Society of Journalists and Authors; WISE; International Association of Scientologists. Literary Agent: Jane Gelfman. Address: PO Box 2401, Clearwater, FL 34617, USA.

CHELES Luciano, b. 7 Sept 1948, Cairo, Egypt. Senior Lecturer in Italian Studies. Education: BA, Italian and French Studies, Reading University, 1973; PGCE, University College, Cardiff, 1974; MPhil, History of Art, Essex University, 1980; PhD, Lancaster University, 1992. Appointments: Senior Lecturer in Italian Studies, Lancaster University, 1994-; Visiting Lecturer, University of Lyons II, 1994-95, 1996. Publications: The Studiolo di Urbino: An Iconographic Investigation, 1986, revised and expanded Italian edition as Lo Studiolo di Urbino: Iconografia di un microcosmo principesco, 1991; Neo-Fascism in Europe (editor with R G Ferguson and M Vaughan), 1991, revised and expanded edition as The Far Right in Western and Eastern Europe, 1995; Grafica Utile: L'affiche d'utilité publique en Italie, 1975-1995, 1995, revised edition, 1997; The Art of Persuasion: Political Communication in Italy, from 1945 to the 1990's, 1999. Contributions to: Scholarly books and journals. Honour: Special Prize, Premio Frontino-Montefeltro, 1992. Memberships: Association for the Study of Modern Italy; Istituto di Studi Rinascimentali; Society for Italian Studies; Society for Renaissance Studies. Address: c/o Department of European Languages and Cultures, Lancaster University, Lancaster, LA1 4YN, England.

CHEN Jo-Hsi, b. 15 Nov 1938, Taiwan. Novelist. Education: BA, Taiwan National University, 1961; MA, Johns Hopkins University, 1965. Appointments: Lecturer, University of California at Berkeley, 1983. Publications: Fiction: Mayor Yin, 1976; Selected works by Jo-Hsi Chen, 1976; The Old Man, 1978; Repatriation, 1978; The Execution of Mayor Yin, and Other Stories from the Great Proletarian Cultural Revolution, 1978; Inside and Outside the Wall, 1981; Tu Wei, 1983; Selected Short Stories by Jo-Hsi Chen, 1983; Foresight, 1984; The Two Hus, 1985; Paper Marriage, 1986; The Old Man and Other Stories, 1986; Woman from Guizhou, Taipei, 1989; Wangzhou's Sorrows, Taipei, 1995; Home of Daughters, 1998; Create a Paradise, 1998. Other: Reminiscences of the Cultural Revolution, 1979; Random Notes, 1981; Democracy Wall and the Unofficial Journals, 1982; Read to Kill Time, 1983; Flower Grown Naturally, 1987; Trip to Tibet, 1988; Trip to Inner Mongolia, 1988; Temptation of the Tibetan Plateau. Honour: Wu Zhuoliu Prize, 1978. Address: 428 Boynton Avenue, Berkeley, CA 94707, USA.

CHENG Tsu-yu, b. 18 Mar 1916, China. Professor; Senior Research Fellow. m. Ting Kwee Choo, 1944, 1 son. Education: Diploma of Rhetoric, Institute of Language Teaching, Waseda University, Tokyo, 1964-65. Appointments: Visiting Professor, Graduate Division of Literature, Waseda University, Tokyo, 1964-65; Professor, Daito Bunka University, 1978-80; Senior Research Fellow, Institute of Chinese Studies, Chinese University of Hong Kong, 1984-; Visiting Professor, Peking University, 1992-. Publications: Poetry and Poetics of Lu Xun, 1951; Criticism of the Works of Huang Zunxian, 1959; Tokyo Lectures, 1963; Evolution of Chinese Rhetoric, 1965; Sinological Research in Japan, 1972; The History of Chinese Rhetoric, 1984; Rhetorical Criticism of the Works of the Eight Prose Masters of the Tang and Song Dynasties, 1992; Self-Selected Academic Works, 1994. Contributions to: Journals. Honours: Advisory Professor, Fudan University, Shanghai, 1986-; Advisor, South China Rhetorical Society, Shanghai, 1986-; Honorary Councillor and Academic Consultant, China Rhetorical Society, Peking, 1987; Honorary Award, Second Chinese National Book Awards. Memberships: China Society, Singapore. Address: Institute of Chinese Studies, Chinese University of Hong Kong, Shatin, NT, Hong Kong.

CHERNOW Ron, b. 3 Mar 1949, New York, New York, USA. Author. m. Valerie Stearn, 22 Oct 1979. Education: BA, Yale College, 1970; MA, Pembroke College, Cambridge, 1972. Publications: The House of Morgan: An American Banking Dynasty and the Rise of Modern Finance, 1990; The Warburgs: The Twentieth-Century Odyssey of a Remarkable Jewish Family, 1993; Titan: The Life of John D Rockefeller Sr, 1998. Contributions to: Various periodicals. Honours: Jack London Award, United Steelworkers of America, 1980; National Book Award, 1990; Ambassador Book Award, English-Speaking Union of the United States, 1990. Memberships: Authors Guild; Phi Beta Kappa. Address: c/o Melanie Jackson, 250 West 57th Street, Suite 1119, New York, NY 10107, USA.

CHERRY Carolyn Janice, (C J Cherryh), b. 1 Sept 1942, St Louis, Missouri, USA. Writer. Education: BA, University of Oklahoma, 1964; MA, Johns Hopkins University, 1965. Publications: The Faded Sun, 1978; Downbelow Station, 1981; The Pride of Chanur, 1982; Chanur's Venture, 1984; Forty Thousand in Gehenna, 1984; Cuckoo's Egg, 1985; Chanur's Homecoming, 1986; Visible Light, 1986; Angel with the Sword, 1987; The Paladin, 1988; Rusalka, 1989; Rimrunners, 1990; Chernevog, 1991; Heavy Time, 1991; Chanur's Legacy, 1992; The Goblin Mirror, 1993; Hellburner, 1993; Faery in Shadow, 1994; Tripoint, 1994; Fortress in the Eye of Time, 1995; Invader, 1995; Rider at the Gate, 1995; Cloud's Rider, 1996; Lois and Clark, 1996; Inheritor, 1996; Fortress of Owls, 1998. Honours: John Campbell Award, 1977; Hugo Awards, 1979, 1982, 1989. Memberships: National Space Society; Science Fiction Writers of America. Address: c/o Warner Books Inc, 1271 Avenue of the Americas, New York, NY 10020, USA.

CHERRY Kelly, b. Baton Rouge, Louisiana, USA. Professor; Writer; Poet. m. Jonathan B Silver, 23 Dec 1966, div 1969. Education: Du Pont Fellow, University of Virginia, 1961-63; MA, University of North Carolina, 1967; Visiting Lecturer, 1977-78, Professor, 1978-79, Assistant Associate Professor, 1979-82, Professor 1982-83, Romnes Professor of English, 1983-88, Evjue-Bascom Professor in the Humanities, 1993-, Eudora Welty Professor of English, 1997-, University of Wisconsin at Madison; Writer-in-Residence, Southwest State University, Marshall, Minnesota, 1974, 1975; Visiting Professor and Distinguished Writer-in-Residence, Western Washington University, 1981; Faculty, MFA Program, Vermont College, 1982, 1983; Distinguished Visiting Professor, Rhodes College, Tennessee, 1985. Publications: Fiction: Sick and Full of Burning, 1974; Augusta Played, 1979; Conversion, 1979; In the Wink of an Eye, 1983; The Lost Traveller's Dream, 1984; My Life and Dr Joyce Brothers, 1990; The Society of Friends, 1999; History, Passion, Freedom, Death and Hope (essays and criticism), forthcomming. Poetry: Lovers and Agnostics, 1975, revised edition, 1995; Relativity: A Point of View, 1977; Songs for a Soviet Composer, 1980; Natural Theology, 1988; Benjamin John, 1993; God's Loud Hand, 1993; Time Out of Mind, 1994; Death and Transfiguration, 1997. Other: The Exiled Heart: A Meditative Autobiography, 1991; Writing the World (essays and criticism), 1995; History, Passion, Freedom, Death and Hope: Prose about Poetry, 1999. Translations:

Octavia, by Seneca; Antigone, by Sophocles. Contributions to: Anthologies and periodicals. Honours: Canaras Award, 1974; Bread Loaf Fellow, 1975; Yaddo Fellow, 1979, 1989; National Endowment for the Arts Fellowship, 1979; Romnes Fellowship, 1983; Wisconsin Arts Board Fellowships, 1984, 1989, 1994; Hanes Prize for Poetry, Fellowship of Southern Writers, 1989; Wisconsin Notable Author, 1991; Hawthornden Fellowship, Scotland, 1994; E B Coker Visiting Writer, Converse, 1996; Leidig Lectureship in Poetry, 1999. Membership: Associated Writing Programs, board of directors, 1990-93. Address: c/o Department of English, University of Wisconsin at Madison, Madison, WI 53706, USA.

CHERRYH C J. See: **CHERRY Carolyn Janice.**

CHESSEX Jacques, b. 1 Mar 1934, Payerne, France. Novelist; Poet. Education: Graduated, University of Lausanne, 1961. Publications: La Tête ouverte, 1962; La Confession du pasteur Burg, 1967; A Father's Love, 1973; L'Ardent Royaume, 1975; Le Séjour des morts, 1977; Les Yeux jaunes, 1979; Où vont mourir les oiseaux, 1980; Judas le transparent, 1983; Jonas, 1987; Morgane Madrigal, 1990. Poetry: Le Jour proche, 1954; Chant du printemps, 1955; Une Voix la nuit, 1957; Batailles dans l'air, 1959; Le Jeûne de huit nuits, 1966; L'Ouvert obscur, 1967; Elégie, soleil du regret, 1976; La Calviniste, 1983; Feux d'orée, 1984; Comme l'os, 1988. Non-Fiction: Maupassant et les autres, 1981; Mort d'un cimetière, 1989; Flaubert, ou, le désert en abîme, 1991. Honour: Prix Goncourt, 1973. Address: Editions Grasset, 61 Rue des Sts-Pères, 75006 Paris, France.

CHESTER Tessa Rose, b. 19 Oct 1950, Stanmore, Middlesex, England. Museum Curator; Writer; Poet. m. (1) Richard James Overy, 18 Apr 1969, 1 son, 2 daughters, (2) Ronald Albert Chester, 8 Aug 1980. Education: Harrow Art College, 1968-69; BA (Hons), Polytechnic of North London, 1981. Appointment: Curator of Childrens Books, Bethnal Green Museum of Childhood, London, 1982-. Publications: A History of Children's Book Illustration; Childrens' Books Research; Sources of Information About Childrens' Books; Provisions of Light, poetry, 1996. Contributions to: Times Educational Supplement; Phaedrus; International Review of Childrens' Literature and Librarianship; Galleries; The Library; Signal; Country Life; Poetry Review; The Rialto. Address: Bethnal Green Museum of Childhood, Cambridge Heath Road, London E2 9PA, England.

CHEYNEY-COKER Syl, b. 28 June 1945, Freetown, Sierra Leone. Senior Lecturer; Poet. Education: University of Oregon, 1967-70; University of California, 1970; University of Wisconsin, 1971-72. Appointments: Visiting Professor of English, University of the Philippines, Quezon City, 1975-77; Senior Lecturer, University of Maiduguri, Nigeria, 1979-. Publications: Concerto for an Exile, 1973; The Graveyard Also Has Teeth, 1974; The Blood in the Desert's Eyes: Poems, 1990. Address: c/o Department of English, University of Maiduguri, PMB 1069, Maiduguri, Nigeria.

CHHETRI Nabin, (Cyril), b. 29 July 1974, Nepal. Academy Principal; Lecturer; Editor. Education: DHM, Australia, 1993; MA, North Bengal University, 1996. Appointments: Principal, Amber Everest Academy; Editor, The O, International Poetic Bi-monthly Journal; MO, Cambridge School of Languages; Advisor to Nepal Poets Council. Publications: Entity, 1997; Our Today, 1997; Zero passion, 1998. Contributions to: Sun, India; The Quest; Writers Forum; Poet; Mawaheb; Wave; Metverse Muse. Honours: Forestell Award; Man of the Year, Nepal Poets Council. Memberships: International Writers Association; Poetry Club of India; World Congress of Poets; World Academy of Arts and Culture; World Poetry Society; Writers Forum; Nepal Poets Council; Kafla Inter-Continental. Literary Agent: Paix Société, Amber Everest Academy. Address: Amber Everest Academy, Bharatpur-10, Chitwan, Nepal.

CHICHETTO James William, b. 5 June 1941, Boston, Massachusetts, USA. Professor; Priest. Education: BA,

Stonehill College, 1964; MA, Holy Cross College, 1968; MA, Wesleyan University, 1978. Appointments: Ordained Priest, Congregation of Holy Cross, 1968; Educator, Missionary, Peru, South America, 1968-72; Associate Editor, Gargoyle Magazine, 1974-80; Editor, 1982-87, Artist, 1990-, The Connecticut Poetry Review; Professor of Writing, Stonehill College, North Easton, Massachusetts, 1982-. Publications: Poems, 1975; Dialogue: Emily Dickinson and Christopher Cauldwell, 1978; Stones: A Litany, 1980; Gilgamesh and Other Poems, 1983; Victims, 1987; Homage to Father Edward Sorin, 1992, 1998; Dream of Norumbega, forthcoming. Contributions to: Boston Phoenix; Colorado Review; Boston Globe; The Manhattan Review; The Patterson Review; The Connecticut Poetry Review; America; Others. Honours: Book Grant, National Endowment for the Arts, 1980, 1983; Sri Chinmoy Poetry Award, 1984. Membership: Connecticut Literary Forum, 1985-. Address: c/o Stonehill College, North Easton, MA 02357, USA.

CHILDS Elizabeth C(atharine), b. 5 July 1954, Denver, Colorado, USA. Associate Professor of Art History and Archaeology. m. John R Klein, 6 June 1987, 1 son. Education: BA, Wake Forest University, 1976; MA, 1980, PhD, 1989, Columbia University. Appointments: Part-time Lecturer, Department of Education, Metropolitan Museum of Art, New York City, 1979-81; Research Associate in Contemporary American Art, Solomon R Guggenheim Museum, New York City, 1979-81; Research Associate in Contemporary American Art, Solomon R Guggenheim Museum, New York City, 1987-91; Lecturer, 1987-89, Assistant Professor Art History, 1987-92, Purchase College, State University of New York; Assistant Professor, 1993-98, Associate Professor, State University of New York; Assistant Professor, 1993-98, Associate Professor of Art History and Archaeology, 1998-, Washington University, St Louis. Publications: Femmes d'esprit: Women in the Caricature of Honoré Daumier (editor and curator with Kirsten Powell), 1990; Suspended License: Censorship and the Visual Arts (editor), 1997; In Search of Paradise: Painting and Photography in Tahiti, 1880-1910, 1999. Contributions to: Scholarly books and journals. Honours: American Council of Learned Societies Fellowship, 1991; Gould Fellow, Princeton University, 1992-93; National Endowment for the Humanities Fellowship, 1996-97; Ailsa Mellon Bruce Senior Visiting Fellowship, National Gallery of Art, Washington, DC, 1997. Memberships: Association of Historians of Nineteenth-Century Art; College Art Association; French Colonial Historical Society; Interdisciplinary Nineteenth-Century Studies; Midwest Art History Society. Address: c/o Department of Art History and Archaeology, Campus Box 1189, Washington University, One Brookings Drive, St Louis, MO 63130, USA.

CHILVER Peter, b. 18 Nov 1933, Southend, Essex, England. Educator; Writer. Education: BA, 1956, MA, 1964, St Edmund Hall, Oxford; Diploma in Speech and Drama, Royal Academy of Dramatic Art, London, 1963; Postgraduate Certificate of Education, 1965, Academic Diploma in Education, 1969, MPhil, 1973, PhD, 1976, University of London. Appointments: Teacher, Inner London Education Authority, 1964-68; Senior Lecturer, Thomas Hucley College, 1968-77; Head of Department of English, Langdon School, 1977-. Publications: Improvised Drama, 1967; Talking Improvisation, 1969; Producing the Play, 1974; Teaching Improvised Dramas, 1978; Learning and Language in the Classroom, 1982; In the Picture Series, 1985; English Coursework for GCSE, 1987. Contributions to: Perspectives on Small Group Learning, 1990. Address: 27 Cavendish Gardens, Barking, Essex, England.

CHINERY Michael, b. 5 June 1938, London, England. Author. Education: MA, Jesus College, Cambridge, 1960. Publications: Pictorial Dictionary of the Animal World, 1966; with Michael Gabb: Human Kind, 1966, The World of Plants, 1966, The Life of Animals with Backbones, 1966; Patterns of Living (with David Larkin), 1966; Breeding and Growing, 1966; Pictorial Dictionary of the Plant World, 1967; Visual Biology, 1968; Purnell's

Concise Encyclopedia of Nature, 1971; Animal Communities, 1972; Animals in the Zoo, 1973; Field Guide to the Insects of Britain and Northern Europe, 1973; Life In the Zoo, 1976; The Natural History of the Garden, 1977; The Family Naturalist, 1977; Nature All Around, 1978; Discovering Animals, 1978; Killers of the Wild, 1979; Garden Birds (with Maurice Pledger), 1979; Collins Gem Guide to Butterflies and Moths, 1981; The Natural History of Britain and Europe, 1982; Collins Guide to the Insects of Britain and Western Europe, 1986; Garden Creepy Crawlies, 1986; The Living Garden, 1986; Collins Gem Guide to Insects, 1986; Exploring the Countryside, 1987; Butterflies and Day-Flying Moths of Britain and Europe, 1989; All About Baby Animals, 1990; Countryside Handbook, 1990; Shark; Butterfly; Ant; Spider; Snake; Frog (6 Children's Books), 1991; All About Wild Animals, 1991; Explore the World of Insects, 1991; Wild World of Animals: Rainforests 1991, Oceans 1991, Deserts 1991, Grasslands and Prairies 1991, Seashores 1992, Forests 1992, Polar Lands 1992, Lakes and Rivers 1992; The Kingfisher Natural History of Britain and Europe, 1992; Spiders, 1993; Garden Wildlife, 1997; Butterflies of Britain and Eurrope, 1998. Address: Mousehole, Mill Road, Hundon, Suffolk C010 8EG, England.

CHINERY William Addo, b. 5 Apr 1934, Ghana. Biomedical Scientist; University Professor. m. Bertha Catherine Laing, 3 Sept 1966, 4 sons. Education: BSc, Hons, 1959; DAP&E, 1961; PhD, 1963, London, England. Appointments: Government Medical Entomologist, Ministry of Health, Ghana, 1959; Research Officer, National Institute of Health and Medical Research, 1964; Lecturer, Senior Lecturer, Associate Professor, Ghana Medical School, 1968-80; Visiting Associate Professor, Harvard School of Public Health, USA, with ranking as Full Professor when participating in teaching at the Harvard Medical School, 1976-77; Professor, Ghana Medical School, 1980-94; Head of Microbiology Department, 1986-94; Member, Expert Advisory Panel, Vector Biol and Cont. World Health Organisation, 1976-85; Member, Editorial Board, Ghana Journal of Science, 1973-76. Publications: Author of over 72 scientific communications in Medical Entomology and Parasitology, Tropical Medicine and Public Health; Author of some 15 literary papers. Honours: Distinguished Student, London School of Hygiene and Tropical Medicine, 1974; One of three leading mosquito vector workers in Africa, WHO, 1985; Life Deputy Governor, ABIRA (ABI), 1989; Member, Advisory Council, IBA (IBC), 1990; KCMSS, 1990; Knight of Humanity KH, 1990; International Order of Merit (IBC), 1991; Fellow, Institute of Biology (UK), 1993; Fellow, World Literary Academy (FWLA-IBC), 1993. Memberships: Fellow, Royal Society of Tropical Medicine and Hygiene; Ghana Science Association; Institute of Biology, UK; Member and Executive Council Member, Ghana Institute for Laboratory Medicine, 1994. Address: PO Box MP 994, Mamprobi, Accra, Ghana.

CHISLETT (Margaret) Anne, b. 22 Dec 1942, St John's, Newfoundland, Canada. Dramatist. BA. Honours, Memorial University of Newfoundland, 1964; Theatre, University of British Columbia. Publications: A Summer Burning, 1977; The Tomorrow Box, 1980; Quiet in the Land, 1981; Another Season's Promise (with K Roulston), 1986; Half a Chance, 1987; The Gift, 1988; Yankee Notions, 1990; Glengarry School Days, 1994; Flippin' In, 1995. Honours: Chalmers Canadian Play Award, 1982; Governor-General's Award for drama, 1983; W C Good Award, 1990. Memberships: Alliance of Canadian Cinema, Television, and Radio Artists; Playwrights Union of Canada. Address: PO Box 46, Auburn, Ontario, Canada N0M 1E0.

CHISSELL Joan Olive, b. 22 May 1919, Cromer, Norfolk, England. Musicologist. Education: ARCM, GRSM, Royal College of Music, 1937-42. Appointments: Piano Teacher, Royal College of Music Junior Department, 1942-53; Lecturer, Extra-Mural Departments, Oxford and London Universities, 1942-48; Broadcaster, BBC, 1943-; Assistant Music Critic, The Times, 1948-79; Reviewer, The Gramophone, 1968-;

Jury Member, International Piano Competitions, Milan, Leeds, Zwickau, Budapest, Sydney, Newport and Dublin. Publications: Robert Schumann, 1948; Chopin, 1965; Schumann's Piano Music, 1972; Brahms, 1977; Clara Schumann: A Dedicated Spirit, 1983. Contributions to: A Companion to the Concerto, 1988; Numerous journals and magazines. Honour: City of Zwickau Robert Schumann Prize, 1991. Memberships: Critics Circle; Royal College of Music Society; Royal Life Boat Society. Address: Flat D, 7 Abbey Road, St Johns Wood, London NW8 9AA, England.

CHITHAM Edward Harry Gordon, b. 16 May 1932, Harborne, Birmingham, England. Education Consultant. m. Mary Patricia Tilley, 29 Dec 1962, 1 son, 2 daughters. Education: BA, MA (Classics), Jesus College, Cambridge, 1952-55; PGCE, University of Birmingham, 1955-56; MA, English, University of Warwick, 1973-77; PhD, University of Sheffield, 1983. Publications: The Black Country, 1972; Ghost in the Water, 1973; The Poems of Anne Brontë, 1979; Brontë Facts and Brontë Problems (with T J Winnifrith), 1983; Selected Brontë Poems (with T J Winnifrith), 1985; The Brontës' Irish Background, 1986; A Life of Emily Brontë, 1987; Charlotte and Emily Brontë (with T J Winnifrith), 1989; A Life of Anne Brontë, 1991; A Bright Start, 1995; The Poems of Emily Brontë (with Derek Roper), 1996; The Birth of Wuthering Heights: Emily Brontë at work, 1998. Contributions to: Byron Journal; Gaskell Society Journal; ISIS Magazine. Memberships: Fellow, Royal Society of Arts, 1997. Joint Association of Classics Teachers; Gaskell Society; Brontë Society. Address: 11 Victoria Road, Harborne, Birmingham B17 0AG, England.

CHITTOCK John (Dudley), b. 29 May 1928, England. Editor; Publisher; Writer. m. Joyce Kate Winter, 23 Aug 1947. Education: South West Technical College. Appointments: Executive Editor, Focal Press, 1954-58; Part-Time Editor, Industrial Screen, 1962-63; Film and Video Columnist, Financial Times, 1963-87; Founder/Publisher, 1971-96, Editor, 1971-74, Screen Digest; Inaugural Editor, Vision (British Academy of Film and Television Arts), 1976; Consultant Editor, Television: Journal of the Royal Television Society, 1978-82; Founder/Publisher, Training Digest, 1978-87; Chairman, Grierson Memorial Trust (documentary film award), 1974-. Chairman, Kraszna-Krausz Foundation (media book awards and grants), 1996-. Publications: Focal Encyclopedia of Photography, executive editor, 1956; How to Produce Magnetic Sound for Films, 1962; Film and Effect, 1967; An International Directory of Stock Shot Libraries, executive editor, 1969; Images of Britain, 1986. Contributions to: Numerous specialist media journals. Honours: Hood Medal, Royal Photographic Society, 1973; Queen's Silver Jubilee Medal, 1977; Presidential Award, Incorporated Institute of Professional Photography, 1983; Video Writer of the Year Award, 1983; Merit Award, British Kinematograph, Sound and Television Society, 1996; Officer of the Order of the British Empire; Fellow, British Kinematograph, Sound, and Television Society; Fellow, Royal Photographic Society; Fellow, Royal Television Society. Memberships: Royal Automobile Club, London; Life Member, Society of Motion Picture and Television Engineers, USA. Address: 37 Gower Street, London WC1E 6HH, England.

CHITTY Sir Thomas Willes (3rd Baronet), (Thomas Hinde), b. 2 Mar 1926, England. Author. m. Susan Elspeth, 1951, 1 son, 3 daughters. Education: University College, Oxford. Appointments: Granada Arts Fellow, University of York, 1964-65; Visiting Lecturer, University of Illinois, 1965-67; Visiting Professor, Boston University, 1969-70. Publications: Fiction: Mr Nicholas, 1952; Happy as Larry, 1957; For the Good of the Company, 1961; A Place Like Home, 1962; The Cage, 1962; Ninety Double Martinis, 1963; The Day the Call Came, 1964; Games of Chance: The Interviewer and the Investigator, 1965; The Village, 1966; High, 1968; Bird, 1970; Generally a Virgin, 1972; Agent, 1974; Our Father, 1975; Daymare, 1980. Non-Fiction: Spain, 1963; On Next to Nothing (with wife), 1976; The Great Donkey Walk (with wife), 1977; The Cottage Book, 1979; Sir Henry and Sons (autobiography), 1980; A Field Guide to the English

Country Parson, 1983; Stately Gardens of Britain, 1983; Capability Brown, 1986; The Domesday Book: England's Heritage, Then and Now (editor), 1986; Courtiers: 900 Years of Court Life, 1986; Tales from the Pumproom: An Informal History of Bath, 1988; Imps of Promise: A History of the King's School, Canterbury, 1990; Looking Glass Letters, 1991; Paths of Progress: A History of Marlborough College, 1993; A History of Highgate School, 1993; A History of King's College School, 1994; Carpenter's Children: A History of the City of London School, 1995; The University of Greenwich: A History, 1996; The Martlet and the Griffen: A History of Abingdon School, 1997. Literary Agent: John Johnson. Address: Bow Cottage, West Hoathly, Sussex RH19 4QF, England.

CHITTY Susan Elspeth, Lady Chitty, b. 18 Aug 1929, London, England. Writer; Journalist; Lecturer. m. Sir Thomas Willes Chitty, 1951, 1 son, 3 daughters. Education: Somerville College, Oxford. Publications: Fiction: The Diary of a Fashion Model, 1958; White Huntress, 1963; My Life and Horses, 1966. Non-Fiction: The Woman Who Wrote Black Beauty, 1972; The Beast and the Monk, 1975; Charles Kingsley and North Devon, 1976; On Next to Nothing (with husband), 1976; The Great Donkey Walk (with husband), 1977; The Young Rider, 1979; Gwen John 1876-1939, 1981; Now to My Mother, 1985; That Singular Person Called Lear, 1988. Editor: The Intelligent Woman's Guide to Good Taste, 1958; The Puffin Book of Horses, 1975; Antonia White: Diaries 1926-1957, 2 volumes, 1991-92; Playing the Game, biography of Henry Newbolt, 1997. Literary Agent: Curtis Brown. Address: Bow Cottage, West Hoathly, Sussex RH19 4QF, England.

CHIU Hungdah, b. 23 Mar 1936, Shanghai, China. Professor of Law; Author; Editor. m. Yuan-yuan Hsieh, 14 May 1966, 1 son. Education: LLB, National Taiwan University, 1958; MA, Long Island University, 1962; LLM, 1962, SJD, 1965, Harvard University. Appointments: Associate in Research, East Asian Research Center, 1964-65, Research Associate in Law, 1966-70, 1972-74, Harvard University; Associate Professor of International Law, National Chengchi University, 1970-72; Associate Professor of Law, 1974-77, Professor of Law, 1977-, University of Maryland at Baltimore; General Editor, Occasional Papers/Reprints Series in Contemporary Asian Studies, 1977-; Editor-in-Chief, Chinese Yearbook of International Law and Affairs, 1981-; Research Member, 1991-95, Member, 1995-, National Unification Council, Republic of China; Minister without Portfolio (Minister of State), Executive Yuan (Cabinet), Republic of China, 1993-94; Affilate Faculty Member, University of Maryland at College Park, 1995-. Publications: China and the Taiwan Issue (editor and contributor), 1979; The Chinese Connection and Normalization (co-editor), 1980; Agreements of the People's Republic of China, 1966-1980: A Calendar, 1981; Multi-system Nations and International Law: The International Status of Germany, Korea and China (co-editor and contributor), 1981; China: 70 Years After the 1911 Hsin-hai Revolution (co-editor and contributor), 1984; Criminal Justice in Post-Mao China: Analysis and Documents (co-author), 1985; The Future of Hong Kong, Toward 1997 and Beyond (co-editor and contributor), 1987; Survey of Recent Developments in China (Mainland and Taiwan) in 1985-86 (editor), 1987; The United States Constitution and Constitutionalism in China (co-editor), 1988; The Draft Basic Law of Hong Kong: Analysis and Documents (editor), 1988; The International Law of the Sea: Cases, Documents and Readings (co-author), 1991; Proceedings of the International Law Association (ILA) First Asian-Pacific Regional Conference (with Su Yun Chang, Chun-i Chen, and Chih-Yu Wu), 1996. Contributions to: Many scholarly journals. Honours: Certificate of Merit, American Society of International Law, 1976; Toulmin Medal, Society of American Military Engineers, 1982; Outstanding Achievement Award, Mid-America Chinese Science and Technology Association, 1991; 1st Class Merit Service Award, Executive Yuan (Cabinet), Republic of China, 1994. Memberships: American Association for Chinese Studies, president, 1985-87; Association of Chinese Social Scientists in North America, president,

1984-86; Chinese Society of International Law, president, 1993-. Address: c/o Department of Government and Politics, University of Maryland at College Park, College Park, MD 20742, USA.

CHODES John Jay, b. 23 Feb 1939, New York, New York, USA. Writer; Dramatist. Education: BA, Hunter College, City University of New York, 1963; Commercial Photography Certificate, Germain School of Photography, 1965. Appointments: Technical Advisor to Dustin Hoffman, Paramount Pictures Film Marathon Man. Publications: The Myth of America's Military Power, 1972; Corbitt, 1973; Bruce Jenner, 1977; Plays: Avenue A Anthology, 1969; Molineaux, 1979; Frederick Two, 1985; The Longboat, 1987; Molineaux (as Musical), 1995; A Howling Wilderness, forthcoming. Contributions to: Various publications. Honours: Journalistic Excellence Award, 1974; Outstanding Service Award, 1988. Memberships: Dramatists Guild; Professors World Peace Academy; Road Runners Club of New York; Libertarian Party of New York; Southern League. Literary Agent: Stephan Rosenberg. Address: 411 East 10th Street, 22G, New York, NY 10009, USA.

CHODRON Pema, b. 14 July 1936, New York City, New York, USA. Author; Buddhist Nun. 1 son, 1 daughter. Publications: The Wisdom of No Escape; Start Where You Are; When Things Fall Apart. Address: Gampo Abbey, Pleasant Bay, NS B0E 2P0, Canada.

CHOMSKY (Avram) Noam, b. 7 Dec 1928, Philadelphia, Pennsylvania, USA. Linguist; Philosopher; Professor; Author. m. Carol Doris Schatz, 24 Dec 1949, 1 son, 2 daughters. Education: BA, 1949, MA, 1951, PhD, 1955, University of Pennsylvania. Appointments: Assistant Professor, 1955-58, Associate Professor, 1958-61, Professor of Modern Languages, 1961-66, Ferrari P Ward Professor of Modern Languages and Linguistics, 1966-76, Institute Professor, 1976-, Massachusetts Institute of Technology; Visiting Professor, Columbia University, 1957-58; National Science Foundation Fellow, Institute for Advanced Study, Princeton, New Jersey, 1958-59; Resident Fellow, Harvard Cognitive Studies Center, 1964-65; Linguistics Society of America Professor, University of California at Los Angeles, 1966; Beckman Professor, University of California at Berkeley, 1966-67; John Locke Lecturer, Oxford University, 1969; Shearman Lecturer, University College, London, 1969; Bertrand Russell Memorial Lecturer, Cambridge University, 1971; Nehru Memorial Lecturer, University of New Delhi, 1972; Whidden Lecturer, McMaster University, 1975; Huizinga Memorial Lecturer, University of Leiden, 1977; Woodbridge Lecturer, Columbia University, 1978; Kant Lecturer, Stanford University, 1979; Jeanette K Watson Distinguished Visiting Professor, Syracuse University, 1982; Pauling Memorial Lecturer, Oregon State University, 1995. Publications: Syntactic Structures, 1957; Current Issues in Linguistic Theory, 1964; Aspects of the Theory of Syntax, 1965; Cartesian Linguistics, 1966; Topics in the Theory of Generative Grammar, 1966; Language and Mind, 1968; Sound Patterns of English (with Morris Halle), 1968; American Power and the New Mandarins, 1969; At War with Asia, 1970; Problems of Knowledge and Freedom, 1971; Studies on Semantics in Generative Grammar, 1972; For Reasons of State, 1973; The Backroom Boys, 1973; Counterrevolutionary Violence (with Edward Herman), 1973; Peace in the Middle East?, 1974; Bains de Sang (with Edward Herman), 1974; Reflections on Language, 1975; The Logical Structure of Linguistic Theory, 1975; Essays on Form and Interpretation, 1977; Human Rights and American Foreign Policy, 1978; Language and Responsibility, 1979; The Political Economy of Human Rights (with Edward Herman), 2 volumes, 1979; Rules and Representations, 1980; Radical Priorities, 1981; Lectures on Government and Binding, 1981; Towards a New Cold War, 1982; Some Concepts and Consequences of the Theory of Government and Binding, 1982; Fateful Triangle: The United States, Israel and the Palestinians, 1983; Modular Approaches to the Study of the Mind, 1984; Turning the Tide, 1985; Barriers, 1986; Pirates and Emperors, 1986; Knowledge of Language: Its

Nature, Origin and Use, 1986; Generative Grammar: Its Basis, Development and Prospects, 1987; On Power and Ideology, 1987; Language in a Psychological Setting, 1987; Language and Problems of Knowledge, 1987; The Chomsky Reader, 1987; The Culture of Terrorism, 1988; Manufacturing Consent (with Edward Herman), 1988; Language and Politics, 1988; Necessary Illusions, 1989; Deterring Democracy, 1991; Chronicles of Dissent, 1992; What Uncle Sam Really Wants, 1992; Year 501: The Conquest Continues, 1993; Rethinking Camelot: JFK, the Vietnam War, and US Political Culture, 1993; Letters from Lexington: Reflections on Propaganda, 1993; The Prosperous Few and the Restless Many, 1993; Language and Thought, 1994; World Orders, Old and New, 1994; The Minimalist Program, 1995; Powers and Prospects, 1996; The Common Good, 1998. Contributions to: Scholarly journals. Honours: Distinguished Scientific Contribution Award, American Psychological Association, 1984; George Orwell Awards, National Council of Teachers of English, 1987, 1989; Kyoto Prize in Basic Science, Inamori Foundation, 1988; James Killian Faculty Award, Massachusetts Institute of Technology, 1992; Lannan Literary Award, 1992; Joel Selden Peace Award, Psychologists for Social Responsibility, 1993; Homer Smith Award, New York University School of Medicine, 1994; Loyola Mellon Humanities Award, Loyola University, Chicago, 1994; Helmholtz Medal, Akademie der Wissenschaft, Berlin-Brandenburg, 1996; Many honorary doctorates. Memberships: American Academy of Arts and Sciences; American Association for the Advancement of Science, fellow; American Philosophical Association; Bertrand Russell Peace Foundation; British Academy, corresponding member; Deutsche Akademie der Naturforscher Leopoldina; Linguistics Society of America; National Academy of Sciences; Royal Anthropological Institute; Utrecht Society of Arts and Sciences. Address: 15 Suzanne Road, Lexington, MA 02420, USA.

CHORLTON David, b. 15 Feb 1948, Spittal-an-der-Drau, Austria. Writer; Poet; Artist. m. Roberta Elliott, 21 June 1976. Education: Stockport College, 1966-69. Publications: Without Shoes, 1987; The Village Painters, 1990; Measuring Time, 1990; Forget the Country You Came From, 1992; Outposts, 1994; The Insomniacs, 1994. Contributions to: Many reviews and journals. Memberships: PEN West; Writer's Voice. Address: 118 West Palm Lane, Phoenix, AZ 85003, USA.

CHOROSINSKI Eugene Conrad, b. 1 Jan 1930, Sienno, Poland (US Citizen). m. Anni Homeier, 23 Mar 1959, 3 daughters. Author; Poet. Education: LLB, Blackstone School of Law, 1968. Appointments: Chief field classifiction AMS, Ethiopia-US Mapping Mission, Addis Ababa, 1965-67; Intelligence Analyst, Combined Intelligence Centre, Vietnam, 1968-69; Senior Intelligence Advisor, DCAT 70, Lai Khe, South Vietnam, 1970-71; Intelligence Analyst, First Armoured Division, Support Command, Nuremberg, Germany, 1971-73; Private Investigator, Alexandria, Virginia, 1973-74; Chief, Zoning Review Department of Consumer and Regulatory Affairs, Government, Washington DC, 1974-85; Chairman, Disaster Damage Assessment ARC, Central Florida chapter, Orlando, 1995-96; Chairman, Parks and Trees Commission, Eustis, Florida, 1998-. Publication: Through the Years. Contributions to: Professional publications. Honours: Bronze Star; Air Medal; Joint Service Commendation Medal; National Defense Service Medal with Oak Leaf Cluster; Vietnam Service Medal with Silver Star; Editor's Choice Award for Outstanding Achievement in Poetry, National Library of Poetry; Honour Award, Special Citation for Exceptional Voluntary Service, ARC., 1994; Best Poet, 1995-96; Award of Recognition for Outstanding Achievement in Poetry, Famous Poets Society, 1998. Memberships: Life Member, International Society of Poets; National Association of Retired Federal Employees; Academy of American Poets, 1997-. Address: 131 Madrona Drive, Eustis, FL 32726, USA.

CHOW Claire, b. 15 Oct 1952, New Brunswick, NJ, USA. Marriage and Family Therapist. m. James L Beattie, 14 June 1980, 1 son, 1 daughter. Education: BA, Occidental College, 1974; MA, University of Chicago, 1975; MA, University of San Francisco, 1989. Appointments: Marriage and Family Therapist, private practice; Adjunct Professor, John F Kennedy University Graduate School of Professional Psychology. Publications: Leaving Deep Water: Lives of Asian-American Women at the Crossroads of Two Cultures, 1998. Contributions to: Too Great a Price: The Psychological Toll of Assimilation, 1994; Raising Children BiCulturally, 1998. Literary Agent: Barbara Lowenstein & Madeleine Morel. Address: 2551 San Ramon Valley Boulevard, Ste 210 San Ramon, CA 94583, USA.

CHOYCE Lesley, b. 21 Mar 1951, Riverside, New Jersey, USA (Canadian citizen). Professor; Writer; Poet; Editor. m. Terry Paul, 19 Aug 1974, 2 daughters. Education: BA, Rutgers University, 1972; MA, Montclair State College, 1974; MA, City University of New York, 1983. Appointments: Editor, Pottersfield Press, 1979-; Professor, Dalhousie University, 1986-. Publications: Adult Fiction: Eastern Sure, 1981; Billy Botzweiler's Last Dance, 1984; Downwind, 1984; Conventional Emotions, 1985; The Dream Auditor, 1986; Coming Up for Air, 1988; The Second Season of Jonas MacPherson, 1989; Magnificent Obsessions, 1991; Ectasy Conspiracy, 1992; Margin of Error, 1992; The Republic of Nothing, 1994; The Trap Door to Heaven, 1996;Beautiful Sadness, 1997, Dance the Rocks Ashore, 1998; World Enough, 1998. Young Adult Fiction: Skateboard Shakedown, 1989; Hungry Lizards, 1990; Wavewatch, 1990; Some Kind of Hero, 1991; Wrong Time, Wrong Place, 1991; Clearcut Danger, 1992; Full Tilt, 1993; Good Idea Gone Bad, 1993; Dark End of Dream Street, 1994; Big Burn, 1995; Falling Through the Cracks, 1996. Poetry: Re-Inventing the Wheel, 1980; Fast Living, 1982; The End of Ice, 1985; The Top of the Heart, 1986; The Man Who Borrowed the Bay of Fundy, 1988; The Coastline of Forgetting, 1995; Beautiful Sadness, 1998. Non-Fiction: An Avalanche of Ocean, 1987; December Six: The Halifax Solution, 1988; Transcendental Anarchy (autobiography), 1993; Nova Scotia: Shaped by the Sea, 1996. Editor: Chezzetcook, 1977; The Pottersfield Portfolio, 7 volumes, 1979-85; Visions from the Edge (with John Bell), 1981; The Cape Breton Collection, 1984; Ark of Ice: Canadian Futurefiction, 1992. Honours: Event Magazine's Creative Nonfiction Competition Winner, 1990; Dartmouth Book Awards, 1990, 1995; Ann Connor Brimer Award for Children's Literature, 1994; Authors Award, Foundation for the Advancement of Canadian Letters, 1995. Address: 83 Leslie Road, East Lawrencetown, Nova Scotia B2Z 1P8, Canada.

CHRAIBI Driss, b. 15 July 1926, El Jadida, Morocco. Novelist; Dramatist. m. Sheena McCallion, 1978. Education: Studied in Casablanca and Paris. Appointment: Professor, University of Laval, Quebec, 1969-70. Publications: The Simple Past, 1954; The Butts, 1955; L'Ane, 1956; De Tous les Horizons, 1958; La Foule, 1961; Heirs to the Past, 1962; Un ami viendra vous voir, 1966; La Mother Comes of Age, 1982; Mort au Canada, 1974; Une Enquête au Pays, 1981; Mother Spring, 1982; Birth at Dawn, 1986; L'Homme du livre, 1994. Other: Radio plays. Honour: Société des Auteurs Prize, 1990. Address: 15 rue Paul Pons, 26400 Crest, France.

CHRISTENSEN Karen Sophia, b. 26 Sept 1957, Lafayette, Indiana, USA. Writer. m. David Levinson, 16 Jan 1994, 1 son, 1 daughter. Education: BA, College of Creative Studies, University of Santa Barbara, 1981. Appointments: Blackwell Scientific Publications, 1980-84; Faber and Faber, London, 1986-88; Co-Owner, Berkshire Reference Works, Great Barrington, Massachusetts, 1994-. Publications: Home Ecology, 1989; Rachel's Roses, 1995; The Green Home, 1995; Global Village Companion, 1996; Encyclopedia of World Sport, 1997; Green Home (Chinese and French editions), 1998; International Encyclopedia of Women and Sport, 1999; Carring on the Work: The Life Story of Sophia Mumford. Contributions to: Daily Telegraph; Daily Express; Health and Fitness; Woman's Realm. Honours: Top 20 Green Books, England, 1989; ALA Best Reference Book, 1997. Membership: Society of Authors, England. Literary Agent: Laura Blake Peterson, Curtis Brown Ltd, New York, USA. Address: 120 Castle Street, Great Barrington, MA 01230, USA.

CHRISTENSEN Thomas Teglgaard, (Thomas Teglgaard), b. 16 Aug 1970, Copenhagen, Denmark. m. Anne Mette Lysholm, 28 Dec 1992. Education: Medicine, University of Copenhagen, 4 years. Publications: Novels: Coffeementality, 1995; Enemy Number One, 1996; A Strange Friendship, 1996; The Princip of Dilution, 1997. Membership: Danish Writers' Union. Address: Frejasvej 46, 8600 Silkeborg, Denmark.

CHRISTENSEN Thyge, b. 13 Sept 1947, Egaa, Denmark. Helle Cohrt, 19 Aug 1994. Education: Social Worker, The Social School of Esbjerg, 1975. Appointment: Social Worker, 1975-79. Publications: Man Kan Ikke Vaske Een Hand, 1984, 1996; Baobabtraet, 1986; Burkina Faso: Vaerdighedens Joro, 1996; Sadan Har Jeg Selv Hort Det, 1997. Contributions to: Information Politiken Samvirke. Honour: Ordre Du Merite Burkinabe. Membership: Dansk Forfatterforening. Address: Vestervej 2, DK 8382 Hinnerup, Denmark.

CHRISTIAN Carol Cathay, b. 15 Nov 1923, Peking, China. Freelance Writer and Editor. m. John Christian, 23 June 1945, 3 sons, 1 daughter. Education: BA, magna cum laude, Smith College, Northampton, Massachusetts, 1944. Publications: Into Strange Country, 1958; God and One Redhead, Mary Slessor of Calabar (with G Plummer), 1970; EFL Readers: Great People of Our Time, 1973; Johnny Ring, 1975; More People of Our Time, 1978; Famous Women of the 20th Century (with Diana Christian), 1982; Save the Goldfish, 1988; In the Spirit of Truth, 1991; Macmillan Bible Stories, 18 titles, 1996-98. Memberships: Society of Authors; Clinical Theology Association. Address: 20 Pitfold Avenue, Shottermill, Haslemere, Surrey GU27 1PN, England.

CHRISTIAN John. See: **DIXON Roger.**

CHRISTIANSEN Rupert, b. 1954, England. Appointments: Writer; Editor, Oxford University Press, 1979-82; Opera Critic, Spectator, Daily Telegraph, opera critic, 1996-. Publications: Prima Donna: A History, 1984; Romantic Affinities: Portraits from an Age 1780-1830, 1988; The Grand Obsession: A Collins Anthology of Opera (editor), 1988; Contemporary Music Review (editor with Paul Driver), 1989; Tales from the New Babylon: Paris 1869-1875, 1994; Cambridge Arts Theatre: Celebrating 60 Years (editor), 1997. Honour: Fellow, Royal Society of Literature, 1997. Address: c/o A D Peters, The Chambers, Chelsea Harbour, Lots Road, London SW10, England.

CHRISTIE-MURRAY David Hugh Arthur, b. 12 July 1913, London, England. m. (1) Ena Louise Elisabeth Mumford, 11 July 1942, (2) Sheila Mary Blackmore (Watson), 15 Apr 1972, 1 son, 3 daughters, 2 stepdaughters. Education: Diploma in Journalism, University College, University of London, 1932-34; BA, 1942, MA, 1945, General Ordination Examination 1942, St Peter's Hall, Oxford University and Wyclif Hall, Oxford. Publications: Beckenham Heraldry, 1954; Armorial Bearings of British Schools, series, 1956-66, collected edition, 1966; Illustrated Children's Bible, 1974; A History of Heresy, 1976, Italian edition, 1997, Japanese edition, 1997; Voices From the Gods, 1978; My First Prayer Book, 1981; Reincarnation: Ancient Beliefs and Modern Evidence, Norwegian Edition, 1989, Spanish Edition 1991; The Practical Astrologer, 1990. Contributions to: Times Literary and Educational Supplements; The Armorial; Christian Parapsychologist; Journal of the Society for Psychical Research; Light; Reincarnation International. Literary Agent: Watson Little Ltd. Address: Capo di Monte, Windmill Hill, Hampstead, London NW3 6RJ, England.

CHRISTOPHER Nicholas, b. 28 Feb 1951, New York, New York, USA. Poet; Writer. m. Constance Barbara Davidson, 20 Nov 1980. Education: AB, Harvard College, 1973. Appointments: Adjunct Professor of English, New York University; Lecturer, Columbia University.

Publications: On Tour with Rita (poems), 1982; A Short History of the Island of Butterflies (poems), 1986; The Soloist (novel), 1986; Desperate Characters (poems), 1988; Under 35: The New Generation of American Poets (editor), 1989; In the Year of the Comet (poems), 1992; 5 Degrees and Other Poems, 1994; Walk and Other Poems, 1995; Veronica (novel), 1996; Somewhere in the Night: Film Noir and the American City, 1997. Contributions to: Anthologies and periodicals. Honours: New York Foundation for the Arts Fellowship, 1986; National Endowment for the Arts Fellowship, 1987; Peter I B Lavan Award, Academy of American Poets, 1991; Guggenheim Fellowship, 1993; Melville Cane Award, 1994. Address: c/o Janklow & Nesbit Associates, 598 Madison Avenue, New York, NY 10022, USA.

CHRISTOPHERSEN Paul (Hans), b. 18 Nov 1911, Copenhagen, Denmark. Emeritus Professor. m. Margaret Travers, 1 Aug 1950, 1 son. Education: MA, 1937, PhD, 1939, University of Copenhagen; PhD, Corpus Christi College, Cambridge, 1943. Appointments: Research Assistant, Royal Institute of International Affairs, London, 1944-46; Professor of English, University of Copenhagen, 1946-48; Professor of English, University of Ibadan, Nigeria, 1948-54; University of Oslo, 1954-68; University of Qatar, 1977-81; Reader in English, 1969-74, Professor 1974-77, Emeritus Professor, 1977-, New University of Ulster, Northern Ireland. Publications: The Articles, 1939; A Modern English Grammar (with O Jespersen), Vol 6, 1942; To Start You Talking (with H Krabbe), 1948; Bilingualism, 1949; The Ballad of Sir Aldingar, 1952; An English Phonetics Course, 1956; Some Thoughts on the Study of English as a Foreign Language, 1957; An Advanced English Grammar (with A Sandved), 1969; Second-Language Learning, 1973; Tina, by Herman Bang, translation, 1984. Contributions to: Oxford Companion to the English Language, 1992. Address: 1 Corfe Close, Cambridge CB2 2QA, England.

CHUN Sook-Hee, b. 15 Mar 1919, Korea. Writer. m. Soon-Ku Kang, 1939, 2 sons, 2 daughters. Education: Graduated, Ewha Women's University, Seoul, 1938. Publications: Apology of the Prodigal Son, 1954; In a Low Voice, 1960; For Our Life, 1978; The Korean PEN - Its Past and Today, 1992; Chun Sook-Hee Essay in Russia, 1993. Contributions to: Magazines and newspapers. Honours: Cultural Medal, Korea, 1977; Grand Literary Award, POK, 1989; Grand Literary Award, Korean Academy of Arts, 1994; Bundesverdienstkruuz, Germany, 1995. Memberships: Korean Women Writer's Association, president, 1980-82; Korean PEN Center, president, 1983-91; International PEN, vice president, 1991-. Address: 302 10 Dong Samho, Apt 759-3, Bangbae-Dong, Seoul, Korea.

CHURCH Robert, b. 20 July 1932, London, England. Author. m. Dorothy June Bourton, 15 Apr 1953, 2 daughters. Education: Beaufoy College, London, 1946-48. Appointments: Metropolitan Police, 1952-78; Probation Service, 1978-88. Publications: Murder in East Anglia, 1987; Accidents of Murder, 1989; More Murder in East Anglia, 1990; Anglian Blood, co-editor, 1995; Well Done Boys, 1996. Contributions to: The Criminologist; Miscellany; Journals. Honour: Winner, Salaman Prize for Non-Fiction, 1997. Memberships: Society of Authors; Crime Writers Association, current judge, Crime Writers' Association Gold Dagger Award for Non-fiction. Address: "Woodside", 7 Crome Walk, Gunton Park, Lowestoft, Suffolk NR32 4NF, England.

CHURCHILL Caryl, b. 3 Sept 1938, London, England. Dramatist. m. David Harter, 1961, 3 sons. Education: BA, Lady Margaret Hall, Oxford, 1960. Publications: Owners, 1973; Light Shining in Buckinghamshire, 1976; Traps, 1977; Vinegar Tom, 1978; Cloud Nine, 1979; Top Girls, 1982; Fen, 1983; Collected Plays, 2 volumes, 1985, 1988; A Mouthful of Birds (with D Lan), 1986; Serious Money, 1987; Ice Cream, 1989; Hot Fudge, 1990; Mad Forest, 1990; Lives of the Great Poisoners (with I Spink and O Gough), 1991; The Skriker, 1994; This is a Chair, 1997; Blue heart, 1997. Other: Various radio and television plays. Address: c/o Casarotto Ramsay Ltd,

National House, 60-66 Wardour Street, London W1V 3HP, England.

CHURCHILL Elizabeth. See: **HOUGH Richard Alexander.**

CIOCHON Russell L, b. 11 Mar 1948, Altadena, California, USA. Paleoanthropologist. m. Noriko Ikeda, 2 Nov 1986. Education: MA, 1974, PhD, 1986, University of California, Berkeley, USA. Appointments: Lecturer, University of North Carolina, Charlotte, 1978-81; Research Paleontologist, University of California, Berkeley, 1982-83; Research Associate, Institute of Human Origins, Berkeley, 1983-85, Stony Brook, 1985-86; Assistant Professor, University of Iowa, Iowa City, 1987-90; Assoc Prof, 1990-96, Prof, 1996-, Chair, 1997-; Visng Lectr, Univ Arizona, Tucson, 1987; Review Board, Journal Human Evolution, 1980-85; Member, editorial board, International Journal of Primatology, 1990; American Journal of Physical Anthropology, 1996-; Series Editor: Advances in Human Evolution, 1991-; Co-Editor, Oxford Series in Human Evolution, 1995-; Publications: Editor, Evolutionary Biology of New World Monkeys, 1980; New Interpretations of Ape and Human Ancestry, 1983; Auth, Ed, Primate Evolution and Human Origins, 1987; The Human Evolution Source Book, 1993; Integrative Paths to the Past, 1994; The Primate Anthology, 1998; Auth, Other Origins: The Search for the Giant Ape, 1990; Evolution of the Cercopithecoid Forelimb, 1993. Honours: Research Grantee, Smithsonian Foreign Currency Program, Washington, 1978; The LSB Leakey Foundation, San Francisco, California, 1987-95; National Geographic Society, Washington, 1988; Wenner-Gren Foundation, New York, 1991. Memberships: AAAS; American Anthropological Association; American Association of Physical Anthropologists; Society of Systematic Biologists; Phi Beta Kappa. Address: 1025 Keokuk St Iowa City, IA 52240-3303, USA.

CISNEROS Antonio, b. 27 Dec 1942, Lima, Peru. Poet. Education: Catholic and National Universities, Lima; PhD, 1974. Appointment: Teacher of Literature, University of San Marcos, 1972-. Publications: Destierro, 1961; David, 1962; Comentarios reales, 1964; The Spider Hangs Too Far from the Ground, 1970; Agua que no has de beber, 1971; Come higuera en un campo de golf, 1972; El libro de Dios y los hungaros, 1978; Cuatro poetas (with others), 1979; Helicopters in the Kingdom of Peru, 1981; La cronica del Nino Jesus de Chilca, 1981; At Night the Cats, 1985; Land of Angels, 1985; Monologo de la casta Susana y otros poemas, 1986; Propios como ajenos poesia 1962-88, 1989; El arte de envolver pescado, 1990; Poesia, una historia de locos: 1962-1986, 1990. Honour: Casa de las Americas Prize, 1968. Address: Department of Literature, Universidad Nacional de San Marcos de Lima, Avda Republica de Chile 295, Of 506, Casilla 454, Lima, Peru.

CISNEROS Sandra, b. 20 Dec 1954, Chicago, Illinois, USA. Writer; Poet. Education: BA, Loyola University, 1976. Publications: Bad Boys, 1980; The House on Mango Street, 1983; The Rodrigo Poems, 1985; My Wicked, Wicked Ways, 1987; Woman Hollering Creek and Other Stories, 1991; Hairs-Pelitos, 1994; Loose Women, 1994. Contributions to: Periodicals. Honours: National Endowment for the Arts Fellowships, 1982, 1987; American Book Award, 1985; Lannan Foundation Award, 1991; John D and Catharine T MacArthur Fellowship, 1995. Address: c/o Alfred A Knopf Inc, 201 East 50th Street, New York, NY 10022, USA.

CISSNA William David, b. 27 July 1952, Evanston, Illinois, USA. Public Relations Manager. m. Kathy Anne Williams, 14 Oct 1978, 1 son. Education: BA, English, Allegheny College, Meadville, Pennsylvania, 1974. Contributions to: Editor, Downtown, Winston Salem News; Short stories and numerous non-fiction articles, 1984-. Memberships: North Carolina Writers' Network, executive committee and board of trustees, 1994-. Address: 275 Post Oak Road, Kernersville, NC 27284, USA.

CIVASQUI José, (Sosuku Shibasaki), b. 2 Jan 1916, Saitama-ken, Japan. Lecturer; Translator; Poet. m. Setsuko Hirose, 18 Sept 1940, 2 sons, 1 daughter. Education: Yokohama Central Army Education Program School. Appointments: Staff, Toshiba-EMI Ltd, 1955-76; Lecturer, Japan Translation Academy, 1978-84, Sunshine Business College, 1985-94. Publications: In His Bosom, 1950; In Thy Grace, 1971; Beyond Seeing, 1977; Living Water, 1984; Invitation to the World of Haiku, 1985; Green Pastures, 1993. Other: Various translations. Contributions to: Anthologies, newspapers and journals. Honours: Excellence in Poetry, 3rd World Congress of Poets, 1976; International Poet Laureate, 8th World Congress of Poets, 1985; Premio Speciale, Pelle di Luna, Italy, 1985; Premio Internazionale San Valentino d'Oro, Italy, 1989; Michael Madhusudan Academy Award, Calcutta, 1992; 4th Order of Merit, Japan, 1993; Silver Medallion Dove in Peace, Poetry Day Australia, 1995. Memberships: Japan Guild of Authors and Composers; Japan League of Poets; PEN; Poetry Society of Japan, president, 1987; United Poets Laureate International, president, 1983-95, honorary president, 1985-. Address: Honcho 2-12-11, Ikebukuro, Toshima-ku, Tokyo 170-0011, Japan.

CIXOUS Hélène, b. 5 June 1937, Oran, Algeria. Professor of English Literature; Writer. 1 son, 1 daughter. Education: Agregation d'Anglais, 1959; Docteur es Lettres, 1968. Appointments: Assistante, University of Bordeaux, France, 1962-65; Maître Assistante, Sorbonne, University of Paris, 1965-67; Maître de Conference, University of Paris X, Nanterre, France, 1967-68; Helped found the experimental University of Paris VIII (Vincennes, St Denis), 1968, Professor of English Literature, 1968-, Founder and Director, Centre de Recherches en Études Feminines, 1974-; Co-founder, Poetique Revue de Theorie d'Analyse Litteraire, 1969; Visiting Professor and Lecturer to many universities in Europe, North America, Japan, India. Publications include: Fiction: Le prénom de Dieu, 1967; Dedans, 1969; Le Troisième corps, 1970; Commencements, 1970; Angst, 1977; Le Livre de Promethea, 1983; Manne, 1988; Jours de l'an, 1990; L'Ange au secret, 1991; Déluge, 1992; Beethoven à jamais, 1993; La fiancée juive, 1995; Or, les lettres de mon père, 1997. Plays: Portrait de Dora, 1976; Le nom d'Oedipe, 1978; L'Indiade ou l'Inde de leurs rêves, 1987; L'Histoire (qu'on ne connaître jamais), 1994; La Ville Parjure ou le Réveil des Erinyes, 1994. Essays: L'exil de James Joyce, ou l'art du remplacement, 1969; Prénoms de personne, 1974; L'heure de Clarice Lispector, 1989; Photos de racines, 1994; Stigmata, Escaping Texts, 1998; Readings: The Poetics of Blanchot, Joyce, Kafka, Lispector, Tsvetaeva, 1992; Three Steps on the Ladder of Writing, 1993. Contributions to: Periodicals. Honours: Prix Medicis, 1969; Southern Cross of Brazil, 1989; Légion d'Honneur, 1994; Prix des critiques, best theatrical work of the Year, 1994; Ambassador of Star Awards, StarGirls and Women Foundation, Pakistan, 1997; Officier de l'Ordre National du Mérite, 1998; Numerous honorary doctorates. Literary Agent: Myriam Diocaretz. Address: Centre d'Études Féminines, Université de Paris VIII, 2 Rue de la Liberte, 93526 St Denis, France.

CIZMAR Paula, b. 30 Aug 1949, Youngstown, Ohio, USA. Playwright; Screenwriter. Education: BA, Ohio University, 1971; Graduate Studies, San Francisco State University, 1972-74. Publications: Plays: The Girl Room, 1979; The Death of a Miner, 1983; Candy and Shelley to the Desert, 1988; Many other plays produced. Contributions to: Periodicals. Honours: Jerome Foundation Commission Fellowship, 1981; National Endowment for the Arts Fellowship, 1982; Rockefeller Foundation International Residency, 1983. Memberships: Dramatists Guild; League of Professional Theatre Women; Writers Guild of America. Address: 2700 North Beachwood Drive, Los Angeles, CA 90068, USA.

CLANCY Joseph Patrick Thomas, b. 8 Mar 1928, New York, New York, USA. College Teacher; Writer; Poet. m. Gertrude Wiegand, 31 July 1948, 4 sons, 4 daughters. Education: BA, 1947, MA, 1949, PhD, 1957, Fordham University. Appointments: Faculty, 1948,

Professor, 1962, Marymount Manhattan College. Publications: The Odes and Epodes of Horace, 1960; Medieval Welsh Lyrics, 1965; The Earliest Welsh Poems, 1970; 20th Century Welsh Poems, 1982; Gwyn Thomas: Living a Life, 1982; The Significance of Flesh: Poems, 1950-83, 1984; Bobi Jones: Selected Poems, 1987. Contributions to: Poetry Wales; Planet; Anglo Welsh Review; Book News from Wales; Epoch; College English; America. Honours: American Philosophical Society Fellowships, 1963, 1968; National Translation Centre Fellowship, 1968; Welsh Arts Council, Literature Award, 1971, Major Bursary, 1972; National Endowment for the Arts Translation Fellowship, 1983; St Davids Society of New York Annual Award, 1986. Memberships: American Literary Translators Association; Dramatists Guild; Yr Academi Gymreig; Eastern States Celtic Association; St Davids Society of New York. Address: 1549 Benson Street, New York, NY 10461, USA.

CLANCY Laurence James, b. 2 Dec 1942, Melbourne, Victoria, Australia. Senior Lecturer; Writer. Div, 2 sons. Education: BA, Melbourne University, 1964; MA, La Trobe University, 1973. Publications: A Collapsible Man, 1975; The Wife Specialist, 1978; Xavier Herber, 1981; Perfect Love, 1983; The Novels of Vladimir Nabokov, 1984; City to City, 1989; A Reader's Guide to Australian Fiction, 1992; The Wild Life Reserve, 1994. Contributions to: Regular Contributor, Reviewer to many Australian journals and newspapers. Honours: Co-Winner, National Book Council Award, 1975;Australian Natives Association Award, 1983. Membership: PEN International. Literary Agent: Curtis Brown Pty Ltd. Address: 227 Westgarth Street, Northcote, Victoria 3070, Australia.

CLANCY Tom, (Thomas L Clancy Jr), b. 1947, Baltimore, Maryland, USA. Author. m. Wanda Thomas, Aug 1969, 1 son, 3 daughters. Education: BA, Loyola College, Baltimore, 1969. Publications: The Hunt for Red October, 1984; Red Storm Rising, 1986; Patriot Games, 1987; The Cardinal of the Kremlin, 1988; Clear and Present Danger, 1989; The Sum of All Fears, 1992; Without Remorse, 1993; Armored Car, 1994; Debut of Honor, 1994; Submarine, 1994; Reality Check: What's Going on Out There?, 1995; Executive Orders, 1996; Into the Storm: A Study in Command (with Fred Franks Jr), 1997; Rainbow Six, 1998. Address: PO Box 800, Huntingtown, MD 20639, USA.

CLAPPS-HERMAN Joanna, b. 23 Feb 1944, USA. 1 son. Publications: Poetry: Autumning In; Each Eary Spring; Open Windows in a Cool Row; After; Mexico for the Last Time; Boy; Uxorious Love; Seasonal; On the Roof. Prose: Certainty and Other Shades of Darkness; Perfect hatred; Seeding Memory; A Voice From Behind; Tidal; Roman Bath; Snow Struck; No Longer and Not Yet; Looking Ahead; Announcements and Other Facts of Life; Amore; As Morning Breaks; Blue; Writing About Photographs; Notes From an Unredeemed Catholic; Listening with Small Ears; One Thing; I Write Because of Early Reading, I Love Because of Love; Hats; Two; Asparagus Soup. Contributions to: Massachusetts Review; Kalliope; The Critic; The Compositor. Literary Agent: Anne Edelstein. Address: 370 Riverside Drive, New York, NY 10025, USA.

CLARE Elizabeth, See: COOK Dorothy Mary.

CLARE Ellen. See: SINCLAIR Olga Ellen.

CLARE Helen. See: HUNTER BLAIR Pauline.

CLARK Alan (Kenneth McKenzie), b. 13 Apr 1928, London, England. Member of Parliament; Writer. m. Caroline Jane Beuttler, 31 July 1958, 2 sons. Education: Eton; BA, 1949, MA, 1950, Christ Church, Oxford. Appointments: Barrister, Inner Temple, 1955; Member, Institute for Strategic Studies, 1963; Member of Parliament, Conservative Party, Plymouth, Sutton, 1974-92, Chelsea, 1997-; Party Under Secretary to State, Department of Employment, 1983-86; Chairman, International Market Council, European Economic Community Ministers, 1986-87; Minister for Trade,

1986-89; Minister of State, Ministry of Defence, 1989-92. Publications: The Donkeys: A History of the BEF in 1915, 1961; The Hall of Crete, 1963; Barbarossa: The Russo-German Conflict, 1941-45, 1965; Aces High: The War in the Air Over the Western Front 1914-18, 1973; A Good Innings: The Private Papers of Viscount Lee of Fareham (editor), 1974; Diaires, 1993. Honour: Privy Councillor, 1991. Membership: Royal United Services Institute for Defence Studies. Address: Saltwood Castle, Kent CT21 4QU, England.

CLARK Anne, See: AMOR Anne Clark.

CLARK Brian Robert, b. 3 June 1932, Bournemouth, England. Dramatist. m. (1) Margaret Paling, 1961, 2 sons, (2) Anita Modak, 1983, 1 stepson, 1 stepdaughter, (3) Cherry Potter, 1990. Education: Redland College of Education, Bristol; Central School of Speech and Drama, London; BA, Honours, English, Nottingham University. Appointments: Staff Tutor in Drama, University of Hull, 1966-70; Founder, Amber Lane Press, 1978. Publications: Group Theatre, 1971; Whose Life is it Anyway?, 1978; Can You Hear Me at the Back?, 1979; Post Mortem, 1979; The Petition, 1986. Other: Over 30 television plays, 1971-; Several stage plays. Honours: Society of West Theatre Award for Best Play, 1977; Royal Society of Literature, fellow, 1985. Address: c/o Judy Daish Associates, 83 Eastbourne Mews, London W2 6LQ, England.

CLARK David. See: HARDCASTLE Michael.

CLARK David R(idgley), b. 17 Sept 1920, Seymour, Connecticut, USA. Professor (retired); Writer. m. Mary Adele Matthieu, 10 July 1948, 2 sons, 2 daughters. Education: BA, Wesleyan University, 1947; MA, 1950, PhD, 1955, Yale University. Appointments: Instructor, 1951-57, Assistant Professor, 1957-58, Associate Professor, 1958-65, Professor, 1965-85, University of Massachusetts; Visiting Professor, St Mary's College, Notre Dame, Indiana, 1985-87; Visiting Professor, Williams College, Williamstown, Massachusetts, 1989-91. Publications: A Curious Quire, 1962; W B Yeats and the Theatre of Desolate Reality, 1965, new edition with Rosalind Clark, 1993; Irish Renaissance, 1965; Dry Tree, 1966; Riders to the Sea, 1970; A Tower of Polished Black Stones: Early Versions of the Shadowy Waters, 1971; Twentieth Century Interpretations of Murder in the Cathedral, 1971; Druid Craft, 1971; That Black Day: The Manuscripts of Crazy Jane on the Day of Judgement, 1980; W B Yeats: The Writing of Sophocles' King Oedipus (with James McGuire), 1989; W B Yeats: The Winding Stair (1929): Manuscript Materials, 1995; W B Yeats: Words for Music Perhaps and Other Poems (1932): Manuscript Materials, 1999. Memberships: American Conference for Irish Studies; International Association for the Support of Anglo-Irish Literature; Modern Language Association of America. Address: 481 Holgerson Road, Sequim, WA 98382, USA.

CLARK Eric, b. 29 July 1937, Birmingham, England. Author; Journalist. m. Marcelle Bernstein, 12 Apr 1972, 1 son, 2 daughters. Appointments: Staff of various newspapers including, Daily Mail, The Guardian, The Observer until 1972; Full-time Author, 1972-. Publications: Len Deighton's London Dossier, Part-author, 1967; Everybody's Guide to Survival, 1969; Corps Diplomatique, 1973, US edition as Diplomat, 1973; Black Gambit, 1978; The Sleeper, 1979; Send in the Lions, 1981; Chinese Burn, 1984, US edition as China Run, 1984; The Want Makers (Inside the Hidden World of Advertising), 1988; Hide and Seek, 1994. Contributions to: Observer; Sunday Times; Daily Mail; Daily Telegraph; Washington Post; Melbourne Age. Memberships: Society of Authors; PEN International UK Centre, fellow; Crime Writers Association; Mystery Writers of America. Address: c/o Child and Company, 1 Fleet Street, London EC4Y 1BD, England.

CLARK Joan, b. 12 Oct 1934, Liverpool, Nova Scotia, Canada. Writer. m. Jack Clark, 3 children. Education: BA, Acadia University, 1957; University of Alberta, 1960. Publications: The Hand of Robin Squires, 1977, 3rd

editioin, 1994; From a High Thin Wire, 1982; Wild Man of the Woods, 1985; The Moons of Madeleine, 1987; The Victory of Geraldine Gill, 1988, 2nd edition, 1994; Swimming Toward the Light, 1990; Eiriksdottir, 1994; The Dream Carvers, 1995. Address: 6 Dover Place, St John's, Newfoundland, A1B 2P5, Canada.

CLARK John Pepper, (J P Clark Bekederemo), b. 6 Apr 1935, Kiagaboo, Nigeria. Dramatist; Poet; Writer. m. Ebun Odutola Clark, 1 son, 3 daughters. Education: Warri Government College, 1948-54; University of Ibadan, 1955-60; BA, Princeton University, 1960. Appointments: Information Officer, Government of Nigeria, 1960-61; Head of Features and Editorial Writer, Lagos Daily Express, 1961-62; Research Fellow, 1964-66, Professor of African Literature, 1966-85, University of Lagos; Co-Editor, Black Orpheus, 1968-. Publications: Poems, 1962; A Reed in the Tide: A Selection of Poems, 1965; Casualties: Poems 1966-68, 1970; Urhobo Poetry, 1980; A Decade of Tongues: Selected Poems 1958-68, 1981; State of the Union, 1985; Mandela and Other Poems, 1988. Other: Plays and other publications. Address: c/o Curtis Brown Ltd, Haymarket House, 28-29 Haymarket, London SW1Y 4SP, England.

CLARK Jonathan Charles Douglas, b. 28 Feb 1951, London, England. Historian. m. Katherine Redwood Penovich, 1996. Education: BA, 1972, PhD, 1981, Cambridge University. Appointments: Research Fellow, Peterhouse, Cambridge, 1977; Leverhulme Trust, 1983; Fellow, All Souls College, Oxford, 1986; Visiting Professor, Committee on Social Thought, University of Chicago, 1993; Senior Research Fellow, All Souls College, Oxford, 1995; Joyce and Elizabeth Hall Distinguished Professor of British History, University of Kansas, 1995-. Publications: The Dynamics of Change, 1982; English Society 1688-1832, 1985; Revolution and Rebellion, 1986; The Memoirs of James 2nd Earl Waldegrave, 1988; Ideas and Politics in Modern Britain, 1990; The Language of Liberty, 1993; Samuel Johnson, 1994. Contributions to: Scholarly books and journals, and to periodicals. Memberships: Royal Historical Society, fellow; Ecclesiastical History Society; Church of England Record Society; American Historical Association; North American Conference on British Studies; British Society for Eighteenth Century Studies. Literary Agent: Michael Shaw. Address: Hall Center for the Humanities, University of Kansas, Lawrence, KS 66045, USA.

CLARK LaVerne Harrell, b. 6 June 1929, Smithville, Texas, USA. Writer; Photographer; Lecturer. m. L D Clark, 15 Sept 1951. Education: BA, Texas Woman's University, 1950; Columbia University, 1951-54; MA, 1962, MFA, 1992, University of Arizona. Appointments: Reporter, Librarian, Fort Worth Press, 1950-51; Sales and Advertising Department, Columbia University Press, 1951-53; Assistant, Promotion News Department, Episcopal Diocese, New York, 1958-59; Founding Director, 1962-66, Photographer, 1966-, Poetry Centre, University of Arizona. Publications: They Sang for Horses, 1966, revised edition, 1999; The Face of Poetry, 1976; Focus 101, 1979; Revisiting the Plains Indians Country of Mari Sandoz, 1979; The Deadly Swarm and Other Stories, 1985; Keepers of the Earth, 1997. Contributions to: Periodicals. Honours: American Philosophical Society Grant, 1967-69; Non Fiction Award, Biennial Letters Contest, 1968; Distinguished Alumna Award, 1973; Julian Ocean Literary Prize, 1984; Philip A Danielson Award, Westerners International, 1992; Best First Novel, Western Writers of America, 1998. Memberships: PEN; National League of American PEN Women; Western Writers of America; Society of Southwestern Authors; Mari Sandoz Heritage Society; Westerners International, honorary board member; Kappa Alpha Mu. Address: 604 Main Street, Smithville, TX 78957, USA.

CLARK Marcelle Ruth, (Marcelle Bernstein), b. 14 June 1945, Manchester, England. Writer; Journalist. m. Eric Clark, 12 Apr 1972, 1 son, 2 daughters. Appointments: Staff, The Guardian, Daily Mirror, Observer. Publications: Nuns, 1976; Sadie, 1983; Salka, 1986; Lili, 1988; Body and Soul, 1991. Contributions to:

Numerous US and UK magazines. Honours: Arts Council Bursary, 1986; Helene Heroys Award, 1988. Memberships: Society of Authors. Address: c/o AP Watt, 20 John Street, London WC1N 2DR, England.

CLARK (Marie) Catherine (Audrey) Clifton, (Audrey Curling), b. London, England. Writer. m. Clifton Clark, 16 Feb 1938. Publications: Novels: The Running Tide, 1963; Sparrow's Yard, 1964. Historical Novels: The Echoing Silence, 1967; Caste for Comedy, 1970; The Sapphire and the Pearl, 1970; Cry of the Heart, 1971; A Quarter of the Moon, 1972; Shadows on the Grass, 1973; Enthusiasts in Love, 1975; The Lamps in the House, 1990; The Saturday Treat, 1993; The Workroom Girls, 1996. Non-fiction: The Young Thackeray, 1966. Contributions to: Periodicals. Honours: Theordora Roscoe Award, 1978; 1st Prize, Wandsworth All London Literary Competition, 1982. Memberships: Society of Authors; Romantic Novelists Association; Society of Women Writers and Journalists, council member. Address: 35 Hadley Gardens, Chiswick, London W4 4NU, England.

CLARK Mary Higgins, b. 24 Dec 1929, New York, New York, USA. Writer. m. Waren F Clark, 26 Dec 1949, 2 sons, 3 daughters. Education: BA, Fordham University; Villanova University, 1983; Rider College, 1986. Publications: Where Are the Children, 1975; A Stranger is Watching, 1978; The Cradle will Fall, 1980; A Cry in the Night, 1982; Weep No More My Lady, 1987; While My Pretty One Sleeps, 1989; All Around the Town, 1991; Loves Music, Loves to Dance, 1991; Remember Me, 1994; All Through the Night, 1998. Contributions to: Ladies Home Journal; Womens Day; Saturday Evening Post. Honour: Grand Priz de Litteratae Policcere, 1980. Memberships: Mystery Writers of America; PEN; American Society of Journalists and Authors. Address: c/o American Society of Journalists and Authors, 1501 Broadway, Suite 302, New York, NY 10036, USA.

CLARK Mavis Thorpe, (M R Clark, Mavis Latham), b. 1909, Melbourne, Victoria, Australia. Children's Author; Biographer. Education: Methodist Ladies College, Melbourne. Publications: Over 30 books, 1930-88. Honours: Highly Commended, Australian Children's Book Council, 1957, 1967; Notable Book, American Library Association, 1969; AM, 1996. Memberships: Australian Society of Authors; Fellowship of Australian Writers; International PEN Club; National Book Council; Order of Australia. Address: Unit 1, 22 Rochester Road, Canterbury, Victoria 3126, Australia.

CLARK Patricia Denise (Claire Lorrimer, Patricia Robins, Susan Patrick), b. 1921, England. Writer; Poet. Publications: As Claire Lorrimer: A Voice in the Dark, 1967; The Shadow Falls, 1974; Relentless Storm, 1975; The Secret of Quarry House, 1976; Mavreen, 1976; Tamarisk, 1978; Chantal, 1980; The Garden (a cameo), 1980; The Chatelaine, 1981; The Wilderling, 1982; Last Year's Nightingale, 1984; Frost in the Sun, 1986; House of Tomorrow (biography), 1987; Ortolans, 1990; The Spinning Wheel, 1991; Variations (short stories), 1991; The Silver Link, 1993; Fool's Curtain, 1994. As Patricia Robins: To the Stars, 1944; See No Evil, 1945; Three Loves, 1949; Awake My Heart, 1950; Beneath the Moon, 1951; Leave My Heart Alone, 1951; The Fair Deal, 1952; Heart's Desire, 1953; So This is Love, 1953; Heaven in Our Hearts, 1954; One Who Cares, 1954; Love Cannot Die, 1955; The Foolish Heart, 1956; Give All to Love, 1956; Where Duty Lies, 1957; He Is Mine, 1957; Love Must Wait, 1958; Lonely Quest, 1959; Lady Chatterley's Daughter, 1961; The Last Chance, 1961; The Long Wait, 1962; The Runaways, 1962; Seven Loves, 1962; With All My Love, 1963; The Constant Heart, 1964; Second Love, 1964; The Night is Thine, 1964; There Is But One, 1965; No More Loving, 1965; Topaz Island, 1965; Love Me Tomorrow, 1966; The Uncertain Joy, 1966; The Man Behind the Mask, 1967; Forbidden, 1967; Sapphire in the Sand, 1968; Return to Love, 1968; Laugh on Friday, 1969; No Stone Unturned, 1969; Cinnabar House, 1970; Under the Sky, 1970; The Crimson Tapestry, 1972; Play Fair with Love, 1972; None But He, 1973; Fulfilment, 1993; Forsaken, 1993; Forever, 1993; The Legend, 1997; Connie's Daughter, 1997; The Reunion, 1997; The Woven Thread, 1998; The Reckoning, 1998. Memberships: Society of Authors; Romantic Novelists Association. Address: Chiswell Barn, Marsh Green, Edenbridge, Kent TN8 5PR, England.

CLARKE Anna, b. 28 Apr 1919, Cape Town, South Africa. Author. Education: BSc, Economics, University of London, 1945; BA, Open University, 1975; MA, University of Sussex, 1975. Appointments: Private Secretary, Victor Gollancz Publishers, 1947-50, Eyre and Spottiswoode, Publishers, 1951-53; Administrative Secretary, British Association for American Studies, London, 1956-63. Publications: The Poisoned Web, 1979; Poison Parsley, 1979; Last Voyage, 1980; Game, Set and Danger, 1981; Desire to Kill, 1982; We the Bereaved, 1982; Soon She Must Die, 1983; Paula Glenning stories: Last Judgement, 1985; Cabin 3033, 1986; The Mystery Lady, 1986; Last Seen in London, 1987; Murder in Writing, 1988; The Whitelands Affair, 1989; The Case of the Paranoid Patient, 1993; The Case of the Ludicrous Letters,1994. Contributions to: Short stories in Ellery Queen Mystery Magazine, New York. Address: c/o Wendy Lipkind, 165 East 66 Street, New York, NY 10021, USA.

CLARKE Arthur C(harles), b. 16 Dec 1917, Minehead, Somerset, England. Author. m. Marilyn Mayfield, 1953, diss 1964. Education: BSc, King's College, London, 1948. Appointments: Assistant Editor, Science Abstracts, 1949-50; Many appearances on UK and US radio and television; Chancellor, Moratuwa University, Sri Lanka, 1979-; Vikram Sarabhai Professor, Physical Research Laboratory, Ahmedabad, 1980. Publications: Non-Fiction: Interplanetary Flight, 1950; The Exploration of Space, 1951; The Exploration of the Moon (with R A Smith), 1954; The Challenge of the Spaceship, 1960; The Challenge of the Sea, 1960; Man and Space (with others), 1964; The Coming of the Space Age, 1967; First on the Moon (with the astronauts), 1970; Beyond Jupiter (with Chesley Bonestell), 1973; Arthur C Clarke's Mysterious World (with Simon Welfare and John Fairley), 1980; Arthur C Clarke's World of Strange Powers (with Simon Welfare and John Fairley), 1984; Arthur C Clarke's Chronicles of the Strange and Mysterious (with Simon Welfare and John Fairley), 1987; Astounding Days, 1988; How the World was One, 1992; Arthur C Clarke's A-Z of Mysteries (with Simon Welfare and John Fairley), 1993; The Snows of Olympus, 1994. Fiction: Prelude to Space, 1951; Against the Fall of Night, 1953; Reach for Tomorrow, 1956; The Other Side of the Sky, 1958; Tales of Ten Worlds, 1962; 2001: A Space Odyssey (with Stanley Kubrick), 1968; The Lost World of 2001, 1972; Rendezvous with Rama, with G Lee, 1973; The Fountains of Paradise, 1979; 2010: Space Odyssey II, 1982; The Songs of Distant Earth, 1986; 2061: Odyssey III, 1988; Rama II, with G Lee, 1989; The Garden of Rama, with G Lee, 1991; Beyond the Fall of Night (with Gregory Benford), 1991; The Hammer of God, 1993; Rama Revealed (with G Lee), 1993; 3001: The Final Odyssey, 1997. Contributions to: Journals and periodicals. Honours: Kalinga Prize, UNESCO, 1961; Stuart Ballantine Medal, Franklin Institute, 1963; Nebula Awards, Science Fiction Writers of America, 1972, 1974, 1979; John Campbell Award, 1974; Hugo Awards, World Science Fiction Convention, 1974, 1980; Vidya Jyothi Medal, 1986; Grand Master, Science Fiction Writers of America, 1986; Charles Lindberg Award, 1987; Commander of the Order of the British Empire, 1989; Lord Perry Award, 1992; Knighted, 1998; Many honorary doctorates. Memberships: Association for the Advancement of Science; International Writers Association, fellow; Royal Astronomical Society, fellow; Society of Authors. Literary Agent: David Higham Associates. Address: 25 Barnes Place, Colombo 7, Sri Lanka.

CLARKE Austin Ardinel Chesterfield, b. 26 July 1934, Barbados, West Indies. Author. m. 14 Sept 1957, 2 daughters. Education: Trinity College, University of Toronto. Appointments: Hoyt Fellow, Yale University, 1968; Margaret Bundy Scott Professor, 1970; Jacob Ziskind Professor, Brandeis University, 1970. Publications: The Meeting Point, 1967; Storm of Fortune, 1972; The Bigger Light, 1972; When He Was Young and Free He Used to Wear Silks, 1972; The Prime Minister, 1977; Growing Up Stupid Under the Union Jack, 1980; When Women Rule, 1985; Nine Men Who Laughed, 1986; Proud Empires, 1986; In This City, 1992; There Are No Eldors, 1993; A Passage Back Home: A Personal Reminiscence of Samuel Selvon, 1994; The Origin of Waves, 1997. Contributions to: Tamarack Review; Canadian Literature. Honours: Presidents Medal, 1965; Canada Council Awards, 1968, 1972; Casa de las Americas Literary Prize, 1980; Arts Council Awards, 1985, 1994; Toronto Arts Award, 1992. Membership: Arts and Letters CLub. Literary Agent: Harold Ober Associates, David Higham Associates, London. Address: 62 McGill Street, Toronto, Ontario M5B 1H2, Canada.

CLARKE Brenda (Margaret Lilian), (Brenda Honeyman, Kate Sedley), b. 30 July 1926, Bristol, England. Author. m. Ronald John Clarke, 5 Mar 1955, 1 son, 1 daughter. Publications: The Glass Island, 1978; the Lofty Banners, 1980; The Far Morning, 1982; All Through the Day, 1983; A Rose in May, 1984; Three Women, 1985; Winter Landscape, 1986; Under Heaven, 1988; An Equal Chance, 1989, US edition as Riches of the Heart, 1989; Sisters and Lovers, 1990; Beyond the World, 1991; A Durable Fire, 1993; Sweet Auburn, 1995; As Brenda Honeyman: Richard by Grace of God, 1968; The Kingmaker, 1969; Richmond and Elizabeth, 1970; Harry the King, 1971; Brother Bedford, 1972; Good Duke Humphrey, 1973; The King's Minions, 1974; The Queen and Mortimer, 1974; Edward the Warrior, 1975; All the King's Sons, 1976; The Golden Griffin, 1976; At the King's Court, 1977; A King's Tale, 1977; Macbeth, King of Scots, 1977; Emma, the Queen, 1978; Harold of the English, 1979. As Kate Sedley: Death and the Chapman, 1991; The Plymouth Cloak, 1992; The Hanged Man, 1993; The Holy Innocents, 1994; The Eve of St Hyacinth, 1995; The Wicked Winter, 1996; The Brothers of Glastonbury, 1997; The Broad Street Inheritance, 1998. Literary Agent: David Grossman Literary Agency Ltd, 118b Holland Park Avenue, London W11 4UA, England. Address: 25 Torridge Road, Keynsham, Bristol, Avon BS31 1QQ, England.

CLARKE Gillian, b. 8 June 1937, Cardiff, Glamorgan, Wales. Poet; Editor; Translator; Tutor of Creative Writing. Education: BA, University College, Cardiff, 1958. Appointments: Lecturer, Gwent College of Art and Design, Newport, 1975-82; Editor, Anglo-Welsh Review, 1976-84; President, Ty Newydd (Welsh creative writers' house), Gwynedd, 1993-. Publications: Poetry: Snow on the Mountain, 1971; The Sundial, 1978; Letter From a Far Country, 1982; Selected Poems, 1985; Letting in the Rumour, 1989; The King of Britain's Daughter, 1993; Collected Poems, 1997; Five Fields, 1998. Editor: The Poetry Book Society Anthology, 1987-88, 1987; The Whispering Room, 1996; I Can Move the Sea (anthology), 1996. Other: Translations. Honours: Fellow, University of Wales, Cardiff, 1984; Honorary Fellow, University of Wales, Aberystwyth, 1995-, University of Wales, Swansea, 1996; Cholmondeley Award for Poetry, 1997. Membership: Welsh Academy, chair, 1988-93. Address: Blaen Cwrt, Talgarreg, Llandysul, Ceredigion SA44 4EU, Wales.

CLARKE Hugh Vincent, b. 27 Nov 1919, Brisbane, Queensland, Australia. Author; Journalist. m. Mary Patricia Ryan, 6 June 1961, 4 sons, 1 daughter. Education: Teachers Training College, Brisbane, 1937; Melbourne Technical College, 1947-48. Appointments: Senior Survey Computer, Department of the Interior, Australia, 1947-56; Director of Information and Publicity, Department of External Territories, Canberra, Australian Capital Territory, 1966-73; Director of Information and Public Relations, Department of Aboriginal Affairs, Canberra, Australian Capital Territory, 1973-75. Publications: The Tub (novel), 1963; Breakout (with Takeo Yamashita), 1965; To Sydney by Stealth (with Takeo Yamashita), 1966; The Long Arm, 1974; Fire One!, 1978; The Broke and the Broken, 1982; Last Stop Nagasaki, 1984; Twilight Liberation, 1985; A Life for Every Sleeper, 1986; Prisoners of War (with Colin Burgess and Russell Braddon), 1988; When the Balloon

Went Up, 1990; Barbed Wire and Bamboo (with Colin Burgess), 1992; Escape to Death, 1994. Contributions to: Anthologies and periodicals; Bulletin Australasian Post. Memberships: National Press Club; Australian Journalists Association; Canberra Historical Society; Australian Society of Authors. Address: 14 Chemside Street, Deakin, Canberra 2600, Australia.

CLARKE Joan Lorraine, b. 23 Aug 1920, Sydney, New South Wales, Australia. Author; Freelance Editor. m. R G Clarke, 1946, div, 1 son. Education: Diploma, Secretarial College, 1938. Appointments: Editor, The Australian Author, 1977-81; Australian Society of Authors, Writers Handbook, 2nd edition, 1980. Publications: The Tracks We Travel: Australian Short Stories (contributing author), 1953; Girl Fridays in Revolt (co-author), 1969; Max Herz, Surgeon Extraordinary, 1976; Australian Political Milestone (contributing author), 1976; Gold (co-author), 1981; The Doctor Who Dared, 1982; Just Us, 1988; Growing Up With Barnardo's (editor), 1990; All on One Good Dancing Leg, 1994. Contributions to: Sydney Morning Herald; Australian Women's Weekly; Flair; Pol; The Australian Author; Overland; Radio talks and features for the Australian Broadcasting Commission and commercial radio. Address: Feros Village, PO Box 585, Byron Bay, New South Wales 2481, Australia.

CLARKE Mary, b. 23 Aug 1923, London, England. Editor; Writer. Appointments: London Correspondent, Dance Magazine, New York, 1943-55; Assistant Editor and Contributor, Ballet Annual, 1952-63; Assistant Editor, 1954-63, Editor, 1963-, Dancing Times; London Editor, Dance News, New York, 1955-70; Dance Critic, The Guardian, 1977-94. Publications: The Sadler's Wells Ballet: A History and Appreciation, 1955; Six Great Dancers, 1957; Dancers of Mercury: The Story of Ballet Rambert, 1962. With Clement Crisp: Ballet: An Illustrated History, 1973, 2nd edition, 1992; Making a Ballet, 1974; Introducing Ballet, 1976; Design for Ballet, 1978; Ballet in Art, 1978; The History of Dance, 1981; Dancer: Men in Dance, 1984; Ballerina, 1987. Editor: Encyclopedia of Dance and Ballet (with David Vaughan), 1977. Contributions to: Encyclopaedia Britannica, newspapers, magazines. Honours: 2nd Prize, Cafe Royal Literary for Best Book on the Theatre, 1955; Queen Elizabeth II Coronation Award, Royal Academy of Dancing, 1990; Knight, Order of Dannebrog, Denmark, 1992; Nijinsky Medal, Polish Ministry of Culture, 1995. Address: 54 Ripplevale Grove, London N1 1HT, England.

CLARKE Pauline. See: **HUNTER BLAIR Pauline**.

CLARKE Thomas Wilfred, b. 25 Sept 1950, Wath-Upon-Dearne, Nr Rotherham, South Yorkshire, England. Music Impresario. Education: Royal Academy of Music, London, 1961-68. Appointments: Manchester Teacher Training College, 1968-71; Director of concerts at the famous pump rooms and assembly rooms, Bath, 1976-. Publications: Over 500 poems published in many anthologies. Contributions to: The Bath Chronicle; Over 600 letters and articles contributed to the press. Honour: Associate, Royal Academy of Music, 1993. Memberships: International Musicians; Fellow, Trinity College of Music in Research; Royal Society of Musicians of Great Britain; Member of the International Society of Poets. Address: 1 North Parade buildings, Bath, Avon BA1 1NS, England

CLARKE Victor Lindsay (Lindsay Clarke), b. 14 Aug 1939, Halifax, W Yorkshire, England. Author. m. Phoebe Clare Mackman, 29 Oct 1980, 1 daughter. Education: BA, English (II/I), King's College, Cambridge, England, 1958-61. Appointments: Senior Master, Akim-Oda Secondary School, Ghana; Lecturer in English, Great Yarmouth CHE; Coordinator of Liberal Studies, Norwich City College; Co-Director, European Centre, Friends World College; Writer-in-Residence, Associate Lecturer in Creative Writing, University of Wales, Cardiff, Wales. Publications: Sunday Whiteman, 1987; The Chymical Wedding, 1989; Alice's Masque, 1994; Essential Celtic Mythology, 1997. Honour: Whitbread Fiction Prize, 1989. Literary Agent: Peters, Fraser & Dunlop. Address: c/o Peters, Fraser & Dunlop, Chelsea Harbour, London SW10 0XF, England.

CLARKE William Malpas, b. 5 June 1922, Ashton-under-Lyne, England. Author. m. Faith Elizabeth (Dawson), 2 daughters. Education: BA Hons, Econ, University of Manchester, England, 1948; Hon DLitt, London Guildhall University, 1992. Appointments: Financial Editor, The Times, 1956-66; Director-General, British Invisible Exports Council, 1967-87; Chairman, ANZ Merchant Bank, 1987-91. Publications: City's Invisible Earnings, 1958; City in the World Economy, 1965; Private Enterprise in Developing Countries, 1966; The World's Money, 1970; Inside the City, 1979; How the City of London Works, 1986; Secret Life of Wilkie Collins. 1988; Planning for Europe, 1989; Lost Fortune of the Tsars, 1994; Letters of Wilkie Collins, 1999. Contributions to: The Banker; Central Banking; Euromoney; Wilkie Collins Society Journal. Honour: CBE, 1976. Memberships: Thackeray Society; Wilkie Collins. Literary Agent: AM Heath & Co. Address: 37 Park Vista, Greenwich, London SE10 9LZ, England.

CLARKSON Ewan, b. 23 Jan 1929, England. Education: MA, University of Exeter, 1984. Publications: Break for Freedom, 1967; Halic: The Story of a Grey Seal, 1970; The Running of the Deer, 1972; In the Shadow of the Falcon, 1973; Wolf Country: A Wilderness Pilgrimage, 1975; The Badger of Summercombe, 1977; The Many Forked Branch, 1980; Wolves, 1980; Reindeer, 1981; Eagles, 1981; Beavers, 1981; In the Wake of the Storm, 1984; Ice Trek, 1986; King of the Wild, 1990; The Flight of the Osprey, 1995. Address: Moss Rose Cottage, Preston, Newton Abbot, Devon TQ12 3PP, England.

CLARKSON J F. See: **TUBB E(dwin) C(harles)**.

CLARKSON Stephen, b. 21 Oct 1937, London, England. Professor of Political Economy; Writer. m. Christina McCall, 1 Sept 1978, 3 daughters. Education: Upper Canada College, 1955; BA, Sorbonne, University of Paris, 1964. Appointments: Lecturer, 1964-65, Assistant Professor, 1965-67, Associate Professor, 1967-80, Professor of Political Economy, 1980-, University of Toronto; Senior Fellow, Columbia University, 1967-68; Policy Chairman, Liberal Party, Ontario, 1969-73; Director, Maison Francaise de Toronto, 1972; Jean Monnet Fellow, European University Institute, 1995-96. Publications: An Independent Foreign Policy for Canada? (editor), 1968; L'Analyse Soviétique des problèmes indiens de sous-développement, 1970; Visions 2020: Fifty Canadians in Search of a Future (editor), 1970; City Lib: Parties and Reform in Toronto, 1972; The Soviet Theory of Development: India and the Third World in Marxist-Leninist Scholarship, 1978; Canada and the Reagan Challenge: Crisis in the Canadian-American Relationship, 1982, 2nd edition, 1985; Trudeau and Our Times (co-author), Vol 1, The Magnificent Obsession, 1990, vol 2, The Heroic Delusion, 1994. Contributions to: Scholarly books and professional journals. Honours: Rhodes Scholar, 1959; Woodrow Wilson Fellow, 1961; John Porter Prize, 1984; Governor-General's Award for Non-Fiction, 1990. Memberships: Canadian Institute of International Affairs; Canadian Political Science Association; International Political Science Association; University League for Social Reform, president. Address: c/o University College, King's College Circle, Toronto, Ontario M5S, Canada.

CLARY Sydney Ann, b. 13 Feb 1948, Auburn, Alabama, USA. Writer. m. Bishop D Clary, 26 Sept 1967, 2 daughters. Education: Palm Beach Community College. Publications: Double Solitaire; Devil and the Duchess; Eye of the Storm; A Touch of Passion; Her Golden Eyes; Fire in the Night; With a Little Spice; Southern Comfort; This Wildlife Magic. Contributions to: Magazines. Honours: Finalist, 1983-84, 1987, 1990, Gold Medallion, Finalist, 1988, Best All Around Series Author, 1989-90, Reviewers Choice. Membership: Romance Writers of America. Address: c/o Maureen Walters, Curtis Brown Ltd., 10 Astor Place, New York, NY 10013, USA.

CLAUSEN Jacob, b. 16 Feb 1937, Denmark. Author; Dramatist. m. Gertrud Grimnitz, 6 July 1963, 2 sons. Appointments: Agriculturist, 1954-69; Teacher, 1969-88;

Author, Dramatist, 1988-. Publications: Klassen, 1979; Laerkehimlen, 1981; Fare, fare krigsmand, 1983; Morgenroden, 1984; Babels Born, 1985; Byen kommer, 1986; Venner for evigt, 1987; Dig og mig og vi to. 1988; Agitatoren, 1988; Vaer ikke bange, 1990; Sidste ar i Timisoara, 1991; Liv og glade dage, 1992; Genforeningsspillene, 1995; Hjertebandet, 1995; Farlig Fredag, 1996; I morgen er det vores dag, 1997; Stene for Brod, 1998. Membership: Dansk Forfatterforening. Literary Agent: Forlaget Forum, Snaregade 4, 1205 Kobenhavn K, Denmark. Address: Aastrupvej 25, 6100 Haderslev, Denmark.

CLAY Linda. See: **JESPERSEN Per**.

CLAYTON John J(acob), b. 5 Jan 1935, New York, New York, USA. Professor of English; Writer. m. (1) Marilyn Hirsch, 31 July 1956, div 1974, 1 son, 1 daughter, (2) Marlynn Krebs, div 1983, 1 son, (3) Sharon Dunn, 26 May 1984, 1 son. Education: AB, Columbia University, 1956; MA, New York University, 1959; PhD, Indiana University, 1966. Appointments: Instructor, University of Victoria, British Columbia, 1962-63; Lecturer, Overseas Division, University of Maryland, 1963-64; Assistant Professor of Humanities, Boston University, 1964-69; Associate Professor, 1969-75, Professor of English, 1975-, University of Massachusetts at Amherst. Publications: Saul Bellow: In Defense of Man, 1968, 2nd edition, 1979; What Are Friends For? (novel), 1979; Bodies of the Rich (short stories), 1984; Gestures of Healing: Anxiety and the Modern Novel, 1991; Radiance (collection of stories), 1998; The Man I Never Wanted To Be (novel), 1998. Editor: The D C Heath Introduction to Fiction. Contributions to: Anthologies and periodicals. Honours: 2nd Prize, O Henry Prize Stories, 1995; Ohio State University Award in short fiction, 1998; Pushcart Prize, 1998. Address: 12 Lawton Road, RFD 3, Amherst, MA 01002, USA.

CLAYTON Martin David, b. 30 Dec 1967, Harrogate, England. Art Historian; Writer. Education: BA, History of Art, 1986-90, MA, 1993, Christ's College, Cambridge. Appointment: Assistant Curator, Royal Library, Windsor Castle. Publications: Leonardo da Vinci: The Anatomy of Man, 1992; Poussin: Works on Paper, 1995; Leonardo da Vinci: A Curious Vision, 1996. Literary Agent: John Johnstone Ltd. Address: Royal Library, Windsor Castle, Berkshire, England.

CLAYTON Mary. See: **LIDE MARY Ruth**.

CLAYTON Michaelwin, b. 20 Nov 1934, Bournemouth, Dorset, England. Journalist; Author. m. Marilyn Crowhurst, 28 Oct 1988, 1 son, 1 daughter. Appointments: News Editor, London Evening Standard, 1962-65; News Correspondent, BBC Radio and Television, 1965-73; Editor, Horse and Hound Magazine, 1973-94; Editor-in-Chief, Country Life, Shooting Times, The Field, 1994-97; Board Director, IPC Magazines, London, 1994-97; Chairman, British Horse Society, 1998-. Publications: A Hunting We Will Go, 1967; The Hunter, 1980; The Golden Thread, 1984; The Chase, 1987; Prince Charles, Horseman, 1987; Foxhunting in Paradise, 1993. Contributions to: Horse and Hound; Country Life; The Field. Honours: British Society of Magazine Editors Award for Services to British Magazine Industry, 1996. Literary Agent: Peters, Fraser and Dunlop. Address: 50/34 The Chambers, Chelsea Harbour, London SW10 0XF, England.

CLAYTON Peter Arthur, b. 27 Apr 1937, London, England. Publishing Consultant; Archaeological Lecturer. m. Janet Frances Manning, 5 Sept 1964, 2 sons. Education: School of Librarianship; North West Polytechnic, London, 1958; Institute of Archaeology, London University, 1958-62; University College, London University, 1958-62; University College, London, 1968-72. Appointments: Librarian, 1953-67; Archaeological Editor, Thames & Hudson, 1963-73; Humanities Publisher, Longmans, 1973; Managing Editor, British Museum's Publications, 1974-79; Publications Director, BA Seaby, 1980-87; Writer, Lecturer, 1987-. Publications: The Rediscovery of Ancient Egypt;

Archaeological Sites of Britain; Seven Wonders of the Ancient World; Treasures of Ancient Rome; Companion to Roman Britain; Great Figures of Mythology; Gods and Symbols of Ancient Egypt; Chronicle of the Pharaohs; Family Life in Ancient Egypt; The Valley of the Kings; Egyption Mythology. Contributions to: Journal of Egyptian Archaeology; Numismatic Chronicle; Coin & Medal Bulletin; Minerva. Memberships: Library Association, fellow; Society of Antiquaries of London, fellow; Royal Numismatic Society, fellow. Address: 41 Cardy Road, Boxmoor, Hemel Hempstead, Hertfordshire HP1 1RL, England.

CLEALL Charles, b. 1 June 1927, Heston, Middlesex, England. Writer. m. Mary Turner, 25 July 1953, 2 daughters. Education: Trinity College of Music, London; BMus, Jordanhill College of Education; MA, University College of North Wales. Appointments: Professor, Solo-Singing and Voice Production, 1949-52; Choral Scholar, Westminster Abbey, 1949-52; Conductor, Morley College Orchestra, 1950-52, Glasgow Choral Union, 1952-54; Music Assistant, BBC Midland Region, 1954-55; Music Master, Glyn County School, 1955-67; Lecturer in Music, Froebel Institute, Roehampton, 1967-68; Music Adviser, London Borough of Harrow, 1968-72; Northern Divisional Music Specialist, Her Majesty's Inspectorate of Schools in Scotland, 1972-87; Editor, Journal of The Ernest George White Society, 1983-87. Publications: Voice Production in Choral Technique, 1955, revised edition, 1970; The Selection and Training of Mixed Choirs in Churches, 1960; Sixty Songs from Sankey, 1960, revised edition, 1966; John Merbecke's Music for the Congregation at Holy Communion, 1963; Music and Holiness, 1964; Plainsong for Pleasure, 1969; Authentic Chanting, 1969; A Guide to Vanity Fair, 1982; Walking Round the Church of St James the Great, Stonehaven, 1993. Contributions to: Master of the Choir; Musical Opinion; Church of England Newspaper; Musical Times; Diapason; Music in Education; Music Teacher; Church and Organ Guide; Methodist Recorder; Organists' Review; Choir and Organ; Promoting Church Music; English Church Music Annual; English Church Music Quarterly; London Quarterly and Holborn Review; Life of Faith; Crusade Monthly; Burrswood Herald; Child Education; Methodist Magazine; Mosaic; Scottish Educational Review; Psychology of Music.Address: 10 Carronhall, Stonehaven, Aberdeen AB39 2QF, Scotland.

CLEARE John Silvey, b. 2 May 1936, London, England. Photographer; Writer. m. (2) Jo Jackson, 12 May 1980, 1 daughter. Education: Wycliffe College, 1945-54; Guildford School of Photography, 1957-60. Appointments: Joint Editor, Mountain Life magazine, 1973-75; Editorial Board, Climber and Rambler magazine, 1975-85. Publications: Rock Climbers in Action in Snowdonia, 1966; Sea-Cliff Climbing in Britain, 1973;Mountains, 1975; World Guide to Mountains, 1979; Mountaineering, 1980; Scrambles Among the Alps, 1986; John Cleare's Best 50 Hill Walks in Britain, 1988; Trekking: Great Walks in the World, 1988; Walking the Great Views, 1991; Discovering the English Lowlands, 1991; On Foot in the Pennines, 1994; On Foot in the Yorkshire Dales, 1996. Contributions to: Times; Sunday Times; Independent; Observer; World; Country Living; Boat International; Intercontinental; Alpine Journal; High; Climber; Great Outdoors. Honour: 35mm Prize, Trento Film Festival, for film The Climbers (as Cameraman), 1971. Membership: Outdoor Writers Guild, executive committee. Literary Agent: Laurel Anderson, Photosynthesis/Offshoot, 180 Harbor Drive No 219, Sausalito, CA 94965, USA. Address: Hill Cottage, Fonthill Gifford, Salisbury, Wiltshire SP3 6QW, England.

CLEARY Beverly Atlee, b. 12 Apr 1916, McMinnville, Oregon, USA. Writer. m. Clarence T Cleary, 6 Oct 1940, 1 son, 1 daughter. Education: BA, University of California at Berkeley, 1938; BA, University of Washington, 1939. Publications: Henry Huggins, 1950; Fifteen, 1956; The Mouse and the Motorcycle, 1965; Ramona the Pest, 1968; Dear Mr Henshaw, 1983; A Girl From Yamhill: A Memoir, 1988; Strider, 1991; Muggie Magic, 1992. Contributions to: Horn Book Magazine. Honours: Laura Ingalls Wilder Award, 1975; Newbery Honor Books, 1978, 1982; Newbery Award, 1984; Christopher Award, 1984; Everychild Award, 1985; Doctor of Humane Letters, 1992. Membership: Authors League of America. Address: Morrow Junior Books, 1350 Avenue of the Americas, New York, NY 10019, USA.

CLEARY Jon (Stephen), b. 22 Nov 1917, Sydney, New South Wales, Australia. Author; Screenwriter. Appointments: Journalist, Australian News and Information Bureau, London, 1948-49 and New York City 1949-51. Publications: The Small Glories (short stories), 1945; You Can't See Round Corners, 1947; The Long Shadow, 1949; Just Let Me Be, 1950; The Sundowners, 1952, screenplay 1961; The Climate of Courage, UK edition as Naked in the Night, 1954; Justin Bayard, 1955; The Green Helmet, 1957, screenplay 1960; Back of Sunset, 1959; The Siege of Pinchgut (screenplay with H Watt), 1959; North from Thursday, 1960; The Country of Marriage, 1961; Forest of the Night, 1962; Pillar of Salt (short stories), 1963; A Flight of Chariots, 1964; The Fall of an Eagle, 1965; The Pulse of Danger, 1966; The High Commissioner, 1967; The Long Pursuit, 1968; Season of Doubt, 1969; Remember Jack Hoxie, 1970; Helga's Webb, 1971; The Liberators (UK edition as Mask of the Andes), 1971; The Ninth Marquess (UK edition as Man's Estate), 1972; Ransom, 1973; Peter's Pence, 1974; Sidecar Boys (screenplay), 1974; The Safe House, 1975; A Sound of Lightning, 1976; High Road to China, 1977; Vortex, 1977; The Beaufort Sisters, 1979; A Very Pirate War, 1980; The Golden Sabre, 1981; The Faraway Drums, 1981; Spearfield's Daughter, 1982; The Phoenix Tree, 1984; The City of Fading Light, 1985; Dragons at the Party, 1987; Now and Then, Amen, 1988; Babylon South, 1989; Murder Song, 1990; Pride's Harvest, 1991; Dark Summer, 1992; Bleak Spring, 1993; Autumn Maze, 1994; Winter Chill, 1995; Endpeace, 1996. Literary Agent: Vivienne Schuster, Curtis Brown Ltd, Haymarket, London, England. Address: c/o Harper Collins, 77-85 Fulham Palace Road, London W6 8JB, England.

CLEESE John (Marwood), b. 27 Oct 1939, Weston-super-Mare, Somerset, England. Author; Actor. m. (1) Connie Booth, 1968, diss 1978, 1 daughter, (2) Barbara Trentham, 1981, diss 1990, 1 daughter, (3) Alyce Faye Eichelberger, 1993. Education: Clifton Sports Academy; MA, Downing College, Cambridge. Appointments: Many stage, television, and film appearances. Publications: Families and How to Survive Them (with Robin Skynner), 1983; The Golden Skits of Wing Commander Muriel Volestrangler FRHS and Bar, 1984; The Complete Fawlty Towers (with Connie Booth), 1989; Life and How to Survive It (with Robin Skynner), 1993. Honour: Honorary LLD, University St Andrews. Address: c/o David Wilkinson, 115 Hazlebury Road, London SW6 2LX, England.

CLEEVE Brian Talbot, b. 22 Nov 1921, Thorpe Bay, Essex, England. Author; Journalist. m. Veronica McAdie, 24 Sept 1945, 2 daughters. Education: BA, University of South Africa, 1954; PhD, University of Ireland, Dublin, 1956. Publications: Cry of Morning, 1970; Sara, 1975; House on the Rock, 1980; The Fourth Mary, 1982; Biographical Dictionary of Irish Writers, 1985; A Woman of Fortune, 1993. Contributions to: Numerous short stories, various magazines. Honours: Award, Mystery Writers of America, 1965; Knight of Mark Twain, 1972-73. Literary Agent: Elaine Markson, 44 Greenwich Avenue, New York, USA. Address: 60 Heytesbury Lane, Ballsbridge, Dublin 4, Ireland.

CLEMENT François, b. 21 Feb 1929, Paris, France. Physician; Writer. m. Jacqueline Tanner, 18 Sept 1986, 2 sons, 1 daughter. Education: Medicine Diploma, 1953; Privat-docent of Haematology, 1969. Appointment: Head of Haematologic Malignancies Unit, CHUV, 1981. Publication: Feuille de Bouleau, 1994. Contributions to: Medical scientific publications. Honours: Viganello Prize, 1964; Samuel Cruchand Prize, 1990. Membership: Société suisse des écrivains. Address: Ave Leman 39, 1005 Lausanne, Switzerland/

CLIFTON (Thelma) Lucille, b. 27 June 1956, Depew, New York, USA. Professor of Literature and Creative Writing; Poet. m. Fred J Clifton, 1958, dec, 1984, 2 sons, 4 daughters. Education: Howard University, Washington, DC, 1953-55; Fredonia State Teachers College, New York, 1955. Appointments: Poet-in-Residence, Coppin State College, Baltimore, 1972-76; Poet Laureate of Maryland, 1976-85; Visiting Writer, George Washington University, Washington DC, 1982-83; Professor of Literature and Creative Writing, University of California at Santa Cruz, 1985-; Distinguished Visiting Professor, St Mary's College, Maryland, 1989-91. Publications: Poetry: Good Times, 1969; Good News about the Earth, 1972; An Ordinary Woman, 1974; Two-Headed Woman, 1980; Good Woman: Poems and a Memoir, 1969-1980, 1987; Next, 1987; Ten Oxherding Pictures, 1989; Quilting: Poems, 1987-1990, 1991; The Book of Light, 1993. Other: Generations, 1976. Children's Books: 14 books, 1970-81. Honours: YM-YWHA Poetry Center Discovery Award, 1969; National Endowment for the Arts Grants,. 1970, 1972; Juniper Prize, 1980; Coretta Scott King Award, 1984. Address: c/o Curtis Brown, 10 Astor Place, New York, NY 10003, USA.

CLIMENHAGA Joel Ray, b. 9 Apr 1922, Bulawayo, Southern Rhodesia. Writer; Teacher. m. Zoe Lenore Motter, 21 Dec 1955, 1 son, 3 daughters. Education: AA, Chaffey College, Ontario, California, 1948-50; BA, 1953, MA, 1958, University of California at Los Angeles. Appointments: Teacher, Central Dauphin High School, Harrisburg, 1956-57, Wilmington College, Ohio, 1958-61, University of North Carolina at Chapel Hill, 1962-63, Culver-Stockton College, Canton, Missouri, 1963-68, Kansas State University, Manhattan, 1968-87, Tarkio College, Missouri, 1987-91, Teikyo Westmar University, LeMars, Iowa, 1991-92, Cochise College, Douglas, Arizona, 1996-. Publications include: Enough Forever, 1996; Exploration of the Great Northwest While Traveling with the Fat Man, 1996; Fragmented Rhythm Becomes Whole Again, 1997; A Peculiar Oleander Blooms, 1997; White Flower Unfeeling, 1997; A Message From the Other Side of the Universe, 1997; Not to Avoid the Rising Sun, 1998; My Face is an Open Book, 1998; Blackboards Soon Become Invisible, 1998; Cold Flowers of the Night, 1998; Early on in the Dance of Dying, 1998; Osmosis for the Unborn, 1998; The Murdering Hand of God, 1998; Death of Desire Along an Ancient Beach, 1998; The Sign for Myself is Infinity, 1998; Blood in the Air, 1998; Shadow of This Red Rock, 1998. Contributions to: Periodicals, journals, anthologies, reviews, quarterlies, newspapers and magazines. Honours include: Samuel Goldwyn Award for Creative Writing; Rockefeller Playwriting Grant; McIntosh Cup. Address: 218 Black Knob View, Bisbee, AZ 85603-1906, USA.

CLINTON Dorothy Louise Randle, b. 6 Apr 1925, Des Moines, Iowa, USA. Poet; Writer. m. Moses S Clinton, 6 June 1950, 1 son. Education: BA, Drake University, 1949. Publications: Ascending Line, 1978; Snobbery in Nuance, 1978; The Look and the See, 1979; Memory Lapse, 1983; The Only Opaque Light, 1989; You Don't Hear the Echo, You Don't Know, 1991. Contributions to: Anthologies and periodicals. Honours: Clover Awards, 1974, 1975; Editors' Choice Award, 1989; Editors' Preference Award of Excellence, 1995, National Library of Poetry; Inducted into the International Poetry Hall of Fame. Memberships: International Society of Authors and Artists; International Society of Poets. Address: 1530 Maple, Des Moines, IA 50316, USA.

CLINTON James, b. 11 Feb 1929, New York, New York, USA. Teaching. m. Shirley Powers, 22 July 1954, 5 daughters. Education: BS, Columbia University, 1950; MBA, University of Washington, 1961; PhD, St Louis University, 1973. Appointments: Navigator, Instructor, Systems Analyst, United States Air Force, 1951-55, 1959-77; Staff Assistant, Procter and Gamble, 1955; Investigator, US Civil Service Commission, 1956-59; Assistant Professor of Management, University of Wisconsin-Whitewater, 1977-80; Professor of Management, University Northern Colorado, 1980-98. Publications: The Loyal Opposition: Americans in North Vietnam, 1965-72; Boulder, Colorado: University Press of Colorado, 1996. Contributions to: Case Research Journal; Society for the Advancement of Management

Journal; Annual Advances in Business Cases. Address: 1720 Highland Drive SE, Puyallup, WA 98372, USA.

CLIVE William. See: BASSETT Ronald Leslie.

CLOUDSLEY Timothy, b. 18 Sept 1948, Cambridge, England. University Lecturer. m. Rhona Cleugh, 18 July 1987, 2 sons. Education: BA, Honours, Cantab, 1971; MA, 1974; Postgraduate Research, Durham University, 1972-74. Appointments: Lecturer, Sociology, Newcastle University, 1972-74, Napier University, Edinburgh, 1974-76, Heriot-Watt University, Edinburgh, 1976-77, Glasgow Caledonian University, 1977-. Publications: Poems to Light (Through Love and Blood), 1980; Mair Licht (anthology), 1988; The Construction of Nature (social philosophy), 1994; Coincidence (anthology), 1995; Incantations From Streams of Fire, 1997; Poems, 1998. Contributions to: Northlight Poetry Review; Understanding Magazine; Interactions; Romantic Heir; The People's Poetry; Cadmium Blue Literary Journal; Le Journal des Poètes. Memberships: Open Circle (Arts and Literature Organization), Glasgow, literary secretary, 1990-96. Address: 1 Hamilton Drive, Glasgow G12 8DN, Scotland.

CLOUDSLEY-THOMPSON John Leonard, b. 23 May 1921, Murree, India. Professor of Zoology Emeritus; Writer. m. Jessie Anne Cloudsley, 1944, 3 sons. Education: BA, 1946, MA, 1948, PhD, 1950, Pembroke College, Cambridge; DSc, London University, 1960. Appointments: Lecturer in Zoology, King's College, 1950-60, Reader in Zoology, 1971-72, Professor of Zoology, 1972-86, Professor of Zoology Emeritus, 1986-, Birkbeck College, University of London; Professor of Zoology, University of Khartoum and Keeper, Sudan Natural History Museum, 1960-71; National Science Foundation Senior Research Fellow, University of New Mexico, 1969; Visiting Professor, University of Kuwait, 1978, 1983, University of Nigeria, 1981, University of Qatar, 1986, Australian National University, 1987, Sultan Qaboos University, Muscat, 1988, Desert Ecological Research Unit of Namibia, 1989, Leverhulme Emeritus Fellow, University College London, 1987-89; Consultantships; Various expeditions. Publications: Biology of Deserts (editor), 1954; Spiders, Scorpions, Centipedes and Mites, 1958, 2nd edition, 1968; Animal Behaviour, 1960; Rhythmic Activity in Animal Physiology and Behaviour, 1961; Land Invertebrates (with John Sankey), 1961; Life in Deserts (with M J Chadwick), 1964; Desert Life, 1965; Animal Conflict and Adaptation, 1965; Animal Twilight: Man and Game in Eastern Africa, 1967; Microecology, 1967; Zoology of Tropical Africa, 1969; The Temperature and Water Relations of Reptiles, 1972; Terrestrial Environments, 1975; Insects and History, 1976; Evolutionary Trends in the Mating of Anthropoda, 1976; Environmental Physiology of Animals (co-editor), 1976; Man and the Biology of Arid Zones, 1977; The Water and Temperature Relations of Woodlice, 1977; The Desert, 1977; Animal Migration, 1978; Why the Dinosaurs Became Extinct, 1978; Wildlife of the Desert, 1979; Biological Clocks: Their Functions in Nature, 1980; Tooth and Claw: Defensive Strategies in the Animal World, 1980; Sahara Desert (editor), 1984; Guide to Woodlands, 1985; Evolution and Adaptation of Terrestrial Arthropods, 1988; Ecophysiology of Desert Arthropods and Reptiles, 1991; The Diversity of Desert Life, 1993; Predation and Defence Amongst Reptiles, 1994; The Nile Quest (novel), 1994; Biotic Interactions in Arid Lands, 1996. Other: Editor-in-Chief, Journal of Arid Environments, Adaptations of Desert Organisms, 1978-87; Teach Yourself Ecology, 1998; The Diversity of Amphibians and Reptiles: An Introduction, forthcoming. Monographs; 11 children's books. Contributions to: Encyclopedias and scholarly journals. Honours: Honorary Captain, 1944; Liveryman, Worshipful Company of Skinners, 1952; Royal African Society Medal, 1969; Silver Jubilee Gold Medal and Honorary DSc, University of Khartoum, 1981; Institute of Biology KSS Charter Award, 1981; Biological Council Medal, 1985; J H Grundy Memorial Medal, Royal Army Medical College, 1987; Foundation for Environmental Conservation Prize, Geneva, 1989; Peter Scott Memorial Award, British Naturalists' Association, 1993; Fellow honoris causa,

Linnean Society, 1997. Memberships: British Arachnological Society, president, 1982-85; British Herpetological Society, president, 1991-96; British Society of Chronobiology, president, 1985-87; World Academy of Arts and Sciences, fellow; Linnean Society, vice-president, 1975-76, 1977-78; Honorary member, Centre Internationale de Documentation Arachnologique, Paris, 1995. Address: 10 Battishill Street, London N1 1TE, England.

CLOUGH Brenda W(ang), b. 13 Nov 1955, Washington, District of Columbia, USA. Writer. m. Lawrence A Clough, 21 May 1977, 1 daughter. Education: BA, Carnegie Mellon University, 1977. Publications: The Crystal Crown, 1984; The Dragon of Mishbil, 1985; The Realm Beneath, 1986; The Name of the Sun, 1988; An Impossible Summer, 1992; How Like a God, 1997. Contributions to: Short stories in anthologies and periodicals. Address: 1941 Barton Hill Road, Reston, VA 20191, USA.

CLOUTIER Cécile, b. 13 June 1930, Quebec, Quebec, Canada. Poet; Writer; Professor Emerita. m. Jerzy Wojciechowski, 27 Dec 1966, 2 daughters. Education: BA, Collège de Sillery, 1951; Licence-ès-Lettres, 1953, Diplôme d'Etudes Supérieures, 1954, Université Laval; Doctorat en Esthétique, Université de Paris, 1962; MA, McMaster University, 1978; MA, University of Toronto, 1981; Doctorat en Psychologie, Université de Tours, 1983. Appointments: Professor of French and Quebec Literature, University of Ottawa, 1958-64; Professor of Aesthetics and French and Quebec Literature, 1964-95, Professor Emerita, 1995-, University of Toronto. Publications: Mains de sable, 1960; Cuivre et soies, 1964; Cannelles et craies, 1969; Paupières, 1970; Câblogrammes, 1972; Chaleuils, 1979; Springtime of Spoken Words, 1979; Près, 1983; Opuscula Aesthetica Nostra: Essais sur L'Esthétique, 1984; La Girafe, 1984; L'Echangeur, 1985; L'Ecouté, 1986; Solitude Rompue, 1986; Lampées, 1990; Périhélie, 1990; La poésie de l'Hexagone, 1990; Ancres d'Encre, 1993; Ostraka. Contributions to: Various publications. Honours: Medal, Société des Ecrivains de France, 1960; Centennial Medal, Canada, 1967; Governor-General's Award for Poetry, 1986; Medal Société des Poètes Français, 1994. Memberships: Association des Ecrivains de Langue Française; PEN Club de France; Société des Ecrivains; Société des Gens de Lettres de Paris; Union des Ecrivains Québécois. Address: 44 Farm Greenway, Don Mills, Ontario, Canada M3A 3M2.

CLOY John Dixon, b. 29 Nov 1955, Greenwood, MS, USA. Bibliographer. m. Margie Smith, 29 May 1988, divorced 15 June 1998. Education: BS, University of Southern Mississippi, 1978; MLS, University of Southern Mississippi, 1985; MA, Mississippi State University, 1990. Appointments: Reference Librarian, Jackson (MS) Public Library, 1985-88; Reference Librarian, Mississippi State University, 1988-90; Bibliographer, University of Mississippi, 1990-. Publication: Pensive Jester: The Literary Career of W W Jcobs, 1996. Contributions to: Barry Pain, Dictionary of Literary Biography, 1994; W W Jacobs, Encyclopedia of British Humourists, 1996. Membership: Lambda Iota Tau. Address: 4 CR 4015, Oxford, MS 38655, USA.

CLUSTER Richard Bruce, (Dick Cluster), b. 17 June 1947, Baltimore, Maryland, USA. Writer, 1 son. Education: BA, Harvard University, 1968; Venceremos Brigade, Cuba, 1970; Auto Mechanics Certificate, Newton Massachusetts High School, 1971. Publications: They Should Have Served That Cup of Coffee, 1979; Shrinking Dollars, Vanishing Jobs, 1980; Return to Sender, 1988; Repulse Monkey, 1989; Obligations of the Bone, 1992. Literary Agent: Gina Maccoby, New York, USA; Gregory & Radice, London, England. Address: 33 Jackson Street, Cambridge, MA 02140, USA.

CLUYSENAAR Anne, (Alice Andrée), b. 15 Mar 1936, Brussels, Belgium (Irish citizen). Lecturer; Poet; Songwriter; Librettist; Painter. m. Walter Freeman Jackson, 30 Oct 1976. Education: BA, Trinity College, Dublin, 1957; University of Edinburgh, 1963.

Appointments: Lecturer, King's College, Aberdeen, 1963-65, University of Lancaster, England, 1965-71, University of Birmingham, England, 1973-76, Sheffield City Polytechnic, England, 1976-87; Part-time Lecturer, University of Wales, Cardiff. Publications: A Fan of Shadows, 1967; Nodes, 1969; Aspects of Literary Stylistics, 1976; Selected Poems of James Burns Singers (editor), 1977; Poetry Introduction 4, 1978; Double Helix, 1982; Time-Slips: New and Selected Poems, 1995; The Life of Metrical and Free Verse by John Silkin (contributor), 1997; Poets on Poets, Henry Vaughan, 1997. Contributions to: Various publications. Memberships: Poetry Society, representative, Gwent, 1994-; Verbal Arts Association, chair, 1983-86. Address: Little Wentworth Farm, Llantrisant, Usk, Gwent NP5 1ND, Wales.

COASE Ronald (Harry), b. 29 Dec 1910, Willesden, London, England (US citizen). Professor Emeritus and Senior Fellow in Law and Economics; Writer. m. Marian Ruth Hartung, 7 Aug 1937. Education: BCom, 1932, DScEcon, 1951, London School of Economics. Appointments: Assistant Lecturer, Dundee School of Economics, 1932-34, University of Liverpool, 1934-35; Assistant Lecturer to Reader, London School of Economics, 1935-40, 1946-51; Head, Statistical Division, Forestry Commission, 1940-41; Statistician, later Chief Statistician, Central Statistical Office, Offices of War Cabinet, 1941-46; Professor, University of Buffalo, 1951-58, University of Virginia, 1958-64; Editor, Journal of Law and Economics, 1964-92; Clifford R Musser Professor, 1964-82, Professor Emeritus and Senior Fellow in Law and Economics, 1982-, University of Chicago. Publications: British Broadcasting: A Study in Monopoly, 1950; The Firm, the Market and the Law, 1988; Essays on Economics and Economists, 1994. Honours: Rockefeller Fellow, 1948; Senior Research Fellow, Hoover Institution, Stanford University, 1977; Nobel Prize for Economic Science, 1991; Honorary doctorates. Memberships: American Academy of Arts and Sciences, fellow; American Economic Association, distinguished fellow; British Academy, corresponding fellow; European Academy; London School of Economics, honorary fellow; Royal Economic Society. Address: 1515 North Astor Street, Chicago, IL 60610, USA.

COATES Kenneth Sidney, b. 16 Sept 1930, Leek, Staffordshire, England. Member, European Parliament; Special Professor in Adult Education. m. Tamara Tura, 21 Aug 1969, 3 sons, 3 daughters. Education: Mature State Scholar, 1956, BA, 1959, Nottingham University. Appointments: Assistant Tutor to Senior Tutor, 1960-80, Reader, 1980-89, Special Professor in Adult Education, 1990-, Nottingham University; Member, Labour Party, then Independent Labour, Nottingham, 1989-94, Nottinghamshire North and Chesterfield, 1994-, European Parliament. Publications: Industrial Democracy in Great Britain (with A J Topham), 1967, 3rd edition, 1976; Poverty: The Forgotten Englishman (with R L Silburn), 1970, 4th edition, 1983; The New Unionism (with A J Topham), 1972, 2nd edition, 1974; Trade Unions in Britain (with A J Topham), 1980, 3rd edition, 1988; Heresies: The Most Dangerous Decade, 1984; Trade Unions and Politics (with A J Topham), 1986; Think Globally, Act Locally, 1988; The Making of the Transport and General Workers' Union (with A J Topham), 1991; A European Recovery Programme, 1993; Full Employment for Europe (with Stuart Holland), 1995; Common Ownership: Clause Four and the Labour Party, 1995; The Right to Work: The Loss of Our First Freedom, 1995; Dear Commissioner, editor, 1996; The Blair Revelation, co-author, 1996; Poverty and Peace (pamphlet), 1997; Community Under Attack: The Struggle for Survival in the Coalfield Communities of Britain, co-author, 1997. Memberships: Bertrand Russell Peace Foundation; Institute of Workers' Control. Address: Bertrand Russell House, Gamble Street, Nottingham NG7 4ET, England.

COBB Vicki, b. 19 Aug 1938, New York, New York, USA. Writer. m. Edward S Cobb, 31 Jan 1960, div 1983, 2 sons. Education: BA, Barnard College, 1958; MA, Columbia University, 1960. Publications: Science

Experiments You Can Eat, 1972; Lots of Rot, 1981; How to Really Fool Yourself, 1981; The Secret Life of School Supplies, 1981; Bet You Can't, Science Impossibilities to Fool You, 1981; Gobs to Goo, 1983; The Monsters Who Died, 1983; Chemically Active, 1985; Inspector Bodyguard, 1986; The Science Safari Series; The Imagine Living Here Series; Inventions Series. Contributions to: Numerous professional journals. Honours: Childrens Science Book Award, 1981; Washington Irving Childrens Book Choice Award, 1984; Eva L Gordon Award, 1985; Commended by COPUS and the London Science Museum, 1989. Memberships: Authors Guild; ASJA; Society of Childrens Book Writers; National Writers Union. Address: 302 Pondside Drive, White Plains, NY 10607, USA.

COBBETT Richard. See: **PLUCKROSE Henry Arthur.**

COBBING Bob, b. 30 July 1920, Enfield, Middlesex, England. Poet. Education: Teacher's Certificate, Bognor Training College, 1949. Appointments: Coordinator, Association of Little Presses, 1971-92; Co-editor, Poetry and Little Press Information, 1980-92. Publications: Bill Jubobe: Selected Poems, 1942-75, 1976; Cygnet Ring: Collected Poems 1, 1977; A Movie Book, 1978; Two-Leaf Book, 1978; Concerning Concrete Poetry (with Peter Mayer) 1978; Found: Sound, 1978; Principles of Movement, 1978; Meet Bournemouth, 1978; Fugitive Poem No X, 1978; Game and Set, 1978; Ginetics, 1978; ABC/Wan do Tree: Collected Poems 2, 1978; Sensations of the Retina, 1978; A Peal in Air: Collected Poems 3, 1978; Fiveways, 1978; Niagara, 1978; Grin, 1979; A Short History of London (with Jeremy Adler), 1979; The Kollekted Kris Kringle: Collected Poems 4, 1979; Pattern of Performance, 1979; The Sacred Mushroom (with Jeremy Adler), 1980; Notes from the Correspondence, 1980; Voicings, 1980; (Soma), Light Song, 1981; Serial Ten (Portraits), 1981; Four Letter Poems, 2 series, 1981; Sound of Jade, 1982; In Line, 1982; Baker's Dozen, 1982; Lightsong Two, 1983; Bob Cobbing's Girlie Poems: Collected Poems 5, 1983; Sockless in Sandals: Collected Poems 6, 1985; Vowels and Consequences: Collected Poems 7, 1985; Lame, Limping, Mangled, Marred and Mutilated: Collected Poems 9, 1986; Metamorphosis, 1986; Variations on a Theme, 1986; Astound and Risible: Collected Poems 8, 1987; Processual: Collected Poems 10, 1987; Entitled: Entitled: Collected Poems 11, 1987; Improvisation is a Dirty Word: Collected Poems 12, 1990; Bob Jubile: Selected Poems 1944-90, 1990; Resonanzas, 1991; Grogram, 1991; Fuerteventura, 1992; Voice Prints: Collected Poems 13, 1993; Poems by RWC for RWC: Collected Poems 14, 1995; Domestic Ambient Noise (with Lawrence Upton) 1994-98; Gibbering His Wares: Collected Poems 15, 1996; Collaborations (with Lawrence Upton), 1997; Cylinder Head (with Jennifer Pike), 1997; 15 Shakespeare Kaku, 1998. Address: 89A Petherton Road, London N5 2QT, England.

COBURN Andrew, b. 1 May 1932, Exeter, New Hampshire, USA. Writer. Education: Suffolk University, Boston, 1954-58. Publications: Novels: The Trespassers, 1974; The Babysitter, 1979; Off Duty, 1980; Company Secrets, 1982; Widow's Walk, 1984; Sweetheart, 1985; Love Nest, 1987; Goldilocks, 1989; No Way Home, 1992; Voices in the Dark, 1994; Birthright, 1997. Contributions to: Transatlantic Magazine. Honour: Honorary DLitt, Merrimack College, USA, 1986. Literary Agent: Smith/Skolnik, 23 East 10th Street, No 712, New York, NY 10003, USA. Address: 303 Walnut Street, Westfield, NJ 07090, USA.

COBURN D(onald) L(ee), b. 4 Aug 1938, Baltimore, Maryland, USA. Dramatist. m. 1) Nazlee Joyce French, 24 Oct 1964, div Sept 1971, 1 son, 1 daughter, 2) Marsha Woodruff Maher, 22 Feb 1975. Education: Public schools, Baltimore. Appointments: Owner, Don Coburn & Associates, Baltimore, 1966-70, Donald L Coburn Corp, Dallas, 1973-75; Member, Stanford Agency, Dallas, 1970-73. Publications: Plays: The Gin Game, 1977; Bluewater Cottage, 1979; The Corporation Man, 1981; Currents Turned Awry, 1982; Guy, 1983; Noble Adjustment, 1986; Anna-Weston, 1988; Return to Blue

Fin, 1991. Screenplays: Flights of Angels, 1987; A Virgin Year, 1992. Honours: Pulitzer Prize in Drama, 1978; Golden Apple, 1978. Memberships: Authors League of America; Dramatists Guild of America; Société des Auteurs et Compositeurs Dramatiques; Texas Institute of Letters; Writers Guild of America. Address: c/o Writers Guild of America, 555 West 57th Street, New York, NY 10019, USA.

COBURN John. See: **COOK Peter John.**

COCHRAN Jeff. See: **DURST Paul.**

COCKETT Mary, b. 1915, England. Children's Author. Appointments: Editor, National Institute of Industrial Psychology, 1943-48, International Congress of Mental Health, 1948-49. Publications: The Marvellous Stick, 1972; The Joppy Stories; Boat Girl, 1972; Bells in Our Lives, 1973; Treasure, 1973; The Rainbow Walk, 1973; Look at the Little One, 1974; Dolls and Puppets, 1974; Walls, 1974; Snake in the Camp, 1975; Tower Raven, 1975; Backyard Bird Hospital, 1975; The Story of Cars, 1976; The Drowning Valley, 1978; The Birthday, 1979; Ladybird at the Zoo, Monster in the River, Pig at the Market, 3 Picture Books, 1979; The Christmas Tree, 1979; Money to Spend, 1980; Shadow at Applegarth, 1981; Hoo Ming's Discovery, 1982; The Cat and the Castle, 1982; The School Donkey, 1982; At the Tower, 1984; Crab Apples, 1984; Strange Hill, 1984; Zoo Ticket, 1985; Rescue at the Zoo, 1986; Winning All the Way, 1987; Kate of Candlewick, 1987; The Day of the Squirrels, 1987; A Place of his Own, 1987; Mystery on the Farm, 1988; Bridesmaids, 1989. Address: 24 Benville Avenue, Bristol BS9 2RX, England.

CODRESCU Andrei, b. 20 Dec 1946, Sibiu, Romania (US citizen, 1981). Professor of English; Author; Poet; Editor; Radio and Television Commentator. m. Alice Henderson, 12 Sept 1969, div 1998, 2 sons. Education: BA, University of Bucharest, 1965. Appointments: Professor of English, Louisiana State University, 1966-; Commentator, All Things Considered, National Public Radio; Editor, Exquisite Corpse, literary journal. Publications: Novels: The Repentence of Lorraine, 1994; The Blood Countess, 1995; Messiah, 1999-. Poetry: Comrade Past and Mister Present, 1991; Belligerence, 1993; Alien Candor: Selected Poems, 1970-1995, 1996. Essays: Raised by Puppets Only to be Killed by Research, 1987; Craving for Swan, 1988; The Disappearance of the Outside: A Manifesto for Escape, 1990; The Hole in the Flag: A Romanian Exile's Story of Return and Revolution, 1991; Road Scholar: Coast to Coast Late in the Century, 1993; The Muse is Always Half-Dressed in New Orleans, 1995; Zombification: Essays from NPR, 1995; The Dog With the Chip in His Neck: Essays from NPR & Elsewhere, 1996. Editor: American Poetry Since 1970: Up Late, 1988; The Stiffest of the Corpse: An Exquisite Corpse Reader, 1983-1990, 1990; American Poets Say Goodbye to the 20th Century, 1996. Film: Road Scholar, Public Broadcasting Service, 1994. Honours: George Foster Peabody Award, 1995; Freedom of Speech Award, American Civil Liberties Union, 1995; Literature Prize, Romanian Cultural Foundation, 1996. Address: 1114 Peniston, New Orleans, LA 70115, USA.

CODY James. See: **ROHRBACH Peter Thomas.**

CODY Sebastian, b. 6 Oct 1956, London, England. Writer; Journalist; Producer. m. Annabel Cole, 1997. Education: Universities of Vienna and York; BA Honours, Mathematics, Music; Trained as Director, National Film School. Appointments: Freelance Writer and Journalist, 1979-; BBC TV, 1979-81; Royal Opera House, Covent Garden, 1985; Editor, After Dark, Channel 4, 1987-98; Executive Producer, numerous television programmes, Open Media, including: The Secret Cabaret, 1990-92; James Randi - Psychic Investigator, 1991, Opinions, 1993-94, Brave New World, 1994, The Mediator, 1995, Is This Your Life?, 1995-96, Natural Causes, 1996, Suez, 1996, Secrets of the Psychics, 1997, Mossad - The Spy Machine, 1998. Address: The Mews Studio, 8 Addison Bridge Place, London W14 8XP, England.

COE Jonathan, b. 19 Aug 1961, Birmingham, England. Author. m. Janine McKeown, 28 Jan 1989. Education: BA, Trinity College, Cambridge, 1983; MA, 1984, PhD, 1986, Warwick University. Publications: The Accidental Woman, 1987; A Touch of Love, 1989; The Dwarves of Death, 1990; Humphrey Bogart: Take It and Like It, 1991; James Stewart: Leading Man 1994; What A Carve Up!, 1994; The House of Sleep, 1997. Contributions to: Periodicals. Honours: John Llewellyn Rhys Prize, 1995; Prix Femina, 1996; Writers' Guild Award, 1997. Address: c/o Peake Associates, 14 Grafton Crescent, London NW1 8LS, England.

COELHO Paulo, b. Aug 1947, Rio de Janeiro, Brazil. Author. Education: Attended law school. Publications: Arquivos do inferno, 1982; O diário de um mago, 1987, English translation as The Diary of a Magus: The Road to Santiago, 1992; O alquimista, 1988, English translation as The Alchemist: A Fable about Following Your Dream, 1993; As valkirias, 1992, English translation as The Valkyries: An Encounter with Angels, 1995; No margem do rio piedra eu sentei e chorei, 1994, English translation as By the River Piedra I Sat Down and Wept, 1996; Frases, 1996; Monte Circo, 1996, English translation, The Fifth Mountain, 1998; Brida, 1990; Veronika decide morrer, 1998. Honours: Several international best-sellers published in more than 41 languages. Address: c/o HarperCollins, 77-85 Fulham Palace Road, Hammersmith, London W6 8JB, England.

COERR Eleanor (Beatrice), (Eleanor B Hicks, Eleanor Page), b. 29 May 1922, Kamsack, Saskatchewan, Canada. Writer. m. Wymberley De Renne Coerr, 10 June 1965. Education: BA, American University, 1969; MLS, University of Maryland, 1971. Appointments: Reporter; Editor; Librarian; Writer. Publications: Many children's books, 1953-93. Address: c/o Harper Collins Childrens Books, Harper Collins Publishers Inc, 10 East 53rd Street, New York, NY 10022, USA.

COERS Donald (Vernon), b. 2 June 1941, San Marcos, Texas, USA. Professor of English; University Administrator; Writer; Editor. m. Mary Jeanne Coers, 30 Dec 1966, 1 son, 1 daughter. Education: BA, 1963, MA, 1969, University of Texas at Austin; PhD, Texas A&M University, 1974. Appointments: Assistant Professor, 1969-79, Associate Professor, 1979-86, Professor of English, 1986-, Coordinator of Graduate Studies, 1992-95, Associate Vice-President for Academic Affairs, 1995-, Sam Houston State University; Associate Editor, 1979-, The Texas Review. Publications: John Steinbeck as Propagandist: The Moon is Down Goes to War, 1991; After the Grapes of Wrath: Essays on John Steinbeck (co-editor with Paul Ruffin), 1995. Contributions to: Books and journals. Honours: Elizabeth Agee Prize, University of Alabama Press, 1990; Burkhardt Award, Ball State University Foundation, 1995. Address: 3799 Summer Lane, Huntsville, TX 77340, USA.

COETZEE John Michael, b. 9 Feb 1940, Cape Town, South Africa. Writer; Professor. 1 son, 1 daughter. Education: BA, 1960, MA, 1963, University of Cape Town; PhD, University of Texas, USA, 1969. Appointments: Assistant Professor, English, 1968-71, Butler Professor of English, 1984, 1986, State University of New York at Buffalo; Lecturer, English, 1972-82, Professor of General Literature, 1984-, University of Cape Town; Hinkley Professor of English, Johns Hopkins University, 1986, 1989; Visiting Professor, English, Harvard University, 1991. Publications: Dusklands, 1974; In the Heart of the Country, 1977; Waiting for the Barbarians, 1980; Life and Times of Michael K, 1983; Foe, 1986; White Writing, 1988; Age of Iron, 1990; Doubling the Point, 1992; The Master of Petersburg, 1994; Giving Offence, 1996; Boyhood: Scenes from Provincial Life, 1997. Contributions to: Essays in various journals. Honours: CNA Literary Awards, 1977, 1980, 1983; James Tait Black Prize, 1980; Geoffrey Faber Award, 1980; Booker McConnell Prize, 1983; Prix Femina Etranger, 1985; Jerusalem Prize, 1987; Sunday Express Award, 1990; Premio Mondello, 1994; Irish Times International Fiction Prize, 1995. Address: PO Box 92,

Rondebosch, 7700, South Africa.

COFFEY Brian, See: **KOONTZ Dean R(ay).**

COFFEY Charles M, (Charles Moore), b. 8 July 1941, Chicago, Illinois, USA. Writer; Researcher. Education: Beloit College, Wisconsin, 1963; Postgraduate, Purdue University, 1980. Appointments: US Air Force, 1963; Editor, WDBJ, Times-World Corporation, Roanoke, Virginia, 1964-66; Editor, Producer, Reporter, WHAS Radio and Television, Louisville, Kentucky, 1967-72; Assistant to Chancellor, Indiana University Southeast, New Albany, 1972-77; Director of Special Events, Indiana University, Bloomington, 1977-82; Director of Alumni Relations, Indiana-Purdue University, 1982-88; Speech Writer, Lt Governor of Indiana, 1989-97; Director of Communication Research, Indiana Department of Administration, 1997-; Reporter, ABC Radio Network Newscasts, CBS Radio Newscasts, CBS Television Newscasts; Producer, Reporter, Air Trafic Control System; Publication: Public Record Destruction Report, 1970. Contributions to: National Observer; NUVO; Indiana Magazine of History; Case Currents. Honours: Associated Press Broadcasters Awards for Excellence, 1964, 1965. Address: 3922 Alsace Place, Indianapolis, IN 46226, USA.

COFFEY Marilyn J(une), b. 22 July 1937, Alma, Nebraska, USA. Writer; Poet; Associate Professor of Creative Writing. m. 15 April 1961, div, 1 son. Education: BA, University of Nebraska, 1959; MFA, Brooklyn College, 1981. Appointments: Faculty, Pratt Institute, Brooklyn, 1966-69, 1973-90; Adjunct Communication Instructor, St Mary's College, Lincoln, Nebraska, 1990-92; Associate Professor of Creative Writing, Ft Hays State University, 1992-. Publications: Marcella (novel), 1973; Great Plains Patchwork (non-fiction), 1989; A Cretan Cycle: Fragments Unearthed From Knossos (poetry), 1991; Creating the Classic Short Story: A Workbook, 1995; Delicate Footsteps: Poems About Real Women, 1995. Contributions to: Anthologies, journals, reviews, and newspapers. Honours: Pushcart Prize, 1976; Master Alumnus, University of Nebraska, 1977; Winner, Newark Public Library Competitions, New Jersey, 1985, 1987-88; Several grants. Memberships: E A Burnett Society, charter member; Poets and Writers. Address: c/o Department of English, Fort Hays State University, Hays, KS 67601, USA.

COFFMAN Virginia (Edith), (Victor Cross, Virginia Du Vaul, Jeanne Duval, Anne Stanfield), b. 30 July 1914, San Francisco, California, USA. Author. Education: AB, University of California at Berkeley, 1938. Publications: Survivor of Darkness, 1973; The Ice Forest, 1976; Looking Glass, 1979; The Lombard Cavalcade, 1982; Dark Winds, 1985; The Royles, 3 volumes, 1991, 1992, 1994. Address: c/o Severn House Publishers Ltd, 41 East 57th Street, 15th Floor, New York, NY 10022, USA.

COGSWELL Frederick William, b. 8 Nov 1917, East Centreville, New Brunswick, Canada. Professor Emeritus; Author; Poet; Editor; Translator. m. (1) Margaret Hynes, 3 July 1944, dec 2 May 1985, 2 daughters, (2) Gail Fox, 8 Nov 1985. Education: BA, 1949, MA, 1950, University of New Brunswick; PhD, University of Edinburgh, 1952. Appointments: Assistant Professor, 1952-57, Associate Professor, 1957-61, Professor, 1961-83, Professor Emeritus, 1983-, University of New Brunswick; Editor, Fiddlehead Magazine, 1952-66, Humanities Association Bulletin, 1967-72. Publications: The Stunted Strong, 1955; The Haloed Tree, 1956; Testament of Cresseid, 1957; Descent from Eden, 1959; Lost Dimensions, 1960; A Canadian Anthology, 1960; Five New Brunswick Poets, 1962; The Arts in New Brunswick, 1966; Star People, 1968; Immortal Plowman, 1969; In Praise of Chastity, 1970; One Hundred Poems of Modern Quebec, 1971; The Chains of Liliput, 1971; The House Without a Door, 1973; Against Perspective, 1979; A Long Apprenticeship: Collected Poems, 1980; Pearls, 1983; The Edge to Life, 1987; The Best Notes Merge, 1988; Black and White Tapestry, 1989; Unfinished Dreams: Contemporary Poetry of Acadie, 1990; Watching an Eagle, 1991; When the Right Light Shines, 1992; In Praise of Old Music, 1992; In My Own Growing, 1993; As I See It, 1994; In Trouble With Light, 1996. Honours: Order of Canada; Medals; Awards. Memberships: League of Canadian Poets; PEN; Writers Federation of New Brunswick. Address: Comp A6, Site 6, RR4, Fredericton, New Brunswick E3B 4X5, Canada.

COHAN Tony, (Anthony Robert Cohan), b. 28 Dec 1939, New York, New York, USA. Writer. m. 1 June 1974, 1 daughter. Education: BA, University of California, 1961. Publications: Nine Ships, 1975; Canary, 1981; The Flame, 1983; Opium, 1984; Agents of Desire, 1997; Mexicolor, 1997. Honour: Notable Book of the Year, 1981. Memberships: Authors Guild; PEN. Address: PO Box 1170, Venice, CA 90294, USA.

COHEN Daniel, b. 12 Mar 1936, Chicago, Illinois, USA. Author. m. Susan Handler, 2 Feb 1958, 1 daughter dec. Education: Journalism degree, University of Illinois, 1959. Appointments: Assistant Editor, 1960-65, Managing Editor, 1965-69, Science Digest. Publications: About 100 books of young adult non-fiction; 10 children's books; 20 other books; Over 25 books in collaboration with wife. Membership: Authors Guild. Address: 24 Elizabeth Street, Port Jervis, NY 12771, USA.

COHEN Leonard (Norman), b. 21 Sept 1934, Montreal, Quebec, Canada. Poet; Singer; Songwriter; Author. Education: BA, English, McGill University, 1955. Appointments: Many poetry readings; Various concert appearances in Canada and abroad. Publications: Let Us Compare Mythologies, 1956; The Spice-Box of Earth, 1961; The Favourite Game, 1963; Flowers for Hitler, 1964; Beautiful Losers, 1966; Parasites of Heaven, 1966; Selected Poems 1956-1968, 1968; The Energy of Slaves, 1972; Death of a Lady's Man, 1978; Book of Mercy, 1984; Stranger Music: Selected Poems and Songs, 1993. Other: Various songs and recordings. Honours: William Harold Moon Award, Recording Rights Organizatioin of Canada Ltd, 1984; Juno Hall of Fame, 1991. Address: c/o Kelley Lynch, 419 North Larchmont Boulevard, Suite 91, Los Angeles, CA 90004, USA.

COHEN Matthew, b. 30 Dec 1942, Kingston, Ontario, Canada. Writer; Poet; Translator. 1 son, 1 daughter. Education: BA, 1964, MA, 1965, Graduate Studies, 1966, University of Toronto. Appointments: Lecturer, McMaster University, 1967-68; Writer-in-Residence, University of Alberta, 1975-76, University of Western Ontario, 1981; Visiting Professor, University of Victoria, 1979-80, University of Bologna, 1984. Publications: Korsoniloff, 1969; Johnny Crackle Sings, 1971; Columbus and the Fat Lady, and Other Stories, 1972; Too Bad Galahad (stories), 1972; The Disinherited, 1974; Peach Melba (poetry), 1975; Wooden Hunters, 1975; The Colours of War, 1977; Night Flights, and Other Stories, New and Selected, 1978; The Sweet Second Summer of Kitty Malone, 1979; Flowers of Darkness, 1981; The Expatriate: Collected Short Stories, 1982; Café Le Dog (stories), 1983; The Spanish Doctor (novel), 1984; Nadine (novel), 1986; Living on Water (stories), 1988; Emotional Arithmetic (novel), 1990; Frued: The Paris Notebooks (stories), 1991; The Bookseller (novel), 1993; Lives of the Mind Slaves: Selected Stories, 1994; Last Seen (novel), 1996. Honours: Senior Canada Council Arts Awards, 1977, 1985; John Glassco Translation Prize, 1991. Membership: Writers' Union of Canada, chairman, 1985-86. Address: PO Box 401, Verona, Ontario, KOH 2W0, Canada.

COHEN Michael Joseph, b. 29 Apr 1940, London, England. Professor of History; Writer. Education: BA, University of London, 1969; PhD, London School of Economics and Political Science, 1971. Appointments: Lecturer, 1972-77, Senior Lecturer, 1977-81, Associate Professor, 1981-86, Professor, 1986-, Lazarus Philips Chair of History, 1990-, Bar Ilan University; Visiting Professor, Stanford University, 1977, 1981, Hebrew University, Jerusalem, 1978-80, 1981-83, Duke University and University of North Carolina, Chapel Hill, 1980-81, University of British Columbia, 1985-86; Bernard and Audre Rapaport Fellow, American Jewish Archives, Cincinnati, 1988-89; Meyerhoff Visiting Professor of Israel Studies, University of Maryland, College Park, 1992-98; Member, Institute of Advanced Studies, Princeton, 1998; Visiting Professor, San Diego State University, 1999. Publications: Palestine: Retreat From the Mandate, 1936-45, 1978; Palestine and the Great Powers, 1982; Churchill and the Jews, 1985; The Origins of the Arab-Zionist Conflict, 1914-1948, 1987; Palestine to Israel: From Mandate to Independence, 1988; Truman and Israel, 1990; Fighting World War Three from the Middle East: Allied Contingency Plans, 1945-1954, 1997, Hebrew edition, 1998. Editor: The Weizmann Letters, Volumes XX, XXI, 1936-1945, 1979; The History of the Founding of Israel, Part III, The Struggle for the State of Israel, 1939-1948,10 vols, 1988; Bar-Ilan Studies in Modern History, 1991; British Security Problems in the Middle East During the 1930s: The Conquest of Abyssinia to World War Two (with Martin Kolinsky), 1992; The Demise of Empire: Britain's Responses to Nationalist Movements in the Middle East, 1943-1955 (with Martin Kolinsky), 1998. Contributions to: Scholarly journals. Address: c/o General History Department, Bar-Ilan University, 52100 Ramat-Gan, Israel.

COHEN Morton Norton, (John Moreton), b. 27 Feb 1921, Calgary, Alberta, Canada. Professor Emeritus; Lecturer; Author. Education: AB, Tufts University, 1949; MA, 1950, PhD, 1958, Columbia University. Appointments: Tutor to Professor, City College, 1952-81, Member, Doctoral Faculty, 1964-81, Deputy Executive Officer, PhD Programme in English, 1976-78, 1979-80, Professor Emeritus, 1981-, City University of New York. Publications: Rider Haggard: His Life and Works, 1960, 2nd edition, revised, 1968; A Brief Guide to Better Writing (co-author), 1960; Rudyard Kipling to Rider Haggard: The Record of a Friendship, 1965; Lewis Carroll's Photographs of Nude Children, 1978, republished as Lewis Carroll, Photographer of Children: Four Nude Studies, 1979; The Russian Journal II, 1979; The Letters of Lewis Carroll (editor), 2 volumes, 1979; Lewis Carroll and the Kitchins, 1980; Lewis Carroll and Alice 1832-1882, 1982; The Selected Letters of Lewis Carroll, 1982, 3rd edition, 1995; Lewis Carroll and the House of Macmillan (co-editor), 1987; Lewis Carroll: A Biography, 1995. Contributions to: Many magazines, journals, papers and books. Honours: Fulbright Fellow, 1954-55, 1974-75; Guggenheim Fellowship, 1966-67; Research Grant, National Endowment for the Humanities, 1974-75; Publication Grant, Guggenheim Foundation, 1979; Royal Society of Literature, fellow. Memberships: Lewis Carroll Society; Lewis Carroll Society of North America; Tennyson Society; Century Association, New York. Address: 55 East 9th Street, Apartment 10-D. New York, NY 10003, USA.

COHEN Sharleen Cooper, b. 11 June 1940, Los Angeles, California, USA. Author. m. Martin L Cohen, 27 Aug 1972, 2 daughters. Education: University of California at Berkeley, 1957-58; University of California at Los Angeles, 1958-60; Los Angeles Valley Film School, 1976-78. Publications: The Day after Tomorrow, 1979; Regina's Song, 1980; The Ladies of Beverly Hills, 1983; Marital Affairs, 1985; Love, Sex and Money, 1988; Lives of Value, 1991; Innocent Gestures, 1994; Sheba (musical stage production), 1995-96. Contributions to: Good Housekeeping. Memberships: Authors Guild; PEN; Writers Guild of America. Address: 24858 Malibu Road, Malibu, CA 90265, USA.

COHEN Stephen F(rand), b. 25 Nov 1938, Indianapolis, Indiana, USA. Professor of Politics and Russian Studies; Writer. m. (1) Lynn Blair, 25 Aug 1962, div, 1 son, 1 daughter, (2) Katrina vanden Heuvel, 4 Aug 1988, 1 daughter. Education: BA, 1960, MA, 1962, Indiana University; PhD, 1969, Russian Institute Certificate, 1969, Columbia University. Appointments: Instructor, Columbia College, 1965-68; Junior Fellow, 1965-68, Senior Fellow, 1971-73, 1976-77, 1985, Associate, 1972-85, Visiting Professor, 1973-84, Visiting Scholar, 1980-81, Columbia University; Assistant Professor, 1968-73, Faculty Associate, Center of International Studies, 1969-, Director, Russian Studies Program, 1973-80, 1989-94, Princeton University;

Consultant and Commentator, CBS News; Associate Editor, World Politics; Professor of Russian Studies and History, New York University, Professor Emeritus, Princeton University, 1998-. Publications: The Great Purge Trial (co-editor), 1965; Bukharin and the Bolshevik Revolution: A Political Biography, 1888-1938, 1973; The Soviet Union Since Stalin (co-editor), 1980; An End to Silence: Uncensored Opinion in the Soviet Union (editor), 1982; Rethinking the Soviet Experience: Politics and History Since 1917, 1985, expanded edition, 1997; Sovieticus: American Perceptions and the Soviet Realities, 1985; Voices of Glasnost: Interviews with Gorbachev's Reformers (co-author and co-editor), 1989; Rethinking Russia, forthcoming. Contributions to: Books, scholarly journals and periodicals; Contributing Editor, The Nation. Honours: Guggenheim Fellowships, 1976-77, 1989; Rockefeller Foundation Humanities Fellowship, 1980-81; National Endowment for the Humanities Fellowship, 1984-85; Fulbright-Hays Faculty Research Abroad Fellowship, 1988-89. Memberships: American Association for the Advancement of Slavic Studies; American Historical Association; American Political Science Association; Council on Foreign Relations. Address: Department of Russian Studies, New York University, 19 University Place, New York, NY 10003-4556, USA.

COHEN Susan, b. 27 Mar 1938, Chicago, Illinois, USA. Author. m. Daniel Cohen, 2 Feb 1958, 1 daughter dec. Education: University of Illinois, 1957-59; BA, New School for Social Research, 1960; MSW, Adelphi University, 1962. Publications: 25 books in collaboration with husband; 8 Gothic books; 4 mystery books. Address: 24 Elizabeth Street, Port Jervis, NY 12771, USA.

COHN Samuel Kline Jr, b. 13 Apr 1949, Birmingham, Alabama, USA. Professor of Medieval History; Writer. m. Genevieve A Warwick, 15 July 1994, 1 son. Education: BA, Union College, 1971; MA, University of Wisconsin at Madison, 1973; Dip di Statistica, Università degli Studi di Firenze, 1976-77; PhD, Harvard University, 1978. Appointments: Assistant Professor, Wesleyan University, 1978-79; Assistant Professor, 1979-85, Associate Professor, 1986-89, Professor of History, 1989-95, Brandeis University; Visiting Professor, Brown University, 1990-91; Professor of Medieval History, University of Glasgow, 1995-. Publications: The Laboring Classes in Renaissance Florence, 1980; Death and Property in Siena 1205-1800: Strategies for the Afterlife, 1988; The Cult of Remembrance and the Black Death: Six Renaissance Cities in Central Italy, 1992; Portraits of Medieval and Renaissance Living: Essays in Memory of David Herlihy (editor), 1996; Women in the Streets: Essays on Sex and Power in the Italian Renaissance, 1996; The Black Death and the Transformation of the West (with David Herlihy), 1996; The Florentine Regional State as seen from the Mountains, forthcoming. Contributions to: Scholarly books and journals. Honours: Honorary Krupp Foundation Fellowship, 1976; Fulbright-Hays Fellowship, Italy, 1977; Fellow, Center for European Studies, Harvard University, 1977-; National Endowment for the Humanities Research Fellowship, 1982-83; Guest Fellow, Villa I Tatti, Settignano, Italy, 1988-89; Howard R Marraro Prize, American Catholic Historical Association, 1989; Outstanding Academic Book Selection, Choice magazine, 1993; Villa I Tatti Fellowship, 1993-94; Guggenheim Fellowship, 1994-95. Memberships: American Historical Association; Society for Italian Historical Studies; Royal Historical Society, fellow. Address: 8 Cleveden Crescent, Glasgow G12 0PB, Scotland.

COLBORN Nigel, b. 20 Feb 1944, Nottingham, England. Journalist; Presenter; Author; Gardener. m. Rosamund F M Hewlett, 10 Nov 1972, 2 sons, 2 daughters. Education: King's School, Ely, Cambs, England; BSc, Cornell University, USA, 1968. Publications: The Classic Horticulturist, 1987; This Gardening Business (Humour), 1989; Leisurely Gardening, 1989; Family Piles (humour), 1990; The Container Garden, 1990; Short Cuts to Great Gardens, 1993; The Good Old Fashioned Gardener, 1993; Annuals and Bedding Plants, 1994; The Kirkland Acres (novel),

1994; The Congregation (novel), 1996; A Flower for Every Day, 1996. Contributions to: Newspapers and magazines. Honour: Royal Society of Arts, fellow. Memberships: Society of Authors; Royal Horticultural Society, standing committee; Hardy Plant Society; Alpine Garden Society; International PEN. Address: Careby Manor, Careby, Stamford, Lincolnshire PE9 4EA, England.

COLE Adrian Christopher Synnot, b. 22 July 1949, Plymouth, England. Local Government Officer; Author. m. 25 May 1977, 1 son, 1 daughter. Publications: The Dream Lords, 1975; Madness Emerging, 1976; Paths in Darkness, 1977; The Lucifer Experiment, 1981; The Sleep of Giants, 1984; A Place Among the Fallen, 1986; The God in Anger, 1988; Mother of Storms, 1989; Thief of Dreams, 1989; Warlord of Heaven, 1990; Labyrinth of Worlds, 1990. Contributions to: Numerous magazines and journals. Membership: British Fantasy Society. Address: The Old Forge, 35 Meddon Street, Bideford, Devon Ex39 2EF, England.

COLE Barry, b. 13 Nov 1936, Woking, Surrey, England. Writer; Poet. m. Rita Linihan, 1959, 3 daughters. Appointments: Northern Arts Fellow in Literature, Universities of Durham and Newcastle-upon-Tyne, England, 1970-72. Publications: Blood Ties, 1967; Ulysses in the Town of Coloured Glass, 1968; A Run Across the Island, 1968; Moonsearch, 1968; Joseph Winter's Patronage, 1969; The Search for Rita, 1970; The Visitors, 1970; The Giver, 1971; Vanessa in the City, 1971; Pathetic Fallacies, 1973; The Rehousing of Scaffardi; Dedications, 1977; The Edge of the Common, 1989; Inside Outside: New and Selected Poems, 1997. Contributions to: New Statesman; Spectator; Listener; Times Educational Supplement; Times Higher Educational Supplement; Critical Survey; Atlantic Monthly; Tribune; London Magazine; Transatlantic Review; Observer; Guardian. Address: 68 Myddelton Square, London EC1R 1XP, England.

COLE Joanna, (Ann Cooke), b. 11 Aug 1944, Newark, New Jersey, USA. Children's Author. m. Philip A Cole, 8 Oct 1965, 1 daughter. Education: University of Massachusetts at Amherst; Indiana University; BA, City College of New York, 1967. Publications: Over 35 non-fiction books for children; 28 fiction books for children; 9 anthologies for children; The Magic School Bus series, 1986-. Honours: Numerous awards and citations. Memberships: Authors Guild; Authors League of America; Society of Children's Book Writers; American Association of the Advancement of Science.

COLE John Morrison, b. 23 Nov 1927, Belfast, Northern Ireland. Journalist; Broadcaster; Writer. m. Margaret Isobel Williamson, 4 Sept 1956, 4 sons. Eduction: London University, 1952. Publications: The Poor of the Earth, 1976; The Thatcher Years, 1987; As It Seemed to Me: Political Memoirs, 1995. Contributions to: Guardian; New Statesman. Honours: Granada Television Newspaper Award, 1960; Royal Television Society Broadcast Journalist of the Year Award, 1990; British Academy of Film and Television Arts Richard Dimbleby Award, 1992; Honorary Doctorates, Open University, 1992, Queen's University, Belfast, 1992, University of Ulster, 1992, University of St Andrews, 1993. Membership: Athenaeum Club. Address: c/o BBC Office, House of Commons, Westminister, London SW1A 0AA, England.

COLE William (Rossa), b. 20 Nov 1919, Staten Island, New York, USA. Author; Poet; Reviewer. m. (1) Peggy Bennett, May 1947, div, 2 daughters, (2) Galen Williams, 10 July 1967, 2 sons. Appointments: Publicity Director, 1946-58, Publicity Director and Editor, 1958-61, Simon & Schuster Inc, New York City; Columnist, Trade Winds, Saturday Review, 1974-79; Book Reviewer, Endless Vacation, 1990-. Publications: A Cat-Hater's Handbook, or, The Ailurophobe's Delight (with Tomi Ungerer), 1963; Uncoupled Couplets: A Game of Rhymes, 1966. Editor: 8 poetry anthologies and 10 other anthologies; 7 anthologies for children; 35 cartoon anthologies. Contributions to: Periodicals. Honour: American Library

Association Notable Books, 1958, 1964, 1965. Memberships: Authors Guild; American PEN; International PEN; Poets and Writers; Poetry Society of America. Address: 201 West 54th Street, New York, NY 10019, USA.

COLEGATE Isabel Diana, b. 10 Sept 1931, London, England. Novelist. m. Michael Briggs, 12 Sept 1953, 2 sons, 1 daughter. Publications: The Blackmailer, 1958; A Man of Power, 1960; The Great Occasion, 1962; Statues in a Garden, 1964; Orlando King, 1968; Orlando at the Brazen Threshold, 1971; Agatha, 1973; News from the City of the Sun, 1979; The Shooting Party, 1980 (filmed 1985); A Glimpse of Sion's Glory, 1985; Deceits of Time, 1988; The Summer of the Royal Visit, 1991; Winter Journey, 1995. Honours: Fellow, Royal Society of Literature, 1981; W H Smith Literary Award, 1981; Honorary MA, University of Bath, 1988. Membership: Author's Society. Literary Agent: Peters Fraser & Dunlop. Address: Midford Castle, Bath BA1 7BU, England.

COLEMAN Jane Candia. See: CANDIA Jane.

COLEMAN Jane (Winthrop) Candia, b. 9 Jan 1939, Pittsburgh, Pennsylvania, USA. Writer. m. (1) Bernard D Coleman, div 1989, (2) Glenn G Boyer, 1989, 2 sons. Education: BA, University of Pittsburgh, 1961. Appointments: Writer-in-Residence, 1980-85, Director, Women's Creative Writing Center, 1985-86, Carlow College, Pittsburgh; Lecturer, University of Pittsburgh, 1981. Publications: Stories from Mesa Country; No Roof But Sky; Deep in His Heart JR is Laughing at Us; Discovering Eve; Shadows in My Hands, 1993; Doc Holliday's Woman, 1995; Moving On, 1997; I, Pearl Hart, 1998. Contributions to: Christian Science Monitor; Horseman; Puerto Del Sol; South Dakota Review; Pennsylvania Review; Yankee; Aqassiz Review; Snowy Egret. Honours: Writing Grant, Pennsylvania Council on the Arts; Western Heritage Award, Poetry, Short Fiction; Grant, Arizona Arts Commission, 1993; Spur Award, Western Writers of America, 1993, 1995. Memberships: Western Writers of America; Authors Guild; PEN. Literary Agent: Golden West Literary Agency. Address: PO Box 40, Rodeo, NM 88056, USA.

COLEMAN Robert Gordon, b. 17 July 1922, Beechworth, Victoria, Australia. Journalist; Author. m. Lilian Gill, 4 June 1949, 1 daughter. Appointments: Working Journalist (reporter, feature writer, cadet counsellor, columnist, leader writer), 1940-86; Freelance Journalist and Author, 1986-. Publications: Reporting for Work (editor), 1970; The Pyjama Girl, 1978; Above Renown, 1988; Seasons in the Sun, 1993. Honours: Australian Automobile Association National Journalism Award, 1967; Highly Commended, Graham Perkin Award for Journalist of the Year, 1980. Memberships: Australian Journalists Association; Victorian Fellowship of Australian Writers. Address: 34 Folkestone Crescent, Beaumaris, Victoria 3193, Australia.

COLEMAN Terry, (Terence Francis Frank), b. 13 Feb 1931, Bournemouth, England; Journalist; Writer. m. (1) Lesley Fox-Strangeways Vane, 1954, div, 2 daughters, (2) Vivien Rosemary Lumsdaine Wallace, 1981, 1 son, 1 daughter. Education: LLB, London University, 1958. Appointments: Editor, Savoir Faire; Sub-Editor, Sunday Mercury, and Birmingham Post; Reporter, then Arts Correspondent, 1961-70, Chief Feature Writer, 1970-74, 1976-79, New York Correspondent, 1980-81, Special Correspondent, 1982-89, Guardian; Special Writer, Daily Mail, 1974-76; Associate Editor, The Independent, 1989-91; Columnist, Guardian and Mail on Sunday, 1992-. Publications: The Railway Navvies, 1965; A Girl for the Afternoons, 1965; Providence and Mr Hardy (with Lois Deacon), 1966; The Only True History: Collected Journalism, 1969; Passage to America, 1971; The Liners, 1976; The Scented Brawl: Collected Journalism, 1978; Southern Cross, 1979; Thanksgiving, 1981; Movers and Shakers: Collected Interviews, 1987; Thatcher's Britain, 1987; Empire, 1993. Contributions to: Various publications. Honours: Yorkshire Post Prize for Best First Book of the Year, 1965; Feature Writer of the Year, British Press Awards, 1982; Journalist of the Year,

Granada Awards, 1987. Membership: Society of Authors. Literary Agent: Peters, Fraser and Dunlop, Chelsea Harbour, London SW10 0XF, England. Address: 18 North Side, London SW4 0RQ, England.

COLEMAN Wanda, b. 13 Nov 1946, Los Angeles, California, USA. Writer; Poet. Publictions: Imagoes, 1983; Heavy Daughter Blues: Poems and Stories, 1987; War of Eyes and Other Stories, 1988; African Sleeping Sickness, 1990; Hand Dance, 1993; Native in a Strange Land, 1996; Bathwater Wine, 1998. Contributions to: Another Chicago Magazine; Callaloo; Poetry International; Poetry New Zealand; Long Shot; Epoch; Phoebe; Zyzzyva. Honours: National Endowment for the Arts, The Guggenheim Foundation, California Arts Council. Membership: WGAW. Address: PO Box 29154, Los Angeles, CA 90029, USA.

COLERIDGE Nicholas David, b. 4 Mar 1957, London, England. Journalist; Author. m. Georgia Elizabeth Metcalfe, 22 July 1989, 2 sons, 1 daughter. Education: Trinity College, Cambridge. Appointments: Editor, Harpers & Queen Magazine, 1986-89; Editorial Director, 1989-91, Managing Director, 1992-, Conde Nast Publishers. Publications: Tunnel Vision, 1981; Around the World in 78 Days, 1984; Shooting Stars, 1984; The Fashion Conspiracy, 1988; How I Met My Wife and Other Stories, 1991; Paper Tigers, 1993; With Friends Like These, 1997. Contributions to: Harpers & Queen; Spectator; Daily Telegraph; Sunday Telegraph; Tatler; Evening Standard; GQ; Vanity Fair. Honour: Young Journalist of the Year, 1983. Literary Agent: Ed Victor. Address: 39 Kensington Park Gardens, London W11, England.

COLES Donald Langdon, b. 12 Apr 1928, Woodstock, Ontario, Canada. Professor; Poet. m. 28 Dec 1958, 1 son, 1 daughter. Education: BA, Victoria College; MA, University of Toronto; MA (Cantab), 1954. Appointments: Fiction Editor, The Canadian Forum, 1975-76; Director, Creative Writing Programme, York University, 1979-85; Poetry Editor, May Studio, Banff Centre for the Fine Arts, 1984-93. Publications: Sometimes All Over, 1975; Anniversaries, 1979; The Prinzhorn Collection, 1982; Landslides, 1986; K in Love, 1987; Little Bird, 1991; Forests of the Medieval World, 1993; Someone Has Stayed in Stockholm: Selected and New Poems, 1994. Contributions to: Saturday Night; Canadian Forum; London Review of Books; Poetry (Chicago); Globe and Mail; Arc; Ariel. Honours: CBC Literary Competition, 1980; Gold Medal for Poetry, National Magazine Awards, 1986; Governor General's Award for Poetry, Canada, 1993. Membership: PEN International. Address: 122 Glenview Avenue, Toronto, Ontario M4R 1P8, Canada.

COLES Robert (Martin), b. 12 Oct 1929, Boston, Massachusetts, USA. Physician; Professor of Psychiatry and Medical Humanities; Writer. m. Jane Hallowell, 3 sons. Education: AB, Harvard College, 1950; MD, Columbia University of Physicians and Surgeons, 1954; Internship, University of Chicago Clinics, 1954-55; Psychiatric Residency, Massachusetts General Hospital, 1955-56, McLean Hospital, 1956-57. Appointments: Research Psychiatrist, Health Services, 1963-, Lecturer on General Education, 1966-, Professor of Psychiatry and Medical Humanities, 1977-, Harvard University; Contributing Editor, New Republic, 1966-, American Poetry Review, 1972-, Aperture, 1974-, Literature and Medicine, 1981-, New Oxford Review, 1981-; Visiting Professor of Public Policy, Duke University, 1973-; Editor, Children and Youth Services Review, 1978-; Visiting Professor of Psychiatry, Dartmouth College, 1989. Publications: Children of Crisis, 5 volumes, 1967, 1972, 1978; The Middle Americans, 1970; The Geography of Faith, 1971; The Old Ones of New Mexico, 1973; William Carlos William, 1975; Walker Percy, 1978; Flannery O'Connor's South, 1980; The Moral Life of Children, 1986; The Political Life of Children, 1986; Simone Weil, 1987; Dorothy Day, 1987; The Call of Stories: Teaching and the Moral Imagination, 1989; Rumors of Another World, 1989; The Spiritual Life of Children, 1990; Anna Freud: The Dream of Psychoanalysis, 1992; Collected Essays: Omnibus, 1993; The Call of Service: A Witness

to Idealism, 1993; The Story of Ruby Bridges, 1995; The Moral Intelligence of Children, 1997; Old and On Their Own, 1998. Contributions to: Numerous books, journals, reviews, magazines, and periodicals. Honours: McAlpin Medal, National Association of Mental Health, 1972; Pulitzer Prize, in General Non-Fiction, 1973; Weatherford Prize, Berea College and Council of Southern Mountains, 1973; Lillian Smith Award, Southern Regional Council, 1973; MacArthur Prize Fellow, 1981; Sarah Josepha Hale Award, 1986; Christopher Medals, 1989, 1991; Gold Medal, College of Physicians and Surgeons, Columbia University, 1991; US Presidential Medal of Freedom, 1998; Numerous honorary doctorates. Memberships: American Academy of Arts and Sciences, fellow; American Orthopsychiatric Association; American Psychiatric Association; Institute of Society, Ethics, and Life Sciences, fellow. Address: 81 Carr Road, Concord, MA 01742, USA.

COLESNIC Jurie, (Jurie Dereneu), b. 1955, Moldova. Editor; Writer. m. Tarus Lidia, 1979, 2 daughters. Education: Technical University, Kishinau, Moldova, 1978. Appointments: Teacher, Technical Collegium No 22, Kishinau, 1979-83; President, Founder, House of the Book Petru Mouila, 1996. Publications: Art of Memory, 1987; The Song of Our Nostalgy, 1990; Unknown Bassarabia, vol 1, 1993, vol 2, 1997; Encyclopaedia Sfatul Tarii, 1998. Contributions to: Literature and Art; Flux; Bassarabia. Honours: Republican Prize, Mihai Eminescu, 1991. Membership: Union of Writers. Address: bd Stefan cel Mare 132 ap 56, Chisinau 2012, Moldova.

COLLIER Catrin. See: **WATKINS Karen Christna.**

COLLIER Richard Hughesdon, b. 8 Mar 1924, London, England. Author. m. Patricia Eveline Russell, 24 July 1953. Appointments: Associate Editor, Phoenix Magazine for the Forces, Southeast Asia, 1945-46; Editor, Town and Country Magazine, 1946-48; Features Staff, Daily Mail, 1948-49. Publications: Ten Thousand Eyes, 1958; The Sands of Dunkirk, 1961; The General Next to God, 1965; Eagle Day, 1966; Duce!, 1971; Bridge Across the Sky, 1978; The City That Wouldn't Die, 1979; 1940: The World in Flames, 1979; 1941: Armageddon, 1981; The War That Stalin Won, 1983; The Rainbow People, 1984; The Warcos, 1989; The Few (co-author), 1989; D-Day: 6 June 1944, 1992; The Past is a Foreign Country, 1996. Contributions to: Reader's Digest; Holiday; The Times. Honour: Knight of Mark Twain, 1972. Memberships: Author's Guild of America; Author's League of America; Society of Theatre Research; Society of Authors. Address: c/o Curtis Brown Group Ltd, 28-29 Haymarket, London, SW1Y 4SP.

COLLIER Zena, (Jane Collier, Zena Shumsky), b. 21 Jan 1926, London, England. Writer. m. (1) Louis Shumsky, 2 sons, 1 dec, (2) Thomas M Hampson, 30 Dec 1969. Appointments: Writer-in-Residence, Just Buffalo, 1984-, Southern Tier Library System, Corning, 1985-, Niagara Erie Writers, Buffalo, 1986; Teacher, Writers Workshop, Nazareth College, Rochester. Publications: Novels: A Cooler Climate, 1990; Ghost Note, 1992. Children's books: As Zena Collier: Next Time I'll Know; Seven for the People - Public Interest Groups at Work. As Jane Collier: The Year of the Dream; A Tangled Web; as Zena Shumsky with Lou Shumsky: First Flight; Shutterbug. Contributions to: Southern Humanities Review; Southwest Review; Prairie Schooner; McCalls; Alfred Hitchcock's Mystery Magazine; Literary Review; New Letters; Upstate; Publishers Weekly; Los Angeles Times Book Review. Honours: Hoepfner Prize; Citation on Honour Roll of Best American Short Stories; Nomination for Pushcart Prize; Resident Fellowships: Yaddo, Macdowell, Virginia Center for the Creative Arts, Alfred University Summer Place. Memberships: Authors Guild; Writers and Books; Poets and Writers. Address: c/o Harvey Klinger, 301 West 53rd Street, New York, NY 10019, USA.

COLLINS Catherine Fisher, b. Apr 1924, Buffalo, New York, USA. Associate Professor. m. Clyde Collins, dec June 1995, 2 sons, 1 daughter. Education: AAS, 1970; BS, 1975, Trocaire College, 1970; MS, 1979, EdD, 1990,

State University of New York. Appointments: Chair, full Professor, Assistant Academic Dean, Erie Community College, 1989-92; Associate Professor, Empire State College, 1992-. Publications: African American Women's Health and Social Issues, 1996; The Imprisonment of African American Women, 1997. Honour: Choice Award for Outstanding Academic Book, 1998. Address: Department of Community Health and Human Services, Empire State College, State University of New York, 617 Main Street, Buffalo, NY 14203, USA.

COLLINS Hunt. See: **LOMBINO Salvatore A.**

COLLINS Jackie, b. England. Novelist; Short Story Writer; Actress. m. Oscar Lerman. Publications: The World is full of Married Men, 1968; The Stud, 1969; Lovehead, 1974; The World is Full of Divorced Women, 1975; The Love Killers, 1977; Lovers and Gamblers, 1977; The Bitch, 1979; Chances, 1981; Sinners, 1981; Hollywood Wives, 1983; Lucky, 1985; Hollywood Husbands, 1986; Rock Star, 1988; Lady Boss, 1990; American Star, 1993. Address: c/o Simon and Schuster, 1230 Avenue of the Americas, New York, NY 10020, USA.

COLLINS Jim, (James Lee Collins), b. 30 Dec 1945, Beloit, Wisconsin, USA. Author; Editor. m. Joan Hertel, 27 Dec 1974, 2 sons. Publications: Comanche Trail, 1984; Gone to Texas, 1984; War Clouds, 1984; Campaigning, 1985; Orphans Preferred, 1985; Riding Shotgun, 1985; Mister Henry, 1986; The Brass Boy, 1987; Spencer's Revenge, 1987; Western Writers Handbook, 1987; Settling the American West, 1993. Contributions to: The Blue and the Gray; Writers Digest Magazine. Memberships: Colorado Authors League; National Writers Club; Western Writers of America. Address: c/o NWC 194500 South Havana Street, Suite 620, Aurora, CO 80014, USA.

COLLINS Joan Henrietta, b. 23 May 1933, London, England. Actress; Writer. m. (1) Maxwell Reed, 1954, div 1957, (2) George Anthony Newley, 1963, div 1970, 1 son, 1 daughter, (3) Ronald S Kass, 1972, div 1983, (4) Peter Holm, 1985, div 1987. Education: Royal Academy of Dramatic Art. Appointments: Actress in numerous stage, film, and television productions. Publications: Past Imperfect, 1978; The Joan Collins Beauty Book, 1980; Katy: A Fight for Life, 1982; Prime Time, 1988; Love and Desire and Hate, 1990; My Secrets, 1994; Too Damn Famous, 1995; Second Act, autobiography, 1997. Honours: Best Television Actress, Golden Globe, 1982; Favourite Television Performer, People's Choice, 1985. Address: c/o Paul Keylock, 16 Bulbecks Walk, South Woodham Ferrers, Essex CM3 5ZN, England.

COLLINS Larry, (John Laurence Collins Jr.), b. 14 Sept 1929, Hartford, Connecticut, USA. Author. Education: BA, Yale University, 1951. Appointments: Correspondent, United Press International, Paris, Rome and Beirut, 1957-59; Correspondent, Beirut, 1959-61; Bureau Chief, Paris, 1961-65, Newsweek magazine. Publications: Is Paris Burning? (with Dominique Lapierre), 1965; Or I'll Dress You in Mourning, 1968; O Jerusalem, 1972; Freedom at Midnight, 1975; The Fifth Horseman, 1980; Fall from Grace, 1985; Maze, 1989; Black Eagles, 1993. Honours: Deauville Film Festival Literary Award, 1985; Mannesman Talley Literary Prize, 1989. Literary Agent: Alan Nevini, Renaissance, 8325 Sunset Boulevard, Los Angeles, CA, USA. Address: c/o E P Dutton, 340 Hudson Street, New York, NY, USA.

COLLINS Michael. See: **LYNDS Dennis.**

COLLINS Philip (Arthur William), b. 28 May 1923, London, England. Professor of English (retired); Author. Education: MA, Emmanuel College, Cambridge, 1947. Appointments: Warden, Vaughan College, 1954-62; Senior Lecturer, 1962-64, Professor of English, 1964-82, University of Leicester; Member, Board of Directors, The National Theatre, 1976-82. Publications: James Boswell,1956; English Christmas (editor), 1956; Dickens and Crime, 1962; Dickens and Education, 1963; The Impress of the Moving Age, 1965; Thomas Cooper the

Chartist: Byron and the Poets of the Poor, 1969; A Dickens Bibliography, 1970; Dickens: A Christmas Carol: The Public Reading Version, 1971; Bleak House: A Commentary, 1971; Dickens: The Critical Heritage (editor), 1971; Reading Aloud: A Victorian Metier, 1972; Charles Dickens: The Public Readings (editor), 1975; Charles Dickens: David Copperfield (editor), 1977; Charles Dickens: Hard Times (editor), 1978; Dickens: Interviews and Recollections (editor), 1981; Thackeray: Interviews and Recollections (editor), 1982; Tennyson, Poet of Lincolnshire, 1985; The Annotated Dickens (editor with Edward Giuliano), 1986; Tennyson: Seven Essays (editor), 1992. Contributions to: Encyclopaedia Britannica; Listener; Times Literary Supplement. Address: 26 Knighton Drive, Leicester LE2 3HB, England.

COLLIS Louise Edith, b. 29 Jan 1925, Arakan, Burma. Writer. Education: BA, History, Reading University, England, 1945. Publications: Without a Voice, 1951; A Year Passed, 1952; After the Holiday, 1954; The Angel's Name, 1955; Seven in the Tower, 1958; The Apprentice Saint, 1964; Solider in Paradise, 1965; The Great Flood, 1966; A Private View of Stanley Spencer, 1972; Maurice Collis Diaries (editor), 1976; Impetuous Heart: The story of Ethel Smyth, 1984. Contributions to: Books and Bookmen; Connoisseur; Art and Artists; Arts Review; Collectors Guide; Art and Antiques. Memberships: Society of Authors; International Association of Art Critics. Address: 65 Cornwall Gardens, London SW7 4BD, England.

COLLOMS Brenda, (Brenda Cross, Brenda Hughes), b. 1 Jan 1919, London, England. Author; Editor. Education: BA, University of London, 1956; MA, University of Liverpool, 1958. Appointment: Editor, The Film Star Diary, Cramp Publishers, London, 1948-63. Publications: Happy Ever After (as Brenda Cross), 1947; The Film Hamlet (as Brenda Cross), 1948; New Guinea Folk Tales (as Brenda Hughes), 1959; Folk Tales from Chile (as Brenda Hughes), 1962; Certificate History, Books 1-4: Britain and Europe, 1966-70; Israel, 1971; The Mayflower Pilgrims, 1973; Charles Kingsley, 1975; Victorian Country Parsons, 1977; Victorian Visionaries, 1982; The Making of Tottie Fox (as Brenda Colloms). Address: 123A Gloucester Avenue, London NW1 8LB, England.

COLLURA Mary-Ellen Lang, b. 1 Aug 1949, Vancouver, Canada. Teacher; Mother. Education: BEd, University of British Columbia, 1972. Publications: Winners, 1984; Sunny, 1988; Dreamers, 1995. Honours: IODE, 1985; SLA, 1985; Ebbel, 1985; Sheila E Goff Award, 1989. Address: 4068 Barclay Road, Campbell River, British Columbia V9W 4Y6, Canada.

COLMAN E(rnest) A(drian) M(ackenzie), b. 8 Dec 1930, Glasgow, Scotland. Professor Emeritus of English; Writer; Editor. Education: MA, University of Glasgow 1952; PhD, University of New South Wales, 1970. Appointments: Lecturer in English, 1962-70, Senior Lecturer, 1970-74, Associate Professor, 1974-78, University of Sydney, New South Wales; Research Associate, Shakespeare Institute, University of Birmingham, England, 1968-69; Professor of English, University of Tasmania, Hobart, 1978-90. Publications: Shakespeare's Julius Caesar, 1965; The Structure of Shakespeare's Antony and Cleopatra, 1971; The Dramatic Use of Bawdy in Shakespeare, 1974; Poems of Sir Walter Raleigh (editor), 1977; King Lear (editor), 1982; Henry IV Part I (editor), 1987; Romeo and Juliet (editor), 1993. Address: 250 Churchill Avenue, Sandy Bay, Tasmania, Tas 7005, Australia.

COLOMBO Furio Marco, b. 1 Jan 1931, Chatillon, Italy. Journalist; Writer. m. Alice Oxman, 16 Aug 1969, 1 daughter. Education: Law Degree, University of Turin, 1954. Appointments: Editor, Communicazione Visiva, University of Bologna, 1970-77, La Stampa, 1972-94, Board of Directors, 1991-94; Communicazioni di Massa, Milan, 1979-84; Century Association, New York, 1981-; Sanpaolo Chair, International Journalism, Graduate School of Journalism, Columbia University, 1991-94; Panorama, 1991-93; Aspen Institute, 1991-; Director, Italian Cultural Institute, New York, 1992-95; L'Espresso, 1993-; La Repubblica, 1994-; Elected to Italian Parliament (Camera dei Deputati), 1996, Member of the Cultural-Scientific Affairs Committee. Publications: Nuovo Teatro Americano, 1963; L'America di Kennedy, 1964; Le Donne Matte, 1964; Il Prigioniero della Torre Velasca, 1965; Cosa Faro da Grande, 1986; Carriera: Vale Una Vita Rizzoli, 1989; Il Destino del Libro e Altri Destini, 1990; Il Terzo Dopoguerra, 1990; Scene da una Vittoria, 1991; Oer Israele, 1991; La Citta Profonda, 1991; Gli Altri, che farne?, 1994; Ultime notizie sul Giornalismo, 1995; Confucio nel Computer, 1996; Ultimas Noticias sobre el Periodismo, 1997; Il Candidato, 1997. Contributions to: Books and journals. Honours: Trumball Lecturer, Yale University, USA, 1964; Chair, Italian Culture, University of California, Berkeley, 1975; Tevere Prize for Literature, Rome, 1986; Amalfi Prize for Best TV Documentary; Capri Prize for Journalism; Valle dei Trulli Award for Literature, 1996; St Vincent Award, 1997. Memberships: Academy of Political Science, New York; Institute for International Affairs, Rome; Council for the United States and Italy, Washington and Rome; Academie des Cultures, Paris; Italian Academy for Advanced Studies, Columbia University, member, board of guarantors, 1992-98. Address: 59 via della Frezza, Rome 00186, Italy.

COLOMBO John (Robert), b. 24 Mar 1936, Kitchener, Ontario, Canada. Author; Poet; Editor; Translator; Communications Consultant. m. Ruth Florence Brown, 11 May 1959, 2 sons, 1 daughter. Education: Waterloo College, 1956-57; BA, 1959, Graduate Studies, 1959-60, University of Toronto; DLitt (h c), York University, Toronto, 1998. Appointments: Author, editor or translator of over 125 varied titles such as collections of quotations, anthologies, poetry, mysteries, folklore. Contributions to: Periodicals and radio programmes. Honours: 1st Writer-in-Residence, Mohawk College, 1979-80; Various prizes and awards. Address: 42 Dell Park Avenue, Toronto, Ontario M6B 2T6, Canada.

COLQUHOUN Keith, b. 5 Aug 1927, London, England. Journalist; Novelist. 3 sons, 3 daughters. Appointments: Chief Sub-Editor, London Daily Herald, Sun, 1959-70; Managing Editor, Observer, 1970-77; News Editor, Far Eastern Economic Review, Hong Kong, 1977-80; Asian Affairs Writer, The Economist, 1980-. Publications: The Money Tree, 1958; Point of Stress, 1960; The Sugar Coating, 1973; St Petersburg Rainbow, 1975; Goebbels and Gladys, 1981; Filthy Rich, 1982; Kiss of Life, 1983; Foreign Wars, 1985; Mad Dog, 1992. Address: The Old Rectory, East Mersea, Essex, England.

COLTON James. See: **HANSEN Joseph.**

COLVIN Sir Howard (Montagu), b. 15 Oct 1919, Sidcup, Kent, England. Historian. m. Christina Edgeworth Butler, 16 Aug 1943, 2 sons. Education: BA, University College, London; MA, Oxford University, 1948. Publications: The White Canons in England, 1951; The History of the King's Works (general editor and part author), 6 volumes, 1962-82; Catalogue of Architectural Drawings in Worcester College Library, 1964; A Biographical Dictionary of British Architects 1600-1840, 1978, 3rd edition, 1995; Unbuilt Oxford, 1983; Calke Abbey, Derbyshire, 1985; The Canterbury Quadrangle: St John's College, Oxford, 1988; All Souls: An Oxford College and its Buildings (with J S G Simmons), 1989; Architecture and the After-Life, 1991. Contributions to: Archaeological Journal; Architectural Review; Country Life. Honours: Fellow, British Academy, 1963; Knighted, 1995. Address: 50 Plantation Road, Oxford OX2 6JE, England.

COLWELL Maxwell Gordon, b. 10 Oct 1926, Brompton, South Australia, Australia. Author. m. Betty Joy Holthouse, 27 Nov 1948, 2 sons. Appointment: Journalist, The Young Australian, 1960-62. Publications: Half Days and Patched Pants; Full Days and Pressed Pants; Glorious Days and Khaki Pants; Whaling Around Australia; Voyages of Matthew Flinders; The Journey of Burke and Wills; Others Big Rivers; Lights Vision the City of Adelaide. Contributions to: Bulletin. Honour: Australian Council Literature Board Senior Fellowship; Order of Australia, 1994. Membership: Australian Society of Authors. Address: 102 8th Avenue, Joslin, South Australia 5070, Australia.

COMAROFF John L(ionel), b. 1 Jan 1945, Cape Town, South Africa (US citizen). Professor of Anthropology and Social Sciences; Writer. m. Jean Rakoff, 15 Jan 1967, 1 son, 1 daughter. Education: BA, University of Cape Town, 1966; PhD, University of London, 1973. Appointments: Lecturer in Social Anthropology, University College of Swansea, 1971-72, University of Manchester, 1972-78; Visiting Assistant Professor of Anthropology, 1978, Associate Professor of Anthropology and Sociology, 1981-87, Professor of Anthropology and Social Sciences, 1987-96, Harold H Swift Distinguished Service Professor of Anthropology and Social Sciences, 1996-, University of Chicago; Directeur d'Études, 1988, Directeur d'Études Associé, 1995, École des Hautes Études en Sciences Sociales, Paris. Publications: The Diary of Sol T Plaatje: An African at Mafeking (editor), 1974; The Structure of Agricultural Transformation in Barolong, 1977; The Meaning of Marriage Payments (editor), 1980; Essays on African Marriage in Southern Africa (editor with E J Krige), 1981; Rules and Processes: The Cultural Logic of Dispute in an African Context (with S A Roberts), 1981; Of Revelation and Revolution: Christianity and Colonialism in South Africa (with J Comaroff), 1991; Ethnography and the Historical Imagination (with J Comaroff), 1992; Modernity and its Malcontents: Ritual and Power in Africa (editor with J Comaroff), 1993; Perspectives on Nationalism and War (editor with Paul C Stern), 1993. Contributions to: Scholarly books and journals. Honours: National Endowment for the Humanities Grants, 1984-85, 1986-87; National Science Foundation Grants, 1986-87, 1993; Spencer Foundation Grant, 1991; Laing Prize, University of Chicago, 1993; American Academy of Arts and Sciences, 1995; Spencer Foundation Mentor Award, 1996. Memberships: Royal Anthropological Institute, fellow; African Studies Association; International African Institute, fellow; Association of Social Anthroplogists; American Anthropological Association, fellow; Association of Political and Legal Anthropology, president, 1995-96. Address: c/o Department of Anthropology, University of Chicago, 1126 East 59th Street, Chicago, IL 60637, USA.

COMFORT Alexander, b. 10 Feb 1920, London, England. Physician; Writer; Poet. m. (1) Ruth Muriel Harris, 1943, div 1973, 1 son, (2) Jane Tristam Henderson, 1973, dec 1991. Education: BA, 1943, MB, BCh, 1944, MA, 1945, Cambridge University; MRCS, LRCP, London Hospital, 1944; DCH, 1946, PhD, 1949, DSc, 1963, University of London. Appointments: House Physician, London Hospital, 1944; Resident Medical Officer, Royal Waterloo Hospital, London, 1944-45; Lecturer in Physiology, London Hospital Medical College, 1948-51; Honorary Research Associate, Department of Zoology, 1951-73, and Director of Research, Gerontology, 1966-73, University College, London; Clinical Lecturer, Department of Psychiatry, Stanford University, 1974-83; Professor, Department of Pathology, University of California School of Medicine at Irvine, 1976-78; Consultant Psychiatrist, Brentwood Veterans Administration Hospital, Los Angeles, 1978-81; Adjunct Professor, Neuropsychiatric Institute, University of California at Los Angeles, 1980-91; Consultant, Ventura County Hospital, California, 1981-91. Publications: Non-Fiction: Art and Social Responsibility: Lectures on the Ideology of Romanticism, 1946; The Novel and Our Time, 1948; Barbarism and Sexual Freedom: Lectures on the Sociology of Sex from the Standpoint of Anarchism, 1948; First Year Physiological Technique, 1948; Sexual Behavior in Society, 1950; Authority and Delinquency in the Modern State: A Criminological Approach to the Problem of Power, 1950; The Biology of Senescence, 1956; Darwin and the Naked Lady: Discursive Essays on Biology and Art, 1961; The Process of Ageing, 1964; The Nature of Human Nature, 1966; The Anxiety Makers: Some Curious Preoccupations of the Medical Profession, 1967; The Joy of Sex: A Cordon Bleu Guide to Lovemaking, 1972; More Joy: A Lovemaking Companion to "The Joy of Sex", 1974; A Good Age, 1975; Sexual

Consequences of Disability, 1978; I and That: Notes on the Biology of Religion, 1979; The Facts of Love (with Jane Comfort), 1979; A Practice of Geriatric Psychiatry, 1980; What Is a Doctor?, 1980; Reality and Empathy: Physics, Mind, and Science in the 21st Century, 1984; Say Yes to Old Age: Developing a Positive Attitude Toward Aging, 1990; The New Joy of Sex, 1991; Writings Against Power and Death, 1993. Fiction: The Silver River, 1937; No Such Liberty, 1941; The Almond Tree, 1943; The Powerhouse, 1945; On This Side of Nothing, 1948; A Giant's Strength, 1952; Come Out to Play, 1961; Tetrach, 1980; Imperial Patient: The Memoirs of Nero's Doctor, 1987; The Philosophers, 1989. Poetry: France and Other Poems, 1942; A Wreath for the Living, 1942; Three New Poets: Roy McFadden, Alex Comfort, Ian Serrailler, 1942; Elegies, 1944; The Song of Lazarus, 1945; The Signal to Engage, 1946; And All But He Departed, 1951; Haste to the Wedding, 1962; Poems for Jane, 1979; Mikrokosmos, 1994. Honours: Ciba Foundation Prize for Research in Gerontology, 1958; Borestone Poetry Award, 2nd Prize, 1962; Karger Memorial Prize, 1969. Memberships: American Association of Sex Educators, Counselors and Therapists; American Medical Association; American Psychiatric Association; British Society for Research on Aging; Gerontological Society; Peace Pledge Union; Royal Society of Medicine. Address: The Manor House, Swalcliffe, Banbury, Oxon.

COMFORT Nicholas Alfred Fenner, b. 4 Aug 1946, London, England. Political Journalist and Consultant. m. (1) 1970, div 1988, 1 son, 1 daughter, (2) Corinne Reed, 1990, 1 son. Education: MA, History (Exhibitioner), Trinity College, Cambridge, 1968. Appointments: Morning Telegraph, Sheffield, 1968-74; Daily Telegraph, 1974-89; Political Editor, The Independent on Sunday, 1989-90, The European, 1990-92, Daily Record, 1992-95; Consultant, Politics International, 1996-97. Publications: Mid-Suffolk Light Railway, 1986, 1997; Brewer's Politics Phrase and Fable Dictionary, 1993, revised edition, 1995; The Lost City of Dunwich, 1994. Contributions to: Numerous political, transport and other journals. Membership: Royal Geographical Society, fellow. Address: The Manor House, Swalcliffe, Banbury, Oxfordshire OX15 5EH, England.

COMINI Alessandra, b. 24 Nov 1934, Winona, Minnesota, USA. Professor of Art History; Author. Education: BA, Barnard College, 1956; MA, University of California, Berkeley, 1964; PhD, Columbia University, 1969. Appointments: Instructor, 1968-69, Assistant Professor, 1969-74, Columbia University; Visiting Assistant Professor, 1970, 1973, Associate Professor, 1974-75, Professor, 1976-, University Distinguished Professor of Art History, 1983-, Southern Methodist University; Alfred Hodder Fellow, Princeton University, 1972-73; Visiting Assistant Professor, Yale University, 1973; Associate Editor, Arts Magazine, 1977-88; Lansdown Professor, University of Victoria, British Columbia, 1981; Visiting Distinguished Professor, California State University, Chico, 1990; Distinguished Visiting Fellow, European Humanities Research Centre, Oxford University, 1996. Publications: Schiele in Prison, 1973; Egon Schiele's Portraits, 1974; Gustav Klimt, 1975; Egon Schiele, 1976; The Fantastic Art of Vienna, 1978; The Changing Image of Beethoven: A Study in Mythmaking, 1987; Egon Schiele's Nudes, 1994. Contributions to: Books, journals, magazines, and exhibition catalogues. Honours: Charles Rufus Morey Book Award, College Art Association of America, 1976; Grand Decoration of Honour for Services to the Austrian Republic, 1990; Lifetime Achievement Award, Women's Caucus for Art, 1995. Memberships: College Art Association of America; Texas Institute of Letters; Women's Caucus for Art. Address: 2900 McFarlin, Dallas, TX 75205, USA.

COMPTON D(avid) G(uy), (Guy Compton, Frances Lynch), b. 19 Aug 1930, London, England. Writer. Education: Cheltenham College, Gloucester, 1941-50. Appointment: Editor, Reader's Digest Condensed Books, London, 1969-81. Publications: Too Many Murderers, 1962; Medium for Murder, 1963; Dead on Cue, 1964;

Disguise for a Dead Gentleman, 1964; High Tide for Hanging, 1965; The Quality of Mercy, 1965; Farewell Earth's Bliss, 1966; The Silent Multitude, 1966; And Murder Came Too, 1966; Synthajoy, 1968; The Palace, 1969; The Electric Crocodile, 1970; Hot Wireless Sets, Aspirin Tablets, the Sandpaper Sides of Used Matchboxes and Something that Might Have Been Castor Oil, 1971; The Missionaries, 1972; The Continuous Katherine Mortenhoe, 1974; Twice Ten Thousand Miles, 1974; The Fine and Handsome Captain, 1975; Stranger at the Wedding, 1977; A Dangerous Magic, 1978; A Usual Lunacy, 1978; Windows, 1979; In the House of Dark Music, 1979; Ascendancies, 1980; Scudder's Game, 1985; Ragnarok (with John Gribbin), 1991; Normansland, 1992; Stammering, 1993; Justice City, 1994; Back of Town Blues, 1996. Address: c/o David Higham Associates, 5-8 Lower John Street, London W1R 4HA, England.

CONDÉ Maryse, b. 11 Feb 1937, Pointe-à-Pitre, Guadeloupe, West Indies. Author; Playwright. m. (1) Mamadou Condé, 1958, div 1981, 3 children, (2) Richard Philcox, 1982. Education: PhD, Sorbonne, University of Paris, 1976. Appointments: Programme Producer, French Services, BBC, London, 1968-70, Radio France Internationale, 1980-; Assistant, Jussieu, 1970-72, Lecturer, Nantes, 1973-80, University of Paris divisions; Chargé de cours, Sorbonne, University of Paris, 1980-85; Professor of Francophone Literature, Columbia University, New York, 1995. Publications: Fiction: Heremakhonon, 1976, English translation, 1982; Une Saison a Rihata, 1981, English translation as A Season in Rihata, 1988; Ségou: Les murailles de terre, 1984, English translation as Segu, 1987; Ségou II: La terre en miettes, 1985, English translation as The Children of Segu, 1989; Pays Melé, short stories, 1985; Moi, Tituba, sorcière noire de Salem, 1986, English translation, 1992; La Vie scelerate, 1987, English translation as Tree of Life, 1992; Traversée de la mangrove, 1990, English translation, 1995; Les Derniers Rois Mages, 1992; La Migration des Coeurs, novel, 1995. Plays: Dieu nous l'a donne, 1972; Mort d'Oluwemi d'Ajumako, 1973; Pension les Alizes, 1988. Other: Anthologie de la litterature africaine d'expression française (editor), 1966; La Poesie antillaise (editor), 1977; La Roman antillais (editor), 1977; La Civilisation du bossale, 1978; Le profil d'une oeuvre: Cahier d'un retour au pays natal, 1978; La Parole des femmes, 1979. Contributions to: Anthologies and journals. Honours: Fulbright Scholar, 1985-86; Prix litteraire de la Femme, 1986; Prix Alain Boucheron, 1986; Guggenheim Fellowship, 1987-88; Académie Française Prize, 1988. Address: Montebello, 97190 Petit Bourg, Guadeloupe, West Indies.

CONE Molly Zelda, b. 3 Oct 1918, Tacoma, Washington, USA. Writer. m. Gerald J Cone, 9 Sept 1939, 1 son, 2 daughters. Education: University of Washington, 1936-38. Publications: For children: Mishmash; Mishmash and the Substitute Teacher; Mishmash and the Sauerkraut Mystery; Mishmash and the Venus Flytrap; Mishmash and the Big Fat Problem; Come Back, Salmon (with photographs by Sidnee Wheelwright), 1992; Listen to the Trees - Jews and the Earth, 1995; Squishy, Misty, Damp & Muddy - The In-Between World of Wetlands, 1996. Biographies: Hurry Henrietta, 1966; Leonard Bernstein, 1970; The Ringing Brothers, 1971; Non-fiction: Stories of Jewish Symbols, 1963; Who Knows Ten, 1965; The Jewish Sabbath, 1966; The Jewish New Year, 1966; Purim, 1967; The Mystery of Being Jewish, 1989. Play: John Bunyan and His Blue Ox, 1966. Honours: Neveh Shalom Centennial Award for Literary Contribution toward Education of Jewish Children, 1970; 2nd Place Award, National Federation of Press Women, 1970; Shirley Kravitz Children's Book Award, Association of Jewish Libraries, 1973; Washington Governor's Writers Award, 1993; Horn Book Fanfare, 1993. Memberships: Authors League of America; Seattle Free Lancers. Literary Agent: McIntosh and Otis Inc, 310 Madison Avenue, New York, NY 10017, USA. Address: 8003 Sand Point Way North East, B-24, Seattle, WA 98115, USA.

CONEY Michael (Greatrex), b. 28 Sept 1932, Birmingham, England. Writer. m. Daphne Coney, 14 May 1957, 1 son, 1 daughter. Publications: King of the Scepter'd Isle, 1969; A Judge of Men, 1969; Whatever Became of the McGowans?, 1971; The Snow Princess, 1971; Susanna! Susanna!, 1971; Mirror Image, 1972; The Bridge on the Scraw, 1973; Syzygy, 1973; Friends Come in Boxes, 1973; The Hero of Downways, 1973; The Hook, the Eye and the Whip, 1974; Winter's Children, 1974; Monitor Found in Orbit, 1974; The Jaws That Bite, The Claws That Catch, 1975; Charisma, 1975; The Hollow Where, 1975; Trading Post, 1976; Hello Summer, Goodbye, 1976; Brontomek!, 1976; Just an Old-Fashioned War Story, 1977; Penny on a Skyhorse, 1979; The Ultimate Jungle, 1979; Neptune's Children, 1981; Cat Karina, 1982; The Celestial Steam Locomotive, 1983; The Byrds, 1983; Gods of the Greataway, 1984; Fang, the Gnome, 1988; No Place for a Sealion, 1993; A Tomcat Called Sabrina, 1993; Sophie's Spyglass, 1993; Die Lorelie, 1993; The Small Penance of Lady Disdain, 1993; Tea and Hamsters, 1994. Honour: Best British Novel Award, British Science Fiction Association, 1976. Memberships: Science Fiction Writers of America; Institute of Chartered Accountants. Literary Agents: MBA Literary Agents, England; Virginia Kidd, USA. Address: 2082 Neptune Road, Sidney, British Columbia V8L 5J5, Canada.

CONGDON Kirby, b. 13 Nov 1924, West Chester, Pennsylvania, USA. Education: BA, Columbia College; MA, Columbia University. Appointment: Poetry Editor, Cayo Magazine, Key West. Publications: Iron Ark. A Bestiary; Juggernaut; A Key West Rebus; Dream-Work; Black Sun; Chain Drive; Contemporary Poets in American Anthologies 1960, 1977; Animals; Fantoccini; Crank Letters; Motorcycle Books, A Critical Survey and Checklist; Here We Are; Aipotu-Utopia. Address: 715 Bakers Lane, Key West, FL 33040, USA.

CONLON Kathleen. See: LLOYD Kathleen Annie.

CONN Stewart, b. 5 Nov 1936, Glasgow, Scotland. Poet; Playwright. Appointments: Radio Producer, Glasgow, 1962-77, Head of Radio Drama, Edinburgh, 1977-92, BBC; Literary Adviser, Royal Lyceum Theatre, Edinburgh, 1972-75. Publications: Poetry: Thunder in the Air, 1967; The Chinese Tower, 1967; Stoats in the Sunlight, US edition as Ambush and Other Poems, 1968; An Ear to the Ground, Poetry Book Society Choice, 1972; PEN New Poems, 1973-74 (editor), 1974; Under the Ice, 1978; In the Kibble Palace: New and Selected Poems, 1987; The Luncheon of the Boating Party, 1992; In the Blood, 1995; At the Aviary, 1995; The Ice Horses (editor), 1996; Stolen Light: Selected Poems, 1999; Drama includes: Thistlewood, 1979; Play Donkey, in A Decade's Drama, 1980. Contributions to: Anthologies, journals, and radio. Honours: E C Gregory Award, 1964; Scottish Arts Council Awards and Poetry Prize, 1968, 1978, 1992; English-Speaking Union Travel Scholarship, 1984; Scottish Arts Council Playwrights Bursary, 1995; Society of Authors Travel Bursary, 1996. Memberships: Knight of Mark Twain; Royal Scottish Academy of Music and Drama, fellow. Address: 1 Fettes Row, Edinburgh EH3 6SF, Scotland.

CONNELL Brian (Reginald), b. 12 Apr 1916, London, England. Author; Journalist; Broadcaster. m. Esmee Jean Mackenzie, 27 Nov 1944. Education: University of Madrid, 1933-36; University of Berlin, 1936-37. Appointments: Reuters, 1940-43, Daily Mail, 1946-50, News Chronicle, 1950-55, Independent Television News, 1955-86, Chairman, Connell Literary Enterprises/Partner, Connell Editors, 1960-; Programme Adviser, Anglia Television, 1961-86. Publications: Manifest Destiny, 1953; Knight Errant, 1955; Portrait of a Whig Peer, 1957; Watcher on the Rhine, 1957; The Plains of Abraham, 1959; Return of the Tiger, 1960; Regina v Palmerston, 1962; The War in the Peninsula, 1973; The Siege of Quebec, 1976; America in the Making, 1977; Editor and compiler of 10 autobiographies. Contributions to: Periodicals. Honours: Producers Guild Award, 1963; Cannes Festival International Award, 1965. Membership:

National Union of Journalists. Address: B2 Marine Gate, Marine Drive, Brighton, Sussex BN2 5TQ, England.

CONNELL Evan S(helby) Jr, b. 17 Aug 1924, Kansas City, Missouri, USA. Author; Poet. Education: Dartmouth College, 1941-43; AB, University of Kansas, 1947; Graduate Studies, Stanford University, 1947-48, Columbia University, 1948-49. Appointment: Editor, Contact magazine, 1960-65. Publications: The Anatomy Lesson and Other Stories, 1957; Mrs Bridge, 1959; The Patriot, 1960; Notes From a Bottle Found on the Beach at Carmel (poems), 1963; At the Crossroads: Stories, 1965; The Diary of a Rapist, 1966; Mr Bridge, 1969; Points for a Compass Rose (poems), 1973; The Connoisseur, 1974; Double Honeymoon, 1976; A Long Desire, 1979; St Augustine's Pigeon, 1980; The White Lantern, 1980; Son of the Morning Star: Custer and the Little Big Horn, 1984; The Alchymist's Journal, 1991; Collected Stories, 1996. Honours: Eugene Saxton Fellow, 1953; Guggenheim Fellowship, 1963; Rockefeller Foundation Grant, 1967; California Literature Silver Medal, 1974; Los Angeles Times Book Award, 1985; American Academy of Arts and Letters Award, 1987. Membership: American Academy of Arts and Letters. Address: c/o Don Cogdon, 156 Fifth Avenue, New York, NY 10010, USA.

CONNELLY Mark, b. 8 July 1951, Philadelphia, PA, USA. Writer; College Instructor. Education: BA, English, Carroll College, 1973; MA, Creative Writing, 1974, PhD, English, 1984, University of Wisconsin, Milwaukee. Appointment: Instructor, Milwaukee Area Technical College, 1986-. Publications: Books: The Diminished Self: Orwell and the Loss of Freedom, 1987; The Sundance Reader, 1997; Orwell and Gissing, 1997; The Sundance Writer, forthcoming. Contributions to: Short stories in Milwaukee Magazine; Wisconsin Review; Indiana Review. Honour: Fiction Award, Milwaukee Magazine, 1982. Membership: Modern Language Association. Address: 700 West State Street, Milwaukee, WI 53233, USA.

CONNOLLY Ray, b. 4 Dec 1940, St Helens, Lancashire, England. Writer. Education: BSc, London School of Economics and Political Science, 1963. Appointments: Columnist, London Evening Standard, 1967-73, 1983-84, The Times, 1989-90. Publications and Screenplays: A Girl Who Came to Stay, 1973; That'll Be the Day, 1973; Stardust, 1974; Trick or Treat?, 1975; James Dean: The First American Teenager, 1975; Newsdeath, 1978; A Sunday Kind of Woman, 1980; Honky Tonk Heroes, 1980; John Lennon 1940-1980, 1981; The Sun Place, 1981; An Easy Game to Play, 1982; Stardust Memories, 1983; Forever Young, 1984; Lytton's Diary, 1985; Defrosting the Fridge, 1988; Perfect Scoundrels, 1989; Sunday Morning, 1992; Shadows on a Wall, 1994; In the Sixties (anthology), 1995; Lost Fortnight, 1996; The Rhythm of Life, 1997. Honour: Stardust, Best Original British Screenplay, Writers Guild of Great Britain, 1974. Address: c/o Rogers, Coleridge and White, 20 Powis Mews, London W11 1JN, England.

CONNOR Fergus. See: MILLER Karl.

CONNORS Bruton. See: ROHEN Edward.

CONQUEST (George) Robert (Acworth), b. 15 July 1917, Malvern, Worcestershire, England. Historian; Writer; Poet. m. (1) Joan Watkins, 1942, div 1948, 2 sons, (2) Tatiana Mihailova, 1948, div 1962, (3), Caroleen Macfarlene, 1964, div 1978, (4) Elizabeth Neece, 1 Dec 1979. Education: University of Grenoble, France, 1935-36; Magdalen College, Oxford, 1936-39. Appointments: Member, Foreign Service, 1946-56; Fellow, London School of Economics and Political Science, 1956-58, Columbia University, 1964-65, Woodrow Wilson International Center, 1976-77, Hoover Institution, 1977-79, 1981-; Visiting Poet, University of Buffalo, 1959-60; Literary Editor, The Spectator, 1962-63; Distinguished Visiting Scholar, Heritage Foundation, 1980-81; Research Associate, Harvard University, 1982-83; Adjunct Fellow, Center for Strategic and International Studies, 1983-; Jefferson Lecturer in

Humanities, 1993. Publications: Poems, 1955; A World of Difference, 1955; New Lines (editor), 1956; Common Sense About Russia, 1960; Power and Policy in the USSR, 1961; Courage of Genius, 1962; Between Mars and Venus, 1962; New Lines II (editor), 1963; The Egyptologists (with Kingsley Amis), 1965; Russia After Khrushchev, 1965; The Great Terror, 1968; Arias from a Love Opera, 1969; The Nation Killers, 1970; Lenin, 1972; Kolyma, 1978; The Abomination of Moab, 1979; Present Danger, 1979; Forays, 1979; We and They, 1980; What to Do When the Russians Come, 1984; Inside Stalin's Secret Police, 1985; The Harvest of Sorrow, 1986; New and Collected Poems, 1988; Tyrants and Typewriters, 1989; Stalin and the Kirov Murder, 1989; The Great Terror Reassessed, 1990; Stalin: Breaker of Nations, 1991. Contributions to: Various publications. Honours: Officer of the Order of the British Empire, 1955; MA, 1972, BLitt, 1975, Oxon; Companion of the Order of St Michael and St George, 1996. Memberships: British Academy, corresponding member, 1994; Royal Society of Literature, fellow, 1972. Address: 52 Peter Coutts Circle, Stanford, CA 94305, USA.

CONRAD Peter, b. 1948, Australia. Education: Australia and England. Writer. Appointment: Fellow in English Literature, Christ Church College, Oxford. Publications: The Victorian Treasure House, 1973; Romantic Opera and Literary Form, 1977; Shandyism: The Character of Romantic Irony, 1978; Imagining America, 1980; Television: The Medium and its Manners, 1984; The Art of the City: Views and Versions of New York, 1984; The Everyman History of English Literature, 1985; A Song of Love and Death: The Meaning of Opera, 1987; The History of English Literature: One Indivisible, Unending Book, 1987; Down Home: Revisiting Tasmania, 1988; Where I Fell to Earth: A Life in Four Cities, 1990; Feasting with Panthers, or the Importance of Being Famous, 1994. Address: c/o Christ Church College, Oxford OX1 1DP, England.

CONRAN Anthony, b. 7 Apr 1931, Kharghpur, India. Poet; Writer. Education: BA, 1953, MA, 1956, University of Wales. Appointments: Research Fellow, 1957-66, Tutor in English, 1966-, University of Wales. Publications: Formal Poems, 1960; Icons, Asymptotes, A String o Blethers, Sequence of the Blu Flower, The Mountain, For the Marriage of Gerald and Linda, 1963; Stalae and Other Poems, 1965; Guernica, 1966; The Penguin Book of Welsh Verse, 1967; Claim, Claim, Claim, A Book of Poems, 1969; Life Fund, On to the Fields of Praise: Essays on the English Poets of Wales, 1979; The Cost of Strangeness, 1982; Welsh Verse, 1987. Address: 1 Frondirion, Glanrafon, Bangor, Carnavanshire, Wales.

CONRAN Shirley (Ida), b. 21 Sept 1932, London, England. Writer. m. Terence Conran, 1955, div 1962, 2 sons. Education: Southern College of Art, Portsmouth, England. Appointments: Founder, Co-Owner, Conran Fabrics Ltd, 1957-62; Design Consultant and Design Writer for various periodicals. Publications: Superwoman: Everywoman's Book of Household Management, 2 volumes, 1975, 1977; Superwoman Yearbook, 1976; Superwoman Yearbook, 1977; Superwoman Two, 1977; Future: How to Survive Life After Thirty, 1979, revised edition as Futurewoman: How to Survive Life, 1981; Lace: A Novel, 1982; The Magic Garden, 1983; Lace II, 1985; The Legend, 1985; Savages, 1987; Down with Superwoman, 1990; The Amazing Umbrella Shop, 1990; Crimson, 1992; Tiger Eyes, 1994. Address: 39 Avenue Princess Grace, Monte Carlo, Monaco.

CONROY (Donald) Pat(rick), b. 26 Oct 1945, Atlanta, Georgia, USA. Writer. m. 1) Barbara Bolling, 1969, div 1977, 3 daughters, 2) Lenore Guerewitz, 1981, 1 son, 2 daughters. Education: BA in English, The Citadel, 1967. Publications: The Boo, 1970; The Water is Wide, 1972; The Great Santini, 1976; The Lords of Discipline, 1980; The Prince of Tides, 1986; Beach Music, 1995. Honours: Ford Foundation Leadership Development Grant, 1971; Anisfield-Wolf Award, Cleveland Foundation, 1972; National Endowment for the Arts Award for Achievement in Education, 1974; Governor's Award for the Arts, Georgia, 1978; Lillian Smith Award for Fiction, Southern

Regional Council, 1981. Memberships: Authors Guild of America; PEN; Writers Guild. Address: c/o Houghton Mifflin Co, 222 Berkeley Street, Boston, MA 02116, USA.

CONROY John, b. 29 Mar 1951, Chicago, Illinois, USA. Writer. m. Colette Davison, May 1986. Education: BA, University of Illinois, 1973. Appointments: Senior Editor, Chicago Magazine, 1974-76; Staff Writer, Chicago Reader, 1978. Publications: Belfast Diary: War as a Way of Life, 1987, UK edition as War as a Way of Life: A Belfast Diary, 1988. Contributions to: New York Times; Boston Globe; Boston Phoenix; Chicago Daily News; Chicago Tribune; Atlanta Constitution; Dallas Morning News; San Diego Union; Village Voice. Honours: Peter Lisagor Awards, 1977, 1991; National Award for Magazine Writing, Society of Professional Journalists, 1978; Alicia Patterson Fellowship, 1980; Society of Midland Authors Award, 1987; Friends of Literature Award, 1987; Carl Sandburg Award, 1987; John D and Catherine T MacArthur Foundation Grant, 1990; John Bartlow Martin Award for Public Interest Magazine Journalism, 1991. Address: c/o Chicago Reader, 11 East Illinois Street, Chicago, IL 60611, USA.

CONSTABLE Trevor James, b. 17 Sept 1925, Wellington, New Zealand. Writer. m. Gloria Garcia, 14 Sept 1983, 1 daughter. Education: Rongotai College, 1936-42. Appointments: Staff Writer, National Commercial Broadcasting Service, 1942-44, International Broadcasting Company, 1950-52; US Correspondent, New Zealand Weekly News, 1958-68. Publications: Fighter Aces, 1966; Horrido, 1968; Blond Knight of Germany, 1970; Hidden Heroes, 1971; Fighter Aces of the USA, 1977; Fighter Aces of the Luftwaffe, 1978; The Cosmic Pulse of Life, 1978; Fighter General: The Life of Adolf Galland, 1988. Contributions to: Numerous. Honour: Aviation, Space Writers Book of the Year Award, 1978. Memberships: Aviation, Space Writers Association; National Maritime Historical Society; American Radio Association. Address: 3726 Bluff Place, San Pedro, CA 90731, USA.

CONSTANTINE David (John), b. 4 Mar 1944, Salford, Lancashire, England. Fellow in German; Poet; Writer; Translator. m. Helen Frances Best, 9 July 1966, 1 son, 1 daughter. Education: BA, 1966, PhD, 1971, Wadham College, Oxford. Appointments: Lecturer to Senior Lecturer in German, University of Durham, 1969-81; Fellow in German, Queen's College, Oxford, 1981-. Publications: Poetry: A Brightness to Cast Shadows, 1980; Watching for Dolphins, 1983; Mappi Mundi, 1984; Madder, 1987; Selected Poems, 1991; Caspar Hauser, 1994; Sleeper, 1995; The Pelt of Wasps, 1998. Fiction: Davies, 1985; Back at the Spike, 1994. Non-fiction: The Significance of Locality in the Poetry of Friedrich Hölderlin, 1979; Early Greek Travellers and the Hellenic Ideal, 1984; Hölderlin, 1988; Friedrich Hölderlin, 1992. Translator: Hölderlin: Selected Poems, 1990, enlarged edition, 1996; Henri Michaux: Spaced, Displaced (with Helen Constantine), 1992; Philippe Jaccottet: Under Clouded Skies/Beauregard (with Mark Treharne), 1994; Goethe: Elective Affinities, 1994; Kleist: Selected Writings, 1998. Editor: German Short Stories 2, 1972. Honours: Alice Hunt Bartlett Prize, 1984; Runciman Prize, 1985; Southern Arts Literature Prize, 1987; European Poetry Translation Prize, 1998. Membership: Poetry Society. Address: 1 Hilltop Road, Oxford OX4 1PB, England.

COOK Christopher Piers, b. 20 June 1945, Leicester, England. Writer; Historian. Education: BA, History, 1967, MA, 1970, Cambridge University; DPhil, Modern History, Oxford University, 1974. Appointment: Editor, Pears Cyclopedia, 1976-. Publications: Sources in British Political History, 6 volumes, 1975-84; The Slump (with John Stevenson), 1976; Dictionary of Historical Terms, 2nd edition, 1989; World Political Almanac, 1989; Longman Handbook of World History Since 1914, 1991; Longman Handbook of Modern European History 1763-1991, 1992; A Short History of the Liberal Party 1900-92, 1993; Britain Since 1945 (with John Stevenson), 1995; Longman Handbook of Modern British History 1714-1995, 1996; What Happened Where (with Diccon

Bewes), 1996; Longman Handbook of Modern American History 1763-1996, with David Waller, 1997. Contributions to: Guardian; Times Literary Supplement; THES. Honour: Fellow, Royal Historical Society, 1977. Literary Agent: Derek Johns, A P Watt & Co, 20 John Street, London WC1, England. Address: c/o Pears Cyclopedia, Penguin Books, 27 Wrights Lane, Kensington, London W8 5TZ, England.

COOK David, b. 21 Sept 1940, Preston, Lancashire, England. Actor; Writer. Education: Royal College of Dramatic Art, 1959-61. Appointments: Professional Actor, 1961-; Writer-in-Residence, St Martin's College, Lancaster, England, 1982-83. Publications: Albert's Memorial, 1972; Happy Endings, 1974; Walter, 1978; Winter Doves, 1979; Sunrising, 1983; Missing Persons, 1986; Crying Out Loud, 1988; Walter and June, 1989; Second Best, 1991. Honours: E M Forster Award, 1977; Hawthornden Prize, 1978; Southern Arts Fiction Prize, 1984; Arthur Welton Scholarship, 1991; Oddfellows Social Concern Award, 1992. Membership: Society of Authors. Literary Agent: Deborah Rogers, 20 Powis Mews, London W11 1JN, England. Address: 7 Sydney Place, London SW7 3NL, England.

COOK Dorothy Mary, (D Y Cameron, D M Carlisle, Elizabeth Clare), b. 13 Feb 1907, Gravesend, England. Author. Education: Grammar School, Rochester, England. Publications: 17 novels as D Y Cameron, 1962-81; 4 novels as D M Carlisle, 1974-86; 12 novels as Elizabeth Clare, 1966-81. Memberships: Fellowship of Reconciliation; Romantic Novelists Association. Address: c/o Hale, 45-47 Clerkenwell Green, London EC1R 0HT, England.

COOK Glen (Charles), b. 9 July 1944, New York, New York, USA. Auto Assembler; Writer. m. 14 June 1971, 3 sons. Publications: The Black Company, series, 1984-89; A Matter of Time, 1985; Pasaage at Arms, 1985; The Garrett Files, series, 1987-; The Dragon Never Sleeps, 1988; The Tower of Fear, 1989. Contributions to: Numerous magazines and journals. Literary Agent: Russell Galen, Scouil-Chichak-Galen, 381 Park Avenue South, Suite 1020, New York, NY 10016, USA. Address: c/o Scott Meredith Inc, 845 Third Avenue, New York, NY 10022, USA.

COOK Lila. See: **AFRICANO Lillian.**

COOK Norman Edgar, b. 4 Mar 1920. Editor; Book Critic. m. Mildred Warburton, 1942, 3 sons. Appointments: Ministry of Information, 1943-45; Editor, Northwich Guardian, 1945-47; Liverpool Daily Post, 1947-49;Information Officer, Air Ministry, 1949-53; Night News Editor, Daily Post, 1953-55; Deputy News Editor, 1955-59, London Editor, 1959-72, Executive News Editor, 1972-77, Editor, 1978-79, 1979, Chief Book Critic, 1980-91, Liverpool Daily Post. Publications: Numerous articles and review. Honour: Commander of the Order of the British Empire, 1980. Address: 7 Trinity Gardens, Southport, Lancashire PR8 1AU, England.

COOK Peter John, (John Coburn) b. 1 Apr 1934, Hertford, England. Yachting Journalist. m. Jill Valerie Moore, 17 Mar 1963, 1 son, 1 daughter. Education: HNC Naval Architecture, 1956. Appointments: UK Boating Industry Management, 1958-66; Assistant Editor, 1966-69, Editor, 1969-91, Yachts and Yachting; Freelance Yachting Journalist, 1991-; Secretary, Yachting Journalists' Association, 1994-. Publications: Boat Building Methods, 1969; The Longest Race, 1972; The Complete Book of Sailing, 1985. Contributions to: Many and various worldwide. Honour: RD. Address: Spinneys, Woodham Mortimer, Maldon, Essex CM9 6SX, England.

COOK Petronelle Marguerite Mary, (Margot Arnold), b. 16 May 1925, Plymouth, Devon, England. Writer; Teacher. m. Philip R Cook, 20 July 1949, 2 sons, 1 daughter. Education: BA, 1946, Diploma in Prehistoric Archaeology and Anthropology, 1947, MA, 1950, Oxford University. Publications: The Officers' Woman, 1972; The Villa on the Palatine, 1975; Marie, 1979; Exit Actors, Dying, 1980; The Cape Cod Caper, 1980; Death of a Voodoo Doll, 1981; Zadok's Treasurer, 1981; Affairs of State, 1981; Love Among the Allies, 1982; Lament for a Lady Laird, 1982; Death on the Dragon's Tongue, 1982; Desperate Measures, 1983; Sinister Purposes, 1985; The Menehune Murders, 1989; Toby's Folly, 1990; The Catacomb Conspiracy, 1991; The Cape Cod Conundrum, 1992; Dirge for a Dorset Druid, 1994; The Midas Murders, 1995. As Petronelle Cook: The Queen Consorts of England, 1993. Contributions to: Numerous short stories to magazines. Honours: Oxford University Archaeological Society, president, 1945; Fiction Prize, National Writers Club, 1983. Memberships: New England Historic and Genealogical Society; Mystery Writers of America, Participant, Mentor programme for fledgling writers. Literary Agent: Collier Associates. Address: 11 High School Road, Hyannis, MA 02601, USA.

COOK Robin, b. 4 May 1940, New York, New York, USA. Physician; Writer. m. Barbara Ellen Mougin, 18 July 1979. Education: BA, Wesleyan University, 1962; MD, Columbia University, 1966; Postgraduate Studies, Harvard University. Appointments: Resident in General Surgery, Queen's Hospital, Honolulu, 1966-68; Resident in Ophthalmology, 1971-75, Staff, 1975-, Massachusetts Eye and Ear Infirmary, Boston. Publications: Novels: The Year of the Intern, 1972; Coma, 1977; Sphinx, 1979; Brain, 1981; Fever, 1982; Godplayer, 1983; Mindbend, 1985; Outbreak, 1987; Mortal Fear, 1988; Mutation, 1989; Harmful Intent, 1990; Vital Signs, 1990; Blindsight, 1991; Terminal, 1992; Fatal Cure, 1994; Acceptable Risk, 1995; Contagion, 1996; Chromosome 6, 1997. Address: c/o Putnam's Sons, 51 Madison Avenue, New York, NY 10010, USA.

COOK Stanley, b. 12 Apr 1922, Austerfield, Yorkshire, England. Retired Lecturer; Poet. m. Kathleen Mary Daly, 1 son, 2 daughters. Education: BA, Christ Church, Oxford, 1943. Appointments: Lecturer, Huddersfield Polytechnic, 1969-81; Editor, Poetry Nottingham, 1981-85. Publications: Form Photograph, 1971; Sign of Life, 1972; Staff Photograph, 1976; Alphabet, 1976; Woods Beyond a Cornfield, 1981; Concrete Poems, 1984; Barnsdale, 1986; Selected Poems, 1972-86, 1986; The Northern Seasons, 1988. Other: Children's poems. Honour: Cheltenham Festival Competition Prize, 1972. Address: 600 Barnsley Road, Sheffield, South Yorkshire S5 6UA, England.

COOK Thomas, b. 19 Sept 1947, Alabama, USA. m. Susan Terner, 17 Mar 1978, 1 daughter. Education: Georgia State College; MA, Hunter College; MPhil, Columbia University. Publications: Blood Innocents, 1980; The Orchids, 1982; Tabernacle, 1983; Elena, 1986; Sacrificial Ground, 1988; Flesh and Blood, 1989; Streets of Fire, 1989; Night Secrets, 1990; Breakheart Hill, 1994. Contributions to: Atlanta Magazine. Honours: Edgar Allan Poe Awards, 1981, 1988. Address: c/o Russell & Volkening, 50 West 29th Street, New York, NY 10001, USA.

COOKE (Alfred) Alistair, b. 20 Nov 1908, Manchester, England (US citizen, 1941). Writer; Broadcaster. m. (1) Ruth Emerson, 1 son, (2) Jane White Hawkes, 1 daughter. Education: 1st Class English Tripos, 1929, BA, 1930, Jesus College, Cambridge; Commonwealth Fund Fellow, Yale University, 1932-33, Harvard University, 1933-34. Appointments: Film Critic, 1934-37, Commentator on American Affairs, 1938-, BBC; London Correspondent, NBC, 1936-37; Special Correspondent on American Affairs, The Times, 1938-42; American Feature Writer, Daily Herald, 1941-43; United Nations Correspondent, 1945-48, Chief US Correspondent, 1948-72, Manchester Guardian, later The Guardian; Host, Omnibus television programme, 1952-61, Masterpiece Theater, PBS series, 1971-92; Writer, Narrator, America: A Personal History of the US, television series, 1972-73. Publications: Garbo and the Night Watchmen (editor), 1937; Douglas Fairbanks, 1940; A Generation on Trial: USA v Alger Hiss, 1950; One Man's America (in UK as Letters from America), 1952; Christmas Eve, 1952; A Commencement Address, 1954; The Vintage Mencken (editor), 1955; Around the World in Fifty Years, 1966; Talk About America, 1968; Alistair Cooke's America, 1973; Six Men, 1977; The Americans: Fifty Letters from America on Our Life and Times, 1979; Above London (with Robert Cameron), 1980; Masterpieces, 1981; The Patient Has the Floor, 1986; America Observed, 1988; Fun and Games with Alistair Cooke, 1994. Honours: George Foster Peabody Awards for International News Reporting, 1952, 1973; 4 Emmy Awards, 1973; Benjamin Franklin Medal, Royal Society of Arts, 1973; Dimbleby Award, 1973; Honorary Knighthood, 1973; Howland Medal, Yale University, 1977; Special George Foster Peabody Award, 1983; Several honorary doctorates. Address: 1150 Fifth Avenue, New York, NY 10128, USA.

COOKE Ann. See: **COLE Joanna.**

COOKE Chantelle Anne, b. 9 Apr 1971, Denver, Colorado, USA. Freelance Writer. Education: Collin County Community College. Publications: Songs From Stars (poetry chapbook), 1995; Poetry Visions series (poetry cassette tape), 1997. Contributions to: Technical, religious, nature, poetry and writing, to various publications. Honours: Award for Library Reading Programme, 1983; Award for Poem, World of Poetry, 1992; Awards for Poems, National Library of Poetry, 1994, 1995; Awards for Poems, Famous Poet Society, 1995, 1996; Awards for Short Stories, Se La Vie Writer's Journal, 1995, 1996; 1st Place, Se La Vie Writer's Journal 8th Anniversary; Anne B Cooke Poetry Award set up in her grandmother's name, Bell's Letters, poetry journal. Memberships: Poetry Connection; Magic Circle; Academy of American Poets. Address: 5003 Birdie Lane, Doylestown, PA 18901, USA.

COOKSON Clive Michael, b. 13 Feb 1952, London, England. Science Journalist. m. Caroline Davidson, 8 Apr 1978, 1 son, 1 daughter. Education: BA, 1st Class Honours, Chemistry, Brasenose College, Oxford, 1974. Appointments: Trainee Journalist, Luton Evening Post, 1974-76; Science Correspondent, 1976-77, American Editor, 1977-81, Times Higher Education Supplement, 1976-77; Technology Editor, The Times, 1981-83; Science Correspondent, BBC Radio, 1983-87; Technology Editor, 1987-91, Science Editor, 1991-, Financial Times. Address: Financial Times, 1 Southwark Bridge, London SE1 9HL, England.

COOLIDGE Clark, b. 26 Feb 1939, Providence, Rhode Island, USA. Poet. m. Susan Hopkins, 1 daughter. Education: Brown University, 1956-58. Publications: Flag Flutter and US Electric, 1966; Poems, 1967; Ing, 1969; Space, 1970; The So, 1971; Moroccan Variations, 1971; Suite V, 1973; The Maintains, 1974; Polaroid, 1975; Quartz Hearts, 1978; Own Face, 1978; Smithsonian Depositions, and Subjects to a Film, 1980; American Ones, 1981; A Geology, 1981; Research, 1982; Mine: The One That Enters the Stories, 1982; Solution Passage: Poems, 1978-1981, 1986; The Crystal Text, 1986; Mesh, 1988; At Egypt, 1988; Sound as Thought: Poems, 1982-1984, 1990; The Book of During, 1991; Odes of Roba, 1991; Baffling Means, 1991; On the Slates, 1992; Lowell Connector: Lines and Shots from Kerouac's Town, 1993; Own Face, 1994; Registers: (People in All), 1994; The ROVA Improvisations, 1994. Honours: National Endowment for the Arts Grant, 1966; New York Poets Foundation Award, 1968. Address: c/o The Figures, 5 Castle Hill, Great Barrington, MA 01230, USA.

COOMBS Lilian, b. 10 Jan 1930, Bristol, England. Housewife. Widow, 5 sons, 4 daughters. Publications: Northern Lights; The Cracked Mirror; The World At My Feet; Under A Southern Sky; Travellers Moon; South West Voices; Words and Work; Life Stills; First Time Poets; Inspration From Southern England; Poets in the West Country; Empty Voices; Poetic Destinations; Threads of Life; The Timeless Collections; The Love Within; United We Stand; Creative Verse; The Power of Love; Poetic Hideaway; Through the Eye of a Poet; West Country Rhythmes; The Marching of Time. Contributions to: PDSA. Honours: Various. Address: 12 Lytton Grove, Horfield, Bristol BS7 0NU, England.

COOMBS Patricia, b. 23 July 1926, Los Angeles, California, USA. Author; Illustrator of Childrens' Books. m. L James Fox, 13 July 1951, 2 daughters. Education: BA, 1947, MA, 1950, University of Washington. Publications: Dorrie and the Blue Witch, 1964; Dorrie and the Haunted House, 1970; Dorrie and the Goblin, 1972; Mouse Cafe, 1972; Molly Mullett, 1975; The Magic Pot, 1977; Dorrie and the Screebit Ghost, 1979; The Magician McTree, 1984; Dorrie and the Pin Witch, 1989; Dorrie and the Haunted Schoolhouse, 1992. Contributions to: Partisan Review; Hudson Review; Poetry. Honours: New York Times Ten Best Books of the Year, 1963; Child Study Association Books of the Year, 1970; New York Times 10 Best Illustrated Books of the Year, 1972. Membership: Authors Guild. Literary Agent: Dorothy Markinko, McIntosh and Otis, New York, USA; Gerald Pollinger, Laurance Pollinger Ltd, London, England. Address: 178 Oswegatchie Road, Waterford, CT 06385, USA.

COONEY Ray(mond George Alfred), b. 30 May 1932, London, England. Actor; Dramatist; Director. m. Linda Dixon, 8 Dec 1962, 2 sons. Publications: Plays, both solo and in collaboration with others: One for the Pot, 1961; Chase Me, Comrade, 1964, Charlie Girl, 1965; Stand by Your Bedouin, 1966; Not Now, Darling, 1967; My Giddy Aunt, 1968; Move Over Mrs Markham, 1969; Why Not Stay for Breakfast?, 1970; There Goes the Bride, 1974; Run For Your Wife, 1984; Two Into One, 1985; Wife Begins at Forty, 1986; It Runs in the Family, 1987; Out of Order, 1990; Funny Money, 1994. Membership: Dramatists Club. Address: Hollowfield Cottage, Littleton, Surrey GU3 1HN, England.

COONTZ Stephanie, b. 31 Aug 1944, Seattle, Washington, USA. Professor of History and Women's Studies; Writer. 1 son. Education: BA, University of California at Berkeley, 1966; MA, University of Washington, Seattle, 1970. Appointments: Faculty, History and Family Studies, Evergreen State College, Olympia, Washington, 1975-; Visiting Faculty, University of Washington, Seattle, 1976; Exchange Professor, Kobe University of Commerce, Japan, 1986; Exchange Professor, 1992, Visiting Associate Professor, 1994, University of Hawaii at Hilo. Publications: Women's Work, Men's Property: On the Origins of Gender and Class (with Peta Henderson), 1986; The Social Origins of Private Life: A History of American Families, 1988; The Way We Never Were: American Families and the Nostalgia Trap, 1992; The Way We Really Are: Coming to Terms with America's Changing Families, 1997; American Families: A Multicultural Reader (with G Raley and M Parson), 1998. Contributions to: Books, professional journals and general periodicals. Honours: Governor's Writers Award, 1988; National Scholar, The National Faculty, 1994-; Dale Richmond Award, American Academy of Pediatrics, 1995. Memberships: American Historical Association; American Studies Association; Organization of American Historians; Council on Contemporary Families. Address: 808 North Rogers, Olympia, WA 98502, USA.

COOPER Beverley Jane, b. 14 June 1958, Vancouver, Canada. Actor; Playwright. m. John Jarvis, 16 Oct 1988, 2 sons. Education: Acting Diploma, Langara College, Vancouver. Appointments: Writer-in-Residence, Theatre Passe Muraille, 1986-87, 1991-92, Theatre Columbus, 1994. Publications: Nelly Bly; Ten Days in a Madhouse; Adventures for (Big) Girls; Seven Radio Plays, 1993; Thin Ice; Wanna Play?, 1993; Out of Body, 1994. Honours: Co-Recipient, Floyd Chalmbers Canadian Play Award, 1988. Memberships: Playwrights Union of Canada; WCG; PEN. Literary Agent: Suzanne DePose. Address: c/o Core Group, 55 Langford Avenue, Toronto, Ontario M4J 3E4, Canada.

COOPER (Brenda) Clare, b. 21 Jan 1935, Falmouth, Cornwall, England. Writer. m. Bill Cooper, 6 Apr 1953, 2 sons, 1 daughter. Publications: David's Ghost; The Black Horn; Earthchange; Ashar of Qarius; The Skyrifters; Andrews and the Gargoyle; A Wizard Called Jones; Kings of the Mountain; Children of the Camps; The Settlement on Planet B; Miracles and Rubies; Timeloft; Marya's Emmets. Honour: Runner Up, Tir Na Nog Award. Memberships: PEN; Society of Authors; Welsh Academy.

Address: Tyrhibin Newydd, Newport, Dyfed SA42 0NT, Wales.

COOPER Bryan, (Robert Wright), b. 6 Feb 1932, Paris, France. Author; Editor; Journalist; Scriptwriter. m. (1) Patricia Barnard, 27 Feb 1954, 2 sons, 2 daughters, (2) Judith Williams, 7 Apr 1979. Appointments: Reporter, Kentish Times, 1948-50; Feature Writer, RAF Flying Review magazine, 1950-52; Sub-editor, Exchange Telegraph, 1953-54; Public Relations Officer, British Petroleum, London, 1954-57, New York, 1957-61; Editor, BP Features and Motor Racing Service, 1961-64; Freelance Author and Scriptwriter, 1964-75; Editor and Publisher, Petroleum Economist, the International Energy Journal, 1975-89; Energy Writer and Consultant, Energy Research Ltd, Cyprus, 1990-94. Publications: North Sea Oil - The Great Gamble, 1966; The Ironclads of Cambrai, 1967; Battle of the Torpedo Boats, 1970; The Buccaneers, 1970; PT Boats, 1970; Alaska - The Last Frontier, 1972; Tank Battles of World War 1, 1973; Fighter, 1973; Bomber, 1974; Stones of Evil (novel) 1974; The E Boat Threat, 1976; The Wildcatters (novel), 1976; The Adventure of North Sea Oil, 1982; The Emigration Handbook, 1997. Contributions to: The Times; Financial Times; Numerous magazines. Memberships: Writer's Guild of Great Britain; Garrick; London Press Club. Literary Agent: Watson, Little Ltd, 12 Egbert Street, London NW1 8LJ, England. Address: Woodbine, 11 Victoria Road, Deal, Kent CT14 7AS, England.

COOPER Colin Symons, (Daniel Benson), b. 5 July 1926, Birkenhead, England. Journalist; Editor. m. Maureen Elizabeth Goodwin, 6 Sept 1966, 2 sons. Appointments: Features Editor, Guitar Magazine, 1972-73; News Editor, Classical Guitar, 1982-84, General Editor, 1984-. Publications: The Thunder and Lightning Man, 1968; Outcrop, 1969; Dargason, 1977; The Epping Pyramid, 1978; The Argyll Killings, 1980. Contributions to: Times Literary Supplement; Times Education Supplement; Guardian; Independent; Gendai Guitar (Tokyo); Asta Journal (USA); European; Raconteur. Address: 24 Blurton Road, London E5 0NL, England.

COOPER Derek Macdonand, b. 25 May 1925. Author; Broadcaster; Journalist. m. Janet Marian Feaster, 1953, 1 son, 1 daughter. Education: University College, Cardiff, Wales; Wadham College, Oxford; MA, Oxon. Appointments: Columnist, Listener, Guardian, Observer Magazine, World Medicine, Scottish Field, Sunday Standard, Homes and Gardens, Saga Magazine, Women's Journal. Publications: The Bad Food Guide, 1967; Skye, 1970, 2nd edition, 1977; The Beverage Report, 1970; The Gullibility Gap, 1974; Hebridean Connection, 1977; Guide to the Whiskies of Scotland, 1978; Road to the Isles, 1979; Enjoying Scotch (with Dione Pattullo), 1980; Wines With Food, 1982, 2nd edition, 1986; The Whisky Roads of Scotland (with Fay Goodwin), 1982; The Century Companion to Whiskies, 1983; Skye Remembered, 1983; The World of Cooking, 1983; The Road to Mingulay, 1985; The Gunge File, 1986; A Taste of Scotch, 1989. Contributions to: In Britain: Signature; Taste; A La Carte; The West Highland Free Press; Television programmes. Honours: Glenfiddich Trophy as Wine and Food Writer, 1973, 1980; Scottish Arts Council Award, 1980; Broadcaster of the Year, 1984; House of Fraser Press Award, 1984. Membership: Guild of Food Writers, 1st chairman. Address: Seafield House, Portree, Isle of Skye, Scotland.

COOPER Helen, b. 6 Feb 1947, Nottingham, England. University Professor. m. M G Cooper, 18 July 1970, 2 daughters. Education: BA, New Hall, Cambridge, 1968; MA, PhD, 1972. Appointments: English Editor, Medium AEvum, 1989. Publications: The Oxford Guides to Chaucer: The Canterbury Tales; The Structure of the Canterbury Tales; Pastoral: Medieval into Renaissance; Great Grand Mother Goose. Contributions to: Numerous. Address: University College, Oxford OX1 4BH, England.

COOPER Jean Campbell, b. 27 Nov 1905, Chefoo, North China. Author; Lecturer. m. V M Cooper, 21 June 1945. Education: Various boarding schools in China, Australia and England; LLA (Hons), 1st Class, Moral

Philosophy, St Andrew's University, 1930. Publications: Taoism, the Way of the Mystic, 1972; An Illustrated Encyclopedia of Traditional Symbols, 1978; Yin and Yang, the Harmony of Opposites, 1982; Fairy Tales, Allegories of the Inner Life, 1983; Chinese Alchemy, 1984; Aquarian Dictionary of Festivals, 1990; Symbolic and Mythological Animals, 1993; Brewer's Myth and Legend, 1993; The Cassell Dictionary of Christianity, 1996. Contributions to: Articles, translations, reviews for Studies in Comparative Religion. Memberships: English PEN; Royal Commonwealth Society, life member; Justice of the Peace. Address: Bobbin Mill, Ulpha, Broughton-in-Furness, Cumbria LA20 6DU, England.

COOPER Jilly (Sallitt), b. 21 Feb 1937, Hornchurch, Essex, England. Writer; Journalist. Appointments: Reporter, Middlesex Independent Newspaper, Brentford, 1957-59; Columnist, The Sunday Times, 1969-85, The Mail on Sunday, 1985-. Publications: How to Stay Married, 1969; How to Survive from Nine to Five, 1970; Jolly Super, 1971; Men and Super Men, 1972; Jolly Super Too, 1973; Women and Super Women, 1974; Jolly Superlative, 1975; Emily (romance novel), 1975; Super Men and Super Women (omnibus), 1976; Bella (romance novel), 1976; Harriet (romance novel), 1976; Octavia (romance novel), 1977; Work and Wedlock (omnibus), 1977; Superjilly, 1977; Imogen (romance novel), 1978; Prudence (romance novel), 1978; Class: A View from Middle England, 1979; Supercooper, 1980; Little Mabel series, juvenile, 4 volumes, 1980-85; Violets and Vinegar: An Anthology of Women's Writings and Sayings (editor with Tom Hartman), 1980; The British in Love (editor), 1980; Love and Other Heartaches, 1981; Jolly Marsupial, 1982; Animals in War, 1983; The Common Years, 1984; Leo and Jilly Cooper on Rugby, 1984; Riders, 1985; Hotfoot to Zabriskie Point, 1985; How to Survive Christmas, 1986; Turn Right at The Spotted Dog, 1987; Rivals, 1988; Angels Rush In, 1990; Polo, 1991; The Man Who Made Husbands Jealous, 1993; Araminta's Wedding, 1993; Appassionata, 1996. Address: c/o Desmond Elliot, 15-17 King Street, St James, London SW1, England.

COOPER Kenneth H(ardy), b. 4 Mar 1931, Oklahoma City, Oklahoma, USA. Physician; Author. m. Mildred Lucille Clark, 7 Aug 1959, 1 son, 1 daughter. Education: BS, 1952, MD, 1956, University of Oklahoma; MPH, Harvard School of Public Health, 1962; Certified Diplomate, American Board of Preventive Medicine, 1966. Appointments: US Air Force, 1957-70, serving as Senior Flight Surgeon and Developer of the 12 minute test and the Aerobics Point System; Founder and Physician, Cooper Aerobics Center, Dallas, 1970-; Consultant and Lecturer on Aerobics. Publications: Aerobics, 1968; The New Aerobics, 1970; Aerobics for Women (with Mildred Cooper), 1972; The Aerobics Way, 1977; The Aerobics Program for Total Well-Being, 1982; Running Without Fear, 1985; Controlling Cholesterol, 1988; The New Aerobics for Women (with Mildred Cooper), 1988; Preventing Osteoporosis, 1989; Overcoming Hypertension, 1990; Kid Fitness, 1991; The Antioxidant Revolution, 1994; It's Better to Believe, 1995, (in paperback as Faith-Based Fitness, 1997); Advanced Nutritional Therapies, 1997; Can Stress Heal?, 1998. Honours: Daniel Webster Award, International Platform Association, 1977; Nurmi Award for Best Scientific Development or Achievement, Runner's World, 1980; Outstanding Texas Citizen, Exchange Clubs of Texas, 1982; Oklahoma Hall of Fame, Oklahoma Heritage Society, 1983; Distinguished Service Citation, University of Oklahoma, 1984; American Academy of Achievement Honoree, 1986; Lifetime Achievement Award, 1988, and Hall of Fame, 1992, International Dance and Exercise Association; Academy of Dentistry International Humanitarian Award, 1991; Order of Eagle Exemplar, Dwight D Eisenhower Fitness Award, United States Sports Academy, 1992; Kenneth Cooper Middle School named in his honour, Oklahoma City, 1993; Harvard University Presidential Citation, 1995; Texas Health, Racquet and Sports Club Award, 1996; International Personality of the Year, Karlsruh, Germany, 1996; Marie Roberts Fisher Distinguished Professor Award, University of North Texas, 1996; Distinguished Alumnus Award,

University of Oklahoma, 1998; several honorary doctorates. Memberships: American College of Preventive Medicine, fellow; American College of Sports Medicine, fellow; American Geriatrics Society, fellow; American Medical Association; American Running and Fitness Association; Texas Medical Association; Texas Medical Foundation; Dallas County Medical Society. Literary Agent: Herb Katz. Address: The Cooper Aerobics Center, 12200 Preston Road, Dallas, TX 75230, USA.

COOPER Richard N(ewell), b. 14 June 1934, Seattle, Washington, USA. Professor of International Economics; Writer. m. Carolyn Cahalan, 5 June 1956, 1 son, 1 daughter. Education: AB, Oberlin College, 1956; MSc, Economics, London School of Economics and Political Science, 1958; PhD, Harvard University, 1962. Appointments: Senior Staff Economist, Council of Economic Advisers to the President of the US, 1961-63; Assistant Professor, 1963-65, Frank Altschul Professor of International Economics, 1966-77, Provost, 1972-74, Yale University; Deputy Assistant Secretary of State for International Affairs, 1965-66, Under-Secretary of State for Economic Affairs, 1977-81, US Department of State; Maurits C Boas Professor of International Economics, Harvard University, 1981-; Chairman, Federal Reserve Bank, Boston, 1990-92, National Intelligence Council, 1995-97. Publications: The Economics of Interdependence, 1968; A Re-ordered World (editor and contributor), 1973; Economic Policy in an Interdependent World, 1986; The International Monetary System, 1987; Can Nations Agree? (co-author), 1989; Economic Stabilization and Debt in Developing Countries, 1992; Boom, Crisis and Adjustment: The Macroeconomic Experience of Developing Countries (co-author), 1993; Environment and Resource Policies for the World Economy, 1994; Macroeconomic Policy and Adjustment in Korea, 1970-1990 (editor and contributor), 1994; Trade Growth in Transition Economies (co-editor and contributor), 1997. Contributions to: Professional journals. Honours: Phi Beta Kappa, 1955; Marshall Scholarship, UK, 1956-58; Brookings Fellow, 1960-61; Ford Foundation Faculty Sciences, 1975-76; Honorary LLD, Oberlin College, 1978; Foreign Affairs Award, US Department of State, 1981; National Intelligence Distinguished Service Medal, 1996. Memberships: American Academy of Arts and Sciences, fellow; Aspen Strategy Group; Council on Foreign Relations; Trilateral Commission. Address: c/o Weatherhead Center for International Affairs, Harvard University, 1737 Cambridge Street, Cambridge, MA 02138, USA.

COOPER Robert Cecil, b. 24 Nov 1917, Wellington, New Zealand. Retired Botanist. m. (1) Jessica Sommerville Scott, 16 Dec 1938, (2) Una Vivienne Cassie, 29 Sept 1984, 1 son, 1 daughter. Education: Accountants' Professional, 1940; BCom, 1948; BA, 1949; MA, 1950; PhD, 1953. Appointment: Botanist, Auckland Museum, 1948-71. Publications: New Zealand Medicinal Plants, 1961-62; Economic Native Plants of New Zealand, 1988, 2nd edition, 1991. Address: 1/117 Cambridge Road, Hillcrest, Hamilton, New Zealand.

COOPER Susan Mary, b. 23 May 1935, Burnham, Buckinghamshire, England. Writer. m. (1) Nicholas J Grant, 1963, div 1982, 1 son, 1 daughter, (2) Hume Cronyn, 1996. Education: MA, Somerville College, Oxford, 1956. Publications: Mandrake, 1964; Over Sea, Under Stone, 1965; Behind the Golden Curtain: A View of the USA, 1968; J B Priestley: Portrait of an Author, 1970; Dawn of Fear, 1970; The Dark is Rising, 1973; Greenwitch, 1974; The Grey King, 1975; Silver on the Tree, 1977; Jethro and the Jumbie, 1979; Seaward, 1983; The Silver Cow, 1983; The Selkie Girl, 1986; Matthew's Dragon, 1990; Danny and the Kings, 1993; The Boggart, 1994; Dreams and Wishes: Essays on Writing for Children, 1996; The Boggart and the Monster, 1997. Contributions to: Periodicals. Honours: Boston Globe-Horn Book Award, 1973; Newbery Medal, 1976; Welsh Arts Council Tir Nan og Awards, 1976, 1978; Hugo Award, 1984; Writers Guild of America Awards, 1984, 1985; Christopher Medal, 1985. Memberships: Authors Guild; Society of Authors; Writers Guild of America. Address: c/o Margaret K McElderry Books, Simon &

Schuster, 1230 Sixth Avenue, New York, NY 10020, USA.

COOPER William. See: HOFF Harry Summerfield.

COOVER Robert (Lowell), b. 4 Feb 1932, Charles City, Iowa, USA. Writer; Dramatist; Poet; University Teacher. m. Maria del Pilar Sans-Mallagre, 3 June 1959, 1 son, 2 daughters. Education: Southern Illinois University; BA, Indiana University, 1953; MA, University of Chicago, 1965. Appointments: Teacher, Bard College, 1966-67, University of Iowa, 1967-69, Princeton University, 1972-73, Brown University, 1980-; Various guest lectureships and professorships. Publications: The Origin of the Brunists, 1966; The Universal Baseball Association, J Henry Waugh, Prop., 1968; Pricksongs & Descants (short fictions), 1969; A Theological Position (plays), 1972; The Public Burning, 1977; A Political Fable (The Cat in the Hat for President), 1980; Spanking the Maid, 1982; Gerald's Party, 1986; A Night at the Movies, 1987; Whatever Happened to Gloomy Gus of the Chicago Bears?, 1987; Pinocchio in Venice, 1991; John's Wife, 1996; Briar Rose, 1997. Contributions to: Plays, poems, fiction, translations, essays and criticism in various publications. Honours: William Faulkner Award for Best First Novel, 1966; Rockefeller Foundation Grant, 1969; Guggenheim Fellowships, 1971, 1974; Obie Awards, 1972-73; American Academy of Arts and Letters Award, 1976; National Endowment for the Arts Grant, 1985; Rhode Island Governor's Arts Award, 1988; Deutscher Akademischer Austauschdienst Fellowship, Berlin, 1990. Memberships: American Academy and Institute of Arts and Letters; PEN International. Address: c/o Department of English, Brown University, Providence, RI 02912, USA.

COPE Robert Knox, (Jack Cope), b. 3 June 1913, Mooi River, Natal, South Africa. Writer; Poet; Editor. m. Lesley de Villiers, 4 June 1942, 2 sons. Appointment: Co-Founder and Editor, Contrast, South African, literary magazine, 1960-80. Publications: Lyrics and Diabtribes, 1948; Selected Poems of Ingrid Jonker (co-translator), 1968, revised edition, 1988; The Rain Maker, 1971; The Student of Zend, 1972; My Son Max, 1977. Editor: Penguin Book of South African Verse. Other: Stage, radio and television adaptations. Contributions to: School textbooks and magazines. Honours: British Council Award, 1960; Carnegie Fellowship, 1966; CNA Prize, Argus Prize, and Gold Medallist for Literature, Veld Trust Prize, 1971; Honorary DLitt, Rhodes. Address: 21 Bearton Road, Hitchin, Herts SG5 1UB, England.

COPE Wendy Mary, b. 21 July 1945, Erith, Kent, England. Poet; Writer; Editor. Education: BA, History, St Hilda's College, Oxford, 1966; Diploma in Education, 1967. Appointments: Teacher, Primary schools, London, 1967-86; Freelance Writer, 1986-. Publications: Across the City, 1980; Hope and the 42, 1984; Making Cocoa for Kingsley Amis, 1986; Poem from a Colour Chart of Housepaints, 1986; Men and Their Boring Arguments, 1988; Does She Like Wordgames?, 1988; Twiddling Your Thumbs, 1988; The River Girl, 1990; Serious Concerns, 1992. Editor: Is That the New Moon?: Poems by Women Poets, 1989; The Orchard Book of Funny Poems, 1993; The Funny Side (editor), 1998; The Faber Book of Bedtime Stories (editor), 1999. Contributions to: Newspapers and reviews. Honours: Cholmondeley Award, 1987; Michael Braude Award for Light Verse, American Academy of Arts and Letters, 1995. Memberships: Royal Society of Literature, fellow, 1993; Society of Authors, management committee, 1992-95. Address: c/o Peters Fraser and Dunlop, 5th Floor, The Chambers, Chelsea Harbour, Lots Road, London SW10 0XF, England.

COPELAND Ann. See: FURTWANGLER Virginia Walsh.

COPELLO Beatriz. Writer. Education: BA, Psychology, 1980, MA, Counselling, 1986, Macquarie University; Graduate Diploma, Communications, Creative Writing, University of Technology, Sydney, 1989; MA, English, Sydney University, 1996. Publications: Short Stories:

Freedom on a Wednesday Morning, 1989; A Game of Cards by the Office Window, 1994; The Women's Pool, 1995; A Tale About a Woman Who Never Existed or Out of a Bird or Dynamic Lifter, 1996; Vita Grama, Vita da Cani, 1998. Poetry Book: Women, Souls and Shadows, 1992. Novel: Forbidden Steps Under the Wisteria, 1999. Non-Fiction: A Call to the Stars, 1999. Play: Malinche's Fire, 1998. Contributions to: Journals, periodicals, quarterlies, reviews, magazines and newspapers. Honours: 1st Prize, Taylor Square Arts Festival Award, 1995; Emerging Writers Grant, Australia Council Literary Fund, 1996; Finalist Certificate, Pave Literary Competition, 1997; Ian Reed Foundation Scholarship, 1998. Address: 14 Finlays Avenue, Earlwood, New South Wales 2206, Australia.

COPLEY Paul, b. 25 Nov 1944, Denby Dale, Yorkshire, England. Actor; Writer. m. Natasha Pyne, 7 July 1972. Education: Teachers Certificate, Northern Counties College of Education. Appointments: Freelance Actor/Writer. Publications: Staged: Pillion, Bush Theatre, London, 1977; Viaduct, Bush Theatre, London, 1979; Tapster, Stephen Joseph Theatre, Scarborough, 1981; Fire-Eaters, Tricycle Theatre, London, 1984; Calling, Stephen Joseph Theatre, Scarborough, 1986; Broadcast: On May-Day, BBC Radio 4 Sunday Play, 1986, repeated World Service, 1987, Radio 4, 1996; Tipperary Smith, BBC Radio 4, 1994; Words Alive, BBC Education Radio, 1996-98; Publication: Odysseus and the Cyclops, 1998. Membership: Writers Guild. Address: Casarotto Ramsey Ltd, 60 Wardour Street, London W1V 4ND, England.

CORBELLA Licia, b. 9 June 1963, Montreal, Quebec, Canada. Journalist. m. James Stephen Gardiner, 25 Apr 1987. Education: Arts and Science Diploma, 1985, Journalism Diploma, Vancouver Community College, 1987. Appointments: Lifestyle/Travel Editor, 1994, Associate Editor, 1996-, Editor, 1998-, Calgary Sun. Publication: For Love and Money: The Tale of the Joudries, 1996. Contributions to: Newspapers. Honours: Edward Dunlop Award of Excellence, 1992; Ontario Reporters Association Award, 1992; Edward Dunlop Award in Feature Writing, 1996. Address: 2615 12th Street North East, Calgary, Alberta T2E 7W9, Canada.

CORBEN Beverly Balkum, b. 6 Aug 1926. Retired Educator; Poet; Writer; Artist. m. Herbert Charles Corben, 25 Oct 1957, 1 stepson, 2 stepdaughters. Education: AA, Santa Monica College, 1950; BA with honours, University of California, Los Angeles, 1960; MA, Case Western Reserve University, 1972. Appointments: Teaching Assistant, 1972-73, Director of Writing Laboratory, 1973-82 (on leave 1978-80), Scarborough College, University of Toronto, Canada; Visiting Scholar, 1978-80, Scholar-in-Residence, 1982-88, Harvey Mudd College. Publication: On Death and Other Reasons for Living (poems), 1972, 2nd printing, 1993. Contributions to: Poetic Justice; Texas Review; Voices International; Prophetic Voices; Modern Haiku; Old Hickory Review. Honours: Cleveland State University Honorary Alumna, 1971; More than 60 awards for poetry and fiction nationwide, 1989-. Memberships: Mississippi Poetry Society; Gulf Coast Writers Association; Writers Unlimited, president, 1991, 1992; Academy of American Poets. Address: 4304 O'Leary Avenue, Pascagoula, MS 39581, USA.

CORBETT William Jesse, b. 21 Feb 1938, Birmingham, England. Childrens Author. Publications: The Song of Pentecost; Pentecost and the Chosen One; The End of the Tale and other stories; Pentecost of Lickey Top; The Bear Who Stood on His Head; Dear Grumble; Toby's Iceberg; Little Elephant; Duck Soup Farm; The Grandson Boy; Hamish; The Dragon's Egg and other stories; The Battle of Chinnbrook Wood; The Arc of the People; Four commissioned short stories and One Poem to various anthologies. Honour: Whitbread Award, 1982. Address: 27 Southam House, Hollybank Road, Billesley, Birmingham B13 0QZ, England.

CORDER Sharon, b. Waco, Texas, USA. Writer; Producer; Actor. m. Jack Blum. Education: BA, Theatre, University of California, USA. Appointments: Writer,

Producer and Actor in Film, Television and Theatre; Wrote and produced feature film, Babyface; Co-Creator of television series, Traders (on Global TV); Written for numerous episodic series and anthologies including Catwalk, Kung Fu: The Legend Continues, Max Glick, Top Cops, Dracula: The Series, The Twilight Zone, and Global Playhouse; Created youth series On Our Own for YTV; Co-Produced two women's comedy anthologies, Life, Liberty and Laughter and Funny Girls, for Women's Television Network; Has co-written & performed in numerous stage productions, including Waves (Theatre Centre) and Bob Gets a Job (Genesis Company Theatre); Co-founded and was Co-Artistic Director of Genesis Company Theatre, Vancouver; Actress, featured in The Outside Chance of Maxmillian Glick (feature). Publications: Jack of Hearts, teleplay. Honours: Dora Mavor Moore Award for Getting Out; Babyface, selected for Director's Fortnight, Cannes Film Festival, 1998. Memberships: Writers Guild of Canada; Writers Guild of America; ACTRA; Actor's Equity (Can & US); PEN; Academy of Canadian Cinema and Television; Artist in the Schools. Address: Burning Past Productions, 10 Sackville Place, Toronto, Ont M4X 144, Canada.

COREN Alan, b. 27 June 1938, London, England. Editor; Author. m. Anne Kasriel, 14 Oct 1963, 1 son, 1 daughter. Education: BA, 1st Class Honours, Wadham College, Oxford, 1961; Harkness Fellowship, Yale University, 1961-62, University of California, Berkeley, 1962-63. Appointments: Assistant Editor, 1963-67, Literary Editor, 1967-69, Deputy Editor, 1969-77, Editor, 1978-87, Punch Magazine; Editor, The Listener, 1988-89. Publications: The Dog It Was That Died, 1965; All Except the Bastard, 1969; The Sanity Inspector, 1974; The Collected Bulletins of Idi Amin, 1974; Golfing for Cats, 1975; The Further Bulletin of Idi Amin, 1975; The Rhinestone as Big as the Ritz, 1977; The Peanut Papers, 1978; The Lady from Stalingrad Mansions, 1979; Tissues for Men, 1980; The Cricklewood Diet, 1982; The Penguin Book of Modern Humour (editor), 1983; Bumf, 1984; Something for the Weekend, 1986; Bin Ends, 1987; 12 novels for children (The Arthur Books, 1979-82); Seems Like Old Times (autobiography), 1989; More Like Old Times, 1990; A Year in Cricklewood, 1991; Toujours Cricklewood?, 1993; Sunday Best, 1993; Animal Passions, 1994; A Bit on the Side, 1995; The Alan Coren Omnibus, 1996; The Cricklewood Dome, 1998. Contributions to: Atlantic Monthly; Tatler; Harper's; Playboy; London Review of Books; Listener; Sunday Times; Observer; Daily Mail; Times; Telegraph; Vogue; Nova; Era; New York Times; Evening Standard. Honours: Editor of the Year, British Society of Magazine Editors, 1986; Hon DLitt, University of Nottingham, 1993. Address: c/o Robson Books, 5 Clipstone Street, London WC1, England.

CORK Richard Graham, b. 25 Mar 1947, Eastbourne, England. Art Critic; Writer. m. Vena Jackson, Mar 1970, 2 sons, 2 daughters. Education: Kingswood School, Bath, 1960-64; MA, PhD, Trinity Hall, Cambridge. Appointments: Art Critic, Evening Standard, 1969-77, 1980-83, The Listener, 1984-90; Editor, Studio International, 1975-79; Durning-Lawrence Lecturer, University College, London, 1987; Slade Professor of Fine Art, Cambridge, 1989-90; Chief Art Critic, The Times, 1991-; Henry Moore Foundation Senior Fellow, Courtauld Institute of Art, London, 1992-95. Exhibitions: organiser of exhibitions at the Tate Gallery, the Hayward Gallery, the Royal Academy. Publications: Vorticism and Abstract Art in the First Machine Age, 2 volumes, 1975-76; The Social Role of Art, 1979; Art Beyond the Gallery in Early Twentieth Century England, 1985; David Bomberg, 1987; Architect's Choice, 1992; A Bitter Truth: Avant-Garde Art and the Great War, 1994; Bottle of Notes: Claes Oldenburg and Coosje van Bruggen, 1997; Jacob Epstein, forthcoming. Contributions to: Catalogues and Periodicals. Honours: John Llewelyn Rhys Memorial Prize, 1976; Sir Banister Fletcher Award, 1986; National Art Collections Fund Award, 1995. Memberships: Arts Council Visual Arts Panel, chairman; British Council Visual Arts Advisory Committee; Contemporary Art Society; South Bank Board Visual Art Advisory Panel. Address: 24 Milman Road, London NW6 6EG, England.

CORKHILL Annette Robyn, (Annette Robyn Vernon), b. 10 Sept 1955, Brisbane, Australia. Writer; Poet; Translator. m. Alan Corkhill, 18 Mar 1977, 2 sons, 1 daughter. Education: BA(Hon), 1977; DipEd, 1978; MA, 1985; PhD, 1993. Publications: The Jogger: Anthology of Australian Poetry, 1987; Destination, Outrider, 1987; Mangoes Encounter - Queensland Summer, 1987; Age 1, LINQ, 1987; Two Soldiers of Tiananmen, Earth Against Heaven, 1990; Australian Writing: Ethnic Writers 1945-1991, 1994; The Immigrant Experience in Australian Literature, 1995. Contributions to: Outrider; Australian Literary Studies. Honours: Honorary Mention, The Creativity Centre, Harold Kesteven Poetry Prize, 1987. Address: 5 Wattletree Place, The Gap, Queensland 4061, Australia.

CORLETT William, b. 8 Oct 1938, Darlington, Durham, England. Children's Author; Dramatist; Actor. Education: Royal Academy of Dramatic Art, London, 1956-58. Publications: The Gentle Avalanche, 1962; Another Round, 1962; Return Ticket, 1962; The Scallop Shell, 1963; Flight of a Lone Sparrow, 1965; Dead Set at Dream Boy, 1965; The Scourging of Matthew Barrow, 1965; Tinker's Curse, 1968; We Never Went to Cheddar Gorge, 1968; The Story Teller, 1969; The Illusionist, 1969; National Trust, 1970; The Deliverance of Fanny Blaydon, 1971; A Memory of Two Loves, 1972; Conversations in the Dark, 1972; The Gate of Eden, 1974; The Land Beyond, 1975; The Ideal Tale, 1975; The Once and Forever Christmas (with John Moore), 1975; Return to the Gate, 1975; Mr Oddy, 1975; The Orsini Emeralds, 1975; Emmerdale Farm series, 1975-77; Orlando the Marmalade Cat Buys a Cottage, adaptation of story by Kathleen Hale, 1975; The Dark Side of the Moon, 1976; Orlando's Camping Holiday, adaptation of a story by Kathleen Hale, 1976; Paper Lads, 1978-79; Question series (The Question of Religion, The Christ Story, The Hindu Sound, The Judaic Law, The Buddha Way, The Islamic Space), 1978-79; Kids series, 1979; Going Back, 1979; The Gate of Eden, 1980; Barriers series, 1980; Agatha Christie Hour, adaptation of 4 short stories, 1982; The Machine Gunners, adaptation of Robert Westall book, 1982; Dearly Beloved, 1983; Bloxworth Blue, 1984; Return to the Gate, 1986; The Secret Line, 1988; The Steps up the Chimney, 1990; The Door in the Tree, 1991; The Tunnel Behind the Waterfall, 1991; The Bridge in the Clouds, 1992; The Gondolier's Cat, 1993; Now and Then, 1995; Two Gentlemen Sharing, 1997. Television and Film: The Watchouse, adaptation of Robert Westall book, 1989; Torch, 6 part family adventure series, BBC TV, 1992; Moonacre, 6 part family adventure series, BBC TV, 1994. Honour: Dillons First Fiction Award, 1995. Memberships: Society of Authors; Writers Guild of Great Britain. Literary Agent: Tessa Sayle Agency, 11 Jubilee Place, London SW3 3TE, England. Address: Churchfields, Hope Mansel, Nr Ross-on-Wye, Herefordshire HR9 5TL, England.

CORLEY Ernest. See: BULMER Henry Kenneth.

CORMAN Avery, b. 28 Nov 1935, New York, New York, USA. Novelist. m. Judith Lishinsky, 5 Nov 1967, 2 sons. Education: BS, New York University, 1952. Publications: Oh God!, 1971; Kramer Vs Kramer, 1977; The Bust-Out King, 1977; The Old Neighborhood, 1980; Fifty, 1987; Prized Possessions, 1991; The Big Hype, 1992. Memberships: PEN American Center; Writers Guild of America. Address: c/o Janklow & Nesbit Associates, 598 Madison Avenue, New York, NY 10022, USA.

CORMAN Cid (Sidney Corman), b. 29 June 1924, Boston, Massachusetts, USA. Poet; Writer; Editor. m. Shizumi Konishi, 1965. Education: AB, Tufts University, 1945; Graduate Studies, University of Michigan, 1946-47, University of North Carolina, 1947, Sorbonne, University of Paris, 1954-55. Appointments: Poetry broadcaster, WMEX, Boston, 1949-51; Editor, Origin Magazine and Origin Press, Kyoto, Japan, 1951-71. Publications: Poetry: Sabluna, 1945; Thanksgiving Eclogue, 1954; The Responses, 1956; Stances and Distances, 1957; A Table in Provence, 1958; The Descent from Daimonji, 1959; For Sure, 1959; For Instance, 1959; For Good, 1961; In Good Time, 1964; In No Time, 1964; All in All, 1965; For

Granted, 1966; At Bottom, 1966; Words for Each Other, 1967; And Without End, 1968; No Less, 1968; No More, 1969; Nigh, 1969; Livingdying, 1970; Of the Breath of, 1970; For Keeps, 1970; For Now, 1971; Out and Out, 1972; A Language Without Words, 1973; So Far, 1973; Breathing, 1973; O/1, 1974; Once and For All, 1976; Auspices, 1978; Aegis: Selected Poems, 1970-1980, 1983; And the Word, 1987. Other: The Gist of Origin: An Anthology (editor), 1973; At Their Word: Essays on the Arts of Language, 2 volumes, 1977-78; Where We Are Now: Essays and Postscription, 1991. Honours: Fulbright Fellowship, 1954; Lenore Marshall Memorial Poetry Award, 1974; National Endowment for the Arts Award, 1974. Address: c/o Black Sparrow Press, PO Box 3993, Santa Barbara, CA 93130, USA.

CORMIER Robert (Edmund), b. 17 Jan 1925, Leominster, Massachusetts, USA. Writer. m. Constance B Senay, 6 Nov 1948, 1 son, 3 daughters. Education: Fitchburg State College, 1943-44. Appointments: Writer, Radio WTAG, Worcester, Massachusetts, 1946-48; Reporter, Columnist, Worcester Telegram and Gazette, 1948-55, Fitchburg Sentinel and Enterprise, 1955-78. Publications: Now and at the Hour, 1960; A Little Raw on Monday Morning, 1963; Take Me Where the Good Times Are, 1965; The Chocolate War, 1974; I Am the Cheese, 1977; After the First Death, 1979; Eight Plus One, 1980; The Bumblebee Flies Anyway, 1983; Beyond the Chocolate War, 1985; Fade, 1988; Other Bells for Us to Ring, 1990; We All Fall Down, 1991; I Have Words to Spend, 1991; Tunes for Bears to Dance to, 1992; In the Middle of the Night, 1995; Tenderness, 1997; Heroes, 1998. Honours: Margaret Edwards Award, American Library Association, School Library Journal, 1981; Alan Award, National Council of Teachers of English, 1982. Membership: PEN. Address: 1177 Main Street, Leominster, MA 01453, USA.

CORN Alfred, b. 14 Aug 1943, Bainbridge, Georgia, USA. Poet; Writer; Critic; Translator. m. Ann Jones, 1967, div 1971. Education: BA, Emory University, 1965; MA, Columbia University, 1967. Appointments: Poet-in-Residence, George Mason University, 1980, Blaffer Foundation, New Harmony, Indiana, 1989, James Thurber House, 1990; Humanities Lecturer, New School for Social Research, New York City, 1988; Ellison Chair in Poetry, University of Cincinnati, 1989; Bell Distinguished Visiting Professor, University of Tulsa, 1992; Hurst Residency in Poetry, Washington University, St Louis, 1994; Numerous college and university seminars and workshops; Many poetry readings. Publications: Poetry: All Roads at Once, 1976; A Call in the Midst of the Crowd, 1978; The Various Light, 1980; Tongues on Trees, 1980; The New Life, 1983; Notes from a Child of Paradise, 1984; An Xmas Murder, 1987; The West Door, 1988; Autobiographies, 1992; Present, 1997. Novel: Part of His Story, 1997. Criticism: The Metamorphoses of Metaphor, 1987; Incarnation: Contemporary Writers on the New Testament (editor), 1990; The Pith Helmet, 1992; A Manual of Prosody, 1997. Contributions to: Books, anthologies, scholarly journals, and periodicals. Honours: Woodrow Wilson Fellow, 1965-66; Fulbright Fellow, Paris, 1967-68; Ingram Merrill Fellowships, 1974, 1981; National Endowment for the Arts Fellowships for Poetry, 1980, 1991; Gustav Davidson Prize, Poetry Society of America, 1983; American Academy and Institute of Arts and Letters Award, 1983; New York Foundation for the Arts Fellowships, 1986, 1995; Guggenheim Fellowship, 1986-87; Academy of American Poets Prize, 1987; Yaddo Corporation Fellowship in Poetry, 1989; Djerassi Foundation Fellowship in Poetry, 1990; Rockefeller Foundation Fellowship in Poetry, Bellagio, Italy, 1992; MacDowell Colony Fellowships in Poetry, 1994, 1996. Memberships: National Book Critics Circle; PEN; Poetry Society of America. Address: 350 West 14th Street, Apt 6A, New York, NY 10014, USA.

CORNER James, b. 27 Dec 1961, Preston, England. Landscape Architect. m. Anne-Marie, 8 Oct 1983, 2 daughters. Education: BA, Honours, Manchester Polytechnic; MLA/UD, University of Pennsylvania. Appointment: Associate Professor of Landscape

Architecture, University of Pennsylvania. Publications: Taking Measures Across the American Landscape, 1996; Recovering Landscape: Essays in Contemporary Landscape Architecture, 1999. Address: 129 Northwestern Avenue, Philadelphia, PA 19118, USA.

CORNWELL Bernard, (Susannah Kells), b. 23 Feb 1944, London, England. Romance/Historical Novelist. m. Judy Acker, 1980. Education: BA, University of London, 1967. Appointments: Producer, BBC Television, London, 1969-76; Head of Current Affairs, BBC Television, Belfast, 1976-79; News Editor, Thames Television, London, 1979-80. Publications: Novels as Bernard Cornwell: Sharpe's Eagle, 1981; Sharpe's Gold, 1981; Sharpe's Company, 1982; Sharpe's Sword, 1983; Sharpe's Enemy, 1984; Sharpe's Honour, 1985; Sharpe's Regiment, 1986; Sharpe's Siege, 1987; Sharpe's Rifles, 1988; Wildtrack, 1988; Sharpe's Revenge, 1989; Sea Lord, 1989; Killer's Wake, 1989; Sharpe's Waterloo, 1990; Crackdown, 1990; Sharpe's Devil, 1991; Stormchild, 1991; Scoundrel, 1992; Rebel, 1993; Copperhead, 1993; The Winter King, 1996. As Susannah Kell: A Crowning Mercy, 1983; The Fallen Angels, 1984; Coat of Arms, 1986. Film adaptations: Sharpe, 1993; Sharpe's Rifles, 1993. Address: c/o Toby Eady Associates, 7 Gledhow Gardens, London SW5 0BL, England.

CORNWELL David John Moore, (John le Carré), b. 19 Oct 1931, Poole, Dorset, England. Writer. m. (1) Alison Ann Veronica Sharp, 1954, div 1971, 3 sons, (2) Valerie Jane Eustace, 1972, 1 son. Education: University of Bern, 1948-49; BA, Lincoln College, Oxford, 1956. Appointments: Teacher, Eton College, 1956-58; Foreign Service, 1959-64. Publications: Call for the Dead, 1961 (filmed as The Deadly Affair, 1967); Murder of Quality, 1962 (filmed for TV, 1995); The Spy Who Came in From the Cold, 1963 (filmed, 1963); The Looking Glass War, 1965 (filmed, 1965); A Small Town in Germany, 1968; The Naive and Sentimental Lover, 1971; Tinker Tailor Soldier Spy, 1974 (TV series, 1972); The Honourable Schoolboy, 1977; Smiley's People, 1979 (TV series, 1980); The Quest for Karla (collected edition of previous 3 titles), 1982; The Little Drummer Girl, 1983 (filmed, 1984); A Perfect Spy, 1986 (TV series, 1987); The Russia House, 1989 (filmed, 1990); The Secret Pilgrim, 1991; The Night Manager, 1993; Our Game, 1995; The Tailor of Panama, 1997; Single and Single, 1999. Honours: Somerset Maugham Award, 1963; Edgar Allan Poe Award, 1965, Grand Master Award, 1986, Mystery Writers of America; James Tait Black Award, 1977; Gold Dagger Award, 1978, Diamond Dagger Award, 1988, Crime Writers Association; Honorary Fellow, Lincoln College, Oxford, 1984; Premio Malaparte, 1987; Nikos Kazanzakis Prize, 1991; Honorary Doctorates, St Andrew's University, Exeter University, Southampton University, Bath University. Address: David Higham Associates, 5-8 Lower John Street, Golden Square, London W1R 4HA, England.

CORNWELL Patricia Daniels, b. 9 June 1956, Miami, Florida, USA. Writer. m. Charles Cornwell, 14 June 1980, div 1990. Education: BA, Davidson College, 1979. Appointments: Police Reporter, Charlotte Observer, North Carolina, 1979-81; Computer Analyst, Office of the Chief Medical Examiner, Richmond, Virginia, 1985-91. Publications: Non-Fiction: A Time for Remembering: The Story of Ruth Bell Graham, 1983. Fiction: Postmortem, 1990; Body of Evidence, 1991; All That Remains, 1992; Cruel and Unusual, 1993; The Body Farm, 1994; From Potter's Field, 1995; Cause of Death, 1996; Hornet's Nest, 1996; Unnatural Exposure, 1997; Point of Origin, 1998. Honours: Investigative Reporting Award, North Carolina Press Association, 1980; Gold Medallion Book Award, Evangelical Christian Publishers Association, 1985; John Creasy Award, British Crime Writers Association, 1990; Macavity Award, Mystery Readers International, 1990; Edgar Award, 1990, Gold Dagger Award, 1993, Mystery Writers of America. Memberships: Authors Guild; International Association of Chiefs of Police; International Association of Identification; International Crime Writers Association; National Association of Medical Examiners. Address: c/o Cornwell Enterprises, PO Box 35686, Richmond, VA 23235, USA.

CORSO Gregory, b. 26 Mar 1930, New York, New York, USA. Poet; Dramatist; Writer. m. (1) Sally November, 7 May 1963, div, 1 daughter, (2) Belle Carpenter, 1968, 1 son, 1 daughter. Education: Elementary school. Publications: Poetry: The Vestal Lady of Brattle, and Other Poems, 1955; Bomb, 1958; Gasoline, 1958, new edition, 1992; A Pulp Magazine for the Dead Generation: Poems (with Henk Marsman), 1959; The Happy Birthday of Death, 1960; Long Live Man, 1962; Selected Poems, 1962; There is Yet Time to Run Back Through Life and Expiate All That's Been Sadly Done, 1965; The Geometric Poem: A Long Experimental Poem, Composite of Many Lines and Angles Selective, 1966; 10 Times a Poem: Collected at Random From 2 Suitcases Filled with Poems: The Gathering of 5 Years, 1967; Elegiac Feelings: American, 1970; Herald of the Autochthonic Spirit, 1981; Wings, Words, Windows, 1982; Mindfield: New and Selected Poems, 1989; Many others. Novel: American Express, 1961. Plays: This Hung-up Age, 1955; Way Out: A Poem in Discord, 1974; Collected Plays, 1980. Non-Fiction: Some of My Beginnings and What I Feel Right Now, 1982. Contributions to: Penguin Modern Poets 5, 1963; A Controversy of Poets, 1965. Honours: Jean Stein Award for Poetry, American Academy and Institute of Arts and Letters, 1986; Longview Award; Poetry Foundation Award. Address: c/o Roger Richards Rare Books, 26 Horatio Street, No 24, New York, NY 10014, USA.

CORTEN Irina H Shapiro,(Renata Starr), b. 15 Feb 1941, Moscow, Russia. Professor of Russian Literature and Culture. m. Barry Corten, 11 Apr 1964, div 1974, 1 daughter. Education: BA, Barnard College, 1962; MA, Harvard University, 1963; PhD, University of California at Berkeley, 1972. Publications: Nicholas Roerich: An Annotated Bibliography, 1984; Flowers of Morya: The Poetry of Nicholas Roerich, 1986; Vocabulary of Soviet Society and Culture, 1992. Contributions to: Periodicals and journals. Honours: Numerous guest lectures and research grants. Memberships: Association of Literary Scholars and Critics; Literary Translators Association. Address: 3725 South 39th Avenue, Minneapolis, MN 55406, USA.

COSGRAVE Patrick, b. 28 Sept 1941, Dublin, Ireland. Writer. m. (1) Ruth Dudley Edwards, 1965, div, (2) Norma Alice Green, 1974, div, 1 daughter, (3) Shirley Ward, 1981. Education: BA, 1964, MA, 1965, University College, Dublin; PhD, Peterhouse, Cambridge, 1968. Appointments: London Editor, Radio Telefis Eireann, 1968-69; Conservative Research Deptarment, 1969-71; Political Editor, The Spectator, 1971-75; Features Editor, Telegraph Magazine, 1974-76; Special Advisor to Rt Hon Mrs Margaret Thatcher, 1975-79; Managing Editor, Quartet Crime (Quartet Books), 1979-81. Publications: The Public Poetry of Robert Lowell, 1969; Churchill at War: Alone, 1974; Cheyney's Law (novel), 1976; Margaret Thatcher: A Tory and her Party, 1978, 2nd edition as Margaret Thatcher: Prime Minister, 1979; The Three Colonels (novel), 1979; R A Butler: An English Life, 1981; Adventure of State (novel), 1984; Thatcher: The First Term, 1985; Carrington: A Life and a Policy, 1985; The Lives of Enoch Powell, 1989; The Strange Death of Socialist Britain, 1992. Contributions to: Various journals and magazines. Literary Agent: Michael Shaw, Curtis Brown, 162-168 Regent Street, London W1R 5TB, England. Address: 21 Thornton Road, London SW12 0JX, England.

COSH Mary, b. Bristol, England. Historian. Education: MA, St Anne's College, Oxford, England. Appointments: Council of Industrial Design; Freelance Journalist and Writer. Publications: The Real World, fiction, 1961; Inveraray and The Dukes of Argyll (with Ian G Lindsay), 1973, 1983; The Squares of Islington, 1990, 1993; Numerous small works on Islington. Contributions to: Country Life; The Times; TLS; TES; Scotsman. Honour: FSA, 1990. Memberships: Society of Authors; Society of Architectural Historians. Address: 10 Albion Mews, Islington, London N1 1JX, England.

COSIC Dobrica, b. 29 Dec 1921, Velika Drenova, Yugoslavia. Writer; Politician. Education: University of Belgrade. Appointments: Journalist, then freelance writer; Founder, Committee for Defence of Freedom of Thought and Speech; President, Federal Republic of Yugoslavia, 1992-93. Publications: Far Away is the Sun, 1951; Roots, 1954; Seven Days in Budapest, 1957; Divisions, 1961; Responsibilities, 1964; A Fairy Tale, 1966; Power and Anxieties, 1971; This Land, This Time, 4 volumes, 1972-79; The Real and the Possible, 1982; Sinner, 1985; Renegade, 1986; Serbian Question: Democratic Question, 1987; Believer, 1990; Changes, 1992; A Time of Power, 1996. Membership: Serbian Academy of Arts and Sciences. Address: c/o Serbian Academy of Arts and Sciences, Belgrade, Yugoslavia.

COSSI Olga, b. St Helena, California, USA. Children's Book Writer. Appointments: Correspondent, columnist, regional newspapers. Publications: Over 15 books. Honours include: US Library of Congress selection, Books for the Blind. Membership: Society of Children's Book Writers and Illustrators. Address: 574 Spinnaker Court, Santa Cruz, CA 95062, USA.

COTES Peter, b. 19 Mar 1912, Maidenhead, Berkshire, England. Actor; Director; Producer; Writer. m. Joan Miller, 19 May 1948, dec 1988. Education: Italia Conti Stage School. Appointments: Lecturer in Drama, Rose Bruford College; Adjudicator and Public Speaker. Publications: No Star Nonsense, 1949; The Little Fellow (with Thelma Niklaus), 1951; Handbook for the Amateur Theatre, 1957; George Robey, 1972; JP: The Man Called Mitch, 1976; Elvira Barney, 1977; World Circus (with R Croft-Cooke), 1978; Performing (Album of the Arts), 1980; Dickie: The Story of Dickie Henderson, 1988; Sincerely Yours, 1989; Thinking Aloud, 1993. Contributions to: Daily Telegraph; Guardian; Independent; Times; Field; Stage; Plays and Players; Irish Times; Spectator. Honours: Fellow, Royal Society of Arts; Knight of Mark Twain. Memberships: Savage Club; Our Society; Society of Authors. Address: 7 Hill Lawn Court, Chipping Norton, Oxon 0X7 5NF, England.

COTTERILL Kenneth Matthew, b. 17 Sept 1950, Sheffield, England. Playwright. m. Marilyn Bokiagon, 6 Oct 1984, 1 son. Education: BA, University of Queensland, 1980; Queensland University of Technology, 1981. Publications: Re-Electing Roger; Richard the Third's Revenge; Perfect Murder; Rhinocerus Hides. Contributions to: Australian Jewish Democrat; British Soccer Week; Flashing Blade; International Association of Agricultural Information Specialists, Quarterly Bulletin. Honours: Australia Bicentennial Award; Australia Day Award for Culture, 1994. Memberships: Australian Writers Guild; Playlab. Address: 44 Martin Avenue, Mareeba, Queensland, Australia.

COTTINGHAM Valery Jean, (Countesse De Cassellet) (Baroness), b. Kingston-upon-Hull, Yorkshire, England. Poet; Writer. m. George Cottingham, 28 Dec 1965, dec 1991. Publications: Memories (poems and short stories), 3 volumes. Contributions to: Various anthologies. Honours: Certificates of Merit, Australia, US. Address: 58 Colliers Close, Horsell, Woking, Surrey GU21 3AW, England.

COTTON John, b. 7 Mar 1925, Hackney, London, England. Poet. m. Peggy Midson, 27 Dec 1948, 2 sons. Education: BA, Honours, English, London University, 1956. Appointments: Editor, Priapus magazine, 1967-72, The Private Library journal, 1969-79; Headmaster, Highfield Comprehensive, Hemel Hempstead, 1963-85. Publications: Fourteen Poems, 1967; Outside the Garden of Eden and Other Poems, 1969; Old Movies and Other Poems, 1971; Roman Wall, 1973; Photographs, 1973; Kilroy Was Here, 1975; Powers, 1977; A Letter for a Wedding, 1980; Somme Man, 1980; The Totleigh Riddles, 1981; Daybook Continued, 1982; The Storyville Portraits, 1984; The Crystal Zoo, 1984; Oh Those Happy Feet, 1986; The Poetry File, 1989; Two by Two (with Fred Sedgwick), 1990; Here's Looking at You Kid: New and Selected Poems, 1992; Oscar the Dog, 1994; This is the Song, 1996. Contributions to: Newspapers and journals.

Honours: Art Council Publication Award, 1971; Deputy Lieutenant of the Country of Hertfordshire, 1989. Memberships: Poetry Society, chairman, 1972-74, 1977, treasurer, 1986-89; Toddington Poetry Society, president, Ver Poets, president. Address: 37 Lombardy Drive, Berkhamstead, Hertfordshire HP4 2LQ, England.

COTTRELL HOULE Mary, b. 1953, USA. Children's Writer. Publications: One City's Wilderness: Portland's Forest Park, 1988; Wings For My Flight: The Peregrine Falcons of Chimney Rock, 1991. Honour: Christopher Award, 1992. Address: c/o Addison Wesley Publishing-Publicity D, 170 Fifth Avenue, New York, NY 10010, USA.

COTTRET Bernard J, b. 23 Apr 1951, Paris, France. Professor of British Studies. m. Monique Astruc, 22 Sept 1951, 1 son. Education: École Normale Superieure de Saint-Cloud, 1971-76. Appointments: Professor, University of Versailles, University of Charleston, South Carolina, 1994; Consultant, Bibliotheque Nationale, Paris, 1988-91. Publications: Glorieuse Révolution d'Angleterre, 1988; Le Christ des Lumières, 1990; The Huguenots in England, 1991; Cromwell, 1992; Bolingbroke, 1992; Histoire des îles Britanniques, 1994; Bolingbroke's Political Writings, 1994; Calvin, Biographie, 1995; Histoire d'Angleterre, 1996. Honours: Docteur ès Lettres; Prix Monseigneur Marcel, Académie Francaise, Silver Medal, 1993. Address: 1 Res du Lac, 94470 Boissy-St-Léger, France.

COTTRINGER Anne Elizabeth, b. 28 May 1952, Niagara Falls, Canada. Film and TV Technician; Writer. Education: BA, Geography, University of Western Ontario, Canada; Dip Ad, Slade School of Fine Art; MA, Film and TV, Royal College of Art, London, England. Publications: Children's Author: Ella and the Naughty Lion; Forthcoming: Danny and the Great White Bear; Gordon; Flip! Flap! Who's That?; Movie Magic. Contributions to: Editorial Board Member, Vertigo, film and tv magazine. Literary Agent: Caroline Walsh, David Higham Associates.

COULOMBE Charles Aquila, b. 8 Nov 1960, New York City, New York, USA. Writer. Education: New Mexico Military Institute, Roswell, 1978-80. Publications: Everyman Today Call Rome, 1987; The White Cockade, 1990; Puritan's Progress, 1996; A Guide to Royal America, 1999. Contributions to: National Catholic Register; All about Issues; All Those Things; Fate; Gnosis; Success; Network Marketing; Angelus; Bourbons; Monarchy Canada; Tradition und Leben; The Irish Democrat; Fidelity, Australia. Honour: Christ the King Award, Christian Law Institute, 1992. Memberships: Author's Guild; Catholic Writer's Guild of Great Britain; The Mayflower; The Drones; The Monarchist League of Toronto; The Keys of London; The Royal Stuart Society of London; Green Room of London. Address: PO Box 660771, Arcadia, CA 91066, USA.

COULSON Juanita Ruth, b. 12 Feb 1933, Anderson, Indiana, USA. Writer. m. Robert Stratton Coulson, 21 Aug 1954, 1 son. Education: BS, 1954, MA, 1961, Ball State University. Publications: Crisis on Cheiron, 1967; The Singing Stones, 1968; Door into Terror, 1972; Dark Priestess, 1976; Space Trap, 1976; Web of Wizardry, 1978; The Death God's Citadel, 1980; Tomorrow's Heritage, 1981; Outward Bound, 1982; Legacy of Earth, 1989; The Past of Forever, 1989; Starsister, 1990; Cold, Hard Silver, in anthology Tales of Ravenloft, 1994; A Matter of Faith, in anthology Women At War, 1995. Contributions to: Magazine of Fantasy and Science Fiction; Fantastic Science Fiction and Fantasy Science Stories; Goldman Fantasy Foliant III. Honour: Co-winner, Hugo, Best Amateur Publication, World Science Fiction Convention, London, 1965. Address: 2677 West 500 North, Hartford City, IN 47348, USA.

COULSON Robert Stratton, (Thomas Stratton), b. 12 May 1928, Sullivan, Indiana, USA. Writer. m. Juanita Ruth Coulson, 21 Aug 1954, 1 son. Publications: The Invisibility Affair, 1967; The Mind-Twisters Affair, 1967; Now You See It/Him/Them, 1975; Gates of the Universe,

1975; But What of Earth?, 1976; To Renew the Ages, 1976; Charles Fort Never Mentioned Wombats, 1977; Nightmare Universe, 1985. Contributions to: Books and periodicals. Address: 2677 West 500 North, Hartford City, IN 47348, USA.

COULTER Harris Livermore, b. 8 Oct 1932, Baltimore, Maryland, USA. Writer; Translator; Interpreter. m. Catherine Nebolsine, 10 Jan 1960, 2 sons, 2 daughters. Education: BA, Yale University, 1954; PhD, Columbia University, 1969. Publications: Divided Legacy: A History of the Schism in Medical Thought, Volume I: The Patterns Emerge, 1975, Volume II: The Origins of Modern Western Medicine, 1977, Volume III: Homeopathy and the American Medical Association, 1981 Volume IV: Twentieth-Century Medicine: The Bacteriological Era, 1994; Homeopathic Science and Modern Medicine, 1981; DPT: A Shot in the Dark (with Barbara Fisher), 1985; Vaccination, Social Violence, and Criminality, 1990; The Controlled Clinical Trial: An Analysis, 1991. Honours: Hahnemann Prize, Société Royale Belge d'Homéopathie, 1985; La Medalla d'Or del Centenari, Academia Medico-Homepatica de Barcelona, 1990. Membership: American Institute of Homeopathy. Address: Center for Empirical Medicine, 4221 45th Street North West, Washington, DC 20016, USA.

COULTON James. See: **HANSEN Joseph.**

COUPLAND Douglas (Campbell), b. 30 Dec 1961, Baden-Sölingen, Germany (Canadian citizen). Author. Education: Emily Carr Institute for Art and Design, Vancouver; Japan; Italy. Publications: Generation X: Tales for an Accelerated Culture, 1991; Shampoo Planet, 1992; Life After God, 1994; Microserfs, 1995; Polaroids from the Dead, 1996. Contributions to: Art Forum; New Republic; New York Times; Wired. Address: c/o Writer's Union of Canada, 24 Ryerson Avenue, Toronto, Ontario M5T 2P3, Canada.

COURLANDER Harold, b. 18 Sept 1908, Indianapolis, Indiana, USA. Author. Education: BA, University of Michigan, 1931; Postgraduate work, Columbia University, 1939-50. Publications: Haiti Singing, 1939; Uncle Bouqui of Haiti, 1942; The Cow-Tail Switch (with George Herzog), 1947; The Fire on the Mountain (with Wolf Leslau), 1950; Ride with the Sun, 1955; Terrapin's Pot of Sense, 1957; The Hat Shaking Dance, 1957; Kantchil's Lime Pit, 1959; The Tiger's Whisker, 1959; On Recognizing the Human Species, 1960; Negro Songs from Alabama, 1960; The Drum and the Hoe, 1960; The King's Drum, 1962; Negro Folk Music USA, 1963; Religion and Politics in Haiti (with Rémy Bastien), 1966; People of the Short Blue Corn, 1970; The Fourth World of the Hopis, 1971; Tales of Yoruba Gods and Heroes, 1973; A Treasury of African Folklore, 1975; A Treasury of Afro-American Folklore, 1976; The Crest and the Hide, 1982; The Heart of the Ngoni, 1982; Hopi Voices, 1982. Novels: The Caballero, 1940; The Big Old World of Richard Creeks, 1962; The African, 1967; The Son of the Leopard, 1974; The Mesa of Flowers, 1977; The Master of the Forge, 1985; The Bordeaux Narrative, 1990. Compiler, Editor, Annotator: Big Falling Snow, 1978. Contributions to:Scholarly journals and periodicals. Honours: Guggenheim Fellowships, 1948, 1955; Various awards and academic grants in aid; Outstanding Achievement Award, University of Michigan, 1984. Address: 5512 Brite Drive, Bethesda, MD 20817, USA.

COURTER Gay, b. 1 Oct 1944, Pittsburgh, Pennsylvania, USA. Writer; Filmmaker. m. Philip Courter, 18 Aug 1968, 2 sons. Education: AB, Drama, Film, Antioch College, Ohio, 1966. Publications: The Bean Sprout Book, 1974; The Midwife, 1981; River of Dreams, 1984; Code Ezra, 1986; Flowers in the Blood, 1990; The Midwife's Advice, 1992; I Speak for This Child, 1995. Contributions to: Parents; Women's Day; Publishers Weekly; Others. Memberships: Authors Guild; Writers Guild of America East; Guardian Ad Litem; International Childbirth Association. Literary Agent: Donald Cutler, Bookmark: The Literary Agency. Address: 121 North West Crystal Street, Crystal River, FL 34428, USA.

COURTNEY Dayle. See: **GOLDSMITH Howard.**

COURTNEY Nicholas Piers ,b. 20 Dec 1944, Berkshire, England. Author. m. Vanessa Hardwicke, 30 Oct 1980. Education: ARICS, Nautical College, Berkshire, 1966; MRAC, Royal Agricultural College, Cirencester. Publications: Shopping and Cooking in Europe, 1980; The Tiger: Symbol of Freedom, 1981; Diana: Princess of Wales, 1982; Royal Children, 1982; Prince Andrew, 1983;Sporting Royals, 1983; Diana, Princess of Fashion, 1984; Queen Elizabeth, The Queen Mother, 1984; The Very Best of British, 1985; In Society: The Brideshead Era, 1986; Princess Anne, 1986; Luxury Shopping in London, 1987; Sisters in Law, 1988; A Stratford Kinshall, 1989; The Mall, 1990; Windsor Castle, 1991; A Little History of Antiques, 1995. Contributions to: Times; Redbook; Spectator; Independent; House and Garden. Membership: Brookes's. Address: 9 Kempson Road, London SW6 4PX, England.

COUSINEAU Philip Robert, b. 26 Nov 1952, Columbia, South Carolina, USA. Writer. Education: BA, cum laude, Journalism, University of Detroit, 1974. Publications: The Hero's Journey: Joseph Campbell on His Life and Work, 1990; The Soul of the World, 1991; Deadlines: A Rhapsody on a Theme of Famous Last Words, 1991; Soul: An Archaeology: Readings from Socrates to Ray Charles, 1994; Prayers at 3am, 1995; Design Outlaws (with Christopher Zelov), 1996. Contributions to: Parabola Magazine; Paris Magazine. Address: c/o Harper San Francisco, 1160 Battery Street, San Francisco, CA 94111, USA.

COUNZYN Jeni, b. 26 July 1942, South Africa (Canadian citizen). Poet; Psychotherapist; Lecturer; Broadcaster. Education: BA, University of Natal, 1963. Appointment: Writer-in-Residence, University of Victoria, British Columbia, 1976. Publications: Flying, 1970; Monkey's Wedding, 1972; Christmas in Africa, 1975; House of Changes, 1978; The Happiness Bird, 1978; Life by Drowning, 1983; In the Skin House, 1993. Editor: Bloodaxe Book of Contemporary Women Poets, 1985; Singing Down the Bones, 1989. Other: Children's books and editions of poetry. Honours: Arts Council of Great Britain Grants, 1971, 1974; Canada Council Grants, 1977, 1983. Memberships: Guild of Psychotherapists; Poetry Society, general council, 1968-75. Literary Agent: Andrew Mann, 1 Old Compton Street, London W1V 5PH, England. Address: c/o Bloodaxe Books, PO Box 1SN, Newcastle upon Tyne NE99, England.

COVARRUBIAS ORTIZ Miguel, b. 27 Feb 1940, Monterrey, Mexico. Writer; Poet; Professor. m. Silvia Mijares, 18 Mar 1967, 2 daughters. Education: Licenciado en letras, 1973, Maestria en letras espagnolas (pasantia), 1987, Universidad Autónoma de Nuevo León, Monterrey. Appointments: Director, Centre for Literary and Linguistic Research, 1976-79, and Institute of Fine Arts, 1976-79, Coordinator, Creative Writing Workshop, 1981-, Universidad Autónoma de Nuevo León, Monterrey. Publications: Fiction: La raiz ausente, 1962; Custodia de silencios, 1965, 2nd edition, 1982; Minusculario, 1966. Poetry: El poeta, 1969; El segundo poeta, 1977, 3rd edition, 1988; Pandora, 1987. Essays: Papeleria, 1970; Olavide o Sade, 1975; Nueva papeleria, 1978; Papeleria en tramite, 1997. Editor: Antologia de autores contemporáneos, 1972, 1974, 1975, 1979, 1980; Desde el Cerro de la Silla, 1992; Traduction: El traidor, 1993; Conversations: Junto a una taza de café, 1994. Contributions to: Various publications. Honours: 2nd Place, Story, Xalapa Arts Festival, 1962; Arts Prize, Literature, Universidad Autónoma de Nuevo León, Monterrey, 1989; Medal of Civic Merit in Literature and Arts, Gobierno del Estado du Nuevo León, 1993; Poetry Translation Prize, National Institute of Fine Arts, Mexico, 1993. Memberships: Deslinde (culture review), director, 1985-; Sociedad General de Escritores de Mexico. Address: Kant 2801, Contry-La Silla, Guadalupe, NL, Mexico City 67170, Mexico.

COVILLE Bruce (Farrington), b. 16 May 1950, Syracuse, New York, USA. Children's Writer; Dramatist. Separated, 2 sons, 1 daughter. Education: Duke

University, 1968-69; State University of New York at Binghamton, 1969-72; BA, State University College of Oswego, 1973. Publications: Fiction: Sarah's Unicorn, 1979; The Monster's Ring, 1982; Sarah and the Dragon, 1984; Operation Sherlock, 1986; Ghost in the Third Row, 1987; My Teacher is an Alien, 1989; Herds of Thunder, Manes of Gold, 1989; Jennifer Murdley's Toad, 1992; Space Brat, 1993; Aliens Ate My Homework, 1993. Plays: The Dragonslayers, 1981; Out of the Blue, 1982; It's Midnight, 1983; Faculty Room, 1988. Honours: 2nd Place, Colorado Children's Book Award, 1984; South Carolina Children's Choice Award, 1984-85; IRA Children's Choice List, 1985, 1987. Memberships: Dramatists Guild; Science Fiction Writers of America; Society of Children's Book Writers. Address: 14 East 11th Street, New York, NY 10003, USA.

COVINGTON Vicki, b. 22 October 1952, Birmingham, Alabama, USA. Writer. m. Dennis Covington, 24 Dec 1977, 2 daughters. Education: BA, 1974, MSW, 1976, University of Alabama. Publications: Gathering Home, 1988; Bird of Paradise, 1990; Night Ride Home, 1992; The Last Hotel for Women, 1996. Honour: National Endowment for the Arts Fellowship, 1988. Address: c/o International Creative Management, 40 West 57th Street, New York, NY 10019, USA.

COWAN Peter, b. 4 Nov 1914, Perth, Western Australia, Australia. Research Fellow; Author. Education: BA, University of Western Australia, 1940. Appointments: Senior English Master, Scotch College, Swanbourne, Western Australia, 1950-62; Member of Faculty, 1962-79, Research Fellow, Department of English, 1979-, University of Western Australia, Nedlands. Publications: Drift Stories, 1944; The Unploughed Land: Stories, 1959; Summer, 1964; Short Story Landscape: The Modern Short Story (editor), 1964; The Empty Street: Stories, 1965; Seed, 1966; Spectrum One To Three (co-editor), 1970-79; Today: Contemporary Short Stories (editor), 1971; The Tins and Other Stories, 1973; A Faithful Picture: Letters of Eliza and Thomas Brown, Swan River Colony 1841-1851 (editor), 1977; A Unique Position: A Biography of Edith Dircksey Cowan, 1978; Westerly 21 (editor), 1978; Mobiles (stories), 1979; Perspectives One (editor), short fiction, 1985; A Window in Mrs X's Place (short stories), 1986; The Color of the Sky (novel), 1986; Voices (short fiction), 1988; Maitland Brown: A View of Nineteenth Century Western Australia (biography), 1988; The Hills of Apollo Bay (novel), 1989; Impressions: West Coast Fiction 1829-1988 (editor), 1989; Western Australian Writing: A Bibliography (co-editor), 1990; The Tenants (novel), 1994. Address: 149 Alfred Road, Mount Claremont, Western Australia 6010, Australia.

COWASJEE Saros, b. 12 July 1931, Secundrabad, India. Professor Emeritus of English; Writer; Editor. Education: BA, St John's College, Agra, 1951; MA, Agra University, 1955; PhD, University of Leeds, 1960. Appointments: Assistant Editor, Times of India Press, Bombay, 1961-63; Teacher, 1963-71, Professor of English, 1971-95, Professor Emeritus, 1995-, University of Regina, Canada; General Editor, Literature of the Raj series, Arnold Publishers, New Delhi, 1984-. Publications: Sean O'Casey: The Man Behind the Plays, 1963; Sean O'Casey, 1966; Stories and Sketches, 1970; Goodbye to Elsa (novel), 1974; So Many Freedoms: A Study of the Major Fiction of Mulk Raj Anand, 1977; Nude Therapy (short stories), 1978; The Last of the Maharajas (screenplay), 1980; Suffer Little Children (novel), 1982; Studies in Indian and Anglo-Indian Fiction, 1993; The Assistant Professor (novel), 1996. Editor: Stories from the Raj, 1982; More Stories from the Raj and After, 1986; Women Writers of the Raj, 1990; The Best Short Stories of Flora Annie Steel, 1995; Orphans of the Storm: Stories on the Partition of India, 1995; The Oxford Anthology of Raj Stories, 1998. Contributions to: Encounter; A Review of English Literature; Journal of Commonwealth Literature; Literary Criterion; World Literature Written in English; Literature East and West; International Fiction Review; Journal of Canadian Fiction. Honours: J N Tata Scholarship, 1957-69; Canada Council and SSHRC Leave Fellowships, 1968-69, 1974-75, 1978-79, 1986-87. Memberships: Cambridge Society; Writers Union of Canada; Association of Commonwealth Literature and Language Studies. Address: Department of English, University of Regina, Regina, Saskatchewan S4S 0A2, Canada.

COWDREY Herbert Edward John, b. 29 Nov 1926, Basingstoke, Hants, England. University Teacher. m. Judith Watson Davis, 14 July 1959, 1 son, 2 daughters. Education: BA, 1949, MA, 1951, Oxford University, 1949. Appointments: Chaplain and Tutor, St Stephen's House, Oxford, 1952-56; Fellow, 1956-94, Fellow Emeritus, 1994-, St Edmund Hall, Oxford. Publications: The Cluniacs and the Gregorian Reform; The Epistolae Vagantes of Pope Gregory VII; Two Studies in Cluniac History; The Age of Abbot Desiderius; Popes, Monks and Crusaders; Pope Gregory VII, 1073-85. Contributions to: Many articles. Honour: British Academy, fellow. Memberships: Royal Historical Society; Henry Bradshaw Society. Address: 30 Oxford Road, Old Marston, Oxford OX3 0PQ, England.

COWDRY Quentin Francis, b. 27 Feb 1956, Bebington, England. Public Relations. m. Zoe Laine McIntyre, 27 Feb 1988, 1 son, 1 daughter. Education: Leicester University, Combined Studies Arts (Hons); NCTJ. Appointments: Reporter, Nottingham Evening Post; Shipping Reporter, Southern Evening Echo; Reporter, Sunday Telegraph; Lobby Correspondent, Daily Telegraph; Home Affairs Correspondent, The Times; Director, Affinity Consulting; Director, Paragon Golin/Harris, current post. Address: Chiswick, London W4, England.

COWELL Stephanie, b. 25 July 1943, New York, New York, USA. Writer. m. Russell O'Neal Clay, 2 Dec 1995, 2 sons. Education: Self-educated. Publications: Nicholas Cooke (actor, soldier, physician, priest), 1993; The Physician of London, 1995; The Players: Shakespeare, 1997. Honour: American Book Award, 1996. Membership: Author's Guild. Address: 585 West End Avenue, New York, NY 10024, USA.

COWEN Athol Ernest, b. 18 Jan 1942, Corbridge, Hexham, England. Writer; Poet; Publisher. Publications: Word Pictures (Brain Soup), 1989; Huh!, 1991. Contributions to: Various anthologies. Memberships: Publishers' Association; Poetry Society; Writers' Guild of Great Britain; Musicians' Union; Guild of International Songwriters and Composers. Address: 40 Gibson Street, Wrexham LL13 7TS, Wales.

COWIE Leonard Wallace, b. 10 May 1919, Brighton, England. Clerk in Holy Orders; Writer. m. Evelyn Elizabeth Trafford, 9 Aug 1949, 1 son. Education: BA 1941, MA, 1946, Pembroke College, Oxford; PhD, University of London, 1954. Publications: Seventeenth-Century Europe, 1960; The March of the Cross, 1962; Eighteenth-Century Europe, 1963; Hanoverian England, 1967; The Reformation, 1968; Martin Luther, 1969; Sixteenth-Century Europe, 1977; Life in Britain, 1980; Years of Nationalism (with R Wolfson), 1985; The French Revolution, 1987; Lord Nelson: A Bibliography, 1990; William Wilberforce: A Bibliography, 1992; Edmund Burke: A Bibliography, 1994; Sir Robert Peel: A Bibliography, 1996. Contributions to: History To-Day; History; Church Times. Memberships: Royal Historical Society, fellow; The Athenaeum. Address: 38 Stratton Road, Merton Park, London SW19 3JG, England.

COWLES Fleur, b. USA. Painter; Writer. Appointments: Associate Editor, Look Magazine, USA, 1949-55; Founder, Editor, Flair Magazine, USA, 1950-51; Editor, Flairbook, USA, 1952. Publications: Bloody Precedent, 1951; The Case of Salvador Dali, 1959; The Hidden World of Hadhramoutt, 1964; I Can Tell It Now, 1965; Treasures of the British Museum, 1966; Tiger Flower, 1969; Lion and Blue, 1974; Friends and Memories, 1975; Romany Free, 1977; The Love of Tiger Flower, 1980; All Too True, 1980; The Flower Game, 1983; Flowers, 1985; People as Animals, 1985; To Be a Unicorn: An Artist's Journey, 1986; The Life and Times of the Rose, 1991; She Made Friends - And Kept Them, 1996; The Best of FLAIR, 1996. Membership: Royal Society of Arts. Membership: Senior Fellow, Royal College of Art. Address: A5 Albany, Piccadilly, London W1, England.

COX Charles Brian, b. 5 Sept 1928, Grimsby, Lincolnshire, England. Professor Emeritus of English Literature; Writer; Poet; Editor. Education: BA, 1952, MA, 1955, MLitt, 1958, Pembroke College, Cambridge. Appointments: Lecturer, Senior Lecturer, University of Hull, 1954-66; Co-editor, Critical Quarterly, 1959-; Professor of English Literature, 1966-93, Professor Emeritus, 1993-, Pro-Vice Chancellor, 1987-91, University of Manchester; Visiting Professor, King's College, London, 1994; Honorary Fellow, Westminster College, Oxford, 1994; Member, Arts Council 1996-98; Chair, North West Arts Board, 1994-. Publications: The Free Spirit, 1963; Modern Poetry (with A E Dyson), 1963; Conrad's Nostromo, 1964; The Practical Criticism of Poetry (with A E Dyson), 1965; Poems of This Century (editor with A E Dyson), 1968; Word in the Desert (editor with A E Dyson), 1968; The Waste Land: A Casebook (editor with A P Hinchliffe), 1968; The Black Papers on Education (editor with A E Dyson), 1971; The Twentieth Century Mind (editor with A E Dyson), 3 volumes, 1972; Conrad: Youth, Heart of Darkness and The End of the Tether (editor), 1974; Joseph Conrad: The Modern Imagination, 1974; Black Paper 1975 (editor with R Boyson), 1975; Black Paper 1977 (editor with R Boyson). 1977; Conrad, 1977; Every Common Sight (verse), 1981; Two Headed Monster (verse), 1985; Cox on Cox: An English Curriculum for the 1990's, 1991; The Great Betrayal: Autobiography, 1992; Collected Poems, 1993; The Battle for the English Curriculum, 1995; African Writers, editor, 1997. Honours: Commander of the Order of the British Empire, 1990; Fellow, Royal Society of Literature, 1993. Address: 20 Park Gates Drive, Cheadle Hulme, Stockport SK8 7DF, England.

COX David Dundas, b. 20 June 1933, Goondiwindi, Australia. Graphic Artist; Author. m. Elizabeth Beath, 21 Feb 1976, 1 son, 2 daughters. Education: St Martin's School of Art, London, England. Appointment: Head Artist, The Courier Mail, Brisbane. Publications: Various children's books, several in collaboration with wife. Honours: Walkeley Award (Illustration), 1978; Highly Commended Children's Book of the Year Awards, 1983, 1985. Memberships: Australian Society of Authors; Opera for Youth, USA; Greek Community of St George, Queensland; Playlab, Queensland. Address: 8 St James Street, Highgate Hill, Queensland 4101, Australia.

COX Sir Geoffrey (Sandford), b. 7 Apr 1910, Palmerston North, New Zealand. Writer; Broadcaster; Editor. m. Cecily Barbara Talbot Turner, 25 May 1935, dec 1993, 2 sons, 2 daughters. Education: Otago University, New Zealand, 1931; Rhodes Scholar, BA, Oriel College, Oxford, 1932-35. Appointments: Reporter, Foreign and War Correspondent, News Chronicle, 1935-37, Daily Express, 1937-40; Served New Zealand Army, Libya, 1940-42, Italy, 1944-45, twice mentioned in despatches; First Secretary and Chargé d'Affaires, New Zealand Legation, Washington, DC, 1943; Political Correspondent, 1945-54, Assistant Editor, 1954-56, News Chronicle; Contributor, BBC Radio and Television, 1945-56; Editor and Chief Executive, Independent Television News, 1956-68; Deputy Chairman, Yorkshire Television, 1968-71; Chairman, Tyne Tees Television, 1971-74, LBC Radio, 1978-81; Independent Director, The Observer, 1981-89. Publications: Defence of Madrid, 1937; The Red Army Moves, 1941; The Road to Trieste, 1946; The Race for Trieste, 1977; See It Happen, 1983; A Tale of Two Battles, 1987; Countdown to War, 1988. Honours: Member of the Order of the British Empire, 1945; Commander of the Order of the British Empire, 1959; Television Producers' Guild Award, 1962; Royal Television Society Silver Medal, 1963, Gold Medal, 1978; Knighted, 1966. Memberships: British Kinematograph and Television Society, fellow; Royal Television Society, Fellow. Address: c/o Garrick Club, London WC2, England.

COX (John) Madison IV, b. 23 Sept 1958, Bellingham, Washington, USA. Garden Designer; Author. Education: BFA, Parson's School of Design, Paris, 1984. Publications: Private Gardens of Paris, 1989; Gardens of the World (co-author), 1991; Artists' Gardens, 1993. Contributions to: Elle Decor, USA; House and Garden, USA. Address: c/o Helen Pratt, 1165 Fifth Avenue, New York, NY 10029, USA.

COX Richard, b. 8 Mar 1931, Winchester, Hampshire, England. Writer. m. 1963, 2 sons, 1 daughter. Honours degree in English, St Catherine's College, Oxford, 1955. Publications: Operation Sealion, 1974; Sam, 1976; Auction, 1978; KGB Directive, 1981; Ground Zero, 1985; An Agent of Influence, 1988; Park Plaza, 1991; Eclipse, 1996. Contributions to: Daily Telegraph (Staff Correspondent, 1966-72); Travel & Leisure; Traveller; Orient Express Magazine. Honour: Territorial Decoration, 1966. Membership: Army and Navy Club; CARE International UK, board member, 1985-; Mystery Writers Association of America. Literary Agent: William Morris Agency, New York. Address: PO Box 88, Alderney, Channel Islands.

COX William Trevor, (William Trevor), b. 24 May 1928, Mitchelstown, County Cork, Ireland. Author. m. Jane Ryan, 26 Aug 1952, 2 sons. Education: St Columba's College, Dublin, 1941-46; BA, Trinity College, Dublin, 1950. Publications: The Old Boys, 1964; The Boarding House, 1965; The Love Department, 1966; The Day We Got Drunk on Cake, 1967; Mrs Eckdorf in O'Neill's Hotel, 1968; Miss Gomez and the Brethren, 1969; The Ballroom of Romance, 1970; Elizabeth Alone, 1972; Angels at the Ritz, 1973; The Children of Dynmouth, 1976; Lovers of Their Time, 1979; Other People's Worlds, 1980; Beyond the Pale, 1981; Fools of Fortune, 1983; A Writer's Ireland: Landscape in Literature, 1984; The News from Ireland, 1986; Nights at the Alexandra, 1987; Family Sins and Other Stories, 1989; The Silence in the Garden, 1989; The Oxford Book of Irish Short Stories (editor), 1989; Two Lives, 1991; Juliet's Story, 1992; Collected Stories, 1992; Felicia's Journey, 1994. Honours: Hawthornden Prize, 1964; Honorary Commander of the Order of the British Empire, 1977; Prize, Royal Society of Literature, 1978; Whitbread Awards and Prizes, 1978, 1983, 1994; Allied Irish Banks Award for Services to Literature, 1978; Honorary DLitt: Exeter, 1984, Dublin, 1986, Queen's University, Belfast, 1989, Cork, 1990; Sunday Express Book of the Year Award, 1994. Membership: Irish Academy of Letters. Address: c/o A D Peters, 5th Floor, The Chambers, Chelsea Harbour, London SW10, England.

COX-JOHNSON Ann. See: SAUNDERS Ann Loreille.

COYLE Harold, b. 6 Feb 1952, New Brunswick, New Jersey, USA. Writer. m. Patricia A Bannon, 5 Oct 1974, 2 sons, 1 daughter. Education: BA, History, Virginia Military Institute, 1974. Appointment: Commissioned Officer, US Army, 1974-91. Publications: Team Yankee, 1987; Sword Point, 1988; Bright Star, 1991; Trial by Fire, 1992; The Ten Thousand, 1993; Code of Honor, 1994. Memberships: Association of Civil War Sites; Reserve Officers Association. Address: c/o Robert Gottlieb, William Morris Agency, 1350 Avenue of the Americas, New York, NY 10019, USA.

CRACE Jim, b. 1 Mar 1946, Brocket Hall, Lemsford, Hertfordshire, England. Author; Dramatist. m. Pamela Ann Turton, 1975, 1 son, 1 daughter. Education: Birmingham College of Commerce, 1965-68; BA (Hons) in English, University of London (external), 1968. Appointments: Freelance Journalist and Writer, 1972-86; Full-time Novelist, 1986-. Publications: Continent, 1986; The Gift of Stones, 1988; Arcadia, 1992; Signals of Distress, 1994; Uncollected short stories: Refugees, 1977; Annie, California Plates, 1977; Helter Skelter, Hang Sorrow, Care'll Kill a Cat, 1977; Seven Ages, 1980; The Slow Digestion of the Night, 1995; Quarantine, 1997. Radio plays. Honours: David Higham Award, 1986; Whitbread Awards, 1986, 1997; Guardian Prize for Fiction, 1986; Antico Fattore Prize, Italy, 1988; GAP International Prize for Literature, 1989; Society of Authors

Travel Award, 1992; Royal Society of Literature Winifred Holty Memorial Prize, 1995; E M Forster Award, 1996; Shortlisted for Booker Prize, 1997. Literary Agent: David Godwin Associates, 14 Goodwins Court, London WC2N 4LL, England.

CRAFT Robert (Lawson), b. 20 Oct 1923, Kingston, New York, USA. Orchestral Conductor; Author. Education: BA, Juilliard School of Music, New York City, 1946; Berkshire Music Center, Tanglewood, Massachusetts; Studied conducting with Pierre Monteux. Appointments: Conductor, Evenings-on-the-Roof and Monday Evening Concerts, Los Angeles, 1950-68; Assistant to, and later closest associate of Igor Stravinsky, 1948-71. Publications: With Igor Stravinsky: Conversations with Igor Stravinsky, 1959; Memories and Commentaries, 1960; Expositions and Developments, 1962; Dialogues and a Diary, 1963; Themes and Episodes, 1967; Retrospections and Conclusions, 1969. Other: Chronicle of a Friendship, 1972; Prejudices in Disguise, 1974; Stravinsky in Photographs and Documents (with Vera Stravinsky), 1976; Current Convictions: Views and Reviews, 1977; Present Perspectives, 1984; Stravinsky: Glimpses of a Life, 1992. Contributions to: Many publications. Address: 1390 South Ocean Boulevard, Pompano Beach, FL 33062, USA.

CRAGGS Robert S, (Jack Creek, Luke Lanside), b. 1920, Manitoba, Canada. Freelance Writer. Publications: Trees for Shade and Beauty, 1961; Sir Adams Archibald, 1967; Ghostwriting for the Mail Order Trade, 1968; Writer Without a By-Line, 1968; Organic Gardening for Profit, 1990; Prophet of the Wheat Fields, in The Almanac for Farmers and City Folk, 1994; Canada's Men of Letters, 1995; Classic Comics on Stamps, 1995. Contributions to: Hundreds of articles, short stories, cartoon gags to Canadian and US publications; Columnist for various publications. Memberships: National Writers Association; Friends of Merril Collection. Address: 25 McMillan Avenue, West Hill, Ontario M1E 4B4, Canada.

CRAGGS Stewart Roger, b. 27 July 1943, Ilkley, West Yorkshire, England. Academic Librarian. m. Valerie J Gibson, 28 Sept 1968, 1 son, 1 daughter. Education: ILA, Leeds Polytechnic, 1968; FLA, 1974; MA, University of Strathclyde, Glasgow, 1978; PhD, University of Strathclyde, 1982. Appointments: Teesside Polytechnic, 1968-69; JA Jobling, 1970-72; Sunderland Polytechnic University, 1973-95. Publications: William Walton: A Thematic Catalogue, 1977; Arthur Bliss: A Bio-Bibliography, 1988; Richard Rodney Bennett: A Bio-Bibliography, 1990; William Walton: A Catalogue, 2nd ed, 1990; John McCabe: A Bio-Bibliography, 1991; William Walton: A Source Book, 1993; John Ireland: A Catalogue, Discography and Bibliography, 1993; Alun Hoddinott: A Bio-Bibliography, 1993; Edward Elgar: A Source Book, 1995; William Mathias: A Bio-Bibliography, 1995; Arthur Bliss: A Source Book, 1996; Soundtracks: An International Dictionary of Composers for Films, 1998; Malcolm Arnold: A Bio-Bibliography, 1998. Honour: Professor of Music Bibliography, University of Sunderland, 1993. Address: 106 Mount Road, High Barnes, Sunderland, SR4 7NN, England.

CRAIG Alisa. See: MACLEOD Charlotte.

CRAIG Amanda Pauline, b. 22 Sept 1959, S Africa. Novelist; Journalist. m. Robin John Cohen, 27 July 1988, 1 son, 1 daughter. Education: Clare College, Cambridge, England, 1979-81. Publications: Foreign Bodies, 1990; A Private Place, 1991; A Vicious Circle, 1996. Contributions to: The Times; The Telegraph; The Observer; The Spectator; The News Statesman; Literary Review. Membership: Authors Society. Literary Agent: Giles Gordon, Curtis Brown. Address: c/o Giles Gordon, Curtis Brown, 28 Haymarket, London W1, England.

CRAIG Gordon A(lexander), b. 26 Nov 1913, Glasgow, Scotland. Retired Professor of History; Writer. m. Phyllis Halcomb, 16 June 1939, 1 son, 3 daughters. Education: AB, 1936, MA, 1939, PhD, 1941, Princeton University; BLitt, Balliol College, Oxford, 1938. Appointments: Instructor, Yale University, 1939-41;

Instructor to Professor, Princeton University, 1941-61; Member, Institute for Advanced Study, Princeton, New Jersey, 1951; Fellow, Center for Advanced Study in the Behavioral Sciences, 1956-57; Shaw Lecturer, Johns Hopkins University, 1958; Haynes Lecturer, University of California at Riverside, 1961; Professor of History, 1961-85, J E Wallace Sterling Professor of Humanities, 1969-85, Stanford University; Curti Lecturer, University of Wisconsin, 1982. Publications: The Politics of the Prussian Army, 1640-1945, 1955; From Bismarck to Adenauer: Aspects of German Statecraft, 1958; Europe Since 1815, 1961, 5th edition, 1979; The Battle of Königgrätz, 1964, new edition, 1996; War, Politics and Diplomacy: Selected Essays, 1966; Germany, 1866-1945, 1978; The Germans, 1982; Force and Statecraft: Diplomatic Problems of Our Time (with Alexander L George), 1983, 3rd edition, revised, 1995; The End of Prussia, 1984; Geld und Geist: Zürich im Zeitalter des Liberalismus, 1830-1869, 1988, English translation as The Triumph of Liberalism: Zürich in the Golden Age, 1830-1869, 1989; Die Politik der Unpolitischen: Deutsche Schriftsteller und die Macht, 1770-1871, 1993, English translation as The Politics of the Unpolitical: German Writers and the Problem of Power, 1770-1871, 1995; Geneva, Zürich, Basel: History, Culture, National Identity (with Nicolas Bouvier and Lionel Grossman), 1994. Editor: Makers of Modern Strategy: Military Thought from Machiavelli to Hitler (with Edward Mead Earle and Felix Gilbert), 1943; The Diplomats, 1919-1939 (with Felix Gilbert), 1953; Treitschke's History of Modern Germany, 1975; Economic Interest, Militarism and Foreign Policy: Essays of Eckart Kehr, 1977; Makers of Modern Strategy: From Machiavelli to the Nuclear Age (with Peter Paret and Felix Gilbert), 1986; The Diplomats, 1939-1979 (with Francis L Loewenheim), 1994; Über Fontane, 1997. Honours: Honorary Professor, Free University of Berlin, 1962-; Guggenheim Fellowships, 1969-70, 1982-83; Commander's Cross of the Legion of Merit, Federal Republic of Germany, 1984; Goethe Medaille, Goethe Gesellschaft, 1987; Honorary Fellow, Balliol College, Oxford, 1989-; Member, Orden Pour le Merité für Wissenschaften und Künste, 1990-. Memberships: American Academy of Arts and Sciences; American Historical Association, president, 1982; American Philosophical Society; British Academy, fellow; Comité International des Sciences Historiques. Address: 451 Oak Grove Avenue, Menlo Park, CA 94025, USA.

CRAIG Jasmine. See: CRESSWELL Jasmine (Rosemary).

CRAIG William. See: BERKSON WILLIAM GRAIG

CRAIK Elizabeth M(ary), b. 25 Jan 1939, Portmoak, Scotland. University Teacher; Writer; Editor. m. Alexander Craik, 15 July 1964, 1 son, 1 daughter. Education: MA, University of St Andrews, 1960; MLitt, Girton College, Cambridge, 1963. Appointments: Research Fellow in Greek, University of Birmingham, 1963-64; Assistant Lecturer to Senior Lecturer in Greek, University of St Andrews, 1964-97; Professor of Classics, Kyoto University, Japan, 1997-. Publications: The Dorian Aegean, 1980; Marriage and Property (editor), 1984; Euripides: Phoenician Women, 1988; Owls to Athens (editor), 1990; Hippocrates: Places in Man, 1998. Contributions to: Scholarly journals. Honours: British Academy Awards, 1981, 1986; Carnegie Trust Award, 1986. Memberships: Classical Society of Japan; Cambridge Philological Society; Hellenic Society. Address: Department of Classics, Faculty of Letters, Kyoto University, Kyoto 606, Japan.

CRAIK Thomas Wallace, b. 17 Apr 1927, Warrington, England. Professor of English Emeritus; Writer; Editor. m. Wendy Ann Sowter, 25 Aug 1955, div 1975, 1 son. Education: BA, English Tripos, Part 1, 1947, Part 2, 1948, MA, 1952, PhD, 1952, Christ's College, Cambridge. Appointments: Assistant Lecturer, 1953, Lecturer, 1954-65, University of Leicester; Lecturer, 1965-67, Senior Lecturer, 1967-73, University of Aberdeen; Professor of English, University of Dundee, 1973-77; Professor of English, 1977-89, Professor of English Emeritus, 1989-, University of Durham. Publications: The

Tudor Interlude, 1958; The Comic Tales of Chaucer, 1964. Editor: Marlowe: The Jew of Malta, 1966; Shakespeare: Twelfth Night, 1975; Beaumont and Fletcher: The Maid's Tragedy, 1988; Shakespeare: The Merry Wives of Windsor, 1989; Shakespeare: King Henry V, 1995. Contributions to: Scholarly journals. Membership: International Shakespeare Association. Address: 58 Albert Street, Western Hill, Durham City DH1 4RJ, England.

CRAMER Richard Ben, b. 12 June 1950, Rochester, New York, USA. Journalist; Writer. Education: BA, Johns Hopkins University, 1971; MS, Columbia University, 1972. Publications: Ted Williams: The Season of the Kid, 1991; What It Takes: The Way to the White House, 1992. Contributions to: Periodicals. Honours: Journalism awards. Address: c/o Sterling Lord Literistic Inc, 65 Bleecker Street, New York, NY 10012, USA.

CRANE Richard Arthur, b. 4 Dec 1944, York, England. Writer. m. Faynia Williams, 5 Sept 1975, 2 sons, 2 step-daughters. Education: BA (Hons), Classics and English, 1966, MA, 1971, Jesus College, Cambridge. Appointments: Fellow in Theatre, University of Bradford, 1972-74; Resident Dramatist, National Theatre, 1974-75; Fellow in Creative Writing, University of Leicester, 1976; Literary Manager, Royal Court Theatre, 1978-79; Associate Director, Brighton Theatre, 1980-85; Dramaturg, Tron Theatre, Glasgow, 1983-84; Visiting Writers Fellowship, University of East Anglia, 1988; Writer-in-Residence, Birmingham Polytechnic, 1990-91, HM Prison Bedford, 1993; Lecturer in Creative Writing, University of Sussex, 1994-. Publications: Thunder, 1976; Gunslinger, 1979; Crippen, 1993; Under the Stars, 1994. Stage Plays: The Tenant, 1971; Crippen, 1971; Decent Things, 1972; Secrets, 1973; The Quest, 1974; Clownmaker, 1975; Venus and Superkid, 1975; Bloody Neighbours, 1975; Satan's Ball, 1977; Gogol, 1979; Vanity, 1980; Brothers Karamazov, 1981; The Possessed, 1985; Mutiny! (with David Essex), 1985; Soldier Soldier (with Tony Parker) 1986; Envy (with Donald Swann), 1986; Pushkin, 1987; Red Magic, 1988; Rolling the Stone, 1989; Phaedra (with Michael Glenny), 1990; Baggage and Bombshells, 1991; Under the Stars, 1993. Editor: Poems from the Waiting Room, 1993; The Last Minute Book, 1995; Pandora's Books, 1997; TV Plays: Rottingdean, 1980; The Possessed, 1985. Radio Plays: Gogol, 1980; Decent Things, 1984; Optimistic Tragedy, 1986; Anna and Marina, 1991; Understudies, 1992; Vlad the Impaler, 1992; The Sea The Sea (classic serial), 1993; Plutopia (with Donald Swann), 1994. Contributions to: Edinburgh Fringe; Guardian; Index on Censorship, Times Literary Supplement. Honours: Edinburgh Fringe First Awards, 1973, 1974, 1975, 1977, 1980, 1986, 1987, 1988, 1989. Address: c/o Casarotto-Ramsay Ltd, National House, 60-66 Wardour Street, London W1V 3HP, England.

CRASTA Richard, (Avatar Prabhu), b. 12 May 1952, Bangalore, India. Author. m Jovita Crasta, 10 Dec 1978, 3 sons. Education: BA, University of Mysore; MA in Literature and Journalism, American University; MFA, Columbia University. Appointments: Indian Administrative Service. Publications: The Revised Kama Sutra: A Novel of Colonialism and Desire, Indian edition, 1993, UK edition, 1994, US edition, 1998; Die Kinder des Kama Sutra, German Edition, 1998; Beauty Queens, Children and the Death of Sex, essay collection, 1997; Eaten by the Japanese (contributor, editor), 1998; Impressing the Whites, 1999. Contributions to: Numerous: Times of India; Newsday, USA; Los Angeles Times. Memberships: National Writers Union, 1995-97; PEN, 1997-. Literary Agent: Harry Smith, Brooklyn, NY 11201, USA. Address: 100 Riverside Drive, Rockville Center, NY 11570, USA.

CRAVENS Hamilton, b. 12 Aug 1938, Evanston, IL, USA. University Professor of History. Div, 1 son, 1 daughter. Education: BA, 1960, MA, 1962, University of Washington; PhD, University Iowa, 1969. Appointments: Instructor, The Ohio State University, 1965-68; Instructor to Professor, Iowa State University, 1968-80; Visiting Professor, University of Washington, University of Maryland, University of Iowa, University of California,

Göttingen University, Bonn University, Heidelberg University (Germany). Publications: The Triumph of Evolution, 1978, 1988; Ideas in America's Cultures, 1982; Before Head Start, 1993; Technical Knowledge in American Culture, 1996; Health Care in Contemporary American, 1997. Contributions to: Over 50 articles in journals and magazines and chapters in books. Honours: Ford Foundation Grant; Fulbright Distinguished Professor Germany, 1988-89, 1997; Stanford University Humanities Center Fellow; National Science Foundation Grants. Address: Department of History, Iowa State University, Ames, IA 50011 1206, USA.

CRAWFORD Linda, b. 2 Aug 1938, Detroit, Michigan, USA. Writer. Education: BA, 1960, MA, 1961, University of Michigan. Publications: In a Class by Herself, 1976; Something to Make Us Happy, 1978; Vanishing Acts, 1981; Ghost of a Chance, 1985. Membership: PEN. Address: 131 Prince Street, New York, NY 10012, USA.

CRAWFORD Robert. See: RAE Hugh Crauford.

CRAWFORD Thomas, b. 6 July 1920, Dundee, Scotland. Honorary Reader in English; Author. m. Jean Rennie McBride, 19 Aug 1946, 1 son, 1 daughter. Education: MA, University of Edinburgh, 1944; MA, University of Auckland, 1953. Appointments: Lecturer, 1953-60, Senior Lecturer, 1961-62, Associate Professor of English, 1962-65, University of Auckland; Lecturer in English, University of Edinburgh, 1965; Commonwealth Research Fellow, McMaster University, Hamilton, Ontario, Canada, 1966-67; Reader in English, 1967-85, Honorary Reader in English, 1985-, University of Aberdeen; Editor, Scottish Literary Journal, 1974-84. Publications: Burns: A Study of the Poems, 1960, revised edition, 1994; Scott, 1965, revised edition, 1982; Sir Walter Scott: Selected Poems (editor), 1972; Love, Labour, and Liberty, 1976; Society and the Lyric, 1979; Longer Scottish Poems 1650-1830, 1987; Boswell, Burns and the French Revolution, 1989; The Correspondence of James Boswell and William Johnson Temple 1756-1795: Volume I, 1756-1777 (editor), 1997. Contributions to: Scholarly journals. Memberships: Association for Scottish Literary Studies, president, 1984-88; Saltire Society; Scots Language Society; Scottish Text Society. Address: 34 Summerhill Terrace, Aberdeen AB15 6HE, Scotland.

CRAWLEY Tony, (Anthony Francis Crawley), b. 26 Mar 1938, Farnham, Surrey, England. Journalist; Writer. m. (1) Janet Wild, 30 Sept 1961, div 17 Feb 1970, (2) Nicole Michelet, 26 Feb 1970, 1 son, 1 daughter. Education: Victoria Technical Institute, Trowbridge, Wiltshire. Appointments: Editor, Cinema X, 1967-78; Founder-Editor, Premiere, 1969, and Cinema Blue, 1975-78. Publications: The Films of Sophia Loren, 1974; Bebe: The Films of Brigitte Bardot, 1975; Screen Dreams: The Hollywood Pin-up, 1982; The Steven Spielberg Story, 1983; Entre deux censures (with François Jouffa), 1989; Chambers Film Quotes, 1992; Brigitte Bardot, 1994. Contributions to: Newspapers and magazines. Membership: National Union of Journalists. Address: 6 Allée Claude Monet, 78160 Marly-le-Roi, France.

CRAWSHAW Jill, b. 13 Oct 1944, Accringon, Lancs, England. Journalist; Travel Writer; Broadcaster. m. Stephen Danos, 20 July 1973, 2 sons. Education: MA (Oxon) Hons. Appointments: Travel Editor, Daily Mail; Travel Editor, EV Standard. Publications: Holidays With Children at Home Abroad. Contributions to: Weekly Column in The Times; Independent on Sunday; Now Magazine; Hello; ABTA News; Travel Show (TV); Russell Grant Programme (Radio). Honour: 4 times Travel Writer of the Year. Address: Pond House, 54 Highgate West Hill, London N6 6DA, England.

CRAY Robert. See: EMERSON Ru.

CREASEY Jeanne. See: WILLIAMS Jeanne.

CRECY Jeanne. See: WILLIAMS Jeanne.

CREE Mary Crowther, b. 19 Mar 1919, Tasmania. Author; Lecturer. m. C E A Cree, 20 Feb 1945, 2 sons, 1 daughter. Education: Toorak College. Appointment: Director, Anglican Newspaper, 1974. Publications: Cumquat May, 1978; Edith May 1895-1974: Life in Early Tasmania, 1983; Looking for Antiques in Tasmania, 1986; Notes of Antiques, 1993; Emily Ida - A Victorian Matriarch in Colonial Tasmania, 1994; Looking for Antiques in Sydney, 1994; Tasmanian and Colonial Furniture in New Zealand, 1996; Herbert John: The Extraordinary Crowther Items, 1998. Honour: Life Governor, Royal Childrens' Hospital, Melbourne, Australia. Membership: Australian Authors. Address: 31 Adelaide St, Armadale, Melbourne 3143, Australia.

CREEK Jack. See: CRAGGS Robert S.

CREELEY Robert White, b. 21 May 1926, Arlington, Massachusetts, USA. Writer; Poet; Professor of English. m. (1) Ann McKinnon, 1946, div 1955, 2 sons, 1 daughter, (2) Bobbie Louise Hall, 1957, div 1976, 4 daughters, (3) Penelope Highton, 1977, 1 son, 1 daughter. Education: BA, Black Mountain College, 1954; MA, University of New Mexico, 1960. Appointments: Professor, 1967-78, David Gray Professor, Poetry, Letters, 1978-89, Samuel P Capen Professor, Poetry, Humanities, 1989, Director, Poetics Programme, 1991-92, State University of New York, Buffalo; Advisory Editor, American Book Review, 1983-, Sagetrieb, 1983-, New York Quarterly, 1984-. Publications: Poetry: For Love, Poems 1950-60, 1962; Words, 1967; Pieces, 1969; A Day Book, 1972; Selected Poems, 1976, revised edition, 1991; Hello, 1978; Later, 1979; Mirrors, 1983; Collected Poems 1945-75, 1983; Memory Gardens, 1986; Windows, 1990; Echoes, 1994; Life and Death, 1998. Prose: The Island, 1963; The Gold Diggers, 1965; Mabel: A Story, 1976; The Collected Prose, 1984; Tales Out of School, 1993. Criticism: A Quick Graph, 1970; Was That a Real Poem and Other Essays, 1976; Collected Essays, 1989. Autobiography, 1990. Co-editor: New American Story, 1965; The New Writng in the USA, 1967. Editor: Selected Writings of Charles Olson, 1967; Whitman, Selected Poems, 1973; The Essential Burns, 1989; Charles Olson, Selected Poems, 1993. Honours: Guggenheim Fellowships, 1964, 1967; Rockefeller Grantee, 1965; Shelley Memorial Award, 1981, Frost Medal, 1987, Poetry Society of America; National Endowment for the Arts Grantee, 1982; Berlin Artists Programme Grants, 1983, 1987; Leone d'Oro Premio Speziale, 1984; Distinguished Fulbright Award, Bicentennial Chair of American Studies, University of Helsinki, 1988; Distinguished Professor, State University of New York, 1989; Walt Whitman Citation, State Poet of New York, 1989-91; Horst Bienek Preis für Lyrik, Munich, 1993; Honorary LittD, University of New Mexico, 1993; America Award in Poetry, 1995; Fulbright Award, University of Auckland, 1995; Lila Wallace-Reader's Digest Writer's Award, 1995. Memberships: American Academy and Institute of Arts and Letters; PEN American Center. Address: 64 Amherst Street, Buffalo, NY 14207, USA.

CREGAN David (Appleton Quartus), b. 30 Sept 1931, Buxton, England. Dramatist; Writer. m. Ailsa Mary Wynne Willson, 1960, 3 sons, 1 adopted daughter. Education: BA, English Tripos, Clare College, Cambridge, 1955. Appointments: Worked with Cambridge Footlights, 1953, 1954, The Royal Court Theatre Studio, London, 1964, 1968, Midlands Art Centre, Birmingham, 1971; Head of English Department, Palm Beach Private School, Florida, USA, 1955-57; Assistant English Master, Burnage Boys Grammar School, Manchester, England, 1957; Assistant English Master, Head of Drama Department, 1958-62, Part-time Drama Teacher, 1962-67, Hatfield School, Herts; Conducted 3 week studio, Royal Shakespeare Company Memorial Theatre, Stratford-upon-Avon, 1971; Tutor in Drama, Southampton University Adult Education Panel. Publications: Ronald Rossiter (novel), 1959. Plays: Miniatures, 1965; The Dancers, 1966; Transcending, 1966; Three Men for Colverton, 1966; Houses by the Green, 1966; numerous other plays and pantomimes. Television plays: Pipkins (children's television series); Events in a Museum, 1984;

A Still Small Shout, 1985; Goodbye Days, 1986; Goodbye and I Hope We Meet Again, 1989. Radio plays: Numerous plays for national radio broadcast. Contributions to: Guardian, New Socialist. Honours: Charles Henry Foyle New Plays Award, 1966; Sony Award, Best Radio Script, 1987; Giles Cooper Radio Drama Award, 1991. Memberships: West Midlands Art Association, 1972-75; Theatre Writers' Union, founder member; Eastern Arts drama panel, 1981-85, 1990-. Address: 76 Wood Close, Hatfield, Hertfordshire, England.

CREGIER Don M(esick), b. 28 Mar 1930, Schenectady, New York, USA. Historian; Writer. m. Sharon Kathleen Ellis, 29 June 1965. Education: BA, Union College, New York, 1951; MA, University of Michigan, 1952. Appointments: Assistant Instructor, Clark University, Worcester, Massachusetts, 1952-54; Instructor, University of Tennessee at Martin, 1956-57; Assistant Professor, Baker University, Baldwin, Kansas, 1958-61; Assistant Professor, Keuka College, Keuka Park, New York, 1962-64; Visiting Assistant Professor, St John's University, Collegeville, Minnesota, 1964-65; Senior Fellow and Tutor, Mark Hopkins College, Brattleboro, Vermont, 1965-66; Associate Professor, St Dunstan's University, Charlottetown, Prince Edward Island, 1966-69; Associate Professor, 1969-85, Professor of History, 1985-86, Adjunct Professor, 1996-, University of Prince Edward Island; Abstractor, ABC/Clio Information Services, 1978-; Foreign Book Review Editor, Canadian Review of Studies in Nationalism, 1996-98. Publications: Bounder from Wales: Lloyd George's Career Before the First World War, 1976; Novel Exposures: Victorian Studies Featuring Contemporary Novels, 1979; Chiefs Without Indians: Asquith, Lloyd George, and the Liberal Remnant, 1916-1935, 1982; The Decline of the British Liberal Party: Why and How?, 1985; Freedom and Order: The Growth of British Liberalism Before 1868, 1988; The Rise of the Global Village (co-author), 1988. Contributions to: Reference works and professional journals. Honours: Mark Hopkins Fellow, 1965; Canada Council Fellow, 1972, Research Grant, Social Sciences and Humanities, Research Council of Canada, 1984-86. Memberships: Historical Society; American Historical Association; Society for Academic Freedom and Scholarship; Canadian Association of University Teachers; Mark Twain Society; North American Conference on British Studies; Phi Beta Kappa; Phi Kappa Phi; Phi Sigma Phi. Address: c/o Department of History, University of Prince Edward Island, 550 University Avenue, Charlottetown, Prince Edward Island C1A 4P3, Canada.

CREMONA John Joseph, b. 6 Jan 1918, Gozo, Malta. Retired Chief Justice; Professor Emeritus of Criminal Law; Historian; POet. m. Marchioness Beatrice Barbaro of St George, 20 Sept 1949, 1 son, 2 daughters. Education: BA, 1939, LLD, cum laude, 1942, University of Malta; DLitt, University of Rome, 1939; BA, 1st Class Honours, 1946, PhD, Law, 1951, University of London. Appointments: Crown Counsel, 1947; Lecturer in Constitutional Law, Royal University of Malta, 1947-65; Attorney General, 1957-64; Professor of Criminal Law, 1959-65, Professor Emeritus, 1965-, Pro-Chancellor, 1971-74, University of Malta; Crown Advocate-General, 1964-65; Attorney General, 1957-64; Professor of Criminal Law, 1959-65, Professor Emeritus, 1965-, Pro-Chancellor, 1971-74, University of Malta; Crown Advocate-General, 1964-65; Vice President, Constitutional Court and Court of Appeal, 1965-71; Judge, 1965-92, Vice President, 1986-92, European Court of Human Rights; Chief Justice and President, Constitutional Court, Court of Appeal, and Court of Criminal Appeal, 1971-81; Judge, 1986-92, Vice President, 1986-92, European Tribunal in Matters of State Immunity. Publications: Non-Fiction: The Treatment of Young Offenders in Malta, 1956; The Malta Constitution of 1835, 1959; The Legal Consequences of a Conviction in the Criminal Law of Malta, 1962; The Constitutional Development of Malta, 1963; From the Declaration of Rights to Independence, 1965; Human Rights Documentation in Malta, 1966; Selected Papers, 1946-89, 1990; The Maltese Constitution and Constitutional History, 1994; Malta and Britain: The Early Constitutions, 1996. Poetry: Eliotropi, 1937; Songbook of the South, 1940; Limestone 84 (with others), 1978; Malta Malta, 1992. Contributions to: Law reviews. Honours: Many, including: Knight of Magisterial Grace, Sovereign Military Order of Malta; Companion of the National Order of Merit of Malta; Chevalier, Legion d'honneur, France; Knight of the Grand Cross, Order of Merit, Italy; Honorary Fellow, London School of Economics and Political Science. Memberships: Royal Historical Society, fellow; Human rights and environmental organizations. Address: Villa Barbaro, Main Street, Attard, Malta.

CRERAR. See: **REANEY James.**

CRESSWELL Helen, b. 11 July 1934, Nottinghamshire, England. Author. m. Brian Rowe, 14 Aug 1962, div 1995, 2 daughters. Education: BA, English, Honours, King's College, London. Publications: Sonya-by-the-Shire, 1961; Jumbo Spencer, 1963; The White Sea Horse, 1964; Pietro and the Mule, 1965; Jumbo Back to Nature, 1965; Where the Wind Blows, 1966; Jumbo Afloat, 1966; The Piemakers, 1967; A Tide for the Captain, 1967; The Signposters, 1968; The Sea Piper, 1968; The Barge Children, 1968; The Nightwatchman, 1969; A Game of Catch, 1969; A Gift from Winklesea, 1969; The Outlanders, 1970; The Wilkses, 1970; The Bird Fancier, 1971; At the Stroke of Midnight, 1971; The Beachcombers, 1972; Lizzie Dripping, 1972; Thee Bongleweed, 1972; Lizzie Dripping Again, 1974; Butterfly Chase, 1975; The Winter of the Birds, 1975; The Bagthorpe Saga, 7 parts, 1977-88; My Aunt Polly, 1979; My Aunt Polly By the Sea, 1980; Dear Shrink, 1982; The Secret World of Polly Flint, 1982; Ellie and the Hagwitch, 1984; Time Out, 1987; Whodunnit, 1987; Moondial, 1987; Two Hoots, 1988; The Story of Grace Darling, 1988; Dragon Ride, 1988; Trouble, 1988; Rosie and the Boredom Eater, 1989; Whatever Happened in Winklesea?, 1989; Meet Posy Bates, 1990; Hokey Pokey Did It!, 1990; Posy Bates Again, 1991; Lizzie Dripping and the Witch, 1991; Posy Bates and the Bag Lady, 1992; The Watchers, 1993; Classic Fairy Tales Retold, 1993; The Little Sea More, 1995; Stonestruck, 1995; Mystery at Winklesea, 1995; Polly Thumb, 1995; Giant, 1996; Puffin Book of Funny Stories (editor), 1993. Literary Agent: A M Heath, London. Address: Old Church Farm, Eakring, Newark, Notts NG22 0DA, England.

CRESSWELL Jasmine (Rosemary), (Jasmine Craig), b. 14 Jan 1941, Dolgelly, Wales (US citizen, 1983). Writer. m. Malcolm Candlish, 15 Apr 1963, 1 son, 3 daughters. Education: BA, University of Melbourne, 1972; BA, Honours, Macquarie University, 1973; MA, Case Western Reserve University, 1975. Publications: Over 50 novels, including: Lord Rutherford's Affair, 1984; Master Touch, 1985; Undercover, 1986; For Love of Christy, 1987; The Devil's Envoy, 1988; Charades, 1989; Nowhere to Hide, 1992; Keeping Secrets, 1993; Eternity, 1994; Desires and Deceptions, 1995; No Sin Too Great, 1996; Secret Sins, 1997; The Daughter, 1998; The Disappearance, 1999. Honours: Colorado Romance Writer of the Year Awards, 1986, 1987. Memberships: Authors Guild; Colorado Authors League; Novelists Inc; Rocky Mountain Fiction Writers. Address: c/o Maureen Walters, 10 Astor Place, New York, NY 10003, USA.

CREW Gary David, b. 23 Sept 1947, Brisbane, Queensland, Australia. Lecturer; Writer. m. Christine Joy Crew, 4 Apr 1970, 1 son, 2 daughters. Education: Civil Engineering Drafting Diploma, 1970; BA, 1979, MA, 1984, University of Queensland. Appointment: Lecturer, Queensland University of Technology, 1987-. Publications: Inner Circle, 1986; The House of Tomorrow, 1988; Strange Objects, 1991; No Such Country, 1992; Tracks, 1992; Lucy's Bay, 1992; The Angel's Gate, 1993. Honours: Australian Children's Book of the Year, New South Wales Premier's Award Alan Marshall Prize, 1991; National Children's Book Award, 1993. Membership: Australian Society of Authors. Literary Agent: Fran Kelly, 23 Main Street, Eastwood, South Australia 5063, Australia. Address: Green Mansions, 66 Picnic Street, Enoggera, Queensland 4051, Australia.

CREWE Quentin Hugh, b. 14 Nov 1926, London, England. Author; Journalist. 2 sons, 3 daughters. Education: Eton College, England, 1940-45; Trinity College, Cambridge, England, 1945-46. Publications: A Curse of Blossom, 1960; The Frontiers of Privilege, 1961; Great Chefs of France, 1978; International Pocket Book of Food, 1980; In Search of the Sahara, 1983; The Last Maharaja, 1985; Touch the Happy Isles, 1987; In the Realms of Gold, 1989-; Well I Forget the Rest, autobiography, 1991; Foods from France, 1993; Crewe House, 1995; Letters from India, 1998. Contributions to: Queen; Vogue; Spectator; Daily Mail; Times; Evening Standard. Membership: FRSL. Literary Agent: Aitken, Stone and Wylie. Address: 9 Bliss Mill, Chipping Norton, Oxfordshire, OX7 5JR, England.

CREWS Frederick (Campbell), b. 20 Feb 1933, Philadelphia, Pennsylvania, USA. Professor Emeritus; Writer. m. Elizabeth Peterson, 9 Sept 1959, 2 daughters. Education: BA, Yale University, 1955; PhD, Princeton University, 1958. Appointments: Instructor, 1958-60, Assistant Professor, 1960-62, Associate Professor, 1962-66, Professor of English, 1966-94, Professor Emeritus, 1994-, University of California at Berkeley; Ward-Phillips Lecturer, University of Notre Dame, 1974-75; Dorothy T Burstein Lecturer, University of California at Los Angeles, 1984; Frederick Ives Carpenter Visiting Professor, University of Chicago, 1985; Nina Mae Kellogg Lecturer, Portland State University, Oregon, 1989; David L Kubal Memorial Lecturer, California State University, Los Angeles, 1994. Publications: The Tragedy of Manners, 1957; E M Forster: The Perils of Humanism, 1962; The Pooh Perplex, 1963; The Sins of the Fathers, 1966; Starting Over, 1970; Psychoanalysis and Literary Process, 1970; The Random House Handbook, 1974, 6th edition, 1992; The Random House Reader, 1981; Out of My System, 1975; The Borzoi Handbook for Writers (co-author), 1985, 3rd edition, 1993; Skeptical Engagements, 1986; The Critics Bear It Away (co-author), 1992; The Memory Wars (co-author), 1995; Unauthorized Freud (editor), 1998. Contributions to: Scholarly journals and to magazines. Honours: Fulbright Lecturer, Turin, 1961-62; American Council of Learned Societies Fellow, 1965-66; Center for Advanced Study in the Behavioral Sciences Fellow, 1965-66; Guggenheim Fellowship, 1970-71; Distinguished Teaching Award, University of California at Berkeley, 1985; Spielvogel Diamonstein PEN Prize, 1992. Membership: American Academy of Arts and Sciences, fellow. Address: 636 Vincente Avenue, Berkeley, CA 94707, USA.

CREWS Harry (Eugene), b. 6 June 1935, Alma, Georgia, USA. Professor of English; Writer. m. Sally Thornton Ellis, 24 Jan 1960, div, 2 sons. Education: BA, 1960, MSEd, 1962, University of Florida. Appointments: Teacher of English, Broward Junior College, Fort Lauderdale, 1962-68; Associate Professor, 1968-74, Professor of English, 1974-, University of Florida, Gainesville. Publications: The Gospel Singer, 1968; Naked in Garden Hills, 1969; This Thing Don't Lead to Heaven, 1970; Karate is a Thing of the Spirit, 1971; Car, 1972; The Hawk is Dying, 1973; The Gypsy's Curse, 1974; A Feast of Snakes, 1976; A Childhood: The Biography of a Place, 1978; Blood and Grits, 1979; The Enthusiast, 1981; Florida Frenzy, 1982; A Grit's Triumph, 1983; Two, 1984; All We Need of Hell, 1987; The Knockout Artist, 1988; Body, 1990; Scar Lover, 1992; Celebrations, 1998. Address: 2820 North West Street, Gainesville, FL 32601, USA.

CRICHTON (John) Michael, (John Michael, Jeffrey Hudson, John Lange), b. 23 Oct 1942, Chicago, Illinois, USA. Film Director; Author. Education: AB summa cum laude, 1964, MD, 1969, Harvard University; Cambridge University, England, 1965; Postdoctoral Fellow, Salk Institute for Biological Sciences, California, 1969-70. Publications: The Andromeda Strain, 1969; Five Patients, 1970; The Terminal Man, 1972; The Great Train Robbery, 1975; Eaters of the Dead, 1976; Jasper Johns, 1977; Congo, 1980; Electronic Life, 1983; Sphere, 1987; Travels, 1988; Jurassic Park, 1990; Rising Sun, 1992; Disclosure, 1994; The Lost World, 1995. Honours: Edgar Awards, Mystery Writers of America, 1968, 1979.

Memberships: Authors Guild; Writers Guild of America; Directors Guild; Academy of Motion Picture Arts and Sciences. Address: International Creative Management, 40 West 57th Street, New York, NY 10025, USA.

CRICK Bernard, b. 16 Dec 1929, England. Education: University College, London. Appointments: Political writer, biographer and journalist; Literary Editor, Political Quarterly; Professor of Politics, Birbeck College, London, 1971-84; Emeritus Professor, University of London, 1993-. Publications: The American Science of Politics, 1958; In Defence of Politics, 1962, 4th edition, 1992; The Reform of Parliament, 1964; Theory and Practice: Essays in Politics, 1972; Basic Forms of Government, 1973; Crime, Rape and Gin: Reflections on Contemporary Attitudes to Violence, Pornography and Addiction, 1977; Political Education and Political Literacy, 1978; George Orwell: A Life, 1980, 3rd edition 1992; Orwell Remembered (co-editor), 1984; Socialism, 1987; Politics and Literature, 1987; Political Thoughts and Polemics, 1990; National Identities (editor), 1991. Honours: Honorary Fellow, Birkbeck College; Honorary Doctorates: Queens University, Belfast; Universities of Sheffield, East London, Kingston. Address: 8A Bellevue Terrace, Edinburgh EH7 4DT, Scotland.

CRICK Donald Herbert, b. 16 July 1916, Sydney, New South Wales, Australia. m. 24 Dec 1943, 1 daughter. Publications: Novels: Bikini Girl, 1963; Martin Place, 1964; Period of Adjustment, 1966; A Different Drummer, 1972; The Moon to Play With, 1981. Screenplays: The Veronica, 1983; A Different Drummer, 1985; The Moon to Play With, 1987. Contributions to: Sydney Morning Herald; The Australian; Overland; The Australian Author. Honours: Mary Gilmore Centenary Award, Novel, 1966; Rigby Anniversary Award, Novel, 1980; Awgie Screenplay Award, 1983-85. Membership: Australian Society of Authors, board of management. Address: 1/1 Elamang Avenue, Kirribilli, New South Wales 2061, Australia.

CRISCUOLO Anthony Thomas, (Tony Crisp), b. 10 May 1937, Amersham, Buckinghamshire, England. Writer; Therapist. 4 sons, 1 daughter. Publications: Yoga and Relaxation, 1970; Do You Dream?, 1971; Yield, 1974; Yoga and Childbirth, 1975; The Instant Dream Book, 1984; Mind and Movement, 1987; Dream Dictionary, 1990; Liberating the Body, 1992; The Hand Book, 1994; Superminds, 1998. Contributions to: Newspapers, journals, radio and television. Address: 79 Aldrich Road, Cutteslowe, Oxford OX2 7SU, England.

CRISP Tony. See: **CRISCUOLO Anthony Thomas.**

CRISPIN Suzy. See: **CARTWRIGHT Justin.**

CRISTIENS Sara. See: **STEIN Clarissa Ingeborg.**

CRITCHLEY Julian (Sir) Michael Gordon), b. 8 Dec 1930, Chelsea, London, England. Member of Parliament; Writer; Broadcaster; Journalist. m. (1) Paula Joan Baron, 1955, div 1965, 2 daughters, (2) Heather Goodrick, 1965, 1 son, 1 daughter. Education: Sorbonne, University of Paris; MA, Pembroke College, Oxford. Appointments: Member of Parliament, Conservative Party, Rochester and Chatham, 1959-64, Aldershot and North Hants, 1970-74, Aldershot, 1974-97; Chairman, Western European Union Defence Committee, 1975-79, Conservative Party Media Committee, 1976-81; Steward, British Boxing Board of Control, 1987-91; Judge, Whitbread Book of the Year Competition, 1996. Publications: Collective Security (with O Pick), 1974; Warning and Response, 1978; The North Atlantic Alliance and the Soviet Union in the 1980s, 1982; Nuclear Weapons in Europe (co-author), 1984; Westminster Blues, 1985; Britain: A View from Westminster (editor), 1986; Heseltine: The Unauthorized Biography, 1987, revised edition, 1994; Palace of Varieties: An Insider's View of Westminster, 1989; Hung Parliament, 1991; Floating Voter, 1992; A Bag of Boiled Sweets (autobiography), 1995-96; Borderlands, 1996; Collapse of Start Party, with Morrison Halnow, 1997/1998; London (with Dave Paterson). Contributions to: Books and periodicals. Honours: Political Journalist of the Year, 1985; Knighted, 1995. Memberships: Various professional organizations. Address: 19 Broad Street, Ludlow SY8 1NG, England.

CRITCHLOW Donald Thomas, b. 18 May 1948, Pasadena, California, USA. Historian; Educator. m. Patricia E Powers, 18 Feb 1978, 2 daughters. Education: BA, San Francisco State University; MA, PhD, University of California at Berkeley. Appointments: Assistant Professor, North Central College, 1978-81; Assistant Professor, University of Dayton, 1981-83; Associate Professor, University of Notre Dame, 1983-91; Professor, Chair, Saint Louis University, 1991-97. Publications: The Brookings Institution, 1916-1952: Expertise and the Public Interest in a Democratic Society, 1985; Studebaker: The Life and Death of an American Auto Company 1852-1963, 1990; Intended Consequences: Birth Control, Abortion and the Federal Government in Modern America, 1999. Honours include: USIA, AmParts Distinguished Lecturer, 1988-89; USIA Grant, 1995; Fellow, Woodrow Wilson International Center for Scholars, 1996-97, Fulbright Scholars Program, University of Hong Kong, 1997-98. Address: 7175 Washington Avenue, St Louis, MO 63031, USA.

CROCOMBE Ronald Gordon, b. 8 Oct 1929, Auckland, New Zealand. m. Marjorie Tuainekore Crocombe, 7 Apr 1959, 3 sons, 1 daughter. Education: BA, Victoria University, 1955; PhD, Australian National University, 1961. Appointments: Director, Institute of Pacific Studies, University of the South Pacific, 1976-85; Chairman of Judges, Asia/Pacific Region, Commonwealth Writers Prize, 1987, 1988. Publications: Land Tenure in the Pacific, 1971, revised edition, 1987; The South Pacific, 1973, 5th edition, revised, 1989; The Pacific Way, 1976; Foreign Forces in Pacific Politics, 1983; Pacific Universities, 1988; Pacific Neighbours, 1992; The Pacific Islands and the USA, 1995. Contributions to: Numerous professional and academic journals. Memberships: South Pacific Social Sciences Association, past president; Pacific History Association, past president; South Pacific Creative Arts Society. Address: Box 309, Rarotonga, Cook Islands.

CROFT Andy, b. 13 June 1956, Handforth, Cheshire, England. Poet; Writer. m. Nikki Wray, 4 sons, 2 daughters. Education: BA Honours, 1978, PhD, 1986, University of Nottingham. Appointment: Full-time Lecturer, University of Leeds, 1983-96. Publications: Red Letter Days, 1990; Out of the Old Earth, 1994; The Big Meeting, 1994; Nowhere Special, 1996; Gaps Between Hills, 1996; A Weapon in the Struggle, 1998. Contributions to: The Guardian; The Independent; London Magazine; Marxism Today; Labour History Review; The Listener; The New Statesman. Membership: Chair, Artistic Director, Write Around Festival, 1989-99. Address: c/o Cleveland Arts, Gurney House, Gurney Street, Middlesbrough TS1 1JL, England.

CROFT Julian (Charles Basset), b. 31 May 1941, Newcastle, New South Wales, Australia. Professor; Writer. m. (1) Loretta De Plevitz, 23 Oct 1967, 1 son, (2) Caroline Ruming, 12 Dec 1987, 1 son. Education: BA, University of New South Wales, 1961; MA, University of Newcastle, New South Wales, 1966. Appointments: Lecturer, University of Sierra Leone, 1968-70; Associate Professor, 1970-94, Professor, 1994-, University of New England, Armidale, Australia. Publications: T J Jones, 1975; The Collected Poems of T Harri James (editor with Don Dale-Jones), 1976; Breakfasts in Shanghai (poems), 1984; Their Solitary Way (novel), 1985; The Portable Robert D FitzGerald (editor), 1987; Confessions of a Corinthian, 1991; The Life and Opinions of Tom Collins, 1991. Membership: Association for the Study of Australian Literature. Address: Department of English, University of New England, Armidale 2351, Australia.

CROIZAT Victor John, b. 27 Feb 1919, Tripoli, Libya. US Marine Corps Officer. m. Meda Mary Fletcher, 14 Aug 1947, 1 son, 1 daughter. Education: BS, Syracuse University, 1940; Ecole Superieure de Guene, Paris, 1950; National War College, Washington, DC, 1960; MA, University of California at Los Angeles, 1967. Appointments: Commissioned US Marine Corps, 1940-. Publications: Across the Reef, 1989; Journey Among Warriors, 1997. Contributions to: Marine Corps Gazette; US Naval Institute Proceedings; US Naval History. Address: 217-21 Street, Santa Monica, CA 90402, USA.

CROMWELL Rue LeVelle, b. 17 Nov 1928, Linton, Indiana, USA. Professor; Clinical Psychologist. m. Ginni H Zhang, 9 July 1987, 2 sons, 1 adopted, 3 daughters. Education: AB Psychology, Indiana University, 1950; MA, Clinical Psychology, 1952, PhD, Clinical Psychology, 1955, Ohio State University. Publications: Stress Factors and Myacordial Infarction: Reaction and Recovery, 1977; The Nature of Schizophrenia, 1978; Schizophrenia, 1993. Contributions to: Over 100 to scientific refereed journals. Address: 1104 Prescott Drive, Lawrence, KS 66049, USA.

CRONIN Anthony, b. 23 Dec 1928, Enniscorthy, County Wexford, Ireland. Author; Poet. m. Theresa Campbell, 1955, 1 daughter. Education: BA, University College, Dublin, 1948. Appointments: Visiting Lecturer, University of Montana, 1966-68; Poet-in-Residence, Drake University, 1968-70; Columnist, Irish Times, 1973-86; Cultural Adviser, Irish Prime Minister. Publications: Poems, 1957; Collected Poems, 1950-73, 1973; Reductionist Poem, 1980; RMS Titanic, 1981; 41 Sonnet Poems, 1982; New & Selected Poems, 1982; Letter to an Englishman, 1985; The End of the Modern World, 1989. Novels: The Life of Riley, 1964; Identity Papers, 1979. Biography: No Laughing Matter: The Life and Times of Flann O'Brian, 1989. Memoir: Dead as Doornails, 1976. Essays: Heritage Now, 1983; An Irish Eye, 1985; Samuel Beckett: The Last Modernist, 1996. Honour: Marten Toonder Award, 1983. Address: Office of the Taoiseach, Government Buildings, Dublin 2, Ireland.

CRONIN Vincent Archibald Patrick, b. 24 May 1924, Tredegar, Wales. Author. m. Chantal De Rolland, 25 Aug 1949, 2 sons, 3 daughters. Education: Harvard University, 1941-43; BA, Trinity College, Oxford, 1947. Publications: The Golden Honeycomb, 1954; The Wise Man from the West, 1955; The Last Migration, 1957; A Pearl to India, 1959; The Letter after Z, 1960; Louis XIV, 1964; Four Women in Pursuit of an Ideal, 1965; The Florentine Renaissance, 1967; The Flowering of the Renaissance, 1970; Napoleon, 1971; Louis and Antoinette, 1974; Catherine, Empress of all the Russias, 1978; The View from Planet Earth, 1981; Paris on the Eve, 1989; Paris: City of Light 1919-1939, 1995. Address: Manor de Brion, Dragey Par, 50530 Sartilly, France.

CRONON William (John), b. 11 Sept 1954, New Haven, Connecticut, USA. Professor of History, Geography, and Environmental Studies; Author. m. Nancy Elizabeth Fey, 27 Aug 1977, 1 son, 1 daughter. Education: BA, University of Wisconsin at Madison, 1976; MA, 1979, MPhil, 1980, PhD, 1990, Yale University; DPhil, Oxford University, 1981. Appointments: Assistant Professor, 1981-86, Associate Professor, 1986-91, Professor of History, 1991-92, Yale University; Frederick Jackson Turner Professor of History, Geography, and Environmental Studies, University of Wisconsin at Madison, 1992-. Publications: Changes in the Land: Indians, Colonists, and the Ecology of New England, 1983; Nature's Metropolis: Chicago and the Great West, 1991; Under an Open Sky: Rethinking America's Western Past (co-editor with George Miles and Jay Gitlin), 1992; Uncommon Ground: Toward Reinventing Nature (editor), 1995. Contributions to: Books and scholarly journals. Honours: Rhodes Scholarship, 1976-78; Francis Parkman Prize, 1984; John D and Catherine T MacArthur Foundation Residences, 1961-62, 1985-90; Bancroft Prize, 1992; George Perkins Marsh Prize, American Society for Environmental History, 1992; Charles A Weyerhaeuser Award, Forest History Society, 1993; Guggenheim Fellowship, 1995. Memberships: Agricultural History Society; American Anthropological Association; American Antiquarian Society; American Historical Association; American Society for Environmental History; American Society for Ethnohistory; American Studies Association; Association of American Geographers; Ecological Society of America; Economic History Association; Forest History Society; Organization of American Historians; Society of American Historians; Urban History Association. Address: c/o Department of History, 3211 Humanities Building, 455 North Park Street, University of Wisconsin at Madison, Madison, WI 53706, USA.

CROOK Joseph Mordaunt, b. 27 Feb 1937, London, England. Professor of Architectural History; Writer. m. (1) Margaret Mullholland, 1964, (2) Susan Mayor, 9 July 1975. Education: Wimbledon College; BA, 1st Class, Modern History, 1958, DPhil, 1961, MA, 1962, Oxford University. Appointments: Research Fellow, Institute of Historical Residences 1961-61, Research Fellow, 1962-63, Bedford College, London, 1962-63, Warburg Institute, London, 1970-71; Assistant Lecturer, University of Leicester, 1963-65; Lecturer, 1965-75, Reader in Architectural History, 1975-81, Bedford College, London; Editor, Architectural History, 1967-75; Slade Professor of Fine Art, Oxford University, 1979-80; Visiting Fellow, Brasenose College, Oxford, 1979-80, Humanities Research Centre, Australian National University, Canberra, 1985, Gonville and Caius College, Cambridge, 1986; Professor of Architectural History, 1981-, Director, Victorian Studies, 1990-, Universityu of London at Royal Holloway; Waynflete Lecturer and Visiting Fellow, Magdalen College, Oxford, 1984-85; Public Orator, University of London, 1988-90; Humanities Fellow, Princeton University, 1990; Director, Victorian Studies, Royal Holloway and Bedford New College, 1990-. Publications: The Greek Revival, 1968; Victorian Architecture: A Visual Anthology, 1971; The British Museum, 1972, 2nd edition, 1973; The Greek Revival: Neo-Classical Attitudes in British Architecture 1760-1870, 1973, 2nd edition, 1995; The Reform Club, 1973; The History of the King' Works (co-author), Vol VI, 1973, Vol V, 1976; William Burges and the High Victorian Dream, 1981; Axel Haig and the Victorian Vision of the Middle Ages (co-author), 1984; The Dilemma of Style: Architectural Ideas from the Picturesque to the Post-Modern, 1987, 2nd edition, 1989; John Carter and the Mind of the Gothic Revival, 1995. Editor: Eastlake: A History of the Gothic Revival, 1970, revised edition, 1978; Emmet: Six Essays, 1972; Kerr: The Gentleman's House, 1972; The Strange Genius of William Burges, 1981; Clark: The Gothic Revival, 1995. Contributions to: Books and scholarly journals. Honours: Hitchcock Medallion, 1974; Freeman, 1979, Liveryman, 1984, Worshipful Company of Goldsmiths. Memberships: British Academy, Fellow, 1988-, council, 1989-92; Historic Buildings Council for England, 1974-80; Society of Architectural Historians of Great Britain, executive committee, 1964-77, President, 1980-84; Victorian Society, executive committee, 1970-77, council, 1978-88. Address: 55 Gloucester Avenue, London NW1 7BA, England.

CROSBY Harry Clifton, (Christopher Anvil), b. 1925, USA. Writer. m. Joy Dolores Douglas, 5 June 1949, 1 son, 1 daughter. Education: Williams College; Juniata College. Publications: Mind Partner, novella, 1960; The Day the Machines Stopped, 1964; Strangers in Paradise, 1969; Pandora's Planet, 1972; Warlord's World, 1975; The Steel, the Mist, and the Blazing Sun, 1980. Contributions to: Magazines and Journals: Analog; Galaxy; Magazine of Fantasy and Science Fiction; Playboy; Ellery Queen's Mystery Magazine; Alfred Hitchcock's Mystery Magazine; Shell Scott's Mystery Magazine; Science Fiction Adventures; Imagination; Venture; Amazing; If; Adam; Worlds of Tomorrow; and others. Literary Agent: Scott Meredith Agency, 1962-96. Address: 300 Crosby Road, Cayuta, NY 14824, USA.

CROSLAND Margaret (McQueen), b. 17 June 1920, Bridgnorth, Shropshire, England. Writer; Translator. m. Max Denis, 1950, div 1959, 1 son. Education: BA, University of London, 1941. Publications: Strange Tempe (poems), 1946; Madame Colette: A Provincial in Paris, 1953; Jean Cocteau, 1955; Ballet Carnival: A Companion to Ballet, 1955, new edition, 1957; Home Book of Opera, 1957; Ballet Lover's Dictionary, 1962; Louise of Stolberg, Countess of Albany, 1962; The Young Ballet Lover's Companion, 1962; Philosophy Pocket Crammer, 1964;

Colette-The Difficulty of Loving: A Biography, 1973; Raymond Radiguet: A Biographical Study with Selections from His Work, 1976; Women of Iron and Velvet: French Women Writers after George Sand, 1976; Beyond the Lighthouse: English Women Novelists in the Twentieth Century, 1981; Piaf, 1985; The Passionate Philosopher: A de Sade Reader, 1991; Simone de Beauvoir, The Woman and Her Work, 1992; Sade's Wife, 1995. Editor: Marquis de Sade: Selected Letters, 1965; A Traveller's Guide to Literary Europe, 1965; Jean Cocteau: My Contemporaries, 1967; Cocteau's World: An Anthology of Major Writings by Jean Cocteau, 1972. Translator: Over 30 books. Honours: Prix de Bourgogne, France, 1973-74; Enid McLeod Prize, Franco-British Society, 1992-93. Membership: Society of Authors. Literary Agent: Jeffrey Simmons. Address: 25 Thornton Meadow, Wisborough Green, Billingshurst RH 14 0BW, England.

CROSS Anthony Glenn, b. 21 Oct 1936, Nottingham, England. Professor of Slavonic Studies; Writer; Editor. m. Margaret Elson, 11 Aug 1960, 2 daughters. Education: BA, 1960, MA, 1964, PhD, 1966, Trinity Hall, Cambridge; AM, Harvard University, 1961; LittD, University of East Anglia, 1981; LittD, Fitzwilliam College, Cardiff, 1997. Appointments: Lecturer, 1964-69, Senior Lecturer, 1969-72, Reader in Russian, 1972-81, University of East Anglia; Visiting Fellow, University of Illinois, 1969-70, All Souls College, Oxford, 1977-78; Reviews Editor, Journal of European Studies, 1971-; Editor, Study Group on Eighteenth-Century Russia Newsletter, 1973-; Roberts Professor of Russian, University of Leeds, 1981-85; Chairman, British Academic Committee for Liaison with Soviet Archives, 1983-95; Professor of Slavonic Studies, 1985-, Fellow, 1986-, Fitzwilliam College, University of Cambridge. Publications: N M Karamzin, 1971; Russia Under Western Eyes 1517-1825, 1971; Russian Literature in the Age of Catherine the Great (editor), 1976; Anglo-Russian Relations in the Eighteenth Century, 1977; Great Britain and Russia in the Eighteenth Century (editor), 1979; By the Banks of the Thames, 1980; Russian and the West in the Eighteenth Century (editor), 1981; The Tale of the Russian Daughter and her Suffocated Lover, 1982; Eighteenth Century Russian Literature, Culture and Thought: A Bibliography (joint editor), 1984; The Russian Theme in English Literature, 1985; Russia and the World of the Eighteenth Century (joint editor), 1988; An English Lady at the Court of Catherine the Great (editor), 1989; Anglophilia on the Throne: The British and the Russians in the Age of Catherine II, 1992; Engraved in the Memory: James Walker, Engraver to Catherine the Great and his Russian Anecdotes (editor), 1993; Anglo-Russian: Aspects of Anglo-Russian Cultural Relations in the Eighteenth and Early Nineteenth Centuries, 1993; Literature, Lives and Legality in Catherine's Russia (joint editor), 1994; By the Banks of the Neva: Chapters From the Lives of the British in Eighteenth-Century Russia, 1996; Russia in the Reign of Peter the Great: Old and New Perspectives (editor), 1998. Contributions to: Scholarly journals. Honours: Frank Knox Fellow, Harvard University, 1960-61; British Academy, fellow, 1989; Academician, Russian Academy of the Humanities, 1995; Antsiferov Prize, St Petersburg, 1998. Membership: British Universities Association of Slavists, president, 1982-84. Address: c/o Department of Slavonic Studies, University of Cambridge, Sidgwick Avenue, Cambridge CB3 9DA, England.

CROSS Brenda. See: COLLOMS Brenda.

CROSS Gillian Clare, b. 10 May 1967. m. Martin Cross, 1967, 2 sons, 2 daughters. Education: BA, Oxford, Class 1, Somerville College, Oxford, 1969; DPhil, University of Sussex, 1973. Publications include: Wolf, 1990; Gobbo the Great, 1991; Rent-A-Genius, 1991; The Great Elephant Chase, 1992; The Furry Maccaloo, 1993; Beware Olga, 1993; The Tree House, 1993; Hunky Parker is Watching You, 1994; What Will Emily Do?, 1994; The Crazy Shoe Shuffle, 1995; Posh Watson, 1995; The Roman Beanfeast, 1996; Pictures in the Dark, 1996; The Demon Headmaster Strikes Again, 1996; The Return of the Demon Headmaster, 1997; The Demon Headmaster Takes Over, 1997; Tightrope, 1999. Honours: Overall Winner, Smarties Prize, The Great

Elephant Chase, 1992; Winner, Whitbread Children's Novel Award, The Great Elephant Chase, 1992; Winner, Library Association's Carnegie Medal for WOLF, 1990. Memberships: Society of Authors; Advisory Council on Libraries. Hobbies: Orienteering; Playing the Piano. Address: c/o Oxford Children's Books, Oxford University Press, Great Clarendon St, Oxford OX2 6DP, England.

CROSS Victor. See: COFFMAN Virginia (Edith).

CROSSAN John Dominic, b. 17 Feb 1934, Nenagh, County Tipperary, Ireland. Theologian; Author; Professor Emeritus. Education: Philosophy and Theology, Stonebridge Priory, Lake Bluff, Illinois, 1951-57; DD, Maynooth College, Kildare, Ireland, 1959; Diploma, Sacred Scripturre Licentiate, Pontifical Biblical Institute, Rome, 1961; Diploma, Ecole Biblique, Jerusalem, 1966. Appointments: Member, Servites religious order, 1950-69; Ordained Roman Catholic Priest, 1957-69; Assistant Professor of Biblical Studies, Stonebridge Priory, Lake Bluff, Illinois, 1961-65; Assistant Professor of Biblical Studies, Stonebridge Priory, Lake Bluff, Illinois, 1961-65; Assistant Professor of Biblical Studies, Mundelein Seminary, Illinois, 1967-68, Catholic Theological Union, Chicago, 1968-69; Associate Professor, 1969-73, Professor of Religious Studies, 1973-95, Professor Emeritus, 1995-, DePaul University, Chicago; Chair, Parables Seminar, 1972-75; Editor, Semeia: An Experimental Journal for Biblical Criticism, 1980-86; Co-Chair, Jesus Seminar, 1985-96; Croghan Bicentennial Visiting Professor of Religion, Williams College, Williamstown, Massachusetts, 1996. Publications: Scanning the Sunday Gospel, 1966; The Gospel of Eternal Life, 1967; In Parables: The Challenge of the Historical Jesus, 1973; The Dark Interval: Towards a Theology of Story, 1975; Raid on the Articulate: Comic Eschatology in Jesus and Borges, 1976; Finding Is the First Act: Trove Folktales and Jesus' Treasure Parable, 1979; Cliffs of Fall: Paradox and Polyvalence in the Parables of Jesus, 1980; A Fragile Craft: The Work of Amos Niven Wilder, 1981; In Fragments: The Aphorisms of Jesus, 1983; Four Other Gospels: Shadows on the Contours of Canon, 1985; Sayings Parallels: A Workbook for the Jesus Tradition, 1986; The Cross that Spoke: The Origins of the Passion Narrative, 1988; The Historical Jesus: The Life of a Mediterranean Jewish Peasant, 1991; Jesus: A Revolutionary Biography, 1994; The Essential Jesus: Original Sayings and Earliest Images, 1994; Who Killed Jesus?: Exposing the Roots of Anti-Semitism in the Gospel Story of the Death of Jesus, 1995; Who is Jesus?: Answers to Your Questions about the Historical Jesus, 1996; The Birth of Christianity, 1998. Contributions to: Many scholarly books and journals. Honours: American Academy of Religion Award for Excellence in Religious Studies, 1989; Via Sapientiae Award, DePaul University, 1995. Memberships: American Academy of Religion; Catholic Biblical Association; Chicago Society of Biblical Research, president, 1978-79; Society of Biblical Literature; Studiorum Novi Testamenti Societas. Address: 608 South Main Avenue, No 31, Clermont, FL 34711, USA.

CROSSLEY-HOLLAND Kevin, (John William), b. 7 Feb 1941, Mursley, Buckinghamshire, England. Professor; Poet; Writer; Editor; Translator. Education: MA, St Edmund Hall, Oxford. Appointments: Editor, Macmillan & Co, 1962-69; Lecturer in English, Tufts-in-London Program, 1967-78, University of Regensburg, 1978-80; Gregory Fellow in Poetry, University of Leeds, 1969-71; Talks Producer, BBC, 1972; Editorial Director, Victor Gollancz, 1972-77; Arts Council Fellow in Writing, Winchester School of Arts, 1983, 1984; Visiting Professor of English and Fulbright Scholar-in-Residence, St Olaf College, Minnesota, 1987-90; Professor and Endowed Chair in Humanities and Fine Arts, University of St Thomas, St Paul, Minnesota, 1991-95; Director, American Composers Forum, 1993-97. Publications: Poetry: The Rain-Giver, 1972; The Dream-House, 1976; Time's Oriel, 1983; Waterslain, 1986; The Painting-Room, 1988; New and Selected Poems, 1991; The Language of Yes, 1996; Poems from East Anglia, 1997. For Children: Havelok the Dane, 1964; King Horn, 1965; The Green Children, 1966;

The Callow Pit Coffer, 1968; Wordhoard (with Jill Paton Walsh), 1969; Storm and Other Old English Riddles, 1970; The Pedlar of Swaffham, 1971; The Sea Stranger, 1973; The Fire-Brother, 1974; Green Blades Rising, 1975; The Earth-Father, 1976; The Wildman, 1976; The Dead Moon, 1982; Beowulf, 1982; The Mabinogion (with Gwyn Thomas), 1984; Axe-Age Wolf-Age, 1985; Storm, 1985; The Fox and the Cat (with Susanne Lugert), 1985; British Folk Tales, 1987; Wulf, 1988; The Quest for the Olwen (with Gwyn Thomas), 1988; Piper and Pooka, 1988; Small Tooth Dog, 1988; Boo!, 1988; Dathera Dad, 1989; Under the Sun and Over the Moon (with Ian Penney), 1989; Sleeping Nanna, 1989; Sea Tongue, 1991; Tales from Europe, 1991; Long Tom and the Dead Hand, 1992; Taliesin (with Gwyn Thomas), 1992; The Labours of Herakles, 1993; Norse Myths, 1993; The Green Children, 1994; The Dark Horseman, 1995; Short!, 1998; The King Who Was and Will Be, 1998. Non-Fiction: Pieces of Land, 1972; The Norse Myths, 1980; The Stones Remain (with Andrew Rafferty, 1989. Editor: Running to Paradise, 1967; Winter's Tales for Children 3, 1967; Winter's Tales 14, 1968; New Poetry 2 (with Patricia Beer), 1976; The Faber Book of Northern Legends, 1977; The Faber Book of Northern Folk-Tales, 1980; The Anglo-Saxon World, 1982; The Riddle Book, 1982; Folk-Tales of the British Isles, 1985; The Oxford Book of Travel Verse, 1986; Northern Lights, 1987; Medieval Lovers, 1988; Medieval Gardens, 1990; Peter Grimes by George Crabbe, 1990; The Young Oxford Book of Folk Tales, 1998. Translations from Old English: The Battle of Maldon (with Bruce Mitchell), 1965; Beowulf (with Bruce Mitchell), 1968; The Exeter Book Riddles, 1978; The Illustrated Beowulf, 1987; The Anglo-Saxon Elegies, 1988. Opera Libretti: The Green Children (with Nicola LeFanu), 1990; The Wildman (with Nicola LeFanu), 1995. Contributions to: Numerous journals and magazines. Honours: Arts Council Awards, Best Book for Young Children, 1966-68; Poetry Book Society Choice, 1976, and Recommendation, 1986; Carnegie Medal, 1985; Royal Society of Literature, fellow, 1998. Address: Clare Cottage, Burnham Market PE31 8HE, Norfolk, England.

CROWDER Ashby Bland Jr, b. 29 June 1941, Richmond, Virginia, USA. Professor; Writer. m. Lynn O'Malley, 10 Mar 1973, 1 son. Education: BA, Randolph-Macon College, 1963; MA, University of Tennessee, 1965; PhD, University of London, 1972. Appointments: Instructor, Centre College, Danville, Kentucky, 1965-67; Assistant Professor, Eastern Kentucky University, 1969-74; Professor, Hendrix College, 1974-; Chairman, Department of English, Hendrix College, 1998-. Publications: Writing in the Southern Tradition, Interviews with Five Contemporary Authors, 1990; Poets and Critics: Their Means and Meanings, 1993; The Complete Works of Robert Browning XIII, 1995. Contributions to: South Dakota Review; Papers on Language and Literature; Studies in Browning and His Circle; Thomas Hardy Review; Victorian Studies; Southern Quarterly; Southern Review; Mississippi Quarterly; Browning Institute Studies; Browning Society Notes; The Wallace Stevens Journal; Explicator; Poetry in English; Cumberland Poetry Review; Adena; Cloverdale Review; Slant. Honours: Andrew Mellon Fellowship; National Endowment for Humanities Fellowships. Memberships: Thomas Hardy Society; South Atlantic Modern Language Association; Arkansas Literary Society. Address: 109 Crystal Court, Little Rock, AR 72205, USA.

CROWE John. See: **LYNDS Dennis.**

CROWLEY John, b. 1 Dec 1942, Presque Isle, Maine, USA. Writer. Education: BA, Indiana University, 1964. Publications: The Deep, 1975; Beasts, 1976; Engine Summer, 1979; Little Big, 1981; Aegypt, 1987; Novelty (short stories), 1989; Great Work of Time, 1991; Antiquities: Seven Stories, 1993; Love and Sleep, 1994. Other: Film Scripts; Television scripts, including America Lost and Found, and No Place to Hide. Contributions to: Periodicals. Honours: American Film Festival Award, 1982; American Academy and Institute of Arts and

Letters Fellow, 1992. Address: Box 395, Conway, MA 01341, USA.

CROZIER Andrew, b. 1943, England. Poet; Senior Lecturer in English. Education: MA, University of Cambridge; PhD, University of Essex. Appointment: Senior Lecturer in English, University of Sussex. Publications: Poetry: Love Litter of Time Spent, 1967; Train Rides: Poems from '63 and '64, 1968; Walking on Grass, 1969; In One Side and Out the Other (with John James and Tom Phillips), 1970; Neglected Information, 1973; The Veil Poem, 1974; Printed Circuit, 1974; Seven Contemporary Sun Dials (with Ian Potts), 1975; Pleats, 1975; Duets, 1976; Residing, 1976; High Zero, 1978; Were There, 1978; Utamaro Variations, 1982; All Where Each Is, 1985; Ghosts in the Corridor (with Donald Davie and C H Sisson), 1992. Other: A Various Art (editor with Tim Longville), 1987. Address: c/o University of Sussex, Falmer, Brighton, Sussex BN1 9RH, England.

CROZIER Brian Rossiter, (John Rossiter), b. 4 Aug 1918, Kuridala, Queensland, Australia. Journalist; Writer; Consultant. m. Mary Lillian Samuel, 7 Sept 1940, dec 1993, 1 son, 3 daughters. Education: Lycée, Montpellier; Peterborough College, Harrow; Trinity College of Music, London. Appointments: Music and Art Critic, London, 1936-39; Reporter, Sub-Editor, Stoke-on-Trent, Stockport, London, 1940-41; Sub-Editor, Reuters, 1943-44, News Chronicle, 1944-48; Sub-Editor and Writer, Sydney Morning Herald, 1948-51; Correspondent, Reuters-AAP, 1951-52; Features Editor, Straits Times, 1952-53; Leader Writer, Correspondent, and Editor, Foreign Report, The Economist, 1954-64; Commentator, BBC English, French, and Spanish Overseas Services, 1954-66; Chairman, Forum World Features, 1965-74; Co-Founder and Director, Institute for the Study of Conflict, 1970-79; Columnist, National Review, New York, 1978-94; Columnist, Now!, 1979-81, The Times, 1982-83, The Free Nation, later Freedom Today, 1982-89; Adjunct Scholar, Heritage Foundation, Washington, DC, 1984-95; Distinguished Visiting Fellow, Hoover Institution, Stanford, California, 1996-. Publications: The Rebels, 1960; The Morning After, 1963; Neo-Colonialism, 1964; South-East Asia in Turmoil, 1965, 3rd edition, 1968; The Struggle for the Third World, 1966; Franco, 1967; The Masters of Power, 1969; The Future of Communist Power (US edition as Since Stalin), 1970; De Gaulle, 2 volumes, 1973, 1974; A Theory of Conflict, 1974; The Man Who Lost China (Chiang Kai-shek), 1976; Strategy of Survival, 1978; The Minimum State, 1979; Franco: Crepúsculo de un hombre, 1980; The Price of Peace, 1980, new edition, 1983; Socialism Explained (co-author), 1984; This War Called Peace (co-author), 1984; The Andropov Deception (novel published under the name John Rossiter), 1984 (published in the US under own name), 1986; Socialism: Dream and Reality, 1987; The Grenada Documents (editor), 1987; The Gorbachev Phenomenon, 1990; Communism: Why Prolong its Death-Throes?, 1990; Free Agent, 1993; The KGB Lawsuits, 1995; Le Phénix Rouge (Paris) (co-author), 1995. Contributions to: Numerous journals. Address: Flat AA, 1 Carlisle Place, London SW1P 1NP, England.

CROZIER Lorna, b. 24 May 1948, Swift Current, Saskatchewan, Canada. Associate Professor; Poet. Education: BA, University of Saskatchewan, 1969; MA, University of Alberta, 1980. Appointments: Creative Writing Teacher, Saskatchewan Summer School of the Arts, Fort San, 1977-81; Writer-in-Residence, Cypress Hills Community College, Swift Current, 1980-81, Regina Public Library, Saskatchewan, 1984-85, University of Toronto, 1989-90; Broadcaster and Writer, CBC Radio, 1986; Guest Instructor, Banff School of Fine Arts, Alberta, 1986, 1987; Special Lecturer, University of Saskatchewan, 1986-91; Associate Professor, University of Victoria, British Columbia, 1991-. Publications: Inside is the Sky, 1976; Crow's Black Joy, 1978; No Longer Two People (with Patrick Lane), 1979; Animals of Fall, 1979; Humans and Other Beasts, 1980; The Weather, 1983; The Garden Going On Without Us, 1985; Angels of Flesh, Angels of Silence, 1988; Inventing the Hawk, 1992; Everything Arrives at the Light, 1995; A Saving Grace: The Collected Poems of Mrs Bentley, 1996. Editor: A

Sudden Radiance: Saskatchewan Poetry (with Gary Hyland), 1987; Breathing Fire: The New Generation of Canadian Poets (with Patrick Lane), 1995. Honours: CBC Prize, 1987; Governor General's Award for Poetry, 1992; Canadian Author's Award for Poetry, 1992; Pat Lowther Awards, League of Canadian Poets, 1992, 1996; National Magazine Award Gold Medal, 1996. Membership: Saskatchewan Writers' Guild. Address: c/o McClelland and Stewart Inc, 481 University Avenue, Suite 900, Toronto, Ontario M5G 2E9, Canada.

CRUMEY Andrew David William Bernard, b. 12 Oct 1961, Glasgow, Scotland. Writer. m. Mary Argyraki, 28 Aug 1993, 1 son. Education: BSc, Honours 1st Class, Imperial College, London, 1983-86; PhD, Physics. Appointments: Care Worker, 1987-88; Research Associate, Imperial College and Leeds University, 1989-92; School Teacher, Newcastle upon Tyne, 1992-96; Writer, 1996-. Publictions: Music in a Foreign Language (novel), 1994; Pfitz (novel), 1995; D'Alembert's Principle (novel), 1996. Honour: Saltire Society Award for Best First Book, 1994. Literary Agent: Bill Hamilton, A M Heath & Co, 79 St Martin's Lane, London WC2N 4AA. Address: 12 Beatty Avenue, Newcastle upon Tyne NE2 3QP, England.

CRYSTAL David, b. 6 July 1941, Lisburn, County Antrim, Northern Ireland. Writer; Editor. m. (1) Molly Stack, 1 Apr 1964, dec 1976, 2 sons, 2 daughters, (2) Hilary Norman, 18 Sept 1976, 1 son. Education: BA, 1962, PhD, 1966, FCST, 1983, University College, London. Appointments: Assistant Lecturer, University College of North Wales, 1963-65; Lecturer and Reader, 1965-76, Professor of Linguistic Science, 1976-85, University of Reading; Professorial Fellow, University of Wales, Bangor, 1985-; Editor, Child Language Teaching and Therapy, 1985-96, Linguistics Abstracts, 1985-96; Consultant Editor, English Today, 1986-94. Publications include: Linguistics, Language and Religion, 1965; What Is Linguistics?, 3rd edition, 1974; The English Tone of Voice, 1975; Child Language, Learning and Linguistics, 1976; Working with LARSP, 1979; Eric Partridge: In His Own Words, 1980; A Dictionary of Linguistics and Phonetics, 1980, 4th edition, 1997; Introduction to Language Pathology, 1980, 4th edition, 1998; Clinical Linguistics, 1981; Directions in Applied Linguistics, 1981; Linguistic Controversies, 1981; Profiling Linguistic Disability, 1982; Linguistic Encounters with Language Handicap, 1984; Language Handicap in Children, 1984; Who Cares About English Usage?, 1984; Listen to Your Child, 1986; The English Language, 1988; Cambridge Encyclopedia of Language, 1987, 2nd edition, 1997; Rediscover Grammar, 1988, 2nd edition, 1996; The Cambridge Encyclopedia, 1990, 3rd edition, 1997; Language A-Z, 1991; Nineties Knowledge, 1992; An Encyclopedic Dictionary of Language and Languages, 1992, 2nd edition, 1999; The Cambridge Factfinder, 1993, 3rd edition, 1998; The Cambridge Biographical Encyclopaedia, 1994, 2nd edition, 1998; The Cambridge Encyclopedia of the English Language, 1995; Discover Grammar, 1996; English as a Global Language, 1997; Language Play, 1998. Children's Non-fiction books. Honour: Officer of the Order of the British Empire, 1995. Address: Akaroa, Gors Avenue, Holyhead, Anglesey, LL65 1PB, Wales.

CSERES Tibor, b. 1 Apr 1915, Gyergyoremete, Tras, Hungary. Writer. m. Nora Ulkey, 15 Nov 1944, 1 daughter. Education: University of Economics, Kolozsvar. Publications: Cold Days, 1964; Players and Lovers, 1970; I, Lajos Kossuth, 1980; Pass of Foksany, 1985; Battles of Vizamua, 1988; Vendeta in Backa, 1991. Honours: Kossuth Prize, 1975; Order of Flag, Hungarian Republic, 1990. Memberships: Hungarian Writers Association, president, 1986-89; Hungarian Writers Chamber, president; Hungarian Academy of Literature and Arts. Address: Orlo 14, 1026 Budapest II, Hungary.

CSOORI Sándor, b. 3 Feb 1930, Zámoly, Hungary. Poet; Writer. Education: Lenin Institute, Budapest, 1951. Appointments: Editor, Uj hang journal, 1955-56; Active in the opposition movement from 1980; Founding member, 1987, Presidium member, 1988-92, Hungarian

Democratic Forum; Chairman, Illyés Gyula Foundation, 1990-94; President, World Federation of Hungarians, 1991-. Publications: In English Translation: Poetry: Wings of Knives and Nails, 1981; Memory of Snow, 1983; Barbarian Prayer: Selected Poems, 1989; Selected Poems of Sándor Csoóri, 1992. Other: Fiction, non-fiction, and screenplays. Contributions to: Various publications. Honours: Attila József, 1954; Cannes Film Festival Prizes, 1964, 1968; Herder Prize, Vienna, 1981; Kossuth Prize, 1990; Eeva Joenpelto Prize, 1995. Address: Semmelweis u. 1-3, 1052 Budapest, Hungary.

CULPER Felix. See: **MCCAUGHREAN Geraldine Margaret.**

CUMBERLEGE Marcus (Crossley), b. 23 Dec 1938, Antibes, France. Poet; Translator. m. (1) Ava Nicole Paranjoti, 11 Dec 1965, div 1972, (2) Maria Lefever, 9 Nov 1973, 1 daughter. Education: BA, St John's College, Oxford, 1961. Appointments: Lecturer, Universities of Hilversum and Lugano, 1978-83. Publications: Oases, 1968; Poems for Quena and Tabla, 1970; Running Towards a New Life, 1973; Bruges, Bruges (with Owen Davis), 1975; Firelines, 1977; The Poetry Millionaire, 1977; La Nuit Noire, 1977; Twintig Vriendelijke Vragen (with Horst de Blaere), 1977; Northern Lights, 1981; Life is a Flower, 1981; Vlaamse Fables, 1982; Sweet Poor Hobo, 1984; Things I Cannot Change, 1993; The Best Is Yet To Be, 1997. Honour: Eric Gregory Award, 1967. Address: Eekhoutstraat 42, 8000 Bruges, Belgium.

CUMMING Peter E, b. 23 Mar 1951, Brampton, Ontario, Canada. Writer; Dramatist; Teacher. m. Mary Shelleen Nelson, 14 Oct 1970. Education: BA, English Literature, 1972; Diploma in Education, 1976; MA, English Literature, 1992. Appointments: Resident Artist in Drama, Wilfrid Laurier University, 1972-73; Executive Director, Atlantic Publishers Association, 1984-85. Publications: Snowdreams, 1982; Ti-Jean, 1983; A Horse Called Farmer, 1984; Mogul and Me, 1989; Out on the Ice in the Middle of the Bay, 1993. Contributions to: Contributing editor, Quill and Quire, 1982-84. Honours: 1st Prize, Children's Prose, 1980, 1st Prize, Adult Fiction, 1981, Writers Federation of Nova Scotia; Toronto Board of Education Canada Day Playwriting Competition, 1981; Our Choice, Children's Book Centre, 1984, 1989, 1993; Hilroy Award for Innovative Teaching, 1990; George Wicken Prize in Canadian Literature, 1994; Tiny Torgi Award, 1995. Memberships: Playwrights Union of Canada; Writers Union of Canada; Canadian Society of Children's Authors, Illustrators, and Performers; Association of Canadian College and University Teachers of English. Address: 201 Front Street, Stratford, Ontario N5A 4H8, Canada.

CUMMINGS David Michael, b. 10 Oct 1942, London, England. Lexicographer; Teacher. m. Anne Marie Zammit-Tabona, 1970, 2 sons, 1 daughter. Education: Dartington Hall School, 1953-60; BEd, Honours, Sidney Webb College, London, 1975. Appointments: School Teacher, 1975-; Lexicographer, 1980-. Publications: The New Everyman Dictionary of Music (editor), 6th edition, 1988; International Who's Who in Music (editor), 12th-16th editions, 1990-98; The Hutchinson Encyclopedia of Music (editor), book and CD versions, 1995; International Authors and Writers Who's Who (consultant editor), 14th-15th editions, 1984; The Oxford Dictionary of Music, 1985, 1994; The Grove Concise Dictionary of Music, 1988; The Penguin Dictionary of Musical Performers, 1990; Grosses Sängerlexikon (Ergänzungsband), 1991-93; The New Grove Dictioinary of Opera, 4 volumes, 1992; The Concise Oxford Dictionary of Opera, 1996. Address: 33 Herga Court, Sudbury Hill, Harrow, HA1 3RS, England

CUMMINS Walter (Merrill), b. 6 Feb 1936, Long Branch, New Jersey, USA. Professor of English; Writer; Editor. m. (1) Judith Gruenberg, 14 June 1957, div 1981, (2) Alison Cunningham, 14 Feb 1981, 2 daughters. Education: BA, Rutgers University, 1957; MA, 1962, MFA, 1962, PhD, 1965, University of Iowa. Appointments: Instructor, University of Iowa, 1962-65; Assistant Professor, 1965-69, Associate Professor, 1969-74, Professor of English, 1974-, Fairleigh Dickinson University; Associate Editor, 1978-83, Editor-in-Chief, 1983-, The Literary Review. Publications: A Stranger to the Deed (novel), 1968; Into Temptation (novel), 1968; The Other Sides of Reality: Myths, Visions and Fantasies (co-editor), 1972; Student Writing Guide (co-editor), 1973; Witness (stories), 1975; Managing Management Climate (with George G Gordon), 1979; Where We Live (stories), 1983; Shifting Borders: East European Poetry of the Eighties (editor), 1993. Contributions to: Stories, articles, and reviews in many publications. Honours: New Jersey State Council on the Arts Fellowship, 1982-83; National Endowment for the Arts Grants, 1987-88, 1990-91. Membership: American Association of University Professors. Address: 6 Hanover Road, Florham Park, NJ 07932, USA.

CUNLIFFE Barrington (Windsor), (Barry Cunliffe), b. 10 Dec 1939, Portsmouth, Hampshire, England. Archaeologist; Professor; Writer. m. Margaret Herdman, 5 Jan 1979, 1 son, 1 daughter. Education: BA, 1961, MA, 1963, PhD, 1966, LittD, 1976, St John's College, Cambridge. Appointments: Lecturer in Classics, University of Bristol, 1963-66; Professor of Archaeology, University of Southampton, 1966-72; Professor of European Archaeology and Fellow of Keble College, Oxford, 1972-; Commissioner, Historic Buildings and Monuments Commission for England, 1987-92; Governor, Museum of London, 1995-97. Publications: Excavations at Richborough, Vol 5, 1968; Roman Bath (editor), 1969; Excavations at Fishbourne, 1961-69, 2 volumes, 1971 Fishbourne: A Roman Palace and its Gardens, 1971; Roman Baths Discovered, 1971, 2nd edition, 1984; Guide to the Roman Remains of Bath, 1971; The Cradle of England, 1972; The Making of the English, 1973; The Regni, 1974; Iron Age Communities in Britain: An Account of England, Scotland, and Wales from the Seventh Century B C until the Roman Conquest, 1974, 3rd edition, 1991; Excavations at Porchester Castle, Hants, 5 volumes, 1975, 1976, 1977, 1985, 1994; Rome and the Barbarians, 1975; Oppida: The Beginnings of Urbanisation in Barbarian Europe (with Trevor Rowley), 1976; Hengistbury Head, 1978; Rome and Her Empire, 1978, 2nd edition, 1994; The Celtic World, 1979, 2nd edition, 1993; Excavating Bath, 1950-75 (editor), 1979; Coinage and Society in Britain and Gaul: Some Current Problems (editor), 1981; Antiquity and Man (editor), 1982; Danebury: Anatomy of an Iron Age Hillfort, 1983; Aspects of the Iron Age in Central Southern Britain (editor with David Miles), 1984; Danebury: An Iron Age Hillfort in Hampshire, Vols 1 and 2, 1984, Vols 4 and 5, 1991; Heywood Sumner's Wessex, 1985; Temple of Sulis Minerva at Bath (with Peter Davenport), Vol I, 1985; The City of Bath, 1986; Hengistbury Head, Darcet, Vol I, 1987; Origins: The Roots of European Civilisation (editor), 1987; Mount Batten, Plymouth: A Prehistoric and Roman Port, 1988; Greeks, Romans & Barbarians: Spheres of Interaction, 1988; Wessex to AD 1000, 1993; The Oxford Illustrated Prehistory of Europe (editor), 1994; Social Complexity and the Development of Towns in Iberia (editor, with S Keay), 1995; The Ancient Celts, 1997; Science and Stonehenge (editor, with C Renfrew), 1997. Contributions to: Periodicals and archaeological journals. Honours: Commander of the Order of the British Empire, 1994; Honorary doctorates. Memberships: British Academy, Fellow; Medieval Society; Prehistoric Society; Royal Archaeological Institute; Society of Antiquaries, fellow, vice president, 1982-86, president 1994-95. Address: Institute of Archaeology, Oxford University, 36 Beaumont Street, Oxford OX1 2PG, England.

CUONZ Romano, b. 25 Aug 1945, Chur, Switzerland. Editor; Publicist. m. Ruth Rothenbühler, 9 Nov 1969, 1 son, 1 daughter. Education: MA, Language Studies, Universities of Zurich, Lausanne, Florence. Appointments: Secondary School Teacher, Cham, Kerns, 1970-78; Editor, Swiss Radio Corporation, and Publicist, 1978-. Publications: Nature Lyric, 1988; Kreuzweg - Wegkreuze, 1990; Abenteuer Nationalpark, for children, 1991; Pax montana - Hotelgeschichten, 1996; Franz Josef Bucher - ein Bauernbub wird Hotelkönig, 1997; Included in various anthologies, 1998-. Contributions to: Regularly to Swiss Radio and various magazines, Switzerland, 1970-. Honours: Federer Books Award, 1988; Jules Gruter Award, 1995. Membership: Author's Guild Group, Olten, Switzerland. Address: Ziegelhuttenstrasse 13, CH-6060 Sarnen, Switzerland.

CURL James Stevens, b. 26 Mar 1937, Belfast, Northern Ireland. Emeritus Professor of Architectural History; Architect; Historian. m. (1) Eileen Elizabeth Blackstock, 1 Jan 1960, div 1986, 2 daughters, (2) Stanisława Dorota Iwaniec 1993. Education: Queen's University, School of Architecture, Belfast, 1954-58; DiplArch, Oxford School of Architecture, 1961-63; Dip TP, Oxford Department of Land Use Studies, 1963-67; PhD, University College, London, 1978-81. Appointment: Emeritus Professor of Architectural History, Senior Research Fellow, De Montfort University, Leicester. Publications: The Victorian Celebration of Death, 1972; City of London Pubs, 1973; The Egyptian Revival, 1982; The Life and Work of Henry Roberts (1803-76), Architect, 1983; The Londonderry Plantation 1609-1914, 1986; English Architecture: An Illustrated Glossary, 1987; Victorian Architecture, 1990; The Art and Architecture of Freemasonry, 1991; Classical Architecture, 1992; Encyclopaedia of Architectural Terms, 1993; Georgian Architecture, 1993; A Celebration of Death, 1993; Egyptomania, 1994; Victorian Churches, 1995. Contributions to: Connaissance des Arts; Country Life; Royal Society of Arts Journal; Architects' Journal; Bauwelt; World of Interiors; Literary Review. Honours: Sir Charles Lanyon Prize, 1956, 1958; Ulster Arts Club Prize, 1958; Baroque Prize, 1962; Society of Antiquaries of London Research Awards, 1979, 1981, 1983; British Academy Research Awards, 1982, 1983; Sir Banister Fletcher Award for Best Book of Year, 1992. Address: 15 Torgrange, Holywood, County Down BT18 0NG, Northern Ireland.

CURLING Audrey. See: **CLARK Marie Catherine Audrey.**

CURNOW (Thomas) Allen (Monro), b. 17 June 1911, Timaru, New Zealand. Poet; Dramatist; Critic; Editor. m. (1) Elizabeth Jaumaud Le Cren, 1936, 2 sons, 1 daughter, (2) Jenifer Mary Tole, 1965. Education: College of St John the Evangelist, 1931-33; BA, University of New Zealand, 1934; LittD, University of Auckland, 1966. Appointments: Staff, The Press, Christchurch, 1935-48, News Chronicle, London, 1949; Senior Lecturer, Associate Professor of English, University of Auckland, 1951-76. Publications: Poetry: Poems 1949-57, 1957; A Small Room with Large Windows: Selected Poems, 1962; Collected Poems 1933-73, 1974; Continuum: New and Later Poems 1971-88, 1988; Selected Poems 1940-89, 1990; Penguin Modern Poets 7 (with Donald Davie and Samuel Menashe), 1996; Early Days Yet: New and Collected Poems, 1941-1997, 1997. Criticism: Look Back Harder, 1987. Editor: A Book of New Zealand Verse, 1945, 2nd edition, 1951; The Penguin Book of New Zealand Verse, 1960. Contributions to: Many journals and reviews. Honours: New Zealand Book Awards for Poetry, 1963, 1975, 1979, 1983, 1987; Katherine Mansfield Memorial Fellowship, 1983; Commander of the Order of the British Empire, 1986; Dillons Commonwealth Poetry Prize, 1989; Queen's Gold Medal for Poetry, 1989; Order of New Zealand, 1990; Cholmondeley Award, 1992. Literary Agent: Curtis Brown. Address: 62 Tohunga Crescent, Parnell, Auckland 1, New Zealand.

CURRAN Colleen, b. 23 Aug 1954, Montreal, Quebec, Canada. Dramatist; Writer; Novelist. Education: BA, Loyola College, Concordia University, 1976; Teacher's Certificate, McGill University, 1981. Appointments: Playwright-in-Residence, Centaur Theatre, Montreal, 1984-85; Co-Artistic Director, Triumvirate Theatre Co, Montreal, 1992-. Publications: Cake-Walk, Villa Eden; Something Drastic, novel. Honours: Dorothy White Playwrighting Award, Ottawa, 1983; Best New Play, Quebec Drama Festival, 1984; Gabriel Radio Award, Texas, 1991; Nominee, Prix Parizeau. Memberships: Writers Guild of Canada; Performers Guild; Playwrights Union of Canada; Playwrights Workshop, Montreal; Siamsa School of Music and Dance. Address: 4955 West Broadway, Montreal, Quebec H4V 1R5, Canada.

CURREY Ralph Nixon, b. 14 Dec 1907, Mafeking, Cape Province, South Africa. Poet; Biographer; Radio Dramatist. Education: BA, Wadham College, Oxford, 1930, MA 1935. Publications: Tiresias and Other Poems, 1940; Poems from India, 1945; War Anthology by Members of the Forces, 1946; This Other Planet, 1945; Indian Landscape: A Book of Descriptive Poems, 1947; Formal Spring, 1950; Poets of the 1939-1945 War, 1960, 1967; Letters of a Natal Sheriff: Thomas Phipson 1815-65, 1968; The Africa We Knew, 1973; Vinnicombe's Trek, 1989. Honours: Viceroy's All-India Poetry Prize, 1944; South Africa Poetry Prize, 1955; Royal Society of Literature, fellow, 1970. Membership: Suffolk Poetry Society, president, 1967-79. Address: 3 Beverley Road, Colchester, Essex CO3 3NG, England.

CURRIE Edwina, b. 13 Oct 1946, England. Writer; Broadcaster. m. Raymond Frank Currie, 1972, sep, 2 daughters. Education: MA, St Anne's College, Oxford; MSc, London School of Economics. Appointments: Teacher, Lecturer, 1972-81; Member of Parliament for Derbyshire South, 1983-97; Minister of Health, 1986-88; Vice Chairman, European Movement, 1995-. Publications: Life Lines, 1989; What Women Want, 1990; Three Line Quips, 1992; A Parliamentary Affair (novel), 1994; A Woman's Place (novel), 1996; She's Leaving Home (novel), 1997. Contributions to: Articles and reviews. Address: c/o Curtis Brown Ltd, 28-29 Haymarket, London SW1Y 4SP, England.

CURRY Jane Louise, b. 24 Sept 1932, East Liverpool, Ohio, USA. Writer. Education: Pennsylvania State University, 1950-51; BA, Indiana University of Pennsylvania, 1954; University of California, Los Angeles, 1957-59; London University, England, 1961-62, 1965-66; AM, 1962, PhD, 1969, Stanford University. Appointments: Teaching Assistant, 1959-61, 1963-65, Acting Instructor, 1967-68, Instructor, 1983-84, Lecturer, 1987, English Department, Stanford University; Freelance Lecturer, Consultant on Children's Books, 1970-. Publications: Beneath the Hill, 1967; The Sleepers, 1968; The Change-Child, 1969; The Day Breakers, 1970; The Housenapper (also published as Mindy's Mysterious Miniature and The Mysterious Shrinking House), 1970; The Ice Ghosts Mystery, 1972; The Lost Farm, 1974; Poor Tom's Ghost, 1977; The Great Flood Mystery, 1985; The Lotus Cup, 1986; Me, Myself and I, 1986; Little Little Sister, 1989; The Big Smith Snatch, 1989; What the Dickens!, 1991; The Christmas Knight, 1993; The Great Smith House Hustle, 1993; Robin Hood and His Merry Men, 1994; Robin Hood in the Greenwood, 1995; Moon Window, 1996. Contributions to: Medium Aevum. Honours: Fulbright Grant, 1961-62; Stanford Leverhulme Fellowship, 1965-66; Book Award, 1971, Special Award, 1979, Southern California Council on Literature for Children; Ohioana Book Awards, 1978, 1987. Memberships: Authors Guild; International Arthurian Society; Southern California Council on Literature for Children and Young People. Address: McElderry Books, Simon & Schuster Children's Publishing Division, 1230 Avenue of the Americas, New York, NY 10020, USA.

CURRY Mary Earle Lowry, b. 13 May 1917, Seneca, South Carolina, USA. Writer. m. Reverend Peden Gene Curry, 25 Dec 1941, 1 son, 1 daughter. Education: Furman University, 1944-45. Publications: Looking Up, 1949; Looking Within, 1961, 1980; Hymn: Church in the Heart of the City, 1973. Contributions to: Numerous anthologies and journals including: Yearbook of Modern Poetry; Poets of America; Poetic Voice of America; We, the People; Poetry Digest; Poetry Anthology of Verse; International Anthology on World Brotherhood and Peace; Parnassus of World Poets, 1994-98, The Greenville News; Inman Times. Honours: World Award for Culture, Centro Studi e Ricerche della Nazioni, Italy, 1985. Memberships: Auxiliary Rotary, Charleston, South Carolina, 1972-74; Centro Studi Scambi Internazionali, Rome; United Methodist Church Women's Organizations; United Methodist Church Ministers; Wives Club, President 1973-74, Charleston; Community clubs. Address: 345 Curry Drive, Seneca, SC 29678, USA.

CURTEIS Ian (Bayley), b. 1 May 1935, London, England. Playwright. m. (1) Joan Macdonald, 1964, diss, 2 sons, (2) Joanna Trollope, 12 Apr 1985, 2 stepdaughters. Appointments: Actor and Director in British Theatres; Playwright. Publications: Numerous television plays and drama series, screenplays, stage plays, and adaptations. Honours: Various nominations. Memberships: Royal Society of Literature; Writers Guild of Great Britain, Chairman, Committee on Censorship, 1981-85; Writers' Guild of Great Britain. president. Address: c/o Coutts & Co, 1 Cadogan Place, London SW1X 9PX, England.

CURTIS Anthony Samuel, b. 12 Mar 1926, London, England. Journalist. m. Sarah Curtis, 3 Oct 1960, 3 sons. Education: BA (Inter MA), 1st Class Honours, English, Merton College, Oxford, 1950. Appointments: Deputy Editor, Times Literary Supplement, 1959-60; Literary Editor, Financial Times, 1970-90. Publications: The Pattern of Maugham, 1974; Somerset Maugham: The Critical Heritage (with John Whitehead), 1987; Lit Ed: on Reviews and Reviewing, 1998. Contributions to: Periodicals and radio. Honour: Harkness Fellowship in Journalism, USA, 1958-59. Memberships: Royal Literary Fund, treasurer, 1975-98; Royal Society of Arts, fellow; Society of Authors, pension fund trustee. Address: 9 Essex Villas, London W8 7BP, England.

CURTIS Edward. See: **PREBBLE John.**

CURTIS Richard Hale. See: **LEVINSON Leonard.**

CURTIS Sarah, b. 21 May 1936, Preston, England. Journalist; Writer. m. 3 Oct 1960, 3 sons. Education: BA, 1958, MA, St Hugh's College, Oxford, England. Appointments: Times Educational Supplement, 1958-59; The Times, 1959-61; Editor, Adoption and Fostering, 1976-87; Editor, RSA Journal and Head of Communications RSA, 1989-95. Publications: Thinkstrip, series, 1976-79; It's Your Life, series, 1983; Juvenile Offending, 1989; The Journals of Woodrow Wyatt, editor, Vol I, 1998. Contributions to: Times Literary Supplement, novel reviewer, since 1960s; Contributor, New Society, Financial Times, BBC Radio 4. Literary Agent: Hilary Rubinstein. Address: 9 Essex Villas, London W8 7BP, England.

CURTIS Tony, b. 26 Dec 1946, Carmathen, Wales. Professor of Poetry; Poet. m. Margaret Blundell, 1970, 1 son, 1 daughter. Education: BA, University College of Swansea, 1968; MFA, Goddard College, Vermont, 1980. Appointment: Professor of Poetry, University of Glamorgan. Publications: Poetry: Walk Down a Welsh Wind, 1972; Home Movies, 1973; Album, 1974; The Deerslayers, 1978; Carnival, 1978; Preparations: Poems, 1974-79, 1980; Letting Go, 1983; Selected Poems, 1970-85, 1986; The Last Candles, 1989; Taken for Pearls, 1993. Other: Islands (radio play), 1975; Out of the Dark Wood: Prose Poems, Stories, 1977; Dannie Abse, 1985; The Art of Seamus Heaney (editor), 1986, 3rd edition, 1994; How to Study Modern Poetry, 1990; How Poets Work (editor), 1996. Honours: National Poetry Competition Winner, 1984; Dylan Thomas Prize, 1993; Cholmondeley Award, 1997. Address: Pentwyn, 55 Colcot Road, Barry, South Glamorgan CF6 8BQ, Wales.

CURZON Daniel, b. Litchfield, Illinois, USA. Writer; Professor. 1 son. Education: MA, Kent State University; PhD, Wayne State University. Appointment: Instructor, City College of San Francisco, California, 1980-. Publications: Something You Do in the Dark, 1971; The World Can Break Your Heart, 1984; Curzon in Love, 1988; Superfag, 1996; Only the Good Parts, 1998; Not Necessarily Nice (stories), 1999. Contributions to: Kansas Quarterly; The Kenyon Review; Descant; The Pannus Index; Christopher Street; Other. Honour: 1st Prize, 1-act competition, Attic Theatre, Hollywood, California, 1992. Address: Box 196, City College of San Francisco, 50 Phelan Avenue, San Francisco, CA 94112, USA.

CUSHMAN Dan, b. 9 June 1909, Marion, Michigan, USA. Writer. m. Elizabeth Louden, 1940, 3 sons, 1 daughter. Education: BS, University of Montana, 1934.

Publications: Montana, Here I Be, 1950; Badlands Justice, 1951; Naked Ebony, 1951; Jewel of the Java Sea, 1951; The Ripper from Rawhide, 1952; Savage Interlude, 1952; Stay Away, Joe, 1953; Timberjack, 1953; Jungle She, 1953; The Fabulous Finn, 1954; Tongking, 1954; Port Orient, 1955; The Fastest Gun, 1955; The Old Copper Collar, 1957; The Silver Mountain, 1957; Tall Wyoming, 1957; The Forbidden Land, 1958; Goodbye, Old Dry, 1959, paperback edition as The Con Man, 1960; The Half-Caste, 1960; Brothers in Kickapoo, 1962, UK edition as Boomtown, US Paperback as On the Make, 1963; 4 for Texas (novelisation of screenplay), 1963; The Grand and the Glorious, 1963; Opium Flower, 1963; North Fork to Hell, 1964; The Long Riders, 1967; The Muskrat Farm, 1977; Rusty Iron, 1984. Non-fiction: The Great North Trail: America's Route of the Ages, 1966; Cow Country Cook Book, 1967; Montana: The Gold Frontier, 1975.Address: 1500 Fourth Avenue North, Great Falls, MT 59401, USA.

CUSSLER Clive (Eric), b. 15 July 1931, Aurora, Illinois, USA. Author; Advertising Executive. m. Barbara Knight, 28 Aug 1955, 3 children. Education: Pasadena City College, 1949-51; Orange Coast College; California State University. Appointments: Advertising Directorships; Author. Publications: The Mediterranean Caper, 1973; Iceberg, 1975; Raise the Titanic, 1976; Vixen O-Three, 1978; Night Probe, 1981; Pacific Vortex, 1982; Deep Six, 1984; Cyclops, 1986; Treasure, 1988; Dragon, 1990; Sahara, 1992; Inca Gold, 1994; Shock Wave, 1996; Flood Tide, 1997. Honours: Numerous advertising awards. Memberships: Explorers Club, fellow; Royal Geographical Society. Address: PO Box 635, Golden, CO 80402, USA.

CYRIL. See: **CHHETRI Nabin.**

CZAJKOWSKI Jerzy Stanislaw, b. 13 Jan 1931, Oscislowo, Mazowsze, Poland. Poet; Essayist; Novelist. Education: History and Sociology, 1961-68; MA, Cultural Sociology, 1968. Appointments: Senior Editor, Artistic and Film Publishing House, 1961-67, State Scientific Publishing House, 1968-71, Polish Contemporary Poetry Series, 1974-80, Kiw Publishing House, 1980-89; Literary Consultant. Publications: Poetry, essays, and novels, 1958-98. Contributions to: Anthologies and journals. Honours: Writer's and editor's awards. Address: ul Swietojerska 4-10 m 57, 00-236 Warsaw, Poland.

CZIGANY Lóránt György,b. 3 June 1935, Sátoraljaújhely, Hungary. m. Magda Salacz, 28 Sept 1957, 1 daughter. Education: University of Szeged, 1954-56; University of Oxford, 1957-58; BA, 1960, PhD, 1964, University of London. Appointments: Szepsi Csombor Literary Circle, 1965-88; Editor, Atelier Hongrois, Paris, 1974; Minister Plenipotentiary for Cultural Affairs, 1990-92. Publications: The Oxford History of Hungarian Literature; The Reception of Hungarian Literature in Victorian England; The Origins of State Control of Hungarian Literature; The Béla Iványi-Grünwald Collection of Hungarica. Contributions to: Times; BBC Overseas Service; Outside Contributor. Honour: Honorary Doctorate, University of Miskolc, Hungary, 1995. Memberships: Szepsi Csombor Literary Circle; International Association of Hungarian Studies. Address: 15 Temple Fortune Lane, London NW11 7UB, England.

CZYKWIN Jan, b. 18 May 1940, Dubicze Cerkiewne, Poland. University Professor; Poet; Translator. m. Tatiana, 26 Dec 1964, 1 daughter. Education: Graduate, Slavonic Studies, Warsaw University, 1964. Appointments: University Teacher, Warsaw University, 1969-; Bialystok University, 1997-. Publications: In Belorussian: Collections of Poetry: I Am Going, 1969; A Holy Well, 1970; Restlessness, 1977; Plexus Solaris, 1988; A Bright Flash, 1989; A Festive Goblet, 1992; The First and the Last World, 1997; In Polish: On the Verge of the World, 1983; A Rest By the Dried Water Spring, 1996; Research: Afanasij Fet Historioliterary Study, 1984; Distant and Near Belorussian Writers of Diaspora, 1997. Contributions to: Editor-in-Chief, Library of Belorussian Literary Society, Bialowieza. Memberships: Union des

Gens de Lettres Polonais, 1970; International PEN Club, 1996. Address: 17-100 Bielsk Podlaski, Ul Strzelnicza 7, Poland.

D

D'AGUIAR Fred, b. 2 Feb 1960, London, England. Poet; Writer; Dramatist; Professor of English. Education: BA, Honours, University of Kent, 1985. Appointments: Writer-in-Residence, London Borough of Lewisham, 1986-87, Birmingham Polytechnic, 1988-89; Instructor in Writing, Arvon Foundation, 1986-; Visiting Fellow, Cambridge University, 1989-90; Northern Arts Literary Fellow, Newcastle and Durham universities, 1990-92; Visiting Writer, Amherst College, Massachusetts, 1992-94; Assistant Professor of English, Bates College, Lewiston, Maine, 1994-95; Professor of English, University of Miami at Coral Gables, Florida, 1995-. Publications: Poetry: Mama Dot, 1985, 2nd edition, 1989; Airy Hall, 1989; British Subjects, 1993; Bill of Rights, 1996. Fiction: The Longest Memory, 1994; Dear Future, 1996; Feeding the Ghosts, 1997. Play: A Jamaican Airman Forsees His Death, 1995. Co-Editor: The New British Poetry, 1988. Contributions to: Journals, magazines, radio and television. Honours: T S Eliot Prize for Poetry, University of Kent, 1984; Malcolm X Prize for Poetry, 1986; Guyana Prize for Poetry, 1989; BBC Race in the Media Award, 1992; Most Innovative Film Award, British Film Institute, 1993; David Higham First Novel Award, 1995; Whitbread Award, 1995. Address: c/o Curtis Brown, Haymarket House, 28-29 Haymarket, London SW1Y 4SP, England.

DABYDEEN Cyril, b. 15 Oct 1945, Guyana. Poet; Writer. m. 6 June 1989, 1 daughter. Education: BA Honours, Lakehead University, Thunder Bay, Ontario, 1973; MA, 1974; MPA, Queen's University, Ottawa. Publications: Poetry; Distances, 1977; Goatsong, 1977; Heart's Frame, 1979; This Planet Earth, 1980; Islands Lovelier Than a Vision, 1988; Dark Swirl, 1989; Stoning the Wind, 1994; Born in Amazonia, 1996; Discussing Columbus, 1997. Fiction: Still Close to the Island, 1980; To Monkey Jungle, 1986; The Wizard Swami, 1989; Dark Swirl, 1989; Jogging in Havana, 1992; Sometimes Hard, 1994; Berbice Crossing (stories), 1996; Black Jesus and Other Stories, 1997. Editor: A Shapely Fire: Changing the Literary Landscape, 1987; Another Way to Dance: Asian-Canadian Poetry, 1990, 2nd edition, 1996. Contributions to: Canadian Forum; Canadian Fiction Magazine; Fiddlehead; Dalhousie Review; Antigonish Review; Canadian Author and Bookman; Toronto South Asian Review; Journal of South Asian Literature; Wascana Review; Literary Review; Globe and Mail; Caribbean Quarterly. Honours: Sandbach Parker Gold Medal; A J Seymour Lyric Poetry Prize; Poet Laureate of Ottawa; Okanagan Fiction Award. Membership: Canadian Association of Commonwealth Language and Literature Studies. Address: 106 Blackburn, Ottawa, Ontario K1N 8A7, Canada.

DABYDEEN David, b. 9 Dec 1955, Guyana. Poet; Writer; Professor of Literature. Education: BA, Cambridge University, 1978; PhD, London University, 1982. Appointments: Junior Research Fellow, Oxford University, 1983-87; Professor of Literature, Warwick University, 1987-. Publications: Slave Song, 1984; Coolie Odyssey, 1988; The Intended, 1991; Disappearance, 1993; Turner, 1994; The Counting House, 1996; Across the Dark Waters: Indian Identity in the Caribbean, 1996; A Harlot's Progress, 1999. Contributions to: Various periodicals. Honours: Commonwealth Poetry Prize, 1984; Guyana Literature Prize, 1992. Memberships: Arts Council of Great Britain, literature panel, 1985-89; Royal Society of the Arts, fellow; Guyana's Ambassador to UNESCO, 1997. Literary Agent: Jane Brandish-Ellames, Curtis Brown Ltd. Address: c/o Warwick University, Coventry, CV4 7AL, England.

DACEY Philip, b. 9 May 1939, St Louis, Missouri, USA. Poet; Teacher. m. Florence Chard, 1963, div 1986, 2 sons, 1 daughter. Education: BA, St Louis University, 1961; MA, Stanford University, 1967; MFA, University of Iowa, 1970. Appointments: Instructor in English, University of Missouri at St Louis, 1967-68; Faculty, Department of English, Southwest State University, Marshall, Minnesota, 1970-; Distinguished Writer-in-Residence, Wichita State University, 1985. Publications: Poetry: The Beast with Two Backs, 1969; Fist, Sweet Giraffe, The Lion, Snake, and Owl, 1970; Four Nudes, 1971; How I Escaped from the Labyrinth and Other Poems, 1977; The Boy Under the Bed, 1979; The Condom Poems, 1979; Gerard Manley Hopkins Meets Walt Whitman in Heaven and Other Poems, 1982; Fives, 1984; The Man with Red Suspenders, 1986; The Condom Poems II, 1989; Night Shift at the Crucifix Factory, 1991. Editor: I Love You All Day: It is That Simple (with Gerald M Knoll), 1970; Strong Measures: Contemporary American Poetry in Traditional Forms (with David Jaus), 1986. Honours: Woodrow Wilson Fellowship, 1961; New York YM-YWHA Discovery Award, 1974; National Endowment for the Arts Fellowships, 1975, 1980; Minnesota State Arts Board Fellowships, 1975, 1983; Bush Foundation Fellowship, 1977; Loft-McKnight Fellowship, 1984; Fulbright Lecturer, 1988. Address: Route 1, Box 89, Lynd, MN 56157, USA.

DACRE Paul Michael, b. 14 Nov 1948. m. Kathleen, 2 sons. Education: BA, University College School, London, University of Leeds. Appointments: Reporter, Daily Express, Manchester, 1970-71; Reporter, Feature Writer and Associate Features Editor, London, 1971-76; New York Correspondent, 1976-79; Bureau Chief, Daily Mail, New York, 1980; Deputy News Editor, London, 1981; News Editor, 1983, Assistant Editor, News and Foreign, 1986; Assistant Editor Features, 1987; Executive Editor, 1988, Associate Editor, 1989-91; Editor, Evening Standard, 1991-92, Daily Mail, 1992-; Editor-in-Chief, Associated Newspapers, 1998-. Address: The Daily Mail, Northcliffe House, 2 Derry St, London, W8 5TT, England.

DAFTARY Farhad, b. 23 Dec 1938, Brussels, Belgium. Academic. m. Fereshteh Kashanchi, Feb 1980, 1 daughter. Education: BA, 1962, MA, 1964, American University; MA, 1966, PhD, 1971, University of California, Berkeley. Appointments: Lecturer, Tehran University, 1972-73, National University, Tehran, 1973-74; Professor, 1988-, Head, Department of Academic Research and Publications, 1992-, Institute of Ismaili Studies, London; Consulting Editor, Encyclopaedia Iranica; General Editor, Ismaili Heritage Series, 1996-; British Institute of Persian Studies, advisory council; Iran Heritage Foundation, academic committee. Publications: The Ismailis: Their History and Doctrines; The Assassin Legends; A Short History of the Ismailis; Mediaeval Ismaili History & Thought; Works translated into French, Hungarian, Portuguese, Russian, Arabic, Persian, Tajik and Urdu. Contributions to: Islamic Culture; Arabica; Iran; Studia Islamica; Encyclopaedia Iranica; Encyclopaedia of Islam; Persian Encyclopaedia of Islam; Turkish Encyclopaedia of Islam; Great Encyclopaedia of Islam; Muslim Almanac; UNESCO History of Civilizations of Central Asia. Honour: Best Book of the Year Award, Iran, 1998. Memberships: American Oriental Society; British Institute of Persian Studies; British Society for Middle Eastern Studies; Society for Iranian Studies. Address: 77 Hamilton Terrace, London NW8, England.

DAICHES David, b. 2 Sept 1912, Sunderland, England. Professor Emeritus; Writer. m. Isobel Janet Mackay, 28 July, 1937, 1 son, 2 daughters. Education: MA, Edinburgh University, 1934; DPhil, Oxford University, 1939. Appointments: Fellow, Balliol College, Oxford, 1936-37; Assistant Professor, University of Chicago, 1939-43; Professor, Cornell University, 1946-51, Sussex University, 1961-77; University Lecturer, 1951-61, Fellow, Jesus College, 1957-62, Cambridge; Director, Institute for Advanced Studies, Edinburgh University, 1980-86. Publications: 45 books including: The Novel and the Modern World, 1939; Robert Burns, 1950; Two Worlds, 1956; A Critical History of English Literature, 1960; The Paradox of Scottish Culture, 1964; God and the Poets, 1984; Edinburgh: A Traveller's Companion, 1986; A Weekly Scotsman and Other Poems, 1994. Honours: Royal Society of Literature, fellow, 1957; Scottish Arts Council Book Award, 1973; Scottish Book of the Year Award, 1984; Commander of the Order of the British Empire, 1991; Various honorary doctorates. Memberships: Association for Scottish Literary Studies, honorary president; Modern Language Association of America, honorary member; Saltire Society, honorary president. Address: 22 Belgrave Crescent, Edinburgh, EH4 3AL, Scotland.

DALE Margaret Jessy, (Margaret J Miller), b. 27 Aug 1911, Edinburgh, Scotland. Writer. m. Clunie Rutherford Dale, 3 Sept 1938, div 1954, 1 son, 2 daughters. Education: 2nd Class Honours BA, English Language and Literature, Lady Margaret Hall, Oxford, 1933. Appointments: Scenario Writer, Associated Screen News, Montreal, Canada, 1935-36; Assistant Editor, Shell Magazine, London, 1937-39. Publications: The Queen's Music, 1961; The Powers of the Sapphire, 1962; Mouse Tails, 1967;Emily, A Life of Emily Brontë, 1969; Knights, Beasts and Wonders, 1969; The Fearsome Road, 1975; The Fearsome Island, 1975; The Fearsome Tide, 1976; The Far Castles, 1978. Contributions to: 200 scripts for Schools Broadcasting; Times; Times Literary Supplement; Scottish Field; Scots Magazine; Scotland's Magazine. Memberships: PEN; National Book League. Address: 26 Grey's Hill, Henley, Oxon RG9 1SJ, England.

DALE Peter John, b. 21 Aug 1938, Addlestone, Surrey, England. Poet; Writer; Translator. m. Pauline Strouvelle, 29 June 1963, 1 son, 1 daughter. Education: BA, Honours, English, St Peter's College, Oxford, 1963. Appointments: Teacher of Secondary Schools, 1963-93; Co-Editor, Agenda, 1972-96. Publications: Poetry: Walk from the House, 1962; The Storms, 1968; Mortal Fire, 1976; One Another (sonnet sequence), 1978; Too Much of Water, 1983; A Set of Darts: Epigrams (with W S Milne and Richard Richardson), 1990; Earth Light: New Poems, 1991; Selected Poems, 1996; Da Capo (poem sequence), 1997; Michael Hamburger in Conversation with Peter Dale, 1998; In Introduction to Rhyme, 1998. Translator: Selected Poems of François Villon, 1978, 4th edition, 1994; Poems of Jules Laforgue, 1986; The Divine Comedy, terza rima version, 1996. Contributions to: Journals and periodicals. Honour: Arts Council Bursary, 1970. Membership: Society of Authors. Address: 10 Selwood Road, Sutton, Surrey SM3 9JU, England.

DALESKI H(illel) M(atthew), b. 19 July 1926, Johannesburg, South Africa. Professor Emeritus of English; Writer. m. (1) Aviva Prop, 29 June 1950, div, 4 children, (2) Shirley Kaufman, 20 June 1974. Education: BA, 1947, BA, Honours, 1949, MA, 1952, University of the Witwatersrand; PhD, Hebrew University, Jerusalem, 1963. Appointments: Assistant Lecturer to Associate Professor, 1958-76, Professor of English 1976-, Chairman, Department of English, 1968-70, 1984-85, Provost, School of Overseas Students, 1973-76, Hebrew University, Jerusalem. Publications: The Forked Flame: A Study of D H Lawrence, 1965; Dickens and the Art of Analogy, 1970; Joseph Conrad: The Way of Dispossession, 1977; The Divided Heroine: A Recurrent Pattern in Six English Novels, 1984; Unities: Studies in the English Novel, 1985; Thomas Hardy and Paradoxes of Love, 1997. Honour: Israel Academy of Sciences and Humanities, 1993. Membership: President, Dickens Society, 1985. Address: Department of English, Hebrew University, Jerusalem, Israel.

DALLEK Robert, b. 16 May 1934, Brooklyn, New York, USA. Professor of History; Author; Biographer. m. (1) Ilse F Shatzkin, 20 Nov 1959, dec Oct 1962, (2) Geraldine R Kronmal, 22 Aug 1965, 1 son, 1 daughter. Education: BA, History, University of Illinois, 1955; MA, History, 1957, PhD, History, 1964, Columbia University. Appointments: Instructor in History, Columbia University, 1960-64; Assistant Professor to Professor of History, University of California at Los Angeles, 1964-94; Research Associate, Southern California Psychoanalytic Institute, 1981-85; Commonwealth Fund Lecturer, University College, London, 1984; Thompson Lecturer, University of Wyoming, 1986; Charles Griffin Lecturer, Vassar College, 1987; Visiting Professor, California Institute of Technology, 1993, LBJ School of Public Affairs, University of Texas, 1996; Harmsworth Visiting Professor, University of Oxford, 1994-95; Professor of History, Boston University, 1996-. Publications: Democrat and Diplomat: The Life of William E Dodd, 1968; Western

Europe (editor), Vol I of The Dynamics of World Power: A Documentary History of United States Foreign Policy, 1945-1973, 1973; Franklin D Roosevelt and American Foreign Policy, 1932-1945, 1979, 2nd edition, 1995; The American Style of Foreign Policy: Cultural Politics and Foreign Affairs, 1983; Ronald Reagan: The Politics of Symbolism, 1984; The Great Republic: A History of the American People (with others), 3rd edition, 1985, 4th edition, 1991; Lone Star Rising: Lyndon Johnson and His Times, 1908-1960, 1991; The Encyclopedia of 20th-Century American History (associate editor with others), 4 volumes, 1995; Hail to the Chief: The Making and Unmaking of American Presidents, 1996; Flawed Giant: Lyndon Johnson and His Times, 1961-1973, 1998. Contributions to: Scholarly books and journals. Honours: Guggenheim Fellowship, 1973-74; Senior Fellow, National Endowment for the Humanities, 1976-77; Bancroft Prize, 1980; Humanities Fellow, Rockefeller Foundation, 1981-82; Notable Book Citations, New York Times Book Review, 1983, 1991, 1998; Fellow, American Council of Learned Societies, 1984-85; Research Grants, Lyndon B Johnson Foundation, 1984-85, 1988-89. Memberships: American Academy of Arts and Sciences, fellow; American Psychoanalytic Association; Society of American Historians, fellow; Society of Historians of American Foreign Relations, president, 1995. Address: 2138 Cathedral Avenue North West, Washington, DC 20008, USA.

DALTON Annie,b. 18 Jan 1948, Weymouth, England. Writer. div. 1 son, 2 daughters. Education: Upper 2nd, English and American Literature, University of Warwick, 1967-70. Publications: Nightmaze: The After Dark Princess; The Real Tilly Beany; The Alpha Box; Swan Sister; The Witch Rose; Demon Spawn; Out of the Ordinary; Naming the Dark, 1992. Honours: East Midlands Arts Bursary, 1987; Nottingham Oak Children's Book Award, 1991; Commended for Carnegie, 1992. Literary Agent: Elizabeth Stevens, Curtis Brown. Address: 13 Selbourne Street, Loughborough, Leics LE11 1BS, England.

DALY Maureen, (Maureen Daly McGivern), b. 15 Mar 1921, Castlecaufield, County Tyrone, Ireland. Journalist; Writer. m. William P McGivern, 28 Dec 1946, dec 1983, 1 son, 1 daughter, dec. Education: BA, Rosary College, 1942. Appointments: Reporter and Columnist, Chicago Tribune, 1941-44; Associate Editor, Ladies' Home Journal, 1944-49; Consultant to the editors, Saturday Evening Post, 1960-69; Reporter and Columnist, Desert Sun, Palm Desert, California, 1987-. Publications: The Perfect Hostess: Complete Etiquette and Entertainment for the Home, 1950; Mention My Name in Mombasa: The Unscheduled Adventures of an American Family Abroad (with William P McGivern), 1958; A Matter of Honour (with William P McGivern), 1984. Young Adult Fiction: Seventeenth Summer, 1942; Sixteen and Other Stories, 1961; Acts of Love, 1986; First A Dream, 1990. Young Adult Non-Fiction: Smarter and Smoother: A Handbook on How To Be That Way, 1944; What's Your P Q (Personality Quotient)?, 1952, revised edition, 1966; Twelve Around the World, 1957; Spanish Roundabout, 1960; Moroccan Roundabout, 1961. Juvenile: Patrick Visits the Library, 1961; Patrick Visits the Zoo, 1963; The Ginger Horse, 1964; Spain: Wonderland of Contrasts, 1965; The Small War of Sergeant Donkey, 1966; Rosie, the Dancing Elephant, 1967. Editor: My Favorite Stories, 1948; My Favorite Mystery Stories, 1966; My Favorite Suspense Stories, 1968. Contributions to: Anthologies and many periodicals. Honours: O Henry Memorial Award, 1938; Dodd, Mead Intercollegiate Literary Fellowship Novel Award, 1942; Freedoms Foundation Award, 1952; Gimble Fashion Award, 1962; Lewis Carroll Shelf Award, 1969; One of 10 great books for teens, Redbook Magazine, 1987. Memberships: Mystery Writers of America; Writers Guild of America. Address: Ironwood Street, Palm Desert, CA 92260, USA.

DALY Niki, (Nicholas Daly), b. 13 June 1946, Cape Town, South Africa. Writer; Illustrator. m. Judith Mary Kenny, 7 July 1973, 2 sons. Education: Diploma, Cape Town Technikon, 1970. Appointments: Graphics Teacher, East Ham Technical College, London, 1976-79; Head, Songololo Books, 1989-. Publications: Children's books: The Little Girl Who Lived Down the Road, 1978; Vim the Rag Mouse, 1979; Joseph's Other Red Sock, 1982; Leo's Christmas Surprise, 1983; Ben's Gingerbread Man, 1985; Teddy's Ear, 1985; Monsters Are Like That, 1985; Just Like Archie, 1986; Look at Me!, 1986; Not So Fast, Songololo, 1985; Thank You Henrietta, 1986; Mama, Papa, and Baby Joe, 1991; Papa Lucky's Shadow, 1991; Mary Mallory and the Baby Who Couldn't Sleep, 1994; One Round Moon, 1995; Why the Sun and the Moon Live in the Sky, 1995; My Dad, 1995; The Dinosaurs are Back and It's Your Fault Edward! (with Wendy Hartmann), 1995, UK edition, 1996. Illustrator: Maybe It's a Tiger, by Kathleen Hersom, 1981; Fly Eagle Fly, by Christopher Gregorowski, 1982; I Want to See the Moon, by Louis Baum, 1994; The Day of the Rainbow, by Ruth Craft, 1988; Charlie's House, by Reviva Schermbrucker, 1989; All the Magic in the World, by Wendy Harmann, 1993; Red Light, Green Light, Mama and Me, by Cari Best, 1995. Honours: British Arts Council Illustration Award, 1978; Parents' Choice Book Award for Literature, 1986; Katrine Harries Awards for Illustration, 1986-87; Horn Book Honor List, 1987; New York Times One of the Best Illustrated Books of the Year Award, 1995; Anne Izard Story Teller's Choice Award, 1996; IBBY Honour List Book, 1996. Membership: Association of Illustrators, London. Address: 36 Strubens Road, 7700 Cape Town, South Africa.

DALY Patricia. See: **BRENNAN Patricia Winifred.**

DALYELL Tam, b. 9 Aug 1932, Edinburgh, Scotland. Member of Parliament; Writer. m. Kathleen Wheatley, 26 Dec 1963, 1 son, 1 daughter. Education: King's College, Cambridge, 1952-56. Appointment: House of Commons, 1962-. Publications: The Case for Ship Schools, 1958; Ship School Dunera, 1961; One Man's Falklands, 1982; A Science Policy for Britain, 1983; Misrule: How Mrs Thatcher Deceived Parliament, 1987; Dick Crossman: A Portrait, 1988. Contributions to: Weekly Columnist, New Scientist, 1967-; Many Obituaries, Independent Newspaper. Honours: Various Awards of Science; Honorary Doctor of Science, University of Edinburgh, 1994; Honorary Degree, City University, London, 1998. Address: House of Commons, London SW1 A0AA, England.

DALZELL Alexander, b. 8 May 1925, Belfast, Northern Ireland. Classical Scholar; Translator. m. Isobel Ann Steel, 21 Aug 1954, 1 son, 1 daughter. Education: BA, 1950, MA, 1955, BLitt, 1956, Trinity College, Dublin. Appointments: Assistant Lecturer, Kings College, London, University of Sheffield; Lecturer, Assistant Professor, Associate Professor, Professor, Honorary Fellow, Toronto, Canada. Publications: Correspondence of Erasmus; The Criticism of Didectic Poetry. Contributions to: Phoenix; Hermathena. Memberships: Classical Association of Canada, president 1980-92. Address: 344 Saunders Street, Fredericton, New Brunswick E3B 1N8, Canada.

DAN Sharon Jaffe, b. 23 Nov 1963, Washington, DC, USA. m. Noah Dan, 10 Apr 1990, 2 daughters. Education: BS, Magazine Journalism, Syracuse University SI Newhouse School of Public Communications, 1985. Appointments: Senior Editor, Caribbean Travel & Life Magazine, 1985-97; Editor, Caribbean Vacation Planner, 1997-; Freelance Writer, at present. Contributions to: Numerous articles in Caribbean Travel & Life, Caribbean Vacation Planner, Bride's, Honeymoon, Family Fun. Address: 5813 Hidden Hill Lane, Potanac, MD 20854, USA.

DANA Robert (Patrick), b. 2 June 1929, Allston, Massachusetts, USA. Emeritus Professor of English; Poet. m. (1) Mary Kowalke, 2 June 1951, div 1973, 3 children, (2) Margaret Sellen, 14 Sept 1974. Education: AB, Drake University, 1951; MA, University of Iowa, 1954. Appointments: Assistant Professor, Associate Professor, Professor of English, Cornell College, Mount Vernon, Iowa, 1953-94; Editor, Hillside Press, Mount Vernon, 1957-67; Editor, 1964-68, Contributing Editor, 1991-, North American Review; Contributing Editor, American Poetry Review, 1973-88, New Letters, 1980-83. Publications: My Glass Brother and Other Poems, 1957; The Dark Flags of Waking, 1964; Journeys from the Skin: A Poem in Two Parts, 1966; Some Versions of Silence: Poems, 1967; The Power of the Visible, 1971; In a Fugitive Season, 1980; What the Stones Know, 1984; Blood Harvest, 1986; Against the Grain: Interviews with Maverick American Publishers, 1986; Starting Out for the Difficult World, 1987; What I Think I Know: New and Selected Poems, 1990; Wildebeest, 1993; Yes, Everything, 1994; Hello, Stranger: Beach Poems, 1996; A Community of Witers: Paul Engle and The Fowa Writers' Workshop, 1999. Contributions to: New Yorker; New York Times; Poetry; Georgia Review; Manoa. Honours: Rainer Maria Rilke Prize, 1984; National Endowment for the Arts Fellowships, 1985, 1993; Delmore Schwartz Memorial Poetry Award, 1989; Carl Sandburg Medal for Poetry, 1994; Pushcart Prize, 1996. Memberships: Academy of American Poets; PEN; Associated Writing Programs; Poetry Society of America. Address: 1466 Westview Drive, Coralville, IA 52241, USA.

DANCE Helen Oakley, b. 15 Feb 1913, Toronto, Ontario, Canada. Writer. m. Stanley Dance, 30 Jan 1947, 2 sons, 2 daughters. Education: University of Toronto; Les Fougéres, Switzerland. Publication: Stormy Monday: The T-Bone Walker Story, 1987. Contributions to: Down Beat; Tempo; Swing; Hot Jazz (Paris); Melody News; Saturday Review; Music Journal; Jazz Times, 1934-96. Address: 1745 Bittersweet Hill, Vista, CA 92084, USA.

DANESHVAR Simin, b. 23 Apr 1921, Shiraz, Iran. Novelist; Translator; Professor Emeritus. Education: PhD, University of Teheran, 1949. Appointments: Professor, Professor Emeritus, 1979-, Department of Archaeology, University of Teheran. Publications: The Extinguished Fire, 1948; A City Like Paradise, 1961; Savushun, 1969; To Whom Shall I Say Hello?, 1980; Jalal's Sunset, 1981; Daneshvar's Playhouse: A Collection of Stories, 1989; Translations of works by Alan Paton, Hawthorne, Chekhov and Shaw. Address: c/o Mage Books, 1032 29th Street North West, Washington, DC 20007, USA.

DANESKJALD Torkel F. See: **ASMUSSEN Jesper.**

DANIEL Colin. See: **WINDSOR Patricia.**

DANIEL Wayne W(endell), b. 14 Feb 1929, Tallapoosa, Georgia, USA. Professor Emeritus of Decision Sciences; Writer. m. Mary Yarbrough, 2 June 1956, 1 son, 2 daughters. Education: BSEd, University of Georgia, 1951; MPH, University of North Carolina, 1959; PhD, University of Oklahoma, 1965. Appointments: Statistical Research Assistant, 1957-58, Research Statistician, 1959-60, Biostatistical Analyst, 1960-63, Chief, Mental Health Statistics Section, Biostatistics Service, 1965-67, Director, Biostatistics Service, 1967-68, Chief Statistician, 1968, Georgia Department of Public Health; Assistant Professor to Professor of Decision Sciences, 1968-91, Professor Emeritus, 1991-, Georgia State University. Publications: Biostatistics: A Foundation for Analysis in the Health Sciences, 1974, 7th edition, 1999; Business Statistics for Management and Economics (with James C Terrell), 1975, 7th edition, 1994; Introductory Statistics with Applications, 1977; Applied Nonparametric Statistics, 1978, 2nd edition, 1990; Essentials of Business Statistics, 1984, 2nd edition, 1988; Pickin' on Peachtree: A History of Country Music in Atlanta, 1990. Contributions to: Numerous journals and periodicals. Memberships: Alpha Iota Delta; American Public Health Association, fellow; Delta Sigma Pi; Phi Kappa Phi. Address: 2943 Appling Drive, Chamblee, GA 30341, USA.

DANIELS Dorothy, (Danielle Dorsett, Angela Gray, Cynthia Kavanaugh, Helaine Ross, Suzanne Somers, Geraldine Thayer, Helen Gray Weston),b. 1 July 1915, Waterbury, Connecticut, USA. Writer. m. 7 Oct 1937. Education: Normal School, New Brittain, Connecticut. Publications: The Magic Ring, 1978; Purple and the Gold, 1978; Yesterday's Evil, 1980; Veil of Treachery, 1980; Legend of Death, 1980; Valley of Shadows, 1980; Monte

Carlo, 1981; Saratoga, 1981; Sisters of Valcour, 1981; For Love and Valcour, 1983; Crisis at Valcour, 1985; Illusion of Haven's Edge, 1990. Memberships: Authors Guild; National League of American Pen Women, honorary member; Ventura County Writers. Address: 6107 Village 6, Camarillo, CA 93010, USA.

DANIELS Lucy. See: **INMAN Lucy Daniels.**

DANIELS Max. See: **GELLIS Roberta Leah.**

DANIELS Molly Ann, (Shouri Daniels), b. 2 July 1932, Kerala, India.Writer; Teacher; Editor. 1 son, 1 daughter. Education: PhD, University of Chicago's Committee on Social Thought, 1986. Appointment: Director, Clothesline School of Writing, Chicago, Illinois, 1984-. Publications: The Yellow Fish, 1966; The Clotheslines Review, 4 issues of anthology of fiction (editor), 1986-90; The Prophetic Novel: A Study of A Passage to India, 1990; Father Gander Rhymes and Other Poems (editor), 1990; The Clothesline Review Manual for Writers, textbook. Contributions to: Indian PEN; Quest; Femina; Chicago Review; Primavera; Carleton Miscellany; Tri-Quarterly; Journal of Literary Studies; Saul Bellow Journal. Honours: Fulbright-Smith-Mundt Grant, 1961-62; Illinois Arts Council Grants, 1978, 1982; Syndicated Fiction Award, PEN. Membership: Midwest Authors. Address: Clothesline School of Writing, Department of Continuing Education, University of Chicago, 5835 South Kimbark, Chicago, IL 60637, USA.

DANIELS Olga. See: **SINCLAIR Olga Ellen.**

DANIELSON Carl. See: **KRUMMACHER Johann Henrich Karl Daniel.**

DANIELSSON Jon, b. 5 Mar 1949, Blonduos, Iceland. Writer; Translator. m. Marion McGreevy, 31 Dec 1993, 3 sons, 2 daughters. Education: Icelandic Student Degree, MA Akureyri, Iceland, 1970; University of Iceland; University of Stockholm, Sweden. Honour: Translator of the Year, Children's Books, 1995. Membership: Icelandic Authors Union. Literary Agent: Skyaldborg Publishers Ltd, Armula 23-15108, Iceland. Address: Skulagata, 62-105 Reykjavik, Iceland.

DANN Colin Michael, b. 10 Mar 1943, Richmond, Surrey, England. Author. m. Janet Elizabeth Stratton, 4 June 1977. Publications: The Animals of Farthing Wood, 1979; In the Grip of Winter, 1981; Fox's Feud, 1982; The Fox Cub Bold, 1983; The Seige of White Deer Park, 1985; The Ram of Sweetriver, 1986; King of the Vagabonds, 1987; The Beach Dogs, 1988; The Flight from Farthing Wood, 1988; Just Nuffin, 1989; In the Path of the Storm, 1989; A Great Escape, 1990; A Legacy of Ghosts, 1991; The City Cats, 1991; Battle for the Park, 1992; The Adventure Begins, 1994; Copycat, 1998. Honour: Arts Council National Award for Children's Literature, 1980. Membership: Society of Authors. Address: Castle Oast, Ewhurst Green, East Sussex, England.

DANN Jack, b. 15 Feb 1945, Johnson City, USA. Author. m. Jeanne Van Buren Dann. Education: BA, State University of New York, Binghamton, 1968. Publications: Wandering Stars (editor), 1974; Starhiker, 1977; Time Tipping, 1980; Junction, 1981; The Man Who Melted, 1984; In the Field of Fire (editor with Jeanne Van Buren Dann), 1987; Unicorns II, 1992; Dragons, 1993. Contributions to: New Dimensions; Orbit; New Worlds; Asimov's Science Fiction Magazines; Fiction Writers Handbook. Honours: Esteemed Knight, Mark Twain Society, 1975-; Co-Winner, Gilgamesh Award, 1986.Memberships: Science Fiction Writers of America; Authors Guild; World Future Society. Address: 825 Front Street, Binghamton, NY 13905, USA.

DANTICAT Edwidge, b. 19 Jan 1969, Port-au-Prince, Haiti. Writer. Education: Barnard College, 1990; MFA, Brown University, 1993. Publications: Breath, Eyes, Memory, 1994; Krik? Krak!, 1995. Honours: National

Book Award Finalist, 1995; Granta's Best of American Novelists Citatioin, 1996. Membership: Alpha Kappa Alpha. Address: c/o Soho Press, 853 Broadway, No 1903, New York, NY 10003, USA.

DANTO Arthur C(oleman), b. 1 Jan 1924, Ann Arbor, Michigan, USA. Professor Emeritus of Philosophy; Writer; Editor. m. (1) Shirley Rovetch, 9 Aug 1946, dec 1978, 2 daughters, (2) Barbara Westman, 15 Feb 1980. Education: BA, Wayne State University, 1948; MA, 1949, PhD, 1952, Columbia University; Postgraduate Studies, University of Paris, 1949-50. Appointments: Teacher, 1952-72, Johnsonian Professor of Philosophy, 1972-92, Chairman, Philosophy Department, 1979-87, Professor Emeritus, 1992-, Columbia University; Editor, Journal of Philosophy, 1975-; Art Critic, The Nation, 1984-. Publications: Analytical Philosophy of History, 1965; Nietzsche as Philosopher, 1965; Analytical Philosophy of Knowledge, 1968; What Philosophy Is, 1968; Mysticism and Morality, 1972; Analytical Philosophy of Action, 1973; Jean-Paul Sartre, 1975; The Transfiguration of the Commonplace, 1981; Narration and Knowledge, 1985; The Philosophical Disenfranchisement of Art, 1986; The State of the Art, 1987; Connections to the World, 1989; Encounters and Reflections, 1990; Beyond the Brillo Box, 1992; Embodied Meaning, 1994; Playing with the Edge, 1995; After the End of Art, 1996. Contributions to: Articles and reviews in many publications. Honours: Fulbright Scholarship, 1949-50; Guggenheim Fellowships, 1969, 1982; Distinguished Fulbright Professor to Yugoslavia, 1976; Lionel Trilling Book Prize, 1982; George S Polk Award for Criticism, 1985; National Book Critics Circle Award in Criticism, 1990; New York Public Library Literary Lion, 1993; Frank Jewett Mather Prize in Criticism, College Art Association, 1996. Address: 420 Riverside Drive, New York, NY 10025, USA.

DARBY Catherine. See: **PETERS Maureen.**

DARBY John, b. 18 Nov 1940, Belfast, Northern Ireland. Professor of Ethnic Studies; Writer. m. Marie Darby, 13 Apr 1966, 2 sons. Education: BA, Honours, Modern History, 1962, Diploma, Education, 1970, Queen's University, Belfast; Certificate, Education, St Joseph's College of Education, Belfast, 1963; DPhil, University of Ulster, 1985. Appointments: Teacher of History, St Malachy's College, Belfast, 1963-71; Research and Publications Officer, Northern Ireland Community Relations Commission, Belfast, 1971-74; Lecturer in Social Administration, New University of Ulster, 1974-85; Associate in Education, Graduate School of Education, Harvard University, 1980; Director, Centre for the Study of Conflict, 1985-91, Professor of Ethnic Studies, 1985-, University of Ulster; Visiting Professor, Center for International Studies, Duke University, 1988; Director, Ethnic Studies Network, 1991-; Director, INCORE (Initiative on Conflict Resolution and Ethnicity), University of Ulster and United Nations University, Japan, 1992-97. Publications: Conflict in Northern Ireland, 1976; Northern Ireland: Background to the Conflict (editor), 1983; Dressed to Kill: Cartoonists and the Northern Irish Conflict, 1983; Intimidation and the Control of Conflict in Northern Ireland, 1986; Political Violence (editor with N Dodge and A C Hepburn), 1990; Scorpions in a Bottle, 1997. Contributions to: Many books and journals. Honours: Outstanding Academic Book Citation, Choice, 1977; Shortlisted, American Sociological Association Distinguished Scholarly Publication Award, 1987; Visiting Scholar, Rockefeller Centre, Bellagio, Italy, 1990; Guest Fellow, Woodrow Wilson Center, Washington, DC, 1992; Officer of the Order of the British Empire, 1997; Honorary Professor, University of Sunderland, 1997; Jennings Randolph Senior Fellow, US Institute of Peace, Washington, DC, 1998. Address: 61 Strand Road, Portstewart, BT55 7LU, Northern Ireland.

DARCY Clare, b. USA. Writer. Publications: Georgia, 1971; Cecily, or A Young Lady of Quality, 1972; Lydia, or Love in Town, 1973; Victoire, 1974; Allegra, 1975; Lady Pamela, 1975; Regina, 1976; Elyza, 1976; Cressida, 1977; Eugenia, 1977; Gwendolen, 1978; Rolande, 1978; Letty, 1980; Caroline and Julia, 1982; Eugenia, 1990;Georgia, 1990; Rolande, 1991; Cressida, 1991.

Address: c/o Walker & Co, 720 Fifth Avenue, New York, NY 10019, USA.

DARDIS Thomas A, b. 19 Aug 1926, New York, New York, USA. Writer; Teacher. m. Jane Buckelew, 25 Oct 1947, div 1982, 2 sons, 1 daughter. Education: AB, New York University, 1949; MA, 1952; PhD 1979, Columbia University. Publications: Some Time in the Sun, 1976; Keaton, 1979; Harold Lloyd, 1983; The Thirsty Muse, 1989; Firebrand: The Life of Horace Liveright, 1995. Contributions to: American Film; Journal of Popular Film and Television; Antioch Review; Vanity Fair. Address: 2727 Palisade Avenue, New York, NY 10463, USA.

DARKE Marjorie Sheila, b. 25 Jan 1929, Birmingham, England. Writer. m. 1952, 2 sons, 1 daughter. Education: Leicester College of Art, 1947-50; Central School of Art, London, 1950-51. Publications: For Young Adults: Ride the Iron Horse, 1973; The Star Trap, 1974; A Question of Courage, 1975; The First of Midnight, 1977; A Long Way to Go, 1978; Comeback, 1981; Tom Post's Private Eye, 1982; Messages and Other Shivery Tales, 1984; A Rose From Blighty, 1990. For Beginner Readers: Mike's Bike, 1974; What Can I Do, 1975; The Big Brass Band, 1976; My Uncle Charlie, 1977; Carnival Day, 1979. For Young Children: Kipper's Turn, 1976; Kipper Skips, 1979; Imp, 1985; The Rainbow Sandwich, 1989; Night Windows, 1990; Emma's Monster, 1992; Just Bear and Friends, 1996. Memberships: Society of Authors; International PEN. Address: c/o Rogers, Coleridge & White, 20 Powis Mews, London W11 1JN, England.

DARLING Julia Rose, b. 21 Aug 1956, Winchester, England. Playwright; Fiction Writer. m. Ivan Sears, div, 2 daughters. Education: BA, Fine Art, Falmouth School of Art. Publications: Sauce, with The Poetry Virgins; Bloodlines, short stories; Crocodile Soup. Contributions to: Printers Devil; British Council New Writing; Penguin Modern Women's Fiction. Honour: Arts Council of England Award, 1996. Literary Agent: Jane Bradish Ellames. Address: 5 Charlotte Square, Newcastle-upon-Tyne NE1 4XF, England.

DARNTON Robert (Choate), b. 10 May 1939, New York, New York, USA. Professor of European History; Writer. m. Susan Lee Glover, 29 June 1963, 1 son, 2 daughters. Education: BA Magna cum Laude, Harvard College, 1960; Bachelor of Philosophy in History, 1962, Doctorate of Philosophy in History, 1964, Oxford University. Appointments: Reporter, New York Times, 1964-65; Junior Fellow, Society of Fellows, Harvard University, 1965-68; Assistant Professor, 1968-71, Associate Professor, 1971-72, Professor, 1972-, Shelby Cullom Davis Professor of European History, 1985-, Director, Program in European Cultural Studies, 1987-95, Princeton University; Director d'Études, École des Hautes Études en Sciences Sociales, Paris, 1971, 1981, 1985; Fellow, Center for Advanced Study in the Behavioral Sciences, Stanford, 1973-74, Netherlands Institute for Advanced Study, 1976-77, Institute for Advanced Study, Berlin, 1989-90, 1993-94; Member, Institute for Advanced Study, Princeton, New Jersey, 1977-81; George Eastman Visiting Professor, Oxford University, 1986-87; Lecturer, Collège de France, 1987; Member, All Souls College, Oxford, 1996-; Honorary Professor, University of Warwick, 1996-. Publications: Mesmerism and the End of the Enlightenment, 1968; The Business of Enlightenment: A Publishing History of the Encyclopédie, 1979; The Literary Underground of the Old Regime, 1982; The Great Cat Massacre and Other Episodes in French Cultural History, 1984; Revolution in Print: The Press in France 1775-1800 (editor with Daniel Roche), 1989; The Kiss of Lamourette: Reflections in Cultural History, 1989; Edition et sédition: L'univers de la littérature clandestine au XVIIIe siècle, 1991; Berlin Journal, 1989-1990, 1991; Gens de Lettres, Gens du Livre, 1992; The Forbidden Best-Sellers of Prerevolutionary France, 1995; The Corpus of Clandestine Literature in France, 1769-1789, 1995. Honours: Koren Prize, Society for French Historical Studies, 1973; Leo Gershoy Prize, American Historical Association, 1979; John D and Catharine T MacArthur Foundation Fellowship, 1982-87; Los Angeles Times Book Prize, 1984; Behrman Humanities Award, Princeton

University, 1987; Chevalier, 1988, Officer, 1993, Ordre des Arts et des Lettres, France; Prix Médicis, 1991; Prix Chateaubriand, 1991; National Book Critics Circle Award, 1996. Memberships: Academia Europaea; Académie Royale de Langue et de Littérature Françaises, Belgium; American Academy of Arts and Sciences, fellow; American Antiquarian Society; American Philosophical Society; American Society for Eighteenth-Century Studies; International Society for Eighteenth-Century Studies, president, 1987-91. Address: c/o Department of History, Princeton University, 129 Dickinson Hall, Princeton, NJ 08544, USA.

DARUWALLA K(eki) N(asserwanji), b. 24 Jan 1937, Lahore, India. Poet; Writer. m. Khorshed Keki Daruwalla, 10 May 1965. Education: MA, English, Punjab University, Chandigarh. Appointment: Visiting Fellow, Queen Elizabeth House, Oxford, 1980-81. Publications: Poetry: Under Oion, 1970; Apparition in April, 1971; Crossing of Rivers, 1976; Winter Poems, 1980; The Keeper of the Dead, 1982; Landscapes, 1987; A Summer of Tigers, 1995. Fiction: Sword and Abyss, 1979. Editor: Two Decades of Indian Poetry, 1960-80, 1981; The Minister for Permanent Unrest, 1996. Contributions to: Anthologies, journals, and periodicals. Honours: Sahitya Akademi Award, 1984; Commonwealth Poetry Award, Asia Region, 1987. Memberships: Sahitya Akademi, advisory board for English, 1983-87. Address: 79 Mount Kailash, Pocket-A, SFS Apartments, New Delhi 110065, India.

DARVI Andrea. See: **PLATE Andrea.**

DARVILL Timothy (Charles), b. 22 Dec 1957, Cheltenham, England. Professor of Archaeology. Education: BA, Honours, Class 2.1, Archaeology, 1979, PhD, 1983, University of Southampton. Appointments: Director, Timothy Darvill Archaeological Consultants, 1985-91; Professor of Archaeology, Bournemouth University, 1991-. Publications: Megalithic Chambered Tombs of the Cotswold-Severn Region, 1982; The Archaeology of the Uplands, 1986; Prehistoric Britain, 1987; Ancient Monuments in the Countryside, 1987; Prehistoric Gloucestershire, 1987; Neolithic Houses in Northwest Europe and Beyond (editor with Julian Thomas), 1996; Prehistoric Britain from the Air, 1996. Contributions to: Scholarly books and journals. Memberships: Cotswold Archaeological Trust, Chairman, 1992-; Council for British Archaeology; Institute of Field Archaeologists, Chairman, 1989-91; Council of the National Trust, 1988-97; Neolithic Studies Group, Coordinator, 1983-; Society of Antiquaries of London, Fellow; Society of Antiquaries of Scotland, Fellow. Address: c/o School of Conservation Sciences, Bournemouth University, Poole House, Talbot Campus, Fern Barrow Poole, Dorset BH12 5BB, England.

DARWISH (Ahmed) Adel (Abed El-Moneim), b. 8 Dec 1945, Alexandria, Egypt. Writer; Journalist. m. Elizabeth Catherine Darwish, div, 1 son, 1 daughter. Education: Graduate, University of Alexandria, 1966, University of London, 1975. Appointments: Editor, Ashara Al-Ansal, London, 1984-86; Reporter, The Independent, London, 1986-; Consultant on the Middle East. Publications: Between the Quill and the Sword: The Political Background to the Rushdie Affair, 1989; Unholy Babylon: The Secret History of Saddam's War, 1991; Water Wars: Coming Conflict in the Middle East, 1993; Rafsanjani's Iran: Iran's Foreign Policy in the 1990's, 1993. Contributions to: Books and periodicals. Memberships: National Union of Journalists; Writers Guild. Address: c/o The Independent, 40 City Road, London E4, England.

DAS Kamala, b. 31 Mar 1934, Malabar, South India. Poetry Editor; Poet; Writer. m. K Madhava Das, 1949, 3 sons. Education: Private. Appointment: Poetry Editor, Illustrated Weekly of India, Bombay, 1971-79. Publications: Poetry: Summer in Calcutta: Fifty Poems, 1965; The Descendants, 1967; The Old Playhouse and Other Poems, 1973; Tonight This Savage Rite: The Love Poetry of Kamala Das and Pritish Nandy, 1979; Collected Poems, 1987. Novels: Alphabet of Lust, 1977; Manomi,

1987; The Sandalwood Tree, 1988. Honours: Kerala Sahitya Academy Award for Fiction, 1969; Asian World Prize for Literature, 1985. Address: Sthanuvilas Bungalow, Sastgamangalam, Trivndrum 10, Kerala, India.

DASSANOWSKY Robert von, b. 28 Jan 1960, New York, New York, USA. Writer; Poet; Dramatist; Editor; University Professor. Education: Graduate, American Academy of Dramatic Arts, Pasadena, California, 1977-78; American Film Institute Conservatory Program, Los Angeles, 1979-81; BA, 1985, MA, 1988, PhD, 1992, University of California at Los Angeles. Appointments: Founding Editor, Rohwedder: International Magazine of Literature and Art, 1986-93; Visiting Assistant Professor of German, 1992-93, University of California at Los Angeles; Writer, Researcher, Disney Channel, 1990-92; Corresponding Editor, Rampike, 1991-.; German Language Editor, Osiris, 1991-; Managing Editor, Writers Forum, 1993-96; Assistant Professor of German, Head, German Studies, Director of Film Studies, University of Colorado at Colorado Springs, 1993-; Founding President, PEN Colorado, 1993-; Vice-President, Austrian American Film Association (AAFA), 1997-; Editorial Board, Modern Austrian Literature, 1997-; Associate Professor of German and Film, University of Colorado at Colorado Springs, 1999-. Publications: Phantom Empires: The Novels of Alexander Lernet-Holenia and the Question of Postimperial Austrian Identity, 1996; Hans Raimund: Verses of a Marriage (translator), 1996; Hans Raimund: Verses of a Marriage (translator), 1996; Telegrams from the Metropole: Selected Poetry, 1999; Alexander Lernet-Holenia: Mars in Aries (translator), forthcoming. Other: Several plays and television scripts. Contributions to: Periodicals and anthologies. Honours: Julie Harris/Beverly Hills Theater Guild Playwrighting Award, 1984; Academico Honoris Causa, Academia Culturale d'Europa, Italy, 1989; City of Los Angeles Cultural Grants, 1990, 1991, 1992; University of Colorado President's Fund for the Humanities Grant, 1996. Memberships: Authors League; Dramatists Guild; Paneuropa Union, Austria; Modern Language Association; PEN; Poet and Writers; Society for Cinema Studies; Screen Actors Guild; Vice president, Austrian American Film Assoc. 1998-; Vice president, International Alexander Lernet-Holenia Society 1998-. Address: c/o Department of Languages and Cultures, University of Colorado, Colorado Springs, CO 80933, USA.

DASZKOWSKI Eugeniusz Andrzei, b. 4 Feb 1930, Wyszkow, Poland. Master Mariner; Writer. m. Danuta Jankowska, 30 May 1958, 1 daughter. Education: Navigation School, Szczecin, 1948-50; Engineering Polytechnical School, Szczecin, 1952-56. Appointment: Rector, Maritime University, Szczecin, 1972-78. Publications: The Watch, 1972; The Sailor's Sea-Line, 1973; To the Port of Design, 1975; The African Meetings, 1975; The Sea Polutions by Ship, 1977; The Sea Doorsteps, 1978; The Fere, 1981; The Last Trip of Narvik, 1982; The Zahi, 1985; The Blinders From San Pedro, 1986; The Monkey Trip, 1988; My Wyszkow, 1996; The Sailor's Knot, 1996; The School of the Sea Wolfs, 1997; First After the God, (two editions), 1997. Contributions to: Periodicals and journals. Honours: Award, Sea Polish Trade Union, 1970; Josef Conrad Award, 1975; Readers Award, 1987; First Award, Szczecin Cultural Association, 1997. Memberships: Polish Writers Association; Société des Auteurs. Address: ul Anhellego 13, 834455 Szczecin, Poland.

DATHORNE O(scar) R(onald), b. 19 Nov 1934, Georgetown, Guyana. Professor of English; Writer; Poet. Education: BA, 1958, MA, 1960, PhD, 1966, University of Sheffield; Graduate Certificate in Education, 1959, Diploma in Education, 1967, University of London; MBA, MPA, 1984, University of Miami. Appointments: Associate Professor, Ahmadu Bello University, Zaria, 1959-63, University of Ibadan, 1963-66; UNESCO Consultant to the Government of Sierra Leone, 1967-68; Professor of English, Njala University College, University of Sierra Leone, 1968-69; Professor of African Literature, Howard University, 1970; Professor of Afro-American Literature, University of Wisconsin, Madison, 1970-71; Professor of

English and Black Literature, Ohio State University, 1975-77; Professor of English, University of Miami, Coral Gables, Florida, 1977-. Publications: Dumplings in the Soup (novel), 1963; The Scholar Man (novel), 1964; Carribean Narrative (editor), 1965; Carribean Verse (editor), 1967; Africa in Prose, 1969; The Black Mind, 1975; African Literature in the Twentieth Century, 1976; Dark Ancestor, 1981; Dele's Child, 1985; Imagining the World: Typical Belief vs Reality in Global Encounters, 1994. Address: Department of English, University of Miami, Coral Gables, FL 33124, USA.

DAUNTON Martin James, b. 7 Feb 1949, Cardiff. University Professor of History. m. Claire Gobbi, 7 Jan 1984. Education: BA, University of Nottingham, 1970; PhD, University of Kent, 1974. Appointments: Lecturer, University of Durham, 1973-79; Lecturer, 1979-85, Reader, 1985-89, Professor of History, 1989-97, University College London; Convenor, Studies in History series, Royal Historical Society, 1995-; Professor Economic History, University of Cambridge, 1997-. Publications: Coal Metropolis: Cardiff; House and Home in the Victorian City, 1850-1914; Royal Mail: The Post office Since 1840; A Property Owning Democracy?; Progress and Poverty. Contributions to: Economic History Review; Past & Present; Business History; Historical Research; Journal of Urban History; Charity, Self-Interest and Welfare in the English Past, 1996; English Historical Review; Twentieth Century British History. Honour: Fellow of the British Academy, 1997. Membership: Royal Historical Society. Address: Churchill College, Cambridge, CB3 0DS, England.

DAVEY Frank(land Wilmot), b. 19 Apr 1940, Vancouver, British Columbia, Canada. Professor of Canadian Literature; Writer; Poet; Editor. m. (1) Helen Simmons, 1962, div 1969, (2) Linda McCartney, 1969, 1 son, 1 daughter. Education: BA, 1961, MA, 1963, University of British Columbia, Vancouver; PhD, University of Southern California at Los Angeles, 1968. Appointments: Founding Editor, Tish Magazine, Vancouver, 1961-63, Open Letter, Toronto, 1965-; Lecturer, 1963-67, Assistant Professor, 1967-69, Royal Roads Military College, Victoria, British Columbia; Writer-in-Residence, Sir George Williams University, Montreal, 1969-70; Assistant Professor, 1970-72, Associate Professor, 1972-80, Professor of English, 1980-90, Chair, Department of English, 1985-88, 1989-90, York University, Toronto; General Editor, Quebec Translations Series, 1973-90, New Canadian Criticism Series, 1977-; Visiting Professor, Shastri Indo-Canadian Institute, Karnatak University, India, 1982; Director, Swift Current Literary Database and Magazine Project, 1984-90; Carl F Klinck Professor of Canadian Literature, University of Western Ontario, London, 1990-. Publications: Poetry: D-Day and After, 1962; City of the Gulls and Sea, 1964; Bridge Force, 1965; The Scarred Hill, 1966; Four Myths for Sam Perry, 1970; Weeds, 1970; Griffon, 1972; King of Swords, 1972; L'An Trentiesme: Selected Poems 1961-70, 1972; Arcana, 1973; The Clallam, 1973; War Poems, 1979; The Arches: Selected Poems, 1981; Capitalistic Affection!, 1982; Edward and Patricia, 1984; The Louis Riel Organ and Piano Company, 1985; The Abbotsford Guide to India, 1986; Postcard Translations, 1988; Popular Narratives, 1991; Cultural Mischief: A Practical Guide to Multiculturalism, 1996. Criticism: Five Readings of Olson's "Maximus", 1970; Earle Birney, 1971; From There to Here: A Guide to English-Canadian Literature Since 1960, 1974; Louis Dudek and Raymond Souster, 1981; The Contemporary Canadian Long Poem, 1983; Surviving the Paraphrase: 11 Essays on Canadian Literature, 1983; Margaret Atwood: A Feminist Poetics, 1984; Reading Canadian Reading, 1988; Post-National Arguments: The Politics of the Anglophone-Canadian Novel Since 1967, 1993; Reading "KIM" Right, 1993; Canadian Literary Power: Essays on Anglophone-Canadian Literary Conflict, 1994; Karla's Web: A Cultural Examination of the Mahaffy-French Murders, 1994, revised edition, 1995. Contributions to: Books and journals. Honours: Macmillan Prize, 1962; Department of Defence Arts Research Grants, 1965, 1966, 1968; Canada Council Fellowships, 1966, 1974;

Humanities Research Council of Canada Grants, 1974, 1981; Canadian Federation for the Humanities Grants, 1979, 1992; Social Sciences and Humanities Research Council Fellowship, 1981. Membership: Association of Canadian College and University Teachers of English, president, 1994-96. Address: 499 Dufferin Avenue, London, Ontario N6B 2A1, Canada.

DAVEY Thomas A, b. 2 Jan 1954, Philadelphia, Pennsylvania, USA. Adult and Child Psychologist; Writer. Education: BA, Duke University, 1976; EdD, Harvard University, 1984. Appointments: Teaching Fellow, Harvard University; Conducts Private Practice in Adult and Child Psychology, Cambridge. Publication: A Generation Divided: German Children and the Berlin Wall, 1987. Contributions to: Articles and reviews to magazines and newspapers. Honours: German Academic Exchange Service Grants, 1981-82, 1988; Lyndhurst Foundation Prize, 1985. Memberships: American Psychological Association; Massachusetts Psychological Association. Address: 23 Bigelow Street, No 2, Boston, MA 02135, USA.

DAVID Hugh Housdon, b. 22 May 1954. Freelance Writer. Education: BEd, Institute of Education, University of London. Appointments: English Teacher, Ramsden School, Orpington, Kent, 1976-82; Director, Fulcrum Theatre, 1982-84; Freelance Writer, 1982-; Columnist, History Today, 1987-93; Charity Consultant, 1996-. Publications: Books: The Fitzrovians, 1988; Heroes, Mavericks and Bounders, 1991; Stephen Spender - A Portrait with Background, 1992; On Queer Street, 1997. Contributions to: The Times; The Independent on Sunday; Times Educational Supplement; London Evening Standard. Membership: Awards Panel, Royal Television Society, 1986, 1988. Address: Flat D, 37 Albert Square, London SW8 1BY, England.

DAVIDSON Basil Risbridger, b. 9 Nov 1914, Bristol, England. Writer. m. Marion Young, 7 July 1943, 3 sons. Publications: Old Africa Rediscovered, 1959; The African Slave Trade, 1961; The Africans, 1969; Africa in Modern History, 1978; Special Operations Europe, 1980; The Fortunate Isles, 1989; African Civilisation Revisited, 1991; The Black Man's Burden: Africa and the Curse of the Nation-State, 1992; The Search for Africa, 1994. Honours: Military Cross, British Army; Bronze Star, US Army; Ansfield Woolf Award, 1959; DLitt, honoris causa, University of Ibadan, 1975, University of Dar-es-Salaam, 1985; DUniv, honoris causa, Open University of Great Britain, 1980; University of Edinburgh, 1981; Agnelli Visiting Professor, University of Turin, 1990. Address: Old Cider Mill, North Wootton, Somerset BA4 4HA, England.

DAVIDSON Donald (Herbert), b. 6 Mar 1917, Springfield, Massachusetts, USA. Philosopher; Professor; Writer. m. (1), 1 daughter, (2), Nancy Hirshberg, 4 Apr 1975, dec 1979, (3) Marcia Cavell, 3 July 1984. Education: BA, 1939, MA, 1941, PhD, 1949, Harvard University. Appointments: Instructor, Queen's College, New York City, 1947-50; Assistant Professor to Professor, Stanford University, 1951-67; Visiting Professor, University of Tokyo, 1955; Professor, 1967-70, Chairman, Department of Philosophy, 1968-70, Lecturer with rank of Professor, 1970-76, Princeton University; Gavin David Young Lecturer, University of Adelaide, 1968; John Locke Lecturer, Oxford University, 1970; Professor, Rockefeller University, New York City, 1970-76, University of Chicago, 1976-81; Willis S and Marion Slusser Professor University of California at Berkeley, 1981-; John Dewey Lecturer, University of Michigan, 1973; George Eastman Visiting Professor, Balliol College, Oxford, 1984-85; Fulbright Distinguished Lecturer, India, 1985-86; S J Keeling Memorial Lecturer in Greek Philosophy, University College, London, 1986; Thalheimer Lecturer, Johns Hopkins University, 1987; John Dewey Lecturer, Columbia University, 1989; Alfred North Whitehead Lecturer, Harvard University, 1990; Kant Lecturer, University of Munich, 1993; Various other lectureships. Publications: Decision Making: An Experimental Approach (with Patrick Suppes), 1957; Words and Objections (editor with J Hintikka), 1969; Semantics for Natural Language (editor with Gilbert Harman), 1970; The Logic of Grammar (co-editor), 1975; Essays on Actions and Events, 1980; Inquiries into Truth and Interpretation, 1983. Honours: Teschemacher Fellow in Classics and Philosophy, 1939-41; Rockefeller Fellowship in the Humanities, 1945-46; American Council of Learned Societies Fellowship, 1958-59; National Science Foundation Research Grants, 1964-65, 1968; Fellow, Center for Advanced Study in the Behavioral Sciences, 1969-70; Guggenheim Fellowship, 1973-74; Fellow, All Souls College, Oxford, 1973-74; Honorary Research Fellow, University College, London, 1978; Sherman Fairchild Distinguished Scholar, California Institute of Technology, 1989; Hegel Prize, City Stuttgart, 1991; DDL Honoris causa, Oxford University, 1995. Memberships: American Academy of Arts and Sciences; American Association of University Professors; American Philosophical Association; American Philosophical Society; British Academy, corresponding member. Address: c/o Department of Philosophy, University of California at Berkeley, Berkeley, CA 94720, USA.

DAVIDSON Lionel, (David Line), b. 31 Mar 1922, Hull, Yorkshire, England. Author. m. (1) Fay Jacobs, 1949, dec 1988, 2 sons, (2) Frances Ullman, 1989. Publications: The Night of Wenceslas, 1960; The Rose of Tibet, 1962; A Long Way to Shiloh, 1966; Run for Your Life, 1966; Making Good Again, 1968; Smith's Gazelle, 1971; Mike and Me, 1974; The Sun Chemist, 1976; The Chelsea Murders, 1978; Under Plum Lake, 1980; Screaming High, 1985; Kolymsky Heights, 1994. Honours: Silver Quill Award, Authors Club, 1961; Gold Dagger Awards, Crime Writers Association, 1961, 1967, 1979. Address: c/o Curtis Brown, Haymarket House, 28/29 Haymarket, London SW1Y 4SP, England.

DAVIDSON Michael, b. 18 Dec 1944, Oakland, California, USA. Professor of Literature; Poet; Writer. m. (1) Carol Wikarska, 1970, div 1974, (2) Lois Chamberlain, 1988, 2 children. Education: BA, San Francisco State University, 1967; PhD, State University of New York at Buffalo, 1971; Post-doctoral Fellow, University of California at Berkeley, 1974-75. Appointments: Visiting Lecturer, San Diego State University, 1973-76; Curator, Archive for New Poetry, 1975-85, Professor of Literature, 1977-, University of California at San Diego. Publications: Poetry: Exchanges, 1972; Two Views of Pears, 1973; The Mutabilities, and the Foul Papers, 1976; Summer Letters, 1976; Grillwork, 1980; Discovering Motion, 1980; The Prose of Fact, 1981; The Landing of Rochambeau, 1985; Analogy of the Ion, 1988; Post Hoc, 1990. Other: The San Francisco Renaissance: Poetics and Community at Mid-Century, 1989. Contributions to: Periodicals. Honour: National Endowment for the Arts Grant, 1976. Address: c/o Department of Literature, University of California at San Diego, La Jolla, CA 92093, USA.

DAVIDSON William H(arley), b. 25 Sept 1951, Albuquerque, New Mexico, USA. Associate Professor; Researcher; Consultant; Writer. m. Anneke Rozendaal, 16 June 1973, 3 sons. Education: AB, Harvard College, 1973; MBA, 1975, DBA, 1979, Harvard Business School. Appointments: Assistant Professor, Amos Tuck School, Dartmouth College, 1978-82; Adjunct Professor, Fletcher School of Law and Diplomacy, Tufts University, 1980; Visiting Professor, INSEAD, Fontainebleau, France, 1981-83, Dalian Institute of Science and Technology, China, 1984, International University of Japan, 1988-90; Associate Professor, Colgate Darden School, University of Virginia, 1982-86; Founder-Chairman, Management Education Services Associates, 1985-; Associate Professor, School of Business Administration, University of Southern California, 1986-; Partner, Deloitte & Touche Management Consulting, 1996-. Publications: Tracing the Multinationals (with J C Curhan and Rajan Suri), 1977; Foreign Production of Technology-Intensive Products by US based Multinational Enterprises (with Raymond Vernon), 1979; Experience Effects in International Investment and Technology Transfer, 1980; Global Strategic Management, 1982; The Amazing Race, 1984; Revitalizing American Industry: Lessons from our Competitors (editor with M S Hochmuth), 1985; US Competiveness: The Case of the Textile Industry (with C Feigenoff and F G Ghadar), 1987; Managing the Global Corporation: Cases in Strategy and Management (with José de la Torre), 1989; 2020 Vision (with Stanley Davis), 1991. Contributions to: Books and journals. Honour: Best Business Book of the Year Selection, Fortune Magazine, 1992. Membership: Academy of International Business. Address: c/o MESA Research, 1874 South Pacific Coast Highway, Suite 710, Redondo Beach, CA 90277, USA.

DAVIE-MARTIN Hugh. See: **McCUTCHEON Hugh.**

DAVIES (Edward) Hunter, b. 7 Jan 1936, Renfrew, Scotland. Writer. m. 11 June 1960, 1 son, 2 daughters. Education: BA, DipEd, University College, Durham, England. Publications: 40 Books including: Here We Go Round the Mulberry Bush, 1965; The Beatles, 1968, 2nd edition, 1985; The Glory Game, 1972, 2nd edition, 1985; A Walk Along the Wall, 1974, 2nd edition, 1986; A Walk Along the Lakes, 1979; Fit for the Sixth, 1989; In Search of Columbus, 1991. Contributions to: Sunday Times, 1960-84; Punch, 1979-89; Independent, London, 1990-. Literary Agent: Giles Gordon. Address: 11 Boscastle Road, London NW5, England.

DAVIES James Atterbury, b. 25 Feb 1939, Llandeilo, Dyfed, Wales. Senior Lecturer; Writer. m. Jennifer Hicks, 1 Jan 1966, 1 son, 1 daughter. Education: BA, 1965; PhD, 1969. Appointments: Visiting Professor, Baylor University, Texas, 1981; Senior Lecturer, University College of Swansea, 1990-; Mellon Research Fellow, University of Texas, 1993. Publications: John Forster: A Literary Life; The Textual Life of Dickens's Characters; Leslie Norris; Dylan Thomas's Places; The Heart of Wales (editor), 1995; A Swansea Anthology (editor), 1996; A Reference Companian to Dylan Thomas, 1998. Membership: University of Wales Association for the Study of Welsh Writing in English. Address: Department of English, University College of Swansea, Swansea SA2 8PP, Wales.

DAVIES Pauline. See: **FISK Pauline.**

DAVIES Peter Joseph, b. 15 May 1937, Terang, Victoria, Australia. Physician; Writer. m. Clare Loughnan, 21 Dec 1960, 1 daughter. Education: MB, 1961; MRACP, 1968; FRACP, 1974; MRCP, 1970; MD, 1991. Publications: Mozart in Person: His Character and Health, 1989; Mozart's Health, Illnesses and Death, 1993; The Cause of Beethoven's Deafness, 1996. Contributions to: Journal of Medical Biography, 1995. Memberships: Royal Australian College of Physicians; Gastro-Enterological Society of Australia; Royal Society of Medicine. Address: 14 Hamilton Street, East Kew, Victoria 3102, Australia.

DAVIES Piers (Anthony David), b. 15 June 1941, Sydney, New South Wales, Australia. Barrister; Solicitor; Screenwriter; Poet. m. Margaret Elaine Haswell, 24 Aug 1973, 1 daughter. Education: LLB, University of Auckland, 1964; Diploma of English and Comparative Law, City of London College, 1967. Appointments: Barrister and Solicitor, Jordan, Smith and Davies, Auckland, New Zealand; Chairperson, Short Film Fund, New Zealand Film Commission, 1987-91; Member, Cultural Heritage Law Committee of the International Law Association, 1997-. Publications: East and Other Gong songs, 1967; The Life and Flight of Rev Buck Shotte (with Peter Weir), screenplay, 1969; Day Trip from Mount Meru, 1969; Homesdale (with Peter Weir), screenplay, 1971; The Cars That Ate Paris (with Peter Weir), screenplay, 1973; Diaspora, 1974; Bourgeois Homage to Dada, 1974; Central Almanac (editor), 1974; Skin Deep, screenplay, 1978; R V Huckleberry Finn, video documentary, 1979; Olaf's Coast, documentary, 1982; Jetsam, 1984; The Lamb of God, screenplay, 1985; A Fair Hearing, screenplay, 1995. Contributions to: Shipping Law Section, Encyclopedia of New Zealand Forms and Precedents, 1994; Anthologies and periodicals. Address: 16 Crocus Place, Remuera, Auckland 5, New Zealand.

DAVIES William Thomas Pennar, b. 12 Nov 1911, Aberpennar, Glamorgan, Wales. Author; Poet. m. Rosemarie Wolff, 26 June 1943, 4 sons, 1 daughter. Education: BA, University of Wales, 1932; BLitt,

University of Oxford, 1938; PhD, Yale University, 1943. Publications: Fiction: Anadl o'r Uchelder, 1958; Caregel Nwyf, 1966; Meibion Darogan, 1968; Llais y Durtur, 1985. Poetry: Cinio'r Cythraul, 1946; Naw Wftt, 1957; Yr Efrydd o lyn Cynon, 1961; Y Tlws yn y Lotws, 1971; Llef, 1987. Non-Fiction: Cudd fy Meiau, 1957; Rhwng Chwedl a Chredo, 1966. Contributions to: Reviews and periodicals. Honours: Commonwealth Fund Fellow, 1936-38; Fellow, 1938-40, Fellow Honoris Causa, 1986, Honorary DD, 1987, University of Wales; Honorary Fellow, Welsh Academy, 1989. Address: 10 Heol Grosvenor, Sgeti, Abertawe, Swansea, SA2 0SP, Wales.

DAVIS Alan, b. 30 June 1950, New Orleans, USA. Writer; Professor. 1 son, 1 daughter. Education: BA, 1973, MA, 1975, University of Louisiana; PhD, University of Denver, 1981. Appointments: Professor, Moorhead State University, 1985-; Editor, American Fiction, 1994-. Publications: Rumours From the Lost World, 1993; Eleven Ways of Breathing, 1999. Contributions to: New York Times Book Review; Hudson Review; San Francisco Chornicle; Denver Quarterly; Cleveland Plain Dealer; North Dakota Review. Honours: Fulbright Awards, 1993, 1996; Loft-McKnight Award, 1995. Memberships: National Book Critics Circle; Authors Guild. Address: PO Box 229, Moorhead State University, MN 56563, USA.

DAVIS Andrew (Wynford), b. 1936, England. Lecturer; Writer; Playwright. Appointments: Teacher, St Clement Danes Grammar School, 1958-61, Woodberry Down School, 1961-63, London; Lecturer, Coventry College of Education and University of Warwick, Coventry College, 1963-. Publications: Plays: Marmalade Atkins in Space, 1982; Also Radio and television plays for children and numerous radio plays for adults. Children's Fiction: The Fantastic Feats of Doctor Box, 1972; Conrad's War, 1978; Marmalade and Rufus, 1979, as Marmalade Atkins Dreadful Deeds, 1982; Marmalade Atkins in Space, 1982; Educating Marmalade, 1983; Danger! Marmalade at Work, 1984; Alfonso Bonzo, 1986; Getting Hurt, 1989; Poonam's Pets, 1990; Dirty Foxes, 1990; B Monkey, 1992. Address: c/o Leinon Unna & Durbridge, 24 Pottery Lane, London W11 4LZ, England.

DAVIS Burke, b. 24 July 1913, Durham, North Carolina, USA. Historian; Biographer. m. (1) Evangeline McLennan, 11 Aug 1940, div 1980, 1 son, 1 daughter, (2) Juliet H Burnett, 6 Feb 1982. Education: Duke University, 1931-32, 1933-34; Guilford College, 1935-36; AB, University of North Carolina, 1937. Appointments: Editor, Feature Writer and Sports Editor, Charlotte News, North Carolina, 1937-47; Reporter, Baltimore Evening Sun, Maryland, 1947-52, Greensboro News, North Carolina, 1951-60; Writer and Historian, Colonial Williamsburg, Virginia, 1960-78. Publications: Whisper My Name, 1949; The Ragged Ones, 1951; Yorktown, 1952; They Called Him Stonewall, 1954; Gray Fox: Robert E Lee and the Civil War, 1956; Jeb Stuart, The Last Cavalier, 1957; To Appomattox, 1959; Our Incredible Civil War, 1960; Marine! The Life of Chesty Puller; The Cowpens-Guilford Courthouse Campaign, 1962; America's First Army, 1962; Appomattox: Closing Struggle of the Civil War, 1963; The Summer Land, 1965; A Rebel Raider (co-author), 1966; The Billy Mitchell Affair, 1967; A Williamsburg Galaxy, 1967; The World of Currier & Ives (co-author), 1968; Get Yamamoto, 1969; Yorktown: The Campaign that won America, 1969; Billy Mitchell Story, 1969; Heroes of the American Revolution, 1971; Jamestown, 1971; Thomas Jefferson's Virginia, 1971; Amelia Earhart, 1972; Biography of a Leaf, 1972; Three for Revolution, 1975; Biography of a Kingsnake, 1975; George Washington and the American Revolution, 1975; Newer and Better Organic Gardening, 1976; Biography of a Fish Hawk, 1976; Old Hickory: A Life of Andrew Jackson, 1977; Mr Lincoln's Whiskers, 1978; Sherman's March, 1980; The Long Surrender, 1985; The Southern Railway, 1985; War Bird: The Life and Times of Elliott White Springs, 1986; Civil War: Strange and Fascinating Facts, 1989. Address: 4100 Well Spring, Greensboro, NC 27410, USA.

DAVIS Christopher, b. 23 Oct 1928, Philadelphia, Pennsylvania, USA. Writer; Teacher. Education: BA, University of Pennsylvania, 1955. Publications: Lost Summer; A Kind of Darkness; A Peep Into the 20th Century; Suicide Note; Waiting For It; The Producer; Dog Horse Rat; Scotty; Belmarch; Ishmael; The Sun in Mid Career. Contributions to: Periodicals. Honours: O Henry Prize Story; American Academy of Arts and Letters Literature Award, 1991. Membership: PEN. Address: Curtis Brown, 10 Astor Place, New York, NY 10003, USA.

DAVIS David Brion, b. 16 Feb 1927, Denver, Colorado, USA. Professer of History; Writer. m. (1), 1 son, 2 daughters, (2) Toni Hahn Davis, 9 Sept 1971, 2 sons. Education: AB, Dartmouth College, 1950; AM, 1953, PhD, 1956, Harvard University. Appointments: Instructor, Dartmouth College, 1953-54; Assistant Professor, 1955-58, Associate Professor, 1958-63, Professor and Ernest I White Professor of History, 1963-69, Cornell University; Fulbright Senior Lecturer, American Studies Research Centre, Hyderabad, India, 1967; Harmsworth Professor, Oxford University, 1969-70; Professor and Farnam Professor of History, 1969-78, Sterling Professor of History, 1978-, Yale University; Fellow, Center for Advanced Study in the Behavioral Sciences, Stanford, 1972-73; Fulbright Lecturer, Universities of Guyana and the West Indies, 1974; French-American Foundation Chair in American Civilization, École des Hautes Études en Sciences Sociales, Paris, 1980-81; Gilder-Lehrman Inaugural Fellow, 1996-97; Director, The Gilder-Lehrman Center at Yale for the Study of Slavery Resistance and Abolition, 1998-2001. Publications: Homicide in American Fiction, 1798-1860: A Study in Social Values, 1957; The Problem of Slavery in Western Culture, 1966, revised edition, 1988; Ante-Bellum Reform (editor), 1967; The Slave Power Conspiracy and the Paranoid Style, 1969; Was Thomas Jefferson an Authentic Enemy of Slavery?, 1970; The Fear of Conspiracy: Images of Unamerican Subversion from the Revolution to to the Present (editor), 1971; The Problem of Slavery in the Age of Revolution, 1770-1823, 1975, revised edition, 1998; The Great Republic (with others), 1977, 4th edition, revised, 1992; Antebellum American Culture; An Interpretive Anthology, 1979, new edition, 1997; The Emancipation Moment, 1984; Slavery and Human Progress, 1984; Slavery in the Colonial Chesapeake, 1986; From Homicide to Slavery: Studies in American Culture, 1986; Revolutions: Reflections on American Equality and Foreign Liberations, 1990; The Antislavery Debate: Capitalism and Abolitionism as a Problem in Historical Interpretation (with Thomas Bender), 1992; The Boisterous Sea of Liberty: A Documentary History of America from Discovery Through the Civil War (with Steven Mintz), 1998. Contributions to: Scholarly journals. Honours: Guggenheim Fellowship, 1958-59; Pulitzer Prize in General Non-Fiction, 1967; Anisfield-Wolf Award, 1967; Albert J Beveridge Award, American Historical Association, 1975; National Book Award, 1976; Bancroft Prize, Columbia University, 1976; President, Organisation of American Historians, 1988-89; Presidential Medal for Outstanding Leadership and Achievement, Dartmouth College, 1991. Memberships: American Academy of Arts and Sciences; American Antiquarian Society; American Philosophical Society; British Academy, corresponding fellow; Institute of Early American History and Culture; Organization of American Historians. Address: c/o Department of History, PO Box 208324, Yale University, New Haven, CT 06520, USA.

DAVIS Dick, b. 18 Apr 1945, Portsmouth, Hampshire, England. Associate Professor of Persian; Poet. m. Afkham Darbandi, 1974, 2 daughters. Education: BA, King's College, Cambridge, 1966; PhD, University of Manchester, 1988. Appointments: Assistant Professor, 1988-93, Associate Professor of Persian, 1993-, Ohio State University. Publications: Shade Mariners, 1970; In the Distance, 1975; Seeing the World, 1980; The Selected Writings of Thomas Traherne (editor), 1980; Visitations, 1983; The Covenant, 1984; What the Mind Wants, 1984; Lares, 1986; Devices and Desires: New and Selected Poems, 1967-87, 1989; The Rubaiyat of Omar Khayyam, Translated by Edward Fitzgerald (editor), 1989; A Kind of Love: New & Selected Poems, 1991; Epic & Sedition: One Case of Ferdonzi's Shahnameh, 1992. Translations: The Conference of the Birds, 1984; The Legend of Seyavash, 1992. Honour: Royal Society of Literature Heinemann Award, 1981. Address: Department of Near Eastern Languages, Ohio State University, 190 North Oval Mall, Columbus, OH 43210, USA.

DAVIS Dorothy Salisbury, b. 26 Apr 1916, Chicago, Illinois, USA. Writer. m. Harry Davis, 25 Apr 1946. Education: AB, Barat College, Lake Forest, Illinois, 1938. Publications: A Gentle Murderer, 1951; Men of No Property, 1956; The Evening of the Good Samaritan, 1961; Enemy and Brother, 1967; Where the Dark Streets Go, 1969; The Little Brothers, 1974; A Death in the Life, 1976; Scarlet Night, 1980; Lullaby of Murder, 1984; Tales for a Stormy Night, 1985; The Habit of Fear, 1987; A Gentleman Called, 1989; Old Sinners Never Die, 1991; Black Sheep, White Lambs, 1993. Contributions to: New Republic. Honours: Grand Master's Award, Mystery Writers of America, 1985; Lifetime Achievement Award, Bouchereon XX, 1989. Memberships: Mystery Writers of America; Crime Writers Association, England; Authors Guild. Address: Palisades, New York, NY 10964, USA.

DAVIS Fred, b. 14 Feb 1947, Columbia, South Carolina, USA. Journalist; Higher Education. m. Joan Sineta Walker, 14 Jan 1967, 2 sons. Education: BS, English Education, North Carolina A&T State University, 1969; MBA, Kennedy-Western University, 1999. Appointments include: Writer, Reporter, KHJ and KCET, Hollywood, 1976-78; Anchor, Editor, WIS-TV, Columbia, South Carolina, 1978-80; Visiting Lecturer, Instructor, Broadcast Journalism, Benedict College, Columbia, 1979-80, 1990; Assistant News Director, Senior Producer, WJXT-TV, Jacksonville, Florida, 1980-81; Staff Writer, Jacksonville Journal, Florida Publishing Co, 1981; News Director, ABC Direction Radio Network, New York City, 1981-88; Visiting Lecturer, College of Journalism and Mass Communication, 1987, Writing Instructor, 1992-95, University of South Carolina, Columbia; Owner, Davis Media Services of Columbia Inc, now DMS & Syndicate Inc, 1989-; Guest Editorial Columnist, USA Today, 1990-94; Weekly Commentator, CBS radio stations, 1992; Self-syndicated Columnist, 1992-; Political Commentator, WPDE-TV, Florence, South Carolina, 1994; Visiting Professor, Lester M Smith Distinguished Professorship in Broadcast Management, Edward R Morrow School of Communication, Washington State University, Pullman, 1995-97; Visiting Professor, Lecturer, Broadcasting, College of Journalism and Mass Communication, University of Nebraska, Lincoln, 1997-. Honours: Awards, International Radio Festival of New York, 1983-88; Best Consumer Journalism, National Press Club Award, 1984, 1985; Ohio State University Award, 1986; Edward R Murrow Brotherhood Award, 1986; Communications Excellence to Black Audiences Award of Distinction, 1987; Distinguished Alumni Award, North Carolina A&T State University, National Association for Equal Opportunity in Higher Education, 1988; Distinguished Achievement Award, College of Liberal Arts, Washington State University, 1996. Address: University of Nebraska-Lincoln, PO Box 85543, Lincoln, NE 68501-5543, USA.

DAVIS Gordon. See: **LEVINSON Leonard.**

DAVIS Jack (Leonard), b. 11 Mar 1917, Perth, Western Australia, Australia; Poet; Dramatist; Writer. m. Madelon Jantine Wilkens, 12 Dec 1987, 1 daughter. Appointment: Writer-in-Residence, Murdoch University, 1982. Publications: The First Born and Other Poems, 1968; Jagardoo Poems from Aboriginal Australia, 1978; The Dreamers (play), 1983; Kullark (play), 1983; John Pat and Other Poems, 1988; Burungin (Smell the Wind) (play), 1989; Plays From Black Australia, 1989. Contributions to: Identity. Honours: Human Rights Award, 1987; BHP Award, 1988; Australian Artists Creative Fellowship, 1989; Honorary doctorates. Memberships: Aboriginal Writers Oral Literature and Dramatists Association; Australian Writers Guild; PEN International. Address: 3 Little Howard Street, Fremantle, Western Australia, Australia.

DAVIS Jon E(dward), b. 28 Oct 192, New Haven, Connecticut, USA. Poet; Writer; Professor of Creative Writing and Literature. m. Terry Lynne Layton, 8 Jan 1978, 1 daughter. Education: University of Bridgeport, 1978-80; BA, High Honours, English, 1984, MFA, Creative Writing, 1985, University of Montana. Appointments: Editor, CutBank, 1982-85; Managing Editor, Shankpainter, 1986-87; Fellow, 1986-87, Coordinator, Writing Program, 1987-88, Fine Arts Work Center, Provincetown, Massachusetts; Visiting Assistant Professor, Salisbury State University, Maryland, 1988-90; Professor of Creative Writing and Literature, Institute of American Indian Arts, Santa Fe, New Mexico, 1990; Co-Editor, Countermeasures, 1993-. Publications: Poetry: West of New England, 1983; Dangerous Amusements, 1987; The Hawk, The Road, The Sunlight After Clouds, 1995; Local Color, 1995; Scrimmage of Appetite, 1995. Contributions to: Anthologies, reviews, quarterlies and journals. Honours: Winner, Connecticut Poetry Circuit Competition, 1980; Academy of American Poets Prize, 1985; INTRO Award for Fiction, 1985; National Endowment for the Arts Fellowship, 1986; Richard Hugo Memorial Award, CutBank, 1988; Maryland Arts Council Fellowship, 1990; Winner, Owl Creek Press Chapbook Contest, 1994; Palanquin Press Chapbook Contest, 1995. Address: c/o Creative Writing Program, Institute of American Indian Arts, Box 20007, Santa Fe, NM 87535, USA.

DAVIS Joy Lynn Edwards, b. 4 Apr 1945, Speedwell, Tennessee, USA. Teacher of English; Writer. m. Joe Mac Davis, 22 July 1969. Education: BA, Lincoln Memorial University, 1969; MA, Union College, 1974; Stokely Fellow, University of Tennessee, 1984. Publications: Immigrants and First Families of America, 1982; Old Speedwell Families, 1983; More Speedwell Families, 1988; American Poetry Anthology, 1990; Great Poets of Our Time, 1993; Distinguished Poets of America, 1993. Honours: Lincoln Memorial University Literary Hall of Fame, 1982; Teacher of the Year, 1991; Delta Kappa Gamma. Memberships: American Federation of Teachers; PETA. Address: Route, 2, Box 302, LaFollette, TN 37766, USA.

DAVIS Kenneth (Sidney), b. 29 Sept 1912, Salina, Kansas, USA. Journalist; Writer. m. Florence Marie Olenhouse, 19 Feb 1938, dec. Education: BS, Kansas State University; MA, University of Wisconsin. Appointments: Journalist; Assistant to Milton S Eisenhower, 1947-49; Personal Staff, Adlai Stevenson, 1955-56. Publications: In the Forests of the Night, 1942; Morning in Kansas, 1952; The Experience of War, 1965; Eisenhower: American Hero, 1969; FDR, 4 volumes, 1972-93; Invincible Summer: An Intimate Portrait of the Roosevelts, 1974; A Sense of History, 1985. Honours: Friend of American Writers Award, 1943; Kansas Centennial Award, 1963; Francis Parkman Prize, 1973; Achievement Award, Kansas Authors Club, 1977. Address: 3330 Arrowhead Drive, Manhattan, KS 66502, USA.

DAVIS Margaret (Thomson), b. 24 May 1926, Bathgate, West Lothian, Scotland. Writer. Div, 1 son. Education: Albert Secondary Modern School, Glasgow. Publications: The Breadmakers, 1972; A Baby Might Be Crying, 1973; A Sort of Peace, 1973; The Prisoner, 1974; The Prince and the Tobacco Lords, 1976; Roots of Bondage, 1977; Scorpion in the Fire, 1977; The Dark Side of Pleasure, 1981; The Making of a Novelist, 1982; A Very Civilized Man, 1982; Light and Dark, 1984; Rag Woman, Rich Woman, 1987; Mothers and Daughters, 1988; Wounds of War, 1989; A Woman of Property, 1991; A Sense of Belonging, 1993; Hold Me Forever, 1994; Kiss Me No More, 1995; A Kind of Immortality, 1996; Burning Ambition, 1997; Gallaghers, 1998; The Glasglow Belle, 1998. Contributions to: 200 short stories in various periodicals. Memberships: PEN; Scottish Labour History Society; Society of Authors. Address: c/o Heather Jeeves Literary Agency, 9 Kingsfield Crescent, Witney, Oxon, OX8 6JB.

DAVIS Nathaniel, b. 12 Apr 1925, Boston, Massachusetts, USA. Diplomat (retired); Professor of Humanities. m. Elizabeth Kirkbride Creese, 24 Nov 1956, 2 sons, 2 daughters. Education: AB, Brown University, 1944; MA, 1947, PhD, 1960, Fletcher School of Law and Diplomacy, Cornell University, 1953; Russian Institute, Columbia University, 1953-54; Middlebury College, Vermont, 1954; Universidad Central de Venezuala, Caracas, 1961-62. Appointments: US Foreign Service: 3rd Secretary, Prague, 1947-49; Vice Consul, Florence, 1949-52; 2nd Secretary, Rome, 1952-53, Moscow, 1954-56; Soviet Desk Officer and Deputy Officer in Charge, USSR Affairs, 1956-60; 1st Secretary, Caracas, 1960-62; Special Assistant to the Director, 1962-63, Deputy Associate Director for Program Development and Operations, 1963-65, Peace Coprs; US Minister to Bulgaria, 1965-66; Senior Staff, National Security Council, 1966-68; US Ambassador to Guatemala, 1968-71, Chile, 1971-73, Switzerland, 1975-77; Director General, US Foreign Service, 1973-75; Assistant Secretary of State for African Affairs, 1975; State Department Advisor, US Naval War College, 1977-83; Teacher: Tufts College, 1947, University Branch, Centro Venezolano-Americano, 1961, Howard University, 1962-68, Salve Regina College, Newport, Rhode Island, 1981-82; Chester W Nimitz Chair of National Security and Foreign Affairs, US Naval War College, 1977-83; Alexander and Adelaide Hixon Chair, Harvey Mudd College and the faculty of Claremont Graduate School, California, 1983-. Publications: The Last Two Years of Salvador Allende, 1985, Spanish edition, 1986, Portuguese edition, 1990; A Long Walk to Church: A Contemporary History of Russian Orthodoxy, 1995. Contributions to: Books, newspapers, journals, and magazines. Honours: Honorary LLD, Brown University, 1970; Distinguished Public Service Award, US Navy, 1983; Fulbright Scholar and Visiting Professor, Russian State University of the Humanities, Moscow, 1996-97. Memberships: American Academy of Diplomacy; American Foreign Service Association; Council on Foreign Relations. Address: c/o Harvey Mudd College, Claremont, CA 91711, USA.

DAVIS Sonia. See: **WILLIAMS Alberta Norine.**

DAVIS William, b. 6 Mar 1933, Hannover, Germany. Editor; Publisher; Writer. m. Sylvette Jouclas, 8 Apr 1967. Education: City of London College. Appointments: Staff, Financial Times, 1954-59; Editor, Investor's Guide, 1959-60, Editor, Punch, 1968-77; City Editor, Evening Standard, 1960-65; Financial Editor, Guardian, 1965-68; Presenter, Money Programme, BBC TV, 1967-69; Editor and Publisher, High Life, 1973-97; Editor-in-Chief, Financial Weekly, 1977-80; Director, Fleet Publishing International, Morgan-Grampian, and Fleet Holdings, 1977-80, Thomas Cook, 1988-, British Invisibles, 1990-93; Chairman, Headway Publications, 1977-90, British Tourist Authority, 1990-93, English Tourist Board, 1990-93, Premier Magazines, 1992-, Allied Leisure, 1993-94. Publications: Three Years Hard Labour: The Road to Devaluation, 1968; Merger Mania, 1970; Money Talks, 1972; Have Expenses, Will Travel, 1975; It's No Sin to be Rich, 1976; The Best of Everything (editor), 1980; Money in the 1980s, 1981; The Rich: A Study of the Species, 1982; Fantasy: A Practical Guide to Escapism, 1984; The Corporate Infighter's Handbook, 1984; The World's Best Business Hotels (editor), 1985; The Supersalesman's Handbook, 1986; The Innovators, 1987; Children of the Rich, 1989; The Lucky Generation: A Positive View of the 21st Century, 1995; Great Myths of Business, 1997. Honour: Knight, Order of Merit, Italian Republic. Address: c/o Premier Magazines, Haymarket House, 1 Oxendon Street, London SW1Y 4EE, England.

DAVIS William (Virgil), b. 26 May 1940, Canton, Ohio, USA. Professor of English; Writer; Poet. m. Carol Demske, 17 July 1971, 1 son. Education: AB, English and American Literature, 1962, MA, English and American Literature, 1965, PhD, American Literature, 1967, Ohio University; MDiv, Pittsburgh Theological Seminary, 1965. Appointments: Teaching Fellow, 1965-67, Assistant Professor of English, 1967-68, Consultant, Creative Writing Program, 1992-, Ohio University; Assistant Professor of English, Central Connecticut State University, 1968-72, University of Illinois, Chicago, 1972-77; Associate Professor of English, 1977-79, Professor of English and Writer-in-Residence, 1979-, Baylor University; Guest Professor, University of Vienna, 1979-80, 1989-90, 1997, University of Copenhagen, 1984; Visiting Scholar-Guest Professor, University of Wales, Swansea, 1983; Writer-in-Residence, University of Montana, 1983; Adjunct MFA Faculty, Southwest Texas State University, 1990-98; Adjunct Member, Graduate Faculty, Texas Christian University, 1992-96. Publications: George Whitefield's Journals, 1737-1741 (editor), 1969; Theodore Roethke: A Bibliography (contributing editor), 1973; One Way to Reconstruct the Scene, 1980; The Dark Hours, 1984; Understanding Robert Bly, 1988; Winter Light, 1990; Critical Essays on Robert Bly (editor), 1992; Miraculous Simplicity: Essays on R S Thomas (editor), 1993; Robert Bly: The Poet and His Critics, 1994. Contributions to: Articles in scholarly journals and poems in numerous anthologies and other publications. Honours: Scholar in Poetry, 1970, John Atherton Fellow in Poetry, 1980, Bread Loaf Writers' Conference; Ordained Minister, Presbyterian Church in the USA, 1971; Yale Series of Younger Poets' Award, 1979; Lilly Foundation Grant, 1979-80; Calliope Press Chapbook Prize, 1984; Nominations, Pushcart Prize, 1991, 1992, 1993, 1995. Memberships: Academy of American Poets; International Association of University Professors of English; Modern Language Association; PEN; Phi Kappa Phi; Poetry Society of America; Poets and Writers; Tau Kappa Alpha; Texas Association of Creative Writing Teachers; Texas Institute of Letters, councilor, 1993-97. Address: 2633 Lake Oaks Road, Waco, TX 76710, USA.

DAVIS-FLOYD Robbie E(lizabeth), b. 26 Apr 1951, Casper, Wyoming, USA. Anthropologist; Writer. m. Robert N Floyd, 30 June 1978, 1 son, 1 daughter. Education: BA, 1972, MA, 1974, PhD, 1986, University of Texas, Austin. Appointments: Adjunct Assistant Professor, University of Tennessee, Chattanooga, 1980-83, Trinity University, 1987-89; Lecturer, University of Texas, Austin, 1990-92; Visiting Lecturer, Rice University, 1993, 1996; Research Fellow, Department of Anthropology, University of Texas, Austin, 1995-99; Associate Faculty, Goddard College, 1999-. Publications: Birth as an American Rite of Passage, 1992; Birth in Four Cultures (revised edition of Brigitte Jordan's 1978 book), 1993; Childbirth and Authoritative Knowledge: Cross-Cultural Perspectives (editor with Carolyn Sargent), 1997; Intuition: The Inside Story (editor with Sven Arvidson), 1997; From Doctor to Healer: The Transformative Journey (with Gloria St. John), 1998; Cyborg Babies: From Techno-Sex to Techno-Tots (editor with J. Dumit), 1998. Contributions to: Books and journals. Honours: National Endowment for the Humanities Grant, 1980; Fetzer Institute Award, 1994; Institute of Noetic Sciences Grant, 1995; Wenner-Gren Foundation for Anthropological Research Grant, 1996. Memberships: American Anthropological Association; American Holistic Medical Association; American Public Health Association; Association for Feminist Anthropology; Association for Pre- and Perinatal Psychology and Health; Council on Anthropology and Reproduction; Midwives' Alliance of North America; Society for Medical Anthropology; Society for the Social Study of Science. Address: 1301 Capital of Texas Highway, B128, Austin, TX 78746, USA.

DAVIS-GARDNER Angela, b. 21 Apr 1942, Charlotte, North Carolina, USA. Writer; Professor. 1 son. Education: BA, Duke University, 1963; MFA, University of North Carolina at Greensboro, 1965. Publications: Felice, 1982; Forms of Shelter, 1991. Contributions to: Short stories in: Kansas Quarterly, Carolina Quarterly; Crescent Review; Greensboro Review; other literary quarterlies. Honours: Phi Beta Kappa, 1963; Artists Fellowship, North Carolina Arts Council, 1981-82; Sir Walter Raleigh Award, 1991; Best Novel by North Carolinian. Membership: Authors Guild, Poets and Writers. Address: Department of English, North Carolina State University, Box 8105, Raleigh, NC 27695, USA.

DAVIS-GOFF Annabel Claire, b. 19 Feb 1942, Ireland. Writer. m. Mike Nichols, 1976, div 1987, 1 son, 1 daughter. Publications: Night Tennis, 1978; Tail Spin, 1980; Walled Gardens, 1989; The Literary Companions to Gambling, 1996; The Dower House, 1998. Literary Agent: Sterling Lord Literistic. Address: 1 West 67th Street, New York, NY 10023, USA.

DAVISON Geoffrey Joseph, b. 10 Aug 1927, Newcastle-upon-Tyne, England. Writer. m. Marlene Margaret Wilson, 15 Sept 1956, 2 sons. Education: TD; FRICS. Publications: The Spy Who Swapped Shoes, 1967; Nest of Spies, 1968; The Chessboard Spies, 1969; The Fallen Eagles, 1970; The Honorable Assassins, 1971; Spy Puppets, 1973; The Berlin Spy Trap, 1974; No Names on Their Graves, 1978; The Bloody Legionnaires, 1981. Membership: Pen and Palette Club. Address: 95 Cheviot View, Ponteland, Newcastle-upon-Tyne NE20 9BH, England.

DAVISON Peter (Hubert), b. 27 June 1928, New York, New York, USA. Poet; Writer; Editor. m. (1) Jane Truslow, 7 Mar 1959, dec 1981, 1 son, 1 daughter, (2) Joan Edelman Goody, 11 Aug 1984. Education: AB, Harvard College, 1949; Fulbright Scholar, St John's College, Cambridge University, 1949-50. Appointments: Assistant Editor, Harcourt, Brace and Co, 1950-51, 1953-55; Assistant to Director, Harvard University Press, 1955-56; Associate Editor, 1956-59, Executive Editor, 1959-64, Director, 1964-79, Senior Editor, 1979-85, Atlantic Monthly Press; Poetry Editor, The Atlantic Monthly, 1972-; Editor, Peter Davison imprint, Houghton Mifflin Co, 1985-98. Publications: Poetry: The Breaking of the Day, 1964; The City and the Island, 1966; Pretending to Be Asleep, 1970; Walking the Boundaries, 1974; A Voice in the Mountain, 1977; Barn Fever, 1981; Praying Wrong: New and Selected Poems, 1959-84, 1984; The Great Ledge: New Poems, 1989; The Poems of Peter Davison, 1957-95, 1995. Prose: Half Remembered: A Personal History, 1973, revised edition, 1991; One of the Dangerous Trades: Essays on the Work and Workings of Poetry, 1991; The Fading Smile: Poets in Boston 1955-60, 1994. Contributions to: Many journals, reviews and periodicals. Honours: Yale Series of Younger Poets Award, 1963; American Academy of Arts and Letters Award, 1972; James Michener Prizes, 1981, 1985; New England Booksellers Award for Literary Excellence, 1995. Address: 70 River Street, No 2, Boston, MA 02108, USA.

DAWE (Donald) Bruce, b. 15 Feb 1930, Geelong, Victoria, Australia. Associate Professor; Poet; Writer. m. Gloria Desley Blain, 27 Jan 1964, 2 sons, 2 daughters. Education: BA, 1969, MLitt, 1973, MA, 1975, PhD, 1980, University of Queensland; Hon. DLitt (USQ), 1995; Hon.DLitt (UNSW), 1997. Appointments: Lecturer, 1971-78, Senior Lecturer, 1978-83, DDIAE; Writer-in-Residence, University of Queensland, 1984; Senior Lecturer, 1985-90, Associate Professor, 1990-93, School of Arts, Darling Heights, Toowoomba. Publications: No Fixed Address, 1962; A Need of Similar Name, 1964; Beyond the Subdivisions, 1968; An Eye for a Tooth, 1969; Heat-Wave, 1970; Condolences of the Season: Selected Poems, 1971; Just a Dugong at Twilight, 1974; Sometimes Gladness: Collected Poems, 1978, 4th edition, revised, 1993; Over Here Harv! and Other Stories, 1983; Towards Sunrise, 1986; This Side of Silence, 1990; Bruce Dawe: Essays and Opinions, 1990; Mortal Instruments: Poems 1990-1995, 1995; A Poets' People, 1999. Contributions to: Various periodicals. Honours: Myer Poetry Prizes, 1966, 1969; Ampol Arts Award for Creative Literature, 1967; Dame Mary Gilmore Medal, Australian Literary Society, 1973; Braille Book of the Year, 1978; Grace Leven Prize for Poetry, 1978; Patrick White Literary Award, 1980; Christopher Brennan Award, 1984; Order of Australia, 1992; Distinguished Alumni Award, UNE, 1996. Memberships: Australian Association for Teaching English, honorary life member; Centre for Australian Studies in Literature; Victorian Association for Teaching of English, honorary life member. Address: 259 Mackenzie Street, Toowoomba, Queensland 4350, Australia.

DAWE Gerald Chartres, b. 22 Apr 1952, Belfast, Northern Ireland. Poet; College Lecturer. m. Dorothea Malvin, 28 Oct 1979, 1 son, 1 daughter. Education: BA, Honours, University of Ulster; MA, University College, Galway. Appointments: Tutor in English, Assistant Lecturer, University College, Galway, 1978-87; Lecturer, 1989-, Director, MPhil in Creative Writing, 1997-, Trinity College, Dublin. Publications: Poetry: Sheltering Places, 1978; The Lundy Letter, 1985; Sunday School, 1991; Heart of Hearts, 1995. Criticism: Across a Roaring Hill: The Protestant Imagination in Modern Ireland (with Edna Longley), 1985; How's the Poetry Going?: Literary Politics and Ireland Today, 1991; The Poet's Place (with John Wilson Foster), 1991; A Real Life Elsewhere, 1993; False Faces: Poetry, Politics and Place, 1994; Against Piety: Essays in Irish Poetry, 1995; The Rest is History, 1998. Editor: The Younger Irish Poets, 1982; Krino (anthology with Jonathan Williams), 1986-96; The Younger Irish Poets, 1991. Contributions to: Newspapers, reviews and journals. Honours: Major State Awards, 1974-77; Arts Council Bursary for Poetry, 1980; Macaulay Fellowship in Literature, 1984; Hawthornden International Writers Fellowship, 1988. Memberships: International Association for the Study of Anglo-Irish Literature; Irish Writers Union; Poetry Ireland. Address: c/o Oscar Wilde Centre, Trinity College, Dublin 2, Ireland.

DAWKINS (Clinton) Richard, b. 26 Mar 1941, Nairobi, Kenya. Zoologist; Professor of the Public Understanding of Science. m. (1) Marian Stamp, 19 Aug 1967, div 1984, (2) Eve Barham, 1 June 1984, 1 daughter. Education: BA, 1962, MA, 1966, DPhil, 1966, Balliol College, Oxford. Appointments: Assistant Professor of Zoology, University of California at Berkeley, 1967-69; Fellow, New College, Oxford, 1970-; Lecturer, 1970-89, Reader in Zoology, 1989-95, Charles Simonyi Reader in the Public Understanding of Science, 1995-96, Professor of the Public Understanding of Science, 1996-, Oxford University; Editor, Animal Behaviour, 1974-78, Oxford Surveys in Evolutionary Biology, 1983-86; Gifford Lecturer, University of Glasgow, 1988; Sidgwick Memorial Lecturer, Newnham College, Cambridge, 1988; Kovler Visiting Fellow, University of Chicago, 1990; Nelson Lecturer, University of California at Davis, 1990. Publications: The Selfish Gene, 1976, 2nd edition, 1989; The Extended Phenotype, 1982; The Blind Watchmaker, 1986; River Out of Eden, 1995; Climbing Mount Improbable, 1996. Contributions to: Scholarly journals. Honours: Royal Society of Literature Prize, 1987; Los Angeles Times Literature Prize, 1987; Honorary Fellow, Regent's College, London, 1988; Silver Medal, Zoological Society, 1989; Michael Faraday Award, Royal Society, 1990; Nakayama Prize, Nakayama Foundation for Human Sciences, 1994; Honorary DLitt, St Andrews University, 1995; Honorary DLitt, Canberra, 1996; International Cosmos Prize, 1997. Literary Agent: John Brockman, Brockman Inc, 5 East 59th Street, New York, NY 10022, USA. Address: c/o Oxford University Museum, Parks Road, Oxford, OX1 3PW, England.

DAWSEY James Marshall, b. 12 Apr 1947, Spartanburg, South Carolina, USA. Professor. m. Dixie Marie Preuss, 27 Aug 1971, 1 son, 1 daughter. Education: BS, Florida Southern College, 1970; MDiv, 1973, PhD, 1983, Emory University. Appointments: Alumni Professor of Religion, Auburn University, 1992-94; Dean of Faculty, Emory & Henry College, 1994-. Publications: The Lukan Voice: Confusion and Irony in the Gospel of Luke, 1986; A Scholar's Guide to Academic Journals in Religion, 1988; Living Waters, 1989; From Wasteland to Promised Land, 1992. Contributions to: Annie Ayres Newman Ranson, 1995. Membership: de Diputadas, Congreso Nacional, Argentina, 1993. Address: Emory & Henry College, Emory, VA 24327, USA.

DAWSON Clay. See: **LEVINSON Leonard.**

DAWSON Jennifer, (Jenny Hinton, Jenny Sargesson), b. 23 Jan 1929, Hertfordshire, England. Writer. m. Michael Hinton, 2 Apr 1964. Education: St Anne's College, Oxford; University College, London. Publications: The Ha-Ha, 1961; Fowlers Snare, 1962; The Queen of Trent (with W Mitchell), 1962; The Cold Country, 1965; Strawberry Boy, 1976; Hospital Wedding, 1978; A Field of Scarlet Poppies, 1979; The Upstairs People, 1988; Judasland, 1989; The Flying Gardens, 1993. Poems in: Ambit. Honours: James Tait Black Award, 1961; Cheltenham Festival Award, 1962; Fawcett Society Fiction Award, 1990. Address: 6 Fisher Lane, Charlbury, Oxon OX7 3RX, England.

DAWSON Jill Dianne, b. 1962, England. Writer; Poet; Editor; Teacher. 1 son. Education: BA, American Studies, University of Nottingham, 1983; MA, Sheffield Hallam University, 1995. Appointments: Fareham College, Hampshire; Tutor of Creative Writing; Literature Development Worker, Eastside, London, 1994-; British Council Fellow-in-Writing, Amherst, USA. Publications: School Tales, 1990; How Do I Look? (non-fiction), 1991; Virago Book of Wicked Verse, 1992; Virago Book of Love Letters, 1994; White Fish with Painted Nails (poetry), 1994; Trick of the Light, 1996; Magpie, 1998. Contributions to: Anthologies and periodicals. Honours: Major Eric Gregory Award, 1992; 2nd Prize, London Writers Short Story Competition, 1994; Blue Nose Poet of the Year, 1995; London Arts Board New Writers, 1998. Memberships: National Association of Writers in Education; Society of Authors. Address: 38 Lockhurst Street, London E5 0AP, England.

DAY Elaine, b. 30 June 1954, Hendon, North London, England. Freelance Writer. m. David John Day, 5 Aug 1994, 1 daughter. Education: Publications include: Natural Tranquility, 1997; Crystal Pillars/Fossil Seas Poetry Book, 1997; Poetry Now East Anglia, 1998; A Celebration of Poets, 1997; Acorn Magazine, 1998; The Secret of Twilight, 1998; A Quiet Storm, anthology, 1998; The Star-Laden Sky, anthology, 1997; Light of the World, anthology, 1997; Beyond the Horizon, anthology, 1997; A Celebration of Friendship (anthology), 1999; A Celebration of Poets (anthology), 1999. Contributions to: Old Yorkshire Magazine; Acorn Magazine; One Magazine; Day By Day Magazine; Forward Press; Freehand Magazine; Poetic Hour Magazine. Honours: 5 Editors Choice Awards for Poetry; British Academy Certificate, 1983. Address: 141 Turpin Avenue, Collier Row, Romford, Essex RM5 2LU, England.

DAY Sir Robin, b. 24 Oct 1923, London, England. Radio and Television Journalist. m. Katherine Mary Ainslie, 1965, div 1986, 2 sons. Education: BA, Honours, Jurisprudence, Oxford University, 1951. Appointments: Called to the Bar, Middle Temple, 1952; Newcaster and Parliamentary Correspondent, Independent Television News, 1955-59; Political Interviewer and Reporter, BBC TV, 1959-89; Presenter, The World at One, BBC Radio, 1979-87. Publications: Television: A Personal Report, 1961; The Case for Televising Parliament, 1963; Day by Day, 1975; Grand Inquistor--Memoirs, 1989; ... But With Respect: Memorable Interviews, 1993. Honours: President, Oxford Union Society, 1950; Guild of Television Producers' Merit Award for Personality of the Year, 1957; Richard Dimbleby Award, 1974; Broadcasting Press Guild Award, 1980; Knighted, 1981; Royal Television Society Judges' Award for 30 Years of Television Journalism, 1985; Honorary Doctorates, Universities of Exeter, 1986, Keele, 1988, Essex, 1988; Honorary Fellow, St Edmund Hall, Oxford, 1989; Honorary Bencher, Middle Temple, 1990; Royal Television Society Hall of Fame, 1995. Address: Royal Automobile Club, Pall Mall, London SW1Y 5HS, England.

DAY Stacey (Biswas), b. 31 Dec 1927, London, England. Physician; Writer; Poet; Editor. m. Ivana Podvalova, 23 Oct 1973, 2 sons. Education: MD, Dublin, 1955; PhD, McGill University, Montreal, 1964; DSc, University of Cincinnati, 1970. Appointments: Editor-in-Chief, Biosciences Communications and Health Communications; Consulting Editor. Publications: Editor of over 50 medical and scientific books; Author of 20 literary books including Hagakure - Spirit of Bushido (with H. Koda), 1993; The Wisdom Of Kagakure (Kyushu), 1995; The Medical Student and the Mission of Medicine in The 21st Century (In Japanese, Oita), 1996; Letters of Owen Wangensteen to a Surgical Fellow: w/a Memoir (Foundation), 1997; Man And Mu, 1998. Contributions to: Numerous journals and magazines. Honours: W.H.O. Medal 1987; Citation, President USA, 1987; First Foreign

Honorary Member Hagakure Society, Japan, 1990; Key to the City of Nashville; Honorary Kentucky Colonel; Medical Honours: Japan, Ecuador, Czech Republic. Memberships: Many professional organizations. Literary Agent: International Foundation, New York. Address: 6 Lomond Avenue, Chestnut Ridge, NY 10977, USA.

DE ARAUGO Sarah Therese, (Tess De Araugo), b. 26 May 1930, Lismore, Victoria, Australia. Writer. m. Maurice De Araugo, 11 Apr 1950, 2 sons, 2 daughters. Education: Notre Dame de Sion College, Warragal, Victoria. Publications: You Are What You Make Yourself To Be, 1980, revised edition, 1989; The Kurnai of Gippsland, 1985; Boonorong on the Mornington Peninsula, 1993. Contributions to: Encyclopaedias and periodicals. Honours: New South Wales Premier's Award for Australian Literature, 1985; Banjo Award, Australian Literature, National Book Council, 1985; Fellowship, 1987, Writer's Grant, 1989, Australian Literature Board; Short Story Award, PEN International, Australia, 1991. Memberships: Australian Society of Authors; Fellowship of Australian Writers; Royal Historical Society of Victoria; Women Writers of Australia; Nepean Historical Society. Address: 19 Grenville Grove, Rosebud West, Victoria 3940, Australia.

DE BELSER Raymond Charles Maria, (Ward Ruyslinck), b. 17 Jun 1929, Antwerp, Belgium. Retired Librarian; Author. m. (1), 1 son, (2) Monika Macken, 18 Dec 1992. Publications: De ontaarde slapers, 1957, English translation as The Deadbeats, 1968; Wierook en tranen, 1958; Het dal van Hinnom, 1961; Het reservaat, 1964, English translation as The Reservation, 1978; Golden Ophelia, 1966; De heksenkring, 1972; Het ganzenbord, 1974; Wurgtechnieken, 1980; Leegstaande huizen, 1983; De uilen van Minerva, 1985; Stille waters, 1987; Ljlings naar nergens, 1989. Contributions to: Periodicals. Honours: Ark Prize for Free Speech, 1960; Flemish Reader Award, 1964; Prize for Literature of the Flemish Provinces, 1967; Europalia Prize for Literature, 1980. Membership: Royal Flemish Academy of Language and Literature, Ex-Chairman. Address: Potaardestraat 25, 1860 Meise, Belgium.

DE BERNIERE-SMART Louis Henry Piers, (Louis de Bernieres), b. 8 Dec 1954, Woolwich, London, England. Novelist. Education: Bradfield College, Berkshire; BA, Manchester University; MA, Leicester Polytechnic and University of London. Publications: The War of Don Emmanuel's Nether Parts; Senior Vivo and the Coea Lord; The Troublesome Offspring of Cardinal Guzman; Captain Corelli's Mandolin. Contributions to: Second Thoughts and Granta. Honours: Commonwealth Writers Prizes, 1991, 1992, 1995; Best of Young British Novelists, 1993; Lannan Award, 1995. Membership: PEN. Address: c/o Secker and Warburg, Michelin House, 81 Fulham Road, London SW3 6RB, England.

DE BERNIERES Louis. See: **DE BERNIERE-SMART Louis Henry Piers.**

DE BLASIS Celeste Ninette, b. 8 May 1946, California, USA. Writer. Education: Wellesley College, 1964-65; Oregon State University, 1965-66; BA cum laude, English, Pomona College, 1968. Publications: The Night Child, 1975; Suffer a Sea Change, 1976; The Proud Breed, 1978; The Tiger's Woman, 1981; Wild Swan, 1984; Swan's Chance, 1985; A Season of Swans, 1989; Graveyard Peaches: A California Memoir, 1991. Contributions to: Writers Digest. Memberships: Authors Guild; Novelists Inc; Nature Conservancy; California State Library Foundation. Address: c/o Witherspoon Associates Inc, 157 West 57th Street, Suite 700, New York, NY 10019, USA.

DE BOISSIERE Ralph (Anthony Charles), b. 6 Oct 1907, Port-of-Spain, Trinidad (Australian citizen, 1970). Novelist. m. Ivy Alcantara, 1935, 2 daughters. Publications: Crown Jewel, 1952; Rum and Coca-Cola, 1956; No Saddles for Kangaroos, 1964. Uncollected short stories: Booze and the Goberdaw, 1979; The Woman on the Pavement, 1979. Play: Calypso Isle, 1955. Literary Agent: Reinhard Sander, Department of Black Studies, Amherst College, Amherst, MA 01002, USA. Address: 10 Vega Street, North Balwyn, Victoria 3104, Australia.

DE BONO Edward (Francis Publius Charles), b. 19 May 1933, Malta. Author; Physician; Inventor; Lecturer. m. Josephine Hall-White, 1971, 2 sons. Education: St Edward's College, Malta; BSc, 1953, MD, 1955, Royal University of Malta; MA, 1957, DPhil, 1961, Oxford University; PhD, Cambridge University, 1963. Appointments: Research Assistant, 1957-60, Lecturer, 1960-61, Oxford University; Assistant Director of Research, 1963-76, Lecturer in Medicine, 1976-83, Cambridge University; Honorary Director and Founding Member, Cognitive Research Trust, 1971-; Secretary-General, Supranational Independent Thinking Organisation, 1983-; Lecturer. Publications: The Use of Lateral Thinking, 1967; The Five-Day Course in Thinking, 1967; The Mechanism of Mind, 1969; Lateral Thinking: A Textbook of Creativity, 1970; The Dog Exercising Machine, 1970; Lateral Thinking for Management: A Handbook of Creativity, 1971; Practical Thinking: Four Ways to Be Right, Five Ways to Be Wrong, 1971; Children Solve Problems, 1972; PO: A Device for Successful Thinking, 1972; Think Tank, 1973; Eureka: A History of Inventions (editor), 1974; Teaching Thinking, 1976; The Greatest Thinkers, 1976; Wordpower: An Illustrated Dictionary of Vital Words, 1977; Opportunities: A Handbook of Business Opportunity Search, 1978; The Happiness Purpose, 1978; Future Positive, 1979; Atlas of Management Thinking, 1981; De Bono's Thinking Course, 1982; Learn to Think, 1982; Tactics: The Art and Science of Success, 1984; Conflicts: A Better Way to Resolve Them, 1985; Six Thinking Hats: An Essential Approach to Business Management from the Creator of Lateral Thinking, 1985; CoRT Thinking Program: CoRT 1-Breadth, 1987; Letters to Thinkers: Further Thoughts on Lateral Thinking, 1987; Masterthinker II: Six Thinking Hats, 1988; Masterthinker, 1990; Masterthinker's Handbook, 1990; Thinking Skills for Success, 1990; I Am Right, You Are Wrong: From This to the New Renaissance: From Rock Logic to Water Logic, 1990; Handbook for the Positive Revolution, 1991; Six Action Shoes, 1991; Serious Creativity: Using the Power of Lateral Thinking to Create New Ideas, 1992; Surpetition: Creating Value Monopolies When Everyone Else is Merely Competing, 1992; Teach Your Child How to Think, 1993; Water Logic, 1993; Parallel Thinking, 1994; Teach Yourself to Think, 1995; Mind Pack, 1995; Edward do Bono's Textbook of Wisdom, 1996. Contributions to: Television series, professional journals, and periodicals. Honour: Rhodes Scholar. Membership: Medical Research Society. Address: 12 Albany, Piccadilly, London W1V 9RR, England.

DE BRISSAC. See: **DOBSON Rosemary.**

DE CADAVAL Rudy. See: **CAMPEDELLI Giancarlo.**

DE CAMP L(yon) Sprague, b. 27 Nov 1907, New York, New York, USA. Writer; Poet. m. Catherine Adelaide Crook, 12 Aug 1939, 2 sons. Education: BS, Aeronautical Engineering, California Institute of Technology, 1930; MS, Engineering and Economics, Stevens Institute of Technology, 1933. Publications: Over 130 books, including science fiction, fantasy, historical novels, history, biography, textbooks and juvenile, among others. Contributions to: Numerous stories, articles and poems in anthologies, periodicals and other publications. Honours: International Fantasy Award, 1953; Grandmaster Fantasy Award, 1976; Nebula Award, Science Fiction Writers of America, 1978; World Fantasy Conference Award, 1984. Memberships: Authors Guild; History of Science Society; Science Fiction and Fantasy Writers of America; Society for the History of Technology. Address: 3453 Hearst Castle Way, Plano, TX 75025, USA.

DE CORMIER Regina, (Regina Shekerjian, Regina Tor), b. Pine Lawn, New York, USA. Writer; Poet. m. Haig Shekerjian, 2 sons. Publications: Growing Toward Peace, 1960; Discovering Israel, 1961; Helicon Nine Reader, 1990; Only Morning in Her Shoes, 1990; Looking for Home, 1990; A Shackle of Days, 1992; Hoofbeats on the Door, 1993; Two Worlds Walking, 1994; Claiming the Spirit Within, 1996. Contributions to: American Poetry Review; Nation; Salmagundi; Parabola; Massachusetts Review; New Virginia Review; Blue Mesa Review; Poetry East; Nimrod. Honours: National Jewish Book Award, 1962; Pablo Neruda Award, 1984; Pulitzer Prize Nomination, 1993. Memberships: Authors Guild; Academy of American Poets; Poetry Society of America. Address: 34 Sparkling Ridge, New Paltz, NY 12561, USA.

DE CRESPIGNY (Richard) Rafe (Champion), b. 16 Mar 1936, Adelaide, South Australia, Australia. m. Christa Charlotte Boltz, 1 son, 1 daughter. Education: BA, 1957, MA, 1961, Cambridge University; BA, University of Melbourne, 1961; BA, 1962, MA, 1964, PhD, 1968, Australian National University. Appointments: Lecturer, 1964-70, Senior Lecturer, 1970-73, Reader in Chinese, 1973-, Australian National University, Canberra; Master, University House, 1991-;Adjunct Professor of Asian Studies, 1999-. Publications: The Biography of Sun Chien, 1966; Official Titles of the Former Han Dynasty (with H H Dubs), 1967; The Last of the Han, 1969; The Records of the Three Kingdoms, 1970; China: The Land and Its People, 1971; China This Century: A History of Modern China, 1975, 2nd edition, 1992; Portents of Protest, 1976; Northern Frontier, 1984; Emperor Huan and Emperor Ling, 1989; Generals of the South, 1990; To Establish Peace, 1996. Membership: Australian Academy of the Humanities, fellow. Address: 5 Rous Crescent, Forrest, ACT 2603, Australia.

DE GRANDIS Rita, b. 16 Feb 1951, Argentina. Professor. Education: BA, Spanish, 1973; Licenciateship, 1975, Universidad Nacional del Litoral; MA, Linguistics, Simon Fraser University, 1981; PhD, Hispanic Literatures, Université de Montréal, 1989. Appointments: TA, Universidad del Litoral, 1975; Lecturer, Universidad Nacional de La Pampa, 1976; Research Assistant, Spanish Literature, 1983, Linguistics, 1982-83, Simon Fraser University; Research Assistant and Teaching Assistant, 1986-89; Postdoctoral Fellow, 1989-90, Université de Montréal; Teaching Assistant, Simon Fraser University, 1977-82; Lecturer, Mount Saint Vincent University, 1983-84, Mount Allison University, 1985-86; Part-time Lecturer, Concordia University and McGill University, 1986-90; Assistant, 1990-94, Associate, 1994-96, Simon Fraser University; Associate Professor, University of British Columbia, 1996-. Publications: Polémica y estrategias narrativas en América Latine, 1993; Imprevisíveis Américas: questoes de Hibridacao Cultural nas Américas (editor with Zilà Bernd), 1995. Contributions to: Refereed journals, conference proceedings and book reviews. Memberships: Canadian Association of Hispanists; Canadian Association of Latin American and Caribbean Studies; International Association of Hispanists; International Ibero-American Literature Institute; Brazilian Association of Comparative Literature; Latin American Studies Association; Institute for the Humanities, associate member, Simon Fraser University. Address: #204 1266 West 13th Avenue, Vancouver, BC V6H 1N6, Canada.

DE GRAVE Kathleen Rose, b. 20 Oct 1950, Green Bay, Wisconsin, USA. English Professor. m. Earl Wayne Lee, 10 Mar 1978, 2 sons, 1 daughter. Education: BA, University of Wisconsin, Green Bay, USA, 1973; MA, University of Arkansas, Fayetteville, 1977; PhD, University of Wisconsin, Madison, 1989. Appointments: Assistant Professor, Pittsburg State University, 1989; Associate Professor, English, Pittsburg State University, 1994. Publications: Swindler, Spy, Rebel: The Confidence Women in 19th-Century America, 1995; Comanpy Women, 1995. Contributions to: Keeping Safe, Valley Women's Voice; We Were Sisters, Potato Eyes. Address: 613 S Olive, Pittsburg, KS 66762, USA.

DE GRAZIA Sebastian, b. 11 Aug 1917, Chicago, Illinois, USA. Retired Professor of Political Philosophy; Writer. m. (1) Miriam Lund Carlson, 1 son, 2 daughters, (2) Anna Maria d'Annunzio di Montenevoso, 2 sons, (3) Lucia Heffelfinger. Education: AB, 1939, PhD, 1947, University of Chicago. Appointments: Faculty, University of Chicago, 1945-50; Visiting Professor, University of Florence, 1950-52, Princeton University, 1957, 1991-92, University of Madrid, 1963, John Jay College of Criminal Justice, 1967-71, Institute for Advanced Study, Princeton, New Jersey, 1983; Professor of Political Philosophy, Rutgers University, 1962-88. Publications: The Political Community, 1948; Errors of Psychotherapy, 1953; Of Time, Work and Leisure, 1962; Masters of Chinese Political Thought, 1973; A Country With No Name, 1987; Machiavelli in Hell, 1989. Honours: Pulitzer Prize for Biography, 1990; Several grants. Memberships: American Political Science Association; American Society and Legal Philosophy; Institut International de Philosophie Politique. Address: 914 Great Road, Princeton, NJ 08540, USA.

DE GUISE Elizabeth (Mary Teresa), (Isobel Chase, Elizabeth Hunter), b. 1934, Nairobi, Kenya. Writer. Education: Open University. Publications: Romance Novels as Elizabeth Hunter: Fountains of Paradise, 1983; London Pride, 1983; Shared Destiny, 1983; A Silver Nutmeg, 1983; Kiss of the Rising Sun, 1984; Rain on the Wind, 1984; Song of Surrender, 1984; A Tower of Strength, 1984; A Time to Wed, 1984; Loving Relations, 1984; Eye of the Wind, 1985; Legend of the Sun, 1985; The Painted Veil, 1986; The Tides of Love, 1988. Romance Novels as Isobel Chase: The House of Scissors, 1972; The Dragon's Cave, 1972; The Edge of Beyond, 1973; A Man of Kent, 1973; The Elban Adventure, 1974; The Cornish Hearth, 1975; A Canopy of Rose Leaves, 1976; The Clouded Veil, 1976; The Desert Castle, 1976; Singing in the Wilderness, 1976; The Whistling Thorn, 1977; The Mouth of Truth, 1977; Second Best Wife, 1978; Undesirable Wife, 1978. Historical Novels as Elizabeth De Guise: Dance of the Peacocks, 1988; Flight of the Dragonfly, 1990; Came Forth the Sun, 1991; Bridge of Sighs, 1992. Contributions to: Women & Home; Woman's Weekly. Memberships: Campaign for Nuclear Disarmament; Pax Christi; Romantic Novelists Association. Literary Agent: June Hall Literary Agents Ltd, 504 The Chambers, Chelsea Harbour, London SW10 0XF, England. Address: 113 Nun Street, St Davids, Haverfordwest, Dyfed SA62 6BP, Wales.

DE LANGE Nicholas (Robert Michael), b. 7 Aug 1944, Nottingham, England. Scholar; Translator. Education: MA, 1969, DPhil, 1970, Christ Church, Oxford. Publications: Apocrypha, 1978; Atlas of the Jewish World, 1984; Judaism, 1986; Illustrated History of the Jewish People, 1997. Other: Many translations. Contributions to: Tel Aviv Review. Honour: George Webber Prize for Translation, 1990. Memberships: British Association of Jewish Studies; Society of Authors; Translators Association; Fellow, Wolfson College, Cambridge. Address: The Divinity School, St John's Street, Cambridge CB2 1TW, England.

DE LAPLANTE Jean, b. 29 Sept 1919, Montreal, Quebec, Canada. Writer; Journalist; Social Researcher. m. Fernande Lachance, 29 Dec 1941, 1 son, 1 daughter. Publications: La Communauté Montréalaise, 1952; Le Petit Juif (novel), 1962; Les Parcs de Montréal (essay), 1990. Contributions to: Journals and newspapers. Membership: Union des Ecrivains du Quebec. Address: 10360 Tolhurst, Montreal, Quebec H3L 3A3, Canada.

DE LINT Charles (Henri Diederick Hoefsmit), b. 22 Dec 1951, Bussum, Netherlands (Canadian citizen, 1961). Editor; Writer; Poet. m. Mary Ann Harris, 15 Sept 1980. Appointments: Owner-Editor, Triskell Press; Writer-in-Residence, Ottawa and Gloucester Public Libraries, 1995. Publications: Drink Down the Moon: A Novel of Urban Faerie, 1990; Death Leaves an Echo, 1991; Dreaming Place, 1992; From a Whisper to a Scream, 1992; Dreams Underfoot: The Newford Collection, 1993; Memory and Dream, 1994; The Ivory and the Horn, 1995; Trader, 1997; Someplace to be Flying, 1998. Contributions to: Anthologies and periodicals. Honours: Various awards. Memberships: Horror Writers of America, vice-president, 1992-93; Science Fiction Writers of America; Small Press Writers and Artists Organization. Address: PO Box 9480, Ottawa, Ontario K1G 3V2, Canada.

DE MADARIAGA Nieves. See: **MATHEWS Nieves H.**

DE MARCO Gino. See: **WEISS Irving.**

DE MILLE Nelson. See: **LEVINSON Leonard.**

DE NATALE Francine. See: **MALZBERG Barry.**

DE NEVERS Marguerite. See: **BOISVERT France.**

DE QUIROS Beltran. See: **ROMEU Jorge Luis.**

DE REGNIERS Beatrice Schenk, (Tamara Kitt), b. 16 Aug 1914, Lafayette, Indiana, USA. Children's Writer, Poet, and Dramatist. m. Francis de Regniers, May 1953. Education: University of Illinois, 1931-33; PhB, 1935, Graduate Studies, 1936-37, University of Chicago; MEd, Winnetka Graduate Teachers College, 1941. Appointments: Copywriter, Scott Foresman & Co, 1943-44, American Book Co, 1948-49; Director, Educational Materials, American Heart Association, 1949-61; Editor, Lucky Book Club, Scholastic Inc, New York City, 1961-81. Publications: Over 50 children's books. Memberships: Authors Guild; Dramatists Guild; PEN; Society of Children's Book Writers and Illustrators. Address: 4530 Connecticut Avenue North West, Apt 302, Washington, DC 20008, USA.

DE ROO Anne (Louise), b. 1931, Gore, New Zealand. Writer. Education: BA, University of Canterbury, Christchurch, 1952. Publications: Juvenile: The Gold Dog, 1969; Moa Valley, 1969; Boy and the Sea Beast, 1971; Cinnamon and Nutmeg, 1972; Mick's Country Cousins, 1974; Scrub Fire, 1977; Traveller, 1979; Because of Rosie, 1980; Jacky Nobody, 1983; The Bat's Nest, 1986; Friend Troll, Friend Taniwha, 1986; Mouse Talk, 1990; The Good Cat, 1990; Hepzibah Mouse's ABC, 1991; Sergeant Sal, 1991; Hepzibah's Book of Famous Mice, 1993. Novels: Hope Our Daughter, 1990; Becoming Fully Human, 1991; And We Beheld His Glory, 1994. Plays: The Dragon Master, 1978; The Silver Blunderbuss, 1984. Honour: ICI Bursary, 1981. Address: 38 Joseph Street, Palmerston North, New Zealand.

DE ROSA Gabriele, b. 24 June 1917, Castellammare de Stabia, Italy. University Professor. m. (1) Gabriella Torrese, 4 Sept 1944, dec 1977, 5 sons, 1 daughter, (2) Carla Sabine Kowohl, 8 Dec 1978. Education: Doctor in Law, 1941. Appointments: Tenured University Lecturer, 1958; Full Professor of Contemporary History; Chancellor, University of Salerno, 1968-75; President, Istituto Luigi Sturzo, Rome; Senator, 1987-94; Deputy, 1994-96; Director, review Ricerche di storia sociale e religiosa, Rome. Publications: Storia politica dell'Azione Cattolica, 1953; Giolitté e il fascismo, 1957; Storia del Partito Popolare Italiano, 1958; Filippo Meda e l'età liberale, 1959; I gesuiti in Sicilia e la rivoluzione del 1848, 1963; Vescovì popolo e magia nel Sud, 1971; Luigi Sturzo, 1977; Tempo religioso e tempo storico, vol I, 1987, vol II, 1994, vol III, 1998; Chiesa e religione popolare nel Mezzogiorno, 1991. Contributions to: Il Tempo; Avvenire; Il Giornale. Honour: Commenda, S Gregorio Magno, Papal Award. Address: Istituto Sturzo, via delle Coppelle 35, 00186 Rome, Italy.

DE ROULET Daniel, b. 1944, Geneva, Switzerland. Writer. m. Chiara Banchini, 1995, 1 son. Education: Architect, University of Geneva, 1971. Publictions: A Nous Deux, Ferdinand, 1991; Virtuellement Votre, 1993; La Vie, Il Y a Des Enfants Pour Ca, 1994; La Ligne Bleue, 1995; Bleu Siecle, 1996; Gris-bleu, 1999. Honours: Prix Dentan, 1994; Prix Alpes-Jura, 1996; Prix de litterature du Canton de Berne, 1999. Membership: Groupe D'Olten des Ecrivains. Address: Editions du Seuil, 27 rue Jacob, 75006 Paris, France.

DE SOUZA Eunice, b. 1 Aug 1940, Poona, India. Reader in English; Poet; Writer. Education: BA, 1960, PhD, 1988, University of Bombay. Appointments: Reader in English, 1969-, Head, Department of English, 1990-, St Xavier's College, Bombay. Publications: Fix, 1979; Women in Dutch Painting, 1988; Ways of Belonging:

Selected Poems, 1990; Selected and New Poems, 1994; Nine Indian Women Poets (editor), 1997; Conversations with Poets, forthcoming. Other: Several children's books. Honour: Poetry Book Society Recommendation, 1990. Address: c/o Department of English, St Xavier's College, Bombay 400 001, India.

DE VRIES Susanna Mary, (Susanna Devries-Evans), b. 6 Oct 1935. Author; Lecturer in Art History. m. Jake de Vries, 25 July 1982. Education: Cours de Civilisation Francaise, Sorbonne, University of Paris, 1953; Universidad Menendez Pelayo, Santander, Spain, 1954; Complutense University, Madrid. Appointments: Lecturer, Continuing Education Department, University of Queensland, 1991. Publications: Historic Sydney: Its Early Artists, 1982, 2nd edition, 1987; The Impressionists Revealed: Masterpieces and Collectors, 1982, 2nd edition 1994; Pioneering Women, Pioneer Land, 1988; Conrad Martens on the Beagle; Strength of Spirit: Pioneering Women of Achievement from the First Fleet to Federation. Contributions to: Periodicals. Honours: Fellowship, Literary Board, Australia Council, 1990; Winston Churchill Fellowship, Arts History, 1994. Memberships: Lyceum Club, Brisbane; Australian Society of Authors. Literary Agent: Selwa Anthony, 10 Loves Avenue, Oyster Bay, New South Wales 2225, Australia. Address: 10 Matingara Street, Chapel Hill, Brisbane 4069, Australia.

DE WEESE Thomas Eugene "Gene", (Jean DeWeese, Thomas Stratton, Victoria Thomas), b. 31 Jan 1934, Rochester, Indiana, USA. Writer. m. Beverly Amers, 1955. Education: Associate Degree, Electronic Engineering, Valparaiso Technical Institute, Indiana, 1953; Indiana University, Kokomo; University of Wisconsin, Milwaukee; Marquette University, Milwaukee. Appointments: Electronics Technician, Delco Radio, Kokomo, 1954-59; Technical Writer, Delco Electronics, Milwaukee, 1959-74. Publications: Fiction: Jeremy Case, 1976; The Wanting Factor, 1980; A Different Darkness, 1982; Something Answered, 1983; Chain of Attack, 1987; The Peacekeepers, 1988; The Final Nexus, 1988; Renegade, 1991; Into the Nebula, 1995; King of the Dead, 1996; Lord of the Necropolis, 1997. (Wth Robert Coulson): The Invisibility Affair, 1967; The Mind-Twisters Affair, 1967; Gates of the Universe, 1975; Now You See It/Him/Them..., 1976; Charles Fort Never Mentioned Wombats, 1977; Nightmare Universe, 1985.(As Jean DeWeese): The Reimann Curse, 1975; The Moonstone Spirit, 1975; The Carnelian Cat, 1975; Cave of the Moaning Wind, 1976; Web of Guilt, 1976; The Doll With Opal Eyes, 1976; Nightmare in Pewter, 1978; Hour of the Cat, 1980; The Backhoe Gothic, 1981. (As Victoria Thomas): Ginger's Wish (with Connie Kugi), 1987. Other: Black Suits From Outer Space; Several other science fiction novels for juveniles. Non-fiction: Fundamentals of Space Navigation, 1968; Fundamentals of Digital Computers, 1972; Fundamentals of Integrated Circuits, 1972; Making American Folk Art Dolls (with Gini Rogowski), 1975; Computers in Entertainment and the Arts, 1984. Contributions to: Anthologies and magazines. Honours: Best Novel Awards, 1976, 1982, Best Juvenile Book Award, 1979, Council for Wisconsin Writers; Notable Science Book of the Year, NSTA, 1984. Address: 2718 North Prospect, Milwaukee, WI 53211, USA.

DE ZEGHER Marie-Catherine, b. 14 Apr 1955, Groningen, The Netherlands. Director, Art Foundation; Curator; Critic. 1 son, 2 daughters. Appointments: Archeologist, and later inventory and restoration of historic monuments, 1977-85; Co-Founder, Director, 1987, Kanaal Art Foundation, centre of contemporary art; Visiting Curator, ICA, Boston, USA. Publications include: Inside the Visible, An Elliptical Traverse of 20th Century Art, in, of, and from the Feminine, 1996; The Os of Orozco, 1996; The Precarious, Art and Poetry of Cecilia Vicuna and Quipoem, 1997; Hatoum's Recollection: About Losing and Being Lost, 1997; Tongue, Torture and Free Rein in Spero's Explicit Series of Paintings, 1988; About Son et Lumière, in Ann Veronica Janssens Sculpture, 1998. Address: Erasmuslaan 32, 8500 Kortrijk, Belgium.

DE'ATH Richard. See: **HAINING Peter Alexander.**

DE-LA-NOY Michael, b. 3 Apr 1934, Hessle, Yorkshire. Author. Appointment: Press Officer, Archbishop of Canterbury, 1967-70. Publications: Elgar: The Man, Denton Welch: The Making of a Writer, The Honours System, Acting as Friends: The Story of the Samaritans, Eddy: The Life of Edward Sackville-West, Michael Ramsey: A Portrait, Windsor Castle: Past & Present, Exploring Oxford, The Church of England: A Portrait, The Queen Behind the Throne, The King Who Never Was; The Story of Frederick, Princes of Wales, Mervyn Stockwood: A Lonely Life (Sutton Pocket Biographies); Scott of the Antarctic; George IV; Bedford School: A History. Literary Agent: Scott Ferris Associates, 15 Gledhow Gardens, London SW5 0AY, England.

DEANE Seamus (Francis), b. 9 Feb 1940, Derry City, Northern Ireland. Professor of Irish Studies; Writer; Poet. m. Marion Treacy, 19 Aug 1963, 3 sons, 1 daughter. Education: BA, Honours, 1st Class, 1961, MA, 1st Class, 1963, Queen's University, Belfast; PhD, Cambridge University, 1966. Appointments: Visiting Fulbright and Woodrow Wilson Scholar, Reed College, Oregon, 1966-67; Visiting Lecturer, 1967-68, Visiting Professor, 1978, University of California at Berkeley; Professor of Modern English and American Literature, University College, Dublin, 1980-93; Walker Ames Professor, University of Washington, Seattle, 1987; Julius Benedict Distinguished Visiting Professor, Carleton College, Minnesota, 1988; Keough Professor of Irish Studies, University of Notre Dame, Indiana, 1993-. Publications: Fiction: Reading in the Dark, 1996. Poetry: Gradual Wars, 1972; Rumours, 1977; History Lessons, 1983; Selected, 1988. Non-Fiction: Celtic Revivals: Essays in Modern Irish Literature, 1880-1980, 1985; A Short History of Irish Literature, 1986, reissued, 1994; The French Revolution and Enlightenment in England, 1789-1832, 1988; Strange Country: Ireland, Modernity and Nationhood, 1790-1970, 1997. Editor: The Adventures of Eminent Persons, Vol IX, 1973; Nationalism, Colonialism and Literature, 1990; The Field Day Anthology of Irish Writing, 3 volumes, 1991; Penguin Twentieth Century Classics: James Joyce, 4 volumes, 1993. Honours: AE Memorial for Literature, 1973; American-Irish Fund, Literature, 1989; Guardian Fiction Prize, 1997; Irish Times International Fiction Award, 1997; Irish Times Fiction Award, 1997; London Weekend Television South Bank Award for Literature, 1997; Ruffino Antico-Fattore International Literature Award, Florence, 1998. Memberships: Aosdana (Irish Artists' Council); Field Day Theatre and Publishing Company, director; Royal Irish Academy. Address: 49 Lombard Street West, Dublin 8, Ireland.

DEAR Nick, b. 11 June 1955, Portsmouth, England. Playwright. Partner: Penny Downie, 2 sons. Education: BA, Honours, European Literature, University of Essex, 1977. Appointments: Playwright-in-Residence, Essex University, 1985, Royal Exchange Theatre, 1987-88. Publications: Temptation, 1984; The Art of Success, 1986; Food of Love, 1988; A Family Affair (after Ostrovsky), 1988; In the Ruins, 1989; The Last Days of Don Juan (after Tirso), 1990; Le Bourgeois Gentilhomme (after Molière), 1992; Pure Science, 1994; Zenobia, 1995. Opera Libretti: A Family Affair, 1993; Siren Song, 1994. Other Several radio plays. Films: The Monkey Parade, 1983; The Ranter, 1988; Persuasion, 1995; The Gambler, 1997. Honours: John Whiting Award, 1987; Olivier Award nominations, 1987, 1988; BAFTA Award, 1996; Broadcasting Press Guild Award, 1996. Membership: Writer's Guild of Great Britain. Address: c/o Rosica Colin Ltd, 1 Clareville Grove Mews, London SW7 5AH, England.

DEARDEN James Shackley, b. 9 Aug 1931, Barrow-in-Furness, England. Appointment: Curator, Ruskin Galleries, Bembridge School, Isle of Wight and Brantwood Coniston, 1957-96. Publications: The Professor: Arthur Severn's Memoir of Ruskin, 1967; A Short History of Brantwood, 1967; Iteriad by John Ruskin (editor), 1969; Facets of Ruskin, 1970; Ruskin and Coniston (with K G Thorne), 1971; John Ruskin, 1973, 2nd edition, 1981; Turner's Isle of Wight Sketch Book, 1979; John Ruskin and Les Alpi, 1989; John Ruskin's Camberwell, 1990; A Tour to the Lakes in Cumberland: John Ruskin's Diary for 1830 (editor), 1990; John Ruskin and Victorian Art, 1993; Ruskin, Bembridge and Brantwood, 1994; Hare Hunting on the Isle of Wight, 1996. Contributions to: Book Collector; Connoisseur; Apollo; Burlington; Bulletin of John Rylands Library; Country Life; Ruskin Newsletter (editor); Ruskin Research Series (general editor); Journal of Pre-Raphaelite Studies (editorial advisory board); Whitehouse Edition of Ruskin's Works (joint general editor). Honour: Hon. D. Litt. (Lancaster), 1998. Memberships: Ruskin Society; Ruskin Association, secretary and treasurer; Turner Society; Companion of the Guild of St George, Director for Ruskin Affairs; Old Bembridgians Association; Isle of Wight Foot Beagles, vice president; Friends of Ruskin's Brantwood, vice president. Address: 4 Woodlands, Foreland Road, Bembridge, Isle of Wight, England.

DEAYTON Angus, b. 6 Jan 1956, Surrey, England. Writer; Performer. Education: BA, Oxon, Modern Languages. Publications: Radio Active Times; The Uncyclopedia of Rock; Have I Got News For You; In Search of Happiness; Have I Got 1997 For You. Literary Agent: Talkback. Address: 36 Percy St, London W1P 0LN, England.

DEBO Yi. See: **BORDAHL Vibeke.**

DEBONIS Steven Larry, b. 10 Jan 1949, Brooklyn, New York, USA. Teacher; Writer. m. Laurie Kuntz, 1 son. Education: BA Psychology, University of Connecticut, 1971. Publication: Children of the Enemy: Oral Histories of Vietnamese Amerasians and their Mothers, 1995. Address: 1-28, 2 chome, Hirahata, Misawa-shi, Aomori-ken 033, Japan.

DEBS Victor Jr, b. 4 Oct 1949, Baseball Author and Lecturer. m. Lola Kashou, 28 June 1980, 1 d. Education: BA, Richmond College, 1970; MA, Richmond College, 1974. Appointment: Teacher, 1970-92. Publications: They Kept Me Loyal to the Yankees, 1993; Baseball Tidbits, 1997; Still Standing After All These Years, 1997; Missed It By That Much, 1998. Contributions to: A Year to Forget for Yankee Fans, 1966; National Pastime, Volume II, 1992. Memberships: Author's Guild; Authors Registry; ASJA. Literary Agent: Stephen Cogil, President; SLC Enterprises. Address: 175 Lewiston Street, Staten Island, NY 10313, USA.

DECLEMENTS Barthe, b. 8 Oct 1920, Seattle, Washington, USA. Writer. m. (1) Don Macri, div, (2) Gordon Greimes, div, 4 children. Education: Western Washington College, 1940-42; BA, 1944, MEd, 1970, University of Washington, Seattle. Appointments: Schoolteacher, 1944-46, 1961-78; High School Counselor, 1978-83. Publications: Nothing's Fair in Fifth Grade, 1981; How Do You Lose Those Ninth Grade Blues?, 1983; Seventeen and In-Between, 1984; Sixth Grade Can Really Kill You, 1985; I Never Asked You to Understand Me, 1986; Double Trouble (with Christopher Greimes), 1987; No Place For Me, 1987; The Fourth Grade Wizards, 1988; Five-Finger Discount, 1989; Monkey See, Monkey Do, 1990; Wake Me at Midnight, 1991; Breaking Out, 1991; The Bite of the Gold Bug, 1992; The Pickle Song, 1993; Tough Loser, 1994. Contributions to: Periodicals. Honours: Over 25 awards. Address: c/o Viking Penguin, 375 Hudson Street, New York, NY 10014, USA.

DEDJA Bedri, b. 20 Nov 1930, Korca, Albania. Writer; Psychologue. m. Pandora Papuciu, 1 son, 1 daughter. Education: Diploma Excellent, Superior Pedagogic Institute Lenin, Moscow, Russia, 1953. Appointments: Taught Psychology, University of Tirana, 1953; Chief Editor, The Teacher, newspaper, 1961; Director, Institute of Studies and School Editions, 1965; Vice Minister of Education and Culture, 1970; Science Secretary of Academy of Sciences, 1973. Publications: Heroism of Specked Fatbardh, 1955; A Dangerous Travel, or Trip, 1962; Children Of My Palace, 1972; School of Forest, 1973; Kacimeri Round the Globe, 1993; How Did for Children Become Businessmen, 1994; Eleven Storey Ed Tale, 1996; The City of Three Castles, 1998; Psychology, 1956, 1967, 1983; Social Psychology, 1998; Towards the Enigma of Physic of Man, 1989; History of Albanian Education, 1990; Secret of Talent, 1998. Honours: Laureate of Republic Prize; Winner, 30 prizes at literature competitions, 1958-98; Prize, Naim Frasheri, 1957; Viktor Eftimiu, 1996; Prize of Career, 1998. Memberships: Academy of Sciences of Albania, 1973-; Head of Association of Psychologist of Albania, 1954-; World League Assembly on Psychological Sciences, 1996-. Address: Lidhja e Shkrimtareve dhe Artisteve, Tirane, Albania.

DEFORD Frank, b. 16 Dec 1938, Baltimore, Maryland, USA. Writer; Editor. m. Carol Penner, 28 Aug 1965, 1 son, 2 daughters. Education: BA, Princeton University, 1962. Appointments: Writer, Commentator, Cable News Network, 1980-86, National Public Radio, 1980-89, 1991-, NBC, 1986-89, ESPN, 1992-; Editor-in-Chief, The National, 1989-91; Writer, Newsweek Magazine, 1991-93, 1996-98; Contributing Editor, Vanity Fair, 1993-96; Sports Illustrated, 1962-89, 1998-. Publications: Five Strides on the Banked Track, 1969; Cut'N'Run, 1971; There She Is, 1972; The Owner, 1974; Big Bill Tilden: The Triumphs and the Tragedy, 1977; Everybody's All-American, 1981; Alex: The Life of a Child, 1982; Spy in the Deuce Court, 1987; World's Tallest Midget, 1988; Casey on the Loose, 1989; Love and Infamy, 1993. Contributions to: Numerous magazines. Honours: Sportswriter of the Year, National Association of Sportswriters and Sportscasters, 1982-88; Emmy, 1988; Cable Ace, 1996; National Association of Sportwriters and Sportscasters, Hall of Fame, 1998. Literary Agent: Sterling Lord Literistic. Address: Box 1109, Greens Farms, CT 06436, USA.

DEGHETT Stephanie Coyne, b. 31 Aug 1951, Saranac Lake, New York, USA. Creative Writing Professor; Poet. m. Victor J DeGhett, 1980, 1 daughter. Education: BA, English, State University College, Potsdam, 1976; MA, English, University of Vermont, Burlington, 1982. Appointments: Graduate Teaching Fellow, University of Vermont; Instructor, English Department, State University of New York at Canton; Instructor, Creative Writing Program, State University College at Potsdam. Publications: Poem: The Physics of Sensation, 1996. Contributions to: Field Notes; North Country; Old Roses; Wordsmith; Airfoil; New England Review. Memberships: SUNY Writers Council, Poets and Writers. Address: English Department, State University College, Potsdam, NY 13676, USA.

DEGTJARJEVA Natalia Ivanovna, b. 6 Aug 1949, Krasny Sulin, Rostov Region, Russia. Musicologist. m. Tchumatchenko Georgy Viktorovitch, 21 June 1977, 1 son. Education: Graduated, 1973, Postgraduate Studies, 1976, St Petersburg Conservatory; Candidate of Science Diploma, 1981; Assistant Professor Certificate, 1991. Appointment: Faculty, Department of Foreign Music, St Petersburg Conservatory. Publications: 6 monographs in Russian, 1977-96. Address: Vosnessensky av 37, apt 65, 190068 St Petersburg, Russia.

DEGUY Michel, b. 25 May 1930, Paris, France. Poet; Writer; Editor. Education: Philosophy Studies, Paris. Appointment: Editor, Poésie, 1972-. Publications: Lese Meurtrières, 1959; Fragments du cadastre, 1960; Poèmes de la presqu'ile, 1961; Thomas Mann, 1962; Approche de Hölderlin, 1962; Le Monde de Thomas Mann, 1963; Biefs, 1964; Actes, 1966; Oui-dire, 1966; Histoire de rechutes, 1968; Figurations, Poèmes, Propositions, Etudes, 1969; Tombeau de Du Bellay, 1973; Poèmes 1960-1970, 1973; Reliefs, 1975; Jumelages suivi de Made in U.S.A., 1978; Donnant, donnant, 1981; La Machine matriomoniale ou Marivaux, 1982; René Girard et le problème du mal (with J-P Dupuis), 1982; Gisants, 1985; Poèmes II; 1970-1980, 1986; Brevets, 1986; Choses de la poésie et affaire culturelle, 1986; Le Comité: Confessions d'un lecteur de grande maison, 1988; La Poésie n'est pas seule: Court traité de Poétique, 1988; Arrets fréquents, 1990; Aux heures d'affluence, 1993; A ce qui n'en finit pas, 1995.

Honour: Grand Prix national de Poésie, 1989. Address: 26 rue Las-Cases, Paris 75007, France.

DEIGHTON Len, (Leonard Cyril Deighton), b. 18 Feb 1929, London, England. Writer. Education: Royal College of Art, 1952-55. Publications: The Ipcress File, 1962; Horse Under Water, 1963; Funeral in Berlin, 1964; Action Cook Book: Len Deighton's Guide To Eating (US edition as Cookstrip Cook Book), 1965; Ou est le Garlic: Len Deighton's French Cook Book, 1965, revised edition as Basic French Cooking, 1978; The Billion Dollar Brain, 1966; An Expensive Place to Die, 1967; London Dossier (editor), 1967; The Assassination of President Kennedy (co-author), 1967; Only When I Larf, 1968; Len Deighton's Continental Dossier: A Collection of Cultural Culinary, Historical, Spooky, Grim and Preposterous Facts, 1968; Bomber, 1970; Declarations of War (stories), 1971; Close-Up, 1972; Spy Story, 1974; Yesterday's Spy, 1975; Twinkle, Twinkle, Little Spy, 1976; Fighter: The True Story of the Battle of Britain, 1977; SS-GB, 1978; Airshipwreck (with Arnold Schwartsman), 1978; Blitzkrieg: From the Rise of Hitler to the Fall of Dunkirk, 1979; Battle of Britain, 1980; XPD 1981; Goodbye Mickey Mouse, 1982; Berlin Game, 1983; Mexico Set, 1984; London Match, 1985; Spy Hook, 1988; Spy Line, 1989; ABC of French Food, 1989; Spy Sinker, 1990; Basic French Cookery Course, 1990; MAMista, 1991; City of Gold, 1992; Violent Ward, 1993; Blood, Tears and Folly, 1993; Faith, 1994; Hope, 1995; Charity, 1996. Literary Agent: Jonathon Clowes Ltd. Address: c/o Jonathon Clowes Ltd, 10 Iron Bridge House, Bridge Approach, London NW1 8BD, England.

DEJEVSKY Nikolai James, b. 22 Sep 1945, Hanau, Germany. Publishing Consultant; Writer; Journalist. m. Mary Peake, 13 Sep 1975. Education: BA, Cornell University, USA, 1968; MA, University of Pennsylvania, USA, 1971; DPhil, Christ Church, University of Oxford, 1977. Appointments: Assistant Editor, Clio Press Ltd, Oxford, 1977-80; Publishing Manager, Pergamon Press Ltd, Oxford, 1980-82; Publisher, Professional Publishing Ltd, London, 1982-84; Editorial Director, Gower Publishing Ltd, Aldershot, 1984-85; Publisher, Longman Group Ltd, Harlow, 1985-88; Freelance writer and journalist, 1990-. Publications: Cultural Atlas of Russia and the Soviet Union, 1989; Free-wheeling in Bear Country, 1994. Contributions to: California Slavic Studies; Cambridge Encyclopaedia of Archaeology; Medieval Scandinavia; Solanus; Modern Encyclopaedia of Russian and Soviet History; Year's Work in Modern Language Studies; Business Eastern Europe, 1991; International Automotive Review, 1991-. Address: 37 Ulysses Road, West Hampstead, London NW6 1ED, England.

DEKKER Carl. See: **LYNDS Dennis.**

DELAGE Denys, b. 2 Apr 1942, Montreal, Quebec, Canada. Historian m. (1), 2 sons, (2) Andrée Gendreau, 26 July 1995. Education: MA, Sociology, University of Montréal, 1968; PhD, Social History, École des Hautes Études en Sciences Sociales, Paris, 1980. Publication: Bitter Feast: Amerindians and Europeans in Northeastern North America, 1600-64, 1993. Contributions to: Recherche Amerindiennes au Quebec: Anthropologie et Sociétés. Honours: John Porter Award, Canadian Association of Sociology and Anthropology; Lionel Groulx Award, Histoire de l'Ameridue Française. Address: 378 Franciscains Quebec City, Quebec, GIS 2P8, Canada.

DELANEY Francis James Joseph (Frank), b. 24 Oct 1942. Broadcaster; Author. m. (1) 1966, dis 1980, 3 sons, (2) 1988, dis 1997. Appointments: Television and Radio Broadcaster, Journalist, RTE News Dublin, Current Affairs with BBC Northern Ireland, BBC TV and BBC Radio 4. Publications: James Joyce's Odyssey, 1981; Betjeman Country, 1983; The Celts, 1986; A Walk in the Dark Ages, 1988; My Dark Rosaleen (novella), 1989; Legends of the Celts, 1989; The Sins of the Mothers, 1992; A Walk to the Western Isles, 1993; Telling the Pictures, 1993; A Stranger in Their Midst, 1995; The Amethysts, 1997. Memberships: Athenaeum; Chelsea Arts. Address: c/o Curtis Brown Ltd, 4th Floor, Haymarket House, 28/29 Haymarket, London W1, England.

DELANEY Shelagh, b. 25 Nov 1939, Salford, Lancashire, England. Playwright. 1 daughter. Education: Broughton Secondary School. Publications: Plays: A Taste of Honey, 1958; The Lion in Love, 1960. Films: A Taste of Honey; The White Bus, 1966; Charlie Bubbles, 1968; Dance with a Stranger, 1985. Television Plays: St Martin's Summer, 1974; Find Me First, 1979. Television Series: The House That Jack Built, 1977 (stage adaptation, New York, 1979). Radio Plays: So Does The Nightingale, 1980; Don't Worry About Matilda, 1983. Honours: Charles Henry Foyle New Play Award; Arts Council Bursary, 1961; New York Drama Critics Award, 1961; British Film Academy Award, Robert Flaherty Award, 1961; Prix Film Jeunesse Etranger, Cannes, 1985. Address: c/o Tessa Sayle, 11 Jubilee Place, London SW3 3TE, England.

DELANY Samuel R(ay), b. 1 Apr 1942, New York, New York, USA. Writer; Professor of Comparative Literature. m. 24 Aug 1961, div 1980, 1 son, 1 daughter. Education: City College, New York City, 1960, 1962-63. Appointments: Editor, Wuark, 1970-71; Senior Fellow, Center for 20th Century Studies, University of Wisconsin, Milwaukee, 1977; Society for the Humanities, Cornell University, 1987; Professor of Comparative Literature, University of Massachusetts, Amherst, 1988-. Publications: The Jewels of Aptor, 1962, unabridged edition, 1968; The Fall of the Towers, Vol 1, Captives of the Flames, 1963, as Out of the Dead City, 1968, Vol 2, The Towers of Toron, 1964, Vol 3, City of a Thousand Suns, 1965; The Ballad of Beta-2, 1965; Empire Star, 1966; Babel-17, 1966; The Einstein Intersection, 1967; Nova, 1968; Driftglass: Ten Tales of Speculative Fiction, 1971; Dhalgren, 1975; Triton, 1976; The Jewel-Hinged Jaw: Notes on the Language of Science Fiction, 1977; The American Shore, 1978; Empire, 1978; Nebula Award Winners 13 (editor), 1979; Distant Stars, 1981; Stars in My Pocket Like Grains of Sand, 1984; Starboard Wine: More Notes on the Language of Science Fiction, 1984; The Splendour and Misery of Bodies, 1985; Flight from Neveryon, 1985; They Fly at Ciron, 1992; Neveryon, 1993; Tales of Neveryon, 1993; The Mad Man, 1994. Literary Agent: Henry Morrison, Box 234, Bedford Hills, NY 10507, USA. Address: c/o Bantam Books, 666 Fifth Avenue, New York, NY 10019, USA.

DELBANCO Andrew (Henry), b. 20 Feb 1952, White Plains, New York, USA. Professor in the Humanities; Writer. m. Dawn Ho Delbanco, 1973, 1 son, 1 daughter. Education: AB, 1973, AM, 1976, PhD, 1980, Harvard University. Appointments: Assistant Professor, Harvard University, 1981-85; Associate Professor, 1985-87, Professor, 1987-, Julian Clarence Levi Professor in the Humanities, 1995-, Columbia University; Adjunct Professor, Yale University, 1989. Publications: William Ellery Channing: An Essay on the Liberal Spirit in America, 1981; The Puritan Ordeal, 1989; The Death of Satan: How Americans Have Lost the Sense of Evil, 1995; Required Reading: Why Our American Classics Matter Now, 1997. Editor: The Puritans in America: A Narrative Anthology (with Alan Heimert), 1985; The Sermons of Ralph Waldo Emerson, Vol II (with Teresa Toulouse), 1990; The Portable Abraham Lincoln, 1992. Contributions to: Professional journals and to general periodicals. Honours: Guggenheim Fellowship; American Council of Learned Societies Fellowship; National Endowment for the Humanities Fellowship; National Humanities Center Fellowship. Membership: Society of American Historians. Address: c/o Department of English and Comparative Literature, Columbia University, 1150 Amsterdam Avenue, New York, NY 10027, USA.

DELBANCO Nicholas Franklin, b. 27 Aug 1942, London, England. Writer. m. Elena Carter Greenhouse, 12 Sept 1970, 2 daughters. Education: BA, History and Literature, Harvard College, 1963; MA, English Comparative Literature, Columbia University, 1966. Appointments: Member, Language and Literature Division, Bennington College, 1966-85; Director, Bennington Writing Workshops, 1977-85; Visiting Professor, Iowa Writers Program, University of Iowa, 1979; Adjunct Professor, School of the Arts, Columbia University, 1979-96; Visiting Artist-in-Residence, Trinity College, 1980; Visiting Professor, Williams College, 1982; Professor of English, Skidmore College, 1984-85; Professor of English, Director, MFA Program, University of Michigan, 1985-; Director, Hopwood Awards Programme, 1988-. Publications: The Martlet's Tale, 1966; Grasse 3/23/66, 1968; Consider Sappho Burning, 1969; News, 1970; In the Middle Distance, 1971; Fathering, 1973; Small Rain, 1975; Possession, 1977; Sherbrookes, 1978; Stillness, 1980; Group Portrait: Conrad, Crane, Ford, James, and Wells, 1982; About My Table and Other Stories, 1983; The Beaux Arts Trio: A Portrait, 1985; Running in Place: Scenes from the South of France, 1989; The Writers' Trade, and Other Stories, 1990; In the Name of Mercy, 1995; Old Scores, 1997. Contributions to: Periodicals. Honours: National Endowment for the Arts Creative Writing Fellowships, 1973, 1982; Guggenheim Fellowship, 1979. Memberships: Authors League; Authors Guild; Signet Society; Phi Beta Kappa; New York State Writers Institute; PEN. Literary Agent: Gail Hochman, Brandt and Brandt. Address: c/o Department of English, University of Michigan, 7601 Haven Hall, Ann Arbor, MI 48109, USA.

DELEHANTY Randolph, b. 5 July 1944, Memphis, Tennessee, USA. University Art Museum Director, Writer, Lecturer. Education: BA, Georgetown University, 1966; MA, University of Chicago, 1968; MA, 1969, PhD, 1992, Harvard University. Publications: San Francisco: Walks and Tours in the Golden Gate City, 1980; California: A Guidebook, 1984; Preserving the West, 1985; In the Victorian Style, 1991; New Orleans: Elegance and Decadence, 1993; San Francisco: The Ultimate Guide, 1995; Classic Natchez, 1996; Art in the American South, 1996; Randolph Delehanty's Ultimate Guide to New Orleans, 1998. Address: 2004 Gough Street, San Francisco, CA 94109, USA

DELGADO James P, b. 11 Jan 1958, San Jose, California, USA. Historian; Museum Director. m. Mary Jean Bremmer, 7 Oct 1978, 1 son, 1 daughter. Education: BA magna cum laude, American History, San Francisco State University, 1981; MA, Maritime History, Underwater Research, East Carolina University, Greenville, North Carolina, 1985. Appointments: Assistant to Regional Historian, Western Region (Hawaii, Guam, American Samoa, California, Arizona), 1978-79; Chief Historian, Golden Gate National Recreation Area, San Francisco, 1979-86; Chief Maritime Historian, National Park Service, Washington, 1987-91; Executive Director, Vancouver Maritime Museum, Canada, 1991-. Publications: Alcatraz Island: The Story Behind the Scenery, 1985; The Log of the Apollo: Joseph Perkins Beach's Log of the Voyage of the Ship Apollo from New York to San Francisco 1849 (editor), 1986; Shipwrecks at the Golden Gate (with Stephen A Haller), 1989; To California By Sea: A Maritime History of the California Gold Rush, 1990; National Parks of America, 1990; Pearl Harbor Recalled: New Images of the Day of Infamy (with Tom Freeman), 1991; Great American Ships (with J Candace Clifford), 1991; Great American Ships (with J Candace Clifford), 1991; Alcatraz Island, 1991; Dauntless St Roch: The Mounties Arctic Schooner, 1992; Shipwrecks of the Northern Shore; Ghost Fleet of the Atomic Age: The Sunken Ships of Bikini Atoll. Contributions to: Pacific Historian; Book Club of California Quarterly; Point Reyes Historian; Public Historian; American History Illustrated; CRM Bulletin. Memberships: Society for Historical Archaeology; California Historical Society; Canadian Nautical Research Society; National Maritime Historical Society; International Committee on Monuments and Sites, Canadian representative; Committee on the International Underwater Heritage; Council of American Maritime Museums, trustee. Address: 4204 West 10th Avenue, Vancouver, British Columbia V6R 2H4, Canada.

DELGADO Ramon Louis, b. 16 Dec 1937, Tampa, Florida, USA. University Professor. Education: BA, Stetson University, 1959; MA, Baylor University, 1960; MFA, Yale School of Drama, 1967; PhD, South Illinois University, 1976. Appointments: Chipola Junior College, 1962-64; Kentucky Wesleyan College, 1967-72; Hardin-Simmons University, 1972-74; St Cloud State

University, 1976-78; Montclair State University, 1978-. Publications: Plays: Waiting for the Bus, 1969; Once Below A Lighthouse, 1972; The Little Toy Dog, 1972; Sparrows of the Field, 1973; The Knight-Mare's Nest, 1974; Omega's Ninth, 1975; A Little Holy Water, 1983. Textbook: Acting With Both Sides of Your Brain, 1986. Honours: 12 national, 5 regional play contests. Memberships: Dramatists Guild; Nashville Songwriters International. Address: c/o Department of Theatre/Dance, Montclair State University, Upper Montclair, NJ 07043, USA.

DeLILLO Don, b. 20 Nov 1936, New York, New York, USA. Author. Education: BA in Communication Arts, Fordham University, 1958. Publications: Americana, 1971; End Zone, 1972; Great Jones Street, 1973; Ratner's Star, 1976; Players, 1977; Running Dog, 1978; Amazons, 1980; The Names, 1982; White Noise, 1985; The Day Room, 1987; Libra, 1988; Mao II, 1991; Underworld, 1997. Contributions to: Periodicals. Honours: American Book Award, 1985; Irish Times-Aer Lingus International Fiction Prize, 1989; PEN/Faulkner Award, 1992. Address: c/o Wallace & Sheil, 177 East 70th Street, New York, NY 10021, USA.

DELIUS Anthony (Ronald Martin), b. 11 June 1916, Simonstown, South Africa; Writer; Poet; Dramatist. Education: BA, Rhodes University, Grahamstown, 1938. Appointment: Writer, BBC Africa Service, London, 1968-77. Publications: Novels: The Young Traveller in South Africa, 1947; The Long Way Round, 1956; Upsurge in Africa, 1960; Border, 1963; The Day Natal Took Off: A Satire, 1963. Poetry: An Unknown Border, 1954; The Last Division, 1959; A Corner of the World: Thirty-Four Poems, 1962; Black South Easter, 1966. Play: The Fall: A Play About Rhodes, 1957. Honour: CNA Literary Award, 1977. Address: 30 Graemesdyke Avenue, London SW14 7BJ, England.

DELORIA Vine (Victor) Jr, b. 26 Mar 1933, Martin, South Dakota, USA. Professor; Writer. Education: BS, Iowa State University, 1958; MST, Lutheran School of Theology, Chicago, 1963; JurD, University of Colorado School of Law, Boulder, 1970. Appointments: Executive Director, National Congress of American Indians, Washington, DC, 1964-67; Professor of Law and Political Science, University of Arizona at Tucson, 1978-80; Professor of American Indian Studies, Professor of History, and Adjoint Professor of Law, Religious Studies, and Political Science, University of Colorado at Boulder, 1990-. Publications: Custer Died For Your Sins: An Indian Manifesto, 1969; We Talk, You Listen: New Tribes, New Turf, 1970; Of Utmost Good Faith, 1971; God is Red: A Native View of Religion, 1973, revised edition, 1992; Behind the Trail of Broken Treaties: An Indian Declaration of Independence, 1974; The Indian Affair, 1974; Indians of the Pacific Northwest: From the Coming of the White Man to the Present Day, 1977; The Metaphysics of Modern Existence, 1979; The World of the American Indian (editor with others), 1979; American Indians, American Justice (with Clifford Lytle), 1983; A Sender of Words: Essays in Memory of John G Neihardt (editor), 1984; The Aggressions of Civilization: Federal Indian Policy Since the 1880s (editor with Sandra Cadwalader, 19984; The Nations Within: The Past and Future of American Indian Sovereignty (with Clifford Lytle), 1984; American Indian Policy in the Twentieth Century (editor), 1985, 2nd edition, 1992; Indian Education in America: Eight Essays, 1991; Frank Waters: Man and Mystic, 1993; Red Earth, White Lies, 1995. Contributions to: Many books, journals, and periodicals. Honours: Anisfield-Wolf Award, 1970; Distinguished Alumni Award, Iowa State University, 1977; Distinguished Alumni in the Field of Legal Education, University of Colorado School of Law, 1985; Lifetime Achievement Award, Mountains and Plains Booksellers Association, 1996; Non-Fiction Book of the Year Award, Colorado Center for the Book, 1996; Lifetime Achievement Award, Native Writers of America, 1996. Memberships: Numerous professional organizations and editorial boards. Address: c/o Department of History, Campus Box 234, University of Colorado at Boulder, Boulder, CO 80309, USA.

DELVIN David George, b. 28 Jan 1939, England. Physician; Radio and Television Broadcaster; Writer. m. (1) Kathleen Sears, 2 sons, 1 daughter, (2) Christine Webber. Education: St Dunstan's College; King's College, University of London; MB, BS, King's College Hospital, 1962; Licentiate, Royal College of Physicians, 1962; Diploma, Royal College of Obstetricians and Gynaecologistsl 1965; Diploma, Child's Health, 1966; Cert, 1972, Instructing Cert, 1974, Family Planning Association; DipVen, Society of Apothecaries, 1977. Appointments: Medical Editor, General Practitioner, 1972-90; Dr Jekyll Columnist, World Medicine, 1973-82; Medical Advisor, BBC and ITV, 1974-; Medical Consultant, Family Planning Association, 1981-90, National Association of Family Planning Doctors, 1990-93; Chairman, Editorial Boards, Medeconomics, Monthly Index of Medical Specialities, and MIM Magazine, 1988-91; Member, Faculty of Family Planning, Royal College of Gynaecologists, 1993-, Editorial Advisory Board, British Journal of Family Planning, 1994-; Medical Columnist, Glasgow Herald, 1995-. Publication: The Good Sex Guide, 1994. Contributions to: Various publications, including books and journals, radio, television, medical films and videos, etc. Honours: Certificates of Special Merit, Medical Journalists' Association, 1974, 1975; Best Book Award, American Medical Writers' Association, 1976; Médaille de la Ville de Paris, 1983; Consumer Columnist of the Year Award, 1986. Memberships: Royal College of General Practitioners; Royal College of Surgeons; Royal Society of Medicine. Address: c/o Coutts, 2 Harley Street, London W1A 1EE, England.

DEMARIA Robert, b. 28 Sept 1928, New York, New York, USA. Professor of English Emeritus; Author; Poet. m. (1) Maddalena Buzeo, (2) Ellen Hope Meyer, 3 sons, 1 daughter. Education: BA, 1948, MA, 1949, PHD, 1959, Columbia University. Appointments: Instructor, University of Oregon, 1949-52; Assistant Professor, Hofstra University, 1952-61; Associate Dean, New School for Social Research, New York City, 1961-64; Professor of English, 1965-97, Professor Emeritus, 1997-, Dowling College; Editor and Publisher, The Mediterranean Review, 1969-73. Publications: Novels: Carnival of Angels, 1961; Clodia, 1965; Don Juan in Lourdes, 1966; The Satyr, 1972; The Decline and Fall of America, 1973; To Be a King, 1976; Outbreak, 1978; Blowout, 1979; The Empress, 1980; Secret Places, 1981; A Passion for Power, 1983; Sons and Brothers, 2 volumes, 1985; Stone of Destiny, 1986. Textbooks: The College Handbook of Creative Writing, 1991, 3rd edition, 1998; A Contemporary Reader for Creative Writing, 1995. Contributions to: Fiction, poetry, and articles in numerous publications. Address: 106 Vineyard Place, Port Jefferson, NY 11777, USA.

DEMARIS Ovid. See: **DESMARAIS Ovide E.**

DEMETILLO Ricaredo, b. 2 June 1920, Dumangas, Philippines. Retired Professor of Humanities; Poet; Writer. Education: AB, Silliman University, 1947; MFA, University of Iowa, 1952. Appointments: Assistant Professor, 1959-70, Chairman, Department of Humanities, 1961-62, Associate Professor, 1970-75, Professor of Humanities, 1975-86, University of the Philippines. Publications: Poetry: No Certain Weather, 1956; La Via: A Spiritual Journey, 1958; Daedalus and Other Poems, 1961; Barter in Panay, 1961; Masks and Signature, 1968; The Scare-Crow Christ, 1973; The City and the Thread of Light, 1974; Lazarus, Troubadour, 1974; Sun, Silhouttes and Shadow, 1975; First and Last Fruits, 1989. Novel: The Genesis of a Troubled Vision, 1976. Play: The Heart of Emptiness is Black, 1973. Non-Fiction: The Authentic Voice of Poetry, 1962; Major and Minor Keys, 1986. Address: 38 Balacan Street, West Avenue, Quezon City, Philippines.

DEMOS John Putnam, b. 2 May 1937, Cambridge, Massachusetts, USA. Professor of History; Writer. m. Elaine Virginia Damis, 27 July 1963, 2 children. Education: BA, 1959, Postgraduate Studies, 1963-68, Harvard University; Postgraduate Studies, University of Oxford, England, 1959-60; MA, University of California at

Berkeley, 1961. Appointments: Teaching Fellow, Harvard University, 1966-68; Assistant Professor, 1968-72, Professor of History, 1972-86, Brandeis University; Professor of History, Yale University, 1986-. Publications: A Little Commonwealth: Family Life in Plymouth Colony, 1970; Remarkable Providences, 1600-1760 (editor). 1972; Turning Points: Historical and Sociological Essays on the Family (editor with Sarane Boocock), 1978; Entertaining Satan: Witchcraft and the Culture of Early New England, 1982; Past, Present, and Personal, 1986; The Unredeemed Captive, 1994. Contributions to: Scholarly journals and other publications. Honours: Bancroft Prize in American History, Columbia University, 1983; Francis Parkman Prize, 1995; Ray Allen Billington Prize, 1995. Membership: American Historical Association. Address: c/o Department of History, Yale University, PO Box 208324, New Haven, CT 06520, USA.

DEMPSTER Nigel Richard Patton, b. 1 Nov 1941, England. Editor; Editorial Executive; Writer. m. (1) Emma de Bendern, 1971, div 1974, (2) Lady Camilla Godolphin Osborne, 1977, 1 daughter. Appointments: Broker, Lloyd's of London, 1958-59, Stock Exchange, 1959-60; PR Account Executive, Earl of Kimberley Associates, 1960-63; Journalist, Daily Express, 1963-71; London Correspondent, Status magazine, USA, 1965-66; Columnist ("Grovel"), Private Eye magazine, 1969-85; Daily Mail, 1971-; Editor, Mail Diary, 1973-, Mail on Sunday Diary, 1986-; Editorial Executive, Mail Newspapers Plc, 1973-; Broadcaster, ABC, USA, CBC, Canada, 1976-; TV-am, 1983-92; Resident Panelist, Headliners, Thames TV, 1987-89. Publications: HRH The Princess Margaret--A Life Unfulfilled, 1981; Heiress: The Story of Christina Onassis, 1989; Nigel Dempster's Address Book, 1990; Behind Palace Doors (with Peter Evans), 1993; Dempster's Secrets, 1998. Address: c/o Daily Mail, Northcliffe House, Derry Street, London W8 5TT, England.

DENGLER Sandy, b. 8 June 1939, Newark, Ohio, USA. Writer. m. William F Dengler, 11 Jan 1963, 2 daughters. Education: BS, Bowling Green State University, Ohio, 1961; MS, Arizona State University, 1967. Publications: Non-Fiction: Fanny Crosby, 1985; John Bunyan, 1986; D L Moody, 1987; Susanna Wesley, 1987; Florence Nightingale, 1988. Fiction: Barn Social, 1978; Yosemite's Marvellous Creatures, 1979; Summer of the Wild Pig, 1979; Melon Hound, 1980; Horse Who Loved Picnics, 1980; Mystery at McGehan Ranch, 1982; Chain Five Mystery, 1984; Summer Snow, 1984; Winterspring, 1985; This Rolling Land, 1986; Jungle Gold, 1987; Code of Honor, 1988; Power of Pinjarra, 1989; Taste of Victory, 1989; East of Outback, 1990; Death Valley, 1993; Cat Killer, 1993; Dublin Crossing, 1993; Mouse Trapped, 1993; Gila Monster, 1994; Last Dinosaur, 1994; Murder on the Mount, 1994; Shamrock Shore, 1994; Emerald Sea, 1994; The Quick and the Dead, 1995; King of the Stars, 1995; Hyaenas, 1998. Contributions to: Journals and magazines. Honours: Writer of the Year, Warm Beach, 1986; Golden Medallion, Romance Writers of America, 1987. Memberships: Mystery Writers of America; Romance Writers of America; Mid-America Palaeontological Society, Writers Guild. Address: 2623 Cypress Avenue, Norman, OK 73072, USA.

DENKER Henry, b. 25 Nov 1912, New York, New York, USA. Writer; Playwright. Education: LLB, New York University, 1934. Publications: I'll Be Right Home, Ma, 1947; My Son, the Lawyer, 1949; Salome: Princess of Galilee, 1951; The First Easter, 1951; The Child is Mine, 1955; The Director, 1970; The Kingmaker, 1972; A Place for the Mighty, 1974; The Physicians, 1975; The Experiment, 1976; The Starmaker, 1977; The Scofield Diagnosis, 1977; The Actress, 1978; Error of Judgement, 1979; Horowitz and Mrs Washington, 1979, as play, 1980; The Warfield Syndrome, 1981; Outrage, 1982, as play, 1983, as film, 1985; The Healers, 1983; Kincaid, 1984; Robert, My Son, 1985; Judge Spence Dissents, 1986; The Choice, 1987; The Retreat, 1988; A Gift of Life, 1989; Payment in Full, 1990; Doctor on Trial, 1991; Mrs Washington and Horowitz, too, 1992; Labyrinth, 1994; This Child is Mine, 1995; To Marcy, With Love,

1996. Plays: Time Limit, 1957; A Far Country, 1961; A Case of Libel, 1963; What Did We Do Wrong?, 1967; The Headhunters, 1976; The Second Time Around, 1977. Memberships: Dramatists Guild, council, 1970-73; Authors Guild; Authors League, council; Writers Guild of America East. Literary Agent: Mitch Douglas, International Creative Management, 40 West 57th Street, New York, NY 10019. USA. Address: 241 Central Park West, New York, NY 10024, USA.

DENNING Mark. See: **STEVENSON John.**

DENNIS Everette Eugene Jr, b. 15 Aug 1942, Seattle, Washington, USA. Foundation Executive; Educator; Author. m. Emily J Smith, 15 June 1988. Education: BS, University of Oregon, 1964; MA, Syracuse University, 1966; PhD, University of Minnesota, 1974. Appointments: Assistant Professor, Journalism, Mass Communication, Kansas State University, Manhattan, 1968-72; Instructor, Assistant Professor, Associate Professor, School of Journalism and Mass Communication, University of Minnesota, 1972-81; Visiting Professor, Medill School of Journalism, Northwestern University, 1976-77; Dean, Professor, School of Journalism, University of Oregon, 1981-84; Executive Director, The Freedom Forum Media Studies Center, Columbia University; Senior Vice-President, The Freedom Forum, Arlington, Virginia; Editor-in-Chief, Media Studies Journal. Publications: Other Voices: The New Journalism in America, 1973; The Media Society, 1978; The Economics of Libel, 1986; Understanding Mass Communication (editor), 1988, 6th edition, 1996; Demystifying Media Technology, 1993; America's Schools and the Mass Media, 1993; The Culture of Crime, 1995; Radio, The Forgotten Medium, 1995; American Communication Research, 1996. Contributions to: Hundreds of articles to popular, professional and scholarly periodicals. Honours: 4 Harvard University Fellowships, 1978-79, 1980, 1981; Other fellowships; Various writing prizes and awards. Memberships: Kappa Tau Alpha;International Communication Association; Eastman House International Museum of Photographs; American Antiquarian Society; Association for Education in Journalism and Mass Communication; International Press Institute; Society of Professional Journalists. Address: 420 Riverside Drive, New York, NY 10027, USA.

DENNIS-JONES Harold, (Paul Hamilton, Dennis Hessing), b. 2 Dec 1915, Port-Louis, Mauritius. Journalist; Author; Photographer. 2 daughters. Education: Open Scholar in Classics, St John's College, Oxford, 1934-38; 1st Class Honours in Classical Honour Moderations; 2nd Class Lt Hum. Appointments: Kensley Newspapers, 1945-47; Travel Correspondent, Geographical Magazine, 1947-56; London Correspondent, Het Geillustreede Pers, Amsterdam, 1947-52; UK Editor, Guide Kleber, Paris, 1963-72. Publications: 56 guide books titles/editions, covering all Europe, Morocco, Israel; Verse translations from Greek, French, Spanish, Romanian; 3 language learning titles, French, Spanish, Italian. Contributions to: Newspapers, magazines, radio and television. Memberships: British Society of Authors; British Guild of Travel Writers. Address: 53 Sunhill Court, High Street, Pembury, Tunbridge Wells TN2 4NT, England.

DENOO Joris, b. 6 July 1953, Torhout, Belgium. Author; Poet. m. Lut Vandemeulebroecke, 23 July 1976, 1 son, 2 daughters. Education: Graduate, German Philology, University of Louvain, 1975; Aggregation PHO, 1976. Publications: Poetry: Binnenscheepvaart, 1988; Staat van Medewerking, 1988; Voltooid Verwarmde Tijd, 1992. Prose: Repelsteel in Bourgondie, 1986; Verkeerde Lieveheer, 1993; Vallen en Opstaan: Diary of an Epileptic Child, 1996; Het Kind van de Rekening: A Christmas Story; Rode Blossen: A Story for Children, 1999. Other: Essays and children's stories. Contributions to: Many Flemish and Dutch magazines and periodicals. Honours: Vlaamse Klub Prize, Brussels, 1979; Premies West-Vlaanderen, 1983, 1991; Prijs Tielt Boekenstad, 1992; Essay Prize, Royal Academy for Dutch Language and Literature, 1996; Poetry Prize Keerbergen, 1998.

Membership: SABAM, Belgium. Address: Oude Ieperseweg 85, B-8501 Heule, Belgium.

DEPAOLA Tomie, (Thomas Anthony Depaola), b. 15 Sept 1934, Meriden, Connecticut, USA. Children's Book Artist and Writer. Education: BFA, Pratt Institute, 1956; MFA, California College of Arts and Crafts, 1969; Doctoral Equivalency, Lone Mountain College, 1970. Publications: Over 200 books including: Country Angel Christmas, 1995; Strega Nona: Her Story, 1996; Bill and Pete to the Rescue, 1998; Big Anthony, His Story, 1998; Honours: Caldecott Honor Book, American Library Association, 1976; Regina Medal, Catholic Library Association, 1983; Honorary Doctor of Letters, Colby-Sawyer College, 1985; Honorary DHL, Saint Anselm College, 1994. Memberships: Authors Guild; Society of Children's Book Writers. Address: c/o Penguin Putnam Books for Young Readers, 375 Hudson Street, New York, NY 10014, USA.

DEPESTRE René, b. 29 Aug 1926, Jacmel, Haiti (French citizen). Poet; Author. m. Nelly Campano, 1962. Education: Sorbonne, University of Paris, 1946-51. Appointment: Attache, Office of Culture, UNESCO, Paris, 1982-86. Publications: Poetry: Etincelles, 1945; Gerbe de sang, 1946; Minerai noir, 1956; Un arc-en-ciel pour l'occident chrétien, 1967; Journal d'un animal marin (selected poems, 1956-90); 1990; Au matin de la négritude, 1990; Anthologie personnelle, 1993. Fiction: Alléluia pour une femme jardin, 1973; Le Mat de cocagne, 1979; Hadriana dans tous mes reves, 1988; Eros dans un train chinois: Neuf histories d'amour et un conte sorcier, 1990. Non-Fiction: Pour la révolution, pour la poésie, 1969; Bonjour et adieu a la négritude, 1980. Honours: Prix Goncourt, 1982; Prix Renaudot, 1988. Address: 31 bis, Route de Roubia, 11200 Lezignan-Corbières, France.

DERENEU Lurie. See: **COLESNIC Lurie.**

DERFLER (Arnold) Leslie, b. 11 Jan 1933, New York, New York, USA. Professor of History; Writer. m. Gunilla Derfler, 25 June 1962, 4 daughters. Education: BA, City College of New York, 1954; University of Chicago, 1956; University of Paris, 1960; MA, 1957, PhD, 1962, Columbia University. Appointments: Faculty, City College of New York, 1959-62, Carnegie Mellon University, 1962-68, University of Massachusetts, Amherst, 1968-69; Professor of History, Florida Atlantic University, 1969-; Visiting Professor, London Center, Florida State University, 1985. Publications: The Dreyfus Affair: Tragedy of Errors, 1963; The Third French Republic, 1870-1940, 1966; Socialism Since Marx, 1973; Alexandre Millerand: The Socialist Years, 1977; President and Parliament: A Short History of the French Presidency, 1984; An Age of Conflict: Readings in 20th Century European History, 1990, 2nd edition, 1996; Paul Lafargue and the Founding of French Marxism, 1842-1882, 1991; Paul Lafargue and the Flowering of French Socialism, 1882-1911, 1998. Honours: American Philosophical Society Grants, 1967, 1976, 1981, 1991; Distinguished Scholar Award, Florida Atlantic University, 1982; National Endowment for the Humanities Fellowship, 1984-85. Address: c/o Department of History, Florida Atlantic University, Boca Raton, FL 33431, USA.

DERIEX Suzanne, (Suzanne Piguet-Cuendet), b. 16 Apr 1926, Yverdon, Switzerland. Writer. m. Jean-François Piguet, 7 May 1949, 3 sons. Education: Lic Math Sc; Semi-lic Theol, University of Lausanne, Switzerland. Publications: Corinne (novel), 1961; San Domenico (novel), 1964; L'enfant et la mort (novel), 1968; L'homme n'est jamais seul (novel), 1983; Les sept vies de Louise Croisier née Moraz (novel), 1096; Un arbre de vie (novel), 1995; Exile (novel), 1997. Honours: Prize of Jubilé de Lyceum Club de Suisse, 1963; Prix Veillon, 1968; Prix Pro Helvetia, 1983; Prix Alpes-Jura and Prix des Murailles, 1988; Prix du Livre vaudois, 1990. Address: Rte de Lausanne 11, 1096 Cully, Switzerland.

DERR Mark (Burgess), b. 20 Jan 1950, Baltimore, Maryland, USA. Writer. m. Gina L Maranto, 11 Sept 1982. Education: AB, 1972, MA, 1973, Johns Hopkins

University. Publications: Some Kind of Paradise: A Chronicle of man and the Land in Florida, 1989; Reprint, 1998; Over Florida, 1992; The Frontiersman: The Real Life and the Many Legends of Davy Crockett, 1993; Dog's Best Friend: Annals of the Dog-Human Relationship, 1997. Contributions to: The Atlantic; Audubon Society; Natural History; The New York Times. Address: 4245 Sheridan Avenue, Miami Beach, FL 33140, USA.

DERRICOTTE Toi, b. 11 Apr 1941, Hamtramck, Michigan, USA. Professor of English; Poet; Author. m. C Bruce Derricotte, 30 Dec 1967, 1 son. Education: BA, Special Education, Wayne State University, 1965; MA, English Literature and Creative Writing, New York University, 1984. Appointments: Master Teacher and Poet in the Schools, New Jersey State Council, on the Arts and Maryland State Council on the Arts, 1973-88; Associate Professor of English Literature, Old Dominion University, 1988-90; Commonwealth Professor, George Mason University, 1990-91; Associate Professor, 1991-97, Professor of English, 1998-, University of Pittsburgh; Visiting Professor, New York University, 1992; Many poetry readings around the world. Publications: The Empress of the Death House, 1978; Natural Birth, 1983; Creative Writing: A Manual for Teachers (with Madeline Bass), 1985; Captivity, 1989; Tender, 1997; The Black Notebooks, 1997. Contributions to: Numerous anthologies and journals. Honours: MacDowell Colony Fellowship, 1982; New Jersey State Council on the Arts Poetry Fellowship, 1983; Lucille Medwick Memorial Award, Poetry Society of America, 1985; National Endowment for the Arts Creative Writing Fellowships, 1985, 1990; Pushcaft Prizes, 1989, 1998; Poetry Committee Book Award, Folger Shakespeare Library, Washington, DC, 1990; Yaddo Residency, 1997; Anisfield-Wolf Book Award for Non-Fiction, 1998; Award in Non-Fiction, Black Caucus, American Library Association, 1998; Paterson Poetry Prize, 1998. Memberships: Academy of American Poets; Associated Writing Programs; Modern Language Association; PEN; Poetry Society of America. Address: c/o Department of English, University of Pittsburgh, Pittsburgh, PA 15260, USA.

DERRIDA Jacques, b. 15 July 1930, El Biar, Algeria. Philosopher; Writer. m. Marguérite Aucouturier, 1957, 2 sons. Education: École Normale Supérieure, Paris, 1952-56; Licence es Lettres, 1953, Licence de Philosophie, 1953, Diplome d'Études Supérieures, 1954, Sorbonne, University of Paris; Certificat d'Ethnologie, 1954, Agregation de Philosophie, 1956, Doctorat en Philosophie, 1967, Doctorat d'Etat es Lettres, 1980; Graduate Studies, Harvard University, 1956-57. Appointments: Professor de lettres supérieures, Lycée du Mans, 1959-60; Professor of Philosophy, Sorbonne, University of Paris, 1960-64, École Normale Supérieure, Paris, 1964-84; Director, École des Hautes Études en Sciences Sociales, Paris, 1984-; Many visiting lectureships and professorships. Publications: La voix et le phénomène: Introduction au probleme du signe dans la phénomènologie de Husserl, 1967, English translation as Speech and Phenomena and Other Essays on Husserl's Theory of Signs, 1973; De la grammatologie, 1967, English translation as Of Grammatology, 1976; L'écriture et la difference, 1967, English translation as Writing and Difference, 1978; La dissémination, 1972, English translation, 1981; Marges de la philosophie, 1972, English translation as Margins of Philosophy, 1982; Glas, 1974, English translation, 1986; L'archeologie du frivole, 1976, English translation as The Archeology of the Frivolous: Reading Condillac, 1980; Eperons: Les styles de Nietzsche, 1976, English translation as Spurs: Nietzsche's Styles, 1979; Limited Inc: abc, 1977; La vérité en peinture, 1978; La carte postale: De Socrate à Freud et au-dela, 1980, English translation as The Post Card: From Socrates to Freud and Beyond, 1987; L'oreille de l'autre: Otobiographies, transferts, traductions: Textes et debats avec Jacques Derrida, 1982, English translation as The Ear of the Other: Otobiography, Transference, Translation, 1985; Signeponge/Signsponge (French and English text), 1984, revised edition, 1988; Mémoires: Lectures for Paul de Man, 1986; De l'esprit: Heidegger et la question, 1987; Psyché: Inventions de l'autre, 1987;

Mémoires: Pour Paul de Man, 1988; Du droit à la philosophie, 1990; Mémoires d'aveugle, 1990; Le problème de la genèse dans la philosophie de Husserl, 1990; L'autre cap, 1991; Donner le temps, 1991; Qu'est-ce que la poésie?, 1991; Reader, 1991; Acts of Literature, 1992; Conders, 1992; Spectres de Marx, 1993; Politiques de l'amitié, 1994; Force de loi, 1994; Aporias, 1996. Honours: Liste d'aptitude a l'enseignement Supérieur, 1968; Chevalier, 1968, Officier, 1980, des Palmes Academiques; Honorary doctorates, Columbia University, 1980, University of Louvain, 1983, University of Essex, 1987, Cambridge University, 1992; Commandeur des Arts et des Lettres, France, 1983; Prix Nietzsche, Association Internationale de Philosophie, 1988. Address: c/o École des Hautes Études en Sciences Sociales, 54 Bouelvard Raspail, 75006 Paris, France.

DERSHOWITZ Alan (Morton), b. 1 Sept 1938, New York, New York, USA. Lawyer; Professor of Law; Writer. m. Carolyn Cohen, 2 sons, 1 daughter. Education: BA, Brooklyn College, 1959; LLB, Yale University, 1962. Appointments: Called to the Bar, Washington, DC, 1963, Massachusetts, 1968, US Supreme Court, 1968; Law Clerk to Chief Judge David L Bazelon, US Court of Appeals, 1962-63, to Justice Arthur J Goldberg, US Supreme Court; Faculty, 1964-, Professor of Law, 1967-, Fellow, Center for Advanced Study of Behavioral Sciences, 1971-72, Felix Frankfurter Professor of Law, 1993-, Harvard University. Publications: Psychoanalysis, Psychiatry and the Law (with others), 1967; Criminal Law: Theory and Process, 1974; The Best Defense, 1982; Reversal of Fortune: Inside the von Bulow Case, 1986; Taking Liberties: A Decade of Hard Cases, Bad Laws and Bum Raps, 1988; Chutzpah, 1991; Contrary to Popular Opinion, 1992; The Abuse Excuse, 1994; The Advocate's Devil, 1994; Reasonable Doubts, 1996. Contributions to: Periodicals. Honours: Guggenheim Fellowship, 1978-79; Honorary doctorates. Memberships: Order of the Coif; Phi Beta Kappa. Address: c/o Harvard University Law School, Cambridge, MA 02138, USA.

DESAI Anita, b. 24 June 1937, Mussoorie, India. Author; Professor of Writing. m. Ashvin Desai, 13 Dec 1958, 2 sons, 2 daughters. Education: BA, Honours, Miranda House, University of Delhi. Appointments: Elizabeth Drew Professor, Smith College, Northampton, Massachusetts, 1987-88; Purington Professor of English, Mount Holyoke College, South Hadley, Massachusetts, 1988-92; Professor of Writing, Massachusetts Institute of Technology, 1993-. Publications: Cry, the Peacock, 1963; Voices in the City, 1965; Bye-Bye Blackbird, 1971; Where Shall We Go This Summer?, 1973; Fire on the Mountain, 1978; Games at Twilight, 1979; Clear Light of Day, 1980; The Village by the Sea, 1983; In Custody, 1984; Baumgartner's Bombay, 1988; Journey to Ithaca, 1995; Fasting, Feasting, 1999. Contributions to: Periodicals. Honours: Winifred Holtby Award, Royal Society of Literature, 1978; Sahitya Akademi Award, 1978; Federation of Indian Publishers Award, 1978; Guardian Prize for Children's Fiction, 1983; Helen Cam Visiting Fellow, 1986-87, Honorary Fellow, 1988, Girton College, Cambridge; Ashby Fellow, 1989, Honorary Fellow, 1991, Clare Hall, Cambridge; Hadassah Prize, Hadassah Magazine, New York, 1989; Padma Sri, India, 1990; Literary Lion, New York Public Library, 1993; Neil Gunn International Writers Fellowship, Scotland, 1994. Memberships: American Academy of Arts and Letters, honorary member; PEN; Royal Society of Literature, fellow; Sahitya Akademi, India. Address: c/o Deborah Rogers Ltd, 20 Powis Mews, London W11 1JN, England.

DESHPANDE Shashi, b. 19 Aug 1938, Dharwad, India. Novelist. m. D H Deshpande, 1962, 2 sons. Education: BA Honours, Economics, 1956, Diploma, Journalism, 1970, MA, English, 1970, University of Bombay; BL, University of Mysore, Karnataka, 1959. Publications: The Dark Holds no Terrors, 1980; If I Die Today, 1982; Roots and Shadows, 1983; Come Up and Be Dead, 1985; That Long Silence, 1988; The Binding Vine, 1993. Short stories: The Legacy and Other Stories, 1978; It Was Dark, 1986; The Miracle and Other Stories, 1986; It Was the Nightingale, 1986; The Intrusion and Other Stories, 1994; A Matter of Time, 1996. Honours:

Rangammal Prize, 1984; Sahitya Academy Award, 1990; Nanjangud Thirumalamba Award, 1991. Address: 409 41st Cross, Jayanagar V Block, Bangalore 560041, India.

DESMARAIS Ovide E, (Ovid Demaris), b. 6 Sept 1919, Biddeford, Maine, USA. Writer; Newspaper Reporter. m. Inez E Frakes, 15 May 1942, 2 daughters. Education: AB, College of Idaho, 1948; Law, Syracuse University; MS, Boston University, 1950. Publications: Mystery novels: Ride the Gold Mare, 1956; The Hoods Take Over, 1957; The Long Night, 1957; The Lusting Drive, 1958; The Slasher, 1959; The Enforcer, 1960; The Extortioners, 1960; The Gold-Plated Sewer, 1960; Candyleg, 1961 (as Machine Gun McCanin, 1970); The Parasite, 1963; The Organization, 1965 (as The Contract 1970); The Overlord, 1972. Other: Lucky Luciano, 1960; The Lindbergh Kidnapping Case, 1961; The Dillinger Story, 1961; The Green Felt Jungle (with Edward Reid), 1963; Jack Ruby (with Gary Wills), 1968; Captive City: Chicago in Chains, 1969; America the Violent, 1970; Poso del Mundo: Inside the Mexican-American Border, 1970; Dirty Business: The Corporate-Political Money-Power Game, 1974; The Director: An Oral Biography of J Edgar Hoover, 1975; Brothers in Blood: The International Terrorist Network, 1977; The Last Mafioso: The Treacherous World of Jimmy Fratianno, 1981; The Vegas Legacy, 1983; The Boardwalk Jungle, 1987; J Edgar Hoover: As They Knew Him, 1994. Contributions to: Professional journals and periodicals. Address: PO Box 6071, Santa Barbara, CA 93111, USA.

DESMEE Gilbert Georges, b. 29 Jan 1951, Suresnes, France. Writer; Editor; Educator. m. Maria Desmee, 28 Jan 1982. Education: Diploma University of Cachan, 1973; Diploma, University of Versailles, 1981. Appointment: Director, Sapriphage literary review, 1988-. Publications: Le Schiste Métamorphique, 1990; L'Infini pour respirer in Histoire de livres d'artistes, 1991; Un Magdalénien Contemporain in Robert Pérot, 1994; En écho des corps d'écriture, 1995; Je m'en dit tu, 1996; Seul le geste serait fécond, 1997; L'eau s'émeut du feu, 1997. Contributions to: Encres Vives; Sapriphage; Agone; Contre-Vox; L'Estracelle; Textuerre; Présage. Address: 118 Avenue Pablo Picasso, 92000 Nanterre, France.

DEUTSCH André, b. 15 Nov 1917. Publisher. Education: Budapest, Vienna and Zürich. Appointments: Founder, Allan Wingate Ltd, publishers, 1945; Founder, Chairman, and Managing Director, 1951-84, Joint Chairman and Joint Managing Director, 1984-87, Joint Chairman, 1987-89, President, 1989-91, André Deutsch Ltd, publishers; Founder, African Universities Press, Lagos, 1962, East Africa Publishing House, Nairobi, 1964; Director, Libra, Budapest, 1991-; Chairman, Aurum Press. Honour: Commander of the Order of the British Empire, 1989. Address: 5 Selwood Terrace, London SW7 3QN, England.

DEVALLE Susana Beatriz Cristina, b. 31 May 1945, Buenos Aires, Argentina. Social and Political Anthropologist. Education: MA, Indian Studies, El Colegio de Mexico, 1973; BA, Honours, Anthropological Science, Buenos Aires National University, 1967; PhD, Social Anthropology, University of London, England, 1989. Appointments: Consultant, PEMEX, Mexican State Oil Company, 1979-80; Visiting Fellow, Faculty of Asian Studies, Australian National University, 1983-84; Consultant, Australian Parliamentary Library, Foreign Affairs, 1984-85; National Researcher, Sistema Nacional de Investigadores, Secretaria de Educacion Publica, Mexico, 1987-; Visiting Fellow, Ethnic Studies Programme, University of Hawaii at Manoa, 1990; Director of Research Group, Ethnicity and Nationalisms in Asia, Africa and Latin America, El Colegio de México, 1994. Publications: La Palabra de la Tierra, Protesta Campesina en India, siglo XIX, 1977; Peasantry and National Integration (co-editor and co-author), 1981; Discourses of Ethnicity, Culture and Protest in Jharkhand, 1992; Power, Violence and Human Rights (editor and co-author), 1996. Contributions to: Various publications. Honours: Fellowships, grants and awards. Memberships: Association for Asian Studies; Asociacion Latinoamericana de Asia y Africa; International Union of

Anthropological and Ethnological Sciences; American Anthropological Association. Address: Centro de Estudios de Asia y Africa, El Colegio de México, Camino al Ajusco No 20, México DF 01000, México.

DEVEREAUX Emily. See: **LEWIS-SMITH Anne Elizabeth.**

DEVERELL Rex Johnson, b. 17 July 1941, Toronto, Ontario, Canada. Playwright. m. Rita Joyce Shelton, 24 May 1967, 1 son. Education: BA, 1963, BD, 1966, McMaster University; STM, Union Theological Seminary, 1967. Appointments: Resident Playwright, Globe Theatre, Regina, 1975-91; President, Playwrights Union of Canada, 1991-93. Publications: Boiler Room Suite, 1978; Superwheel, 1979; Drift, 1981; Black Powder, 1981. Other: Deverell of the Globe (anthology), television and radio scripts, opera libretti and children's plays. Contributions to: Canadian Theatre Review; Canadian Children's Literature; Canadian Drama; Prairie Fire; Grain. Honours: McMaster University Honour Society, 1963; Ohio State Award, 1974; Canadian Authors Association Medal, 1978; Major Armstrong Award, 1986; Nominee, Chalmers Award, 1994. Memberships: Saskatchewan Writers Guild; Playwrights Union of Canada; Saskatchewan Playwrights Centre; Amnesty International. Address: 36 Oneida Avenue, RR 4, Coldwater, Ontario L0K 1E0, Canada.

DEVERELL William H(erbert), b. 4 Mar 1937, Regina, Saskatchewan, Canada. Author. m. Tekla Melnyk, 1 son, 1 daughter. Education: BA, LLB, University of Saskatchewan, 1962. Appointments: Staff, Saskatoon Star-Phoenix, 1956-60, Canadian Press, Montreal, 1960-62, Vancouver Sun, 1963; Partner in law firm, Vancouver, 1964-79; Writer, 1979-. Publications: Fiction: Needles, 1979; High Crimes, 1979; Mecca, 1983; Dance of Shiva, 1984; Platinum Blues, 1988; Mindfield, 1989; Kill All the Lawyers, 1994. Non-fiction: Fatal Cruise: The Trial of Robert Frisbee, 1991; Street Legal - The Betrayal, 1995; Trial of Passion, 1997. Honours: McClelland and Stewart/Seal First Novel Award, 1979; Book of the Year Award, Periodical Distributors Association of Canada, 1980; Arthur Ellis Canadian Crime Writer Award, 1998; Dashiel Hammett International Crime Writers Association Award, 1998. Memberships: British Columbia Bar Association; British Columbia Civil Liberties Association; British Crime Writers Association; Crime Writers of Canada; Writers Union of Canada, chairman, 1994-95. Address: Box 14, Rural Route 1, North Pender Island, British Columbia V0N 2M0, Canada.

DEVEREUX Eve. See: **BARNETT Paul le Page.**

DEVINE Thomas Martin, b. 30 July 1945, Motherwell, Scotland. Professor; Writer. m. Catherine Mary Lynas, 6 Jul 1971, 2 sons, 3 daughters. Education:BA, University of Strathclyde, 1968; PhD, 1971; D Litt, 1991. Appointments: Assistant Lecturer, 1969-71, Lecturer, Senior Lecturer, 1971-83, Reader, 1983-88, Professor, 1988-, Dean of Faculty of Arts and Social Studies, 1993-94; Deputy Principal, 1994-97, University of Strathclyde. Publications: The Tobacco Lords, Ireland and Scotland 1700-1850; The Great Highland Famine; People and Society in Scotland; Farm Servants and Labour in Lowland Scotland; Irish Immigrants and Scottish Society in the Eighteenth and Nineteenth Centuries; Scottish Emigration and Scottish Society; Clanship to Crofters' War: The Social Transformation of the Scottish Highlands; The Transformation of Rural Scotland: Agrarian and Social Change 1680-1815; Glasgow, Vol 1, Beginnings to 1930, 1995; Scotland in the Twentieth Century, 1996; Eighteenth Century Scotland: New Perspectives, 1998. Contributions to: Times Literary Supplement; Times Higher Education Supplement; Economic History Review; Social History; Scottish Historical Review; History Today; Scottish Economic and Social History. Honours: Fellow, Royal Society of Edinburgh; Fellow, British Academy, 1994; Henry Duncan Prize Lectureship, Royal Society of Edinburgh, 1995. Memberships: Economic and Social History Society of Scotland; Scottish Catholic Historical Association; Royal Society; Royal Historical Society;

Trustee, National Museums of Scotland. Address: University of Strathclyde, 16 Richmond Street, Glasgow G1 1XQ, Scotland.

DEVIOUS B K. See: **HERRING Peggy J.**

DEVLIN Timothy, b. 28 July 1944. Public Relations Director. m. Angela Denise Laramy, 31 Jan 1967, 2 sons, 2 daughters. Education: University College, Oxford, 1963-66. Appointments: Feature Writer, Aberdeen Press and Journal, 1966-67; Reporter, Scotsman, 1967; Education Reporter, Evening Echo, Watford, England, 1967-69; Reporter, TES, 1969-71; Reporter, Times, 1971-73; Education Correspondent, The Times, 1973-77; National Director, ISIS, 1977-84; Head of Public Relations, IOD, 1984-86; Associate Director, Charles Barker, 1986-89; Founder and MD, of Tim Devlin Enterprises, 1989-. Publications: What Must We Teach?, with Mary Warnock, 1977; Public Relations and Marketing for Schools, with Brian Knight, 1990; Old School Ties (with Hywel Williams), 1992; Anybody's Nightmare, with Angela Devlin, 1998; Public Relations & Marketing Manual, 1998. Contributions to: TES, Independent. Address: Ramsons, Maidstone Road, Staplehurst, Kent TN12 0RD, England.

DEVRIES Susanna. See: **DE VRIES-EVANS Susanna Mary.**

DEW Robb (Reavill) Forman, b. 26 Oct 1946, Mount Vernon, Ohio, USA. Writer. m. Charles Burgess Dew, 26 Jan 1968, 2 sons. Education: Louisiana State University. Publications: Dale Loves Sophie to Death, 1982; The Time of Her Life, 1984; Fortunate Lives, 1991; A Southern Thanksgiving: Recipes and Musings for a Manageable Feast, 1992; The Family Heart: A Memoir of When Our Son Came Out, 1994. Honour: American Book Award 1st Novel, 1982. Address: c/o Russell and Volkening, 50 West 29th Street, Apt 7E, New York, NY 10001, USA.

DEWAR Colin Scott, b. 20 July 1963, Dundee, Scotland. Scientist. m. Hui Lu Dewar, 30 Nov 1993, 1 son, 1 daughter. Education: BSc, Hons Physiology; MBChB. Appointments: Crosshouse Hospital, West Highland Hospital, Christchurch Public Hospital, Tongji Medical University, Bundaberg Base Hospital, NCB English Language Institute, Crichton Royal Hospital. Contributions to: Aural Images, Dandelion Arts Magazine, First Time, The Magazine, Community of Poets. Address: 1 Mountainhill Cottages, Bankend Road, Dumfries, DG1 4TS, England.

DEWDNEY Christopher, b. 9 May 1951, London, Ontario, Canada. Poet; Writer. m. (1) Suzanne Dennison, 1971, div 1975, 1 daughter, (2) Lise Downe, 1977, div 1990, 1 son, (3) Barbara Gorrdy. Education: South and Westminster Collegiate Institutes, London, Ontario; H B Beal Art Annex, London, Ontario. Appointments: Associate Fellow, Winters College, York University, Toronto, 1984; Poetry Editor, Coach House Publishing, Toronto, 1988. Academic Advisor, Col);umet College, York University, 1997- Publications: Poetry: Golders Green, 1972; A Paleozoic Geology of London, Ontario, 1973; Fovea Centralis, 1975; Spring Trances in the Control Emerald Night, 1978; Alter Sublime, 1980; The Cenozoic Asylum, 1983; Predators of the Adoration: Selected Poems 1972-1982, 1983; Permugenesis, 1987; The Radiant Inventory, 1988; Demon Pond, 1994. Other: The Immaculate Perception, 1986; Recent Artifacts from the Institute of Applied Fiction, 1990; Concordant Proviso Ascendant: A Natural History of Southwestern Ontario, Book III, 1991; The Secular Grail, 1993; Demon Pond, 1994; Last Flesh, 1998. Contributions to: Periodicals. Honours: Design Canada Award, 1974; CBC Prize, 1986. Address: c/o McClelland and Stewart Inc, 481 University Avenue, Suite 900, Toronto, Ontario M5G 2E9, Canada.

DeWEESE Jean. See: **DE WEESE Thomas Eugene "Gene".**

DEWEY Jennifer Owings, b. 2 Oct 1941, Chicago, Illinois, USA. Writer; Illustrator. Div, 1 daughter. Education: University of New Mexico, 1960-63; Rhode Island School of Design. Publications: CLEM: The Story of a Raven, 1986; At the Edge of the Pond, 1987; Birds of Antarctica, The Adelie Penguin, 1989; Can You Find Me: A Book About Animal Camouflage, 1989; Animal Architecture, 1991; Night & Day in the Desert, 1991; Mud Matters; Bugs in our House; Navajo Summer; Poison Dart Frogs; Various illustrated books. Honours: Several awards for book illustrations; Spur Award, Juvenile Non-Fiction, 1998. Memberships: San Francisco Society of Illustrators; American Society of Scientific Illustrators; No Poets Society, founder-president. Address: 607 Old Taos Highway, Santa Fe, NM 87501, USA.

DEWHIRST Ian, b. 17 Oct 1936, Keighley, Yorkshire, England. Retired Librarian; Writer; Poet. Education: BA Honours, Victoria University of Manchester, 1958. Appointment: Staff, Keighley Public Library, 1960-91. Publications: The Handloom Weaver and Other Poems, 1965; Scar Top and Other Poems, 1968; Gleanings From Victorian Yorkshire, 1972; A History of Keighley, 1974; Yorkshire Through the Years, 1975; Gleanings from Edwardian Yorkshire, 1975; The Story of a Nobody, 1980; You Don't Remember Bananas, 1985; Keighley in Old Picture Postcards, 1987; In the Reign of the Peacemaker, 1993; Down Memory Lane, 1993; Images of Keighley, 1996; Co-editor, A Century of Yorkshire Dialect, 1997. Contributions to: Yorkshire Ridings Magazine; Lancashire Magazine; Dalesman; Cumbria; Pennine Magazine; Transactions of the Yorkshire Dialect Society; Yorkshire Journal. Honour: Honorary Doctor of Letters, University of Bradford, 1996. Memberships: Yorkshire Dialect Society; Brontë Society; Edward Thomas Fellowship; Associate of the Library Association. Address: 14 Raglan Avenue, Fell Lane, Keighley, West Yorkshire BD22 6BJ, England.

DEWHURST Eileen Mary, b. 27 May 1929, Liverpool, England. Author. Div. Education: BA (Hons) English Language and Literature, St Anne's College, Oxford, 1951. Publications: Crime novels: Death Came Smiling, 1975; After the Ball, 1976; Curtain Fall, 1977; Drink This, 1980; Trio in Three Flats, 1981; Whoever I Am, 1982; The House That Jack Built, 1983; There Was a Little Girl, 1984; Playing Safe, 1985; A Private Prosecution, 1986; A Nice Little Business, 1987; The Sleeper, 1988; Dear Mr Right, 1990; The Innocence of Guilt, 1991; Death in Candie Gardens, 1992; Now You See Her, 1995; The Verdict on Winter, 1996; Alias the Enemy, 1997; Roundabout, 1998; Death of a Stranger, 1999. Contributions to: Various newspapers, journals and anthologies. Memberships: Crime Writers Association; Society of Authors. Address: c/o Gregory and Radice, 3 Barb Mews, London W6 7PA, England.

DEWHURST Keith, b. 24 Dec 1931, Oldham, England. Writer. m. (1) Eve Pearce, 14 July 1958, div 1980, 1 son, 2 daughters, (2) Alexandra Cann, 4 Nov 1980. Education: BA, Peterhouse, Cambridge, 1953. Appointments: Sports Writer, Evening Chronicle, Manchester, 1955-59; Presenter, Granada Television, 1968-69, BBC2 Television, London, 1972; Arts Columnist, The Guardian, London, 1969-72; Writer-in-Residence, Western Australia APA, Perth, 1984. Publications: Lark Rise to Candleford (2 plays), 1980; Captain of the Sands (novel), 1981; Don Quixote (play), 1982; McSullivan's Beach (novel), 1986; Black Snow, 1992; War Plays (plays), 1997; Philoctetes (translated play), 1998. Address: 12 Abingdon Road, London W8 6AF, England.

DEXTER Colin, b. 29 Sept 1930, Stamford, Lincolnshire, England. Writer. Education: Christ's College, Cambridge; MA (Cantab): MA (Oxon). Publications: Last Bus to Woodstock, 1975; Last Seen Wearing, 1976; The Silent World of Nicholas Quinn, 1977; Service of All the Dead, 1979; The Dead of Jericho, 1981; The Riddle of the Third Mile, 1983; The Secret of Annexe 3, 1983; The Wench is Dead, 1989; The Jewel That Was Ours, 1991; The Way Through the Woods, 1992; Morse's Greatest Mystery, 1993; The Daughters of Cain, 1994; Death is Now My Neighbour, 1996. Honours: Silver Dagger, 1979, 1981, Gold Dagger, 1989, 1992, Diamond Dagger, 1997; Crime Writers Association; Macavity Award, Best Short Story, 1995; Lotos Club Medal of Merit, New York, 1996. Memberships: Crime Writers Association; Detection Club. Address: 456 Banbury Road, Oxford OX2 7RG, England.

DEXTER Pete(r Whittemore), b. 22 July 1943, Pontiac, Michigan, USA. Columnist; Author. m. Dian McDonough, 1 child. Education: BA, University of South Dakota, 1969. Appointments: Columnist, Philadelphia Daily News, 1976-86, Esquire magazine, 1985-86, Sacramento Bee, 1986-. Publications: God's Pocket, 1983; Dead Wood, 1986; Paris Trout, 1988; The Paperboy, 1994. Honours: Mark Twain Award, Associated Press, California-Nevada, 1987; National Book Award, 1988; Penn West Award, Los Angeles, 1988; Bay Area Book Reviewers Award, 1988. Address: c/o Sacramento Bee, 21st and Q Streets, Sacramento, CA 95852, USA.

DEY-BERGMOSER THOMPSON Olga Maria, b. 7 Dec 1938, Lindenheuvel, Geleen, The Netherlands. Author; Retired Multilingual Translator. m. (1), 1 daughter, (2) Rev Cecil L Thompson, 26 Feb 1994. Education: Translation Diplomas, Germany, 1956; MA, University of Toronto, Canada, 1978; Academic Excellence Award in 1975. Appointments: Multilingual Translator, Government of Ontario, 25 years; VIP Hostess, Montreal Olympics, 1976. Publications: Under the Spell of India, 1978; People, 1981; Many Faces, Many Spaces - Artists in Ontario (co-author), 1988; More Faces, More Spaces - Artists in Canada, 1991. Contributions to: The Spires Cultural Community Focus quarterly; Rikka; Canadian Author and Bookman; Nuevo Diario; Arts in Action. Memberships: The Arts and Letters Club of Toronto; The Writers Union of Canada; Canadian Authors Association. Address: 23 Cronin Drive, Etobicoke, Ontario M9B 4T7, Canada.

DI CICCO Pier Giorgio, b. 5 July 1949, Arezzo, Italy. Roman Catholic Priest; Poet. Education: BA, 1972, BEd, 1973, Master of Divinity, 1990, University of Toronto; Bachelor of Sacred Theology, St Paul's University, 1990. Appointments: Founder-Poetry Editor, Poetry Toronto Newsletter, 1976-77; Associate Editor, Books in Canada, 1976-79; Co-Editor, 1976-79, Poetry Editor, 1980-82, Waves; Ordained Roman Catholic Priest and Associate Pastor, St Anne's Church, Brampton, Ontario, 1993-. Publications: We Are the Light Turning, 1975; The Sad Facts, 1977; The Circular Dark, 1977; Dancing in the House of Cards, 1977; A Burning Patience, 1978; Roman Candles: An Anthology of 17 Italo-Canadian Poets (editor), 1978; Dolce-Amaro, 1979; The Tough Romance, 1979; A Straw Hat for Everything, 1981; Flying Deeper into the Century, 1982; Dark to Light: Reasons for Humanness: Poems 1976-1979, 1983; Women We Never See Again, 1984; Twenty Poems, 1984; Post-Sixties Nocturne, 1985; Virgin Science: Hunting Holistic Paradigms, 1986; The City of Hurried Dreams, 1993. Honours: Canada Council Awards, 1974, 1976, 1980; Carleton University Italo-Canadian Literature Award, 1979. Address: PO Box 344, King City, Ontario L0G 1K0, Canada.

DI MICHELE Mary, b. 6 Aug 1949, Lanciano, Italy (Canadian citizen). Poet; Author; Associate Professor. div, 1 daughter. Education: BA, University of Toronto, 1972; MA, University of Windsor, 1974. Appointments: Poetry Editor, Toronto Life, 1980-81, Poetry Toronto, 1982-84; Writer-in-Residence, University of Toronto, 1985-86, Metro Reference Library, Toronto, 1986, Regina Public Library, 1987-88; Writer-in-Residence, 1990, Associate Professor, Creative Writing Programme, Concordia University. Publications: Poetry: Tree of August, 1978; Bread and Chocolate, 1980; Mimosa and Other Poems, 1981; Necessary Sugar, 1984; Immune to Gravity, 1986; Luminous Emergencies, 1990; Stranger in You: Selected Poems & New, 1995; Debriefing the Rose, 1998. Novel: Under My Skin, 1994. Editor: Anything is Possible, 1984. Contributions to: Anthologies and periodicals. Honours: 1st Prize for Poetry, CBC Literary Competition, 1980; Silver Medal, DuMaurier Poetry Award, 1982; Air Canada Writing Award, 1983. Memberships: Italian-Canadian Writers Association; Writers Union. Address: c/o Department of English,

Concordia University, 1455 de Maisonneuve Boulevard West, Montreal, Quebec H3G 1M8, Canada.

DI PRIMA Diane, b. 6 Aug 1934, New York, New York, USA. Poet; Writer; Dramatist; Artist. m. (1) Alan S Marlowe, 1962, div 1969, (2) Grant Fisher, 1972, div 1975, 2 sons, 3 daughters. Education: Swarthmore College, 1951-53. Appointments: Co-Founder, New York Poets Theater, 1961-65; Co-Editor (with LeRoi Jones), 1961-63, Editor, 1963-69, Floating Bear magazine; Publisher, Poets Press, 1964-69, Eidolon Editions, 1974-; Faculty, Naropa Institute, 1974-, New College of California, San Francisco, 1980-87; Co-Founder, San Francisco Institute of Magical and Healing Arts, 1983-91; Senior Lecturer, California College of Arts and Crafts, Oakland, 1990-92; Visiting Faculty, San Francisco Art Institute, 1992; Adjunct Faculty, California Institute of Integral Studies, 1994-95. Publications: Poetry: This Kind of Bird Flies Backward, 1958; The Monster, 1961; The New Handbook of Heaven, 1963; Poets Vaudeville, 1964; Combination Theatre Poem and Birthday Poem for Ten People, 1965; Haiku, 1967; Earthsong: Poems 1957-59, 1968; Hotel Albert, 1968; New Mexico Poem, June-July 1967, 1968; The Star, the Child, the Light, 1968; LA Odyssey, 1969; New As..., 1969; The Book of Hours, 1970; Kerhonkson Journal 1966, 1971; Prayer to the Mothers, 1971; So Fine, 1971; XV Dedications, 1971; Revolutionary Letters, 1971; The Calculus of Variation, 1972; Loba, Part 1, 1973; Freddie Poems, 1974; Brass Furnace Going Out: Song, After an Abortion, 1975; Selected Poems 1956-1975, 1975, revised edition, 1977; Loba as Eve, 1975; Loba, Part 2, 1976; Loba, Parts 1-8, 1978; Wyoming Series, 1988; The Mysteries of Vision, 1988; Pieces of a Song: Selected Poems, 1990; Seminary Poems, 1991; The Mask is the Path of the Star, 1993. Fiction: Dinners and Nightmares, 1961, revised edition, 1974; The Calculus of Variation, 1966; Memoirs of a Beatnik, 1969. Plays: Zip Code: Collected Plays, 1994. Other: Various Fables from Various Places (editor), 1960; War Poems (editor), 1968; Notes on the Summer Solstice, 1969. Contributions to: Various publications. Honours: National Endowment for the Arts Grants, 1966, 1973; Coordinating Council of Little Magazines Grants, 1967, 1970; Lapis Foundation Awards, 1978, 1979; Institute for Aesthetic Development Award, 1986; Lifetime Service Award, National Poetry Association, 1993. Address: 584 Castro Street, Suite 346, San Francisco, CA 94114, USA.

DI STEFANO BUSA Ninnj, b. 28 Jan 1941, Partanna (TP), Italy. Teacher of Literature; Writer; Poet; Journalist; Critic; Essayist. m. Alberto Busà, 15 Aug 1969, 2 sons. Education: Diploma in Literature, University of Genoa. Appointments: Participant, numerous national and international conferences and meetings. Publications: Many books of poetry including: Oltre il segno tangibile, 1987; Lo spazio di un pensiero, 1988; Quel lucido delirio, 1989; Sortilegio di riflessi, 1989; La parola essenziale, 1990; Abitare la polvere, 1990; L'area di Broca, 1993; L'attimo che conta, 1994; Anche l'ipotesi, 1995; Quella dolcezza inquieta, 1997; Le lune oltre il cancello, 1998; Essays: Il valore di un rito onirico, 1989; L'Estetica crociana e i problemi dell'arte, 1996; Translations of Argentinian poets. Contributions to: Corriere di Roma; Portofranco; Procellaria; La Ballata; La Clessidra. Honours: Cinque Terre Prize, La Spezia, 1989, 1994; Diploma of Cultural Merit, Argentinian Society of Authors, Buenos Aires, 1990; Editoriale Agemina Prize, Florence, 1990; Città di Pontinia Prize, 1993; Histonium di Vasto Prize, 1995; La Magra Prize, Spezia, 1996; G Parise Prize, Bolzano, 1997; Prize for New Literature, Istituto Italiano di Cultura, Naples, 1997; Libero de Libero Prize, Fondi, 1998. Address: Via Mattarella No 2, 20090 Segrate (Milano), Italy.

DICKENSON C Reginald, b. 22 June 1912, Shaftesbury, England. Retired. m. Anneliese Ursula Frenkel, 9 Feb 1951, 2 daughters. Education: Bornemouth Municipal College. Appointments: Senior Executive Engineer, British Post Office; Controller, British Foreign Office; Managing Director, Jamaica Telephone Company; Senior Staff Member, Division Chief, World Bank; Consultant, various international agencies. Publications: African Ambit, 1995; The Brotherhood, 1996; Telecommunications in Developing Countries; The Relation to the Economy and the Society; Telecommunications in the Developing World. Contributions to: IPOEE Journal. Honours: Officer of the Order of the British Empire; London City and Guilds; Insignia Award; CGIA Fellow of Institute of Electrical Engineers. Address: 643 Smithfield Street, Pittsburgh, PA 15222, USA.

DICKEY Christopher, b. 31 Aug 1951, Nashville, Tennessee, USA. Journalist; Writer. m. (1) Susan Tuckerman, 29 Nov 1969, div Dec 1979, (2) Carol Salvatore, 22 Mar 1980, 1 son. Education: BA, University of Virginia, 1972; MS, Boston University, 1974. Appointments: Staff, Washington Post, 1974-86; Cairo Bureau Chief, 1986-88, Paris Bureau Chief, 1988-93, Middle East Regional Editor, 1993-95, Paris Bureau Chief, 1995-, Newsweek. Publications: With the Contras: A Reporter in the Wilds of Nicaragua, 1986; Expats: Travels in Arabia, from Tripoli to Teheran, 1990; Innocent Blood (novel), 1997; Summer of Deliverance: A Memoir of Father and Son, Contributions to: Periodicals. Honours: Interamerican Press Association Award, 1980; Mary Hemingway Award, Overseas Press Club, 1983; Edward Weintal Award for Diplomatic Reporting, Georgetown University. Membership: Council on Foreign Relations. Literary Agent: Kathy Robbins. Address: c/o Newsweek, 251 West 57th Street, New York, NY 10019, USA.

DICKINSON Donald Percy, b. 28 Dec 1947, Prince Albert, Saskatachewan, Canada. Writer; Teacher. m. Chellie Eaton, 1 May 1970, 2 sons, 1 daughter. Education: BA, University of Saskatachewan, 1973; MFA, University of British Columbia, 1979. Appointments: Fiction Editor, Prism International, 1977-79; Teacher of English, Lillooet Secondary School, 1981-98. Publications: Novel: The Crew, 1993. Short Stories: Third Impressions, 1982; Fighting the Upstream, 1987; Blue Husbands, 1991. Contributions to: Best Canadian Short Fiction, 1984; Words We Call Home, 1990; The New Writers, 1992; The Porcupine Quill Reader, 1996. Honours: Bankson Award, 1979; Governor-General Award of Canada Nominee, 1991; Ethel Wilson Fiction Prize, 1991; Books in Canada 1st Novel Nominee, 1993. Membership: Oldtimers' Hockey Association. Address: 554 Victoria Street, Box 341, Lillooet, British Columbia V0K 1V0, Canada.

DICKINSON Margaret. See: **MUGGESON Margaret Elizabeth.**

DICKSON Gordon (Rupert), b. 1 Nov 1923, Edmonton, Alberta, Canada. Writer. Education: BA, 1948, Graduate Studies, 1948-50, University of Minnesota. Publications include: Alien From Arcturus, 1956; Mankind on the Run, 1956; Earthman's Burden (with Poul Anderson), 1957; Secret Under the Sea, 1960; Time to Teleport, 1960; The Genetic General, 1960; Delusion World, 1960; Spacial Delivery, 1961; Naked to the Stars, 1961; Necromancer, 1962; Secret Under Antarctica, 1963; Secret Under the Carribean, 1964; Space Winners, 1965; The Alien Way, 1965; Mission to Universe, 1965; Planet Run, 1967; Soldier Ask Not, 1967; The Space Swimmers, 1967; None But Man, 1969; Spacepaw, 1969; Wolfing, 1969; Hour of the Horde, 1970; Danger - Human (also known as The Book Of Gordon R Dickson), 1970; Mutants, 1970; Sleepwalker's World, 1971; The Tactics of Mistake, 1971; The Outposter, 1971; The Pritcher Mass, 1972; The Star Road, 1973; Alien Art, 1973; The R-Master, 1973; Gremlins Go Home! (with Ben Bova), 1974; Ancient My Enemy, 1974; Three to Dorsai, 1975; Combat SF (editor), 1975; Star Prince Charlie (with P Anderson), 1975; The Lifeship (with Harry Harrison), 1976; The Dragon and The George, 1976; Time Storm, 1977; Nebula Award Stories Twelve (editor), 1978; The Far Call, 1978; Home From the Shore, 1978; Spirit of Dorsai, 1980; Masters of Everon, 1980; Lost Dorsai, 1980; In Iron Years, 1981; Love Not Human, 1981; Dragon at War, 1992; Dragon on The Border, 1992; The Magnificent Wilf, 1995; The Dragon and the Gnarly King, 1997; The Dragon in Lyonesse, 1998. Honours: Hugo Award, 1965, 1981 (2); Nebula Award, 1966; British Fantasy Award, 1976; Jupiter Award, 1977. Memberships: Science Fiction Writers of America, president, 1969-71; Authors Guild; Mystery Writers of America. Literary Agent: The Pimlico Agency, Box 20447, 1539 First Avenue, New York, NY 10028.Address: PO Box 11569, St Paul, MN 55111, USA.

DICKSON Mora Agnes, b. 20 Apr 1918, Glasgow, Scotland. Author; Artist. Education: Diploma of Art, Edinburgh College of Art, 1941; Certificate, Byam Shaw School of Drawing and Painting, London, 1950. Publications: New Nigerians, 1960; Baghdad and Beyond, 1961; A Season in Sarawak, 1962; A World Elsewhere, 1964; Israeli Interlude, 1966; Count Us In, 1968; Longhouse in Sarawak, 1971; Beloved Partner, 1974; A Chance to Serve (editor), 1977; The Inseparable Grief, 1977; Assignment in Asia, 1979; The Powerful Bond, 1980; Nannie, 1988. Address: 19 Blenheim Road, London W4, England.

DIDIK Frank X, b. 1956, New York City, New York, USA. Investor; Designer; Engineer. Publications: Eastern European Business Directory; Didik's Directory of American Businesses; Complete Director of Electric Vehicles; History and Guide Book to Lenticular Images; Eastern Europe for Exporters; Didik's Guide Book to the Broadcast Television Industry. Contributions to: Numerous publications. Address: GPO Box 7426, New York, NY 10116, USA.

DIDION Joan, b. 5 Dec 1934, Sacramento, California, USA. Author; Screenwriter. m. John Gregory Dunne, 30 Jan 1964, 1 daughter. Education: BA, University of California at Berkeley, 1956. Appointments: Associate Feature Editor, Vogue magazine, 1956-63; Columnist, Esquire, Life, and Saturday Evening Post magazines. Publications: Run River, 1963; Slouching Towards Bethlehem, 1968; Play It as It Lays, 1970; A Book of Common Prayer, 1977; Telling Stories, 1978; The White Album, 1979; Salvador, 1983; Democracy, 1984; Miami, 1987; After Henry, 1992; The Last Thing He Wanted, 1996. Screenplays (all with John Gregory Dunne): The Panic in Needle Park), 1971; Play It as It Lays, 1972; A Star is Born, 1976; True Confessions, 1981; Hills Like White Elephants, 1991; Broken Trust, 1995; Up Close and Personal, 1996. Contributions to: Periodicals. Honours: 1st Prize, Prix de Paris, Vogue magazine, 1956; Morton Dauwen Zabel Prize, American Academy of Arts and Letters, 1978. Memberships: American Academy of Arts and Letters; American Academy of Arts and Sciences; Council on Foreign Relations. Address: c/o Janklow & Nesbit Associates, 598 Madison Avenue, New York, NY 10022, USA.

DIECKMANN Friedrich, b. 25 May 1937, Landsberg, Germany. Writer. m. Christine Decker, 1976, 1 daughter. Education: University of Leipzig, 1983. Publications: Karl von Appens Bühnenbilder am Berliner Ensemble, 1971; Streifzüge (essays), 1977; Theaterbilder (essays), 1979; Richard Wagner in Venedig, 1983, 2nd edition, 1994; Hilfsmittel wider die alternde Zeit (essays), 1990; Die Geschichte Don Giovannis, 1991; Temperatursprung/Deutsche Verhältnisse, 1995; Der Irrtum des Verschwindens (essays), 1996. Honours: Heinrich Mann Prize, Berlin, 1983; Richard Wagner Prize, 1983. Memberships: Deutsche Akademie für Sprache und Dichtung; Freie Akademie der Künste, Leipzig; German PEN; Sächsische Akademie der Künste, vice president; Schriftstellerverband. Address: Moosdorfstrasse 13, D-12435 Berlin, Germany.

DIGBY John (Michael), b. 18 Jan 1938, London, England. Emigrated, USA, 1978. Poet; Collagist. m. (1) Erica Susan Christine Berwick-Stephens, 1963, div, 1 son, (2) Joan Hildreth Weiss, 3 Mar 1979. Publications: The Structure of Biofocal Distance, poems, 1974; Sailing Away From Night, poems, collages, 1978; To Amuse a Shrinking Sun, poems, collages, 1985; The Collage Handbook (with wife, Joan Digby), 1985; Miss Liberty, collages, 1986; Incantation, poems, collages, 1987; A Parliament of Owls, poems, collages, 1989; Editor with Joan Digby: Inspired by Drink, 1988; The Wood

Engravings of John de Pol, 1988. Address: 30 Kellogg Street, Oyster Bay, NY 11771, USA.

DIGREGORIO Charlotte Antonia, b. 30 Aug 1953, Portland, Oregon, USA. Author; Editorial Consultant; Professional Speaker. Education: BA, Pomona College, 1975; MA, University of Chicago, 1979. Appointment: Host, Poetry Beat, Oregon Public Broadcasting, 1995-. Publications: Beginners' Guide to Writing and Selling Quality Features, 1990; You Can Be a Columnist, 1993; Your Original Personal Ad, 1995. Contributions to: Magazines and journals. Memberships: International Women's Writing Guild; Northwest Association of Book Publishers; Publishers Marketing Association; International Women's Writing Guild, regional representative, 1995-96; Judge, Non-fiction Writing Contest, Willamette Writers, Portland, Oregon, 1997. Address: 2770 South West Old Orchard Road, Portland, OR 97201, USA.

DILLARD Annie, b. 30 Apr 1945, Pittsburgh, Pennsylvania, USA. Adjunct Professor; Writer-in-Residence. m. (1) Richard Dillard, 4 June 1964, (2) Gary Clevidence, 12 Apr 1980, (3) Robert D Richardson Jr, 1988. Education: BA, 1967, MA, 1968, Hollins College. Appointments: Scholar-in- Residence, Western Washington University, 1975-79; Visiting Professor, 1979-81, Adjunct Professor, 1983-, Writer-in-Residence, 1987-, Wesleyan University. Publications: Pilgrim at Tinker Creek, 1974; Holy the Firm, 1977; Teaching a Stone to Talk, 1983; Encounters with Chinese Writers, 1984; An American Childhood, 1987; The Writing Life, 1989; The Living, 1992; The Annie Dillard Reader, 1994; Tickets for a Prayer Wheel, 1994; Mornings Like This, 1995. Honours: Pulitzer Prize, 1975; New York Press Club Award, 1975; Washington Governor's Award, 1977; National Endowment for the Arts Grant, 1985; Guggenheim Fellowship, 1986; Appalachian Gold Medallion, 1989; Ambassador Book Award, 1990; Campion Award, 1994; Milton Prize, 1994. Memberships: PEN International; Poetry Society of America; Western Writers of America; Century Association; National Association for the Advancement of Colored People; Society of American Historians. Address: c/o Tim Seldes, Russel & Volkening, 50 West 29th, New York 10001, USA.

DILLARD R(ichard) H(enry) W(ilde), b. 11 Oct 1937, Roanoke, Virginia, USA. Professor of English; Writer; Poet; Editor. m. (1) Annie Doak, 1965, div 1972, (2) Cathy Hankla, 1979. Education: BA, Roanoke College, Salem, Virginia, 1958; MA, 1959, PhD, 1965, University of Virginia. Appointments: Instructor, Roanoke College, 1961, University of Virginia, 1961-64; Assistant Professor, 1964-68, Associate Professor, 1968-74, Professor of English, 1974-, Hollins College, Virginia; Contributing Editor, Hollins Critic, 1966-77; Editor-in-Chief, Children's Literature, 1992-. Publications: Fiction: The Book of Changes, 1974; The First Man on the Sun, 1983; Omniphobia, 1995. Poetry: The Day I Stopped Dreaming About Barbara Steele and Other Poems, 1966; News of the Nile, 1971; After Borges, 1972; The Greeting: New and Selected Poems, 1981; Just Here, Just Now, 1994. Non-Fiction: Horror Films, 1976; Understanding George Garrett, 1988. Editor: The Experience of America: A Book of Readings (with Louis D Rubin Jr), 1969; The Sounder Few: Essays from "The Hollins Critic" (with George Garrett and John Rees Moore), 1971. Contributions to: Periodicals. Honours: Academy of American Poets Prize, 1961; Ford Foundation Grant, 1972; O B Hardison, Jr Poetry Award, Folger Shakespeare Library, Washington, DC, 1994. Address: Box 9671, Hollins College, CA 24020, USA.

DILLINGHAM William Byron, b. 7 Mar 1930, Atlanta, Georgia, USA; Emeritus Professor of American Literature; Writer. m. Elizabeth Joiner, 3 July 1952, 1 son, 2 daughters. Education: BA, 1955, MA, 1956, Emory University; PhD, University of Pennsylvania, 1961. Appointments: Instructor, 1956-58, Assistant Professor, Associate Professor, Professor, Charles Howard Candler Professor of American Literature, 1959-96, Emeritus Professor 1996-; Emory University; Editorial Boards,

Nineteenth-Century Literature, South Atlantic Bulletin. Publications: Humor of the Old Southwest, 1965, 3rd edition, 1994; Frank Norris: Instinct and Art, 1969; An Artist in the Rigging: The Early Work of Herman Melville, 1972; Melville's Short Fiction, 1853-1856, 1977; Melville's Later Novels, 1986; Practical English Handbook, 9th edition, 1992, 10th edition, 1996; Melville and His Circle: The Last Years, 1996. Contributions to: Many articles and reviews to scholarly journals. Address: 1416 Vistaleaf Drive, Decatur, GA 30033, USA.

DILLON Millicent Gerson, b. 24 May 1925. New York, New York, USA. Writer. m. (1) Murray Lesser, 1 June 1948, div 1959, 2 daughters, (2) David F Dillon, 1 Jan 1974, div. Education: BA, Hunter College, 1944; MA, San Francisco State University, 1966. Publications: Baby Perpetua and Other Stories, 1971; The One in the Back is Medea (novel), 1973; A Little Original Sin: The Life and Work of Jane Bowles, 1981; After Egypt, 1990; The Dance of the Mothers (novel), 1991; You Are Not I: A Portrait of Paul Bowles, 1998. Contributions to: Southwest Review; Witness; Threepenny Review; The New Yorker; Raritan. Honours: 5 O. Henry Short Story Awards; Best American Short Stories, 1992; Guggenheim Fellowship; National Endowment for the Humanities Fellowship. Memberships: PEN; Authors Guild. Address: 83 6th Avenue, San Francisco, CA 94118, USA.

DILSAVER Paul, b. 8 Dec 1949, Colorado, USA. Poet; Writer; Editor. Education: BA, Philosophy, University of Southern Colorado, 1972; MA, English, 1973, Additional Graduate Studies, 1974, 1975, Colorado State University; MFA, Creative Writing, Bowling Green State University, Ohio, 1979; BS, Accounting, State University of New York, 1996. Appointments: Instructor, Laramie County Community College, Cheyenne, Wyoming, 1973-74; Casper College, Wyoming, 1974-77, Western Illinois University, Macomb, 1979-81; Poetry Editor, Rocky Mountain Creative Arts Journal and Chapbook Series, 1974-78; Poet-in-Residence, Wyoming Arts Council, 1977-78; Editor, Blue Light Books, 1979-, Blue Light Review, 1983-91; Assistant Professor of English, Carroll College, Helena, Montana, 1981-84; Lecturer in English, University of Southern Colorado, 1986-91; Visiting Instructor of English, Anoka-Ramsey College, Coon Rapids, Minnesota, 1991-92. Publications: Malignant Blues (poems), 1976; Words Wyoming (anthology), 1976; A Brutal Blacksmith, An Anvil of Bruised Tissue (poems), 1979; Encounters with the Antichrist (prose poems), 1982; Character Scatology (poems), 1984; Stories of the Strange (fiction), 1985; Nurtz! Nurtz! (novel), 1989; A Cure for Optimism (poems), 1993; The Toilet Papers (anthology), 1994. Contributions to: Various anthologies and periodicals. Address: PO Box 1621, Pueblo, CO 81002, USA.

DIMBLEBY David, b. 28 Oct 1938, London England. Broadcaster; Newspaper Proprietor. m. Josceline Gaskell, 1967, 1 son, 2 daughters, Education: Christ Church, Oxford; Universities of Paris and Perugia. Appointments: News Reporter, BBC Bristol, 1960-61; Presenter, Interviewer, current affairs and political programmes, BBC TV 1961-; Managing Director, 1966-86, Chairman, 1986-, Dimbleby & Sons Ltd. Publication: An Ocean Apart (with David Reynolds), 1988. Honours: Supreme Documentary Award, 1979; Emmy Award, 1991; Golden Nymph Award, 1991; BAFTA Richard Dimbleby Award, 1997. Address: c/o BBC, Broadcasting House, Portland Place, London W1 1AA, England.

DIMBLEBY Jonathan, b. 31 July 1944, Aylesbury, Buckinghamshire, England. Broadcaster; Journalist; Writer. m. Bel Mooney, 1968, 1 son, 1 daughter. Education: BA, Honours, Philosophy, University College, London. Appointments: Reporter, BBC Bristol, 1969-70, BBC Radio, 1970-71, Thames TV, 1972-78, 1986-88, Yorkshire TV, 1980-86; Presenter, TV-am, 1985-86, BBC Radio, 1987-, BBC TV, 1988-1993, London Weekend TV, 1995-. Publications: Richard Dimbleby, 1975; The Palestinians, 1979; The Prince of Wales: A Biography, 1994; The Last Governor, 1997. Honour: Richard Dimbleby Award, Society of Film and Television Arts,

1974. Memberships: Council for Protection of Rural Engalnd, vice president, 1997-; Soil Association, president, 1997-; Richard Dimbleby Cancer Fund, board member; Voluntary Service Overseas, president, 1998-; Bath Festivals Trust, chairman, 1998-. Address: c/o David Higham Associates, 5 Lower Street, London W1R 4HA, England.

DIMBLEBY Josceline Rose, b. 1 Feb 1943, Oxford, England. Cookery Writer and Editor. m. David Dimbleby, 20 Jan 1967, 1 son, 2 daughters. Education: Guildhall School of Music, London. Appointments: Contributor, Daily Mail, 1976-78; Cookery Writer, Sainsbury's, 1978-; Cookery Editor, Sunday Telegraph, 1982-97. Publications: A Taste of Dreams, 1976, 3rd edition, 1984; Party Pieces, 1977; Cooking for Christmas, 1978; Josceline Dimbleby's Book of Puddings, Desserts and Savouries, 1979, 2nd edition, 1983; Family Meat and Fish Cookery, 1979; Cooking with Herbs and Spices, 1979; Curries and Oriental Cookery, 1980; Salads for all Seasons, 1981; Marvellous Meals with Mince, 1982; Festive Food, 1982; Favourite Food, 1983, 2nd edition, 1984; Sweet Dreams, 1983; First Impressions, 1984; The Josceline Dimbleby Collection, 1984; Main Attractions, 1985; A Traveller's Tastes, 1986; The Josceline Dimbleby Christmas Book, 1987; The Josceline Dimbleby Book of Entertaining, 1988; The Essential Josceline Dimbleby, 1989; The Cook's Companion, 1991; The Almost Vegetarian Cookbook, 1994; The Christmas Book, 1994; Josceline Dimbleby's Complete Cookbook, 1997. Contributions to: Numerous magazines and television programmes. Honours: André Simon Memorial Award, 1979; Glenfiddich Cookery Writer of the Year Award, 1993. Address: 14 King Street, Richmond, Surrey TW9 1NF, England.

DIMITROFF Pashanko, b. 22 Mar 1924, Stanimaka, Bulgaria. Journalist. m. Margaret Greenwood, 18 July 1959, 2 sons. Education: Law, University of Sofia, 1943-46; Music, Cello, Academy of Music, Sofia, 1943; Doctor of Law, Faculte de Droit, Paris, 1959. Publications: Boris III of Bulgaria, 1986; The Silent Bulgarians (in Bulgarian), 1991; King of Mercy, 1993; Princess Clementine, 1994. Address: 20 Old Station Way, Wooburn Green, Buckinghamshire HP10 0HZ, England.

DIMONT Penelope. See: MORTIMER Penelope (Ruth).

DINNERSTEIN Leonard, b. 5 May 1934, New York, New York, USA. Professor of History; Writer. m. Myra Anne Rosenberg, 20 Aug 1961, 1 son, 1 daughter. Education: BA, City College of New York, 1955; MA, 1960, PhD, 1966, Columbia University. Appointments: Instructor, New York Institute of Technology, 1960-65; Assistant Professor, Fairleigh Dickinson University, 1967-70; Associate Professor, 1970-72, Professor of American History,1972-, University of Arizona, Tucson. Publications: The Leo Frank Case, 1968; The Aliens (with F C Jaher), 1970, as Uncertain Americans, 1977; American Vistas (with K T Jackson), 1971, 7th edition, 1995; Antisemitism in the United States, 1971; Jews in the South (with M D Palsson), 1973; Decisions and Revisions (with J Christie), 1975; Ethnic Americans: A History of Immigration and Assimilation (with D M Reimers), 1975, 3rd edition, 1988; Natives and Strangers (with R L Nichols and D M Reimers), 1979, 2nd edition, 1990; America and the Survivors of the Holocaust, 1982; Uneasy at Home, 1987; Antisemitism in America, 1994. Address: 1981 Miraval Cuarto, Tusson, AZ 85718, USA

DISCH Thomas M(ichael), (Leonie Hargrave, Dobbin Thorpe), b. 2 Feb 1940, Des Moines, Iowa, USA. Writer; Poet; Dramatist; Librettist; Lecturer. Education: Cooper Union, New York; New York University. Appointments: Lecturer at colleges and universities; Artist-in-Residence, College of William and Mary, 1996. Publications: Novels: The Genocides, 1965; Mankind Under the Leash, 1966; The House That Fear Built (with John Sladek), 1966; Echo Round His Bones, 1967; Black Alice (with John Sladek), 1968; Camp Concentration, 1968; The Prisoner, 1969; 334, 1974; Clara Reeve, 1975;

On Wings of Song, 1979; Triplicity, 1980; Neighboring Lives (with Charles Naylor), 1981; The Businessman: A Tale of Terror, 1984; Amnesia 1985; The M.D.: A Horror Story, 1991; The Priest: A Gothic Romance, 1995. Poetry: The Right Way to Figure Plumbing, 1972; ABCDEFG HIJKLM NOPQRST UVWXYZ, 1981; Orders of the Retina, 1982; Burn This, 1982; Here I Am, There You Are, Where Were We, 1984; Yes, Let's: New and Selected Poetry, 1989; Dark Verses and Light, 1991; The Dark Old House, 1995. Criticism: The Castle of Indolence, 1995; The Dreams Our Stuff is Made of: How Science Fiction Conquered the World, 1998. Other: Short story collections; plays; opera libretti; juvenile books. Contributions to: Many anthologies and periodicals. Honours: O Henry Prizes, 1975, 1979; John W Campbell Memorial Award, 1980; British Science Fiction Award, 1981. Memberships: National Book Critics Circle; PEN; Writers Guild. Address: Box 226, Barryville, NY 12719, USA.

DISIPIO Rocco Thomas, b. 17 Dec 1949, Philadelphia, Pennsylvania, USA. Writer. m. Jane Heeres Newell, 1974, div. Education: BSc, Police Administration, Michigan State University, 1971. Appointments: Probation/Parole Officer, Commonwealth of Pennsylvania, 1971. Publication: Arcadia Ego, 1995; Darkness Paradise, 1998. Contributions to: Exile; Canadian Literary Journal. Honour: USA Today Award, 1998. Address: PO Box 414, Alburg, VT 05540-0414, USA.

DIVINE Robert A(lexander), b. 10 May 1929, New York, New York, USA. Professor of American History Emeritus; Author. m. (1) Barbara Christine Renick, 6 Aug 1955, 3 sons, 1 daughter, dec 1993, (2) Darlene S Harris, 1 June 1996. Education: BA, 1951, MA, 1952, PhD, 1954, Yale University. Appointments: Instructor, 1954-57, Assistant Professor, 1957-61, Associate Professor, 1961-63, Professor, 1963-80, George W Littlefield Professor of American History, 1981-96, Professor Emeritus, 1996-, University of Texas at Austin; Fellow, Center for Advanced Study in the Behavioural Sciences, Stanford, 1962-63; Albert Shaw Lecturer, Johns Hopkins University, 1968. Publications: American Immigration Policy 1924-1952, 1957; The Illusion of Neutrality, 1962; The Reluctant Belligerent: American Entry into World War II, 1965, 2nd edition, 1979; Second Chance: The Triumph of Internationalism in America During World War II, 1967; Roosevelt and World War II, 1969; Foreign Policy and US Presidential Elections, 1940-1960, 2 volumes, 1974; Since 1945: Politics and Diplomacy in Recent American History, 1975, 3rd edition, 1985; Blowing on the Wind, 1978; Eisenhower and the Cold War, 1981; America: Past and Present (with T H Breen, George Fredrickson and R Hal Williams), 1984, 5th edition, 1999; The Sputnik Challenge, 1993. Editor: American Foreign Policy, 1960; The Age of Insecurity: America 1920-1945, 1968; Twentieth-Century America: Contemporary Documents and Opinions (with John A Garraty), 1968; American Foreign Policy Since 1945, 1969; Causes and Consequences of World War II, 1969; The Cuban Missile Crisis, 1971, 2nd edition, 1988; Exploring the Johnson Years, 1981; The Johnson Years: Vol Two, Vietnam, the Environment and Science, 1987; The Johnson Years: Vol Three, LBJ at Home and Abroad, 1994. Contributions to: Scholarly books and journals. Honours: Rockefeller Humanities Fellowship, 1976-77; Graduate Teaching Award, University of Texas, 1986; Eugene E Emme Astronomical Literature Award, 1993. Memberships: Phi Beta Kappa; Society for Historians of American Foreign Relations. Address: 10617 Sans Souci Place, Austin, TX 78759, USA.

DIVINSKY Nathan J(oseph), b. 29 Oct 1925, Winnipeg, Manitoba, Canada. Mathematician. 3 daughters. Education: BSc, University of Manitoba, 1946; SM, 1947, PhD, 1950, University of Chicago, USA. Appointment: Editor, Canadian Chess Chat, 1959-74. Publications: Around the Chess World in 80 Years, 1963; Rings and Radicals, 1965; Linear Algebra, 1970; Warriors of the Mind (with R Keene), 1988; Chess Encyclopedia, 1990; Life Maps of the Great Chessmasters, 1994. Memberships: Life Master, ACBL (Bridge League); Commonwealth Chess Association, president, 1988-94; Canada's Representative to FIDE (World Chess Federation), 1987-94. Address: 5689 McMaster Road, Vancouver, British Columbia V6T 1K1, Canada.

DIVOK Mario J, b. 22 Sept 1944, Benus, Czechoslovakia. Real Estate Broker; Investments Executive; Poet; Dramatist. m. Eva Pytlova, 1 son, 2 daughters. Education: MA, Pedagogic Institute, Martin, Czechoslovakia, 1967; MPA, California State University, Long Beach, 1977; Management, University of California, Irvine, 1995. Publications: The Relations, 1975; The Voice, 1975; The Wind of Changes, 1978; Equinox, 1978; The Collection, 1978; I Walk the Earth, 1980; The Blind Man, 1980; Looking for the Road to the Earth, 1983; The Birthday, 1984; Stranger in the Land, 1989; Selected Works, 1992. Contributions to: Various periodicals. Honours: Schlossar Award, Hall Publishers, Switzerland, 1980; American Poetry Association Award, 1988; World of Poetry Award, 1990. Memberships: American Association of Poets; American Playwrights Association. Address: 5 Misty Meadow Drive, Irvine, CA 92612, USA.

DIXON Dougal, b. 3 Mar 1947, Dumfries, Scotland. Writer. m. Jean Mary Young, 3 Apr 1971, 1 son, 1 daughter. Education: BSc, 1970, MSc, 1972, University of St Andrews. Appointments: Researcher, Editor, Mitchell-Beazley Ltd, 1973-78, Blandford Press, 1978-80; Part-time Tutor, Earth Sciences, Open University, 1976-78; Chairman, Bournemouth Science Fiction and Fantasy Group, 1981-82. Publications: Doomsday Planet (comic strip), 1980; After Man: A Zoology for the Future, 1981; Discovering Earth Sciences, 1982; Science World: Geology, 1982; Science World: Geography, 1983; Picture Atlas: Mountains, 1984; Picture Atlas: Forests, 1984; Picture Atlas: Deserts, 1984; Find Out About Prehistoric Reptiles, 1984; Find Out About Jungles, 1984; The Age of Dinosaurs (with Jane Burton), 1984; Nature Detective Series: Minerals, Rocks and Fossils, 1984; Time Machine 7: Ice Age Explorer, 1985; Secrets of the Earth, 1986; Find Out About Dinosaurs, 1986. Address: c/o Hamlyn, 69 London Road, Twickenham, Middlesex TW1 3SB, England.

DIXON Jean Clarence, b. 9 Apr 1915, Sydney, New South Wales, Australia. Writer; Editor. m. Douglas Lindsay Dixon, 12 Dec 1936, dec 1995, 2 sons, 1 daughter. Education: Writers' Retreat, New England University, Armidale, New South Wales, 1968; Creative Writing Course, Sydney University, 1969; Pilot Group, Women Playwrights, 1974. Appointments: Editor, Bushland News, 1974-88, PEN Quarterly, 1981-86, New South Wales Society of Women Writers Newsletter, 1995-96. Publications: That Way Madness, 1964; The Poison Tree, 1968; Death Takes the Chair, 1973; Blue Fire Lady, 1977; The Riddle of Powder Works Road, 1980; Hello Mr Melody Man (editor), 1983; The Climber, 1987. Contributions to: Periodicals. Memberships: Australian Society of Authors; International PEN; New South Wales Society of Women Writers; New South Wales State Library Society; New South Wales Writers' Centre. Address: PO Box 431, Mona Vale, New South Wales 2103, Australia.

DIXON Roger, (John Christian, Charles Lewis), b. 6 Jan 1930, Portsmouth, England. Author; Playwright. m. Carolyn Anne Shepheard, 28 June 1966, 2 sons, 4 daughters. Publications: Noah II, 1970; Christ on Trial, 1973; The Messiah, 1974; Five Gates to Armageddon (as John Christian), 1975; The Cain Factor (as Charles Lewis), 1975; Going to Jerusalem, 1977; Georgiana, 1984; Return to Nebo, 1991; Musical: The Commander of New York (with Phil Medley and Basil Bova), 1987. Other: Over 50 radio plays and series. Adddress: Badgers, Warren Lane, Croos-in-Hand, Heathfield, Sussex, England.

DIXON Stephen, b. 6 June 1936, New York, New York, USA. Writer; University Teacher. m. Anne Frydman, 17 Jan 1982, 2 daughters. Education: BA, City College of New York, 1958. Publications: No Relief, 1976; Work, 1977; Too Late, 1978; Quite Contrary, 1979; 14 Stories, 1980; Movies, 1983; Time to Go, 1984; Fall and Rise, 1985; Garbage, 1988; Love and Will, 1989; The Play and Other Stories, 1989; All Gone, 1990; Friends, 1990; Frog, 1991; Long Made Short, 1993; The Stories of Stephen Dixon, 1994; Interstate, 1995; Man on Stage, 1996; Gould, 1997; Sleep, 1999; 30, 1999. Contributions to: 400 short stories to magazines and journals including Atlantic; Harper's; Esquire; Playboy; Paris Review; Triquarterly; Western Humanities Review; Ambit; Bananas; Boulevard; Glimmer Train; Partisan Review; O. Henry Prize Stories, 1977, 1982, 1993; Best American Stories, 1993, 1996. Honours: Stegner Fiction Fellowship, Stanford University, 1964-65; National Endowment of the Arts Grants, 1974-75, 1990-91; American Academy and Institute of Arts and Letters Award, 1983; John Train Prize, Paris Review, 1984; Guggenheim Fellowship, 1985-86. Address: 1315 Boyce Avenue, Baltimore, MD 21204, USA.

DJERASSI Carl, b. 29 Oct 1923, Vienna, Austria. Professor of Chemistry; Author; Poet. m. Diane Wood Middlebrook, 20 June 1985, 1 son. Education: AB summa cum laude, Kenyon College, 1942; PhD, University of Wisconsin, 1945. Appointments: Associate Professor, 1952-53, Professor of Chemistry, 1953-59, Wayne State University; Professor of Chemistry, Stanford University, 1959-. Publications: Optical Rotatory Dispersion, 1959; Steroid Reactions, 1963; Mass Spectrometry of Organic Compounds (with H Budzikiewicz and D H Williams), 1967; The Politics of Contraception, 1979; The Futurist and Other Stories, 1988; Cantor's Dilemma (novel), 1989; Steroids Made It Possible, 1990; The Clock Runs Backward (poetry), 1991; The Pill, Pygmy Chimps, and Degas' Horse (autobiography), 1992; The Bourbaki Gambit (novel), 1994; From the Lab into the World (collected essays), 1994; Marx, Deceased (novel), 1996; Menachem's Seed (novel), 1997; NO (novel), 1998; An Immaculate Misconception (drama), Edinburgh Festival Fringe, 1998. Contributions to: Kenyon Review; Southern Review; Grand Street; New Letters; Exquisite Corpse; Michigan Quarterly Review; South Dakota Review; Frank; Midwest Quarterly. Memberships: National Academy of Sciences; American Academy of Arts and Sciences; Swedish, German, Brazilian and Mexican Academies of Science; Royal Society of Chemistry. Literary Agents: Andrew Nurnberg Associates, 45-47 Clerkenwell Green, London EC1R 0HT, England. Address: Department of Chemistry, Stanford University, Stanford, CA 94305, USA.

DJURDJEVICH Milos, b. 2 Aug 1961, Rab, Croatia. Critic; Editor; Translator; Poet. Education: BA, Philosophy and Comparative Literature, 1991, MA Literature, 1997, University of Zagreb. Appointments: Literary Critic, Radio 101, Radio Zagreb; Literary Critic and Translator, Croatian Radio; Poetry Editor, Vijenac magazine. Publications: Landscapes or Circling for Words, 1989; In the Mirror, 1994; Harvest, 1997. Contributions to: Journals, reviews and periodicals. Memberships: Croatian Association of Writers; International PEN. Address: 1 Ferenscica 27, 10000 Zagreb, Croatia

DOAN Eleanor Lloyd, (Lloyd E Werth), b. 4 June 1914, Idaho, USA. Journalist; Writer; Publicist. Education: University of Nevada, 1936; Graduate Work, Wheaton College, Illinois, 1937; Marketing Research, University of California, Los Angeles, 1956, 1957. Publications: VBS Courses, 57 books, 1944, 1950; Mother's Day Source Book, 1973; Child's Treasury of Verse, 1977; Complete Speakers Source Book, 1996. Contributions to: Periodicals and journals. Address: 10749 Galvin Street, Ventura, CA 93004, USA.

DOBAI Péter, b. 12 Aug 1944, Budapest, Hungary. Author; Poet; Screenwriter. m. 1) Donatella Failioni, 1972, 2) Maria Mate, 1992. Education: Teacher's Diploma, University of Budapest, 1970. Publications: Novels: Csontmolnárok, 1974; Tartozó élet, 1975; Lavina, 1980; Vadon, 1982; Háromszögtan, 1983; A birodalom ezredese, 1985; Iv, 1988; Lendkerék, 1989. Short Stories: Játék a szobákkal, 1976; Sakktábla két figurával, 1978. Poetry: Kilovaglás egy őszi erődből, 1973; Egy arc módosulásai, 1976; Hanyatt, 1978; Az éden vermei, 1985 Válogatott versek, 1989; Vitorlák emléke, 1994;

Onmultszád, 1996. Other: 15 screenplays, 1971-95. Honours: József Attila Prize, 1976; Several Awards, Hungarian Literary Foundation and Minister of Culture; Various screenplay awards. Memberships: Hungarian Academy of Artists; Hungarian Writers' Association, Executive Board; PEN Club, Hungary. Address: Közraktár u 12/B, 1093 Budapest, Hungary.

DOBBS Michael, b. 14 Nov 1948, England. Author. Education: MA, Oxford University, 1968-71; MALD, PhD, Fletcher School of Law and Diplomacy, USA, 1971-75. Appointments: Deputy Chairman, Saatchi and Saatchi, 1983-91, Conservative Party, 1994-95. Publications: House of Cards, 1989; Wall Games, 1990; Last Man to Die, 1991; To Play the King, 1992; The Touch of Innocents, 1994; The Final Cut, 1995; Goodfellowe M.P., 1997; The Buddha of Brewer Street, 1998. Contributions to: Mail on Sunday. Address: Bilshay Dairy Farmhouse, Dottery, Bridport, Dorset DT6 5HR, England.

DOBROVENSKY Roald, b. 2 Sept 1936, Yelets, Russia. Writer. m. Velta Kaltina, 28 June 1975, 1 daughter. Education: Moscow Conservatory, 1955; Higher Literary School, 1975. Appointments: Newspaperman, Chabarovsk, Yuzhnosahalinsk, 1958-73; Editor, Editor-in-Chief, Daugava magazine, Riga, 1977-95. Publications: Novels: My Kitezh-town, 1971; Up There on the Second Floor, 1974; Alche-mist, or Life of Composer Alexander Borodin, 1984; Poore Knight (Mussorgsky story), 1986; Rainis and His Brothers, 1999. Membership: Latvian Writers Union, 1975. Address: Diku str 19-1, Riga, LV-1004, Latvia.

DOBSON Andrew Nicholas Howard, b. 15 Apr 1957, Doncaster, England. University Lecturer in Politics; Writer. Education: BA, 1st Class, Politics, Reading University, 1979; DPhil, Politics, Oxford University, 1983. Appointments: Editorial Board, Environmental Values, 1991-, Environmental Politics, 1991-, Anarchist Studies, 1991-; Chair of Politics, Keele University, 1993-. Publications: Introduction to the Politics and Philosophy of José Ortega y Gasset, 1989; Green Political Thought, 1990, 2nd edition, 1995; The Green Reader, 1991; The Politics of Nature: Explorations in Green Political Theory (editor with Paul Lucardie), 1993; Jean-Paul Sartre and the Politics of Reason: A Theory of History, 1993; Justice and the Environment, 1998; editor, Fairness and Futurity, forthcoming. Contributions to: Numerous articles and book reviews to magazines and journals. Honours: Spanish Government Scholar, 1983-84; ERSC Postdoctoral Fellow, 1984-87. Address: Department of Politics, Keele University, Keele, Staffs ST5 5BG, England.

DOBSON Julia Lissant, (Julia Tugendhat), b. 23 Sept 1941, Tanzania. Writer. m. Christopher Tugendhat, 8 Apr 1967, 2 sons. Education: BA, Lady Margaret Hall, Oxford, 1963. Publications: The Children of Charles I, 1975; The Smallest Man in England, 1977; Mountbatten Sailor Hero, 1978; Children of the Tower, 1978; They Were at Waterloo, 1979; The Ivory Poachers: A Crisp Twins Adventure, 1981; The Tomb Robbers, 1981; The Wreck Finders, 1982; The Animal Rescuers, 1982; Danger in the Magic Kingdom, 1983; The Chinese Puzzle, 1984; As Julia Tugendhat: What Teenagers Can Tell Us About Divorce and Step Families, 1990; The Adoption Triangle, 1992. Address: 35 Westbourne Park Road, London W2, England.

DOBSON Rosemary (de Brissac), b. 18 June 1920, Sydney, New South Wales, Australia. Poet; Editor; Translator. m. A T Bolton, 1951, 2 sons, 1 daughter. Education: Frensham, Mittagong, New South Wales. Publications: In a Convex Mirror, 1944; The Ship of Ice & Other Poems, 1948; Child with a Cockatoo and Other Poems, 1955; Poems, 1963; Cock Crow, 1965; Selected Poems, 1973, revised edition, 1980; Greek Coins: A Sequence of Poems, 1977; Over the Frontier, 1978; The Three Fates and Other Poems, 1984; Collected Poems, 1991; Untold Lives: A Sequence of Poems, 1992. Honours: Patrick White Award, 1984; Officer, Order of Australia, 1987; Honorary DLitt, Sydney University, 1996; Emeritus Award, Literature Fund of the Australia Council, 1996. Memberships: Patron, ACT Writers Centre, 1996. Address: 61 Stonehaven Crescent, Deakin, Canberra, Australian Capital Territory 2600, Australia.

DOBYNS Stephen, b. 19 Feb 1941, Orange, New Jersey, USA. Professor of Creative Writing; Poet; Writer. m. 2 children. Education: Shimer College, Mount Carroll, Illinois, 1959-60; BA, Wayne State University, 1964; MFA, University of Iowa, 1967. Appointments: Instructor, State University of New York College at Brockport, 1968-69; Reporter, Detroit News, 1969-71; Visiting Writer, University of New Hampshire, 1973-75, University of Iowa, 1977-79, Boston University, 1978-79, 1980-81, Syracuse University, 1986; Faculty, Goddard College, Plainfield, Vermont, 1978-80, Warren Wilson College, Swannanoa, North Carolina, 1982-87; Professor of Creative Writing, Syracuse University, New York, 1987-. Publications: Poetry: Concurring Beasts, 1972; Griffon, 1976; Heat Death, 1980; The Balthus Poems, 1982; Black Dog, Red Dog, 1984; Cemetery Nights, 1987; Body Traffic, 1991; Velocities: New and Selected Poems, 1966-1992, 1994. Fiction: A Man of Little Evils, 1973; Saratoga Longshot, 1976; Saratoga Swimmer, 1981; Dancer with One Leg, 1983; Saratoga Headhunter, 1985; Cold Dog Soup, 1985; Saratoga Snapper, 1986; A Boat Off the Coast, 1987; The Two Deaths of Señora Puccini, 1988; Saratoga Bestiary, 1988; The House of Alexandrine, 1989; Saratoga Hexameter, 1990; After Shocks/Near Escapes, 1991; Saratoga Haunting, 1993; The Wrestler's Cruel Study, 1993; Saratoga Backtalk, 1994; Saratoga Fleshpot, 1995; Saratoga Trifecta, 1995. Honours: Lamont Poetry Selection Award, 1971; MacDowell Colony Fellowships, 1972, 1976; Yaddo Fellowships, 1972, 1973, 1977, 1981, 1982; National Endowment for the Arts Grants, 1974, 1981; Guggenheim Fellowship, 1983; National Poetry Series Prize, 1984. Address: 208 Brattle Road, Syracuse, NY 13203, USA.

DOCHERTY John. See: **SILLS-DOCHERTY Jonathon John.**

DOCTOROW E(dgar) L(awrence), b. 6 Sept 1931, New York, New York, USA. Writer; Professor of American and English Letters. m. Helen Setzer, 20 Aug 1954, 1 son, 2 daughters. Education: AB, Kenyon College, 1952; Graduate Study, Columbia University, 1952-53. Appointments: Script Reader, Columbia Pictures, 1959-59; Senior Editor, New American Library, 1960-64; Editor-in-Chief, Dial Press, 1964-69; Writer-in-Residence, University of California, Irvine, 1969-70; Member of Faculty, Sarah Lawrence College, 1971-78; Creative Writing Fellow, Yale School of Drama, 1974-75; Visiting Senior Fellow, Council on the Humanities, Princeton University, 1980; Glucksman Professor of American and English Letters, New York University, 1987-. Publications: Welcome to Hard Times, 1960; Big as Life, 1966; The Book of Daniel, 1971; Ragtime, 1975; Drinks Before Dinner (play), 1979; Loon Lake, 1980; Lives of the Poets, 1984; World's Fair, 1985; Billy Bathgate, 1989; Jack London, Hemingway and the Constitution, 1993; The Waterworks, 1994. Honours: Guggenheim Fellowship, 1973; American Academy of Arts and Letters Award, 1976, and Howells Medal, 1990; National Book Critics Circle Awards, 1976, 1989; National Book Award, 1985; PEN/Faulkner Award, 1990; National Humanities Medal, 1998. Memberships: PEN, American Center; Writers Guild of America; Authors Guild; Century Association. Literary Agent: Arlene Donovan, International Creative Management, 40 West 57th Street, New York, NY 10022, USA. Address: c/o Random House, 201 East 50th Street, New York, NY 10019, USA.

DODSON James Yarnell, b. 11 Sept 1978, Port Chester, New York, USA. College Student. Education: University of Florida. Publications: Kids' Little Instruction Book, 1997. Contributions to: Wise Workds to Kids; Kidzette. Honours: USA Today All-Academic Team, 1996; Top 20 High School Students in US Award. Literary Agent: Robert Diforio. Address: 1016 Country Club Drive, North Palm Beach, FL 33408, USA.

DODSON Steven Yarnell, b. 17 July 1981, Philadelphia, Pennsylvania, USA. Student. Education: University of Florida. Publication: Kid's Little Instruction Book, 1997. Contributions to: Kidzette. Literary Agent: Robert Diforio. Address: 1016 Country Club Drive, North Palm Beach, FL 33408, USA.

DOGRA Rajiv, b. 2 Apr 1948, India. Diplomat. m. Meenakshi Dogra, 28 Feb 1979, 1 son, 1 daughter. Education: BSc, Electrical Engineering, Institute of Technology, Varanasi, India. Appointments: Joined Indian Foreign Service, 1974; Second Secretary, Embassy of India, Stockholm, 1976-78; Under Secretary, Ministry of External Affairs, New Delhi, 1978-81; First Secretary, Embassy of India, Rome, 1981-85; Counsellor/Charge d'Affaires, Embassy of India, Doha(Qatar), 1985-88; Director, Ministry of External Affairs, New Delhi, 1988-92; Consul General of India, Karachi, Pakistan, 1992-94; Minister, High Commission of India, London, 1994-1997; Ambassador of India to Romania, 1997-. Publications: Foot Prints in Foreign Sands, 1997. Contributions to: Occasional columns for Hindustan Times, India; Short stories in magazines in India and other countries; Articles on international affairs in specialised journals. Memberships: Habitat India; United Service, Institution of India. Address: Ambassador of India, No 11, Uruguay Street, Bucharest, Romania.

DOHERTY Berlie, b. 6 Nov 1943, Liverpool, England. Writer; Dramatist; Poet. m. Gerard Doherty, 17 Dec 1966, div 1996, 1 son, 2 daughters. Education: BA, Honours, English, Durham University, 1964; Postgraduate Certificate, Social Studies, Liverpool University, 1965; Postgraduate Certificate, Education, Sheffield University, 1976. Publications: Novels: Requiem, 1991; The Vinegar Jar, 1994. Children's Books: How Green You Are, 1982; The Making of Fingers Finnigan, 1983; White Peak Farm, 1984; Children of Winter, 1985; Granny Was a Buffer Girl, 1986; Tilly Mint Tales, 1986; Tilly Mint and the Dodo, 1988; Paddiwak and Cosy, 1988; Tough Luck, 1988; Spellhorn, 1989; Dear Nobody, 1990; Snowy, 1992; Big, Bulgy, Fat Black Slug, 1993; Old Father Christmas, 1993; Street Child, 1993; Walking on Air (poetry), 1993; Willa and Old Miss Annie, 1994; The Snake-Stone, 1995; The Golden Bird, 1995; Dear Nobody (play), 1995; The Magical Bicycle, 1995; Our Field, 1996; Morgan's Field (play), 1996; Daughter of the Sea, 1996. Contributions to: Periodicals. Honours: Boston Globe-Horn Book Award, 1987. Burnley Children's Book of the Year Award, 1987; Carnegie Medals, 1987, 1991; Writer's Guild of Great Britain Children's Play Award, 1994. Membership: Arvon Foundation, Lumb Bank, chairperson, 1988-93. Address: 222 Old Brompton Road, London, England.

DOKIC Jérôme André, b. 19 Aug 1965, Fribourg, Switzerland. Researcher; Teaching Assistant. Education: Licence Lettres (BA), 1989, DES (MA), 1990, PhD, 1995, University of Geneva. Publications: La Philosophie Du Son (with R Casati); Penser en Contexte (with E Corazza), 1993; Why is Fregi's Puzzle Still Puzzling? (with E Corazza), Sense and Reference 100 Years Later, 1995. Address: Department of Philosophy, University of Geneva, 2 Rue Candolle, CH-1211 Geneva 4, Switzerland.

DOLIS John, b. 25 Apr 1945, St Louis, Missouri, USA. Professor; Writer; Poet. Education: BA, English, St Louis University, 1967; MA, English, 1969; PhD, English, 1978, Loyola University, Chicago. Appointments: Teaching Assistant, 1967-69, 1970-73, Lecturer, 1974-75, 1978-80, Loyola University, Chicago; Instructor, Columbia College, 1970-71, Northeastern Illinois University, 1978-80, University of Kansas, 1981-85; Fulbright Lecturer, University of Turin, 1980-81; Assistant Professor, 1985-92, Associate Professor, 1992-, Penn State University, Scranton; Senior Fulbright Lecturer, University of Bucharest, 1989-90; Visiting Professor of American Culture and Literature, Bilkent University, Ankara, 1995-96. Publications: The Style of Hawthorne's Gaze: Regarding Subjectivity, 1993; Bl( )nk Space, 1993. Contributions to: Articles in scholarly journals; Poems in anthologies and magazines. Honours: National Endowment for the Humanities Fellowships, 1979-88; Pharmakon Research International Award for Excellence in Scholarly Activities, Penn State University, 1991;

Various grants. Memberships: American Culture Association; American Literature Association; American Philosophical Association; Association for Applied Psychoanalysis; International Association for Philosophy and Literature; International Husserl and Phenomenological Research Society; International Society for Phenomenology and the Human Sciences; International Society for Phemomenology and Literature; Modern Language Association; Nathaniel Hawthorne Society; National Social Science Association; Society for the Advancement of American Philosophy; Society for Phenomenology and Existential Philosophy; Society for Philosophy and Psychiatry; Society for Romanian Studies; Thoreau Society; World Phenomenology Institute. Address: 711 Summit Pointe, Scranton, PA 18508, USA.

DOLL Mary Aswell, b. 4 June 1940, New York, New York, USA. Professor of English. m. William Elder Doll Jr, 25 June 1966, div 1994, 1 son (William Campbell). Education: BA, Connecticut College, New London, 1962; MA, Johns Hopkins University, 1970; PhD, Syracuse University, 1980. Appointments: Assistant Professor, State University of New York, Oswego, 1978-84; Lecturer, University of Redlands, California, 1985-88; Assistant Professor, Loyola University, 1988; Visiting Assistant Professor, Tulane University, 1988; Associate Professor, 1989-93, Professor, 1993-, Our Lady of Holy Cross College. Publications: Rites of Story: The Old Man at Play, 1987; Beckett and Myth: An Archetypal Approach, 1988; In the Shadow of the Giant: Thomas Wolfe, 1988; Walking and Rocking, 1989; Joseph Campbell and the Power of the Wilderness, 1992; Stoppard's Theatre of Unknowing, 1993; To the Lighthouse and Back, 1996. Contributions to: Periodicals. Honours: Outstanding Book Citation Choice, 1989; Sears-Roebuck Teaching Excellence Award. Memberships: Modern Language Association; Thomas Wolfe Society, board of directors; American Academy of Religion. Address: 4154 State Street Drive, New Orleans, LA 70125, USA.

DOMARADZKI Théodore Felix, (Felice), b. 27 Oct 1910, Warsaw, Poland. Retired University Professor; Writer. m. Maria Dobija, 20 Apr 1954. Education: Diploma, Political Science, Warsaw, 1933; MA, Warsaw University, 1939; LittD, Rome University, 1941. Appointments: Member, Doctoral Examination Commissions, Literature, University of Ottawa, 1950-53, University of Montreal, 1950-76; Editor-in-Chief, Slavic and East European Studies/Etudes Slaves et Est-Européennes, Montreal-Quebec, 1956-76; Director-General, Institute of Comparative Civilization, Montreal. Publications: Le Culte de la Vierge Marie et le Catholicisme de C K Norwid, 1961; La réalité du mal chez C Baudelaire et C Norwid, 1973; Les post-Romantiques polonais, 1973; Le symbolisme et l'universalisme de C K Norwid, 1974; Personalités ethniques au Québec, 1991. Contributions to: Journals and encyclopaedias. Honours: Order of Merit, Polish Literature, University of Lublin, 1969; Order of Canada, 1989; Award of Merit, Canadian Multilingual Press Federation, 1991; Order of Polonia Restituta, 1991; Commemorative Medal, Literary Society of Warsaw, 1992. Memberships: PEN Club International, Quebec Section; Société des Ecrivains Canadiens; Polish Scientific Society, London; Société Historique et Littéraire Polonaise, Paris; Honorary Life Member: Canadian Association of Slavists; Canadian Society for Comparative Study of Civilizations; Quebec Ethnic Press Association; Polish Institute of Arts and Sciences in Canada; Istituto Italiano di Cultura. Address: 60 Avenue Willowdale, Outremont (Montréal) H3T 2A3, Canada.

DONALD Brian Bernard, b. 27 Feb 1942, Edinburgh, Scotland. Retired Lecturer in English. m. Iris Rintoul, 28 Aug 1965, 1 son, 1 daughter. Education: BA, Strathclyde University, Glasgow, 1969; Master's degree, Edinburgh University, 1977. Appointments: Baker and Confectioner, 1957-62; Police Officer, 1963-64; Lecturer in English, 1970-96; Journalist, Author, 1986-. Publications: Fight Game in Scotland, 1st volume of Scottish professional boxing history, 1988; British Boxing Yearbook (contributor), 1989-92; Scottish Boxing Hall of Fame

Yearbook. Contributions to: General history, literary and cultural articles to The Scotsman, Guardian, Aberdeen Evening Express; Weekly column, Edinburgh Evening News. Membership: PEN, Scottish Branch. Address: 7 Arran Crescent, Kirkcaldy, Fife KY2 6DJ, Scotland.

DONALD David Herbert, b. 1 Oct 1920, Goodman, Mississippi, USA. Professor of History Emeritus; Author. m. Aida DiPace, 1955, 1 son. Education: AB, Millsaps College, Jackson, Mississippi, 1941; Graduate Study in History, University of North Carolina, 1942; MA, 1942, PhD, 1945, in History, University of Illinois. Appointments: Teaching Fellow, University of North Carolina, 1942; Research Assistant, 1943-45, Research Associate, 1946-47, University of Illinois; Fellow, Social Science Rsearch Council, 1945-46; Instructor, 1947-49, Assistant Professor, 1951-52, Associate Professor, 1952-57, Professor of History, 1957-59, Columbia University; Associate Professor of History, Smith College, 1949-51; Visiting Associate Professor, Amherst College, 1950; Fulbright Lecturer in American History, University College of North Wales, 1953-54; Member, Institute for Advanced Study, 1957-58; Harmsworth Professor of American History, Oxford University, 1959-60; Professor of History, Princeton University, 1959-62; Harry C Black Professor of American History and Director of the Institute of Southern History, Johns Hopkins University, 1962-73; Charles Warren Professor of American History and Professor of American Civilization, 1973-91, Professor Emeritus, 1991-, Harvard University; Walter Lynwood Fleming Lecturer, Louisiana State University, 1965; Commonwealth Lecturer, University College of London, 1975; Samuel Paley Lecturer, Hebrew University of Jerusalem, 1991. Publications: Lincoln's Herndon, 1948; Divided We Fought: A Pictorial History of the War, 1861-1865, 1952; Inside Lincoln's Cabinet: The Civil War Diaries of Salmon P Chase, 1954; Lincoln Reconsidered: Essays on the Civil War Era, 1956, revised edition, 1961; Charles Sumner and the Coming of the Civil War, 1960; Why the North Won the Civil War, 1960; The Civil War and Reconstruction (with J G Randall), 2nd edition, 1961, revised edition, 1969; The Divided Union, 1961; The Politics of Reconstruction, 1863-1867, 1965; The Nation in Crisis, 1861-1877, 1969; Charles Sumner and the Rights of Man, 1970; The South Since the War (with Sidney Andrews), 1970; Gone for a Soldier: The Civil War Memoirs of Private Alfred Bellard, 1975; The Great Republic: A History of the American People (with others), 1977, 4th edition, 1992; Liberty and Union: The Crisis of Popular Government, 1830-1890, 1978; Look Homeward: A Life of Thomas Wolfe, 1987; Lincoln, 1995. Contributions to: Scholarly journals. Honours: George A and Eliza G Howard Fellow, 1957-58; Pulitzer Prizes in Biography, 1960, 1988; Guggenheim Fellowships, 1964-65, 1985-86; American Council of Learned Societies Fellow, 1969-70; Center for Advanced Study in the Behavioral Sciences Fellow, 1969-70; National Endowment for the Humanities Fellow, 1971-72; C Hugh Holman Prize, Modern Language Association, 1988; Distinguished Alumnus Award, University of Illinois, 1988; Benjamin L C Wailes Award, Mississippi Historical Society, 1994; Lincoln Prize, 1996; Christopher Award, 1996; Distinguished Non-Fiction Award, American Library Association, 1996. Memberships: American Academy of Arts and Sciences, fellow; American Antiquarian Society; American Historical Association; Massachusetts Historical Association; Omicron Delta Kappa; Organization of American Historians; Southern Historical Association, president, 1969; Honorary doctorates. Address: 41 Lincoln Road, Po Box 6158, Lincoln, MA 01773, USA.

DONALDSON Stephen Reeder, (Reed Stephens), b. 13 May 1947, Cleveland, Ohio, USA. Writer. 1 son, 1 daughter. Education: BA, English, Wooster College, 1968; MA, Kent State University, 1971. Appointments: Associate Instructor, Ghost Ranch Writers Workshops, 1973-77; Contributing Editor, Journal of the Fantastic in the Arts. Publications: Lord Foul's Bane, 1977; The Earth War, 1977; The Power That Preserves, 1977; The Wounded Land, 1980; The One Tree, 1982; White Gold Wielder, 1983; Daughter of Regals, 1984; The Mirror of Her Dreams, 1986; A Man Rides Through, 1987; The

Real Story, 1991; Forbidden Knowledge, 1991; A Dark and Hungry God Arises, 1992; The Gap Into Madness: Chaos and Order, 1994. As Reed Stephens: The Man Who Killed His Brother, 1980; The Man Who Risked His Partner, 1984; The Man Who Tried to Get Away, 1990. Honours: Best Novel, British Fantasy Society, 1979; Best New Writer, John W Campbell, 1979; Honorary DLitt, College of Wooster, 1993. Address: c/o Howard Morhaim, 175 Fifth Avenue, New York, NY 10010, USA.

DONALDSON William, b. 19 July 1944, Fraserburgh. Teacher; Writer. m. Loraine Challis-Sowerby, 1 Apr 1970, 2 sons, 1 daughter. Education: MA, 1968, PhD, 1974, Aberdeen University. Appointments: Registrar of the North East Survey; Teacher of English; Associate Lecturer, Open University. Publications: Popular Literature in Victorian Scotland, 1986; The Jacobite Song, 1988; The Language of the People, 1989. Honours: Blackwell Prize, 1988; Scottish Arts Council Book Award, 1989. Memberships: Association for Scottish Literary Studies, secretary of schools committee. Address: c/o Tuckwell Press, The Mill House, Phantassie, East Linton EH40 3DG, England.

DONGLI Jiefu. See: ZHANG Changxin.

DONKIN Nance (Clare), b. 1915, West Maitland, New South Wales, Australia. Children's Fiction Writer; Journalist. m. Victor Donkin, 14 Jan 1939, 1 son, 1 daughter. Appointments: Journalist, Daily Mercury, Maitland, Morning Herald, Newcastle; President, Children's Book Council, Victoria, 1968-76. Publications: Araluen Adventures, 1946; No Medals For Meg, 1947; Julie Stands By, 1948; Blue Ribbon Beth, 1951; The Australian's Children's Annual, 1963; Sheep, 1967; Sugar, 1967; An Emancipist, 1968; A Currency Lass, 1969; House By the Water, 1969; An Orphan, 1970; Johnny Neptune, 1971; The Cool Man, 1974; A Friend for Petros, 1974; Margaret Catchpole, 1974; Patchwork Grandmother, 1975; Green Christmas, 1976; Yellowgum Girl, 1976; A Handful of Ghosts, 1976; The Best of the Bunch, 1978; The Maidens of Pefka, 1979; Nini, 1979; Stranger and Friend, 1983; We of the Never Retold for Children, 1983; Two at Sullivan Bay, 1985; Blackout, 1987; A Family Affair, 1988; The Women Were There, 1988; Always a Lady, 1990. Honours: Member of the Order of Austalia, 1986; Alice Award for Distinguished Contribution to Australian Literature, Society Women Writers, 1990. Memberships: Fellowship of Australian Writers; Australian Society of Authors; Society of Women Writers of Australia; Royal Historical Society; Children's Book Council; Gallery Society; National Trust; Melbourne Theatre Company. Address: 18/26 Rochester Road, Canterbury, Victoria 3126, Australia.

DONLEAVY J(ames) P(atrick), b. 23 Apr 1926, New York, New York, USA (Irish citizen, 1967). Author; Dramatist. m. (1) Valerie Heron, div, 1 son, 1 daughter, (2) Mary Wilson Price, div, 1 son, 1 daughter. Education: Trinity College, Dublin. Publications: Fiction: The Ginger Man, 1955, unexpurgated edition, 1963; A Singular Man, 1963; Meet My Maker the Mad Molecule (short stories), 1964; The Saddest Summer of Samuel S, 1966; The Beastly Beatitudes of Balthazar B, 1968; The Onion Eaters, 1971; A Fairy Tale of New York, 1973; The Destinies of Darcy Dancer, Gentleman, 1977; Schultz, 1979; Leila: Further in the Destinies of Darcy Dancer, Gentleman, 1983; Are You Listening Rabbi Löw, 1987; That Darcy, That Dancer, That Gentleman, 1990; The Lady Who Liked Clean Rest Rooms, 1996. Plays: The Ginger Man, 1961; Fairy Tales of New York, 1961; A Singular Man, 1964; The Plays of J P Donleavy, 1973; The Beastly Beatitudes of Balthazar B, 1981. Other: The Unexpurgated Code: A Complete Manual of Survival and Manners, 1975; De Alfonce Tennis: The Superlative Game of Eccentric Champions, Its History, Accoutrements, Rules, Conduct, and Regimes, 1984; J P Donleavy's Ireland: In All Her Sins and in Some of Her Graces, 1986; A Singular Country, 1989; The History of the Ginger Man, 1994; Wrong Information Is Being Given Out At Princeton. Contributions to: Periodicals. Honours: Most Promising Playwright Award, Evening Standard, 1960; Brandeis University Creative Arts Award, 1961-62;

American Academy of Arts and Letters Grant, 1975; Worldfest Houston Gold Award, 1992; Cine Golden Eagle Award, 1993. Address: Levington Park, Mullingar, County Westmeath, Ireland.

DONOGHUE Denis, b. 1928, Ireland. Writer. Appointments: Henry James Professor of English and American Letters, New York University. Publications: The Third Voice: Modern British and American Verse Drama, 1959; Conoisseurs of Chaos: Ideas of Order in Modern American Literature, 1965; An Honoured Guest: New Essays on W B Yeats (with J R Mulryne), 1965; Swift Revisited, 1968; The Ordinary Universe: Soundings in Modern Literature, 1968; Jonathan Swift: A Critical Introduction, 1969; Emily Dickinson, 1969; William Butler Yeats, 1971; Jonathan Swift: A Critical Anthology, 1971; Memoirs, by W B Yeats, 1973; Thieves of Fire, 1973; The Sovereign Ghost: Studies in Imagination, 1976; Ferocious Alphabets, 1981; The Ants Without Mystery, 1983; Being Modern Together, 1991; The Pure Good of Theory, 1992; The Old Moderns; Warrenpoint, 1993; Walter Pater: Lover of Strange Souls, 1995; The Practice of Reading, 1998. Contributions to: New York Review of Books. Address: Department of English, New York University, New York, NY 10003, USA.

DONOGHUE Emma, b. 24 Oct 1969, Dublin, Ireland. Writer. Education: BA Honours, English, French, University College, Dublin, 1990; PhD, English, University of Cambridge, 1997. Publications: Passions Between Women, history, 1993; Stir-Fry, novel, 1994; Hood, novel, 1995; Kissing the Witch, interlinked fairytales, 1997; What Sappho Would Have Said, US edition as Poems Between Women, anthology, 1997; We Are Michael Field, biography, 1998; Ladies and Gentlemen, play, 1998. Honour: American Library Association for Gay, Lesbian and Bisexual Book Award, for Hood, 1997. Membership: Authors' Society. Literary Agent: Caroline Davidson. Address: c/o Caroline Davidson, 5 Queen Anne's Gardens, London W4 1TU, England.

DONOVAN Paul James Kingsley, b. 8 Apr 1949, Sheffield, Yorkshire, England. Author; Journalist. m. Hazel Case, 27 Oct 1979, 1 son, 2 daughters. Education: MA, Oriel College, Oxford. Appointments: Reporter and TV Critic, Daily Mail, 1978-85; Showbusiness Editor and Critic, Today, 1986-88; Radio Columnist, Sunday Times, 1988-. Publications: Roger Moore, 1983; Dudley, 1988; The Radio Companion, 1991; All Our Todays, 1997. Contributions to: Newspapers including The Times, Sunday Times, Observer, Guardian; New Dictionary of National Biography. Literary Agent: John Pawsey. Address: 11 Stile Hall Gardens, London W4 3BS, England.

DOR Moshe, b. 9 Dec 1932, Tel Aviv, Israel. Poet; Journalist. m. Ziona Dor, 29 Mar 1955, 2 sons. Education: Hebrew University of Jerusalem, 1949-52; BA, Political Science, University of Tel Aviv, 1956. Appointments: Counsellor for Cultural Affairs, Embassy of Israel, London, England, 1975-77; Distinguished Writer-In-Residence, American University, Washington, DC, 1987. Publications: From the Outset, 1984; On Top of the Cliff (in Hebrew),1986; Crossing the River, 1989; From the Outset (selected poems in Dutch translation), 1989; Crossing the River (selected poems in English translation), 1989; Love and Other Calamities (poems in Hebrew), 1993; Khamsin (memoirs and poetry in English translation), 1994; The Silence of the Builder (poems in Hebrew), 1996. Other books of poetry, children's verse, literary essays, interviews with writers, translations of poetry and literature from English into Hebrew. Honours: Honourable Citation, International Hans Christian Andersen Prize for Children's Literature, 1975; Holon Prize for Literature, 1981; Prime Minister's Award for Creative Writing, 1986; Balik Prize for Literature, 1987. Memberships: Association of Hebrew Writers, Israel; National Federation of Israel Journalists; Israel Pen Centre, president, 1988-90. Address: 6623 Fairfax Road, Chevy Chase, Mary Bld, 20815, USA.

DORESKI William, b. 10 Jan 1946, Stafford, Connecticut, USA. Professor of English; Writer; Poet. m. Carole Doreski, 17 June 1981. Education: BA, 1975, MA, 1977, Goddard College; PhD, Boston University, 1983; Postdoctoral Studies, Princeton University, 1987, Dartmouth College, 1994. Appointments: Writer-in-Residence, Emerson College, 1973-75; Instructor in Humanities, Goddard College, 1975-80; Assistant Professor, 1982-87, Associate Professor, 1988-91, Professor of English, 1992-, Keene State College, New Hampshire. Publications: The Testament of Israel Potter, 1976; Half of the Map, 1980; Earth That Sings: The Poetry of Andrew Glaze, 1985; How to Read and Interpret Poetry, 1988; The Years of Our Friendship: Robert Lowell and Allen Tate, 1990 Ghost Train, 1991; The Modern Voice in American Poetry, 1995; Sublime of the North and Other POems, 1997; Pianos in the Woods, 1998; Shifting Colors: The Public and the Private in the Poetry of Robert Lowell, 1999. Contributions to: Books, journals, reviews, quarterlies, and magazines. Honours: Poet Lore Translation Prize, 1975; Black Warrior Prize, 1979; National Endowment for the Humanities Grants, 1987, 1995; Whiting Foundation Fellowship, 1988; Clay Potato Fiction Prize, 1997; Frith Press Poetry Award, 1997. Memberships: American Studies Association; Associated Writing Programs; Association of Scholars and Critics; Modern Language Association; New Hampshire Writers' Project; Robert Frost Society; Wallace Stevens Society. Address: c/o Department of English, Keene State College, Keene, NH 03435, USA.

DORET Michel, b. 5 Jan 1938, Petion-Ville, Haiti. Architect; Writer; Poet. m. Liselotte Bencze, 30 Nov 1970. Education: BA, Pace University, 1970; MA, New York University, 1972; BS, State University of New York, 1978; MPhil, 1980, PhD, 1982, George Washington University. Appointment: Founder and Director, Les Editions Amon Ra, 1982-97. Publications: Isolement, 1979; La Poésie francophone, 8 volumes, 1980; Panorama de la poésie feminine Suisse Romande, 1982; Panorama de la poésie feminine francophone, 1984; La negritude dans la poésie haitienne, 1985; Poétesses Genevoises francophones, 1985; Haiti en Poésie, 1990; Les Mamelles de Lutèce, 1991; Lyrisme du Moi, 1992; The History of the Architecture of Ayiti, 2 volumes, 1995. Contributions to: Numerous books, journals, reviews and other publications. Honours: Various medals, diplomas, and honorable mentions. Memberships: Several literary organizations. Address: 26 Mellow Lane, Westbury, NY 11590, USA.

DORFMAN Ariel, b. 6 May 1942, Buenos Aires, Argentina (Chilean citizen). Research Professor of Literature and Latin; Author; Dramatist; Poet. Education: Graduated, University of Chile, Santiago, 1967. Appointment: Walter Hines Page Research Professor of Literature and Latin, Center for International Studies, Duke University, Durham, North Carolina, 1984-. Publications: Fiction: Hard Rain, 1973; My House is On Fire, 1979; Widows, 1983; Dorando la pildora, 1985; Travesia, 1986; The Last Song of Manuel Sendero, 1986; Mascara, 1988; Konfidenz, 1996. Poetry: Last Waltz in Santiago and Other Poems of Exile and Disappearance, 1988. Plays: Widows, 1988; Death and the Maiden, 1991; Reader, 1992; Who's Who (with Rodrigo Dorfman), 1997. Films: Death and the Maiden, 1994; Prisoners in Time, 1995; My House is on Fire, 1997. Non-Fiction: How to Read Donald Duck (with Armand Mattelart), 1971; The Empire's Old Clothes, 1983; Some Write to the Future, 1991; Heading South, Looking North: A Bilingual Journey, 1998. Honours: Olivier Award, London 1991; Time Out Award, 1991; Literary Lion, New York Public Library, 1992; Dora Award, 1994; Charity Randall Citation, International Poetry Forum, 1994; Best Film for Television, Writers Guild of Great Britain, 1996. Address: c/o Center for International Studies, Duke University, Durham, NC 27708, USA.

DORJI Chen-Kyo Tshering (City), b. 11 June 1949, Uma, Bhutan. Civil Servant; Academician; Historian. m. Sangay Xam, 4 sons, 5 daughters. Education: MA; PhD, Magadh University, India; Studied, London School of Economics and Political Science. Appointments: Bhutan Civil Service, 1968; Joint Director and Registrar, Royal Institute of Management, Thimphu. Publications: The Development of Road Transport Communication in Bhutan, 1973; A Historical Analysis of Civil Service Training in SAARC Member Countries, 1992; The Guarantee of Buddhism in Bhutan, 1993; An Introduction to Modern Bhutanese Administrative System, 1994; History of Bhutan Based on Buddhism, 1994; A Political and Religious History of Bhutan (1651-1907), 1995; An Introduction to Bhutanese Languages, 1996; Blue Annals of Bhutan, 1996; A Brief History of Bhutan, 1996. Contributions to: Professional journals. Address: Post Box No 417, Thimphu, Bhutan.

DORMAN Michael L, b. 9 Oct 1932, New York, New York, USA. Writer. m. Jeanne Darrin O'Brien, 25 June 1955, 2 daughters. Education: BS, Journalism, New York University, 1953. Appointments: Correspondent, New York Times, 1952-53; Reporter, Editor, Houston Press, 1953-58; Newsday, Long Island, New York, 1959-64; Freelance Writer, 1965-. Publications: We Shall Overcome, 1964; The Secret Service Story, 1967; King of the Courtroom, 1969; The Second Man, 1969; Under 21, 1970; Payoff: The Role of Organized Crime in American Politics, 1972; The Making of a Slum, 1972; Confrontation: Politics and Protest, 1974; Vesco: The Infernal Money-Making Machine, 1975; The George Wallace Myth, 1976; Witch Hunt, 1976; Detectives of the Sky, 1976; Dirty Politics, 1979; Blood and Revenge, 1991. Contributions to: Periodicals. Address: 7 Lauren Avenue South, Dix Hills, NY 11746, USA.

DORN Ed(ward Merton), b. 2 Apr 1929, Villa Grove, Illinois, USA. Poet; Writer; Translator; Anthropologist; Ethnologist; Professor. m. Jennifer Dunbar, 1969. Education: University of Illinois at Urbana-Champaign, 1949-50; BA, Black Mountain College, 1954. Appointments: Lecturer, Idaho State University, Pocatello, 1961-65; Co-Editor, Wild Dog, Pocatello, 1964-65; Visiting Professor, University of Kansas, Lawrence, 1968-69; Fulbright Lecturer in American Literature, Member English Department, 1969-70, 1974-75, University of Essex, Colchester, England; Regent's Lecturer, University of California at Riverside, 1973-74; Writer-in-Residence, University of California at San Diego, La Jolla, 1976; Professor, University of Colorado at Boulder, 1977-. Publications: Poetry: The Newly Fallen, 1961; Hands Up!, 1964; From Gloucester Out, 1964; Idaho Out, 1965; Geography, 1965; The North Atlantic Turbine, 1967; Gunslinger I, 1968, II, 1969; The Midwest Is That Space Between the Buffalo Statler and the Lawrence Eldridge, 1969; The Cosmology of Finding Your Spot, 1969; Twenty-Four Love Songs, 1969; Songs: Set Two, A Short Count, 1970; Spectrum Breakdown: A Microbook, 1971; By the Sound, 1971; The Cycle, 1971; A Poem Called Alexander Hamilton, 1971; The Hamadyas Baboon at the Lincoln Park Zoo, 1972; Gunslinger, Book III: The Winterbook, Prologue to the Great Book IV Kornerstone, 1972; Recollections of Gran Apacheria, 1974; Manchester Square, (with Jennifer Dunbar), 1975; Collected Poems: 1956-1974, 1975; Hello, La Jolla, 1978; Selected Poems, 1978; Abhorrences, 1989. Fiction: Some Business Recently Transacted in the White World (short stories), 1971. Non-Fiction: What I See in the Maximum Poems, 1960; Prose 1 (with Michail Rumaker and Warren Tallamn), 1964; The Rites of Passage: A Brief History, 1965; The Shoshoneans: The People of the Basin-Plateau, 1966; Way West: Essays and Verse Accounts 1963-1993, 1993. Translations: Our Word: Guerilla Poems From Latin America (with Gordon Brotherston), 1968; Tree Between Two Walls (with Gordon Brotherston), 1969; Selected Poems of Cesar Vallejo, 1976. Honours: D H Lawrence Fellow, 1969. Address: 1035 Mapleton, Boulder, CO 80302, USA.

DORNER Majorie, b. 21 Jan 1942, Luxembourg, Wisconsin, USA. Professor of English Literature; Writer; 2 daughters. Education: BA, English, St Norbert College, 1964; MA, English, Marquette University, 1965; PhD, English, Purdue University, 1971. Appointment: Professor of English Literature, Winona State University, Minnesota, 1971-. Publications: Nightmare, 1987; Family Closets, 1989; Freeze Frame, 1990; Winter Roads, Summer Fields, 1992; Blood Kin, 1992. Contributions to: Various publications. Honours: Minnesota Book Awards, 1991, 1993. Address: 777 West Broadway, Winona, MN 55987, USA.

DORR James Suhrer, b. 12 Aug 1941, Pensacola, Florida, USA. Writer; Poet. m. Ruth Michelle Clark, 1975, div 1982. Education: BS, Massachusetts Institute of Technology, 1964; MA, Indiana University, 1968. Appointments: Technical Writer, Editor, Wrubel Computing Center, Bloomington, Indiana, 1969-81; Writer, Marketing Consultant, The Stackworks, 1982; Associate Editor, Bloomington Area Magazine, 1983-86; Freelance Writer, 1982-. Publications: Towers of Darkness (poetry), 1990; Borderlands II, 1991; Grails, 1992; Dark Destiny I and II, 1994-95; Dante's Disciples, 1996; Darkside: Horror for the Next Millennium, 1996; Dark Tyrants, 1997; Gothic Ghosts, 1997; Asylums and Labyrinths, 1997; The Best of Cemetery Dance, 1998; New Mythos Legends, 1999. Contributions to: Anthologies, periodicals, journals, reviews, magazines, quarterlies, and newspapers. Honours include: Rhysling Honorary Mention, 1993, 1995, 1996; Darrell Nominee, 1998. Memberships: Science Fiction and Fantasy Writers of America; Horror Writers Association; Science Fiction Poetry Association; Short Mystery Fiction society. Address: 1404 East Atwater, Bloomington, IN 47401, USA.

DORSETT Danielle. See: **DANIELS Dorothy.**

DORST Tankred, b. 19 Dec 1925, Oberlind, Thuringia. Germany. Dramatist; Writer. Education: German Language and Literature, Dramaturgy, and History of Art, Bamberg and University of Munich. Publications: Gesellschaft im Herbst, 1961; Die Kurve, 1962; Freiheit für Clemens, 1962; Grosse Schmährede an der Stadtmauer, 1962; Toller, 1968; Sang: Ein Szenarium, 1971; Eiszeit, 1973; Auf dem Chimborazo, 1974; Dorothea Merz, 1976; Klaras Mutter, 1978; Die Villa, 1980; Mosch, 1980; Heinrich oder die Schmerzen der Phantasie, 1981; Merlin oder Das wüste Land, 1981; Eisenhaus, 1983; Ich, Feuerbach, 1986; Korbes, 1988; Parzival, 1989; Herr Paul, 1994. Honours: Gerhart Hauptmann Prize, 1964; Co-Winner, Prize of the City of Florence, 1970; Carl Zuckmayer Award, Rhineland-Palatinate, 1987; Buchner Prize, 1990; Prize of the German Centre of the International Theatre Institute, Berlin, 1994; Heinrich Heine Society Prize, 1994; Co-Winner, Drama Prize of the Goethe Institute, 1994; Munchen leuchtet Award in Gold, 1995. Memberships: Bavarian Academy of Fine Arts, Munich; Deutsche Akademie für Sprache und Dichtung e.V., Darmstadt; PEN Club. Address: Schleissheimerstrasse 218, D-80809 Munich, Germany.

DOTY Mark, b. 10 Aug 1953, Maryville, Tennessee, USA. Writer; Poet; Professor. Education: BA, Drake University, 1978; MFA, Goddard College, 1980. Appointments: Faculty, MFA Writing Program, Vermont College, 1981-94, Writing and Literature, Goddard College, 1985-90; Guest Faculty, Sarah Lawrence College, 1990-94, 1996; Fannie Hurst Visiting Professor, Brandeis University, 1994; Visiting Faculty, University of Iowa, 1995, 1996, Columbia University, 1996; Professor, Creative Writing Program, University of Utah, 1997-. Publications: Turtle, Swan, 1987; Bethlehem in Broad Daylight, 1991; My Alexandria, 1993; Atlantis, 1995; Heaven's Coast (memoir), 1996. Contributions to: Many anthologies and journals. Honours: Theodore Roethke Prize, 1986; National Endowment for the Arts Fellowships in Poetry, 1987, 1995; Pushcart Prizes, 1987, 1989; Los Angeles Times Book Prize, 1993; Ingram Merrill Foundation Award, 1994; National Book Critics Circle Award, 1994; Guggenheim Fellowship, 1994; Whiting Writers Award, 1994; Rockefeller Foundation Fellowship, Bellagio, Italy, 1995; New York Times Notable Book of the Year, citations, 1995, 1996; American Library Association Notable Book of the Year, 1995; T S Eliot Prize, 1996; Bingham Poetry Prize, 1996; Ambassador Book Award, 1996; Lambda Literary Award, 1996. Address: c/o Creative Writing Program, University of Utah, Salt Lake City, UT 84112, USA.

DOUBTFIRE Dianne Joan, b. 18 Oct 1918, Leeds, Yorkshire, England. Author. m. Stanley Doubtfire, 1946, 1 son. Education: Diploma, Slade School of Fine Art, 1941; ATD, Institute of Education, University of London, 1947. Appointments: Lecturer, Creative Writing, Isle of Wight County Council Adult Education, 1965-85, University of Surrey, 1986-. Publications: Lust for Innocence, 1960; Reason for Violence, 1961; Kick a Tin Can, 1964; The Flesh is Strong, 1966; Behind the Screen, 1969; Escape on Monday, 1970; This Jim, 1974; Girl in Cotton Wool, 1975; A Girl Called Rosemary, 1977; Sky Girl, 1978; The Craft of Novel Writing, 1978; Girl in a Gondola, 1980; Sky Lovers, 1981; Teach Yourself Creative Writing, 1983, revised edition, 1996; The Wrong Face, 1985; Overcoming Shyness, 1988; Getting Along With People, 1990. Contributions to: Radio Times; Guardian; Homes and Gardens; Writers' Monthly; Vogue. Memberships: Society of Authors; PEN English Centre. Literary Agent: Curtis Brown Ltd. Address: April Cottage, Beech Hill, Headley Down, Hampshire GU35, 8EQ, England.

DOUGALL Robert Neill, b. 27 Nov 1913, Croydon, England. Retired BBC TV Newscaster; Writer. m. N A Byam, 7 June 1947, 1 son, 1 stepdaughter. Publications: In and Out of the Box, 1973; A Celebration of Birds, 1978; Now for the Good News, 1976; British Birds, 1983; Years Ahead, 1984; Birdwatch Round Britain, 1985. Contributions to: Periodicals. Honour: Member of the Order of the British Empire, 1965. Memberships: Garrick Club; Royal Society for the Protection of Birds, president 1970-75. Address: Kendal House, 62 New Street, Woodbridge, Suffolk IP12 1DX, England.

DOUGHTY Louise, b. 4 Sept 1963, Melton Mobray, England. Novelist; Playwright. Education: BA Hons, English Literature, Leeds University, 1981-84; MA, Creative Writing, University of East Anglia, 1986-87. Publications: Novels: Crazy Paving, 1995; Dance With Me, 1996; Honey-Dew, 1998; Radio Plays: Maybe, 1991; The Koala Bear Joke, 1994; Nightworkers, 1999. Honours: Radio Times Drama Award, 1991; Ian St James Award, 1991. Membership: Writers Guild, 1998-. Literary Agent: Merric Davidson. Address: c/o Merric Davidson Literary Agency, 12 Priors Heath, Goudhust, Kent TN17 2RG, England.

DOVE Rita (Frances), b. 28 Aug 1952, Akron, Ohio, USA. Poet; Writer; Professor. m. Fred Viebahn, 23 Mar 1979, 1 daughter. Education: BA, summa cum laude, Miami University, Oxford, Ohio, 1973; Postgraduate studies, University of Tübingen, 1974-75; MFA, University of Iowa, 1977. Appointments: Assistant Professor, 1981-84, Associate Professor, 1984-87, Professor of English, 1987-89, Arizona State University, Tempe; Writer-in-Residence, Tuskagee Institute, 1982; Associate Editor, Callaloo, 1986-; Advisor and Contributing Editor, Gettysburg Review, 1987-, TriQuarterly, 1988-, Georgia Review, 1994, Bellingham Review, 1996-; Professor of English, 1989-93, Commonwealth Professor, 1993-, University of Virginia; Poet Laureate of the USA, 1993-95. Publications: Poetry: Ten Poems, 1977; The Only Dark Spot in the Sky, 1980; The Yellow House on the Corner, 1980; Mandolin, 1982; Museum, 1983; Thomas and Beulah, 1986; The Other Side of the House, 1988; Grace Notes, 1989; Selected Poems, 1993; Lady Freedom Among Us, 1994; Mother Love, 1995; On the Bus with Rosa Parks (poems), 1999. Other: Fifth Sunday (short stories), 1985; Through the Ivory Gate (novel), 1992; The Darker Face of Earth (verse play), 1994; The Poet's World (essays), 1995. Contributions to: Numerous magazines and journals. Honours: Fulbright Fellow, 1974-75; National Endowment for the Arts Grants, 1978, 1989; Portia Pittman Fellow, Tuskegee Institute, 1982; Guggenheim Fellowship, 1983-84; Peter I B Lavan Younger Poets Award, Academy of American Poets, 1986; Pulitzer Prize in Poetry, 1987; General Electric Foundation Award for Younger Writers, 1987; Rockefeller Foundation Residency, Bellagio, Italy, 1988; Ohio Governor's Award, 1988; Mellon Fellow, National Humanities Center, 1988-89; Fellow, Center for Advanced Studies, University of Virginia, 1989-92; NAACP Great American Artist Award, 1993; Renaissance

Forum Award, Folger Shakespeare Library, 1994; Charles Frankel Prize, 1996; National Medal in the Humanities, 1996; Heinz Award in the Arts and Humanities, 1996; Sara Lee Frontrunner Award, 1997; Barnes and Noble writers for Writers Award, 1997; Levinson Prize, 1998; Phi Beta Kappa; Many honorary doctorates. Memberships: Academy of American Poets; Associated Writing Programs; Poetry Society of America; Poets and Writers. Address: Department of English, Bryan Hall, University of Virginia, Charlottesville, VA 22903, USA.

DOVRING Karin Elsa Ingeborg, b. 5 Dec 1919, Stenstorp, Sweden (US citizen, 1968). Writer; Poet; Dramatist. m. Folke Dovring, 30 May 1943. Education: Graduated, College of Commerce, Göteborg, 1936; MA, 1943, PhD, 1951, Lund University; PhilLic, Göteborg University, 1947. Appointments: Journalist, 1940-60; Research Associate, Harold D Lasswell, Yale University, 1953-78, University of Illinois at Urbana-Champaign, 1968-69; Visiting Lecturer, many universities and colleges. Publications: Songs of Zion, 1951; Road of Propaganda, 1959; Land Reform as a Propaganda Theme, 3rd edition, 1965; Optional Society, 1972; Frontiers of Communication, 1975; No Parking This Side of Heaven (short stories), 1982; Harold D Lassell: His Communication with a Future, 1987, 2nd edition, 1988; Heart in Escrow (novel), 1990; Faces in a Mirror (poems), 1995; Shadows on a Screen (poems), 1996; Whispers on a Stage (poems), 1996; English as Lingua Franca, 1997; Invoices in a Drama (poems), 1998. Other: Film and television plays. Contributions to: Anthologies and professional journals. Honour: International Poetry Hall of Fame, 1996. Memberships: International Society of Poets; The Poetry Guild, New York, 1998. Address: 613 West Vermont Avenue, Urbana, IL 61801, USA.

DOWLING Basil Cairns, b. 29 Apr 1910, Southbridge, Canterbury, New Zealand. Retired English Master; Poet. m. Margaret Wilson, 11 June 1938, 1 son, 2 daughters. Education: St Andrew's College, Christchurch, New Zealand; MA, Canterbury University College, Christchurch, 1933; Library Diploma, Wellington University, 1946. Appointments: Reference Librarian, 1947-49, Deputy Librarian, 1950-51, Otago University; Assistant Master, Downside School, Surrey, England, 1952-54; Assistant Master, 1954-75, Head, English Department, 1965-75, Raine's Foundation School, London. Publications: A Day's Journey, 1941; Signs and Wonders, 1944; Canterbury and Other Poems, 1949; Hatherley: Recollective Lyrics, 1968; A Little Gallery of Characters, 1971; Bedlam: A Mid-Century Satire, 1972; The Unreturning Native, 1973; The Stream: A Reverie of Boyhood, 1979; Windfalls, 1983. Contributions to: Periodicals. Honour: Jessie Mackay Memorial Award, 1961. Membership: International PEN. Address: 12 Mill Road, Rye, East Sussex, TN31 7NN, England.

DOWNER Lesley Ann, b. 9 May 1949, London, England. Writer; Journalist; Broadcaster. Education: St Anne's College, Oxford, 1968-71; BA Honours, MA, English Language and Literature, Oxford University; MA, Area Studies, South Asia, School of Oriental and African Studies, University of London, 1974. Publications: Step-by-Step Japanese Cooking, 1986; Japanese Vegetarian Cookery, 1986; Economist Business Traveller's Guide to Japan (consultant editor, co-author), 1986; On the Narrow Road to the Deep North, 1989; A Taste of Japan, 1991; The Brothers: The Saga of the Richest Family in Japan, 1994; Hard Currency in Amazonian, the Penguin Book of New Travel Writing, editors, Dea Burkett and Sara Wheeler, 1998. Contributions to: Independent; Financial Times; Observer; Sunday Times Magazine; Telegraph Magazine; New York Times Magazine; Wall Street Journal Europe; Fortune Magazine. Honour: Glenfiddich Food Book of the Year, 1986; Shortlisted for Thomas Cook Travel Book of the Year, 1990. Memberships: Society of Authors; Groucho Club; PEN; Women in Journalism. Literary Agent: Gill Coleridge. Address: 40 Beresford Road, London N5 2HZ, England.

DOWNES David Anthony, b. 17 Aug 1927, Victor, Colorado, USA. Professor of English Emeritus; Writer. m. Audrey Romaine Ernst, 7 Sep 1949, 1 son, 3 daughters. Education: BA, cum laude, Regis University, 1949; MA, Marquette University, 1950; PhD, University of Washington, 1956. Appointments: Assistant Professor, Professor, Chairman of Department, University of Seattle, 1953-68; Professor of English, Dean of Humanities and Fine Arts, 1968-72, Director of Educational Development Projects, 1972-73, Director of Humanities Programme, 1973-74, Director of Graduate English Studies, 1975-78, Chairman of Department, 1978-84, Professor Emeritus, 1991, California State University, Chico; Consultant Cowles Rare Book Library, Gonzaga University, 1997. Publications: Gerard Manley Hopkins: A Study of His Ignatian Spirit, 1959; Victorian Portraits: Hopkins and Pater, 1965; Pater, Kingsley and Newman, 1972; The Great Sacrifice: Studies in Hopkins, 1983; Ruskin's Landscape of Beatitude, 1984; Hopkins' Sanctifying Imagination, 1985; The Ignatian Personality of Gerard Manley Hopkins, 1990; Hopkins' Achieved Self, 1996. Contributions to: Scholarly books and journals. Honours: Exceptional Merit Awards for Scholarship, 1984, 1988, 1990, 1992; Honorary Doctor of laws, Gonzaga University, 1997. Address: 1076 San Ramon Drive, Chico, CA 95973, USA.

DOWNES Mary Raby, (Jayne Noble), b. 31 May 1920, Calcutta, India. Writer; Poet. m. (1)Henry May Poade Ashby , 25 Nov 1942, dec, (2) Eric Mytton Downes, 28 Dec 1963, dec, 2 daughters. Education: Countryside Conservation Course, Department of Continuing Education, University of Oxford, 1990-91. Appointment: Village Correspondent, Andover Midweek Advertiser. Publications: Loving is Living, 1965; Out of Evil, novel, 1975; Emma's Family Pony Delight, 1992. Contributions to: Contributions to: Various publications. Honour: 1st Prize, National Newspaper Competition. Memberships: PEN; Society of Authors; College of Psychic Studies; National Federation of Spiritual Healers; BHS, Dressage Group; Danebury Riding Club; Overseas League; Poetry Society; Mike Shields Poetry Society. Address: Wheat Cottage, Barton Stacey, Winchester, Hants SO21 3RS, England.

DOWNIE Leonard, b. 1 May 1942, Cleveland, Ohio, USA. Newpaper Editor; Author. m. (1) Barbara Lindsey, 1960, div 1971, (2) Geraldine Rebach, 1971, 3 sons, 1 daughter, div 1997, (3) Janice Galin, 1997. Education: MA, Ohio State University. Appointments: Reporter, Editor, 1964-74, Metropolitan Editor, 1974-79, London Correspondent, 1979-82, National Editor, 1982-84, Managing Editor, 1984-91, Executive Editor, 1991-, Washington Post. Publications: Justice Denied, 1971; Mortgage on America, 1974; The New Muckrakers, 1976. Membership: American Society of Newspaper Editors. Address: Washington Post, 1150 15th Street North West, Washington, DC 20071, USA.

DOWNIE Mary Alice Dawe (nee Hunter), b. 12 Feb 1934, Alton, Illinois, USA. Writer; Poet. m. John Downie, 27 June 1959, 3 daughters. Education: BA, Honours, English Language and Literature, Trinity College, University of Toronto. Appointment: Book Review Editor, Kingston Whig-Standard, 1973-78. Publications: The Wind Has Wings: Poems from Canada (with Barbara Robertson), 1968; Scared Sarah, 1974; Dragon on Parade, 1974; The Last Ship, 1980; Jenny Greenteeth, 1981; A Proper Acadian (with George Rawlyk), 1982; The Wicked Fairy-Wife, 1983; Alison's Ghost (with John Downie), 1984; Stones and Cones (with Jillian Gilliland), 1984; The Window of Dreams: New Canadian Writing for Children, 1986; The Well-Filled Cupboard (with Barbara Robertson), 1987; How the Devil Got His Cat, 1988; The Buffalo Boy and the Weaver Girl, 1989; Doctor Dwarf and Other Poems for Children, 1990; Cathal the Giant-Killer and the Dun Shaggy Filly, 1991; Written in Stone: A Kingston Reader (with M A Thompson), 1993; The Cat Park, 1993; Snow Paws, 1996. Contributions to: Hornbook Magazine; Pittsburgh Press; Kingston Whig-Standard; Ottawa Citizen; Globe and Mail; United Church Observer; OWL Magazine; Chickadee; Crackers.

Memberships: Writers Union of Canada; PEN. Address: 190 Union Street, Kingston, Ontario K7L 2P6, Canada.

DOWNING Angela, b. 28 Sept 1933, Liverpool, England. Professor of English. m. Enrique Hidalgo, 22 Aug 1959, 2 sons, 3 daughters. Education: BA, Modern Languages, 1956, MA, 1962, University of Oxford; Licenciatura in English Philology, 1973; PhD, 1976, Universidad Complutense de Madrid. Appointments: Professor of English, Universidad Complutense, Madrid, Spain; Editor, Estudios Ingleses de la Universidas Complutense, 1991. Publications: La metáfora gramatical de M A K Halliday y su motivación funcional en el discurso, 1991; An Alternative Approach to Theme: A Systemic Functional Perspective, 1991; A University Course in English Grammar (with Philip Locke), 1992. Honours: Mary Ewart Scholar, Somerville College, Oxford, 1952-55; Duke of Edinburgh's Award, 1992. Memberships: Philological Society; European Society for the Study of English; Sociedad Española de Linguistica; Asociación Española de Linguistica Aplicada; Asociación Española de Estudios Ingleses Medievales; International Association of University Professors of English. Address: Arascues 43, 28023 Madrid, Spain.

DOYLE Charles Desmond, (Mike Doyle), b. 18 Oct 1928, Birmingham, England. Professor Emeritus of English; Author; Poet. m. (1) Doran Ross Smithells, 1959, div, (2) Rita Jean Brown, 1992, 3 sons, 1 daughter. Education: Diploma of Teaching, 1956, BA, 1957, MA, 1959, University of New Zealand; PhD, University of Auckland, 1968. Appointments: Associate Professor, 1968-76, Professor of English, 1976-93, Professor Emeritus, 1993-, University of Victoria, British Columbia, Canada. Publications: A Splinter of Glass, 1956; The Night Shift: Poems on Aspects of Love (with others), 1957; Distances, 1963; Messages for Herod, 1965; A Sense of Place, 1965; Quorum-Noah, 1970; Abandoned Sofa, 1971; Earth Meditations, 1971; Earthshot, 1972; Preparing for the Ark, 1973; Pines (with P K Irwin), 1975; Stonedancer, 1976; A Month Away from Home, 1980; A Steady Hand, 1982; The Urge to Raise Hats, 1989; Separate Fidelities, 1991; Intimate Absences: Selected Poems 1954-1992, 1993; Trout Spawning at the Lardeau River, 1997. Non-Fiction: James K Baxter, 1976; William Carlos Williams and the American Poem, 1982; William Carlos Williams: The Critical Heritage (editor), 1982; The New Reality (co-editor), 1984; Wallace Stevens: The Critical Heritage (editor), 1985; Richard Aldington: A Biography, 1989; Richard Aldington: Reappraisals (editor), 1990. Contributions to: Journals, reviews, and periodicals. Honours: UNESCO Creative Arts Fellowships, 1958-59; ACLS Fellowship, 1967-68. Memberships: New Canterbury Literary Society; Writers Union of Canada. Address: 641 Oliver Street, Victoria, British Columbia V8S 4W2, Canada.

DOYLE Roddy, b. 1958, Dublin, Ireland. Novelist; Playwright; Screenwriter. m. Belinda, 2 sons. Appointments: Lecturer at universities. Publications: Novels: The Commitments, 1988; The Snapper, 1990; The Van, 1991; Paddy Clarke Ha Ha Ha, 1993; The Woman Who Walked into Doors, 1996. Plays: Brown Bread, 1992; USA, 1992. Screenplays: The Commitments (with Dick Clement and Ian La Frenais), 1991; The Snapper, 1993. Honours: Shortlisted, 1991, Recipient, 1993, Booker Prize; People's Choice Award, Best Film, Toronto Film Festival. Literary Agent: Secker & Warburg. Address: c/o Patti Kelly, Viking Books, 375 Hudson Street, New York, NY 10014, USA.

DOZOIS Gardner R(aymond), b. 23 July 1947, Salam, Massachusetts, USA. Writer; Editor. Appointments: Reader, Dell and Award Publishers, Galaxy, If, Worlds of Fantasy, Worlds of Tomorrow, 1970-73; Co-Founder and Associate Editor, 1976-77, Editor, 1985-, Isaac Asimov's Science Fiction Magazine. Publications: A Day in the Life, 1972; Beyond the Golden Age: Nightmare Blue (with George Alec Effinger), 1975; Future Power (with Jack Dann), 1976; Another World (juvenile), 1977; The Visible Man (short stories), 1977; The Fiction of James Tiptree, Jr, 1977; Best Science Fiction Stories of the Year 6-9, 4 volumes, 1977-80; Strangers, 1978; Aliens! (with Jack

Dann), 1980; The Year's Best Science Fiction (with Jim Frankell) 1984; Modern Classics of Science Fiction (editor), 1991; Isaac Asimov's Science Fiction Lite (editor), 1993. Address: 401 Quince Street, Philadelphia, PA 19147, USA.

DRABBLE Margaret, b. 5 June 1939, Sheffield, England. Author; Biographer; Editor. m. (1) Clive Walter Swift, 1960, div 1975, 2 sons, 1 daughter, (2) Michael Holroyd, 1982. Education: BA, Newnham College, Cambridge, 1960. Publications: Novels: A Summer Bird-Cage, 1963; The Garrick Year, 1964; The Millstone, 1965; Jerusalem the Golden, 1967; The Waterfall, 1969; The Needle's Eye, 1972; The Realms of Gold, 1975; The Ice Age, 1977; The Middle Ground, 1980; The Radiant Way, 1987; A Natural Curiosity, 1989; The Gates of Ivory, 1991; The Witch of Exmoor, 1996. Dramatic: Laura (television play), 1964; Isadora (screenplay), 1968; Thank You All Very Much (screenplay), 1969; Bird of Paradise (play), 1969. Non-fiction: Wordsworth, 1966; Arnold Bennett, 1974; The Genius of Thomas Hardy (editor), 1976; For Queen and Country: Britain in the Victorian Age, 1978; A Writer's Britain: Landscape and Literature, 1979; The Oxford Companion to English Literature (editor), 5th edition 1985, revised edition, 1995; The Concise Oxford Companion to English Literature (editor with Jenny Stringer), 1987; Angus Wilson: A Biography, 1995. Honours: John Llewelyn Rhys Memorial Award, 1966; James Tait Black Memorial Book Prize, 1968; Book of the Year Award, Yorkshire Post, 1972; E M Forster Award, American Academy and Institute of Arts and Literature, 1973; Honorary Doctorates, Universities of Sheffield, 1976, Manchester, 1987, Bradford, 1988, Keele, 1988, Hull, 1992, East Anglia, 1994 and York, 1995; Commander of the Order of the British Empire, 1980. Membership: National Book League, chairperson, 1980-82. Address: c/o A D Peters, Fifth Floor, The Chambers, Chelsea Harbour, Lots Road, London, SW10 0XF, England.

DRACKETT Phil(ip Arthur), (Paul King), b. 25 Dec 1922, Finchley, Middlesex, England. Writer; Broadcaster. m. Joan Isobel Davies, 19 June 1948. Education: Woodhouse School, 1934-39; Junior County Award, Cambridge University; General Schools, London University. Publications include: You and Your Car, 1957; Great Moments in Motoring, 1958; Automobiles Work Like This, 1958; Like Father Like Son, 1969; Rally of the Forests, 1970; The Classic Mercedes-Benz, 1984; Flashing Blades, 1988; They Call it Courage: The Story of the Segrave Trophy, 1990; Benetton and Ford: A Racing Partnership, 1991; Vendetta on Ice, 1992; Just Another Incident, 1994; Total Ice Hockey Encyclopedia (contributor), 1998. Contributions to: Newspapers and magazines. Memberships: Sports Writers Association; Guild of Motoring Writers; British Ice Hockey Writers Association; Friends of Mundesley Library. Address: 9 Victoria Road, Mundesley, Norfolk NR11 8RG, England.

DRAGONWAGON Crescent, b. 25 Nov 1952, New York, New York, USA. Writer. m. Ned Shank, 20 Oct 1978. Publications: Always, Always, 1984; The Year it Rained, 1985; The Dairy Hollow House Cookbook, 1986; Half a Moon and One Whole Star, 1986; Alligator Arrived with Apples: A Thanksgiving Potluck Alphabet, 1987; Margaret Zeigler, 1988; This is the Bread I Baked for Ned, 1988; Home Place, 1990; The Itch Book, 1990; Winter Holding Spring, 1990; Dairy Hollow House Soup and Bread: A Country Inn Cookbook, 1992; Annie Flies the Birthday Bike, 1993; Alligators and Others, All Year Long: A Book of Months, 1993; Brass Button, 1997; Bat in the Dining Room, 1997. Contributions: Mode Magazine. Honours: Porter Fund Prize for Literary Excellence, 1991; William Allen White Children's Book Award Master List, 1992-93; Neumans Own Professional Category, 1997. Memberships: Author's Guild; Society of Children's Book Writers; IACP; Professional Society of Innkeepers International; The Eureka Group. Literary Agent: Edite Kroll. Address: Route 4 Box 1, Eureka Springs, AR 72632, USA.

DRAKE Albert Dee, b. 26 Mar 1935, Portland, Oregon, USA. Professor; Writer. div. 1 son, 2 daughters.

Education: Portland State College, 1956-59; BA, Englaish, 1962, MFA, English, 1966, University of Oregon. Appointments: Research Assistant, 1965, Teaching Assistant, 1965-66, University of Oregon; Assistant Professor, 1966-70, Associate Professor, 1970-79, Professor, 1979-, Michigan State University, East Lansing. Publications: Michigan Signatures (editor), 1968; Riding Bike, 1973; Roadsalt, 1975; Returning to Oregon, 1975; The Postcard Mysteries, 1976; Tillamook Burn, 1977; In the Time of Surveys, 1978; One Summer, 1979; Garage, 1980; Beyond the Pavement, 1981; The Big Little GTO Book, 1982; Street Was Fun in '51, 1982; I Remember the Day That James Dean Died, 1983; Homesick, 1988; Herding Goats, 1989. Contributions to: Numerous periodicals. Honours: 1st Ernest Haycox Fiction Award, 1962; National Endownment for the Arts Grants, 1974-75, 1983-84; 1st Prize, Writer's Digest Fiction Contest, 1979; Michigan Council for the Arts Grant, 1982. Address: Department of English, Michigan State University, East Lansing, MI 48824, USA.

DRAPER Alfred Ernest, b. 26 Oct 1924, London, England. Author. m. Barbara Pilcher, 31 Mar 1951, 2 sons. Education: North West London Polytechnic. Publications: Swansong for a Rare Bird, 1969; The Death Penalty, 1972 (made into a French Film); Smoke Without Fire, 1974; The Prince of Wales, 1975; The Story of the Goons, 1976; Operation Fish, 1978; Amritsar, 1979; Grey Seal, 1981; Grey Seal: The Restless Waves, 1983; The Raging of the Deep, 1985; Storm over Singapore, 1986; The Con Man, 1987; Dawns Like Thunder, 1987; The Great Avenging Day, 1989; A Crimson Splendour, 1991; Operation Midas, 1993. Contributions to: Numerous periodicals. Memberships: National Union of Journalists, life member. Address: 31 Oakridge Avenue, Radlett, Herts WD7 8EW, England.

DRAPER Ronald Philip, b. 3 Oct 1928, Nottingham, England. Professor Emeritus of English; Author. m. Irene Margaret Aldridge, 19 June 1950, 3 daughters. Education: BA, 1950, PhD, 1953, University of Nottingham. Appointments: Lecturer in English, University of Adelaide, 1955-56; Lecturer, 1957-68, Senior Lecturer, 1968-73, University of Leicester; Professor, 1973-86, Regius Chalmers Professor of English, 1986-94, Professor Emeritus, 1994-, University of Aberdeen. Publications: D H Lawrence, 1964, 3rd edition, 1984. D H Lawrence: The Critical Heritage (editor), 1970, 3rd edition, 1986; Hardy: The Tragic Novels (editor), 1975, revised edition, 1991; George Eliot, The Mill on the Floss and Silas Marner, 1977, 3rd edition, 1984; Tragedy, Developments in Criticism (editor), 1980; Lyric Tragedy, 1985; The Winter's Tale: Text and Performance, 1985; Hardy: Three Pastoral Novels, 1987; The Literature of Region and Nation, 1989; An Annotated Critical Bibliography of Thomas Hardy (with Martin Ray), 1989; The Epic: Developments in Criticism (editor), 1990; A Spacious Vision: Essays on Hardy, (co-editor), 1994; An Introduction to Twentieth-Century Poetry in England, 1999. Contributions to: Books and scholarly journals. Address: Maynestay, Chipping Camden, Gloucestershire, GL55 6DJ, England.

DRAVA Rita. See: **RUNCE Rute.**

DRECKI Zbigniew Bogdan, b. 20 Nov 1922, Warsaw, Poland. Artist. m. Cynthia Josephine Scott, 22 Feb 1961. Education: Humanistic Gymnasium (High School), Warsaw, 1928-39; Art Diploma, Darmstadt Academy of Art, 1952. Publication: Freedom and Justice Spring From the Ashes of Auschwitz, 1992, Polish version in Auschwitz Museum. Contributions to: Polish medical journals; British and US newspapers. Memberships: West Country Writers Association, life member; Association of Little Presses. Address: Winterhaven, 23 Albion Street, Exmouth, Devon EX8 1JJ, England.

DREIER Ole, b. 15 Apr 1946, Nyborg, Denmark. Professor of Personality Psychology; Author. m. Dorthe Bukh, 5 Sept 1983, 1 son, 1 daughter. Education: MA, Psychology, 1970; PhD, 1979; DPhil, 1993. Appointment: Professor of Personality Psychology, University of Copenhagen. Publications: Society and Psychology, 1978; Critical Psychology, 1979; Familiäres Sein und Jamiliäres Bewusstaein, 1980; Psychosocial Treatment, 1993; Contributions to: Books and professional journals. Honours: Visiting Professor, Mexico City, Berkeley, Leipzig, 1984-86. Memberships: Danish Authors Association; Boards of several journals; Danish Psychological Association; International Society of Theoretical Psychology. Address: Dr Olgas Vej 37, 2000 Frederiksberg, Denmark.

DREIKA Dagnija, b. 2 May 1951, Riga, Latvia. Poet; Writer; Translator. m. Janis Cekuls, 19 July 1985. Education: School of Applied Arts, Latvian University, Faculty of Foreign Languages. Appointment: Professional Freelance Writer and Translator. Publications: Brown Stars, poetry, 1971; Lunatics, poetry, 1975; Delta, poetry, 1982; Saga's and Stories, 1981; The Walley at Flowers, poetry, 1986; The Country of the Soul, essays, 1988; This Side of Wind, That Side of Rain, short prose, 1989; The Snow and the Full Moon; Pidgeontime Stories, prose for children; The Time Before Fest, poetry; The Mole and the Egg of Big Big Bird, children's, 1994; Enigma, 1998; Witch Doctor; My Witch Doctor. Memberships: Latvian Writers Union; Latvian Journalists Society. Address: Riga 50, PO Box 157, LV 1050, Riga, Latvia.

DREW Bettina, b. 23 Apr 1956, New York, New York, USA. Writer; Poet; Teacher. Education: BA, Philosophy, University of California, Berkeley, 1977; MA, Creative Writing, City College of New York, 1983; MA, American Studies, Yale University, 1995. Appointments: Lecturer in English, College of New York; Lecturer in Humanities, New York University, 1990-93; Part-time Acting Instructor, Yale University, 1995-97. Publications: Nelson Algren: A Life on the Wild Side, 1989; The Texas Stories of Nelson Algren (editor), 1995; Travels in Expendable Landscapes, forthcoming. Contributions to: Boulevard; The Writer; Chicago Tribune; Threepenny Review; Washington Post Book World; Chicago Tribune Book World; Ms; Black American Literature Forum; Michigan Quarterly Review; Poems to various magazines. Memberships: PEN American Center; Biography Seminar, New York University. Literary Agent: Theresa Park, Sanford J Greenberg Associates, 55 Fifth Avenue, New York, NY 10003, USA. Address: 87 Olive Street, New Haven, CT 06511, USA.

DREWE Robert (Duncan), b. 9 Jan 1943, Melbourne, Victoria, Australia. Author; Dramatist. m. (3) Candida Baker, 4 sons, 2 daughters. Education: Hale School, Perth, Western Australia. Appointments: Literary Editor, The Australian, 1972-75; Writer-in-Residence, University of Western Australia, Nedlands, 1979, La Trobe University, Bundoora, Victoria, 1986; Columnist, Mode, Sydney, and Sydney City Monthly, 1981-83. Publications: The Savage Crows, 1976; A Cry in the Jungle Bar, 1979; Fortune, 1986; Our Sunshine, 1991; The Picador Book of the Beach (editor), 1993; The Drowner (novel), 1996; The Penguin Book of the City (editor), 1997; Walking Ella (non-fiction), 1998. Short stories: The Bodysurfers, 1983; The Bay of Contented Men, 1989. Plays: The Bodysurfers, 1989; South American Barbecue, 1991. Contributions to: The Bulletin; The Australian; Times Literary Supplement; Granta. Honours: National Book Council Award, 1987; Commonwealth Writers' Prize, 1990; Australian Creative Artists' Fellowship, 1993-96; Hon DLitt, Queensland, 1997; New South Wales, Victorian, West Australian and South Australian premieres' literary prizes, 1997; Book of the Year, 1997; Adelaide Festival Prize for Literature, 1998. Membership: Australian Society of Authors. Literary Agent: Hickson Associates. Address: Hickson Associates, 128 Queen Street, Wollahra, New South Wales 2025, Australia.

DRISCOLL Peter (John), b. 4 Feb 1942, London, England. Writer; Journalist. m. Angela Hennessy, 14 Jan 1967, 1 son, 1 daughter. Education: BA, University of the Witwatersrand, 1967. Appointments: Reporter, Rand Daily Mail, Johannesburg, South Africa, 1959-67; Sub-editor, Scriptwriter, ITV News, London, 1969-73. Publications: The White Lie Assignment, 1971; The Wilby Conspiracy, 1972; In Connection with Kilshaw, 1974; The Barboza Credentials, 1976; Pangolin, 1979; Heritage, 1982; Spearhead, 1987; Secrets of State, 1991. Address: c/o David Higham Associates, 5-8 Lower John Street, London W1R 4HA, England.

DRIVER Charles Jonathan, (Jonty), b. 19 Aug 1939, Cape Town, South Africa. Headmaster; Writer; Poet. m. Ann Elizabeth Hoogewerf, 1967, 2 sons, 1 daughter. Education: BA (Hons), BEd, University of Cape Town, 1958-62; MPhil, Trinity College, Oxford, 1967. Appointments: The Master, Wellington College, Crowthorne, Berkshire; Editor, Conference and Common Room, 1993-. Publications: Elegy for a Revolutionary, 1968; Send War in Our Time, O Lord, 1970; Death of Fathers, 1972; A Messiah of the Last Days, 1974; I Live Here Now (poems), 1979; Occasional Light (poems, with Jack Cope), 1979; Patrick Duncan (biography), 1980; Hong Kong Portraits (poems), 1985; In the Water-Margins (poems), 1994; Holiday Haiku (poems), 1996; Requiem (poems), 1998. Contributions to: Numerous magazines and journals. Honour: Royal Society of Arts, fellow. Memberships: Headmasters' Conference. Address: c/o The Master's Lodge, Wellington College, Crowthorne, Berkshie, RG45 7PU, England.

DRIVER Deana J, b. 26 Feb 1956, Athabasca, Alberta, Canada. Freelance Journalist; Photographer. m. Allan Driver, 17 Jan 1976, 1 son, 2 daughters. Education: Journalism Administration, Diploma of Applied Arts, Southern Alberta Institute of Technology, Calgary, Alberta, 1973-75. Publications: Church Photo Directory for Heritage United Church The Yes Factor: New Life and Renewal in 16 Churches (photograph), 1996; First Book of Saints (chapter), 1988. Contributions to: The Medical Post, United Church Observer, The Bottom Line, Pharmacy Post. Address: 91 Minot Drive, Regina. Saskatchewan, S4X 1B6, Canada.

DRIVER Paul William, b. 14 Aug 1954, Manchester England. Music Critic; Writer. Education: MA, Honours, Oxford University, 1979. Appointments: Music Critic, The Boston Globe, 1983-84, Sunday Times, 1985-; Member, Editorial Board, Contemporary Music Review. Publications: A Diversity of Creatures (editor), 1987; Music and Text (editor), 1989; Manchester Pieces, 1996. Contributions to: Sunday Times; Financial Times; Tempo; London Review of Books; New York Times; numerous others. Membership: Critics Circle. Literary Agent: Toby Eady Associates. Address: 15 Victoria Road, London NW6 6SX, England.

DROBOT Eve Joanna, b. 7 Feb 1951, Crakow, Poland (US citizen, 1968). Journalist; Author. m. Jack Kapica, 9 Apr 1983, 1 daughter. Education: Baccalaureat, Universite d'Aix Marseilles, Aix-en-Provence, France, 1971; BA, magna cum laude, Tufts University, Medford, Massachussetts, USA, 1973. Appointments: Columnist, Globe and Mail, 1980-82, 1990-; Contributing Editor, Saturday Night Magazine, 1988-; Toronto Correspondent, L'Actualite Magazine, 1989-. Publications: Words for Sale (co-editor), 1979, 3rd edition, 1989; Class Acts, 1982; Zen and Now, 1985; Amazing Investigations: Money, 1987; Chicken Soup and Other Nostrums, 1987. Contributions to: Hundreds, including book reviews, to magazines and journals. Honours: Gold Medal, Canadian National Magazine Award, 1989; Canadian Authors Award, 1989. Membership: International PEN. Address: 17 Simpson Avenue, Toronto, Ontario M4K 1A1, Canada.

DROWER G(eorge) M(atthew) F(rederick), b. 21 July 1954, London, England. Feature Writer. Education; BA, Honours, Politics and Government, City of London Polytechnic, 1979; MA, Area Studies, University of London, 1980; PhD, London School of Economics, 1989. Publications: Neil Kinnock: The Path to Leadership, 1984; Britain's Dependent Territories: A Fistful of Islands, 1992. Contributions to: The Times; The Sunday Times; Financial Times; Independent Mail on Sunday; Sun; House and Garden; Traditional Homes. Honours: University of London Central Research Fund Travelling Scholarship to Hong Kong; London School of Economics Director's Fund Scholarship. Membership: Inner Temple Rowing Club. Literay Agent: Serafina Clarke, 98 Tunis

Road, London W12, England. Address: 480A Church Road, Northolt, Middlesex UB5 5AU, England.

DRUCKER Henry Matthew, b. 29 Apr 1942, Paterson, New Jersey, USA. Managing Director; Visiting Professor of Government. m. Nancy Livia Neuman, 29 Mar 1975. Education: BA, Philosophy, Allegheny College, Meadville, Pennsylvania, 1964; PhD, Political Science, London School of Economics and Political Science, 1967. Appointments: Lecturer, 1964-76, Senior Lecturer, 1976-86, Politics, Univesity of Edinburgh; Director, University Development Office, Oxford University, 1987-93, Campaign for Oxford, 1988-93; Managing Director, Oxford Philanthropic, 1994-; Visiting Professor of Government, London School of Economics and Political Science, 1994-. Publications: Political Uses of Ideology, 1974; Our Changing Scotland (editor with M G Clarke), 1977; Breakaway: The Scottish Labour Party, 1978; Scottish Government Yearbook (editor with Nancy Drucker), 1978-82; Doctrine and Ethos in the Labour Party, 1979;Multi-Party Britain (editor), 1979; The Politics of Nationalism and Devolution (with Gordon Brown), 1980; John P Mackintosh on Scotland (editor), 1982; Developments in British Politics (general editor), 1, 1983, 2, 1986, revised edition, 1988. Address: c/o Oxford Philanthropic Ltd, 36 Windmill Road, Oxford OX3 7BX, England.

DRUCKER Peter (Ferdinand), b. 19 Nov 1909, Vienna, Austria. Management Consultant; Professor of Social Science; Writer. m. Doris Schmitz, 1937, 1 son, 3 daughters. Education: Austria, Germany and England. Appointments: Investment Banker, London, 1933-36; Professor of Philosophy and Politics, Bennington College, Vermont, 1942-49; International Management Consultant to businesses and governments, 1943-; Professor of Management, New York University, 1950-72; Clarke Professor of Social Science, Claremont Graduate University, California, 1971-; Professorial Lecturer in Oriental Art, Claremont Colleges, California, 1980-86. Publications include: The End of Economic Man, 1939, new edition, 1995; The Future of Industrial Man, 1942, new edition, 1994; The Concept of the Corporation, 1946, new edition, 1992; Society, Economics, Politics: The New Society, 1949, 1992; The Frontiers of Management (essays), 1986, 1997; The New Realities, 1989; Drucker on Asia: A Dialogue with Isao Nakauchi, 1996; Peter Drucker on the Profession of Management, 1998; Management Challenges for the 21st Century, forthcoming. Novels: The Last of All Possible Worlds, 1982, The Temptation to to Good, 1984; Autobiography: Adventures of a Bystander, 1979, 1998. Contributions: Frequent contributions to magazines; Columnist, Wall Street Journal, 1975-95.Honours: Order of the Sacred Treasure of Japan; Grand Cross of Austria; 25 honorary doctorates. Memberships: American Academy of Management, fellow; International Academy of Management, fellow. Address: 636 Wellesley Drive, Claremont, CA 91711, USA.

DRUMMOND June, b. 15 Nov 1923, Durban, South Africa. Author. Education: BA, English, University of Cape Town. Publications: Slowly the Poison, 1975; The Patriots, 1979; The Trojan Mule, 1982; The Bluestocking, 1985; Junta, 1989; The Unsuitable Miss Pelham, 1990. Memberships: Soroptimist International; Writers Circle of South Africa. Address: 24 Miller Grove, Durban 4001, South Africa.

DRYSDALE Helena Claire, b. 6 May 1960, London, England. Writer. m. Richard Pomeroy, 21 May 1987, 2 daughters. Education: Trinity College, Cambridge, 1978-82; BA, Honours, History, Art History, Cambridge. Publications: Alone Through China and Tibet, 1986; Dancing With the Dead, 1991; Looking for Gheorghe: Love and Death in Romania, 1995; Looking for George, 1996. Contributions to: Vogue; Marie Claire; Independent; Independent on Sunday; Harpers and Queen; Cosmopolitan; World. Honours: Exhibitioner, Trinity College; Shortlisted, Esquire/Waterstones Non-Fiction Award, 1995; PEN/J R Ackerley Award for Autobiograhy, 1995. Membership: Royal Geographical Society. Literary

Agent: A P Watt. Address: 22 Stockwell Park Road, London SW9 OAJ, England.

DU VAUL Virginia. See: COFFMAN Virginia (Edith).

DUBE Marcel, b. 3 Jan 1930, Montreal, Quebec, Canada. Dramatist; Author; Poet; Translator. m. Nicole Fontaine, Apr 1956. Education: BA, Collège Sainte-Marie, 1951; University of Montreal; Theatre schools, Paris, 1953-54. Publications: Over 30 plays, including: Zone, 1955, English translation, 1982; Un simple soldat, 1958; Le temps des lilas, 1958, English translation as Time of the Lilacs, 1990; Florence, 1958; Bilan, 1968; Les beaux dimanches, 1968; Au retour des oies blanches, 1969, English translation as The White Geese, 1972; Hold-up! (with Louis-George Carrier), 1969; Un matin commes les autres, 1971; Le neufrage, 1971; De l'autre coté du mur, 1973; L'impromptu de Québec, ou Le testament, 1974; L'été s'appelle Julie, 1975; Le réformiste, ou L'honneur des hommes, 1977; Le trou, 1986; L'Amérique a sec, 1986. Other: Television series. Poetry: Poèmes de sable, 1974. Non-Fiction: Textes et documents, 1968; La tragédie est un acte de foi, 1973; Jean-Paul Lemieux et le livre, 1988, revised edition, 1993; Andrée Lachapelle: Entre ciel et terre, 1995. Honours: Prix Victor-Morin, Saint-Jean-Baptiste Society, 1966; Prix David, Quebec, 1973; Molson Prize Canada Council, 1984; Académie canadienne-francaise Medal, 1987. Memberships: Académie canadienne-francaise, fellow; Federation of Canadian Authors and Artists, president, 1959; Royal Society of Canada, fellow. Address: c/o Société professionalle des auteurs et des compositeurs du Québec, 759 Square Victoria, No 420, Montreal, Quebec H2Y 2J7, Canada.

DUBERMAN Martin (Bauml), b. 6 Aug 1930, New York, New York, USA. Professor of History; Writer. Education: BA, Yale University, 1952; MA, 1953, PhD, 1957, Harvard University. Appointments: Teaching Fellow, Harvard University, 1955-57; Instructor, 1957-61, Morse Fellow, 1961-62, Yale University; Bicentennial Preceptor and Assistant Professor, 1962-65, Associate Professor, 1965-67, Professor, 1967-71, Princeton University; Distinguished Professor of History, Lehman College and the Graduate Center, City University of New York, 1972-; Founder-Director, Center for Lesbian and Gay Studies, Graduate Center, City University of New York, 1991-; Visiting Randolph Distinguished Professor, Vassar College, 1992; Associate Editor, Journal of The History of Sexuality, 1993-; Masculinities: interdisciplinary studies on gender, 1993-. Publications: Charles Francis Adams, 1807-1886, 1960; In White America, 1964; The Antislavery Vanguard: New Essays on the Abolitionists (editor), 1965; James Russell Lowell, 1966; The Uncompleted Past, 1969; The Memory Bank, 1970; Black Mountain: An Exploration in Community, 1972; Male Armor: Selected Plays, 1968-1974, 1975; Visions of Kerouac, 1977; About Time: Exloring the Gay Past, 1986, revised edition, 1991; Hidden from History: Reclaiming the Gay and Lesbian Past (co-editor), 1989; Paul Robeson, 1989; Cures: A Gay Man's Odyssey, 1991; Mother Earth: An Epic Play on the Life of Emma Goldman, 1991; Stonewall, 1993; Midlife Queer, 1996; A Queer World: The Center for Lesbian and Gay Studies Reader (editor), 1997; Queer Representations: Reading Lives, Reading Cultures (editor), 1997. Contributions to: Journals and newspapers. Honours: Bancroft Prize, 1961; Vernon Rice/Drama Desk Award, 1965; President's Gold Medal in Literature, Borough of Manhattan, 1988; 2 Lambda Book Awards, 1990; Distinguished Service Award, Association of Gay and Lesbian Psychiatrists, 1996. Address: c/o Graduate School and University Center of the City University of New York, 33 West 42nd Street, Room 404N, NEw York, NY 10036, USA.

DUBERSTEIN Larry, b. 18 May 1944, New York, New York, USA. Writer; Cabinetmaker. 3 daughters. Education: BA, Wesleyan University, 1966; MA, Harvard University, 1971. Publications: Nobody's Jaw, 1979; The Marriage Hearse, 1983; Carnovsky's Retreat, 1988; Postcards From Pinsk, 1991; Eccentric Circles, 1992; The Alibi Breakfast, 1995; The Handsome Sailor, 1998. Contributions to: Articles, essays, reviews to: Saturday

Review: Boston Review; The National; The Phoenix; New York Times Book Review; others. Honours: New American Writing Award, 1987, 1991. Address: Box 609, Cambridge, MA 02139, USA.

DUBIE Norman (Evans, Jr), b. 10 Apr 1945, Barre, Vermont, USA. Professor of English; Writer; Poet. Education: BA, Goddard College, 1969; MFA, University of Iowa, 1971. Appointments: Teaching Assistant, Goddard College, 1967-69; Teaching Assistant, 1969-70, Writing Fellow, 1970-71, Distinguished Lecturer and Member of the Graduate Faculty, 1971-74, University of Iowa; Poetry Editor, Iowa Review, 1971-72, Now Magazine, 1973-74; Assistant Professor, Ohio University, 1974-75; Lecturer, 1975-76, Director, Creative Writing, 1976-77, Associate Professor, 1978-81, Professor of English, 1982-, Arizona State University. Publications: The Horsehair Sofa, 1969; Alehouse Sonnets, 1971; Indian Summer, 1973; The Prayers of the North American Martyrs, 1975; Popham of the New Song, 1975; In the Dead of the Night, 1975; The Illustrations, 1977; A Thousand Little Things, 1977; Odalisque in White, 1978; The City of the Olesha Fruit, 1979; Comes Winter, the Sea Hunting, 1979; The Everlastings, 1989; The Window in the Field, 1982; Selected & New Poems, 1983, new edition, 1996; The Springhouse, 1986; Groom Falconer, 1989; Radio Sky, 1991; The Clouds of Magellan, 1991; The Choirs of June and January, 1993. Contributions to: Anthologies and periodicals. Honours: Bess Hokin Prize, 1976; Guggenheim Fellowship, 1977-78; Pushcart Prize, 1978-79; National Endowment for the Arts Grant, 1986; Ingram Merrill Grant, 1987. Address: c/o Department of English, Arizona State University, Tempe, AZ 85281, USA.

DUBIEC Antoni, b. 19 Aug 1937, Horostyta, Poland. Lawyer; Writer. m. Bozena Kolodrubiec, 1 June 1963, 2 daughters. Education: BA, University of Lodz, Poland, 1962. Publications: The Feast of Voltures, 1993; A Talk With a Sea, 1994; Penetrations, 1995; Migration, 1996; Thoughts Full of Sadness, 1997; The Cross Roads, 1998; Selected Poems, 1998. Contributions to: Metafora Literary Magazine. Membership: Union of Polish Writers. Literary Agent: Festinus Publishing House. Address: ul Lecznicza 17 m 23, 93-173 Lodz, Poland.

DUBOIS J E. See: PARKES Joyce Evelyne.

DUBOIS M. See: KENT Arthur (William Charles).

DUBOIS DU NILAC Frédéric, (Julien Dunilac), b. 24 Sept 1923, Neuchatel, Switzerland. m. Lydia Induni, 12 Apr 1947, 1 son, 2 daughters. Education: Human Sciences, Paris. Appointments: Swiss Department of Foreign Affairs; Secretary, Swiss Ambassy in Paris; Head, Federal Office for Culture. Publications: La Vue Courte, 1952; La Part du Feu, 1954; Corps et Biens, 1957; Les Mauvaises Têtes, 1958; Passager Clandestin, 1962; Futur Mémorable, 1970; George Sand sous la loupe, 1977; François Mitterand sous la loupe, 1981; Plein ciel, 1985; La Passion Selon Belle, 1985; Mythologiques, 1987; Le Conseil fédéral sous la loupe, 1991; Precaire Victoire, 1993; Hotel le Soleil, 1995; L'Habit eet Le Moine, 1996; Le Coup de Grace, 1998. Honour: Prix Ondas, Barcelone (radio). Membership: Société Swisse des Ecrivaineset Ecrivains. Address: Rue des Paris 5, CH 2000 Neuchatel, Switzerland.

DUCHARME Réjean, b. 12 Aug 1941, Saint-Félix-de-Valois, Quebec, Caanda. Novelist; Dramatist; Screenwriter; Sculptor; Painter. Education: Ecole Polytechnique, Montreal. Publications: Novels: L'avalée des avalés, 1966; English translation as The Swallower Swallowed, 1968; Le nez qui voque, 1967; L'océantume, 1968; La fille de Christophe Colomb, 1969; L'huver de force, 1973; Les enfantomes, 1976; Dévadé, 1990; Va savoir, 1994. Plays: Le Cid maghané, 1968; Le marquis qui perdit, 1970; Inès Pérée et Inat Tendu, 1976; HA! ha! ..., 1982. Screenplays: Les bons débarras (with Francis Manckiewicz), 1979; Les beaux souvenirs (with Francis Manckiewicz), 1981. Honours: Governor-General's Awards for Fiction, 1966, and Drama, 1982. Address: Montreal, Quebecn, Canada.

DUCKWORTH Marilyn, b. 10 Nov 1935, Auckland, New Zealand. Writer. m. (1) Harry Duckworth, 28 May 1955, (2) Ian MacFarlane, 2 Oct 1964, (3) Dan Donovan, 9 Dec 1974, (4) John Batstone, 8 June 1985, 4 daughters. Publications: A Gap in the Spectrum, 1959; The Matchbox House, 1960; A Barbarous Tongue, 1963; Over the Fence is Out, 1969; Disorderly Conduct, 1984; Married Alive, 1985; Rest for the Wicked, 1986; Pulling Faces, 1987; A Message From Harpo, 1989; Explosions on the Sun, 1989; Unlawful Entry, 1992; Seeing Red, 1993; Leather Wings, 1995; Cherries on a Plate, editor, 1996; Studmuffin, 1997. Contributions to: Landfall; New Zealand Listener; Critical Quarterly; Islands; others. Honours: New Zealand Literary Fund Scholarships in Letters, 1961, 1994; Katherine Mansfield Fellowship, 1980; New Zealand Book Award for Fiction, 1985; Shortlisted, Wattie Book of the Year Award, 1985; Officer of the Order of the British Empire, 1987; Fulbright Visiting Writers Fellowship, 1987; Australia-New Zealand Writers Exchange Fellowship, 1989; Victoria University of Wellington Writers Fellowship, 1990; Auckland University Literary Fellowship, 1996; Shortlisted, Commonwealth Writers Prize, 1996. Membership: PEN. Literary Agent: Tim Curnow, Curtis Brown, Australia. Address: 41 Queen Street, Wellington, New Zealand.

DUCORNET Erica Lynn, (Rikki Ducornet), b. 19 Apr 1943, New York, New York, USA. Writer; Artist; Teacher. 1 son. Education: Bard College, 1964. Appointments: Novelist-in-Residence, University of Denver, 1988-; Visiting Professor, University of Trento, Italy, 1994. Publications: The Stain, 1984; Entering Fire, 1986; The Fountains of Neptune, 1989; Eben Demarst, 1990; The Jade Cabinet, 1993; The Butcher's Tales, 1994; Phosphor in Dreamland, 1995; The Word "Desire", 1997; The Fan-Maker's Inquisition, 1999. Contributions to: Periodicals. Honours: National Book Critics Circle Award Finalist, 1987, 1990, 1993; Critics Choice Award, 1995; Charles Flint Kellogg Award in Arts and Letters, 1998. Membership: PEN. Address: c/o Department of English, University of Denver, Denver, CO 80208, USA.

DUDEK Louis, b. 6 Feb 1918, Montreal, Quebec, Canada. Professor of English Emeritus; Poet; Writer. m. (1) Stephanie Zuperko, 1943, div 1965, 1 son, (2) Aileen Collins, 1970. Education: BA, McGill University, 1939; MA, History, 1947, PhD, English and Comparative Literature, 1955, Columbia University, New York City. Appointments: Lecturer to Assistant Professor, 1951-68, Greenshield Professor of English, 1969-84, Professor Emeritus, 1984-, McGill University. Publications: East of the City, 1946; The Searching Image, 1952; Twenty-Four Poems, 1952; Europe, 1954; The Transparent Sea, 1956; Literature and the Press, 1956; Laughing Stalks, 1958; En Mexico, 1958; Poetry of Our Time (editor), 1965; The Making of Modern Poetry in Canada (co-editor), 1967; Atlantis, 1967; The First Person in Literature, 1967; Collected Poetry, 1971; Selected Essays and Criticism, 1978; Technology and Culture, 1979; Cross Section: Poems 1940-1980, 1980; Poems from Atlantis, 1980; Louis Dudek: Open Letter Nos 8-9, 1981; Continuation I, 1981, II, 1990; In Defence of Art, 1988; Infinite Worlds, 1988; Small Perfect Things, 1991; Paradise: Essays on Art, Myth and Reality, 1992; Notebooks 1960-1994, 1994; The Birth of Reason, 1994; The Caged Tiger, 1998; Reality Games, 1998; The Poetry of Louis Dudek: Definitive Edition, 1998. Contributions to: Various journals. Honours: Order of Canada, 1984; Various honorary doctorates, including Doctor of Laws, St Thomas University, Fredericton, 1996, Lakehead University, 1996. Address: 5 Ingleside Avenue, Montreal, Quebec H3Z 1N4, Canada.

DUDLEY Helen. See: HOPE-SIMPSON Jacynth (Ann).

DUEMER Joseph, b. 31 May 1951, San Diego, California, USA. Associate Professor of Humanities; Poet; Writer. m. Carole A Mathery, 31 Dec 1987. Education: BA, University of Washington, 1978; MFA, University of Iowa, 1980. Appointments: Lecturer, Western Washington University, 1981-83, San Diego State University, 1983-87; Associate Professor of Humanities,

Clarkson University, 1987-; Poet-in-Residence, St Lawrence University, 1990. Publications: Poetry: Fool's Paradise, 1980; The Light of Common Day, 1985; Customs, 1987; Static, 1996; Primitive Alphabets, 1998. Editor: Dog Music (with Jan Simmerman), 1996. Contributions to: Reference books, anthologies, reviews, journals, magazines and radio. Honours: National Endowment for the Arts Creative Writing Fellowships, 1984, 1992, and National Endowment for the Humanities Grants, 1985, 1995. Membership: Associated Writing Programs, board of directors, 1998-2002. Address: c/o Clarkson University, Potsdam, NY 13699, USA.

DUFF Alan, b. 26 Oct 1950, Rotorua, New Zealand. Columnist; Writer. m. Joanna Robin Harper, Sept 1990. Appointment: Syndicated newspaper columnist, 1971-. Publications: Once Were Warriors, 1994; One Night Out Stealing, 1995. Address: 51 Busby Hill, Havelock North, New Zealand.

DUFF-WARE Freddie. See: BARNETT Paul (le Page).

DUFFEY John Patrick, b. 19 Nov 1963, Dallas, TX, USA. Assistant Professor of Spanish. m. Magdalena Duffey, 3 Feb 1988, 2 daughters. Education: AB, Washington University in St Louis, 1985; BA, University of Texas, Arlington, 1990; MA & PhD, University of Texas, Austin, USA, 1994. Appointments: Assistant Professor of Spanish, Austin College, Sherman, Texas, USA, 1994-. Publications: De la pantalla al texto: La influencia del cine en la narrativa mexicana del siglo XX (From Screen to Text: The Influence of Film on 20th Century Mexican Narrative), 1997. Memberships: Modern Language Association; Latin American Studies Association.

DUFFY Carol Ann, b. 23 Dec 1955, Glasgow, Scotland. Poet; Dramatist. Education: BA, Honours, Philosophy, University of Liverpoool, 1977. Publications: Standing Female Nude, 1985; Selling Manhattan, 1987;The Other Country, 1990. Other: Plays. Contributions to: Numerous magazines and journals. Honours: C Day-Lewis Fellowships, 1982-84; Eric Gregory Award, 1985; Scottish Arts Council Book Awards of Merit, 1985, 1987; Somerset Maugham Award, 1988; Dylan Thomas Award, 1990. Address: c/o Liz Graham, 4 Camp View, London SW19 4VL, England.

DUFFY Maureen Patricia, b. 21 Oct 1933, Worthing, Sussex, England. Writer; Poet. Education: BA, Honours, English, King's College, University of London, 1956. Publications: That's How It Was, 1962; The Microcosm, 1966; Lyrics for the Dog Hour, 1968; Rites, 1969; Wounds, 1969; Love Child, 1971; The Venus Touch, 1971; The Erotic World of Faery, 1972; I Want to Go to Moscow, 1973; A Nightingale in Bloomsbury Square, 1974; Capital, 1975; Evensong, 1975; The Passionate Shepherdess, 1977; Housespy, 1978; Memorials for the Quick and the Dead, 1979; Illuminations, 1992; Ocean's Razor, 1993. Memberships: Copywright Licencing Agency, chairman, 1996; European Writers Congress; Royal Society of Literature, fellow; Writer's Action Group, co-founder; Writer's Guild of Great Britain. Address: 18 Fabian Road, London SW6 7TZ, England.

DUGAN Alan, b. 12 Feb 1923, Brooklyn, New York, USA. Poet. m. Judith Shahn. Education: Queens College; Olivet College; BA, Mexico City College. Appointments: Teacher, Sarah Lawrence College, 1967-71, Fine Arts Work Center, Provincetown, Massachusetts, 1971-. Publications: General Prothalamion in Populous Times, 1961; Poems, 1961; Poems 2, 1963; Poems 3, 1967; Collected Poems, 1969; Poems 4, 1974; Sequence, 1976; Collected Poems, 1961-1983, 1983; Poems 6, 1989. Contributions to: Several magazines. Honours: Yale Series of Younger Poets Award, 1961; National Book Award, 1961; Pulitzer Prizes in Poetry, 1962, 1967; Rome Fellowship, American Academy of Arts and Letters, 1962-63; Guggenheim Fellowship, 1963-64; Rockefeller Foundation Fellowship, 1966-67; Levinson Poetry Prize, 1967. Address: Box 97, Truro, MA 02666, USA.

DUGGER Ronnie, b. 16 Apr 1930, Chicago, Illinois, USA. Writer; Publisher. m. (1) Jean Wilson, 13 June 1950, div 1978, 1 son, 1 daughter, (2) Patricia Blake, 29 June 1982. Education: BA, 1950, 1951-52, 1954, University of Texas; Oxford University, 1950-51. Appointments: Owner-Publisher, The Texas Observer, 1965-94; Visiting Professor, Hampshire College, 1976, University of Illinois, 1976, University of Virginia. Publications: Dark Star: Hiroshima Reconsidered, 1967; Three Men in Texas, 1967; Our Invaded Universities, 1974; The Politician: The Life and Times of Lyndon Johnson, 1982; On Reagan: The Man and His Presidency, 1983. Contributions to: Periodicals. Honours: Rockefeller Foundation Fellowship, 1969-70; National Endowment for the Humanities Fellowship, 1978; Woodrow Wilson Center for Scholars Fellow, 1983-84; Alicia Patterson Fellowship, 1994. Memberships: Authors Guild; PEN; Philosophical Society of Texas; Texas Institute of Letters. Address: Box 311, 70A Greenwich Avenue, New York, NY 10011, USA.

DUKE Elizabeth. See: WALLINGTON Vivienne Elizabeth.

DUKES Carol Muske. See: MUSKE Carol.

DUKORE Bernard F(rank), b. 11 July 1931, New York, New York, USA. Professor of Theatre Arts and Humanities Emeritus; Writer. 1 son, 2 daughters. Education: BA, Brooklyn College, 1952; MA, Ohio State University, 1953; PhD, University of Illinois, 1957. Appointments: Instructor, Hunter College in the Bronx, 1957-60; Assistant Professor, University of Southern California, Los Angeles, 1960-62; Assistant to Associate Professor, California State University, Los Angeles, 1962-66; Associate Professor to Professor of Theatre, City University of New York, 1966-72; Professor of Drama and Theatre, University of Hawaii, 1972-86; University Distinguished Professor of Theatre Arts and Humanities, 1986-97, Professor Emeritus, 1997-, Virginia Polytechnic Institute and State University, Blacksburg. Publications: Bernard Shaw, Director, 1971; Bernard Shaw, Playwright, 1973; Dramatic Theory and Criticism, 1974; Where Laughter Stops: Pinter's Tragicomedy, 1976; Collected Screenplays of Bernard Shaw, 1980; Money and Politics in Ibsen, Shaw and Brecht, 1980; The Theatre of Peter Barnes, 1981; Harold Pinter, 1982; Alan Ayckbourn: A Casebook, 1991; The Drama Observed (editor and annotator), 4 volumes, 1993; 1992: Shaw and the Last Hundred Years (editor), 1994; Barnestorm: The Plays of Peter Barnes, 1995; Bernard Shaw and Gabriel Pascal, 1996; Not Bloody Likely: The Columbia Book of Bernard Shaw Quotations, 1997; Shaw on Cinema (editor and annotator), 1997. Honours: Guggenheim Fellowship, 1969-70; National Endowment for the Humanities Fellowships, 1976-77, 1984-85, 1990; Fulbright Research Scholarship, England and Ireland, 1991-92. Memberships: American Theatre Association, fellow; Pinter Society. Address: 2581 Forest Run Ct., Clearwater, FL 33761, USA.

DUMAS Claudine. See: MALZBERG Barry.

DUMMETT Michael (Anthony Eardley), b. 27 June 1925, London, England. Professor of Logic Emeritus; Writer. m. Ann Chesney, 1951, 3 sons, 2 daughters. Education: Winchester College; Christ Church, Oxford. Appointments: Fellow, 1950-79, Emeritus Fellow, 1979-, Senior Research Fellow, 1974-79, All Souls College, Oxford; Commonwealth Fund Fellow, University of California, Berkeley, 1955-56; Reader in the Philosophy of Mathematics, 1962-74, Wykeham Professor of Logic, 1979-92, Professor of Logic Emeritus, 1992-, Oxford University; Fellow, 1979-92, Fellow Emeritus, 1992-, New College, Oxford; Various visiting lectureships and professorships. Publications: Frege: Philosophy of Language, 1973, 2nd edition, 1981; The Justification of Deduction, 1973; Elements of Intuitionism, 1977; Truth and Other Enigmas, 1978; Immigration: Where the Debate Goes Wrong, 1978; Catholicism and the World Order, 1979; The Game of Tarot, 1980; Twelve Tarot Games, 1980; The Interpretation of Frege's Philosophy, 1981; Voting Procedures, 1984; The Visconti-Sforza

Tarot Cards, 1986; Ursprünge der analytischen Philosophie, 1988, revised edition as Origins of Analytical Philosophy, 1993; Frege and Other Philosophers, 1991; The Logical Basis of Metaphysics, 1991; Frege: Philosophy of Mathematics, 1991; Grammar and Style for Examination Candidates and Others, 1993; The Seas of Language, 1993; Il Mondo e l'Angelo, 1993; I Tarocchi siciliani (with R Dedcer and T Depaulis), 1995; A Wicked Pack of Cards, 1996; Principles of Electoral Reform, 1997. Contributions to: Various books and scholarly journals. Honours: Lakatos Award in the Philosophy of Science, 1994; Roy Schock Prize for Philosophy and Logic, 1995; Honorary DLitt, Oxford, 1989; other honorary doctorates. Memberships: American Academy of Arts and Sciences, honorary member; British Academy, fellow; Academia Europaea. Address: 54 Park Town, Oxford OX2 6SJ, England.

DUMONT André, b. 12 Apr 1929, Campbellton, New Brunswick, Canada. Writer. m. Germaine Richard, 1958, 2 sons, 2 daughters. Education: BA, 1961; BEd, 1964. Publications: Francais Renouvele I, 1964, II, 1966; Le Parti Acadien (co-author), 1972; Jeunesse Mouvementée, 1979; Quand Je Serai Grand, 1989; Pour un Francais Moderne, 1990; Avancez en arrière, 1996. Contributions to: Over 100 articles on different topics, mostly political. Address: 1445-A boul de l'Entente, Quebec, (Quebec), G15 2V1

DUMONT Pascal, b. 18 Jan 1954, Dijon, France. Professor. m. Virginie Ballif, 24 Aug 1985. 4 daughters. Education: Agrégation, Philosophy, 1984; Doctor of Philosophy, University of Paris-Sorbonne, 1993. Appointments: Saint-Dizier High School, 1983; French High School, Rabat, Morocco, 1987; University of Dijon, France, 1992; Khâgne, Dijon, 1995. Publications: L'abrégé de musique de Descartes, 1990; Descartes et l'esthétique, l'art d'émerveiller, 1997; Essais de culture générale, 1998. Contributions to: Revue de métaphysique et de morale; Revue philosophique; Milieux; Revue de l'enseignement philosophique; Philomèle; Temps mêlés; Cahiers du Collège de Pataphysique. Memberships: Société Bourguignonne de Philosophie; Société de Philosophie au Maroc; AARPPH, 1977; Cymbalum Pataphysicum, 1980. Address: 49 avenue Victor Hugo, 21000 Dijon, France.

DUNANT Sarah, (Peter Dunant), b. 8 Aug 1950, London. England. Writer; Broadcaster. Partner of Ian David Willox, 2 daughters. Education: Newnham College, Cambridge, 1969-72; BA, 2:1 History, Cambridge University, 1972. Publications: As Peter Dunant: Exterminating Angels (co-author), 1983; Intensive Care (co-author), 1986. As Sarah Dunant: Snow Falls in a Hot Climate, 1988; Birth Marks, 1991; Fatlands, 1993; The War of the Words: Essays on Political Correctness (editor), 1994; Under My Skin, 1995; The Age of Anxiety (editor), 1996; Transgressions, 1997. Contributions to: Various London magazines; Listener; Guardian. Honours: Shortlisted for Crime Writers Golden Dagger, 1987, 1991; Silver Dagger Award, 1993. Address: c/o Gillon Aitken, 29 Fernshaw Road, London SW10 OTG, England.

DUNBAR Andrea, b. 22 May 1961, Bradford, Yorkshire, England. Playwright. 1 son, 2 daughters. Education: Buttershaw Comprehensive School, Bradford. Publications: Plays: The Arbor (produced, London 1980, New York, 1983), 1980; Rite, Sue and Bob Too (produced London 1982), 1982; Shirley (produced London 1986). Screenplay, Rite, Sue and Bob Too, 1987. Honour: George Devine Award, 1981. Address: 7 Edge End Gardens, Buttershaw, Bradford, West Yorkshire BD6 2BB, England.

DUNBAR-HALL Peter, b. 15 July 1951, Sydney, New South Wales, Australia. Lecturer; Writer. Education: BA, Honours, 1972; MMus, 1989; PhD, 1995. Publications: Music - A Practical Teaching Guide, 1987; A Guide to Rock'n'Pop, 1988; Music in Perspective, 1990; A Guide to Music Around the World, 1991; Teaching Popular Music, 1992; Discography of Aboriginal and Torres Strait Islander Performers, 1995; Strella Wilson: The Career of an Australian Singer, 1997. Contributions to: Many

articles in Education Australia; Papers in International Review of Aesthetics and Sociology of Music; British Journal of Music Education; International Journal of Music Education; Research Studies in Music Education; Perfect Beat. Honours: Frank Albert Prize, Sydney University, 1971; Busby Music Scholarship, Sydney University, 1971; Lady Henley Award for Excellence in Teaching, Sydney Conservatorium of Music, 1993. Address: 5/198 Kurraba Road, Neutral Bay, New South Wales 2089, Australia.

DUNCAN Lois, b. 28 Apr 1934, Philadelphia, Pennsylvania, USA. Writer. m. Donald W Arquette, 15 July 1965, 2 sons, 3 daughters. Education: Duke University, 1952-53; BA, University of New Mexico, 1977. Publications: Ransom, 1966; A Gift of Magic, 1971; I Know What You Did Last Summer, 1973; Down a Dark Hall, 1974; Summer of Fear, 1976; Killing Mr Griffin, 1978; Daughters of Eve, 1979; Stranger With My Face, 1981; My Growth as a Writer, 1982; The Third Eye, 1984; Locked in Time, 1985; Horses of Dreamland, 1986; The Twisted Window, 1987; Songs From Dreamland, 1989; The Birthday Moon, 1989; Don't Look Behind You, 1989; Who Killed My Daughter?, 1992; The Circus Comes Home, 1993; Psychic Connections: A Journey into the Mysterious World of Psi (co-author William Roll, Phd), 1995; The Magic of Spider Woman, 1996; Gallows Hill, 1997; Night Terrors (edited anthology), 1997; Trapped (edited anthology), 1998. Literary Agent: Wendy Schmalz, Harold Ober Associates. Address: c/o Dell Publishing, 1540 Broadway, New York, NY 10036, USA.

DUNCAN Paul Edwin, b. 20 Aug 1959, Cape Town, South Africa. Writer; Journalist. Education: MA, Honours, History of Art, University of Edinburgh, 1984. Appointments: London Correspondent, Casa Vogue, 1989-92; Writer, Researcher, Royal Fine Art Commission, England, 1991-95; Speech Writer, President's Office, IBM Europe, Middle East, Africa, 1995-96; Editor-in-Chief, Condé Nast House & Garden, South Africa, 1998-. Publications: Scandal: Georgian London in Decay (co-author), 1986; Insight Guide Tuscany (contributor), 1989; Discovering the Hill Towns of Italy, 1991; AA Tour Guide Rome, 1991; AA Tour Guide South Africa, 1991; AA Tour Guide Italy, 1991; Sicily, A Traveller's Companion, 1991; The Traditional Architecture of Rural Italy, 1993; Nelson Mandela's Illustrated Walk to Freedom (editor), 1996; Italy (contributor), 1996; London Living, co-author, 1997; On the Roads Round Southern Africa, 1997. Contributions to: Italian Vogue; Condé Nast Traveler (USA); Vogue Glamour; Casa Vogue; GQ; World of Interiors; Independent; Sunday Times; Evening Standard; Harpers and Queen, Architect's Journal; Elle; Elle Decoration: L'Uomo Vogue; Country Life; Cosmopolitan; Sunday Life (South Africa). Literary Agent: Anne Engel. Address: 7 Moray Place, Oranjezicht, Cape Town 8001, South Africa.

DUNCKER Patricia, b. 29 June 1951, Kingston, Jamaica. Writer; University Lecturer. Education: Cambridge, 1970-73; Oxford, 1973-78; MA, Cambridge, England; DPhil (Oxford). Appointments: University Lecturer; Roehampton Institute, 1978-80; Oxford Polytechnic, 1980-86; IUT Angoulême, University of Poitiers, France, 1987-91; University of Wales, Aberystwyth, 1991-. Publications: Sisters and Strangers: An Introduction to Contemporary Feminist Fictions, 1992; Hallucinating Foucault, 1996; Cancer Through the Eyes of Ten Women, 1996; Monsieur Shoushana's Lemon Trees, 1997. Contributions to: Critical Quarterly; Stand Magazine, Women: A Cultural Review. Honours: Dillons First Fiction Award; McKittericke Prize. Membership: Society of Authors. Literary Agent: Toby Eady Associates. Address: Third Floor, 9 Orme Court, London W2 4RL, England.

DUNHAM William Wade, b. 8 Dec 1947, Pittsburgh, Pennsylvania, USA. Professor of Mathematics. m. Penelope Higgins, 26 Sept 1970, 2 sons. Education: BS, University of Pittsburgh, 1969; MS, 1970, PhD, 1974, Ohio State University. Appointment: Truman Koehler Professor of Mathematics, Muhlenberg College, 1992-. Publications: Journey Through Genius: The Great

Theorems of Mathematics, 1990; The Mathematical Universe, 1994; Euler: The Master of Us All, 1999. Contributions to: American Mathematical Monthly; Mathematics Magazine; College Mathematics Journal; Mathematics Teacher. Honours: Phi Beta Kappa, 1968; M M Culver Award, University of Pittsburgh, 1969; Master Teacher Award, Hanover College, 1981; National Endowment for the Humanities Summer Seminars on Great Theorems, 1988-96;, Humanities Achievement Award for Scholarship, Indiana Humanities Council, 1991; George Pólya Award, Mathematical Association of America, 1993; Trevor Evans Award, Mathematical Association of America, 1997. Memberships: Mathematical Association of America; National Council of Teachers of Mathematics Civil War Roundtable. Address: Department of Mathematics, Muhlenberg College, Allentown, PA 18104, USA.

DUNILAC Julien. See: DUBOIS DU NILAC Frédéric.

DUNKERLEY James, b. 15 Aug 1953, Wokingham, England. Reader in Politics; Writer. Education: BA, University of York, 1974; BPhil, Hertford College, Oxford, 1977; PhD, Nuffield College, Oxford, 1979. Appointments: Researcher, Latin America Bureau, London, 1979-80, 1983-84; Research Fellow, Institute for Latin American Studies, University of London, 1981-82, Centre for Latin American Studies, University of Liverpool, 1982-83; Fellow, Kellogg Institute, University of Notre Dame, Indiana, 1985; Reader in Politics, Queen Mary and Westfield College, University of London, 1986-. Publications: Unity is Strength: Trade Unions in Latin America (with C Whitehouse), 1980; Bolivia: Coup d'Etat, 1980; The Long War: Dictatorship and Revolution in El Salvador, 1982; Rebellion in the Veins: Political Struggle in Bolivia, 1952-1982, 1984; Granada: Whose Freedom? (with F Amburseley), 1984; Origenes del podermilitair on Bolivia, 1879-1935, 1987; Power in the Isthmus: A Political History of Central America, 1988; Political Suicide in Latin America and Other Essays, 1992; The Pacification of Central America, 1994. Contributions to: Scholarly journals, newspapers, and magazines. Address: c/o Department of Political Studies, Queen Mary and Westfield College, University of London, Mile End Road, London E1 4NS, England.

DUNKLEY Christopher, b. 22 Jan 1944, Scarborough, Yorkshire, England. Critic; Broadcaster. m. Carolyn Elizabeth Lyons, 18 Feb 1967, 1 son, 1 daughter. Appointments: Mass media correspondent, Television critic, The Times, 1968-73; Television critic, Financial Times, 1973-; Presenter, Feedback, BBC Radio 4, 1986-99. Publication: Television Today and Tomorrow: Wall to Wall Dallas?, 1985. Contributions to: Telegraph Magazine; Listener; Sunday Times; Stills; Television World; Electronic Media. Honours: Critic of the Year, British Press Awards, 1976, 1986; Broadcaster Journalist of the Year, 1989 and Judges Award, 1990, TV-AM Awards. Memberships: Commodore; Theta Club. Address: 38 Leverton Street, London NW5 2PG, England.

DUNLAP Leslie W(hittaker), b. 3 Aug 1911, Portland, Oregon, USA. Dean of Library Administration Emeritus; Writer. m. Marie Neese, 15 Apr 1933, 1 son, 1 daughter. Education: BA, University of Oregon, 1933; Graduate Studies, University of Freiburg, 1933-34; AM, 1938, BS, 1939, PhD, 1944, Columbia University. Appointments: Associate Director, University of Illinois Libraries, 1951-58; Director of Libraries, 1958-70, Dean of Library Administration, 1970-82, Dean Emeritus, 1982-, University of Iowa. Publications: The Letters of Willis Gaylord Clark and Lewis Gaylord Clark, 1940; American Historical Societies, 1944; Readings in Library History, 1972; The Wallace Papers: An Index, 1975; The Publication of American Historical Manuscripts, 1976; Your Affectionate Husband, J F Culver, 1978; Our Vice-Presidents and Second Ladies, 1988. Address: 640 Stuart Court, Iowa City, IA 52245, USA.

DUNLOP Eileen Rhona, b. 13 Oct 1938, Alloa, Scotland. Children's Writer. m. Antony Kamm, 27 Oct 1979. Education: Alloa Academy, 1943-56; Diploma

Education, Moray House College of Education, Edinburgh, 1956-59. Appointments: Assistant Teacher, various schools, 1959-69; Deputy Head, Sunnyside School, Alloa, 1969-79; Headmistress Preparatory School of Dollar Academy, 1980-90. Publications: Robinsheugh, 1975; A Flute in Mayferry Street, 1976; Fox Farm, 1978; The Maze Stone, 1982; Clementina, 1985; The House on the Hill, 1987; The Valley of Deer, 1989; Finn's Island, 1991; Green Willow's Secret, 1993; Castle Gryffe, 1995; The Ghost by the Sea, 1997; Scottish Verse to 1800 (with Antony Kamm), 1985. Honours: Scottish Arts Council Book Awards, 1983, 1986. Memberships: PEN Scottish Centre; Society of Authors. Literary Agent: Antony Kamm. Address: 46 Tarmangie Drive, Dollar, FK14 7BP, Scotland.

DUNLOP Richard, b. 20 June 1921, Chicago, Illinois, USA. Writer. Education: BS, Northwestern University, 1945. Publications: The Mississippi River, 1956; St Louis, 1957; Burma, 1958; The Young David (novel), 1959; Doctors of the American Frontier, 1965; Great Trails of the West, 1971; Outdoor Recreation Guide, 1974; Backpacking and Outdoor Guide, 1977; Wheels West, 1977; Behind Japanese Lines: With the OSS in Burma, 1979; Donovan: America's Master Spy, 1982; On the Road in an RV, 1987. Honour: Midland Author's Best Biography Award. Memberships: Society of American Travel Writers, president, 1971; Society of Midland Authors, 1980. Address: 1115 Mayfair Road, Arlington Heights, IL 60004, USA.

DUNMORE Helen, b. 1952, Yorkshire, England. Poet; Novelist. m. 1 son, 1 stepson. Education: BA, York University, 1973. Publications: Poetry: The Apple Fall, 1983; The Sea Skater, 1986; The Raw Garden, 1988; Short Days, Long Nights: New & Selected Poems, 1991; Secrets, 1994; Recovering a Body, 1994. Novels: Going to Egypt, 1992; Zennor in Darkness, 1993; In the Money, 1993; Burning Bright, 1994; A Spell of Winter, 1995. Honours: Poetry Book Society Recommendation, 1991; Alice Hunt Bartlett Award; 1st Orange Prize, 1996. Address: c/o Bloodaxe Books Ltd, PO Box 1SN, Newcastle upon Tyne, NE99 1SN, England.

DUNMORE John, b. 6 Aug 1923, Trouville, France. University Professor. m. Joyce Megan Langley, 22 April 1946, 1 son, 1 daughter. Education: BA, Honours, London University, 1950; PhD, University of New Zealand, 1962. Publications: French Explorers in the Pacific, 1966-69; The Fateful Voyage of the St Jean Baptiste, 1969; Norman Kirk: A Portrait, 1972; Pacific Explorer, 1985; New Zealand and the French, 1990; The French and the Maoris, 1992; Who's Who in Pacific Navigation, 1992; The Journal of La Perouse, 1994-95; I Remember Tomorrow, 1998. Contributions to: Numerous learned journals and periodicals. Honours: New Zealand Book of the Year, 1970; Legion of Honour, 1976; Academic Palms, 1986; New Zealand Commemoration Medal, 1990; Massey Medal, 1993. Membership: Australasian Language and Literature Association, president, 1980-82. Address: 35 Oriwa Street, Waikanae, New Zealand.

DUNN Douglas (Eaglesham), b. 23 Oct 1942, Inchinnan, Scotland. Professor of English; Writer; Poet. m. Lesley Jane Bathgate, 10 Aug 1985, 1 son, 1 daughter. Education: BA, University of Hull, 1969. Appointments: Writer-in-Residence, University of Hull, 1974-75, Duncan of Jordanstone College of Art, Dundee District Library, 1986-88; Writer-in-Residence, 1981-82, Honorary Visiting Professor, 1987-88, University of Dundee; Fellow in Creative Writing, 1989-91, Professor of English, 1991-, Head, School of English, 1994-, University of St Andrews. Publications: Terry Street, 1969; The Happier Life, 1972; Love or Nothing, 1974; Barbarians, 1979; St Kilda's Parliament, 1981; Europea's Lover, 1982; Elegies, 1985; Secret Villages, 1985; Selected Poems, 1986; Northlight, 1988; New and Selected Poems, 1989; Poll Tax: The Fiscal Fake, 1990; Andromache, 1990; Scotland: An Anthology (editor), 1991; The Faber Book of 20th Century Scottish Poetry (editor), 1992; Dante's Drum-Kit, 1993; Boyfriends and Girlfriends, 1994; The Oxford Book of Scottish Short Stories (editor), 1995; Norman MacCaig: Selected Poems (editor), 1997. Contributions to: Newspapers, reviews, and journals. Honours: Somerset Maugham Award, 1972; Geoffrey Faber Memorial Prize, 1975; Hawthornden Prize, 1982; Whitbread Poetry Award, 1985; Whitbread Book of the Year Award, 1985; Honorary LLD, University of Dundee, 1987; Cholmondeley Award, 1989; Honorary DLitt, University of Hull, 1995. Membership: Scottish PEN. Address: c/o School of English, University of St Andrews, St Andrews, Fife KY16 9AL, Scotland.

DUNN Durwood, b. 30 Nov 1943, Chickamauga, Georgia, USA. Professor of History. Education: BA, 1965, MA, 1968, PhD, 1976, University of Tennessee, Knoxville. Appointments: Instructor, Hiwassee College, 1970-74; Instructor, Assistant Professor, Associate Professor, Professor, Chairman, Department of History, Tennessee Wesleyan College, 1975-. Publications: Cades Cove: The Life and Death of a Southern Appalachian Community, 1818-1937, 1998; An Abolitionist in the Appalachian South: Ezekiel Birdseye on Slavery, Capitalism, and Separate Statehood in East Tennessee, 1841-1846, 1997. Contributions to: Appalachian Journal, 1979; West Tennessee Historical Society's Publications, 1982. Honour: Thomas Wolfe Memorial Literary Award, 1988. Address: PO Box 1941, Athens, Tennessee, USA.

DUNN Stephen, b. 24 June 1939, New York, New York, USA. Poet; Writer. m. Lois Kelly, 1964, 2 daughters. Education: BA, History, Hofstra University, 1962; New School for Social Research, New York City, 1964-66; MA, Creative Writing, Syracuse University, 1970. Appointments: Assistant Professor, Southwest Minnesota State College, Marshall, 1970-73; Visiting Poet, Syracuse University, 1973-74, University of Washington at Seattle, 1980; Associate Professor to Professor, 1974-90, Stockton State College, New Jersey; Adjunct Professor of Poetry, Columbia University, 1983-87. Publications: Poetry: Five Impersonations, 1971; Looking for Holes in the Ceiling, 1974; Full of Lust and Good Usage, 1976; A Circus of Needs, 1978; Work and Love, 1981; Not Dancing, 1984; Local Time, 1986; Between Angels, 1989; Landscape at the End of the Century, 1991; New and Selected Poems, 1974-1994, 1994; Loosestrife, 1996; Double Standards, 1998. Other: Walking Light: Essays and Memoirs, 1993. Contributions to: Periodicals. Honours: Academy of American Poets Prize, 1970; National Endowment for the Arts Fellowships, 1973, 1982, 1989; Bread Loaf Writers Conference Robert Frost Fellowship, 1975; Theodore Roethke Prize, 1977; New Jersey Arts Council Fellowships, 1979, 1983; Helen Bullis Prize, 1982; Guggenheim Fellowship, 1984; Levinson Prize, 1988; Oscar Blumenthal Prize, 1991; James Wright Prize, 1993; American Academy of Arts and Letters Award, 1995. Address: 445 Chestnut Neck Road, Port Republic, NJ 08241, USA.

DUNNE Dominick, b. 29 Oct 1925, Hartford, Connecticut, USA. Novelist; Essayist. m. Ellen Griffin, 24 Apr 1952, div, 2 sons, 1 daughter, dec. Education: BA, Williams College, 1949. Appointments: Television and film producer; Co-Founder, Dunne-Didion-Dunne film production company. Publications: The Winners: Part II of Joyce Haber's "The Users", 1982; The Two Mrs Grenvilles, 1985; Fatal Charms, and Other Tales of Today, 1986; People Like Us, 1988; An Inconvenient Woman, 1990; The Mansions of Limbo, 1991; A Season in Purgatory, 1993; Another City, Not My Own: A Novel in the Form of a Memoir, 1997. Contributions to: Vanity Fair. Address: c/o Curtis Brown Ltd, 575 Madison Avenue, New York, NY 10022, USA.

DUNNETT Dorothy, (Dorothy Halliday), b. 25 Aug 1923, Dunfermline, Scotland. Novelist; Portrait Painter. m. Sir Alastair M Dunnett, 17 Sept 1946, 2 sons. Publications: The Game of Kings, 1961, 13th edition, 1999; Queens' Play, 1964, 13th edition 1999; The Disorderly Knights, 1966, 12th edition, 1997; Dolly and the Singing Bird (also the Photogenic Soprano), 1968, 5th edition, 1991; Pawn in Frankincense, 1969, 13th edition, 1999; Dolly and the Cookie Bird (also Murder in the Round), 1970, 5th edition, 1993; The Ringed Castle, 1971, 13th edition, 1998; Dolly and the Doctor Bird (also Match for a Murder), 1971, 5th edition, 1985; Dolly and the Starry Bird, 1973, 5th edition, 1993; Checkmate, 1975, 13th edition, 1997; King Hereafter, 1982, 6th edition, 1999; Dolly and the Bird of Paradise, 1983, 5th edition, 1991; Niccolo Rising, 1986, 6th edition, 1999; The Spring of the Ram, 1987, 7th edition, 1999; The Scottish Highlands (with Alastair M Dunnett and David Paterson), 1988, 2nd edition, 1997; Race of Scorpions, 1989, 5th edition, 1999; Moroccan Traffic, 1991, 3rd edition, 1993; Scales of Gold, 1991, 5th edition, 1999; The Unicorn Hunt, 1993, 5th edition, 1999; To Lie with Lions, 1995, 5th edition, forthcoming; Caprice and Rando, 1997, 4th edition 1999; A Scottish Childhood vol II, 1998. Honours: Officer of the Order of the British Empire, 1992; Royal Society of the Arts, fellow; National Library of Scotland, trustee; Scottish PEN, honorary vice president. Literary Agent: Curtis Brown. Address: 87 Colinton Road, Edinburgh EH10 5DF, Scotland.

DUPONT (Jean) Louis, b. 17 Jan 1924, Shawinigan, Canada. Retired School Principal; Writer. m. Beaulieu Madeleine, 1 Aug 1953, 2 sons, 3 daughters. Education: Superior Diploma, Primary Teaching, 1948; MA, 1952; Master of Public Administration, 1967. Publications: La Guerre du Castor, 1984; La Légende de Thogoruk, 1993. Contributions to: La Presse; Lettres Québécoises. Memberships: La Société Littéraire de Laval; L'Union des Ecrivains Québécois. Address: 1255 Montpellier, Laval, Quebec H7E 3C8, Canada.

DUPUIS Sylviane, b. 20 Mar 1956, Geneva, Switzerland. Teacher of French Literature; Writer. Education: MA, University of Geneva, 1979; Appointments: Assistant, University of Geneva, 1979-80; Teacher of French Literature, 1980-; Writer, 1985-; Dramatist, 1995-. Publications: Poetry: D'un lieu l'autre, 1985; Creuser la Nuit, 1985; Figures d'Egarées, 1989; Odes brèves, 1995; Travaux du voyage, essay, 1992; A quoi sert le théâtre?, essay, 1998; Plays: La seconde Chute, 1993; Moi, Maude (ou) La Malvivante, 1997. Honours: Prix C F Ramuz, 1986; Jasmin d'Argent francophone, 1997. Membership: Groupe d'Olten, Switzerland. Address: 45 rue Terrassière, 1207 Geneva, Switzerland.

DURANG Christopher (Ferdinand), b. 2 Jan 1949, Montclair, New Jersey, USA. Dramatist; Actor. Education: BA, Harvard University, 1971; MFA, Yale University, 1974. Publications: Plays (with dates of production and publication): The Nature and Purpose of the Universe, 1971, 1979; Robert, 1971, as 'dentity Crisis, 1975; Better Dead Than Sorry, 1972; I Don't Generally Like Poetry, But Have You Read "Trees"? (with Albert Innaurato), 1972; The Life Story of Mitzi Gaynor, or Gyp (with Albert Innaurato), 1973; The Marriage of Bette and Boo, 1973, 1985; The Idiots Karamazov (with Albert Innaurato), 1974, 1980; Titanic, 1974, 1983; Death Comes to Us All, Mary Agnes, 1975; When Dinah Shore Ruled the Earth (with Wendy Wasserstein), 1975; Das Lusitania Songspiel (with Sigourney Weaver), 1976; A History of the American Film, 1976, 1978; The Vietnamization of New Jersey, 1976, 1978; Sister Mary Ignatius Explains it All for You, 1979, 1980; Beyond Therapy, 1981, 1983; The Actor's Nightmare, 1981, 1982; Baby with the Bathwater, 1983, 1984; Sloth, 1985; Laughing Wild, 1987; Cardinal O'Connor, 1988; Woman Stand-up, 1988; Chris Durang & Dawne, 1990; Naomi in the Living Room, 1991; Media Amok, 1992; Putting it Together, 1993; For Whom the Southern Belle Tolls, 1994. Honours: CBS Fellow, 1975-76; Rockefeller Foundation Grant, 1976-77; Guggenheim Fellowship, 1978-79; Obie Award, 1980; Lecomte du Nouy Foundation Grant, 1980-81; Kenyon Festival Playwriting Award, 1983; Hull-Warriner Award, Dramatists Guild, 1985; Lila Wallace-Reader's Digest Fund Writer's Award, 1994. Memberships: Actors' Equity Association; American Society of Composers, Authors, and Publishers; Dramatists Guild of America. Address: c/o Writers Guild of America, 555 West 57th Street, New York, NY 10019, USA.

DURANTI Francesca. See: **ROSSI Maria Francesca.**

DURBAND Alan, b. 3 June 1927, Liverpool, England. Writer. m. Audrey Atherton, 26 July 1952, 1 son, 1 daughter. Education: BA, 1951, MA, 1956, Downing College, Cambridge. Publications: English Workshop, books 1-3, 1959; New Directions: Five One-Act Plays in the Modern Idiom, 1961; Contemporary English Books 1-2, 1962; Shorter Contemporary English, 1964; New English Books, 1-4, 1966; Playbill 1-3, 1969; Second Playbill, 1-3, 1973; Prompt 1-3, 1975; Wordplays 1-2, 1982; Shakespeare Made Easy (12 plays), 1984-89. Address: Ty-Nant, Lansilin, Near Oswestry, Salop SY10 7QQ, England.

DURCAN Paul, b. 16 Oct 1944, Dublin, Ireland. Poet. m. Nessa O'Neill, 8 May 1969, 2 daughters. Education: BA, Honours, Archaeology and Mediaeval History, University College, Cork. Appointment: Writer-in-Residence, Trinity College, Dublin. Publications: Endsville, 1967; O Westport in the Light of Asia Minor, 1975; Teresa's Bar, 1976; Sam's Cross, 1978; Jesus, Break His Fall, 1980; Ark of the North, 1982; Jumping the Train Tracks With Angela, 1983; The Selected Paul Durcan, 1985; The Berlin Wall Cafe, 1985; Going Home to Russia, 1987; In the Land of Punt, 1988; Jesus and Angela, 1988; Daddy, Daddy, 1990; Crazy About Women, 1991; A Snail in My Prime, 1993; Give Me Your Hand, 1994. Contributions to: Irish Press; Irish Times; Hibernia; Magill; Cyphers; Honest Ulsterman; Gorey Detail; Cork Examiner; Aquarius. Honours: Patrick Kavanagh Poetry Award, 1974; Arts Council of Ireland Bursaries for Creative Writing, 1976, 1980-81; Poetry Book Society Choice 1985; Irish- American Cultural Institute Poetry Award, 1989; Whitbread Poetry Award, 1990; Heinemann Award, 1995. Membership: Aosdána. Address: 14 Cambridge Avenue, Ringsend, Dublin 4, Ireland.

DURGNAT Raymond Eric, (O O Green), b. 1 Sept 1932, London, England. Writer; Lecturer. Education: BA, Honours, English Literature, Pembroke College, Cambridge, 1957; MA, 1970. Appointments: Visiting Professor, UCLA, Dartmouth College, Columbia University; Visiting Professor, University of East London. Publications: A Mirror for England, 1973; The Strange Case of Alfred Hitchcock, 1973; Durgnat on Film, 1976; Luis Bunuel, 1988; Michael Powell and the English Genius, forthcoming. Contributions to: British Journal of Aesthetics. Membership: British Society of Aesthetics. Address: 84 Saint Thomas's Road, London N4 2QW, England.

DURKIN Barbara (Rae Wernecke), b. 13 Jan 1944, Baltimore, Maryland, USA. Writer. m. William J Durkin, 20 May 1973, 2 sons. Education: AA, Essex Community College, 1964; BS, Towson State College, 1966; Graduate Studies, Morgan State College, 1968, John Hopkins University, 1968-70. Publications: Oh, You Dundalk Girls, Can't You Dance the Polka?, 1984; Visions and Viewpoints (editor), 1993. Honour: Best of 1984 List, American Library Association, 1984. Memberships: American PEN Women; International Women's Writing Guild. Address: 531 Phillips Road, Webster, NY 14580, USA.

DÜRRSON Werner, b. 12 Sept 1932, Schwenningen am Neckar, Germany. Poet; Writer; Dramatist; Translator. Education: Music Studies, Trossingen, 1953; German and French Literature Studies, Tübingen, Munich, 1957; PhD, 1962. Publications: Schubart (play), 1980; Stehend Bewegt (play), 1980; Der Luftkünstler (prose), 1983; Wie ich lese? (essay), 1986; Ausleben (poems of 12 years), 1988; Abbreviaturen (aphorisms), 1989; Werke (works: poetry and prose), 4 volumes, 1992; Ausgewählte d'Aquitaine, Marguerite de Navarre, Stéphane Mallarmé, Arthur Rimbaud, Yvan Goll, René Char, and Henri Michaux. Contributions to: Anthologies and radio. Honours: Lyric Poetry Prize, South West German Press, 1953; German Awards for Short Stories, 1973, 1983; Literary Prize, Stuttgart, 1978; Literary Prize, Überlingen, 1985. Memberships: Association Internationaleides Critiques littéraires, Paris; Association of German Writers; PEN. Address: Schloss Neufra, D-88499 Riedlingen, Germany.

DURST Paul, (John Shane), b. 23 Apr 1921, Archbald, Pennsylvania, USA. Writer. Education: Colorado State College, 1938-40; Northwest Missouri State College, 1940-41. Publications: Die! Damn You, 1952; Bloody River, 1953; Trail Herd North, 1953; Guns of Circle 8 (as Jeff Cochran), 1954; Along the Yermo Rim (as John Shane), 1954; My Deadly Angel (as John Chelton), 1955; Showdown, 1955; Justice, 1956; Kid From Canadian, 1956; Prairie Reckoning, 1956; Sundown in Sundance (as John Shane), 1956; Six-Gun Thursday (as John Shane), 1956; Gunsmoke Dawn (as John Shane), 1957; John Law, Keep Out, 1957; Ambush at North Platte, 1957; The River Flows West, 1957; If They Want Me Dead (as Peter Bannon), 1958; If I Should Die (as Peter Bannon), 1958; Kansas Guns, 1958; Dead Man's Range, 1958; The Gun Doctor, 1959; Johnny Nation, 1960; Whisper Murder Softly (as Peter Bannon), 1963; Backlash, 1967; Badge of Infamy (crime), 1968; Intended Treason: What Really Happened to the Gunpowder Plot, 1970; A Roomful of Shadows (autobiography), 1975; The Florentine Table, 1980; Paradiso Country, 1985. Address: The Keep, West Wall, Presteigne, Powys LD8 2BY, Wales.

DUSKY Lorraine Blanche, b. 13 June 1942, Detroit, Michigan, USA. Author. m. Anthony Scott Brandt, 20 Sept 1981, 1 daughter. Education: BA, Wayne State University, 1964. Publications: Total Vision, 1978; Birthmark, 1979; The Best Companies for Women, 1988; Still Unequal, 1996. Contributions to: The New York Times Magazine, Newsweek; On the Issues; USA Today Board of Contributions. Honours: American Optemetric Association for Reporting and Writing, 1979; Empire State Award for Excellence in Medical Reporting, 1996; Exceptional Merit Media Award, National Women's Political Caucus, 1991, 1997. Literary Agent: Suzanne Gluck, International Creative Management. Address: Box 968, Sag Harbor, NY 11963, USA.

DUTESCU Mircea, b. 28 Apr 1938, Bucharest, Romania. Physician. m. Isolde Prediger, 2 sons. Education: Medical University, Iasi, Romania. Appointments: Ophthalmological Clinic, Coltea, Bucharest; Ophthalmological Clinic, Aachen, Germany; Luisen Hospital, Aachen, Germany. Publication: Hydrodynamic of the Intraocular Liquids in Normal and Glaucoma Eyes. Contributions to: Medical and Ophthalmological journals. Memberships: European Society for PHACO and Laser Surgery. Address: Starenweg 10, 52078 Aachen, Germany.

DUTHIE Gilbert William Arthur, b. 21 May 1912, Nhill, Victoria, Australia. Uniting Church Minister. m. Jeannette E Blake, 8 Mar 1941, 3 daughters. Publication: The Jesus Tale Words Never Knew. Contributions to: In Parliament with 8 Prime Ministers; How Did They Shape Up? Honours: BA, 1937; LTH, 1936. Honour: Order of Australia Award, 1986. Address: 03 63442611, Launceston, Tasmania, Australia.

DUTHOY Pascal, b. 13 May 1927, Menen, Belgium. Ethnographer. m. Mireille Ruscart, 27 Mar 1955. Education: Master in Economics and Aggregation for Teaching Economics at Highest Degree, University of Gent, 1950. Appointments: Artillery Officer, 1951-52; Expert, Court of Justice, Lusambo, Belgian Congo, 1953-55; Professor of Economics, Overpelt High, 1956-87; Member, Commission of Book Selection for State Departments, 1960-75; Introducer of art exhibitions, including African Art, 1960-98; Lecturer on African Art, Neerpelt Cultural Centre, 1988, Rotary and Lions Service Clubs, 1988-98. Publications: Tonaliteiten van Mireille Duthoy, 1987; Several articles relating to African Art, registered by African Library, Smithsonian Institution, Washington DC, USA. Contributions to: Permanent Contributor to Beleggen Magazine, 1986-98, Investir Magazine, 1982 and Dutch Magazine Ethnographic Newspapers, 1986-98. Honours: Knight of the Order of the Crown, 1966; Knight of the Order of Leopold, 1979. Membership: Heikracht Art Association, Chairman, 1979. Address: Bemvaartstr 128, 3900 Overpelt, Belgium.

DUTOIT Bernard, b. 18 Jan 1933, Lausanne, Switzerland. Professor; Writer; Poet. m. Carine Borner, 8 Dec 1962, 5 daughters. Education: Licence and Doctorate in Law, Lausanne University, 1958; Diploma, Institude of High International Studies, Paris, 1961; Diploma in Russian, School of Oriental Languages, Paris, 1962. Appointments: Permanent Office, The Hague Conference of Private International Law, 1966-67; Professor of Comparative Law and Director, Center of Comparative and European Law, Law Faculty, Lausanne, 1967-. Publications: Poetry: Les cals au coeur, 1977; Le tain et le miroir, 1978; Transhumances, 1979; En filigrane, 1981; La manne des jours, 1982; Et chantent les oasis, 1987; Poésiades, Florilège, 1989; Comme une brise légère, 1989; Poésiades, Florilège, 1993; Le désert refleurira, 1993; Poésiades, Florilège, 1995; Les poètes et la foi, 1996; Séquences, 1996; D'espace et de silence, 1997; Poésiades, Florilège, 1998. Novels: L'automne musicien, 1986; Aube naissante, 1991. Various juridical works. Honours: 2 3rd Prizes, 1990, 2nd Prize, 1994, Poètes suisses de langue française; Honourable Mention, 1989, 1992, 1995, 1998; Prix de la Délégation générale de la SPAF, 1997. Memberships: Société suisse des écrivains; Association vaudoise des écrivains. Address: Sentier de Bellevue, CH-1603 Grandvaux, Switzerland.

DUTTON Geoffrey (Piers Henry), b. 2 Aug 1922, Anlaby, South Australia. Writer; Poet; Editor. m. (1) Ninette Trott, 31 July 1944, 2 sons, 1 daughter. (2) Robin Lucas, 1985. Education: University of Adelaide; BA, Magdalen College, Oxford, 1949. Appointments: Co-Editor, Australian Letters, 1957-68, Australian Book Review, 1961-70; Editorial Director, Sun Books Ltd, 1965-83; Editor, The Bulletin Literary Supplement, 1980-85, The Australian Literary Magazine, 1985-88. Publications: Night Flight and Sunrise, 1944; Antipodes in Shoes, 1958; Walt Whitman: Patrick White, 1961; Flowers and Fury, 1962; The Hero as Murderer, 1967; On My Island; Poems for Children, 1967; Poems Soft and Loud, 1967; Andy, 1968; Findings and Keepings: Selected Poems 1940-70, 1970; New Poems to 1972, 1972; Queen Emma of the South Seas, 1976; A Body of Words, 1977; Patterns of Australia, 1978; White on Black, 1978; Snow on the Saltbush, 1984; Selective Affinities, 1985; The Innovators, 1986; Kenneth Slessor, 1991; Flying Low, 1992; New and Selected Poems, 1993; Out in the Open: An Autobiography, 1994. Contributions to: Journals, magazines, and broadcasting services. Honour: Officer of the Order of Australia, 1976. Address: c/o Curtis Brown Ltd, PO Box 19, Paddington, New South Wales, 2021, Australia.

DUTTON Ninette Clarice Bernadette, b. 24 July 1923, Adelaide, South Australia, Australia. Enameller; Artist; Author. m. Geoffrey Dutton, 31 July 1944, 2 sons, 1 daughter. Education: University of Adelaide. Publications: The Beautiful Art of Enamelling, 1966; Portrait of a Year, 1976; An Australian Wildflower Diary, 1982; Wildflower Journeys, 1985; Probabilities, short stories, 1987; A Passionate Gardener, 1990; Firing, a Memoir, 1994. Contributions to: Adelaide Advertiser; Your Garden magazine; Regular broadcasts. Honours: Medal, Order of Australia. Memberships: Australian Society of Authors; Fellowship of Australian Writers. Address: PO Box 342, Williamstown, South Australia 5351, Australia.

DUVAL Jeanne. See: **COFFMAN Virginia (Edith).**

DWORKIN Ronald (Myles), b. 11 Dec 1931, Worcester, Massachusetts, USA. Professor of Jurisprudence; Writer. m. Betsy Ross, 18 July 1958, 1 son, 1 daughter. Education: BA, 1953, LLB, 1957, Harvard University; BA, Oxford University, 1955. Appointments: Admitted to the Bar, New York, 1959; Faculty, 1962-69, Hohfeld Professor of Jurisprudence, 1968-69, Yale Law School; Visiting Professor of Philosophy, 1963, 1974-75, Gauss Seminarian, 1966, Princeton University; Master, Trumbull College, 1966-69; Visiting Professor of Law, Stanford University, 1967; Professor of Jurisprudence, Oxford University, 1969-98; Professor of Law, New York University, 1975-; Academic Freedom Lecturer, University of the Witwatersrand, 1976; Professor-at-Large, Cornell University, 1976-; Visiting

Professor of Law and Philosophy, 1977, Visiting Professor of Philosophy, 1979, Harvard University; Quain Professor of Jurisprudence, University College, London, 1998-. Publications: Taking Rights Seriously, 1977; Philosophy of Law (editor), 1977; A Matter of Principle, 1985; Law's Empire, 1986; A Bill of Rights for Britain, 1990; Life's Dominion, 1993; Freedom's Law, 1996. Contributions to: Professional journals. Memberships: American Academy of Arts and Sciences; British Academy, fellow. Address: c/o School of Law, New York University, 40 Washington Square South, New York, NY 10012, USA.

DWYER Deanna. See: **KOONTZ Dean R(ay).**

DWYER K R. See: **KOONTZ Dean R(ay).**

DYBEK Stuart, b. 10 Apr 1942, Chicago, Illinois, USA. Poet; Writer; Professor of English. m. Caren Bassett, 1966, 1 son, 1 daughter. Education: BS, 1964, MA, 1967, Loyola University; MFA, University of Iowa, 1973. Appointments: Teaching Assistant, 1970-72, Teaching and Writing Fellow, 1972-73, University of Iowa; Professor of English, Western Michigan University, 1973-; Guest Writer and Teacher, Michigan Council for the Arts' Writer in the Schools Program, 1973-92; Faculty, Warren Wilson MFA Program in Creative Writing, 1985-89; Visiting Professor of Creative Writing, Princeton University, 1990, University of California, Irvine, 1995; Numerous readings, lectures and workshops. Publications: Brass Knuckles (poems), 1979; Childhood and Other Neighbourhoods (stories), 1980; The Coast of Chicago (stories), 1990; The Story of Mist (short fiction and prose poems), 1994. Contributions to: Many anthologies and magazines. Honours: Award in Fiction, Society of Midwest Authors, 1981; Cliffdwellers Award for Fiction, Friends of American Literature, 1981; Special Citation, PEN/Hemingway Prize Committee, 1981; Michigan Council for the Arts Grants, 1981, 1992; Guggenheim Fellowship, 1982; National Endowment for the Arts Fellowships, 1982, 1994; Pushcart Prize, 1985; 1st Prize, O Henry Award, 1985; Nelson Algren Prize, 1985; Whiting Writers Award, 1985; Michigan Arts Award, Arts Foundation of Michigan, 1986; American Academy of Arts and Letters Award for Fiction, 1994; PEN/Malamud Award, 1995; Rockefeller Residency, Bellagio, Italy, 1996. Address: 310 Monroe, Kalamazoo, MI 49006, USA.

DYER Charles, b. 17 July 1928, Shrewsbury, England. Playwright. m. Fiona, 20 Feb 1960, 3 sons. Publications: Turtle in the Soup, 1948; Who On Earth, 1950; Poison in Jest, 1952; Jovial Parasite, 1955; Red Cabbage and Kings, 1958; Rattle of a Simple Man, novel, play, film, 1962; Staircase, novel, play, film, 1966; Mother Adam, 1970; Lovers Dancing, 1982; various screenplays. Address: Old Wob, Gerrards Cross, Buckinghamshire SL9 8SF, England.

DYER James Frederick, b. 23 Feb 1934, Luton, England. Archaeological Writer. Education: MA, Leicester University, 1964. Appointment: Editor, Shire Archaeology, 1974-. Publications: Southern England: An Archaeological Guide, 1973; Penguin Guide to Prehistoric England and Wales, 1981; Discovering Archaeology in England and Wales, 1985, 6th enlarged edition, 1997; Ancient Britain, 1990; Discovering Prehistoric England, 1993; The Stopsley Book, 1998. Contributions to: Bedfordshire Magazine; Illustrated London News; Archaeological Journal. Memberships: Society of Authors; Royal Archaeological Institute; Society of Antiquaries. Address: 6 Rogate Road, Luton, Bedfordshire LU2 8HR, England.

DYMOKE Juliet, b. 28 June 1919, Enfield, England. Writer. m. Hugo de Schanschieff, 9 May 1942, 1 son, 1 daughter. Publications: The Cloisterman, 1969; Norman Trilogy, 1970-74; The White Cockade, 1979; Plantagenet Series, 6 volumes, 1978-80; A King of Warfare, 1981; March to Corunna, 1985; The Queen's Diamond, 1985; Aboard the Mary Rose, 1985; Two Flags for France, 1986; A Border Knight, 1987; Ride to Glencoe, 1989; Portrait of Jenny, 1990; Hollander's House, 1991; Cry of

the Peacock, 1992; Winter's Daughter, 1994. Contribution to: The Lady. Membership: Romantic Novelists Association. Literary Agent: Jane Conway-Gordon, 1 Old Compton Street, London W1, England. Address: Heronswood, Chapel Lane, Forest Row, East Sussex RH18 5BS, England.

DYSON A(nthony) E(dward), b. 28 Nov 1928, London, England. Writer. Education: MLitt, Pembroke College, Cambridge, 1952. Appointments: Co-Founder, Director, Critical Quarterly Society, 1960-84; Visiting Professor, Concordia University, Montreal, Canada, 1967, 1969, University of Connecticut, USA, 1976; General Editor, Macmillan Casebooks, England, 1968-; Director, Norwich Tapes Ltd, England, 1979-; Honorary Fellow, former Reader in English, University of East Anglia, Norwich. Publications: Modern Poetry (with C B Cox), 1963; The Crazy Fabric: Essays in Irony, 1965; The Practical Criticism of Poetry (with C B Cox), 1965; Modern Judgements on Dickens, 1968; Word in the Desert (with C B Cox), 1968; Casebook on Bleak House, 1969; Black Papers on Education, 3 volumes, 1969-70; The Inimitable Dickens, 1970; Between Two Worlds: Aspects of Literary Form, 1972; Twentieth Century Mind, 3 volumes (with C B Cox), 1972; English Poetry: Select Bibliographical Guides, 1973; English Novel: Select Bibliographical Guides, 1974; Casebook on Paradise Lost (with Julian Lovelock), 1974; Masterful Images: Metaphysicals to Romantics (with Julian Lovelock), 1975; Education and Democracy (with Julian Lovelock), 1975; Yeats, Eliot and R S Thomas: Riding the Echo, 1981; Poetry Criticism and Practice, 1986; Thom Gunn, Ted Hughes and R S Thomas, 1990; The Fifth Dimension, 1996. Contributions to: Over 100 articles in world of English criticism to various, US, UK and European Community journals; 8 teaching tapes. Address: c/o Macmillan Publishers, Hampshire RG21 2XS, England.

DYSON Freeman J(ohn), b. 15 Dec 1923, Crowthorne, England (US citizen, 1957). Professor of Physics Emeritus. m. (1) Verena Haefeli-Huber, 11 Aug 1950, div 1958, 1 son, 1 daughter, (2) Imme Jung, 21 Nov 1958, 4 daughters. Education: BA, Cambridge University, 1945; Graduate Studies, Cornell University, 1947-48, Institute for Advanced Study, Princeton, New Jersey, 1948-49. Appointments: Research Fellow, Trinity College, Cambridge, 1946-49; Warren Research Fellow, University of Birmingham, England, 1949-51; Professor of Physics, Cornell University, 1951-53; Professor of Physics, 1953-94, Professor Emeritus, 1994-, Institute for Advanced Study. Publications: Symmetry Groups in Nuclear and Particle Physics, 1966; Neutron Stars and Pulsars, 1971; Disturbing the Universe, 1979; Values at War, 1983; Weapons and Hope, 1984; Origins of Life, 1986; Infinite in All Directions, 1988; From Eros to Gaia, 1992; Imagined Worlds, 1997. Honours: Heineman Prize, American Institute of Physics, 1966; Lorentz Medal, Royal Netherlands Academy of Sciences, 1966; Hughes Medal, Royal Society, 1968; Max Planck Medal, German Physical Society, 1969; J Robert Oppenheimer Memorial Prize, Center for Theoretical Studies, 1970; Harvey Prize, Israel Institute of Technology, 1977; Wolf Prize, Wolf Foundation, 1981; National Book Critics Circle Award, 1984; Honorary doctorates. Memberships: American Physical Society; National Academy of Sciences; Royal Society, fellow. Address: 105 Battle Road Circle, Princeton, NJ 08540, USA.

E

EADY F R. See: **KERNER Fred**

EAGLETON Terence Francis, b. 22 Feb 1943, Salford, England. Professor of English Literature; Author. m. Elizabeth Rosemary Galpin, 1966, 2 daughters. Education: MA, Trinity College, Cambridge, 1964; PhD, Jesus College, Cambridge, 1967. Appointments: Fellow in English, Jesus College, Cambridge, 1964-69; Tutorial Fellow, Wadham College, 1969-89, Lecturer in Critical Theory, 1989-92, Fellow, Linacre College, 1989-92, Thomas Warton Professor of Literature and Fellow of St Catherine's College, Oxford, 1992-. Publications: Criticism and Ideology, 1976; Marxism and Literary Criticism, 1976; Walter Benjamin, 1981; Literary Theory: An Introduction, 1983; The Function of Criticism, 1984; The Rape of Clarissa, 1985; Against the Grain, 1986; William Shakespeare, 1986; The Ideology of the Aesthetic, 1990; Ideology: An Introduction, 1993; Heathcliff and the Great Hunger: Studies in Irish Culture, 1995; The Illusions of Postmodernism, 1996. Contributions to: Periodicals. Honours: Irish Sunday Tribune Arts Award, 1990; Honorary DLitt, Salford, 1993; Honorary DLitt, National University of Ireland, 1997. Address: St Catherine's College, Oxford, Oxford OX1 3UJ, England.

EARL Maureen J, b. 4 Sept 1944, Cairo, Egypt (British nationality). Writer; Journalist; Screenwriter; Documentary Maker. m. Clifford Irving, 1984, 1 son, 1 daughter. Publications: Gulliver Quick, 1992; Boat of Stone, 1993. Contributions to: Various magazines and journals worldwide. Honours: Best Young Journalist Award, New Zealand, 1967; Exceptional Political Reporting Award, Australia, 1970; Best Independent Documentary, Australia, 1972; Emmy Award, 1975; Emmy Award Nominee, 1976; Jewish Book of the Year, 1993; Runner Up Critics Circle Award, 1993. Memberships: Authors' Guild; New York Writers' Guild; PEN International; Author's League. Literary Agent: Clyde Taylor, Curtis Brown Ltd, New York, NY 10003, USA. Address: Aldama 1, San Miguel de Allende, GTO 37700, Mexico.

EARLY Gerald, b. 21 Apr 1952, Philadelphia, Pennsylvania, USA. Professor of English and Afro-American Studies; Writer; Poet. m. Ida Haynes, 27 Aug 1977, 2 daughters. Education: BA cum laude, English, University of Pennsylvania, 1974; MA, English, 1980, PhD, English, 1982, Cornell University. Publications: Tuxedo Junction: Essays on American Culture, 1990; My Soul's High Song, 1991; Lure and Loathing, 1993; Daughters: One Family and Fatherhood, 1994; Culture of Bruising, 1994; How the War in the Streets is Won, 1995. Contributions to: Essays and reviews to many journals; Poetry: American Poetry Review; Northwest Review; Tar River Poetry; Raccoon; Seneca Review; Obsidian II; Black American Literature Forum. Honours: Whiting Foundation Writer's Award, 1988; CCLM-General Electric Foundation Award for Younger Writers, 1988; Several Fellowships. Address: Washington University, Campus Box 1109, One Brookings Drive, St Louis, MO 63130, USA.

EAST Morris. See: **WEST Morris.**

EASTAUGH Kenneth, b. 30 Jan 1929, Preston, England. Appointments: Television Critic, 1965-67, Show Business Writer, 1967-70, Daily Mirror, London; Chief Show Business Writer, The Sun, London, 1970-73; TV Columnist, The Times, London, 1977; Film Critic, Prima Magazine, Music Critic, Classical Music Weekly, 1976-; Chief Show Business Executive, Daily Star, London, 1978-83. Publications: The Event (television play), 1968; Better Than a Man (televsion play), 1970; Dapple Downs (radio serial), 1973-74; Awkward Cuss (play), 1976; Havergal Brian: The Making of a Composer (biography), 1976; Coronation Street (television series), 1977-78; The Carry On Book (cinema), 1978; Havergal Who? (television documentary), 1980; Mr Love (novel, screenplay), 1986; Dallas (television serial), 1989; Three

film contract with David Puttman/Warner Brothers, 1992; Embers (play), 1998; The New Carry On Book, 1998. Address: c/o Michael Shaw, Curtis Brown Group Ltd, Haymarket House, 28-29 Haymarket, London SW1Y 4SP, England.

EASTHOPE Antony Kelynge Revington, b. 14 Apr 1939, Portsmouth, England. Professor. m. Diane Garside, 1 Feb 1972, 1 son, 2 daughters. Education: BA, 1961, MA, 1965, MLitt, 1967, Christ's College, Cambridge. Appointments: Brown University, Rhode Island, USA, 1964-66; Warwick University, England, 1967-68; Manchester Metropolitan University, 1969-. Publications: Poetry as Discourse, 1983; What a Man's Gotta Do, 1986; British Post-Structuralism, 1988; Poetry and Phantasy, 1989; Literary into Cultural Studies, 1991; Wordsworth, Now and Then, 1993; Englishness and National Culture, 1999. Contributions to: Numerous magazines and journals. Honours: Charter Fellow, Wolfson College, Oxford, 1985-86; Visiting Fellow, University of Virginia, 1990. Address: 27 Victoria Avenue, Didsbury, Manchester M20 8QX, England.

EASTON Robert Olney, b. 4 July 1915, San Francisco, California, USA. Writer. m. Jane Faust, 24 Sept 1940, 4 daughters. Education: Stanford University, 1933-34; SB, Harvard University, 1938; MA, University of California, 1960. Publications: The Happy Man, 1943; Lord of Beasts (co-author), 1961; The Book of the American West (co-author), 1963; The Hearing, 1964; Californian Condor (co-author), 1964; Max Brand, 1970; Black Tide, 1972; This Promised Land, 1982; China Caravans, 1982; Life and Work (co-author), 1988; Power and Glory, 1989; Love and War (co-author), 1991. Contributions to: Magazines. Literary Agent: Jon Tuska. Address: 2222 Las Canoas Road, Santa Barbara, CA 93105, USA.

EATON Charles Edward, b. 25 June 1916, Winston-Salem, North Carolina, USA. Poet; Writer. m. Isabel Patterson, 1950. Education: Duke University, 1932-33; BA, University of North Carolina at Chapel Hill, 1936; Princeton University, 1936-37; MA in English, Harvard University, 1940. Appointments: Instructor in Creative Writing, University of Missouri, 1940-42; Vice Consul, American Embassy, Rio de Janeiro, 1942-46; Professor of Creative Writing, University of North Carolina, 1946-52. Publications: Poetry: The Bright Plain, 1942; The Shadow of the Swimmer, 1951; The Greenhouse in the Garden, 1956; Countermoves, 1963; On the Edge of the Knife, 1970; The Man in the Green Chair, 1977; Colophon of the Rover, 1980; The Thing King, 1983; The Work of the Wrench, 1985; New and Selected Poems 1942-1987, 1987; A Guest on Mild Evenings, 1991; The Country of the Blue, 1994; The Fox and I, 1996. Novel: A Lady of Pleasure, 1993. Short Stories: Write Me From Rio, 1959; The Girl From Ipanema, 1972; The Case of the Missing Photographs, 1978; New and Selected Stories 1959-1989, 1989. Honours: Bread Loaf Writers Conference Robert Frost Fellowship, 1941; Ridgely Torrence Memorial Award, 1951; Gertrude Boatwright Harris Award, 1955; Arizona Quarterly Awards, 1956, 1975, 1977, 1979, 1982; Roanoke-Chowan Awards, 1970, 1987, 1991; Oscar Arnold Young Award, 1971; O Henry Award, 1972; Alice Faye di Castagnola Award, 1974; Arvon Foundation Award, 1980; Hollins Critic Award, 1984; Brockman Awards, 1984, 1986; Kansas Quarterly Awards, 1987; North Carolina Literature Award, 1988; Fortner Award, 1993. Contributions to: Periodicals. Membership: American Academy of Poets. Address: 808 Greenwood Road, Chapel Hill, NC 27514, USA.

EATON Trevor Michael William, b. 26 Mar 1934, Harrow, London, England. Writer; Editor; Professional Performer of Chaucer. m. Beryl Elizabeth Rose Conley, 29 Sept 1958, 2 sons, 2 daughters. Education: New College, Oxford University, 1955-58; MA, English Language and Literature, Oxford; MA, Applied Linguistics, University of Kent, Canterbury, 1988. Appointments: Founder-Editor, Journal of Literary Semantics, 1972-; Founder, International Association of Literary Semantics, 1992. Publications: The Semantics of

Literature, 1966; Theoretical Semics, 1972; Editor, Essays in Literary Semantics (editor), 1978. Other: Recordings in Middle English: the Canterbury Tales, 1986-93; Sir Gawain and the Green Knight, 1995. Contributions to: Linguistics; Cahier Roumains d'Etudes Littéraires; Style; Educational Studies. Memberships: International Association of Literary Semantics; International PEN; Linguistics Association of Great Britain; PALA. Address: Honeywood Cottage, 35 Seaton Avenue, Hythe, Kent CT21 5HH, England.

EBARA Jun. See: **SHIMOKAWA Hideo.**

EBEJER Francis, b. 28 Aug 1925, Malta. Author; Dramatist; Poet. m. Jane Couch, 5 Sept 1947, separated 1957, 2 sons, 1 dec, 1 daughter. Education: Matriculated, Malta Lyceum, 1939; Fulbright Grant, USA, 1961-62. Appointments: Drama and Literature Lecturer. Publications: A Wreath of Maltese Innocents, 1958; Evil of the King Cockroach, 1960; In the Eye of the Sun, 1969; Requiem for a Maltese Fascist, 1980; Come Again in Spring, 1980; Leap of Malta Dolphins, 1982. Plays: Over 40 in Maltese, 7 volumes, 1950-85; 11 in English, 3 volumes, 1950-85. Contributions: Short stories, poems, essays etc. in various Maltese publications; Contributed chapter to book No Longer Silent, 1995. Honours: Cheyney Award for Drama, 1964; 4 Malta Literary Awards, 1972-; Phoenicia Trophy Award for Culture, 1982; Médaille d'Honneur de la Ville d'Avignon, France, 1986. Memberships: English PEN; fellow; French Academy of Vaucluse; Malta Literary Society, honorary president; Maltese Academy of Letters, council member, 1984-88. Address: Nivea Court, Sweigqi Valley, Swieqi STJ05, Malta.

EBEL Suzanne, (Suzanne Goodwin, Cecily Shelbourne), Writer. Publications: Love, The Magician, 1956; Journey from Yesterday, 1963; The Half-Enchanted, 1964; The Love Campaign, 1965; The Dangerous Winter, 1965; A Perfect Stranger, 1966; A Name in Lights, 1968; A Most Auspicious Star, 1968; Somersault, 1971; Portrait of Jill, 1972; Dear Kate, 1972; To Seek a Star, 1973; The Family Feeling, 1973; Girl by the Sea, 1974; Music in Winter, 1975; A Grove of Olives, 1976; River Voices, 1976; The Double Rainbow, 1977; A Rose in Heather, 1978; Julia's Sister, 1982; The Provencal Summer, 1982; House of Nightingales, 1986; The Clover Field, 1987. As Suzanne Goodwin: The Winter Spring, 1978 (USA - Stage of Love, as Cecily Shelbourne, 1978); The Winter Sisters, 1980; Emerald, 1980; Floodtide, 1983; Sisters, 1985; Cousins, 1986; Daughters, 1987; Lovers, 1988; To Love a Hero, 1989; A Change of Season, 1990; The Rising Storm, 1992; While the Music Lasts, 1993; The Difference, 1995; Sheer Chance, 1997. Non-fiction: Explore the Cotswolds by Bicycle (with Doreen Impey), 1973; London's Riverside: From Hampton Court in the West to Greenwich Palace in the East (with Doreen Impey), 1975. Literary Agent: Curtis Brown. Address: 52A Digby Mansions, Hammersmith Bridge Road, London W6 9DF, England.

EBER Irene, b. 29 Dec 1929, Germany. Professor. 1 son, 1 daughter. Education: BA, Pomona College, 1955; MA, Sacramento State University, 1961; PhD, Claremont Graduate University, 1966. Appointments: Assistant Professor of History, Whittier College, California, 1966-68; Professor of East Asian Studies, Hebrew University of Jerusalem, 1969-98, Emeritus, 1998-. Publications: Voices From Afar: Modern Chinese Writers on Oppressed Peoples and Their Literature, 1980; Confucianism, the Dynamics of Tradition (editor), 1986; The Bible in Modern China: The Literary and Intellectual Impact (co-editor), 1998; The Jewish Bishop and the Chinese Bible, S.I.Y. Schereschewsky 1831-1906, 1999. Contributions to: China Quarterly; Bulletin of SOAS; Monumenta Serica; Feminist Studies; Judaism; Revue Bibliographique de Sinologie. Address: c/o Truman Research Institute, Hebrew University, Mount Scopus, 91905 Jerusalem, Israel.

EBERSOHN Wessel (Schalk), b. 6 Mar 1940, Cape Town, South Africa. Writer. Publications: A Lonely Place to Die (mystery novel), 1979; The Centurion (mystery novel), 1979; Store up the Anger (novel), 1981; Divide the Night (mystery novel), 1981; Klara's Visitors (novel), 1987. Address: 491 Long Avenue, Ferndale 2194, Transvaal, South Africa.

EBERT Alan, b. 14 Sept 1935, New York, New York, USA. Author. Education: BA, Brooklyn College, 1957; MA, Fordham University, 1975. Publications: The Homosexuals, 1977; Every Body is Beautiful (with Ron Fletcher), 1978; Intimacies, 1979; Traditions (novel), 1981; The Long Way Home (novel), 1984; Marriages (novel), 1987. Contributions to: Family Circle; Essence; Look; Us; Good Housekeeping. Membership: American Society of Journalists and Authors. Address: 353 West 56th Street, New York, NY 10019, USA.

EBERT Roger (Joseph), b. 18 June 1942, Urbana, Illinois, USA. Film Critic; Writer; Lecturer. m. Chaz Hammelsmith, 18 July 1992. Education: BS, University of Illinois, 1964; University of Cape Town, 1965; University of Chicago, 1966-67. Appointments: Reporter, News Gazette, Champaign-Urbana, Illinois, 1958-66; Instructor, Chicago City College, 1967-68; Film Critic, Chicago Sun-Times, 1967-, US Magazine, 1978-79, WMAQ-TV, Chicago, 1980-83, WLS-TV, Chicago, 1984-, New York Post, 1986-88, New York Daily News, 1988-92, Compu Serve, 1991-, Microsoft Cinemania, 1994-; Lecturer, University of Chicago, 1969-; Co-Host, Sneak Previews, WTTW-TV, Chicago, 1977-82; At the Movies, syndicated television programme, 1982-86; Siskel and Ebert, syndicated television programme, 1986-99. Publications: An Illini Century, 1967; A Kiss is Still a Kiss, 1984; Roger Ebert's Movie Home Companion (annual volumes), 1986-93, subsequently Roger Ebert's Video Companion, 1994-; The Perfect London Walk (with Daniel Curley), 1986; Two Weeks in the Midday Sun: A Cannes Notebook, 1987; The Future of the Movies: Interviews with Martin Scorses, Steven Spielberg, and George Lucas (with Gene Siskel), 1991; Behind the Phantom's Mask, 1993; Ebert's Little Movie Glossary, 1994; The Future of the Movies: The Computer Insectiary (co-author), 1994; Roger Ebert's Book of Film, 1996; Questions for the Movie Answer Man, 1997. Contributions to: Newspapers and magazines. Honours: Overseas Press Club Award, 1963; Rotary Fellow, 1965; Pulitzer Prize for Criticism, 1975; Chicago Emmy Award, 1979; Honorary Doctorate, University of Colorado, 1993; Kluge Fellow in Film Studies, University of Virginia, 1995-96. Memberships: Academy of London; American Newspaper Guild; National Society of Film Critics; Phi Delta Theta; Sigma Delta Chi; Writers Guild of America. Address: c/o ChicagoSun-Times, 401 North Wabash, Chicago, IL 60611, USA.

EBERT Tibor, b. 14 Oct 1926, Bratislava, Czechoslovakia. Writer; Poet; Dramatist. m. Eva Gati, 11 Feb 1968, 1 daughter. Education: BA, Music, Ferenc Liszt Academy of Music, 1952; Law, Philosophy, Literature Studies, Department of Law and Philosophy, Eötvös Lórand University, Budapest, 1951-53. Appointments: Dramaturg, József Attila Theatre, Budapest, Hungary, 1984-85; Editor-in-Chief, Agora Publishers, Budapest, 1989-92; Editor, Hirvivo Literary Magazine, 1990-92. Publications: Mikrodrámák, 1971; Rosarium, 1987; Kobayashi, 1989; Legenda egy fúvószenekarról, 1990; Jób kőnyve, 1991; Fagyott Orpheusz (poems), 1993; Esõ, 1996; Egy város glóriája, 1997; Bartók, 1997; Eredők, 1998; Éltem, 1998. Several plays performed on stage including: Les Escaliers; Musique de Chambre; Demosthenes; Esterházy. Contributions to: Numerous short stories, poems, dramas, and essays to several leading Hungarian literary journals and magazines. Honours: Honorary Member, Franco-Hungarian Society, 1980-; Bartók Prize, 1987; Commemorative Medal, City of Pozsony-Pressburg-Bratislava, 1991; Esterházy Prize, 1993; Order of Hungarian Republic, 1996. Memberships: PEN Club; Association of Hungarian Writers; Literary Association Berzsenyi. Literary Agent: Artisjus Budapest, Hungary. Address: Csévi u 15c, 1025 Budapest, Hungary.

ECO Umberto, b. 5 Jan 1932, Alessandria, Italy. Professor of Semiotics; Author. m. Renate Ramge, 24 Sept 1962, 1 son, 1 daughter. Education: PhD, University of Turin, 1954. Appointments: Assistant Lecturer, 1956-63, Lecturer 1963-64, University of Turin; Lecturer, University of Milan, 1964-65; Professor, University of Florence, 1966-69; Visiting Professor, New York University, 1969-70, 1976, Northwestern University, 1972, Yale University, 1977, 1980, 1981, Columbia University, 1978, 1984; Professor of Semiotics, Milan Polytechnic, 1970-71, University of Bologna, 1971-. Publications: Il Problema Estetico in San Tommaso, 1956, English translation as The Aethetics of Thomas Aquinas, 1988; Sviluppo dell'Estetica Medioevale, 1959, English translation as Art and Beauty in the middle Ages, 1986; Diario Minimo, 1963; La Struttura Assente, 1968; Il Costume di Casa, 1973; Trattato di Semiotica Generale, 1976; Il Nome della Rosa (novel), 1981, English translation as The Name of the Rose; Sette anni di desiderio 1977-83, 1984; Il Pendolo di Foucault, 1988; L'isola del giorno prima (novel), 1995, English translation as The island of the day Before. Contributions to: various publications. Honours: Medici Prize, 1982; McLuhan Teleglobe Prize, 1985; Honorary DLitt, University of Glasgow, 1990, University of Kent, 1992. Membership: International Association for Semiotic Studies. Address: Piazza Castello 13, 20121 Milan, Italy.

ECO-LOGIJA. See: **XERRI Raymond Christian.**

EDDINGS David, b. 7 July 1931, Spokane, Washington, USA. Writer. m. Judith Leigh Schall, 27 Oct 1962. Education: Everett Junior College, 1950-52; BA, Reed College, 1954; MA, University of Washington, Seattle, 1961. Publications: High Hunt, 1973; Pawn of Prophecy, 1982; Queen of Sorcery, 1982; Magician's Gambit, 1983; Castle of Wizardry, 1984; Guardians of the West, 1987; King of the Margos, 1988; Demon Lord of Karanda, 1988; The Diamond Throne, 1989; The Sorceress of Darshiva, 1989; The Ruby Knight, 1990; The Seeress of Kell, 1991; The Losers, 1992; The Sapphire Rose, 1992; Domes of Fire, 1993; The Hidden City, 1994; The Shining Ones, 1994. Address: c/o Ballantine Books Inc, 201 East 50th Street, New York, NY 10022, USA.

EDELMAN Bernard, b. 14 Dec 1946, Brooklyn, New York, USA. Editor; Consultant. m. Ellen M Leary, 31 May 1985. Education: BA, Brooklyn College, 1968; MA, John Jay College of Criminal Justice, 1983. Publication: Dear America: Letters Home From Vietnam (editor), 1985. Contributions to: Periodicals. Honours: 2 Emmy Awards and many film citations. Address: Mount Joy Road, Finesville, NJ 08865, USA.

EDGAR David, b. 26 Feb 1948, Birmingham, England. Playwright. Education: BA, Honours, Drama, Manchester University, 1969. Appointments: Lecturer in Playwriting, 1974-78, Honorary Senior Research Fellow, 1988-, Honorary Professor, 1992-, Birmingham University; Resident Playwright, Birmingham Repertory Theatre, 1985-. Publications: The Second Time as Farce, 1988; Edgar Shorts (Blood Sports with Ball Boys, Baby Love, The National Theatre, The Midas Connection), 1990. Plays: Maydays, London, 1983, revised edition, 1984; Entertaining Strangers: A Play for Dorchester, Dorchester, Dorset, 1985, revised version, London, 1987; That Summer, London, 1987; Plays I (includes The Jail Diary of Albie Sachs, Mary Barnes, Saigon Rose, O Fair Jerusalem, Destiny), 1987; Heartlanders (with Stephen Bill and Anne Devlin), 1989; The Shape of the Table, 1990; Dr Jekyll and Mr Hyde, 1991. Screenplay: Lady Jane, 1986; Radio Plays: Ecclesiastes, 1977; A Movie Starring Me, 1991. Television Plays: The Eagle Has Landed, 1973; Sanctuary From His Play Gangsters, 1973; I Know What I Meant, 1974; The Midas Connection, 1975; Censors (with Hugh Whitemore and Robert Muller), 1975; Voe For Them (with Neil Grant), 1989; Buying a Landslide, 1992. Honours: John Whiting Award, 1976; Bicentennial Exchange Fellowship, 1978; Society of West End Theatre Award, 1980; New York Drama Critics Circle Award, 1982; Tony Award, 1982. Address: c/o Michael Imison Playwrights, 28 Almeida Street, London, N1 1TD, England.

EDGECOMBE Jean Marjorie, b. 28 Feb 1914, Bathurst, New South Wales, Australia. Author. m. Gordon Henry Edgecombe, 2 Feb 1945, 2 sons, 2 daughters. Education: BA, Honours, Sydney University, 1935. Publications: Discovering Lord Howe Island, (with Isobel Bennett), 1978; Discovering Norfolk Island, (with Isobel Bennett), 1983; Flinders Island, the Furneaux Group, 1985; Flinders Island and Eastern Bass Strait, 1986, 2nd edition, 1994; Lord Howe Island, World Heritage Area, 1987; Phillip Island and Western Port, 1989; Norfolk Island, South Pacific: Island of History and Many Delights, 1991; Discovering Flinders Island, 1992; Discovering King Island, Western Bass Strait, 1993. Contributions to: Articles and poems. Honour: Medal of the Order of Australia, 1995. Membership: Australian Society of Authors. Address: 7 Oakleigh Avenue, Thornleigh, 2120 New South Wales, Australia.

EDMOND Lauris Dorothy, b. 2 Apr 1924, Dannevirke, New Zealand. University Tutor; Poet; Writer; Editor. m. Trevor Charles Edmond, 16 May 1945, 1 son, 5 daughters. Education: Certificate, Wellington Teachers' College, 1943; Speech Therapy Diploma, Christchurch Teachers' College, 1944; BA, Honours, Waikato University, 1968; MA, 1st Class Honours, Victoria University, Wellington, 1972. Appointments: High School Teacher, 1967-73; Editor, Post Primary Teachers' Journal, 1973-81; Tutor, Massey University, 1980-; Writer-in-Residence, Deakin University, 1985; Many poetry readings. Publications: Poetry: In Middle Air, 1975; The Pear Tree and Other Poems, 1977; Wellington Letter: A Sequence of Poems, 1980; Catching It, 1983; Selected Poems, 1984; Seasons and Creatures, 1986; Summer Near the Arctic Circle, 1988; New and Selected Poems, 1991; Scenes from a Small City, 1994; Selected Poems, 1975-94, 1994; A Matter of Timing, 1996; In Position, 1996. Non-Fiction: Autobiography: Vol 1, Hot October 1989, Vol 2, Bonfires in the Rain, 1991, Vol 3, The Quick World, 1992. Editor: Women in Wartime, 1986. Contributions to: Many anthologies, journals and magazines. Honours: Best First Book Award, 1975, Lilian Ida Smith Award for Poetry, 1987; PEN New Zealand Centre; Katherine Mansfield Memorial Fellowship, 1981; Commonwealth Poetry Prize, 1985; Officer of the Order of the British Empire, 1986; Writers Fellowship, Victoria University, Wellington, 1987; Honorary DLitt, Massey University, 1988. Memberships: PEN New Zealand Centre; Wellington Poetry Society. Address: 22 Grass Street, Oriental Bay, Wellington, New Zealand.

EDMOND Murray (Donald), b. 1949, New Zealand. Director; Actor; Poet. Appointments: Director and Actor, Town and Country Players, Wellington; Lecturer in Drama, University of Auckland, 1991. Publications: Entering the Eye, 1973; Patchwork, 1978; End Wall, 1981; Letters and Paragraphs, 1987; The New Poets of the 80's: Initiatives in New Zealand Poetry (co-editor), 1987; From the Word Go, 1992; The Switch, 1994. Address: c/o Department of English, University of Auckland, Private Bag 92019, Auckland, New Zealand.

EDRIC Robert. See: **ARMITAGE G E.**

EDSON Russell, b. 9 Apr 1935, USA. Poet; Writer. m. Frances Edson. Education: Art Students League, New York City; New School for Social Research, New York City; Columbia University; Black Mountain College, North Carolina. Publications: Poetry: Appearances: Fables and Drawings, 1961; A Stone is Nobody's: Fables and Drawings, 1964; The Boundry, 1964; The Very Thing That Happens: Fables and Drawings, 1964; The Brain Kitchen: Writings and Woodcuts, 1965; What a Man Can See, 1969; The Childhood of an Equestrian, 1973; The Calm Theatre, 1973; A Roof with Some Clouds Behind It, 1975; The Intuitive Journey and Other Works, 1976; The Reason Why the Closet-Man is Never Sad, 1977; Edson's Mentality, 1977; The Traffic, 1978; The Wounded Breakfast: Ten Poems, 1978; With Sincerest Regrets, 1981; Wuck Wuck Wuck!, 1984; The Wounded Breakfast, 1985; Tick Tock, 1992; The Tunnel: Selected Poems,

1994. Fiction: Gulping's Recital, 1984; The Song of Percival Peacock, 1992. Honours: Guggenheim Fellowship, 1974; National Endowment for the Arts Grant, 1976, and Fellowship, 1982; Whiting Foundation Award, 1989. Address: 29 Ridgeley Street, Darien, CT 06820, USA.

EDWARDS Anne, b. 20 Aug 1927, Porchester, New York, USA. Writer. Education: University of California at Los Angeles, 1943-46; Southern Methodist University, 1947-48. Publications: A Child's Bible (adaptor) 1967; The Survivors, 1968; Miklos Alexandrovitch is Missing, 1969; Shadow of a Lion, 1970; The Hesitant Heart, 1974; Judy Garland: A Biography, 1974; Haunted Summer, 1974; The Inn and Us (with Stephen Citron), 1975; Child of Night, 1975; P T Barnum, 1976; The Great Houdini, 1977; Vivien Leigh: A Biography, 1977; Sonya: The Life of the Countess Tolstoy, 1981; The Road to Tara: The Life of Margaret Mitchell, 1983; Matriarch: Queen Mary and the House of Windsor, 1984; A Remarkable Woman: Katherine Hepburn, 1985; Early Reagan: The Rise to Power, 1986; The Demilles: An American Dynasty, 1987; American Princess: A Biography of Shirley Temple, 1988; Royal Sisters: Queen Elizabeth and Princess Margaret, 1990; Wallis - the Novel, 1991; The Grimaldis of Monaco: Centuries of Scandals, Years of Grace, 1992; La Divina, 1994; Throne of Gold: The Lives of the Aga Khans, 1995; Streisand: It Only Happens Once, 1996. Address: c/o International Creative Management Inc, 40 West 57th Street, New York, NY 10019, USA.

EDWARDS Clive D, b. 24 Mar 1947, England. University Lecturer. m. Lynne Green, 3 July 1993. Education: BA, Open University; MA, PhD, Royal College of Art. Appointments: Loughborough University, 1990-. Publications: Victorian Furniture, 1993; Twentieth Century Furniture, 1994; Eighteenth Century Furniture, 1996; Encyclopaedia of Interior Design (contributor), 1997. Contributions to: Design History Journal; Studies in Decorative Arts; Furniture History; County Life; Antique Collecting; History of Technology. Membership: Fellow, Royal Society of Arts. Address: c/o Loughborough University School of Art, Loughborough, Leics, England.

EDWARDS Elizabeth, b. 13 Oct 1920, Holmfirth, Yorkshire, England. Retired Lecturer. m. Harry L Edwards, 28 Dec 1968. Education: BA, Admin, Teachers Diploma, Manchester University, 1945-49. Appointments: Broadway Secondary Modern School, Cheadle; Leamington Spa College of Further Education; Buxton College of Further Education; Bournemouth College of Technology. Publications: A History of Bournemouth, 1981; Tails of the Famous, 1987; Famous Women in Dorset, 1992; Margaret Brown - Shelley Was Her Life, 1994; Rebbeck Bros, 150 Years and Still Going Strong, 1995; Bournemouth Past, 1998. Contributions to: Dorset Life; Hampshire Life; Choice; Yours; Gentlemen's Magazine. Membership: Friends Literary Society; Tutor, French Conversation, University of the Third Age. Address: 24 St Mary's Court, 59 Belle Vue Ruad, Bournemouth BH6 3DF, England.

EDWARDS Josh. See: LEVINSON Leonard.

EDWARDS L M T. See: LLOYD Linda Mary Teressa.

EDWARDS Norman. See: CARR Terry (Gene).

EDWARDS Page Lawrence Jr, b. 15 Jan 1941, Gooding, Idaho, USA. Archivist. m. Diana Selser, 26 Aug 1986, 2 sons, 2 daughters. Education: BA, Stanford University, 1963; MFA, University of Iowa, 1974; MLS, Simmons College, 1982. Appointments: Staff, Breadloaf Writers' Conference, 1982-84; Writer-in-Residence, Flagler College, St Augustine, Florida, 1985-. Publications: Mules That Angels Ride, 1972; Touring, 1974; Staking Claims, 1976; Peggy Salte, 1984; Scarface Joe, 1985; The Lake, 1986; American Girl, 1990. Contributions to: Redbook; Woman's World; Bananas; Iowa Review. Address: c/o Marion Boyars Ltd, 26 East 33rd Street, New York, NY 10016, USA.

EDWARDS Philip Walter, b. 7 Feb 1923, Cumbria, England. Retired Professor of English; Writer. m. Sheila Mary Wilkes, 8 May 1952, 3 sons, 1 daughter. Education: BA, 1942, MA, 1946, PhD, 1960, University of Birmingham. Appointments: Lecturer, University of Birmingham, 1946-60; Professor, Trinity College, Dublin, 1960-66, University of Essex, 1966-74, University of Liverpool, 1974-90. Publications: Sir Walter Ralegh, 1953; Kyd, The Spanish Tragedy, 1959; Shakespeare and the Confines of Art, 1968; Massinger: Plays and Poems, 1976; Shakespeare's Pericles, 1976; Threshold of a Nation, 1979; Hamlet, 1985; Shakespeare: A Writers Progress, 1986; Last Voyages, 1988; The Story of the Voyage, 1994; Sea-Mark, 1997. Membership: British Academy, fellow, 1986-. Address: High Gillinggrove, Gillinggate, Kendal, Cumbria LA9 4JB, England.

EDWARDS Rebecca Jane, b. 4 Apr 1969, Batlow, New South Wales, Australia. Writer; Poet; Artist. 1 daughter. Education: BA with double major in Japanese Language and Culture, University of Queensland, 1992. Appointment: Writer-in-Residence, James Cook University, Townsville, Queensland, 1996. Publications: Eating the Experience, 1994; Eat the Ocean (contributor), 1996. Contributions to: Anthologies and journals. Honours: Red Earth Award, Northern Territories Section, 1989; Ford Memorial Medal, University of Queensland, 1991, 1992; 5th Regional Illustrated Poetry Competition, 1995. Memberships: Fellowship of Australian Writers; New South Wales Poets' Union; Queensland Artworkers' Alliance; Queensland Writers' Centre. Address: PO Box 1055, Spring Hill, Brisbane, Queensland 4004, Australia.

EDWARDS Robert Philip, b. 13 Oct 1953, Liverpool, England. Journalist; Writer. m. Fiona Riddoch, 2 daughters. Education: MA, English Literature, Jesus College, Cambridge, England. Appointments: Organiser, Scottish Campaign to Resist Atomic Menace, 1977-78; Campaigner Organiser, Shelter (Scotland), 1978-80; Freelance Journalist Writing for Social Work Today, New Statesman, The Scotsman, The Guardian, Edinburgh Evening News, Scotland on Sunday, The Observer, New Scientist, 1980-. Publications: Fuelling the Nuclear Arms Race: The Links Between Nuclear Power and Nuclear Weapons (with Sheila Durie), 1982; Britain's Nuclear Nightmare (with Janes Cutler), 1988; Still Fighting for Gemma (with Susan D'Arcy), 1995. Honours: Many for environmental journalism. Memberships: Society of Authors; National Union of Journalists. Literary Agent: Sheil Land Associates. Address: 53 Nile Grove, Edinburgh EH10 4RE, Scotland.

EDWARDS Rowan (Judith), b. 19 Nov 1945, India. Writer; Journalist; Creative Writing Tutor. m. Martin Brian Edwards, 18 Dec 1965, 1 son, 1 daughter. Education: BA, King's College, University of London, 1966; RSA Certificate in ESL, 1976. Appointments: Teacher to Adults, Inner London Education Authority; Personal Assistant to Labour MP; Examiner; Creative Writing Tutor. Publications: 16 Romantic novels, 1983-94. Contributions to: Newspapers and magazines. Honours: Bristol Poetry Competition, 1988; ORBIS, 1989; 1st Prize, South West Arts, for Radio Play, 1989. Memberships: Society of Authors; Romantic Novelists Association. Address: 66 Cooden Drive, Bexhill-on-Sea, East Sussex TN39 3AX, England.

EDWARDS Ted (Brian), b. 25 Apr 1939, Leigh, Lancashire, England. Explorer; Author; Teacher; Song Writer. Education: BEd, Manchester Polytechnic, 1979. Publications: A Slutchy Brew, 1971; The Empty Quarter, 1984; Beyond the Last Oasis, 1985; Fight the Wild Island, 1986. Contributions to: Journals and magazines. Address: The Garret, 6 Westminster Road, Eccles, Manchester M30 9HF, England.

EFFINGER George Alec, b. 10 Jan 1947, Cleveland, Ohio, USA. Writer. Education: Yale University, 1965, 1969; New York University, 1968. Appointment: Teacher, Tulane University, New Orleans, 1973-74. Publications: What Entropy Means to Me, 1972; Relatives, 1973; Mixed Feelings (short stories), 1974; Nightmare Blue (with G Dozois), 1975; Irrational Numbers (short stories), 1976;

Those Gentle Voices, 1976; Felicia, 1976; Death in Florence, 1978, as Utopia Three, 1980; Dirty Tricks (short stories), 1978; Heroics, 1979; The Wolves of Memory, 1981; Idle Pleasures (short stories), 1983; The Nick of Time, 1986; The Bird of Time, 1986; When Gravity Fails, 1987; Exile Kiss, 1991; Maureen Birnbaum, Barbarian Swordsperson, 1993. Address: Box 15183, New Orleans, LA 70175, USA.

EGAN Gregory Mark, b. 20 Aug 1961, Perth, Western Australia. Writer. Education: BSc, University of Western Australia, 1981. Appointments: Computer Programmer, Garvan Institute of Medical Research, 1983-87, Royal Perth Hospital, Department of Medical Physics, 1989-91. Publications: Novels: An Unusual Angle, 1983; Quarantine, 1992; Permutation City, 1994; Distress, 1995; Diaspora, 1997. Short Fiction: Axromatic, 1995; Luminous, 1998. Contributions to: Interzone Magazine; Asimovs Science Fiction Magazine. Honour: John W Campbell Memorial Award, 1995. Literary Agent: Peter Robinson. Address: c/o Curtis Brown, Haymarket House, 28/29 Haymarket, London SW1Y 4SP, England.

EGERIC Miroslav, b. 23 Feb 1934, Ridjevstica, Yugoslavia. Professor; Writer. m. Ljubinka Egeric, 13 Nov 1961, 1 daughter. Education: Graduated, Yugoslav Literature, Serbian Language, 1960, Doctorate, 1970, University of Philosophy. Appointments: Assistant, 1963, Docent, 1971, Associate Professor, 1976, Full Professor, 1981, University of Philosophy. Publications: Portraits and Pamphlets, 1963; Prayers on Chegar, 1967; Anthology of Modern Serbian Satire, 1970; People, Books and Dates, 1971; Word in Time, 1974; Works and Days, 1975; Lucky Choice, 1979; The Well, 1980; Works and Days II, 1982; Voices and Silences, 1984; Letters to Family Men, 1986; Works and Days III, 1990; Voices, Values, 1995; Serbia and Memory, 1996; Works and Days IV, 1997. Contributions to: Horizons; The Student; Works; Politika; NIN; Dnevnik; Letopis Matice Srpske; Izraz; Savremenik; Knjizevna Rec; Knjizene Novine; Indeks; Knjizevne Kritika. Honours: Djordje Jovanovic; Milan Bogdanovic; Laza Kostic. Memberships: Association of Serbian Writers, 1965; Serbian PEN Centre, 1989. Address: Brace Jovandic 17, 21 000 Novi Sad, Yugoslavia.

EGGERTSSON Thorsteinn, b. 25 Feb 1942, Keflavik, Iceland. Author; Lyricist; Journalist. Education: Graphic Design, Akademiet for Friog Merkantil Kunst, Copenhagen, 1964. Appointment: Most Prolific Pop-Lyricist in Scandinavian Countries. Publications: The Paper King's Subjects, 1991; Va (Danger), 1993; Cartoonists and Their Inventions, 1997. Contributions to: Short stories and poetry in several magazines in Iceland and Denmark, numerous articles in dailies and magazines in Iceland. Honour: Best Pop Lyricist in Iceland, 1968, 1969; Represented Iceland, Poetry Hall of Fame, International Poets' Society, 1997. Memberships: Writers Union of Iceland, 1995-; STEF in Iceland, 1965-; FTT in Iceland, 1983-; International Poets' Society, Kent, England, 1997. Address: Skipholt 18, 105 Reykjavik, Iceland.

EGLETON Clive Frederick William, (Patrick Blake, John Tarrant), b. 25 Nov 1927. Author; Retired Army Officer; Retired Civil Servant. m. Joan Evelyn Lane, 9 Apr 1949, dec 22 Feb 1996, 2 sons. Education: Staff College, Camberley, 1957. Publications: Backfire, 1979; The Winter Touch, 1982; Conflict of Interests, 1984; The October Plot, 1985; Picture of the Year, 1987; Gone Missing, 1988; Seven Days to a Killing, 1988; In the Red, 1990; Last Act, 1991; A Double Deception, 1992; Hostile Intent, 1993; A Killing in Moscow, 1994; Death Throes, 1994; A Lethal Involvement, 1995; Warning Shot, 1996; Blood Money, 1997. Memberships: Crime Writers Association; Society of Authors. Literary Agent: Anthony Goff, David Higham Associates Ltd. Address: Dolphin House, Beach House Lane, Bembridge, Isle of Wight PO35 5TA, England.

EHLE John Marsden Jr, b. 13 Dec 1925, Asheville, North Carolina, USA. Writer. m. 1) Gail Oliver, 30 Aug 1952, div Apr 1967, 2) Rosemary Harris, 22 Oct 1967, 1 daughter. Education: BA, University of North Carolina at Chapel Hill, 1949. Appointments: Faculty, University of North Carolina at Chapel Hill, 1951-63; Special Assistant to Governor Terry Sanford, North Carolina, 1963-64; Programme Officer, Ford Foundation, New York City, 1964-65; Member, White House Group for Domestic Affairs, 1964-66; Special Consultant, Duke University, 1976-80. Publications: Fiction: Move Over, Mountain, 1957; Kingstree Island, 1959; Lion on the Hearth, 1961; The Land Breakers, 1964; The Road, 1967; Time of Drums, 1970; The Journey of August King, 1971; The Changing of the Guard, 1975; The Winter People, 1981; Last One Home, 1983; The Widows Trial, 1989. Non-Fiction: The Free Men, 1965; The Survivor, 1968; Trail of Tears: The Rise and Fall of the Cherokee Nation, 1988; Dr Frank: Living with Frank Porter Graham, 1993. Screenplay: The Journey of August King, 1995. Honours: Walter Raleigh Prizes for Fiction, North Carolina Department of Cultural Affairs, 1964, 1967, 1970, 1975, 1984; Mayflower Society Cup, 1965; State of North Carolina Award for Literature, 1972; Governor's Award for Distinguished Meritorious Service, North Carolina, 1978; Lillian Smith Prize, Southern Regional Council, 1982; Distinguished Alumnus Award, University of North Carolina at Chapel Hill, 1984; Thomas Wolfe Memorial Award, Western North Carolina Historical Association, 1984; W D Weatherford Award, Berea College, 1985; Caldwell Award, North Carolina Humanities Council, 1995. Memberships: Authors League; PEN; State of North Carolina Awards Commission, 1982-93. Address: 125 Westview Drive North West, Salem, NC 27104, USA.

EHRENBERG Miriam Colbert, b. 6 Mar 1930, New York, New York, USA. Psychologist. m. Otto Ehrenberg, 20 Sept 1956, 2 daughters. Education: BA, Queens College; MA, City University of New York; PhD, New School for Social Research, New York City. Publications: The Psychotherapy Maze, 1977, 2nd edition, 1986; Optimum Brain Power, 1985; The Intimate Circle, 1988. Contributions to: Ready Reference: Women's Issues; Transforming the Categories; Gay and Lesbian Mental Health. Membership: American Psychological Association. Address: 118 Riverside Drive, New York, NY 10024, USA.

EHRENREICH Barbara, b. 26 Aug 1941, Butte, Montana, USA. Feminist; Critic; Novelist. m. (1) John Ehrenreich, 6 Aug 1966, 1 son, 1 daughter, (2) Gary Stevenson, 10 Dec 1983. Education: BA, Reed College, 1963; PhD, Rockefeller University, 1968. Appointments: Essayist, Time Magazine, 1990-; Columnist, The Guardian (London), 1991-. Publications: Long March, Short Spring, 1969; For Her Own Good, 1978; The Hearts of Men, 1983; Remaking Love, 1986; The Mean Season, 1987; Fear of Falling, 1989; The Worst Years of Our Lives, 1990; Kipper's Game, 1993. Contributions to: New York Times; Mother Jones; Atlantic; MS; New Republic; Radical America. Honours: National Magazine Award, 1980; Ford Foundation Award for Humanistic Perspectives on Contemporary Issues, 1981; Guggenheim Fellowship, 1987, Long Island NOW Women's Equality Award, 1988; National Book Critics' Award Nominee; National Magazine Award Finalist for Essays, 1992. Address: c/o Time, Time-Life Building, Rockefeller Center, New York, NY 10020, USA.

EHRLICH Eugene, b. 21 May 1922, New York, New York, USA. Lexicographer; Writer. Education: BS, City College, 1942; MA, Columbia University, 1948. Appointments: Assistant Professor, Fairleigh Dickinson University, 1946-48; Associate in English, Columbia University, 1949-87. Publications: How to Study Better, 1960; The Art of Technical Writing (with D Murphy), 1962; Researching and Writing Term Papers and Reports (with D Murphy), 1964; College Developmental Reading (with D Murphy and D Pace), 1966; Basic Grammar for Writing (with D Murphy), 1970; Concise Index to English (with D Murphy), 1974; Basic Vocabulary Builder, 1975; English Grammar, 1976; Punctuation, Capitalization and Spelling, 1977; Oxford American Dictionary (with others), 1980; The Oxford Illustrated Literary Guide to the United States (with Gorton Carruth), 1982; Speak for Success, 1984; Amo, Amas, Amat and More, 1985; The Bantam Concise Handbook of English, 1986; Harper's Dictionary of Foreign Terms, number 3, 1990; Collins Gem Dictionary, 1990; Collins Gem Thesaurus, 1990; Choose the Right Word (with S I Hayakawa), 1994; Veni, Vidi, Vici, 1995; The Highly Selective Dictionary for the Extraordinarily Literate, 1997; Les Bons Mots, 1997. Address: c/o HarperCollins, 10 East 53rd Street, New York, NY 10022, USA.

EHRLICH Paul (Ralph), b. 29 May 1932, Philadelphia, Pennsylvania, USA. Biologist; Professor; Writer. m. Anne Fitzhugh Howland, 18 Dec 1954, 1 daughter. Education: AB, University of Pennsylvania, 1953; AM, 1955, PhD, 1957, University of Kansas. Appointments: Research Associate, University of Kansas, 1958-59; Assistant Professor, 1959-62, Associate Professor, 1962-66, Professor, 1966-, Bing Professor of Population Studies, 1976-, Stanford University; President, Center for Conservation Biology, 1988-; Correspondent, NBC News, 1989-92. Publications: How to Know the Butterflies, 1961; Process of Evolution, 1963; Principles of Modern Biology, 1968; Population Bomb, 1968, 2nd edition, 1971; Population, Resources, Environment: Issues in Human Ecology, 1970, 2nd edition, 1972; How to be a Survivor, 1971; Global Ecology: Readings Toward a Rational Strategy for Man, 1971; Man and the Ecosphere, 1971; Introductory Biology, 1973; Human Ecology: Problems and Solutions, 1973; Ark II: Social Response to Environmental Imperatives, 1974; The End of Affluence: A Blueprint for the Future, 1974; Biology and Society, 1976; Race Bomb, 1977; Ecoscience: Population, Resources, Environment, 1977; Insect Biology, 1978; The Golden Door: International Migration, Mexico, and the US, 1979; Extinction: The Causes and Consequences of the Disappearance of Species, 1981; The Machinery of Nature, 1986; Earth, 1987; The Science of Ecology, 1987; The Birder's Handbook, 1988; New World/New Mind, 1989; The Population Explosion, 1990; Healing the Planet, 1991; Birds in Jeopardy, 1992; The Birdwatchers Handbook, 1994; The Stork and the Plow, 1995; Betrayal of Science and Reason, 1996. Contributions to: Scholarly journals. Honours: World Wildlife Federation Medal, 1987; Co-winner, Crafoord Prize in Population Biology and Conservation Biology Diversity, 1990; John D and Catherine T MacArthur Foundation Fellowship, 1990-95; Volvo Environmental Prize, 1993; United Nations Sasakawa Environmental Prize, 1994; Heinz Prize for the Environment, 1995; Tyler Prize for Environmental Achievement, 1998; Heineken Prize for Environmental Sciences, 1998. Memberships: American Academy of Arts and Sciences, fellow; American Philosophical Society, fellow; American Society of Naturalists; Entomological Society of America; Lepidopterists Society; National Academy of Sciences; Society for the Study of Evoloution; Society of Systematic Zoology. Address: c/o Department of Biological Sciences, Stanford University, Stanford, CA 94305, USA.

EHRLICHMAN John (Daniel), b. 20 Mar 1925, Tacoma, Washington, USA. Lawyer; Writer; Radio and Television Commentator. m. (1) Jeanne Fisher, 21 Aug 1949, div, 5 children, (2) Christy McLaurine, Nov 1978. Education: AB, University of California at Los Angeles, 1948; LLB, Stanford University, 1951. Appointments: Founder-Partner, Hullin, Erlichman, Roberts, and Hodge law firm, Seattle, Washington, 1952-68; Instructor in Law, University of Washington, 1967; Counsel to Richard Nixon, 1968-69; Assistant to the President for Domestic Affairs, Washington, DC, 1969-73; Convicted of conspiracy, obstruction of justice, and 2 counts of perjury in the wake of the Watergate investigation and served time in the Federal Prison Camp, Safford, Arizona, 1976-78; Radio and Television Commentator, Mutual Broadcasting System, 1978-; Executive, Law Cos Group, Atlanta, Georgia, 1991-. Publications: The Company (also published as Washington Behind Closed Doors), (novel), 1976; The Whole Truth (novel), 1979; Witness to Power: The Nixon Years (memoirs), 1982; The China Card (novel), 1986; Sketches and Notes, 1987; The Rigby File, 1989. Contributions to: Periodicals. Address: c/o Law Cos Group, 1000 Abernathy Road, Atlanta, GA 30328, USA.

EIBEL Deborah, b. 25 June 1940, Montreal, Quebec, Canada. Poet. Education: BA, McGill University, 1960; AM, Radcliffe College, 1962; MA, Johns Hopkins University, 1971. Publications: Kayak Sickness, 1972; Streets Too Narrow for Parades, 1985; Making Fun of Travellers, 1992; Gold Rush, 1996; Purple Passages, 1998; A Poet's Notebook, 1999. Contributions to: Anthologies and periodicals. Honours: Arthur Davison Ficke Sonnet Award, Poetry Society of America, 1965; Arts Bursary, Canada Council, 1967; Residency, Leighton Artists' Colony, 1988. Memberships: League of Canadian Poets; Poetry Society of America. Address: 6657 Wilderton Avenue, Montreal, Quebec H3S 2L8, Canada.

EICHENBAUM Luise Ronni, b. 22 July 1952, New York, New York, USA. Psychotherapist; Lecturer; Writer. m. Jeremy Pikser, 1 son, 1 daughter. Education: BA, City College of the City University of New York, 1973; MSW, State University of New York at Stony Brook, 1975. Appointments: Co-founder and Director, Women's Therapy Centre Institute, New York City, 1980-. Publications: Understanding Women: A Feminist Psychoanalytic Approach, 1983; What Do Women Want?: Exploring the Myth of Dependency, 1983; Between Women: Love, Envy, and Competition in Women's Friendships, 1989. Address: 562 West End Avenue, New York, NY 10024, USA.

EINARSDOTTIR Solveig Kristin, b. 24 Nov 1939, Reykjavik, Iceland. Writer. m. (1) Thorsteinn Oskarsson, 24 July 1959, div 1980, 1 son, 1 daughter, (2) Lindsay O'Brien, 6 July 1989. Education: BA, University of Iceland. Appointments: Teacher, Iceland, 1962-89; Writer, Australia, 1990-. Publications: Sögur Solveigar (The Stories of Solveig), short stories, 1991; A Danish-Icelandic Dictionary, with Peter Rasmussen, 1995; Snaedis i Solskinslandinu (Snaedis in the Land of Sunshine), children's book, 1997. Contributions to: Various articles, poems and short stories in magazines and newspapers, Iceland, 1989-. Honour: Literary Award for Short Stories, AB Publishers, Iceland, 1991. Membership: Writers Union of Iceland, 1997-. Address: The University of Sudney, PO Box 219, Narrabri, New South Wales 2390, Australia.

EINARSSON Sveinn, b. 18 Sept 1934, Reykjavík, Iceland. Writer; Dramatist; Theatre Director; Theatre Historian. m. Thora Kristjánsdóttir, 17 Oct 1964, 1 daughter. Education: Stockholm University; Sorbonne. Appointments: Artistic Director, Reykjavik Theatre Company, 1963-72; National Theatre of Iceland, 1972-83; Icelandic State Television, 1989-93; The Bandamenn Theatre Company, 1992-; Vice President, International Theatre Institute, 1979-81; Various appointments for The Council of Europe, 1985-; President, National Commission for UNESCO in Iceland, 1994-; Director, Reykjavík Arts Festival 2000. Publications: Novel: The Electricity Man, 1998; Plays: The Egg of Life, 1984; I'm Gold and Treasure, 1985; Búkolla (for children), 1989; Bandamanna saga, 1992; The Amlodi Saga, 1996; The Daughter of the Poet, 1998; Several TV and radio plays; Children's Books: Gabriella in Portugal, 1985; Dordingull, 1994; Books on the theatre: The Theatre by the Lake, 1972; Nine Years Down There, 1985; Icelandic Theatre, Vol I, 1991, Vol II, 1996. Honours: Children's Book of the Year Award, 1985; Nordic Clara Lachman Prize, 1990; 1st Prize, Icelandic Radio Short Story Competition, 1984; The Jon Sigurdson Legacy, 1997. Memberships: Icelandic Writers' Union; Playwrights' Union (former President). Address: Tjarnargata 26, 101 Reykavik, Iceland.

EIRIKSSON Asgeir Hannes, b. 19 May 1947, Reykjavik, Iceland. Columnist; Writer. m. Valgerdur Hjartardottir, 14 Apr 1974, 1 son, 2 daughters. Education: Dane End House College, Herts, England, 1963-65; Commercial College, 1967; Hotel and Catering College, 1971. Appointments: Former Member of Parliament; Member, North Atlantic Assembly, NATO, 1989-91; Alternative Member, Reykjavik City Council, 1990-94; Columnist, Timinn newspaper, 1992-. Publications: Thad Er Allt Haegt Vinvr!, 1989; Ein Med Ollu, 1990; Sogur Ur Reykjavik, 1992. Contributions to: Newspapers and magazines. Honour: Icelandic Mission, UN General Assembly, New York City, 1990. Address: Klapparberg 16, 111 Reykjavik, Iceland.

EISELE Robert, b. 9 June 1948, Altadena, California, USA. Playwright. Education: BA, 1971, MFA, 1974, University of California at Los Angeles. Appointments: Playwrighting Fellow and Actor, American Conservatory Theatre, 1975-76; Associate Professor of Theatre Arts, Rio Hondo College, California, 1976-87. Publications: Plays. Other: Many television scripts. Honours: Samuel Goldwyn Writing Award, 1973; Oscar Hammerstein Playwrighting Fellowship, 1973-74; Donald Davis Dramatic Writing Award, 1974; American Conservatory Theatre Playwrighting Fellowship, 1975-76; 1st Prize, Theatre Arts Corporation Contest, 1979; Humanitas Award, 1986; Writers Guild Award Nominations, 1994, 1996. Memberships: Academy of Television Arts and Sciences; Actors Equity Association; Dramatists Guild; Screen Actors Guild; Writers Guild of America. Address: c/o Ken Shearman & Associates, 99507 Santa Monica Boulevard, No 212, Beverly Hills, CA 90210, USA.

EISEN Sydney, b. 5 Feb 1929, Poland. University Professor; Writer. m. Doris Kirschbaum, 22 Jan 1957, 2 sons, 2 daughters. Education: Harbord Collegiate Institute, Toronto, 1946; BA, University of Toronto, 1950; PhD, Johns Hopkins University, 1957. Appointments: Instructor, 1955-58, Assistant Professor, 1958-61, Williams College, Williamstown, Massachusetts; Assistant Professor, City College of the City University of New York, 1961-65; Associate Professor, 1965-68, Professor of History and Humanities, 1968-93, Director, Centre for Jewish Studies, 1989-95, University Professor, 1993-, York University, Ontario. Publications: The Human Adventure: Readings in World History (with M Filler), 2 volumes, 1964; Victorian Science and Religion: A Bibliography with Emphasis on Evolution, Belief, and Unbelief, Comprised of Works Published from c.1900-75 (with Bernard Lightman), 1984. Contributions to: Victorian Faith in Crisis (edited by Richard Helmadter and Bernard Lightman), 1990; Articles and reviews in scholarly journals. Honours: Grant, 1967, Fellowship, 1968-69, Canada Council; Sydney Eisen Prize for General Honors Students established in his honour by York University, 1978; Shem Tov Award, Toronto Jewish Federation, 1988; Faculty of Arts Teaching Award, 1989; Ben Sadowski Award, Toronto Jewish Federation, 1994. Memberships: American Historical Association; Conference on British Studies; Victorian Studies Association. Address: 5 Renoak Drive, Willowdale, Ontario M2R 3E1, Canada.

EISENBERG Gerson G, b. 5 Mar 1909. Author. m. 15 Sept 1967, Baltimore, Maryland, USA. Education: AB, George Washington University, 1930; Graduate Student, John Hopkins University, 1937-38; MBA, New York University, 1944; Jewish and Christian Studies, St Mary's Ecumenical Institute. Publications: Learning Vacations, 1977, 6th edition, 1986; Marylanders Who Served the Nation, 1990. Contributions to: Baltimore Views the Great Depression, to Maryland Historical Society, 1976; Impressionist paintings to Baltimore Museum of Art; Seminar Room to Johns Hopkins University Library (Milton Eisenhower Library). Memberships: Baltimore Writers Association; Authors Guild of America; Board member of numerous organizations. Address: 11 Slade Avenue 116, Baltimore, MD 21208, USA.

EISENMANN-WESTPHAL Eva Elsa Dorothea, b. 1 May 1910, Beuthen, Silesia. Writer. m. Will Eisenmann, 17 June 1948, 5 sons. Education: Matura, 1930. Studied violin, singing and acting. Publications: Die Freunde, 1986; Von Zeit zu Zeit regnet es in der Wüste, 1988; Zaghafte Hoffnung, 1991. Other: Schach (television play), 1994. Contributions to: Numerous magazines. Memberships: Swiss Pen-Club; Swiss Writers' Club; German Writers' Club. Address: Rigistrasse 37, CH-6353 Weggis, Switzerland.

EKINS Paul (Whitfield), b. 24 July 1950, Djakarta, Indonesia (British Citizen). Economist; Writer. m. Susan Anne Lofthouse, 24 Sept 1979, 1 son. Education: BSc,

Imperial College, London University, 1971; MSc, Economics, 1988, PhD, Economics, 1996, Birkbeck College, University of London; MPhil, Peace Studies, University of Bradford, 1990; Level III, SEDA, Keele University, 1997. Appointments: General Secretary, Ecology Party, 1979-82; Director, Warminster Arts Center, 1982-83; The Other Economic Summit, 1984-87, Sustainable Economy Unit of the Forum of the Future, 1996-; Research Fellow, School of Peace Studies, University of Bradford, 1987-90; Founder and Coordinator, Living Economy Network, 1989-92; Founder and Trustee, New Consumer Charitable Trust, 1989-96; Research Fellow, 1990-95, Member National Consumer Council, 1996-; Research Associate, Department of Applied Economics, University of Cambridge, 1991-98; Senior Lecturer, 1996-98, Reader, 1998-, Department of Environmental Social Sciences, Keele University. Publications: The Living Economy: A New Economics in the Making (editor), 1986; A New World Order: Grassroots Movements for Global Change, 1992; Wealth Beyond Measure: An Atlas of New Economics (with Mayer Hillman and Robert Hutchison), 1992; US Edition as The Gaia Atlas of Green Economics; Real-Life Economics: Understanding Wealth Creation (editor with Manfred Max-Neef), 1992; Real Wealth: Green Economics in the Classroom (with Ken Webster), 1994; Global Warming and Energy Demand (editor with Terry Barker and Nick Johnstone), 1995; Environmentally Sustainable Economic Growth: Resolving the Contradictions, forthcoming. Contributions to: Books, journals, reviews, and newspapers. Honours: Honorary Fellow, Centre for Social and Environmental Accounting Research, University of Dundee, 1992-; Global 500 Award for Environmental Achievement, United Nations Environmental Programme, 1994. Memberships: European Association for Environmental and Resource Economists; European Association of Evolutionary Political Economists, Founder-Member; Global 500 Forum; International Society for Ecological Economics; Society for International Development; Society for the Advancement of Socioeconomics. Address: c/o Department of Environmental Social Sciences, Keele University, Staffordshire, ST5 5BG, England.

EKLUND Gordon (Stewart), b. 24 July 1945, Seattle, Washington, USA. Writer. 1 daughter. Education: Contra Costra College, 1973-75. Publications: The Eclipse of Dawn, 1971; A Trace of Dreams, 1972; Beyond the Resurrection, 1973; All Times Possible, 1974; Serving in Time, 1975; Falling Toward Forever, 1975; If the Stars are Gods, 1976; The Dance of the Apocalypse, 1976; The Grayspace Beast, 1976; Find the Changeling, 1980; The Garden of Winter, 1980; Thunder on Neptune, 1989. Contributions to: Analog; Galaxy; If Science Fiction; Fantasy and Science Fiction; Universe; New Dimensions; Amazing Stories; Fantastic. Honour: Nebula Award, 1975. Membership: Science Fiction Writers of America. Address: 6305 East D Street, Tacoma, WA 98404, USA.

EKSTRÖM (Sigrid) Margareta, b. 23 Apr 1930, Stockholm, Sweden. Writer. 1 son, 1 daughter. Education: BA, University of Stockholm, 1958. Publications: Death's Midwives, 1985; The Day I Begun My Studies in Philosophy, and Other Stories, 1989; Food for Memory, 1993; Olga on Olga, 1994; One Alive for Dead, 1995. Contributions to: Periodicals. Membership: International PEN. Address: Styrmansg 41, 11454 Stockholm, Sweden.

EKWENSI Cyprian, (Odiatu Duaka), b. 26 Sept 1921, Minna, Nigeria. Pharmacist; Author. Education: Government College, Ibadan; Achimota College, Ghana; School of Forestry, Ibadan; Chelsea School of Pharmacy, University of London; University of Iowa. Appointments: Lecturer, Igbobi College, Lagos, 1947-49; Lecturer, Pharmacy, Lagos, 1949-56; Pharmacist, Nigerian Medical Service, 1956; Head, Features, Nigerian Broadcasting Corporation, 1956-61; Director of Information, Federal Ministry of Information, Lagos, 1961-66; Director, Information Services, Enugu, 1966; Managing Director, Star Printing and Publishing Company Ltd, 1975-79, Niger Eagle Press, 1981-. Publications: When Love Whispers, Ikolo the Wrestler, 1947; The Leopard's Claw,

1950; People of the City, 1954; Passport of Mallam Ilia; The Drummer Boy, 1960; Jagua Nana, 1961; Burning Grass: An African Night's Entertainment, 1962; Yaba Round About Murder, 1962; Beautiful Feathers, 1963; Great Elephant Bird, 1965; Rainmaker, 1965; Lokotown Juju Rock, 1966; Trouble in Form VI, 1966; Iska, 1966; Boa Suitor, 1966; Coal Camp Boy, 1973; Samankwe in the Strange Forest, 1974; Samankwe and the Highway Robbers, 1975; Restless City, 1975; Christmas Gold, 1975; Survive the Peace, 1976; Divided We Stand, 1980; Motherless Baby, 1980; Jaguanana's Daughter, 1986; For a Roll of Parchment, 1986. Address: 12 Hillview Crescent, Independence Layout, PO Box 317, Enugu, Nigeria.

ELBERG Yehuda, (Y L Berg, Y Renas), b. 15 May 1912, Poland. Novelist. 2 sons, 1 daughter. Education: Rabbinnical Ordination, 1929; Textile Engineering, 1932. Appointments: Author-in-Residence, Bar-Ilan University Israel, 1988; Lecturer in Hebrew Studies, Oxford University, 1990, 1994. Publications: Under Copper Skies, 1951; On the Tip of a Mast, 1974; Scattered Stalks, 1976; Tales, 1980; The Empire of Kalman the Cripple, 1983; In Clay Houses, I and II, 1983; A Man Is But a Man, 1983; Between Morning and Evening, 1983; The Fifteen Powers, 1989; Ship of the Hunted (novel), 1988; The Empire of Kalman the Cripple (novel), 1988. Honours: Feffer Prize, Congress for Jewish Culture, Sao Paulo, Brazil, 1951; J I Segal Awards, Montreal, 1975, 1988; Wasjslic-Cymerman Award, Sydney, Australia, 1975; Gonopolsky Prize, Paris, 1977; Manger Prize, Yiddish Literature, Government of Israel, City of Tel Aviv and Manger Prize Foundation, 1977; Prime Minister's Award, Yiddish Literature, Israel, 1984; I M Wisenberg Prize, Congress for Jewish Culture, New York, 1984. Membership: PEN International. Address: 1745 Cedar Avenue, Montreal, Quebec H3G 1A7, Canada.

ELDRIDGE Colin Clifford, b. 16 May 1942, Walthamstow, England. University Reader in History; Writer. m. Ruth Margaret Evans, 3 Aug 1970, 1 daughter. Education: BA, 1963, PhD, 1966, Nottingham University. Appointments: Lecturer, 1968-75, Senior Lecturer in History, 1975-92, Reader, 1992-, University of Wales. Publications: England's Mission: The Imperial Idea in the Age of Gladstone and Disraeli, 1973; Victorian Imperialism, 1978; Essays in Honour of C D Chandaman, 1980; British Imperialism in the 19th Century, 1984; Empire, Politics and Popular Culture, 1989; From Rebellion to Patriation: Canada & Britain in the Nineteenth & Twentieth Centuries, 1989; Disraeli and the Rise of a New Imperialism, 1996; The Imperial Experience: From Carlyle to Forster, 1996; The Zulu War, 1879, 1996; Kith and Kin: Canada, Britain and the United States form the Revolution to the Cold War, 1997. Contributions to: Various learned journals. Honour: Royal Historical Society, fellow. Memberships: Historical Association; Association of History Teachers in Wales; British Association of Canadian Studies; British Australian Studies Association. Address: Tanerdy, Cilau Aeron, Lampeter, Dyfed SA48 8DL, Wales.

ELEGANT Robert Sampson, b. 7 Mar 1928, New York, New York, USA. Author; Journalist; Novelist. m. Moira Clarissa Brady, 16 Apr 1956, 1 son, 1 daughter. Education: AB, University of Pennsylvania, 1946; Japanese Army Language School, 1947-48; Yale University, 1948; MA, 1950, MS, 1951, Columbia University. Appointments: War, Southeast Asia Correspondent, Various Agencies, 1951-61; Central European Bureau, Newsweek, 1962-64; Others, Los Angeles Times, Washington Post, 1965-70; Foreign Affairs Columnist, 1970-76; Independent Author and Journalist, 1977-. Publications: China's Red Masters, 1951; The Dragon's Seed, 1959; The Centre of the World, 1961; The Seeking, 1969; Mao v Chiang: The Battle for China, 1972; The Great Cities, Hong Kong, 1977; Pacific Destiny, 1990. Novels: A Kind of Treason, 1966; The Seeking, 1969; Dynasty, 1977; Manchu, 1980; Mandarin, 1983; White Sun, Red Star, 1987; Bianca, 1992; The Everlasting Sorrow, 1994; Last Year in Hong Kong, 1997; The Big Brown Bears, 1998. Contributions to: Newspapers and periodicals. Honours: Phi Beta

Kappa; Pulitzer Fellow, 1951-52; Ford Foundation Fellowship, 1954-55; Overseas Press Club Awards, 1963, 1966, 1967, 1972; Edgar Allan Poe Award, 1967; Sigma Delta Chi Award, 1967; Fellow, American Institute for Public Policy Research, Washington, DC, 1976-78; Senior Fellow, Institute for Advanced Study, Berlin, 1993-94. Memberships: Authors League of America; Hong Kong Foreign Correspondents Club. Literary Agent: Christopher Sinclair Stevenson. Address: c/o Sarah Cook, 6 Wheeler Avenue, Penn, Buckinghamshire HP10 8EH, England.

ELEY Barry Michael, b. 6 Mar 1940, London, England. Dental Surgeon; Professor of Peridontology. m. Julie Chistina, 1 June 1963, dec, 4 Jan 1997, 1 son, 1 daughter. Education: LDSRCS (Eng), 1982; BDS, University of London, England, 1963; FDSRCS (Eng); PhD, Faculty of Medicine, University of London, 1980. Appointments: Full and Part time, General Dental Practice, 1962-65; House Surgeon, LHDS, 1963; Assistant Lecturer, Registrar, King's College Hospital, DS, 1963-65; Lecturer, Conservative Dentistry KCSMD, 1965-74; Senior Lecturer Periodontology KESMD, 1974-80; Senior Lecturer/Honorary Consultant, Periodontology KCSMD, 1980-89; Director of School Dental Hygiene; Reader/Consultant, 1984-97; Professor of Periodontology, 1997-; Chairman, Division of Periodontology & Preventive Dentistry Guy/King's/St Thomas' (GRT), 1998-. Publications: Amalgam Tattoos, 1982; Outline of Periodontics, 2nd edition, 1989; Dental Diamond, 1993; Dental Amalgam, a Review of Safety, 1993; The Future of Dental Amalgam - a Review of the Literature, 1998. Contributions to: Over 80 refereed articles in professional and scientific journals; Referee for several journals. Address: 10 Grosvenor Road, Petts Wood, Orpington, Kent BR5 1QU, England.

ELIAS Victor Jorge, b. 21 July 1937, Tucuman, Argentina. Economist. m. Ana M Ganum, 21 May 1966, 1 son, 2 daughters. Education: PhD Economics, University of Chicago, Illinois, USA, 1969. Appointments: Full Professor, 1965-, Director Magister of Economics, 1988-, University of Tucuman; Director, Institute of Applied Economics, FBET, 1994-. Publications: Estimacion del Capital, Trabajo, Producto de la Industria en Argentina: 1935-1965, 1969; Sources of Growth: A Study of Seven Latin American Economies, 1992. Contributions to: The Role of Total Factor Productivity on Economic Growth, 1993. Honour: Guggenheim Fellowship, 1974. Membership: Full Member, National Academy of Economics Science of Argentina. Address: Balcarce 740, Tucuman 4000, Argentina.

ELIOT Karen. See: **HOME Stewart Ramsay.**

ELISHA Ron, b. 19 Dec 1951, Jerusalem, Israel. Medical Practitioner; Playwright. m. Bertha Rita Rubin, 6 Dec 1981, 1 son, 1 daughter. Education: BMed, BSurg, Melbourne University, 1975. Publications: In Duty Bound, 1983; Two, 1985; Einstein, 1986; The Levine Comedy, 1987; Pax Americana, 1988; Safe House, 1989; Esterhaz, 1990; Impropriety, 1993; Choice, 1994; Pigtales, 1994; Unknown Soldier, 1996; Too Big, 1997. Contributions to: Business Review Weekly; The Age; Vogue Australia; Generation Magazine; Australian Book Review; Centre Stage Magazine; Melbourne Jewish Chronicle; The Westerly. Honours: Best Stage Play, 1982; Major Award, 1982; Best Stage Play, 1984; Gold Award, Best Screenplay, 1990; Best TV Feature, Australian Writers Guild Award, 1992. Memberships: Australian Writers Guild; International PEN; Fellowship of Australian Writers. Address: 2 Molonga Court, North Caulfield, Victoria 3161, Australia.

ELIZABETH Von S. See: **FREEMAN Gillian.**

ELKINS Aaron, b. 24 July 1935, New York, New York, USA. Writer. m. (1) Toby Siev, 1959, div 1972, 2 sons, (2) Charlotte Trangmar, 1972. Education: BA, Hunter College, 1956; Graduate Studies, University of Wisconsin at Madison, 1957-59; MA, University of Arizona, 1960; MA, California State University at Los Angeles, 1962; EdD, University of California at Berkeley, 1976.

Appointments: Director, Management Development, Contra Costa County Government, 1971-76, 1980-83; Lecturer, University of Maryland at College Park, European Division, 1976-78, 1984-85; Management Analyst, US Office of Personnel Management, San Francisco, 1979-80; Member, Clallam County Civil Service Commission, 1987-. Publications: Fellowship of Fear, 1982; The Dark Place, 1983; Murder in the Queen's Armes, 1985; A Deceptive Clarity, 1987; Old Bones, 1987; Dead Men's Hearts, 1994. Honour: Edgar Allan Poe Award, Mystery Writers of America, 1988. Address: c/o Karpfinger Agency, 500 Fifth Avenue, Suite 2800, New York, NY 10110, USA.

ELLEN Margaret. See: **OSBORNE Maggie.**

ELLIA William E, b. 1 Jan 1940, Danville, Kentucky, USA. Professor; Author; Editor. m. Charlotte Frances Rohrer, 30 July 1960, 1 son, 1 daughter. Education: BA, Georgetown College, 1962; MA, Education, Georgetown College, 1966; MA, Eastern Kentucky University, 1967; PhD, University of Kentucky, 1974. Appointment: Eastern Kentucky University, 1970-99. Publications: A Man of Books and A Man of the People: E Y Mullins and the Crisis of Moderate Southern Baptist Leadership, 1985; Patrick Henry Callahan: Progressive Catholic Layman in the American South, 1989; Robert Worth Bingham and the Southern Mystique, 1999. Contributions to: Articles in The Historian, The Catholic Historical Review, The Social Science Journal, The Register of the Kentucky Historical Society. Honour: Fulbright Grant to New Zealand, 1989. Address: 123 Pleasant Ridge Drive, Richmond, KY 40475, USA.

ELLIOT Alistair, b. 13 Oct 1932, Liverpool, Lancashire, England. Poet; Translator; Editor; Retired Librarian. m. 1956, 2 sons. Education: Fettes College, Edinburgh; BA, MA, Christ Church, Oxford. Appointments: Librarian, Kensington Public Library, London, 1959-61, Keele University, 1961-65, Pahlavi University, Iran, 1965-67, Newcastle University, 1967-82. Publications: Air in the Wrong Place, 1968; Contentions, 1977; Kisses, 1978; Talking to Bede, 1982; Talking Back, 1982; On the Appian Way, 1984; My Country: Collected Poems, 1989; Turning the Stones, 1993; Facing Things, 1997. Editor: Poems by James I and Others, 1970; Virgil, The Georgics with John Dryden's Translation, 1981. Editor and Translator: French Love Poems (bilingual), 1991; Italian Landscape Poems (bilingual), 1993. Translator: Alcestis, by Euripides, 1965; Peace, by Aristophanes, 1965; Femmes Hombres, by Paul Verlaine, 1979; The Lazarus Poems, by Heinrich Heine, 1979; Medea, by Euripides, 1993; La Jeune Parque, by Paul Valéry, 1997. Contributions to: Many journals, reviews, and magazines. Honours: Arts Council of Great Britain Grant, 1979; Ingram Merrill Foundation Fellowships, 1983, 1989; Prudence Farmer Awards, New Statesman, 1983, 1991; Djerassi Foundation Fellowship, 1984. Address: 27 Hawthorn Road, Newcastle-upon-Tyne NE3 4DE, England.

ELLIOT Bruce. See: **FIELD Edward.**

ELLIOT Zena Marjorie, b. 13 June 1922, New Zealand. Retired Art Teacher. m. A J Elliot, 10 Aug 1946, div 1958, 2 sons, 1 daughter. Education: Certified Teacher, New Zealand, 1942, New South Wales, 1960; Diploma, Home Economics, 1969; Diploma, Art Education, 1974. Appointments: Graduate Assistant, New South Wales, Australia, 1974; Teacher of Art. Publications: Concise Coppercraft Book, 1975; Creative Weaving with Art to Wear, 1995. Memberships: Telopea Gallery; Craft at the Rocks; Handweavers and Spinners Guild; National Parks and Wild Life; New South Wales Trust Fund; Blue Mountains Creative Art Centre; Textile Fibre Forum. Address: 15 Hopewell Street, Paddington, New South Wales 2021, Australia.

ELLIOTT David Stuart, b. 29 Apr 1949, Prestbury, England. Director, Modema Museet, Stockholm, 2 sons. Education: BA Hons, Modern History, University of Durham, England, 1967-70; MA History of Art, Courtauld Institute of Art, University of London, England, 1972-73.

Appointments: Member of Purchasing Sub-Committee, The British Council, 1982-96; On Council of Great Britain, USSR, 1983-96; Purchaser, Arts Council of Great Britain collection, 1984-85; Associate Tutor in Visual Arts, Department of External Studies, Oxford University, 1984-86; Member, British Delegation to the CSCE Conference, Budapest, 1985; Course Tutor for Oxford, Berkeley University Summer School, 1985-87. Publications include: The Battle for Art in the 1930s, 1995; Doubles, 1996; Home Should Be Where the Art Is..., 1996; Strong Women, 1997; Let's Talk About Art, 1997; Dangerous Spaces, 1997, 1998; The State-of-the-Art Museum, 1998; Sponge, Mirror, Knife, 1998; No Pain No Gain, 1998. Memberships: ICOM, 1980-; Comité International des Musées d'Art Moderne; International Exhibitions groupo of ICOM; former member, British Museums Association; Association of Art Historians; Art Galleries' Association; British Film Institute; Great Britain-Russia Association; Hispano-Luzo American Council. Address: Moderna Museet, Box 16382, S 103 27 Stockholm, Sweden.

ELLIS (Christopher) Royston (George), (Richard Tresilian), b. 10 Feb 1941, Pinner, Middlesex, England. Author; Travel Writer; Cruise Ship Lecturer; Poet. 1 son. Appointments: Assistant Editor, Jersey News and Features Agency, 1961-63; Associate Editor, Canary Islands Sun, Las Palmas, 1963-66; Editor, The Educator, Director, Dominica Broadcasting Services and Reuters, Cana Correspondent, 1974-76; Managing Editor, Wordsman Features Agency, 1977-86; Editorial Consultant, Explore Sri Lanka, 1990-95; Travel and Colonial Property Correspondent, Sunday Times, Colombo, 1991-; Managing Director, Wordsman Inc, 1997-; Maldives (Rit) Ltd, 1997. Publications: Jiving to Gyp, 1959; Rave, 1960; The Big Beat Scene, 1961; The Rainbow Walking Stick, 1961; Rebel, 1962; Burn Up, 1963; The Mattress Flowers, 1963; The Flesh Merchants, 1966; The Rush at the End, 1967; The Bondmaster Series (7 books), 1977-83; The Fleshtrader Series (3 books), 1984-85; The Bloodheart Series (3 books), 1985-87; Giselle, 1987; Guide to Mauritius, 1988-98; India By Rail, 1989-97; Sri Lanka By Rail, 1994; A Maldives Celebration (with Gemunu Amarasinghe), 1997; The Book of Ceylon Tea (with Gemunu Amarasinghe), 1997; A Man For All Islands, 1998; Sri Lanka at Fifty, 1998; Guide to Maldives (with Gemunu Amarasinghe), forthcomng; Guide to Sri Lanka, forthcoming. Contributions to: Newspapers and magazines. Honours: Dominica National Poetry Awards, 1967, 1971. Memberships: Institute of Rail Transport, India; Royal Commonwealth Society. Address: Royal Cottage, Bentota, Sri Lanka.

ELLIS Alice Thomas. See. **HAYCRAFT Anna (Margaret).**

ELLIS Bret Easton, b. 7 Mar 1964, Los Angeles, California, USA. Writer. Education: BA, Bennington College, 1986. Publications: Less Than Zero, 1985; The Rules of Attraction, 1987; American Psycho, 1993; The Informers, 1994; Glamorama (Knopf), 1998. Contributions to: Rolling Stone; Vanity Fair; Elle; Wall Street Journal; Bennington Review. Membership: Authors Guild. Address: c/o Amanda Urban, International Creative Management, 40 West 57th Street, New York, NY 10019, USA.

ELLIS David George, b. 23 June 1939, Swinton, Lancashire, England. University Teacher. m. 24 Sept 1966, 2 daughters. Education: MA, 1964, PhD, 1970, University of Cambridge. Appointments: Lecturer, La Trobe University, Melbourne, Victoria, Australia, 1968-72; Lecturer, Senior Lecturer, Professor, University of Kent at Canterbury, England, 1972-. Publications: Stendhal, Memoirs of an Egotist, translation, 1975; Wordsworth, Freud and the Spots of Time: Interpretation in 'The Prelude', 1985; D H Lawrence's Non-Fiction: Art, Thought and Genre (with Howard Mills), 1988; Imitating Art: Essays in Biography, editor, 1993; Dying Game, vol 3, New Cambridge Biography of D H Lawrence, 1998. Address: English School, University of Kent at Canterbury, Canterbury CT2 7NX, England.

ELLIS Ella Thorp. b. 14 July 1928, Los Angeles, California, USA. Childrens Writer. m. Leo Herbert Ellis, 17 Dec 1949, 3 sons. Education: BA, English, University of California at Los Angeles; MA, English and Creative Writing, San Francisco State University. Appointments: Lecturer, San Francisco State University, University of California at Berkeley. Publications: Swimming With the Whales, 1995; Hugo and the Princess Nina; Hallelujah; Sleepwalker's Moon; Where The Road Ends; Celebrate the Morning; Riptide; Roam the Wild Country. Contributions to: Cosmopolitan. Memberships: Authors Guild; SCB Writers. Literary Agent: Susan Cohen. Address: 1438 Grizzly Peak, Berkeley, CA 94708, USA.

ELLIS Mark Karl, b. 1 Aug 1945, Musoorie, India. Training Consultant; Author. m. Printha Jane, 30 Aug 1969, 2 sons. Education: MA, Christ's College, Cambridge, 1967; Postgraduate Diploma, University of Leeds, 1970. Publications: Bannerman; Adoration of the Hanged Man; Fatal Charade; Survivors Beyond Babel; Nelson Counterpoint Series; Nelson Skill of Reading Series; Longman Business Skills Series; Professional English; The Economist: An English Language Guide; Giving Presentations; Teaching Business English; Kiss in the Dark. Address: 39 St Martins, Marlborough, Wiltshire SN8 1AS, England.

ELLIS Richard J, b. 27 Nov 1960, Leicester, England. Associate Professor of Political Science. m. Juli Takenaka, 18 July 1987. Education: BA, with highest honours, University of California, Santa Cruz, 1982; MA, Political Science, 1984, PhD, Political Science, 1989, University of California, Berkeley. Appointments: Assistant Professor, 1990-95, Associate Professor, 1995-, Willamette University, Salem, Oregon, Professor, 1999-. Publications: Dilemmas of Presidential Leadership (co-author), 1989; Cultural Theory (co-author), 1990; American Political Cultures, 1993; Presidential Lightning Rods: The Politics of Blame Avoidance, 1994; Politics, Policy and Culture (co-editor), 1994; Culture Matters: Essays in Honour of Aaron Wildavsky (co-editor), 1997; The Dark Side of the Left: Illiberal Egalitarianism in America, 1997; Speaking to the People: The Rhetorical Presidency in Historical Perspective, 1998. Contributions to: Comparative Studies in Society and History; Journal of Behavioural Economics; Presidential Studies Quarterly; Journal of Theoretical Politics: Studies in American Political Development; Review of Politics; Polity; Western Political Quarterly; Critical Review; American Political Science Review. Honours: Regents Fellowship, University of California, 1983-85; I G S Harris Fellowship, 1986-88; Summer Stipend, National Endowment for the Humanities, 1991; Fellowship, George and Eliza Howard Foundation, 1993-94; Arnold L and Lois S Graves Award in the Humanities, 1998. Memberships: American Political Science Association; Organization of American Historians. Address: Willamette University, Salem, OR 97301, USA.

ELLISON Harlan Jay, b. 27 May 1934, Cleveland, Ohio, USA. Author. m. Susan Toth, Sept 1986. Education: Ohio State University, 1953-55. Appointments: Instructor, Clarion Writer's Workshop, Michigan State University, 1969-77, 1984; Book Critic, Los Angeles Times, 1969-82; Editorial Commentator, Canadian Broadcasting Corp, 1972-78, Sci-Fi Channel, USA, 1993-; President, Kilimanjaro Corp, 1979-. Publications: 74 books including: Harlan Ellison's Dream Corridor (comic book), 1995; The City on the Edge of Forever, 1995; Slippage, 1997; Edgeworks Vols I-V, 1996-98. Contributions to: Newspapers. Motion Pictures and Television: Over 60 Screenplays and Teleplays. Honours: Nebula Awards, 1965, 1969, 1977; Various Hugo Awards, 1966-86; Edgar Allan Poe Awards, 1974, 1988; British Fanatasy Award, 1978; American Mystery Award, 1987; Bram Stoker Awards, 1987, 1989, 1994, 1995; Life Achievement Award, World Fantasy Convention, 1993; Only four-times winner, Writers Guild Award; Brandeis University (National Women's Committee): Words, Wit and Wisdom Award, 1998. Memberships: Science Fiction Writers of America, vice-president, 1965-66; Writers Guild of America. Literary Agent: Richard Curtis Associates. Address: PO Box 55548, Sherman Oaks, CA 91413, USA.

ELLWOOD Edith Elizabeth, b. 18 Aug 1947, New York City, USA. Freelance Writer. m. William A Ellwood, 15 Sept 1988, 1 son, 2 daughters. Education: BA, Political Science, 1965-69; MA, Political Science, 1969-71. Publications: The Alternative to Technological Culture; US Democracy: Myth vs Reality; The Individual High-Tech Society. Contributions to: Haiku; Dragonfly. Address: RR 1 Box 178, Bushkill, PA 18324-9727, USA.

ELMSLIE Kenward Gray, b. 27 Apr 1929, New York, New York, USA. Poet; Librettist. Education: BA, Harvard University, 1950. Publications: Poetry: The Champ, 1968, new edition, 1994; Album, 1969; Circus Nerves, 1971; Motor Disturbance, 1971; The Orchid Stories, 1972; Tropicalism, 1976; The Alphabet Work, 1977; Communications Equipment, 1979; Moving Right Along, 1980; Bimbo Dirt, 1981; 26 Bars, 1986; Sung Sex, 1989; Pay Dirt (with Joe Brainard), 1992; Champ Dust, 1994; Bare Bones, 1995; Routine Disruptions; Selected Poems and Lyrics, 1998. Opera Libretti: Lizzie Borden, 1966; Miss Julie, 1966; The Sweet Bye and Bye, 1973; The Seagull, 1974; Washington Square, 1976; Three Sisters, 1986. Play: City Junket, 1987. Musical Plays: The Grass Harp, 1971; Lola, 1982; Postcards on Parade, 1993. Contributions to: Many anthologies, reviews, and journals. Honour: Frank O'Hara Poetry Award, 1971. Membership: American Society of Composers, Authors and Publishers. Address: Box 38, Calais, VT 05648, USA.

ELPHINSTONE Francis. See: **POWELL-SMITH Vincent.**

ELSOM John Edward, b. 31 Oct 1934, Leigh on Sea, Essex, England. Author; Dramatist; Journalist; Broadcaster; Lecturer. m. Sally Mays, 3 Dec 1956, 2 sons. Education: BA, 1956; PhD, City University, London, 1991. Appointments: Script Advisor, Paramount Pictures, 1960-68; Theatre Critic, London Magazine, 1963-68, The Listener, 1972-82; Correspondent, Contemporary Review, 1978-88; Lecturer, Course Leader, Arts Criticism, City University, London, 1986-96; Consultant, South Bank University, 1996-97, School for Oriental and African Studies, University of London, 1997. Publications: Theatre Outside London, 1969; Erotic Theatre, 1972; Post-War British Theatre, 1976, 2nd edition, 1979; The History of the National Theatre, 1978; Change and Choice, 1978; Post-War British Theatre Criticism (editor), 1981; Is Shakespeare Still Our Contemporary? (editor), 1989; Cold War Theatre, 1992. Other: Plays published and produced. Contributions to: Observer; Mail on Sunday; Encounter; Times Literary Supplement; The World and I; Sunday Telegraph; Plays International; Plays & Players; San Diego Union; Numerous others. Memberships: Liberal Party of Great Britain, Art and Broadcasting Committee; International Association of Theatre Critics, 1985-92, now honorary president; Chair and Convenor, Liberal Party's Arts and Broadcasting Committee, 1978-88. Literary Agent: John McLaughlin. Address: Stella Maris, Anglesea Road, Kingston Upon Thames, Surrey KT1 2EW, England.

ELSTOB Peter, b. 22 Dec 1915, London, England. Writer. Education: University of Michigan, 1934-35. Appointments: Director, Arts Theatre Club, London, 1946-54, Trade Wind Films, 1958-62, Archive Press Ltd, 1965-; Press Officer, 1970-74, Secretary General, 1974-82, Vice-President, 1982-, International PEN. Publications: Spanish Prisoner, 1938; The Flight of the Small World (co-author), 1959; Warriors for the Working Day, 1960; The Armed Rehearsal, 1964; Bastogne: The Road Block, 1968; The Battle of Reichswald, 1970; Hitler's Last Offensive, 1971; A Register of the Regiments and Corps of the British Army (editor), 1972; Condor Legion, 1973; The Survival of Literature (editor), 1979; Scoundrel, 1986. Memberships: English and International PEN; Society of Authors; Writers Guild. Address: Pond Cottage, Burley Lawn, Hampshire BH24 4DL, England.

ELSY (Winifred) Mary, b. England. Freelance Travel Journalist; Writer. Education: Teaching Diploma, Oakley Training College for Teachers, Cheltenham, 1945. Appointments: Teacher, 1946-51; Realist Film Unit, 1953-55; Editorial Assistant, Children's Encyclopedia, 1959-62; British Publishing Corp, 1963; Evans Brothers, 1965-66; Children's Book Editor, Abelard Schuman, 1967-68. Publications: Travels in Belgium and Luxembourg, 1966; Brittany and Normandy, 1972; Travels in Brittany, 1988; Travels in Normandy, 1988; Travels in Alsace and Lorraine, 1989; Travels in Burgundy, 1989. Contributions to: Daily Telegraph; Sunday Telegraph; Observer; Irish Times; Universe; Womans Journal; In Britain; Illustrated London News; Travel; Ham and High; Camping and Walking; My Family; Voyager; Family Life; Christian Herald; Home and Country; Overseas Review; The Key. Memberships: PEN International; Society of Authors; Institute of Journalists; British Guild of Travel Writers; Camden History Society; Hampstead Authors Society. Address: 519c Finchley Road, London NW3 7BB, England.

ELTIS Walter (Alfred), b. 23 May 1933, Warnsdorf, Czechoslovakia. Economist. m. Shelagh Mary Owen, 5 Sept 1959, 1 son, 2 daughters. Education: Emmanuel College, Cambridge; BA, Cambridge University; MA, Nuffield College, 1960; DLitt, Oxford University, 1990. Appointments: Fellow, Tutor, Economics, 1963-88, Emeritus Fellow, 1988-, Exeter College, Oxford; Director General, National Economic Development Office, London, 1988-92; Chief Economic Adviser to the President of the Board of Trade, 1992-95; Visiting Professor, 1992-, University of Reading. Publications: Growth and Distribution, 1973; Britain's Economic Problem: Too Few Producers (with Robert Bacon), 1976; The Classical Theory of Economic Growth, 1984; Keynes and Economic Policy (with Peter Sinclair), 1988; Classical Economics, Public Expenditure and Growth, 1993; Britain's Economic Problem Revisited, 1996; Condillac, Commerce and Government (editor, with Shelagh M Eltis). Contributions to: Economic journals and bank reviews. Memberships: Reform Club, chairman, 1994-95; Royal Automobile Club; Political Economy Club. Address: Danesway, Jarn Way, Boars Hill, Oxford OX1 5JF, England.

ELTON Ben(jamin Charles), b. 3 May 1959, England. Writer; Comedian. Education: BA, Drama, University of Manchester. Appointments: Writer of television series and for British comedians; Stand-up comedian; Host, Friday Night Live television comedy showcase; Co-writer and presenter, South of Watford documentary television series, 1984-85. Publications: Bachelor Boys, 1984; Stark, 1989; Gridlock, 1992; This Other Eden, 1994; Popcorn, 1996; Blast from the Past, 1998. Plays: Gasping, 1990; Silly Cow, 1991; Popcorn, 1996; Blast from the Past, 1999. Other: Recordings: The Young Ones, 1986; Motormouth, 1987; Motorvation, 1989; This Other Eden, 1994; The Thin Blue Line (sitcom), 1995-96; Popcorn, 1996. Videos: The Man From Auntie, 1991; Ben Elton Live, 1989, 1993, 1997; The Man From Auntie 2, 1994. Honours: Best Comedy Show Awards, British Academy, 1984, 1987; Best New Comedy Laurence Olivier Award, 1998; Various other awards. Address: c/o Phil McIntyre, 35 Soho Square, London W1V 50G, England.

EMECHETA (Florence Onye) Buchi, b. 21 July 1944, Lagos, Nigeria. Writer; Visiting Professor; Lecturer. m. S Onwordi, 7 May 1960, 2 sons, 3 daughters. Education: BSc, London University, 1974. Appointments: Professional Senior Research Fellow, University of Calabar, Nigeria; Visiting Professor, many US Universities, 1982-87; Fellow, University of London, 1986-. Publications: Second Class Citizen, 1975; The Bride Price, 1976; The Slave Girl, 1977; Joys of Motherhood, 1979; Naura Power, 1981; Double Yoke, 1982; Destination Biafra, 1982; A Land of Marriage, 1983; Head Above Water, 1987; Gwendoline, 1989. Contributions to: New Statesman; New Society; New International Sunday Times Magazine. Honours: Jack Campbell Award; New Statesman, 1979; One of Best Young British Writers, 1983. Membership: PEN

International. Address: Collins Publishers, 8 Grafton Street, London W1X 3LA, England.

EMENYONU Ernest NNeji, b. Nigeria. Professor of English. m, 4 children. Education: University of Nigeria, Nsuka; Teachers College, Columbia University, New York; London University, England; University of Wisconsin, Madison; BA, 1t Class Honours, English and Education; MA, Teaching of English as a Foreign Language; PhD, African Literature. Appointments: Teacher, Knoxville College, Tennessee,Virginia State College, Petersburg,College of William and Mary, Williamsburg, Virginia,University of Colorado, Boulder, University of Montana, Head, Department of English and Literary Studies, Dean, Faculty of Arts, Chairman, Committee of Deans, Deputy Vice-Chancellor of University, University of Calabar, Nigeria, 1988-90. Publications: Cyprian Ekwensi, 1974; The Rise of the Igbo Novel, 1978; African Literature for Schools and Colleges, 1985; The Essential Ekwensi, 1987; Studies on the Nigerian Novel, 1991; Current Trends in Literature and Language Studies in West Africa, 1994; Ideas and Challenges in Nigerian Education, 1994. Children's Books: Bed Time Stories for African Children, Vol I, Stories About Animals, 1989; Vol II: The Adventures of Ebeleako, 1991; UZO Remembers His Father, 1991; Calabar Studies in African Literature. Memberships: Literary Society of Nigeria, president; West African Association for Commonwealth Literature and Language Studies, president, 1965-95; Nigerian Academy of Education, 1995-; President, Association for Commonwealth Literature and Language Studies. Address: c/o Department of English Language and Literature, Alvan Ikoku College of Education, P M B 1033, Owerri, Imo State, Nigeria.

EMERSON Ru, (Robert Cray), b. 15 Dec 1944, Monterey, California, USA. Writer. Education: University of Montana, 1963-66. Publications: Princess of Flames, 1986; To the Haunted Mountains, 1987; In the Caves of Exile, 1988; On the Seas of Destiny, 1989; Spell Bound, 1990; Trilogy: Night Threads, 1990, 1991, 1992; The Bard's Tale: Fortress of Frost and Fire (with Mercedes Lackey), 1993; Night Threads: The Craft of Light, 1993; The Sword and the Lion, 1993; The Art of the Sword, 1994; The Science of Power, 1995; Xena: Warrior Princess, The Empty Throne, 1996; Xena: Warrior Princess, The Huntress and the Sphynx, 1997; Xena: Warrior Princess, The Thief of Hermes (with A C Crispin), 1997; Voices of Chaos, 1998; Beauty and the Beast: Masgues, 1998. Contributions to: Anthologies and magazines. Membership: Science Fiction Writers of America. Address: 2600 Reuben Boise, Dallas, OR 97338, USA.

EMERY Fred, b. 19 Oct 1933, Ilford, Essex, England. Author; Broadcaster. m. E Marianne Nyberg, 23 Aug 1958, 2 sons. Education: St John's College, Cambridge; MA Cantab. Appointments: National Service as Fighter Pilot, RAF, 266 and 234 Squadrons, 1953; Radio Bremen, 1955-56; Joined The Times, 1958: Foreign Correspondent, Paris, Algeria, Tokyo, Indonesia, Vietnam, Cambodia, Malaysia, Singapore, 1961-70; Chief Washington Correspondent, 1970-77, Political Editor, 1977-81, Assistant Editor, Home, 1981-82, Executive Editor, Home and Foreign, Acting Editor 1982; Presenter, BBC-TV Panorama, 1978-80, 1982-92; Reporter, Watergate, TV series, 1994; Freelance contributions to BBC-TV, CBC-TV, others. Publication: Watergate, The Corruption and Fall of Richard Nixon, 1994, paperback 1995. Honour: US Emmy, 1995. Address: 5 Woodsyre, Sydenham Hill, London SE26 6SS, England.

EMERY Thomas J, b. 27 July 1971, Urbana, Illinois, USA. Freelance Writer. Education: BA, Blackburn College, 1993; MBA, Southern Illinois University, Edwardsville, 1995. Appointments: Sports Information Director, Blackburn College, 1993-94; Reporter, Macoupin County Enquirer, 1994-96; Journalist, Monterey Coal Company, 1994-95; Owner, History in Print, 1997-. Publications: Richard Rowett: Thoroughbreds, Beagles and "The" Civil War, 1997; The Other John Logan: Col John Logan and the 32nd Illinois, 1998; Hold the Fort: A Catchphrase with Evangelical Background, 1999. Honours: Blackburn College Ziegler Service Award, 1996. Memberships: Illinois State Historical Society; Macoupin County Genealogical Society; National Trust for Historic Preservation; College Sports Information Directors of America; Melberger Award Selection Panel; USA III Football Panel. Address: 337 E Second South, Carlinville, IL 62626, USA.

EMMETT Nicholas, b. 22 July 1935, Dublin, Ireland. Writer; Translator. m. Anne Brit Emmett, 20 May 1965. Education: Philosophy course, Oslo University; Literature course, Galway University. Appointments: Taxi-Owner and Driver, 6 years; Interpreter-Translator, Indian Embassy, Oslo, Norway, 1973; Founding Co-Editor, Ragtime, English cultural magazine, Norway. Publications: The Cave, novel, 1987; The Red Mist and Other Stories, 1988; Brains on the Dump, short story, 1991. Contributions to: 80 short stories and articles in newspapers, anthologies and magazines, England, USA, Ireland, Norway. Honour: Writing Grant, Irish Arts Council. Memberships: Society of Authors; The Irish Writers Union. Address: Rathcoffey North, Donadea, Co Kildare, Ireland.

EN-NEHAS Jamal, b. 11 May 1961, Casablanca, Morocco. m. Sheri En-nehas, 23 Sept 1995, 2 daughters. Education: BA, English Language and Literature, University of Hassan II, Casablanca, Morocco, 1985; Postgraduate Diploma, Comparative Literature, 1986, MA, 19th and 20th Century English and United States Literature, University of Essex, Colchester, England, 1987; PhD, English, University of New Brunswick, Fredericton, Canada. Appointments: Assistant Editor, Maknasat, 1991-92; Book Reviewer, World Literature Today, 1995-. Publications: The Writing Guide for Students of English in Moroccan Universities, 1997; Laurens Van Der Post's Ventures to the Interior: A Study in Travel, Cultural Quests and Self-Exploration, forthcoming.Contributions to: Maknasat; International Fiction Review; World Literature Today; Chimo: The News-Journal of the Canadian Association for Commonwealth Literature and Language Studies; Interculturel: Quaderni dell'Alliance Française. Honours: Moroccan Government Scholarship for Higher Education, 1985; Honorary Visiting Fellowship, Rhodes University, 1995; DWL Earl Fellowship, University of New Brunswick, 1995; Honourary Visiting Scholarship, Columbia University, 1996; Fulbright Visiting Scholar, Yale University, 1998. Address: Cité Ifriquia Rue 30 No 54, Casablanca 20450, Morocco.

ENG Stephen Richard, b. 31 Oct 1940, San Diego, California, USA. Biographer; Poet; Literary Journalist; Scholar. m. Anne Jeanne Kangas, 15 May 1969, 2 sons, 2 daughters. Education: AB, English Literature, George Washington University, Washington, DC, 1963; MS, Education (Counselling), Portland State University, Oregon, 1973. Appointments: Poetry Editor, The Diversifier, 1977-78; Associate Editor, Triads, 1985; Director and Editor, Nashville House, 1991-; Staff Book Reviewer, Nashville Banner, 1993-98. Publications: Elusive Butterfly and Other Lyrics (editor), 1971; The Face of Fear and Other Poems (editor), 1984; The Hunter of Time: Gnomic Verses (editor), 1984; Toreros: Poems (editor), 1990; Poets of the Fantastic (co-editor), 1992; A Satisfied Mind: The Country Music Life of Porter Wagoner, 1992; Jimmy Buffett: The Man From Margaritaville Revealed, 1996; Yellow Rider and Other Lyrics, 1999. Contributions to: Lyric; Night Cry; Journal of Country Music; Tennessee Historical Quarterly; Bookpage; Nashville Banner; Music City Blues; Space & Time. Honours: American Poets' Fellowship Society Certificate of Merit, 1973; Co-Winner, Rhysling Award, Science Fiction Poetry Association, 1979; Best Writer, 1979, 1983, Special Achievement, 1985, Small Press Writers and Artists Organization. Memberships: Broadcast Music Inc, 1972-; Syndic, F Marion Crawford Memorial Society, 1978-; Country Music Association, 1990-; Science-Fiction Poetry Association, 1990-. Address: PO Box 111864, Nashville, TN 37222, USA.

ENGEL Howard, b. 2 Apr 1931, Toronto, Ontario, Canada. Writer. m. (1) Marian Ruth Passmore, 1962, 1 son, 1 daughter, (2) Janet Evelyn Hamilton, 1978, 1 son. Education: St Catherine's College Institute; BA, McMaster University, 1955; Ontario College of Education, 1956. Appointments: Writer-in-Residence, Hamilton Public Library, 1989; Barker Fairley Distinguished Visitor in Canadian Culture, University College, University of Toronto, 1995-96. Publications: The Suicide Murders, 1980; The Ransom Game, 1981; Murder on Location, 1982; Murder Sees the Light, 1984; A City Called July, 1986; A Victim Must Be Found, 1988; Dead and Buried, 1990; Murder in Montparnasse, 1992; Criminal Shorts: Mysteries by Canadian Crime Writers (editor with Eric Wright), 1992; There Was an Old Woman, 1993; Getting Away With Murder, 1995; Lord High Executioner: An Unashamed Look at Hangmen, Headsmen, and Their Kind, 1996. Contributions to: Radio and television. Honours: Arthur Ellis Award for Crime Fiction, 1994; Harbourfront Festival Prize, 1990; LLD, Brock University, 1994. Memberships: Crime Writers of Canada, chairman, 1986-87; International Association of Crime Writers; Mystery Writers of America; Writers Guild of Canada. Address: 281 Major Street, Toronto, Ontario, Canada M5S 2L5.

ENGEL Matthew Lewis, b. 11 June 1951, Northampton, England. Journalist; Editor. m. Hilary Davies, 27 Oct 1990, 1 son, 1 daughter. Education: BA, Economics, University of Manchester, 1972. Appointments: Reporter, Northampton Chronicle and Echo, 1972-75, The Guardian, 1979-; Cricket Correspondent, 1982-87; Feature Writer, Political, Foreign and War Correspondent, 1987-98; Columnist, 1998-. Publications: Ashes '85, 1985; Guardian Book of Cricket, 1986; Wisden Cricketers' Almanack (editor), 1993; Wisden (editor), 1993-; Tickle The Public, 1996. Honours: Sports Writer of the Year, 1985, 1991. Address: The Oaks, Newton St Margarets, Herefordshire HR2 0QN, England.

ENGELS John (David), b. 19 Jan 1931, South Bend, Indiana, USA. Professor of English; Poet; Writer. m. Gail Jochimsen, 1957, 4 sons, 2 daughters. Education: AB, University of Notre Dame, 1952; University College, Dublin, 1955; MFA, University of Iowa, 1957. Appointments: Instructor, Norbert College, West De Pere, Wisconsin, 1957-62; Assistant Professor, 1962-70, Professor of English, 1970-, St Michael's College, Winooski Park, Vermont; Visiting Lecturer, University of Vermont, 1974, 1975, 1976; Slaughter Lecturer, Sweet Briar College, 1976; Writer-in-Residence, Randolph Macon Women's College, 1992. Publications: Poetry: The Homer Mitchell Place, 1968; Signals from the Safety Coffin, 1975; Blood Mountain, 1977; Vivaldi in Early Fall, 1981; The Seasons in Vermont, 1982; Weather-Fear: New and Selected Poems 1958-1982, 1983; Cardinals in the Ice Age, 1987; Walking to Cootehill: New and Selected Poems 1958-1992, 1993; Big Water, 1995. Other: Writing Techniques (with Norbert Engels), 1962; Experience and Imagination (with Norbert Engels), 1965; The Merrill Checklist of William Carlos Williams (editor), 1969; The Merrill Studies in Paterson (editor), 1971. Honours: Bread Loaf Writers Conference Scholarship, 1960, and Robert Frost Fellowship, 1976; Guggenheim Fellowship, 1979. Address: c/o Department of English, St Michaels' College, Winooski Park, VT 05404, USA.

ENGLE Margarita, b. 2 Sept 1951, Pasadena, California, USA. Novelist; Poet. m. Curtis Engle, 18 Apr 1978, 1 son, 1 daughter. Education: BS, Agronomy, California Polytechnic University, Pomona, 1974; MS, Botany, Iowa State University, Ames, 1977. Publications: Singing to Cuba, 1993; Skywriting, 1995. Contributions to: Numerous. Honour: Cintas Fellowship, San Diego Book Award. Membership: PEN USA West. Literary Agent: Julie Castiglia. Address: c/o Julie Castiglia, 1155 Camino Del Mar, Suite 510, Del Mar, CA 92014, USA.

ENGLISH Sir David, b. 26 May 1931, England. Journalist; Editor; Media Chairman. m. Irene Mainwood, 1954, 1 son, 2 daughters. Education: Bournemouth School. Appointments: Daily Mirror, 1951-53; Feature

Editor, 1956, Editor, 1969-71, Daily Sketch; Foreign Correspondent, 1961-63, Chief American Correspondent, 1963-65, Foreign Editor, 1965-67, Associate Editor, 1967-69, Express; Editor, Daily Mail, 1971-92, Mail on Sunday, 1982; Vice-Chairman, 1986-88, Joint Deputy Chairman, 1989-92, Editor-in-Chief, 1989-, Chairman, 1992-, Associated Newspapers, Teletext UK, 1993-, Channel One TV, 1993-; Chairman, Editors of Editors Code Committee, 1993-; President, Commonwealth Press Union, 1995-; Chairman, Independent Television News, 1997-. Publication: Divided They Stand (A British View of the 1968 American Presidential Election), 1969. Honour: Knighted, 1982. Memberships: Association of British Editors, board, 1985-; Commonwealth Press Union, president, 1994-. Address: Northcliffe House, 2 Derry Street, London W5 5TT, England.

ENQUIST Per Olov, b. 23 Sept 1934, Bureå, Västerbotten, Sweden. Novelist; Playwright. m. Lone Bastholm. Education: PhD, University of Uppsala, 1964. Appointment: Critic, Expressen, Stockholm, 1967-. Publications: The Crystal Eye, 1962; The Route, 1963; The Casey Brothers, 1964; The Magnetist's Fifth Winter, 1964; Hess, 1966; The Legionnaires, 1968; The Seconder, 1971; Tales from the Age of Cancelled Rebellions, 1974; The March of the Musicians, 1978; Dr Mabuse's New Will, 1982; Downfall: A Love Story, 1985; Protagora's Theory, 1987; Captain Nemo's Library, 1991. Plays: The Night of the Tribades, 1975; Chez Nous: Pictures from Swedish Community Life, 1976; Man on the Pavement, 1979; To Phaedra, 1980; The Rain Snakes, 1981; The Hour of the Lynx, 1988. Other: Strindberg - A Life, 1984. Honour: Nordic Council Prize, 1969. Address: c/o Norstedts Forlag, Box 2052, 103 12 Stockholm 2, Sweden.

ENRIGHT D(ennis) J(oseph), b. 11 Mar 1920, Leamington, Warwickshire, England. Writer; Poet; Editor. m. Madeleine Harders, 3 Nov 1949, 1 daughter. Education: BA, Honours, 1944, MA, 1946, Downing College, Cambridge; DLitt, University of Alexandria, Egypt, 1949. Appointments: Professor of English, Far East, 1947-70; Co-Editor, Encounter, 1970-72; Director, Chatto and Windus Publishers, 1974-82. Publications: The Laughing Hyena and Other Poems, 1953; Academic Year, 1955; Bread Rather Than Blossoms, 1956; Some Men are Brothers, 1960; Selected Poems, 1969; Memoirs of a Mendicant Professor, 1969; Daughters of Death, 1972; The Terrible Shears: Scenes From a Twenties Childhood, 1974; Sad Ires and Others, 1975; Paradise Illustrated, 1978; A Faust Book, 1979; The Oxford Book of Death (editor), 1983; A Mania for Sentences, 1983; The Alluring Problem, 1986; Collected Poems, 1987; Fields of Vision, 1988; The Faber Book of Fevers and Frets (editor), 1989; Selected Poems, 1990; Under the Circumstances, 1991; The Oxford Book of Friendship (editor with David Rawlinson), 1991; The Way of the Cat, 1992; Old Men and Comets, 1993; The Oxford Book of the Supernatural (editor), 1994; Interplay: A Kind of Commonplace Book, 1995; The Sayings of Goethe (editor), 1996; Collected Poems 1948-1998, 1998; Play Resumed: A Journal, 1999. Contributions to: Journals, reviews, and magazines. Honours: Cholomondeley Award, 1974; Queen's Gold Medal for Poetry, 1981; Honorary Doctorates, University of Warwick, 1982, University of Surrey, 1985; Officer of the Order of the British Empire, 1991; Companion of Literature, 1998. Membership: Royal Society of Literature, Fellow. Address: 35A Viewfield Road, London SW18 5JD, England.

ENSLIN Theodore (Vernon), b. 25 Mar 1925, Chester, Pennsylvania, USA. Poet; Writer. m. (1) Mildred Marie Stout, 1945, div 1961, 1 son, 1 daughter, (2) Alison Jane Jose, 1969, 1 son. Education: Public and Private; Studied composition with Nadia Boulanger. Appointment: Columnist, The Cape Codder, Orleans, Massachusetts, 1949-56. Publications: Poetry: The Work Proposed, 1958; New Sharon's Prospect, 1962; The Place Where I Am Standing, 1964; To Come to Have Become, 1966; The Diabelli Variations and Other Poems, 1967; 2/30-6/31: Poems 1967, 1967; The Poems, 1970; Forms, 5 volumes, 1970-74; The Median Flow: Poems 1943-73,

1974; Ranger, Ranger 2, 2 volumes, 1979, 1980; Music for Several Occasions, 1985; Case Book, 1987; Love and Science, 1990; A Sonare, 1994. Fiction: 2 + 12 (short stories), 1979. Play: Barometric Pressure 29.83 and Steady, 1965. Other: Mahler, 1975; The July Book, 1976. Honours: Nieman Award for Journalism, 1955; National Endowment for the Arts Grant, 1976. Address: RFD Box 289, Kansas Road, Milbridge, MA 04658, USA.

ENSMINGER Audrey Helen, b. 30 Dec 1919, Winnipeg, Manitoba, Canada (US Citizen). Nutrition Consultant; Author. m. Marion Eugene Ensminger, 11 June 1941, 1 son, 1 daughter. dec. Education: BSc, University of Manitoba, 1940; MSc, Washington State University, 1943; Certified Nutrition Specialist. Publications: Foods and Nutrition Encyclopedia, 2nd edition, 1995; The Concise Encyclopedia of Foods & Nutrition, 1995; China - The Impossible Dream. Honours: American Medical Writers Association; Distinguished Service Award, American Medical Association; Humanitarian Award, Academy of Dentistry International. Address: 648 West Sierra Avenue, Clovis, CA 93612, USA.

ENTMAN Robert Mathew, b. 7 Nov 1949, New York, New York, USA. Professor of Communications; Consultant; Writer. m. Frances Seymour, 1 June 1979, 1 son, 1 daughter. Education: AB, Duke University, 1971; PhD, Yale University, 1977; M in Public Policy, University of California at Berkeley, 1980. Appointments: Assistant Professor, Dickinson College, Carlisle, Pennsylvania, 1975-77, Duke University, 1980-89, Postdoctoral Fellow, University of California, 1978-80; Consultant, US House of Representatives Subcommittee on Telecommunications, 1982, National Telecommunications and Information Administration, Washington, DC, 1984-85, Aspen Institute, 1986-; Guest Scholar, Woodrow Wilson Center, Washington, DC, 1989; Associate Professor of Communication, Northwestern University, 1989-94; Professor of Communication, North Carolina State University, 1994-; Adjunct Professor, University of North Carolina at Chapel Hill, 1995-. Publications: Media Power Politics (co-author), 1981; Democracy Without Citizens, 1989; Blacks in the News, 1991; Privatization of Broadcast Media, 1997. Contributions to: Journals. Honours: Markle Foundation Research Grants, 1984, 1986, 1988, 1995; Ameritech Research Fellow, 1989-90; McGannon Award for Communications Policy Research, 1993. Memberships; American Political Science Association; International Communication Association. Address: c/o Department of Communications, North Carolina State University, Box 8104, Raleigh, NC 27695, USA.

ENYEART James L(yle), b. 13 Jan 1943, Auburn, Washington, USA. Photographer; Adjunct Professor; Writer. m. Roxanne Malone, 3 children. Education: BFA, Kansas City Art Institute, 1965; MFA, University of Kansas, 1972. Appointments: Director, Albrecht Galley of Art, Instructor, Drawing and Design, Missouri Western University, 1967-68; Curator of Photography, Spencer Museum of Art, Associate Professor, Department Art History, University of Kansas, 1968-76; Director, Center for Creative Photography, Adjunct Professor of Art, University of Arizona, 1977-89; Director, George Eastman House, 1989-. Publications: Kansas Album (editor), 1977; Francis Brugiere, 1977; George Fiske: Yosemite Photographer, 1980; Photography of the Fifties: An American Perspective, 1980; Heineckan (editor), 1980; W Eugene Smith: Master of the Photographic Essay, 1981; Jerry Uelsmann: Twenty-five Years, a Retrospective, 1982; Aaron Siskind: Terrors and Pleasures 1931-80, 1982; Three Classic American Photographs: Texts and Contexts (with R D Monroe and Philip Stoker), 1982; Edward Weston Omnibus (with others), 1984; Edward Weston's California Landscapes, 1984; Judy Dater: Twenty Years, 1986; Andreas Feininger: A Retrospective (editor with Henry Holmes Smith) 1986. Honours: Photokina Obelisk Award, Cologne, Germany, 1982; Guggenheim Fellowship, 1987; Josef Sudek Medal, Ministry of Culture, Prague, Czechoslovakia, 1989. Memberships: American Association of Art Museum Directors; American Association of Art Museums; Oracle,

co-founder. Address: George Eastman House, 900 East Avenue, Rochester, NY 14607, USA.

ENZENSBERGER Hans Magnus, b. 11 Nov 1929, Kaufbeuren/Allgäu, Germany. Author; Poet; Dramatist. m. Katharina Bonitz, 2 children. Education: German Literature, Philosophy, and Linguistics, University of Erlanger, University of Hamburg, University of Freiburg im Breisgau, Sorbonne, University of Paris; PhD, 1955. Publications: verteidigung der wölfe, 1957; landessprache, 1957; Museum der modernen Poesie (editor and translator), 1960; Clemens Brentanos Poetik, 1961; Einzelheiten, 1964; blindenschrift, 1964; Politik und Verbrechen, 1964; Das Verhör von Habana, 1970; Klassenbuch (co-editor), 3 volumes, 1972; Der kurze Sommer der Anarchie: Buenaventura Durrutis Leben und Tod, 1972; Gespräche mit Marx und Engels (editor), 1973; Mauseleum: Siebenunddreissig Balladen aus der Geschichte des Fortschritts, 1975; Der Untergang der Titanic, 1978; Die Furie des Verschwindens, 1980; Politische Brosamen, 1982; Der Menschenfeind, 1984; Gedichte 1950-1985, 1986; Ach Europa!: Wahrnemung aus sieben Landern, 1987; Mittelmass und Wahn: Gesammelte Zerstreuungen, 1988; Requiem für eine romantische Frau: Die Geschichte von Auguste Bussmann und Clemens Brentano, 1988; Zukunftsmusik, 1991; Die Grosse Wangering: 33 Markierungen, 1992; Aussichten des Bürgerkriegs, 1993; Kiosk, 1995. Honours: German Critics' Literature Prize, 1962; Büchner Prize, 1963; Cultural Prize of the City of Nuremberg, 1967; Bavarian Academy of Fine Arts Literature Award, Munich, 1987; Erich Maria Remarque Peace Prize, Osnabrück, 1993; Cultural Prize of the City of Munich, 1994. Address: c/o Suhrkamp Verlag, Lindenstrasse 29-35, D-60325 Frankfurt am Main, Germany.

EPHRON Nora, b. 19 May 1941, New York, New York, USA. Writer. m. 1) Dan Greenburg, div, 2) Carl Bernstein, div, 2 sons, 3) Nicholas Pileggi. Education: BA, Wellesley College, 1962. Appointments: Reporter, New York Posts, 1963-68; Contributing Editor, Columnist, 1972-73, Senior Editor, Columnist, 1974-78, Esquire magazine; Contributing Editor, New York magazine, 1973-74. Publications: Wallflower at the Orgy, Crazy Salad, 1975; Scribble, Scribble, 1978; Heartbearn, 1983; Nora Ephron Collected, 1991. Screenplays: Silkwood, 1983; Heartbearn, 1986; Cookie, 1989; When Harry Met Sally, 1989; My Blue Heaven, 1990; This is My Life, 1992; Sleepless in Seattle, 1993; Mixed Nuts, 1994. Honours: Academy Award Nominations, 1983, 1989, 1993. Memberships: Academy of Motion Picture Arts and Sciences; Authors Guild; Directors Guild of America; Writers Guild of America. Address: c/o International Creative Management, 40 West 57th Street, New York, NY 10019, USA.

EPSTEIN Joseph, b. 9 Jan 1937, Chicago, Illinois, USA. Editor; Writer; Lecturer. m. Barbara Maher, 27 Feb 1976, 1 son. Education: BA, University of Chicago, 1959. Appointments: Associate Editor, The New Leader, 1962-63; Senior Editor, Encyclopaedia Britannica, 1965-69, Quadrangle/New York Times Books, 1969-70; Lecturer, Northwestern University, 1974-; Editor, The American Scholar, 1975-. Publications: Divorced in America, 1975; Ambition, 1979; Familiar Territory, 1980; The Middle of My Tether, 1983; Plausible Prejudices, 1985; Once More Around the Block, 1987; Partial Payments, 1989; A Line Out for A Walk, 1991; The Golden Boys: Stories, 1991; Pertinent Players, 1993; With My Trousers Rolled, 1995; Life Sentences, 1997. Editor: Masters: Portraits of Teachers, 1980; Best American Essays, 1993; Norton Book of Personal Essays, 1997. Contributions to: Many books and journals. Address: 522 Church Street, Evanston, IL 60201, USA.

EPSTEIN Seymour, (Sy Epstein), b. 2 Dec 1917, New York, New York, USA. Writer; Retired Professor. M. Miriam Kligman, 5 May 1956, 2 sons. Education: College, 2 years. Publications: Pillar of Salt, 1960; Leah, 1964; Caught in That Music, 1967; The Dream Museum, 1971; Looking for Fred Schmidt, 1973; A Special Destiny, 1986; September Faces, 1987; Light, 1989. Contributions to: Periodicals. Honour: Edward Lewis Wallant Memorial

Award, 1965; Guggenheim Fellowship, 1965. Memberships: Author's Guild; PEN. Address: 750 Kappock Street, Apt 608, Riverdale, Bronx, NY 10463, USA.

ERBA Luciano, b. 18 Sept 1922, Milan, Italy. Poet; Translator; Writer; Dramatist; Retired Professor of French Literature. Education: PhD, Catholic University, Milan, 1947. Appointments: Professor of French Literature, University of Padua, 1973-82, University of Verona, 1982-87, Catholic University, Milan, 1987-97. Publications: Linea K, 1951; Il bel paese, 1956; Il prete di Ratanà, 1959; Il male minore, 1960; Il prato più verde, 1977; Il nastro di Moebius, 1980; Il cerchio aperto, 1983; L'ippopotamo, 1989; L'ipotesi circense, 1995. Other: Françoise (novel), 1982; Radio and television plays; Translations. Honours: Viareggio Prize, 1980; Bagutta Prize, 1988; Librex-Guggenheim Eugenio Montale Prize, 1989; Italian Pen Club Prize, 1995. Address: Via Giason del Maino 16, 20146 Milan, Italy.

ERDRICH (Karen) Louise, b. 7 June 1954, Little Falls, Minnesota, USA. Writer; Poet. m. Michael Anthony Dorris, 10 Oct 1981, dec 1997, 6 children. Education: BA, Dartmouth College, 1976; MA, Johns Hopkins University, 1979. Appointments: Visiting Poet and Teacher, North Dakota State Arts Council, 1977-78; Writing Instructor, Johns Hopkins University, 1978-79; Communications Director and Editor of Circle of the Boston Indian Council, 1979-80. Publications: Fiction: Love Medicine, 1984, augumented edition, 1993; The Beet Queen, 1986; Tracks, 1988; The Crown of Columbus (with Michael Anthony Dorris), 1991; The Bingo Palace, 1994; The Antelope Wife, 1998. Poetry: Jacklight, 1984; Baptism of Desire, 1989. Other: Imagination, textbook, 1980. Contributions to: Anthologies; American Indian Quarterly; Atlantic; Frontiers; Kenyon Review; Ms; New England Review; New York Times Book Review; New Yorker; North American Review; Redbook; Others. Honours: MacDowell Colony Fellowship, 1980; Yaddo Colony Fellowship, 1981; Dartmouth College Visiting Fellow, 1981; National Magazine Fiction Awards, 1983, 1987; National Book Critics Circle Award for Best Work of Fiction, 1984; Virginia McCormick Scully Prize for Best Book of the Year, 1984; Best First Fiction Award, American Academy and Institute of Arts and Letters, 1985; Guggenheim Fellowship, 1985-86; 1st Prize, O Henry Awards, 1987. Address: c/o Rambar & Curtis, 19 West 45th Street, New York, NY 10036, USA.

ERICKSON Peter Brown, b. 11 Aug 1945, Worcester, Massachusetts, USA. Literary Critic; Librarian. m. Tay Gavin, 30 June 1968, dec, 2 sons, 1 daughter. Education: BA, Amherst College, 1967; Centre for Contemporary Cultural Studies, University of Birmingham, England, 1967-68; PhD, University of California, Santa Cruz, 1975; MSLS, Simmons College, 1984. Appointments: Assistant Professor, Williams College, 1976-81; Visiting Assistant Professor, Wesleyan University, 1982-83; Research Librarian, Clark Art Institute, 1985-. Publications: Patriarchal Structures in Shakespeare's Drama, 1985; Shakespeare's Rough Magic: Renaissance Essays in Honor of C L Barber, 1985; Rewriting Shakespeare, Rewriting Ourselves, 1991, paperback, 1994; Making Trifles of Terrors: Redistributing Complicities in Shakespeare, 1997. Contributions to: Books and journals. Honours: Phi Beta Kappa, 1967; Amherst Memorial Fellowship, 1967-68; Kent Fellowship, Wesleyan University, 1981-82. Memberships: Shakespeare Association of America; Renaissance Society of America; Modern Language Association. Address: Clark Art Institute, PO Box 8, Williamstown, MA 01267, USA.

ERICKSON Stephen (Michael), (Steve Erickson) b. 20 Apr 1950, Santa Monica, California, USA. Novelist. Education: BA, 1972, Master of Journalism, 1973, University of California, Los Angeles. Appointments: Arts Editor, 1989-91, Film Editor, 1992-93, Los Angeles Weekly. Publications: Days Between Stations, 1985; Rubicon Beach, 1986; Tours of the Black Clock, 1989; Leap Year, 1989; Arc d'X, 1993; Amnesiascope, 1996; American Nomad, 1997. Contributions to: New York Times; Esquire; Rolling Stone; Details; Elle; Los Angeles Times; Los Angeles Style; Los Angeles Weekly. Honours: Samuel Goldwyn Award, 1972; National Endowment for the Arts Fellowship, 1987. Address: c/o Melanie Jackson, 250 West 57th Street, Suite 1119, New York 10107, USA.

ERMAN Jack. See: **ACKERMAN Forrest J.**

ERMANSONS Egils, b. 13 Oct 1940, Riga, Latvia. Science Fiction Writer; Journalist. Div. Education: Moscow State Institute of Cinematography, 1969. Appointments: Cameraman and Documentary Film Director, Television Studio, Riga, 1966-78, Film Studio Eesti Reklaam Films, Riga, 1986-94; Writer, 1993-; Correspondent, Newspaper Neatkariga Rita Avize, 1994-97. Publications: Cilveks ar bernu ratiniem, English translation as The Man With a Pram (novel), 1994; Teicejs, English translation as The Speaker (play), 1995; Short stories in different newspapers and magazines. Honours: Karogs and R Gerkens Award, 1993; Children's Play Award, 1994. Memberships: Latvian Filmmakers' Union, 1977; Writers' Union of Latvia, 1994. Address: Auglu iela 8a dz 5, Riga, LV-1002, Latvia.

ERMAYNE Laurajean. See: **ACKERMAN Forrest J.**

ERSA-LIBIETE Mirdza, b. 22 Mar 1924, Riga, Latvia. Translator. 1 son. Education: French Lyceum of Riga, 1931-43; Romance Department, Philological Faculty, University of Latvia, 1944-49. Appointments: Pianist, Riga Puppet Theatre, 1957-61; Translator from French and Italian into Latvian, 1961-98. Publications: French into Latvian, the works by F Mauriac, George Sand, Jules Verne, Georges Simenon, A de Vigny, S de Beauvoir, Marcel Aymé, H de Balzac, Emil Zola and other authors. From Italian into Latvian: Il Maestro, by Goffredo Parise, 1969; La luna e il falo, Selected Works by Cesare Pavese, 1978. Honour: Order of Arts and Literature, France, 1993. Membership: Writers' Union of Latvia, 1997. Address: Maskavas iela 311-101, LV 1063, Riga, Latvia.

ERSKINE Barbara, b. 10 Aug 1944, Nottingham, England. Writer. m. 2 sons. Education: MA Honours, Edinburgh University, 1967. Publications: Lady of Hay, 1986; Kingdom of Shadows, 1988; Encounters, 1990; Child of the Phoenix, 1992; Midnight is a Lonely Place, 1994; House of Echoes, 1996; Distant Voices, 1996; On the Edge of Darkness, 1998. Contributions to: Numerous short stories to magazines and journals. Membership: Society of Authors; Scientific and Medical Network. Address: c/o Blake Friedmann, 122 Arlington Road, London, NW1 7HP.

ERSPAMER Peter Roy, b. 28 Sept 1959, Minnesota, USA. University Lecturer. Education: BA, Grinnell College, Iowa, 1982; MA, 1986, PhD, cum laude, 1992, University of Wisconsin at Madison. Appointments: Teaching Assistant in German, University of Wisconsin at Madison, 1984-89; Visiting Assistant Professor of German, Winona State University, 1992-93, University of Missouri-Columbia, 1993-94, Fort Hays State University, Kansas, 1994-96; NEH Visiting Scholar, University Professors Program, Boston University, 1997; Visiting Lecturer in German, Indiana University/Purdue University of Indianapolis, 1997-98. Publications: the Elusiveness of Tolerance: The Jewish Question From Lessing to the Napoleonic Wars (book), 1997. Contributions to: The Yale Companion to Jewish Writing and Thought; Literature and Ethnic Discrimination. Honour: Fulbright Grantee; Lucius N Littauer Grantee. Choice Magazine Outstanding Academic Book of 1997. Address: Box 48, Chetek, WI 54728, USA.

ERWIN Douglas Hamilton, b. 1958, Los Angeles, California, USA. Paleontologist. m. Cheryl Adams, 1993. Education: AB, Colgate University, 1980; PhD, Geological Science, University of California at Santa Barbara, 1985. Appointments: Assistant Professor, Associate Professor, Department of Geological Science, Michigan State University, 1985-90; Associate Curator, Curator, Department of Paleobiology, National Museum of Natural History, Smithsonian Institute, Washington, DC, 1990-. Publications: The Great Paleogic Crisis, 1993; The Fossils of the Burgess Shale, 1994; New Approaches to Speciation in the Fossil Record, 1995; Euolutionary Paleobiology, 1996. Contributions to: Science; Nature; Scientific American. Honour: Schuchett Award, 1996. Address: Department of Paleobiology, MRC-121, Smithsonian Institute, Washington, DC 20560, USA.

ESAIN Simon Salvador, (Uyariwak), b. 30 Aug 1945, Maipú, Province of Buenos Aires, Argentina. Painter of Letters. m. Irene Luján Pérez, 2 Apr 1971, div., 1 daughter. Appointments: Founder Member, MAYA, Chascomús' movement of artists and artisans; Director, Editor, La Silla Tibia, artisanal literary magazine. Publications: November Indignation (editor), 1995; May of 1989 or the smoke, 1996; Superviser Muse, 1997; The Moment of Drowning, forthcoming. Contributions to: Several underground magazines, Argentina, Colombia, Mexico, Peru, Brasil, Belgium, Spain.. Address: Obligado No 133, 7130 Chascomús, Buenos Aires, Argentina.

ESBER ali Ahmad Said, (Adonis), b. 1930, Oassabin, Syria. Poet; Educator. Education: BA, University of Damascus, 1954; PhD, University of St Joseph, Beirut, 1973. Appointments: Professor of Arabic Literature, Lebanese University, Beirut, 1971-85; PhD Advisor, University of St Joseph, Beirut, 1971-85; Visiting Lecturer, Collège de France, Paris, 1983, Georgetown University, Washington, DC, 1985; Associate Professor of Arab Poetry, University of Geneva, 1989-95. Publications: Poetry in French: Chants de Mihyar le Damascene, 1983; Tombeau pour New York suivi de Prologue a l'histoire des rois des ta'ifa et de Ceci est mon nom, 1986; Le Temps les Villes, 1990; Célébrations, 1991; Chronique des branches, 1991; Mémoire du vent (anthology), 1991; Soleils Seconds, 1994; Singuliers, 1995. In English: An Introduction to Arab Poetics, 1990; The Pages of Day and Night, 1994. Other: Much poetry in Arabic. Honours: Prix des Amis du Livre, Beirut, 1968; Syria-Lebanon Award, International Poetry Forum, 1971; National Prize for Poetry, Lebanon, 1974; Officier des Arts et des Lettres, France, 1993; Grand Prix des Biennales Internationales de la Poésie de Liège, Belgium, 1986; Prix Jean Malrieu-Etranger, Marseille, 1991; Feronia-Cita di Fiano, Rome, 1993; Nazim Hikmat Prize, Istanbul, 1994; Prix Méditerranée-Etranger, France, 1995; Prize of the Lebanese Culture Form, France, 1995. Memberships: Académie Stéphane Mallarmé, Paris; Haut Conseil de Réflexion du Collège International de Philosophie, Paris. Address: 1 Square Henri Regnault, 92400 Courbevoie, France.

ESCANDELL Noemi, b. 27 Sept 1936, Havana, Cuba. Professor of Spanish Language and Literature; Poet. m. Peter Knapp, 1 June 1957, div 1972, 2 sons, 2 daughters. Education: Bachiller en Letras, Instituto de la Vibora, 1955; BA, Queens College of the City University of New York, 1968; MA, 1971, PhD, 1976, Harvard University. Appointments: Assistant Professor, Bard College, 1976-83; Language Programme Director, Nuevo Instituto de Centroamerica, Esteli, Nicaragua, 1987-88; Professor of Spanish, Westfield State College, 1983-93; Director, Afterschool Preogramme, Ross School, Washington, DC, 1995-96. Publications: Cuadros, 1982; Ciclos, 1982; Palabras/Words, 1986. Contributions to: Anthologies and periodicals. Honours: Poet-in-Residence, Millay Colony for the Arts, Austerlitz, New York, 1983, 1991; Special Mention, Certamen Poetico Federico Garcia Lorca Poetry Contest, 1995; 1st Prize in Poetry, XXXII Certamen Literario International Odon Betanzos Palacio, 1996. Membership: Academia Iberoamericana de Poesia, Washington, DC, Chapter. Address: 1525 Q Street Northwest, No 11, Washington, DC 20009, USA.

ESHLEMAN Clayton, b. 1 June 1935, Indianapolis, Indiana, USA. Professor of English; Poet; Writer; Translator. m. 1) Barbara Novak, 1961, div 1967, 1 son, 2) Caryl Reiter, 1969. Education: BA, Philosophy, 1958, MA, Creative Writing, 1961, Indiana University. Appointments: Editor, Folio, 1959-60; Instructor, University of Maryland Eastern Overseas Division, 1961-62, New York University American Language Institute, 1966-68; Publisher, Caterpillar Books, 1966-68; Founder-Editor-Publisher, Caterpillar magazine, 1967-73;

Faculty, School of Critical Studies, California Institute of the Arts, Valencia, 1970-72; Dreyfuss Poet-in-Residence and Lecturer, California Institute of Technology, Pasadena, 1979-84; Visiting Lecturer in Creative Writing, University of California at San Diego, Los Angeles, Santa Barbara, and Riverside, 1979-86; Reviewer, Los Angeles Times Book Review, 1979-86; Founder-Editor, Sulfur magazine, 1981-; Professor of English, Eastern Michigan University, 1986-. Publications: Mexico & North, 1962; Brother Stones, 1968; Indiana, 1969; The House of Ibuki, 1969; Altars, 1971; A Caterpillar Anthology: A Selection of Poetry and Prose from Caterpillar Magazine (editor), 1971; Coils, 1973; The Gull Wall, 1975; Grotesca, 1975; On Mules Sent from Chavin, 1977; What She Means, 1977; Our Lady of the Three-Pronged Devil, 1977; Nights We Put the Rock Together, 1980; Hades in Manganese, 1981; Fracture, 1983; The Name Encanyoned River: Selected Poems, 1960-85, 1986; Hotel-Cro-Magnon, 1989; Antiphonal Swing: Selected Prose, 1962-87, 1989; Novices: A Study of Poetic Apprenticeship, 1989; Under World Arrest, 1994; Nora's Roar, 1996; From Scratch, 1998. Translations: 13 books, 1962-95. Contributions to: Numerous anthologies, magazines, and newspapers. Honours: PEN Translation Prize, 1977; Guggenheim Fellowship, 1978; National Book Award for Translation, 1979; National Endowment for the Arts Fellowship, 1979; National Endowment for the Humanities Grant, 1980, and Fellowships, 1981, 1988; Michigan Arts Council Grant, 1988; Eastern Michigan University Research Grants, 1990, 1997. Address: 210 Washtenaw Avenue, Ypsilanti, MI 48197, USA.

ESLER Gavin William James, b. 27 Feb 1953, Glasgow, Scotland. Broadcaster; Author. m. Patricia Warner, 1 son, 1 daughter. Education: BA, Honours, Kent; MA, Leeds. Appointments: BBC Television News Presenter; Columnston The Scotsman Newspaper. Publications: Novels: Loyalties, 1990; Deep Blue, 1992; The Blood Brother, 1995. Non-Fiction: The United States of Anger, 1997. Contributions to: Anthologies, journals, periodicals, quarterlies, newspapers and magazines. Literary Agent: Jonathan Lloyd. Address: c/o Curtis Brown, Haymarket House, London.

ESMOND Harriet. See: **BURKE John Frederick.**

ESPOSITO Nancy (Giller), b. 1 Jan 1942, Dallas, Texas, USA. Poet; Writer; Editor; Adjunct Assistant Professor. Education: University of Wisconsin; BA, English, MA, English, New York University. Appointments: Associate Professor, Illinois Central College, East Peoria, 1968-70; Instructor, Harvard University, 1976-80, 1981-84, Wellesley College, 1980; Lecturer, Tufts University, 1986-93, Boston College, 1994; Adjunct Assistant Professor, Bentley College, 1986-. Publication: Changing Hands, 1984. Contributions to: Anthologies: Two Decades of New Poets, 1984, Ixok-Amar-Go, 1987, Quarterly Review of Literature 50th Anniversary Anthology, 1993, and Poetry from Sojourner, 1999; Reviews, journals, and periodicals. Honours: Discovery/The Nation Award, 1979; Virginia Center for the Creative Arts Fellow, 1979-80, 1981, 1990; Yaddo Fellow, 1981; Colladay Award, 1984; MacDowell Colony Fellow, 1986-87; Gordon Barber Memorial Award, Poetry Society of America, 1987; Fulbright-Hays Grant to Egypt, 1988; Publishing Award, 1988, Faculty Development Fund Grant, 1997, Bentley College; Ragdale Foundation Fellow, 1990. Memberships: Academy of American Poets; Associated Writing Programs; Poetry Society of America; Poets and Writers. Address: 34 Trowbridge Street, Belmont, MA 02478, USA.

ESSLIN Martin (Julius), b. 8 June 1918, Budapest, Hungary (British citizen). Professor of Drama Emeritus; Writer. m. Renate Gerstenberg, 1947, 1 daughter. Education: Vienna University. Appointments: Head of Drama, BBC Radio, 1963-77; Professor of Drama, 1977-88, Professor Emeritus, 1988- Stanford University; now Professor Emeritus. Publications: Brecht: A Choice of Evils: A Critical Study of the Man, His Work and His Opinions, 1959; The Theatre of the Absurd, 1961, 1968; Samuel Beckett: A Collection of Critical Essays (editor), 1965; Harold Pinter, 1967; The Genius of the German Theatre (editor), 1968; Berthold Brecht, 1969; Brief Chronicles: Essays on Modern Theatre, 1970; The Peopled Wound: The Work of Harold Pinter, 1970; The New Theatre of Europe, Vol 4 (editor), 1970; An Anatomy of a Drama, 1976; Artaud, 1976; Mediation, 1980; The Age of Television, 1982; The Field of Drama, 1987; Antonin Artaud, 1992. Address: 64 Loudoun Road, London NW8, England.

ESSOP Ahmed, b. 1 Sept 1931, Dabhel, India. m. Writer. 17 Apr 1960, 1 son, 3 daughters. Education: BA Honours, English, University of South Africa, 1964. Publications: The Hajii and Other Stories, 1978; The Visitation, 1980; The Emperor, 1984; Noorjehan and Other Stories, 1990; The King of Hearts and Other Stories, 1997. Honour: Olive Schyeiner Award, English Academy of Southern Africa, 1979. Address: PO Box 1747, Lenasia 1820, Johannesburg, South Africa.

ESTERHAZY Péter, b. 14 Apr 1950, Budapest, Hungary. Novelist. m. Gitta Reen. Education: Graduated, University of Budapest and Eötvös Lorand University, 1974. Publications: Fancsiko and Pinta, 1976; Don't Be a Pirate on Papal Waters, 1977; Production Novel, 1979; Indirect, 1981; Who Can Guarantee the Lady's Safety?, 1982; Hauliers, 1983; Little Hungarian Pornography, 1984; Helping Verbs of the Heart, 1985; Seventeen Swans, 1987; The Stuffed Swan, 1988; Certain Adventure, 1989; Hrabal's Book, 1990; The Glance of Countess Hahn-Hahn, 1991; The Wonderful Life of the Little Fish, 1991; From the Ivory Tower, 1991; Notes of a Blue Stocking, 1994; Farewell Symphony, 1994; She Loves Me, 1995. Honour: Attila József Prize; Lajos Kossuth Prize. Address: c/o Hungarian Writers' Federation, Bajza-utca 18, 1962 Budapest, Hungary.

ESTLEMAN Loren D, b. 15 Sept 1952, Ann Arbor, Michigan, USA. Writer. Education: BA, English Literature/Journalism, Eastern Michigan University, 1974; Vice President, President Elect, Western Writers of America, 1998. Publications: Novels: The Oklahoma Punk, 1976; The Hider, 1978; Sherlock Holmes vs Dracula, 1978; The High Rocks, 1979; Dr Jekyll and Mr Holmes, 1979; Stamping Ground, 1980; Motor City Blue, 1980; Aces and Eights, 1981; Angel Eyes, 1981; The Wolfer, 1981; Murdock's Law, 1982; The Midnight Man, 1982; Mister St John, 1983; This Old Bill, 1984; Kill Zone, 1984; Sugartown, 1984; Roses are Dead, 1985; Gun Man, 1985; Every Brilliant Eye, 1986; Any Man's Death, 1986; Lady Yesterday, 1987; Downriver, 1988; Bloody Season, 1988; Silent Thunder, 1989; Peeper, 1989; Sweet Women Lie, 1990; Whiskey River, 1990; Sudden Country, 1991; Motown, 1991; King of the Corner, 1992; City of Widows, 1994; Edsel, 1995; Stress, 1996; Billy Gashade, 1997; Never Street, 1997; The Witchfinderm 1998. Non-Fiction: The Wister Trace, 1987; The Witchfinder, 1998; Journey of the Dead, 1998; Jitterbug, 1998. Contributions to: Journals. Honours: Golden Spur Awards, 1981, 1987, Stirrup Award, 1983, Western Writers of America; Shamus Awards, 1984, 1985, 1988; Stirrup Award, 1985; Private Eye Writers of America; Michigan Arts Foundation Award, 1987; American Mystery Awards, 1988, 1990; Golden Spur Award, 1996; Michigan Author Award, 1997. Literary Agent: Dominick Abel Literary Agency Inc. Address: 5552 Walsh Road, Whitmore Lake, MI 48189, USA.

ESTORIL Jean. See: **ALLAN Mabel Esther.**

ETCHEMENDY Nancy Howell, b. 19 Feb 1952, Reno, Nevada, USA. Writer; Graphic Designer. m. 14 Apr 1973, 1 son. Education: BA, University of Nevada, Reno, 1974. Publications: The Watchers of Space, 1980; Stranger From the Stars, 1983; The Crystal City, 1985. Contributions to: Anthologies and magazines. Memberships: Science Fiction Writers of America; Society of Children's Book Writers; Horror Writers Association, treasurer, 1996-97. Address: 410 French Court, Menlo Park, CA 94025, USA.

ETTER Dave, (David Pearson Etter), b. 18 Mar 1928, Huntington Park, California, USA. Poet; Writer; Editor. m. Margaret A Cochran, 8 Aug 1959, 1 son, 1 daughter. Education: BA, History, University of Iowa, 1953. Appointments: Promotion Department, Indiana University, 1959-60; Rand McNally Publishing Co, 1960-61; Assistant Editor, Encyclopaedia Britannia, Chicago, 1964-73; Editor, Northern Illinois University Press, 1974-80; Freelance Writer, Poet, and Editor, 1981-. Publications: Go Read the River, 1966; The Last Train to Prophetstown, 1968; Open the Wind, 1978; Riding the Rock Island Through Kansas, 1979; Cornfields, 1980; West of Chicago, 1981; Boondocks, 1982; Alliance, Illinois, 1983; Home Stat, 1985; Live at the Silver Dollar, 1986; Selected Poems, 1987; Midlanders, 1988; Electric Avenue, 1988; Carnival, 1990; Sunflower Country, 1994; How High the Moon, 1996. Contributions to: Many journals, reviews, and periodicals. Honours: Society of Midlands Authors Poetry Prize, 1967; Friends of Literature Poetry Prize, 1967; Bread Loaf Writers' Conference Fellowship in Poetry, 1967; Illinois Sesquicentennial Poetry Prize, 1968; Theodore Roethke Poetry Prize, 1971; Carl Sandburg Poetry Prize, 1982. Address: 414 Gates Street, PO Box 413, Elburn, IL 60119, USA.

ETZIONI Amitai, b. 4 Jan 1929, Cologne, Germany (US citizen, 1963). Sociologist; Professor; Writer. m. 1) Minerva Morales, 14 Sept 1965, dec 20 Dec 1985, 5 sons, 2) Patricia Kellogg, 6 Nov 1992. Education: BA, 1954, MA, 1956, Hebrew University, Jerusalem; PhD in Sociology, University of California at Berkeley, 1958. Appointments: Faculty, 1958-67, Professor of Sociology, 1967-78, Chairman, Department of Sociology, 1969-78, Columbia University; Fellow, Center for Advanced Study in the Behavioral Sciences, 1965-66; Founder-Director, Center for Policy Research, 1968-; Guest Scholar, Brookings Institution, 1978-79; Senior Advisor, White House, Washington, DC, 1979-80; University Professor, 1980-, Director, Center for Communitarian Studies, 1995-, George Washington University; Thomas Henry Carroll Ford Foundation Visiting Professor, Graduate School of Business, Harvard University, 1987-89; Editor, The Responsive Community: Rights and Responsibilities quarterly, 1990-; Founder-Director, The Communitarian Network, 1993-. Publications: A Comparative Analysis of Complex Organizations, 1961; Modern Organizations, 1964; Political Unification: A Comparative Study of Leaders and Forces, 1965; Studies in Social Change, 1966; The Active Society, 1968; Genetic Fix, 1973; Social Problems, 1975; An Immodest Agenda, 1982; Capital Corruption, 1984; The Moral Dimension, 1988; The Spirit of Community: Rights, Responsibilities and the Communitarian Agenda, 1993; The New Golden Rule: Community and Morality in a Democratic Society, 1996; The Limits of Privacy, 1999. Contributions to: Scholarly journals, newspapers, periodicals, and television. Honours: Social Science Research Council Fellowship, 1960-61; Guggenheim Fellowship, 1968-69; Certificate of Appreciation, American Revolution Bicentennial Commission, 1976; Tolerance Book Award, Simon Wiesenthal Center, 1997; Honorary doctorates. Memberships: American Academy of Arts and Sciences, fellow; American Sociological Association, president, 1995; Society for the Advancement of Socio-Economics, founder-president, 1989-90, honorary fellow. Address: c/o The Gelman Library, George Washington University, 2130 H Street North West, Washington, DC 20052, USA.

ETZIONI HALEVY Eva, b. 21 Mar 1934, Vienna, Austria. Political Sociologist; Professor. m. Zvi Halevy, 2 sons, 1 daughter. Education: PhD, Tel Aviv University, 1971. Appointment: Professor, Bar Ilan University, Ramat Gan, Israel. Publications: Social Change, 1981; Bureaucracy and Democracy, 1985; The Knowledge Elite and the Failure of Prophecy, 1985; National Broadcasting Under Siege, 1987; Fragile Democracy, 1989; The Elite Connection, 1992; The Elite Connection and Democracy in Israel, 1993; A Place at the Top: Elites and Elitism in Israel, 1997; Classes and Elites in Democracy and Democratization, 1997; Place at the Top, 1997. Contributions to: Numerous magazines and journals. Honour: Fellow, Academy of Social Sciences in Australia. Address: Department of Sociology, Bar Ilan University, Ramat Gan 52900, Israel.

EULO Ken, b. 17 Nov 1939, Newark, New Jersey, USA. Playwright; Director; Novelist. m. 1 son. Education: University of Heidelberg, 1961-64. Appointments: Artistic Director, Courtyard Playhouse, New York; Staff Writer, Paramount. Publications: Plays: Bang?, 1969; Zarf, I Love You, 1969; SRO, 1970; Puritan Night, 1971; Billy Hofer and the Quarterback Sneak, 1971; Black Jesus, 1972; The Elevator, 1972; 48 Spring Street, 1973; Final Exams, 1975; The Frankenstein Affair, 1979; Say Hello to Daddy, 1979. Novels: Bloodstone, 1982; The Brownstone, 1982; The Deathstone, 1982; Nocturnal, 1983; The Ghost of Veronica, 1985; House of Caine, 1988. Other: Television scripts. Contributions to: Magazines and newspapers. Memberships: Dramatists Guild; Italian Playwrights of America; Writers Guild of America. Address: 14633 Valley Vista Boulevard, Sherman Oaks, CA 91403, USA.

EVANS Alan. See: **STOKER Alan.**

EVANS Aled Lewis, b. 9 Aug 1961, Machynlleth, Wales. Poet; Teacher; Broadcaster. Education: Joint Honours Degree, Welsh, English, University College of North Wales, Bangor. Publications: Border Town, 1983; Whispers, 1986; Waves, 1989; Can I Have a Patch of Blue Sky?, 1991; Between Two September Tides, 1994. Contributions to: Welsh Language Periodicals, Golwg; Barn; Tu Chwith; English Language, Chester Poets Anthologies. Honour: National Eisteddfod of Wales Award for Poetry, 1991. Memberships: Gorsedd Bards; Chester Poets. Address: 28 Jubilee Road, Pentrefelin, Wrexham, Clwyd LL13 7NN, Wales.

EVANS Donald, (Onwy), b. 12 June 1940, Cardiganshire, Wales. Welsh Specialist; Poet. m. Pat Thomas, 29 Dec 1972, 1 son. Education: Honours Degree, Welsh, 1962, Diploma, Education, 1963, University College of Wales Aberystwyth. Appointments: Welsh Master, Ardwyn Grammar School, Aberystwyth, 1963-73, Penglais Comprehensive School, Aberystwyth, 1973-84; Welsh Specialist, Cardigan Junior School, 1984-91. Publications: Egin, 1976; Haidd, 1977; Grawn, 1979; Y Flodeugerodd O Gywyddau (editor), 1981; Machlud Canrif, 1983; Cread Crist, 1986; O'r Bannau Duon, 1987; Iasau, 1988; Seren Poets 2 (with others), 1990; The Life and Work of Rhydwen Williams, 1991; Wrth Reddf, 1994; Asgwrn Cefen (Backbone), 1997. Contributions to: Several publications. Honours: National Eisteddfod Crown and Chair, 1977, 1980; Welsh Arts Council Poetry Prizes, 1977, 1983, 1989; Welsh Academy Literary Award, 1989. Memberships: Welsh Academy; Welsh Poetry Society. Address: Y Plas, Talgarreg, Llandysul, County of Ceredigion SA44 4XA, Wales.

EVANS Harold Matthew, b. 28 June 1928, Manchester, England. Editor; Publisher; Writer. m. (1) Enid Muriel Evans, 15 Aug 1953, div 1979, 1 son, 2 daughters, (2) Cristina Hamley Brown, 20 Aug 1982, 1 son, 1 daughter. Education: BA, Durham University, 1952; MA, Dunelm, 1966. Appointments: Ashton-under-Lyne, Reporter Newspapers, 1944-46, 1949; Manchester Evening News, 1952; Commonwealth Fund Fellow in Journalism, University of Chicago and Stanford University, 1956-57; Assistant Editor, Manchester Evening News, 1958-61; Editor, Northern Echo, 1961-66; Editor-in-Chief, North of England Newspaper Co, 1963-66; Managing Editor, 1966-67, Editor, 1967-81, Sunday Times; Editor, The Times, 1981-82; Editor-in-Chief, Atlantic Monthly Press, 1984-86; Editorial Director, 1984-86, Contributing Editor, 1986-97, US News & World Report; Vice-President and Senior Editor, Weidenfeld & Nicolson, 1986-87; Founder-Editor, Condé-Nast Traveler Magazine, 1986-90; President and Publisher, Random House Trade Group, 1990-97; Editorial Director and Vice Chairman, Atlantic Monthly, Daily News, New York, US News & World Report, 1997-. Publications: The Active Newsroom, 1961; Editing and Design, 5 volumes, 1972-77; We Learned to Ski, 1974; The Story of Thalidomide, 1978; Eye Witness (editor), 1981; How We Learned to Ski, 1983; Good Times, Bad Times (autobiography), 1983; Front Page History, 1984. Contributions to: Periodicals. Honours: International

Editor of the Year, 1975; Gold Medal Award, Institute of Journalists, 1979; Hood Medal, Royal Photographic Society, 1981; Honorary Doctorate, University of Stirling, 1981; Editor of the Year, 1982; Lotos Club Medal, New York, 1993. Membership: Society of American Historians. Address: c/o US News & World Report, 2400 N Street North West, Washington, DC 20037, USA.

EVANS Jonathan. See: **FREEMANTLE Brian.**

EVANS Mari, b. 16 July 1923, Toledo, Ohio, USA. Poet; Writer. Div, 2 sons. Education: University of Toledo. Appointments: Writer, producer and director, The Black Experience television programme, Indianapolis, 1968-73; Writer-in-Residence and Instructor in Black Literature, Indiana University-PUrdur University at Indianapolis, 1969-70; Assistant Professor of Black Literature and Writer-in-Residence, Indiana University, 1970-78, Purdue University, 1978-80; Writer-in-Residence and Visiting Assistant Pofessor, Northwestern University, 1972-73; Visiting Professor, Washington University, 1980, Cornell University, 1981-84, University of Miami at Coral Gables, 1989; Associate Professor, State University of New York at Albany, 1985-86; Writer-in-Residence, Spelman College, Atlanta, 1989-90. Publications: Poetry: Where Is All the Music?, 1968; I Am A Black Woman, 1970; Whisper, 1979; Nightstar, 1981; A Dark and Splendid Mass, 1992. Other: Rap Stories, 1973; J D, 1973; I Look at Me, 1974; Singing Black, 1976; Jim Flying High, 1979; Black Women Writers 1950-1980: A Critical Evaluation (editor), 1984. Honours: John Hay Whitney Fellowship, 1965; Woodrow Wilson Foundation Grant, 1968; Black Academy of Arts and Letters Award, 1971; MacDowell Fellowship, 1975; Copeland Fellowship, 1980; National Endowment for the Arts Award, 1981; Yaddo Fellowship, 1984. Address: PO Box 483, Indianapolis, IN 4606, USA.

EVANS Max, b. 29 Aug 1925, USA. Writer; Painter. Publications: Southwest Wind (short stories), 1958; Long John Dunn of Taos, 1959; The Rounders, 1960; The Hi Lo Country, 1961; Three Short Novels: The Great Wedding, The One-Eyed Sky, My Pardner, 1963; The Mountain of Gold, 1965; Shadow of Thunder, 1969; Three West: Conversations with Vardis Fisher, Max Evans, Michael Straight, 1970; Sam Peckinpah, Master of Violence, 1972; Bobby Jack Smith, You Dirty Coward!, 1974; The White Shadow, 1977; Xavier's Folly and Other Stories, 1984; Super Bull and Other True Escapades, 1985. Address: 1111 Ridgecrest Drive South East, Albuquerque, NM 87108, USA.

EVANS Michael Stephen James, b. 5 Jan 1945, Worthing, Sussex, England. Journalism. m. Nicky Coles, 19 June 1971, 3 sons. Education: BA Hons, English, Queen Mary College, London University. Appointments: Daily Express, Action Line Reporter, 1970-72; General Reporter, 1972-77; Home Affairs Correspondent, 1977-82; Defence and Diplomatic Correspondent, 1982-86; The Times: Whitehall Correspondent, 1986-87; Defence Correspondent, 1987-88; Defence Editor, 1998-. Publications: A Crack in the Dam, 1978; False Arrest, 1979; Great Disasters, 1981; South Africa, 1987; The Gulf Crisis, 1988. Honour: Desmond Wettern Maritime Media Award, 1998. Address: The Times, 1 Pennington Street, London E1 9XN, England.

EVANS Richard Rowland, b. 26 May 1936, Tabor, Dolgellau, Wales. Retired Headteacher; Writer; Poet. m. Bronwen Edwards, 21 Aug 1965, 1 daughter. Education: Teacher's Certificate, 1958; Diploma in Bilingual Education, 1964; BEd, 1980, University College of Wales; BA, University of Wales, 1998. Appointment: Welsh Editor, The Normalite/Y Normalydd, 1957-58. Publication: Mynd i'r Lleuad, 1973. Contributions to: Articles and poetry to Dalen; Godre'r Gader; The Normalite/Y Normalydd; Y Cyfnod; Y Dydd. Honour: Winner, Book Writing Competition, 1970, Bardic Chair, 1988. Memberships: Barddas; Cymdeithas Bob Owen; Undeb Awduron Cymru. Address: Rhandir Mwyn, Cae Deintur, Dolgellau, Gwynedd, North Wales.

EVENSON Brian, b. 12 Aug 1966, Ames, Iowa, USA. Fiction Writer. m. Connie Joyce Evenson, 16 Aug 1989,

2 daughters. Education: BA, English, Brigham Young University, 1989; MA, English, 1990; PhD, Critical Theory/English Literature, University of Washington, 1994. Appointments: Assistant Professor, English, Brigham Young University, 1994-96; Assistant Professor, English, Oklahoma State University, 1996-. Publications: Altmann's Tongue, 1994; The Din of Celestial Birds, 1997; Prophets and Brothers, 1997; Father of Lies, 1998. Contributions to: Fiction Editor, Cimarron Review, 1996-; Editor, Conjunctions, 1997-. Honour: National Endowment for the Arts Grant, 1995. Literary Agent: Giles Gordon. Address: Giles Gordon, c/o Curtis Brown, 6 Ann Street, Edinburgh EH4 1PJ, Scotland.

EVERETT Graham, b. 23 Dec 1947, Oceanside, New York, USA. Adjunct Professor; Poet; Writer. m. Elyse Arnow, 27 Dec 1981, 1 son. Education: BA, English, Canisius College, 1970; MA, English, 1987, PhD, English, 1994, State University of New York at Stony Brook. Appointments: Editor and Publisher, Street Press and Magazine, 1972-86; Adjunct Instructor, Southampton College, 1979-81; Dowling College, 1987; Teaching Assistant, 1986-90, Adjunct, Graduate English Department, 1996-, State University of New York at Stony Brook; Adjunct Instructor, 1987-91, Adjunct Assistant Professor, 1991-, Suffolk County College; Adjunct Assistant Professor, Long Island University, 1988-92; Adjunct Professor, 1991-, Academic Tutor, 1992-, Adelphi University. Publications: Trees, 1978; Strange Coast, 1979; Paumanok Rising: An Anthology of Eastern Long Island Aesthetics (co-editor), 1981; Sunlit Sidewalk, 1985; Minus Green, 1992; Minus Green Plus, 1995. Contributions to: Anthologies, reviews, quarterlies, and journals. Memberships: Modern Language Association; National Council of Teachers of English. Address: PO Box 772, Sound Beach, NY 11789, USA.

EVERS Gene, b. 26 Mar 1951, Manhattan, New York, USA. Independent Writer. Education: AA, Humanities, Nassau Community College, 1973; BA, Humanities, State University of New York, Old Westbury; Philosophy, Stony Brook University, 1973. Publications: Over 15 published poems, 1995-: The Poems Rainbow, Man in the Moon, Angel at Noon, Heavens Dawn, Big Red Mountain, She Sat upon the Cloud; Songs: Cindy Girl, 1996; Ohio, 1997; Northern Wind, 1998; Where my Heart lies, 1998; A Christmas Journey, movie, to be published; Collection of short stories. Contributions to: National Library of Poetry; Poetry Guild. Honours: Editor's Choice Poems, 1995, 1996, Outstanding Achievement Award, 1995, 1996, 1997, National Library of Poetry; Poet of the Year 1996, International Society of Poets; International Society of Poets Hall of Fame, 1996; Distinguished Member, International Society of Poets, 1996, 1997; Invited to join International Platform Association, 1998. Membership: New York Writer's Guild. Address: 33 Hayden Drive, Bethpage, NY 11714, USA.

EVERS Lawrence Joseph (Larry), b. 15 Aug 1946, Grand Island, Nebraska, USA. Professor of English. m. Barbara Zion Grygutis, 20 Dec 1982, 1 son, 1 daughter. Education: BA, 1968, MA, 1969, PhD, 1972, University of Nebraska, Lincoln; Postdoctoral Fellow, University of Chicago, 1973-74. Appointments: Assistant to Full Professor, 1974-86, Full Professor, 1986-, of English, University of Arizona, Tucson. Publications: Words and Place: Native Literature from the American Southwest, 1979; The South Corner of Time, 1980; With Felipe S Molina: Yaqui Deer Songs - Maso Bwrikam, 1987; Woi Bwikam - Coyote Songs, 1990; Hiakim: The Yaqui Homeland, 1992; Homeplaces, 1995. Honours: National Endowment for the Humanities Fellowship, 1972-73; 1st Place, Chicago Folklore Prize, 1987; Burlington Foundation Award, 1992. Membership: Modern Language Association. Address: 273 North Main Avenue, Tucson, AZ 85701, USA.

EXTON Clive b. 11 Apr 1930, London, England. Scriptwriter; Playwright. m. (1) Patricia Fletcher Ferguson, 1951, d. Dec 1983, 2 daughters, (2) Margaret Josephine Reid, 1957, 1 son, 2 daughters. Education: Christ's Hospital. Publications: Over 15 television plays; Many television series; Numerous screenplays; Several stage plays. Honour: Writers Guild Award, 1994. Address: c/o Rochell Stevens & Co, 2 Terrets Place, London N1 1QZ, England.

EYNON Robert (Bob), b. 20 Mar 1941, Tynewydd, Rhondda, Wales. Retired University Lecturer; Self-employed. Education: BA Honours, Spanish, 1962, External BA Honours, French, 1969, London University. Appointments: Bedford High School, England; Lycée Foch, Rodez, France; Ecole Technique de la Salle, Lille; Peter Symons School, Winchester, England; Pontypridd Girls Grammar School, Wales; University College, Cardiff; Park Keeper, Rhondda Borough Council; Currently self-employed. Publications: Bitter Waters, 1988; Texas Honour, 1988; Johnny One Arm, 1989; Gunfight at Simeons Ridge, 1991; Gun Law Legacy, 1991; Sunset Reckoning, 1993; Anderton Justice, 1997; Pecos Vengeance, 1998; Various Welsh novels for learners including: Perygl Yn Sbaen, 1987; Yr Asiant Cudd, 1997. Honour: Short-listed for Tir Na N'Og Prize, 1998. Address: 5 Troedyrhiw Terrace, Treorchy, Rhondda CF42 6PG, Wales.

EYTHORSDOTTIR Sigridur, b. 21 Aug 1940, Selvogur, Iceland. Teacher; Writer; Poet; Dramatist. m. Jon Laxdalarnalds, 24 Aug 1963, 1 son, 1 daughter. Education: Diploma in Drama, 1968; Professional Skills in Special Education; Diploma in Teaching, University of Teaching. Publications: Gunnar Eignast Systur, 1979; Lena Sol, 1983. Other: Stage plays, radio dramas, short stories, and poems. Contributions to: Several publications. Honours: Malog Menning Award, 1982; Kramhusio Award, 1992; Ibbx Award, 1996. Membership: Writer's Association of Iceland. Asvallagata 26, 101 Reykjavik, Iceland.

EZEKIEL Nissim, b. 16 Dec 1924, Bombay, India. Retired Professor of English; Poet. m. Daisy Jacob, 1952, 1 son, 2 daughters. Education: M, University of Bombay, 1947. Appointments: Reader, 1972-81, Professor, 1981-85, English, University of Bombay; Writer-in-Residence, National University of Singapore, 1988-89. Publications: A Time to Change and Other Poems, 1952; Sixty Poems, 1953; The Third, 1958; The Unfinished Man: 1959, 1960; The Exact Name, 1960-64, 1965; A Martin Luther King Reader (editor), 1969; Pergamon Poets 9, 1970; Hymns in Darkness, 1976; Collected Poems, 1952-88, 1990. Honours: National Academy Award, 1983; Padma Shree, 1988. Address: 18 Kala Niketan, 6th Floor, 47C, Bhulabhai Desai Road, Bombay 400 026, India.

F

FABEND Firth Haring, (Firth Haring), b. 12 Aug 1937, Tappan, New York, USA. Writer; Historian. m. Carl Fabend, 12 Feb 1966, 2 daughters. Education: BA, Barnard College, 1959; PhD, New York University, 1988. Publications: As Firth Haring: The Best of Intentions, 1968; Three Women, 1972; A Perfect Stranger, 1973; The Woman Who Went Away, 1981; Greek Revival, 1985; As Firth Haring Fabend: A Dutch Family in the Middle Colonies, 1660-1800. Contributions to: de Halve Maen; New York History. Honours: Ms Award, New York State Historical Association, 1989; Hendricks Prize, 1989; Fellow, Holland Society of New York, 1993; Fellow, New Netherland Project, 1996. Address: Upper Montclair, NJ 07043, USA.

FABRI Peter, b. 21 Dec 1953, Budapest, Hungary. Writer; Poet; Librettist. m. (1) 1 son, (2) Kriszta Kováts, 7 June 1986, 1 daughter. Education: Eötvös Lóránd University, Budapest, 1973-78. Publications: Folytatásos regény (novel), 1981; Napforduló, 1987; Bámészkodásaim könyve (short stories), 1991; Kolumbusz, az örült spanyol (rock opera), 1992. Other: Librettos for musicals; Lyrics for songs. Contributions to: Periodicals. Honour: Emerton Prize, Best Lyricist of the Year, 1990. Memberships: ARTISJUS, Hungarian Copyright Agency, member presidential board, 1996-; Hungarian PEN, 1980-. Address: Rippl Ronai u 27, 1068 Budapest, Hungary.

FACOS James, b. 28 July 1924, Lawrence, USA. Professor Retired. m. Cleo J Chigos, 1 Dec 1956, 1 son, 2 daughters. Education: AB, Bates College, 1949; MA, Florida State University, 1958; DHL, Norwich University, 1989. Publications: The Silver Lady (novel), 1972; Fugitives' Fair (novella), 1985. Contributions to: Stories; Negative Capability; New Press Literary Quarterly. Address: 333 Elm Street, Montpelier, VT 05602-2213, USA.

FAES Urs, b. 13 Feb 1947, Aarau. Writer. Education: MA, University of Zurich. Appointments: Journalist, 1979-81; Dramatist, 1982-86; Writer, 1982-. Publications: Eine Kerbe im Mittag (poems), 1975; Heidentum und Aberglaube (essay), 1979; Regenspur (poems), 1979; Webfehler (novel), 1983; Zugluft (play), 1983; Der Traum vom Leben (short stories), 1984; Kreuz im Feld (play), 1984; Bis ans Ende der Erinnerung (novel), 1986; Wartzimmer (play), 1986; Partenza (radio play), 1986; Sommerwende (novel), 1989; Alphabet des Abschieds, 1991; Eine andere Geschichte (radio play), 1993; Augenblicke im Paradies (novel), 1994; Ombra (novel), 1997. Honours: Prize, City of Zurich, 1986; Prize for Literature, 1991. Memberships: Swiss Authors Group; PEN. Literary Agent: Suhrkamp Frankfurt. Address: Feigelstrasse 25, CH-4600 Olten, Switzerland.

FAGAN Brian Murray, b. 1 Aug 1936, Birmingham, England. Professor of Anthropology; Writer. m. Lesley Ann Newhart, 16 Mar 1985, 2 children. Education: BA, 1959, MA, 1962, PhD, 1963, Pembroke College, Cambridge. Appointments: Keeper of Prehistory, Livingstone Museum, Zambia, 1959-65; Former Director, Bantu Studies Project, British Institute in Eastern Africa; Visiting Associate Professor, University of Illinois, 1965-66; Associate Professor, 1967-69, Professor of Anthropology, 1969-, University of California at Santa Barbara. Publications: Victoria Falls Handbook, 1964; Southern Africa During the Iron Age (editor), 1966; Iron Age Cultures in Zambia (with S G H Daniels and D W Phillipson), 2 volumes, 1967, 1969; A Short History of Zambia, 1968; The Hunter-Gatherers of Gwisho (with F Van Noten), 1971; In the Beginning, 1972, 7th edition, 1991; People of the Earth, 1974, 7th edition, 1992; The Rape of the Nile, 1975; Elusive Treasure, 1977; Quest for the Past, Archaeology: A Brief Introduction, 1978, 4th edition, 1991; Return to Babylon, 1979; The Aztecs, Clash of Cultures, 1984; Adventures in Archaeology, Bareboating, Anchoring, 1985; The Great Journey, 1987; The Journey From Eden, 1990; Ancient North America,

1991; Kingdoms of Jade, Kingdoms of Gold, 1991; Time Detectives, 1995; Oxford Companion to Archaeology, 1996; Into the Unknown, 1997; From Black Land to Fifth Sun, 1998; Floods, Famines and Emperors, 1999. Address: Department of Anthropology, University of California at Santa Barbara, CA 93106, USA.

FAGLES Robert, b. 11 Sept 1933, Philadelphia, PA, USA. Professor; Translator; Poet. m. Marilyn Fagles, 17 June 1956, 2 children. Education: AB, Amherst College, 1955; MA, 1956, PhD, 1959, Yale University. Appointments: Instructor, Yale University, 1959-60; Instructor, 1960-62, Assistant Professor, 1962-65, Associate Professor, 1965-70, Director, Program in Comparative Literature, 1965-, Professor, 1970-, Princeton University. Publications: Translations: Complete Poems, by Bacchylides, 1961; The Oresteia, by Aeschylus, 1975; The Three Theban Plays, by Sophocles, 1984; The Iliad, by Homer, 1990; The Odyssey, by Homer, 1996. Poetry: I, Vincent: Poems from the Pictures of Van Gogh, 1978. Co-Editor: Homer: A Collection of Critical Essays, 1962; Pope's Iliad and Odyssey, 1967. Contributions to: Books and journals. Honours: Harold Morton Landon Translation Award, Academy of American Poets, 1991; American Academy of Arts and Letters Award, 1996; PEN/Ralph Manheim Medal for Life-time Achievement in Translation, 1997. Memberships: American Academy of Arts and Letters; American Academy of Arts and Sciences; American Philosophical Society. Address: c/o Program in Comparative Literature, Princeton University, Princeton, NJ 08540, USA.

FAINLIGHT Ruth (Esther), b. 2 May 1931, New York, New York, USA. Writer; Poet; Translator; Librettist. m. Alan Sillitoe, 19 Nov 1959, 1 son, 1 daughter. Education: Colleges of Arts and Crafts, Birmingham, Brighton. Appointment: Poet-in-Residence, Vanderbilt University, 1985, 11990. Publications: Poetry: Cages, 1966; To See the Matter Clearly, 1968; The Region's Violence, 1973; Another Full Moon, 1976; Sibyls and Others, 1980; Climates, 1983; Fifteen to Infinity, 1983; Selected Poems, 1987, 2nd edition, revised, 1995; The Knot, 1990; Sibyls, 1991; This Time of Year, 1994; Sugar-Paper Blue, 1997; Visitacao: Selected Poems in Portuguese translation, 1995; Encore La Pleine Lune, Selected Poems in French translation, 1997. Translations: All Citizens Are Soldiers, from Lope de Vega, 1969; Navigations, 1983; Marine Rose: Selected Poems of Sophia de Mello Breyner, 1988. Short Stories: Daylife and Nightlife, 1971; Dr Clock's Last Case, 1994. Libretti: The Dancer Hotoke, 1991; The European Story, 1993; Bedlam Britannica, 1995. Contributions to: Atlantic Monthly; Critical Quarterly; English; Hudson Review; Lettre Internationale; London Magazine; London Review of Books; New Yorker; Poetry Review; Threepenny Review; Times Literary Supplement. Honours: Cholmondeley Award for Poetry, 1994; Hawthornden Award for Poetry, 1994. Memberships: PEN; Writers in Prison Committee. Address: 14 Ladbroke Terrace, London W11 3PG, England.

FAIRBAIRNS Zoe Ann, b. 20 Dec 1948, England. Writer. Education: MA, Honours, University of St Andrews, Scotland, 1972. Appointments: C Day-Lewis Fellowship, Rutherford School, London, 1977-78; Writer-in-Residence, Deakin University, Australia, 1983; Sunderland Polytechnic, 1983-85. Publications: Live as Family, 1968; Down, 1969; Benefits, 1979; Stand We at Last, 1983; Here Today, 1984; Closing, 1987; Daddy's Girls, 1991; Other Names, 1998. Contributions to: New Scientist; Guardian; Women's Studies International Quarterly; Spare Rib; Arts Express. Honour: Fawcett Book Prize, 1985. Membership: Writer's Guild. Address: c/o A M Heath, 79 St Martins Lane, London, WC2N 4AA, England.

FAIRBURN Eleanor M, (Catherine Carfax, Emma Gayle, Elena Lyons), b. 23 Feb 1928, Ireland. Author. m. Brian Fairburn, 1 daughter. Appointments: Past Member, Literary Panel for Northern Arts; Tutor, Practical Writing, University of Leeds Adult Education Centre. Publications: The Green Popinjays, 1962; New edition, 1998; The White Seahorse, 1964, 3rd edition, 1996; The Golden

Hive, 1966; Crowned Ermine, 1968; The Rose in Spring, 1971; White Rose, Dark Summer, 1972; The Sleeping Salamander, 1973, 3rd edition, 1986; The Rose at Harvest End, 1975; Winter's Rose, 1976. As Catherine Carfax: A Silence with Voices, 1969; The Semper Inheritance, 1972; To Die a Little, 1972. As Emma Gayle: Cousin Caroline, 1980; Frenchman's Harvest, 1980. As Elena Lyons: The Haunting of Abbotsgarth, 1980; A Scent of Lilacs, 1982. Biographies (as Eleanor Fairburn): Edith Cavell, 1985; Mary Hornbeck Glyn, 1987; Grace Darling, 1988. Honour:Winner, Mail on Sunday novel-opening competition, 1989. Membership: Middlesbrough Writers Group, president, 1988. Address: 27 Minsterley Drive, Acklam, Middlesbrough, Cleveland TS5 8QU, England.

FAIRFAX John, b. 9 Nov 1930, London, England. Writer, Poet. 2 sons. Appointments: Co-Founder and Member of Council of Management, Arvon Foundation; Director, Phoenix Press, Arts Workshop, Newbury; Poetry Editor, Resurgence. Publications: The Fifth Horseman of the Apocalypse, 1969; Double Image, 1971; Adrift on the Star Brow of Taliesin, 1974; Bone Harvest Done, 1980; Wild Children, 1985; The Way to Write, 1981; Creative Writing, 1989; Spindrift Lp, 1981; 100 Poems, 1992; Zuihitsu, 1996; Poem Sent to Satellite E2F3, 1997; Poem on Sculpture, 1998; Poem in Hologram, 1998. Contributions to: Most major literary magazines. Literary Agent: A D Peters. Membership: The Arvon Foundation. co-founder, 1968. Address: The Thatched Cottage, Eling, Hermitage, Newbury, Berkshire RG16 9XR, England.

FAIRLEY John Alexander, b. 15 Apr 1939, Liverpool, England. Broadcasting Executive; Writer. 3 daughters. Education: MA, Queen's College, Oxford. Appointments: Journalist, Bristol Evening Post, 1963, London Evening Standard, 1964; Producer, BBC Radio, 1965-68; Producer, 1968-78, Director of Programmes, 1984-92; Managing Director, 1992-95, Yorkshire TV; Chairman, ITV Broadcast Board, 1995-. Publications: The Coup, 1975; The Monocled Mutineer (with W Allison), 1975; Arthur C Clarke's Mysterious World, 1980; Great Racehorses in Art, 1984; Chronicles of the Strange and Mysterious, 1987; Racing in Art, 1990; The Cabinet of Curiosities, 1991; A Century of Mysteries, 1993; The Art of the Horse, 1995. Address: 539 Willoughby House, Barbican, London EC2Y 8BN, England.

FALCK (Adrian) Colin, b. 14 July 1934, London, England. Associate Professor; Writer; Poet. 1 daughter. Education: BA, 1957, MA, 1986, University of Oxford; PhD, University of London, 1988. Appointments: Lecturer in Sociology, London School of Economics and Political Science, 1961-62; Associate Editor, The Review, 1962-72; Lecturer in Literature, Chelsea College, 1964-84; Poetry Editor, The New Review, 1974-78; Associate Professor, York College, Pennsylvania, 1989-. Publications: The Garden in the Evening, 1964; Promises, 1969; Backwards into the Smoke, 1973; Poems Since 1900: An Anthology (editor with Ian Hamilton), 1975; In This Dark Light, 1978; Robinson Jeffers: Selected Poems (editor), 1987; Myth, Truth and Literature, 1989, 2nd edition, 1994; Edna St Vincent Millay: Selected Poems (editor), 1991; Memorabilia, 1992; Post-Modern Love, 1997. Contributions to: Many professional journals and general periodicals. Address: 20 Thurlow Road, London NW3 5PP, England.

FALDBAKKEN Knut (Robert), b. 31 Aug 1941, Oslo, Norway. Novelist; Playwright. Appointment: Literary Reviewer, Dagbladet, Oslo, 1972-. Publications: The Grey Rainbow, 1967; His Mother's House, 1969; Fairytales, 1970; The Sleeping Prince, 1971; E 18, 1980; The Honeymoon, 1982; Glahn, 1985; Bad Boy, 1988; Forever Yours, 1990; To the End of the World, 1991. Plays: The Bull and the Virgin, 1976; Life with Marilyn, 1987. Honour: Riksmal Prize, 1978. Address: Gyldendal Norsk Forlag, Postboks 6860, St Olavs Plass, 0130 Oslo 1, Norway.

FALKENLÖWE Michael Sixten Joachim, Baron of Rützt, (Michael Rützt), b. 2 Aug 1942, Copenhagen, Denmark. Writer. m. Kiell Otto Falkenlöwe of Rützt, 15

Aug 1998. Education: Historian, University of Århus; Journalist; Writer. Appointment: President, Falkenlöwe Group of Publishing Firms, Scandinavia and Netherlands. Publications: 20 books, 1964-, including Famous Gay, 1998. Contributions to: Numerous to magazines and journals. Honour: Brother, Danish Cullenton Society. Literary Agent: K O Løken. Address: Postbox 82, 9560 Hadsund, Denmark.

FALKIRK Richard. See: **LAMBERT Derek (William).**

FALLACI Oriana, b. 29 June 1930, Florence, Italy. Writer; Journalist. Education: Liceo Classico Galileo Galilei; Faculty, Medicine, University of Florence, 1946-48. Appointments: Editor, Special Correspondent, Europeo Magazine, Milan, 1958-77; Special Correspondent, Corriere della Sera, Milan. Publications: The Seven Sins of Hollywood, 1958; The Useless Sex (Voyage Around the Woman), 1962; The Egotists, 1965; Penelope at War (novel), 1966; If the Sun Dies, 1967; Nothing and So Be It, 1972; Interview With History, 1976; Letter to a Child Never Born (novel), 1977; A Man (novel), 1979; Inshallah, 1990. Contributions to: Look; Life; Washington Post; New York Times; London Times; Corriere della Sera; Europeo; Der Spiegel; L'Express. Honours: St Vincent Awards for Journalism, 1971, 1973; Bancarella Award, 1972; Honorary LittD, Columbia College, Chicago, 1977; 2 Variegggio Prize Awards, 1979; Hemingway Prize for Literature, 1991; Super Bancarella Prize, 1991; Prix d'Antibes, 1993. Address: c/o RCS Rizzoli Corp, 31 West 57th Street, New York, NY 10019, USA

FALLON Ivan Gregory, b. 26 June 1944, Wexford, Ireland. Deputy Editor; Writer. m. (1), 1 son, 2 daughters, (2) Elizabeth Rees-Jones, 1997. Education: St Peter's College, Wexford, 1952-62; BBS, Trinity College, Dublin, 1966. Appointments: Irish Times, 1964-66; Thomson Provincial Newspapers, 1966-67; Daily Mirror, 1967-68; City Editor, Sunday Telegraph, 1968-70; Deputy City Editor, Sunday Express, 1970-71; City Editor, Sunday Telegraph, 1979-84; Deputy Editor, Sunday Times, 1984-94; Editorial Director, Chief Executive, Editorial Director, Independent Newspapers Holdings Ltd, 1995-, Chief Executive, 1997-; Director, N Brown Holdings, 1994-, Independent Newspapers Plc, 1995-, Independent Newspapers of South Africa,1996-. Publications: Delorean: The Rise and Fall of a Dream Maker (with James L Srodes), 1983; Takeovers (with James L Srodes), 1987; The Brothers - The Rise of Saatchi and Saatchi, 1988; Billionaire: The Life and Times of Sir James Goldsmith, 1991; Paperchase, 1993; The Player: The Life of Tony O'Reilly, 1994. Memberships: Fellow, Royal Society of Arts, 1989; Beefsteak; Political Economy; Rand Club, Johannesburg. Literary Agent: Vivienne Schuster, Curtis Brown. Address: c/o Independent Newspapers Holdings Ltd, PO Box 1014, 47 Sauer Street, Johannesburg 2000, South Africa.

FALLON Martin. See: **PATTERSON Harry.**

FALLON Peter, b. 26 Feb 1951, Osnabruck, Germany (Irish citizen). Editor; Poet. 2 children. Education: BA, 1975, H Dip Ed, 1976, MA, 1979, Trinity College, Dublin. Appointments: Founder, Editor, Gallery Press, Dublin, 1970-; Poet-in-Residence, Deerfield Academy, Massachusetts, 1976-77; International Writer-in-Residence at various Indiana Schools, 1979; Fiction Editor, O'Brien Press, Dublin, 1980-85; Teacher, Contemporary Irish Poetry, School of Irish Studies, Dublin, 1985-89; Writing Fellow, Poet-in-Residence, Trinity College, Dublin, 1994; Poet-in-Residence, Deerfield Academy, Massachusetts, USA, 1996-97. Publications: Among the Walls, 1971; Co-incidence of Flesh, 1972; The First Affair, 1974; Finding the Dead, 1978; The Speaking Stones, 1978; Winter Work, 1983; The News and Weather, 1987; The Penguin Book of Contemporary Irish Poetry (editor with Derek Mahon), 1990. Other: Editor of prose and poems by Irish writers; Eye to Eye, 1992; News of the World: Selected and New Poems, 1998. Contributions to: Poetry anthologies, periodicals and journals. Honours: Irish Arts Council Bursary, 1981; National Poetry Competition, England,

1982; Meath Merit Award, Arts and Culture, 1987; O'Shaughnessy Poetry Award, 1993. Address: Gallery Press, Loughcrew, Oldcastle, County Meath, Ireland.

FALLOWELL Duncan Richard, b. 26 Sept 1948, London, England. Writer. Education: Magdalen College, Oxford. Publications: Drug Tales, 1979; April Ashley's Odyssey, 1982; Satyrday, 1986; The Underbelly, 1987; To Noto, 1989; Twentieth Century Characters, 1994; One Hot Summer in St Petersburg, 1994; Gormenghast, 1998. Literary Agent: Gillon Aitken, London. Address: 44 Leamington Road Villas, London W11 1HT, England.

FANE Julian, b. 25 May 1927, London, England. Writer. m. Gillian Swire, 6 Jan 1976. Publications: Morning; A Letter; Memoir in the Middle of the Journey; Gabriel Young; Tug-of-War; Hounds of Spring; Happy Endings; Revolution Island; Gentleman's Gentleman; Memories of My Mother; Rules of Life; Cautionary Tales for Women; Hope Cottage; Best Friends; Small Change; Eleanor; The Duchess of Castile; His Christmas Box; Money Matters; The Social Comedy; Evening; The Collected Works of Julian Fane, Vols I and II; The Harlequin Edition of Shorter Writings. Contributions to: Vogue; London Magazine; Queen; Others. Honour: Fellow, Royal Society of Literature, 1974. Membership: Society of Authors. Address: Rotten Row House, Lewes, East Sussex BN7 1TN, England.

FANG Qi. See: **WANG Zhecheng.**

FANICA Gheorghe N, b. 1915, Romania. Professor; Writer. Publications: Mihai Eminescu - analize si sinteze, 1972, 3rd edtion, 1993; Eternele reintoarceri, 1989; Glose eminesciene, 1996. Contributions to: Journals, periodicals and magazines, chapters in books. Address: str Cristian Tell 9-11, Bucharest 70 171, Romania.

FANTHORPE Robert Lionel, b. 9 Feb 1935, Dereham, Norfolk, England. Priest; Author; Broadcaster; Consultant; Lecturer; Tutor. m. Patricia Alice Tooke, 7 Sept 1957, 2 daughters. Education: BA; FIMgt; FCP; Anglican Ordination Certificate. Appointments: Consultant and Festival Co-ordinator, UK Year of Literature and Writing, 1995; Presenter, Fortean TV, Channel 4, 1997. Publications: The Black Lion, 1979; The Holy Grail Revealed, 1982; Life of St Francis, 1988; God in All Things, 1988; Thoughts and Prayers for Troubled Times, 1989; Birds and Animals of the Bible, 1990; Thoughts and Prayers for Lonely Times, 1990; The First Christmas, 1990; Rennes-le-Château, 1992; The Oak Island Mystery, 1995; The Abbot's Kitchen, 1995; The World's Greatest unsolved Mysteries, 1997; The World's most Mysterious People, 1998. Contributions to: Purnells History of World War 1; Las Enigmas, Madrid; The X-Factor. Honours: Electrical Development Association Diploma, 1958; Holder of Four World Championships for Professional Authors: Prose, Drama, Poetry and Autobiography; Finalist, Bard of the Year, Poetry Digest. Memberships: MENSA; Society of Authors; Welsh Academy. Address: Rivendell, 48 Claude Road, Roath Cardiff, Wales.

FANTHORPE U(rsula) A(skham), b. 22 July 1929, Kent, England. Writer; Poet. Education: BA, MA, Oxford University. Appointments: Writer in Residence, St Martin's College, Lancaster, 1983-85; Northern Arts Literary Fellow, Universities of Durham and Newcastle, 1987-88. Publications: Side Effects, 1978; Standing To, 1982; Voices Off, 1984; Selected Poems, 1986; A Watching Brief, 1987; Neck Verse, 1992; Safe as Houses, 1995; Penguin Modern Poets 6, 1996. Contributions to: Times Literary Supplement; Encounter; Outposts; Firebird; Bananas; South West Review; Quarto; Tribune; Country Life; Use of English; Poetry Review; Poetry Book Society Supplement; Writing Women; Spectator; BBC. Honours: Travelling Scholarship, Society of Authors, 1983; Hawthornden Scholarship, 1987, 1997; Arts Council Writers Award, 1994; Chomondeley Award, Society of Authors, 1995; Honorary DLitt, the West of England, 1995. Memberships: PEN; Royal Society of Literature, fellow. Address: Culverhay House, Wotton-under-Edge, Gloucestershire GL12 7LS, England.

FANUS. See: **AL-KHATIB Burhan.**

FARAH Nuruddin, b. 24 Nov 1945, Baidoa, Somalia. Writer. m. (1), 1 son, 1 daughter, (2) Amina Mama, 18 Sept 1992. Education: Panjab University, 1966-70; University of London, 1974-75; Essex University, 1975-76. Appointments: Writer-in-Residence, University of Jos, Nigeria, 1981-83, University of Minnesota, 1989, Brown University, 1991; Professor, Makerere University, Uganda, 1989-91. Publications: From a Crooked Rib, 1970; A Naked Needle, 1976; Sweet and Sour Milk, 1979; Sardines, 1981; Close Sesame, 1983; Maps, 1986; Gifts, 1992; Secrets, 1998. Contributions to: Guardian; New African; Transition Magazine; New York Times; Observer; Times Literary Supplement; London Review of Books. Honours: English Speaking Literary Award, 1980; Deutscher Akademischer Austauschdienst Residency, 1990; Tucholsky Award, 1991; Premio Cavour Award, 1992; Zimbabwe Annual Award, 1993; Neustadt International Prize for Literature, 1998; Festival Étonnant Voyageur St Malo, France, 1998. Memberships: Union of Writers of the African People; PEN International; Somali-Speaking PEN Centre. Address: c/o Rogers, Coleridge & White, 20 Powis Mews, London W11 1JN, England.

FARELY Alison. See: **POLAND Dorothy Elisabeth Hayward.**

FARIAS Victor, b. 4 May 1940, Santiago, Chile. Philosopher; Writer. m. Teresa Zurita, 31 Dec 1960, 1 son, 2 daughters. Education: Catholich University, Santiago, 1957-60; Dr Phil, University of Freiburg, 1967; Dr Hab, University, Berlin, 1985. Appointment: Freie University, Berlin. Publications: Sein und Gegenstand, 1967; Los Manuscriptos de Melquiades, 1981; La Estetica de la Agresion: Diálogo de J L Borges and Ernst Jünger, 1986; Heidegger et le Nazisme, 1987; Logica, Lecciones de Verano de Martin en el legado de Helene Weiss, 1991; La Metaficicia del Arrabel: El tamaño de mi Esperanza, un Libro Desconocido de Jorge Luis Borges, 1992; Las Actas Secretas, 1994. Address: c/o Freie University, Rudesheimerstrasse 52-56, 14197 Berlin, Germany.

FARICY Robert, b. 29 Aug 1926, St Paul, Minnesota, USA. Professor Emeritus of Spiritual Theology; Writer. Education: BS, United States Naval Academy, 1949; PhL, 1954, MA, 1955, St Louis University; STL, Lyon-Fourvière University, 1963; STD, Catholic University of America, 1966. Appointments: Society of Jesus; Assistant Professor, Catholic University of America, 1965-71; Professor of Spiritual Theology, 1971-96, Professor Emeritus, 1996-, Pontifical Gregorian University, Rome. Publications: Seeking Jesus in Contemplation and Discernment, 1983, 2nd edition, 1987; Medjugorje Up Close: Mary Speaks to the World (with L Rooney), 1985; Contemplating Jesus (with R Wicks), 1986; The Contemplative Way of Prayer (with L Rooney), 1986; The Healing of the Religious Life (with S Blackborow), 1986; Lord, Teach Us to Pray (with L Rooney), 1986; Wind and Sea Obey Him: Approaches to a Theology of Nature, 1986; Medjugorje Journal (with L Rooney), 1987; Lord Jesus, Teach Me to Pray (with L Rooney), 1988; The Lord's Dealing, 1988; Mary Among Us, 1989; Medjugorje Retreat (with L Rooney), 1989; Pilgrim's Journal, 1990; Our Lady Comes to Scottsdale (with L Rooney), 1991; Return to God (with L Rooney), 1993; Knowing Jesus in the World, 1996; Your Wounds I Will Heal, 1998. Contributions to: Numerous theological and philosophical journals. Address: c/o Pontifical Gregorian University, Piazza della Pilotta 4, 00187 Rome, Italy.

FARKAS Oliver, b. 14 May 1955, Miskolc, Hungary. Chief Editor. m. Judit Barabas, 15 July 1978, 1 son, 1 daughter. Education: Theology Diploma, 1980. Appointments: Editor, 1985-; Chief Editor, 1989-. Publications: Üvegpres, poems, 1991; Az Aranyag Mesel, story-book, 1996. Contributions to: Kapu; Fel; Aranyag. Membership: Hungarian Writers' Association. Address: Metro u 40, H-1163 Budapest, Hungary

FARLEY Carol, b. 20 Dec 1936, Ludington, Michigan, USA. Children's Book Writer. m. 21 June 1954, 1 son, 3 daughters. Education: Western Michigan University, 1956; BA, Michigan State University, 1980; MA, Children's Literature, Central Michigan University, 1983. Publications: Mystery of the Fog Man, 1974; The Garden is Doing Fine, 1976; Mystery in the Ravine, 1976; Mystery of the Melted Diamonds, 1985; Case of the Vanishing Villain, 1986; Case of the Lost Look Alike, 1988; Korea, Land of the Morning Calm, 1991; Mr Pak Buys A Story, 1997. Contributions to: The Writer; Society of Children's Book Writer's Bulletin; Cricket; Disney Adventures; Challenge; Spider; Pockets; Appleseeds. Honours: Best Book of Year, Child Study Association, 1976; Best Juvenile Book by Mid-West Writer, Friends of the Writer, 1978; IRA/CBC Children's Choice Book, 1987. Memberships: Mystery Writers of America; Authors Guild: Children's Book Guild; Society of Children's Book Writers; Chicago Childrens Reading Round Table. Address: 5448 Desert Paradise Drive, Las Vegas, NV 89130, USA.

FARMER Beverley, b. 1941, Australia. Novelist. Publications: Alone, 1980; Short stories: Milk, 1983; Home Time, 1985; A Body of Water: A Year's Notebook, 1990; Place of Birth, 1990; The Seal Woman, 1992; The House in the Light, 1995; Collected Stories, 1996. Address: c/o University of Queensland Press, PO Box 42, St Lucia, Queensland 4067, Australia.

FARMER David Hugh, b. 30 Jan 1923, Ealing, London, England. Lecturer; Reader; Writer. m. Pauline Ann Widgery, 1966, 2 sons. Education: Linacre College, Oxford. Appointments: Lecturer, 1967-77, Reader, 1977-88, Reading University. Publications: Life of St Hugh of Lincoln, 1961, 2nd edition, 1985; The Monk of Fame, 1962; The Rule of St Benedict, 1968; The Oxford Dictionary of Saints, 1978, 4th edition, 1997; Dizionari dei Santi, 1989; Benedict's Disciples, 1980, 2nd edition, 1995; The Age of Bede, 1983, 4th edition, 1997; St Hugh of Lincoln, 1985, 2nd edition, 1987; Bede's Ecclesiastical History, 1990; Christ Crucified and Other Meditations, 1994. Contributions to: St Augustine's Abbey (English Heritage), 1997; Benedictines in Oxford, 1997; Dictionnaire D'Histoire Ecclesiastique; New Catholic Encyclopedia; Bibliotheca Sanctorum; Lexikon der Christlichen Ikonographie; Studia Monastica; Studia Anselmiana; Journal of Ecclesistical History; The Tablet. Honours: Fellow, Society of Authors, 1962; Fellow, Royal Historical Society, 1967. Address: 26 Swanston Field, Whitchurch, Reading, Berks RG8 7HP, England.

FARMER James, b. 12 Jan 1920, Marshall, Texas, USA. Civil Rights Leader; Professor; Writer. m. Lula Peterson, 21 May 1949, dec May 1977, 2 daughters. Education: BS, Wiley College, Marshall, Texas, 1938; BD, Howard University, 1941. Appointments: Founder-National Chairman, 1942-44, 1950, National Director, 1961-66, Congress of Racial Equality; Race Relations Secretary, Fellowship of Reconciliation, 1941-45; Organizer, Upholsterer's International Union of North America, 1945-47; Student Field Secretary, League of Industrial Democracy, 1950-54; International Representative, State, County, and Municipal Employees Union, 1954-59; Program Director, National Association for the Advancement of Colored People, 1959-61; Leader, Congress of Racial Equality Freedom Ride, 1961; Professor of Social Welfare, Lincoln University, Pennsylvania, 1966-67; Adjunct Professor, New York University, 1969; Assistant Secretary for Administration, US Department of Health, Education, and Welfare, Washington, DC, 1969-70; Executive Director, Coalition of American Public Employees, 1977-82; Visiting Professor, Antioch University, 1983-84; Distinguished Visiting Professor, 1985-94, Distinguished College Professor, 1994-, Mary Washington College, Fredericksburg, Virginia. Publications: Freedom-When? 1965; Lay Bare the Heart: An Autobiography, 1985. Contributions to: Many publications. Honours: Omega Psi Phi Awards, 1961, 1963; John Dewey Award, League of Industrial Democarcy, 1962; Distinguished Postgraduate Achievement Alumni Award, Howard Unversity, 1964; US Presidential Medal of Freedom, 1998. Memberships: American Civil Liberties Union; Americans for Democratic Action; Black World Foundation; Friends of the Earth; League of Industrial Democracy. Address: c/o Mary Washington College, Frdericksburg, VA 22401, USA.

FARMER Penelope (Jane), b. 14 June 1939, Westerham, Kent, England. Writer. m. (1) Michael John Mockridge, 16 Aug 1962, div 1977, 1 son, 1 daughter, (2) Simon Shorvon, 20 Jan 1984. Education: Degree in History, St Anne's College, Oxford, 1960; Diploma in Social Studies, Bedford College, London, 1962. Publications: Novels: Standing in the Shadow, 1984; Eve: Her Story, 1985; Away from Home, 1987; Glasshouses, 1988; Snakes and Ladders, 1993. Children's Books: The China People, 1960; The Summer Birds, 1962, revised edition, 1985; The Magic Stone, 1964; The Saturday Shillings, 1965; The Seagull, 1965; Emma in Winter, 1966; Charlotte Sometimes, 1969, revised edition, 1985; Dragonfly Summer, 1971; A Castle of Bone, 1972; William and Mary, 1974; Heracles, 1975; August the Fourth, 1975; Year King, 1977; The Coal Train, 1977; Beginnings: Creation Myths of the World (editor), 1979; The Runaway Train, 1980; Thicker Than Water, 1989; Stone Croc, 1991; Penelope, 1994; Twin Trouble, 1996. Other: Anthology: Two: The Book of Twins and Doubles, 1996; Short stories; Radio and television scripts. Contributions to: Periodicals. Honours: American Library Association Notable Book, 1962; Carnegie Medal Commendation, 1963. Memberships: PEN; Society of Authors. Address: 12 Dalling Road, London W6 0JB, England.

FARR Diana, (Diana Pullein-Thompson), b. 1 Oct 1925, Wimbledon, Surrey, England. Author. m. Dennis L A Farr, June 1959, 1 son, 1 daughter. Appointments: Director, Grove Riding Schools, 1939-52; Assistant, Rosica Colin (lit agencies, 1953-55); Assistant Editor, Faith Press, 1957-59. Publications: I Wanted a Pony, 1946; Three Ponies and Shannan, 1947; The Pennyfields, 1949; A Pony to School, 1950; A Pony for Sale, 1951; Janet Must Ride, 1953; Horses at Home, 1954; Riding with Lyntons, 1956; The Boy and The Donkey, 1958; The Secret Dog, 1959; The Hidden River, 1960; The Boy Who Came to Stay, 1960; The Hermit's Horse, 1974; Ponies in the Valley, 1976; Ponies on the Trail, 1978; Gilbert Cannan, 1978; Ponies in Peril, 1979; Only a Pony, 1980; The Ponyseekers, 1981; A Foal for Candy, 1981; A Pony Found, 1983; Cassidy in Danger, 1979; Five at 10, 1985; Choosing, 1988; Dear Pup, 1988; Fair Girls & Grey Horses (with sisters), 1996; The Long Ride Home, 1996. Contributions to: The Guardian; Pony Riding; Good Housekeeping. Membership: Society of Authors; PEN. Literary Agent: Jennifer Luithlen Agency. Address: Orchard Hill, Swan Barn Road, Haslemere, Surrey GU27 2HY, England.

FARRELL Pamela Barnard, b. 11 Oct 1943, Mt Holly, New Jersey, USA. Writer; Poet; Teacher. m. Joseph Donald Farrell, 1 Sept 1968. Education: BA, English, Radford College, 1965; MS, English, Radford University, 1975; MA, Writing, Northeastern University, 1988. Appointments: Editor, The Grapevine, Northeastern University Writing Progam Newsletter, 1986-90; Poetry Teacher/Consultant, Geraldine R Dodge Foundation, 1986-; Editorial Board, Computers and Composition, 1987-90, The Writing Center Journal, 1988-; Caldwell Chair of Composition, The McCallie School, 1991-. Publications: Waking Dreams (poems), 1989; The High School Writing Center: Establishing and Maintaining One, 1989; Waking Dreams II (poems), 1990; National Directory of Writing Centres, 1992. Contributions to: Anthologies, books, and journals. Honours: Woodrow Wilson National Fellowship Foundation Fellow, 1985; Golden Poet Award, 1986. Memberships: Modern Language Association; National Writing Center Association, president; Assembly of Computer in English, treasurer. Address: The McCallie School, 2850 McCallie Avenue, Chattanooga, TN 37404, USA.

FARRINGTON David Philip, b. 7 Mar 1944, Ormskirk, Lancashire, England. Psychologist; Criminologist. m. Sally Chamberlain, 30 July 1966, 3 daughters. Education: BA, 1966, MA, 1970, PhD, 1970, Cambridge University. Appointment: Institute of Criminology, Cambridge, England. Publications: Who Becomes Delinquent, 1973; The Delinquent Way of Life, 1977; Psychology, Law and Legal Processes, 1979; Behaviour Modification with Offenders, 1979; Abnormal Offenders, Delinquency and the Criminal Justice System, 1982; Prediction in Criminology, 1985; Reactions to Crime, 1985; Aggression and Dangerousness, 1985; Understanding and Controlling Crime, 1986; Human Development and Criminal Behaviour, 1991; Offenders and Victims, 1992; Integrating Individual and Ecological Aspects of Crime, 1993; Psychological Explanations of Crime, 1994; Building a Safer Society, 1995; Understanding and Preventing Youth Crime, 1996; Biosocial Bases of Violence, 1997; Serious and Violent Juvenile Offenders, 1998; Evaluating Criminology and Criminal Justice, 1998; Antisocial Behaviour and Mental Health Problems, 1998; Crime and Justice in the United States and in England and Wales 1981-96, 1998. Contributions to: Over 240 articles to journals. Honours: Sellin Glueck Award for International Contributions to Criminology, 1984. Memberships: Fellow, British Academy; British Society of Criminology; British Psychological Society; European Association of Psychology and Law; American Society of Criminology; American Psychological Association; Association for Child Psychology and Psychiatry. Address: Institute of Criminology, 7 West Road, Cambridge CB3 9DT, England.

FARROW James S. See: **TUBB E(dwin) C(harles).**

FAST Howard (Melvin), b. 11 Nov 1914, New York, New York, USA. Author; Dramatist. m. Betty Cohen, 6 June 1937, 1 son, 1 daughter. Appointments: Staff, Office of War Information, 1942-44; Chief Newswriter, Orginator, Voice of America, 1982-83; Columnist, New York Observer, 1989-92, Greenwich Time, 1992-. Publications: Fiction: Two Valleys, 1933; Conceived in Liberty, 1939; The Last Frontier, 1941; The Unvanquished, 1942; Citizen Tom Paine, 1943; Freedom Road, 1944; The American, 1946; Clarkton, 1947; My Glorious Brothers, 1948; Spartacus, 1952; Moses, Prince of Egypt, 1958; The Winston Affair, 1959; April Morning, 1961; Power, 1962; Agrippa's Daughter, 1964; Torquemada, 1966; The Crossing, 1971; The Hessian, 1972; The Immigrants, 1977; Second Generation, 1978; The Establishment, 1979; The Legacy, 1981; The Outsider, 1984; The Immigrant's Daughter, 1985; The Dinner Party, 1986; The Pledge, 1988; The Confession of Joe Cullen, 1989; The Trial of Abigail Goodman, 1995; An Independent Woman, 1997. Other: Many other books of fiction, short stories, dramas, and screenplays. Non-Fiction: Being Red (autobiography), 1990; War and Peace (essays), 1992. Contributions to: Various periodicals. Honours: Breadloaf Award, New York Public Library, 1945; Newspaper Guild Racial Equality Award, 1947; Jewish Book Council Award, 1947; Stalin Peace Prize, 1954; Secondary Education Book Award, 1962; Notable Book Citation, American Library Association, 1972. Membership: World Peace Council, 1950-55. Address: c/o Sterling Lord, 65 Bleeker Street, New York, NY 10012, USA.

FATCHEN Maxwell Edgar, b. 3 Aug 1920, Adelaide, South Australia. Author. m. Jean Wohlers, 15 May 1942, 2 sons, 1 daughter. Appointments; Journalist, Feature Writer, Adelaide News, 1946-55; Special Writer, 1955, 1981-84, Literary Editor, 1971-81, The Advertiser. Publications: The River Kings, 1966; Conquest of the River, 1970; The Spirit Wind, 1973; Chase Through the Night, 1977; Closer to the Stars, 1981; Wry Rhymes, 1987; A Country Christmas, 1990; Tea for Three, 1994. Contributions to: Denver Post; Sydney Sun; Regional South Australian Histories. Honours: Commendation, 1967, Runner Up, 1974, Australian Childrens Book of Year; Member of the Order of Australia, 1980; Honour Award, 1988; Advance Australia Award for Literature, 1991; AMP-Walkley Award for Journalism, 1996. Memberships: Australian Society of Authors; Australian Fellowship of Writers; South Australian Writers Centre; Australian Journalists Association. Literary Agent: John Johnson, London EC1R 0HT, England. Address: 15 Jane Street, Box 6, Smithfield, South Australia 5114, Australia.

FAULK Odie, b. 26 Aug 1933, Winnsboro, Texas, USA. Professor of History Emeritus; Writer. m. Laura Ella Whalen, 22 Aug 1959, 1 son, 1 daughter. Education: BS, 1958, MA, 1960, PhD, 1962, Texas Tech University. Appointments: Professor, Texas A & M University, 1962, University of Arizona, 1963; Professor of History, 1968-88, Professor Emeritus, 1988-, Okalhoma State University. Publications: Author, co-author, or editor of over 50 books. Contributions to: Over 100 scholarly history journals. Honour: Best Non-Fiction Book of the Year, Southwestern Border Library Association, 1973. Memberships: Oklahoma Historical Society; Texas State Historical Association, fellow; Westerners International. Address: 5008 Sturbridge, Temple, TX 76502, USA.

FAULKS Sebastian, b. 20 Apr 1953, Newbury, England. Writer. m. Veronica Toulten, 16 Dec 1989, 2 sons, 1 daughter. Education: Emmanuel College; Scholar, Wellington College; BA, Exhibitioner, Cambridge University. Appointments: Reporter, Daily & Sunday Telegraph; Literary Editor, The Independent; Deputy Editor, The Independent on Sunday. Publications: A Trick of the Light, 1984; The Girl at the Lion D'or, 1989; A Fool's Alphabet, 1992; Bird Song, 1993; The Fatal Englishman, 1996; Charlotte Gray, 1998. Contributions to: Columnist, The Guardian, 1992-98; Evening Standard, 1996-. Honour: Fellow, Royal Society Literature, 1994. Literary Agent: Gillon Aitken. Address: 29 Fernshaw Road, London SW10 0TG, England.

FAUST Naomi F(lowe), b. Salisbury, North Carolina, USA. Professor of English; Writer; Poet. m. Roy M Faust. Education: AB, Bennett College, Greensboro, North Carolina; MA, University of Michigan; PhD, New York University, 1963. Appointments: Instructor of English, Bennett College and Southern University; Professor of English, Morgan State Collee, Baltimore; Professor of English Education, Queens College of the City University of New York. Publications: Poetry: Speaking in Verse, 1974; All Beautiful Things, 1983; And I Travel by Rhythms and Words, 1990. Other: Discipline and the Classroom Teacher, 1977. Contributions to: Anthologies and journals. Honours: Cooper Hill Writers Conference Prize and Certificate of Merit, 1970; Cyclo Flame Magazine Prize, 1970; The Creative Record, 1989. Memberships: Alpha Epsilon; Alpha Kappa Mu; American Association of University Professors; National Council of Teachers of English; National Women's Book Association; New York Poetry Forum; World Poetry Society Intercontinental. Address: 112-01 175th Street, Jamaica, NY 11433, USA.

FAWKES Richard Brian, b. 31 July 1944, Camberley, Surrey, England. Writer; Dramatist; Film Director. m. Cherry Elizabeth Cole, 17 Apr 1971, 2 sons, 1 daughter. Education: BA, Honours, St David's University College, 1967. Publications: The Last Corner of Arabia (with Michael Darlow), 1976; Fighting for a Laugh, 1978; Dion Boucicault: A Biography, 1979; Notes from a Low Singer (with Michael Langdon), 1982; Welsh National Opera, 1986. Other: Plays for stage, radio, and television; Documentary film scripts. Contributions to: Journals and magazines including, BBC Music Magazine, Opera Now, Classical Music and Daily Telegraph. Honour: West Midlands Arts Association Bursary, 1978. Memberships: Society of Authors; Society for Theatre Research. Address: 5-8 Lower John Street, Golden Square, London W1R 4HA, England.

FEDER Kenneth, b. 1 Aug 1952, New York, New York, USA. Archaeologist. m. Melissa Jean Kalogeros, 30 Aug 1981, 2 sons. Education: BA, Anthropology, University of New York, 1973; MA, Anthropology, 1975, PhD, 1982, University of Conecticut. Appointment: Professor of Anthropology, Central Conecticut State University, 1977-. Publications: Human Antiquity (with Michael Park), 1989; Frauds, Myths and Mysteries: Science and Pseudoscience in Archaeology, 1990; The Past In Perspective: An Introduction to Human Prehistory, 1996; Field Methods in Archaeology (with Tom Hester and Harry Shafer), 1997; Lessons From the Past, 1999; A Village of Outcasts: Historical Archaeology and Documentary Research at the Lighthouse, 1999. Honour: Excellence in Teaching, Central Conecticut State University. Address: c/o Department of Anthropology, Central Conecticut State University, New Britain, CT 06050, USA.

FEDERMAN Raymond, b. 15 May 1928, Paris, France. Distinguished Professor; Novelist; Poet; Translator. m. Erica Hubscher, 14 Sept 1960, 1 daughter. Education: BA cum laude, Columbia University, 1957; MA, 1958, PhD, 1963, University of California at Los Angeles. Appointments: Assistant Professor, University of California at Los Angeles, 1960-64; Associate Professor of French and Comparative Literature, 1964-68, Professor of Comparative Literature, 1968-73, Professor of English and Comparative Literature, 1973-90, Distinguished Professor, 1990-, State University of New York at Buffalo. Publications: Novels: Double or Nothing, 1971; Amer Eldorado, 1974; Take It or Leave It, 1976; The Voice in the Closet, 1979; The Twofold Vibration, 1982; Smiles on Washington Square, 1985; To Whom It Many Concern, 1990; Aunt Rachel's Fur. Non-Fiction: Journey to Chaos, 1965; Samuel Beckett, 1970; Surfiction, 1976. Poetry: Temporary Landscapes, 1965; Among the Beasts, 1967; Me Too, 1975; Duel, 1989; Autobiographic Poems, 1991. Contributions to: Reviews, journals, and magazines. Honours: Guggenheim Fellowship, 1966-67; Frances Steloff Fiction Prize, 1971; Panache Experimental Prize, 1972; American Book Award, 1986. Memberships: American PEN Centre; Fiction Collective, board member, 1988-, director, 1989-94. Address: 46 Four Seasons West, Eggertsville, NY 14226, USA.

FEIFFER Jules (Ralph), b. 26 Jan 1929, New York, New York, USA. Cartoonist; Writer; Dramatist; Screenwriter. m. Judith Sheftel, 1961, 1 daughter. Education: Art Students League; Pratt Institute. Appointments: Contributing cartoonist, Village Voice, New York City, 1956-; Cartoons nationally syndicated in USA, 1959-. Publications: Sick, Sick, Sick, 1959; Passionella and Other Stories, 1960; The Explainers, 1961; Boy, Girl, Boy, Girl, 1962; Hold Me!, 1962; Harry, The Rat With Women (novel), 1963; Feiffer's Album, 1963; The Unexpurgated Memoirs of Bernard Mergendeiler, 1965; The Great Comic Book Heroes, 1967; Feiffer's Marriage Manual, 1967; Pictures at a Prosecution, 1971; Ackroyd (novel), 1978; Tantrum, 1980; Jules Feiffer's America: From Eisenhower to Reagan, 1982; Marriage is an Invasion of Privacy, 1984; Feiffer's Children, 1986. Other: Plays and screenplays. Honours: Academy Award for Animated Cartoon, 1961; Special George Polk Memorial Award, 1962. Address: c/o Universal Press Syndicate, 4900 Main Street, Kansas City, MO 64112, USA.

FEINBERG Joan Miriam, (Joan Schuchman), b. 13 Oct 1934, Far Rockaway, New York, USA. Freelance Writer. m. Arnold I Feinberg, 4 Oct 1986, 2 sons. Education: Brooklyn College, 1952-54; BA, University of Minnesota, 1970. Publications: Astrology: Science or Hoax?, 1978; Help for Your Hyperactive Child, 1978; Two Places to Sleep, 1979; Broken Dreams, 1992. Contributions to: Today's Family; Conquest Magazine; Horoscope Guide; World Book and Travel; New York Times Syndicate; International Travel News. Memberships: Conservatory of American Letters; Women in Communication; Florida Freelance Writers Association; International Women's Writer's Guild. Address: 4725 Excelsior Boulevard, Suite 300, Minneapolis, MN 55416, USA.

FEINBERG Joel, b. 19 Oct 1926, Detroit, Michigan, USA. Professor of Philosophy and Law; Writer. m. Betty Grey Sowers, 29 May 1955, 1 son, 1 daughter. Education: BA, 1949, MA, 1951, PhD, 1957, University of Michigan. Appointments: Instructor, 1955-57, Assistant Professor, 1957-62, Brown University; Assistant Professor, 1962-64, Associate Professor, 1964-66, Princeton University; Professor, University of California at Los Angeles, 1966-67; Professor, 1967-77, Chairman, Department of Philosophy, 1971-77, Rockefeller University; Professor, 1977-, Head, 1978-81, Acting Head, 1983-84, Department of Philosophy, Professor of Philosophy and Law, 1985-, Regents Professor of Philosophy and Law, 1988-94, Regents Professor Emeritus, 1994-, University of Arizona; Numerous visiting appointments. Publications: Reason and Responsibilty (editor), 1965, 9th edition, 1995; Moral Concepts (editor), 1970; Doing and Deserving: Essays in the Theory of Responsibilty, 1970, revised edition, 1974; Social Philosophy, 1973; The Problem of Abortion (editor), 1973, 2nd edition, 1983; Philosophy of Law (editor with Hyman Gross), 1975, 5th edition, 1994; Moral Philosophy: Classic Texts and Contemporary Problems (editor with Henry West), 1977; Philosophy and the Human Condition (editor with Tom L Beauchamp and William T Blackstone), 1980, 2nd edition, 1988; Rights, Justice, and the Bounds of Liberty, 1980; The Moral Limits of the Criminal Law, Vol I, Harm to Others, 1984, Vol II, Offense to Others, 1985, Vol III, Harm to Self, 1986, Vol IV, Harmless Wrongdoing, 1988; Freedom and Fulfilment, 1992. Contributions to: Reference works, books, and professional journals. Honours: Fellow, Center for Advanced Study in the Behavioral Sciences, Stanford, 1960-61; Liberal Arts Fellow, Harvard Law School, 1963-64; Guggenheim Fellowship, 1974-75; National Endowment for the Humanities Fellowship, 1977; Rockefeller Foundation Fellowship, 1981-82; Romanell-Phi Beta Kappa Professorship in Philosophy, 1989-90. Memberships: American Academy of Arts and Sciences, fellow; American Philosophical Association; American Society for Political and Legal Philosophy, president, 1989-92; Council for Philosophical Studies. Address: 5322 North Via Entrada, Tucson, AZ 85718, USA.

FEINSTEIN (Allan) David, b. 22 Dec 1946, Brooklyn, New York, USA. Psychologist; Writer. m. Donna Eden, 7 Oct 1984. Education: BA, Whittier College, 1968; MA, US International University, 1970; PhD, Union Institute, 1973. Publications: Personal Mythology, 1988; Rituals for Living and Dying, 1990; The Mythic Path, 1997. Contributions to: Common Boundary; Magical Blend; Psychotherapy; American Journal of Orthopsychiatry; American Journal of Hypnosis; The Futurist. Honour: William James Award, 1968. Memberships: American Psychological Association; Association for Humanistic Psychology. Literary Agent: Susan Schulman Agency, New York. Address: 777 East Main Street, Ashland, OR 97520, USA.

FEINSTEIN Elaine Barbara, b. 24 Oct 1930, Bootle, Lancashire, England. Poet. 3 sons. Education: Newnham College, Cambridge, 1949-52. Appointments: Editorial Staff, Cambridge University Press, 1960-62; Lecturer, Bishops Stortford College, 1963-66; Assistant Lecturer, University of Essex, 1967-70. Publications: In A Green Eye, 1966; The Circle, 1970; The Magic Apple, 1971; At the Edge, 1972; The Celebrants and Other Poems, 1973; The Glass Alembic, 1973; The Children of the Rose, 1974; The Ecstasy of Miriam Garner, 1976; Some Unease and Angels: Selected Poems, 1977; The Silent Areas, 1980; The Feast of Euridice, 1980; The Survivors, 1982; The Border, 1984; Badlands, 1987; Bessie Smith, 1985; A Captive Lion: The Life of Marina Tsvetayeva, 1987; Mother's Girl, 1988; All You Need, 1989; City Music, 1990; Loving Brecht, 1992; Lawrence's Women, 1993; Dreamers, 1994; Selected Poems, 1994; Daylight, 1997. Contributions to: Periodicals. Honours: Fellow, Royal Society of Literature, 1980; Chomondeley Award, 1990; Honorary DLitt, Leicester University, 1990. Membership: International PEN, Executive Committee. Address: c/o Rogers, Coleridge and White, 20 Powis Mews, London W11, England.

FEKETE John, b. 7 Aug 1946, Budapest, Hungary. Professor of English and Cultural Studies; Writer. Education: BA, Honours, English Literature, 1968, MA, English Literature, 1969, McGill University; PhD, Cambridge University, 1973. Appointments: Visiting Assistant Professor, English, McGill University, Montreal, Quebec, 1973-74; Associate Editor, Telos, 1974-84; Visiting Assistant Professor, Humanities, York University, Toronto, Ontario, 1975-76; Assistant Professor, 1976-78, Associate Professor, 1978-84, Professor, English, Cultural Studies, 1984-, Trent University, Peterborough, Ontario. Publications: The Critical Twilight: Explorations in the Ideology of Anglo-American Literary Theory from Eliot to McLuhan, 1978; The Structural Allegory: Reconstructive Encounters With the New French Thought, 1984; Life After Postmodernism: Essays on Culture and Value, 1987; Moral Panic: Biopolitics Rising, 1994. Contributions to: Canadian Journal of Political and Social Theory; Canadian Journal of Communications; Science-Fiction Studies. Address: 181 Wallis Drive, Peterborough, Ontario K9J 6C4, Canada.

FELDMAN Alan Grad, b. 16 Mar 1945, New York, New York, USA. Writer; Poet; Teacher. m. Nanette Hass, 22 Oct 1972, 1 son, 1 daughter. Education: AB, Columbia College, 1966; MA, Columbia University, 1969; PhD, State University of New York, Buffalo, 1973. Publications: The Household, 1966; The Happy Genius, 1978; Frank O'Hara, 1978; The Personals, 1982; Lucy Mastermind, 1985; Anniversary, 1992. Contributions to: New Yorker; Atlantic; Kenyon Review; Mississippi Review; Ploughshares; North American Review; Threepenny Review; Boston Review; Tendril; College English. Honours: Award for Best Short Story in a College Literary Magazine, Saturday Review-National Student Association, 1965; Elliston Book Award for Best Book of Poems by a Small Press in US, 1978. Address: 399 Belknap Road, Framingham, MA 01701, USA.

FELDMAN Gerald D(onald), b. 24 Apr 1937, New York, New York, USA. Professor of History; Writer. m. (1), 1 son, 1 daughter, (2) Norma von Ragenfeld, 30 Nov 1983. Education: BA, Columbia College, 1958; MA, 1959, PhD, 1964, Harvard University. Appointments: Assistant Professor, 1963-68, Associate Professor, 1968-70, Professor of History, 1970-, Director, Center for German and European Studies, 1994-, University of California at Berkeley; Historisches Kolleg, 1982-83; Karl W Deutsch Guest Professor, Wissenschaftszentrum, Berlin, 1997; Fellow, American Academy in Berlin, 1998-99. Publications: Army, Industry and Labor in Germany, 1914-1918, 1966; Iron and Steel in the German Inflation, 1916-1923, 1977; Industrie und Inflation: Studien und Dokumente zur Politik der deutschen Unternehmer 1916 bis 1923 (with Heidrun Homburg), 1977; Vom Weltkrieg zur Weltwirtschaftskrise: Studien zur deutschen Wirtschafts-und Sozialgeschichte 1914-1932, 1984; Industrie und Gewerkschaften 1918-1924: Die überforderte Zentralarbeitsgemeinschaft (with Irmgard Steinisch), 1985; Hugo Stinnes: Biographie eines Industriellen, The 1988; Great Disorder: Politics, Economics, and Society in the German Inflation, 1914-1924, 1993. Editor: German Imperialism, 1914-1918, 1972; A Documentary History of Modern Europe (with Thomas G Barnes), 4 volumes, 1972; Historische Prozesse der deutschen Inflation 1914-1924 (with Otto Büsch), 1978; The German Inflation Reconsidered: A Preliminary Balance (with Carl-Ludwig Holtfrerich, Gerhard A Ritter, and Peter-Christian Witt), 1982; The Experience of Inflation: International Comparative Studies (with Carl-Ludwig Holtfrerich, Gerhard A Ritter, and Peter-Christian Witt), 1984; Die Nachwirkungen der Inflation auf die deutsche Geschichte 1924-1933 (with Elizabeth Müller-Luckner), 1985; Die Anpassung and die Inflation/The Adaption to Inflation (with Carl-Ludwig Holtfrerich, Gerhard A Ritter, and Peter-Christian Witt), 1986; Konsequenzen der Inflation/Consequences of Inflation (with Carl-Ludwig Holtfrerich Gerhard A Ritter and Peter-Christian Witt), 1989; Arbeiter, Unternehmer und Staat im Bergbau: Industrielle Beziehungen im internationalen Vergleich (with Klaus Tenfelde), 1989, English translation as Workers, Owners and Politics in Coal Mining: An International Comparison of Industrial Relations, 1990; The Evolution of Modern Financial Institutions in the Twentieth Century: Proceedings: Eleventh International Economic History congress: Milan, September 1994 (with Ulf Olssen, Michael D Bordo, and Youssef Cassis), 1994; The Evolution of Financial Institutions and Markets in Twentieth-Century Europe (with Youssef Cassis and Ulf Olsson), 1995; How to Write the History of a Bank (with Martin M G Fase and Manfred Pohl), 1995. Contributions to: Many scholarly books and journals. Honours: American Council of Learned Societies Fellowships, 1966-67, 1970-71; Guggenheim Fellowship, 1973-74; National Endowment for the Humanities Fellowship, 1977-78; German Marshall Fund Fellow, 1981-82; Historische, Holleg Munich, 1982-83; Rockefeller Foundation Center Residency, Bellagio, Italy, 1987; Wissenschaftskolleg, Berlin, 1987-88; Woodrow Wilson Center Fellow, 1991-92; Book Prize, Conference Group for Central European History, American Historical Association, 1995; DAAD Book Prize, German Studies Association, 1995; Co-Winner, Financial Times/Booz-Allen & Hamilton Business Book Award, 1995; Apprintal Chancellor's Professor, University of California at Berkeley, 1997-2000. Address: c/o University of California at Berkeley, Department of History, Berkeley, CA 94720, USA.

FELDMAN Irving (Mordecai), b. 22 Sept 1928, Brooklyn, New York, USA. Professor of English; Poet. m. Carmen Alvarez del Olmo, 1955, 1 son. Education: BS, City College, New York City, 1950; MA, Columbia University, 1953. Appointments: Teacher, University of Puerto Rico, Rio Piedras, 1954-56, University of Lyons, France, 1957-58, Kenyon College, Gambier, Ohio, 1958-64; Professor of English, State University of New York at Buffalo, 1964-. Publications: Poetry: Work and Days and Other Poems, 1961; The Pripet Marshes and Other Poems, 1965; Magic Papers and Other Poems, 1970; Lost Originals, 1972; Leaping Clear, 1976; New and Selected Poems, 1979; Teach Me, Dear Sister, and Other Poems, 1983; All of us Here and Other Poems, 1986. Other: The Life and Letters, 1994. Honours: Kovner Award, Jewish Book Council of America, 1962; Ingram Merrill Foundation Grant, 1963; American Academy of Arts and Letters Grant, 1973; Guggenheim Fellowship, 1973; Creative Artists Public Service Grant, 1980; Academy of American Poets Fellowship, 1986; John D and Catharine T MacArthur Foundation Fellowship, 1992. Address: c/o Department of English, State University of New York at Buffalo, Buffalo, NY 14260, USA.

FELDMAN Paula R, b. 4 July 1948, Washington, District of Columbia, USA. Professor of English; Writer. Education: BA, Bucknell University, 1970; MA, 1971, PhD, 1974, Northwestern University. Appointments: Assistant Professor, English, 1974-79, Associate Professor, English, 1979-89, Professor, English, 1989-, Director, Graduate Studies in English, 1991-93, University of South Carolina, Columbia. Publications: The Microcomputer and Business Writing (with David Byrd and Phyllis Fleishel), 1986; The Journals of Mary Shelley (editor with Diana Scott-Kilvert), 2 volumes, 1987; The Wordworthy Computer: Classroom and Research Applications in Language and Literature (with Buford Norman), 1987; Romantic Women Writers: Voices and Countervoices (editor with Theresa Kelley), 1995; British Women Poets of the Romantic Era: An Anthology, 1997; A Century of Sonnets: The Romantic Era Revival 1750-1850 (Editor with Daniel Robinson), 1999; Records of Woman, (Editor), 1999. Contributions to: Studies in English Literature; Keats-Shelley Journal; Papers of the Bibliographical Society of America; Approaches to Teaching Shelley's Frankenstein, 1990; Blake: An Illustrated Quarterly, 1994. Address: Department of English, University of South Carolina, Columbia, SC 29208, USA.

FELICE. See: **DOMARADZKI Théodore Felix.**

FELICE Cynthia, b. 10 Oct 1942, Chicago, Illinois, USA. Writer. m. Robert E Felice Sr, 23 Dec 1961, 2 sons. Publications: Godsfire, 1978; The Sunbound, 1981; Water Witch (with Connie Willis), 1982; Eclipses, 1983; Downtime, 1985; Double Nocturne, 1986; Light Raid (with Connie Willis), 1988. Contributions to: Anthologies and periodicals. Membership: Science Fiction Writers Association. Address: 5025 Park Vista Boulevard, Colorado Springs, CO 80918, USA.

FELINTO Marilene Barbosa de Lima, b. 5 Dec 1957, Recife, Brazil. Writer; Journalist. Education: Bachelor in Portuguese and English Language, Brazilian, American and English Literatures, University of São Paulo, 1981. Appointments: Visiting Writer, University of California in Berkeley, 1992, Haus der Kulturen der Welt, 1994. Publications: As Mulheres de Tijucopapo (novel), 1982, English translation as The Women of Tijucopapo, 1992, Dutch translation as De Vrouwen van Tijucopapo, 1997; O Lago Encantado de Grongonzo (novel), 1987; Postcard (short stories), 1991. Other: Outros Herois e Esse Graciliano (essay), 1983. Honour: Jabuti Prize in Literature, Brazil, 1983. Address: Av Afonso Mariano Fagundes, 472/32 04054-000 São Paulo SP Brazil.

FELL Derek John, b. 28 Sept 1939, Morecambe, England. Garden Writer; Photographer. m. Carolyn Heath, 1 son, 2 daughters. Appointments: News Reporter, Newport Advertiser, England, 1956-58; Account Executive, OD Gallagher Ltd, England, 1958-64; Catalog Manager, W Atlee Burpee Co (USA), 1964-70; Executive Director, All-America Selections (USA), 1970-73; Executive Director, National Garden Bureau (USA), 1970-73; Director, Garden Writers Association of America (USA), 1970-73; Television Garden Show Host, QVC, Step-by-Step Gardening (USA), 1992-98. Publications: 550 Home Landscaping Ideas, 1991; Renoir's Garden, 1994; The Impressionist Garden, 1994; Secrets of Monet's Garden, 1997; Impressionist Bouquets, 1998; Impressionist Roses, 1999. Contributions to: Frequent contributor to Architectural Digest, Journal of the Royal Horticultural Society. Honours: Best Book Award, Garden Writers Association America, 1982, 1986, 1987, 1988, 1991; Best Photography Award, 1988, 1990, 1998. Memberships: Fellow, Garden Writers Association of America; Active Member, Society of American Travel Writing. Address: Box 1, Gardenville, PA 18926, USA.

FENG Jicai, b. 9 Feb 1942, Tianjin, China. Novelist; Dramatist. Education: Graduate, High School, Tanggu, Tianjin. Publications: The Boxers, 1977; Flowering Branch Road, 1979; A Letter, 1980; The Magic Lantern, 1981; The Carved Pipe, 1981; Man in the Fog, 1983; Into the Storm, 1983; The Miraculous Pigtail, 1984; The Tall Woman and her Short Husband, 1984; Chrysanthemums, 1985; Thanks to Life, 1985; Three-Inch Golden Lotus, 1986; The Eight Diagrams of Yin and Yang, 1988; Voices from the Whirlwind, 1991. Other: Radio and television plays. Address: 801 Yun-Feng-Lou A, Nanjing Road, Tianjin, China.

FENNARIO David, b. 26 Apr 1947, Verdun, Quebec, Canada. Playwright. m. Elizabeth Fennario, 1976, 1 child. Education: Dawson College, Montreal, 1969-71. Appointments: Playwright-in-Residence, Centaur Theatre, Montreal, 1973-; Co-Founder, Cultural Workers Association. Publications: Plays: On the Job, 1976; Nothing to Lose, 1977; Without a Parachute, 1978; Balconville, 1980; Changes, 1980; Moving, 1983; Joe Beef, 1991; Doctor Thomas Weill Cream, 1994; Placeville Marie, 1996. Honours: Canada Council Grant, 1973; Chalmers Award: 1976, 1979; Prix Pauline Julien, 1986. Membership: International Socialist. Address: 627 Beatty, Verdun, Quebec H4H 1X9, Canada.

FENNELLY Tony, (Antonia Fennelly), b. 25 Nov 1945, Orange, New Jersey, USA. Author. m. James Richard Catoire, 24 Dec 1972. Education: BA, Drama and Communications, University of New Orleans, 1976. Publications: The Glory Hole Murders, 1985; The Closet Hanging, 1987; Kiss Yourself Goodbye, 1989; Der Hippie in Der Wand, 1992; Hurenglanz, 1993; 1(900) D-E-A-D, 1997. Honour: Edgar Allan Poe Special Award, Mystery Writers of America, 1986. Memberships: Mystery Writers of America; Authors Guild; International Association of Crime Writers; Sisters in Crime. Address: 921 Clouet Street, New Orleans, LA 70117, USA.

FENNER Carol (Elizabeth), b. 30 Sept 1929, Almond, New York, USA. Children's Writer; Illustrator. m. Jiles B Williams, 3 July 1965. Publications: Tigers in the Cellar, 1963; Christmas Tree on the Mountain, 1966; Lagalag, the Wanderer, 1968; Gorilla, Gorilla, 1973; The Skates of Uncle Richard, 1978; Saving Amelia Earhart, 1982; A Summer of Horses, 1989; Randall's Wall, 1991; Yolonda's Genius, 1995; The King of Dragons, 1998. Contributions to: Magazines. Honours: Notable Book Citations, 1963, 1973, Newbery Honor Book, 1996, American Library Association; Runnerup, Coretta Scott

King Freedom Award, 1970; Christopher Medal, 1973; Library of Congress Book of the Year, 1973; Outstanding Science Trade Book for Children Citation, 1973; Michigan Council for the Arts Literature Grant, 1982; Readers' Choice Master Lists Citations, 1991-92; Maryland Children's Book Award, 1997. Memberships: Society of Children's Book Writers and Illustrators. Address: 190 Rebecca Road, Battle Creek, MI 49015, USA.

FENNER James R. See: **TUBB E(dwin) C(harles).**

FENNO Jack. See: **CALISHER Hortense.**

FENTON James (Martin), b. 25 Apr 1949, Lincoln, England. Professor of Poetry; Poet; Writer. Education: MA, Magdalen College, Oxford, 1970. Appointments: Assistant Literary Editor, 1971, Editorial Assistant, 1972, Political Columnist, 1976-78, New Statesman; Freelance Correspondent, Indo-China, 1973-75; German Correspondent, Guardian, 1978-79; Theatre Critic, Sunday Times, 1979-84; Chief Book Reviewer, Times, 1984-86; Far East Correspondent, 1986-88; Columnist, 1993-95, Independent; Professor of Poetry, University of Oxford, 1994-. Publications: Our Western Furniture, 1968; Terminal Moraine, 1972; A Vacant Possession, 1978; A German Requiem, 1980; Dead Soldiers, 1981; The Memory of War, 1982; Rigoletto, by Giuseppe Verdi (translator), 1982; You Were Marvellous, 1983; The Original Michael Frayn, 1983; Children in Exile, 1984; Poems 1968-83, 1985; Simon Boccanegra, by Giuseppe Verdi (translator), 1985; The Fall of Saigon, 1985; The Snap Revolution, 1986; Cambodian Witness: The Autobiography of Someth May (editor), 1986; Partingtime Hall (poems with John Fuller), 1987; All the Wrong Places: Adrift in the Politics of Asia, 1988; Manila Evelope, 1989; Underground in Japan, by Rey Ventura (editor), 1992; Out of Danger (poems), 1993. Honour: Royal Society of Literature, Fellow, 1983. Address: c/o Peters Fraser & Dunlop, 5th Floor, The Chambers, Chelsea Harbour, Lots Road, London SW10 0XF, England.

FERDINANDY György, (Georges Ferdinandy), b. 11 Oct 1935, Budapest, Hungary. Professor; Author. m. (1) Colette Peyrethon, 27 May 1958, (2) Maria Teresa Reyes-Cortes, 3 Jan 1981, 3 sons, 1 daughter. Education: Doctorate in Literature, University of Strasbourg, France, 1969. Appointments: Freelance Literary Critic, Radio Free Europe, 1977-86; Professor, University of Puerto Rico, Cayey, Puerto Rico. Publications: In French: L'ile sous l'eau, 1960; Famine au Paradis, 1962; Le seul jour de l'annèe, 1967; Itinéraires, 1973; Chica, Claudine, Cali, 1973; L'oeuvre hispanoaméricaine de Zs Remenyik, 1975; Fantomes magnétiques, 1979; Youri, 1983; Hors jeu, 1986; Mémoires d'un exil terminé, 1992; Entre chien et loup, 1996. In Hungarian: Latoszemueknek, 1962; Tizenharom Töredék, 1964; Futoszalagon, 1965; Nemezio Gonzalex, 1970; Valencianal a tenger, 1975; Mammuttemetõ, 1982; A Mosoly Albuma, 1982; Az elveszett gyermek, 1984; A Vadak Utjan, 1986; Szerecsenségem Története, 1988; Furcsa, idegen szerelem, 1990; Uzenöfüzet, 1991; Szomorü Szigetek, 1992; A Francia Völegény, 1993; Ta'vlattan, 1994; Az Amerikai telefon, 1996. Contributions to: Le Monde; NRF; Europe; Elet és Irodalom; Kortars; Uj Hold; Magyar Naplo. Honours: Del Duca Prix, 1961; St Exupéry Literary Award, 1964; Book of the Year, 1993; Prize Jòzsef Attila, Budapest, 1995; Prize Ma'rai Sàndor, Budapest, 1997. Memberships: Société des Gens de Lettres, France; Hungarian Writers Association; International PEN. Address: Joaquin Lopez Lopez 1056, Sta Rita, Rio Piedras, PR 00925, USA.

FERGUSON Joseph (Francis), b. 11 Feb 1952, Yonkers, New York, USA. Critic; Writer; Poet. m. Janice Robinson, 30 July 1986, 1 son. Education: BA, State University of New York at New Paltz, 1979; MS (not completed), Pace University. Appointment: Critic for various publications. Contributions to: Fiction and poetry in many anthologies and other publications; Articles and columns in numerous publications. Honours: Honorable Mention, American Poetry Association Contest, 1989; Finalist, American Book Series, San Diego Poets Press, 1990; Honorable Mention, World of Poetry Contest, 1990; Golden Poet, World of Poetry, 1990; Distinguished Poet of America, 1993; Semi-Finalist, North American Open Poetry Contest, 1993. Address: 26 Bank Street, Cold Spring, NY 10516, USA.

FERGUSON Robert Thomas, b. 2 June 1948, Stoke on Trent, England. Writer. m. 3 Apr 1987. Education: BA, University College, London, 1980. Publications: Enigma: The Life of Knut Hamsun, 1987; Henry Miller: A Life, 1991; Henrik Ibsen: A New Biography, 1996. Contributions to: Best Radio Drama, 1984; Best Radio Drama, 1986. Honours: BBC Methuen Giles Cooper Awards, 1984, 1986; J G Robertson Prize, 1985-87. Address: Trudvangvn 25, 0363 Oslo, Norway.

FERGUSON William (Rotch), b. 14 Feb 1943, Fall River, Massachusetts, USA. Associate Professor of Spanish; Writer; Poet. m. Nancy King, 26 Nov 1983. Education: BA, 1965, MA, 1970, PhD, 1975, Harvard University. Appointments: Instructor, 1971-75, Assistant Professor, 1975-77, Boston University; Visiting Professor, 1977-79, Assistant Professor, 1979-83, Associate Professor of Spanish, 1983-, Adjunct Professor of English, 1989-, Chairman, Foreign Languages, 1990-, Clark University, Worcester, Massachusetts; Visiting Lecturer in Spanish Renaissance Literature, University of Pennsylvania, 1986-87; Associate Editor, Hispanic Review, 1986-87. Publications: Dream Reader (poems), 1973; Light of Paradise (poems), 1973; La versificación imitativa en Fernanado de Herrera, 1981; Freedom and Other Fictions (stories), 1984; The Conference (novel), 1990. Contributions to: Scholarly journals, anthologies, periodicals and magazines. Memberships: American Association of University Professors; International Institute in Spain; Modern Language Association; Phi Beta Kappa; Sigma Delta Pi. Address: 1 Tahanto Road, Worcester, MA 01602, USA.

FERLINGHETTI Lawrence (Monsanto), b. 24 Mar 1920, Yonkers, New York, USA. Poet; Writer; Dramatist; Publisher; Editor; Painter. m. Selden Kirby-Smith, Apr 1951, div, 1 son, 1 daughter. Education: AB, University of North Carolina, 1941; MA, Columbia University, 1948; Doctorat (with honours), Sorbonne, University of Paris, 1951. Appointments: Co-Owner, City Lights Pocket Bookshop, later City Lights Books, San Francisco, 1953-; Founder-Editor, City Lights Books, publishing, San Francisco, 1955-; Many poetry readings; Participation in many national and international literary conferences; Retrospective exhibition of paintings, Palazzo delle Esposizione, Rome, Italy, 1996. Publications: Poetry: Pictures of the Gone World, 1955; A Coney Island of the Mind, 1958; Berlin, 1961; Starting from San Francisco, 1961, revised edition, 1967; Where is Vietnam?, 1965; An Eye on the World: Selected Poems, 1967; After the Cries of the Birds, 1967; The Secret Meaning of Things, 1969; Tyrannus Nix?, 1969; Back Roads to Far Places, 1971; Open Eye, Open Heart, 1973; Who Are We Now?, 1976; Landscapes of Living and Dying, 1979; A Trip to Italy and France, 1980; Endless Life: Selected Poems, 1984; Over All the Obscene Boundaries: European Poems and Transitions, 1985; Inside the Trojan Horse, 1987; When I Look at Pictures, 1990; These Are My Rivers: New and Selected Poems, 1955-1993, 1993. Novels: Her, 1960; Love in the Days of Rage, 1988. Other Writings: The Mexican Night: Travel Journal, 1970; Northwest Ecolog, 1978; Literary San Francisco: A Pictorial History from the Beginning to the Present (with Nancy J Peters), 1980; The Populist Manifestos, 1983; Seven Days in Nicaragua Libre, journal, 1985. Editor: Beatitude Anthology, 1960; City Lights Anthology, 1974; City Lights Review, No 1, 1987, and No 2, 1988. Plays: Unfair Arguments with Existence: Seven Plays for a New Theatre, 1963; Routines, (13 short plays), 1964. Contributions to: Numerous books and periodicals. Honours: National Book Award Nomination, 1970; Notable Book of 1979 Citation, Library Journal, 1980; Silver Medal for Poetry, Commonwealth Club of California, 1986,1998; Poetry Prize, City of Rome, 1993; 1st Poet Laureate of San Francisco, 1998. Address: c/o City Lights Books, 261 Columbus Avenue, San Francisco, CA 94133, USA.

FERLITA Ernest Charles, b. 1 Dec 1927, Tampa, Florida, USA. Jesuit Priest. Education: BS, Spring Hill College, 1950; STL, St Louis University, 1964; DFA, Yale University, 1969. Publications: The Theatre of Pilgrimage, 1971; Film Odyssey (co-author), 1976; The Way of the River, 1977; The Parables of Lina Wertmuller (co-author), 1977; Religion in Film (contributor), 1982; Gospel Journey, 1983; The Mask of Hiroshima in Best Short Plays, 1989; The Uttermost Mark, 1990; The Road to Bethlehem, 1997. Honours: 1st Prize, Christian Theatre Artists Guild, 1971; American Radio Scriptwriting Contest, 1985; Miller Award, 1986. Memberships: Dramatists Guild; International Hopkins Society. Address: Loyola University, New Orleans, LA 70118, USA.

FERNANDEZ DIAZ Natalia, b. 12 Mar 1967, Suria, Barcelona, Spain. Researcher; Writer; Poet. m. Maximo R Mewe, 28 Feb 1994. Education: BA, Germanic Languages and Linguistics, University of Barcelona, 1990; Master, Human Sexuality, UNED University, Madrid, 1994; PhD, Critical Discourse Analysis, University of Amsterdam and Universidad Autonoma, Madrid. Publications: Preludios de Juventud, 1983; La Profesión del Espejo o el Tierno Oasis, 1989; El Arbol que mira nacia la Luz, 1992; Quaderns de Poesia (with others), 1993; Poemas de la Luz (with others), 1994; La Blanca Estatue de tu Ausencia (Querido Pablo), 1996. Contributions to: Newspapers, magazines, and Radio Nederland. Honour: El Taller, Ex-Equo, Poetry, Barcelona, 1995. Memberships: International Writers and Artists Association, USA; PEN Club, Netherlands; School of Criminology, Barcelona. Address: Lepelaarlaan 17, 1241 EE Kortenhoef, Netherlands.

FERNANDEZ-ARMESTO Felipe Fermin Ricardo, b. 6 Dec 1950, London, England. Historian. m. Lesley Patricia Hook, 16 July 1977, 2 sons. Education: Magdalen College, Oxford, 1969-72; 1st Class Honours, Modern History, 1972, MA, 1976, DPhil, 1977, Oxford University. Appointment: Journalist, The Diplomatist, 1972-74; Senior Visiting Fellow, John Carter Brown Library, Brown University, USA, 1997-98. Publications: The Canary Islands after the Conquest, 1982; Before Columbus, 1987; The Spanish Armada, 1988; Barcelona, 1991; The Times Atlas of World Exploration (general editor), 1991; Columbus, 1991; Edward Gibbon's Atlas of the World, 1992; Millennium, 1995; The Times Guide to the People of Europe, 1995; The Times Illustrated History of Europe, 1995; Reformation (with Derek Wilson), 1996; Truth, 1997. Contributions to: English Historical Review; History; History Today; Anuarto de Estudios Atlanticos; Sunday Times Magazines. Honours: Arnold Modern History Prize, 1971; Leverhulme Research Fellowship, 1981; Commendation, Library Association, 1992. Caird Medal, for services to maritime history, National Maritime Museum, 1997; Honorary Doctor of Letters, La Trobe University, Australia, 1997. Memberships: Royal Historical Society, fellow; Hakluyt Society; Society of Authors; PEN; Athenaeum; Historical Association; Association of Hispanists; Society of Antiquaries. Literary Agent: Serafina Clarke. Address: High Gables, Oxford OX3 0DW, England.

FERRARI Ronald Leslie, b. 3 Feb 1930, Romford, Essex, England. Electrical Engineer. m. Judith Wainwright, 5 Sept 1959, 1 son, 3 daughters. Education: BSc, DIC, Imperial College, London; MA, ScD. Appointments: Lecturer, Cambridge University, 1965; Fellow, Trinity College, Cambridge, 1966. Publications: Problems in Physical Electronics, 1973; Introduction to Electromagnetic Fields, 1975; Finite Elements for Electrical Engineers, 1983, 3rd edition, 1996. Contributions to: Special Issue of IEE Proceedings. Membership: Fellow, Institution Electrical Engineers. Address: Trinity College, Cambridge CB2 1T, England.

FERRE Rosario, b. 28 July 1942, Ponce, Puerto Rico, USA. m. Benigno Trigo, 1960, div, 2 sons, 1 daughter. Education: MA, University of Puerto Rico; PhD, University of Maryland, 1986. Appointment: Founder-Director, Zona de carga y descarga, Puerto Rican literary journal. Publications (in English): The Youngest Doll, 1991; The House on the Lagoon, 1995; Sweet Diamond Dust and

Other Stories, 1996. Contributions to: Anthologies. Honour: National Book Award Nomination, 1996. Address: c/o Tomas Colchie, 5 rue de la Villette, Paris 75019, France.

FERRIS Paul (Frederick), b. 15 Feb 1929, Swansea, Wales. Writer; Dramatist. Publications: A Changed Man, 1958; The City, 1960; Then We Fall, 1960; The Church of England, 1962; A Family Affair, 1963; The Doctors, 1965; The Destroyer, 1965; The Nameless Abortion in Britain Today, 1966; The Dam, 1967; Men and Money: Financial Europe Today, 1968; The House of Northcliffe, 1971; The New Militants, 1972; The Detectives, 1976; Dylan Thomas, 1977; Talk to Me about England, 1979; Richard Burton, 1981; A Distant Country, 1983; Gentlemen of Fortune, 1984; Collected Letters of Dylan Thomas, 1985; Children of Dust, 1988; Sex and the British, 1993; Caitlin, 1993; The Divining Heart, 1995. Television Plays: The Revivalist, 1975; Dylan, 1978; Nye, 1982; The Extremist, 1983; The Fasting Girl, 1984; Dr Freud: A Life, 1997; Dylan Thomas: The Biography, 1999; The Infidelity, 1999. Address: c/o Curtis Brown Ltd, Haymarket House, 28/29 Haymarket, London SW14 4SP, England.

FERRON Madeleine, b. 24 July 1922, Louiseville, Quebec, Canada. Writer. m. Robert Cliche, 22 Sept 1945, 2 sons, 1 daughter. Publications: Short Stories: Coeur de Sucre, 1966; Le Chemin des Dames, 1977; Histoires Edifiantes, 1981; Un Singulier Amour, 1987; Le Grand Theatre, 1989. Novels: La Fin des Loups-Garous, 1966; Le Baron Ecarlate, 1971; Sur le Chemin Craig, 1982. Essays: Quand le Peuple fait la loi, 1972; Les Beaucerons, ces insoumis, 1974; Adrienne, une saga familiale, 1993. Honour: Ordre National du Quebec, Chevalier, 1992. Address: 1130 de la Tour, Quebec G1R 2W7, Canada.

FERRY Charles Allen, b. 8 Oct 1927, Chicago, Illinois, USA. Writer. m. Ruth Louise Merz, 26 Sept 1958, 1 stepson. Education: Attended University of Illinois. Publications: Novels, children's and juvenile: Up in Sister Bay, 1975; O Zebron Falls!, 1977; Raspberry One, 1983; One More Time!, 1985; Binge, 1992; A Fresh Start, 1996; Love, 1998. Contribution to: Political analysis, to The New Republic magazine, 24 Jan 1964. Honours: Best Book of 1983, Friends of American Writers; A Best Book, American Library Association, 1983, 1992; A Best Book, National Council of Teachers of English, 1983, 1992, 1996; Best Book of the Year, Daisy Hill Press, 1992; A Best Book, New York Public Library, 1992, 1996. Address: PO Box 1681, Rochester, MI 48308, USA.

FESTA Georges, b. 17 Apr 1956, Algeria. Professor; Writer. Education: DLitt, Universite Blaise Pascal, 1991. Publications: L'image de la femme dans l'oeuvre de Gabriele d'Annunzio, 1979; Les Études sur le Prince de Ligne du XVIIIe siecle a nos jours, 1979; Les Études sur le marquis de Sade: Contribution a une bibliographie analytique, 1981; Le Voyage d'Italie de Sade 1775-1776: Genese d'un immoralisme visionnaire, 1991. Contributions to: Professional journals. Address: 75 bd Gambetta, F-93130 Noisy-Le-Sec, France.

FEVERSHAM (Charles Antony) Peter, Right Honorable Lord, b. 3 Jan 1945, England. Journalist. m. Polly Mary Antonia Aldridge, 6 Oct 1979, 3 sons, 1 daughter. Education: Middle Temple. Appointments: Chairman, Standing Conference of Regional Arts Associations, 1969-76; Yorkshire Arts Association, 1969-80; Yorkshire Sculpture Park, 1981-; President, The Arvon Foundation, 1976-86; The National Association of Local Councils, 1986-. Publications: Novel: A Wolf in Tooth, 1967; Great Yachts, 1970. Contributions to: Daily Telegraph, Yorkshire Post, Country Life, Motor Boat Yachting. Address: Duncombe Park, Helmsley, York YO62 5EB, England.

FICKERT Kurt Jon, b. 19 Dec 1920, Pausa, Germany. Professor of Languages. m. Lynn Barbara Janda, 8 Aug 1946, 2 sons, 1 daughter. Education: BA, Hofstra University, 1941; MA, 1947, PhD, 1952, New York University. Appointments: Instructor, Hofstra University, 1947-52; Assistant Professor, Florida State University,

1953-54; Assistant Professor, Kansas State University, 1954-56; Assistant Professor, Associate Professor, Professor, Wittenberg University, 1956-86; Professor of Languages Emeritus, 1986-. Publications: To Heaven and Back, 1972; Hermann Hesse's Quest, 1978; Kafka's Doubles, 1979; Signs and Portents, 1980; Franz Kafka: Life, Work, Criticism, 1984; End of a Mission, 1993; Dialogue With the Reader, 1995. Contributions to: Journals and magazines. Membership: Ohio Poetry Day Association, president, 1970-75. Address: 33 South Kensington Place, Springfield, OH 45504, USA.

FIEDLER Leslie A(aron), b. 8 Mar 1917, Newark, New Jersey, USA. Professor of English; Writer; Poet. m. (1) Margaret Ann Shipley, 7 Oct 1939, div 1972, 3 sons, 3 daughters; (2) Sally Andersen, 1973, 2 stepsons. Education: BA, New York University, 1938; MA, 1939, PhD, 1941, University of Wisconsin; Postgraduate Studies, Harvard University, 1946-47. Appointments: Instructor to Associate Professor, 1941-53, Professor of English, 1953-64, Chairman, Department of English, State University of New York at Buffalo, 1965-; Various visiting professorships. Publications: Waiting for God (with S Weil), 1952; Leaves of Grass: 100 Years After (with others), 1955; An End to Innocence, 1955; The Art of the Essay, 1959, revised edition, 1969; The Image of the Jew in American Fiction, 1959; Love and Death in the American Novel, 1960, revised edition, 1966; Pull Down Vanity (short stories), 1962; The Second Stone (novel), 1963; The Continuing Debate (with J Vinocur), 1964; Waiting for the End, 1964; Back to China, 1965; The Girl in the Black Raincoat (with others), 1966; The Last Jew in America, 1966; The Return of the Vanishing American, 1967; O Brave New World (with A Zeiger), 1967; Nude Croquet and Other Stories, 1969; Being Busted, 1970; Collected Essays, 1971; The Stranger in Shakespeare, 1972; The Messengers Will Come No More, 1974; In Dreams Awake, 1975; Freaks, 1977; A Fiedler Reader, 1977; The Inadvertent Epic, 1979; Olaf Stapledon, 1982; What Was Literature?; Fiedler on the Roof, 1991; Stranger in a Strange Land (collected essays), 1994; Tyranny of the Normal, 1996. Contributions to: Many journals, reviews, and magazines. Honours: Furioso Prize for Poetry, 1951; Christian Gauss Lecturer, 1956; Guggenheim Fellowship, 1970-71; Lifetime Achievement Award, National Book Critics Circle, 1998. Memberships: American Academy of Arts and Letters; American Association of University Professors; Dante Society of America; Modern Language Association; PEN; Phi Beta Kappa. Address: c/o Department of English, Clemens Hall, State University of New York at Buffalo, Buffalo, NY 14260, USA.

FIELD D M. See: **GRANT Neil.**

FIELD Edward, (Bruce Elliot), b. 7 June 1924, Brooklyn, New York, USA. Writer; Poet. Education: New York University, 1946-48. Publications: Stand Up, Friend, With Me, 1963; Variety Photoplays, 1967; Eskimo Songs and Stories, 1973; A Full Heart, 1977; A Geography of Poets (editor), 1979, revised edition as A New Geography of Poets, 1992; New and Selected Poems, 1987; Counting Myself Lucky, 1992; Afrieze for a Temple of Love, 1998; Magic Words, 1998. Contributions to: Reviews, journals, and periodicals. Honours: Lamont Award, 1963; Shelley Memorial Award, 1978; Lambda Award, 1993. Memberships: American Academy of Rome, Fellow. Address: 463 West Street, A323, New York, NY 10014, USA.

FIELDS Abbey. See: **BERMEN Raeann.**

FIENNES Ranulph (Twisleton-Wykeham), b. 7 Mar 1944, Windsor, England. Explorer; Writer. m. Virginia Pepper, 9 Sept 1970. Education: Eton College. Appointments: British Army, 1965-70; Special Air Service, 1966; Sultan of Muscat's Armed Forces, 1968-70; Led British Expeditions to White Nile, 1969, Jostedalsbre Glacier, 1970, Headless Valley, British Columbia, 1970; Transglobal expedition, first circumpolar journey round the world, 1979-82, North Pole (5 expeditions), 1985-90; Ubar Expedition (discovered the lost city of Ubar, Oman), 1992, First unsupported crossing of Antarctic continent,

1993; Lectures; Television and film documentary appearances. Publications: A Talent for Trouble, 1970; Ice Fall on Norway, 1972; The Headless Valley, 1973; Where Soldiers Fear to Tread, 1975; Hell on Ice, 1979; To the Ends of the Earth: The Transglobe Expedition - The First Pole-to-Pole Circumnavigation of the Globe, 1983; Bothie the Polar Dog (with Virginia Fiennes), 1984; Living Dangerously (autobiography), 1988; The Feather Men, 1991; Atlantis of the Sands, 1992; Mind Over Matter: The Epic Crossing of the Antarctic Continent, 1994; The Sett, 1996; Ranulph Fiennes: Fit For Life, 1998. Honours: Dhofar Campaign Medal, 1969; Sultan of Muscat Bravery Medal, 1970; Krug Award for Excellence, 1980; Gold Medal and Honorary Life Membership, Explorer's Club of New York, 1983; Livingstone's Gold Medal, Royal Scottish Geographic Society, 1983; Founder's Medal, Royal Geographic Society, 1984; Guiness Hall of Fame, 1987; Polar Medal and Bar, 1987, 1994; ITN Award, 1990; Officer of the Order of the British Empire, 1993. Membership: Honorary Membership, Royal Institute of Navigation, 1997. Literary Agent: Ed Victor Ltd. Address: Greenlands, Exford, Somerset TA24 7NU, England.

FIERSTEIN Harvey (Forbes), b. 6 June 1954, Brooklyn, New York, USA. Dramatist; Actor. Appointments: Debut as actor in Andy Warhol's Pork, New York City, 1971; Various stage, film and television appearances. Publications: Theatre Pieces: In Search of the Cobra Jewels, 1973; Freaky Pussy, 1975; Flatbush Tosca, 1976; Cannibals Just Don't Know Better, 1978; La Cage Aux Folles, 1983; Spookhouse, 1984; Safe Sex, 1987; Forget Him, 1988; Legs Diamond (with Peter Allen and Charles Suppon), 1989. As Dramatist and Actor: The International Stud, 1978; Fugue in a Nursery, 1979; Widows and Children First!, 1979; (3 previous works as Torch Song Trilogy, 1981). As Screenwriter and Actor: Torch Song Trilogy, 1988; Tidy Endings, 1988. Honours: Villager Award, 1980; Obie Award, 1982; 2 Drama Desk Awards, 1982; Tony Awards (2), 1982, (2), 1984; Theatre World Award, 1983; Fund for Human Dignity Award, 1983; Dramatist Guild Award, 1984; Los Angeles Drama Critics Circle Award, 1984; 2 Ace Awards, 1988. Address: c/o AGF Inc, 30 West 21st Street, New York, NY 10010, USA.

FIFIELD Christopher (George), b. 4 Sept 1945, Croydon, England. Musician; Writer. m. Judith Weyman, 28 Oct 1972, div. Education: Associate, Royal College of Organists, 1967; MusB, 1968; Graduate, Royal Schools of Music, 1969; Associate, Royal Manchester College of Music, 1969. Publications: Max Bruch: His Life and Works, 1988; Wagner in Performance, 1992; True Artist and True Friend: A Biography of Hans Richter, 1993. Contributions to: Musical Times; Strad; Classical Music; Music and Letters; BBC Music Magazine. Address: 162 Venner Road, London SE26 5JQ, England.

FIGES Eva, b. 15 Apr 1932, Berlin, Germany. Writer. 1 son, 1 daughter. Education: BA, Honours, English Language and Literature, University of London, 1953. Publications: Winter Journey, 1967; Patriarchal Attitudes, 1970; B, 1972; Nelly's Version, 1977; Little Eden, 1978; Waking, 1981; Sex and Subterfuge, 1982; Light, 1983; The Seven Ages, 1986; Ghosts, 1988; The Tree of Knowledge, 1990; The Tenancy, 1993; The Knot, 1996. Honour: Guardian Fiction Prize, 1967. Membership: Society of Authors. Address: 24 Fitzjohns Avenue, London NW3 5NB, England.

FIGUEROA John (Joseph Maria), b. 4 Aug 1920, Kingston, Jamaica. Professor (retired); Writer; Poet. m. Dorothy Grace Murray Alexander, 3 Aug 1944, 4 sons, 3 daughters. Education: AB, College of the Holy Cross, 1942; Teachers Diploma, 1947, MA, 1950, University of London; Graduate Studies, Indiana University, 1964. Appointments: Lecturer, University of London, 1948-53; Senior Lecturer, 1953-57, Professor of Education, 1957-73, Dean of the Faculty of Education, 1966-69, University College of the West Indies, Kingston; Professor of English and Consultant to the President, University of Puerto Rico, 1971-73; Professor of Humanities, El Centro Caribeno de Estudios

Postgraduados, Puerto Rico, 1973-76; Professor of Education, University of Jos, Nigeria, 1976-80; Visiting Professor of Humanities, Bradford College, Yorkshire, England, 1980; Fellow, Centre of Caribbean Studies, Warwick University, 1988. Publications: Blue Mountain Peak (poems and prose), 1944; Love Leaps Here (poems), 1962; (editor), Caribbean Voices: An Anthology of West Indian Poetry, 2 volumes, 1966, 1970; Society, Schools and Progress in the West Indies, 1971; Ignoring Hurts: Poems, 1976; Dreams and Realities: Six One-Act Comedies (editor), 1978; Caribbean Writers (editor with others), 1979; An Anthology of African and Caribbean Writing in English (editor) 1982; Third World Studies: Caribbean Sampler (editor), 1983; The Chase: The Collected Poems of John Figuero, 1991. Contributions to: Journals and periodicals. Honours: British Council Fellowship, 1946-47; Carnegie Fellowship, 1960; Guggenheim Fellowship, 1964; Lilly Foundation Grant, 1973; Institute of Jamaica Medal, 1980. Address: 77 Station Road, Woburn Sands, Buckinghamshire MK17 8SH, England.

FINALE Frank (Louis), b. 10 Mar 1942, Brooklyn, New York, USA. Editor; Poet. m. Barbara Long, 20 Oct 1973, 3 sons. Education: BS, Education: Ohio State University, 1964; MA, Human Development, Fairleigh Dickinson University, 1976. Appointments: Founding Editor, 1983, Editor-in-Chief, 1985-95, Without Halos; Poetry Editor, the new renaissance, 1996-. Publication: Under a Gull's Wing: Poems and Photographs of the Jersey Shore (co-editor), 1996. Contributions to: Various anthologies, reviews, and journals. Honour: Literacy Award, International Reading Association and Ocean County Reading Council, 1993. Memberships: Poetry Society of America; National Education Association; New Jersey Education Association; Ocean County Poets Collective. Address: 19 Quail Run, Bayville, NJ 08721, USA.

FINCH Matthew. See: **FINK Merton.**

FINCH Merton. See: **FINK Merton.**

FINCH Peter, b. 6 Mar 1947, Cardiff, Wales. Poet; Writer; Chief Executive: Academic Literature Promotion Agency. 2 sons, 1 daughter. Education: Glamorgan Polytechnic. Appointment: Editor, Second Aeon, 1966-75. Publications: Wanted, 1967; Pieces of the Universe, 1968; How to Learn Welsh, 1977; Between 35 and 42 (short stories), 1982; Some Music and a Little War, 1984; How to Publish Your Poetry, 1985; Reds in the Bed, 1986; Selected Poems, 1987; How to Publish Yourself, 1988; Make, 1990; Poems for Ghosts, 1991; Five Hundred Cobbings, 1994; The Spe Ell, 1995; The Poetry Business, 1995; Antibodies, 1997; Useful, 1997 Contributions to: Magazines and journals. Memberships: Welsh Academy; Welsh Union of Writers. Address: 19 Southminster Road, Roath, Cardiff CF2 5AT, Wales.

FINCKE Gary (William), b. 7 July 1945, Pittsburgh, Pennsylvania, USA. Professor of English; Poet; Writer. m. Elizabeth Locker, 17 Aug 1968, 2 sons, 1 daughter. Education: BA, Thiel College, 1967; MA, Miami University, 1969; PhD, Kent State University, 1974. Appointments: Instructor in English, Pennsylvania State University of Monaca, 1969-75; Chair, Department of English, LeRoy Central School, New York, 1975-80; Administrator, 1980-93, Professor of English and Director of the Writers' Institute, 1993-, Susquehanna University; Editor, The Apprentice Writer, 1982-98; Syndicated Columnist, 1996-. Publications: Poetry: Breath, 1984; The Coat in the Heart, 1985; The Days of Uncertain Health, 1988; Handing the Self Back, 1990; Plant Voices, 1991; The Public Talk of Death, 1991; The Double Negatives of the Living, 1992; Inventing Angels, 1994; The Technology of Paradise, 1998. Fiction: For Keepsies, 1993; Emergency Calls, 1996; The Inadvertent Scofflaw, 1999; Blood Ties, 1999. Contributions to: Many anthologies, reviews, quarterlies, journals, and magazines. Honours: Various grants and fellowships; Beloit Fiction Journal Short-Story Prize, 1990; Bess Hokin Prize, Poetry Magazine, 1991; Book-of-the-Month, Vietnam Veterana' Magazine, 1993; Notable Fiction Book of the Year, Dictionary of Literary Biography, 1993; Pushcart Prize, 1995; Rose Lefcowitz Prize, Poet Lore, 1997. Address: 3 Melody Lane, Selinsgrove, PA 17870, USA.

FINDLEY Timothy (Irving Frederick), b. 30 Oct 1930, Toronto, Ontario, Canada. Author; Dramatist. Education: Mainly audiodidact. Appointments: Playwright-in-Residence, National Arts Centre, Ottawa, 1974-75; Writer-in-Residence, University of Toronto, 1978-79, Trent University, 1984, University of Winnipeg, 1985. Publications: The Last of the Crazy People, 1967; The Butterfly Plague, 1969; Can You See Me Yet? (play), 1977; The Wars, 1977; John A...Himself (play), 1979; Famous Last Words, 1981; Not Wanted on the Voyage, 1984; Dinner Along the Amazon (stories), 1984; The Telling of Lies, 1986; Stones (stories), 1988; Inside Memory: Pages From a Writer's Workbook, 1990; Headhunter, 1993; The Stillborn Lover (play), 1993; The Piano Man's Daughter, 1995; The Trials of Ezra Pound, 1995; You Went Away, 1996; Dust to Dust (stories), 1997; From Stone Orchard: A Collection of Memories, 1998. Other: Screenplays; Radio, film and television documentaries. Contributions to: Newspapers and periodicals. Honours: Major Armstrong Award, 1970; Association of Canadian Television and Radio Artists Award, 1975; Governor-General's Award for Fiction, 1977; City of Toronto Book Award, 1977; Canada Council Senior Arts Award, 1978; Canadian Authors Association Literary Awards, 1985, 1991, 1994; Officer of the Order of Canada, 1986; Order of Ontario, 1991; Chevalier de l'Ordre des Arts et des Lettres, 1996; From Stone Orchard: A Collection of memories, 1998. Memberships: Association of Canadian Television and Radio Artists; Authors Guild; Authors League of America; Writers' Union of Canada, chairman, 1977-78; English-Canadian Centre, International PEN, president, 1986-87. Address: Westwood Creative Artist, 94 Harbord Street, Toronto, Ontario M5S 1G6, Canada.

FINE Anne, b. 7 Dec 1947, Leicester, England. Writer. m. Kit Fine, 3 Aug 1968, 2 daughters. Education: BA Honours, University of Warwick. Publications: Novels: The Killjoy, 1986; Taking the Devil's Advice, 1990; In Cold Domain, 1994. For Older Children: The Summer House Loon, 1978; The Other Darker Ned, 1979; The Stone Menagerie, 1980; Round Behind the Ice House, 1981; The Granny Project, 1983; Madame Doubtfire, 1987; Goggle Eyes, 1989; The Book of the Banshee, 1991; Flour Babies, 1992; Step by Wicked Step, 1995; The Tulip Touch, 1996. Honours: Guardian Children's Award, 1989; Carnegie Medals, 1989, 1993; Smarties Prize, 1990; Guardian Children's Literature Award, 1990; Publishing News, Children's Author of Year, 1990, 1993; Whitbread Children's Novel Awards, 1993, 1996. Membership: Society of Authors. Address: 222 Old Brompton Road, London SW5 0BZ, England.

FINER Alexander, b. 12 Mar 1947, London, England. Journalist. m. Linda Anne Barnard, 13 Sept 1974, 1 daughter. Education: LLB, LSE, London University, 1965-68; LLM, Berkley University of California, 1968-69; Barister-at-Law, 1970. Appointments: Journalist, Sunday Times, Sunday Times Magazine, Evening Standard, Sunday Telegraph, Telegraph Magazine, Launch Editor, Esquire, England; Editor, Hot Air; Editorial Director, John Brown Publishing, 1994-97. Publications: Deepwater, 1983, 1984. Honours: BSME Editor of the Year, 1994, 1997. Membership: Garrick Club. Address: c/o The Garrick Club, Garrick Street, London WC1, England.

FINK Merton, (Matthew Finch, Merton Finch), b. 17 Nov 1921, Liverpool, England. Author. m. (1) 15 Mar 1953, 1 son, 1 daughter, (2) 24 Nov 1981. Education: School of Military Engineers, 1942; School of Military Intelligence, 1943; LDS, Liverpool University, 1952. Publications: Dentist in the Chair, 1953; Teething Troubles, 1954; The Third Set, 1955; Hang Your Hat on a Pension, 1956; The Empire Builder, 1957; Solo Fiddle, 1959; Matchbreakers, 1961; Five Are the Symbols, 1962; Chew this Over, 1965; Eye with Mascara, 1966; Eye Spy, 1967; Simon Bar Cochba, 1971; A Fox Called Flavius, 1973; Open Wide, 1976. Contributions to: Dental Practice, 1956-; Bath Chronicle, 1995. Honour: Richard Edwards Scholar, 1950. Memberships: Civil Service Writers; Deputy Chairman, Bath Literary Society; British Dental Association; Chairman, Service Committee, Bath British Legion. Address: 27 Harbutts, Bathampton, Bath BA2 6TA, England.

FINK-JENSEN Jens, b. 19 Dec 1956, Copenhagen, Denmark. Author; Poet; Photographer; Composer; Architect MAA. 1 daughter. Education: Architect MAA, Royal Academy of Fine Arts, Copenhagen, 1986; Multimedia Designer, 1997. Publications: The World in An Eye, poetry, 1981; Travels in Sorrow, poetry, 1982; Dancing Under the Gallows, poetry, 1983; The Beasts, short stories, 1986; Near the Distance, poetry, 1988; Jonas and the Conch Shell, childrens book, 1994; The Sea of Change, poetry, 1995; Jonas and the Sky Tent, childrens book, 1998;The Jonas books illustrated by Mads Stage. Contributions to: Poems, short stories and articles in Danish and international magazines and journals. Honours: Danish Arts Foundation, 1982; The Ministry of Culture's Commission for the Illustrated Danish Book, 1992; The Danish Literature Council, 1997 and 1998. Memberships: Danish PEN; The Danish Writer's Association. Address: Holger Danskes Vej 56 2tv, DK-2000 Frederiksberg, Denmark.

FINKEL Donald, b. 21 Oct 1929, New York, New York, USA. Poet; University Teacher (retired). m. Constance Urdang, 1956, 1 son, 2 daughters. Education: BA, 1952, MA, 1953, Columbia University. Appointments: Teacher, University of Iowa, 1957-58, Bard College, 1958-60; Faculty, 1960-92, Poet-in-Residence, 1965-92, Poet-in-Residence Emeritus, 1992-, Washington University, St Louis; Visiting Lecturer, Bennington College, 1966-67, Princeton University, 1985. Publications: The Clothing's New Emperor and Other Poems, 1959; Simeon, 1964; A Joyful Noise, 1966; Answer Back, 1968; The Garbage Wars, 1970; Adequate Earth, 1972; A Mote in Heaven's Eye, 1975; Going Under, and Endurance: An Arctic Idyll: Two Poems, 1978; What Manner of Beast, 1981; The Detachable Man, 1984; Selected Shorter Poems, 1987; The Wake of the Electron, 1987; Beyond Despair, 1994; A Question of Seeing, 1998. Honours: Helen Bullis Prize, 1964; Guggenheim Fellowship, 1967; National Endowment for the Arts Grants, 1969, 1973; Ingram Merrill Foundation Grant, 1972; Theodore Roethke Memorial Prize, 1974; Morton Dauwen Zabel Award, American Academy of Arts and Letters, 1980; Dictionary of Literary Biography Yearbook Award, 1994. Membership: Phi Beta Kappa. Address: 2051 Park Avenue, Apt D, St Louis, MO 63104, USA.

FINLAY William. See: **MACKAY James Alexander.**

FINNIGAN Joan, b. 23 Nov 1925, Ottawa, Ontario, Canada. Writer. m. Charles Grant Mackenzie, 23 May 1949, 2 sons, 1 daughter. Education: BA, Queens University, 1967. Publications: Through the Glass, Darkly, 1963; A Dream of Lilies, 1965; Entrance to the Greenhouse, 1968; It Was Warm and Sunny When We Set Out, 1970; In The Brown Cottage on Loughborough Lake, 1970; Living Together, 1976; A Reminder of Familiar Faces, 1978; This Series Has Been Discontinued, 1980; The Watershed Collection, 1988; Wintering Over, 1992. Other Genres: Old Scores: New Goals, History of Ottawa Senators 1891-1992, 1992; Lisgar Collegiate Institute 1843-1993, 1993; Witches, Ghosts and Loups-Garous, 1994; Dancing at the Crossroads, 1995; Down the Unmarked Roads, 1997; Second Wind, Second Sight, 1998; Tallying the Tales of the Old-Timers, 1998. Screenplay: The Best Damn Fiddler from Calabogie to Kaladar, 1967. CBC Radio Scripts: Songs for the Bible Belt; May Day Rounds; Children of the Shadows; There's No Good Time Left - None at All. Membership: League of Canadian Poets; Writers Union of Canada. Address: Hartington, Ontario K0H 1W0, Canada.

FINNIS John (Mitchell), b. 28 July 1940, Adelaide, South Australia, Australia. Professor of Law and Legal Philosophy; Writer. m. Marie Carmel McNally, 1964, 3 sons, 4 daughters. Education: St Peter's College, Adelaide; LLB, St Mark's College, University of Adelaide,

1961; Rhodes Scholar, 1962, DPhil, 1965, University College, Oxford. Appointments: Associate in Law, University of California, Berkeley, 1965-66; Fellow and Praelector in Jurisprudence, 1966-, Stowell Civil Law Fellow, 1973-, University College, Oxford; Called to the Bar, Gray's Inn, 1970; Rhodes Reader in the Laws of the British Commonwealth and the United States, 1972-89, Professor of Law and Legal Philosophy, 1989-, Oxford University; Professor and Head, Department of Law, University of Malawi, 1976-78; Consultor, Pontifical Commission, Iustitia et Pax, 1977-89; Huber Distinguished Visiting Professor, Boston College, 1993-94; Biolchini Professor of Law, University of Notre Dame, Indiana, 1995-. Publications: Commonwealth and Dependencies (Halsbury's Laws of England), Vol 6, 4th edition, 1974, revised edition, 1991; Natural Law and Natural Rights, 1980; Fundamentals of Ethics, 1983; Nuclear Deterrence, Morality and Realism (with Joseph Boyle and Germain Grisez), 1987; Moral Absolutes, 1991; Aquinas: Moral, Political and Legal Theory, 1998. Memberships: Catholic Bishops' Joint Committee on Bio-Ethical Issues, 1981-88; International Theological Commission, Vatican, 1986-92; Pontifical Council de Iustitia et Pace, 1990-96; Fellow of the British Academy, 1990. Address: University College, Oxford, OX1 4BH, England.

FINSCHER Ludwig, b. 14 Mar 1930, Kassel, Germany. Professor of Musicology (retired); Editor; Lexicographer. Education: PhD, University of Göttingen, 1954; Habilitation, University of Saarbrücken, 1967. Appointments: Assistant Lecturer, University of Kiel, 1960-65, University of Saarbrücken, 1965-68; Editor, 1961-68, Co-Editor, 1968-74, Die Musikforschung; Professor of Musicology, University of Frankfurt am Main, 1968-81, University of Heidelberg, 1981-95. Publications: Loyset Compère (c.1450-1518): Life and Works, 1964; Geschichte der Evangelischen Kirchenmusik (editor with others), 2nd edition, 1965, revised English translation as Protestant Church Music: A History, 1974; Studien zur Geschichte des Streichquartetts: I, Die Entstehung des klassischen Streichquartetts: Von den Vorformen zur Grundlegung durch Joseph Haydn, 1974; Renaissance-Studien: Helmuth Osthoff zum 80. Geburtstag (editor), 1979; Quellenstudien zu Musik der Renaissance (editor), 2 volumes, 1981, 1983; Ludwig van Beethoven (editor), 1983; Claudio Monteverdi: Festschrift Reinhold Hammerstein zum 70. Geburtstag (editor), 1986; Die Musik des 15. und 16. Jahrhunderts: Neues Handbuch der Musikwissenschaft (editor), Vol 3/1-2, 1989-90; Die Mannheimer Hofkapelle im Zeitalter Carl Theodors (editor), 1992; Die Musik in Geschichte und Gegenwart (editor), 2nd edition, 20 volumes, 1994-. Other: Editor of the complete works of Gaffurius, 2 volumes, 1955, 1960, Compère, 4 volumes, 1958-72, and Hindemith (co-editor), 1976 et seq. Contributions to: Complete works of Mozart and Gluck, and scholarly books and journals. Honours: Akademie der Wissenschaften Prize, Göttingen, 1968; Order Pour le mérite, 1994; Great Order of Merit, Germany, 1997. Memberships: Akademie der Wissenschaften, Heidelberg; Akademie der Wissenschaften und der Literatur, Mainz; Academia Europaea; International Musicological Society, honorary member; Royal Musical Association, London, honorary foreign member. Address: Am Walde 1, D-38302 Wolfenbuttel, Germany.

FINSTAD Suzanne, b. 14 Sept 1955, Minneapolis, Minnesota, USA. Author; Attorney (non-practising). Education: University of Texas, Austin, 1973-74; BA, French, University of Houston, 1976; University of Grenoble, France, 1979; JD, Bates College of Law, 1980; London School of Economics, 1980. Publications: Heir Not Apparent, 1984; Ulterior Motives, 1987; Sleeping with the Devil, 1991. Contributions to: Magazines. Honours: American Jurisprudence Award in Criminal Law, Bancroft-Whitney Publishing Co, 1979; Order of the Barons, 1980; Frank Wardlaw Award, 1985. Address: c/o Joel Gotler, 152 North La Peer Drive, Beverly Hills, CA 90048, USA.

FIRER Susan, b. 14 Oct 1948, Milwaukee, Wisconsin, USA. Adjunct Assistant Professor of English; Poet. 1 son,

2 daughters. Education: BA, 1973, MA, 1982, University of Wisconsin at Milwaukee. Appointments: Teaching Assistant, 1981-82, Lecturer, 1982, Adjunct Assistant Professor of English, 1988-, University of Wisconsin at Milwaukee. Publications: My Life with the Tsar and Other Poems, 1979; The Underground Communion Rail, 1992; The Lives of the Saints and Everything, 1993. Contributions to: Numerous anthologies, reviews, journals, and magazines. Honours: Academy of American Poets Prize, University of Wisconsin at Milwaukee, 1977; Best American Poetry, 1992; Cleveland State University Poetry Center Prize, 1992; Wisconsin Council of Writers Posner Poetry Award, 1993; 1st Place, Writer's Place Literary Awards, 1995; Milwaukee County Artist Fellowship, 1996; Work included in Midwest Express Center, 1998. Address: 1514 East Kensington, Milwaukee, WI 53211, USA.

FIRST Tina Lincer, b. 6 Aug 1955, Brooklyn, New York, USA. Writer; Editor. 1 son, 1 daughter. Education: BA in English and Art, magna cum laude, University of Albany, 1976. Appointments: Feature Writer, The Troy Record, New York, 1976-81; Drama Critic, Albany Times Union, New York, 1981-87; Senior Writer, Sawchuk, Brown Associates, 1992-. Publications: Guidebooks: Dutchess County: The New Business Frontier, 1994; Your Business, 1995. Essay: Confessions of a Reluctant Mockey Mom, 1999. Contributions to: Writers Digest; Los Angeles Times Syndicate; Jewish Monthly; Womens Times; Albany Times Union; Family Weekly. Honours: International Labor Communication Awards, 1981, 1985, 1988, 1995, 1998; Writers Digest Awards, 1996, 1997, 1998. Membership: Hudson Valley Writers Guild. Address: 41 State Street, Albany, NY 12207, USA.

FIRTH Anne Catherine, (Anne Valery), b. 24 Feb 1926, London, England. Scriptwriter; Autobiographer; Novelist; Theatre Playwright. Education: Matriculation (Honours), Badminton Public School. Publications: The Edge of a Smile, 1974; Baron Von Kodak, Shirley Temple and Me, 1973; The Passing Out Parade (theatre), 1979; Tenko Reunion, 1984; Talking About the War... (non-fiction), 1991. Other: Over 50 television plays. Contributions to: Radio Times. Honours: Book of the Month, Telegraph; BAFTA Award, Tenko (TV Series), 1984. Memberships: PEN International; Fawcett Society. Literary Agent: Linda Seifut (plays), Jacintha Alexander (books). Address: 5 Abbot's Place, London NW6 4NP, England.

FISCHER Lynn Helen, b. 2 June 1943, Red Wing, Minnesota, USA. Writer; Poet; Editor; Inventor. Education: College Studies; Doctor of Genius Degree, 1986. Appointments: Editor, Genius Newsletter, 1990-, Welcome Neighbor Newsletter, 1995-. Publications: The 1, 2, 4 Theory: A Synthesis, 1971; Sexual Equations of Electricity, Magnetism and Gravitation, 1971; Human Sexual Evolution, 1971; Middle Concept Theory, 1972; A Revised Meaning of Paradox, 1972; Unitary Theory, 1973; An Introduction to Circular or Fischerian Geometry, 1976; Two Four Eight Theory, 1976; Fischer's Brief Dictionary of Sound Meanings, 1977; Introducing the Magnetic Sleeve: A Novel Sexual Organ, 1983; The Expansion of Duality, 1984; The Inger Poems, 1987; Circular Geometry, 1990; The Four Inventions, 1990; The Expansion of Dualism: A 2 4 8 System, 1990; The Early Poems of Musical Lynn, 1990; The Musical Lynn Song Lyrics, 1991; The Musical Lynn Essays, 1992; Caveman Talk, 1992; The Three in One Ring (and) The Magnetic Woman, 1992; Music that Sings, 1993; Apple Skies, 1993; Math of Poetry, 1994; A Triversal Woman, 1997. Membership: National Association for Female Executives. Address: 1415 East 22nd Street, Apt 1108, Minneapolis, MN 55404-3015, USA.

FISDEL Steven Alan, b. 26 July 1948, Chicago, Illinois, USA. Rabbi. Education: BA, Hebrew University of Jerusalem, 1973; Bachelor of Hebrew Letters, Spertus College, Chicago, USA, 1977; MA, Spertus College; Rabbinic Ordination, Pnai Or Fellowship, Philadelphia, Pennsylvania, 1992. Appointments: Educator, Hebrew Academy of Northwest Indiana, Hammond, Indiana, USA, 1976; Educational Director, Temple Chai, Long Grove,

Illinois, USA, 1982; Administrative Director, Drs Cohen and Minana, San Francisco, California, USA, 1988; Rabbi, Congregation Beth Israel, Chico, California, USA, 1992; Core Faculty, Chochmat HaLev Institute, Berkeley, California, USA, 1997; Rabbi, Congregation Bnai Torah, Antioch, California, USA, 1997. Publications: The Practice of Kabbalah: Meditation in Judaism, 1996; The Dead Sea Scrolls: Understanding Their Spiritual Message, 1997. Contributions to: Proceedings of the International Association of New Science, 1995.

FISH Stanley (Eugene), b. 19 Apr 1938, Providence, Rhode Island, USA. Arts and Sciences Professor of English and Professor of Law. m. 1) Adrienne Aaron, 23 Aug 1959, div 1980, 1 daughter, 2) Jane Parry Tompkins, 7 Aug 1982. Education: BA, University of Pennsylvania, 1959; MA, 1960, PhD, 1962, Yale University. Appointments: Assistant Professor, 1963-67, Associate Professor, 1967-69, Professor of English, 1969-74, University of California at Berkeley; Visiting Associate Professor, Washington University, 1967; Visiting Professor, Sir George Williams University, 1969, State University of New York, 1991, Columbia Law School, 1995, Cardozo School of Law, 1996; Visiting Professor, 1971, Professor of English, 1974-78, William Kenan Jnr Professor of English and Humanities, 1978-85, Chairman, Department of English, 1983-85, Johns Hopkins University; Visiting Bing Professor of English, University of Southern California, 1973-74; Adjunct Professor, University of Maryland Law School, 1976-85; Arts and Sciences Professor of English and Professor of Law, 1985-98, Chairman, Department of English, 1986-92, Associate Vice Provost, 1993-98, Executive Director, University Press, 1993-98, Duke University. Dean-Designate, College of Liberal Arts and Sciences, University of Illinois at Chicago, 1999-. Publications: John Skelton's Poetry, 1965; Surprised by Sin: The Reader in Paradise Lost, 1967, new edition, 1997; Seventeenth Century Prose: Modern Essays in Criticism (editor), 1971; Self-Consuming Artifacts: The Experience of Seventeenth Century Literature, 1972; The Living Temple: George Herbert and Catechizing, 1978; Is There a Text in This Class?: Interpretive Communities and the Sources of Authority, 1980; Doing What Comes Naturally: Change, Rhetoric, and the Practice of Theory in Literary and Legal Studies, 1989; There's No Such Thing as Free Speech, and It's a Good Thing, Too, 1994; Professional Correctness: Literary Studies and Political Change, 1995. Contributions to: Scholarly books and journals. Honours: American Council of Learned Societies Fellowship, 1966; Humanities Research Professorship, University of California at Berkeley, 1966, 1970; 2nd Place, Explicator Prize, 1968; Guggenheim Fellowship, 1969-70; Nomination, National Book Award, 1972; Fellow, Humanities Research Institute, University of California at Irvine, 1989; Honored Scholar, Milton Society of America, 1991; PEN/Spielvogel-Diamonstein Award, 1994; Hanford Book Award, 1998. Memberships: American Academy of Arts and Sciences; Milton Society of American, President, 1980; Modern Language Association. Address: c/o University of Illinois at Chicago, College of Liberal Arts and Science, Office of the Dean, M/C 228, 601 S. Morgan Street, Chicago, IL 60607-7104, USA.

FISHER Allen, b. 1 Nov 1944, Norbury, Surrey, England. Painter; Poet; Art Historian. Education: BA, University of London; MA, University of Essex. Appointment: Head of Art, Roehampton Institute. Publications: Over 100 books including: Place Book One, 1974; Brixton Fractals, 1985; Unpolished Mirrors, 1985; Stepping Out, 1989; Future Exiles, 1991; Fizz, 1994; Civic Crime, 1994; Breadboard, 1994; Now's the Time, 1995. Contributions to: Various magazines and journals. Honour: Co-Winner, Alice Hunt Bartlett Award, 1975. Address: 14 Hopton Road, Hereford HR1 1BE, England.

FISHER Leonard Everett, b. 24 June 1924, New York, New York, USA. Artist; Author. m. Margery Meskin, 21 Dec 1952, 1 son, 2 daughters. Education: BFA, 1949, MFA, 1950, Yale University. Publications: 80 books written and illustrated including: Non Fiction: Colonial Americans, 19 volumes, 1964-76; Ellis Island, 1986; Look

Around, 1987; The Tower of London, 1987; Galileo, 1992; Tracks Across America, 1992; Stars and Stripes, 1993; Marie Curie, 1994; Moses, 1995; Gandhi, 1995; Niagara Falls, 1996; Anasazi, 1997. Fiction: Death of Evening Star, 1972; Across the Sea from Galway, 1975; Sailboat Lost, 1991; Cyclops, 1991; Kinderdike, 1994; William Tell, 1996. Illustrator of more than 250 books for young readers. Honours: Premio Grafico Fiera di Bologno, Italy, 1968; Medallion, University of Southern Mississippi, 1979; Christopher Medal, 1980; National Jewish Book Award for Children's Literature, 1981; Children's Book Guild, Washington Post Non-Fiction Award, 1989; Regina Medal, Catholic Library Association, 1991; Kerlan Award, University of Minnesota, 1991; Arbuthnot Honour Lecture Citation, American Library Association, 1994. Memberships: PEN; Authors Guild; Society of Illustrators; Society of Children's Book Authors and Illustrators. Address: 7 Twin Bridge Acres Road, Westport, CT 06880, USA.

FISHER Roy, b. 11 June 1930, Birmingham, England. Poet; Musician. Education: BA, 1951, MA, 1970, Birmingham University. Publications: City, 1961; Interiors, 1966; The Ship's Orchestra, 1967; The Memorial Fountain, 1968; Matrix, 1971; Cut Pages, 1971; Metamorphoses, 1971; The Thing About Joe Sullivan, 1978; A Furnace, 1986; The Left-Handed Punch, 1987; Poems 1955-1987, 1988; Birmingham River, 1994; The Dow Low Drop: New and Selected Poems, 1996. Contributions to: Numerous journals and magazines. Honours: Andrew Kelus Prize, 1979; Cholmondeley Award, 1981. Memberships: Musicians Union; Society of Authors. Address: Four Ways, Earl Sterndale, Buxton, Derbyshire SK17 0EP, England.

FISHKIN Shelley Fisher, b. 9 May 1950, New York, New York, USA. Professor of American Studies and English; Writer; Editor. m. James Steven Fishkin, 27 May 1973, 2 sons. Education: Swarthmore College, 1967-69; BA in English, 1971, MA in English, 1974, MPhil in American Studies, 1974, PhD in American Studies, 1977, Yale University. Appointments: Visiting Lecturer, Yale University, 1981-84; Senior Lecturer, 1985-89, Associate Professor, 1989-92, Professor of American Studies, 1993-, Professor of American Studies and English, 1994-, University of Texas at Austin; Associate Editor, American National Biography, 1989-. Publications: From Fact to Fiction: Journalism and Imaginative Writing in America, 1985; Was Huck Black? Mark Twain and African-American Voices, 1993; Listening to Silences: New Essays in Feminist Criticism (editor with Elaine Hedges), 1994; The Oxford Mark Twain (editor), 29 volumes, 1996; Lighting Out for the Territory: Reflections on Mark Twain and American Culture, 1997. Contributions to: Books, journals, newspapers and periodicals. Honours: Mellon Fellow, 1979, Rockefeller Humanist Fellow, 1984, Aspen Institute; Frank Luther Mott-Kappa Tau Alpha Research Book Award, National Journalism Scholarship Society, 1986; American Council of Learned Societies Fellowship, 1987-88; Humanities Scholar, Connecticut Humanities Council, 1987, 1989-91; Visiting Fellow, 1992-93; Life Member, 1993-, Clare Hall, Cambridge University; Outstanding Academic Book Citation, Choice, 1994. Memberships: American Literature Association; American Studies Association; Authors Guild; Charlotte Perkins Gilman Society, co-founder and executive director, 1990-; International Theodore Dreiser Society; Mark Twain Circle of America, president, 1997-; Modern Language Association; Research Society for American Periodicals, board of directors, 1991-94. Address: c/o American Studies Program, University of Texas at Austin, Austin, TX 78712, USA.

FISHLOCK Trevor, b. 21 Feb 1941, Hereford, England. Journalist; Author. m. Penelope Symon, 1978. Appointments: Portsmouth Evening News, 1957-62; Freelance News Agency Reporter, 1962-68; Staff Correspondent, Wales and West England, 1968-77, South Asia Correspondent, 1980-83, New York Correspondent, 1983-86, Times; Roving Foreign Correspondent, 1986-89, 1993-96, Moscow Correspondent, 1989-91, Roving Correspondent,

1993-96, Daily Telegraph; Roving Foreign Correspondent, Sunday Telegraph, 1991-93. Publications: Wales and the Welsh, 1972; Discovering Britain - Wales, 1975; Talking of Wales, 1975; Americans and Nothing Else, 1980; India File, 1983; The State of America, 1986; Indira Gandhi (children's book), 1986; Out of Red Darkness, 1992; My Foreign Country, 1997; Wild Tracks, 1998. Honours: David Holden Award for Foreign Reporting, 1983, International Reporter of the Year, 1986, British Press Awards. Memberships: Society of Authors; World Press Institute. Address: 56 Dovercourt Road, London SE22 8ST, England.

FISHMAN Charles (Munro), b. 10 July 1942, Oceanside, New York, USA. Distinguished Service Professor and Professor Emeritus; Poet; Writer; Editor. m. Ellen Marci Haselkorn, 25 June 1967, 2 daughters. Education: BA, English Literature, 1964, MA, English Literature, 1965, Hofstra University; DA, Creative Writing, State University of New York at Albany, 1982. Appointments: Founder-Director, Visiting Writers Program, 1979-97, Distinguished Service Professor, 1989-, Professor Emeritus, 1997-, State University of New York at Farmingdale; Founder-Editor, Xanadu, 1975-78; Poetry Editor, Gaia, 1993-95, The Genocide Forum, 1997-, The Cistercian Studies Quarterly, 1998-. Publications: An Index to Women's Magazines and Presses (editor), 1977; Mortal Companions, 1977; The Death Mazurka, 1989; Catlives, by Sarah Kirsch (translator with Marina Roscher), 1991; Blood to Remember: American Poets on the Holocaust (editor), 1991; Nineteenth-Century Rain, 1994; The Firewalkers, 1996. Contributions to: Many anthologies and over 300 periodicals. Honours: Gertrude B Claytor Memorial Award, Poetry Society of America, 1987; Outstanding Academic Book of the Year, American Library Association, 1989; Firman Houghton Poetry Award, New England Poetry Club, 1995; New York Foundation for the Arts Fellowship in Poetry, 1995; Winner, Anabiosis Press Chapbook Competition, 1996; Ann Stanford Poetry Prize, Southern California Anthology, 1996. Memberships: Associated Writing Programs; PEN; Poetry Society of America; Poets and Writers. Address: 2956 Kent Road, Wantagh, NY 11793, USA.

FISHMAN Lisa, b. 14 Dec 1966, Michigan, USA. Professor; Poet. m. Henry Morren, 31 July 1992. Education: BA in English, Michigan State University, 1988; MFA in Creative Writing, Western Michigan University, 1992; PhD in English, University of Utah, 1998. Appointment: Assistant Professor, English Department, Beloit College, Wisconsin, 1998-. Publication: The Deep Heart's Core is a Suitcase, 1996. Contributions to: Antioch Review; Indiana Review; Wallace Stevens Journal; Prairie Schooner; Cutbank. Address: c/o English Department, Beloit College, Beloit, WI 53511, USA.

FISK Pauline, (Pauline Davies), b. 27 Sept 1948, London, England. Writer. m. David Davies, 12 Feb 1972, 2 sons, 3 daughters. Publications: Midnight Blue, 1990; Telling the Sea, 1992; Tyger Pool, 1994; Beast of Whixall Moss, 1997; The Candle House, 1999. Contributions to: Homes and Gardens, 1989; Something to Do With Love (anthology), 1996. Honours: Smarties Grand Prix Prize, 1990; Shortlisted, Whitbread Award. Address: c/o Laura Cecil, 17 Alwyne Villas, London N1 2HG, England.

FISKE Sharon. See: HILL Pamela.

FITCH Noel Riley, b. 24 Dec 1937, New Haven, USA. Author; Educator. m. Albert Sonnenfeld, 23 Aug 1987, 1 daughter. Education: PhD, Washington State University, 1969; Postdoctoral Study, Princeton University, 1976, Yale University, 1979. Appointments: Lecturer, University of Southern California; Visiting Professor, American University of Paris. Publications: Anais: The Erotic Life of Anais Nin; Sylvia Beach and the Lost Generation: A History of Literary Paris in the Twenties and Thirties; Faith and Imagination: Essays on Evangelicals and Literature; Literary Cafés of Paris; Walks in Hemingway's Paris; Djuna Barnes; The Elusive Seamless Whole: A Biographer Treats or Fails to Treat Lesbianism; The

Literate Passion of Anais Nin and Henry Miller; Appetite for Life: The Biography of Julia Child. Contributions to: Los Angeles Magazine; Arete; James Joyce Literary Supplement; Journal of Library Science, Princeton University Chronicle. Honours: NEH Fellow; Certificate of Merit, DLB. Memberships: PEN; Authors Guild of America. Literary Agent: Kristine Dahl, ICM, 40 West 57th Street, New York City, USA. Address: 11829 Mayfield Avenue, Los Angeles, CA 90049, USA.

FITTER Richard (Sidney Richmond), b. 1 Mar 1913, London, England. Naturalist; Writer; Editor. m. Alice Mary Stewart Park, 1938, dec, 2 sons, 1 daughter. Education: Eastbourne College; BSc, London School of Economics and Political Science, 1933. Appointments: Editor, London Naturalist, 1942-46, Kingfisher, 1965-72; Assistant Editor, Countryman, 1946-59; Open Air Correspondent, Observer, 1958-66. Publications: London's Natural History, 1945; London's Birds, 1949; The Pocket Guide to British Birds, 1952; revised edition as Collins Pocket Guide to Birds, 1966; Birds of Town and Village, 1953; The Pocket Guide to Nests and Eggs (with Guy Charteris), 1954, revised edition as The Collins Pocket Guide to Nests and Eggs, 1968; The Guide to Wild Flowers (with David McClintock), 1956; The Ark in Our Midst: The Story of the Introduced Animals of Britain: Birds, Beasts, Reptiles, Amphibians, Fishes, 1959; Six Great Naturalists: White, Linnaeus, Waterton, Audubon, Fabre, Huxley, 1959; Collins Guide to Bird-watching, 1963, 2nd edition, 1970; Fitter's Rural Rides: The Observer Illustrated Map-Guide to the Countryside, 1963; Wildlife in Britain, 1963; Wildlife and Death, 1964; British Wildlife: Rarities and Introductions, 1966; The Penguin Dictionary of British Natural History (with Alice Fitter), 1967; Vanishing Wild Animals of the World, 1968; The Birds of Britain and Europe with North Africa and the Middle East (with Hermann Heinzel and J L F Parslow), 1972; Finding Wild Flowers, 1972; The Wild Flowers of Britain and Northern Europe (with Alastair Fitter), 1974; The Penitent Butchers (with Sir Peter Scott), 1978; Handguide to the Wild Flowers of Britain and Europe (with Marjorie Blamey), 1979; Wild Flowers, 1980; The Complete Guide to British Wildlife (with Alastair Fitter), 1981; John Clare's Birds (editor with Eric Robinson), 1982; Collins Guide to the Countryside (with Alastair Fitter), 1984; The Grasses, Sedges, Rushes and Fens of Britain and Northern Europe (with Alastair Fitter), 1984; Wildlife for Men: How and Why We Should Conserve Our Species, 1986; Field Guide to the Freshwater Life of Britain and Northwest Europe (with R Manuel), 1986; The Road to Extinction: Problems of Categorizing the Status of Taxa Threatened with Extinction (editor with Maisie Fitter), 1987; Guide to the Countryside in Winter (with Alastair Fitter), 1988. Honour: Officer, Order of the Golden Ark, Netherlands, 1978. Memberships: British Trust for Ornithology; Fauna and Flora Preservation Society, chairman, 1983-88; International Union for Conservation of Nature, Royal Society for the Protection of Birds; World Wildlife Fund; Zoological Society of London; Society of Authors. Address: Drifts, Chinnor Hill, Oxford OX9 4BS, England.

FITZGERALD Frances, b. 21 Oct 1940, New York, New York, USA. Writer. Education: BA, Radcliffe College, 1962. Publications: Fire in the Lake: The Vietnamese and Americans in Vietnam, 1972; America Revised: History Schoolbooks in the Twentieth Century, 1979; Cities on a Hill: A Journey Through Contemporary American Culture, 1986. Contributions to: New Yorker; Atlantic Monthly; New York Review of Books; Harper's; Vogue; Look; Nation; New Times. Honours: Pulitzer Prize for General Non-Fiction, 1973; National Book Award, 1973; Bancroft Prize, 1973; Christopher Award, 1973; American Academy of Arts and Letters Award, 1973; National Institute of Arts and Letters Award, 1973. Address: c/o Lescher & Lescher Ltd, 67 Irving Place, New York, NY 10003, USA.

FITZGERALD Judith (Ariana), b. 11 Nov 1952, Toronto, Ontario, Canada. Poet; Critic. Education: BA, Honours, 1976, MA, 1977, York University. Appointments: Teacher, Erindale College, 1978-81; Professor, Laurentian University, 1981-83; Poetry Editor,

Black Moss Press, 1981-87; Entertainment Journalist, The Globe, 1983-84; Poetry Critic, The Toronto Star, 1984-88; Writer-in-Residence, University of Windsor, 1993-94; Creator, Today's Country, Satellite Radio Network, 1993-; Professor of English, Université Canadienne en France, 1994-95. Publications: Poetry: City Park, 1972; Journal Entries, 1975; Victory, 1975; Lacerating Heartwood, 1977; Easy Over, 1981; Split/Levels, 1983; Heart Attacks, 1984; Beneath the Skin of Paradise, 1984; Given Names, 1985; Diary of Desire, 1987; Rapturous Chronicles, 1991; Ultimate Midnight, 1992; Walkin' Wounded, 1993; River, 1995; AKA Paradise, 1996. Children's Poetry: My Orange Gorange, 1985; Whale Waddleby, 1986; Editor: Un Dozen: Thirteen Canadian Poets, 1982; Sp/Elles: Poetry by Canadian Women/Poesie de femmes canadiennes, 1986; First Person Plural, 1988. Contributions to: Various anthologies and other publications. Honours: Fiona Mee Award, 1983; Writers' Choice Award, 1986; Shortlisted, Governor-General's Award for Poetry, 1991; Several grants. Memberships: League of Canadian Poets; Society of Composers, Authors and Music Publishers of Canada. Address: RR 1, South River, Ontario POA 1XO, Canada.

FITZGERALD Maureen Elizabeth, b. 24 Dec 1920, Mumbles, Glamorgan, Wales. Journalist. Education: Pensionnat des Servites, Brussels, Belgium; BSc, Economics, University College, London, 1949. Appointments: Associate Editor, 1952-62, Editor, 1963-73, Director, 1968-77, Managing Editor, 1973-77, Editorial Adviser, 1978-80, Consultant and Profile Writer, 1981-85, Profile Writer, 1985-88, Local Government Chronicle. Publication: The Story of a Parish, 1990. Contributions to: Local Government Chronicle; District Council Review; Rating and Valuation; Chamber's Encyclopaedia, Review of the Year; Local Government Review. Honour: Member of the Order of the British Empire, 1979. Memberships: Society of Women Writers and Journalists; Chartered Institute of Journalists; New Cavendish Club. Address: 5 Buckingham Court, Chestnut Lane, Amersham, Buckinghamshire HP6 6EL, England.

FITZGERALD Penelope Mary, b. 17 Dec 1916, Lincoln, England. Teacher; Writer. m. Desmond Fitzgerald, 1942, 1 son, 2 daughters. Education: BA, Somerville College, Oxford. Appointment: English Tutor, Westerminster Tutors, London, 1965-. Publications: The Knox Brothers, 1977; The Bookship, 1978; The Golden Child, 1978; Offshore, 1979; Human Voices, 1980; At Freddies, 1982; Charlotte New and Her Friends, 1984; Innocence, 1986; The Beginning of Spring, 1989; The Gate of Angels, 1990; The Blue Flower, 1995. Honours: Booker McConnell Prize, 1979; National Book Critics Circle Award, USA, for Fiction, 1998. Membership: Royal Society of Literature, fellow; International PEN. Address: Harpercollins, 77-85 Fulham Rd, London W6 8BJ, England.

FITZHARDINGE Joan Margaret, (Joan Phipson), b. 16 Nov 1912, Warrawee, New South Wales, Australia. Freelance Writer; Grazier. Publications: Good Luck to the Rider, 1953; Six and Silver, 1954; It Happened One Summer, 1957; The Boundary Riders, 1962; The Family Conspiracy, 1962; Threat to the Barkers, 1963; Birkin, 1965; The Crew of the Merlin, 1966; A Lamb in the Family, 1966; Peter and Butch, 1969; The Haunted Night, 1970; The Way Home, 1973; Polly's Tiger, 1973; Helping Horse, 1974; Bennelong, 1975; The Cats, 1976; Fly into Danger, 1977 (Australian edition as The Bird Smugglers, 1979); Hide Till Daytime, 1977; Keep Calm, 1978; No Escape, 1979; Mr Pringle and the Prince, 1979; A Tide Flowing, 1981; The Watcher in the Garden, 1982; Beryl the Rainmaker, 1984; The Grannie Season, 1985; Dinko, 1985; Hit and Run, 1985; Bianca, 1988. Literary Agent: A P Watt, London. Address: Wongalong, Mandurama, New South Wales 2792, Australia.

FITZMAURICE Gabriel John, b. 7 Dec 1952, Moyvane, County Kerry, Ireland. Primary Teacher; Poet. m. Brenda Downey, 17 Aug 1981, 1 son, 1 daughter. Education: Leaving Certificate, Honours, St Michael's College, Listowel, County Kerry, 1970; Diploma, Primary Teaching, Mary Immaculate College, Limerick, 1972. Appointments: Assistant Teacher, Avoca National School, County Wicklow, 1972-74; Teacher, Christ the King National School, Limerick City, 1974-75, Moyvane National School, 1975-. Publications: Poetry in English: Rainsong, 1984; Road to the Horizon, 1987; Dancing Through, 1990; The Father's Part, 1992; The Space Between: New and Selected Poems 1984-92, 1993; The Village Sings, 1996; Poetry in Irish: Nocht, 1989; Ag Siobshiul Chun An Rince, 1995. Other: Children's poetry in English and Irish. Translations: The Purge, by Michéal O Airtnéide, 1989; Pomes I Wish I'd Written, 1996; Editor: The Flowering Tree, 1991; Between the Hills and Sea: Songs and Ballads of Kerry, 1991; Irish Poetry Now: Other Voices, 1993; Kerry Through Its Writers, 1993. Contributions to: Newspapers, reviews, and journals. Honours: Represented Ireland, Europees Poeziefestival, Leuven, Belgium, 1987, 1991; Award Winner, Gerard Manley Hopkins Centenary Poetry Competition, 1989. Address: Applegarth, Moyvane, County Kerry, Ireland.

FITZPATRICK Janine, b. Glasgow, Scotland. Teacher; Lecturer; Writer; Poet; Translator. 1 son, 1 daughter. Education: University of Paris, 1961-62; University of Friburg-im-Breisgan, 1963; MA, Honours, University of Glasgow, 1964; University of Munich, 1967; University of Michigan, 1982. Appointments: Researcher in modern German Poetry, Bilingualism, Jewish Mysticism, German Resistance. Translator; Tutor; Teacher; Researcher to Scottish Examination Board; Arvon Poetry Foundation, Bursar, 1998. Publications: Egon Schiele, 1971; Brecht's Lyrics (translator) A Refugee Kurd in Berlin (drama); Zen in the Hokoku-Ji, 1980; Maestri a Roma nel Cinquecento (translator). Many contributions to: Journals, reviews, periodicals, quarterlies, newspapers and magazines. Poems in 16 anthologies. Honours: Woman of Europe Award, 1998, 1999. Memberships: Writers Guild of Great Britain; Educational Institute of Scotland. Address: 21 Havelock Street, Glasgow G11 5JF, Scotland.

FITZSIMMONS Thomas, b. 21 Oct 1926, Lowell, Massachusetts, USA. Poet; Writer; Translator; Editor; Publisher; Professor Emeritus of English and Comparative Literature. m. Karen Hargreaves, 2 sons. Education: Fresno State College, 1947-49; Sorbonne and Institut de Sciences Politiques, Paris, 1949-50; BA, English Literature and Creative Writing, Stanford University, 1951; MA, English and Comparative Literature, Columbia University, 1952. Appointments: Writer and Editor, The New Republic magazine, 1952-55; Research Team Chairman, 1955-56, Director of Research for Publication, 1956-58, Director and Editor, 1958-59, HRAF Press, Yale University; Assistant Professor, 1959-61, Associate Professor, 1961-66, Professor of English and Comparative Literature, 1966-89, Professor Emeritus, 1989-, Oakland University, Rochester, Michigan; Fulbright Lecturer, Tokyo University of Education, 1962-64, Tsuda University, Tokyo, 1962-64, University of Bucharest, 1967-68, University of Nice, 1968; Visiting Lecturer, Japan National Women's University, Tokyo, 1973-75, Keio University, Tokyo, 1973-75, Detroit Institute of Arts, 1986; Visiting Professor, Tokyo University of Education, 1973-75, Kyushu National University, Fukuoka, 1979; Visiting Poet and Scholar, Sophia University, Tokyo, 1988-89; Editor-Publisher, Katydid Books. Publications: Poetry: This Time This Place, 1969; Mooning, 1971; Meditation Seeds, 1971; With the Water, 1972; Playseeds, 1973; The Big Huge, 1975; The Nine Seas and the Eight Mountains, 1981; Rocking Mirror Daybreak, 1982; Water Ground Stone (poems and essays), 1994; The Dream Machine, 1996; Fencing the Sky, 1998; Iron Harp, 1999. Author or Translator: Over 60 volumes, 1955-98. Honours: National Endowment for the Arts Fellowships, 1967, 1982, 1989-90, and Grants, 1984, 1986; Oakland University Research Fellowship, 1982; Japan-US Friendship Foundation Grant, 1983; Michigan Council for the Arts Award, 1986; Fulbright Research Fellowship, Japan, 1988-89. Address: 1 Balsa Road, Santa Fe, NM 87505, USA.

FLAGG Fannie, (Patricia Neal), b. 21 Sept 1941, Birmingham, Alabama, USA. Writer; Actress. Education: University of Alabama; Pittsburgh Playhouse; Town and Gown Theatre. Publications: Coming Attractions: A Wonderful Novel, 1981; Fried Green Tomatoes at the Whistle Stop Cafe, 1987; Welcome to the World, Baby Girl!, 1988. Other: Fried Green Tomatoes at the Whistle Stop Cafe (screenplay with Jon Avnet), 1991. Contributions to: Magazines and newspapers. Address: c/o Random House Inc, 201 East 50th Street, New York, NY 10022, USA.

FLAM Jack (Donald), b. 2 Apr 1940, Paterson, New Jersey, USA. Professor of Art History; Writer. m. Bonnie Burnham, 7 Oct 1972, 1 daughter. Education: BA, Rutgers University, 1961; MA, Columbia University, 1963; PhD, New York University, 1969. Appointments: Instructor in Art, Newark College of Arts and Sciences, Rutgers University, 1962-66; Assistant Professor of Art, 1966-69, Associate Professor of Art, 1969-72, University of Florida; Associate Professor of Art, 1975-79, Professor of Art, 1980-91, Distinguished Professor of Art, 1991-, Brooklyn College of the City University of New York; Associate Professor of Art History, 1979-80, Professor of Art History, 1980-91, Distinguished Professor of Art History, 1991-, Graduate School and University Center of the City University of New York; Art Critic, The Wall Street Journal, 1984-92. Publications: Matisse on Art, 1973, revised edition, 1995; Zoltan Gorency, 1974; Bread and Butter, 1977; Henri Matisse Paper Cut-Outs (co-author), 1977; Robert Motherwell (co-author), 1983; Matisse: The Man and His Art 1869-1918, 1986; Fernand Léger, 1987; Matisse: A Retrospective, 1988; Motherwell, 1991; Richard Diebenkorn: Ocean Park, 1992; Matisse: The Dance, 1993; Western Artists/African Art, 1994; The Paine Webber Art Collection (co-author), 1995; Robert Smithson: The Collected Writings (editor), 1996; Judith Rotheschild an Artist's Search, 1998; Le Peiutures Picasso: Un Théâtre Meutal, 1998. Contributions to: Apollo. Honours: Guggenheim Fellowship, 1979-80; National Endowment for the Humanities Fellowship, 1987-88. Memberships: International Association of Art Critics; PEN. Address: 35 West 81st Street, New York, NY 10024, USA.

FLANAGAN Mary, b. 20 May 1943, Rochester, New Hampshire, USA. Novelist; Critic. Education: BA, History of Art, Brandeis University, Waltham, MA, USA. Appointment: Creative Writing Seminars (two terms), University of East Anglia, England. Publications: Bad Girls, 1984; Trust, 1987; Rose Reason, 1991; The Blue Woman, 1994; Adèle, 1997. Memberships: PEN; Society of Authors. Literary Agent: Lisa Eveleigh. Address: 62 Camden Lock Place, London NW1 8AF, England.

FLANAGAN Thomas (James Bonner), b. 5 Nov 1923, Greenwich, Connecticut, USA. Distinguished Professor; Author. m. Jean Parker, 10 June 1949, 2 children. Education: BA, Amherst College, 1945; MA, 1949, PhD, 1958, Columbia University. Appointments: Instructor, 1949-52, Assistant Professor, 1952-59, Columbia University; Assistant Professor, 1960-67, Associate Professor, 1967-73, Professor of English Literature, 1973-78, University of California at Berkeley; Professor of English Literature, 1978-92, Distinguished Professor, 1993-, State University of New York at Stony Brook. Publications: Novels: The Year of the French, 1979; The Tenants of Time, 1988; The End of the Hunt, 1994. Non-Fiction: The Irish Novelists, 1800-1850, 1959. Contributions to: Professional journals, reviews, and periodicals. Honours: American Council of Learned Societies Grant, 1962; Guggenheim Fellowship, 1962-63; National Book Critics Circle Award for Fiction, 1979; American Irish Historical Society Gold Medal, 1982. Memberships: American Committee for Irish Studies; International Association for the Study of Anglo-Irish Literature; Modern Language Assocation; Phi Beta Kappa. Address: c/o Department of English, State University of New York at Stony Brook, Stony Brook, NY 11794, USA.

FLEET Kenneth George, b. 12 Sept 1929, Cheshire, England. Journalist. m. (Alice) Brenda Wilkinson, 28 Mar 1953, 3 sons, 1 daughter. Education: BSc, Economics, London School of Economics and Political Science. Appointments: Journal of Commerce, Liverpool, 1950-52;

Sunday Times, 1955-56; Deputy City Editor, Birmingham Post, 1956-58; Deputy Financial Editor, Guardian, 1958-63; Deputy City Editor, 1963, City Editor 1966-77, Daily Telegraph; City Editor, Sunday Telegraph, 1963-66; Editor, Business News, Sunday Times, 1977-78; City Editor, Sunday Express, 1978-82; City Editor-in-Chief, Express Newspapers plc, 1982-85; Executive Editor, Finance and Industry, The Times, 1983-87; Chairman, Chichester Festival Theatre, 1985-; Governor, London Schools of Economics, 1989-; Director, TUS Entertainment plc, 1990-93. Honour: Wincott Award, 1974. Address: c/o 20 Farrington Road, London EC1M 3NH, England.

FLEISCHMAN Paul, b. 5 Sept 1952, Monterey, California, USA. Children's Writer and Poet. m. Becky Mojica, 15 Dec 1978, 2 sons. Education: University of California at Berkeley; BA, University of New Mexico. Publications: The Birthday Tree, 1979; The Half-a-Moon Inn, 1980; Graven Images, 1982; Path of the Pale Horse, 1983; Finzel the Farsighted, 1983; Coming-and-Going Men, 1985; I Am Phoenix: Poems for Two Voices, 1985; Rondo in C, 1988; Joyful Noise: Poems for Two Voices, 1989; Saturnalia, 1990; Shadow Play, 1990; The Borning Room, 1991; Time Train, 1991. Honours: Silver Medal, Commonwealth Club of California, 1980; Newberry Medals, American Library Association, 1983, 1989; Parents Choice Award, 1983; Numerous citations by Society of Children's Book Writers, American Library Association, New York Times. Memberships: Authors Guild; Society of Children's Book Writers. Address: 855 Marin Pines, Pacific Grove, CA 93950, USA.

FLEISCHMAN (Albert) Sid(ney), b. 16 Mar 1920, New York, New York, USA. Writer. Education: BA, San Diego State College, 1949. Publications: 10 adult novels, 1948-63; Over 40 juvenile books, 1962-95. Address: 305 Tenth Street, Santa Monica, CA 90402, USA.

FLEMING Laurence William Howie, b. 8 Sept 1929, Shillong, Assam, India. Author; Artist; Landscape Designer. Education: The New School, Darjeeling, India, 1941-44; Repton School, Derbyshire, 1945-47; Royal Air Force, 1947-49; St Catharine's College, Cambridge, 1949-52. Publications: A Diet of Crumbs, 1959; The English Garden, 1979; The One Hour Garden, 1985; Old English Villages, 1986; Roberto Burle Marx: A Portrait, 1996. Contributions to: Journals. Memberships: International PEN; Writers Guild; Anglo-Brazilian Society. Address: c/o Lloyds Bank Plc, 112 Kensington High Street, London W8 4SN, England.

FLEMING Robert Paterson Howe, (R Paterson-Howe), b. 12 Apr 1927, Lucknow, India. Lecturer; Metallurgist. m. Patricia Parker, 9 Mar 1950, 2 sons, 1 daughter. Education: BSc Eng Met; PhD; Dip BIM; Cert Ed; CEng. Appointments: Royal Arsenal, Woolwich; English Electric Ltd, Stafford; GEC, Wembley, Middlesex; Rolls Royce Ltd, Bristol; City Polytechnic, Jewry St, London. Publications: Butterflies from my Brain; A Boy from Calcutta; The Great Win; Merv: Railway Wallah; The House, poems; Kitty: Life and Times, novel; The Indigo Hour, poems; Hush: Shakespeare Sahib, novel; Conversations with my Cat. Contributions to: Numerous. Honours: Fellow, Institute of Metals; FIBF. Memberships: Authors Society; Writers; STAMD. Address: 23 Birch Crescent, Holtwood, Aylesford, Kent ME20 7QE, England.

FLETCHER John (Walter James, Jonathan Fune), b. 23 June 1937, Barking, Essex, England. Emeritus Professor of European Literature; Writer; Translator. m. Beryl Sibley Connop, 14 Sept 1961, 2 sons, 1 daughter. Education: BA, 1959, MA, 1963, University of Cambridge; MPhil, 1961, PhD, 1964, University of Toulouse. Appointments: Lecturer, University of Toulouse, 1961-64, University of Durham, 1964-66; Lecturer in French, 1966-68; Reader in French, 1968-69, Professor of Comparative Literature, 1969-89, Professor of European Literature, 1989-98, University of East Anglia; Visiting Professor, University of Odense, 1971, University of Salzburg, 1971, University of Konstanz, 1976, 1978; University of Yaoundé, Cameroon, 1979, 1981, Griffith University, Brisbane, 1981, University of Toulouse, 1984-85, University of Lille, 1993, University of Brest, 1996-97, University of Bordeaux, 1998; Visiting Fellow, Australian National University, 1988. Publications: The Novels of Samuel Beckett, 1964, 2nd edition, revised, 1970; Samuel Beckett's Art, 1967; A Critical Commentary on Flaubert's Trois Contes, 1968; New Directions in Literature: Critical Approaches to a Contemporary Phenomenon, 1968; Samuel Beckett: Fin de Partie (editor with Beryl S Fletcher), 1970; Samuel Beckett: His Works and His Critics, An Essay in Bibliography (with Raymond Federman), 1970; Beckett: A Study of His Plays (with John Spurling), 1972, 3rd edition, revised, 1985; Claude Simon and Fiction Now, 1975; A Student's Guide to the Plays of Samuel Beckett (with others), 1978, 2nd edition, revised, 1985; Novel and Reader, 1980; Alain Robbe-Grillet, 1983; The Nouveau Roman Reader (editor with John Calder), 1986; The Georgics by Claude Simon (translator with Beryl S Fletcher), 1989; Iris Murdoch: A Descriptive Primary and Annotated Secondary Bibliography (with Cheryl Bove), 1994. Contributions to: Scholarly journals, newspapers and periodicals. Honours: Scott Moncrieff Prize, 1990; Honourable Mention, Florence Gould Foundation Translation Prize, 1990; Shortlisted, European Translation Prize, 1991. Memberships: Association of University Teachers; Society of Authors; Translators' Association. Address: 16 Mill Hill Road, Norwich NR2 3DP, England.

FLETCHER Richard. See: **BUTLIN Martin.**

FLEXNER James Thomas, b. 13 Jan 1908, New York, New York, USA. Historian; Biographer. m. Beatrice Hundson, 1 Aug 1950, 1 daughter. Education: BS, Harvard University, 1929. Publications: Doctors on Horseback: Pioneers of American Medicine, 1937; America's Old Masters, 1939, 2nd edition, revised, 1980; William Henry Welch and the Heroic Age of American Medicine (with Simon Flexner), 1941; Steamboats Come True, 1944; History of American Painting, 3 volumes, 1947, 1954, 1962; John Singleton Copley, 1947; A Short History of American Painting, 1950; The Traitor and the Spy: Benedict Arnold and John André, 1953, revised edition, 1975; Gilbert Stuart, 1955; Mohawk Baronet: Sir William Johnson of New York, 1959, revised edition as Lord of the Mohawks: A Biography of Sir William Johnson, 1979; George Washington: A Biography, 4 volumes, 1965, 1968, 1970, 1972; The World of Winslow Homer, 1836-1910, 1966; The Double Adventure of John Singleton Copley, 1969; Nineteenth Century Painting, 1970; Washington: The Indispensable Man, 1974; The Face of Liberty, 1975; The Young Hamilton, 1978; States Dyckman: American Loyalist, 1980; Asher B Durand: An Engraver's and a Farmer's Art, 1983; An American Saga: The Story of Helen Thomas and Simon Flexner, 1984; Poems of the Nineteen Twenties, 1991; On Desperate Seas: Biography of Gilbert Stuart, 1995. Contributions to: Many publications. Honours: Life in America Prize, 1946; Guggenheim Fellowships, 1953, 1979; Francis Parkman Prize, 1963; National Book Award, 1972; Special Pulitzer Prize Citation, 1972; Christopher Award, 1974; Archives of American Art Award, Smithsonian Institution, 1979; Peabody Award, 1984; Gold Medal for Eminence in Biography, American Academy and Institute of Arts and Letters, 1988. Memberships: American Academy and Institute of Arts and Letters; Authors League of America; PEN; Society of Historians, president, 1976-77. Address: 530 86th Street, New York, NY 10028, USA.

FLINT John. See: **WELLS Peter Frederick.**

FLOGSTAD Kjartan, b. 7 June 1944, Sauda, Norway. Writer, Poet. m. Kathrine Norre, 1977. Education: MA, University of Oslo, 1971. Publications: Mooring Lines, 1972; Rasmus, 1974; Not Even Death, 1975; One for All, 1976; Dollar Road, 1977; Fire and Flame, 1980; U3, 1983; The Seventh Climate: Salim Mahmood in Media Thule, 1986; The Knife at the Throat, 1991. Other: Verse: Pilgrimage, 1968; Ceremonies, 1969; The Secret Cheering, 1970; The Law West of Pecos and Other Essays on Popular Art and the Culture Industry, 1981; Wording, 1983; Tyrannosaurus Text, 1988; Portrait of a Magic Life: The Poet Claes Gill, 1988; The Light of Work, 1990. Honour: Melsom Prize, 1980. Address: Gyldendal Norsk Forlag, Postboks 6860, St Olave Plass, 0130 Oslo 1, Norway.

FLORA Joseph Martin, b. 9 Feb 1934, Toledo, Ohio, USA. Professor; Writer; Editor. m. Glenda Christine Flora, 30 Jan 1959, 4 sons. Education: BA, English, 1956, MA, English, 1957, PhD, English, 1962, University of Michigan. Appointments: Teaching Fellow to Instructor, University of Michigan, 1957-62; Instructor, 1962-64, Assistant Professor, 1964-66, Associate Professor, 1966-77, Professor, 1977-, University of North Carolina at Chapel Hill; Visiting Professor, University of New Mexico, 1976, 1996; Senior Editor, American Literature, 1915-1945, Twayne Publishers, 1989-. Publications: Vardis Fisher, 1965; William Ernest Henley, 1970; Frederick Manfred, 1974; Southern Writers: A Biographical Dictionary (editor with Robert Bain and Louis D Rubin Jr), 1979; Hemingway's Nick Adams, 1982; The English Short Story 1880-1945: A Critical History (editor), 1985; Fifty Southern Writers After 1900 (editor with Robert Bain), 1987; Fifty Southern Writers Before 1900 (editor with Robert Bain), 1987; Ernest Hemingway: A Study of the Short Fiction, 1989; Contemporary Fiction Writers of the South (editor with Robert Bain), 1993; Contemporary Poets, Dramatists, Essayists, and Novelists of the South (editor with Robert Bain), 1994. Contributions to: Books and journals. Honours: Kenan Research Award, 1978; Mayflower Award, North Carolina Literary and Historical Association, 1982. Memberships: American Literature Association; James Branch Cabell Society; Hemingway Society; Modern Language Association; Society for the Study of Southern Literature; South Atlantic Modern Language Association, president, 1998-99; Thomas Wolfe Society, president, 1995-97; Western Literature Association, president, 1992. Address: 505 Caswell Road, Chapel Hill, NC 27514, USA.

FLOREN Lee, (Brett Austin, Lisa Franchon, Claudia Hall, Wade Hamilton, Matt Harding, Matthew Whitman Harding, Felix Lee Horton, Stuart Jason, Grace Lang, Marguerite Nelson, Lew Smith, Maria Sandra Sterling, Lee Thomas, Len Turner, Will Watson, Dave Wilson), b. 22 Mar 1910, Hinsdale, Montana, USA. Author. Education: BA, Santa Barbara State College; Teacher's Certificate, Occidental College; MA, Texas Western College, 1964. Publications: Over 300 novels, 1944-. Address: c/o Hale, 45-47 Clerkenwell Green, London EC1R 0HT, England.

FLORICA Bud, b. 21 Mar 1957, Ulmeni, Maramures, Romania. Engineer. m. Bud Nicolae, 25 Oct 1980, 1 son, 1 daughter. Education: Gheorghe Sincai College; Mining Institute of Petrosani; Computer Analyst. Appointments: Baia Borsa; Baia Sprie Mine; Baia Mare Territorial Computing Center; Writer. Publications: Love, I Am a Not Flying Object, 1992; The Adventures of NO-TOMCAT at the Courtyard of Ca-Fe-Mini Dragon, fairytales, 1994; NO-TOMCAT and the Paper Dragon, fairytales, 1995; Running Inside the Self, short stories, 1996; Who Loves School?, meditations and short stories, 1997; NO-TOMCAT and the Red-Yellow-Green Semaphor Dragon, tales, 1998. Contributions to: local and national newspapers and magazine (Graiul Maramuresului, Art Panorama. Honours: Chestnut Festival Awards; Sorin Titel Award. Membership: Romanian Union of Writers, 1997. Address: Oituz Str 6B, sc A, Ap 7, RO-4800 Baia Mare.

FLYNN Robert (Lopez), b. 12 Apr 1932, Chillicothe, Texas, USA. Professor; Writer. m. Jean Sorrels, 1 June 1953, 2 daughters. Appointments: Assistant Professor, Baylor University, Waco, Texas, 1959-63; Professor, Novelist-in-Residence, Trinity University, San Antonio, Texas, 1963-. Publications: North to Yesterday, 1967; In the House of the Lord, 1969; The Sounds of Rescue, The Signs of Hope, 1970; Seasonal Rain and Other Stories, 1986; Wanderer Springs, 1987; A Personal War in Vietnam, 1989; When I Was Just Your Age, 1992; The Last Klick, 1994; Living with the Hyenas, 1996. Address: 101 Cliffside Drive, San Antonio, TX 78231, USA.

FLYNT Candace, b. 12 Mar 1947, Greensboro, North Carolina, USA. Author. m. John Franklin Kime, 29 Jan 1992, 1 son. Education: BA, Greensboro College, 1969; MFA, University of North Carolina, 1974. Publications: Mother Love; Sins of Omission; Chasing Dad. Memberships: Authors Guild; PEN. Address: c/o Rhoda A Weyr, 151 Bergen Street, Brooklyn, NY 11217, USA.

FO Dario, b. 24 Mar 1926, Leggiuno-Sangiamo, Italy. Dramatist; Actor. m. Franca Rame, 1954. Education: Academy of Fine Arts, Milan. Appointments: Dramatist and Actor in agitprog theatre and television; Co-Founder (with Franca Rame), Dramatist, Actor, Nuova Scena acting groupe, 1968, Collettivo Teatrale la Comune, 1970. Publications: Numerous plays, including: Morte accidentale di un anarchico (Accidental Death of an Anarchist), 1974; Non si paga, non si paga! (We Can't Pay? We Won't Pay!), 1974; Tutta casa, letto e chiesa (Adult Orgasm Escapes From the Zoo), 1978; Female Parts (with Franca Rame), 1981; Il papa e la stega (The Pope and the Witch), 1989; Le commedie, I-IX, 1966-91, 1992; Il diavolo con le zinne, 1997. Honour: Nobel Prize for Literature, 1997. Address: c/o CTFR, Viale Piave 11, 20129 Miland, Italy.

FOERSTER Richard Alfons, b. 29 Oct 1949, New York, New York, USA. Editor; Writer; Poet. m. Valerie Elizabeth Malinowski, 28 Oct 1972, div 1985. Education: BA, English, Fordham University, 1971; MA, English, University of Virginia, 1972; Teacher's Certificate, Manhattanville College, 1975. Appointments: Assistant Editor, Clarence L Barnhart Inc, 1973-75; Editor, Prentice Hall Inc, 1976-78; Associate Editor, 1978-94, Editor, 1994-, Chelsea Magazine. Publications: Transfigured Nights, 1990; Sudden Harbor, 1992; Patterns of Descent, 1993; Trillium, 1998. Contributions to: Boulevard; Epoch; Kenyon Review; Nation; New Criterion; Poetry; Shenandoah; Southern Review; Southwest Review. Honours: Discovery/The Nation Award, 1985; Bess Hokin Prize, 1992; Hawthornden Fellow, 1993; National Endowment for the Arts Creative Writing Fellowship, 1995; Maine Arts Commission Individual Artist Fellowship, 1997. Memberships: Academy of American Poets; Maine Writers and Publishers Alliance; Poetry Society of America; Society for the Arts, Religion and Contemporary Culture. Address: PO Box 1040, York Beach, ME 03910, USA.

FOGEL Robert William, b. 1 July 1926, New York, New York, USA. Economic Historian; Professor. m. Enid Cassandra Morgan, 2 Apr 1949, 2 sons. Education: AB, Cornell University, 1948; AM, Columbia University, 1960; PhD, Johns Hopkins University, 1963. Appointments: Instructor, Johns Hopkins University, 1958-59; Assistant Professor, 1960-64, Professor of Economics, 1968-71, Professor of Economics and History, 1972-75, University of Rochester; Ford Foundation Visiting Research Professor, 1963-64, Associate Professor, 1964-65, Professor of Economics, 1965-69, Professor of Economics and History, 1970-75, Charles R Walgreen Distinguished Service Professor of American Institutions, 1981-, University of Chicago; Taussig Research Professor, 1973-74, Harold Hitchings Burbank Professor of Political Economy and Professor of History, 1975-81, Harvard University; Pitt Professor of American History and Institutions, University of Cambridge; Research Associate, 1978-, Director, DAE program, 1978-91, National Bureau of Economic Research. Publications: The Union Pacific Railroad: A Case in Premature Enterprise, 1960; Railroads and American History (with others), 1971; The Dimensions of Quantitative Research in History (with others), 1972; Time on the Cross: The Economics of American Negro Slavery (with S L Engerman), 1974; Ten Lectures on the New Economic History, 1977; Which Road to the Past?: Two Views of History (with G R Elton), 1983; Long-Term Changes in Nutrition and the Standard of Living (editor), 1986; Without Consent or Contract: The Rise and Fall of American Slavery (with others), 4 volumes, 1989, 1992; Egalitarianism: The Economic Revolution of the 20th Century, 1994; The Escape from Hunger and Premature Death: Europe, America, and the Third World: 1700-2100, 1995; The Political Realignment of the 1850s:

A Socioeconomic Analysis, 1996. Contributions to: Numerous book and scholarly journals. Honours: Gilman Fellowship, 1957-60; National Science Foundation Grants, 1967, 1970, 1972, 1975-76, 1978, 1992-96; Fulbright Grant, 1968; Arthur H Cole Prize, 1968; Schumpeter Prize, 1971; Bancroft Prize, 1975; Gustavus Myers Prize, 1990; National Institutes of Health Grants, 1991-96; Nobel Prize in Economic Science, 1993; Several honorary degrees. Memberships: American Academy of Arts and Sciences; American Economic Society, president, 1998-; American Historical Association; Association of American Historians; British Academy, corresponding fellow; Econometric Society, fellow; Economic History Association, president, 1977-78; Economic History Society; National Academy of Sciences; Phi Beta Kappa; Royal Economic Society; Royal Historical Society; Social Science History Association, president, 1980-81. Address: c/o Graduate School of Business, University of Chicago, 1101 East 58th Street, Chicago, IL 60637, USA.

FOLEY (Mary) Louise Munro, b. 22 Oct 1933, Toronto, Ontario, Canada, (US citizen). Author. m. Donald J Foley, 9 Aug 1957, 2 sons. Education: University of Western Ontario, 1951-52; Ryerson Institute of Technology, 1952-53; BA, California State University, Sacramento, 1976. Appointments: Columnist, News-Argus, Goldsboro, North Carolina, 1971-73; Editor of Publications, Institute for Human Service Management, California State University, Sacramento, 1975-80. Publications: The Caper Club, 1969; No Talking, 1970; Sammy's Sister; A Job for Joey, 1970; Somebody Stole Second, 1972; Stand Close to the Door (editor), 1976; Tackle 22, 1978; Women in Skilled Labor (editor), 1980; The Train of Terror, 1982; The Sinister Studies of KESP-TV, 1983; The Lost Tribe, 1983; The Mystery of the Highland Crest, 1984; The Mystery of Echo Lodge, 1985; Danger at Anchor Mine, 1985; The Mardi Gras Mystery, 1987; Mystery of the Sacred Stones, 1988; Australia! Find the Flying Foxes, 1988; The Cobra Connection, 1990; Ghost Train, 1991; Poison! Said the Cat, 1992; Blood! Said the Cat, 1992; Thief! Said the Cat, 1992; In Search of the Hidden Statue, 1993; Moving Target, 1993; Stolen Affections, 1995; Running Into Trouble, 1996; The Vampire Cat Series: My Substitute Teacher's Gone Baity, 1996, The Bird-Brained Fiasco, 1996, The Phoney Baloney Professor, 1996, The Cat-Nap Cat-Astrophe, 1997. Memberships: Authors Guild; California Writers Club; National League of American Pen Women; Society of Children's Book Writers and Illustrators; Novelists Inc. Address: 5010 Jennings Way, Sacramento, CA 95819, USA.

FOLLETT Ken(neth Martin), b. 5 June 1949, Cardiff, Wales. Author. m. (1) 5 Jan 1968, 1 son, 1 daughter, (2) 8 Nov 1985. Education: BA, Honours, University College, London; Apprenticeship in Journalism. Appointment: Fellow, University College, London; President, The Dyslexia Institute; Council Member, National Literacy Trust; Chair, National Year of Reading, 1998-99. Publications: The Shakeout, 1975; The Bear Raid, 1976; The Modigliani Scandal, 1976; The Power Twins and the Worm Puzzle, 1976; The Secret of Kellerman's Studio, 1976; Paper Money, 1977; Eye of the Needle, 1978; Triple, 1979; The Key to Rebecca, 1980; The Man from St Petersburg, 1982; On Wings of Eagles, 1983; Lie Down with Lions, 1986; The Pillars of the Earth, 1989; Night Over Water, 1991; A Dangerous Fortune, 1993; A Place Called Freedom, 1995; The Third Twin, 1996; The Hammer of Eden, 1998. Other: Various Screenplays. Contributions to: Book reviews and essays. Honours: Edgar Award for Best Novel, Mystery Writers of America, 1979; Fellow, University College, London, 1995. Memberships: National Union of Journalists, UK; Writers Guild, USA. Literary Agent: Writers House Inc, New York. Address: PO Box 708, London SW10 0DH, England.

FONER Eric, b. 7 Feb 1943, New York, New York, USA. Professor of History; Writer. m. Lynn Garafola, 1 May 1980, 1 daughter. Education: BA, Columbia College, 1963; BA, Oriel College, Oxford, 1965; PhD, Columbia University, 1969. Appointments: Professor, City College and Graduate Center, City University of New York,

1973-82; Pitt Professor of American History and Institutions, Cambridge University, 1980-81; Professor, 1982-88, DeWitt Clinton Professor of History, 1988-, Columbia University; Fulbright Professor of American History, Moscow State University, 1990; Harmsworth Professor of American History, Oxford University, 1993-94. Publications: Free Soil, Free Labor, Free Men: The Ideology of the Republican Party Before the Civil War, 1970, new edition, 1995; America's Black Past: A Reader in Afro-American History, 1971; Nat Turner, 1971; Tom Paine and Revolutionary America, 1976; Politics and Ideology in the Age of the Civil War, 1980; Nothing But Freedom: Emancipation and Its Legacy, 1983; Reconstruction: America's Unfinished Revolution 1863-1877, 1988; A Short History of Reconstruction, 1990; A House Divided: America in the Age of Lincoln (with Olivia Mahoney), 1990; The New American History (editor), 1990; Reader's Companion to American History (editor with John A Garraty), 1991; Freedom's Lawmakers: A Directory of Black Officeholders During Reconstruction, 1993, revised edition, 1996; Thomas Paine, 1995; America's Reconstruction: People and Politics After the Civil War (with Olivia Mahoney), 1995. Contributions to: Scholarly journals and periodicals. Honours: American Council of Learned Societies Fellowship, 1972-73; Guggenheim Fellowship, 1975-76; National Endowment for the Humanities Senior Fellowship, 1982-83, 1996-97; Los Angeles Times Book Award for History, 1989; Bancroft Prize, 1989; Parkman Prize, 1989; Lionel Trilling Award, 1989; Owsley Prize, 1989; James Harvey Robinson Prize, American Historical Association, 1991; Literary Lion, New York Public Library, 1994; Scholar of the Year Award, New York Council for the Humanities, 1995. Memberships: American Academy of Arts and Sciences; British Academy, corresponding fellow; Organization of American Historians, president, 1993-1994. Address: 606 West 116th Street, New York, NY 10027, USA.

FONSECA James W(illiam), b. 13 Oct 1947, Fall River, Massachusetts, USA. Professor of Geography; University Administrator; Writer. m. Elaine Rae Hart, 20 Nov 1971, 1 son. Education: BA, MA, Bridgewater State College, 1969; PhD, Geography, Clark University, 1974. Appointments: Instructor, 1973-74, Assistant Professor, 1974-79, Associate Professor, 1979-95, Associate Dean, Graduate School, 1986-92, Director, Prince William Campus, 1992-98, Professor of Geography, 1996-98, George Mason University; Campus Dean, Ohio University at Zanesville, 1998-. Publications: World Regional Map Skills: Student Supplement to De Blij's Geography: Regions and Concepts (with Alice Andrews), 1981; The Urban Rank-Size Hierarchy: A Mathematical Intepretation, 1989; Atlas of American Higher Education (with Alice Andrews), 1993; Atlas of American Society (with Alice Andrews), 1995; Community Colleges in the United States: A Geographical Perspective (with Alice Andrews), 1998. Contributions to: Reference works and journals. Membership: Association of American Geographers. Address: c/o Office of the Dean, Ohio University at Zanesville, Zanesville, OH 43701, USA.

FONSS Nina, b. 20 Nov 1935, Copenhagen, Denmark. Author. m. Eric Grinstead. Education: Cand mag, Chinese, Japanese, Copenhagen University. Appointments: Copenhagen University, 12 years. Publications: Kinesisk Poesi fra T'ang-tiden, 1968; Kina Parlor, 1978; Kina Parlor, Dansk-kinesisk parlor, 1983. Membership: Danish Society of Authors. Address: Henrik Steffensvej 5, 1866 Frederiksberg C, Denmark.

FONTINEL Nancy, b. 26 Sept 1957, Chico, California, USA. Administrative Assistant. 1 son, 1 daughter. Education: AA, Christian Arts, San Jose Bible College, 1977; Floral Design Diploma, ICS, Scranton, Pennsylvania, 1994. Publications: Heat Wave, 1993; Futility, 1995. Address: 611 Wexford Way, Telford, PA 18969, USA.

FOOT Michael, b. 23 July 1913, Plymouth, England. Journalist; Politician. m. Jill Craigie, 1949. Education: Wadham College, Oxford. Appointments: Assistant Editor, 1937-38, Joint Editor, 1948-52, Editor, 1952-59,

Managing Editor, 1952-74, Tribune; Staff, 1938, Acting Editor, 1942-44, Evening Standard; Political Columnist, Daily Herald, 1944-64; Member of Parliament, Labour Party, Devonport Division of Plymouth, 1945-55, Ebbw Vale, 1960-83, Blaenau Gwent, 1983-92; Secretary of State for Employment, 1974-76; Lord President of the Council and Leader of the House of Commons, 1976-79; Deputy Leader, 1976-80, Leader, 1980-83, Labour Party. Publications: Guilty Men (with Frank Owen and Peter Howard), 1940; Armistice 1918-1939, 1940; Trial of Mussolini, 1943; Brendan and Beverley, 1944; Who Are the Patriots?, 1949; Still at Large, 1950; Full Speed Ahead, 1950; The Pen and the Sword, 1957; Parliament in Danger, 1959; Anuerin Bevan, 2 volumes, 1962, 1973; Harold Wilson: A Political Biography, 1964; Debts of Honour, 1980; Another Heart and Other Pulses, 1984; Loyalists and Loners, 1986; The Politics of Paradise, 1988; H G: The History of Mr Wells, 1995. Honours: Honorary Fellow, Wadham College, 1969; Honorary DLitt, University of Wales, 1985. Address: 308 Gray's Inn Road, London WC1X 8DY, England.

FOOT Michael (Richard Daniell), b. 14 Dec 1919, London, England. Professor of Modern History; Writer. Education: New College, Oxford. Appointments: Teacher, Oxford, 1947-59; Professor of Modern History, University of Manchester, 1967-73; Director of Studies, European Discussion Centre, 1973-75. Publications: Gladstone and Liberalism (with J L Hammond), 1952; British Foreign Policy Since 1898, 1952; Men in Uniform, 1961; SOE in France, 1966; The Gladstone Diaries (editor), 4 volumes, 1968, 1974; War and Society, 1973; Resistance, 1976; Six Faces of Courage, 1978; M19 (with J M Langley), 1979; SOE: An Outline History, 1984; Art and War, 1990; Holland at War Against Hitler (editor), 1990; The Oxford Companion to the Second World War (joint editor), 1995. Honours: French Croix de Guerre, 1945; Officer of the Order of Orange Nassau, Netherlands, 1989. Literary Agent: Peters, Fraser & Dunlop, London. Address: Martins Cottage, Bell Lane, Nuthampstead, Hertfordshire SG8 8ND, England.

FOOT Paul (Mackintosh), b. 8 Nov 1937, Haifa, Palestine. Writer; Journalist. 3 sons, 1 daughter. Education: BA, University College, Oxford, 1961. Appointments: Editor, Isis, 1961, Socialist Worker, 1974-75; President, Oxford Union, 1961; TUC Delegate, National Union of Journalists, 1967, 1971; Staff, Daily Mirror, 1979-93, Private Eye, 1993-. Publications: Immigration and Race in British Politics, 1965; The Politics of Harold Wilson, 1968; The Rise of Enoch Powell, 1969; Who Killed Hanratty?, 1971; Why You Should Be a Socialist, 1977; Red Shelley, 1981; The Helen Smith Story, 1983; Murder at the Farm: Who Killed Carl Bridgewater?, 1986; Who Framed Colin Wallace?, 1989; Words as Weapons, 1990; Quicksand, 1997; The Memory of all That, 1999. Honours: Journalist of the Year Awards, 1972, 1989; Campaigning Journalist of the Year, British Press Awards, 1980; George Orwell Prize for Journalism, 1994. Address: c/o Private Eye, 6 Carlisle Street, London W1V 5RG, England.

FOOT Philippa Ruth, b. 3 Oct 1920. Professor Emmeritus of Philosophy; Writer. m. M R D Foot, 1945, div 1960. Education: BA, 1942, MA, 1946, Somerville College, Oxford. Appointments: Lecturer in Philosophy, 1947, Fellow and Tutor, 1950-69, Vice Principal, 1967-69, Senior Research Fellow, 1970-88, Honorary Fellow, 1988-, Somerville College, Oxford; Professor of Philosophy, 1974-91, Griffin Professor, 1988-91, Professor Emeritus, 1991-, University of California, Los Angeles; Fellow, Center for Advanced Studies in the Behavioral Sciences, Stanford, California, 1981-82; Various visiting professorships. Publications: Theories of Ethics (editor), 1967; Virtues and Vices, 1978; Die Wirklichkeit des Guten, 1997. Contributions to: Scholarly journals and periodicals. Memberships: British Academy; American Academy of Arts and Sciences, fellow. Address: 15 Walton Street, Oxford OX1 2HG, England.

FOOTE (Albert) Horton (Jr), b. 14 Mar 1916, Wharton, Texas, USA. Dramatist; Scriptwriter. m. Lillian Valish, 4 June 1945, 2 sons, 2 daughters. Education: Pasadena Playhouse School Theatre, California, 1933-35; Tamara Daykarhanova School Theatre, New York City, 1937-39. Appointments: Actor, American Actors Theatre, New York City, 1939-42; Theatre Workshop Director and Producer, King-Smith School of Creative Arts, Washington, DC, 1944-45; Manager, Productions Inc, Washington, DC, 1945-48. Publications: Novel: The Chase, 1956. Plays: Texas Town, 1942; Out of My House, 1942; Only the Heart, 1944; Celebration, 1948; The Chase, 1952; The Trip to Bountiful, 1953; The Midnight Caller, 1953; A Young Lady of Property, 1954; The Traveling Lady, 1955; The Roads to Home, 1955; Tomorrow, 1960; Roots in a Parched Ground, 1962; The Road to the Graveyard, 1985; Blind Date, 1986; Habitation of Dragons, 1988; Dividing the Estate, 1989; Talking Pictures, 1990; The Young Man from Atlanta, 1994; Night Seasons, 1994; Laura Dennis, 1994. *Screenplays: Storm Fear*, 1956; *To Kill a Mockingbird*, 1962; Baby, the Rain Must Fall, 1965; Hurry Sundown, 1966; Tomorrow, 1971; Tender Mercies, 1983; 1918, 1984; On Valentine's Day, 1985; The Trip to Bountiful, 1985; Spring Moon, 1987; Convicts, 1991; Of Mice and Men, 1992. Other: Many television scripts. Honours: Academy Awards, 1962, 1983; Writers Guild of America Awards, 1962, 1989; Pulitzer Prize in Drama, 1995; American Academy of Arts and Letters Gold Medal, 1998. Membership: American Academy of Arts and Letters. Address: c/o Lucy Kroll Agency, 390 West End Avenue, New York, NY 10024, USA.

FOOTE Patricia Sandra, b. 2 Oct 1948, Nigeria. Health Writer. m. Ken Kohlen, 16 Oct 1972. Education: MA, Education, California State University at San Luis Obispo; BA, Liberal Studies, California State University at Northridge. Appointments: Board of Directors, VHL Family Alliance, California, 1993-96, Chair, California Chapter, 1993-97; Education and Consumer Committees, Pacific Southwest Regional Genetics Network, 1994-; Board of Directors, San Luis Obispo Mozart Festival, 1995-98. Publication: How Are You? Manage Your Own Medical Journey, 1998. Contributions to: Coping Magazine; Parents Helping Parents; Genetically Speaking; VHL Family Forum. Honour: Youth Outreach for the Performing Arts Award. Address: PO Box 3612, San Luis Obispo, CA 93403, USA.

FOOTE Shelby, b. 17 Nov 1916, Greenville, Mississippi, USA. Author; Historian; Dramatist. m. Gwyn Rainer, 5 Sept 1956, 1 son, 1 daughter. Education: University of North Carolina, 1935-37. Appointments: Guest Lecturer, University of Virginia, 1963; Playwright-in-Residence, Arena Stage, Washington, DC, 1963-64; Writer-in-Residence, Hollins College, Virginia, 1968; Academic Advisory Board, US Naval Academy, 1988-89. Publications: Fiction: Tournament, 1949; Follow Me Down, 1950; Love in a Dry Season, 1951; Shiloh, 1952; Jordan County: A Landscape in Narrative, 1954; September September, 1977. Non-Fiction: The Civil War: A Narrative: Vol I: Fort Sumter to Perryville, 1958, Vol II: Fredericksburg to Meridian, 1963, Vol III: Red River to Appomattox, 1974; The Novelist's View of History, 1981; Stars in Their Courses, 1994; The Beleaguered City, 1995. Play: Jordan County: A Landscape in the Round, 1964. Editor: The Night Before Chancellorsville and Other Civil War Stories, 1957; Chickamauga and Other Civil War Stories, 1993. Other: The Civil War, adapted for PBS telecast, 1990. Honours: Guggenheim Fellowships, 1955-57; Ford Foundation Grant, 1963; Fletcher Pratt Awards, 1963, 1974; Distinguished Alumnus, University of North Carolina, 1975; Dos Passos Prize for Literature, 1988; Charles Frankel Award, 1992; St Louis Literary Award, 1992; Nevins-Freeman Award, 1992; Several honorary doctorates. Memberships: American Academy of Arts and Letters; Fellowship of Southern Writers; Society of American Historians. Address: 542 East Parkway South, Memphis, TN 38104, USA.

FORAN Charles William, b. 2 Aug 1960, North York, Ontario, Canada. Writer. m. Mary, 2 daughters. Education: BA, University of Toronto, 1983; MA, University College, Dublin, 1984. Appointments: Librarian and Freelance Journalist, New York State, 1985-88; Teacher, Beijing College, 1988-90; Freelance Writer and Journalist, 1990-. Publications: Coming Attractions (5 short stories), 1987; Sketches in Winter (non-fiction), 1992; Kitchen Music (novel), 1994; The Last House of Ulster (non-fiction), 1995; Butterfly Lovers (novel), 1996; The Story of My Life (So Far) (non-fiction), 1998. Contributions to: Globe; Mail; Montreal Gazette; Saturday Night Magazine. Honours: Finalist, QSpell Award and National Magazine Award, 1992, 1994, 1996; Winner, QSpell Award, Non-Fiction, 1995; Finalist, Governor General's Literary Award, Non-Fiction, 1995; Winner, QSpell Award, Fiction, 1990. Memberships: PEN Canada; Writers Union of Canada. Address: 298 Boswell Avenue, Peterborough, Ontario K9J 5G3, Canada.

FORBES Bryan, b. 22 July 1926, Stratford, London, England. Film Executive; Director; Screenwriter. m. Nanette Newman, 1955, 2 daughters. Education: West Ham Secondary School; Royal Academy of Dramatic Art. Publications: Truth Lies Sleeping, 1951; The Distant Laughter, 1972; Notes for a Life, 1974; The Slipper and the Rose, 1976; Ned's Girl, 1977; Familiar Strangers, 1979; The Despicable Race, 1980; The Rewrite Man, 1983; The Endless Game, 1986; A Song at Twlight, 1989; A Divided Life, 1992; The Twisted Playground, 1993; Partly Cloudy, 1995. Honours: Best Screenplay Awards; UN Award; Many film festival prizes; Honorary DL, University of London, 1987. Memberships: Beatrix Potter Society; National Youth Theatre of Great Britain; Writers Guild of Great Britain. Address: c/o The Bookshop, Virginia Water, Surrey, England.

FORBES John, b. 1 Sept 1950, Melbourne, Victoria, Australia. Poet; Writer. Education: BA, University of Sydney, 1973. Appointment: Editor, Surfer's Paradise, 1974-83. Publications: Tropical Skiing, 1976; On the Beach, 1977; Drugs, 1980; Stalin's Holidays, 1981; The Stunned Mullet and Other Poems, 1988; New and Selected Poems, 1992. Contributions to: Newspapers and magazines. Honours: New Poetry Prize, 1973; Southerly Prize, 1976; Grace Leverson Prize, 1993. Membership: Australian Society of Authors. Address: 54 Morris Street, Summerhill, New South Wales, Australia.

FORBES (DeLoris Florine) Stanton, (Forbes Rydell, Tobias Wells), b. 29 July 1923, Kansas City, Missouri, USA. Writer. m. William James Forbes, 29 Oct 1948, 2 sons, 1 daughter. Appointment: Associate Editor, Wellesley Townsmen, Massachusetts, 1960-72. Publications: Over 40 mystery novels. Contributions to: Magazines. Honour: Best Mystery of the Year, 1963. Membership: Mystery Writers of America. Address: Sanford, FL 32771, USA.

FORCHE Carolyn (Louise), b. 28 Apr 1950, Detroit, Michigan, USA. Poet; Writer; Associate Professor. m. Henry E Mattison, 27 Dec 1984, 1 son. Education BA, Michigan State University, 1972; MFA, Bowling Green State University, 1975. Appointments: Visiting Lecturer in Poetry, Michigan State University, Justin Morrill College, East Lansing, 1974; Visiting Lecturer, 1975, Assistant Professor, 1976-78, San Diego State University; Journalist and Human Rights Activist, El Salvador, 1978-80; Visiting Lecturer, 1979, Visiting Associate Professor, 1982-83, University of Virginia; Assistant Professor, 1980, Associate Professor, 1981, University of Arkansas at Fayetteville; Visiting Writer, New York University, 1983, 1985, Vassar College, 1984; Adjunct Associate Professor, Columbia University, 1984-85; Visiting Associate Professor, University of Minnesota, 1985; Writer-in-Residence, State University of New York at Albany, 1985; Associate Professor, George Mason University, 1994-. Publications: Poetry: Gathering the Tribes, 1976; The Country Between Us, 1981; The Angel of History, 1994. Non-Fiction: Women in the Labor Movement, 1835-1925: An Annotated Bibliography (with Martha Jane Soltow), 1972; Women and War in El Salvador (editor), 1980; El Salvador: The Work of Thirty Photographers (with others), 1983. Other: Claribel Alegria: Flowers from the Volcano (translator), 1982; Against Forgetting: Twentieth-Century Poetry of Witness (editor), 1993. Contributions to: Anthologies and periodicals. Honours: Devine Memeorial Fellowship in Poetry, 1975; Yale Series of Younger Poets Award, 1975;

Tennessee Williams Fellowship in Poetry, Bread Loaf Writers Conference, 1976; National Endowment for the Arts Fellowships, 1977, 1984; Guggenheim Fellowship, 1978; Emily Clark Balch Prize, Virginia Quarterly Review, 1979; Alice Fay di Castagnola Award, Poetry Society of America, 1981; Lamont Poetry Selection Award, Academy of American Poets, 1981; Los Angeles Times Book Award for Poetry, 1994. Memberships: Academy of American Poets; Amnesty International; Associated Writing Programs, president, 1994-; PEN American Centre; Poetry Society of America; Theta Sigma Phi. Address: c/o Department of English, George Mason University, 4400 University Drive, Fairfax, VA 22030, USA.

FORD David. See: **HARKNETT Terry.**

FORD Kirk. See: **SPENCE William (John Duncan).**

FORD Peter, b. 3 June 1936, Harpenden, Hertfordshire, England. Author; Editorial Consultant. Div, 2 sons, 1 daughter. Education: St George's School, 1948-52. Appointments: Editor, Cassell, 1958-61; Senior Copy Editor, Penguin Books, 1961-64; Senior Editor, Thomas Nelson, 1964-70. Publications: The Fool on the Hill, 1975; Scientists and Inventors, 1979; The True History of the Elephant Man, 1980; Medical Mysteries, 1985; The Picture Buyer's Handbook, 1988; A Collector's Guide to Teddy Bears, 1990; Rings and Curtains: Family and Personal Memoirs, 1992; The Monkey's Paw and Other Stories by W W Jacobs, 1994; A Willingness to Die: Memoirs of Brian Kingcome, 1999. Memberships: Society of Authors; New York Academy of Sciences; Folklore Society. Address: The Storehouse, Longhope, Orkney KW16 3PQ, Scotland.

FORD Richard, b. 16 Feb 1944, Jackson, Mississippi, USA. Writer. m. Kristina Hensley, 1968. Education: BA, Michigan State University, 1966; MFA, University of California, Irvine, 1970. Appointments: Lecturer, University of Michigan, Ann Arbor, 1974-76; Assistant Professor of English, Williams College, Williamstown, Massachusetts, 1978-79; Lecturer, Princeton University, 1979-80. Publications: Fiction: A Piece of My Heart, 1976; The Ultimate Good Luck, 1981; The Sportswriter, 1986; Rock Springs: Stories, 1987; Wildlife, 1990; Independence Day, 1995; Women with Men, 1997. Play: American Tropical, 1983. Screenplay: Bright Angel, 1991. Editor: The Best American Short Stories (with Shannon Ravenal), 1990; The Granta Book of the American Short Story, 1992. Contributions to: Various periodicals. Honours: Guggenheim Fellowship, 1977-78; National Endowment for the Arts Fellowships, 1979-80, 1985-86; Mississippi Academy of Arts and Letters Literature Award, 1987; American Academy and Institute of Arts and Letters Award, 1989; Echoing Green Foundation Award, 1991; Pulitzer Prize in Fiction, 1996; PEN-Faulkner Award, 1996. Memberships: American Academy of Arts and Letters; PEN; Writers Guild. Address: c/o Amanda Urban, International Creative Management, 40 West 57th Street, New York, NY 10019, USA.

FORDHAM William. See: **SEARLE Ronald.**

FOREMAN Richard, b. 10 June 1937, New York, New York, USA. Dramatist; Director. m. (1) Amy Taubin, 1961, div 1972. (2) Kate Manhelm, 1986. Education: BA, Brown University, 1959; MFA, Yale University, 1962. Appointments: Artistic Director, Ontological-Hysteric Theatre, New York City, 1968-, Theatre O H, Paris, 1973-85; Director-in-Residence, New York Shakespeare Festival, 1975-76; Director, Broadway and Off-Broadway plays. Publications: Dr Selavy's Magic Theater, 1972; Rhoda in Potatoland, 1976; Theatre of Images, 1977; Reverberation Machines, 1985; Film is Evil: Radio is Good, 1987; Unbalancing Acts: Foundations for a Theater, 1992; My Head Was a Sledgehammer, 1995. Honours: Creative Artists Public Service Fellow, New York State Arts Council, 1971, 1974; Guggenheim Fellowship, 1972; Rockefeller Foundation Fellow, 1974; Lifetime Achievement Award, National Endowment for the Arts, 1990; American Academy of Arts and Letters Prize

in Literature, 1992; Honorary DArts, Brown University, 1993; John D and Catharine T MacArthur Foundation Fellow, 1995-2000. Memberships: Dramatists Guild: PEN; Society of Stage Directors. Address: 152 Wooster Street, New York, NY 10012, USA.

FORGAS Joseph Paul, b. 16 May 1947, Budapest, Hungary. University Professor. m. Letitia Jane Carr, 16 Mar 1974, 2 sons. Education: BA, Honours, Macquarie University, 1974; DPhil, 1977; DSc, 1990, University of Oxford. Appointments: Associate Editor, Cognition and Emotion, 1995-; Consulting Editor, Journal of Personality and Social Psychology, 1996-. Publications: Social Episodes, 1979; Social Cognition, 1981; Interpersonal Behavior, 1985; Affect, Cognition - Social Behaviour (with K Fiedler), 1988; Emotion and Social Judgement, 1991; Soziale Kognition und Kommunikation, 1993. Contributions to: Over 100 articles - chapters published. Honours: APS Early Career Award, 1983; Alexander von Humboldt Prize, 1994; Fellow, Academy of Social Sciences in Australia, 1987-; Fellow, American Psychological Society, 1994-; Fellow, Society for Personality and Social Psychology, 1994. Address: c/o Department of Psychology, University of New South Wales, Sydney 2052, Australia.

FORIO Robert. See: **WEISS Irving.**

FORKER Charles R(ush), b. 11 Mar 1927, Pittsburgh, Pennsylvania, USA. Professor Emeritus; Writer. Education: AB, Bowdoin College, 1951; BA, 1953, MA, 1955, Merton College, Oxford; PhD, Harvard University, 1957. Appointments: Instructor, University of Wisconsin, 1957-59; Instructor, 1959-61, Assistant Professor, 1961-65, Associate Professor, 1965-68, Professor, 1968-92, Professor Emeritus, 1992-, Indiana University; Visiting Professor, University of Michigan, 1969-70, Dartmouth College, 1982-83, Concordia University, Montreal, 1989. Publications: James Shirley: The Cardinal (editor), 1964; William Shakespeare: Henry V (editor), 1971; Edward Phillips's "History of the Literature of England and Scotland": A Translation from the "Compendiosa Enumeratio Poetarum" with an Introduction and Commentary (with Daniel G Calder), 1973; Visions and Voices of the New Midwest (associate editor), 1978; Henry V: An Annotated Bibliography (with Joseph Candido), 1983; Skull Beneath the Skin: The Achievement of John Webster, 1986; Fancy's Images: Contexts, Settings, and Perspectives in Shakespeare and His Contemporaries, 1990; Christopher Marlowe: Edward the Second (editor), 1994; Richard II: The Critical Tradition, 1998. Contributions to: Scholarly books and journals. Honours: Fulbright Fellowship, England, 1951-53; Folger Fellow, 1963; Huntington Library Fellow, 1969; National Endowment for the Humanities Senior Research Fellow, 1980-81. Memberships: American Association of University Professors; Guild of Anglican Scholars, president; International Shakespeare Association; Malone Society; Marlowe Society; Modern Language Association; Renaissance Society of America; Shakespeare Society of America; World Centre for Shakespeare Studies, advisory board. Address: 1219 East Maxwell Lane, Bloomington, IN 47401, USA.

FORMAN Robert K(raus) C(onrad), b. 3 Aug 1947, Baltimore, Maryland, USA. Associate Professor of Religion; Writer; Editor. m. Yvonne Forman, 20 Nov 1975, 2 children. Education: BA in Philosophy, University of Chicago, 1969; MA in Religion, 1981, MPhil in Religion, 1985, PhD in Religion, 1988, Columbia University. Appointments: Adjunct Professor, New School for Social Research, New York City, 1985-88; Instructor, Union Theological Seminary, New York City, 1987; Visiting Assistant Professor, Vassar College, 1989-90; Associate Professor of Religion, Hunter College, 1990-; Founder-Executive Editor, Journal of Consciousness Studies: Controversies in Science and the Humanities, 1991-. Publications: The Problem of Pure Consciousness (editor), 1990; Meister Eckhart: Mystic as Theologian: An Experiment in Methodology, 1991; The Religions of Asia, 3rd edition (general editor), 1993; Religions of the World, 3rd edition (general editor), 1993; The Innate Capacity (editor), 1997; Mysticism, Mind, Consciousness,

forthcoming. Contributions to: More than 30 scholarly books and journals. Honours: New World Foundation Grants, 1992, 1993, 1994; Senior Fellow, Columbia University Writing Program, 1993; City University of New York Research Grant, 1996; Fetzer Institute Grant, 1997. Memberships: American Academy of Religion; Association for Asian Studies; Association for Transpersonal Psychology; Institute for Noetic Sciences; United States Millennium Commission; Sankat Mocan (Save the Ganges) Foundation. Address: 383 Broadway, Hastings-on-Hudson, NY 10706. USA.

FORREST Richard (Stockton), (Stockton Woods), b. 8 May 1932, Orange, New Jersey, USA. Writer. m. (1) Frances Anne Reese, 20 Dec 1952, div 1955, 1 son, (2) Mary Bolan Brumby, 11 May 1955, dec 1996, 5 children. Education: New York Dramatic Workshop, 1950; University of South Carolina, 1953-55. Publications: Who Killed Mr Garland's Mistress?, 1974; A Child's Garden of Death, 1975; The Wizard of Death, 1977; Death Through the Looking Glass, 1978; The Death in the Willows, 1979; The Killing Edge, 1980; The Laughing Man, 1980; Death at Yew Corner, 1981; Game Bet, 1981; The Man Who Heard Too Much, 1983; Death Under the Lilacs, 1985; Lark, 1986; Death on the Mississippi, 1989; The Complete Nursing Home Guide (with Mary Forrest), 1990; Retirement Living (with Mary Forrest), 1991; Pied Piper of Death, 1997. Contributions to: Periodicals. Honour: Edgar Allan Poe Award, Mystery Writers of America, 1975. Membership: Mystery Writers of America. Address: 108 Park Lane West, Charlottesville, VA 22903, USA.

FORSLOFF Carol Marie Matthews, b. 31 Mar 1941. Executive Vocational Consultant. m. Delbert R Forsloff, 14 Feb 1984, 2 sons, 1 daughter. Education: BA, University of Washington, 1967; MA, State University of New York, 1968. Appointments: Teacher, Saddle River, New Jersey, 1968; Education Director, ACLD, Pittsburgh, 1969-74; Learning Disability Consultant, Bethel Park Schools, Alleghony Community College, 1974-76; Education Director, Three Rivers Youth, Pittsburgh, 1976-77; Director, Student Services and Instructor, Hawaii Pacific College, 1977-79; Teacher, Kaisen High School, Honolulu, 1980-81; Senior Counselor, Supervisor, Crawford Rehabilitation, 1984-92; Executive Consultant, Administrator, Heritage Counseling, 1992-. Publications: Learning Disabilities in Adolescents and Adults, South Campus Allegheny Community College, 1974; Vocational Profiling: Workplace Solutions, 1998. Contributions to: A Community Program for the Learning Disabled, Academic Therapy, 1973; Language and Learning Therapy in a Community College, Bulletin of the Orton Society, 1977; Case Study of an Adult Dyslexic, Perspectives on Dyslexia, 1977. Membership: National Education Writers Association. Literary Agent: Rusty Walker. Address: 84-680 Kili Dr #7101 Waianoie, HI 96792, USA.

FORSTER Margaret, b. 25 May 1938, Carlisle, Cumberland, England. Writer. m. Hunter Davies, 11 June 1960, 1 son, 2 daughters. Education: BA, Sommerville College, Oxford, 1960. Appointments: Teacher, Barnbury Girls School, London, 1961-63; Chief Non-Fiction Reviewer, London Evening Standard, 1977-80. Publications: Georgy Girl, 1963; The Bogeyman, 1966; The Park, 1968; Mr Bone's Retreat, 1971; Mother, Can You Hear Me?, 1979; Marital Rites, 1981; Private Papers, 1986; Lady's Maid, 1989; The Battle for Christobel, 1991. Membership: Royal Society of Literature. Address: 11 Boscastle Road, London NW5, England.

FORSYTH Frederick, b. 25 Aug 1938, Ashford, Kent, England. Author. m. Carole Forsyth, Sept 1973, 2 sons. Education: Tonbridge School. Appointments: Reporter, Eastern Daily Press, Norfolk, 1958-61; Reporter, Paris, 1962-63, Chief of Bureau, East Berlin, 1963-64, Reuters; Radio and Television Reporter, BBC, 1965-66; Assistant Diplomatic Correspondent, BBC TV, 1967-68; Freelance Journalist, Nigeria and Biafra, 1968-69. Publications: Non-Fiction: The Biafra Story, 1969, revised edition as The Making of an African Legend: The Biafra Story, 1977; Emeka, 1982; I Remember: Reflections on Fishing in

Childhood, 1995. Novels: The Day of the Jackal, 1971; The Odessa File, 1972; The Dogs of War, 1974; The Shepherd, 1975; The Devil's Alternative, 1979; The Fourth Protocol, 1984; The Negotiator, 1988; The Deceiver, 1991; The Fist of God, 1994; Icon, 1996. Other: No Comebacks: Collected Short Stories, 1982; Great Flying Stories (editor), 1991. Contributions to: Newspapers and magazines. Honour: Edgar Allan Poe Award, Mystery Writers of America, 1971. Address: c/o Bantam Books, 62-63 Uxbridge Road, London W5 5SA, England.

FOSSE Jon, b. 29 Sept 1959, Haugesund, Norway. Author; Dramatist. m. (1) 1980, div. 1991, 1 son, (2) Grethe Fatima Syéd, 9 Oct 1993, 1 daughter. Education: Cand philol, Comparative Literature, University of Bergen. Appointments: Teacher of Creative Writing, Academy of Writing, Bergen, 1987-93; Professional Writer, 1993-. Publications include: Novels: Raudt, svart, 1983; Stengd gitar, 1985; Naustet, 1989; Flaskesamlaren, 1991; Bly og vatn, 1992; Melancholia I, 1995; Melancholia II, 1996; Shorter prose: Blod. Steinen er. Forteljing, 1987; To forteljingar, 1993; Prosa frå ein oppvekst. Kortprosa, 1994; Eldre kortare prosa, 1997; Books of poems: Engel med vatn i augene, 1986; Hundens bevegelsar, 1990; Hund og engel, 1992; Nye dikt, 1997; Plays: Og aldri skal vi skiljast, 1994; Namnet, 1995; Nokon kjem til å komme, 1996; Barnet, Mor og barn, Sonen. Tre skodespel, 1997; Natta syng sine songar, Ein sommars dag. To skodespel, 1998; Draum om hausten, 1999; Essays: Frå telling via showing til writing, 1989; Gnostiske essays, 1999; Books for children. Honours: Noregs Mållags Prize for Children's Books, 1990; Andersson-Rysst Fondet, 1992; Prize for Literature in New Norwegian, 1993; Samlags Prize, 1994; Ibsen Prize, 1996; Sunnmoers Prize, 1996; Melsom Prize, 1997; Asehoug Prize, 1997. Memberships include: Norwegian Society of Authors; Norwegian Society of Dramatists. Literary Agents: For books: Samlaget, Boks 4672 Sofienberg, 0506 Oslo, Norway; For plays: Colombine Teaterförlag, Skeppargatan 70, 11459 Stockholm, Sweden. Address: Storetveitvegen 47, 5032 Minde, Norway.

FOSTER Cecil Adolphus, b. 26 Sept 1954, Barbados, West Indies. Writer; Journalist. 3 sons. Education: Diploma, Mass Communications, University of the West Indies, 1978; BA Adminastrative Studies, York University, Toronto, 1982; BA Hons, Economics, York University, Toronto, 1984. Publications: No Man in the House, 1992; Sleep on Beloved, 1994; Caribana: The Greatest Celebration, 1995; A Place Called Heaven: The Meaning of Being Black, 1996; Slammin' Tar, 1998; Island Wing, 1998. Honour: Gordon Mantador Award, 1997. Membership: PEN Canada. Literary Agent: Bev Slopen, Toronto, Canada. Address: 111 Davisville Ave, Apt 208, Toronto, M45 1G4, Canada.

FOSTER David (Manning), b. 15 May 1944, Sydney, New South Wales, Australia. Novelist. Education: BSc, Chemistry, University of Sydney, 1967; PhD, Australian National University, Canberra, 1970. Publications: The Pure Land, 1974; The Empathy Experiment, 1977; Moonlite, 1981; Plumbum, 1983; Dog Rock: A Postal Pastoral, 1985; The Adventures of Christian Rosy Cross, 1986; Testostero, 1987; The Pale Blue Crochet Coathanger Cover, 1988; Mates of Mars, 1991; Self Portraits (editor), 1991; A Slab of Fosters, 1994; The Glade Within the Grove, 1996; The Ballad of Erinungarah, 1997; Crossing the Blue Montain (contributor), 1997; In the New Country, 1999. Short Stories: North South West: Three Novellas, 1973; Escape to Reality, 1977; Hitting the Wall: Two Novellas, 1989. Honours: The Age Award, 1974; Australian National Book Council Award, 1981; New South Wales Premier's Fellowship, 1986; Keating Fellowship, 1991-94; James Joyce Foundation Award, 1996; Miles Franklin Award, 1997; Shortlisted, International Dublin IMPAC Award, 1998. Address: PO Box 57, Bundanoon, New South Wales 2578, Australia.

FOSTER Donald Wayne, b. 22 June 1950, Chicago, Illinois, USA. Associate Professor; Writer. m. Gwen Bell Foster, 29 Dec 1974, 2 sons. Education: BA, Wheaton College, 1972; MA, 1983, PhD, 1985, University of California. Appointments: Visiting Lecturer, University of California, Santa Barbara, 1984-85; Assistant Professor, 1986-90, Associate Professor, 1990-, Jean Webster Chair of Dramatic Literature, 1991-, Vassar College. Publications: Eleg, by W S: A Study in Attribution; Women's Works: An Anthology of British Literature; SHAXICON: A lexical database for Shakespeare studies, 1995. Contributions to: Books and scholarly journals. Honours: William Riley Parker Prize; Delaware Shakespeare Prize. Memberships: Modern Language Association; Shakespeare Association of America; Renaissance English Text Society; American Association of University Professors. Address: Box 388, Vassar College, Poughkeepsie, NY 12601, USA.

FOSTER J(ames) A(nthony), (Tony Foster), b. 2 Aug 1932, Winnipeg, Manitoba, Canada. Writer. m. 10 Oct 1964, 1 son, 2 daughters. Education: University of Brunswick, 1950. Publications: Zig Zag to Armageddon, 1978; By-Pass, 1982; The Money Burn, 1984; A coeur ouvert, 1985; Heart of Oak: A Pictorial History of the Royal Canadian Navy, 1985; Meeting of Generals, 1986; Sea Wings: A Pictorial History of Canada's Waterborne Defence Aircraft, 1986; Muskets to Missiles, 1987; Rue du Bac, 1987; For Love and Glory, 1989; The Bush Pilots: A Canadian Phenomena, 1990; Ransom for a God, 1990; The Sound and the Silence, 1990. Memberships: Canadian Authors Association; PEN; Writers Guild of America; Writers' Union of Canada. Address: 67 Briarwood Crescent, Halifax, Nova Scotia B3M 1P2, Canada.

FOSTER Jeanne See: **WILLIAMS Jeanne.**

FOSTER John Bellamy, b. 19 Aug 1953, Seattle, Washington, USA. Writer. m. Laura Tamkin, 30 Aug 1987, 1 son, 1 daughter. Education: BA, The Evergreen State College, 1975; MA, York University, 1977; PhD, York University, 1984. Publications: The Faltering Economy (editor with Henryk Szlaifer), 1984; The Theory of Monopoly Capitalism, 1986; The Limits of Environmentalism Without Class (pamphlet), 1993; The Vulnerable Planet, 1994. Contributions to: Monthly Review; Quarterly Journal of Economics; Capitalism, Nature, Socialism; Review of Radical Political Economy; Science and Society; Dollars and Sense. Address: c/o Department of Sociology, University of Oregon, Eugene, OR 97403, USA.

FOSTER Linda Nemec, b. 29 May 1950, Garfield Heights, Ohio, USA. Poet; Writer; Teacher. m. Anthony Jesse Foster, 26 Oct 1974, 1 son, 1 daughter. Education: BA, Aquinas College, Grand Rapids, 1972; MFA, Goddard College, Plainfield, Vermont, 1979. Appointments: Teacher of Creative Writing and Poetry, Michigan Council for the Arts, 1980-98; Instructor of English Composition, Ferris State University, 1983-84; Director of Literature Programming, Urban Institute for Contemporary Arts, Grand Rapids, 1989-95; Lecturer in Poetry, Aquinas College, 1999-; Guest Lecturer and Speaker, various schools, colleges, and conferences. Publications: A History of the Body, 1987; A Modern Fairy Tale: The Baba Yaga Poems, 1992; Trying to Balance the Heart, 1993; Living in the Fire Nest, 1996. Contributions to: Reviews, journals, and magazines. Honours: Creative Artist Grants in Poetry, Michigan Council for the Arts, 1984, 1990, 1996; Grand Prize, American Poetry Association, 1986; Honourable Mention, Writers' Digest, 1987; Prizewinner, McGuffin Poetry Contest, 1987, 1994; Passages North National Poetry Competition, 1988; Poetry/Visual Art Selections, Sage College, New York, 1994, 1995; Arts Foundation of Michigan Fellowship in Poetry, 1996. Memberships: Academy of American Poets; Detroit Women Writers; Poetry Resource Center of Michigan, executive committee; Urban Institute for Contemporary Arts. Address: Wilshire Drive South East, Grand Rapids, MI 49506, USA.

FOSTER Paul, b. 15 Oct 1931, Pennsgrove, New Jersey, USA. Dramatist; Screenwriter. Education: BA, Rutgers University; LLB, New York University Law School. Publications: 25 books of plays including: Tom Paine, 1971; Madonna in the Orchard, 1971; Satyricon, 1972; Elizabeth I, 1972; Marcus Brutus, 1976; Silver Queen Saloon, 1976; Mellon and the National Art Gallery, 1980; A Kiss is Just a Kiss, 1984; 3 Mystery Comedies, 1985; The Dark and Mr Stone, 1985; Odon von Horvath's Faith, Hope and Charity, translation, 1987; Make Believe (with music by Solt Dome), musical book and lyrics, 1994; Films: Smile, 1980; Cop and the Anthem, 1982; When You're Smiling, 1983; Cinderella, 1984; Home Port, 1984. Contributions to: Off-Off Broadway Book, 1972; Best American Plays of the Modern Theatre, 1975; New Stages magazine. Honours: Rockefeller Foundation Fellowship, 1967; British Arts Council Award, 1973; J S Guggenheim Fellowship, 1974; Theater Heute Award, 1977. Memberships: Dramatists Guild; Society of Composers and Dramatic Authors, France; Players Club, New York City. Address: 44 West 10th Street, New York, NY 10011, USA.

FOULKE Robert Dana, b. 25 Apr 1930, Minneapolis, USA. Professor; Author; Travel Writer. m. Patricia Ann Nelson, 29 Dec 1953, 1 son, 2 daughters. Education: AB, Princeton University, 1952; MA, 1957, PhD, 1961, University of Minnesota. Appointments: Instructor in English, University of Minnesota, 1956-59, 1960-61; Assistant Professor of English, 1961-66, Associate Professor, 1966-70, Trinity College, Hartford; Professor of English, 1970-92, Chair of Department, 1970-80, Skidmore College; Visiting Associate and Life Member, Clare Hall, Cambridge, 1976-77, 1990-91; Visiting Fellow, Department of English, Princeton University, 1988. Publications: An Anatomy of Literature (co-author and editor), 1972; The Writer's Mind (co-editor), 1983; The Sea Voyage Narrative, 1997. Travel Guides: Europe Under Canvas, 1980; Fielding's Motoring and Camping Europe, 1986; Day Trips and Getaway Vacations in New England, 1983; Day Trips and Getaway Vacations in Mid-Atlantic States, 1986; Exploring Europe By Car, 1991; Fielding's Great Sights of Europe, 1994; Colonial America, 1995; Romantic Weekends, New England, 1998. Honours: Fulbright Fellow, University of London, 1959-60; Alexander O Vietor Fellow, John Certor Brown Library, Brown University, 1993. Memberships: College English Association; Modern Language Association; Joseph Conrad Society; Melville Society; American Society of Journalists and Authors; Society of American Travel Writers; Travel Journalists Guild. Literary Agent: Denise Marcil, New York, USA. Address: 25 Dark Bay Lane, Lake George, NY 12845, USA.

FOWLER Alastair (David Shaw), b. 17 Aug 1930, Glasgow, Scotland. Professor of English; Writer; Editor. m. Jenny Catherine Simpson, 23 Dec 1950, 1 son, 1 daughter. Education: MA, University of Edinburgh, 1952; MA, 1955, DPhil, 1957, DLitt, 1972, University of Oxford. Appointments: Junior Research Fellow, Queen's College, Oxford, 1955-59; Instructor, Indiana University, 1957; Lecturer, University College, Swansea, 1959; Fellow and Tutor in English Literature, Brasenose College, Oxford, 1962-71; Visiting Professor, Columbia University, 1964; Member, Institute for Advanced Study, Princeton, New Jersey, 1966, 1980; Visiting Professor, 1969, 1979, 1985-90, Professor of English, 1990-, University of Virginia; Professor of English, 1990-, University of Virginia; Regius Professor of Rhetoric and English Literature, 1972-84, Professor Emeritus, 1984-, University Fellow, 1985-87, University of Edinburgh; Advisory Editor, New Literary History, 1972-; Visiting Fellow, Council of the Humanities, Princeton University, 1974, Humanities Research Centre, Canberra, 1980; Visiting Fellow, All Souls College, Oxford, 1984; General Editor, Longman Annotated Anthologies of English Verse, 1977-80; Member, Editorial Board, English Literary Renaissance, 1978-, Word and Image, 1984-91, The Seventeenth Century, 1986-, Connotations, 1990-, English Review, 1990-, Translation and Literature, 1990-. Publications: De re poetica, by Richard Wills (editor and translator), 1958; Spenser and the Numbers of Time, 1964; Spenser's Images of Life, by C S Lewis (editor), 1967; The Poems of John Milton (editor with John Carey), 1968; Triumphal Forms, 1970; Silent Poetry (editor), 1970; Topics in Criticism (editor with Christopher Butler), 1971;

Seventeen, 1971; Conceitful Thought, 1975; Catacomb Suburb, 1976; Edmund Spenser, 1977; From the Domain of Arnheim, 1982; Kinds of Literature, 1982; A History of English Literature, 1987; The New Oxford Book of Seventeenth Century Verse (editor), 1991; The Country House Poem, 1994; Time's Purpled Masquers, 1996; Milton: Paradise Lost (editor), 1998. Contributions to: Scholarly books and journals. Membership: Fellow, British Academy, 1974. Address: 11 East Claremont Street, Edinburgh EH7 4HT, Scotland.

FOWLER Don D, b. 24 Apr 1936, Torrey, Utah, USA. Professor of Anthropology; Writer. m. Catherine Sweeney, 14 June 1963. Education: Weber State College, 1954-55; BA, 1959, Graduate Studies, 1959-62, University of Utah; PhD, University of Pittsburgh, 1965. Appointments: Instructor, 1964-65, Assistant Professor, 1965-67, Associate Professor of Anthropology and Executive Director of Human Systems Center of the Desert Research Institute, 1968-71, Research Professor and Executive Director of the Social Sciences Center of the Desert Research Institute, 1971-78, Mamie Kelberg Professor of Historic Preservation and Anthropology, 1978-, Chairperson, Department of Anthropology, 1990-98, University of Nevada, Reno; Visiting Postdoctoral Fellow, 1967-68, Research Associate, 1970-, Smithsonian Institution, Washington, DC. Publications: Down the Colorado: John Wesley Powell's Diary of the First Trip Through the Grand Canyon (with Eliot Porter), 1969; The Anthropology of the Numa: John Wesley Powell's Manuscripts on Great Basin Indians, 1968-1980 (with C S Fowler), 1971; "Photographed all the Best Scenery": Jack Hillers' Diary of the Powell Expedition, 1871-1875 (editor), 1971; In Sacred Manner We Live: Edward S Curtis' Indian Photographs, 1972; Material Culture of the Numa: The John Wesley Powell Collection, 1867-1880 (with J F Matley), 1979; American Archaeology Past and Future: A Celebration of the Society for American Archaeology, 1935-1985 (editor with D J Metzger and J A Sabloff), 1986; Anthropology of the Desert West: Essays in Honor of Jesse D Jennings (editor with Carol J Condie), 1986; Regional Conferences: Summary Report, Society for American Archaeology (editor with Cynthia Irwin-Williams), 1986; The Western Photographs of Jack Hillers, "Myself in the Water", 1989; Others Knowing Others: Perspectives on Ethnographic Careers (editor with Donald L Hardesty), 1994. Contributions to: Many scholarly journals. Honours: Many private and government grants; Distinguished Graduate Medal, University of Pittsburgh, 1986. Memberships: American Anthropological Association, fellow; American Society for Ethnohistory; Current Anthropology; Society for American Archaeology, president, 1985-87; Southwestern Anthropological Association. Address: 1010 Foothill Road, Reno, NV 89511, USA.

FOWLER Marian Elizabeth, b. 15 Oct 1929, Newmarket, Ontario, Canada. Writer. m. Dr Rodney Singleton Fowler, 19 Sept 1953, div 1977, 1 son, 1 daughter. Education: BA, Honours, English, 1951, MA, English, 1965, PhD, English, 1970, University of Toronto, Canada. Publications: The Embroidered Tent: Five Gentlewomen in Early Canada, 1982; Redney: A Life of Sara Jeannette Duncan, 1983; Below the Peacock Fan: First Ladies of the Raj, 1987; Blenheim: Biography of a Palace, 1989; In a Gilded Cage: From Heiress to Duchess, 1993; The Way She Looks Tonight: Five Women of Style, 1996. Contributions to: English Studies in Canada; University of Toronto Quarterly; Dalhousie Review; Ontario History; Dictionary of Canadian Biography; Oxford Companion to Canadian Literature; New Canadian Encyclopaedia. Honours: Governor-General's Gold Medal in English, 1951; Canadian Biography Award, 1979. Address: Apt 505, 77 St Clair Avenue East, Toronto, Ontario M4T 1M5, Canada.

FOWLES John (Robert), b. 31 Mar 1926, Leigh-on-Sea, Essex, England. Writer; Poet; Dramatist. m. (1) Elizabeth Whitton, 1956, dec 1990, (2) Sarah Smith, 1998. Education: University of Edinburgh, 1949; BA, Honours, French, New College, Oxford, 1950. Appointments: Lecturer in English, University of Poitiers, France, 1950-51; Teacher, Anargyrios College, Spetsai, Greece, 1951-52, and London, 1953-63. Publications: The Collector, 1963; The Aristos, 1965; The Magus, 1966, revised edition, 1977; The French Lieutenant's Woman, 1969; Poems, 1973; The Ebony Tower, 1974; Shipwreck, 1975; Daniel Martin, 1977; Islands, 1978; The Tree (with Frank Horvat), 1979; John Aubrey's Monumenta Britannica (editor), Parts 1 and 2, 1980, Part 3 and Index, 1982; The Enigma of Stonehenge, 1980; Mantissa, 1982; Thomas Hardy's England, 1984; Land, 1985; A Maggot, 1985. Honours: Silver Pen Award, PEN English Centre, 1969; W H Smith Award, 1970; Honorary Fellow, New College, Oxford, 1997. Address: c/o Sheil Land Associates Ltd, 43 Doughty Street, London WC1N 2LF, England.

FOX Constance (Connie), b. 12 Feb 1932, Chicago, USA. Writer; Entertainer. m. Nono Grimes, 15 Sept 1971, 1 son, 2 daughters. Education: BS, MA, Loyola, Chicago, 1955; PhD, University of Illinois, 1958. Publications: Blood Cocoon, 1980; Dream of the Black Topaze Chamber, 1981; 10 to the 170th Power, 1986; Babicka, 1986; Schreckliche Engel, 1986. Contributions to: Tri Quarterly; Santa Barbara Review; Portland Review; Exquisite Corpse; Centennial Review. Address: 1876 Melrose, East Lansing, MI 48823, USA.

FOX Geoffrey Edmund, b. 3 Apr 1941, Chicago, Illinois, USA. Writer; Sociologist; Translator. m. (1) Sylvia Herrera, 8 Aug 1966, (2) Mirtha Quintanales, 15 June 1975, (3) Susana Torre, 5 Oct 1979, 2 sons. Education: BA, Harvard University, 1963; PhD, Northwestern University, 1975. Appointments: Editor, Hispanic Monitor, 1983-84; Guest Editor, NACLA Report on the Americas, 1989; Publications Director, New York City Commission on Human Rights, 1994-95; Publications Consultant, College of Urban, Labor and Metropolitan Affairs, Wayne State University, 1996-. Publications: Welcome to My Country; The Land and People of Argentina; The Land and People of Venezuela; Working Class Emigres from Cuba; Hispanic Nation; Culture, Politics and the Constructing of Ideality, 1996. Contributions to: New York Times; Nation; Village Voice; Yellow Silk; Fiction International; Central Park; Newsday; Solidarity. Memberships: Authors Guild; National Writers Union; Latin American Studies Association. Literary Agent: Colleen Mohyde. Address: 8120 East Jefferson, Apt 4E, Detroit, MI 48214, USA.

FOX Hugh (Bernard), b. 12 Feb 1932, Chicago, Illinois, USA. Professor; Author; Poet; Dramatist. m. (1) Lucia Alicia Ungaro, 9 June 1957, div 1969, 1 son, 2 daughters, (2) Nona W Werner, June 1970, 1 son, 2 daughters, (3) Maria Bernadette Costa, 14 Apr 1988. Education: BS, Humanities, 1955, MA, 1956, Loyola University, Chicago; PhD, University of Illinois, Urbana-Champaign, 1958. Appointments: Professor of American Literature, Loyola Marymount University, Los Angeles, 1958-68; Fulbright Professor, Mexico, 1961, Venezuela, 1964-66, Brazil, 1978-80; Editor, Ghost Dance: The International Quarterly of Experimental Poetry, 1968-95; Professor, Michigan State University, 1968-; Lecturer, Spain, Portugal, 1975-76. Publications: Novels: Honeymoon/Mom, 1978; Leviathan, 1980; Shaman, 1993; The Last Summer, 1995. Poetry: The Face of Guy Lombardo, 1975; Almazora 42, 1982; Jamais Vu, 1991; The Sacred Cave, 1992; Once, 1995; Techniques, 1997. Non-Fiction: Henry James, 1968; Charles Bukowski: A Critical and Bibliographical Study, 1969; The Gods of the Cataclysm, 1976; First Fire: Central and South American Indian Poetry, 1978; Lyn Lifshin: A Critical Study, 1985; The Mythological Foundations of the Epic Genre: The Solar Voyage as the Hero's Journey, 1989; Stairway to the Sun, 1996. Contributions to: Many journals, reviews, quarterlies, and periodicals. Honours: John Carter Brown Library Fellowship, Brown University, 1968; Organization of American States Grants, Argentina, 1971, Chile, 1986. Address: 1876 Melrose, East Langsing, MI 48823, USA.

FOX Levi, b. 28 Aug 1914, Leicestershire, England. Author. m. Jane Richards, 1 son, 2 daughters. Education: BA, 1936, MA, 1938, Oriel College, Oxford; MA, University of Manchester, 1938. Appointments: General Editor, Dugdale Society, 1945-80; Director and Secretary, 1945-89, Director Emeritus, 1990-, Shakespeare Birthplace Trust. Publications: Leicester Abbey, 1938; Administration of the Honor of Leicester in the Fourteenth Century, 1940; Leicester Castle, 1943; Leicester Forest (with P Russell), 1945; Coventry's Heritage, 1946; Stratford-upon-Avon, 1949; Shakespeare's Town, 1949; Oxford, 1951; Shakespeare's Stratford-upon-Avon, 1951; Shakespeare's Country, 1953; The Borough Town of Stratford-upon-Avon, 1953; English Historical Scholarship in the 16th and 17th Centuries (editor), 1956; Shakespeare's Town and Country, 1959, 3rd edition, 1990; Stratford-upon-Avon: An Appreciation, 1963, 2nd edition, 1976; The 1964 Shakespeare Anniversary Book, 1964; Celebrating Shakespeare, 1965; Correspondence of the Reverend Joseph Greene, 1965; A Country Grammar School, 1967; The Shakespeare Book, 1969; Shakespeare's Sonnets (editor), 1970; Shakespeare's England, 1972; In Honour of Shakespeare, 1972, 2nd edition, 1982; The Shakespeare Treasury, compiler, 1972; The Stratford-upon-Avon Shakespeare Anthology, compiler, 1975; Stratford: Past and Present, 1975; Shakespeare's Flowers, 1978, 2nd edition, 1990; Shakespeare's Birds, 1978; The Shakespeare Centre, 1982; Shakespeare in Medallic Art, 1982; Shakespeare's Magic, 1982; The Early History of King Edward VI School, Stratford-upon-Avon, 1984; Coventry Constables' Presentments, 1986; Historic Stratford-upon-Avon, 1986; Shakespeare's Town and Country, 1986; Minutes and Accounts of the Corporation of Stratford-upon-Avon (1592-96), 1990; The Shakespeare Birthplace Trust: A Personal Memoir, 1997. Address: The Shakespeare Centre, Stratford-upon Avon CV37 6QW, England.

FOX Mem, (Merrion Frances Fox), b. 5 Mar 1946, Melbourne, Victoria, Australia. Writer. m. Malcolm, 2 Jan 1969, 1 daughter. Education: BA, Flinders University, 1978; B Ed, Sturt College, 1979; Graduate Diploma, Underdale College, 1981. Publications: Children's books: Possum Magic, 1983; Wilfrid Gordon McDonald Partridge, 1984; How to Teach Drama to Infants, 1984; A Cat Called Kite, 1985; Zoo-Looking, 1986; Hattie and the Fox, 1986; Sail Away, 1986; Arabella, 1986; Just Like That, 1986; A Bedtime Story, 1987; The Straight Line Wonder, 1987; Goodnight Sleep Tight, 1988; Guess What?, 1988; Koala Lou, 1988; Night Noises, 1989; Shoes for Grandpa, 1989; Sophie, 1989; Memories, 1992; Tough Boris, 1994; Wombat Divine, 1995; Boo to a Goose, 1996; Feathers and Fools, 1996; Adult Books: Mem's the Word, 1990; Dear Mem Fox, I Have Read All Your Books, Even the Pathetic Ones, 1992. Co-Author: English Essentials: The Wouldn't-be-without-it Handbook on Writing Well, 1993; Radical Reflections: Passionate Opinions on Teaching, Learning, and Living, 1993. Contributions to: Language Arts; Horn Book; Australian Journal of Language and Literacy; Reading Teacher; Reading and Writing Quarterly; Dragon Lode. Honours: New South Wales Premier's Literary Award, Best Children's Book, 1984; KOALA First Prize, 1987; The Dromkeen Medal for Outstanding Services to Children's Literature, 1990; Advance Australia Award, 1990; Order of Australia, 1994; Alice Award, Fellowship of Australian Women Writers, 1994; Honorary Doctorate, University of Wollongong, 1996. Memberships: Australian Society of Authors; Australian Children's Book Council. Address: c/o Australian Literary Management, 2A Armstrong Street, Middlepark, Victoria 3206, Australia.

FOX Paula, b. 22 Apr 1923, New York, New York, USA. Author. m. (1) Richard Sigerson, 1948, div 1954, 2 sons, 1 daughter, (2) Martin Greenberg, 9 June 1962. Education: Columbia University, 1955-58. Appointments: State University of New York, 1974; University of Pennsylvania, 1980-85; New York University, 1989. Publications: How Many Miles to Babylon?, 1967; Desperate Characters, 1970; The Western Coast, 1972; The Slave Dancer, 1974; The Widow's Children, 1976; A Servant's Tale, 1983; One-Eyed Cat, 1984; The Village by the Sea, 1989; The God of Nightmares, 1990. Honours: Guggenheim Fellowship, 1972; American Academy of Arts and Letters Award, 1972; National

Endowment for the Arts Award, 1973; Newbery Medals, 1974, 1986; American Book Award, 1980; Hans Christian Andersen Medal, 1983; Brandeis Fiction Citation, 1984; Rockefeller Foundation Residency Fellow, 1985; Boston Globe-Horn Book Award, 1989. Membership: PEN. Address: c/o Robert Lescher, 67 Irving Place, New York, NY 10003, USA.

FOX-GENOVESE Elizabeth (Ann Teresa), b. 28 May 1941, Boston, Massachusetts, USA. Historian; Professor. m. Eugene Dominick Genovese, 6 June 1969. Education: BA, Bryn Mawr College, 1963; Institut d'Etudes Politiques, Paris, 1961-62; MA, 1966, PhD, 1974, Harvard University; Special Candidate, Center for Psychoanalytic Training and Research, Columbia University, 1977-79; Institute in Quantitative Methods, Newberry Library, Chicago, 1979. Appointments: Teaching Fellow, Harvard University, 1965-66, 1967-69; Assistant Professor, 1973-76, Associate Professor, 1976-80, University of Rochester; Professor, State University of New York at Binghamton, 1980-86; Professor, 1986-, Eleonore Raoul Professor of Humanities, 1988-, Emory University; Adjunct Professor, Auburn University, Alabama, 1987; Eudora Welty Professor, Millsaps College, 1990. Publications: The Origins of Physiocracy: Economic Revolution and Social Order in 18th Century France, 1976; Fruits of Merchant Capital: Slavery and Bourgeois Property in the Rise and Expansion of Capitalism (with Eugene Dominick Genovese), 1983; Within the Plantation Household: Black and White Women of the Old South, 1988; Feminism without Illusions: A Critique of Individualism, 1991; Feminism is Not the Story of My Life: How Today's Feminist Elite Has Lost Touch with the Real Concerns of Women, 1996. Contributions to: professional journals and general periodicals. Honour: Honorary LittD, Millsaps College, 1992. Memberships: American Academy of Liberal Education; American Antiquarian Society; American Comparative Literature Association; American Historical Association; American Political Science Association; American Studies Association; Association of Literary Scholars and Critics; Modern Language Association; Organization of American Historians, life member; Social Science Historical Association; Society for the Study of Southern Literature; Society of American Historians; Southern Association for Women Historians, life member; Southern Historical Association, life member. Address: c/o Department of History, Emory University, Atlanta, GA 30322, USA.

FRAILE Medardo, b. 21 Mar 1925, Madrid, Spain. Writer; Emeritus Professor in Spanish. Education: DPh, DLitt, University of Madrid, 1968. Publications: Cuentos con Algun Amor, 1954; A La Luz Cambian las Cosas, 1959; Cuentos de Verdad, 1964; Descubridor de Nada y Otros Cuentos, 1970; Con Los Dias Contados, 1972; Samuel Ros Hacia una Generacion Sin Critica, 1972; La Penultima Inglaterra, 1973; Poesia y Teatro Espanoles Contemporaneos, 1974; Ejemplario, 1979; Autobiografia, 1986; Cuento Espanol de Posguerra, 1986; El gallo puesto en hora, 1987; Entre parentesis, 1988; Santa Engracia, numero dos o tres, 1989; Teatro Espanol en un Acto, 1989; El rey y el pais con granos, 1991; Cuentos Completos, 1991; Claudina y los cacos, 1992; La Familia irreal inglesa, 1993; Los brazos invisibles, 1994; Documento Nacional, 1997; Contrasombras, 1998; Ladrones del Paraiso, 1999. Translation: El Weir de Hermiston by R L Stevenson, 1995. Contributions to: Many publications. Honours: Sesamo Prize, 1956; Literary Grant, Fundacion Juan March, 1960; Critics Book of the Year, 1965; La Estafeta literaria Prize, 1970; Hucha de Oro Prize, 1971; Research Grant, Carnegie Trust for Universities of Scotland, 1975; Colegiado de Honor del Colegio heraldico de España y de las Indias, 1995. Memberships: General Society of Spanish Authors; Working Community of Book Writers, Spain; Association of University Teachers. Address: 24 Etive Crescent, Bishopbriggs, Glasgow G64 1ES, Scotland.

FRAJLICH-ZAJAC Anna, b. 10 Mar 1942, Osz, Kyrgyzstan. Adjunct Assistant Professor; Writer. m. Wladyslaw Zajac, 31 July 1965, 1 son. Education: Masters of Polish Literature, Warsaw University, 1965; PhD, Slavic Literatures, New York University, 1991. Appointment: Adjunct Assistant Professor, Department of Slavic Languages, Columbia University. Publications: Indian Summer, 1982; Ktory las, 1986; Between Dawn and the Wind, 1991; Ogrodem i ogrodzeniem (The Garden and the Fence), 1993; Jeszcze w drodze (Still on its Way), 1994. Contributions to: Terra Poetica; Artful Dodge; The Polish Review; Wisconsin Review; Mr Cogito; The Jewish Quarterly; Poésie Premiére. Honour: Koscielski Foundation Award, Switzerland, 1981. Memberships: PEN Club International, executive board; Association of Polish Writers. Address: 345 East 81st Street, Apt 11J, New York, NY 10028-4018, USA.

FRAME Janet (Paterson), (surname legally changed to Clutha), b. 28 Aug 1924, Dunedin, New Zealand. Author. Education: University of Otago Teachers Training College. Publications: The Lagoon Stories, 1951; Faces in the Water, 1961; The Edge of the Alphabet, 1961; Scented Gardens for the Blind, 1963; The Reservoir Stories and Sketches, 1963; Snowman, 1963; The Adaptable Man, 1965; A State of Siege, 1966; The Reservoir and Other Stories, 1966; The Pocket Mirror, 1967; The Rainbirds, 1968; Mona Minim and the Small of the Sun, 1969; Daughter Buffalo, 1972; Living in the Maniototo, 1979; To the Island, 1982; You Are Now Entering the Human Heart, 1984; The Envoy from the Mirror City, 1985; The Carpathians, 1988. Address: 276 Glenfield Road, Auckland 10, New Zealand.

FRANCE (Evelyn) Christine, b. 23 Dec 1939, Sydney, New South Wales, Australia. Art Historian. m. Stephen Robert Bruce France, 22 Dec 1962, 1 daughter. Education: BA, University of Sydney. Publications: Justin O'Brien: Image and Icon, 1987; Margaret Olley, 1990; Marea Gazzard: Form and Clay, 1994; Jean Appleton: A Lifetime with Art, 1998. Contributions to: Art and Australia; Australian newspapers. Address: Old Baerami, Baerami, Wales 2333, Australia.

FRANCHON Lisa. See: FLOREN Lee.

FRANCIS Alexander. See: HEATH-STUBBS John.

FRANCIS Clare, b. 17 Apr 1946, Surrey, England. Writer. 1 son. Education: Economics Degree, University College, London. Publications: Come Hell or High Water, 1977; Come Wind or Weather, 1978; The Commanding Sea, 1981; Night Sky, 1983; Red Crystal, 1985; Wolf Winter, 1987; Requiem, 1991; Deceit, 1993; Betrayal, 1995; A Dark Devotion, 1997. Honours: Member, Order of British Empire; University College, London, honorary fellow; University of Manchester Institute of Technology, honorary fellow. Membership: Society of Authors, chairman, 1997-99. Address: c/o John Johnson Agency, Clerkenwell House, 45-47 Clerkenwell Green, London EC1R 0HT, England.

FRANCIS Elphinstone. See: POWELL-SMITH Vincent.

FRANCIS Dick, (Richard Stanley Francis), b. 31 Oct 1920, Pembrokeshire, South Wales. Ex Steeplechase Jockey; Author. m. Mary Margaret Brenchley, 21 June 1947, 2 sons. Appointment: Racing Correspondent, London Sunday Express, 1957-63. Publications: Dead Cert, 1962; Nerve, 1964; For Kicks, 1965; Odds Against, 1965; Flying Finish, 1966; Blood Sport, 1967; Forfeit, 1968; Enquiry, 1969; Rat Race, 1970; Bonecrack, 1971; Smokescreen, 1972; Slay-Ride, 1973; Knock Down, 1974; High Stakes, 1975; In the Frame, 1976; Risk, 1977; Trial Run, 1978; Whip Hand, 1979; Reflex, 1980; Twice Shy, 1981; Banker, 1982; The Danger, 1983; Proof, 1984; Break In, 1985; Bolt, 1986; Hot Money, 1987; The Edge, 1988; Straight, 1989; Longshot, 1990; Comeback, 1991; Driving Force, 1992; Decider, 1993; Wild Horses, 1994; Come to Grief, 1995; To the Hilt; 1996; Field of Thirteen, 1998. Autobiography: The Sport of Queens, 1957. Biography: Lester, 1986. Contributions to: Sunday Express; Daily Express; Sunday Times; Daily Mail; New York Times; Washington Post; The Age, Melbourne; Horse & Hound; Sports Illustrated; Classic. Honours: Officer of the Order of the British Empire, 1954; Gold

Dagger Awards, Crime Writers Association, 1966, 1980; Edgar Allan Poe Best Novel Awards, Mystery Writers of America, 1970, 1981; Honorary LHD, Tufts University, 1991. Memberships: Crime Writers Association, chairman, 1965-66; Mystery Writers of America; Society of Authors; Racecourse Association. Address: c/o John Johnson Agency, 45/47 Clerkenwell Green, London EC1R 0HT, England.

FRANCISCO Nia, b. 2 Feb 1952, Fort Defiance, Arizona, USA. Poet. m. Dec 1975, 5 children. Education: Institute of American Indian Arts, 1970-71; Navajo Community College, 1971-77. Publications: Blue Horses for Navajo Women, 1988; Carried Away by the Black River, 1994. Contributions to: Anthologies. Honours: Arizona Commission on the Arts Grant; National Endowment for the Arts Grant; New York Commission on the Arts Grant. Membership: Arizona Commission on Humanities, 1978-79. Address: PO Box 794, Navajo, NM 87328, USA.

FRANCK Thomas M(artin), b. 14 July 1931, Berlin, Germany (US citizen, 1977). Professor of Law; Writer. Education: BA, 1952, LLB, 1953, University of British Columbia; LLM, 1954, SJD, 1959, Harvard Law School. Appointments: Assistant Professor, University of Nebraska College of Law, 1954-56; Associate Professor, 1960-62, Professor of Law, 1962-, Director, Center for International Studies, 1965-, New York University School of Law; Visiting Professor, Stanford Law School, 1963, University of East Africa Law School, Dar es Salaam, 1963-66, Osgood Hall Law School, York University, Toronto, 1972-76, Woodrow Wilson School, Princeton University, 1979; Director, International Law Program, Cargenie Endowment for International Peace, 1973-79; Director of Research, United Nations Institute for Training and Research, 1980-82; Lecturer, The Hague Academy of International Law, 1993; Visiting Fellow, Trinity College, Cambridge, 1996-97. Publications: Race and Nationalism, 1960; The Role of the United States in the Congo (co-author), 1963; African Law (co-author), 1963; East African Unity Through Law, 1964; Comparative Constitutional Process: Cases and Materials in the Comparative Constitutional Process of Nation Building, 1968; The Structure of Impartiality, 1968; A Free Trade Association (with others), 1968; Why Federations Fail (co-author), 1968; Word Politics: Verbal Strategy Among the Superpowers (co-author), 1971; Secrecy and Foreign Policy (co-author), 1974; Resignation in Protest: Political and Ethical Choices Between Loyalty to Team and Loyalty to Conscience in American Public Life (co-author), 1975; Control of Sea Resources by Semi-Autonomous States: Prevailing Legal Relationships Between Metropolitan Governments and Their Overseas Commonwealths, Associated States, and Self-Governing Dependencies, 1978; Foreign Policy by Congress (co-author), 1979; United States Foreign Relations Law: Documents and Sources (co-author), 5 volumes, 1980-84; The Tethered Presidency, 1981; Human Rights in Third World Perspective, 3 volumes, 1982; Nation Against Nation: What Happened to the U.N. Dream and What the U.S. Can Do About It, 1985; Judging the World Court, 1986; Foreign Relations and National Security Law, 1987; The Power of Legitimacy Among Nations, 1990; Political Questions/Judicial Answers: Does the Rule of Law Apply to Foreign Affairs?, 1992; Fairness in the International Legal and Institutional System, 1993; Fairness in International Law and Institutions, 1995; International Law Decisions in National Courts (co-editor), 1996. Contributions to: Scholarly journals. Honours: Guggenheim Fellowships, 1973-74, 1982-83; Christopher Medal, 1976; Certificates of Merit, American Society of International Law, 1981, 1986, 1994, 1996; John E Read Medal, Canadian Council on International Law, 1994; Honorary LLD, University of British Columbia, 1995. Memberships: Africa Watch; American Society of International Law; Canadian Council on International Law; Council on Foreign Relations; French Society of International Law; German Society of International Law; Institut du Droit International; International Law Association, vice-president, 1973-94, honorary vice-president, 1994-; International Peace Academy.

Address: c/o New York University School of Law, 40 Washington Square South, New York, NY 10012, USA.

FRANCO Tomaso, b. 23 May 1933, Bologna, Italy. Poet; Writer. div, 2 sons. Education: Classical Studies, 1952; Doctorate in Law, 1959; Art Studies. Publications: Poetry: Uno Scatto dell'Evoluzione, 1984; Parole d'Archivio, 1986; Il Libro dei Torti, 1988; Casa di Frontiera, 1990; Novel: Soldato dei Sogni, 1995; Essay: Lettere a un Fuoruscito, 1988; Essay: Sila-Torino, 1961, 1998. Contributions to: Various anthologies, newspapers, and journals. Honours: 1st Award, Clemente Rèbora, Milan, 1986; Gold Medal, City of Como, 1990; 1st Award, National, Associazione Promozione Cultura in Toscana, 1992. Address: Via San Domenico 2, I-36100 Vicenza, Italy.

FRANÇOIS Marie. See: **BUTOR Michel.**

FRANK Joseph Nathaniel, b. 6 Oct 1918, New York, New York, USA. Professor Emeritus of Comparative Literature and Slavic Languages and Literatures. m. Marguerite J Straus, 11 May 1953, 2 daughters. Education: New York University, 1937-38; University of Wisconsin 1941-42; University of Paris, 1950-51; PhD, University of Chicago, 1960. Appointments: Editor, Bureau of National Affairs, Washington,DC, 1942-50; Assistant Professor, Department of English, University of Minnesota, 1958-61; Associate Professor, Rutgers University, 1961-66; Professor of Comparative Literature, 1966-85, Director of Christian Gauss Seminars, 1966-83, Princeton University; Visiting Member, Institute for Advanced Study, 1984-87; Professor of Comparative Literature and Slavic Languages and Literatures, 1985-89, Professor Emeritus, 1989-, Stanford University. Publications: The Widening Gyre: Crisis and Mastery in Modern Literature, 1963; A Primer of Ignorance Dostoevsky: The Seeds of Revolt, 1821-1849, 1976; Dostoevsky: The Years of Ordeal, 1850-1859, 1983; Dostoevsky: The Stir of Liberation, 1860-1865, 1986; Selected Letters of Fyodor Dostoevsky (co-editor), 1987; Through the Russian Prism, 1989; The Idea of Spatial Form, 1991; Dostoevsky: The Miraculous Years, 1865-1871, 1995. Contributions to: Southern Review; Sewanee Review; Hudson Review; Partisan Review; Art News; Critique; Chicago Review; Minnesota Review; Russian Review; Le Contrat Social; Commentary; Encounter; New York Review. Honours: Fulbright Scholar, 1950-51; Rockefeller Fellow, 1952-53, 1953-54; Guggenheim Fellowships, 1956-57, 1975-76; Award, National Institute of Arts and Letters, 1958; Research Grants, American Council of Learned Societies, 1964-65, 1967-68, 1970-71; James Russell Lowell Prize, 1977; Christian Gauss Awards, 1977, 1996; Rockefeller Foundation Fellowships, 1979-80, 1983-84; National Book Critics Circle Award, 1984. Membership: American Academyof Arts and Sciences, fellow. Address: c/o Department of Slavic Languages and Literatures, Stanford University, Stanford, CA 94305, USA.

FRANK Terence Francis. See: **COLEMAN Terry.**

FRANKEL Ellen, b. 22 May 1951, New York, New York, USA. Editor; Writer; Story Teller. m. Herbert Levine, 3 Aug 1975, 1 son, 1 daughter. Education: BA, University of Michigan, 1973; PhD, Princeton University, 1978. Appointment: Editor-in-Chief, Jewish Publication Society, 1991-. Publications: Choosing to Be Chosen, Ktav; The Classic Tales: 4000 Years of Jewish Lore; The Encyclopedia of Jewish Symbols, with Betsy Teutsch; George Washington and the Constitution; Tell It Like It Is: Tough Choices for Today's Teens, with Sarah Levine; The Five Books of Miriam: A Woman's Commentary on the Torah; The Jewish Spirit (Stewart, Tabor and Chang), 1997; The Illustrated Jewish Bible (Stewart, Tabor and Chang), 1999. Contributions to: Judaism; Jewish Spectator; Moment; Jewish Monthly; Shofar Magazine. Memberships: Association of Jewish Studies; Phi Beta Kappa. Address: 6670 Lincoln Drive, Philadelphia, PA 19119, USA.

FRANKFURT Harry, b. 29 May 1929, Langhorne, Pennsylvania, USA. Professor of Philosophy; Writer. m. Joan Gilbert. Education: BA, 1949, MA, 1953, PhD, 1954, Johns Hopkins University; Cornell University, 1949-51. Appointments: Instructor, 1956-59, Assistant Professor, 1959-62, Ohio State University; Associate Professor, State University of New York at Binghamton, 1962-63; Research Associate, 1963-64, Associate Professor, 1964-71, Professor of Philosophy, 1971-76, Rockefeller University, New York City; Visiting Fellow, All Souls College, Oxford, 1971-72; Visiting Professor, Vassar College, 1973-74, University of Pittsburgh, 1975-76, University of California at Los Angeles, 1990; Professor of Philosophy, 1976-89, Chairman, Department of Philosophy, 1978-87, John M Schiff Professor, 1989, Yale University; Professor of Philosophy, Princeton University, 1990-. Publications: Demons, Dreamers, and Madmen: The Defense of Reason in Descartes's Meditations, 1970; Leibniz: A Collection of Critical Essays (editor), 1972; The Importance of What We Care About, 1988. Contributions to: Many scholarly books and journals. Honours: National Endowment for the Humanities Fellowships, 1981-82, 1994; Guggenheim Fellowship, 1993; American Philosophical Association (Eastern Division), president, 1991-92. Memberships: American Academy of Arts and Sciences, fellow; American Philosophical Association. Address: c/o Department of Philosophy, 1879 Hall, Princeton University, Princeton, NJ 08544, USA.

FRANKLAND (Anthony) Noble, b. 4 July 1922, Ravenstonedale, England. Historian; Biographer. m. (1) Diana Madeline Fovargue Tavernor, 28 Feb 1944, dec 1981, 1 son, 1 daughter, (2) Sarah Katharine Davies, 7 May 1982. Education: Open Scholar, MA, 1948, DPhil, 1951, Trinity College, Oxford. Appointments: Official British Military Historian, 1951-60; Deputy Director of Studies, Royal Institute of International Affairs, 1956-60; Director, Imperial War Museum, 1960-82. Publications: Crown of Tragedy: Nicholas II, 1960; The Strategic Air Offensive Against Germany (co-author), 4 volumes, 1961; The Bombing Offensive Against Germany: Outlines and Perspectives, 1965; Bomber Offensive: The Devastation of Europe, 1970; Prince Henry, Duke of Gloucester, 1980; Witness of a Century: Prince Arthur, Duke of Connaught, 1850-1942, 1993; History at War: The Campaigns of an Historian, 1998; Encyclopedia of Twentieth Century Warfare (general editor and contributor), 1989; The Politics and Strategy of the Second World War (joint editor), 9 volumes. Contributions to: Encyclopaedia Britannica; Times Literary Supplement; The Times; Daily Telegraph; Observer; Military journals. Honours: Companion of the Order of the Bath; Commander of the Order of the British Empire; Holder of the Distinguished Flying Cross. Address: Thames House, Eynsham, Witney, Oxon OX8 1DA, England.

FRANKLIN John Hope, b. 2 Jan 1915, Rentiesville, Oklahoma, USA. Historian; Professor; Author. m. Aurelia E Whittington, 11 June 1940, 1 son. Education: AB, Fisk University, 1935; AM, 1936, PhD, 1941, Harvard University. Appointments: Instructor, Fisk University, 1936-37; Professor of History, St Augustine's College, 1939-43, North Carolina College at Durham, 1943-47, Howard University, 1947-56; Chairman, Department of History, Brooklyn College, 1956-64; Professor of American History, 1964-82, Chairman, Department of History, 1967-70, John Matthews Manly Distinguished Service Professor, 1969-82, University of Chicago; James B Duke Professor of History, 1982-85, Professor of Legal History, 1985-92, Duke University; Various visiting professorships. Publications: Free Negro in North Carolina, 1943; From Slavery to Freedom: A History of American Negroes, 1947, 7th edition, 1994; Militant South, 1956; Reconstruction After the Civil War, 1961; The Emancipation Proclamation, 1963; Land of the Free (with others), 1966; Illustrated History of Black Americans (with others), 1970; A Southern Odyssey, 1976; Racial Equality in America, 1976; George Washington Williams: A Biography, 1985; The Color Line: Legacy for the 21st Century, 1993. Editor: Civil War Diary of James T Ayres, 1947; A Fool's Errand by Albion Tourgee, 1961; Army Life in a Black Regiment by Thomas Higginson, 1962; Color and Race, 1968; Reminiscences of an Active Life by John R Lynch, 1970; Black Leaders in the Twentieth Century (with August Meier), 1982. Contributions to: Scholarly journals. Honours: Edward Austin Fellow, 1937-39; Guggenheim Fellowships, 1950-51, 1973-74; President's Fellow, Brown University, 1952-53; Center for Advanced Study in the Behavioral Sciences Fellow, 1973-74; Senior Mellon Fellow, National Humanities Center, 1980-82; Cleanth Brooks Medal, Fellowship of Southern Writers, 1989; Gold Medal, Encyclopaedia Britannica, 1990; North Carolina Medals, 1992, 1993; Charles Frankel Medal, 1993; Bruce Catton Award, Society of American Historians, 1994; Sidney Hook Award, Phi Beta Kappa Society, 1994; Over 100 honorary doctorates. Memberships: American Academy of Arts and Sciences, fellow; American Association of University Professors; American Historical Association, president, 1978-79; American Philosophical Society; American Studies Association; Association for the Study of Negro Life and History; Phi Alpha Theta; Phi Beta Kappa, president, 1973-76; Organization of American Historians, president, 1974-75; Southern Historical Association, president, 1970-71. Address: c/o Department of History, Duke University, Durham, NC 27707, USA.

FRAPPELL Ruth Meredith (Ruth Teale), b. 8 Mar 1942, Bathurst, New South Wales, Australia. Historian; Biographer; Editor. m. Leighton Frappell, 15 Aug 1970, 1 son, 2 daughters. Education: BA, 1963; LMusA, 1964, Australian Music Examination Board; MA, 1968, PhD, 1992, University of Sydney. Appointments: Writer, Australian Dictionary of Biography, 1968-, Journal of the Royal Australian Historical Society, 1994-; Editor, Journal of Religious History, 1995-. Publications: Thomas Brisbane, 1971; Colonial Eve, 1979. Contributions to: Reference books and scholarly journals. Memberships: Australian Historical Association; Royal Australian Historical Society, life member, senior vice president. Address: 22 Ingalara Avenue, Wahroonga 2076, Australia.

FRASER Lady Antonia, (Lady Antonia Pinter), b. 27 Aug 1932, London, England. Author. m. (1) Sir Hugh Fraser, 1956, diss 1977, 3 sons, 3 daughters, (2) Harold Pinter, 1980. Education: MA, Lady Margaret Hall, Oxford. Appointment: General Editor, Kings and Queens of England series. Publications: King Arthur and the Knights of the Round Table, 1954; Robin Hood, 1955; Dolls, 1963; A History of Toys, 1966; Mary Queen of Scots, 1969; Cromwell, Our Chief of Men, 1973; King James: VI of Scotland, I of England, 1974; Kings and Queens of England (editor), 1975; Scottish Love Poems: A Personal Anthology (editor), 1975; Love Letters: An Anthology (editor), 1976, revised edition, 1989; Quiet as a Nun, 1977; The Wild Island, 1978; King Charles II, 1979; Heroes and Heroines (editor), 1980; A Splash of Red, 1981; Mary Queen of Scots: Poetry Anthology (editor), 1981; Oxford and Oxfordshire in Verse: An Anthology (editor), 1982; Cool Repentance, 1982; The Weaker Vessel: Woman's Lot in Seventeenth Century England, 1984; Oxford Blood, 1985; Jemima Shore's First Case, 1986; Your Royal Hostage, 1987; Boadicea's Chariot: The Warrior Queens, 1988; The Cavalier Case, 1990; Jemima Shore at the Sunny Grave, 1991; The Six Wives of Henry VIII, 1992; The Pleasure of Reading (editor), 1992; Political Death, 1994; The Gunpowder Plot, 1996. Other: Several books adapted for television. Contributions to: Anthologies. Honours: James Tait Black Memorial Prize, 1969; Wolfson History Award, 1984; Prix Caumont-La Force, 1985; Honorary DLitt, Universities of Hull, 1986, Sussex, 1990, Nottingham, 1993 and St Andrews, 1994; Shortlisted for NCR Award, 1997. Memberships: Society of Authors, chairman, 1974-75; Crimewriters' Association, chairman, 1985-86; Writers in Prison Committee, chairman, 1985-88, 1990; English PEN, vice president, 1990-. Address: c/o Curtis Brown Ltd, 162-168 Regent Street, London W1R 5TB, England.

FRASER Conon, b. 8 Mar 1930, Cambridge, England. Retired Documentary Film Producer and Director; Writer. m. Jacqueline Stearns, 17 Mar 1955, 5 sons. Education: Marlborough College, 1943-47; Royal Military Academy, Sandhurst, 1948-50. Publications: The Underground Explorers, 1957; Oystercatcher Bay, 1962; Looking at New Zealand, 1969; Beyond the Roaring Forties, 1986.

Contributions to: New Zealand's Heritage; Argosy (UK); New Zealand Listener. Honours: Silver Medal for Documentary Film, Coal Valley, Festival of the Americas, 1979; Silver Screen Award, United States Industrial Film Festival, 1980; Mitra Award of Honour, 26th Asian Film Festival, 1980. Address: Matapuna Road, RD6 Raetihi, New Zealand.

FRASER George MacDonald, b. 2 Apr 1925, Carlisle, England. Author; Journalist. m. Kathleen Margarette Hetherington, 1949, 2 sons, 1 daughter. Education: Glasgow Academy. Appointment: Deputy Editor, Glasgow Herald newspaper, 1964-69. Publications: Flashman, 1969; Royal Flash, 1970, screenplay, 1975; The General Danced at Dawn, 1970; Flash for Freedom, 1971; Steel Bonnets, 1971; Flashman at the Charge, 1973; The Three Musketeers, screenplay, 1973; The Four Musketeers, screenplay, 1974; McAuslan in the Rough, 1974; Flashman in the Great Game, 1975; The Prince and the Pauper, screenplay, 1976; Flashman's Lady, 1977; Mr American, 1980; Flashman and the Redskins, 1982; Octopussy, screenplay, 1983; The Pyrates, 1983; Flashman and the Dragon, 1985; Casanova, television screenplay, 1987; The Hollywood History of the World, 1988; The Sheikh and the Dustbin, 1988; The Return of the Musketeers, screenplay, 1989; Flashman and the Mountain of Light, 1990; Quartered Safe Out Here, 1992; The Candlemass Road, 1993; Flashman and the Angel of the Lord, 1994; Black Ajax, 1997; Flashman and the Tiger, 1999. Address: Baldrine, Isle of Man, Britain.

FRASER Kathleen, b. 22 Mar 1937, Tulsa, Oklahoma, USA. Professor; Poet. m. Jack Marshall, 1961, div 1970, 1 son. Education: BA, Occidental College, Los Angles, 1959; Columbia University, 1960-61; New School for Social Research, New York City, 1960-61; Doctoral Equivalency in Creative Writing, San Francisco State University, 1976-77. Appointments: Visiting Professor, University of Iowa, 1969-71; Writer-in-Residence, Reed College, Portland, Oregon, 1971-72; Director, Poetry Center, 1972-75, Associate Professor, 1975-78, Professor, 1978-92, San Francisco State University. Publications: Poetry: Change of Address and Other Poems, 1966; In Defiance of the Rains, 1969; Little Notes to You from Lucas Street, 1972; What I Want, 1974; Magritte Series, 1978; New Shoes, 1978; Each Next, 1980; Something (Even Human Voices) in the Foreground, A Lake, 1984; Notes Preceding Trust, 1987; Boundayr, 1988; Giotto, Arena, 1991; When New Time Folds Up, 1993; Wing, 1995; Il Cuore: The Heart, New and Selected Poems 1970-95, 1997; Translating the Unspeakable (essays), forthcoming. Editor: Feminist Poetics; A Consideration of Female Construction of Language, 1984. Honours: YMM-YWHA Discovery Award, 1964; National Endowment for the Arts Grant, 1969, and Fellowship, 1978; Guggenheim Fellowship in Poetry, 1981. Address: 1936 Leavenworth Street, San Francisco, CA 94133, USA.

FRASER Sylvia Lois, b. 8 Mar 1935, Hamilton, Ont, Canada. Writer. div. Education: BA, University of Western Ontario, 1957. Appointments: Writer, Toronto Star Weekly, 1957-68; Guest Lecturer, Banff Centre, 1973-79, 1985, 1987-88; Writer-in-Residence, University of Western Ontario, 1980; Instructor, Maritime Writers' Workshop, 1986. Publications: Pandora, 1972; The Candy Factory, 1975; A Casual Affair, 1978; The Emperor's Virgin, 1980; Berlin Solstice, 1984; My Father's House, memoir, 1987; The Book of Strange, 1992; The Ancestral Suitcase, 1996; A Woman's Place: seventy years in the lives of Canadian women (editor), 1997; Tom and Francine (children's book), 1998. Honours: Women Press Club Awards, 1967, 1968; President's Medal for Canadian Journalism, 1969; Canadian Authors' Association Award for Non-Fiction, 1987; National Magazine Award, 1994, 1996. Memberships: Writers' Development Trust. Address: 701 King Street West, No 302, Toronto, Ontario M5V 2W7, Canada.

FRATTI Mario, b. 5 July 1927, L'Aquila, Italy. (US citizen, 1974). Playwright; Educator. 3 children. Education: PhD, Ca Foscari University, 1951. Appointments: Drama Critic, 1963-, Paese, 1963-, Progresso, 1963-, Ridotto, 1963; Adelphi College, teacher, 1964-65; Faculty, Columbia University, 1965-66; Professor of Literature, New School, Hunter College, 1967-; Faculty, Hofstra University, 1973-74. Publications: Plays: Cage-Suicide, 1964; Academy-Return, 1967; Mafia, 1971; Bridge, 1971; Races, 1972; Eleven Plays in Spanish, 1977; Refrigerators, 1977; Eleonora Duse-Victim, 1981; Nine, 1982; Biography of Fratti, 1982; AIDS, 1987;Porno, 1988, Encounter, musical, 1989; Family, 1990; Friends, 1991; Lovers, 1992; Leningrad Euthanasia, 1993; Holy Father, 1994; Sacrifices, 1995; Jurors, 1996. Honours: Tony Award, 1982; Other awards for plays and musicals. Memberships: Drama Desk; American Theatre Critics; Outer Critics Circle, Vice-President. Literary Agent: Susan Schulman, 454 West 44th Street, New York, NY 10036, USA. Address: 145 West 55th Street, Apt 15D, New York, NY 10019, USA.

FRAYN Michael, b. 3 Sept 1933, London, England. Author; Dramatist; Translator; Journalist. Education: BA, Emmanuel College, Cambridge University. Publications: Novels: The Tin Men, 1966; The Russian Interpreter, 1967; A Very Private Life, 1968; Towards the End of the Morning, 1969; Sweet Dreams, 1973; The Trick of It, 1989; A Landing on the Sun, 1991; Now You Know, 1992. Philosophy: Constructions, 1974. Plays: The Two of Us, 1970; Alphabetical Order and Donkeys Years, 1977; Clouds, 1977; Make and Break, 1980; Noises Off, 1982; Benefactors, 1984; Here, 1993; Now You Know, 1995; La Belle Vivette (libretto), 1995; Copenhagen, 1998; Alarms and Excursions, 1998. Screenplays and TV: Clockwise, 1986; First and Last, 1989; A Landing on the Sun, 1994; Remember Me?, 1997. Translations: Chekhov: The Cherry Orchard, 1978; Tolstoy: The Fruits of Enlightenment, 1979; Chekhov: Three Sisters, 1983; Wild Honey, 1984; Anouilh: Number One, 1985; The Seagull, 1987; Uncle Vanya, 1989; The Sneeze, 1989; Trifonov: Exchange, 1990; Documentaries include: Laurence Sterne Lived Here, BBC, 1973; Vienna: The Mask of Gold, BBC, 1977; The Long Straight (in Great Railway Journeys of the World), BBC, 1980. Honours: Somerset Maugham Award, 1966; Hawthornden Prize, 1967; National Press Award, 1970; 3 SWET/Olivier Awards; 4 Evening Standard Drama Awards; Sunday Express Book of the Year Award, 1991. Memberships: Royal Society of Literature, fellow; Emmanuel College, Cambridge University, England, honorary fellow. Address: c/o Greene & Heaton Ltd, 31 Newington Green, London N16 9PU, England.

FRAZER Andrew. See: **MARLOWE Stephen.**

FRAZER Vernon, b. 2 Oct 1945, Middleton, USA. Writer. m. Elaine Kass, 3 Aug 1998. Education: BA, English, University of Connecticut. Publications: A Slick Set of Wheels (poetry book); Sex Queen of the Berlin Turnpike (recording); Slam! (recording); Demon Dance (poetry book); Song of Baobab (recording); Sing Me One Song of Evolution (poetry book). Contributions to: Plain Brown Wrapper; Hartford Advocate. Address: 132 Woodycrest Drive, East Hartford, CT 06118, USA.

FRAZEUR Joyce Jaeckle, b. 17 Jan 1931, Lewisburg, Pennsylvania, USA. Poet; Writer. m. Theodore C Frazeur Jr, 24 July 1954, 1 son, 2 daughters. Education: BA, William Smith College, 1952. Publications: Poetry: A Slip of Greenness, 1989; The Bovine Affliction, 1991; Flower Soup, 1993; Chirruping, 1994; Cycles, 1996; Novel: By Lunar Light, 1995. Contributions to: Newspapers, reviews, magazines, and journals. Address: 390 Juniper Drive, Sedona, AZ 86336, USA.

FRAZIER Arthur. See: **BULMER Henry Kenneth.**

FRAZIER Charles, b. 1950, Asheville, North Carolina, USA. Author. m. Katherine Frazier, 1 daughter. Education: PhD, University of North Carolina at Chapel Hill. Appointments: Former faculty member, University of Colorado at Boulder and North Carolina State University. Publications: Adventuring in the Andes: The Sierra Club Travel Guide to Ecuador, Peru, Bolivia, the Amazon Basin, and the Galapagos Islands (with Donald Secreast), 1985; Cold Mountain: Odyssey in North Carolina (novel), 1997. Honour: National Book Award, 1997. Address: c/o Atlantic Monthly Press, 19 Union Square West, New York, NY 10003, USA.

FREDERICKS Frohm. See: **KERNER Fred.**

FREEBORN Richard (Harry), b. 19 Oct 1926, Cardiff, Wales. Professor of Russian Literature Emeritus; Writer; Translator. m. Anne Davis, 14 Feb 1954, 1 son, 3 daughters. Education: BA, 1950, MA, 1954, DPhil, 1957, Oxford University. Appointments: University Lecturer in Russian and Hulme Lecturer in Russian, Brasenose College, Oxford, 1954-64; Visiting Professor, University of California at Los Angeles, 1964-65; Sir William Mather Chair of Russian Studies, University of Manchester, 1965-67; Professor of Russian Literature, 1967-88, Professor Emeritus, 1988-, University of London. Publications: Fiction: Two Ways of Life, 1962; The Emigration of Sergey Ivanovich, 1963; Russian Roulette, 1979; The Russian Crucifix, 1987. Non-Fiction: Turgenev: A Study, 1960; A Short History of Modern Russia, 1966; The Rise of the Russian Novel, 1974; Russian Literary Attitudes from Pushkin to Solzhenitsyn (editor), 1976; Russian and Slavic Literature to 1917, Vol I (editor with Charles Ward), 1976; The Russian Revolutionary Novel: Turgenev to Pasternak, 1982; Ideology in Russian Literature (editor with Jane Grayson), 1990. Translator: Sketches from a Hunter's Album, by Turgenev, 1967; Home of the Gentry, by Turgenev, 1970; Rudin, by Turgenev, 1974; Love and Death: Six Stories by Ivan Turgenev, 1983; First Love and Other Stories, by Turgenev, 1989; Fathers and Sons, by Turgenev, 1991; A Month in the Country, by Turgenev, 1991; An Accidental Family, by Dostoevsky, 1994. Editor: Anton Chekhov: The Steppe and Other Stories, 1991; Ivan Goncharov: Oblomov, 1992; Reference Guide to Russian Literature: Articles on the Classic Russian Novel, Gor'kii, Kuzmin, Pasternak et al, 1998. Contributions to: Various publications. Honour: Honorary DLitt, University of London, 1984. Memberships: Association of Teachers of Russian, honorary vice president; British Universities Association of Slavists, president, 1969-72. Address: 24 Park Road, Surbiton, Surrey KT5 8QD, England.

FREEDLAND Michael Rodney, b. 14 Dec 1934, London, England. Biographer; Journalist; Broadcaster. m. Sara Hockerman, 3 July 1960, 1 son, 2 daughters. Publications: Al Jolson: Irving Berlin, James Cagney, Fred Astaire, Sophie, Errol Flynn, Danny Kaye, Leonard Bernstein; Jerome Kern, The Warner Brothers; The Goldwyn Touch; Gregory Peck; Katharine Hepburn; So Let's Hear the Applause; Sean Connery, All the Way - A Biography of Frank Sinatra, Bob Hope, Bing Crosby. Contributions to: The Times; The Guardian; The Observer; Daily Mail. Literary Agent: Curtis Brown & Jonathon Lloyd. Address: Bays Hill Lodge, Barnet Lane, Elmtree, Herts W06 3QU, England.

FREEDMAN David N(oel), b. 12 May 1922, New York, New York, USA. Professor of Biblical Studies; Writer; Editor. m. Cornelia Anne Pryor, 16 May 1944, 2 sons, 2 daughters. Education: City College of New York, 1935-38; AB, University of California at Los Angeles, 1938-39; ThB, Old Testament, Princeton Theological Seminary, 1944; PhD, Semitic Languages and Literature, Johns Hopkins University, 1948. Appointments: Ordained Minister, Presbyterian Church USA, 1944; State Supply Minister, Acme and Deming, Washington, Presbyterian Churches, 1944-45; Teaching Fellow, 1946-47, Assistant Instructor, 1947-48, Johns Hopkins University; Assistant Professor of Old Testament, 1948-51, Professor of Hebrew and Old Testament, 1951-60, Western Theological Seminary, Pittsburgh; Associate Editor, 1952-54, Editor, 1955-59, Journal of Biblical Literature; Professor of Hebrew and Old Testament, 1960-61, James A Kelso Professor of Hebrew and Old Testament, 1961-64, Pittsburgh Theological Seminary; Professor of Old Testament, 1964-70, Dean of Faculty, 1966-70, Gray Professor of Old Testament Exegesis, 1970-71, San Francisco Theological Seminary; Professor of Old Testament, Graduate Theological Union, 1964-71; Vice President, 1970-82, Director of Publications, 1974-82,

American Schools of Oriental Research; Editor, Biblical Archaeologist, 1976-82; Professor of Biblical Studies, 1971-92, Director, Program on Studies in Religion, 1971-91, Arthur F Thurnau Professor in Old Testament Studies, 1984-92, University of Michigan; Visiting Professor in Old Testament Studies, 1985-86, Professor in Hebrew Biblical Studies, 1987, Endowed Chair in Hebrew Biblical Studies, 1987-, University of California at San Diego; Numerous visiting lectureships and professorships. Publications: God Has Spoken (with J D Smart), 1949, Studies in Ancient Yahwistic Poetry (with Frank M Cross), 1950; Early Hebrew Orthography (with Frank M Cross), 1952; The People of the Dead Sea Scrolls (with J M Allegro), 1958; The Secret Saying of Jesus (with R M Grant), 1960; Ashdod I (with M Dothan), 1967; The Published Works of W F Albright (with R B MacDonald and D L Mattson), 1975; William Foxwell Albright: Twentieth Century Genius (with L G Running), 1975, 2nd edition, 1991; The Mountain of the Lord (with B Mazar and G Cornfeld), 1975; An Explorer's Life of Jesus (with W Phillips), 1975; Hosea (Anchor Bible Series; with F I Andersen), 1980; Pottery, Poetry, and Prophecy, 1981; The Paleo-Hebrew Leviticus Scroll (with K A Mathews), 1985; Amos (Anchor Bible Series; with F I Andersen), 1989; The Unity of the Hebrew Bible, 1991; Studies in Hebrew and Aramaic Orthography (with D Forbes and F I Andersen), 1992; The Relationship Between Herodotus' History and Primary History (with Sara Mandell), 1993. Other: The Biblical Archaeologist Reader (co-editor), 4 volumes, 1961, 1964, 1970, 1982; Anchor Bible Series (co-editor), 18 volumes, 1964-72; 50 volumes, (general editor), 1972-; Computer Bible Series (co-editor), 18 volumes, 1971-80; Anchor Bible Reference Library (general editor), 16 volumes, 1988-96; Anchor Bible Dictionary (editor-in-chief), 6 volumes, 1992. Honours: Guggenheim Fellowship, 1958-59; AATS Fellowship, 1965; Honorary doctorates. Memberships: American Academy of Religion; American Archaeological Institute; American Oriental Society; American Schools of Oriental Research; Explorers Club; Society of Biblical Literature. Address: c/o Department of History, No 0104, University of California at San Diego, La Jolla, CA 92093, USA.

FREEDMAN Lawrence (David), b. 7 Dec 1948, Northumberland, England. Professor of War Studies; Writer; Editor. m. Judith Anne Hill, 1974, 1 son, 1 daughter. Education: BA, Economics, University of Manchester, 1970; BPhil, University of York, 1971; DPhil, University of Oxford, 1975. Appointments: Teaching Assistant, University of York, 1971-72; Research Fellow, Nuffield College, Oxford, 1974-75; Lecturer in Politics, Balliol College, Oxford, 1975; Research Associate, 1975-76, Member of the Council, 1983-92, 1993-, International Institute for Strategic Studies; Research Fellow, 1976-78, Head of Policy Studies, 1978-82, Royal Institute of International Affairs; Professor of War Studies, King's College, University of London, 1982-; Chairman, Committee on International Peace and Security, Social Science Research Council, USA, 1993-96. Publications: US Intelligence and the Soviet Strategic Threat, 1977, new edition, 1986; Britain and Nuclear Weapons, 1980; The Evolution of Nuclear Strategy, 1981, 2nd edition, 1989; Nuclear War and Nuclear Peace (with Edwina Moreton, Gerald Segal, and John Baylis), 1983, 2nd edition, 1988; The Troubled Alliance: Atlantic Relations in the 1980s (editor), 1983; The Atlas of Global Strategy, 1985; The Price of Peace: Living with the Nuclear Dilemma, 1986; Britain and the Falklands War, 1988; US Nuclear Strategy: A Reader (editor with Philip Bobbitt and Gregeory Treverton), 1989; Signals of War: The Falklands Conflict of 1982 (with Virginia Gamba-Stonehouse), 1990; Europe Transformed (editor), 1990; Military Power in Europe: Essays in Memory of Jonathon Alford (editor), 1990; Britain in the world (editor with Michael Clarke), 1991; Population Change and European Security (editor with John Saunders), 1991; War, Strategy and International Politics: Essays in Honour of Sir Michael Howard (editor with Paul Hayes and Robert O'Neill), 1992; The Gulf Conflict 1990-91; Diplomacy and War in the New World Order (with Efraim Karsh), 1993; War: A Reader (editor), 1994; Military Intervention in Europe (editor), 1994; Strategic Coercion (editor), 1998. Contributions to: Various publications. Honours: Fellow, Royal Society of Arts, 1991; Fellow, King's College, University of London, 1992; Fellow, British Academy, 1995; Commander of the Order of the British Empire, 1996. Address: c/o Department of War Studies, King's College, University of London, Strand, London WC2R 2LS, England.

FREEDMAN (Bruce) Russell, b. 11 Oct 1929, San Francisco, California, USA. Children's Book Writer. Education: San Jose State University; BA, University of California at Berkeley. Publications: Thomas Alva Edison, 1961; 2000 Years of Space Travel, 1963; Scouting with Baden-Powell, 1967; The First Days of Life, 1974; How Animals Defend Their Young, 1978; Immigrant Kids, 1980; When Winter Comes, 1981; Dinosaurs & Their Young, 1983; Children of the Wild West, 1984; Lincoln: A Photobiography, 1985; Cowboys of the Wild West, 1985; Sharks, 1985; The First Fifty Years, 1985; Indian Chiefs, 1987; The Wright Brothers, 1991; Eleanor Roosevelt, 1993. Contributions to: Reference books and periodicals. Honours: Notable Book of the Year Citation; American Library Association, 1980, 1983, 1985; Western Heritage Award, 1984; Newberry Medal, 1988; Newberry Honour Citation, American Library Association, 1992; Boston Globe/Horn Book Award, 1994. Memberships: Authors League of America; American Civil Liberties Union. Address: 280 Riverside Drive, New York, NY 10025, USA.

FREELING Nicolas, b. 3 Mar 1927, London, England. Writer. m. Cornelia Termes, 1954, 4 sons, 1 daughter. Education: University of Dublin. Publications: Fiction: Love in Amsterdam, 1961; Because of the Cats, 1962; Gun Before Butter, 1963; Valparaiso, 1964; Double Barrel, 1964; Criminal Conversation, 1965; The King of the Rainy Country, 1966; The Dresden Green, 1966; Strike Out Where Not Applicable, 1967; This is the Castle, 1968; Tsing-Boum, 1969; Over the High Side, 1970; A Long Silence, 1971; Dressing of Diamond, 1974; What Are the Bugles Blowing For?, 1975; Lake Isle, 1976; Gadget, 1977; The Night Lords, 1978; The Widow, 1979; Castang's City, 1980; One Damned Thing After Another, 1981; Wolfnight, 1982; The Back of the North Wind, 1983; No Part in Your Death, 1984; A City Solitary, 1985; Cold Iron, 1986; Not as Far as Velma, 1989; Sand Castles, 1989; Those in Peril, 1990; Flanders Sky, 1992; You who Know, 1994; The Seacoast of Bohemia, 1995; A Dwarf Kingdom, 1996; One More River, 1998. Other: The Kitchen: A Delicious Account of the Author's Years as a Grand Hotel Cook, 1970; Criminal Convictions: Errant Essays on Perpetrators of Literary License, 1994. Honours: Crime Writers Award, 1963; Grand Prix de Roman Policier, 1965; Edgar Allan Poe Award, Mystery Writers of America, 1966. Address: Grandfontaine, 67130 Schirmeck, Bas Rhin, France.

FREEMAN Anne Hobson, b. 19 Mar 1934, Richmond, Virginia, USA. Fiction Writer; Essayist. m. George Clemon Freeman Jr, 6 Dec 1958, 2 sons, 1 daughter. Education: AB, Bryn Mawr College, 1956; MA, University of Virginia, 1973. Appointments: Reporter, International News Service, Russia and Eastern Europe, 1957; Editor, Member's Bulletin, Virginia Museum of Fine Arts, 1958-63; Lecturer, English, University of Virginia, 1973-88. Publication: The Style of a Law Firm: Eight Gentlemen from Virginia, 1990; A Hand Well Played: The Life of Jim Wheat, Jr, 1994. Contributions to: Anthologies and periodicals. Address: Oyster Shell Point Farm, Callao, VA 224356, USA.

FREEMAN Gillian (Elizabeth Von S), b. 5 Dec 1929, London, England. Writer. m. Edward Thorpe, 12 Sept 1955, 2 daughters. Education: BA, Honours, University of Reading, 1951. Publications: The Liberty Man, 1955; Fall of Innocence, 1956; Jack Would be a Gentleman, 1959; The Story of Albert Einstein, 1960; The Leather Boys, 1961; The Campaign, 1963; The Leader, 1965; The Undergrowth of Literature, 1969; The Alabaster Egg, 1970; The Marriage Machine, 1975; The Schoolgirl Ethic: The Life and Work of Angela Brazil, 1976; Nazi Lady, (1st edition as Elizabeth von S), 1979; An Easter Egg Hunt, 1981; Lovechild, 1984; Ballet Genius (with Edward Thorpe), 1988; Termination Rock, 1989. Other: Screenplays and adaptations; Ballet scenarios. Contributions to: Periodicals. Memberships: Arts Council; Writers Guild of Great Britain. Address: c/o Richard Scott Simon, 48 Doughty Street, London WC1N 2LP, England.

FREEMAN James M(ontague), b. 1 Dec 1936, Chicago, Illinois, USA. Professor of Anthropology; Writer. Education: BA, Northwestern University, 1958; MA, 1964, PhD, 1968, Harvard University. Appointments: Assistant Professor to Professor of Anthropology, San Jose State University, 1966-. Publications: Scarcity and Opportunity in an Indian Village, 1977; Untouchable: An Indian Life History, 1979; Hearts of Sorrow: Vietnamese-American Lives, 1989; Changing Identities: Vietnamese Americans 1975-1995, 1996. Contributions to: Scholarly books and journals. Honours: Choice Outstanding Academic Book, 1979; Phi Kappa Phi Distinguished Academic Achievement Award, 1982; National Endowment for the Humanities Fellowship, 1983-84; President's Scholar, San Jose State University, 1984; Before Columbus Foundation American Book Award, 1990; Association for Asian-American Studies Outstanding Book Award, 1990; Austin D Warburton Award for Outstanding Scholarship, 1991. Memberships: Aid to Refugee Children Without Parents, 1988-95, and its successor, Aid to Children Without Parents, Inc, chairman of the board, 1995-; Southwestern Anthropological Association, president, 1991-92. Address: c/o Department of Anthropology, San Jose State University, San Jose, CA 95192, USA.

FREEMAN Judith, b. 1 Oct 1946, Ogden, Utah, USA. Writer; Critic. m. Anthony Hernandez, 1986, 1 son. Appointment: Contributing Critic, Los Angeles Times Book Review. Publications: Family Attractions, 1988; The Chinchilla Farm, 1989; Set for Life, 1991; A Desert of Pure Feeling, 1996. Honour: Western Heritage Award for Best Western Novel, 1991. Membership: PEB West. Address: c/o The Lantz Office, 888 Seventh Avenue, New York, NY 10106, USA.

FREEMAN-GRENVILLE Greville Stewart Parker, b. 29 June 1918, Hook Norton, Oxfordshire, England. Historian; Writer. Education: BLitt, 1940, MA, 1943, DPhil, 1957, Worcester College, Oxford. Publications: The Medieval History of the Coast of Tanganyika, 1962; The East African Coast: Select Documents (editor and translator), 1962, 2nd edition, 1975; The Muslim and Christian Calendars, 1963, 2nd edition, 1977; French at Kilwa Island, 1965; Chronology of African History, 1973; Chronology of World History, 1975; A Modern Atlas of African History, 1976; The Queen's Lineage, 1977; Atlas of British History, 1979; The Mombasa Rising Against the Portuguese 1631, 1980; The Beauty of Cairo, 1981; Buzurg ibn Shahriyar: The Book of Wonders of India (c 953) (editor and translator), 1982; Emily Said-Ruete: Memoirs of an Arabian Princess (1888) (editor), 1982, 2nd edition, 1994; The Beauty of Jerusalem and the Holy Places of the Gospels, 1982, 2nd edition, 1987; The Stations of the Cross, 1982; The Beauty of Rome, 1988; The Swahili Coast: Islam, Christianity and Commerce in Eastern Africa, 1988; A New Atlas for African History, 1991; Historical Atlas of the Middle East, 1993; The Basilica of the Nativity at Bethlehem, 1993; The Basilica of the Holy Sepulchre in Jerusalem, 1993; The Basilica of the Annunciation at Nazareth and other nearby shrines, 1993; The Holy Land: A Pilgrim's Guide to Israel, Jordan and the Sinai, 1995; Islamic and Christian Calendars, AD 622-2222, 1995; Wordsworth's Kings and Queens of Great Britain, 1997. Contributions to: Numerous journals, reviews and encyclopaedias including Journal of the Royal Asiatic Society; Numismatic Chronocle; Encyclopaedia of Islam; Encyclopaedia Britannica. Memberships: Society of Antiquaries, fellow; Royal Asiatic Society, fellow; Palestine Exploration Fund, executive committee, 1992-; Royal Asiatic Society, vice president, 1997-. Address: North View House, Sheriff Hutton, York Y060 6ST, England.

FREEMANTLE Brian (Harry), (Jonathan Evans, Richard Gant, John Maxwell, Jack Winchester), b. 10 June 1936, Southampton, England. Author. m. Maureen Hazel Tipney, 8 Dec 1957, 3 daughters. Education:

Secondary school, Southampton. Appointments: Reporter, New Milton Advertiser, 1953-58, Bristol Evening News, 1958, Evening News, London, 1959-61; Reporter, 1961-63, Assistant Foreign Editor, 1963-69, Daily Express; Foreign Editor, Daily Sketch, London, 1969-70, Daily Mail, London, 1971-75. Publications: Novels: The Touchables, 1968; Goodbye to an Old Friend, 1973; Face Me When You Walk Away, 1974; The Man Who Wanted Tomorrow, 1975; The November Man, 1976; Deaken's War, 1982; Rules of Engagement, 1984; Vietnam Legacy, 1984; The Lost American, 1984; The Laundryman, 1986; The Kremlin Kiss, 1986; The Bearpit, 1988; O'Farrell's Law, 1990; The Factory, 1990; The Choice of Eddie Franks, 1990; Betrayals, 1991; Little Grey Mice, 1992; The Button Man, 1993; No Time for Heroes, 1995. Other: 11 books in the Charlie Muffin mystery series. Non-Fiction: KGB, 1982; CIA, 1983; The Fix: Inside the World Drug Trade, 1985; The Steal: Counterfeiting and Industrial Espionage, 1987; The Octopus: Europe in the Grip of Organised Crime, 1996. Contributions to: Periodicals. Address: c/o Jonathan Clowes, 10 Iron Bridge House, Bridge Approach, London NW1 8BD, England.

FREISINGER Randall R(oy), b. 6 Feb 1942, Kansas City, Missouri, USA. Professor of Rhetoric, Literature and Creative Writing; Poet. m. 2 sons. Education: BJ, Journalism, 1962, MA, English Literature, 1964, PhD, English Literature, 1975, University of Missouri. Appointments: Instructor, Jefferson College, 1964-68; Resident Lecturer, University of Maryland Overseas Program, 1968-69, 1975-76; Assistant Professor, Columbia College, 1976-77; Assistant, Associate Professor, 1977-93, Professor of Rhetoric, Literature and Creative Writing, 1993-, Michigan Technological University; Associate Editor, Laurel Review, 1989-. Publications: Running Patterns, 1985; Hand Shadows, 1988; Plato's Breath, 1997. Contributions to: Anthologies, journals, reviews, and quarterlies. Honours: Winner, Flume Press National Chapbook Competition, 1985; 4 Pushcart Prize Nominations, 1985-97; May Swenson Poetry Award, 1996. Memberships: Associated Writing Programs; National Council of Teachers of English. Address: 200 Prospect Street, Houghton, MI 49931, USA.

FRENCH David, b. 18 Jan 1939, Coleys Point, Newfoundland, Canada. m. Leslie Gray, 5 Jan 1978. Dramatist; Writer. Education: Studied Acting, Pasadena Playhouse, Toronto, Canada; Roy Lawler Acting School, Toronto, Canada. Publications: A Company of Strangers (novel), 1968; Leaving Home, 1972; Of the Fields, Lately, 1973; One Crack Out, 1976; The Seagull, by Anton Chekov, translation, 1978; Jitters, 1980; Salt-Water Moon, 1985; "1949", 1989. Contributions to: Montrealer; Canadian Boy. Honours: Chalmers Award, Best Canadian Play, Ontario Arts Council, 1973; Lieutenant Governor's Award, 1974; Canada Council Grants, 1974, 1975. Address: c/o Tarragon Theatre, 30 Bridgman Avenue, Toronto, Ontario M5R 1X3, Canada.

FRENCH Linda. See: **MARIZ Linda Catherine French.**

FRENCH Marilyn, b. 21 Nov 1929, New York, New York, USA. Writer; Critic. m. Robert M French Jr, 4 June 1950, div 1967, 2 children. Education: BA, 1951, MA, 1964, Hofstra University; PhD, Harvard University, 1972. Appointments: Lecturer, Hofstra University, 1964-68; Assistant Professor, Holy Cross College, Worcester, Massachusetts, 1972-76; Mellon Fellow, Harvard University, 1976-77. Publications: Fiction: The Women's Room, 1977; The Bleeding Heart, 1980; Her Mother's Daughter, 1987; Our Father: A Novel, 1994. Non-Fiction: The Book as World: James Joyce's Ulysses, 1976; Shakespeare's Division of Exprience, 1981; Beyond Power: On Women, Men and Morals, 1986; The War Against Women, 1992. Contributions to: Books and periodicals. Memberships: James Joyce Society; Modern Language Association; Virginia Woolf Society. Address: c/o Random House Value Publishing Inc, 40 Engelhard Avenue, Avenal, NJ 07001, USA.

FRENCH Philip (Neville), b. 28 Aug 1933, Liverpool, England. Writer; Broadcaster; Film Critic. m. Kersti Elisabet Molin, 1957, 3 sons. Education: BA, Exeter College, Oxford; Indiana University. Appointments: Reporter, Bristol Evening Post, 1958-59; Producer, North American Service, 1959-61, Talks Producer, 1961-67, Senior Producer, 1968-90, BBC Radio; Theatre Critic, 1967-68, Arts Columnist, 1967-72, New Statesman; Film Critic, The Observer, 1978-. Publications: The Age of Austerity, 1945-51 (editor with Michael Sissons), 1963; The Novelist as Innovator (editor), 1966; The Movie Moguls, 1969; Westerns: Aspects of a Movie Genre, 1974, revised edition, 1977; Three Honest Men: Portraits of Edmund Wilson, F R Leavis, Lionel Trilling, 1980; The Third Dimension: Voices from Radio Three (editor), 1983; The Press: Observed and Projected (editor with Deac Rossell), 1991; Malle on Malle, (editor), 1992; The Faber Book of Movie Verse (editor with Ken Wlaschin), 1993; Wild Strawberries (with Kersti French), 1995. Contributions to: Many anthologies and periodicals. Address: 62 Dartmouth Park Road, London NW5 1SN, England.

FRENCH Warren Graham, b. 26 Jan 1922, Philadelphia, Pennsylvania, USA. Retired College Professor. Education: BA, University of Pennsylvania, 1943; MA, 1948, PhD, American Literature 1954, University of Texas. Publications: John Steinbeck, 1961, revised edition, 1974; Frank Norris, 1962; J D Salinger, 1963; The Social Novel at the End of an Era, 1966; Jack Kerouac, 1986; J D Salinger, Revisited, 1988; The San Francisco Poetry Renaissance, 1955-1960, 1991. Editor: The Thirties, 1967; The Forties, 1969; The Fifties, 1971; The South in Film, 1981; The Twenties, 1975. Contributions to: Numerous American academic journals. Honour: DHL, Ohio University, 1985. Memberships: International John Steinbeck Society; American Literature; Modern Language Association of America; American Studies Association; Western American Literature Association. Address: 23 Beechwood Road, Uplands, Swansea, West Glamorgan SA2 0HL, Wales.

FREUD Esther Lea, b. 2 May 1963, London, England. Writer. 1 son, 1 daughter. Education: Trained as an actress, Drama Centre, London, 1981-83. Publications: Hideous Kinky, 1992; Peerless Flats, 1993; Gaglow, 1997. Literary Agent: Toby Eady Assoc. Address: Third Floor, 9 Orme Court, London W2 4RL, England.

FREWER Glyn Mervyn Louis, (Mervyn Lewis), b. 4 Sept 1931, Oxford, England. Author; Scriptwriter. m. Lorna Townsend, 11 Aug 1956, 2 sons, 1 daughter. Education: MA, English Language and Literature, St Catherine's College, Oxford, 1955. Publications: The Hitch-Hikers (BBC Radio Play), 1957; Adventure in Forgotten Valley, 1962; Adventure in the Barren Lands, 1964; The Last of the Wispies, 1965; Death of Gold (as Mervyn Lewis), 1970; The Token of Elkin, 1970; Crossroad, 1970; The Square Peg, 1972; The Raid, 1976; The Trackers, 1976; Tyto: The Odyssey of an Owl, 1978; Bryn of Brockle Hanger, 1980; Fox, 1984; The Call of the Raven, 1987. Other scripts for children's television series, industrial films, etc. Contributions to: Birds; Imagery. Honours: Junior Literary Guild of America Choice, for Adventure in Forgotten Valley, 1964; Freeman of the City of Oxford, 1967. Literary Agent: Watson, Little Ltd. Address: Cottage Farm, Taston, Oxford OX7 3JN, England.

FREY Bruno S, b. 4 May 1941, Basel, Swtizerland. University Professor. Education: Lizentiat, 1964; PhD, 1965, Habilitation, 1969, University of Basel, Switzerland. Appointments: Full Professor, University of Zürich, 1977-; Full Professor, University of Konslanz, 1970-77; Associate Professor, University of Basel, 1969-. Publications: Umweltoekonomie, 3rd edition, 1972-92; Modern Political Economy; Democratic Economic Policy, 1983; Schallenwirtschaft, 1984; Muses and Markets Explorations in the Economics of Arts, 1989; Economics as a Science of Human Behaviour, 1990; Not Just for the Money, a Theory of Personal Motivation, 1997; A New Proposal of Federalism in Europe, 1999. Honour: DHon, University of St Gallen, 1998; DHon, University of Gothenburg, 1998. Address: Institute for Empirical Economic Research, University of Zurich, Bluemlisalystr 10, CH-8006, Zurich, Switzerland.

FRIDRIKSSON Gudjon, b. 9 Mar 1945, Reykjavík, Iceland. Historian; Writer; Journalist. m. Hildur Kjartanspottir, 26 Mar 1983, 2 daughters. Education: BA, University of Iceland, 1970. Appointments: Teacher in Litterature, 1972-75; Journalist, 1976-80, Editor, Sunday edition, 1980-84, Thjodvilsinn newspaper; Editor, Offical History of Reykjavik, 1985-91; Freelance Writer. Publications: Togarasaga Magnusar Runólfssonar, 1983; Baerin Vaknar Saga Reykjavikur 1870-1940 (Awakening of a Town: History of Reykjavik 1870-1940), 2 volumes, 1991, 1994; Saga Jonasar Jonssonar Fra Hriflu (The Biography of the Politician Jonas Jonsson from Hrifla), 1991-93; Indaela Reykjavik (Wonderful Reykjavik), 1995. Contributions to: Heimsmynd, 1989-94. Honours: Mother Tongue Prize for Journalists, 1985; Icelandic Literature Prize, 1991. Membership: Icelandic Writers Union, board of directors, 1994-. Address: Tjarnargata 44, 101 Reykjavík, Iceland.

FRIEDAN Betty (Naomi), b. 4 Feb 1921, Peoria, Illinois, USA. Feminist Activist; Writer. m. Carl Friedan, June 1947, div May 1969, 2 sons, 1 daughter. Education: AB, Smith College, 1942. Appointments: Research Fellow, University of California at Berkeley, 1943; Founder-1st President, National Organization for Women, 1966-70; Contributing Editor, McCall's magazine, 1971-74; Senior Research Associate, Columbia University, 1979-81; Research Fellow, Harvard University, 1982-83; Chubb Fellow, Yale University, 1985; Guest Scholar, Woodrow Wilson Center for International Scholars, 1995-96; Many other lectureships. Publications: The Feminine Mystique, 1963; It Changed My Life: Writings on the Women's Movement, 1976; The Second Stage, 1981; The Fountain of Age, 1993. Contributions to: Periodicals. Honours: Humanist of the Year Award, 1974; Mort Weisinger Award for Outstanding Magazine Journalism, 1979; Author of the Year, 1982, American Society of Journalists and Authors; Eleanor Roosevelt Leadership Award, 1989; Various honorary doctorates. Memberships: American Society of Journalists and Authors; American Sociology Association; Association of Humanistic Psychology; Authors Guild; National Organizatioin for Women; National Press Club; PEN; Phi Beta Kappa. Address: 420 7th Street North West, Apt 1010, Washington, DC 20004, USA.

FRIEDBERG Maurice, b. 3 Dec 1929, Rzeszow, Poland. Professor of Russian Literature; Writer; Translator. m. Barbara Bisguier, 1956, 2 daughters. Education: BA, Brooklyn College, 1951; AM, 1953, PhD, 1958, Columbia University. Appointments: Associate Professor of Russian, Chairman, Russian Division, Hunter College, City University of New York, 1955-65; Fulbright Professor of Russian Literature, Hebrew University, Jerusalem, Israel, 1965-66; Professor of Slavic Languages and Literatures, 1966-75, Director, Russian and East European Institute, 1967-71, Indiana University; Professor of Slavic Languages and Literatures, Department Head, University of Illinois, Urbana, 1975-95; Directeur d'Etudes Associés, Ecole des Hautes Etudes en Sciences Sociales, Paris, 1984-85; Center for Advanced Study Professor of Russian Literature, University of Illinois, 1995-. Publications: Russian Classics in Soviet Jackets, 1962; A Bilingual Edition of Russian Short Stories, Vol II (editor and translator with R A Maguire), 1965; The Jew in Post-Stalin Soviet Literature, 1970; Encyclopedia Judaica (editor and co-author), 16 volumes, 1971-72; The Young Lenin, by Leon Trotsky (editor), 1972; A Decade of Euphoria: Western Literature in Post-Stalin Russia, 1977; Russian Culture in the 1980's, 1986; Soviet Society under Gorbachev (editor with Heyward Isham), 1987; The Red Pencil (editor with Marianna Tax Choldin), 1989; How Things Were Done in Odessa, 1991. Honours: Guggenheim Fellowships; National Endowment for the Humanities Fellowship. Address: 3001 Meadowbrook Court, Champaign, IL 61821, USA.

FRIEDEN Bernard J(oel), b. 11 Aug 1930, New York, New York, USA. Professor of Urban Development; Writer. m. Elaine Leibowitz, 23 Nov 1958, 1 daughter. Education: BA, Cornell University, 1951; MA, Pennsylvania State University, 1953; MCP, 1957, PhD, 1962, Massachusetts Institute of Technology. Appointments: Assistant Professor, 1961-65, Associate Professor, 1965-69, Professor of Urban Studies and Planning, 1969-, Chairman, Faculty, 1987-89, Ford Professor of Urban Development, 1989-, Associate Dean, Architecture and Planning, 1993-, Massachusetts Institute of Technology; Research Fellow, 1978-89, Senior Fellow, 1989-, Urban Land Institute; Visiting Scholar, University of California, Berkeley, 1990-91. Publications: The Future of Old Neighborhoods, 1964; Metropolitan America, 1966; Urban Planning and Social Policy (with Robert Morris), 1968; Shaping an Urban Future (with William W Nash), 1969; The Politics of Neglect (with Marshall Kaplan), 1975, 2nd edition, 1977; Managing Human Services (with Wayne E Anderson and Michael J Murphy), 1977; The Environmental Protection Hustle, 1979; Downtown, Inc (with Lynne B Sagalyn), 1989. Contributions to: Books and encyclopaedias. Honour: Guggenheim Fellowship, 1975-76. Memberships: American Institute of Certified Planners; American Planning Association; Senior Fellow, Urban Land Institute, 1989-98. Address: 245 Highland Avenue, Newton, MA 02165, USA.

FRIEDMAN Alan Howard, b. 4 Jan 1928, New York City, USA. Writer. m. (1) Leonore Ann Helman, 1 Aug 1950, div, 1 son, (2) Kate Miller Gilbert, 30 Oct 1977. Education: BA, Harvard College, 1949; MA, Columbia University, 1950; PhD, University of California at Berkeley, 1964. Publications: The Turn of the Novel, 1966; Hermaphrodeity: The Autobiography of a Poet (novel), 1972. Contributions to: Hudson Review; Mademoiselle; Partisan Review; New American Review; Paris Review; Fiction International; Kansas Quarterly; Denver Quarterly; Formations. Honours: D H Lawrence Fellowship, 1974; National Endowment for the Arts Award, 1975; Pen Syndicated Fiction Award, 1987. Literary Agent: Lynn Nesbit, New York City. Address: 3530 Monte Real, Escondido, CA 92029, USA.

FRIEDMAN Bruce Jay, b. 26 Apr 1930, New York, New York, USA. Writer; Dramatist; Screenwriter. m. (1) Ginger Howard, 13 June 1954, div 1978, 3 sons, (2) Patricia O'Donohue, 3 July 1983, 1 daughter. Education: BJ, University of Missouri, 1951. Appointment: Editorial Director, Magazine Management Co, New York City, 1953-64. Publications: Stern, 1962; Far From the City of Class, and Other Stories, 1963; A Mother's Kisses, 1964; Black Humour (editor), 1965; Black Angels, 1966; Pardon Me, Sir, But Is My Eye Hurting Your Elbow? (with others), 1968; The Dick, 1970; About Harry Towns, 1974; The Lonely Guys Book of Life, 1978; Let's Hear It for a Beautiful Guy, and Other Works of Short Fiction, 1984; Tokyo Woes, 1985; Violencia, 1988; The Current Climate, 1990; Collected Short Fiction of Bruce Jay Friedman, 1995; The Slightly Older Guy, 1995. Other: Plays and screenplays including Have You Spoken to Any Jews Lately, 1995; A Father's Kisses, 1996. Memberships: PEN; Sigma Delta Chi. Literary Agent: Candida Denadio, 121 West 27th Street, New York, NY 10001, USA. Address: PO Box 746, Water Mill, NY 11976, USA.

FRIEDMAN Dennis, b. 23 Feb 1924, London, England. Psychiatrist. m. Rosemary Tibber, 2 Feb 1949, 4 daughters. Education: Licentiate, Royal College of Physicians, London, 1948. Publication: Inheritance: A Psychological History of the Royal Family, 1993; Darling Georgie: The Enigma of King George V, 1998. Contributions to: Books and other publications. Memberships: Royal College of Psychiatrists, Fellow; Royal College of Psychiatrists; Royal Society of Medicine. Address: 2 St Katharine's Precinct, Regent's Park, London NW1 4HH, England.

FRIEDMAN Lawrence J, b. 8 Oct 1940, Cleveland, Ohio, USA. Professor of History; Writer. m. Sharon Bloom, 3 Apr 1966, 1 daughter. Education: BA, University of California at Riverside, 1962; MA, 1965, PhD, 1967, University of California at Los Angeles; Postdoctoral

Fellow, Menninger Foundation Interdisciplinary Studies Program, 1981. Appointments: Assistant Professor, Arizona State University, 1967-71; Associate Professor, 1971-77, Professor of History and American Studies, 1977-91, Distinguished University Professor, 1991-93, Bowling Green State University; Visiting Scholar, Harvard University, 1991; Professor of History, Indiana University, 1993-. Publications: The White Savage: Racial Fantasies in the Postbellum South, 1970; Inventors of the Promised Land, 1975; Gregarious Saints: Self and Community in American Abolitionism, 1830-1870, 1982; Menninger: The Family and the Clinic, 1990; Identity's Architect: A Biography of Erik Erikson, 1999. Contributions to: Books and professional journals. Honours: National Endowment for the Humanities Fellowships, 1979-80, 1986-87, 1994-95; Ohioana Library Association Book Award in History, 1983; Paul and Ruth Olscamp Distinguished Research Award, 1989-92; John Adams Fellow, Institute of United States Studies, University of London. Memberships: American Association of University Professors; American Historical Association; Cheiron; Organization of American Historians; Society of American Historians. Literary Agent: Gerard McCauley. Address: c/o Department of History, Indiana University, Bloomington, IN 47405, USA.

FRIEDMAN Lawrence Meir, b. 2 Apr 1930, Chicago, Illinois, USA. Professor of Law; Writer. m. Leah Feigenbaum, 27 Mar 1955, 2 daughters. Education: AB, 1948, JD, 1951, MLL, 1953, University of Chicago. Appointments: Assistant to Associate Professor 1957-61, Childress Memorial Lecturer, 1987, St Louis University; Associate Professor to Professor of Law, University of Wisconsin, Madison, 1961-68; Professor of Law, 1968-76, Marion Rice Kirkwood Professor of Law, 1976-, Stanford University; David Stouffer Memorial Lecturer, Rutgers University, 1969; Fellow, Center for Advanced Study in the Behavioral Sciences, 1973-74; Sibley Lecturer, University of Georgia, 1976; Wayne Morse Lecturer, University of Oregon, 1985; Fellow, Institute for Advanced Study, Berlin, 1985; Jefferson Lecture, University of California at Berkeley, 1995; Ruston Lecture, Cumberland School of Law, 1997. Publications: Contract Law in America, 1965; Government and Slum Housing: A Century of Frustration, 1968; Law and the Behavioral Sciences (with Stewart Macaulay), 1969, 2nd edition, 1977; A History of American Law, 1973, 2nd edition, 1985; The Legal System: A Social Science Perspective, 1975; Law and Society: An Introduction, 1978; The Roots of Justice: Crime and Punishment in Alameda County, California, 1870-1910, 1981; American Law, 1984, 2nd edition, 1998; Total Justice: What Americans Want from the Legal System and Why, 1985; Your Time Will Come: The Law of Age Discrimination and Mandatory Retirement, 1985; American Law and the Constitutional Order Historical Perspectives (editor with Harry N Schrieber), 1988; The Republic of Choice: Law, Authority and Culture, 1990; Crime and Punishment in American History, 1993; Law and Society: Readings on the Study of Law (co-editor), 1995; Legal Culture and the Legal Profession (co-editor), 1996; The Crime Conundrum (co-editor), 1997. Honours: Scribes Award, 1974; Triennial Award, Order of Coif, 1976; Willard Hurst Prize, 1982; Harry Kalven Prize, 1992; Silver Gavel Award, ABA, 1994; Five Honorary Doctorates, 1977-98. Memberships: American Academy of Arts and Sciences; Law and Society Association, president, 1979-81; American Society for Legal History, president, 1990-91; Society of American Historians. Address: c/o School of Law, Stanford University, Stanford, CA 94305, USA.

FRIEDMAN Milton, b. 31 July 1912, Brooklyn, New York, USA. Professor of Economics Emeritus; Senior Research Fellow; Writer. m. Rose Director, 25 June 1938, 1 son, 1 daughter. Education: BA, Rutgers University, 1932; AM, University of Chicago, 1933; PhD, Columbia University, 1946. Appointments: Associate Economist, Natural Resources Committee, Washington, DC, 1935-37; National Bureau of Economic Research, New York, 1937-40; Principal Economist, Tax Research Division, US Treasury Department, Washington, DC, 1941-43; Associate Director, Statistical Research Group, Division of War Research, Columbia University, 1943-45;

Professor of Economics, 1948-82, Professor Emeritus, 1982-, University of Chicago; Member, Research Staff, National Bureau of Economic Research, 1948-81; Fulbright Lecturer, Cambridge University, 1953-54; Columnist, 1966-84, Contributing Editor, 1974-84, Newsweek magazine; Senior Research Fellow, Hoover Institution, Stanford University, 1976-. Publications: Income from Independent Professional Practice (with Simon Kuznets), 1946; Sampling Inspection (with others), 1948; Essays in Positive Economics, 1953; Studies in the Quantity Theory of Money (editor), 1956; A Theory of the Consumption Function, 1957; A Program for Monetary Stability, 1960; Capitalism and Freedom, 1962; Price Theory: A Provisional Text, 1962; A Monetary History of the United States 1867-1960 (with Anna J Schwartz), 1963; Inflation: Causes and Consequences, 1963; The Balance of Payments: Free Versus Flexible Exchange Rates (with Robert V Roosa), 1967; Dollars and Deficits, 1968; Optimum Quantity of Money and Other Essays, 1969; Monetary Policy Versus Fiscal Policy (with Walter W Heller), 1969; Monetary Statistics of the United States (with Anna J Schwartz), 1970; A Theoretical Framework for Monetary Analysis, 1971; Social Security: Universal or Selective? (with Wilbur J Cohen), 1972; An Economist's Protest, 1972; Money and Economic Development, 1973; There's No Such Thing as a Free Lunch, 1975; Price Theory, 1976; Free to Choose (with Rose Friedman), 1980; Monetary Trends in the United States and the United Kingdom (with Anna J Schwartz), 1982; Bright Promises, Dismal Performance, 1983; Tyranny of the Status Quo (with Rose Friedman), 1984; Money Mischief, 1992; Two Lucky People: Memoirs (with Rose D Friedman), 1998. Honours: John Bates Clark Medal, American Economic Association, 1951; Nobel Prize for Economic Science, 1976; Grand Cordon, Sacred Treasure, Japan, 1986; US Presidential Medal of Freedom, 1988; National Medal of Science, 1988; Institution of World Capitalism Prize, Jacksonville University, 1993; Goldwater Award, Goldwater Institute, 1997; Robert Maynard Hutchins History Maker Award for Distinction in Education, Chicago Historical Society, 1997; Templeton Honour Rolls Lifetime Achievement Award, 1997; Various fellowships, awards and honorary doctorates. Memberships: American Economic Association, president, 1967; Mont Pelerin Society, president, 1970-72; Royal Economic Society. Address: c/o Hoover Institution, Stanford, CA 94305-6010, USA.

FRIEDMAN Richard Elliott, b. 5 May 1946, USA. Scholar; Professor. Education: BA, Philosophy, University of Miami, 1968; MHL, Hebrew Literature, Jewish Theological Seminary, 1971; ThM, Hebrew Bible, 1974; ThD, Hebrew Bible, 1978, Harvard University. Appointments: Professor of Hebrew & Comparative Literature, Katzin Professor of Jewish Civilization, University of California, San Diego, USA. Publications: The Exile and Biblical Narrative, 1981; The Creation of Sacred Literature, editor, 1981; The Poet and the Historian, editor, 1983; The Future of Biblical Studies, co-editor, 1987; Who Wrote the Bible?, first ed, 1987; Who Wrote the Bible, second edition, 1996; The Disappearance of God, 1995; The Hidden Face of God, 1997; The Hidden Book in the Bible, 1998. Honours: BA cum laude; ThM cum laude; ThD distinction; American Council of Learned Societies Fellow, 1982; Elected to membership, The Biblical Colloquium, 1987; Life Member, Clare Hall, University of Cambridge, England; University of California President's Research Fellowship in the Humanities, 1997; University of California Research Awards, 1978, 1979, 1984, 1988, 1997; New York Times Editors' Recommended Selection, 1987; New York Times Notable Books of 1987; The Times, London, Editors' Recommended Selection, 1988; Laymen's National Bible Association Citation, 1988; New York Times Editors' Recommended Paperback Selection, 1989; New York Times Notable Paperback Books of 1989; Publishers Weekly Best Books of 1995. Memberships: Society of Biblical Literature; The Authors Guild. Literary Agent: Elaine Markson, Literary Agency, New York, USA. Address: Department of Literature, UCSD, La Jolla, CA 92093, USA.

FRIEDMAN (Eve) Rosemary, (Robert Tibber, Rosemary Tibber), b. 5 Feb 1929, London, England. Writer. m. Dennis Friedman, 2 Feb 1949, 4 daughters. Education: Queen's College, Harley Street, London; Law Faculty, University College, London University. Publications: The Life Situation, 1977; The Long Hot Summer, 1980; Proofs of Affection, 1982; A Loving Mistress, 1983; Rose of Jericho, 1984; A Second Wife, 1986; To Live in Peace, 1987; An Eligible Man, 1989; Golden Boy, 1994; Vintage, 1996. As Robert Tibber: No White Coat, 1957; Love on My List, 1959; We All Fall Down, 1960; Patients of a Saint, 1961; The Fraternity, 1963; The Commonplace Day, 1964; The General Practice, 1967; Practice Makes Perfect, 1969. Others: Home Truths, (stage play), 1997; The Writing Game, 1999. Several screenplays and television dramas. Contributions to: Reviewer; Sunday Times; Times Literary Supplement; Guardian; Sunday Times; Jewish Quarterly. Memberships: Fellow, PEN; Royal Society of Literature; Society of Authors; Writers' Guild of Great Britain; British Association of Film and Television Arts; PEN, fellow; Royal Society of Literature; Society of Authors; Writers' Guild of Great Britain. Literary Agent: Sonia Land, Sheil Land, 43 Doughty Street, London WC1 2LF, England. Address: 2 St Katherine's Precinct, Regents Park, London NW1 4HH, England.

FRIEDMAN Thomas (Loren), b. 20 July 1953, Minneapolis, Minnesota, USA. Journalist. m. Ann Louise Bucksbaum, 23 Nov 1978, 2 daughters. Education: BA, Brandeis University, 1975; MPhil, St Anthony's College, Oxford, 1978. Appointments: Correspondent, London and Beirut, United Press International, 1978-81; Business Reporter, 1981-82, Beirut Bureau Chief, 1982-84, Jerusalem Bureau Chief, 1984-89, Chief Diplomatic Correspondent, Washington, DC, Bureau, 1989-, New York Times. Publications: War Torn, 1984; From Beirut to Jerusalem, 1989. Contributions to: New York Times Magazine. Honours: Overseas Press Club Award, 1980; George Polk Award, 1982; Livingston Award for Young Journalists, 1983; Pulitzer Prize, for Journalism, 1983, 1988; Page One Award, New York Newspaper Guild, 1984; Colonel Robert D Heinl Jr: Memorial Award in Marine Corps History, Marine Corps Historical Foundation, 1985; National Book Award, National Book Foundation, 1989. Membership: Phi Beta Kappa. Address: c/o New York Times, Washington, DC, Bureau, 1627 I Street North West, Washington, DC 20006, USA.

FRIEDRICH Paul (William), b. 22 Oct 1927, Cambridge, Massachusetts, USA. Professor of Anthropology, Linguistics, and Social Thought; Writer; Poet; Linguist. m. 1) Lore Bucher, 6 Jan 1950, div Jan 1960, 1 son, 2 daughters, 2) Margaret Hardin, 26 Feb 1966, div June 1974, 3) Deborah Joanna Gordon, 9 Aug 1975, div Nov 1996, 2 daughters, 4)Domnica Raduclescu, 10 Nov 1996, 1 son. Education: Williams College, 1945-46; BA, Harvard College, 1951; MA, Harvard University, 1951; PhD, Yale University, 1957. Appointments: Instructor, University of Connecticut, 1956-57, Harvard University, 1957-58; Junior Linguist Scholar, Deccan College, India, 1958-59; Assistant Professor, University of Pennsylvania, 1959-62; Visiting Assistant Professor, University of Michigan, 1960, 1961; Associate Professor, 1962-67, Professor of Anthropology, Linguistics, and Social Thought, 1967-, University of Chicago; Visiting Professor, Indiana University, 1964. Publications: Agrarian Revolt in a Mexican Cillage, 1970; Proto-Indo-European Trees, 1970; The Tarascan Suffices of a Locative Space: Meaning and Morphotactics, 1971; A Phonology of Tarascan, 1973; On Aspect Theory and Homeric Aspect, 1974; Proto-Indo-European Syntax: The Order of Meaningful Elements, 1975; Neighboring Leaves Ride This Wind (poems), 1976; The Meaning of Aphrodite, 1978; Bastard Moons (poems), 1978, 2nd edition, revised, 1979; Language, Context, and the Imagination: Essays by Paul Friedrich (edited by A S Dil), 1979; Redwig (poems), 1982; The Language Parallax: Linguistic Relativism and Poetic Indeterminacy, 1986; The Princes of Naranja: An Essay in Anthrohistorical Method, 1987; Sonata (poems), 1987; Russia and Eurasia: Encyclopedia of World Cultures, Vol 6 (Editor), 1994; Music in Russian Poetry, 1998. Contributions to:

Books and journals. Honours: Ford Foundation Grant, 1957; Social Science Research Council Grant, 1966-67; National Endowment for the Humanities Grant, 1974-76; Guggenheim Fellowship, 1982-83. Memberships: Academy of American Poets; American Academy of Arts and Sciences; American Anthropological Association; American Association for Teachers of Slavic and East European Languages; American Association for the Advancement of Science; Linguistic Society of America, life member; Linguistic Society of India, life member; Modern Language Association; Poetry Society of America; Sigma Xi. Address: c/o Committee on Social Thought, University of Chicago, 1130 East 59th Street, Chicago, IL 60637, USA.

FRIEL Brian, b. 9 Jan 1929, Killyclogher, County Tyrone, Ireland. Writer; Dramatist. m. Anne Morrison, 1954, 1 son, 4 daughters. Education: St Columb's College, Derry; St Patrick's College, Maynooth; St Joseph's Training College, Belfast. Appointments: Taught in various schools, 1950-60; Writer, 1960-. Publications: Collected Stories: The Saucer of Larks, 1962; The Gold in the Sea, 1966; Plays: Philadelphia Here I Come!, 1965; The Loves of Cass McGuire, 1967; Lovers, 1968; The Mundy Scheme, 1969; Crystal and Fox, 1970; The Gentle Island, 1971; The Freedom of the City, 1973; Volunteers, 1975; Living Quarters, 1976; Aristocrats, 1979; Faith Healer, 1979; Three Sisters, translation, 1981; The Communication Cord, 1983; Fathers and Sons, translation, 1987; Making History, 1988; Dancing at Lughnara, 1990; The London Vertigo, adaptation of a play by Charles Macklin, 1992; A Month in the Country, adaptation of Turgenev, 1992. Honours: Honorary DLitt, National University of Ireland, 1983; Ewart Biggs Memorial Prize, British Theatre Association Award. Address: Drumaweir House, Greencastle, County Donegal, Ireland.

FRIMAN Alice (Ruth), b. 20 Oct 1933, New York, New York, USA. Professor of English; Poet; Writer. m. (1) Elmer Friman, 3 July 1955, 2 sons, 1 daughter, (2) Marshall Bruce Gentry, 24 Sept 1989. Education: BA, Brooklyn College, 1954; Indiana University, 1964-66; MA, English, Butler University, 1971. Appointments: Lecturer of English, Indiana University-Purdue University of Indianapolis, 1971-74; Faculty, 1971-90, Professor of English, 1990-, University of Indianapolis; Visiting Professor of Creative Writing, Indiana State University, 1982; Ball State University, 1996; Writer-in-Residence, Curtin University, Perth, Australia, 1989. Publications: A Question of Innocence, 1978; Song to My Sister, 1979; Loaves and Fishes: A Book of Indiana Women Poets (editor), 1983; Reporting from Corinth, 1984; Insomniac Heart, 1990; Driving for Jimmy Wonderland, 1992; Inverted Fire, 1997. Contributions to: Several anthologies and numerous reviews, quarterlies, and journals. Honours: Virginia Center for the Creative Arts Fellowships, 1983, 1984, 1993, 1996. Consuelo Ford Award, 1988, Cecil Hemley Memorial Award, 1990; Lucille Medwick Memorial Award, 1993, Poetry Society of America; Midwest Poetry Award, Society for the Study of Midwestern Literature, 1990; Millay Colony for the Arts Fellowship, 1990; Yaddo Fellowship, 1991; Teacher of the Year Award, University of Indianapolis, 1993; 1st Prize, Abiko Quarterly International Poetry Contest, 1994; Individual Arts Fellowship, Indiana Arts Commission, 1996-97; Ezra Pound Poetry Award, Truman State University, 1997-98. Memberships: Associated Writing Programs; Modern Language Association; Poetry Society of America; Writers' Center of Indianpolis, board member, 1984-89, honorary life member, 1993-. Address: 6312 Central Avenue, Indianapolis, IN 46220, USA.

FRISBIE Richard, b. 27 Nov 1926, Chicago, Illinois, USA. Writer; Consultant. m. Margery Rowbottom, 3 June 1950, 3 sons, 5 daughters. Education: University of Chicago, 1944-45; BA, University of Arizona, 1948. Appointments: Reporter, Editor, Chicago Daily News; Copy Chief, Cunningham and Walsh; Creative Director, Campbell-Ewald; Editor, Chicago Magazine; Owner, Frisbie Communications, 1966-. Publications: The Do-It-Yourself Parent (co-author with Margery Frisbie; Family Fun and Recreation; How to Peel a Sour Grape;

Who Put the Bomb in Father Murphy's Chowder?; It's a Wise Woodsman Who Knows What's Biting Him; Basic Boat Building; Daily Meditations for Busy Grandpas. Honours: Best Article, Catholic Press Association, 1954. Memberships: Society of Midland Authors, president, 1985-88; Illinois Center for the Book, president, 1991-92. Address: 631 North Dunton Avenue, Arlington Heights, IL 60004, USA.

FRITH David (Edward John), b. 16 Mar 1937, London, England. Cricket Writer. m. 11 May 1957, 2 sons, 1 daughter. Education: Canterbury High School, Sydney, 1949-53. Appointments: Editor, The Cricketer, 1973-78, Wisden Cricket Monthly, 1979-96. Publications: Runs in the Family, 1969; A E Stoddart: Biography, 1970; The Archie Jackson Story, 1974; The Fast Men, 1975; Cricket Gallery (editor), 1976; England v Australia Pictorial History, 1977; The Ashes '77, 1977; The Golden Age of Cricket 1890-1914, 1978; Ashes '79, 1979; Jeff Thomson: Biography, 1980; The Slow Men, 1984; Cricket's Golden Summer, 1985; England v Australia Test Match Records, 1986; Pageant of Cricket, 1987; By His Own Hand, 1991; Stoddy's Mission, 1994; Test Match Year, 1997; Caught England, Bowled Australia (autobiography), 1997 Contributions to: Periodicals. Honours: Cricket Society Jubilee Literary Awards, 1970, 1987; Cricket Writer of the Year, Wombwell Cricket-Lovers Society, 1984; British Magazine Sportswriter of the Year, 1988. Memberships: Association of Cricket Statisticians; Cricket Society; Cricket Writers Club, honorary life member. Address: 6 Beech Lane, Guildford, Surrey GU2 5ES, England.

FRITZ Jean, b. 16 Nov 1915, Hankow, China. Writer. m. Michael Fritz, 1 Nov 1941, 1 son, 1 daughter. Education: BA, Wheaton College, Norton, Massachusetts. 1937. Publications: The Cabin Faced West, 1957; And Then What Happened, Paul Revere, 1973; Stonewall, 1979; Homesick: My Own Story, 1982; The Double Life of Pocahontas, 1983; The Great Little Madison, 1989; Bully for You, Teddy Roosevelt, 1991; Around the World in a Hundred Years, 1994; Harriet Beecher Stowe and the Beecher Preachers, 1994; You Want Women to Vote, Lizzie Stanton?, 1995. Contributions to: New Yorker; Redbook; New York Times; Washington Post; Seventeen; Horn Book; Children's Literature in Education. Honours: National Book Award, 1982; Laura Ingalls Wilder Award, 1986. Literary Agent: Gina MacCaby. Address: 50 Bellewood Avenue, Dobbs Ferry, NY 10522, USA.

FRITZ Walter Helmut, b. 26 Aug 1929, Karlsruhe, Germany. Author; Poet. Education: Literature and Philosophy, University of Heidelberg, 1949-54. Publications: Achtsam sein, 1956; Veranderte Jahre, 1963; Umwege, 1964; Zwischenbemerkungen, 1965; Abweichung, 1965; Die Verwechslung, 1970; Aus der Nahe, 1972; Die Beschaffenheit solcher Tage, 1972; Bevor uns Horen und Sehen Vergeht, 1975; Schwierige Uberfahrt, 1976; Auch jetzt und morgen, 1979; Gesammelte Gedichte, 1979; Wunschtraum alptraum, 1981; Werkzeuge der Freiheit, 1983; Cornelias Traum und andere Aufzeichnungen, 1985; Immer einfacher, immer schwieriger, 1987; Zeit des Sehens, 1989; Die Schlüssel sind vertauscht, 1992; Gesammelte Gedichte 1979-94, 1994. Contributions to: Journals and periodicals. Honours: Literature Prize, City of Karlsruhe, 1960; Prize, Bavarian Academy of Fine Arts, 1962; Heine-Taler Lyric Prize, 1966; Prize, Culture Circle, Federation of German Industry, 1971; Literature Prize, City of Stuttgart, 1986; Georg Trakl Prize, 1992. Memberships: Academy for Sciences and Literature; Bavarian Academy of Fine Arts; German Academy for Speech and Poetry; PEN; Union of German Writers. Address: Kolbergerstrasse 2a, 76139 Karlsruhe, Germany.

FROHM Frederika. See: KERNER Fred.

FROMMER Harvey, b. 10 Oct 1937, Brooklyn, New York, USA. Professor Emeritus; Author. m. Myrna Katz, 23 Jan 1960, 2 sons, 1 daughter. Education: BS, Journalism, MA, English, PhD, Communications, New

York University. Appointments: Professor, Writing, Speech, New York City Technical College, City University of New York, 1970-96; Professor Emeritus, City University, New York; Professor, Liberal Studies, Dartmouth College, 1992-; Graduate Liberal Studies, Wesleyan University, 1994; Reviewer, Yankees Magazine, Library Journal, Choice, Kliatt Paperback Book Guide, Dodger Blue; Frequent Lecturer. Publications: Growing Up At Bat: 50 Years of Little League Baseball, 1989; Running Tough: The Autobiography of Tony Dorsett, 1989; Throwing Heat: The Autobiography of Nolan Ryan, 1989; It Happened in the Catskills: An Oral History of the Catskill Resorts (with Myrna Katz Frommer), 1990; Behind the Lines: The Autobiography of Don Strock, 1991; Holzman on Hoops, 1991; Shoeless Joe and Ragtime Baseball, 1992; It Happened in Brooklyn: An oral history of growing up in the borough in the 1940s, 1950s and 1960s, 1993; Big Apple Baseball, 1995; Growing Up Jewish in America (with Myrna Katz Frommer), 1995; It Happened On Broadway (with Myrna Katz Frommer), 1997; New York Yankees Encyclopaedia, 1997. Contributions to: New York Times; Red Book Magazine. Address: 83 Franklin Hill Road, Lyme, NH 03768, USA.

FROST Sir David (Paradine), b. 7 Apr 1939, Beccles, Suffolk, England. Television Personality; Author. m. (1) Lynn Frederick, 1981, div 1982, (2) Lady Carina Fitzlan-Howard, 1983, 3 sons. Education: MA, Gonville and Caius College, Cambridge. Appointments: Various BBC TV series, 1962-; Many ITV series, 1966-; Chairman and Chief Executive, David Paradine Ltd, 1966-; Joint Founder and Director, TV-am, 1981-93; Regular appearances on US television. Publications: That Was the Week That Was, 1963; How to Live Under Labour, 1964; Talking with Frost, 1967; To England With Love, 1967; The Presidential Debate 1968, 1968; The Americans, 1970; Whitlam and Frost, 1974; I Gave Them a Sword, 1978; I Could Have Kicked Myself, 1982; Who Wants to be a Millionaire?, 1983; The Mid-Atlantic Companion (jointly), 1986; The Rich Tide (jointly), 1986; The World's Shortest Books, 1987; David Frost: An Autobiography, Part I: From Congregations to Audiences, 1993. Honours: Golden Rose Award, Montreux, 1967; Richard Dimbleby Award, 1967; Silver Medal, Royal Television Society, 1967; Officer of the Order of the British Empire, 1970; Religious Heritage of America Award, 1970; Emmy Awards, 1970, 1971; Albert Einstein Award, 1971; Knighted, 1993. Address: c/o David Paradine Ltd, 5 St Mary Abbots Place, London W8 6LS, England.

FROST Jason. See: **OBSTFELD Raymond.**

FRUCHTMANN Benno, b. 5 Sept 1913, Meuselwitz, Germany. Writer; Poet; Dramatist. m. Mirjam David, 2 Nov 1951, 2 sons. Publications: Poetry in anthologies in German and Hebrew translation; short stories; ballads; metric prose. Other: Radio plays. Contributions to: German and Hebrew newspapers and periodicals. Honours: Stipend Atelierhaus, Worpswede, Germany, 1986; Participant, International Colloquium of Jewish Authors, Osnabruck, 1991. Memberships: Association of German Writers; Israel Writers Association. Address: 10 Liesin Street, 62977, Tel Aviv, Israel.

FRUMKIN Gene, b. 29 Jan 1928, New York, New York, USA. Poet; Professor. m. Lydia Samuels, 3 July 1955, 1 son, 1 daughter. Education: BA, English, University of California, Los Angeles. Appointments: Professor, University of New Mexico; Editor, Coastlines Literary Magazine, 1958-62; Guest Editor, New Mexico Quarterly, 1969; Visiting Professor, Modern Literature, State University of New York, Buffalo, 1975; Co-Editor, San Marcos Review, 1978-83; Exchange Professor, 1980-81, 1984-85, Writer-in-Residence, 1989, University of Hawaii. Publications: Hawk and the Lizard, 1963; Orange Tree, 1965; Rainbow-Walker, 1969; Dostoyevsky and Other Nature Poems, 1972; Locust Cry: Poems 1958-65, 1973; Mystic Writing-Pad, 1977; Indian Rio Grande: Recent Poems from 3 Cultures (co-editor), anthology, 1977; Clouds and Red Earth, 1982; Lover's Quarrel With America, 1985; Sweetness in the Air, 1987;

Comma in the Ear, 1991; Saturn Is Mostly Weather, 1992. Contributions to: Paris Review; Prairie Schooner; Yankee; Conjunctions; Sulfur; Poetry; Saturday Review; Nation; Evergreen Review; Dacotah Territory; Malahat Review; Minnesota Review. Honour: 1st Prize for Poetry, Yankee magazine, 1979. Memberships: Past President, Rio Grande Writers Association; Hawaii Literary Arts Council; PEN West. Address: 3721 Mesa Verde North East, Albuquerque, NM 87110, USA.

FRY Christopher, b. 18 Dec 1907, Bristol, England. Dramatist. m. Phyllis Marjorie Hart, 1936, dec 1987, 1 son. Education: Bedford Modern School. Publications: The Boy with a Cart, 1939; The Firstborn, 1946; A Phoenix too Frequent, 1946; The Lady's Not for Burning, 1949; Thor, with Angels, 1949; Venus Observed, 1950, revised edition, 1992; A Sleep of Prisoners, 1951; The Dark is Light Enough, 1954; The Lark, 1955; Tiger at the Gates, 1955; Duel of Angels, 1958; Curtmantle, 1961; Judith, 1962; A Yard of Sun, 1970; Peer Gynt, 1970. Television Plays: The Brontës at Haworth, 1973; Sister Dora, 1977; The Best of Enemies, 1977; Can You Find Me: A Family History, 1978; Editor: Charlie Hammond's Sketch Book, 1980; Selected Plays, 1985; Genius, Talent and Failure, 1986 (Adam Lecture); One Thing More of Caedmon Construed, 1987; A Journey into the Light, 1992. Films: The Queen is Crowned, 1953; The Beggar's Opera, 1953; Ben Hur, 1958; Barabbas, 1960; The Bible: In the Beginning, 1962. Honours: Fellow, Royal Society of Literature, 1950; Queen's Gold Medal for Poetry, 1962; Honorary Fellow, Manchester Metropolitan University, 1988; DLitt, Lambeth, 1988; Hon DLitt, Sussex University, 1994; Hon DLitt, De Montfort University, 1994. Membership: Garrick Club. Address: The Toft, East Dean, Chichester, West Sussex PO18 0JA, England.

FRYE Roland Mushat, b. 3 July 1921, Birmingham, Alabama, USA. Literary and Theological Scholar. m. Jean Elbert Steiner, 11 Jan 1947, 1 son. Education: AB, 1943, PhD, 1952, Princeton University; Special Student, Theology, Princeton Theological Seminary, 1950-52. Appointments: Emory University , 1952-61; L P Stone Foundation Lecturer, Princeton Theological Seminary, 1959; Reverend Professor, Folger Shakespeare Library, 1961-65; Faculty, 1965-83, Emeritus Professor, 1983-, National Phi Beta Kappa Visiting Scholar, 1985-86, University of Pennsylvania; Stone Foundation Lecturer, Princeton Theological Seminary, 1959; Chairman, 1989-91, Chairman Emeritus, 1991-, Center of Theological Inquiry, Princeton, New Jersey. Publications: God, Man and Satan: Patterns of Christian Thought and Life, 1960; Shakespeare and Christian Doctrine, 1963; Shakespeare's Life and Times: A Pictorial Record, 1967; Milton's Imagery and the Visual Arts: Iconographic Tradition in the Epic Poems, 1978; Is God a Creationist? The Religious Case Against Creation-Science, 1983; The Renaissance Hamlet: Issues and Responses in 1600, 1984. Contributions to: The Dissidence of Dissent and the Origins of Religious Freedom in America: John Milton and the Puritans, to Proceedings of the American Philosophical Society, 1989; Numerous other articles in learned journals, literary and theological. Address: 226 West Valley Road, Strafford-Wayne, PA 19087, USA.

FRYER Jonathan, (G L Morton), b. 5 June 1950, Manchester, England. Writer; Broadcaster; University Lecturer. Education: Diplome D'Etudes Françaises, Université de Poitiers, France, 1967; BA, Honours, Chinese with Japanese, 1973, MA, St Edmund Hall, University of Oxford, 1980. Appointments: Visiting Lecturer, School of Journalism, University of Nairobi, Kenya, 1976; Subject Teacher, School of Oriental and African Studies, University of London, 1993-. Publications: The Great Wall of China, 1975; Isherwood, 1977, updated edition as Eye of the Camera, 1993; Brussels as Seen by Naif Artists (with Rona Dobson), 1979; Food for Thought, 1981; George Fox and the Children of the Light, 1991; Dylan, 1993; The Sitwells (with Sarah Bradford and John Pearson), 1994; André and Oscar, 1997; Soho in the Fifties and Sixties, 1998; Numerous political pamphlets, mainly on Third World themes. Contributions to: Economist; Tablet; Geographical Magazine; London Magazine; Andy

Warhol's Interview Magazine; Guardian; Independent; Times; Observer; European. Memberships: English PEN; Association Foreign Affairs Journalists, president, 1997-; Royal Society of Literature; Society of Authors. Literary Agent: Laura Longrigg, MBA, 62 Grafton Way, London W1P 5LD, England. Address: 140 Bow Common Lane, London E3 4BH, England.

FUCHS Sir Vivian (Ernest), b. 11 Feb 1908, Freshwater, Isle of Wight. Geologist; Explorer. m. (1) Joyce Connell, 6 Sept 1933, dec 1990, 1 son, 2 daughters, (2) Eleanor Honnywill, 8 Aug 1991. Education: BA, 1929, MA, 1935, PhD, 1936, Cambridge University. Appointments: Geologist, Cambridge East Greenland Expedition, 1929, Cambridge East African Lakes Expedition, 1930-31, East African Archaeological Expedition, 1931-32; Leader, Lake Rudolf Rift Valley Expedition, 1933-34, Lake Rukwa Expedition, 1937-38; Military Service, 1939-46; Leader, Falkland Islands Dependencies Survey, Antarctica, 1947-50, Commonwealth Trans-Antarctic Expedition, 1955-58; Director, British Antarctic Survey, 1958-73. Publications: The Crossing of Antarctica (with Sir Edmund Hillary), 1958; Antarctic Adventure, 1959; Forces of Nature (editor), 1977; Of Ice and Men, 1982; A Time to Speak (autobiography), 1990. Contributions to: Scientific journals. Honours: Knighted, 1958; Many UK and foreign medals and awards; Honorary doctorates. Memberships: British Association for the Advancement of Science; International Glaciological Society, president, 1963-66; Royal Geological Society, vice president, 1961-64, president, 1982-84, honorary vice president, 1985-, Royal Society, fellow, 1974. Address: 106 Barton Road, Cambridge CB3 9LH, England.

FUENTES Carlos, b. 11 Nov 1928, Panama City, Panama. Professor of Latin American Studies; Writer. m. (1) Rita Macedo, 1957, 1 daughter, (2) Sylvia Lemus, 24 Jan 1973, 1 son, 1 daughter. Education: Law School, National University of Mexico; Institute de Hautes Études Internationales, Geneva. Appointments: Head, Cultural Relations Department, Ministry of Foreign Affairs, Mexico, 1955-58; Mexican Ambassador to France, 1975-77; Professor of English and Romance Languages, University of Pennsylvania, 1978-83; Professor of Comparative Literature, 1984-86, Robert F Kennedy Professor of Latin American Studies, 1987-, Harvard University; Simon Bolivar Professor, Cambridge University, 1986-87. Publications: La Region Mas Transparente, 1958; Las Buenas Conciencias, 1959; Aura, 1962; La Muerte de Artemio Cruz, 1962; Cantar de Ciegos, 1964; Cambio de Piel, 1967; Zona Sagrada, 1967; Terra Nostra, 1975; Una Familia Lejana, 1980; Agua Quemada, 1983; Gringo Viejo, 1985; Cristóbal Nonato, 1987; Myself with Others (essays), 1987; Orchids in the Moonlight (play), 1987; The Campaign, 1991; The Buried Mirror, 1992; El Naranjo, 1993; Geography of the Novel: Essays, 1993; La frontera de cristal (stories), 1995. Contributions to: Periodicals. Honours: Biblioteca Breva Prize, Barcelona, 1967; Rómulo Gallegos Prize, Caracas, 1975; National Prize for Literature, Mexico, 1984; Miguel de Cervantes Prize for Literature, Madrid, 1988; Légion d'Honneur, France, 1992; Honorary doctorates. Memberships: American Academy and Institute of Arts and Letters; El Colegio Nacional, Mexico; Mexican National Commission on Human Rights. Address: c/o Harvard University, 401 Boylston Hall, Cambridge, MA 02138, USA.

FUENTES Martha Ayers, b. 21 Dec 1923, Ashland, Alabama, USA. m. Manuel Solomon Fuentes, 11 Apr 1943. Education: BA, Education University of South Florida, USA, 1969. Appointments: Playwright/Author, at present; Jewellery Sales, Tampa, Florida, 1940; Later served in various business positions; Author, 1953. Publications: Pleasure Button, full length play, 1995-96; Jordan's End, 1998. Honours: Iona Lester Scholarship, Creative Writing, University Southern Florida, George Sergel Drama Award, University of Chicago, Southeastern Writers Conference; Instructor, Playwriting and TV; Feature Writer for national magazines. Memberships: Dramatist Guild; Authors Guild; Florida Theatre Conference; North Carolina Writers' Network;

Florida Studio Theatre, Sarasota, Florida; United Daughters of the Confederacy; Southern Heritage Society. Hobbies: Theatre; Swimming; Travel; Animal Rights; Environmental Protection; Gardening. Address: 102 Third Street, Belleair Beach, FL 33786-2311, USA.

FUGARD (Harold) Athol, b. 11 June 1932, Middelburg Cape, South Africa. Playwright. m. Sheila Meiring, 22 Sept 1956, 1 daughter. Appointments: Playwright; Director; Actor. Publications: Three Port Elizabeth Plays, 1974; Statements: Three Plays (co-author), 1974; Sizwi Banzzi is Dead, and The Island (co-author), 1976; Dimetos and Two Early Plays, 1977; Boesman and Lena and Other Plays, 1978; Tsotsi (novel), 1980; A Lesson from Aloes, 1981; Master Harold and the Boys, 1982; The Road to Mecca, 1985; Notebooks 1960-1977, 1983. Film Scripts: The Guest, 1977; Marigolds in August, 1981; My Children! My Africa!, 1990; Playland, 1991. Other: Cousins: A Memoir, 1997. Honours: New York Drama Critics Circle Award for Best Play, 1981; Evening Standard Award, Best Play of the Year, 1984. Memberships: Royal Society of Literature, fellow; American Academy of Arts and Sciences. Address: PO Box 5090 Walmer, Port Elizabeth 6065, South Africa.

FUKUYAMA Francis, b. 27 Oct 1952, Chicago, Illinois, USA. Political Scientist; Consultant; Writer. m. Laura Holmgren, 8 Sept 1986, 2 sons, 1 daughter. Education: BA, Cornell University, 1974; Graduate Studies, Yale University, 1974-75; PhD, Harvard University, 1981. Appointments: Consultant, Pan Heuristics Inc, Los Angeles, 1978-79; Associate Social Scientist, 1979-81, Senior Staff Member, Department of Political Science, 1983-89, Consultant, 1990-, RAND Corp; Policy Planning Staff Member, 1981-82, Deputy Director, 1989-90, Consultant, 1990-, US Department of State; Visiting Lecturer in Political Science, University of California at Los Angeles, 1986, 1989. Publications: The Soviet Union and the Third World: The Last Three Decades (editor with Andrzej Korbonski), 1987; The End of History and the Last Man, 1992. Contributions to: Books and journals. Honour: Los Angeles Times Book Critics Award, 1992; Premio Capri International Award, 1992. Address: c/o RAND Corp, 2100 M Street North West, Washington, DC 20037, USA.

FULFORD Robert (Marshall Blount), b. 13 Feb 1932, Ottawa, Ontario, Canada. Journalist; Writer. m. (1) Jocelyn Jean Dingman, 16 June 1956, div 1970, 1 son, 1 daughter, (2) Geraldine Patricia Sherman, 28 Nov 1970, 2 daughters. Education: Malvern Collegiate, Toronto. Appointments: Reporter, 1950-53, 1956-57, Columnist, 1992-, Globe and Mail; Assistant Editor, Canadian Homes and Gardens, 1955, Mayfair, 1956, Maclean's, 1962-64; Columnist, Toronto Star, 1958-62, 1964-68, 1971-87; Editor, Saturday Night, 1968-87; Barker Fairley Distinguished Visitor in Canadian Culture, University College, University of Toronto, 1987-88; Columnist and Contributing Editor, Financial Times, 1988-92; Chair, Banff Centre Program in Arts Journalism, 1989-91, Maclean Hunter Program in Communications Ethics, Ryerson Polytechnical Institute, Toronto, 1989-93. Publications: This Was Expo, 1968; Crisis at the Victory Burlesk, 1968; Marshall Delaney at the Movies, 1974; An Introduction to the Arts in Canada, 1977; Canada: A Celebration, 1983; Best Seat in the House: Memoirs of a Lucky Man, 1988; Accidental City: The Transformation of Toronto, 1995. Honours: Prix d'Honneur, Canadian Conference of the Arts, 1981; Officer of the Order of Canada, 1984; Honorary doctorates, McMaster University, 1986, York University, 1987, University of Western Ontario, 1988, University of Toronto, 1994. Membership: Canadian Civil Liberties Association. Address: 19 Lynwood Avenue, Toronto, Ontario, Canada M4V 1K3.

FULLER Charles, b. 5 Mar 1939, Philadelphia, Pennsylvania, USA. Dramatist. m. Miriam A Nesbitt, 4 Aug 1962, 2 sons. Education: Villanova University, 1956-58; LaSalle College, 1965-67. Appointments: Co-Founder and Co-Director, Afro-American Arts Theatre, Philadelphia, 1967-71; Writer and Director, The Black Experience, WIP Radio, Philadelphia, 1970-71; Professor of African-American Studies, Temple University, until 1993. Publications: Plays: The Village: A Party, 1968, revised version as The Perfect Party, 1969; In My Names and Days, 1972; Candidate, 1974; In the Deepest Part of Sleep, 1974; First Love, 1974; The Lay Out Letter, 1975; The Brownsville Raid, 1976; Sparrow in Flight, 1978; Zooman and the Sign, 1981; A Soldier's Play, 1982; We: Part I, Sally, 1988, Part II, Prince, Part III, Jonquil, 1989, Part IV, Burner's Frolic, 1990; Songs of the Same Lion, 1991. Other: Screenplays and television series. Honours: National Endowment for the Arts Grant, 1976; Rockefeller Foundation Grant, 1976; Guggenheim Fellowship, 1977-78; Obie Award, 1981; Pulitzer Prize in Drama, 1982; New York Drama Critics Circle Award, 1982; Edgar Allan Poe Mystery Award, 1985. Memberships: Dramatists Guild; PEN; Writers Guild of America. Address: c/o William Morris Agency, 1350 Avenue of the Americas, New York, NY 10019, USA.

FULLER Cynthia Dorothy, b. 13 Feb 1948, Isle of Sheppey, England. Poet; Adult Education Tutor. div, 2 sons. Education: BA Honours, English, Sheffield University, 1969; Postgraduate Certificate of Education, Oxford University, 1970; MLitt, Aberdeen University, 1979. Appointments: Teacher of English, Redborne School, 1970-72; Freelance in Adult Education, University Departments at Durham and Newcastle Universities, also Open University and Workers Education Association. Publications: Moving towards Light, 1992; Instructions for the Desert, 1996. Contributions to: Poems in various magazines including: Other Poetry; Iron; Poetry Durham; Literary Review. Honour: Northern Arts Financial Assistance. Address: 28 South Terrace, Esh Winning, Co Durham DH7 9PR, England.

FULLER Jean Violet Overton, b. 7 Mar 1915, Iver Heath, Bucks, England. Author. Education: Brighton High School, 1927-31; Royal Academy of Dramatic Art, 1931-32; BA, University of London, 1944; University College of London, 1948-50. Publications: The Comte de Saint Germain, 1988; Blavatsky and Her Teachers, 1988; Dericourt: The Chequered Spy, 1989; Sickert and the Ripper Crimes, 1990; Cats and other Immortals, 1992. Honour: Writers Manifold Poems of the Decade, 1968. Membership: Society of Authors. Address: Fuller D'Arch Smith Ltd, 37B New Cavendish Street, London, England.

FULLER John Leopold, b. 1 Jan 1937, Ashford, Kent, England. Poet; Writer. m. Cicely Prudence Martin, 20 July 1960, 3 daughters. Education: BA, BLitt, MA, New College, Oxford, 1957-62. Publications: Fairground Music, 1961; The Tree That Walked, 1967; Cannibals and Missionaries, 1972; The Sonnet, 1972; Epistles to Several Persons, 1973; Penguin Modern Poets 22, 1974; The Mountain in the Sea, 1975; Lies and Secrets, 1979; The Illusionists, 1980; The Dramatic Works of John Gay (editor), 1983; The Beautiful Inventions, 1983; Flying to Nowhere, 1983; The Adventures of Speedfall, 1985; Selected Poems, 1954-82, 1985; The Grey Among the Green, 1988; Tell it Me Again, 1988; The Burning Boys, 1989; Partingtime Hall (with James Fenton), 1989; The Mechanical Body and Other Poems, 1991; Look Twice, 1991; The Worm and the Star, 1993; The Chatto Book of Love Poetry, 1994; Stones and Fires 1996; Collected Poems, 1996; A Skin Diary, 1997; W.H. Auden: A Commentary, 1998. Contributions to: Periodicals, reviews, and journals. Honours: Newdigate Prize, 1960; Richard Hillary Award, 1962; E C Gregory Award, 1965; Geoffrey Faber Memorial Prize, 1974; Southern Arts Prize, 1980; Whitbread Prize, 1983; Shortlisted, Booker Prize, 1983; Forward Prize, 1996. Memberships: Magdalen College, Oxford, Fellow; Royal Society of Literature, Fellow. Address: 4 Benson Place, Oxford OX2 6QH, England.

FULLERTON Alexander Fergus, b. 20 Sept 1924, Saxmundham, Suffolk, England. Writer. m. Priscilla Mary Edelston, 10 May 1956, 3 sons. Education: Royal Naval College, Dartmouth, 1938-41; School of Slavonic Studies, Cambridge University, 1947. Appointments: Editorial Director, Peter Davies Ltd, 1961-64; General Manager, Arrow Books, 1964-67. Publications: Surface!, 1953; A Wren Called Smith, 1957; The White Men Sang, 1958; The Everard Series of naval novels: The Blooding of the Guns, 1976; Sixty Minutes for St George, 1977; Patrol to the Golden Horn, 1978; Storm Force to Narvik, 1979; Last Lift from Crete, 1980; All the Drowning Seas, 1981; A Share of Honour, 1982; The Torch Bearers, 1983; The Gatecrashers, 1984. Special Deliverance, 1986; Special Dynamic, 1987; Special Deception, 1988; Bloody Sunset, 1991; Look to the Wolves, 1992; Love for an Enemy, 1993; Not Thinking of Death, 1994; Into the Fire, 1995; Band of Brothers, 1996; Return to the Field, 1997; Final Dive, 1998;In at the Kill, 1999; Never Not Say Goodbye, forthcoming. Address: c/o John Johnson Ltd, 45 Clerkenwell Green, London EC1R 0HT, England.

FULTON Alice, b. 25 Jan 1952, Troy, New York, USA. Professor of English; Poet. m. Hank De Leo, 1980. Education: BA, Empire State College, Albany, New York, 1978; MFA, Cornell University, 1982. Appointments: Assistant Professor, 1983-86, Willam Willhartz Professor, 1986-89, Associate Professor, 1989-92, Professor of English, 1992-, University of Michigan; Visiting Professor of Creative Writing, Vermont College, 1987, University of California at Los Angeles, 1991. Publications: Anchors of Light, 1979; Dance Script with Electric Ballerina, 1983; Palladium, 1986; Powers of Congress, 1990; Sensual Math, 1995. Honours: Macdowell Colony Fellowships, 1978, 1979; Millay Colony Fellowship, 1980; Emily Dickinson Award, 1980; Academy of American Poets Prize, 1982; Consuelo Ford Award, 1984; Rainer Maria Rilke Award, 1984; Michigan Council for the Arts Grants, 1986, 1991; Guggenheim Fellowship, 1986-87; Yaddo Colony Fellowship, 1987; Bess Hokin Prize, 1989; Ingram Merrill Foundation Award, 1990; John D and Catharine T MacArthur Foundation Fellowship, 1991-96; Elizabeth Matchett Stover Award, 1994. Address: 2370 Le Forge Road, RR2, Ypsilanti, MI 48198, USA.

FULTON Len, b. 15 May 1934, Lowell, Massachusetts, USA. Author; Publisher. 1 son, 1 daughter. Education: BA, University of Wyoming, 1961. Appointments: Member, Literary Advisory Panel, National Endowment for the Arts, 1976-78; Member, Advisory Board, Center for the Book, Library of Congress, 1978-80. Publications: The Grassman, novel, 1974; Dark Other Adam Dreaming, novel, 1976, play, 1984; American Odyssey, travelogue, 1978; For the Love of Pete, play, 1988; Grandmother Dies, play, 1989; Headlines, play, 1990. Membership: PEN. Address: PO Box 100, Paradise, CA 95967, USA.

FULTON Robin, b. 6 May 1937, Arran, Scotland. Writer. Education: MA, Hons, 1959, PhD, 1972, Edinburgh; LittD. Appointment: Editor, Lines Review, 1967-76. Publications: Poetry: Instances, 1967; Inventories, 1969; The Spaces Between the Stones, 1971; The Man with the Surbahar, 1971; Tree-Lines, 1974; Music and Flight, 1975; Between Flights, 1976; Places to Stay In, 1978; Following a Mirror, 1980; Selected Poems, 1963-78, 1980; Fields of Focus, 1982; Coming Down to Earth and Spring is Soon, 1990. Criticism: Contemporary Scottish Poetry: Individuals and Contexts, 1974; The Way the Words are Taken, Selected Essays, 1989. New Poets from Edinburgh (editor), 1971; Iain Crichton Smith: Selected Poems, 1955-80, 1982; Robert Garioch: The Complete Poetical Works with Notes, 1983; Robert Garioch: A Garioch Miscellany, Selected Prose and Letters, 1986. Translations: An Italian Quartet, 1966; Blok's Twelve, 1968; Five Swedish Poets, 1972; Lars Gustafsson, Selected Poems, 1972; Gunnar Harding: They Killed Sitting Bull and Other Poems, 1973; Tomas Tranströmer: Citoyens, 1974; Tomas Tranströmer: Selected Poems, 1974, editor, 1980; Osten Sjöstrand: The Hidden Music & Other Poems, 1975; Toward the Solitary Star: Selected Poetry and Prose, 1988; Werner Aspenström: 37 Poems, 1976; Tomas Tranströmer: Baltics, 1980; Johannes Edfelt: Family Tree, 1981; Werner Aspenström: The Blue Whale and Other Prose Pieces, 1981; Kjell Espmark: Béla Bartók Against the Third Reich and Other Poems, 1985; Olva Hauge: Don't Give Me the Whole Truth and Other Poems, 1985; Tomas Tranströmer: Collected Poems, 1987; Stig Dagerman: German Autumn, 1988; Par Lagervist: Guest of Reality, 1989; Preparations for Clight, and other Swedish Stories, 1990; Four Swedish Poets (Kjell

Espmark, Lennart Sjögren, Eva Ström & Tomas Transtromer), 1990; Olva Hauge: Selected Poems, 1990; Hermann Starheimstaeter: Stone-Shadows, 1991. Contributions to: Various journals and magazines. Honours: Gregory Award, 1967; Writers Fellowship, Edinburgh University, 1969; Scottish Arts Council Writers Bursary, 1972; Arthur Lundquist Award for translations from Swedish, 1977; Swedish Academy Award, 1978. Address: Postboks 467, N 4001, Stavanger, Norway.

FUNE Jonathan. See: **FLETCHER John Walter James.**

FURTWÄNGLER Virginia Walsh, (Ann Copeland), b. 16 Dec 1932, Hartford, Connecticut, USA. Writer; Teacher. m. Albert Furtwangler, 17 Aug 1968, 2 sons. Education: BA, College of New Rochelle, 1954; MA, Catholic University of America, 1959; PhD, Cornell University, Kent, 1970. Appointments: Writer-in-Residence, College of Idaho, 1980, Linfield College, 1980-81, University of Idaho, 1982, 1986, Wichita State University, 1988, Mt Allison University, 1990, St Mary's University, 1993; Hallie Brown Ford Chair of English, Willamette University, 1996. Publications: At Peace, 1978; The Back Room, 1979; Earthen Vessels, 1984; The Golden Thread, 1989; Strange Bodies on a Stranger Shore, 1994; The ABC's of Writing Fiction, 1996. Contributions to: Anthologies and magazines. Honours: Kent Fellowship; Canada Council Grant; National Endowment for the Arts Writing Fellowship, 1994; Ingram Merrill Award. Memberships: Authors Guild; Writers Union of Canada; International Womens Writing Guild. Literary Agent: Barbara Kouts, New York. Address: 235 Oak Way North East, Salem, OR 97301, USA.

FUSSELL Paul, b. 22 Mar 1924, Pasadena, California, USA. Professor Emeritus of English Literature; Writer. m. 1) Betty Ellen Harper, 17 June 1949, div 1987, 1 son, 1 daughter, 2) Harriette Behringer, 11 Apr 1987. Education: BA, Pomona College, 1947; MA, 1949, PhD, 1952, Harvard University. Appointments: Instructor, Connecticut College, 1951-55; Faculty, 1955-76, John DeWitt Professor of English Literature, 1976-83, Rutgers University; Consultant Editor, Random House, 1963-64; Contributing Editor, Harper's, 1979-83, The New Republic, 1979-85; Donald T Regan Professor of English Literature, 1983-94, Professor Emeritus, 1994-, University of Pennsylvania; Visiting Professor, King's College, London, 1990-92. Publications: The Rhetorical World of Augustan Humanism, 1965; Poetic Meter and Poetic Form, 1965, revised edition, 1979; Samuel Johnson and the Life of Writing, 1971; The Great War and Modern Memory, 1975; Abroad: British Literary Traveling Between the Wars, 1980; The Boy Scout Handbook and Other Observations, 1982; Class: A Guide Through the American Status System, 1983; Thank God for the Atom Bomb and Other Essays, 1988; Wartime: Understanding and Behavior in the Second World War, 1989; BAD: Or the Dumbing of America, 1991; The Anti-Egoist: Kingsley Amis, Man of Letters, 1994. Contributions to: Scholarly journals. Honours: James D Phelan Award, 1964; Lindback Foundation Award, 1971; Senior Fellow, National Endowment for the Humanities, 1973-74; Ralph Waldo Emerson Award, Phi Beta Kappa, 1976; Guggenheim Fellowship, 1977-78; Rockefeller Foundation Fellow, 1983-84. Memberships: Academy of Literary Studies; Modern Language Association; Royal Society of Literature, fellow; Society of American Historians. Address: 2020 Walnut Street, Philadelphia, PA 19103, USA.

G

GAARDER Jostein, b. 1952, Oslo, Norway. Writer. m. 2 sons. Publications: Kabalmysteriet, 1990, English translation as The Solitaire Mystery, 1996; Sofies verden: Roman on filosofiens historie, 1991, English translation as Sophie's World: A Novel about the History of Philosophy, 1994; Julemysteriet, 1992, English translation as The Christmas Mystery, 1996. Honours: Norwegian Literary Critics Award, 1991; Norwegian Ministry of Cultural and Scientific Affairs Literary Prize, 1991; Number One International Fiction Bestseller, Publishing Trends, 1995. Address: c/o Farrar, Straus & Giroux Inc, 19 Union Square West, New York, NY 10003, USA.

GADGIL Gangadhar, b. Bombay, India. Writer; Economic Adviser. m. Vasanti Gadgil, 12 Dec 1948, 1 son, 2 daughters. Education: MA, Bombay University, 1944. Appointments: Director, Ravalagaon Sugar Farm Ltd, Walchand Capitol Ltd, Deposit Insurance and Credit Guarantee Corp. Publications: Several books and stories. Contributions to: Many newspapers, reviews, journals, and magazines. Honours: Sahitya Akademy Award; Janasthan Award. Memberships: Asiatic Society of Bombay; Indian PEN; Sahitya Akademi, vice president, 1988-93; Marathi Sahitya Sammelan, president. Address: 4 Abhang, Sahitya Sahawas, Bandra, Bombay 400051, India.

GAERTNER Kenneth Clark, b. 18 Jan 1933, Saginaw, MI, USA. Playwright; Poet. m. Mary Ann Vega, 15 Aug 1972, 1 son, 1 daughter. Publications: Koan Bread, poetry and plays, 1978; Produced Plays: Blood Money, The Old Man's Death; The Lady and God, 1975; The Moon on Snow, 1978; The Open Eye Theatre, 1978; Dog's Tooth, 1985; American Theatre of Actors; Seventeen Hoofbeats, 1992; Actors Institute; Lives Over Easy, 1994; Three Hands Clapping, 1995; Dominica's Smile, 1997; The Mystic Theatre. Honours: Dog's Tooth, Winner National One-Act Play Contest, 1985; American Theatre of Actors, New York, 1992; Winner, American Treasures One-Act Contest, Actors Institute, New York, 1994. Membership: The Dramatists Guild, USA. Address: 211 McCotter Lane, Ann Arbor, MI 48103, USA.

GAGLIANO Frank, b. 18 Nov 1931, New York, New York, USA. Playwright; Screenwriter; Novelist; Professor of Playwriting. Education: Queens College, New York City, 1949-53; BA, University of Iowa, 1954; MFA, Columbia University, 1957. Appointments: Playwright-in-Residence, Royal Shakespeare Company, London, 1967-69; Assistant Professor of Drama, Playwright-in-Residence, Director of Contemporary Playwrights Center, Florida State University, Tallahassee, 1969-73; Lecturer in Playwriting, Director of Conkie Workshop for Playwrights, University of Texas, Austin, 1973-75; Distinguished Visiting Professor, University of Rhode Island, 1975; Benedum Professor of Theatre, West Virginia University, 1976-; Artistic Director, Carnegie Mellon, Showcase of New Plays, 1986-. Publications: The City Scene (2 plays), 1966; Night of the Dunce, 1967; Father Uxbridge Wants to Marry, 1968; The Hide-and-Seek Odyssey of Madeleine Gimple, 1970; Big Sur, 1970; The Prince of Peasantmania, 1970; The Private Eye of Hiram Bodoni (television play), 1971; Quasimodo (musical), 1971; Anywhere the Wind Blows (musical), 1972; In the Voodoo Parlour of Marie Laveau, 1974; The Comedia World of Lafcadio Beau, 1974; The Resurrection of Jackie Cramer (musical), 1974; Congo Square (musical), 1975, revised, 1989; The Total Immersion of Madelaine Favorini, 1981; San Ysidro (dramatic cantata), 1985; From the Bodoni County Songbook Anthology, Book I, 1986, musical version, 1989; Anton's Leap (novel), 1987. Address: West Virginia University Creative Arts Center, Morgantown, WV 26506 USA.

GAGNON Madeleine, b. 27 July 1938, Amqui, Quebec, Canada. Author; Poet. Div, 2 sons. Education: BA, Literature, Université Saint-Joseph du Nouveau-Brunswick, 1959; MA, Philosophy, University of Montreal, 1961; PhD, Literature, Université d'Aix-en-Provence, 1968. Appointments: Teacher of Literature, Université du Québec a Montréal, 1969-82; Various guest professorships and writer-in-residencies. Publications: Les morts-vivants, 1969; Pour les femmes et tous les autres, 1974; Poélitique, 1975; La venue a l'écriture (with Hélène Cixous and Annie Leclerc), 1977; Retailles (with Denise Boucher), 1977; Antre, 1978; Lueur; Roman archéologique, 1979; Au coeur de la lettre, 1981; Autographie 1 and 2: Fictions, 1982; Les fleurs du catapla, 1986; Toute écriture est amour, 1989; Chant pour un Québec lointain, 1991; La terre est remplie de langage, 1993; Les cathédrales sauvages, 1994; Le vent majeur, 1995. Contributions to: Many periodicals. Honours: Grand Prize, Journal de Montréal, 1986; Governor-General's Award for Poetry, 1991. Membership: Union des écrivaines et écrivains Québecois. Address: c/o Union des écrivaines et écrivains québecois, La Maison des écrivains, 3492 Avenue Laval, Montreal, Quebec H2X 3C8, Canada.

GAIDUK Ilya Valer'evich, b. 6 July 1961, Krasnovodsk, Turkmenistan. Historian. Education: Graduated, Moscow State Pedagogical Institute, 1980-84; Postgraduate, 1987-90, PhD, 1990, Institute of World History. Appointments: Junior Research Fellow, 1990-93, Research Fellow, 1993-97, Senior Research Fellow, 1997-, Institute of World History, Russian Academy of Sciences, Moscow. Publications: Book: The Soviet Union and the Vietnam War, 1996; Articles: Soviet-American Commercial Relations during the Period of Non-Recognition. The View of the US Modern Sovietology, 1990; George F Kennan as a Historian of Soviet-American Relations, 1990; The Vietnam War and Soviet-American Relations, 1964-73: New Russian Evidence, 1995-96; The Soviet Union and the Vietnam War, 1996; Soviet Policy towards US Participation in the Vietnam War, 1996; Turnabout? The Soviet Policy Dilemma in the Vietnamese Conflict, 1997. Honours: Fellowship, Cold War International History Project, Woodrow Wilson Center, Washington DC, 1993; Fellowship, Norwegian Nobel Institute, Oslo, 1995. Address: Institute of World History, 32a Leninskii pr, Moscow 117334, Russia.

GAINES Ernest J(ames), b. 15 Jan 1933, River Lake Plantation, Pointe Coupee Parish, Louisiana, USA. Professor of English; Writer. Education: BA, San Francisco State College, 1957; Graduate Studies, Stanford University, 1958-59. Appointments: Writer-in-Residence, Denison University, 1971, Stanford University, 1981; Visiting Professor, 1983, Writer-in-Residence, 1986, Whittier College; Professor of English and Writer-in-Residence, University of Southwestern Louisiana, 1983-. Publications: Catherine Carmier, 1964; Of Love and Dust, 1967; Bloodline (short stories), 1968; The Autobiography of Miss Jane Pittman, 1971; In My Father's House, 1978; A Gathering of Old Men, 1983; A Lesson Before Dying, 1993. Contributions to: Anthologies and periodicals. Honours: National Endowment for the Arts Award, 1967; Rockefeller Grant, 1970; Guggenheim Fellowship, 1971; Black Academy of Arts and Letters Award, 1972; Fiction Gold Medals, Commonwealth Club of California, 1972, 1984; 9 Emmy Awards, 1975; American Academy and Institute of Arts and Letters Award, 1987; John D and Catharine T MacArthur Foundation Fellowship, 1993; National Book Critics Circle Award, 1994; Honorary doctorates. Membership: American Academy of Arts and Letters. Address: 932 Divosadero Street, San Francisco, CA 94115, USA.

GAINHAM Sarah, b. 1 Oct 1922, London, England. Writer. m. Kenneth Robert Ames, 14 Apr 1964, dec 1975. Publications: Time Right Deadly, 1956; Cold Dark Night, 1957; The Mythmaker, 1957; Stone Roses, 1959; Silent Hostage, 1960; Night Falls on the City, 1967; A Place in the Country, 1968; Takeover Bid, 1970; Private Worlds, 1971; Maculan's Daughter, 1973; To the Opera Ball, 1975; The Habsburg Twlight, 1979; The Tiger, Life, 1983; A Discursive Essay on the Presentation of Recent History in English, 1998. Contributions to: Encounter; Atlantic;

BBC. Address: Altes Forsthaus,Schlosspark, A2404 Petronell, Austria.

GAITHER Carl Clifford, b. 3 June 1944, San Antonio, Texas, USA. Freelance Writer. m. Alma E Cavazos, 14 Dec 1995, 3 sons. Education: BA, Psychology, University of Hawaii, 1972; MA, Psychology, McNeese State University, 1974; MA, Criminal Justice, Northeast Louisiana University, 1980; MS, Mathematical Statistics, Southwest Louisiana University, 1984; Command and General Staff College, 1993. Appointments: Anti Submarine Warfare Technology, US navy, 1960-66; Texas Department of Corrections, 1974-77; Researcher, Louisiana Criminal Justice Information Systems, 1977-78; Hospital Administrator, Louisiana Department of Corrections, 1978-82; Instructor of Statistics, 1985-86; Operations Research Analyst, Department of Army, 1987-95; Freelance Writer, 1995-. Publications: Statistically Speaking: A Dictionary of Quotations, 1996; Physically Speaking: A Dictionary of Quotations on Physics and Astronomy, 1997; Mathematically Speaking: A Dictionary of Quotations, 1998; Practically Speaking: A Dictionary of Qotations on Engineering, Technology and Architecture, 1999; Medically Speaking: A Dictionary of Quotations on Dentistry, Medicine and Nursing, 1999; Scientifically Speaking: A Dictionary of Quotations, 1999. Literary Agent: Institute of Physics Publishing. Address: Dirac House, Temple Back, Bristol BS1 6BE, England.

GALBRAITH James Kenneth, b. 29 Jan 1952, Boston, Massachusetts, USA. Professor. m. (1) Lucy Ferguson, 28 July 1979, div, 1 son, 1 daughter, (2) Ying Tang, 17 July 1993. Education: AB, Harvard College, 1974; University of Cambridge, 1974-75; MA, 1976, MPhil, 1977, PhD, 1981, Yale University. Appointment: Professor, LBJ School of Public Affairs, University of Texas at Austin, 1985-. Publications: Balancing Acts; The Economic Problem; Macroeconomics. Contributions to: Numerous. Honours: Marshall Scholar, University of Cambridge. Memberships: American Economic Association; Association for Public Policy Analysis and Management. Address: LBJ School of Public Affairs, University of Texas at Austin, Austin, TX 78713, USA.

GALBRAITH John Kenneth, b. 15 Oct 1908, Iona Station, Ontario, Canada (US citizen, 1937). Professor of Economics Emeritus; Author. m. Catherine Atwater, 17 Sept 1937, 3 sons. Education: BS, University of Guelph, 1931; MS, 1933, PhD, 1934, University of California; Postgraduate Studies, Cambridge University, 1937-38. Appointments: Research Fellow, University of California, 1931-34; Instructor and Tutor, 1934-39, Lecturer 1948-49, Professor of Economics, 1949-75, Paul M Warburg Professor of Economics, 1959-75, Professor Emeritus, 1975-, Harvard University; Assistant Professor of Economics, Princeton University, 1939-42; Economic Adviser, National Defense Advisory Commission, Washington, DC, 1940-41; Assistant Administrator, Price Division, 1941-42, Deputy Administrator, 1942-43, Office of Price Administration, Washington, DC; Director, US Strategic Bombing Survey, 1945, Office of Economic Security Policy, US State Department, Washington, DC, 1946; US Ambassador to India, 1961-63; Adviser to Presidents John F Kennedy and Lyndon B Johnson. Publications: Modern Competition and Business Policy (with Henry Sturgis Dennison), 1938; American Capitalism: The Concept of Countervailing Power, 1952; A Theory of Price Control, 1952; The Great Crash, 1929, 1955; Marketing Efficiency in Puerto Rico (with others), 1955; Journey to Poland and Yugoslavia, 1958; The Affluent Society, 1958, 4th edition, 1984; The Liberal Hour, 1960; Economic Development in Perspective, 1962, revised edition as Economic Development, 1964; The McLandress Dimension (satire published under the name Mark Epernay), 1963, revised edition, 1968; The Scotch (memoir), 1964, 2nd edition, 1985; The New Industrial State, 1967, 4th edition, 1985; How to Get Out of Vietnam: A Workable Solution to the Worst Problem of Our Time, 1967; The Triumph: A Novel of Modern Diplomacy, 1968; Indian Painting: The Scene, Themes and Legends (with Mohinder Singh Randhawa), 1968; How to Control the Military, 1969; Ambassador's Journal: A Personal Account of the Kennedy Years, 1969; Who

Needs the Democrats, and What It Takes to Be Needed, 1970; A Contemporary Guide to Economics, Peace, and Laughter (essays), 1971; A China Passage, 1973; Economics and the Public Purpose, 1973; Money: Whence It Came, Where It Went, 1975; The Age of Uncertainty, 1977; Almost Everyone's Guide to Economics (with Nicole Salinger), 1978; Annals of an Abiding Liberal, 1979; The Nature of Mass Poverty, 1979; A Life in Our Times: Memoirs, 1981; The Anatomy of Power, 1983; The Voice of the Poor: Essays in Economic and Political Persuasion, 1983; A View from the Stands: Of People, Politics, Military Power, and the Arts, 1986; Economics in Perspective: A Critical History, 1987; Capitalism, Communism and Coexistence: From the Bitter Past to the Bitter Present (with Stanislav Menshikov), 1988; A Tenured Professor (novel), 1990; The Culture of Contentment, 1992; A Short History of Financial Euphoria, 1993; A Journey Through Economic Time, 1994. Contributions to: Books and scholarly journals. Honours: Social Science Research Council Fellow, 1937-38; US Medal of Freedom, 1964; Many honorary doctorates. Memberships: American Academy of Arts and Sciences, fellow; American Academy and Institute of Arts and Letters, president, 1984-87; American Economic Association, president, 1972; American Agricultural Economics Association; Americans for Democratic Action, chairman, 1967-68. Address: 30 Francis Avenue, Cambridge, MA 02138, USA.

GALE Gwendoline Fay, b. 13 June 1932, Balaklava, Australia. University Academic. Div, 1 son, 1 daughter. Education: BA, Honours, 1954, PhD, 1962, Adelaide University. Appointments: Professor of Geography, University of Adelaide; Pro-Vice-Chancellor, University of Adelaide; Vice-Chancellor, University of Western Australia; President, Australian Vice-Chancellors Committee; President, Academy of the Social Sciences in Australia. Publictions: Woman's Role in Aboriginal Society; Urban Aborigines; Race Relations in Australia; The Aboriginal Situation; Poverty Among Aboriginal Families in Adelaide; Adelaid Aborigines: A Case Study of Urban Life 1966-81; We Are Bosses Ourselves: The Status and Role of Aboriginal Women; Tourists and the National Estate: Procedures to Protect Australia's Heritage; Aboriginal Youth and the Criminal Justice System; Changing Australia; Inventing Places; Juvenile Justice; Debating the Issues; Tourism and the Protection of Aborginal Cultural Sites; Cultural Geography. Honours include: John Lewis Medal; ASSA; AO; Honorary DLitt. Membership: Queen Qdelaide Club. Address: c/o Academy of the Social Sciences in Australia, Canberra, ACT 2601, Australia.

GALEF David, Associate Professor. Education: BA, summa cum laude, Princeton University, 1977-81; MA, PhD, English, Columbia University, 1983-89. Appointments: English Teacher, Overseas Training Center, Osaka, Japan, 1981-82; English and Mathematics Instructor, Stanley H Kaplan Educational Centers, Boston and New York, 1983-85; English Teacher, Japanese Business Seminars, New York Area, 1985-86; Logic and Rhetoric Teacher, 1986-88, Preceptor, Literature Humanities, 1988-89, Columbia University; Head, Creative Writing Workshop, Masters School, Dobbs Ferry, New York, 1990; Assistant Professor of English, 1989-95, Assistant Director of English Graduate Studies, 1993-95, Associate Professor of English, 1995-, University of Mississippi. Publications: Books: Even Monkeys Fall From Trees, and Other Japanese Proverbs, 1987; The Little Red Bicycle, 1988; The Supporting Cast: A Study of Flat and Minor Characters, 1993; Flesh, 1995; Tracks, 1996; Second Thoughts: A Focus on Rereading, 1998; Turning Japanese, 1998. Honours: Several grants and scholarships. Memberships: Associated Writing Programs; Modern Language Association; National Council of Teachers of English; South Central Modern Language Association. Address: c/o Department of English, College of Liberal Arts, University of Mississippi, MS 38677, USA.

GALIOTO Salvatore, b. 6 June 1925, Italy. Retired Professor of Humanities; Poet. m. Nancy Morris, 8 July 1978, 1 son. Education: BA, University of New Mexico, 1952; MA, University of Denver, 1955; John Hay Fellow, Yale University, 1959-60; Catskill Area Project Fellow, Columbia University, 1961-62; Mediaeval and Renaissance Doctoral Programme, University of New Haven. Publications: The Humanities: Classical Athens, Renaissance Florence and Contemporary New York, 1970; Bibliographic Materials on Indian Culture, 1972; Let Us Be Modern (poems), English, Italian, 1985; INAGO Newsletter (poems), 1988; Is Anybody Listening (poems), English, 1990; Flap Your Wings (poems), English, 1992; Rosebushes and the Poor (poems), Italian, 1993. Contributions to: Antologies and periodicals. Honours: Purple Heart, Bronze Star, 1944; John Hay Fellowship, 1958-59; Asian Studies Fellow, 1965-66; Mole of Turin, 1st Prize, Foreign Writer, 1984; 1st Prize, Chapbook Competition, The Poet, 1985, 1986; 1st Prize, Poetry, Gli Etrusci, Italy, 1985; Trofeo delle Nazioni, Poetry, Italy; Gold Medal, Istituto Carlo Capodieci, 1987; INAGO Newspaper Poet, 1989. Memberships: Long Island Historians Society; Asian Society; California State Poetry Society; Poets and Writers of America; International Society of Poets. Address: Via Bruno Buozzi 15, Montecatini Terme 51016 (Pistoia), Italy.

GALL Henderson Alexander (Sandy Gall), b. 1 Oct 1927, Penang, Malaysia. Television Journalist. m. Aug 1958, 1 son, 3 daughters. Education: MA, Aberdeen University, Scotland, 1952. Publications: Gold Scoop, 1977; Chasing the Dragon, 1981; Don't Worry about the Money Now, 1983; Behind Russian Lines: An Afghan Journal, 1983; Afghanistan: Agony of a Nation, 1988; Salang, 1989; George Adamson: Lord of the Lions, 1991; News From the Front: The Life of a Television Reporter, 1994. Honours: Rector, 1978-81, Honorary LLD, 1981, Aberdeen University; Sitara-i-Pakistan, 1986; Lawrence of Arabia Medal, 1987; Commander of the Order of the British Empire, 1988. Address: Peters, Fraser and Dunlop, 503/4 The Chambers, Chelsea Harbour, London SW10 0XF, England.

GALL Sally Moore, b. 28 July 1941, New York, New York, USA. Librettist. m. William Einar Gall, 8 Dec 1967. Education: BA cum laude, Harvard University, 1963; MA, 1971, PhD, 1976, New York University. Appointments: Poetry Editor, Free Inquiry, 1981-84; Founding Editor, Eidos, The International Prosody Bulletin, 1984-88. Publications: The Modern Poetic Sequence: The Genius of Modern Poetry (co-author), 1983; Maximum Security Ward and Other Poems (editor), 1984; Poetry in English: An Anthology (versification editor), 1987; Kill Bear Comes Home, 1994; Opera Libretti: The Singing Violon,1995; Eleanor Roosevelt, 1996; The Little Thieves of Bethlehem, 1997; Musical Theatre: The Lysistrata affair, 1995. Contributions to: Reference books, professional journals and literary magazines. Honours: Penfield Fellow, New York University, 1973-74; Academy of American Poets Award, New York University, 1975; Key Pin and Scroll Award, New York University, 1976; Co-Winner, Explicator Literary Foundation Award, 1984. Memberships: American Music Center; American Society of Composers, Authors and Publishers; Dramatists Guild; National Opera Association; Opera For Youth; Opera America; International Alliance for Women in Music; Poets and Writers; Various wildlife societies and community music groups. Address: 5820 Folsom Drive, La Jolla, CA 92037, USA.

GALLAGHER Richard. See: **LEVINSON Leonard.**

GALLAGHER Tess, b. 21 July 1943, Port Angeles, Washington, USA. Poet; Writer. m. (1) Lawrence Gallagher, 1963, div 1968, (2) Michael Burkard, 1973, div 1977, (3) Raymond Carver, 1988, dec. Education: BA, 1969, MA, 1970, University of Washington, Seattle; MFA, University of Iowa, 1974. Appointments: Instructor, St Lawrence University, Canton, New York, 1974-75; Assistant Professor, Kirkland College, Clinton, New York, 1975-77; Visiting Lecturer, University of Montana, 1977-78; Assistant Professor, University of Arizona, Tucson, 1979-80; Professor of English, Syracuse University, 1980-89; Visiting Fellow, Williamette University, Salem, Oregon, 1981; Cockefair Chair

Writer-in-Residence, University of Missouri, Kansas City, 1994; Poet-in-Residence, Trinity College, Hartford, Connecticut, 1994; Edward F Arnold Visiting Professor of English, Whitman College, Walla Walla, Washington, 1996-97; Bucknell University, 1998. Publications: Poetry: Stepping Outside, 1974; Instructions to the Double, 1976; Under Stars, 1978; Portable Kisses, 1978; On Your Own, 1978; Willingly, 1984; Amplitude: New and Selected Poems, 1987; Moon Crossing Bridge, 1992; The Valentine Elegies, 1993; Portable Kisses Expanded, 1994; My Black Horse: New and Selected Poems, 1995. Short Stories: The Lover of Horses, 1986; At the Owl Woman Saloon, 1997. Non-Fiction: A Concert of Tenses: Essays on Poetry, 1986. Translator: The Sky Behind the Forest, by Liliana Ursu (with Liliana Ursu and Adam Sorkin), 1997. Other: Screenplay: Dostoevsky (with Raymond Carver), 1985; Many introductions to the work of Raymond Carver, 1988-97. Contributions to: Many anthologies. Honours: Elliston Award, 1976; National Endowment for the Arts Grants, 1977, 1981, 1987; Guggenheim Fellowship, 1978; American Poetry Review Award, 1981; Washington State Governor's Awards, 1984, 1986, 1987, 1993; New York State Arts Grant, 1988; Maxime Cushing Gray Foundation Award, 1990; American Library Association Most Notable Book List, 1993; Lyndhurst Prize, 1993; Translation Award, 1997; Honorary DHL, Whitman College, Walla Walla, Washington, 1998. Address: c/o ICM/Amanda Urban, 40 West 57th Street, New York, NY 10019, USA.

GALLAHER John G(erard), b. 28 Dec 1928, St Louis, Missouri, USA. Professor of History Emeritus. m. C Maia Hofacker, 2 June 1956, 1 son, 2 daughters. Education: University of Paris, 1950-51; University of Grenoble, 1951-52; BA, Washington University, 1954; MA, 1957, PhD, 1960, St Louis University. Appointments: Professor to Professor of History Emeritus, Southern Illinois University at Edwardsville. Publications: The Iron Marshal: A Biography of Louis N Davout, 1976; The Students of Paris and the Revolution of 1848, 1980; Napoleon's Irish Legion, 1993; General Alexandre Dumas: Soldier of the French Revolution, 1997. Contributions to: Reference works, books and scholarly journals. Honours: Fulbright Research Scholar, France, 1959-60; University Research Fellow, Southern Illinois University at Edwardsville, 1978-79. Address: c/o College of Arts and Sciences, Department of History, Southern Illinois University at Edwardsville, Edwardsville, IL 62026, USA.

GALLANT Jennie. See: **SMITH Joan Gerarda.**

GALLANT Mavis, b. 11 Aug 1922, Montreal, Quebec, Canada. Novelist. Education: Schools in Montreal and New York. Appointment: Writer-in-Residence, University of Toronto, 1983-84. Publications: Green Water, Green Sky, 1959; The Other Paris (stories), 1956; My Heart is Broken: Eight Short Stories and a Short Novel, 1964; A Fairly Good Time, 1970; From the Fifteenth District: A Novel and Eight Short Stories, 1979; Home Truths: Selected Canadian Stories, 1981; In Transit, Twenty Stories, 1988; Across the Bridge (stories), 1993. Honours: Officer, Order of Canada, 1981; Governor General's Award, 1982; Canada-Australia Literary Prize, 1984; Honorary Degree, University Sainte Anne, Pointe de Eglise, Nova Scotia, 1984. Address: 14 Ruse Jean Ferrandi, 75006 Paris, France.

GALLANT Roy Arthur, b. 17 Apr 1924, Portland, Maine, USA. Author; Teacher. m. Kathryn Dale, 1952, 2 sons. Education: BA, 1948, MS, 1949, Bowdoin College; Doctoral work, Columbia University, 1953-59. Appointments: Managing Editor, Scholastic Teachers Magazine, 1954-57; Author-in-Residence, Doubleday, 1957-59; Editorial Director, Aldus Books, London, 1959-62; Editor-in-Chief, The Natural History Press, 1962-65; Consultant, The Edison Project, Israel Arts and Sciences Academy. Publications: Our Universe, 1986, 1994; Private Lives of the Stars, 1986; Rainbows, Mirages and Sundogs, 1987; Before the Sun Dies, 1989; Ancient Indians, 1989; The Peopling of Planet Earth, 1990; Earth's Vanishing Forests, 1991; A Young Person's Guide to Science, 1993; The Day the Sky Split Apart,

1995; Geysers, 1997; Sand Dunes, 1997; Limestone Caves, 1998; Planet Earth, 1998; When the Sun Dies, 1998; Glaciers, 1999. Honours: Thomas Alva Edison Foundation Mass Media Award, 1955; John Burroughs Award for Nature Writing, 1995. Address: PO Box 228, Beaver Mountain Lake, Rengeley, ME 04990, USA.

GALLINER Peter, b. 19 Sept 1920, Berlin, Germany. Publisher. m. (1) Edith Marguerite Goldsmidt, 1948, 1 daughter, (2) Helga Stenschke, 1990. Education: Berlin and London. Appointments: Worked for Reuters, London, England, 1944-47; Foreign Man, Financial Times, London, 1947-60; Chairman of Board, Managing Director, Illstein Publishing Group, Berlin, Germany, 1969-64; Vice-Chairman, Managing Director, British Printing Corporation, 1965-70; International Publishing Consultant, 1965-67, 1970-75; Chairman, Peter Galliner Associates, 1970-; Director, International Press Institute, 1975-93; Director Emeritus, International Press Institute, 1993-; Chairman, International Encounters, 1995-. Honours: Order of Merit, 1st Class, Germany, 1965; Ecomienda, Orden de Isabel la Catolica, Spain, 1982; Commander's Cross, Order of Merit, Germany, 1990. Address: Untere Zaüne 9, 9001 Zürich, Switzerland.

GALLO John, b. 16 Aug 1966, New York City, New York, USA. Writer; Musician. Publications: Standing on Lorimer Street Awaiting Crucifixion, 1996; Street Gospel Intellectual Mystical Survival Codes, 1999; To Be Joyous Is To Be A Madman in a World of Sad Ghosts, 1999. Contributions to: Only the Dead Know Brooklyn, 1998; India, 1998; Don't Let the Green Grass Fool Ya, 1998; Various poems to: Christ in a Wheelchair, Lucio Moon, Hayden's Poetry Review, ZZZ Zyne, Blind Man's Rainbow; Dream International Quarterly; Crackrock; Caizine; Plain Jane; Soul Fountain; Various journals. Address: 61-36 160th Street, Flushing, New York 11365, USA.

GALLOWAY David Darryl, b. 5 May 1937, Memphis, Tennessee, USA. Journalist; Novelist; Professor; Art Consultant. m. Sally Lee Gantt, dec, 1 son. Education: BA, Harvard College, 1959; PhD, State University of New York, 1962. Appointments: Lecturer, State University of New York, 1962-64; University of Sussex, 1964-67; Chair of American Studies, University of Hamburg, 1967-68; Associate Professor, Case Western Reserve University, 1968-72; Chair of American Studies, Ruhr University, Germany, 1972-; Editor-in-Chief, German-American Cultural Review, 1993-. Publications: The Absurd Hero; Lamaar Ransom; Calamus; Artware; A Family Album; Tamsen; The Selected Writings of Edgar Allan Poe; Melody Jones. Contributions to: International Herald Tribune; Art in America; Art News. Memberships: Royal Society of Arts; Harvard Club. Address: Band Strasse 13, 42105 Wuppertal, Germany.

GALLOWAY Janice, b. 2 Dec 1956, Ayrshire, Scotland. Writer. 1 son. Education: Ardrossan Academy, University of Glasgow, Scotland, 1974-78. Appointments: Singing Waitress, 1972-74; Welfare Rights Worker, 1976; Teacher of English, 1980-90. Publications: The Trick in Keep Breathing, 1990; Blood, 1991; Foreign Parts, 1994; Where You Find It, 1996. Honours: Shortlisted, Whitbread First Novel, Scottish First Book and Aer Lingus Awards; Won MIND/Alan Lane Prize and Scottish Arts Council Award; Shortlisted for the Guardian Fiction Prize, People's Prize and Saltire Award, New York Times Notable Book of the Year, Won Scottish Arts Council Award; Shortlisted for Saltire Award, Won McVitie's Prize and Scottish Arts Council Award, 1994; American Academy of Arts and Letters EM Forster Award, 1994. Literary Agent: Derek Johns, AP Watt. Address: 20 John Street, London WC1N 2DR, England.

GALTON Herbert, b. 1 Oct 1917, Vienna, Austro-Hungary. University Professor; Writer. m. 28 Jan 1992. Education: High School, Vienna, 1935; University of Vienna, 1935-38; PhD, Russian Philology, University of London, 1951. Appointment: Professor, University of Kansas, 1962-88. Publications: Aorist und Aspekt im Slavischen, 1962; The Main Functions of the Slavic Verbal Aspect, 1976; Der Einfluss des Altaischen auf die

Entsehung des Slavischen (The Influence of Altaic on the origin of Slavic), 1997; Reisetagebuch,(poetry), 1990; Balkanisches Tagebuch (Balkan Diary), novel, 1998. Contributions to: The Equality Principle, (anthology), 1974; Freedom - from Illusions, 1994; Lyrische Annalen, 1994, 1995. Contributions: Over 100 linguistic articles in various periodicals. Honour: Gold Medal, Macedonian Academy of Sciences, 1987. Memberships: Austrian Writers' Union; Austrian PEN Club; Societas Linguistica Europaea. Address: Kaiserstrasse 12/18, A-1070 Vienna, Austria.

GALTON Raymond Percy, b. 17 July 1930, England. Author; Scriptwriter. m. Tonia Phillips, 1956, 1 son, 2 daughters. Contributions to: Television with Alan Simpson: Hancock's Half House, 1954-61; Comedy Playhouse, 1962-63; Steptoe and Son, 1962-74; Galton-Simpson Comedy, 1969; Clochermerle, 1971; Casanova, '74, 1974; Dawson's Weekly, 1975; The Galton and Simpson Playhouse, 1976-77. With Johnny Speight: Tea Ladies, 1979; Spooner's Patch, 1979-80. With John Antrobus: Room at the Bottom, 1986. Films with Alan Simpson: The Rebel, 1960; The Bargee, 1963; The Wrong Arm of the Law, 1963; The Spy with a Cold Nose, 1966; Loot, 1969; Steptoe and Son, 1971; Steptoe and Son Ride Again, 1973; Den Siste Fleksnes, 1974; Die Skraphandlerne, 1975. Theatre with Alan Simpson: Way Out in Piccadilly, 1969; The Wind in the Sassfras Trees, 1968; Albert och Herbert, 1981; Fleksnes, 1983; Mordet pa Skolgatan 15, 1984. With John Antrobus: When Did You Last See Your Trousers?, 1986. Address: The Ivy House, Hampton Court, Middlesex, England.

GALVIN Brendan, b. 20 Oct 1938, Everett, Massachusetts, USA. Professor of English; Poet. m. Ellen Baer, 1968, 1 son, 1 daughter. Education: BS, Boston College, 1960; MA, Northeastern University, 1964; MFA, 1967, PhD, 1970, University of Massachusetts. Appointments: Instructor, Northeastern University, 1964-65; Assistant Professor, Slippery Rock State College, 1968-69; Assistant Professor, 1969-74, Associate Professor, 1974-80, Professor of English, 1980-, Central Connecticut State University; Visiting Professor, Connecticut College, 1975-76; Editor (with George Garrett), Poultry: A Magazine of Voice, 1981-; Coal Royalty Chairholder in Creative Writing, University of Alabama, 1993. Publications: The Narrow Land, 1971; The Salt Farm, 1972; No Time for Good Reasons, 1974; The Minutes No One Owns, 1977; Atlantic Flyway, 1980; Winter Oysters, 1983; A Birder's Dozen, 1984; Seals in the Inner Harbour, 1985; Wampanoag Traveler, 1989; Raising Irish Walls, 1989; Great Blue: New and Selected Poems, 1990; Early Returns, 1992; Saints in Their Ox-Hide Boat, 1992; Islands, 1993. Honours: National Endowment for the Arts Fellowships, 1974, 1988; Connecticut Commission on the Arts Fellowships, 1981, 1984; Guggenheim Fellowship, 1988; Sotheby Prize, Arvon International Foundation, 1988; Levinson Prize, Poetry magazine, 1989; O B Hardison Jr Poetry Prize, Folger Shakespeare Library, 1991; Charity Randall Citation, International Poetry Forum, 1994. Address: PO Box 54, Durham, CT 06422, USA.

GALVIN James, b. 8 May 1951, Chicago, Illinois, USA. Poet. Education: BA, Antioch College; MFA, University of Iowa. Appointments: Professor; Editor, Crazyhorse, 1979-81. Publications: Imagining Timber, 1980; God's Mistress, 1984; Elements, 1988. Contributions to: New Yorker; Nation; Antioch Review; Poetry Now; Antaeus; Sewanee Review. Honours: Discovery Award, Nation/Young Men's Hebrew Association, 1977; Co-Winner, National Poetry Series Open Competition, 1984. Address: Iowa Writers Workshop, Univesity of Iowa, 436 EPB, Iowa City, IA 52242, USA.

GALVINS Davis. See: **RAUHVARGERS Eizens.**

GAMBARO Griselda, b. 28 July 1928, Buenos Aires, Argentina. Playwright; Novelist. m. Juan Carlos Distefano. Appointments: Drama Teacher; Lecturer. Publications: Matrimonio, 1965; El desatino, 1966; Las paredes, 1966; Los siameses, 1967; The Camp, 1968; Nada que ver, 1972; Solo un aspecto, 1974; El viaje a

Bahia Blanca, 1975; El hombre, 1976; Putting Two and Two Together, 1976; Decir si, 1981; La malasangre, 1982; Real envido, 1983; Del sol naciente, 1984; Teatro, 4 volumes, 1984-90; Information for Foreigners, 1986; The Impenetrable Madam X, 1991. Fiction: Cuentos, 1953; Madrigal en ciudad, 1963; Un Felicidad con menos pena, 1968; Nada que ver con ora historia, 1972; Ganarse la muertel, 1976; Lo impenetrable, 1984. Honour: Guggenheim Fellowship, 1982. Address: c/o Argentores, Virrey Pacheo De Melo, 1126 Buenos Aires, Argentina.

GAMBONE Philip Arthur, b. 21 July 1948, Melrose, Massachusetts, USA. Teacher; Writer. Education: AB, Harvard University, 1970; MA, Episcopal Divinity School, 1976. Publications: Author or contributing author of 10 books including Men on Men III, 1990; Sister and Brother, 1994; Men on Men VI, 1996. Contributions to: Book reviews to New York Times; Lambda Book Report; Bay Windows. Honours: MacDowell Colony Fellow; Nominee, Lambda Literary Award; Helene Wurlitzer Foundation Award, 1996. Membership: PEN. Literary Agent: Edward Hibbert. Address: 47 Waldeck Street, Dorchester, MA 02124, USA.

GAMST Frederick Charles, b. 24 May 1936, New York, New York, USA. Professor of Anthropology. m. Marilou Swanson, 28 Jan 1961, 1 daughter. Education: AB, University of California, Los Angeles, 1961; PhD, University of California, Berkeley, 1967. Appointments: Instructor, Anthropology, 1966-67, Assistant Professor, Anthropology, 1967-71, Associate Professor, Anthropology, 1971-75, Rice University; Professor of Anthropology, University of Massachusetts, Boston, 1975-. Publications: Travel and Research in Northwestern Ethiopia, 1965; The Qemant: A Pagan-Hebraic Peasantry of Ethiopia, 1969; Peasants in Complex Society, 1974; Studies in Cultural Anthropology, 1975; Ideas of Culture: Sources and Uses, 1976; The Hoghead: An Industrial Ethnology of the Locomotive Engineer, 1980; Highballing with Flimsies: Working under Train Orders on the Espee's Coast Line, 1990; Meanings of Work: Considerations for the Twenty-first Century, 1995; Early American Railroads: Franze Anton Ritter von Gerstner's Die innern Communicationen 1842-1843, 2 volumes, 1997. Contributions to: Magazines and journals. Honour: Conrad Arensberg Award, 1995. Memberships: Society for the Anthropology of Work of the American Anthropological Association; Railroad and Locomotive Historical Society; Society for Applied Anthropology; Royal Anthropology Institute. Address: 73 Forest Avenue, Cohasset, MA 02025, USA.

GANDER Forrest, b. 21 Jan 1956, Barstow, California, USA. Professor; Poet; Editor. m. C D Wright, 1983, 1 son. Education: BS, BA, College of William and Mary; MA, San Francisco State University; Brown University. Appointments: Co-Editor, Lost Road Publishers, 1982-; Professor, Providence College, Rhode Island, 1985-. Publications: Rush to the Lake, 1988; Eggplants and Lotus Root, 1991; Lynchburg, 1993; Mouth to Mouth: Poems by 12 Contemporary Mexican Women (editor), 1993; Deeds of Utmost Kindness, 1994; Science of Steepleflower, 1998. Contributions to: Periodicals. Honour: Whiting Award for Writers, 1996. Membership: Associated Writing Programs. Address: 351 Nyatt Road, Barrington, RI 02806, USA.

GANESAN Indira, b, 5 Nov, Srirangam, India. Education: Stella Maris College, Madras, 1978-79; BA, Vassar College, 1979-82; MFA, University of Iowa, 1982-84. Appointments: Ticket Sales, McCarter Theatre, 1990; Assistant Professor, University of Missouri, 1991-92; Lecturer, University of California at San Diego, 1992-95; Assistant Professor, University of California at Santa Cruz, 1995-96; Fellow, Bunting Institute, Radcliffe College, 1997-98; Assistant Professor, Long Island University, Southampton, 1997-. Publications: The Journey, 1990; Inheritance, 1998. Contributions to: Seventeen; Glamour; Antaeus. Honours: Fellow, Fine Arts Work Center; MacDowell Colony Wk Rose Fellowship; Best American Novelist Finalist. Literary

Agent: Sandra Dijkstra. Address: c/o 1155 Camino Del Mar, Ste 515, Del Mar, CA 92014, USA.

GANNETT Ruth Stiles, b. 12 Aug 1923, New York, New York, USA. Author. m. Hans Peter Kahn, 21 Mar 1947, 7 daughters. Education: AB, Vassar College, 1944. Publications: My Father's Dragon, 1948; The Wonderful House-Boat-Train, 1949; Elmer and the Dragon, 1950; The Dragons of Blueland, 1951; Katie and the Sad Noise, 1961. Honours: Herald Tribune Spring Book Award, 1948; Honour Book, Newberry, 1948; Junior Literary Guild Selections. Address: 8315 Route 227, Trumansburg, NY 14886, USA.

GANNON Robert, b. 5 March 1931, White Plains, NY, USA. Writer; Educator. m. Melady Kehm, 25 Oct 1991. Education: Miami University, NYU, Columbia, 1949-55. Appointments: Various in broadcasting and public relations; Freelance Writer, 1989-; Penn State English Department, Associate Professor of nonfiction writing, 1974-; Contributing Editor, Popular Science, 1963-. Publications: Books: The Complete Book of Archery, 1963; Time is Short and the Water Rises, 1967; What's Under a Rock?, 1971; Great Survival Adventures, 1973; Pennsylvania Burning, 1976; Why Your House Many Endanger Your Health, with Alfred Zamm, 1980; Half Mile Up Without an Engine-the Excitement, the Essentials of Soaring, 1982; Article Writing, 1989; Best Science Writing, Readings and Insights, 1991; Hellions of the Deep: The Development of American Torpedoes in World War II, 1996. Contributions to: 300 magazine articles, including in: Reader's Digest; Audubon; Popular Mechanics; Saturday Evening Post; Glamour; Family Circle; TV Guide. Memberships: ASJA; NASW. Literary Agent: Theron Raines, 71 Park Avenue, NYC 10016, USA.

GANO Lila Lee, b. 25 Sept 1949, Ft Benning, Georgia, USA. Writer; Editor. Education: BA, Sociology, Psychology, Anthropology, 1971; MA, Counseling and Psychology, Writing Courses, Public Relations Courses, TV Production Courses, Scripting, 1975. Publications: Smoking, 1989; Television - Electronic Pictures, 1990; Hazardous Waste, 1994. Contributions to: San Diego Women's Magazine; Housewife Writer's Forum; San Diego Homes and Gardens. Honours: Society for Technical Communication Achievement Awards, 1994-96. Memberships: Society for Technical Communications; Tallahassee Writer's Association. Address: 2528 Pretty Bayou Island, Panama City, FL 32405, USA.

GANS Bruce, b. 23 Aug 1951. Professor of English. m. 8 Jan 1994, 2 daughters. Education: MFA, University of Iowa, 1975. Appointments: Lecturer, Lake Forest College, Roosevelt University, 1978-79; Associate Professor of English, City Colleges of Chicago, Wright College, 1995-; City Colleges of Chicago, Washington College, 1981-95; Founder and Director, Great Books Curriculum, Wright College, 1996-. Publications include: What Does Ruthie Have To Do With It?, 1986; What Do You Want From Me?, 1988; He Never Got the Message, 1988; Jak Jest Shura, 1991; The Duell, 1993. Contributuons to: Playboy Magazine; American Scholar; Kansa Quarterly, Chicago Magazine. Honours include: Madmoiselle Fiction Prize, 1972; National Endowment for Arts grant for Fiction, 1973; Best Non-Fiction Book for 1978, 1978; Citation for A Collection of Short Stories of Outstanding Merit Iowa School of Letter; Illinois Arts Council Awards for the Essay, 1979, 1993; Heatherstone Press Fiction Award, 1984. Memberships: Authors Guild; National Writers Union; Society of Midland Authors; Associated Writing Programs; National Association of Scholars; Illinois Association of Scholars. Address: 5324 Hyde Park Blvd #1, Chicago, IL 60615, USA.

GANT Jonathon. See: **ADAMS Clifton.**

GANT Richard. See: **FREEMANTLE Brian.**

GARAFOLA Lynn, b. 12 Dec 1946, New York, New York, USA. Dance Critic; Historian. m. Eric Foner, 1 May 1980, 1 daughter. Education: AB, Barnard College, 1968; PhD, City University of New York, 1985. Appointment: Editor, Studies in Dance History, 1990-. Publications: Diaghilev's Ballets Russes; André Levinson on Dance: Writings from Paris in the Twenties; The Diaries of Marius Petipa. Contributions to: Dance Magazine; Ballet Review; Dancing Times; Dance Research Journal; Raritan; Nation; Women's Review of Books; Times Literary Supplement; New York Times Book Review. Honour: Torre de lo Bueno Prize. Memberships: Society of Dance History Scholars; Dance Critics Association; Association Européenne des Historiens de la Danse. Address: 606 West 116th Street, New York, NY 10027, USA.

GARCIA MÁRQUEZ Gabriel (José), b. 6 Mar 1928, Aracataca, Colombia. Author. m. Mercedes Barch, Mar 1958, 2 sons. Education: Universidad Nacional de Colombia, 1947-48; Universidad de Cartagena, 1948-49. Appointments: Journalist, 1947-65; Founder-President, Fundacion Habeas, 1979-. Publications: Fiction: La hojarasca, 1955; El coronel no tiene quien le escriba, 1961, English translation as No One Writes to the Colonel and Other Stories, 1968; La mala hora, 1961, English translation as In Evil Hour, 1979; Los funerales de la Mama Grande, 1962; Cien anos de soledad, 1967, English translation as One Hundred Years of Solitude, 1970; Isabel viendo llover en Macondo, 1967; La incredible y triste historia de la candida Erendira y su abuela desalmada, 1972; El negro que hizo esperar a los angeles, 1972; Ojos de perro azul, 1972; Leaf Storm and Other Stories, 1972; El otono del patriarca, 1975, English translation as The Autumn of the Patriarch, 1976; Todos los cuentos de Gabriel García Marquez: 1947-1972, 1975; Cronica de una muerte anunciada, 1981, English translation as Chronicle of a Death Foretold, 1982; El rastro de tu sangre en la nieve: El verano feliz de la senora Forbes, 1982; Collected Stories, 1984; El amor en los tiempos del colera, 1985, English translation as Love in the Time of Cholera, 1988; El general en su labertino, 1989, English translation as The General in His Laybyrinth, 1990; Collected Novellas, 1990; Doce cuentos peregrinos, 1992, English translation as Strange Pilgrims: Twelve Stories, 1993; Del amor y otros demonios, 1994, English translation as Of Love and Other Demons, 1995. Non-Fiction: La novela en America Latina: Dialogo (with Mario Vargas), 1968; Relato de un naufrago, 1970, English translation as The Story of a Shipwrecked Sailor, 1986; Cuando era feliz e indocumentado, 1973; Cronicas y reportajes, 1978; Periodismo militante, 1978; De viaje por los paises socialistas: 90 dias en la "Cortina de hierro", 1978; Obra periodistica, 4 volumes, 1981-83; El olor de la guayaba: Conversaciones con Plinio Apuleyo Mendoza, 1982, English translation as The Fragrance of Guava, 1983; Persecucion y muerte de minorias: Dos perspectivas, 1984; La aventura de Miguel Littin, clandestino en Chile: Un reportaje, 1986, English translation as Clandestine in Chile: The Adventures of Miguel Littin, 1987; Primeros reportajes, 1990; Notas de prensa, 1980-1984, 1991; Elogio de la utopia: Una entrevista de Nahuel Maciel, 1992; Noticia de un secuestro, 1996. Honours: Colombian Association of Writers and Artists Award, 1954; Premio Literario Esso, Colombia, 1961; Chianciano Award, Italy, 1969; Prix de Meilleur Livre Etranger, France, 1969; Ròmulo Gallegos Prize, Venezuela, 1971; Honorary LLD, Columbia University, New York City, 1971; Books Abroad/Neustadt International Prize for Literature, 1972; Nobel Prize for Literature, 1982; Los Angeles Times Book Prize for Fiction, 1988; Serfin Prize, 1989. Membership: American Academy of Arts and Letters, honorary fellow. Address: PO Box 20736, Mexico City DF, Mexico.

GARDAM Jane Mary, b. 11 July 1928, Yorkshire, England. Writer. m. David Hill Gardam, 20 Apr 1954, 2 sons, 1 daughter. Education: BA, Bedford College, London University, 1949. Appointments: Sub-Editor, Weldon's Ladies Journal, 1952; Assistant Literary Editor, Time and Tide, 1952-54. Publications: Fiction: A Long Way From Verona, 1971; The Summer After the Funeral, 1973; Bilgewater, 1977; God on the Rocks, 1978; The Hollow Land, 1981; Bridget and William, 1981; Horse, 1982; Kit, 1983; Crusoe's Daughter, 1985; Kit in Boots, 1986; Swan, 1987; Through the Doll's House Door, 1987; The Queen of the Tambourine, 1991; Faith Fox, 1995. Short Stories: A Few Fair Days, 1971; Black Faces, White Faces, 1975; The Sidmouth Letters, 1980; The Pangs of Love, 1983; Showing the Flag, 1989; Going Into a Dark House, 1994; Missing the Midnight, 1997; The Green Man (with painting by Mary Fedder, 1998. Non-Fiction: The Iron Coast, 1994. Contributions to: Newspapers and magazines. Honours: David Higham's Award, 1978; Winifred Holtby Award, 1978; Whitbread Literary Award, 1983, Novel Award, 1991, and Fiction Award, 1992; Katherine Mansfield Award, 1984; Silver Pen Award, PEN, 1995. Memberships: PEN; Royal Society of Literature, fellow (FRSL). Address: Haven House, Sandwich, Kent CT13 9ES, England.

GARDAPHE Fred Louis, b. 7 Sept 1952, Chicago, Illinois, USA. Writer; Professor. m. Susan Rose Stolder, 18 Sept 1982, 1 son, 1 daughter. Education: BS, Education, University of Wisconsin-Madison, 1976; AM, English, University of Chicago, 1982; PhD, English, University of Illinois at Chicago, 1993. Appointments: Columbia College, Chicago, 1979-98; Editor, FráNoi, 1984-, Voices in Italian Anericana, 1990-; SUNY, Stony Brook, 1998-. Publications: Italian-American Ways, 1989; New Chicago Stories (editor), 1991; The Italian-American Writer, 1995; Italian Signs, American Streets, 1996; Dagos Read, 1996; From the Margin (contributing editor); Moustache Pete is Dead, 1998. Contributions to: Voices in Italian America; MELUS; Borderlines; FráNoi; Altre Italie; Italian-American Review; Forkroads; Italian America. Honours: UNICO National Prize, 1987; Illinois Arts Council, 1988. Memberships: Modern Language Association; American Italian Historical Association, president, 1997-99; Society of Midland Authors; National Book Critics Circle. Literary Agent: Caroline Frances Carney, Book Deals Inc. Address; c/o Department of European Studies, SUNY Stony Brook, Stony Brook, New York, NY 11794, USA.

GARDEN Bruce. See: **MACKAY James Alexander.**

GARDEN Nancy, b. 15 May 1938, Boston, Massachusetts, USA. Writer; Editor; Teacher. Education: BFA, Columbia University School of Dramatic Arts, 1961; MA, Teachers College, Columbia University, 1962. Appointments: Actress, Lighting Designer, 1954-64; Teacher of Speech and Dramatics, 1961-64; Editor, educational materials, textbooks, 1964-76; Teacher of Writing, Adult Education, 1974; Correspondence School, 1974-. Publications: What Happened in Marston, 1971; The Loners, 1972; Maria's Mountain, 1981; Fours Crossing, 1981; Annie on My Mind, 1982; Favourite Tales from Grimm, 1982; Watersmeet, 1983; Prisoner of Vampires, 1984; Peace, O River, 1986; The Door Between, 1987; Lark in the Morning, 1991; My Sister, the Vampire, 1992; Dove and Sword, 1995; My Brother, the Werewolf, 1995; Good Moon Rising, 1996; The Year They Burned the Books, 1999. The Monster Hunter series: Case No 1, Mystery of the Night Raiders, 1987; Case No 2: Mystery of the Midnight Menace, 1988; Case No 3: Mystery of the Secret Marks, 1989; Case No 4: Mystery of the Kidnapped Kidnapper, 1994; Case No 5: Mystery of the Watchful Witches, 1995. Non-Fiction: Berlin: City Split in Two, 1971; Vampires, 1973; Werewolves, 1973; Witches, 1975; Devils and Demons, 1976; Fun with Forecasting Weather, 1977; The Kids' Code and Cipher Book, 1981. Contributions to: Lambda Book Report. Membership: Society of Children's Book Writers and Illustrators. Address: c/o McIntosh and Otis Inc, 310 Madison Avenue, New York, NY 10017, USA.

GARDNER Herb(ert), b. 1934, New York, New York, USA. Dramatist; Writer. Education: Carnegie Institute of Technology; Antioch College. Publications: Plays: The Elevator, 1952; A Thousand Clowns, 1962; The Goodbye People, 1974; Thieves, 1977; I'm Not Rappaport, 1986; Conversations with My Father, 1993. Other: A Piece of the Action (novel), 1958; One Night Stand (book and lyrics for the Jules Styne musical), 1980. Contributions to: Magazines. Honour: Screenwriters Guild Award, 1965. Membership: Dramatists Guild. Address: c/o International Creative Management, 40 West 57th Street, New York, NY 10019, USA.

GARDNER Sandra, b. 22 May 1940, Everett, Massachusetts, USA. Author of Young/Adult Books. m. Lewis Gardner, 16 Feb 1969, 1 son, 2 daughters. Education: BA, magna cum laude, English Literature, Hunter College, New York, 1979. Publications: Six Who Dared, 1981; Street Gangs, 1983; Street Gangs in America, 1992; Teenage Suicide, 1985, 2nd edition, 1990. Contributions to: New York Times New Jersey Weekly Section, 1981-86, 1991-93. Honours: Honourable Mention, Poetry Award, Hunter College, 1979; Juvenile Book Award, National Federation of Press Women, 1993. Literary Agent: Claudia Menza, New York, New York. Address: 16 Cedar Way, Woodstock, NY 12498, USA.

GARDONS S S. See: **SNODGRASS W D.**

GARFINKEL Patricia Gail, b. 15 Feb 1938, New York, New York, USA. Poet; Writer. 2 sons. Education: BA, New York University. Publications: Ram's Horn, poems, 1980; From the Red Eye of Jupiter (poems), 1990. Contributions to: Numerous anthologies and other publications. Honours: Poetry in Public Places Award for New York State, 1977; 1st Prize, Lip Service Poetry Competition, 1990; Book Competition, Washington Writers Publishing House, 1990. Membership: Poets and Writers. Address: 900N Stuart Street, # 1001, Arlington, Virginia, 22203, USA.

GARFITT Roger, b. 12 Apr 1944, Melksham, Wiltshire, England. Poet; Writer. Education: BA, Honours, Merton College, Oxford, 1968. Appointments: Arts Council Creative Writing Fellow, University College of North Wales, Bangor, 1975-77, and Poet-in-Residence, Sunderland Polytechnic, 1978-80; Editor, Poetry Review, 1977-82; Welsh Arts Council Poet-in-Residence, Ebbw Vale, 1984; Poet-in-Residence, Pilgrim College, Boston, 1986-87, Blyth Valley Disabled Forum, 1992. Publications: Caught on Blue, 1970; West of Elm, 1974; The Broken Road, 1982; Rowlstone Haiku (with Frances Horovitz), 1982; Given Ground, 1989; Border Songs, 1996. Contributions to: Journals, reviews, and magazines. Honours: Guinness International Poetry Prize, 1973; Gregory Award, 1974. Memberships: National Association of Writers in Education: Poetry Society; Welsh Academy. Address: c/o Jane Turnbull, 13 Wendell Road, London W12 9RS, England.

GARLICK Helen Patricia, b. 21 Apr 1958, Doncaster, England. Writer; Solicitor. m. Richard Howard, 1 daughter. Education: LLB Class 2i Honours, University of Bristol, 1979; Solicitor of Supreme Court, 1983. Appointments: TV and radio appearances. Publications: The Separation Survival Handbook, 1989; The Good Marriage, 1990; The Which? Good Divorce Guide, 1992; Penguin Guide to the Law, 1992. Contributions to: Independent; Guardian; Various magazines. Memberships: National Council for One Parent Families; Consumers Association, family law adviser. Address: c/o Carolyn Brunton, Studio 8, 125 Moore Park Road, London SW6 4PS, England.

GARLICK Raymond, b. 21 Sept 1926, London, England. Poet; Retired Lecturer. m. Elin Jane Hughes, 1948, 1 son, 1 daughter. Education: BA, University College of North Wales, Bangor, 1948. Appointment: Principal Lecturer, Trinity College, Carmarthen, 1972-86. Publications: Poetry: Poems from the Mountain-House, 1950; Requiem for a Poet, 1954; Poems from Pembrokeshire, 1954; The Welsh-Speaking Sea, 1954; Blaenau Observed, 1957; Landscapes and Figures: Selected Poems, 1949-63, 1964; A Sense of Europe: Collected Poems, 1954-68, 1968; A Sense of Time: Poems and Antipoems, 1969-72, 1972; Incense: Poems, 1972-75, 1975; Collected Poems, 1946-86, 1987; Travel Notes: New Poems, 1992. Other: An Introduction to Anglo-Welsh Literature, 1970; Anglo-Welsh Poetry, 1480-1980 (editor), 1982. Honours: Welsh Arts Council Prizes; Honorary Fellow, Trinity College, Carmarthen; Fellow, Welsh Academy; DLitt, Central University, Pella, Iowa, 1998. Address: 26 Glannant House, College Road, Carmarthen SA31 3EF, Wales.

GARLINSKI Jozef, b. 14 Oct 1913, Poland. Writer. Education: MA, University of Warsaw, 1942; PhD, London School of Economics and Political Science, 1973. Appointments: Chairman, Executive Committee, Polish Home Army Circle, London, England, 1954-65; Cultural Vice-Chairman, Polish Cultural and Social Centre, London, 1970-79; Chairman, Union of Polish Writers Abroad, 1975-. Publications: Dramat i Opatrznosc, 1961; Matki i zony, 1962; Ziemia, novel, 1964; Miedzy Londynem i Warszawa, 1966; Polish SOE and the Allies, 1969; Fighting Auschwitz, 1975; Hitler's Last Weapons, 1978; Intercept: Secrets of the Enigma War, 1979; The Swiss Corridor, 1981; Polska w Drugiej Wojnie Swiatowej, 1982; Poland in the Second World War, 1985; Szwajcarski Kryterz, 1987; Niezapomniane lata, 1987. Address: 94 Ramillies Road, London W4 1JA, England.

GARNER Alan, b. 17 Oct 1934, Cheshire, England. Author. m. (1) Ann Cook, 1956, div, 1 son, 2 daughters, (2) Griselda Greaves, 1972, 1 son, 1 daughter. Education: Magdalen College, Oxford, 1955-56. Appointment: Member, International Editorial Board, Detskaya Literatura Publishers, Moscow, 1991-. Publications: The Weirdstone of Brisingamen, 1960; The Moon of Gomrath, 1963; Elidor, 1965; Holly from the Bongs, 1966; The Owl Service, 1967; The Book of Goblins, 1969; Red Shift, 1973; The Guizer, 1975; The Stone Book Quartet, 1976-78; Fairy Tales of Gold, 1979; The Lad of the Gad, 1980; British Fairy Tales, 1984; A Bag of Moonshine, 1986; Jack and the Beanstalk, 1992; Once Upon a Time, 1993; Strandloper, 1996; The Voice that Thunders, 1997; The Well of the Wind, 1998. Honours: Carnegie Medal, 1967; Guardian Award, 1968; Lewis Carroll Shelf Award, USA, 1970; Gold Plaque, Chicago International Film Festival, 1981; Children's Literature Association International Phoenix Award, 1996. Membership: Portico Library, Manchester. Literary Agent: Sheil Land Associates Ltd. Address: Blackden, Holmes Chapel, Crewe, Cheshire CW4 8BY, England.

GARNER Helen, b. 7 Nov 1942, Geelong, Victoria, Australia. Novelist; Journalist. m. (3) Murray Bail, 1992. Education: BA, Melbourne University, 1965. Publications: Monkey Grip, 1977; Honour, and Other People's Children, 1980; The Children's Bach, 1984; Postcards from Surfers, 1985; Cosmo Cosmolino, 1992; The Last Days of Chez Nous, 1993; The First Stone, 1995; True Stories, 1996. Honours: Australia Council Fellowships; National Book Council Award, 1978; New South Wales Premiers Award, 1986. Address: c/o Barbara Mobbs, PO Box 126, Edgecliff, New South Wales 2027, Australia.

GARNETT Michael Pearson, b. 24 Nov 1938, Essex, England. Writer. m. 2 sons. Education: Framlingham College, Suffolk; Diploma, Business Management, British Institute of Careers, New South Wales, Australia. Appointments: Flight Lieutenant, Royal Air Force in Far East during Malaya emergency, RAAF Reserve; Executive, Australian Real Tennis Association. Publications: A History of Royal Tennis in Australia, 1983; The Garnett Family: A History, 1985; Tennis, Rackets and Other Ball Games, 1986; Royal Tennis - For the Record, 1991. Contributions to: Periodicals. Membership: Melbourne Press Club. Literary Agent: Historical Publications, Melbourne. Address: The Chase, Romsey, Victoria 3434, Australia.

GARNETT Richard (Duncan Carey), b. 8 Jan 1923, London, England. Writer; Publisher; Translator. Education: BA, King's College, Cambridge, 1948; MA, 1987. Appointments: Production Manager, 1951-59, Director, 1957-66, Rupert Hart-Davis Ltd; Director, Adlard Coles Ltd, 1963-66; Editor, 1966-82, Director, 1972-82, Macmillan London; Director, Macmillan Publishers, 1982-87. Publications: Goldsmith: Selected Works (editor), 1950; Robert Gruss: The Art of the Aqualung (translator), 1955; The Silver Kingdom (in US as The Undersea Treasure), 1956; Bernard Heuvelmans: On the Track of Unknown Animals (translator), 1958; The White Dragon, 1963; Jack of Dover, 1966; Bernard Heuvelmans: In the Wake of the Sea-Serpents (translator), 1968; Joyce (editor with Reggie Grenfell), 1980; Constance Garnett: A Heroic Life, 1991; Sylvia and David, The Townsend Warner/Garnett Letters (editor), 1994. Literary Agent: A.P. Watt Ltd., 20 John Street, London WC1N 2DR. Address: Hilton Hall, Hilton, Huntingdon, Cambridgeshire PE18 9NE, England.

GARRATT Sheryl, b. 29 Mar 1961, Birmingham, England. Journalist. m. Mark McGuire, 1 son. Education: BA Hons, English, University College London, England. Appointments: Music & Clubs Editor, City Limits, 1984-86; Music Editor, The Face, 1987-89; Editor, The Face, 1989-95; Editor, The Observer Magazine, 1998-. Publications: Adventures in Wonderland, 1998; Signed, Scaled and Delivered, 1985; Published in anthologies including The Faber Book of Pop; Love is the Drug. Contributions to: City Limits; The Face; Arena; The Guardian; Independent; Mail on Sunday; Sunday Times; Red; The Big Issue; Gay Times; Evening Standard; Cosmo. Literary Agent: Cat Ledger. Address: 56c St Thomas' Road, London N4 2QW, England.

GARRETT George (Palmer Jr), b. 11 June 1929, Orlando, Florida, USA. Professor of English; Writer; Poet; Editor. m. Susan Parrish Jackson, 1952, 2 sons, 1 daughter. Education: BA, 1952, MA, 1956, PhD, 1985, Princeton University. Appointments: Assistant Professor, Wesleyan University, 1957-60; US Poetry Editor, Transatlantic Review, 1958-71; Visiting Lecturer, Rice University, 1961-62; Associate Professor, 1962-67, Hoyns Professor of English, 1984-, University of Virginia; Writer-in-Residence, Princeton University, 1964-65, Bennington College, Vermonty, 1979, University of Michigan, 1979-80, 1983-84; Co-Editor, Hollins Critic, 1965-71, Worksheet, 1972-, Poultry: A Magazine of Voice, 1981-; Professor of English, Hollins College, Virginia, 1967-71; Professor of English and Writer-in-Residence, University of South Carolina, 1971-73; Senior Fellow, Council of the Humanities, Princeton University, 1974-78; Adjunct Professor, Columbia University, 1977-78. Publications: Novels: The Finished Man, 1959; Which Ones Are the Enemy?, 1961; Do, Lord, Remember Me, 1965; Death of the Fox, 1971; The Succession: A Novel of Elizabeth and James, 1983; Poison Pen, or, Live Now and Pay Later, 1986; Entered from the Sun, 1990; The Old Army Game, 1994; The King of Babylon Shall Not Come Against You, 1996. Short Stories: King of the Mountain, 1958; In the Briar Patch, 1961; Cold Ground Was My Bed Last Night, 1964; A Wreath for Garibaldi and Other Stories, 1969; The Magic Striptease, 1973; To Recollect a Cloud of Ghosts: Christmas in England, 1979; An Evening Performance: New and Selected Short Stories, 1985. Poetry: The Reverend Ghost, 1957; The Sleeping Gypsy and Other Poems, 1958; Abraham's Knife and Other Poems, 1961; For a Bitter Season: New and Selected Poems, 1967; Welcome to the Medicine Show: Postcards, Flashcards, Snapshots, 1978; Luck's Shining Child: A Miscellany of Poems and Verses, 1981; The Collected Poems of George Garrett, 1984. Other: James Jones, 1984; Understanding Mary Lee Settle, 1988; The Sorrows of Fat City, 1992; Whistling in the Dark, 1992; My Silk Purse and Yours, 1993. Editor: 18 books, 1963-93. Honours: Sewanee Review Fellowship, 1958; American Academy in Rome Fellowship, 1958; Ford Foundation Grant, 1960; National Endowment for the Arts Grant, 1967; Contempora Award, 1971; Guggenheim Fellowship, 1974; American Academy of Arts and Letters Award, 1985; Cultural Laureate of Virginia, 1986; T S Eliot Award, 1989. Membership: Fellowship of Southern Letters, vice-chancellor, 1987-93, chancellor, 1993-. Address: 1845 Wayside Place, Charlottesville, VA 22903, USA.

GARRETT Richard, b. 15 Jan 1920, London, England. Author; Journalist. m. Margaret Anne Selves, 20 Aug 1945, 2 sons, 1 daughter. Education: Bradfield College. Publications: Fast and Furious: The Story of the World Championship of Drivers, 1968; Cross Channel, 1972; Scharnhorst and Gneisenau: The Elusive Sisters, 1978; Mrs Simpson, 1979; The Raiders, 1980; POW, 1981; Royal Travel, 1982; Atlantic Disaster: The Titanic and Other Victims, 1986; Flight Into Mystery, 1986; Voyage Into Mystery, 1987; Great Escapes of World War II, 1989; The Final Betrayal: The Armistice, 1918 ... And

Afterwards, 1990; Sky High, 1991. Other: Biographies of Generals Gordon Wolfe and Clive, and a number of children's books. Contributions to: Magazines and radio. Membership: Society of Authors. Address: c/o Watson, Little Ltd, Capo di Monte, Windmill Hill, London, NW3 6RJ, England.

GARRISON Omar V, b. 2 June 1913, LaJunta, Colorado, USA. Author. m. Virginia Leah Herrick, 11 Sept 1952. Education: PhD, 1938. Publications: Tantra, philosophy, 1964; Spy Government, 1967; Howard Hughes in Las Vegas, 1970; Balboa Conquistador, biography, 1971; Lost Gems of Secret Knowledge, 1973; Hidden Story of Scientology, 1974; Secret World of Interpol, 1977; Playing Dirty, 1980; The Baby That Laughed All Night (novel), 1989. Membership: Authors Guild. Address: 26812 Cherry Hills Boulevard, No 224, Sun City, CA 92586, USA.

GARROW David J(effries), b. 11 May 1953, New Bedford, Massachusetts, USA. Author; Professor. m. Susan Foster Newcomer, 18 Dec 1984. Education: BA magna cum laude, Wesleyan University, 1975; MA, 1978, PhD, 1981, Duke University. Appointments: Senior Fellow, Twentieth Century Fund, 1991-93; Visiting Distinguished Professor, Cooper Union, 1992-93; James Pinckney Harrison Professor of History, College of William and Mary, 1994-95; Distinguished Historian-in-Residence, American University, Washington, DC, 1995-96; Presidential Distinguished Professor, Emory University, 1997-. Publications: Protest at Selma, 1978; The FBI and Martin Luther King Jr, 1981; Bearing the Cross, 1986; The Montgomery Bus Boycott and the Women Who Started It (editor), 1987; Liberty and Sexuality, 1994. Contributions to: New York Times; Washington Post; Newsweek; Dissent; Journal of American History; Constitutional Commentary. Honours: Pulitzer Prize in Biography, 1987; Robert F Kennedy Book Award, 1987; Gustavus Myers Human Rights Book Award, 1987. Address: Emory University Law School, Atlanta, GA 30322, USA.

GARTNER Chloe Maria, b. 21 Mar 1916, Troy, Kansas, USA. Writer. m. Peter Godfrey Trimble, 22 Jan 1942, div 1957, 1 daughter. Education: University of California; Mesa College, Grand Junction, Colorado; College Marin, Kentfield, California. Publications: The Infidels, 1960; Drums of Khartoum, 1967; Die Lange Sommer, 1970; Woman From the Glen, 1973; Mistress of the Highlands, 1976; Anne Bonney, 1977; The Image and the Dream, 1980; Still Falls the Rain, 1983; Greenleaf, 1987; Lower Than the Angels, 1989. Contributions to: Magazines. Honour: Silver Medal, Commonwealth Club of California, 1960. Membership: Authors Guild. Address: c/o Kidde, Hoyt and Picard, 355 East 51st Street, New York, NY 10022, USA.

GARTON ASH Timothy (John), b. 12 July 1955, London, England. Writer. m. Danuta Maria, 24 Dec 1982, 2 sons. Education: BA, 1st Class Honours, Modern History, 1977, MA, 1984, Exeter College, Oxford; Graduate Studies, St Antony's College, Oxford, 1978-80. Appointments: Editorial Writer, The Times, 1984-86; Foreign Editor, The Spectator, 1984-90; Fellow, Woodrow Wilson International Center for Scholars, Washington, DC, 1986-87; Senior Associate Member, 1987-89, Fellow and Senior Research Fellow in Contemporary European History, 1990-, St Antony's College, Oxford; Columnist, The Independent, 1988-90. Publications: 'Und willst du nicht mein Bruder sein...': Die DDR heute, 1981; The Polish Revolution: Solidarity, 1983, new edition, 1991; The Uses of Adversity: Essays on the Fate of Central Europe, 1989, new edition, 1991; We the People: The Revolution of '89 Witnessed in Warsaw, Budapest, Berlin and Prague, 1990; In Europe's Name: Germany and the Divided Continent, 1993; Freedom for Publishing for Freedom: The Central and East European Publishing Project (editor), 1995; The File: A Personal History, 1997. Contributions to: Books, newspapers, and magazines. Honours: Somerset Maugham Award, Society of Authors, 1984; Prix Européen de l'Essai, Veillon Foundation, 1989; David Watt Memorial Prize, 1989; Commentator of the Year, Granada Awards, 1989; Friedrich Ebert Stiftung

Prize, 1991; Golden Insignia of the Order of Merit, Poland, 1992; Knight's Cross of the Order of Merit, Germany, 1995; Imre Nagy Memorial Plaque, Hungary, 1995; Premio Napoli, 1995. Memberships: Academy of Sciences, Berlin-Brandenburg, fellow; European Academy of Arts and Sciences, fellow; Institute for Human Sciences, Vienna, corresponding fellow; PEN; Royal Society of Arts, fellow; Society of Authors. Address: St Antony's College, Oxford OX2 6JF, England.

GASCOIGNE Bamber, b. 24 Jan 1935, London, England. Author; Broadcaster. m. Christina Ditchburn, 1965. Education: Scholar, Magdalene College, Cambridge; Commonwealth Fund Fellow, Yale University, 1958-59. Appointments: Theatre Critic, Spectator, 1961-63, Observer, 1963-64; Co-Editor, Theatre Notebook, 1968-74; Founder, Saint Helena Press, 1977; Chairman, Ackermann Publishing, 1981-85; Presenter, television programmes and documentaries. Publications: Twentieth Century Drama, 1962; World Theatre, 1968; The Great Moghuls, 1971; Murgatreud's Empire, 1972; The Heyday, 1973; The Treasures and Dynasties of China, 1973; Ticker Khan, 1974; The Christians, 1977; Images of Richmond, 1978; Images of Twickenham, 1981; Why the Rope went Tight, 1981; Fearless Freddy's Magic Wish, 1982; Fearless Freddy's Sunken Treasure, 1982; Quest for the Golden Hare, 1983; Cod Streuth, 1986; How to Identify Prints, 1986; Encyclopedia of Britain, 1993; Milestones in Colour Printing, 1997. Address: Saint Helena Terrace, Richmond, Surrey TW9 1NR, England.

GASCOIGNE John, b. 20 Jan 1951, Liverpool, England. Associate Professor of History; Writer. m. Kathleen May Bock, 6 Apr 1980, 1 son, 1 daughter. Education: BA, University of Sydney, 1972; MA, Princeton University, 1974; PhD, University of Cambridge, 1981. Appointments: Lecturer, St Paul's Teachers' College, Rabaul, 1973, University of Papua New Guinea, Port Moresby, 1977-78; Tutor, 1980-84, Lecturer, 1984-87, Senior Lecturer, 1987-96, Associate Professor of History, 1997-, University of New South Wales; Reviews Editor, Journal of Religious History, 1996-. Publications: Cambridge in the Age of Enlightenment: Science, Religion and Politics from the Restoration to the French Revolution, 1988; Joseph Banks and the English Enlightenment: Useful Knowledge and Polite Culture, 1994; Science in the Service of Empire: Sir Joseph Banks and the British State in the Age of Revolution, 1998. Contributions to: Scholarly books and journals. Honours: Hancock Prize, Australian Historical Society, 1991; Fellow, Royal Historical Society, London, 1992. Address: c/o School of History, University of New South Wales, Sydney, New South Wales 2052, Australia.

GASCOIGNE Marguerita See: **LAZARUS Marguerite.**

GASCOYNE David Emery, b. 10 Oct 1916, Harrow, Middlesex, England. Poet; Writer; Translator. m. Judy Tyler Lewis, 17 May 1975, 2 stepsons, 2 stepdaughters. Education: Salisbury Cathedral Choir School; Regent Street Polytechnic Secondary, London, 1930-32. Publications: A Short Survey of Surrealism, 1936; Holderlin's Madness, 1938; A Vagrant and Other Poems, 1950; Collected Poems, 1954, revised edition, 1988; Night Thoughts, 1956, revised edition, 1995; Collected Verse Translations, 1970, revised edition, 1996; Collected Journals, 1936-42, 1990; Selected Poems, 1995; Collected Prose, 1998. Contributions to: Many reviews, journals, and periodicals. Honours: Premio Biella Europae, 1982; Chevalier des Arts et Lettres, France, 1995. Memberships: Biennales Internationales de Poesie, committee, Belgim; Royal Society of Literature, fellow; World Organization for Poets, cultural committee. Address: 48 Oxford Street, Northwood, Cowes, Isle of Wight PO31 8PT, England.

GASH Jonathan See: **GRANT John.**

GASKELL Jane, b. 7 July 1941, Lancashire, England. Writer. Appointments: Staff, Daily Express, 1961-65,

Daily Sketch, 1965-71, Daily Mail, 1971-84. Publications: Strange Evil, 1957; King's Daughter, 1958; Attic Summer, 1958; The Serpent, 1963; The Shiny Narrow Grin, 1964; The Fabulous Heroine, 1965; Atlan, 1965; The City, 1966; All Neat in Black Stockings, 1966 (filmed); A Sweet Sweet Summer, 1969; Summer Coming, 1974; Some Summer Lands, 1977; Sun Bubble, 1990. Honour: Somerset Maugham Award, 1970. Address: c/o Michael Sharland Organization, 9 Marlbourough Crescent, Bedford Park, London W4 1HE, England.

GASKIN Catherine Marjella, b. 2 Apr 1929, County Louth, Dundalk, Ireland. Novelist. m. Sol Cornberg, 1 Dec 1955. Education: Holy Cross College, Sydney, Australia; Conservatorium of Music, Sydney. Publications: This Other Eden, 1946; With Every Year, 1947; Dust in Sunlight, 1950; All Else is Folly, 1951; Daughter of the House, 1952; Sara Dane, 1955; Blake's Reach, 1958; Corporation Wife, 1960; I Know My Love, 1962; The Tilsit Inheritance, 1963; The File on Devlin, 1965; Edge of Glass, 1967; Fiona, 1970; A Falcon for a Queen, 1972; The Property of a Gentleman, 1974; The Lynmara Legacy, 1975; The Summer of the Spanish Woman, 1977; Family Affairs, 1980; Promises, 1982; The Ambassador's Women, 1985; The Charmed Circle, 1988. Memberships: Society of Authors; Author's Guild of America. Address: White Rigg, Church Road, Maughold IM7 1AR, Isle of Man.

GASKIN J(ohn) C(harles) A(ddison), b. 4 Apr 1936, Hitchin, Hertfordshire, England. Professor of Philosophy; Writer. m. Diana Dobbin, 20 May 1972, 1 son, 1 daughter. Education: MA, 1963, BLitt, 1965, St Peter's College, Oxford; MA, Trinity College, Dublin, 1967; D. Litt., Dublin University, 1997. Appointments: Lecturer, 1965-78, Fellow, 1978-, Professor of Philosophy, 1982-97, Trinity College, Dublin. Publications: Hume's Philosophy of Religion, 1978, revised edition, 1988; The Quest for Eternity: An Outline of the Philosophy of Religion, 1984; Varieties of Unbelief From Epicurus to Sarte, 1989; David Hume: Dialogues Concerning Natural Religion and the Natural History of Religion (editor), 1993; The Epicurean Philosophers (editor), 1994; Thomas Hobbes: Human Nature and the De Corpore (editor), 1994; Hobbes: Leviathan, 1996. Contributions to: Scholarly journals and periodicals. Membership: Royal Institute of Philosophy. Address: Hatfield College, University of Durham, Durham, DH1 3RQ, England.

GASPARIKOVA Viera, b. 15 Apr 1928, Martin-Priekopa, Slovakia. Senior Research Worker of Slovak Academy of Sciences. Education: High School Gymnasium, 1948; Philosophical Faculty, University of Bratislava, 1949-53; University of Prague, 1956-60; PhD, Philosophical Faculty, University of Bratislava, 1953; DSc, Slovak Academy of Sciences, 1992. Publications: Humor and Satire in the Slovak People's Folktales, 1960; The Singing Linden Tree, 1972; The Sun Horse, 1981; Miraculous Tales of the Slovak People, 1984-85; Slovak Folk Prose and Its Evolutionary Tendencies, 1987; Catalogue of Slovak Folk Prose I-II, 1991-92; Slovak Folk Tales, Vol I (with B Filova), 1993; The Garden of Miracles - Central European Fairy Tales, together with O Sirovatka, 1996. Contributions to: About 300 contributions to: Slovak and foreign journals in the fields of ethnology, folklore and literature. Honours: Member of Executive Committee, International Society for Folk Narrative Research; Member, Polish Ethnological Society; Gold Medal, Presidium of the Slovak Academy of Sciences, 1988. Memberships: International Society for Ethnology & Folklore; Slovak Ethnologic Society; Member of Presidium of Slovak Committee of Slavists. Address: Mikoviniho 9, Bratislava 831-02, Slovakia.

GASS William H(oward), b. 30 July 1924, Fargo, North Dakota, USA. Distinguished Professor in the Humanities; Author; Critic. m. (1) Mary Pat O'Kelly, 1952, 2 sons, 1 daughter, (2) Mary Henderson, 1969, 2 daughters. Education: AB, Philosophy, Kenyon College, 1947; PhD, Philosophy, Cornell University, 1954. Appointments: Instructor in Philosophy, College of Wooster, 1950-54; Assistant Professor, 1955-58; Associate Professor, 1960-65, Professor of Philosophy,

1966-69, Purdue University; Visiting Lecturer in English and Philosophy, University of Illinois, 1958-59; Professor of Philosophy, 1969-78, David May Distinguished Professor in the Humanities, 1979-, Director, International Writers Centre, 1990-, Washington University. Publications: Novels: Omensetter's Luck, 1966; Willie Masters' Lonesome Wife, 1968; The Tunnel, 1995. Stories: In the Heart of the Heart of the Country, 1968; Cartesian Sonata, 1998. Essays: Fiction and the Figures of Life, 1971; On Being Blue, 1976; The World Within the Word, 1978; The Habitations of the Word, 1984; Finding a Form, 1996; Cartesian Sonata (Knopf), 1998. Editor: The Writer in Politics (with Lorin Cuoco), 1996. Translator: Reading Rilke, 1999. Contributions to: Essays, criticism, poems, stories, and translations in various publications. Honours: Longview Foundation Prize for Fiction, 1959; Rockefeller Foundation Grant, 1965-66; Guggenheim Fellowship, 1970-71; American Academy and Institute of Arts and Letters Award, 1975, and Medal of Merit, 1979; Pushcart Prizes, 1976, 1983, 1987, 1992; National Book Critics Circle Awards, 1985, 1996; Getty Scholar, 1991-92; American Book Award, Before Columbus Foundation, 1996; Lannan Lifetime Achievement Award, 1997. Memberships: American Academy of Arts and Letters; American Academy of Arts and Sciences. Address: 6304 Westminster Place, St Louis, MO 63130, USA.

GATENBY Greg, b. 5 May 1950, Toronto, Ontario, Canada. Artistic Director; Poet. Education: BA, English Literature, York University, 1972. Appointments: Editor, McClelland and Stewart, Toronto, 1973-75; Artistic Director, Harbourfront Reading Series and concomitant festivals, 1975-, Humber College School of Creative Writing, 1992-93. Publications: Imaginative Work: Rondeaus for Erica, 1976; Adrienne's Blessing, 1976; The Brown Stealer, 1977; The Salmon Country, 1978; Growing Still, 1981. Anthologies: 52 Pickup, 1977; Whale Sound, 1977; Whales: A Celebration, 1983; The Definitive Notes, 1991; The Wild Is Always There, 1993. Translator: Selected Poems, by Giorgio Bassani, 1980; The Wild Is Always There, Vol 2, 1995; The Very Richness of that Past, 1995. Honours: City of Toronto Arts Award for Literature, 1989; League of Canadian Poets Honorary Lifetime Member, 1991; Jack Award for Lifetime Promotion of Canadian Books, 1994; E J Pratt Lifetime Fellow, 1995. Memberships: PEN, Canadian Centre; Writers Union of Canada. Address: c/o Harbourfront Reading Series, 410 Queen's Quay West, Toronto, Ontario M5V 2Z3, Canada.

GATES Henry Louis Jr, b. 16 Sept 1950, Keyser, West Virginia, USA. Professor of Humanities and English; Writer; Editor. m. Sharon Lynn Adams, 1 Sept 1979, 2 daughters. Education: BA summa cum laude, History, Yale University, 1973; MA, English Language and Literature, 1974, PhD, English Language and Literature, 1979, Clare College, University of Cambridge, England. Appointments: Lecturer and Director of Undergraduate Studies, 1976-79, Assistant Professor, 1979-84, Associate Professor of English and Afro-American Studies, 1984-85, Yale University; Professor of English, Comparative Literature, and Africana Studies, 1985-88, W E B Du Bois Professor of Literature, 1988-90, Cornell University; Virginia Commonwealth Professor, 1987; Richard Wright Lecturer, University of Pennsylvania, 1990; John Spencer Bassett Professor of English and Literature, Duke University, 1990-91; W E D Du Bois Professor of Humanities, 1991-, Professor of English, 1991-, Chair, Department of Afro-American Studies, 1991-, Director, W E D Du Bois Institute for Afro-American Research, 1991-, Harvard University; Clarendon Lecturer, University of Oxford, 1992. Publications: Figures in Black: Words, Signs, and the Racial Self, 1987; The Signifying Monkey: Towards a Theory of Afro-American Literary Criticism, 1988; Loose Canons: Notes on the Culture Wars, 1992; Colored People: A Memoir, 1994; The Future of the Race (with Cornel West), 1996; Thirteen Ways of Looking at a Black Man, 1997. Editor: Numerous books, including: Black Literature and Literary Theory, 1984; "Race", Writing, and Difference, 1986; In the House of Osugbo: Critical Essays on Wole Soyinka, 1988; The Oxford-Schomburg Library

of Nineteenth-Century Black Women Writers (series editor), 30 volumes, 1988; The Schomburg Library of Nineteenth-Century Black Women Writers, 10 volumes, 1991; Critical Perspectives Past and Present (with K A Appiah), 1993; Richard Wright: Critical Perspectives Past and Present (with K A Appiah), 1993; Zora Neale Hurston: Critical Perspectives Past and Present (with K A Appiah), 1993; Toni Morrison: Critical Perspectives Past and Present (with K A Appiah), 1993; Gloria Naylor: Critical Perspectives Past and Present (with K A Appiah, 1993; Alice Walker: Critical Perspectives Past and Present (with K A Appiah), 1993; Langston Hughes: Critical Perspectives Past and Present (with K A Appiah), 1993; The Norton Anthology of African American Literature, 1996; The Dictionary of Global Cultural, 1997. Contributions to: Numerous scholarly and other publications. Honours: Ford Foundation National Fellowship, 1976-77; Rockefeller Foundation Fellowship for Minority Scholars, 1980-81; John D and Catharine T MacArthur Foundation Fellowship, 1981-86; Zora Neale Hurston Society Award for Cultural Scholarship, 1986; Woodrow Wilson National Fellowship, 1988-90; Anisfield-Wolf Book Award for Race Relations, 1989; American Book Award, American Jewish Committee, 1994; Chicago Tribune Heartland Award, 1994; Lillian Smith Book Award, 1994; West Virginian of the Year, 1995; Tikkun National Ethics Award, 1996; New England Award for Editorial Excellence, 1997; National Humanities Medal, 1998. Numerous honorary degrees. Memberships: African Literature Association; Afro-American Academy; American Antiquarian Society; American Philosophical Society; American Studies Association; Association for the Study of Afro-American Life and History, life member; Caribbean Studies Association; College Language Association, life member; Council on Foreign Relations; Modern Language Association. Address: c/o Department of Afro-American Studies, Harvard University, Barker Center, 12 Quincy Street, Cambridge, MA 02128, USA.

GATHORNE-HARDY Jonathan, b. 15 May 1933, Edinburgh, Scotland. Author. m. (1) Sabrina Tennant, 1962, 1 son, 1 daughter, (2) Nicolette Sinclair Loutit, 12 Sept 1985. Education: BA, Arts, Trinity College, Cambridge, 1957. Publications: One Foot in the Clouds (novel), 1961; Chameleon (novel), 1967; The Office (novel), 1970; The Rise and Fall of the British Nanny, 1972; The Public School Phenomenon, 1977; Love, Sex, Marriage and Divorce, 1981; Doctors, 1983; The Centre of the Universe is 18 Baedeker Strasse (short stories), 1985; The City Beneath the Skin (novel), 1986; The Interior Castle: A Life of Gerald Brenan (biography), 1992; Particle Theory (novel), 1996; Alfred C. Kinsey - Sex The Measure of All Things, A Biography, 1998. Other: 11 novels for children. Contributions to: Numerous magazines and journals. Literary Agents: Sinclair Stevenson; For Children's books: Laura Cecil. Address: 31 Blacksmith's Yard, Binham, Fakenham, Norfolk NR21 0AL, England.

GATLAND Elizabeth. See: WEIN Elizabeth Eve.

GATTEY Charles Neilson, b. 3 Sept 1921, London, England. Author; Playwright; Lecturer. Education: London University. Publications: The Incredible Mrs Van Der Eist, 1972; They Saw Tomorrow, 1977; Queens of Song, 1979; The Elephant that Swallowed a Nightingale, 1981; Peacocks on the Podium, 1982; Foie Gras and Trumpets, 1984; Excess in Food, Drink and Sex, 1987; Prophecy and Prediction in the 20th Century, 1989; Luisa Tetrazzini, 1995. Other: Television Play: The White Falcon, 1955. Film: The Love Lottery, 1954. Memberships: Society of Civil Service Authors, president, 1980; The Garrick. Address: 15 St Lawrence Drive, Pinner, Middlesex HA5 2RL, England.

GATTI Armand, b. 26 Jan 1924, Monaco (French citizen). Playwright. Education: Seminary of Saint Paul, near Cannes. Publications include: Le Poisson noir, 1958; La crapaud-buffle, 1959; Le Voyage de Grand Chou, 1960; Chant public devant deux chaises électriques, 1966; V comme Vietnam, 1967; Le Passion du Général Franco, 1968; Un homme seul, 1969; Petit

manuel de guérilla urbaine, 1971; La colonne Durutti, 1974; Die Hälfte des Himmels und wir, 1975; Le labyrinthe, 1982; Opéra avec titre long, 1987; Oeuvres théâtrales, 3 tomes regroupant 44 pièces de 1958 à 1990, 1991; Ces em Pe reurs Troue's, 1991; Le chant d'amour des alphabets d'Auschwitz, 1992; Gatti à Marseilles, 1993; Adam quoi?, 1993; La journée d'une infirmière, 1995; Notre tranchée de chaque jour, 1996; L'Inconnu no 5, 1996; Les personnages de théâtre meurent dans la rue, 1997. Honours: Prix Fénéon, 1959; Grand prix national du théâtre, 1988; Officier des Arts et des Lettres, 1989; Médaille de vermeil Picasso, UNESCO, 1994. Address: La Parole Errante, 5/7 rue François Debergue, 931000 Montreuil, France.

GAUNT Graham. See: GRANT John.

GAVIN Catherine, b. Aberdeen, Scotland. Author. m. John Ashcraft, 1948. Education: MA, PhD, University of Aberdeen; Sorbonne, University of Paris. Publications: Liberated France, 1955; Madeleine, 1957; The Cactus and the Crown, 1962; The Fortress, 1964; The Moon Into Blood, 1966; The Devil in Harbour, 1968; The House of War, 1970; Give Me the Daggers, 1972; The Snow Mountain, 1973; Traitors' Gate, 1976; None Dare Call It Treason, 1978; How Sleep the Brave, 1980; The Sunset Dream, 1983; The Glory Road, 1987; A Dawn of Splendour, 1989; The French Fortune, 1991; One Candle Burning, 1996. Contributions to: Time magazine; Kemsley newspapers; Daily Express. Honours: University Medal of Honour, Helsinki, 1970: Honorary DLitt, University of Aberdeen, 1986. Literary Agent: Scott Ferris Associates, London, England. Address: 21 Bret Harte Road, San Rafael, CA 94901, USA.

GAVIN Thomas Michael, b. 1 Feb 1941. Newport News, Virginia, USA. Emeritus Professor of English; Writer. m. Susan Holahan, 5 July 1991, 2 daughters. Education: BA, MA, University of Toledo. Appointments: Delta College, University Center, Michigan, 1972-75; Middlebury College, Vermont, 1975-80; University of Rochester, New York, 1980-97. Publications: Breathing Water; Kingkill; The Last Film of Emile Vico; "The Truth Beyond Facts". Contributions to: Georgia Review; TriQuarterly. Honours: National Endowment for the Arts Fellowship; Andrew W Mellon Fellowship; Lillian Fairchild Award. Address: PO Box 155, East Middlebury, Vermont 05740, USA.

GAY Peter (Jack), b. 20 June 1923, Berlin, Germany. Writer. m. Ruth Slotkin, 30 May 1959, 3 stepdaughters. Education: AB, University of Denver, 1946; MA, 1947, PhD, 1951, Columbia University; Psychoanalytic training, Western New England Institute for Psychoanalysis, 1976-83; Sterling Professor of History Emeritus; Director, Center for Scholars and Writers, New York Public Library. Publications: The Dilemma of Democratic Socialism: Eduard Bernstein's Challenge to Marx, 1952; The Question of Jean Jacques Rousseau (editor), 1954; Voltaire's Politics: The Poet as Realist, 1959; Voltaire: Philosophical Dictionary (translator), 1962; Voltaire: Candide (translator) 1963; The Party of Humanity: Essays in the French Enlightenment, 1964; John Locke on Education (editor), 1964; The Enlightenment: An Interpretation, Vol I: The Rise of Modern Paganism, 1966, Vol II: The Science of Freedom, 1969; A Loss of Mastery: Puritan Historians in Colonial America, 1966; Weimar Culture: The Outsider as Insider, 1968; Deism: An Anthology, 1968; Columbia History of the World (with John A Garraty), 1972; Modern Europe (with R K Webb), 2 volumes, 1973; The Enlightenment: A Comprehensive Anthology, 1973, revised edition, 1985; Style in History, 1974; Art and Act: On Causes in History - Manet, Gropius, Mondrian, 1976; The Bourgeois Experience, Victoria to Freud, Vol I, Education of the Senses, 1984, Vol II, The Tender Passion, 1986, Vol III, The Cultivation of Hatred, 1993, Vol IV, The Naked Heart, 1995, Vol V, Pleasure Wars, 1998; Freud: A Life for Our Time, 1989; Reading Freud, 1990; My German Question: Growing Up in Nazi Berlin, 1998. Honours: Frederic G Melcher Book Award, 1967; National Book Award, 1967; Guggenheim Fellowships, 1967-68, 1977-78; Gold Medal, American Academy of Arts and Letters. Membership: Phi Beta

Kappa. Address: 105 Blue Trail, Hamden, CT 06518, USA.

GAYLE Emma. See: **FAIRBURN Eleanor M.**

GEBAUER Phyllis, b. 17 Oct 1928, Chicago, Illinois, USA. Novelist; Writer; Teacher. m. Frederick A Gebauer, 2 Dec 1950. Education: BS, Northwestern University, 1950; MA, University of Houston, 1966; Postgraduate, several universities. Appointments: Workshop Leader, Santa Barbara Writers' Conference, 1980-; Instructor, University of California at Los Angeles Extension Writers' Program, 1989-; Lecturer, San Diego State University Writers Conference, 1995-. Publictions: The Pagan Blessing, 1979; The Cottage, 1985; The Final Murder of Monica Marlowe, 1986; Criticism, The Art of Give and Take, 1987. Honours: 1st Prize for Fiction, Santa Barbara City College, 1972; 1st and 2nd Prizes for Fiction, Santa Barbara City College, 1973. Memberships: PEN Center, USA; Mystery Writers of America. Address: 515 West Scenic Drive, Monrovia, CA 91016-1511, USA.

GÉBLER Carlo, b. 21 Aug 1954, Dublin, Ireland. Writer; Film-Maker. m. Tyga Thomason, 23 Aug 1990, 3 sons, 2 daughters. Education: BA, English and Related Literature, University of York, 1976; Graduate, National Film & Television School, 1979. Appointments: Part-time Teacher, Creative Writing, HMP Maze, Co Antrim, 1993-95; Appointed Writer-in-Residence, HMP Maghaberry, Co Antrim, 1997. Publications: The Eleventh Summer, 1985; August in July, 1986; Work & Play, 1987; Driving through Cuba, 1988; Malachy and His Family, 1990; The Glass Curtain: Inside an Ulster Community, 1991; Life of a Drum, 1991; The Cure, 1994; W9 and Other Lives, 1998; How to Murder a Man, 1998; Frozen Out, 1998. Membership: Elected to Aosdána, Ireland, 1990. Literary Agent: Antony Harwood. Address: c/o Antony Harwood, Aitken & Assocs, 29 Fernshaw Road, London SW10 0TG, England.

GEDDES Gary, b. 9 June 1940, Vancouver, British Columbia, Canada. Professor of English; Writer; Poet. m. (1) Norma Joan Fugler, 1963, div 1969, 1 daughter, (2) Jan Macht, 2 May 1973, 2 daughters. Education: BA, University of British Columbia, 1962; Diploma in Education, University of Reading, 1964; MA, 1966, PhD, 1975, University of Toronto. Appointments: Visiting Assistant Professor, Trent University, Peterborough, Ontario, Canada, 1968-69; Lecturer, Carleton University, Ottawa, Ontario, 1971-72; Lecturer, University of Victoria, British Columbia, 1972-74; Writer-in-Residence, 1976-77, Visiting Associate Professor, 1977-78, University of Alberta, Edmonton; Visiting Associate Professor, 1978-79, Professor of English, 1979-98, Concordia University, Montreal, Quebec; General Editor, Studies in Canadian Literature series; Distinguished Professor of Canadian Culture, Western Washington University, 1999-. Publications: 20th Century Poetry and Poets, 1969, 4th edition, 1996; 15 Canadian Poets (editor with Phyllis Bruce), 1970, 3rd edition, 1988; Poems, 1970; Rivers Inlet (verse), 1972; Snakeroot (verse), 1973; Letter of the Master of Horse (verse), 1973; Skookum Wawa: Writings of the Canadian Northwest (editor), 1975; The Inner Ear: An Anthology of New Canadian Poets (editor), 1983; The Terracotta Army (verse), 1984; I Didn't Notice the Mountain Growing Dark (co-translator), 1985; Changes of State (verse), 1986; Vancouver: Soul of a City (editor), 1986; The Unsettling of the West (stories), 1986; Hong Kong (verse), 1987; Letters from Managua, 1990; Light of Burning Towers (verse), 1990; The Art of Short Fiction: An International Anthology, 1992; Girl By the Water, 1994; The Perfect Cold Warrior, 1995; Active Trading: Selected Poems, 1996; Flying Blind (verse), 1998 Honours: E J Pratt Medal; National Poetry Prize, Canadian Authors Association; America's Best Book Award; Writers Choice Award; National Magazine Award; Archibald Lampman Prize; Milton Acorn Competition; Gabriela Mistral Prize, 1996. Address: 975 Seaside Drive, RR 2, Socke, B.C., VO5 INO, Canada.

GEE Maggie (Mary), b. 2 Nov 1948, Poole, Dorset, England. Novelist. m. Nicholas Rankin, 1983. Education: BA, 1969; BLitt, 1972, Somerville College, Oxford; PhD,

Wolverhampton Polytechnic, 1980. Appointments: Research Assistant, Wolverhampton Polytechnic, 1975-79; Eastern Arts Writing Fellow, University of East Anglia, 1982; Honorary Visiting Fellow, Sussex University, 1986-; Northern Arts Writer-in-Residence, University of Northumbria, 1996; Teaching Fellow, Sussex University, 1996-. Publications: Dying, In Other Words, 1981; The Burning Book, 1983; Light Years, 1985; Grace, 1988; Where Are the Snows?, 1991; Lost Children, 1994; The Ice People, 1998. Honours: Hawthornden Fellow, 1989; Fellow, Royal Society of Literature, 1994. Membership: Society of Authors, management committee, 1991-94. Address: c/o The Society of Authors, 84 Drayton Gardens, London SW10 9SB.

GEE Maurice Gough, b. 22 Aug 1931, Whakatane, New Zealand. Writer. Education: MA, University of Auckland, 1954. Appointments: Robert Burns Fellow, University of Otago, 1964; Writing Fellow, Victoria University of Wellington, 1989; Katherine Mansfield Fellow, Menton, France, 1992. Publications: Plumb, 1978; Meg, 1981; Sole Survivor, 1983; Collected Stories, 1986; Prowlers, 1987; The Burning Boy, 1990; Going West, 1993; Crime Story, 1994;Loving Ways, 1996. Other 8 novels for children. Honours: New Zealand Book Awards, 1976, 1979, 1981, 1991, 1993; James Tait Black Memorial Prize, 1979; Honorary DLitt, Victoria University of Wellington, 1987. Membership: PEN New Zealand Centre, national vice president, 1990-91. Address: 41 Chelmsford Street, Ngaio, Wellington, New Zealand.

GEE Shirley, b. 25 Apr 1932, London, England. Dramatist. m. Donald Gee, 30 Jan 1965, 2 sons. Education: Webber-Douglas Academy of Music and Drama. Publications: Stones, 1974; Moonshine, 1977; Typhoid Mary, 1979; Bedrock, 1982; Never in My Lifetime, 1983; Flights, 1984; Long Live the Babe, 1985; Ask for the Moon, 1986; Against the Wind, 1988; Warrior, 1989. Other: Stage adaptations, including The Forsyte Saga (co-adapter); Children's poems, stories and songs. Honours: Radio Times Drama Bursary Award, 1974; Pye Award, 1979; Jury's Special Commendation, Prix Italia, 1979; Giles Cooper Awards, 1979, 1983; Sony Award, 1983; Samuel Beckett Award, 1984; Susan Smith Blackburn Prize, 1985. Memberships: Society of Authors; Writers Guild. Address: c/o Shiel Land Associates Ltd, 43 Doughty Street, London WC1N 2LF, England.

GEERTZ Clifford (James), b. 23 Aug 1926, San Francisco, California, USA. Professor of Social Science; Writer. m. (1) Hildred Storey, 30 Oct 1948, div 1982, 1 son, 1 daughter, (2) Karen Blu, 1987. Education: AB, Antioch College, 1950; PhD, Harvard University, 1956. Appointments: Research Assistant, 1952-56, Research Associate, 1957-58, Massachusetts Institute of Technology; Instructor and Research Associate, Harvard University, 1956-57; Fellow, Center for Advanced Study in the Behavioral Sciences, Stanford, 1958-59; Assistant Professor of Anthropology, University of California at Berkeley, 1958-60; Assistant Professor, 1960-61, Associate Professor, 1962-64, Professor, 1964-68, Divisional Professor, 1968-70, University of Chicago; Senior Research Career Fellow, National Institute for Mental Health, 1964-70; Professor of Social Science, 1970-, Harold F Linder Professor of Social Science, 1982-, Institute for Advanced Study, Princeton, New Jersey; Visiting Lecturer with Rank of Professor, Princeton University, 1975-; Various guest lectureships. Publications: The Religion of Java, 1960; Old Societies and New States (editor), 1963; Agricultural Involution: The Processes of Ecological Change in Indonesia, 1963; Peddlers and Princes, 1963; The Social History of an Indonesian Town, 1965; Person, Time and Conduct in Bali: An Essay in Cultural Analysis, 1966; Islam Observed: Religious Development in Morocco and Indonesia, 1968; The Interpretation of Cultures: Selected Essays, 1973; Myth, Symbol and Culture (editor), 1974; Kinship in Bali (with Hildred Geertz), 1973; Meaning and Order in Moroccan Society (with Hildred Geertz and Lawrence Rosen), 1979; Negara: The Theatre State in Nineteenth Century Bali, 1980; Local Knowledge: Further Essays in Interpretive Anthropology, 1983; Bali,

interprétation d'une culture, 1983; Works and Lives: The Anthropologist as Author, 1988; After the Fact: Two Countries, Four Decades, One Anthropologist, 1995. Contributions to: Scholarly books and journals. Honours: Talcott Parsons Prize, American Academy of Arts and Sciences, 1974; Sorokin Prize, American Sociological Association, 1974; Distinguished Lecturer, American Anthropological Association, 1983; Huxley Memorial Lecturer and Medallist, Royal Anthropological Institute, 1983; Distinguished Scholar Award, Association for Asian Studies, 1987; National Book Critics Circle Prize in Criticism, 1988; Horace Mann Distinguished Alumnus Award, Antioch College, 1992; Fukuoka Asian Cultural Prize, 1992. Memberships: American Academy of Arts and Sciences, fellow; American Association for the Advancement of Science, fellow; American Philosophical Society, fellow; British Academy, corresponding fellow; Council on Foreign Relations, fellow; National Academy of Sciences, fellow; Royal Anthropological Institute, honorary fellow. Address: c/o School of Social Science, Institute for Advanced Study, Princeton, NJ 08540, USA.

GEIKINS Arijs, b. 14 Feb 1936, Riga, Latvia. Writer; Theatre Director. m. Laima Geikina, 17 Aug 1993, 5 children. Education: Diploma, 3rd Daile Theatre Studio, Riga, 1962; Diploma of Theatre Director, Lunacharsky Institute of Theatre Art, Moscow, 1970. Appointments: Actor, Liepaja Theatre, 1963-64; Producer, Riga Youth Theatre, 1968-70; Actor, Dailes Theatre, 1976-79; Producer, Amateur Theatre, Armatura, 1974-95; Producer, Students Theatre University of Latvia, 1974-92; Producer, Amateur Theatre, Sarkandaugava, 1996-. Publications: Explosion; The Murder at Saul Starini - Criminal Novel Mystery, 1998; The First Season of Rihards Buss, 1998. Severl plays and stories. Honours: Grand Prix, Story Competition, 1994; Award, Novel Competition, Karogs magazine, 1994; Jury Award, Karogs magazine, 1996, 1997. Membership: Writers Union of Latvia. Literary Agent: Copyright Agency of Latvia. Address: 3-104 Saulu Street, Riga, LV-1055, Latvia.

GEISMAR L(udwig) L(eo), b. 25 Feb 1921, Mannheim, Germany. Retired Professor of Social Work and Sociology; Writer. m. Shirley Ann Cooperman, 18 Sept 1948, 3 daughters. Education: BA, 1947, MA, 1950, University of Minnesota; PhD, Hebrew University, Jerusalem, 1956. Appointments: Coordinator of Social Research, Ministry of Social Welfare, Israel, 1954-56; Research Director, Family Centred Project, St Paul, Minnesota, USA, 1956-59; Associate Professor, 1959-62, Professor, Social Work and Sociology, Director, Social Work Research Center, Graduate School of Social Work and Department of Sociology, 1963-91, Rutgers University. Publications: Understanding the Multi-Problem Family: A Conceptual Analysis and Exploration in Early Identification (with M A LaSorte), 1964; The Forgotten Neighborhood: Site of an Early Skirmish in the War on Poverty (with J Krisberg), 1967; Preventive Intervention in Social Work, 1969; Family and Community Functioning, 1971; Early Supports for Family Life, 1972; 555 Families: A Social Psychological Study of Young Families in Transition, 1973; Families in an Urban Mold (with S Geismar), 1979; A Quarter Century of Social Work Education (editor with M Dinerman), 1984; Family and Delinquency: Resocializing the Young Offender (with K Wood), 1986; Families at Risk (with K Wood), 1989; The Family Functioning Scale: A Guide to Research and Practice (with M Camasso), 1993. Address: 347 Valentine Street, Highland Park, NJ 08904, USA.

GELBART Larry (Simon), b. 25 Feb 1928, Chicago, Illinois, USA. Writer; Dramatist; Screenwriter; Producer. m. Pat Marshall, 25 Nov 1956, 3 sons, 2 daughters. Education: Chicago and Los Angeles public Schools. Publication: Laughing Matters, 1998. Other: Dramatic: A Funny Thing Happened on the Way to the Forum, 1962; Sly Fox, 1976; One, Two, Three, Four, Five, 1988; City of Angels, 1989; Mastergate, 1989; Jerome Robbins' Broadway (co-author), 1989. Screenplays: The Notorious Landlady, 1962; The Thrill of It All, 1963; The Wrong Box, 1966; Not With My Wife You Don't, 1966; The Chastity Belt, 1968; A Fine Pair, 1969; Oh, God, 1977; Movie,

Movie, 1978; Neighbors, 1981; Tootsie, 1982; Blame It On Rio, 1984; Barbarians at the Gate, 1993. Television: M*A*S*H, 1972-76; After M*A*S*H, 1983-84; Weapons of Mass Distraction, 1997. Honours: Tony Awards, 1963, 1990; Writers Guild Awards, 1972, 1974, 1977, 1978; Christopher Award, 1978; Los Angeles Film Critics Award, 1982; National Society of Film Critics Award, 1982; New York Film Critics Award, 1982; Honorary LittD, Union College, Schenectady, New York, 1986; Drama Desk Award, 1989; Lee Strasberg Lifetime Achievement in the Arts and Sciences Award, 1990. Memberships: American Society of Composers, Authors, and Publishers; Dramatists Guild; Writers Guild of America. Address: 807 North Alpine Drive, Beverly Hills, CA 90210, USA.

GELBER Jack, b. 12 Apr 1932, Chicago, Illinois, USA. Professor; Dramatist; Director. m. Carol Westenberg, 22 Dec 1957, 1 son, 1 daughter. Education: BS in Journalism, University of Illinois, 1953. Appointments: Adjunct Associate Professor, Columbia University, 1967-72; Professor, Brooklyn College, 1972-. Publications: Plays: The Connection, 1959; The Apple, 1961; Square in the Eye, 1965; The Cuban Thing, 1968; Sleep, 1972; Barbary Shore (adapter), 1974; Jack Gelber's New Play: Rehearsal, 1976; Starters, 1982; Big Shot, 1988; Magic Valley, 1990. Other: On Ice (novel), 1964. Honours: Vernon Rice Award, 1959-60; Obie Awards, 1960, 1972, 1979; Guggenheim Fellowships, 1963-64, 1966-67; Rockefeller Grant, 1972; Directing Award, Village Voice, 1972-73; National Endowment for the Arts Fellow, 1974; CBS Fellow, Yale University, 1974-75. Address: 230 East 18th Street, Apt 1C, New York, NY 10003, USA.

GÉLINAS Gratien, b. 8 Dec 1909, Saint-Tite, Quebec, Canada. Dramatist; Actor; Director. m. (1) Simone Lalonde, 1935, dec 1967, 4 sons, 1 daughter, (2) Huguette Oligny, 1973. Education: Graduated, Collège de Montréal, 1929. Appointments: Actor, creator of the character Fridolin in 9 revues, 1938-46; Founder, Comédie-Canadienne, Montreal, 1957. Publications: Tit-Coq, 1950, English translation, 1967; Bousille et les justes, 1960, English translation as Bousille and the Just, 1961; Yesterday the Children Were Dancing, 1967; Les Fridolinades, 1945 et 1946, 1980; Les Fridolinades, 1943 et 1944, 1981; Les Fridolinades, 1941 et 1942, 1981; La Passion de Narcisse Mondoux, 1987, English translation as The Passion of Narcisse Mondoux, 1992; Les Fridolinades, 1938, 1939, 1940, 1988. Honours: Grand Prix, Dramatists Society, 1949; Film of the Year Award, 1953; Honorary LLD, University of Saskatchewan, 1966, McGill University, 1968, University of New Brunswick, 1969, Trent University, 1970, Mount Allison University, 1973; Victor Morin Prize, 1967. Memberships: Canada Film Development Corporation, chairman, 1969-78; Canada Theatre Institute, president, 1959-60; National Theatre School of Canada, founding member, 1960; Royal Society of Canada. Address: 316 Girouard Street, Box 207, Oka, Quebec J0N 1E0, Canada.

GELLIS Roberta Leah, (Max Daniels, Priscilla Hamilton, Leah Jacobs), b. 27 Sept 1927, Brooklyn, New York, USA. Author. m. Charles Gellis, 14 Apr 1947, 1 son. Education: BA, Hunter College, 1947; MS, Brooklyn Polytechnic Institute, 1952. Publications: Knight's Honor, 1964; Bond of Blood, 1965; The Dragon and the Rose, 1977; The Sword and the Swan, 1977; The Space Guardian (as Max Daniels), 1978; The Roselynde Chronicles series: Roselynde, 1978, Alinor, 1978, Joanna, 1979, Gilliane, 1980, Rhiannon, 1982, Sybelle, 1983; Offworld (as Max Daniels), 1979; The Love Token (as Priscilla Hamilton), 1979; The Royal Dynasty series: Siren Song, 1980, Winter Song, 1982, Fire Song, 1984, A Silver Mirror, 1989; The Napoleonic Era series: The English Heiress, 1980, The Cornish Heiress, 1981, The Kent Heiress, 1982, Fortune's Bride, 1983, A Woman's Estate, 1984; The Tales of Jernaeve series: Tapestry of Dreams, 1985, Fires of Winter, 1986, Irish Magic, 1995, Shimmering Splendor, 1995, Enchanted Fire, 1996, Irish Magic II, 1997; Dazzling Brightness, 1994. Literary Agent: Ms Lucienne Diver, Spectrum Literary Agency, 111

Eighth Avenue, New York, NY 10011, USA. Address: PO Box 483, Roslyn Heights, NY 11577, USA.

GENOVESE Eugene D(ominick), b. 19 May 1930, New York, New York, USA. Retired Professor of History; Writer. m. Elizabeth Ann Fox, 6 June 1969. Education: BA, Brooklyn College, 1953; MA, 1955, PhD, 1959, Columbia University. Appointments: Assistant Professor, Polytechnical Institute, Brooklyn, 1958-63; Associate Professor, Rutgers University, 1963-67; Professor of History, 1967-69, Social Science Research Fellow, 1968-69, Sir George Williams University, Montreal; Visiting Professor, Columbia University, 1967, Yale University, 1969; Professor of History, 1969-90, Distinguished Professor of Arts and Sciences, 1985-90, University of Rochester; Pitt Professor of American History and Institutions, University of Cambridge, England, 1976-77; Sunderland Fellow and Visiting Professor of Law, University of Michigan, 1979; Visiting Mellon Professor, Tulane University, 1986; Distinguished Scholar-in-Residence, University Center, Georgia, 1990-95. Publications: The Political Economy of Slavery, 1965; The World the Slaveholders Made, 1969; In Red and Black, 1971; Roll, Jordan, Roll, 1974; From Rebellion to Revolution, 1979; Fruits of Merchant Capital (with Elizabeth Fox-Genovese), 1983; The Slaveholders Dilemma, 1991; The Southern Tradition, 1994; The Southern Front, 1995; A Consuming Fire, 1998. Contributions to: Scholarly journals. Honours: Richard Watson Gilder Fellow, Columbia University, 1959; Center for Advanced Study in the Behavioral Sciences Fellow, Stanford, California, 1972-73; National Humanities Center Fellow, Research Triangle Park, North California, 1984-85; Mellon Fellow, 1987-88; Guggenheim Fellowship, 1987-88; Bancroft Prize, 1994. Memberships: Historical Society, president; American Academy of Arts and Sciences, fellow; National Association of Scholars. Address: 1487 Sheridan Walk North East, Atlanta, GA 30324, USA.

GENSLER Kinereth Dushkin, b. 17 Sept 1922, New York, New York, USA. Poet. Widow, 2 sons, 1 daughter. Education: BA, University of Chicago, 1943; MA, Columbia University, 1946. Appointment: Editor, Alice James Books, 1976-90. Publications: Threesome Poems, 1976; The Poetry Connection (co-author), 1978; Without Roof, 1981; Journey Fruit, 1997.Contributions to: Anthologies, books, journals, and periodicals. Honours: Members Award, Poetry Society of America, 1969; Power Dalton Award, New England Poetry Club, 1971; Borestone Mountain Award, 1973; Residency, Ragdale, 1981; Residency, MacDowell Colony, 1982, 1983. Memberships: Academy of American Poets; Alice James Poetry Cooperative Society; New England Poetry Club; Poetry Society of America. Address: 221 Mt Auburn Street, Cambridge, MA 02138, USA.

GENTLE Mary Rosalyn, b. 29 Mar 1956, Sussex, England. Writer. Education: BA, English, Politics, Geography, 1985, MA, 17th Century Studies, 1988; MA, War Studies, 1995. Publications: A Hawk in Silver, 1977; Golden Witchbreed, 1983; Ancient Light, 1987; Scholars and Soldiers, 1989; Rats and Gargoyles, 1990; The Architecture of Desire, 1991; Grunts!, 1992; Left to His Own Devices, 1994; Co-Editor: The Weerde Book 1, 1992; Villains!, 1992; The Weerde Book 2, The Book of the Ancients, 1993. Contributions to: Reviews. Memberships: Society of Authors; British Science Fiction Association. Literary Agent: Maggie Noach, The Maggie Noach Literary Agency, 21 Redan Street, London W14 0AB, England. Address: 29 Sish Lane, Stevenage, Herts, England.

GENTRY Robert Bryan, b. 21 July 1936, Knoxville, Tennessee, USA. Writer; Educator. m. Mary Sue Koeppel, 31 May 1980, 2 sons. Education: BS, 1958, MA, 1966, University of Tennessee; US Army Language School, 1959; Graduate work, University of Georgia, 1968-72, University of New Hampshire, 1977. Appointments: Professor of Humanities, 1972-, College Historian, 1988-91, Florida Community College; Editor, Riverside-Avondale Historic Preservation Publication, 1975-76.Publications: The Rise of the Hump House,

novel, 1976; A College Tells Its Story: An Oral History of Florida Community College at Jacksonville, 1963-1991, 1991; Insights into Love and Freedom, A Humanities Text, 1997; An Introduction to Twentieth-Century Western Culture, A Humanities Text, 1998. Contributions to: A Diarist's Journal; Kalliope: A Journal of Women's Art; Teaching English in the Two-Year College; The State Street Review. Honours: Professor of the Year, Florida Community College, 1985; Prize Winner, Quest for Peace Writing Contest, University of California, 1988; Nominated for National Pushcart Award, 1989; Award, National Endowment for the Humanities, 1993; Prize Winner for Satire, Prose Contest of the International Institution of Elvisology, 1994; Winner, Short Fiction Contest, Florida First Coast Writers' Festival, 1997. Memberships: Community College Humanities Association; US English. Address: 3879 Oldfield Trail, Jacksonville, FL 32223, USA.

GEORGE Elizabeth, b. 26 Feb 1949, Warren, Ohio, USA. Author. m. Jay Toibin, 28 May 1971, div 11 Nov 1995. Education: AA, Foothill Community College, 1969; BA, University of California at Riverside, 1970; MS, California State University, 1979. Appointment: Teacher of Creative Writing, Coastline College, Costa Mesa, California, 1988-. Publications: A Great Deliverance, 1988; Payment in Blood, 1989; Well-Schooled in Murder, 1990; A Suitable Vengeance, 1991; For the Sake of Elena, 1992; Missing Joseph, 1993; Playing for the Ashes, 1994; In the Presence of the Enemy, 1996; Deception on his Mind, 1997; In Pursuit of the Proper Sinner, 1998. Honours: Anthony Award, 1989; Agatha Award, 1989; Grand Prix de Littérature Policière, 1990. Address: c/o Deborah Schneider, 250 West 57th Street, New York, NY 10107, USA.

GEORGE Jean Craighead, b. 21 July 1919, Washington, District of Columbia, USA. Author; Illustrator. m. John L George, 28 Jan 1944, div 1963, 2 sons, 1 daughter. Education: BA, Pennsylvania State University. Appointments: Reporter, Washington Post, 1943-46; Roving Editor, Reader's Digest, 1965-84. Publications: My Side of the Mountain, 1959; Summer of the Falcon, 1962; The Thirteen Moons, 1967-69; Julie of the Wolves, 1972; Going to the Sun, 1976; Wounded Wolf, 1978; The American Walk Book, 1978; River Rats, 1979; The Grizzly Bear with the Golden Ears, 1982; The Cry of the Crow, 1982; Journey Inward, 1982; Talking Earth, 1983; How to Talk to Your Animals, 1985; Water Sky, 1987; One Day in the Woods, 1988, as musical, 1989; Shark Beneath the Reef, 1989; On the Far Side of the Mountain, 1990; One Day in a Tropical Rain Forest, 1990; Missing 'Gator of Gumbo Limbo, 1992; The Fire Bug Connection, 1993; Dear Rebecca Winter is Here, 1993; The First Thanksgiving, 1993; Julie, 1994; Animals Who Have Won Our Hearts, 1994; The Tarantula in My Purse, 1996; Look to the North, 1997; Julie's Wolf Pack, 1997. Address: 20 William Street, Chappaqua, NY 10514, USA.

GEORGE Jonathan. See: BURKE John Frederick.

GEORGE Kathleen (Elizabeth), b. 7 July 1943, Johnstown, Pennsylvania, USA. Associate Professor of Theatre Arts; Director; Dramatist; Writer. Education: BA, English, 1964, MA, Theatre Arts, 1966, PhD, Theatre Arts, 1975; MFA, Creative Writing, 1988, University of Pittsburgh. Appointments: Assistant Professor, Carlow College, 1968-76; Associate Professor, University of Pittsburgh, 1976-. Publications: Rhythm in Drama, 1980; Playwriting: The First Workshop, 1994; The Man in the Buick and Other Stories, forthcoming. Other: Various short fiction. Contributions to: Reviews and journals. Honours: Virginia Center for the Arts Fellowships, 1980-83; Pennsylvania Arts Council Grants, 1982, 1987; MacDowell Colony Fellowship, 1996; Mary Anderson Center Fellowship, 1996. Address: 1213 Monterey Street, Pittsburgh, PA 15212, USA.

GEORGE Sydney. See: HATTERSLEY Roy.

GEORGEOGLOU Nitsa-Athina, b. 4 Sept 1922, Athens, Greece. Author. m. 9 Nov 1947, 2 sons.

Education: Graduate, Greek Gymasium, 1938; Superior Studies, French Institute of Athens. Publications: Once in Missolonghi, 1971; The Secret Society, 1973; A Ship Called Hope, 1975; Enterprise Archemides, 1977; Toto is My Guest, 1977; Waves and Islands, 1978; The Wrath of the Earth, 1978; Up the Hill, 1979; Vravron, before the Christian Era, 1980; Chronicle of Thyateira, 1981; The Horse Farm, 1981; The Golden Coin, 1982; Saturn Calling, 1984; On Foreign Land, 1985; The Will of Youth, 1987; Uranus Calling, 1987; Walking Through the Centuries, 1987; Difficult Steps, 1988; The Gods of Olympus, 1988; The Three S's, 1989; Adventure in Athens, 1990; Soldiers for Fun, 1991; Sealed Envelopes, 1992; Sunrise, 1993; On the Wings of Youth, 1993; Written on the Waves, 1994; Storm and Lull, 1994. Contributions to: Numerous journals and magazines. Honours: Woman's Literary Committee of Athens Awards, 1969-71, 1979-81, 1985, 1992; Circle of Greek Children's Book Authors Awards, 1970, 1977, 1978; Hans Christian Anderson Honour List, 1982; National Award for the best book for Youth for the year 1989, awarded 1992. Memberships: National Society of Greek Authors; Greek IBBY; Greek Union, International Soroptimist; Hestia Cultural Club. Address: 83 Plastira Street, 171 21 Nea Smirni, Athens, Greece.

GERDES Eckhard, b. 17 Nov 1959, Atlanta, Georgia, USA. Novelist; Playwright; Educator. m. Persis Alisa Wilhelm, 30 Jan 1988, 3 sons. Education: BA, Honours, English, University of Dubuque, Iowa, 1988; MA, English, Roosevelt University, Chicago, 1994; MFA, Writing, School of the Art Institute of Chicago, 1998. Appointments: Instructor, University of Alaska, Anchorage, 1988-90; Co-Director, Dreamerz' Fiction Reading Series, Chicago, 1991-92; Lecturer, Roosevelt University, 1994-; Instructor, Macon State College, 1998-; Editor, Journal of Experimental Fiction, 1994-. Publications: Projections, 1986; Truly Fine Citizen, 1989; Ring in a River, 1994. Contributions to: Rampike; Oyez Review; Coe Review; Tomorrow Magazine; Planet Roc; Strong Coffee; No Magazine; Random Weirdness. Honours: Richard Pike Bissell Creative Writing Awards, 1987, 1988. Membership: COSMEP. Address: 1352 Hardeman Avenue, Macon, Georgia 31201, USA.

GERMOZ Alain, b. 31 July 1920, Antwerp, Belgium. Writer; Editor. m. 1950-79, 1 daughter. Education: Royal Academy of Fine Arts, Antwerp, 1940-44. Appointments: Journalist, Theater and Art Critic, Le Matin, 1944-63; Chief, Cultural Section, La Métropole, 1963-65, in Antwerp, idem in Brussels, Spécial, 1965-77; Pourguoi Pas?, 1977-85; Publisher and Chief Editor, Archipel, half-yearly International Book of Literature. Publications: Ecorce De Chair, 1952; Le Transfuge, 1956; Les Guillemets, 1962; Le Témoin, Les Résidus, 1969; Le Cinquième Mur, 1965; Le Carré de L'Hypoténuse, 1988; Le Chat de Schrödinger, Fragments D'une Identité, 1989; Les Cercles de La Liberté, 1990; Fin de Régime, 1991; Petite Zoologie Portative, 1994; Créations: Ballets and Plays in Antwerp, Brussels, Paris, Kinshasa; Translations: Prose and Poetry. Contributions to: US Art Correspondent for Artés, Antwerp, 1946-47; Correspondent and Collaborator, several magazines. Honours: Prix Michel de Ghelderode, 1962; Prix Auguste Michot, 1963. Memberships: PEN Club; AICA; AEB; AGJPB; SABAM. Address: Jan Van Rijswijcklaan 7 B2, B-2078, Antwerp, Belgium.

GERRIOR William Dawson, b. 6 Aug 1944, Halifax, Nova Scotia, Canada. School Principal. m. Audrey Gray, 6 June 1969, 1 son, 1 daughter. Education: BA, 1967, BEd, 1971, St Mary's University, Halifax; MEd, Mount St Vincent University, Halifax, 1989. Appointments: Director of Residence, St Mary's University, 1967-70; Mathematics Teacher, 1971-79, Head, Mathematics Department, 1975-79, Brookside Junior High, Brookside, Nova Scotia; Vice-Principal, Herring Cove Elementary School, 1979-80; Teaching Principal, Shatford Memorial Elementary School, Hubbards, Nova Scotia, 1980-82; Principal, Shatford, Boutilier's Point and St Margaret's Bay Elementary Schools, Nova Scotia, 1983-87; Principal, Timberlea Junior High School, Timberlea, Nova Scotia, 1987-92; Principal, Harry R Hamilton Elementary School, Sackville, Nova Scotia, 1993-97. Memberships: Writers Federation of Nova Scotia, 1997; Genealogical Association of Nova Scotia, 1997-98. Literary Agent: Henri-Dominique Paratte, Publisher-Editor, Editions de Grand-Pré. Address: c/o Box 298, Acadia University, Wolfville, Nova Scotia, Canada B0P 1X0.

GERRISH Brian Albert, b. 14 Aug 1931, London, England. Distinguished Service Professor of Theology; Writer. m. (1) 1 son, 1 daughter, (2) Dawn Ann De Vries, 3 Aug 1990, 1 daughter. Education: BA, 1952, MA, 1956, Queens' College, Cambridge; STM, Union Theological Seminary, New York City, 1956; PhD, Columbia University, 1958. Appointments: Associate Professor, 1965-68, Professor, 1968-85, John Nuveen Professor, 1985-96, Professor Emeritus, 1996-, Divinity School, University of Chicago; Co-Editor, Journal of Religion, 1972-85; Distinguished Service Professor of Theology, Union Theological Seminary, Virginia, 1996-. Publications: Grace and Reason: A Study in the Theology of Luther, 1962, Japanese translation, 1974, reprint, 1979; Tradition and the Modern World: Reformed Theology in the Nineteenth Century, 1978; The Old Protestantism and the New: Essays on the Reformation Heritage, 1982; A Prince of the Church: Schleiermacher and the Beginnings of Modern Theology, 1984, Korean translation, 1988; Grace and Gratitude: The Eucharistic Theology of John Calvin, 1993; Continuing the Reformation: Essays on Modern Religious Thought, 1993. Editor: The Faith of Christendom: A Source Book of Creeds and Confessions, 1963; Reformers in Profile, 1967; Reformatio Perennis: Essays on Calvin and the Reformation in Honor of Ford Lewis Battles, 1981. Address: 9142 Sycamore Hill Place, Mechanicsville, VA 23116, USA.

GERROLD David, (born Jarrold David Friedman), b. 24 Jan 1944, Chicago, Illinois, USA. Author; Screenwriter; Computer Columnist. Education: University of Southern California at Los Angeles; BA, California State University at Northridge. Appointments: Story Editor, Land of the Lost, television series, 1974; Computer Columnist, CIT Profiles, 1984-; Columnist, Starlos and Galileo magazines. Publications: The Flying Sorcerers (with Larry Niven), 1971; Generation (editor), 1972; Space Skimmer, 1972; Yesterday's Children, 1972; When Harlie Was One, 1972; With a Finger in My I (short stories), 1972; Battle for the Planet of the Apes (novelisation of screenplay), 1973; The Man Who Folded Himself, 1973; The Trouble with Tribbles, 1973; The World of Star Trek, 1973; Deathbeast, 1978; The Galactic Whirlpool, 1980; The War Against the Chtorr: A Matter for Man, 1983; A Day for Damnation, 1984; When Harlie Was One, 1987; When Harlie Was Two, 1987. Other: Editor with Stephen Goldin: Protostars, 1971; Science Fiction Emphasis I, 1974; Alternities, 1974; Ascents of Wonder, 1977. Address: Box 1190, Hollywood, CA 90028, USA.

GERSTLER Amy, b. 24 Oct 1956, San Diego, California, USA. Poet; Writer. Education: BA, Pitzer College. Publications: Poetry: Yonder, 1981; Christy's Alpine Inn, 1982; White Marriage/Recovery, 1984; Early Heavens, 1984; The True Bride, 1986; Bitter Angel, 1990; Nerve Storm, 1993. Fiction: Martine's Mouth, 1985; Primitive Man, 1987. Other: Past Lives (with Alexis Smith), 1989. Contributions to: Magazines. Honour: National Book Critics Circle Award, 1991. Address: c/o Viking Penguin, 375 Hudson Street, New York, NY 10014, USA.

GERVAIS Charles Henry Martin, b. 20 Oct 1946, Windsor, Ontario, Canada. Poet; Writer; Editor. m. Donna Wright, 1968, 2 sons, 1 daughter. Education: BA, University of Guelph, 1971; MA, University of Windsor, 1972. Appointments: Staff, Toronto Globe and Mail, 1966, Canadian Press, Toronto, 1967; Reporter, Daily Commercial News, Toronto, 1967, Chatham Daily News, 1972-73; Teacher of Creative Writing, St Clair College, Windsor, 1969-71; Publisher, Black Moss Press, Windsor, 1969-; Editor, Sunday Standard, Windsor, 1972; General News Reporter, 1973-74, 1976-81, Bureau Chief, 1974-76, Religion Editor, 1979-80, Book Editor, 1980-, Entertainment Writer, 1990-, Windsor Star. Publications: Poetry: Sister Saint Anne, 1968; Something, 1969; Other Marriage Vows, 1969; A Sympathy Orchestra, 1970; Bittersweet, 1972; Poems for American Duaghters, 1976; The Believable Body, 1979; Up Country Lines, 1979; Silence Comes with Lake Voices, 1980; Into a Blue Morning: Selected Poems, 1982; Public Fanatasy: The Maggie T Poems, 1983; Letters From the Equator, 1986; Autobiographies, 1989; Playing God: New Poems, 1994. Other: The Rumrunners: A Prohibition Scrapbook, 1980; Voices Like Thunder, 1984; The Border Police: One Hundred and Twenty-Five Years of Policing in Windsor, 1992; Seeds in the Wilderness: Profiles of World Religious Leaders, 1994; From America Sent: Letters to Henry Miller, 1995. Editor: The Writing Life: Historical and Critical Views of the Tish Movement, 1976. Children's Books: How Bruises Lost His Secret, 1975; Doctor Troyer and the Secret in the Moonstone, 1976; If I Had a Birthday Everyday, 1983. Honours: Western Ontario Newspaper Awards, 1983, 1984, 1987. Address: 1939 Alsace Avenue, Windsor, Ontario N8W 1M5, Canada.

GERY John Roy Octavius, b. 2 June 1953, Reading, Pennsylvania, USA. Professor of English; Poet. Education: AB, Honours, Princeton University, 1975; MA, English, University of Chicago, 1976; MA, Creative Writing, Stanford University, 1978. Appointments: Lecturer, Stanford University and San Jose State University, 1977-79; Instructor, 1979-84, Assistant Professor, 1984-88, Associate Professor, 1988-95, Professor of English, 1995-, University of New Orleans; Visiting Professor, University of Iowa, 1991-92. Publications: Charlemagne: A Song of Gestures, 1983; The Burning of New Orleans, 1988; Three Poems, 1989; The Enemies of Leisure, 1995; Nuclear Annihilation and Contemporary American Poetry, 1996. Contributions to: Reviews and journals. Honours: Deep South Writers Poetry Award, 1987; Charles William Duke Long Poem Award, 1987; Wesleyan Writers Conference Poetry Fellowship, 1989; W B Yeats Chair in Poetry, Italy, 1990; National Endowment for the Arts Creative Fellowship, 1992-93. Memberships: Academy of American Poets; Associated Writing Programs; Modern Poetry Association; Poets and Writers. Address: c/o Department of English, University of New Orleans, New Orleans, LA 70148, USA.

GERZAN Everest. See: **VERZEA Ernest-George.**

GETHING Phillip John David, b. 22 Aug 1929, Luton, Beds, England. Physicist. m. Helen Mary Slater, 14 Feb 1953, 2 sons. Education: BSc, 1948, MSc, 1949, PhD, 1951, Imperial College, London, 1946-51. Appointments: Scientific Civil Service, 1951-87; Assistant Director, Procurement Executive, Ministry of Defence, 1983-87; Management Consultant, Admiral Group plc, 1988-89. Publications: Radio Direction Finding and the Resolution of Multicomponent Wave-Fields, 1978; Radio Direction Finding and Superesolution, 1991. Contributions to: Numerous articles in New Scientist, Physics World, The Friend. Memberships: Slough Writers Circle, 1975-76; Portsdown Writers Circle, 1976-83; Farnborough Writers Circle, 1983-. Address: 26 Dukes Mead, Fleet, Hants GU13 8HE, England.

GEVE Thomas, b. 1929, Germany. Engineer; Writer. m. 1963, 1 son, 2 daughters. Education: National Diploma of Building, 1950; BSc, 1957. Publications: Youth in Chains, 1958, enlarged edition, 1981; Guns and Barbed Wire, 1987; There Are No Children Here, 1997; Aufbrueche, 1998. Literary Agent: M J Wald, New York, USA. Address: PO Box 4727, Haifa, Israel.

GEVIRTZ Susan, b. 27 Oct 1955, Los Angeles, California, USA. Poet; Writer. m. David Delp, 15 Aug 1992. Education: BA, Literature, Cultural Theory, Poetics, Evergreen State College, 1977; MA, Classical Literature, Philosophy, St John's Graduate Institute, Santa Fe, New Mexico, 1980; PhD, History of Consciousness, University of California at Santa Cruz, 1990. Appointments: Teaching Assistant, University of California at Santa Cruz, 1983-87; Teacher-Poet, California Poets in the

Schools, San Francisco, 1984-86; Teacher, Aegean College of Fine Arts, Paros, Greece, 1985; Associate Editor HOW(ever) journal, 1985-90; Instructor, University of San Francisco, 1988-89, California College of Arts and Crafts, Oakland, 1989-91; Assistant Professor, Hutchins School of Liberal Studies, Sonoma State University, Rohnert Park, California, 1989-98. Publications: Poetry: Korean and Milkhouse, 1991; Domino: Point of Entry, 1992; Linen minus, 1992; Taken Place, 1993; Prosthesis:: Caesarea, 1994; Black Box Cutaway, 1998. Other: Feminist Poetics: A Consideration of the "Female" Construction of Language (associate editor), 1984; Narrative's Journey: The Fiction and Film Writing of Dorothy Richardson, 1995. Contributions to: Anthologies, journals, and magazines. Honours: Awards, grants, and fellowships. Address: 1939 Jones Street, San Francisco, CA 94133, USA.

GEYER Georgie Anne, Author. Education: BS, Medill School of Journalism, Northwest University, Evanston, Illinois, 1952-56. Appointments: Society Desk Reporter, Chicago Daily News, 1959-60; General Assignment Reporter, 1960-64; Foreign Correspondent, 1964-75; Syndicated Columnist, Los Angeles Times Syndicate, 1975-80, Universal Press Syndicate and Washington Star, 1980-81, Universal Press Syndicate, 1981-; Senior Fellow, Annenberg Washington Program, 1992-94. Publications: Books: The New Latins: Fateful Chance in South and Central America; The New 100 Years' War, 1972; The Young Russians, 1975; Buying the Night Flight: Autobiography of a Woman Foreign Correspondent, 1983; Guerrilla Prince: The Untold Story of Fidel Castro, 1991; Waiting for Winter to End: An Extraordinary Voyage Through Soviet Central Asia, 1994; Americans No More: The Death of Citizenship, 1996; Buying the Night Flight, 1996. Honours: Weintal Prize, Georgetown University, 1984; Chicago Foundation Literature Award, 1984. Memberships: Cosmos Club, Washington, DC; Tavern Club, Chicago; Cliff Dwellers Club; Gridiron Club; Council on Foreign Relations; Washington Institute on Foreign Affairs; International Press Institute. Address: The Plaza, 800 25th Street North West, Washington, DC 20037, USA.

GEYER Georgie Anne, b. 2 Apr 1935, Chicago, Illinois, USA. Syndicated Columnist; Author; Foreign Correspondent; Speaker; Educator. Education: BS, Journalism, Northwestern University, 1956; Fulbright Scholar, University of Vienna, 1956-57. Appointments: Reporter, 1959-64, Foreign Correspondent, 1964-75, Chicago Daily News; Syndicated Columnist: Los Angeles Times, 1975-80, Universal Press, 1980-. Publications: New Latins, 1970; The New 100 Years' War, 1972; The Young Russians, 1976; Buying the Night Flight, 1983, new edition, 1996; Guerrilla Prince, 1991; Waiting for Winter to End, 1994; Americans No More: The Death of Citizenship, 1996. Chapters in: The Responsibilities of Journalism, 1984; Beyond Reagan: The Politics of Upheaval, 1986; The Conceit of Innocence, 1997. Contributions to: Numerous journals, including: Reader's Digest, People, Kiwanis. Honours: 21 honorary degrees and doctorates; More than 12 other honours including: Chicago Journalism Hall of Fame, 1991; Northwestern University Alumni Association Award, 1991; Society of Professional Journalists, fellow, 1992. Memberships: Center for Strategic and International Studies, Advisory Board member; Washington Institute on Foreign Affairs; Council on Foreign Relations; Cosmos Club, D.C.; Gridiron Club, D.C. Tavern Club, Chicago. Address: The Plaza, 800 25th Street N.W., Washington, DC 20037, USA.

GHOSE Zulfikar, b. 13 Mar 1935, Sialkot, Pakistan (British citizen). Professor of English; Poet; Writer. Education: BA, Keele University, 1959. Appointment: Professor of English, University of Texas at Austin, 1969-. Publications: Poetry: The Loss of India, 1964; Jets from Orange, 1967; The Violent West, 1972; A Memory of Asia, 1984; Selected Poems, 1991. Fiction: The Contradictions, 1966; The Murder of Aziz Khan, 1967; The Incredible Brazilian the Native, 1972; The Beautiful Empire, 1975; Crump's Terms, 1975; A Different World, 1978; Hulme's Investigations into the Bogan Script, 1981; A New History of Torments, 1982; Don Bueno, 1983; Figures of Enchantment, 1986; The Triple Mirror of the Self, 1992. Criticism: Hamlet, Prufrock and Language, 1978; The Fiction of Reality, 1983; The Art of Creating Fiction, 1991; Shakespeare's Mortal Knowledge, 1993; Veronica and the Góngora Passion, 1998. Autobiography: Confessions of a Native-Alien, 1965. Address: c/o Department of English, University of Texas at Austin, Austin, TX 78712, USA.

GHOSH Manas, b. 27 Sept 1959, Calcutta, India. Eye Doctor; Contact Lens Specialist. m. 22 Nov 1991, 1 son. Education: BSc, Bangabasi College; BIAM, Medical College of Alt Medicines & Institute of Ocular Science. Publications: Eye Care; Choke Gire Rog; Ra Patrika, Calcutta. Contributions to: Sambad Darpam; Saptalaik Bartaman; Arikalpa. Memberships: Indian Science Congress Association; Indian Sc News Association, Calcutta. Address: 41/B Ashutosh Mukherjee Road, Budge Budge, 24 Parganas WB (South), 743319, India.

GIBBONS Kaye, b. 1960, Nash County, North Carolina, USA. Writer. m. div, 3 daughters. Education: North Carolina State University; University of North Carolina at Chapel Hill. Publications: Ellen Foster, 1987; A Virtuous Woman, 1989; A Cure for Dreams, 1991; Charms for the Easy Life, 1993; Sights Unseen, 1995; On the Occasion of My Last Afternoon, 1998. Honours: Sue Kaufman Prize for First Fiction, American Academy and Institute of Arts and Letters, 1988; Citation, Ernest Hemingway Foundation, 1988; National Endowment for the Arts Fellowship, 1989; Nelson Algren Heartland Award for Fiction, Chicago Tribune, 1991; PEN/Revson Foundation Fellowship, 1991. Address: Putnam Publishing Group, 200 Madison Avenue, New York, NY 10016, USA.

GIBBONS (William) Reginald (Jr), b. 7 Jan 1947, Houston, Texas, USA. Professor of English; Poet; Writer; Translator. m. Cornelia Maude Spelman, 18 Aug 1983, 1 stepson, 1 stepdaughter. Education: AB, Spanish and Portuguese, Princeton University, 1969; MA, English and Creative Writing, 1971, PhD, Comparative Literature, 1974, Stanford University. Appointments: Lecturer, Livingston College, Rutgers University, 1975-76, Princeton University, 1976-80, Columbia University, 1980-81; Editor, TriQuarterly magazine, 1981-97; Professor of English, Northwestern University, 1981-; Core Faculty, MFA Program for Writers, Warren Wilson College, 1989-. Publications: Poetry and Fiction: Roofs Voices Roads (poems), 1979; The Ruined Motel (poems), 1981; Saints (poems), 1986; Maybe It Was So (poems), 1991; Five Pears or Peaches (short stories), 1991; Sweetbitter (novel), 1994; Sparrow: New and Selected Poems, 1997; Homage to Longshot O'Leary (poems), 1998. Other: Criticism in the University (editor with Gerald Graff), 1985; The Writer in Our World (editor), 1986; Writers from South Africa (editor), 1988; William Goyen: A Study of the Short Fiction, 1991; Thomas McGrath: Life and the Poem (editor with Terrence Des Pres), 1991; New Writings from Mexico (editor and principal translator), 1992. Contributions to: Many journals, reviews, quarterlies, and magazines. Honours: Fulbright Fellowship, Spain, 1971-72; Co-Winner, Denver Quarterly Translation Award, 1977; Guggenheim Fellowship, 1984; National Endowment for the Arts Fellowship, 1984-85; Texas Institute of Letters Short Story Award, 1986; Illinois Arts Council Fellowship, 1987; John Masefield Memorial Award, Poetry Society of America, 1991; Carl Sandburg Award, Friends of the Chicago Public Library, 1992; Anisfield-Wolf Book Award, 1995; Pushcart Prize XXII, 1997; Thomas H Carter Prize, Shenandoah magazine, 1998; Balcones Poetry Prize, 1998. Memberships: Associated Writing Programs; The Guild Complex, co-founder; PEN American Center; Poetry Society of America; Texas Institute of Letters; Society of Midland Authors. Address: 1428 Crain Street, Evanston, IL 60202, USA.

GIBBS Hope Katz, b. 8 July 1964, Philadelphia, Pensylvania, USA. Journalist. m. Michael Gibbs, 1 Feb 1995, 1 daughter. Education: BA Communications, University of Pennsylvania, 1986; MA Educational Leadership, George Washington University, 1993. Appointments: Reporter, The Dominion Post, Morgantown, West Virginia, USA, 1986-87; Assistant Editor, The Miami Herald, Miami, Florida, USA, 1987-89; Associate Editor, New Miami Magazine, Miami, Florida, 1989-91; Senior Publications Coordinator, The George Washington University, Washington, DC, 1991-93; Founder and President, The Writing's on the Wall Inc, Alexandria, Virginia, 1993-; Self-Employed Journalist, Alexandria, Virginia, USA, 1993-. Publications: The Politics of Preservation, 1990; Hotshots, 1991; Auth, Glorious Reunion, The Erotic Edge: Erotica for Couples, 1994. Honours: Silver Award, Florida Magazine Association; First Place Award, Florida Magazine Association. Membership: Florida Magazine Association. Address: 7 W Braddock Road, Alexandria, VA 22301, USA.

GIBSON Charles E(dmund), b. 16 Dec 1916, England. Children's Writer. Education: Wandsworth Training College, London. Publications: The Story of the Ship, 1948; The Secret Tunnel, 1948; Wandering Beauties, 1960; The Clash of Fleets, 1961; Knots and Splices, 1962; Plain Sailing, 1963; Daring Prows, 1963; Be Your Own Weatherman, 1963; The Two Olafs of Norway, 1964; With a Cross on Their Shields, 1964; The Ship with Five Names, 1965; Knots and Splices, 1979; Death of a Phantom Raider, 1987. Literary Agent: A M Heath & Co Ltd. Address: 59 Victoria Road, Shoreham-by-Sea, Sussex BN43 5WR, England.

GIBSON Colin Raymond, b. 9 Feb 1957, Manchester, England. Journalist (Sports Editor). m. Patricia Mary Coxon, 6 June 1987, 1 son, 1 daughter. Education: William Holmes GS, Manchester; NCTJ Course, Preston, England. Appointments: St Regis Newspapers, 1976-79; Messenger Newspapers, 1979-80; Daily Telegraph, 1980-84; Daily Mail, 1984-86; Daily Telegraph, 1986-93; Sunday Telegraph, 1993-. Publications: Football Association Handbooks; Golf Course Guides; History of Tottenham Hotspur in Europe; Glory, Glory Nights. Contributions to: Daily Telegraph; Sunday Telegraph. Address: 1 Canada SQ, London E1W 5DT, England.

GIBSON Graeme, b. 9 Aug 1934, London, Ontario, Canada. Author. m. Margaret Atwood, 2 sons, 1 daughter. Education: University of Waterloo, 1953-54; University of Edinburgh, 1955-56; BA, University of Western Ontario, 1958. Publications: Five Legs, 1969; Communion, 1971; Eleven Canadian Novelists, 1973; Perpetual Motion, 1982; Gentleman Death, 1993. Honours: Toronto Arts Award, 1990; Member of the Order of Canada, 1992; Harbourfront Festival Prize, 1993. Memberships: International PEN, Canadian Centre, president, 1987-89; Writers' Union of Canada, chairman, 1974-75. Address: c/o McClelland and Stewart, 481 University Avenue, Suite 900, Toronto, Ontario M5G 2E9, Canada.

GIBSON Margaret, b. 2 Feb 1944, Philadelphia, Pennsylavania, USA. Poet. m. David McKain. Education: Hollins College, University of Virginia. Publications: Lunes, 1973; On the Cutting Edge, 1976; Signs, 1979; Long Walks in the Afternoon, 1982; Memories in the Future: The Daybooks of Tina Modotti, 1986; Out in the Open, 1989; The Vigil, A Poem in Four Voices, 1993; Earth Elegy: New and Selected Poems, 1997. Honours: Lamont Poetry Selection, 1982; Melville Cane Award, 1986; Finalist, National Book Award in Poetry, 1993. Address: c/o Louisiana State University Press, PO Box 25053, Baton Rouge, Louisiana 70894, USA.

GIBSON Morgan, b. 6 June 1929, Cleveland, Ohio, USA. Professor; Poet; Writer. m. (1) Barbara Gibson, 1950, div 1972, 2 daughters, (2) Keiko Matsui Gibson, 14 Sept 1978, 1 son. Education: BA, English Literature, Oberlin College, 1950; MA, English and American Literature and Creative Writing, 1952, PhD, 1959, University of Iowa. Appointments: Assistant, then Associate Professor of English, University of Wisconsin at Milwaukee, 1961-72; Chair, Graduate Faculty, Goddard College, Vermont, 1972-75, Osaka University, 1975-79; Visiting Professor, Michigan State University,

1979, University of Illinois, 1982, Knox College, 1989-91; Professor, Chukyo University, 1987-89, Japan Women's University, Tokyo, 1993-96; Kanda University of International Studies, 1997-; Lecturer, Pennsylvania State University, 1991-93. Publications: Stones Glow Like Lovers' Eyes, 1970; Crystal Sunlake, 1971; Kenneth Rexroth, 1972; Dark Summer, 1977; Wakeup, 1978; Speaking of Light, 1979; Kokoro: Heart-Mind, 1979; The Great Brook Book, 1981; Revolutionary Rexroth: Poet of East-West Wisdom, 1986; Among Buddhas in Japan, 1988; Winter Pilgrim, 1993. Editor: Several books and journals. Contributions to: Anthologies, books, journals and reviews. Honours: Awards and grants. Membership: Buddhist Peace Fellowship. Address: 202 Excel Negishi, 3-chome 148-2, Negishi-cho, Naka-ku, Takohama-shi, 231-0836, Japan.

GIBSON Walter Samuel, b. 31 Mar 1932, Columbus, Ohio, USA. Professor of the Humanities; Writer. Education: BFA, 1957, MA, 1960, Ohio State University; PhD, Harvard University, 1969. Appointments: Assistant Professor, 1966-71, Associate Professor, 1971-78, Acting Chairman, 1970-71, Chairman, 1971-79, Department of Art, Andrew W Mellon Professor of the Humanities, 1978-97, Andrew W Mellon Professor of the Humanities Emeritus, 1997-, Case Western Reserve University; Murphy Lecturer, University of Kansas and the Nelson-Atkins Museum of Art, 1988; Clark Visiting Professor of Art History, Williams College, 1989, 1992. Publications: Hieronymus Bosch, 1973; The Paintings of Cornelis Engebrechtsz, 1977; Bruegel, 1977; Hieronymus Bosch: An Annotated Bibliography, 1983; "Mirror of the Earth": The World Landscape in Sixteenth-Century Flemish Painting, 1989; Pieter Bruegel the Elder: Two Studies, 1991. Contributions to: Scholarly books and journals. Honours: Fulbright Scholarships, 1960-61, 1984; Guggenheim Fellowship, 1978-79; Fellow-in-Residence, Netherlands Institute for Advanced Study, Wasenaar, 1995-96. Memberships: American Association of Netherlandic Studies; College Art Association; Historians of Netherlandish Art; Midwest Art History Society; Renaissance Society of America; Society for Emblem Studies; Société Internationale pour l'Etude du Théâtre Medieval; Vereeniging van Nederlandse Kunsthistorici. Address: R R 2, #461 H, Pownal, VT 05261-9767, USA.

GIBSON William, b. 13 Nov 1914, New York, New York, USA. Dramatist; Writer; Poet. m. 1), div, 2) Margaret Brenman, 6 Sept 1940, 2 sons. Education: College of the City of New York. Publications: Plays (with dates of production and publication): I Lay in Zion, 1943, 1947; A Cry of Players, 1948, 1969; The Ruby, 1955; The Miracle Worker, 1957, 1957; Two for the Seesaw, 1958, 1960; Dinny and the Witches, 1959, 1960; Golden Boy (with Clifford Odets), 1964, 1965; John and Abigail, 1969, 1972; The Body and the Wheel, 1974, 1975; The Butterfingers Angel, Mary and Joseph, Herod the Nut, and the Slaughter of 12 Hit Carols in a Pear Tree, 1974, 1975; Golda, 1977, 1977; Goodly Creatures, 1980, 1986; Monday After the Miracle, 1982, 1983; Handy Dandy, 1984, 1986; Raggedy Ann: The Musical Adventure, 1985, 1986. Novel: The Cobweb, 1954. Poetry: Winter Crook, 1948; A Mass for the Dead, 1968. Criticism: Shakespeare's Game, 1978. Contributions to: Magazines. Honours: Harriet Monroe Memorial Prize for Poetry, 1945; Sylvania Award, 1957. Memberships: Authors League of America; Dramatists Guild; PEN. Address: c/o Flora Roberts, 157 West 57th Street, New York, NY 10022, USA.

GIBSON William (Ford), b. 17 Mar 1948, Conway, South Carolina, USA. Writer. m. Deborah Thompson, June 1972, 1 son, 1 daughter. Education: BA, University of British Columbia, 1977. Publications: Neuromancer, 1984; Count Zero, 1986; Burning Chrome (short stories with John Shirley, Bruce Sterling, and Michael Swanwick), 1986; Mona Lisa Overdrive, 1988; The Difference Engine (with Bruce Sterling), 1990; Agrippa: A Book of the Dead (with Dennis Ashbaugh and Keven Begos Jr), 1992; Virtual Light, 1993. Other: Dream Jumbo (performance art text), 1989; Johnny Mnemonic (screenplay), 1995. Contributions to: Anthologies and journals. Honours: Ditmar Award, Australian National

Science Fiction Foundation, 1984; Hugo Award, World Science Fiction Society, 1984; Nebula Award, Science Fiction Writers of America, 1984; Porgie Award, West Coast Review of Books, 1984. Address: c/o Martha Millard Literary Agency, 204 Park Avenue, Madison, NJ 07940, USA.

GIFFORD Barry Colby, b. 18 Oct 1946, Chicago, Illinois, USA. Writer. m. Mary Lou Nelson, 23 Oct 1970, 1 son, 1 daughter. Education: University of Missouri, 1964-65; Cambridge University, 1966. Publications: Jack's Book (co-author), biography, 1978; Port Tropique, 1980; Landscape with Traveler, 1980; The Neighborhood of Baseball, 1981; Devil Thumbs a Ride, 1988; Ghosts No Horse Can Carry, 1989; Wild at Heart, 1990; Sailor's Holiday, 1991; New Mysteries of Paris, 1991; A Good Man to Know, 1992; Night People, 1992; Arise and Walk, 1994; Hotel Room Trilogy, 1995; Baby Cat-Face, 1995; The Phantom Father, 1997; Lost Highway (co-author), 1997; Flaubert at Key West, 1997; Perdita Durango, 1997; The Sinaloa Story, 1998; Bordertown, 1998; The Wild Life of Sailor & Lula, 1998; My Last Martini, 1999. Contributions to: Punch; Esquire; Rolling Stone. Honours: Notable Book Awards, American Library Association, 1978, 1988; National Endowment for the Arts Fellowship, 1982; Maxwell Perkins Award, 1983; Syndicated Fiction Award, 1987, PEN; Premio Brancati, Italy, 1993. Literary Agent: Peter Ginsberg, President, Curtis Brown Ltd, 10 Astor Place, New York, NY 10003, USA. Address: c/o Curtis Brown Ltd.

GIFFORD Denis, b. 26 Dec 1927, London, England. Author; Cartoonist. Div., 1 daughter. Appointment: Art Assistant, Reynolds News, 1944-45. Publications: Pictorial History of Horror Movies, 1973; British Comic Catalogue 1874-1974, 1974; British Film Catalogue 1895-1980, 1980; International Book of Comics, 1984; Golden Age of Radio, 1985; Encyclopaedia of Comic Characters, 1987; Best of Eagle Annual 1951-59, 1989; Comic Art of Charlie Chaplin, 1989; The American Comic Book Catalogue, 1990; Books and Plays in Films, 1991. Contributions to: TV Times; Radio Times; Guardian; Times; Observer; Sunday Times; Independent; Collectors Fayre; Book Collector. Memberships: Association of Comics Enthusiasts, founder; Society of Strip Illustration, co-founder; Edgar Wallace Society; Old Bill Society; Savers of Television and Radio Shows, founder, 1940 Society. Address: 80 Silverdale, Sydenham, London SE26 4SJ, England.

GIGGAL Kenneth, (Henry Marlin, Angus Ross), b. 19 Mar 1927, Dewsbury, Yorkshire, England. Writer. Publications: The Manchester Thing, 1970; The Huddersfield Job, 1971; The London Assignment, 1972; The Dunfermline Affair, 1973; The Bradford Business, 1974; The Amsterdam Diversion, 1974; The Leeds Fiasco, 1975; The Edinburgh Exercise, 1975; The Ampurias Exchange, 1976; The Aberdeen Conundrum, 1977; The Congleton Lark, 1979; The Hamburg Switch, 1980; A Bad April, 1980; The Menwith Tangle, 1982; The Darlington Jaunt, 1983; The Luxembourg Run, 1985; Doom Indigo, 1986; The Tyneside Ultimatum, 1988; Classic Sailing Ships, 1988; The Greenham Plot, 1989; The Leipzig Manuscript, 1990; The Last One, 1992; John Worsley's War, 1992. Other: Television scripts and films. Contributions to: Many magazines, national and international. Honour: Truth Prize for Fiction, 1954. Memberships: Savage Club; Arms and Armour Society. Literary Agent: Andrew Mann Ltd. Address: The Old Granary, Bishop Monkton, Near Harrogate, North Yorkshire, England.

GIGUERE Diane Liliane, b. 6 Dec 1937, Montreal, Quebec, Canada. Author. Education: College Marie de France, 1941; Conservatory of Dramatic Arts, 1954-56. Publications: Le Temps des Jeux, 1961; L'eau est Profonde, 1965; Dans Les Ailes du vent, 1976; L'Abandon, 1993. Honours: Prix du Cercle du Livre de France, 1961; Guggenheim Fellowship, 1969; France Quebec Prize, 1977. Memberships: Writers' Union, Quebec; Association of French Speaking Writers at Home and Overseas. Address: 60 rue William Paul 304, Ile des Soeurs, Quebec H3E 1M6, Canada.

GIL David Georg, b. 16 Mar 1924, Vienna, Austria. Professor of Social Policy; Author. m. Eva Breslauer, 2 Aug 1947, 2 sons. Education: Certificate in Psychotherapy with Children, Israeli Society for Child Psychiatry, 1952; Diploma in Social Work, School of Social Work, 1953, BA, 1957, Hebrew University, Jerusalem, Israel; MSW, 1958, DSW, 1963, University of Pennsylvania. Appointment: Professor of Social Policy, Brandeis University. Publications: Violence Against Children, 1970; Unraveling Social Policy, 1973, 5th edition, 1992; The Challenge of Social Equality, 1976; Beyond the Jungle, 1979; Child Abuse and Violence (editor), 1979; Toward Social and Economic Justice (editor with Eva Gil), 1985; The Future of Work (editor with Eva Gil), 1987; Confronting Injustice and Opression, 1998. Contributions to: Over 50 articles to professional journals, book chapters, book reviews. Address: Heller Graduate School, Brandeis University, Waltham, MA 02254, USA.

GILB Dagoberto G, b. 31 July 1950, Los Angeles, California, USA. Writer. m. Rebeca Santos, 1978, 2 sons. Education: BA, MA, University of California. Appointments: Visiting Writer, University of Texas, 1988-89, University of Arizona, 1992-93, University of Wyoming, 1994. Publications: Winners on the Pass Line, 1985; The Magic of Blood, 1993; The Last Known Residence of Mickey Acuña, 1994. Honours: James D Phelan Award; Dobie Paisano Fellowship; Creative Writing Fellowship, National Endowment for the Arts; Whiting Writers Award, 1993; Best Book of Fiction Award, Texas Institute of Letters, 1993; Ernest Hemingway Foundation Award, 1994. Memberships: Texas Institute of Letters; PEN. Literary Agent: Kim Witherspoon. Address: PO Box 31001, El Paso, TX 79931, USA.

GILBERT Anna. See: LAZARUS Marguerite.

GILBERT Bentley Brinkerhoff, b. 5 Apr 1924, Mansfield, Ohio, USA. Writer. Education: AB, Honours, History, Miami University, Oxford, Ohio, 1949; MA, University of Cincinnati, 1950; PhD, University of Wisconsin, 1954. Appointments: Faculty, University of Cincinnati, Colorado College, 1955-67; Faculty, 1967-70, Professor of History, 1967-, University of Illinois at Chicago; Editor, Journal of British Studies, 1978-83. Publications: The Evolution of National Insurance in Great Britain: The Origins of the Welfare State, 1966, reprinted, 1996; Britain Since 1918, 1967, revised edition, 1980; British Social Policy, 1970; David Lloyd George: A Political Life, Vol I, The Architect of Change 1863-1912, 1987, Vol II, The Organiser of Victory, 1912-1916, 1992; Britain, 1914-1945: The Aftermath of Power, 1996. Contributions to: Reference works and professional journals. Honours: Guggenheim Fellowship, 1973-74; Society of Midland Authors Biography Prize, 1993; Various grants. Memberships: North American Conference on British Studies; Royal Historical Society, fellow. Address: c/o Department of History University of Illinois at Chicago, Chicago, IL 60607, USA.

GILBERT Harriett Sarah, b. 25 Aug 1948, London, England. Writer. Education: Diploma, Rose Bruford College of Speech and Drama, 1966-69. Appointments: Co-Books Editor, City Limits magazine, 1981-83; Deputy Literary Editor, 1983-86, Literary Editor, 1986-88, New Statesman; Presenter, Meridian Books Programme, BBC World Service Radio, 1991-; Lecturer in Journalism, City University, London, 1992-. Publications: I Know Where I've Been, 1972; Hotels with Empty Rooms, 1973; An Offence Against the Persons, 1974; Tide Race, 1977; Running Away, 1979; The Riding Mistress, 1983; A Women's History of Sex, 1987; The Sexual Imagination (editor), 1993. Contributions to: Time Out; City Limits; New Statesman; Guardian; BBC; Australian Broadcasting Corporation; Washington Post; BBC World Service Radio. Membership: Writers Guild of Great Britain. Literary Agent: Richard Scott Simon. Address: 2 Oaktree Court, Valmar Road, London SE5 9NH, England.

GILBERT Ilsa, b. 27 Apr 1933, Brooklyn, New York, USA. Poet; Playwright; Librettist; Lyricist. Education: University of Michigan, 1951-52; BA, Brooklyn College,

1955. Appointments: Editor, Copywriter, Creative Director, various companies, 1955-68; Freelance Copywriter, Vantage Press, 1962-79. Publications: Pardon the Prison, 1976; Survivors and Other New York Poems, 1985. Other: Numerous productions, staged readings, verse plays, musicals, concert pieces, etc. Contributions to: Numerous magazines. Honours: Honourable Mention, Atlantic Monthly College Poetry Contest, 1955; Best Subjective Poem, Poet Lore, 1968; Writers Colony Residencies, Dorset, Vermont, 1982, 1986-87. Memberships: Authors League of America; Dramatists Guild; PEN American Center; Pentangle Literary Society; Poets and Writers; Women's Salon. Address: 203 Bleecker Street, Apt 9, New York, NY 10012, USA.

GILBERT Jack, b. 17 Feb 1925, Pittsburgh, Pennsylvania, USA. Poet; Writer. Education: BA, University of Pittsburgh, 1954; MA, San Francisco State University, 1962. Appointments: University of California's at Berkeley, 1958-59, San Francisco State University, 1962-63, 1965-67, 1971, Syracuse University, 1982-83, University of San Francisco, 1985; Professor, Kyoto University, Tokyo, 1974-75; Chair, Creative Writing, University of Alabama, Tuscaloosa, 1986. Publications: Poetry: Views of Jeopardy, 1962; Monolithos, 1982; The Great Fires: Poems, 1982-1992, 1994. Contributions to: Various reviews, journals, and periodicals. Honours: Yale Younger Award, 1962; Guggenheim Fellowship, 1964; National Endowment for the Arts Award, 1974; 1st Prize, American Poetry Review, 1983; Stanley Kunitz Prize, 1983; Lannan Award, 1995. Address: 136 Montana Street, San Francisco, CA 94112, USA.

GILBERT John (Raphael), b. 8 Apr 1926, London, England. Writer. m. 3 sons. Education: Columbia University, 1941-42; BA, King's College, London, 1945. Publications: Modern World Book of Animals, 1947; Cats, Cats, Cats, 1961; Famous Jewish Lives, 1970; Myths of Ancient Rome, 1970; Pirates and Buccaneers, 1971; Highwaymen and Outlaws, 1971; Charting the Vast Pacific, 1971; National Costumes of the World, 1972; World of Wildlife, 1972-74; Miracles of Nature, 1975; Knights of the Crusades, 1978; Vikings, 1978; Prehistoric Man, 1978; Leonardo da Vinci, 1978; La Scala, 1979; Dinosaurs Discovered, 1980; Macdonald Guide to Trees, 1983; Macdonald Encyclopedia of House Plants, 1986; Theory and Use of Colour, 1986; Macdonald Encyclopedia of Roses, 1987; Gardens of Britain, 1987; Macdonald Encyclopedia of Butterflies and Moths, 1988; Trekking in the USA, 1989; Macdonald Encyclopedia of Orchids, 1989; Macdonald Encyclopedia of Bulbs, 1989; Trekking in Europe, 1990; Macdonald Encyclopedia of Herbs and Spices, 1990; Macdonald Encyclopedia of Bonsai, 1990; Macdonald Encyclopedia of Amphibians and Reptiles, 1990; Macdonald Encyclopedia of Saltwater Fishes, 1992; Decorating Chinese Porcelain, 1994. Address: 28 Lyndale Avenue, London NW2, England.

GILBERT Sir Martin (John), b. 25 Oct 1936, London, England. Historian. m. (1) Helen Constance, 1963, 1 daughter, (2) Susan Sacher, 2 sons. Education: Magdalen College, Oxford. Appointments: Senior Research Scholar, St Antony's College, Oxford, 1960-62; Visiting Lecturer, University of Budapest, 1961; Research Assistant to Senior Research Assistant to Randolph S Churchill, 1962-67; Fellow, 1962-94, Honorary Fellow, 1994-, Merton College, Oxford; Visiting Professor, University of South Carolina, 1965, University of Tel Aviv, 1979, Hebrew University of Jerusalem, 1980-, University College, London, 1995-96; Official Biographer of Sir Winston Churchill, 1968-. Publications: The Appeasers (with Richard Gott), 1963; Britain and Germany Between the Wars, 1964; The European Powers, 1900-1945, 1965; Plough My Own Furrow: The Life of Lord Allen of Hurtwood, 1965; Servant of India: A Study of Imperial Rule, 1905-1910, 1966; The Roots of Appeasement, 1966; Recent History Atlas 1860-1960, 1966; Winston Churchill, 1966; British History Atlas, 1968, 2nd edition, 1993; American History Atlas, 1968, 3rd edition, 1993; Jewish History Atlas, 1969, 5th edition, 1993; First World War Atlas, 1970, 2nd edition, 1994; Winston S Churchill, Vol III, 1914-1916, 1971, companion volume, 1973, Vol

IV, 1917-1922, 1975, companion volume, 1977, Vol V, 1922-1939, 1976, companion volumes, 1980, 1981, 1982, Vol VI, Finest Hour, 1939-1941, 1983, Vol VII, Road to Victory, 1986, Vol VIII, "Never Despair", 1945-1965, 1988; Russian History Atlas, 1972, 2nd edition, 1993; Sir Horace Rumbold: Portrait of a Diplomat, 1973; Churchill: A Photographic Portrait, 1974, 2nd edition, 1988; The Arab-Israeli Conflict: Its History in Maps, 1974, 6th edition, 1993; The Jews in Arab Lands: Their History in Maps, 1975; The Jews of Russia: Illustrated History Atlas, 1976; Jerusalem Illustrated History Atlas, 1977, 2nd edition, 1994; Exile and Return: The Emergence of Jewish Statehood, 1978; Children's Illustrated Bible Atlas, 1979; Final Journey, the Fate of the Jews of Nazi Europe, 1979; Auschwitz and the Allies, 1981; Churchill's Political Philosophy, 1981; Atlas of the Holocaust, 1982, 2nd edition, 1993; The Jews of Hope: The Plight of Soviet Jewry Today, 1984; Jerusalem: Rebirth of a City, 1985; The Holocaust: The Jewish Tragedy, 1986; Shcharansky: Hero of Our Time, 1986; Second World War, 1989; Churchill: A Life, 1991; Atlas of British Charities, 1993; The Churchill War Papers, 3 volumes, 1993, 1995, 1996; In Search of Churchill, 1994; First World War, a History, 1994; The Day the War Ended: VE Day, 1945, 1995; Jerusalem in the 20th Century, 1996; The Boys: Triumph Over Adversity, 1996; A History of the Twentieth Century, 3 volumes, 1997 et seq. Editor: A Century of Conflict: Essays Presented to A J P Taylor, 1966; Churchill, 1967; Lloyd George, 1968; Jackdaws: Winston Churchill, 1970; The Coming of War in 1939, 1973. Other: Script designer and co-author of the film Genocide, 1981; Writer and narrator, Churchill, BBC TV, 1989-91; The Day the War Ended: (VE Day, 1995; Jerusalem in the Twentieth Century, 1996; A History of the Twentieth Century, volume 1, 1997, volume 2, 1998. Contributions to: Periodicals. Honours: Academy Award, 1981; Wolfson Award, 1983; Commander of the Order of the British Empire, 1990; Knighted, 1995. Membership: Royal Society of Literature, fellow. Address: Merton College, Oxford OX1 4JD, England.

GILBERT Michael (Francis), b. 17 July 1912, Billinghay, Lincolnshire, England. Author; Solicitor. m. Roberta Mary Marsden, 26 July 1947, 2 sons, 5 daughters. Publications: Close Quarters, 1947; They Never Looked Inside, 1948; The Doors Open, 1949; Smallbone Deceased, 1950; Death has Deep Roots, 1951; Death in Captivity, 1952; Fear to Tread, 1953; Sky High, 1955; Be Shot for Sixpence, 1956; The Tichborn Claimant, 1957; Blood and Judgement, 1958; After the Fine Weather, 1963; The Crack in the Teacup, 1965; The Dust and the Heat, 1967; Game Without Rules (stories), 1967; The Etruscan Net, 1969; The Body of a Girl, 1972; The Ninety Second Tiger, 1973; Amateur in Violence (stories), 1973; Flash Point, 1975; The Night of the Twelfth, 1976; Petrella at Q (stories), 1977; The Empty House, 1978; Death of a Favourite Girl (in US as The Killing of Katie Steelstock), 1980; Mr Calder and Mr Behrens (stories), 1982; The Final Throw (in US as End-Game), 1982; The Black Seraphim, 1983; The Long Journey Home, 1985; The Oxford Book of Legal Anecdotes, 1986; Trouble, 1987; Paint Gold & Blood, 1989; Anything for a Quiet Life, 1991; Prep School (anthology), 1991; Roller-Coaster, 1993; Into Battle, 1997; Ring of Terror, 1998; Over and Out, 1998. Honours: Lauréat de Grand Prix de Littérature Policière, 1957; Grand Master, Swedish DeKarademins, 1981; Grand Master, Mystery Writers of America, 1987; Crime Writers Association Cartier Diamond Dagger, 1994. Memberships: Garrick Club; HAC, Crime Writers Association. Address: Luddesdown Old Rectory, Gravesend, Kent DA13 0XE, England.

GILBERT Robert Andrew, b. 6 Oct 1942, Bristol, England. Antiquarian Bookseller; Editor; Writer. m. Patricia Kathleen Linnell, 20 June 1970, 3 sons, 2 daughters. Education: BA, Honours, Philosophy, Psychology, University of Bristol, 1964. Appointment: Editor, Ars Quatuor Coronatorum, 1994-. Publications: The Golden Dawn: Twilight of the Magicians, 1983; A E Waite: A Bibliography, 1983; The Golden Dawn Companion, 1986; A E Waite: Magician of Many Parts, 1987; The Treasure of Montsegur (with W N Birks), 1987;

Elements of Mysticism, 1991; World Freemasonry: An Illustrated History, 1992; Freemasonry: A Celebration of the Craft (J M Hamil), 1992; Casting the First Stone, 1993. Editor with M A Cox: The Oxford Book of English Ghost Stories, 1986; Victorian Ghost Stories: An Oxford Anthology, 1991; The Golden Dawn Scrapbook, 1997. Contributions to: Ars Quatuor Coronatorum; Avallaunius; Christian Parapsychologist; Gnosis; Hermetic Journal; Cauda Pavonis; Yeats Annual. Memberships: Society of Authors; librarian, Societas Rosicruciana in Anglia. Address: 4 Julius Road, Bishopston, Bristol BS7 8EU, England.

GILBERT Virginia, b. 19 Dec 1946, Elgin, Illinois, USA. Associate Professor of English; Poet; Writer. Education: BA, English, Iowa Wesleyan College, 1969; MFA, Creative Writing and Poetry, University of Iowa, 1971; PhD, Creative Writing, Poetry and English, University of Nebraska, 1991. Appointments: Instructor, College of Lake County, Illinois, 1979; Teaching Assistant, University of Nebraska, 1984-87; Assistant Professor, 1990-92, Associate Professor, 1992-, of English, Alabama A&M University. Publications: To Keep at Bay the Hounds, 1985; The Earth Above, 1993. That Other Brightness, 1996. Contributions to: Journals, reviews, and quarterlies. Honours: National Endowment for the Arts Fellowship, 1976-77; 2nd Place, Hackney Awards, 1990; 1st Place, Sakura Festival Haiku Contest, 1992. Memberships: Associated Writing Programs; Modern Language Association; Peace Corps Volunteer Association; Peace Corps Volunteer Readers and Writers Association; Poetry Society of America; Poets and Writers. Address: c/o Department of English, Alabama A&M University, Box 453, Normal, AL 35762, USA.

GILCHRIST Ellen, b. 20 Feb 1935, Vicksburg, Mississippi, USA. Author; Poet. Education: BA, Millsaps College, Jackson, Mississippi, 1967; Postgraduate Studies, University of Arkansas, 1976. Publications: The Land Surveyor's Daughter (poems), 1979; The Land of Dreamy Dreams (stories), 1981; The Annunciation (novel), 1983; Victory Over Japan: A Book of Stories, 1984; Drunk With Love (stories), 1986; Riding Out the Tropical Depression (poems), 1986; Falling Through Space: The Journals of Ellen Gilchrist, 1987; The Anna Papers (novel), 1988; Light Can Be Both Wave and Particle: A Book of Stories, 1989; I Cannot Get You Close Enough (3 novellas), 1990; Net of Jewels (novel), 1992; Anabasis: A Journey to the Interior, 1994; Starcarbon: A Meditation on Love, 1994; An Age of Miracles (stories), 1995; Rhoda: A Life in Stories, 1995; Sarah Conley, 1997. Contributions to: Many journals and periodicals. Honours: National Endowment for the Arts Grant in Fiction, 1979; Pucshcart Prizes, 1979-80, 1983; Louisiana Library Association Honor Book, 1981; Mississippi Academy of Arts and Sciences Awards, 1982, 1985; Saxifrage Award, 1983; American Book Award for Fiction, 1984; J William Fulbright Award for Literature, University of Arkansas, 1985; Mississippi Institute of Arts and Letters Literature Award, 1985. Memberships: Authors Guild; Authors League of America. Address: 834 Eastwood Drive, Fayetteville, AR 72701, USA.

GILES Frank (Thomas Robertson), b. 31 July 1919, London, England. Journalist (retired); Writer. m. Lady Katharine Sackville, 29 June 1946, 1 son, 2 daughters. Education: Wellington College; MA, Open Scholar in History, Brasenose College, Oxford, 1946. Appointments: Assistant Correspondent, Paris Bureau, 1947-50, Chief Correspondent, Rome Bureau, 1950-53, and Paris Bureau, 1953-61, The Times, London; Foreign Editor, 1961-77, Deputy Editor, 1967-81, Editor, 1981-83, The Sundry Times, London; Director, The Times Newspapers, 1981-85. Publications: A Prince of Journalists: The Life and Times of Henri de Blowitz, 1962; Sundry Times, (autobiography), 1986; Forty Years On, (editor), 1990; The Locust Years: History of the 4th French Republic, 1991; Corfu: The Garden Isle, editor, 1994. Contributions to: Books, newspapers and periodicals. Honour: Franco-British Society Prize. Address: 42 Blomfield Road, London W9 2PF, England.

GILES Richard Lawrence, b. 24 May 1937, Petersham, New South Wales, Australia. Teacher; Writer. m. Faye Laurel, 3 May 1969. Education: BA, 1957; DipEd, 1969; ATCL, 1971; AMusA, 1973. Publications: Technology, Employment and the Industrial Revolution, 1984; For and Against, 1989, 2nd edition, 1993; Debating, 1992; Understanding Our Economy, 1995. Contributions to: Good Government; Progress; The Individual; Australian Land Economics Review. Membership: Australian School for Social Science. Literary Agent: Jacaranda Press, director. Address: PO Box 443, Enfield, New South Wales 2136, Australia.

GILL Anton, b. 22 Oct 1948, Essex, England. Writer. m. Nicola Susan Browne, 6 Nov 1982. Education: Clare College, Cambridge, 1967-70. Publications: The Journey Back From Hell; Berlin to Bucharest; City of the Horizon; City of Dreams; A Dance Between Flames; City of the Dead; An Honourable Defeat; The Devil's Mariner, 1997; . Honour: HH Wingate Award. Address: c/o Mark Lucas, L.A.W., Elsinore House, 77 Fulham Road, London, W6 8JA, UK.

GILL Bartholomew. See: **McGARRITY Mark.**

GILL David Lawrence William, b. 3 July 1934, Chislehurst, Kent, England. Poet; Writer. m. Irene Henry, 5 July 1958, 2 sons, 1 daughter. Education: BA, Honours, German, University College, London, 1955; Certificate in Education, Birmingham University, 1958; BA, Honours, English, London External, 1970. Appointments: Lecturer, 1971-79, Senior Lecturer, 1979-87, Newland Park College of Education, later incorporated into Bucks College of Higher Education. Publications: Men Without Evenings, 1966; The Pagoda and Other Poems, 1969; In the Eye of the Storm, 1975; The Upkeep of the Castle, 1978; Karel Klimsa, by Ondra Lysohorsky (translator), 1984; One Potato, Two Potato (with Dorothy Clancy), 1985; Legends, Please, 1986; The White Raven, 1989; The New Hesperides, 1991. Contributions to: Many journals, reviews, and magazines. Address: 38 Yarnells Hill, Botley, Oxford OX2 9BE, England.

GILL Evalyn Pierpoint, Writer; Editor. 2 daughters. Education: BA cum laude, University of Colorado; MA, Central Michigan University, 1968. Appointments: Humanities, English, Saginaw Valley College, 1968-72; English, University of North Carolina, Greensboro, 1973-74; Founder, 1975, Editor, 1975, International Poetry Review. Publications: Poetry by French Women, 1930-1980, 1980; Dialogue, 1985; Southeast of Here: Northwest of Now, 1986; Entrances, 1996. Honours: 1st Prize in Poetry, Tar Heel Writers Round Table, 1977; Fortner Writing and Community Award, St Andrews College, 1995; Altrusa International Community Artists Award, Greensboro, 1998. Memberships: Phi Beta Kappa; North Carolina Poetry Society; North Carolina Writers Network; Founder, The Greensboro Group. Address: 2900 Turner Grove Drive N, Greensboro, NC 27455, USA.

GILL Jerry Henry, b. 7 Feb 1933, Lynden, Washington, USA. College Teacher; Writer. m. M Sorri, 3 Sept 1982. Education: BA, Westmont College, 1956; MA, University of Washington, 1957; MDiv, New York Theological Seminary, 1960; PhD, Duke University, 1966. Publications: Philosophy Today, 3 volumes, 1968-70; Essays on Kierkegaard, 1969; Possibility of Religious Knowledge, 1971; Wittgenstein and Metaphor, 1980, revised edition, 1996; On Knowing God, 1981; Faith in Dialogue, 1985; Mediated Transcendence, 1989; Post-Modern Epistemology (with M Sorri), 1989; Enduring Questions (with M Rader), 1990; Merleau-Ponty and Metaphor, 1991, Learning to Learn, 1992; At the Threshold of Language, 1996. Contributions to: Theology Today; Soundings; International Philosophical Quarterly; Mind; Philosophy and Phenomenological Research; Journal of Aesthetics. Honour: Danforth Teacher Grant, 1964-66. Address: 521 West Shadow Place, Tucson, AZ 85737, USA.

GILL Stephen Matthew, b. 25 June 1932, Sialkot, Pakistan. Poet; Author; Editor. m. Sarala Gill, 17 Feb 1970, 1 son, 2 daughters. Education: BA, Panjab University, 1956; MA, Meerut College, Agra University, 1963; University of Ottawa, 1967-70; University of Oxford, 1971. Appointments: Editor, Canadian World Federalist, 1971-73, 1977-79, Writer's Lifeline, 1982-; President, Vesta Publications Ltd, 1974-90. Publications: Poetry: Reflections and Wounds, 1978; Moans and Waves, 1989; The Dove of Peace, 1989; The Flowers of Thirst, 1991; Songs for Harmony, 1992; Flashes, 1994; Aman Di Ghuggi, 1994; Divergent Shades, 1995; Shrine, forthcoming. Fiction: Life's Vagaries (short stories), 1974; Why, 1976; The Loyalist City, 1979; Immigrants, 1982. Non-Fiction: Six Symbolist Plays of Yeats, 1974; Discovery of Bangladesh, 1975; Scientific Romances of H G Wells, 1975; English Grammar for Beginners, 1977; Political Convictions of G B Shaw, 1980; Sketches of India, 1980. Editor: Various anthologies. Contributions to: Over 250 publications. Honours: Honorary DLitt, World University, 1986, World Academy of Arts and Culture, 1990; International Eminent Poet, International Poets Academy, Madras, 1991; Pegasus International Poetry for Peace Award, Poetry in the Arts, Austin, Texas, 1991; Laureate Man of Letters, United Poets Laureate International, 1992; Poet of Peace Award, Pakistan Association, Orleans, Ontario, 1995; Mawaheb Culture Friendship Medal, Mawaheb Magazine (Canada), 1997. Memberships: Christian Cultural Association of South Asians, vice-president; International Academy of Poets, fellow; PEN International; World Academy of Arts and Culture; World Federalists of Canada; Amnesty International; The Writers Union of Canada. Address: PO Box 32, Cornwall, Ontario K6H 5R9, Canada.

GILLARD David Owen, b. 8 Feb 1947, Croydon, Surrey, England. Arts Writer and Critic. m. Valerie Ann Miles, 13 June 1994. Education: Tavistock School, Croydon, England. Appointments: Scriptwriter, Assistant Director, Associated British Pathé, 1967-70; Film and Theatre Critic, Daily Sketch, 1971; Opera Critic, Daily Mail, 1971-; Ballet Critic, Daily Mail, 1971-88; Radio Correspondent, BBC Radio Times, 1984-91; Founder Editor, ENO Friends Magazine, 1983-93. Publication: Beryl Grey: A Biography, 1977. Contributions to: Writer, My Kind of Day; BBC Radio Times, 1992-; Instituted Drama Review Pages, The Listener, 1982. Address: 16 Grasmere Road, Bromley, Kent BR1 4BA, England.

GILLESPIE Robert B(yrne), b. 31 Dec 1917, Brooklyn, New York, USA. Writer. m. Marianna Albert, 26 June 1957, dec, 1 daughter. Education: Brooklyn College, 1935-37; LLB, St John's Law School, 1940. Publications: The Crossword Mystery, 1979; Little Sally Does It Again, 1982; Print-Out, 1983; Heads You Lose, 1985; Empress of Coney Island, 1986; The Hell's Kitchen Connections, 1987; The Last of the Honeywells, 1988; Deathstorm, 1990; Many crossword books. Contributions to: St John's Law Review; Discovery 6. Memberships: Authors Guild; Mystery Writers of America. Address: 226 Bay Street, Douglaston, NY 11363, USA.

GILLIES Valerie, b. 4 June 1948, Edmonton, Alberta, Canada (British citizen). Poet; Writer. m. William Gillies, 24 June 1972, 1 son, 2 daughters. Education: MA, 1970, MLitt, 1974, University of Edinburgh. Appointments: Writer-in-Residence, Duncan of Jordanstone College of Art, Dundee, 1988-90, University of Edinburgh, 1995-98. Publications: Trio: New Poets from Edinburgh, 1971; Each Bright Eye: Selected Poems, 1977; Bed of Stone, 1984; Leopardi: A Scottish Quair, 1987; Tweed Journey, 1989; The Chanter's Tune, 1990; The Jordanstone Folio, 1990; The Ringing Rock, 1995. Contributions to: Radio, television, reviews, and journals. Honours: Scottish Arts Council Bursary, 1976, and Book Award, 1996; Eric Gregory Award, 1976. Membership: Society of Authors, Scotland, fellow. Address: c/o Scottish Cultural Press, Unit 14, Leith Walk Business Centre, 130 Leith Walk, Edinburgh EH6 5DT, Scotland.

GILLIS Launa. See: **PARTLETT Launa.**

GILLON Adam, b. 17 July 1921, Poland. Professor of English Emeritus; Writer; Poet. m. Isabella Zamojre, 1946, 1 son, 1 daughter. Education: MA, Hebrew University of Jerusalem, 1949; PhD, English and Comparative Literature, Columbia University, 1954. Appointments: Professor of English, Acadia University, Nova Scotia, 1957-62, University of Haifa, 1979-84; Professor of English and Comparative Literature, 1962-81, Professor Emeritus, 1981-, State University of New York at New Paltz. Publications: Poetry: Selected Poems and Translations, 1962; In the Manner of Haiku: Seven Aspects of Man, 1967; Daily New and Old: Poems in the Manner of Haiku, 1971; Strange Mutations in the Manner of Haiku, 1973; Summer Morn...Winter Weather: Poems 'Twist Haiku and Senryu, 1975; The Withered Leaf: A Medley of Haiku and Snryu, 1982. Novels: A Cup of Fury, 1962; Jared, 1986. Non-Fiction: The Eternal Solitary: A Study of Joseph Conrad, 1960; Joseph Conrad: Commemorative Essays (editor), 1975; Conrad and Shakespeare and Other Essays, 1976; Joseph Conrad, 1982; Joseph Conrad: Comparative Essays, 1994. Other: Translations, radio plays, and screenplays. Contributions to: Journals, reviews, and periodicals. Honours: Alfred Jurzykowski Foundation Award, 1967; Joseph Fels Foundation Award, 1970; National Endowment for the Humanities Grant, 1985; Gold Award, Worldfest International Film Festival, 1993. Memberships: Haiku Society of America; Joseph Conrad Society of America; Modern Language Association; Polish Institute of Arts and Sciences. Address: Lake Illyria, 490 Rt 299 West, New Paltz, NY 12561, USA.

GILMAN Dorothy, (Dorothy Gilman Butters), b. 25 June 1923, New Brunswick, New Jersey, USA. Author; Children's Writer. m. Edgar A Butters, 15 Sept 1945, div 1965, 2 sons. Education: Pennsylvania Academy of Fine Arts, 1940-45; University of Pennsylvania and Art Students League, 1963-64. Publications: Novels: The Unexpected Mrs Pollifax, 1966, in UK as Mrs Pollifax, Spy, 1971; Uncertain Voyage, 1967; The Amazing Mrs Pollifax, 1970; The Elusive Mrs Pollifax, 1971; A Palm for Mrs Pollifax, 1973; A Nun in the Closet, 1975, in UK as A Nun in the Cupboard, 1976; The Clairvoyant Countess, 1975; Mrs Pollifax on Safari, 1977; A New Kind of Country, 1978; The Tightrope Walker, 1979; Mrs Pollifax on the China Station, 1983; The Maze in the Heart of the Castle, 1983; Mrs Pollifax and the Hong Kong Buddha, 1985; Mrs Pollifax and the Golden Triangle, 1988; Incident at Badamya, 1989; Mrs Pollifax and the Whirling Dervish, 1990; Mrs Pollifax and the Second Thief, 1993; Mrs Pollifax Pursued, 1995. For children: Enchanted Caravan, 1949; Carnival Gypsy, 1950; Ragamuffin Alley, 1951; The Calico Year, 1953; Four-Party Line, 1954; Papa Dolphin's Table, 1955; Girl in Buckskin, 1956; Heartbreak Street, 1958; Witch's Silver, 1959; Masquerade, 1961; Ten Leagues to Boston Town, 1962; The Bells of Freedom, 1963. Contributions to: Magazines. Honour: Catholic Book Award, 1975. Membership: Authors Guild. Address: c/o Howard Morhaim Agency, 175 Fifth Avenue, New York, NY 10010, USA.

GILMAN George G. See: **HARKNETT Terry.**

GILMAN Sander L(awrence), b. 21 Feb 1944, Buffalo, New York, USA. Professor; Writer. m. Marina von Eckardt, 28 Dec 1969. Education: BA, PhD, Tulane University; University of Munich; Free University of Berlin. Appointments: Professor of German Language and Literature; Professor of Psychiatry. Publications: Nietzchean Parody, 1976; The Face of Madness: Hugh W Diamond and the Origin of Psychiatric Photography, 1976; Bertold Brecht's Berlin, 1976; Seeing the Insane, 1981; Sexuality: An Illustrated History, 1989; The Jew's Body, 1991; Freud, Race and Gender, 1993; The Case of Sigmund Freud: Medicine and Identity at Fin de Siècle, 1994; Re-emerging Jewish Culture in Today's Germany, 1994; Franz Kafka, The Jewish Patient, 1995; Jews in Today's German Culture, 1995; Also scholarly editions of German texts and monographs. Address: c/o Department of Modern Languages, Cornell University 203 Merrill Hall, Ithaca, NY 14853-0001, USA.

GILMOUR David, b. 14 Nov 1952, London, England. Writer. m. Sarah Anne Bradstock, 25 September 1975, 1 son, 3 daughters. Education: BA, Balliol College, Oxford, 1974. Appointments: Deputy Editor and Contributing

Editor, Middle East International, London, 1978-85; Research Fellow, St Antony's College, Oxford, 1996-97. Publications: Dispossessed: The Ordeal of the Palestinians, 1980; Lebanon: The Fractured Country, 1983; The Transformation of Spain: From Franco to the Constitutional Monarchy, 1985; The Last Leopard: A Life of Giuseppe di Lampedusa, 1988; The Hungry Generations, 1991; Cities of Spain, 1992; Curzon, 1994. Contributions to: Periodicals. Honours: Marsh Biography Award, 1988; Scottish Arts Council Spring Book Award, 1988; Duff Cooper Prize, 1994. Address: c/o Aitken, Stone, and Wylie, 29 Fernshaw Road, London SW10 0TG, England.

GILMOUR Robin, b. 17 June 1943, Hamilton, Scotland. Reader in English; Writer; Editor. m. Elizabeth Simpson, 29 Dec 1969, 2 sons, 2 daughters. Education: BA, St John's College, Cambridge, 1964; PhD, University of Edinburgh, 1969. Appointments: Lecturer, University of Ulster, 1969-73; Lecturer, 1973-84, Senior Lecturer, 1984-90, Reader in English, 1990-, University of Aberdeen; Founder-General Editor, Edward Arnold's Modern Fiction series. Publications: The Idea of the Gentleman in the Victorian Novel, 1981; The Novel in the Victorian Age, 1986; The Victorian Period: The Intellectual and Cultural Context of English Literature 1830-1890, 1993. Editor: Barchester Towers, by Anthony Trollope, 1983; The Warden, by Anthony Trollope, 1984; Great Expectations, by Charles Dickens, 1994. Contributions to: Scholarly books and journals. Address: 9 Brighton Place, Aberdeen AB10 6RT, England.

GILROY Frank D(aniel), b. 13 Oct 1925, New York, New York, USA. Dramatist; Screenwriter; Author; Producer; Director. m. Ruth Dorothy Gaydos, 13 Feb 1954, 3 sons. Education: BA magna cum laude, Dartmouth College, 1950; Yale School of Drama, 1950-51. Publications: Novels: Private, 1970; Little Ego (with Ruth Gilroy), 1970; Little Ego (with Ruth Gilroy), 1970; From Noon Till Three, 1973. Non-Fiction: I Wake Up Screening: Everything You Need to Know About Making Independent Films Including a Thousand Reasons Not To, 1993. Other: Plays: Who'll Save the Plowboy?, 1957; The Subject was Roses, 1962; That Summer, That Fall, 1967; The Only Game in Town, 1968; The Next Contestant, 1978; Last Licks, 1979; Real to Reel, 1987; Match Point, 1990; A Way with Words, 1991; Give the Bishop My Faint Regards, 1992; Any Given Day, 1993. Films: The Fastest Gun Alive (with Russell House), 1956; Gallant Hours (with Beirne Lay Jr), 1960; Desperate Characters, 1970; From Noon till Three, 1977; Once in Paris, 1978; The Gig, 1985; The Luckiest Man in the World, 1989. Honours: Obie Award, 1962; Outer Circle Award, 1964; Drama Critics Circle Award, 1964; New York Theatre Club Award, 1964-65; Tony Award, 1965; Pulitzer Prize for Drama, 1965; Best Screenplay Award, Berlin Film Festival, 1970. Memberships: Directors Guild of America; Dramatists Guild, president, 1969-71; Writers Guild of America. Address: c/o Dramatists Guild, 1501 Broadway, New York, NY 10036, USA.

GILSON Estelle, b. 16 June 1926, New York, New York, USA. Author; Translator. m. Saul B Gilson, 21 Dec 1950, 2 sons. Education: AB, Brooklyn College, 1946; MSSW, Columbia University, 1949. Appointment: Teacher, College of Mt St Vincent Seton Seminars. Publications: Gabriel Preil: To Be Recorded (translator), 1992; Umberto Saba: The Stories and Recollections of Umberto Saba (translator), 1993. Contributions to: Anthologies. Honours: Italo Calvino Award, Translation Center, 1991; Renato Poggioli Award, PEN, 1992; Aldo and Jeanne Scaglione Award, Modern Language Association, 1994; National Endowment for the Arts Grant, 1995. Memberships: American Literary Translators Association; PEN. Address: 7 Sigma Place, Riverside, NY 10471, USA.

GINSBURG Mark Barry, b. 9 Dec 1949, Los Angles, California, USA. Professor. m. Barbara Iris Chasin, 5 Sept 1971, 1 son, 2 daughters. Education: BA, Sociology, Dartmouth College, 1972; MA, Sociology, 1974, PhD, Education, 1976, University of California at Los Angeles. Publications: Contradictions in Teacher Education and Society, 1988; Understanding Educational Reform in Global Context, 1991; The Politics of Educators' Work and Lives, 1995; The Political Dimension in Teacher Education, 1995. Contributions to: Comparative Education Review; Educational Foundations; Journal of Education; Oxford Review of Education, Honours: AESA Critics Choice (Book Award), 1990. Memberships: American Educational Studies Association, board of directors, 1990-93; Comparative and International Education Society, president, 1991-92. Address: 1125 Wightman Street, Pittsburgh, PA 15217, USA.

GINZBURG Carlo, b. 1939, Turin, Italy. Historian; Professor. m. 1) div, 2) Luisa Ciammitti, 2 daughters. Education: Degree, Scuola Normale Superiore, Pisa; Warburg Institute, London. Appointments: Professor of Modern History, University of Bologna, 1970-; Several visiting fellowships. Publications: I benandanti: Stregoneria e culti agrari tra Cinquecento e Seicento, 1966, English translation as The Night Battles: Witchcraft and Agrarian Cults in the Sixteenth and Seventeenth Centuries, 1983; Il nicodemismo: Simulazione e dissimulazione religiosa nell'Europa del '500, 1970; Giochi di pazienza: Un seminario sul Beneficio di Cristo (with Adriano Prosperi), 1975; Il formaggio e i vermi: Il cosmo di un mugnaio del '500, 1976, English translation as The Cheese and the Worms: The Cosmos of a Sixteenth-Century Miller, 1980; Indagini su Piero: Il Battesimo, il Ciclo di Arezzo, la Flagellazione di Urbino, 1981, English translation as Clues, Myths, and the Historical Method, 1989; Storia notturna: Una decifrazione del sabba, 1989, English translation as Ecstatcies: Deciphering the Witches' Sabbath, 1991; Il giudice e lo storico: Considerazioni in margine al processo sofri, 1991; Il registro: Carcere politico di Civitavecchia (editor with Aldo Natoli and Vittorio Foa), 1994. Honour: Citta di Montesilvano, 1989. Address: c/o Departimento di Storia, Universita degli Studi, Piazza San Giovanni in Monte 2, I-40124 Bologna, Italy.

GIOIA (Michael) Dana, b. 24 Dec 1950, Los Angeles, California, USA. Writer; Poet. m. Mary Hiecke, 23 Feb 1980, 3 sons, 1 dec. Education: BA, English, 1973, MBA, 1977, Stanford University; MA, Comparative Literature, Harvard University, 1975. Publications: The Ceremony and Other Stories, 1984; Poems from Italy (anthology), 1985; Daily Horoscope, 1986; Mottetti: Poems of Love (translator), 1990; The Gods of Winter, 1991; Can Poetry Matter?, 1992; An Introduction to Poetry, 1994. Contributions to: Reviews, journals, and periodicals. Honours: Best of New Generation Award, Esquire, 1984; Frederick Bock Prize for Poetry, 1985. Memberships: Poetry Society of America, board; Wesleyan University Writers Conference. Address: 7190 Faught Road, Santa Rosa, CA 95403, USA.

GIOSEFFI Daniela, b. 12 Feb 1941, Orange, New Jersey, USA. Singer; Actress; Dancer; Poet; Writer; Lyricist. m. (1) Richard J Kearney, 5 Sept 1965, div 1982, 1 daughter, (2) Dr Lionel B Luttinger, 1986. Education: BA, Montclair State College; MFA, Drama, Catholic University of America. Appointments: Editorial Board, VIA, magazine of literature and culture at Purdue University; Skylands Writers Association Inc, president; Wise Womans Web, editor-in-chief: Electronic magazine of Literature and Graphics. Publications: The Great American Belly Dance (novel), 1977; Eggs in the Lake (poems), 1979; Earth Dancing: Mother Nature's Oldest Rite, 1980; Women on War, 1990; On Prejudice: A Global Perspective, 1993; Words, Wounds and Flowers, 1995; Dust Disappears by Corilda Oliver Labra, (translator), 1995; In Bed With the Exotic Enemy: Stories and Novella, 1997. Contributions to: Nation; Chelsea; Ambit; Poetry Review; Modern Poetry Studies; Anteus; The Paris Review; American Book Review; The Hungry Mind Review. Honours: New York State Council on the Arts Award Grants in Poetry, 1972, 1977; American Book Award, 1990; PEN American Centre Short Fiction Award, 1990. Memberships: PEN; Academy of American Poets; National Book Critics Circle; Poetry Society of America; Poets House, NYC. Literary Agent: Shelley Roth Agency. Address: P O Box 15, Andover, NJ 07821, USA.

GIOVANNI Nikki, (Yolande Cornelia Giovanni), b. 7 June 1943, Knoxville, Tennessee, USA. Poet; Writer; Professor of Creative Writing. 1 son. Education: BA, Fisk University, 1967; School of Social Work, University of Pennsylvania, 1967; Columbia University, 1968. Appointments: Assistant Professor, Queens College of the City University of New York, 1968; Associate Professor, Livingston College, Rutgers University, 1968-72; Founder-Publisher, Niktom Publishers, 1970-74; Visiting Professor, Ohio State University, 1984; Professor of Creative Writing, Mount St Joseph on the Ohio, 1985-. Publications: Poetry: Black Judgement, 1968; Black Feeling, Black Talk, 1968; Re: Creation, 1970; Poem for Angela Yvonne Davis, 1970; My House, 1972; The Women and the Men, 1975; Cotton Candy on a Rainy Day, 1978; Those Who Ride the Night Winds, 1983. Children's Poetry: Spin a Soft Black Dog, 1971, revised edition, 1985; Ego Tripping and Other Poems for Young Readers, 1973; Vacation Time, 1980; Knoxville, Tennessee, 1994. Non-Fiction: Gemini: An Extended Autobiographical Statement on My First Twenty-Five Years of Being a Black Poet, 1971; A Dialogue: James Baldwin and Nikki Giovanni, 1973; A Poetic Equation: Conversations Between Nikki Giovanni and Margaret Walker, 1974; Sacred Cows ... and Other Edibles, 1988; Conversations with Nikki Giovanni, 1992; Racism 101, 1994. Editor: Night Comes Softly: An Anthology of Black Female Voices, 1970; Appalachian Elders: A Warm Hearth Sampler (with Cathee Dennison), 1991; Grandmothers: Poems, Reminiscences, and Short Stories About the Keepers of Our Traditions, 1994. Honours: Ford Foundation Grant, 1968; National Endowment for the Arts Grant, 1969; Honorary doctorates. Address: c/o William Morrow Inc, 105 Madison Avenue, New York, NY 10016, USA.

GIRST Jack Alan, b. 27 April 1948, Pontiac, Michigan, USA. m. Kathie Walter, 27 Dec 1973, 1 son, 2 daughters. Education: BS, Sterling College, 1970. Publications: Dear Rufus, Your A Bull, 1989; A Mighty, Muddy Lesson, 1989; Renfro Would Rather Rest, 1989; Every Bunny Needs A Bear Friend, 1989. Address: 2409 North Waldron, Hutchinson, KS 67502, USA.

GISSURARSON Hannes H, b. 19 Feb 1953, Reykjavik, Iceland. Education: BA, MA, University of Iceland; DPhil, Oxford University, 1985. Appointments: Assistant Professor, 1988-92, Associate Professor, 1992-95, Professor of Politics, 1995-, University of Iceland, Reykjavik. Publications: Hayek's Conservative Liberalism, 1987; Island. Arvet från Thingvellir, 1990; Jon Thorlaksson, 1992; Benjamin Eriksson, 1996; Overfishing: The Icelandic Solution, 1998; 7 other books. Contributions to: Journal of Economic Affairs; Wall Street Journal; Others. Honours: 1st Prize, Essay Competition, Mont Pelerin Society, 1984; Collingwood Scholar, Pembroke College, 1984-85. Address: University of Iceland, 101 Reykjavik, Iceland.

GIULIANO Maurizio, b. 24 Feb 1975, Milan, Italy. Writer; Journalist. Education: University College, Oxford, 1993-96; BA, Oxford University, 1996; Fitzwilliam College, Cambridge, 1996-97; MPhil, Cambridge University, 1997. Appointments: President, Oxford International Forum, Oxford University, 1994-96; Treasurer, Oxford University L'Chaim Society, 1995. Publications: La Transicion Cubana y el Bloqueo Norteamericano, 1996; El Caso CEA, 1997. Contributor to: El Mundo, Spain; ABC, Spain; Publico, Portugal; Il Sabato, Italy; Ha'Aretz, Israel; Mensaje, Chile; Somos, Argentina; Cosas, Chile; Eleftherotypia, Greece. Address: Via della Commenda 41, 20122 Milan, Italy.

GIVNER Joan (Mary), b. 5 Sept 1936, Manchester, England. Retired Professor of English; Writer. m. David Givner, 15 Apr 1965, 2 daughters. Education: BA, 1958, PhD, 1972, University of London; MA, Washington University, St Louis, 1962. Appointments: Professor of English, University of Regina, 1965-95; Editor, Wascana Review, 1984-92. Publications: Katherine Anne Porter: A Life, 1982, revised edition, 1991; Tentacles of Unreason, 1985; Katherine Anne Porter: Conversations (editor), 1987; Unfortunate Incidents, 1988; Mazo de la Roche:

The Hidden Life, 1989; Scenes from Provincial Life, 1991; The Self-Portrait of a Literary Biographer, 1993; In the Garden of Henry James, 1996. Membership: Saskatchewan Writers' Guild. Address: 2587 Seaview Road, RR 1, Mill Bay, British Columbia, Canada V0R 2P0.

GLADSTONE Mrs Arthur M. See: **WORTH Helen.**

GLADSTONE William. See: **WICKHAM Glynne.**

GLAISTER Lesley Gillian, b. 4 Oct 1956, Wellinborough, Northamptonshire, England. Writer. 3 sons. Education: MA, University of Sheffield. Publications: Honour Thy Father; Trick or Treat; Digging to Australia; Limestone and Clay, 1993; Partial Eclipse, 1994; The Private Parts of Women, 1996; Easy Peasy, 1997. Honours: Somerset Maugham Award; Betty Trask Award; Yorkshire Author of Year Award, 1993. Membership: Royal Society of Literature, fellow. Address: 43 Walton Road, Sheffield S11 8RE, England.

GLANVILLE Brian Lester, b. 24 Sept 1931, London, England. Author; Journalist. m. Elizabeth Pamela De Boer, 19 Mar 1959, 2 sons, 2 daughters. Appointments: Football Correspondent and Sports Columnist, Sunday Times, 1958-92; Sports Columnist, The People, 1992-96, The Times 1996-98; Sunday Times, 1998-. Publications: The Reluctant Dictator, 1952; Henry Sows the Wind, 1954; Along the Arno, 1956; The Bankrupts, 1958; After Rome Africa, 1959; A Bad Streak, short stories, 1961; Diamond, 1962; The Director's Wife, short stories, 1963; The King of Hackney Marshes, short stories, 1965; The Olympian, 1969; A Cry of Crickets, 1970; Goalkeepers are Different, children's novel, 1971; The Thing He Loves, 1973; Never Look Back, 1980; Kissing America, 1985; Love Is Not Love, 1985; The Catacomb, 1988. Sporting Books: Soccer Nemesis, 1955; Footballer's Companion, editor, 1962; The Joy of Football, editor, 1986; Champions of Europe, 1991; Story of the World Cup, 1993; Football Memories, 1999. Contributions to: New Statesman; Spectator. Honour: Thomas Y Coward Award, New York, 1969. Hobby: Playing Football. Address: 160 Holland Park Avenue, London W11 4UH, England.

GLAZEBROOK Philip Kirkland, b. 3 Apr 1937, London, England. Writer. m. Clare Rosemary Gemmell, 5 Oct 1968, 2 sons, 2 daughters. Education: MA, Trinity College, Cambridge. Publications: Try Pleasure, 1968; The Eye of the Beholder, 1975; Byzantine Honeymoon, 1978; Journey to Kars, 1985; Captain Vinegar's Commission, 1988; The Walled Garden, 1989; The Gate at the End of the World, 1989; Journey to Khiva, 1992. Contributions to: Spectator; Sunday Times; New York Times; Washington Post; Daily Telegraph. Literary Agent: Richard Scott Simon. Address: Strode Manor, Bridport, Dorset, England.

GLEASNER Diana (Cottle), b. 26 Apr 1936, New Brunswick, New Jersey, USA. Writer. m. G William Gleasner, 12 July 1958, 1 son, 1 daughter. Education: BA cum laude, Ohio Wesleyan University, 1958; MA, University of Buffalo, 1964. Publications: The Plaid Mouse, 1966; Pete Polar Bear's Trip Down the Erie Canal, 1970; Women in Swimming, 1975; Women in Track and Field, 1977; Hawaiian Gardens, 1978; Kauai Traveler's Guide, 1978; Oahu Traveler's Guide, 1978; Big Island Traveler's Guide, 1978; Maui Traveler's Guide, 1978; Breakthrough: Women in Writing, 1980; Illustrated Dictionary of Surfing, Swimming and Diving, 1980; Sea Islands of the South, 1980; Rock Climbing, 1980; Callaway Gardens, 1981; Inventions That Changed Our Lives: Dynamite, 1982; Inventions That Changed Our Lives: The Movies, 1983; Breakthrough: Women in Science, 1983; Charlotte: A Touch of Gold, 1983; Woodloch Pines - An American Dream, 1984; Windsurfing, 1985; Lake Norman - Our Inland Sea, 1986; Governor's Island - From the Beginning, 1988; R Ving America's Backroads - Florida, 1989; Touring by Bus at Home and Abroad, 1989; The Strange and Terrible Adventures of Popoki, The Hawaiian Cat, 1996; Florida off the Beaten Path, 5th edition, 1998. Contributions to: Numerous magazines and newspapers. Memberships: American Society of Journalists and Authors; Society of American Travel Writers; Travel Journalists Guild. Address: 7994 Holly Court, Denver, NC 28037, USA.

GLECKNER Robert F(rancis), b. 2 Mar 1925, Rahway, New Jersey, USA. Professor of English; Writer; Editor. m. Glenda Jean Karr, 7 Feb 1946, 1 son, 1 daughter. Education: BA, magna cum laude, Williams College, 1948; PhD, Johns Hopkins University, 1954. Appointments: Editor, Research Studies Institute, Maxwell Air Force Base, Alabama, 1951-52; Instructor in English, University of Cincinnati, 1952-54, University of Wisconsin at Madison, 1954-57; Assistant Professor, Associate Professor of English, Wayne State University, 1957-62; Associate Editor, 1959-62, Advisory Editor, 1962-76, Criticism; Professor of English, 1962-78, Chairman, Department of English, 1962-66, Associate Dean, College of Letters and Sciences, 1968-70, Dean, College of Humanities and Fine Arts, 1970-75, University of California at Riverside: Professor of English, 1978-, Acting Chairman, Department of English, 1982, Director, Graduate Studies, 1986-88, Duke University; Advisory Editor, Romanticism Past and Present, 1979-87, Byron Journal, 1990-, South Atlantic Review, 1997-. Publications: The Piper and the Bard: A Study of William Blake, 1957; Romanticism: Points of View (editor with G Enscoe), 1962, 2nd edition, revised as sole editor, 1970; Selected Writings of William Blake (editor), 1967, revised edition, 1970; Byron and the Ruins of Paradise, 1967; The Poetical Works of Byron (editor), 1975; Blake's Prelude: "Poetical Sketches", 1982; Blake and Spenser, 1985; Approaches to the Teaching of Blake's "Songs" (author and editor with Mark Greenberg), 1989; Critical Essays on Lord Byron, 1991; Gray Agonistes: Thomas Gray, Milton, and Masculine Friendship, 1996; Critical Essays on Byron's Plays (editor with Bernard Beatty), 1997; The Lessons of Romaniticism (editor with Thomas Pfau), 1998. Contributions to: Scholarly books and journals. Honours: Poetry Society of America Award, 1957; Faculty Research Lecturer, University of California, 1973; National Endowment for the Humanities Research Fellowship, 1980-81; Visiting Fellow, 1987, Mellon Fellow, 1991, Henry E Huntington Library; Distinguished Scholar, Keats-Shelley Association of America, 1991; Honorary Fellow, Center for Ideas and Society, University of California at Riverside, 1991, 1993. Memberships: International Byron Society; American Society for Eighteenth-Century Studies; Association of Scholars and Literary Critics; Keats-Shelley Association; Modern Language Association; Wordsworth-Coleridge Association. Address: c/o Department of English, Box 90015, Duke University, Durham, NC 27708, USA.

GLEN Duncan Munro, (Ronald Eadie Munro), b. 11 Jan 1933, Cambuslang, Lanarkshire, Scotland. Retired Professor; Poet; Writer. m. Margaret Eadie, 4 Jan 1958, 1 son, 1 daughter. Education: Rutherglen Academy; Edinburgh College of Art. Appointments: Lecturer to Principal Lecturer, South Lancashire University, 1965-78; Professor and Head of the Department of Visual Communication, Nottingham Trent University, 1972-87. Publications: Hugh MacDiarmid and the Scottish Renaissance, 1964; Selected Essays of Hugh MacDiarmid (editor), 1969; In Appearances: A Sequence of Poems, 1971; The Individual and the Twentieth Century Scottish Literary Tradition, 1971; Buits and Wellies: A Sequence of Poems, 1976; Gaitherings (poems), 1977; Realities (poems), 1980; The Turn of the Earth: A Sequence of Poems, 1985; The Autobiography of a Poet, 1986; Tales to Be Told, 1987; European Poetry in Scotland (editor), 1990; Selected Poems, 1965-90, 1991; The Poetry of the Scots, 1991; Hugh MacDiarmid: Out of Langhoom and Into the World, 1992; Echoes: Frae Classical and Italian Poetry, 1992; The Bright Writers' Guides to Scottish Culture, 1995; A Nation in a Parish: A New Historical Prospect of Scotland, 1995; Splendid Lanarkshire, 1997; Selected New Poems 1987-1996, 1998; Illustrious Fife, 1998. Contributions to: Numerous journals and magazines. Honours: Special Prize for Services to Scottish Literature, Scottish Arts Council, 1975; Howard Sergeant Poetry Award, 1993. Membership: Chartered Society of Designers, fellow. Address: 33 Lady Nairn Avenue, Kirkcaldy, Fife KY1 2AW, Scotland.

GLENDINNING Victoria, b. 23 Apr 1937, Sheffield, England. Author; Journalist. m. (1) O N V Glendinning, 1958, 4 sons, (2) Terence de Vere White, 1981, (3) K P O'Sullivan, 1996. Education: BA, Honours, Modern Languages, Somerville College, Oxford, 1959; Diploma, Social Administration, 1969. Appointment: Editorial Assistant, Times Literary Supplement, 1970-74. Publications: A Suppressed Cry: Life and Death of a Quaker Daughter, 1969; Elizabeth Bowen: Portrait of a Writer, 1977; Edith Sitwell: A Unicorn Among Lions, 1981; Vita: The Life of Victoria Sackville-West, 1983; Rebecca West: A Life, 1987; The Grown-ups (novel), 1989; Hertfordshire, 1989; Trollope, 1992; Electricity (novel), 1995; Sons and Mothers (co-editor), 1996; Jonathan Swift, 1998. Contributions to: Various journals, newspapers and magazines. Honours: Duff Cooper Memorial Award, 1981; James Tait Black Prize, 1981; Whitbread Awards, 1983, 1992; Whitbread Award, Trollope, 1992; Honorary DLitt, Southampton University, 1994, University of Ulster, 1995, Trinity College, Dublin, 1995; Commander of the Order of the British Empire, 1998. Memberships: Royal Society of Literature; PEN. Address: David Higham Associates, 5/8 Lower John Street, Golden Square, London W1, England.

GLENDOWER Rose. See: **HARRIS Marion Rose.**

GLISSANT Édouard, b. 21 Sept 1928, Sainte-Marie, Martinique. Distinguished Professor; Writer; Dramatist; Poet. Education: DPhil, 1953, State Doctorate, 1977, Sorbonne, Université de Paris; Musée de l'homme, Paris. Appointments: Instructor in Philosophy, Lycée des Jeunes Filles, Fort-de-France, Martinique, 1965; Founder, 1967, Director, 1967-78, Institut Martiniquais d'Études, Fort-de-France; Co-Founder, ACOMA Review, 1970; Editor, UNESCO, Paris, France, 1981-88; Distinguished Professor and Director of Center for French and Francophone Studies, Louisiana State University, Baton Rouge, USA, 1988-. Publications: Poetry: Un champ d'îles, 1953; La terre inquiète, 1954; Les Indes: Poèmes de l'une et l'autre terre, 1955; Le sel noir, 1959; Le sang rivé, 1960; Poèmes, 1963; Boises, 1979; Pays rêvé, pays réel, 1985; Fastes, 1992. Non-Fiction: Soleil de la conscience, 1956; L'intention poétique, 1969; Le discours antillais, 1981, English translation as Caribbean Discourse: Selected Essays, 1989; Poétique de la relation, 1990. Fiction: La Lézarde, 1958; Le quatrième siècle, 1964; Malemort, 1975; La case du commandeur, 1981; Mahagony, 1987; Tout-monde, 1993. Play: Monsieur Toussaint, 1961, revised version, 1978. Honours: Ordre des Francophones d'Amérique, Quebec; Prix Rénaudot, 1958; Prix Charles Veillon, 1965; Award, 12th Putterbaugh Conference, Norman, Oklahoma, 1989; Honorary LittD, York University, 1989; Roger Callois International Prize, 1991. Address: 213 Prescott, Baton Rouge, LA 70803, USA.

GLOAG Julian, b. 2 July 1930, London, England. Novelist. 1 son, 1 daughter. Education: Exhibitioner, BA, 1953, MA, 1959, Magdalene College, Cambridge. Publications: Our Mother's House, 1963; A Sentence of Life, 1966; Maundy, 1969; A Woman of Character, 1973; Sleeping Dogs Lie, 1980; Lost and Found, 1981; Blood for Blood, 1985; Only Yesterday, 1986; Love as a Foreign Language, 1991; Le passeur de la nuit, 1996; Chambre d'ombre, 1996. Teleplays: Only Yesterday, 1986; The Dark Room, 1988. Memberships: Royal Society of Literature, fellow; Authors Guild. Address: c/o Michelle Lapautre, 6 rue Jean Carriès, 75007 Paris, France.

GLOVER Douglas (Herschel), b. 14 Nov 1948, Simcoe, Ontario, Canada. Writer; Editor. Education: BA, York University, 1969; MLitt, University of Edinburgh, 1971; MFA. University of Iowa, 1982. Appointments: Various writer-in-residencies; Lecturer, Skidmore College, 1992, 1993; Visiting Professor, Colgate University, 1995. Publications: The Mad River, 1981; Precious, 1984; Dog Attempts to Drown Man in Saskatoon, 1985; The South Will Rise at Noon, 1988; A Guide to Animal Behaviour, 1991; Coming Attractions (co-editor), 5 volumes,

1991-95; The Life and Times of Captain N, 1993; The Journey Prize Anthology (editor), 1994; Best Canadian Stories (editor), 1996, 1997. Contributions to: Numerous journals and magazines. Honours: Contributor's Prize, Canadian Fiction Magazine, 1985; Literary Press Group Writers Choice Award, 1986; National Magazine Award for Fiction, 1990. Membership: Writers' Union of Canada. Address: RR 1, Waterford, Ontario, Canada N0E 1Y0.

GLOVER Judith, b. 31 Mar 1943, Wolverhampton, England. Author. 2 daughters. Education: Wolverhampton High School for Girls, 1954-59; Aston Polytechnic, 1960. Publications: Drink Your Own Garden (non-fiction), 1979; The Sussex Quartet: The Stallion Man, 1982, Sisters and Brothers, 1984, To Everything a Season, 1986; Birds in a Gilded Cage, 1987; The Imagination of the Heart, 1989; Tiger Lilies, 1991; Mirabelle, 1992; Minerva Lane, 1994; Pride of Place, 1995. Address: c/o Artellus Ltd, 30 Dorset House, Gloucester Place, London NW1 5AD, England.

GLÜCK Louise (Elisabeth), b. 22 Apr 1943, New York, New York, USA. Author; Poet. m. (1) Charles Hertz, div; (2) John Dranow, 1 Jan 1977, div 1996. 1 son. Education: Sarah Lawrence College, 1962; Columbia University, 1963-66, 1967-68. Appointments: Artist-in-Residence, 1971-72, Faculty Member, 1973-74, Goddard College, Plainfield, Vermont; Poet-in-Residence, University of North Carolina at Greensboro, 1973; Visiting Professor, University of Iowa, 1976-77, Columbia University, 1979, University of California at Davis, 1983; Faculty Member, Board Member, MFA Writing Program, 1976-80; Ellison Professor of Poetry, University of Cincinnati, 1978; Faculty Member, Board Member, MFA Writing Program, Warren Wilson College, Swannoa, North Carolina, 1980-84; Holloway Lecturer, University of California at Berkeley, 1982; Scott Professor of Poetry, 1983, Senior Lecturer in English, part-time, 1984-, Williams College, Williamstown, Massachusetts; Parrish Professor, Williams, 1997-; Regents Professor of Poetry, University of California at Los Angeles, 1985-88; Phi Beta Kappa Poet, 1990, Visiting Professor, 1995, Harvard University; Hurst Professor, Brandeis University, 1996. Publications: Poetry: Firstborn, 1968; The House on the Marshland, 1975; The Garden, 1976; Descending Figure, 1980; The Triumph of Achilles, 1985; Ararat, 1990; The Wild Iris, 1992; The First Four Book of Poems, 1995; Meadowlands, 1996. Other: Proofs and Theories: Essays on Poetry, 1994; Vita Nova, forthcoming. Contributions to: Many anthologies and periodicals. Honours: Academy of American Poets Prize, 1967; Rockefeller Foundation Grant, 1968-69; National Endowment for the Arts Fellowships, 1969-70, 1979-80, 1988-89; Eunice Tietjens Memorial Prize, 1971; Guggenheim Fellowships, 1975-76, 1987-88; Vermont Council for the Arts Grant, 1978-79; American Academy and Institute of Arts and Letters Award, 1981; National Book Critics Circle Award, 1985; Melville Cane Award, Poetry Society of America, 1985; Sara Teasdale Memorial Prize, Wellesley College, 1986; Co-recipient, Bobbitt National Prize, 1992; Pulitzer Prize in Poetry, 1993; William Carlos Williams Award, 1993; LLD, Williams College, 1993; Poet Laureate of Vermont, 1994; PEN/Martha Albrand Award, 1995; LLD, Skidmore College, 1995; LLD, Middlebury College, 1996. Memberships: American Academy of Arts and Sciences, fellow; PEN; American Academy and Institute of Arts and Letters. Address: 14 Ellsworth Park, Cambridge, MA 02139, USA.

GOAD Johnny. See: PHILANDERSON Flavian Titus.

GODBER John (Harry), b. 18 May 1956, Upton, Yorkshire, England. Dramatist. m. Jane Thornton, 1993, 2 daughters. Education: Bretton Hall College, West Bretton, Yorkshire, 1974-78; CertEd, 1977, BEd, Honours, 1978, MA, Theatre, 1979, PhD, 1979-83, Leeds University. Appointment: Artistic Director, Hull Truck Theatre Co, 1984-. Publications: Up 'N' Under, 1985; Bouncers, 1986; Shakers (with Jan Thornton), 1986; John Godber: 5 Plays, 1989; Teachers, 1990; On the Piste, 1991; April in Paris, 1992; Blood, Sweat and Tears, 1995; Lucky Sods, 1995; Passion Killers, 1995; Gym and Tonic, 1996; Weekend Breaks, 1997; It Started With A Kiss!, 1997; Perfect Pitch, 1998; Up 'n' Under (feature

film), 1998. Contributions to: Stage, film, and television. Honours: Sunday Times Playwriting Award, 1981; Edinburgh Festival Awards, 1981, 1982, 1984, 1988; Olivier Award for Comedy of the Year, 1984; Los Angeles Drama Critics Circle Award, 1986; Honorary DLitt, Hull University, 1988, Humberside University, 1997. Address: 64 Riverview Avenue, North Ferriby, Humberside HU14 3DT, England.

GODBOUT Jacques, b. 27 Nov 1933, Montreal, Quebec, Canada. Author; Poet; Filmmaker. m. Ghislaine Reiher, 31 July 1954, 2 children. Education: BA, 1953, MA, 1954, University of Montreal. Appointments: Lecturer, 1969, Writer-in-Residence, 1991-92, University of Montreal; Visiting Lecturer, University of California at Berkeley, 1985. Publications: Novels: L'aquarium, 1962; Le couteau sur la table, 1965; English translation as Knife on the Table, 1968; Salut Galarneau!, 1967; English translation as Hail Galarneau!, 1970; D'Amour, PQ, 1972; L'ile au dragon, 1976; English translation as Dragon Island, 1979; Les tetes a Papineau, 1981; Une histoire americaine, 1986; English translation as an American Story, 1988; Le temps des Galarneau, 1993. Poetry: Carton-pate, 1956; Les pavés secs, 1958; La chair est un commencement, 1959; C'est la chaude loi des hommes, 1960; La grande muraille de Chine (with J R Colombo), 1969. Essays: Le réformiste, 1975; Le murmure marchand, 1984; L'écran du bonheur, 1990. Journal: Ecrivain de province, 1991. Other: many films. Honours: Prix France-Canada, 1962; Prix de l'Académie Francaise, 1965; Governor-General's Award for Fiction, 1968; Various film prizes. Address: 815 Pratt, Montreal, Quebec H2V 2T7, Canada.

GODFREY (William) Dave, b. 9 Aug 1938, Winnipeg, Manitoba, Canada. Novelist. m. Ellen Swartz, 1963, 2 sons, 1 daughter. Education: BA, 1960, MFA, 1963, PhD, 1966, University of Iowa; MA, Stanford University, 1963; University of Chicago, 1965. Appointments: General Editor, Canadian Writers Series, McClelland and Stewart, 1968-72; Co Founding Editor, News Press, Toronto, 1969-73; Editor, Press Porcepic, Erin, Ontario, 1972-; Vice President, Inter Provincial Association for Telematcis and Telidon, 1982-. Publications: The New Ancestors, 1970; Short Stories: Death Goes Better with Coca Cola, 1967; New Canadian Writing, 1968, 1969; Dark Must Yield, 1978; Other Non Fiction Works. Honours: University of Western Ontario Presidents Medal, 1965; Canada Council Award, 1969; Governor-General's Award, 1971. Address: Porcepic Books, 4252 Commerce Circle, Vancouver, British Columbia V87 4M2, Canada.

GODFREY Martyn N, b. 17 Apr 1949, Birmingham, England. (Naturalised Canadian citizen). Writer. m. Carolyn Boswell, 1973, div 1985, 2 children. Education: BA, Honours, 1973, BEd, 1974, University of Toronto. Appointments: Elementary School Teacher, in Kitchener and Waterloo, Ontario, Canada, 1974-77, Mississauga, Ontario, 1977-80, Assumption, Alberta, 1980-82; Junior High School Teacher, Edson, Alberta, 1983-85; Writer, 1985-. Publications: Children: The Last War, 1986; It Isn't Easy Being Ms Teeny-Wonderful, 1987; Wild Night, 1987; More Than Weird, 1987; Rebel Yell, 1987; It Seemed Like a Good Idea at the Time, 1987; Baseball Crazy, 1987; Sweat Hog, 1988; Send in Ms Teeny-Wonderful, 1988; In the Time of the Monsters, 1988; The Day the Sky Exploded, 1991; Don't Worry About Me, I'm Just Crazy, 1992; Wally Stutzgummer, 1992. Honours: Award for Best Children's Short Story, Canadian Authors Association, 1985; Award for Best Children's Book, University of Lethbridge, 1987. Memberships: Writers Union of Canada; Canadian Authors Association; Canadian Society of Children's Authors, Illustrators and Performers; Writers Guild of Alberta, vice president, 1986, president, 1987. Canada. Address: c/o Killock and Associates, 11017-80 Avenue, Edmonton, Alberta T6G 0R2, Canada.

GODFREY Paul, b. 16 Sept 1960, Exeter, Devon, England. Playwright; Director. Publications: Inventing a New Colour, 1988; A Bucket of Eels, 1989; Once in a While the Odd Thing Happens, 1990; The Blue Ball, 1993; The Modern Husband, 1994; The Candidate, 1995;

The Invisible Woman, 1996; Catalogue of Misunderstanding, 1997; Collected Plays, Volume One, 1998. Literary Agent: Julia Kreitman, The Agency, 24 Pottery Lane, W11, England. Address: c/o The Agency, 24 Pottery Lane, W11, England.

GODKIN Celia Marilyn, b. 15 Apr 1948, London, England, Teacher; Illustrator; Children's Author; Biologist. Education: BSc, London University, 1969; MSc, University of Toronto, 1983; AOCA, Ontario College of Art, 1983. Publications: Wolf Island; Ladybug Garden; Sea Otter Inlet, 1997; Illustrator, Black Nell: The Adventures of a Coyote, by Shirley Woods, 1998; Flying Lessons, 1999. Contributions to: Bulletin of Marine Science; Environmental Biology of Fishes; Guild of Natural Science Illustrators Newsletter. Honours: Best Information Book Award; Honour Book, Children's Literature Round Tables of Canada, 1995. Memberships: Guild of Natural Science Illustrators; Canadian Society of Children's Authors, Illustrators and Performers; Writer's Union of Canada. Literary Agent: Jill Greenberg, Scovil Chichak Galen Literary Agency, 381 Park Ave South, Suite 1020, New York, NY 10016. Address: Division of Biomedical Communications, University of Toronto, Medical Sciences Building, 1 King's College Circle, Toronto, Ontario M5S 1A8, Canada.

GODLEY John Raymond, 3rd Lord Kilbracken, b. 17 Oct 1920, London, England. Author; Journalist; Labour Backbencher, House of Lords. m. (1) Penelope Reyne, 22 May 1943, div, 2 sons, 1 dec, (2) Susan Heazlewood, 15 May 1981, div, 1 son. Education: BA, MA, 1948, Balliol College, Oxford. Appointments: Served in RNVR (Air Branch) as Pilot, 1940-46; Lt-Commander, 1945; Commander, 835 Naval Air Squadron; Reporter, Daily Mirror, 1947-49, Sunday Express, 1949-51; Foreign Correspondent, Evening Standard, 1960-65; Editorial Director, Worldwatch, 1984-85. Publications: Even For an Hour (poems), 1940; Tell Me the Next One, 1951; Letters from Early New Zealand (editor), 1951; Living Like a Lord, 1955; A Peer Behind the Curtain, 1959; Shamrocks and Unicorns, 1962; Van Meegeren, 1967; Bring Back My Stringbag, 1979; The Easy Way to Bird Recognition, 1982; The Easy Way to Tree Recognition, 1983; The Easy Way to Wild Flower Recognition, 1984. Contributions to: As writer and photographer to British, US and overseas journals. Honours: Distinguished Service Cross, Royal Navy, 1945; Times Educational Supplement Senior Information Book Award, 1982. Address: Killegar, County Leitrim, Ireland.

GODMAN Arthur, b. 10 Oct 1916, Hereford, England. Educationalist. m. Jean Barr Morton, 24 June 1950, 2 sons, 1 daughter. Education: BSc, 1937, BSc Hons, Chemistry, 1938, University College, London; Dip Ed, Institute of Education, London, 1939; Malay Government Exam Standard III, 1948; CChem. Appointments: Colonial Education Service, 1946-63; Educational Consultant, Longman Group, 1966-77; Honorary Fellow, University of Kent, Eliot College, 1978-; Research Fellow, Department of South East Asian Studies, 1978-94. Publications: Chemistry: A New Certificate Approach (with S T Bajah), 1969; Human and Social Biology, 1973; Dictionary of Scientific Usage (with E M F Payne), 1979; Illustrated Science Dictionary, 1981; Illustrated Dictionary of Chemistry, 1981; Illustrated Thesaurus of Computer Sciences, 1984; Energy Supply, 1990. Contributions to: Babel, 1990. Memberships: Society of Authors; Royal Society of Chemistry; Royal Asiatic Society. Address: Sondes House, Patrixbourne, Canterbury, Kent CT4 5DD, England.

GODWIN Gail Kathleen, b. 18 June 1937, Birmingham, Alabama, USA. Writer. m. 1) Douglas Kennedy, 1960, div 1961, 2), Ian Marshall, 1965, div 1966. Education: Peace Junior College, Raleigh, North Carolina, 1955-57; BA in Journalism, University of North Carolina, 1959; MA in English, 1968, PhD, 1971, University of Iowa. Appointments: Staff, Miami Herald, 1959-60, US Travel Service, London, 1961-65; Editorial Assistant, Saturday Evening Post, 1966; Instructor, University of Iowa, 1967-71; Lecturer, Iowa Writer's Workshops, 1972-73; Vassar College, 1977, Columbia

University Writing Program, 1978, 1981. Publications: Novels: The Perfectionists, 1970; Glass People, 1972; The Odd Woman, 1974; Violet Clay, 1978; A Mother and Two Daughters, 1982; The Finishing School, 1984; A Southern Family, 1987; Father Melancholy's Daughter, 1991; The Good Husband, 1994. Librettos: The Last Lover, 1975; Journals of a Songmaker, 1976; Apollonia, 1979; Anna Margarita's Will, 1981; Remembering Felix, 1987. Editor: The Best American Short Stories, 1985 (with Shannon Ravenel), 1985. Honours: Fellow, Center for Advanced Study, University of Illinois, 1971-72; National Endowment for the Arts Grant, 1974-75; Guggenheim Fellowship, 1975-76; American Academy and Institute of Arts and Letters Award, 1981; Janet Kafka Award, University of Rochester, 1988; Thomas Wolfe Memorial Award, Lipinsky Endowment of the Western North Carolina Historical Association, 1988. Memberships: American Society of Composers, Authors, and Publishers; Authors Guild; Authors League; PEN. Address: PO Box 946, Woodstock, NY 12498, USA.

GODWIN Peter (Christopher), b. 4 Dec 1957, Rhodesia. Journalist; Writer. Education: MA, Cambridge University. Appointments: East European Correspondent, 1984-86, Africa Correspondent, 1986-, The Sunday Times, London. Publication: Rhodesians Never Die: The Impact of War and Political Change on White Rhodesia, 1970-1980 (with Ian Hancock), 1993. Contributions to: Newspapers and periodicals. Honour: Commended, British Press Awards, 1984. Membership: Foreign Correspondents Association. Address: c/o The Sunday Times, Foreign Department, 1 Pennington Street, London E1, England.

GODWIN Rebecca Thompson, b. 9 July 1950, Charleston, South Carolina, USA. Writer. m. (1) 2 daughters, (2) Deane Bogardus, 24 Aug 1988. Education: BA, Coastal Carolina College, 1977; MA, Middlebury College, 1988. Appointments: Teacher, Bennington Writing Workshops, 1995; Wildacres Writing Workshops, 1996. Publications: Private Parts, 1992; Keeper of the House, 1994. Contributions to: South Carolina Review; Paris Review; Iris; Crescent Review; First Magazine. Honours: Winner, S C Fiction Project, 1988; National Endowment for the Arts Grant, 1994-95. Membership: Associate Writing Programme. Literary Agent: Colleen Mohyde, Doe Coover Agency, Winchester, MA, USA. Address: PO Box 211, Poestenkill, NY 12140, USA.

GOEDICKE Patricia, b. 21 June 1931, Boston, Massachusetts, USA. Professor of Creative Writing; Poet. m. Leonard Wallace Robinson, 3 June 1971. Education: BA, Middlebury College, 1953; MA, Ohio University, 1965. Appointments: Lecturer in English, Ohio University, 1963-68, Hunter College, 1969-71; Associate Professor of Creative Writing, Instituto Allende, 1972-79; Visiting Writer-in-Residence, Kalamazoo College, 1977; Guest Faculty, Writing Programme, Sarah Lawrence College, 1980; Visiting Poet-in-Residence, 1981-83, Associate Professor, 1983-90, Professor of Creative Writing, 1990-, University of Montana. Publications: Between Oceans, 1968; For the Four Corners, 1976; The Trail That Turns on Itself, 1978; The Dog That Was Barking Yesterday, 1980; Crossing the Same River, 1980; The King of Childhood, 1984; The Wind of Our Going, 1985; Listen Love, 1986; The Tongues We Speak: New and Selected Poems, 1989; Paul Bunyan's Bearskin, 1992; Invisible Horses, 1996. Contributions to: Reviews, journals, and periodicals. Honours: National Endowment for the Arts Fellowship, 1976; Pushcart Prize, 1977-78; Honourable Mention, Arvon International Poetry Competition, 1987; Honourable Award, Memphis State Review, 1988; Research Grant, 1989, Distinguished Scholar, 1991, University of Montana. Memberships: Academy of American Poets; Associated Writing Programs; Poetry Society of America. Address: 310 McLeod Avenue, Missoula, MT 59801, USA.

GOFF James Rudolph Jr, b. 9 Jan 1957, Goldsboro, North Carolina, USA. Historian; Writer. m. Connie Goff, 22 Dec 1978, 1 son, 1 daughter. Education: BA, Wake Forest University, 1978; MDiv, Duke University, 1981; PhD, University of Arkansas, 1987. Appointments:

Teaching Assistant, University of Arkansas, 1982-86; Lecturer, 1986-87, 1988-89, Instructor, 1987-88, Assistant Professor, 1989-94, Associate Professor, 1994-, Appalachian State University, Boone, North Carolina. Publication: Fields White Unto Harvest. Contributions to: Christianity Today; Kansas History; Ozark Historical Review; Pentecostals from The Inside Out. Honours: Faculty Award; Phi Theta Kappa; Gordon H McNeil Award; Charles Oxford Scholar. Memberships: Organization of American Church Historians; Organization of American Historians; Society for Pentecostal Studies; Southern Historical Association. Address: Department of History, Appalachian State University, Boone, NC 28608, USA.

GOLD Herbert, b. 9 Mar 1924, Cleveland, Ohio, USA. Author. m. (1) Edith Zubrin, Apr 1948, div 1956, 2 daughters, (2) Melissa Dilworth, Jan 1968, div 1975, 2 sons, 1 daughter. Education: BA, 1946, MA, 1948, Columbia University; Licences-Lettres, Sorbonne, University of paris, 1951. Appointments: Lecturer, Western Reserve University, 1951-53; Faculty, Wayne State University, 1954-56; Visiting Professor, Cornell University, 1958, University of California at Berkeley, 1963, 1968, Harvard University, 1964, Stanford University, 1967; Mcguffey Lecturer in English, Ohio University, 1971; Regents Professor, 1973, Visiting Professor, 1974-79, 1985, University of California at Davis. Publications: Fiction: Birth of a Hero, 1951; The Prospect Before Us, 1954; The man Who Was Not With It, 1956; 15 x 3 (stories with R V Cassill and James B. Hall), 1957; The Optimist, 1959; Therefore Be Bold, 1960; Love and Like (stories), 1960; Salt, 1963; Father: A Novel in the Form of a Memoir, 1967; The Great American Jackpot, 1969; Biafra Goodbye, 1970; The Magic Will: Stories and Essays of a Decade, 1971; My Last Two Thousand Years, 1972; Swiftie the Magician, 1974; Waiting for Cordelia, 1977; Slave Trade, 1979; He/She, 1980; Family: A Novel in the Form of a Memoir, 1981; True Love, 1982; Mister White Eyes, 1984; Stories of Misbegotten Love, 1985; A Girl of Forty, 1986; Lovers and Cohorts: Twenty Seven Stories, 1986; Dreaming, 1988; She Took My Arm as if She Loved Me, 1997. Non-Fiction: The Age of Happy Problems, 1962; A Walk on the West Side: California on the Brink, 1981; Travels in San Francisco, 1990; Best Nightmare on Earth: A Life In Haiti, 1991; Bohemia: Where Art, Angst, Love and Strong Coffee Meet, 1993. Contributions to: Various periodicals. Honours: Guggenheim Fellowship, 1957; Ohioana Book Award, 1957; National Institute of Arts and Letters Grant, 1958; Longview Foundation Award, 1959; California Literature Medal Award, 1968; Commonwealth Club Award for Best Novel, San Francisco, 1982; Honorary LHD, Baruch College of the City University of New York, 1988; Sherwood Anderson Prize for Fiction, 1989. Address: 1051-A Broadway, San Francisco, CA 94133, USA

GOLD Ivan, b. 12 May 1932, New York, New York, USA. Writer. m. Vera Cochran, 22 Oct 1968, 1 son. Education: BA, Columbia College, New York City, 1953; MA, University of London. Appointments: Writer-in-Residence, Austin Peay State University, 1991, University of Massachusetts, Boston, 1992. Publications: Nickel Miseries; Sick Friends; Sams in a Dry Season. Address: c/o Many Yost Associates, 59 East 54th Street, New York, NY 10022, USA.

GOLD Robert Stanley, b. 19 June 1924, New York City, USA. Professor of English. m. Liliane, 18 Jan 1980, 1 son, 1 daughter. Education: BS, Syracuse University, 1949; MA, 1955, PhD, 1962, New York University. Appointments: Lecturer, English Department, Queens College, 1958-63; English Department, Hunter College, 1962; Professor of English, Jersey City College, 1963-94; Instructor, English Department, Rutgers University, 1995. Publications: A Jazz Lexicon, 1964; Point of Departure (editor), 1967; Controversy (with Stanford Radner), 1969; The Rebel Culture (editor), 1971; Jazz Talk, 1975, reprint 1981; The Roar of the Sneakers (editor), 1977. Contributions to: Reviews. Honour: Outstanding Reference Work, Library Journal, 1964. Address: 167 Orange Road, Montclair, NJ 07042, USA.

GOLDBARTH Albert, b. 31 Jan 1948, Chicago, Illinois, USA. Poet; Writer; Assistant Professor of Creative Writing. Education: BA, University of Illinois, 1969; MFA, University of Iowa, 1971; University of Utah, 1973-74. Appointments: Instructor, Elgin Community College, Illinois, 1971-72, Central YMCA Community College, Chicago, 1971-73, University of Utah, 1973-74; Assistant Professor, Cornell University, 1974-76; Visiting Professor, Syracuse University, 1976; Assistant Professor of Creative Writing, University of Texas at Austin, 1977-. Publications: Poetry: Under Cover, 1973; Coprolites, 1973; Opticks: A Poem in Seven Sections, 1974; Jan 31, 1974; Keeping, 1975; A Year of Happy, 1976; Comings Back: A Sequence of Poems, 1976; Curve: Overlapping Narratives, 1977; Different Flashes, 1979; Eurekas, 1980; Ink Blood Semen, 1980; The Smugglers Handbook, 1980; Faith, 1981; Who Gathered and Whispered Behind Me, 1981; Goldbarth's Book of Occult Phenomena, 1982; Original Light: New and Selected Poems 1973-1983, 1983; Albert's Horoscope Alamanac, 1986; Arts and Sciences, 1986; Popular Culture, 1989; Delft: An Essay Poem, 1990; Heaven and Earth: A Cosmology, 1991; Across the Layers: Poems Old and New, 1993; The Gods, 1993. Fiction: Marriage and Other Science Fiction, 1994. Essays: A Sympathy of Souls, 1990; Great Topics of the World: Essays, 1994. Editor: Every Pleasure: The "Seneca Review" Long Poem Anthology, 1979. Honours: Theodore Roethke Prize, 1972; Ark River Review Prizes, 1973, 1975; National Endowment for the Arts Grants, 1974, 1979; Guggenheim Fellowship, 1983. Address: c/o Department of English, University of Texas at Austin, Austin, TX 78712, USA.

GOLDBERG Barbara June, b. 26 Apr 1943, Wilmington, Delaware, USA. Writer; Poet; Editor. m. (1) J Peter Kiers, 1963, div 1970, (2) Charles Goldberg, 1971, div 1990, 2 sons. Education: BA, Mount Holyoke College, 1963; MA, Yeshiva University, 1969; MEd, Columbia University, 1971; MFA, American University, 1985. Appointments: Director, Editorial Board, The World Works publishers, 1987-; Executive Editor, Poet Lore, 1990-. Publications: Berta Broad Foot and Pepin the Short; Cautionary Tales; The Stones Remember. Contributions to: American Scholar; Antioch Review; New England Review; Bread Loaf Quarterly. Honours: Work in Progress Grant; National Endowment for the Arts Fellowship; Armand G Erpf Award; Writter Bynner Foundation Award. Memberships: Poetry Society of America; Poets and Writers; Poetry Committee, Greater Washington Area. Address: 6623 Fairfax Road, Chevy Chase, MD 20815, USA.

GOLDBERG Bruce, b. 18 Nov 1948, New York City, New York, USA. Dentist; Hypnotherapist; Author. Education: BA, Southern Connecticut State University, 1970; Doctor of Dental Surgery, University of Maryland School of Dentistry, 1974; MS, Counseling Psychology, Loyola College, 1984. Appointments: General practice residency in dentistry, 1974-76; Private practice in general dentistry, 1976-89; Private practice in hypnotherapy, specializing in past life regression/future life progression and conscious dying, 1974-; Consulting Editor, Columnist, FATE magazine, Hypnotic Highways, 1996-. Publications: Past Lives-Future Lives: Accounts of Regressions and Progressions Through Hypnosis, 1982; Past Lives-Future Lives, 1988; The Search for Grace: A Documented Case of Murder and Reincarnation, 1994, 1997; Soul Healing, 1996; Peaceful Transition: The Art of Conscious Dying and the Liberation of the Soul, 1997; Look Younger: Add 25 to 50 Years to Your Life, Naturally, 1998; New Age Hypnosis, 1998; Protected by the Light: The Complete Book of Psychic Self-Defense, 1998; Time Travelers From Our Future: An Explanation of Alien Abductions, 1998. Membership: American Association of Applied and Preventive Psychology; American Psychological Society; Academy of Psychosomatic Medicine. Address: 4300 Natoma Avenue, Woodland Hills, CA 91364, USA.

GOLDBERG Hillel, b. 10 Jan 1946, Denver, Colorado, USA. Writer; Editor; Rabbi. m. Elaine Silberstein, 19 May 1969, 2 sons, 4 daughters. Education: BA, Yeshiva University, 1969; MA, 1972, PhD, 1978, Brandeis

University; Rabbinical Ordination, 1976. Appointments: Co-Publisher and Co-Editor, Tempo, 1964; Executive Editor and Editor of Literary Supplement, Intermountain Jewish News, 1966-; Editor, Pulse, 1968-69; Contributing Editor, Jewish Action, 1987-; Associate Editor, Tradition, 1988-. Publications: Israel Salanter: Text, Structure, Idea, the Ethics and Theology of an Early Psychologist of the Unconscious, 1982; The Fire Within: The Living Heritage of the Musar Movement, 1987; Between Berlin and Slobodka: Jewish Transition Figures from Eastern Europe, 1989; Illuminating the Generations: From the Middle of the Patriarch and Matriarchs to the Musar Thinkers of Our Time, 1992. Contributions to: Newspapers and journals. Honours: Academic Book of the Year Citation, Choice, 1982; Rockower Awards for Distinguished Editorial Writing, 1983, 1986, 1987, 1994; Distinguished New Reportage, 1988; Distinguished personality Profiles, 1996; Distinguished International News Reporting, 1993, 1997; Joseph Polakoff Award, 1994. Memberships: American Jewish Press Association, corresponding secretary; Colarado Press Association. Address: 1275 Sherman Street, Denver, CO 80203, USA.

GOLDBERG Lester, b. 3 Feb 1924, Brooklyn, New York, USA. Real Estate Official; Writer; Poet. m. Dorothy Weinstein, June 1947, 1 son, 3 daughters. Education: BS, City College, 1946. Appointments: Worked in Real Estate, affiliated with State Division of Housing, 1988-. Publications: One More River, stories, 1978; In Siberia It Is Very Cold, (novel), 1987. Contributions to: Anthologies and periodicals. Honours: National Endowment for the Arts, 1979, Fellowship; New Jersey Arts Council Awards, 1982, 1986; Short Story Award, International PEN Syndicated Fiction Project, 1984. Memberships: Poets and Writers; Metropolitan Association of Housing and Redevelopment Officials. Address: 18 Woods Hole Road, Cranford, NJ 07016, USA.

GOLDEN Mark, b. 6 Aug 1948, Winnipeg, Manitoba, Canada. Professor of Classics; Writer. m. Monica Becker, 6 Jan 1985, 1 son. Education: BA, Honours, University College, Toronto, 1970; MA, 1976, PhD, 1981, University of Toronto. Appointments: Lecturer, Assistant Professor, University of British Columbia, 1980-82; Assistant Professor, Professor of Classics, University of Winnipeg, 1982-. Publications: Children and Childhood in Classical Athens, 1990; Inventing Ancient Culture: Historicism, Periodization and the Ancient World (editor with Peter Toohey), 1997; Sport and Society in Ancient Greece, 1998. Contributions to: Scholarly books and journals. Honours: National Humanities Center Fellow, Research Triangle Park, North Carolina, 1987-88; Visiting Research Fellow, University of New England, Armidale, New South Wales, Australia, 1992; Visiting Fellow, Clare Hall, Cambridge, 1995; Center for Hellenic Studies Summer Scholar, Washington, DC, 1996. Address: c/o Department of Classics, University of Winnipeg, Manitoba R3B 2E9, Canada.

GOLDIN Barbara Diamond, b. 4 Oct 1946, New York, New York, USA. Writer; Teacher. m. Alan Goldin, 31 Mar 1968, div 1990, 1 son, 1 daughter. Education: BA, University of Chicago, 1968; Teacher's Certificate, Primary and Secondary Education, Boston University, 1970; Western Washington University, 1970. Publications: Just Enough Is Plenty: A Hanukkah Tale, 1988; The World's Birthday: A Story About Rosh Hashanah, 1990; The Family Book of Midrash: Fifty-two Stories from the Sages, 1990; Cakes and Miracles: A Purim Tale, 1991; Fire!: The Beginnings of the Labor Movement, 1992; The Magician's Visit: A Passover Tale, 1993; The Passover Journey: A Seder Companion, 1994; Red Means Good Fortune: A Story of San Francisco's China Town, 1994; Night Lights: A Sukkot Story, 1994; Bat Mitzvah: A Jewish Girl's Coming of Age, 1995; Creating Angels: Stories of Tzedakah, 1996; Coyote and the Fire Stick: A Pacific Northwest Indian Tale, 1996; While the Candles Burn: Eight Stories for Hanukkah, 1996; The Girl Who Lived with the Bears, 1997. Contributions to: Various publications. Honours: National Jewish Book Award, 1989; Sydney Taylor Book Award, 1991, and Body-of-Work Award, 1997; Association of Jewish Libraries Award, 1992 American Library Association Notable Book Citation, 1995. Address: PO Box 981, Nothampton, MA 01061, USA.

GOLDIN Stephen, b. 28 Feb 1947, Philadelphia, Pennsylvania, USA. Writer. Education: BA, University of California at Los Angeles, 1968. Appointments: Editor, Jaundice Press, Van Nuys, California, 1973-74, San Francisco Ball, 1973-74, Science Fiction Writers of America Bulletin, 1975-77; Director, Merrimont House Creative Consultations. Publications: The Alien Condition (editor), 1973; Herds, 1975; Caravan, 1975; Scavenger Hunt, 1975; Finish Line, 1976; Imperial Stars, 1976; Strangler's Moon, 1976; The Clockwork Traitor, 1976; Assault on the Gods, 1977; Getaway World, 1977; Mindfight, 1978; Appointments at Bloodstar, UK edition as The Bloodstar Conspiracy, 1978; The Purity Plot, 1978; Trek to Madworld, 1979; The Eternity Brigade, 1980; A World Called Solitude, 1981; And Not Make Dreams Your Master, 1981; Planet of Treachery, 1982; The Business of Being a Writer (with Kathleen Sky), non-fiction, 1982; Eclipsing Binaries, 1984; The Omicron Invasion, 1984; Revolt of the Galaxy, 1985, Editor with David Gerrold: Protostars, 1971; Science Fiction Emphasis 1, 1974; Alternities, 1974; Ascents of Wonder, 1977. Address: 389 Florin Road, No 22, Sacramento, CA 95831, USA.

GOLDMAN Paul H(enry) J(oseph), b. 3 Apr 1950, London, England. Art Historian. m. Corinna Maroulis, 11 July 1987. Education: BA, Honours, English, London University, 1971; Postgraduate Diploma, Art Gallery and Museum Studies, University of Manchester, 1972; Diploma, Museums Association in Art, 1978. Appointment: Assistant Keeper, Department of Prints and Drawings, British Museum, London, 1974-97. Publications: Sporting Life: An Anthology of British Sporting Prints, 1983; Looking at Prints, Drawings and Watercolours, 1988; Victorian Illustrated Books 1850-1870: The Heyday of Wood-Engraving, 1994; Victorian Illustration: The Pre-Raphaelites, the Idyllic School and the High Victorians, 1996; Retrospective Adventures, Forrest Reid, Author and Collector (editor with Brian Taylor, 1998. Contributions to: Journals, reviews, and quarterlies. Memberships: Royal Society of Arts, fellow; Museums Association; Society of Authors; Founder, committee member, Imaginative Book Illustration Society; Trustee, Cartoon Art Trust. Address: c/o 45 Mitford Road, London N19 4HJ, England.

GOLDMAN William, b. 12 Aug 1931, Chicago, Illinois, USA. Author; Screenwriter. m. Ilene Jones, 15 Apr 1961, 2 daughters. Education: BA, Oberlin College, 1952; MA, Columbia University, 1956. Publications: The Temple of Gold, 1957; Your Turn to Curtsy, My Turn to Bow, 1958; Soldier in the Rain, 1960; Boys and Girls Together, 1964; No Way to Treat a Lady, 1964; The Thing of It Is, 1967; The Season: A Candid Look at the Broadway, 1969; Father's Day, 1971; The Princess Bride, 1973; Marathon Man, 1974; Wigger, 1974; Magic, 1976; Tinsel, 1979; Control, 1982; Adventures in the Screen Trade, 1983; The Silent Gondoliers, 1983; The Color of Light, 1984; Heat, 1985; Brothers, 1987; Wait Until Next Year, 1988; Hype and Glory, 1990; Four Screenplays, 1995. Screenplays: Masquerade, 1965; Harper, 1966; Butch Cassidy and the Sundance Kid, 1969; The Hot Rock, 1972; The Stepford Wives, 1974; The Great Waldo Pepper, 1975; Marathon Man, 1976; All the President's Men, 1976; A Bridge Too Far, 1977; Magic, 1978; The Princess Bridge, 1987; Heat, 1987; Misery, 1990; The Year of the Comet, 1992; Memoirs of an Invisible Man, 1992; Chaplin, 1992; Maverick, 1994. Play: Blood, Sweat and Stanley Poole (with James Goldman), 1961. Musical Comedy: A Family Affair (with James Goldman and John Kander), 1962. Honours: Academy Award for Best Original Screenplay, 1970, and for Best Screenplay Adaptation, 1977; Laurel Award for Lifetime Achievement in Screenwriting, 1983. Address: c/o CAA, 9830 Wilshire Boulevard, Beverly Hills, CA 90212, USA.

GOLDREIN Iain Saville, b. 10 Aug 1952, Crosby, Liverpool, England. Barrister; Writer. m. Margaret de Haas, 18 May 1980, 1 son, 1 daughter. Education: Hebrew University of Jerusalem; Pembroke College, Cambridge. Appointments: Called to the Bar, Inner Temple, 1975; Joint Head, Corn Exchange Chambers, Liverpool, 1989-; Visiting Professor, Nottingham Law School, 1991; Assistant Recorder, 1995-. Publications: Property Distribution on Divorce (with Margaret de Haas), 1983, 2nd edition, 1985; Personal Injury Litigation: Practice and Precedents, 1985; Ship Sale and Purchase, Law and Technique, 1985, 3rd edition (editor-in-chief), 1998; Commercial Litigation: Pre-Emptive Remedies (with K H P Wilkinson), 1987, 3rd edition (with K H P Wilkinson and P M Kershaw), 1996; Butterworths Personal Injury Litigation Service (with Margaret de Haas), 1988-; Bullen and Leake and Jacob's Precedents of Pleadings of Pleadiongs (with Sir J Jacob), 12th edition, 1990; Pleadings, Principles and Practice (with Sir J Jacob), 1990; Structured Settlements (with Margaret de Haas), 1993, 2nd edition, 1997; Medical Negligence: Cost Effective Case Management (with Margaret de Haas), 1997. Honours: Fellow, Royal Society of Arts, 1994; Queen's Counsel, 1997. Address: Corn Exchange Chambers, Fenwick Street, Liverpool, L2 7QS, England.

GOLDSCHEIDER Gabriele Maria, b. 7 Mar 1929, Vienna, Austria. Bookseller; Author; Publisher. Education: Blunt House, Oxted, 1947-49; Ruskin School of Art, Oxford, 1949-53; Dip French, Neuchâtel University, 1953. Appointments: Editor, Hamlyn Publications, Feltham, England, 1967-74; General Editor, Medallion Collectors' Series, Constable, 1979-83. Publications: A Bibliography of Sir Arthur Conan Doyle, 1977; Dolls, 1979; Richard Jeffries: A Modern Appraisal, (editor), 1984; A Sheaf of Verses by Radclyffe Hall (editor), 1985. Contributions to: Journals. Address: Deep Dene, Baring Road, Cowes, Isle of Wight PO31 8DB, England.

GOLDSMITH Edward Rene David, b. 8 Nov 1928. England. Author; Publisher; Editor. m. (1) Gillian Marion Pretty, 1953, 1 son, 2 daughters, (2) Katherine Victoria James, 1981, 2 sons. Education: MA, Magdalen College, Oxford. Appointments: Publisher, Editor, The Ecologist, 1970-; Adjunct Associate Professor, University of Michigan, 1975; Visiting Professor, Sangamon State University, 1984. Publications: Can Britain Survive? (editor), 1971; A Blueprint for Survival (with R Allen), 1972; The Future of an Affluent Society: The Case of Canada, 1976; The Stable Society, (editor with J M Brunett), 1977; La Medecine a la Question (editor with J M Brunett), 1981; The Social and Environmental Effects of Large Dams, (with N Hildyard), 2 volumes, 1984, 1986; Green Britain or Industrial Wasteland? (with N Hildyard), 1986; The Earth Report (editor with N Hildyard), 1988; The Great U-Turn, 1988. Address: Whitehay, Witiel, Bodmin, Cornwall, England.

GOLDSMITH Howard, (Ward Smith, Dayle Courtney), b. 24 Aug 1945, New York City, USA. Author; Editor. Education: BA, Honours, CUNY, 1965; MA, Honours, University of Michigan, 1966. Appointments: Editorial Consultant, Mountain View Center for Environmental Education, University of Colorado, 1970-85; Senior Editor, Santillana Publishing Company, 1980-85; Contributing Editor, Children's Magic Window, 1987-90. Publictions: The Whispering Sea, 1976; What Makes a Grumble Smile?, 1977; The Shadow and Other Strange Tales, 1977; Terror by Night, 1977; Spine-Chillers, 1978; Sooner Round the Corner, 1979; Invasion: 2200 A.D., 1979; Into the Timid Turtle, 1980; The Ivy Plot, 1981; Three-Ring Inferno, 1982; Plaf Le Paresseux, 1982; Ninon, Miss Vison, 1982; Toulou Le Ilibou, 1982; Fourteu Le Kangourou, 1982; The Tooth Chicken, 1982; Mireille l'Abeille, 1982; Little Dog Lost, 1983; Stormy Day Together, 1983; The Sinister Circle, 1983; Shadow of Fear, 1983; Treasure Hunt, 1983; The Square, 1983; The Circle, 1983; The Contest, 1983; Welcome Makoto!, 1983; Helpful Julin, 1984; The Secret of Success, 1984; Pedro's Puzzling Birthday, 1984; Rosa's Prank, 1984; A Day of Fun, 1984; The Rectangle, 1984; Kirby the Kangaroo, 1985; Ollie the Owl, 1985; The Twiddle Twins Haunted House, 1985; Young Ghosts, 1985; Von Geistern Besessen, 1987; The Further Adventures of Halman, 1989; Visions of Fantasy, 1989; The Pig and the Witch, 1990; The Mind-Stalkers, 1990; Spooky Stones, 1990; Little Quack and Baby Duckling,

1991; The Prousl Syndrome, 1992; The President Train, 1991; The Future Light of the World, 1993; Evil Tales of Evil Things, 1991; The Twiddle Twins Music Box My Sky, 1996; The Gooey Dewy Bubble Gum Contest, 1996; The Twiddle Twins Amusement Park Mystery, 1997; McGraw-Hill Science Through Stories Series, 1998; The Twiddle Twins Single Footprint Mystery, 1999; The Tooth Fairy Mystery, 1999. Contributions to: Periodicals, journals, magazines, reviews and newspapers. Honours: Several. Memberships: Poets and Writers; Science Fiction Writers of America; Society of Childrens Book Writers and Illustrators; Phi Beta Kappa. Address: 41-07 Bowne Street #6B, Flushing, NY 11355-5629, USA.

GOLDSTEIN Laurence (Alan), b. 5 Jan 1943, Los Angeles, California, USA. Professor of English; Writer; Poet; Editor. m. Nancy Jo Copeland, 28 Apr 1968, 2 sons. Education: BA, University of California at Los Angeles, 1965; PhD, Brown University, 1970. Appointments: Instructor, Brown University, 1968-70; Assistant Professor, 1970-78, Associate Professor, 1978-85, Professor of English, 1985-, University of Michigan; Editor, Michigan Quarterly Review, 1977-. Publications: Ruins and Empire: The Evolution of a Theme in Augustan and Romantic Literature, 1977; Altamira, 1978; The Automobile and American Culture (editor with David L Lewis), 1983; The Flying Machine and Modern Literature, 1986; The Three Gardens, 1987; Writers and Their Craft: Short Stories and Essays on the Narrative (editor with Nicholas Delbanco), 1991; Seasonal Performances: A Michigan Quarterly Review Reader (editor), 1991; The Female Body: Figures, Styles, Speculations (editor), 1992; The American Poet at the Movies: A Critical History, 1994; The Male Body: Features, Destinies, Exposures (editor), 1994; Cold Reading, 1995; The Movies: Texts, Receptions, Exposures (editor with Ira Konigsberg), 1996. Contributions to: Books, anthologies, reviews, and journals. Honours: Distinguished Service Award, University of Michigan, 1977; University of Michigan Press Book Award, 1995. Address: c/o Department of English, University of Michigan, Ann Arbor, MI 48109, USA.

GOLDSTEIN Rebecca, b. 23 Feb 1950, New York, New York, USA. Novelist; Philosopher. m. Sheldon Goldstein, 25 June 1969, 2 daughters. Education: BA, Barnard College, Columbia University, 1972; PhD, Princeton University, 1976. Publications: The Mind Body Problem, 1983; The Late Summer Passion of a Woman of Mind, 1989; The Dark Sister, 1991; Strange Attractors: Stories, 1993; Mazel, 1995. Honours: Whiting Writers Award, 1991; John D and Catharine T MacArthur Foundation, Fellow, 1996. Membership: PEN. Address: 15th North 7th Avenue, Highland Park, NJ 08904, USA.

GOLDSTEIN Robert Justin, b. 28 Mar 1947, Albany, New York, USA. College Professor. Education: BA, University of Illinois, 1969; MA, 1971, PhD, 1976, University of Chicago. Appointments: Research and Administrative Assistant, University of Illinois, 1972-73; Lecturer, San Diego State University, 1974-76; Assistant Professor, Associate Professor, Full Professor, Oakland University, Rochester, Michigan, 1976-. Publications: Political Repression in Modern America, 1978; Political Repression in Nineteenth Century Europe, 1983; Political Censorship of the Press and the Arts in Nineteenth Century Europe, 1989; Censorship of Political Caricature in Nineteenth Century France, 1989; Saving "Old Glory": The History of the American Flag Desecration Controversy, 1995; Burning the Flag: The Great 1989-90 American Flag Desecration Controversy, 1996; Descrating the American Flag: Key Documents from the Controversy from the Civil War to 1995, 1996. Address: Department of Political Science, Oakland University, Rochester, MI 48309, USA.

GOLDSTEN Benjamin. See: **KATZIR Benjamin.**

GOLDSWORTHY Peter, b. 12 Oct 1951, Minlaton, South Australia, Australia. Poet; Writer. m. Helen Louise Wharldall, 1972, 1 son, 2 daughters. Education: BMed, BSurg, 1974, University of Adelaide. Publications: Number Three Friendly Street: Poetry Reader (co-editor), 1979; Readings from Ecclesiastes, 1982; This Goes With This, 1988; Maestro (novel), 1989; This Goes With That, 1991. Honours: Commonwealth Poetry Prize, 1982; South Australia Poetry Award, 1988. Address: 8 Rose Street, Prospect, South Australia 5082, Australia.

GOLICK Jill A, b. 23 May 1956, Montreal, Canada. Screenwriter. 1 son, 1 daughter. Education: BA, Psycholinguistics, Brown University, 1977. Publications: Writer for following television series: Noddy; The Magical Adventures of Mumfie; Wimzie's House; Zoboomafoo; Skinnamarink TV; Sesame Park; Kratts Creatures; Shining Time Station; Max the Cat; Groundling Marsh; Wizadora; Fred Penners Place; Smoggies. Membership: Writers Guild of Canada, National Councillor, 1996-99. Literary Agent: Suzanne De Poe. Address: 3 Church Street, Suite 507, Toronto, Ontario M5E 1M2, Canada.

GOLIN Milton, b. 2 Apr 1921, Oak Park, Illinois, USA. Writer; Editor; Publisher. m. Carol Brierly, 13 Dec 1975, 2 sons, 1 daughter. Education: Wright City College, Chicago; Central YMCA College, Chicago. Appointments: Radio-TV News Editor, City News Bureau of Chicago; Assistant Editor, Journal of the American Medical Association; Editor, OB-GYN News, Pediatric News, Diagnosis News; Editor, Medicolegal Digest; Editor, Medical Group News, Surgical Update, Adolescent Medicine; Editor, Computers and Medicine. Publication: The Business Side of Medical Practice. Contributions to: Journal of the American Medical Association; Reader's Digest; Saturday Evening Post; Mechanix Illustrated; Mademoiselle; Changing Times; Seventeen; Catholic Digest; Others. Memberships: American Society of Journalists and Authors; National Association of Science Writers; SDX Society of Journalists. Address: 400 E Ohio Street, # 1802, Chicago. IL 60611, USA.

GOMERY Douglas, b. 5 Apr 1945, New York, New York, USA. Professor; Writer. m. Marilyn Moon, 1973. Education: BS, Lehigh University, 1967; MA, 1970, PhD, 1975, University of Wisconsin at Madison. Appointments: Instructor to Associate Professor, University of Wisconsin at Milwaukee, 1974-81; Visiting Professor, University of Wisconsin at Madison, 1977, Northwestern University, 1981, University of Iowa, 1982, University of Utrecht, 1990, 1992; Associate Professor, 1981-86, Professor, Department of Radio-Television-Film, 1987-92, then College of Journalism, 1992-, University of Maryland; Senior Researcher, Woodrow Wilson Center for International Scholars, Washington, DC, 1988-92. Publications: High Sierra: Screenplay and Analysis, 1979; Film History: Theory and Practice (with Robert C Allen), 1985; The Hollywood Studio System, 1986; The Will Hays Papers, 1987; American Media (with Philip Cook and Lawrence W Lichty), 1989; The Art of Moving Shadows (with Annette Michelson and Patrick Loughney), 1989; Movie History: A Survey, 1991; Shared Pleasures, 1992; The Future of News (with Philip Cook and Lawrence W Lichty), 1992; A Media Studies Primer (with Michael Cornfield and Lawrence W Lichty), 1997; Media in America, editor, 1998. Contributions to: Books and scholarly journals. Honours: Jeffrey Weiss Literary Prize, Theatre Historical Society, 1988; Prize, Theatre Library Association, 1992. Address: 4817 Drummond Avenue, Chevy Chase, MD 20815, USA.

GOMEZ Jewelle Lydia, b. 11 Sept 1948, Boston, Massachusetts, USA. Writer; Poet. Education: BA, Northeastern University, 1971; MS, Columbia Graduate School of Journalism, 1973. Appointments: Associate, 1984-91, Director of Literature, 1991-93, New York State Council on the Arts; Adjunct Professor, New College of California, 1994, Menlo College, California, 1994; Writer-in-Residence, California Arts Council, 1995-96. Publications: The Gilda Stories, 1991; Forty-Three Septembers, 1993; Oral Tradition, 1995. Contributions to: Various publications. Memberships: American Center of Poets and Writers; PEN. Address: c/o Frances Goldin Literary Agency, 57 East 11th Street, New York, NY 10003, USA.

GONCZ Arpad, b. 10 Feb 1922, Budapest, Hungary. President of the Republic of Hungary; Writer; Dramatist; Translator. m. Maria Zsuzsanna Göntér, 1947, 2 sons, 2 daughters. Education: DJ, Pázmány Péter University, 1944; University of Agricultural Sciences. Appointments: Active with Independent Smallholders' Party, 1947-48; Imprisoned for political activities, 1957-63; Founding Member, Free Initiative Network, Free Democratic Federation, Historic Justice Committee; Member and Speaker of Parliament, 1990; Acting President, 1990, President, 1990-, Republic of Hungary. Publications: Men of God (novel), 1974; Hungarian Medea (play), 1979; Iron Bars (play), 1979; Encounters (short stories), 1980; 6 plays, 1990; Homecoming (short stories), 1991; Shavings (essays), 1991. Honours: Honorary Knight Commander of the Order of St Michael and St George, England, 1991. Membership: Hungarian Writers' Union, President, 1989-90. Address: Office of the President, Kossuth tér 1-3, 1357 Budapest, Hungary.

GONZALEZ Luis Daniel, b. 5 Apr 1955, El Rosal, Pontevedra, Spain. Writer. Education: Graduate, Physical Sciences, Valladolid, Spain, 1977. Publications: Deporte y Educación, 1993; Los Mejores: La Ambición y el Liderazgo en el Deporte, 1993; Islas Llenas de Tesoros: Elogio de Los Clásicos Juveniles (co-author and editor), 1994; Guía de Clásicos de la Literatura Infantil y Juvenil (1) - hasta 1950-,1997; Guía de Clásicos de la Literatura Infantil y Juvenil (2) -desde 1950-, 1998; Guía de Clásicos de la Literatura Infantil y Juvenil (3) -libros ilustrados cómic, teatro, poesía-, 1998. Address: Gamazo 12 30, 47004 Valladolid, Spain.

GONZALEZ-CRUSSI Frank, b. 4 Oct 1936, Mexico City, Mexico. Professor of Pathology; Writer. m. (1) Ana Luz, div, 2 sons, 1 daughters, (2) Wei Hsueh, 7 Oct 1978. Education: BA, 1954, MD, 1961, Universidad Nacional Autonoma de Mexico. Appointments: Intern, Penrose Hospital, Colorado Springs, 1962; Resident in Pathology, St Lawrence Hospital, Lansing; Shands Teaching Hospital, University of Florida, Gainesville, 1963-67; Assistant Professor of Pathology, Queens University, Kingston, 1967-73; Associate Professor of Pathology, Indiana University-Purdue University at Indianapolis, 1973-78; Professor of Pathology, Northwestern University, Chicago, 1978-; Head of Laboratories, Children's Memorial Hospital,, Chicago. Publications: Notes of an Anatomist, 1985; Other Reflections on the Grandeur and Misery of the Body, 1986; On the Nature of Things Erotic, 1988, Suspended Animation, 1995; There is a World Elsewhere. Contributions to: Numerous specialized medial journals. Honour: Best Non-Fiction Award, Society of Midland Authors, 1985; Nominee, PEN Award for the Art of Essay, 1996. Memberships: International Academy of Pathology; Society for Pediatric Patholgy; American Society of Clinical Pathologists; Royal College of Physicians and Surgeons of Canada; Chicago Pathology Society; Authors Guild; Society of Midland Authors. Address: 2626 North Lakeview Avenue, Chicago, IL 60614, USA.

GOOCH John, b. 25 Aug 1945, Weston Favell, England. Professor of International History; Writer. m. Catharine Ann Staley, 1967, 1 son, 1 daughter. Education: BA, 1st Class Honours, History, 1966, PhD, War Studies, 1969, King's College, University of London. Appointments: Assistant Lecturer in History, 1966-67, Assistant Lecturer in War Studies, 1969, King's College, University of London; Lecturer in History, 1969-81, Senior Lecturer, 1981-84, Reader in History, 1984-88, Professor of History, 1988-92, University of Lancaster; Editor, Journal of Strategic Studies, 1978-; Secretary of the Navy Senior Research Fellow, US Naval War College, 1985-86; Visiting Professor of Military and Naval History, Yale University, 1988; Professor of International History, University of Leeds, 1992-. Publications: The Plans of War: The General Staff and British Military Strategy c.1900-1916; Armies in Europe, 1980; The Prospect of War: Studies in British Defence Policy 1847-1942, 1981; Politicians and Defence: Studies in the Formulation of British Defence Policy 1847-1970, 1981; Strategy and the Social Sciences, 1981; Strategy and the Social Sciences, 1981; Military Deception and Strategic Surprise, 1982;

Soldati e Borghesi nell' Europa Moderna, 1982; Army; State and Society in Italy 1870-1915, 1989; Decisive Campaigns of the Second World War, 1989; Military Misfortunes: The Antomy of Failure in War (with Eliot A Cohen), 1990; Airpower: Theory and Practice, 1995. Contributions to: Scholarly journals. Memberships: Army Records Society, chairman of the council, 1983-; Royal Historical Society, fellow, vice president, 1990-94. Honours: Premio Internazionale di Cultura, Citta di Anghiari, 1983; Knight, Royal Military Order of Vila Vicosa, Portugal, 1991. Address: Coverhill House, Coverhill Road, Oldham OL4 5RE, England.

GOOCH Stanley Alfred, b. 13 June 1932, London, England. Writer. m. Ruth Senior, 1 Apr 1961. Education: BA, Honours, Modern Languages, King's College, London, 1955; Diploma in Education, Institute of Education, London, 1957; BSc, Honours, Psychology, Birkbeck College, University of London, 1962. Publications: Four Years On, 1966; Total Man, 1972; Personality and Evolution, 1973; The Neanderthal Question, 1977; The Paranormal, 1978; Guardians of the Ancient Wisdom, 1979; The Double Helix of the Mind, 1980; The Secret Life of Humans, 1981; Creatures from Inner Space, 1984; The Child with Asthma, 1986; Cities of Dreams, 1989, revised edition, 1995. Contributions to: New Scientist; New Society; British Journal of Psychology; British Journal of Social and Clinical Psychology; British Journal of Educational Psychology; International Journal of Human Development. Honours: Royal Literary Fund Awards, 1984, 1987, 1994. Address: c/o David Percy, 25 Belsize Park, Hampstead, London NW3 4DU, England.

GOOCH Steve, b. 22 July 1945, Surrey, England. Dramatist. Education: BA, Trinity College, 1967; Graduate Studies, St John's College, Cambridge, 1967-68, University of Birmingham, 1968-69. Appointments: Assistant Editor, Plays and Players magazines, London, 1972-73; Resident Dramatist, Half Moon Theatre, London, 1973-74, Greenwich Theatre, London, 1974-75, Solent People's Theatre, Southampton, 1982, Theatre Venture, London, 1983-84, Warehouse Theatre, Croydon, 1986-87, Gate Theatre, Notting Hill, 1990-91. Publications: Big Wolf (translator), 1972; The Mother (translator), 1973; Female Transport, 1974; The Motor Show (with Paul Thompson), 1974; Will Wat, If Not, What Will, 1975; Wolf Biermann's Poems and Ballads (translator), 1977; The Women Pirates, 1978; Wallraff: The Undesirable Journalist (translator), 1978; Fast One, 1982; Landmark, 1982; All Together Now, 1984; Taking Liberties, 1984; Mr Fun, 1986; Writing a Play, 1988, new edition, 1995; Lulu and the Marquis of Keith (translator), 1990; Stages of Translation (essay), 1996. Contributions to: Time Out; Theatre Quarterly; Drama. Honours: Harper-Wood Scholarship, 1968; Arts Council of Great Britain Bursaries, 1980, 1987, 1992. Address: c/o Micheline Steinberg Playwrights, 409 Triumph House, 187-191 Regent Street, London W1R 7WF, England.

GOODFIELD (Gwyneth) June, b. 1 June 1927, Stratford-on-Avon, England. Professor of Health Science and Health Policy; Writer. Education: BSc, Honours, Zoology, University of London, 1949; PhD, History and Philosophy of Science, University of Leeds, 1959. Appointments: Leverhulme Research Fellow, 1956-57, Lecturer in the History and Philosophy of Science, 1957-60, University of Leeds; Visiting Professor, Hebrew University of Jerusalem, 1965; Rebecca Bacarach Treves Professor of the History and Philosophy, Wellesley College, Michigan State University, 1968-70; Professor, College of Medicine, 1970-72, 1972-76; Adjunct Professor, Cornell University Medical College, 1977-82; Senior Research Associate and Adjunct Professor, 1977-82, Co-Director, Life Sciences and Public Policy Program, 1980-82, Rockefeller University; President, International Health and Biomedicine Ltd, 1982-; Professor of Health Science and Health Policy, School of Nursing, George Mason University, 1990-; President, International Health and Biomedicine, 1982-86; Various visiting lectureships. Publications: The Growth of Scientific Physiology, 1960; The Fabric of the Heavens (co-author), 1961; The Architecture of Matter (co-author),

1962; The Discovery of Time (co-author), 1965; Courier to Peking, 1973; The Siege of Cancer, 1975; Playing God: Genetic Engineering and the Manipulation of Life, 1977; Reflections on Science and the Media, 1981; An Imagined World: A Study of Scientific Creativity, 1981; Quest for the Killers, 1985; A Chance to Live, 1991; The Nomad Scientist, forthcoming. Contributions to: Scholarly books and professional journals. Other: Scripts for 9 scientific films. Memberships: American Association for the Advancement of Science; PEN Club. Address: The Manor House, Alfriston, East Sussex BN26 5SY, England.

GOODHEART Eugene, b. 26 June 1931, New York, New York, USA. Professor of Humanities; Writer. m. Joan Bamberger, 1 son, 1 daughter. Education: BA, English, Columbia College, 1953; MA, English, University of Virginia, 1954; Sorbonne, University of Paris, 1956-57; PhD, English and Comparative Literature, Columbia University, 1961. Appointments: Instructor, 1958-60, Assistant Professor, 1960-62, Bard College; Assistant Professor, University of Chicago, 1962-66; Associate Professor, Mount Holyoke College, 1966-67; Associate Professor, 1967-70, Professor, 1970-74, Massachusetts Institute of Technology; Visiting Professor, Wellesley College, 1968; Professor, Boston University, 1974-83; Corresponding Editor, Partisan Review, 1978-; Edytha Macy Gross Professor of Humanities, 1983-, Director, Center for the Humanities, 1986-, Brandeis University; Adjunct Professor of English, Columbia Unversity, 1986. Publications: The Utopian Vision of D H Lawrence, 1963; The Cult of the Ego: The Self in Modern Literature, 1968; Culture and the Radical Conscience, 1978; The Failure of Criticism, 1978; The Skeptic Disposition in Contemporary Criticism, 1984, new edition, 1991; Pieces of Resistance, 1987; Desire and Its Discontents, 1991; The Reign of Ideology, 1996. Contributions to: Journals and periodicals. Honours: Fulbright Scholarship, Paris, 1956-57; American Council of Learned Societies Fellowship, 1965-66; Guggenheim Felowship, 1970-71; National Endowment for the Humanities Senior Fellowship, 1981; National Humanities Center Fellow, 1987-88; Rockefeller Foundation Fellowship, Bellagio, Italy, 1989; Phi Beta Kappa. Membership: PEN. Address: c/o Department of English, Brandeis University, Waltham, MA 02254, USA.

GOODISON Lorna (Gaye), b. 1 Aug 1947, Kingston, Jamaica. Poet; Painter; Writer. Education: Art schools, Kingston and New York, 1967-69. Appointments: Teacher of Creative Writing, USA and Canada. Publications: Poetry: Poems, 1974; Tamarind Season, 1980; I Am Becoming My Mother, 1986; Heartease, 1988; To Us All Flowers Are Roses, 1992; Selected Poems, 1992. Short Stories: Baby Mother and the King of Swords, 1989. Honours: Institute of Jamaica Centenary Prize, 1981; Commonwealth Poetry Prize, 1986. Address: 8 Marley Close, Kingston 6, Jamaica, West Indies.

GOODMAN David G, b. 12 Feb 1946, Racine, Wisconsin, USA. Professor; Writer. m. Kazuko Fujimoto, 24 June 1968, 2 children. Education: BA, cum laude, Yale University, 1969; MA, 1980, PhD, 1982, Cornell University. Appointments: Visiting Assistant Professor, University of Kansas, 1981-82; Associate Professor, 1982-86, 1986-90, Professor, 1990-, University of Illinois. Publications: Isuraeru--koe to kao, English translation as Israel: Voices and Faces, 1979; Fujisan mieta--Satoh Makoto ni okeru kakumei no engeki, English translation as Mount Fuji Perceived: The Revolutionary Theatre of Satoh Makoto, 1983; Land of Volcanic Ash, 1986; After Apocalypse: Four Japanese Plays of Hiroshima and Nagasaki, 1986; Japanese Drama and Culture in the 1960s: The Return of the Gods, 1988; Five Plays by Kishida Kunio, 1989; Hashiru, English translation as Running, 1989; Long, Long Autumn Nights: Selected Poems of Oguma Hideo, 1901-1940, 1989; Jews in the Japanese Mind: The History and Uses of a Cultural Stereotype, 1995. Honours: NEH Fellowship for Independent Study and Research, 1985-86; Fulbright Scholar, 1980-81, 1990-91; Translation Center Award, Columbia University, 1990. Address: c/o Department of

East Asian Languages and Cultures, University of Illinois, 608 South Mathews Avenue, Urbana, IL 61801, USA.

GOODMAN Jonathan, b. 17 Jan 1931, London, England. Author; Publisher; Editor. Appointments: Theatre Director and Television Producer, various companies, United Kingdom, 1951-64; Director, Anmbar Publications Ltd, London, 1967-; General Editor, Celebrated Trials Series, David & Charles (Publishers) Ltd, Newton Abbott, Devon, 1972-. Publications: Martinee Idylls (poetry), 1954; Instead of Murder (novel), 1961; Criminal Tendencies (novel), 1964; Hello Cruel World Goodbye (novel), 1964; The Killing of Julia Wallace, 1969; Bloody Versicles, 1971; Posts-Mortem, 1971; Trial of Ian Brady and Myra Hindley (editor), 1973; Trial of Ian Ruth Ellis (editor), 1975; The Burning of Evelyn Foster, 1977; The Last Sentence (novel), 1978; The Stabbing of George Harry Storrs, 1982; Pleasure of Murder, 1983; Railway Murders, 1984; Who-He, 1984; Seaside Murders, 1985; The Crippen File (editor) 1985; The Underworld (with I Will), 1985; Christmas Murders (editor) 1986; The Moors Murders, 1986; Acts of Murder, 1986; Murder in High Places, 1986; The Slaying of Joseph Bowne Elwell, 1987. Address: 43 Ealing Village, London W5 2LZ, England.

GOODMAN Michael Lawrence, b. 26 May 1947, London, England. Journalist. Education: BA, Sussex University. Appointments: City Press; Post Magazine; Money Week. Contributions to: Daily Telegraph; Weekly Telegraph. Membership: Association of British Insurers Directory. Address: 63 Hartham Road, Isleworth, Middlesex, TW7 5EY, England.

GOODRICK-CLARKE Nicholas, b. 15 Jan 1953, Lincoln, England. Author; Historian. m. Clare Radene Badham, 11 May 1985. Education: Jagdschloss Glienicke, Berlin, 1971; University of Bristol, 1971-74; University of Oxford, 1975-78. Appointments: Editor, Essential Readings, 1983-; Director, IKON Productions Ltd, 1988-. Publications: The Occult Roots of Nazism; Paracelsus; The Enchanted City; Hitler's Priestess; The Rosicrucian Enlightenment Revisited (contributions); The Nazi Underground; Heavenstormers. Contributions to: The Times; Durham University Journal; Theosophical History; Images of War; Decadence and Innovation; Ambix; Politica Hermetica; Le Nouvel Observateur; Gnostika; Lapis. Memberships: Society of Authors; Scientific & Medical Network; Keston College. Address: Manor Farm House, Manor Road, Wantage OX12 8NE, England.

GOODWIN Doris (Helen) Kearns, b. 4 Jan 1943, Rockville Centre, New York, USA. Historian. m. Richard Goodwin, 1973, 3 sons. Education: BA, Colby College, 1964; PhD, Harvard University, 1968. Appointments: Research Associate, US Department of Health, Education, and Welfare, 1966; Special Assistant, US Department of Labor, 1967, and to President Lyndon B Johnson, 1968; Assistant Professor, 1969-71, Assistant Director, Institute of Politics, 1971, Associate Professor of Government, 1972, Harvard University; Special Consultant to President Lyndon B Johnson, 1969-73. Publications: Lyndon Johnson and the American Dream, 1976; The Fitzgeralds and the Kennedys: An American Saga, 1987; No Ordinary Time: Franklin and Eleanor Roosevelt: The Home Front in World War II, 1994. Contributions to: Books and television. Honours: Fulbright Fellow, 1966; White House Fellow, 1967; Pulitzer Prize for History, 1995. Memberships: Amnerican Political Science Association; Council on Foreign Relations; Group for Applied Psychoanalysis; Phi Beta Kappa; Phi Sigma Iota; Signet Society; Women Involved. Address: c/o Simon & Schuster Trade Division, 1230 Avenue of the Americas, New York, NY 10020, USA.

GOODWIN SUZANNE. See: EBEL Suzanne.

GOODWIN (Trevor) Noël, b. 25 Dec 1927, Fowey, Cornwall, England. Music and Dance Critic. m. Anne Mason Myers, 23 Nov 1963, 1 stepson. Education: BA, London. Appointments: Music Critic, News Chronicle, 1952-54, Manchester Guardian, 1954-56; Music and

Dance Critic, Daily Express, 1956-78; Music critic panel, The Times, 1978-98; Associate Editor, Dance and Dancers, 1958-; Executive Editor, Music and Musicians, 1963-71; London Dance Critic, International Herald Tribune, Paris, 1978-83; London Correspondent, Opera News, New York City, 1980-91; Overseas News Editor, 1985-91, Editorial Board, 1991-, Opera, London. Publications: London Symphony: Portrait of an Orchestra, 1954; Royal Opera and Royal Ballet Yearbooks (editor), 1978, 1979, 1980; A Ballet for Scotland, 1979; The New Grove Dictionary of Music and Musicians (area editor and contributor), 1980; A Portrait of the Royal Ballet (editor), 1988; The New Grove Dictionery of opera (contibutor), 1992; Cambridge Encyclopedia of Russia and the former Soviet Union (contributor), 1994. Contributions to: Various reference books, journals, and magazines. Memberships: Critics' Circle of Great Britain, president, 1977; International Dance Course for Professional Choreographers and Composers, trustee director, Address: 87 Skeena Hill, London SW18 5PN, England.

GOONERATNE Malini Yasmine, b. 22 Dec 1935, Colombo, Sri Lanka. Writer; Poet; Editor; Professor. m. Brendon Gooneratne, 31 Dec 1962, 1 son, 1 daughter. Education: BA, 1st Class Honours, Ceylon, 1959; PhD, English Literature, Cambridge University, 1962; DLitt, English and Commonwealth Literature, Macquarie University, Australia, 1981. Appointments: Editor, New Ceylon Writing, 1971-; Director, Post-Colonial Literature and Language Research Centre, 1988-93, Personal Chair in English Literature, 1991, Macquarie University; Visiting Professor of English, University of Michigan, USA, Edith Cowan University, Western Australia, 1991; External Advisor, Department of English, University of the South Pacific, 1993, 1995. Publications: English Literature in Ceylon 1815-1878: The Development of an Anglo-Ceylonese Literature, 1968; Jane Austen, 1970; Word Bird, Motif, 53 Poems, 1971; The Lizard's Cry and Other Poems, 1972; Alexander Pope, 1976; Poems from India, Sri Lanka, Malaysia and Singapore (editor), 1979; Stories from Sri Lanka (editor), 1979; Diverse Inheritance: A Personal Perspective on Commonwealth Literature, 1980; 6000 Foot Death Dive, poems, 1981; Silence, Exile, and Cunning: The Fiction of Ruth Prawer Jhabvala, 1983; Relative Merits (memoir), 1986; Celebrations and Departures, poems, 1991; A Change of Skies, novel, 1991; The Pleasures of Conquest (novel), 1995. Contributions to: Various publications. Honours: Order of Australia, 1990; Eleanor Dark Writers Fellowship, 1991; Marjorie Barnard Literary Award for Fiction, 1992; Several research and travel grants. Memberships: Australian Society of Authors; Fédération Internationales des Langues et Littératures Modernes, vice-president, 1990-96; International Association of University Professors of English; Jane Austen Society of Australia, patron; Friends of Macquarie University Library; New South Wales Writers Centre; South Asian Studies Association of Australia; South Pacific Branch of the Association for Commonwealth Literature and Language Studies. Address: c/o School of English, Linguistics and Media, Macquarie University, North Ryde, New South Wales 2109, Australia.

GOONETILLEKE Devapriya Chitra Ranjan Alwis, b. 9 Oct 1938, Colombo, Sir Lanka. Professor of English. m. Chitranganie Lalitha Dalpatadu, 23 Nov 1967, 2 sons. Education: BA, 1961; PhD, 1970. Appointments: Regional Representative, The Journal of Commonwealth Literature, 1978; Associate Editor, Journal of South Asian Literature, 1980; National Editor, The Routledge Encyclopaedia of Commonwealth Literature, 1990; Advisor, Contemporary Novelists, 1990, 1995; Advisor, Reference Guide to Short Fiction, 1992. Publications: Developing Countries in British Fiction; Images of the Raj; Joseph Conrad: Beyond Culture and Background; The Penguin New Writing in Sri Lanka; Between Cultures: Essays on Literature, Language and Education; Joseph Conrad: Heart of Darkness, 1995; The Penguin Book of Modern Sri Lankan Stories, 1996; Sri Lankan Literature in English 1948-1998, 1998; Salman Rushdie, 1998; Contemporary Novelists (advisor), 1995. Contributions to: 82 articles. Honours: Commonwealth Scholar; Foundation Visiting Fellow, Clare Hall; Henry Charles

Chapman Visiting Fellow, University of London. Memberships: International Chairperson, the Association for Commonwealth Literature and Language Studies, 1992-97; Vice-president, International Federation for Modern Languages and Literature, 1993-97; Member, American Studies Association; Member, The New York Academy of Sciences. Address: No 1 Kandewatta Road, Nugegoda, Sri Lanka.

GORAK Jan, b. 12 Oct 1952, Blackburn, Lancashire, England. Professor of English; Writer. m. Irene Elizabeth Mannion, 12 Dec 1983. Education: BA, University of Warwick, 1975; MA, 1981, PhD, 1983, University of Southern California, Los Angeles. Appointments: Lecturer, 1984-87, Senior Lecturer, 1988, University of the Witwatersrand; Associate Professor, 1988-92, Professor of English, 1992-, University of Denver. Publications: God the Artist: American Novelists in a Post-Realist Age, 1987; Frank Kermode: Critic of Crisis, 1987; The Alien Mind of Raymond Williams, 1988; The Making of the Modern Canon: Genesis and Crisis of a Literary Idea, 1991; "Canons, 1660-1800", in The Cambridge History of Literary Criticism, Vol I, 1996. Contributions to: Books and scholarly journals. Honours: Thomas Pringle Award for Literary Articles, English Academy of Southern Africa, 1986; Andrew W Mellon/ Eighteenth-Century Society Fellowship, University of Texas at Austin, 1994; External Fellowship, Oregon State University, 1994-95. Memberships: American Society for Eighteenth-Century Studies; T S Eliot Society. Address: c/o Department of English, University of Denver, Denver, CO 80208, USA.

GORBACHEV Valeri, b. 10 June 1944, Kiev, Ukraine. Fulltime Artist; Writer. m. Victoria, 18 Oct 1970, 1 son, 1 daughter. Education: Art Academy, Kiev, Ukraine. Publications: So Much in Common, 1994; Young Mouse and Elephant, An East African Folktale, 1996; Arnie the Brave, 1997; Nicky and the Big, Bad Wolves, 1998; The Fool of the World and the Flying Ship, 1998; Little Bunny's Sleepless Night, 1999. Contributions to: Highlights for Children; Turtle; Playmate; Ladybug. Honours: Award, A Parent's Guide Children's Media, 1998. Membership: Society of Children's Book Writers and Illustrators. Address: 1440 E14th Street, Apt F-5, Brooklyn, NY 11230, USA.

GORDIMER Nadine, b. 20 Nov 1923, Springs, South Africa. Author. m. (1) Gerald Gavronsky, 4 Mar 1949, div 1952, 1 daughter, (2) Reinhold Cassirer, 29 Jan 1954, 1 son. Publications: The Soft Voice of the Serpent, 1953; The Lying Days, 1953; Six Feet of the Country, 1956; A World of Strangers, 1958; Friday's Footprint, 1960; Occasion for Loving, 1963; Not for Publication, 1965; The Late Bourgeois World, 1966; South African Writing Today (co-editor), 1967; A Guest st of Honour, 1970; Livingstone's Companions, 1972; The Black Interpreters (literary criticism), 1973; The Conservationist, 1974; Selected Stories, 1975; Some Monday for Sure, 1976; Burger's Daughter, 1979; A Soldier's Embrace, 1980; July's People, 1981; Something Out There, 1984; Six Feet of Country, 1986; A Sport of Nature, 1987; The Essential Gesture (essays), 1988; My Sons' Story (novel), 1991; Jump (story collection), 1992; None to Accompany Me (novel), 1994; Writing and Being, 1995; The House Gun (novel), 1998. Honours: W H Smith Literary Award, 1961; Thomas Pringle Award, 1969; James Tait Black Memorial Prize, 1971; Co-Winner, Booker Prize, 1974; Grand Aigle d'Or Prize, France, 1975; Scottish Arts Council Neil M Gun Fellowship, 1981; Modern Language Association Award, USA, 1981; Nobel Prize for Literature, 1991. Memberships: American Academy of Arts and Sciences, honorary fellow; American Academy and Institute of Arts and Letters, honorary member; Congress of South African Writers; International PEN; Modern Language Association of America, honorary fellow; Royal Society of Literature, fellow. Address: c/o A.P. Watt Ltd, 20 John Street, London WC1N 2DR.

GORDON April, b. 12 Apr 1947, Evansville, Indiana, USA. Professor of Sociology. m. Donald L Gordon, 7 Oct 1984, 2 sons. Education: MA, University of Evansville; MA, PhD, University of Missouri-Columbia. Appointments:

Francis Marion College, 1975-76; Coker College, 1977-86; Winthrop University, 1987-. Publications: Soviet Family Policy: 1944 to the Present, 1979; Understanding Contemporary Africa, 1992; Transforming Capitalism and Patriarchy: Gender and Development in Africa, 1997. Address: c/o Winthrop University, Rock Hill, SC 29733, USA.

GORDON Diana. See: **ANDREWS Lucilla Matthew**.

GORDON Donald. See: **PAYNE Donald Gordon**.

GORDON Donald Ramsay, b. 14 Sept 1929, Toronto, Ontario, Canada. Writer. m. Helen E Currie, 21 Dec 1952, 3 sons. Education: BA, Honours, Political Science, Economics, Queen's University, Kingston, 1953; MA, Political Economy, University of Toronto, 1955; Predoctoral studies, Political Science, London School of Economics and Political Science, England, 1956-63. Appointments: Writer, Filing Editor, The Canadian Press, Toronto, Montreal, Edmonton, 1955; Assistant Editor, The Financial Post, Toronto, 1955-57; European Correspondent, Canadian Broadcasting Corporation, London, 1957-63; Assistant Professor, Associate Professor, Political Science, University of Calgary, Alberta, 1963-66. University of Waterloo, Ontario, 1966-75; Self-employed Writer, Consultant, 1975-81; Chief Writer, The Image Corporation, Waterloo, 1983-92; Instructor, Conestoga College, Kitchener, Ontario, 1991-, Long Ridge Writers Group, West Redding, Connecticut, USA, 1992-. Publications: Language, Logic and the Mass Media, 1966; The New Literacy, 1971; The Media, 1972; Fineswine, 1984; The Rock Candy Bandits, 1984; S.P.E.E.D, 1984; The Prosperian Papers, 1989; The Choice, 1990; The Sex Shoppe, 1991. Address: 134 Iroquois Place, Waterloo, Ontario N2L 2S5, Canada.

GORDON Giles, b. 23 May 1940. Edinburgh, Scotland. Writer; Literary Agent; Editor; Lecturer. m. (1) Margaret Eastoe, dec, 2 sons, 1 dec, 1 daughter, (2) Maggie McKernan, 2 daughters. Education: Edinburgh Academy. Appointments: Editor, Hutchinson & Co, and Penguin Books; Editorial Director, Victor Gollancz Ltd; Lecturer, Tufts and Hollins Universities; Editor, Short Story Collections, Bloomsbury Classics, 1995-, Clarion Tales, 1996-. Publications: Two and Two Makes One, 1966; Two Elegies, 1968; Pictures from an Exhibition, 1970; The Umbrella Man, 1971; Twelve Poems for Callum, 1972; About a Marriage, 1972; Girl with Red Hair, 1974; Farewell Fond Dreams, 1975; Beyond the Words (editor), 1975; 100 Scenes from Married Life, 1976; Members of the Jury (editor with Dulan Barber), 1976; Enemies, 1977; Modern Scottish Short Stories (editor with Fred Urquhart), 1978; Ambrose's Vision, 1980; Modern Short Stories, 1940-1980 (editor), 1982; Shakespeare Stories (editor), 1982; Best Short Stories (editor with David Hughes), 10 volumes, 1986-95; English Short Stories: 1900 to the Present (editor), 1988; The Twentieth Century Short Story in English, 1989; Aren't We Due a Royalty Statement?, 1993; Scottish Ghost Stories (editor), 1996; Scotland from the Air, 1996. Contributions to: Times; Scotsman; Spectator; London Daily News; Observer. Memberships: Royal Society of Literature, fellow; Society of Authors; PEN; Society of Authors in Scotland, committee, 1997-. Address: 6 Ann Street, Edinburgh EH4 1PJ, Scotland.

GORDON Graeme, b. 21 June 1966, Epsom, England. Author. Education: BA, Honours, University of Sussex, 1988; DEJF, University of Strasbourg, III, 1987. Publications: Novels: Bayswater Bodycount, 1995; Barking Mad. Membership: Writers' Guild of Great Britain. Literary Agent: Yvonne Baker. Address: c/o Yvonne Baker Associates, 8 Temple Fortune Lane, London NW11 7UD, England.

GORDON Jaimy, b. 4 July 1944, Baltimore, Maryland, USA. Professor of English; Writer. m. Peter Blickle, 1988. Education: BA, Antioch College, 1966; MA, 1972, DA, 1975, Brown University. Appointments: Writer-in-Residence, Rhode Island State Council on the Arts, 1975-77; Director, Creative Writing Program, Stephens College, Columbia, Missouri, 1980-81;

Assistant Professor, 1981-87, Associate Professor, 1987-92, Professor of English, 1992-, Western Michigan University, Kalamazoo. Publications: Shamp of the City-Solo, 1974; The Bend, the Lip, the Kid (narrative poem), 1978; Circumspection from an Equestrian Statue, 1979; Maria Beig: Lost Weddings (translator with Peter Blickle), 1990; She Drove Without Stopping, 1990. Contributions to: Magazines. Honours: National Endowment for the Arts Fellowships, 1979, 1991; American Academy and Institute of Arts and Letters Award, 1991. Address: 1803 Hazel Street, Kalamazoo, MI 49008, USA.

GORDON John Fraser, b. 18 Feb 1916, London, England. Writer. Education: City of London College. Appointments: Managing Director, Dongora Mill Co Ltd, London and J F Gordon London, Ltd, 1963-. Publications: Staffordshire Bull Terrier Handbook, Bull Terrier Handbook, Bulldog Handbook, Dandie Dinmont Terrier Handbook, 1952-59; Staffordshire Bull Terriers, 1964; Miniature Schnauzers, 1966; Spaniel Owner's Encyclopaedia, 1967; Staffordshire Bull Terrier Owner's Encyclopaedia, 1967; The Beagle Guide, 1968; The Miniature Schnauzer Guide, 1968; All About the Boxer, 1970; The Staffordshire Bull Terrier, 11 editions, 1970; All About the Cocker Spaniel, 1971; The Pug, 1973; The German Shepherd, 1978; World of Dogs Atlas Pictorials, 1978; The Pyrenean Mountain Dog, 1978; The Alaskan Malamute, 1979; Schnauzers, 1982; All About the Staffordshire Bull Terrier, 1984; All About the Cairn Terrier, 1987. Honours: Freeman of the City of London and Member of the Guild of Freemen, 1938; Horticultural Hybridist of Fuchsia Gordon's China Rose, 1953. Membership: Society of Authors, 1969; Southern Counties Staffordshire Terrier Society of London, life vice president; Antiquarian Horological Society. Address: The Moat House, 4 St Martins Mews, Chipping Ongar, Essex CM5 9HY, England.

GORDON John William, b. 19 Nov 1925, Jarrow-on-Tyne, England. Writer. m. Sylvia Young, 9 Jan 1954, 1 son, 1 daughter. Publications: The Giant Under the Snow, 1968, sequel, Ride the Wind, 1989; The House on the Brink, 1970; The Ghost on the Hill, 1976; The Waterfall Box, 1978; The Spitfire Grave, 1979; The Edge of the World, 1983; Catch Your Death, 1984; The Quelling Eye, 1986; The Grasshopper, 1987; Secret Corridor, 1990; Blood Brothers, 1991; Ordinary Seaman (autobiography), 1992; The Burning Baby, 1992; Gilray's Ghost, 1995; The Flesh Eater, 1998; The Midwinter Watch, 1998; Skinners, forthcoming. Contributions to: Beginnings (Signal 1989); Ghosts & Scholars 21. Membership: Society of Authors. Literary Agent: A.P. Watt, 20 Johns Street, London, WC1N 2DR. Address: 99 George Borrow Road, Norwich, NR4 7HU, England.

GORDON Lois, b. 13 Nov 1938, Englewood, New Jersey, USA. Professor of English; Writer. m. Alan Lee Gordon, 13 Nov 1961, 1 son. Education: BA, Honours, University of Michigan, 1960; MA, 1962, PhD, 1966, University of Wisconsin. Appointments: Lecturer in English, City College of the City University of New York, 1964-66; Assistant Professor of English, University of Missouri, Kansas City, 1966-68; Assistant Professor, 1968-71, Associate Professor, 1971-75, Professor of English, 1975-, Chairman, Department of English and Comparative Literature, 1982-90, Fairleigh Dickinson University; Visiting Exchange Professor, Rutgers University, 1994. Publications: Stratagems to Uncover Nakedness: The Dreams of Harold Pinter, 1969; Donald Barthelme, 1981; Robert Coover: The Universal Fictionmaking Process, 1983; American Chronicle: Six Decades in American Life, 1920-1980, 1987; American Chronicle: Seven Decades in American Life, 1920-1990, 1990; Harold Pinter Casebook, 1990; The Columbia Chronicles of American Life, 1910-1992, 1995; The Columbia World of Quotations, 1996; The World of Samuel Beckett, 1906-1946, 1996. Contributions to: Journals, reviews, and newspapers. Memberships: Academy of American Poets; Authors Guild; Harold Pinter Society; International League for Human Rights; Modern Language Association; PEN; Samuel Beckett

Society. Address: c/o Department of English, Fairleigh Dickinson University, Teaneck, NJ 07666, USA.

GORDON Michael. See: **CRITCHLEY Sir Julian.**

GORDON Reva Jo Kerns, (Reva Jo Kerns), b. 16 Feb 1928, Harrison County, Missouri, USA. Former English and Business Teacher; Librarian; Writer. m. Roland K Gordon 24 Nov 1949, 1 son, 1 daughter. Education: BS, Northwest Missouri State University, Maryville, 1949; MA, Library Science, University of Michigan, Ann Arbor, Michigan, 1970. Appointments: Editor, Northwest Missourian, college newspaper, 1948-49; Maryville, Missouri; High School Teacher, LeRoy, Iowa, Malvern Iowa; Business Teacher, Platt Business College, St Joseph, Missouri; English Teacher, Librarian, Flushing Community Schools, Michigan, 27 1/2 years; Genesee District Library, Genesee County, Michigan. Publications: The Goodwins and Hensleys (book); A Bevy of Biographies (non-fiction); Newspaper articles. Contributions to: Mature Living; Senior Herald; Senior World; CAPPERS; Fiction under pseudonym. Address: 3379 Ambleside Drive, PO Box 406, Flushing, MI 48433-0406, USA.

GORDON Rex. See: **HOUGH Stanley Bennett.**

GORES Joseph (Nicholas), b. 25 Dec 1931, Rochester, Minnesota, USA. Writer; Novelist; Screenwriter. m. Dori Corfitzen, 16 May 1976, 1 son, 1 daughter. Education: BA, University of Notre Dame, 1953; MA, Stanford University, 1961. Appointment: Story Editor, B L Stryker Mystery Movie Series, ABC-TV, 1988-89. Publications: A Time of Predators, 1969; Marine Salvage (non-fiction), 1971; Dead Skip, 1972; Final Notice, 1973; Interface, 1974; Hammett, 1975; Gone, No Forwarding, 1978; Come Morning, 1986; Wolf Time, 1989; Mostly Murder (short story collection), 1992; 32 Cadillacs, 1992; Dead Man, 1993; Menaced Assassin, 1994; Contract Null and Void, 1996; Cases, 1998. Contributions to: Numerous magazines and anthologies; 8 film scripts; 25 hours of television drama. Honours: Best First Novel, 1969, Best Short Story, 1969, Edgar, Best Episodic TV Drama, 1975, Mystery Writers of America; Falcon, Maltese Falcon Society of Japan, 1986. Memberships: Mystery Writers of America, president, 1986; International Association of Crime Writers; Crime Writers Association; Private Eye Writers of America. Literary Agent: Henry Morrison. Address: PO Box 446, Fairfax, CA 94978, USA.

GOREY Edward (St John), b. 22 Feb 1925, Chicago, Illinois, USA. Writer; Artist. Education: BA, Harvard University, 1950. Publications: The Unstrung Harp, 1953; The Doubtful Guest, 1957; The Hapless Child, 1961; The Willowdale Handcar, 1962; The Wuggly Ump, 1963; The Remembered Visit, 1965; The Bilded Bat, 1966; The Blue Aspic, 1968; The Other Statue, 1968; The Epiplectic Bicycle, 1969; The Awdrey-Gore Legacy, 1972; Amphigorey, 1972; The Glorious Nosebleed, 1975; Amphigorey Too, 1975; The Broken Spoken, 1976; The Loathsome Couple, 1977; The Dwindling Party, 1982; The Water Flowers, 1982; Amphigorey Also, 1983; The Raging Tide, 1987; The Helpless Doorknob, 1989; The Betrayed Confidence, 1992; The Pointless Book, 1993; Figbash Acrobate, 1994. Theatre Pieces: Tinned Lettuce, 1985; Lost Shoelaces, 1987; Useful Urns, Stuffed Elephants, 1990; Flapping Ankles, 1991; Crazed Teacups, 1992; Amphigorey: The Musical, 1992; Blithering Christmas, 1992; Chinese Gossip, 1994; Inverted Commas, 1995; Stumbling Christmas, 1995. Address: PO Box 146, Yarmouth Port, MA 02675, USA.

GORMAN Ed, b. 29 Nov 1941, Cedar Rapids, Iowa, USA. Writer. m. Carol Maxwell, 2 Jan 1982, 1 son. Education: Coe College, 1962-66. Appointment: Editor, Mystery Scene Magazine. Publications: Night Kills; The Autumn Dead; The Night Remembers; Prisoners Collection of Short Stories; A Cry of Shadows; Blood Moon, 1994. Contributions to: Redbook; Ellery Queen; Mayayne of Poetry. Address: 3601 Skylark Lane, Cedar Rapids, IA 52403, USA.

GORZELSKI Roman, b. 12 Apr 1934, Luck, Poland. Writer; Journalist. Education: College, Lodz, 1954; University of Warsaw, 1962. Appointments: Former Teacher. Publications: Three Blues's, 1964; Western, 1970; Metamorphosis, 1973; The Town and the Poem, 1975; Pronunciation of Words, 1977; Little Proverbs, 1977; Bitterman, 1982; Policeman Brandy, 1982; The Silver Thoughts, 1986; The Warta River, 1988; Catching Heads, 1990; The Grain of Anxiety, 1991; The Thoughts in Section, 1995; The Fears of Cupido, 1996. Contributions to: Metfora monthly magazine; Przekroj weekly magazine. Honour: Merit of Polish Culture, 1982. Membership: Union of Polish Writers. Literary Agent: Festinus Publishing House, Poland. Address: ul Chodkiewicza 6, 94-028 Lodz, Poland.

GOSDEN Roger Gordon, b. 23 Sept 1948, Ryde, Isle of Wight, England. Professor. m. Carole Ann Walsh, 7 Aug 1971, 2 sons. Education: BSc, University of Bristol; PhD, University of Cambridge; DSc, Edinburgh University. Appointments: Medical Research Council, Cambridge, 1973-74, 1975-76; Duke University, USA, 1974-75; Edinburgh University, 1976-94;Professor, Honorary Consultant, Leeds Teaching Hospitals NHS Teaching Trust, Leeds University, 1994-. Publications: Biology of Menopause, 1985; Transplantation of Ovarian and Testicular Tissues (with Y Avbard), 1996; Cheating Time (with Freeman), 1996; Designing Babies (with Freeman) (published in rest or world as Designer Babies), 1999. Contributions to: Daily Telegraph; The Independent. Literary Agent: Maggie Pearlstine, 31 Ashley Gardens, Ambrosden Avenue, London, England. Address: Division of Obstetrics and Gynaecology, Clarendon Wing, D Floor, Leeds General Infirmary, Leeds LS2 9NS, England.

GOSLING-HARE Paula Louise, (Ainslie Skinner), b. 12 Oct 1939, Michigan, USA. Author; Crime and Suspense Fiction. m. (1) Christopher Gosling, Sept 1968, div 1978, 2 daughters, (2) John Hare, 1982. Education: BA, Wayne State University. Appointments: Copywriter, Campbell Ewald, USA; Copywriter, Mitchell & Co, London; Copywriter, Pritchard Wood, London: Freelance Copywriter, 1974-. Publications: A Running Duck, 1976; Zero Trap, 1978; The Woman in Red, 1979; Losers Blues, 1980; Minds Eye (as Ainslie Skinner), 1980; Monkey Puzzle, 1982; The Wychford Murders, 1983; Hoodwink, 1985; Backlash, 1987; Death Penalties, 1990; The Body in Blackwater Bay, 1992; A Few Dying Words, 1994; The Dead of Winter, 1995; Death and Shadows, 1999. Honours: Gold Dagger, Crime Writers' Association; Arts Achievement Award, Wayne State University. Memberships: Crimewriters' Association, chairman, 1982; Society of Authors. Address: c/o Greene & Heaton Ltd, 37 Goldhawk Road, London W12 8QQ, England.

GOTO Hiromi, b. 31 Dec 1966, Chiba-ken, Japan. Writer. 2 children. Education: BA, Humanities, University of Calgary, 1989. Publications: Chorus of Mushrooms, 1994. Honours: Co-Winner, Canada-Japan Book Award, 1995; Commonwealth Writers Prize, Best First Book, Canada-Caribbean Region, 1995. Memberships: Writers Union of Canada, co-chair, racial minority committee, 1995-97. Literary Agent: Anne McDermid and Associates. Address: PO Box 67038, Northland Village, Calgary AB T2L 2L2, Canada.

GOULD Alan David, b. 22 Mar 1949, London, England. Poet; Writer. m. Anne Langridge, 17 Jan 1984, 2 sons. Education: BA, Honours, 1971; DipEd, 1974. Appointments: Creative Fellow, Australian National University, 1978; Writer-in-Residence, Geelong College, 1978, 1980, 1982, 1985, Australian Defence Forces Academy, 1986, Lincoln Humberside Arts Centre, 1988. Publications: Icelandic Solitaries, 1978; Astral Sea, 1981; The Pausing of the Hours, 1984; The Twofold Place, 1986; Years Found in Likeness, 1988; Former Light (selected poems), 1992; Momentum, 1992; Mermaid, 1996. Fiction: The Man Who Stayed Below, 1984; The Enduring Disguises, 1988; To The Burning City, 1991; Close Ups, 1994; The Tazyrik Year, 1998. Essays: The Totem Ship, 1996. Contributions to: Various Australian publications. Honours: New South Wales Premier's Prize for Poetry, 1981; Prizes for Fiction, 1985, 1992. Address: 6 Mulga Street, O'Connor, Australian Capital Territory 2602, Australia.

GOULD James L, b. 31 July 1945, Tulsa, Oklahoma, USA. Professor. m. Carol Holly Grant, 6 June 1970, 1 son, 1 daughter. Education: BS, California Institute of Technology, 1970; PhD, Rockefeller University, 1975. Appointment: Professor, Princeton University. Publications: Ethology, 1982; Biological Science, 6th edition, 1996; Honey Bee, 1988, 2nd edition, 1995; Life at the Edge, 1988; Sexual Selection, 1989, 2nd edition, 1996; The Animal Mind, 1994. Contributions to: More than 100 articles to journals and magazines. Honours: Guggenheim Fellowship, 1987; Fellow, American Association for the Advancement of Science, 1989; Animal Behavior Society, Fellow, 1991; New Jersey Professor of the Year, 1996; Animal Behaviour Society Distinguished Teaching Award, 1997. Address: Department of Ecology and Evolutionary Biology, Princeton University, Princeton, NJ 08544, USA.

GOULD Stephen Jay, b. 10 Sept 1941, New York, New York, USA. Professor of Geology and Zoology; Curator; Writer. m. Deborah Ann Lee, 3 Oct 1965, 2 sons. Education: AB, Antioch College, 1963; PhD, Columbia University, 1967. Appointments: Assistant Professor, 1967-71, Associate Professor, 1971-73, Professor of Geology, 1973-, Alexander Agassiz Professor of Zoology, 1982-, Assistant Curator, 1967-71, Associate Curator, 1971-73, Curator, 1973-, Invertebrate Paleontology, Museum of Comparative Zoology, Harvard University; Lecturer, Cambridge University, 1984, Yale University, 1986, Stanford University, 1989. Publications: Ontogeny and Phylogemy, 1977; Ever Since Darwin, 1977; The Panda's Thumb, 1980; The Mismeasure of Man, 1981; Hen's Teeth and Horse's Toes, 1983; The Flamingo's Smile, 1985; Time's Arrow, Time's Cycle, 1987; An Urchin in the Storm, 1987; Wonderful Life, 1989; Bully for Brontosaurus, 1991; Finders, Keepers (with R W Purcell), 1992; Eight Little Piggies, 1993; Questioning the Millennium: A rationalist's Guide to a Precisely Arbitrary Countdown, 1997; Leonardo's Mountain of Clams and the Diet of Worms, 1998. Contributions to: Journals. Honours: American Book Award, 1981; National Book Award, 1981; John D and Catharine T MacArthur Foundation Fellowship, 1981-86; National Book Critics Circle Award, 1982; Outstanding Book Award, American Educational Research Association, 1983; Phi Beta Kappa Book Awards, 1983, 1990; Brandeis University Creative Arts Award, 1986; Medal, City of Edinburgh, 1990; Forkosch Award, 1990; Rhone-Poulenc Prize, 1991; Silver Medal, Linnean Society, 1992; Over 35 honorary doctorates; Numerous other awards, medals, etc. Memberships: American Academy of Arts and Sciences, fellow; American Society of Naturalists, president, 1977-80; History of Science Association; National Academy of Sciences; Paleontological Society, president, 1985-; Sigma Xi; Society for the Study of Evolution, president, 1990; Society for the Systematic Study of Zoology. Address: c/o Museum of Comparative Zoology, Department of Earth Sciences, Harvard University, Cambridge, MA 02138, USA.

GOULDEN Joseph C, (Henry S A Becket), b. 23 May 1934, Marshall, Texas, USA. Writer. m. (1), 2 sons, (2) Leslie Cantrell Smith, 23 June 1979. Education: University of Texas, 1952-56. Appointments: Staff Writer, Dallas Morning News, Philadelphia Inquirer, 1958-68. Publications: The Curtis Caper, 1965; Monopoly, 1968; Truth is the First Casualty, 1969; The Money Givers, 1971; The Superlawyers, 1972; Meany: The Unchallenged Strong Man of American Labor, 1972; The Benchwarmers, 1974; Mencken's Last Campaign (editor), 1976; The Best Years, 1976; The Million Dollar Lawyers, 1978; Korea: Untold Story of War, 1982; Myth-Informed (with Paul Dickson), 1983; The News Manipulators (with Reed Irvine and Cliff Kincaid), 1983; Jerry Wurf: Labor's Last Angry Man, 1982; The Death Merchant, 1984; There Are Alligators in Our Sewers (with Paul Dickson), 1984; Dictionary of Espionage (as Henry S A Becket), 1987; Fit to Print: A M Rosenthal and His Times, 1988. Contributions to: Over 200 articles to magazines.

Address: 1534 29th Street North West, Washington, DC 20007, USA.

GOVIER Katherine Mary, b. 4 July 1948, Edmonton, Alberta, Canada. Writer. m. John Allen, 27 Feb 1981, 2 children. Education: BA, University of Alberta, 1970; MA, York University, 1972. Appointments: Lecturer in English, Ryerson Polytechnic, 1973-74; Contributing Editor, Toronto Life Magazine, 1975-77; Visiting Lecturer in Creative Writing, York University, 1982-85; Research Fellow, University of Leeds, 1986; Writer-in-Residence, Toronto Public Library, 1994-95. Publications: Random Descent, 1979; Going Through the Motions, 1981; Fables of Brunswick Avenue, 1985; Between Men, 1987; Before and After, 1989; Hearts of Flame, 1991; The Immaculate Conception Photography Gallery, 1994; Without a Guide (editor), 1994; Angel Walk, 1996. Contributions to: Numerous anthologies and periodicals. Honours: Authors Award, Foundation for the Advancement of Canadian Letters, 1979; National Magazine Award, 1979; City of Toronto Book Award, 1992; Shortlisted, Trillium Award, 1995. Memberships: PEN Canada; Writers Development Trust, chairman, 1990-91; Writers in Electronic Residence, chairman, 1991-94; Writers Union of Canada. Address: 54 Farnham Avenue, Toronto, Ontario, M4V 1H4, Canada.

GOWDY Barbara Louise, b. 25 June 1950, Windsor, Ontario, Canada. Novelist and Short Story Writer. Div. Education: York University, 1969-70. Publications: Through the Green Valley (novel), 1988; Falling Angels (novel), 1989; We So Seldom Look on Love (short stories), 1992; Mister Sandman (novel), 1995; The White Bone (novel), 1998. Contributions to: Best American Short Stories; The New Oxford Book of Canadian Short Stories; The Penguin Anthology of Stories by Canadian Women. Honours: Finalist, Giller Prize; Finalist, Governor General's Award; Recipient, The Marian Engel Award. Memberships: PEN Canada; The Writer's Union of Canada. Literary Agent: Jan Whitford. Address: c/o Jan Whitford, Westwood Creative Artists, 94 Harbord Street, Toronto, Ontario M5S 1G6, Canada.

GOYTISOLO Juan, b. 5 Jan 1931, Barcelona, Spain. Novelist. Education: Universities of Madrid and Barcelona, 1948-52. Appointments: Visiting Professor at universities in the USA. Publications: The Young Assassins, 1954; Children of Chaos, 1955; El Circo, 1957; La resaca, 1958; Fiestas, 1958; Para vivir aquí, 1960; Island of Women, 1961; The Party's Over: Four Attempts to Define a Love Story, 1962; Marks of Identity, 1966; Count Julian, 1970; Juan the Landless, 1975; Complete Works, 1977; Makbara, 1980; Landscapes after the Battle, 1982; The Virtues of the Solitary Bird, 1988; La Cuarentena, 1991; Other: The Countryside of Najir, 1960; Forbidden Territory (autobiography), 1985; Realms of Strife, 1986; Space in Motion, 1987. Honour: Europalia International Prize, 1985. Address: c/o Balcells, Diagonal 580, 08021, Barcelona, Spain.

GRABBE Crockett Lane, b. 3 Dec 1951, Silverton, Texas, USA. Research Scientist in Physics. Education: BSc, Physics, 1972, MA, Physics and Mathematics, 1973, University of Texas at Austin; PhD, Applied Physics, California Institute of Technology, Pasadena, 1978. Appointments: Visiting Assistant Professor, University of Tennessee, 1978-79; Research Scientist, Naval Research Laboratories, Washington, DC, 1979-81, University of Iowa, 1981-. Publications: Advances in Space Research (co-author), 1985; Plasma Waves and Instabilities, 1986; Space Weapons and the Strategic Defense Initiative, 1991; Trends in Geophysical Research 2 (co-author), 1993. Contributions to: Scientific journals. Honour: National Science Foundation Postdoctoral Fellowship, 1977-78. Memberships: American Association of Physics Teachers; American Geophysical Union; American Physical Society; Federation of American Scientists; International Union of Radio Science. Address: c/o Department of Physics and Astronomy, University of Iowa, Iowa City, IA 52242, USA.

GRACE Patricia (Frances), b. 1937, Wellington, New Zealand. Novelist. m. 7 children. Education: St Mary's

College; Wellington Teachers College. Appointments: Teacher, Primary and Secondary Schools, King Country, Northland and Porirua; Writing Fellow, Victoria University, Wellington, 1985. Publications: Mutuwhenua: The Moon Sleeps, 1978; Potiki, 1986; Cousins, 1992. Short Stories: Waiariki, 1975; The Dream Sleepers and Other Stories, 1980; Electric City and Other Stories, 1980; Selected Stories, 1991; The Sky People, 1994; Collected Stories, 1994. Other: Several books for children. Honours: New Zealand Fiction Award, 1987; HLD, Victoria University, 1989. Address: c/o Longman Paul Ltd, Private Bag, Takapuna, Auckland 9, New Zealand.

GRAEF Roger Arthur, b. 18 Apr 1936, New York, New York, USA. Writer; Television Producer; Filmmaker. m. Susan Mary Richards, 20 Nov 1985, 1 son, 1 daughter. Education: BA, Honours, Harvard University; Actors Studio, New York City. Appointments: Consultant, Collins Publishers, 1982-88; Media Columnist, The Times, 1993-95; Chairman, Signals International Trust: Book Aid (1 million books to Russia); Over 80 films and television programmes for British and International television. Publications: Talking Blues, 1989; Living Dangerously, 1993. Contributions to: Telegraph; Sunday Telegraph; Observer; Guardian; Independent; Independent on Sunday; Sunday Times; Evening Standard; Mail on Sunday. Honours: Royal Televison Society Award, 1979; British Academy of Televison and Film Arts, 1982; European Television Magazine Award. Membership: Writers' Guild; Mannheim Centre of Criminology, fellow; Royal Television Society, fellow; European Analytical College of Crime Prevention; Fulbright Commission. Address: Films of Record, 2 Elgin Avenue, London, A9 3QP.

GRAFF Henry F(ranklin), b. 11 Aug 1921, New York, New York, USA. Professor of History Emeritus; Writer. m. Edith Krantz, 16 June 1946, 2 daughters. Education: BSS, City College, New York City, 1941; MA, 1942, PhD, 1949, Columbia Unversity. Appointments: Fellow in History, 1941-42, Tutor in History, 1946, City College, New York City; Lecturer, 1946-47, Instructor to Associate Professor, 1946-61, Chairman, Department of History, 1961-64, Professor of History, 1961-91, Professor Emeritus, 1991-, Columbia University; Lecturer, Vassar College, 1953, Yale School of Medicine, 1993; Presidential appointee, National Historical Publications Commission, 1965-71, President John F Kennedy Assassination Records Review Board, 1993-; Senior Fellow, Freedom Foundation Media Studies Center, New York City, 1991-92; Dean's Distinguished Lecturer in the Humanities, Columbia University College of Physicians and Surgeons, 1992. Publications: Bluejackets with Perry in Japan, 1952; The Modern Researcher (with Jacques Barzun), 1962, 5th edition 1992; American Themes (with Clifford Lord), 1963; Thomas Jefferson, 1968; American Imperialism and the Philippine Insurrection, 1969; The Tuesday Cabinet: Deliberation and Decision on Peace and War under Lyndon B Johnson, 1970; The Call of Freedom (with Paul J Bohannan), 1978; The Promise of Democracy, 1978; This Great Nation, 1983; The Presidents: A Reference History, 1984, 2nd edition, 1996; America: The Glorious Republic, 1985, revised edition, 1990. Contributions to: Scholarly journals and to general periodicals. Honours: Townsend Harris Medal, City College of the City University of New York, 1966; Mark Van Doren Award, 1981, Great Teacher Award, 1982; Columbia University; Kidger Award, New England History Teachers Association, 1990; Phi Beta Kappa. Memberships: American Historical Association; Author's Guild; Council on Foreign Relations; Organization of American Historians; PEN; Society of American Historians; Corresponding member, Massachusetts Historical Society. Address: 47 Andrea Lane, Scarsdale, NY 10583, USA.

GRAFTON Sue, b. 24 Apr 1940, Louisville, Kentucky, USA. Writer. m. (1), 1 child, (2), 2 children, (3) Steven F Humphrey, 1 Oct 1978. Education: BA, University of Louisville, 1961. Appointments: Many guest lectureships at colleges and universities. Publications: Keziah Dane, 1967; The Lolly-Madonna War, 1969; "A" is for Alibi, 1982; "B" is for Burglar, 1985; "C" is for Corpse, 1989; "D" is for Deadbeat, 1987; "E" is for Evidence, 1988; "F" is for Fugitive, 1989; "G" is for Gumshoe, 1990; "H" is for Homicide, 1991; "I" is for Innocent, 1992; Kinsey and Me, 1992; "J" is for Judgement, 1994; "K" is for Killer, 1994; "L" is for Lawless, 1995; "M" is for Malice, 1996; "N" is for Noose, 1998. Editor: Writing Mysteries, 1992. Contributions to: Magazines, films and television. Honours: Shamus Awards, 1986, 1991, 1994; Anthony Awards, 1987, 1991; Doubleday Mystery Guild Awards, 1989, 1990, 1991, 1992; Falcon Award, 1990. Memberships: Crime Writers Association, president, 1989-90; Writers Guild of America. Address: PO Box 41447, Santa Barbara, CA 93140, USA.

GRAHAM Ada, b. 22 Aug 1931, Dayton, Ohio, USA. Writer. m. Frank Graham Jr, 31 Oct 1953. Education: Bowling Green State University, 1949-52; AB, Hunter College, New York City, 1957. Appointments: Vice-Chairman, Maine State Commission on the Arts, 1975-80; Board Memebr, New England Foundation for the Arts, 1977-80; Developer, Writer, Adventures, National Audubon Society, 1984-. Publications: The Great American Shopping Cart (with F Graham), 1969; Wildlife Rescue (with F Graham) 1970; Puffin Island (with F Graham), 1971; The Mystery of the Everglades, 1972; Dooryard Garden, 1974; Let's Discover the Winter Woods, 1974; Discover Changes Everywhere, 1974; Let's Discover Birds in Our World, 1974; The Careless Animal, 1974; The Milkweed and Its World of Animals (wth F Graham), 1976; Foxtails, Ferns and Fishscales: A Handbook of Art and Nature Projects, 1976; Whale Watch, 1978; Bug Hunters, 1978; Coyote Song, 1978; Falcon Flight, 1978; Audubon Readers (with F Graham), 6 volumes, 1978-81; Alligators (with F Graham), 1979; Careers in Conservation (with F Graham), 1980; Birds of the Northern Seas (with F Graham), 1980; Bears, 1981; The Changing Desert (with F Graham), 1981; Jacob and the Owl (with F Graham) 1981; Three Million Mice (with F Graham), 1981; Six Little Chicadees, 1982; Busy Bugs (with F Graham), 1983; The Big Stretch (with F Graham), 1985; We Watch Squirrels (with F Graham), 1985. Honours: 1st Prize, Annual Children's Science Book Award, New York Academy of Sciences, 1986; Eva L Gordon Award, American Nature Study Society, 1989. Address: Milbridge, ME 04658, USA.

GRAHAM Charles S. See: **TUBB E(dwin) C(harles).**

GRAHAM Frank Jr, b. 31 Mar 1925, New York, New York, USA. Writer. m. Ada Graham, 31 Oct 1953. Education: AB, Columbia University, 1950. Appointment: Field Editor, Audubon magazine, 1968-. Publications: It Takes Heart (with M Allen), 1959; Disaster by Default, 1966; The Great American Shopping Cart (with A Graham), 1969; Since Silent Spring, 1970; Wildlife Rescue (with A Graham), 1970; Puffin Island (with A Graham), 1971; Man's Dominion, 1971; The Mystery of the Everglades (with A Graham), 1972; Where the Place Called Morning Lies, 1973; Audubon Primers (with A Graham), 4 volumes, 1974; The Careless Animal (with A Graham), 1975; Gulls: A Social History, 1975; Potomac: The Nation's River, 1976; The Milkweed and its World of Animals (with A Graham), 1976; The Adirondack Park: A Political History, 1978; Audubon Readers (with A Graham), 6 volumes, 1978-81; Careers in Conservation (with A Graham) 1980; Birds of the Northern Seas (with A Graham), 1981; A Farewell to Heroes, 1981; The Changing Desert (with A Graham), 1981; Jacob and Owl (with A Graham), 1981; Three Million Mice (with A Graham), 1981; Busy Bugs (with A Graham), 1983; The Dragon Hunters, 1984; The Big Stretch (with A Graham), 1985; We Watch Squirrels (with A Graham), 1985; The Audubon Ark, 1990. Address: Milbridge, ME 04658, USA.

GRAHAM Henry, b. 1 Dec 1930, Liverpool, England. Lecturer; Poet. Education: Liverpool College of Art, 1950-52. Appointment: Poetry Editor, Ambit, London, 1969-. Publications: Good Luck to You Kafka/You'll Need It Boss, 1969; Soup City Zoo, 1969; Passport to Earth, 1971; Poker in Paradise Lost, 1977; Europe After Rain, 1981; Bomb, 1985; The Very Fragrant Death of Paul Gauguin, 1987; Jardin Gobe Avions, 1991; The Eye of the Beholder, 1997. Contributions to: Ambit; Transatlantic Review; Prism International Review; Evergreen Review; Numerous anthrologies worldwide. Honours: Arts Council Literature Awards, 1969, 1971, 1975. Address: Flat 5, 23 Marmion Road, Liverpool L17 8TT, England.

GRAHAM James. See: **PATTERSON Harry.**

GRAHAM Jorie, b. 9 May 1951, New York, New York, USA. Poet; Teacher. m. James Galvin. Education: BFA, New York University, 1973; MFA, University of Iowa, 1978. Appointments: Poetry Editor, Crazy Horse, 1978-81; Assistant Professor, Murray State University, Kentucky, 1978-79, Humboldt State University, Arcata, California, 1979-81; Instructor, Columbia University, 1981-83; Staff, University of Iowa, 1983-. Publications: Hybrids of Plants and of Ghosts, 1980; Erosion, 1983; The End of Beauty, 1987; The Best American Poetry (editor with David Lehman), 1990; Region of Unlikeness, 1991; Materialism, 1993; The Dream of the Unified Field, 1995; Errancy. 1997. Honours: American Academy of Poets Award, 1977; Young Poets Prize, Poetry Northwest, 1980; Pushcart Prizes, 1980, 1982; Ingram Merrill Foundation Grant, 1981; Great Lakes Colleges Association Award, 1981; American Poetry Review Prize, 1982; Bunting Fellow, Radcliffe Institute, 1982; Guggenheim Fellowship, 1983-84; John D and Catharine T MacArthur Foundation Fellowship, 1990; Pulitzer Prize in Poetry, 1996. Address: c/o Department of Creative Writing, University of Iowa, Iowa City, IA 52242, USA.

GRAHAM Robert Donald, (Bob Graham), b. 20 Oct 1942, Sydney, Australia. Author; Illustrator. m. Carolyn Smith, 26 Aug 1968, 1 son, 1 daughter. Education: Julian Ashton School of Fine Art, Sydney. Publications: Pete and Roland, 1981; Here Comes John, 1983; Here Comes Theo, 1983; Pearl's Place, 1983; Libby, Oscar and Me, 1984; Bath Time for John, 1985; First There Was Frances, 1985; Where Is Sarah?, 1985; The Wild, 1986; The Adventures of Charlotte and Henry, 1987; Crusher is Coming!, 1987; The Red Wollen Blanket, 1987; Has Anyone Here Seen William?, 1988; Sitting Ducks and The Duck's Revenge, 1988; Bringing Home the New Baby, 1989; Grandad's Magic, 1989; Greetings From Sandy Beach, 1990; Rose Meets Mr Wintergarten, 1992; Brand New Baby, 1992; Spirit of Hope, 1993; Zoltan the Magnificent, 1994; Queenie the Bantam, 1997. Honours: Australian Picture Book of the Year, 1988, 1991, 1993. Membership: Australian Society of Authors. Address: Greystones, Vale Street, Henstridge, Somerset BA8 0SQ, England.

GRAHAM Sonia. See: **SINCLAIR Sonia Elizabeth.**

GRAHAM Toni, b. 24 June 1945, San Francisco, CA, USA. Writer (fiction); College Lecturer. m. 23 Nov 1972, Div 1986, 1 son. Education: BA, Humanities, New College of California, San Francisco, CA, USSA, 1989; BA, English, 1992; MFA, Creative Writing, San Francisco State University, 1996. Appointments: Lecturer, San Francisco State University, 1992; Lecturer, University of San Francisco, 1995-; Lecturer, University of California, Santa Cruz, 1995-97, Lecturer, Santa Clara University, Santa Clara, CA, USA, 1997-. Publication: The Daiquiri Girls, 1998. Contributions to: American Fiction; Mississippi Review; Ascent; Five Fingers Review; many others. Honours: Associated Writing Programs, Short Fiction Award, 1997. Memberships: Hemingway Society; Modern Language Association; Associated Writing Programs. Address: 345 Prospect Avenue, San Francisco, CA 94110, USA.

GRAHAM Winston Mawdsley, b. 30 June 1910, Victoria Park, Manchester, England. m. Jean Mary Williamson, 1939, dec 1992, 1 son, 1 daughter. Publications: Night Journey, 1941, revised edition, 1966; The Merciless Ladies, 1944, revised edition, 1979; The Forgotten Story, 1945 (ITV production, 1983); Ross Poldark, 1945; Demelza, 1946; Take My Life, 1947 (filmed, 1947); Cordelia, 1949; Night Without Stars, 1950 (filmed, 1950); Jeremy Poldark, 1950; Fortune is a Woman, 1953 (filmed, 1958); Greek Fire, 1957; The Tumbled House, 1959; Marnie, 1961 (filmed, 1963); The Grove of Eagles, 1963; After the Act, 1965; The Walking Stick, 1967 (filmed, 1970); The Spanish Armadas, 1972; The Black Moon, 1973; Woman in the Morror, 1975; The Four Swans, 1976; The Angry Tide, 1977; The Stranger from the Sea, 1981; The Miller's Dance, 1982; Poldark's Cornwall, 1983; The Loving Cup, 1984; The Green Flash, 1986; Cameo, 1988; The Twisted Sword, 1990; Stephanie, 1992; Tremor, 1995; The Ugly Sister, 1998. Other: BBC TV Series Poldark (the first 4 Poldark novels), 1975-76, second series (the next 3 Poldark novels), 1977; Circumstantial Evidence, play, 1979. Honours: Officer of the Order of the British Empire, 1983; Fellow, Royal Society of Literature. Address: Abbotswood House, Buxted, East Sussex TN22 4PB, England.

GRAHAM-YOOLL Andrew Michael, b. 5 Jan 1944, Buenos Aires, Argentina. Journalist; Writer. m. 17 Jan 1966, 1 son, 2 daughters. Appointments: News Editor and Political Columnist, Buenos Aires Herald, 1966-76; Freelance Writer, San Francisco Chronicle, 1967-70, 1976, Baltimore Sun, 1967-69, 1976, Miami Herald, 1969, Kansas City Star, 1969-73, New York Times, 1970, Newsweek, 1970; Broadcaster, BBC World Service, London, 1976; Occasional News Commentary, London Broadcasting Company; Sub Editor, Foreign News, Daily Telegraph, London, 1976-77; Foreign Correspondent, The Guardian, London, 1977-84; Editor, Writers News, London, 1983-85; Deputy Editor, 1984-85, Editor, 1985-88, South Magazine, London; Editor, Index on Censorship, 1989-93; Senior Visiting Fellow, Queen Mary and Westfield College, London, 1990-94; Press Fellow, Wolfson College, University of Cambridge, 1994; Editor-in-Chief, Buenos Aires Herald, 1994-, President of the Board, 1995-98. Publications: The Press in Argentina, 1973-78, 1979; Portrait of an Exile, 1981; The Forgotten Colony, 1981; Small Wars You May Have Missed (in South America), 1983; A State of Fear, 1986; Argentina, Peron to Videla 1955-1976, 1989; After the Despots, 1991; Point of Arrival, 1992; Committed Observer, 1995. Short Stories: The Date Might Be Forgotten, 1967; The Premonition, 1968; Twenty Pages of Garcia, 1974; Money Cures Melancholy, 1974; Sirens, 1980; Goodbye Buenos Aires (novel), 1997; Rosas in British Eyes (History), 1997; Poetry in Spanish. Honours: Poetry Prize, El Vidente Ciego Magazine Rosario, Argentina, 1975; British Council Visitorship to Britain, 1976; Nicholas Tomalin Memorial Award for Journalists, 1977. Memberships: PEN, press officer, 1979-87; Writers Guild of Great Britain, executive council, 1983; Argentine Writers Society; Anglo-Argentine Society, committee member, 1989-90; Royal Literary Fund, life member, 1987; Association of British Editors, board member, 1990-93; Arts Council Literature Touring Panel, 1992-94. Address: c/o Buenos Aires Herald, Azopardo 455, 1107 Buenos Aires, Argentina.

GRAMLEY Judith, b. 22 Oct 1941, Mansfield, Ohio, USA. Professor of Spanish. m. Harold Dean Gramley, 18 Jan 1969, 2 sons. Education: BS, 1963, MA, 1966, Kent State University, Ohio; AS, 1984, BS, 1986, Edinboro University of Pennsylvania; ABD, University of Pittsburgh. Publications: Human Sacrifice and Cannibalism Among the Aztecs: A Moral or Barbaric Act?, 1993; Clémence Ravaçon Mershon: A Life-long Commitment, 1994; Adapting the Novel to Film: The Case of Galdós's Doña Perfecta, 1995; Crossing Borders Through Language, 1995. Contributions to: Periodicals and journals. Honours: Sigma Delta Pi; Phi Sigma Iota; Alpha Chi. Address: 126B Biggers House, Edinboro University of Pennsylvania, Edinboro, PA 16444, USA.

GRANADOS Paul. See: **KENT Arthur (William Charles).**

GRANDOWER Elissa. See: **WAUGH Hillary Baldwin.**

GRANGE Peter. See: **NICOLE Christopher Robin.**

GRANT Anthony. See: **PARES Marion.**

GRANT Charles, b. 12 Sept 1942, Newark, New Jersey, USA. Writer. Education: BA, Trinity College, Hartford, Connecticut, 1964. Publications: The Shadow of Alpha, 1976; The Curse, 1976; The Hour of the Oxrum

Dead, 1977; Writing and Selling Science Fiction (editor), 1977; The Ravens of the Moon, 1978; The Sound of Midnight, 1978; Shadows (editor), 9 volumes, 1978-86; Nightmares (editor), 1979; The Last Call of Mourning, 1979; Legion, 1979; Tales from the Nightside, 1981; Glow of Candles and Other Stories, 1981; Nightmare Seasons, 1982; Night Songs, 1984; The Tea Party, 1985; The Pet, 1986; The Orchards, 1987; Something Stirs, 1992. Address: c/o Tor Books, 175 Fifth Avenue, New York, NY 10010, USA.

GRANT Ellen Catherine Gardner, b. 29 Sept 1934, Scotland. Physician. m. David Norman Grant, 12 Sept 1959, 1 son, 2 daughters. Education: Bachelor of Medicine, Bachelor of Surgery, St Andrews University, 1958; Diploma, Royal College of Obstetricians and Gynaecologists, London, 1959. Contributions to: Books and journals. Memberships: British Society for Allergy and Environmental Medicine; British Society for Nutritional Medicine; Doctors Against Abuse from Steroid Sex Hormones, honorary secretary; Dyslexia Institute; Foresight (Association for the Promotion of Preconception Care). Address: 20 Coombe Ridings, Kingston-upon-Thames, Surrey KT2 7JU, England.

GRANT James Shaw, b. 22 May 1910, Stornoway, Scotland. Author; Journalist. m. Catherine Mary Stewart, 25 May 1951. Education: MA; LLD (Aberdeen); Nicolson Institute; Glasgow University, Scotland. Appointments: Editor, Stornoway Gazette, 1932-63; Chairman, Crofters Commission, 1963-78; Member, Highlands and Islands Development Board, 1970-82; Director, Grampian TV, 1969-80; Member, Scottish Advisory Committee of the British Council, 1972-94; Chairman, Pitlochry Festival Theatre, 1971-82; Vice Chairman, Eden Court Theatre, 1987-96. Publications: Plays: Tarravore; The Magic Rowan; Legend is Born; Comrade the King; Books: Highland Villages; Their Children Will See; The Hub of My Universe; Surprise Island; The Gaelic Vikings; Stornoway and the Lews; Discovering Lewis and Harris; Enchanted Island; A Shilling for Your Scowl; Morrison of the Bounty. Honours: OBE; CBE; FRAGS; LLD; FRSE. Address: Ardgrianach, Culloden Road, Inverness IV2 5BQ, Scotland.

GRANT John, (Jonathan Gash, Graham Gaunt), b. 30 Sept 1933, Bolton, Lancashire, England. Physician; Author. m. Pamela Richard, 19 Feb 1955, 3 daughters. Education: MB, 1958, BS, 1958, University of London; MRCS, 1958, LRCP, 1958, Royal College of Surgeons and Physicians. Appointments: General Practitioner, London, 1958-59; Pathologist, London and Essex, 1959-62; Clinical Pathologist, Hannover and Berlin, 1962-65; Lecturer in Clinical Pathology and Head of the Pathology Division, University of Hong Kong, 1965-68; Microbiologist in Hong Kong and London, 1968-71; Head of the Bacteriology Unit, School of Hygiene and Tropical Medicine, University of London, 1971-88. Publications: As Jonathan Gash: The Judas Pair, 1977; Gold by Gemini, 1978; The Grail Tree, 1979; Spend Game, 1981; The Vatican Rip, 1981; The Sleepers of Erin, 1983; Firefly Gadroom, 1984; The Gondola Scam, 1984; Pearlhanger, 1985; The Tartan Ringers, 1986; Moonspender, 1987; Jade Woman, 1989; The Very Last Gambado, 1990; The Great California Game, 1991; The Lies of Fair Ladies, 1992; Paid and Loving Eyes, 1993. As Graham Gaunt: The Incomer, 1982. Honour: Crime Writers' Association Award, 1977. Memberships: International College of Surgeons, fellow; Royal Society of Tropical Medicine, fellow. Address: Silver Willows, Chapel Lane, West Bergholt, Colchester, Essex CO6 3EF, England.

GRANT John. See: BARNETT Paul le Page.

GRANT Maxwell. See: LYNDS Dennis.

GRANT Michael, b. 21 Nov 1914, London, England. Retired Educator; Writer. m. Anne Sophie Beskow, 2 Aug 1944, 2 sons. Education: BA, 1936, MA, 1940, Trinity College, Cambridge. Appointments: Fellow, Trinity College, Cambridge, 1938-49; Professor of Latin Literature, University of Edinburgh, 1948-59; Vice-Chancellor, University of Khartoum, 1956-58;

President and Vice-Chancellor, Queen's University, Belfast, 1959-66; Chairperson, Advisory Council for Education in Northern Ireland, 1959-66, and Commonwealth Conference on English as a Second Language, 1960. Publications: From Imperium to Auctoritas: A Historical Study of Aes Coinage in the Roman Empire, 49 BC-AD 14, 1946; Aspects of the Principate of Tiberius: Historical Comments on the Colonial Coinage Issued Outside Spain, 1950; Roman Anniversary Issues: An Exploratory Study of the Numismatic and Medallic Commemoration and Anniversary Years, 49 BC-AD 375, 1950; Ancient History, 1952; The Six Main Aes Coinages of Augustus, 1953; Roman Imperial Money, 1954; Roman Literature, 1954, revised edition, 1964; Roman Readings (editor), 1958; Roman History from Coins, 1958; Greeks (with Don Pottinger), 1958; Romans (with Don Pottinger), 1960; The World of Rome, 1960; Myths of the Greeks and Romans, 1962; The Birth of Western Civilization: Greece and Rome, 1964; The Civilizations of Europe, 1966, revised edition, 1971; Cambridge, 1966; Gladiators, 1967, revised edition, 1971; The Climax of Rome: The Final Achievements of the Ancient World, AD 161-337, 1968; The Ancient Mediterranean, 1969; Julius Caesar, 1969; The Ancient Historians, 1970; The Rome Forum, 1970; Nero: Emperor in Revolt, 1970; Cities of Vesuvius: Pompeii and Herculaneum, 1971; Herod the Great, 1971; Roman Myths, 1971; Cleopatra, 1972; Ancient History Atlas, 1972; The Jews in the Roman World, 1973; Gods and Mortals in Classical Mythology (with John Hazel), 1973; Greek Literature in Translation (editor), 1973; Who's Who in Classical Mythology (with John Hazel), 1973; Caesar, 1974; The Army of the Caesars, 1974; The Twelve Caesars, 1975; Eros in Pompeii: The Secret Rooms of the National Museum of Naples, 1975; The Fall of the Roman Empire: A Reappraisal, 1976; Saint Paul, 1976; Jesus: An Historian's Review of the Gospels, 1977; The History of Rome, 1978; The Art and Life of Pompeii and Herculaneum, 1979; Latin Literature: An Anthology (editor), 1979; The Etruscans, 1980; Greek and Latin Authors, 800 BC-AD 1000, 1980; Dawn of the Middle Ages, 1981; From Alexander to Cleopatra: The Hellenistic World, 1980; History of Ancient Israel, 1984; The Roman Emperors: A Biographical Guide to the Rulers of Ancient Rome, 31 BC-AD 476, 1985; Guide to the Classical World: A Dictionary of Place-Names, 1986; The Rise and Fall of the Greeks, 1988; The Classical Greeks, 1988; A Short History of Classical Civilization, 1991; A Social History of Greece and Rome, 1992; Saint Peter, 1994; My First Eighty Years, 1994; The Antonines, 1994; The Sayings of the Bible, 1994; Art in the Roman Empire, 1995; Greek and Roman Historians: Information and Misinformation, 1995; The Severans, 1996; From Rome to Byzantium, 1998; The Collapse and Recovery of the Roman Empire, 1999. Other: Editor and translator of various Roman writers. Honours: Officer of the Order of the British Empire, 1946; Commander of the Order of the British Empire, 1958; Leverhulme Research Fellow, 1958; Premio Latina, 1981. Memberships: British Institute of Archaeology at Ankara, vice-president, 1961-; Classical Association, president, 1977-78; Roman Society, vice-president, 1961-; Royal Numismatic Society, president, 1953-56; Virgil Society, president, 1963-66. Address: Le Pitturacce, 351 Via Della Chiesa, Gattaiola, 55050 Lucca, Italy.

GRANT Neil, (David Mountfield, D M Field, Gail Trenton), b. 9 June 1938, England. Writer. m. Vera Steiner, 23 Sept 1977, 2 daughters. Education: MA, Honours, St John's College, Cambridge, 1961. Publications: A History of Polar Exploration, 1974; Neil Grant's Book of Spies and Spying, 1975; A History of African Exploration, 1976; Children's History of Britain, 1977; Greek and Roman Erotica, 1982; The White Bear, fiction, 1983; American Folktales and Legends, 1988; London's Villages, 1990. Membership: Royal Geographical Society. Address: 2 Avenue Road, Teddington, Middlesex TW11 0BT, England.

GRANT Nicholas. See: NICOLE Christopher Robin.

GRANT Roderick, b. 16 Jan 1941, Forres, Morayshire, Scotland. Author. Appointment: Sub Editor, Weekly

Scotsman, 1965-67. Publications: Adventure in My Veins, 1968; Seek Out the Guilty, 1969; Where No Angels Dwell, 1969; Gorbals Doctor, 1970; The Dark Horizon (with Alexander Highlands), 1971; The Lone Voyage of Betty Mouat, 1973; The Stalking of Adrian Lawford, 1974; The Clutch of Caution, 1975, 2nd edition, 1985; The 51st Highland Division at War, 1976; Strathalder: A Highland Estate, 1978, 2nd edition, 1989; A Savage Freedom, 1978; The Great Canal, 1978; A Private Vendetta, 1978; But Not in Anger (with C Cole), 1979; Clap Hands for the Singing Molecatcher, 1989. Address: 3 Back Lane Cottages, Bucks Horn Oak, Farmham, Surrey, England.

GRANT-ADAMSON Lesley Ann, b. 26 Nov 1942, London, England. Writer. m. Andrew Grant-Adamson, 14 Dec 1968. Education: Schools in Trealaw, Rhondda & Islington, London. Appointments: Journalist, Trade & Technical Magazines in London; Reporter for Southgate & Palmers Green Gazette, London; Reporter for the Citizen, Gloucester, Rugby Advertiser, Coventry Telegraph & News Editor of Herts Advertizer. Publications: Fiction: Patterns in the Dust; The Face of Death; Guilty Knowledge; Wild Justice; Threatening Eye; Curse the Darkness; Flynn; A Life of Adventure; The Dangerous Edge; Dangerous Games; Wish You Were Here; Evil Acts; The Girl in the Case; Lipstick and Liese; Undertow; Non-Fiction: A Season in Spain; Writing Crime TV Suspense Fiction. Contributions to: Stories and Features in numerous British Magazines. Memberships: Crime Writers' Association; Society of Authors; RSL; PEN. Literary Agent: Gregory & Radice. Address: 30 Bewdley St, London N1 1HB, England.

GRASS Günter (Wilhelm), b. 16 Oct 1927, Danzig, Germany. Author; Dramatist; Poet; Sculptor; Printmaker. m. (1) Anna Schwartz, 1954, 3 sons, 1 daughter, (2) Utte Grunert, 1979. Education: Art School, Düsseldorf. Publications: Novels: Die Blechtrommel, 1959, English translation as The tin Drum: Katz und Maus, 1961, English translation as Cat and Mouse; Hundejahre, 1963, English translation in Telgte, 1979, English translation as The Meeting at Telgte: Kopfgeburten: Oder die Deutschen sterben aus, 1980, English translation as Headbirths: Or the Germans Are Dying Out; Unkenrufe, 1992, English translation as The Call of the Toad; Ein weites Feld, 1995. Plays: Hochwasser, 1956; Noch 10 Minuten bis Buffalo, 1958; Onkel, Onkel, 1958; Die bösen Köche, 1961; Die Plebejer probem den aufstand, 1965; Davor, 1968. Poetry: Dokumente zur politischen Wirkung, 1972; Aufsätze zur Literatur, 1980; Zeichen und Schreiben, 1982; Widerstand lernen-Politische Gegenreden, 1980-83, 1984; On Writing and Politics, 1967-1983, 1985; Two States--One Nation?, 1990; Vier Jahrzehnte, 1992. Honours: Lyric Prize, Süddeutscher Rundfunk, 1955; Group 47 Prize, 1959; Literary Prize, Association of German Critics, 1960; Georg Büchner Prize, 1965; Theodor Heuss Prize, 1969; International Feltrinelli Prize, 1982; Karel Capek Prize, 1994. Memberships: Akademie der Künste, Berlin, president, 1983-86; American Academy of Arts and Sciences. Address: Niedstrasse 13, 12159, Berlin, Germany.

GRASSBY Albert Jaime, b. 12 July 1926, Brisbane, Queensland, Australia. Author. m. Ellnor Judith Louez, 3 Feb 1962, 1 daughter. Education: Special Studies, University of California, Berkeley; PhD, University of Munich. Publications: Griffith of the Four Faces, 1960; Morning After, 1979; The Spanish Contribution to Australia, 1983; Six Australian Battlefields, 1988; Oodgeroo Noonuccal, 1990; The Australian Republic, 1992; The Tyranny of Prejudice, 1994. Contributions to: Australia's Italians; Republican Australia; Pacific Islander Migration; Many journals. Honours: Knight Commander of Order of Solidarity, Italy, 1971; Special Citation, University of Santo Tomas, Manila, 1974; Honorary Citizenship, Plati and Sinopoli, Italy, 1974; Akrata and Platynos, Greece, 1977; Knight Commander, Order of Santa Agata, Malta, 1979; Honorary PhD, University of Munich, 1979; Order of Australia, 1985; UN Peace Medal, 1986; Knight Commander of the Order of Isabella La Catolica, Spain, 1986; Medal of Merit, Ecuador, 1997; Medal of Sarajevo, Bosnia, 1998. Address: GPO Box 1611, Canberra 2601, Australia.

GRAU Shirley Ann, b. 8 July 1929, New Orleans, Louisiana, USA. Writer. m. James Feibleman, 4 Aug 1955, 2 sons, 2 daughters. Education: BA, Tulane University. Publications: The Black Prince, 1955; The Hard Blue Sky, 1958; The House on Coliseum Street, 1961; The Keepers of the House, 1964; The Condor Passes, 1971; The Wind Shifting West, 1973; Evidence of Love, 1977; Nine Women, 1985; Roadwalkers, 1994. Contributions to: New Yorker; Saturday Evening Post; Others. Honour: Pulitzer Prize for Fiction, 1965. Address: 210 Baronne Street, Suite 1120, New Orleans, LA 70112, USA.

GRAVER Elizabeth, b. 2 July 1964, Los Angeles, California, USA. Writer; Teacher. Education: BA, Wesleyan University, 1986; MFA, Washington University, 1990. Appointments: Visiting Professor of English and Creative Writing, 1993-95, Assistant Professor of Creative Writing and English, 1995-, Boston College. Publication: Have You Seen Me?; Unravelling (novel), 1997; The Honey Thief, 1999; Best American Essays, 1998. Contributions to: Best American Short Stories; Story; Southern Review; Antaeus; Seventeen; Southwest Review; O Henry Prize Stories, 1994, 1996; Louder Than Words; Ploughshares; Best American Essays, 1998. Honours: Fulbright Fellowship; Drue Heinz Literature Prize; National Endowment for the Arts Fellowship; Writers Exchange Winner; Guggenheim Memorial Fellowship, 1997. Membership: Phi Beta Kappa. Address: c/o Richard Parks Agency, 138 East 16th Street 5B, New York, NY 10003, USA.

GRAVER Lawrence Stanley, b. 6 Dec 1931, New York, New York, USA. Professor of English. m. Suzanne Levy Graver, 28 Jan 1960, 2 daughters. Education: BA, City College of New York, 1954; PhD, University of California, Berkeley, 1961. Appointments: Assistant Professor, University of California, Los Angeles, 1961-64; Associate Professor, 1964-71, Professor, 1971-, Williams College. Publications: Conrad's Short Fiction, 1968; Carson McCullers, 1969; Mastering the Film, 1974; Beckett: The Critical Heritage, 1979; Beckett: Waiting for Godot, 1989; An Obsession with Anne Frank: Meyer Levin and The Diary, 1995. Contributions to: New York Times Book Review: Saturday Review: New Republic: New Leader; 19th Century Fiction. Membership: Modern Language Association. Address: Department of English, Williams College, Williamstown, MA 01267, USA.

GRAVES Richard Perceval, b. 21 Dec 1945, Brighton, England. Author. 2 sons, 1 daughter. Education: St John's College Oxford, 1964-67; MA, Modern History. Appointments: Arnold Lodge School, 1968; Harrow School, 1969; Holme Grange School, 1969-71; Ellesmere College, 1971-73. Publications: Lawrence of Arabia and His World, 1976; A E Houseman: The Scholar-Poet, 1979; The Brothers Powys, 1983; Robert Graves: The Assault Heroic, 1986; Robert Graves: The Years with Laura Riding, 1990; Richard Hughes, 1994; Robert Graves and The White Goddess, 1995. Honour: Hawthornden Fellowship, 1999. Memberships: Housman Society; Powys Society; Society of Authors. Literary Agent: Rachel Calder of Tessa Sayle, 11 Jubilee Place, London SW3 3TE, England. Address: 26 Hill's Lane, Shrewsbury SY1 1QU, England.

GRAVES Roy Neil, b. 2 Feb 1939, Medina, Tennessee, USA. Professor of English; Poet; Writer. m. Sue Lain Hunt, 5 June 1965, div July 1982, 1 son, 2 daughters. Education: BA, Honours, English, Princeton University, 1961; MA, English, Duke University, 1964; DA, English, University of Mississippi, 1977. Appointments: Assistant Professor of English, Lynchburg Branch, University of Virginia, 1965-67; Assistant Professor, 1967-68, Associate Professor of English, 1968-69, Central Virginia Community College, Lynchburg; Assistant Professor, 1969-77, Associate Professor, 1977-82, Professor of English, 1982-, University of Tennessee at Martin. Publications: River Region Monographs: Reports on People and Popular Culture (editor), 1975; "Medina" and Other Poems, 1976; Hugh John Massey of the Royal Hall: The Lost Master Poet of Forteenth-Century England and the Lost Runes, 1977; Out of Tennessee: Poems, with an Introduction, 1977; The Runic "Beowulf" and Other Lost Anglo-Saxon Poems, Reconstructed and Annotated, 1979; Shakespeare's Lost Sonnets: The 154 Runic Poems Reconstructed and Introducted, 1979; Somewhere on the Interstate (poems), 1987; Shakespeare's Sonnets Upside Down, 1995; Always at Home Here: Poems and Insights from Six Tennessee Poets (edited by Ernest Lee), 1997. Contributions to: Articles in reference works and scholarly journals; Poems in anthologies and periodicals. Honours: National Endowment for the Humanities Grant, 1975; Cunningham Teacher/Scholar Award, University of Tennessee at Martin, 1997. Address: c/o Department of English, University of Tennessee at Martin, Martin, TN 38238, USA.

GRAY Alasdair (James), b. 28 Dec 1934, Glasgow, Scotland. Writer; Painter. 1 son. Education: Diploma, Glasgow Art School, 1957. Appointments: Artist-recorder, People's Palace, history museum, 1977; Writer-in-Residence, University of Glasgow, 1977-79; Freelance painter and maker of books, 1979-; Mural in Abbots House Local History Museum, Dunfermline, 1995. Publications: Lanark, 1981, revised edition, 1985; Unlikely Stories, 1983, revised edition, 1984; Janine, 1984, revised edition, 1985; The Fall of Kelvin Walker: A Fable of the Sixties, 1985; Lean Tales (with James Kelman and Agnes Owens), 1985; Saltire Self-Portrait 4, 1988; McGrotty and Ludmilla, or The Harbinger Report: A Romance of the Eighties, 1989; Old Negatives, Four Verse Sequences, 1989; Something Leather, 1990; Poor Things, 1992; Ten Tales Tall and True, 1993; A History Maker, 1994; Maris Belfrage, a Romantic Novel with Five Shorter Tales, 1996; Working Legs, a Play for People Without Them, 1997; Why Scots Should Rule Scotland, 1997. Honours: Saltire Society, 1982; Whitbread Award, 1992. Memberships: Society of Authors; Various organizations supporting coal miners and nuclear disarmament. Literary Agent: Giles Gordon, 6 Ann Street, Edinburgh, EH4 1PJ. Address: 2 Marchmont Terrace, Glasgow G12 9LT, Scotland.

GRAY Alice Wirth, b. 29 Apr 1934, Chicago, Illinois, USA. Writer; Poet. m. Ralph Gareth Gray, 16 July 1954, 2 daughters. Education: BA, 1958, MA, 1960, University of California. Publication: What the Poor Eat, 1993. Contributions to: Atlantic; American Scholar; Poetry; Breakfast Without Meat; Little Magazine; Helicon Nine; Primavera; Sequoia. Honours: Illinois Arts Council Literary Award; Gordon Barber Memorial Award; Duncan Lawrie Award. Memberships: Poetry Society of America; PEN Center USA West. Address: 1001 Merced Street, Berkeley, CA 94707, USA.

GRAY Angela. See: **DANIELS Dorothy.**

GRAY Anne, b. 26 Oct 1941, Vienna, Austria (US citizen, 1948). Author; Professor of Music, Speech, and Drama; Musicologist. m. Charles R Bubb III, 7 Aug 1966, 2 sons. Education: BA cum laude in Music, Speech, and Drama, Hunter College of the City University of New York, 1963; MA, Honours, in English and Education, San Diego State University, 1968; PhD summa cum laude in Humanities, University of California at San Diego, 1982. Appointments: Teacher, San Diego Public Schools, 1963-68; Professor of English, Mesa College, California, 1968-71. Publications: The Wonderful World of San Diego, 1971, 2nd edition, 1976; Where Have You Been All Your Life?, 1990; How to Hang Onto Your Husband!, 1990; The Popular Guide to Classical Music, 1993; The Popular Guide to Women in Classical Music, 1999. Contributions to: Reference books, journals, periodicals, and newspapers. Honours: Music Award, San Diego Public Schools, 1968; Award of Merit, San Diego Historical Society, 1976; Outstanding Leadership Award, Toastmasters of America, 1981; Certificates of Appreciation, San Diego Symphony Orchestra, 1983, 1985, 1987; Achievement Award, San Diego Writers Guild, 1989; Literary Medals, San Diego Public Library, 1990, 1993, 1995; Outstanding Author of the Year Award, National League of American Penwomen, 1996. Memberships: American Association of University Women; National League of Penwomen; International Platform Speakers Association; International Alliance of Women in Music; College Music Society. Address: c/o WordWorld, PO Box 91496, San Diego, CA 92169-3496, USA.

GRAY Caroline. See: **NICOLE Christopher Robin.**

GRAY Douglas, b. 17 Feb 1930, Melbourne, Victoria, Australia. Professor of English; Writer. m. 3 Sept 1959, 1 son. Education: MA, Victoria University of Wellington, New Zealand, 1952; BA, 1956, MA, 1960, Merton College, Oxford. Appointment: J R R Tolkien Professor of English, Oxford, 1980-97, Emeritus, 1997-. Publications: Themes and Images in the Medieval English Religious Lyric, 1972; Robert Henryson, 1979; The Oxford Book of Late Medieval Verse and Prose (editor), 1985; Selected Poems of Robert Henryson and William Dunbar (editor), 1998. Contributions to: Scholarly journals. Honours: British Academy, fellow, 1989; Honorary LitD, Victorian University of Wellington, 1995. Memberships: Early English Text Society; Society for the Study of Medieval Languages and Literatures, president, 1982-86. Address: Lady Margaret Hall, Oxford OX2 6QA, England.

GRAY Dulcie (Winifred Catherine), b. 20 Nov 1920, England. Actress; Dramatist; Writer. m. Michael Denison, 29 Apr 1939. Education: England and Malaysia. Appointments: Numerous stage, film, radio, and television appearances. Publications: Murder on the Stairs, 1957; Baby Face, 1959; For Richer, for Richer, 1970; Ride on a Tiger, 1975; Butterflies on My Mind, 1978; Dark Calypso, 1979; The Glanville Women, 1982; Mirror Image, 1987; Looking Forward, Looking Backward (autobiography), 1991. Contributions to: Periodicals. Honours: *Queen's Silver Jubilee Medal*, 1977; *Times* Educational Supplement Senior Information Book Prize, 1978; Commander of the Order of the British Empire, 1983. Memberships: British Actors Equity; Linnean Society, fellow; Royal Society of Arts, fellow; Society of Authors. Address: Shardeloes, Amersham, Bucks HP7 0RL, England.

GRAY Francine du Plessix, b. 25 Sept 1930, Warsaw, Poland. Author. m. Cleve Gray, 23 Apr 1957, 2 sons. Education: Bryn Mawr College, 1948-50; Black Mountain College, 1951, 1952; BA, Barnard College, 1952. Appointments: Reporter, United Press International, New York City, 1952-54; Assistant Editor, Realites Magazine, Paris, 1954-55; Book Editor, Art in America, New York City, 1962-64; Visiting Professor, City University of New York, 1975, Yale University, 1981, Columbia University, 1983; Ferris Professor, Princeton University, 1986; Annenberg Fellow, Brown University, 1997. Publications: Divine Disobedience: Profiles in Catholic Radicalism, 1970; Hawaii: The Sugar-Coated Fortress, 1972; Lovers and Tyrants, 1976; World Without End, 1981; October Blood, 1985; Adam and Eve and the City, 1987; Soviet Women: Walking the Tightrope, 1991; Rage and Fire: A Life of Louise Colet, 1994; At Home with the Marquis de Sade: A Life, 1998. Membership: American Academy of Arts and Letters. Address: c/o Georges Borchardt Inc, 136 East 57th Street, New York, NY 10022, USA.

GRAY Marianne Claire, b. 21 Sept 1947, Cape Town, South Africa. Journalist; Biographer. Education: Certificat d'Assiduite, University of Aix-Marseille, 1966; Cambridge Polytechnic, 1967; BA, UNISA, 1972. Appointments: Reporter, Argus Group, South Africa, 1968-70, Cape Times, 1970-73; Editor, Athens News, 1974; Syndication Assistant, South African National Magazines, London, 1975-77; Freelance Journalist, 1977-. Publications: Depardieu; La Moreau; Freelance Alternative; The Other 'Arf; Working from Home; Thoughts About Architecture. Contributions to: Various Magazines and Journals internationaly. Memberships: Women in Publishing; Critics Circle; Lawrence Durrell Research Centre; Women in Film International. Literary Agent: Blake Friedmann. Address: 32 Eburne Road, London N7 6AU, England.

GRAY (John) Richard, b. 7 July 1929, Weymouth, England. Professor of African History Emeritus; Writer. m. Gabriella Gray, 1957, 1 son, 1 daughter. Education:

Downing College, Cambridge; BA, Cantab, 1951; PhD, University of London, 1957. Appointments: Lecturer, University of Khartoum, 1959-61; Resident Fellow, 1961-63, Reader, 1963-72, School of Oriental and African Studies, London; Visiting Professor, University of California at Los Angeles, 1967; Editor, Journal of African History, 1968-71; Professor African History, 1972-89; Professor Emeritus, 1989-, University of London. Publications: The Two Nations: Aspects of the Development of Race Relations in the Rhodesias and Nyasaland, 1960; A History of the Southern Sudan, 1839-1889, 1961; Materials for West African History in Italian Archives (with D Chambers), 1965; Pre-Colonial African Trade (editor with D Birmingham), 1970; The Cambridge History of Africa, Vol 4 (editor), 1975; Christianity in Independent Africa (editor with others), 1978; Black Christians and White Missionaries, 1990. Contributions to: Professional journals. Honour: Order of St Silvester, 1966. Membership: Pontifical Committee of the Historical Sciences, 1982-. Address: 39 Rotherwick Road, London NW11 7DD, England.

GRAY Simon (James Holliday), (Hamish Reade), b. 21 Oct 1936, Hayling Island, Hants, England. Playwright; Writer. m. Beryl Mary Keven, 1965, 1 son, 1 daughter. Education: Dalhousie University; MA, Trinity College, Cambridge. Appointments: Senior Instructor in English, University of British Columbia, 1963-64; Lecturer in English, London University, 1965-85; Co-Director, The Common Pursuit, Promenade Theatre, New York, 1986; Director, Phoenix Theatre, 1988. Publications: Novels: Colmain, 1963; Simple People, 1965; Little Portia, 1967; A Comeback for Stark, 1968. Plays: Wise Child, 1968; Sleeping Dog, 1968; Dutch Uncle, 1969; The Idiot, 1971; Spoiled, 1971; Butley, 1971; Otherwise Engaged, 1975; Plaintiffs and Defendants, 1975; Two Sundays, 1975; Dog Days, 1976; Molly, 1977; The Rear Column, 1978; Close of Play, 1979; Stage Struck, 1979; Quartermaine's Terms, 1981 (televised, 1987); The Common Pursuit, 1984 (televised, 1992); Plays One, 1986; Melon, 1987; Hidden Laughter, 1990; Cell Mates, 1995; Life Support, 1997; Just the Three of us, 1997. Television Plays: After Pilkington, 1987; Old Flames, 1990; They Never Slept, 1991; Running Late, 1992; Unnatural Pursuits, 1993; Femme Fatale, 1993. Screenplay: A Month in the Country, 1987. Radio Plays: The Rector's Daughter, 1992; Suffer the Little Children, 1993; With a Nod and a Bow, 1993; Cell Mates, 1995. Non-Fiction: An Unnatural Pursuit and Other Pieces, 1985; How's That for Telling 'Em, Fat Lady?, 1988; Fat Chance, 1995. Fiction: Breaking Hearts, 1997. Honours: Several drama awards in the UK and US. Address: c/o Judy Daish Associates, 2 St Charles Place, London W10 6EG, England.

GRAY Tony (George Hugh), b. 23 Aug 1922, Dublin, Ireland. Writer. m. Patricia Mary Walters, 1 Oct 1946, 1 son, 1 daughter. Education: St Andrews College, Dublin, 1935-39. Appointment: Features Editor, Daily Mirror, London, 1959-62. Publications: Starting from Tomorrow, 1965; The Real Professionals, 1966; Gone the Time, 1967; The Irish Answer, 1967; The Record Breakers (with L Villa), 1970; The Last Laugh, 1972; The Orange Order, 1972; Psalms and Slaughter, 1972; The White Lions of Timbavati (with C McBride), 1977; Some of My Best Friends Are Animals (with T Murphy), 1979; Operation White Lion (with C McBride), 1981; The Irish Times Book of the 20th Century, 1985; The Road to Success: Alfred McAlpine, 1935-85, 1987; Fleet Street Remembered, 1990; Mr Smyllie, Sir, 1991; Ireland This Century, 1994; Saint Patrick's People, 1996; A Peculiar Man: A Life of George Moore. Address: 3 Broomfield Road, Kew Gardens, Richmond, Surrey, England.

GREALY Lucy, b. 1963, Dublin, Ireland. Writer; Poet. Education: Sarah Lawrence College, Bronxville, New York. Publication: Autobiography of a Face, 1994, UK edition as In the Mind's Eye, 1994. Contributions to: Periodicals. Honours: Fine Arts Work Centre Fellow, Provincetown, Massachusetts, 1993; National Magazine Award, 1994. Address: c/o Houghton Mifflin Company, 222 Berkeley Street, Boston, MA 02116, USA.

GREELEY Andrew (Moran), b. 5 Feb 1928, Oak Park, Illinois, USA. Professor; Author. Education: AB, 1950, STB, 1952, STL, 1954, St Mary of the Lake Seminary; MA, 1961, PhD, 1962, University of Chicago. Appointments: Ordained, Roman Catholic Priest, 1954; Assistant Pastor, Church of Christ the King, Chicago, 1954-64; Senior Study Director, 1961-68, Program Director for Higher Education, 1968-70, Director of Center for the Study of American Pluralism, 1971-85, Research Associate, 1985-, Professor of Social Science, 1991-, University of Chicago; Professor of Sociology, University of Arizona at Tucson, 1978-. Publications: Non-Fiction includes: Letters to a Young Man, 1964; Letters to Nancy, from Andrew M Greeley, 1964; The Catholic Experience: An Interpretation of the History of American Catholicism, 1967; Uncertain Trumpet: The Priest in Modern America, 1968; What Do We Believe?: The Stance of Religion in America (with Martin E Marty and Stuart E Rosenberg), 1968; Life for a Wanderer: A New Look at Christian Spirituality, 1969; Come Blow Your Mind with Me (essays), 1971; The Jesus Myth, 1971; What a Modern Catholic Believes about God, 1971; The Denominational Society: A Sociological Approach to Religion in America, 1972; The Sinai Myth, 1972; The Devil, You Say! Man and His Personal Devils and Angels, 1974; The Sociology of the Paranormal: A Reconnaissance, 1975; Death and Beyond, 1976; The Great Mysteries: An Essential Catechism, 1976; The Mary Myth: On the Femininity of God, 1977; No Bigger Than Necessary: An Alternative to Socialism, Capitalism, and Anarchism, 1977; The Best of Times, The Worst of Times (with J N Kotre), 1978; Religion: A Secular Theory, 1982; How to Save the Catholic Church, 1984; Confessions of a Parish Priest: An Autobiography, 1986; Patience of a Saint, 1986; God in Popular Culture, 1989; Myths of Religion, 1989; Complaints Against God, 1989; Andrew Greeley (autobiography), 1990; The Bible and Us: A Priest and a Rabbi Read Scripture Together (with Jacob Neusner), 1990; Faithful Attraction: Discovering Intimacy, Love and Fidelity in American Marriage, 1991; Love Affair: A Prayer Journal, 1992; The Sense of Love, 1992; I Hope You're Listening God, 1997. Fiction includes: Nora Maeve and Sebi, 1976; The Magic Cup: An Irish Legend, 1979; Death in April, 1980; The Cardinal Sins, 1981; Thy Brother's Wife, 1982; Ascent into Hell, 1984; Virgin and Martyr, 1985; Happy Are the Meek, 1985; Angels of September, 1986; God Game, 1986; The Final Planet, 1987; Happy Are Those Who Thirst For Justice, 1987; Lord of the Dance, 1987; Rite of Spring, 1987; Angel Fire, 1988; Happy Are the Clean of Heart, 1988; Love Song, 1988; All About Women, 1989; St Valentine's Night, 1989; The Search for Maggie Ward, 1991; The Cardinal Virtues, 1991; An Occasion of Sin, 1992; Happy Are the Merciful, 1992; Wages of Sin, 1992; Fall from Grace, 1993; Happy Are the Peacemakers, 1993; Happy Are the Poor in Spirit, 1994; Star Bright: A Christmas Story, 1997; The Bishop at Sea, 1997; Irish Whiskey, 1998; Contract with an Angel, 1998; A Midwinter's Tale, 1998; The Bishop and the Three Kings, 1998. Honours: C Albert Kobb Award, National Catholic Education Association, 1977; Mark Twain Award, Society for the Study of Midwestern Literature, 1987; Several honorary doctorates. Memberships: American Catholic Sociological Society; American Sociological Association; Religious Research Association; Society for the Scientific Study of Religion. Address: 1012 East 47th Street, Chicago, IL 60653, USA.

GREEN O O. See: **DURGNAT Raymond Eric.**

GREEN Benjamin, b. 17 July 1956, San Bernardino, California, USA. Writer. Education: BA, Humboldt State University, Arcata, 1985. Publications: The Field Notes of a Madman; The Lost Coast; From a Greyhound Bus; Monologs from the Realm of Silence; Green Grace, 1993; This Coast of Many Colors, 1993. Honours: Ucross Fellow. Address: 3415 Patricks Point Drive 3, Trinidad, CA 95570, USA.

GREEN Benny (Bernard), b. 9 Dec 1927, Leeds, Yorkshire, England. Critic; Writer. m. Antoinette Kanal, 1962, 3 sons, 1 daughter. Appointments: Saxophonist, 1947-60; Jazz Critic, Observer, 1958-77; Literary Critic, Spectator, 1970-; Film Critic, Punch, 1972-77; Television

Critic, 1977-. Publications: Books and Lyrics: Boots with Strawberry Jam, 1968; Cole, 1974; Oh Mr Porter, 1977; D D Lambeth, 1985. Books: The Reluctant Art, 1962; Blame it on My Youth, 1967; 58 Minutes to London, 1969; Drums in my Ears, 1973; I've Lost My Little Willie, 1976; Swingtime in Tottenham 1976; Cricket Addict's Archive, 1977; Shaw's Champions, 1978; Fred Astaire, 1979; Wisden Anthology, vol 1 1864-1900, 1979, vol II, 1900-1940, 1983; P G Woodhouse: A literary Biography, 1981; Wisden Book of Obituaries, 1986; A Histroy of Cricket, 1988; Let's Pace the Music,1989. Address: c/o BBC Broadcasting House, Portland Place, London, W1, England.

GREEN Brian. See: **CARD Orson Scott.**

GREEN Clifford, b. 6 Dec 1934, Melbourne, Victoria, Australia. Author; Screenwriter. m. Judith Irene Painter, 16 May 1959, 1 son, 3 daughters. Education: Primary Teachers Certificate, Toorak Teachers' College, 1959. Publications: Marion, 1974; The Incredible Steam-Driven Adventures of Riverboat Bill, 1975; Picnic at Hanging Rock: A Film, 1975; Break of Day, 1976; The Sun is Up, 1978; Four Scripts, 1978; Burn the Butterflies, 1979; Lawson's Mates, 1980; The Further Adventures of Riverboat Bill, 1981; Plays for Kids, 1981; Cop Out! Riverboat Bill Steams Again, 1985; Boy Soldiers, 1990. Honours: Australian Writers Guild Awards, 1973, 1974, 1976, 1978, 1979, 1990, 1992; Television Society of Australia Awards, 1974, 1976, 1978, 1980; Variety Club of Australia Award, 1978. Membership: Australian Writers Guild. Address: c/o Rick Raftos Management, PO Box 445, Paddington, New South Wales 2021, Australia.

GREEN Hannah. See: **GREENBERG Joanne.**

GREEN John F, b. 5 June 1943, Saskatoon, Saskatchewan, Canada. Teacher. m. Maureen Anne Horne, 1 Feb 1969, 3 sons, 1 daughter. Education: Ryerson Institute, 1964-67; Teachers Certificate, Red River Community College, 1976. Appointments: Professor, Arts and Sciences, Durham College, Oshawa, Ontario, 1976-; Writer and producer for western Canadian broadcasting companies. Publications: There are Trolls, 1974; The Bargain, 1974; The House on Geoffrey Street, 1981; The Gadfly, 1983; There's a Dragon in My Closet, 1986; Alice and The Birthday Giant, 1989; Junk-Pile Jennifer, 1991; The House that Max Built, 1991. Honour: Canadian Children's Book Centre Gold Seal Award, 1990. Address: 966 Adelaide Street East, No 70, Oshawa, Ontario L1K 1L2, Canada.

GREEN Jonathon, b. 20 Apr 1948, Kidderminster, Worcestershire, England. Writer; Broadcaster. 2 sons. Educatioin: BA, Brasenose College, Oxford, 1969. Publications: Book of Rock Quotes I, 1977; Famous Last Words, 1979; The Book of Sports Quotes (with D Atyeo), 1979; Directory of Infamy, 1980; Don't Quote Me: The Other Famous Last Words (with D Atyeo), 1981; The Book of Royal Quotes (with D Atyeo), 1981; Book of Political Quotes, 1982; Book of Rock Quotes II, 1982; Contemporary Dictionary of Quotations, 1982, revised edition, 1989; What a Way to Go, 1983; Newspeak: A Dictionary of Jargon, 1983, revised edition as The Dictionary of Jargon, 1987; The Dictionary of Contemporary Slang, 1984, revised edition, 1992; The Cynics' Lexicon, 1984; Sweet Nothings: A Book of Love Quotes, 1985; Consuming Passions: A Book of Food Quotes, 1985; It Takes All Sports: Sporting Anecdotes (with D Atyeo), 1986; The Slang Thesaurus, 1986; The A to Z of Nuclear Jargon, 1986; Says You: A Twentieth-Century Quotation Finder, 1988; Day in the Life: Voices from the English Underground, 1961-71, 1988; The Bloomsbury Good Word Guide, 1988, 2nd edition, 1990; The Encyclopedia of Censorship, 1990; Them: Voices from the Immigrant Community in Contemporary Britain, 1990; The Dictionary of Political Language, 1991; Neologisms: A Dictionary of Contemporary Coinage, 1991; It: The State of Sex Today, 1992; All Dressed Up: The Sixties and the Counter-Culture, 1998; Cassell Dictionary of Slang, 1998. Literary Agent: Lucas Alexander Whitey, Elsinore House,

77 Fulham Palace Road, London, W6 8JA. Address: 117 Ashmore Road, London W9 3DA, England.

GREEN Kenneth Hart, b. 13 Mar 1953, Toronto, Ontario, Canada. Associate Professor. m. Sharon Mintz, 28 Aug 1979, 3 sons. Education: BA, University of Toronto, 1977; MA, 1981, PhD, 1989, Brandeis University. Appointments: Lecturer, 1978, Assistant Professor, 1991, Associate Professor, 1995, University of Toronto; Series Editor, State University of New York Press, 1992-97. Publications: Jew and Philosopher: The Return to Maimonides in the Jewish Thought of Leo Strauss, author, 1993; Leo Strauss's Philosophy and Law: Contributions to the Understanding of Maimonides and His Predecessors, editor, 1995; Leo Strauss's Jewish Philosophy and the Crisis of Modernity: Essays and Lectures in Modern Jewish Thought, editor, 1997. Contributions to: Interpretation: A Journal of Political Philosophy, 1986; Modern Judaism, 1987, 1992; Journal of the American Academy of Religion, 1993; Jewish Political Studies Review, 1997; Studies in Religion, 1997; Books in Canada: The Canadian Review of Books, 1998; Several books. Honours: Short-listed Finalist, 3rd Annual Hans Rosenhaupt Memorial Book Award for Best Dissertation Accepted for Publication, Woodrow Wilson National Fellowship Foundation, 1991; University of Toronto Connaught Grant for Series Editor work, 1992-97; Dean's Excellence Award, Faculty of Arts and Science, University of Toronto, 1992-93, 1996-97; 17 reviews of book Jew and Philosopher, 1994-97; Doctoral Fellowships. Memberships: American Academy of Religion; Association for Jewish Studies. Address: University College, Rm 318, University of Toronto, Toronto, Ontario, Canada M5S 3H7.

GREEN Martin (Burgess), b. 21 Sept 1927, London, England. Professor of English; Writer. m. Carol Elizabeth Hurd, 1967, 1 son, 2 daughters. Education: BA, 1948, MA, 1952, St John's College, Cambridge; Teachers Diploma, King's College, London, 1951; Certificat d'Etudes Françaises, Sorbonne, Paris, 1952; PhD, University of Michigan, 1957. Apppointments: Instructor, Wellesley College, Massachussetts, USA, 1957-61; Lecturer, Birmingham University, England, 1965-68; Professor of English, Tufts University, Medford, Massachusetts, 1968-. Publications: Mirror for Anglo-Saxons, 1960; Reappraisals, 1965; Science and the Shabby Curate of Poetry, 1965; Yeat's Blessings on von Hugel, 1968; Cities of Light and Sons of the Morning, 1972; The von Richthofen Sisters, 1974; Children of the Sun, 1975; The Earth Again Redeemed (novel), 1976; Transatlantic Patterns, 1977; The Challenge of the Mahatmas,1978; Dreams of Adventure, Deeds of Empire, 1980; The Old English Elegies, 1983; Tolstoy and Gandhi, 1983; The Great American Adventure, 1984; Montains of Truth, 1986; The Triumph of Pierrot (with J Swan), 1986. Address: 8 Boylston Terrace, Medford, MA 02144, USA.

GREEN Michael Frederick, b. 2 Jan 1927, Leicester, England. Writer. Education: BA, Honours, Open University. Publications: The Art of Coarse Rugby, 1960; The Art of Coarse Sailing, 1962; Even Coarser Rugby, 1963; The Art of Coarse Acting, 1964; The Art of Coarse Golf, 1967; The Art of Coarse Moving, 1969 (TV serial, 1977); The Art of Coarse Drinking, 1973; Squire Haggard's Journal, 1976 (TV serial, 1990 and 1992); Four Plays For Coarse Actors, 1978; The Coarse Acting Show Two, 1980; Tonight Josephine, 1981; The Art of Coarse Sex, 1981; Don't Swing from the Balcony Romeo, 1983; The Art of Coarse Office Life, 1985; The Third Great Coarse Acting Show, 1985; The Boy Who Shot Down an Airship, 1988; Nobody Hurt in Small Earthquake, 1990. Memberships: Society of Authors; Equity; National Union of Journalists. Literary Agent: Anthony Sheil Associates. Address: 14 St Mary's Avenue, Southall, Middlesex UB2 4LS, England.

GREEN Sharon, b. 6 July 1942, New York, New York, USA. Writer. div, 3 sons. Education: BA, New York University, 1963. Publications: The Crystals of Mida, 1982; The Warrior Within, 1982; The Warrior Enchained, 1983; An Oath to Mida, 1983; Chosen of Mida, 1984; The Warrior Rearmed, 1984; Mind Guest, 1984; Gateway to Xanadu, 1985; The Will of the Gods, 1985; To Battle the Gods, 1986; The Warrior Challenged, 1986; Rebel Prince, 1986; The Far Side of Forever, 1987; The Warrior Victorious, 1987; Lady Blade, Lord Fighter, 1987; Mists of the Ages, 1988; Hellhound Magic, 1989; Dawn Song, 1990; Haunted House, 1990; Silver Princess, Golden Knight, 1993; The Hidden Realms, 1993; Werewolfmoon, 1993; Fantasy Man, 1993; Flame of Fury, 1993; Dark Mirror, Dark Dreams, 1994; Silken Dreams, 1994; Enchanting, 1994; Wind Whispers, Shadow Shouts, 1995. Contributions to: Anthologies and magazines. Membership: Science Fiction Writers of America. Address: 110 Bellevue Road, No 28, Nashville, TN 37221, USA.

GREEN Timothy (Seton), b. 29 May 1936, Beccles, England. Writer. m. Maureen Snowbald, Oct 1959, 1 daughter. Education: BA, Christ's College, Cambridge, 1957; Graduate Diploma in Journalism, University of Western Ontario, 1958. Appointments: London Correspondent, Horizon, and American Heritage, 1959-62, Life, 1962-64; Editor, Illustrated London News, 1964-66. Publications: The World of God, 1968; The Smugglers, 1969; Restless Spirit, UK edition as The Adventurers, 1970; The Universal Eye, 1972; World of Gold Today, 1973; How to Buy Gold, 1975; The Smuggling Business, 1977; The World of Diamonds, 1981; The New World of Gold, 1982, 2nd edition, 1985; The Prospect for Gold, 1987; The World of Gold, 1993; The Good Water Guide, 1994; New Frontiers in Diamonds: The Mining Revolution, 1996; The Gold Companion, 1997. Address: 8 Ponsonby Place, London, SW1P 4PT, England.

GREEN Vivian Hubert Howard, b. 18 Nov 1915, Wembley, Middlesex, England. Writer. Education: BA, 1937, BD, 1941, Cambridge University; DD, Oxford and Cambridge, 1957. Publications: Renaissance and Reformation, 1952; Oxford Common Room, 1957; The Young Mr Wesley, 1961; Religion at Oxford and Cambridge, 1964; The Commonwealth of Lincoln College 1427-1977, 1979; Love in a Cool Climate: The Letters of Mark Pattison and Meta Bradley, 1985; The Madness of Kings, 1993; A New History of Christianity, 1996; The European Reformation, 1998. Honours: Thirlwall Prize and Medal, Cambridge University, 1940; Honorary Fellow, Lincoln College, Oxford. Membership: Royal Historical Society, fellow. Address: Calendars, Sheep Street, Burford, Oxford OX8 4LS, England.

GREENBERG Alvin (David), b. 10 May 1932, Cincinnati, Ohio, USA. Professor of English; Poet; Writer. 2 sons, 1 daughter, m. Janet Holmes, 1993. Education: BA, 1954, MA, 1960, University of Cincinnati; PhD, University of Washington, 1964. Appointments: Faculty, University of Kentucky, 1963-65; Professor of English, 1965-, Chair, Department of English, 1988-93, Macalester College; Fulbright Lecturer, University of Kerala, India, 1966-67; Editor, Minnesota Review, 1967-71. Publications: Poetry: The Metaphysical Giraffe, 1968; The House of the Would-Be Gardner, 1972; Dark Lands, 1973; Metaform, 1975; In/Direction, 1978; And Yet, 1981; Heavy Wings, 1988; Why We Live with Animals, 1990. Novels: The Small Waves, 1965; Going Nowhere, 1971; The Invention of the West, 1976. Short Stories: The Discovery of America and Other Tales of Terror, 1980; Delta q, 1983; The Man in the Cardboard Mask, 1985; How the Dead Live, 1998. Play: A Wall, 1971; Opera Libretti: Horspfal, 1969; The Jealous Cellist, 1979; Apollonia's Circus, 1994. Contributions to: Many reviews, journals, and quarterlies. Honours: National Endowment for the Arts Fellowships, 1972, 1992; Bush Foundation Artist Fellowships, 1976, 1981; Associated Writing Programs Short Fiction Award, 1982; Nimrod/Pablo Neruda Prize in Poetry, 1988; Loft-McKnight Poetry Award, 1991, and Distinction in Poetry Award, 1994; Chelsea Award for Poetry, 1994; Minnesota State Arts Board Fellowship, 1996. Address: 1113 Lincoln Avenue, St Paul, MN 55105, USA.

GREENBERG Joanne, (Hannah Green), b. 24 Sept 1932, Brooklyn, New York, USA. Author; Teacher. m. Albert Greenberg, 4 Sept 1955, 2 sons. Education: BA, American University. Publications: The King's Persons, 1963; I Never Promised You a Rose Garden, 1964; The Monday Voices, 1965; Summering: A Book of Short Stories, 1966; In This Sign, 1970; Rites of Passage, 1972; Founder's Praise, 1976; High Crimes and Misdemeanors, 1979; A Season of Delight, 1981; The Far Side of Victory, 1983; Simple Gifts, 1986; Age of Consent, 1987; Of Such Small Differences, 1988; With the Snow Queen (short stories), 1991; No Reck'ning Made, 1993; Where the Road Goes, 1998. Contributions to: Articles, reviews, short stories to numerous periodicals. Honours: Harry and Ethel Daroff Memorial Fiction Award, 1963; William and Janice Epstein Fiction Award, 1964; Marcus L Kenner Award, 1971; Christopher Book Award, 1971; Freida Fromm Reichman Memorial Award, 1971; Rocky Mountain Women's Institute Award, 1983; Denver Public Library Bookplate Award, 1990; Colorado Author of the Year. Memberships: Authors Guild; PEN: Colorado Authors League; National Association of the Deaf. Literary Agent: Lois Wallace, Wallace Literary Agency, New York, NY. Address: 29221 Rainbow Hill Road, Golden, CO 80401, USA.

GREENBERG Martin, b. 3 Feb 1918, Norfolk, Virginia, USA. Retired Professor of English; Writer; Translator. m. Paula Fox, 9 June 1962, 1 son. Education: BA, University of Michigan. Appointments: Editor, Schocken Books, 1946-49; Commentary magazine, 1953-60; Lecturer, New School for Social research, New York City, 1961-67; Assistant Professor to Professor of English, C W Post College, 1963-88. Publications: The Terror of Art: Kafka and Modern Literature, 1968; The Hamlet Vocation of Coleridge and Wordsworth, 1986; Translations: The Diaries of Franz Kafka 1914-23, 1948-49; The Marquise of O & Other Stories, 1960; Five Plays (von Kleist), 1988; Faust, Part One, 1992; Faust, Part Two, 1996. Honours: Literature Award, American Academy and Institute of Arts and Letters, 1989; Harold Morton Lansdon Translation Award, 1989. Membership: Academy of American Poets. Address: 306 Clinton Street, Brooklyn, NY 11201, USA.

GREENBLATT Stephen (Jay), b. 7 Nov 1943, Cambridge, Massachusetts, USA. Professor of English; Writer. m. Ellen Schmidt, 27 Apr 1969, 2 sons. Education: BA, 1964, MPhil, 1968, PhD, 1969, Yale University; BA, 1966, MA, 1969, Pembroke College, Cambridge. Appointments: Assistant Professor, 1969-74, Associate Professor, 1974-79, Professor of English, 1979-84, Class of 1932 Professor, 1984-, University of California at Berkeley; Visiting Professor, University of California at Santa Cruz, 1981, University of Beijing, 1982, Northwestern University, 1984, University of Bologna, 1988, University of Chicago, 1989, École des Hautes en Sciences Sociales, Paris, 1989, Harvard University, 1990, 1991, 1993, 1994, University of Trieste, 1991, Dartmouth College, 1992, University of Florence, 1992, Wissenschaftskolleg zu Berlin, 1996-97, University of Turin, 1997; Clarendon Lecturer, Oxford University, 1988. Publications: Three Modern Satirists: Waugh, Orwell and Huxley, 1965; Sir Walter Raleigh: The Renaissance Man and His Roles, 1973; Renaissance Self-Fashioning: From More to Shakespeare, 1980; Shakespearean Negotiations: The Circulation of Social Energy in Renaissance England, 1988; Learning to Curse: Essays in Early Modern Culture, 1990; Marvelous Possessions: The Wonder of the New World, 1991. Editor: Allegory and Representation, 1981; The Power of Forms in the English Renaissance, 1982; Representing the English Renaissance, 1988; Essays in Memory of Joel Fineman, 1989; Redrawing the Boundaries: The Transformation of English and American Literary Studies (with Giles Gunn), 1992; New World Encounters, 1992; Norton Shakespeare, 1997. Contributions to: Scholarly journals. Honours: Fulbright Scholarship, Cambridge, 1964-66; National Endowment for the Humanities Fellowship, 1971-72; Guggenheim Fellowships, 1975, 1983; British Council Prize in the Humanities, 1981; James Russell Lowell Prize, Modern Language Association, 1989. Memberships: American Academy of Arts and Sciences, fellow; International Association of University Professors of English; Modern Language Association; Renaissance

Society of America; Wissenschaftskolleg zu Berlin, fellow. Address: 1004 Oxford Street, Berkeley, CA 94707, USA.

GREENE A(lvin) C(arl), b. 4 Nov 1923, Abilene, Texas, USA. Professor; Historian; Author. m. (1) Betty Jo Dozier, 1 May 1950, 3 sons, 1 daughter, (2) Judy Dalton, 20 Jan 1990. Education: Phillips University, 1942; Kansas State College, 1943; BA, Abilene Christian College, 1948; Graduate Studies, Hardin-Simmons University, 1951, University of Texas at Austin, 1968-70. Appointment: Co-Director, Centre for Texas Studies, University of North Texas. Publications: A Personal Country, 1969; The Santa Claus Bank Robbery, 1972; The Last Captive, 1972; Dallas: The Deciding Years, 1972; The Highland Park Woman, 1984; Taking Heart, 1990. Contributions to: Atlantic; McCalls; Southwestern History Quarterly; New York Times Book Review. Honours: National Conference of Christians and Jews, 1964; Dobie-Paisano Fellow, 1968; Fellow, Texas State History Association, 1990. Memberships: Texas Institute of Letters, president, 1969-71, fellow 1981-; Writers Guild of America, West; PEN International. Address: 4359 Shirley Drive, Dallas, TX 75229, USA.

GREENE Constance C(larke), b. 27 Oct 1924, New York, New York, USA. Writer. m. Philip M Greene, 8 June 1946, 2 sons, 3 daughters. Education: Skidmore College, 1942-44. Publications: A Girl Called Al, 1969; Leo the Lioness, 1970; The Good-Luck Bogie Hat, 1971; Unmaking of Rabbit, 1972; Isabelle the Itch, 1973; The Ears of Louis, 1974; I Know You, Al, 1975; Beat the Turtle Drum, 1976; Getting Nowhere, 1977; I and Sproggy, 1978; Your Old Pal, Al, 1979; Dotty's Suitcase, 1980; Double-Dare O'Toole, 1981; Al(exandra) the Great, 1982; Ask Anybody, 1983; Isabelle Shows Her Stuff, 1984; Star Shine, 1985; Other Plans, 1985; The Love Letters of J Timothy Owen, 1986; Just Plain Al, 1986; Isabelle and Little Orphan Frannie, 1988; Monday I Love You, 1988; Al's Blind Date, 1989; Funny You Should Ask, 1992; Odds on Oliver, 1992. Contributions to: Magazines and newspapers. Honours: American Library Association Notable Books, 1970, 1977, 1987. Address: c/o Viking Press Inc, 40 West 23rd Street, New York, NY 10010, USA.

GREENE Jonathan (Edward), b. 19 Apr 1943, New York, New York, USA. Poet; Writer; Editor; Publisher; Book Designer. m. (1) Alice-Anne Kingston, 5 June 1963, div, 1 daughter, (2) Dobree Adams, 23 May 1974, 1 daughter. Education: BA, Bard College, 1965. Publications: The Reckoning, 1966; Instance, 1968; The Lapidary, 1969; A 17th Century Garner, 1969; An Unspoken Complaint, 1970; The Poor in Church, by Arthur Rimbaud (translator), 1973; Scaling the Walls, 1974; Glossary of the Everyday, 1974; Peripatetics, 1978; Jonathon Williams: A 50th Birthday Celebration (editor), 1979; Once a Kingdom Again, 1979; Quiet Goods, 1980; Idylls, 1983, revised edition, 1990; Small Change for the Long Haul, 1984; Trickster Tales, 1985; Les Chambres des Poètes, 1990; The Man Came to Haul Stone, 1995; Of Moment, 1998; Inventions of Necessity: Selected Poems, 1998; Incidents of Travel in Japan, 1999. Contributions to: Anthologies, reviews, quarterlies, and journals. Honours: National Endowment for the Arts Fellowships, 1969, 1978; Southern Federation of State Arts Agencies Fellowship, 1977. Address: PO Box 475, Frankfort, KY 40692, USA.

GREENER Michael John, b. 28 Nov 1931, Barry, Wales. Chartered Accountant Company Director. m. May 1964, div 1972, 1 son. Education: BA, University of South Wales and Monmouthshire, 1949-53; Articled, Deloitte Plender Griffiths, Cardiff, Wales, 1949-57; Qualified as Chartered Accountant, 1957; FCA, 1967; BA, Open University, 1991. Publications: Between the Lines of the Balance Sheet, 1968, revised edition, 1980; Penguin Dictionary of Commerce, 1970, revised, 1980, new revised, Penguin Business Dictionary, 1987, revised edition, 1994; Problems for Discussion in Mercantile Law, 1970; The Red Bus, 1973. Contributions to: Many articles in business and professional journals. Membership: Fellow, Institute of Chartered Accountants, 1967. Address: 33 Glan Hafren, Maes-y-Coed, Barry, South Glamorgan CF62 6TA, Wales.

GREENFIELD Jeanette, b. Melbourne, Australia. International Lawyer; Author. Education: LLB, University of Melbourne, 1968; Called to the Bar, Supreme Court of Victoria, 1969; LLB, 1973, PhD, 1976, Wolfson College, Cambridge University. Publications: China and the Law of the Sea, Air and Environment, 1979; The Return of Cultural Treasures, 1989, 2nd edition, 1996; China's Practice in the Law of the Sea, 1991; Papers in: The Law of the Sea in the Asian Pacific Region, 1995; The Spoils of War, 1997. Contributions to: Chambers Biographical Dictionary; Antiquity; Apollo; Australian Outlook. Honour: British Academy Grant, 1986. Address: 59 River Court, Upper Ground, London SE1 9PB, England.

GREENFIELD Jerome, b. 25 May 1923, Siberia, Russia. Writer; Associate Professor of English. Education: BA, English, New School, New York, 1952; MA, English, Columbia University, 1953. Appointments: Currently Associate Professor of English, State University of New York, New Paltz. Publications: The Chalkine, novel, 1963; Wilhelm Reich vs The USA, 1974, German translation, 1994. Contributions to: Numerous in Village Voice, Psychology Today, others. Honour: Monetary Grant, Chapelbrook Foundation, 1970. Literary Agent: Max Gartenberg. Address: English Department, State University of New York, New Paltz, NY 12561, USA.

GREENHILL Basil Jack, b. 26 Feb 1920, Weston-super-Mare, Somerset, England. Author. m. (1) Gillian Stratton, 1950, dec 1959, 1 son, (2) Ann Giffard, 1961, 1 son. Education: BA, 1946, PhD, 1981,Bristol University. Appointments: Diplomatic Service, 1946-66; Director, 1967-83, Caird Research Fellow, 1983-86, National Maritime Museum, Greenwich; Chairman, 1982-92, Vice-President, 1992-, SS Great Britain Project; Consultant, Gerald Duckworth & Co, 1998-; Chairman, Centre for Maritime Historical Studies, University of Exeter, 1991-. Publications: The Merchant Schooners, Vol I, 1951, Vol II, 1957, 4th edition, revised, 1988; Sailing for a Living, 1962; Westcountrymen in Prince Edward's Isle (with Ann Giffard), 1967, 3rd edition, 1974; The Merchant Sailing Ship: A Photographic History (with Ann Giffard), 1970; Women Under Sail (with Ann Giffard), 1970; Captain Cook, 1970; Boats and Boatmen of Pakistan, 1971; Travelling by Sea in the Nineteenth Century (with Ann Giffard), 1972; Sail and Steam (with P W Brock), 1973; West Country Coasting Ketches (with W J Slade), 1974; A Victorian Maritime Album, 1974; A Quayside Camera, 1975; The Coastal Trade: Sailing Craft of British Waters 900-1900 (with L Willis), 1975; Archaeology of the Boat, 1976; Victorian and Edwardian Ships and Harbours (with Ann Giffard), 1976, 4th edition, revised 1987; Victorian and Edwardian Ships and Harbours (with Ann Giffard), 1978; Victorian and Edwardian Merchant Steamships (with Ann Giffard), 1979; Schooners, 1980; The Life and Death of the Sailing Ship, 1980; The British Seafarer (with Michael Mason), 1980; Seafaring Under Sail (with Denis Stonham), 1981; Karlsson, 1982; The Woodshipbuilders, 1986; The Grain Races, 1986; The British Assault on Finland, 1854-55 (with Ann Giffard), 1988; The Evolution of the Wooden Ship, 1988; The Herzogin Cecilie (with John Hackman), 1991; The New Maritime History of Devon (co-editor), 2 volumes, 1993, 1994; The Advent of Steam (editor), 1993; The Last Century of Sail (editor), 1993; The Årby Boat (with Owain Roberts), 1993; Steam, Politics and Patronage (with Ann Giffard), 1994; The Bertha L Downs, 1995; The Archaeology of Boats and Ships, 1995; The Evolution of the Sailing Ship, 1995; Paddle Wheels, Sail and Screw (with Peter Allington), 1997; The Chatham Directory of Inshore Craft (editor), 1997. Contributions to: Many publications. Honours: Companion of the Order of St Michael and St George, 1967; Knight Commander of the Order of the White Rose, Finland, 1980; Companion of the Order of the Bath, 1981; Honorary Fellow, University of Exeter, 1985; Honorary D Litt, University of Plymouth, 1996. Memberships: Ancient Monuments Board for England, 1972-84; Devon Historical Society, president, 1993-96; Maritime Trust, council, 1977-83, honorary vice-president, 1984-; Royal Historical Society, fellow; Society for Nautical Research, vice-president, 1975-; Society of Antiquaries, fellow. Address: West Boetheric Farmhouse, St Dominic, Saltash, Cornwall Pl 12 6SZ, England.

GREENLAND Colin, b. 17 May 1954, Dover, Kent, England. Writer. Education: MA, 1978, DPhil, 1981, Pembroke College, Oxford. Appointments: Writer-in-Residence, North East London Polytechnic, 1980-82. Publications: The Entropy Exhibition, 1983; Daybreak on a Different Mountain, 1984; Magnetic Storm (with Roger and Martyn Dean), 1984; Interzone: The First Anthology (co-editor), 1985; The Freelance Writer's Handbook (with Paul Kerton), 1986; The Hour of the Thin Ox, 1987; Storm Warnings (co-editor), 1987; Other Voices, 1988; Take Back Plenty, 1990; Michael Moorcock: Death is No Obstacle, 1992; Harm's Way, 1993; Seasons of Plenty, 1995; The Plenty Principle, 1997; Mother of Plenty, 1998. Contributions to: Many anthologies and periodicals. Honours: Eaton Award for Science Fiction Criticism, 1985; Arthur C Clarke Award, 1992; British Science Fiction Association Award, 1992; Eastercon Award, 1992; Guest of Honour, Evolution, National Science Fiction Easter Convention, 1996. Memberships: Science Fiction Foundation; Science Fiction Writers' Conference, Milford; British Science Fiction Association, Council Member. Literary Agent: Maggie Noach, 21 Redan Street, London, W14 0AB. Address: 98 Sturton Street, Cambridge CB1 2QA, England.

GREENLEAF Stephen (Howell), b. 17 July 1942, Washington, District of Columbia, USA. Attorney; Writer. m. Ann Garrison, 20 July 1968, 1 son. Education: BA, Carleton College, 1964; JD, University of California, at Berkeley, 1967; Creative Writing, University of Iowa, 1978-79. Appointments: Admitted to the Bar, California, 1968, Iowa, 1977. Publications: Grave Error, 1979; Death Bed, 1980; State's Evidence, 1982; Fatal Obsession, 1983; The Ditto List, 1985; Beyond Blame, 1986; Toll Call, 1987; Impact, 1989; Book Case, 1991; Blood Type, 1992; Southern Cross, 1993; False Conception, 1994. Honour: Maltese Falcon Award, Japan, 1993. Address: c/o Esther Newberg, International Creative Management, 40 West 57th Street, New York, NY 10019, USA.

GREENSLADE Roy, b. 31 Dec 1946, London, England. Journalist. m. Noreen Taylor, 28 July 1984, 1 stepson, 1 stepdaughter. Education: BA Hons, Sussex University, 1976-79. Appointments: Reporter, Barking Advertiser, 1962-66; Sub-Editor, Lancashire Evening Telegraph, 1966-67; Sub-Editor, Daily Mail, 1967-69; Sub-Editor, The Sun, 1969-71; Sub-Editor, The Daily Mirror, 1971; Deputy Chief Sub, The Sun, 1971-73; Sub-Editor, Daily Star, 1979-80, and Editor, Daily Express, 1980; Feature Editor, Daily Star, 1980-81; Assistant Editor, The Sun, 1981-86; Managing Editor (News), The Sunday Times, 1987-90; Editor, Daily Mirror, 1990-91; Consultant Editor, Sunday Times & today, 1991-; Freelance Writer, 1991-. Publications: Goodbye to the Working Class, 1975; Maxwell's Fall, 1992. Contributions to: The Guardian; British Journalism Review, Media & Culture. Literary Agent: Charles Walker, Peters, Fraser & Dunlop. Address: Chelsea Harbour, London SW10 0XF, England.

GREENWOOD Ted, (Edward Alister Greenwood), b. 4 Dec 1930, Melbourne, Victoria, Australia. Children's Writer. m. Florence Lorraine Peart, 15 Jan 1954, 4 daughters. Education: Primary Teacher's Certificate, Melbourne Teacher's College, 1949; Diploma of Art, Royal Melbourne Institute of Technology, 1959. Publications: Sly Old Wardrobe (with Ivan Southall), 1968; Obstreperous, 1969; Alfred, 1970; Curious Eddie, 1970; VIP: Very Important Plant, 1971; Joseph and Lulu and the Prindiville House Pigeons, 1972; Terry's Brrrmmm GT, 1974; The Pochetto Coat, 1978; Ginnie, 1979; The Boy Who Saw God, 1980; Everlasting Circle, 1981; Flora's Treasurers, 1982; Marley and Friends, 1983; Warts and All (with S Fennessy), 1984; Ship Rock, 1985; I Don't Want to Know (with S Fennessy), 1986; Windows, 1989; Uncle Theo is a Number Nine, 1990; Spooner or Later, 1992; Duck for Cover, 1994, Freeze a Crowd, (with Paul Jennings and Terry Denton), 1996; The

Ventriloquist, 1994; What Do We Do With Dawson?, (with Terry Denton), 1996; After Dusk (with A. James), 1997. Honour: Churchill Fellow, 1972. Address: 50 Hilton Road, Ferny Creek, Victoria 3786, Australia.

GREENWOOD Theresa Winifrey, b. 28 Dec 1936, Cairo, Illinois, USA. Writer; Poet; Educator. m. Charles H Greenwood, 26 June 1960, 1 son, 1 daughter. Education: BMusic Education, Millikin University, 1959; Master of Arts in Education, Ball State University, 1963; EdD, Education, Ball State University, 1976. Publications: Journals: THE Journal; Principal; The Technology Teacher; The Teddy Bear Review; Books: Psalms of a Black Mother; Gospel Graffiti; Magazines: Saturday Evening Post; Upper Boom. Honours: Elizolly; Christa McHuloffe, Disney; Teacher of the Year (Indiana) Geraldine Dodge; Fulbright Memorial Scholar. Address: Ball State University, 2000 University Avenue, Muncie, Indiana 47306, USA.

GREER Germaine b. 29 Jan 1939, Melbourne, Victoria, Australia. Writer; Broadcaster. Education: BA, Honours, Melbourne University, 1959; MA, Honours, Sydney University, 1962; PhD, Cambridge University, 1967. Appointments: Senior English Tutor, Sydney University, 1963-64; Assistant Lecturer and Lecturer, English, University of Warwick, 1967-72; Lecturer, American Program Bureau, 1973-78; Visiting Professor, Graduate Faculty of Modern Letters, 1979, Professor of Modern Letters, 1980-83, University of Tulsa; Founder-Director, Tulsa Centre for Studies in Women's Literature, 1981; Proprietor, Stump Cross Books, 1988-; Special Lecturer and Unofficial Fellow, Newnham College, Cambridge, 1989-98. Publications: The Female Eunuch, 1969; The Obstacle Race: The Fortunes of Women Painters and Their Work, 1979; Sex and Destiny: The Politics of Human Fertility, 1984; Shakespeare (editor), 1986; The Madwoman's Underclothes (selected journalism), 1986; Daddy, We Hardly Knew You, 1989; The Change: Women, Ageing and the Menopause, 1991; Slip-Shod Sybils: Recognition, Rejection and the Woman Poet, 1995; The Whole Woman, 1999. Editor: The Uncollected Verse of Aphra Behn, 1989. Co-Editor: Kissing the Rod: An Anthology of Seventeenth Century Verse, 1988; Surviving Works of Annne Wharton, 1997. Contributions to: Journalist, columnist, reviewer, 1972-79. Honours: Scholarships, 1952, 1956; Commonwealth Scholarship, 1964; J R Ackerly Prize and Premio Internazionale Mondello, 1989. Address: c/o Aitken and Stone Associates Ltd, 29 Fernshaw Road, London SW10 0TG, England.

GREGORIOU Gregory, b. 20 May 1929, Athens, Greece. Physician; Psychiatrist; Writer. Education: Diploma, Psychiatry, McGill University, 1965; Specialist Certificate, Royal College of Physicians of Surgeons of Canada, 1965, and College of Physicians and Surgeons of the Province of Quebec, 1968. Appointments: Lecturer in Psychiatry, McGill University, 1968-; Psychiatrist, Queen Elizabeth Hospital, Montreal. Publications: Le Devin du Village: Un coté peu connu de l'oeuvre de Jean-Jacques Rousseau, 1984; Le livret de l'opéra de Jean-Jacques Rousseau: Le Devin du Village une expression lyrique de sa philosophie, 1989; Actes du Colloque International J J Rousseau de Montmorency, 1989; Nostalgies (poems), 1990; Musicothérapie, 1992; La Renaissance de la Psychiatrie, 1992; La Moisson Litteraire, 1993; Le Danger des Paranoiaques et des Sociopathes Pour La Société, 1993; Le Passé et L'Avenir de l'Humanisme Medical, 1994. Honours: Cesare Pavese Prize, 1990; International Man of the Year, International Biographical Centre, 1995-96. Memberships: Royal College of Physicians and Surgeons of Canada, fellow; Professional Corporation of Physicians of Quebec; Quebec Medical Association; Federation of Medical Specialists of Quebec; American Physicians Poetry Association; Canadian Writers Association; American Association of French Philosophy; North American Association for the Study of J J Rousseau; Société Américaine de Philosophie de Langue Francaise, founding member; World Literary Academy; vice president, The International Association of Greek Writers, Canada, 1998-. Address: 2155 Stevens St, St Laurent, Quebec, H4A 1G6, Canada.

GREGORY Joan. See: **POULSON Joan.**

GREGORY Richard (Langton), b. 24 July 1923, London, England. Professor of Neuropsychology Emeritus; Writer. m. (1) Margaret Hope Pattison Muir, 1953, div 1966, 1 son, 1 daughter, (2) Freja Mary Balchin, div 1976. Education: Downing College, Cambridge, 1947-50; DSc, University of Bristol, 1983. Appointments: Research, MRC Applied Psychology Research Unit, Cambridge, 1950-53; University Demonstrator, later Lecturer, Department of Psychology, Cambridge, 1953-67; Fellow, Corpus Christi College, Cambridge, 1962-67; Professor of Bionics, University of Edinburgh, 1967-70; Professor of Neuropsychology and Director of the Brain and Perception Laboratory, 1970-88, Professor Emeritus, 1988-, University of Bristol; Founder and Chairman of the Trustees, 1983-91, President, 1991-, Exploratory Hands-on Science Centre; Advisory Committee, Royal Society Representative, The British Library, 1996-97. Publications: Recovery from Early Blindness (with Jean Wallace), 1963; Eye and Brain, 1966, 5th edition, 1998; The Intelligent Eye, 1970; Illusion in Nature and Art (co-editor), 1973; Concepts and Mechanisms of Perception, 1974; Mind in Science, 1981; Odd Perceptions (essays), 1986; The Oxford Companion to the Mind (editor), 1987; Evolution of the Eye and Visual System (co-editor), Vol II of Vision and Visual Dysfunction, 1991; Even Odder Perceptions (essays), 1994; The Artful Eye, 1995; Mirrors in Mind, 1996; Mind-Makers, 1998. Contributions to: Scientific journals; Founder and Editor of the Journal Perception, 1972-. Honours: Commander of the Order of the British Empire, 1989; Michael Faraday Medal, Royal Society, 1993; Lord Crook Medal, Spectacle Makers' Co, 1996; Corpus Christi College, Cambridge, honorary fellowship; Honorary doctorates. Memberships: Royal Institution; Royal Society, fellow. Address: 23 Royal York Crescent, Clifton, Bristol BS8 4JX, England.

GRENDEL Lajos, b. 6 Apr 1948, Levice, Czechoslovakia. Writer. m. Agota Sebok, 6 July 1974, 1 son, 1 daughter. Education: University Komens Keho. Appointments: Editor, Publishing House, Medech Brehsleva; Editor-in-Chief, Literary Monthly, Kalligram; Chairman, Publishing House, Kalligram, 1992. Publications: Elesloveszet; Attetelil; Borondok Tartalma; Theszevz eș a Pekete ozvegy; Einstien harangjai; Galeir; Hutleneck; Es Eljön az Ö Országa (novel). Contributions to: Hungarian and Slovak magazines. Honours: Dery Prize; József Attila Prize; Cryslal Vilenica; Füst Milan Award, 1995. Membership: Union of Hungarian Writers; President, Slovak Centre PEN. Address: Vazovova 15, 81107 Bratislava, Slovak Republic.

GRENNAN Eamon, b. 13 Nov 1941, Dublin, Ireland. Professor; Poet. 1 son, 2 daughters. Education: BA, 1963, MA, 1964, University College, Dublin; PhD, Harvard University, 1973. Appointments: Lecturer in English, University College, Dublin, 1966-67; Assistant Professor, Herbert Lehman College, City University of New York, 1971-74; Assistant Professor, 1974-83, Associate Professor, 1983-89, Professor, 1989-, Vassar College. Publications: Wildly for Days, 1983; What Light There Is, 1987; Twelve Poems, 1988; What Light There Is and Other Poems, 1989; As If It Matters, 1991; So It Goes, 1995; Selected Poems of Giacomo Leopardi (translator), 1995; Relations: New and Selected Poems, 1998. Contributions to: Anthologies and periodicals. Honours: National Endowment for the Humanities Grant, 1986; National Endowment for the Arts Grant, 1991; Guggenheim Fellowship, 1995. Address: c/o Department of English, Vassar College, Poughkeepsie, NY 12604, USA.

GRENVILLE John A(shley) S(oames), b. 11 Jan 1928, Berlin, Germany. Historian; Professor. m. (1) Betty Anne Rosenberg, 1960, dec 1974, 3 sons, (2) Patricia Carnie, 1975, 1 daughter, 1 stepdaughter. Education: Correspondence courses, Birbeck College, and London School of Economics and Political Science; BA, Yale University; PhD, London University. Appointments: Postgraduate Scholar, London University, 1951-53; Assistant Lecturer to Lecturer, 1953-64, Reader in Modern History, 1964-65, Nottingham University; Commonwealth Fund Fellow, 1958-59; Postdoctoral Fellow, Yale University, 1960-63; Professor of International History, Leeds University, 1965-69; Editor, Fontana History of War and Society, 1969-78, Leo Baeck Year Book, 1992-; Professor of Modern History, 1969-94, Professorial Research Fellow, Institute of German Studies, 1994-, University of Birmingham. Publications: The Coming of the Europeans (with J G Fuller), 1962; Lord Salisbury and Foreign Policy, 1964, 2nd edition, 1970; Politics, Strategy and American Diplomacy: Studies in Foreign Policy 1873-1917 (with G B Young), 1966, 2nd edition, 1971; The Major International Treaties 1914-1973: A History and Guide, 1974, enlarged edition, 2 volumes, 1987; Europe Reshaped 1848-1878, 1975; Nazi Germany, 1976; World History of the Twentieth Century, Vol I, 1900-1945, 1980; Collins World History of the Twentieth Century, 1994, second edition, 1998. Other: Films with N Pronay: The Munich Crisis, 1968; The End of Illusion: From Munich to Dunkirk, 1970. Contributions to: Scholarly journals. Address: c/o Institute of German Studies, University of Birmingham, Birmingham B15 2TT, England.

GREY Anthony (Keith), b. 5 July 1938, Norwich, England. Author; Television and Radio Presenter/Reporter; Publisher. m. Shirley McGuinn, 4 Apr 1970, 2 daughters. Appointments: Journalist, Eastern Daily Press, 1960-64; Foreign Correspondent, Reuters, East Berlin and Prague, 1965-67, Beijing, 1967-69; Established imprint, Tagman Press, London. Publications: Hostage in Peking, 1970; A Man Alone, 1971; Some Put Their Trust in Chariots, 1973; Crosswords from Peking, 1975; The Bulgarian Exclusive, 1976; Himself (radio play), 1976; The Chinese Assassin, 1978; Saigon, 1982; The Prime Minister was a Spy, 1983; Peking, 1988; The Naked Angels, 1990; The Bangkok Secret, 1990; Tokyo Bay, 1996. Other: BBC World Service radio documentary series, UFO's: Fact, Fiction or Fantasy, 1997. Honours: Officer of the Order of the British Empire, 1969; UK Journalist of the Year, 1970. Memberships: PEN International; Royal Institute of International Affairs; Society of Authors; Groucho Club. Address: c/o Peters, Fraser and Dunlop Group, The Chambers, 5th Floor, Chelsea Harbour, Lots Road, London SW10 0XF, England.

GREY Belinda. See: **PETERS Maureen.**

GREY Charles. See: **TUBB E(dwin) C(harles).**

GRIDBAN Volsted. See: **TUBB E(dwin) C(harles).**

GRIFFIN Keith (Broadwell), b. 6 Nov 1938, Colón, Panama (British Citizen). Distinguished Professor of Economics; Writer. m. Dixie Beth Griffin, 2 Apr 1956, 2 daughters. Education: BA, Williams College, Williamstown, Massachusetts, 1960; BPhil, 1965, University of Oxford. Appointments: Visiting Professor, University of Chile, 1962-63, 1964-65; Fellow and Tutor in Economics, 1965-76, President, 1979-88, Magdalen College, Oxford, Cecil and Ida Green Visiting Professor, University of British Columbia, 1986; Distinguished Professor of Economics, 1988-, Chair, Department of Economics, 1988-93; University of California at Riverside. Publications: Undevlopment in Spanish America, 1969, 2nd edition, 1971; Planning Development (with John Enos), 1970; Financing Development in Latin America (editor), 1971; Growth and Inequality in Pakistan (editor with Azizur Rahman Khan), 1972; The Green Revolution: An Economic Analysis, 1972; The Economic Development of Bangladesh (editor with E A G Robinson), 1974; The Political Economy of Agrarian Change, 1974, 2nd edition, 1979; Land Concentration and Rural Poverty, 1976, 2nd edition, 1981; Poverty and Landlessness in Rural Asia (editor with Azizur Rahman Khan), 1977; International Inequality and National Poverty, 1978; The Transition to Egalitarian Development (with Jeffrey James), 1981; Growth and Equality in Rural China (with Ashwani Saith), 1981; Institutional Reform and Economic Development in the Chinese Countryside (editor), 1984; World Hunger and the World Economy, 1987; Alternative Strategies for Economic Development, 1989; Human Development and the International Development Strategy for the 1990s (editor with John Knight), 1990; The Economy of Ethiopia (editor), 1992; Globalization and the Developing World (with Azizur Rahman Khan), 1992; The Distribution of Icome in China (editor with Zhao Renwei), 1993; Implementing a Human Development Strategy (with Terry McKinley), 1994; Poverty and the Transition to a Market Economy in Mongolia (editor), 1995; Social Policy and Economic Transformation in Uzbekistan (editor), 1996; Studies in Globalization and Economic Transitions, 1996; Economic Reform in Vietnam (editor), 1998. Contributions to: Scholarly books and journals. Honours: Honorary DLitt, Williams College, 1980; Honorary Fellow, Magdalen College, Oxford, 1988. Membership: American Association for the Advancement of Science, Fellow, 1997. Address: c/o Department of Economics, University of California at Riverside, Riverside, CA 92521, USA.

GRIFFIN RESS Patricia, (Bernadette Bay O'Shaughnessy), b. 7 Aug 1945, Sioux City, Iowa, USA. Journalist; Teacher; Laboratory Medical Technician. m. Fred Callsen Ress, 7 Sept 1969, 1 son, 2 daughters. Education: BS, Education, University of South Dakota; South Dakota Graduate College; University of Iowa. Appointments: Teacher, Omaha Public Schools; Staff, Midlands Business Journal, Sun Newspapers of Lincoln, Nebraska Voice, Walton County Tribune. Publications: Alien Abductions and Encounters in the American Midwest; Armageddon - the Last Alien Battle; She Talks to Angels. Contributions to: Prediction Magazine; Uri Geller's Encounters; Alien Encounters; Fate Magazine; Spectra; Crystal Tower Magazine; Farm and Ranch Living Magazine. Memberships: National Writers Club. Address: 618 North 172nd Ct Circle, Omaha, NE 68118, USA.

GRIFFITH A(rthur) Leonard, b. 19 Mar 1920, Lancashire, England. Retired Minister of Religion; Writer. m. Anne Merelie Cayford, 17 June 1947, 2 daughters. Education: BA, McGill University, 1942; BD, Queen's University, Kingston, Ontario, 1958. Publications: The Roman Letter Today, 1959; God and His People, 1960; Beneath the Cross of Jesus, 1961; What is a Christian, 1962?, Barriers to Christian Belief, 1962; A Pilgrimage to the Holy Land, 1962; The Eternal Legacy, 1963; Pathways to Happiness, 1964; God's Time and Ours, 1964; The Crucial Encounter, 1965; This is Living, 1966; God is Man's Experience, 1968; Illusions of Our Culture, 1969; The Need to Preach, 1971; Hang on to the Lord's Prayer, 1973; We Have This Ministry, 1973; Ephesians: A Positive Affirmation, 1975; Gospel Characters, 1976; Reactions to God, 1979; Take Hold of the Treasure, 1981; From Sunday to Sunday, 1987. Address: 71 Old Mill Road, 105 Etobicoke, Ontario M8X 1G9, Canada.

GRIFFITH Patricia Browning, b. 9 Nov 1935, Ft Worth, Texas, USA. Writer; Dramatist. m. William Byron Griffith, 6 June 1960, 1 daughter. Education: BA, Baylor University, 1958. Appointments: Associate Adjunct Professor, George Washington University; President, PEN/Faulkner Foundation Award for Fiction. Publications: Novels: The Future is Not What it Used to Be, 1970; Tennessee Blue, 1981; The World Around Midnight, 1991; Supporting the Sky, 1996. Plays: Outside Waco, 1984; Safety, 1987; Risky Games, 1992; Contributions to: Anthologies and periodicals. Honours: National Endowment for the Arts Grant, 1978; American Library Association Notable Book, 1992. Address: 1215 Geranium Street North West, Washington, DC 20012, USA.

GRIFFITHS Helen, (Helen Santos), b. 8 May 1939, London, England. Writer. Publications: Horse in the Clouds, 1957; Wild and Free, 1958; Moonlight, 1959; Africano, 1960; The Wild Heart, 1962; The Greyhound, 1963; Wild Horse of Santander, 1965; Dark Swallows, 1965; Leon, 1966; Stallion of the Sands, 1967; Moshie Cat, 1968; Patch, 1969; Federico, 1970; Russian Blue, 1973; Just a Dog, 1974; Witch Fear, 1975; Pablo, 1976; Kershaw Dogs, 1978; The Last Summer, 1979; Blackface Stallion, 1980; Dancing Horses, 1981; Hari's Pigeon, 1982; Rafa's Dog, 1983; Jesus, As Told By Mark, 1983; Dog at the Window, 1984; As Helen Santos: Caleb's Lamb, 1984; If Only, 1987; Pepe's Dog, 1996. Honours: Daughter of Mark Twain, 1966; Highly Commended, Carnegie Medal Award, 1966; Silver Pencil Award, for Best Children's Book, Netherlands, 1978. Address: 9 Ashley Terrace, Bath, Avon, BA1 3DP, England.

GRIFFITHS Paul (Anthony), b. 24 Nov 1947, Bridgend, Glamorgan, Wales. Music Critic; Writer. m. Sally Mclaughlin, 1979. Education: BA, MSc, Lincoln College, Oxford. Appointments: Area Editor, The New Grove Dictionary of Music and Musicians, 1973-76; Music Critic, The Times, 1982-92, The New Yorker, 1992-. Publications: A Concise History of Modern Music, 1978; Boulez, 1978; A Guide to Electronic Music, 1979; Modern Music, 1980; Cage, 1981; Peter Maxwell Davies, 1982; The String Quartet, 1983; György Ligeti, 1983; Bartók, 1984; Olivier Messiaen, 1985; New Sounds, New Personalities, 1985; The Thames & Hudson Encyclopedia of 20th Century Music, 1986; Myself and Marco Polo (novel), 1987; The Life of Sir Tristram (novel), 1991; The Jewel Box (opera libretto), 1991; Stravinsky, 1992; Modern Music and After, 1995. Address: The Old Bakery, Lower Heyford, Oxford OX6 3NS, England.

GRIFFITHS Trevor, b. 4 Apr 1935, Manchester, Lancashire, England. Playwright. m. (1) Janice Elaine Stansfield, 1960, dec 1977, 1 son, 2 daughters, (2) Gillian Cliff, 1992. Education: St Bede's College, Manchester, 1945-52; BA, English, Manchester University, 1955. Appointments: Lecturer in Liberal Studies, Stockport Technical College, Cheshire, 1962-65; Co-Editor, Labour's Northern Voice, 1962-65; Series Editor, Workers Northern Publishing Society; Further Education Officer, BBC, Leeds, 1965-72. Theatre plays include: Occupations, 1970; The Party, 1973; Comedians, 1975; The Cherry Orchard, 1977; Oi for England,1982; Real Dreams, 1984; Piano, 1990; The Gulf between Us, 1992; Thatcher's Children, 1993; Who Shall Be Happy....?, 1995. Television plays and films include: All Good Men, 1974; Through the Night, 1975; Bill Brand, 1976; Sons and Lovers, 1981; Country, 1981; The Last Place on Earth, 1985; Hope in the Year Two, 1994; Food for Ravens, 1997. Cinema: Reds, 1981; Fatherland, 1986. Other publications include; Collected Plays for Television, 1988; Trevor Griffiths: Plays, 1996; Honours: BAFTA Writer's Award, 1982; Writers' Guild of America Award for Best Screenplay, 1982; Oscar Nomination, 1982; Royal Television Society Award for the Best Regional Programme, 1998. Address: c/o Peters, Fraser & Dunlop Group Ltd, The Chambers, 503-4 Chelsea Harbour, Lots Road, London SW10 0XF, England.

GRIFO Lionello. See: **VAGGE Ornello.**

GRIGG John (Edward Poynder), b. 15 Apr 1924, London, England. Writer. m. Marion Patricia Campbell, 3 Dec 1958, 2 sons. Education: MA, New College, Oxford, 1948. Appointments: Grenadier Guards, 1943-45; Editor, National and English Review, 1954-60; Columnist, The Guardian, 1960-70. Publications: Two Anglican Essays, 1958; The Young Lloyd George, 1973; Lloyd George: The People's Champion, 1978; The Victory That Never Was, 1980; Nancy Astor: Portrait of a Pioneer, 1980; Lloyd George: From Peace to War 1912-1916, 1985; The Thomson Years (vol VI in The History of the Times), 1993. Contributions to: Various books of essays, magazines and journals. Honours: Whitbread Award, 1978; Wolfson Literary Prize, 1985. Memberships: Blackheath Society, president; London Library, chairman, 1985-91, president, 1996-; Royal Society of Literature, fellow. Address: 32 Dartmouth Row, London SE10, England.

GRIGSON Sophie, b. 19 June 1959. Food Writer; Broadcaster. m. William Black, 1 son, 1 daughter. Education: BSc, Honours, 1978-82. Appointments: Colomnist. Publications include: Fish; Sophie Grigson's Taste of the Times; Sophie Grigson's Meat Course; Travels a la Carte; Eat Your Greens; Food for Friends; Sophie's Table; The Carved Angel Cook Book; Sophie Grigson's Ingredients Book; the Student's Cookbook; Sophie Grigson's Herbs. Contributions to: Country Living; Food and Travel; BBC Good Food Magazine; Taste; Sunday Express Magazine; Cosmopolitan; New Woman; Sunday Telegraph; Woman; Family Circle; Daily Mail; Bon Appetit. Honours include: Caroline Walker Prize. Membership: Jane Grigson Library, trustee. Literary Agent: Borra Gabon. Address: c/o Deborah McKenna Ltd, Claridge House, 29 Barnes High Street, London SW13 9LW, England.

GRILLO Odhise, (Odeta Guri, Oltion Gurra, Odi Kristo, Ograja), b. 21 Mar 1933, Vuno, Himare, Vlore, Albania. Editor; Journalist. m. Vangjelo Veizi, 2 Sept 1960, 1 son, 1 daughter. Education: Faculty of Philology & Juridical and Political Sciences, Tirana University, 1960-64. Appointments: Senior Editor, Hosteni, Humourist Magazine, 1953-60; Senior Editor for Children Literature publishing house, Naim Frasheeri, 1964-94; University Teacher in Tirana, 1971-94; Elbasan University, Aleksander Xhuvani, 1975-81. Publications: 84 works published; 35 works re-published; Gun Shots on the Coast, novel, 1967; The One Who Conquered the Emperor, triptych poems, 1978; The Errors of Veshkaush, tales, 4 vols, 1984, 1988, 1990, 1995; Literary Panorama, 1 and 2, studies and critics, 1986, 1997; Don Quixote de la Mancha, novel adapted for children, 1992; Lexicon: Albanian Writers, 1872-1995; The Echoes of Childhood, verses in Greek, Athens, 1991; The Butterfly and the Flowers, tales and stories in Arabik, Damasque, 1987; History of Skanderbeg, novel in Italian, Genova, 1998. Contributions to: Magazines: Fatosi; Pionieri; Gezimi; Mrekullia; Filizat; Drita; Nentori; Ipuwais Journals, Zeri i Rinise, Hosteni, Flaka e vellazerimit. Honours: Migjeni; Asdreni; La Fontaine; Aesopi; Giani Rodari. Membership: Chairman, Albanian Society of Writers for Children; Board Chairman, magazines: Filizat; Mrekullia; Fllad; Univers. Address: Rruga Gjin Bua Shpata, pallati 7, shkalla 2/25, Tirana, Albania.

GRIMM Barbara Lockett, (Cherry Wilder), b. 3 Sept 1930, Auckland, New Zealand. Writer. m. Horst Grimm, 1963, 2 daughters. Education: BA, Canterbury University College, Christchurch, 1952. Publications: The Luck of Brin's Five, 1977; The Nearest Fire, 1979; The Tapestry Warriors, 1982; Second Nature, 1982; A Princess of the Chameln, 1983; Yorath the Wolf, 1984; The Summer's King, 1985; Cruel Designs, 1988; Dealings in Light and Darkness, 1994. Contributions to: Anthologies, magazines and newspapers. Honours: Australia Council Literary Grants, 1973, 1975; Dimar, Australian Science Fiction Award, 1978. Memberships: British Science Fiction Association; Science Fiction Club of Germany; Science Fiction Writers of America; Women Writers of Australia. Address: Kurt Schumacher Strasse 36, D-6070 Langen/Hessen, Germany.

GRINSELL Leslie Valentine, b. 14 Feb 1907, Hornsey, North London, England. Museum Curator (retired). Education: Highgate School, 1921-23. Appointments: Clerk, Barclays Bank, 1925-49; Staff, Victoria County History of Wiltshire, 1949-52; Curator in Archaeology, Bristol City Museum, 1952-72. Publications: Ancient Burial Mounds of England, 1936, 3rd edition, 1975; Egyptian Pyramids, 1947; Archaeology of Wessex, 1958; Archaeology of Exmoor, 1970; Barrow, Pyramid and Tomb, 1975. Contributions to: Proceedings of various societies. Honours: MA, Bristol University, 1971; Officer of the Order of the British Empire, 1972. Memberships: County Archaeological Societies in Southern England; Society of Antiquaries, London; Prehistoric Society, treasurer, 1947-70. Address: 32 Queens Court, Clifton, Bristol BS8 1ND, England.

GRISEZ Germain, b. 30 Sept 1929, University Heights, Ohio, USA. Professor of Christian Ethics; Writer. m. Jeannette Selby, 9 June 1951, 4 sons. Education: BA, John Carroll University, University Heights, Ohio, 1951; MA and PhL, Dominican College of St Thomas Aquinas, River Forest, Illinois, 1951; PhD, University of Chicago, 1959. Appointments: Assistant Professor to Professor, Georgetown University, 1957-72; Lecturer in Medieval

Philosophy, University of Virginia at Charlottesville, 1961-62; Special Assistant to Patrick Cardinal O'Boyle, Archbishop of Washington, DC, 1968-69; Consultant, Archdiocese of Washington, DC, 1969-72; Professor of Philosophy, Campion College, University of Regina, Saskatchewan, Canada, 1972-79; Archbishop Harry J Flynn Professor of Christian Ethics, Mount Saint Mary's College, Emmitsburg, Maryland, 1979-. Publications: Contraception and the Natural Law, 1964; Abortion: The Myths, the Realities, and the Arguments, 1970; Beyond the New Morality: The Responsibilities of Freedom (with Russell Shaw), 1974, 3rd edition, 1988; Beyond the New Theism: A Philosophy of Religion, 1975; Free Choice: A Self-Referential Argument (with Joseph M Boyle Jr and Olaf Tollefsen), 1976; Life and Death with Liberty and Justice: A Contribution to the Euthanasia Debate (with Joseph M Boyle Jr), 1979; The Way of the Lord Jesus, Vol I, Christian Moral Principles (with others), 1983, Vol II, Living a Christian Life (with others), 1993, Vol III, Difficult Moral Questions (with others), 1997; Nuclear Deterrence, Morality and Realism (with John Finnis and Joseph M Boyle Jr), 1987; Fulfilment in Christ: A Summary of Christian Moral Principles (with Russell Shaw), 1991. Contributions to: Many scholarly journals. Honours: Pro ecclesia et pontifice Medal, 1972; Special Award for Scholarly Work, 1981, Cardinal Wright Award for Service to the Church, 1983, Fellowship of Catholic Scholars; Various other fellowships and grants. Memberships: American Catholic Philosophical Association, president, 1983-84; Catholic Theological Society of America; Fellowship of Catholic Scholars, founding member. Address: Mount Saint Mary's College, Emmitsburg, MD 21727, USA.

GRISHAM John, b. 8 Feb 1955, Jonesboro, Arkansas, USA. Writer. m. Renee Jones, 1 son, 1 daughter. Education: BS, Mississippi State University; JD, University of Mississippi. Appointments: Admitted to the Bar, Mississippi, 1981; Attorney, Southaven, Mississippi, 1981-90; Member, Mississippi House of Representatives, 1984-90. Publications: A Time to Kill, 1988; The Firm, 1989; The Pelican Brief, 1990; The Client, 1993; The Chamber, 1994; Rainmaker, 1995; The Runaway Jury, 1996; The Partner, 1997; The Street Lawyer, 1998. Address: c/o Jay Garon-Brooke Associates Inc, 101 West 55th Street, Suite 5K, New York, NY 10019, USA.

GRODS Arvis, b. 20 Sept 1933, Tukums, Latvia. Editor; Writer. m. Tamara, 7 Jan 1983, 1 son. Education: Latvian State University, 1957; Moscow Institute of Poligraphy, 1968. Appointments: Teacher, 1957-59, Lecturer, 1959-60, Department Manager, 1961-66, 1971-81; Journalist, 1966-68, 1970-75; Proof-Reader, 1969-70; Editor, 1982-92; State Language Inspector, 1992-93. Publications: All Happy Families, 1973; Tudalin, Tagadin, English translation as Latvian Folk Dance, 1977; Orchard Nearby, 1990; Darovoye, Part I - Everybody's Pain, 1993, Part II - That Killing Work, 1994; See You, 1994; The Klavnieki, 1998. Contributions to: Karogs; Sieviete; Liesma; Daugava; Lauku Dzive; Literatura un Maksla. Honour: Best Book of the Year, 1973; Membership: Writers' Union of Latvia, 1991-. Address: Degoles iela 6, Tukums, LV-3104, Latvia.

GROSS John (Jacob), b. 12 Mar 1935, London, England. Writer; Critic; Editor. m. Miriam May, 1965, div 1988, 1 son, 1 daughter. Education: MA, Wadham College, Oxford, 1955; Graduate Studies, Princeton University, 1958-59. Appointments: Editor, Victor Gollancz Ltd, 1956-58, Times Literary Supplement, 1974-81; Assistant Lecturer, Queen Mary College, University of London, 1959-62; Fellow, King's College, Cambridge, 1962-65; Literary Editor, New Statesman, 1973; Director, Times Newspapers Holdings, 1982; Staff, New York Times, 1983-89; Theatre Critic, Sunday Telegraph, 1989-. Publications: Dickens and the Twentieth Century (editor with Gabriel Pearson), 1962; John P Marquand, 1963; The Rise and Fall of the Man of Letters: Aspects of English Literary Life since 1800, 1969; James Joyce, 1970; Rudyard Kipling: The Man, His Work, and His World (editor), 1972; The Oxford Book of Aphorisms (editor), 1983; The Oxford Book of Essays (editor), 1991; Shylock, 1992; The Modern Movement

(editor), 1992; The Oxford Book of Comic Verse (editor), 1994. Contributions to: Periodicals and newspapers. Honours: Harkness Fellow, Princeton University, 1958-59; Duff Cooper Memorial Prize, 1969; Honorary DHL, Adelphi University, 1995. Address: 74 Princess Court, Queensway, London W2 4RE, England.

GROSS Miriam (Marianna), (Lady Owen), b. 12 May 1939, England. Literary Editor. m. (1) John Gross, 1965, div 1988, (2) Sir Geoffrey Owen, 1993. Education: Dartington Hall School; MA, St Anne's College, Oxford. Appointments: Deputy Literary Editor, The Observer, 1969-81; Arts Editor, The Daily Telegraph, 1986-91; Editor, Book Choice, Channel 4 Television, 1986-91; Literary Editor, Sunday Telegraph, 1991-. Publications: The World of George Orwell (editor), 1971; The World of Raymond Chandler (editor), 1976. Address: 24 St Peterborough Place, London W2 4LB, England.

GROSS Natan, b. 16 Nov 1919, Kraków, Poland. Film Director; Journalist; Translator; Poet. m. Shulamit Lifszyc, 1 son, 1 daughter. Education: Law and Art Studies; Diploma, Film Directing, Polish Film Institute, 1946. Appointment: Film Critic, Al Hamishmar, 1962-82. Publications: Over 15 books, including poetry, anthologies, monographs, criticism, and translations, 1947-97. Contributions to: Journals and magazines. Honours: Numerous Israeli and international film festival awards. Memberships: Film and Television Directors Guild of Israel; Israel Federation of Writers; Israeli Film Union, secretary, 1951-71; Israel Journalists Association. Address: 14 Herzog Street, Givatayim 53586, Israel.

GROSSKURTH Phyllis, b. 16 Mar 1924, Toronto, Ontario, Canada. Professor Emeritus; Author. m. (1) Robert A Grosskurth, 2 sons, 1 daughter, (2) Mavor Moore, 1968, div 1980, (3) Robert McMullan, 1986. Education: BA, University of Toronto, 1946; MA, University of Ottawa, 1960; PhD, University of London, 1962. Appointments: Lecturer, Carleton University, 1964-65; Professor of English, 1965-87, Faculty, Humanities and Psychoanalysis Programme, 1987-95, University of Toronto. Publications: John Addington Symonds: A Biography, 1964; Notes on Browning's Works, 1967; Leslie Stephen, 1968; Gabrielle Roy, 1969; Havelock Ellis: A Biography, 1980; The Memoirs of John Addington Symonds (editor), 1984; Melanie Klein: Her World and Her Work, 1986; Margaret Mead: A Life of Controversy, 1988; The Secret Ring: Freud's Inner Circle and the Politics of Psychoanalysis, 1991; Byron: The Flawed Angel, 1997. Contributions to: Periodicals. Honours: Governor-General's Award for Non-Fiction, 1965; University of British Columbia Award for Biography, 1965; Guggenheim Fellowships, 1977-78, 1983; Rockefeller Foundation Fellowship, 1982; Canada Council Arts award, 1989-90; Social Science and Humanities Research Grant, 1982-92; Honorary DSL, Trinity College, University of Toronto, 1992. Membership: PEN. Address: 147 Spruce Street, Toronto, Ontario M5A 26J, Canada.

GROSSMAN David, b. 25 Jan 1954, Jerusalem, Israel. Writer. m. Michal Grossman, 2 sons, 1 daughter. Education: BA, Hebrew University, Jerusalem, 1979. Publications: Hiyukh ha-gedi, 1983, English translation as The Smile of the Lamb, 1991; 'Ayen 'erekh--ahavah, 1986, English translation as See Under: Love, 1989; Ha-Zeman ha-tsahov, 1987, English translation as The Yellow Wind, 1988; Gan Riki: Mahazeh bi-shete ma'arakhot (play), 1988, English translation as Rikki's Kindergarten, 1988; Sefer hakikduk hapnimi, 1991, English translation as Book of Internal Grammar, 1993; Hanochachim hanifkadim, 1992, English translation as Sleeping on a Wire, 1992. Other: Short stories; children's books. Contributions to: Periodicals. Honours: Children's Literature Prize, Ministry of Education, 1983; Prime Minister's Hebrew Literature Prize, 1984; Israeli Publisher's Association Prize for Best Novel, 1985; Vallombrosa Prize, Italy, 1989; Nelly Sachs Prize, Germany, 1992; Premio Mondelo, Italy. Address: c/o Deborah Harris, The Harris/Elon Agency, PO Box 4143, Jerusalem 91041, Israel.

GROTH Carl Joakim, b. 21 Dec 1953, Stockholm, Sweden. Writer. Publications: Blindfönster Vidare, poetry, 1979; Världen Enligt Edi, novel, 1986; Harlig Ar Jorden, play, 1995. Address: Flemingsgatan 25 D 61, 00500 Helsingfors, Finland.

GROTRIAN Simon Herskind, b. 21 Dec 1961, Aarhus, Denmark. Poet. Education: Literature Studies, Universities of Aarhus and Copenhagen. Appointments: Poet, 1984-. Publications: Collections of Poems: Through My Hand, 1987; Collage, 1988; Next Heaven, 1989; Fire, 1990; Lifetraps, 1993; Snakeharvest, 1994; A Box for Lot, 1995; Magnets and Ambrosia, 1996; The Pulse of Ossian, 1997; Ten, 1998; China Letters, 1999. Contributions to: Die Horen; Hjärnstorm; Poesia; Action Poetique. Honours: Michael Strunge Award, 1990; Emil Aarestrup Medal, 1998. Literary Agent: Jens Christiansen, Borgen Publishers. Address: Lemming Brovej 13B, 8632 Lemming, Denmark.

GRUENWALD George Henry, b. 23 Apr 1922, Chicago, Illinois, USA. Writer; Management Consultant. m. Corrine Rae Linn, 16 Aug 1947, 1 son, 1 daughter. Education: Evanston Academy of Fine Arts, 1937-38; Chicago Academy of Fine Arts, 1938-39; Grinnell College, 1940-41; Medill School of Journalism, Northwestern University, 1941-43, 1945-47; BSc. Appointments include: Public Relations Writer, Mediterranean Tactical Air Force, 1943-44; Night Editor, Daily Northwestern newspaper, 1946; Editor-in-Chief, The Purple Parrot magazine, 1946-47; Editor-in-Chief, The Willys-Overland Motors Salesbuilder magazine, 1949-51; Hudson Family Magazine, 1955-56; Oldsmobile Rocket Circle magazine, 1956-65. Publications include: Books: New Product Development - What Really Works, 1985; New Product Development, 1986, 1988, 1991; New Products: Seven Steps to Success, video, 1988; New Product Development, video, 1989; New Product Checklists - System Workbook, 1991; New Product Development - Responding to Market Demand, 1992; How to Create Profitable New Products - from Mission to Market, 1997; Creative Choices: How to Make Them, 1999. Contributions to: Books: Advertising Age Yearbook, 1982; Feature in How to Development and Market New Products...Better and Faster, 1985; Appetite for Life, Biography of Julia Child, 1997; Contributing feature writer: Advertising Age, 1972, 1981, 1984, 1987, 1995, 1997, 1998; New Product Development Newsletter, 1984, 1986, 1987; Feature writer: The Quill; American Institute of Wine and Food Monthly; Marketing News, publication of American Marketing Association, 1985, 1986, 1988, 1989, 1990-97; Your Company, 1997-98; Business Start-Ups, 1994; San Diego Magazine, 1998; Epicurean Tattler, 1995-96; The Rountree Report; Intrepreneurial Excellence, publication of American Management Association, 1986; Northwestern Remembrances - The War Years, 1993-96; Television commercials, 1951-84; Corporate Communications, 1953-84. Honours include: Hermes Award, 1963; Educational Television Awards, 1969, 1971, 1986; Northwestern University Medill School of Journalism Hall of Achievement, 1997; Best of San Diego Book Award, 1997. Memberships include: President, Northwestern University Chapter, National Society of Professional Journalists, 1946-47; President, Deru, 1946-47; Trustee, The Linus Pauling Institute of Science and Medicine, 1984-; Director, American Institute of Wine and Food, 1985-92; Management Committee, American Association of Advertising Agencies, 1976-84; Director, Executive Committee, Public Broadcasting Service, 1978-86, Director, 1988-94; Trustee, Chicago Public Television, 1969-78; Chairman, President, Twin Cities Public Television, 1972-84; Vice-Chairman, Minnesota Public Radio, 1974-75; Board Member, San Diego Public Broadcasting, 1986-; Southern California Advertising Media Society, 1992-. Address: PO Box 1696, Rancho Santa Fe, CA 92067, USA.

GRUFFYDD Peter, b. 12 Apr 1935, Liverpool, England. Writer; Poet; Translator; Actor. m. (1), 1 son, 1 daughter, (2) Susan Soar, 28 Dec 1974, 2 sons. Education: BA, Honours, University of Wales, Bangor, 1960. Publications: Triad, 1963; Welsh Voices, 1967; Poems, 1969; The Lilting House, 1970; Poems, 1972;

The Shivering Seed, 1972; On Censorship, 1985; Environmental Teletex, 1989; Damned Braces, 1993. Contributions to: Anthologies and periodicals. Honours: Eric Gregory Trust, 1963; 2nd Prize, Young Poets Competition, Welsh Arts Council, 1969; 1st Prizes, 1984, 1994, 3rd Prizes, 1986, 1991, 1993, Aberystwyth Open Poetry Competitions; Duncan Lawrie Prize, Arvon-Observer International Poetry Competition, 1993. Memberships: Equity; PEN International, founder-member, Welsh Branch, 1993; Welsh Union of Writers; Yr Academi Gymraeg. Address: 21 Beech Road, Norton, Stourbridge, West Midlands DY8 2AS, England.

GRUMBACH Doris (Isaac), b. 12 July 1918, New York, New York, USA. Author; Critic; Retired Professor of English. m. Leonard Grumbach, 15 Oct 1941, div 1972, 4 daughters. Education:AB, Washington Square College, 1939; MA, Cornell University, 1940. Appointments: Associate Editor, Architectural Forum, 1942-43; Teacher of English, Albany Academy for Girls, New York, 1952-55; Instructor, 1955-58, Assistant Professor, 1958-60, Associate Professor, 1960-69, Professor of English, 1969-73, College of Saint Rose, Albany; Visiting University Fellow, Empire State College, 1972-73; Literary Editor, New Republic, 1973-75; Adjunct Professor of English, University of Maryland, 1974-75; Professor of American Literature, American University, Washington, DC, 1975-85; Columnist and reviewer for various publications, radio, and television. Publications: The Spoil of the Flowers, 1962; The Short Throat, the Tender Mouth, 1964; The Company She Kept (biography of Mary McCarthy), 1967; Chamber Music, 1979; The Missing Person, 1981; The Ladies, 1984; The Magician's Girl, 1987; Coming Into the End Zone, 1992; Extra Innings: A Memoir, 1993; Fifty Days of Solitude, 1994; The Book of Knowledge: A Novel, 1995. Contributions to: Books and periodicals. Memberships: PEN; Phi Beta Kappa. Address: c/o Maxine Groffsky, 2 Fifth Avenue, New York, NY 10011, USA.

GRUN Max von der, b. 25 May 1926, Bayreuth, Germany. Author. m. Elke Hüser, 1 son, 1 daughter. Education: Commercial Studies; Bricklayer Apprenticeship. Publications: Männer in zweifacher Nacht, 1962; Irrlicht und Feuer, 1963; Zwei Briefe an Pospischiel, 1968; Stellenweise Glatteis, 1973; Menschen in Deutschland, 1973; Leben im gelobten Land, 1975; Wenn der rote Rabe von Baum fällt, 1975; Vorstadtkrokodile, 1976; Wie war das eigentlich?: Kindheit und Jugend im Dritten Reich, 1979; Flächenbrand, 1979; Etwas ausserhalb der Legalität, 1980; Meine Fabrik, 1980; Klassengespräche, 1981; Späte Liebe, 1982; Friedrich und Friederlike, 1983; Die Lawine, 1986; Springflut, 1990; Die Saujagd und andere Vorstadtgeschichten, 1995. Honours: Grand Cultural Prize of the City of Nuremberg, 1974; Wilhelm Lubke Prize, 1979; Gerrit Engelke Prize, Hannover, 1985. Memberships: PEN Club; Verband Deutscher Schriftsteller. Address: Bremsstrasse 40, D-44239, Dortmund, Germany.

GRÜNBAUM Adolf, b. 15 May 1923, Cologne, Germany (US citizen, 1944). Professor of Philosophy; Research Professor of Psychiatry; Writer. m. Thelma Braverman, 26 June 1949, 1 daughter. Education: BA, Wesleyan University, 1943; MS, Physics, 1948, PhD, Philosophy, 1951, Yale University. Appointments: Faculty, 1950-55, Professor of Philosophy, 1955-56, Selfridge Professor of Philosophy, 1956-60, Lehigh University; Visiting Research Professor, Minnesota Center for the Philosophy of Science, 1956, 1959; Andrew Mellon Professor of Philosophy, 1960-, Director, 1960-78, later Chairman, Center for the Philosophy of Science, Research Professor of Psychiatry, 1979-, University of Pittsburgh; Werner Heisenberg Lecturer, Bavarian Academy of Sciences, 1985; Gifford Lecturer, University of St Andrews, 1985; Visiting Mellon Professor, California Institute of Technology, 1990. Publications: Philosophical Problems of Space and Time, 1963, 2nd edition, 1973; Modern Science and Zeno's Paradoxes, 2nd edition, 1968; Geometry and Chronometry in Philosophical Perspective, 1968; The Foundations of Psychoanalysis: A Philosophical Critique, 1984; Psicoanalisi: Obiezioni e Risposte, 1988; Validation in the Clinical Theory of Psychoanalysis, 1993; La Psychanalyse à l'Épreuve, 1993. Contributions to: Books and scholarly journals. Honours: J Walker Tomb Prize, Princeton University, 1958; Honour Citation, Wesleyan University, 1959; Festschriften published in his honour, 1983, 1993; Senior US Scientist Prize, Alexander von Humboldt Foundation, 1985; Fregene Prize for Science, Italian Parliament, 1989; Master Scholar and Professor Award, University of Pittsburgh, 1989; Wilbur Lucius Cross Medal, Yale University, 1990; Honorary Doctorate, University of Konstanz, Germany, 1995. Memberships: American Academy of Arts and Sciences; American Philosophical Association; Academie Internationale de Philosophie des Sciences; International Academy of Humanism; Philosophy of Science Association, president, 1965-70; American Association for the Advancement of Science. Address: 7141 Roycrest Place, Pittsburgh, PA 15208, USA.

GRYNBERG Henryk, b. 4 July 1936, Warsaw, Poland. m. Writer. Krystyna Walczak, 30 July 1967, 1 son, 1 daughter. Education: Master's, Journalism, Warsaw University, 1959; MA, Slavic Languages and Literatures, University of California, Los Angeles, 1971. Appointment: Literary Workshop, Warsaw University, 1993-94. Publications: Zydowska wojna, 1965, 2nd edition, 1989; Zwyciestwo, 1969, 2nd edition, 1990; Kadisz, 1987, 2nd edition, 1992; Prawda Nieartystyczna, 1984, 2nd edition, 1994; Rysuje w Pamieci, 1995. Contributions to: Commentary; Midstream; Tygodnik Powszechny; Odra; Kresy; Tel-Aviv Review; Gazeta Wyborcza; Midrash; East European Jewish Affairs. Honours: Various awards. Memberships: ZLP; ZPPO; Pen American Center; SPP. Address: 6251 N Kensington Street, McLean, VA 22101-4902, USA.

GSTEIGER Manfred, b. 7 June 1930. Writer. m. Favarger Pierrette, 4 Feb 1960, 2 daughters. Education: PhD, University of Berne. Appointments: Journalist, Swiss Radio; Assistant Lecturer, University of Neuchâtel; Visiting Professor, University of Illinois; Professor, University of Lausanne. Publications: Inselfahrt, 1955; Literatur des Übergangs, 1962; Französische Gedichte aus neun Jahrhunderten, 1959; Die Zeitgenössischen Literaturen der Schweiz, 1974; Wandlungen Werthers and Other Essays, 1980; Einstellungen, 1982; Den Vater begraben (novel), 1993; Littératures Suisses - Littérature Européenne (essays), 1996. Memberships: Swiss Writers Association; International and Swiss Comparative Literature Associations; PEN. Address: Pertuis du Sault 10, CH-2000 Neuchâtel, Switzerland.

GUARE John, b. 5 Feb 1938, New York, New York, USA. Dramatist. m. Adele Chatfield-Taylor, 20 May 1981. Education: AB, Georgetown University, 1961; MFA, Yale University, 1963. Appointments: Co-Founder, Eugene O'Neill Theater Center, Waterford, Connecticut, 1965; Resident Playwright, New York Shakespeare Festival, 1976; Seminar-in-Writing Fellow, 1977-78, Adjunct Professor, 1978-81, Yale University; Co-Editor, Lincoln Center New Theatre Review, 1977-; Visiting Artist, Harvard University, 1990-91; Fellow, Juilliard School, 1993-94. Publications: Plays: Theatre Girl, 1959; The Toadstool Boy, 1960; The Golden Cherub, 1962; Did You Write My Name in the Snow?, 1962; To Wally Pantoni, We Leave a Credenza, 1964; The Loveliest Afternoon of the Year, 1966; Something I'll Tell You Tuesday, 1966; Muzeeka, 1967; Cop-Out, 1968; A Play by Brecht, 1969; Home Fires, 1969; Kissing Sweet, 1969; The House of Blue Leaves, 1971, as a musical, 1986; Two Gentlemen of Verona, 1971; A Day for Surprises, 1971; Un Pape a New York, 1972; Marco Polo Sings a Solo, 1973; Optimism, or the Adventures of Candide, 1973; Rich and Famous, 1974; Landscape of the Body, 1977; Take a Dream, 1978; Bosoms and Neglect, 1979; In Fireworks Lie Secret Codes, 1981; Lydie Breeze, 1982; Gardenia, 1982; Stay a While, 1984; Women and Water, 1984; Gluttony, 1985; The Talking Dog, 1985; Moon Over Miami, 1989, revised version as Moon Under Miami, 1995; Six Degrees of Separation, 1990; Four Baboons Adoring the Sun, 1992; Chuck Close, 1995; The War Against the Kitchen Sink (volume of plays), 1996. Honours: Obie Awards, 1968, 1971, 1990; New York Drama Critics Circle Awards, 1969, 1971, 1972, 1990; Drama Desk Awards, 1972; Tony Awards, 1972, 1986; Joseph Jefferson Award, 1977; Award of Merit, American Academy of Arts and Letters, 1981; Los Angeles Film Critics Award, 1981; National Society of Film Critics Circle Award, 1981; New York Film Critics Award, 1981; Venice Film Festival Grand Prize, 1981; Olivier Best Play Award, 1993; New York State Governor's Award, 1996. Memberships: American Academy of Arts and Letters; Dramatists Guild. Address; c/o R Andrew Boose, 1 Dag Hammarskjöld Plaza, New York, NY 10017, USA.

GUARNIERI Patrizia, b. 16 June 1954, Florence, Italy. Historian; Lecturer in Italian and History of Science; Narrative Translator. m. Franco Cardini, 2 Aug 1991, 1 son, 1 daughter. Education: MA, Philosophy, University of Florence, 1977; PhD, University of Urbino, 1979; Fulbright Visiting Scholar, Harvard University, Massachusetts, 1981. Appointments: Lecturer in Italian Culture and Language, University of Florence, 1978-81, Stanford University Programme in Italy, 1982-93; Professor, History of Science, University of Trieste, 1988-91. Publications: Introduzione a James, 1985; Individualita' Difformi, 1986; L'Ammazzabambini, 1988, English edition as A Case of Child Murder, 1992; Between Soma and Psyche, 1988; Theatre and Laboratory, 1988; The Psyche in Trance, 1990; Carta Penna e Psiche, 1990; La Storia della Psichiatria, 1991; Per Una Storia delle Scienze del Bambino, 1996; Dangerous Girls, Family Secrets and Incest Law in Italy, 1998. Contributions to: Kos; Physis; Nuncius; Belfagor. Honours: CNR-NATO Fellow, 1983; Jean Monnet Fellow, 1989. Membership: Scientific Council, European Association of the History of Psychiatry. Address: Via A. Baldesi 12, 50131 Florence, Italy.

GUASCH Anna Maria, b. 15 Oct 1953, Barcelona, Spain. Teacher; University Lecturer. m. Joan Sureda, 22 Dec 1975, 2 sons. Education: History of Art, University of Barcelona; Doctorate, History of Art, University of Seville. Appointments: Professor, History of Contemporary Art, University of Barcelona, 1986-. Publications: Arte e Ideologia en el País Vasco 1940-1980, 1985; La Trama de lo Moderno, 1987; El Arte del Siglo XX en sus Exposiciones 1945-1995, 1997; Del Postminimalismo a lo Multicultural (1968-1999), 1999; El Arte Ultimo a Través de sus Exposiciones-Manifiesto 1980-1995, 1999; Critica de arte: Hisoria, Teoria y praxis (editor) forthcoming; Guia del Arte Contemporareo 1970-2000, forthcoming. Contributions to: Guadalimar; Artes Plasticas; Batik; D'Art; Rehüll; Egin; El País; Diari de Barcelona; Liberacion; Ya; Ad; Tekné; La Vauguardia; Others. Honour: Espais a la Critica d'Art Prize, 1998; Editor of a series on Contemporary Art for Ediciones Akal (Madrid). Literary Agent: José Maria Riaño, Ed del Serbal. Address: Francesc Tarrega 32, 08027 Barcelona, Spain.

GUDMUNDSDOTTIR Kristjana Emilia, b. 23 Apr 1939, Stykkishólmur, Iceland. Writer; Poet. m. 10 June 1957, 3 sons, 3 daughters. Education: Three years in college in Iceland; Journeyman's Certificate Bookbinding, 1985. Publications: Ljóðnálar, 1982; Ljóðblik, 1993; Ljóðgeislar, 1995; Ljóðárur, 1998. With other writers: Ljóðspeglar, 1989; Ljóð Dagsins, 1995; Gluggi, 1996; Lifið Sjálft, 1996; Blánótt, The Iclandic Art Festival Book of Poems, 1996; Ljóð eftir okkur, 1997; Ljós Mál, 1997. Contributions to: Poems and articles in newspapers. Membership: Rithöfundasamband Islands. Address: Borgarholtsbraut 27, 200 Kópavogur, Iceland.

GUERARD Albert Joseph, b. 2 Nov 1914, Houston, Texas, USA. m. 11 July 1941, 3 daughters. Education: BA, 1934, PhD, 1938, Stanford University; MA, Harvard University, 1996. Appointments: Instructor, Amherst College, 1935-36; Instructor to Professor of English, Harvard University, 1938-61; Professor of English, Stanford University, 1961-85. Publications: Robert Bridges, 1942; Joseph Conrad, 1947; Thomas Hardy, 1949; Night Journey, 1950; Andre Gidis, 1951; Conrad The Novelist, 1958; The Touch of Time, 1980; Christine/Annette, 1985; Gabrielle, 1993; The Hotel in the

Jungle, 1995; Suspended Sentences, 1999. Contributions to: Journals, periodicals, reviews and magazines. Membership: American Academy of Arts and Sciences. Address: c/o Department of English, Stanford University, Stanford, CA 94305, USA.

GUERARD Mary Maclin, b. 21 Dec 1920, Baton Rouge, LA, USA. m. Albert J Guerard, 11 July 1941, 3 daughters. Education: BA, Radcliffe College, 1942. Publications: Heaven Lies About, southern stories, 1995; Citizen of the World, short stories, 1999. Contributions to: Southern Review; Denver Quarterly; Sequoiy. Honour: PEN Award. Address: 635 Gerona Road, Stanford, CA 94305, USA.

GUEST Harry, (Henry Bayly Guest), b. 6 Oct 1932, Glamorganshire, Wales. Poet; Writer. m. Lynn Doremus Dunbar, 28 Dec 1963, 1 son, 1 daughter. Education: BA, Trinity Hall, Cambridge, 1954, DES, Sorbonne, University of Paris, 1955. Appointments: Lecturer, Yokohama National University, 1966-72; Head of Modern Languages, Exeter School, 1972-91; Teacher of Japanese, Exeter University, 1979-95. Publications: Arrangements, 1968; The Cutting-Room, 1970; Post-War Japanese Poetry, (editor and translator), 1972; A House Against the Night, 1976; The Distance, the Shadows, 1981; Lost and Found, 1983; The Emperor of Outer Space (radio play), 1983; Lost Pictures, 1991; Coming to Terms, 1994; Traveller's Literary Companion to Japan, 1994; So Far, 1998; Contributions to: Reviews, quarterlies, and journals. Honours: Hawthornden Fellow, 1993; Honorary Research Fellow, Exeter University, 1994-; Honorary Doctor of Letters, Plymouth University, 1998. Membership: Poetry Society, General Council, 1972-76. Address: 1 Alexandra Terrace, Exeter, Devon EX4 6SY, England.

GUNN James Edwin, b. 12 July 1923, Kansas City, Kansas, USA. Professor Emeritus; Writer. m. Jane Frances Anderson, 6 Feb 1947, 2 sons. Education: BS, Journalism, 1947, MA, English, 1951, University of Kansas. Appointments: Assistant Instructor, 1950-51, 1955, Instructor, 1958-70, Lecturer, 1970-74, Professor, 1974-93, Professor Emeritus, 1993-, University of Kansas. Publications: This Fortress World, 1955; Star Bridge (with Jack Williamson), 1955; Station in Space, 1958; The Joy Makers, 1961; The Immortals, 1962; Future Imperfect, 1964; The Witching Hour, 1970; The Burning, 1972; Breaking Point, 1972; The Listeners, 1972; Alternate Worlds: The Illustrated History of Science Fiction, 1975; The Magicians, 1976; Kampus, 1977; The Dreamers, 1981; Isaac Asimov: The Foundations of Science Fiction, 1982; Crisis, 1986; Inside Science Fiction, 1992; The Unpublished Gunn, Part 1, 1992, Part 2, 1996; The Joy Machine, 1996; Isaac Asimov: The Foundations of Science Fiction (revised), 1996 Editor: The Road to Science Fiction, 6 volumes, 1977, 1979, 1979, 1982, 1998; The New Encyclopedia of Science Fiction, 1988; The Best of Astounding: Classic Short Novels from the Golden Age of Science Fiction, 1992; Contributions to: Many magazines and journals. Honours: Byron Caldwell Smith Prize, 1971; Pilgrim Award, Science Fiction Research Association, 1976; Hugo Awards, 1976, 1983; Edward Grier Award, 1989; Eaton Award for Lifetime Achievement, 1992. Memberships: Authors Guild; Science Fiction Research Association, president, 1980-82; Science Fiction Writers of America, president, 1971-72. Address: 2215 Orchard Lane, Lawrence, KS 66049, USA.

GUNN Robin Jones, b. 18 Apr 1955, Baraboo, Wisconsin, USA. Writer. m. Ross Gunn III, 13 Aug 1977, 1 son, 1 daughter. Education: Biola University, 1973-75. Appointment: Host, Kids Korner program, KNIS, Carson City, Nevada, 1993-94. Publications: 37 books; 14 picture books. Honours: First Place, Article Writing Contest, Biola Writer's Conference, 1988; Sherwood E Wirt Award, 1989; Mount Hermon Christian Writer's Conference Poetry Award, 1993, and Pacesetter Award, 1996; EPA Article of the Year, 1994. Address: 8002 North East Highway 99, Suite 52, Vancouver, WA 98665, USA.

GUNN Thom(son William), b. 29 Aug 1929, Gravesend, England. Poet. Education: Trinity College, Cambridge. Appointments: Taught English, 1958-66; Lecturer, 1977-, Senior Lecturer, 1988-, University of California, Berkeley, USA. Publications: Fighting Terms, 1954; The Sense of Movement, 1957; My Sad Captains, 1961; Positives (with Ander Gunn), 1966; Touch, 1967; Moly, 1971; Jack Straw's Castle, 1976; Selected Poems, 1979; The Passages of Joy, 1982; The Occasions of Poetry (prose), 1982, expanded edition, 1985; The Man with Night Sweats, 1992; Collected Poems, 1993; Shelf Life (prose), 1993. Honours: Levinson Prize, 1955; Somerset Maugham Prize, 1959; National Institute of Arts and Letters Grant, 1964; Rockefeller Foundation, 1966; Guggenheim Fellowship, 1972; Lila Wallace/ Reader's Digest Fund Award, 1991; Forward Poetry Prize, 1992; MacArthur Fellowship, 1993; Lenore Marshall Prize, 1993. Address: 1216 Cole Street, San Francisco, CA 94117, USA.

GUNNARSSON Baldur, b. 22 Dec 1953, Reykjavik, Iceland. University Lecturer; Writer. 1 son, 1 daughter. Education: BA, University of Iceland, 1981; Cand mag, 1984; MA, State Univeristy of New York at Stony Brook, 1987. Publications: The Labyrinth (novel), 1990; Seaside-Cafe (novel), 1992; Full Fathom Five (novel), 1993; Perpetuum Mobile (novel), 1994. Membership: Writers' Union of Iceland. Literary Agent: Fjölvi, Njörvasundi 15a, 104 Reykjavik, Iceland. Address: Neshagi 9, 107 Reykjavik, Iceland.

GUNSTON Bill, (William Tudor Gunston), b. 1 Mar 1927, London, England. Author. m. Margaret Anne, 10 Oct 1964, 2 daughters. Education: University College, Durham, 1945-46; City University, London, 1948-51. Appointments: Editorial Staff, 1951-55, Technical Editor, 1955-64, Flight; Technology Editor, Science Journal, 1964-70; Freelance author, 1970-; Director, So Few Ltd. Publications: Over 300 books including: Aircraft of The Soviet Union, 1983; Jane's Aerospace Dictionary, 1980, 4th edition, 1998; Encyclopaedia of World Aero Engines, 1986, 3rd edition, 1995; Encyclopaedia of Aircraft Armament, 1987; Giants of the Sky, 1991; Faster Than Sound, 1992; World Encyclopaedia of Aircraft Manufacturers, 1993; Jet Bombers, 1993; Piston Areo Engines, 1994, 2nd edition, 1998; Encyclopaedia of Russian Aircraft, 1995; Jet and Turbine Aero Engines, 1995, 2nd edition, 1997. Contributions to: 188 periodicals; 18 partworks; 75 video scripts. Honours: Royal Aeronautical Society, fellow; Officer of the Order of the British Empire. Address: High Beech, Kingsley Green, Haslemere, Surrey GU27 3LL, England.

GUNTER Peter A Y, b. 20 Oct 1936, Hammond, Indiana, USA. Professor of Philosophy; Writer. m. Elizabeth Ellington Gunter, 2 Apr 1969, 1 daughter. Education: BA, Philosophy and English, University of Texas at Austin, 1958; Marshall Scholar, University of Cambridge, England, 1958-60; PhD, Philosophy, Yale University, 1963. Appointments: Faculty, Auburn University, 1962-65, University of Tennessee at Knoxville, 1965-69; Chairman, Department of Philosophy, 1969-76, Professor of Philosophy, 1969-, Regents' University Professor, 1990-, North Texas State University, renamed University of North Texas at Denton. Publications: Bergson and the Evolution of Physics, 1969; The Big Thicket, 1972; Henri Bergson: A bibliography, 1974, 2nd edition, revised and enlarge, 1987; PRocess Philosophy: Basic Writings (with J R Sibley), 1978; W R Strong: His Memoirs (with R A Calvert), 1981; River in Dry Grass (Novel), 1985; Present, Tense, Future, Perfect (editor), 1985; Bergson and Modern Thought: Towards a Unified Science (editor with A Papanicolaou), 1989; Creativity in George Herbert Mead, 1990; Founders of Constructive Postmodernism (with D Griffin, J Cobb, M Fod, and P Ochs), 1993; The Big Thicket: An Ecological Reconsideration, 1993; Texas Land Ethics (with Max Oelschlaeger), 1998. Contributions to: Many scholarly books and journals. Honours: National Endowment for the Humanities Young Scholar Grant, 1968; North Texas State University Honors Professor, 1972-73; Regents' Faculty Lecturer, 1985, and Toulouse Scholar, 1992; Sierra Club Lone Star Chapter Special Service Award,

1997. Memberships: Society for Process Philosophy of Education; Texas Institute of Letters, 1973-. Address: c/o Department of Philosophy and Religion Studies, College of Arts and Sciences, University of North Texas, PO Box 310920, Denton, TX 76203, USA.

GUNTRUM Suzanne Simmons, (Suzanne Simms), b. 29 Aug 1946, Storm Lake, Iowa, USA. Writer. m. Robert Ray Guntrum, 9 Sept 1967, 1 son. Education: BA, English Literature, Pennsylvania State University, 1967. Publications: Moment in Time, 1982; Of Passion Born, 1982; A Wild Sweet Magic, 1983; All the Night Long, 1983; Dream Within a Dream, 1984; Only This Night, 1984; Moment of Truth, 1986; Nothing Ventured, 1986; Christmas in April, 1986; The Genuine Article, 1987; Made in Heaven, 1988. Contributions to: Magazines. Memberships: Authors Guild; Romance Writers of America. Address: 5245 Willowview Road, Racine, WI 53402, USA.

GURGANUS Allan, b. 11 June 1947, Rocky Mount, North Carolina, USA. Writer; Artist. Education: Monterey Language School, 1966; Radioman and Cryptography School, 1966; University of Pennsylvania, 1966-67; Pennsylvania Academy of Fine Arts, 1966-67; Harvard University, 1969-70; BA, Sarah Lawrence College, 1972; MFA, University of Iowa Writers' Workshop, 1974; Stanford University, 1974-76. Appointments: Professor of Fiction Writing, 1972-74, Writer's Workshop, 1989-90, University of Iowa; Professor of Fiction Writing, Stanford University, 1974-76; Duke University, 1976-78; Sarah Lawrence College, 1978-86; Artist. Publications: Oldest Living Confederate Widow Tells All, 1989; White People: Stories and Novellas, 1991; Practical Heart, 1993; Plays Well With Others, 1997. Contributions to: Periodicals. Honours: National Endowment for the Arts Grants, 1976-77, 1987-88; Ingram Merrill Grant, 1986; Sue Kaufman Prize for First Fiction, American Academy and Institute of Arts and Letters, 1990; Books Across the Sea Ambassador Book Award, English-Speaking Union of the United States, 1990; Los Angeles Times Book Prize, 1991. Address: c/o Amanda Urban, International Creative Management, 40 West 57th Street, New York, NY 10019, USA.

GURI Odeta. See: GRILLO Odhise.

GURNEY A(lbert) R(amsdell), b. 1 Nov 1930, Buffalo, New York, USA. Professor of Literature; Dramatist; Writer. m. Mary Goodyear, 1957, 2 sons, 2 daughters. Education: BA, Williams College, 1952; MFA, Yale University School of Drama, 1958. Appointments: Faculty, 1960-, Professor of Literature, 1970-, Massachusetts Institute of Technology. Publications: Plays: Children, 1974; The Dining Room, 1982; The Perfect Party, 1986; Another Antigone, 1986; Sweet Sue, 1986; The Cocktail Hour, 1988; Love Letters, 1989; The Old Boy, 1991; The Fourth Wall, 1992; Later Life, 1993; A Cheever Evening, 1994; Sylvia, 1995; Overtime, 1995. Novels: The Gospel According to Joe, 1974; The Snow Ball, 1985. Screenplay: The House of Mirth, 1972. Television Play: O Youth and Beauty (from a story by John Cheever), 1979. Honours: Drama Desk Award, 1971; Rockefeller Foundation Grant, 1977; National Endowment for the Arts Award, 1982; Theatre Award, American Academy of Arts and Sciences, 1990; Honorary doctorates. Address: 40 Wellers Bridge Road, Roxbury, CT 06783, USA.

GURR Andrew (John), b. 23 Dec 1936, Leicester, England. Professor; Writer. m. Elizabeth Gordon, 1 July 1961, 3 sons. Education: BA, 1957, MA 1958, University of Auckland, New Zealand; PhD, University of Cambridge, 1963. Appointments: Lecturer, Leeds University, 1962; Professor, University of Nairobi, 1969; University of Reading, 1976-. Publications: The Shakespeare Stage 1574-1642, 1970, 3rd edition, 1992; Writers in Exile, 1982; Katherine Mansfield, 1982; Playgoing in Shakespeare's London, 1987, 2nd edition, 1996; Studying Shakespeare, 1988; Rebuilding Shakespeare's Globe, 1989; The Shakespearian Playing Companies, 1996. Editor: Plays of Shakespeare and Beaumont and Fletcher. Contributions to: Scholarly journals and periodicals. Memberships: International Shakespeare Association; Association of Commonwealth Literature and Language Studies; Society for Theatre Research; Malone Society. Address: c/o Department of English, University of Reading, PO Box 218, Reading, Berkshire RG6 2AA, England.

GURR David, b. 5 Feb 1936, London, England. Writer. m. Judith Deverell, 30 Aug 1958, 2 sons, 1 daughter. Education: Canadian Naval College, 1954-56; BSc, University of Victoria, British Columbia, 1965. Appointments: Career Officer, Royal Canadian Navy, 1954-70; House Designer and Builder, 1972-81. Publications: Troika, 1979; A Woman Called Scylla, 1981; An American Spy Story, 1984; The Action of the Tiger, 1984; On the Endangered List, 1985; The Ring Master, 1987; The Voice of the Crane, 1989; Arcadia West: The Novel, 1994. Memberships: Crime Writers of Canada; Writers' Guild of America; Writers' Union of Canada. Address: c/o Henry Morrison, Henry Morrison Inc, Box 235, Bedford Hills, NY 10507, USA.

GURRA Oltion. See: **GRILLO Odhise.**

GUSTAFSSON Lars, b. 17 May 1936, Västeras, Sweden. Writer; Poet; Dramatist; Professor. Education: Magdalene College, Oxford, 1957; Licentiate, Philosophy, 1960, DPhil, 1978, University of Uppsala. Appointments: Associate Editor, 1960-65, Editor-in-Chief, 1965-72, Bonniers Litterära Magasin; Deutscher Akademischer Austauschdienst Fellow, Berlin, 1972-73; Research Fellow, Bielefeld Institute of Advanced Studies, Germany, 1981-82; Adjunct Professor of German Studies, 1982-, Jamail Distinguished Professor, 1998-, University of Austin at Texas; Aby Warburg Foundation Professor, Warburg Stiftung, Hamburg, 1997. Publications: Over 50 works, including fiction, non-fiction, poetry, and drama, 1957-99. Contributions to: Various publications. Honours: Swedish Novel Prize, 1979; Prix International Charles Veillon des Essais, 1983; Officier de l'Ordre des Arts et des Lettres, France, 1986; Heinrich Steffens Prize, Germany, 1986; Kommendör des Bundesverdienstzeichens, Germany, 1988; Bellman Prize, Royal Swedish Academy, 1990; Poetry Prize, Swedish Broadcasting Corp, 1993; Guggenheim Fellowship, 1994; Pilot Prize, Sweden, 1996. Memberships: Akademie der Künste, Berlin; Akademie der Wissenschaften und der Literatur, Mainz; Royal Swedish Academy of Engineering; Author's Guild of America; International Parliament of Writers; PEN International, Sweden; Swedish Writer's Union. Address: 2312 Tower Drive, Austin, TX 78703, USA.

GUT-RUSSENBERGER Margrit, (Greta Rosenberg, Gret Stamm), b. 29 Apr 1938, CH, Switzerland. Secondary Teacher; Writer. m. Robert Gut, 5 Aug 1966, 3 sons, 3 daughters. Education: Secondary Teacher, University of Zürich, Switzerland. Publications: Jakob, 1976; Ich Glaube, 1978; Ein Wort für CHB, 1993; Bilder, (in German and English), 1996. Memberships: Innerschweizer Schriftstellerverein; Schweizerischer Schriftstellerverband. Address: Mattweid 12, 6204 Sempach, Switzerland.

GUTERSON David, b. 4 May 1956, Seattle, Washington, USA. Writer. m. Robin Ann Radwick, 1979, 3 sons, 1 daughter. Education: BA, 1978, MA, 1982, University of Washington. Appointment: High School Teacher of English, Bainbridge Island, Washington, 1984-94. Publications: The Country Ahead of Us, The Country Behind, 1989; Family Matters: Why Home Schooling Makes Sense, 1992; Snow Falling on Cedars, 1994. Honour: PEN/Faulkner Award for Fiction, 1995. Address: c/o Georges Borchardt Inc, 136 East 57th Street, New York, NY 10022, USA.

GUTHRIE Alan. See: **TUBB E(dwin) C(harles).**

GUTIERREZ José Ismael, b. 7 Aug 1964, Tenerife, Canary Islands, Spain. Teacher of Spanish Language and Literature; Writer. Education: Doctor, Hispanic Philology, 1996. Publication: Manuel Gutierrez Nájesa y sus cuentos. Contributions to: Articles about Spanish-American literature in several professional journals. Memberships: Instituto Literario y Cultural Hispánico; Instituto Internacional de Literatura Iberoamericana. Address: Calle Los Bajos, No 36, 38380 La Victoria, Tenerife, Canary Islands, Spain.

GUTTERIDGE Don(ald George), b. 30 Sept 1937, Sarnia, Ontario, Canada. Poet: Author; Professor of English Methods Emeritus. m. Anne Barnett, 30 June 1961, 1 son, 1 daughter. Education: Chatham College Institute, Ontario, 1956; BA, Honours, University of Western Ontario, London, 1960. Appointments: Assistant Professor, 1968-75, Associate Professor, 1975-77, Professor of English Methods, 1977-93, Professor Emeritus, 1993-, University of Western Ontario. Publications: Poetry: Riel: A Poem for Voices, 1968: The Village Within, 1970; Death at Quebec and Other Poems, 1972; Saying Grace: An Elegy, 1972; Coppermine: The Quest for North, 1973; Borderlands, 1975; Tecumseh, 1976; A True History of Lambton County, 1977; God's Geography, 1982; The Exiled Heart: Selected Narratives, 1986; Love in the Wintertime, 1982; Flute Music in the Cello's Belly, 1997. Fiction: Bus-Ride, 1974; All in Good Time, 1980; St Vitus Dance, 1986; Shaman's Ground, 1988; How the World Began, 1991; Summer's Idyll, 1993; Winter's Descent, 1996. Honours: President's Medal, University of Western Ontario, 1971; Canada Council Travel Grant, 1973. Address: 114 Victoria Street, London, Ontario N6A 2B5, Canada.

GUTTMANN Allen, b. 13 Oct 1932, Chicago, Illinois, USA. Professor of English and American Studies; Writer. m. (1) Martha Britt Ellis, 1955, div 1972, 1 son, 1 daughter, (2) Doris Bargen, 1974. Education: BA, University of Florida, 1953; MA, Columbia University, 1956; PhD, University of Minnesota, 1961. Appointments: Instructor, 1959-62, Assistant Professor, 1962-66, Associate Professor, 1966-71, Professor of English and American Studies, 1971-, Amherst College. Publications: The Wound in the Heart: America and the Spanish Civil War 1962; The Removal of the Cherokee Nation (editor with Louis Filler), 1962; American Neutrality and the Spanish Civil War (editor) 1963; Communism, the Constitution, and the Courts (editor with Benjamin Ziegler), 1964; The Conservative Tradition in America, 1967; Jewish Writer in America: Assimilation and the Crisis of Identity, 1971; Korea: Cold War and Limited War (editor), 1972; From Ritual to Record: The Nature of Modern Sport, 1978; The Games Must Go On: Avery Brundage and the Olympic Movement, 1984; Sports Spectators, 1986; A Whole New Ball Game, 1988; Women's Sports, 1991; The Olympics: A History of the Modern Games, 1992; Games and Empires, 1994; The Erotic in Sports, 1996. Honours: Carnegie Fellowship; Guggenheim Fellowship. Memberships: American Studies Association; British Association for Sport History; International Committee for Sport Sociology; North American Association for Sport Sociology. Address: c/o Department of English, Amherst College, Amherst, MA 01002, USA.

GUY Rosa (Cuthbert), b. 9 Jan 1928, Trinidad, West Indies. Writer. Appointment: Writer-in-Residence, Michigan Technical University. Publications: The Friends, 1973; Edith Jackson, 1978; Ruby, 1976; Edith Jackson, 1978; The Disappearance, 1979; A Measure of Time, 1983; New Guys Around the Block, 1983; Pee Wee and Big Dog, 1984; I Heard a Bird Sing, 1986; Music of Summer, 1992; My Love My Love, 1996; The Sun, The Sea, a Touch of the Wind (novel). Play: Once on This Island (adaptation of My Love My Love), 1990. Contributions to: New York Times Sunday Magazine; Red Book; Cosmopolitan. Honours: The Other Award, England; Best of the Best, New York Times. Memberships: Harlem Writers Guild, president; PEN. Literary Agent: Ellen Levine Literary Agency. Address: 20 West 72nd Street, New York, NY 10023, USA.

GWYN Richard, b. 22 July 1956, Pontypool, Wales. Poet; Lecturer. m. Rosemary Pallot, 2 June 1992, 2 daughters. Education: London School of Economics, 1975-77; MA, 1991, PhD, 1997, Cardiff University. Appointments: Lecturer in Communication Studies, University of Glamorgan, 1992-93; Tutor in Language and Communication, 1993-96, Researcher, Lecturer in Health Communication, 1996-, Cardiff University. Publications: Defying Gravity (poems), 1992; One Night in Icarus Street (poems), 1995; Stone Dog, Flower Red, (poems), 1995; Tales From Christo's Taverna (poems), 1999. Contributions to: Poetry Wales; Prose Poem, USA; Totem; Yellow Crane. Membership: Welsh Union of Writers. Address: c/o School of English, Communication and Philosophy, Cardiff University, Wales.

GYARFAS Endre, b. 6 May 1936, Szeged, Hungary. Poet; Novelist; Playwright. m. Edit Kincses, 7 Dec 1963, 1 son. Education: Hungarian and English Literature, Elte University, Budapest, 1961. Publications: Partkozelben (poems), 1964; Pazarlo Skotok (travel book), 1970; Apaczai (novel), 1978; Varazslasok (poems), 1984; Hosszu Utnak Pora (novel), 1988; Zsuzsanna Kertje (novel), 1989; Zoldag-Parittya (poems), 1990; Cowboyok, Aranyasok, Csavargok, (Folk Poetry of North America), 1992; Szölöhegyi varazslat, 1995. Honours: Gold Medal for Children's Literature, 1976; Fulbright Grant, 1988. Memberships: PEN Club of Hungary; Union of Hungarian Writers. Address: I Attila ut 133, Budapest 1012, Hungary.

GYLLENSTEN Lars Johan Wictor, b. 12 Nov 1921, Stockholm, Sweden. Former Professor of Histology; Author. Education: MD. Publications: Barnabok, 1952; Senilia, 1956; Sokratod, 1960; Desparados (short stories), 1962; Juvenilia, 1965; Palatset i parken, 1970; Ur min offentliga sektor (essays), 1971; Grottan i oknen, 1973; I skuggan av Don Juan, 1975; Baklangesminnen, 1978; Skuggans aterkomst, 1985; Sju vise mastare om kanlek (short stories), 1986; Just sa elle kahske det (short stories), 1989; Det himmelska gästabudet, 1991; Anteckningar fån en vindskupa, 1993. Memberships: Royal Swedish Academy of Sciences; Royal Swedish Academy of Letters, History and Antiquities. Address: Karlavagen 121, 115 26 Stockholm, Sweden.

GYORE Balazs, b. 8 May 1951, Hungary. Writer. m. Adrienn Scheer, 25 Sept 1980, 1 daughter. Education: Eotvos Lorand University, Budapest, 1971-76. Publications: The Hand of Humble Abbot Paphnutius (poems), 1982; I Can Safely Sleep on the 91 Bus (novel), 1989; One Has to Search For His Own Death (short novels), 1993; To Call Somebody is Illusion (short stories), 1994; If He Doesn't Live, Please Burn It Without Reading, 1996; It Is In Reality Too, (novel), 1997; Crises (short novels), 1998. Contributions to: Ujhold; Liget; Elet es Irodalom. Honours: Greve - award, 1996; Füst Milan - award, 1997. Memberships: Association of Hungarian Writers; Hungarian PEN Club. Address: Bartok B 52, 1111 Budapest, Hungary.

H

HAAKANA Anna-Liisa, b. 30 Jan 1937, Rovaniemi, Finland. Author. m. Veikko Olavi Haakana, 24 Feb 1963, 1 son, 1 daughter. Education: Literature studies, University of Tampere. Publications: 7 books for youth, 1978-86; 4 novels, 1 collection of short stories, 1989-97. Honours: National Award for Literature, 1981; Anni Swan Medal, 1982; H C Andersen's Certificate of Honour, 1982; Church's Award for Literature, 1982; Arvid Lydecken Award, 1984. Memberships: Association of Finnish Writers for Children and Youth; Finnish Society of Authors. Address: 99600 Sodankylä, Savikankaantie 11, Finland.

HAAVIKKO Paavo (Juhani), b. 25 Jan 1931, Helsinki, Finland. Poet; Dramatist; Writer. Education: University of Helsinki, 1951. Publications: Poetry: Several volumes, including: Poems 1949-74, 1975; Bridges: Selected Poems, 1984; Winter Poems, 1990; Poems, Poems, 1992. Other: Various plays for the stage, radio, and television; Several short stories. Honour: Knight 1st Class, White Rose of Finland, 1978. Address: c/o Arthouse Publishing Group, Bulevardi 19C, 00120 Helsinki, Finland.

HABERMAS Jürgen, b. 18 June 1929, Düsseldorf, Germany. Professor of Philosophy Emeritus; Writer. m. Ute Wesselhoeft, 1955, 1 son, 2 daughters. Education: PhD, University of Bonn, 1954; Habilitation, University of Marburg, 1961. Appointments: Assistant, Institute of Social Research, Frankfurt am Main, 1956-59; Associate Professor, University of Heidelberg, 1961-64; Professor of Philosophy and Sociology, 1964-71, Professor of Philosophy, 1983-94, Professor Emeritus, 1994-, University of Frankfurt am Main; Director, Max Planck Institute, Frankfurt am Main, 1971-81; Member, Max Planck Institute of Psychological Research, Munich, 1983-. Publications: Das Absolute und die Geschichte: Von der Zwiespältigkeit in Schellings Denken, 1954; Student und Politik: Eine soziologische Untersuchung zum politischen Bewusstsein Frankfurter Studenten (with Ludwig von Friedeburg, Christoph Oehler, and Friedrich Weltz), 1961; Strukturwandel der Offentlichkeit: Untersuchungen zu einer Katergorie der bürgerlichen Gesellschaft, 1962, new edition, 1990; Theorie und Praxis: Sozialphilosophische Studien, 1963; Technik und Wissenschaft als Ideologie, 1968; Erkenntnis und Interesse, 1968; Protestbewegung und Hochschulreform, 1969; Zur Logik der Sozialwissenschaften, 1970; Philosophisch-politische Profile, 1971; Theorie der Gesellschaft oder Sozialtechnologie (with Niklas Luhmann), 1971; Legitimationsprobleme im Spätkapitalismus, 1973; Zur Rekonstruktion des Historischen Materialismus, 1976; Politik, Kunst, Religion, 1978; Kleine Politische Schriften I-IV, 1981; Theorie des kommunikativen Handelns, 1981; Moralbewusstsein und kommunikatives Handeln, 1983; Vorstudien und Ergänzungen zur Theorie des kommunikativen Handelns, 1984; Der Philosophische Diskurs der Moderne, 1985; Die Neue Unübersichtlichkeit, 1985; Eine Art Schadensabwicklung, 1987; Nachmetaphysisches Denken, 1988; Die nachholende Revolution, 1990; Texte und Kontexte, 1991; Erläuterungen zur Diskursethik, 1991; Faktizität und Geltung, 1992; Vergangenheit als Zukunft, 1993; Die Normalität einer Berliner Republik, 1995; Die Einbeziehung des Anderen, 1996; Vom sinnlichen Eindruck zum symbolischen Ausdruck, 1997; Die postnationale Konstellation, 1998. Contributions to: Scholarly journals. Honours: Hegel Prize, Stuttgart, 1973; Sigmund Freud Prize, 1976; Theodor W Adorno Prize, 1980; Geschwister Scholl Prize, 1985; Leuschner Medal, 1985; Sonning Prize, 1987; Various honorary doctorates from German and foreign universities. Memberships: Academia Europaea, London; American Academy of Arts and Sciences; British Academy of Science; Deutsche Akademie für Sprache und Dichtung e. v. Darmstadt. Address: Ringstrasse 8b, D-82319 Starnberg, Germany.

HABGOOD John Stapylton, Baron of Habgood Calverton, b. 23 June 1927. Retired Archbishop of York;

Author. m. Rosalie Mary Ann Boston, 7 June 1961, 2 sons, 2 daughters. Education: BA, 1948, MA, 1951, PhD, 1952, King's College, Cambridge; Cuddesdon College, Oxford. Appointments: Demonstrator in Pharmacology, Cambridge, 1950-53; Fellow, King's College, Cambridge, 1952-55; Curate, St Mary Abbots, Kensington, 1954-56; Vice Principal, Westcott House, Cambridge, 1956-62; Rector, St John's Church, Jedburgh, 1962-67; Principal, Queen's College, Birmingham, 1967-73; Bishop of Durham, 1973-83; Archbishop of York, 1983-95; Pro Chancellor, University of York, 1985-90; Hulsean Preacher, University of Cambridge, 1987-88. Publications: Religion and Science, 1964; A Working Faith: Essays and Addresses on Science, Medicine and Ethics, 1980; Church and Nation in a Secular Age, 1983; Confessions of a Conservative Liberal, 1988; Making Sense, 1993; Faith and Uncertainty, 1997; Being a Person: Where Faith and Science Meet, 1998. Honours: Honorary DD, Universities of Durham, 1975, Cambridge, 1984, Aberdeen, 1988, Huron, 1990, Hull, 1991, Oxford, 1996, Manchester, 1996, York, 1996; Privy Counsellor, 1983; Honorary Fellow, King's College, Cambridge, 1986; Life Peer, 1995. Address: 18 The Mount, Malton, North Yorkshire YO17 7ND, England.

HACKER Marilyn, b. 27 Nov 1942, New York, New York, USA. Poet; Writer; Critic; Editor; Teacher. 1 daughter. Education: BA, Romance Languages, New York University, 1964. Appointments: Editor, Quark: A Quarterly of Speculative Fiction, 1969-71, The Kenyon Review, 1990-94; Jenny McKean Moore Chair in Writing, George Washington University, 1976-77; Member, Editorial Collective, 1977-80, Editor-in-Chief, 1979, The Little Magazine; Teacher, School of General Studies, Columbia University, 1979-81; Visiting Artist, Fine Arts Work Center, Provincetown, Massachusetts, 1981; Visiting Professor, University of Idaho, 1982; Editor-in-Chief, Thirteenth Moon: A Feminist Literary Magazine, 1982-86; Writer-in-Residence, State University of New York at Albany, 1988, Columbia University, 1988; George Elliston Poet-in-Residence, University of Cincinnati, 1988; Distinguished Writer-in-Residence, American University, Washington, DC, 1989; Visiting Professor of Creative Writing, State University of New York at Binghamton, 1990, University of Utah, 1995, Barnard College, 1995, Princeton University, 1997; Fannie Hurst Poet-in-Residence, Brandeis University, 1996. Publications: Presentation Piece, 1974; Separations, 1976; Taking Notice, 1980; Assumptions, 1985; Love, Death and the Changing of the Seasons, 1986; The Hang-Glider's Daughter: New and Selected Poems, 1990; Going Back to the River, 1990; Selected Poems: 1965-1990, 1994; Winter Numbers, 1994; Edge (translator of poems by Claire Malroux), 1996. Contributions to: Numerous anthologies and other publications. Honours: National Endowment for the Arts Grants, 1973-74, 1985-86, 1995; National Book Award in Poetry, 1975; Guggenheim Fellowship, 1980-81; Ingram Merrill Foundation Grant, 1984-85; Robert F Winner Awards, 1987, 1989, John Masefield Memorial Award, 1994, Poetry Society of America; Lambda Literary Awards, 1991, 1995; Lenore Marshall Award, Academy of American Poets, 1995; Poets' Prize, 1995. Address: 230 West 105th Street, New York, NY 10025, USA.

HACKER Peter Michael Stephan, b. 15 July 1939, London, England. Academic. m. Sylvia Dolores Imhoff, 31 Aug 1963, 2 sons, 1 daughter. Education: BA, Queens College, Oxford, 1960-63; DPhil, St Antony's College, Oxford, 1963-65. Appointments: Balliol College, Oxford, 1965-66; St John's College, Oxford, 1966-. Publications: Insight and Illusion, 1972, revised edtion, 1986; Wittgenstein: Understanding and Meaning (co-author with G P Baker), 1980; Frege: Logical Excavations (co-author with G P Baker), 1984; Language, Sense and Nonsense (co-author with G P Barker), 1984; Specticism, Rules and Language, 1984; Wittgenstein: Rules Grammar and Necessity (co-author with G P Baker), 1985; Appearance and Reality, 1987; The Renaissance of Gravure: The Art of S W Hayter, 1988; Wittgenstein: Meaning and Mind, 1990; Gravure and Grace: The Engravings of Roger Vieillard, 1993; Wittgenstein: Mind and Will, 1996; Wittgenstein's Place in Twentieth Century Analytic

Philosophy, 1996; Wittgenstein on Human Nature, 1997. Address: St John's College, Oxford OX1 3JP, England.

HACKETT General Sir John Winthrop, b. 5 Nov 1910, Perth, Australia. Soldier; Academic; Author. m. Margaret Frena, 21 Mar 1942, 1 daughter, dec, 2 adopted stepdaughters. Education: MA, BLitt, New College, Oxford, 1929-33. Appointments: Regular Army, Commissioned 8th King's Royal Hussars, 1931; Service before, during, and after World War II, wounded, 1941, 1942; Commandant, Royal Military College of Science, 1958-61; Deputy Chief, Imperial General Staff, 1963-64, and Ministry of Defence, 1964-66; Commander-in-Chief, British Army of the Rhine, and Commander, Northern Army Group in NATO, 1966-68; Principal, 1968-75, Visiting Professor in Classics, 1977-, King's College, London. Publications: I Was a Stranger, 1977; The Third World War (co-author), 1978; The Untold Story (co-author), 1982; The Profession of Arms, 1983; Warfare in the Ancient World (editor), 1989. Contributions to: Books and periodicals. Honours: Member of the Order of the British Empire, 1938; Commander of the Order of the British Empire, 1953; Knighted, 1962; Honorary Liveryman, Worshipful Company of Dyers, 1975; Freeman of the City of London, 1976; Honorary doctorates. Memberships: English Association, president, 1973; Royal Society of Literature, fellow; UK Classical Association, president, 1971. Address: Coberley Mill, Cheltenham, Glos GL53 9NH, England.

HADAS Rachel, b. 8 Nov 1948, New York, New York, USA. Professor of English; Poet; Writer. m. (1) Stavros Kondilis, 7 Nov 1970, div 1978, (2) George Edwards, 22 July 1978, 1 son. Education: BA, Classics, Radcliffe College, 1969; MA, Poetry, Johns Hopkins University, 1977; PhD, Comparative Literature, Princeton University, 1982. Appointments: Assistant Professor, 1982-87, Associate Professor, 1987-92, Professor of English, 1992-, Rutgers University; Adjunct Professor, Columbia University, 1992-93; Visiting Professor, Princeton University, 1995, 1996. Publications: Starting From Troy, 1975; Slow Transparency, 1983; A Son from Sleep, 1987; Pass It On, 1989; Living in Time, 1990; Unending Dialogue, 1991; Mirrors of Astonishment, 1992; Other Worlds Than This, 1994; The Empty Bed, 1995; The Double Legacy, 1995; Halfway Down the Hall (New and Selected Poems), 1998. Contributions to: Periodicals. Honours: Ingram Merrill Foundation Fellowship, 1976-77; Guggenheim Fellowship, 1988-89; American Academy and Institute of Arts and Letters Award, 1990. Memberships: American Academy of Arts and Sciences, fellow; Modern Greek Studies Association; Modern Language Association; PEN; Poetry Society of America. Address: 838 West End Avenue, No 3A, New York, NY 10025, USA.

HAGELIN Aiban, b. 24 Dec 1934, Atacama, Chile. Physician; Philosopher of Science. m. Nora Stigol, 10 June 1965, 1 son, 1 daughter. Education: MD, University of Buenos Aires, 1961. Publications: Infantile Psichosis, 1980; Narcissism, 1985; Autism, 1995. Contributions to: Professional journals. Address: Ayacucho 2030 70, 1112 Buenos Aires, Argentina.

HAGERTY William John Gell, b. 23 Apr 1939, Ilford, Essex, England. Writer; Broadcaster; Editor. m. (1) 1 son, 1 daughter, (2) Elizabeth Vercoe, 8 Sept 1991, 1 son. Appointments: Assistant Editor, Daily Mirror; Associate Editor, Today; Editor, Sunday Today; Deputy Editor, Sunday Mirror; Deputy Editor, Daily Mirror; Editor, The People, 1991-92; Theatre and Film Critic, Today; Theatre Critic, News of the World, 1996-. Publication: Flash Bang Wallop! Literary Agent: Abner Styne. Address: Bull Cottage, 10/11 Strand-On-the-Green, Chiswick, London W4 3PQ, England.

HAGGER Nicholas Osborne, b. 22 May 1939, London, England. British Poet; Verse Dramatist; Short Story Writer; Lecturer; Author; Man of Letters; Philosopher; Cultural Historian. m. Madeline Ann Johnson, 22 Feb 1974, 2 sons, 1 daughter. Education: MA English Literature, Worcester College, Oxford, 1958-61. Appointments: Lecturer in English, University of

Baghdad, 1961-62; Professor of English Literature, Tokyo University of Education and Keio University, Tokyo, 1963-67; Lecturer in English, University of Libya, Tripoli, 1968-70; Freelance Features for Times, 1970-72. Publications: The Fire and the Stones: A Grand Unified Theory of World History and Religion, 1991; Selected Poems: A Metaphysical's Way of Fire, 1991; The Universe and the Light: A New View of the Universe and Reality, 1993; A White Radiance: The Collected Poems 1958-93, 1994; A Mystic Way: A Spiritual Autobiography, 1994; Awakening to the Light: Diaries, Vol 1, 1958-67, 1994; A Spade Fresh with Mud: Collected Stories, Vol 1, 1995; The Warlords: From D-Day to Berlin, A Verse Drama, 1995; A Smell of Leaves and Summer: Collected Stories, Vol 2, 1995; Overlord, The Triumph of Light 1944-1945: An Epic Poem, Books 1 & 2, 1995, Books 3-6, 1996, Books 7-9, 10-12, 1997; The One and the Many, 1999; Wheeling Bats and a Harvest Moon: Collected Stories, Vol 3, 1999; Prince Tudor, A Verse Drama, 1999; The Warm Glow of the Monastery Courtyard: Collected Stories, Vol 4, 1999. Address: Otley Hall, Otley, Nr Ipswich, IP6 9PA, England.

HAGON Priscilla. See: **ALLAN Mabel Esther.**

HAIBLUM Isidore, b. 23 May 1935, New York, New York, USA. Writer. Education: BA, City College, New York City, 1958. Publications: The Tsaddik of the Seven Wonders, 1971; The Return, 1973; Transfer to Yesterday, 1973, revised edition, 1981; The Wilk Are Among Us, 1975, revised edition, 1979; Interworld, 1977; Outerworld, 1979; Nightmare Express, 1979; Faster Than a Speeding Bullet: An Informal History of Radio's Golden Age (with Stuart Silver), 1980; The Mutants Are Coming, 1984; The Identity Plunderers, 1984; The Hand of Gantz, 1985; Murder in Yiddish, 1988; Bad Neighbors, 1990; Out of Sync, 1990; Specterworld, 1991; Crystalword, 1992. Contributions to: Periodicals. Address: 160 West 77th Street, New York, NY 10024, USA.

HAIDA. See: **NAGARAJA RAO C K.**

HAIGH Christopher, b. 28 Aug 1944, Birkenhead, England. Lecturer in Modern History; Writer. 2 daughters. Education: BA, Cambridge University, 1966; PhD, Victoria University of Manchester, 1969. Appointments: Lecturer in History, Victoria University of Manchester, 1969-79; Lecturer in Modern History, Christ Church, Oxford, 1979-. Publications: The Last Days of the Lancashire Monasteries, 1969; Reformation and Resistance in Tudor Lancashire, 1975; The Cambridge Historical Encyclopaedia of Great Britain and Ireland, 1984; The Reign of Elizabeth I, 1985; The English Reformation Revised, 1987; Elizabeth I: A Profile in Power, 1988; English Reformations: Religion, Politics and Society Under the Tudors, 1993; The Church of England and Its People, 1559-1642, forthcoming. Membership: Royal Historical Society, fellow. Address: c/o Christ Church, Oxford, OX1 1DP, England.

HAIGH Jack, b. 21 Feb 1910, West Hartlepool, England. Journalist. m. Josephine Agnes Mary McLoughlin, 7 July 1949. Appointments: Editor, Jerusalem Services Magazine, 1941-42; Staff, The Racing Calendar, 1956-68; Sport Sub Editor, Daily Mail, 1972-84; Proprietor, Greenfriar Press. Publications: Theory of Genius, 1972; Constellation of Genius, 1982; Phillimore: The Postcard Art of R P Phillimore, 1985; Psychology of Genius, 1991. Membership: Institute of Journalists. Address: 28 Manville Road, London SW17 8JN, England.

HAILEY Arthur, b. 5 Apr 1920, Luton, England (British and Canadian citizen). Author; Screenwriter. m. (1) Joan Fishwick, 1944, div 1950, 3 sons, (2) Sheila Dunlop, 1951, 1 son, 2 daughters. Education: British elementary schools. Appointments: Pilot, Flight Lieutenant, Royal Air Force, 1939-47; Flight Lieutenant, Royal Canadian Air Force Reserve, 1951; Industry and sales positions; Writer, 1956-. Publications: Runway-Zero Eight (with John Castle), 1958; The Final Diagnosis, 1959; Close-up (collected plays), 1960; In High Places, 1962; Hotel, 1965; Airport, 1968; Wheels, 1971; The Moneychangers, 1975; Overload, 1979; Strong Medicine, 1984; The Evening News, 1990; Detective, 1997. Films: Zero Hour, 1956; Time Lock, 1957; The Young Doctors, 1961; Hotel, 1966; Airport, 1970; The Moneychangers, 1976; Wheels, 1978; Strong Medicine, 1986. Honours: Royal Air Force Air Efficiency Award; Canadian Council of Artists and Authors Award, 1956; Best Canadian TV Playwright Awards, 1957, 1959; Doubleday Prize Novel Award, 1962. Memberships: Alliance of Canadian Cinema, Television and Radio Artists, honorary life member; Authors League of America; Writers Guild of America, life member. Address: Lyford Cay, PO Box N7776, Nassau, Bahamas.

HAILEY Elizabeth Forsythe, b. 31 Aug 1938, Dallas, Texas, USA. Writer; Dramatist. m. Oliver Daffan Hailey, 25 June 1960, dec 1993, 2 daughters. Education: Diploma, Sorbonne, University of Paris, 1959; BA, Hollins College, Virginia, 1960. Publications: Fiction: A Woman of Independent Means, 1978; Life Sentences, 1982; Joanna's Husband and David's Wife, 1986; Home Free, 1991. Plays: A Woman of Independent Means, 1984; Joanna's Husband and David's Wife, 1989. Contributions to: Books and periodicals. Honours: Siver Medal for Best First Novel, Commonwealth Club of California, 1978; Los Angeles Drama Critics Award, 1983. Memberships: Authors League of America; PEN; Writers Guild of America West. Address: 11747 Canton Place, Studio City, CA 91604, USA.

HAILSHAM OF SAINT MARYLEBONE, Baron of Herstmonceux, Quintin McGarel Hogg, b. 9 Oct 1907, London, England. Lawyer; Politician. m. (1) Mary Evelyn Martin, 18 Apr 1944, dec 1978, 2 sons, 3 daughters, (2) Deirdre Shannon, 1986. Education: 1st Class Honour Moderatous, 1928, 1st Class Literae Humanicores, 1930, Christ Church, Oxford. Appointments: Fellow, All Souls College, Oxford, 1931-38, 1961-; Barrister, 1932, Bencher, 1956, Treasurer, 1975, Lincoln's Inn; Member of Parliament, Conservative Party, Oxford City, 1938-50, Saint Marylebone, 1963-70; Military service, World War II, 1939-45, wounded, 1941; First Lord of the Admiralty, 1956-57; Minister of Education, 1957; Lord President of the Council, 1957-59, 1960-64; Deputy Leader, 1957-60, Leader, 1960-63, House of Lords; Lord Privy Seal, 1959-60; Rector, Glasgow University, 1959-62; Minister for Science and Technology, 1959-64; Lord High Chancellor of Great Britain, 1970-74, 1979-87; Chancellor, University of Buckingham, 1983-92. Publications: The Law of Arbitration, 1935; One Year's Work, 1944; The Law and Employers' Liabilty, 1944; The Times We Live In, 1944; Making Peace, 1945; The Left Was Never Right, 1945; The Purpose of Parliament, 1946; The Case for Conservatism, 1947; The Law of Monopolies, Restrictive Practices and Resale Price Maintenance, 1956; The Conservative Case, 1959; Interdependence, 1961; Science and Politics, 1963; The Devil's Own Song, 1968; Halsbury's Laws of England (editor), 4th edition, 1972; The Door Wherein I Went, 1975; Elective Dictatorship, 1976; The Dilemma of Democracy, 1978; Hamlyn Revisited: The British Legal System, 1983; A Sparrow's Flight (autobiography), 1990; On the Constitution, 1992; Values: Collapse and Cure, 1994. Honours: Companion of Honour, 1974; Knight of the Garter, 1988; Honorary doctorates. Memberships: Classical Association, president, 1960-61; Royal Society, fellow. Address: House of Lords, London SW1A OPW, England.

HAINES John (Meade), b. 29 June 1924, Norfolk, Virginia, USA. Poet; Writer; Teacher. m. (1) Jo Ella Hussey, 10 Oct 1960, (2) Jane McWhorter, 23 Nov 1970, div 1974, (3) Leslie Sennett, Oct 1978, div, 4 children. Education: National Art School, Washington, DC, 1946-47; American University, 1948-49; Hans Hoffman School of Fine Art, New York City, 1950-52; University of Washington, 1974. Appointments: Poet-in-Residence, University of Alaska, 1972-73; Visiting Professor in English, University of Washington, 1974; Visting Lecturer in English, University of Montana, 1974; Writer-in-Residence, Sheldon Jackson College, 1982-83, Ucross Foundation, 1987, Montalvo Center for the Arts, 1988, Djerassi Foundation, 1988; Visiting Lecturer, University of California at Santa Cruz, 1986; Wordsworth Conference, Grasmere, England, 1996; Visting Writer, The Loft Mentor Series, 1987, George Washington University, 1991-92; Visiting Professor, Ohio University, 1989-90; Elliston Fellow in Poetry, University of Cincinnati, 1992; Chair in Creative Arts, Austin Peay State University, Clarksville, Tennessee, 1993. Publications: Poetry: Winter News, 1966, revised edition, 1983; Suite for the Pied Piper, 1968; The Legend of Paper Plates, 1970; The Mirror, 1970; The Stone Harp, 1971; Twenty Poems, 1971, 3rd edition, 1982; Leaves and Ashes, 1975; In Five Years, 1976; Cicada, 1977; In a Dusty Light, 1977; The Sun on Your Shoulder, 1977; News From the Glacier: Selected Poems, 1960-80, 1982; New Poems: 1980-1988, 1990; Rain Country, 1990; The Owl in the Mask of a Dreamer, 1993. Non-Fiction: Minus Thirty-One and the Wind Blowing: Nine Reflections About Living on the Land (with others), 1980; Living Off the Country: Essays on Poetry and Place, 1981; Other Days, 1982; Of Traps and Snares, 1982; Stories We Listened To, 1986; You and I and the World, 1988; The Stars, the Snow, the Fire, 1989; Fables and Distances: New and Selected Essays, 1996; A Guide to the Four-Chambered Heart, 1996. Contributions to: Gettysburg Review; Graywolf Annual; Harper's; Hudson Review; Michigan Quarterly Review; Nation; New Criterion; New England Review; Northwest Review; Ohio Review; TriQuarterly; Manoa. Honours: Guggenheim Fellowships, 1965-66, 1984-85; National Endowment for the Arts Grant, 1967-68; Amy Lowell Scholarship, 1976-77; Alaska State Council on the Arts Grant, 1979, and Fellowship, 1987; Governor's Award for lifetime contributions to the arts in Alaska, 1982; Honorary LD, University of Alaska, 1983; Ingram Merrill Foundation Grant, 1987; Western States Federation Award, 1990; Lenore Marshall Nation Award, 1991; Literary Award, American Academy of Arts and Letters, 1995. Memberships: Academy of American Poets; Alaska Conservation Society; Natural Resources Defense Council; PEN American Center; Poetry Society of America; Sierra Club; Wilderness Society. Address: PO Box 103431, Anchorage, AL 99510, USA.

HAINING Peter (Alexander), (Peter Alex, Jim Black, Richard De'ath, William Patrick, Richard Peters, Richard Peyton, Sean Richards), b. 2 Apr 1940, Enfield, Middlesex, England. Writer. Publications: The Ghost Ship, 1985; Tune in for Fear, 1985; Vampire, 1985; Stories of the Walking Dead, 1986; Supernatural Sleuths, 1986; Tales of Dungeons and Dragons, 1986; Poltergeist, 1987; Werewolf, 1987; Irish Tales of Terror, 1988; The Mummy, 1988; The Scarecrow: Fact and Fable, 1988; Bob Hope: Thanks for the Memory, 1989; The Day War Broke Out, 1989; Hook Line and Laughter, 1989; The Legend of Garbo, 1990; The Legend That is Buddy Holly, 1990; Spitfire Summer, 1990; The English Highwayman, 1991; Sinister Gambits, 1991; Great Irish Stories of the Supernatural, 1992; The Supernatural Coast, 1992; The Television Detectives Omnibus, 1992; The Armchair Detectives, 1993; Great Irish Detective Stories, 1993; The MG Log, 1993; Masters of the Macabre, 1993; Tombstone Humour, 1993; The Complete Maigret, 1994; London After Midnight, 1995; Murder at the Races, 1995; Agatha Christie's Poirot, 1996; Murder on the Railways, 1996; The Wizards of Odd, 1997; The Un-Dead: The Legend of Bram Stoker and Dracula, 1997; Great Irish Humorous Stories, 1998; Sweeney Todd: The Real Story of the Demon Barber of Fleet Street, 1998; Invasion: Earth, 1998. Membership: PEN International. Address: Peyton House, Boxford, Suffolk, England.

HAKE Theodore Lowell, b. 30 Aug 1943, York, Pennsylvania, USA. Owner, American Collectibles Auction House. m. Jonell A Robinson, 25 Aug 1973, 1 son. Education: BA, Political Science, University of Pittsburgh; MA, Communications, University of Pennsylvania. Publications: Hake's Price Guide to Character Toys; Hake's Price Guide to Cowboy Character Collectibles; Hake's Price Guide to Comic Character Collectibles; Hak's Price Guide to Presidential Campaign Items; Collectible Pin-Back Buttons 1896-1986; The Encyclopedia of Political Buttons, 3 volumes 1789-1976. Contributions to: Collectibles Flea Market Finds. Address: PO Box 1444, York, PA 17405-1444, USA.

HAKIM Seymour (Sy) b. 23 Jan 1933, New York, New York, USA. Poet; Writer; Artist; Educator. m. Odetta Roverso, 18 Aug 1970. Education: AB, Eastern New Mexico University, 1954; MA, New York University, 1960; Postgraduate work, various universities. Appointments: Consultant Editor, Poet Gallery Press, New York, 1970; Editor, Overseas Teacher, 1997. Publications: The Sacred Family, 1970; Manhattan Goodbye (poems), 1970; Under Moon, 1971; Museum of the Mind, 1971; Wine Theorem, 1972; Substituting Memories, 1976; Iris Elegy, 1979; Balancing Act, 1981; Birth of a Poet, 1985; Eleanor, Goodbye, 1988; Michaelangelo's Call, 1999. Contributions to: Overseas Educator; California State Poetry Quarterly; American Writing; Dan River Anthology; Its On My Wall; Older Eyes; Art Exhibition Reading, New York, 1999. Honours: Exhibits with accomanying writings: 1970, 1973, 1982-3, 1985; Poems and Prints, New York, 1995; Art works in public collections in various countries including prints in collections in Taiwan, Korea and Japan; Solo exhibition, New York, 1998-99. Memberships: Association of Poets and Writers; National Phot Instructors Association; Italo-Brittanica Association, 1972-80. Address: Via Chiesanuova No 1, 36023 Langare, VI 36023, Italy.

HAKIMZADEH. See: **ZAND Roxane.**

HALBERSTAM David, b. 10 Apr 1934, New York, New York, USA. Writer. m. 1) Elizabethj Tchizerska, 13 June 1965, div, 2) Jean Sanders, 29 June 1979, 1 daughter. Education: AB, Harvard University. Appointments: Staff, Daily Times Leader, West Point, Mississippi, 1955-56; Nashville Tennessean, 1956-60; Foreign Correspondent, New York Times, 1960-67; Contributing Editor, Harper's Magazine, 1967-71. Publications: The Noblest Roman, 1961; The Making of a Quagmire, 1965, 2nd edition as The Making of a Quagmire: America and Vietnam During the Kennedy Era, 1987; One Very Hot Day, 1968; The Unfinished Odyssey of Robert Kennedy, 1969; Ho, 1971; The Best and the Brightest, 1972; The Powers That Be, 1979; The Breaks of the Game, 1981; The Amateurs, 1985; The Reckoning, 1986; The Summer of '49, 1989; The Next Century, 1991; The Fifties, 1993; October 1964, 1994; The Children, 1998. Contributions to: Newspapers and magazines. Honours: Page One Award, Newspaper Guild of America, 1962; Co-Winner, Pulitzer Prize for International Reporting, 1964; George Polk Award, 1964; Louis M Lyons Award, 1964; Overseas Press Club Award, 1973. Address: c/o Random House, 201 East 50th Street, New York, NY 10022, USA.

HALDEMAN Joe William, b. 9 June 1943, Oklahoma City, Oklahoma, USA. Novelist. m. Mary Gay Potter, 21 Aug 1965. Education: BS, Physics and Astronomy, University of Maryland, 1967; MFA, English, University of Iowa, 1975. Appointment: Associate Professor, writing programme, Massachusetts Institute of Technology, 1983-. Publications: War Year, 1972; Cosmic Laughter (editor), 1974; The Forever Year, 1975; Mindbridge, 1976; Planet of Judgement, 1977; All My Sins Remembered, 1977; Study War No More (editor), 1977; Infinite Dreams, 1978; World Without End, 1979; Worlds, 1981; There is No Darkness (co-author), 1983; Worlds Apart, 1983; Nebula Awards 17, 1983; Dealing in Futures, 1985; Body Armour 2000, 1986; Tool of the Trade, 1987; Supertanks (co-editor), 1987; Starfighters (co-editor), 1988; The Long Habit of Living, 1989; The Hemingway Hoax, 1990; Worlds Enough and Time, 1992; 1968, 1995; None So Blind, 1996; Forever Peace, 1997; Saul's Death and Other Poems, 1997. Honours: Purple Heart, US Army, 1969; Nebula Awards, 1975, 1990, 1993; Hugo Awards, 1976, 1977, 1991, 1995, 1998; Rhysling Awards, 1984, 1990; World Fantasy Award, 1993. Memberships: Science Fiction and Fantasy Writers of America; Author's Guild; Poets and Writers National Space Institute; Writers Guild. Literary Agent: Ralph Vicinanza. Address: 5412 North West 14th Avenue, Gainesville, FL 32605, USA.

HALE Julian Anthony Stuart, (Anthony Stuart), b. 27 Nov 1940, Llandrindod Wells. Radio Producer. m. Helen Likierman, 18 Apr 1987, 1 son, 2 daughters. Education: Winchester College, 1954-59; Christ Church, Oxford, England, 1959-63. Appointments: G G Harrap, 1963-65; UN, Geneva, 1963-67; BBC World Service, 1968-73; BBC Network Radio, 1978-94. Publications: Ceauescu's Romania, 1971; Radio Power, 1975; Slack Summer, 1982; Anthony Stuart: Snap Judgement, 1977; Vicious Circles, 1978; Force Play, 1979; Midwinter Madness, 1979; The London Affair, 1981; Russian Leave, 1981. Contributions to: Telegraph Magazine. Literary Agent: Hilary Rubinstein. Address: 11 Alexander Street, London W2 5NT, England.

HALEY Kenneth Harold Dobson, b. 19 Apr 1920, Southport, England. Professor of Modern History Emeritus; Writer. m. Iris Houghton, 22 Mar 1948, 1 son, 2 daughters. Education: MA, 1940, BLitt, Balliol College, Oxford. Appointments: Professor of Modern History, 1962-82, Professor Emeritus, 1982-, Sheffield University. Publications: William of Orange and the English Opposition 1672-74, 1953; The First Early of Shaftesbury, 1968; The Dutch in the Seventeenth Century, 1972; Politics in the Reign of Charles II, 1985; An English Diplomat in the Low Countries: Sir William Temple and John de Witt, 1986; The British and the Dutch, 1988. Contributions to: Scholarly journals. Honour: Fellow, British Academy, 1987. Memberships: Historical Association, Honorary Vice President, 1994. Address: 15 Haugh Lane, Sheffield S11 9SA, England.

HALIM Huri. See: **OFFEN Yehuda.**

HALL Angus, b. 24 Mar 1932, Newcastle upon Tyne, England. Author; Editor. Appointments: Editor, IPC Publishers, London, 1971-, BPC Publishers, London, 1972-. Publications: London in Smoky Region, 1962, High-Bouncing Lover, 1966; Live Like a Hero, 1967; Comeuppance of Arthur Hearne, 1967; Qualtrough, 1968; Late Boy Wonder, 1969; Devilday, 1970; To Play the Devil, 1971; Scars of Dracula, 1971; Long Way to Fall, 1971; On the Run, 1974; Signs of Things to Come: A History of Divination, 1975; Monsters and Mythic Beasts, 1976; Strange Cults, 1977; The Rigoletto Murder, 1978; Self-Destruct, 1985. Address: 96 High Street, Old Town, Hastings, Sussex, England.

HALL Claudia. See: **FLOREN Lee.**

HALL Donald (Andrew Jr), b. 20 Sept 1928, New Haven, Connecticut, USA. Poet; Writer; Professor of English (retired). m. (1) Kirby Thompson, 1952, div 1969, 1 son, 1 daughter, (2) Jane Kenyon, 1972, dec 1995. Education: BA, Harvard University, 1951; BLitt, Oxford University, 1953; Stanford University, 1953-54. Appointments: Poetry Editor, Paris Review, 1953-62; Junior Fellow, Society of Fellows, Harvard University, 1954-57; Assistant Professor, 1957-61, Associate Professor, 1961-66, Professor of English, 1966-75, University of Michigan. Publications: Poetry: Poems, 1952; Exile, 1952; To the Loud Wind and Other Poems, 1955; Exiles and Marriages, 1955; The Dark Houses, 1958; A Roof of Tiger Lilies, 1964; The Alligator Bride: Poems New and Selected, 1969; The Yellow Room: Love Poems, 1971; A Blue Tit Tilts at the Edge of the Sea: Selected Poems 1964-1974, 1975; The Town of Hill, 1975; Kicking the Leaves, 1978; The Toy Bone, 1979; The Twelve Seasons, 1983; Brief Lives, 1983; Great Day at the Cows' House, 1984; The Happy Man, 1986; The One Day: A Poem in Three Parts, 1988; Old and New Poems, 1990; The One Day and Poems (1947-1990), 1991; The Museum of Clear Ideas, 1993; The Old Life, 1996. Short Stories: The Ideal Bakery, 1987. Other: String Too Short to Be Saved, 1961; Henry Moore: The Life and Work of a Great Sculptor, 1966; Marianne Moore: The Cage and the Animal, 1970; As the Eye Moves: A Sculpture by Henry Moore, 1970; The Gentleman's Alphabet Book, 1972; Writing Well, 1973, 7th edition, revised, 1991; Playing Around: The Million-Dollar Infield Goes to Florida (with others), 1974; Dock Ellis in the Country of Baseball (with Dock Ellis), 1976; Remembering Poets: Reminiscences and Opinions--Dylan Thomas, Robert Frost, T S Eliot, Ezra Pound, 1978; Goatfoot Milktongue Twinbird: Interviews, Essays and Notes on Poetry 1970-76, 1978; To Keep Moving, 1980; To Read Literature: Fiction, Poetry, Drama, 1981, 3rd edition, revised, 1987; The Weather for Poetry: Essays, Reviews and Notes on Poetry 1977-81, 1982; Fathers Playing Catch with Sons: Essays on Sports (Mostly Baseball), 1985; Winter, 1986; Seasons at Eagle Pond, 1987; Poetry and Ambition: Essays 1982-1988, 1988; Anecdotes of Modern Art (with Pat Corrigan Wykes), 1990; Here at Eagle Pond, 1990; Their Ancient Glittering Eyes, 1992; Life Work, 1993; Death to Death of Poetry, 1994; Principal Products of Portugal, 1995. Editor: The Harvard Advocate Anthology, 1950; New Poets of England and America (with Robert Pack and Louis Simpson), 1957; Whittier, 1961; Contemporary American Poetry, 1962, revised edition, 1971; A Poetry Sampler, 1962; The Concise Encyclopedia of English and American Poets and Poetry (with Stephen Spender), 1963, revised edition, 1970; Poetry in English (with Warren Taylor), 1963, revised edition, 1970; The Faber Book of Modern Verse, 1965; A Choice of Whitman's Verse, 1968; The Modern Stylists: Writers on the Art of Writing, 1968; Man and Boy: An Anthology, 1968; American Poetry: An Introductory Anthology, 1969; The Pleasures of Poetry, 1971; A Writer's Reader (with D L Emblem), 1976, 5th edition, revised, 1988; To Read Literature, 1980; To Read Poetry, 1981; The Oxford Book of American Literary Anecdotes, 1981; Claims for Poetry, 1982; The Contemporary Essay, 1984; The Oxford Book of Children's Verse in America, 1985; To Read Fiction, 1987; The Best American Poetry (with David Lehman), 1989; The Essential Andrew Marvell, 1991; The Essential E A Robinson, 1993. Honours: Edna St Vincent Millay Memorial Prize, 1956; Longview Foundation Award, 1960; Guggenheim Fellowships, 1963, 1972; Sarah Josepha Hale Award, 1983; Poet Laureate of New Hampshire, 1984-89; Lenore Marshall Award, 1987; National Book Critics Circle Award, 1989; Los Angeles Times Book Award, 1989; Robert Frost Silver Medal, Poetry Society of America, 1991; Lifetime Achievement Award, New Hampshire Writers and Publishers Project, 1992; New England Book Award for Non-Fiction, 1993; Ruth Lilly Prize for Poetry, 1994; Honorary doctorates. Address: Eagle Pond Farm, Danbury, NH 03230, USA.

HALL Hugh Gaston, b. 7 Nov 1931, Jackson, Mississippi, USA. Reader Emeritus; Writer. m. Gillian Gladys Lund, 16 July 1955, 1 son, 2 daughters. Education: BA, Millsaps College, 1952; Diplome pour l'Enseignement, University of Toulouse, 1953; MA, Oxon, 1959; PhD, Yale University, 1959. Appointments: Faculty, Yale University, 1958-60; Lecturer, University of Glasgow, 1960-64; Assistant Professor, University of California at Berkeley, 1963; Senior Lecturer, 1966-74, Reader, 1974-89, Reader Emeritus, 1989-, University of Warwick; Special Lecturer, Monash University, 1965, 1968; Professor of Romance Languages, City University of New York, 1970-72; Fellow, Humanities Research Centre, Canberra, 1984; Camargo Foundation, Cassis, 1987, 1990. Publications: Molière: Tartuffe, 1960; Quadruped Octaves, 1983; Comedy in Context, 1984; Alphabet Aviary, 1987; Richelieu's Desmarets and the Century of Louis XIV, 1990; Molière's Le Bourgeois Gentilhomme, 1990. Contributions to: Reference books and scholarly journals. Address: 18 Abbey End, Kenilworth, Warwickshire, England.

HALL James B(yron), b. 21 July 1918, Midland, Ohio, USA. Author; Poet; University Provost Emeritus. m. Elizabeth Cushman, 14 Feb 1946, 1 son, 4 daughters. Education: Miami University, Oxford, Ohio, 1938-39; University of Hawaii, 1938-40; BA, 1947, MA, 1948, PhD, 1953, University of Iowa; Postgraduate Studies, Kenyon College, 1949. Appointments: Writer-in-Residence, Miami University, Oxford, Ohio, 1948-49, University of North Carolina at Greensville, 1954, University of British Columbia, 1955, University of Colorado, 1963; Instructor, Cornell University, 1952-54; Assistant Professor, 1954-57, Associate Professor, 1958-60, Professor of English, 1960-65, University of Oregon; Professor of English and Director, Writing Center, University of California at Irvine, 1965-68; Provost, 1968-75, Provost Emeritus, 1983-88, University of California at Santa Cruz. Publications: Novels: Not by the Door, 1954; Racers to the Sun, 1960; Mayo Sergeant, 1968. Short Story

Collections: 15 x 3 (with Herbert Gold and R V Cassill), 1957; Us He Devours, 1964; The Short Hall, 1980; I Like It Better Now, 1992. Poetry: The Hunt Within, 1973; Bereavements (collected and selected poems), 1991. Non-Fiction: Perspectives on William Everson (co-editor), 1992; Art and Craft of the Short Story, 1995. Contributions to: Anthologies and other publications. Honours: Octave Thanet Prize, 1950; Rockefeller Foundation Grant, 1955; Oregon Poetry Prize, 1958; Emily Clark Balch Fiction Prize, 1967; Chapelbrook Award, 1967; James B Hall Gallery named in his honour, University of California Regents, 1985; James B Hall Traveling Fellowship founded in his honour, University of California at Santa Cruz, 1985. Memberships: Founder and Past President, American Associated Writing Program, 1965-66; American Assocation of University Professors; National Writers Union. Address: 1413 Oak Street, Lake Oswego, OR 97034, USA.

HALL Jane Anna, b. 4 Apr 1959, New London, CT, USA. Education: Professional model, Barbizon School, 1976; Diploma, Westbrook High School, 1977. Appointments: Model Barbizon Agency, 1977; Employed by Director of Career Planning, Wesleyan University, 1985-86; Freelance Poet/Writer, 1986-; Artist, 1989-. Publications: Poems published in: The Bell Bouy; Expressions I; Expressions II; The Pictoria Gazette; The Connecticut River Review; Connecticut Chapt Romance Writers of Am Newsletter; Chapbooks: Cedar and Lace, 1986; Satin and Pinstripe, 1987; Fireworks and Diamonds, 1988; Stars and Daffodils, 1989; Sunrises and Stone Walls, 1990; Mountains and Meadows, 1991; Moonlight and Water Lillies, 1992; Sunsets and Beaches, 1993; New and Selected Poems, 1986-94, 1995; Poems for Children, 1986-95, 1995; Butterflies and Roses, 1996; Hummingbirds and Hibiscus, 1997; Swans and Azaleas, 1998; Damselflies and Peonies, 1999; Egrets and Cattails, 2000; Under Par Recipes, book, 1994. Honours include: Second Prize, Connecticut Poetry Society Contest, 1983; Second Prize, Connecticut Poetry Society Contest, 1986; Certificate for Contributions to Arts from Personalities of America, 1989; Certificate for Service to Community, Two Thousand Notable American Women Hall of Fame, 1989; Third Honorable Mention, Connecticut Poetry Society Contest, 1996. Memberships include: Platform Association, 1989-90; Romance Writers of America, 1989-; Romance Writers of American Connecticut Chapter, 1989-; Book Cover Board Designer, Connecticut Chapter Romance Writers of America, 1991-93; Friends of the Guilford Free Lib, 1998-. Address: PO Box 629, Westbrook, CT 06498-0629, USA.

HALL Joan Wylie, b. 2 Sept 1947, Port Allegany, Pennsylvania, USA. English Instructor; Literary Critic. m. J R Hall, 17 Aug 1974, 1 son, 1 daughter. Education: BA, Saint Mary-of-the-Woods College, 1969; MA, 1970, PhD, 1976, University of Notre Dame. Appointments: General Reporter, News-Herald, Franklin, Pennsylvania, summers 1966-69; Teaching Assistant, 1971-72, Instructor, part-time, 1973-74, University of Notre Dame; Instructor, Saint Mary-of-the-Woods College, 1974-78; Instructor, part-time, 1979-83, 1984-, University of Mississippi; Preceptor for English tutorials, Harvard University, 1983-84. Publication: Literary criticism: Shirley Jackson: A Study of the Short Fiction, 1993. Contributions to: Essays of literary criticism in Papers on Language and Literature, College Language Association Journal, Faulkner Journal, Studies in Short Fiction, Colby Library Quarterly, Willa Cather Yearbook, Legacy: A Journal of American Women Writers, Mississippi Quarterly, Renascence, others; Many book reviews and reference work entries. Honours: Dissertation Fellowship, University of Notre Dame, 1973-74; Travel Fellowship, National Endowment for the Humanities, 1990; Research Fellowship Earhart Foundation, 1998. Memberships include: Sigma Tau Delta; Modern Language Association; Society for the Study of Southern Literature; American Literature Association. Address: English Department, University of Mississippi, University, MS 38677, USA.

HALL J(ohn) C(live), b. 12 Sept 1920, London, England. Poet. Education: Oriel College, Oxford. Appointments: Staff, Encounter Magazine, 1955-91; Editor, Literary Executor of Keith Douglas. Publications: Poetry: Selected Poems, 1943; The Summer Dance and Other Poems, 1951; The Burning Hare, 1966; A House of Voices, 1973; Selected and New Poems 1939-84, 1985. Other: Collected Poems of Edwin Muir, 1921-51 (editor), 1952; New Poems (co-editor), 1955; Edwin Muir, 1956. Address: 9 Warwick Road, Mount Sion, Tunbridge Wells, Kent TN1 1YL, England.

HALL Oakley Maxwell, (Jason Manor), b. 1 July 1920, San Diego, California, USA. Author. m. Barbara Erdinger, 28 June 1945, 1 son, 3 daughters. Education: BA, University of California, Berkeley, 1943; MFA, University of Iowa, 1950. Appointments: Director, Programs in Writing, University of California, Irvine, 1969-89, Squaw Valley Community of Writers, 1969-. Publications: So Many Doors, 1950; Corpus of Joe Bailey, 1953; Mardios Beach, 1955; Warlock, 1958; The Downhill Racers, 1962; The Pleasure Garden, 1962; A Game for Eagles, 1970; Report from Beau Harbor, 1971; The Adelita, 1975; The Badlands, 1978; Lullaby, 1982; The Children of the Sun, 1983; The Coming of the Kid, 1985; Apaches, 1986; The Art and Craft of Novel Writing, 1989. Honours: Nomination for Pulitzer Prize, 1953; Commonwealth Club of California Silver Medal, 1954; Western Writers of America Golden Spur Award, 1984; Cowboy Hall of Fame Wrangler Award, 1989. Address: Department of English, University of California at Irvine, CA 92717, USA.

HALL Peter (Geoffrey), b. 19 Mar 1932, London, England. Professor of Planning; Writer. m. (1) Carla Maria Wartenberg, 1962, div 1966, (2) Magdalena Mróz, 1967. Education: MA, PhD, St Catharine's College, Cambridge. Appointments: Assistant Lecturer, 1957-60, Lecturer, 1960-66, Birkbeck College, University of London; Reader in Geography, London School of Economics and Political Science, 1966-68; Professor of Geography, 1968-89, Professor Emeritus, 1989-, University of Reading; Professor of City and Regional Planning, 1980-92, Professor Emeritus, 1992-, University of California at Berkeley; Professor of Planning, 1992-, Director, School of Public Policy, 1995-, University College, London. Publications: The Industries of London, 1962; London 2000, 1963, revised edition, 1969; Labour's New Frontiers, 1964; Land Values (editor), 1965; The World Cities, 1966, 3rd edition, 1984; Von Thunen's Isolated State (editor), 1966; An Advanced Geography of North West Europe (co-author), 1967; Theory and Practice of Regional Planning, 1970; Containment of Urban England: Urban and Metropolitan Growth Processes or Megapolis Denied (co-author), 1973; Containment of Urban England: The Planning System: Objectives, Operations, Impacts (co-author), 1973; Planning and Urban Growth: An Anglo-American Comparison (with M Clawson), 1973; Urban and Regional Planning: An Introduction, 1974, 2nd edition, 1982; Europe 2000, 1977; Great Planning Disasters, 1980; Growth Centres in the European Urban System, 1980; Transport and Public Policy Planning (editor with D Banister), 1980; The Inner City in Context (editor), 1981; Silicon Landscapes (editor), 1985; Can Rail Save the City? (co-author), 1985; High-Tech America (co-author), 1986; Western Sunrise (co-author), 1987; The Carrier Wave (co-author), 1988; Cities of Tomorrow, 1988; London 2001, 1989; The Rise of the Gunbelt, 1991; Technoples of the World, 1994; Sociable Cities (co-author), 1998; Cities in Civilisation, 1998. Honours: Honorary Fellow, St Catharine's College, Cambridge, 1988; British Academy, fellow, 1983; Member of the Academia Europea, 1989; Knight Bachelor, 1998. Memberships: Fabian Society, chairman, 1971-72; Tawney Society, chairman, 1983-85. Literary Agent: Peters, Fraser, Dunlap. Address: c/o Bartlett School, University College, London, Wates House, 22 Gordon Street, London WC1H 0QB, England.

HALL Sir Peter (Reginald Frederick), b. 22 Nov 1930, Bury St Edmunds, Suffolk, England. Director and Producer for Stage, Film, Television, and Opera; Associate Professor of Drama. m. 1) Leslie Caron, 1956, div 1965, 1 son, 1 daughter, 2) Jacqueline Taylor, 1965, div 1981, 1 son, 1 daughter, 3) Maria Ewing, 1982, div 1990, 1 daughter, 4) Nicola Frei, 1990, 1 daughter. Education: BA, Honours, St Catharine's College, Cambridge. Appointments: Director, Arts Theatre, London, 1955-56, Royal Shakespeare Theatre, 1960, National Theatre, 1973-88; Founder-Director-Producer, International Playwright's Theatre, 1957, Peter Hall Co, 1988; Managing Director, Stratford-on-Avon and Aldwych Theatre, London, 1960-68; Associate Professor of Drama, Warwick University, 1966-; Co-Director, Royal Shakespeare Co, 1968-73; Artistic Director, Glyndebourne Festival, 1984-90, Old Vic, 1997. Publications: The Wars of the Roses, adaptation after Shakespeare (with John Barton), 1970; John Gabriel Borkman, by Ibsen (translator with Inga-Stina Ewbank), 1975; Peter Hall's Diaries: The Story of a Dramatic Battle (edited by John Goodwin), 1983; Animal Farm, adaptation after Orwell, 1986; The Wild Duck, by Ibsen (translator with Inga-Stina Ewbank), 1990; Making an Exhibition of Myself (autobiography), 1993; An Absolute Turkey, by Feydeau (translator with Nicola Frei), 1994. Honours: Commander of the Order of the British Empire, 1963; Honorary Fellow, St Catharine's College, Cambridge, 1964; Chevalier de l'Ordre des Arts et Des Lettres, France, 1965; Tony Award, USA, 1966; Shakespeare Prize, University of Hamburg, 1967; Knighted, 1977; Standard Special Award, 1979; Special Award for Outstanding Achievement in Opera, 1981, and Awards for Best Director, 1981, 1987; Several honorary doctorates. Membership: Theatre Directors' Guild of Great Britain, founder-member, 1983-. Address: c/o Old Vic, Waterloo Road, London SE1 8NB, England.

HALL Rodney, b. 18 Nov 1935, Solihull, Warwickshire, England. Writer; Poet. m. Bet MacPahil, 3 daughters. Education: BA, University of Queensland, Brisbane, 1971. Appointments: Poetry Editor, The Australian, 1967-78; Creative Arts Fellow, Australian National University, 1968-69. Publications: Novels: The Ship on the Coin, 1972; A Place Among People, 1975; Just Relations, 1982; Kisses of the Enemy, 1987; Captivity Captive, 1988; The Second Bridgegroom, 1991; The Grisly Wife, 1993; Poetry: Penniless Till Doomsday, 1962; The Law of Karma: A Progression of Poems, 1968; A Soapbox Omnibus, 1973; Selected Poems, 1975; Black Bagatelles, 1978; The Most Beautiful World: Fictions and Sermons, 1981; Journey Through Australia, 1989. Contributions to: Newspapers, magazines, reviews, and journals. Honours: Grace Leven Prize for Poetry, 1973; Australia, 1982, 1994; Order of Australia, 1990. Address: PO Box 7, Bermagui South, New South Wales, 2546, Australia.

HALL Roger Leighton, b. 17 Jan 1939, Woodford, Wells, Essex, England. Dramatist. m. Dianne Sturm, 20 Jan 1968, 1 son, 1 daughter. Education: BA, 1966, MA, 1968, Victoria University, Wellington, New Zealand; Diploma of Teaching. Publications: Plays: Glide Time, 1976; Middle Age Spread, 1977; State of the Play, 1978; Prisoners of Mother England, 1979; The Rose, 1981; Hot Water, 1982; Fifty-Fifty, 1982; Multiple Choice, 1984; Dream of Sussex Downs, 1986; The Hansard Show, 1986; The Share Club, 1987; After the Crash, 1988; Conjugal Rites, 1990; By Degrees, 1993. Other: Musicals with Philip Norman and A K Grant; Many plays for radio, television, and children. Honours: Robert Burns Fellow, Otago University, 1977, 1978; Fulbright Travel Award, 1982; QSO, 1987; Turnovsky Award, Outstanding Contribution to the Arts, 1987. Memberships: PEN; New Zealand; Scriptwriters Guild. Address: c/o Playmarket, PO Box 9767, Wellington, New Zealand.

HALL Willis, b. 6 Apr 1929, Leeds, England. Writer; Dramatist. m. Valerie Shute, 1973, 1 son, 3 sons by previous marriages. Education: Cockburn High School, Leeds. Publications: Football Classified (with Michael Parkinson), 1974; My Sporting Life, 1975; Football Final, 1975. Children's Books: The Last Vampire, 1982; The Inflatable Shop, 1984; The Return of the Antelope, 1985; Dragon Days, 1986; The Antelope Company Ashore, 1987; Spooky Rhymes, 1987; The Antelope Company at Large, 1987; Doctor Jekyll and Mr Hollins, 1988; The Vampire's Holiday, 1992; The Vampire's Christmas, 1994; The Vampire Vanishes, 1995; Vampire Park, 1996; The

Vampire Hunt, 1998; Vampire Island, 1999. Plays: The Long and the Short and the tall, 1959; The Play of the Royal Astrologers, 1960;Kidnapped at Christmas, 1975; Christmas Crackers, 1976; Walk On, Walk On, 1976; A Right Christmas Caper, 1978; Jane Eyre (adaptation from C. Brontë), 1992; Mansfield Park (adaptation from Jane Austen), 1993; The Three Musketeers (adaptation from Dumas), 1994. Plays written in collaboration with Keith Waterhouse: Billy Liar, 1960; Celebration, 1961; All Things Bright and Beautiful, 1962; Squat Betty and the Sponge Room, 1963; Say Who You Are, 1965; Whoops A Daisy, 1968; Children's Day, 1969; Who's Who, 1972; Saturday, Sunday, Monday (adaptation from de Filippo), 1973; Filumena (adaptation from de Filippo), 1978. Musicals: Treasure Island (with Denis king), 1985; The Wind in the Willows (with Denis King), 1985, The Water Babies (with John Cooper) 1987; The Card (with Keith Waterhouse, Tony Hatch and Anthony Drewe), 1994; Peter Pan (with George Stiles and Anthony Drewe), 1998. Address: c/o Alexandra Cann Representation, 12 Abingdon Road, London W8 6AF, England

HALLDORSSON Omar Thor, b. 26 May 1954, Reykjavik, Iceland. Writer. 3 daughters. Education: BS, Selfoss, 1971. Appointments: Bus and Truck Driver, 1970-79; Pop and Rock Musician, 1970-80; Writer of poems, novels, short stories, articles, interviews, 1970-98. Publications: Horfin Sky, poems, 1970; Novels: Hversdagsleikur, 1973; Thetta var nú í fyllirii, 1982; Blindflug, 1987. Contributions to: Icelandic magazines. Address: Birkivollum 1, 800 Selfoss, Iceland.

HALLIDAY Dorothy. See: **DUNNETT Dorothy.**

HALLMUNDSSON Hallberg, b. 29 Oct 1930, Iceland. Poet; Writer; Translator. m. May Newman, 29 July 1960. Education: BA, University of Iceland, 1954; University of Barcelona, 1955-56; New York University, 1961. Appointments include: Columnist, Frjals Thjod, Iceland, 1954-60; Assistant, Associate, Senior Editor, Encyclopedia International, New York, 1961-76; Senior Editor, Americana Annual, 1976-78, Funk & Wagnalls New Encyclopedia, 1979-82; Production Copy Editor, Business Week, 1984-. Publications: Poetry: Haustmal, 1968; Neikvaeda, 1977; Spjaldvisur, 1985; Thraetubók, 1990; Spjaldvisur II, 1991; Skyggnur, 1993; Vandraedur, 1995; Umhendur, 1997. Other: Anthology of Scandinavian Literature, 1966; Icelandic Folk and Fairy Tales (with May Hallmundsson), 1987; Short stories; Translations. Contributions to: Reviews and journals. Honours: 1st Prize, Short Story Contest, Reykjavik, 1953; 1st Prize, Translation of Norwegian Poetry, Minneapolis, 1966; Grants, Translation Center, New York, 1975; Government of Iceland, 1976-79; American Scandinavian Society, 1991, Translation Fund, Iceland, 1994, 1996, 1998; Award, Iceland Writers Fund, 1985. Memberships: American Literature Translators Association; Writers Union of Iceland. Address: 30 Fifth Avenue, New York, NY 10011, USA.

HALLWORTH Grace Norma Leonie Byam, b. 4 Jan 1928, Trinidad, West Indies. Ex-Librarian; Author; Storyteller. m. Trevor David Hallworth, 31 Oct 1964. Education: Exemptions from Matriculation, 1946; Associate of Library Association, 1956; Diploma in Education, London University, 1976; Editorial Board Member, Institute of Education, University of London, 1995. Publications: Listen to this Story, 1977; Mouth Open Story Jump Out, 1984; Web of Stories, 1990; Cric Crac, 1990; Buy a Penny Ginger, 1994; Poor-Me-One, 1995; Rythm and Rhyme, 1995; Down By The River, 1997 Contributions to: Books and journals. Honours: Runner-up for Greenaway Medal. 1997. Membership: Society for Storytelling, patron, 1993-94. Literary Agent: Marilyn Malin. Address: Tranquillity, 36 Lighthouse Road, Bacolet Point, Scarborough, Tobago, West Indies.

HALPERN Daniel, b. 11 Sept 1945, Syracuse, New York, USA. Associate Professor; Poet; Writer; Editor. m. Jeanne Catherine Carter, 31 Dec 1982, 1 daughter. Education: San Francisco State College, 1963-64; BA, California State University at Northridge, 1969; MFA, Columbia University, 1972. Appointments:

Founder-Editor, Antaeus literary magazine, 1969-95; Instructor, New School for Social Research, New York City, 1971-76; Editor-in-Chief, Ecco Press, 1971-; Visiting Professor, Princeton University, 1975-76, 1987-88, 1995-96; Associate Professor, Columbia University, 1976-. Publications: Poetry: Traveling on Credit, 1978; Seasonal Rights, 1982; Tango, 1987; Foreign Neon, 1991; Selected Poems, 1994. Other: The Keeper of Height, 1974; Treble Poets, 1975; Our Private Lives: Journals, Notebooks and Diaries, 1990; Not for Bread Alone: Writers on Food, Wine, and the Art of Eating, 1993; The Autobiographical Eye, 1993; Holy Fire: Nine Visionary Poets and the Quest for Enlightenment, 1994. Editor: Borges on Writing (co-editor), 1973; The American Poetry Anthology, 1975; The Antaeus Anthology, 1986; The Art of the Tale: An International Anthology of Short Stories, 1986; On Nature, 1987; Writers on Artists, 1988; Reading the Fights (with Joyce Carol Oates), 1988; Plays in One Act, 1990; The Sophisticated Cat (with Joyce Carol Oates), 1992; On Music (co-editor), 1994. Contributions to: Various anthologies, reviews, journals, and magazines. Honours: Jesse Rehder Poetry Award, Southern Poetry Review, 1971; YMHA Discovery Award, 1971; Great Lakes Colleges National Book Award, 1973; Borestone Mountain Poetry Award, 1974; Robert Frost Fellowship, Bread Loaf, 1974; National Endowment for the Arts Fellowships, 1974, 1975, 1987; Pushcaft Press Prizes, 1980, 1987, 1988; Carey Thomas Award for Creative Publishing, Publishers Weekly, 1987; Guggenheim Fellowship, 1988; PEN Publisher Citation, 1993. Address: c/o The Ecco Press, 100 West Broad Street, Hopewell, NJ 08525, USA.

HALVORSEN Richard Toralf, b. Stockholm, Sweden. Medical Practitioner (GP). m. Charlotte Knox Wright, 9 Feb 1978, 1 son, 1 daughter. Education: MBBS, Middlesex Hospital, University of London. Appointments: Full Time GP Principle, 1988; GP Trainer, 1995. Contributions to: Regular contributor, Director magazine; Contributor to variety of medical magazines. Address: The Holborn Medical Centre, 64 Lambs Conduit Street, London WC1N 3LW, England.

HAM Debra Lynn Newman, b. 27 Aug 1948, York, Pennsylvania, USA. Professor; Black History Specialist. m. Lester James Ham, 29 Apr 1989, 1 son, 1 daughter. Education: BA, 1970, PhD, 1984, Howard University; MA, Boston University, 1971. Appointments: Professor of History, Morgan State University, 1994-. Publications: Black History: A Guide to Civilian Records in the National Archives, 1984; The African-American Mosaic: A Library of Congress Resource Guide for the Study of Black History and Culture, 1993; Jesus and Justice: Nannie Helen Burroughs and Her Struggle for Civil Rights, Society and Humanity; The African American Odyssey, 1998. Contributions to: They Left With the British: Black Women in the Evacuation of Philadelphia, Pennsylvania Heritage, 1978. Honour: Coker Prize, Society of American Archivists, 1985. Membership: Association for the Study of Afro-American Life and History, executive council member, 1989. Address: Morgan State University, Cold Spring Lane and Hillen Road, Baltimore, MD 21251, USA.

HAMBRICK-STOWE Charles Edwin, b. 4 Feb 1948, Worcester, Massachusetts, USA. m. Elizabeth Anne Hambrick-Stowe, 11 Sept 1971, 2 sons, 1 daughter. Education: BA, Hamilton College, 1970; MA and MDiv, Pacific School of Religion, 1973; PhD, Boston University Graduate School, 1980. Appointment: Religion Columnist, Evening Sun Newspaper, Carrol County, MD, 1982-85. Publications: Massachusetts Militia Companies and the Officers of the Lexington Alarm, 1976; Practice of Piety: Puritan Devotional Disciplines in 17th Century New England, 1982; Early New England Meditative Poetry: Anne Bradstreet and Edward Taylor, 1988; Theology and Identity: Traditions, Movements and Issues in the United Church of Christ, 1990; Charles G Finney and The Spirit of American Evangelicalism, 1996; Living Theological Heritage: Colonial and Early National Beginnings, 1998. Contributions to: Reference works, books and journals. Honour: Jamestown Prize for Early American History, 1980. Memberships: American

Historical Association; American Society of Church History; American Academy of Religion; Address: 1101 Davis Drive, Lancaster, PA 17603, USA.

HAMBURGER Anne (Ellen), (Anne Beresford), b. 10 Sept 1928, Redhill, Surrey, England. Poet; Writer; Actress; Teacher. m. Michael Hamburger, 28 July 1951, 1 son, 2 daughters. Education: Central School of Dramatic Art, London, 1944-46. Appointments: Actress, various repertory companies, 1946-48, BBC Radio, 1960-78; Teacher; General Council, Poetry Society, 1976-78; Committee Member, 1989, Advisor on Agenda, Editorial Board, 1993-, Aldeburgh Poetry Festival. Publications: Poetry: Walking Without Moving, 1967; The Lair, 1968; The Courtship, 1972; Footsteps on Snow, 1972; The Curving Shore, 1975; Songs a Thracian Taught Me, 1980; The Songs of Almut, 1980; The Sele of the Morning, 1988; Charm with Stones,(Lyrik im Hölderlinturm), 1993; Landscape With Figures, 1994; No Place for Cowards, 1998. Other: Struck by Apollo, radio play (with Michael Hamburger), 1965; The Villa, radio short story, 1968; Alexandros Poems of Vera Lungu, translator, 1974; Duet for Three Voices, dramatised poems for Anglia TV, 1982; Snapshots from an Album, 1884-1895, 1992; Selected and New Poems, 1997. Contributions to: Periodicals. Address: Marsh Acres, Middleton, Saxmundham, Suffolk IP17 3NH, England.

HAMBURGER Michael (Peter Leopold), b. 22 Mar 1924, Berlin, Germany (British Citizen). Poet; Writer; Translator; Editor. m. Anne Ellen File, 1951, 1 son, 2 daughters. Education: MA, Christ Church, Oxford, England. Appointments: Assistant Lecturer in German, University College, London, 1952-55; Lecturer, then Reader in German, University of Reading, 1955-64; Florence Purington Lecturer, Mount Holyoke College, South Hadley, Massachusetts, 1966-67; Visiting Professor, State University of New York at Buffalo, 1969, and at Stony Brook, 1971, University of South Carolina, 1973, Boston University, 1975-77; Visiting Fellow, Wesleyan University, Middletown, Connecticut, 1970; Regent's Lecturer, University of California at San Diego, 1973; Professor (part-time), University of Essex, 1978. Publications: Poetry: Flowering Cactus, 1950; Poems 1950-51, 1952; The Dual Site, 1958; Weather and Season, 1963; Feeding the Chickadees, 1968; Penguin Modern Poets (with A Brownjohn and C Tomlinson), 1969; Travelling, 1969; Travelling I-V, 1973; Ownerless Earth, 1973; Travelling VI, 1975; Real Estate, 1977; Moralities, 1977; Variations, 1981; Collected Poems, 1984; Trees, 1988; Selected Poems, 1988; Roots in the Air, 1991; Collected Poems, 1941-94, 1995, paperback, 1998; Late, 1997. Prose: Reason and Energy, 1957; From Prophecy to Exorcism, 1965; The Truth of Poetry, 1970, new edition, 1996; A Mug's Game (memoirs), 1973, revised edition as String of Beginnings, 1991; Hugo von Hofmannsthal, 1973; Art as a Second Nature, 1975; A Proliferation of Prophets, 1983; After the Second Flood: Essays in Modern German Literature, 1986; Testimonies: Selected Shorter Prose 1950-1987, 1989. Translator: Many books, including: Poems of Hölderlin, 1943, revised edition as Hölderlin: Poems, 1952; JCF Holderlin: Selected Verse, 1961; H von Hofmannsthal: Poems and Verse Plays (with others), 1961; H von Hofmannsthal: Selected Plays and Libretti (with others), 1964; J C F Hölderlin: Poems and Fragments, 1967, new edition, enlarged, 1994; The Poems of Hans Magnus Enzenberger (with others), 1968; The Poems of Günter Grass (with C Middleton), 1969; Paul Celan: Poems, 1972, new edition, enlarged as Poems of Paul Celan, 1988, 3rd edition, 1995; Selected Poems and Fragments, 1994; Kiosk, 1997; Günter Grass: Selected Poems and Fragments, 1998. Contributions to: Numerous publications. Honours: Bollingen Foundation Fellow, 1959-61, 1965-66; Translation Prizes, Deutsche Akademie für Sprache und Dichtung, Darmstadt, 1964; Arts Council of Great Britain, 1969; Medal, Institute of Linguistics, 1977; Schlegel-Tieck Prizes, 1978, 1981; Goethe Medal, 1986; Austrian State Prize for Literary Translation, 1988; Honorary LittD, University of East Anglia, 1988; European Translation Prize, 1990; Officer of the Order of the British Empire, 1992; Honorary DPhil, Technical University, Berlin, 1995. Address: c/o John

Johnson Ltd, Clerkenwell House, 45-47 Clerkenwell Green, London EC1 0HT, England.

HAMBURGER Philip (Paul), b. 2 July 1914, Wheeling, West Virginia, USA. Writer. m. (1) Edith Iglauer, 24 Dec 1942, (2) Anna Walling Matson, 27 Oct 1968, 2 sons. Education: BA, Johns Hopkins University, 1935; MS, Graduate School of Journalism, Columbia University, 1938. Appointment: Staff Writer, The New Yorker, 1939-. Publications: The Oblong Blur and Other Odysseys, 1949; J P Marquand, Esquire, 1952; Mayor Watching and Other Pleasures, 1958; Our Man Stanley, 1963; An American Notebook, 1965; Curious World, A New Yorker at Large, 1987; Friends Talking in the Night, forthcoming. Contributions to: The New Yorker. Honours: New York Public Library Literary Lion Award, 1986; George Polk Career Award, 1994; Columbia Journalism Alumni Award, 1997. Memberships: Authors League of America; PEN USA; Board of Directors, Authors League Fund and National Press Club, Washington; Century Association. Literary Agent: Sterling Lord Literistic. Address: c/o The New Yorker, 20 West 43rd Street, New York, NY 10036, USA.

HAMELIN Claude, b. 25 Aug 1943, Montreal, Quebec, Canada. Poet; Writer; Scientist. m. Renée Artinian, 11 Sept 1970, 1 son, 1 daughter. Education: BPed, 1965; BSc, 1970; MSc, 1972; PhD, 1975. Publications: Poetry: Fables des quatre-temps, 1990; Lueurs froides, 1991; Nef des fous, 1992; Néant bleu/Nada azul/Blue Nothingness, 1994; Novel: Roman d'un quartier, 1993. Contributions to: Anthologies and journals. Address: 4630 Avenue Lacombe, Montreal, Quebec H3W 1R3, Canada.

HAMILL (William) Pete, b. 24 June 1934, New York, New York, USA. Journalist; Columnist; Writer. m. (1) Ramona Negron, 3 Feb 1962, div 1970, 2 daughters, (2) Fukiko Aoki, 23 May 1987. Education: Pratt Institute, 1952; Mexico City College, 1956-57. Appointments: Reporter, later columnist, 1960-74, 1988-93, New York Post; Contributing Editor, Saturday Evening Post, 1963-64; Contributor, Village Voice and New York Magazine, 1974-; Columnist, New York Daily News, 1975-79, 1982-84, Esquire Magazine, 1989-91; Editor, Mexico City News, 1986-87. Publications: Fiction: A Killing for Christ, 1968; The Gift, 1973; Flesh and Blood, 1977; Loving Women, 1990; Tokyo Sketches, 1993. Non-Fiction: Irrational Ravings, 1972; The Invisible City: A New York Sketchbook, 1980; A Drinking Life: A Memoir, 1994; News is a Verb, 1998; Why Sinatra Matters, 1998. Screenplays: Doc, 1971; Badge 373, 1973; Liberty, 1986; Neon Empire, 1987. Contributions to: Many periodicals. Honours: Meyer Berger Award, Columbia School of Journalism, 1962; Newspaper Reporters Association Award, 1962; 25 Year Achievement Award, Society of Silurians, 1989; Peter Kihss Award, 1992. Membership: Writers Guild of America. Address: c/o New York Magazine, 755 Second Avenue, New York, NY 10017, USA.

HAMILTON Donald B(engtsson), b. 24 Mar 1916, Uppsala, Sweden. Writer. m. Kathleen Stick, 12 Sep 1941, dec Oct 1989, 2 sons, 2 daughters. Education: BS, University of Chicago, 1938. Publications: 5 mystery novels, 1947-56; 4 western novels, 1954-60; The big Country, 1958; 25 novels featuring agent Matt Helm, 1960-93; On Guns and Hunting, 1970; Cruises with Kathleen, 1980. Contributions to: Periodicals. Honour: Western Writers of America; Spur, 1967. Memberships: Author's Guild; Mystery Writers of America; Western Writers of America; Outdoor Writer's Association of America. Address: PO Box 1141, Old Saybrook, CT 06475, USA.

HAMILTON Eleanor, b. Oct 1909, Portland, Oregon, USA. Marriage Counselor; Sex Therapist; Journalist. m. A E Hamilton, 11 Aug 1932, 1 son, 3 daughters. Education: AB, University of Oregon, 1930; MA, Teachers College, 1939, PhD, 1955, Columbia University. Appointments: Director, Hamilton School Inc, 1934-45; Director, Hamilton School Counselling Center, 1948-83; Inverness Ridge Counselling Center, 1983-95.

Publications: Books: Partners in Love, 1961; Sex Before Marriage, 1969; Sex With Love, 1978; Intimacy, 1991; What Made Me?. Contributions to: Grand Times Magazine. Honours: American Library Award, Best Book for Teens. Membership: AAJA. Address: 2069 Marylhurst Drive, West Linn, OR 97068, USA.

HAMILTON (Robert) Ian, b. 24 Mar 1938, King's Lynn, Norfolk, England. Lecturer; Writer; Poet. Education: BA, Keble College, Oxford, 1962. Appointments: Poetry and Fiction Editor, Times Literary Supplement, 1965-73; Presenter, Bookmark, BBC TV, 1984-87. Publications: Poetry: Pretending Not to Sleep, 1964; The Visit, 1970; Anniversary and Vigil, 1971; Returning, 1976; Fifty Poems, 1988. Other: A Poetry Chronicle: Essays and Reviews, 1973; The Little Magazines: A Study of Six Editors, 1976; Robert Lowell: A Biography, 1983; In Search of J D Salinger, 1988; Editions of contemporary poetry. Honours: Eric Gregory Award, 1963; English-Speaking Union Award, 1984. Address: 54 Queen's Road, London SW19, England.

HAMILTON Jane, b. 1957, Oak Park, Illinois, USA. Writer. m. Robert Willard, June 1982, 2 children. Education: BA, Carleton College, Northfield, Minnesota, 1979. Publications: The Book of Ruth, UK edition as The Frogs Are Still Singing, 1989; A Map of the World, 1994; The Short History of a Prince, 1998. Honour: Ernest Hemingway Foundation Award, PEN American Center, 1989. Address: c/o Doubleday Publishers, 1540 Broadway, New York, 10036, USA.

HAMILTON John Maxwell, b. 28 Mar 1947, Evanston, Illinois, USA. Journalist; Lecturer. m. Regina N, 19 Aug 1975, 1 s. Education: BA, Journalism, Marquette University, 1969; MS, Journalism, Boston University, 1974; PhD, American Civilization, George Washington University, 1983. Appointments: The Milwaukee Journal, 1967-69; Marine Corps, 1969-73; Freelance Writer, ABC Radio correspondent, 1973-78; Agency for International Development (political appointee) 1979-81; House Foreign Affairs Committee, 1981-83; World Bank, 1983-84, 1982-92; Visiting Professor, Journalism, Northwestern University, 1985-87; Dean, Manship School of Mass Communication, Louisiana State University. Publications: Main Street America and the Third World, 1986, revised, enlarged edition, 1988; Edgar Snow: A Biography, 1988; Entangling Alliances, 1990; Hold The Press: The Inside Story on Newspapers (co-author), 1996. Contributions to: Numerous books and periodicals. Honours: Ford Fondation, German Marshall Fund, Carnegie Corporation and Benton Foundation Grants, 1985-88; Frank Luther Mott Journalism Research Award, 1989; By-line Award, Marguette University, 1993. Memberships: Society of Professional Journalists; Society of International Development; Director, Board of Directors, International Centre for Journalists. Address: 567 LSU Avenue, Baton Rouge, LA 70808, USA.

HAMILTON Paul. See: **DENNIS-JONES Harold.**

HAMILTON Priscilla. See: **GELLIS Roberta Leah.**

HAMILTON Virginia, b. 12 Mar 1936, Yellow Springs, Ohio, USA. Writer. m. Arnold Adoff, 19 Mar 1960, 2 sons. Education: Antioch College, 1952-55; Ohio State University, 1957-58; New School for Social Research, New York City. Publications: Zeely, 1967; The House of Dies Drear, 1968; The Time-Ago Tales of Jadhu, 1969; The Planet of Junior Brown, 1971; W E B DuBois: A Biography, 1972; Time-Ago Lost: More Tales of Jadhu, 1973; M C Higgins, the Great, 1974; Paul Robeson: The Life and Times of a Free Black Man, 1974; The Writings of W E B DuBois (editor), 1975; Arilla Sun Down, 1976; Illusion and Reality, 1976; Justice and Her Brothers, 1978; Jahdu, 1980; Dustland, 1980; The Gathering, 1981; Sweet Whispers, Brother Rush, 1982; The Magical Adventures of Pretty Pearl, 1983; Willie Bea and the Time the Martians Landed, 1983; A Little Love, 1984; Junius Over Far, 1985; The People Could Fly: American Black Folktales, 1985; The Mystery of Drear House, 1987; A White Romance, 1987; In the Beginning: Creation Stories from Around the World, 1988; Anthony Burns: The Defeat

and Triumph of a Fugitive Slave, 1988; The Bells of Christmas, 1989; The Dark Way: Stories from the Spirit World, 1990; Cousins, 1990; The All Jahdu Storybook, 1991; Many Thousands Gone, 1992; Plain City, 1993; Jaguarundi, 1994; Her Story: African American Folktales, 1995. Honours: Edgar Allan Poe Award, 1969; Newbery Honor Books Awards, 1971, 1983, 1989; Boston Globe/Horn Book Awards, 1974, 1983, 1988; John Newbery Medal, 1975; National Book Award, 1975; Coretta Scott King Awards, 1983, 1986, 1989; Horn Book Fanfare Award, 1985; Regina Medal, Catholic Library Association, 1990; Laura Ingalls Wilder Award, American Library Association, 1995. Address: c/o Arnold Adoff Agency, PO Box 293, Yellow Springs, OH 45387, USA.

HAMILTON Wade. See: **FLOREN Lee.**

HAMLYN David W(alter), b. 1 Oct 1924, Plymouth, England. Professor of Philosophy Emeritus; Writer. m. Eileen Carlyle Litt, 2 July 1949, 1 son, 1 daughter. Education: BA, in Literae Humanores with 1st Class Honours, 1948, BA in Philosophy and Psychology with 1st Class Honours, 1950, MA 1949 Exeter College, Oxford. Appointments: Research Fellow, Corpus Christi College, Oxford, 1950-53; Lecturer, Jesus College, Oxford, 1953-54; Lecturer, 1954-63, Reader, 1963-64, Professor of Philosophy and Head of the Department of Philosophy, 1964-88, Head of the Department of Classics, 1981-86, Vice-Master, 1983-88, Fellow, 1988, Professor of Philosophy Emeritus, 1988-, Birbeck College, University of London; Editor, Mind, 1972-84; Consulting Editor, Journal of Medical Ethics, 1981-90. Publications: The Psychology of Perception, 1957, new edition, 1969; Sensation and Perception, 1961; Aristotle's De Anima, Books II-III, 1968; The Theory of Knowledge, 1970; Experience and the Growth of Understanding, 1978; Schopenhauer, 1980; Perception, Learning and the Self, 1983; Metaphysics, 1984; History of Western Philosophy, 1987; In and Out of the Black Box, 1990; Being a Philosopher, 1992; Understanding Perception, 1996. Contributions to: Books and professional journals. Memberships: Aristotelian Society, president, 1977-78; London University Senate, 1981-87; National Committee for Philosophy, 1986-92, honorary Vice-president, 1992-; Royal Institute of Philosophy, council, 1968-, executive committee, 1971-97, vice-chairman, 1991-95. Address: 38 Smithy Knoll Road, Hope Valley, Calver, Derbyshire S32 3XW, England.

HAMMER David Lindley, b. 6 June 1929, Newton, Iowa, USA. Advocate; Writer. m. Audrey Lowe Hammer, 20 June 1953, 1 son, 2 daughters. Education: BA, Grinnell College, 1947-51; JD, University of Iowa Law School, 1953-56. Publications: Poems From the Ledge, 1980; The Game is Afoot, 1983; For the Sake of the Game, 1986; The 22nd Man, 1989; To Play the Game, 1990; Skewed Sherlock, 1992; The Worth of the Game, 1992; The Quest, 1993; My Dear Watson, 1994; The Before Breakfast Pipe, 1995; A Dangerous Game, 1997. Contributions to: American Journal of Philately; Baker Street Journal; Sherlock Holmes Journal. Address: Laurel Cottage, 720 Laurel Park Road, Dubuque, IA 52003, USA.

HAMMICK Georgina, b. 24 May 1939, Hampshire, England. Writer; Poet. m. 24 Oct 1961, 1 son, 2 daughters. Education: Academie Julian, Paris, 1956-57; Salisbury Art School, 1957-59. Publications: A Poetry Quintet (poems), 1976; People for Lunch, 1987; Spoilt (short stories), 1992; The Virago Book of Love and Loss (editor), 1992; The Arizona Game, 1996. Contributions to: Journals and periodicals. Membership: Writers Guild. Address: Bridgewalk House, Brixton, Deverill, Warminster, Wiltshire BA12 7EJ, England.

HAMMOND Jane. See: **POLAND Dorothy Elizabeth Hayward.**

HAMPSHIRE Sir Stuart (Newton), b. 1 Oct 1914, Healing, Lincolnshire, England. Professor of Philosophy (retired); Writer. m. (1) Renee Ayer, 1961, dec 1980, (2) Nancy Cartwright, 1985, 2 daughters. Education: Balliol College, Oxford. Appointments: Fellow and Lecturer in

Philosophy, 1936-40, Domestic Bursar and Research Fellow, 1955-60, All Souls College, Oxford; Service in the British Army, 1940-45; Personal Assistant to the Minister of State, British Foreign Office, 1945; Lecturer in Philosophy, University College, London, 1947-50; Fellow, New College, Oxford, 1950-55; Grote Professor of Philosophy of Mind and Logic, University of London, 1960-63; Professor of Philosophy, Princeton University, 1963-70; Warden, Wadham College, Oxford, 1970-84; Professor, Stanford University, 1985-91. Publications: Spinoza, 1951; Thought and Action, 1959; Freedom of the Individual, 1965; Modern Writers and Other Essays, 1969; Freedom of Mind and Other Essays, 1971; The Socialist Idea (co-editor), 1975; Two Theories of Morality, 1977; Public and Private Morality (editor), 1978; Morality and Conflict, 1983; Innocence and Experience, 1989. Contributions to: Philosophical journals. Honours: Honorary DLitt, University of Glasgow, 1973; Knighted, 1979. Memberships: American Academy of Arts and Sciences, fellow; British Academy, fellow. Address: 7 Beaumont Road, The Quarry, Headington, Oxford, OX3 8JN, England.

HAMPSHIRE Susan, b. 12 May 1942, London, England. Actress; Writer. m. (1) Pierre Granier-Deferre, div 1974, 1 son, (2) Eddie Kulukundis, 1980. Education: Knightsbridge, England. Appointments: Actress on the London stage, 1959-; Film and television appearances; Writer. Publications: Susan's Story: An Autobiographical Account of My Struggle with Dyslexia, 1982; The Maternal Instinct, 1985; Lucy Jane at the Ballet, 1987; Trouble Free Gardening, 1989; Lucy Jane on Television, 1989; Every Letter Counts, 1990; Lucy Jane and the Dancing Competition, 1990; Easy Gardening, 1992; Lucy Jane and the Russian Ballet, 1993; Rosie's First Ballet Lesson, 1995. Honours: Emmy Awards, 1970, 1971, 1973; Honorary doctorates, London University, 1984, St Andrew's University, 1986, Kingston University, 1994, Pine Manor College, Boston, Massachusetts, 1994; Officer of the Order of the British Empire, 1995. Memberships: Dyslexia Institute; Royal Society of Authors. Address: c/o Chatto and Linnit Ltd, 123a Kings Road, London SW3 4PL, England.

HAMPSON Norman, b. 8 Apr 1922, Leyland, Lancashire, England. Retired University Professor. m. Jacqueline Gardin, 22 Apr 1948, 2 daughters. Education: University College Oxford, 1940-41, 1945-47. Publications: La Marine de l'An II, 1959; A Social History of The French Revolution, 1963; The First European Revolution, 1963; The Enlightenment, 1968; The Life and Opinions of Maximilien Robespierre, 1974; A Concise History of the French Revolution, 1975; Danton, 1978; Will and Circumstance: Montesquieu, Rousseau and The French Revolution, 1983; Prelude to Terror, 1988; Saint-Just, 1991. Contributions to: Numerous magazines and journals. Honour: D Litt (Edinburgh), 1989. Memberships: Fellow, British Academy; Fellow, Royal Historical Society. Address: 305 Hull Road, York, YO1 3LB, England.

HAMPTON Angeline Agnes, (A A Kelly), b. 28 Feb 1924, London, England. Writer. m. George Hughan Hampton, 31 Dec 1944, 1 son, 3 daughters. Education: BA, External, Honours, English, University of London, 1965; Licencié è lettres, 1969, Docteur ès lettres , 1973, University of Geneva, Switzerland. Publications: Liam O'Flaherty the Storyteller, 1976; Mary Lavin: Quiet Rebel, 1980; Joseph Campbell, 1879-1944, Poet and Nationalist, 1988; The Pillars of the House (editor), 1987; Wandering Women, 1994; The Letters of Liam O'Flaherty (editor), 1996. Contributions to: English Studies; Comparative Education; Eire, Ireland; Hibernia; Linen Hall Review; Geneva News and International Report; Christian. Honour: British Academy Grant, 1987. Memberships: International Association for the Study of Anglo-Irish Literature; Society of Authors; PEN International. Address: Gate Cottage, Pilley Green, Lymington, Hampshire SO41 5QQ, England.

HAMPTON Christopher (James), b. 26 Jan 1946, Fayal, The Azores. Playwright. m. Laura de Holesch, 1971, 2 daughters. Education: Lancing College, Sussex,

1959-63; BA, Modern Languages, 1968, MA, New College, Oxford. Appointment: Resident Dramatist, Royal Court Theatre, London, 1968-70. Publications: Tales from Hollywood, 1983; Tartuffe or The Imposter (adaptation of Moliére's play), 1984; Les Liaisons Dangereuses (adaptation of C de Laclos's novel), 1985; Hedda Gabler and A Doll's House (translations of Ibsen's plays), 1989; Faith, Hope and Charity (translator), 1989; The Ginger Tree (adaptation of Oscar Wynd's novel), 1989; White Chameleon, 1991; The Philanthropist and Other Plays, 1991. Other: Screenplays, radio and television plays. Membership: Royal Society of Literature, fellow. Address: National House, 60-66 Wardour Street, London W1V 3HP, England.

HAN Suyin, b. 12 Sept 1917, Sinyang, China. Novelist; Physician. Education: Yenching University, Beijing; University of Brussels; London University; Royal Free Hospital, London. Publications: A Many Splendoured Thing, 1952; The Mountain is Young, 1958; The Crippled Tree, 1965; Lhassa, the Open City, 1977; My House Has Two Doors,1980; Till Morning Comes, 1982; The Enchantress, 1985; A Share of Loving, 1987; Han Suyin's China, 1987. Contributions to: Periodicals. Honours: Bancaralla Prize, Italy, 1956; McGill Beatty Prize, Canada, 1968; Nutting Prize, Canada, 1980; Woman Reader Prize, Italy, 1983. Address: c/o Jonathan Cape, 32 Bedford Square, London WC1, England.

HANBURY-TENISON (Airling) Robin, b. 7 May 1936, London, England. Writer; Farmer. Education: BA, MA, Magdalen College, Oxford. Appointment: Chief Executive, British Field Sports Society/Countryside Alliance, 1995-98. Publications: The Rough and the Smooth, 1969; A Question of Survival for the Indians of Brazil, 1973; A Pattern of Peoples: A Journey Among the Tribes of the Outer Indonesian Islands, 1975; Mulu: The Rain Forest, 1980; The Aborigines of the Amazon Rain Forest: The Yanomami, 1982; Worlds Apart (autobiography), 1984; White Horses Over France, 1985; A Ride Along the Great Wall, 1987; Fragile Eden: A Ride Through New Zealand, 1989; Spanish Pilgrimage: A Canter to St James, 1990; The Oxford Book of Exploration, 1993; Jake's Escape, 1996; Jake's Treasure, Jake's Safari, 1998. Contributions to: Frontiers Column, Geographical Magazine, 1995-. Honours: Royal Geographical Society Gold Medal, 1979; Officer of the Order of the British Empire, 1981; Thomas Cook Travel Book Award, 1984. Memberships: Royal Geographical Society, council member, 1968-82, 1995- vice president, 1982-86; Survival International, president, 1969-; Society of Authors. Address: Cabilla Manor, Cardinham, Bodmin, Cornwall PL30 4DW, England.

HANCOCK Geoffrey White, b. 14 Apr 1946, New Westminster, New Brunswick, Canada. Writer; Literary Journalist. m. Gay Allison, 6 Aug 1983, 1 daughter. Education: BFA, 1973, MFA, University of British Columbia, 1975. Appointments: Editor in Chief, Canadian Fiction Magazine, 1975; Consulting editor, Canadian Author and Bookman, 1978; Fiction editor, Cross-Canada Writers Quarterly, 1980; Literary consultant, CBC Radio, 1980. Publications: Magic Realism, 1980; Illusion: Fables Fantasies and Metafictions, 1983; Metavisions, 1983; Shoes and Shit: Stories for Pedestrians, 1984; Moving Off the Map: From Story to Fiction, 1986; Invisible Fictions: Contemporary Stories from Quebec, 1987; Canadian Writers at Work: Interviews, 1987; Singularities, 1990; Fast Travelling, 1995. Contributions to: Toronto Star; Writer's Quarterly; Canadian Author and Bookman; Books In Canada; Canadian Forum. Honour: Fiona Mee Award for Literary Journalism, 1979. Membership: Periodical Writers of Canada; Address: c/o Canadian Fiction Magazine, Box No 1061, Kingston, Ontario K7L 4Y5, Canada.

HANCOCK Lyn, b. 5 Jan 1938, Fremantle, West Australia. Writer; Photographer; Lecturer. Education: Teaching Diploma, 1955, 1977; ASDA, 1955; LTCL, 1959; LSDA, 1957; LRAM (mime), 1961; LRAM (Speech), 1961; BEduc, Simon Fraser University, 1977; MA, Communications, 1981. Appointments: Twelve years teaching in three countries (Grade 3 to university level); Principal of a privately-owned Academy of Speech and

Drama in Western Australia, 1954-59. Publications: There's a Seal in My Sleeping Bag, 1972; There's a Raccoon in My Parka, 1977; Looking for the Wild, 1986; Northwest Territories, 1993; Nunavut, 1995; Winging It in the North, 1996; Yukon, 1996; Destination Vancouver, 1997; Great Canadian Fishing Stories that Didn't Get Away, 1998; Western Canada, Travel Smart, 1998. Contributions to: Frequent Contributor to Above and Beyond; Globe and Mail; numerous other magazines. Honours: Pacific Northwest Booksellers Award, 1973; Francis H Kortnight Conservation Award, 1978, 1987; American Express Travel Writing Awards, 1981, 1983. Address: 8270 Sabre Road, Lantzville, British Columbia VOR 2HO, Canada.

HANDKE Peter, b. 6 Dec 1942, Griffen-Altenmarkt, Austria. Writer; Dramatist; Poet. 1 daughter. Education: Law Studies, University of Graz. Publications: Die Hornissen, 1966; Publikumsbeschimpfung, 1966; Der Hausierer, 1967; Kaspar, 1968; Deutsche Gedichte, 1969; Die Innenwelt der Aussenwelt der Innenwelt, 1969; Die Angst des Tormanns beim Elfmeter, 1970; Ich bin ein Bewohner des Elfenbeinturms, 1972; Kurzer Briefzum langen Abschied, 1972; Stücke, 2 volumes, 1972-73; Wunschloses Unglück, 1972; Als das Wünschen noch geholfen hat, 1974; Falsche Bewegung, 1975; Der Rand der Wörter, 1975; Die linkshändige Frau, 1975; Die Stunde der wahren Empfindung, 1975; Das Ende des flanierens, 1977; Das Gewichte der Welt: Ein Journal, 1977; Langsame Heimkehr, 1979; Die Lehrer der Sainte Victoire, 1980; Kindergeschichte, 1981; Uber die Dörfer, 1981; Die Geschichte des Bleistifts, 1982; Der Chinese des Schmerzes, 1983; Die Wiederholung, 1986; Die Abwesenheit, 1987; Nachmittag eines Schriftstellers, 1987; Versuch über die Müdigkeit, 1989; Noch einmal für Thukydides, 1990; Versuch über die Jukebox, 1990; Versuch über den geglückten Tag: Ein Wintertagtraum, 1991; Abschied des Träumers von Neunten Land: Eine Wirklichkeit, die vergangen ist: Erinnerung an Slowenien, 1991; Langsam in Schatten: Gesammelte Verzettelungen 1980-91, 1993; Theaterstücke in einem Band, 1993; Mein Jahre in der Niemandsbucht, 1994; Letzte Bilder?, 1995; Eine winterliche Reise zu den Flüssen Donau, Save, Morawa und Drina oder Gerechtigkeit für Serbien, 1996. Honours: Gerhart Hauptmann Prize, 1967; Schiller Prize, Mannheim, 1972; Büchner Prize, 1973; Kafka Prize, 1979; Salzburg Literary Prize, 1986; Franz Grillparzer Prize, Hamburg, 1991; Drama Prize, Goethe Institute, Munich, 1993; Prize of Honour of the Schiller Memorial Prize, 1995. Address: c/o Suhrkamp Verlag, Lindenstrasse 29, D-60325 Frankfurt am Main, Germany.

HANDLIN Oscar, b. 29 Sept 1915, New York, New York, USA. Professor of History; Writer. m. (1) Mary Flug, 18 Sept 1937, 1 son, 2 daughters, (2) Lilian Bombach, 17 June 1977. Education: AB, Brooklyn College, 1934; AM, 1935, LLD, 1940, Harvard University. Appointments: Instructor, Brooklyn College, 1936-38; Instructor, 1939-44, Assistant Professor, 1944-48, Associate Professor, 1948-54, Professor, 1954- , of History, Director, Center for the Study of Liberty in America, 1958-66, Winthrop Professor of History, 1962-65, Charles Warren Professor of History, 1965-72, Director, Charles Warren Center for Studies in American History, 1965-72, Carl H Pforzheimer University Professor, 1972-84, Director, University Library, 1979-84, Carl M Loeb University Professor, 1984-86, Harvard University; Harmsworth Professor, Oxford University, 1972-73. Publications: Boston's Immigrants, 1941; Commonwealth, 1947; This Was America, 1949; The Uprooted, 1951, 2nd edition, 1973; The American People in the Twentieth Century, 1954; Adventure in Freedom, 1954; Chance or Destiny, 1955; Race and Nationality in American Life, 1956; Readings in American History, 1957, revised edition, 1970; Al Smith and His America, 1958; Immigration as a Factor in American History, 1959; The Newcomers: Negroes and Puerto Ricans in a Changing Metropolis, 1959; American Principles and Issues, 1961; The Dimensions of Liberty, 1961; The Americans, 1963; Fire-Bell in the Night, 1964; Children of the Uprooted, 1966; Popular Sources of Political Authority, 1967; History of the United States, 1967; America: A History, 1968; The American College and American Culture,

1970; Statue of Liberty, 1971; Facing Life: Youth and the Family in American History, 1971; A Pictorial History of Immigration, 1972; The Wealth of the American People, 1975; Truth in History, 1979, revised edition, 1997; Abraham Lincoln and the Union, 1980; The Distortion of America, 1981, revised edition, 1996; Liberty and Power, 1986; Liberty in Expansion, 1989; Liberty in Peril, 1992; Liberty and Equality, 1994; From the Outer Worlds, 1997. Contributions to: Scholarly journals. Honours: J H Dumning Prize, American History Association, 1941; Award of Honor, Brooklyn College, 1945; Pulitzer Prize in History, 1952; Guggenheim Fellowship, 1954; Christopher Award, 1958; Robert H Lord Award, 1972; Many honorary doctorates. Memberships: American Academy of Arts and Sciences, fellow; American Jewish Historical Society; Colonial Society of Massachusetts; Massachusetts Historical Society. Address: 18 Agassiz Street, Cambridge, MA 02140, USA.

HANKINSON Alan, b. 25 May 1926, Gatley, Cheshire, England. Writer. m. Roberta Lorna Gibson, 15 Dec 1951, div 1985, 1 son. Education: MA, History, Magdalen College, Oxford, 1949. Publications: The First Tigers, 1972; Camera on the Crags, 1975; The Mountain Men, 1977; Man of Wars, 1982; The Blue Box, 1983; The Regatta Men, 1988; A Century on the Crags, 1988; Coleridge Walks the Fells, 1991; Geoffrey Winthrop Young, 1995; Twelve Miles from a Lemon, 1996. Contributions to: Cumbria Life. Honours: Runner-Up, BP Arts Journalism, 1991; Portico Prize, 1991; Cumbria Book of the Year, 1992; Boardman Tasker Award, 1995. Address: 30 Skiddaw Street, Keswick, Cumbria CA12 4BY, England.

HANLEY Clifford (Henry Calvin), b. 28 Oct 1922, Glasgow, Scotland. Writer; Dramatist. m. Anna Clark, 10 Jan 1948, 1 son, 2 daughters. Education: Eastbank Academy, Glasgow. Appointments: Professor of Creative Writing, York University, Toronto, 1979. Publications: Dancing in the Streets, 1958; The Taste of Too Much, 1960; Nothing But the Best, 1964; Prissy, 1978; The Scots, 1980; Another Street Another Dance, 1983. Plays: The Durable Element, 1961; Oh For an Island, 1966; Dick McWhittie, 1967; Jack O'The Cudgel, 1969; Oh Glorious Jubilee, 1970; The Clyde Moralities, 1972. Contributions to: Numerous articles in magazines and journals. Honour: Oscar for Best Foriegn Documentary, 1960. Memberships: Ours Club, Glasgow, president; PEN, Scottish president, 1975. Address: 35 Hamilton Drive, Glasgow, Scotland.

HANNAH Barry, b. 23 Apr 1942, Meridian, Mississippi, USA. Author. Div, 3 sons. Education: BA, Mississippi College, Clinton, 1964; MA, 1966, MFA, 1967, University of Arkansas. Appointments: Teacher, Clemson University, 1967-73, University of Alabama, Tuscaloosa, 1975-80; Writer-in-Residence, Middlebury College, Vermont, 1974-75, University of Iowa, 1981, University of Mississippi, University, 1982, 1984-85, University of Montana, Missoula, 1982-83. Publications: Geronimo Rex, 1972; Nightwatchmen, 1973; Airships, 1978; Ray, 1981; Two Stories, 1982; Black Butterfly, 1982; Power and Light, 1983; The Tennis Handsome, 1983; Captain Maximus, 1985; Hey Jack!, 1987; Boomerang, 1989; Never Die, 1991; Bats Out of Hell, 1993. Contributions to: Magazines. Honours: Bellaman Foundation Award, 1970; Atherton Fellowship, Bread Loaf Writers Conference, 1971; Arnold Gingrich Award, Esquire Magazine, 1978; American Academy of Arts and Letters Award, 1978. Address: c/o NAL/Dutton, 375 Hudson Street, New York, NY 10014, USA.

HANNAM June, b. 10 Nov 1947, Southampton, England. University Lecturer. div, 1 son, 1 daughter. Education: BA, History, Warwick University, 1969; MA, Labour History, Warwick, 1970; PhD, Sheffield University, 1984. Appointments: Associate Lecturer, North East London Polytechnic, 1971-73; Lecturer, Bristol Poly, 1973-86; Principal Lecturer, Bristol Poly/UWE, Bristol, 1987-. Publications: In the Comradeship of the Sekes... Women in the West Riding ILP, 1890-1914, 1987; Isabella Ford, 1855-1924, 1989; Women, History and Protest, 1993, 1997; Women and Politics, 1995. Address: Faculty Humanities, St Mathias, Uwe, Bristol BS16 2JP, England.

HANNON Ezra. See: **LOMBINO Salvatore A.**

HANSEN Joseph, (Rose Brock, James Colton, James Coulton), b. 19 July 1923, Aberdeen, South Dakota, USA. Author. m. Jane Bancroft, 4 Aug 1943, 1 daughter. Education: Public Schools. Publications: Lost on Twilight Road, 1964; Strange Marriage, 1965; The Corruptor and Other Stories, 1968; Known Homosexual, 1968, revised edition as Stranger to Himself, 1977, republished as Pretty Boy Dead, 1984; Cocksure, 1969; Gard, 1969; Hang-Up, 1969; Fadeout, 1970; The Outward Side, 1971; Tarn House, 1971; Todd, 1971; Death Claims, 1973; Longleaf, 1974; Troublemaker, 1975; One Foot in the Boat (poems), 1977; The Man Everybody Was Afraid Of, 1978; Skinflick, 1979; The Dog and Other Stories, 1979; A Smile in His Lifetime, 1981; Gravedigger, 1982; Backtrack, 1982; Job's Year, 1983; Nightwork, 1984; Brandsetter and Others: Five Fictions, 1984; Steps Going Down, 1985; The Little Dog Laughed, 1986; Early Graves, 1987; Bohannon's Book: Five Mysteries, 1988; Obedience, 1988; The Boy Who Was Buried This Morning, 1990; A Country of Old Men, 1991; Living Upstairs, 1993; Bohannon's Country (short stories), 1993. Contributions to: Anthologies and periodicals. Honours: National Endowment for the Arts Grant, 1974; Outstanding Literary Contribution to the Lesbian and Gay Communities Citation, Out/Look Foundation, San Francisco, 1991. Memberships: Mystery Writers of America; PEN; Private Eye Writers of America. Address: 2638 Cullen Street, Los Angeles, CA 90034, USA.

HANSEN Poul Einer, b. 24 Mar 1939, Hoeve, Denmark. Associate Professor of Mathematics; Writer; Translator. m. Jette Cassias, 29 May 1993, dec. Education: Cand Mag et Mag Scient, 1962. Publications: The Count of Monte Cristo (translation), 1991; Various books for children and adolescents (in translation), 1992-98; Af Gammel Jehannes hans Bivelskistarri, modern part, 1993; Politisk Korrekt (with Roald Als), 1995; Fodfejl og Pletskud (with Roald Als), 1997. Contributions to: Periodicals. Address: Vester Soegade 18, 2 th, DK-1601 Copenhagen V, Denmark.

HANSEN Ron, b. 8 Dec 1947, Omaha, Nebraska, USA. Writer. Education: BA, Creighton University, 1970; MFA, University of Iowa, 1974; Stanford University, 1977-78. Appointment: Former Professor of English, Cornell University. Publications: The Desperadoes, 1979; The Assassination of Jesse James by the Coward Robert Ford, 1983; The Shadowmaker, 1986; You Don't Know What Love Is, 1987; Nebraska Stories, 1989; Mariette in Ecstacy: A Novel, 1992; Atticus, 1996. Address: c/o Grove-Atlantic, 841 Broadway, 4th Floor, New York, NY 10003, USA.

HANSON William Stewart, b. 22 Jan 1950, Doncaster, Yorkshire, England. University Lecturer; Archaeologist. m. Lesley Macinnes. Education: BA Ancient History/Archaeology, 1972, PhD Archaeology, 1982, University of Manchester. Publications: Rome's North-West Frontier: The Antonine Wall (co-author), 1983; Agricola and the Conquest of the North, 1987; Scottish Archaeology: New Perceptions (co-editor), 1991. Contributions to: Major academic archaeological and antiquarian journals and collected works. Memberships: Fellow, Societies of Antiquaries of London and Scotland. Address: 4 Victoria Road, Stirling, Scotland.

HANVIK Jan Michael, b. 9 Nov 1950, Minnesota, USA. Arts Administrator; Writer. Education: BFA, City College, City University of New York, 1982; MA, New York University, 1985. Appointments: Executive Director, Pan-American Musical Art Research, 1986; Guest Lecturer, National Institute of Fine Arts, Mexico, 1995-96. Publication: Twentieth Century Cultures. Contributions to: Caribbean Review; Americas; Dance Magazine; Zona de Danza; International Encyclopedia of Dance. Honours; Fulbright Scholar Award, 1990-91, 1999. Literary Agent: Mitchell Rose. Address: 179 East 3rd Street #24, NY 10009, USA.

HARBINSON-BRYANS Robert, (Robin Bryans), b. 24 Apr 1928, Belfast, Northern Ireland. Author. Publications: Gateway to the Khyber, 1959; Madeira, 1959; Summer Saga, 1960; No Surrender, 1960; Song of Erne, 1960; Up Spake the Cabin Boy, 1961; Danish Episode, 1961; Tattoo Lily, 1962; Fanfare for Brazil, 1962; The Protégé, 1963; The Azores, 1963; Ulster, 1964; Lucio, 1964; Malta and Gozo, 1966; The Field of Sighing, 1966; Trinidad and Tobago, 1967; Faber Best True Adventure Stories (editor), 1967; Sons of El Dorado, 1968; Crete, 1969; The Dust Has Never Settled, 1992; Let the Petals Fall, 1993; Checkmate, 1994, Blackmail and Whitewash, 1996. Address: 90 Ferrymead Avenue, Greenford, Middlesex, UB6 9TN, England.

HARCOURT Geoffrey (Colin), b. 27 June 1931, Melbourne, Australia. Academic; Professor Emeritus; Economist; Writer. m. Joan Margaret Bartrop, 30 July 1955, 2 sons, 2 daughters. Education: BCom, Honours, 1954, MCom, 1956, University of Melbourne; PhD, 1960, LittD, 1988, Cambridge University. Appointments: Professor Emeritus, University of Adelaide, 1988; President, Jesus College, Cambridge, 1988-89, 1990-92; Reader in the History of Economic Theory, Cambridge University, 1990. Publications: Economic Activity (with P.H. Karmel and R.H. Wallace), 1967; Readings in the Concept and Measurement of Income (editor, with R.H. Parker), 1969; Capital and Growth: Selected Readings (editor, with N.F. Laing), 1971; Some Cambridge Controversies in the Theory of Capital, 1972; The Microeconomic Foundations of Macroeconomics (editor), 1977; The Social Science Imperialists (selected essays), 1982; Controversies in Political Economy (selected essays), 1986; Readings in the Concept and Measurement of Income (editor, with R H Parker and G Whittington), 2nd edition, 1986; Keynes and His Contemporaries: The Sixth and Centennial Keynes Seminar Held in the University of Kent at Canterbury (editor), 1983; On Political Economists and Modern Political Economy (selected essays), 1992; Post-Keynesian Essays in Biography: Portraits of Twentieth Century Political Economists, 1993; The Dynamics of the Wealth of Nations: Essays in Honour of Luigi Pasinetti (editor, with Mauro Baranzino), 1993; Income and Employment in Theory and Practice (editor with Alessandro Ronlaglia and Robin Rowley), 1994; Capitalism, Socialism and Post-Keynesianism: Selected Essays, 1995; A "Second Edition" of The General Theory (editor, with P A Riach), 2 volumes, 1997. Contributions to: Many books and scholarly journals. Honours: Economic Society of Australia, distinguished fellow, 1996; Honorary DLitt, De Montfort University, 1997; Honorary Fellow, Queen's College, University of Melbourne, 1998. Memberships: Fellow, Academy of the Social Sciences in Australia, 1971; President, Economic Society of Australia and New Zealand, 1974-77; Officer in the General Division of the Order of Australia (AO), 1994; Royal Economic Society. Address: Jesus College, Cambridge CB5 8BL, England.

HARCOURT Palma, Author. Publications: Climate for Conspiracy, 1974; A Fair Exchange, 1975; Dance for Diplomats, 1976; At High Risk, 1977; Agents of Influence, 1978; A Sleep of Spies, 1979; Tomorrow's Treason, 1980; A Turn of Traitors, 1981; The Twisted Tree, 1982; Shadows of Doubt, 1983; The Distant Stranger, 1984; A Cloud of Doves, 1985; A Matter of Conscience, 1986; Limited Options, 1987; Clash of Loyalties, 1988; Cover for a Traitor, 1989; Double Deceit, 1990; The Reluctant Defector, 1991; Cue for Conspiracy, 1992; Bitter Betrayal, 1993; The Vermont Myth, 1994; Shadows of the Past, 1996. Address: c/o Murray Pollinger, Literary Agent, 222 Old Brompton Road, London, SW5 0BZ, England.

HARDCASTLE Michael (David Clark), b. 6 Feb 1933, Huddersfield, England. Author. m. Barbara Ellis Shepherd, 30 Aug 1979, 4 daughters. Appointment: Literary Editor, Bristol Evening Post, 1960-65. Publications: Author of over 100 children's books, 1966-; One Kick, 1986; James and the TV Star, 1986; Mascot, 1987; Quake, 1988; The Green Machine, 1989; Walking the Goldfish, 1990; Penalty, 1990; Advantage Miss Jackson, 1991; Dog Bites Goalie, 1993; One Good

Horse, 1993; Soccer Captain, 1994; Puzzle, 1995; Please Come Home, 1995; Matthew's Goals, 1997; Carole's Camel, 1997; The Price of Football, 1998; Shoot-Out, 1998; Eye for a Goal, 1998; Goal-Getter, 1999; Injury Time, 1999; Rivals United, 1999. Contributions to: Numerous articles in magazines and journals. Honour: Member of the Order of the British Empire, 1988. Memberships: Federation of Children's Book Groups, national chair, 1989-90; Society of Authors; Society for Storytelling. Address: 17 Molescroft Park, Beverley, East Yorkshire HU17 7EB, England.

HARDEN Blaine (Charles), b. 4 Apr 1952, Moses Lake, Washington, USA. Journalist. Education: BA, Philosophy and Political Science, Gonzaga University, 1974; MA, Journalism, Syracuse University, 1976. Appointments: Africa Correspondent, 1985-89, East European Correspondent, 1989-93, Reporter, 1995-, Washington Post. Publications: Africa: Dispatches From a Fragile Continent, 1990; A River Lost: The Life and Death of Columbia, 1996. Contributions to: Washington Post. Honours: Livingston Award for Young Journalists, 1986; Martha Albrand Citation for First Book of Non-Fiction, PEN, 1991; Ernie Pyle Award for Human Interest Reporting, 1993. Address: c/o Washington Post, 1150 15th Street North West, Washington, DC 20071, USA.

HARDIE (Katherine) Melissa, b. 20 Apr 1939, Houston, Texas, USA. Writer; Publisher; Collector. m. (1) J W Woelfel, 1958, 2 daughters, (2) M C Hardie, 1974, (3) Philip Graham Budden, 8 Jan 1986. Education: BA, English Language and Literature, Boston University, 1961; SRN, St Thomas Hospital, England, 1969; PhD, Social Science, Edinburgh University, 1980. Appointments: Publisher, Patten Press, 1981-; Director, Jamieson Library of Women's History, 1986-; Editor and Publisher, Hypatia Publications Forum. Publications: Understanding Ageing, Facing Common Family Problems, 1978; Nursing Auxiliaries in Health Care, 1978; In Time & Place, Lamorna, Life of E Lamorna Kerr, 1990; A Mere Interlude, Some Literary Visitors to Lyonnesse (editor), 1992; One Hundred Years at Newlyn, Diary of a Gallery (editor), 1995. Contributions to: Nursing Times; International Hospitals; Social Work Today; Health & Social Service Journal. Honours: Winston Churchill Travelling Fellow, 1975; YWCA Woman of the West, 1994; Honorary Fellow, Exeter University. Memberships: Thomas Hardy Society; West Country Writers Association; Private Libraries Association; Trustee, Company Secretary, The Hypatia Trust 1996-; Director, The Hypatia Institute, 1998-. Address: The Old Post Office, New Mill, Penzance TR20 8XN, England.

HARDING James, b. 1929, England. Appointments: Senior Lecturer in French, University of Greenwich, 1966-94. Publications: Saint-Saëns and His Circle, 1965; The Duke of Wellington, 1968; Massenet, 1970; Rossini, 1971; The Ox on the Roof, 1972; Lord Chesterfield's Letters to his Son, 1973; Erik Satie, 1975; Poulenc: My Friends and Myself (translator), 1978; Folies de Paris: The Rise and Fall of the French Operetta, 1979; Offenbach, 1980; Maurice Chevalier, 1982; Jacques Tati: Frame by Frame, 1984; James Agate, 1986; Ivor Novello, 1987; The Rocky Horror Show Book, 1987; Gerald du Maurier, 1989; George Robey and the Music Hall, 1991; Emlyn Williams, A Life, 1993. Membership: Fellow, The Royal Society of Literature. Literary Agent: Peake Associates, 14 Grafton Crescent, London NW1 8SL. Address: 100 Ridgmount Gardens, Torrington Place, London WC1E 7AZ, England.

HARDING Karl Gunnar, b. 11 June 1940, Sundsvalla, Sweden. Poet; Translator; Critic; Editor. m. Ann Charlotte Jending, Sept 1966, 1 son, 3 daughters. Education: BA, University of Uppsala, 1967. Appointments: Editor, FIB: Lyrikklabb and Magazine, Lyrikvannen, 1971-74; Poetry Critic, Expressen, Daily Paper, 1970-88; Editor, Artes Magazine, 1989. Publications: Blommortil James Dean, 1969; Ballander, 1975; Starnberger See, 1977; Stjarndykaren, 1987; Mitt Vinterland, 1991; Vortex, 1990; Kreol, 1991. Contributions to: Evergreen Review; Ambit. Honours: Lifetime Scholarship, Swedish Writer's Union;

Several Poetry Prizes. Memberships: Vice President, Swedish PEN, 1975-78; Swedish Writer's Union; Swedish Bunk Johnson Society. Address: Vasterled 206, S-16142, Bromma, Sweden.

HARDING Matt. See: **FLOREN Lee.**

HARDWICK Elizabeth, b. 27 July 1916, Lexington, Kentucky, USA. Writer; Critic; Teacher. m. Robert Lowell, 28 July 1949, div 1972, 1 daughter. Education: AB, 1938, MA, 1939, University of Kentucky; Columbia University. Appointments: Co-Founder and Advisory Editor, New York Review of Books, 1963-; Adjunct Associate Professor of English, Barnard College. Publications: Fiction: The Ghostly Lover, 1945; The Simple Truth, 1955; Sleepless Nights, 1979. Non-fiction: The Selected Letters of William James (editor), 1960; A View of My Own: Essays on Literature and Society, 1962; Seduction and Betrayal: Women and Literature, 1974; Rediscovered Fiction by American Women: A Personal Selection (editor), 18 volumes, 1977; Bartleby in Manhattan (essays), 1984; The Best American Essays 1986 (editor), 1986; Sight Readings: American Fictions (essays), 1998. Contributions to: Periodicals. Honour: Gold Medal, American Academy and Institute of Arts and Letters, 1993. Address: 15 West 67th Street, New York, NY 10023, USA.

HARDY Barbara (Gladys), b. England. Writer; Lecturer. Appointments: Emeritus Professor, University of London, Birkbeck College; Honorary Professor, University of Wales, Swansea; Honorary Fellowship, Birkbeck College; Honorary Fellowship, Royal Holloway College; Honorary Fellowship, University of Wales, Swansea. Publications: The Novels of George Eliot: A Study in Form, 1959; Wuthering Heights, 1963; The Appropriate Form: An Essay on the Novel, 1964; Jane Eyre, 1964; Middlemarch: Critical Approaches to the Novel, 1967; Charles Dickens: The Later Novels, 1968; Critical Essays on George Eliot, 1970; The Moral Art of Dickens, 1970; The Exposure of Luxury: Radical Themes in Thackeray, 1972; Tellers and Listeners: The Narrative Imagination, 1975; A Reading of Jane Austen, 1976; The Advantage of Lyric: Essays on Feeling in Poetry, 1976; Particularities: Readings in George Eliot, 1983; Forms of Feeling in Victorian Fiction, 1985; Narrators and Novelists, 1989; Swansea Girl, 1994; London Lovers, 1996; Henry James: The Later Writing, 1996; Shakespeares Storytellers, 1997. Honours: Rose Mary Crawshay Prize, 1962; Sagittarius Award, 1997. Memberships: Modern Language Association, honorary member; Welsh Academy, fellow; George Eliot Fellowship; Thomas Hardy Society; Royal Society of Literature, fellow. Address Birkbeck College, Malet Street, London, WC1E 7HX, England

HARDY Frank, b. 21 Mar 1917, Southern Cross, Victoria, Australia. Novelist. Appointments: President, Realist Writers Group, Melbourne, Sydney, 1954-74; Co-Founder, Australian Society of Authors, Sydney, 1968-74; President, Carringbush Writers, Melbourne, 1980-83. Publications: The Four Legged Lottery, 1958; Power Without Glory, 1962; The Outcasts of Follgarah, 1971; Who Shot George Kirkland?, 1981; Warrant of Distress, 1983; The Obsession of Oscar Oswald, 1983. Short Stories: The Loser Now Will be Later to Win, 1985; Hardy's People, 1986. Plays: Black Diamonds, 1956; The Ringbolter, 1964; Who Was Harry Larse, 1985; Faces in the Street: An Epic Drama, 1990. Address: 9/76 Elizabeth Bay Road, Elizabeth Bay, New South Wales 2011, Australia.

HARE David, b. 5 June 1947, St Leonards, Sussex, England. Dramatist; Director. m. (1) Margaret Matheson, 1970, div 1980, 2 sons, 1 daughter, (2) Nicole Farhi, 1992. Education: Lancing College; MA, Honours, Jesus College, Cambridge. Appointments: Founder, Portable Theatre, 1968, Joint Stock Theatre Group, 1975, Greenpoint Films, 1982; Literary Manager and Resident Dramatist, Royal Court, 1969-71; Resident Dramatist, Nottingham Playhouse, 1973; Associate Director, National Theatre, 1984-88, 1989-. Publications: Slag, 1970; The Great Exhibition, 1972; Knuckle, 1974;

Brassneck, 1974; Fanshen, 1976; Teeth 'n' Smiles, 1976; Plenty, 1978; Licking Hitler, 1978; Dreams of Leaving, 1980; A Map of the World, 1982; Saigon, 1983; The History Plays, 1984; Pravda, 1985; Wetherby, 1985; The Asian Plays, 1986; The Bay at Nice and Wrecked Eggs, 1986; The Secret Rapture, 1988; Paris by Night, 1989; Straples, 1990; Racing Demon, 1990; Writing Lefthanded, 1991; Heading Home, 1991; The Early Plays, 1991; Murmuring Judges, 1991; The Absence of War, 1993; Asking Around, 1993; Skylight, 1995; Mother Courage, 1995. Honours: John Llewellyn Rhys Award, 1974; BAFTA Award, 1978; New York Drama Critics' Circle Award, 1983; London Standard Award, 1985; Plays and Players Awards, 1985, 1990; Drama Award, 1988; Olivier Award, 1990; Critic's Circle Best Play of the Year, 1990; Time Out Award, 1990. Membership: Royal Society of Literature, fellow. Address: c/o Margaret Ramsay Ltd, 14a Goodwins Court, St Martins Lane, London WC2, England.

HARFIELD Alan, b. 12 Dec 1926, Gosport, Hampshire, England. Author. m. June Bowler, 6 June 1966, 1 daughter. Publications: A History of the Village of Chilmark, 1961; The Royal Brunei Malay Regiment, English and Malay, 1977; Headdress and Badges of the Royal Signals, 1982; British and Indian Armies in the East Indies, 1984; Blandford and the Military, 1984; Christian Cemeteries and Memorials in Malacca, 1984; Bencoolen, the Christian Cemetery and the Fort Marlborough Monuments, 1986; Early Signalling Equipment, 1986; Christian Cemeteries of Penang and Perak, 1987; Early Cemeteries in Singapore, 1988; Pigeon to Packhorse, 1989; British and Indian Armies on the China Coast 1785-1985, 1990; Indian Army of the Empress 1861-1903, 1990; Meerut: The First Sixty Years 1815-1875, 1992; Bencoolen, A History of the East India Company's Garrison on the West Coast of Sumatra 1685-1825, 1994. Contributions to: Military journals. Honours: Fellow, Royal Historical Society; Fellow, Company of Military Historians, USA; Military, British Empire Medal, 1953; Most Blessed Order of the Setia Negara Brunei 3rd Class. Memberships: Royal Asiatic Society; Company of Military Historians; Military Historical Society; Society for Army Historical Research; Orders and Medals Research Society; Indian Military Historical Society. Address: Plum Tree Cottage, Royston Place, Barton-on-Sea, Hampshire BH25 7AJ, England.

HARGITAI Peter, b. 28 Jan 1947, Budapest, Hungary. Writer. m. Dianne Kress, 24 July 1967, 1 son, 1 daughter. Education: MFA, University of Massachusetts, 1988. Appointments: Lecturer in English, University of Miami, 1980-85, University of Massachusetts, 1987-88; Professor and Writing Specialist, Florida International University, 1990-. Publications: Forum: Ten Poets of the Western Reserve, 1976; Perched on Nothings Branch, 1986; Magyar Tales, 1989; Budapest to Bellevue, 1989; Budapesttöl New Yorkig és tovább..., 1991; Fodois Budget Zion, 1991; The Traveler, 1994; Attila: A Barbarian's Bedtime Story, 1994. Contributions to: North Atlantic Review; Colorado Quarterly; Nimrod; College English; California Quarterly; Spirit; Prairie Schooner; Poetry East; Cornfield Review; Blue Unicorn. Honours: Academy of American Poets Translation Award, 1988; Fulbright Grant, 1988; Florida Arts Council Fellowship, 1990; Fust Milan Award, Hungarian Academy of Sciences, 1994. Memberships: PEN International; Literary Network, New York. Address: Katalin Katai, Artisjus, Budapest, Hungary.

HARGRAVE Leonie. See: **DISCH Thomas M(ichael).**

HARING Firth. See: **FABEND Firth Haring.**

HARITAS. See: **NAGARAJA RAO C K.**

HARJO Joy, b. 9 May 1951, Tulsa, Oklahoma, USA. Poet; Author; Screenwriter; Educator; Musician. 1 son, 1 daughter. Education: BA, University of New Mexico, 1976; MFA, University of Iowa, 1978; Anthropology Film Center, 1982. Appointments: Instructor, Institute of American Indian Arts, 1978-79, 1983-84, Santa Fe Community College, 1983-84; Lecturer, Arizona State

University, 1980-81; Assistant Professor, University of Colorado at Boulder, 1985-88; Associate Professor, University of Arizona at Tucson, 1988-90; Professor, University of New Mexico, 1991-97. Publications: The Last Song, 1975; What Moon Drove Me To This?, 1980; She Had Some Horses, 1983; Secrets From the Center of the World (with Stephen Strom), 1989; In Mad Love and War, 1990; Fishing, 1992; The Woman Who Fell From the Sky, 1994; Reinventing the Enemy's Language, 1997. Contributions to: Many anthologies, magazines, and recordings. Honours: National Endowment for the Arts Creative Writing Fellowships, 1978, 1992; Pushcart Prize, Poetry XIII, 1987-88, and Poetry Anthology XV, 1990; Arizona Commission on the Arts Poetry Fellowship, 1989; American Indian Distinguished Achievement in the Arts Award, 1990; American Book Award, Before Columbus Foundation, 1991; Delmore Schwartz Memorial Award, New York University, 1991; Mountains and Plains Booksellers Award for Best Book of Poetry, 1991; William Carlos Williams Award, Poetry Society of America, 1991; Honorary Doctorate, Benedictine College, 1992; Woodrow Wilson Fellowship, 1993; Witter Bynner Poetry Fellowship, 1994; Lifetime Achievement Award, Native Writers Circle of the Americas, 1995; Oklahoma Book Arts Awards, 1995; Governor's Award for Excellence in the Arts, State of New Mexico, 1997; Lila Wallace-Reader's Digest Writers Award, 1998-2000. Membership: PEN, advisory board; National Council of the Arts. Address: c/o Two Red Horses Inc, 1140 Alewa Drive, Honolulu, HI 96817, USA.

HARKEY Ira Brown Jr, b. 15 Jan 1918, New Orleans, Louisiana, USA. Journalist; Executive; Writer. m. (1) Marie Ella Gore, 1939, div 1962, 3 sons, 3 daughters, (2) Marion Marks Drake, 10 Dec 1963, div 1976, 1 daughter, (3) Virgia Quin Mioton, 24 Feb 1977. Education: BA, Tulane University, 1941; MA, Journalism, PhD, Political Science, Ohio State University. Appointments: Staff, Times-Picayune, New Orleans, 1939-42, 1946-49; Editor, Publisher, and President, The Chronicle, Pascagoula, Mississippi, 1949-63; President, Gulf Coast Times, Ocean Springs, Mississippi, and Advertiser Printing Inc, Pascagoula, 1949-63; Faculty, Ohio State University, 1965-66; Secretary, Vice President, and Director, Oklahoma Coca-Cola Bottling Co Inc, Oklahoma City, 1965-80, and Great Plains Industries, 1979-80; Carnegie Visiting Professor, University of Alaska, 1968-69; Lecturer, University of Montana, 1970, University of Oregon, 1972; President, Indian Creek Co Inc, 1981-83. Publications: Dedicated to the Proposition..., 1963; The Smell of Burning Crosses, 1967; Pioneer Bush Pilot: The Story of Noel Wien, 1974; Alton Ochsner: Surgeon to the South (co-author), 1990. Contributions to: Periodicals. Honours: Puitzer Prize for Distinguished Editorial Writing, 1963; Sidney Hillman Foundation Award, 1963; Sigma Delta Chi National Award for Distinguished Public Service in Newspaper Journalism, 1963; Civil Libertarian of the Year Award, Mississippi Civil Liberties Union, 1992; Hall of Fame, Mississippi Press Association, 1993. Memberships: American Political Science Association; Authors Guild; Delta Kappa Epsilon; Kappa Tau Alpha; Phi Beta Kappa; Pi Sigma Alpha. Address: HCR 5, Box 574-540, Kerrville, TX 78028, USA.

HARKNETT Terry, (Frank Chandler, David Ford, George G Gilman, William M James, Charles R Pike, James Russell, William Terry), b. 14 Dec 1936, Rainham, Essex, England. Writer. Appointments: Editor, Newspaper Features Ltd, 1958-61; Reporter and Features Editor, National Newsagent, 1961-72. Publications: (as George G Gilman), Edge series: The Godforsaken, 1982; Arapaho Revenge, 1983; The Blind Side, 1983; House of the Range, 1983; Edge Meets Steele No 3 Double Action, 1984; The Moving Cage, 1984; School for Slaughter, 1985; Revenge Ride, 1985; Shadow of the Gallows, 1985; A Time for Killing, 1986; Brutal Border, 1986; Hitting Paydirt, 1986; Backshort, 1987; Uneasy Riders, 1987. Adam Steele series: Canyon of Death, 1985; High Stakes, 1985; Rough Justice, 1985; The Sunset Ride, 1986; The Killing Strain, 1986; The Big Gunfight, 1987; The Hunted, 1987; Code of the West, 1987. The Undertaker series: Three Graves to a Showdown, 1982; Back from the Dead, 1982; Death in the Desert, 1982. As William Terry: Red Sun (novelization of screenplay), 1972. As Frank Chandler: A Fistful of Dollars (novelization of screenplay), 1972. As Charles R Pike: Jubal Cade series: The Killing Trail, 1974; Double Cross, 1974; The Hungary Gun, 1975. As William M James: Apache series: The First Death, 1974; Duel to the Death, 1974; Fort Treachery, 1975. As Terry Harknett: The Caribbean, 1972. As James Russell: The Balearic Islands, 1972. As David Ford: Cyprus, 1973. Address: Spring Acre, Springhead Road, Uplyme, Lyme Regis, Dorset DT7 3RS, England.

HARLAN Louis R(udolph), b. 13 July 1922, West Point, Mississippi, USA. Professor Emeritus; Historian. m. Sadie Morton, 6 Sept 1947, 2 sons. Education: BA, Emory University, 1943; MA, Vanderbilt University, 1948; PhD, Johns Hopkins University, 1955. Appointments: Assistant to Associate Professor, East Texas State College, 1950-59; Associate Professor to Professor, University of Cincinnati, 1959-66; Professor of History, 1966-84, Distinguished Professor of History, 1984-92, Professor Emeritus, 1992-, University of Maryland, College Park. Publications: Separate and Unequal, 1958; The Booker T Washington Papers (editor), 14 volumes, 1972-89; Booker T Washington: Volume I, The Making of a Black Leader, 1972, Volume II, The Wizard of Tuskegee, 1983; Booker T Washington in Perspective, 1988. Contributions to: Periodicals. Honours: Bancroft Prizes, 1973, 1984; Guggenheim Fellowship, 1975; Pulitzer Prize in Biography, 1984; Albert J Beveridge Award, 1984; Julian P Boyd Award, 1989; National Historical Publications and Records Commission Award, 1991. Memberships: American Historical Association, president, 1989; Association for the Study of Afro-American Life and History; National Historical Publications and Records Commission; Organization of American Historians, president, 1989-90; Phi Beta Kappa; Phi Kappa Phi; Society of American Historians, fellow. Address: 6924 Pineway, Hyattsville, MD 20782, USA.

HARLE Elizabeth. See: **ROBERTS Irene.**

HARLEMAN Ann, b. 28 Oct 1945, Youngstown, Ohio, USA. Writer; Educator. m. Bruce A Rosenberg, 20 June 1981, 1 daughter. Education: BA, English Literature, Rutgers University, 1967; PhD, Linguistics, Princeton University, 1972; MFA, Creative Writing, Brown University, 1988. Appointments: Assistant Professor of English, Rutgers University, 1973-74; Assistant Professor, 1974-79, Associate Professor of English, 1979-84, University of Washington; Visiting Professor of Rhetoric, Massachusetts Institute of Technology, 1984-86; Visiting Scholar, Programme in American Civilisation, Brown University, 1986-; Cole Distinguished Professor of English, Wheaton College, 1992; Professor of English, Rhode Island School of Design, 1994-. Publications: Graphic Representation of Models in Linguistic Theory, 1976; Ian Fleming: A Critical Biography (with Bruce A Rosenberg), 1989; Mute Phone Calls, (translation of fiction by Ruth Zernova), 1992; Happiness, 1994; Bitter Lake, 1996. Contributions: More than 50 scholarly articles, short stories, poems, reviews. Honours: Guggenheim Fellowship, 1976; Fulbright Fellowship, 1980; Raymond Carver Contest, 1986; MacDowell Colony Fellow, 1988; National Endowment for the Humanities Fellowship, 1989; Rhode Island State Council on the Arts Fellowship, 1990, 1997; PEN Syndicated Fiction Award, 1991; Iowa Short Fiction Prize, 1993; Senior Fellow, American Council of Learned Societies, 1993; Bogliasco Foundation Fellowship, 1998. Memberships: Modern Language Association, chair, general linguistics executive committee; Poets and Writers; PEN American Center. Literary Agent: Richard P. McDonough. Address: 55 Summit Avenue, Providence, RI 02906, USA.

HARMON Maurice, b. 21 June 1930, Dublin, Ireland. Professor Emeritus; Writer; Editor. Education: BA, 1951, HDE, 1953, MA, 1955, PhD, 1961, University College, Dublin; AM, Harvard University, 1957. Appointments: Lecturer in English, 1964-76, Associate Professor of Anglo-Irish Literature and Drama, 1976-90, Professor Emeritus, 1990-, University College, Dublin; Editor, University Review, 1964-68, Irish University Review, 1970-. Publications: Sean O'Faolain: A Critical Introduction, 1966; Modern Irish Literature 1800-1967: A Reader's Guide, 1967; Fenians and Fenianism: Centenary Papers (editor), 1968; The Celtic Master: Contributions to the first James Joyce Symposium, 1969; Romeo and Juliet, by Shakespeare (editor), 1970; J M Synge Centenary Papers 1971 (editor), 1971; King Richard II, by Shakespeare (editor), 1971; Coriolanus, by Shakespeare (editor), 1972; The Poetry of Thomas Kinsella, 1974; The Irish Novel in Our Time (editor with Patrick Rafroidi), 1976; Select Bibliography for the Study of Anglo-Irish Literature and Its Backgrounds, 1976; Richard Murphy: Poet of Two Traditions (editor), 1978; Irish Poetry After Yeats: Seven Poets (editor), 1979, 3rd edition, 1997; Image and Illusion: Anglo-Irish Literature and Its Contexts (editor), 1979; A Short History of Anglo-Irish Literature From Its Origins to the Present (with Roger McHugh), 1982; The Irish Writer and the City (editor), 1985; James Joyce: The Centennial Symposium (with Morris Beja et al), 1986; Austin Clarke: A Critical Introduction, 1989; The Book of Precedence (poems), 1994; Sean O'Faolain: A Life, 1994; A Stillness at Kiowah (poems), 1996; No Author Better Served: The Correspondence of Samuel Becket & Alan Schneider, 1998. Address: 20 Sycamore Road, Mount Merrion, Blackrock, County Dublin, Ireland.

HARPER Marjory-Ann Denoon, b. 6 Apr 1956, Blackpool, Lancashire, England. University Lecturer. m. Andrew J Shere, 22 Aug 1991. Education: MA, Honours, History, 1978, PhD, 1984, University of Aberdeen. Publications: Emigration from North East Scotland: Willing Exiles, 1988; Emigration from North East Scotland: Beyond the Broad Atlantic, 1988; Emigration from Scotland between the Wars: Opportunity or Exile, forthcoming Contributions to: History Today; British Journal of Canadian Studies; Northern Scotland; Southwestern Historical Quarterly; Aberdeen Leopard; The Weekend Scotsman; Glasgow Herald; The Highlander. Memberships: Royal Historical Society, fellow; British Association of Canadian Studies. Address: Department of History, University of Aberdeen, Old Aberdeen AB9 2UB, Scotland.

HARPER Michael S(teven), b. 18 Mar 1938, New York, New York, USA. Professor of English; Poet. m. 3 children. Education: BA, 1961, MA, 1963, California State University at Los Angeles; MA, University of Iowa Writers Workshop, 1963; ad eundem, Brown University, 1972. Appointments: Visiting Professor, Lewis and Clark College, 1968-69, Reed College, 1968-69, Harvard University, 1974-77, Yale University, 1976; Professor of English, Brown University, 1970-; Benedict Distinguished Professor, Carleton College, 1979; Elliston Poet and Distinguished Professor, University of Cincinnati, 1979; National Endowment for the Humanities Professor, Colgate University, 1985; Distinguished Minority Professor, University of Delaware, 1988, Macalester College, 1989; 1st Poet Laureate of the State of Rhode Island, 1988-93; Phi Beta Kappa Visiting Scholar, 1991; Berg Distinguished Visiting Professor, New York University, 1992. Publications: Dear John, Dear Coltrane, 1970; History is Your Own Heartbeat, 1971; History as Apple Tree, 1972; Song: I Want a Witness, 1972; Debridement, 1973; Nightmare Begins Responsibility, 1975; Images of Kin, 1977; Chant of Saints (co-editor), 1979; Healing Song for the Inner Ear, 1985; Songlines: Mosaics, 1991; Every Shut Eye Ain't Asleep, 1994; Honorable Admendments, 1995; Collected Poems, 1996. Honours: Black Academy of Arts and Letters Award, 1972; National Institute of Arts and Letters Grants, 1975, 1976, 1985; Guggenheim Fellowship, 1976; Melville Cane Award, Poetry Society of America, 1978; Governor's Poetry Award, Rhode Island Council of the Arts, 1987; Robert Hayden Memorial Poetry Award, United Negro College Fund, 1990; Literary Lion, New York Public Library, 1992; Honorary doctorates. Membership: American Academy of Arts and Sciences. Address: c/o Department of English, Brown University, Providence, RI 02912, USA.

HARPER Stephen (Dennis), b. 15 Sept 1924, Newport, Monmouthshire, Wales. Journalist; Writer. Publications: Novels: A Necessary End, 1975; Mirror Image, 1976; Live Till Tomorrow, 1977. Non-Fiction: Last Sunset, 1978; Miracle of Deliverance, 1985. Membership: Society of Authors. Address: Green Dene Lodge, Greene Dene, East Horsley, Surrey, England.

HARRIS Bruce Wayne, b. 19 Nov 1953, San Antonio, Texas, USA. Mining Consultant. m. Sharon L Huddleston, 4 Apr 1978. Education: GED, 1970. Publictions: Gold Miner's Handbook, 1994; Modern Gold Dredging, 1998. Address: c/o Heavy Metal Mining Company, PO Box 8256, Springfield, MO 65801-8256, USA.

HARRIS Eddy, b. 26 Jan 1956, Indiana, USA. Author; Travel Writer; Essayist; Professor. Education: BA, Stanford University, 1977. Appointments: Writer in Residence, Visiting Professor of African and African American Studies, Washington University, St Louis, MO, USA. Publications: Missiissppi Solo, 1988; Native Stranger, 1992; South of Haunted Dreams, 1993; Still Life in Harlem, 1996. Address: Sterling Lord Literistic. Address: 65 Bleecker Street, New York, NY 10012, USA.

HARRIS Francis C, b. 25 Sept 1957, Brooklyn, New York, USA. Author; Historian. Education: Masters of Education/Management, Cambridge College, Massachusetts, 1992-. Publication: The Amistad Pictorial History of the African American Athlete (with Charles F Harris Jr), 1999. Contribution to: Paul Robeson: Artist and Citizen (essays), 1998. Address: 140-35 Burden Crescent, No 207, Briarwood, New York 11435, USA.

HARRIS Harry, b. 30 May 1952, London, England. Journalist; Chief Football Writer. Education: Harlow College; Newcastle Chronical - London Evening News. Appointments: Daily Mail Football Reporter; Daily Mirror Chief Football Writer. Publications: Terry Neill Autobiography; Steve McMahon Autobiography; Bill Nicholson Autobiography; Glenn Hoddle Autobiography: Spurred to Success; The Jurgen Klinsmann Diary; Against All Odds: Gary Mabbutt Autobiography; Rock Bottom: The Paul Merson Autobiography; Portrait of a Genius, The Ruud Gullit Biography; Gullit - The Chelsea Diary - Zola Biography; Ruud Gullit Autobiography - The Road to France (World Cup Book). Honours: Race in the Media Awards, Runner Up, 1993; British Sports Writer of the Year, 1993, 1998; Sports Council Reporter of the Year, 1993, Runner Up, 1998. Memberships: Football Writers Association, Sports Writers Association. Literary Agent: Robert Kirby, Peters, Fraser, Dunlop.

HARRIS Jana, b. 21 Sept 1947, San Francisco, California, USA. Writer; Poet; Instructor. m. Mark Allen Bothwell. Education: BS, University of Oregon, 1969; MA, San Francisco State University, 1972. Appointments: Instructor, Creative Writing, New York University, 1980, University of Washington, 1986-, Pacific Lutheran University, 1988. Publications: This House That Rocks with Every Truck on the Road, 1976; Pin Money, 1977; The Clackamas, 1980; Alaska (novel), 1980; Who's That Pushy Bitch?, 1981; Running Scared, 1981; Manhattan as a Second Language, 1982; The Sourlands: Poems by Jana Harris, 1989; Oh How Can I Keep on Singing: Voices of Pioneer Women (poems), 1993; The Dust of Everyday Life (poems); The Pearl of Ruby City (novel), 1998. Contributions to: Periodicals. Honours: Berkeley Civic Arts Commemoration Grant, 1974; Washington State Arts Council Fellowship, 1993. Memberships: Feminist Writers Guild; Associated Writing Programs; Women's Salon; PEN: Poetry Society of America; National Book Critics Club. Address: 32814 120th Street South East, Sultan, WA 98294, USA.

HARRIS Jocelyn Margaret, b. 10 Sept 1939, Dunedin, New Zealand. University Teacher; Writer. 1 son, 1 daughter. Education: MA, University of Otago; PhD, University of London. Appointments: Personal Chair, Department of English, University of Otago. Publications: Samuel Richardson: Sir Charles Grandison (editor), 1972; Samuel Richardson, 1989; Jane Austen's Art of Memory, 1989; Samuel Richardson's Published Commentary on Clarissa, 1747-1765, Vol I (editor with Tom Keymer). Contributions to: Scholarly journals. Membership: Australian and South Pacific 18th Century Society. Address: c/o Department of English, University of Otago, Box 56, Dunedin, New Zealand.

HARRIS Kenneth, b. 11 Nov 1919. Journalist; Author; Business Executive. m. (1) Doris Young-Smith, 1949, dec 1970, (2) Jocelyn Rymer, 1987. Education: Wadham College, Oxford. Appointments: War Service, R.A, 1940-45; Washington Correspondent, 1950-53, Associate Editor, 1976-, Director, 1978, The Observer; Radio and TV work (mainly for BBC), 1957-; Chairman, George Outram Ltd, The Observer Group, 1981-. Publications: Travelling Tongues: Debating Across America, 1949; About Britain, 1967; Conversations, 1968; Life of Attlee, 1982; The Wildcatter: The Life of Robert O Anderson; David Owen, 1987; Thatcher, 1988. Address: The Observer, Chelsea Bridge House, Queenstown Road, London SW8, England.

HARRIS Marion Rose, (Rose Glendower, Marion Rose), b. 12 July 1925, Cardiff, South Wales. Author. m. Kenneth Mackenzie Harris, 18 Aug 1943, 2 sons, 1 daughter. Appointments: Editor/Owner, Regional Feature Service, 1964-74; Editorial Controller, W Foulsham and Co Ltd, 1974-82. Publications: Captain of Her Heart, 1976; Just a Handsome Stranger, 1983; The Queen's Windsor, 1985; Soldiers' Wives, 1986; Officers' Ladies, 1987; Nesta, 1988; Amelda, 1989; Sighing for the Moon (as Rose Glendower), 1991; To Love and Love Again (as Rose Young), 1993. Memberships: Society of Authors; Romantic Novelists Association; Welsh Academy. Address: Walpole Cottage, Long Drive, Burnham, Slough SL1 8AJ, England.

HARRIS Mark, b. 19 Nov 1922, Mount Vernon, New Hork, USA. Professor of English (Retired); Author. m. Josephine Horen, 17 Mar 1946, 2 sons, 1 daughter. Education: BA, 1950, MA, 1951, University of Denver; PhD, University of Minnesota, 1956. Appointments: Newsman, Daily Item, Port Chester, New York, 1944; PM, New York City, 1945, International News Service, St Louis, 1945-46; Writer, Negro Digest, Ebony, 1946-51; Faculty, Department of English, University of Minnesota, 1951-54, San Francisco State College, 1954-68, Prudue University, 1968-70, California Institute of the Arts, 1970-73, Immaculate Heart College, 1973-74, University of Southern California at Los Angeles, 1974-75; Fulbright Professor, University of Hiroshima, 1957-58; Visiting Professor, Brandeis University, 1963; Professor of English, University of Pittsburgh, 1975-80, Arizona State University, Tempe, 1980-94. Publications: Trumpet to the World, 1946; City of Discontent: An Interpretive Biography of Vachel Lindsay, Being Also the Story of Springfield, Illinois, USA, and of the Love of the Poet for That City, That State, and That Nation, 1952; The Southpaw, by Henry W Wiggen: Punctuation Freely Inserted and Spelling Greatly Improved by Mark Harris, 1953, new edition, 1963; Bang the Drum Slowly, by Henry W Wiggen: Certain of His Enthusiams Restrained by Mark Harris, 1956; Something About a Soldier, 1957; A Ticket for a Seamstich, by Henry W Wiggen: But published for the Printer by Mark Harris, 1957; Wake Up, Stupid, 1959; Mark the Glove Boy, or, The Last Days of Richard Nixon, 1964, new edition, 1972, Twentyone Twice: A Journal, 1966; The Goy, 1970; Killing Everybody, 1973; Best Father Ever Invented: The Autobiography of Mark Harris, 1976; The Design of Fiction (editor with Josephine Harris and Hester Harris), 1976; It Looked Like for Ever, 1979; Short Work of It: Selected Writings by Mark Harris, 1980; The Heart of Boswell: Six Journals in One Volume (editor), 1980; Saul Bellow: Drumlin Woodchuck, 1980; Lying in Bed, 1984; Speed, 1990; The Tale Maker, 1994; Diamond; Baseball Writings of Mark Harris, 1994. Honours: Ford Foundation Grant, 1960; National Institute of Arts and Letters Award, 1961; Guggenheim Fellowships, 1965-66, 1974; National Endowment for the Arts Grant, 1966; DHL, Illinois Wesleyan University, 1974. Address: 2014 East Balboa Drive, Tempe, AZ 85282, USA.

HARRIS Philip Robert, b. 22 Jan 1926, New York, New York, USA. Management Consultant; Writer; Editor. m. Dorothy Lipp, 3 July 1965, dec 30 December 1997. Education: BBA, St John's University, 1949; New York University, 1948-49; MS Psychology, 1952, PhD, 1956, Fordham University; Syracuse University, 1961. Appointments: Director of Guidance, St Francis Preparatory School, New York City, 1952-56; Director of Student Personnel and Vice-President, St Francis College, New York City, 1956-63; Fulbright Professor to India, 1962-63; Visiting Professor, Pennsylvania State University, 1965-66; Senior Associate, Leadership Resources Inc, 1966-69; Vice-President, Copley International Corp, 1970-71; President, Management and Organizational Development Inc, and its successor, Harris International Ltd, La Jolla, California, 1971-; Research Associate, California Space Institute, University of California at San Diego, 1984-90; Senior Scientist, Netrologic Inc, La Jolla, 1990-93; Founding Editor Emeritus, Space Governance Journal, 1993-98; Executive Vice President, Director Emeritus, United Societies in Space Inc, 1994-98. Publications: Organizational Dynamics, 1973; Effective Management of Change, 1976; Improving Management Communication Skills (with D Harris), 1978; Managing Cultural Differences (with R Moran), 1979, 4th edition, 1996; Innovations in Global Consultation (with G Malin), 1980; Managing Cultural Synergy (with R Moran), 1982; New Worlds, New Ways, New Management, 1983; Global Strategies for Human Resource Development, 1984; Management in Transition, 1985; High Performance Leadership, 1989, 2nd edition, 1994; Living and Working in Space, 1992, 2nd edition, 1996; Transcultural Leadership (with G M Simmons and C Vaquez), 1993; Multicultural Management (with F Elashmarie), 1993, 2nd edition, 1997; Developing Global Organizations (with R Moran and W Stripp), 1993; Multicultural Law Enforcement (co-author), 1994; High Performance Leadership, 1989, 2nd edition, 1994; The New Work Culture Series, 3 volumes, 1994-98; Multicultural Management 2000, 2nd edition, 1998 Contributions to: 200 articles published in numerous professional journals. Honours: Journalism Awards, Aviation Space Writers Association, 1986, 1988, 1989, 1993; Gulf Publishing Authors Hall of Fame, 1998. Memberships: American Institute of Aeronautics and Astronautics, associate fellow; European Business Review, editorial advisory board, 1990-; Society for Human Performance in Extreme Environments; Literate Club. Address: 2702 Costebelle Drive, La Jolla, CA 93037, USA.

HARRIS Randy Allen, b. 6 Sept 1956, Kitimat, British Columbia, Canada. Professor; Author. m. Indira Naidoo-Harris, 4 Aug 1984. Education: BA, Honours, English Literature, Queen's University, 1980; MA, English Literature, Dalhousie University, 1982; MSc, Linguistics, University of Alberta, 1985; MS, Technical Communication, 1986; PhD, Communication and Rhetoric, 1990, Rensselaer Polytechnic Institute. Publications: Acoustic Dimensions of Functor Comprehension in Broca's Aphasia, 1988; Linguistics Wars, 1993; Landmark Essays in Rhetoric of Science, 1997. Contributions to: College English; Perspectives on Science; Rhetoric Review; Historiographia Linguistica; Rhetoric Society Quarterly; Neuropsychologia. Honours: Heritage Scholar; Rensselaer Scholar; Killam Scholar; Killam Fellow. Memberships: Authors Guild; Linguistic Society of America. Address: Department of English, University of Waterloo, Waterloo, Ontario N2L 3G1, Canada.

HARRIS Robert (Dennis), b. 7 Mar 1957, Nottingham, England. Writer. m. Gillian Hornby, 1988, 1 son, 1 daughter. Education: BA, Honours, Selwyn College, Cambridge, 1978. Appointments: Researcher and Film Director, Tonight, Nationwide and Panorama, 1978-81, Reporter, Newsnight, 1981-85, Panorama, BBC, 1985-87; Political Editor, Observer, London, 1987-89; Political Reporter, This Week, Thames Television, 1988-89; Political Columnist, Sunday Times, London, 1989-92. Publications: A Higher Form of Killing: The Secret of Gas and Germ Warfare (with Jeremy Paxman),

1982; Form of Killing: The Secret Story of Chemical and Biological Warfare, 1982; Gotcha!: The Media, the Government, and the Falklands Crisis, 1983; The Making of Neil Kinnock, 1984; Selling Hitler, 1987; Good and Faithful Servant: The Unauthorized Biography of Bernard Ingham, 1990; Fatherland (novel), 1992; Enigma (novel), 1996. Address: The Old Vicarage, Kintbury, Berkshire R915 0TR, England.

HARRIS Robert William (Bob), b. 9 Nov 1944, Birmingham, England. Sports Journalist; Broadcaster; Company Director. m. Carol Ann, 2 Oct 1975, 2 s, 1 d. Appointments: Sports Editor and Sports Writer, Birmingham Planet; Sports Editor and Chief Sports Writer, Thomson Regional Newspapers; Sports Writer and Chief Football Writer Today; Sports Editor and Executive Sports Editor, Sunday Mirror; Editorial Director and Editor-in-Chief, Sport First. Publications: No Half Measures (with Graeme Souness); Touch and Go (with Steve Coppell); More than Somewhat (with Bruce Grobbelaar); World Cup Diary (with Bobby Robson); Bring on the Clown (with Bruce Grobbelaar); Against the Odds (with Bobby Robson); Kevin Keegan Autobiography; An Englishman Abroad (with Bobby Robson). Contributions to: Various football, Olympic, Commonwealth Games books and magazines. Literary Agent: Jonathon Harris. Address: 25 Broadheath Drive, Chislehurst, Kent BR7 6EU, England.

HARRIS Rosemary (Jeanne), b. 23rd February 1923, London, England. Author. Appointments: Children's Book Reviewer, The Times, London, 1970-73. Publications: The Summer-House, 1956; Voyage to Cythera, 1958; Venus with Sparrows, 1961; All My Enemies, 1967; The Nice Girl's Story, 1968 (in USA as Nor Evil Dreams, 1974); The Moon in the Cloud, 1968; A Wicked Pack of Cards, 1969; The Shadow on the Sun, 1970; The Seal-Singing, 1971; The Child in the Bamboo Grove, 1972; The Bright and Morning Star, 1972; The King's White Elephant, 1973; The Double Snare, 1974; The Lotus and the Grail: Legends from East to West (abridged edition in USA as Sea Magic and Other Stories of Enchantment), 1974; The Flying Ship, 1975; The Little Dog of Fo, 1976; Three Candles for the Dark, 1976; I Want to Be a Fish, 1977; A Quest for Orion, 1978; Beauty and the Beast (folklore), 1979; Green Finger House, 1980; Tower of the Stars, 1980; The Enchanted Horse, 1981; Janni's Stork, 1981; Zed, 1982; Summers of the Wild Rose, 1987; Love and the Merry-Go-Round, 1988; Ticket to Freedom, 1991; The Wildcat Strike, 1995; The Haunting of Joey M'basa, 1996. Honour: Library Association Carnegie Medal, 1967. Membership: Society of Authors. Address: c/o A P Watt Ltd, 20 John Street, London WC1N 2DR, England.

HARRIS Ruth Elwin, b. 22 June 1935, Bristol, England. Writer. m. Christopher J L Bowes, 24 July 1964, 2 sons, 1 daughter. Education: Bristol, England. Publications: The Quantocks Quartet: The Silent Shore, 1986; The Beckoning Hills, 1987; The Dividing Sea, 1989; Beyond the Orchid House, 1994; Billie: The Nevill Letters 1914-1916, 1991. Membership: Society of Authors. Address: c/o Random House, 20 Vauxhall Bridge Road, London SW1V 2SA, England.

HARRIS Thomas, b. 1940, USA. Writer. Publications: Black Sunday, 1975; Red Dragon, 1981; Silence of the Lambs, 1988. Address: c/o St Martin's Press, 175 Fifth Avenue, New York, NY 10010, USA.

HARRIS William M(cKinley) Sr, b. 29 Oct 1941, Richmond, Virginia, USA. Professor of City Planning; Writer. 3 daughters. Education: BS, Physics, Howard University, 1964; Master of Urban Planning, 1972, PhD, 1974, University of Washington, Seattle. Appointments: Director, Center for Urban Studies, Western Washington State University, Seattle, 1974; Assistant Professor, Portland State University, 1974-76; Associate Professor, 1976-82, Professor of City Planning, 1982-, University of Virginia; Adjunct Professor of Urban Planning, Virginia State University, 1979-85; Visiting Professor, Cornell University, 1986. Publications: A Design for Desegregation Evaluation, 1976; Black Community

Development, 1976; Perspectives on Black Studies (with Darrell Millner), 1977. Contributions to: The Ethics of Social Intervention, 1978; Lectures: Black Scholars on Black Issues, 1979; The Housing Status of Black Americans, 1992; Confronting Environmental Racism: Voices from the Grassroots, 1993; Also articles in professional journals. Honour: NDEA Fellow, University of Washington, 1992-94. Memberships: American Planning Association; American Institute of Certified Planners; Association for the Study of Afro-American Life and History; International Association of Community Development; APA Community Planning Team, team leader, 1995-96; Urban Affairs Association. Address: 485 14th Street North West, Charlottesville, VA 22903, USA.

HARRIS (Theodore) Wilson, b. 24 Mar 1921, New Amsterdam, British Guiana. Poet; Novelist. m. (1) Cecily Carew, 1945, (2) Margaret Whitaker, 1959. Education: Graduated, Queen's College, Georgetown, 1939. Appointments: Visiting Lecturer, State University of New York, Buffalo, 1970; Writer-in-Residence, University of West Indies, Kingston, Jamaica, Scarborough College, University of Toronto, 1970, University of Newcastle, New South Wales, 1979; Commonwealth Fellow in Caribbean Literature, Leeds University, Yorkshire, 1971; Visiting Professor, University of Texas, Austin, 1972, 1981-82, University of Mysore, 1978; Yale University, 1979; Regents Lecturer, University of California, Santa Cruz, 1983. Publications: Poetry: Fetish, 1951; The Well and the Land, 1952; Eternity to Season, 1954, revised edition 1979. Novels: The Guyana Quartet, 1960-63; Tumatumari, 1968; Black Marsden, 1972; Companions of the Day and Night, 1975; Da Silva's Cultivated Wilderness, 1977; Genesis of the Clowns, 1977; The Tree of the Sun, 1978; The Angel at the Gate, 1982; The Carnival Trilogy, 1985-90; Resurrection at Sorrow Hill, 1993. Other: Short stories and other publications. Address: c/o Faber and Faber Ltd, 3 Queen Square, London WC1N 3AU, England.

HARRISON Christopher, b. 20 Jan 1971, Manchester, England. Student. Education: History, Open University. Publication: Take It As You Find It, Or Whatever You Like, 1998. Address: 2 Winchester Court, Macclesfield, Cheshire SK10 1PJ, England.

HARRISON Edward Hardy, (Ted Harrison), b. 28 Aug 1926, Wingate, County Durham, England. Artist; Writer. m. Robina McNicol, 12 Nov 1960, 1 son. Education: Hartlepool College of Art, 1943-45, 1948-50; National Diploma, Design, King's College, Newcastle upon Tyne, 1951; BEd, University of Alberta, Canada, 1977. Publications: Children of the Yukon, 1977; The Last Horizon, 1980; A Northern Alphabet, 1982; The Blue Raven (television story), 1987, Canada, 1992. Honours: Best Childrens Book, A Child Study Association of Canada, 1977; Choice Book, Childrens Book Centre, Toronto, 1978; Ibby - Certificate of Honour for Illustration, 1984; Order of Canada; Honorary Doctorate, Athabasca University, 1991; Honorary Doctor of Fine Arts, University of Victoria, 1998. Memberships: Writers Union of Canada; PEN, Canada. Address: 2029 Romney Place, Victoria, British Columbia V8S 4J6, Canada.

HARRISON Elizabeth Fancourt, b. 12 Jan 1921, Watford, Hertfordshire, England. Author. Publications: Coffee at Dobree's, 1965; The Physicians, 1966; The Ravelston Affair, 1967; Corridors of Healing, 1968; Emergency Call, 1970; Accident Call, 1971; Ambulance Call, 1972; Surgeon's Call, 1973; On Call, 1974; Hospital Call, 1975; Dangerous Call, 1976; To Mend a Heart, 1977; Young Dr Goddard, 1978; A Doctor Called Caroline, 1979; A Surgeon Called Amanda, 1982; A Surgeon's Life, 1983; Marrying a Doctor, 1984; Surgeon's Affair, 1985; A Surgeon at St Mark's, 1986; The Surgeon She Married, 1988; The Faithful Type, 1993; The Senior Partner's Daughter, 1994; Made for Each Other, 1995. Honours: Runner-up, 1970, shortlisted, 1971, 1972, 1973, Romantics Novelists Association. Memberships: Society of Authors; Romantic Novelists Association. Address: 71 Wingfield Road, Kingston on Thames, Surrey KT2 5LR, England.

HARRISON James (Thomas), b. 11 Dec 1937, Grayling, Michigan, USA. Author; Poet. m. Linda May King, 10 Oct 1959, 2 daughters. Education: BA, 1960, MA, 1964, Michigan State University. Appointment: Instructor, State University of New York at Stony Brook, 1965-66. Publications: Fiction: Wolf: A False Memoir, 1971; A Good Day to Die, 1973; Farmer, 1976; Legends of the Fall, 1979; Warlock, 1981; Sundog, 1984; Dalva, 1988; The Woman Lit by Fireflies, 1990; Sunset Limited, 1990; Julip, 1994. Poetry: Plain Song, 1965; Locations, 1968; Walking, 1969; Outlyer and Ghazals, 1971; Letters to Yesinin, 1973; Returning to Earth, 1977; New and Selected Poems, 1961-81, 1982; The Theory and Practice of Rivers, 1986; Country Stores, 1993. Screenplays: Cold Feet (with Tom McGuane), 1989; Revenge (with Jeffrey Fishkin), 1990; Wolf (with Wesley Strick), 1994. Non-Fiction: Just Before Dark, 1991. Honours: National Endowment for the Arts Grant, 1967-69; Guggenheim Fellowship, 1968-69. Address: PO Box 135, Lake Leelanau, MI 49653, USA.

HARRISON John Arthur, b. 14 Oct 1952, Liverpool, England. Town Planner; Writer. Education: MA 1st Class Hons, Geography, Jesus College, Cambridge, England, 1974; Master of Civic Design, Liverpool, England, 1977. Appointments: Planner, Wyn Thomas & Partners, 1977-79; Senior Planning Officer, Vale of Glamorgan, BC, 1979-86; SPO Welsh Office, 1986-88; SPO Sports Council for Wales, 1988-98; Secretary, Welsh Union of Writers, 1993-98. Publications include: Extracts from Where the Earth Ends, 1998. Contributions to: New Welsh Review; many stories and reviews, travel pieces, Planet stories, Cambrensis stories. Honours: Welsh Union of Writers, 1992-; Associate Member, Welsh Academy, 1996-; PEN, Wales, 1994-. Address: 4 Teilo Street, Pontcanna, Cardiff CF1 9JN, Wales.

HARRISON Keith, b. Vancouver, Canada. Writer. Education: University of British Columbia; PhD, McGill University. Appointment: Teacher, Malaspina University College. Publications: Dead Ends, 1981; After Six Days, 1985; Eyemouth, 1990; Crossing the Gulf, 1998. Honours: Okanagan Short Story Award, 1991. Address: High Salal 1-10, Hornby Island, British Columbia V0R 1Z0, Canada.

HARRISON Raymond Vincent, b. 28 Oct 1928, Chorley, Lancashire, England. Inspector of Taxes; Financial Consultant; Writer. m. 7 Apr 1977. Education: BA, Honours, 1952; MA, 1954, Magdalene College, Cambridge. Publications: French Ordinary Murder, 1983; Death of An Honourable Member, 1984; Deathwatch, 1985; Death of a Dancing Lady, 1985; Counterfeit of Murder, 1986; A Season for Death, 1987; Harvest of Death, 1988; Tincture of Death, 1989; Sphere of Death, 1990; Patently Murder, 1991; Akin to Murder, 1992; Murder in Petticoat Square, 1993; Murder by Design, 1996. Address: Forthill, Kinsale, County Cork, Eire.

HARRISON Sarah, b. 7 Aug 1946, Exeter, England. Author. Education: BA, University of London, 1967. Appointment: Journalist, IPC Magazines, London, 1967-71. Publications: The Flowers of the Field, 1980; In Granny's Garden (children's book), 1980; A Flower That's Free, 1984; Hot Breath, 1985; Laura From Lark Rise, series (children's books), 4 volumes, 1986; An Imperfect Lady, 1987; Cold Feet, 1989; Foreign Parts, 1991; The Forests of the Night, 1992; Be An Angel, 1993; Both Your Houses, 1995; Life After Lunch, 1996; Flowers Won't Fax, 1997; That Was Then, 1998. Non-Fiction: How to Write a Blockbuster, 1995. Address: 17 Station Road, Steeple Morden, Royston, Hertfordshire, England.

HARRISON Sue (Ann McHaney), b. 29 Aug 1950, Lansing, Michigan, USA. Novelist. m. Neil Douglas Harrison, 22 Aug 1969, 1 son, 2 daughters, 1 dec. Education: BA, English, 1971. Publications: Mother Earth, Father Sky, 1990; My Sister the Moon, 1992; Brother Wind, 1994; Sisu, 1997; Song of the River, 1997; Cry of the Wind, 1998. Membership: Society of Midland Authors. Literary Agent: Rhoda Weyr. Address: PO Box 6, 18 Mile Road, Pickford, MI 49774, USA.

HARRISON Tony, b. 30 Apr 1937, Leeds, England. Poet; Dramatist. Publications: Earthworks, 1964; Aikin Mata (play with J Simmons), 1965; Newcastle is Peru, 1969; The Loiners, 1970; Voortrekker, 1972; The Misanthrope (translation of Molière's play), 1973; Poems of Palladas of Alexandria (editor and translator), 1973; Phaedra Britannica (translation of Racine's Phèdre), 1975; Bow Down (music theatre), 1977; The Passion (play), 1977; The Bartered Bride (libretto), 1978; From the "School of Eloquence" and Other Poems, 1978; Continuous, 1981; A Kumquat for John Keats, 1981; The Oresteia (translation), 1981; US Martial, 1981; Selected Poems, 1984, revised edition, 1987; Dramatic Verse, 1973-1985, 1985; The Fire-Gap, 1985; The Mysteries, 1985; V, 1985; Theatre Works, 1973-1985, 1986; Loving Memory, 1987; The Blasphemers' Banquet, 1989; The Trackers of Oxyrhynchus, 1990; V and Other Poems, 1990; A Cold Coming: Gulf War Poems, 1991; The Common Chorus, 1992; The Gaze of the Gorgon, 1992; Square Rounds, 1992; Black Daisies for the Bride, 1993; Poetry or Bust, 1993; A Maybe Day in Kazakhstan, 1994; The Shadow of Hiroshima, 1995; Permanently Bard, 1995; The Prince's Play, 1996; The Labourers of Herakles, 1996; Plays 3, 1996; Prometheus, 1998; Plays 1, forthcoming. Address: c/o 2 Crescent Grove, London, SW4 7AH, England.

HARROWER Jennifer Hilary, (Jenny Johnson), b. 2 Nov 1945, Bristol, England. Writer. m. Noel David Harrower, 28 Apr 1990, 1 son. Publications: Poetry: The Wisdom Tree, 1993; Neptune's Daughters, 1999. Contributions to: The Poet's Voice; Salzburg University Press; Stand Magazine. Honours: 4 Literary Awards, Southwest Arts, 1978-92. Membership: Poetry Society. Address: "Culross", 11 The Crescent, Woodthorpe, Nottingham NG5 4FX, England.

HARRS Margaret Norma, b. 15 Sept 1935, Releast, N Ireland. Writer. m. Leonard Michael Harrs, 2 sons. Publications: A Certain State of Mind, 1980; Love Minus One & Other Stories, 1994; Where Dreams Have Gone, 1997; Ladies Start Your Engines, anthology, 1997. Contributions to: Pittsburgh Review; Kairos; Antigonish Review; Room of One's Own. Honours: Ontario Literary Grant, 1988; Canada Council Travel Grant, 1997. Memberships: Writers Union of Canada; Playwrights Union of Canada, Treasurer, 1997, 1998, 1999. Literary Agent: Elspeth Cochrane Agency, London, England. Address: 95 Old Mill Drive, Toronto, M6S 4K2, Ontario, Canada.

HARRY J S, b. 1939, Adelaide, South Australia, Australia. Poet. Appointments: Writer-in-Residence, Australian National University, Canberra, 1989, Narrabundah College, Canberra, 1995. Publications: The Deer Under the Skin, 1970; Hold for a Little While, and Turn Gently, 1979; A Dandelion for Van Gogh, 1985; The Life on Water and the Life Beneath, 1995; Selected Poems, 1995. Honours: Harri Jones Memorial Prize, 1971; PEN International Lynne Phillips Prize, 1987; Kenneth Slessor Poetry Prize, 1996. Memberships: Australian Society of Authors; N.S.W. Writers' Centre; Poets' Union. Address: PO Box 184, Randwick, New South Wales 2031, Australia.

HARSENT David, b. 9 Dec 1942, Devonshire, England. Poet; Writer. m. (1), div, 2 sons, 1 daughter, (2), 1 daughter. Appointments: Fiction Critic, Times Literary Supplement, London, 1965-73; Poetry Critic, Spectator, London, 1970-73. Publications: Poetry: Tonight's Lover, 1968; A Violent Country, 1969; Ashridge, 1970; After Dark, 1973; Truce, 1973; Dreams of the Dead, 1977; Mister Punch, 1984; Selected Poems, 1989; News From the Front, 1993; Playback, 1997. Novel: From an Inland Sea, 1985. Libretto: Gawain (for Harrison Birtwistle's opera), 1991. Editor: New Poetry 7, 1981; Poetry Book Society Supplement, 1983; Savremena Britanska Poezija, 1988. Other: The Sorrow of Sarajevo (translation of poems by Goran Simic). Honours: Eric Gregory Award, 1967; Cheltenham Festival Prize, 1968; Arts Council Bursaries, 1969, 1984; Geoffrey Faber Memorial Prize, 1978; Society of Authors Travel Fellowship, 1989. Address: c/o Oxford University Press, Walton Street,

Oxford OX2 6DP, England.

HART Ellen, b. 10 Aug 1949, Minneapolis, Minnesota, USA. Writer. 2 daughters. Education: BA, Theology, Ambassador University. Publications: Hallowed Murder, 1989; Vital Lies, 1991; Stage Fright, 1992; A Killing Cure, 1993; The Little Piggy Went to Murder, 1994; A Small Sacrifice, 1994; Faint Praise, 1995; For Every Evil, 1995; Robbers Wine, 1996; The Oldest Sin, 1996; Murder in the Air, 1997; Wicked Games, 1998. Honours: Lambda Literary Award, 1994, 1996; Minnesota Book Award, 1995, 1996. Membership: Sisters in Crime. Literary Agent: Deborah Schneider, Gelfman Schneider Literary Agents, New York. Address: 4623 Blaisdell Avenue South, Minneapolis, MN 55409, USA.

HART Jonathan Locke, b. 30 June 1956, Halifax, Nova Scotia, Canada. Professor. m. Mary Alice Marshall, 15 Aug 1981, 1 son, 1 daughter. Education: BA, 1978; MA, 1979; PhD, 1984. Publications: Theater and World, 1992; Northrop Five, 1994; Explorations in Difference, 1996; Reading the Renaissance, 1996; Imagining Culture, 1996; Breath and Dust, 1996. Contributions to: Harvard Review; Quarry; Antigonish Review; Mattoid; Grain; Dalhousie Review. Honours: Senior Fellow, Toronto, 1986; Visiting Scholar, 1986-87; Fulbright Fellow, 1996-97, Harvard University; Visiting Fellow, Cambridge, 1993-94. Address: Department of English, University of Alberta, Edmonton, Alberta T6G 2E5, Canada.

HART Kevin, b. 5 July 1954, London, England (Australian citizen). Professor of English; Poet. Education: Australian National University; Stanford University, California, and University of Melbourne; PhD, 1987. Appointments: Lecturer in English, Melbourne University, Australia, 1986-87; Lecturer in Literary Studies, Deakin University, Victoria, 1987-91; Senior Lecturer, 1991-95; Associate Professor, 1991-95, Professor of English, 1995-, Monash University; Foundation Professor of Australian and New Zealand Studies, Georgetown University, Washington, DC, 1996-97. Publications: Nebuchadnezzar, 1976; The Departure, 1978; The Lines of the Hand: Poems 1976-79; Your Shadow, 1984; The Trespass of the Sign, 1989; Peniel, 1990; The Buried Harbour (translator), 1990; A D Hope, 1992; The Oxford Book of Australian Religious Verse (editor), 1994; New and Selected Poems, 1995; Dark Angel, 1996; Economic Acts, 1998. Contributions: Contibuting Editor: Arena Journal, The Critical Review, Boxkite, Heat. Honours: Australian Literature Board Fellowship, 1977; New South Wales Premier's Award, 1985; Victorian Premier's Award for Poetry, 1985; Grace Levin Award for Poetry, 1991, 1995. Memberships: Vice-President, Johnson Society of Australia; Fellow, Australian Academy of the Humanities. Address: 247 Richardson Street, North Carlton, Victoria 3054, Australia.

HART Veronica. See: KELLEHER Victor.

HART-DAVIS Duff, b. 3 June 1936, London, England. Author. Education: BA, Oxford University, 1960. Appointments: Feature Writer, 1972-76, Literary Editor, 1976-77, Assistant Editor, 1977-78, Sunday Telegraph, London; Country Columnist, Independent, 1986-. Publications: The Megacull, 1968; The Gold of St Matthew (in USA as The Gold Trackers), 1968; Spider in the Morning, 1972; Ascension: The Story of a South Atlantic Island, 1972; Peter Fleming (biography), 1974; Monarchs of the Glen, 1978; The Heights of Rimring, 1980; Fighter Pilot (with C Strong), 1981; Level Five, 1982; Fire Falcon, 1984; The Man-Eater of Jassapur, 1985; Hitler's Games, 1986; Armada, 1988; The House the Berrys Built, 1990; Horses of War, 1991; Country Matters, 1991; Wildings: The Secret Garden of Eileen Soper, 1992; Further Country Matters, 1993; When the Country Went to Town, 1997; Raoul Millais, 1998. Address: Owlpen Farm, Uley, Dursley, Gloucestershire GL11 5BZ, England.

HART-DAVIS Sir Rupert (Charles), b. 28 Aug 1907, London, England. Author; Editor; Former Publisher. m.

(1) Peggy Ashcroft, 1929, div, (2) Catherine Comfort Borden-Turner, 1933, 2 sons, 1 daughter, div, (3) Winifred Ruth Simon, 1964, dec 1967, (4) June Clifford, 1968. Education: Balliol College, Oxford; Student, Old Vic, 1927-28. Appointments: Actor, Lyric Theatre, Hammersmith, 1928-29; Office Boy, William Heinemann Ltd., 1929-31; Manager, Book Society, 1932; Director, Jonathan Cape Ltd., 1933-40; Served in Coldstream Guards, 1940-45; Founder, 1946, Director, 1946-64, Rupert Hart-Davis Ltd. Publications: Hugh Walpole, a Biography, 1952; The Arms of Time, a memoir, 1979; The Power of Chance, 1991. Editor: The Essential Neville Cardus, 1949; E.V. Lucas: Cricket all his Life, 1950; George Moore: Letters to Lady Cunard, 1957; The Letters of Oscar Wilde, 1962; Max Beerbohm: Letters to Reggie Turner, 1964; Max Beerbohm: More Theatres, 1969; Max Beerbohm: Last Theatres, 1970; Max Beerbohm: A Peep into the Past, 1972; A Catalogue of the Caricatures of Max Beerbohm, 1972; The Autobiography of Arthur Ransome, 1976; William Plomer: Electric Delights, 1978; The Lyttelton Hart-Davis Letters, 6 volumes 1978-84; Selected Letters of Oscar Wilde, 1979; Two Men of Letters, 1979; Siegfried Sassoon Diaries: 1920-1922, 1981, 1915-1918, 1983, 1923-1925, 1985; The War Poems of Siegfried Sassoon, 1983; A Beggar in Purple: A Commonplace Book, 1983; More Letters of Oscar Wilde, 1985; Siegfried Sassoon: Letters to Max Beerbohm, 1988; Letters of Max Beerbohm 1892-1956, 1989; The Power of Chance, 1991; Praise from the Past, 1996; Halfway to Heaven, 1998. Honours: Honorary DLitt, Reading University. 1964, Durham University, 1981. Address: The Old Rectory, Marske-in-Swaledale, Richmond, North Yorkshire DL11 7NA, England.

HARTCUP Adeline, b. 26 Apr 1918, Isle of Wight, England. Writer. m. John Hartcup, 11 Feb 1950, 2 sons. Education: MA, Classics and English Literature, Oxon. Appointments: Editorial Staff, Times Educational Supplement; Honorary Press Officer, Kent Voluntary Service Council. Publications: Angelica, 1954; Morning Faces, 1963; Below Stairs in the Great Country Houses, 1980; Children of the Great Country Houses, 1982; Love and Marriage in the Great Country Houses, 1984; Spello: Life Today in Ancient Umbria, 1985. Contributions to: Times Educational Supplement; Harper's; Queen; Times Higher Educational Supplement. Address: Swanton Court, Sevington, Ashford, Kent TN24 0LL, England.

HARTE Marjorie. See: McEVOY Marjorie.

HARTILL Rosemary Jane, b. 11 Aug 1949, Oswestry, England. Writer; Broadcaster; Independent Producer. Education: BA Hons, English, University of Bristol, 1970. Appointments: Religious Affairs Correspondent, 1982-88, Presenter of World Service's Meridian Books Programme, 1990-92, 1994, BBC. Publications: Emily Brontë: Poems (editor), 1973; Wild Animals, 1976; In Perspective, 1988; Writers Revealed, 1989; Were You There?, 1995; Visionary Women: Florence Nightingale, editor, 1996. Contributions to: Times Educational Supplement; Saga magazine. Honours: Nominated, Sony Award for Radio Reporter of the Year, 1988 and Best Arts Radio Feature, 1990; Sandford St Martin Trust Personal Award, 1994; Honorary D. Litt. University of Hull, 1995; Finalist in New York Festivals International Radio Competition, 1996. Address: Old Post Office, 24 Eglingham Village, Alnwick, Northumberland NE66 2TX, England.

HARTLAND Michael, b. 7 Feb 1941, Cornwall, England. Writer; Broadcaster. m. Jill Tarjan, 1975, 2 daughters. Education: Christ's College, Cambridge, 1960-63. Appointments: British Diplomatic and Civil Service, 1963-78; United Nations, 1978-83; Full-time Writer, 1983-; Book Reviewer and Feature Writer, The Sunday Times, The Times, Guardian and Daily Telegraph; Resident Thriller Critic, The Times, 1989-90; Daily Telegraph, 1993-; Travel Correspondent: The Times, 1993-; Presenter, Masterspy, BBC Radio 4, 1991-; Chairman, Wade Hartland Films Ltd. Publications: Down Among the Dead Men; Seven Steps to Treason (dramatized for BBC Radio 4, 1990); The Third Betrayal; Frontier of Fear; The Year of the Scorpion; As Ruth Carrington: Dead Fish. Honours: Fellow, Royal Society of

Arts; Honorary Fellow, University of Exeter; South West Arts Literary Award. Memberships: Executive Committee of PEN, 1997-; Detection Club; Crime Writers Association; Mystery Writers of America; Society of Authors. Address: Cotte Barton, Branscombe, Devon, EX12 3BH, England.

HARTLING Peter, b. 13 Nov 1933, Chemnitz, Germany. Author; Poet; Critic. m. Mechthild Maier, 2 sons, 2 daughters. Education: Grammar School, Nürtingen. Appointments: Editor and Co-Publisher, Der Monat, 1967-70; Editor and Managing Director, S Fischer Verlag, Frankfurt am Main, 1968-74; Professor of Poetry, University of Frankfurt am Main, 1984. Publications: Spielgeist, Spielgeist, 1962; Niembsch oder Der Stillstand: Eine Suite, 1964; Janek: Porträt einer Erinnerung, 1966; Das Familienfest oder Das Ende einer Geschichte, 1969; Neue Gedichte, 1972; Zwettl: Nachprüfung einer Erinnerung, 1973; Eine Frau, 1974; Hölderlin, 1976; Hubert oder Die Rückkehr nach Casablanca, 1978; Meine Lekture: Literatur als Widerstand, 1980; Nachgetragene Liebe, 1980; Die dreifache Maria, 1982; Vorwarnung, 1983; Sätze von Liebe, 1983; Das Windrad, 1983; Ich rufe die Wörter zusammen, 1984; Der spanische Soldat oder Finden und Erfinden: Frankfurter Poetik-Vorlesungen, 1984, 1984; Die Mörsinger Pappel, 1987; Waiblingers Augen, 1987; Gedichte 1953-1987, 1989; Herzwand: Mein Roman, 1990; Zwischen Untergang und Aufbruch: Aufsätze, Reden, Gespräche, 1990; Brüder und Schwestern: Tagebuch eines synodalen, 1991; Schubert, 1992; Bozena, 1994; Schumanns Schatten, 1996; Grosse, kleine Schwester, 1998. Honours: Literary Prize, German Critics' Association, 1964; Gerhart Hauptmann Prize, 1971; Friedrich Hölderlin Prize, 1987; Andreas Gryphius Prize, 1990; Lion Feutchtwanger Prize, Academy of Arts, Berlin, 1992; Honorary Professor, Stuttgart, 1994; Grand Cross of Merit, Federal Republic of Germany, 1995. Memberships: Academy of Arts, Berlin; Academy of Science and Literature, Mainz; Deutsche Akademie für Sprache und Dichtung e.V., Darmstadt; PEN. Address: Finkenweg 1, D-46546 Mörfelden-Walldorf, Germany.

HARTMAN Geoffrey H, b. 11 Aug 1929, Frankfurt am Main, Germany (US citizen, 1946). Professor of English and Comparative Literature; Writer. m. Renee Gross, 21 Oct 1956, 1 son, 1 daughter. Education: BA, Queens College, New York City, 1949; PhD, Yale University, 1953. Appointments: Fulbright Fellow, University of Dijon, 1951-52; Faculty, Yale University, 1955-62; Associate Professor, 1962-64, Professor of English, 1964-65, University of Iowa; Professor of English, 1965-67, Sterling Professor, 1994-, Cornell University; Professor of English and Comparative Literature, 1967-, Karl Young Professor, 1974-94, Yale University; Gauss Seminarist, Princeton University, 1968; Director, School of Theory and Criticism, Dartmouth College, 1982-87; Associate Fellow, Center for Research in Philosophy and Literature, University of Warwick, 1993; Fellow, Woodrow Wilson International Center, 1995; Various guest lectureships and professorships. Publications: The Unmediated Vision, 1954; André Malraux, 1960; Wordsworth's Poetry, 1964; Beyond Formalism, 1970; The Fate of Reading, 1975; Akiba's Children, 1978; Criticism in the Wilderness, 1980; Saving the Text, 1981; Easy Pieces, 1985; The Unremarkable Wordsworth, 1987; Minor Prophecies, 1991. Editor: Hopkins: A Collection of Critical Essays, 1966; Selected Poetry and Prose of William Wordsworth, 1970; Romanticism: Vistas, Instances, Continuities, 1973; Psychoanalysis and the Question of the Text, 1978; Shakespeare and the Question of Theory, 1985; Bitburg in Moral and Political Perspective, 1986; Midrash and Literature, 1986; Holocaust Remembrance: The Shapes of Memory, 1993; The Longest Shadow: In the aftermath of the Holocaust, 1996; The Fateful Question of Culture, 1997. Honours: Christian Gauss Award, Phi Beta Kappa, 1965; Guggenheim Fellowships, 1969, 1986; Honorary LHD, Queens College, New York City, 1990; Distinguished Scholar Award, 1997. Memberships: American Academy of Arts and Sciences; Modern Language Association. Address: 260 Everit Street, New Haven, CT 06511, USA.

HARTMAN Jan, b. 23 May 1938, Stockholm, Sweden. Professor; Dramatist; Writer. Education: Phillips Andover Academy, 1956; BA, Harvard College, 1960. Appointments: Resident Playwright, The Theatre of The Living Arts, Philadelphia, 1964-65; Director, Founder, Playwrights Theatre Project Circle in the Square, 1967-69, Eleventh Hour Productions, 1977; Resident Playwright, Theatre St Clements, 1977-78; Visiting Professor, Syracuse University, 1985-94; Professor of Dramatic Writing and Shakespeare, New York University, 1981-93. Publications: More than 100 plays for film, television and radio including: Mother Teresa: In the Name of God's Poor; The Next War; Geneology of Evil; The Great Wallendas; Second Sight; Song of Myself; Theatrical productions include: Kepler's Room; Abelard and Heloise; Flight 981; The American War Crimes Trial; Fragment of a Last Judgement; Freeman! Freeman!; The Legend of Daniel Boone. Fiction: Joshua; Envy; The Wail, 1998. Contributions to: Dramatists Guild Quarterly. Honours: Guggenheim Fellowship for Playwriting; 2 Emmies; 2 Christophers; Writers Guild of America Award, Numerous grants. Memberships: PEN; Writers Guild of America; Eugene O'Neill Memorial Theatre Foundation; American National Theatre and Academy; Dramatists Guild; British Academy of Film and Television Arts; Address: c/o Robert A Freeman Dramatic Agency Inc, 1501 Broadway, Suite 2310, NY 10036, USA.

HARTNETT David William, b. 4 Sept 1952, London, England. Writer; Poet; Editor. m. Margaret R N Thomas, 26 Aug 1976, 1 son, 1 daughter. Education: Scholarship, English Language and Literature, 1971, 1st Class Honour Moderations, 1973, 1st Class BA, English Language and Literature, 1975, MA, 1981, DPhil, 1987, Oxford University. Appointment: Co-Editor, Poetry Durham magazine. Publications: Poetry: A Signalled Love, 1985; House of Moon, 1988; Dark Ages, 1992; At the Wood's Edge, 1997. Novels: Black Milk, 1994; Brother to Dragons, 1998. Contributions to: Times Literary Supplement. Honour: Times Literary Supplement/Cheltenham Festival Poetry Competition, 1989. Literary Agent: David Higham Associates, 5-8 Lower John Street, Golden Square, London, W1R 4HA. Address: c/o Jonathan Cape, 20 Vauxhall Bridge Road, London SW1V 2SA, England.

HARTNETT Michael, b. 18 Sept 1941, County Limerick, Ireland. Poet. Education: University College and Trinity College, Dublin. Appointment: Teacher of Physical Education, National College, Limerick. Publications: Anatomy of a Cliche, 1968; Selected Poems, 1971; Culuide: The Retreat of Ita Cagney, 1975; A Farewell to English and Other Poems, 1975; Poems in English, 1977; Prisoners, 1978; Collected Poems, 2 volumes, 1985, 1987; A Necklace of Wrens: Poems in English and Irish, 1987; House of Moon, 1989. Address: c/o Gallery Press, Loughcrew, Oldcastle, County Meath, Ireland.

HARTSTON W(illiam) R(oland), b. 12 Aug 1947, London, England. Writer. Education: MA, Jesus College, 1972. Appointment: Chess Columnist, The Mail on Sunday. Publications: The King's Indian Defence (with L Barden and R Keene), 1969; The Benoni, 1969; The Grunfeld Defence, 1971; Karpov-Korchnoi (with R Keene), 1974; The Best Games of C H O'D Alexander (with H Golombek), 1975; How to Cheat at Chess, 1976; The Battle of Baguio City, 1978; Soft Pawn, 1979; The Penguin Book of Chess Openings, 1980; Play Chess 1 and 2, 2 volumes, 1980-81; London (with S Reuben), 1980; The Master Game Book Two (with J James), 1981; Karpov v Korchnoi, 1981; The Psychology of Chess (with P C Wason), 1983; The Ultimate Irrelevant Encyclopaedia (with J Dawson), 1984; Teach Yourself Chess, 1985; Kings of Chess, 1985; Chess: The Making of a Musical, 1986. Address: 48 Sotheby Road, London N5 2UR, England.

HARUKI Murakami, b. 12 June 1949, Kyôto, Japan. Writer. Education: Waseda University. Publications: Novels: Kaze no Uta o Kike/Hear the Wind Sing, 1979; Hitsuji o Meguru Bôken/A Wild Sheep Chase, 1982; Sekai no Owari to Haado-Boirudo Wandaarando/Hard-Boiled Wonderland and the End of the World, 1985; Nruwei no Mori/Norwegian Wood, 1987; Dansu, Dansu, Dansu/Dance Dance Dance, 1988; Kokkyô no Minami, Taiyô no Nishi/South of the Border, West of the Sun, 1992; Nejimakidori kuronikuru/The Wind-Up Bird Chronicle, 3 volumes, 1994-95. Short Stories: Elephant Vanishes, 1986; Kureta Kanô, 1989. Honours: New Writer Award, Gunzô Magazine, 1979; Noma Award for New Writers, 1982; Tanizaki Jun'ichiro Award, 1985; Yomiuri Literary Award, 1996. Address: c/o International Creative Management, 40 West 57th Street, New York, NY 10019, USA.

HARVEY Anne (Berenice), b. 27 Apr 1933, London, England. Actress; Writer; Poet; Editor. m. Alan Harvey, 13 Apr 1957, 1 son, 1 daughter. Education: Guildhall School of Music and Drama, London, 1950-54. Publications: A Present for Nellie, 1981; Poets in Hand, 1985; Of Caterpillars, Cats and Cattle, 1987; In Time of War: War Poetry, 1987; Something I Remember (selected poetry of Eleanor Farjeon), 1987; A Picnic of Poetry, 1988; The Language of Love, 1989; Six of the Best, 1989; Faces in the Crowd, 1990; Headlines from the Jungle (with Virginia McKenna), 1990; Occasions, 1990; Flora's Red Socks, 1991; Shades of Green, 1991; Elected Friends (poems for and about Edward Thomas), 1991; He Said, She Said, They Said (conversation poems, editor), 1993; Solo Audition Speeches for Young Actors, 1993; Criminal Records: Poetry of Crime (editor), 1994; Methuen Book of Duologues, 1995; Starlight, Starbright: Poems of Night, 1995; Swings and Shadows: Poems of Times Past and Present, 1996. Series Editor: Poetry Originals, 1992-95. Contributions to: Radio, journals, and magazines. Honour: Signal Poetry Award, 1992. Memberships: Poetry Society; Friends of the Dymock Poets; Eighteen Nineties Society; Imaginative Book Illustration Society. Address: 37 St Stephen's Road, Ealing, London W13 8HJ, England.

HARVEY Brett, b. 28 Apr 1936, New York, New York, USA. Writer; Critic. 1 son, 1 daughter. Education: Northwestern University, 1956-59. Appointments: Drama and Literature Director, WBAI-FM, 1971-74; Publicity and Promotion Director, The Feminist Press, Old Westbury, New York, 1974-80. Publications: My Prairie Year, 1986; Immigrant Girl, 1987; Cassie's Journey, Various Gifts: Brooklyn Fiction, 1988; My Prairie Christmas, 1990; The Fifties: A Women's Oral History, 1993. Contributions to: Village Voice; New York Times Book Review; Psychology Today; Voice Literary Supplement; Mirabella; Mother Jones; Mademoiselle. Address: 305 8th Avenue, Brooklyn, NY 11215, USA.

HARVEY Caroline. See: **TROLLOPE Joanna.**

HARVEY John Barton, b. 21 Dec 1938, London, England. Writer; Poet. Education: Goldsmith College, University of London; Hatfield Polytechnic; University of Nottingham. Publications: What about it, Sharon, 1979; Lonely Hearts, 1989; Rough Treatment, 1990; Cutting Edge, 1991; Off Minor, 1992; Ghosts of a Chance (collected poems), 1992; Wasted Years, 1993; Cold Light, 1994; Living Proof, 1995. Other: Numerous radio and television scripts. Address: 37-41 Gower Street, London WC1E 6HH, England.

HARVEY John Robert, b. 25 June 1942, Bishops Stortford, Hertfordshire, England. University Lecturer; Writer. m. Julietta Chloe Papadopoulou, 1968, 1 daughter. Education: BA, Honours Class 1, English, 1964, MA, 1967, PhD, 1969, University of Cambridge. Appointments: English Faculty, Emmanuel College, Cambridge; Editor, Cambridge Quarterly, 1978-86. Publications: Victorian Novelists and Their Illustrators, 1970. Novels: The Plate Shop, 1979; Coup d'Etat, 1985; The Legend of Captain Space, 1990; Men in Black, 1995. Contributions to: London Review of Books; Sunday Times; Sunday Telegraph; Listener; Encounter; Cambridge Quarterley; Essays in Criticism. Honour: David Higham Prize, 1979. Literary Agent: Curtis Brown. Address: Emmanuel College, Cambridge, England.

HARVEY Julia. See: **JAMES Mary.**

HARVOR Elisabeth, (Erica Elisabeth Arendt), b. 26 June 1936, Saint John, NB, Canada. Writer; Teacher. m. Stig Harvor, 16 Nov 1957, 2 sons. Publications: Women and Children, eleven stories, 1973; If Only We Could Drive Like This Forever, six stories, 1988; Our Lady of All the Distances, 1991; Fortress of Chairs, 1992; Let Me Be the One, 1996; The Long Cold Green Evenings of Spring, 1997; Editor, A Room at the Heart of Things, 1998. Honours include: Malahat Long Poem Prize, 1990; Ottawa Short Story Competition, 1970; League of Canadian Poets' National Poetry PRize, 1989; League of Canadian Poets' National Poetry Prize, 1991; Governor-General's Award, Finalist, 1996. Address: c/o The Writers' Union of Canada.

HARWOOD Lee, b. 6 June 1939, Leicester, England. Poet; Writer; Translator. Div, 2 sons, 1 daughter. Education: BA, Honours, English, Queen Mary College, University of London, 1961. Publications: Title Illegible, 1965; The Man with Blue Eyes, 1966; The White Room, 1968; The Beautiful Atlas, 1969; Landscapes, 1969; The Sinking Colony, 1970; Penguin Modern Poets 19 (with John Ashbery and Tom Raworth), 1971; The First Poem, 1971; New Year, 1971; Captain Harwood's Log of Stern Statements and Stout Sayings, 1973; Freighters, 1975; H.M.S. Little Fox, 1976; Boston-Brighton, 1977; Old Bosham Bird Watch and Other Stories, 1977; Wish You Were Here (with A Lopez), 1979; All the Wrong Notes, 1981; Faded Ribbons, 1982; Wine Tales (with Richard Caddel), 1984; Crossing the Frozen River: Selected Poems 1965-1980, 1984, revised edition, 1994; Monster Masks, 1985; Dream Quilt (stories), 1985; Rope Boy to the Rescue, 1988; The Empty Hill: Memories and Praises of Paul Evans 1945-1991 (editor with Peter Bailey), 1992; In the Mists: Mountain Poems, 1993. Other: Translations of works by Tristan Tzara. Contributions to: Journals, reviews, and magazines. Honours: Poetry Foundation Award, New York, 1966; Alice Hunt Bartlett Prize, Poetry Society, London, 1976. Memberships: National Poetry Secretariat, Chairman, 1974-76; Poetry Society, London, Chairman, 1976-77. Address: 2 Ivy Place, off Waterloo Street, Hove, Sussex BN3 1AP, England.

HARWOOD Ronald, b. 9 Nov 1934, Cape Town, South Africa. Dramatist; Writer. m. Natasha Riehle, 1959, 1 son, 2 daughters. Education: Royal Academy of Dramatic Art. Appointments: Actor, 1953-60; Presenter, Kaleidoscope, BBC, 1973, Read All About It, BBC TV, 1978-79; Artistic Director, Cheltenham Festival of Literature, 1975; Visitor in Theatre, Balliol College, Oxford, 1986. Publications: Stage Plays: Country Matters, 1969; The Ordeal of Gilbert Pinfold (after Evelyn Waugh), 1977; A Family, 1978; The Dresser, 1980; After the Lions, 1982; Tramway Road, 1984; The Deliberate Death of a Polish Priest, 1985; Interpreters, 1985; J J Farr, 1987; Ivanov (after Anton Chekov), 1989; Another Time, 1989; Reflected Glory, 1992; Poison Pen, 1993; Taking Sides, 1995. Television Plays: The Barber of Stamford Hill, 1960; Private Potter (with Casper Wrede), 1961; The Guests, 1972; Breakthrough at Reykjavik, 1987; Countdown to War, 1989. Television Series: All the World's a Stage, 1984. Screenplays: A High Wind in Jamaica, 1965; One Day in the Life of Ivan Denisovich, 1971; Evita Perón, 1981; The Dresser, 1983; Mandela, 1987; The Browning Version, 1994; Cry, Beloved Country, 1995. Novels: All the Same Shadows, 1961; The Guilt Merchants, 1963; The Girl in Melanie Klein, 1969; Articles of Faith, 1973; The Genoa Ferry, 1976; Cesar and Augusta, 1978; Home, 1993;The Handyman, 1996; Equally Divided, 1998. Non-Fiction: Sir Donald Wolfit, CBE: His Life and Work in the Unfashionable Theatre, 1971. Editor: A Night at the Theatre, 1983; The Ages of Gielgud, 1984; Dear Alec: Guinness at Seventy-Five, 1989; The Faber Book of Theatre, 1993. Honours: New Standard Drama Award, 1981; Drama Critics Award, 1981; Molière Award for Best Play, Paris, 1993; Chevalier Dans L'Orore National des Arts and Lettres, 1996; Commander of the Order of the British Empire, 1999. Memberships: Arts Council of Great Britain, literature panel, 1978-79; English PEN, president, 1989-93; International PEN, president, 1993-; Royal Society of Literature, fellow; Writers Guild of Great Britain, chairman, 1969. Address: c/o Judy Daish Associates, 2 St Charles Place, London W10 6EG, England.

HASHMI (Aurangzeb) Alamgir, b. 15 Nov 1951, Lahore, Pakistan. Professor; Poet; Writer; Editor; Broadcaster. m. Beatrice Stoerk, 15 Dec 1978, 2 sons, 1 daughter. Education: MA, University of Louisville, 1977. Appointments: Broadcaster, Pakistan Broadcasting Corp, Lahore, 1968-74, 1988-; Staff, Government College, Lahore, 1971-73; Lecturer, Forman Christian College, Lahore, 1973-74, University of Berne, University of Basel, 1982; Davidson International Visiting Scholar from Pakistan, University of North Carolina, 1974-75; Lecturer in English, University of Louisville, 1975-78, University of Zürich and Volkshochschule, Zürich, 1980-85; Assistant Professor of English, University of Bahawalpur, Pakistan, 1979-80; Associate Professor of Englsh, International Islamic University, Islamabad, 1985-86; Course Director, Foreign Service Training Institute, Pakistan Ministry of Foreign Affairs, Islamabad, 1988-; Professor of English and Comparative Literature, Pakistan Futuristics Institute, Islamabad, 1990. Publications: Poetry: The Oak and Amen: Love Poems, 1976; America is a Punjabi Word, 1979; An Old Chair, 1979; My Second in Kentucky, 1981; This Time in Lahore, 1983; Neither This Time/Nor That Place, 1984; Inland and Other Poems, 1988; The Poems of Alamgir Hashmi, 1992; Sun and Moon and Other Poems, 1992; Others to Sport with Amaryllis in the Shade, 1992. Other: Pakistani Literature (editor), 2 volumes, 1978, 2nd edition as Pakistani Literature: The Contemporary English Writers, 1987; Commonwealth Literature, 1983; Ezra Pound in Melbourne (editor with others), 1983; The Worlds of Muslim Imagination (editor), 1986; The Commonwealth, Comparative Literature and the World, 1988; Pakistani Short Stories in English (editor), 1992; Studies in Pakistani Literature (editor), 1992; Encyclopedia of Post-Colonial Literatures (co-editor), 1994; Where Coyotes Howl and Wind Blows Free (editor with Alexandra Haslam), 1995; The Great Tejon Club Jubilee, 1996. Contributions to: Many books, journals, and periodicals. Honours: Honorary DLitt, Centre Universitaire de Luxembourg, 1984, San Francisco State University, 1984; Patras Bokhari Award, Pakistan Academy of Letters, 1985; Rockefeller Foundation Fellow, 1994; Roberto Celli Memorial Award, 1994. Memberships: Associated Writing Programs; Association for Asian Studies; Commonwealth Club; Association for Commonwealth Literature and Language Studies; International Association of University Professors of English; International Centre for Asian Studies, fellow; International PEN, fellow; Modern Language Association of America. Address: House 162, Street 64, Ramna 8/1, Islamabad, Pakistan.

HASKINS James, b. 19 Sept 1941, Demopolis, Alabama, USA. Professor of English; Writer. Education: BA, Psychology, Georgetown University, 1960; BS, History, Alabama State University, 1962; MA, Social Psychology, University of New Mexico, 1963. Appointments: Teacher, Board of Education, New York City, 1966-69; Visiting Lecturer, New School for Social Research, New York City, 1966-69, State University of New York at New Paltz, 1970-72, Manhattanville College, Purchase, New York, 1972-76, Indiana University-Purdue University at Indianapolis, 1973-76; Associate Professor, S I Community College, New York City, 1972-76; Visiting Professor, College of New Rochelle, New York, 1977; Professor of English, University of Florida at Gainesville, 1977-. Publications: Diary of a Harlem Schoolteacher, 1969; The War and the Protest, 1970; Resistance: Profiles in Nonviolence, 1970; Revolutionaries: Agents of Change, 1971; Profiles in Black Power, 1972; Religions, 1973; Ralph Bunche: A Most Reluctant Hero, 1974; Adam Clayton Powell: Portrait of a Marching Black, 1974; Witchcraft, Mysticism and Magic in the Black World, 1974; Babe Ruth and Hank Aaron: The Home Run Kings, 1974; The Creoles of Color of New Orleans, 1975; Fighting Shirley Chisholm, 1975; Dr J: A Biography of Julius Erving, 1975; The Story of Stevie Wonder, 1976; Always Movin' On: A Biography of Langston Hughes, 1976; A Long Struggle: American Labor, 1976; Pele: A Biography, 1976; The Life and Death of Martin Luther King, Jr, 1977; Barbara Jordan, 1977; Voodoo and Hoodoo, 1978; James Van DerZee: The Picture Takin' Man, 1979; Andrew Young: Man with a Mission, 1979; I'm Gonna Make You Love Me: The Story of Diana Ross, 1980; Werewolves, 1981; Sugar Ray Leonard, 1982; Black Theater in America, 1982; Lena Horne, 1983; Diana Ross: Star Supreme, 1985; Black Music in America: A History Through its People, 1987; Queen of the Blues: The Story of Dinah Washington, 1987; Mabel Mercer: A Life, 1988; Corazon Aquino: Leader of the Philippines, 1988; India Under Indira and Rajiv Gandhi, 1989; Outward Dreams: Black Inventors and Their Inventions, 1991; The Day That Martin Luther King Jr was Shot, 1992; Amazing Grace: The Story Behind the Song, 1992; Jesse Jackson, 1992; Against All Opposition: Black Explorers in America, 1992; Colin Powell, 1992; Thurgood Marshall: A Life for Justice, 1992; Get on Board: The Story of the Underground Railroad, 1992; I Have a Dream: The Life of Martin Luther King Jr, 1992; The Methodist Church, 1992; The March on Washington, 1993; Freedom Rides, 1994; The Headless Haunt and Other African-American Ghost Stories, 1994; Black Eagles: African Americans in Aviation, 1995; The Day They Fired on Fort Sumter, 1995. With Others: Scott Joplin, 1978; Nat King Cole, 1984; Mr Bojangles: Biography of Bill Robinson, 1988; The Sixties Reader, 1988; Scatman, 1991; Hippocrene Guide to the Historic Black South, 1993. Honours: Coretta Scott King Award, 1976; ASCAP-Deems Taylor Award, 1979; Washington Post/Children's Book Guild Award, 1994. Address: 325 West End Avenue, No 7D, New York, NY 10023, USA.

HASLAM Gerald William, b. 18 Mar 1937, Bakersfield, California, USA. Writer; Educator. m. Janice E Pettichord, 1 July 1961, 3 sons, 2 daughters. Education: BA, 1963, MA, 1965, San Francisco State University; PhD, Union Graduate School, 1980. Appointments: Associate Editor, ETC: A Review of General Semantics, 1967-69; Editor, Ecolit, 1971-73; General Editor, A Literary History of the American West, 1973-76; Columnist, California English, 1987-93, San Francisco Chronicle, 1992-93. Publications: Okies, 1973; Masks, 1976; The Wages of Sin, 1980; Snapshots, 1985; The Man Who Cultivated Fire, 1987; Voices of a Place, 1987; Coming of Age in California, 1990; That Constant Coyote, 1990; The Other California, 1990, revised edition, 1994; The Great Central Valley: California's Heartland, 1993; Condor Dreams and Other Fictions, 1994; Teh Great Tejon Club Jubilee, 1996. Editor: Forgotten Pages of American Literature, 1970; Western Writing, 1974; California Heartland (with James D Houston), 1978; Many Californias, 1992. Honours: Josephine Miles Award, 1990; Bay Area Book Reviewers' Award, 1993; Benjamin Franklin Award, 1993; Commonwealth Club Medal, 1994; Award of Merit, Association of State and Local History, 1995; Laureate, San Fransico Public Library, 1998. Membership: National Writers' Union. Address: Box 969, Penngrove, CA 94951, USA.

HASLUCK Nicholas (Paul), b. 17 Oct 1942, Canberra, Australian Capital Terretory, Australia. Writer; Poet. Education: University of Western Australia, 1960-63; Oxford University, 1964-66. Appointments: Barrister, Solicitor, Supreme Court of Western Australia, 1968; Deputy Chairman, Australia Council, 1978-82. Publications: Fiction: Quarantine, 1978; The Blue Guitar, 1980; The Hand that Feeds You: A Satiric Nightmare, 1982; The Bellarmine Jug, 1984; The Country without Music, 1990; The Blosseville File, 1992; Offcuts From a Legal Literary Life, 1993; A Grain of Truth, 1994. Stories: The Hat on the Letter O and Other Stories, 1978. Poetry, Anchor and Other Poems, 1976; On the Edge, 1980; Chinese Journey, 1985. Honours: Age Book of the Year Award, 1984; Member of the Order of Australia, 1986. Address: 14 Reserve Street, Claremont, Western Australia 6010, Australia.

HASNAIN S Imtiaz, b. 20 Dec 1957, Gaya, India. Teaching. m. Shagufta Imtiaz, 31 July 1987. Education: MA Linguistics, JNU, 1980; PhD Linguistics, JNU; Research Intern, East West Center, Hawaii, USA. Appointments: Research Intern, EWC, Hawaii, 1986; Research Associate, Department of Anth Linguistics, PU, Patiala, 1987; Lecturer, AMU, 1987; Senior Lecturer, AMU, 1992. Publications: Structuralism and

Post-structuralism, 1992; Standardization & Modernization: Dynamics of Language Planning, 1996; Linguistics and Language Teaching, 1991. Contributions to: Language Science (Pergamon); IJAL; Language Forum; South Asian Language Review; IJDL; Indian Linguistics. Honours: East West Center Fellowship, 1986; UGC Fellowship, 1981-85. Memberships: ISI; IJDL. Address: Department of Linguistics, AMU, Aligarh 202002, India.

HASS Robert (Louis), b. 1 Mar 1941, San Francisco, California, USA. Poet; Writer; Translator; Editor; Professor. m. Earlene Joan Leif, 1 Sept 1962, div 1986, 2 sons, 1 daughter. Education: BA, St Mary's College of California, 1963; MA, 1965, PhD, 1971, Stanford University. Appointments: Assistant Professor, State University of New York, Buffalo, 1967-71; Professor of English, St Mary's College of California, 1971-89, University of California, Berkeley, 1989-; Visiting Lecturer, University of Virginia, 1974, Goddard College, 1976, Columbia University, 1982, University of California, Berkeley, 1983; Poet-in-Residence, The Frost Place, Franconia, New Hampshire, 1978; Poet Laureate of the USA, 1995-97. Publications: Poetry: Field Guide, 1973; Winter Morning in Charlottesville, 1977; Praise, 1979; The Apple Tree at Olema, 1989; Human Wishes, 1989; Sun under Wood, 1996. Other: Twentieth Century Pleasures: Prose on Poetry, 1984; Into the Garden - A Wedding Anthology: Poetry and Prose on Love and Marriage, 1993. Translations: Czeslaw Milosz's The Separate Notebooks (with Robert Pinsky), 1983; Czeslaw Milosz's Unattainable Earth (with Czeslaw Milosz), 1986; Czeslaw Milosz's Collected Poems, 1931-1987 (with Louis Iribane and Peter Scott), 1988. Editor: Rock and Hawk: A Selection of Shorter Poems by Robinson Jeffers, 1987; The Pushcart Prize XII (with Bill Henderson and Jorie Graham), 1987; Tomaz Salamun: Selected Poems (with Charles Simic), 1988; Selected Poems of Tomas Tranströmer, 1954-1986 (with others), 1989; The Essential Haiku: Versions of Basho, Buson and Issa, 1994. Contributions to: Anthologies and other publications. Honours: Woodrow Wilson Fellowship, 1963-64; Danforth Fellowship, 1963-67; Yale Series of Younger Poets Award, Yale University Press, 1972; US-Great Britain Bicentennial Exchange Fellow in the Arts, 1976-77; William Carlos Williams Award, 1979; National Book Critics Circle Award, 1984; Award of Merit, American Academy of Arts and Letters, 1984; John D and Catherine T MacArthur Foundation Grant, 1984. Address: PO Box 807, Inverness, CA 94937, USA.

HASSEL Sven, b. 19 Apr 1917, Denmark. Author. m. Dorthe Jensen, 6 Jan 1951, 1 son. Education: Officer's Academy. Publications: The Legion of the Damned; Wheels of Terror; Comrades of War; Marchbattalion; Assignment Gestapo; Monte Cassino; Liquidate Paris; SS General; Reign of Hell; Blitzfreeze; The Bloody Road to Death; Court Martial; OGPU Prison; The Commissar. Honours: Author of the Year, Italy, twice. Memberships: Danish Authors Society; Authors Union, Germany. Literary Agent: Michael Hassel. Address: Calle Francesc Pérez Cabrero 2, 08021 Barcelona, Spain.

HASTE Cate, b. 6 Aug 1945, Leeds, England. Writer; Television Documentary Producer; Director. m. Melvyn Bragg, 18 Dec 1973, 1 son, 1 daughter. Education: BA Hons, English, University of Sussex, 1963-66; Diploma Adult Education, Manchester University, 1967. Appointments: Freelance Television Documentary Producer/Director. Publications: Keep the Home Fires Burning: Propaganda to the Home Front in the First World War, 1977; Rules of Desire: Sex in Britain World War I to the Present, 1992. Literary Agent: Faith Evans Associates. Address: 12 Hampstead Hill Gardens, London NW3 2PL, England.

HASTINGS March. See: **LEVINSON Leonard.**

HASTINGS Max Macdonald, b. 28 Dec 1945, London, England. Author; Broadcaster; Journalist. m. Patricia Edmondson, 27 May 1972, 2 sons, 1 daughter. Education: Exhibitioner, University College, Oxford, 1964-65; Fellow, World Press Institute, St Paul, Minnesota, USA, 1967-68. Appointments: Researcher, BBC TV, 1963-64; Reporter, London Evening Standard, 1965-67, BBC TV Current Affairs, 1970-73; Editor, Evening Standard Londoner's Diary, 1976-77, Daily Telegraph, 1986-95, Evening Standard, 1996-; Columnist, Daily Express, 1981-83, Sunday Times, 1985-86; Editor-in-Chief and a Director, Daily Telegraph Plc, 1989-96. Publications: The Fire This Time, 1968; Ulster, 1969; The Struggle for Civil Rights in Northern Ireland, 1970; Montrose: The King's Champion, 1977; Yoni: The Hero of Entebbe, 1979; Bomber Command, 1979; The Battle of Britain (with Lee Deighton), 1980; Das Reich, 1981; Battle for the Falklands (with Simon Jenkins), 1983; Overlord: D-Day and the Battle for Normandy, 1984; Oxford Book of Military Anecdotes (editor), 1985; Victory in Europe, 1985; The Korean War, 1987; Outside Days, 1989. Contributions to: Country Life; The Field. Honours: Somerset Maugham Prize, 1979; British Press Awards, Journalist of the Year, 1982; Granada TV Reporter of the Year, 1982; Yorkshire Post Book of the Year Awards, 1983, 1984; Editor of the Year, 1988; Honorary DLitt. Leicester University, 1992; Royal Society of Literature, fellow, 1996. Literary Agent: Peters, Fraser and Dunlop Group Ltd. Address: Northcliffe House, 2 Derry Street, London W8 5EE, England.

HASTINGS Michael (Gerald), b. 2 Sept 1938, London, England. Dramatist; Author. m. (1), 2 sons, 1 daughter, (2) Victoria Hardie, 1975. Publications: Plays: Three Plays (Don't Destroy Me, Yes and After, and The World's Baby), 1966; The Silence of Saint-Just, 1970; Tom and Viv, 1985; Three Political Plays (The Silence of Lee Harvey Oswald, For the West, and the Emperor), 1990; A Dream of People, 1992; Unfinished Business and Other Plays, 1994. Fiction: The Game, 1957; The Frauds, 1960; Tussy Is Me: A Romance, 1970; The Nightcomers, 1972; And in the Forest the Indians, 1975; Bart's Mornings and Other Tales from Modern Brazil, 1975; A Spy in Winter, 1984. Poetry: Love Me Lambeth and Other Poems, 1961. Non-Fiction: The Handsomest Young Man in England: Rupert Brooke, 1967; Sir Richard Burton: A Biography, 1978. Contributions to: Films and television. Honours: Arts Council Award, 1956; Emmy Award, 1972; Writers Guild Award, 1972; Somerset Maugham Award, 1972; Comedy of the Year Award, Evening Standard, 1978. Address: 2 Helix Gardens, Brixton Hill, London SW2, England.

HASTINGS Lady Selina, b. 5 Mar 1945, Oxford, England. Writer. Education: St Hugh's College, Oxford, England. Appointments: Daily Telegraph, books page, 1968-82; Harper's & Queen Literary Editor, 1986-94. Publications: Nancy Mitford, biography, 1985; Evelyn Waugh, 1994; various children's books. Contributions to: Daily & Sunday Telegraph; Spectator; TLS; New Yorker; Harper's & Queen. Honour: Marsh Biography Award, 1993-96. Memberships: Royal Society of Literature Committee, 1994-. Literary Agent: Rogers Coleridge & White. Address: c/o Rogers Coleridge & White, 20 Powis Mews, London W11, England.

HASWELL Chetwynd John Drake, b. 18 July 1919, Penn Buckinghamshire, England. Soldier; Author. m. Charlotte Annette Petter, 25 Oct 1947, 2 sons, 1 daughter. Education: Winchester College, 1933-37; Royal Military College, Sandhurst, 1938-39. Appointments: Soldier, 1939-60; Author, Service Intelligence, Intelligence Centre, Ashford, 1966-84. Publications: (As George Foster) Indian File, 1960; Soldier on Loan, 1961; (As Jock Haswell) The Queen's Royal Regiment, 1967; The First Respectable Spy, 1969; James II, Soldier and Sailor, 1972; British Military Intelligence, 1973; Citizen Armies, 1973; The British Army, 1975; The Ardent Queen, Margaret of Anjou, 1976; The Battle for Empire, 1976; Spies and Spymasters, 1977; The Intelligence and Deception of the D Day Landings, 1979; The Tangled Web, 1985; The Queen's Regiment, 1986; Spies and Spying, 1986. Membership: Regimental Historian for the Queen's Regiment. Address: The Grey House, Lyminge, Folkestone, Kent CT18 8ED, England.

HATALA Marián, b. 11 Sept 1958, Holíč. Teacher. div June 1998, 1 son. Education: Language School; Studied German and Literature, Comenius University in Bratislava. Appointments: Teacher, German, Private Grammar School; Translator, German and Austrian Poetry, Mercury in Bratislava; egularly publishes reviews on new books. Publications: Moje Udalosti (My Events), 1990; Zatišie S Nočnými Výkrikm (Still Life With Night Sreams), 1993; Všetky Moje Smútky Ainé Výtržnosti (All My Sadness and Other Disturbances, 1996. Contributions to: Obrys, München; Sudetenland, München; Lichtungen-Graz, Österreich; Podium, Wien; Sodobnost, Lyublanja; Orfeus, Sofia; Romboid, Bratislava; Knižná Revue, Bratislava. Membership: Klub Nezárislych Spisovatelöv. Address: Púpavová 28, 841 04 Bratislava, Slovakia.

HATCH Lynda, b. 19 Feb 1950, Portland, OR, USA. Professor. Education: BA, Washington State University, 1972; MS, Portland State University, 1975; EdD, Oregon State University, 1984. Appointments: Teacher, Clover Park School District, Tacoma, WA, 1971-72; Hillsboro Elementary School District, 1971-72; Hillsboro Elementary School District, 1972-78; Bend-La Pine School District, 1978-80; Professor, Northern Arizona University, 1990-. Publications: Pathways of America: The Oregon Trail, 1993; Pathways of America: Lewis & Clark, 1993; Pathways of America: The Santa Fe Trail, 1995; Fifty States, 1997; US Presidents, 1997; US Map Skills, 1997; Human Body, 1998; National Parks and Other Park Service Sites, 1999. Contributions to: Journals include: Teacher Magazine; Elementary English; Social Studies and the Young Learner; LESI Science; Mountain Living Magazine; The New Teacher Advocate; Science & Children; Tools for Teachers; Childhood Education. Honours include: Oregon Teacher of the Year, 1982. Address: Center for Excellence in Education, PO Box 5774, Northern Arizona University, Flagstaff, AZ 86001-5774, USA.

HATCHER Robin Lee, b. 10 May 1951, Payette, Idaho, USA. Novelist. m. Jerrold W Neu, 6 May 1989, 2 daughters. Education: General High School Diploma, 1969. Publications: Stormy Surrender, 1984; Heart's Landing, 1984; Thorn of Love, 1985; Passion's Gamble, 1986; Heart Storm, 1986; Pirate's Lady, 1987; Gemfire, 1988; The Wager, 1989; Dream Tide, 1990; Promised Sunrise, 1990; Promise Me Spring, 1991; Rugged Splendor, 1991; The Hawk and the Heather, 1992; Devlin's Promise, 1992; Midnight Rose, 1992; A Frontier Christmas, 1992; The Magic, 1993; Where the Heart Is, 1993; Forever, Rose, 1994; Remember When, 1994; Liberty Blue, 1995; Chances ARe, 1996; Kiss me Katie, 1996; Dear Lady, 1997; Patterns of Love, 1998; In His Arms, 1998; The Forgiving Hour, 1999; Hometown Girl; For Such a Time as This, 1999. Contributions to: Various publications. Honours: Emma Merritt Award, 1998; Heart of Romance Readers Choice Award, 1996. Memberships: Romance Writers of America, former president 1992-1994; The Authors Guild. Address: PO Box 4722, Boise, ID 83711, USA.

HATOUM Milton, b. 19 Aug 1952, Manaus, Brazil. Professor; Writer. Education: Architecture Diploma, University of Sao Paulo, Brazil; MA, Comparative Literature, Sorbonne, Paris. Appointments: Freelance Journalist on culture, ISTOÉ Magazine, 1978-79; Professor, French and Latin American Literature. Publications: Novel: The Tree of the Seventh Heaven, Transl into French, 1992, German, 1992, Italian, 1992, transl by Ellen Watson, 1994. Contributions to: Grand Street, short story; Europe, short story; Anthologies published in Germany, Mexico. Honours: Most Prestigious Prize in Brazil, 1990. Literary Agent: Luiz Schwarcz. Address: Av Sete de Setembro 687, 69005-140 Manaus, AM, Brazil.

HATTENDORF John Brewster, b. 22 Dec 1941, Hinsdale, Illinois, USA. Naval and Maritime Historian. m. Berit Sundell, 15 Apr 1978, 3 daughters. Education: AB, Kenyon College, 1964; AM, Brown University, 1971; DPhil, University of Oxford, 1979. Appointments: Serving Officer, US Navy, 1964-73; Professor of Military History, National University of Singapore, 1981-83; Ernest J King Professor of Maritime History, US Naval War College,

1984-. Publications: The Writings of Stephen B Luce, 1975; On His Majesty's Service, 1983; Sailors and Scholars, 1984; A Bibliography of the Works of A T Mahan, 1986; England in the War of the Spanish Succession, 1987; Maritime Strategy and the Balance of Power, 1989; The Limitations of Military Power, 1990; Mahan on Naval Strategy, 1990; Mahan is Not Enough, 1993; British Naval Documents (co-editor), 1993; Ubi Sumnus: The State of Maritime and Naval History, 1994; Doing Naval History, 1995; Sea of Words (with Dean King), 1995; Maritime History: The Age of Discovery, 1996; Maritime History: The Eighteenth Century, 1996. Contributions to: Naval War College Review; International History Review. Memberships: Navy Records Society; Hakluyt Society; Academie du Var; Royal Historical Society, fellow; Royal Swedish Academy of Naval Science; Society for Nautical Research Address: 28 John Street, Newport, RI 02840, USA.

HATTERSLEY Roy, (Sydney George), b. 28 Dec 1932, Sheffield, England. Politician; Writer. m. Molly Hattersley, 1956. Education: BSc, Economics, University of Hull. Appointments: Journalist and Health Service Executive, 1956-64; Member, City Council, Sheffield, 1957-65; Member of Parliament, Labour Party, Sparkbrook Division, Birmingham, 1964-97; Parliamentary Private Secretary, Minister of Pensions and National Insurance, 1964-67; Director, Campaign for a European Political Community, 1966-67; Joint Parliamentary Secretary, Ministry of Labour, 1967-69, Minister of Defence for Administration, 1969-70; Visiting Fellow, Harvard University, 1971, 1972, Nuffield College, Oxford, 1984-; Labour Party Spokesman on Defence, 1972, and on Education and Science, 1972-74; Minister of State, Foreign and Commonwealth Office, 1974-76; Secretary of State for Prices and Consumer Protection, 1976-79; Principal Opposition Spokesman on the Environment, 1979-80, Home Affairs, 1980-83, Treasury and Economics Affairs, 1983-87, Home Affairs, 1987-92; Deputy Leader, Labour Party, 1983-92. Publications: Nelson: A Biography, 1974; Goodbye to Yorkshire (essays), 1976; Politics Apart, 1982; Press Gang, 1983; A Yorkshire Boyhood, 1983; Choose Freedom: The Future for Democratic Socialism, 1987; Economic Priorities for a Labour Government, 1987; The Maker's Mark (novel), 1990; In That Quiet Earth (novel), 1991; Skylark Song (novel), 1994; Between Ourselves (novel), 1994; Who Goes Home?, 1995; 50 Years On, 1997. Contributions to: Newspapers and journals. Honours: Privy Counsellor, 1975; Columnist of the Year, Granada, 1982; Honorary doctorates. Address: House of Lords, London SW1A 0PW, England.

HAUCK Dennis William, b. 8 Apr 1945, Hammond, Indiana, USA. Writer. Education: Indiana University, 1963-66; University of Vienna, Austria, 1969-72. Appointments: Editor, Infor Services Inc, 1973-76, Countrywide Publications, New York, 1976-79; Writer, Oldenberg Group Inc, Sacramento, 1983-91; Columnist, Today's Supervisor, Sacramento, 1991-. Publications: The UFO Handbook, 1974; Ufology, 1975; The Secret of the Emerald Tablet, 1991; The Haunted Places Guidebook, 1991; William Shatner: A Biography, 1992; Jewish Alchemy, 1992; Haunted Places Directory, 1996; The Emerald Tablet, 1998. Contributions to: Magazines and periodicals including: New Age Retailer; Whole Life Times; Fate. Honour: Appeared in and wrote script for theatrical release, Mysteries of the Gods, 1976. Memberships: Authors Guild; National Writers Union; Society for Technical Communication; California Writers Club; Association for Transpersonal Psychology; Institute of Noetic Sciences. Literary Agent: Michael Larsen/Elizabeth Pomada, San Fransico, California. Address: PO 22201, Sacramanto, CA 95822, USA.

HAUGAARD Erik Christian, b. 13 Apr 1923, Copenhagen, Denmark. Author. m. (1) Myra Seld, 23 Dec 1949, dec 1981, 1 son, 1 daughter, (2) Masako Taira, 27 July 1986, dec 1996. Publications: The Little Fishes, 1967; Orphas of the Wind, 1969; The Untold Tale, 1972; Hans Christian Andersen's Fairy Tales (translator), 1973; Chase Me Catch Nobody, 1980; Leif the Unlucky, 1982; The Samurai's Tale, 1984; Princess Horrid, 1990; The Boy and the Samurai, 1991; The Death of Mr Angel, 1992; Under the Black Flag, 1993; The Revenge of the Forty-Seven Samurai, 1995. Honours: Herald Tribune Award; Boston Globe-Horn Book Award; Jane Addams Award; Danish Cultural Ministry Award; Phoenix Award. Memberships: Authors Guild; Society of Authors; British PEN; Danish Authors Union. Address: Toad Hall, Ballydehob, West Cork, Ireland.

HAUGEN Paal-Helge, b. 26 Apr 1945, Valle, Norway. Poet; Writer; Dramatist. Appointments: Chairman, Norwegian State Film Production Board, 1980-85, Board of Literary Advisors, Association of Norwegian Authors, 1984-88, International Pegasus Prize Committee, 1988. Publications: 28 books including: Anne (novel), 1968; Stone Fences, 1986; Meditasjonar over Georges de la Tour (poetry), (1990); Sone O (poetry), 1992; Wintering with the Light, 1995; Poesi: Collected Poems, 1965-1995, 1995. Other: Plays for stage, radio and television; Opera libretti. Contributions to: Professional journals. Honours: Dobloug Prize, 1986; Richard Wilbur Prize, USA, 1986; Norwegian Literary Critics Prize, 1990; The Brage Prize, Norway, 1992; Norwegian National Brage Prize, 1994. Address: Skrefjellv 5, 4645 Nodeland, Norway.

HAUPTMAN William (Thornton), b. 26 Nov 1942, Wichita Falls, Texas, USA. Dramatist; Writer. m. (1) Barbara Barbat, 1968, div 1977, 1 daughter, (2) Marjorie Endreich, 1985, 1 son. Education: BFA, Drama, University of Texas at Austin, 1966; MFA, Playwrighting, Yale University School of Drama, 1973. Publications: Plays: Hear, 1977; Domino Courts/Comanche Cafe, 1977; Big River (with Roger Miller), 1986; Gillette, 1989. Television Drama: A House Divided (series), 1981. Fiction: Good Rockin' Tonight and Other Stories, 1988; The Storm Season, 1992. Honours: National Endowment for the Arts Grant, 1977; Boston Theatre Critics Circle Award, 1984; Tony Award, 1985; Drama-Lounge Award, 1986; Jesse Jones Award, Texas Institute of Letters, 1989. Address: 240 Warren Street, Apt E, Brooklyn, NY 11201, USA.

HAUTZIG Esther Rudomin, (Esther Rudomin), b. 18 Oct 1930, Vilna, Poland (US Citizen). Publications: Let's Cook Without Cooking (as E Rudomin), 1955; Let's Make Presents, 1961; Redecorating Your Room for Practically Nothing, 1967; The Endless Steppe, 1968; In the Park, 1968; At Home 1969; In School, 1971; Let's Make More Presents, 1973; Cool Cooking, 1974; I L Peretz: The Case Against the Wind and Other Stories (translator and adaptor), 1975; Life with Working Parents, 1976; A Gift for Mama, 1981; Holiday Treats, 1983; I L Peretz: The Seven Good Years and Other Stories (translator and adaptor), 1984; Make It Special, 1986; Christmas Goodies, 1989; Remember Who You Are, 1990; On the Air, 1991; Riches, 1992; New Introduction to a fascimile edition of Vilna by Israel Cohen, 1992. Contributions to: Periodicals. Memberships: Authors Guild; Authors League of America. Address: 505 West End Avenue, New York, NY 10024, USA.

HAVEL Václav, b. 5 Oct 1936, Prague, Czechoslovakia. President of the Czech Republic; Writer; Dramatist. m. (1) Olga Splichová, 1964, dec 27 Jan 1996, (2) Dagmar Havlová, January 4 1997. Education: Faculty of Economy, 1955-57; Drama Department, Academy of Arts, Prague, 1966. Appointments: ABC Theatre Prague, 1959-68, Editorial Board, Tvár, 1965, Lidové noviny, 1987-89; Co-founder, Charter 77, 1977, VONS, 1978, Civic Forum, 1989; President of Czechoslovakia, 1989-1992; President, Czech Republic, 1993-. Publications: 13 Plays; 10 books: Many essays; English translations include: The Garden Party, 1969; The Increased Difficulty of Concentration, 1972; Václav Havel or Living in Truth, 1986; Letters to Olga, 1988; Disturbing the Peace, 1990; Open Letters: Selected Writings 1965-90, 1991; Selected Plays by Václav Havel, 1991; Summer Meditations, 1992; Toward a Civil Society, 1994; The Art of the Impossible, 1997. Honours: The Olof Palme Prize, 1989; Simon Bolívar Prize, UNESCO, 1990; Political Book of the Year, 1990. Memberships: Czech PEN, 1989; PEN-Centre, Germany; PEN, Sweden; Hamburg Academy of Liberal Arts; Austrian PEN; Royal British Legion; Associé éntranger Académie des sciences morales et politiques Institut de France. Literary Agent: Aura Pont Agency, Prague. Address: Kancelár prezidenta republiky, 119 08 Praha-Hrad, Czech Republic.

HAVIARAS Stratis, b. 28 June 1935, Nea Kios, Greece. Librarian; Poet; Writer; Editor. m. Heather E Cole, 30 Mar 1990, 1 daughter. Education: BA, 1973, MFA, 1976, Goddard College. Appointments: Librarian, Harvard University Library; Editor, Harvard Review, 1992-. Publications: Poetry: 4 books in Greek, 1963, 1965, 1967, 1972; Crossing the River Twice, 1976. Novels: When the Tree Sings, 1979; The Heroic Age, 1984. Editor: Seamus Heaney: A Celebration, 1996. Contributions to: Newspapers and magazines. Honours: National Book Critics Circle Awards. Memberships: PEN New England; Phi Beta Kappa; Signet; Societe Imaginaire. Address: c/o Poetry Room, Harvard University Library, Cambridge, MA 02138, USA.

HAVLAND Finn, b. 1 Apr 1934, Solbjerg Sogn, Denmark. Adviser. 5 sons, 3 daughters. Appointments: Blacksmith; Tramp, 3 years; Fisherman; Navigator, Expedition to Greenland, Leader of Biological Station; Architect. Publications: Europas Vandvejes Historie; Lods for Europas Vandveje; Maremindet: A Sea Lexicon. Membership: Dansk Forfatterforening. Address: Skt. Annagade 64 Helsingor, Denmark.

HAWKESWORTH John Stanley, b. 7 Dec 1920, London, England. Television and Film Writer and Producer; Painter. m. 10 Apr 1943, 1 son. Education: Académie Julien, Paris; BA, Queen's College, Oxford. Appointments: Army Service, 1940-47; London Films; Freelance Designer; Producer, Scriptwriter, Tiger Bay, then became TV and Film Scriptwriter, 1962; Many TV productions; Freelance Writer and Producer. Publications: Upstairs Downstairs, 1972; In My Lady's Chamber, 1973. Contributions to: Many and various. Honours: Writer's Guild of Great Britain, 1967, 1973, 1974; Academy of Arts and Sciences, USA, 1974, 1979, 1980; Critics Circle, USA, 1976, 1977; Peabody Award, USA. Membership: Writer's Guild of Great Britain. Address: c/o Jenne Casarotto, National House, 60-66 Wardour Street, London W1V 3HP, England.

HAWKING Stephen (William), b. 8 Jan 1942, Oxford, England. Professor of Mathematics; Writer. m. Jane Wilde, 1965, div, 2 sons, 1 daughter. Education: BA, University College, Oxford; PhD, Trinity Hall, Cambridge. Appointments: Research Fellow, 1965-69, Fellow for Distinction in Science, 1969-, Gonville and Caius College, Cambridge; Member, Institute of Theoretical Astronomy, Cambridge, 1968-72; Research Assistant, Institute of Astronomy, Cambridge, 1972-73; Research Assistant, Department of Applied Mathematics and Theoretical Physics, 1973-75, Reader in Gravitational Physics, 1975-77, Professor, 1977-79, Lucasian Professor of Mathematics, 1979-, Cambridge University. Publications: The Large Scale Structure of Space-Time (with G F R Ellis), 1973; General Relativity: An Einstein Centenary Survey (editor with W W Israel), 1979; Is the End in Sight for Theoretical Physics?: An Inaugural Lecture, 1980; Superspace and Supergravity: Proceedings of the Nuffield Workshop (editor with M Roček), 1981; The Very Early Universe: Proceedings of the Nuffield Workshop (co-editor), 1983; Three Hundred Years of Gravitation (with W W Israel), 1987; A Brief History of Time: From the Big Bang to Black Holes, 1988; Black Holes and Baby Universes and Other Essays, 1993. Contributions to: Scholarly journals. Honours: Eddington Medal, 1975, Gold Medal, 1985, Royal Academy of Science; Pius XI Gold Medal, Pontifical Academy of Sciences, 1975; William Hopkins Prize, Cambridge Philosophical Society, 1976; Maxwell Medal, Institute of Physics, 1976; Dannie Heinemann Prize for Mathematical Physics, American Physical Society and American Institute of Physics, 1976; Honorary fellow, University College, Oxford, 1977; Trinity Hall, Cambridge, 1984; Commander of the Order of the British Empire, 1982; Paul Dirac Medal and Prize, Institute of Physics, 1987; Wolf Foundation Prize for Physics, 1988; Companion of Honour, 1989; Honorary doctorates. Memberships: American Academy of Arts and

Sciences; American Philosophical Society; Pontifical Academy of Sciences; Royal Society, fellow. Address: c/o Department of Applied Mathematics and Theoretical Physics, Cambridge University, Silver Street, Cambridge CB3 9EW, England.

HAWKINS Angus Brian, b. 12 Apr 1953, Portsmouth, England. Historian. m. Esther Armstrong, 20 May 1980, 2 daughters. Education: BA Hons, Reading University, 1975; PhD, London School of Economics, 1980. Publications: Parliament, Party and the Art of Politics in Britain, 1987; Victorian Britain: An Encyclopaedia, 1989; British Party Politics, 1852-1886, 1998; The Political Journals of the First Earl of Kimberley, 1862-1902, 1998. Contributions to: English Historical Review, Parliamentary History, Journal of British Studies, Victorian Studies; Nineteenth Century Prose, Archive. Honours: McCann Award, 1972; Gladstone Memorial Prize, 1978. Memberships: Reform Club. Address: Rewley House, University of Oxford, 1 Wellington Square, Oxford, England.

HAWORTH John, b. 13 Apr 1942, Bury, Lancashire, England. Retired General Medical Practitioner. m. Winifred Eleanor Roan, 28 July 1969, 1 daughter. Education: MBChB, University St Andrews, 1966; D Obst RCog, 1970; MRCGP, 1974; FRCGP, 1991. Appointments: House Physician, Maryfield Hospital, Dundee, 1966; House Surgeon, Perth Royal Infirmary, 1967; SHO Medicine, Cumberland Infirmary, Carlisle, 1967; SHo, Obstetrics, City Maternity Hospital, Carlisle, 1968; SHO Accident and Emergency, Cumberland Infirmary Carlisle, 1969, retired 1997. Publications: Chapter in "Alimentary My Dear Doctor", 1988; Chapter in "Nervous Laughter", 1991. Contributions to: Several papers, variety of medical publications including Update, The Practitioner. Membership: General Practice Writers Association. Address: 40 Brampton Road, Carlisle, Cumbria CA3 9AT, England.

HAWORTH-BOOTH Mark, b. 20 Aug 1944, Westow, Yorks, England. Writer. m. Rosemary Joanna Miles, 19 July 1979, 2 daughters. Education: English Tripos, parts I and II, Cambridge University, 1963-66; Postgraduate Diploma in Fine Art, Edinburgh University, 1967-69. Publications: E McKnight Kauffer: A Designer and his Public, 1979; The Golden Age of British Photography 1839-1900, 1983; Bill Brandt's Literary Britain, 1984; Photography Now, 1989; Camille Silvy: River Scene, France, 1992; Photography: An Independent Art. Photographs from the Victoria and Albert Museum, 1839-1996, 1997; Photography: An Independent Art, 1997. Contributions to: Times Literary Supplement; London Magazine; The Spectator; New Statesman; Aperture. Honours: Hood Medal, 1988; Sudek Medal, 1989. Address: Victoria & Albert Museum, London SW7 2RL, England.

HAWTHORNE Susan, b. 30 Nov 1951, Wagga Wagga, New South Wales, Australia. University Lecturer; Publisher; Poet; Writer. Education: Diploma, Primary Teaching, Melbourne Teachers College, 1972; BA, Honours, Philosophy, La Trobe University, 1976; MA, Prelim, Classics, University of Melbourne, 1981. Appointments: Tutor, Koori Teacher Education Programme, Deakin University, 1986; Editor and Commissioning Editor, Penguin Books, Australia, 1987-91; Publisher, Spinifex Press, 1991-; Lecturer, Department of Communication and Language Studies, Victoria University of Technology, 1995-. Publications: Difference (editor), 1985; Moments of Desire, 1989; The Exploring Frangipani, 1990; Angels of Power, 1991; The Spinifex Book of Answer's Answers, 1991; The Falling Women, 1992; The Language in My Tongue: Four New Poets, 1993; The Spinifex Quiz Book, 1993; Australia for Women (co-editor), 1994; Car Maintenance, Explosives and Love (co-editor), 1997; Cyberfeminism, forthcoming. Contributions to: Journals, reviews, and periodicals. Honours: Shortlisted, Mattara Poetry Prize, 1991, ABC Radio National Poetry Award, 1994. Memberships: Australian Society of Authors; Fellowship of Australian Authors; PEN International; Victoria Writers Centre. Address: c/o Spinifex Press, 504 Queensbury Street, North Melbourne, Victoria 3051, Australia.

HAYCRAFT Anna (Margaret), (Alice Thomas Ellis, Brenda O'Casey). Writer. Appointments: Director, Duckworth, publishers, London; Columnist (Home life), The Spectator, 1984-90, The Universe, 1989-90, The Catholic Herald, 1990-95; The Oldie, 1995-; The Catholic Herald, 1998-. Publications: Natural Baby Food: A Cookery Book (as Brenda O'Casey), 1977; The Sin Eater (novel), 1977; Darling You Shouldn't Have Gone to So Much Trouble (cookery) (as Anna Haycraft with Caroline Blackwood), 1980; The Birds of the Air (novel), 1980; The 27th Kingdom (novel), 1982; The Other Side of the Fire (novel), 1983; Unexplained Laughter (novel), 1985; Home Life (collected columns from the Spectator), 1986; Secrets of Strangers (with Tom Pitt Aikens) (psychiatry), 1986; The Clothes in the Wardrobe (novel), 1987; More Home Life (collection), 1987; The Skeleton in the Cupboard (novel), 1988; Home Life III (collection), 1988; The Loss of the Good Authority (with Tom Pitt Aikens), (psychiatry), 1989; Wales: An Anthology, 1989; The Fly in the Ointment (novel), 1989; Home Life IV (collection), 1989; The Inn at the Edge of the World (novel), 1990; A Welsh Childhood (autobiography), 1990; Pillars of Gold, 1992; Serpent on the Rock, 1994; The Evening of Adam, 1994; Cat Among the Pigeons: Collected Columns from the Catholic Herald, 1994; Fairy Tale, 1996. Honours: Welsh Arts Council Award, 1977; Yorkshire Post Novel of the Year, 1983; Writers Guild Award for Best Fiction, 1991. Literary Agent: Robert Kirby, Peters Fraser & Dunlop, 5th Floor, 503/4 The Chambers, Chelsea Harbour, Lots Road, London SW 10 0XF. Address: 22 Gloucester Crescent, London NW1 7DS, England.

HAYDEN Dolores, b. 15 Mar 1945, New York, USA. Architect; Professor; Author. m. Peter Marris, 18 May 1975, 1 daughter. Education: BA, Mount Holyoke College, 1966; Diploma, English Studies, Girton College, Cambridge, 1967; M.Arch, Harvard Graduate School of Design, 1972. Publications: Seven American Utopias, 1976; The Grand Domestic Revolution, 1981; Redesigning the American Dream, 1984; The Power of Place, 1995; Playing House, 1998. Contributions to: Numerous journals. Honours: National Endowment for the Humanities Fellowship, 1976; National Endowment for the Arts Fellowship, 1980; Guggenheim Fellowship, 1981; Rockefeller Foundation Fellowship, 1981; American Council of Learned Societies/Ford Foundation Fellowship, 1988. Memberships: American Studies Association; Organization of American Historians. Address: School of Architecture, Yale University, PO Box 208242, New Haven, CT 06520, USA.

HAYES Charles Langley. See: **HOLMES Bryan John.**

HAYLOCK John Mervyn, b. 22 Sept 1918, Bournemouth, England. Writer. Education: Diploma français, Institut de Touraine, Tours, France, 1937; Certificat d'Immatriculation, Grenoble University, France, 1938; BA Honours, 1940, MA Honours, 1946, Pembroke College, Cambridge. Publications: New Babylon, A Portrait of Iraq (with Desmond Stewart), 1956; See You Again, 1963; It's All Your Fault, 1964; Flight into Egypt, by Philippe Jullian (translator), 1970; Choice and Other Stories, 1979; One Hot Summer in Kyoto, 1980; Tokyo Sketch Book, 1980; Japanese Excursions 1981; Japanese Memories, 1987; Romance Trip and Other Stories, 1988; A Touch of the Orient, 1990; Uneasy Relations, 1993; Eastern Exchange: Memoirs of People and Places, 1997; Doubtful Partners, 1998. Contributions to: Magazines and periodicals. Memberships: Royal Society of Literature, fellow; Oriental Club, London. Literary Agent: Rivers Scott, 15 Gledhow Gardens, London SW5 0AY, England. Address: Flat 28, 15 Grand Avenue, Hove, BN3 2NG, England.

HAYMAN David, b. 7 Jan 1927, New York, New York, USA. Professor of Comparative Literature; Emeritus; Writer; Editor. m. Loni Goldschmidt, 28 June 1951, 2 daughters. Education: BA, New York University, 1948; PhD, University of Paris, 1955. Appointments: Instructor, 1955-57, Assistant Professor, 1957-58, Associate Professor of English, 1958-65, University of Texas; Professor of English and Comparative Literature, University of Iowa, 1965-73; Professor of Comparative Literature, 1973-95, Professor Emeritus, 1995-, University of Wisconsin, Madison. Publications: Joyce et Mallarmé, 1956; A First-Draft Version of Finnegans Wake, 1963; Configuration Critique de James Joyce (editor), 1965; Ulysses: The Mechanics of Meaning, 1970; Form in Fiction (with Eric Rabkin), 1974; Ulysses: Critical Essays (with Clive Hart), 1974; The James Joyce Archive (editor), 1978; Philippe Sollers: Writing and the Experience of Limits (editor and co-translator), 1980; Re-forming the Narrative, 1987; The Wake in Transit, 1990; Probes: Genetic Studies in Joyce (with Sam Slote), 1994; James Joyce: Epiphanias (editor), 1996. Contributions to: Many scholarly books and journals. Honours: Guggenheim Fellowship, 1958-59; National Endowment for the Humanities Fellowship, 1979-80; Harry Levin Prize, American Comparative Literature Association, 1989. Address: 2913 Columbia Road, Madison, WI 53705, USA.

HAYMAN Richard, b. 13 Oct 1959, Taunton, England. Archaeologist. Education: BA, University College, Cardiff, 1981. Appointments: Archaeologist, The National Trust, 1983-85; Archaeologist, Merthyr Tydfil Heritage Trust, 1985-88; Freelance Photographer, 1988-94; Archaeologist, Ironbridge Gorge Museum, 1994-. Publications: Riddles in Stone, 1997. Contributions to: The Archaeologist As Witness, Industrial Archaeology Review, 1997. Address: Ty Wen, Falstaff St, Shrewsbury, SY1 2QN, England.

HAYMAN Ronald, b. 4 May 1932, Bournemouth, England. Writer. Education: BA, 1954, MA, 1963, Trinity Hall, Cambridge. Publications: Harold Pinter, 1968; Samuel Beckett, 1968; John Osborne, 1968; John Arden, 1968; Robert Bolt, 1969; John Whiting, 1969; Collected Plays of John Whiting (editor), 2 volumes, 1969; Techniques of Acting, 1969; The Art of the Dramatist and Other Pieces, by John Whiting (editor), 1970; Arthur Miller, 1970; Tolstoy, 1970; Arnold Wesker, 1970; John Gielgud, 1971; Edward Albee, 1971; Eugène Ionesco, 1972; Playback, 1973; The Set-Up, 1974; Playback 2, 1974; The First Thrust, 1975; The German Theatre (editor), 1975; How to Read a Play, 1977; The Novel Today, 1967-75, 1976; My Cambridge (editor), 1977; Tom Stoppard, 1977; Artaud and After, 1977; De Sade, 1978; Theatre and Anti-Theatre, 1979; British Theatre Since 1955: A Reassessment, 1979; Nietzsche: A Critical Life, 1980; K: A Biography of Kafka, 1981; Brecht: A Biography, 1983; Fassbinder: Film Maker, 1984; Brecht: The Plays, 1984; Günter Grass, 1985; Secrets: Boyhood in a Jewish Hotel, 1932-54, 1985; Writing Against: A Biography of Sartre, 1986; Proust: A Biography, 1990; The Death and Life of Sylvia Plath, 1991; Tennessee Williams: Everyone Else is an Audience, 1994; Thomas Mann, 1995; Hitler and Geli, 1997; Nietzsche's Voices, 1997; Jung, forthcoming. Membership: Society of Authors. Literary Agent: Peters, Fraser & Dunlop, 503-4 The Chambers, Chelsea Harbour, London, SW10 0XF. Address: Flat D, 3 Chesterford Gardens, London NW3 7DD, England.

HAYS Robert Glenn, b. 23 May 1935, Carmi, Illinois, USA. Journalism Educator. m. Mary Elizabeth Corley, 21 Dec 1957, 2 sons. Education: BS, Jounalism, 1961, MS, Journalism, 1972, PhD, 1976, Southern Illinois University. Appointments: Reporter, Granite City Press-Record, 1961-63; Public Relations Writer, 1963-66, Alumni Editor, 1966-71, Southern Illinois University; Assistant Scientist, Illinois Board of Natural Resources and Conservation, 1971-73; Journalism Faculty, Sam Houston State University, 1974-75, University of Illinois, 1975-86, 1987-; Chair, Department of Mass Communications, Southeast Missouri University, 1986-87. Publications: G-2: Intelligence for Patton, 1971; Country Editor, 1974; State Science in Illinois, 1980; Early Stories From the Land, 1995; A Race at Bay: New York Times Editorials on the 'Indian Problem', 1860-1900, 1997. Contributions to: Periodicals and journals. Honours: International ACE Award of Excellence, 1993, 1994; University of Illinois

Academy of Teaching Excellence Award, 1996. Membership: Research Society of American Periodicals, founding member. Address: 2314 Glenoak Drive, Champaign, IL 61821, USA.

HAYTER Alethea Catharine, b. 7 Nov 1911, Cairo, Egypt. Former British Council Representative and Cultural Attache; Writer. Education: BA, MA, University of Oxford. Publications: Mrs Browning: A Poet's Work and Its Setting, 1962; A Sultry Month: Scenes of London Literary Life in 1846, 1965; Elizabeth Barrett Browning, 1965; Opium and the Romantic Imagination, 1968; Horatio's Version, 1972; A Voyage in Vain, 1973; Fitzgerald to His Friends: Selected Letters of Edward Fitzgerald, 1979; Portrait of a Friendship, Drawn From New Letters of James Russell Lowell to Sybella Lady Lyttelton 1881-1891, 1990; The Backbone: Diaries of a Military Family in the Napoleonic Wars, 1993; Charlotte Yonge, 1996; A Wise Woman: A Memoir of Lavinia Mynors from her Diaries and Letters, 1996. Contributions to: Oxford Companion to English Literature; Sunday Times; Times Literary Supplement; Spectator; New Statesman; History Today; Ariel; London Review of Books; Longman Encyclopedia. Honours: W.H. Heinemann Prize, Royal Society of Literature, 1963; Rose Mary Crawshay Prize, British Academy, 1968; Officer of the Order of the British Empire. Memberships: Royal Society of Literature, fellow; Society of Authors, committee of management, 1975-79; PEN. Address: 22 Aldebert Terrace, London SW8 1BJ, England.

HAZEN Robert M(iller), b. 1 Nov 1948, Rockville Centre, New York, USA. Scientist; Musician; Writer. m. Margaret Hindle, 9 Aug 1969, 1 son, 1 daughter. Education: BS, SM, Massachusetts Institute of Technology, 1971; PhD, Harvard University, 1975. Appointments: NATO Fellow, Cambridge University, 1975-76; Research Scientist, Geophysical Laboratory, Carnegie Institution, Washington, DC, 1976-; Clarence Robinson Professor, George Mason University; Trumpeter with many orchestras. Publications: Comparative Crystal Chemistry, 1982; Poetry of Geology, 1982; Music Men, 1987; The Breakthrough, 1988; Science Matters, 1990; Keepers of the Flame, 1991; The New Alchemist, 1993; The Sciences, 1995; Why Aren't Black Holes Black?, 1997. Contributions to: Many scientific journals and to periodicals. Honours: Mineralogical Society of America Award, 1981; Ipatief Prize, 1984; ASCAP-Deems Taylor Award, 1988; Education Press Association Award, 1992. Memberships: American Chemistry Society; American Geophysical Union; History of Science Society; International Guild of Trumpeters; Mineralogical Society of America; Phi Lambda Upsilon; Sigma Xi; Education Press Award. Address: c/o Geophysical Laboratory, Carnegie Institution, 5251 Broad Branch Road North West, Washington, DC 20015, USA.

HAZLETON Lesley, b. 20 Sept 1945, Reading, England. Writer. Education: BA, Honours in Psychology, Manchester University, 1966; MA, Psychology, Hebrew University of Jerusalem, 1972. Appointment: Automotive Columnist, Detroit Free Press. Publications: Israeli Women, 1978; Where Mountains Roar, 1980; In Defence of Depression, 1984; Jerusalem, Jerusalem, 1986; England, Bloody England, 1989; Confessions of a Fast Woman, 1992; Everything Women Always Wanted to Know About Cars, 1995; Driving to Detroit, 1998. Contributions to: Many periodicals and magazines. Memberships: International Motor Press Association; PEN American Center. Address: c/o Watkins-Loomis Inc, 133 East 35th Street, New York, NY 10016, USA.

HAZO Samuel (John), b. 19 July 1928, Pittsburgh, Pennsylvania, USA. Professor of English; Writer; Poet. Education: BA, University of Notre Dame, 1948; MA, Duquesne University, 1955; PhD, University of Pittsburgh, 1957. Appointments: Faculty, 1955-65, Dean, College of Arts and Sciences, 1961-66, Professor of English, 1965-, Duquesne University; Director, International Forum, 1966-. Publications: Discovery and Other Poems, 1959; The Quiet Wars, 1962; Hart Crane: An Introduction and Interpretation, 1963, new edition as Smithereened Apart: A Critique of Hart Crane, 1978; The Christian Intellectual Studies in the Relation of Catholicism to the Human Sciences (editor), 1963; A Selection of Contemporary Religious Poetry (editor), 1963; Listen With the Eye, 1964; My Sons in God: Selected and New Poems, 1965; Blood Rights, 1968; The Blood of Adonis (with Ali Ahmed Said), 1971; Twelve Poems (with George Nama), 1972; Seascript: A Mediterranean Logbook, 1972; Once for the Last Bandit: New and Previous Poems, 1972; Quartered, 1974; Inscripts, 1975; The Very Fall of the Sun, 1978; To Paris, 1981; The Wanton Summer Air, 1982; Thank a Bored Angel, 1983; The Feast of Icarus, 1984; The Color of Reluctance, 1986; The Pittsburgh That Starts Within You, 1986; Silence Spoken Here, 1988; Stills, 1989; The Rest is Prose, 1989; Lebanon, 1990; Picks, 1990; The Past Won't Stay Behind You, 1993; The Pages of Day and Night, 1995; The holy Surprise of Right Now, 1996. Address: 785 Somerville Drive, Pittsburgh, PA 15243, USA.

HAZZARD Shirley, b. 30 Jan 1931, Sydney, New South Wales, Australia. Writer. m. Francis Steegmuller, 22 Dec 1963, dec 1994. Education: Queenwood School, Sydney. Appointments: Member, Combined Services Intelligence, Hong Kong, 1947-48, UK High Commissioner's Officer, Wellington, New Zealand, 1949-50; General Service Post, United Nations, New York City, 1952-62; Boyer Lecturer, Australia, 1984, 1988. Publications: Fiction: The Evening of the Holiday, 1966; The Bay of Noon, 1970; The Transit of Venus, 1980. Stories: Cliffs of Falls and Other Stories, 1963; People in Glass Houses, 1967. Non-Fiction: Defeat of an Ideal: A Study of the Self-Destruction of the United Nations, 1973; Countenance of Truth, 1990. Contributions to: Magazines. Honours: National Institute of Arts and Letters Award, 1966; Guggenheim Fellowship, 1974; 1st Prize, O Henry Short Story Awards, 1976; National Book Critics Award for Fiction, 1981. Membership: American Academy and National Institute of Arts and Letters. Address: 200 East 66th Street, New York, NY 10021, USA.

HEADLEY John Miles, b. 23 Oct 1929, New York, New York, USA. Historian; Professor. Education: BA, Princeton University, 1951; MA, 1953, PhD, 1960, Yale University. Appointments: Instructor, University of Massachusetts, Amherst, 1959-61; Instructor to Assistant Professor, University of British Columbia, Vancouver, 1962-64; Assistant Professor, 1964-66, Associate Professor, 1966-69, Professor, 1969-, University of North Carolina at Chapel Hill. Publications: Luther's View of Church History, 1963; Medieval and Renaissance Studies, Vol III (editor), 1968; Responsio ad Lutherum, Complete Works of St Thomas More, Vol V (editor), 1969; The Emperor and his Chancellor: A Study of the Imperial Chancellery under Gattinara, 1983; San Carlo Borromeo: Catholic Reform and Ecclesiastical Politics in the Second Half of the Sixteenth Century (editor and contributor), 1988; The Oxford Encyclopedia of the Reformation (associate editor), 1996; Tommaso Campanella and the Transformation of the World, 1997; Empire, Church and World: The Quest for Universal Order, 1997. Contributions to: Various scholarly books and journals. Honours: Guggenheim Fellowship, 1974; Institute for Arts and Humanities Fellowship, 1989. Address: c/o Department of History, University of North Carolina at Chapel Hill, Chapel Hill, NC 27599, USA.

HEALD Tim(othy Villiers), (David Lancaster), b. 28 Jan 1944, Dorset, England. Journalist; Writer. m. Alison Martina Leslie, 30 Mar 1968, sep, 2 sons, 2 daughters. Education: MA, Honours, Balliol College, Oxford, 1965. Appointments: Reporter, Sunday Times, 1965-67; Feature Editor, Town magazine, 1967; Feature Writer, Daily Express, 1967-72; Associate Editor, Weekend Magazine, Toronto, 1977-78; Columnist, Observer, 1990. Publications: It's a Dog's Life, 1971; Unbecoming Habits, 1973; Blue Book Will Out, 1974; Deadline, 1975; Let Sleeping Dogs Die, 1976; The Making of Space, 1999, 1976; John Steed: An Authorized Biography, 1977; Just Desserts, 1977; H.R.H: The Man Who Will be King (with M Mohs), 1977; Murder at Moose Jaw, 1981; Caroline R, 1981; Masterstroke, 1982; Networks, 1983; Class Distinctions, 1984; Red Herrings, 1985; The Character of Cricket, 1986; Brought to Book, 1988; The Newest London Spy (editor), 1988; Business Unusual, 1989; By Appointments: 150 Years of the Royal Warrant, 1989; A Classic English Crime (editor), 1990; My Lord's (editor), 1990; The Duke: A Portrait of Prince Philip, 1991; Honourable Estates, 1992; Barbara Cartland: A Life of Love, 1994; Denis: The Authorized Biography of the Incomparable Compton, 1994; Brian Johnston: The Authorized Biography, 1995; A Classic Christmas Crime (editor), 1995; Beating Retreat: Hong Kong Under the Last Governor, 1997; Stop Press, 1998. Memberships: Crime Writers Association, Chairman, 1987-88; PEN; Society of Authors. Address: 66 The Esplanade, Fowey, Cornwall PL23 1JA, England.

HEALEY Denis (Baron of Riddlesden in the County of West Yorkshire), (Winston), b. 30 Aug 1917, Mottingham, England. Politician; Writer. Education: Balliol College, Oxford; First Class Hon Mods, 1938; Jenkyns Exhib, 1939; Harmsworth Senior Scholar, First Class Lit.Hum, BA, 1940, MA, 1945. Appointments: Secretary, International Department, Labour Party, 1945-52; Member of Parliament, Labour Party, South East Leeds, 1951-55, Leeds East, 1955-92; Shadow Cabinet, 1959-64, 1970-74, 1979-87; Secretary of State for Defence, 1964-70; Chancellor of the Exchequer, 1974-79; Deputy Leader, Labour Party, 1980-83; President, Birkbeck College, 1993. Publications: The Curtain Falls, 1951; New Fabian Essays, 1952; Neutralism, 1955; Fabian International Essays, 1956; A Neutral Belt in Europe, 1958; NATO and American Security, 1959; The Race Against the H Bomb, 1960; Labour Britain and the World, 1963; Healey's Eye, 1980; Labour and a World Society, 1985; Beyond Nuclear Deterrence, 1986; The Time of My Life (autobiography), 1989; When Shrimps Learn to Whistle (essays), 1990; My Secret Planet, 1992; Denis Healey's Yorkshire Dales, 1996. Honours: Member of the Order of the British Empire, 1945; Companion of Honour, 1979; Grand Cross of the Order of Merit, Federal Republic of Germany, 1979; Created Baron Healey of Riddlesden, 1992; Freeman, City of Leeds, 1992; Honorary doctorates. Membership: Royal Society of Literature, fellow. Address: Pingles Place, Alfriston, East Sussex BN26 5TT, England.

HEALEY Robin Michael, b. 16 Feb 1952, London, England. Historian; Biographer. Education: BA, 1974, MA, 1976, University of Birmingham. Appointments: Documentation Officer, Tamworth Castle and Cambridge Museum of Archaeology and Anthropology, 1977-80; Research Assistant, History of Parliament, 1985-92; Visiting Research Fellow, Manchester University, 1997-. Publications: Books: Hertfordshire, 1982; Diary of George Mushet (1805-13), 1982; Grigson at Eighty, 1985; A History of Barley School, 1995; Entries in: Biographical Dictionary of Modern British Radicals, 1984; Domesday Book, 1985; Secret Britain, 1986; Dictionary of Literary Biography, 1991; Encyclopaedia of Romanticism, 1992; Consumer Magazines of the British Isles, 1993; Postwar Literatures in English, 1998-. Contributions to: Country Life; Guardian; Literary Review; Book and Magazine Collector; Learned journals. Honour: 1st Prize, Birmingham Post Poetry Contest, 1974. Memberships: Executive, Charles Lamb Society, 1983-; Press Officer, Alliance of Literary Societies, 1989-. Address: 80 Hall Lane, Great Chishill, Royston, Herts SG8 8SH, England.

HEANEY Seamus (Justin), b. 13 Apr 1939, County Londonderry, Northern Ireland. Poet; Writer; Professor. m. Marie Devlin, 1965, 2 sons, 1 daughter. Education: St Columb's College, Derry; BA 1st Class, Queen's University, Belfast, 1961. Appointments: Teacher, St Thomas's Secondary School, Belfast, 1962-63; Lecturer, St Joseph's College of Education, Belfast, 1963-66, Queen's University, Belfast, 1966-72, Carysfort College, 1975-81; Senior Visting Lecturer, 1982-85, Boylston Professor of Rhetoric and Oratory, 1985-97, Harvard University; Professor of Poetry, Oxford University, 1989-94. Publications: Eleven Poems, 1965; Death of a Naturalist, 1966; Door Into the Dark, 1969; Wintering Out,

1972; North, 1975; Field Work, 1979; Selected Poems, 1965-1975, 1980; Sweeney Astray, 1984, revised edition as Sweeney's Flight, 1992; Station Island, 1984; The Haw Lantern, 1987; New Selected Poems, 1966-1987, 1990; Seeing Things, 1991; The Spirit Level, 1996; Opened Ground: Selected Poems, 1966-1996, 1998. Prose: Preoccupations: Selected Prose, 1968-1978, 1980; The Government of the Tongue, 1988; The Place of Writing, 1989; The Redress of Poetry: Oxford Lectures, 1995. Honours: Somerset Maugham Award, 1967; Cholmondeley Award, 1968; W H Smith Award, 1975; Duff Cooper Prize, 1975; Whitbread Awards, 1987, 1996; Nobel Prize for Literature, 1995; Whitbread Book of the Year Award, 1997. Membership: Irish Academy of Letters. Address: c/o Faber & Faber, 3 Queen Square, London WC1N 3RU, England.

HEARD Anthony Hazlitt, b. 20 Nov 1937, Johannesburg, South Africa. Journalist. m. (1) Valerie Joy Hermanson, 1959, (2) Mary Ann Barker, 1988, 1 son, 3 daughters. Education: BA, Honours, 1st class, Political Science, University of Cape Town, 1964. Appointments: Editor, The Cape Times, 1971-87; Freelance writer for international newspapers, 1987-94. Publication: The Cape of Storms: A Personal History of the Crisis in South Africa, 1990. Contributions to: Many newspapers. Honour: Golden Pen of Freedom, World Association of Newspapers, 1986. Address: PO Box 12189, Mill Street, Gardens 8010, South Africa.

HEARDEN Patrick Joseph, b. 17 Sept 1942, Green Bay, Wisconsin, USA. Historian. m. Carol J Morgan, 27 July 1991. Education: BS, 1965, MS, 1966, PhD, 1971, University of Wisconsin, Madison. Appointments: Case Western Reserve University, 1971-72; University of South Dakota, 1973-75; University of Missouri, 1975-78; University of Arizona, 1979-80; University of Wisconsin, 1981-82; Purdue University, 1983-. Publications: Independence and Empire, 1982; Roosevelt Confronts Hitler, 1987; Vietnam: Four American Perspectives (editor), 1990; The Tragedy of Vietnam, 1991. Contributions to: American Historical Review; Journal of Southern History; Journal of Interdisciplinary History; South Atlantic Quarterly. Memberships: Organization of American Historians; Society for Historians of American Foreign Relations. Address: 7613 N 300 East, Battleground, IN 47920, USA.

HEARLE Kevin (James), b. 17 Mar 1958, Santa Ana, California, USA. University Lecturer; Poet; Writer. m. Elizabeth Henderson, 26 Nov 1983. Education: AB, English with Distinction, Stanford University, 1980; MFA, University of Iowa, 1983; MA, Literature, 1990; PhD, Literature, 1991, University of California at Santa Cruz. Appointments: Poetry Co-Editor, Quarry West, 1988-92; Instructor, 1991, Lecturer, 1993, 1998, University of California at Santa Cruz; Lecturer, San Jose State University, 1992-94; Instructor, University of California at Los Angeles Extension, 1995-96; Lecturer, California State University at Los Angeles, 1995-96. Publications: Each Thing We Know Is Changed Because We Know It, and Other Poems, 1994, 2nd edition, 1996; John Steinbeck: The Grapes of Wrath: Text and Criticism (editor with Peter Lisca), revised edition, 1997; Beyond Boundaries: Steinbeck and the World - Papers from the Fourth International Steinbeck Congress (editor with Susan Shillinglaw), forthcoming. Contributions: Steinbeck Newsletter, editorial board, 1994; Various books, reviews, quarterlies, and journals. Honours: Peninsula Community Foundation Individual Artist Grant, 1986; Millay Colony for the Arts Residency, 1990. Memberships: American Literature Association; International John Steinbeck Society; Modern Language Association; Robinson Jeffers Association; Western Literature Association. Address: 102 Hobart Avenue, San Mateo, CA 94402, USA.

HEARON Shelby, b. 18 Jan 1931, Marion, Kentucky, USA. Author. m. (1) Robert Hearon Jr, 15 June 1953, div 1976, 1 son, 1 daughter, (2) Billy Joe Lucas, 19 Apr 1981, div 1995, (3) William Halpern, 19 Aug 1995. Education: BA, University of Texas at Austin, 1953. Appointments: Visiting Lecturer, University of Texas at Austin, 1978-80; Visiting Associate Professor, University of Houston, 1981,

Clark University, 1985, University of California at Irvine, 1987; Visiting Professor, University of Illinois at Chicago, 1993, Colgate University, 1993, University of Massachusetts at Amherst, 1994-96, Middlebury College, 1996-98. Publications: Armadillo in the Grass, 1968; The Second Dune, 1973; Hannah's House, 1975; Now and Another Time, 1976; A Prince of a Fellow, 1978; Painted Dresses, 1981; Afternoon of a Faun, 1983; Group Therapy, 1984; A Small Town, 1985; Five Hundred Scorpions, 1987; Owning Jolene, 1989; Hug Dancing, 1991; Life Estates, 1994; Footprints, 1996. Other: Best Friends for Life (based on Life Estates), CBS-TV, 1998. Contributions to: Magazines. Honours: Guggenheim Fellowship in Fiction, 1982; National Endowment for the Arts Fellowship in Fiction, 1983; Ingram Merrill Grant, 1987; American Academy of Arts and Letters Literature Award, 1990. Memberships: Associated Writing Program; Authors Guild; Authors League; PEN American Centre; Poets and Writers; Texas Institute of Letters. Address: 246 South Union Street, Burlington, VT 05401, USA.

HEATER Derek Benjamin, b. 28 Nov 1931, Sydenham, England. Writer. m. Gwyneth Mary Owen, 12 Mar 1982, 1 son, 1 daughter. Education: BA, Honours, History, University College London, 1953; Postgraduate Certificate in Education, Institute of Education, University of London, 1954. Appointments: Editor, Teaching Politics, 1973-79; Co-Editor (with Bernard Crick), Political Realities Series, 1974-93. Publications: Political Ideas in the Modern World, 1960; Order and Rebellion, 1964; World Affairs (with Gwyneth Owen), 1972; Contemporary Political Ideas, 1974; Britain and the Outside World, 1976; Essays in Political Education (with Bernard Crick), 1977; World Studies, 1980; Our World This Century, 1982; Peace Through Education, 1984; Reform and Revolution, 1987; Refugees, 1988; Case Studies in Twentieth-Century World History, 1988; Citizenship: The Civic Ideal in World History, Politics and Education, 1990; The Idea of European Unity, 1992; The Remarkable History of Rottingdean, 1993; Introduction to International Politics (with G.R. Berridge), 1993; Foundations of Citizenship (with Dawn Oliver), 1994; National Self-Determination, 1994; World Citizenship and Government, 1996; The Theory of Nationhood: A Platonic Symposium, 1998; Keeping Faith 1899-1999; Histoy of Sutton Grammar School, 1998. Contributions to: Reference works, scholarly journals, and other publications. Honours: Children's Book of the Year Award for Refugees, 1988; Fellow, Politics Association, 1994. Memberships: The Politics Association, founder-member, 1969-73; Council for Education in World Citizenship, honorary life member. Address: 3 The Rotyngs, Rottingdean, Brighton, BN2 7DX, England.

HEATH Roy A(ubrey) K(elvin), b. 13 Aug 1926, Georgetown, British Guiana. Author. m. Aemilia Oberli, 3 children. Education: BA, University of London, 1956. Appointments: Teacher, London, 1959-; Called to the Bar, Lincoln's Inn, 1964. Publications: Fiction: A Man Come Home, 1974; The Murderer, 1978; From the Heat of the Day, 1979; One Generation, 1980; Genetha, 1981; Kwaku, or, The Man Who Could Not Keep His Mouth Shut, 1982; Orealla, 1984; The Shadow Bridge, 1988. Non-Fiction: Art and History, 1983; Shadows Round the Moon (memoirs), 1990. Play: Inez Combray, 1972. Honours: Drama Award, Theatre Guild of Guyana, 1971; Fiction Prize, The Guardian, London, 1978; Guyana Award for Literature, 1989. Address: c/o Harper/Collins, 77 Fulham Palace Road, London W6 8J, England.

HEATH-STUBBS John (Francis Alexander), b. 9 July 1918, London, England. Poet; Writer; Translator; Editor. Education: Worcester College for the Blind; Queen's College, Oxford. Appointments: English Master, Hall School, Hampstead, 1944-45; Editorial Assistant, Hutchinson's 1945-46; Gregory Fellow in Poetry, University of Leeds, 1952-55; Visiting Professor of English, University of Alexandria, 1955-58, University of Michigan, 1960-61; Lecturer in English Literature, College of St Mark and St John, Chelsea, 1963-73. Publications: Poetry: Wounded Thammuz, 1942; Beauty and the Beast, 1943; The Divided Ways, 1946; The Swarming of the Bees, 1950; A Charm Against the Toothache, 1954;

The Triumph of the Muse, 1958; The Blue Fly in His Head, 1962; Selected Poems, 1965; Satires and Epigrams, 1968; Artorius, 1973; A Parliament of Birds, 1975; The Watchman's Flute, 1978; Mouse, the Bird and the Sausage, 1978; Birds Reconvened, 1980; Buzz Buzz, 1981; Naming the Beasts, 1982; The Immolation of Aleph, 1985; Cat's Parnassus, 1987; Time Pieces, 1988; Collected Poems, 1988; A Partridge in a Pear Tree, 1988; A Ninefold of Charms, 1989; Selected Poems, 1990; The Parson's Cat, 1991; Sweetapple Earth, 1993; Chimeras, 1994; Galileo's Salad, 1996; The Torriano Sequences, 1997. Play: Helen in Egypt, 1958. Autobiography: Hindsights, 1993. Criticism: The Darkling Plain, 1950; Charles Williams, 1955; The Pastoral, 1969; The Ode, 1969; The Verse Satire, 1969. Translator: Hafiz of Shiraz (with Peter Avery), 1952; Leopardi: Selected Prose and Poetry (with Iris Origo), 1966; The Poems of Anyte (with Carol A Whiteside), 1974; The Rubaiyat of Omar Khayyam (with Peter Avery), 1979. Editor: Several books, including: Faber Book of Twentieth Century Verse (with David Wright), 1953; Poems of Science (with Phillips Salman), 1984. Honours: Queen's Gold Medal for Poetry, 1973; Oscar Williams/Jean Durwood Award, 1977; Officer of the Order of the British Empire, 1989; Commonwealth Poetry Prize, 1989; Cholmondeley Award, 1989; Howard Sargeant Award, 1989. Membership: Royal Society of Literature, Fellow. Address: 22 Artesian Road, London W2 5AR, England.

HEATHCOTT Mary. See: KEEGAN Mary Constance.

HEATON Tom, (Thomas Peter Starke), b. 16 Nov 1928, Celle, Germany. BBC Editor and Arabic Monitor. m. Jackie Noble, 20 Dec 1972, 1 son. Education: BA, Honours, 1955, MA Distinction, 1960, School of Oriental and African Studies, London; Postgraduate Certificate in Education, London, 1957. Publication: In Teleki's Footsteps: A Walk Across East Africa, 1990. Contributions to: World Tax Report of the Financial Times. Address: PO Box 24945, Nairobi, Kenya.

HEBALD Carol, b. 6 July 1934, New York, New York, USA. Writer. Education: MFA, University of Iowa, 1971; BA, City College of City University of New York, 1969. Publications: Three Blind Mice, 1989; Clara Kleinschmidt, 1989; Martha (play), 1991. Contributions to: Antioch Review; Kansas Quarterly; Texas Quarterly; Massachusetts Review; The Humanist; New Letters; Confrontation; North American Review; New York Tribune; PEN International. Honours: Pushcart Nominations, 1987, 1994. Memberships: PEN American Centre; Authors Guild of America; Poet and Writers. Literary Agent: Thomas C. Wallace, c/o Harold Ober Associates. Address: 463 West Street, No 660, New York, NY 10014, USA.

HEBERT Anne, b. 1 Aug 1916, Sainte-Catherine-de-Fossambault, Quebec, Canada. Author; Poet; Dramatist. Education: Collège Notre Dame, Bellevue, Quebec. Publicatioins: Fiction: Le torrent (short stories), 1950, English translation as The Torrent, 1967, new edition, 1963; Les chambres de bois, 1958, English translation as The Silent Rooms, 1975; Kamouraska, 1970, English translation, 1974; Les enfants du sabbat, 1975, English translation as Children of the Black Sabbath, 1978; Héloise, 1980, English translation, 1982; Les fous de Bassan, 1982, English translation as In the Shadow of the Wind, 1983; Le premier jardin, 1988, English translation as The First Garden, 1991; L'enfant chargé de songes, 1992; Aurélien, Clara, Mademoiselle et le lieutenant anglais, 1995. Poetry: Les songes en équilibre, 1942; Le tombeau des rois, 1953; Mystère de la parole, 1960; Poems, 1975; Oeuvre poétique, 1993. Plays: Le temps sauvage (3 plays: Le temps sauvage, La mercière assassinée, and Les invités au procès), 1967; La cage and L'ile de la demoiselle (2 plays), 1990. Honours: Governor-General's Awards, 1960, 1975; Molson Prize, 1967; Académie Francaise Award, 1976; Prix Femina, 1982; Honorary doctorates. Address: 24 rue de Pontoise, 75005 Paris, France.

HECHT Anthony (Evan), b. 16 Jan 1923, New York, New York, USA. Poet; Professor. m. (1) Patricia Harris,

27 Feb 1954, div 1961, 2 sons, (2) Helen D'Alessandro, 12 June 1971, 1 son. Education: BA, Bard College, 1944; MA, Columbia University, 1950. Appointments: Teacher, Kenyon College, 1947-48, State University of Iowa, 1948-49, New York University, 1949-56, Smith College, 1956-59; Associate Professor of English, Bard College, 1961-67; Faculty, 1967-68, John D Deane Professor of English of Rhetoric and Poetry, 1968-85, University of Rochester, New York; Hurst Professor, Washington University, St Louis, 1971; Visiting Professor, Harvard University, 1973, Yale University, 1977; Faculty, Salzburg Seminar in American Studies, 1977; Professor, Georgetown University, 1985-93; Consultant in Poetry, Library of Congress, Washington, DC, 1982-84; Andrew Mellon Lecturer in Fine Arts, National Gallery of Art, Washington, DC, 1992. Publications: A Summoning of Stones, 1954; The Seven Deadly Sins, 1958; A Bestiary, 1960; The Hard Hours, 1968; Millions of Strange Shadows, 1977; The Venetian Vespers, 1977; Obbligati: Essays in Criticism, 1986; The Transparent Man, 1990; Collected Earlier Poems, 1990; The Hidden Law: The Poetry of W H Auden, 1993; On the Laws of the Poetic Art, 1995; The Presumption of Death, 1995; Flight Among the Tombs, 1996. Co-Author and Co-Editor: Jiggery-Pokery: A Compendium of Double Dactyls (with John Hollander), 1967. Editor: The Essential Herbert, 1987. Translator: Seven Against Thebes (with Helen Bacon), 1973. Contributions to: Many anthologies; Hudson Review; New York Review of Books; Quarterly Review of Literature; Transatlantic Review; Voices. Honours: Prix de Rome Fellowship, 1950; Guggenheim Fellowships, 1954, 1959; Hudson Review Fellowship, 1958; Ford Foundation Fellowships, 1960, 1968; Academy of American Poets Fellowship, 1969; Bollingen Prize, 1983; Eugenio Montale Award, 1983; Harriet Monroe Award, 1987; Ruth Lilly Award, 1988; Aiken Taylor Award, Sewanee Review, 1988; National Endowment for the Arts Grant, 1989; Phi Beta Kappa. Memberships: Academy of American Poets, honorary chancellor, 1971-97; American Academy of Arts and Sciences; American Academy of Arts and Letters; Phi Beta Kappa. Address: 4256 Nebraska Avenue North West, Washington, DC 20016, USA.

HECKLER Jonellen, b. 28 Oct 1943, Pittsburgh, Pennsylvania, USA. Writer; Poet. m. Lou Heckler, 17 Aug 1968, 1 son. Education: BA, English Literature, University of Pittsburgh, 1965. Publications: Safekeeping, 1983; A Fragile Peace, 1986; White Lies, 1989; Circumstances Unknown, 1993; Final Tour, 1994. Contributions to: Numerous poems and short stories in Ladies Home Journal Magazine, 1975-83. Membership: Authors Guild. Address: 5562 Pernod Drive South West, Ft Myers, FL 33919, USA.

HEDIN Mary Ann, b. 3 Aug 1929, Minneapolis, Minnesota, USA. Writer; Poet. m. Roger Willard Hedin, 3 sons, 1 daughter. Education: BS, University of Minnesota; MA, University of California. Appointments: Fellow, Yaddo, 1974; Writer-in-Residence, Robinson Jeffers Town House Foundation, 1984-85. Publications: Fly Away Home, 1980; Direction, 1983. Contributions to: Anthologies and journals. Honours: John H McGinnis Memorial Award, 1979; Iowa School of Letters Award for Short Fiction, 1979. Memberships: Authors Guild; PEN; American Poetry Society. Address: 182 Oak Avenue, San Anselmo, CA 94960, USA.

HEDLEY Annie. See: **HUNT Fay Ann.**

HEDMAN Dag Sven Gustav, (Julius Mosca), b. 11 June 1953, Lahäll, Sweden. Professor of Literature; Writer. m. Eva Ingrid Sabler, 1 Sept 1990, 1 son. Education: PhD, 1985. Appointment: Professor of Literature, University of Linköping. Publications: Eleganta eskapader: Frank Hellers författarskap till och med Kejsarens gamla kläder, 1985; Gunnar Serner (Frank Heller), bibliography, 1987; Stanislaw Ignacy Witkiewicz: Fem dramer (with A N Uggla), 1988; Brott, kärlek, äventyr, 1995; Två polska dramatiker: S Wyspianski, S I Witkiewicz (with A N Uggla), 1996; Prosaberättelser om brott på den svenska bokmarknaden 1885-1920, 1997. Contributions to: Various periodicals. Honours: Prize from the Swedish Academy of Mystery and Detection for the Best Non-Fiction Book, 1997. Address: c/o Department of Literature, University of Linköping, 581 83 Linköping, Sweden.

HEDRICK Joan D(oran), b. 1 May 1944, Baltimore, Maryland, USA. Associate Professor of History; Writer. m. Travis K Hedrick, 26 Aug 1967, 2 daughters. Education: AB, Vassar College, 1966; PhD, Brown University, 1974. Appointment: Associate Professor of History, Trinity College, Hartford, Connecticut. Publications: Solitary Comrade: Jack London and His Work, 1982; Harriet Beecher Stowe: A Life, 1994. Honour: Pulitzer Prize in Biography, 1995. Address: c/o Department of History, Trinity College, Hartford, CT 06106, USA.

HEFFERNAN Thomas (Patrick Carroll), b. 19 Aug 1939, Hyannis, Massachusetts, USA. American and English Studies Educator; Writer; Poet. m. Nancy E Iler, 15 July 1972, div 1977. Education: AB, Boston College, 1961; MA, English Literature, University of Manchester, England, 1963; Universita per Stranieri, Perugia, Italy, 1965; PhD, English Literature, Sophia University, Tokyo, 1990. Appointments: Poet in Schools, North Carolina Department of Public Instruction, Raleigh, 1973-77; Visiting Artist, Poetry, North Carolina Department of Community Colleges, 1977-81, South Carolina Arts Commission, 1981-82; Co-Editor, The Plover (Chidori), bilingual haiku journal, Japan, 1989-92; Professor of English, Kagoshima Prefectural University, Japan. Publications: Mobiles, 1973; A Poem is a Smile You Can Hear (Editor), 1976; A Narrative of Jeremy Bentham, 1978; The Liam Poems, 1981; City Renewing Itself, 1983; Art and Emblem: Early Seventeenth Century English Poetry of Devotion, 1991; Gathering in Ireland, 1996. Contributions to: Anthologies and other publications. Honours: National Endowment for the Arts Literary Fellowship, 1977; Gordon Barber Memorial Award, 1979; Portfolio Award, 1983; Roanoke Chowan Prize, 1982. Memberships: Modern Language Association; Japan English Literary Society; Japan American Literary Society. Address: Kagoshima Prefectural University, 1-52-1 Shimo-Ishiki-cho, Kagoshima-shi, Japan 890-0005.

HEFFRON Dorris, b. 18 Oct 1944, Noranda, Quebec, Canada. Writer. m. (1) William Newton-Smith, 29 June 1968, div, 2 daughters, (2) D L Gauer, 29 Oct 1980, 1 son, 1 daughter. Education: BA, 1967, MA, 1969, Queen's University, Kingston, Ontario. Appointments: Tutor, Oxford University, 1970-80, The Open University, 1975-78, University of Malaysia, 1978; Writer-in-Residence, Wainfleet Public Library, 1989-90. Publications: A Nice Fire and Some Moonpennies, 1971; Crusty Crossed, 1976; Rain and I, 1982; A Shark in the House, 1996. Contributions to: Various publications. Honour: Canada Council Arts Grant, 1974. Memberships: Authors Society; PEN; Writers Union of Canada. Address: 202 Riverside Drive, Toronto, Ontario M6S 4A9, Canada.

HEGI Ursula (Johanna), b. 23 May 1946, Büderich, Germany. Professor of English; Writer; Poet; Critic. 2 sons. Education: BA, 1978, MA, 1979, University of New Hampshire. Appointments: Instructor, University of New Hampshire, 1980-84; Book Critic, Los Angeles Times, New York Times, Washington Post, 1982-; Assistant Professor, 1984-89, Associate Professor, 1989-95, Professor of English, 1995-, Eastern Washington University; Visiting Writer, various universities. Publications: Fiction: Intrusions, 1981; Unearned Pleasures and Other Stories, 1988; Floating in My Mother's Palm, 1990; Stones from the River, 1994; Salt Dancers, 1995. Non-Fiction: Tearing the Silence: On Being German in America, 1997. Contributions to: Anthologies, newspapers, journals and magazines. Honours: Indiana Fiction Award, 1988; National Endowment for the Arts Fellowship, 1990; New York Times Best Books Selections, 1990, 1994; Pacific Northwest Booksellers Association Award, 1991; Governor's Writers Awards, 1991, 1994. Memberships: Associated Writing Programs; National Book Critics Circle, board of directors, 1992-94. Address: c/o Department of English, Eastern Washington University, Cheney, WA 99004, USA.

HEIDELBERGER Michael (Johannes), b. 9 Aug 1947, Karlsruhe, Germany. Professor of Philosophy; Writer. m. Nicole Jeannet, 16 Sept 1978, 1 son, 1 daughter. Education: PhD, Philosophy and the History of Science, University of Munich, 1978; Habilitation, Philosophy of Science, University of Göttingen, 1989. Appointment: Professor of Philosophy, Humboldt-University of Berlin. Publications: Natur und Erfahrung, 1981; The Probabilistic Revolution, 1987; Die innere Seite der Natur: Gustav Fechners wissenschaftlich-philosophische Weltauffassung, 1993. Contributions to: Many anthologies, journals, and other publications. Address: Humboldt-Universität zu Berlin, Institut für Philosophie, Unter den Linden 6, D-10099 Berlin, Germany.

HEIGHTON Steven, b. 14 Aug 1961, Toronto, Canada. Writer; Editor; Translator. Education: BA, 1985, MA, 1986, Queens. Appointment: Editor, Quarry Magazine, 1988-94. Publications: Fiction: Flight Paths of the Emperor, 1992; On Earth as it is, 1995. Non-Fiction: The Admen Move on Lhasa (writing and culture in a virtual world), 1997. Poetry: Stalin's Carnival, 1989; Foreign Ghosts, 1989; The Ecstasy of Skeptics, 1994. Honours: Air Canada Award, 1988; Gold Medal for Fiction, National Magazine Awards, 1991; Finalist, Trillium Award, 1993; Finalist, Governor General's Award, 1995. Memberships: PEN; Writers Union of Canada; League of Canadian Poets. Literary Agent: Anne McDermid. Address: PO Box 382, Kingston, Ontario K7L 4W2, Canada.

HEIKENFELD Rita Nader, b. 15 July 1946, Cincinnati, Ohio, USA. Food Writer. m. Frank Heikenfeld Jr, 7 Mar 1970, 2 sons, 1 stepson. Education: International Association of Cooking Professionals, Culinary Professor, Level 3. Appointments: Food Editor, Clermont Sun, Batavia, Ohio, 1987-96; Food and Historical Cooking Series, Gannett Papers, Cincinnati, Ohio, 1989-93; Columnist, Food, Press Community Newspapers, Cincinnati, Ohio. Contributions to: Eastside Weekend News Magazine; Women Alive. Honour: Cincinnati's Best Kept Secret in Culinary Writing and Teaching, 1997. Memberships: Society of Professional Journalists. Address: c/o Community Press Newspapers, 395 Wards Corner Road, Loveland, OH 45140, USA.

HEILBRONER Robert L(ouis), b. 24 Mar 1919, New York, New York, USA. Professor of Economics; Writer. m. (1) Joan Knapp, div, 2 sons, (2) Shirley E T Davis. Education: BA, Harvard University, 1940; PhD, New School for Social Research, New York City. Appointments: Economist in government and business; Norman Thomas Professor of Economics, New School for Social Research, New York City, 1972-; Lecturer to various organizations. Publications: The Worldly Philosophers, 1953, 6th edition, 1986; The Quest for Wealth, 1956; The Future as History, 1960; The Making of Economic Society, 1962, 9th edition, 1993; The Great Ascent, 1963; A Primer on Government Spending (with P L Bernstein), 1963, 2nd edition, 1971; Understanding Macroeconomics (with James Galbraith), 1965, 9th edition, 1990; The Limits of American Capitalism, 1966; The Economic Problem (with James Galbraith), 1968, 9th edition, 1990; Understanding Microeconomics (with James Galbraith), 1968, 9th edition, 1990; Economic Means and Social Ends (editor with others), 1969; Between Capitalism and Socialism: Essays in Political Economics, 1970; Is Economics Relevant? (editor with A M Ford), 1971; In the Name of Profit (with others), 1972; Corporate Social Policy (editor with Paul London), 1975; An Inquiry into the Human Prospect, 1975, 3rd edition, 1991; Business Civilization in Decline, 1976; Economic Relevance: A Second Look (with A M Ford), 1976; The Economic Transformation of America (with Aaron Singer), 1977, 3rd edition, 1994; Beyond Boom and Crash, 1978; Marxism: For and Against, 1980; Five Economic Challenges (with Lester C Thurow), 1981; Economics Explained (with Lester C Thurow), 1982, 3rd edition, 1994; The Nature and Logic of Capitalism, 1985; The Essential Adam Smith (editor), 1986; Beyond the Veil of

Economics, 1988; Twenty-First Century Capitalism, 1993; The Crisis of Vision in Modern Economic Thought (with William Milberg), 1995; Teachings from the Worldly Philosophy (editor), 1996. Contributions to: Many periodicals. Honours: Guggenheim Fellowship, 1983; Scholar of the Year, 1995; Honorary doctorates. Memberships: American Economic Association; Council on Economic Priorities; Phi Beta Kappa. Address: 830 Park Avenue, New York, NY 10021, USA.

HEILBRUN Carolyn (Gold), b. 13 Jan 1926, East Orange, New Jersey, USA. Professor of English Literature Emerita; Writer. m. James Heilbrun, 20 Feb 1945, 1 son, 2 daughters. Education: BA, Wellesley College, 1947; MA, 1951, PhD, 1959, Columbia University. Appointments: Instructor, Brooklyn College, 1959-60; Instructor, 1960-62, Assistant Professor, 1962-67, Associate Professor, 1967-72, Professor of English Literature, 1972-86, Avalon Foundation Professor of Humanities, 1986-93, Professor Emerita, 1993-, Columbia University; Visiting Professor, University of California at Santa Cruz, 1979, Princeton University, 1981, Yale Law School, 1989. Publications: The Garrett Family, 1961; In the Last Analysis, 1964; Christopher Isherwood, 1970; Toward a Recognition of Androgyny, 1973; Lady Ottoline's Album, 1976; Reinventing Womanhood, 1979; Representation of Women in Fiction (editor), 1983; Writing a Woman's Life, 1988; Hamlet's Mother and Other Women, 1990; The Education of a Woman: The Life of Gloria Steinem, 1995. Honours: Guggenheim Fellowship, 1966; Rockefeller Foundation Fellowship, 1976; Senior Research Fellow, National Endowment for the Humanities, 1983; Alumnae Achievement Award, Wellesley College, 1984; Award of Excellence, Graduate Faculty of Columbia University Alumni, 1984; Many honorary doctorates. Memberships: Modern Language Association, President, 1984; Mystery Writers of America; Phi Beta Kappa. Address: c/o Department of English, Columbia University, New York, NY 10027, USA.

HEIN Christoph, b. 8 Apr 1944, Heinzendorf/Schlesien, Germany. Novelist; Playwright. Education: University of Leipzig; Humboldt University, Berlin. Appointments: Dramaturg and Playwright, Deutsches Theater, East Berlin, 1971-79. Publications: Nachfahrt und früher Morgen, 1980; The Distant Lover, 1982; Horns Ende, 1985; Der Tangospieler, 1989. Plays: Cromwell, 1977; Lassalle fragt Herrn Herbert nach Sonja, 1981; Der neue Mendoza, 1981; Schlotel, oder was solls, 1981; The True Story of Ah Q, 1983; Passage, 1987; Die Ritter der Tafelrunde, 1989. Also: Jamie and his Friends (for children), 1984; I Saw Stalin as a Child, 1990. Honours: City of Hamburg Prize, 1986; Lessing Prize, 1989. Address: c/o Aufbau-Verlag, Postfach 1217, 1086 Berlin, Germany.

HEINESEN Jens Pauli, b. 12 Nov 1932, Torshavn, Faroe Islands. Novelist. Education: University of Copenhagen, 1953-54. Appointment: Teacher, Torshavn, 1957-70. Publications: The Dawn Shower, 1953, second edition, 1978; The Beautiful Calm, 1959; You, World of Origin, 3 volumes, 1962-64; The Waves Play on the Shore, 1969; In the Garden of Eden, 1971; The Serpent's Name is Fraenir, 1973; The Beachcomber, 1977; Drops in the Ocean of Life, 1978; They Carve Their Idols, 1979; Now You are a Child of Man on Earth, 1980; The World Now Shines Before You, 1981; Your Playing is Like the Bright Day, 1982; The World Now Stretches Boundless Before You, 1983; A Depth of Precious Time, 1984; The Mysteries of Love, 1986; Exposed to the Wind, 1986; Blue Mountain, 1992; Rosemary, 1995. Honours: Nominated for the Nordic Council Prize, 1987. Address: Stoffalag 18, Torshavn, The Faroe Islands, via Denmark.

HEITMILLER David, b. 14 Dec 1945, San Pedro, California, USA. Writer. m. Jacqueline Blix, 19 July 1986, 1 son, 1 daughter. Education: BA, History, University of Washington, Seattle, 1969. Publication: Getting a Life: Real Lives Transformed by "Your Money or Your Life". Contributions: Simple Living Quarterly; Yes! A Journal of Positive Futures. Literary Agent: Beth Vesél, Greenburger and Associates, New York, USA. Address: c/o

Greenburger and Associates, 55 5th Avenue, New York, NY 10003, USA.

HEJINIAN Lyn, b. 17 May 1941, Alameda, California, USA. Poet; Writer. m. 1) John P Hejinian, 1961, div 1972, 1 son, 1 daughter, 2) Larry Ochs, 1977. Education: BA, Harvard University, 1963. Appointments: Founder-Editor, Tuumba Press, 1976-84; Faculty, Graduate Poetics Program, New College of California. Publications: A Great Adventure, 1972; A Thought is the Bride of What Thinking, 1976; A Mask of Motion, 1977; Gesualdo, 1978; Writing is an Aid to Memory, 1978; My Life, 1980, revised and enlarged edition, 1987; The Guard, 1984; Redo, 1984; Individuals, 1988; Leningrad: American Writers in the Soviet Union (with Michael Davidson, Ron Silliman, and Barrett Watten), 1991; The Hunt, 1991, revised and enlarged edition as Oxota: A Short Russian Novel, 1991; The Cell, 1992; The Cold of Poetry, 1994; Two Stein Talks, 1995. Contributions to: Journals. Address: c/o Sun & Moon Press, 6026 Wilshire Boulevard, Los Angeles, CA 90036, USA.

HEJMADI Padma, b. 30 Dec 1939, Madras, India. Writer; Photographer; Visual Artist. m. Peter S Beagle, 1998. Education: BA, Hons, University of Delhi; MA, University of Michigan, 1961. Publications: Coigns of Vantage, 1972; Doctor Salaam and Other Stories, 1978; Birthday Deathday, 1985, 1992; Room to Fly, forthcoming 1999. Contributions to: The New Yorker Horizon; The Southern Review; Parabola; The American Book Review; The Iowa Review; The Massachusetts Review; Frontiers. Honour: The Hopwood Award for Major Fiction. Membership: Poets & Writers PEN West. Address: 2135 Humboldt Avenue, Davis, CA 95616, USA.

HELGADOTTIR Gudrun, b. 7 Sept 1935, Hafnarfiordur, Iceland. Writer. div, 2 sons, 2 daughters. Education: Graduate, Reykjavik Grammar School, 1955. Appointments: Member, Icelandic Parliament, 1979-95; Member, Nordic Council, 1982-88; Speaker, House of Parliament, 1988-91. Publications: Jon Oddur og Jon Bjarni, 1974-80, 3 vols, 1981; Sitji guds englar 1983-1987, 3 vol, 1990; Ekkert ad thakka 1995-1998, 3 vol, 1997. Honours: Thorbjorn Egner Fond Award, 1980; Nordic Children's Book Award, 1992. Literary Agent: Vaka-Helgafell hf Sidumula 8, IS-108 Reykjavik, Iceland.

HELIANOS Orestis. See: **STYLIANOPOULOS Orestis.**

HELLENGA Robert, b. 5 Aug 1941, USA. Teacher; Writer. m. Virginia Killion, 31 Aug 1963, 3 daughters. Education: BA, University of Michigan, 1963; Queens University, Belfast, 1963-64; PhD, Princeton University, 1969. Appointment: Knox College, 1968-. Publications: Novels: The Sixteen Pleasures, 1994; The Fall of a Sparrow, 1998. Contributions to: Iowa Review; Chicago Review; California Quarterly; Columbia; Ascent; Farmer's Market; Chicago Tribue Magazine; TriQuarterly; Crazyhorse; Mississippi Valley Review; Black Warrior Review; New York Times Magazine. Honours: Several fellowships and grants; Illinois Arts Council Artist's Literary Award, 1985; PEN Syndicated Fiction Award, 1988; Society of Midland Authors Award for Fiction, 1995; Knox College Faculty Achievement Award, 1997-98. Memberships: Society of Midland Authors; Illinois Arts Alliance. Address: 343 North Prairie Street, Galesburg, IL 61401, USA.

HELLER Joseph, b. 1 May 1923, New York, New York, USA. Author. m. (1) Shirley Held, 3 Sept 1945, div 1984, 1 son, 1 daughter, (2) Valerie Humphries, 1987. Education: University of Southern California, Los Angeles; BA, New York University, 1948; MA, Columbia University, 1949; Graduate Studies, Oxford University, 1949-50. Appointments: Teacher, Pennsylvania State University, Yale University, University of Pennsylvania; Distinguished Professor of English, City College of the City University of New York; Full-time Author, 1975- . Publications: Fiction: Catch-22, 1961; Something Happened, 1974; Good as Gold, 1979; God Knows, 1984; Picture This, 1988; Closing Time, 1994. Plays: We Bombed in New Haven, 1968; Catch-22: A Dramatization,

1971; Clevinger's Trial, 1971. Screenplays: Sex and the Single Girl (with David R Schwartz), 1964; Casino Royale, 1967; Dirty Dingus Magee (with Tom Waldman and Frank Waldman), 1970; Of Men and Women (with others), 1972. Non-Fiction: No Laughing Matter (with Speed Vogel), 1986; Now and Then: From Coney Island to Here (memoir), 1998. Contributions to: Magazines. Honours: Fulbright Scholar, 1949-50; National Institute of Arts and Letters Grant, 1963; Prix Interallie, France, 1985; Prix Medicis Etranger, France, 1985. Memberships: National Institute of Arts and Letters; Phi Beta Kappa. Address: c/o Simon and Schuster, 1230 Avenue of the Americas, New York, NY 10020, USA.

HELLER Michael, b. 11 May 1937, New York, New York, USA. Poet; Writer; Teacher. m. 1) Doris Whytal, 1962, div 1978, 2) Jane Augustine, 5 Mar 1979, 1 son. Education: BS in Engineering, Rensselaer Polytechnic Institute, 1959; MA in English, New York University, 1986. Appointments: Faculty, 1967, Acting Director, 1986-87, Academic Coordinator, 1987-91, American Language Institute, New York University; Poet and Teacher, New York State Poets in the Schools, 1970-. Publications: Two Poems, 1970; Accidental Center, 1972; Figures of Speaking, 1977; Knowledge, 1979; Marble Snows, Origin, 1979; Conviction's Net of Branches: Essays on the Objectivist Poets and Poetry, 1985; Marginalia in a Desperate Hand, 1986; In the Builded Place, 1990; Carl Rakosi: Man and Poet (editor), 1993; Wordflow: New and Selected Poems, 1997. Contributions to: Anthologies, reference books, and journals. Honours: Coffey Poetry Prize, New School for Social Research, 1964; Poetry in Public Places Award, 1975; New York State Creative Artists Public Service Fellowship in Poetry, 1975-76; National Endowment for the Humanities Grant, 1979; Di Castagnola Award, Poetry Society of America, 1980; Outstanding Writer Citations, Pushcart Press, 1983, 1984, 1992; New York Fellowship in the Arts, 1989. Memberships: American Academy of Poets; Modern Language Association; New York State Poets in Public Service; PEN; Poetry Society of America; Poets and Writers; Poets House. Address: PO Box 1289, Stuyvesant Station, New York, NY 10009, USA.

HELLMANN Rainer, b. 9 Sept 1930, Freiburg, Germany. Journalist; Economist. m. Johanna Hellmann, 30 July 1955, 2 sons, 1 daughter. Education: Diplom - Volkswirt - Dr rer pol, Univerity of Heidelberg. Appointments: Brussels Bureau Chief, German Economic News Agency, Vwd, 1959-97; Correspondent, EU-Magazin Nomos Verlagsgesellschaft, Brussels, 1997. Publications: Transnational Control of Multinational Corporations, 1977; La Guerre des Monnaies, 1977; Gold, the Dollar and the European Currency Systems, 1979; Weltwirtschaftsgipfel, 1983; Europäische Industriepolitik, 1994. Contributions to: EU Magazin - Nomos Verlag; Europaische Zeitung, Bonn; EU-Kommentar - Nomos; Euro Guide - Deutscher Wirtschaftsdienst. Address: 61 Av Baron d'Huart, B1150 Brussels, Belgium.

HELPRIN Mark, b. 28 June 1947, New York, New York, USA. Writer. m. Lisa Kennedy, 28 June 1980, 2 daughters. Education: AB, 1969, AM, 1972, Harvard University; Postgraduate Studies, Magdalen College, Oxford, 1976-77. Appointments: Contributing Editor, The Wall Street Journal; Speechwriter for Senator Robert J Dole, 1996. Publications: A Dove of the East and Other Stories, 1975; Refiner's Fire, 1977; Ellis Island and Other Stories, 1981; Winter's Tale, 1983; Swan Lake, 1989; A Soldier of the Great War, 1991; Memoir from Antproof Case, 1995; A City in Winter, 1996. Honours: Prix de Rome, American Academy and Institute of Arts and Letters, 1982; National Jewish Book Award, 1982. Membership: Council on Foreign Relations. Address: c/o The Wall Street Journal, 200 Liberty Street, New York, NY 10281, USA.

HELWIG David (Gordon), b. 5 Apr 1938, Toronto, Ontario, Canada. Poet; Writer; Editor. m. Nancy Keeling, 1959, 2 daughters. Education: Graduated, Stamford Collegiate Institute, 1956; BA, University of Toronto, 1960; MA, University of Liverpool, 1962. Appointments:

Faculty, Department of English, Queen's Unversity, Kingston, Ontario, 1962-80; Co-Editor, Quarry magazine. Publications: Poetry: Figures in a Landscape, 1967; The Sign of the Gunman, 1969; The Best Name of Silence, 1972; Atlantic Crossings, 1974; A Book of the Hours, 1979; The Rain Falls Like Rain, 1982; Catchpenny Poems, 1983; The Hundred Old Names, 1988; The Beloved, 1992. Fiction: The Day Before Tomorrow, 1971; The Glass Knight, 1976; Jennifer, 1979; The King's Evil, 1981; It Is Always Summer, 1982; A Sound Like Laughter, 1983; The Only Son, 1984; The Bishop, 1986; A Postcard From Rome, 1988; Old Wars, 1989; Of Desire, 1990; Blueberry Cliffs, 1993; Just Say the Words, 1994. Editor: Fourteen Stories High: Best Canadian Stories of 71 (with Tom Marshall), 1971; 72, 73, 74 and 75: New Canadian Stories (with Joan Harcourt), 4 volumes, 1972-75; Words From Inside, 1972; The Human Elements: Critical Essays, 2 volumes, 1978, 1981; Love and Money: The Politics of Culture, 1980; 83, 84, 85 and 86: Best Canadian Stories (with Sandra Martin), 4 volumes, 1983-86; Coming Attractions 1983, 1984, 1985, and 1986 (with Sandra Martin), 4 volumes, 1983-86; Coming Attractions 1987 and 1988 (with Maggie Helwig), 2 volumes 1987, 1988; 87, 88, 89, and 91: Best Canadian Stories (with Maggie Helwig), 4 volumes, 1987-91. Honour: CBC Literary Prize, 1983. Address: c/o Viking Penguin, 375 Hudson Street, New York, NY 10014, USA.

HELYAR Jane Penelope Josephine, (Josephine Poole), b. 12 Feb 1933, London, England. Writer. m. (1) T R Poole, 1956, (2) V J H Helyar, 1975, 1 son, 5 daughters. Publications: A Dream in the House, 1961; Moon Eyes, 1965; The Lilywhite Boys, 1967; Catch as Catch Can, 1969; Yokeham, 1970; Billy Buck, 1972; Touch and Go, 1976; When Fishes Flew, 1978; The Open Grave, The Forbidden Room (remedial readers), 1979; Hannah Chance, 1980; Diamond Jack, 1983; The Country Dairy Companion (to accompany Central TV series), 1983; Three For Luck, 1985; Wildlife Tales, 1986; The Loving Ghosts, 1988; Angel, 1989; This is Me Speaking, 1990; Paul Loves Amy Loves Christo, 1992. Television scripts: The Harbourer, 1975; The Sabbatical, 1981; The Breakdown, 1981; Miss Constantine, 1981; Ring a Ring a Rosie, 1983; With Love, Belinda, 1983; The Wit to Woo, 1983. Stories: Fox, 1984; Buzzard, 1984; Dartmoor Pony, 1984; Snow White (picture book), 1991; Pinocchio (re-written), 1994; Scared to Death, 1994; Deadly Inheritance, 1995; Hero, 1997; Joan of Arc (picture book), 1998; Run Rabbit, 1999. Address: Poundisford Lodge, Poundisford, Taunton, Somerset TA3 7AE, England.

HEMLEY Robin, b. 28 May 1958, New York, New York, USA. Assistant Professor of English; Writer. m. Beverly Bertling Hemley, 18 July 1987, 2 daughters. Education: BA, Indiana University, 1980; MFA, University of Iowa, 1982. Appointments: Associate Professor of English, University of North Carolina at Charlotte, 1986-94; Assistant Professor of English, Western Washington University, Bellingham, 1994-. Publications: The Mouse Town, 1987; All You Can Eat, 1988; The Last Studebaker, 1992; Turning Life into Fiction, 1994. Address: c/o Elizabeth Grossman, Sterling Lord Literistic, 1 Madison Avenue, New York, NY 10010, USA.

HEMMING John Henry, b. 5 Jan 1935, Vancouver, British Columbia, Canada. Author; Publisher. m. Sukie Babington-Smith, 1979, 1 son, 1 daughter. Education: McGill and Oxford Universities; MA; D.Litt. Appointments: Explorations in Peru and Brazil, 1960, 1961, 1971, 1972, 1986-87; Director and Secretary, Royal Geographical Society, 1975-96; Joint Chairman, Hemming Publishing Ltd, 1976-; Chair, Brintex Ltd., Newman Books Ltd. Publications: The Conquest of the Incas, 1970; Tribes of the Amazon Basin in Brazil (with others), 1973; Red Gold: The Conquest of the Brazilian Indians, 1978; The Search for El Dorado, 1978; Machu Picchu, 1982; Monuments of the Incas, 1983; Change in the Amazon Basin, (editor), 2 volumes, 1985; Amazon Frontier: The Defeat of the Brazilian Indians, 1987; Maracá, 1988; Roraima: Brazil's Northernmost Frontier, 1990; The Rainforest Edge (editor), 1994; The Golden Age of Discovery, 1998. Honours: CMG; Pitman Literary Prize, 1970; Christopher

Award, NY, 1971; Order of Merit (Peru) 1991; Order of the Southern Cross (Brazil), 1998; Honorary doctorates , University of Warwick, University of Stirling; Medals from Royal Geographical Society, Boston Museum of Science, Royal Scottish Geographical Society; Citation of Merit, New York Explorers' Club. Address: Hemming Publishing Ltd, 32 Vauxhall Bridge Road, London SW1V 2SS, England.

HEN Jozef (Korab), b. 8 Nov 1923, Warsaw, Poland. Writer. m. Irena Lebewal, 15 Apr 1946, 1 son, 1 daughter. Education: Largely educated by life. Publications: April (Kwiecien), 1961, novel, 1961; Herod's Theatre, 2 novels, 1966, 1967; The Boxer and Death, stories, 1975, 15 translations; Crimen, historical novel, 1975; I, Michel De Montaigne, literary biography, 1978; Silence between Us, novel, 1985; I'm Not Afraid of Sleepless Nights, notes and reflections, 1987; Royal Dreams, historical novel, 1989; Dayan's Eye, 3 short stories, 1990; No-one Calls, novel, 1990; Nowolipie Street, memoirs, 1991; Aphrodite Has Gone, (Odejscie Afrodyty), novel, 1995; Jester - The Great Man, literary biography, 1998. Contributions to: SWIAT Weekly, 1953-68; Les Temps Modernes, 1970; Dialog and Tworczosc monthlies. Honours: Book of the Year, 1961; Book of the Month, 4 times, 1987-; Over 20 books translated into foreign languages. Memberships: Polish Union of Writers, Warsaw Branch, Vice-Chairman, 1966-69, 1978-80, Chairman, 1981-83; PEN Club, 1966; Board, Union of Authors and Composers-ZAIKS, 1971-; Association of Polish Film Makers; Société Internationale des Amis de Montaigne; Corresponding Member, Académie des Beaux Arts, Sciences et Lettres, Bordeaux, 1986. Address: Al Ujazdowskie 8/2, 00-478 Warsaw, Poland.

HENDERSON Graeme John, b. 8 Feb 1947, Perth, Western Australia. Museum Director. m. Kandy-Jane Hodgson, 15 Apr 1977, 1 son. Education: BA, 1968; Diploma of Education, 1970; MA, 1975; Diploma of Public Sector Management, 1992. Publications: Last Voyage of the James Matthews, 1979; Western Australians and the Sea, 1981; Maritime Archaeology in Australia, 1986. Contributions to: over 100 articles in journals and magazines. Honour: Australian Heritage Award, 1988. Address: 3B Braunton St Bicton, Western Australia 6157, Australia.

HENDERSON Hamish, b. 11 Nov 1919, Blairgowrie, Perthshire, Scotland. Poet; Lecturer. Education: MA, Downing College, Cambridge. Appointments: Senior Lecturer and Research Fellow, School of Scottish Studies, University of Edinburgh, 1951-. Publications: Elegies for the Dead in Cyrenaica, 1948; Freedom Come-All-Ye, 1967; Alias MacAlias, 1990; Collected Essays, 1990. Contributions to: Ballads of World War II. Honours: Somerset Maugham Award, 1949. Address: c/o School of Scottish Studies, University of Edinburgh, 27 George Square, Edinburgh EH8 9LD, Scotland.

HENDERSON Kathy Caecilia, b. 22 Apr 1949, Oxford, England. Writer; Illustrator; Editor. 2 sons, 1 daughter. Education: BA Honours, English Language and Literature, Oxford University, 1969. Publications: My Song is My Own, 1979; Sam and the Big Machines, 1985; 15 Ways to go to Bed, 1986; Series, Where does it come from? Water, 1986, Sweater, 1986, Lego, 1986, Banana, 1986, Bread, 1987, Letter, 1987; Sam and the Box, 1987; The Babysitter, 1988; Don't Interrupt, 1988; The Baby's Book of Babies, 1988; 15 Ways to get Dressed, 1989; Sam, Lizzie and the Bonfire, 1989; Baby Knows Best, 1991; Annie and the Birds, 1991; Second Time Charley, 1991; In the Middle of the Night, 1992; Pappy Mashy, 1992; Annie and the Tiger, 1992; Jim's Winter, 1992; Bumpety Bump, 1994; Bounce, Bounce, Bounce, 1994; Counting Farm, 1995; The Little Boat, 1995; Motorway Madness, 1995; Dotty the hen, 1996; A Year in the City, 1996; Metal Muncher, 1996; Crow Talk, 1996; The Baby Dances, 1999; The Storm, 1999. Honours: Book Trust's Childrens Books of the Year (list and exhibition of 100 best children's books), 1987, 1989, 1990, 1993, 1996; Shortlisted for the Smarties Prize, 1986 and 1995; Parents' Magazine Best Books for babies, 1987; Emil/Kurt Maschler Award, 1995; Primary

English Award: Best Children's Picture Book, 1996. Address: Muswell Hill, London N1O 3UN, England.

HENDERSON Kent William, b. 29 Jan 1954, Geelong, Victoria, Australia. Author; Teacher. m. Marise de Quadros, 19 Dec 1993, 1 daughter. Education: Deakin University and Victoria University of Technology; Diploma of Teaching; BEd; Graduate Certificate of Education; Graduate Diploma of Education; MEd. Publications: Masonic World Guide, 1984; Naracoorte Caves - South Australia, 1986; Masonic Grand Masters of Australia, 1989; Jenolan Caves, 1989; Buchan and Murrindal Caves, 1992. Contributions to: Australasian Cave and Karst Management Association Journal (editor); Transactions, Victorian Lodge of Masonic Research Annual Book; Numerous to journals and magazines. Membership: Fellowship of Australian Writers. Address: PO Box 332, Williamstown, Victoria 3016, Australia.

HENDERSON Nancy Wallace, b. 21 July 1916, Wilmington, North Carolina, USA. Social Worker; Freelance Writer. m. William Henderson, 9 Aug 1942, 1 son. Education: MA, Christian Education, Union Theological Seminary, 1938; MA, Dramatic Art, University of North Carolina, Chapel Hill, 1950. Publications: Speed, Bonnie Boat, 1954; The Scots Helped Build America, 1969; Medusa of 47th Street, published play; Circle of Life, story of the Miccosukee Indian Tribe (with Jane Dewey), 1974; The Twelfth Lantern, play, produced 1989, published 1990; Story of North Carolina's admission to United States, bicentennial play; Alice Unwanted, story of Alice in Wonderland, play; Penelope, Act II, play. Contributions to: Voice, scholastic magazine. Honour: Engstrom Award, for The Twelfth Lantern. Memberships: Authors Guild; Dramatists Guild. Address: 13 Bank Street, New York, NY 10014, USA.

HENDERSON Neil Keir, b. 7 Mar 1956, Glasgow, Scotland. Education: MA, English Language, English Literature and Scottish Literature, Glasgow University, 1977. Publication: Maldehyde's Discomfiture, or A Lady Churned, 1997. Contributions to: Loveable Warts: A Defence of Self-Indulgence, 1997; Mystery of the City, poetry anthology, 1997; The Red Candle Treasury, 1998; Mightier Than the Sword: The Punch of the Poses, 1998. Address: 46 Revoch Drive, Knightswood, Glasgow G13 4SB, Scotland.

HENDRIKS A(rthur) L(emiere), b. 7 Apr 1922, Kingston, Jamaica. Poet; Writer. Education: Open University. Publications: The Independence Anthology of Jamaican Literature (editor with C Lindo), 1962; On This Mountain and Other Poems, 1965; These Green Islands, 1971; Muet, 1971; Madonna of the Unknown Nation, 1974; The Islanders and Other Poems, 1983; Archie and the Princess and the Everythingest Horse (for children), 1983; The Naked Ghost and Other Poems, 1984; Great Families of Jamaica, 1984; To Speak Slowly: Selected Poems, 1961-86, 1988. Address: Box 265, Constant Spring, Kingston 8, Jamaica.

HENDRY Diana (Lois), b. 2 Oct 1941, Meols, Wirral, Cheshire, England. Poet; Children's Writer. m. George Hendry, 9 Oct 1965, div 1981, 1 son, 1 daughter. Education: BA, Honours, 1984, MLitt, 1986, University of Bristol. Appointments: Assistant to Literature Editor, Sunday Times, London, 1958-60; Reporter and Feature Writer, Western Mail, Cardiff, 1960-65; Freelance journalist, 1965-80; Part-time English Teacher, Clifton College, 1984-87; Part-time Lecturer, Bristol Polytechnic, 1987; WEA, Modern Poets Course, 1987-; Tutor, Open University, 1991-92; Part-time Tutor, Creative Writing, University of Bristol, 1993-. Publications: Midnight Pirate, 1984; Fiona Finds Her Tongue, 1985; Hetty's First Fling, 1985; The Not Anywhere House, 1989; The Rainbow Watchers, 1989; The Carey Street Cat, 1989; Christmas on Exeter Street, 1989; Sam Sticks and Delilah, 1990; A Camel Called April, 1990; Double Vision, 1990; Harvey Angell, 1991; Kid Kibble, 1992; The Thing-in-a-Box, 1992; Wonderful Robert and Sweetie-Pie Nell, 1992; Back Soon, 1993; Making Blue, 1995; Strange Goings-on, 1995; The Awesome Bird, 1995; The Thing on Two Legs, 1995; Harvey Angell and the Ghost Child, 1997; Mindus,

1998. Contributions to: Anthologies and periodicals. Honours: Stoud Festival International Poetry Competition, 1976; 3rd Prize, 1991, 2nd Prize, 1993, Peterloo Poetry Competition; Whitbread Award, 1991; 1st Prize, Housman Poetry Society, 1996. Membership: Society of Authors; PEN. Address: 52 York Road, Montpelier, Bristol BS6 5QF, England.

HENDRY Joy McLaggan, b. 3 Feb 1953, Perth, Scotland. Editor; Writer; Poet; Dramatist; Broadcaster. m. Ian Montgomery, 25 July 1986. Education: MA, Honours, Mental Philosophy, 1976, Diploma, Education, 1977, University of Edinburgh. Appointments: Editor, Chapman magazine, 1972-; Radio Critic, The Scotsman newspaper, 1987-; Chair, Scottish Actors Studio, 1994-. Publications: Scots: The Way Forward, 1981; Poems and Pictures by Wendy Wood (editor), 1985; Critical Essays on Sorley MacLean (editor with Raymond J Ross), 1986; Critical Essays on Norman MacCraig (editor with Raymond J Ross), 1991. Plays: Gang down wi' a Sang, 1990; The Wa' at the Warld's End, 1993. Contributions to: Newspapers, journals, periodicals, radio, and television. Memberships: Advisory Council for the Arts in Scotland; National Union of Journalists; Scottish PEN. Address: 4 Broughton Place, Edinburgh EH1 3RX, Scotland.

HENLEY Elizabeth Becker, b. 8 May 1952, Jackson, Mississippi, USA. Playwright. Education: BFA, Southern Methodist University. Publications: Crimes of the Heart, 1981; The Wake of Jamey Foster, 1982; Am I Blue, 1982; The Miss Firecracker Contest, 1984; The Lucky Spot, 1987; The Debutante Ball, 1988; Abundance, 1990; Control Freaks, 1993. Honours: Pulitzer Prize for Drama, 1981; New York Drama Critics Circle Best Play Award, 1981; George Oppenheimer/Newsday Playwriting Award, 1981. Address: c/o The William Morris Agency, 1350 Avenue of the Americas, New York, NY 10019,USA.

HENNEBERG PEDERSEN Else Hannegram Iversen, b. 3 Aug 1937, Brorup, Denmark. Translator. m. Herluf Henneberg Pedersen, 19 Apr 1962, div 1986, 2 daughters. Education: MA, University of Copenhagen, Denmark. Publications: The Complete Essays of Michel de Montaign, 1992; Henri Bergson: Le Rire, 1994; Jean Giono: Le Hussard Sur Le Toit, 1996; Le Prince Henrik De Danemark: Destin Oblige, 1996; Others: Colette, Anne Marie Garat, Judith L Herman, Malraux. Contributions to: Bonniers Litteråra Magasin, Essay ABT Translating Montaigne, 1996; Marginal, Essay ABT La Coalition De Emmanuel Bove, 1997. Honours: The Translators' Award of Danish Academy, 1993; Grant, His Royal Highness Prince Henrik's Foundation; 3 Year Grant, Danish State Art Foundation. Address: Amagerbrogade 133, 4 TV, DK-2300 Copenhagen 5, Denmark.

HENNESSY Helen. See: **VENDLER Helen.**

HENNESSY Peter John, b. 28 Mar 1947, London, England. Professor of Contemporary History; Writer. m. Enid Mary Candler, 14 June 1969, 2 daughters. Education: BA, St John's College, Cambridge, 1969; London School of Economics and Political Science, 1969-71; Kennedy Memorial Scholar, Harvard University, 1971-72; PhD, Cantab, 1990. Appointments: Reporter, Times Higher Education Supplement, 1972-74; Reporter, 1974-76, Whitehall Correspondent, 1976-82, Home Leader Writer and Columnist, 1982-84, The Times: Journalist, The Economist, 1982; Visiting Lecturer, 1983-84, Visiting Professor of Government, 1989-, University of Strathclyde; Senior Fellow, 1984-85; Visiting Fellow, 1986-91; Policy Studies Institute; Columnist, New Statesman, 1986-87, The Independent, 1987-91; Co-Founder and Co-Director, 1986-89, Member of the Board, 1989-98, Institute of Contemporary British History; Visiting Fellow, University of Reading, 1988-94, Royal Institute of Public Administration, 1989-92, University of Nottingham, 1989-95; Partner, Intellectual R and D, 1990-; Visiting Scholar, Griffith University, Brisbane, 1991; Professor of Contemporary History, Queen Mary and Westfield College, University of London, 1992-; Gresham Professor of Rhetoric, 1994-97, Gresham College, London; Chairman Kennedy Memorial Trust, 1995-. Publications: States of Emergency (with Keith Jeffery), 1983; Sources Close to the Prime Minister (with Michael Cockerell and David Walker), 1984; What the Papers Never Said, 1985; Cabinet, 1986; Ruling Performance (editor with Anthony Seldon), 1987; Whitehall, 1989; Never Again: Britain, 1945-51, 1992; The Hidden Wiring: Unearthing the British Constitution, 1995; Muddling Through: Power, Politics and the Quality of Government in Postwar Britain, 1996. Contributions to: Scholarly books and journals, and to radio and television. Honours: Duff Cooper Prize, 1993; NCR Book Award for Non-Fiction, 1994; Hon DLitt, University of West of England 1995; Hon DLitt University of Westminster, 1996; Hon DLitt Kingston University, 1998. Memberships: Royal Historial Society, Fellow, Vice President, 1996-; Royal Society of Arts, Fellow; Johnian Society, President, 1995. Address: c/o Department of History, Queen Mary and Westfield College, University of London, Mile End Road, London E1 4NS, England.

HENNING Jocelyn Ann Margareta Maria (Countess of Roden), b. 5 Aug 1948, Göteborg, Sweden. Author; Playwright; Translator. m. Earl of Roden, 13 Feb 1986, 1 son. Education: BA, Lund University, Sweden, 1975. Appointments: Artistic Director, Connemara Theatre Company. Publications: Modern Astrology, 1983, 1985, 1993. The Connemara Whirlwind, 1990; The Connemara Stallion, 1991; The Connemara Champion, 1994; Honeylove the Bearcub, 1995; The Cosmos and You, 1995; Plays: Baptism of Fire (Connemara Theatre Co), 1997; The Alternative (Connemara Theatre Co), 1998. Contributions to: Magazines including Vogue. Memberships: Translators Association; Society of Authors; Irish Writer's Union; Society of Irish Playwrights. Address: 4 The Boltons, London SW10 9TB, England.

HENRI Adrian (Maurice), b. 10 Apr 1932, Birkenhead, England. Poet; Dramatist; Painter. m. Joyce Wilson, 28 October 1959, div June 1974. Education: BA, Honours, Fine Arts, King's College, Newcastle, 1955. Appointments: Teacher, Manchester College of Art, 1961-64, Liverpool College of Art, 1964-67; Writer-in-Residence, Tattenhall Centre, Cheshire, 1980-82; Writer-in-Residence, 1989, Visiting Lecturer, 1995, University of Liverpool. Publications: The Mersey Sound: Penguin Modern Poets 10 (with Roger McGough and Brian Patten), 1967; Tonight at Noon, 1968; Poems for Wales and Six Landscapes for Susan, 1970; Autobiography, 1971; The Best of Henri: Selected Poems 1968-70, 1970; City Hedges: Poems 1970-76, 1976; From the Loveless Motel: Poems 1976-79, 1980; Penny Arcade 1978-82, 1983; New Volume with Roger Mcgough and Brian Patten: Collected Poems 1967-85, 1986; Wish You Were Here, 1990; Not Fade Away, 1994; Liverpool Accents: Seven Poets and a City, 1996; Poems for children: The World's Your Lobster, 1998; Robocat, 1998. Honour: Honorary DLitt, Polytechnic, 1990. Literary Agent: Rogers, Coleridge & White, 20 Powis Mews, London W11 1JN, England. Address: 21 Mount Street, Liverpool L1 9HD, England.

HENRY Desmond Paul, b. 5 July 1921, Almondbury, Yorks, England. Philosopher; Artist. m. Louise H J Bayen, 19 May 1945, 3 daughters. Education: BA Honours, Philosophy, University of Leeds, 1949; PhD, University of Manchester, 1960. Appointments: Philosophy Teacher, University of Manchester, 1949-82; Visiting Professor, Brown University, 1966, University of Pennsylvania, 1970. Publications: The Logic of St Anselm, 1967; Medieval Logic and Metaphysics, 1972; Commentary on De Grammatico, 1974; That Most Subtle Question, 1984; Medieval Meréology, 1991. Contributions to: Various publications. Membership: Manchester Medieval Society. Address: 4 Burford Drive, Whalley Range, Manchester M16 8FJ, England.

HENRY Stuart (Dennis), b. 18 Oct 1949, London, England. Professor of Sociology; Writer; Editor. m. Lee Doric, 5 Mar 1988. Education: BA, Honours, Sociology, 1972, PhD, Sociology, 1976, University of Kent. Appointments: Research Sociologist, London University, 1975-78; Research Fellow, Middlesex University, 1978-79; Senior Lecturer, Nottingham Trent University, 1979-83; Assistant Professor, Old Dominion University, Norfolk, Virginia, 1984-87; Professor, Eastern Michigan University, 1987-98; Co-Editor, Critical Criminologist, 1997-; Professor of Sociology and Chairman of Department of Sociology, Valparaiso University, 1998-. Publications: Self-help and Health: Mutual Aid for Modern Problems (with D Robinson), 1977; The Hidden Economy: The Context and Control of Borderline Crime, 1978; Private Justice: Toward Integrated Theorizing in the Sociology of Law, 1983; Making Markets: An Interdisciplinary Perspective on Economic Exchange (with R Cantor and S Rayner), 1992; The Deviance Process (with E H Pfuhl), 3rd edition, 1993; Criminological Theory (with W Einstadter), 1995; Constitutive Criminology: Beyond Postmodernism (with D Milovanovic), 1996; Essential Criminology (with M Lanier), 1998. Editor: Informal Institutions: Alternative Networks in the Corporate State, 1981; The Informal Economy (with L Ferman and M Hoyman), 1987; Degrees of Deviance: Student Accounts of their Deviant Behavior, 1989; Work Beyond Employment in Advanced Capitalist Countries: Classic and Contemporary Perspectives on the Informal Economy (with L Ferman and L Berndt), 2 volumes, 1993; Social Control: Aspects of Non-State Justice, 1994; Employee Dismissal: Justice at Work, 1994; Inside Jobs: A Realistic Guide to Criminal Justice Careers for College Graduates, 1994; The Criminology Theory Reader (with W Einstadter), 1998; The Criminology Theory Reader, 1998. Contributions to: Scholarly books and journals. Memberships: American Sociological Association, American Society of Criminology. Address: c/o Department of Sociology, Valparaiso University, Valparaiso, IN 46383, USA.

HENSEL Klaus, b. 14 May 1954, Brasov, Transylvania, Romania. Writer; Journalist; Filmmaker. Education: Lic Phil, German and English Literature, University of Bucharest. Publications: Das Letzte Fruehstueck mit Gertrude, 1980; Oktober Lichtspiel, 1988; Stradivarius Geigenstein, 1990; Summen im Falsett, 1995. Honours: Kranichsteiner Literaturpreis, Germany, 1988; Villa-Massimo-Grant, Rome, Italy, 1994-95. Address: Humboldstrasse 56, D-60318 Frankfurt, Germany.

HEPBURN Ronald William, b. 16 Mar 1927, Aberdeen, Scotland. Retired Professor of Moral Philosophy; Writer. m. Agnes Forbes Anderson, 16 July 1953, 2 sons, 1 daughter. Education: MA, 1951, PhD, 1955, University of Aberdeen. Appointments: Assistant, 1952-55, Lecturer, 1955-60, Department of Moral Philosophy, University of Aberdeen; Visiting Associate Professor, New York University, 1959-60; Professor of Philosophy, University of Nottingham, 1960-64; Professor of Philosophy, 1964-75, Professor of Moral Philosophy, 1975-96, University of Edinburgh; Stanton Lecturer in the Philosophy of Religion, Cambridge University, 1965-68. Publications: Metaphysical Beliefs (jointly), 1957; Christianity and Paradox: Critical Studies in Twentieth-Century Theology, 1958; Wonder and Other Essays: Eight Studies in Aesthetics and Neighbouring Fields, 1984. Contributions to: Scholarly books and journals. Address: 8 Albert Terrace, Edinburgh EH10 5EA, Scotland.

HERALD Kathleen. See: **PEYTON Kathleen Wendy.**

HERBERT Brian Patrick, b. 29 June 1947, Seattle, Washington, USA. Author. Education: BA, Sociology, University of California at Berkeley, 1968. Publications: Classic Comebacks, 1981; Incredible Insurance Claims, 1982; Sidney's Comet, 1983; The Garbage Chronicles, 1984; Sudanna, Sudanna, 1985; Man of Two Worlds (with Frank Herbert), 1986; Prisoners of Arionn, 1987; The Notebooks of Frank Herbert's Dune (editor), 1988; Memorymakers (with Marie Landis), 1991; The Race for God, 1990; Never As It Seems (editor), 1992; Songs of Muad' Dib (editor), 1992; Blood on the Sun (with Marie Landis), 1996; House Atreides (with Kevin J Anderson), 1999; A Whisper of Caladan Seas (with Kevin J Anderson), 1999; House Harkonnen (with Kevin J Anderson), forthcoming; The Spice War (with Kevin J Anderson), forthcoming. Contributions to: Short stories in various anthologies and other publications. Memberships: L-5 Society; National Writers Club; Science Fiction Writers of America; Horror Writers Association. Address: PO Box 10164, Bainbridge Island, WA 98110, USA.

HERBERT (Edward) Ivor (Montgomery), b. 20 Aug 1925, Johannesburg, South Africa. Author; Journalist; Scriptwriter. Education: MA, Trinity College, Cambridge, 1949. Appointments: Travel Editor, Racing Editor, The Mail on Sunday, 1982-. Publications: Eastern Windows, 1953; Point to Point, 1964; Arkle: The Story of a Champion, 1966, 2nd edition, 1975; The Great St Trinian's Train Robbery (screenplay), 1966; The Queen Mother's Horses, 1967; The Winter Kings (co- author), 1968, enlarged edition, 1989; The Way to the Top, 1969; Night of the Blue Demands, play (co-author), 1971; Over Our Dead Bodies, 1972; The Diamond Diggers, 1972; Scarlet Fever (co-author), 1972; Winter's Tale, 1974; Red Rum: Story of a Horse of Courage, 1974; The Filly (novel), 1977; Six at the Top, 1977; Classic Touch (TV documentary), 1985; Spot the Winner, 1978, updated, 1990; Longacre, 1978; Horse Racing, 1980; Vincent O'Brien's Great Horses, 1984; Revolting Behaviour, 1987; Herbert's Travels, 1987; Reflections on Racing (co-author), 1990; Riding Through My Life (with HRH The Princess Royal), 1991. Address: The Old Rectory, Bradenham, Buckinghamshire HP14 4HD, England.

HERBERT James (John), b. 8 Apr 1943, London, England. Author. Education: Hornsey College of Art, 1959. Publications: The Rats, 1974; The Fog, 1975; The Survivor, 1976; Fluke, 1977; The Spear, 1978; Lair, 1979; The Dark, 1980; The Jonah, 1981; Shrine, 1983; Domain, 1984; Moon, 1985; The Magic Cottage, 1986; Sepulchre, 1987; Haunted, 1988; Creed, 1990; Portent, 1992; James Herbert: By Horror Haunted, 1992; James Herbert's Dark Places, 1993; The City, 1994; The Ghosts of Sleath, 1994; '48, 1996; Others, 1999. Films: The Rats, 1982; The Survivor, 1986; Fluke, 1995; Haunted, 1995. Address: c/o Bruce Hunter, David Higham Associates, 5-8 Lower John Street, London W1R 4HA, England.

HERBST Philip H, b. 1 June 1944, Peoria, Illinois, USA. Editor; Writer; Researcher. Education: BA, University of Illinois, 1966; PhD, Cornell University, 1976. Appointments: Instructor in Anthropology, State University of New York at Potsdam, 1971-74; Visiting Scholar, Northwestern University, 1989-92. Publications: A Multicultural Dictionary: A Guide to Ethnic and Racial Words, 1993; The Color of Words: An Encyclopedic Dictionary of Ethnic Bias in the United States, 1997. Contributions to: Several publications. Address: 2415 Central Street, Evanston, IL 60201, USA.

HERDMAN John MacMillan, b. 20 July 1941, Edinburgh, Scotland. Writer. m. Dolina MacLennan, 30 July 1983, div. Education: BA, 1963, MA, 1967, PhD, 1988, Magdalene College, Cambridge, England. Appointments: Creative Writing Fellow, Edinburgh University, Scotland, 1977-79; William Soutar Fellow, Perth, Scotland, 1990-91. Publications: Descent, 1968; A Truth Lover, 1973; Memoirs of My Aunt Minnie/Clapperton, 1974; Pagan's Pilgrimage, 1978; Stories Short and Tall, 1979; Voice Without Restraint: Bob Dylan's Lyrics, 1982; Three Novellas, 1987; The Double in Nineteenth-Century Fiction, 1990; Imelda and Other Stories, 1993; Ghostwriting, 1996; Cruising (play), 1997. Honours: Scottish Arts Council Book Awards, 1978, 1993. Address: Roselea, Bridge of Tilt, Pitlochry, Perthshire PH18 5SX, Scotland.

HERMODSSON Elisabet, b. 20 Sept 1927, Göteborg, Sweden. Writer; Artist; Songwriter. m. (1) Ingemar Olsson, 1951, (2) Olof Hellstrom, 1956, 2 daughters. Publications: Poem-things, 1966; Human Landscape Unfairly, 1968; Rite and Revolution, 1968; Swedish Soul-life, 1970; Culture at the Bottom, 1971; Voices in the Human Landscape, 1971; What Shall We Do With The Summer, Comrades? (songs), 1973; Disa Nilsons Songs, 1974; Through the Red Waist Coat of the Ground, 1975; Visional Turning Point, 1975; Words in Woman's Time, 1979; Wake Up With a Summer Soul, 1979; Make Yourself Visible, 1980; Discources Meanwhile, 1983;

Stones, Shards, Layers of Earth, 1985; Creation Betrayed, 1986; Streams of Mist, 1990; Cloud Steps, 1994. Contributions to: Anthologies, journals and magazines; Editor, several anthologies. Honour: Royal Medal, Litteris et Artibus, 1994. Memberships: PEN Club. Address: Ostra Agatan 67, 75322 Uppsala, Sweden.

HERNANDEZ Consuelo, b. Colombia. Poet; Critic; Professor. Education: BA, Languages and Literature, University of Antioquica, Columbia, 1978; MA, Latin American Literature, Simon Bolivar University, 1982; PhD, Latin American Literature, New York University, 1991. Appointments: Simon Rodriquez University, 1981-87; New York University, 1987-95; Manhattanville College, New York, 1991-95; Professor, American University, Washington, DC, 1995-. Publications: Books: Voces de la soledad, 1982; Alvaro Mutis: Una estética del deterioro, 1996; Solo de violin. Poemario para musicos y pintores, 1997. Contributions to: Literary journals. Honours include: Finalist, International Poetry Contest, Spain, 1997. Address: c/o American University, Language and Foreign Studies Department, Washington, DC 20016, USA.

HERNDON Nancy Ruth, b. 29 May 1934, St Louis, Missouri, USA. Novelist. m. William C Herndon, 27 Dec 1956, 2 sons. Education: BA, distinction, English; Bachelor of Journalism, 1956; MA, English, 1958. Appointments: English Lecturer, Rice, 1996-98, New York University, 1959-61, University of Mississippi, 1962-63; Florida Atlantic University, 1966, University of Texas at El Paso, 1976-81; Novelist, 1989-. Publications include: Widow's Fire, 1990; All Bets Are Off, Women of the West, 1990; Saloon Girls, New Frontiers, 1990; Pinata Tycoon Weds Western Style, West Texas Sun, 1990; Murder by Snail, Third Woman Sleuth Anthology, 1990; Virgin Fire, 1991; Bride Fire, 1992; November, 1993; Reluctant Lovers, 1993; Elusive Lovers, 1994; Acid Bath, 1995; Widows' Match, 1995; Lethal Statues, 1996; Hunting Game, 1996; Time Bombs, 1997; C.O.P. Killers, 1998; Casanova Crimes, 1999. Honours: Phi Beta Kappa, 1954; Regent's Scholarship, 1952-53; Mortar Board, 1955; Rice Fellowship, 1956-58; Winner Rice Faculty Student Play Contest, 1957; DYU Fellowship; El Paso Writers Hall of Fame, 1997. Memberships: NOW; Planned Parent Head, University of Texas at El Paso Women's Club; Smithsonian Associates; South West Writer's Workshop; Sisters in Crime. Hobbies: Reading; Travel; Opera; History; Baroque Music. Address: 6504 Pino Road, El Paso, TX 79912, USA.

HERR Pamela (Staley), b. 24 July 1939, Cambridge, Massachusetts, USA. Writer. 2 daughters. Education: BA, magna cum laude, Harvard University, 1961; MA, George Washington University, 1971. Appointments: Writer and Editor, Field Educational Publications, 1973; Editor, Sullivan Associates, 1973-74; Project Manager, Sanford Associates, Education Development Corp, Menlo Park, 1974-76; Managing Editor, American West, Cupertino, California, 1976-79; Historian and Writer, 1980-. Publications: Jessie Benton Fremont: A Biography, 1987; Letters of Jessie Benton Fremont (with Mary Lee Spence), 1993. Honour: Phi Beta Kappa. Address: 559 Seale Avenue, Palo Alto, CA 94301, USA.

HERRA Maurice. See: ASSELINEAU Roger Maurice.

HERRING Peggy J, (B K Devious), b. 18 Jan 1953, Beeville, Texas, USA. Civil Service. Publications: Once More With Feeling; Love's Harvest; Hot Check; A Moments Indiscretion, one short story in the Naiad Anthologies titled - The First Time Ever; Dancing In the Dark; Lady Be Good. Address: PO Box 120024, San Antonio, TX 78212, USA.

HERSEY April (Maeve), b. 4 Apr 1924, Australia. Writer; Editor. Appointments: Consultant Scriptwriter, Pilgrim International; Editor: Craft Australia, 1974-81; POL, 1976, Oz Arts Magazine, 1990-. Publications: Australian Style, 1968; New Zealand, 1969; Hooked On God, 1970; The Insulted Heart: Recovery from Bypass Surgery, 1996. Contributions to: Bulletin; Sun Herald; Women's Day; Home and Family; Home; House and

Garden; Life; Sunday Times; Reader's Digest. Memberships: Australian Society of Authors; Fellowship of Australian Writers. Address: 12 Wright Street, Glenbrook, New South Wales 2773, Australia.

HERSH Burton David, b. 18 Sept 1933, Chicago, Illinois, USA. Author; Biographer. m. Ellen Eiseman, 3 Aug 1957, 1 son, 1 daughter. Education: BA magna cum laude, Harvard College, 1955; Fulbright Scholar, 1955-56. Publications: The Ski People, 1968; The Education of Edward Kennedy, 1972; The Mellon Family, 1978; The Old Boys, 1992; The Shadow President, 1997. Contributions to: Many magazines. Honours: Book Find Selection, 1972; Book-of-the-Month Club, 1978. Memberships: Authors Guild; American Society of Journalists and Authors; PEN. Address: PO Box 433, Bradford, NH 03221, USA.

HERSH Seymour, b. 8 Apr 1937, Chicago, Illinois, USA. Journalist; Writer. m. Elizabeth Sarah Klein, 30 May 1964, 2 sons, 1 daughter. Education: BA in History, University of Chicago, 1958. Appointments: Correspondent, United Press International, 1962-63, Associated Press, 1963-67, The New Yorker, 1992-; Staff, New York Times, 1972-79; National Correspondent, Atlantic Monthly, 1983-86. Publications: Chemical and Biological Warfare: America's Hidden Arsenal, 1968; My Lai 4: A Report on the Massacre and Its Aftermath, 1970; Cover-Up: The Army's Secret Investigation of the Massacre of My Lai, 1972; The Price of Power: Kissinger in the Nixon White House, 1983; The Target is Destroyed: What Really Happened to Flight 007 and What America Knew About It, 1986; The Samson Option: Israel's Nuclear Arsenal and America's Foreign Policy, 1991; The Dark Side of Camelot, 1997. Contributions to: Various magazines. Honours: Pulitzer Prize for International Reporting, 1970; Sigma Delta Chi Distinguished Service Awards, 1970, 1981; George Polk Memorial Awards, 1970, 1973, 1974, 1981; Scripps-Howard Public Service Award, 1973; Sidney Hillman Award, 1974; John Peter Zenger Freedom of the Press Award, 1975; Los Angeles Times Book Prize, 1983; National Book Critics Circle Award, 1983; Investigate Reporters and Editors Prizes, 1983, 1992. Address: 1211 Connecticut Avenue North West, Suite 320, Washington, DC 20036, USA.

HERZBERG Judith, b. 4 Nov 1934, Amsterdam, Netherlands. Poet; Playwright. Education: Graduated, Montessori Lyceum, 1952. Appointments: Teacher at film schools in Netherlands and Israel. Publications: Slow Boat, 1964; Meadow Grass, 1968; Flies, 1970; Grazing Light, 1971; 27 Love Songs, 1973; Botshol, 1980; Remains of the Day, 1984; Twenty Poems, 1984; But What: Selected Poems, 1988; The Way, 1992; What She Meant to Paint, 1998; Small Catch, 1999. Plays: Near Archangel, 1971; It Is Not a Dog, 1973; That Day May Dawn, 1974; Lea's Wedding, 1982; The Fall of Icarus, 1983; And/Or, 1984; The Little Mermaid, 1986; Scratch, 1989; Lulu (adaptation of Wedekind), 1989; A Good Head, 1991; The Nothing-factory, 1997. Other: Texts for the Stage and Film, 1972-88; Screenplays and Television plays; Translations, including The Trojan Women, by Euripides, and Ghosts, by Ibsen. Honours: Netherlands-Vlaamse Drama Prize, 1989; Constantijn Huyens Prize, 1995; P C Hooft Prize for Poetry, 1997. Address: c/o De Harmonie, Postbus 3547, 1001 AH Amsterdam, Netherlands.

HESKETH Phoebe, b. 29 Jan 1909, Preston, Lancashire, England. Retired Lecturer; Poet; Writer. Appointments: Lecturer, Bolton Women's College, 1967-69; Teacher of Creative Writing, Bolton School, 1977-79. Publications: Poetry: Lean Forward, Spring, 1948; No Time for Cowards, 1952; Out of the Dark, 1954; Between Wheels and Stars, 1956; The Buttercup Children, 1958; Prayer for Sun, 1966; A Song of Sunlight, 1974; Preparing to Leave, 1977; The Eighth Day, 1980; A Ring of Leaves, 1985; Over the Brook, 1985; Netting the Sun: New and Collected Poems, 1989; Sundowner, 1992; The Leave Train, New and Selected Poems, 1994; A Box of Silver Birch, 1997. Prose: My Aunt Edith, 1966; Rivington: The Story of a Village, 1972; What Can the

Matter Be?, 1985; Rivington: Village of the Mountain Ash, 1989. Honour: Honorary Fellow, University of Central Lancashire, 1992. Address: 10 The Green, Heath Charnock, Chorley, Lancashire PR6 9JH, England.

HESSAYON David Gerald, b. 13 Feb 1928, Manchester, England. Author. m. Joan Parker Gray, 2 Apr 1951, 2 daughters. Education: BSC, Leeds University, 1950; PhD, Manchester University, 1954. Publications: The House Plant Expert, 1980; The Armchair Book of the Garden, 1983; The Tree and Shrub Expert, 1983; The Flower Expert, 1984; The Indoor Plant Spotter, 1985; The Garden Expert, 1986; The Home Expert, 1987; The Fruit Expert, 1990; Be Your Own Greenhouse Expert, 1990; The New House Plant Expert, 1991; The Garden DIY Expert, 1992; The Rock and Water Garden Expert, 1993; The Flowering Shrub Expert, 1994; The Greenhouse Expert, 1994; The Flower Arranging Expert, 1994; The Container Expert, 1995; The Bulb Expert, 1995; The Easy-Care Gardening Expert, 1996; The New Bedding Plant Expert, 1996; The New Rose Expert, 1996; The New Vegetable and Herb Expert, 1997; The New Lawn Expert, 1997; The Evergreen Expert, 1998; The New Flower Expert, 1999. Honours: Lifetime Achievement Trophy, National British Book Awards, 1992; Gold Veitch Memorial Medal, Royal Horticultural Society, 1992; Gardening Book of the Year Award, 1993; Roy Hay Memorial Award, 1998. Membership: Society of Authors. Address: Sloe House, Halstead, Essex CO9 1PA, England.

HESSAYON Joan Parker, b. 21 Jan 1932, Louisville, Kentucky, USA. Author. m. David Hessayon, 2 Apr 1951, 2 daughters. Publications: All Kinds of Courage, 1983; For All Good Men, 1984; Little Maid All Unwary, 1985; Sybilla, 1986; Thorsby, 1987; Lady from St Louis, 1989; Belle's Daughter, 1990; Roxanne's War, 1991; House on Pine Street, 1992; Capel Bells, 1995; Helmingham Rose, 1997; The Paradise Garden, 1999. Memberships: Romantic Novelists Association; Society of Authors. Address: Sloe House, Halstead, Essex CO9 1PA, England.

HESSING Dennis. See: **DENNIS-JONES Harold.**

HESTER William,b. 6 June 1933, Detroit, Michigan, USA. Author; Lyricist. Div, 1 daughter. Education: Brown University, 1951-52; University of Detroit, 1956; BA, Mesa College, 1970; MA, Special Studies, University of California at Los Angeles, New York University. Appointments: Staff, Warner Brothers Pictures, 1961-62, Playboy Magazine, 1966-68; Creative Staff, Sierra Productions, 1962-65; Associate Director, Vance Publications, 1970-73. Publications: Please Don't Die In My House, 1965; Selections, 1967; Running Off, 1970; Not the Right Season, 1984; Another Town, 1984; Still Not the Right Season, 1985; Our Place, 1986; Sleeping Neighbours, 1986; Tyranny/2000, 1988. Also music. Contributions to: Pulpsmith; Confrontation; Amelia; Easy Riders; The Poet; Playboy; Witness; Golf Magazine; Fortune News; Wind. Honours: Eisner Fellowship, 1984; 1st and 2nd Awards, fiction and non-fiction, PEN American Centre, 1985, 1986; Various awards, American Song Festival. Memberships: Authors Guild; Conservatory of American Letters; Broadcast Music Inc. Address: c/o James McDonald Inc, 1130-20th Street, No 5 Santa Monica, CA 90403, USA.

HETHERINGTON (Hector) Alastair, b. 31 Oct 1919, Llanishen, Glamorganshire, Wales. Journalist; Writer. Professor Emeritus. m. (1) Helen Miranda Oliver, 1957, div 1978, 2 sons, 2 daughters, (2) Sheila Cameron, 1979. Education: MA, Corpus Christi College, Oxford. Appointments: Staff, Glasgow Herald, 1946-50, BBC, 1975-80; Staff, 1950-53, Foreign Editor, 1953-56, Editor, 1956-75, Manchester Guardian; Director, Guardian Newspapers Ltd, 1967-75; Controller, BBC Scotland, 1975-78; Manager, BBC Highland, 1979-80; Research Professor, 1982-88, Professor Emeritus, 1988-, Stirling University. Publications: Guardian Years, 1981; News, Newspapers and Television, 1985; Perthshire in Trust, 1988; News in the Regions, 1989; Highlands and Islands, a Generation of Progress, 1990; Cameras in the Commons, 1990; Inside BBC Scotland, 1975-1980, 1992; A Walker's Guide to Arran, 1994. Address: High Corrie, Isle of Arran KA27 8GB, Scotland, also: 38 Chalton Road, Bridge of Allan, Stirling, FK9 4EF.

HETHERINGTON Norriss Swigart, b. 30 Jan 1942, Berkeley, California, USA. University Research Associate, Writer. m. Edith Wiley White, 10 Dec 1966, 1 son, 1 daughter. Education: BA, 1963, MA, 1965, MA, 1967, University of California, Berkeley; PhD, Indiana University, 1970. Appointments: Lecturer in Physics and Astronomy, Agnes Scott College, Decatur, Gorgia 1967-68; Assistant Professor of Mathematics and Science, York University, Toronto, Ontario, 1970-72; Administrative Specialist, National Aeronautics and Space Aministration, 1972; Assistant Professor of History, University of Kansas, 1972-76; Assistant Professor of Science, Technology and Society, Razi University, Sanandaj, Iran, 1976-77; Visiting Scholar, Cambridge University, England, 1977-78; Research Associate, Office for History of Science and Technology, University of Calfornia, Berkeley, 1978-; Associate Professor of the History of Science, University of Oklahoma at Norman, 1981; Director, Institute for the History of Astronomy, 1988-. Publications: Ancient Astronomy and Civilization, 1987; Science and Objectivity: Episodes in the History of Astronomy, 1988; The Edwin Hubble Papers, 1990; Encyclopedia of Cosmology, 1993; Cosmology: Historical, Literary, Philosophical, Religious and Scientific Perspectives, 1993; Hubble's Cosmology: A Guided Study of Selected Texts, 1996. Honour: Goddard Historical Essay Award, 1974. Address: Office for History of Science and Technology, 543 Stephens Hall, University of California at Berkeley, Berkeley, CA 94720, USA.

HETTICH Michael, b. 25 Sept 1953, Brooklyn, New York, USA. Professor. m. Colleen Ahern, 7 Feb 1980, 1 son, 1 daughter. Education: BA, Hobart College, 1975; MA, University of Denver, 1979; PhD, University of Miami, 1990. Publications: Lathe, 1987; White Birds, 1989; A Small Boat, 1990; Immaculate Bright Rooms, 1994; Many Simple Things, 1997. Contributions to: Poetry East; Witness; Literary Review; Miami Herald; Salt Hills Journal. Honour: Mac Smith Endowed Chair. Address: 561 North East 95th Street, Miami Shores, FL 33138, USA.

HEWETT Dorothy (Coade), b. 21 May 1923, Perth, Western Australia. Poet; Writer; Dramatist. Education: BA, 1961, MA, 1963, University of Western Australia. Publications: Bobbin Up (novel), 1959; What About the People (poems with Merv Lilly), 1962; The Australians Have a Word for It (stories), 1964; Windmill Country (poems), 1968; The Hidden Journey (poems), 1969; The Chapel Perilous, or The Perilous Adventures of Sally Bonner, 1971; Sandgropers: A Western Australian Anthology, 1973; Rapunzel in Suburbia (poems), 1975; Miss Hewett's Shenanigans, 1975; Greenhouse (poems), 1979; The Man from Mukinupin (play), 1979; Susannah's Dreaming (play), 1981; The Golden Oldies (play), 1981; Selected Poems, 1990; Wild Card (autobiography), 1990. Honour: Member of the Order of Australia, 1986. Address: 195 Bourke Street, Darlinghurst, New South Wales 2011, Australia.

HEYEN William (Helmuth), b. 1 Nov 1940, Brooklyn, New York, USA. Professor of English; Poet; Writer. m. Hannelore Greiner, 7 July 1962, 1 son, 1 daughter. Education: BS, Education, State University of New York College at Brockport, 1961; MA, English, 1963, PhD, English, 1967, Ohio University. Appointments: Instructor, State University of New York College at Cortland, 1963-65; Assistant Professor to Professor of English and Poet-in-Residence, State University of New York College at Brockport, 1967-; Teacher, University of Hannover, Germany, 1971-72; Visiting Creative Writer, University of Wisconsin at Milwaukee, 1980; Visiting Writer, Hofstra University, 1981, 1983, Southampton College, 1984, 1985; Visiting Professor of English, University of Hawaii, 1985. Publications: Depth of Field, 1970; A Profile of Theodore Roethke (editor), 1971; Noise in the Trees: Poems and a Memoir, 1974; American Poets in 1976 (editor), 1976; The Swastika Poems, 1977; Long Island Light: Poems and a Memoir, 1979; The City Parables, 1980; Lord Dragonfly: Five Sequences, 1981; Erika: Poems of the Holocaust, 1984; The Generation of 2000: Contemporary American Poets (editor), 1984; Vic Holyfield and the Class of 1957: A Romance, 1986; The Chestnut Rain: A Poem, 1986; Brockport, New York: Beginning with "And", 1988; Falling From Heaven (co-author), 1991; Pterodactyl Rose: Poems of Ecology, 1991; Ribbons: The Gulf War, 1991; The Host: Selected Poems 1965-1990, 1994; With Me Far Away: A Memoir, 1994; Crazy Horse in Stillness: Poems, 1996; Pig Notes and Dumb Music: Prose on Poetry, 1998; Diana, Charles and the Queen: Poems, 1998. Contributions to: Many books, chapbooks, journals and magazines. Honours: Borestone Mountain Poetry Prize, 1965; National Endowment for the Arts Fellowships, 1973-74, 1984-85; American Library Association Notable American Book, 1974; Ontario Review Poetry Prize, 1977; Guggenheim Fellowship, 1977-78; Eunice Tietjens Memorial Award, 1978; Witter Bynner Prize for Poetry, 1982; New York Foundation for the Arts Poetry Fellowship, 1984-85; Lillian Fairchild Award, 1996; Small Press Books Award for Poetry, 1997. Address: c/o Department of English, State University of New York College at Brockport, Brockport, NY 14420, USA.

HEYERDAHL Thor, b. 6 Oct 1914, Larvik, Norway. Author; Anthropologist. m. (1) Liv Coucheron Torp, 1936, dec 1969, 2 sons, (2) Yvonne Dedekam-Simonsen, 1949, 3 daughters. Education: University of Oslo, 1933-36. Appointments: Organised and Led, Kon-Tiki Expedition, 1947; Made Crossing from Safi, Morocco to West Indies in Papyrus Boat, RAII, 1970. Publications: Paa Jakt efter Paradiset, 1938; The Kon-Tiki Expedition, 1948; American Indians in the Pacific: The Theory Behind the Kon-Tiki Expedition, 1952; Archaeological Evidence of Pre-Spanish Visits to the Galapagos Islands (with A Skjolsvold), 1956; Aku-Aku: The Secrets of Easter Island, 1961, Vol II, Miscellaneous Papers, 1965; Indianer und Alt-Asiaten im Pazifik: Das Abenteuer einer heorie, 1965; Sea Routes to Polynesia, 1968; The Ra Expeditions, 1970; Fatu-Hiva Back to Nature, 1974; Art of Easter Island, 1975; Zwischen den Kontinenten, 1975; Early Man and the Ocean, 1978; The Tigris Expedition, 1980; The Mystery of the Maldives, 1986; Easter Island, 1990; Pyramids of Tucme: The Quest for Peru's Forgotten City, 1995; Green Was the Earth on the Seventh Day, 1996; Seafaring in Ancient Peru, 1996; Let the Conquered Speak, 1997. Contributions to: Numerous professional journals. Honours: Gold Medal, Royal Geographical Society, London, 1964; Commander with Star, Order of St Olav, Norway, 1970; Order of Merit, Egypt, 1971; Grand Officer, Royal Alaouites Order, Morocco, 1971; Honorary Citizen, Larvik, Norway, 1971; International Pahlavi Environment Prize, UN, 1978; Order of Golden Ark, Netherlands, 1980. Address: Apartado de Correos 80, Guimar, 38500 Tenerife, Canary Islands.

HEYM Stefan, b. 10 Apr 1913, Chemnitz, Germany. Writer. Education: Universities of Berlin and Chicago; MA, 1935. Publications: Hostages, 1942; Of Smiling Peace, 1944; The Crusaders, 1948; The Eye of Reason, 1951; Goldsborough, 1953; The Cannibals and Other Stories, 1953; Shadows and Light: Eight Short Stories, 1960; The Lenz Papers, 1964; Uncertain Friend, 1969; The Queen Against Defoe and Other Stories, 1972; The King David Report, 1972; Five Days in June, 1974; Collin, 1980; The Wandering Jew, 1984; Schwarzenberg, 1984; Collected Stories, 1984; Nachruf (autobiography), 1988; Selected prose, 1990; Built on Sand, 1990; Filz (essays), 1991; Radek, 1995. Honours: DLitt, University of Cambridge, 1991; Dr Theol.h.c, University of Berne; Jerusalem Prize, 1993. Memberships: German Academy of Arts; PEN.

HIBBARD Bill (Curt William Jr), b. 20 Sept 1927, Milwaukee, WI, USA. Writer; Photographer; Editor. m. Edith Molinaro, 2 Sept 1961, 1 son, 1 daughter. Education: BS, Journalism, University of Wisconsin, Madison, 1950; Graduate studies in journalism, history, political science. Appointments: Police, City Hall Reporter, Dubuque Telegraph Herald, Dubuque, Iowa, 1951-52; Reporter, Feature Writer, Milwaukee Journal,

Milwaukee, Wisconsin, 1952-65; Ski Writer, 1958-80; Travel Editor, 1965-80; Feature Writer, Copy Editor, Auto Editor, 1983-90, retired 1990 to go freelance; Correspondent for US Information Service, late 50's, early 60's; Writing Instructor, Marquette University Continuing Education, late 50's; Midwest Editor, SKI Magazine, 1970-80; Freelance Travel Writer, 1965-; Milwaukee Section of book Walking Tours of America, 1977; Five photos in Children's Press Book on Hungary; Retired in 1980, after 30 years in US Naval Reserve with Rank of Commander. Contributions to: Freelance contributions to Better Homes and Gardens, Midwest Living, Odyssey, Open Road, Where to Retire, Airline In-Flight Magazines; SKI; Skiing; S Area Management, S Racing and many newspaper travel sections. Honours: Midwest Travel Writers Travel Writer of the Year Award, 1967; Hedman Top Newspaper Travel Writer Award, 1968; US S Writers S Writer of the Year Award, 1972; several Society of American Travel Writers and Midwest Travel Writers Writing and Photography Awards; Milwaukee Journal Editor of the Year Award, 1990. Membership: Midwest Travel Writers Association; Society of American Travel Writers, President, 1978. Address: 3333 N Shepard Avenue, Milwaukee, WI 53211, USA.

HIBBERD Jean, (J O McDonald), b. 11 Oct 1931, London, England. Writer; Editor. m. Reginald George Hibberd, 8 Mar 1952, 2 sons, 2 daughters. Education: Diploma, Short Story Writing, 1980. Appointments: Coordinator, Nepean Community College; Editor, Compiler, Nepean Community College Annual Anthology, 1985-; Holiday and Travel Writer, Western Weekender, 1991-93. Publications: The Adventures of Peter Possum and His Friends; Further Adventures of Peter Possum and His Friends; Duty to My God; On the Sea of the Moon, romance; Ordeal by Love; The Artist and the Gypsy; Poetry of the Sun; Short Stories from Around the World. Contributions to: Periodicals. Honours: Medal of Merit, Scout Association, 1971; Order of Australia Medal, 1994. Memberships: Fellowship of Australian Writers; Australian Society of Authors; Order of Australia. Address: 7 Rusden Road, Blaxland, New South Wales 2774, Australia.

HIBBERT Christopher, b. 5 Mar 1924, Enderby, Leicestershire, England. Author. m. Susan Piggford, 1948, 2 sons, 1 daughter. Education: MA, Oriel College, Oxford. Appointments: Served in Italy, 1944-45; Captain, London Irish Rifles; Military Cross; Partner, firm of land agents, auctioneers and surveyors, 1948-59. Publications: The Road to Tyburn, 1957; King Mob, 1958; Wolfe at Quebec, 1959; The Destruction of Lord Raglan, 1961; Corunna, 1961; Benito Mussolini, 1962; The Battle of Arnhem, 1962; The Roots of Evil, 1963; The Court at Windsor, 1964; Agincourt, 1964; The Wheatley Diary (editor), 1964; Garibaldi and His Enemies, 1965; The Making of Charles Dickens, 1967; Waterloo: Napoleon's Last Campaign (editor), 1967; An American in Regency England: The Journal of Louis Simond (editor), 1968; Charles I, 1968; The Grand Tour, 1969; London: Biography of a City, 1969; The Search for King Arthur, 1970; Anzio: The Bid for Rome, 1970; The Dragon Wakes: China and the West, 1793-1911, 1970; The Personal History of Samuel Johnson, 1971; George IV, Prince of Wales 1762-1811, 1972; George IV, Regent and King 1812-1830, 1973; The Rise and Fall of the House of Medici, 1974; Edward VII: A Portrait, 1976; The Great Mutiny: India, 1857, 1978; The French Revolution, 1981; Africa Explored: Europeans in the Dark Continent, 1796-1889, 1982; The London Encyclopaedia (editor), 1983; Queen Victoria in Her Letters and Journals, 1984; Rome: The Biography of a City, 1985; Critics and Civilizations, 1985; The English: A Social History, 1987; Venice: Biography of a City, 1988; The Encyclopaedia of Oxford (editor), 1988; Redcoats and Rebels: The War for America 1760-1781, 1990; The Virgin Queen: The Personal History of Elizabeth I, 1990; Captain Gronow: His Reminiscences of Regency and Victorian Life (editor), 1991; Cavaliers and Roundheads: The English at War 1642-1649, 1993; Florence: Biography of a City, 1993; Nelson: A Personal History, 1994; Wellington: A Personal History, 1997; George III: A Personal History. Honours: Heinemann Award for Literature, 1962; McColvin Medal,

1989; Honorary DLitt, Leicester University, 1996. Address: c/o David Higham Associates, 5-8 Lower John Street, Golden Square, London W1R 4HA, England.

HICK John (Harwood), b. 20 Jan 1922, Scarborough, Yorkshire, England. Professor of the Philosophy of Religion (retired); Writer. m. Joan Hazel Bowers, 30 Aug 1953, 3 sons, 1 daughter. Education: MA, 1948, DLitt, 1975, University of Edinburgh; DPhil, Oxford University, 1950; Postgraduate Studies, Westminster Theological College, 1950-53; PhD, by incorporation, Cambridge University, 1964. Appointments: Ordained to the Ministry, United Reformed Church, England, 1953; Minister, Belford Presbyterian Church, Northumberland, England, 1953-56; Assistant Professor of Philosophy, Cornell University, 1956-59; Stuart Professor of Christian Philosophy, Princeton Theological Seminary, 1959-64; Lecturer, 1964-67, Arthur Stanley Eddington Memorial Lecturer, 1972, Stanton Lecturer, 1974-77, Cambridge University; H G Wood Professor of Theology, Birmingham University, 1967-82; Ingersoll Lecturer, Harvard University, 1977; Danforth Professor of the Philosophy of Religion, Claremont Graduate University, California, 1979-92; Gifford Lecturer, University of Edinburgh, 1986-87; Resler Lecturer, Ohio State University, 1991. Publications: Faith and Knowledge, 1957, 2nd edition, 1966; The Philosophy of Religion, 1963, 4th edition, 1990; Evil and the God of Love, 1966, 2nd edition, 1977; God and the Universe of Faiths, 1973; Death and Eternal Life, 1976; God Has Many Names, 1980; Problems of Religious Pluralism, 1985; An Interpretation of Religion, 1989; Disputed Questions in Theology and the Philosophy of Religion, 1993; The Metaphor of God Incarnate, 1993; The Rainbow of Faiths, 1995. Honours: Guggenheim Fellowships, 1963-64, 1985-86; Leverhulme Research Fellowships, 1976, 1990; Grawemeyer Award in Religion, 1991. Memberships: American Academy of Religion; American Philosophical Association. Address: 144 Oak Tree Lane, Selly Oak, Birmingham, B29 6HU, U.K.

HICKOK Gloria Vando, b. 21 May 1934, New York, New York, USA. Poet; Publisher; Editor. m. (1) Maurice Peress, 2 July 1955, 1 son, 2 daughters, (2) William Harrison Hickok, 4 Oct 1980. Education: BA, Texas A & I College, Corpus Christi, 1975; Graduate Studies, Southampton College, Long Island University, New York. Appointments: Founding Publisher, editor, Helicon Nine Editions, 1977-. Publications: Caprichos, 1987; Promesas: Geography of the Impossible, 1993; Touching the Fire: Fifteen Poets of Today's Latino Renaissance (anthology), 1998; Spud Songs: An Anthology of Potato Poems (co-editor), 1998. Contributions to: Cottonwood Magazine, Gloria Vando Issue, Summer 1994; Kenyon Review; Western Humanities Review; Seattle Review. Honours: Billee Murray Denny Prize, 1991; Thorpe Menn Book Award, 1994; River Styx International Poetry Award, second place, 1997; Poetry Society of America's Alice Fay Di Castagnola Award, 1998. Memberships: PEN International; Poetry Society of America; Writers Place, Kansas City, Missouri, co-founder; Cockefair Chair, Universty of Missouri-Kansas City, board; Clearing House for Midcontinent Foundations, art chair, 1988-90; Midwest Center for the Literary Arts Inc, board vice-president; Academy of American Poets. Address: c/o Helicon Nine Editions, PO Box 22412, Kansas City, MO 64113, USA.

HICKS Eleanor B. See: **COERR Eleanor (Beatrice)**.

HIGDON Hal, b. 17 June 1931, Chicago, Illinois, USA. Writer. Education: BA, Carleton College, 1953. Appointment: Assistant Editor, The Kiwanis Magazine, 1957-59. Publications: The Union vs Dr Mudd, 1964; Heroes of the Olympics, 1965; Pro Football USA, 1967; The Horse That Played Center Field, 1967; The Business Healers, 1968; Stars of the Tennis Courts, 1969; 30 Days in May, 1969; The Electronic Olympics, 1969; On the Run from Dogs and People, 1969; Finding the Groove, 1973; Find the Key Man, 1974; The Last Series, 1974; Six Seconds to Glory, 1974; The Crime of the Century, 1976; Summer of Triumph, 1977; Fitness after Forty, 1977; Beginner's Running Guide, 1978; Runner's Cookbook,

1979; Johnny Rutherford, 1980; The Marathoners, 1980; The Team That Played in the Space Bowl, 1981; The Masters Running Guide, 1990; Run Fast, 1992; Marathon: The Ultimate Training and Racing Guide, 1993; Falconara: A Family Odyssey, 1993; Ideas for Rent: The UOP Story, 1994; Boston: A Century of Running, 1995; Hal Higdon's How to Train, 1997; Hal Higdon's Smart Running, 1998. Memberships: American Society of Journalists and Authors; Authors Guild; North American Ski Journalists Association. Address: Box 1034, Michigan City, IN 46360, USA.

HIGGINBOTHAM (Prieur) Jay, b. 16 July 1937, Pascagoula, Mississippi, USA. Archivist; Writer. m. Alice Louisa Martin, 27 June 1970, 2 sons, 1 daughter. Education: BA, University of Mississippi, 1960; Graduate Studies, Hunter College of the City University of New York, American University, Washington, DC. Appointments: Head, Local History Department, Mobile Public Library, 1973-83; Director, Mobile Municipal Archives, 1983-. Publications: The Mobile Indians, 1966; The World Around, 1966; Family Biographies, 1967; The Pascagoula Indians, 1967; Pascagoula: Singing River City, 1968; Mobile: City by the Bay, 1968; The Journal of Sauvole, 1969; Fort Maurepas: The Birth of Louisiana, 1969; Brother Holyfield, 1972; A Voyage to Dauphin Island, 1974; Old Mobile: Fort Louis de la Louisiane, 1702-1711, 1977; Fast Train Russia, 1983; Autumn in Petrishchevo, 1986; Discovering Russia, 1989; Mauvila, 1990; Kazula (play), 1991; Man, Nature and the Infinite, 1998. Contributions to: Periodicals. Honours: General L Kemper Williams Prize, Louisiana Historical Association, 1977; Award of Merit, Mississippi Historical Society, 1978; Non-Fiction Award, Alabama Library Association, 1978; Gilbert Chinard Prize, Institute Français de Washington and Society for French Historical Studies, 1978. Memberships: Authors League of America; Franklin Society; Smithsonian Associates. Address: c/o Mobile Municipal Archives, 457 Church Street, Mobile, AL 36602, USA.

HIGGINS Aidan, b. 3 Mar 1927, Celbridge, County Kildare, Ireland. Writer. Education: Clongowes Wood College, County Kildare. Publications: Stories Felo De Se, 1960; Langrishe, Go Down, 1966; Balcony of Europe, 1972; Scenes from a Receding Past, 1977; Bornholm Night Ferry, 1983; Helsingor Station and Other Departures, 1989; Ronda Gorge and Other Precipices: Travel Writings, 1959-90; Lions of The Grunewald (novel), 1993; Donkey's Years (Memories of a Life as Story Told), 1995; Secker, Flotsam and Jetsam (collected stories), 1997; Dog Days, 1998. Honours: British Arts Council Grant; James Tait Black Memorial Prize, 1967; Irish Academy of Letters Award, 1970; American Ireland Fund, 1977. Address: c/o Secker and Warburg, Michelin House, 91 Fulham Road, London SW3 6RB, England.

HIGGINS George V(incent), b. 13 Nov 1939, Brockton, Massachusetts, USA. Writer; Lawyer; Professor. m. 1) Elizabeth Mulkerin, 4 Sept 1965, div, 1 son, 1 daughter, 2) Loretta Lucas Cubberley, 23 Aug 1979. Education: AB, English, Boston College, 1961; MA, English, Stanford University, 1965; JD, Boston College Law School, 1967. Appointments: Staff, Journal and Evening Bulletin, Providence, Rhode Island, 1962-63; Associate Press, 1963-66; Legal Assistant, 1967, Deputy Assistant Attorney General, Assistant Attorney General, Organized Crime Section, Criminal Division, 1967-70, Massachusetts; Lecturer, Lincoln College, Northeastern University, 1968-70; Assistant United States Attorney, 1970-73; Special Assistant United States Attorney, 1973, District of Massachusetts; Instructor, Boston College Law School, 1971-72, 1979; Special Correspondent, Atlantic Monthly, 1973-76; Attorney at law, George V Higgins Inc, Boston, 1973-83; Columnist, Boston Phoenix, 1974-76; Boston Herald-American, 1976-79, Boston Globe, 1979-85; Writer-in-Residence, Washington Star, 1977; Television Critic, Wall Street Journal, 1984-87; Visiting Professor of English, State University of New York at Buffalo, 1988; Professor of Creative Writing, Boston University, 1988-. Publications: Fiction: The Friends of Eddie Coyle, 1972; The Digger's Game, 1973; Cogan's Trade, 1974; A City on a Hill, 1975; The Judgement of

Deke Hunter, 1976; Dreamland, 1977; A Year or So with Edgar, 1978; Kennedy for the Defense, 1980; The Rat on Fire, 1981; The Patriot Game, 1982; A Choice for Enemies, 1984; Penance for Jerry Kennedy, 1985; Imposters, 1986; Outlaws, 1987; The Sins of the Fathers, 1988; Wonderful Years, Wonderful Years, 1988; Trust, 1989; Victories, 1990; The Mandeville Talent, 1991; Defending Billy Ryan: A Jerry Kennedy Novel, 1992; Bomber's Law, 1993; Swan Boats at Four, 1995; Sandra Nichols Found Dead, 1996; A Change of Gravity, 1997; The Agent, 1998. Non-Fiction: The Friends of Richard Nixon, 1976; Style Versus Substance, 1985; The Progress of the Seasons, 1989; On Writing, 1990. Honour: Honorary DHL, Westfield State College, Massachusetts, 1986. Address: 15 Brush Hill Lane, Milton, MA 02186, USA.

HIGGINS Jack. See: **PATTERSON Harry.**

HIGH Peter Brown, b. 6 Sept 1944, New York, New York, USA. Professor; Writer. m. 21 Oct 1972, 1 son. Education: BA, American University, 1966; MA, California State University, 1982; PhD, Nagoya University, 1985. Appointments: Columnist, Asahi Shimbun, Japanese Language, 1987-92; Professor of Film and Literature, Nagoya University, 1987-. Publications: An Outline of American Literature, 1985; Read All About It, 1986; A Journalist Looks At Popular Culture, 1991; The Imperial Screen: Japanese Cinema and the 15 Year War, 1995; A History of Cinema, 1997; Assorted language textbooks in the ESL field. Contributions to: Journals. Address: 43 Meidai Shukusha, Kogawa-cho, Chikusa-ku, Nagoya, Japan.

HIGHAM Charles, b. 18 Feb 1931, London, England. Writer. Appointments: Film Critic, Nation, Sydney, 1961-63; Literary Editor, The Bulletin, Sydney, 1963-68; Hollywood Feature Writer, New York Times, 1971-80; Visiting Regents' Professor, University of California at Santa Cruz, 1990. Publications: The Earthbound and Other Poems, 1959; Noonday Country: Poems 1954-1865, 1966; The Celluloid Muse: Hollywood Directors Speak (editor with J Greenberg), 1969; Hollywood in the Forties (editor with J Greenberg), 1969; The Films of Orson Welles, 1970; The Voyage to Brindisi and Other Poems 1966-1969, 1970; Ziegfeld, 1972; Cecil B DeMille, 1973; The Art of the American Film, 1900-1971, 1973; Ava, 1974; Kate: The Life of Katharine Hepburn, 1975; Warner Brothers, 1975; Charles Laughton: An Intimate Biography, 1976; Marlene: The Life of Marlene Dietrich, 1977; Errol Flynn: The Untold Story, 1980; Star Maker: The Autobiography of Hal B Wallis, 1980; Bette: The Life of Bette Davis, 1981; Trading with the Enemy: An Exposae of the Nazi-American Money Plot 1933-1949, 1983; Princess Merle (with Roy Moseley), 1983; Sisters: The Story of Olivia de Haviland and Joan Fontaine, 1984; Audrey: The Life of Audrey Hepburn, 1984; American Swastika, 1985; Orson Welles: The Rise and Fall of an American Genius, 1986; Palace: My Life in the Royal Family of Monaco (with Baron C de Massy), 1986; Brando: The Unauthorized Biography, 1987; Wallis: The Secret Lives of the Duchess of Windsor, 1988; Cary Grant: The Lonely Heart (with Roy Moseley), 1989; Elizabeth and Philip: The Untold Story of the Queen of England and Her Prince (with Roy Moseley), 1991; Rose: The Life of Rose Fitzgerald Kennedy, 1994. Contributions to: Newspapers, reviews, and magazines. Address: John Hawkins and Sons, 71 West 23rd Street, New York, NY 100010.

HIGHAM Robin (David Stewart), b. 20 June 1925, London, England (US citizen, 1954). Professor of History; Writer; Editor. m. Barbara Davies, 5 Aug 1950, 1 son, 3 daughters, 2 dec. Education: AB, 1950, PhD, 1957, Harvard University; MA, Claremont Graduate School, California, 1953. Appointments: Instructor, University of Massachusetts, 1954-57; Assistant Professor, University of North Carolina at Chapel Hill, 1957-63; Associate Professor, 1963-66, Professor of History, 1966-, Kansas State University; Editor, 1968-88, Editor Emeritus, 1989-, Military Affairs; Editor, 1970-88, Editor Emeritus, 1989-, Aerospace Historian; Founder-President, Sunflower University Press, 1977-; Editor and Co-Publisher, Journal of the West, 1977-. Publications: Britain's Imperial Air Routes, 1918-39, 1960; The British Rigid Airship, 1908-31, 1961; Armed Forces in Peacetime: Britain, 1918-39, 1963; The Military Intellectuals in Britain, 1918-39, 1966; A Short History of Warfare (with David H Zook), 1966; Air Power: A Concise History, 1973, 3rd edition, enlarged, 1988; The Compleat Academic, 1975; A Brief Guide to Scholarly Editing (with Mary Cisper and Guy Dresser), 1982; Diary of a Disaster: British Aid to Greece, 1940-41, 1986; The Bases of Air Strategy 1915-1945, 1998. Editor: Various books, including: Civil Wars in the Twentieth Century, 1972; A Guide to the Sources of British Military History, 1971; A Guide to the Sources of US Military History, 1975, 3rd supplement, 1993; The Rise of the Wheat State: A History of Kansas Agriculture (with George E Ham), 1986; Russian Aviation and Air Power (with John T Greenwood and Von Handesty), 1998. Contributions to: Reference works, scholarly books, and professional journals. Honours: Social Science Research Council National Security Policy Research Fellow, 1960-61; Victor Gondos Award, 1983, Samuel Eliot Morison Award, 1986, American Military Institute. Memberships: Several aviation and military history organizations. Address: 2961 Nevada Street, Manhattan, KS 66502, USA.

HIGHLAND Monica. See: **SEE Carolyn.**

HIGHWATER Jamake, Writer; Poet; Lecturer. Appointments: Senior Editor, Fodor Travel Guides, 1970-75; Classical Music Editor, Soho Weekly News, 1975-79; Graduate Lecturer, School of Continuing Education, New York University, 1979-83; Assistant Adjunct Professor, Graduate School of Architecture, Columbia University, 1983-84; Contributing Arts Critic, Christian Science Monitor, 1988-92; Lecturer, UCLA Extension, 1998; Contributing Editor to several periodicals; Guest Lecturer in colleges and universities in North America. Publications: Indian America: A Cultural and Travel Guide, 1975; Song from the Earth: American Indian Painting, 1976; Ritual of the Wind: North American Indian Ceremonies, Music and Dances, 1977; Anpao: An American Indian Odyssey, 1977; Journey to the Sky, 1978; Many Smokes, Many Moons, 1978; Dance: Rituals of Experience, 1978; Masterpieces of American Indian Painting, 2 volumes, 1978, 1980; The Sun, He Dies, 1980; The Sweet Grass Lives On: Fifty Contemporary North American Indian Artists, 1980; The Primal Mind: Vision and Reality in Indian America, 1981; Moonsong Lullaby (poems), 1981; Eyes of Darkness, 1983; Leaves From the Sacred Tree: Arts of the Indian Americas, 1983; Words in the Blood: Contemporary Indian Writers of North and South America, 1984; Legend Days, 1984; I Wear the Morning Star, 1986; Native Land: Sagas of American Civilizations, 1986; Shadow Show: An Autobiographical Insinuation, 1987; Kill Hole, 1988; Myth and Sexuality, 1990; The World of 1492, 1992; Dark Legend, 1994; The Language of Vision, 1994; Rama, 1994; Songs for the Seasons (poems), 1995; The Mythology of Transgression, 1997. Other: Writer, Host and Narrator, PBS TV series, Native Land, 1986. Honours: Newbery Honor Award, 1978; Best Book for Young Adults Awards, American Library Association, 1978, 1986; Virginia McCormick Scully Literary Award, 1982; National Educational Film Festival Best Film of the Year Award, 1986; Ace Award, Discovery Channel, 1991; Best Book for Young Adults Award, New York Public Library, 1994. Memberships: American Federation of Television and Radio Artists; American Poetry Center, board member, 1991-; Authors Guild; Authors League; Dramatists Guild; Indian Art Foundation, founder-member, 1980-87; Native American Rights Fund, national advisory board member, 1980-87; PEN. Address: Native Lands Foundation, 1201 Larrabee Street, Suite 202, Los Angeles, CA 90069, USA.

HIGSON Philip (John Willoughby), b. 21 Feb 1933, Newcastle-under-Lyme, Staffordshire, England. Poet; Translator; Editor; Historian; Art Historian. Education: BA, Honours, 1956, MA, 1959, PhD, 1971, Liverpool University; PGCE, Keele University, 1972. Appointments: Lecturer to Senior Lecturer in History, 1972-89, Visiting Lecturer, 1989-90, University College, Chester; Chairman, President, Anthology Editor, Chester Poets, 1974-92, President, La Société Baudelaire, Paris, 1992-. Publications: Poems of Protest and Pilgrimage, 1966; The Riposte and Other Poems, 1971; Baudelaire: The Flowers of Evil and All Other Authenticated Poems (editor and co-translator), 1974; Sonnets to My Goddess, 1983; Maurice Rollinat's Les Névroses: Selected English Versions (translator), 1986; A Warning to Europe: The Testimony of Limouse (co-author), 1992; The Complete Poems of Baudelaire with Selected Illustrations by Limouse (principal translator), 1992; Limouse Nudes, 1992; Childhood in Wartime Keele: Poems of Reminiscence, 1995; Sonnets to My Goddess in This Life and the Next, 1995; Poems on the Dee, 1997; Inner City Liebestod: a love-story in verse, 1998. Contributions to: Scholarly journals, anthologies, and periodicals. Honours: Brian O'Connor Trophy for Poetry, 1981, 1982, 1983; 1st Prize, Eclectic Muse Competition, Vancouver, 1990; David St John Thomas Poetry Publication Prize, 1996; Prizewinner, Lexikon Poetry Competition, 1996. Memberships: Society of Antiquaries of London, fellow; Royal Society of Arts, fellow; Society of Authors. Address: 1 Westlands Avenue, Newcastle-under-Lyme, Staffordshire, ST5 2PU, England.

HIJUELOS Oscar, b. 24 Aug 1951, New York, New York, USA. Writer. Education: BA, 1975, MA, 1976, City College of the City University of New York. Publications: Our House in the Last World, 1983; The Mambo Kings Play Songs of Love, 1989; The Fourteen Sisters of Emilio Montez O'Brien, 1993; Mr Ive's Christmas, 1995. Honours: Outstanding Writer, Pushcart Press, 1978; Bread Loaf Writers Conference Scholarship, 1980; Ingram Merrill Foundation Grant, 1983; National Endowment for the Arts Fellowship, 1985; American Academy in Rome Fellowship, 1985; Pulitzer Prize in Fiction, 1990. Address: c/o Harriet Wasserman Literary Agency, East 36th Street, New York, NY 10016, USA.

HILDICK (Edmund) Wallace, (E W Hildick), b. 29 Dec 1925, Bradford, England. Author. m. Doris Clayton, 9 Dec 1950. Education: Teacher's Certificate, City of Leeds Training College, 1950. Appointment: Visiting Critic and Associate Editor, The Kenyon Review, Gambier, Ohio, 1966-67. Publications: Fiction: Bed and Work, 1962; A Town on the Never, 1963; Lunch with Ashurbanipal, 1965; Bracknell's Law, 1975; The Weirdown Experiment, 1976; Vandals, 1977; The Loop, 1977. Non-Fiction: Word for Word: A Study of Authors' Alterations, with Exercises, 1965; Writing with Care: Two Hundred Problems in the Use of English, 1967; Thirteen Types of Narrative, 1968; Children and Fiction: A Critical Study in Depth of the Artistic and Psychological Factors Involved in Writing Fiction for and about Children, 1971, revised edition, 1974; Storypacks: A New Concept in English Teaching, 1971; Only the Best: Six Qualities of Excellence, 1973. Other: Many books for juvenile readers, including the Jim Starling series, 7 books, 1958-63, the Birdy Jones series, 6 books, 1963-74, the Lemon Kelly series, 3 books, 1963-68, the Louie series, 4 books, 1965-78, the Questers series, 3 books, 1966-67, the McGurk Mystery series, 26 books, 1973-96, the Ghost Squad series, 6 books, 1984-88; The Felicity Snell Mysteries, 2 Books, 1997. Contributions to: Numerous periodicals. Honours: Tom-Gallon Trust Award, 1957; Honour Book Citation, International Hans Christian Andersen Award, 1968; American Ambassador Books Booklist Selection, 1970; Honour Book Citation, Austrian Children and Youth Book Prize Award, 1976; Edgar Allan Poe Special Awards, Mystery Writers of America, 1979, 1995. Memberships: Authors Guild; Mystery Writers of America; Society of Authors. Address: c/o Coutts & Co, 440 Strand, London WC2R 0QS, England.

HILL Anthony Robert, b. 24 May 1942, Melbourne, Victoria, Australia. Writer; Journalist. m. Gillian Mann, 15 Oct 1965, 1 daughter. Publications: The Bunburyists, 1985; Antique Furniture in Australia, 1985; Birdsong, 1988; The Burnt Stick, 1994; Spindrift, 1996; The Grandfather Clock, 1996; Growing Up and Other Stories, 1999. Honour: Children's Book Council of Australia Honour Book, 1995. Membership: Australian Society of

Authors. Address: PO Box 85, Yarralumla, Australian Capital Terretory 2600, Australia.

HILL (John Edward) Christopher, (K E Holme), b. 6 Feb 1912, York, England. Historian. Education: BA, 1934, MA, 1938, Balliol College, Oxford. Publications: The English Revolution 1640, 1940; Two Commonwealths, 1945; Lenin and the Russian Revolution, 1947; The Good Old Cause (with E Dell), 1949; Economic Problems of the Church, 1956; Puritanism and Revolution, 1958; The Century of Revolution, 1961; Society and Puritanism, 1964; Intellectual Origins of the English Revolution, 1965; Reformation to Industrial Revolution, 1967; God's Englishman, 1970; Antichrist in Seventeenth Century England, 1971; The World Turned Upside Down, 1972; The Law of Freedom and Other Writings by Gerrard Winstanley, 1973; Change and Continuity in Seventeenth Century England, 1975; Milton and the English Revolution, 1978; Some Intellectual Consequences of the English Revolution, 1980; The Experience of Defeat, 1983; Writing and Revolution, 1985; Religion and Politics in Seventeenth Century England, 1986; People and Ideas in Seventeenth Century England, 1986; A Turbulent and Factious People: John Bunyan and his Church, 1988, 5 editions; A Nation of Change and Novelty, 1990; The English Bible and the Seventeenth Century Revolution, 1993. Address: Woodway House, Sibford Ferris, Oxon, England.

HILL Douglas Arthur, (Martin Hillman), b. 6 Apr 1935, Brandon, Manitoba, Canada. Author. m. Gail Robinson, 8 Apr 1958, div, 1 son. Education: BA, University of Saskatchewan, 1957. Appointment: Literary Editor, Tribune, London, 1971-84. Publications: The Supernatural, 1965; The Opening of the Canadian West, 1967; John Keats, 1969; The Scots to Canada, 1972; Galactic Warlord, 1980; The Huntsman, 1982; The Last Legionary Quartet, 1985; Penelope's Pendant, 1990; The Unicorn Dream, 1992; The Lightless Dome, 1993; The Voyage of Mudjack, 1993; World of the Stiks, 1994; The Leafless Forest, 1994; CADE: Galaxy's Edge, 1996; The Dragon Charmer, 1997; Eyewitness Witch and Wizard, 1997; Space Girls Don't Cry, 1998. Memberships: Society of Authors; Children's Book Circle. Address: 3 Hillfield Avenue, London N8 7DU, England.

HILL Elizabeth Starr, b. 4 Nov 1925, Lynn Haven, Florida, USA. Writer. m. Russell Gibson Hill, 28 May 1949, 1 son, 1 daughter. Education: Finch Junior College; Columbia University. Publications: The Wonderful Visit to Miss Liberty, 1961; The Window Tulip, 1964; Evan's Corner, 1967; Master Mike and the Miracle Maid, 1967; Pardon My Fangs, 1969; Bells: A Book to Begin On, 1970; Ever-After Island, 1977; Fangs Aren't Everything, 1985; When Christmas Comes, 1989; The Street Dancers, 1991; Broadway Chances, 1992; The Banjo Player, 1993; Curtain Going Up!, 1995. Contributions to: Magazines. Honours: Notable Book for Children Citation, American Library Association, 1967; Junior Literary Guild Selections, 1977, 1989; Pick of the Lists Citation, American Book Association, 1992. Memberships: Authors Guild; Authors League; University Club of Winter Park. Address: Langford Apartments, PO Box 940, Winter Park, FL 32790, USA.

HILL Errol Gaston, b. 5 Aug 1921, Trinidad, West Indies. College Professor Emeritus. m. Grace Lucille Eunice Hope, 11 Aug 1956, 1 son, 3 daughters. Education: Graduate Diploma, Royal Academy of Dramatic Art, London, 1951; Diploma in Dramatic Art with distinction, London University, 1951; BA summa cum laude, 1962, MFA, Playwriting, 1962, DFA, Theatre History, 1966, Yale University. Publications: Man Better Man: A Musical Comedy, 1964, reprinted, 1985; The Trinidad Carnival, 1972, 2nd edition, updated, 1997; The Theatre of Black Americans, 1980, reprinted, 1987; Shakespeare in Sable: A History of Black Shakespearean Actors, 1984; The Jamaican Stage, 1655-1900, 1992. Editor: Caribbean Plays, Vol 1, 1958, Vol 2, 1965; A Time and a Season: 8 Caribbean Plays, 1976, reprinted, 1997; Plays for Today, 1985; Black Heroes: Seven Plays, 1989; The Cambridge Guide to African and Caribbean Theatre (co-author), 1994. Contributions to: McGraw Encyclopaedia of World Drama, 1984; Theatre Journal; Theatre History Studies; American Literature Forum; Caribbean Quarterly; Cambridge Guide to World Theatre; Cambridge Guide to American Theatre; World Encyclopedia of Contemporary Theatre, Vol. 2. Honours: British Council Scholarship, 1949-51; Rockefeller Foundation Fellowships, 1958-60, 1965; Theatre Guild of America Fellowship, 1961; Barnard Hewitt Award for Theatre History, 1985; Guggenheim Fellowship, 1985-86; Fulbright Fellowship, 1988; National Endowment for the Humanities Fellowship, 1997; Honorary DLitt, University of the West Indies, 1998. Memberships: American Society for Theatre Research; American Theatre and Drama Society; Phi Beta Kappa; International Federation for Theatre Research; College of Fellows of the American Theatre. Address: 3 Haskins Road, Hanover, NH 03755, USA.

HILL Geoffrey (William), b. 18 June 1932, Bromsgrove, Worcestershire, England. Professor of Literature and Religion; Poet; Writer. m. (1) Nancy Whittaker, 1956, div 1983, 3 sons, 1 daughter, (2) Alice Goodman, 1987, 1 daughter. Education: BA, 1953, MA, 1959, Keble College, Oxford. Appointments: Staff, 1954-76, Professor of English Literature, 1976-80, University of Leeds; Churchill Fellow, University of Bristol, 1980; University Lecturer in English and Fellow, Emmanuel College, Cambridge, 1981-88; Clark Lecturer, Trinity College, Cambridge, 1986; University Professor and Professor of Literature and Religion, Boston University, 1988-. Publications: Poetry: Poems, 1952; For the Unfallen: Poems, 1952-58, 1959; Preghiere, 1964; King Log, 1968; Mercian Hymns, 1971; Somewhere is Such a Kingdom: Poems 1952-72, 1975; Tenebrae, 1978; The Mystery of the Charity of Charles Péguy, 1983; New and Collected Poems 1952-92, 1994; Canaan, 1996. Criticism: The Lords of Limit, 1984; The Enemy's Country, 1991. Other: Brand (adaptation of Henrik Ibsen's play), 1978. Honours: Gregory Award, 1961; Hawthornden Prize, 1969; Alice Hunt Bartlett Award, 1971; Geoffrey Faber Memorial Prize, 1971; Whitbread Award, 1971; Duff Cooper Memorial Prize, 1979; Honorary Fellow, Keble College, Oxford, 1981, Emmanuel College, Cambridge, 1990; Loines Award, American Academy and Institute of Arts and Letters, 1983; Ingram Merrill Foundation Award, 1988; Honorary DLitt, University of Leeds, 1988. Memberships: Royal Society of Literature, fellow; American Academy of Arts and Sciences, fellow. Address: The University Professors, Boston University, 745 Commonwealth Avenue, Boston, MA 02215, USA.

HILL Jane (Bowers), b. 17 Oct 1950, Seneca, South Carolina, USA. Assistant Professor; Editor; Writer; Poet. m. Robert W Hill, 16 Aug 1980, 1 daughter. Education: BA, 1972, MA, 1978, Clemson University; PhD, University of Illinois, 1985. Appointments: Associate Editor, Peachtree Publishers, 1986-88; Senior Editor, Longstreet Press, 1988-91; Director, Kennesaw Summer Writers Workshop, 1988-92; Assistant Professor, West Georgia College, 1992-. Publications: Gail Godwin, 1992. Editor: An American Christmas: A Sampler of Contemporary Stories and Poems, 1986; Our Mutual Room: Modern Literary Portraits of the Opposite Sex, 1987; Songs: New Voices in Fiction, 1990; Cobb County: At the Heart of Change, 1991. Contributions to: Numerous stories, poems, essays and reviews. Honours: Frank O'Connor Prize for Fiction, 1989; Syvenna Foundation Fellow, 1991; Monticello Fellowship for Female Writers, 1992. Membership: Modern Language Association. Address: 1419 Arden Drive, Marietta, GA 30060, USA.

HILL John. See: **KOONTZ Dean R(ay).**

HILL John Spencer, b. 22 Oct 1943, Brantford, Ontario, Canada. Professor English Literature. m. 25 June 1966, 2 sons, 1 daughter. Education: BA, 1966, MA, 1968, Queen's University, Canada; PhD, University of Toronto, Canada, 1972. Appointments: Assistant Professor, English, Royal Military College of Canada, 1967-69, 1972-73; Lecturer University of Western Australia, 1973-79; Professor, University of Ottawa, 1979-. Publications: Imaginations in Coleridge, 1978; John Milton: Poet, Priest and Prophet, 1979; The Last Castrato, novel, 1995; Ghirlandaio's Daughter, novel, 1996; Infinity, Faith and Time, 1997. Contributions to: Milton Studies; The Wordsworth Circle; Journal of Biblical Literature. Honours: Critics' Choice Award, San Francisco Review of Books, 1995; Arthur Ellis Award, Crime Writers of Canada, 1996. Literary Agent: Frances Hanna, Toronto. Address: Department of English, University of Ottawa, Ottawa, Ontario, K1N 6N5, Canada.

HILL Pamela, (Sharon Fiske), b. 26 Nov 1920, Nairobi, Kenya. Writer. Education: DA, Glasgow School of Art, 1943; BSc, Equivalent, University of Glasgow, 1952. Publications include: Flaming Janet, 1954; The Devil of Aske, 1972; The Malvie Inheritance, 1973; Homage to a Rose, 1979; Fire Opal, 1980; This Rough Beginning, 1981; My Lady Glamis, 1981; Summer Cypress, 1981; The House of Cray, 1982; The Governess, 1985; Venables, 1988; The Sutburys, 1987; The Brocken, 1991; The Sword and the Flame, 1991; Mercer, 1992; The Silver Runaways, 1992; O Madcap Duchess, 1993; The Parson's Children, 1993; The Man from the North, 1994; Journey Beyond Innocence, 1994; The Charmed Descent, 1995; The Inadvisable Marriages, 1995; Saints' Names for Confirmation, 1995; Alice the Palace, 1996; Murder in Store, 1996; The Supplanter; The Small Black Knife; Countess Isobel. Contributions to: Argosy; Chambers Journal. Memberships: Royal Society of Literature; Crime Writers' Association; Historical Association; Keats Shelley Memorial Association. Address: 89A Winchester Street, London SW1V 4NU.

HILL Patricia S, b. 27 Oct 1954, Taipei, Taiwan. Journalist. Education: BA, Oberlin College, 1976. Appointments: Associate Editor, Inside Washington Publications, 1982-85; Reporter, The Daily Bond Buyer, 1986-94; Chief Economics Correspondent, The Washington Times, 1994-. Membership: National Press Club, 1980-. Address: 3600 New York Ave NE, Washington, DC 20002, USA.

HILL Reginald (Charles), (Dick Morland, Patrick Ruell, Charles Underhill), b. 3 Apr 1936, West Hartlepool, England. Author; Playwright. Education: BA, St Catherine's College, Oxford, 1960. Publications: As Reginald Hill: A Clubbable Woman, 1970; Fell of Dark, 1971; An Advancement of Learning, 1972; A Fairly Dangerous Thing, 1972; An Affair of Honour (play), 1972; Ruling Passion, 1973; A Very Good Hater, 1974; An April Shroud, 1975; Another Death in Venice, 1976; A Pinch of Snuff, 1978; Pascoe's Ghost (stories), 1979; A Killing Kindness, 1980; The Spy's Wife, 1980; Who Guards a Prince, 1981; Traitor's Blood, 1983; Deadheads, 1983; Exit Lines, 1984; No Man's Land, 1984; Child's Play, 1987; The Collaborators, 1987; There Are No Ghosts in the Soviet Union, 1987; Under World, 1988; Bones and Silence, 1990; One Small Step (novella), 1990; Recalled to Life, 1992; Blood Sympathy, 1993; Pictures of Perfection, 1994; Born Guilty, 1995; The Wood Beyond, 1996; Killing the Lawyers, 1997; On Beulah Height, 1998; Singing the Sadness, 1999. As Dick Morland: Heart Clock, 1973; Albion! Albion!, 1974. As Patrick Ruell: The Castle of Demon, 1971; Red Christmas, 1972; Death Takes the Low Road, 1974; Urn Burial, 1976; The Long Kill, 1986; Death of a Dormouse, 1987; Dream of Darkness, 1989; The Only Game, 1991. As Charles Underhill: Captain Fantom, 1978; The Forging of Fantom, 1979. Honours: Gold Dagger Award, 1990; Diamond Dagger Award, 1995. Address: c/o A P Watt Ltd, 20 John Street, London WC1N 2DR, England.

HILL Richard Fontaine, b. St Petersburgh, Florida, USA. Writer. Education: MA, English, University of South Florida, Tampa, 1968; PhD, English, Florida State University, 1990. Appointments: Professor, Writers Workshop, Eckerd College, St Petersburgh, Florida, 1979; Visiting Artist, Community College System, North Carolina, 1983-85; Professional Writer, University of North Carolina, 1990-92. Publictions: Ghost Story, 1971; What Rough Beast?, 1992; Riding Solo With the Golden Horde, 1994; Shoot the Piper, 1994; Kill the Hundredth Monkey, 1995. Contributions to: Kenyon Review; North Carolina Humanities Review. Honours include: O Henry

Short Story Prize, 1974; National Endowment for the Arts, Individual Fellowship for Literature, 1976; Honorable Mention, PEN/Nelson Algren Prize, 1989; US Panel First Choice Nominee for the Raymond Chandler Fulbright Scholarship in Mystery Writing, Oxford University, 1990-91; Fellow, Hawthornden Castle, Scotland, 1992. Address: 500 South Himes Avenue #39, Tampa, FL 33609, USA.

HILL Selima (Wood), b. 13 Oct 1945, London, England. Poet. 2 sons, 2 daughters. Education: New Hall College, Cambridge. Appointments: Writing Fellow, University of East Anglia, 1991; Writer-in-Residence, Exeter and Devon Arts Centre, 1996; Poet-in-Residence, Royal Festival Hall, 1998; Reader-in-Residence, South Bank Centre, 1998-. Publications: Saying Hello at the Station, 1984; My Darling Camel, 1988; The Accumulation of Small Acts of Kindness, 1989; A Little Book of Meat, 1993; Trembling Hearts in the Bodies of Dogs, 1994; My Sister's Horse, 1996; Violet, 1997; Paradise for Sale, 1998; Bunny, 1999. Honours: Cholmondeley Prize, 1986; Arvon Observer Poetry Competition Prize, 1988; Arts Council Writers Bursary, 1993; H K Travel Scholarship to Mongolia, 1994; Judge, Kent, Exeter, 1995, Bournemouth, 1996; Nominated for T.S. Eliot, Whitbread, Forward Prizes, 1998. Address: c/o Bloodaxe Books, PO Box 1SN, Newcastle upon Tyne, NE99 1SN, England.

HILL Susan Elizabeth, b. 5 Feb 1942, Scarborough, Yorkshire, England. Novelist; Playwright. m. Stanley W Wells, 3 daughters, 1 dec. Education: BA, University of London, 1963. Appointments: Literary Critic, Various Journals, 1963; Numerous Plays for BBC, 1970-. Publications: The Enclosure, 1961; Do Me a Favour, 1963; Gentleman and Ladies, 1969; A Change for the Better, 1969; I'm the King of the Castle, 1970; Strange Meeting, 1971; The Bird of Night, 1972; The Cold Country and Other Plays for Radio, 1975; The Magic Apple Tree, 1982; The Woman in Black, 1983; Through the Garden Gate, 1986; Mothers Magic, 1986; Lanterns Across the Snow, 1987; Can It Be True?, 1988. Membership: Royal Society of Literature, fellow. Address: Midsummer Cottage, Church Lane, Beckley, Oxon, England.

HILLERMAN Tony, b. 27 May 1925, USA. Professor of Journalism Emeritus; Author. m. Mary Unzner, 16 Aug 1948, 3 sons, 3 daughters. Education: Oklahoma State University, 1943; BA, University of Oklahoma, 1946; MA, University of New Mexico, 1966. Appointments: Reporter, Borger News Herald, Texas, 1948; City Editor, Morning Press-Constitution, Lawton, Oklahoma, 1948-50; Political Reporter, Oklahoma City, 1950-52; Bureau Manager, Santa Fe, 1952-54, United Press International; Political Reporter and Executive Editor, New Mexican, Santa Fe, 1954-63; Associate Professor, 1965-66, Professor of Journalism, 1966-85, Professor Emeritus, 1985-, University of New Mexico. Publications: Fiction: The Blessing Way, 1970; The Fly on the Wall, 1971; Dance Hall of the Dead, 1973; Listening Woman, 1977; The People of Darkness, 1978; The Dark Wind, 1981; Ghostway, 1984; A Thief of Time, 1985; Skinwalkers, 1986; The Joe Leaphorn Mysteries (collection), 1989; Talking God, 1989; Coyote Waits, 1990; Best of the West: An Anthology of Classic Writing from the American West (editor), 1991; The Jim Chee Mysteries (collection), 1992; Sacred Clowns, 1993; Finding Moon, 1994; The Fallen Man, 1996; The First Eagle. Non-Fiction: The Spell of New Mexico (editor), 1984; Indian Country: America's Sacred Land, 1987; Hillerman Country: A Journey through the Southwest with Tony Hillerman, 1991; Talking Mysteries: A Conversation with Tony Hillerman (with Ernie Bulow), 1991; New Mexico, Rio Grande, and Other Essays, 1992. Other: The Oxford Book of the American Detective Story, 1996. Contributions to: Magazines. Honour: Edgar Allan Poe Award, Mystery Writers of America, 1974. Memberships: Phi Kappa Phi; Sigma Delta Chi. Address: 1632 Francisca North, Albuquerque, NM 87107, USA.

HILLERY Mary Jane, b. 15 Sept 1931, Boston, Massachusetts, USA. Writer. m. Thomas H Hillery, 25 Feb 1961, 1 son. Education: BS, Northeastern University,

1953; Command and General Staff College, 1982. Appointments include: Linguist, Pan American Airways, Boston, 1955-61; Interpreter, International Conference of Fire Chiefs, Boston, 1966; Teacher, Spanish, YWCA, Natick, Massachusetts, 1966-67; Community Relations Consultant, Advisory Board of Directors, Lecturer for Migrant Education, Project Division, Massachusettes Department of Community Affairs, Boston, 1967-69; Editor-in-Chief, Sudbury (Mass) Citizen, 1967-76; Assicoate Editor, The Beacon, 1976-79, Contributing Editor, 1979-83; Area Editorial Advisor, Beacon Publishing Company, Acton, Massachusetts, 1970-80, Editor, 1976-80; Columnist, Town Crier, 1987-; Producer, Host, Television Interview Show, For the Record, 1985-; Public Affairs Officer, Federal Emergency Management Agency, 1995-. Publications: Annual History Special Forces, 1989; Separtment of Defense Dependents Schools, 1992. Contributions to: Sudbury Town Crier; Federal Emergency Management Magazine; National League of American Pen Women Magazine; Massachusetts Bicentennial Times. Honours: George Washington Honor Medal, 1998. Memberships: National League of American Pen Women. Address: 66 Willow Road, Sudbury, MA 01776-2663, USA.

HILLES Robert (Edward), b. 13 Nov 1951, Kenora, Ontario, Canada. Poet; Writer; Senior Professor of Computer Programming. m. Rebecca Susan Knight, 16 Aug 1980, 2 children. Education: BA, 1976, MSc, 1984, University of Calgary. Appointments: Professor, 1983-94, Senior Professor, 1994-, of Computer Programming, DeVry Institute of Technology, Calgary. Publications: Poetry: Look the Lovely Animal Speaks, 1980; Angel in the Works, 1983; Outlasting the Landscape, 1989; Finding the Lights On, 1991; A Breath at a Time, 1992; Cantos from a Small Room, 1993; Nothing Vanishes, 1996. Fiction: Raising of Voices, 1993; Near Morning, 1995. Non-Fiction: Kissing the Smoke, 1996. Honours: Governor-General's Literary Award for Poetry, 1994; Writers Guild of Alberta Best Novel Award, 1994. Memberships: League of Canadian Poets; Writers Guild of Alberta; Writers' Union of Canada. Address: 802 21 Avenue North West, Calgary, Alberta T2M 1K4, Canada.

HILLIKER Grant, b. 26 June 1921, Tomah, WI, USA. Diplomat (Retired); Educator. m. Adele C Hilliker, 9 Dec 1979, 1 son, 1 daughter. Education: BA, University of Wisconsin, 1942. Appointments: Foreign Service Officer, US Department of State, 1946-71; Adjunct Professor, Ohio State University, 1971-74; President or Director of several non-profit organizations, 1982-92. Publications: The Politics or Reform in Peru, 1971; Hunger Here and There, 1982, 1983; Citizen Power in US Foreign Policy, 1990; Various articles & book reviews in journals & newspapers. Honours: Phi Beta Kappa; other academic honours. Address: 5268 Rush Avenue, Columbus, OH 43214-1218, USA.

HILLIS Rick, b. 3 Feb 1956, Nipawin, Saskatchewan, Canada. Writer; Poet; Teacher. m. Patricia Appelgren, 29 Aug 1988, 1 son, 1 daughter. Education: University of Victoria, 1977-78; BEd, University of Saskatchewan, 1979; Graduate Studies, Concordia University, 1983; MFA, University of Iowa, 1984; Stanford University, 1988-90. Appointments: Stegner Fellow, 1988-90, Jones Lecturer, 1990-92 Stanford University;, Lecturer, California State University at Hayward, 1990; Chesterfield Film Writer's Fellowship, 1991-92; Visiting Assistant Professor of English, Reed College, 1992-96. Publications: The Blue Machines of Night (poems), 1988; Coming Attractions (co-author), 1988; Canadian Brash (co-author), 1990; Limbo Stories, 1990. Contributions to: Anthologies and periodicals. Honours: Canada Council Grants, 1985, 1987, 1989; Drue Heinz Literature Prize, 1990. Address: c/o Department of English, Lewis and Clark College, Portland, OR 97202, USA.

HILLMAN Ellis Simon, b. 17 Nov 1928, London, England. Lecturer in Environmental Studies; Writer. m. Louise Hillman, 10 Dec 1967, 1 son. Education: University College School, 1942-46; BSc, Chelsea College of Science and Technology. Appointments: Chairman, London Subterranean Survey Association,

1968-; Governor, Imperial College of Science and Technology, later Imperial College of Science, Technology and Medicine, 1969-91, Queen Mary College, 1973-82; Principal Lecturer in Environmental Studies, North East London Polytechnic, later Polytechnic of East London, and finally University of East London, 1972-; Councillor, Labour Party, Colindale, 1986-, Mayor, London Borough of Barnet, 1994-95. Publications: Essays in Local Government Enterprise, 1964-67; Towards a Wider Use (editor), 1976; Space for the Living or Space for the Dead (editor), 1977; Novellae on the Scroll of Esther, 1982; London Under London, 1985. Contributions to: Professional journals. Honour: National Book League Prize, 1986. Memberships: Green Alliance; Lewis Carroll Society, founder-honorary president, 1969-; Royal Society of Architects, fellow; Society of Educational Consultants. Address: 29 Haslemere Avenue, London NW4 2PU, England.

HILLMAN Martin. See: Hill Douglas Arthur.

HILTON Suzanne McLean, b. 3 Sept 1922, Pittsburgh, Pennslyvania, USA. Writer. m. Warren Mitchell Hilton, 15 June 1946, 1 son, 1 daughter. Education: BA, Beaver College, 1946. Appointments: Editor, Bulletin of Old York Road Historical Society, 1976-92, Bulletin of Historical Society of Montgomery County, 1987-89; Associate Editor, Montgomery County History, 1983. Publications: How Do They Get Rid of It?, 1970; How Do They Cope with It?, 1970; Beat It, Burn It and Drown It, 1974; Who Do You Think You Are?, 1976; Yesterday's People, 1976; Here Today and Gone Tomorrow, 1978; Faster than a Horse: Moving West with Engine Power, 1983; Montgomery County: The Second Hundred Years, 1983; The World of Young Tom Jefferson, 1986; The World of Young George Washington, 1986; The World of Young Herbert Hoover, 1987; The World of Young Andrew Jackson, 1988; A Capital Capitol City, 1991; Miners, Merchants and Maids, 1995. Contributions to: Historical journals. Honours: Legion of Honour, Chapel of the Four Chaplains, 1978; Award for Excellence in Non-Fiction, Drexel University, 1979; Golden Spur, Western Writers of America, 1980; Gold Disc, Beaver College, 1981. Memberships: Society of Children's Book Writers and Illustrators; Philadelphia Childrens Reading Round Table. Address: 3320 108th Street North West, Gig Harbour, WA 98332, USA.

HILTS-GOSSETT Ellen Michele, b. 1947, New York City, New York, USA. Thoroughbred Racing Journalist; Columnist; Magazine Feature Writer. m. Kenneth Gossett, 1 Jan 1989. Education: AA, El Camino College, 1973; BA, California State University, Long Beach, 1975. Appointments: Director, California Breeding Bureau, Daily Racing Form, 1982-94; Features Writer, 1983-89, California Racing Correspondent, 1987-89, Pacemaker International. Contributions to: Breeders' Cup Magazine; Owner/Breeder, Thoroughbred of California, The Florida Horse, The Blood-Horse, The Thoroughbred Record, Backstretch Magazine, 1983-91. Honour: Honoree, Japan Racing Association, 1987. Membership: National Turf Writers Association. Address: 2104 Grant Avenue #2, Redondo Beach, CA 90278, USA.

HIMMELFARB Gertrude, b. 8 Aug 1922, New York, New York, USA. Professor of History Emerita; Writer. m. Irving Kristol, 18 Jan 1942, 1 son, 1 daughter. Education: Jewish Theological Seminary, 1939-42; BA, Brooklyn College, 1942; MA, 1944, PhD, 1950, University of Chicago; Girton College, Cambridge, 1946-47. Appointments: Professor, 1965-78, Distinguished Professor of History, 1978-88, Professor Emerita, 1988-, Graduate School of the City University of New York. Publications: Lord Acton: A Study in Conscience and Politics, 1952; Darwin and the Darwinian Revolution, 1959, revised edition, 1968; Victorian Minds: Essays on Nineteenth Century Intellectuals, 1968; On Liberty and Liberalism: The Case of John Stuart Mill, 1974; The Idea of Poverty: England in the Industrial Age, 1984; Marriage and Morals Among the Victorians and Other Essays, 1986; The New History and the Old, 1987; Poverty and Compassion: The Moral Imagination of the Late Victorians, 1991; On Looking Into the Abyss: Untimely

Thoughts on Culture and Society, 1994; The De-Moralization of Society, 1995; Vuctorian Minds, 1995. Contributions to: Scholarly books and journals. Honours: American Association of University Women Fellowship, 1951-52; American Philosophical Society Fellowship, 1953-54; Guggenheim Fellowships, 1955-56, 1957-58; National Endowment for the Humanities Senior Fellowship, 1968-69; American Council of Learned Societies Fellowship, 1972-73; Phi Beta Kappa Visiting Scholarship, 1972-73; Woodrow Wilson Center Fellowship, 1976-77; Rockefeller Humanities Fellowship, 1980-81. Memberships: American Academy of Arts and Sciences; American Historical Association; American Philosophical Society; British Academy, fellow; Royal Historical Society, fellow; Society of American Historians. Address: 2510 Virginia Avenue, NW, Washignton, DC 20037, USA.

HIND Sulaima, b. 27 Aug 1969, Arhus, Denmark. Author; Lecturer. Publications: Noxeverk, novel, 1997; Lille Dame, short story, 1998; Hjemve, short story, 1998. Contributions to: Svanger, short story in Politiken, 1998. Honour: Awarding of Prize, Danish State Fond for Endowment of the Arts, The Literary Section), 1998. Membership: Danish Author's Association. Literary Agent: Hostogsson Kobenhavn. Address: Faergestedet, Badsmandsstraede 43, 1407 KBH K, Denmark.

HINDE Thomas. See: **CHITTY Sir Thomas Willes.**

HINE (William) Daryl, b. 24 Feb 1936, Burnaby, British Columbia, Canada. Poet; Writer; Translator. Education: McGill University, 1954-58; MA, 1965, PhD, 1967, University of Chicago. Appointments: Assistant Professor of English, University of Chicago, 1967-69; Editor, Poetry magazine, Chicago, 1968-78. Publications: Poetry: Five Poems, 1954; The Carnal and the Crane, 1957; The Devil's Picture Book, 1960; Heroics, 1961; The Wooden Horse, 1965; Minutes, 1968; Resident Alien, 1975; In and Out: A Confessional Poem, 1975; Daylight Saving, 1978; Selected Poems, 1980; Academic Festival Overtures, 1985; Arrondissments, 1988; Postscripts, 1992. Novel: The Prince of Darkness & Co, 1961. Other: Polish Subtitles: Impressions from a Journey, 1962; The "Poetry" Anthology 1912-1977 (editor with Joseph Parisi), 1978. Translator: The Homeric Hymns and the battle of the Frogs and the Mice, 1972; Theocritus: Idylls and Epigrams, 1982; Ovid's Heroines: A Verse Translation from the Heroides, 1991. Honours: Canada Foundation-Rockefeller Fellowship, 1958; Canada Council Grants 1959, 1979; Ingram Merrill Foundation Grants, 1962, 1963, 1983; Guggenheim Fellowship, 1980; American Academy of Arts and Letters Award, 1982; John D and Catharine T McArthur Foundation Fellowship, 1986. Address: 2740 Ridge Avenue, Evanston, IL 60201, USA.

HINES Barry Melvin, b. 30 June 1939, Barnsley, Yorkshire, England. Writer. Div, 1 son, 1 daughter. Education: Loughborough College of Education, 1958-60, 1962-63. Appointments: Yorkshire Arts Association Fellow, Sheffield University, 1972-74; East Midlands Art Association Fellow, Matlock College of Higher Education, 1975-77; Arts Council of Great Britain Fellow, Sheffield City Polytechnic, 1982-84. Publications: The Blinder, 1966; A Kestrel for a Knave, 1968; First Signs, 1972; The Gamekeeper, 1975; The Price of Coal, 1979; Unfinished Business, 1983; Looks and Smiles, 1981; The Heart of It, 1994; Elvis over England, 1998. Television and film: Two Men from Derby, 1967; Kes, 1969; The Price of Coal, 2 films, 1975; The Gamekeeper, 1976; Looks and Smiles, 1979; A Question of Leadership, 1981; Threads, 1984; Shooting Stars, 1990; Born Kicking, 1992; Elvis over England, 1998. Address: 323 Fulwood Road, Sheffield S10 3BJ, England.

HINES Donald (Merrill), b. 23 Jan 1931, St Paul, Minnesota, USA. Writer; Teacher. m. Linda Marie Arnold, 10 June 1961, 3 sons. Education: BS, Lewis and Clark College, Portland, Oregon, 1953; MAT, Reed College, Portland, Oregon, 1960; PhD, Indiana University, 1969. Appointments: Faculty, Washington State University, 1968-77, King Saud University, Abha, Saudi Arabia,

1982-90, Blue Mountain Community College, Pendleton, Oregon, 1990-91. Publications: Cultural History of the Inland Pacific Northwest Frontier, 1976; Tales of the Okanogans, 1976; Tales of the Nez Perce, 1984; The Forgotten Tribes: Oral Tales of the Tenino and Adjacent Mid-Columbia River Indian Nations, 1991; Ghost Voices: Yakima Indian Myths, Legends, Humour and Hunting Stories, 1992; Celilo Tales: Wasco Myths, Legends, Tales of Magic and the Marvelous, 1996. Contributions to: Journals. Honours: Ford Foundation Fellowship, 1965; 3rd Prize, Chicago Folklore Contest, University of Chicago, 1970. Membership: American Folklore Society. Address: 3623 219th Place South East, Issaquah, WA 98029, USA.

HINES Joanna, b. London, England. Writer. m. Derrek Hines, 1 son, 2 daughters. Education: BA, History, Somerville College, Oxford, England; Diploma, Social Administration, LSE. Publications: Dora's Room, 1993; The Cornish Girl, 1994; The Fifth Secret, 1995; The Puritan's Wife, 1996; Autumn of Strangers, 1997. Memberships: WCWA; Society of Authors. Literary Agent: Laura Longrigg, MBA, 62 Grafton Way, W1P 5LD, London. Address: c/o MBA, 62 Grafton Way, W1P 5LD, London, England.

HINOJOSA-SMITH Rolando, b. 21 Jan 1929, Mercedes, Texas, USA. Author; Professor. 1 son, 2 daughters. Education: BS, University of Texas at Austin, 1953; MA, New Mexico Highlands University, Las Vegas, 1963; PhD, University of Illinois, 1969. Appointments: Assistant Professor, Trinity University, San Antonio, 1968-70; Associate Professor, 1970-74, Dean, College of Arts and Sciences, 1974-76, Vice President for Academic Affairs, 1976-77, Texas A and I University, Kingsville; Chair, Department of Chicano Studies, 1977-80, Professor, 1980-81, University of Minnesota; Professor, University of Texas at Austin, 1981-. Publications: Estampas del valle y otras obras, 1972, bilingual edition as Sketches of the Valley and Other Works, 1980, revised English edition as The Valley, 1983; Klail City y sus alrededores, 1976, English translation as Klail City, 1987; Korean Love Songs from Klail City Death Trip, 1978; Claros varones de Belken, 1981, bilingual edition as Fair Gentlemen of Belken County, 1987; Mi querido Rafa, 1981, English translation as Dear Rafe, 1985; Rites and Witnesses, 1982; Partners in Criime, 1985; Los amigos de Becky, 1990, English translation as Becky and Her Friends, 1990; The Useless Servants, 1993; Ask a Policeman, 1998. Contributions to: Anthologies, reviews, journals, and periodicals. Honours: Quinto Sol Literary Award for Best Novel, 1972; Casa de las Américas Award for Best Novel, 1976; Southwest Studies on Latin America Award for Best Writing in the Humanities, 1981; University of Illinois College of Liberal Arts Award, 1987, and Alumni Achievement Award, 1998; Lon C Tinkle Award, Texas Institute of Letters, 1998. Memberships: Modern Language Association; PEN; Salado Institute. Address: c/o Department of English, PAR 108, University of Texas at Austin, Austin, TX 78712, USA.

HINRIKSSON Larus, b. 28 Feb 1956, Reykjavik, Iceland. Writer; Poet. m. Freyja Baldursdottir, Aug 1982, 1 son, 1 daughter. Education: Industrial School of Iceland. Publications: Enigma Well, 1993; The Lupin, 1994; Echo of Time, Broken Glass (poems), 1995. Membership: Writers' Union of Iceland. Address: Box 410, 602 Akureyri, Iceland.

HINSON E(dward) Glenn, b. 27 July 1931, St Louis, Missouri, USA. Professor of Spirituality and of Church History; Writer. m. Martha Anne Burks, 1 Sept 1956, 1 son, 1 daughter. Education: BA, Washington University, St Louis, 1954; BD, 1957, ThD, 1962, Southern Baptist Theological Seminary, Louisville; DPhil, University of Oxford, 1973. Appointments: Professor, Southern Baptist Theological Seminary, 1959-92, Wake Forest University, 1982-84; Visiting Professor, St John's University, Collegeville, Minnesota, 1983, Catholic University of America, 1987, University of Notre Dame, 1989; Professor of Spirituality and John F Loftis Professor of Church History, Baptist Theological Seminary, Richmond, Virginia, 1992-. Publications: The Church: Design for

Survival, 1967; Seekers after Mature Faith, 1968; A Serious Call to a Contemplative Life-Style, 1974, revised edition, 1993; Soul Liberty, 1975; The Early Church Fathers, 1978; The Reaffirmation of Prayer, 1979; A History of Baptists in Arkansas, 1980; The Evangelization of the Roman Empire, 1981; Are Southern Baptists Evangelicals?, 1983; Religious Liberty, 1991; Spirituality in Ecumenical Perspective, 1993; The Church Triumphant: A History of Christianity up to 1300, 1995; The Early Church, 1996; Love at the Heart of Things: A Biography of Douglas V Steere, 1998. Contributions to: Festschriften, reference works, and journals. Honours: American Association of Theological Schools Fellowship, 1966-67; Professor of the Year, Southern Baptist Theological Fellowship, 1975-76; Johannes Quasten Medal, Catholic University of America; Cuthbert Allen Award, Ecumenical Institute of Belmont Abbey/Wake Forest University, 1992. Memberships: American Society of Church History; Association Internationale des Patristique; International Thomas Merton Society; National Association of Baptist Professor of Religion, president, 1993-94; North American Patristics Society; Societas Liturgica. Address: 3400 Brook Road, Richmond, VA 23227, USA.

HINTON Jenny. See: **DAWSON Jennifer.**

HINTON S(usan) E(loise), b. 1948, Tulsa, Oklahoma, USA. Writer. m. David Inhofe, 1970, 1 son. Education: BS, University of Tulsa, 1970. Publications: The Outsiders, 1967; That Was Then, This is Now, 1971; Rumble Fish, 1975; Tex, 1979; Taming the Star Runner, 1988; Big David, Little David, 1994. Screenplay: Rumble Fish (with Francis Ford Coppola), 1983. Honours: Media and Methods Maxi Award, 1975; Golden Archer Award, 1983; Sue Hefly Award, 1983; Author's Award, American Library Association Young Adult Services Division/School Library Journal, 1988. Address: c/o Delacorte Press, 1540 Broadway, New York, NY 10036, USA.

HIRO Dilip. Writer. Education: MS, State University of Virginia, USA, 1962. Publications: A Triangular View, 1969; Black British, White British, 1971, revised edition, 1991; To Anchor a Cloud, 1972; The Untouchables of India, 1975; Inside India Today, 1976; Clean Break (play), 1978; Apply, Apply, No Reply (play), 1978; Interior, Exchange, Exterior, 1980; Inside the Middle East, 1982; Iran Under the Ayatollahs, 1985; Three Plays, 1987; Iran: The Revolution Within, 1988; Islamic Fundamentalism, 1988; The Longest War: The Iran-Iraq Military Conflict, 1989; Desert Shield to Desert Storm: The Second Gulf War, 1992; Lebanon, Fire and Embers: A History of the Lebanese Civil War, 1993; Between Marx and Muhammed: The Changing Face of Central Asia, 1994; Dictionary of the Middle East, 1996; The Middle East, 1996; Sharing the Promised Land: An Interwoven Tale of Israelis and Palestinians, 1996. Contributions to: Newspapers and journals. Honour: Silver Hugo, Chicago Film Festival, 1975. Memberships: Middle East Studies Association of North America; Centre for Iranian Research and Analysis. Literary Agent: David Higham Associates, 5 Lower John Street, London W1R 4HA. Address: 31 Waldegrave Road, Ealing, London W5 3HT, England.

HIROKO Takenishi, b. 1929, Hiroshima, Japan. Writer. Education: Graduated in Japanese Literature, Waseda University, Tokyo. Appointments: Worked in publishing company; Writer, 1963-. Publications: Essays: Oukan no ki - Nihon no Koten ni omou; Yamakawa Tomiko - Myoujô no kajin. Novels: Tsuru, 1976; Kangen sai, 1978; Heitai yado, 1981; Gishiki; Mizu-umi; Aisatsu; Choujô no kaze. Honours: Tamura Tishiko Literary Prize, 1964; Hirabayashi Prize of Literature, 1973; Minister of Education Prize for Young Writers, 1976; Women's Literary Award, 1978; Kawabata Yasunari Literary Award, 1981; Mainichi Art Award, 1986; Japan Art Academy Prize, 1994. Memberships: Japan Art Academy; Japan PEN Club; Board of Directors, Japan Writers' Association. Address: c/o Japan Writers' Association, Bungei Shunjyu Building, 9th Floor, 3-23 Kioi-cho, Chiyoda-ku, Tokyo 102, Japan.

HIRSCH Edward (Mark), b. 20 Jan 1950, Chicago, Illinois, USA. Professor of English; Poet; Writer. m. Janet Landay, 29 May 1977, 1 son. Education: BA, Grinnell College, 1972; PhD, University of Pennsylvania, 1979. Appointments: Teacher, Poetry in the Schools Program, New York and Pennsylvania, 1976-78; Assistant Professor, 1978-82, Associate Professor of English, 1982-85, Wayne State University; Associate Professor, 1985-88, Professor of English, 1988-, University of Houston. Publications: For the Sleepwalkers, 1981; Wild Gratitude, 1986; The Night Parade, 1989; Earthly Measures, 1994; Transforming Vision (editor), 1994; On Love, 1998; How to read a Poem and Fall in Love with Poetry, 1999; Responsive Reading, 1999. Contributions to: Many anthologies, books, journals, and periodicals. Honours: Awards, 1975-77, Peter I B Lavan Younger Poets Award, 1983, Academy of American Poets; Ingram Merrill Foundation Award, 1978; American Council of Learned Societies Fellow, 1981; National Endowment for the Arts Fellowship, 1982; Delmore Schwartz Memorial Poetry Award, New York University, 1985; Guggenheim Fellowship, 1986-87; Texas Institute of Letters Award in Poetry, 1987; National Book Critics Circle Award, 1987; Rome Prize, American Academy and Institute of Arts and Letters, 1988; Robert and Hazel Ferguson Memorial Award for Poetry, Friends of Chicago Literature, 1990; Lila Wallace-Reader's Degest Writing Fellow, 1993; Woodrow Wilson Fellow, 1994, 1995; Lyndhurst Prize, 1994-96. Memberships: Authors Guild; Modern Language Association; PEN; Phi Beta Kappa; Poetry Society of America; Texas Institute of Letters. Address: 1528 Sul Ross, Houston, TX 77006, USA.

HIRSCHFELD Vizhar, b. 6 Feb 1950, Jerusalem. Archaeologist. m. Hannah, 4 Jan 1983, 3 daughters. Education: PhD, Classical Archaeology, Hebrew University of Jerusalem. Publications: The Judean Desert Monasteries in the Byzantine Period,1992; The Palestinian Dwelling in the Roman-Byzantine Period, 1995. Address: Institute of Archaeology, Hebrew University, Jersualem.

HIRSCHHORN Clive Errol, b. 20 Feb 1940, Johannesburg, South Africa. Critic. Education: BA, University of the Witwatersrand, Johannesburg. Appointment: Film and Theatre Critic, London Sunday Express, 1966-. Publications: Gene Kelly: A Biography, 1974; Films of James Mason, 1976; The Warner Brothers' Story, 1978; The Hollywood Musical, 1981; The Universal Story, 1983; The Columbia Story, 1989. Address: 42a South Audley Street, Mayfair, London W1, England.

HIRSCHMAN Jack, b. 13 Dec 1933, New York, New York, USA. Poet; Translator. m. Ruth Epstein, 1954, 1 son, 1 daughter. Education: BA, City College of New York, 1955; AM, 1957, PhD, 1961, Indiana University. Publications: Poetry: Fragments, 1952; Correspondence of Americans, 1960; Two, 1963; Interchange, 1964; Kline Sky, 1965; Yod, 1966; London Seen Directly, 1967; Wasn't Like This in the Woodcut, 1967; William Blake, 1967; A Word in Your Season (with Asa Benveniste), 1967; Ltd Interchangeable in Eternity: Poems of Jackruthdavidcelia Hirschman, 1967; Jerusalem, 1968; Aleph, Benoni and Zaddik, 1968; Jerusalem Ltd, 1968; Shekinah, 1969; Broadside Golem, 1969; Black Alephs: Poems 1960-68, 1969; NHR, 1970; Scintilla, 1970; Soledeth, 1971; DT, 1971; The Burning of Los Angeles, 1971; HNYC, 1971; Les Vidanges, 1972; The R of the Ari's Raziel, 1972; Adamnan, 1972; K'wai Sing: The Origin of the Dragon, 1973; Cantillations, 1973; Aur Sea, 1974; Djackson, 1974; Cockroach Street, 1975; The Cool Boyetz Cycle, 1975; Kashtaniyah Segodnyah, 1976; Lyripol, 1976; The Arcanes of Le Comte de St Germain, 1977; The Proletarian Arcane, 1978; The Jonestown Arcane, 1979; The Caliostro Arcane, 1981; The David Arcane, 1982; Class Questions, 1982; Kallatumba, 1984; The Necessary Is, 1984; The Bottom Line, 1988; Sunsong, 1988; The Tirana Arcane, 1991; The Satin Arcane, 1991; Endless Threshold, 1992; The Back of a Spoon, 1992; The Heartbeat Arcane, 1993; The Xibalba Arcane, 1994. Editor: Artaud Anthology, 1965; Would You Wear My Eyes: A Tribute to Bob Kaufman, 1989.

Translator: Over 25 volumes, 1970-95. Address: PO Box 26517, San Francisco, CA 94126, USA.

HIRSHFIELD Jane, b. 24 Feb 1953, New York, New York, USA. Poet; Writer; Editor; Lecturer. Education: AB magna cum laude, Princeton University, 1973. Appointments: California Poet in the Schools, 1980-85; Faculty, various writers conferences, 1984-; Lecturer, University of San Francisco, 1991-; Visiting Poet-in-Residence, University of Alaska, Fairbanks, 1993; Adjunct Professor, Northern Michigan University, 1994; Associate Faculty, Bennington College, 1995; Visiting Associate Professor, University of California at Berkeley, 1995; Core Faculty, Bennington College, MFA Writing Seminars, 1999-. Publications: Poetry: Alaya, 1982; Of Gravity & Angels, 1988; The October Palace, 1994; The Lives of the Heart, 1997. Other: The Ink Dark Moon: Poems by Ono no Komachi and Izumi Shikibu (translator with Aratani), 1988, expanded edition, 1990; Women in Praise of the Sacred: 43 Centuries of Spiritual Poetry by Women (editor), 1994; Nine Gates: Entering the Mind of Poetry (essays), 1997. Contributions to: Many anthologies, journals, and reviews. Honours: Yaddo Fellowships, 1983, 1985, 1987, 1989, 1992, 1996; Guggenheim Fellowship, 1985; Joseph Henry Jackson Award, San Francisco Foundation, 1986; Columbia University Translation Center Award, 1987; Poetry Society of America Awards, 1987, 1988; Artist-in-Residence, Djerassi Foundation, 1987-90; Pushcart Prize, 1988; Commonwealth Club of California Poetry Medals, 1988, 1994; Dewar's Young Artists Recognition Award in Poetry, 1990; MacDowell Colony Fellowship, 1994; Poetry Center Book Award, 1995; Rockefeller Foundation Fellowship, Bellagio Study Center, Italy, 1995. Memberships: Associated Writing Programs; Authors Guild; Djerassi Resident Artist Program, board member, 1996-; Lindisfarne Association, fellow, 1995-; PEN American Center. Address: c/o Michael Katz, 367 Molino Avenue, Mill Valley, CA 94941, USA.

HISLOP Ian (David), b. 13 July 1960, England. Editor; Writer; Broadcaster. m. Victoria Hamson, 1 son, 1 daughter. Education: BA, Honours, English Language and Literature, Magdalen College, Oxford. Appointments: Staff, 1981-85, Deputy Editor, 1985-86, Editor, 1986-, Private Eye; Columnist, The Listener, 1985-89, Sunday Telegraph, 1996-; Television Critic, The Spectator, 1994-96. Publications: Private Eye collections, 1985-. Other: Television scripts. Contributions to: Newspapers, magazines, radio, and television. Honours: Editor's Editor Award, British Society of Magazine Editors, 1991; Magazine of the Year, 1991; Best Light Entertainment, British Academy of Film and Television Arts, 1992. Address: c/o Private Eye, 6 Carlisle Street, London W1V 5RG, England.

HISSEY Jane Elizabeth, b. 1 Sept 1952, Norwich, Norfolk, England. Author; Illustrator. m. Ivan James Hissey, 1 Aug 1979, 2 sons, 1 daughter. Education: Art Foundation Course, Great Yarmouth College of Art and Design, 1970; BA, 1974, Art Teachers Certificate, Brighton Polytechnic, 1975. Publications: Old Bear, 1986; Little Bears Trousers, 1987; Little Bear Lost, 1989; Jolly Tall, 1990; Jolly Snow, 1991; Old Bear Tales, 1991; Little Bear's Day, Little Bear's Bedtime, 1992; Ruff, 1994; Hoot, 1996. Address: c/o Hutchinson Childrens Books, Random House, 20 Vauxhall Bridge Road, London SW1V 2SA, England.

HJORTSBERG William Reinhold, b. 23 Feb 1941, New York, New York, USA. Author. Education: BA, Dartmouth College, 1962; Postgraduate Studies, Yale Drama School, 1962-63; Stanford University, 1967-68. Publications: Alp, 1969; Gray Matters, 1971; Symbiography, 1973; Toro! Toro! Toro!, 1974; Falling Angel, 1978; Tales and Fables, 1985; Nevermore, 1994. Films: Thunder and Lightning, 1977; Georgia Peaches (co-author), 1980; Legend, 1986. Contributions to: Various journals, magazines and newspapers. Honours: Wallace Stegner Fellowship, 1967; National Endownment for the Arts Grant, 1976; Playboy Editorial Award, 1971, 1978. Memberships: Writers Guild of America; The

Authors Guild. Literary Agent: Harold Matson Company, New York City, NY, USA. Address: Main Boulder Route, McLeod, MT 59052, USA.

HOAGLAND Edward, b. 21 Dec 1932, New York, New York, USA. Author; Teacher. m. (1) Amy J Ferrara, 1960l, div 1964, (2) Marion Magid, 28 Mar 1968, 1 daughter. Education: AB, Harvard University, 1954. Appointments: Faculty, New School for Social Research, New York City, 1963-64, Rutgers University, 1966, Sarah Lawrence College, 1967, 1971, City University of New York, 1967, 1968, University of Iowa, 1978, 1982, Columbia University, 1980, 1981, Bennington College, 1987-97, Brown University, 1988, University of California at Davis, 1990, 1992. Publications: Cat Man, 1956; The Circle Home, 1960; The Peacock's Tail, 1965; Notes from the Century Before: A Journal from British Columbia, 1969; The Courage of Turtles, 1971; Walking the Dead Diamond River, 1973; The Moose on the Wall: Field Notes from the Vermont Wilderness, 1974; Red Wolves and Black Bears, 1976; African Calliope: A Journey to the Sudan, 1979; The Edward Hoagland Reader, 1979; The Tugman's Passage, 1982; City Tales, 1986; Seven Rivers West, 1986; Heart's Desire, 1988; The Final Fate of the Alligators, 1992; Balancing Acts, 1992; Tigers and Ice, 1999. Contributions to: Periodicals. Honours: Houghton Mifflin Literary Fellowship, 1954; Longview Foundation Award, 1961; Prix de Rome, 1964; Guggenheim Fellowships, 1964, 1975; O Henry Award, 1971; New York State Council on the Arts Award, 1972; National Book Critics Circle Award, 1980; Harold D Vursell Award, 1981; National Endowment for the Arts Award, 1982; Literary Lion Award, New York Public Library, 1988; National Magazine Award, 1989; Lannon Foundation Literary Award, 1993; Literary Lights Award, Boston Public Library, 1995; American Academy of Arts and Letters, 1982. Address: c/o Simon and Schuster, 1230 Avenue of the Americas, New York, NY 10020, USA.

HOBAN Russell (Conwell), b. 4 Feb 1925, Lansdale, Pennsylvania, USA. Writer. m. (1) Lillian Aberman, 31 Jan 1944, div, 1 son, 3 daughters, (2) Gundula Ahl, 14 Aug 1975, 3 sons. Education: High School, Philadelphia. Appointments: General Illustrator, Wexton Co, New York City, 1950-52; Television Art Director, Batten, Barton, Durstine & Osborne, New York City, 1952-57; Copywriter, Doyle Dane Bernbach, New York City, 1965-67. Publications: The Lion of Boaz-Jachin and Jachin-Boaz, 1973; Kleinzeit, 1974; Turtle Diary, 1975; Riddley Walker, 1980, 2nd edition, 1986; Pilgermann, 1983; The Medusa Frequency, 1987; The Moment Under the Moment, 1992; The Court of the Winged Serpent, 1994. Libretto: The Second Mrs Kong (for Harrison Birtwistle's Opera), 1994. Children's Books: Over 55 books, 1959-94. Honours: Whitbread Children's Book Award, 1974; John W Campbell Memorial Award for Best Science Fiction Novel, 1981; Science Fiction Achievement Award, 1981. Memberships: PEN; Royal Society of Literature, fellow; Society of Authors. Address: c/o David Higham Associates Ltd, Golden Square, 5-8 Lower John Street, London W1R 4HA, England.

HOBFOLL Stevan E(arl), b. 25 Sept 1951, Chicago, Illinois, USA. Psychologist; Writer; Editor. m. Ivonne Heras, 18 May 1977, 2 sons, 1 daughter. Education: King's College, London, 1971-72; BS, Psychology, University of Illinois, 1973; MA, 1975, PhD, 1977, Psychology, University of South Florida. Appointments: Senior Lecturer, Ben Gurion University, Beersheba, Israel, 1980-83; Fellow Professor in Psychology, Tel Aviv University, 1983-87; Director, Applied Psychology Center, Kent State University, Ohio, 1987-; Editor, Anxiety, Stress and Coping: An International Journal, 1992-. Publications: Stress, Social Support, and Women, 1986; The Ecology of Stress, 1988; Conservation of Resources, 1989; War-Related Stress, 1991; Work Won't Love You Back: The Dual Career Couple's Survival Guide (with Ivonne Hobfoll), 1994. Contributions to: Many books and journals. Honour: Peer recognition award for work in the HIV/AIDS Ohio racial and ethnic communities, 1990. Memberships: American Psychological Association, fellow; International Society for the Study of Personal Relationships; Stress and Test Anxiety Research Society.

Address: c/o Applied Psychology Centre, 106 Kent Hall, Kent State University, Kent, OH 44242, USA.

HOBHOUSE (Mary) Hermione, b. 1934, Somerset, England. Conservationist; Writer. m. Henry Trevenen Davidson Graham, 1958, div 1988, 1 son, 1 daughter. Education: Honours Modern History, Lady Margaret Hall, Oxford. Appointments: Researcher/Writer, Associated-Rediffusion Television, 1956-58, Granada Television, 1958-63; General Editor, Survey of London RCHME, 1983-94. Publications: The Ward of Cheap in the City of London, 1963; Thomas Cubitt: Master Builder, 1971, 2nd edition, 1995; Lost London, 1971; History of Regent Street, 1975; Oxford and Cambridge, 1980; Prince Albert: His Life and Work, 1983; County Hall, 1991; Poplar, Blackwall and the Isle of Dogs, 1994; London Survey'd: The Work of the Survey of London 1894-1994, 1994. Contributions to: Journals. Honours: Member of the Order of the British Empire, 1981; Hitchcock Medallion, 1972. Memberships: National Trust, council, 1983-; Society of Antiquaries, council, 1984-87. Address: 61 St Dunstan's Road, London W6 8RE, England.

HOBHOUSE Penelope, (Penelope Malins), b. 20 Nov 1929, Castledawson, Northern Ireland. Writer; Designer. m. (1) Paul Hobhouse, 1952, 2 sons, 1 daughter, (2) John Malins, 1 Nov 1983. Education: Honours, Economics, University of Cambridge, 1951. Publications: The Country Gardener; Colour in Your Garden; Garden Style; Flower Gardens; Guide to the Gardens of Europe; The Smaller Garden; Painted Gardens; Private Gardens of England; Borders; Flower Gardens; Plants in Garden History; Garden Style. Contributions to: The Garden; Horticulture; Vogue; Antiques; Plants and Gardens. Honour: Awarded Royal Horticultural Society Victoria Medal of Honour, 1996. Address: The Coach House, Bettiscombe, Bridport, Dorset DT6 5NT, England.

HOBSBAUM Philip (Dennis), b. 29 June 1932, London, England. Writer; Poet; Emeritus Professor of English Literature. m. (1) Hannah Hobsbaum, 1957, div 1968, (2) Rosemary Phillips, 20 July 1976. Education: BA, 1955, MA, 1961, Downing College, Cambridge; Licentiate, Royal Academy of Music, London, 1956; PhD, University of Sheffield, 1968. Appointments: Editor, Delta, 1954-55; Co-Editor, Poetry from Sheffield, 1959-61; Lecturer in English, Queen's University, Belfast, 1962-66; Lecturer, 1966-72, Senior Lecturer, 1972-79, Reader, 1979-85, Professor of English Literature, 1985-97, Honorary Professorial Research Fellow, 1997-, University of Glasgow. Publications: A Group Anthology (editor with E Lucie-Smith), 1963; The Place's Fault and Other Poems, 1964; Snapshots, 1965; In Retreat and Other Poems, 1966; Ten Elizabethan Poets (editor), 1969; Coming Out Fighting, 1969; Some Lovely Glorious Nothing, 1969; A Theory of Communication: A Study of Value in Literature, 1970; Women and Animals, 1972; A Reader's Guide to Charles Dickens, 1973; Tradition and Experiment in English Poetry, 1979; A Reader's Guide to D H Lawrence, 1981; Essentials of Literary Criticism, 1983; A Reader's Guide to Robert Lowell, 1988; Wordsworth: Selected Poetry and Prose (editor), 1989; Channels of Communication (editor with P Lyons and J McGhie), 1993; Metre, Rhythm and Verse Form, 1996. Contributions to: Anthologies, journals, reviews, and magazines. Honour: Honorary DLitt, University of Glasgow, 1994. Address: c/o Department of English Literature, University of Glasgow, Glasgow G12 8QQ, Scotland.

HOBSBAWM Eric John Ernest, b. 9 June 1917, Alecandria, Egypt (British citizen). Professor of Economic and Social History Emeritus; Writer. m. Marlene Schwarz, 1962, 1 son, 1 daughter. Education: BA, 1939, MA, 1943, PhD, 1951, University of Cambridge. Appointments: Lecturer in History, 1947-59, Reader in History, 1959-70, Professor of Economic and Social History, 1970-82, Professor Emeritus, 1982-, Birkbeck College, University of London; Fellow in History, King's College, Cambridge, 1949-55. Publications: Labour's Turning Point, 1880-1900 (editor), 1948; Primitive Rebels, 1959, US edition as Social Bandits and Primitive Rebels, 1959; The Jazz Scene, 1959, revised edition, 1993; The Age of Revolution, 1789-1848, 1962; Labouring Men, 1964; Industry and Empire: An Economic History of Britain since 1750, 1968, US edition as Industry and Empire: The Making of Modern English Society, 1968; Captain Swing (with George Rudé), 1969; Bandits, 1969, revised edition, 1981; Revolutionaries, 1973; The Age of Capital, 1848-1875, 1975; Marxism in Marx's Day (editor), 1982; The Invention of Tradition (editor with Terence Ranger), 1983; Worlds of Labour: Further Studies in the History of Labour, 1984, US edition as Workers: Worlds of Labor, 1984; The Age of Empire, 1875-1914, 1987; Politics for a Rational Left: Political Writing, 1977-1988, 1989; Echoes of the Marseillaise: Two Centuries Look Back on the French Revolution, 1990; Nations and Nationalism since 1780: Programme, Myth, Reality, 1990, 2nd edition, 1992; Age of Extremes: The Short Twentieth Century, 1914-1991, 1994, US edition as The Age of Extremes: A History of the World, 1914-1991, 1994; On History, 1997. Uncommon People, 1998. Contributions to: Scholarly journals and general publications. Honours: Palmes Académiques, France, 1993; Lionel Gelber Prize, 1995; Commander, Order of the Southern Cross, Brazil, 1996; Companion of Honour, 1998. Memberships: American Academy of Arts and Sciences, honorary member; British Academy, fellow; Economic History Society; Hungarian Academy of Sciences, honorary member. Address: Birkbeck College, University of London, Malet Street, London WC1E 7HX, England.

HOBSON Fred Colby Jr, b. 23 Apr 1943, Winston-Salem, North Carolina, USA. Professor of Literature; Writer. m. 17 June 1967, div, 1 daughter. Education: AB, English, University of North Carolina, 1965; MA, History, Duke University, 1967; PhD, English, University of North Carolina, 1972. Appointments: Professor of English, University of Alabama, 1972-86; Professor of English and Co-Editor, Southern Review, Louisiana State University, 1986-89; Professor of English; Lineberger Professor in the Humanities and Co-Editor, Southern Literary Journal, University of North Carolina at Chapel Hill, 1989-. Publications: Serpent in Eden: H L Mencken and the South, 1974; Literature at the Barricades: The American Writer in the 1930's (co-editor), 1983; Tell About the South: The Southern Rage to Explain, 1984; South-Watching: Selected Essays of Gerald W Johnson (editor), 1984; The Southern Writer in the Post-Modern World, 1990; Mencken: A Life, 1994; Thirty-Five Years of Newspaper Work by H L Mencken (co-editor), 1994. Contributions to: Virginia Quarterly Review; Sewanee Review; Kenyon Review; New York Times Book Review; American Literature; Times Literary Supplement. Address: Department of English, University of North Carolina at Chapel Hill, NC 27514, USA.

HOCH Edward D, b. 22 Feb 1930, Rochester, New York, USA. Writer. m. Patricia McMahon, 5 June 1957. Education: University of Rochester, 1947-49. Appointment: Guest of Honour, Bouchercon 22, 1991. Publictions: The Thefts of Nick Velvet, 1978; The Quests of Simon Ark, 1984; Leopold's Way, 1985; The Night My Friend, 1992; Diagnosis: Impossible, 1996; The Ripper of Storyville, 1997. Contributions to: Ellery Queen's Mystery Magazine. Honours: MWA Edgar Award, 1968; Boughercon Award, 1998. Membership: Mystery Writers of America, president, 1982-83. Address: 2941 Lake Avenue, Rochester, NY 14612, USA.

HOCHHUTH Rolf, b. 1 Apr 1931, Eschwege, Germany. Dramatist; Writer; Poet; Critic. m. 3 sons. Education: Extramural Studies, University of Heidelberg, University of Munich. Appointment: Chief Cultural Correspondent, Die Welt newspaper, Berlin, 1989-. Publications: Der Stellvertreter, 1963; Die Berliner Antigone, 1966; Soldaten, 1967; Guerrillas, 1970; Die Hebamme, 1971, revised edition, 1973; Lysistrate und die NATO, 1973; Tod eines Jägers, 1976; Eine Liebe in Deutschland, 1978; Juristen, 1979; Arztinnen, 1980; Spitze des Eisbergs: Ein Reader, 1982; Judith, 1984; Atlantik, 1985; Der Berliner Antigone: Erzählungen und Gedichte, 1986; War hier Europa?: Reden, Gedichte, Essays, 1987; Tater und Denker: Profile und Probleme von Cäaser bis Jünger, 1987; Unbefleckte Empfängnis: Ein Kreidekreis, 1988; Sommer 14: Ein Totentan, 1989; Alle Dramen, 2 volumes, 1991; Panik im Mai: Sämtliche Gedichte und Erzählungen, 1991; Wessis in Weimar: Szenen aus einem besetzten Land, 1993; Julia oder Weg zur Macht, 1994. Honours: Gerhart Hauptmann Prize, 1962; Berlin Art Prize, 1963; Basel Art Prize, 1976; Literature Prize, City of Munich and Association of Bavarian Publishers, 1980; Lessing Prize, Hamburg, 1981; Jacob Burckhardt Prize, 1991. Memberships: Academy of Fine Arts; PEN Club. Address: c/o Die Welt, Kochstrasse 50, D-10069 Berlin, Germany.

HOCHSCHILD Adam, b. 5 Oct 1942, New York, New York, USA. Writer. m. Arlie Russell, 26 June 1965, 2 sons. Education: AB cum laude, Harvard University, 1963. Appointments: Reporter, San Francisco Chronicle, 1965-66; Editor and Writer, Ramparts Magazine, 1966-68, 1973-74; Co-Founder, Editor, Writer, Mother Jones Magazine, 1974-81, 1986-87; Commentator, National Public Radio, 1982-83, Public Interest Radio, 1987-88; Regents Lecturer, University of California at Santa Cruz, 1987; Lecturer, Graduate School of Journalism, University of California at Berkeley, 1992, 1995, 1997-. Fulbright Lecturer, India, 1997-98. Publications: Half the Way Home: A Memoir of Father and Son, 1986; The Mirror at Midnight: A South African Journey, 1990; The Unquiet Ghost: Russians Remember Stalin, 1994; Finding the Trapdoor: Essays, Portraits, Travels, 1997; King Leopold's Ghost: A Story of Greed, Terror and Heroism In Colonial Africa, 1998. Contributions to: New Yorker; Harper's; New York Times; Los Angeles Times; Washington Post; Progressive; Village Voice; New York Review of Books; Mother Jones. Honours: Thomas Storke Award, World Affairs Council, 1987; Madeleine Dane Ross Award, Overseas Press Club of America, 1995; Lowell Thomas Award, Society of American Travel Writers, 1995; PEN/Spielvogel-Diamonstein Award for the Art of the Essay, 1998. Memberships: PEN; National Writers Union; National Book Critics Circle. Address: 84 Seward Street, San Francisco, CA 94114, USA.

HOCKENSMITH Sean, b. 4 Jan 1972, Johnstown, Pennsylvania, USA. Motivational Speaker; Author. m. Gina Leis, 7 May 1998. Education: University of Tampa, Florida. Publication: Smashing the Wall of Fear, 1998. Address: 3310 Graham Avenue, Windber, PA 15963, USA.

HOCKING Mary (Eunice), b. 8 Apr 1921, Acton, London, England. Writer. Appointment: Local government officer, 1946-70. Publications: The Winter City, 1961; Visitors to the Crescent, 1962; The Sparrow, 1964; The Young Spaniard, 1965; Ask No Question, 1967; A Time of War, 1968; Checkmate, 1969; The Hopeful Traveller, 1970; The Climbing Frame, 1971; Family Circle, 1972; Daniel Come to Judgement, 1974; The Bright Day, 1975; The Mind Has Mountains, 1976; Look, Stranger!, 1978; He Who Plays the King, 1980; March House, 1981; Good Daughters, 1984; Indifferent Heroes, 1985; Welcome Strangers, 1986; An Irrelevant Woman, 1987; A Particular Place, 1989; Letters from Constance, 1991; The Very Dead of Winter, 1993; The Meeting Place, 1996. Memberships: Royal Society of Literature, fellow; Society of Authors. Address: 3 Church Row, Lewes, Sussex, England.

HODGE Jane Aiken, b. 4 Dec 1917, Watertown, Massachusetts, USA. Author. m. Alan Hodge, 3 Jan 1948, dec 1979, 2 daughters. Education: BA, Somerville College, Oxford, 1938; AM, Radcliffe College, 1939. Publications: Fiction: Maulever Hall, 1964; The Adventurers, 1965; Watch the Wall, My Darling, 1966; Here Comes a Candle, 1967; The Winding Stair, 1968; Marry in Haste, 1970; Greek Wedding, 1970; Savannah Purchase, 1971; Strangers in Company, 1973; Shadow of a Lady, 1974; One Way to Venice, 1975; Rebel Heiress, 1975; Runaway Bridge, 1976; Judas Flowering, 1976; Red Sky at Night: Lover's Delight?, 1978; Last Act, 1979; Wide is the Water, 1981; The Lost Garden, 1981; Secret Island, 1985; Polonaise, 1987; First Night, 1989; Leading Lady, 1990; Windover, 1992; Escapade, 1993; Whispering, 1995; Bride of Dreams, 1996; Unsafe Hands,

1997; Susan in America, 1998; Caterina, 1999. Non-Fiction: The Double Life of Jane Austen, 1972; The Private World of Georgette Heyer, 1984; Passion and Principle: The Loves and Lives of Regency Women, 1996. Contributions to: Newspapers and journals. Membership: Society of Authors. Address: 23 Eastport Lane, Lewes, East Sussex BN7 1TL, England.

HODGE Paul William, b. 8 Nov 1934, Seattle, Washington, USA. Professor of Astronomy; Writer. m. Ann Uran, 14 June 1962, 2 sons, 1 daughter. Education: BS, Yale University, 1956; PhD, Harvard University, 1960. Appointments: Physicist, Smithsonian Astrophysical Observatory, Cambridge, Massachusetts, 1956-74; Lecturer, Harvard University, 1960-61; Fellow, Mount Wilson Palomar Observatory, California Institute of Technology, Pasadena, 1960-61; Assistant Professor of Astronomy, University of California at Berkeley, 1961-65; Associate Professor, 1965-69, Professor of Astronomy, 1969-, Chairman, Department of Astronomy, 1987-91, University of Washington; Editor, The Astronomical Journal, 1984-. Publications: Solar System Astrophysics, 1964; Galaxies and Cosmology, 1966; The Large Magellanic Cloud, 1967; Concepts of the Universe, 1969; Revolution in Astronomy, 1970; Galaxies, 1972; Concepts of Contemporary Astronomy, 1974; The Small Magellanic Cloud, 1977; An Atlas of the Andromeda Galaxy, 1981; Interplanetary Dust, 1982; The Universe of Galaxies, 1985; Galaxies, 1986; The Andromeda Galaxy, 1992; Meteorite Craters and Impact Structures of the World, 1994; Atlas of Local Group Galaxies, 1998. Contributions to: Astronomical journals. Honours: Beckwith Prize in Astronomy, 1956; Bart Bok Prize in Astronomy, 1962; Best Physical Science Book Award, 1986. Memberships: American Astronomical Society, vice president, 1990-93; Astronomical Society of the Pacific, vice-president, 1974-75; International Astronomical Union. Address: c/o Department of Astronomy, Box 351580, University of Washington, Seattle, WA 98195, USA.

HODGINS Jack Stanley, b. 3 Oct 1938, Vancouver Island, British Columbia, Canada. Novelist; Teacher. m. Dianne Child, 17 Dec 1960, 2 sons, 1 daughter. Education: BEd, University of British Columbia. Publications: Spit Delaney's Island, 1976; The Invention of the World, 1977; The Resurrection of Joseph Bourne, 1979; The Honorary Patron, 1987; Innocent Cities, 1990; Over Forty in Broken Hill, 1992; A Passion for Narrative, 1993; The Macken Charm, 1995; Broken Ground, 1998. Honours: Gibson First Novel Award, 1978; Governor General's Award for Fiction, 1980; Canada-Australia Literature Prize, 1986; Commonwealth Literature Prize, 1988; DLitt, University of British Columbia, 1995; DLitt, Malaspina University, 1998. Memberships: PEN; Writers Union of Canada. Address: Department of Writing, University of Victoria, PO Box 1700, Victoria, British Columbia V8W 2Y2, Canada.

HOE Susanna Leonie, b. 14 Apr 1945, Southampton, England. Women's Historian. m. Derek Roebuck, 18 Aug 1981. Education: London School of Economics, 1980-82; BA, University of Papua, New Guinea, 1983-84. Appointments: Campaign Coordinator, British Section, Amnesty International, 1977-80; Tutor, Department of Anthropology and Sociology, University of Papua New Guinea, 1985-86; TEFL Teacher, Women's Centre, Hong Kong, 1991-97. Publications: Lady in the Chamber (novel), 1971; God Save the Tsar (novel), 1978; The Man Who Gave His Company Away (biography), 1978; The Private Life of Old Hong Kong (history), 1991; Chinese Footprints (history), 1996; Stories for Eva (reader for Chinese women learning English), 1997. Contributions to: Times (Papua New Guinea); Liverpool Post; Women's Feature Service. Honour: Rangi Hiroa Pacific History Prize, 1984. Membership: Centre of Asian Studies, University of Hong Kong, research associate. Address: 20A Plantation Road, Oxford OX2 6JD, England.

HOEFSMIT Henri Diederick. See: DE LINT Charles.

HOEG Peter, b. 1957, Denmark. Writer. 2 daughters. Appointments: Former Drama Teacher and Sailor; Writer.

Publications: Forestilling om det tyvende arhundrede (novel), 1988, English translation as The History of Danish Dreams, 1995; Fortaellinger om natten, 1990, English translation as Tales of the Snow by Barbara Haveland, 1998; Froken Smillas fornemmelse for sne (novel), 1992, English translation as Miss Smilla's Feeling for Snow by F. David, American translation as Smilla's Sense of Snow by Tiina Nunnally, 1993; De Maske Egnede, 1993, English translation as Borderliners by Barbara Haveland; Kvinden og Aben, 1996, English translation as The Woman and The Ape by Barbara Haveland, 1996. Address: c/o Munksgaard Rosinante, Norre Sogade 35, Postbox 2148, DK-1016 Copenhagen K, Denmark.

HOERR John Peter III, b. 12 Dec 1930, McKeesport, Pennsylvania, USA. Writer. m. Joanne Lillig, 24 Nov 1960, 2 sons. Education: AB, Pennsylvania State University, 1953. Appointments: Reporter, United Press International, 1956-57, 1958-60, The Daily Tribune, Royal Oak, Michigan, 1957-58, Business Week, 1960-63, 1964-69; Reporter and Commentator, WQED-TV, Pittsburgh, 1969-74; Labour Editor, Senior Writer, Business Week, 1975-91. Publications: The Reindustrialization of America (co-author), 1981; And The Wolf Finally Came: The Decline of the American Steel Industry, 1988. Contributions to: Atlantic; American Prospect; Pittsburgh Magazine; Harvard Business Review. Honours: Page One Awards, New York Newspaper Guild, 1985, 1988; Richard A Lester Award, Princeton University, 1988. Memberships: National Writers Union; Industrial Relations Research Association. Address: 12 Parker Lane, Teaneck, NJ 07666, USA.

HOFF Harry Summerfield, (William Cooper), b. 4 Aug 1910, Crewe, England. Novelist. m. Joyce Barbara Harris, 1951, 2 daughters. Education: MA, Christ's College, Cambridge, 1933. Appointments: Assistant Commissioner, Civil Service Commission, 1945-56; Personnel Consultant, UKAEA, 1958-72, CEGB, 1958-72; Commission of European Communities, 1972-73; Assistant Director, Civil Service Selection Board, 1973-76; Member, Board of Crown Agents, 1975-77; Personnel Advisor, Millbank Technical Services, 1975-77; Adjunct Professor, Syracuse University, 1977-90. Publications: Rhea, 1935; Three Marriages, 1946; Scenes From Provincial Life, 1950; The Struggles of Albert Woods, 1952; Young People, 1958; Scenes from Married Life, 1961; Memoirs of a New Man, 1966; Shall We Ever Know?, 1971; Love on the Coast, 1973; Scenes From Metropolitan Life, 1982; Scenes From Later Life, 1983; From Early Life, 1990; Immortality At Any Price, 1991. Memberships: Royal Society of Literature; International PEN. Address: 22 Kenilworth Court, Lower Richmond Road, London SW15 1EW, England.

HOFFMAN Alice, b. 16 Mar 1952, New York, New York, USA. Author; Screenwriter. m. Tom Martin, 2 sons. Education: BA, Adelphi University, 1973; MA, Stanford University, 1975. Publications: Property Of, 1977; The Drowning Season, 1979; Angel Landing, 1980; White Horses, 1982; Fortune's Daughter, 1985; Illumination Night, 1987; At Risk, 1988; Seventh Heaven, 1990; Second Nature, 1993; Here on Earth, 1997. Other: Various screenplays. Contributions to: Redbook; American Review; Playgirl. Address: c/o G P Putnam, 200 Madison Avenue, New York, NY 10016, USA.

HOFFMAN Daniel (Gerard), b. 3 Apr 1923, New York, New York, USA. Professor of English Emeritus; Poet; Writer. m. Elizabeth McFarland, 1948, 2 children. Education: AB, 1947, MA, 1949, PhD, 1956, Columbia University. Appointments: Instructor, Columbia University, 1952-56; Visiting Professor, University of Dijon, 1956-57; Assistant Professor, 1957-60, Associate Professor, 1960-65, Professor of English, 1965-66, Swarthmore College; Fellow, School of Letters, Indiana University, 1959; Elliston Lecturer, University of Cincinnati, 1964; Lecturer, International School of Yeats Studies, Sligo, Ireland, 1965; Professor of English, 1966-83, Poet-in-Residence, 1978-, Felix E Schelling Professor of English, 1983-93, Professor Emeritus, 1993-, University of Pennsylvania; Consultant in Poetry, 1973-74, Honorary

Consultant in American Letters, 1974-77, Library of Congress, Washington, DC; Poet-in-Residence, Cathedral of St John the Divine, New York City, 1988-; Visiting Professor of English, King's College, London, 1991-92. Publications: Poetry: An Armada of Thirty Whales, 1954; A Little Geste and Other Poems, 1960; The City of Satisfactions, 1963; Striking the Stones, 1968; Broken Laws, 1970; Corgi Modern Poets in Focus 4 (with others), 1971; The Center of Attention, 1974; Able Was I Ere I Saw Elba: Selected Poems 1954-1974, 1977; Brotherly Love, 1981; Hang-Gliding from Helicon: New and Selected Poems 1948-1988, 1988; Middens of the Tribe, 1995. Other: Paul Bunyan: Last of the Frontier Demigods, 1952; The Poetry of Stephen Crane, 1957; Form and Fable in American Fiction, 1961; Barbarous Knowledge: Myth in the Poetry of Yeats, Graves and Muir, 1967; Poe Poe Poe Poe Poe Poe Poe, 1972. Others: Shock Troops of Stylistic Change, 1975; "Moonlight Dries No Mittens": Carl Sandburg Reconsidered, 1979; Faulkner's Country Matters: Folklore and Fable in Yoknapatawpha, 1989; Words to Create a World: Interviews, Essays and Reviews of Contemporary Poetry, 1993. Editor: American Poetry and Poetics: Poems and Critical Documents from the Puritans to Robert Frost, 1962; English Literary Criticism: Romantic and Victorian (with Samuel Hynes), 1966; Harvard Guide to Contemporary American Writing, 1979; Ezra Pound and William Carlos Williams: The University of Pennsylvania Conference Papers, 1983. Honours: Yale Series of Younger Poets Award, 1954; Ansley Prize, 1957; American Council of Learned Societies Fellowships, 1961-62, 1966-67; Columbia University Medal for Excellence, 1964; American Academy of Arts and Letters Grant, 1967; Ingram Merrill Foundation Grant, 1971; National Endowment for the Humanities Fellowship, 1975-76; Hungarian PEN Medal, 1980; Guggenheim Fellowship, 1983; Hazlett Memorial Award, 1984; Paterson Poetry Prize, 1989. Membership: Academy of American Poets, Chancellor 1973-97, Chancellor Emeritus 1997-. Address: c/o Department of English, University of Pennsylvania, Philadelphia, PA 19104, USA.

HOFFMAN Eva Alfreda, b. 1 July 1945, Cracow, Poland. Writer. Appointment: Editor, The New York Times Book Review, 1987-90. Publications: Lost in Translation: A Life in a New Language, 1989; Exit Into History: A Journey Through the New Eastern Europe, 1993. Contributions to: Newspapers and periodicals. Honours: American Academy of Arts and Letters Award, 1990; Whiting Award, 1992; Guggenheim Fellowship, 1993. Memberships: PEN; New York University Institute for the Humanities. Address: c/o Georges Barchardt, 136 East 57th Street, New York, NY 10022, USA.

HOFFMAN Mary Margaret Lassiter, b. 20 Apr 1945, Eastleigh, Hampshire, England. Writer; Journalist. m. Stephen James Barber, 22 Dec 1972, 3 daughters. Education: BA, 1967, MA, 1973, Newnham College, Cambridge; University College, London, 1970. Publications: 60 Children's Books including, My Grandma Has Black Hair, 1989; Amazing Grace, 1991; Henry's Baby, 1993; Grace and Family, 1995; Song of the Earth, 1995; An Angel Just Like Me, 1997; Sun, Moon and Stars, 1998. Contributions to: Daily Telegraph; Guardian; Independent; Sunday Times; Specialist Children's Book Press. Honour: Waldenbooks Best Children's Book Honor Award, 1991; Primary English Award, 1995; Honorary Fellow of the Library Association, 1998. Membership: Society of Authors. Address: c/o Rogers, Coleridge & White, 20 Powis Mews, London W11 1JN, England.

HOFFMAN Valerie Jon, b. 27 Apr 1954, NY, USA. Associate Professor of Islamic Studies. m. (1) Steven Ladd, 26 May 1984, div 21 Mar 1995, (2) Dr Kirk Hauser, 10 Jan 1998, 1 son, 2 daughter. Education: BA, University of Pennsylvania (Anthropology), 1975; MA, 1979, PhD, 1986, University of Chicago (Arabic & Islamic Studies). Appointments: Visiting Lecturer, Ecole des Hautes en Scis Sociales, Paris, 1993; Associate Professor, 1994-; Assistant Professor 1986-94; Lecturer, 1983-86. Publications: Sufica, Mystics and Saints in Modern Egypt, 1995; Polemics on the Modesty and

Segregation of Women in Contemporary Egypt, 1987; Mysticism and Sexuality in Sufi Thought and Life, 1992; Devotion to the Prophet and His Family in Egyptian Sufism, 1992; Eating and Fasting for God in Sufi Tradition, 1995. Honour: Fulbright, 1987-88; NEH, 1991-92; University Scholar, 1996. Memberships: Middle East Studies Association of North America, Board of Directors, 1995-98; American Academy of Religion, Islam Sect Steering Committee, Editl Bd of JAAR; Assn of Middle E Women in Studies. Address: Program for the Study of Religion, University of Illinois, 3014 FLB, 70715 Mathews Ave, Urbana, IL 61801, USA.

HOFFMAN William, b. 12 Apr 1939, New York, New York, USA. Writer. Education: BA, City College of the City University of New York. Publications: As Is, 1985; The Ghosts of Versailles (libretto for opera by John Corigliano), 1991. Editor: New American Plays 2, 3, 4, 1968, 1970, 1971; Gay Plays, 1977. Contributions to: Journals and magazines. Honours: Drama Desk Award, 1985; Obie, 1985; International Classical Music Award, 1991; Emmy, 1992; WGA Award, 1992; Erwin Piscator, 1994. Memberships: American Society of Composers, Authors, and Publishers; Dramatists Guild; PEN; Writers Guild of America. Address: c/o International Creative Management, 40 West 57th Street, New York, NY 10019, USA.

HOFFMANN Donald, b. 24 June 1933, Springfield, Illinois, USA. Architectural Critic; Historian. m. Theresa McGrath, 12 Apr 1958, 4 sons, 1 daughter. Education: University of Chicago, University of Kansas City. Appointments: General Assignment Reporter, 1956-65, Art Critic, 1965-90, Kansas City Star; Assistant Editor, Journal of the Society of Architectural Historians, 1970-72. Publications: The Meanings of Architecture: Buildings and Writings by John Wellborn Root (editor), 1967; The Architecture of John Wellborn Root, 1973; Frank Lloyd Wright's Fallingwater, 1978, 2nd edition, 1993; Frank Lloyd Wright's Robie House, 1984; Frank Lloyd Wright: Architecture and Nature, 1986; Frank Lloyd Wright's Hollyhock House, 1992; Understanding Frank Lloyd Wright's Architecture, 1995; Frank Lloyd Wright's Dana House, 1996; Frank Lloyd Wright, Louis Sullivan and the Skyscraper, 1998. Honours: National Endowment for the Humanities Fellowship, 1970-71; National Endowment for the Arts Fellowship, 1974; Graham Foundation Grant, 1981. Membership: The Art Institute of Chicago, life member. Address: 6441 Holmes Street, Kansas City, MO 64131-1110, USA.

HOFMAN David, b. 26 Sept 1908, Poona, India. Author; Editor; Publisher. 1 son, 1 daughter. Appointments: Editor, New World Order, 1937-39, The Baha'i World, 1963-88; Founder, George Ronald Publishers, 1984. Publications: The Renewal of Civilization, 1946; A Commentary on the Will and Testament of Abdul Baha, 1950; George Townshend, 1983; Baha u'i llah: The Prince of Peace, a Portrait, 1992. Membership: Publishers Association. Address: 28 Kirk Close, North Oxford OX2 8JN, England.

HOFMANN Michael, b. 25 Aug 1957, Freiburg, Germany. Poet; Dramatist; Translator. Education: BA, Magdalene College, Cambridge, 1979. Appointments: Visiting Associate Professor, Creative Writing Department, University of Michigan, Ann Arbor, 1994; Visiting Distinguished Lecturer, University of Florida, Gainesville, 1994-. Publications: Nights in the Iron Hotel, 1983; Acrimony, 1986; K S in Lakeland: New and Selected Poems, 1990; Corona, Corona, 1993; After Ovid: New Metamorphoses (co-editor with James Lasdun), 1994; Penguin Modern Poets 13, 1998; Approximately Nowhere, forthcoming. Plays: The Double Bass (adaptation of a play by Patrick Suskind), 1987; The Good Person of Sichuan (adaptation of a play by Brecht), 1989. Other: Translations. Contributions to: The London Review of Books; The Times Literary Supplement; The Times, poetry critic. Honours: Cholmondeley Award, 1984; Geoffrey Faber Memorial Prize, 1988; Schlegel Tieck Prize, 1988, 1992; Arts Council Writers Bursary, 1997. Address: c/o Faber and Faber, 3 Queen Square, London WC1N 3AU, England.

HOFSTADTER Douglas R(ichard), b. 15 Feb 1945, New York, New York, USA. Professor of Computer Science and Cognitive Science; Writer. m. Carol Ann Brush, 1985, dec 1993, 1 son, 1 daughter. Education: BS in Mathematics, Stanford University, 1965; MS in Physics, 1972, PhD in Physics, 1975, University of Oregon. Appointments: Visiting Scholar, Stanford University, 1975-77, 1980-81, 1997; Assistant Professor of Computer Science, 1977-80, Associate Professor of Computer Science, 1980-83, College Professor of Computer Science and Cognitive Science, and Director, Center for Research on Concepts and Cognition, 1988-, Indiana University; Visiting Scientist, Massachusetts Institute of Technology, 1983-84, Istituto per la Ricerca Scientifica e Technologica, Povo, Trento, 1993-94; Walgreen Professor for the Study of Human Understanding and Professor of Psychology and Cognitive Science, University of Michigan, 1984-88. Publications: Gödel, Escher, Bach: an Eternal Golden Braid, 1979; The Mind's I: Fantasies and Reflections on Self and Soul (editor with Daniel C Dennett), 1981; Metamagical Themas: Questing for the Essence of Mind and Pattern, 1985; Ambigrammi: Un microcosmo ideale per lo studio della creativita, 1987; Fluid Concepts and Creative Analogies: Computer Models of the Fundamental Mechanisms of Thought, 1995; Rhapsody on a Theme by Clément Marot, 1996; Le Ton beau de Marot: In Praise of the Music of Language, 1997. Contributions to: Scholarly books and journals. Honours: Pulitzer Prize for General Non-Fiction, 1980; American Book Award, 1980; Guggenheim Fellowship, 1980-81; Senior Fellow, Michigan Society of Fellows, 1985; Arts and Sciences Alumni Fellows Award, University of Oregon, 1997. Memberships: American Association for Artificial Intelligence; Committee for the Scientific Investigation of Claims of the Paranormal; Cognitive Science Society; Golden Key National Honor Society. Address: c/o Center for Research on Concepts and Cognition, Indiana University, 510 North Fess Street, Bloomington, IN 47408, USA.

HOGAN Desmond, b. 10 Dec 1950, Ballinasloe, Ireland. Writer; Teacher. Education: BA, 1972, MA, 1973, University College, Dublin. Appointment: Strode Fellow, University of Alabama, 1989. Publications: The Ikon Maker, 1976; The Leaves on Grey, 1980; A Curious Street, 1984; A New Shirt, 1984; A Link with the River, 1989; The Edge of the City, 1993. Honours: John Llewellyn Memorial Prize, 1980; Irish Post Award, 1985; Deutscher Akademischer Austauschdienst Fellowship, Berlin, 1991. Address: Basement, 6 Stanstead Grove, London SE6 4UD, England.

HOGAN James P(atrick), b. 27 June 1941, London, England. Writer. m. (1) Iris Crossley, 1961, div 1977, 3 daughters, (2) Lynda Shirley Dockerty, div 1980, (3) Jackie Price, 1983, 3 sons. Education: Certificates, Royal Aircraft Establishment Technical College, 1963, Reading Technical College, 1965. Publications: Inherit the Stars, 1977; The Genesis Machine, 1978; The Gentle Giants of Ganymede, 1978; The Two Faces of Tomorrow, 1979; Thrice Upon a Time, 1980; Giants' Star, 1981; Voyage from Yesteryear, 1982; Code of the Lifemaker, 1983; The Proteus Operation, 1985; Minds, Machines and Evolution (short stories), 1986; Endgame Enigma, 1987; The Mirror Maze, 1989; The Infinity Gambit, 1991; The multiplex Man, 1992; Entoverse, 1992; Realtime Interrupt, 1995; The Immortality Option, 1995; Paths to Otherwhere, 1996; Bug Park, 1997; Mind Matters, 1998. Contributions to: Anthologies and magazines. Address: 96 Main Street, Bray, County Wicklow, Republic of Ireland.

HOGAN Kathleen Margaret, (Kay Hogan), b. 13 Feb 1935, Bronx, New York, USA. Writer. m. James P Hogan, 4 sons, 1 daughter. Education: High School Graduate, 1952. Publications: The El Train, 1882; The Silent Men, 1984; Widow Women, 1985; Little Green Girl, 1986; Of Saints and Other Things, 1992; The Women Wore Black, 1993. Contributions to: Descant; Long Pond Review; Journal of Irish Literature; North Country Anthology; Catholic Girls Antholgoy; Glens Falls Review. Address: 154 East Avenue, Saratoga Springs, NY 12866, USA.

HOGAN Linda Chickasaw Nation, b. 16 July 1947, Denver, Colorado, USA. Poet: Novelist; Essayist; Professor of English. m. Pat Hogan, div, 2 daughters. Education: MA, University of Colorado at Boulder, 1978. Appointments: Associate, Rocky Mountain Women's Institute, University of Denver, 1979-80; Poet-in-the-Schools, Colorado and Oklahoma, 1980-84; Assistant Professor, Tribes Program, Colorado College, 1982-84; Associate Professor of American and American Indian Studies, University of Minnesota, 1984-89; Professor of English, University of Colorado at Boulder, 1989-. Publications: Poetry: Calling Myself Home, 1979; Eclipse, 1983; Seeing Through the Sun, 1985; Savings, 1988; The Book of Medicines, 1993. Fiction: That Horse, 1985; Mean Spirit, 1990; Solar Storms, 1995; Power, 1998. Other: A Piece of Moon (play), 1981; The Stories We Hold Secret: Tales of Women's Spiritual Development (editor with Carol Bruchac and Judith McDaniel), 1986; Dwellings: A Spiritual History of the Natural World, 1995; Intimate Nature: The Bond Between Women and Animals, 1998. Honours: Guggenheim Fellowship; Lannan Award for Poetry; National Endowment for the Arts Grant; American Book Award, 1986; Oklahoma Book Award for Fiction, 1990; Colorado Book Awards, 1994, 1997. Memberships: Authors Guild; Modern Language Association; National American Studies Program; National Council of Teachers of English; PEN West; Writers Guild. Address: c/o Department of English, University of Colorado at Boulder, Boulder, CO 80302, USA.

HOGAN Robert (Goode), b. 29 May 1930, Boonville, Missouri, USA. Professor of English; Writer. m. (1) Betty Mathews, 1 Dec 1950, div 1978, 2 sons, 3 daughters, (2) Mary Rose Callaghan, 21 Dec 1979. Education: BA, 1953, MA, 1954, PhD, 1956, University of Missouri. Appointments: Publisher, Proscenium Press, 1964-; Professor of English, University of Delaware, 1970-; Editor, Journal of Irish Literature, 1972-, George Spelvin's Theatre Book, 1978-85. Publications: Experiments of Sean O'Casey, 1960; Feathers from the Green Crow, 1962; Drama: The Major Genres (editor with S Molin), 1962; Arthur Miller, 1964; Independence of Elmer Rice, 1965; Joseph Holloway's Abbey Theatre (editor with M J O'Neill), 1967; The Plain Style (with H Bogart), 1967; After the Irish Renaissance, 1967; Seven Irish Plays (editor), 1967; Joseph Holloway's Irish Theatre (editor with M J O'Neill), 3 volumes, 1968-70; Dion Boucicault, 1969; The Fan Club, 1969; Betty and the Beast, 1969; Lost Plays of the Irish Renaissance (with J Kilroy), 1970; Crows of Mephistopheles (editor), 1970; Towards a National Theatre (editor), 1970; Eimar O'Duffy, 1972; Mervyn Wall, 1972; Conor Cruise O'Brien (with E Young-Bruehl), 1974; A History of the Modern Irish Drama, Vol 1, The Irish Literary Theatre (with J Kilroy), 1975, Vol II, Laying the Foundation (with J Kilroy), 1976, Vol III, The Abbey Theatre 1905-09 (with J Kilroy), 1978, Vol IV, The Rise of the Realists, 1910-1915 (with R Burnham and D P Poteet), 1979, Vol V, The Art of the Amateur 1916-1920 (with R Burnham), 1984, Vol VI, The Years of O'Casey (with R Burnham), 1992; The Dictionary of Irish Literature (editor), 1979; Since O'Casey, 1983; The Plays of Frances Sheridan (edited with J C Beasley), 1984; Guarini's The Faithful Shepherd, translated by Thomas Sheridan (edited and completed with E Nickerson), 1990; Murder at the Abbey (with J Douglas), 1993. Address: PO Box 361, Newark, DE 19711, USA.

HOGG James Dalby, b. 9 July 1937, London, England. Writer; Broadcaster. m. Joan Blackledge, 19 Aug 1964, 2 sons. Appointments: Reporter, Bolton Evening News; Reporter, Morning Telegraph, Sheffield; Presenter, Reporter, BBC Television. Publication: Lord Emsworth's Annotated Whiffle. Contributions to: Daily Telegraph; Listener; Country Living; Jazz Express; Jazz Journal. Memberships: Wodehouse Society; Johnson Society. Literary Agent: Peter S Fraser and Dunlop. Address: Noon's Folly Cottage, Noon's Folly, Melbourn, Cambs SG8 7NG, England.

HOGGARD James (Martin), b. 21 June 1941, Whichita Falls, Texas, USA. Professor of English; Poet;

Writer; Translator. m. Lynn Taylor Hoggard, 23 May 1976, 1 son, 1 daughter. Education: BA, Southern Methodist University, 1963; MA, University of Kansas, 1965. Appointments: Teaching Assistant, University of Kansas, 1963-65; Instructor to Professor of English, Midwestern State University, 1966-; Guest Professor, Instituto Allende, San Miguel de Allende, Mexico, 1977, 1978, University of Mosul, Iraq, 1990; Exchange Professor, Instituto Tecnologico de Estudias Superiores de Monterrey, Chihuahua, Mexico, 1993. Publications: Poetry: Eyesigns: Poems on Letters and Numberes, 1977; The Shaper Poems, 1983; Two Gulls, One Hawk, 1983; Breaking an Indelicate Statue, 1986. Fiction: Trotter Ross, 1981; Riding the Wind and Other Tales, 1997. Non-Fiction: Elevator Man, 1983. Contributions to: Anthologies, reviews, quarterlies, journals, and magazines. Honours: Several awards, grants, and citations. Memberships: American Literary Translators Association; American Studies Association of Texas; Conference of College Teachers of English; Texas Institute of Letters, president, 1994-. Address: c/o Department of English, Midwestern State University, Wichita Falls, TX 76308, USA.

HOGGART Richard, b. 24 Sept 1918, Leeds, England. Writer. m. Mary Holt France, 18 July 1942, 2 sons, 1 daughter. Education: BA, 1939, MA 1940, University of Leeds, 1978. Appointments: Senior Lecturer, University of Leicester, 1959-62; Professor of English, Birmingham University, 1962-73; Director, Centre for Contemporary Cultural Studies, 1964-73; Assistant Director General, UNESCO, 1970-75; Warden, Goldsmiths' College, London, 1976-84; Chairman, National Advisory Council for Adult and Continuing Education; Chairman, Book Trust, 1995-97. Publications: Auden, 1951; The Uses of Literacy, 1957; W H Auden, 1957; Teaching Literature, 1963; Speaking to Each Other, 2 volumes, 1970; Only Connect (Reith Lectures), 1972; An Idea and Its Servants, 1978; An English Temper, 1982; An Idea of Europe (co-author), 1987; Autobiography, 3 Volumes: A Local Habitation, 1988, A Sort of Clowning, 1990, An Imagined Life, 1992; Townscape with Figures, 1994; The Way We Live Now, 1995. Honours: Honorary Doctorates from Universities in France, Canada and England. Address: Mortonsfield, Beavers Hill, Farnham, Surrey GU9 7DF, England.

HOGGART Simon David, b. 26 May 1946, Ashton, England. Journalist. m. Alyson Corner, 9 July 1983, 1 son, 1 daughter. Education: Kings College, Cambridge, England; MA, 1965-68. Appointments: N Ireland Correspondent, 1971-73, Pariamentary Sketch Writer, 1993-, The Guardian, 1971-73; Political Correspondent, 1973-81; Feature Writer, The Observer, 1981-85; US Correspondent, The Observer, 1985-89. Publications: The Pact, with Alastair Michie, 1977; Michael Foot, with David Leigh; On the House, 1981; Back on the House, 1982; House of Ill Fame, 1985; House of Cards, 1988; America - A User's Guide, 1990; Punch, House of Correction, 1994; Bizarre Beliefs, with Michael Hutchinson, 1996; Live Briefs, with Steve Bell, 1996. Contributions to: The Spectator; New York Times; Times Literary Supplement; LRB. Honours: Granada Political Writer of the Year, 1985; BPA Resident for Correspondence, 1987. Literary Agent: Curtis Brown, London SW1Y 4SP, England. Address: The Guardian, 119 Farringdon Road, London EC1R 3ER, England.

HOGNAS Kurt Carl Alexander, b. 2 Feb 1931, Jakobstad, Finland. Writer. m. Siv Gunnel, 30 Dec 1956, 4 sons. Education: BA, 1955, MA, 1960, University of Helsinki, 1960. Publications: Glashus, 1972; Överskridningar, 1978; Italiensk Svit (prose poems), 1979; En handfull Ljus, 1981; Nattens lökar, 1985; Tunnelbana, 1987; Monvass, 1992; Röster fran en gräns, 1995.Contributions to: Vasabladet; Hufvudstadsbladet; Horisont; Café Existens. Honours: Prizes, Svenska Litteratursällskapet, 1983, 1995, Svenska Akademin, 1988. Membership: Finland's Svenska Författarförening. Literary Agent: Söderströms Förlag, Helsinki, Finland. Address: Sibeliusgatan 3, 67100 Kristinestad, Finland.

HOGWOOD Christopher (Jarvis Haley), b. 10 Sept 1941, Nottingham, England. Harpischordist; Conductor; Musicologist; Writer; Editor; Broadcaster. Education: BA, Pembroke College, Cambridge, 1964; Charles University, Prague; Academy of Music, Prague. Appointments: Founder-Member, Early Music Consort of London, 1967-76; Founder-Director, The Academy of Ancient Music, 1973-; Faculty, Cambridge University, 1975-; Artistic Director, Handel and Haydn Society, Boston, 1986-; Honorary Professor of Music, University of Keele, 1986-89; Music Director, 1988-92, Principal Guest Conductor, 1992-98, St Paul Chamber Orchestra, Minnesota; International Professor of Early Music Performance, Royal Academy of Music, London, 1992-96; Visiting Professor, King's College, London, 1992-. Publications: Music at Court, 1977; The Trio Sonata, 1979; Haydn's Visits to England, 1980; Music in Eighteenth-Century England (editor), 1983; Handel, 1984; Holme's Life of Mozart (editor), 1991. Contributions to: The New Grove Dictionary of Music and Musicians, 1980. Honours: Walter Wilson Cobbett Medal, 1986; Commander of the Order of the British Empire, 1989; Honorary Fellow, Jesus College, Cambridge, 1989, Pembroke College, Cambridge, 1992; Freeman, Worshipful Company of Musicians, 1989; Incorporated Society of Musicians Distinguished Musician Award, 1997. Membership: Royal Society of Authors, fellow. Address: 10 Brookside, Cambridge CB2 1JE, England.

HOLBROOK David (Kenneth), b. 9 Jan 1923, Norwich, England. Author. m. 23 Apr 1949, 2 sons, 2 daughters. Education: BA, Honours, English, 1946, MA, 1951, Downing College, Cambridge. Appointments: Fellow, King's College, Cambridge, 1961-65; Senior Leverhulme Research Fellow, 1965, Leverhulme Emeritus Research Fellow, 1988-90; Writer-in-Residence, Dartington Hall, 1972-73; Fellow and Director of English Studies, 1981-88, Emeritus Fellow, 1988, Downing College; Publications: English for Maturity, 1961; Imaginings, 1961; Against the Cruel Frost, 1963; English for the Rejected, 1964; The Secret Places, 1964; Flesh Wounds, 1966; Children's Writing, 1967; The Exploring Word, 1967; Object Relations, 1967; Old World New World, 1969; English in Australia Now, 1972; Chance of a Lifetime, 1978; A Play of Passion, 1978; English for Meaning, 1980; Selected Poems, 1980; Nothing Larger than Life, 1987; The Novel and Authenticity, 1987; A Little Athens, 1990; Edith Wharton and the Unsatisfactory Man, 1991; Jennifer, 1991; The Gold in Father's Heart, 1992; Where D H Lawrence Was Wrong About Women, 1992; Creativity and Popular Culture, 1994; Even If They Fail, 1994; Tolstoy, Women and Death, 1996; Wuthering Heights: a Drama of Being, 1997; Getting it Wrong with Uncle Tom, 1998; More Selected Poems, 1999. Contributions to: Numerous professional journals. Honour: Festschrift, 1996. Membership: Society of Authors. Address: Denmore Lodge, Brunswick Gardens, Cambridge CB6 8DQ, England.

HOLDEN Anthony (Ivan), b. 22 May 1947, Southport, England. Journalist; Author. m. (1) Amanda Warren, 1971, div 1988; (2) Cynthia Blake, 1990. Education: MA, Merton College, Oxford, 1970. Appointments: Correspondent, Sunday Times, 1973-77; Columnist (Atticus), 1977-79, Chief US Correspondent, 1979-81, The Observer; Features Editor and Assistant Editor, The Times, 1981-82; Freelance journalist and author; Broadcaster on radio and television. Publications: Agememnon of Aeschylus, 1969; The Greek Anthology, 1973; The St Albans Poisoner, 1974; Charles, Prince of Wales, 1979; Their Royal Highnesses, 1981; Of Presidents, Prime Ministers and Princes, 1984; The Queen Mother, 1985; Charles, 1988; Olivier, 1988; Big Deal, 1990; The Last Paragraph (editor), 1990; A Princely Marriage, 1991; The Oscars, 1993; The Tarnished Crown, 1993; Power and the Throne (contributor), 1994; Tchaikovsky, 1995. Honour: Columnist of the Year, British Press Awards, 1977. Address: c/o Rogers, Coleridge and White, 20 Powis Mews, London W11 1JN, England.

HOLDEN Joan, b. 18 Jan 1939, Berkeley, California, USA. Dramatist. m. 1) Arthur Holden, 1958, div, 2) Daniel Chumley, 1968, 3 daughters. Education: BA, Reed College, Portland, Oregon, 1960; MA, University of California at Berkeley, 1964. Appointments: Editor, Pacific News Service, 1973-75; Instructor in Playwriting, University of California at Davis, 1975, 1977, 1979, 1983, 1985, 1987. Publications: Americans, or, Last Tango in Huahuatenango (with Daniel Chumley), 1981; Factwindo Meets the Moral Majority (with others), 1981; Factwino vs Armaggedonman, 1982; Steeltown, 1984; Spain/36, 1986; The Mozangola Caper (with others), 1986; Seeing Double, 1989; Back to Normal, 1990; Offshore, 1993. Honours: Obie Awards, 1973, 1990; Rockefeller Foundation Grant, 1985; Edward G Robbins Playwriting Award, 1992. Address: c/o San Francisco Mime Troupe, 855 Treat Street, San Francisco, CA 94110, USA.

HOLDSTOCK Pauline Jane, b. Gravesend, England. Writer; Novelist. Education: BA, London University, 1969; Postgraduate Teacher's Certificate, Goldsmiths' College, 1970. Appointment: Teacher, England, Bahamas, Canada, 1970-79. Publications: The Blackbird's Song, 1987; The Burial Ground, 1990; House, 1994; Swimming From the Flames, 1995; The Turning, 1996. Contributions to: True North Down Under; Snapshots; New Canadian Fiction; Ambit; Iron; Critical Quarterly; This Magazine; Flare; Exile; Rampike. Honours: Finalist, Books in Canada/W H Smith Best First Novel Award, 1988. Memberships: Writers' Union of Canada; Federation of British Columbia Writers. Address: 24 Ryerson Avenue, Toronto, Ontario M5T 2P3, Canada.

HOLDSTOCK Robert, b. 2 Aug 1948, Hythe, Kent, England. Writer. Education: BSc, University College of North Wales, 1970; MSc, London School of Hygiene and Tropical Medicine, 1971. Publications: Eye Among the Blind, 1976; Earthwind, 1977; Octopus Encyclopaedia of Science Fiction, 1978; Stars of Albion, 1979; Alien Landscapes, 1979; Tour of the Universe, 1980; Where Time Winds Blow, 1981; Mythago Wood, Emerald Forest, 1985; The Labyrinth, 1987; Other Edens, 1987; Lavondyss, 1988; The Fetch, 1991; The Bone Forest, 1992; The Hollowing, 1993; Merlin's Wood, 1994; Gate of Ivory, Gate of Horn, 1997. Honours: World Fantasy Awards, 1985, 1993. Address: 54 Raleigh Road, London N8, England.

HOLINGER Richard, b. 20 Mar 1949, Chicago, Illinois, USA. Teacher. m. Tia Rush, 16 June 1979, 1 son, 1 daughter. Education: BA, Hartwick College, 1971; MA, Washington University, 1975; PhD, University of Illinois at Chicago, 1993. Appointment: Marmion Academy, 1979-. Contributions to: Boulevard; Chelsea; Iowa Review; Southern Review; Witness; ACM; Oasis. Honour: Illinois Arts Council Artists Grant for Poetry. Address: c/o Marmion Academy, 1000 Butterfield Road, Aurora, IL 60504, USA.

HOLLAND Cecelia (Anastasia), b. 31 Dec 1943, Henderson, Nevada, USA. Author. Education: Pennsylvania State University; BA, Connecticut College, 1965. Publications: The Firedrake, 1966; Rakosy, 1967; Kings in Winter, 1968; Until the Sun Falls, 1969; Ghost on the Steppe, 1969; The King's Road, 1970; Cold Iron, 1970; Antichrist, 1970; Wonder of the World, 1970; The Earl, 1971; The Death of Attila, 1973; The Great Maria, 1975; Floating Worlds, 1976; Two Ravens, 1977; The Earl, 1979; Home Ground, 1981; The Sea Beggars, 1982; The Belt of Gold, 1984; Pillar of the Sky, 1985; The Bear Flag, 1992; Jerusalem, 1996. Honour: Guggenheim Fellowship, 1981-82. Address: c/o Alfred A Knopf, 201 East 50th Street, New York, NY 10022, USA.

HOLLAND Isabelle, (Francesca Hunt), b. 16 June 1920, Basel, Switzerland (US citizen). Writer. Education: University of Liverpool; BA, Tulane University, 1942. Appointments: Publicity Director, Crown Publishers, New York City, 1956-60, J B Lippincott Co, New York City, 1960-66, G P Putnam's Sons, New York City, 1968-69; Assistant to the Publisher, Harper's, New York City, 1967-68. Publications: Kilgaren, 1974; Trelawny, 1974; Moncrieff, 1975; Darcourt, 1976; Grenelle, 1976; The deMaury Papers, 1977; Tower Abbey, 1978; The Marchington Papers, 1980; Counterpoint, 1980; The Lost

Madonna, 1981; A Death at St Anselm's, 1984; Flight of the Archangel, 1985; A Lover Scorned, 1986; Bump in the Night, 1988; A Fatal Advent, 1989; The Long Search, 1990; Love and Inheritance, 1991; Family Trust, 1994. Other: About 35 books for children and young adults, 1967-96. Honour: Ott Award, Church and Synagogue Library Association, 1983. Memberships: Authors Guild; Authors League of America; PEN. Address: c/o JCA Literary Agency, 27W 20th St, Suite 1103, New York, New York 10011, USA.

HOLLAND Margaret Ann, b. 28 July 1956, Wimbledon, London, England. Legal Secretary. Education: Holy Family Convent, Tooting. Appointments: Legal Secretary, Family Practice of Solicitors in Croydon, Surrey. Publications: Growing Hope, anthology, 1995; And God Created Woman, anthology, 1996; The Lighter Side, anthology, 1996; Christian Poetry Companion, anthology, 1996; What A Wonderful World, anthology, 1996; Triumph House Poets of 1996, anthology, 1996; Along The Way, anthology, 1998.

HOLLAND Norman N(orwood), b. 29 Sept 1927, New York, New York, USA. Scholar; Writer. m. Jane Kelley, 17 Dec 1954, 1 son, 1 daughter. Education: BS, Massachusetts Institute of Technology, 1947; LLB, 1950, PhD, 1956, Harvard University. Appointments: Instructor to Associate Professor, Massachusetts Institute of Technlogy, 1955-66; McNulty Professor of English, State University of New York at Buffalo, 1966-83; Associate Professor, University of Paris, 1971-72, 1985; Marston-Milbauer Eminent Scholar, University of Florida at Gainesville, 1983-. Publications: The First Modern Comedies, 1959, 2nd edition, 1967; The Shakespearean Imagination, 1964, 2nd edition, 1968; Psychoanalysis and Shakespeare, 1966, 2nd edition, 1975; The Dynamics of Literary Response, 1968, 2nd edition, 1989; Poems in Persons: An Introduction to the Psychoanalysis of Literature, 1973; 5 Readers Reading, 1975; Laughing: A Psychology of Humor, 1982; The I, 1985; The Brain of Robert Frost: A Cognitive Approach to Literature, 1988; Holland's Guide to Psychoanalytic Psychology and Literature-and-Psychology, 1990; The Critical I, 1992; Death in a Delphi Seminar, 1995. Honours: American Council of Learned Societies Fellow, 1974-75; Guggenheim Fellowship, 1979-80. Memberships: American Academy of Psychoanalysis; Boston Psychoanalytic Society; Modern Language Association. Address: c/o Department of English, University of Florida at Gainesville, Gainesville, FL 32611, USA.

HOLLANDER John, b. 28 Oct 1929, New York, New York, USA. Professor of English; Poet; Critic; Editor. m. (1) Anne Loesser, 15 June 1953, div, 2 daughters, (2) Natalie Charkow, 17 Dec 1982. Education: AB, 1950, MA, 1952, Columbia University; PhD, Indiana University, 1959. Appointments: Junior Fellow, Society of Fellows, Harvard University, 1954-57; Lecturer, Connecticut College, 1957-59; Poetry Editor, Partisan Review, 1959-65; Instructor to Associate Professor, 1959-66, Professor of English, 1977-86, A Bartlett Giametti Professor of English, 1986-95, Sterling Professor of English, 1995-, Yale University; Christian Gauss Seminarian, Princeton University, 1962; Visiting Professor, 1964, Patten Lecturer, 1986, Fellow, Institute for Advanced Study, 1986, Indiana University; Faculty, Salzburg Seminar in American Studies, 1965; Professor of English, Hunter College and the Graduate Center of the City University of New York, 1966-77; Overseas Fellow, Churchill College, Cambridge, 1967-68; Elliston Professor of Poetry, University of Cincinnati, 1969; Resident Guest Writer, City of Jerusalem, 1980; Phi Beta Kappa Lecturer, 1981-82; Glasgow Lecturer, Washington and Lee University, 1984. Publications: Poetry: A Crackling of Thorns, 1958; Movie-Going and Other Poems, 1962; Visions from the Ramble, 1965; Types of Shape, 1968, expanded edition, 1991; The Night Mirror, 1971; Town and Country Matters, 1972; Selected Poems, 1972; Tales Told of the Fathers, 1975; Reflections on Espionage, 1976; Spectral Emanations: New and Selected Poems, 1978; Blue Wine, 1979; Flowers of Thirteen, 1983; In Time and Place, 1986; Harp Lake, 1988; Selected Poetry, 1993; Tesserae, 1993. Criticism:

The Untuning of the Sky, 1960; Images of Voice, 1970; Vision and Resonance, 1975, 2nd edition, 1985; The Figure of Echo, 1981; Rhyme's Reason, 1981, 2nd edition, revised and expanded, 1989; Melodious Guile, 1988; William Bailey, 1990; The Gazer's Spirit, 1995; The Work of Poetry, 1997; The Poetry of Everyday Life, 1998; Figurehen, 1999. Editor: The Wind and the Rain (with Harold Bloom), 1961; Jiggery-Pokery (with Anthony Hecht), 1966, 2nd edition, 1984; Poems of Our Moment, 1968; Modern Poetry: Essays in Criticism, 1968; American Short Stories Since 1945, 1968; The Oxford Anthology of English Literature (with Frank Kermode, Harold Bloom, J B Trapp, Martin Price and Lionel Trilling), 1973; I A Richards: Essays in His Honor (with R A Brower and Helen Vendler), 1973; Literature as Experience (with David Bromwich and Irving Howe), 1979; The Poetics of Influence (selected essays of Harold Bloom), 1988; The Essential Rossetti (selected poetry of Dante Gabriel Rossetti), 1990; Nineteenth-Century American Poetry, 2 volumes, 1993; Animal Poems, 1994; Garden Poems, 1996; Committed to Memory, 1997. Other: The Death of Moses (libretto for Alexander Goehr's opera), 1992. Honours: Poetry Chapbook Award, 1962; Melville Cane Award, 1990, Poetry Society of America; National Institute of Arts and Letters Award, 1963; National Endowment for the Humanities Senior Fellowship, 1973-74; Levinson Prize, 1974; Washington Monthly Prize, 1976; Guggenheim Fellowship, 1979-80; Mina P Shaughnessy Award, Modern Language Association, 1982; Bollingen Prize, 1983; Shenandoah Prize, 1985; John D and Catharine T MacArthur Foundation Fellowship, 1990-95; Robert Penn Warren-Cleanth Brooks Award, 1998. Memberships: Academy of American Poets; American Academy of Arts and Letters; American Academy of Arts and Sciences, fellow. Address: c/o Department of English, Yale University, PO Box 208302, New Haven, CT 06520, USA.

HOLLANDER Paul, b. 3 Oct 1932, Budapest, Hungary (US citizen, 1968). Professor of Sociology; Writer. m. Mina Harrison, 26 June 1977, 1 daughter. Education: BA, Sociology, London School of Economics and Political Science, 1959; MA, Sociology, University of Illinois, 1960; PhD, Sociology, Princeton University, 1963. Appointments: Assistant Professor, 1963-68, Research Fellow, Associate, Russian Research Center, 1963-, Harvard University; Associate Professor, 1968-73, Professor of Sociology, 1973-, University of Massachusetts at Amherst. Publications: American and Soviet Society: A Reader in Comparative Sociology and Perception (editor), 1969; Soviet and American Society: A Comparison, 1973, 2nd editon, 1978; Political Pilgrims: Travels of Western Intellectuals to the Soviet Union, China and Cuba 1928-1978, 1981, 1983, 1990, 1997; The Many Faces of Socialism, 1983, 2nd edition, 1990; The Survival of the Adversary Culture, 1988; Decline and Discontent: Communism and the West Today, 1992; Anti-Americans: Critiques at Home and Abroad 1965-1990, 1992; Anti-Americanism: Irrational and Rational, 1995; Political Power and Personal Belief: The Loss of Will in the Fall of Soviet Communism, forthcoming. Contributions to: Scholarly and general publications. Honours: Guggenheim Fellowship, 1974-75; Scholar-in-Residence, Rockefeller Study and Conference Center, Bellagio, Italy, 1984; Visiting Scholar, Hoover Institution, 1985, 1986, 1993. Membership: National Association of Scholars. Address: 35 Vernon Street, Northampton, MA 01060, USA.

HOLLANDS Roy Derrick, b. 20 July 1924, Canterbury, Kent, England. Mathematics; Writer. m. Sarah Carroll, 14 Apr 1945, 1 daughter. Education: BSc, Southampton University, 1951; Certificate in Education, 1952; Advanced Certificate in Education, 1969; MA, Exeter University, 1969; MSc, Newcastle University, 1980; PhD (Educ), 1998. Appointments: Adviser to Longman, Ginn, Blackwell, MacMillan, and others, 1969-. Publications: SMP 7-13, 1973; Headway Maths, 1979; Ginn Mathematics, 1983; Let's Solve Problems, 1986; National Curriculum Ginn Mathematics, 1995. Other: Author or co-author of over 200 books. Contributions to: Articles and reviews in many journals. Honours: Fellow, College of Preceptors, 1979; Mensa Chess Champion,

1992. Membership: Society of Authors Educational Writers Group, past chairman. Address: Flat 62, Berkeley Court, Wilmington Square, Eastbourne, East Sussex BN21 4DX, England.

HOLLAR David Wason, b. 17 July 1960, Yadkinville, North Carolina, USA. Biologist; Educator. m. Virginia Paige Dean, 28 Nov 1992, 1 daughter. Education: BS, Biology, University of North Carolina at Chapel Hill, 1982; MS, Molecular Biology, Vanderbilt University, 1984; PhD Dissertation in Progress, University of North Carolina, Greensboro, 1997. Publication: The Origin and Evolution of Life on Earth, 1992. Membership: American Educational Research Association. Address: 911 South Elm Street, Eden, NC 27288, USA.

HOLLES Robert Owen, b. 11 Oct 1926, London, England. Author; Playwright. m. Philippa Elmer, 12 July 1952, 2 sons, 1 daughter. Appointment: Artist-in-Residence, Central State University of Oklahoma, 1981-82. Publications: Now Thrive the Armourers, 1952; The Bribe Scorners, 1956; Captain Cat, 1960; The Siege of Battersea, 1962; Religion and Davey Peach, 1962; The Nature of the Beast, 1965; Spawn, 1978; I'll Walk Beside You, 1979; Sunblight, 1981; The Guide to Real Village Cricket, 1983; The Guide to Real Subversive Soldiering, 1985. Other: 30 plays in television series. Contributions to: Magazines and journals. Honour: Best Novel of the Year Citation, Time magazine, 1960. Address: Crown Cottage, 14 Crown Street, Castle Hedingham, Essex, England.

HOLLEY Irving Brinton Jr, b. 8 Feb 1919, Hartford, Connecticut, USA. Historian. m. Janet Carlson, 9 Oct 1945, 3 daughters. Education: BA, Amherst College. 1940; MA, 1942, PhD, 1947, Yale University. Publications: Ideas and Weapons, 1953, 4th edition, 1997; Buying Aircraft, 1964, new edition, 1989; General John M Palmer, Citizen Soldiers and the Army of a Democracy, 1982. Contributions to: Aerospace Historian; Military Review; Technology and Culture; Defense Analysis; Air Force Journal of Logistics. Honours: US Airforce Distinguished Service Medal, Legion of Merit; Civilian Service Medal, US Army and US Airforce. Memberships: American Historical Society; Society for the History of Technology; Society for Military History. Address: 2701 Pickett Road, Apt 3028, Durham, NC 27705, USA.

HOLLINGDALE Reginald John, b. 20 Oct 1930, London, England. Writer. Appointment: Sub Editor, The Guardian Newspaper, 1968-91. Publications: Thus Spoke Zarathustra, 1961; One Summer on Majorca, 1961; The Voyage to Africa, 1964; Nietzsche: The Man and His Philosophy, 1965; revised edition, 1999; Western Philosophy: An Introduction, 1966, 2nd edition, 1979; Essays and Aphorisms of Schopenhauer, 1970; Thomas Mann, 1971; A Nietzsche Reader, 1977; Aphorisms of Lichtenberg, 1990. Other: Editions of Nietzsche's Writings. Contributions to: Three Essays by Wolfgang Müller-Lauter, 1993; Nietzsche: A Critical Reader, 1995; The Cambridge Companion to Nietzsche, 1996. Honour: Visiting Fellow, Trinity College, Melbourne, 1991. Memberships: Nietzsche Society, honorary president; National Union of Journalists. Address: 32 Warrington Crescent, London W9 1EL, England.

HOLLINGHURST Alan, b. 26 May 1954, Stroud, Gloucestershire, England. Novelist. Education: BA, 1975, MLitt, 1979, Magdalen College, Oxford. Appointments: Assistant Editor, 1982-84, Deputy Editor, 1985-90, Poetry Editor, 1991-95, Times Literary Supplement, London. Publications: Novels: The Swimming-Pool Library, 1988; The Folding Star, 1994; The Spell, 1998. Poetry: Confidential Chats with Boys, 1982. Translator: Bajazet, by Jean Racine, 1991. Honours: Somerset Maugham Award, 1988, E.M. Forster Award of the American Academy of Arts and Letters, 1990; James Taite Black Award, 1995. Memberships: Fellow, The Royal Society of Literature. Literary Agent: Aitken & Stone. Address: c/o Aitken & Stone, 29 Fernshaw Road, London SW10 OTG.

HOLLINGSHEAD Greg(ory Albert Frank), b. 25 Feb 1947, Toronto, Ontario, Canada. Professor of English; Writer. m. Rosa Spricer, 1 son. Education: BA, 1968, MA, 1970, University of Toronto; PhD, University of London, 1974. Appointments: Assistant Professor, 1975-81, Associate Professor, 1981-93, Professor of English, 1993-, University of Alberta. Publications: Famous Players, 1982; White Buick, 1992; Spin Dry, 1992; The Roaring Girl, 1995; The Healer, 1998. Honours: George Bugnet Award for Excellence in the Novel, 1993; Howard O'Hagan Award for Excellence in Short Fiction, 1993-96; Governor General's Award for Fiction, 1995. Memberships: PEN Canada; Writers Guild of Alberta; Writers' Union of Canada. Address: c/o Department of English, University of Alberta, Edmonton, Alberta T6G 2E5, Canada.

HOLLINS Amy, b. Birkenhead, Merseyside, England. Poet; Novelist. m. T H B Hollins, 2 sons, 2 daughters. Education: BA, Honours, Modern Languages, Diploma in Education, University of Liverpool. Appointment: Assistant Editor, New Poetry. Publications: Axe and Tree, 1973; Many People, Many Voices (co-editor), 1978; partial reprint, 1997; The Quality, 1985; Centrepiece, 1994. Contributions to: International Poets, Madras, special issue, 1997; Many anthologies, other publications, and BBC broadcasts. Memberships: National Poetry Society; Royal Society of Literature; Society of Authors; Women Writers Network. Address: 2 Lidgett Park Avenue, Leeds, West Yorkshire, LS8 1DP, England.

HOLLO Anselm, b. 12 Apr 1934, Helsinki, Finland. Associate Professor of Poetry, Poetics, and Translation; Poet; Writer; Translator; Editor. m. Jane Dalrymple-Hollo. Education: Modern Languages and Literature, University of Helsinki, University of Tübingen. Appointments: Programme Assistant and Producer, BBC European Services, 1958-66; Visiting Professor, State University of New York at Buffalo, 1967, University of Iowa, 1968-73, Bowling Green State University, Ohio, 1971-73, Hobart and William Smith Colleges, Geneva, New York, 1973-75, Southwest Minnesota State College, Marshall, 1977-78; Poetry Editor, Iowa Review, 1971-72, Par Rapport, 1978-80, Baltimore Sun Sunday Magazine, 1983-85; Translation Editor, Seneca Review, 1973-74; Distinguished Visiting Poet, Michigan State University, 1974; Associate Professor of Literature and Creative Writing, University of Maryland, 1975-77; Margaret Bannister Distinguished Writer-in-Residence, Sweet Briar College, 1978-81; Poet-in-Residence, 1981, Visiting Lecturer, 1985-89, Kerouac School of Poetics, Boulder; Visiting Lecturer in Poetics, New College of California, San Francisco, 1981-82; Book Reviewer, Baltimore Sun, 1983-85; Distinguished Visiting Professor of Poetry, University of Colorado at Boulder, 1985; Contributing Editor, The New Censorship, 1989-; Associate Professor of Poetry, Poetics and Translation, Naropa Institute, Boulder, 1989-. Publications: Poetry: Sojourner Microcosms: New and Selected Poems, 1959-77, 1978; Finite Continued, 1981; Pick Up the House: New and Selected Poems, 1986; Outlying Districts: New Poems, 1990; Near Miss Haiku, 1990; Blue Ceiling, 1992; High Beam: 12 Poems, 1993; West is Left on the Map, 1993; Survival Dancing, 1995; Corvus: New Poems, 1995; Hills Like Purple Pachyderms, 1997; AHOE: And How on Earth, 1997. Translator: Pentti Saarikoski: Selected Poems, 1959-1980, 1984; August Strindberg: A Biography, by Olof Lagercrantz, 1984; Egon Schiele: The Poems, 1988; Franz Werfel: The Story of a Life, by Peter Stephan Jungk, 1990; Paavo Haavikko: Selected Poems 1949-1989, 1991; The Czar's Madman, by Jaan Kross, 1993. Contributions to: New York State Creative Artists' Public Service Award, 1976; Yaddo Residency Fellowship, 1978; National Endowment for the Arts Fellowship in Poetry, 1979; Witter Bynner/Poetry Society of America Translation Grant, 1979; PEN/American-Scandinavian Foundation Award for Poetry in Translation, 1980; Finnish Literature Society Translation Fellowships, 1982, 1986; Lahti International Writers' Conference Residency, 1985; American-Scandinavian Foundation Award for Poetry in Translation, 1989; Fund for Poetry Award for Contributions to: Contemporary Poetry, 1989, 1991; Stein

Award in Innovative American Poetry, 1996. Address: 3336 14th Street, Boulder, CO 80304, USA.

HOLLOWAY John, b. 1 Aug 1920, Croydon, Surrey, England. Professor of Modern English (retired); Writer; Poet. m. (1) Audrey Gooding, 1946, 1 son, 1 daughter, (2) Joan Black, 1978. Education: 1st Class Modern Greats, New College, Oxford, 1941; DPhil, Oxon, 1947. Appointments: Temporary Lecturer in Philosophy, New College, Oxford, 1945; Fellow, All Souls College, Oxford, 1946-60; Lecturer in English, University of Aberdeen, 1949-54, University of Cambridge, 1954-66; Fellow, 1955-82, Life Fellow, 1982-, Queens' College, Cambridge; Reader, 1966-72, Professor of Modern English, 1972-82, University of Cambridge; Various visiting lectureships and professorships. Publications: Language and Intelligence, 1951; The Victorian Sage, 1953; Poems of the Mid-Century (editor), 1957; The Charted Mirror (essays), 1960; Selections from Shelley (editor), 1960; Shakespeare's Tragedies, 1961; The Colours of Clarity (essays), 1964; The Lion Hunt, 1964; Widening Horizons in English Verse, 1966; A London Childhood, 1966; Blake: The Lyric Poetry, 1968; The Establishment of English, 1972; Later English Broadside Ballads (editor with J Black), 2 volumes, 1975, 1979; The Proud Knowledge, 1977; Narrative and Structure, 1979; The Slumber of Apollo, 1983; The Oxford Book of Local Verses (editor), 1987. Poetry: The Minute, 1956; The Fugue, 1960; The Landfallers, 1962; Wood and Windfall, 1965; New Poems, 1970; Planet of Winds, 1977; Civitatula: Cambridge, the Little City, 1994. Contributions to: Professional journals. Membership: Royal Society of Literature, fellow, 1956. Address: c/o Queens' College, Cambridge CB3 9ET, England.

HOLLOWAY (Percival) Geoffrey, b. 23 May 1918, Birmingham, Warwickshire, England. Retired Mental Welfare Officer; Poet. m. 1), 2 daughters, 2) Patricia Pogson, 27 Aug 1977. Education: University of Southampton, 1946-48. Publications: To Have Eyes, 1972; Rhine Jump, 1974; All I Can Say, 1978; The Crones of Aphrodite, 1985; Salt, Roses, Vinegar, 1986; Precepts Without Deference, 1987; My Ghost in Your Eye, 1988; The Strangest Thing, 1991; Mongoose on My Shoulder, 1992; The Leaping Pool, 1993; A Sheaf of Flowers, 1994. Contributions to: Numerous publications. Honour: Poetry Book Choice, 1974. Memberships: Brewery Poets, Brewery Arts Centre, Highgate, Kendal; Keswick Poetry Group. Address: 4 Gowan Crescent, Staveley, near Kendal, Cumbria LA8 9NF, England.

HOLLY David C, b. 17 Oct 1915, Baltimore, Maryland, USA. Retired Naval Officer; University Professor. m. Carolyn King, 15 June 1949, 3 sons. Education: BS, John Hopkins University, 1938; MA, University of Maryland, 1939; PhD, American University, 1964. Publications: Exodus, 1947, 2nd edition, 1969; Steamboat on the Chesapeake, 1987; Tidewater by Steamboat, 1991; Chesapeake Steamboats: Vanished Fleet, 1994. Contributions to: Numerous articles to professional journals. Honours: Phi Kappa Phi; Pi Sigma Alpha; Pi Gamma Mu; Legion of Merit; Bronze Star; Order of Merit. Address: 918 Schooner Circle, Annapolis, MD 21401, USA.

HOLME K E. See: HILL (John Edward) Christopher.

HOLMES Bryan John, (Charles Langley Hayes, Ethan Wall), b. 18 May 1939, Birmingham, England. Lecturer; Writer. m. 1962, 2 sons. Education: BA, University of Keele, 1968. Publications: The Avenging Four, 1978; Hazard, 1979; Blood, Sweat and Gold, 1980; Gunfall, 1980; A Noose for Yanqui, 1981; Shard, 1982; Bad Times at Backwheel, 1982; Guns of the Reaper, 1983; On the Spin of a Dollar, 1983; Another Day, Another Dollar, 1984; Dark Rider, 1987; I Rode with Wyatt, 1989; Dollars for the Reaper, 1990; A Legend Called Shatterhand, 1990; Loco, 1991; Shatterhand and the People, 1992; The Last Days of Billy Patch, 1992; Blood on the Reaper, 1992; All Trails Leads to Dodge, 1993; Montana Hit, 1993; A Coffin for the Reaper, 1994; Comes the Reaper, 1995; Utah Hit, 1995; Dakota Hit, 1995; Viva Reaper, 1996; The Shard Brand, 1996; High

Plains Death, 1997; Smoking Star, 1997. Contributions to: Professional journals and general magazines. Address: c/o Robert Hale Ltd, Clerkenwell Green, London EC1R 0HT, England.

HOLMES Charlotte (Amalie), b. 26 Apr 1956, Georgia, USA. Associate Professor; Writer. m. James Brasfield, 7 Mar 1983, 1 son. Education: BA, Louisiana State University, 1977; MFA, Columbia University, 1980; Appointments: Editorial Assistant, Paris Review, 1979-80; Associate and Managing Editor, Ecco Press, 1980-82; Instructor, Western Carolina University, 1984-87; Assistant Professor, 1987-93, Associate Professor, 1993-, Pennsylvania State University. Publication: Gifts and Other Stories, 1994. Contributions to: Periodicals. Honours: Stegner Fellowship, Stanford University, 1982; North Carolina Arts Council Grant, 1986; Pennsylvania Council on the Arts Fellowships, 1988, 1993; Bread Loaf Writer's Conference National Arts Club Scholarship, 1990; Poets and Writers Award, 1993. Membership: Associated Writing Programs. Address: c/o Department of English, Pennsylvania State University, University Park, PA 16802, USA.

HOLMES John, b. 12 May 1913, Bishopton, Renfrewshire, Scotland. Farmer; Dog Breeder/Trainer; Writer. m. Kathleen Mary Trevethick, 6 Dec 1955. Education: Edinburgh and East of Scotland College of Agriculture, 1929-30. Publications: The Family Dog, 1957, 13 editions; The Farmers Dog, 1960, 13 editions; The Obedient Dog, 1975, 6 editions; Looking After Your Dog (with Mary Holmes), 1985; The Complete Australian Cattle Dog (with Mary Holmes), 1993; The Pet Owners Guide to Puppy Care and Training (with Mary Holmes), 1995; Reading the Dog's Mind (with Mary Holmes), 1998. Contributions to: Kennel Gazette; Dog World; Our Dogs; The Field; Carriage Driving; Horse and Hound; Pedigree Digest. Honour: Maxwell Award for Short Books, Dog Writers Association of America, 1995. Memberships: Society of Authors; British Actors Equity Association; UK Registry of Canine Behaviourists. Address: Formakin Farm, Cranborne, Dorset BH21 5QY, England.

HOLMES John. See: SOUSTER Raymond (Holmes).

HOLMES Leslie Templeman, b. 5 Oct 1948, London, England. Professor of Political Science. m. Susan Mary Bleasby, 4 Sept 1971, div Oct 1989. Education: BA Honours Russian Studies and German, Hull University, 1971; MA, Soviet Government and Politics, 1974, PhD, Comparative Government, 1979, Essex University. Appointment: Professor of Political Science, University of Melbourne. Publications: The Policy Progress in Communist States, 1981; The Withering Away of the State? (editor), 1981; Politics in the Communist World, 1986; The End of Communist Power, 1993; Post-Communism, 1996. Honour: Fellow, Academy of the Social Sciences in Australia, 1995. Address: Department of Political Science, University of Melbourne, Parkville, Victoria 3052, Australia.

HOLMES Marjorie Rose, b. 22 Sept 1910, Storm Lake, Iowa, USA. Author. m. (1) Lynn Mighell, 9 Apr 1932, 2 sons, 2 daughters, (2) George Schmieler, 4 July 1981. Education: Buena Vista College, 1922-29; BA, Cornell College, 1931. Publications: World by the Tail, 1943; Ten O'Clock Scholar, 1946; Saturday Night, 1959; Cherry Blossom Princess,1960; Follow Your Dream, 1961; Love is a Hopscotch Thing; 1963; Senior Trip, 1962; Love and Laughter, 1967; I've got to talk to Somebody, God, 1969; Writing the Creative Article, 1969; Who Am I, God?, 1969; To Treasure our Days, 1971; Two from Galilee, 1972; Nobody Else Will Listen, 1973; You and I and Yesterday, 1973; As Tall as My Heart, 1974; How Can I Find You God?,: 1975; Beauty in Your Own Back Yard, 1976; Hold Me Up a Little Longer, Lord, 1977; Lord, Let Me Love, 1978; God and Vitamins, 1980; To Help You Through the Hurting, 1983; Three from Galilee, 1985; Secrets of Health, Energy and Staying Young, 1987; The Messiah, 1987; At Christmas the Heart Goes Home, 1991; The Inspirational Writings of Marjorie Holmes, 1991; Gifts Freely Given, 1992; Second Wife, Second Life, 1993; Writing Articles from the Heart, 1993;

Still By Your Side: How I Know a Great Love Never Dies, 1996. Contributions to: Numerous journals and magazines.

HOLMES Richard (Gordon Heath), b. 5 Nov 1945, London, England. Writer; Poet. Education: BA, Churchill College, Cambridge. Appointments: Reviewer and Historical Features Writer, The Times, London, 1967-92; Earnest Jones Memorial Lecturer, British Institute of Psycho-Analysis, 1990; John Keats Memorial Lecturer, Royal College of Surgeons, 1995. Publications: Thomas Chatterton: The Case Re-Opened, 1970; One for Sorrows (poems), 1970; Shelley: The Pursuit, 1974; Shelley on Love (editor), 1980; Coleridge, 1982; Nerval: The Chimeras (with Peter Jay), 1985; Footsteps: Adventures of a Romantic Biographer, 1985; Mary Wollstonecraft and William Godwin (editor), 1987; Kipling: Something Myself (editor with Robert Hampson), 1987; Coleridge: Early Visions, 1989; Dr Johnson and Mr Savage, 1993; Coleridge: Selected Poems (editor), 1996. Honours: Somerset Maugham Award, 1977; Whitbread Book of the Year Prize, 1989; Officer of the Order of the British Empire, 1992; James Tait Black Memorial Prize, 1994. Membership: Royal Society of Literature, fellow. Address: c/o HarperCollins, 77 Fulham Palace Road, London W6 8JB, England.

HOLROYD Michael (de Courcy Fraser), b. 27 Aug 1935, London, England. Biographer; Writer. m. Margaret Drabble, 17 Sept 1982. Appointment: Visiting Fellow, Pennsylvania State University, 1979. Publications: Hugh Kingsmill: A Critical Biography, 1964; Lytton Strachey: A Critical Biography, 2 volumes, 1967, 1968, revised edition, 1994; A Dog's Life (novel), 1969; The Best of Hugh Kingsmill (editor), 1970; Lytton Strachey by Himself: A Self-Portrait (editor), 1971, new edition, 1994; Unreceived Opinions (essays), 1973; Augustus John, 2 volumes, 1974, 1975, revised edition, 1996; The Art of Augustus John (with Malcolm Easton), 1974; The Genius of Shaw (editor), 1979; The Shorter Strachey (editor with Paul Levy), 1980; William Gerhardie's God Fifth Column (editor with Robert Skidelsky), 1981; Essays by Diverse Hands (editor), Vol XLII, 1982; Peterley Harvest: The Private Diary of David Peterley (editor), 1985; Bernard Shaw: Vol I, The Search for Love 1856-1898, 1988, Vol II, The Pursuit of Power 1898-1918, 1989, Vol III, The Lure of Fantasy 1918-1950, 1991, Vol IV, The Last Laugh 1950-1991, 1992, Vol V, The Shaw Companion, 1992, one-volume abridged edition, 1997; Basil Street Blues, 1999. Contributions to: Radio, television, and periodicals. Honours: Saxton Memorial Fellowship, 1964; Bollingen Fellowship, 1966; Winston Churchill Fellowship, 1971; Commander of the Order of the British Empire, 1989; Honorary DLitts, Universities of Ulster, 1992, Sheffield, 1993, Warwick, 1994, and East Anglia, 1994. Memberships: Arts Council, chairman, literature panel, 1992-95; National Book League, chairman, 1976-78; PEN, president, British branch, 1985-88; Royal Historical Society, fellow; Royal Society of Literature, chairman, 1998-; Society of Authors, chairman, 1973-74; Royal Society of Arts, fellow; Strachey Trust, chairman, 1990-95; Public Lending Right Advisory Committee, chairman, 1997-; Royal Literary Fund, vice-chairman, 1997-. Address: c/o A P Watt Ltd, 20 John Street, London WC1N 2DR, England.

HOLT George. See: **TUBB E(dwin) C(harles).**

HOLUIGUE B Diane, b. 22 Oct 1942, Melbourne, Australia. Teacher; Journalist; Author. m. Gérard Holuigue, 30 Aug 1963, 1 son, 1 daughter. Education: BA, Melbourne University. Appointments: Started Cooking School, The French Kitchen, 1969, 54,000 students, closed 1996; Food Editor, 1973-. Publications: Home Beautifuls Best Recipes; The French Kitchen, 1983; Master Class, 1988; France, A Culinary Journey, 1992; Clever Cook, 1994; Clever Cook, 1995. Contributions to: 16 years at House Beautiful; Melbourne Herald Weekend Magazine; Australian Weekend Magazine. Address: 3 Avondale Road, Armadale, Vic 3143, Australia.

HOMBERGER Eric (Ross), b. 30 May 1942, Philadelphia, Pennsylvania, USA. Reader in American Literature; Writer. m. Judy Jones, 2 June 1967, 2 sons, 1 daughter. Education: BA, University of California at Berkeley, 1964; MA, University of Chicago, 1965; PhD, Cambridge University, 1972. Appointments: Temporary Lecturer in American Literature, University of Exeter, 1969-70; Lecturer, 1970-88, Reader in American Literature, 1988-, University of East Anglia; Visiting Faculty, University of Minnesota, 1977-78; Visiting Professor of American Literature, University of New Hampshire, 1991-92. Publications: The Cambridge Mind: Ninety Years of the "Cambridge Review", 1879-1969 (editor with William Janeway and Simon Schama), 1970; Ezra Pound: The Critical Heritage (editor), 1972; The Art of the Real: Poetry in England and America since 1939, 1977; The Second World War in Fiction (editor with Holger Klein and John Flower), 1984; Scenes from the Life of a City: Corruption and Conscience in Old New York, 1984; John le Carre, 1986; American Writers and Radical Politics, 1900-1939: Equivocal Commitments, 1987; The Troubled Face of Biography (editor with John Charmley), 1987; John Reed, 1990; John Reed and the Russian Revolution: Uncollected Articles, Letters and Speeches in Russia, 1917-1920 (editor with John Biggart), 1992; The Historical Atlas of New York City, 1994; Scenes from the Life of a City: Corruption and Conscience in Old New York, 1994; The Penguin Historical Atlas of North America, 1995. Contributions to: Periodicals. Honour: Leverhulme Fellowship, 1978-79. Membership: British Association for American Studies. Address: 74 Clarendon Road, Norwich NR2 2PN, England.

HOME Stewart Ramsay,(Karen Eliot, Monty Cantsin, Harry Bates), b. 24 Mar 1962, Merton, South London, England. Writer. Publications: Assault on Culture, 1988; Pure Mania, 1989; Defiant Pose, 1991; No Pity, 1993; Red London, 1994; Neoism, Plagiarism & Praxis, 1995; Cranked Up Really High, 1995; Slow Death, 1996; Come Before Christ & Murder Love, 1997; Blow Job, 1997; Cunt, 1999; Confusion Incorporated: A Collection of Lies, Hoaxes and Hidden Truths, 1999. Contributions to: Big Issue; Independent; Art Monthly; Edinburgh Review; New Art Examiner; Konkret. Membership: Society of Authors. Address: BM Senior, London WC1N 3XX, England.

HONAN Park, b. 17 Sept 1928, Utica, New York, USA. Biographer. Education: MA, University of Chicago, 1951; PhD, University of London, 1959. Appointments: Professor of English and American Literature, University of Leeds, 1984-93. Publications: Browning's Characters: A Study in Poetic Technique, 1961; Shelley (editor), 1963; Bulwer Lytton's Falkland (editor), 1967; The Complete Works of Robert Browning (co-editor), 9 volumes, 1969-; The Book, The Ring and The Poet: A Biography of Robert Browning (co-author), 1975; Matthew Arnold: A Life, 1981; Jane Austen: Her Life, 1987; The Beats: An Anthology of "Beat" Writing (editor), 1987; Authors' Lives: On Literary Biography and the Arts of Language, 1990; Shakespeare: A Life, 1998. Honours: Britsih Academy Awards; Leverhulme Award; Huntington Library Fellowship; Folger Shakespeare Library Fellowship, 1991. Address: School of English, University of Leeds, Leeds LS2 9JT, England.

HONAN William Holmes, b. 11 May 1930, New York, New York, USA. Journalist. m. Nancy Burton, 22 June 1975, 2 sons, 1 daughter. Education: BA, Oberlin College, 1952; MA, University of Virginia, 1955. Appointments: Editor, The Villager, New York, 1957-60; Assistant Editor, New Yorker Magazine, 1960-64; Associate Editor, Newsweek, New York City, 1969; Assistant Editor, New York Times Magazine, 1969-70; Travel Editor, 1970-72, 1973-74, Arts and Leisure Editor, 1974-82, Culture Editor, 1982-88, Chief Cultural Correspondent, 1988-93, National Higher Education Correspondent, 1993-, New York Times; Managing Editor, Saturday Review, 1972-73. Publications: Greenwich Village Guide, 1959; Ted Kennedy: Profile of a Survivor, 1972; Bywater: The Man Who Invented the Pacific War, 1990; Visions of Infamy: The Untold Story of

How Journalist Hector C Bywater Devised the Plans that Led to Pearl Harbour, 1991; Fire When Ready, Gridley! - Great Naval Stories from Manila Bay to Vietnam (editor), 1992; Treasure Hunt: A New York Times Reporter Tracks the Quedlinburg Treasures, 1997. Contributions to: Periodicals. Address: c/o New York Times, 229 West 43rd Street, New York, NY 10036. USA.

HONE Joseph, b. 25 Feb 1937, London, England. Writer; Broadcaster. m. Jacqueline Mary Yeend, 5 Mar 1963, 1 son, 1 daughter. Education: Kilkenny College, Sandford Park School, Dublin; St Columba's College, Dublin. Publications: The Flowers of the Forest, 1982; Children of the Country, 1986; Duck Soup in the Black Sea, 1988; Summer Hill, 1990; Firesong, 1997. Contributions to: Periodicals. Membership: Upton House Cricket Club. Address: c/o Aitken & Stone Ltd, 29 Fernshaw Road, London SW10, England.

HONEYCOMBE Gordon, b. Sept 1936, Karachi, British India. Writer; Dramatis; Television Presenter. Education: MA, English, Edinburgh Academy and University College, Oxford, England. Appointments: TV Newscaster, ITN, 1965-77; Chief Newsreader, TVam, 1984-89; Presented, appeared and narrated many television programmes including: Something Special, Scottish TV; The Late Late Show, TVS; Family History; Arthur C Clarke's Mysterious World, YTV; A Shred of Evidence, Thames TV; Sick as a Parrot, Channel 4; Appeared in many TV plays and series including: The Foundation; The Brack Report; CQ; First Among Equals; Bad Company; Ransom; The Medusa Touch; Castaway; The Fourth Protocol; Bullseye; Recorded voice-overs or narrations of many TV and other documentaries, training films, commercials and cinema shorts. Publications: Neither the Sea Nor the Sand, 1969; Dragon under the Hill, 1972; Adam's Tale, 1974; Red Watch, 1976; Royal Wedding, 1981; Nagasaki 1945, 1981; The Edge of Heaven, 1981; The Year of the Princess, 1982; The Murders of the Black Museum, 1982; Selfridges, 1984; The TVam Celebration of the Royal Wedding, 1986; Siren Song, 1992; More Murders of the Black Museum, 1993; Written several stage & radio dramatisations including: The Redemption; Lancelot and Guinevere and Paradise Lost; 3 TV Plays: The Golden Vision, BBC1, 1968; Time and Again, Westward TV, 1974; The 13th Day of Christmas, Granada TV, 1985; The Princess and the Goblins, musical, book and lyrics, 1994; Starred in Suspects, Swansea, 1989; Toured in Run for Your Wife, with Les Dawson, 1990; Played Emperor of China, in Aladdin, Wimbledon Theatre, with Cilla Black, 1989-90; Played Emperor, in Aladdin at Pavillion Theatre, Bournmouth, with Sue Pollard, 1990-91; Produced and directed own play, The Redemption, Festival of Perth in Western Australia, March 1990; Appeared in: Pricess Ida, 1998; The Taming of the Shrew, 1998-99; The Mikado, 1999. Address: c/o Jules Bennett, PO Box 25, Moreton in Marsh, Glos GL56 9YJ, England.

HONEYMAN Brenda. See: **CLARK Brenda (Margaret Lilian).**

HONG Yonghong, b. 6 May 1930, Xiamen, Fujian, China. Associate Professor. m. Qiongyun Wu, 17 Nov 1958, 1 son, 1 daughter. Education: Graduated, Xiamen Englo-Chinese College, 1947; Graduated, Xiamen University, 1951. Appointments: Chorus Leader, Fujian Song and Dance Ensemble, 1957; Professional Writer of Fujian Writers' Association, 1981; Director of the Fifth Council, Chinese Film Artists' Association, 1985; Vice Chairman, General Secretary, Fujian Television Artists' Association, 1985; Director, University History Department, Xiamen University, 1986; Deputy Chief, Art Institute of Xiamen University, 1991. Publications: A Song About the Golden Cup, opera play, 1970; The Prisoners on the Sea, novel, 1980; The Prisoners on the Sea, senario of the film, 1981; Lady Jin, opera play, 1982; Tan Kah Kee, TV senario, 1984; A Story About Going Abroad, novel, 1984; A Tale About Return, novel 1985; The Legendary Madam, TV senario, 1987; The History of Xiamen University, vol 1, 1990. Contributions to: Talk on the History of the Remarkable Personages Moved by Hands, Treatise, 1979. Memberships: Chinese Writers'

Association; Chinese Film Artists' Association; Chinese Television Artists' Association. Address: President Office, Xiamen University, Xiamen, Fujing, China.

HONIG Edwin, b. 3 Sept 1919, New York, New York, USA. Retired Professor of English and of Comparative Literature; Poet; Writer; Dramatist; Translator. m. (1) Charlotte Gilchrist, 1 Apr 1940, dec 1963, (2) Margot Dennes, 15 Dec 1963, div 1978, 2 sons. Education: BA, 1939, MA, 1947, University of Wisconsin at Madison. Appointments: Poetry Editor, New Mexico Quarterly, 1948-52; Instructor, Claremont College, California, 1949; Faculty, 1949-57, Assistant Professor of English, Harvard University; Faculty, 1957-60, Professor of English, 1960-82, Professor of Comparative Literature, 1962-82, Brown University; Visiting Professor, University of California at Davis, 1964-65; Mellon Professor, Boston University, 1977. Publications: Poetry: The Moral Circus, 1955; The Gazabos: 41 Poems, 1959; Survivals, 1964; Spring Journal, 1968; Four Springs, 1972; At Sixes, 1974; Shake a Spear with Me, John Berryman, 1974; Selected Poems 1955-1976, 1979; Interrupted Praise, 1983; Gifts of Light, 1983; The Imminence of Love: Poems 1962-1992, 1993. Stories: Foibles and Fables of an Abstract Man, 1979. Non-Fiction: García Lorca, 1944, revised edition, 1963; Dark Conceit: The Making of Allegory, 1959; Calderón and the Seizures of Honor, 1972; The Poet's Other Voice: Conversations on Literary Translation, 1986. Plays: Ends of the World and Other Plays, 1984. Translations: Over 10 books, 1961-93. Contributions to: books, anthologies, reviews, journals, and periodicals. Honours: Guggenheim Fellowships, 1948, 1962; National Academy of Arts and Letters Grant, 1966; Amy Lowell Traveling Poetry Fellowship, 1968; Rhode Island Governor's Award for Excellence in the Arts, 1970; National Endowment for the Humanities Fellowship, 1975, and Grants, 1977-80; National Endowment for the Arts Fellowship, 1977; Translation Award, Poetry Society of America, 1984; National Award, Columbia University Translation Center, 1985; Decorated by the President for translation of Pessoa, 1989; Decorated by the King of Spain for translation of Calderón, 1996. Memberships: Dante Society of America; Poetry Society of America. Address: 229 Medway Street, Ap 305, Providence, RI 02906, USA.

HOOD Hugh (John Blagdon), b. 30 Apr 1928, Toronto, Ontario, Canada. Writer;Teacher. m. Noreen Mallory, 22 Apr 1957, 2 sons. Education: BA, 1952, MA, 1952, PhD, 1955, University of Toronto. Appointment: Professor Titulaire, Department of English Studies, University of Montreal, 1961-. Publications: Flying a Red Kite, 1962; The Swing in the Garden, 1975; Black and White Keys, 1982; You'll Catch Your Death, 1992; Be Sure to Close Your Eyes, 1993; Dead Men's Watches, 1995. Honours: City of Toronto Literary Award, 1975; SQPELL Literary Award, 1988; Officer of the Order of Canada, 1988. Membership: Arts and Letters Club of Toronto. Address: 4242 Hampton Avenue, Montreal, Quebec H4A 2K9, Canada.

HOOKER Jeremy (Peter), b. 23 Mar 1941, Warsash, Hampshire, England. Lecturer in English; Poet; Writer. Education: BA, 1963, MA, 1965, University of Southampton. Appointments: Arts Council Creative Writing Fellow, Winchester School of Art, 1981-83; Lecturer in English, Bath College of Higher Education, 1988-. Publications: The Elements, 1972; Soliloquies of a Chalk Giant, 1974; Solent Shore: New Poems, 1978; Landscape of the Daylight Moon, 1978; Englishman's Road, 1980; Itchen Water, 1982; Poetry of Place, 1982; A View from the Source: Selected Poems, 1982; Master of the Leaping Figures, 1987; The Presence of the Past, 1987; In Praise of Windmills, 1990; Their Silence a Language (with Lee Grandjean), 1994; Writers in a Landscape, 1996; Our Lady of Europe, 1997; Groundwork (with Lee Grandjean), 1998. Contributions to: Reviews and journals. Honours: Eric Gregory Award, 1969; Welsh Arts Council Literature Prize, 1975. Memberships: Academi Gymreig, English language section; Powys Society; Richard Jefferies Society; Salisbury Poetry Circle, honorary president. Address: Old School House, 7 Sunnyside, Frome, Somerset, BA11 1LD, England.

HOOPER John Edward Francis, b. 17 July 1950, Westminster, London, England. Journalist; Author. m. Hon Lucinda Evans, 19 July 1980. Education: BA, St Catharine's College, Cambridge. Appointments: Reporter, BBC Radio, 1971-73; Diplomatic Correspondent, IRN, 1973-74; Correspondent on Cyprus, BBC, Guardian and Economist, 1974-76; Correspondent, Spain and Portugal, 1976-79, London Staff, 1979-88, The Guardian; Correspondent, Western Mediterranean. Economist, Guardian and Observer, 1988-94; Correspondent, Southern Europe, Guardian and Observer, 1994-. Publications: The Spaniards, 1986; The New Spaniards, 1995. Contributions to: The New Spain, 1993; Wilson Quarterly, 1993, 1998; A New Italian Renaissance. Honour: Allen Lane Award, 1987. Membership: Society of Authors. Literary Agent: Gill Coleridge, Rodgers, Coleridge and White, 20 Powis Mews, London W11 1JN, England. Address: c/o La Stampa, Via Barberini 50, 00187 Rome, Italy.

HOOVER Carol Faith, b. 24 Jan 1921, Eagle Grove, Iowa, USA. Publisher. div, 1 daughter. Education: AB, Duke University, 1940; MS Social Work, University of North Carolina, 1947; DSW, Catholic University, 1973. Appointment: President, Ariadne Press, 1976. Publication: How to Write an Uncommonly Good Novel. Contributions to: Denver Quarterly; Story; Texas Quarterly; Potomac Review; Crescent Review. Honour: Fiction Prize, Baltimore Festival of the Arts. Memberships: Montgomery Arts Council; Writers Mentor Group. Address: 4817 Tallahassee Avenue, Rockville, MD 20853, USA.

HOOVER Helen Mary, (Jennifer Price), b. 5 Apr 1935, Stark County, Ohio, USA. Writer. Publications: Children of Morrow, 1973; The Lion Cub, 1974; Treasures of Morrow, 1976; The Delikon, 1977; The Rains of Eridan, 1977; The Lost Star, 1979; Return to Earth, 1980; The Time of Darkness, 1980; Another Heaven, Another Earth, 1981; The Bell Tree, 1982; The Shepherd Moon, 1984; Orvis, 1987; The Dawn Palace, 1988; Away is a Strange Place to Be, 1989. Contributions to: Language Arts; Top of the News; Journal of American Library Association. Honours: Ohioana Award, 1982; Outstanding Contribution to Children's Literature Award, Central Missouri State University, 1984; Parents Choice Awards, 1987, 1988; Library of Congress Best Book, 1988; American Library Association, Best Young Adult Book, 1988. Memberships: Authors Guild. Address: c/o Viking Penguin Children's Books, 40 West 23rd Street, New York, NY 10010, USA.

HOOVER Paul Andrew, b. 30 Apr 1946, Harrisonburg, Virginia, USA. Poet-in-Residence; Professor of English. m. Maxine Chernoff, 5 Oct 1974, 2 sons, 1 daughter. Education: BA, Manchester College; MA, University of Illinois. Appointment: Poet-in-Residence, Columbia College, Chicago, 1974-. Publications: Letter to Einstein Beginning Dear Albert, 1979; Somebody Talks a Lot, 1983; Nervous Songs, 1986; Idea, 1987; Saigon, Illinois (novel), 1988; The Novel: A Poem, 1990; Postmodern American Poetry (anthology), 1994; Viridian, 1997; Totem and Shadow: New and Selected Poems, 1999; New American Writing (editor). Contributions to: New Republic; American Poetry Review; TriQuarterly; Paris Review; Common Knowledge; Green Mountains Review. Honours: NEA Fellowship in Poetry, 1980; GE Award, 1984. Memberships: MLA; Poetry Center of Chicago, 1974-88. Address: 369 Molino Avenue, Mill Valley, CA 94941, USA.

HOPCRAFT Arthur (Edward), b. 29 Nov 1932, Essex, England. Writer; Dramatist. Appointments: Staff, Daily Mirror, 1956-59, Guardian, 1959-64. Publications: Born to Hunger, 1968; The Football Man, 1968; The Great Apple Raid, 1970; World Cup 70 (editor with H McIlvanney), 1970; Mid-Century Men, 1982. Other: Screenplay: Agatha (with K Tynan), 1979. Television Dramatisations: The Mosedale Horseshoe, 1971; The Panel, 1971; The Birthday Run, 1972; Buggins Ermine, 1972; The Reporters, 1972; Said the Preacher, 1972; Jingle Bells, 1973; Katapult, 1973; The Nearly Man, 1974; Humbug, Finger or Thumb?, 1974; Journey to London, 1974; Baa, Baa, Blacksheep, 1974; Wednesday Love, 1975; Nightingale's Boys, 1975; Hannah, 1976; Hard Times, 1977; Tinker, Tailor, Soldier, Spy, 1979; Bleak House, 1985; A Perfect Spy, 1987; A Tale of Two Cities, 1988; Hostage, 1992; Rebecca, 1997. Honours: Several drama awards. Membership: Writers Guild of Great Britain. Address: c/o The Rod Hall Agency, 7 Goodge Place, London, W1P 1FL.

HOPE Catherine Jane Margaret, (Cathy Hope), b. 15 Sept 1945, Waikari, South Island, New Zealand. Primary School Teacher; Educational Author. m. Terry Hope, 30 Dec 1966, 2 daughters. Education: Trained Infant School Teacher, Coburg Teachers College, Victoria, 1965. Publications: Thematic Approach to Tadpoles 'N' Things, 1978; Themes through the Year, 1980; Ideas for Excursions, 1981; Everyone's Different, 1981; Seasons: Themes through the Year, 1982; Everyone Ages, 1983; Themes from the Playground, 1984; All Australian Themes, 1987; Ideas for Multicultural Education, 1992; Fundraising for Schools, 1994. Membership: Fellowship of Australian Writers. Address: 98A Gould Street, Frankston, Victoria 3199, Australia.

HOPE Christopher David Tully, b. 26 Feb 1944, Johannesburg, South Africa. Writer. m. Eleanor Marilyn Margaret Klein, 1967, 2 sons. Education: BA, Natal University, 1969; MA, University of the Witwatersrand, 1972. Publications: Cape Drives, 1974; A Separate Development, 1981; The Country of the Black Pig, 1981; The King, the Cat and the Fiddle, 1983; Kruger's Alp, 1984; The Dragon Wore Pink, 1985; White Boy Running, 1988; My Chocolate Redeemer, 1989; Serenity House, 1992; The Love Songs of Nathan J Swirsky, 1993; Darkest England, 1996; Me, The Moon and Elvis Presley, 1997; Signs of the Heart, 1999. Contributions to: Times Literary Supplement; London Magazine; Les Temps Modernes. Honours: Cholmondeley Award, 1974; David Higham Prize, 1981; International PEN Award, 1983; Whitbread Prize, 1985. Memberships: Royal Society of Literature, fellow; Society of Authors. Address: c/o Rogers, Coleridge & White Ltd, 20 Powis Mews, London W11 1JN, England.

HOPE Ronald (Sidney), b. 4 Apr 1921, London, England. Writer. Education: BA, 1941, MA, 1946, DPhil, New College, Oxford. Appointments: Fellow, Brasenose College, Oxford, 1945-47, Seafarer's Education Service, London, 1947-76; Director, The Marine Society, 1976-86. Publications: Spare Time at Sea, 1954; Economic Geography, 1956; Dick Small in the Half Deck, Ships, 1958; The British Shipping Industry, 1959; The Shoregoer's Guide to World Ports, 1963; Seamen and the Sea, 1965; Introduction to the Merchant Navy, 1965; Retirement from the Sea, 1967; In Cabined Ships at Sea, 1969; Twenty Singing Seamen, 1979; The Seamen's World, 1982; A New History of British Shipping, 1990. Address: 2 Park Place, Dollar, FK14 7AA.

HOPE-SIMPSON Jacynth (Ann), (Helen Dudley), b. 10 Nov 1930, Birmingham, England. Writer. Education: University of Lausanne, 1949; MA and Diploma in Education, Oxford University, 1953. Publications: The Stranger in the Train, 1960; The Bishop of Kenelminster, 1961; The Man Who Came Back, 1962; The Bishop's Picture, 1962; The Unravished Bridge, 1963; The Witch's Cave, 1964; The Hamish Hamilton Book of Myths and Legends, 1965; The Hamish Hamilton Book of Witches, 1966; Escape to the Castle, 1967; The Unknown Island, 1968; They Sailed from Plymouth, 1970; Elizabeth I, 1971; Tales in School, 1971; The Gunner's Boy, 1973; Save Tarranmoor!, 1974; Always on the Move, 1975; The Hijacked Hovercraft, 1975; Black Madonna, 1976; Vote for Victoria, 1976; The Making of the Machine Age, 1978; The Hooded Falcon, 1979; Island of Perfumes, 1985; Cottage Dreams, 1986. Address: Franchise Cottage, Newtown, Milborne, Port Sherborne, Dorset, England.

HOPKINS Antony, b. 21 Mar 1921, London, England. Composer; Conductor; Lecturer; Writer. m. Alison Purves,

1947, dec 1991. Education: Royal College of Music, London. Appointments: Director, Intimate Opera Co, 1952-64; Presenter, Talking About Music, BBC, 1954-92; Lecturer, Royal College of Music, London. Publications: Talking About Symphonies, 1961, reprinted, 1996; Talking About Concertos, 1964; Music All Around Me, 1967; Music Face to Face, 1971; Talking About Sonatas, 1971; Downbeat Guide, 1977; Understanding Music, 1979; The Nine Symphonies of Beethoven, 1980; Songs for Swinging Golfers, 1981; Sounds of Music, 1982; Beating Time, 1982; Pathway to Music, 1983; The Concertgoer's Companion, 2 volumes, 1984, 1986, reprinted as single volume, 1994; The Seven Concertos of Beethoven, 1996. Honours: Gold Medal, Royal College of Music, 1943; Italia Prizes, 1951, 1957; Medal for Services to Music, City of Tokyo, 1973; Commander of the Order of the British Empire, 1976. Address: Woodyard, Ashridge, Berkhamsted, Hertfordshire HP4 1PS, England.

HOPKINS Bruce R, b. 25 Apr 1941, Sault Ste Marie, Michigan, USA. Lawyer. 1 son. Education: BA, University of Michigan, 1964; JD, 1967, LLM, 1971, George Washington University. Publications: The Law of Tax-Exempt Organizations, 6th edition, 1992; A Legal Guide to Starting and Managing a Nonprofit Organization, 2nd edition, 1993; The Legal Answer Book for Nonprofit Organizations, 1996; The Law of Fund-Raising, 2nd edition, 1996; Nonprofit Law Dictionary, 1994; The Law of Tax-Exempt Healthcare Organizations, 1995; Intermediate Sanctions: Curbing Nonprofits' Abuse, 1997; Private Foundations: Tax Law and Compliance, 1997. Contributions to: Over 100 articles in law, management, and fund raising journals. Honour: First National Society of Fund Raising Executives/Staley/Robeson/Ryan/St Lawrence Research Award. Literary Agent: Martha Cooley, John Wiley & Sons Inc, New York, NY, USA. Address: 700 West 47th Street, Suite 1000, Kansas City, MO 64112, USA.

HOPKINS Lee Bennett, b. 13 Apr 1938, Scranton, Pennsylvania, USA. Writer; Editor; Educational Consultant. Education: BA, Kean College, 1960; MS, Bank St College, 1964; Diploma, Hunter College of the City University of New York, 1966. Appointments: Curriculum Specialist, Scholastic Inc, 1968-75; Educational Consultant, 1975-. Publications: Author and/or editor of numerous children's books. Contributions to: Professional journals and to magazines. Honours: Educational Leadership Award, Phi Delta Kappa, 1980; Award, International Reading Association, 1983; Children's Literature Award, University of Southern Mississippi, 1989. Address: Kemeys Cove, 307, Scarborough, NY 10510, USA.

HOPKIRK Joyce, b. 2 Mar 1937, England. Writer; Journalist. 1 son, 1 daughter. Appointments: Reporter, Gateshead Post, 1955; Founder Editor, Majorcan News, 1959; Reporter, Daily Sketch, 1960; Royal Reporter, Daily Express, 1961; Editor, Fashion Magazine, 1967; Woman's Editor, The Sun launch, 1969; Launch Editor, Cosmopolitan, 1971-72; Assistant Editor, Daily Mirror, 1973-78; Women's Editor, Sunday Times, 1982; Editorial Director, Elle launch, 1984; Assistant Editor, Sunday Mirror, 1985; Editor-in-Chief, She Magazine, 1986-89; Director, Editors' Unlimited, 1990-; Founder Editor, Chic Magazine, 1994. Publications: Successful Slimming, 1976; Successful Slimming Cookbook, 1978; Splash! (co-author), 1995; Best of Enemies, 1996; Double Trouble, 1997; Unfinished Business, 1998. Honours: Editor of the Year, 1972, Women's Magazines Editor of the Year, 1988, British Society of Magazine Editors; Woman of Achievement Award, Women's Advertising Club of London, 1998; Co-Chairman, Periodical Publishers Association Magazine Awards, 1998. Membership: Fellow, Royal Society of Arts. Address: Gadespring, 109 Piccotts Eng, Hemel Hempstead, Herts HP1 3AT, England.

HOPPE Matthias, b. 5 Dec 1952, Schluechtern, Germany. Editor; Writer. 1 daughter. Education: Studies, German Language and Literature, History and Politics. Publications: Muenchen, 1982; Was macht Arno im Sommer, 1989; Mouse and Elephant, 1991; Muenchen, Fit and Fun, 1995; Exploring Germany, 1996; Verrueckt ist ganz normal, 1996. Contributions to: Abendzeitung Muenchen; Stern; Die Zeit; Frankfurter Rundschau; TV Stations. Memberships: IG Medien; Verband Deutscher Schriftsteller VS. Address: Post Box 900526, 81505 Munich, Germany.

HORNBY Nick, b. 1957, London, England. Freelance Journalist; Novelist. Publications: Contemporary American Fiction (essays), 1992; Fever Pitch (memoirs), 1992; My Favourite Year: A Collection of New Football Writing (editor), 1993; High Fidelity (novel), 1995. Screenplay: Fever Pitch, 1997; About a Boy. Contributions to: Sunday Times; Times Literary Supplement; Literary Review. Address: c/o Victor Gollancz Ltd, Villiers House, 41-47 The Strand, London WC2N 5JE, England.

HORNE Alistair Allan, b. 9 Nov 1925, London, England. Author; Journalist; Lecturer. m. (1) Renira Margaret Hawkins, 3 daughters, (2) The Hon Mrs Sheelin Eccles, 1987. Education: MA, Jesus College, Cambridge. Appointments: Foreign Correspondent, Daily Telegraph, 1952-55; Official Biographer, Prime Minister Harold Macmillan, 1979. Publications: Back into Power, 1955; The Land is Bright, 1958; Canada and the Canadians, 1961; The Fall of Paris 1870-1871, 1965; To Lose a Battle: France 1940, 1969; Death of a Generation, 1970; The Paris Commune, 1971; Small Earthquake in Chile, 1972; Napoleon, Master of Europe 1805-1807, 1979; The French Army and Politics 1870-1970, 1984; Macmillan, Vol I, 1894-1956, 1985,; Vol II, 1957-1986, 1989; A Bundle from Britain, 1993; The Lonely Leader: Monty 1944-45, 1994; How Far From Austerlitz: Napoleon 1805-1815, 1996. Contributions to: Various periodicals. Honours: Hawthornden Prize, 1963; Yorkshire Post Book of Year Prize, 1978; Wolfson Literary Award, 1978; Enid Macleod Prize, 1985; Commander of the Order of the British Empire, 1992; Chevalier, Legion d'Honneur, 1993; LittD. Memberships: Society of Authors; Royal Society of Literature. Literary Agent: Andrew Wylie Inc. Address: The Old Vicarage, Turville, Nr Henley on Thames, Oxon RG9 6QU, England.

HORNE Donald Richmond, b. 26 Dec 1921, Sydney, New South Wales, Australia. Author; Lecturer; Professor Emeritus. m. 22 Mar 1960, 1 son, 1 daughter. Education: Sydney University, Canberra University College, 1944-45. Appointments: Editor, The Observer, 1958-61, The Bulletin, 1961-62, 1967-72, Quadrant, 1963-66; Contributing Editor, Newsweek International, 1973-76; Chancellor, University of Canberra, 1992-96. Publications: The Lucky Country, 1964; The Permit, 1965; The Education of Young Donald, 1967; God is an Englishman, 1969; The Next Australia, 1970; But What If There Are No Pelicans?, 1971; Money Made Us, 1976; The Death of the Lucky Country, 1976; His Excellency's Pleasure, 1977; Right Way Don't Go Back, 1978; In Search of Billy Hughes, 1979; Time of Hope, 1980; Winner Take All, 1981; The Great Museum, 1984; Confessions of New Boy, 1985; The Story of the Australian People, 1985; The Public Culture, 1986, 1994; The Lucky Country Revisited, 1987; Portrait of an Optimist, 1988; Ideas for a Nation, 1989; The Intelligent Tourist, 1993; The Avenue of the Fair Go, 1997; An Interrupted Life, 1998. Contributions to: Numerous professional journals. Honours: AO, 1982; Honorary doctorates; Fellow, Australian Academy of Humanities. Memberships: Australian Society of Authors; Copyright Agency Ltd. Address: 53 Grosvenor Street, Woollahra, Sydney, New South Wales 2025, Australia.

HOROVITZ Michael, b. 4 Apr 1935, Frankfurt am Main, Germany. Writer; Poet; Editor; Publisher. Education: BA, 1959, MA, 1964, Brasenose, College, Oxford. Appointments: Editor and Publisher, New Departures International Review, 1959-; Founder, Coordinator and Torchbearer, Poetry Olympics Festivals, 1980-. Publications: Europa (translator), 1961; Alan Davie, 1963; Declaration, 1963; Strangers: Poems, 1965; Poetry for the People: An Essay in Bop Prosody, 1966; Bank Holiday: A New Testament for the Love Generation, 1967; Children of Albion (editor), 1969; The Wolverhampton Wanderer: An Epic of Football, Fate and Fun, 1970; Love Poems, 1971; A Contemplation, 1978; Growing Up: Selected Poems and Pictures 1951-1979, 1979; The Egghead Republic (translator), 1983; A Celebration of and for Frances Horovitz, 1984; Midsummer Morning Jog Log, 1986; Bop Paintings, Collages and Drawings, 1989; Grandchildren of Albion (editor), 1992; Wordsounds and Sightlines: New and Selected Poems, 1994; Grandchildren of Albion Live (editor), 1996; The POW! Anthology, 1996; A New Waste Land, forthcoming. Honours: Arts Council of Great Britain Writers Award, 1976; Poetry Book Society Recommendation, 1986. Address: PO Box 9819, London, W11 2GG.

HOROWITZ Donald (Leonard), b. 27 June 1939, New York, New York, USA. Professor of Law and Political Science; Writer. m. Judith Anne Present, 4 Sept 1960, 2 sons, 1 daughter. Education: AB, 1959, LLB, 1961, Syracuse University; LLM, 1962, AM, 1965, PhD, 1967, Harvard University. Appointments: Admitted to the Bar, New York, 1962; Research Associate, Center for International Affairs, Harvard University, 1967-69; Brookings Institution, Washington, DC, 1972-75; Attorney, US Department of Justice, Washington, DC, 1969-71; Fellow, Council on Foreign Relations and Woodrow Wilson International Center for Scholars, Washington, DC, 1971-72; Senior Fellow, Research Institute on Immigration and Ethnic Studies, Smithsonian Institution, Washington, DC, 1975-81; McDonald-Currie Memorial Lecturer, McGill University, Montreal, 1980; Professor of Law and Political Science, 1980-, Charles S Murphy Professor, 1988-93, James B Duke Professor, 1994-, Duke University; Visiting Professor and Charles J Merriam Scholar, University of Chicago, 1988; Visiting Fellow, Cambridge University, 1988; Visiting Scholar, Universiti Kebangsaan, Malaysia, 1991. Publications: The Courts and Social Policy, 1977; The Jurocracy: Government Lawyers, Agency Programs and Judicial Decisions, 1977; Coup Theories and Officers' Motives, 1980; Ethnic Groups in Conflict, 1985; A Democratic South Africa?: Constitutional Engineering in a Divided Society, 1991. Contributions to: Professional journals, newspapers, and periodicals. Honours: Louis Brownlow Prize, National Academy of Public Administration, 1977; Guggenheim Fellowship, 1980-81; Ralph J Bunche Award, American Political Science Association, 1992. Membership: American Academy of Arts and Sciences, fellow. Address: School of Law, Duke University, Durham, NC 27706, USA.

HOROWITZ Irving (Louis), b. 25 Sept 1929, New York, New York, USA. Professor of Social and Political Theory; Writer; Editor; Publisher. m. (1) Ruth Lenore Horowitz, 1950, div 1964, 2 sons, (2) Mary Curtis Horowitz, 9 Oct 1979. Education: BSS, City College, New York City, 1951; MA, Columbia University, 1952; PhD, University of Buenos Aires, 1957; Postgraduate Fellow, Brandeis University, 1958-59. Appointments: Associate Professor, University of Buenos Aires, 1955-58; Visiting Professor of Sociology, University of Caracas, 1957, University of Buenos Aires, 1959, 1961, 1963, State University of New York at Buffalo, 1960, Syracuse University, 1961, University of Rochester, 1962, University of California at Davis, 1966, University of Wisconsin at Madison, 1967, Stanford University, 1968-69, American University, 1972, Queen's University, Canada, 1973, Princeton University, 1976, University of Miami, 1992; Assistant Professor, Bard College, 1960; Chairman, Department of Sociology, Hobart and William Smith Colleges, 1960-63; Visiting Lecturer, London School of Economics and Political Science, 1962; Editor-in-Chief, Transaction Society, 1962-94; Associate Professor to Professor of Sociology, Washington University, St Louis, 1963-69; President, Transaction Books, 1966-94; Chairman, Department of Sociology, Livingston College, Rutgers University, 1969-73; Professor of Sociology, Graduate Faculty, 1969-, Hannah Arendt Professor of Social and Political Theory, 1979-, Rutgers University; Bacardi Chair of Cuban Studies, Miami University, 1992-93; Editorial Chairman and President Emeritus, Transaction/USA and

Transaction/UK. Publications: Idea of War and Peace in Contemporary Philosophy, 1957; Philosophy, Science and the Sociology of Knowledge, 1960; Radicalism and the Revolt Against Reason: The Social Theories of Georges Sorel, 1962, 2nd edition, 1968; The War Game: Studies of the New Civilian Militarists, 1963; Professing Sociology: The Life Cycle of a Social Science, 1963; The New Sociology: Essays in Social Science and Social Values in Honor of C Wright Mills (editor), 1964; Revolution in Brazil: Politics and Society in a Developing Nation, 1964; The Rise and Fall of Project Camelot, 1967, revised edition, 1976; Three Worlds of Development: The Theory and Practice of International Stratification, 1967, revised edition, 1972; Latin American Radicalism: A Documentary Report on Nationalist and Left Movements, 1969; Sociological Self-Images, 1969; The Knowledge Factory: Masses in Latin America, 1970; Cuban Communism, 1970, 9th edition, 1998; Foundations of Political Sociology, 1972; Social Science and Public Policy in the United States, 1975; Ideology and Utopia in the United States, 1977; Dialogues on American Politics, 1979; Taking Lives: Genocide and State Power, 1979, 4th edition, 1997; Beyond Empire and Revolution, 1982; C Wright Mills: An American Utopian, 1983; Winners and Losers, 1985; Communicating Ideas, 1987; Daydreams and Nightmares: Reflections of a Harlem Childhood, 1990; The Decomposition of Sociology, 1993; Behemoth: Main Currents in the History and Theory of Political Sociology, 1999. Contributions to: Professional journals. Honours: Harold D Lasswell Award; Festschrift, 1994; National Jewish Book Award in Biography/Autobiography. Memberships: American Academy of Arts and Sciences; American Association of University Professors; American Political Science Association; Authors Guild; Council on Foreign Relations; International Society of Political Psychology, founder; National Association of Scholars. Literary Agent: Brandt and Brandt. Address: 1247 State Road, Route 206, Blanwenberg Road, Rocky Hill Intersection, Princeton, NJ 08540, USA.

HORTON Felix Lee. See: **FLOREN Lee.**

HORWOOD Harold (Andrew), b. 2 Nov 1923, St John's, Newfoundland, Canada. Author. m. Cornelia Lindismith, 1 July 1973, 1 son, 1 daughter. Education: Prince of Wales College, St John's, Newfoundland. Appointments: Member, House of Assembly, Newfoundland, Liberal Party, 1949-51; Columnist, Evening Telegram, St John's, Newfoundland, 1952-58; Writer-in-Residence, University of Western Ontario, 1976-77, University of Waterloo, 1980-82. Publications: Tomorrow Will be Sunday (novel), 1966, revised edition, 1992; The Foxes of Beachy Cove, 1967; Newfoundland, 1969, 2nd edition, 1977; White Eskimo: A Novel of Labrador, 1972; Beyond the Road: Portraits and Visions of Newfoundlands, 1976; Bartlett: The Great Canadian Explorer, 1977; The Colonial Dream 1497/1760, 1978; Only the Gods Speak (short stories), 1979; Tales of the Labrador Indians, 1981; A History of Canada, 1984; Pirates and Outlaws of Canada 1610-1932 (with E Butts), 1984; A History of the Newfoundland Ranger Force, 1986; Corner Brook: A Social History of a Paper Town, 1986; Historic Newfoundland (with John de Visser), 1986; Remembering Summer (novel), 1987; Dancing on the Shore, 1987; Bandits and Privateers: Canada in the Age of Gunpowder (with E Butts), 1987; Joey: The Life and Political Times of Joey Smallwood, 1989; The Magic Ground, 1996; A Walk in the Dream Time: Growing Up in Old St John's, 1997. Contributions to: Numerous journals and magazinees. Honours: Beta Sigma Phi First Novel Award, 1966; Best Scientific Book of the Year, 1967; Canada Council Senior Arts Award, 1975; Member of the Order of Canada, 1980. Membership: Writers' Union of Canada, chairman, 1980-81. Address: PO Box 489, Annapolis Royal, Nova Scotia BOS 1A0, Canada.

HOSAKA Kazushi, b. 1956, Yamanashi Prefecture, Japan. Writer. Education: Graduated, Political Science, Waseda University, Tokyo, 1981. Publications: Plainsong, 1990; Breakfast on the Grass, 1993; Time Passes on Cats, 1994; A Person's Limit, 1995; Memories of Seasons, 1996. Honours: Noma Literary Award for New Writers, 1993; Akutagawa Literary Prize, 1995. Address: c/o Japan PEN Club, 265 Akasaka Residential Hotel, 9-1-7 Akasaka, Minato-ku, Tokyo 107, Japan.

HOSEIN Hosenuddin, b. 28 Feb 1941, Krishna Nagar, Jhikargacha, Bangladesh. Farmer. m. Hasina Aktar, 8 Nov 1963, 2 sons, 2 daughters. Education: Matriculation, Dhaka Education Board, 1957. Appointments: Reporter, Daily Sangbad, 1960; Exexutive Editor, Natun Desh weekly, 1968-71. Publications: Jessoreaddadesh, 1974; Jessore Zillar Kimbodanti, 1974; Amrito Baideshik, 1975; Nasto Manush (novel), 1975; Plaban Abong Akzan (novel), 1979; Voltaire-Flower-Tolstoy, Troye Upannasho Jugmanash (analytical criticism), 1988; Autiya, Adhunikata and Ahasan Habib (analytical criticism), 1996; Banglar Bidroho (thesis on revolt of Bengal from 600-1947), 1998. Contributions to: Dainik Bangla; Dainik Ittefaque; Dainik Sangbad; Shaily. Honours: Chanderhat Literary Award, 1990; Mohammad Shidulla Literary Award, 1996. Address: Vill Krishna Nagar, Post Jhikargacha, Dist Jessore, Bangladesh.

HOSILLOS Lucila V,b. 29 June 1931, Tanza, Iloilo City, Philippines. Cultural Consultant; Writer. Education: AB, English, Far Eastern University, Manila, 1958; AM, Comparative Literature, 1962, PhD 1964, Indiana University, USA. Appointments: Instructor, State University of New York at Buffalo, 1963-64; Assistant Professor, Full Professor of Comparative Literature, University of the Philippines, 1966-85; Visiting Professor, National University of Singapore, 1983-84; Cultural Consultant, 1985-. Publications: The Concentric Sphere and Other Essays in Comparative Literature, 1968; Philippine American Literary Relations 1898-1941, 1969; Philippine Literature and Contemporary Events, 1970; Anthology of Third World Poetry, 1978; Originality as Vengeance in Philippine Literature, 1984; Perempuam (editor), 1987; Hiligaynon Literature: Texts and Contexts, 1992. Contributions to: Poems, short-stories, essays and scholarly papers. Honours: 1st Prize, Hiligaynon Short Story Writing Contest, Liwayway Publications, 1969; 1st Prize, ASEAN Literary Contest, Manila, 1977; Grand Prize, Literary Criticism in English, Cultural Centre of the Philippines 10th Anniversary Literary Contest, 1979; 2nd Prize, UNESCO Contest on Least Developed Countries, 1981; National Winner, UNESCO Essay Competition, Columbus Quincentenery, 1993. Memberships: Federation Internationale des Langues et Literatures Modernes; Association Internationale de Litterature Comparée; American Comparative Literature Association; ASEAN Writers Association; Illonggo Language and Literature Foundation, founder, chairman, and president . Address: 24/25 Block 3, Fatima Village, Sta. Cruz, Arevalo, 5000 Iloilo City, Philippines.

HOSPITAL Janette Turner, b. 12 Nov 1942, Melbourne, Victoria, Australia. Novelist. Education: BA, University of Queensland, Brisbane, 1965; MA, Queen's University, Canada, 1973. Appointments: Lecturer, Queen's University, St Lawrence College, Kingston, Ontario, 1971-82; Writer-in-Residence, Massachusetts Institute of Technology, 1985-89; Adjunct Professor, La Trobe University, 1991-93; Visiting Fellow and Writer-in-Residence, University of East Anglia, Norwich, 1996. Publications: The Ivory Swing, 1982; The Tiger in the Tiger Pit, 1983; Borderline, 1985; Charades, 1988; A Very Proper Death, 1990; The Last Magician, 1992; Oyster, 1996. Contributions to: Times Literary Supplement; London Review of Books; Independent; New York Times; Boston Globe. Honours: Seal Award, 1982; Fellowship of Australian Writers Award, 1988. Address: c/o Mic Cheetham, 138 Buckingham Palace Road, London SW1W 9SA, England.

HOSTE Pol, b. 25 Mar 1947, Lokeren, Belgium. Writer. Education: Licentiate, Germanic Philology, State University of Ghent, 1970. Publications: De Veranderingen, 1979; Vrouwelijk Enkelvoud, 1987; Een Schoon Bestaan, 1989; Brieven aan Mozart, 1991; Ontroeringen van een Forens, 1993; High Key, 1995; Foto's met de Aap, 1997; De Lucht naar Mirabel, 1999. Address: Kortedagsteeg 31, B-9000 Gent, Belgium.

HOTCHNER Aaron Edward, b. 28 June 1920, St Louis, Missouri, USA. Author; Dramatist. Education: LLB, Washington University, St Louis, 1941. Publications: The Dangerous American, 1958; The White House (play), 1964; Papa Hemingway: A Personal Memoir, 1966; The Hemingway Hero (play), 1967; Treasure, 1970; Do You Take This Man? (play), 1970; King of the Hill, 1972; Looking for Miracles, 1974; Doris Day: Her Own Story, 1976; Sophia: Living and Loving, 1979; Sweet Prince (play), 1980; The Man Who Lived at the Ritz, 1982; Choice People, 1984; Hemingway and His World, 1988; Welcome to the Club (musical), 1989; Blown Away, 1990 Louisiana Purchase, 1996; Exactly Like You (musical), 1998. Contributions to: Magazines. Honours: Honorary DHL, Washington University, 1992; Distinguished Alumni Award, Washington University Law School, 1992. Memberships: Authors League; Dramatists Guild; PEN. Address: 14 Hillandale Road, Westport, CT 06880, USA.

HOUGH (Helen) Charlotte, b. 24 May 1924, Hampshire, England. Writer. m. (1) Richard Hough, 17 July 1941, div 1973, 4 daughters, (2) Louis Ackroyd 24 April 1997. Publications: Jim Tiger, 1956; Morton's Pony, 1957; The Hampshire Pig, 1958; The Story of Mr Pinks, 1958; The Animal Game, 1959; The Homemakers, 1959; The Trackers, 1960; Algernon, 1962; Three Little Funny Ones, 1962; The Owl in the Barn, 1964; More Funny Ones, 1965; Red Biddy, 1966; Anna and Minnie, 1967; Sir Frog, 1968; My Aunt's Alphabet, 1969; A Bad Child's Book of Moral Verse, 1970; The Bassington Murder, 1980. Memberships: Crime Writers Association; PEN; Society of Authors. Address: 1A Ivor Street, London NW1 9PL, England.

HOUGH Julia Marie. See: **TAYLOR Judy.**

HOUGH Richard Alexander, (Bruce Carter, Elizabeth Churchill, Pat Strong), b. 15 May 1922, Brighton, Sussex, England. Writer. m. (1) Helen Charlotte, 1943, div, 4 daughters, (2) Judy Taylor, 1980. Appointments: Publisher, 1947-70; Director and Managing Director, Hamish Hamilton Children's Books Ltd, 1955-70. Publications: Non-Fiction: The Fleet that Had to Die, 1958; Admirals in Collision, 1959; The Potemkin Mutiny, 1960; The Hunting of Forze Z, 1963; Dreadnought, 1964; The Big Battleship, 1966; First Sea Lord: An Authorized Life of Admiral Lord Fisher, 1969; The Pursuit of Admiral von Spee, 1969; The Blind Horn's Hate, 1971; Captain Bligh and Mr Christian, 1972; Louis and Victoria: The First Mountbattens, 1974; One Boy's War: Per astra ad ardua, 1975; Advice to a Grand-daughter (Queen Victoria's letters, editor), 1975; The Great Admirals, 1977; The Murder of Captain James Cook, 1979; Man o' war, 1979; Nelson, 1980; Mountbatten: Hero of Our Time, 1980; Edwina: Countess Mountbatten of Burma, 1983; The Great War at Sea 1914-1918, 1983; Former Naval Person: Churchill and the Wars at Sea, 1985; The Longest Battle, 1986; The Ace of Clubs: A History of the Garrick, 1986; Born Royal, 1988; The Battle of Britain: The Jubilee History (with Denis Richards), 1989; Winston and Clementine: The Triumph of the Churchills, 1990; Bless Our Ship: Mountbatten and HMS Kelly, 1991; Other days Around Me: A Memoir, 1992; Edward and Alexandra: The Private and Public Lives, 1992; Captain James Cook: A Biography, 1994; Victoria and Albert, 1996; Sister Agnes: A History of King Edward VII's Hospital for Officers, 1998. Fiction: Angels One Five, 1978; The Fight of the Few, 1979; The Fight to the Finish, 1979; Buller's Guns, 1981; Razor Eyes, 1981; Buller's Dreadnought, 1982; Buller's Victory, 1984; The Raging Sky, 1989. Other: Several children's books. Contributions to: Newspapers and magazines. Honour: Daily Express Best Book of the Sea Award, 1972. Membership: Navy Records Society, vice president, 1977-82. Address: 31 Meadowbank, Primrose Hill, London, NW3 1AY, England.

HOUGH Stanley Bennett, (Rex Gordon, Bennett Stanley), b. 25 Feb 1917, Preston, Lancashire, England. Author. m. Justa E C Wodschow, 1938. Publications: Frontier Incident, 1951; Moment of Decision, 1952; Mission in Guemo, 1953; The Seas South, 1953; The Primitives, 1954; Sea to Eden, 1954; Extinction Bomber,

1956; A Pound a Day Inclusive, 1957; Expedition Everyman, 1959; Beyond the Eleventh Hour, 1961; The Tender Killer, 1962; Where?, 1965; Dear Daughter Dead, 1965; Sweet Sister Seduced, 1968; Fear Fortune Father, 1974. Honour: Infinity Award for Science Fiction, 1957. Membership: Royal Cornwall Polytechnic Society, 1985-88. Address: 21 St Michael's Road, Ponsanooth, Truro TR3 7ED, England.

HOUGHTON Eric, b. 4 Jan 1930, West Yorkshire, England. Teacher; Author. m. Cecile Wolffe, 4 June 1954, 1 son, 1 daughter. Education: Sheffield City College of Education, 1952. Publications: The White Wall, 1961; Summer Silver, 1963; They Marched with Spartacus, 1963; A Giant Can Do Anything, 1975; The Mouse and the Magician, 1976; The Remarkable Feat of King Caboodle, 1978; Steps Out of Time, 1979; Gates of Glass, 1987; Walter's Wand, 1989; The Magic Cheese, 1991; The Backwards Watch, 1991; Vincent the Invisible, 1993; Rosie and the Robbers, 1997. Honour: American Junior Book Award, 1964. Memberships: Society of Authors; Childrens Writers Group. Address: The Crest, 42 Collier Road, Hastings, East Sussex TN34 3JR, England.

HOUK Margaret, (Patricia Hughes), b. 8 Jan 1932, Grand Rapids, Michigan, USA. Freelance Writer. m. John Peter Houk, 16 Aug 1952, 1 son, 3 daughters. Education: BS, Honours, Home Economics, Valparaiso University, 1953. Appointments: Homemaker, Substitute Home Economics, 1957-58; Nursery School Teacher, 1962-63; Writer, 1971-. Publications: That Very Special Person Me!, 1990; 100 Easy Ways to Teach Your Child to Love God's World (mini book), 1994; Lighten Up and Enjoy Life More, 1996. Contributions to: Anthologies and periodicals. Honours: 2nd Place, Michigan Bar Association, 1949; Several other awards. Memberships: Wisconsin Region Writers Association; Associated Church Press Association; Evangelical Press Association; PEN; Christian Writers Club; Fox Valley Writers Club. Address: W 2355 Valleywood Lane, Appleton, WI 54915, USA.

HOUSTON James, b. 10 Nov 1933, San Francisco, California, USA. Author. m. Jeanne Toyo Wakatsuki, 1957, 1 son, 2 daughters. Education: BA, San Jose State College, 1956; MA, Stanford University, 1962. Appointments: Instructor in English, Cabrillo College, 1962-64; Lecturer in English, Stanford University, 1967-68; Lecturer in Writing, 1969-88, Visiting Professor in Literature, 1989-93, University of California at Santa Cruz; Writer-in-Residence, Villa Montalvo, Saratoga, California, 1980, 1992, Centrum Foundation, Port Townsend, Washington, 1992; Distinguished Visiting Writer, University of Hawaii, 1983; Allen T Gilliland Chair in Telecommunications, San Jose State University, 1985; Visiting Writer, University of Michigan, 1985, University of Oregon, 1994. Publications: Novels: Between Battles, 1968; Gig, 1969; A Native Son of the Golden West, 1971; Continental Drift, 1978; Love Life, 1987; The Last Paradise, 1998. Stories: Gasoline: The Automotive Adventures of Charlie Bates, 1980. Non-Fiction: Farewell to Manzanar (with Jeanne Wakatsuki Houston), 1973; Open Field (with John R Brodie), 1974; Three Songs for My Father, 1974; Californians: Searching for the Golden State, 1982; One Can Think About Life After the Fish is in the Canoe, and Other Coastal Sketches, 1985; The Men in My Life, and Other More or Less True Recollections of Kinship, 1987; In the Ring of Fire: A Pacific Basin Journey, 1997. Editor: Writing From the Inside, 1973; California Heartland: Writing From the Great Central Valley (with Gerald Haslam), 1978; West Coast Fiction: Modern Writing From California, Oregon and Washington, 1979. Films: Farewell to Manzanar (with Jean Wakatsuki Houston and John Korty), 1976; Li'a: The Legacy of a Hawaiian Man, 1988; Listen to the Forest, 1991; The Hawaiian Way: The Art and Family Tradition of Slack Key, 1993; Words, Earth and Aloha: The Sources of Hawaiian Music, 1995. Contributions to: Various anthologies. Honours: Wallace Stegner Writing Fellow, Stanford University, 1966-67; Joseph Henry Jackson Award, 1967; Humanitas Prize, 1976; National Endowment for the Arts Grants, 1976-77; Research Fellow, East-West Center, Honolulu, 1984; American Book Award, 1983; Hawaii International Film Festival Special Award, 1989; Rockefeller Foundation Writer's Residency, Bellagio, Italy, 1995. Memberships: PEN Center West; Writers Guild of America West. Address: 2-1130 East Cliff Drive, Santa Cruz, CA 95062, USA.

HOUSTON James A(rchibald), b. 12 June 1921, Toronto, Ontario, Canada. Author. m. (1) Alma G Bardon, 1950, div 1966, (2) Alice Daggett Watson, 9 Dec 1967, 2 sons. Education: Ontario College of Art, 1938-40; Academie de la Grande Chaumiere, Paris, 1947-48; Unichi-Hiratsuka, Tokyo, 1958-59; Atelier 17, Paris, 1961. Appointments: Arctic Adviser, Canadian Guild of Crafts, 1949-52; Civil Administrator, West Baffin, Northwest Territories, Canada, 1952-62; Associate Director, 1962-72, Master Designer, 1972-, Steuben Glass, New York City; President, Indian and Eskimo Art of the Americas. Publications: Fiction: The White Dawn: An Eskimo Saga, 1971; Ghost Fox, 1977; Spirit Wrestler, 1980; Eagle Song, 1983; Running West, 1989. Children's Books: Over 15 books, 1965-92. Non-Fiction: Canadian Eskimo Art, 1955; Eskimo Graphic Art, 1960; Eskimo Prints, 1967, 2nd edition, 1971; Songs of the Dream People: Chants and Images from the Indians and Eskimos of North America, 1972; Ojibwa Summer, 1972; Confessions of an Igloo Dweller, 1995. Screenplays: The White Dawn, 1973; The Mask and the Drum, 1975; So Sings the Wolf, 1976; Kalvak, 1976. Contributions to: Magazines; Canadian Encyclopedia. Honours: American Indian and Eskimo Cultural Foundation Award, 1966; Canadian Library Association of the Year Awards, 1966, 1968, 1980; American Library Association Notable Books Awards, 1967, 1968, 1971; Officer of the Order of Canada, 1972; Inuit Kuavati Award of Merit, 1979; Citation of Merit Award, Royal Canadian Academy of Arts, 1987; Max and Gretta Ebel Award, Canadian Society of Children's Authors, Illustrators, and Performers, 1989; Honorary doctorates. Memberships: American Indian Arts Center; Canadian Arctic Producers; Canadian Eskimo Arts Center; Explorers Club; Producers Guild of America; Royal Society of the Arts, fellow; Writers Union of Canada; Writers Guild of Canada. Address: 24 Main Street, Stonington, CT 06378, USA.

HOUSTON R B. See: **RAE Hugh Crauford.**

HOUTH Henriette, b. 8 July 1967, Grenaa, Denmark, Architect. Education: Architect, School of Architecture, Aarhus, Denmark, 1997. Publications: Samling, poetry, 1997; Levende Dode Ting, essays on organic design, 1999. Contributions to: Poems to Hvedekorn, 1996; Den Bla Port; Ildfisken, 1998. Membership: The Danish Writers' Union. Address: Gyldendalis Forlag, Klareboderne 3, DK-1115 Kobenhaun, Denmark.

HOVANNISIAN Richard G, b. 9 Nov 1932, Tulare, California, USA. Professor of Armenian and Near Eastern History; Writer. m. Vartiter Kotcholosian, 2 Mar 1957, 4 children. Education: BA in History, 1954, MA in History, 1958, University of California at Berkeley; Certificate in Armenian, Collège Armènien, Beirut, 1956; PhD in History, University of California at Los Angeles, 1966. Appointments: Lecturer, 1962-69, Professor of Armenian and Near Eastern History, 1969-, Associate Director, G E von Grunebaum Center of Near Eastern Studies, 1979-95, University of California at Los Angeles; Associate Professor of History, St Mary's College, Los Angeles, 1965-69; Chairman, Modern Armenian History, Armenian Educational Foundation, 1987-; Guest Lecturer; Consultant. Publications: Armenia on the Road to Independence, 1967, 4th edition, 1984; The Republic of Armenia, Vol I, 1971, 2nd edition, 1996, Vol II, 1982, 2nd edition, 1996, Vols III-IV, 1996; The Armenian Holocaust, 1980; The Armenian Genocide in Perspective, 1986; The Armenian Genocide: History, Politics, Ethics, 1992; The Armenian People from Ancient to Modern Times, Vol I, The Dynastic Periods: From Antiquity to the Fourteenth Century, Vol II, Foreign Dominion to Statehood: The Fifteenth to Twentieth Century, 1997. Co-Author: Transcaucasia: Nationalism and Social Change, 1983; Le Crime de Silence: Le Gènocide des Armèniens, 1984; Toward the Understanding and Prevention of Genocide, 1984; A Crime of Silence, 1985; Genocide: A Critical Bibliographic Review, 1988; Embracing the Other: Philosophical, Psychological, and Historical Perspectives on Altruism, 1992; Diasporas in World Politics, 1993; Genocide and Human Rights, 1993; Genocide: Conceptual and Historical Dimensions, 1994; The Legacy of History in Russia and the New States of Eurasia, 1994. Editor: The Armenian Image in History and Literature, 1981; Islam's Understanding of Itself, 1983; Ethics in Islam, 1985; Poetry and Mysticism in Islam: The Heritage of Rumi, 1994. Contributions to: Many professional journals and to periodicals. Honours: Humanities Institute Fellow, 1972; Guggenheim Fellowship, 1974-75; National Endowment for the Humanities Grant, 1981-82; California Council for the Humanities Grant, 1985-86; Numerous awards, citations, and recognitions. Memberships: American Association for the Advancement of Slavic Studies; American Historical Association; Armenian Academy of Science; Middle East Studies Association, fellow; National Association of Armenian Studies; Oral History Association; Society for Armenian Studies, founder-president, 1974-75, 1990-92. Address: 101 Groverton Place, Los Angeles, CA 90077, USA.

HOWARD Anthony Michell, b. 12 Feb 1934, London, England. Biographer; Reviewer; Writer. m. Carol Anne Gaynor, 26 May 1965. Education: BA, Christ Church, Oxford, 1955. Appointments: Called to the Bar, Inner Temple, 1956; Political Correspondent, Reynolds News, 1958-59; Editorial Staff, Manchester Guardian, 1959-61; Political Correspondent, 1961-64, Assistant Editor, 1970-72, Editor, 1972-78, New Statesman; Whitehall Correspondent, 1965, Sunday Times, Washington; Chief Political Correspondent, 1966-69, Deputy Editor, 1981-88, Observer; Editor, The Listener, 1979-81; Reporter, BBC TV News and Current Affairs, 1989-92; Obituaries Editor, The Times, 1993-99. Publications: The Making of the Prime Minister (with Richard West), 1965; The Crossman Diaires: Selections from the Diaries of a Cabinet Minister (editor), 1979; Rab: The Life of R A Butler, 1987; Crossman: The Pursuit of Power, 1990; The Times Lives Remembered (editor with David Heaton), 1990. Contributions to: Books, newspapers, and journals. Honours: Harkness Fellowship, USA, 1960; Commander of the Order of the British Empire, 1997. Address: 11 Campden House Court, 42 Gloucester Walk, London W8 4HU, England.

HOWARD Catherine Audrey, b. 5 Feb 1953, Huddersfield, England. Retired Government Officer. m. Leslie Howard, 3 Apr 1987. Education: Harold Pitchforth School of Commerce; Ashlar and Spen Valley Further Education Institute; Royal Society of Arts Diplomas. Appointments: Clerk, Treasury Department, 1969-70, Clerk, Housing Department, 1970-74, Elland Urban District Council; Clerk, Telephonist, Housing Department, Calderdale Metropolitan Borough Council, 1974-83; Social Work Assistant; Social Services Department, Calderdale, 1983-88. Publications: Elland in Old Picture Postcards, 1983; Poetry: Down By the Old Mill Stream, 1993; The Flamborough Longsword Dance, 1994; Sacrifice for Christianity, 1994; My Pennine Roots, 1994; The Old and the New, 1994; Having Faith, 1994; The Might of the Meek, 1995; Tough as Old Boots, 1995; Portrait of All Hallows, 1996; Childhood Memories, 1996; Old Ways in Modern Days, 1996; Northern Cornucopia, 1996; A Glimpse of Spring, 1998; Poetry From Yorkshire, 1999. Contributions to: Mercedes-Benz Gazette, 1996. Honours: National Poet of the Year Commendations, 1996 (3 times); National Open Competition Commendations, 1996, 1997; Robert Bloomfield Memorial Awards Commendation, 1998. Address: 17 Woodlands Close, Bradley Grange, Bradley, Huddersfield, West Yorkshire, England.

HOWARD Clark, b. 1934, USA. Author. Publications: The Arm, 1967; A Movement Toward Eden, 1969; The Doomsday Squad, 1970; The Killings, 1973; Last Contract, 1973; Summit Kill, 1975; Mark the Sparrow, 1975; The Hunters, 1976; The Last Great Death Stunt, 1976; Six Against the Rock, 1977; The Wardens, 1979; Zebra: The True Account of the 179 Days of Terror in San Francisco, 1979, UK edition as The Zebra Killings,

1980; American Saturday, 1981; Brothers in Blood, 1983; Dirt Rich, 1986; Hard City, 1990; Love's Blood, 1993; City Blood, 1994. Honours: Edgar Allan Poe Award, 1980; Ellery Queen Awards, 1985, 1986, 1988, 1990. Membership: Mystery Writers of America. Address: Box 1527, Palm Springs, CA 92263, USA.

HOWARD Deborah (Janet), b. 26 Feb 1946, London, England. Architectural Historian; Writer. m. Malcolm S Longair, 26 Sept 1975, 1 son, 1 daughter. Education: BA, Honours, 1968, MA, 1972, Newnham College, Cambridge; MA, 1969, PhD, 1973, University of London. Appointments: Reader in Architectural History, University of Cambridge; Fellow, St John's College, Cambridge. Publications: Jacopo Sansovino: Architecture and Patronage in Renaissance Venice, 1975, 2nd edition, 1987; The Architectural History of Venice, 1980, 3rd edition, 1987; Scottish Architecture from the Reformation to the Restoration, 1560-1660, 1995. Contributions to: Professional journals. Honour: Honorary Fellow, Royal Incorporation of Architects of Scotland. Memberships: Royal Commission on the Ancient and Historical Monuments of Scotland, commissioner; Society of Antiquarians of Scotland, fellow; Society of Antiquaries, fellow; Address: St John's College, Cambridge CB2 1TP, England.

HOWARD Elizabeth Jane, b. 26 Mar 1923, London, England. Author. m. (1) Peter Scott, 1941, 1 daughter, (2) Kingsley Amis, 1965, div 1983. Education: Trained as Actress, London Mask Theatre School, Scott Thorndike Student Repertory. Appointments: Honorary Director, Cheltenham Literary Festival, 1962; Co-Director, Salisbury Festival, 1973. Publications: The Beautiful Visit, 1950; The Long View, 1956; The Sea Change, 1959; After Julius, 1965; Odd Girl Out, 1972; Mr Wrong, 1975; Getting It Right, 1982; The Light Years, 1990; Marking Time, 1991; Confusion, 1993; Casting Off, 1995. Other: 14 television plays; 3 film scripts. Contributions to: The Times; Sunday Times; Telegraph; Encounter; Vogue; Harper's; Queen. Honours: Yorkshire Post Novel of the Year, 1982. Memberships: Royal Society of Literature, fellow; Authors Lending and Copyright Society. Address: c/o Jonathan Clowes, Ivan Bridge House, Bridge Approach, London NW1 8BD, England.

HOWARD Ellen, b. 8 May 1943, New Bern, North Carolina, USA. Writer. m. Charles Howard Jr, 29 June 1975, 4 daughters. Education: University of Oregon, 1961-63; BA, Honours, English, Portland State University, 1979. Publications: Circle of Giving, 1984; When Daylight Comes, 1985; Gillyflower, 1986; Edith Herself, 1987; Her Own Song, 1988; Sister, 1990; The Chickenhouse House, 1991; The Cellar, 1992; The Tower Room, 1993; The Big Seed, 1993; Murphy and Kate, 1995; The Log Cabin Quilt, 1996; A Different Kind of Courage, 1996. Honours: Golden Kite Honor Book, 1984; Christopher Award, 1997. Memberships: Authors Guild; Society of Children's Book Writers and Illustrators. Address: 1811 Montview Boulevard, Greeley, CO 80631, USA.

HOWARD Lynette Desley, (Lynsey Stevens), b. 28 Sept 1947, Sherwood, Queensland, Australia. Writer. Publications: Ryan's Return, 1981; Terebori's Gold, 1981; Race for Revenge, 1981; Play Our Song Again, 1981; Tropical Knight, 1982; Starting Over, 1982; Man of Vengeance, 1982; Closest Place to Heaven, 1983; Forbidden Wine, 1983; The Ashby Affair, 1983; Lingering Embers, 1984; Leave Yesterday Behind, 1986; But Never Love, 1988; A Rising Passion, 1990; Touched by Desire, 1993; A Physical Affair, 1994; His Cousin's Wife, 1996; Close Relations, 1997; Male for Christmas, 1998. Honour: Arty, Romantic Times, Worldwide Romance, 1984. Memberships: Romantic Novelists Association, UK; Queensland Writers Centre; Australian Society of Authors; Romance Writers of America; Romance Writers of Australia. Address: PO Box 400, Red Hill, Queensland 4259, Australia.

HOWARD Maureen, b. 28 June 1930, Bridgeport, Connecticut, USA. Lecturer; Writer. m. (1) Daniel F Howard, 28 Aug 1954, div 1967, 1 daughter, (2) David J Gordon, 2 Apr 1968, div, (3) Mark Probst, 1981.

Education: BA, Smith College, 1952. Appointments: Lecturer, New School for Social Research, New York City, 1967-68, 1970-71, 1974-, University of California at Santa Barbara, 1968-69, Amherst College, Brooklyn College of the City University of New York, Columbia University. Publications: Fiction: Not a Word About Nightingales, 1961; Bridgeport Bus, 1966; Before My Time, 1975; Grace Abounding, 1982; Expensive Habits, 1986; Natural History, 1992; A Lover's Almanac, 1998. Non-Fiction: Facts of Life (autobiography), 1978. Editor: Seven American Women Writers of the Twentieth Century, 1977; Contemporary American Essays, 1984. Honours: Guggenheim Fellowship, 1967-68; Radcliffe Institute Fellow, 1967-68; National Book Critics Circle Award, 1980; Ingram Merrill Foundation Fellow, 1988; Literary Lion Award, New York Public Library, 1993. Address: c/o Simon and Schuster, 1230 Avenue of the Americas, New York, NY 10020, USA.

HOWARD Philip Nicholas Charles, b. 2 Nov 1933, London, England. Editor; Columnist; Writer. m. Myrtle Janet Mary Houldsworth, 17 Oct 1959, 2 sons, 1 daughter. Education: MA, Trinity College, Oxford, 1957. Appointments: Staff, Glasgow Herald, 1959-64; Staff, 1964-, Literary Editor, 1978-92, Leader Writer and Columnist, 1992-, The Times; London Editor, Verbatim, 1977-. Publications: The Black Watch, 1968; The Royal Palaces, 1970; London's River, 1975; New Words for Old, 1977; The British Monarchy, 1977; Weasal Words, 1978; Words Fail Me, 1980; A Word in Your Ear, 1983; The State of the Language: English Observed, 1984; The Times Bicentenary Stamp Book (co-author), 1985; We Thundered Out: 200 Years of the Times, 1785-1985, 1985; Winged Words, 1988; Word-Watching, 1988; London: The Evolution of a Great City (co-author), 1989; A Word in Time, 1990; The Times Bedside Book (editor), 1991; Reading a Poem, 1992. Honour: Fellow, Royal Society of Literature, 1987. Memberships: Classical Association; Friends of Classics, founder-patron; Horatian Society; Literary Society; Society of Bookmen. Address: Flat 1, 47 Ladbroke Grove, London W11 3AR, England.

HOWARD Richard (Joseph), b. 13 Oct 1929, Cleveland, Ohio, USA. Poet; Critic; Editor; Translator. Educaton: BA, 1951, MA, 1952, Columbia University; Postgraduate Studies, Sorbonne, University of Paris, 1952-53. Appointments: Lexicographer, World Publishing Co, 1954-58; Poetry Editor, New American Review, New Republic, Paris Review, Shenandoah; Rhodes Professor of Comparative Literature, University of Cincinnati. Publications: Poetry: Quantities, 1962; The Damages, 1967; Untitled Subjects, 1969; Findings, 1971; Two-Part Inventions, 1974; Fellow Feelings, 1976; Misgivings, 1979; Lining Up, 1984; Quantities/Damages, 1984; No Traveller, 1989; Like Most Revelations: New Poems, 1994. Criticism: Alone With America, 1969; Passengers Must Not Ride on Fenders, 1974. Editor: Preferences: Fifty-One American Poets Choose Poems from Their Own Work and from the Past, 1974; The War in Algeria, 1975. Translator: Over 65 books. Contributions to: Magazines and journals. Honours: Guggenheim Fellowship, 1966-67; Harriet Monroe Memorial Prize, 1969; Pulitzer Prize in Poetry, 1970; Levinson Prize, 1973; Cleveland Arts Prize, 1974; American Academy and Institute of Arts and Letters Medal for Poetry, 1980; American Book Award for Translation, 1984; PEN American Center Medal for Translation, 1986; France-American Foundation Award for Translation, 1987; National Endowment for the Arts Fellowship, 1987. Address: c/o Alfred A Knopf Inc, 201 East 50th Street, New York, NY 10022, USA.

HOWARD Roger, b. 19 June 1938, Warwick, England. Dramatist; Poet; Author; Senior Lecturer in Literature. m. Anne Mary Zemaitis, 13 Aug 1960, 1 son. Education: Royal Academy of Dramatic Art, London, 1956-57; University of Bristol, 1958; MA, University of Essex, 1976. Appointments: Teacher, Nankai University, Tientsin, China, 1965-67; Lecturer, University of Beijing, 1972-74; Fellow in Creative Writing, University of York, 1976-78; Writing Fellow, University of East Anglia, 1979; Lecturer, 1979-93, Founder-Director, Theatre Underground, 1979-, Editor, New Plays series, 1980-, Senior Lecturer in

Literature, 1993-, University of Essex. Publications: A Phantastic Satire (novel), 1960; From the Life of a Patient (novel), 1961; To the People (poems), 1966; Praise Songs (poems), 1966; The Technique of the Struggle Meeting, 1968; The Use of Wall Newspapers, 1968; New Plays I, 1968; Fin's Doubts, 1968; Episodes from the Fighting in the East, 1971; The Hooligan's Handbook, 1971; Slaughter Night and Other Plays, 1971; Method for Revolutionary Writing, 1972; Culture and Agitation: Theatre Documents (editor), 1972; Contemporary Chinese Theatre, 1977; Mao Tse-tung and the Chinese People, 1978; The Society of Poets, 1979; A Break in Berlin, 1980; The Siege, 1981; Partisans, 1983; Ancient Rivers, 1984; The Speechifier, 1984; Contradictory Theatres, 1985; Senile Poems, 1988; The Tragedy of Mao and Other Plays, 1989; Britannia and Other Plays, 1990; Selected Poems 1966-96, 1997; Contributions to: Anthologiese, newspapers and journals. Address: c/o Theatre Underground, Department of Literature, University of Essex, Wivenhoe Park, Colchester, Essex CO4 3SQ, England.

HOWATCH Susan, b. 14 July 1940, Leatherhead, Surrey, England. Writer. Education: LLB, Kings College, University of London, 1958-61. Publications: The Dark Shore, 1965; The Waiting Sands, 1966; Call in the Night, 1967; The Shrouded Walls, 1968; April's Grave, 1969; The Devil on Lammas Night, 1970; Penmarric, 1971; Cashelmara, 1974; The Rich are Different, 1977; Sins of the Fathers, 1980; The Wheel of Fortune, 1984; Glittering Images, 1987; Glamorous Powers, 1988; Ultimate Prizes, 1989; Scandalous Risks, 1991; Mystical Paths, 1992; Absolute Truths, 1994; A Question of Integrity (published in USA as: The Wonder Worker). 1997. Contributions to: Writer; Church Times; Tablet. Honour: Winifred Mary Stanford Memorial Prize, 1992. Memberships: PEN; Society of Authors; Royal Overseas League. Address: c/o Aitken & Stone, 29 Fernshaw Road, London SW10 0TG, England.

HOWCROFT Wilbur Gordon, b. 28 Aug 1917, Kerang, Victoria Australia. Writer. m. Barbara Innes McLennan, 17 Aug 1942. Publications: Outback Observations, 1970; This Side of the Rabbit Proof Fence, 1971; The Clancy That Overflowed, 1971; Random Ramblings, 1972; The Farm that Blew Away, 1973; Facts, Fables and Foolery, 1973; Sand in the Stew, 1974; The Old Working Hat, 1975; The Eucalypt Trail, 1975; Black with White Cockatoos, 1977; Dungarees and Dust, 1978; Nonsery Rhymes, 1978; Bush Ballads and Buffoonery, 1979; Bush Ballads and Buldust, 1982; Hello Cocky, 1982; The Bushman Who Laughed, 1982; The Bushman Who Laughed Again, 1983; The Wilbur Howcroft Omnibus, 1985; Bush Characters, 1986; Aussie Odes, 1988; Billabongs and Billy Tea, 1989; Mopokes and Mallee Roots, 1989; Whimsical Wanderings. Contributions to: Professional journals, newspapers and magazines. Memberships: Australian Society of Authors. Address: PO Box 36, Culgoa, Victoria 3530, Australia.

HOWE Fanny, b. 15 Oct 1940, Buffalo, New York, USA. Professor of Writing and American Literature; Author; Poet; Dramatist. 1 son, 2 daughters. Education: Stanford University, 1958-61. Appointments: Lecturer, Tufts University, 1968-71, Emerson College, 1974, Columbia University Extension and School of the Arts, 1975-78, Yale University, 1976, Harvard University Extension, 1977, Massachusetts Institute of Technology, 1978-87; Professor of Writing and American Literature, University of California at San Diego, 1987-; Associate Director, Study Center, University College, London, 1993-95; Distinguished Visiting Writer-in-Residence, Mills College, 1996-97. Publications: Novels: Forty Whacks, 1969; First Marriage, 1975; Bronte Wilde, 1976; Holy Smoke, 1979; The White Slave, 1980; In the Middle of Nowhere, 1984; Taking Care, 1985; The Lives of a Spirit, 1986; The Deep North, 1988; Famous Questions, 1989; Saving History, 1992; Nod, 1998. Young Adult Novels: The Blue Hills, 1981; Yeah, But, 1982; Radio City, 1983; The Race of the Radical, 1985. Poetry: Eggs, 1980; The Amerindian Coastline Poem, 1976; Poem from a Single Pallet, 1980; Alsace Lorraine, 1982; For Erato, 1984; Introduction to the World, 1985; Robeson Street, 1985;

The Vineyard, 1988; The Quietist, 1992; The End, 1992; O'Clock, 1995; One Crossed Out, 1997; Q, 1998. Contributions to: Many anthologies, reviews, quarterlies, journals, and magazines. Honours: MacDowell Colony Fellowships, 1965, 1990; National Endowment for the Arts Fellowships in Fiction, 1969, and in Poetry, 1991; Bunting Institute Fellowship, 1974; St Botolph Award for Fiction, 1976; Writer's Choice Award for Fiction, 1984; Village Voice Award for Fiction, 1988; California Council on the Arts Award for Poetry, 1993. Address: 5208 La Jolla Hermosa, La Jolla, CA 92037, USA.

HOWE James, b. 2 Aug 1946, Oneida, New York, USA. Children's Writer. m. Betsy Imershein, 5 Apr 1981, 1 daughter. Education: BFA, Boston University, 1968; MA, Hunter College, 1977. Publications: Bunnicula, 1979; Teddy Bear's Scrapbook, 1980; The Hospital Book, 1981; Howliday Inn, 1982; A Night Without Stars, 1983; The Celery Stalks at Midnight, 1983; Morgan's Zoo, 1984; The Day the Teacher Went Bananas, 1984; What Eric Knew, 1985; Stage Fright, 1986; When You Go to the Kindergarten, 1986; There's a Monster Under My Bed, 1986; Babes in Toyland, 1986; Eat Your Poison, Dear, 1987; Nighty-Nightmare, 1987; I Wish I Were a Butterfly, 1987; The Fright Before Christmas, 1988; Scared Silly, 1989; Hot Fudge, 1990; Dew Drop Dead, 1990; Pinky and Rex, 1990; Pinky and Rex Get Married, 1990; Pinky and Rex and the Spelling Bee, 1991; Pinky and Red and the Mean Old Witch, 1991; Greepy-Crawly Birthday, 1991; Dances With Wolves: A Story for Children, 1991; Return to Howliday Inn, 1992; Pinky and Rex Go To Camp, 1992; Pinky and Rex and the New Baby, 1993; Rabbit-Cadabral, 1993; Bunnicula Fun Book, 1993; Bunnicula Escapes! A Pop-up Adventure, 1994; There's a Dragon in My Sleeping Bag, 1994; Playing With Words, 1994; Pinky and Rex and the Double-Dad Weekend, 1995. Contributions to: Journals and magazines. Address: Writers House, 21 West 26th Street, New York, NY 10010, USA.

HOWE Susan, b. 10 June 1937, USA. Poet. Education: BFA, Painting, Museum of Fine Arts, Boston, 1961. Appointments: Butler Fellow in English, 1988, Professor of English, 1989, State University of New York at Buffalo; Visiting Scholar and Professor of English, Temple University, Philadelphia, 1990, 1991; Visiting Poet and Leo Block Professor, University of Denver, 1993-94; Visiting Brittingham Scholar, University of Wisconsin at Madison, 1994; Visiting Poet, University of Arizona, 1994. Publications: Poetry: Hinge Picture, 1974; The Western Borders, 1976; Secret History of the Dividing Line, 1978; Cabbage Gardens, 1979; The Liberties, 1980; Pythagorean Silence, 1982; Defenestration of Prague, 1983; Articulation of Sound Forms in Time, 1987; A Bibliography of the King's Book, or Eikon Basilike, 1989; The Europe of Trusts: Selected Poems, 1990; Singularities, 1990; The Nonconformist's Memorial, 1993; Frame Structures: Early Poems 1974-1979, 1996. Other: My Emily Dickinson, 1985; Incloser, 1990; The Birthmark: Unsettling the Wilderness in American Literary History, 1993. Honours: Before Columbus Foundation American Book Awards, 1980, 1986; New York State Council of the Arts Residency, 1986; Pushcart Prize, 1987; New York City Fund for Poetry Grant, 1988; Roy Harvey Pearce Award, 1996; Guggenheim Fellowship, 1996-97. Address: 115 New Quarry Road, Guilford, CT 06437, UA.

HOWE Tina, b. 21 Nov 1937, New York, New York, USA. Playwright; Professor. m. Norman Levy, 1961, 1 son, 1 daughter. Education: BA, Sarah Lawrence College, Bronxville, New York, 1959. Appointments: Adjunct Professor, New York University, 1983-; Visiting Professor, Hunter College, New York, 1990-. Publications: The Nest, 1969; Museum, 1979; The Art of Dining, 1980; Painting Churches, 1984; Coastal Disturbances, 1987. Productions: One Shoe Off, New York, 1993; Approaching Zanzibar and Other Plays, Theatre Communications Group, 1995; Birth and After Birth, Philadelphia and Washington, DC, 1995-96; Prides Crossing, 1997; Honours: Obie for Distinguished Playwriting, 1983; Outer Critics Circle Award, 1983; Rockefeller Grant, 1984; National Endowment for the Arts Fellowships, 1985, 1995; Guggenheim Fellowship, 1990; American Academy of Arts and Letters Award in Literature, 1993; Honorary Degree, Whittier College, 1997; Honorary Degree Bowdoin College, 1998. Memberships: Dramatists Guild, council, 1990-; PEN. Address: Flora Roberts Inc, 157 West 57th Street, New York, NY 10019, USA.

HOWELL Anthony, b. 20 Apr 1945, London, England. Poet; Writer; Editor. Education: Leighton Park School; Royal Ballet School, London. Appointments: Lecturer, Grenoble University, Cardiff School of Art; Editor, Softly, Loudly Books, London, Grey Suit. Publications: Poetry: Inside the Castle, 1969; Femina Deserta, 1971; Oslo: A Tantric Ode, 1975; The Mekon, 1976; Notions of a Mirror: Poems Previously Uncollected, 1964-82, 1983; Winter's Not Gone, 1984; Why I May Never See the Walls of China, 1986; Howell's Law, 1990; Near Cavalry: Selected Poems of Nick Lafitte (editor), 1992. Fiction: In the Company of Others, 1986; First Time in Japan, 1995. Honour: Welsh Arts Council Bursary, 1989. Address: 21 Augusta Street, Adamsdown, Cardiff CF2 1EN, Wales.

HOWELLS Coral Ann, b. 22 Oct 1939, Maryborough, Queensland, Australia. Professor of English and Canadian Literature. m. Robin Jonathan Howells, 17 Dec 1963, 2 daughters. Education: BA, 1962, MA, 1965, University of Queensland; PhD, University of London, 1969. Appointment: Professor of English and Canadian Literature, University of Reading, 1996-. Publications: Love, Mystery and Misery: Feeling in Gothic Fiction, 1978, 2nd edition, 1995; Private and Fictional Words: Canadian Women Novelists of the 1970s and 80s, 1987; Jean Rhys, 1991; Margaret Atwood, 1996; Alice Munro, 1998. Contributions to: Many academic journals. Membership: British Association for Canadian Studies, president, 1992-94. Address: Department of English, University of Reading, Whiteknights, Reading RG6 6AA, Berkshire, England.

HOWER Edward, b. 10 Jan 1941, New York, USA. Writer. m. Alison, 10 May 1995. Education: BA, Cornell University; Diploma of Education, MaKerere; MA, University of California at Los Angeles. Publications: The New Life Hotel; Wolf Tickets; The Pomegranate Princess; Night Train Blues; Queen of the Silver Dollar. Contributions to: TLS; New York Times; Smithsonian. Membership: PEN. Address: 1409 Hanshaw Road, Ithaca, NY 14850, USA.

HOWLAND Bette, b. 28 Jan 1937, Chicago, Illinois, USA. Writer. 2 sons. Education: AB, University of Chicago, 1955. Appointment: Visiting Professor, University of Chicago, 1993. Publications: W3, 1974; Blue in Chicago, 1978; Things to Come and Go, 1983; German Lessons, 1993. Contributions to: Newspapers, journals, and magazines. Honours: Rockefeller Foundation Grant, 1969; Marsden Foundation Grant, 1973; Guggenheim Fellowship, 1978; John D and Catharine T MacArthur Foundation Fellowship, 1984-89. Address: 102 Mulbarger Lane, Bellefonte, PA 16823, USA.

HØY Thorkild, b. 18 Nov 1918, Vindblæs, Løgstør, Denmark. Chartered Surveyor; Writer. m. Christel Jutta Boysen, 15 Oct 1976, 1 son, 3 daughters. Education: Ranum Teachers College; University of Copenhagen; Agricultural University of Copenhagen. Appointments: Community of Frederiksberg, Copenhagen, 1954-80. Publications: Surveying and Mapping in Southern Peary Land, North Greenland (with 4 maps), 1970; Danmarks Soer, 4 volumes (co-author), 1991-97. Contributions to: Major articles in: Thoreau as a Surveyor, in Surveying and Mapping, 1976; Danish Lakes with some Considerations on Cartometry, in Geografisk Tidsskrift, 1988; Several more. Membership: Danish Writers Union. Address: Sjælsøparken 7, DK-3460 Birkerød, Denmark.

HOYLAND Michael (David), b. 1 Apr 1925, Nagpur, India. Retired Art Lecturer; Author. m. Marette Nicol Fraser, 21 July 1948, 2 sons, 2 daughters. Appointments: School Teacher, 1951-63; Lecturer, 1963-65, Senior Lecturer in Art, 1963-80, Kesteven College of Education. Publications: Introduction Three, 1967; Art for Children, 1970; Variations: An Integrated Approach to Art, 1975; A Love Affair with War, 1981; The Bright Way In, 1984; Dominus-Domina (play); Poems in journals and a collection; 6 Short Stories. Contributions to: Reviewing for Ore; Jade. Memberships: Stamford Writers Group; PEN; Welland Valley Art Society; East Anglian Potters Association. Address: Foxfoot House, South Luffenham, Nr Oakham Rutland, Leicestershire LE15 8NP, England.

HOYLE Sir Fred, b. 24 June 1915, Bingley, Yorkshire, England. Scientist; Honorary Research Professor; Author. m. Barbara Clark, 1939, 1 son, 1 daughter. Education: Emmanuel College, Cambridge. Appointments: Fellow, St John's College, Cambridge, 1939-72; University Lecturer in Mathematics, 1945-58, Plumian Professor of Astronomy and Experimental Philosophy, 1958-72, Director, Institute of Theoretical Astronomy, 1967-73, Cambridge; Staff, Mount Wilson and Palomar Observatories, 1957-62; Visiting Associate in Physics, California Institute of Technology, 1963-; Andrew D White Professor-at-Large, Cornell University, 1972-78; Honorary Research Professor, University of Manchester, 1972-, University College, Cardiff, 1975-. Publications: Non-Fiction: Some Recent Researches in Solar Physics, 1949; The Nature of the Universe, 1951; A Decade of Decision, 1953; Frontiers of Astronomy, 1955; Man and Materialism, 1956; Astronomy, 1962; Star Formation, 1963; Of Men and Galaxies, 1964; Encounter with the Future, 1965; Galaxies, Nuclei and Quasars, 1965; Man in the Universe, 1966; From Stonehenge to Modern Cosmology, 1972; Nicolaus Copernicus, 1973; The Relation of Physics and Cosmology, 1973; Action-at-a-Distance in Physics and Cosmology (with J V Narlikar), 1974; Astronomy and Cosmology, 1975; Astronomy Today, 1975; Ten Faces of the Universe, 1977; On Stonehenge, 1977; Energy or Extinction, 1977; Lifecloud (with N C Wickramasinghe), 1978; The Cosmogony of the Solar System, 1978; Diseases From Space (with N C Wickramasinghe), 1979; Commonsense and Nuclear Energy (with G Hoyle), 1979; The Physics-Astronomy Frontier (with J V Narlikar), 1980; Space Travellers: The Bringers of Life (with N C Wickramasinghe), 1981; Ice, 1981; Evolution from Space (with N C Wickramasinghe), 1981; The Intelligent Universe, 1983; The Small World of Fred Hoyle, 1986; Archaeopteryx, the Primordial Bird: A Case of Fossil Forgery (with N C Wickramasinghe), 1986; Cosmic Life Force (with N C Wickramasinghe), 1988; The Theory of Cosmic Grains (with N C Wickramasinghe), 1991; Our Place in the Cosmos (with N C Wickramasinghe), 1993; Home is Where the Wind Blows, 1994. Fiction: The Black Cloud, 1957; Ossian's Ride, 1959; A for Andromeda (with J Elliot), 1962; Fifth Planet (with G Hoyle), 1963; Andromeda Breakthrough (with J Elliot), 1964; October the First is Too Late, 1966; Element 79, 1967; Rockets in Ursa Major (with G Hoyle), 1969; Seven Steps to the Sun (with G Hoyle), 1970; The Molecule Men (with G Hoyle), 1971; The Inferno (with G Hoyle), 1973; Into Deepest Space (with G Hoyle), 1974; The Incandescent Ones (with G Hoyle), 1977; The Westminster Disaster (with G Hoyle), 1978. Other: Children's stories. Contributions to: Professional journals. Honours: Gold Medal, Royal Astronomical Society, 1968; Knighted, 1972; Royal Medal, Royal Society, 1974; Dag Hammarskjöld Gold Medal, Académie Diplomatique de la Paix, 1986; Karl Schwarzehild Medal, German Astronomical Society, 1992; Balzan Prize, 1994; Crayfoord Prize, 1997; Honorary doctorates. Memberships: American Academy of Arts and Sciences, honorary member; American Philosophical Society; Royal Astronomical Society, president, 1971-73; Royal Society, fellow. Address: c/o The Royal Society, 6 Carlton House Terrace, London SW1Y 5AG, England.

HOYLE Geoffrey, b. 12 Jan 1942, Scunthorpe, Lancashire, England. Author. Education: St John's College, Cambridge, 1961-62. Publications: (with Fred Hoyle): Fifth Planet, 1963; Rockets in Ursa Major, 1969; Seven Steps to the Sun, 1970; The Molecule Men, 1971; The Inferno, 1973; Into Deepest Space, 1974; The Incandescent Ones, 1977; The Westminster Disaster, 1978; Commonsense and Nuclear Energy, 1979. Other:

The Energy Pirate, 1982; The Giants of Universal Park, 1982; The Frozen of Azuron, 1982; The Planet of Death, 1982; Flight, 1984. Address: RMYC, RMYCS Enchantress, Sandbanks, Poole, Dorset BH13 7RE, England.

HOYLE Trevor, (Joseph Rance, Larry Milne), b. 25 Feb 1940, Rochdale, England. Writer. m. 15 Sept 1962, 1 son, 1 daughter. Appointments: Panel Judge, Constable Novel Competition and Portico Literary Prize. Publications: Novels: The Relatively Constant Copywriters, 1972; The Adulterer, 1972; Rule of Night, 1975; Rock Fix, 1977; Seeking the Mythical Future, science fiction, 1977, 1982; Through the Eye of Time, science fiction, 1977, 1982; The Gods Look Down, science fiction, 1978, 1982; The Man Who Travelled on Motorways, 1979; Earth Cult, science fiction, 1997; The Stigma, 1980; Bullet Train, 1980; The Last Gasp, 1983, 1984; Vail, 1984; K.I.D.S., 1988, 1990; Blind Needle, 1994; Mirrorman, 1999; Film and TV adaptations: Blake's 7, 1977; Blake's 7: Project Arrow, 1979; Blake's 7: Scorpio Attack, 1981; Ghostbusters, 1985; Biggles, 1985; Civvies, 1992; Prime Suspect 2, 1992; Prime Suspect, 1993; The Governor, 1995. Contributions to: Short stories in: Transatlantic Review; Montrose Review; BBC Morning Story; New Fiction Society Magazine; New Yorkshire Writing; Fireweed; Double Space; Wordworks; Pennine Magazine; Artful Reporter. Honours: Winner, Radio Times Drama Award, for Gigo radio play, 1991; Sony Best Actor Award, 1992; Winner, British Short Story, Transatlantic Review; Ray Mort Northern Novel Award. Membership: Society of Authors. Literary Agent: Sheil Land Associates Ltd. Address: c/o Sheil Land Associates Ltd, 43 Doughty Street, London WC1N 2LF, England.

HOYT Erich, b. 28 Sept 1950, Akron, Ohio, USA. Writer. m. Sarah Elizabeth Wedden, 4 Mar 1989, 1 son, 2 daughters. Education: Vannevar Bush Fellow in Science Journalism, Massachusetts Institute of Technology, 1985-86. Appointments: Contributing Editor, Equinox Magazine, Canada, 1982-87; Field Correspondent, Defenders Magazine, USA, 1985-; Visiting Lecturer, Massachusetts Institute of Technology, Cambridge, 1986-87; Ohio State University, 1992-; University of Edinburgh, Medical School, 1994-95; Consultant for science and botanical museums and conservation organizations, 1987-; Co-Producer and Writer, Vega Films, Berlin, 1996-; Lectures to European Cetacean Society Annual General Meeting, 1994; Encounters with Whales '95, Australia, 1995; International Whale Watching Meeting, Ogata, Japan, 1994; International Whale Watching Forum, Zamami, Japan, 1996; Reviewer, Good Book Guide, London, 1998-. Publications: Orca: The Whale Called Killer, 1981, 3rd edition, 1990; The Whale Watcher's Handbook, 1984; Conserving the Wild Relatives of Crops, 1988; Seasons of the Whale, 1990, 2nd edition, 1997; Extinction A-Z, 1991; Meeting the Whales, 1991; Riding with the Dolphins, 1992; The Earth Dwellers, 1996; The Nature Company Guide to Whales, Dolphins and Porpoises, 1998; Collins Whales and Dolphins, 1998. Contributions to: Anthologies and textbooks; National Geographic; New York Times; Globe and Mail, Toronto; Discover; Guardian; Over 100 other journals. Honours: Francis H Kortwright Award, 1st place, Magazines, 1983; Environment Canada Award for Best Magazine Article, 1986; BBC Wildlife Award for Nature Writing, 2nd place for Essay, 1988; James Thurber Writer-in-Residence, Thurber House, 1992; 1st Place, Magazines, Outdoor Writers of Canada, 1994; Finalist, Outstanding Article Award, American Society of Journalists and Authors, 1994; Animal Rights Writing Award, Best Book, 1994; Finalist, Science-in-Society Book Awards, 1996; 1996 Book to Remember, New York Public Library Association. Memberships: Writers Guild; American Society of Journalists and Authors; Society of Authors; International Science Writers Association; National Association of Science Writers; Outdoor Writers of Canada; Society for Marine Mammalogy; European Cetacean Society; Association of British Science Writers; Society for Economic Botany; Xerces Society. Address: The Gannetry, 11 Bramerton Court, North Berwick EH39 4BE, Scotland.

HU Zha La Ga, b. 4 Feb 1930. Writer. m. 28 Dec 1951, 2 sons, 2 daughters. Education: Graduate, Research Class of Literature & Art, Inner Mongolia University, 1961-65; Graduate, Engineering School of Zhalantun, 1948. Appointments: Party Committee of Buteha County, Hunan League and the East Area Committee of Inner Mongolia, 1948-55; Journalist, Editor, Inner Mongolia Daily, 1955-60; Vice Chairman, Writer's Association of Inner Mongolia, 1965; Victim of Cultural Revolution, 1966-71; Chief Editor, Grassland, magazine, 1971-73; Secretary, Party Committee, Association of Literature and Art of Inner Mongolia and Director of Propaganda Department of Party Committee of Inner Mongolia, 1983-90; Chairman, Writer's Association of Inner Mongolia, 1990-. Publications: The Story of the Little White Horse, short story collection, 1956; Spring in Grassland, novelette, 1956; Red Road, novel, 1959; Fog in Grassland, novel, 1982; Selection of Zha La Ga Hu, novelette, 1986; Legend of Gada Meilin, novel, 1986; Research Collection on Zha La Ga Hu, 1988; Variation at Dawn, 1993; Pondering on the Literature World, 1994. Contributions to: People's Literature; Literature and Art Press; Guangming Press; Grassland; Inner Mongolia Press, the literature of Minority Nationality. Honours: First Prize, Inner Mongolia Literature Creation for Novels for three times, the Story Awards of Inner Mongolia twice, the Literature Review Awards of Inner Mongolia once, the Novel Awards of Minority Nationality Literature of China twice; Literature Review Awards of National Minority Nationality. Memberships: Vice President, Socialist Literature and Art Association, China; Vice President, Minority Nationality Writer's Association of China; Vice President, Jianggeer Research Society of China; Standing Council, Mongolia Literature Society of China; National Committee Member, Writer's Association of China; Committee Member, Minority Nationality Literature; Editorial Board Member, Minority Nationality Literature. Address: Writer's Association of Inner Mongolia, Hohehot Inner Mongolia, 010010, China.

HUANG Harry J(unxiong), (Freeman J Wong, Will Strength), b. 1956, Jieyang, Guangdong, China. Teacher; Writer; Translator. m. Wendy. Education: BA, Beijing Foreign Languages University; MEd, University of Toronto. Appointments: Lecturer, Sun Yatsen University, 1983; Advisor for a Translator, 1988; Professor, Seneca College, 1991. Publications: As Freeman J Wong: Nothing Comes of Nothing: A Treasury of Chinese Mini-Stories, 1990; Morality, Eh?..A Pocketful of Canadian Short Stories, 1998; A Bride in Washington: North American Short Stories. As Harry J Huang: How to Punctuate the English Sentence, 1986; Shantou, 1989; A Course of Chinese-English Translation, 1989; Selected Translation by Huang Junxiong, 1989; A Cultural Tour Across China, 1993; Refining the Sentence, 1993; Essential College Writing Skills, 1993. As Will Strength: An Easy Way to Teach the Alphabet to Your Small Child, 1996; An Easy Way to Teach Mathematics to Your Small Child, 1996; An Easy Way to Tell Bedtime Stories to Your Small Child, 1996. Contributions to: Magazines and journals. Honour: Guangdong Province Outstanding Social Science Research Award, 1989. Membership: Writers Union of Canada. Address: c/o Seneca College, 1750 Finch Avenue East, North York, Ontario M2J 2X5, Canada.

HUARACHE Pablo. See: **MURUA CONTRERAS Dámaso.**

HUBER-ABRAHAMOWICZ Elfriede, b. 19 Dec 1922, Vienna, Austria. Gerhard Huber, 7 Sept 1948, 2 daughters. Education: DPhil, University Basle, Switzerland, 1950. Publications: Das Problem der Kunst bei Platon, thesis, 1954, 2nd ed 1997; Verhängnis Gedichte, 1957; Der unendliche Weg. Prosa u. Gedichte, 1964; Seiltanz und Waage. Gedichte, 1974; Parallel. Roman, 1979, 4 eds; Spiegelspannung. Sonette, 1981; Muttergestirn. Gedichte, 1984; Hoffnungslos hoffend. Gedichte, 1989; Die Nabelschnur. Roman, 1990, 2nd ed 1991; Treibstoff Sehnsucht. Roman, 1992; Tödliche Geborgenheit. Autobiographische Geschichten, 1995. Contributions to: Neue Zürcher Zeitung, Badener Tagblatt; Zur Sprache der Dichtung in: Was

Philosophinnen denken, II, 1986; Analogisch-intuitives Denken in Robin Morgans Anatomy of Freedom, in Symposium der Internationalen Assoziation von Philosophinnen, 1989. Honours: Preis des Basler Literaturkredits, 1960; C F Meyer-Preis, 1965. Memberships: Schweiz Schriftstellerinnen-u. Schriftstellerverband; IAPh Internationale Assoziation von Philosophinnen. Address: Berghaldenstrasse 36c, CH-8053 Zürich, Switzerland.

HUCKER Hazel Zoë, (Hazel Hucker), b. 7 Aug 1937, London, England. Novelist; Justice of the Peace. m. Michael Hucker, 7 Jan 1961, 2 sons, 1 dec, 1 daughter. Education: BSc, Honours, Economics, London School of Economics and Political Science, 1960. Publications: The Aftermath of Oliver, 1993; La Herencia del Recuerdo, 1994; A Dangerous Happiness, 1994; Cousin Susannah, 1995; Trials of Friendship, 1996; The Real Claudia Charles, 1998. Membership: Society of Authors. Address: c/o MBA Literary Agents Ltd, 62 Grafton Way, London W1P 5LD, England.

HUDDLE David, b. 11 July, 1942, Ivanhoe, Virginia, USA. Professor of English; Writer; Poet. m. Lindsey M Huddle, 2 daughters. Education: BA, Foreign Affairs, University of Virginia, 1968; MA, English, Hollins College, 1969; MFA, Writing, Columbia Unversity, 1971. Appointments: Faculty, Warren Wilson College, 1981-85; Professor of English, University of Vermont, 1982-; Editor, New England Review, 1993-94. Publications: A Dream With No Stump Roots In It, 1975; Paper Boy, 1979; Only the Little Bone, 1986; Stopping by Home, 1988; The High Spirits, 1992; The Writing Habit: Essays on Writing, 1992; The Nature of Yearning, 1992; Intimates, 1993; Tenormen, 1995. Contributions to: Esquire; Harper's; New York Times Book Review; Kentucky Poetry Review; Texas Quarterly; Poetry; Shenandoah; American Poetry Review. Honours: Honorary Doctorate of Humanities, Shenandoah College and Conservatory, Virginia, 1989; Bread Loaf School of English Commencement Speaker, 1989; Robert Frost Professor of American Literature, 1991. Address: Department of English, University of Vermont, Burlington, VT 05405, USA.

HUDGINS Andrew (Leon Jr), b. 22 Apr 1951, Killeen, Texas, USA. Professor of English; Poet; Writer. Education: BA, Huntingdon College, 1974; MA, University of Alabama, 1976; Postgraduate Studies, Syracuse University, 1976-78; MFA Writers' Workshop, University of Iowa, 1981-83. Appointments: Adjunct Instructor, Auburn University, 1978-81; Teaching-Writing Fellow, University of Iowa, 1981-83; Lecturer, Baylor University, 1984-85; Professor of English, University of Cincinnati, 1985-. Publications: Poetry: Saints and Strangers, 1985; After the Lost War: A Narrative, 1988; The Never-Ending: New Poems, 1991; The Glass Hammer: A Southern Childhood, 1994; Babylon in a Jar, 1998. Non-Fiction: The Glass Anvil (essays), 1997. Contributions to: Numerous journals. Honours: Wallace Stegner Fellow in Poetry, Stanford University, 1983-84; Yaddo Fellowships, 1983, 1985, 1987, 1988, 1991; Academy of American Poets Award, 1984; MacDowell Colony Fellowship, 1986; National Endowment for the Arts Fellowships, 1986, 1992; Ingram Merrill Foundation Grant, 1987; Poets' Prize, 1988; Witter Bynner Award, American Academy and Institute of Arts and Letters, 1988; Alfred Hodder Fellow, Princeton University, 1989-90; Poetry Award, Texas Institute of Letters, 1991; Ohioana Poetry Award, 1997. Membership: Texas Institute of Letters. Address: c/o Department of English, ML 69, University of Cincinnati, Cincinnati, OH 45221, USA.

HUDSON Christopher, b. 29 Sept 1946, England. Writer. m. Kirsty McLeod, 10 Mar 1978, 1 son. Education: Scholar, Jesus College, Cambridge. Appointments: Editor, Faber & Faber, 1968; Literary Editor, The Spectator, 1971, The Standard, 1981; Editorial Page Editor, The Daily Telegraph, 1992. Publications: Overlord, 1975; The Final Act, 1980; Insider Out, 1982; The Killing Fields, 1984; Colombo Heat, 1986; Playing in the Sand, 1989; Spring Street Summer, 1993. Address: Little Dame, Biddendem, Kent TN27 8JT, England.

HUDSON Helen. See: **LANE Helen.**

HUDSON Jeffrey. See: **CRICHTON Michael.**

HUDSON Liam, b. 20 July 1933, London, England. Psychologist; Writer. m. Bernadine Jacot de Boinod, 2 July 1965, 3 sons, 1 daughter. Education: MA, Exeter College, 1957; PhD, Cambridge University, 1961. Publications: Contrary Imaginations, 1966; Frames of Mind, 1968; The Ecology of Human Intelligence, 1970; The Cult of the Fact, 1972; Human Beings, 1975; The Nympholepts, 1978; Bodies of Knowledge, 1982; Night Life, 1985; The Way Men Think, 1991; Intimate Relations, 1995. Contributions to: Times Literary Supplement. Honour: Tanner Lectures, Yale University, 1997. Membership: British Psychological Society. Address: Balas Copartnership, 34 North Park, Gerrards Cross, Bucks, England.

HUFANA Alejandrino, b. 22 Oct 1926, San Fernando, La Union, Philippines. Editor; Writer; Poet; Dramatist. Education: AB, 1952, MA, 1961, University of the Philippines; University of California at Berkeley, 1957-58; MS, Columbia University, 1969. Appointments: Co-Founding Editor, Signatures Magazine, 1955; Comment Magazine, 1956-67; Heritage Magazine, 1967-68; Editor, Panorama Magazine, 1959-61; Managing Editor, University of the Philippines Press, 1965-66; Director, Cultural Center of the Philippines Library, 1970-85; Editor, 1971, Pamana Magazine; Professor, 1975, Director, Creative Writing Center, 1981-85, University of the Philippines; Literary Editor, Heritage Magazine, 1987-. Publications: 13 Kalisud, 1955; Man in the Moon, 1956; Sickle Season, 1948-58, 1959; Poro Point, 1955-60, 1961; Curtain Raisers: First Five Plays, 1964; A Philippine Cultural Miscellany, 1970; The Wife of Lot and Other New Poems, 1971; Notes on Poetry, 1973; Sieg Heil (epic on the Third Reich), 1975; Philippine Writing, 1977; Shining On, 1985; Dumanon, 1994; No Facetious Claim: Notes on Writers and Writing, 1995; Enuegs (extracts of tributes to my Civilization), 1999; Survivor (spinoffs from the Enuegs), 1999; Kaputt (sequel to Sieg Heil), 1999. Address: c/o Heritage Magazine, 20218 Tajauta Avenue, Carson, CA 90746, USA.

HUGHES Brenda. See: **COLLOMS Brenda.**

HUGHES David (John), b. 27 July 1930, Alton, Hampshire, England. Writer; Critic; Editor. m. (1) Mai Zetterling, 1957, (2) Elizabeth Westoll, 1980, 1 son, 1 daughter. Education: MA, Christ Church, Oxford. Appointments: Editorial Assistant, London Magazine, 1953-55; Reader, Rupert Hart-Davis, 1956-60; Editor, Town Magazine, 1960-61, New Fiction Society, 1975-78, 1981-82, Letters, journal of the Royal Society of Literature, 1992-96; Assistant Visiting Professor, University of Iowa, 1978-79, 1987, University of Alabama, 1979; Film Critic, Sunday Times, 1982-83; Fiction Critic, Mail on Sunday, 1982-; Visiting Associate Professor, University of Houston, 1986; Editor, Letters, 1992-96; Theatre Critic, 1996, Mail on Sunday. Publications: Fiction: A Feeling in the Air, 1957; Sealed with a Loving Kiss, 1958; The Horsehair Sofa, 1961; The Major, 1964; The Man Who Invented Tomorrow, 1968; Memories of Dying, 1976; A Genoese Fancy, 1979; The Imperial German Dinner Service, 1983; The Pork Butcher, 1984, film version as Souvenir, 1989; But for Bunter, 1985; The Little Book, 1996. Non-Fiction: J B Priestley: An Informal Study, 1958; The Road to Stockholm, 1964; The Seven Ages of England, 1967; The Rosewater Revolution, 1971; Evergreens, 1976; Himself and Other Animals, 1997. Editor: Winter's Tales: New Series I, 1985; Best Short Stories (with Giles Gordon), 10 volumes, 1986-95; The Best of Best Short Stories 1986-1995, 1995. Honours: Welsh Arts Council Fiction Prize, 1984; W H Smith Literary Award, 1985. Membership: Royal Society of Literature, fellow and vice president. Literary Agent: Giles Gordon, Curtis Brown. Address: 163 Kennington Road, London SE11 6SF, England.

HUGHES Glyn, b. 25 May 1935, Middlewich, Cheshire, England. Author; Poet. 1 son. Education: Regional College of Art, Manchester, 1952-56; Qualified Art Teacher, 1959. Appointments: Teacher, Lancashire and Yorkshire, 1956-72; Arts Council Fellow, Bishop Grosseteste College, Lincoln, 1979-81; Southern Arts Writer-in-Residence, Farnborough, 1982-84; Arts Council Writer-in-Residence, D H Lawrence Centenary Festival, 1985. Publications: Novels: Where I Used to Play on the Green, 1982; The Hawthorn Goddess, 1984; The Antique Collector, 1990; Roth, 1992; Bronte, 1996. Autobiography: Millstone Grit, 1975; Fair Prospects, 1976. Poetry: Neighbours, 1970; Rest the Poor Straggler, 1972; Best of Neighbours, 1979. Plays: Mary Hepton's Heaven, 1984; Various plays for BBC school broadcasts on radio and television. Honours: Welsh Arts Council Poets Prize, 1970; Guardian Fiction Prize, 1982; David Higham Fiction Prize, 1982. Address: Mors House, 1 Mill Bank Road, Mill Bank, Sowerby Bridge, West Yorkshire HX6 3DY, England.

HUGHES Ian. See: **PATERSON Alistair.**

HUGHES Matilda. See: **MACLEOD Charlotte.**

HUGHES Monica (Ince), b. 3 Nov 1925, Liverpool, England. Writer. m. Glen Hughes, 22 Apr 1957, 2 sons, 2 daughters. Publications: Crisis on Conshelf Ten, 1975; The Keeper of the Isis Light, 1980; Hunter in the Dark, 1982; Ring-Rise, Ring-Set, 1982; Invitation to the Game, 1991; The Crystal Drop, 1992; The Golden Aquarians, 1994; Castle Tourmandyne, 1995; Where Have You Been, Billy Boy?, 1995; The Seven Magpies, 1996; The Faces of Fear; The Story Box, 1998; What if...?, 1998. Contributions to: Various publications. Literary Agent: Pamela Paul, 253 High Park Avenue, Toronto, Ontario M6P 2S5, Canada. Address: 13816-110A Avenue, Edmonton, Alberta T5M 2M9, Canada.

HUGHES Patricia. See: **HOUK Margaret.**

HUGHES Richard Joseph, b. 8 July 1931, Melbourne, Australia. Journalist; Jazz Pianist. m. Fay Parsons, 5 June 1962, 3 daughters. Education: BA Honours, University of Melbourne, 1951. Publications: Daddy's Practising Again, 1977; Don't You Sing!, 1994. Contributions to: Quadrant; The Bulletin; Australian Jazz Quarterly; Australian Blues and Jazz Journal. Literary Agent: Curtis Brown. Address: Conga Brava, 11 Girilang Avenue, Vaucluse, New South Wales 2030, Australia.

HUGHES Robert (Studley Forrest), b. 28 July 1938, Sydney, New South Wales, Australia. Art Critic; Writer. m. Victoria Whistler, 30 May 1981, 1 son. Education: Saint Ignatius College, Sydney; University of Sydney, 1956-61. Appointments: Staff, Time magazine, New York City, 1970-; Writer and Narrator, art documentaries, BBC-TV, London, 1974-. Publications: The Art of Australia, 1966; Heaven and Hell in Western Art, 1970; The Fatal Shore, 1987; Nothing If Not Critical, 1990; Frank Auerbach, 1990; Barcelona, 1992; Culture of Complaint, 1993; American Visions: The Epic History of Art in America, 1997. Contributions to: Various publications. Honours: Frank Jewett Mather Awards, College Art Association of America, 1982, 1985; Duff Cooper Prize, 1987; W H Smith Literary Award, 1987; Officer, Order of Australia, 1991; 1st Prize, Olimpiada Cultural, Spain, 1992. Address: c/o Time Magazine, Time-Life Building, Rockefeller Center, New York, NY 10020, USA.

HUGHES Shirley, b. 16 July 1927, Hoylake, England. Children's Fiction Writer and Illustrator. Education: Liverpool Art School; Ruskin School of Drawing and Fine Arts, Oxford. Appointments: Public Lending Right Registrars Advisory Committee, 1984-88; Library and Information Services Council, 1989-92. Publications: Lucy & Tom Series, 6 volumes, 1960-87; The Trouble with Jack, 1970; Sally's Secret, 1973; It's too Frightening for Me, 1977; Moving Molly, 1978; Up and Up, 1979; Charlie Moon and the Big Bonanza Bust Up, 1982; An Evening at Alfies, 1984; The Nursery Collection, 6 volumes, 1985-86; Another Helping of Chips, 1986; The Big Alfie and Annie Rose Story Book, 1988; Out and About, 1989; The Big Alfie Out of Doors Story Book, 1992; Giving, 1993; Bouncing, 1993; Stories by Firelight, 1993; Chatting Hiding, 1994; Rhymes for Annie Rose, 1995; Enchantment in the Garden, 1996. Honours: Kate Greenaway Medal for Dogger, 1977; Eleanor Farjeon Award, 1984. Membership: Society of Authors. Address: c/o Bodley Head, Randon/Century, 20 Vauxhall Bridge Road, London SW1V 2SA, England.

HUGHES William, b. 25 Aug 1964, Liverpool, England. University Lecturer. m. Elaine Marie Hartnell, 8 Apr 1989. Education: BA, Honours, 1985, MA in Modern Literature, 1988, PhD, 1994, University of East Anglia. Appointment: Lecturer in English, Bath Spa University College, 1993-. Publications: Contemporary Writing and National Identity (co-editor), 1995; Bram Stoker: A Bibliography, 1997; Bram Stoker: History, Psychoanalysis and the Gothic (co-editor), 1998; Beyond Dracula: Bram Stoker's Fiction and its Cultural Context (editor), 1999; The Lady of the Shroud, 1999. Contributions to: European and American journals. Memberships: International Gothic Association; Bram Stoker Society; Association for Research in Popular Fictions. Address: c/o Faculty of Humanities, Bath Spa University College, Bath BA2 9BN, England.

HUHNE Christopher Murray Paul, b. 2 July 1954, London, England. Economist. m. Vasiliki Courmouzis, 19 May 1984, 2 sons, 1 daughter. Education: Sorbonne, University of Paris, 1972; BA, Oxford University, 1975. Publications: Debt and Danger, 1985; Real World Economics, 1990; The ECU Report, 1991. Honours: Wincott Awards for Financial Journalism, 1981, 1990. Membership: Royal Economics Society. Address: 8 Crescent Grove, London SW4 7AH, England.

HULL Robin, b. 21 Oct 1931, Harpenden, Hertfordshire, England. Retired Professor of General Practice. m. Gillian Edwards, 4 Oct 1958, 3 daughters. Education: Christ's Hospital; St Mary's Hospital Medical School, London. Appointments: General Practitioner, Stratford-upon-Avon, 1960-85; Senior Lecturer, Department of General Practice, Birmingham Medical School, 1972-92; Professor of General Practice, Vrije Universiteit, Amsterdam, Netherlands, 1985-87. Publications: Introduction to General Practice (with Drury), 1974; Infective Disease in Primary Care, 1987; Teamwork in Palliative Care (with Ellis and Sargent), 1989; Just a GP Biography - Prof Sir Michael Drury, 1994; A Pocket Book of Palliative Care, 1994; Two Centuries of Scottish Birds, 1999. Contributions to: Some 600 articles and papers in medical and lay press. Membership: General Practitioner Writers' Association, Chairman, 1985-92, President, 1992-. Literary Agent: Ocean Books, Sulgrave, Warwickshire, England. Address: West Carnliath, Strathtay, Perthshire PH9 0PG, Scotland.

HULME Keri, b. 9 Mar 1947, Christchurch, New Zealand. Writer. Education: Canterbury University, Christchurch. Publications: The Silences Between, 1982; The Bone People, 1984; Lost Possessions, 1986; Te Kaihau, the Windeater, 1986; Homeplaces, 1989; Strands, 1992; Bait, 1996. Contributions to: Various publications. Honours: New Zealand Writing Bursary, 1983; New Zealand Book of the Year, 1984; Mobil Pegasus Prize, 1984; Booker McConnell Award, 1985; Special Scholarship in Letters, 1990. Memberships: New Zealand Society of Authors; Nga Puna Wailhanga. Address: PO Box 1, Whataroa, South Westland, Aotearoa, New Zealand.

HULSE Michael (William), b. 12 June 1955, Stoke-on-Trent, Staffordshire, England. Poet; Writer; Translator; Lecturer. Education: MA, German, University of St Andrews, 1977. Appointments: Lecturer, University of Erlangen/Nuremberg, 1977-79; Catholic University, Eichstätt, 1981-83, University of Zurich, 1994; Part-time Lecturer, University of Cologne, 1985-; Translator, Deutsche Welle TV, Cologne, 1986-. Publications: Poetry: Monochrome Blood, 1980; Dole Queue, 1981; Knowing and Forgetting, 1981; Propaganda, 1985; Eating Strawberries in the Necropolis, 1991; Mother of Beetles, 1991. Editor: The New Poetry (with D Kennedy and D Morley), 1993. Translator: Tumult, by Botho Strauss, 1987; The Sorrows of Young Werther, by Johann von

Goethe, 1989; The Complete Paintings of van Gogh, by I F Walther and R Metzger, 2 volumes, 1990; Wonderful, Wonderful Times, by Elfried Jelinek, 1990; Jan Lobel from Warsaw, by Luise Rinser, 1991; Picasso, by I F Walther, 2 volumes, 1992; Gauguin in Tahiti, by Günter Metken, 1992; Caspar Hauser, by Jakob Wassermann, 1992; Lust, by Elfriede Jelinek, 1992; Impressionism, by Peter H Feist, 2 volumes, 1993; Written in the West, by Wim Wenders, 1993; Salvador Dali: The Paintings, by Gilles Néret, 2 volumes, 1994. Honours: 1st Prize, National Poetry Competition, 1978; Eric Gregory Award, 1980; Bridport Poetry Competition Prizes, 1988, 1994; Hawthorden Castle Fellowship, 1991; Cholmondeley Award, 1991. Address: c/o Collins Harvill, London W6 8JB, England.

HUME George Haliburton, (Basil Hume), b. 2 Mar 1923, Newcastle upon Tyne, England. Archbishop of Westminster; Theologian; Author. Education: M, St Benets Hall, 1947; STL, University of Fribourg, 1951. Appointments: Entered Ordo Sancti Benedicti, 1941; Ordained Priest, Ampleforth, 1950; Senior Master in Modern Languages, 1952-63; Housemaster, St Bede's, 1955-63; Professor of Dogmatic Theology, 1955-63; Magister Scholarum, English Benedictine Congregation, 1957-63; Abbot of Ampleforth, 1963-76; Chairman, Benedictine Ecumenical Commission, 1972-76; Installed as Archbishop of Westminster, 1976; Created Cardinal-Priest of the Title San Silvestro in Capite, 1976; President, Council of Christians and Jews. Publications: Searching for God, 1977; In Praise of Benedict, 1981; To Be a Pilgrim: A Spiritual Notebook, 1984; Towards a Civilisation of Love, 1988; Light in the Lord, 1991; Remaking Europe, 1994; Footprints of the Northern Saints, 1996; The Mystery of Love, 1996; Basil in Blunderland, 1997; The Mystery of the Cross, 1998. Contributions to: Periodicals. Honours: Honorary DD: Cambridge, 1979, Newcastle upon Tyne, 1979, London, 1980, Oxon, 1981, York, 1982, Kent, 1983, Durham, 1987, Hull, 1989, Keele, 1990; Hon DHL, Manhattan College, New York, 1980, Catholic University of America, 1980; Hon Doctor of Law, University of Northumbria at Newcastle, 1992; Honorary D, University of Surrey, 1992; Many other honours. Memberships: Bishops' Conference of England and Wales, president, 1979; Council of European Bishops' Conferences, president, 1978-87; Churches Together in England, joint president, 1990-; Congregation for the Sacraments and Divine Worship; Congregation for Religious and Secular Institutes; Congregation for Eastern Churches; Pontifical Council for the Promotion of Christian Unity; Pontifical Council for Pastoral Assistance to Health Care Workers; Relator for the Synod on Consecrated Life, 1994. Address: Archbishop's House, Ambrosden Avenue, Westminster, London SW1P 1QJ, England.

HUME John Robert, b. 26 Feb 1939, Glasgow, Scotland. Lecturer; Writer. Education: BSc, University of Glasgow, 1961. Appointments: Lecturer, 1964-82, Senior Lecturer, 1982-, University of Strathclyde; Treasurer, 1968-71, Editor, 1971-79, Scottish Society for Industrial Archaeology; Director, Scottish Industrial Archaeology Survey, 1978-85; Seconded to Historic Scotland as Principal Inspector of Ancient Monuments, 1984-91, Principal Inspector of Historic Buildings, 1991-93, Chief Inspector of Historic Buildings, 1993-. Publications: Industrial History in Pictures: Scotland, 1968; Glasgow as it Was, 3 volumes, 1975-76; A Plumber's Pastime, 1975; The Workshop of the British Empire, 1976; The Industrial Archaeology of Scotland: The Lowlands and Borders, 1976; The Highlands and the Islands, 1977; Beardmore: History of a Scottish Industrial Giant, 1979; A Bed of Nails, 1983; Shipbuilders to the World: A History of Harland Wolff, Belfast, 1986; Various Guidebooks to Historic Scotland Monuments in Care. Honour: Andre Simon Prize, 1981; Honarary FRIAS (Incorporation of Architects in Scotland), 1997; Office of the Order of the British Empire, 1998. Memberships: Society of Antiquaries: Society of Antiquaries of Scotland. Address: 28 Patrick Hill Road, Glasglow, G11 5BP, Scotland.

HUMPHREY Paul, b. 14 Jan 1915, New York City, USA. Commercial Writer. m. Eleanor Nicholson, 2 sons, 1 daughter. Education: Graduate, De Veaux Academy, University of Rochester. Appointments: Teacher, High School and University of Rochester, 1948-64. Publications: Several books. Contributions to: Magazines, periodicals and journals. Address: 2329 South Union Street, Spencerport, NY 14559, USA.

HUMPHREYS Emyr Owen, b. 15 Apr 1919, Clwyd, Wales. Author. m. Elinor Myfanwy, 1946, 3 sons, 1 daughter. Education: University College, Aberystwyth; University College, Bangor. Publications: The Little Kingdom, 1946; The Voice of a Stranger, 1949; A Change of Heart, 1951; Hear and Forgive, 1952; A Man's Estate, 1955; The Italian Wife, 1957; A Toy Epic, 1958; The Gift, 1963; Outside the House of Baal, 1965; Natives, 1968; Ancestor Worship, 1970; National Winner, 1971; Flesh and Blood, 1974; Landscapes, 1976; The Best of Friends, 1978; The Kingdom of Bran, 1979; The Anchor Tree, 1980; Pwyll a Riannon, 1980; Miscellany Two, 1981; The Taliesin Tradition, 1983; Salt of the Earth, 1985; An Absolute Hero, 1986; Open Secrets, 1988; The Triple Net, 1988; Bonds of Attachment, 1990; Outside Time, 1991; Unconditional Surrender, 1996; The Gift of a Daughter, 1998. Honours: Somerset Maugham Award, 1953; Hawthornden Prize, 1959; Society of Authors Travel Award, 1978; Welsh Arts Council Prize, 1983; Honorary DLitt, University of Wales, 1990; Welsh Book of the Year, 1992; Honorary Professor of English, University College of North Wales, Bangor. Membership: Fellow, The Royal Society of Literature, 1991. Literary Agent: Richard Scott Simon. Address: Llinon, Penyberth, Llanfairpwll, Ynys Môn, Gwynedd LL61 5YT, Wales.

HUMPHREYS Josephine, b. 2 Feb 1945, Charleston, South Carolina, USA. Novelist. m. Thomas A Hutcheson, 30 Nov 1968, 2 sons. Education: AB, Duke University, 1967; MA, Yale University, 1968. Publications: Dreams of Sleep, 1984; Rich in Love, 1987; The Fireman's Fair, 1991. Contributions to: Newspapers and periodicals. Honours: PEN, Ernest Hemingway Foundation, 1985; Guggenheim Fellowship, 1985; Lyndhurst Prize, 1986. Address: c/o Harriet Wasserman, 137 East 36th Street, New York, NY 10016, USA.

HUMPHRIES (John) Barry, b. 17 Feb 1934, Australia. Actor; Writer. m. 2 sons. Education: University of Melbourne. Appointments: Various one-man shows; film appearances. Publications: Bizarre I, 1965; Innocent Australian Verse, 1968; Wonderful World of Barry McKenzie, 1968; Bazza Pulls It Off, 1972; Adventures of Barry McKenzie, 1973; Bazza Holds His Own, 1974; Dame Edna's Coffee Table Book, 1976; Bazza Comes Into His Own, 1978; Les Patterson's Australia, 1979; Barry Humphries' Treasury of Australian Kitsch, 1980; Dame Edna's Bedside Companion, 1982; Les Patterson: The Traveller's Tool, 1985; Dame Edna: My Gorgeous Life, 1989; Women in the Backyard, 1996. Honour: Society of West End Managements Award, 1979. Address: c/o The John Reid Organisation, Singes House, 32 Galena Road, London W6 0LT, England.

HUMPHRY Derek John, b. 29 Apr 1930, Bath, England. Journalist; Author; Broadcaster. Appointments: Messenger Boy, Yorkshire Post, London, 1945-46; Cub Reporter, Evening World, Bristol, 1946-51; Junior Reporter, Evening News, Manchester, 1951-55; Reporter, Daily Mail, 1955-61; Deputy Editor, The Luton News, 1961-63; Editor, Havering Recorder, 1963-67, Hemlock Quarterly, 1983-92, Euthanasia Review, 1986-88, World Right to Die Newsletter, 1992-94; Home Affairs Correspondent, The Sunday Times, 1966-78; Special Writer, Los Angeles Times, 1978-79. Publications: Because They're Black, 1971; Police Power and Black People, 1972; Passports and Politics, 1974; The Cricket Conpiracy, 1976; False Messiah, 1977; Jean's Way, 1978; Let Me Die Before I Wake, 1982; The Right to Die!: Understanding Euthanasia, 1986; Final Exit, 1991; Dying with Dignity, 1992; Lawful Exit, 1993; Freedon to Die, 1998. Contributions to: New Statesman; Independent, London; USA Today. Literary Agent: Robert I Ducas, The Barn House, 244 Westside Road, Norfolk, CT 06058, USA. Address: 24829 Norris Lane, Junction City, OR 97448-9559, USA.

HUNT Bruce J(ames), b. 23 June 1956, Walla Walla, Washington, USA. Associate Professor of History; Writer. m. Elizabeth Hedrick, 17 July 1992, 1 son, 1 daughter. Education: BA, History and BS, Physics, University of Washington, Seattle, 1979; PhD, History of Science, Johns Hopkins University, 1984. Appointments: Assistant Professor, 1985-92, Associate Professor of History, 1992-, University of Texas at Austin; Visiting Fellow, Clare Hall, Cambridge, 1989-90. Publication: The Maxwellians, 1991. Contributions to: Scholarly books and journals, 1983-98. Honours: Fulbright Fellowship, England, 1981-82; Smithsonian Institution Postdoctoral Fellowship, 1984; National Science Foundation Grant, 1989. Memberships: British Society for the History of Science; History of Science Society; Society for the History of Technology. Address: c/o Department of History, University of Texas at Austin, Austin, TX 78712, USA.

HUNT Fay Ann, (Annie Hedley), b. 18 July 1935, Cornwall, England. Farmer; Teacher; Writer. div, 3 sons. Education: Redland College of Education. Publications: Listen: Let's Make Music, 1980; Look at Home Before you Look Away, 1983; Creative Activities for the Mentally Handicapped, 1986; Motherin' Sunday, 1990. Contributions to: Times Educational Supplement; Lancet; Special Education; Cornish Scene; Observer; Correspondent; Western Morning News; Cornish Times. Honour: 1st Prize, Ian S James Award, 1990. Membership: West Country Writers Association. Address: Clift Farmhouse, Anthony, Torpoint, Cornwall PL11 2PH, England.

HUNT Francesca, See: **HOLLAND Isabelle.**

HUNT Gill. See: **TUBB E(dwin) C(harles).**

HUNT Morton M(agill), b. 20 Feb 1920, Philadelphia, Pennsylvania, USA. Writer. m. (3)Bernice Weinick, 10 Sept 1951. Education: AB, Temple University, 1941. Publications: The Natural History of Love, 1959; Her Infinite Variety: The American Woman as Lover, Mate and Rival, 1962; The Affair: A Portrait of Extramarital Love in Contemporary America, 1969; The Mugging, 1972; Sexual Behaviour in the 1970's, 1974; Prime Time: A Guide to the Pleasures and Opportunities of the New Middle Age, 1975; The Divorce Experience, 1977; Profiles of Social Research: The Scientific Study of Human Interaction, 1985; The Compassionate Beast: What Science is Discovering About the Humane Side of Humankind, 1990; The Story of Psychology, 1993. Contributions to: Newspapers and periodicals. Honours: American Association for the Advancement of Science Westinghouse Award, 1952; Claude Bernard Award, 1971; American Society of Journalists and Authors, 1983. Address: 15 Kingstown Avenue, East Hampton, NY 11937, USA.

HUNT Sam, b. 4 July 1946, Auckland, New Zealand. Poet. Publications: Between Islands, 1964; A Fat Flat Blues, 1969; Selected Poems, 1965-69, 1970; A Song About Her, 1970; Postcard of a Cabbage Tree, 1970; Bracken Country, 1971; Letter to Jerusalem, 1971; Bottle Creek Blues, 1971; Bottle Creek, 1972; Beware the Man, 1972; Birth on Bottle Creek, 1972; South into Winter, 1973; Roadsong Paekakariki, 1973; Time to Ride, 1976; Drunkards Garden, 1978; Collected Poems, 1963-80, 1980; Three Poems of Separation, 1981; Running Scared, 1982; Approaches to Paremata, 1985; Selected Poems, 1987. Address: PO Box 1, Mana, Wellington, New Zealand.

HUNT Tim(othy Arthur), b. 22 Dec 1949, Calistoga, California, USA. College Teacher. m. Susan D Spurlock, 1 son, 1 daughter. Education: AB cum laude, 1970, MA, 1974, PhD, 1975, Cornell University. Appointments: Assistant, Associate Professor, English Department, Indiana-Purdue University, Fort Wayne, 1985-87; Academic Dean, Deep Springs College, California, 1987-90; Associate Professor of English, Coordinator for Humanities, Washington State University, Vancouver, 1990-. Publications: Kerouac's Crooked Road: *Development of a Fiction*, 1981; *The Collected Poetry of*

Robinson Jeffers: 3 volumes, 1988, 1989, 1991. Contributions to: Various publications, Address 323 North West 74th Street, Vancouver, WA 98665, USA.

HUNTER Alan James Herbert, b. 25 June 1922, Hoveton St John, Norwich, England. Author. m. Adelaide Elizabeth Cecily Cubitt, 6 Mar 1944, 1 daughter. Education: Royal Air Force, 1940-46. Appointments: Crime Reviewer, Eastern Daily Press, 1955-71. Publications: The Norwich Poems, 1945; Gently Go Man, 1961; Vivienne: Gently Where She Lay, 1972; The Honfleur Decision, 1980; Gabrielles Way, 1981; The Unhung Man, 1984; Traitors End, 1988; Bomber's Moon, 1994; Jackpot!, 1995; The Love of Gods, 1997; Over Here, 1998. Author of 46 crime novels featuring Chief Superintendent George Gently to 1999. Contributions to: Magazines and journals. Memberships: Society of Authors; Crime Writers Association; Authors Licensing and Collecting Society. Address: 3 St Laurence Avenue, Brundall, Norwich NR13 5QH, England.

HUNTER Dave, b. 3 June 1941, Brighton, England. Travel Author. m. Kathaline Steers, 17 Mar 1963. Publications: 7 Annual editions of Along Interstate-75. Honours: 97 Excellence in Book Design, Alcuin Society, Vancouver, Canada; 97 Certificate of Merit, Writer's Digest, Cincinnati, USA. Address: #81 20 Mineola Road E, Mississauga, Ont, L5G 4N9, Canada.

HUNTER Elizabeth. See: **DE GUISE Elizabeth (Mary Teresa).**

HUNTER Evan. See: **LOMBINO Salvatore A.**

HUNTER BLAIR Pauline, (Pauline Clarke, Helen Clare). Author. m. Peter Hunter Blair, Feb 1969. Education: BA Honours, Somerville College, Oxford. Publications: As Pauline Clarke: The Pekinese Princess, 1948; The Great Can, 1952; The White Elephant, 1952; Smith's Hoard, 1955; The Boy with the Erpingham Hood, 1956; Sandy the Sailor, 1956; James, the Policeman, 1957; James and the Robbers, 1959; Torolv the Fatherless, 1959, 2nd edition 1974, re-issued 1991; The Lord of the Castle, 1960; The Robin Hooders, 1960; James and the Smugglers, 1961; Keep the Pot Boiling, 1961; The Twelve and the Genii, 1962; Silver Bells and Cockle Shells, 1962; James and the Black Van, 1963; Crowds of Creatures, 1964; The Bonfire Party, 1966; The Two Faces of Silenus, 1972; As Helen Clare: Five Dolls in a House, 1953; Merlin's Magic, 1953; Bel, the Giant and Other Stories, 1956; Five Dolls and the Monkey, 1956; Five Dolls in the Snow, 1957; Five Dolls and Their Friends, 1959; Seven White Pebbles, 1960; Five Dolls and the Duke, 1963; The Cat and the Fiddle and Other Stories from Bel, the Giant, 1968. Honours: Library Association Carnegie Medal, 1962; Lewis Carroll Shelf Award, 1963; Deutsche Jugend Buchpreis, 1968. Address: Church Farm House, Bottisham, Cambridge CB5 9BA, England.

HUNTINGTON R P Vince, b. 20 Aug 1934, Ohio, USA. Psychotherapist. m. Sally Cutler, 21 Mar 1982, 3 sons. Education: BA, US International University, San Diego; 3 Masters Degrees in Human Behavior. Publication: Huntington Sexual Behavior Scales. Contributions to: Numerous. Honour: Best Single Story, San Diego Press Club, 1994. Literary Agent: Jas Wiedner. Address: c/o Wiedner Publications, PO Box 2178, Riverton, NJ 08077, USA.

HUNTINGTON Samuel (Phillips), b. 18 Apr 1927, New York, New York, USA. Political Scientist; Writer. m. Nancy Alice Arkelyan, 8 Sept 1957, 2 sons. Education: BA, Yale University, 1946; MA, University of Chicago, 1948; PhD, Harvard University, 1951. Appointments: Instructor, 1950-53, Assistant Professor, 1953-58, Professor of Government, 1962-, Research Associate, 1963-64, Faculty, 1964-, Associate Director, 1973-78, Acting Director, 1975-76, Director, 1978-89, Center for International Affairs, Thomson Professor of Government, 1967-81, Clarence Dillon Professor of International Affairs, 1981-82, Eaton Professor of the Science of Government, 1982-, Director, John M Olin Institute for Strategic Studies, 1989-, Albert J Weatherhead University Professor, 1995-, Harvard University; Research Associate, Brookings Institution, Washington, DC, 1952-53; Research Fellow, Social Science Research Council, New York City, 1954-57; Assistant Director, 1958-59, Research Associate, 1958-63, Associate Director, 1959-62, Associate Professor of Government, 1959-62, Institute of War and Peace Studies, Columbia University; Fellow, Center for Advanced Study in the Behavioral Sciences, Stanford, California, 1969-70; Co-Editor, Foreign Policy Quarterly, 1970-77; Visiting Fellow, All Souls College, Oxford, 1973; Coordinator, Security Planning, National Security Council, 1977-78; Chairman, Havard Academy for International and Area Studies, 1996-. Publications: The Soldier and the State: The Theory and Politics of Civil-Military Relations, 1957; The Common Defense: Strategic Programs in National Politics, 1961; Changing Patterns of Military Politics (co-editor), 1962; Political Power: USA/USSR (co-author), 1964; Political Order in Changing Societies, 1968; Authoritarian Politics in Modern Society: The Dynamics of Established One-Party Systems (co-editor), 1970; The Crisis of Democracy (co-author), 1975; No Easy Choice: Political Participation in Developing Countries (with J M Nelson), 1976; American Politics: The Promise of Disharmony, 1981; The Strategic Imperative: New Policies for American Security, 1982; Living with Nuclear Weapons (co-author), 1983; Global Dilemmas (co-editor), 1985; Reorganizing America's Defense (co-editor), 1985; Understanding Political Development (co-editor), 1987; The Third Wave: Democratization in the Late Twentieth Century, 1991; The Clash of Civilizations and the Remaking of the World Order, 1996. Contributions to: Professional journals. Honours: Silver Pen Award, 1960; Grawemayer World Order Award, 1992. Memberships: American Academy of Arts and Sciences, fellow; American Political Science Association, president, 1986-87; Council on Foreign Relations; International Institute for Strategic Studies; International Political Science Association. Address: c/o John M Olin Institute for Strategic Studies, Harvard University, 1737 Cambridge Street, Cambridge, MA 02138, USA.

HURD Douglas (Richard), b. 8 Mar 1930, Marlborough, England. Politician; Diplomat; Writer. m. (1) Tatiana Elizabeth Michelle, 1960, div, 3 sons, (2) Judy Smart, 1982, 1 son, 1 daughter. Education: Eton; Trinity College, Cambridge. Appointments: HM Diplomatic Service, 1952-66; Joined Conservative Research Department, 1966, Head, Foreign Affairs Section, 1968; Private Secretary to the Leader of the Opposition, 1968-70; Political Secretary to the Prime Minister, 1970-74; Member of Parliament, Conservative Party, Mid-Oxon, 1974-83, Witney, 1983-97; Opposition Spokesman on European Affairs, 1976-79; Visiting Fellow, Nuffield College, 1978-86; Minister of State, Foreign and Commonwealth Office, 1979-83, Home Office, 1983-84; Secretary of State for Northern Ireland, 1984-85, Home Secretary, 1985-89, Foreign Secretary, 1989-95; Director Natwest Group, 1995-; Deputy Chairman, NatWest Markets, 1995-98; Deputy Chairman, Coutts & Co, 1998-; Chairman, Hawkpoint Advisory Committee, 1998-; Chairman British Invisibles, 1998-; Chairman Prison Reform Trust, 1998-;Chairman, The Booker Prize Panel, 1998. Publications: The Arrow War, 1967; Send Him Victorious (with Andrew Osmond), 1968; The Smile on the Face of the Tiger (with Andrew Osmond), 1969; Scotch on the Rocks (with Andrew Osmond), 1971; Truth Game, 1972; Vote to Kill, 1975; An End to Promises, 1979; War Without Frontiers (with Andrew Osmond), 1982; Palace of Enchantments (with Stephen Lamport), 1985; The Search for Peace (BBC TV Series), 1997; The Shape of Ice, 1998. Honours: Commander of the Order of the British Empire, 1974; Privy Counsellor, 1982; Companion of Honour, 1995; Baron Hurd of Westwell, 1997. Address: c/o Hawkpoint Partners Limited, Crosby Court, 4 Great St Helens, London, EC3A 6HA.

HURD Michael John, b. 19 Dec 1928, Gloucester, England. Composer; Author. Education: BA, 1953, MA, 1957, Pembroke College, Oxford. Appointment: Professor of Theory, Royal Marines School of Music, 1953-59. Publications: Immortal Hour: The Life and Period of Rutland Boughton, 1962, revised edition as Rutland Boughton and the Glastonbury Festivals, 1993; The Composer, 1968; An Outline History of European Music, 1968, revised edition, 1988; Elgar, 1969; Vaughan Williams, 1970; Mendelssohn, 1970; The Ordeal of Ivor Gurney, 1978; The Oxford Junior Companion to Music, 1979; Vincent Novello and Company, 1981; The Orchestra, 1981. Contributions to: Reference books. Address: 4 Church Street, West Liss, Hampshire GU33 6JX, England.

HURST Frances. See: **MAYHAR Ardath.**

HUSTON Margo, b. 2 Dec 1943, Waukesha, Wisconsin, USA. Journalist. 1 son. Education: AB, College of Journalism, Marguette University, 1965. Appointment: Milwaukee Journal Sentinel. Publication: I'd Nebver Leave My Home, Would You?. Honour: Pulitzer Prize, 1977. Address: c/o Milwaukee Journal Sentinel, 333 West State Street, Milwaukee, WI 53202, USA.

HUSTON Nancy Louise, b. 16 Sept 1953, Calgary, Alberta, Canada. Writer. m. Tzvetan Todorov, 18 May 1981, 1 son, 1 daughter. Education: BA, Sarah Lawrence College, 1975; Diploma, École des Hautes Études, 1977. Appointments: Writer-in-Residence, American University, Paris, 1989; Facilitator, South African Writers Workshop, 1994; Visiting Professor, Harvard University, 1994. Publications: Les Variations Goldberg, 1981; Histoire d'Omaya, 1985; The Story of Omaya 1987; Journal de la Création, 1990; Cantique des Plaines, 1993; Plainsong, 1993; La Virevolte, 1994; The Goldberg Variations: Slow Emergencies, 1996; Instruments of Darkness, 1997; L'Empriente de l'ange, 1998. Honours: Prix, Binet Sangle de l'Académie Française, 1980; Prix Contrepoint, 1981; Prix du Gouverneur-Général, 1993; Prix Louis Hémon, 1995; Pix Goncourt des Lycéens, 1996; Prix du Livre Inter, 1997. Address: c/o Mary Kling, La Nouvelle Agence, 7 Rue Corneille, 75006 Paris, France.

HUTCHEON Linda Ann Marie, b. 24 Aug 1947, Toronto, Ontario, Canada. Professor; Writer. m. Michael Alexander Hutcheon, 30 May 1970. Education: BA, Modern Language and Literature, 1969, PhD, Comparative Literature, 1975, University of Toronto; MA, Romance Studies, Cornell University, 1971. Appointments: Assistant, Associate and full Professor of English, McMaster University, 1976-88; Professor of English and Comparative Literature, University of Toronto, 1988-96; University Professor, University of Toronto, 1996-. Publications: Narcissistic Narrative, 1980; Formalism and the Freudian Aesthetic, 1984; A Theory of Parody, 1985; A Poetics of Postmodernism, 1988; The Canadian Postmodern, 1988; The Politics of Postmodernism, 1989; Splitting Images, 199l; Irony's Edge, 1995. Opera: Desire, Disease, Death (with Michael Hutcheon), 1996. Editor: Other Solitudes, 1990; Double-Talking, 1992; Likely Stories, 1992; A Postmodern Reader, 1993. Contributions to: Diacritics; Textual Practice; Cultural Critique and other journals. Honours: Fellow, Royal Society of Canada, 1990; LLD, 1995. Membership: Second Vice-President, Modern Language Association of America, 1998. Address: University of Toronto, Ontario M5S 1A1, Canada.

HUTCHINS Pat, b. 18 June 1942, Yorkshire, England. Writer; Illustrator. m. 20 Aug 1966, 2 sons. Education: Darlington School of Art, 1958-61; Leeds College of Art, 1961-63; National Diploma in Design. Publications: Rosie's Walk, 1968; Tom and Sam, 1968; The Surprise Party, 1969; Clocks and More Clocks, 1970; Changes, Changes, 1971; Titch, 1971; Goodnight Owl, 1972; The Wind Blew, 1974; The Very Worst Monster, 1975; The House That Sailed Away, 1975; The Tale of Thomas Mead, 1980; King Henry's Palace, 1983; One Hunter, 1982; You'll Soon Grow into Them Titch, 1983; The Curse of the Egyptian Mummy, 1983; The Doorbell Rang, 1986; Where's the Baby?, 1988; Which Witch is Which?, 1989; Rats, 1989; What Game Shall We Play?, 1990; Tidy Titch, 1991; Silly Billy, 1992; My Best Friend, 1992; Little Pink Pig, 1993; Three Star Billy, 1994; Titch and Daisy, 1996. Honour: Kate Greenaway Medal, 1975.

HUTCHINSON Gregory Owen, b. 5 Dec 1957, London, England. Writer. m. Yvonne Downing, 4 Aug 1979, 1 daughter. Education: City of London School, 1968-74; BA, MA, DPhil, Oxford University (Balliol and Christ Church), 1975-83. Publications: Aeschylus, Septem Contra Thebas (edited with introduction and commentary), 1985; Hellenistic Poetry, 1988; Latin Literature from Seneca to Juvenal: A Critical Study, 1993; Cicero's Correspondence: A Literary Study, 1998. Address: Exeter College, Oxford OX1 3DP, England.

HUTTERLI Kurt, b. 18 Aug 1944, Bern, Switzerland. Writer; Artist. m. Marianne Büchler, 7 July 1966, 1 son, 1 daughter. Education: Secondary School Teacher Diploma, University of Bern, 1966. Publications: Aber, 1972; Herzgrün, 1974; Felsengleich, 1976; die Faltsche, 1977; Das Matterköpfen, 1978; Ein Hausmann, 1980; Finnlandisiert, 1982; Uberlebenslust, 1984; Elchspur, 1986; Baccala, 1989; Gaunerblut, 1990; Mir Kommt Kein Tier ins Haus, 1991; Stachelflieder, 1991; Katzensprung, 1993; Die sanfte Piratin, 1994; Im Fischbauch, 1998. Contributions to: Der Bund; Stuttgarter Zeitung; Drehpunkt; Einspruch. Honours: Poetry Prize, City of Bern, 1971; Book Prizes, City of Bern, 1972, 1978; Theatre Awards, 1976, 1982, 1987. Memberships: PEN Switzerland; Autorengruppe Olten; Berner Schriftsteller-Verein. Address: RR2, S53/C9, Oliver, British Columbia, V0H 1T0, Canada.

HUTTON Alasdair Henry, b. 19 May 1940, London, England. Narrator; Script Writer. m. Deirdre Mary, 2 sons. Appointments: Non-Executive Chairman, Calchou Electronics, Kelso; European Adviser, Scottish Police College and Isle of Man Parliament; Senior Adviser, Career Associates, Edinburgh; Consultant, Antenna Audio. Publication: 15 Para 1947, 1993. Contributions to: Flodden; Second Chance. Honours: TD, 1977; MBE, 1986; OBE, 1980; Winner, Alexander Graham Bell Short Story Competition, 1997. Memberships: John Buchan Society, vice chairman, life member, 1985-; Edinburgh Sir Walter Scott Club, life member, 1994-. Address: Rosebank, Shedden Park Road, Kelso, Roxburghshire TD5 7PX, England.

HUTTON Ronald Edmund, b. 19 Dec 1953, Ootacamund, India. Historian. m. Lisa Radulovic, 5 Aug 1988. Education: BA, Cantab, 1976; MA, 1980; DPhil, 1980. Appointments: Professor of British History, Bristol University, 1996-. Publications: The Royalist War Effort, 1981; The Restoration, 1985; Charles II, 1989; The British Republic, 1990; The Pagan Religions of the Ancient British Isles, 1991; The Rise and Fall of Merry England, 1994; The Stations of the Sun, 1996. Contributions to: Journals. Honour: Benjamin Franklin Prize, 1993. Memberships: Royal Historical Society; Folklore Society. Address: 13 Woodland Road, Bristol BS8 1TB, England.

HUXTABLE Ada Louise, b. New York, New York, USA. Architecture Critic; Writer. m. L Garth Huxtable. Education: AB, magna cum laude, Hunter College, New York City; Postgraduate Studies, Institute of Fine Arts, New York University. Appointments: Assistant Curator of Achitecture and Design, Museum of Modern Art, New York, 1946-50; Contributing Editor, Progressive Architecture and Art in America, 1950-63; Architecture Critic, The New York Times, 1963-82; The Wall Street Journal, 1996-; Cook Lecturer in American Institutions, University of Michigan, 1977; Hitchcock Lecturer, University of California at Berkeley, 1982. Publications: Pier Luigi Nervi, 1960; Classic New York, 1964; Will They Ever Finish Bruckner Boulevard?, 1970; Kicked a Building Lately?, 1976; The Tall Building Artistically Reconsidered: The Search for a Skyscraper Style, 1985; Goodbye History, Hello Hamburger, 1986; Architecture Anyone?, 1986; The Unreal America: Architecture and Illusion, 1997. Contributions to: Various publications. Honours: Many honorary doctorates; Fulbright Fellowship, 1950-52; Guggenheim Fellowship, 1958; Architectural Medal for Criticism, American Institute of Architects, 1969; 1st Pulitzer Prize for Distinguished Criticism, 1970; Medal for Literature, National Arts Club, 1971; Diamond Jubilee Medallion, City of New York,

1973; Secretary's Award for Conservation, US Department of the Interior, 1976; Thomas Jefferson Medal, University of Virginia, 1977; John D and Catharine T MacArthur Foundation Fellowship, 1981-86; Henry Allen Moe Prize in the Humanities, American Philosophical Society, 1992. Memberships: American Academy of Arts and Letters; American Philosophical Society; American Academy of Arts and Sciences, fellow; New York Public Library, director's fellow; Society of Architectural Historians. Address: 969 Park Avenue, New York, NY 10028, USA.

HUYLER Jean Wiley, b. 30 Mar 1935, Seattle, Washington, USA. Communications Management Consultant; Writer; Editor; Photojournalist. Div, 1 son, 1 daughter. Education: Business Administration, University of Washington, 1953-55; BA, Maryhurst College, 1979; MA, Pacific Lutheran University, 1979; D Litt, Fairfax University, 1989. Appointments: Various newspaper and magazine editorships, 1963-96; Editor, books for Education System Managers, Washington School Directors Association, 1977-81; Designer and Editor, For the Record: A History of Tacoma Public Schools, Tacoma School District, 1985-. Publications: Demystifying the Media, 1980; Campaign Savvy: School Support, 2nd edition, 1981; Communications is a People Process, 1981; Crisis Communications, 1983; How to Get Competent Communications Help, 1983; Sharing a Vision for Gifted Education with Business and Education Leaders, 1988; Lifespan Learning on Centerstage of the Future, 1988; Learning to Learn: New Techniques for Corporate Education, 1989.

HW. See: **WIVEL Henrik.**

HWANG David Henry, b. 11 Aug 1957, Los Angeles, California, USA. Dramatist; Screenwriter. m. 1) Ophelia Chong, 1985, 2) Kathryn Layng, 17 Dec 1993, 1 son. Education: BA, English, Stanford University, 1979; Postgraduate Studies, Yale Drama School, 1980-81. Appointment: Dramaturg, Asian American Theatre Centre, San Francisco, 1987-. Publications: Plays: FOB, 1980; The Dance and the Railroad, 1981; Family Devotions, 1981; Sound and Beauty, 1983; The Sound of a Voice, 1984; As the Crow Flies, 1986; Rich Relations, 1986; M Butterfly, 1988; Bondage, 1992; Face Value, 1993; Trying to Find Chinatown, 1996; Golden Child, 1996. Screenplays: M Butterfly, 1993; Golden Gate, 1993. Other: 1000 Airplanes on the Roof (musical), 1988; Forbidden Nights (television play), 1990; The Voyage (libretto), 1992. Honours: Drama-Logue Awards, 1980, 1986; Obie Award, 1981; Rockefeller Foundation Fellowship, 1983; Guggenheim Fellowship, 1984; National Endowment for the Arts Fellowship, 1987; Tony Award for Best Play, 1988; Outer Critics Circle Award for Best Broadway Play, 1988; John Gassner Award, 1988. Memberships: Dramatists Guild, board of directors, 1988-. Address: c/o Writers and Artists Agency, 19 West 44th Street, suite 1000, New York, NY 10036, USA.

HYKISCH Anton, b. 23 Feb 1932, Ban Stiavnica, Slovakia. Economist Manager; Diplomat; Journalist. m. Eva Suchonova, 19 Oct 1957, 1 son, 1 daughter. Education: Economical University, Bratislava, 1956. Appointments: Managing Director, Mlada Leta Publishers; Member of Parliament, Slovak Parliament, 1990-92; Ambassador of Slovakia to Canada, 1993-97. Publications include: A Step in the Unknown, 1959; The Square in the Town Mahring, 1965; The Time of Masters, 1977; Lets Love the Queen, 1984; Defending Mysteries, 1990; I've Met You, 1963; Canada in Not a Fun, 1968; Atomic Summers, 1988; My Little Chippy, 1989. Contributions to: Slovak and Czech literary magazines and weeklies. Honours: Award for Fiction, 1988; Childrens Book Award, 1989. Memberships: Union of Slovak Writers; Committee for Education and Culture; Pan Europa Union; Christian Social Union; Society of the Slovak Writers, Chairman; Slovak Centre PEN Club. Literary Agent: Lita Slovak Literary Agency, Mozartova 9, 815 30 Bratislava, Slovakia. Address: Lachova 18, 851 03 Bratislava, Slovakia.

HYLAND Paul Robert, b. 15 Sept 1947, Poole, Dorset, England. Poet; Travel Writer. Education: BSc, Honours, Bristol University, 1968. Publications: Purbeck: The Ingrained Island, 1978; Wight: Biography of an Island, 1984; The Black Heart, 1988; Indian Balm, 1994; Backwards Out of the Big World, 1996; Poetry: Poems Ofz, 1982; The Stubborn Forest, 1984; Getting into Poetry, 1992 , 2nd edition, 1996; Kicking Sawdust, 1995. Honours: Eric Gregory Award, 1976; Authors Foundation, 1995; Discover Dorset: Isle of Purbeck, 1998. Memberships: Society of Authors; Poetry Society. Literary Agent: David Higham Associates Ltd. Address: 32 Colliton Street, Dorchester, Dorset DT1 1XH, England.

HYMAN Harold M(elvin), b. 24 July 1924, New York, New York, USA. Professor of History Emeritus; Author. m. Ferne Beverly Handelsman, 11 Mar 1946, 2 sons, 1 daughter. Education: BA, University of California at Los Angeles, 1948; MA, 1950, PhD, 1952, Columbia University. Appointments: Instructor, City College, New York City, 1950-52; Columbia University, 1953, University of Washington, 1960, Brooklyn College, 1962, University of Chicago, 1965; Assistant Professor, Earlham College, 1952-55; Visiting Assistant Professor, 1955-56, Professor, 1963-68, University of California at Los Angeles; Associate Professor, Arizona State University, Tempe, 1956-57; Professor of History, University of Illinois, 1963-68; William P Hobby Professor of History, 1968-96, Professor Emeritus, 1997-, Rice University; Graduate Faculty in Political Science, University of Tokyo, 1973; Faculty of Law, Keio University, 1973; Adjunct Professor of Legal History, Bates College of Law, University of Houston, 1977, and of American Legal History, School of Law, University of Texas, 1986; Meyer Visiting Distinguished Professor of Legal History, School of Law, New York University, 1982-83. Publications: Era of the Oath: Northern Loyalty Tests During the Civil War and Reconstruction, 1954; To Try Men's Souls: Loyalty Tests in American History, 1959; Stanton: The Life and Times of Lincoln's Secretary of War (with Benjamin P Thomas), 1962; Soldiers and Spruce: The Loyal Legion of Loggers and Lumbermen, the Army's Labor Union of World War I, 1963; A More Perfect Union: The Impact of the Civil War and Reconstruction on the Constitution, 1973; Union and Confidence: The 1860s, 1976; Equal Justice Under Law: Constitutional History, 1835-1875 (with William Wiecek), 1982; Quiet Past and Stormy Present?: War Powers in American History, 1986; American Singularity: The 1787 Northwest Ordinance, the 1862 Homestead-Morrill Acts, and the 1944 G I Bill, 1986; Oleander Odyssey: The Kempners of Galveston, 1870-1980, 1990; The Reconstruction Justice of Salmon P Chase: In Re Turner and Texas v White, 1997; Craftsmanship and Character: A History of the Vinson & Elkins Law Firm of Houston, 1917-1990s, 1998. Editor: Several books and reprint editions. Contributions to: Scholarly journals. Honours: Albert J Beveridge Award, American Historical Association, 1952; Coral H Tullis Memorial Prize, Texas A & M University Press, 1990; T R Fehrenbach Book Award, Texas Historical Commission, 1990; Ottis Lock Endowment Award, East Texas Historical Association, 1991. Memberships: American Historical Association; American Society of Legal History, president, 1994-95; Organization of American Historians; Southern Historical Association. Address: c/o Department of History - M5 42, Rice University, 6100 Main Street, Houston, TX 77005, USA.

I

IBSEN Arni. See: **THORGEIRSSON Arni Ibsen.**

ICTERUS. See: **WRIGHT David James Thomas.**

IESMANTAS Gintautas, b. 1 Jan 1930, Lithuania. Journalist; Poet. m. Dalija, 16 Mar 1990, 2 sons. Education: Diploma in Lithuanian Language and Literature, Vilnius Pedagogical Institute, 1953. Appointments: Journalist, 1953-74, 1989-90, 1992-; Bibliographer, 1974-80; Imprisoned and exiled, 1980-88; Deputy, Lithuanian Republic Supreme Council, Restoration, Seimas, 1990-92. Publications: Witnessings (book),; 15 poetry books. Contributions to: Liotuvos aidas; Voruta; Lietuvos zinios; Dienovidis. Honours: P Lauritzen, Freedom Award, Copenhagen University, 1990. Memberships: PEN; Lithuanian Journalists Union. Address: Simulionio 4-232, LT 2050 Vilnius, Lithuania.

IGGERS Georg Gerson, b. 7 Dec 1926, Hamburg, Germany. Historian; Distinguished Professor; Writer. m. Wilma Abeles, 23 Dec 1948, 3 sons. Education: BA, University of Richmond, Virginia, 1944; AM, 1945, PhD, 1951, University of Chicago; Graduate Studies, New School for Social Research, New York City, 1945-46. Appointments: Instructor, University of Akron, 1948-50; Associate Professor, Philander Smith College, 1950-56; Visiting Professor, University of Arkansas, 1956-57, 1964, University of Rochester, New York, 1970-71, University of Leipzig, 1992; Associate Professor, Dillard University, New Orleans, 1957-63; Visiting Associate Professor, Tulane University, 1957-60, 1962-63; Associate Professor, Roosevelt University, Chicago, 1963-65; Professor, 1965-; Distinguished Professor, 1978-, State University of New York at Buffalo; Visiting Scholar, Technische Hochschule, Darmstadt, 1991; Universität Leipzig, 1992; Forschungsschwerpunkt Zeithistorische Studien, Potsdam, 1993, 1998; University of Aarhus, Denmark, 1998. Publications: Cult of Authority: Political Philosophy of the Saint Simonians, 1958; German Conception of History, 1968; Leopold von Ranke: the Theory and Practice of History (co-editor), 1973; New Directions in European Historiography, 1975; International Handbook of Historical Studies (co-editor), 1979; Social History of Politics (editor), 1985; Aufklärung und Geschichte (co-editor), 1986; Leopold von Ranke and the Shaping of the Historical Discipline (co-editor), 1990; Marxist Historiography in Transition: Historical Writings in East Germany in the 1980's (editor), 1991; Geschichtswissenschaft 20 Jahrhundert, 1993; Historiography in the Twentieth Century: From Scientific Objectivity to the Postmodern Challenge, 1997. Contributions to: Scholarly journals. Honour: Recipient of Research Prize, Alexander von Humboldt Foundation, 1995-96; International Commission for the History and Theory of Historiography, president, 1995-. Address: c/o Department of History, State University of New York at Buffalo, Buffalo, NY 14260, USA.

IGGULDEN John Manners, (Jack), b. 12 Feb 1917, Brighton, Victoria, Australia. Author; Industrialist. m. Helen Carroll Schapper, 1 son dec, 2 daughters. Appointments: Manager, family-owned manufacturing companies, 1940-59; Writer, 1959-70; Businessman, 1970-; Part-time writer, 1980-; Currently, Chief Executive, Planet Lighting, Lucinda Glassworks, Bellingen, New South Wales, Australia. Publications: Breakthrough, 1960; The Storms of Summer, 1960; The Clouded Sky, 1964; Dark Stranger, 1965; Summer's Tales 3, 1966; Manual of Standard Procedures, Gliding Federation of Australia, 1964; Gliding Instructor's Handbook, 1968; The Promised Land Papers Vol 1, The Revolution of the Good, 1986, Vol 2, How Things Are Wrong and How to Fix Them, 1988; Vol 3, The Modification of Freedom, 1993; Silent Lies, 1997; Good World, 1998. Address: "Evandale", Promised Land, Bellingen, NSW 2454, Australia.

IGNATIEFF Michael, b. 12 May 1947, Toronto, Ontario, Canada. Writer; Historian. m. Susan Barrowclough, 20 Dec 1977, 1 son, 1 daughter. Education: BA, University of Toronto, 1969; PhD, Harvard University, 1975; MA, University of Cambridge, 1978. Appointments: Reporter, Globe and Mail, Toronto, 1966-67; Teaching Fellow, Harvard University, 1971-74; Assistant Professor, University of British Columbia, Vancouver, 1976-78; Senior Research Fellow, King's College, Cambridge, 1978-84; Visiting Professor, Ecole des Hautes Etudes, Paris, 1985; Host, Thinking Aloud, BBC-TV, 1986-, Voices, Channel Four, 1986, The Late Show, BBC-2, 1989-; Editorial Columnist, The Observer, London, 1990-93. Publications: A Just Measure of Pain: The Penitentiary in the Industrial Revolution, 1978; Wealth and Virtue: The Shaping of Classical Political Economy in the Scottish Enlightenment (editor with Istvan Hont), 1983; The Needs of Strangers, 1984; The Russian Album, 1987; Asya, 1991; Scar Tissue, 1993; Blood and Belonging: Journeys Into the New Nationalism, 1994. Honours: Governor-General's Award, 1988; Heinemann Prize, Royal Society of Literature, 1988; Booker Prize Nomination, 1993; Whitbread Award Nomination, 1993; Lionel Gelber Award, 1994; Honorary Doctorate, Bishop's University, 1995. Address: 37 Baalbec Road, London N5 1QN, England.

IHIMAERA Witi, b. 7 Feb 1944, Gisborne, New Zealand. Author. Education: University of Auckland, 1963-66; Victoria University, 1968-72. Publications: Pounamu, Pounamy, 1972; Tangi, 1973; Whanau, 1974; Maori, 1975; The New Net Goes Fishing, 1977; Into the World of Light, 1980; The Matriarch, 1986; The Whale Rider, 1987; Dear Miss Mansfield, 1989. Address: c/o Ministry of Foreign Affairs, Private Bag, Wellington 1, New Zealand.

IKEDA Daisaku, b. 2 Jan 1928, Tokyo, Japan. Buddhist Philosopher; Poet; Peace Activist. Education: Fuji College. Publications include: Human Revolution, Volumes 1-6, 1972-99; Choose Life: A Dialogue with Arnold Toynbee, 1976; The Living Buddha: An Interpretative Biography, 1976, 1995; Buddhism, the First Millennium, 1977; Songs From My Heart, 1978; Glass Children and Other Essays, 1979, 1983; Life: An Enigma, a Precious Jewel, 1982; Buddhism and the Cosmos, 1985; The Flower of Chinese Buddhism, 1986; Human Values in a Changing World (with Bryan Wilson), 1987; Unlocking the Mysteries of Birth and Death: Buddhism in the Contemporary World, 1988, 1995; The Snow Country Prince, 1990; A Lifelong Quest for Peace (with Linus Pauling), 1992; Choose Peace (with Johan Galtung), 1995; A New Humanism: The University Addresses of Daisaku Ikeda, 1996; Kanta and the Deer, 1997; Space and Eternal Life (with Chandra Wickramasinghe), 1998; Numerous titles and essays in Japanese. Contributions to: Seikyo, Nihon-Keizai, Yomiuri newspapers; Ushio, Poet (World Poetry Society), Mirror magazines; Others. Honours include: Poet Laureate, World Academy of Arts and Culture, 1981; UN Peace Award, 1983; Kenya Oral Literature Award, 1986; Honorary Doctorate, University of Glasgow, 1994; Tagore Peace Award, 1997. Memberships include: Non-resident Member, Brazilian Academy of Letters; Honorary Founding Member, Pan-African Writers Association; Honorary Member, The Club of Rome; Honorary Senator, European Academy of Sciences and Arts. Address: c/o Soka Gakkai International, 15-3 Samon-cho, Shinjuku-ku, Tokyo 160-0017, Japan.

ILIOPOULOS Vagelis, b. 15 Sept 1964, Athens, Greece. Teacher. m. Georgia Panagiotopoulos, 24 Jan 1998. Education: BA, Paegogic Academy of Athens, 1984; BA, Department of Theology, University of Athens, 1990. Appointments: Teacher, Manessis Primary School, 1984-86; Teacher, 1986, Acting Principal, 1994-, J M Panagiotopoulos Primary School. Publications: The Adventure of the Crumpled Sock, story for children, 1995; The Little Triangle-Fish, story for children, 1997; The Awakening of the Strawberry, novel, 1997; Adaptation of 20,000 Leagues under the Sea (Jules Verne), educational CD-ROM, 1997; The Galaxy of Numbers (with Damianakis), educational CD-ROM, 1997; The Secret of the Golden Limpet, fairy tale, 1998. Contributions to: Club of Educators, Patakis Publications, magazine, 1996-97. Honour: Antigone Metaxas Honour, Greek Department of IBBY. Membership: International Reading Association, 1997. Address: Themistokleous 37, 15342 Aghia Paraskevi, Athens, Greece.

IMPEY Rose(mary June), b. 7 June 1947, Northwich, Cheshire, England. Writer. 2 daughters. Education: Teacher's Certificate, 1970. Publications: Who's a Clever Girl, Then, 1985; The Baked Bean Queen, 1986; The Girls Gang, 1986; Desperate for a Dog, 1988; The Flat Man, 1988; Letter to Father Christmas, 1988; Instant Sisters, 1989; Joe's Cafe, 1990; Revenge of the Rabbit, 1990; First Class, 1992; Trouble with the Tucker Twins, 1992; Orchard Book of Fairytales, 1992; Animal Crackers, 1993; Sir Billy Bear and Other Friends, 1996; Potbelly and the Haunted House, 1996; Fireballs from Hell. 1996; Sleepover Club, 1997; Feather Pillows, 1997. Address: 6 The Homestead, Mountsorrel, Loughborough, Leicestershire LE12 7HS, England.

INDICK Benjamin Philip, b. 11 Aug 1923, New Jersey, USA. Pharmacist; Writer. m. 23 Aug 1953, 1 son, 1 daughter. Education: BS, Biology, Rutgers University, 1947; BS, Pharmacy, Ohio State University, 1951; New School for Social Research, New York, 1960-61, no degree. Publications: Plays: Incident at Cross Plains, 1976; He, She and the End of the World, 1982; The Children of King, 1989; Books: A Gentleman from Providence Pens a Letter, 1975; The Drama of Ray Bradbury, 1976; Ray Bradbury: Dramatist, 1989. Non Fiction: Exploring Fantasy Worlds, 1985; Discovering Modern Horror Fiction, 1, 1985, II, 1988; Kingdon of Fear, 1986; Discovering H P Lovecraft, 1987; Reign of Fear, 1988; Penguin Encyclopaedia of Horror and the Supernatural, 1986; George Alec Effinger: From Entropy to Budayeen, 1993. Contributions to: Books and magazines. Honours: First Prizes, Playwright Contests, 1962, 1964, 1965. Memberships: Dramatists Guild; Horror Writers of America; Rho Chi; Phi Lambda Epsilon. Address: 428 Sagamore Avenue, Teaneck, NJ 07666, USA.

INGALLS Jeremy, b. 2 Apr 1911, Gloucester, Massachusetts, USA. Poet; Translator; Professor (retired). Education: AB, 1932, AM, 1933, Tufts University; Student, 1938, 1939, Research Fellow, Classical Chinese, 1945-46, University of Chicago. Appointments: Assistant Professor, Western College, Oxford, Ohio, 1941-43; Resident Poet, 1947, Assistant Professor, 1948-50, Associate Professor, 1953-55, Professor of English and Asian Studies, 1955-60, Rockford College, Illinois; Visiting Lecturer at numerous colleges and universities. Publications: A Book of Legends (stories), 1941; The Metaphysical Sword (poems), 1941; Tahl (narrative poem), 1945; The Galilean Way, 1953; The Woman from the Island (poems), 1958; These Islands Also (poems), 1959; This Stubborn Quantum: Sixty Poems, 1983; Summer Liturgy (verse play), 1985; The Epic Tradition and Related Essays, 1988. Contributions to: Various publications. Honours: Yale Series of Younger Poets Prize, 1941; Guggenheim Fellowship, 1943-44; American Academy of Arts and Letters Grant, 1944-45; Shelley Memorial Award for Poetry, 1950; Lola Ridge Memorial Awards for Poetry, 1951, 1962; Ford Foundation Faculty Fellow, 1952-53; Fulbright Lecturer, Kobe, Japan, 1957-58; Rockefeller Foundation Lecturer, Kyoto, Japan, 1960; Honorary Epic Poet Laureate, United Poets Laureate International, 1965; Honorary doctorates. Memberships: Dante Society; Modern Language Association; Phi Beta Kappa; Poetry Society of America. Address: 6269 East Rosewood, Tucson, AZ 85711, USA.

INGALLS Rachel (Holmes), b. 13 May 1940, Boston, Massachusetts, USA. Author. Education: BA, Radcliffe College, 1964. Publications: Theft, 1970; The Man Who Was Left Behind, 1974; Mediterranean Cruise, 1973; Mrs Caliban, 1982; Binstead's Safari, 1983; I See a Long Journey, 1985; The Pearlkillers, 1987; The End of the Tragedy, 1987; Something to Write Home About, 1990; Black Diamond, 1992; Be My Guest, 1992. Honours: First Novel Award, Author's Club, England, 1971; British Book Marketing Council Best Book Award, 1986. Membership:

American Academy and Institute of Arts and Letters, fellow. Address: c/o Georges Borchardt Inc, 136 East 57th Street, New York, NY 10022, USA.

INGHAM Bernard, b. 21 June 1932, Halifax, W Yorkshire, England. Journalist; Broadcaster. m. Nancy Hilda Hoyle, 3 Nov 1956, 1 son. Education: Godmorden, Halifax and Bradford Technical College; Certificate of Training, Junior Journalist, 1954. Appointments: Reporter, Hebden Bridge Times, 1948-52; Reporter, Yorkshire Evening Post and Yorkshire Post, 1952-59; Reporter, The Yorkshire Post, 1959-60; Northern Industrial Correspondent, The Yorkshire Post, 1961-62; Reporter, The Guardian, 1962-65; Labour Staff, The Guardian, 1965-67; Press and PR Adviser, National Board for Prices and Incomes, 1967-68; Head of Information, Department of Employment & Productivity, 1968-72; Director, Information Department of Employment, 1972-73; Director, Information, Department of Energy, 1974-78; Head, Energy Conservation Division, Department of Energy, 1978-79; Chief, Press Secretary to the Prime Minister, 1979-90; Columnist, Daily Express, Sunday Express, 1991-98; Columnist, PR Week, 1994-; Columnist, Retail Week, 1998-; Non Executive Director, Hill & Knowlton (UK) Ltd, 1991-; Non Executive Director, McDonald's Restaurants, 1991-; Chairman, Bernard Ingham Communications, 1991-; Member, Council of University of Huddersfield, 1994-; Visiting Fellow, Politics Department, University of Newcastle upon Tyne, 1988-; Visiting Professor, University Business School, Middlesex University, 1998-; FCAM, 1997. Publication: Kill the Messenger, 1991. Honours: Knight Bachelor, 1990; Magazine '95 Columnist of the Year; Hon DLitt, University of Buckingham, 1997. Literary Agent: Peters, Fraser and Dunlop. Address: 9 Monahan Avenue, Purley, Surrey CR8 3BB, England.

INGHAM Daniel. See: LAMBOT Isobel Mary.

INGHAM Kenneth, b. 9 Aug 1921, Harden, England. Professor of History Emeritus; Writer. m. Elizabeth Mary Southall, 18 June 1949, 1 son, 1 daughter. Education: Exhibitioner, Keble College, Oxford, 1940; Frere Exhibitioner in Indian Studies, 1947, DPhil, 1950, Oxford University. Appointments: Lecturer, 1950-56, Professor, 1956-62, Makerere College, Uganda; Director of Studies, Royal Military Academy, Sandhurst, 1962-67; Professor of History, 1967-84, Head, Department of History, 1970-84, Part-time Professor of History, 1984-86, Professor Emeritus, 1986-, University of Bristol. Publications: Reformers in India, 1956; The Making of Modern Uganda, 1958; A History of East Africa, 1962; The Kingdom of Toro in Uganda, 1975; Jan Christian Smuts: The Conscience of a South African, 1986; Politics in Modern Africa, 1990; Obote: A Political Biography, 1994. Contributions to: Reference books and professional journals. Honours: Military Cross, 1946; Officer of the Order of the British Empire, 1961. Memberships: British Institute in Eastern Africa; Royal African Society; Royal Historical Society. Address: The Woodlands, 94 West Town Lane, Bristol BS4 5DZ, England.

INGLE Stephen James, b. 6 Nov 1940, Ripon, Yorkshire, England.University Professor. m. Margaret Anne Farmer, 5 Aug 1964, 2 sons, 1 daughter. Education: BA, 1962, DipEd, 1963, MA, 1965, University of Sheffield; PhD, Victoria University, New Zealand, 1967. Appointment: Professor, University of Stirling. Publications: Socialist Thought in Imaginative Literature, 1979; Parliament and Health Policy, 1981; British Party System, 1989; George Orwell: A Political Life, 1993. Contributions to: Many in Fields of Politics and Literature. Honours: Commonwealth Scholar, 1964-67; Erasmus Scholar, 1989; Visiting Research Fellow, Victoria University, New Zealand, 1993. Memberships: Political Studies Association. Address: Department of Politics, University of Stirling, Stirling FK9 4LA, Scotland.

INGRAMS Richard Reid, (Philip Reid), b. 11 Aug 1937, London, England. Journalist. m. 1962, 2 sons, 1 dec, 1 daughter. Education: University College, Oxford. Appointments: Editor, 1963-86, Chairman, 1974-, Private Eye; TV Critic, The Spectator, 1976-84; Editor, The Oldie,

1993-94. Publications: Private Eye on London, 1962; Private Eye's Romantic England, 1963; Mrs Wilson's Diary, 1966; The Tale of Driver Grope, 1968; The Life and Times of Private Eye, 1971; Harris in Wonderland, 1973; Cobbets's Country Book, 1974; The Best of Private Eye, 1974; God's Apology, 1977; Goldenballs, 1979; The Other Hald, 1981; Piper's Places, 1983; Down the Hatch, 1985; Just the One, 1986; John Stewart Collis: A Memoir, 1986; The Best of Dear Bill, 1986; Mud in Your Eye, 1987; You Might as Well Be Dead, 1988; Number 10, 1989; On and On, 1990. Address: c/o Private Eye, 6 Carlisle Street, London W1, England.

INMAN Lucy Daniels, (Lucy Daniels), b. 24 Mar 1934, Durham, North Carolina, USA. Clinical Psychologist. 3 sons, 1 daughter. Education: AB, Psychology, 1972, PhD, Clinical Psychology, 1977, University of North Carolina. Publications: Caleb, My Son, 1956; High on a Hill, 1961; A Room of One's Own Revisited; Socarides, 1995. Contributions to: Journals and magazines. Honour: Guggenheim Fellowship, 1957. Literary Agent: Carl D Brandt, 1501 Broadway, New York, NY 10036, USA. Address: 2636 Tatton Drive, Raleigh, NC 27608, USA.

INNAURATO Albert (Francis), b. 2 June 1947, Philadelphia, Pennsylvania, USA. Playwright; Director. Education: BA, Temple University; BFA, California Institute of the Arts, 1972; MFA, Yale University, 1975. Appointments: Playwright-in-Residence, Public Theatre, New York City, 1977, Circle Repertory Theatre, New York City, 1979, Playwright's Horizons, New York City, 1983; Adjunct Professor, Columbia University, Princeton University, 1987-89; Instructor, Yale School of Drama, 1993. Publications: Plays: Earthworms, 1974; Gemini, 1977; The Transfiguration of Bennon Blimpie, 1977; Verna the USO Girl, 1980; Gus and Al, 1988; Magda and Callas, 1988. Other: Coming of Age in Soho, 1985. Contributions to: Newspapers and journals. Honours: Guggenheim Fellowship, 1976; Rockefeller Foundation Grant, 1977; Obie Awards, 1977, 1978; Emmy Award, 1981; National Endowment for the Arts Grants, 1986, 1989; Drama League Award, 1987. Memberships: Dramatists Guild; Writers Guild of America. Address: 325 West 22nd Street, New York, NY 10011, USA.

INNES Brian, b. 4 May 1928, Croydon, Surrey, England. Writer; Publisher. m. (1) Felicity McNair Wilson, 5 Oct 1956, (2) Eunice Lynch, 2 Apr 1971, 3 sons. Education: BSc, King's College, London, 1946-49. Appointments: Assistant Editor, Chemical Age, 1953-55; Associate Editor, The British Printer, 1955-60; Art Director, Hamlyn Group, 1960-62; Director, Temperance Seven Ltd, 1961-; Proprietor, Brian Innes Agency, 1964-66; Immediate Books, 1966-70; FOT Library, 1970-; Creative Director, Deputy Chairman, Orbis Publishing Ltd, 1970-86; Editorial Director, Mirror Publishing, 1986-88. Publications: Book of Pirates, 1966; Book of Spies, 1967; Book of Revolutions, 1967; Book of Outlaws, 1968; Flight, 1970; Saga of the Railways, 1972; Horoscopes, 1976; The Tarot, 1977; Book of Change, 1979; The Red Baron Lives, 1981; Red Red Baron, 1983; The Havana Cigar, 1983; Crooks and Conmen, 1993; Catalogue of Ghost Sightings, 1996; The History of Torture, 1998; Death and The Afterlife, 1999. Contributions to: Man, Myth & Magic; Take Off; Real Life Crimes; Fire Power; The Story of Scotland; Discover Scotland; Marshall Cavendish Encyclopaedia of Science; Numerous recordings, films, radio and television broadcasts; Many photographs published. Honour: Royal Variety Command Performance, 1961. Memberships: Chartered Society of Designers; Royal Society of Arts; Institute of Printing; Crime Writers Association; British Actors' Equity. Address: Les Forges de Montgaillard, 11330 Mouthoumet, France.

IOANNOU Noris, b. 22 Feb 1947, Larnaca, Cyprus. Cultural Historian; Critic; Writer. Education: BSc, Honours, 1969, DipEd, 1971, University of Adelaide; PhD, Visual Arts, Archaeology, Flinders University, South Australia, 1989; Writer in Residence, Migration Museum. Publications: Ceramics in South Australia 1836-1986, 1986; The Culture Brokers, 1989; Craft in Society (editor),

1992; Australian Studio Glass, 1995; The Barossa Folk: Germanic Furniture and Craft Traditions in Australia, 1995; Masters of their Craft; Barossa Journeys: Into a Valley of Tradition, 1997; Barossa Journeys, 1997. Contributions to: Books and journals. Honours: Australian Heritage Award, 1987; Writing Fellowship, Australian Council, 1989; Churchill Fellow, 1996; Visiting Fellow, History Department, Flinders University, 1998. Memberships: Association of Professional Historians, president; Australiana Society, 1995-98; Australian Society of Authors; Independent Scholars Association of Australia. Address: 28 Osmond Terrace, Norwood, Adelaide, South Australia 5067, Australia.

IOANNOU Susan, b. 4 Oct 1944, Toronto, Ontario, Canada. Writer; Editor. m. Lazaros Ioannou, 28 Aug 1967, 1 son, 1 daughter. Education: BA, 1966; MA, 1967, University of Toronto. Appointments: Managing Editor, Coiffure du Canada, 1979-80; Associate Editor, Cross-Canada Writers' Magazine, 1980-89; Poetry Editor, Arts Scarborough Newsletter, 1980-85; Poetry Instructor, Toronto Board of Education, 1982-94, University of Toronto, 1989-90; Director, Wordwrights Canada, 1985-. Publications: Spare Words, 1984; Motherpoems, 1985; The Crafted Poem, 1985; Familiar Faces, Private Griefs, 1986; Ten Ways To Tighten Your Prose, 1988; Writing Reader-Friendly Poems, 1989; Clarity Between Clouds, 1991; Read-Aloud Poems: For Students from Elementary through Senior High School, 1993; Polly's Punctuation Primer, 1994; Where the Light Waits, 1996; A Real Farm Girl, 1998. Honours: Arts Scarborough Poetry Award, 1987; Media Club of Canada Memorial Award, 1990; Okanagan Short Story Award, 1997. Memberships: League of Canadian Poets; Writers' Union of Canada; Arts and Letters Club of Toronto; Canadian Poetry Association. Address: c/o Wordwrights Canada, PO Box 456, Station O, Toronto, Ontario M4A 2P1, Canada.

IPSEN David Carl, b. 15 Feb 1921, Schenectady, New York, USA. Freelance Writer. m. Heather Marian Zoccola, 28 Aug 1949, 2 sons. Education: BS, Engineering, University of Michigan, 1942; PhD, Mechanical Engineering, University of California, 1953. Publications: Units, Dimensions and Dimensionless Numbers, 1960; The Riddle of the Stegosaurus, 1969; Rattlesnakes and Scientists, 1970; What Does a Bee See?, 1971; The Elusive Zebra, 1971; Eye of the Whirlwind: The Story of John Scopes, 1973; Isaac Newton: Reluctant Genius, 1985; Archimedes: Greatest Scientist of the Ancient World, 1988. Membership: Authors Guild. Address: 655 Vistamont Avenue, Berkeley, CA 94708, USA.

IQBAL Obadiah. See: ZEPHANIAH Benjamin.

IRBY Kenneth (Lee), b. 18 Nov 1936, Bowie, Texas, USA. Writer; Poet; Teacher. Education: BA, Univerity of Kansas; MA, 1960, PhD Studies, 1962-63, Harvard University; MLS, University of California, 1968. Appointment: Currently Associate Professor of English, University of Kansas, Lawrence. Publications: The Roadrunner Poem, 1964; Kansas-New Mexico, 1965; Movements/Sequences,1965; The Flower of Having Passed Through Paradise in a Dream, 1968; Relation,1970; To Max Douglas, 1971; Archipelago, 1976; Catalpa, 1977; Orexis, 1981; Riding the Dog, 1982; A Set, 1983; Call Steps, 1992; Antiphonal and Fall to Fall, 1994. Contributions to: Anthologies and magazines. Address: N-311 Regency Place, Lawrence, KS 66049, USA.

IRELAND David, b. 24 Aug 1927, Lakemba, New South Wales, Australia. Novelist. Education: State Schools, New South Wales. Publications: The Chantic Bird, 1968; The Unknown Industrial Prisoner, 1971; The Flesheaters, 1972; Burn, 1974; The Glass Canoe, 1976; A Woman of the Future, 1979; City of Women, 1981; Archimedes and the Eagle, 1984; Bloodfather, 1987. Short Story: The Wild Colonial Boy, 1979. Play: Image in the Clay, 1962. Honours: Adelaide Advertiser Award, 1966; Age Book of the Year Award, 1980; Member, Order of Australia, 1981.Address: c/o Curtis Brown Ltd, 27 Union Street, Paddington, New South Wales 2021, Australia.

IRELAND Kevin Mark, b. 18 July 1933, Auckland, New Zealand. Writer; Poet. m. Phoebe Caroline Dalwood, 2 sons. Appointments: Writer-in-Residence, Canterbury University, 1986; Sargeson Fellow, 1987, Literary Fellow. 1989, Auckland University. Publications: Poetry: Face to Face, 1964; Educating the Body, 1967; A Letter From Amsterdam, 1972; Poems, 1974, A Grammar of Dreams, 1975; Literary Cartoons, 1978; The Dangers of Art: Poems 1975-80, 1980; Practice Night in the Drill Hall, 1984; The Year of the Comet, 1986; Selected Poems, 1987; Tiberius at the Beehive, 1990; Skinning a Fish, 1994. Other: Sleeping with the Angels (stories), 1995; Blowing My Top (novel), 1996; Anzac Day: Selected Poems, 1997; The Man Who Never Lived (novel), 1997; Under the Bridge and Over the Moon (memoir), 1998. Honours: New Zealand National Book Award for Poetry, 1979; Commemorative Medal, 1990; Officer of the Order of the British Empire, 1992. Membership: PEN. Address: 8 Domain Street, Devonport, Auckland 9, New Zealand.

IROD Corneliu, b. 24 Aug 1937, Maritei, Suceava County, Romania. Teacher; Priest. m. Genoveva Mocanu, 8 July 1970, 1 daughter. Education: Graduated, Ukrainian Medium Highschool, Siret, Suceava County, 1955; Faculty of Philology, Ukrainian, Romanian, University of Bucharest, 1960; Faculty of Orthodox Theology, Bucharest, Graduated, 1974. Appointments: Reader and Editor, The Didactic & Pedagogical Publishing House; High School Teacher of Political Economy, Bucharest, 1960-62; Methodologist, 1966-68; Chief Inspector, State Committee for Art and Culture, 1968-72; Orthodox Priest, 1976-; Archpriest of Oltenita, 1990-; Member, National Assembly of The Romanian Orthodox Church; The Ukrainian Literary Encyclopaedia, 2nd vol, 1990; Dictionary of Contemporary Romanian Literature, 1977. Publications: Short Stories: August, 1964; Our Springtimes, 1972; Light and Shade, 1973; The White Piano, 1990. Novels: The Eve, 1975; The Morning, 1984; Blinded by rhe Sun, 1988; Poetry: Lyrical Strings, 1968; Vesperal Prayers, 1973. Reportages: Earth and Bread, 1972. Contributions: Poetry; Short stories; Essays; Reportages; Memories; Translations to various Romanian and Ukrainian Periodicals. Honour: Prize, The Romanian Writers' Union, 1990. Address: Str Irimicului 3, Bloc 3, Sc 4, ap 99, Sector 2, Bucharest 72216, Romania.

IRVING Clifford (Michael), (John Luckless), b. 5 Nov 1930, New York, New York, USA. Author; Screenwriter. Education: BA, Cornell University, 1951. Publications: On a Darkling Plain, 1956; The Losers, 1957; The Valley, 1962; The 38th Floor, 1965; Spy, 1969; The Battle of Jerusalem, 1970; Fake, 1970; Global Village Idiot, 1973; Project Octavio, 1978; The Death Freak, 1979; The Hoax, 1981; Tom Mix and Pancho Villa, 1982; The Sleeping Spy, 1983; The Angel of Zin, 1984; Daddy's Girl, 1988; Trial, 1990; Final Argument, 1993. Address: c/o Frank Cooper, 10100 Santa Monica Boulevard, Los Angeles, CA 90067, USA.

IRVING John Winslow, b. 2 Mar 1942, Exeter, New Hampshire, USA. Novelist. m. (1) Shyla Leary, 1964, div 1981, 2 sons, (2) Janet Turnbull, 1987, 1 son. Education: BA, University of New Hampshire, 1965; MFA, University of Iowa, 1967. Publications: Setting Free the Bears, 1969; The Water-Method Man, 1972; The 158 Pound Marriage, 1974; The World According to Garp, 1978; The Hotel New Hampshire, 1981; The Cider House Rules, 1985; A Prayer for Owen Meany, 1989; A Son of the Circus, 1994; Trying to Save Piggy Sneed, 1996; A Widow for One Year, 1998. Contributions to: New York Times Book Review; New Yorker; Rolling Stone; Esquire; Playboy. Honours: Pushcart Prize, Best of the Small Presses, 1978; American Book Award, 1979; O Henry Prize, 1981. Membership: PEN American Centre. Address: c/o The Turnbull Agency, PO Box 757, Dorset, VT 05251, USA.

ISAACS Alan, (Alec Valentine), b. 14 Jan 1925, London, England. Writer; Lexicographer. m. Alison Coster, 1 son, 3 daughters. Education: Imperial College, 1942-50. Publications: Penguin Dictionary of Science, 1964; Introducing Science, 1965; Survival of God in the Scientific Age, 1967; Longman Dictionary of Physics,

1975; Collins English Dictionary, 1978; Macmillan Encyclopedia, 1981-2000; Brewer's Twentieth Century Phrase and Fable, 1991; Sex and Sexuality: A Thematic Dictionary of Quotations, 1993; Thematica, Larousse 6 Volume Encyclopaedia, 1995; Penguin Biographical Dictionary of Women, 1998; Oxford Dictionary for International Business, 1998. Contributions to: Nature; New Scientist. Address: 74 West Street, Harrow on the Hill HA1 3ER, England.

ISAACS Susan, b. 7 Dec 1943, Brooklyn, New York, USA. Novelist; Screenwriter. m. 11 Aug 1968, 1 son, 1 daughter. Education: Queens College of the City University of New York. Publications: Compromising Positions, 1978; Close Relations, 1980; Almost Paradise, 1984; Shining Through, 1988; Magic Hour, 1991; After All These Years, 1993; Lily White, 1996; Red, White and Blue, 1998; Lily White, 1997; Red, White and Blue, 1998;Brave Dames and Wimpettes: What Women are really doing on Page and Screen, 1999. Contributions to: Newspapers and magazines. Honours: Honorary Doctor of Letters, Dowling College, 1988; Honorary Doctor of Humane Letters, Queens College, 1996; Barnes & Noble Writers for Writers Award, 1996; John Steinbeck, 1999. Memberships: Authors Guild; International Crime Writers Association; Mystery Writers of America; National Book Critics Circle; PEN; Poets and Writers, Chairman of the Board; Creative Coalition. Address: c/o Harper Collins, 10 East 53rd Street, New York, NY 10022, USA.

ISHIGURO Kazuo, b. 8 Nov 1954, Nagasaki, Japan. Writer; Resettlement Worker. Education: BA, University of Kent, 1978; MA, University of East Anglia. Appointment: Residential Social Worker, London, 1970-. Publications: A Pale View of Hills, 1982; A Profile of Arthur J Mason, 1985; An Artist of the Floating World, 1986; The Gourmet, 1987; The Remains of the Day, 1989; The Unconsoled Heart, 1995. Honours: Winifred Holtby Prize; Whitbread Book of Year Award; Booker Prize, 1989; Fellow, Royal Society of Literature, 1989; Honorary Doctor of Letters, 1990; Officer of the Order of the British Empire, 1995; Cheltenham Prize, 1995. Membership: Royal Society of Arts, fellow, 1990. Address: c/o Faber & Faber Ltd, 3 Queen Square, London WC1N 3AU, England.

ISLER Ursula, b. 26 Mar 1923, Zürich, Switzerland. Writer; Doctor; Critic. Education: Gymnasium and University of Zürich. Publications: Nadine: Eine Reise, 1967; Landschaft mit Regenbogen, 1975; Madame Schweizer, 1982; Die Ruinen von Zürich, 1985; Frauen aus Zürich, 1991; Der Künstler und sein Fälscher, 1992. Contributions to: Staff, Neue Zürcher Zeitung, 1950-. Honours: Numerous literary awards. Address: Hornweg 14, 8700 Küsnacht, Switzerland.

IVANOVA Natalia, b. 17 May 1945, Moscow, Russia. Literary Critic. m. Alexander Rybakov, 28 Apr 1973, 1 daughter. Education: Philological Faculty, Moscow State University. Appointments: Editorial House Sovkemennik, 1971-72; Literary Monthlies, Znamya, 1972-86, Drushba Narodov, 1986-91, Znamya, 1991-. Publications: The Prose of Yrij Trifonov, 1984; The Point of View. Notes on the Prose of the Last Years, 1989; Laugh Against Terror or Fasil Iskander, 1990; The Death of Gods, 1990; Revival of Nessesary Things, 1991. Contributions to: Znamya; Novy Mir; Drushba Narodov; Voprosy Literatury; Literaturnaja Gazeta. Membership: PEN. Address: 129110 Prospect Mira 49-86, Moscow, Russia.

IVIMY May. See: BADMAN May Edith.

IYAYI Festus, b. 29 Sept 1947, Ibadan, Nigeria. Novelist. Education: Annunciation Catholic College; Kiev Institute of Economics; PhD, University of Bradford, Yorkshire, 1980. Appointment: Lecturer, University of Benin. Publications: Violence, 1979; The Contract, 1982; Heroes, 1986; Awaiting Court Martial, 1996. Honours: Association of Nigerian Authors Prize, 1987; Commonwealth Writers Prize, 1988; Pius Okigbo Africa Prize for Literature, 1996; Nigerian Author of the Year, 1996. Address: Department of Business Administration,

University of Benin, PMB 1145, Ugbowo Campus, Benin City, Nigeria.

IZAWA Motohiko, b. 1 Feb 1954, Nagoya City, Japan. Author. m. 1980. Education: Graduate, Law Department, Waseda University, 1961. Publications: Sarumaru Genshiko, 1980; The Hidden Mikado, 1990; The Court of Hatred, 1991; Soul of Language, 1991; The Paradox of Japanese History, 5 volumes, 1993-97. Honour: Edogawa Ranpo Award, 1980. Memberships: Japan Writers Association; Japan PEN Club; Mystery Writers of Japan; Mystery Writers of America; Science Fiction Writers Club of Japan. Literary Agent: Woodbell Co Ltd. Address: 437-29 Nanabayashi-cho, Funabashi, Chiba, Japan.

IZON Lucy Ann, b. 17 Aug 1953, Toronto, Canada. Travel Journalist; Author. Publications: Travellers' Trip Planner, 1993; Izon's Backpacker Journal, 1998; Touring Eastern Canada (with others), 1998; Weekly syndicated column for young travellers, many North American newspapers. Honour: President's Bowl, Society of American Travel Writers. Membership: Society of American Travel Writers. Address: PO Box 1043, Station Q, Toronto M4T 2L7, Canada.

J

JABEEN N, b. 21 May 1969, Burnley, England. Student Designer; Artist. Education: Mansfield High School, Brierfield, England. Publications: Poems in: Poetry Now, North West, 1992; A Break in the Clouds, 1993; Northern Lights, 1994; Poetry Now, War, 1994; Poetry Now, Obsessions, 1996; Arrival Press, Happiness Is, 1996; Gripes & Grumbles, 1996; A Passage in Time, 1996; Jewels of Imagination, 1997; The Killing Fields, 1997; Poetry Now, North West 1998, 1997; Secret of Twilight, 1998. Contributions to: The Daily Jang, poem, 1994; Designs in Cross Stitch Magazine, Jan 1995, Dec 1995, Mar 1996, July 1996, Nov 1997; Cross Stitcher Magazine, Jan 1999. Honour: Editor's Choice Award, 1996. Address: 2A Chapel Street, Brierfield, Nr Nelson, Lancashire BB9 5HJ, England.

JACCOTTET Philippe, b. 30 June 1925, Moudon, Switzerland. Poet. Education: Graduated, University of Lausanne, 1946. Publications: Poetry: Requiem, 1947; L'Effraie et autres poésies, 1953; L'ignorant: Poèmes 1952-56. Airs: Poèmes 1961-64; Poésie 1946-67; Leçons, 1969; Chants d'en bas, 1974; Breathings, 1974; Pensées sous les nuages, 1983; Selected Poems, 1987; Cahier de verdure, 1990; Libretto, 1990; Other: Through the Orchard, 1975; Des Histoires de passage: Prose 1948-78; Autres Journées, 1987; Translator of works by Robert Musil, Thomas Mann, Leopardi, Homer and Hölderlin. Honour: Larbaud Prize, 1978. Address: c/o Editions Gallimard, 5 rue Sebastien-Bottin, 75007 Paris, France.

JACK Dana Crowley, b. 19 Mar 1945, Texas, USA. Professor; Psychologist. m. Rand Jack, 16 Mar 1968, 1 son, 1 daughter. Education: BA, Mount Holyoke College, 1963-67; MSW, University of Washington, 1970-72; EdD, Harvard University, 1979-84. Publications: Moral Vision and Professional Decisions: The Changing Values of Women and Men Lawyers (with Rand Jack), 1989; Silencing The Self: Women and Depression, 1991; The Silencing the Self Scale (with D Dill), 1992; Behind the Mask: Destruction and Creativity in Women's Aggression, 1999. Contributions to: 5 chapters in various edited books. Address: 5790 Schornbush Road, Deming, WA 98244, USA.

JACK Ian, (Robert James), b. 5 Dec 1923, Edinburgh, Scotland. Professor of English Literature Emeritus; Writer. m. (1) Jane Henderson MacDonald, 1948, div, 2 sons, 1 daughter, (2) Margaret Elizabeth Crone, 1972, 1 son. Education: George Watson's College; MA, University of Edinburgh, 1947; DPhil, Merton College, Oxford, 1950; Honorary Fellow, 1999. Appointments: Lecturer in English Literature, 1950-55, Senior Research Fellow, 1955-61, Brasenose College, Oxford; Visiting Professor, University of Alexandria, 1960, University of Chicago, 1968-69, University of California at Berkeley, 1968-69, University of British Columbia, 1975, University of Virginia, 1980-81, Tsuda College, Tokyo, 1981, New York University, 1989; Lecturer in English Literature, 1961-73, Reader in English Poetry, 1973-76, Professor of English Literature, 1976-89, Professor Emeritus, 1989-, University of Cambridge; Fellow, 1961-89, Librarian, 1965-75, Fellow Emeritus, 1989-, Pembroke College, Cambridge; de Carle Lecturer, University of Otago, 1964; Warton Lecturer in English Poetry, British Academy, 1967. Publications: Augustan Satire, 1952; English Literature 1815-1832, Vol X of The Oxford History of English Literature, 1963; Keats and the Mirror of Art, 1967; Browning's Major Poetry, 1973; The Poet and His Audience, 1984. General Editor: Brontë novels, Clarendon edition, 7 volumes, 1969-72; The Poetical Works of Browning, 1983, Vols I-V, 1983-95. Contributions to: Scholarly books and professional journals. Honour: Leverhulme Emeritus Fellow, 1990, 1991. Memberships: British Academy, fellow; Brontë Society, vice-president, 1973-; Browning Society, president, 1980-83; Charles Lamb Society, president,

1970-80; Johnson Society, Lichfield, president, 1986-87. Address: Highfield House, High Street, Fen Ditton, Cambridgeshire CB5 8ST, England.

JACK Ronald Dyce Sadler, b. 3 Apr 1941, Ayr, Scotland. University Professor. m. Kirsty Nicolson, 8 July 1967, 2 daughters. Education: MA, Glasgow, 1964; PhD, Edinburgh, 1968; DLitt, Glasgow. Appointments: Lecturer, Department of English Literature, Edinburgh University, 1965; Reader, 1978; Professor, 1987; Visiting Professor, University of Virginia, 1973-74; Director, Universities Central Council on Admissions, 1988-94; Visiting Professor, University of Strathclyde, 1993; Distinguished Visiting Professor, University of Connecticut, 1998. Publications: Scottish Prose 1550-1700, 1972; The Italian Influence on Scottish Literature, 1972; A Choice of Scottish Verse 1560-1660, 1978; The Art of Robert Burns (co-author), 1982; Sir Thomas Urquhart (co-author), 1984; Alexander Montgomerie, 1985; Scottish Literature's Debt to Italy, 1986; The History of Scottish Literature, Vol I, 1988; Patterns of Divine Comedy, 1989; The Road to the Never Land, 1991; Of Lion and Unicorn, 1993; The Poems of William Dunbar, 1997; Mercat Anthology of Early Scottish Literature, 1997. Contributions to: Review of English Studies; Modern Language Review; Comparative Literature; Studies in Scottish Literature. Memberships: Medieval Academy of America; Scottish Text Society. Address: David Hume Tower, George Square, Edinburgh EH8 9JX, Scotland.

JACKMAN Brian, b. 25 Apr 1935, Epsom, Surrey, England. Freelance Journalist; Writer. m. (1) 14 Feb 1964, div Dec 1992, 1 daughter, (2) Jan 1993. Education: Grammar School. Appointment: Staff, Sunday Times, 1970-90. Publications: We Learned to Ski, 1974; Dorset Coast Path, 1977; The Marsh Lions, 1982; The Countryside in Winter, 1986; My Serengeti Years, 1987; Roaring at the Dawn, 1996; The Big Cat Diary, 1996. Contributions to: Sunday Times; The Times; Daily Telegraph; Daily Mail; Country Living; Country Life; BBC Wildlife. Honours: TTG Travel Writer of Year, 1982; Wildscreen Award, 1982. Memberships: Royal Geographical Society; Fauna and Flora Preservation Society. Address: Spick Hatch, West Milton, Nr Bridport, Dorset DT6 3SH, England.

JACKMAN Stuart (Brooke), b. 22 June 1922, Manchester, England. Clergyman; Editor; Writer. Education: Appointments: Congregational Minister, Barnstaple, Devon, 1948-52, Pretoria, 1952-55, Caterham, Surrey, 1955-61, Auckland, 1961-65, Upminster, Essex, 1965-67, Oxford, Surrey, 1969-; Editor, Council for World Mission, 1967-71, Oxted, Surrey, 1969-81, Melbourne, Cambridgeshire, 1981-87. Publications: Portrait in Two Colours, 1948; But They Won't Lie Down, 1954; The Numbered Days, 1954; Angels Unawares, 1956; One Finger for God, 1957; The Waters of Dinyanti, 1959; The Daybreak Boys, 1961; The Desirable Property, 1966; The Davidson Affair, 1966; The Golden Orphans, 1968; Guns Covered with Flowers, 1973; Slingshot, 1975; The Burning Men, 1976; Operation Catcher, 1980; A Game of Soldiers, 1981; The Davidson File, 1981; Death Wish, 1998. Address: c/o Curtis Brown Ltd, Haymarket House, 28-29 Haymarket, London SW1Y 4SP, England.

JACKONT Amnon, b. 3 Oct 1948, Ramat-Gan, Israel. Insurance Underwriter; Broker; Analyst; Editor; Writer. m. Varda Rasiel Jackont, 30 Sep 1990, 1 son. Education: Hebrew University of Jerusalem; Israel Insurance Academy; Bar Ilan University. Appointment: Editor, Keter Publishing House, Jerusalem. Publications: Borrowed Time, 1982; The Rainy Day Man, 1987; The Last of the Wise Lovers, 1991; Honey Trap, 1994. Contributions to: Magazines and journals. Memberships: Israel Authors Association; Israel's Chamber of Insurance Brokers. Address: 20 Manne Street, Tel Aviv 64363, Israel.

JACKOWSKA Nicki, b. 6 Aug 1942, Brighton, Sussex, England. Poet; Novelist; Writer; Teacher. m. Andrzej Jackowski, 1 May 1970, div, 1 daughter. Education: ANEA Acting Diploma, hons, 1965; BA, 1977, MA, 1978, University of Sussex. Appointments: Founder-Tutor,

Brighton Writing School; Writer-in-Residence at various venues; Readings; Radio and television appearances. Publications: The House That Manda Built, 1981; Doctor Marbles and Marianne, 1982; Earthwalks, 1982; Letters to Superman, 1984; Gates to the City, 1985; The Road to Orc, 1985; The Islanders, 1987; News from the Brighton Front, 1993; Write for Life, 1997; Lighting a Slow Fuse, New and Selected Poems, 1998. Contributions to: Various publications. Honours: Winner, Stroud Festival Poetry Competition, 1972; Continental Bursary, South East Arts, 1978; C Day-Lewis Fellowship, 1982; Arts Council Writer's Fellowship, 1984-85; Arts Council of England Writer's Bursary, Arts Council, 1994. Membership: Poetry Society. Address: c/o Judy Martin Agency, 94 Goldhurst Terrace, London, NW6 3HS, England.

JACKSON Alan, b. 6 Sept 1938, Liverpool, Lancashire, England. Poet. m. Margaret Dickson, 1963, 2 sons. Education: Edinburgh University, 1956-59, 1964-65. Appointments: Founding Director, Kevin Press, Edinburgh, 1965; Director, Live Readings, Scotland, 1967-. Publications: Under Water Wedding, 1961; Sixpenny Poems, 1962; Well Ye Ken Noo, 1963; All Fall Down, 1965; The Worstest Beast, 1967; Penguin Modern Poets, 1968; The Grim Wayfarer, 1969; Idiots are Freelance, 1973; Heart of the Sun, 1986; Salutations: Collected Poems, 1960-89, 1990. Honours: Scottish Arts Council Bursaries. Address: c/o Polygon, 22 George Square, Edinburgh EH8 9LF, Scotland.

JACKSON E F. See: **TUBB E(dwin) C(harles).**

JACKSON Everatt. See: **MUGGESON Margaret Elizabeth.**

JACKSON Guida. See: **JACKSON-LAUFER Guida Myrl Miller.**

JACKSON Jane See: **POLLARD Jane.**

JACKSON (William) Keith, b. 5 Sept 1928, Colchester, Essex, England. Emeritus Professor. m. (1), 3 children, (2) Jennifer Mary Louch, 21 Dec 1990. Education: London University Teaching Certificate, 1947; BA, Honours, University of Nottingham, 1953; PhD, University of Otago, New Zealand, 1967. Publications: New Zealand Politics in Action (with A V Mitchell and R M Chapman), 1962; New Zealand (with J Harré), 1969; Editor, Fight for Life, New Zealand, Britain and the EEC, 1971; New Zealand Legislative Council, 1972; Politics of Change, 1972; The Dilemma of Parliament, 1987; Historical Dictionary of New Zealand (with A D McRobie), 1996; New Zealand Adopts Proportional Representation: Accident? Design? Evolution? (with Alan McRobie), 1998. Contributions to: Numerous professional journals. Honours: Mobil Award for Best Spoken Current Affairs Programme, Radio New Zealand, 1979; Henry Chapman Fellow, Institute of Commonwealth Studies, London, 1963; Canterbury Fellowship, 1987; Asia 2000 Fellowship, 1996. Address: 92A, Hinau Street, Christchurch 4, New Zealand.

JACKSON Keith. See: **KELLY Tim.**

JACKSON Kenneth T(erry), b. 27 July 1939, Memphis, Tennessee, USA. Professor of History; Writer. m. Barbara Ann Bruce, 25 Aug 1962, 2 sons, 1 dec. Education: BA, University of Memphis, 1961; MA, 1963, PhD, 1966, University of Chicago. Appointments: Assistant Professor, 1968-71, Associate Professor, 1971-76, Professor, 1976-87, Mellon Professor, 1987-90, Barzun Professor of History and Social Sciences, 1990-, Chairman, Department of History, 1994-97, Columbia University; Visiting Professor, Princeton University, 1973-74, George Washington University, 1982-83, University of California at Los Angeles, 1986-87; Chairman, Bradley Commission on History in the Schools, 1987-90, National Council for History Education, 1990-92. Publications: The Ku Klux Klan in the City 1915-1930, 1967; American Vistas (editor with L Dinnerstein), 2 volumes, 1971, 7th edition, 1995; Cities in American History (editor with S K Schultz), 1972; Atlas of

American History, 1978; Columbia History of Urban Life (general editor), 1980-; Crabgrass Frontier: The Suburbanization of the United States, 1985; Silent Cities: The Evolution of the American Cemetery (with Camilo Verqara), 1989; Dictionary of American Biography (editor-in-chief), 1991-95; Encyclopaedia of New York City, 1995. Contributions to: Scholarly books and professional journals. Honours: Woodrow Wilson Foundation Fellow, 1961-62; National Endowment for the Humanities Senior Fellow, 1979-80; Guggenheim Fellowship, 1983-84; Bancroft Prize, 1986; Francis Parkman Prize, 1986; Mark Van Doren Grant Teaching Award, Columbia University, 1989; Outstanding Alumni Award, University of Memphis, 1989. Memberships: American Historical Association; Organization of American Historians, president, 1999; Urban History Association, president, 1994; Society of American Historians, president, 1998-. Address: c/o Department of History, 603 Fayerweather Hall, Columbia University, New York, NY 10027, USA.

JACKSON MacDonald Pairman, b. 13 Oct 1938, Auckland, New Zealand. University Professor. m. Nicole Philippa Lovett, 2 Sept 1964, 1 son, 2 daughters. Education: MA, University of New Zealand, 1960; BLitt, Oxford University, 1964. Appointments: Lecturer, 1964-89, Professor, 1989-, University of Auckland. Publications: Studies in Attribution: Middleton and Shakespeare, 1979; The Revenger's Tragedy, 1983; The Oxford Book of New Zealand Writing Since 1945, 1983; The Selected Plays of John Marston, 1986; A R D Fairburn: Selected Poems, 1995. Contributions to: Chapters in Cambridge Companion to Shakespeare Studies, 1986; The Oxford History of New Zealand Literature in English, 1991, revised 1998; Academic and literary journals. Honours: Folger Shakespeare Library Fellowship, 1989; Huntington Library Fellowship, 1993. Membership: International Shakespeare Association. Address: 21 Te Kowhai Place, Remuera, Auckland 5, New Zealand.

JACKSON Richard Paul, b. 17 Nov 1946, Lawrence, Massachusetts, USA. Writer; College Professor; Editor. m. Margaret McCarthy, 28 June 1970, 1 daughter. Education: BA, Merrimack College, 1969; MA, Middlebury College, 1972; PhD, Yale University, 1976. Appointments: Journal Editor, University of Tennessee at Chattanooga Faculty and Mala Revija. Publications: Part of the Story, 1983; Acts of Mind, 1983; Worlds Apart, 1987; Dismantling Time in Contemporary Poetry, 1989; Alive All Day, 1993. Contributions to: Georgia Review; Antioch Review; North American Review; New England Review. Honours: National Endowment for the Humanities Fellowship, 1980; National Endowment for the Arts Fellowship, 1985; Fulbright Exchange Fellowships, 1986, 1987; Agee Prize, 1989; CSU Poetry Award, 1992. Memberships: Sarajevo Committee of Slovene; PEN; Associated Writing Programs. Address: 3413 Alta Vista Drive, Chattanooga, TN 37411, USA.

JACKSON Robert Howard, b. 31 Dec 1955, Alameda, California, USA. Assistant Professor of History; Writer. m. Ana Solorio Rodriguez, 17 Dec 1977, 2 sons, 1 daughter. Education: BA, History, University of California, Santa Cruz, 1980; MA, History, University of Arizona, 1982; PhD History, University of California, Berkeley, 1988. Appointment: Assistant Professor of History, Texas Southern University, 1990. Publications: Indian Population Decline: The Missions of Northwestern New Spain 1687-1840, 1994; Regional Markets and Agrarian Transformation in Bolivia: Cochabamba 1539-1960, 1995; Indians, Franciscans and Spanish Colonization: The Impact of the Mission System on California Indians (with Ed Castillo), 1995; The New Latin American Mission History (editor with Erick Langer), 1995. Contributions to: Numerous journals. Membership: Conference on Latin American History. Address: 22830 Thadds Trail, Spring, TX 77373, USA.

JACKSON Robert L(ouis), b. 10 Nov 1923, New York, New York, USA. Professor of Slavic Languages and Literatures; Writer; Editor. m. Elizabeth Mann Gillette, 18 July 1951, 2 daughters. Education: BA, Cornell University, 1944; MA, 1949, Certificate, Russian Institute, 1949, Columbia University; PhD, University of California at Berkeley, 1956. Appointments: Instructor, 1954-58, Assistant Professor, 1958-67, Professor of Russian Literature, 1967-91, B E Bensinger Professor of Slavic Languages and Literatures, 1991-, Yale University. Publications: Dostoevsky's Underground Man in Russian Literature, 1958; Dostoevsky's Quest for Form: A Study of His Philosophy of Art, 1966; The Art of Dostoevsky, 1981; Dialogues with Dostoevsky: The Overwhelming Questions, 1993. Editor: Chekov: Collected Critical Essays, 1967; Crime and Punishment: Collected Critical Essays, 1974; Dostoevsky: Collected Critical Essays, 1984; Reading Chekov's Text, 1993. Contributions to: Professional journals. Honours: Distinguished Scholarly Career Award, American Association of Teachers of Slavic and East European Languages (AATSEEL), 1993; Honorary Doctor's Degree, Moscow State University, 1994; AATSEEL Prize for Outstanding Work in the field of Slavic Languages and Literature, 1994. Memberships: North American Dostoevsky Society, president, 1971-77; International Dostoevsky Society, president, 1977-83; North American Chekhov Society, founder and president, 1988-; Vyacheslav Ivanov Convivium, founder and president, 1981-. Address: c/o Department of Slavic Languages and Literatures, PO Box 208236, New Haven, CT 06520, USA.

JACKSON Sir William Godfrey Fothergill, b. 28 Aug 1917, Lancashire, England. Retired, British Army; Historian. m. Joan Mary Buesden, 7 Sept 1946, 1 son, 1 daughter. Education: Shrewsbury School; King's College, Cambridge; Staff College, Camberley; Imperial Defence College. Appointments: British Army; Governor and Commander-in-Chief of Gibraltar, 1978-82. Publications: Attack in the West, 1953; Seven Roads to Moscow, 1957; Battle for Italy, 1967; Battle for Rome, 1968; North African Campaigns, 1975; Overlord: Normandy, 1944, 1978; Rock of the Gibraltarians, 1986; Withdrawal from Empire, 1986; British Official History of the Mediterranean and Middle East Campaigns, 1940-45, Vol VI, 1986-88; The Alternative Third World War, 1987; Rock of Gibraltarians, 1989; Britain's Defence Dilemmas, 1990; The Chiefs, 1992; Governor's Cat, 1992; The Pomp of Yesterday, 1994; As Ninevah and Tyre, 1995; Fortress to Democracy: A Political Biography of Sir Joshua Hassan, 1996. Honours: King's Medal, 1937; Military Cross, 1940, Bar, 1944; Officer of the Order of the British Empire, 1958; Knight Commander of the Order of the Bath, 1971; Knight, Grand Cross of the British Empire, 1975. Address: West Stowell, Marlborough, Wiltshire SN8 4JU, England.

JACKSON-LAUFER Guida Myrl Miller, (Guida Jackson), b. Clarendon, Texas, USA. Author; University Lecturer; Editor. m. (1) Prentice Lamar Jackson, 3 sons, 1 daughter, 1954, (2) William Hervey Laufer, 1986. Education: BA, Texas Tech University, 1954; MA, California State University, 1986; PhD, Greenwich University International Institute of Advanced Studies, 1989. Appointments: Managing Editor, Touchstone Literary Journal, 1976-; Lecturer in Writing, 1986-. Publications: Passing Through, 1979; The Lamentable Affair of the Vicar's Wife, 1981; The Three Ingredients (co-author), 1981; Heart to Heart, 1988; Women Who Ruled, 1990; African Women Write (compiler), 1990; Virginia Diaspora, 1992; Encyclopaedia of Traditional Epic, 1994; Legacy of the Texas Plains, 1994. Contributions to: Books and periodicals. Address: c/o Touchstone, PO Box 8308, Spring, TX 77387, USA.

JACOB John, b. 27 Aug 1950, Chicago, Illinois, USA. Assistant Professor; Writer. 1 son, 1 daughter. Education: AB, University of Michigan, 1972; MA, 1973, PhD, 1989, University of Illinois. Appointments: Instructor, 1974-79, 1984-, Northwestern University; Lecturer, Roosevelt University, 1975-; Assistant Professor, North Central College, 1987-. Publications: Scatter: Selected Poems, 1979; Hawk Spin, 1983; Wooden Indian, 1987; Long Ride Back, The Light Fandango, 1988. Contributions to: Margins; ALB Booklist. Honours: Carl Sandburg Award, 1980; Illinois Arts Council Grants, 1985, 1987. Memberships: International PEN; Modern Languages Association; Associated Writing Programs; Authors Guild; Multi Ethnic Literature Society of the US. Address: 527 Lyman Street, Oak Park, IL 60304, USA.

JACOBS Barbara, b. 6 Feb 1945, St Helens, England. Journalist; Writer. m. Mark Jacobs, 26 Feb 1968, div, 1 son. Education: BA, 1966, PGCE, 1967, Leicester University. Appointment: Freelance journalist, 1978-. Publications: Ridby Graham, 1982; Two Times Two, 1984; The Fire Proof Hero, 1986; Desperadoes, 1987; Listen to My Heartbeat, 1988; Stick, 1988; Goodbye My Love, 1989; Just How Far, 1989; Loves a Pain, 1990; Not Really Working, 1990. Contributions to: Periodicals. Address: 29 Gotham Street, Leicester LE2 0NA, England.

JACOBS Leah. See: **GELLIS Roberta Leah.**

JACOBSEN Rich Shirley Marie, (Marie Lee), b. 8 Jan 1944, Sioux City, Iowa, USA. Writer; Songwriter. m. Gerald Lee Jacobsen, 6 Jan 1974, 2 sons. Education: Bachelor of Career Arts, Business Administration; Bachelor Degree, SAGU. Appointments: Board of Governors, Deputy Governor, nominated by American Biographical Institute, 1999. Publications: Feelings of the Heart, 1998; Cancer Review, 1983; Published works: Poetry: The Prettiest Rose of All, 1998; Sweet Sombre Nights, 1998; The Eloquence of the Quill and the Soul; I Just Stood There, 1997; Bunny Habitat, 1994; A Second Start of Life, 1993. Honours: Semi Finalist, The Popside Stick, 1998; The Eloquence of the Quill and the Soul, 1998; Editor's Choice Award, I Just Stood There, 1997. Memberships: Distinguished Member, International Society of Poets; International Poetry Hall of Fame, 1998. Address: 780 Beachside, Chandler, TX 75758, USA.

JACOBSON Dan, b. 7 Mar 1929, Johannesburg, South Africa. Professor Emeritus; Writer. m. Margaret Pye, 3 sons, 1 daughter. Education: BA, University of the Witwatersrand; Honarary Ph.D., University of Witwatersrand. Appointments: Professor, Syracuse University, New York, 1965-66; Lecturer, 1975-80, Reader, 1980-87, Fellow, 1981, Australian National University; Professor, 1988-94, Professor Emeritus, 1994-, University College, London. Publications: The Trap, 1955; A Dance in the Sun, 1956; The Price of Diamonds, 1957; The Evidence of Love, 1960; The Beginners, 1965; The Rape of Tamar, 1970; The Confessions of Josef Baisz, 1979; The Story of the Stories, 1982; Time and Time Again, 1985; Adult Pleasures, 1988; Hidden in the Heart, 1991; The God Fearer, 1992; The Electronic Elephant, 1994; Heshels's Kingdom, 1998. Contributions to: Periodicals and newspapers. Honours: John Llewelyn Rhys Memorial Award, 1958; W Somerset Maugham Award, 1964; H H Wingate Award, 1979; J R Ackerley Award, 1986; Honorary DLitt, University of the Witwatersrand, 1987; Mary Elinore Smith Prize, 1992. Address: c/o A M Heath & Co Ltd, 79 St Martins Lane, London WC2, England.

JACOBSON Howard, b. 25 Aug 1942, Manchester, England. Novelist. m. Rosalin Sadler, 1978, 1 son. Education: BA, Downing College, Cambridge. Appointments: Lecturer, University of Sydney, 1965-68; Supervisor, Selwyn College, Cambridge, 1969-72; Senior Lecturer, Wolverhampton Polytechnic, 1974-80; Television Critic, The Sunday Correspondent, 1989-90; Into the Land of Oz, (Channel 4), 1991; Writer/Presenter, Yo, Mrs Askew! (BBC2), 1991, Roots Schmoots (Channel 4 TV), 1993, Sorry, Judas (Channel 4 TV), 1993, Seriously Funny: An Argument for Comedy (Channel 4 TV), 1997. Publications: Shakespeare's Magnanimity: Four Tragic Heroes, Their Friends and Families, 1978; Coming From Behind, 1983; Peeping Tom, 1984; Redback, 1986; In the Land of Oz, 1987; The Very Model of a Man, 1992; Roots Schmoots, 1993; Seeing With the Eye: The Peter Fuller Memorial Lecture, 1993; Seriously Funny, 1997; No More Mister Nice Guy, 1998. Membership: Modern Painters, editorial board. Address: Peters Fraser & Dunlop Group Ltd, 503-4 The Chambers, Chelsea Harbour, Lots Road, London SW10 0XF, England.

JACOBUS Lee A, b. 20 Aug 1935, Orange, New Jersey, USA. Professor of English; Writer. m. Joanna Jacobus, 1958, 2 children. Education: BA, 1957, MA, 1959, Brown University; PhD, Claremont Graduate University, 1968. Appointments: Faculty, Western Connecticut State University, 1960-68; Assistant Professor, 1968-71, Associate Professor, 1971-76, Professor of English, 1976-, University of Connecticut; Visiting Professor, Brown University, 1981; Visiting Fellow, Yale University, 1983, 1996. Publications: Improving College Reading, 1967, 6th edition, 1993; Issues and Responses, 1968, revised edition, 1972; Developing College Reading, 1970, 5th edition, 1995; Humanities Through the Arts (with F David Martin), 1974, 5th edition, 1997; John Cleveland: A Critical Study, 1975; Sudden Apprehension: Aspects of Knowledge in Paradise Lost, 1976; The Paragraph and Essay Book, 1977; The Sentence Book, 1980; Humanities: The Evolution of Values, 1986; Writing as Thinking, 1989; Shakespeare and the Dialectic of Certainty, 1993; Substance, Style and Strategy, 1998. Editor: Aesthetics and the Arts, 1968; 17 From Everywhere: Short Stories from Around the World, 1971; Poems in Context (William T Moynihan), 1974; Longman Anthology of American Drama, 1982; The Bedford Introduction to Drama, 3rd edition, 1997; A World of Ideas, 4th edition, 1994; Teaching Literature: An Introduction to Critical Reading, 1996; Co-editor: LIT: Literature Interpretation Theory. Contributions to: Scholarly books, journals, and other publications. Address: Department of English, U-25, University of Connecticut, Storrs, CT 06269, USA.

JACOBUS Mary, b. 4 May 1944, Cheltenham, Gloucestershire, England. Professor of English; Writer. Education: BA, 1965, MA, 1970, DPhil, 1970, Oxford University. Appointments: Lecturer, Department of English, Manchester University, 1970-71; Fellow, Tutor in English, Lady Margaret Hall, Oxford, 1971-80; Lecturer in English, Oxford University, 1971-80; Associate Professor, 1980-82, Professor, 1982-, John Wendell Anderson Professor of English, 1989, Department of English, Cornell University, Ithaca, New York, USA. Publications: Tradition and Experiment in Wordsworth's Lyrical Ballads (1798), 1976; Women Writing and Women about Women (editor), 1979; Reading Women, 1986; Romanticism, Writing, and Sexual Difference: Essays on The Prelude, 1989; Body/Politics: Women and the Discourses of Science (co-editor), 1989; First Things: Thinking the Maternal Body, 1995. Contributions to: Numerous magazines and journals. Honour: Guggenheim Fellowship, 1988-89. Membership: Modern Language Association. Address: Department of English, Cornell University, Ithaca, NY 14853, USA.

JADAV Kishore, b. 15 Apr 1938, Gujarat, India. Writer. m. Smt Kumsangkola Ao, 4 Mar 1967, 2 sons, 3 daughters. Education: BCom, 1960, MCom, 1963. Publications: Suryarohan, 1972; Nishachakra, 1979; Chhadmavesh, 1982; Kishore Jadavni Vartao, 1984; Riktaraag, 1989; Aatash, 1993; Kathatrayi, 1998; Folklore and Its Motifs in Modern Literature, 1998; Contemporary Gujarati Short-Stories, forthcomming. Other: Novels, short stories and essays. Contributions to: Kishore Jadav Sathe Vartalap; Kishore Jadavni; Sahityik Goshthi; Kishore Jadav Sathe Cartakala Vishe Vartalap. Honours: Gujarat Goverment Award, 1972; Gujarati Sahitya Parishad Award, 1988; Critics Sandham Award, 1988. Memberships: Gujarati Sahitya Parishad; Indian PEN; Lions Club. Address: PO Box 19 Nagaland, PO Kohima 797 001, India.

JAFFA Robert Harvey, b. 4 Mar 1953, Leeds, W Yorkshire, England. Head of Media Relations. m. Celia Barlow, 27 Aug 1988, 2 sons, 1 daughter. Education: BSc Hons II, Geography, University of Hull, England, 1973-76; MA, History, University of London, England, 1992; Diploma in Journalism, University of Wales, 1978-79; Visiting Fellow, Wolfson College, Cambridge, 1991. Appointments: BBC National Radio Reporter, 1984-94; BBC North America Business Correspondent based in New York, 1994-96; Head of Media Relations, Price Waterhouse Cooper, Europe, Middle East, Africa. Publications: Maxwell Stories, Safe as Houses; Detective Novel, forthcoming; Helping wife with a screenplay. Address: The Old Rectory, Bookers Lane, Earnley, West Sussex PO20 7JH, England.

JAFFEE Annette Williams, b. 10 Jan 1945, Abilene, Texas, USA. Novelist. Div, 1 son, 1 daughter. Education: BS, Boston University, 1966. Publications: Adult Education, 1981; Recent History, 1988; The Dangerous Age, 1999. Contributions to: Ploughshares; Missouri Review; Ontario Review. Honours: New Jersey Arts Council Grant, 1986; Dodge Fellow, Yaddo, 1991. Memberships: Authors Guild; PEN. Address: PO Box 26, River Road, Lumberville, PA 18933, USA.

JAGLOM Henry David, b. 26 Jan 1943, London, England. Film Writer; Film Director; Actor. m. Victoria Foyt Jaglom, 22 Oct 1991, 1 son, 1 daughter. Education: University of Pennsylvania; Actors Studio. Publications: Writer, Director, films: A Safe Place, 1971; Tracks, 1976; Sitting Ducks, 1980; Can She Bake a Cherry Pie, 1983; Always But Not Forever, 1985; Someone to Love, 1987; New Year's Day, 1989; Eating, 1990; Venice/Venice, 1992; Babyfever, 1994; Last Summer in the Hamptons, 1995. Books: Eating (A Very Serious Comedy about Women and Food), 1992; Babyfever (For Those Who Hear Their Clock Ticking), 1994. Address: Rainbow Film Company, 9165 Sunset Boulevard, The Penthouse, Los Angeles, CA 90069, USA.

JAKES John (William), b. 31 Mar 1932, Chicago, Illinois, USA. Author. m. Rachel Ann Payne, 15 June 1951, 1 son, 3 daughters. Education: AB, DePauw University, 1953; MA, Ohio State University, 1954. Appointment: Research Fellow, University of South Carolina, 1989. Publications: Brak the Barbarian, 1968; Brak the Barbarian Versus the Sorceress, 1969; Brak Versus the Mark of the Demons, 1969; Six Gun Planet, 1970; On Wheels, 1973; The Bastard, 1974; The Rebels, 1975; The Seekers, 1975; The Titans, 1976; The Furies, 1976; The Best of John Jakes, 1977; The Warriors, 1977; Brak: When the Idols Walked, 1978; The Lawless, 1978; The Americans, 1980; Fortunes of Brak, 1980; North and South, 1982; Love and War, 1984; Heaven and Hell, 1988; California Gold, 1989; The Best Western Stories of John Jakes, 1991; Homeland, 1993; New Trails (co-editor), 1994; American Dreams, 1998. Contributions to: Magazines. Honours: Honorary LLD, Wright State University, 1976; Honorary LittD, DePauw University, 1977; Porgie Award, 1977; Ohioana Book Award, 1978; Honorary LDH, Winthrop College, 1985, University of South Carolina, 1993; Distinguished Alumni Award, Ohio State University, 1995; Western Heritage Literature Award, Cowboy Hall of Fame, 1995; Honorary Doctor of Humanities, Ohio State University, 1996; Professional Achievement Award, Ohio State University Alumni Association, 1997. Memberships: Authors Guild; Authors League of America; Dramatists Guild; PEN; Western Writers of America. Address: c/o Rembar and Curtis, 19 West 44th Street, New York, NY 10036, USA.

JAKOBSONS Valentins, b. 27 May 1922, Riga, Latvia. Writer. m. Annemarija, 1 Sept 1956, 2 daughters. Appointments: State Puppet Theatre, Riga; Producer, Animation Film, Riga Film Studio. Publications: Breakfast in the Wild; Breakfast in the North; Breakfast at Midnight; St Peter's Day's Evening. Translations: Kolima Tales; Narina Chronicle. Contributions to: Literature and Art, Daugava; The Flag; The Voce of Riga. Membership: Writers Union of Latvia. Address: Ieriku iela 25-90, Riga, LV-1084, Latvia.

JAMES Alan, b. 22 Aug 1943, Guilford, England. Educator; Writer. Education: St John's College, York; BSc, Economics, London University; MEd, PhD, Newcastle University. Appointments: Master, Junior School, Royal Grammar School, Newcastle upon Tyne, 1968-78; Deputy Head, Runnymede First School, Ponteland, 1979-. Publications: Animals Hospital, 1969; Tunnels, 1969; Buses and Coaches, 1971; Sir Rowland Hilland the Post Office, 1972; Living Light Book Two, 1972; Clock and Watches, Zoos, 1974; Keeping Pets, 1975; Newspapers, Buildings, 1975; Living Light Book Five, 1975; Spiders and Scorpions, The Telephone Operator, 1976; The Vet, 1976; Stocks and Shares, 1977; Circuses, 1978; Let's Visit Finland, 1979; Let's Visit Austria, 1984; Let's Visit Denmark, 1984; Homes in Hot Places, 1987; Homes in Cold Places, 1987; Castles and Mansions, 1988; Homes on Water, 1988; Gilbert and Sullivan: Their Lives and Time, 1990. Address; The Stable, Market Square, Holy Island, Northumberland TD15 2RU, England.

JAMES Anthony, (A R James), b. 17 Mar 1931, London, England. Literary Researcher; Author. m. (1) Jacqueline, 19 Apr 1952, dec, (2) Anne, 27 Sept 1997, 1 son, 2 daughters. Appointments: General Manager, Wimbledon Stadium, 1956-91; Secretary, NGRC Racecourse Promoters, 1989-. Publications: W W Jacobs Companion, 1990; Wimbledon Stadium - The First, 1990; Sixty Years, 1993; Informing the People, 1996; W W Jacobs (biography), 1999. Contributions to: Frequent contributions to Book and Magazine Collector; Antiquarian Book Monthly; W W Jacobs Appreciation Society Newsletter; WWII HMSO Paperbacks Society Newsletter. Memberships: Secretary and Editor, W W Jacobs Appreciation Society, WWII HMSO Paperbacks Society.. Address: 3 Roman Road, Southwick, W Sussex BN42 4TP, England.

JAMES Anthony Stephen, b. 27 Oct 1956, Penllergaer, South Wales. Writer; Poet. m. Penny Windsor, 24 May 1987, div 1994, 1 daughter. Education: BA, University College of Swansea, 1991. Publications: Novel: A House with Blunt Knives, 1991. Poetry: All That the City Has to Offer; Introducing Kivi; We Rescued a Dog Called Gordon, 1997. As Antonia James: The Serpent in April. Contributions to: Numerous publications. Honour: Eileen Illtyd David Award, 1983. Membership: Literature for More than One Year Group. Address: 16 Buckingham Road, Bonymaen, Swansea SA1 7AL, Wales.

JAMES Clive (Vivian Leopold), b. 7 Oct 1939, Kogarah, New South Wales, Australia. Writer; Poet; Broadcaster; Journalist. Education: BA, Sydney University, 1960; MA, Pembroke College, Cambridge, 1967. Appointments: Assistant Editor, Morning Herald, Sydney, 1961; Television Critic, 1972-82, Feature Editor, 1972-, Observer, London; Various television series and documentaries. Publications: Poetry: Peregrine Prykke's Pilgramage Through the London Literary World, 1974, revised edition, 1976; The Fate of Felicity Fark in the Land of the Media, 1975; Britannia Bright's Bewilderment in the Wilderness of Westminster, 1976; Fan-Mail, 1977; Charles Charming's Challenges on the Pathway to the Throne, 1981; Poem of the Year, 1983; Other Passports: Poems, 1958-1985, 1986. Fiction: Brilliant Creatures, 1983; The Remake, 1987; Brrm! Brrm!, 1991. Non-Fiction: The Metropolitan Critic, 1974; Visions Before Midnight, 1977; At the Pillars of Hercules, 1979; Unreliable Memoirs, 1980; The Crystal Bucket, 1981; From the Land of Shadows, 1982; Glued to the Box, 1983; Flying Visits, 1984; Falling Towards England (Unreliable Memoirs Continued), 1985; Snakecharmers in Texas, 1988; May Week Was in June: Unreliable Memoirs III, 1990; Fame in the 20th Century, 1993. Contributions to: Commentary; Encounter; Listener; London Review of Books; Nation; New Review; New Statesman; New York Review of Books; New Yorker; Times Literary Supplement; Others. Address: c/o Observer, 8 St Andrew's Hill, London EC4V 5JA, England.

JAMES Dana. See: POLLARD Jane.

JAMES Mary, (Julia Harvey, Julia Nicholas), b. 2 Oct 1923, Birmingham, England. m. Writer. m. James James CDR, RN, MBE, 25 Aug 1951, 1 son, 1 daughter. Education: Sacred Heart High School, Harrow, Middlesex, England, 1926-39; Matriculation Distinction English. Contributions to: Articles for leading newspapers, magazines, journals, specialising in travel, religion, children & profile pieces. Membership: Society of Authors, 1993-. Address: 13 Lankton Close, Beckenham, Kent BR3 5DZ, England.

JAMES P(hyllis) D(orothy) (Baroness James of Holland Park). b. 3 Aug 1920, Oxford, England. Author. m. Ernest Conner Bantry White, 9 Aug 1941, dec 1964, 2 daughters. Appointments: Member, BBC General Advisory Council, 1987-88, Arts Council, 1988-92, British Council, 1988-93; Chairman, Booker Prize Panel of Judges, 1987; Governor, BBC, 1988-93; President, Society of Authors, 1997-. Publications: Cover Her Face, 1962; A Mind to Murder, 1963; Unnatural Causes, 1967; Shroud for a Nightingale, 1971; The Maul and the Pear Tree (with T A Critchley), 1971; An Unsuitable Job for a Woman, 1972; Innocent Blood, 1980; The Skull Beneath the Skin, 1982; A Taste for Death, 1986; Devices and Desires, 1989; The Children of Men, 1992; Original Sin, 1994; A Certain Justice, 1997. Honours: Officer of the Order of the British Empire; Honorary Doctor of Letters, University of Buckingham, 1992, University of Hertfordshire, 1994, University of Glasgow, 1995, University of Durham, 1988; Honorary Doctor of Literature, University of London, 1993, University of Hertfordshire, 1994; Honorary Doctor, University of Essex, 1996. Memberships: Royal Society of Literature, fellow; Royal Society of Arts, fellow. Address: c/o Greene & Heaton Ltd, 37 Goldhawk Road, London W12 8QQ, England.

JAMES Robert. See: JACK Ian.

JAMES Sir R(obert) V(idal) Rhodes, b. 10 Apr 1933, Murree, India. Politician; Writer. m. Angela Margaret Robertson, 1956, 4 daughters. Education: Private schools, India; Sedbergh School; Worcester College, Oxford. Appointments: Assistant Clerk, 1955-61, Senior Clerk, 1961-64, House of Commons; Fellow, All Souls College, Oxford, 1965-68, 1979-81, Wolfson College, Cambridge, 1991-; Kratter Professor of European History, Stanford University, 1968; Director, Institute for the Study of International Organisation, University of Sussex, 1968-73; Principal Officer, Executive Office of the Secretary-General of the United Nations, 1973-76; Member of Parliament, Conservative Party, Cambridge, 1976-92; Parliamentary Private Secretary, Foreign and Commonwealth Office, 1979-82; Chairman, History of Parliament Trust, 1983-92; Visiting Professor, Baylor University, 1922-. Publications: Lord Randolph Churchill, 1959; An Introduction to the House of Commons, 1961; Rosebery, 1963; Gallipoli, 1965; Standardization and Production of Military Equipment in NATO, 1967; Churchill: A Study in Failure, 1900-1939, 1970; Ambitions and Realities: British Politics 1964-1970, 1972; Victor Cazalet: A Portrait, 1976; Albert, Prince Consort, 1983; Anthony Eden, 1986; Bob Boothby: A Portrait, 1991; Henry Wellcome, 1994. Editor: Chips: The Diaries of Sir Henry Channon, 1967; The Czechoslovak Crisis 1968, 1969; The Complete Speeches of Sir Winston Churchill 1897-1963, 1974. Contributions to: Books and periodicals. Honours: John Llewelyn Rhys Memorial Prize, 1962; Royal Society of Literature Award, 1964; Knighted, 1991; Angel Literature Award, 1992. Memberships: Anglo-Israel Association, vice-president, 1990-; Conservative Friends of Israel, chairman, 1989-95, president, 1995-; Royal Historical Society, fellow; Royal Society of Literature, fellow. Address: The Stone House, Great Gransden, near Sandy, Bedfordshire SG19 3AF, England.

JAMES Tegan. See: ODGERS Sally Farrell.

JAMES William M. See: HARKNETT Terry.

JANDL Ernst, b. 1 Aug 1925, Vienna, Austria. Writer. Education: Teachers Diploma, 1949, PhD, 1950, University of Vienna. Publications: Laut und Luise, 1966; Fünf Mann Menschen, 1968; Der künstliche Baum, 1970; Aus der Fremde, 1980; Gesammelte Werke, 3 volumes, 1985; Idyllen, 1989; Stanzen, 1992; Peter und die Kuh, 1996. Honours: Hörspielpreis der Kriegsblinden, 1968; Georg Trakl Prize, 1974; Prize of the City of Vienna, 1976; Austrian State Prize, 1984; Georg Büchner Preis, 1984; Medal of Honour in Gold of the City of Vienna, 1986; Peter Huchel Preis, 1990; Heinrich von Kleist Preis, 1993. Memberships: Academy of Arts, Berlin; Deutsche Akademie für Sprache und Dichtung, Darmstadt;

Academy of Fine Arts, Munich; Forum Stadtpark, Graz; Grazer Autorenversammlung. Address: PO Box 227, A-1041 Vienna, Austria.

JANES J(oseph) Robert, b. 23 May 1935, Toronto, Ontario, Canada. Writer. m. Gracia Joyce Lind, 16 May 1958, 2 sons, 2 daughters. Education: BSc, Mining Engineering, 1958, MEng, Geology, 1967, University of Toronto. Publications: Children's books: The Tree-Fort War, 1976; Theft of Gold, 1980; Danger on the River, 1982; Spies for Dinner, 1984; Murder in the Market, 1985. Adult books: The Toy Shop, 1981; The Watcher, 1982; The Third Story, 1983; The Hiding Place, 1984; The Alice Factor, 1991; Mayhem, 1992; Carousel, 1992; Kaleidoscope, 1993; Salamander, 1994; Mannequin, 1994; Dollmaker, 1995; Stonekiller, 1995; Sandman, 1996; Gypsy, 1997. Non-Fiction: The Great Canadian Outback, 1978. Textbooks: Holt Geophoto Resource Kits, 1972; Rocks, Minerals and Fossils, 1973; Earth Science, 1974; Geology and the New Global Tectonics, 1976; Searching for Structure (co-author), 1977. Teacher's Guide: Searching for Structure (co-author), 1977; Airphoto Interpretation and the Canadian Landscape (with J D Mollard), 1984. Contributions to: Toronto Star; Toronto Globe and Mail; The Canadian; Winnipeg Free Press; Canadian Children's Annual. Honours: Grants: Canada Council; Ontario Arts Council; J P Bickell Foundation; Thesis Award, Canadian Institute of Mining and Metallurgy; Works-in-progress Grant, Ontario Arts Council, 1991. Memberships: Crime Writers of Canada; Historical Novel Society; International Association of Crime Writers (North American Branch). Literary Agent: Acacia House, 51 Acacia Road, Toronto, Ontario M4S 2K6, Canada. Address: PO Box 1590, Niagara-on-the-Lake, Ontario L0S 1J0, Canada.

JANOWITZ Phyllis, b. 3 Mar 1940, New York, New York, USA. Poet. Div, 1 son, 1 daughter. Education: BA, Queens College; MFA, University of Massachusetts, Amherst, 1970; Appointments: Hodder Fellow in Poetry, Princeton University, 1979-80; Associate Professor in English, then Professor, Cornell University, 1980-. Publications: Rites of Strangers, 1978; Visiting Rites, 1982; Temporary Dwellings, 1988. Contributions to: Poems to New Yorker; Atlantic; Nation; New Republic; Paris Review; Ploughshares; Radcliffe Quarterly; Prairie Schooner; Esquire; Andover Review; Harvard Magazine Backbone; Literary Review; Mid-Atlantic Review. Honour: National Endowment for the Arts Fellowship, 1989. Honour: National Endowment for the Arts Fellowship, 1989. Address: Department of English, Cornell University, Ithaca, NY 14853, USA.

JANOWSKA Anita Halina, b. 2 Feb 1933, Lódz, Poland. Writer; Musician; Sociologist. widowed, 1 daughter. Education: Class of Piano, Warsaw Conservatoire, 1960; MD, 1965, PhD, 1974, Warsaw University. Appointments: Accompanist, Teacher in School Music, 1951-65; Assistant, Department Criminology, Polish Academy of Sciences, 1965-72; Adjunct and Director, Department of Education, Warsaw, Poland, 1973-92. Publications: 7 books including 3 brochures: Zabójstwa i ich sprawcy, 1974; Funkcjonowanie szkolne modziezy i jego uwarunkowania, 1982; Mój diabel stróz, 1988, 1996; Krzyzowka, 1996, 1997. Criminological and sociological periodicals. Contributions to: Various magazines for woman. Honours: Booksellers Literary Award, Warsaw Literary Premiere, April, 1997. Memberships: Stowarzyszenie Autorów Polskich, 1989; Stowarzyszenie Pisarzy Polskich, 1997. Address: ul Grzybowska 16/22 m 1327, 00-132 Warszawa, Poland.

JANSEN Garfield (Auburn Mariano), (Mariananda), b. 15 Aug 1967, Coimbatore, India. Monk; Writer; Poet. Education: BA, Psychology, 1989; PhD, Mariology, International University of California, 1997. Publications: Assumption of Our Lady Mary, 1994; Mary: Mother and Queen, 1995; Hail Mary: Full of Grace, 1996; Mystic Woman, 1997. Contributions to: Many publications. Honours: May Ash Prize, 1985; Winged Word Award, 1996. Memberships: International Socio-Literary Foundation; Stop the Killing, Indian Chapter, president;

United Writers Association. Address: 1275 Trichy Road, Near Sreepathy, Theatre, Coimbatore 641018, Tamil Nadu, India.

JANUS Ludwig, b. 21 Aug 1939, Essen, Germany. Psychoanalyst; Psychotherapist. m. Brigitte Janus-Stanek, 17 Nov 1972, 3 sons, 3 daughters. Education: Dr Med, 1969, Psychoanalyst, 1974. Publications: Die Psychoanalyse der vorgeburtlichen Lebenszeit und der Geburt, 1991; Ungewollte Kinder (with Helga Haesing), 1994; The Enduring Effects of Prenatal Life, 1997; Editor of several books on prenatal psychology. Contributions to: Professional journals. Memberships: German Psychoanalytical Society; International Society of Prenatal and Perinatal Psychology and Medicine. Address: 69118 Heidelberg, Koepfelweg 52, Germany.

JAQUES Elliott, b. 18 Jan 1917, Toronto, Ontario, Canada. Social Analyst; Professor Emeritus. Education: BA, Honours in Science, 1936, MA, Psychology, 1937, University of Toronto; MD, Johns Hopkins Medical School, 1940; PhS, Social Relations, Harvard University, 1950. Appointments: Social Analyst, Professor Emeritus, Brunel University; Visiting Research Professor, Management Science, George Washington University. Publications: Changing Culture of a Factory, 1951; Time-Span Handbook, 1964; General Theory of Bureaucracy, 1976; Form of Time, 1982; Requisite Organization, 1989, revised edition, 1996; Creativity and Work, 1990; Executive Leadership, 1991; Human Capability, 1994. Contributions to: Harvard Business Review; Quality and Participation; The World and I; Human Relations. Address: c/o Rebecca Cason, Cason Hall & Co Ltd., 51 Monroe Street, Suite 608, Rockville, MD 20850, USA.

JARC Katarina. See: MILCINSKI Jana.

JARMAN Mark (Foster), b. 5 June 1952, Mt Sterling, Kentucky, USA. Professor of English; Poet. m. Amy Kane Jarman, 28 Dec 1974, 2 daughters. Education: BA, University of California at Santa Cruz, 1974; MFA, University of Iowa, 1976. Appointments: Teacher and Writing Fellow, University of Iowa, 1974-76; Instructor, Indiana State University, Evansville, 1976-78; Visiting Lecturer, University of California at Irvine, 1979-80; Assistant Professor, Murray State University, Kentucky, 1980-83; Assistant Professor, 1983-86, Associate Professor, 1986-92, Professor of English, 1992-, Vanderbilt University. Publications: Poetry: North Sea, 1978; The Rote Walker, 1981; Far and Away, 1985; The Black Riviera, 1990; Iris, 1992; Questions for Ecclesiastes, 1997. Other: The Reaper Essays (with Robert McDowell), 1996; Rebel Angels: 25 Poets of the New Formalism (editor with David Mason), 1996; The Secret of Poetry, forthcoming; Unmoly Sonnets, forthcoming. Contributions to: Journals, periodicals, and magazines. Honours: Joseph Henry Jackson Award, 1974; Academy of American Poets Prize, 1975; National Endowment for the Arts Grants, 1977, 1983, 1992; Robert Frost Fellowship, Bread Loaf Writers' Conference, 1985; Poets' Prize, 1991; Guggenheim Fellowship, 1991-92; Finalist, National Book Critics Circle Award in Poetry, 1997; Lenore Marshall Poetry Prize, 1998. Memberships: Associated Writing Programs; Modern Language Association; Poetry Society of America; Poets Prize Committee. Address: 509 Broadwell Drive, Nashville, TN 37220, USA.

JARVIS Martin, b. 4 Aug 1941, Cheltenham, Gloucestershire, England. Actor; Writer. m. (1), div, 2 sons, (2) Rosalind Ayres, 23 Nov 1974. Education: Diploma, Honours, Royal Academy of Dramatic Art, 1962. Appointments: Numerous appearances as an actor on stage and in films, radio, and television; Founder-Director, Jarvis and Ayres Productions, 1986-; Active as a producer and director; Co-star in the film Buster, 1988, and as Monsieur de Renal in the BBC-TV production Scarlet and Black, 1993. Publications: Play: Bright Boy, 1977. Short Stories: Name Out of a Hat, 1967; Alphonse, 1972; Late Burst, 1976; Autobiography: Acting Strangly, forthcoming. Other: Adaptations for BBC

Radio, stories by Richmal Crompton, Grant Allen, Dennis Potter; Produced radio programme/audio cassette, A Night To Remember; Autobiographical works for radio; Just William, adapted and performed 6 audio cassettes, 1990-98. Honours: Vanbrugh Award, Silver Medal, Royal Academy of Dramatic Art, 1968; Emmy Award, 1991; Sony Silver Award, 1992; British Spoken Word Association Talkies Awards, 1995, 1997; NY Award for contribution to broadcasting; BPI Gold Award, 1998. Memberships: Children's Film Unit, board member; Oscar Wilde Society; P G Wodehouse Society. Literary Agent: Green & Heaton. Address: c/o London Management, 2-4 Noel Street, London W1V 3RB, England.

JARVIS Sharon, b. 1 Oct 1943, Brooklyn, New York, USA. Literary Agent; Editor; Writer. Education: BFA, Hunter College, 1964. Appointments: Copy Editor, Ace Books, 1969; Assistant Managing Editor, Popular Library, 1971; Editor, Ballantine Books, 1972, Doubleday and Co, 1975; Senior Editor, Playboy Books, 1978. Publications: The Alien Trace (with K Buckley), 1984; Time Twister, 1984; Inside Outer Space, 1985; True Tales of the Unknown, 1985; True Tales of the Unknown: The Uninvited, 1989; True Tales of the Unknown: Beyond Reality, 1991; Dead Zones, 1992; Dark Zones, 1992. Memberships: International Fortean Organization; Association of Authors Representatives; American Booksellers Association; Endless Mountains Council of the Arts. Address: RR2, Box 16B, Laceyville, PA 18623, USA.

JASCOLL John, b. 17 Dec 1949, Surbiton, England. Writer; Anthologist; Publisher. m. Dorie Luttringer, 29 Dec 1974, 1 daughter. Education: BSc, Economics, 1971, MSc, 1973, London School of Economics. Appointments: Currently: Owner, Hazelwood Press; Correspondent, Lancaster Newspapers Inc; Buyer, Lancaster General Hospital. Publications: A Hundred Necessary Rules of Conduct for Children, editor, 1993; How to Win at the Healthcare Salesgame, author, 1994; The New Mozart Compendium Mass, author, 1995; W W Jacobs Uncollected Cargoes, editor, 1996; The W W Jacobs Periodical Bibliography, compiler, 1996; The Monkey's Paw, editor, manuscript facsimile, 1998. Contributions to: Antiquarian Book Monthly; Biblio; Book and Magazine Collector; Materials Management in Healthcare. Honours: 2 Awards, Women in Communications Inc, 1997. Address: 2633 Hazelwood Road, Lancaster, PA 17601, USA.

JASON Kathrine, b. 9 Feb 1953, New York, New York, USA. Instructor; Writer. m. Peter Rondinone, 23 Apr 1984. Education: AB, Bard College, 1975; MF, Columbia University, 1978; Doctoral Study, Graduate Center of the City University of New York, 1980-81. Appointment: Instructor, Hunter College, City University of New York, 1981-. Publications: Racers, What People, 1984; Words in Commotion and Other Stories, 1986; Name and Tears: Forty Years of Italian Fiction, 1990. Contributions to: Anthologies and periodicals. Honour: Fulbright Fellowship, 1978-79; Finalist, Renato Poggioli Award, 1984; Finalist, Nation Award, 1985. Address: 348 West 11th Street, No 38, New York, NY 10014, USA.

JASON Stuart. See: **FLOREN Lee.**

JASPER David, b. 1 Aug 1951, Stockton on Tees, England. University Teacher; Clergyman. m. Alison Elizabeth Collins, 29 Oct 1976, 3 daughters. Education: Dulwich College, 1959-69; Jesus College, Cambridge, 1969-72; BA, MA, 1976, BD, 1980, Keble College, Oxford; PhD, Hatfield College, Durham, 1983. Appointments: Director, Centre for the Study of Literature and Theology, Durham University, 1986-91, Glasgow University, 1991-; Editor, Literature and Theology; Professor of Literature and Theology, University of Glasgow, 1998-. Publications: Coleridge as Poet and Religious Thinker, 1985; The New Testament and the Literary Imagination, 1987; The Study of Literature and Religion, 1989; Rhetoric Power and Community, 1992; Reading in the Canon of Scripture, 1995; The Sacred and Secular Canon in Romanticism, 1999; General Editor, Macmillan Series, Studies in Literature and Translation.

Honours: Dana Fellow, Emory University, Atlanta, 1991; Honorary Fellow, Research Foundation, Durham University, 1991. Memberships: European Society for Literature and Religion, secretary; American Academy of Religion; Modern Language Association. Address: Netherwood, 124 Old Manse Road, Wishaw, Lanarkshire ML2 0EP, Scotland.

JAY Sir Antony (Rupert), b. 20 Apr 1930, London, England. Writer; Producer. m. Rosemary Jill Watkins, 15 June 1957, 2 sons, 2 daughters. Education: BA, 1st Class Honours, Classics and Comparative Philology, 1952, MA, 1955, Magdalene College, Cambridge. Appointments: Staff, BBC, 1955-64; Chairman, Video Arts Ltd, 1972-89; Writer (with Jonathan Lynn), Yes, Minister and Yes, Prime Minister, BBC-TV series, 1980-88. Publications: Management and Machiavelli, 1967, 2nd edition, 1987; To England With Love (with David Frost), 1967; Effective Presentation, 1970; Corporation Man, 1972; The Householder's Guide to Community Defence Against Bureaucratic Aggression, 1972; Yes, Minister (with Jonathan Lynn), 3 volumes, 1981-83; The Complete Yes, Minister (with Jonathan Lynn), 1984; Yes, Prime Minister (with Jonathan Lynn), 2 volumes, 1986-87; The Complete Yes, Prime Minister (with Jonathan Lynn), 1989; Elizabeth R, 1992; Oxford Dictionary of Political Quotations (editor), 1996; How to Beat Sir Humphrey, 1997. Contributions to: Understanding Laughter: Proceedings of the Royal Institution, Vol 62, 1990. Honours: Honorary MA, Sheffield University, 1987; Knighted, 1988; Doctor of Business Administration, International Management Centre, Buckingham, 1988; Royal Society of Arts, fellow, 1992; Companion, Institute of Management, 1992; Commander of the Royal Victorian Order, 1993. Address: c/o Video Arts Ltd, 68 Oxford Street, London W1N 9LA, England.

JAY Martin (Evan), b. 4 May 1944, New York, New York, USA. Professor of History; Writer. m. Catherine Gallagher, 6 July 1974, 2 daughters. Education: BA, Union College, 1965; PhD, Harvard University, 1971. Appointments: Assistant Professor, 1971-76, Associate Professor, 1976-82, Professor of History, 1982-, Sidney Hellman Ehrman Professor, 1997-, University of California at Berkeley. Publications: The Dialectical Imagination: A History of the Frankfurt School and the Institute of Social Research, 1923-1950, 1973, new edition, 1996; Adorno, 1984; Marxism and Totality, 1984; Permanent Exiles, 1985; Fin de Siècle Socialism, 1989; Downcast Eyes, 1993; Force Fields, 1993; Cultural Semantics, 1997-98. Contributions to: Salmagundi. Honour: Herbert Baxter Adams Award, American Academy of Arts and Sciences, 1996. Memberships: American Historical Association; Society for Exile Studies. Address: 718 Contra Costa Avenue, Berkeley, CA 94707, USA.

JEAL Tim, b. 27 Jan 1945, London, England. Author. m. Joyce Timewell, 11 Oct 1969, 3 daughters. Education: MA, Christ Church, Oxford. Publications: For Love of Money, 1967; Livingstone, 1973; Cushing's Crusade, 1974; Until the Colours Fade, 1976; A Marriage of Convenience, 1979; Baden-Powell, 1989; The Missionary's Wife, 1997. Honours: Joint Winner, Llewelyn Rhys Memorial Prize, 1974; Writers Guild Laurel Award. Membership: Society of Authors. Literary Agent: Toby Eady Associates. Address: 29 Willow Road, London NW3 1TL, England.

JEBB Miles (Lord Gladwyn), Education: MA, Magdalen College, Oxford. Publictions: The Thames Valley Heritage Walk, 1980; A Guide to the South Downs Way, 1984; Walkers, 1986; A Guide to the Thames Path, 1988; East Anglia, 1990; A Guide to the Colleges of Oxford, 1992; Suffolk, 1995; The Diaries of Cynthia Gladwyn, 1995. Address: E I Albany, Piccadilly, London W1V 9RH, England.

JEFFERSON Alan (Rigby), b. 20 Mar 1921, Ashstead, Surrey, England. Writer. m. (1), 1 son, 2 sons, 1 daughter (3) Antonia Dora Raeburn, 24 Sept 1976, 2 sons. Education: Rydal School, Colwyn Bay, 1935-37; Old Vic Theatre School, 1947-48. Appointments:

Administrator, London Symphony Orchestra, 1968-69; Visiting Professor of Vocal Interpretation, Guildhall School of Music and Drama, London, 1968-74; Manager, BBC Concert Orchestra, London, 1969-73; Editor, The Monthly Guide to Recorded Music, 1980-82. Publications: The Operas of Richard Strauss in Great Britain 1910-1963, 1964; The Lieder of Richard Strauss, 1971; Delius, 1972; The Life of Richard Strauss, 1973; Inside the Orchestra, 1974; Strauss, 1975; The Glory of Opera, 1976, 2nd edition, 1983; Discography of Richard Strauss's Operas, 1977; Strauss, 1978; Sir Thomas Beecham, 1979; The Complete Gilbert and Sullivan Opera Guide, 1984; Der Rosenkavalier, 1986; Lotte Lehmann: A Centenary Biography, 1989; CD ROM: An Introduction to Classical Music, 1996; Elisabeth Schwarzkopf, 1996. Contributions to: Periodicals. Memberships: Royal Society of Musicians; Society of Authors. Address: c/o Society of Authors, 84 Drayton Gardens, London SW10 9SB, England.

JEHU Jeremy Charles Rhys, b. 31 Aug 1955, Southampton, England. Journalist; Critic. Education: BA, English, University College, Durham, England, 1976. Appointments: Staff Writer and News Executive, Surrey Daily Advertiser, 1976-79; The Stage and Television Today, 1979-94, Deputy Editor, 1986-92, Editor, 1992-94; Book Critic/Columnist, Teletext on ITV and Channel 4, 1997-; Book Critic/Commentator, Talk Radio, 1998-. Publication: The Monday Lunchtime of the Living Dead, 1999. Address: 11 Rita Road, London SW8 1JX, England.

JELINEK Elfriede, b. 20 Oct 1946, Mürzzuschlag, Austria. Author; Dramatist; Poet. m. Gottfried Hüngsberg. Education: Piano and Organ, Vienna Conservatory; Theatre and Art History, University of Vienna. Publications: Lisas Schatten, 1967; wir sind lockvögel baby!, 1970; Michael: Ein Jugendbuch für die Infantilgesell-schaft, 1973; Die Liebhaberinnen, 1975; bukolit, 1979; ende: gedichte, 1966-1968, 1980; Die Ausgesperrten, 1980; Die Klavierspielerin, 1983; Burgtheater, 1984; Clara S, 1984; Was geschah, nachdem Nora ihren Mann verlassen hatte oder Stützen der Gesellschaft, 1984; Oh Wildnis, oh Schutz vor ihr, 1985; Krankeit oder Moderne Frauen, 1987; Lust, 1989; Wolken: Heim, 1990; Malina, 1991; Totenauberg, 1991; Die Kinder der Toten, 1995. Honours: Prize for Poetry and Prose, Innsbrucker Jugendkulturwoche, 1969; National Scholarship for Writers, Austria, 1972; Roswitha von Gandersheim Memorial Medal, 1979; Drehbuchpreis, Ministry of the Interior, Austria, 1979; Heinrich Böll Prize, 1986; Styrian Literature Prize, 1987; Bremen Prize for Literature, Rudolf Alexander Schroder Foundation, 1996. Memberships: Graz Writers' Association. Address: Sendlingerstrasse 43, D-80331 Munich, Germany, and Jupiterweg 40, A-1140 Vienna, Austria.

JELLICOE (Patricia) Ann, b. 15 July 1927, Middlesborough, Yorkshire, England. Dramatist; Director. m. (1) C E Knight-Clarke, 1950, div 1961, (2) Roger Mayne, 1962, 1 son, 1 daughter. Education: Polam Hall, Darlington; Queen Margaret's, York; Central School of Speech and Drama. Appointments: Actress, stage manager, and director, 1947-51; Founder-Manager, Cockpit Theatre Club, 1952-54; Teacher and Director of Plays, Central School of Speech and Drama, 1954-56; Literary Manager, Royal Court Theatre, 1973-75; Founder-Director, 1979-85, President, 1986, Colway Theatre Trust. Publications: Plays: The Sport of My Mad Mother, 1958; The Knack, 1962; Shelley or The Idealist, 1966; The Rising Generation, 1969; The Giveaway, 1970; 3 Jelliplays, 1975. Other: Some Unconscious Influences in the Theatre, 1967; Shell Guide to Devon (with Roger Mayne), 1975; Community Plays: How to Put Them On, 1987. Honour: Officer of the Order of the British Empire, 1984. Address: Colway Manor, Lyme Regis, Dorset DT7 3HD, England.

JENCKS Charles Alexander, b. 21 June 1939, Baltimore, Maryland, USA. Writer; Architect; Professor. m. Margaret Keswick, 3 sons, 1 daughter. Education: BA, 1961, BA, MA, 1965, Harvard University; PHP, London University. Appointment: Editorial Advisor, Architectural

Design, London, 1979. Publications: Ad Hocism, 1972; Modern Movements in Architecture, 1973, 2nd edition, 1984; Le Corbusier and the Tragic View of Architecture, 1974; The Language of Post Modern Architecture, 1977; Daydream Houses of Los Angeles, 1978; Late Modern Architecture, 1980; Architecture Toady, 1982, 2nd edition, 1988. Contributions to: Architectural Design; Times Literary Supplement; Encounter. Honours: Melbourne Oration, 1974; Boston Lectures, Royal Society of Arts. Literary Agent: Ed Victor. Address: Architectural Association, 36 Bedford Square, London WC1, England.

JENKINS John (Geraint), b. 4 Jan 1929, Llangrannog, Ceredigion, Wales. Museum Curator; Writer. m. 8 Jan 1954, 3 sons. Education: BA, 1952, MA, 1953, DSc, 1980, University of Wales, Swansea and Aberystwyth. Appointments: Museum Curator; Editor, Folk Life, 1963-78; Chairman, Language and Culture Committee, Ceredigion County Council, 1998-. Publications: The English Farm Wagon, 1963; Traditional Country Craftsmen, 1965; Agricultural Transport in Wales, 1966; The Welsh Woollen Industry, 1969; Life and Tradition in Rural Wales, 1973; Nets and Coracles, 1974; The Coracle, 1985; Exploring Museums, Wales, 1990; Interpreting the Heritage of Wales, 1990; Getting Yesterday Right, 1993; The In-Shore Fishermen of Wales, 1993; Interpreting the Heritage of a Coastal Village, 1998. Contributions to: Journals and magazines. Honour: Druid Gorsedd of Bards, National Eisteddfod of Wales, 1969. Memberships: Society for Folk Life Studies, president, 1983-86; Society for the Interpretation of Britain's Heritage, chairman, 1975-81; Coracle Society, 1990-; Wales Arts Council, West Wales Region, chairman, 1996-; Ceredigion County Council, councillor; Language and Culture Committe, 1998. Address: Cilhaul, Sarnau, Ceredigion SA44 6QT, Wales.

JENKINS (John) Robin, b. 11 Sept 1912, Cambusland, Lanarkshire, England. Teacher (retired); Writer. Education: BA, Glasgow University, 1935. Appointments: Teacher, Gjazi College, Khabul, 1957-59, British Institute, Barcelona, 1959-61, Gaya School, Sabah, 1963-68. Publications: Go Gaily Sings the Lark, 1951; Happy for the Child, 1953; The Thistle and the Grail, 1954; The Cone-Gatherers, 1955; Guests of War, 1956; The Missionaries, 1957; The Changeling, 1958; Love is a Fervent Fire, 1959; Some Kind of Grace, 1960; Dust on the Paw, 1961; The Tiger of Gold, 1962; A Love of Innocence, 1963; The Sardana Dancers, 1964; A Very Scotch Affair, 1968; The Holly Tree, 1969; The Expatriates, 1971; A Toast to the Lord, 1972; A Figure of Fun, 1974; A Would-Be-Saint, 1978; Fergus Lamont, 1979; The Awakening of George Darroch, 1985; Poverty Castle, 1991. Address: Fairhaven, Toward by Dunoon, Argyll PA23 7UE, Scotland.

JENKINS Roy (Harris) (Lord Jenkins of Hillhead), b. 11 Nov 1920, Abersychan, Monmouthshire, Wales. Politician; Writer. m. Jennifer Morris, 2 sons, 1 daughter. Education: BA, Balliol College, Oxford, 1941. Appointments: Member of Parliament, Labour Party, Central Southwark, London, 1948-50, Stechford, Birmingham, 1950-77; Home Secretary, 1965-67, 1974-76; Chancellor of the Exchequer, 1967-70; President, European Commission, 1977-81; Co-Founder, 1981, Leader, 1982-83, Member of Parliament, Hillhead, Glasgow, 1982-87, Social Democratic Party; Chancellor, Oxford University, 1987-. Publications: Purpose and Policy (editor), 1947; Mr Attlee: An Interim Biography, 1948; New Fabian Essays (contributor), 1952; Pursuit of Progress, 1953; Mr Balfour's Poodle, 1954; Sir Charles Dilke: A Victorian Tragedy, 1958; The Labour Case, 1959; Asquith, 1964; Essays and Speeches, 1967; Afternoon on the Potomac?, 1972; What Matters Now, 1973; Nine Men of Power, 1974; Partnership of Principle, 1985; Truman, 1986; Baldwin, 1987; Twentieth Century Portraits, 1988; European Diary, 1989; A Life at the Centre, 1991; Portraits and Miniatures, 1993; Gladstone, 1995; The Chancellors, 1998. Honours: Privy Councillor, 1964; Life Peer, 1987-; Chancellor, Oxford University, 1987-; Order of Merit, 1993; President, Royal Society of Literature, 1998-; Numerous honorary doctorates, awards

and prizes. Address: 2 Kensington Park Gardens, London W11, England.

JENKINS Simon David, b. 10 June 1943, Birmingham, England. Journalist; Editor. m. Gayle Hunnicutt, 1978. Education: BA, St John's College, Oxford. Appointments: Staff, Country Life Magazine, 1965; News Editor, Times Educational Supplement, 1966-68; Leader Writer, Columnist, Features Editor, 1968-74, Editor, 1977-78, Evening Standard; Insight Editor, Sunday Times, 1974-76; Political Editor, The Economist, 1979-86; Director, Faber and Faber (Publishers) Ltd., 1981-90. Publications: A City at Risk, 1971; Landlords to London, 1974; Newspapers: The Power and the Money, 1979; The Companion Guide to Outer London, 1981; Images of Hampstead, 1982; The Battle for the Falklands, 1983; With Respect, Ambassador, 1985; Market for Glory, 1986; The Selling of Mary Davies, 1993. Address: 174 Regents Park Road, London NW1, England.

JENNINGS Charles Anthony, b. 6 Dec 1956, London, England. m. Susie Fisher, 2 sons. Education: St John's College Oxford University, England. Publications: The Confidence Trick; Up North; People Like Us; Fathers' Race. Contributions to: The Times; Sunday Times; Guardian; Observer; Sunday Telegraph; Independent; Daily Mail; Evening Standard, Harper's & Queen; GQ; Tatler; Cosmopolitan. Literary Agent: David Higham Associates. Address: David Higham Associates, 5-8 Lower John Street, Golden Square, London W1R 4HA, England.

JENNINGS Elizabeth (Joan), b. 18 July 1926, Boston, Lincolnshire, England. Education: MA, St Anne's College, Oxford. Appointments: Assistant, Oxford City Library, 1950-58; Reader, Chatto & Windus Ltd, 1958-60. Publications: Poetry: Poems, 1953; A Way of Looking, 1955; A Sense of the World, 1958; Song for a Birth or a Death, 1961; Recoveries, 1964; The Mind has Mountains, 1966; The Secret Brother, 1966; Collected Poems, 1967; The Animals' Arrival, 1969; Lucidities, 1970; Relationships, 1972; Growing Points, 1975; Consequently I Rejoice, 1977; After the Ark, 1978; Selected Poems, 1980; Moments of Grace, 1980; Celebrations and Elegies, 1982; Extending the Territory, 1985; Collected Poems, 1953-86, 1986; Tributes, 1989; Times and Seasons, 1992; Familiar Spirits, 1994; A Spell of Words, 1997. Editor: The Batsford Book of Children's Verse, 1958; A Choice of Christina Rossetti's Verse, 1970; The Batsford Book of Religious Verse, 1981. Other: Let's Have Some Poetry, 1960; Every Changing Shape, 1961; Robert Frost, 1964; Christianity and Poetry, 1965; Seven Men of Vision, 1976. Contributions to: Newspapers, journals, and magazines. Honours: Arts Council Prize, 1953, and Bursary, 1969; Somerset Maugham Award, 1956; Richard Hillary Prize, 1966; W H Smith Award, 1987; Commander of the Order of the British Empire, 1992; Paul Hamlyn Award, 1997. Memberships: Society of Authors. Address: c/o David Higham Associates Ltd, 5-8 Lower John Street, London W1R 4HA, England.

JENSEN De Lamar, b. 22 Apr 1925, Roseworth, Idaho, USA. Professor of History; Writer. Education: BA, Brigham Young University, 1952; MA, 1953, PhD, 1957, Columbia University. Appointments: Instructor in History, New York University, 1954-57; Professor of History, Brigham Young University, 1957-. Publications: Machiavelli: Cynic, Patriot or Political Scientist? (compiler, editor), 1960; Diplomacy and Dogmatism: Bernardino de Mendoza and the French Catholic League, 1964; The Expansion of Europe: Motives, Methods and Meanings (compiler, editor), 1967; The World of Europe: The Sixteenth Century; Confrontation at Worms: Martin Luther and the Diet of Worms, 1973; Renaissance Europe, 1980, 2nd edition, 1991; Reformation Europe, 1981, 2nd edition, 1991. Address: 1079 Briar Avenue, Provo, UT 84604, USA.

JENSEN Laura Linnea, b. 16 Nov 1948, Tacoma, Washington, USA. Poet. Education: BA, University of Washington, 1972; MFA, University of Iowa, 1974. Appointments: Occasional Teacher; Visiting Poet,

Oklahoma State University, 1978. Publications: After I Have Voted, 1972; Anxiety and Ashes, 1976; Bad Boats, 1977; Tapwater, 1978; The Story Makes Them Whole, 1979; Memory, 1982; Shelter, 1985; A Sky Empty of Orion, 1985. Contributions to: Periodicals. Honours: National Endowment for the Arts Fellowship, 1980-81; Ingram Merrill Foundation Grant, 1983; Theodore Roethke Award, 1986; Guggenheim Fellowship, 1989-90; Lila Wallace-Reader's Digest Writers Award, 1993. Memberships: Academy of American Poets; Associated Writing Programs; Poets and Writers. Address: 302 North Yakima, No C3, Tacoma, WA 98403, USA.

JENSEN Ruby Jean, b. 1 Mar 1930, USA. Author. m. Vaughn Jensen, 1 daughter. Publications: The House That Samuel Built, 1974; The Seventh All Hallows Eve, 1974; Dark Angel, 1978; Hear the Children Cry, 1981; Such a Good Baby, 1982; Mama, 1983; Home Sweet Home, 1985; Annabelle, 1987; Chain Letter, 1987; House of Illusions, 1988; Jump Rope, 1988; Death Stone, 1989; Baby Dolly, 1991; Celia, 1991; The Reckoning, 1992; The Living Exile, 1993; The Haunting, 1994. Address: 41 West 82nd Street, New York, NY 10024, USA.

JERSILD Per Christian, b. 14 Mar 1935, Katrineholm, Sweden. Writer. m. Ulla Jersild, 1960, 2 sons. Education: MD. Publications: The Animal Doctor, 1975, 2nd edition, 1988; After the Flood, 1986; Children's Island, 1987; The House of Babel, 1987; A Living Soul, 1988; also 29 books published in Sweden. Honours: Swedish Grand Novel Prize, 1981; Swedish Academy Award, 1982; De Nios Grand Prize, 1998. Membership: Swedish PEN, board. Address: Rosensdalsv. 20, 5-19454 Uppl. Vasby, Sweden.

JESPERSEN Per, (Linda Clay), b. 14 Jan 1938, Copenhagen, Denmark. Author; Philosopher; Theologian; Teacher. m. Anne Jespersen, 28 Mar 1962, 1 son, 1 daughter. Education: Graduated, University of Copenhagen, 1965. Publications: Filosofi for born, 1988; Naar svanen dor, 1987; Born og filosofi, 1993. Contributions to: Philosophy, children and the schools, 1986, How to do philosophy with children, 1987, The Wonder Dough, 1988, Benjamin, 1990, Hope, 1990, A Strange Experience, 1990, It is strange, 1990, I Had a Dream, 1991, A Nightly Talk, 1991, in Analytic Teaching. Membership: Danish Authors. Address: Randerup 40, 6261 Bredebro, Denmark.

JESSUP Frances, b. 29 July 1936, England. Novelist; Poet; Playwright. m. Clive Turner, 1960, div 1996, 1 son, 3 daughters. Education: BA, Honours, Philosophy, King's College, University of London, 1958. Appointment: Organiser, Theatre Writing, Halesmere, UNA, 1992. Publication: The Fifth Child's Conception, 1970, 1972. Contributions to: Anthologies and magazines. Honours: 1st Prize for Fiction and Poetry, Moor Park College, 1972; UNA Trust Award, 1988; University of Surrey Arts Committee Literary Festival Award, 1991. Membership: PEN. Address: 20 Heath Road, Haslemere, GU27 3QN England.

JHABVALA Ruth Prawer, b. 7 May 1927, Cologne, Germany. Writer. m. 16 June 1951, 3 daughters. Education: BA, 1948, MA, 1951, DLitt, London. Publications: The Householder, 1960; A New Dominion, 1971; Heat and Dust, 1975; Out of India, 1986; Three Continents, 1987; Poet and Dancer, 1993; Shards of Memory, 1995. Honours: Booker Prize, 1975; Neil Gunn International Fellowship, 1979; John D and Catharine T MacArthur Foundation Fellowship, 1984-89; Academy Awards, 1987, 1993; American Academy of Arts and Letters Literature Award, 1992; Commander of the Order of the British Empire, 1998. Memberships: Royal Society of Literature, fellow; Authors Guild; Writers Guild of America. Address: 400 East 52nd Street, New York, NY 10022, USA.

JIANG Da-Ya, b. 2 June 1928, Jiangxi, China. Childrens Journalist. m. Zhao Weitian, May 1951, 1 son, 2 daughters. Education: Graduate, Sociology Department, Nanking University. Appointments: Editor, 1954, Senior Editor, 1990, China Childrens News;

Professor, 1989-. Publications: Words From Bosom Sister, 1981; A Child With Wings, 1986; Unrevealed Love From the Heart, 1987; Eleven Little Genius, 1988; Hong Xiuquan, 1993; Ups and Downs of Young Sons, 1994; Young Pearls of China, 1997; Talented Children of the World, 1998. Honours: 1st Prize, 1980, 2nd Prize, 1988, Nation's Best News. Address: 601 23rd Tower Liu Fang, Nan Li Chao Young District, Beijing 100027, China.

JIANG AN DAO. See: **PARKIN Andrew Terence Leonard.**

JILES Paulette, b. 1943, Salem, Missouri, USA. Poet; Writer. Education: BA, University of Missouri, 1968. Appointments: Teacher, David Thompson University, Nelson, British Columbia, 1984-85; Writer-in-Residence, Phillips Academy, Andover, Massachusetts, 1987-. Publications: Poetry: Waterloo Express, 1973; Celestial Navigation, 1983; The Jesse James Poems, 1987; Flying Lessons: Selected Poems, 1995. Other: Sitting in the Club Car Drinking Rum & Karma-Kola, 1986; The Late Great Human Roadshow, 1986; Blackwater, 1988; Song to the Rising Sun, 1989; Cousins, 1991; North Spirit, 1995. Honours: Governor-General's Award, 1984; Gerald Lampert Award, 1984; Pat Lowther Award, 1984; ACTRA Award for Best Original Drama, 1989. Membership: Writers' Union of Canada. Address: c/o Writers Union of Canada, 24 Ryerson Avenue, Toronto, Ontario M5T 2P3, Canada.

JNK. See: **KAUSHIK J N.**

JOHANSEN Birgit Dagmar Johansen, b. 14 Sept 1942, Viborg, Denmark. Psychiatrist; Sexologist; Writer. 1 son, 1 daughter. Education: MD, 1973; Psychiatrist, Teacher in Sexology, Advanced Level, University of Göteborg, Sweden, 1984. Publications: Den Skjulte Lyst, 1988; Incest, 1989; Dit Seksuelle Indre, 1990; Smertens Lyst, 1990; Love Has No Age, 1997; Co-author of several books in field. Contributions to: Periodicals. Memberships: National Press Club of Denmark; Danish Writers' Union. Address: Ved Stranden 16, DK-1061 Copenhagen, Denmark.

JOHANSSON-BACKE Karl Erik, b. 24 Nov 1914, Stockholm, Sweden. Retired Teacher; Writer; Dramatist; Poet. m. Kerstin Gunhild Bergquist, 21 Nov 1943, 1 son, 3 daughters. Education: High School Teacher's Degree. Publications: Novels: A Pole in the River, 1950; Daybreak, 1954; The Mountain of Temptation, 1983; The Tree and the Bread, 1987; King of Mountains, 1993. Poetry: Lust and Flame, 1981. Honours: Many literary awards, 1961-93. Memberships: Swedish Authors Federation; Swedish Playwrights Federation, honorary member. Address: Kopmangstan 56, 83133 Ostersund, Sweden.

JOHN Katherine. See: **WATKINS Karen Christna.**

JOHN Nicholas. See: **VIDOR Miklos Janos.**

JOHNS Kenneth. See: **BULMER Henry Kenneth.**

JOHNS Richard Alton Jr, b. 17 July 1929, Tyler, Texas, USA. Commerical Artist; Writer. m. Joan Turner, 8 Nov 1958, 1 son, 1 daughter. Education: AA, Tyler Junior College, 1948; BA, North Texas University, 1950. Publications: The Legacy, 1963; Thirteenth Apostle, 1966; Garden of the Okapi, 1968; Return to Heroism, 1969; The Andrews Center (history), 1992; Jarvis College (history), 1994. Contributions to: Chronicles; Cable Guide. Honour: Grand Prize, Short Story, 1994. Address: 3324 Teakwood Drive, Tyler, TX 75701, USA.

JOHNSON Alison Findlay, b. 19 Nov 1947, Stafford, England. Author. m. Andrew J D Johnson, 1973, 1 daughter. Education: MA, Aberdeen University, 1968; BPhil, Oxford University, 1970. Publications: A House by the Shore, 1986; Scarista Style, 1987; Children of Disobedience, 1989; Islands in the Sound, 1989; The Wicked Generation, 1992. Contributions to: West Highland Press; The Times. Address: c/o Vivien Green,

43 Doughty Street, London WC1N 2LF, England.

JOHNSON Charles, b. 1 Jan 1942, Erdington, Birmingham, England. Poet. m. Rosalind Mora MacInnes, 15 July 1977, 1 daughter. Education: Newcastle upon Tyne College of Commerce, 1964-65. Publication: A Box of Professional Secrets: Poems, 1995. Contributions to: Anthologies, journals, and periodicals. Memberships: Droitwich Poetry Groups; Redditch Poets Workshop, founder; St John's Poetry Workshop. Address: 41 Buckleys Green Alvechurch, Birmingham B48 7NG, England.

JOHNSON Charles (Richard), b. 23 Apr 1948, Evanston, Illinois, USA. Professor of English; Writer. m. Joan New, June 1970, 1 son, 1 daughter. Education: BA, 1971, MA, 1973, Southern Illinois University; Postgraduate Studies, State University of New York at Stony Brook, 1973-76. Appointments: Assistant Professor, 1976-79, Associate Professor, 1979-82, Professor of English, 1982-, University of Washington, Seattle. Publications: Faith and the Good Thing, 1974; Oxherding Tale, 1982; The Sorcerer's Apprentice: Tales and Conjurations, 1986; Being and Race: Black Writing Since 1970, 1988; Middle Passage, 1990; All This and Moonlight, 1990; In Search of a Voice (with Ron Chernow), 1991; Dreamer, 1998. Honours: Governor's Award for Literature, State of Washington, 1983; National Book Award, 1990. Address: c/o Department of English, University of Washington, Seattle, WA 98105, USA.

JOHNSON Colin, b. 23 July 1939, Beverley, Western Australia. Novelist. Appointment: Lecturer, University of Queensland, St Lucia. Publications: Wild Cat Falling, 1965; Long Live Sandawara, 1979; Before the Invasion: Aboriginal Life to 1788, 1980; Doctor Wooreddy's Prescription for Enduring the End of the World, 1983; Doin' Wildcat, 1988; Dalwurra: The Black Bittern, 1988; Writing from the Fringe, 1990. Honours: Wieckhard Prize, 1979; Western Australia Literary Award, 1989. Address: c/o Department of English, University of Queensland, St Lucia, Queensland 4067, Australia.

JOHNSON David, b. 26 Aug 1927, Meir, Staffordshire, England. Historian. Education: Repton; Sandhurst. Publications: Sabre General, 1959; Promenade in Champagne, 1960; Lanterns in Gascony, 1965; A Candle in Aragon, 1970; Regency Revolution, 1974; Napoleon's Cavalry and its Leaders, 1978; The French Cavalry 1792-1815, 1989. Contributions to: The Armourer (1914: The Riddle of the Marine). Address: 16 Belgrave Gardens, London NW8 0RB, England.

JOHNSON Denis, b. 1949, Munich, Germany. Writer; Poet. Publications: The Man Among the Seals, 1969; Inner Weather, 1976; The Incognito Lounge and Other Poems, 1982; Angels, 1983; Fiskadoro, 1985; The Stars at Noon, 1986; Jesus' Son, 1993; Already Dead, 1997. Honour: American Academy of Arts and Letters Literature Award, 1993. Address: Alfred A Knopf Inc, 201 East 50th Street, New York, NY 10022, USA.

JOHNSON Diane Lain, b. 28 Apr 1934, Moline, Illinois, USA. Writer. m. John Frederick Murray, 9 Nov 1969, 4 children. Education: AA, Stephens College, 1953; BA, University of Utah, 1957; MA, PhD, 1968, University of California at Los Angeles. Appointment: Faculty, Department of English, University of California, 1968-87. Publications: Fair Game, 1965; Loving Hands at Home, 1968; Lesser Lives, 1972; The Shadow Knows, 1975; Terrorists and Novelists, 1982; Dashiell Hammett, 1983; Perian Nights, 1987; Health and Happiness, 1990; Natural Opium, 1993. Contributions to: Newspapers and magazines. Honours: Several awards. Memberships: PEN; Writers Guild of America. Address: Attorney Lizbeth Hasse, 2000 Center Street, Suite 300, Berkeley, CA 94704, USA.

JOHNSON Frank Robert, b. 20 Jan 1943, London, England. Editor, The Spectator. Appointments: Messenger Boy, Sunday Express, 1959-60; Reporter on Local and Regional Newspapers, 1960-69; Political Staff, Sun, 1969-72; Parliamentary Sketch Writer and Leader

Writer, Daily Telegraph, 1972-79; Columnist, Now! Magazine, 1979-81; The Times: Parliamentary Sketchwriter, 1981-83; Paris Diarist, 1984; Bonn Correspondent, 1985-86; Parliamentary Sketch Writer, 1986-87; Associate Editor, 1987-88; The Sunday Telegraph: Associate Editor, 1988-93; Deputy Editor, Comment, 1993-94; Deputy Editor, 1994-95; Editor, The Spectator, 1995-. Publications: Out of Order, 1982; Frank Johnson's Election Year, 1983. Honours: Sketch Writer of the Year, Granada; What the Papers Say, 1977; Columnist of the Year, British Press Awards, 1981. Membership: The Garrick Club; Beefsteak Club. Address: The Spectator, 56 Doughty Street, London WC1N 2LL, England.

JOHNSON George (Laclede), b. 20 Jan 1952, Fayetteville, Arkansas, USA. Writer. Education: BA, University of New Mexico, 1975; MA, American University, 1979. Publications: Architects of Fear, 1984; Machinery of the Mind, 1986; In the Places of Memory, 1991. Contributions to: Newspapers and magazines. Honour: Alicia Patterson Journalism Fellow, 1984. Address: c/o International Creative Management, 40 West 57th Street, New York, NY 10019, USA.

JOHNSON Hugh Eric Allan, b. 10 Mar 1939, London, England. Author; Editor. m. Judith Eve Grinling, 1965, 1 son, 2 daughters. Education: MA, King's College, Cambridge. Appointments: Feature Writer, Condé Nast Magazines, 1960-63; Editor, Wine and Food Magazine, 1962-63; Wine Correspondent, Sunday Times, 1963-67; Travel Editor, 1967; Editor, Queen Magazine, 1968-70; Wine Editor, Cuisine Magazine, New York, 1983-84; Editorial Consultant, The Garden, 1975-. Publications: Wine, 1966; The World Atlas of Wine, 1971, 4th edition, 1994; The International Book of Trees, 1973, 2nd edition, 1994; The California Wine Book (with Bob Thompson), 1975; Hugh Johnson's Pocket Wine Book, annually, 1977-; The Principles of Gardening, 1979, revised edition, 1996; Hugh Johnson's Wine Companion, 1983, latest edition, 1997; Hugh Johnson's Cellar Book, 1986; The Atlas of German Wines, 1986; Understanding Wine (A Sainsbury Guide), 1986; Atlas of the Wines of France (with Hubrecht Duijker), 1987; The Story of Wine, 1989, reissued, 1998; The Art and Science of Wine (with James Halliday), 1992; Hugh Johnson on Gardening, 1993. Other: How to Handle a Wine (video), 1984; A History of Wine (Channel 4 TV series), 1989. Membership: Circle of Wine Writers, President 1997-. Address: Saling Hall, Great Saling, Essex CM7 5DT, England.

JOHNSON James (Henry), b. 19 Nov 1930, Coleraine, Northern Ireland. Professor of Geography; Writer. m. Jean McKane, 31 Mar 1956, 2 sons, 2 daughters. Education: BA, Queen's University of Belfast, 1953; MA, University of Wisconsin, 1954; PhD, University of London, 1962. Appointments: Professor of Geography; Editor, Aspects of Geography series, 1980-96. Publications: Urban Geography: An Introductory Analysis, 1967; Trends in Geography (editor), 1969; Geographical Mobility of Labour in England and Wales (co-author), 1974; Suburban Growth (editor), 1974; Urbanisation, 1980; The Structure of Nineteenth Century Cities (co-editor), 1982; Labour Migration (co-editor), 1990; Population Migration (co-author), 1990; The Human Geography of Ireland, 1994. Contributions to: Geographical journals. Address: The Coach-house, Wyreside Hall, Dolphinholme, Lancaster LA2 9DH, England.

JOHNSON Jenny. See: **HARROWER Jennifer Hilary.**

JOHNSON Linton Kwesi, b. 1952, Chapeltown, Jamaica. Poet; Writer. Education: BA, Sociology, Goldsmith's College, University of London, 1973. Publications: Voices of the Living and the Dead, 1974; Dread, Beat, and Blood, 1975; Inglan is a Bitch, 1980; Tings an Times: Selected Poems, 1991. Contributions to: Recordings and television. Honour: C Day-Lewis Fellowship, 1977. Address: PO Box 623, Herne Hill, London SE24 0L5, England.

JOHNSON Mel. See: **MALZBERG Barry.**

JOHNSON Nora, b. 31 Jan 1933, Hollywood, California, USA. Author.m. (1) Leonard Siwek, 1955, (2) John A Milici, 1965, 2 sons, 2 daughters. Education: BA, Smith College, 1954. Publications: The World of Henry Orient, 1958; A Step Beyond Innocence, 1961; Love Letter in the Dead Letter Office, 1966; Flashback, 1979; You Can Go Home Again, 1982; The Two of Us, 1984; Tender Offer, 1985; Uncharted Places, 1988; Perfect Together, 1991. Contributions to: Newspapers and magazines. Honours: McCall's Short Story Prize, 1962; O Henry Award Story, 1982; New York Times Best Book Citations, 1982, 1984. Memberships: Author's Guild; PEN. Address: c/o PEN American Center, 568 Broadway, New York, NY 10012, USA.

JOHNSON Norman Lloyd, b. 9 Jan 1917, Ilford, Essex, England. Retired University Professor. m. Regina Cecylia Elandt, 4 Jan 1964. Education: BS, Mathematics, 1936, BS, Statistics, 1937, MS, Statistics, 1938, PhD, Statistics, 1948, DSc, Statistics, 1963, University College, London. Appointments: Assistant Lecturer, 1938-39, 1945-46, Lecturer, 1946-56, Reader, 1956-62, University College, London; Experimental Officer, Ordnance Board, London, 1939-45; Professor of Statistics, University of North Carolina at Chapel Hill, 1962-82, Alumni Distinguished Professor, 1979-82, Retired, 1982. Publications: Statistics and Experimental Design in Engineering and Physical Sciences (with F C Leone), 1964; Distributions in Statistics: Discrete Distributions (with S Kotz), 1969; Distributions in Statistics: Continuous Univariate Distributions, 2 volumes (with S Kotz), 1970; Distributions in Statistics: Multivariate Distributions (with S Kotz), 1972; URN Models (with S Kotz), 1978; Survival Models and Data Analysis (with Regina C Elandt Johnson), 1980. Honours: Shewhart Medal, 1985; Wilks Memorial Award, 1993. Address: c/o Department of Statistics, University of North Carolina, Chapel Hill, NC 27599-3260, USA.

JOHNSON Owen Verne, b. 22 Feb 1946, Madison, Wisconsin, USA. Historian; Associate Professor. m. Marta Kucerova, 17 July 1969, 2 daughters. Education: BA, Washington State University, 1968; MA, 1970, Certificate, 1978, PhD, 1978, University of Michigan. Appointments: Sports Editor, General Assignment Reporter, Pullman Washington Herald, 1961-67; Reporter, Editor, Producer, WUOM, Ann Arbor, Michigan, 1969-77; Administrative Assistant, Russian and East European Center, University of Michigan, 1978-79; Assistant Professor, Journalism, Southern Illinois University, 1979-80; Assistant Professor, Journalism, 1980-87, Associate Professor, Journalism, 1987-, Acting Director, Polish Studies Center, 1989-90, Director, Russian and East European Institute, 1991-95, Indiana University, Bloomington; Director, Russian and East European Institute, 1991-95; Adjunct Professor, Department of History, Indiana University, 1996-. Publications: Slovakia 1918-1938: Education and the Making of a Nation, 1985. Editor: Czech Marks, 1982-84; Clio Among the Media, 1983-84; Eastern European Journalism: Before, During and After Communism, 1998. Address: School of Journalism, Indiana University, Bloomington, IN 47405, USA.

JOHNSON Paul (Bede), b. 2 Nov 1928, Barton, England. Historian; Journalist; Broadcaster. m. Marigold Hunt, 1957, 3 sons, 1 daughter. Education: BA, Magdalen College, Oxford. Appointments: Assistant Executive Editor, Realites, Paris, 1952-55; Assistant Editor, 1955-60, Deputy Editor, 1960-64, Editor, 1965-70, Director, 1965-75, New Statesman; DeWitt Wallace Professor of Communications, American Enterprise Institute, Washington, DC, 1980; Freelance Writer; Daily Mail Columnist. Publications: The Offshore Islanders, 1972; Elizabeth I: A Study in Power and Intellect, 1974; Pope John XXIII, 1975; A History of Christianity, 1976; Enemies of Society, 1977; The National Trust Book of British Castles, 1978; The Civilization of Ancient Egypt, 1978; Civilizations of the Holy Land, 1979; British Cathedrals, 1980; Ireland: Land of Troubles, 1980; The Recovery of Freedom, 1980; Pope John Paul II and the Catholic Restoration, 1982; History of the Modern World: From 1917 to the 1980s, 1984; The Pick of Paul Johnson, 1985; A History of the Jews, 1986; The Oxford Book of Political Anecdotes (editor), 1986; The Intellectuals, 1989; The Birth of the Modern World Society, 1815-30, 1991. Honours: Book of the Year Prize, Yorkshire Post, 1975; Francis Boyer Award for Services to Public Policy, 1979; Krag Award for Excellence, Literature, 1980. Memberships: Royal Commission on the Press, 1974-77; Cable Authority, 1984-. Address: 29 Newton Road, London W2, England.

JOHNSON Ronald, b. 25 Nov 1935, Ashland, Kansas, USA. Poet; Writer. Education: BA, Columbia University, 1960. Appointments: Writer-in-Residence, University of Kentucky; Roethke Chair for Poetry, University of Washington; Director, Wallace Stegner Advanced Workshop, Stanford University, 1991; Poet-in-Residence, University of California at Berkeley, 1994. Publications: A Line of Poetry, A Row of Trees, 1964; Io and the Ox-Eye Daisy, 1965; Assorted Jungles: Rousseau, 1966; GORSE/GOOSE/ROSE and Other Poems, 1966; Sun Flowers, 1966; The Book of the Green Man, 1967; The Round Earth on Flat Paper, 1968; Reading 1 and Reading 2, 1968; Valley of the Many-Coloured Grasses, 1969; Balloons for Moonless Nights, 1969; Songs of the Earth, 1970; Maze/Mane/Wane, 1973; Eyes & Objects, 1976; RADI OS I-IV, 1977; ARK: The Foundations 1-33, 1980; ARK 50: Spires 34-50, 1984; ARK, 1996. Contributions to: Many periodicals. Address: c/o Living Batch Books, 106 Cornell Drive South East, Albuquerque, NM 87108, USA.

JOHNSON (John) Stephen, b. 3 June 1947, Mansfield, England. Writer. Education: MA, 1976, DPhil, 1976, Oxford University. Publications: The Roman Fort of the Saxon Shore, 1976; Later Roman Britain, 1980; Late Roman Fortifications, 1983; Hadrian's Wall, 1989; Rome and its Empire, 1989. Address: 50 Holmdere Avenue, London SE24 9LF, England.

JOHNSON Terry, b. 20 Dec 1955, England. Dramatist; Screenwriter. Education: BA, Drama, University of Birmingham, 1976. Publications: Insignificance, 1982; Unsuitable for Adults, 1985; Tuesday's Child (with Kate Lock), 1987; Imagine Drowning, 1991. Screenplays: Insignificance, 1985; Killing Time, 1985; Way Upstream, 1987. Television Plays: Time Trouble, 1985; Tuesday's Child (with Kate Lock), 1985. Honour: Evening Standard Drama Award, 1983. Address: c/o Curtis Brown Ltd, Haymarket House, 28-29 Haymarket, London SW14 4SP, England.

JOHNSSON Esther Klara Marie, b. 3 June 1926, Copenhagen, Denmark. m. Bengt Johnsson, 25 Sept 1948, 1 daughter. Education: Certificate d'Assiduité, Cours International de Vacances, Universitié de Caen, 1965. Appointments: Avec Les Compliments du Directeur de l'Institut Français, Copenhagen, 1965. Publications: Digte, poems, Collection of Poems, 1981, 1982; Collection: Inventions; Bow and Strings, 1997. Others: Several articles, chronicles, essays, short stories and poems in Danish journals & Danish Broadcast. Membership: The Danish Writers Union. Address: Porsevaenget 18, DK-2800 Lyngby, Denmark.

JOHNSTON George (Benson), b. 7 Oct 1913, Hamilton, Ontario, Canada. Poet; Translator. m. Jeanne McRae, 1944, 3 sons, 3 daughters. Education: BA, 1936, MA, 1945, University of Toronto. Appointments: Faculty, Department of English, Mount Allison University, Sackville, New Brunswick, 1947-49, Carleton College, later University, Ottawa, 1949-79. Publications: Poetry: The Cruising Auk, 1959; Home Free, 1966; Happy Enough: Poems 1935-1972, 1972; Between, 1976; Taking a Grip, 1979; Auk Redivivus: Selected Poems, 1981; Ask Again, 1984; Endeared by Dark: The Collected Poems, 1990; What is to Come: Selected and New Poems, 1996. Prose: Carl: Portrait of a Painter, 1986. Translator: Over 10 volumes, 1963-94. Honours: Honorary doctorates. Address: PO Box 1706, Huntingdon, Quebec J0S 1H0, Canada.

JOHNSTON Jennifer, b. 12 Jan 1930, Ireland. Author; Dramatist. m. (1) Ian Smyth, 1951, 2 sons, 2 daughters, (2) David Gilliland, 1976. Publications: Fiction: The Captains and the Kings, 1972; The Gates, 1973; How Many Miles to Babylon?, 1974; Shadows on our Skin, 1978 (dramatised for TV, 1979); The Old Jest, 1979; The Invisible Worm, 1991. Plays: Nightingale and Not the Lark, 1980; Indian Summer, 1983; The Porch, 1986; The Invisible Man, 1986; The Desert Lullaby, 1996. Monologues: The Illusionist, 1995. Contributions to: BBC Radio. Honours: Honorary doctorates. Address: Brook Hall, Culmore Road, Derry BT48 8JE, Northern Ireland.

JOHNSTON Julia (Ann), b. 21 Jan 1941, Smith Falls, Ontario, Canada. Writer. m. Basil W Johnston, 12 Oct 1963, 4 daughters. Education: University of Toronto, 1963; Trent University, 1984. Publications: There's Going to be a Frost, 1979; Don't Give Up the Ghosts, 1981; Tasting the Alternative, 1982; After 30 Years of Law, Ken Starvis Sculpts New Career, 1990; Hero of Lesser Causes, 1992; The Interiors of Pots, 1992; Adam and Eve and Pinch Me, 1994. Honours: Governor-General's Literary Award, 1992; School Library Best Book, 1993; Joan Fassler Memorial Award, 1994; Ruth Schwartz Young Adult Book Award, 1995; Canadian Library Association Young Adult Book Award, 1995. Memberships: Canadian Society of Childrens Authors; Writers Union of Canada. Address: 463 Hunter Street West, Peterborough, Ontario K9H 2M7, Canada.

JOHNSTON Ronald John, b. 30 Mar 1941, Swindon, Wiltshire, England. Professor of Geography; Writer. m. Rita Brennan, 16 Apr 1963, 1 son, 1 daughter. Education: BA, 1962, MA, 1964, University of Manchester; PhD, Monash University, 1967. Appointments: Teaching Fellow, 1964, Senior Teaching Fellow, 1965, Lecturer, 1966, Monash University; Lecturer, 1967-68, Senior Lecturer, 1969-72, Reader, 1973-74, University of Canterbury, New Zealand; Professor of Geography, 1974-92, Pro-Vice Chancellor for Academic Affairs, 1989-92, University of Sheffield; Vice-Chancellor, Essex University, 1992-95; Professor of Geography, Bristol University, 1995-. Publications: Retailing in Melbourne (with P J Rimmer), 1970; Urban Residential Patterns: An Introductory Review, 1971; Spatial Structures: An Introduction to the Study of Spatial Systems in Human Geography, 1973; The New Zealanders: How They Live and Work, 1976; The World Trade System: Some Enquiries Into Its Spatial Structure, 1976; Geography and Inequality (with B E Coates and P L Knox), 1977; Multivariate Statistical Analysis in Geography: A Primer on the General Linear Model, 1978; Political, Electoral and Spatial Systems, 1979; Geography of Elections (with P J Taylor), 1979; Geography and Geographers: Anglo-American Human Geography Since 1945, 1979, 5th edition, 1997; City and Society: An Outline for Urban Geography, 1980; The Geography of Federal Spending in the United States of America, 1980; The American Urban System: A Geographical Perspective, 1982; Geography and the State, 1982; Philosophy and Human Geography: An Introduction to Contemporary Approaches, 1983, 2nd edition, 1986; Residential Segregation, the State and Constitutional Conflict in American Urban Areas, 1984; The Geography of English Politics: The 1983 General Election, 1985; On Human Geography, 1986; Bell-Ringing: The English Art of Change-Ringing, 1986; Money and Votes: Constituency Campaign Spending and Election Results, 1987; The United States: A Contemporary Human Geography (co-author), 1988; A Nation Dividing?: The Electoral Map of Great Britain, 1979-1987 (with C J Pattie and J G Allsopp), 1988; Environmental Problems: Nature, Economy and State, 1989, 2nd edition, 1996; The Dictionary of Human Geography (editor), 1989, 3rd edition, 1993; An Atlas of Bells (co-author), 1990; A Question of Place: Exploring the Practice of Human Geography, 1991. Contributions to: Various books and professional journals. Honours: Murchison Award, 1985; Victoria Medal, Royal Geographical Society, 1990; Honors Award for Distinction in Research, Association of American Geographers, 1991. Memberships: Institute of British Geographers, secretary, 1982-85, president, 1990. Address: School of Geographical Studies, Bristol University, Bristol BS8 1SS, England.

JOHNSTON William, b. 30 July 1925, Belfast, Northern Ireland. Jesuit Roman Catholic Priest; Professor of Theology; Writer. Education: Theological studies. Appointments: Ordained a Roman Catholic Priest, 1957; Professor of Theology, Sophia University, Tokyo, 1960-. Publications: The Mysticism of the Cloud of Unknowing, 1967, 2nd edition, 1975; S Endo: Silence (translator), 1969; The Still Point: On Zen and Christian Mysticism, 1970; Christian Zen, 1971; The Cloud of Unknowing and the Book of Privy Counselling (editor), 1973; Silent Music, 1974; The Inner Eye of Love, 1978; The Mirror Mind, 1981; T Nagai, The Bells of Nagasaki (translator), 1984; The Wounded Stag, 1985; Being in Love: The Practice of Christian Prayer, 1988; Letters to Contemplatives, 1991; Mystical Theology, 1995. Address: c/o S J House, 7 Kioi-Cho, Chiyodaku, Tokyo 102, Japan.

JOHNSTONE Iain Gilmour, b. 8 Apr 1943, Reading, England. Film Critic. m. Maureen Hammond, 1957, 1 son, 2 daughters. Education: LLB Honours; Distinction, Solicitor's finals. Appointment: Film Critic, The Sunday Times. Publications: The Arnhem Report, 1977; The Men With No Name, 1980; Dustin Hoffman, 1984; Cannes: The Novel, 1990; Wimbledon 2000, 1992. Address: 16 Tournay Road, London SW6, England.

JOLLEY (Monica) Elizabeth, b. 4 June 1923, Birmingham, England. Writer; Tutor. m. Leonard Jolley, 1 son, 2 daughters. Education: Nursing Training, 1940-46. Appointment: Writer-in-Residence, Western Australia Institute of Technology, later Curtin University of Technology, Perth, 1980-. Publications: Five Acre Virgin and Other Stories, 1976; The Travelling Entertainer, 1979; Palomino, 1980; The Newspaper of Claremont Street, 1981; Mr Scobie's Riddle, 1983; Woman in a Lampshade, 1983; Miss Peabody's Inheritance, 1983; Milk and Honey, 1984; The Well, 1986; The Sugar Mother, 1988; My Father's Moon, 1989; Cabin Fever, 1990; Central Mischief, 1992; The Georges' Wife, 1993; Diary of a Weekend Farmer (poems), 1993; The Orchard Thieves, 1995; Lovesong, 1997. Honours: Honorary Doctorate, Western Australia Institute of Technology, 1986; Officer of the Order of Australia, 1988; Honorary Doctor of Literature, Macquarie University, Sydney, 1995; Honorary Doctorate, University of Queensland, 1997. Literary Agent: Jenny Darling, Australian Literary Management. Address: 28 Agett Road, Claremont, Western Australia 6010, Australia.

JONAS Manfred, b. 9 Apr 1927, Mannheim, Germany. Historian. m. Mancy Jane Greene, 19 July 1952, 2 sons, 2 daughters. Education: BS, City College of New York, 1949; AM, 1951, PhD, 1959, Harvard University. Appointments: Visiting Professor for North American History, Free University of Berlin, 1959-62; Assistant Professor to Professor of History, 1963-81, Washington Irving Professor in Modern Literary and Historical Studies, 1981-86, John Bigelow Professor of History, 1986-96, Union College, Schenectady, New York, USA; Dr Otto Salgo Visiting Professor of American Studies, Eötvös Lorand University, Budapest, Hungary, 1983-84. Publications: Die Unabhängigkeitserklärung der Vereingten Staaten, 1964; Isolationism in America 1935-1941, 1966, 2nd edition, 1990; American Foreign Relations in the 20th Century, 1967; Roosevelt and Churchill: Their Secret Wartime Correspondence, 1975, 2nd edition, 1990; New Opportunities in the New Nation, 1982; The United States and Germany: A Diplomatic History, 1984. Contributions to: The Historian; Mid-America; American Studies; Maryland Historical Magazine; Essex County Historical Collections; Jahrbuch für Amerikastudien. Address: Department of History, Union College, Schenectady, NY 12308, USA.

JONES Alun Arthur Gwynne. See: CHALFONT Baron.

JONES Alys, b. 15 Sept 1944, Newborough, Anglesey, North Wales. Teacher. m. Robin Jones, 28 Apr 1973, 1 son, 1 daughter. Education: BA, Honours, University College, Bangor, North Wales. Appointments: Teacher in Welsh, Maesteg Comprehensive School, 1966-67, Manchynlleth Secondary School, Powys,

1967-70, Ysgol Dyffryn Conny, Llanrwst, 1970-73. Publications: Ysbrydion y môr, 1982; Storiau Non, 1982; Storiau Huw a'i Frindiau, 1987; Dirgelwch Neuadd Hentfordd, 1987; Mac Pync, 1987; Storiau Cornel y Cae, 1988; Yr Ysbryd Arian, 1989; Y Gadwyn, 1989; Jetsam, 1991; Straeon Cornel y Stryd, 1994; Cuthbert Caradog, 1998; Pwlyn Escapes, 1998. Contributions to: CIP. Address: Llys Alaw, 18 Ystad Eryri, Bethel, Gwynedd, North Wales.

JONES Ann (Maret), b. 3 Sept 1937, Eau Claire, Wisconsin, USA. Author; Teacher. Education: University of Vienna, 1958; BS, 1960, PhD, 1970, University of Wisconsin; MA, University of Michigan, 1961. Appointments: Assistant Professor of English, City College of the University of New York, 1970-73; Assistant Professor of English and Coordinator of Women's Studies, University of Massachusetts at Amherst, 1973-75; Senior Contributor, Kirkus Reviews, 1978-83; Visiting Professor, University of South Maine, 1985; Writer-in-Residence, Lake George Arts Council, 1986; Writing Faculty, Mount Holyoke College, 1986-97. Publications: Uncle Tom's Campus, 1973; Women Who Kill, 1980; Everyday Death: The Case of the Bernadette Powell, 1985; When Love Goes Wrong: What to Do When You Can't to Anything Right (with Susan Schechter), 1992; Next Time, She'll be Dead: Battering and How to Stop It, 1994. Contributions to: Books and periodicals. Honour: Author/Journalist of the Year, National Prisoners Rights Union, 1986. Memberships: Authors Guild; National Book Critics Circle; National Coalition Against Domestic Violence; National Writers Union; PEN. Address: c/o Charlotte Sheedy Agency, 65 Bleecker Street, New York, NY 10012, USA.

JONES Brian, b. 1938, London, England. Poet; Writer. Publications: Poems, 1966; A Family Album, 1968; Interior, 1969; The Mantis Hand and Other Poems, 1970; For Mad Mary, 1974; The Spitfire on the Northern Line, 1975; The Island Normal, 1980; The Children of Separation, 1985; Freedom John, 1990. Honours: Cholmondeley Award, 1967; Eric Gregory Award, 1968. Address: c/o Carcanet Press, 208-212 Corn Exchange Buildings, Manchester M4 3BQ, England.

JONES Christopher Dennis, b. 13 Dec 1949, New York, USA. Playwright. m. Gwendoline Shirley Rose, 18 Aug 1979. Education: BA, English Literature, University of Pittsburgh. Appointments: Resident Playwright, Carnaby Street Theatre, London, 1975-76; New Hope Theatre, London, 1977- 78. Publications: Plays: Passing Strangers, 1975; Nasty Corners, 1977; New Signals, 1978; In Flight Reunion, 1979; Sterile Landscape, 1982; Ralph Bird's River Race, 1985; Dying Hairless With a Rash, 1985; Bitter Chalice, 1987; Begging the Ring, 1989; Burning Youth, 1989. Contributions to: Country Life; Arts Review. Membership: Writer's Guild of Great Britain. Address: Peters, Fraser and Dunlop Group Ltd, 503/504 The Chambers, Chelsea Harbour, Lots Road, London SW10 0XF, England.

JONES David James. See: ANNWN David.

JONES Diana Wynne, b. 16 Aug 1934, London, England. Writer. m. J A Burrow, 22 Dec 1956, 3 sons. Education: BA, Oxford University, 1956. Publications: Wilkin's Tooth, 1973; The Ogre Downstairs, 1974; Cart and Cwidder, 1975; Dogsbody, 1975; Eight Days of Luke, 1975; Power of Three, 1976; Charmed Life, 1977; Drowned Ammet, 1977; Who Got Rid of Angus Flint?, 1978; The Spellcoats, 1979; The Magicians of Caprona, 1980; The Four Grannies, 1980; The Homeward Bounders, 1981; The Time of the Ghost, 1981; Witch Week, 1982; Archer's Goon, 1984; Warlock at the Wheel, 1984; The Skiver's Guide, 1984; Fire and Hemlock, 1985; Howl's Moving Castle, 1986; A Tale of Time City, 1987; The Lives of Christopher Chant, 1988; Chair Person, 1989; Hidden Turning (editor), 1989; Wild Robert, 1989; Castle in the Air, 1990; Black Maria, 1991; Yes Dear, 1992; A Sudden Wild Magic, 1992; The Crown of Dalemark, 1993; Hexwood, 1993; Fantasy Stories (editor), 1994; Everard's Ride, 1995; The Tough Guide to Fantasyland, 1996; Minor Arcana, 1996; Deep Secret,

1997; Dark Lord of Derkholm, 1998. Contributions to: Newspapers. Honours: Guardian Award for Children's Books, 1978; Honour Book, Boston Globe, 1984; Horn Book Award, 1986. Memberships: Society of Authors; BSFA. Address: 9 The Polygon, Bristol BS8 4PW, England.

JONES Douglas Gordon, b. 1 Jan 1929, Bancroft, Ontario, Canada. Retired Professor; Poet. Education: MA, Queen's University, Kingston, Ontario, 1954. Appointment: Professor, University of Sherbrooke, Quebec, 1963-94. Publications: Poetry: Frost on the Sun, 1957; The Sun Is Axeman, 1961; Phrases from Orpheus, 1967; Under the Thunder the Flowers Light Up the Earth, 1977; A Throw of Particles: Selected and New Poems, 1983; Balthazar and Other Poems, 1988; The Floating Garden, 1995; Wild Asterisks in Cloud, 1997. Other: Butterfly on Rock: A Study of Themes and Images in Canadian Literature, 1970. Honours: President's Medal, University of Western Ontario, 1976; Governor General's Award for Poetry, 1977, and for Translation, 1993; Honorary DLitt, Guelph University, 1982. Address: PO Box 356, North Hatley, Quebec J0B 2C0, Canada.

JONES Elwyn Ashford, b. 7 Mar 1941, Cynwyd, Wales. Teacher; Writer. Education: BEd, University of Wales, Bangor. Publications: Y Baal Barfog, 1971; Picell Mewn Cefn, 1978; Nain Ar Goll, 1986; Cicio Nyth Cacwn, 1987; Straeon Hanner Nos, 1989; Heb El Fai, 1992. Contributions to: Various magazines. Address: Pen y Ddol, Cynwyd, Corwen, Clwyd LL21 0ET, Wales.

JONES Evan (Lloyd), b. 20 Nov 1931, Preston, Victoria, Australia. Poet; Writer. m. (1) Judith Anne Dale, 1954, 1 son, (2) Margot Sanguinetti, 1966, 3 daughters. Education: BA, Honours, History, MA, History, University of Melbourne; AM, Creative Writing, Stanford University. Publications: Poetry: Inside the Whale, 1960; Understandings, 1967; Recognitions, 1978; Left at the Post, 1984; Alone at Last!, forthcoming. Other: Kenneth Mackenzie, 1969; The Poems of Kenneth Mackenzie (editor with Geoffrey Little), 1972. Contributions to: Innumerable essays and reviews in venues ranging from learned journals to newspapers, on topics ranging from literature to physics. Address: PO Box 122, North Carlton, Victoria, 3054, Australia.

JONES Frederick Malcolm Anthony, b. 14 Feb 1955, Middlesex, England. University Lecturer in Classics and Ancient History; Writer; Poet. m. Christina Jones, 2 sons. Education: BA, Classics, University of Newcastle-upon-Tyne, 1977; MA, Medieval Studies, University of Leeds, 1979; PhD, St Andrews University, 1987. Appointments: Assistant Lecturer, University of Cape Town, 1982-86; Teacher of Classics, Cobham Hall, Kent, 1987-89; Lecturer in Classics and Ancient History, University of Liverpool, 1989-. Publication: Congreve's Balsamic Elixir, 1995. Contributions to: Journals, reviews, and periodicals. Honours: 1 of 10 joint winners, Northern Poetry Competition, 1991; Felicia Hemans Prize for Lyrical Poetry, 1991. Memberships: Cambridge Philological Society; Society for the Promotion of Roman Studies. Address: c/o Department of Classics and Ancient History, University of Liverpool, Liverpool L69 3BX, England.

JONES (Morgan) Glyn, b. 28 Feb 1905, Merthyr Tydfill, Glamorgan, Wales. Teacher of English (retired); Poet; Writer; Translator. m. Phyllis Doreen Jones, 19 Aug 1935. Education: St Paul's College, Cheltenham. Appointment: Teacher of English, South Wales Schools. Publications: Poetry: Poems, 1939; The Dream of Jake Hopkins, 1954; Selected Poems, 1975; Selected Poems, Fragments and Fictions, 1988. Fiction: The Blue Bed, 1937; The Water Music, 1944; The Valley, the City, the Village, 1956; The Learning Lark, 1960; The Island of Apples, 1965; Selected Short Stories, 1977. Other: Books of criticism; Translations. Contributions to: Journals and periodicals. Honours: Honorary DLitt, University of Wales, 1974; Honorary Fellow, Trinity College, Carmarthen, Wales, 1993. Membership: Welsh Academy, fellow. Address: 158 Manor Way, Whitchurch, Cardiff CF4 1RN, Wales.

JONES Gwyn, b. 24 May 1907, Blackwood, Monmouthshire, Wales. Author. m. (1) Alice Rees, 1928, dec 1979, (2) Mair Sivell, 1979. Education: BA, 1927, MA, 1929, University of Wales. Appointments: Schoolmaster, 1929-35; Lecturer, University College of South Wales and Monmouthshire, 1935-40; Editor, Welsh Review, 1939-48; Director, Penmark Press, 1939-; Professor of English Language and Literature, 1940-64, Fellow, 1987, University College of Wales, Aberystwyth; Professor of English Language and Literature, 1965-75, Fellow, 1980, University College, Cardiff; Visiting Professor, University of Iowa, 1982. Publications: Novels: Richard Savage, 1935; Times Like These, 1936, reprint, 1979; Garland of Bays, 1938; The Green Island, 1946; The Flowers Beneath the Scythe, 1952; The Walk Home, 1962. Short Stories: The Buttercup Field, 1945; The Still Waters, 1948; Shepherd's Hey, 1953; Selected Short Stories, 1974. Non-Fiction: A Prospect of Wales, 1948; Welsh Legends and Folk-Tales, 1955; Scandinavian Legends and Folk-Tales, 1956; The Norse Atlantic Saga, 1964, new edition, 1986; A History of the Vikings, 1968, revised and enlarged, 1984; Being and Belonging, 1977; Kings, Beasts and Heroes, 1982; Background to Dylan Thomas and Other Explorations, 1992. Translator: The Vatndalers' Saga, 1942; The Mabinogion (with Thomas Jones), 1948; Egil's Saga, 1960; Eirik the Red, 1961. Editor: Short Stories, 1956; Twenty-Five Welsh Short Stories (with I Ff Elis), 1971; The Oxford Book of Welsh Verse in English, 1977; Fountains of Praise, 1983. Contributions to: Learned and literary journals. Honours: Commander of the Order of the British Empire, 1965; Christian Gauss Award, Institut International des Arts et des Lettres, 1973; Honorary DLitt, Universities of Wales, 1977, Nottingham, 1978, Southampton, 1983; Commander's Cross, Order of the Falcon, Iceland, 1987; Honorary Freeman of Islwyn, 1988. Memberships: Learned societies; Viking Society for Northern Research, president, 1950-52. Address: Castle Cottage. Sea View, Aberystwyth, Dyfed SW23 1DZ, Wales.

JONES Hettie, b. 16 July 1934, Brooklyn, New York, USA. Writer. Div, 2 daughters. Education: BA, Washington College, University of Virginia, 1955; Graduate Studies, Columbia University. Appointments: Faculty, Hunter College of the City University of New York, 1984, State University of New York, 1989-91, New School for Social Research, 1991, University of Wyoming, 1993. Publications: Longhouse Winter, 1974; Big Star Fallin' Mama, 1975; Coyote Tales, 1976; How to Eat Your ABCs, 1978; I Hate to Talk About Your Mother, 1980; How I Became Hettie Jones, 1991. Contributions to: Periodicals. Honours: Best Book for Young Adults Award, New York Public Library, 1975; Best Book of the Year Selection, New York Times, 1991. Memberships: PEN, prison writing committee; Phi Beta Kappa. Address: c/o Berenice Hoffman Literary Agency, 215 West 75th Street, New York, NY 10022, USA.

JONES Ivor Wynne, b. 28 Mar 1927, Liverpool, England. Journalist; Author; Company Director; Book Designer. m. Marion-Jeannette Wrighton, 19 July 1958, 1 son, 1 daughter. Education: BBC Engineering Training School. Appointment: Editor, Caernarvon and Denbigh Herald, 1953; Columnist, 1955-, Welsh Political Correpondent, 1969-92, Chief Welsh Correspondent, 1980-92, Liverpool Daily Post; Research Editor, Llechwedd Slate Caverns, Blaenau Ffestiniog, 1972-. Publications: Money for All, 1969; Betws-y-coed, The Mountain Resort, 1972; Shipwrecks of North Wales, 1973; Betws-y-coed and the Conway Valley, 1974; Llandudno, Queen of the Welsh Resorts, 1975; America's Secret War in Welsh Waters, 1976; Luftwaffe Over Clywd, 1977; U-Boat Rendezvous at Llandudno, 1978; Minstrels and Miners, 1986; Wales and Israel, 1988; Baden-Powell, The Welsh Dimension, 1992; The Order of St John in Wales, 1993; Colwyn Bay: A Brief History, 1995; Gold, Frankenstein and Manure, 1997; Alice in Llechweddland, 1998. Contributions to: Various historical journals. Honour: European Architectural Year Book Design Award, 1975. Memberships: Undeb Awduron Cymru (Union of Welsh Authors); Lewis Carroll Society, UK; Lewis Carroll Society of North America. Address: Pegasus, 71 Llandudno Road, Penrhyn Bay, Llandudno LL30 3HN, Wales.

JONES J Farragut. See: **LEVINSON Leonard.**

JONES Jem, b. 7 Feb 1954, New York City, USA. Writer; Evangelist; Researcher. 2 sons. Education: AB, Psychology, Douglass College. Appointments: House Chairman, by Dean's Appointment; Poet, Harlem Writers Guild. Publications: Travelin on Faith/Travelin on Credit; Veiled Truths; No Résumé at My Funeral. Contributions to: 38 states and 5 foreign countries. Honours: D. Rosenberg Award, Starr King School for the Ministry; Outstanding Young Woman of America. Membership: Highland Church; Harlem Writers Guild. Address: The Picture Poet, PO Box 23144, Hollis, NY 11423, USA.

JONES Joanna. See: **BURKE John Frederick.**

JONES John Idris, b. 9 Mar 1938. Company Director. m. Denise, 17 July 1986, 2 sons, 1 daughter. Education: BA, Keele; Certificate of Education, Leeds; MA, Cornell University. Appointments: Various teaching positions. Publications: Way Back to Ruthin; Barry Island and Other Poems; Football Match and Other Events; Revisions. Contributions to: Poetry Wales; New Welsh Review. Honours: FRSA; Welsh Academy, fellow. Address: Borthwen, Wrexham Road, Ruthin LL15 1DA, Wales.

JONES John Owain, b. 13 June 1921, Borthygest, Wales. Retired Surveyor of Customs and Excise. m. 5 May 1951, 1 daughter. Education: BA, Aberystwyth. Publications: Fuoch Chi Rioed Yn Morio, 1965; Dalfa Deg, 1967; Cam Gwag, 1971; Capten Pererin, 1979; Pleidiol Wyf Im Gwlad, 1987; Y Mor a'i Dollau, 1994. Literary Agent: Gomer Press. Address: Ardwyn, 86 Wimmerfield Crescent, Cila, Abertawe, Gorllewin Morgannwg SA2 7DB, Wales.

JONES John R(obert), (John Dalmas), b. 3 Sept 1926, Chicago, Illinois, USA. Author. m. Gail Hill, 15 Sept 1954, 1 son, 1 daughter. Education: BSc, Michigan State College, 1954; Master of Forestry, University of Minnesota, 1955; PhD, Colorado State University, 1967. Publications: The Yngling, 1969; The Varkaus Conspiracy, 1983; Touch the Stars: Emergence (with Carl Martin), 1983; Homecoming, 1984; The Scroll of Man, 1985; Fanglith, 1985; The Reality Mix, 1986; The Walkaway Clause, 1986; The Regiment, 1987; The Playmasters (with Rodney Martin), 1987; Return to Fanglith, 1987; The Lantern of God, 1987; The General's President, 1988; The Lizard War, 1989; The White Regiment, 1990; The Kalif's War, 1991; Yngling and the Circle of Power, 1992; The Orc Wars (collection), 1992; The Regiment's War, 1993; The Yngling in Yamato, 1994; The Lion of Farside, 1995; The Bavarian Gate, 1997. Contributions to: Journals and magazines. Honours: Xi Sigma Pi Forestry Honorary Society, 1953; Phi Kappa Phi Scholastic Honorary Society, 1954; Sigma Xi Scientific Research Society, 1963. Memberships: Science Fiction Writers of America; Vasa Order of America. Address: 1425 Glass Street, Spokane, WA 99206, USA.

JONES Julia, b. 27 March 1923, Liverpool, England. Writer; Dramatist. m. Edmund Bennett, 10 Oct 1950, 1 son, 1 daughter. Education: Royal Academy of Dramatic Art, London, 1946-48. Publication: The Navigators, 1986. Other: Over 50 plays for stage, film, radio and television. Honour: 1st Prize for Drama, Prague Television Festival, 1970. Memberships: Dramatist Club; Writers Guild of Great Britain. Address: c/o Jill Foster Ltd, 35 Brompton Road, London SW3 1DE, England.

JONES Kenneth Westcott, b. 11 Nov 1921, London, England. Editor; Writer. Appointments: Travel Editor, East Anglian Daily Times, 1951-93; Group Travel Correspondent, United Newspapers, 1960-83. Publications: To the Polar Sunrise, 1957; New York, 1958; America Beyond the Bronx, 1961; Great Railway Journeys of the World, 1964; Exciting Railway Journeys of the World, 1967; By Rail to the Ends of the Earth, 1970; Business Air Travellers Guide, 1970; Romantic Railways, 1971; Steam in the Landscape, 1972; Railways for Pleasure, 1981; Scenic America, 1984; Where to Go in America, 1991; Rail Tales of the Unexpected, 1992. Contributions to: Magazines. Honours: Canton of Valais Award, 1964; Thomson Travel Award Travel Writer of the Year, 1971. Memberships: British Guild of Travel Writers, chairman, 1975-76; Royal Geographical Society, fellow. Address: Hillswick, Michael Road, London SE25 6RN, England.

JONES (Everett) LeRoi, b. 7 Oct 1934, Newark, New Jersey, USA. Professor of Africana Studies; Poet; Dramatist; Writer. m. (1)Hettie Roberta Cohen, 1958, div 1965, 2 daughters, (2) Sylvia Robinson, 1967, 6 children and 2 stepdaughters. Education: Rutgers University, 1951-52; BA, English, Howard University, 1954. Appointments: Founder-Director, Yugen magazine and Totem Press, New York, 1958-62; Co-Editor, Floating Bear magazine, New York, 1961-63; Teacher, New School for Social Research, New York City, 1961-64, 1977-79, State University of New York at Buffalo, 1964, Columbia University, 1964, 1980; Founder-Director, Black Arts Repertory Theatre, Harlem, New York, 1964-66, Spirit House, Newark, 1966-; Visiting Professor, San Francisco State College, 1966-67, Yale University, 1977-78, George Washington University, 1978-79; Chair, Congress of Afrikan People, 1972-75; Assistant Professor, 1980-82, Associate Professor, 1983-84, Professor of Africana Studies, 1985-, State University of New York at Stony Brook. Publications: Poetry: April 13, 1959; Spring and Soforth, 1960; Preface to a Twenty Volume Suicide Note, 1961; The Disguise, 1961; The Dead Lecturer, 1964; Black Art, 1966; A Poem for Black Hearts, 1967; Black Magic: Collected Poetry 1961-1967, 1970; It's Nation Time, 1970; In Our Terribleness: Some Elements and Meaning in Black Style (with Billy Abernathy), 1970; Spirit Reach, 1972; African Revolution, 1973; Hard Facts, 1976; Selected Poetry, 1979; AM/TRAK, 1979; Spring Song, 1979; Reggae or Not!, 1982; Thoughts for You!, 1984; The LeRoi Jones/Amiri Baraka Reader, 1993. Plays: A Good Girl is Hard to Find, 1958; Dante, 1961; The Toilet, 1964; Dutchman, 1964; The Slave, 1964; The Baptism, 1964; Jello, 1965; Experimental Death Unit #1, 1965; A Black Mass, 1966; Arm Yrsell or Harm Yrsell, 1967; Slave Ship: A Historical Pageant, 1967; Madheart, 1967; Great Goodness of Life (A Coon Show), 1967; Home on the Range, 1968; Police, 1968; The Death of Malcolm X, 1969; Rockgroup, 1969; Insurrection, 1969; Junkies Are Full of (SHHH...), 1970; BA-RA-KA, 1972; Black Power Chant, 1972; Columbia the Gem of the Ocean, 1973; A Recent Killing, 1973; The New Ark's a Moverin, 1974; The Sidnee Poet Heroical, 1975; S-1, 1976; The Motion of History, 1977; What Was the Relationship of the Lone Ranger to the Means of Production?, 1979; At the Dim'cracker Convention, 1980; Boy and Tarzan Appear in a Clearing, 1981; Weimar 2, 1981; Money: A Jazz Opera (with George Gruntz), 1982; Primitive World, 1984; General Hag's Skeezag, 1992. Fiction: The System of Dante's Hell (novel), 1965; Tales (short stories), 1967. Other: Cuba Libre, 1961; Blues People: Negro Music in White America, 1963; Home: Social Essays, 1966; Black Music, 1968; Trippin': A Need for Change (with Larry Neal and A B Spellman), 1969; A Black Value System, 1970; Gary and Miami: Before and After, 1970; Raise Race Rays Raze: Essays Since 1965, 1971; Strategy and Tactics of a Pan African Nationalist Party, 1971; Beginning of National Movement, 1972; Kawaida Studies: The New Nationalism, 1972; National Liberation and Politics, 1974; Crisis in Boston!!!!, 1974; African Free School, 1974; Toward Ideological Clarity, 1974; The Creation of the New Ark, 1975; Selected Plays and Prose, 1979; Daggers and Javelins: Essays 1974-1979, 1984; The Autobiography of LeRoi Jones/Amiri Baraka, 1984; The Artist and Social Responsibility, 1986; The Music: Reflections on Jazz and Blues (with Amina Baraka), 1987; A Race Divided, 1991; Conversations with Amiri Baraka, 1994. Editor: Four Young Lady Poets, 1962; The Moderns: New Fiction in America, 1963; Black Fire: An Anthology of Afro-American Writing (with Larry Neal), 1968; African Congress: A Documentary of the First Modern Pan-African Congress, 1972; Confirmation: An Anthology of African American Women (with Amina Baraka), 1983. Honours: Obie Award, 1964; Guggenheim Fellowship,

1965; Yoruba Academy Fellowship, 1965; Dakar Festival Prize, 1966; Grant, 1966, Award, 1981, National Endowment for the Arts; DHL, Malcolm X College, Chicago, 1972; Rockefeller Foundation Grant, 1981; American Book Award, Before Columbus Foundation, 1984. Membership: Black Academy of Arts and Letters. Address: c/o Department of Africana Studies, State University of New York at Stony Brook, Stony Brook, NY 11794, USA.

JONES Madison Percy, b. 21 Mar 1925, Nashville, Tennessee, USA. Author; Professor of English (retired). m. Shailah McEvilley, 5 Feb 1951, 3 sons, 2 daughters. Education: BA, Vanderbilt University, 1949; MA, University of Florida, 1953. Appointments: Instructor, Miami University of Ohio, 1953-54; University of Tennessee, 1955-56; Professor of English and Writer-in-Residence, Auburn University, 1956-67. Publications: The Innocent, 1957; Forest of the Night, 1960; A Buried Land, 1963; An Exile, 1967; A Cry of Absence, 1971; Passage Through Gehenna, 1978; Season of the Stranger, 1983; Last Things, 1989; To the Winds, 1996; Nashville 1864 - the Dying of the Light, 1997. Contributions to: Journals and magazines. Honours: Sewanee Review Writing Fellowship, 1954-55; Rockefeller Foundation Fellowship, 1968; Alabama Library Association Book Award, 1968; Guggenheim Fellowship, 1973-74. Memberships: Alabama Academy of Distinguished Authors; Fellowship of Southern Writers. Address: 800 Kudena Acres, Auburn, AL 36830, USA.

JONES Malcolm Vince, b. 7 Jan 1940, Stoke-sub-Hamdon, England. Emeritus Professor of Slavonic Studies; Writer. m. Jennifer Rosemary Durrant, 27 July 1963, 1 son, 1 daughter. Education: Graduate, 1962, Postgraduate Studies, 1962-65, University of Nottingham. Appointment: Emeritus Professor of Slavonic Studies, University of Nottingham. Publications: Dostoyevsky: The Novel of Discord, 1976; New Essays on Tolstoy (editor), 1978; New Essays on Dostoyevsky (editor with Garth M Terry), 1983; Dostoyevsky After Bakhin, 1990; The Cambridge Companion to the Classic Russian Novel (editor with Robin Feuer Miller), 1998. Contributions to: Scholarly journals. Memberships: British Association for Slavonic and East European Studies, vice-president, 1988-91; British Universities' Association of Slavists, president, 1986-88; International Dostoyevsky Society, president, 1995-98. Address: c/o Department of Slavonic Studies, University of Nottingham, University Park, Nottingham NG7 2RD, England.

JONES Mervyn, b. 27 Feb 1922, London, England. Writer. Education: New York University, 1939-41. Appointments: Assistant Editor, 1955-60, Drama Critic 1958-66, Tribune; Assistant Editor, New Statesman, London, 1966-68. Publications: No Time to Be Young, 1952; The New Town, 1953; The Last Barricade, 1953; Helen Blake, 1955; Guilty Men (with Michael Foot), 1957; Suez and Cyprus, 1957; On the Last Day, 1958; Potbank, 1961; Big Two (in US as The Antagonists), 1962; Two Ears of Corn: Oxfam in Action (in US as In Famine's Shadow: A Private War on Hunger), 1965; A Set of Wives, 1965; John and Mary, 1966; A Survivor, 1968; Joseph, 1970; Mr Armitage Isn't Back Yet, 1971; Life on the Dole, 1972; Holding On (in US as Twilight of the Day), 1973; The Revolving Door, 1973; Lord Richard's Passion, 1974; Strangers, 1974; K S Karol: The Second Chinese Revolution (translator), 1974; The Pursuit of Happiness, 1975; The Oil Rush (with Fay Godwin), 1976; Scenes from Bourgeois Life, 1976; Nobody's Fault, 1977; Today the Struggle, 1978; The Beautiful Words, 1979; A Short Time to Live, 1980; Two Women and Their Men, 1982; Joanna's Luck, 1985; Coming Home, 1986; Chances, 1987; That Year in Paris, 1988; A Radical Life, 1991; Michael Foot, 1994. Address: 1 Evelyn Mansions, Carlisle Place, London SW1P 1NH, England.

JONES Owen Marshall, (Owen Marshall), b. 17 Aug 1941, Te Kuiti, New Zealand. Writer. m. Jacqueline Hill, Dec 1965, 2 daughters. Education: MA, Honours, University of Canterbury, 1964; Diploma in Teaching, Christchurch Teachers College, 1965. Publications: Supper Waltz Wilson, 1979; The Master of Big Jingles,

1982; The Day Hemingway Died, 1984; The Lynx Hunter, 1987; The Divided World, 1989; Tomorrow We Save the Orphans, 1991; A Many Coated Man, 1995; Coming Home in the Dark, 1995; The Best of Owen Marshall, 1997. Contributions to: Numerous magazines and journals. Honours: New Zealand Literary Fund Scholarship in Letters, 1988; Robert Burns Fellowship, 1992; Katherine Mansfield Fellowship in Menton, France, 199. Address: 10 Morgans Road, Timaru, New Zealand.

JONES Richard (Andrew III), b. 8 Aug 1953, London, England. Professor of English; Poet; Writer; Editor. Education: BA, English, 1975, MA, English, 1976, University of Virginia; MFA, Poetry, Vermont College, 1987. Appointments: Production Editor, CBS Books, 1978-80; Editor, Poetry East, 1979-, Scandinavian Review, 1982-83; Adjunct Faculty, Piedmont College, 1981-82; Director of Publications, American-Scandinavian Foundation, 1982-83; Lecturer, University of Virginia, 1982-86; Teaching Fellow, Vermont College, 1985-87; Assistant Professor, Ripon College, 1986-87; Professor of English, DePaul University, 1987-. Publications: Windows and Walls, 1982; Innocent Things, 1985; Walk On, 1986; Country of Air, 1986; Sonnets, 1990; At Last We Enter Paradise, 1991; A Perfect Time, 1994; The Abandoned Garden, 1997; 48 Questions, 1998; The Stone It Lives On, 1999; New and Collected Poems: 1980-2000, 2000. Editor: Of Solitude and Silence: Writings on Robert Bly (with Kate Daniels), 1982; Poetry and Politics, 1984; The Inward Eye: The Photographs of Ed Roseberry (with S Margulies), 1986; The Last Believer in Words, 1998. Contributions to: Numerous publications. Honours: Many grants; Swedish Writers Union Excellence Prize, 1982; Coordinating Council of Literary Magazines Editors Award, 1985, and Citation of Special Commendation, 1988; Posner Award for Best Book of Poetry, Council for Wisconsin Writers, 1986; Illinois Artists Fellowship, 1990-91; Illinois Arts Council Awards, 1991, 1995, 1996, 1997. Memberships: Coordinating Council of Literary Magazines; Poetry Society of America. Address: c/o Department of English, DePaul University, 802 West Belden Avenue, Chicago, IL 60614, USA.

JONES Robert C, b. 7 Apr 1936, Detroit, Michigan, USA. Writer; Columnist. Education: Diploma, Technical High School, 1954; Associate Engineering School, Diploma, 1957; College, BS, 1967; Post degree courses. Contributions to: Reader's Digest Magazine; Concepts Magazine; Newspaper Columns; MPathy (Mensa Magazine). Membership: Society of the Black Bull. Address: 353 Lysander, Rochester, MI 48307-1526, USA.

JONES Robert Gerallt Hamlet, b. 11 Sept 1934, Nefyn, Gwynedd, Wales. Writer; Poet; Editor. m. Susan Lloyd Griffith, 15 Sept 1962, 2 sons, 1 daughter. Education: BA, 1954, MA, 1956, University College of North Wales. Appointments: Creative Writing Fellow, University of Wales, 1976-78; Senior Lecturer in Welsh Studies, University College, Aberystwyth, 1979-89; Editor, Taliesin, Welsh Academy Quarterly, 1988-, Books From Wales, 1992-. Publications: Over 35 books, including novels, poetry and criticism, many in Welsh. Honours: Prose Medals, National Eisteddfod of Wales, 1977, 1979; Hugh McDiarmid Award, 1984; Welsh Arts Council Poetry Award, 1990. Memberships: Wales Film Council, chairman, 1992-; Welsh Academy, chairman, 1982-87. Address: c/o Welsh Academy, Mount Stuart House, 3rd Floor, Mount Stuart Square, Cardiff CF1 6DQ, Wales.

JONES Robert Maynard, b. 20 May 1929, Cardiff, Wales. Professor Emeritus. m. Anne Elizabeth (James), 27 Dec 1952, 1 son, 1 daughter. Education: BA First Class, 1949, MA, 1951, PhD, 1965, DLitt, 1979, University of Wales, Cardiff. Appointments: Lecturer, Trinity College Carmarthen, 1956-58; Lecturer, University of Wales, Aberystwyth, 1959-67 (Senior Lecturer, Reader, 1967-79); Professor of Welsh and Head of Department, 1980-89. Publications: Y Gân Gyntaf, 1956; Nid yŵ Dŵr Yn Plygu, 1958; Rhwng Taf A Thaf, 1960; Allor Wydn, 1971; Tafod Y Llenor, 1974; Llên Cymru A Chrefydd, 1977; Seiliau Beirniadaeth, 1984-85; Hunllef

Arthur, 1986; Llenyddiaeth Gymraeg, 1902-1936, 1987; Casgliad o Gerddi, 1989; Crio Chwerthin, 1990; Cyfriniaeth Gymraeg, 1994; Canu Arnaf, 1994, 1995; Ysbryd Y Cwlwm, 1998; Ynghylch Tawelwch, 1998; Tair Rhamant Arthuraidd, 1998; Or Bedd ir Crud, 1999. Honours: Welsh Arts Council Prizes, 1956, 1959, 1971, 1987, 1990; FBA, 1992. Membership: Chairman, Yr Academi Gymreig, 1975-79. Address: Tandderwen, Ffordd Llanbadarn, Aberystwyth, SY23 1HB, Wales.

JONES Rodney, b. 11 Feb 1950, Hartselle, Alabama, USA. Poet; Writer. m. (1) Virginia Kremza, 1972, div 1979, (2) Gloria Nixon de Zepeda, 21 June 1981, 2 children. Education: BA, University of Alabama, 1971; MFA, University of North Carolina at Greensboro, 1973. Publications: Going Ahead, Looking Back, 1977; The Story They Told Us of Light, 1980; The Unborn, 1985; Transparent Gestures, 1989; Apocalyptic Narrative and Other Poems, 1993. Contributions to: Periodicals. Honours: Lavan Younger Poets Award, Academy of American Poets, 1986; Younger Writers Award, General Electric Foundation, 1986; Jean Stein Prize, American Academy and Institute of Arts and Letters, 1989; National Book Critics Circle Award, 1989. Memberships: Associated Writing Programs; Modern Language Association. Address: c/o Houghton Mifflin Co, 222 Berkeley Street, Boston, MA 02116, USA.

JONES Sally Roberts, b. 30 Nov 1935, London, England. Author; Publisher. Education: BA, University College of North Wales, 1957; ALA, North-Western Polytechnic, 1964. Appointments: Senior Assistant, Reference Library, London Borough of Havering, 1964-67; Reference Librarian, Borough of Port Talbot, Wales, 1967-70; Publisher, Alun Books, 1977-. Publications: Turning Away, 1969; Elen and the Goblin, 1977; The Forgotten Country, 1977; Books of Welsh Interest, 1977; Allen Raine, 1979; Relative Values, 1985; The History of Port Talbot, 1991; Pendaruis, 1992. Honour: Welsh Arts Council Literature Prize, 1970. Memberships: Welsh Academy, chairman, 1993-97; Afan Poetry Society; Welsh Union of Writers; Port Talbot Historical Society. Address: 3 Crown Street, Port Talbot SA13 1BG, Wales.

JONES Volcano. See: MITCHELL Adrian.

JONG Erica Mann, b. 26 Mar 1942, NY, USA. Author; Poet. m. Kenneth David Burrows, 1 daughter. Education: BA, Barnard College, 1963; MA, Columbia University, 1965. Appointments: Faculty, English Department, CUNY, 1964-65; Overseas Division of Maryland, 1969-70; Member, Literary Panel, NY State Council on Arts, 1972-74; Faculty Bread Loaf Writers Conference, Middlesex, VT, USA, 1982; Mbr, Faculty Salzburg Seminar, Salzburg, Austria, 1993. Publications: Author: (poems) Fruits and Vegetables, 1971, reissued, 1997; Half Lives, 1973; Loveroot, 1975; At the Edge of the Body, 1979; Ordinary Miracles, 1983; Becoming Light: Poems New and Selected, 1992; (Novels) Fear of Flying, 1973; How to Save Your Own Life, 1977; Fanny: Being the True History of Fanny Hackabout-Jones, 1980; Parachutes and Kisses, 1984; Serenissima, 1987, reissued as Shylock. Honours: Woodrow Wilson Fellow; Recipient Bess Hokin Prize Poetry Magazine, 1971; Named Mother of the Year, 1982; National Endowment Arts Grantee, 1973. Literary Agent: Ed Victor Ltd. Address: 6 Bayley St, Bedford Square, London WC1B 3HB, England.

JÓNSSON Elias Snaeland, b. 8 Jan 1943, Iceland. Journalist; Author. m. Brynjulfsdottir, Anna Kristin, 24 June 1967, 3 sons. Education: Samvinnuskolinn, 1962. Publications: Novels: Davíd og Krókódílarnir, 1991; Brak og brestir, 1993; Haltu mér fast, 1994; Krókódílar gráta ekki, 1995; Draumar undir gaddavír, 1996; Töfradalurinn, 1997; Návígi á hualaslód, 1998. Plays: Myrkraverk, 1996; Non-Fiction: Aldarspegill - Atök milli Strida, 1984; Aldarspegill - Undir högg ad saekja, 1985; Lydveldid Island 50 ára, 1994. Honour: Iceland Childrens Literature Prize, 1993. Membership: National Union of Icelandic Writers. Literary Agent: Vaka-Helgafell, Sidumula 6, 108

Reykjavík, Iceland. Address: Brekkutun 18, 200 Képavogur, Iceland.

JONTY. See: **DRIVER Charles Jonathan.**

JOOS Steven L, b. 7 Feb 1955, USA. Sportswriter; Poet. Education: BSc, Bradley University, 1978. Appointments: Staff, F M Havana, Illinois, 1979-88; Reporter, Times-Advocate, West Salem, 1988-89; Sports Editor, Posey County News, 1989-. Contributions to: Weekend Journal; Moments, Moods and Memories; Sparrowgrass; Poetry Forum. Membership: Press Association. Address: PO Box 372, Poseyville, IN 47633, USA.

JORDAN June, b. 9 July 1936, New York, New York, USA. Professor of African-American Studies; Poet; Writer. m. Michael Meyer, 5 Apr 1955, div 1966, 1 son. Education: Barnard College, 1953-55, 1956-57; University of Chicago, 1955-56. Appointments: Faculty, City College of the City University of New York, 1967-69, Sarah Lawrence College, 1969-70, 1973-74; Professor of English, State University of New York at Stony Brook, 1978-79; Visiting Poet-in-Residence, MacAlester College, 1980; Chancellor's Distinguished Lecturer, 1986, Professor of Afro-American Studies and Women's Studies, 1989-93, Professor of African-American Studies, 1994-, University of California at Berkeley; Playwright-in-Residence, 1987-88, Poet-in-Residence, 1988, New Dramatists, New York City; Visiting Professor, University of Wisconsin at Madison, 1988; Poet-in-Residence, Walt Whitman Birthplace Association, 1988; Professor of Education, University of California at Berkeley. Publications: Who Look at Me, 1969; Soulscript, 1970; The Voice of the Children, 1970; Fannie Lou Hamer, 1971; His Own Where, 1971; Dry Victories, 1972; New Days: Poems of Exile and Return, 1974; New Life: New Room, 1975; Passion: New Poems 1977-80, 1980; Civil Wars: Selected Essays 1963-80, 1981; Kimako's Story, 1981; Things I Do in the Dark: Selected Poems 1954-77, 1981; Living Room: New Poems 1980-84, 1985; On Call: New Political Essays, 1981-85, 1985; Lyrical Campaigns: Selected Poems, 1989; Moving Towards Home: Selected Political Essays, 1989; Naming Our Destiny: New and Selected Poems, 1989; Technical Difficulties: New Political Essays, 1992; The Haruko/Love Poetry of June Jordan, 1993. Other: I Was Looking at the Ceiling and Then I Saw the Sky, 1995; Affirmative Acts: New Political Essays, 1998; Portrait of the Poet as a Little Black Girl, forthcomng. Contributions to: Professional journals and magazines. Honours: Rockefeller Foundation Grant, 1969; Prix de Rome, 1970; CAPS Grant in Poetry, 1978; Yaddo Fellow, 1979, 1980; National Endowment for the Arts Fellowship, 1982; Achievement Award for International Reporting, National Association of Black Journalists, 1984; New York Foundation for the Arts Fellowship, 1985; MADRE Award for Leadership, 1989; Freedom to Write Award, PEN West, 1991; Lila Wallace-Reader's Digest Writers Award, 1995; Lifetime Achievement Award, National Black Writers' Conference, 1998. Memberships: American Writers Congress; PEN American Center; Poets and Writers. Address: Department of Education, University of California at Berkeley, Berkeley, CA 94720, USA.

JORDAN Leonard. See: **LEVINSON Leonard.**

JORDAN Neil Patrick, b. 25 Feb 1950, Sligo, Ireland. Author; Director. 3 sons, 2 daughters. Education: BA, 1st Class Honours, History/English Literature, University College, Dublin, 1972. Appointment: Co-Founder, Irish Writers Cooperative, Dublin, 1974. Publications: Night in Tunisia, 1976; The Past, 1979; The Dream of a Beast, 1983; The Past, 1979; Sunrise with Sea Monster, 1995. Films as a Director: Angel, 1982; Company of Wolves, 1984; Mona Lisa, 1986; High Spirits, 1988; We're No Angels, 1989; The Miracle, 1990; The Crying Game, 1992; Interview With the Vampire, 1994; Michael Collins, 1995; The Butcher Boy, 1996. Honours: Guardian Fiction Prize, 1979; Los Angeles Film Critics Award, 1986; New York Film Critics Award, 1986; London Critics Circle Award, 1986; Oscar, 1992; Golden Lion, Venice Film Festival, 1997; Silver Bear, Berlin Film Festival, 1998. Address: c/o Jenne Casarotto Co Ltd, National House, 60-66 Wardour Street, London W1V 3HP, England.

JOSEPH Jenny, b. 7 May 1932, Birmingham, England. Writer; Poet; Lecturer. m. C A Coles, 29 Apr 1961, dec 1985, 1 son, 2 daughters. Education: BA, Honours, English, St Hilda's College, Oxford, 1953. Publications: The Unlooked-for Season, 1960; Warning, 1961; Boots, 1966; Rose in the Afternoon, 1974; The Thinking Heart, 1978; Beyond Descartes, 1983; Persephone, 1986; The Inland Sea, 1989; Beached Boats, 1991; Selected Poems, 1992; Ghosts and Other Company, 1995; Extended Smiles, 1997. Other: 6 children's books. Contributions to: Anthologies and magazines. Honours: Eric Gregory Award, 1962; Cholmondeley Award, 1974; Arts Council of Great Britain Award, 1975; James Tait Black Award for Fiction, 1986; Society of Authors Travelling Scholarship, 1995; Forward Prize, 1995. Memberships: Centre for the Spoken Word, patron; National Poetry Society of Great Britain, council, 1975-78. Literary Agent: John Johnson Ltd, London, England. Address: 17 Windmill Road, Minchinhampton, Gloucestershire GL6 9DX, England.

JOSEPHY Alvin M Jr, b. 18 May 1915, Woodmere, New York, USA. Author; Editor. m. Elizabeth C Peet, 13 Mar 1948, 1 son, 3 daughters. Education: Harvard University, 1932-34. Appointments: Reporter and Correspondent, New York Herald-Tribune, 1937-38; Staff, WOR-Mutual Radio, New York City, 1938-42, Radio Bureau, Office of War Information, Washington, DC, 1942-43; Screenwriter, Metro-Goldwyn-Mayer Studios, Culver City, California, 1945-51; Associate Editor, Time magazine, 1951-60; Vice-President and Senior Editor, American Heritage Books, 1960-76; Editor, 1976-78, Editor-in-Chief, 1978-79, American Heritage magazine. Publications: The US Marines on Iwo Jima (co-author), 1945; The Long, the Short and the Tall: The Story of a Marine Combat Unit in the Pacific, 1946; Uncommon Valor (co-author), 1946; The American Heritage Book of the Pioneer Spirit (co-author), 1959; The Patriot Chiefs: A Chronicle of American Indian Leadership, 1961; Chief Joseph's People and Their War, 1964; The Nez Perce Indians and the Opening of the Northwest, 1965; The American Heritage Pictorial Atlas of United States History (co-author), 1966; The Artist Was a Young Man, 1970; Red Power: The American Indians' Fight for Freedom, 1971; The Pictorial History of the American Indian (revised edition of the book by Oliver La Farge), 1974; History of the Congress of the United States, 1975; Black Hills, White Sky, 1979; On the Hill, 1979; Now That the Buffalo's Gone: A Study of Today's American Indians, 1982; The Civil War in the American West, 1991; 500 Nations, 1994. Editor: The American Heritage Book of Indians, 1961; The American Heritage History of Flight, 1962; The American Heritage Book of Natural Wonders, 1962; The American Heritage History of World War I, 1964; The American Heritage History of the Great West, 1965; RFK: His Life and Death, 1968; The Horizon History of Africa, 1971; The American Heritage History of Business and Industry, 1972; The Horizon History of Vanishing Primitive Man, 1973; The Law in America, 1974; The Cold War, 1982; America in 1492, 1992. Contributions to: Many books, newspapers and magazines. Honours: National Cowboy Hall of Fame and Western Heritage Center Awards, 1961, 1965; Gold Spur and Golden Saddleman Awards, Western Writers of America, 1965; New York Westerners Buffalo Awards, 1965, 1968; National Award of Merit, American Association for State and Local History, 1966; Guggenheim Fellowship, 1966-67; National Magazine Award for Excellence in Reporting, 1976; Charles E S Wood Award, Oregon Institute of Literary Arts, 1993; Wallace Stegner Award, Century of the American West, Colorado, 1995; Governor's Arts Award, Oregon, 1996. Memberships: American Antiquarian Society; Association on American Indian Affairs; Institute of the American West; Institute of the North American West; New York Westerners; US Capitol Historical Association; Western History Association, president, 1993-94; National Museum of the American Indian, Smithsonian Institution, founding chairman, 1990-93. Address: 4 Kinsman Lane, Greenwich, CT 06830, USA.

JOSET Jacques, b. 10 July 1943, Liège, Belgium. Professor University. m. Yolanda Montalvo-Aponte, 1 daughter. Education: Doctor of Philosophy and Literatures, University of Liège, Belgium, 1970. Appointments: Professor, University of Antwerp, 1972; Professor, University of Liège, 1990. Publications: La Littérature Hispano-Américaine, 1979; Les Geôles de Papier, 1971; Nuevas Investigaciones Sobre El Libro De Buen Amor, 1988; Gabriel García Márquez: Coetáneo de la Eternidad, 1984; Historias Cruzadas De Novelas Hispanoamericanas, 1995; G García Márquez, Cien Años De Soledad, J Joset, editor, 1997. Honour: Orden de Andrés Bello, 1996. Memberships: Vice President, Asociación International De Hispanistas, 1998. Address: Quai Mativa 54/082 - 4020 Liege, Belgium.

JOSIPOVICI Gabriel David, b. 8 Oct 1940, Nice, France. Professor of English; Writer; Dramatist. Education: BA, Honours, 1st Class, St Edmund Hall, Oxford, 1961. Publications: Novels: The Inventory, 1968; Migrations, 1977; The Air We Breath, 1981; Contre-Jour, 1986; The Big Glass, 1990; In a Hotel Garden, 1993; Moo Pak, 1994; Now, 1998. Essays: The World and the Book, 1971; The Book of God: A Response to the Bible, 1988; Text and Voice, 1992; Touch, 1996; NOw, 1998. Contributions to: Encounter; New York Review of Books; London Review of Books; Times Literary Supplement. Honours: BBC nominations for Italia Prize, 1977, 1989; Lord Northcliffe Lectures, University of London, 1981; Lord Weidenfeld Visiting Professor of Comparative Literature, University of Oxford, 1996-97; Fellow of the Royal Society of Literature, 1997. Address: 60 Prince Edwards Road, Lewes, Sussex, England.

JOUDRY Patricia, b. 18 Oct 1921, Spirit River, Canada. Playwright; Novelist. m. (1) Delmar Dinsdale, div 1952, 2 daughters, (2) John Steele, div 1975, 3 daughters. Publications: Script Writings: Henry Aldrich Show; Penny's Diary. Other Works: The Sand Castle (comedy); Three Rings for Michele (play); The Song of Louise in the Morning (one act drama); Stranger in My House (play); Walk Alone Together (comedy); Valerie (comedy); Don The Dinted Armour (comedy); God Goes Heathen (drama); Think Again (comedy); Now (science fiction, multi-media drama), 1970; I Ching (drama), 1971; The Dweller on the Threshold (novel), 1973; And the Children Played (non-fiction), 1975; Spirit River to Angels' Roost (non-fiction), 1977; The Selena Tree (novel), 1980; A Very Modest Orgy (play), 1981; Sound Therapy for the Walk Man (non-fiction), 1984; Twin Souls (with Maurie D Pressman, non-fiction), 1993. Honours: Prize, Stratford-Globe Playwriting Competition and London West End, 1959. Address: PO Box 105, Lund, British Columbia V0N 2G0, Canada.

JOY David (Anthony Welton), b. 14 June 1942, Ilkley, England. Writer; Editor. Education: Leeds College of Commerce, 1961-62. Appointments: General Reporter, Yorkshire Post Newspapers, 1962-65; Editorial Assistant, 1965-70, Books Editor, 1970-88, Editor, 1988-93, Dalesman Publishing Co Ltd; Managing Editor, Atlantic Transport Publishers, 1995-. Publications: Settle-Carlisle Railway (with W R Mitchell), 1966; Main Line Over Shap, 1967; Cumbrain Coast Railways, 1968; Whitby-Pickering Railway, 1969; Railways in the North, 1970; Traction Engines in the North, 1970; George Hudson of York (with A J Peacock), 1971; Railways of the Lake Countries, 1973; Regional History of the Railways of Great Britain: South and West Yorkshire, 1975; Railways in Lancashire, 1975; Settle-Carlisle Centenary, 1975; Railways of Yorkshire: The West Riding, 1976; North Yorkshire Moors Railway (with P Williams), 1977; Steam on the North York Moors, 1978; Yorkshire Railways (with A Haigh), 1979; Steam on the Settle and Carlisle, 1981; Yorkshire Dales Railway, 1983; Settle-Carlisle in Colour, 1983; Regional History of the Railways of Great Britain: The Lake Countries, 1984; Portrait of the Settle: Carlisle, 1984; Yorkshire Dales in Colour, 1985; The Dalesman: A Celebration of 50 Years, 1989; Life in the Yorkshire Coalfield, 1989; Settle-Carlisle Celebration, 1990; Best Yorkshire Tales, 1991; Uphill to Paradise, 1991; Yorkshire's Christmas, 1992; The Dalesman Bedside Book, 1993; Yorkshire's Farm Life, 1994; Railways in

Your Garden, 1995; Painters of the Dlaes, 1997. Address: Hole Bottom, Hebden, Skipton, North Yorkshire BD23 5D1, England.

JOYAUX Philippe. See: **SOLLERS Philippe.**

JOYCE Graham, b. 22 Oct 1954, Keresley, Coventry. Author. m. Suzanne Lucy Johnsen, 6 May 1988, 1 daughter. Education: MA, BEd, Cert Ed, Leicester University. Publications: Dreamside, 1991; Dark Sister, 1992; House of Lost Dreams, 1993; Requiem, 1995; The Tooth Fairy, 1996; The Stormwatcher, 1998. Honours: Derleth Award, 1993, 1996, 1997. Membership: Society of Authors. Literary Agent: Lugi Bonomi. Address: c/o Sheil Land Associates, 43 Doughty St, London WC1N 2LF, England.

JUDD Denis (O'Nan), b. 28 Oct 1938, Byfield, Northamptonshire, England. Historian; Writer. m. Dorothy Woolf, 10 July 1964, 3 sons, 1 daughter. Education: BA, Honours, Modern History, Oxford University, 1961; PGCEd, 1962, PhD, 1967, London University. Publications: Balfour and the British Empire, 1968; The Boer War, 1977; Radical Joe: Joseph Chamberlain, 1977; Prince Philip, 1981; Lord Reading, 1982; Alison Uttley, 1986; Jawaharlal Nehru, 1993; Empire: The British Imperial Experience, 1996; 2 novels/books and stories for children; Other history books and biographies. Contributions to: History Today; History; Journal of Imperial and Commonwealth History; Literary Review; Daily Telegraph; New Statesman; International Herald Tribune; Independent. Honours: Fellow, Royal Historical Society, 1977; Awarded Professorship, 1990. Literary Agent: Bruce Hunter at David Higham Associates. Address: 20 Mount Pleasant Road, London NW10 3EL, England.

JUDSON John, b. 9 Sept 1930, Stratford, Connecticut, USA. Educator; Editor; Writer; Poet. Education: AB, Colby College, 1958; University of Maine, 1962-63; MFA, University of Iowa, 1965. Appointments: Editor, Juniper Press, Northeast/Juniper Books, literary magazine and chapbook series, 1961-; Professor of English, University of Wisconsin, La Crosse, 1965-93. Publications: Two from Where It Snows (co-author), 1963; Surreal Songs, 1968; Within Seasons, 1970; Voyages to the Inland Sea, 6 volumes, 1971-76; Finding Worlds in Winter; West of Burnam South of Troy, 1973; Ash Is the Candle's Wick, 1974; Roots from the Onion's Dark, 1978; A Purple Tale, 1978; North of Athens, 1980; Letters to Jirac II, 1980; Reasons Why I Am Not Perfect, 1982; The Carrabassett Sweet William Was My River, 1982; Suite for Drury Pond, 1989; Muse(sic), 1992; The Inardo Poems, 1996. Address: 1310 Shorewood Drive, La Crosse, WI 54601, USA.

JUERGENSEN Hans, b. 17 Dec 1919, Myslowitz, Germany (US citizen). Professor of Humanities Emeritus; Poet; Writer; Editor; Graphic Artist. m. Ilse Dina Loebenberg, 27 Oct 1945, 1 daughter. Education: BA, Upsala College, New Jersey, 1942; PhD, Johns Hopkins University, 1951. Appointments: Instructor, University of Kansas, Lawrence, 1951-53; Assistant Professor to Associate Professor of English, Quinnipiac College, Hamden, Connecticut, 1953-61; Lecturer in Humanities, 1958-61, Acting Dean, 1960-61, Silvermine College of Art; Co-Editor, Orange Street Poetry Journal, 1958-62, University of South Florida Language Quarterly, 1961-74; Assistant Professor, 1961-63, Associate Professor, 1963-68, Professor of Humanities, 1968-92, Professor Emeritus, 1992-, University of South Florida, Tampa; Editor, Gryphon, 1974-89; Member, Nominating Committee, Nobel Prize for Literature, 1975-80. Publications: I Feed You From My Cup, 1958; In Need for Names, 1961; Existential Canon, and Other Poems, 1965; Florida Montage, 1966; Sermons from the Ammunition Hatch of the Ship of Fools, 1968; From the Divide, 1970; Hebraic Modes, 1972; Children's Poetry Anthology (editor), 1975; Journey Toward the Roots, 1976; California Frescoes, 1980; General George H Thomas: A Summary in Perspective, 1980; The Record of a Green Planet, 1982; Fire-Tested, 1983; Beachheads and Mountains: Campaigning from Sicily to Anzio: A

Journal, 1986; Roma, 1987; Testimony: Selected Poems, 1954-1986, 1989. Contributions to: Anthologies and other publications. Honours: Florida Poet of the Year Award, 1965; Award for Services to American Literature, Hayden Library, Arizona State University, 1970; Stephen Vincent Benet Awards, 1970, 1974; Special Arts Award, State of Florida, 1980. Memberships: Academy of American Poets; International Poetry Society, fellow; National Federation of State Poetry Societies, president, 1968-70; Poetry Society of America; Poetry Society of Florida. Address: 7815 Pine Hill Drive, Tampa, FL 33610, USA.

JULIAN Jane. See: **WISEMAN David.**

JUNKINS Donald (Arthur), b. 19 Dec 1931, Saugus, Massachusetts, USA. Poet; Writer; Professor. m. (1), 2 sons, 1 daughter, (2) Kaimei Zheng, 18 Dec 1993, 1 stepson. Education: BA, University of Massachusetts, 1953; STB, 1956, STM, 1957, AM, 1959, PhD, 1963, Boston University. Appointments: Instructor, 1961-62, Assistant Professor, 1962-63, Emerson College, Boston; Assistant Professor, Chico State College, California, 1963-66; Assistant Professor, 1966-69, Associate Professor, 1969-74, Director, Master of Fine Arts Program in English, 1970-78, 1989-90, Professor of English, 1974-95, Professor Emeritus, 1995-, University of Massachusetts, Amherst. Publications: The Sunfish and the Partridge, 1965; The Graves of Scotland Parish, 1969; Walden, One Hundred Years After Thoreau, 1969; And Sandpipers She Said, 1970; The Contemporary World Poets (editor), 1976; The Uncle Harry Poems and Other Maine Reminiscences, 1977; Crossing By Ferry: Poems New and Selected, 1978; The Agamenticus Poems, 1984; Playing for Keeps: Poems, 1978-1988, 1989; Andromache, by Euripides (translator), 1998; Journey to the Corrida, 1998; Lines from Bimini Waters, 1998; Contributions to: Longman Anthology of American Poetry: Colonial to Contemporary; reviews, journals and magazines. Honours: Bread Loaf Writers Conference Poetry Scholarship, 1959; Jennie Tane Award for Poetry, 1968; John Masefield Memorial Award, 1973; National Endowment for the Arts Fellowships, 1974, 1979. Memberships: PEN; Hemingway Society; Fitzgerald Society. Address: 63 Hawks Road, Deerfield, MA 01342, USA.

JUNOD Jean-Michel, b. 2 May 1916, Corgemont, Switzerland. Surgeon. m. Yolene Thomet, 9 Oct 1954, 3 sons, 1 daughter. Education: Universities of Neuchatel, Lausanne, Berlin, Germany. Appointment: Chief of Surgery, Bienne, Beer Shera, Dacca. Publications: Le Blé de la Mer; Si la Tour m'appelle; Iris et les mirages; Archipel; Pindari; La Poudre d'escampette; Le Cone-Elisabeth; Le Mont de Vénus. Honour: Prix Cesase Pavese. Membership: Société des Ecrivains Suisses. Literary Agent: Editions L'Age d'Homme, Lausanne. Address: Editions L'Age d'Homme, 10 route de Genève, Lausanne, Switzerland.

JUST Ward (Swift), b. 5 Sept 1935, Michigan City, Indiana, USA. Writer. Education: Lake Forest Academy, Illinois, 1949-51; Cranbrook School, Michigan, 1951-53; Trinity College, Hartford, Connecticut, 1953-57. Appointments: Reporter, Waukegan News-Sun, Illinois, 1957-59; Reporter, 1962-63, Correspondent, 1963-65, Newsweek magazine; Correspondent, Washington Post, 1965-70. Publications: To What End: Report from Vietnam, 1968; A Soldier of the Revolution, 1970; Military Men, 1970; The Congressmen Who L:oved Flaubert and Other Washington Stories, 1973; Stringer, 1974; Nicholson at Large, 1975; A Fmily Trust, 1978; Honor, Power, Riches, Fame and the Love of Women, 1979; In the City of Fear, 1982; The American Blues, 1984; The American Ambassador, 1987; Jack Glance, 1989; Twenty-One Selected Stories, 1990; The Translator, 1991; Ambition and Love, 1994; Echo House, 1997. Contributions to: Anthologies and periodicals. Honours: O Henry Awards, 1985, 1986; Berlin Prize Fellowship, 1998. Address: Vineyard Haven, MA 02568, USA.

JUSTICE Donald (Rodney), b. 12 Aug 1925, Miami, Florida, USA. Professor (retired); Poet; Writer. m. Jean Catherine Ross, 22 Aug 1947, 1 son. Education: BA,

University of Miami, 1945; MA, University of North Carolina, 1947; Postgraduate Studies, Stanford University, 1948-49; PhD, University of Iowa, 1954. Appointments: Instructor, University of Miami, 1947-51; Assistant Professor, Hamline University, 1956-57; Lecturer, 1957-60, Assistant Professor, 1960-63, Associate Professor, 1963-66, Professor, 1971-82, University of Iowa; Professor, Syracuse University, 1966-70, University of Florida at Gainesville, 1982-92. Publications: Poetry: The Summer Anniversaries, 1960; Night Light, 1967; Departures, 1973; Selected Poems, 1979; The Sunset Maker, 1987; A Donald Justice Reader, 1992; New and Selected Poems, 1995. Other: The Collected Poems of Weldon Kees (editor), 1962; Platonic Scripts (essays), 1984; Oblivion: On Writers and Writing, 1998; Orpheus Hesitated Beside the Black River, 1998. Contributions to: Journals and magazines. Honours: Rockefeller Foundation Fellowship, 1954; Lamont Award, 1959; Ford Foundation Fellowship, 1964; National Endowment for the Arts Grants, 1967, 1973, 1980, 1989; Guggenheim Fellowship, 1976; Pulitzer Prize in Poetry, 1980; Academy of American Poets Fellowship, 1988; Co-Winner, Bollingen Prize, 1991; Lannan Literary Award, 1996. Memberships: Academy of American Poets, board of chancellors, 1997-; American Academy of Arts and Letters. Address: 338 Rocky Shore Drive, Iowa City, IA 52246, USA.

JUSTICIAR. See: **POWELL-SMITH Vincent.**

JUTEAU Monique, b. 8 Jan 1949, Montreal, Quebec, Canada. Poet; Author; University Teacher. Education: MA, French Literature, 1987. Appointments: Teacher, University of Quebec, Trois-Rivières, 1987-. Publications: Poetry: La Lune Aussi, 1975; Regard Calligraphes, 1986; Trop Plein D'Angles, 1990; Des jours de chemins perdus et retrouvés, 1997. Novels: En Moins de Deux, 1990; L'Emporte-Clé, 1994. Contributions to: Various publications. Honour: Prix Litteraire, Societe des Ecrivains de la Mauricie; Prix Gerald-Godin, 1998. Memberships: Société des Ecrivains de la Mauricie; Union des Ecrivains du Quebec. Address: 19200 Forest, Saint-Gregoire, Quebec, Canada.

K

KADMON Jean Ball Kosloff, b. 1 Aug 1922, Denver, Colorado, USA. Poet; Novelist; Sculptor; Painter. m. 18 Aug 1945, 2 sons. Education: BA, University of Alberta, 1943; Graduate Studies, Anthropology, University of Chicago, 1944-46. Appointments: Anthropologist, International Centre for Community Development, Haifa, Israel, 1964-65; Sociologist, Jewish Agency, Israel, 1966-68. Publications: Moshav Segev, 1972; Clais and Clock, 1988; Peering Out, 1996; MacKenzie Breakup, 1997. Contributions to: Anthologies and periodicals. Honour: 2nd Prize, New Zealand International Writers Workshop, 1981. Membership: Israel Association of Writers in English. Address: 12 Zerubbabel Street, Jerusalem 93505, Israel.

KADOHATA Cynthia Lynn, b. 7 Feb 1956, Chicago, Illinois, USA. Writer. m. 30 Aug 1992. Education: Los Angeles City College; University of South Carolina; University of Pittsburgh; Columbia University. Publications: The Floating World, 1989; In the Heart of the Valley of Love, 1992. Contributions to: Newspapers and magazines. Honours: National Endowment for the Arts Grant, 1991; Whiting Writers Award, 1991. Address: c/o Wylie, Aitken and Stone Inc, 250 West 57th Street, Suite 2106, New York, NY 10107, USA.

KADOTA Paul Akira, b. 15 Mar 1930, Kobe, Japan. Retired College Teacher; Writer. m. Theresa Yoko Ishikawa, 27 Dec 1961, 3 sons, 1 daughter. Education: Kobe University, 1949; BEcons, 1955; BEduc, 1957. Appointments: Faculty, Kagoshima Prefectural College, 1966-95; Visiting Scholar, St Edmond College, Cambridge, England, 1975, Sonoma State University, California, 1988. Publications: Kariforunia No Shikon (Samurai Spirit in California), 1983; Kanaye Nagasawa: A Biography of Satsuma Student, 1990; Wakaki Satsuma No Gunzo (Young Satsuma Students), 1991. Contributions to: Several publications. Honours: Minami Nippon Broadcasting Company Prize, 1987; Toyota Minoru Prize, 1992. Membership: Nihon Eigakushi Gakkai (Historical Society of English Studies in Japan). Address: 37-6 Shimoishiki 3-chome, Kagoshima-shi 890, Japan.

KAEL Pauline, b. 19 June 1919, Sonoma County, California, USA. Movie Critic; Writer. Education: University of California, Berkeley, 1936-40. Appointment: Movie Critic, The New Yorker, 1968-91. Publications: I Lost it at the Movies, 1965; Kiss Kiss Bang Bang, 1968; Going Steady, 1970; Raising Kane in The Citizen Kane Book, 1971; Deeper into Movies, 1973; Reeling, 1976; When the Lights Go Down, 1980; 5001 Nights at the Movies, 1982; Taking It All In, 1984; State of the Art, 1985; Hooked, 1989; Move Love, 1991; For Keeps, 1994. Contributions to: Partisan Review; Vogue; New Republic; McCall's; Atlantic; Harper's. Honours: Guggenheim Fellowship, 1964; George Polk Memorial Award for Criticism, 1970; National Book Award, 1974; Front Page Awards, Newswomen's Club of New York, Best Magazine Column, 1974, Distinguished Journalism, 1983; 8 honorary degrees. Address: c/o The New Yorker, 20 West 43rd Street, New York, NY 10036, USA.

KAESER Ewald, b. 19 Aug 1942, Basle, Switzerland. Poet. Publications: Bei der Sprache genommen, 1982; Zeit der wilden Wespen, 1983; Antransport des Sprachmulls taglich, 1984; Jahreszeiten, 1988; Salecina Gedichte, 1997. Address: Hegenheimerstr 197, CH-4055 Basel, Switzerland.

KAFF Albert E, b. 14 June 1920, Atchison, Kansas, USA. Journalist; Author; Columnist. m. Diana Lee-chuan Fong, 15 Oct 1960, 2 sons. Education: BA, Economics, University of Colorado, 1942. Appointments: Summer Reporter, Atchison (Kansas) Daily Globe, 1939-41; Reporter, Ponca City (Oklahoma) News, 1946-48, Daily Oklahoman, 1948-50; Editor, 45th Division News, Louisiana, Japan and Korea, 1950-52; Reporter, United Press, Korea, Japan, 1952-56; Bureau Manager, United Press International, Saigon, Taipei, Manila, 1956-63; Editor, United Press International, Tokyo, Hong Kong, 1963-75; Personnel Director, United Press International, New York, 1975-78; Vice President, United Press International, Hong Kong, New York, 1978-85; Managing Editor, Business and International Editor, Cornell University News Service, Ithaca, New York, 1986-93; Freelance Writer, 1993-. Publications: Fire Arrows Over Quemoy, 1967; Crash: Ten Days in October...Will It Strike Again?, 1989; Black Monday: Boraku wa Kanarazu Kuru?, 1990; Ping-Pong Diplomacy, 1997. Honour: US Army Bronze Star for Meritorious Service, 1952. Memberships: Overseas Press Club of America; Tokyo Foreign Correspondents Club; Hong Kong Foreign Correspondents Club. Address: 393 Unquowa Road, Fairfield, CT 06430, USA.

KAGAN Andrew Aaron, b. 22 Sept 1947, St Louis, Missouri, USA. Art Historian; Art Adviser. m. Jayne Wilner, 17 May 1987. Education: BA, Washington University; MA, 1971, PhD, 1977, Harvard University. Appointments: Advisory Editor, Arts Magazine, 1975-89; Critic of Art, Music, Architecture, St Louis Globe Democrat, 1978-81. Publications: Paul Klee/Art and Music, 1983; Rothko, 1987; Trova, 1988; Marc Chagall, 1989; Paul Klee at the Guggenheim, 1993; Absolute Art, 1995. Contributions to: McMillan Dictionary of Art; Arts Magazine; Burlington Magazine; Others. Honours: Phi Beta Kappa, 1969; Harvard Prize Fellowship, 1970-77; Kingsbury Fellowship, 1977-78; Goldman Prize, 1985. Membership: Wednesday Night Society, founder, director. Address: 232 North Kingshighway, No 1709, St Louis, MO 63108, USA.

KAGRAMANOV Youri Michailovitch, b. 1 July 1934, Baku, USSR. Man of Letters; Writing on Culture. m. Irina Marinetz, 8 July 1983, deceased 1986. Education: Faculty of History, Moscow University, 1965. Appointment: Freelance, 1965-. Publications: Without Banner, 1979; many essays and reviews in literary magazines. Honour: Novy Mir Prize, 1995; Laureate of Znanie, 1988. Memberships: Union of Russian Men of Letters; Council of Novy Mir Magazine. Address: Moscow 115407, Sudostroitelnaya 51 ap 76, Russia.

KAHN James, b. 30 Dec 1947, Chicago, Illinois, USA. Physician; Writer. Education: BA, 1970, MD, 1974, University of Chicago. Appointments: Resident, Los Angeles County Hospital, 1976-77; University of California at Los Angeles, 1978-79; Physician, Emergency Room, Rancho Encino Hospital, Los Angeles, 1978-. Publications: Diagnosis Murder, 1978; Nerves in Patterns (with Jerome McGann), 1978; World Enough and Time, 1982; Time's Dark Laughter, 1982; Poltergeist, 1982; Return of the Jedi, 1983; Indiana Jones and the Temple of Doom, 1984; Goonies, 1985; Timefall, 1986; Poltergeist II, 1986. Address: c/o Jane Jordan Browne, 410 South Michigan Avenue, Suite 724, Chicago, IL 60605, USA.

KAHN Michele Anne, b. 1 Dec 1940, Nice, France. Writer; Journalist. m. Pierre-Michel Kahn, 8 Jan 1961, 1 son. Education: Diploma, Social Sciences, University of Paris, 1976. Publications: Contes du jardin d'Eden, 1983; Un Ordinateur pas Ordinaire, 1983; Juges et Rois, 1984; Hotel Riviera, 1986; Rue du Roi-dore, 1989; La vague noire, 1990; Boucles d'Or et Bebe Ours, 1990; Contes et légendes de la Bible, 2 volumes, 1994, 1995; Shanghaï-la-juive, 1997; Les Fantômes de Zurich, 1998. Contributions to: Magazine Litteraire; L'Arche; Honours: Diplomes Loisirs Jeunes, 1971, 1983. Memberships: International PEN Club; Société des Gens des Lettres de France; Société Civile des Auteurs Multimedia. Address: Residence Belloni, 192A Rue de Vaugirard, Paris 75015, France.

KAHN Robert (Bob), b. USA. Journalist; Photographer. Education: Master Degree, Graduate School and University Center, New York City; Honorary MA, Brooks College, Santa Barbara, California. Publications include: The Papal Trip; Eight Ways to Ruin Your Records; Victor By Borge; Norman Mailer Speaks; Goren Gentele, A Memorial; Kahn and the Future; The Swiss Riviera Exposed; Vanderbilt Reunion; JFK/Oswald; Tattooing Secrets; Bianca Jagger; Rome's Playing Cards; LA Wealth; The Great Battles - Toy Soldiers; Gunnar Myrdal, Nobel Winner; Empty Nest Syndrome; Comic Art in America; How Gentele Died; Sexist Reader; The Jokes of Goodman Ace; Kekkonen of Finland; Senator Eugene McCarthy; James Jones/Author; Burt Lancaster, Hah!. Memberships: American Society of Magazine Photographers; Royal Photographic Society of Great Britain, associate; Sigma Delta Chi. Address: 156 East 79th Street, New York, NY 10021-0435, USA.

KAHN Sy, b. 15 Sept 1924, New York, New York, USA. Professor Emeritus; Writer; Poet. Div. 1 son. Education: BA, Honours, University of Pennsylvania, 1948; MA, University of Connecticut, 1951; PhD, University of Wisconsin, 1957. Appointments: Assistant Professor, Beloit College, 1955-60, University of South Florida, 1960-63; Fulbright Professor of American Literature, University of Salonika, Greece, 1958-59, University of Warsaw, 1966-67, University of Vienna, 1970-71, University of Porto, Portugal, 1985-86; Professor of English and Humanities, Raymond College, 1963-68; Professor of Drama and English, 1968-86, Chairman, Department of Drama, 1970-81, Professor Emeritus, 1986-, University of the Pacific. Publications: Our Separate Darkness, 1963, 3rd edition, 1968; Triptych, 1964; The Fight is With Phantoms, 1966; A Later Sun, 1966; Another Time, 1968; Facing Mirrors, 1981; Devour the Fire: Selected Poems of Harry Crosby (editor), 1984; Between Tedium and Terror: A Soldier's World War II Diary, 1993. Contributions to: Various anthologies, journals, reviews and quarterlies. Honours: Gardner Writing Awards, University of Wisconsin, 1954, 1955; Crosby Writing Fellowships, 1962, 1963; Borestone Poetry Award, 1964; Promethean Lamp Prize, 1966; Grand Prize in Poetry, University of the Pacific, 1985. Membership: Modern Language Association. Address: Ravenshill House, 1212 Holcomb Street, Port Townsend, WA 98368, USA.

KALB Jonathan, b. 30 Oct 1959, Englewood, New Jersey, USA. Theatre Critic; Associate Professor of Theatre. m. Julie Heffernan, 18 June 1988, 2 sons. Education: BA, English, Wesleyan University; MFA, Dramaturgy, Dramatic Criticism, 1985, DFA, Dramaturgy, Dramatic Criticism, 1987, Yale School of Drama. Appointments: Theatre Critic, The Village Voice, 1987-97; Chief Theatre Critic, New York Press, 1997-. Assistant Professor of Performance Studies, 1990-92, Assistant Professor of Theatre, 1992-95, Associate Professor of Theatre, 1996-, Hunter College, City University of New York. Publications: Beckett in Performance, 1989; Free Admissions: Collected Theater Writings, 1993; The Theater of Heiner Müller, 1998. Contributions to: Newspapers and journals. Honours: Fulbright Hays Grant, 1988-89; T C G Jerome Fellowship, 1989-90; George Jean Nathan Award for Dramatic Criticism, 1990-91. Memberships: Modern Language Association; PEN American Centre. Address: c/o Department of Theatre, Hunter College of the City University of New York, 695 Park Avenue, New York, NY 10021, USA.

KALECHOFSKY Roberta, b. 11 May 1931, New York, New York, USA. Writer; Publisher. m. Robert Kalechofsky, 7 June 1953, 2 sons. Education: BA, Brooklyn College, 1952; MA, 1957, PhD, 1970, English, New York University. Appointments: Literary Editor, Branching Out, Canada, 1973-74; Contributing Editor, Margins, 1974-77, On the Issues, 1987-94. Publications: Stephen's Passion, 1975; La Hoya, 1976; Orestes in Progress, 1976; Solomon's Wisdom, 1978; Second edition, 1999; Rejected Essays and Other Matters, 1980; The 6th Day of Creation, 1986; Bodmin 1349, 1988; Haggadah for the Liberated Lamb, 1988; Autobiography of a Revolutionary: Essays on Animals and Human Rights, 1991; Justice, My Brother, reissued, 1993; Haggadah for the Vegetarian Family, 1993; K'tia: A Savior of the Jewish People, 1995; A Boy, a Chicken and the Lion of Judah: How Ari Became a Vegetarian (children's book), 1995; Vegetarian Judaism - A Guide for Everyone, 1998. Contributions to: Confrontation; Works; Ball State University Forum; Western Humanities Review;

Rocky Mountain Review; Between the Species; So'western; Response; Reconstructionist. Honours: National Endowment for the Arts Fellowship, 1962; Cited for Distinctive Writing in Best American Short Stories, 1976, 1977; Honorary Member Israel Bibliophile Society, 1982; Literary Fellowship in Fiction, Massachusetts Council on the Arts, 1987. Memberships: National Writers Union, Charter member; Authors Guild; Israel Bibliophile Society. Address: 255 Humphrey Street, Marblehead, MA 01945, USA.

KALNINS Viktors, (Viks, Silvija Vo, Karlo Kassini), b. 1 Apr 1939, Riga, Latvia. Poet. m. V Egle, 26 Nov 1971, div 1980, 3 sons, 1 daughter. Education: BPH, Latvian State University, 1972. Appointments: Locksmith, Riga Radioworks, 1955-58; Architect Assistant, 1961-62; Courier, State Bank, 1966-68; Teacher of English, Latvian University, 1972-73; Laboratory Assistant, Botanical Gardens, 1973-75. Publications: Poems: Communications, 1978; the Complicated Sparrow, 1982; Klaids in the Land of Fairies, 1983; The Great Day of Underwater Pack, 1985; Poems: Electronic Pagan, 1986; Poems: Bana Bana Bala Bala, 1987; Dinits Coming, 1990; I Cry Over You, Nik, 1990; O,15, 1993; The Summer Castle, 1994; The Jungle Night Rainbow, 1994; The "California" Course, 1995; Nuks the Little Tiger, 1996; Poems: Give Me a Kiss, 1996; Tornado Nuks, 1996; Angel in the Zone, 1997; Pocket-Size Paradises, 1997. Honours: Pastarina Prize, All-Union Award, USSR, 1986. Membership: Writers' Union, Latvia, 1982. Address: Kleistu iela 21, dz 95, Riga, LV-1067, Latvia.

KALTINA Velta, b. 28 June 1931, Jekabpils District, Latvia. Poet; Writer. m. Roald Dobrovensky, 28 June 1975. Education: Medical Institute, Riga, 1955; Higher Literary School, Moscow, 1975. Appointments: Pharmacist, Ventspils, 1955-65; Librarian, Riga, 1965-73. Publications: Signature, 1967; Trumpets of the Blue Elephants, 1970; Redearthen Glaze, 1973; Egretta Alba, 1978; Echo in the Well, 1981; Arrival of Love, 1985; Sign of Cross, 1995; Lifestory and 33 Fatal Rhymes, 1997; Madness of Love or Great Cabbage Celebration (novel), 1999. Membership: Latvian Writers Union, 1971. Address: Diku str 19-1, Riga, LV-1004, Latvia.

KAMANDA Kama, b. 11 Nov 1952, Luebo, Beligian Congo. Poet; Writer; Critic; Lecturer. Education: State Diploma, Literary Humanities, 1968; Degree, Journalism School, Kinshasa, 1969; Political Science Degree, University of Kinshasa, 1973; Law Degrees, University of Liège, 1981, University of Strasbourg, 1988. Publications: Les Contes des Veillées Africaines, 1967, 2nd edition, 1985; Chants de Brumes, 1986; Les Résignations, 1986; Eclipse d'Etoiles, 1987; Les Contes du Griot, 2 volumes, 1988, 1991; La Somme du Néant, 1989; L'Exil des Songes, 1992; Les Myriades des Temps Vécus, 1992; Lointaines sont les Rives du Destin, 1992; Les Vents de l'Epreuve, 1993; L'Etreinte des Mots, 1995; Quand dans l'âme les mers s'agitent, 1998. Contributions to: Many newspapers. Honours: Prix Paul Verlaine, 1987, Louise Labé Award, 1990, Théophile Gautier Award, 1993, French Academy; Literature Award, Black African Association of French-Speaking Writers, 1991; Special Poetry Award, Academy Institute, Paris, 1992. Memberships: Association of African Writers; Association of French Language Authors; Association of French Poets; International PEN Club; Société des Gens de Lettres en France. Address: 18 Am Moul, 7418 Buschdorf, Luxembourg.

KAMINSKI Ireneusz Gwidon, b. 1 March 1925, Gniezno, Poland. Writer; Dramatist; Poet. m. Alicja Gardocka, 26 Aug 1960, 2 sons, 2 daughters. Education: MA, Liberal Arts, Mickiewicz University, Poznan, 1952. Appointments: Journalist, Teacher, Librarian, 1950-70; War Correspondent, Vietnam, 1968, 1972; Editor-in-Chief, Morze (Sea), monthly, 1971-85. Publications: 10 novels, short stories, essays, radio plays and poems. Honours: Literary Awards, City of Szczecin, 1958, 1975, 1985. Membership: Polish Writers Union. Address: 70-791 Szczecin, ul Kozia 16, Poland.

KAMINSKY Stuart M(elvin), b. 29 Sept 1934, Chicago, Illinois, USA. Professor of Radio, Television and Film; Writer. Education: BS, 1957, MA, 1959, University of Illinois; PhD, Northwestern University, 1972. Appointments: Director of Public Relations and Assistant to the Vice President for Public Affairs, University of Chicago, 1969-72; Faculty, later Professor of Radio, Television, and Film, Northwestern University, 1972-. Publications: Non-Fiction: Don Siegal: Director, 1973; Clint Eastwood, 1974; American Film Genres: Approaches to a Critical Theory of Popular Film, 1974; Ingmar Bergman: Essays in Criticism (editor with Joseph Hill), 1975; John Huston: Maker of Magic, 1978; Basic Filmmaking (with Dana Hodgdon), 1981; American Television Genres (with Jeffrey Mahan), 1984. Fiction: Bullet for a Star, 1977; Murder on the Yellow Brick Road, 1978; You Bet Your Life, 1979; The Howard Hughes Affair, 1979; Never Cross a Vampire, 1980; Death of a Dissident, 1981; High Midnight, 1981; Catch a Falling Clown, 1981; He Done Her Wrong, 1983; When the Dark Man Calls, 1983; Black Knight on Red Square, 1983; Down for the Count, 1985; Red Chameleon, 1985; Exercise in Terror, 1985; Smart Moves, 1987; A Fine Red Rain, 1987; Lieberman's Day, 1994. Address: c/o School of Speech, Northwestern University, Evanston, IL 60201, USA.

KAN Sergei, b. 31 Mar 1953, Moscow, Russia (US citizen). Associate Professor of Anthropology and of Native American Studies; Writer. m. Alla Glazman, 19 Dec 1976, 1 daughter. Education: Moscow State University, 1970-73; BA, Boston University, 1976; MA, 1978, PhD, 1982, University of Chicago. Appointments: Lecturer, Sheldon Jackson College, Sitka, Alaska, 1979-80, University of Massachusetts, Boston, 1982-83; Part-time Assistant Professor, Northeastern University, 1981-83; Assistant Professor, University of Michigan, 1983-89; Assistant Professor, 1989-92, Associate Professor of Anthropology and of Native American Studies, 1992-, Dartmouth College. Publications: Symbolic Immortality: The Tlingit Potlatch of the Nineteenth Century, 1989; Memory Eternal: Tlingit Culture and Russian Orthodox Christianity, 1794-1994, 1999. Contributions to: Books and scholarly journals. Honours: Robert F Heizer Prize, American Society for Ethnohistory, 1987; American Book Award, Before Columbus Foundation, 1990; American Council of Learned Societies Fellowship, 1993-94; National Endowment for the Humanities Fellowship, 1993-94. Memberships: Alaska Anthropological Association; American Association for the Advancement of Slavic Studies; American Ethnological Society; American Society for Ethnohistory; International Arctic Social Science Association. Address: 18 Wellington Circle, Lebanon, NH 03766, USA.

KANE Paul, b. 23 Mar 1950, Cobleskill, New York, USA. Poet; Critic; Professor of English. m. Christine Reynolds, 21 June 1980. Education: BA, 1973, MA, 1987, MPhil, 1988, PhD, 1990, Yale University; MA, University of Melbourne, 1985. Appointments: Instructor, Briarcliff College, 1975-77; Associate, Institute for World Order, 1982; Director of Admissions and Instructor, Wooster School, 1982-84; Part-time Instructor, Yale University, 1988-90; Professor of English, Vassar College, 1990-. Publications: The Farther Shore, 1989; A Hudson Landscape (with William Cliff), 1993; Ralph Waldo Emerson: Collected Poems and Translations, 1994; Poetry of the American Renaissance, 1995; Australian Poetry: Romanticism and Negativity, 1996; Emerson: Essays and Poems, 1996. Contributions to: Articles, poems, and reviews in New Republic; Paris Review; Poetry; Sewanee Review; Partisan Review; Raritan; Antipodes. Honours: Fulbright Scholar, 1984-85; National Endowment for the Humanities Grant, 1998; Guggenheim Fellowship, 1999. Memberships: Academy of American Poets; PEN; Poetry Society of America. Address: 8 Big Island, Warwick, NY 10990, USA.

KANE Penny. See: **RUZICKA Penelope Susan.**

KANIGEL Robert, b. 28 May 1946, Brooklyn, New York, USA. Writer. m. Judith Schiff Pearl, 28 June 1981, 1 son. Education: BS, Rensselaer Polytechnic Institute, Troy, New York. Appointments: Freelance Writer, 1970-; Instructor, Johns Hopkins University School of Continuing Studies, 1985-91; Visiting Professor of English, University of Baltimore, and Senior Fellow, Institute of Publications Design, 1991-. Publications: Apprentice to Genius: The Making of a Scientific Dynasty, 1986, 2nd edition, 1993; The Man Who Knew Infinity: A Life of the Genius Ramanujan, 1991, 2nd edition, 1992; The One Best Way: Frederick Winslow Taylor and the Enigma of Efficency, 1997; Paperback edition, 1999; Vintage Reading: From Pluto to Bradbury, a Personal Tour of some of the World's Best Books, 1998; . Contributions to: New York Times Magazine; The Sciences; Health; Psychology Today; Science 85; Johns Hopkins Magazine; Washington Post; Civilization. Honours: Grady-Stack Award, 1989; Alfred P Sloan Foundation Grant. 1991; Elizabeth Eisenstein Prize, 1994; Author of the Year, American Society of Journals and Authos, 1998. Memberships: Authors Guild; American Society of Journalists and Authors. Literary Agent: Vicky Bijur. Address: 202 Dunkirk Road,Baltimore, MD 21212, USA.

KANN Mark E, b. 24 Feb 1947, Chicago, Illinois, USA. Professor of Political Science. m. Kathy Michael, 13 Feb 1969, 1 son. Education: BA, 1968, MA, 1972, PhD, 1975, University of Wisconsin, Madison. Appointments: Assistant Professor, 1975-81, Associate Professor, 1981-88, Professor of Political Science, 1988-, University of Southern California at Los Angeles. Publications: Thinking About Politics: Two Political Sciences, 1980; The American Left: Failures and Fortunes, 1983; Middle Class Radicals in Santa Monica, 1986; On the Man in Question: Gender and Civic Virtue in America, 1991; A Republic of Men: The American Founders, Gendered Language, and Political Patriachy, 1998. Contributions to: Numerous newspapers, journals and magazines. Honours: Various research and teaching awards. Address: Department of Political Science, University of Southern California, Los Angeles, CA 90089, USA.

KANNAN Lakshmi (Kaaveri), b. 13 Aug 1947, Mysore, India. Writer. m. L V Kannan, 2 sons. Education: BA, Honours, MA, PhD, all in English. Appointment: Writer-in-Residence, University of Kent at Canterbury, 1993. Publications: Glow and the Grey, 1976; Exiled Gods, 1985; Rhythms, 1986; India Gate, 1993; Going Home, 1999; other books in Hindi and Tamil. Honours: Honarary Fellow in Writing, University of Iowa, USA; Ilakkiya Chintanai Award for Best Short-story. Memberships: The Poetry Society, India, Founder-member and Treasurer, 1986-; Indian Association for American Studies; Life member India International Centre, Delhi; American Studies Research Centre, Hyderabad. Address: B-11/8193, Vasant Kunj, New Delhi 110030, India.

KANT Hermann Paul Karl, b. 14 June 1926, Hamburg, Germany. Writer. m. Marion Meyer, 1 Mar 1982, 2 sons, 2 daughters. Education: A-Level Workers and Peasants Faculty, Greifswald University, 1951; BA, Philosophy, University of Berlin, 1956. Appointments: Electrician, 1940-49; Assistant Professor, 1956-57; Editor, 1957-60; Freelance Writer, 1960-. Publications: Books: Einbisschen Südsee, short stories, 1962; Die Aula, novel, 1965; Eine Liebertretung, 1971, short stories, 1971; Das Impressum, novel, 1972; Der Aufenthalt, novel, 1977; Der dritte Nagel, short stories, 1980; Bronzezeit, short stories, 1984; Kormoran, novel, 1992; Anspann, memoir, 1992; Escape, novel, 1994. Contributions to: Numerous. Honours: Heinrich Heine Prize, 1962; Heinrich Mann Prize, 1967; National Prize, 1973, 1977; Goethe Prize, 1985; Dr honoris causa, 1980. Memberships: Writers Association, President 1979-89; German PEN Centre, East. Address: Dorfstrasse 4, 17235 Prälank, Germany.

KANTARIS Sylvia, b. 9 Jan 1936, Grindleford, Derbyshire, England. Poet; Writer; Teacher. m. Emmanuel Kantaris, 11 Jan 1958, 1 son, 1 daughter. Education: Diplome d'Etudes Civilisation Française, Sorbonne, University of Paris, 1955; BA, Honours, 1957, CertEd, 1958, Bristol University; MA, 1967, PhD, 1972,

University of Queensland, Australia. Appointments: Tutor, University of Queensland, Australia, 1963-66, Open University, England, 1974-84; Extra-Mural Lecturer, Exeter University, 1974-. Publications: Time and Motion, 1975; Stocking Up, 1981; The Tenth Muse, 1983; News From the Front (with D M Thomas), 1983; The Sea at the Door, 1985; The Air Mines of Mistila (with Philip Gross), 1988; Dirty Washing: New and Selected Poems, 1989; Lad's Love, 1993. Contributions to: Many anthologies, newspapers, and magazines. Honours: National Poetry Competition Award, 1982; Honorary Doctor of Letters, Exeter University, 1989; Major Arts Council Literature Award, 1991; Society of Authors Award, 1992. Memberships: Poetry Society of Great Britain; South West Arts, literature panel, 1983-87, literary consultant, 1990-. Address: 14 Osborne Parc, Helston, Cornwall TR13 8PB, England.

KANTOR Peter, b. 5 Nov 1949, Budapest, Hungary. Poet. Education: MA, English and Russian Literature, 1973, MA, Hungarian Literature, 1980, Budapest ELTE University. Appointment: Literary Editor, Kortars magazine, 1984-86; Poetry Editor, Élet és Irodalom, magazine, 1997-. Publications: Kavics, 1976; Halmadar, 1981; Sebbel Lobbal, 1982; Gradicsok, 1985; Hogy no az eg, 1988; Naplo, 1987-89, 1991; Font lomb, lent avar, 1994; Mentafü (selected poems), 1994; Bucsu és Megérkezés, 1997. Contributions to: Various publications. Honours: George Soros Fellowship, 1988-89; Wessely Laszlo Award, 1990; Dery Tibor Award, 1991; Fulbright Fellowship, 1991-92; Fust Milan Award, 1992; József Attila Award, 1994. Memberships: Hungarian Writers Union; International PEN Club. Address: Stollar Bela u 3/a, Budapest 1055, Hungary.

KAPLAN Harold, b. 3 Jan 1916, Chicago, Illinois, USA. Professor Emeritus. m. Isabelle M Ollier, 29 July 1962, 1 son, 2 daughters. Education: BA, 1937, MA, 1938, University of Chicago. Appointments: Instructor of English, Rutgers University, 1946-49; Professor of English, Bennington College, 1950-72; Professor of English, 1972-86, Professor Emeritus, 1986-, Northwestern University. Publications: The Passive Voice, 1966; Democratic Humanism and American Literature, 1972; Power and Order, 1981; Conscience and Memory: Meditations in a Museum of the Holocaust, 1994. Honours: Fulbright Lecturer, 1967, 1981; Rockefeller Foundation Humanities Fellowship, 1982. Address: Turnabout Lane, Bennington, VT 05201, USA.

KAPLAN Justin, b. 5 Sept 1925, New York, New York, USA. Biographer; Editor. m. Anne F Bernays, 29 July 1954, 3 daughters. Education: BS, 1944, Postgraduate Studies, 1944-46, Harvard University. Appointments: Senior Editor, Simon & Schuster Inc, New York City, 1954-59; Lecturer in English, Harvard University, 1969, 1973, 1976, 1978; Writer-in-Residence, Emerson College, Boston, 1977-78; Visiting Lecturer, Griffith University, Brisbane, Australia, 1983; Jenks Professor of Contemporary Letters, College of the Holy Cross, Worcester, Massachusetts, 1992-95. Publications: Mr Clemens and Mark Twain, 1966; Lincoln Steffens: A Biography, 1974; Mark Twain and His World, 1974; Walt Whitman: A Life, 1980. Editor: Dialogues of Plato, 1948; With Malice Toward Women, 1949; The Pocket Aristotle, 1956; The Gilded Age, 1964; Great Short Works of Mark Twain, 1967; Mark Twain: A Profile, 1967; Walt Whitman: Complete Poetry and Collected Prose, 1982; The Harper American Literature, 1987, new edition, 1994; Best American Essays, 1990. General Editor: Bartlett's Familiar Quotations, 16th edition, 1992. Contributions to: Newspapers, journals and magazines. Honours: Pulitzer Prize for Biography, 1967; National Book Award, 1967; Guggenheim Fellowship, 1975-76; American Book Award, 1981; DHL, Marlboro College, 1984; Bellagio Study and Conference Center Residency, 1990. Memberships: American Academy of Arts and Letters; American Academy of Arts and Sciences, fellow; Phi Beta Kappa; Society of American Historians, fellow. Address: 16 Francis Avenue, Cambridge, MA 02138, USA.

KAPLAN Morton A, b. 9 May 1921, Philadelphia, Pennsylvania, USA. Political Scientist; Distinguished Service Professor Emeritus; Writer; Editor; Publisher. m. Azie Mortimer, 22 July 1967. Education: BS, Temple University, 1943; PhD, Columbia University, 1951. Appointments: Instructor, Ohio State University, 1951-52; Fellow, 1952-53, Research Associate, 1958-62, Center of International Studies, Princeton, New Jersey; Assistant Professor, Haverford College, 1953-54; Staff, Brookings Institution, Washington, DC, 1954-55; Fellow, Center for Advanced Study in the Behavorial Sciences, Stanford, California, 1955-56; Assistant Professor, 1956-61, Associate Professor, 1961-65, Professor of Political Science, 1965-89, Distinguished Service Professor, 1989-91, Professor Emeritus, 1991-, University of Chicago; Visiting Associate Professor, Yale University, 1961-62; Associate Editor (with others), Journal of Conflict Resolution, 1961-79; Staff, 1961-78, Consultant, 1978-80, Hudson Institute; Director, Center for Strategic and Foreign Policy Studies, 1976-85; Editor and Publisher, The World and I, 1985-. Publications: System and Process in International Politics, 1957; Some Problems in the Strategic Analysis of International Politics, 1959; The Communist Coup in Czechoslovakia (co-author), 1960; The Political Foundations of International Law, 1961; Macropolitics: Essays on the Philosophy and Science of Politics, 1969; On Historical and Political Knowing: An Enquiry into Some Problems of Universal Law and Human Freedom, 1971; On Freedom and Human Dignity: The Importance of the Sacred in Politics, 1973; The Rationale for NATO: Past and Present, 1973; Alienation and Identification, 1976; Justice, Human Nature and Political Obligation (co-author), 1976; Towards Professionalism in International Theory: Macrosystem Analysis, 1979; Science, Language and the Human Condition, 1984, revised edition, 1989; Consolidating Peace in Europe (editor), 1987; The Soviet Union and the Challenge of the Future (co-editor), 4 volumes, 1988-89; Morality and Religion (co-editor), 1992; Law in a Democratic Society, 1993; The World of 2044: Technological Development and the Future of Society (co-editor), 1994; Character and Identity: Philosophical Foundations of Political and Sociological Perspectives (editor and co-author), 1998. Contributions to: Many books and professional journals. Memberships: American Academy of Arts and Sciences; American Political Science Association; Institute of Strategic Studies, London. Address: 5446 South Ridgewood Court, Chicago, IL 60615, USA.

KAPLAN Robert David, b. 23 June 1952, New York, New York, USA. Author; Journalist. m. Maria Cabral, 26 Aug 1983, 1 son. Education: BA, University of Connecticut, 1973. Publications: Surrender or Starve: The Wars Behind the Famine, 1988; Soldiers of God: With the Mujahidin in Afghanistan, 1990; Balkan Ghosts: A Journey Through History, 1993; The Arabists: The Romance of an American Elite, 1993; The Ends of the Earth, 1996. Contributions to: Newspapers and magazines. Memberships: Authors Guild; Authors League of America.

KARAHALIOU-TOKA Melita, b. 17 June 1940, Thessaloniki, Greece. Teacher of French. m. Konstantinos Karahalios, 1 son, 1 daughter. Education: Degree in French Philology. Appointment: Taught ideograms, many schools. Publications: Passages, poetry, 1980; Wanderings, poetry, 1983; Ideograms, poetry, 1995; From Theokritos to logogram, essay on schematic poetry, 1995; The night is born, poetry, 1997; Light outfit, translation from Italian to Greek of Vito d'Armento's poetry, 1998. Contributions to: Connaisance Hellénique; N Europa magazine, Luxembourg; Doc(k)s; Sentiers Poêtiques. Honours: Giovanni Gronchi, 1998; French-speaking Poet's Award, Allauch, France, 1998; Special Award, Poets and Authors Society, Nîmes, France, 1998. Membership: Thessaloniki Literary Society. Address: 5 Kapeton Dogra Street, Ano Toumba, Thessaloniki 54352, Greece.

KARAVIA Lia Headzopoulou, b. 27 June 1932, Athens, Greece. Writer; Poet; Dramatist. m. Vassillis Karavias, 20 Sept 1953, 2 sons. Education: Diploma, English Literature, Pierce College, Athens, 1953; Diploma, French Literature, Institute of France, Athens, 1954; Diploma, Acting School, Athens, 1962; Classical Literature, University of Athens, 1972; Doctorat Nouveau Regime, Comparative Literature, Sorbonne, Paris, 1991. Appointments: Actress; Teacher of Acting and History of the Theatre, Public Schools, 1984-94. Publications: 12 novels; 10 poetry collections; 12 stage and radio plays; television scripts. Contributions to: Anthologies, journals, and magazines; Numerous translations of novels and plays. Honours: Menelaos Loudemis Prize, 1980; Michaela Averof Prize, 1981; Prizes for plays for Young People, 1986, 1987, 1988; National Prize for Best Play for Young People, 1989; National Playwrights Prizes, 1990, 1991. Memberships: Actors League of Greece; European Institute for Theater Research, president, Greek section; International Theatre Institute; Maison International de Poesie, Liège; Society of Greek Writers; Union of Greek Playwrights; Steering Committee of Women Playwrights' Conferences; Board of International Playwrights' Forum. Address: 51 Aghiou Polycarpou Street, Nea Smyrni 17124, Athens, Greece.

KARIM Fawzi, b. 1 July 1945, Baghdad, Iraq. Poet; Writer; Editor; Publisher. m. 31 Dec 1980, 2 sons. Education: BA, Arabic Literature, College of Arts, Baghdad, 1967. Appointment: Editor-in-Chief and Publisher, Al-Lahda Al-Shiriya, quarterly, London. Publications: Where Things Begin, 1968; I Raise My Hand in Protest, 1973; Madness of Stone, 1977; Stumbling of a Bird, 1985; We Do Not Inherit the Earth, 1988; Schemes of Adam, 1991; Pestilential Continents, 1992; Collected Poems, 1968-1992, 1993. Other: Essays and short stories. Contributions to: Reviews and periodicals. Memberships: Poetry Society, England; Union of Iraqi Writers. Address: PO Box 2137, London W13 0TY, England.

KARL Frederick R(obert), b. 10 Apr 1927, New York, New York, USA. Professor; Literary Scholar. m. Dolores Mary Oristaglio, 8 June 1951, 3 daughters. Education: BA, Columbia College, 1948; MA, Stanford University, 1949; PhD, Columbia University, 1957. Appointments: Faculty, 1957-81, Director of Graduate Programs in English, 1970-76, City College, New York City; Professor, New York University, 1982-; Several guest professorships and lectureships. Publications: A Reader's Guide to Joseph Conrad, 1960; The Quest (novel), 1961; The Contemporary English Novel, 1962; The Adversary Literature, 1974; Joseph Conrad: The Three Lives, 1979; American Fictions: 1940-1980, 1983; Modern and Modernism: The Sovereignty of the Artist, 1885-1925, 1983; The Collected Letters of Joseph Conrad (general editor), 1983 et seq.; William Faulkner: American Writer, 1989; Franz Kafka: Representative man, 1991; George Eliot: Voice of a Century, 1995. Contributions to: Scholarly books and journals. Honours: Fulbright Grant, 1965-66; Guggenheim Fellowship, 1966-67; National Endowment for the Humanities Senior Research Grants, 1979, 1988. Address: 2 Settlers Landing Lane, East Hampton, NY 11937, USA.

KARLIN Wayne Stephen, b. 13 June 1945, Los Angeles, California, USA. Writer; Teacher. m. Ohnmar Thein, 27 Oct 1977, 1 son. Education: BA, American College, Jerusalem, 1972; MA, Goddard College, 1976. Appointments: President, Co-Editor, First Casualty Press, 1972-73; Visiting Writer, William Joiner Center for the Study of War and Social Consequences, University of Massachusetts, Boston, 1989-93; Director, Fiction, Literary Festival, St Mary's College, 1994-; Editor, Curbstone Press, Vietnamese Writers Series, 1996-. Publications: Free Fire Zone (co-editor, contributor), 1973; Crossover, 1984; Lost Armies, 1988; The Extras, 1989; US, 1993; The Other Side of Heaven: Postwar Fiction by Vietnamese and American Writers (co-editor with Le Minh Khve, contributor); Rumors and Stones: A Journey, 1996; Prisoners, 1998. Contributions to: Anthologies and periodicals. Honours: Fellowship in Fiction and Individual Artist Award, Maryland State Arts Council, 1988, 1991, 1993; National Endowment for the Arts Fellowship, 1993; The Critics' Choice Award, 1995-96. Membership: Associated Writing Programs. Address: PO Box 239, St Mary's City, MD 20686, USA.

KARNOW Stanley, b. 4 Feb 1925, New York, New York, USA. Journalist; Writer. m. (1) Claude Sarraute, 15 July 1948, div 1955, (2) Annette Kline, 21 Apr 1959, 2 sons, 1 daughter. Education: BA, Harvard University, 1947; University of Paris, 1948-50. Appointments: Correspondent, Time magazine, Paris, 1950-57; Bureau Chief, North Africa, 1958-59, Hong Kong, 1959-62, Time-Life; Special Correspondent, Observer, London, 1961-65, Time Inc, 1962-63, NBC News, 1973-75; Far East Correspondent, Saturday Evening Post, 1963-65; Far East Correspondent, 1965-71, Diplomatic Correspondent, 1971-72, Washington Post; Associate Editor, New Republic, 1973-75; Columnist, King Features, 1975-88, Le Point, Paris, 1976-83, Newsweek International, 1977-81; Editor, International Writers Service, 1976-86; Chief Correspondent, PBS series, Vietnam: A Television History, 1983; Chief Correspondent and Narrator, PBS series The US and the Philippines: In Our Image, 1989. Publications: Southeast Asia, 1963; Mao and China: From Revolution to Revolution, 1972; Vietnam: A History, 1983; In Our Image: America's Empire in the Philippines, 1989; Asian Americans in Transition (co-author), 1992; Paris in the Fifties, 1997. Contributions to: Books, newspapers, journals, and magazines. Honours: Neiman Fellow, 1957-58; East Asian Research Center Fellow, 1970-71; Peabody Award, 1984; Pulitzer Prize in History, 1990. Memberships: Asia Society; Council on Foreign Relations; PEN American Centre; Society of American Historians. Address: 10850 Spring Knowlls Drive, Rockville, MD 20854, USA.

KAROL Alexander. See: **KENT Arthur (William Charles).**

KARSEN Sonja Petra, b. 11 Apr 1919, Berlin, Germany (US citizen). Professor of Spanish Emerita. Education: BA, Carleton College, 1939; MA, Bryn Mawr College, 1941; PhD, Columbia University, 1950. Appointments: Reviewer, Books Abroad, 1959-76, World Literature Today, 1977-92; Editor, Language Association Bulletin, 1980-82. Publications: Guillermo Valencia, Colombian Poet, 1873-1943, 1951; Educational Development in Costa Rica with UNESCO's Technical Assistance, 1951-54, 1954; Jaime Torres Bodet: A Poet in a Changing World, 1963; Selected Poems of Jaime Torres Bodet, 1964; Versos y prosas de Jaime Torres Bodet, 1966; Jaime Torres Bodet, 1971; Essays on Iberoamerican Literature and History, 1988; Leopoldo Zea, The Role of the Americas in History (translator), 1992; Bericht über den Vater: Fritz Karsen (1885-1951), 1993. Contributions to: Over 100 articles and book reviews to professional journals. Honours: Faculty Research Lecturer, Skidmore College, 1963; Chevalier dans l'Ordre des Palmes Académiques, Ministère de l'Education Nationale, Paris, 1964; Fulbright Lecturer, Free University, Berlin, 1968; Alumni Achievement Award, Carleton College, 1982; International Women of the Year, IBC, 1991-92. Memberships: Asociación Internacional de Hispanistas; Hispanic Institute, Columbia University; Modern Language Association; National Geographic Society. Address: 1755 York Avenue, No 37-A, New York, NY 10128, USA.

KARVAS Peter, b. 25 Apr 1920, Banska Bystrica, Czechoslovakia. Writer; Professor. m. Eva Ruman, 15 May 1969, 1 son. Education: PhD, 1946. Publications: 15 books, 1969-93. Contributions to: Various books and journals. Honours: Czechoslovak State Prize, 1960; Czechoslovak Writers Union Prize, 1991. Memberships: Slovak Writers Association; Slovak Writers Union. Address: Vlckova 7, 81106 Bratislava, Slovak Republic.

KASISCHKE Laura, b. 5 Dec 1961, Lake Charles, Louisiana, USA. Poet; Writer; Teacher. m. William Abernethy, Aug 1994, 1 son. Education: BA, 1984, MFA, 1987, University of Michigan; Graduate Studies, Columbia University. Appointments: Instructor in Writing, South Plains College, Levelland, Texas, 1987-88; Visiting Lecturer in Creative Writing and Literature, Eastern Michigan University, 1989-90; Instructor in Creative Writing and Literature, Washtenaw Community College, Ann Arbor, 1990-; Associate Professor, University of Nevada, Las Vegas, 1994-95. Publications: Poetry: Brides, Wives, and Widows, 1990; Wild Brides, 1992; Housekeeping in a Dream, 1995. Fiction: Suspicious River, 1996. Contributions to: Numerous periodicals. Honours: Michael Gutterman Poetry Award, 1983; Marjorie Rapaport Poetry Award, 1986; Michigan Council for the Arts Individual Artist Grant, 1990; Ragdale Foundation Fellowships, 1990-92; Elmer Holmes Bobst Award for Emerging Writers, 1991; Bread Loaf Fellow in Poetry, 1992; MacDowell Colony Fellow, 1992; Creative Artists Award, Arts Foundation of Michigan, 1993; Alice Fay DiCastagnola Award, 1993; Pushcart Prize, 1993; Barbara Deming Memorial Award, 1994; National Endowment for the Arts Fellowship, 1994; Poets & Writers Exchange Fellowship, 1994. Address: 2997 South Fletcher Road, Chelsea, MI 48118, USA.

KASSEM Lou(ise Sutton Morrell), b. 10 Nov 1931, Elizabethton, Tennessee, USA. Author. m. Shakeep Kassem, 17 June 1951, 4 daughters. Education: East Tennessee State University, 1949-51; Short courses, University of Virginia, 1982, Vassar College, 1985. Publications: Dance of Death, 1984; Middle School Blues, 1986; Listen for Rachel, 1986; Secret Wishes, 1989; A Summer for Secrets, 1989; A Haunting in Williamsburg, 1990; The Treasures of Witch Hat Mountain, 1992; Odd One Out, 1994; The Druid Curse, 1994; The Innkeeper's Daughter, 1996; Sneeze on Monday, 1997. Contributions to: Alan Review; Signal. Honours: Notable Book in Social Studies, American Library Association, 1986; Best Book for Young Readers, Virginia State Reading Association. Memberships: Society of Children's Book Writers; Writers in Virginia; Appalachian Writers; National League of American Pen Women. Address: 715 Burruss Drive North West, Blacksburg, VA 24060, USA.

KASSINI Karlo. See: **KALNINS Viktors.**

KASTELY James, b. 6 Nov 1947, Detroit, USA. Professor of English. m. Amy Hilsman, 5 Sept 1975, 1 son, 1 daughter. Education: AB, University of Michigan; MA, PhD, University of Chicago. Appointments: Assistant Professor, University of Hawaii at Manoa; Associate Professor, University of Houston. Publication: Rethinking the Rhetorical Tradition. Contributions to: PMLA; College English; Rhetoric Society Quarterly; Philosophy and Literature; Philosophy and Rhetoric; Nineteenth-Century Literature. Address: c/o Department of English, University of Houston, Houston, TX 77204-3012, USA.

KATO Shuichi, b. 19 Sept 1919, Tokyo, Japan. Writer; Professor. Education: Graduate, Faculty of Medicine, 1943, MD 1950, Tokyo University. Publications: Form, Style, Tradition: Reflexions on Japanese Art and Society, 1969; Japan-China Phenomenon, 1973; Six Lives/Six Deaths: Portraits from Modern Japan (with Robert Lifton and Michael Reich), 1979; Chosakushu (Collected Works), 15 volumes, 1978-80; A History of Japanese Literature, 3 volumes, 1979-83; Japan, Spirit and Form, 1995. Contributions to: Asahi Shimbun; Many Japanese, French and American periodicals. Honours: Osaragi Jiro Prize, 1980; Ordre des Arts et des Lettres, 1985. Membership: PEN Club, Japanese Branch. Address: Kaminage 1-8-16, Setagaya-ku, Tokyo 158, Japan.

KATTAN Naim, b. 26 Aug 1928, Baghdad, Iraq. Writer. m. 21 July 1961, 1 son. Education: Law College, Baghdad, 1945-47; Sorbonne, Paris, 1947-52. Appointments: Head of Writing and Publishing, Associate Director, Canada Council, Ottawa, 1990-91; Writer-in-Residence, 1991-93, Associate Professor, 1993-, University of Quebec, Montreal. Publications: Reality and Theatre, 1970; Farewell Babylon, 1974; La Memoire de la Promesse, 1980; Le Père, 1988; Farida, 1989; La Réconciliation, 1993; Portraits d'un Pays, 1994; A M Klein, 1994; La distraction, 1994; Culture: Alibi ou liberté, 1996; Idoles et images, 1996; La Célébration, 1997; Figures bibliques, 1997. Contributions to: Critique; Quaizaire; Nouvelle Revue Française; Passages; Le Devoir; Canadian Literature. Honours: Prix France, Canada, 1971; Segal Awards, 1975, 1998; Order of Canada, 1987; Order of Arts and Letters, France, 1989; Order of Quebec, 1990. Memberships: Royal Society of Canada; Académie des Lettres, Montreal; Union des Ecrivains du Quebec. Address: 3463 Rue Ste Famille 2114, Montreal, Quebec H2X 2K7, Canada.

KATUNARIC Drazen, b. 25 Dec 1954, Zagreb, Croatia. Writer. 1 son. Education: BA, Maitrise; ES, Lettres, Universite des Sciences Humaines, Strasbourg. Appointments: Editor, literary journal, Lettre Internationale, Croatian Edition, 1991-93; Editor in Chief, literary journal, The Bridge, 1993-. Publications: Poems: Bacchus in Marble, 1983; Sand Trap, 1985; Imposture, 1987; At Sea, 1988; Psalms, 1990; Imposing Voice, 1991; Sky Earth, 1993; Prose: Church, Street 200, 1994; The Story of Cavern, 1998; Essays: The House of Decadence, 1992; Return of the Barbarogenius, 1995. Contributions to: Esprit; Le Messager; European, Paris. Honours: Tin Ujevic, 1994; Delhi Telugu Academy Award, 1995. Memberships: Croatian Writer's Association; PEN Club, Croatia. Address: Gracanske Duzice 21, 1000 Zagreb, Croatia.

KATZ Bobbi, b. 2 May 1933, Newburgh, New York, USA. Writer; Poet; Editor. m. H D Katz, 1956, div 1979, 1 son, dec, 1 daughter. Education: BA, Goucher College, 1954. Appointment: Editor, Books for Young Readers, Random House, New York City, 1982-. Publications: Over 80 books for children; Over 700 poems. Contributions to: Cousteau Almanac; First Teacher; Highlights for Children; Ladybug Magazine; Ranger Rick; Various textbooks. Memberships: Authors Guild, PEN; SCBWI. Address: 65 West 96th Street, 21H, New York, NY 10025, USA.

KATZ Steve, b. 14 May 1935, New York, New York, USA. Novelist; Short Story Writer; Poet; Screenwriter; Professor. m. Patricia Bell, 10 June 1956, div, 3 sons. Education: BA, Cornell University, 1956; MA, University of Oregon, 1959. Appointments: English Language Institute, Lecce, Italy, 1960; Overseas Faculty, University of Maryland, Lecce, Italy, 1961-62; Assistant Professor of English, Cornell University, 1962-67; Lecturer in Fiction, University of Iowa, 1969-70; Writer-in-Residence, 1970-71, Co-Director, Projects in Innovative Fiction, 1971-73, Brooklyn College, City University of New York; Adjunct Assistant Professor, Queens College, City University of New York, 1973-75; Associate Professor of English, University of Notre Dame, 1976-78; Associate Professor of English, 1978-82, Professor of English, 1982-, University of Colorado at Boulder. Publications: Novels: The Lestriad, 1962; The Exagggerations of Peter Prince, 1968; Posh, 1971; Saw, 1972; Moving Parts, 1977; Wier and Pouce, 1984; Florry of Washington Heights, 1987; Swanny's Ways, 1995. Short Stories: Creamy and Delicious: Eat my Words (in Other Words), 1970; Stolen Stories, 1985; 43 Fictions, 1991. Poetry: The Weight of Antony, 1964; Cheyenne River Wild Track, 1973; Journalism, 1990. Screenplay: Grassland, 1974. Honours; PEN Grant, 1972; Creative Artists Public Service Grant, 1976; National Educational AssociationGrants, 1976, 1982; GCAH Book of the Year, 1991; America Award in Fiction, 1995. Memberships; Authors League of America; PEN International; Writers Guild. Address: 669 Washington Street, No 602, Denver, CO 80203, USA.

KATZIR Benjamin, (Dril Stern, Benjamin Goldsten), b. 16 Apr 1941, Copenhagen, Denmark. Writer; Translator; Painter; Gastronome. 1 son, 4 daughters. Education: Law Studies, University of Århus. Appointments: Teacher, Adult Education; Publisher; Journalist; Cook; President, The Katzir Family Foundation, Israel and Denmark. Publications: Jødiske vitaminer; Thi kendes for ret; Man tage en orred; Du er hvad, du spiser; Yemenittisk-jodisk mad og kultur; Black and White; Den gyldne pige; Sange fra Zion og der ømkring; 198 Gammeldags danske frokostretter; Kunsternerliv i Faaborg; Den fynske bladkrig; Mine cykelture på Hedebo-egnen; Rapport fra beskyttelsesrummet; Lav selv dine oste; Pagtens tegn; Judaism and Sex; Verdens eneste vegetariske landsby; Hul i hovedet; Mit elskede Safed; Man tager en kartoffel; Blandingsgods; Vi er et folk alene; Sporg Benjamin; Neot Kedumin; Gittan på landet; Advokat for avocadoen;

Segertrønen; Man tager en struds; Das Forellenkochbuch; The Miracle of Love; The Ostrich Cookbook; Anleitung zur herstellung von Öko-Käse. Contributions to: Svenska Journalen; Helse; Sundhedsbladet. Honours: Danish Ministry of Culture, 1981; Danish Author's Association, 1991, 1993; Frøken Suhr's Literary Award, 1993; Travel Award, Danish Ministry of Culture, 1996; Ellen and Nils Nilssons' Literary Award, 1998; The Poet Poul Sørensen's Literary Award, 1998. Memberships: Danish Author's Association; Union of Israeli Writers. Address: KUNSTHUSET 67, Sejerslevvej 67, DK-6260 Hojer, Denmark.

KAUFMAN Gerald (Bernard), b. 21 June 1930, Leeds, England. Member of Parliament; Writer. Education: MA, Queen's College, Oxford, 1953. Appointments: Assistant General Secretary, Fabian Society, 1954-55; Staff, Daily Mirror, 1955-64; Political Correspondent, New Statesman, 1964-65; Parly Press Liaison Officer, 1965-70, Member of Parliament, Manchester, Ardwick, 1970-83, Manchester, Gorton, 1983-, Labour Party; Parliamentary Under-Secretary of State, Department of the Environment, 1974-75; Department of Industry, 1975; Minister of State, Department of Industry, 1975-79; Shadow Environment Secretary, 1980-83; Shadow Home Secretary, 1983-87; Shadow Foreign Secretary, 1987-92; Chairman, Select Committee on the National Heritage, 1992-97, and on Culture, Media and Sport, 1997-. Publications: How to Live Under Labour (co-author), 1964; The Left (editor), 1966; To Build the Promised Land, 1973; How to Be a Minister, 1980, 2nd edition, 1997; Renewal: Labour's Britain in the 1980s, 1983; My Life in the Silver Screen, 1985; Inside the Promised Land, 1986; Meet Me in St Louis, 1994. Honour: Privy Councillor, 1978. Address: 87 Charlbert Court, Eamont Street, London NW8 7DA, England.

KAUFMANN Myron S, b. 27 Aug 1921, Boston, Massachusetts, USA. Novelist. m. Paula Goldberg, 6 Feb 1960, div 1980, 1 son, 2 daughters. Education: AB, Harvard University, 1943. Publications: Novels: Remember Me To God, 1957; Thy Daughter's Nakedness, 1968; The Love of Elspeth Baker, 1982. Address: 111 Pond Street, Sharon, MA 02067, USA.

KAUFMANN Thomas DaCosta, b. 7 May 1948, New York, New York, USA. Professor of Art History; Writer. m. Virginia Burns Roehrig, 1 June 1974, div 17 July 1998, 1 daughter. Education: BA, MA, 1970, Yale University; MPhil, Warburg Institute, University of London, 1972; PhD, Harvard University, 1977. Appointments: Assistant Professor, 1977-83, Associate Professor, 1983-89, Professor of Art History, 1989-, Princeton University; Visiting professorships and curatorships. Publications: Variations on the Imperial Theme, 1978; Drawings From the Holy Roman Empire 1540-1650, 1982; L'Ecole de Prague, 1985; Art and Architecture in Central Europe 1550-1620, 1985; The School of Prague: Painting at the Court of Rudolf II, 1988; Central European Drawings 1680-1800, 1989; The Mastery of Nature, 1993; Court, Cloister and City, 1995. Contributions to: Books and professional journals. Honours: Marshall-Allison Fellow, 1970; David E Finley Fellow, National Gallery of Art, Washington, DC, 1974-77; American Council of Learned Societies Award, 1977-78, and Fellowship, 1982; Senior Fellow, Alexander von Humboldt Stiftung, Berlin and Munich, 1985-86, 1989-90; Guggenheim Fellowship, 1993-94; Herzog August Bibliothek Fellow, Wolfenbüttel, 1994. Memberships: College Art Association of America; Renaissance Society of America; Verband Deutscher Kunsthistorien. Address: c/o Department of Art and Archeology, McCormick Hall, Princeton University, Princeton, NJ 08544, USA.

KAUSHIK J N, (JNK), b. 4 Nov 1935, Haryana, India. Educator. m. Vimla Kaushik, 21 June 1961, 1 son, 2 daughters. Education: MA, Hindi, Delhi University, 1963; MA, English, Aligarh University, 1968; JD, Punjab University, 1959; MEd, 1969, PhD, Education, 1974, Kurukshetra University; Advanced course in Applied Linguistics, Osmania University/NCERT, 1972. Appointments: Teaching, 1955-65; Headmaster, 1965-75;

Teacher Educator, 1975-88; Director, 1988-90, Vice-Principal, 1991-, Haryana Sahitya Academy. Publications: Books: Basic Hindi Vocabulary; Haryanavi Hindi Kosh; Vedic Haryanavi Kosh; Sukti Sudha Kosh; Uchcharan ki Siksha; Hindi Shikshan; Lesson Plan Manual; Maati Ka Mol; Budha Suhagin, novel; Asha Kiran, novel; Ped Kiskahaui; Yatra ke Padava, poem; Dhara ke Geet, poem; Budda Vani, poem; Fasts of the Hindus, Parts i, ii, iii; Krishna Katha Aur Lok Sahitya; Ram Katha or Lok Sahitya; Delhi Anchel ki Lok Samskriti; Dilli Ki Kahaui; Kailash Mansarouer ki Yatsa; Children's literature: Chunmun ki Kahaniyan, Anhon ki Kahani; Rashtriya Saba Samvat ki Kahani; Vaigyanib Kahaniyan; Pradusan ki Kahani; Others. Contributions to: Editor, Harigandha, Haryana Sahitys Akademy Magazine; Editor, Naval Kusum; Regular columns in Sevagram weekly, 10 years. Honours: 2 National Awards for books; Delhi Teacher Award; National Award for Teachers; Teacher Educator Awards, 8 times. Memberships: Secretary, Delhi Hindi Sahitya Sammelan; Saraswati Vihar Mandal; Founder, Bhartiya Samskriti Chitra Mandal; Secretary, New Delhi Evening Institute of Hindi. Literary Agents: Hindi Book Centre, Asaf Ali Rd, New Delhi 2, India; National Publishing House, Dasye Ganj, New Delhi 2, India. Address: C-605 Saraswati, Vihar, Delhi 110034, India.

KAVALER Lucy Estrin, b. 29 Aug 1930, New York, New York, USA. Author. m. 9 Nov 1948, 1 son, 1 daughter. Education: BA magna cum laude, Oberlin College, Ohio; Fellowship, Advanced Science Writing, Columbia University Graduate School. Publications: Private World of High Society, 1960; Mushrooms, Molds and Miracles, 1965; The Astors, 1966; Freezing Point, 1970; Noise the New Menace, 1975; A Matter of Degree, 1981; The Secret Lives of the Edmonts, 1989; Heroes and Lovers, 1995. Contributions to: Smithsonian; Natural History; McCall's; Reader's Digest; Redbook; Primary Cardiology; Woman's Day (encyclopaedia); Skin Cancer Foundation Journal; Memories; Female Patient. Address: c/o Noah Lukeman, 501 Fifth Avenue, New York, NY 10017, USA.

KAVALER Rebecca, b. 26 July 1930, Atlanta, Georgia, USA. Writer. m. Frederic Kavaler, 1955, 2 sons. Education: AB, University of Georgia. Publications: Further Adventures of Brunhild, 1978; Doubting Castle, 1984; Tigers in the Woods, 1986. Contributions to: Anthologies and magazines. Honours: Short stories included in Best of Nimrod, 1957-69; Best American Short Stories, 1972; Award for Short Fiction, Association of Writers and Poets, 1978; National Endowment for the Arts Fellowships, 1979, 1985. Membership: PEN. Address: 425 Riverside Drive, New York, NY 10025, USA.

KAVANAGH Dan. See: BARNES Julian Patrick.

KAVANAGH Jake, b. 8 Jan 1962, Beaconsfield, England. Journalist. Education: Wycombe College, 1982. Appointments: Police Officer, Thames Valley, 1979-81; Ambulance Driver, 1983; Lock-keeper, River Thames, 1985-89; Features Editor, Link House Magazines, 1996-. Publication: The Ups and Downs of a Lockkeeper. Contributions to: Features and cartoons to Motorboats Monthly, Taxation, Sailing Today, 1990-. Memberships: Cartoonists Club of Great Britain; Yachting Journalists Association. Address: 7B Woodside Road, Sutton, Surrey SM1 3SU, England.

KAVANAGH P(atrick) J(oseph), b. 6 Jan 1931, Worthing, Sussex, England. Poet; Writer; Editor. m. (1) Sally Philipps, 1956, dec, (2) Catherine Ward, 1965, 2 sons. Education: MA, Merton College, Oxford. AppointmentS: Columnist, The Spectator, 1983-96; Times Literary Supplement, 1996-. Publications: Poetry: One and One, 1960; On the Way to the Depot, 1967; About Time, 1970; Edward Thomas in Heaven, 1974; Life Before Death, 1979; Selected Poems, 1982; Presences: New and Selected Poems, 1987; An Enchantment, 1991; Collected Poems, 1992. Fiction: A Song and Dance, 1968; A Happy Man, 1972; People and Weather, 1978; Scarf Jack: The Irish Captain, 1978; Rebel for Good,

1980; Only By Mistake, 1980. Non-Fiction: The Perfect Stranger, 1966; People and Places, 1988; Finding Connections, 1990; Voices in Ireland: A Traveller's Literary Companion, 1994. Editor: The Collected Poems of Ivor Gurney, 1982; The Oxford Book of Short Poems (with James Michie), 1985; The Bodley Head G K Chesterton, 1985; Selected Poems of Ivor Gurney, 1990; A Book of Consolations, 1992. Honours: Richard Hillary Prize, 1966; Guardian Fiction Prize, 1968; Cholmondeley Poetry Prize, 1993. Membership: Fellow, Royal Society of Literature. Address: c/o A D Peters, The Chamber, Chelsea Harbour, London SW10 0XF, England.

KAVANAUGH Cynthia. See: DANIELS Dorothy.

KAWALEC Julian, b. 11 Oct 1916, Wrzawy, Poland. Writer. m. Irene Wierzbanowska, 2 June 1948, 1 daughter. Education: Graduate, Jagellonian University, Kraków. Publications: Paths Among Streets, 1957; Scars, 1960; Bound to the Land, 1962; Overthrown Elms, 1963; The Dancing Hawk, 1964; Black Light, 1965; Wedding March, 1966; Appeal, 1968; Searching for Home, 1968; Praise of Hands, 1969; To Cross the River, 1973; Gray-Aureole, 1974; Great Feast, 1974; To Steal the Brother, 1982; Among the Gates, 1989; Dear Sadness (poems), 1992. Contributions to: Literary Life, Kraków; Literary Monthly, Warsaw. Honours: Prize of Polish Editors, 1962; Prizes of Minister of Culture and Art, 1967, 1985; Prize of State, 1975. Memberships: Polish Pen Club; Polish Writers Association; Society European Culture. Address: 39 Zaleskiego, 31-525 Kraków, Poland.

KAWINSKI Wojciech, b. 22 May 1939, Poland. Poet. m. Helena Lorenz, 17 Apr 1964, 1 son, 1 daughter. Education: MA, 1964. Appointments: Sub-Director, Pismo Literacko-Artystyczne, 1985-90. Publications: Odleglosci Posluzne, 1964; Narysowane We Wnetrzu, 1965; Ziarno Rzeki, 1967; Pole Widzewnia, 1970; Spiew Bezimienny, 1978; Pod Okiem Slonca, 1980; Listy Do Ciebie, 1982; Milosc Nienawistna, 1985; Ciemna strona jasnosci, 1989; Wieczorne sniegi, 1989; Czysty zmierzch, 1990; Pamiec zywa, 1990; Zwierciadlo sekund, 1991; Powrity Stów, 1991; Srebro Lisci, 1993; Zelazna Rosa, 1995; Planeta Ognia, 1997. Contributions to: Numerous journals and magazines. Honours: Prize, City of Kraków, 1985; Red Rose for Poetry, Gdansk, 1985; Prize of Klemens Jornicki, 1995. Membership: Polish Writers Association. Address: ul Stachiewicza 22a, 31-303 Kraków, Poland.

KAY Guy Gavriel, b. 7 Nov 1954, Weyburn, Saskatchewan, Canada. Author. m. Laura Beth Cohen, 15 July 1984, 2 sons. Education: BA, University of Manitoba, 1975; LLB, University of Toronto, 1978. Appointment: Principal Writer and Associate Producer, The Scales of Justice, CBC Radio Drama, 1981-90. Publications: The Summer Tree, 1984; The Darkest Road, 1986; The Wandering Fire, 1986; Tigana, 1990; A Song for Arbonne, 1992; The Lions of Al-Rassan, 1995. Contributions to: Journals. Honours: Aurora Prizes, 1986, 1990. Memberships: Association of Canadian Radio and TV Artists; Law Society of Upper Canada. Address: c/o Curtis Brown Agency, Haymarket House, 28/29 Haymarket, London SW1Y 4SP, England.

KAYE Geraldine (Hughesdon), b. 14 Jan 1925, Watford, Herts, England. Writer. m. 1948, div 1975, 1 son, 2 daughters. Education: BSc, Economics, London School of Economics and Political Science, 1949. Publications: Comfort Herself, 1985; A Breath of Fresh Air, 1986; Summer in Small Street, 1989; Someone Else's Baby, 1990; A Piece of Cake, 1991; Snowgirl, 1991; Stone Boy, 1991; Hands Off My Sister, 1993; Night at the Zoo, 1995; Forests of the Night, 1995; Late in the Day, 1997; The Dragon Upstairs, 1997; My Second Best Friend, 1998; Between Us (adult novel), 1998. Honour: The Other Award, 1986. Memberships: PEN; West Country Writers; Society of Authors. Address: 39 High Kingsdown, Bristol BS2 8EW, England.

KAYE Marvin Nathan, b. 10 Mar 1938, Philadelphia, Pennsylvania, USA. Writer. m. Saralee Bransdorf, 4 Aug 1963, 1 daughter. Education: BA, MA, Pennsylvania State University; Graduate study, University of Denver,

Colorado. Appointments: Senior Editor, Harcourt Brace Jovanovich; Artistic Director, The Open Book Theatre Company 1975-; Adjunct Professor of Creative Writing, New York University, 1975-; Seminar Director, The Smithsonian Institute, 1998-. Publications: The Histrionic Holmes, 1971; A Lively Game of Death, 1972; A Toy is Born, 1973; The Stein and Day Handbook of Magic, 1973; The Grand Ole Opry Murders, 1974; The Handbook of Mental Magic, 1974; Bullets for Macbeth, 1976; The Incredible Umbrella, 1977; Catalog of Magic, 1977; My Son the Druggist, 1977; The Laurel and Hardy Murders, 1977; My Brother the Druggist, 1979; The Amorous Umbrella, 1981; The Possession of Immanuel Wolf, 1981; The Soap Opera Slaughters, 1982; Ghosts of Night and Morning, 1985; Fantastique, 1993. With Parke Godwin: The Masters of Solitude, 1978; Wintermind, 1982; A Cold Blue Light, 1983. Editor: Fiends and Creatures, 1975; Brother Theodore's Chamber of Horrors, 1975; Ghosts, 1981; Masterpieces of Terror and the Supernatural, 1985; Ghosts of Night and Morning, 1987; Devils and Demons, 1987; Weird Tales, the Magazine That Never Dies, 1988; Witches and Warlocks, 1989; 13 Plays of Ghosts and the Supernatural, 1990; Haunted America, 1991; Lovers and Other Monsters, 1991; Sweet Revenge, 1992; Masterpieces of Terror and the Unknown, 1993; Frantic Comedy, 1993; The Game is Afoot, 1994; Angels of Darkness, 1995; Readers Theatre: How to Stage It, 1995; The Resurrected Holmes, 1996; Page to Stage, 1996; The Best of Weird Tales, 1923, 1997; The Confidential Casebook of Sherlock Holmes, 1998; Don't Open This Book, 1998. Contributions to: Amazing; Fantastic; Galileo; Family Digest; Columnist, Science Fiction Chronicle. Honour: 1st runner-up, Best Novella, British Fantasy Awards, 1978. Memberships: Several professional organisations. Address: c/o Donald C Maass, 157 West 57th Street, Suite 703, New York, NY 10019, USA.

KAYE Mary Margaret, b. 1909, Simla, India. Author. Publications: Six Bars at Seven, 1940; Death Walks in Kashmir, 1954; Death Walks in Berlin, 1955; Death Walks in Cyprus, 1956, as Death in Cyprus, 1984; Shadow of the Moon, revised edition, 1979; Later Than You Think, 1958, as Death in Kenya, 1983; House of Shade, 1959, as Death in Zanzibar, 1983; Night on the Island, 1960; Trade Wind, 1963, revised edition, 1981; The Far Pavilions, 1978; The Ordinary Princess, 1980; The Golden Calm (editor), 1980; Thistledown, 1981; Autobiography: Vol 1, The Sun in the Morning, 1990. Address: c/o St Martin's Press, 175 Fifth Avenue, New York, NY 10010, USA.

KAZAN Elia, b. 7 Sept 1909, Constantinople, Turkey (US citizen). Writer; Director. m. (1) Moly Day Thacher, 12 Dec 1983, dec, 2 sons, 2 daughters, (2) Barbara Loden, 5 June 1967, dec, 1 son, (3) Frances Rudge, 28 June 1982. Education: Williams College, 1930; Postgraduate School of Drama, 1932. Publications: America, America, 1962; The Arrangement, 1967; The Assassins, 1972; The Understudy, 1975; Acts of Love, 1978; The Anatolian, 1982; Elia Kazan: A Life, 1988; Beyond the Aegean, 1994. Contributions to: Periodicals. Honours: Honorary doctorates. Address: c/o Alfred A Knopf, 201 East 50th Street, New York, NY 10022, USA.

KAZANTZIS Judith, b. 14 Aug 1940, Oxford, England. Poet; Fiction Writer. 1 son, 1 daughter. Education: Honours Degree, Modern History, Oxford, 1961. Appointments: General Council, Poetry Society, member, 1991-94. Publications: Poetry Collections: Minefield, 1977; The Wicked Queen, 1980; Touch Papers (co-author), 1982; Let's Pretend, 1984; Flame Tree, 1988; A Poem for Guatemala, pamphlet, 1988; The Rabbit Magician Plate, 1992; Selected Poems 1977-92, 1995; Swimming Through the Grand Hotel, 1997; The Odysseus Papers: Fictions of the Odyssey of Homer, 1999. Contributions to: Stand; London Magazine; New Statesman; Poetry Review; Ambit; Verse; Honest Ulsterman; Bete Noire; Key West Reader; Faber Book of Blue Verse; Virago Book of Love Poetry; Comparative Criticism; Mind Readings, anthology. Honours: Judge, Sheffield Hallam Poetry Competition, 1995-96; Judge, Stand International Poetry Competition, 1998.

Memberships: Poetry Society; Society of Authors; English PEN; Labour Party. Address: PO Box 1671, Key West, FL 33041, USA.

KAZIN Alfred, b. 5 June 1915, Brooklyn, New York, USA. Distinguished Professor of English; Writer. m. (1) Caroline Bookman, 23 May 1947, div, 1 son, (2) Ann Birstein, 26 June 1953, div, 1 daughter, (3) Judith Dunford, 21 May 1983. Education: BSS, College of the City of New York, 1935; MA, Columbia University, 1938. Appointments: Literary Editor, 1942-43, Contributing Editor, 1943-45, The New Republic; Associate Editor, Fortune, 1943-44; William Allan Neilson Research Professor, Smith College, 1953-54; Professor of American Studies, Amherst College, 1955-58; Berg Professor of Literature, New York University, 1957; Christian Gauss Lecturer, Princeton University, 1961; Buell Gallagher Professor, City College of the City University of New York, 1962; Beckman Professor, University of California at Berkeley, 1963; Distinguished Professor of English, State University of New York at Stony Brook, 1963-73; Distinguished Professor of English, 1973-84, Distinguished Professor Emeritus, 1984-, Hunter College of the City University of New York; Distinguished Professor of English, City University Graduate Center, 1973-; William White Professor of English, University of Notre Dame, 1978-79; Various other visiting lectureships and professorships. Publications: On Native Grounds, 1942; A Walker in the City, 1951; The Inmost Leaf, 1955; Contemporaries, 1962; Starting Out in the Thirties, 1965; Bright Book of Life, 1973; New York Jew, 1978; An American Procession, 1984; A Writer's America: Landscape in Literature, 1988; Our New York, 1990; A Lifetime Burning in Every Moment, 1996; God and the American Writer, 1997. Editor: The Portable William Blake, 1946; F Scott Fitzgerald: The Man and His Work, 1951; The Stature of Theodore Dreiser (with Charles Shapiro), 1955; Ralph Waldo Emerson: A Modern Anthology (with Daniel Aaron); The Works of Ann Frank (with Ann Birstein), 1959; The Open Form: Essays for Our Time, 1965; Selected Short Stories of Nathaniel Hawthorne, 1966; Writers at Work: The Paris Review Interviews, Third Series, 1967. Other: The Emmy Parrish Lectures in American Studies, 1992. Contributions to: Books and periodicals. Honours: Guggenheim Fellowships, 1940, 1947; Rockefeller Fellowship, 1945; Fulbright Lecturer, University of Cambridge, 1952; George Polk Memorial Award for Criticism, 1966; Brandeis University Creative Arts Award, 1973; Center for the Advanced Study of Behavioral Studies Fellow, 1977-78; National Endowment for the Humanities Senior Fellow, 1977-78; Modern Language Association Medal, 1983; Several honorary doctorates. Memberships: American Academy of Arts and Letters; Phi Beta Kappa. Address: c/o Department of English, Graduate Center, City University of New York, 33 West 42nd Street, New York, NY 10036, USA.

KEANE John B(rendan), b. 21 July 1928, Listowel, County Kerry, Ireland. Author. Education: Graduated, St Michael's College, Listowel, 1946. Publications: Sive, 1959; Sharon's Grave, 1960; The Highest House on the Mountain, 1961; Many Young Men of Twenty, 1961; The Street and Other Poems, 1961; Hut 42, 1963; The Man From Clare, 1963; Strong Tea, 1963; The Year of the Hiker, 1964; Self-Portrait, 1964; The Field, 1965; The Rain at the End of the Summer, 1967; Letters of a Successful T D, 1967; Big Maggie, 1969; The Change in Mame Fadden, 1971; Moll, 1971; Letters of an Irish Parish Priest, 1972; Letters of an Irish Publican, 1973; Values, 1973; The Crazy Wall, 1973; The Gentle Art of Matchmaking, 1973; Letters of a Love-Hungry Farmer, 1974; Letters of a Matchmaker, 1975; Death Be Not Proud, 1976; Letters of a Civic Guard, 1976; Is the Holy Ghost Really a Kerryman, 1976; The Good Thing (play), 1976; Letters of a Country Postman, 1977; Unlawful Sex and Other Testy Matters, 1978; The Buds of Ballybunion, 1979; Stories From a Kerry Fireside, 1980; The Chastitute, 1981; More Irish Short Stories, 1981; Letters of Irish Minister of State, 1982; Man of the Triple Name, 1984; Owl Sandwiches, 1985; The Bodhran Makers, 1986; Love Bites, 1991; Duraneo, 1992; The Ram of God, 1992; Christmas Short Stories, 1996. Honours:

Honorary D Litt, Trinity College, Dublin, 1984; Honorary DFA, Marymount Manhatten College, 1984; Independent Irish Life Award, 1986; Sunday Tribune Award, 1986; Irish American Literary Award, 1988; Person of the Year Award, 1991. Memberships: Irish PEN, president, 1973-74; Royal Dublin Society, honorary life member, 1991. Address: 37 William Street, Listowel, County Kerry, Ireland.

KEATING Frank, b. 4 Oct 1937, Hereford, England. Journalist. m. Jane Anne Sinclair, 8 Aug 1987. Appointments: Editor, Outside Broadcasts, ITV, 1964-70; Columnist, The Guardian, 1975-, Punch, 1980-. Publications: Bowled Over, 1979; Up and Under, 1980; Another Bloody Day in Paradise, 1981; High, Wide, and Handsome, 1985; Long Days, Late Nights, 1986; Gents and Players; Half-Time Whistle, 1992; Band of Brothers, 1996. Contributions to: Punch; New Statesman; Listener; Cricketer. Honours: Sportswriter of the Year, 1978, 1980, 1989; Magazine Writer of the Year, 1987; Sports Journalist of the Year, British Press Awards, 1988. Address: Church House Marden, Hereford HR1 3EN, England.

KEATING Henry Reymond Fitzwalter, b. 31 Oct 1926, St Leonards-on-Sea, Sussex, England. Author. m. 1953, 3 sons, 1 daughter. Education: BA, Trinity College, Dublin. Publications: The Perfect Murder, 1964; Inspector Ghote Trusts the Heart, 1972; The Lucky Alphonse, 1982; Under a Monsoon Cloud, 1986; Dead on Time, 1989; The Iciest Sin, 1990; The Man Who (editor), 1992; The Rich Detective, 1993; Doing Wrong, 1994; The Good Detective, 1995; The Bad Detective, 1996; Asking Questions, 1996; The Soft Detective, 1997; Bribery, Corruption Also, 1999. Contributions to: Crime books reviews, the Times, 1967-83. Honours: Gold Dagger Awards, 1964, 1980, Diamond Dagger Award, 1996, Crime Writers Association. Memberships: Crime Writers Association, chairman, 1970-71; Detection Club, president, 1986; Royal Society of Literature, fellow; Society of Authors, chairman, 1982-84. Address: 35 Northumberland Place, London W2 5AS, England.

KEAY John (Stanley Melville), b. 18 Sept 1941, Devon, England. Author. Education: BA, Magdalen College, Oxford, 1963. Publications: Into India, 1973; When Men and Mountains Meet, 1977; The Gilgit Game, 1979; India Discovered, 1981; Eccentric Travellers, 1982; Highland Drove, 1984; Explorers Extraordinary, 1985; The Royal Geographical Society's History of World Exploration, 1991; The Honourable Company, 1991; Collins Encyclopaedia of Scotland, 1994; Indonesia: From Sabang to Meranke, 1995; The Explorers of the Western Himalayas, 1996; Last Post, 1997. Address: Succoth, Dalmally, Argyll, Scotland.

KEBL Anna-Luise, (A L Weiss, Lu Borows, Marielu Winter), b. 5 Feb 1922, Neustettin, Germany. Retired. m. George W Kebl, 1 daughter. Education: Business College, Berlin, 1941. Appointments: Office Clerk, Stars and Stripes, Würzburg, 1954-55; School Secretary, Landerziehungsheim Schloss Thüngen, Unterfranken, 1955-59; Bookkeeper, Versicherungen Michael Böhm, Würzburg, 1959-60; Australian Citizen, 1965-. Publications: Novels: Maurisches Filigran, 1949; Chanson für Corinna, 1950; Morgen ist alles Vergangenheit, 1952; Wild Geese, Swans and Nightingales (autobiographical novel), 1998. Contributions to: Daily Newspapers of Coburg, Bamberg, Würzburg, Lübeck. Address: 7 Nathalia Road, Belgrave South, Victoria 3160, Australia.

KEEBLE Neil Howard, b. 7 Aug 1944, London, England. University Reader in English Literature. m. Jenny Bowers, 20 July 1968, 2 sons, 1 daughter. Education: BA, University of Lampeter, 1966; DPhil, University of Oxford, 1974; D Litt, University of Stirling, 1994. Publications: Richard Baxter: Puritan Man of Letters, 1982; The Literary Culture of Nonconformity, 1987; Calendar of the Correspondence of Richard Baxter (co-author), 1991. Editor: The Autobiography of Richard Baxter, 1974; The Pilgrim's Progress, 1984; John Bunyan: Conventicle and Parnassus, 1988; The Cultural Identity of Seventeenth-Century Women (a reader), 1994;

Lucy Hutchinson, Memoirs of the Life of Colonel Hutchinson, 1995. Contributions to: Numerous articles on cultural history 1500-1700, in academic journals. Honour: Fellow, Royal Historical Society, 1990. Address: Duncraggan House, Airthrey Road, Stirling FK9 5JS, Scotland.

KEEFFE Barrie (Colin), b. 31 Oct 1945, London, England. Playwright. m. (1) Dee Truman, 1969, div 1979, (2) Verity Bargate, 1981, dec 1981, 2 stepsons, (3) Julia Linday, 1983, div 1993. Appointments: Actor; Reporter, Stratford and London Express; Dramatist-in-Residence, Shaw Theatre, London, 1977, Royal Shakespeare Company, 1978; Associate Writer, Theatre Royal Stratford East, London, 1986-91. Publications: Plays: A Mad World, My Masters, 1977, revised version, 1984; Eyre Methuen, 1977; Gimme Shelter, 1977; Barbarians, 1977; Frozen Assets, 1978, revised version, 1987; Sus, 1979; Heaven Scent, 1979; Bastard Angel, 1980; Black Lear, 1980; She's So Modern, 1980; Chorus Girls, 1981; A Gentle Spirit (with Jules Croiset), 1981; The Long Good Friday (screenplay), 1984; Better Times, 1985; King of England, 1986; My Girl, 1989; Not Fade Away, 1990; Wild Justice, 1990; I Only Want to Be With You, 1997. Radio Plays: Good Old Uncle Jack, 1975; Pigeon Skyline, 1975; Self-Portrait, 1977; Paradise, 1990; Barrie Keeffe Plays I, forthcoming. Television Plays: Gotcha, 1977; Champions, 1978; Hanging Around, 1978; Waterloo Sunset, 1979; No Excuses Series, 1983; King, 1984; The Gary Oldman Fan Club, 1998. Honours: French Critics Prix Revelation, 1978; Giles Cooper Award, Best Radio Plays, 1978; Edgar Allan Poe Award, Mystery Writers of America, 1982; Ambassador for United Nations 5oth Anniversary, 1995. Address: 110 Annandale Road, London SE10 0JZ, England.

KEEGAN John (Desmond Patrick), b. 15 May 1934, London, England. Editor; Writer; Defence Correspondent. m. Susanne Everett, 1960, 2 sons, 2 daughters. Education: BA, 1957, MA, 1962, Balliol College, Oxford. Appointments: Senior Lecturer in Military History, Royal Military Academy, Sandhurst, 1960-68; Defence Editor, Daily Telegraph, 1986-. Publications: The Face of Battle, 1976; Who's Who in Miltary History (co-author), 1976; World Armies (editor), 1979, new edition, 1982; Six Armies in Normandy, 1982; Zones of Conflict (co-author), 1986; The Mask of Command, 1987; The Price of Admiralty, 1988, reissued as Battle at Sea, 1993; The Times Atlas of the Second World War, 1989; Churchill's Generals (editor), 1991; A History of Warfare, 1993; Warpaths: Travels of a Military Historian in North America, 1995. Honours: Officer of the Order of the British Empire, 1991; Duff Cooper Prize, 1994. Address: The Manor House, Kilmington, near Warminster, Wilts BA12 6RD, England.

KEEGAN Mary Constance, (Mary Heathcott, Mary Raymond), b. 30 Sept 1914, Manchester, England. Author. Appointments: Editorial positions, London Evening News, 1934-40, Straits Times and Singapore Free Press, 1940-42, MOI All-India Radio, 1944, Time and Tide, 1945, John Herling's Labor Letter, 1951-54. Publications: As Mary Keegan, Mary Heathcott or Mary Raymond: If Today Be Sweet, 1956; Island of the Heart, 1957; Love Be Wary, 1958; Her Part of the House, 1960; Hide My Heart, 1961; Thief of My Heart, 1962; Never Doubt Me, 1963; Shadow of a Star, 1963; Take-Over, 1965; Girl in a Mask, 1965; The Divided House, 1966; The Long Journey Home, 1967; I Have Three Sons, 1968; That Summer, 1970; Surety for a Stranger, 1971; The Pimpernel Project, 1972; The Silver Girl, 1973; Villa of Flowers, 1976; April Promise, 1980; Grandma Tyson's Legacy, 1982. Address: Cockenskell, Blawith, Ulverston, Cumbria, England.

KEEGAN William James, b. 3 July 1938, London, England. Journalist. m. (1) Tessa Ashton, 7 Feb 1967, div 1982, 2 sons, 2 daughters, (2) Hilary Stonefrost, 1992, 1 son, 2 daughters. Appointments: Economics Editor, 1977, Associate Editor, 1983-, The Observer; Visiting Professor of Journalism, Sheffield University, 1989-. Publications: Consulting Father Wintergreen (novel), 1974; A Real Killing (novel), 1976; Who Runs the Economy?, 1979;

Mrs Thatcher's Economic Experiment, 1984; Britain Without Oil, 1985; Mr Lawson's Gamble, 1989; The Spectre of Capitalism, 1992. Contributions to: The Tablet; Frequent Broadcaster. Honours: Honorary D.Litt. City University, 1998; Honorary D.Litt. Sheffield. Membership: Department of Applied Economics, Cambridge, advisory board, 1988-93. Address: c/o Garrick Club, London WC2, England.

KEELEY Edmund (Leroy), b. 5 Feb 1928, Damascus, Syria (US citizen). Professor of Creative Writing and English Emeritus; Author; Translator. m. Mary Stathatos-Kyris, 18 Mar 1951. Education: BA, Princeton University, 1949; DPhil, University of Oxford, 1952. Appointments: Instructor, Brown University, 1952-53; Instructor, 1954-57, Assistant Professor, 1957-63, Associate Professor, 1963-70, Professor of English and Creative Writing, 1970-92, Charles Barnwell Straut Class of 1923 Professor of English, 1992-94, Professor Emeritus, 1994-, Princeton University; Visiting Lecturer, University of Iowa, 1962-63, University of the Aegean, 1988; Writer-in-Residence, Knox College, 1963; Visiting Professor, New School for Social Research, New York City, 1980, Columbia University, 1981, King's College, University of London, 1996; Fulbright Lecturer, University of Thessaloniki, 1986; Fulbright Lecturer, 1985, and Research Fellow, 1987, University of Athens; Senior Associate Member, St Antony's College, Oxford, 1996. Publications: Fiction: The Libation, 1958; The Gold-Hatted Lover, 1961; The Imposter, 1970; Voyage to a Dark Island, 1972; A Wilderness Called Peace, 1985; School for Pagan Lovers, 1993. Non-Fiction: Cavafy's Alexandria, 1976, new edition, 1995; Modern Greek Poetry: Voice and Myth, 1982; The Salonika Bay Murder: Cold War Politics and the Polk Affair, 1989; Albanian Journal: The Road to Elbasan, 1997; George Seferis and Edmund Keeley: Correspondence, 1951-71, 1997; Translator: George Seferis: Collected Poems (with Philip Sherrard), 1967, revised edition, 1995; Odysseus Elytis: The Axion Esti (with George Savidis), 1974; C P Cavafy: Collected Poems (with Philip Sherrard and George Savidis), 1975, revised edition, 1992; Angelos Sikelianos: Selected Poems (with Philip Sherrard), 1979, revised edition, 1997; Odysseus Elytis: Selected Poems (with Philip Sherrard), 1981; Yannis Ritsos: Repetitions, Testimonies, Parentheses, 1991; A Greek Quintet (with Philip Sherrard), 1992; Translation: Reflections and Conversations, 1998; Inventing Paradise: The Greek Journey 1937-47, forthcoming. Contributions to: Books and journals. Honours: Rome Prize Fellow, American Academy of Arts and Letters, 1959-60; Guggenheim Fellowships, 1959-60, 1973; Columbia University Translation Center-PEN Award, 1975; Harold Morton Landon Translation Award, 1980; National Endowment for the Arts Fellowships, 1981, 1988-89; Rockefeller Foundation Scholar, Bellagio Study Center, Italy, 1982, 1989; Research Fellow, Virginia Center for the Creative Arts, 1983, 1984, 1986, 1990; Pushcart Prize Anthology Award, 1984; European Prize for Translation of Poetry, 1987; Honorary Doctorate, University of Athens, 1994. Memberships: American Academy of Arts and Sciences; American Literary Translators Association; Authors Guild; Modern Greek Studies Association, president, 1969-73; PEN American Center, president, 1991-93; Poetry Society of America. Address: 140 Littlebrook Road, Princeton, New Jersey, USA.

KEEN Geraldine. See: NORMAN Geraldine.

KEENAN Brian, b. 28 Sept 1950, Belfast, Northern Ireland. Author. m. Audrey Doyle, 20 May 1993. Education: BA, 1974, MA, 1984, Ulster University; PhD, Queen's University, Belfast, 1993. Appointments: Instructor in English, American University, Beirut, Lebanon, 1985-86; Writer-in-Residence, Trinity College, Dublin, 1993-94. Publications: An Evil Cradling: The Five-Year Ordeal of a Hostage, 1992; Blind Fight (screenplay), 1995. Address: c/o Elaine Steel, 110 Gloucester Avenue, London NW1 8JA, England.

KEENE Dennis, b. 10 July 1934, London, England. Retired Professor of English Literature; Poet; Writer; Translator. m. Keiko Kurose, 5 May 1962, 1 daughter.

Education: BA, Honours, English Literature and Language, 1957, MA, 1961, DPhil, 1973, University of Oxford. Appointments: Assistant Lecturer in English Literature, University of Malaya, 1958-60; Lecturer in English Language and Literature, Kyoto University, 1961-63; Lecturer in English Literature, Kyushu University, 1965-69; Assistant Professor, 1970-76, Professor of English Literature, 1976-81, 1983-93, Japan Women's University. Publications: Poetry: Surviving, 1980; Universe and Other Poems, 1984. Prose: Problems in English, 1969; Yokomitsu Riichi, Modernist, 1980; Wasurerareta Kuni, Nippon, 1995. Editor: Selected Poems of Henry Howard, Earl of Surrey, 1985. Translator: Over 10 books of Japanese poems, novels and short stories, 1974-97. Honours: Independent Foreign Fiction Special Award, 1990; Noma Translation Prize, 1992. Address: 77 Staunton Road, Headington, Oxford OX3 7TL, England.

KEENE Donald, b. 18 June 1922, New York, New York, USA. Professor of Japanese Emeritus; Writer; Translator. Education: BA, 1942, MA, 1947, PhD, 1951, Columbia University; MA, 1949, DLitt, 1978, Cambridge University. Appointments: Lecturer, Cambridge University, England, 1948-53; Guest Editor, Asahi Shimbun, Tokyo, Japan; Shincho Professor Emeritus of Japanese, Columbia University. Publications: The Battles of Coxinga, 1951; The Japanese Discovery of Europe, 1952, 2nd edition, 1969; Japanese Literature: An Introduction for Western Readers, 1953; Living Japan, 1957; Bunraku, the Puppet Theater of Japan, 1965; No: The Classical Theatre of Japan, 1966; Landscapes and Portraits, 1971; Some Japanese Portraits, 1978; World Within Walls, 1978; Meeting with Japan, 1978; Travels in Japan, 1981; Dawn to the West, 1984; Travellers of a Hundred Ages, 1990; Seeds in the Heart, 1993; On Familiar Terms, 1994; Modern Japanese Diaries, 1995. Editor: Modern Japanese Literature, 1956; Sources of Japanese Tradition, 1958; Twenty Plays of the No Theater, 1970. Translations: The Setting Sun, 1956; Five Modern No Plays, 1957; No Longer Human, 1958; Major Plays of Chikamatsu, 1961; The Old Woman, the Wife and the Archer, 1961; After the Banquet, 1965; Essays in Idleness, 1967; Madame de Sade, 1967; Friends, 1969; The Man Who Turned into a Stick, 1972; Three Plays of Kobo Abe, 1993; The Narrow Road to Oku, 1997; The Tale of the Bamboo Cutter, 1998. Honours: D.Litt. Tohoku, 1997; D.Litt. Waseda, 1998. Memberships: Japan Society, New York, director, 1979-82; American Academy of Arts and Letters; Japan Academy, foreign member. Literary Agent: Georges Borchardt. Address: 407 Kent Hall, Columbia University, New York, NY 10027, USA.

KEIGER John Frederick Victor, b. 7 Dec 1952, Wembley, England. University Pofessor. Education: Institut d'etudes Politiques d'Aix-en Provence, University of Aix Marseille III, France, 1971-74; PhD, University of Cambridge, 1975-78. Appointments: Professor, Salford University, Manchester. Publications: France and the Origins of the First World War; Europe 1848-1914 (19 volumes in British Documents on Foreign Affairs, Reports and Papers from the Foreign Office Confidential Print), 1988-92; Raymond Paircare, 1997. Contributions to: Times Higher Education Supplement; History; International History Review. Address: Department of Languages, Salford University, Manchester M5 4WT, England.

KEILLOR Garrison, (born Gary Edward Keillor), b. 7 Aug 1942, Anoka, Minnesota, USA. Writer; Radio Host. Education: BA, University of Minnesota, 1966. Appointments: Creator-Host, national public radio programmes, A Prairie Home Companion and American Radio Company. Publications: Happy to Be Here, 1982; Lake Wobegon Days, 1985; Leaving Home, 1987; We Are Still Married: Stories and Letters, 1989; WLT: A Radio Romance, 1991; The Book of Guys, 1993; Wobegon Days, 1997. Children's Books: Cat, You Better Come Home, 1995; The Old Man Who Loved Cheese, 1996; Sandy Bottom Orchestra, 1997. Contributions to: Newspapers and magazines. Honours: George Foster Peabody Award, 1980; Grammy Award, 1987; Ace

Award, 1988; Best Music and Entertainment Host Awards, 1988, 1989; American Academy and Institute of Arts and Letters Medal, 1990; Music Broadcast Communications Radio Hall of Fame, 1994. Address: c/o Minnesota Public Radio, 45 East 7th Street, St Paul, MN 55101, USA.

KEITH W(illiam) J(ohn), b. 9 May 1934, London, England (Canadian citizen, 1974). Professor of English Emeritus; Literary Critic; Poet. m. Hiroko Teresa Sato, 26 Dec 1965. Education: BA, Jesus College, Cambridge, 1958; MA, 1959, PhD, 1961, University of Toronto. Appointments: Lecturer, 1961-62, Assistant Professor, 1962-66, McMaster University; Associate Professor, 1966-71, Professor of English, 1971-95, Professor Emeritus, 1995-, University of Toronto; Editor, University of Toronto Quarterly, 1976-85. Publications: Richard Jefferies: A Critical Study, 1965; Charles G D Roberts, 1969; The Rural Tradition, 1974; Charles G D Roberts: Selected Poetry and Critical Prose (editor), 1974; The Poetry of Nature, 1980; The Arts in Canada: The Last Fifty Years (co-editor), 1980; Epic Fiction: The Art of Rudy Wiebe, 1981; A Voice in the Land: Essays by and About Rudy Wiebe (editor), 1981; Canadian Literature in English, 1985; Regions of the Imagination, 1988; Introducing The Edible Woman, 1989; A Sense of Style: Studies in the Art of Fiction in English-Speaking Canada, 1989; An Independent Stance: Essays on English-Canadian Criticism and Fiction, 1991; Echoes in Silence (poems), 1992; Literary Images of Ontario, 1992; The Jefferies Canon, 1995. Contributions to: Journals. Honour: Fellow, Royal Society of Canada, 1979. Membership: Richard Jefferies Society, honorary president, 1974-91. Address: University College, University of Toronto, Toronto, Ont M5S 3H7, Canada.

KELL Richard (Alexander), b. 1 Nov 1927, Youghal, County Cork, Ireland. Retired Senior Lecturer in English; Poet; Editor. m. Muriel Adelaide Nairn, 31 Dec 1953, 2 sons, 2 daughters. Education: BA, 1952, Higher Diploma in Education, 1953, University of Dublin. Appointments: Lecturer in English, Isleworth Polytechnic, England, 1960-70; Senior Lecturer in English, Newcastle upon Tyne Polytechnic, 1970-83; Joint Editor, Other Poetry, 1994. Publications: Poems, 1957; Control Tower, 1962; Six Irish Poets, 1962; Differences, 1969; Humours, 1978; Heartwood, 1978; The Broken Circle, 1981; Wall (with others), 1981; In Praise of Warmth, 1987; Rock and Water, 1993. Contributions to: Newspapers and periodicals. Address: 18 Rectory Grove, Gosforth, Newcastle upon Tyne NE3 1AL, England.

KELLEGHAN Kevin Michael, b. 23 Sept 1934, Chicago, Illinois, USA. Writer; Trainer. m. Beatriz Monges, 23 Aug 1957, 2 sons. Education: BA, English, De Paul Law School, Illinois; University of the Americas, Mexico. Publications: I Earn Now You Can Invest or Retire in Mexico; Periodismo Economico. Contributions to: Magazines and newspapers. Membership: Authors Guild. Address; 504 Fairview Boulevard, Rockford, IL 61107-4861, UA.

KELLEHER Victor, (Veronica Hart), b. 19 July 1939, London, England. Writer. m. Alison Lyle, 2 Jan 1962, 1 son, 1 daughter. Education: BA, University of Natal, 1961; Diploma in Education, University of St Andrews, 1963; BA, Honours, University of the Witwatersrand, 1969; MA 1970, DLitt et Phil 1973, University of South Africa. Appointments: Junior Lecturer in English, University of the Witwatersrand, 1969; Lecturer, 1970-71, Senior Lecturer in English, 1972-73, University of South Africa, Pretoria; Lecturer in English, Massey University, Palmerston North, New Zealand, 1973-76; Lecturer, 1976-79, Senior Lecturer, 1980-83, Associate Professor of English, 1984-87, University of New England, Armidale, Australia. Publications: Voices from the River, 1979; Forbidden Paths of Thual, 1979; The Hunting of Shadroth, 1981; Master of the Grove, 1982; Africa and After, 1983; The Beast of Heaven, 1983 Papio, 1983; The Green Piper, 1984; Taronga, 1986; The Makers, 1987; Em's Story, 1988; Baily's Bones, 1988; The Red King, 1989; Wintering, 1990; Brother Night, 1990; Del-Del, 1991; To the Dark Tower, 1992; Micky Darlin, 1992; Where the Whales Sing, 1994; Parkland, 1994; Earthsong, 1995; Storyman, 1996; Fire Dancer, 1996; Slow Burn, 1997 Double God (as Veronica Hart), 1994; The House That Jack Built (as Veronica Hart), 1994. Contributions to: Anthologies and magazines. Membership: Australian Society of Authors. Literary Agent: Margaret Connolly. Address: 1 Avenue Road, Glebe, New South Wales 2037, Australia.

KELLER David (Michael), b. 26 May 1941, Berkeley, California, USA. Poet. m. Eloise F Bruce, 7 Aug 1994. Education: AB, Harvard College, 1964; Iowa State University, 1961-62; University of Iowa, 1963; PhD, University of Wisconsin, 1974. Appointments: Director of Admissions, Frost Place Festival of Poetry, Franconia, New Hampshire, 1980-; Assistant Poetry Coordinator, Geraldine R Dodge Foundation, 1986-90; American Guest Poet, Poets' House, Islandmagee, Northern Ireland, 1991-95; Teacher, University of Vermont, 1995, College of New Jersey, 1997. Publications: Circling the Site, 1982; A New Room, 1987; Land That Wasn't Ours, 1989. Contributions to: 8 anthologies, 1981-94, and various journals and magazines. Honours: Prize for Best Poem, Indiana Review, 1985; Artistic Merit Grant for Poetry, 1985, Fellowship for Poetry, 1991, New Jersey State Council on the Arts; Colladay Award, Quarterly Review of Literature, 1987; Lucille Medwick Memorial Award, Poetry Society of America, 1993; Carolyn Kizer Prize, Poetry Northwest, 1993. Memberships: Frost Place, Franconia, New Hampshire, advisory board, 1994-; Poetry Society of America, board of governors, 1989-92; Poets' House, Islandmagee, Northern Ireland, advisory board, 1993-; Roosevelt Arts Project, New Jersey, board of directors, 1988-. Address: 151 Hughes Avenue, Lawrenceville, NJ 08648, USA.

KELLER Evelyn Fox, b. 20 Mar 1936, New York, New York, USA. Professor of History and Philosophy of Science; Writer. 1 son, 1 daughter. Education: BA, Brandeis University, 1957; MA, Radcliffe College, 1959; PhD, Harvard University, 1963. Appointments: Professor of Mathematics and Humanities, Northeastern University, 1982-88; Senior Fellow, Cornell University, 1987; Member, Institute for Advanced Study, Princeton, New Jersey, 1987-88; Professor, University of California at Berkeley, 1988-92; Professor of History and Philosophy of Science, Massachusetts Institute of Technology, 1992-. Publications: A Felling for the Organism: The Life and Work of Barbara McClintock, 1983, 2nd edition, 1993; Reflections on Gender and Science, 1985, new edition, 1995; Women, Science and the Body (editor with Mary Jacobus and Sally Shuttleworth), 1989; Conflicts in Feminism (editor with Marianne Hirsch), 1990; Keywords in Evolutionary Biology (editor with Elisabeth Lloyd), 1992; Secrets of Life, Secrets of Death: Essays on Language, Gender, and Science, 1992; Refiguring Life: Metaphors of Twentieth Century Biology, 1995; Feminism and Science (editor with Helen Longino), 1996. Contributions to: Scholarly journals. Honours: Distinguished Publication Award, Association for Women in Psychology, 1986; Alumni Achievement Award, Brandeis University, 1991; Honorary Doctorates, Holyoke College, 1991, University of Amsterdam, 1995, Simmons College, 1995, Rensselaer Polytechnic Institute, 1995, Technical University of Lulea, Sweden, 1996; John D and Catharine T MacArthur Foundation Fellowship, 1992-97. Address: c/o Program in Science, Technology and Society, Massachusetts Institute of Technology, 77 Massachusetts Avenue, Cambridge, MA 02139, USA.

KELLERMAN Jonathan Seth, b. 9 Aug 1949, New York, New York, USA. Clincial Child Psychologist; Medical School Professor; Author. m. Fate Marder, 23 July 1972, 1 son, 3 daughters. Education: AB, University of California at Los Angeles, 1971; AM, 1973, PhD, 1974, University of Southern California at Los Angeles. Appointments: Freelance Illustrator, 1966-72, Director, Psychsocial Program, 1976-81, Staff Psychologist, 1975-81, Children's Hospital of Los Angeles; Clinical Associate Professor, University of Southern California School of Medicine, Los Angeles, 1979-; Head, Jonathan Kellerman PhD and Associates, Los Angeles, 1981-88. Publications: Psychological Aspects of Childhood Cancer, 1980; Helping the Fearful Child: A Parents' Guide to Everyday Problem Anxieties, 1981; When the Bough Breaks, 1985; Blood Test, 1986; Over the Edge, 1987; The Butcher's Theatre, 1988; Silent Partner, 1989; Time Bomb, 1990; Private Eyes, 1992; Devil's Waltz, 1993; Bad Love, 1994; Daddy, Daddy Can You Touch the Sky?, 1994; Self-Defense, 1995; The Web, 1996; Survival of the Fittest, 1997. Honours: Edgar Allan Poe Award, Mystery Writers of America, 1985; Anthony Boucher Award, 1986. Address: c/o Barney Karpfinger, 500 Fifth Avenue, New York, NY 10110, USA.

KELLEY Leo P(atrick), b. 10 Sept 1928, Wilkes Barre, Pennsylvania, USA. Author. Education: BA, New School for Social Research, New York City, 1957. Publications: The Counterfeits, 1967; Odyssey to Earthdeath, 1968; Time Rogue, 1970; The Coins of Murph, 1971; Brother John, 1971; Mindmix, 1972; Time: 110100, 1972, UK edition as The Man From Maybe, 1974; Themes in Science Fiction: A Journey Into Wonder (editor), 1972; The Supernatural in Fiction (editor), 1973; Deadlocked (novel), 1973; The Earth Tripper, 1973; Fantasy: The Literature of the Marvellous (editor), 1974. Science fiction novels for children: The Time Trap, 1977; Backward in Time, 1979; Death Sentence, 1979; Earth Two, 1979; Prison Satellite, 1979; Sunworld, 1979; Worlds Apart, 1979; Dead Moon, 1979; King of the Stars, 1979; On the Red World, 1979; Night of Fire and Blood, 1979; Where No Star Shines, 1979; Vacation in Space, 1979; Star Gold, 1979; Goodbye to Earth, 1979. Western novels: Luke Sutton series, 9 volumes, 1981-90; Cimarron series, 20 volumess, 1983-86; Morgan, 1986; A Man Named Dundee, 1988; Thunder Gods Gold, 1988. Address: 702 Long Boulevard, Long Beach, NY 11561, USA.

KELLMAN Steven G, b. 15 Nov 1947, Brooklyn, New York, USA. Critic; Professor of Comparative Literature. Education: BA, State University of New York, 1967; MA, 1969, PhD, 1972, University of California, Berkeley. Appointments: Editor- in-Chief, Occident, 1969-70; Assistant Professor, Bemidji State University, Minnesota, 1972-73; Lecturer, Tel-Aviv University, Israel, 1973-75; Visiting Lecturer, University of California, Irvine, 1975-76; Assistant Professor, 1976-80, Associate Professor, 1980-85, Professor, 1985-, Ashbel Smith Professor of Comparative Literature, 1995-, University of Texas, San Antonio; Fulbright Senior Lecturer, USSR, 1980; Visiting Associate Professor, University of California, Berkeley, 1982; Literary Scene Editor, USA Today; Partners of the Americas Lecturer, Peru, 1988, 1995; Fulbright Travel Grant, China, 1995; National Endowment for the Humanities Summer Seminar, Natal, South Africa, 1996; John E Sawyer Fellow, Longfellow Institute, Harvard University, 1997. Publications: The Self-Begetting Novel, 1980; Approaches to Teaching Camus's The Plague (editor), 1985; Loving Reading: Erotics of the Text, 1985; The Modern American Novel, 1991; The Plague: Fiction and Resistance, 1993; Perspectives on Raging Bull, 1994; Into The Tunnel (co-editor), 1998; Leslie Fiedler and American Culture (co-editor), 1999. Contributions to: San Antonio Light; Village Voice; Nation; Georgia Review; Moment; Newsweek; Modern Fiction Studies; Midstream; New York Times Book Review; Washington Post Book World; Gettysburg Review; The American Scholar; Film Critic, Texas Observer; San Antonio Current. Honour: H L Mencken Award, 1986. Membership: National Book Critics Circle, board of directors, 1996-99. Address: 302 Fawn Drive, San Antonio, TX 78231, USA.

KELLOGG Steven, b. 26 Oct 1941, Norfolk, Connecticut, USA. Children's Writer. Education: BFA, Rhode Island School of Design, 1963; American University. Publications: The Wicked Kings of Bloon, 1970; Can I Keep Him?, 1971; The Mystery Beast of Ostergeest, 1971; The Orchard Cat, 1972; Won't Somebody Play With Me, 1972; The Island of the Skog, 1973; The Mystery of the Missing Red Mitten, 1974; There was an Old Woman, 1974; Much Bigger Than Martin, 1976; Steven Kellogg's Yankee Doodle, 1976; The Mysterious Tadpole, 1977; The Mystery of the Magic Green Ball, 1978; Pinkerton Behave, 1979; The Mystery of the Flying Orange Pumpkin, 1980; A Rose for

Pinkerton, 1981; The Mystery of the Stolen Blue Paint, 1982; Tallyho Pinkerton, 1982; Ralph's Secret Weapon, 1983; Paul Bunyan, 1984; Chicken Little, 1985; Best Friends, 1986; Pecos Bill, 1986; Aster Aardvark's Alphabet Adventure, 1987; Prehistoric Pinkerton, 1987; Johnny Appleseed, 1990; Mike Fink, 1992; The Christmas Witch, 1992. Address: Bennett's Bridge Road, Sandy Hook, CT 06482, USA.

KELLS Susannah. See: CORNWELL Bernard.

KELLY A A. See: HAMPTON Angeline Agnes.

KELLY Christopher Paul, b. 24 Apr 1940, Cuddington, Cheshire, England. Writer; Producer. m. Vivien Ann Day, 22 Dec 1962, 1 son, 1 daughter. Education: Clare College, Cambridge, 1959-62; MA, Modern Languages. Publications: The War of Covent Garden, 1989; The Forest of the Night, 1991; Taking Leave, 1995. Literary Agent: Anthony Harwood, Gillon Aitken Associates. Address: 24 Harmood St, London NW1 8DJ, England.

KELLY M(ilton) T(errence), b. 30 Nov 1946, Toronto, Ontario, Canada. Writer; Poet; Dramatist. Education: BA, York University, 1970; BEd, University of Toronto, 1976. Appointments: Reporter, Moose Jaw Times Harald, 1974-75; Columnist, Globe and Mail, 1979-80; Teacher of Creative Writing, York University, 1987-92, 1995; Writer-in-Residence, North York Public Library, 1992, Metropolitan Toronto Reference Library, 1993. Publications: Fiction: I Do Remember the Fall, 1978; The More Loving One, 1980; The Ruined Season, 1982; A Dream Like Mine, 1987; Breath Dances Between Them, 1990; Out of the Whirlwind, 1995; Save Me, Joe Louis, 1998. Poetry: Country You Can't Walk In, 1979; Country You Can't Walk In and Other Poems, 1984. Other: The Green Dolphin (play), 1982; Wildfire: The Legend of Tom Longboat (screenplay), 1983. Contributions to: Many anthologies, reviews, quarterlies, and journals. Honours: Canada Council Grants; Ontario Arts Council Grants; Toronto Arts Council Award for Poetry, 1986; Governor-General's Award for Fiction, 1987; Award for Journalism, 1995. Memberships: International PEN; Writers' Union of Canada. Address: 60 Kendal, Toronto, Ontario M5R 1L9, Canada.

KELLY Patrick. See: ALLBEURY Theodore Edward le Bouthilliers.

KELLY Robert, b. 24 Sept 1935, Brooklyn, New York, USA. Professor of Literature; Poet; Writer. Education: AB, City College, New York City, 1955; Columbia University, 1955-58. Appointments: Editor, Chelsea Review, 1957-60, Matter magazine and Matter publishing, 1964-, Los 1, 1977; Lecturer, Wagner College, 1960-61; Founding Editor (with George Economou), Trobar magazine, 1960-64, Trobar Books, 1962-65; Instructor, 1961-64, Assistant Professor, 1964-69, Associate Professor, 1969-74, Porfessor of English, 1974-86, Director, Writing Programme, 1980-93, Asher B Edelman Professor of Literature, 1986-, Bard College; Assistant Professor, State University of New York at Buffalo, 1964; Visiting Lecturer, Tufts University, 1966-67; Poet-in-Residence, California Institute of Technology, Pasadena, 1971-72, University of Kansas, 1975, Dickinson College, 1976. Publications: Poetry: Armed Descent, 1961; Her Body Against Time, 1963; Round Dances, 1964; Tabula, 1964; Entasy, 1964; Matter/Fact/Sheet/1, 1964; Matter/Fact/Sheet/2, 1964; Lunes, 1964; Lectiones, 1965; Words in Service, 1966; Weeks, 1966; Songs XXIV, 1967; Twenty Poems, 1967; Devotions, 1967; Axon Dendron Tree, 1967; Crooked Bridge Love Society, 1967; A Joining: A Sequence for H D, 1967; Alpha, 1968; Finding the Measure, 1968; From the Common Shore, Book 5, 1968; Songs I-XXX, 1968; Sonnets, 1969; We Are the Arbiters of Beast Desire, 1969; A California Journal, 1969; The Common Shore, Books I-V: A Long Poem About America in Time, 1969; Kali Yuga, 1971; Flesh: Dream: Book, 1971; Ralegh, 1972; The Pastorals, 1972; Reading Her Notes, 1972; The Tears of Edmund Burke, 1973; Whaler Frigate Clippership, 1973; The Bill of Particulars, 1973; The Belt,

1974; The Loom, 1975; Sixteen Odes, 1976; The Lady of, 1977; The Convections, 1978; The Book of Persephone, 1978, revised edition, 1983; The Cruise of the Pnyx, 1979; Kill the Messenger Who Brings the Bad News, 1979; Sentence, 1980; The Alchemist to Mercury, 1981; Spiritual Exercises, 1981; Mulberry Women, 1982; Under Words, 1983; Thor's Thrush, 1984; Not This Island Music, 1987; The Flowers of Unceasing Coincidence, 1988; Oahu, 1988; A Strange Market, 1992; Mont Blanc, 1994. Fiction: The Scorpions, 1967; Cities, 1971; Wheres, 1978; A Transparent Tree: Ten Fictions, 1985; Doctor of Silence, 1988; Cat Scratch Fever: Fictions, 1990; Queen of Terrors: Fictions, 1994. Other: A Controversy of Poets: An Anthology of Contemporary American Poetry (editor with Paris Leary), 1965; Statement, 1968; In Time, 1971; Sulphur, 1972; A Line of Sight, 1974. Honours: Los Angeles Times Book Prize, 1980; American Academy of Arts and Letters Award, 1986. Address: c/o Department of English, Bard College, Annandale-on-Hudson, NY 12504, USA.

KELLY Tim, (Keith Jackson, J Moriarty, Vera Morris, Robert Swift), b. 2 Oct 1937, Saugus, Massachusetts, USA. Playwright; Screenwriter. Education: BA, 1956, MA, 1957, Emerson College; American Broadcasting Fellow, Yale University, 1965. Publications: Over 300 plays. Honours: Numerous awards and grants. Memberships: Authors League; Dramatists Guild; Writers Guild of America; College of Fellows of the American Theatre. Literary Agent: William Talbot, Samuel French Inc., West 25th Street, New York NY 10010, USA. Address: 8730 Lookout Mountain Avenue, Hollywood, CA 90046, USA.

KELMAN James, b. 9 June 1946, Glasgow, Scotland. Author; Dramatist. m. Marie Connors, 2 daughters. Education: University of Strathclyde, 1975-78, 1981-82. Publications: The Busconductor Hines, 1984; A Chancer, 1985; A Disaffection, 1989. Short Stories: An Old Pub Near the Angel, 1973; Short Tales from the Nightshift, 1978; Not Not While the Giro and Other Stories, 1983; Lran Tales, 1985; Greyhound for Breakfast, 1987; The Burn, 1991; How Late it Was, How Late, 1994. Plays: The Busker, 1985; Le Rodeur, 1987; In the Night, 1988; Hardie and Baird, The Last, 1990. Screenplay: The Return, 1990. Honours: Scottish Arts Council Fellowships; Scottish Arts Council Bursaries, Book Awards, 1983, 1987, 1989; Cheltenham Prize, 1987; James Tait Black Memorial Prize, 1989; Booker Prize, 1994. Address: 244 West Princess Street, Glasgow G4 9DP, Scotland.

KELSALL Malcolm Miles, b. 27 Feb 1938, London, England. Professor of English. m. Mary Emily Ives, 5 Aug 1961. Education: BA, Oxon, 1961; BLitt, Oxon, 1964; MA, Oxon, 1965. Appointments: Staff Reporter, The Guardian newspaper, 1961; Assistant Lecturer, Exeter University, 1963-64; Lecturer, Reading University, 1964-75; Professor, University of Wales, Cardiff, 1975-. Publications: Editor, Sarah Fielding, David Simple, 1969; Editor, Thomas Otway, Venice Preserved, 1969; Christopher Marlowe, 1981; Congreve: The Way of the World, 1981; Studying Drama, 1985; Byron's Politics, 1987; Editor, Encyclopedia of Literature and Criticism, 1990; The Great Good Place: The Country House and English Literature, 1992; Editor, J M Synge, The Playboy of the Western World, 1997; Editor, William Congreve, Love For Love, 1999; Jefferson and the Iconography of Romanticism, 1999. Contributions to: Byron Journal; Essays in Criticism; Irish University Review; Theatre Research International; Review of English Studies; Studies in Romanticism. Honours: Elma Dangerfield Prize, 1991; British Academy Warton Lecturer, 1992. Address: School of English, University of Wales, PO Box 94, Cardiff CF1 3XB, Wales.

KELTON Elmer Stephen, (Lee McElroy), b. 29 Apr 1926, Andrews, Texas, USA. Novelist; Agricultural Journalist. m. Anna Lipp, 3 July 1947, 2 sons, 1 daughter. Education: BA, Journalism, University of Texas, 1948. Publications: The Day the Cowboys Quit, 1971; The Time It Never Rained, 1973; The Good Old Boys, 1978; The Wolf and the Buffalo, 1980; Stand Proud, 1984; The Man

Who Rode Midnight, 1987; Honour at Daybreak, 1991; Slaughter, 1992; The Far Canyon, 1994; The Pumpkin Rollers, 1996; Cloudy in the West, 1997; The Smiling Country, 1998; The Buckskin Line, 1999. Contributions to: Numerous articles to magazines and newspapers. Honours: 6 Spur Awards, Western Writers of America; 4 Western Heritage Awards, National Cowboy Hall of Fame; Tinkle-McCombs Achievement Award, Texas Institute of Letters; Lifetime Achievement, Western Literature Association; Larry McMurtry Lone Star Lifetime Achievement Award. Memberships: Western Writers of America, president, 1963-64; Texas Institute of Letters; Sigma Delta Chi. Address: 2460 Oxford, San Angelo, TX 76904, USA.

KEMAL Yashar, b. 1923, Adana, Turkey. Writer; Journalist. m. Thilda Serrero, 1952, 1 son. Education: Self-educated. Publications: (in English) Memed, My Hawk, 1961; The Wind From the Plain, 1963; Anatolian Tales, 1968; They Burn the Thistles, 1973; Iron Earth, Copper Sky, 1974; The Legend of Ararat, 1975; The Legend of a Thousand Bulls, 1976; The Undying Grass, 1977; The Lords of Akchasaz, Part I, Murder in the Ironsmiths Market, 1979; The Saga of a Seagull, 1981; The Sea-Crossed Fisherman, 1985; The Birds Have Also Gone, 1987; To Crush the Serpent, 1991; Salman The Solitary, 1997; novels, short stories, plays and essays in Turkish. Honours: Commander, Legion d'honneur, 1984; Doctor Honoris Causa, Universite de Sciences Humaines, Strasbourg, 1991; VIIIe Premi International Catalunya, Barcelona, 1996; Hellman-Hammett Award, 1996; Peace Prize of the German Book Trade, Frankfurt Book Fair, 1997; The Stig Dagerman Prize, Sweden, 1997; Nonio Prize, Italy, 1997; Kenne Fant Foundation Award, Sweden, 1997; The Norwegian Authors Prize, 1997; Prix Ecureuil, 1998; Salon du Livre de Bordeaux. Literary Agent: Lucien Leitess, Unionsverlag, Zurich. Address: PK 14, Basinkoy, Istanbul, Turkey.

KEMP Gene, b. 27 Dec 1926, Wigginton, England. Children's Author; Educator. Education: Graduated, University of Exeter, 1945. Appointments: Teacher, St Sidwell's School, Exeter, 1962-74; Lecturer, Rolle College, 1963-79. Publications: Tamworth Pig series, 4 volumes, 1972-78; The Turbulent Term of Tyke Tiler, 1977; Gowie Corby Plays Chicken, 1979; Ducks and Dragons (editor), 1980; Dog Days and Cat Naps, 1980; The Clock Tower Ghost, 1981; No Place Like, 1983; Charlie Lewis Plays for Time, 1984; The Well, 1984; Jason Bodger and the Priory Ghost, 1985; McMagus is Waiting for You, 1986; Juniper, 1986; I Can't Stand Losing, 1987. Honours: Children's Awards, 1977; Carnegie Medal, 1978; Honorary MA, Exeter University, 1984; Runner-up, Whitbread Award, 1985. Address: c/o Laurence Pollinger Ltd, 18 Maddox Street, London W1R OEU, England.

KEMP Harry Vincent, b. 11 Dec 1911, Singapore. Poet; Mathematician. m. Alix Eiermann, 9 July 1941, 1 son, 1 daughter. Education: Clare College, Cambridge, 1931-34. Publications: The Left Hersey (with Laura Riding and Robert Graves), 1939; Ten Messengers (with Witold Kawalec), 1977; Verses for Heidi, 1978; Poems for Erato, 1980; Collected Poems, 1985; Poems for Mnemosyne, 1993. Address: 6 Western Villas, Western Road, Crediton, Devon EX17 3NA, England.

KEMP (Patricia) Penny, b. 1944, Strathroy, Ontario, Canada. Writer. 1 son, 1 daughter. Education: Honours in English Language and Literature, 1966, MEduc, 1988, University of Toronto. Appointments: Various Writer-in-Residencies. Publications: Bearing Down, 1972; Binding Twine, 1984; Some Talk Magic, 1986; Eidolons, 1990; Throo, 1990; The Universe is One Poem, 1990; What the Ear Hears Last, 1994. Contributions to: Magazines. Honours: Canada Council Arts Grants, 1979-80, 1981-82, 1991-92; Ontario's Graduate Scholarship, 1987-88. Memberships: League of Canadian Poets; Playwright's Union; Writer's Union. Address: C-7 2163 Queen Street E, Toronto, Ontario M4L 1J1, Canada.

KEMPER Troxey, b. 29 Apr 1915, Oklahoma, USA. Editor; Novelist; Poet. m. Jeanne Doty, 31 July 1954, div 1964, 2 daughters. Education: BA, University of New Mexico, Albuquerque, 1951. Appointments: Newspaper Reporter, Albuquerque Journal, 1951-69; Editor, Tucumcari Literary Review, 1988-. Publications: Mainly on the Plain, 1982; Whence and Whither, 1983; Folio and Signature, 1983; Part Comanche, 1991; Comanche Warbonnet, 1991; Under a Sky of Azure, 1993; Lean into the Wind, 1997; Shallow Graves, 1997; Texas for the Duration, 1998; New Mexico: Tough and Tender, 1998; Bloom of the Years: Indian Territory into Oklahoma, 1998; Dear Editor: Cranky Letters, 1998. Contributions to: Poets and Writers Magazine; Small Press Review; Amarillo News Globe; Los Angeles Daily News; Los Angeles Times; American Film Magazine; Tucumcari Literary Review. Honour: Honourable Mention, National Writers Club, 1990. Memberships: National Writers Union; Sigma Delta Chi. Address: 3108 West Bellevue Avenue, Los Angeles, CA 90026, USA.

KEMSKE Floyd, b. 11 Mar 1947, Wilmington, Delaware, USA. Writer. m. Alice Geraldine Morse, 21 Dec 1968. Education: BA, University of Delaware, 1970; MA, Michigan State University, 1971. Publications: Novels: Lifetime Employment, 1992; The Virtual Boss, 1993; Human Resources, 1995; The Third Lion, 1997; Non-Fiction: Co-author with Donna Baier Stein, Write on Target: The Direct Marketer's Copywriting Handbook, 1997; Jigsaw Puzzles: Hole in One, 1997; Unbridled Fear, 1997; Cooking Commando, 1997; Cat Scan, 1998. Memberships: National Writers Union. Address: PO Box 563, Pepperell, MA 01463, USA.

KENDALL Carol (Seeger), b. 13 Sept 1917, Bucyrus, Ohio, USA. Writer. m. Paul Murray Kendall, 15 June 1939, 2 daughters. Education: AB, Ohio University, 1939. Publications: The Black Seven, 1946; The Baby Snatcher, 1952; The Other Side of the Tunnel, 1956; The Gammage Cup, 1959, as The Minnipins, 1960; The Big Splash, 1960; The Whisper of Glocken, 1965; Sweet and Sour Tales from China, retold by Carol Kendall and Yao-Wen Li, 1978; The Firelings, 1981; Haunting Tales from Japan, 1985; The Wedding of the Rat Family, 1988. Honours: Ohioana Award, 1960; Newbery Honour Book, 1960; American Library Association Notable Book, 1960; Parents Choice Award, 1982; Aslan Award, Mythopoeic Society, 1983. Memberships: PEN American Center; Authors League of America; Authors Guild. Address: 928 Holiday Drive, Lawrence, KS 66049, USA.

KENEALLY Thomas (Michael), b. 7 Oct 1935, Sydney, New South Wales, Australia. Author; Screenwriter; Distinguished Professor. m. Judith Mary Martin, 1965, 2 daughters. Education: St Patrick's College, Strathfield, New South Wales. Appointments: Lecturer in Drama, University of New England, 1968-69; Visiting Professor, 1985, Distinguished Professor, 1991-, University of California at Irvine; Berg Professor, New York University, 1988. Publications: The Place at Whitton, 1964; The Fear, 1965, 2nd edition, 1973; Bring Larks and Heroes, 1967, 2nd edition, 1973; Three Cheers for the Paraclete, 1968; The Survivor, 1969; A Dutiful Daughter, 1971; The Chant of Jimmie Blacksmith, 1972; Blood Red, Sister Rose, 1974; Gossip From the Forest, 1975; The Lawgiver, 1975; Season in Purgatory, 1976; A Victim of the Aurora, 1977; Ned Kelly and the City of the Bees, 1978; Passenger, 1979; Confederates, 1979; Schindler's Ark, 1982, reissued as Schindler's List, 1994; Outback, 1983; The Cut-Rate Kingdom, 1984; A Family Madness, 1985; The Playmaker, 1987; Towards Asmara, 1989; Flying Hero Class, 1991; The Place Where Soles Are Born, 1992; Now and in Time to Be, 1992; Woman of the Inner Sea, 1992; Memoirs From a Young Republic, 1993; Jacko, 1993; The Utility Player, 1994; A River Town, 1995; Homebush Boy: A Memoir, 1995. Honours: Commonwealth Literary Fellowships, 1966, 1968, 1972; Booker Prize, 1983; Los Angeles Times Fiction Prize, 1983; Member of the Order of Australia, 1983; Honorary DLitt, University of Queensland, 1993, National University of Ireland, 1994, Fairleigh Dickinson University, 1994. Memberships: American Association for the Advancement of Science, fellow; Australian Society of Authors, council member, 1985-, chairman, 1987-90; National Book Council of Australia, president, 1985-89; Royal Society of Literature, fellow. Address: c/o Department of English and Comparative Literature, University of California at Irvine, Irvine, CA 92697, USA.

KENNAN George (Frost), b. 16 Feb 1904, Milwaukee, Wisconsin, USA. Retired Diplomat; Professor Emeritus; Author. m. Annelise Sorenson, 1 son, 3 daughters. Education: AB, Princeton University, 1925. Appointments: Various diplomatic posts, 1926-45; Deputy for Foreign Affairs, National War College, Washington, DC, 1946; Director, Policy Planning Staff, US Department of State, 1947; Deputy Counselor and Chief Long Range Adviser to the US Secretary of State, 1949-50; Member, 1950-53, Professor, 1956-74, Professor Emeritus, 1974-, Institute for Advanced Study, Princeton, New Jersey; US Ambassador to the USSR, 1952, Yugoslavia, 1961-63; George Eastman Visiting Professor, Oxford University, 1957-58; Fellow, Harvard University, 1965-70, All Souls College, Oxford, 1969. Publications: American Diplomacy 1900-1950, 1951; Realities of American Foreign Policy, 1954; Soviet-American Relations 1917-1920, 2 volumes, 1956, 1958; Russia, the Atom and the West, 1958; Soviet Foreign Policy 1917-1945, 1960; Russia and the West Under Lenin and Stalin, 1961; On Dealing with the Communist World, 1963; Memoirs 1925-1950, 1967; Democracy and the Student Left, 1968; From Prague After Munich: Diplomatic Papers 1938-1940, 1968; The Marquis de Custine and His Russia in 1839, 1971; Memoirs 1950-1963, 1972; The Cloud of Danger: Current Realities of American Foreign Policy, 1977; The Decline of Bismarck's European Order: Franco-Russian Relations 1875-1890, 1979; The Nuclear Delusion: Soviet-American Relations in the Atomic Age, 1982; The State Department Policy Planning Staff Papers, 1983; The Fateful Alliance: France, Russia and the Coming of the First World War, 1984; Sketches from a Life, 1989; Around the Cragged Hill, 1993; At a Century's End, 1996. Contributions to: Scholarly journals. Honours: Freedom House Award, 1951; Bancroft Prize, 1956; National Book Awards, 1957, 1968; Francis Parkman Prize, 1957; Pulitzer Prizes, 1957, 1968; Albert Einstein Peace Prize, 1981; Gold Medal in History, American Academy and Institute of Arts and Letters, 1984; Literary Lion Award, New York Public Library, 1985; Creative Arts Award, Brandeis University, 1986; Toynbee Prize, 1988; Presidential Medal of Freedom, 1989; Ambassador Book Award, 1993; Distinguished Service Award, US Department of State, 1994; Excellence in Diplomacy Award, 1997; Numerous honorary doctorates. Memberships: American Academy of Arts and Letters, president, 1967-71; American Philosophical Society; National Institute of Arts and Letters, president, 1964-67; Royal Society of Arts. Address: 146 Hodge Road, Princeton, NJ 08540, USA.

KENNEDY Adrienne (Lita), b. 13 Sept 1931, Pittsburgh, Pennsylvania, USA. Dramatist. m. Joseph C Kennedy, 15 May 1953, div 1966, 2 sons. Education: BS, Ohio State University, 1953; Columbia University, 1954-56; New School for Social Research, American Theatre Wing, Circle in the Square Theatre School, New York City, 1957-58, 1962. Appointments: Playwright, Actors Studio, New York City, 1962-65; Lecturer, Yale University, 1972-74, Princeton University, 1977; CBS Fellow, School of Drama, New York City, 1973; Visiting Associate Professor, Brown University, 1979-80; Distinguished Lecturer, University of California, Berkeley, 1980, 1986; Visiting Lecturer, Harvard University, 1990, 1991; Visiting Professor, Harvard, 1997. Publications: Plays: Funnyhouse of a Negro, 1964; Cities in Bezique, 1965; A Rat's Mass, 1966; A Lesson in Dead Language, 1966; The Lennon Plays, 1968; Sun, 1969; A Movie Star Has to Star in Black and White, 1976; She Talks to Beethoven, 1990; The Alexander Plays, 1992; Sleep Deprivation Chamber: A Theatre Piece (co-written with Adam Kennedy), 1996. Other: People Who Led to My Plays, 1987; Letter to My Students, 1992. Contributions to: Anthologies. Honours: Obie Award, 1964, 1996; Guggenheim Fellowship, 1968; Rockefeller Foundation Fellowships, 1968, 1974; National Endowment for the Arts Fellowships, 1973, 1993; Manhattan Borough President's Award, 1988; American Academy of Arts and Letters Award, 1994; Lila Wallace-Reader's Digest Award, 1994; Pierre Lecomte du Novy Award, Lincoln Center for the Performing Arts, New York City, 1994; Visiting Professor, Harvard University, 1999-2000. Membership: PEN. Address: c/o University of Minnesota Press, 111 Third Avenue South, Suite 290, Minneapolis, MN 55401, USA.

KENNEDY Alison Louise, b. 22 Oct 1965, Dundee, Scotland. Writer. Education: BA Hons, Theatre Studies and Drama, Warwick University, England. Appointments include: Community Arts Worker for Clydebank & District, 1988-89; Writer in Residence, Hamilton & East Kilbride Social Work Department, 1989-91; Writer in Residence for Project Ability, Arts & Special Needs, 1989-95; Book Reviewer for Scotsman, Glasgow Herald, BBC, STV, Telegraph, 1990-; Writer in Residence, Copenhagen University, 1995; Editor of New Writing Scotland, 1993-95; Booker Prize Judge, 1996. Publications: Night Geometry and the Garscadden Trains, 1991; Looking for the Possible Dance, 1993; Now That You're Back, 1994; So I Am Glad, 1995; Tea and Biscuits, 1996; Original Bliss, 1997; The Life and Death of Colonel Blimp, 1997; Everything You Need, 1999. Film/Drama includes: Delicate, performance piece for Motionhouse dance company, 1995; Ghostdancing, BBC TV drama/documentary, writer and presenter, 1995; Bathory, feature film in development with Hungry Eye, Trijbits and Worrell, 1997; True, performance project for Fiere Productions and Tramway Theatre, 1998; Never Say No, feature film in development with The Producers, 1998. c/o The Antony Harwood, Aitken & Stone, 29 Fernshaw Road, London SW10 0TG, England.

KENNEDY John Hines, b. 1 Nov 1925, Washington, District of Columbia, USA. Cardiothoracic Surgeon (retired); Physiologist; Poet. m. (1), 2 sons, 2 daughters, (2) Shirley Angela Josephine Watson. Education: Princeton University, 1943-45; MD, Harvard Medical School, 1945-49; FACS, 1957; MPhil, Imperial College, London, 1990. Publications: Carnet Parisien, 1987; Vieux Colombier, 1987-88; Les Images, 1991. Contributions to: Books and journals. Honours: Medal of Vishnevsky, Moscow, 1962; Medal, Un Liège, Belgium, 1978. Memberships: PEN Club; Cercle de l'Union Interliée, Paris. Address: Old Court, Clare, Sudbury, Suffolk CO10 8NP, England.

KENNEDY Joseph Charles, (X J Kennedy), b. 21 Aug 1929, Dover, New Jersey, USA. Poet; Writer. m. Dorothy Mintzlaff, 31 Jan 1962, 4 sons, 1 daughter. Education: BSc, Seton Hall University, 1950; MA, Columbia University, 1951; University of Paris, 1956. Appointments: Teaching Fellow, 1956-60, Instructor, 1960-62, University of Michigan; Poetry Editor, The Paris Review, 1961-64; Lecturer, Women's College of the University of North Carolina, 1962-63; Assistant Professor to Professor, Tufts University, 1963-79. Publications: Nude Descending a Staircase, 1961; An Introduction to Poetry (with Dana Gioia), 1968, 8th edition, 1994; The Bedford Reader, 1982, 6th edition (with Dorothy Kennedy and Jane Aarron), 1996; Cross Ties, 1985; Dark Horses, 1992. Contributions to: Newspapers and journals. Honours: Lamont Award, 1961; Los Angeles Times Book Award, 1985. Memberships: Authors Guild; John Barton Wolgamot Society; Modern Language Association; PEN. Address: 4 Fern Way, Bedford, MA 01730, USA.

KENNEDY Sir Ludovic (Henry Coverley), b. 3 Nov 1919, Edinburgh, Scotland. Writer; Broadcaster. m. Moira Shearer King, 1950, 1 son, 3 daughters. Education: MA, Christ Church, Oxford. Appointments: Broadcaster, numerous radio and television programmes, 1955-90; Columnist, Newsweek International, 1974-75, Sunday Standard, 1981-82; Director, The Spectator, 1988-90. Publications: Sub-Lieutenant, 1942; Nelson's Band of Brothers, 1951; One Man's Meat, 1953; Murder Story, 1956; Ten Rillington Place, 1961; The Trial of Stephen Ward, 1964; Very Lovely People, 1969; The British War (general editor), 1973-77; Pursuit: The Chase and Sinking of the Bismarck, 1974; A Presumption of

Innocence: The Amazing Case of Patrick Meehan, 1979; Menace: The Life and Death of the Tirpitz, 1979; The Portland Spy Case, 1979; Wicked Beyond Belief, 1980; A Book of Railway Journeys (editor), 1980; A Book of Sea Journeys (editor), 1981; A Book of Air Journeys (editor), 1982; The Airman and the Carpenter, 1985; On My Way to the Club (autobiography), 1989; Euthanasia: The Good Death, 1990; Truth to Tell (collected writings), 1991; In Bed with an Elephant: A Journey Through Scotland's Past and Present, 1995; All in the Mind: A Farewell to God, 1999. Honours: Rockefeller Foundation Atlantic Award in Literature, 1950; Winner, Open Finals Contest, English Festival of Spoken Poetry, 1953; Cross, 1st Class, Order of Merit, Germany, 1979; Richard Dimbleby Award, British Association of Film and Television Arts, 1988; Knighted, 1994; F.R.S.L., 1998; Several honorary doctorates. Memberships: Russian Convoy Club, patron, 1989-; Voluntary Euthanasia Society, president, 1995-. Address: c/o Rogers, Coleridge and White, 20 Powis Mews, London W11 1JN, England.

KENNEDY (George) Michael (Sinclair), b. 19 Feb 1926, Manchester, England. Music Critic; Author. m. Eslyn Durdle, 16 May 1947. Education: Berkhamsted School. Appointments: Staff, 1941-, Northern Music Critic, 1950-, Northern Editor, 1960-86, Joint Chief Music Critic, 1986-89, The Daily Telegraph; Music Critic, The Sunday Telegraph, 1989-. Publications: The Hallé Tradition: A Century of Music, 1960; The Works of Ralph Vaughan Williams, 1964, revised edition, 1980; Portrait of Elgar, 1968, 3rd edition, 1987; Elgar: Orchestral Music, 1969; Portrait of Manchester, 1970; A History of the Royal Manchester College of Music, 1971; Barbirolli: Conductor Laureate, 1971; Mahler, 1974, revised edition, 1990; The Autobiography of Charles Hallé, with Correspondence and Diaries (editor), 1976; Richard Strauss, 1976, revised edition, 1995; The Concise Oxford Dictionary of Music (editor), 1980, revised edition, 1995; Britten, 1981, revised edition, 1993; The Hallé 1858-1983, 1983; Strauss: Tone Poems, 1984; The Oxford Dictionary of Music (editor), 1985, 2nd edition, revised, 1994; Adrian Boult, 1987; Portrait of Walton, 1989; Music Enriches All: The First 21 Years of the Royal Northern College of Music, Manchester, 1994; Richard Strauss, Man, Musician, Enigma, 1999. Contributions to: Newspapers and magazines. Honours: Fellow, Institute of Journalists, 1967; Officer of the Order of the British Empire, 1981; Fellow, Royal Northern College of Music, 1981; Commander of the Order of the British Empire, 1998. Address: 3 Moorwood Drive, Sale, Cheshire, M33 4QB, England.

KENNEDY Moorhead, b. 5 Nov 1930, New York, New York, USA. Foundation Administrator; Writer. m. Louisa Livingston, 8 June 1955, 4 sons. Education: AB, Princeton University, 1952; JD, Harvard University, 1959; National War College, 1974-75. Appointments: Foreign Service Officer, 1961-69, 1975-78, Director, Office of Investment Affairs, 1971-74, US Department of State; Executive Director, Cathedral Peace Institute, New York City, 1981-83, Council for International Understanding, New York City, 1983-90; President, Moorhead Kennedy Institute, New York City, 1990-97. Publications: The Ayatollah in the Cathedral, 1986; Terrorism: The New Warfare, 1988; Hostage Crisis, 1989; Death of a Dissident, 1990; Fire in the Forest, 1990; Metalfabriken, 1993; Grocery Store, 1993; Nat-Tel, 1995. Contributions to: Books and professional journals. Honours: Medal for Valor, US Department of State, 1981; Gold Medal, National Institute of Social Sciences, 1991; Many honorary doctorates. Memberships: American Foreign Service Association; Americans for Middle East Understanding; Episcopalian; Freemason. Address: POB 751, Mount Desert, Maine 04660, USA.

KENNEDY Paul M(ichael), b. 17 June 1945, Wallsend, Northumberland, England. Professor of History; Writer. m. Catherine Urwin, 2 Sept 1967, 3 sons. Education: BA, University of Newcastle, 1966; PhD, Oxford University, 1970. Appointments: Research Assistant to Sir Basil Liddell Hart, 1966-70; Lecturer, 1970-75, Reader, 1975-82, Professor, 1982-83, University of East Anglia; Visiting Fellow, Institute for Advanced Study, Princeton, New Jersey, 1978-79; J Richardson Dilworth Professor of History, 1983-, Director, International Security Studies, 1990-, Yale University; Various guest lectureships including the first Nobel Peace Foundation Lecture, Oslo, 1992. Publications: Pacific Onslaught 1941-1943, 1972; Conquest: The Pacific War 1943-1945, 1973; The Samoan Tangle: A Study in Anglo-German-American Relations 1878-1900, 1974; The Rise and Fall of British Naval Mastery, 1976; The Rise of the Anglo-German Antagonism 1860-1914, 1980; The Realities Behind Diplomacy: Background Influences on British External Policy 1865-1980, 1981; Strategy and Diplomacy 1870-1945: Eight Essays, 1983; The Rise and Fall of the Great Powers: Economic Change and Military Conflict from 1500-2000, 1988; Preparing for the Twenty-First Century, 1993. Editor: Germany in the Pacific and Far East 1870-1914 (with John A Moses), 1977; The War Plans of the Great Powers 1880-1914, 1979; Appeasement (with Jack Spence), 1980; Nationalist and Racialist Movements in Britain and Germany Before 1914 (with A J Nicholls), 1981; Grand Strategies in War and Peace, 1991; Global Trends: The World Almanac of Development and Peace (with Ingomar Hauchler), 1994; The Pivotal States (with R Chase and E Hill), 1998. Contributions to: Professional journals and to general magazines and newspapers. Honours: Various research awards, fellowships, and honorary doctorates. Memberships: American Academy of Arts and Sciences; American Philosophical Society; Royal Historical Society, fellow; Society of American Historians. Address: 409 Humphrey Street, New Haven, CT 06511, USA.

KENNEDY Thomas Eugene, b. 9 Mar 1944, New York, USA. Writer; Editor; Translator; Teacher; Administrator. m. Monique M Brun, 28 Dec 1974, div 1997, 1 son, 1 daughter. Education: BA (summa cum laude), Fordham University, New York, 1974; MFA, Vermont College, Norwich University, USA, 1985; PhD, Copenhagen University, 1988. Appointments: Guest Editor, Nordic Section, Frank magazine, 1987; European Editor, Rohwedder, 1988-89; International Editor, Cimarron Review, 1989-, Potpourri, 1993-; Contributing Editor, Pushcart Prize, 1990-; Advisory Editor, Short Story, 1990-, Literary Review, 1996-; Editorial Board, International Quarterly, 1994. Publications: Andre Dubus: A Study, 1988; Crossing Borders (novel), 1990; The American Short Story Today, 1991; Robert Coover: A Study, 1992; Index, American Award Stories, 1993; A Weather of the Eye (novel), 1996; Unreal City (stories) 1996; New Danish Fiction (editor), 1995; The Book of Angels, novel, 1997; Drive, Dive, Dance and Fight (stories), 1997; New Irish Writing (editor), 1997; Stories and Sources (editor), 1998. Address: Oster Sogade 52, I, DK 2100 Copenhagen, Denmark.

KENNEDY William (Joseph), b. 16 Jan 1928, Albany, New York, USA. Novelist; Professor of English. m. Ana Daisy Dana Segarra, 31 Jan 1957, 1 son, 2 daughters. Education: BA, Siena College, Loudonville, New York, 1949. Appointments: Assistant Sports Editor and Columnist, Glens Falls Post Star, 1949-50; Reporter, 1952-56, Special Writer, 1963-70, Albany Times-Union; Assistant Managing Editor and Columnist, Puerto Rico World Journal, San Juan, 1956; Reporter, Miami Herald, 1957; Correspondent, Time-Life Publishers in Puerto Rico, 1957-59; Reporter, Knight Newspapers, 1957-59; Founding Managing Editor, San Juan Star, 1959-61; Lecturer, 1974-82, Professor of English, 1983-, State University of New York at Albany; Visiting Professor, Cornell University, 1982-83; Founder, New York State Writers Institute, 1983. Publications: The Ink Truck, 1969; Legs, 1975; Billy Phelan's Greatest Game, 1978; O Albany!, 1983; Ironweed, 1983; The Cotton Club (with Francis Ford Coppola), film script, 1984; Charlie Malarkey and the Belly Button Machine (with Brenden Christopher Kennedy), 1986; Quinn's Book, 1988; Very Old Bones, 1992; Riding the Yellow Trolley Car, 1993; Charlie Malarkey and the Singing Moose (with Brenden Christopher Kennedy), 1994; The Flaming Corsage, 1996. Contributions to: Numerous periodicals. Honours: National Endowment for the Arts Fellowship, 1981; John D and Catherine T MacArthur Foundation Fellowship, 1983; Pulitzer Prize in Fiction, 1984; National Book Critics Circle Award in Fiction, 1984; Creative Arts Award, Brandeis University, 1986; Commander of the Order of Arts and Letters, France, 1993. Memberships: American Academy of Arts and Letters; PEN Club; Writers Guild of America. Address: New York State Writers Institute, 1400 Washington Avenue, Albany, NY 12222, USA.

KENNEDY William S, b. 23 Jan 1926, South Norfolk, Virginia, USA. Journal Editor and Publisher; Short Fiction Genre Founder and Promoter. Appointments: Founder, Editor, Publisher, Reflect literary journal; Founder, The Spiral Mode (spiral fiction), 1982. Publications: Johnny Mowbrough, spiral novel, published as serial in Puck and Pluck, 1994-; Manuals: Paranormal Writing; Music Writing. Contributions to: Journals. Memberships: Norfolk Musicians Union; American Federation of Musicians. Address: 3306 Argonne Avenue, Norfolk, VA 23509, USA.

KENNEDY X J. See: **KENNEDY Joseph Charles.**

KENNELLY Brendan, b. 17 Apr 1936, Ballylongford, County Kerry, Ireland. Professor of Modern Literature; Senior Fellow; Poet; Author; Dramatist. Education: BA, 1st Class Honours, English and French, 1961, MA, 1963, PhD, 1966, Trinity College, Dublin. Appointments: Professor of Modern Literature and Senior Fellow, Trinity College, Dublin, 1973-. Publications: Poetry: Cast a Cold Eye (with Rudi Holzapfel), 1959; The Rain, The Moon (with Rudi Holzapfel), 1961; The Dark About Our Loves (with Rudi Holzapfel), 1962; Green Townlands: Poems (with Rudi Holzapfel), 1963; Let Fall No Burning Leaf, 1963; My Dark Fathers, 1964; Up and At It, 1965; Collection One: Getting Up Early, 1966; Good Souls to Survive, 1967; Dream of a Black Fox, 1968; Selected Poems, 1969, enlarged edition, 1971; A Drinking Cup: Poems From the Irish, 1970; Bread, 1971; Love Cry, 1972; Salvation, the Stranger, 1972; The Voices, 1973; Shelley in Dublin, 1974, revised edition, 1982; A Kind of Trust, 1975; New and Selected Poems, 1976; Islandman, 1977; The Visitor, 1978; A Girl: 22 Songs, 1978; A Small Light, 1979; In Spite of the Wise, 1979; The Boats Are Home, 1980; The House That Jack Didn't Build, 1982; Cromwell: A Poem, 1983, corrected edition, 1987; Moloney Up and At It, 1984; Selected Poems, 1985; Mary: From the Irish, 1987; Love of Ireland: Poems From the Irish, 1989; A Time for Voices: Selected Poems 1960-1990, 1990; The Book of Judas: A Poem, 1991; Breathing Spaces: Early Poems, 1992; Poetry My Arse, 1995; The Man Made of Rain, 1998. Novels: The Crooked Cross, 1963; The Florentines, 1967. Plays: Medea, 1991; The Trojan Women, 1993; Antigone, 1996; Blood Wedding, 1996. Criticism: Journey into Joy: Selected Prose, 1994. Anthologies: The Penguin Book of Irish Verse, 1970, 2nd edition, enlarged, 1981; Landmarks of Irish Drama, 1988; Joycechoyce: The Poems in Verse and Prose of James Joyce (with A Norman Jeffares), 1992; Irish Prose Writings: Swift to the Literary Renaissance (with Terence Brown), 1992; Between Innocence and Peace: Favourite Poems of Ireland, 1993; Dublines (with Katie Donovan), 1994; Ireland's Women: Writings Past and Present (with Katie Donovan and A Norman Jeffares), 1994. Other: Real Ireland, 1984; Ireland Past and Present (editor), 1985. Honours: AE Monorial Prize for Poetry, 1967; Fellow, Trinity College, Dublin, 1967; Critics' Special Harveys Award, 1988. Address: c/o School of Engish, Trinity College, Dublin 2, Ireland.

KENNER (William) Hugh, b. 7 Jan 1923, Peterborough, Ontario, Canada. Professor of English; Writer. m. (1) Mary J Waite, 30 Aug 1947, dec 1964, 2 sons, 3 daughters, (2) Mary A Bittner, 13 Aug 1965, 1 son, 1 daughter. Education: Peterborough Collegiate Institute, 1936-41; BA, 1945, MA, 1946, University of Toronto; PhD, Yale University, 1950. Appointments: Assistant Professor, Assumption College, Windsor, Ontario, Canada, 1946-48; Instructor, 1950-51, Assistant Professor, 1951-56, Associate Professor, 1956-58, Chairman, Department of English, 1956-63, Professor of English, 1958-73, University of California, Santa Barbara; Professor of English, 1973-75, Andrew W Mellon Professor of the Humanities, 1975-91, Chairman,

Department of English, 1980-83, Johns Hopkins University; Franklin and Callaway Professor of English, University of Georgia, 1992-; Several visiting appointments. Publications: Paradox in Chesterton, 1948; The Poetry of Ezra Pound, 1951; Wyndham Lewis, 1954; Dublin's Joyce, 1956; Gnomon: Essays in Contemporary Literature, 1958; The Invisible Poet: T S Eliot, 1958; The Art of Poetry, 1959; Seventeenth Century Poetry: The Schools of Donne and Jonson (editor), 1965; Samuel Beckett: A Critical Study, 1961; The Stoic Comedians, 1963; The Counterfeiters, 1968; The Pound Era, 1971; Bucky: A Guided Tour of Buckminster Fuller, 1973; A Reader's Guide to Samuel Beckett, 1973; A Homemade World: The American Modernist Writers, 1975; Geodesic Math and How to Use It, 1976; Joyce's Voices, 1978; Ulysses, 1982; A Colder Eye: The Modern English Writers, 1983; The Mechanic Muse, 1987; A Sinking Island: The Modern Irish Writers, 1988; Mazes (essays), 1989; Historical Fictions (essays), 1990; Chuck Jones: A Flurry of Drawings, 1994; The Elsewhere Community, 1997. Contributions to: About 600 articles and reviews in many periodicals. Honours: American Council of Learned Societies Fellow, 1956; Guggenheim Fellowships, 1956, 1964; Royal Society of Literature Fellow, 1957; National Institute of Arts and Letters Award, 1969; Christian Gauss Prize, 1972; A D Emmart Award, 1977; Several honorary doctorates. Address: 203 Plum Nelly Road, Athens, GA 30606, USA.

KENNET Lady, (Elizabeth Ann Young), b. 14 Apr 1923, London, England. Writer; Poet. m. Wayland Hilton Young, 2nd Baron Kennet, 24 Jan 1948, 1 son, 5 daughters. Education: MA, Oxford University. Publications (with husband): Old London Churches, 1956; London's Churches, 1986; Northern Lazio, 1990. Other: Time is as Time Does (poems), 1958. Contributions to: Anthologies and other publications. Honour: European Federation Tourist Press Overall Prize, 1990. Address: 100 Bayswater Road, London W2 3HJ, England.

KENNET 2nd Baron, (Wayland Hilton Young, b. 2 Aug 1923, England. Politician; Writer; Journalist. m. Elizabeth Ann Adams, 24 Jan 1948, 1 son, 5 daughters. Education: Trinity College, Cambridge. Appointments: Staff, Foreign Office, 1946-47, 1949-51; Delegate, Parliamentary Assemblies, Western European Union and Council of Europe, 1962-65; Editor, Disarmament and Arms Control, 1962-65; Parly Secretary, Ministry of Housing and Local Government, 1966-70; Opposition Spokesman on Foreign Affairs and Science Policy, 1971-74; Member, European Parliament, 1978-79; Chief Whip, 1981-83, Spokesman on Foreign Affairs and Defence, 1981-90, Social Democratic Party, House of Lords; Vice President, Parly and Scientific Committee, 1989-. Publications: As Wayland Young: The Italian Left, 1949; The Deadweight, 1952; Now or Never, 1953; Old London Churches (with Elizabeth Young), 1956; The Montesi Scandal, 1957; Still Alive Tomorrow, 1958; Strategy for Survival, 1959; The Profumo Affair, 1963; Eros Denied, 1965; Thirty-Four Articles (editor), 1965; Existing Mechanisms of Arms Control, 1965. As Wayland Kennet: Preservation, 1972; The Futures of Europe, 1976; The Rebirth of Britain, 1982; London's Churches (with Elizabeth Young), 1986; Northern Lazio (with Elizabeth Young), 1990; Parliaments and Screening, 1995. Honour: Created 2nd Baron Kennet, 1935. Address: c/o House of Lords, London SW1A 0PW, England.

KENNEY Catherine, b. 3 Oct 1948, Memphis, Tennessee, USA. Writer; Professor. m. John Patrick Kenney, 1 June 1968, 1 son. Education: BA, English, Siena College, 1968; MA, English, 1970, PhD, English, 1974, Loyola University, Chicago. Publications: Thurber's Anatomy of Confusion, 1984; The Remarkable Case of Dorothy L Sayers, 1990; Dorothy L (play), 1993. Contributions to: Books, scholarly journals and newspapers. Address: 228 Stanley Avenue, Park Ridge, IL 60068, USA.

KENNY Adele, b. 28 Nov 1948, Perth Amboy, New Jersey, USA. Poet; Writer; Editor; Consultant. Education: BA, English, Newark State College, 1970; MS, Education,

College of New Rochelle, 1982. Appointments: Artist-in-Residence, Middlesex County Arts Council, 1979-80; Poetry Editor, New Jersey Art Form, 1981-83; Associate Editor, Muse-Pie Press, 1988-. Publications: An Archaeology of Ruins, 1982; Illegal Entries, 1984; The Roses Open, 1984; Between Hail Marys, 1986; Migrating Geese, 1987; The Crystal Keepers Handbook, 1988; Counseling Gifted, Creative and Talented Youth Through the Arts, 1989; Castles and Dragons, 1990; Questi Momenti, 1990; Starship Earth, 1990; We Become By Being, 1994; Staffordshire Spaniels, 1997; Staffordshire Animals, 1998. Contributions to: Periodicals. Honours: Writer's Digest Award, 1981; New Jersey State Council on the Arts Fellowships, 1982, 1987; Merit Book Awards, 1983, 1985, 1987, 1990; Roselip Award, 1988; Haiku Quarterly Award, 1989; Allen Ginsberg Poetry Award, 1993. Memberships: Haiku Society of America, president, 1987-88, 1990; Poetry Society of America. Address: 207 Coriell Avenue, Fanwood, NJ 07023, USA.

KENRICK Tony, b. 23 Aug 1935, Sydney, New South Wales, Australia. Author. Appointments: Advertising Copywriter, Sydney, Toronto, San Francisco, New York, London, 1953-72. Publications: The Only Good Body's a Dead One, 1970; A Tough One to Lose, 1972; Two for the Price of One, 1974; Stealing Lillian, 1975; The Seven Day Soldiers, 1976; The Chicago Girl, 1976; Two Lucky People, 1978; The Nighttime Guy, 1979; The 81st Site, 1980; Blast, 1983; Faraday's Flowers, 1985; China White, 1986; Neon Tough, 1988; Glitterbug, 1991; Round Trip, 1996. Address: c/o 216 East 75th Street, New York, NY 10021, USA.

KENT Alexander. See: **REEMAN Douglas Edward.**

KENT Arthur (William Charles), (James Bradwell, M DuBois, Paul Granados, Alexander Karol, Alex Stamper, Brett Vane), b. 31 Jan 1925, London, England. Author. Education: City Literary Institute, London. Appointments: Journalist, News Chronicle, London, 1943-46, Australian Daily Mirror, 1947-53, Beaverbook Newspapers, UK, 1957-69, BBC, London, 1970-71. Publications: Sunny (as Bret Vane), 1953; Gardenia (as Bret Vane), 1953; Broadway Contraband (as Paul Granados), 1954; El Tafile (as M DuBois), 1954; Legion Etrangere (as M DuBois), 1954; March and Die (as M DuBois), 1954; Revolt at Zaluig (as Alex Stamper), 1954; Inclining to Crime, 1957; Special Edition Murder, 1957; Kansas Fast Gun, 1958; Stairway to Murder, 1958; Wake Up Screaming, 1958; The Camp on Blood Island (with G Thomas), 1958; Last Action, 1959; Broken Doll, 1961; Action of the Tiger, 1961; The Weak and the Strong, 1962; The Counterfeiters, 1962; Long Horn, Long Grass, 1964; Black Sunday, 1965; Plant Poppies on My Grave, 1966; Red Red Red, 1966; Fall of Singapore (with I Simon), 1970; The Mean City (as James Bradwell), 1971; A Life in the Wind (with Z de Tyras), 1971; Sword of Vengeance (as Alexander Karol), 1973; Dark Lady (as Alexander Karol), 1974; The King's Witchfinder (as Alexander Karol), 1975; Maverick Squadron, 1975; The Nowhere War, 1975. Address: 26 Verulam Avenue, London E17, England.

KENT Helen. See: **POLLEY Judith Anne.**

KENT Peter. See: **ST PIERRE Roger.**

KENT Philip. See: **BULMER Henry Kenneth.**

KENYON Bruce (Guy), (Meredith Leigh), b. 16 Aug 1929, Cadillac, Michigan, USA. Writer. m. Marian Long, 1950, div 1954. Publications: Rose White, Rose Red, 1983; The Forrester Inheritance, 1985; Fair Game, 1986; A Marriage of Inconvenience, 1986; Wild Rose, 1986; The Counterfeit Lady, 1987; An Elegant Education, 1987; A Lady of Qualities, 1987; Return to Cheyne Spa, 1988; A Certain Reputation, 1990. Contributions to: Periodicals. Memberships: Authors Guild; Authors League. Address: c/o Kearns and Orr, 686 Lexington Avenue, New York, NY 10022, USA.

KENYON Kate. See: **ADORJAN Carol.**

KENYON Michael, b. 26 June 1931, Huddersfield, Yorkshire, England. Author. 3 daughters. Education: Wadham College, Oxford, 1951-54; MA (Oxon), History. Publications: May You Die in Ireland, 1965; The 100,000 Welcomes, 1970; Mr Big, 1973; The Rapist, 1976; A Healthy Way to Die, 1986; Peckover Holds the Baby, 1988; Kill the Butler!, 1991; Peckover Joins the Choir, 1992; A French Affair, 1992; Peckover and the Bog Man, 1994. Contributions to: 50 articles to Gourmet Magazine. Membership: Detection Club. Address: 164 Halsey Street, Southampton, NY 11968, USA.

KENZLE Linda Fry, b. 22 May 1950, Wisconsin, USA. Artist; Author. m. Don Carlo, 1 son. Education: Privately educated. Publications: Third Coast Press Imprint: Fine Time Craft, 1972; Gathering: A Free Will Anthology, 1978; Stylecloth, 1984; Stylecloth 2, 1985; Belts, 1985; Scented Geraniums: Enchanted Plants for Today's Garden, 1986; Vines for America, 1987; The Joy of Herbs, 1988; Be Your Own Boss Now!, 1988; New World Adventures, 1990; Chilton Book Company Imprint: Embellishments, 1993; Dazzle, 1995; The Irresistible Bead, 1996; Krause Publications; Imprint: Pages: Innovative Book Making Techniques, 1997; Gathering: Cleanings from the Garden, 1998. Address: PO Box 177, Fox River Grove, IL 60021, USA.

KEOGH Dermot Francis, b. 12 May 1945, Dublin, Ireland. Professor; Historian. m. Ann, 22 Aug 1973, 2 sons, 2 daughters. Education: BA, 1970, MA, 1974, University College, Dublin; PhD, 1980, European University Institute, Florence, 1980. Appointments: Lecturer, Department of History, 1970-, Jean Monnet Professor of Modern Integration, 1990-, University College, Cork; Acting Head of Department, 1999-. Publications: The Vatican, the Bishops and Irish Politics 1919-1939, 1985; The Rise of the Irish Working Class 1890-1914, 1983; Ireland and Europe 1919-1989, 1989; Church and Politics in Latin America, 1990; Ireland, 1922-1993, 1993; Jews in Twentieth Century Ireland, 1998. Contributions to: Academic journals and national press. Honour: Fellow, Woodrow Wilson Centre for Scholars, Washington, DC, 1988. Address: Department of Modern History, University College, Cork, Ireland.

KERMODE Sir (John) Frank, b. 29 Nov 1919, Douglas, Isle of Man, England. Professor of English Literature (Retired); Writer; Editor. m. Maureen Eccles, 1947, div 1970, 1 son, 1 daughter. Education: BA, 1940, MA, 1947, University of Liverpool. Appointments: Lecturer, King's College, Newcastle, 1947-49, University of Reading, 1949-58; John Edward Taylor Professor of English Literature, University of Manchester, 1958-65; Winterstoke Professor of English, University of Bristol, 1965-67; Co-Editor, Encounter, 1966-67; Lord Northcliffe Professor of Modern England Literature, 1967-74, Honorary Fellow, 1996, University College, London; Editor, Fontana Masterguides and Modern Masters series, 1969-, Oxford Authors, 1984-; King Edward VII Professor of English Literature, University of Cambridge, 1974-82; Fellor, 1974-87, Honorary Fellow, 1988, King's College, Cambridge; Charles Eliot Norton Professor of Poetry, Harvard University, 1977-78; Visiting Professor, Columbia University, 1984, 1985; Henry Luce Professor, Yale University, 1994. Publications: Romantic Image, 1957; John Donne, 1957; The Living Milton, 1960; Wallace Stevens, 1960; Puzzles & Epiphanies, 1962; The Sense of an Ending, 1967; Continuities, 1968; Shakespeare, Spenser, Donne, 1971; Modern Essays, 1971; D H Lawrence, 1973; Oxford Anthology of English Literature (editor with John Hollander), 1973; The Classic, 1975; Selected Prose of T S Eliot (editor), 1975; The Genesis of Secrecy, 1979; Essays on Fiction, 1971-82, 1983; Forms of Attention, 1985; The Literary Guide to the Bible (editor with Robert Alter), 1987; History and Value, 1988; An Appetite for Poetry, 1989; Poetry, Narrative, History, 1990; Andrew Marvell (editor with Keith Walker), 1990; The Uses of Error, 1991; The Oxford Book of Letters (editor with Anita Kermode), 1995; Not Entitled (memoirs), 1996. Contributions to: Journals and periodicals. Honours: Officier de l'Ordre des Arts et des Sciences, France, 1973; Knighted, 1991; Honorary doctorates. Memberships: American Academy of Arts and

Sciences, honorary member; British Academy, fellow; Royal Society of Literature, fellow. Address: 27 Luard Road, Cambridge CB2 2PJ, England.

KERN E R. See: **KERNER Fred.**

KERN Gregory. See: **TUBB E(dwin) C(harles).**

KERNAGHAN Eileen (Shirley), b. 6 Jan 1939, Enderby, British Columbia, Canada. Writer. m. Patrick Walter Kernaghan, 22 Aug 1959, 2 sons, 1 daughter. Education: Elementary Teaching Certificate, University of British Columbia. Publications: The Upper Left-Hand Corner: A Writer's Guide for the Northwest (co-author), 1975, revised edition, 1986; Journey to Aprilioth, 1980; Songs for the Drowned Lands, 1983; Sarsen Witch, 1988; Walking After Midnight, 1991. Contributions to: Journals and periodicals. Honours: Silver Porgy Award, West Coast Review of Books, 1981; Canadian Science Fiction and Fantasy Award, 1985. Memberships: Burnaby Writers Society; Federation of British Columbian Writers; Writers Union of Canada. Address: 5512 Neville Street, Burnaby, British Columbia V5J 2H7, Canada.

KERNER Fred, (F R Eady, Frohm Fredericks, Frederika Frohm, E R Kern, Frederick Kerr, D F Renrick, M N Thaler), b. 15 Feb 1921, Montreal, Quebec, Canada. Writer. m. Sally Dee Stouten, 18 May 1959, 2 sons, 1 daughter. Education: BA, Sir George Williams University (Concordia University), Montreal, 1942. Appointments: Creative Writing Departments, Stanford University, Long Island University, American River University (USA), University of Western Ontario, University of Toronto, (Canada). Publications: Eat, Think and Be Slender (with L Kotkin), 1954; The Magic Power of Your Mind (with W Germain), 1956; Ten Days to a Successful Memory (with J Brothers), 1957; Love is a Man's Affair, 1958; Stress and Your Heart, 1961; Watch Your Weight Go Down (as Frederick Kerr), 1962; A Treasury of Lincoln Quotations, 1965; Secrets of Your Supraconscious, 1965; What's Best For Your Child... and You (with D Goodman), 1966; Buy Higher, Sell Higher (with J Reid), 1966; It's Fun to Fondue (as M N Thaler), 1968; Nadia (with I Grumeza), 1977; Mad About Fondue, 1986; Folles, folles les fondues, 1987; Prospering Through the Coming Depression (with Andrew Willman), 1988; Home Emergency Handbook, 1990; The Writer's Essential Desk Reference, 1991, 2nd edition, 1996; Lifetime: A Treasury of Uncommon Wisdoms, 1992; Idées and Tendances: Des trésors de sagesse, 1993. Contributions to: Numerous magazines and journals. Honours: American Heritage Foundation Award, 1952; Queen's Silver Jubilee Medal, 1977; Allen Sangster Award, 1982; Canadian Book Publishers Council Award, 1984; Air Canada Award, 1984; International Mercury Award, 1990. Memberships: Canadian Authors Association; Academy of Canadian Writers; The Writes' Union of Canada; The Authors' Guild (U.S.); The Author's League (U.S.); Periodical Writers Association of Canada. Address: 1405-1555 Finch Avenue East, Willowdale, Ontario M2J 4X9, Canada.

KERNFELD Barry Dean, b. 11 Aug 1950. Freelance Jazz Writer. m. Sally McMurry, 15 Aug 1981, 2 sons. Education: BA, Music, University of California at Davis, 1975; MA, Musicology, 1978, PhD, Musicology, 1981, Cornell University. Publications: The New Grove Dictionary of Jazz (editor), 1988, 2nd edition, forthcoming; The Blackwell Guide to Recorded Jazz (editor), 1991, 2nd edition, 1995; What to Listen for in Jazz (author), 1995. Contributions to: Extensive to reference works including: The New Harvard Dictionary of Music, 1986; American National Biography, 1998. Address: 506 W Foster Avenue, State College, PA 16801-4039, USA.

KERNS Reeva. See: **GORDON Reva Jo Kerns.**

KERR Carole. See: **CARR Margaret.**

KERR Frederick. See: **KERNER Fred.**

KERR (Anne) Judith, b. 14 June 1923, Berlin, Germany. Children's Fiction Writer. Appointments: Secretary, Red Cross, London, England, 1941-45; Teacher and Textile Designer, 1948-53; Script Editor, Script Writer, BBC-TV, London, 1953-58. Publications: The Tiger Who Came to Tea, 1968; Mog the Forgetful Cat, 1970; When Hitler Stole Pink Rabbit, 1971; When Willy Went to the Wedding, 1972; The Other Way Round, 1975; Mog's Christmas, 1976; A Small Person Far Away, 1978; Mog and the Baby, 1980; Mog in the Dark, 1983; Mog and Me, 1984; Mog's Family of Cats, 1985; Mog's Amazing Birthday Caper, 1986; Mog and Bunny, 1988; Mog and Barnaby, 1990; How Mrs Monkey Missed the Ark, 1992; The Adventures of Mog, 1993; Mog on Fox Night, 1993; Mog in the Garden, 1994; Mog's Kittens, 1994; Mog and the Vee Ee Tee, 1996; The Big Mog Book, 1997; Birdie Halleluyah, 1998. Address: c/o Harper Collins Publishers, 77-85 Fulham Palace Road, London W6 8JB, England.

KERSHAW Peter. See: **LUCIE-SMITH (John) Edward (McKenzie).**

KERVIN Alison Cristine, b. 18 Feb 1967, Birmingham, England. Magazine Editor. Appointments: Regular Sports Writer, The Times; Feature Writer, Country Life, Health and Fitness, Rugby World. Publication: Sports Writing - The ultimate guide to becoming a sports writer, 1997. Honours: Cosmopolitan Woman of Achievement, 1993; British Sports Journalist of the Year Award, 1993; Writer of the Year, Independent Press Council, 1996. Address: 1 Poulett Lodge, Cross Deep, Twickenham TW1 4QJ, England.

KESSLER Jascha (Frederick), b. 27 Nov 1929, New York, New York, USA. Professor; Poet; Writer; Dramatist. m. 17 July 1950, 2 sons, 1 daughter. Education: BA, University of Heights College of New York University, 1950; MA, 1951, PhD, 1955, University of Michigan. Appointments: Faculty, University of Michigan, 1951-54, New York University, 1954-55, Hunter College, 1955-56, Hamilton College, 1957-61; Professor, University of California at Los Angeles, 1961-. Publications: Poetry: Whatever Love Declares, 1969; After the Armies Have Passed, 1970; In Memory of the Future, 1976. Fiction: An Egyptian Bondage, 1967, 2nd edition, 1998; Death Comes for the Behaviorist, 1983; Classical Illusions: 28 stories, 1985; Transmigrations: 18 Mythologemes, 1985; Siren Songs and Classical Illusions (50 stories), 1992; A New Verse Translation of Oedipus Tyrannus: King Oedipus, with an intoductory essay: An Open Secret, 1998; Collected Poems, 1998. Other: Plays: The Cave (opera libretto); Selected Plays, 1998; Rapid Transit: 1948, 1998; Christmas Carols and Other Plays, 1998. Translations. Honours: National Endowment for the Arts Fellowship, 1974; Rockefeller Foundation Fellowship, 1979; Hungarian PEN Club Memorial Medal, 1979; George Soros Foundation Prize, 1989; California Arts Council Fellowship, 1993-94. Memberships: Association of Literary Scholars and Critics; American Society of Composers, Authors, and Publishers; Poetry Society of America. Address: c/o Department of English, University of California at Los Angeles, Los Angeles, CA 90095, USA.

KESSLER Lauren Jeanne, b. 4 Apr 1951, New York, New York, USA. Author; Professor. m. Thomas Hager, 7 July 1984, 2 sons, 1 daughter. Education: BS, Northwestern University, 1971; MS, University of Oregon, 1975; PhD, University of Washington, 1980. Appointment: Faculty, School of Journalism and Communications, University of Oregon. Publications: The Dissident Press: Alternative Journalism in American History, 1984; When Worlds Collide, 1984, 5th edition, 1999; Aging Well, 1987; Mastering the Message, 1989; After All These Years: Sixties Ideals in a Different World, 1990; The Search, 1991; Stubborn Twig: A Japanese Family in America, 1993; Full Court Press, 1997; Full Throttle: The Life and Times of Pancho Barnes, 1999. Contributions to: Scholarly journals. Honours: Excellence in Periodical Writing Award, Council for the Advancement of Secondary Education, 1987; Excellence in Journalism Award, Sigma Delta Chi, 1987; Frances Fuller Victor

Award for Literary Non-Fiction, 1994. Memberships: American Journalism Historians Association; Association for Education in Journalism and Mass Communications. Address: c/o School of Communications, Allen Hall, University of Oregon, Eugene, OR 97403, USA.

KEYES Daniel, b. 9 Aug 1927, New York, New York, USA. Author. m. Aurea Georgina Vazquez, 14 Oct 1952, 2 daughters. Education: BA, 1950; MA, 1962. Appointments: Lecturer, Wayne State University, 1962-66; Professor, English, Ohio University, 1966-. Publications: Flowers for Algernon, 1966, filmed as Charly; The Touch, 1968; The Fifth Sally, 1980; The Minds of Billy Milligan (non-fiction), 1986; Daniel Keyes Short Stories, 1993; Daniel Keyes Reader, 1994; The Milligan Wars, 1995. Address: c/o William Morris Agency, 1350 Avenue of the Americas, New York, NY 10019, USA.

KEYES Ralph Jeffrey, b. 12 Jan 1945, Cincinnati, Ohio, USA. Writer. m. Muriel Gordon, 13 Feb 1965, 2 sons. Education: BA, Antioch College, 1967; Graduate Study, International History, London School of Economics and Political Sciences, 1968-69. Appointment: Board of Trustees, Antioch Writers' Workshops. Publications: The Courage to Write: How Writers Transcend Fear; The Wit and Wisdom of Oscar Wilde; Is There Life After High School?; The Height of Your Life; Chancing It: Why We Take Risks; Timelock: How Life Got So Hectic and What You Can Do About It; Nice Guys Finish Seventh: False Phrases, Spurious Sayings and Familiar Misquotations; The Wit and Wisdom of Harry Truman; We, The Lonely People: Searching for Community; Sons on Fathers: A Book of Men's Writing. Contributions to: Journals, anthologies, and periodicals. Honours: Headliner of the Year, Literature, San Diego Press Club, 1976; Citation for Nonfiction, 1985. Membership: Authors Guild. Literary Agent: Colleen Mohyde. Address: 690 Omar Circle, Yellow Springs, OH 45387, USA.

KHAIR Tabish, b. 21 Mar 1966, Ranchi, India. Journalist; Writer; Poet. Education: BA, Honours, 1988; Diploma, Journalism, 1988; MA, 1992. Appointments: District Correspondent, 1986-87, Staff Correspondent, 1990-92, Times of India; Co-Editor, Cultural Academy, Gaya, 1987-89. Publications: My World, 1991; A Reporter's Diary, 1993; The Book of Heoros, 1995; An Angel in Pyjamas, 1996. Contributions to: Numerous newspapers, reviews, journals, and magazines. Honour: British Council's All India Prize, 1996. Membership: Poetry Society of India. Address: Roarsvej 14 St tv, 2000 Frederiksberg, Denmark.

KHALVATI Mimi, b. 28 Apr 1944, Tehran, Iran. Poet; Writer. 1 son, 1 daughter. Education: University of Neuchatel, Switzerland, 1960-62; Drama Centre, London, 1967-70; University of London, 1991. Appointments: Lecturer, Goldsmith's College, University of London, 1995; Coordinator, The Poetry School, 1997-. Publications: Persian Miniatures, 1990; In White Ink, 1991; Mirrorwork, 1995; Entries on Light 1997. Contributions to: Anthologies, reviews and journals. Honours: Joint Winner, Poetry Business Pamphlet Competition, 1989; Joint Winner, Afro Caribbean-Asian Prize, Peterloo Poets, 1990; Writers Award, Arts Council of England, 1994. Membership: Council of Poetry Society, 1998-. Address: 130C Evering Road, London N16 7BD, England.

KHAN Ismith, b. 16 Mar 1925, Trinidad, West Indies. Writer; University Lecturer. m. M Ghose, 14 Feb 1949, 1 son, 1 daughter. Education: BA, New School for Social Research, New York City, 1960; MA, Johns Hopkins University, 1970. Appointments: Freelance Manuscript Consultant; Senior Lecturer, California State University, Long Beach, 1978-83; Adjunct Professor, Humanities Division, Medgar Evers College of the City University of New York, Brooklyn, New York, 1986-. Publications: Novels: The Jumbie Bird, UK edition, 1961, American edition, 1962, 2nd UK edition, 1985; The Obeah Man, 1964, radio adaptation, BBC London, 1970; The Crucifixion, 1987; A Day in the Country (short stories), 1994. Contributions to: Journals and magazines. Honour:

National Endowment for the Humanities Fellowship, 1972. Membership: PEN.

KHATCHADOURIAN Haig, b. 22 July 1925, Old City, Jerusalem, Palestine. Professor of Philosophy; Writer; Poet. m. Arpiné Yaghlian, 10 Sept 1950, 2 sons, 1 daughter. Education: BA, MA, American University of Beirut, Lebanon; PhD, Duke University, USA. Appointments: American University of Beirut, Lebanon, 1948-49, 1951-67; Professor of Philosophy, University of Southern California at Los Angeles, 1968-69, University of Wisconsin, Milwaukee, 1969-94; Emeritus Professor, 1994- Publications: The Coherence Theory of Truth: A Critical Evaluation, 1961; Traffic with Time (co-author, poems), 1963; A Critical Study in Method, 1967; The Concept of Art, 1971; Shadows of Time, poetry, 1983; Music, Film and Art, 1985; Philosophy of Language and Logical Theory: Collected Papers, 1996; The Morality of Terrorism, 1998; Community and Communitarianism, 1999. Contributions to: Numerous professional and literary journals including Armenian Mind. Memberships: Fellow of the Royal Society for the Encouragement of Arts, Manufacture and Commerce; Foreign Member of the Armenian Academy of Philosophy, Republic of Armenia. Address: Department of Philosophy, University of Wisconsin, Milwaukee, WI 53201, USA.

KHAYAM Massoud, b. 5 May 1947, Tehran, Iran. Consultant Engineer; Writer. 2 sons, 1 daughter. Education: BSc, Engineering, 1971; MSc, Engineering, 1975. Appointment: Lecturer, Tehran University of Science, 1990. Publications: Over 15 books, 1982-98. Contributions to: Private Iranian journals. Address: PO Box 1587, Tehran 3168, Iran.

KHEIRABADI Masoud, b. 28 Feb 1951, Sabzevar, Iran. Lecturer; Researcher. Education: BS, Geography, University of Tehran, 1973; MS, Agricultural Mechanization, Texas A & M University, 1978; MA, 1983, PhD, Geography, 1987, University of Oregon. Appointments: Lecturer, University of Oregon, 1987-89, Lewis and Clark College, 1989-, Portland State University, 1989-, Clackamas Community College, 1990-. Publication: Iranian Cities: Formation and Development, 1991, 2nd edition, 1993. Contributions to: Books, scholarly journals, newspapers, and magazines. Memberships: Association of American Geographers; Middle East Association of North America; National Geographic Society. Address: 67 South West Oswego Summit, Lake Oswego, OR 97035, USA.

KHERDIAN David, b. 17 Dec 1931, Racine, Wisconsin, USA. Author; Poet. m. (1) Kato Rozeboom, 1968, div 1970, (2) Nonny Hogrogian, 17 Mar 1971. Education: BS, University of Wisconsin, 1965. Appointments: Literary Consultant, Northwestern University, 1965; Founder-Editor, Giligia Press, 1966-72, Press at Butterworth Creek, 1987-88, Fork Roads: Journal of Ethnic American Literature, 1995-96; Rare Book Consultant, 1968-69, Lecturer, 1969-70, Fresno State College; Poet-in-the-Schools, State of New Hampshire, 1971; Editor, Ararat magazine, 1971-72; Director, Two Rivers Press, 1978-86. Publications: On the Death of My Father and Other Poems, 1970; Homage to Adana, 1970; Looking Over Hills, 1972; The Nonny Poems, 1974; Any Day of Your Life, 1975; Country Cat, City Cat, 1978; I Remember Root River, 1978; The Road from Home: The Story of an Armenian Girl, 1979; The Farm, 1979; It Started With Old Man Bean, 1980; Finding Home, 1981; Taking the Soundings on Third Avenue, 1981; The Farm Book Two, 1981; Beyond Two Rivers, 1981; The Song of the Walnut Grove, 1982; Place of Birth, 1983; Right Now, 1983; The Mystery of the Diamond in the Wood, 1983; Root River Run, 1984; The Animal, 1984; Threads of Light: The Farm Poems Books III and IV, 1985; Bridger: The Story of a Mountain Man, 1987; Poems to an Essence Friend, 1987; A Song for Uncle Harry, 1989; The Cat's Midsummer Jamboree, 1990; The Dividing River/The Meeting Shore, 1990; On a Spaceship with Beelzebub: By a Grandson of Gurdjieff, 1990; The Great Fishing Contest, 1991; Junas's Journey, 1993; Asking the River, 1993; By Myself, 1993; Friends: A Memoir, 1993; My Racine, 1994; Lullaby for Emily,

1995. Editor: Visions of America by the Poets of Our Time, 1973; Settling America: The Ethnic Expression of 14 Contemporary Poets, 1974; Poems Here and Now, 1976; Traveling America with Today's Poets, 1976; The Dog Writes on the Window with His Nose and Other Poems, 1977; If Dragon Flies Made Honey, 1977; I Sing the Song of Myself, 1978; Beat Voices: An Anthology of Beat Poetry, 1995; Seven Poems for Mikey, 1997; I called it Home, 1997; The Roses Smile, 1997; The Golden Bracelet, 1998; Chippecotton: Root River Tales of Racine. Co-Editor: Down at the Santa Fe Depot: 20 Fresno Poets, 1970. Other: Various translations. Honours: Jane Addams Peace Award, 1980; Banta Award, 1980; Boston Globe/Horn Book Award, 1980; Lewis Carroll Shelf Award, 1980; Newbery Honor Book Award, 1980; Friends of American Writers Award, 1982. Membership: PEN. Address: 7121 Palm Avenue, Sebastopol, CA 95472, USA.

KHOSLA Gurdial Singh, b. 15 Jan 1912, Lahore, India. Writer; Dramatist. m. Manorama Khosla, 16 Oct 1941, 1 son, 1 daughter. Education: BA, Honours, 1931, MA, 1933, English, Punjab University, Lahore. Appointments: Lecturer in English, Khalsa College, Amritsar, 1934-35; General Manager, Western Railway, 1967-70; Adviser and Head, Department of Dramatic Arts, Punjab University, 1970-72. Publications: The Auction of a City: Literary and Other Essays, 1951; Railway Management in India, 1972; A History of Indian Railways, 1988; Road to Nowhere (novel), 1993. Contributions to: Newspapers and journals. Honours: Eminent Theatreman Citation, Delhi Natya Sangh, 1980, and World Punjabi Conference, 1983; Drama Award, Punjabi Academy, Delhi, 1988, and Sahitya Academy, Punjab, 1989. Memberships: Authors Guild of India; Conservation Society, Delhi, president, 1983-86; General Indian Heritage Society, honorary president, 1987-93; PEN International. Address: D103 Defence Colony, New Delhi 110-024, India.

KHRUSHCHEV Sergei Nikitich, b. 2 July 1935, Moscow, Russia. Control Systems Engineer. m. Valentina N Golenko, 3 Aug 1985, 3 sons. Education: Moscow Electrical Power Institute, 1952-68; PhD, Engineering, 1967, Assistant Professor, 1968, Moscow Technical University; Doctorate, Ukrainian Academy of Sciences, 1988. Appointments: Professor, Control Computer Institute, 1989; Senior Fellow, Thomas J Watson Jr Institute for International Studies, Brown University, Providence, Rhode Island, 1991; Columnist, Asia Times, 1995-, Asia Inc, 1992-97. Publications: Khrushchev on Khrushchev, 1990; Pensioner Sousnogo Znachenia, 1991; Nikita Khrushchev: Crises and Missiles, 1994. Contributions to: Publications worldwide. Honours: Lenin Prize for Engineering, 1959; Hero of Soviet Labour, 1963; Council of Ministers Prize, USSR, 1985. Memberships: International Informatization Academy; Russian Computer Society. Address: 3 Laurelhurst Road, Cranston, RI 02920, USA.

KIANG John, b. 10 May 1931, Shaoyung, Hunan, China. Publisher. m. S Y Kiang, 20 Aug 1959. Education: BA, Hunan University, Changsha; MA, 1952, PhD, Political Science, 1956, University of Nebraska, Lincoln, USA; MA, Library Science, University of Michigan, Ann Arbor, 1955. Appointments: President, Chiang Small Duplicator, South Bend, Indiana, USA, 1958-75; Manager, One World Publishing, South Bend, 1975-; Founder, Director, One World Movement, Notre Dame, Indiana, 1984-. Publications: The Sea is Wide and the Sky is High, in Chinese, 1972; Dr Y C James Yen, in English, 1876; One World, the Approach to Permanent Peace on Earth and General Happiness of Mankind, in English, 1984, revised and enlarged edition in English, 1992, revised and enlarged edition in Chinese, 1996; The Early One World Movement, in English, 1984, in Chinese, 1994, Volume 2 in English, 1997, Volume 2 in Chinese, to be published; Two Years After, in English, 1986; Our World, in Chinese, 1994; My Memoir, in Chinese, 1996, Supplement, to be published; The Story of Kings Family, in progress. Honours: One World reviewed favourably worldwide and nominated for Nobel Peace Prize, 1986,

1987, 1988, 1994. Address: One World Publishing, PO Box 423, Notre Dame, IN 46556, USA.

KIDD Jane, b. 3 June 1943, England. Writer. divorced. Education: 2.1 Honours Degree in Economics & Government, Bristol University. Appointments: Chairman, International Teams in Dressage, 1997-; Chairman, Dressages U-21, 1992-96; Vice Chairman, British Horse Foundation, 1999. Publications: Breeds & Breeding; The International Warmblood Horse; Goodwood Champions Dressage; Young Persons Guide to Dressage; The Gilbeys; Dressage Essentials. Contributions to: Horse & Hound; Breeding News; Dressage News. Address: The Barn House, Aldsworth, Glos GL54 3RE, England.

KIDDER Tracy, b. 12 Nov 1945, New York, New York, USA. Writer. m. Frances T Toland, 2 Jan 1971, 1 son, 1 daughter. Education: AB, Harvard University, 1967; MFA, University of Iowa, 1974. Appointment: Contributing Editor, Atlantic Monthly, 1982-. Publications: The Road to Yuba City: A Journey into the Juan Corona Murders, 1974; The Soul of a New Machine, 1981, revised edition, 1997; House, 1985; Among Schoolchildren, 1989; Old Friends, 1993. Contributions to: Newspapers and magazines. Honours: Atlantic First Award, Atlantic Monthly, 1978; Sidney Hillman Foundation Prize, 1978; Pulitzer Prize in General Non-Fiction, 1982; American Book Award, 1982; Ambassador Book Award, 1990; Robert F Kennedy Award, 1990; New England Book Award, 1994. Address: c/o George Borchardt Inc, 136 East 47th Street, New York, NY 10019, USA.

KIDMAN Fiona (Judith), b. 26 Mar 1940, Hawera, New Zealand. Writer; Poet. m. Ernest Ian Kidman, 20 Aug 1960, 1 son, 1 daughter. Publications: Novels: A Breed of Women, 1979; Mandarin Summer, 1981; Paddy's Puzzle, 1983, US edition as In the Clear Light, 1985; The Book of Secrets, 1987; True Stars, 1990; Ricochet Baby, 1996; The House Within, 1997; The Best of Fiona Kidman's Short Stories, 1998. Poetry: Honey and Bitters, 1975; On the Tightrope, 1978; Going to the Chathams, Poems: 1977-1984, 1985; Wakeful Nights: Poems Selected and New, 1991. Other: Search for Sister Blue (radio play), 1975; Gone North (with Jane Ussher), 1984; Wellington (with Grant Sheehan), 1989; Palm Prints, 1994. Contributions to: Periodicals. Honours: Scholarships in Letters, 1981, 1985, 1991, 1995; Mobil Short Story Award, 1987; Queen Elizabeth II Arts Council Award for Achievement, 1988; Officer of the Order of the British Empire, 1988; New Zealand Book Council Fiction Award, 1988; Victorian University Writing Fellowship, 1988; President of Honour, New Zealand Book Council, 1997; Dame Companion of the New Zealand Order of Merit, for services to literature, 1998. Memberships: International PEN; Media Women; New Zealand Book Council, president, 1992-95; New Zealand Writers' Guild. Address: 28 Rakau Road, Hataitai, Wellington 3, New Zealand.

KIELY Benedict, b. 15 Aug 1919, Dromore, County Tyrone, Ireland. Journalist; Writer. Education: National University of Ireland. Appointments: Journalist, Dublin, 1940-65; Visiting Professor and Writer-in-Residence, several US universities. Publications: Land Without Stars, 1946; In a Harbour Green, 1949; Call for a Miracle, 1950; Honey Seems Bitter, 1952; The Cards of the Gambler: A Folktale, 1953; There Was an Ancient House, 1955; The Captain With the Whiskers, 1960; Dogs Enjoy the Morning, 1968; Proxopera: A Novella, 1977; Nothing Happens in Carmincross, 1985; Drink to the Bird (memoir), 1991; Selected Stories, 1993; As I Rode By Granard Moat: A Personal Anthology, 1997; Memoirs: The Waves Behind Us, Clay Gods and Men (collection of essays), both to celebrate his eightieth birthday. Honours: American Irish Foundation Award, 1980; Irish Academy of Letters Award, 1980; Irish Independent Literary Award, 1985; Honorary DLitt, National University of Ireland and Queen's University, Belfast. Literary Agent: Derek Johns, A.P. Watt, John Street, London. Address: 119 Morehampton Road, Donnybrook, Dublin 4, Ireland.

KIENZLE William X(avier), b. 11 Sept 1928, Detroit, Michigan, USA. Author. m. Javan Herman Andrews, Nov

1974. Education: BA, Sacred Heart Seminary College, 1950; St John's Seminary, 1950-54. Appointments: Editor, The Michigan Catholic, 1962-74, MPLS Magazine, 1974-76. Publications: The Rosary Murders, 1979; Death Wears a Red Hat, 1980; Mind Over Murder, 1981; Assault with Intent, 1982; Shadow of Death, 1983; Kill and Tell, 1984; Sudden Death, 1985; Deathbed, 1986; Deadline for a Critic, 1987; Marked for Murder, 1988; Eminence, 1989; Masquerade, 1990; Chameleon, 1991; Body Count, 1992; Dead Wrong, 1993; Bishop as Pawn, 1994; Call No Man Father, 1995; Requiem for Moses, 1996; The Man Who Loved God, 1997; The Greatest Evil, 1998. Honours: Journalism Award for General Excellence, Michigan Knights of Columbus, 1963; Honourable Mention for Editorial Writing, Catholic Press Association, 1974. Membership: Authors Guild; International Association of Crime Writers. Address: PO Box 80942, Rochester, MI 48308, USA.

KIHLMAN Christer Alfred, b. 14 June 1930, Helsinki, Finland. Writer; Dramatist. m. Selinda Enckell, 7 Jan 1956, 1 son, 1 daughter. Education: University of Helsinki, 1948-53. Appointments: Columnist, Finnish and Swedish newspapers; Artist Professor, 1975. Publications: Several books. Other: Various plays. Address: Diktarhemmet, 06100 Borga, Finland.

KILJUNEN Kimmo Roobert, b. 13 June 1951, Rauha, Finland. Member of Parliament; Development Researcher and Director. m. Marja Liisa Kiljunen, 17 Jan 1972, 2 sons, 2 daughters. Education: MA, Helsinki University, 1973; MPhil, 1977, DPhil, 1985, Sussex University, England. Appointment: Member of Parliament, Finland. Publications: Nambia, The Last Colony (editor), 1981; Kampuchea: Decade of the Genocide, 1984; Region to Region Cooperation Between Developed and Developing Countries, 1990; Finland and the New International Division of Labour, 1992; Finns in the United Nations, 1996. Other: 9 books in Finnish, 1976-99. Honour: President, Urho Kekkonen Foundation Literary Award, 1992. Membership: European Association of Development Research and Training Institutes, executive committee, 1987-95. Address: Linnoittajanpolku 3 g 15, 01280 Vantaa, Finland.

KILLANIN Michael Morris, Lord, b. 30 July 1914, London, England. Writer; Film Producer; Company Director. m. Mary Sheila Dunlop, 17 Dec 1945, 3 sons, 1 daughter. Education: Eton, 1928-31; Sorbonne, University of Paris, 1931-32; BA, 1935, MA, 1939, Magdalene College, Cambridge. Publications: Four Days, 1938; Sir Godfrey Kneller, 1947; Shell Guide to Ireland (with M V Duigan), 1956; The Olympic Games (with John Rodda), 1976, 3rd edition, 1984; My Ireland: A Personal Impression, 1987. Honours: Various UK and foreign honours. Memberships: French Academy of Sports; International Olympic Committee, president, 1972-80; Olympic Council of Ireland, president, 1950-73, honorary life president, 1981-; Royal Society of Antiquaries of Ireland, fellow; Royal Society of Arts, fellow; National Heritage Council, president, 1988-. Address: 9 Lower Mount Pleasant Avenue, Dublin 6, Ireland.

KILLDEER John. See: **MAYHAR Ardath.**

KILLINGER Barbara Elizabeth, b. 6 June 1934, London, Ontario, Canada. Clinical Psychologist; Author. m. Dr Donald, 11 May 1957, 1 son, 2 daughters. Education: BA, University of Western Ontario, 1955; BA Hons, 1972, MA, 1974, PhD, 1977, York University. Publications include: The Place of Humour in Adult Psychotherapy, 1977; Humour in Psychotherapy - A Shift to a New Perspective, 1987; Workaholics: The Respectable Addicts, 1991; L'Ergomamie, L'Obsession Du Travail, 1992; Workaholics: The Respectable Addicts, 1992; Workaholics: The Respectable Addicts, 1992; Workaholics: the Respectable Addicts, 1997; La Adiccion Al Trabajo, 1995; Ich Habe Leider Keine Zeit, 1994; Toonarkomaanid, 1994; Accros du boulot, 1996; Workaholics: The Respectable Addicts, 1998; The Balancing Act, Rediscovering Your Feelings, 1995; Workaholismus (Czech edition), 1998. Contributions to: The Globe; The Mail; Article in workaholism. Literary

Agent: M Beverley Slopen. Address: 131 Bloor St W, #711, Toronto M5S 1S3, Canada.

KILLOUGH (Karen) Lee, b. 5 May 1942, Syracuse, Kansas, USA. Science Fiction Writer. Publications: A Voice Out of Ramah, 1979; The Doppelganger Gambit, 1979; The Monitor, the Miners, and the Shree, 1980; Aventine, 1981; Deadly Silents, 1982; Liberty's World, 1985; Spider Play, 1986; Blood Hunt, 1987; The Leopard's Daughter, 1987; Bloodlinks, 1988; Dragon's Teeth, 1990; Bloodwalk, 1997; Bridling Chaos, 1998. Memberships: Science Fiction and Fantasy Writers of America; Mystery Writers of America. Address: Box 1821, Manhattan, KS 66505, USA.

KILROY Thomas, b. 23 Sept 1934, Callan, Ireland. Writer; Dramatist; University Teacher. m. (1) 3 sons, (2) Julia Lowell Carlson, 9 Dec 1981, 1 daughter. Education: BA, 1956, MA, 1959, University College, Dublin. Publications: Death and Resurrection of Mr Roche (play), 1968; The Big Chapel (novel), 1971; Talbots' Box (play), 1977; The Seagull (play adaptation), 1981; Double Cross (play), 1986; Ghosts, 1989; The Madame McAdam Travelling Theatre (play), 1990; Gold in the Streets (television), 1993; Six Characters in Search of An Author (adaption), 1996; The Secret Fall of Constance Wilde (play), 1997. Contributions to: Radio, television, journals, and magazines. Honours: Guardian Fiction Prize, 1971; Heinnmann Award for Literature, 1971; Irish Academy of Letters Prize, 1972; American-Irish Foundation Award for Literature, 1974. Memberships: Fellow, Royal Society of Literature, 1971, Irish Academy of Letters, 1973. Literary Agent: Casarotto Ramsay Ltd, National House, 60-66 Wardour Street, London W1V 3HP, England. Address: Kilmaine, County Mayo, Ireland.

KILWORTH Garry, b. 5 July 1941, York, England. Writer. m. Annette Jill Bailey, 30 June 1962, 1 son, 1 daughter. Education: Business Studies, 1974; Honours Degree in English, 1985. Publications: Songbirds of Pain, 1984; Spiral Winds, 1987; Hunter's Moon, 1989; In the Hollow of the Deep-Sea Wave, 1989; Standing on Samshan, 1992; The Navigator Kings (Trilogy), 1996-98; Crimean War (Trilogy), 1997-99. Contributions to: Magazines and newspapers. Honours: Gollancz Short Story Award, Sunday Times, 1974; Carnegie Medal Commendation, Librarian Association, 1991; Lancashire Childrens Book of the Year Award, 1995. Membership: PEN; Crimean War Society. Address: Wychwater, The Chase, Ashington, Essex, England.

KIMBALL Roger, b. 13 Aug 1953, Ohio, USA. Writer; Editor. m. Alexandra Mullen, 1993. Education: BA, Bennington College, 1975; MA, 1977, MPhil, 1978, Yale University. Publications: Tenured Radicals: How Politics has Corrupted our Higher Education, 1990; Against the Grain: The New Criteria on Art and Intellect at the End of the Twentieth Century (editor), 1994; The Future of the European Parliment (editor), 1997. Contributions to: New Criterion; Wall Street Journal; Times Literary Supplement; Commentary; American Scholar; Architectural Record. Address: 850 Seventh Avenue, New York, NY 10019, USA.

KIMBROUGH Robert (Alexander III), b. 26 June 1929, Philadelphia, Pennsylvania, USA. Professor of English; Writer. Education: BA, Williams College, 1951; MA, Stanford University, 1955; PhD, Harvard University, 1959. Appointments: Instructor to Associate Professor, 1959-68, Professor of English, 1968-, Chair, Integrated Liberal Studies Department, 1970-75, University of Wisconsin, Madison. Publications: Joseph Conrad: Heart of Darkness: An Authoritative Text, Backgrounds and Sources (editor), 1963, 3rd edition, 1987; Shakespeare's Troilus and Cressida and Its Setting, 1964; Henry James: The Turn of the Screw: An Authoritative Text, Backgrounds and Sources (editor), 1966; Troilus and Cressida: A Scene by Scene Analysis with Critical Commentary, 1966; Sir Philip Sidney: Selected Prose and Poetry (editor), 1969, 2nd edition, 1982; Sir Philip Sidney, 1971; Joseph Conrad: The Nigger of the Narcissus (editor), 1984; Shakespeare and the Art of Human Kindness: The Essay Toward Androgyny, 1990.

Contributions to: Professional journals. Address: 3206 Gregory Street, Madison, WI 53711, USA.

KIMMEL Eric Alan, b. 30 Oct 1946, Brooklyn, New York, USA. Author of children's books. m. Doris Ann Dunlap, 16 June 1978, 1 daughter. Education: BA, Lafayette College, 1967; MA, New York University, 1970; PhD, University of Illinois, 1973. Publications: Anansi and Moss-Covered Rock, 1988; Hershel and the Hanukkah Goblins, 1989; I Took My Frog to the Library, 1990; Four Dollars and Fifty Cents, 1990; Anansi and the Talking Melon, 1994; The Adventures of Hershel of Ostropol, 1995; Bar Mitzvah, 1995; The Magic Dreidels, 1996; Billy Lazroe and the King of the Sea, 1996; One Eye, Two Eyes and Three Eyes, 1996; Ali Baba and the Forty Thieves, 1996; Squash It!, 1997. Contributions to: Children's magazines. Honours: Caldecott Honor, 1990; Washington State Children's Choices. Memberships: Authors Guild; PEN Northwest; Society of Childrens Book Writers. Address: c/o Sharon Friedman, Ralph M Vicinauza Ltd, 111 8th Avenue. New York, NY 10011, USA.

KINCAID Jamaica, b. 25 May 1949, St John's, Antigua, West Indies. Writer. Publications: At the Bottom of the River (short stories), 1984; Annie John (novel), 1985; A Small Place (non-fiction), 1988; Lucy (novel), 1990; Autobiography of My Mother, 1996; My Brother (memoir), 1997. Contributions to: Periodicals. Honours: Morton Dauwen Zabel Award, 1983; Address: c/o Farrar Straus Giroux, Inc., 19 Union Square West, New York, NY 10003-3304, USA

KING Betty Alice, b. 17 June 1919, Enfield, England. Novelist. m. D James King, 14 June 1941, 2 sons, 1 daughter. Education: Queenswood School, Hertfordshire; Open University. Publications: The Lady Margaret, 1965; The Lord Jasper, 1967; The King's Mother, 1969; Margaret of Anjou, 1974; Emma Hamilton, 1976; Nell Gwyn, 1979; Claybourn, 1980; The French Countess, 1982; We Are Tomorrow's Past, 1984. Contributions to: Hertfordshire Countryside; Enfield Gazette. Memberships: Society of Authors; Samuel Pepys Association. Address: Crescent House, 31 North Road, Hertford, Herts SG14 1LN, England.

KING (David) Clive, b. 28 Apr 1924, Richmond, Surrey, England. Author. m. (1) Jane Tuke, 1948, 1 son, 1 daughter, (2) Penny Timmins, 1974, 1 daughter. Education: Downing College, 1947. Publications: The Town That Went South, 1959; Stig of the Dump, 1963; The Twenty-Two Letters, 1966; The Night the Water Came, 1973; Snakes and Snakes, 1975; Me and My Million, 1976; Ninny's Boat, 1980; The Sound of Propellers, 1986; The Seashore People, 1987; 7 other books. Honour: Boston Globe-Horn Book Award, Honour Book, 1980. Membership: Society of Authors. Address: Pond Cottage, Low Road, Thurlton, Norwich NR14 6PZ, England.

KING Cynthia, b. 27 Aug 1925, New York, New York, USA. Writer. m. Jonathan King, 26 July 1944, 3 sons. Education: Bryn Mawr College, 1943-44; University of Chicago, 1944-45; New York University Writers Workshop, 1964-67. Appointments: Associate Editor, Hillman Periodicals, 1945-50; Managing Editor, Fawcett Publications, 1950-55. Publications: In the Morning of Time, 1970; The Year of Mr Nobody, 1978; Beggars and Choosers, 1980; Sailing Home, 1982. Contributions to: Book Reviews: New York Times Book Review; Detroit News; Houston Chronicle; LA Daily News; Short Fiction: Good Housekeeping, Texas Stories & Poems, Quartet. Honour: Michigan Council for the Arts Grant, 1986. Memberships: Authors Guild; Poets and Writers; Detroit Women Writers, President 1979-81. Address: 5306 Institute Lane, Houston, TX 77005, USA.

KING Francis Henry, (Frank Cauldwell), b. 4 Mar 1923, Adelboden, Switzerland. Author; Drama Critic. Education: BA, 1949, MA, 1951, Balliol College, Oxford. Appointment: Drama Critic, Sunday Telegraph, 1978-88. Publications: Novels: To the Dark Tower, 1946; Never Again, 1947; An Air That Kills, 1948; The Dividing

Stream, 1951; The Dark Glasses, 1954; The Firewalkers, 1956; The Widow, 1957; The Man on the Rock, 1957; The Custom House, 1961; The Last of the Pleasure Gardens, 1965; The Waves Behind the Boat, 1967; A Domestic Animal, 1970; Flights, 1973; A Game of Patience, 1974; The Needle, 1975; Danny Hill, 1977; The Action, 1978; Act of Darkness, 1983; Voices in an Empty Room, 1984; Frozen Music, 1987; The Woman Who Was God, 1988; Punishments, 1989; Visiting Cards, 1990; The Ant Colony, 1991; Secret Lives (with Tom Wakefield and Patrick Gale), 1991; The One and Only, 1994; Ash on an Old Man's Sleeve, 1996; Dead Letters, 1997. Short Stories: So Hurt and Humiliated, 1959; The Japanese Umbrella, 1964; The Brighton Belle, 1968; Hard Feelings, 1976; Indirect Method, 1980; One is a Wanderer, 1985; A Hand at the Shutter, 1996. Other: E M Forster and His World, 1978; A Literary Companion to Florence, 1991; Autobiography: Yesterday Came Suddenly, 1993. Honours: Somerset Maugham Award, 1952; Katherine Mansfield Short Story Prize, 1965; Officer, 1979, Commander, 1985, of the Order of the British Empire. Memberships: English PEN, president, 1976-86; International PEN, president, 1986-89, vice-president, 1989-; Royal Society of Literature, fellow. Address: 19 Gordon Place, London W8 4JE, England.

KING Janey. See: **THOMAS Rosie.**

KING Larry L, b. 1 Jan 1929, Putnam, Texas, USA. Playwright; Author; Actor. m. Barbara S Blaine, 2 sons, 3 daughters. Education: Texas Technical University, 1949-50; Nieman Fellow, Harvard University, 1969-70; Duke Fellow of Communications, Duke University, 1975-76. Appointments: Visiting Ferris Professor of Journalism and Political Science, Princeton University, 1973-74; Poet Laureate (life), Monahans (Texas) Sandhills Literary Society, 1977-. Publications: Plays: The Kingfish, 1979; The Best Little Whorehouse in Texas, 1978; Christmas: 1933, 1986; The Night Hank Williams Died, 1988; The Golden Shadows Old West Museum, 1989; The Best Little Whorehouse Goes Public, 1994; The Dead Presidents' Club, 1996; Books: The One-Eyed Man, novel, 1966; ...And Other Dirty Stories, 1968; Confessions of a White Racist, 1971; The Old Man and Lesser Mortals, 1974; Of Outlaws, Whores, Conmen, Politicians and Other Artists, 1980; Warning: Writer at Work, 1985; None But a Blockhead, 1986; Because of Lozo Brown, 1988. Contributions to: Harper's; Atlantic Monthly; Life; New Republic; Texas Monthly; Texas Observer; New York; Playboy; Parade; Esquire; Saturday Evening Post; National Geographic. Address: 3025 Woodland Drive, North West, Washington, DC 20008, USA.

KING Laurie R, b. 19 Sept 1952, Oakland, California, USA. Writer. m. Noel Q King, Nov 1977, 1 son, 1 daughter. Education: BA, University of California, Santa Cruz, 1977; MA, Graduate Theological Union, Berkeley, 1984. Publications: A Grave Talent, 1993; The Beekeeper's Apprentice, 1994; To Play the Fool, 1995; A Monstrous Regiment of Women, 1995; With Child, 1996; A Letter of Mary, 1997; The Moor, 1998; The Birth of a New Moon (in US, A Darker Place), 1999; O Jerusalem, 1999. Honours: Edgar Award for Best First Novel, 1993; Creasey Award for Best First Novel, 1995; Nero Wolfe Award, Best Novel, 1996; Honorary Doctorate, Church Divinity School of the Pacific, 1997. Memberships: Mystery Writers of America; Sisters in Crime; International Association of Crime Writers; Crime Writers Association. Literary Agent: Linda Allen. Address: PO Box 1152, Freedom, CA 95019, USA.

KING Lawrence, b. 18 Nov 1967, St Louis, Missouri, USA. Electrical Engineer; Writer. Education: Southern Illinois University at Edwardsville, 1986-90; Rochester Institute of Technology, 1989; BSEE, Howard University, 1992. Publications: Recism and Blaxploitation within the American Film Industry, 1994; The Return of Blaxploitation within the American Film Industry, 1995; Pulp Fiction: The Long-Awaited 80-Year Sequel to The Birth Of A Nation, 1995. Contributions to: Philadelphia Tribune; Philadelphia Inquiries. Address: 937 Chester Pike, Apt 1 J, Prospect Park, PA 19076, USA.

KING Michael, b. 15 Dec 1945, Wellington, New Zealand. Writer. m. 17 Oct 1987, 1 son, 1 daughter. Education: BA, Victoria University, 1967; MA, 1968, DPhil, 1978, Waikato University. Appointments: Katherine Mansfield Fellow, 1976; Writing Fellow, Victoria University, 1983; National Library Fellow, 1990; Fellowship in Humanities, Waikato University, 1991-; Senior Research Fellow, Arts Faculty, University of Auckland, 1996-97; Robert Burns Fellow, Otago University, 1998. Publications: Te Puea, 1977; Maori, 1983; Being Pakeha, 1985; Death of the Rainbow Warrior, 1986; Moriori, 1989; Frank Sargeson, A Life, 1995. Contributions to: Columnist and feature writer for variety of newspapers and magazines including New Zealand Listener, New Zealand Sunday Times and Metro. Honours: Feltex Award, 1975; Cowan Prize, 1976; New Zealand Book Award, 1978; Wattie Book of the Year Prizes, 1984, 1990; Officer of the Order of the British Empire, 1988; Literary Fund Achievement Award, 1989; Buckland Literary Award, 1996; Honorary DLitt, Victoria University, 1997. Memberships: PEN New Zealand, president, 1979-80; New Zealand Authors Fund Advisory Committee, 1980-92; Frank Sargeson Trust, 1982-; Auckland Institute Museum Council, 1986-91; Chatham Islands Conservation Board, 1990-; Hon DLitt, Victoria Univ, 1997. Literary Agent: Curtis Brown, Australia. Address: PO Box 109, Whangamata, New Zealand.

KING Paul. See: **DRACKETT Phil(ip Arthur).**

KING Stephen (Edwin), (Richard Bachman), b. 21 Sept 1947, Portland, Maine, USA. Author; Screenwriter. m. Tabitha jane Spruce, 2 Jan 1971, 2 sons, 1 daughter. Education: BS, University of Maine, 1970. Appointments: Teacher of English, Hampden Academy, Maine, 1971-73; Writer-in-Residence, University of Maine at Orono, 1978-79. Publications (including those as Richard Bachman): Novels and Short Stories: Carrie, 1974; Salem's Lot, 1975; The Shining, 1976; Night Shift, 1978; Rage, 1978; The Stand, 1978; The Dead Zone, 1979; The Long Walk, 1979; Firestarter, 1980; Cujo, 1981; Danse macabre, 1981; Roadwork, 1981; Different Seasons, 1982; The Running Man, 1982; The Dark Tower Stories: Vol 1, The Gunslinger, 1982, Vol 2, The Drawing of the Three, 1987, Vol 3, The Waste Lands, 1991, Vol 4, Wizard and Glass, 1997; Christine, 1983; Pet Cematary, 1983; The Talisman (with Peter Straub), 1984; Thinner, 1984; Cycle of the Werewolf, 1985; Skeleton Crew, 1985; It, 1986; The Eyes of the Dragon, 1987; Misery, 1987; The Tommyknockers, 1987; The Dark Half, 1989; Four Past Midnight, 1990; Needful Things, 1991; Gerald's Game, 1992; Dolores Claiborne, 1993; Nightmares and Dreamscapes, 1993; Insomnia, 1994; Desperation, 1996; The Green Mile, 1996; The Regulators, 1996; Bag of Bones, 1998. Other: Screenplays and television plays. Memberships: Author's Guild of America; Screen Artists Guild; Screen Writers of America; Writer's Guild. Address: c/o Simon and Schuster, 1230 Avenue of the Americas, New York, NY 10020, USA.

KING-HELE Desmond George, b. 3 Nov 1927, Seaford, Sussex, England. Scientist; Author; Poet. m. Marie Therese Newman, 1954, separated 1992, 2 daughters. Education: BA, 1st Class Honours, Mathematics, 1948, MA, 1952, Trinity College, Cambridge. Appointments: Staff, 1948-68, Deputy Chief Scientific Officer, Space Department, 1968-88, Royal Aerospace Establishment; Editor, Notes and Records of the Royal Society, 1989-96; Various lectureships. Publications: Shelley: His Thought and Work, 1960, 3rd edition, 1984; Satellites and Scientific Research, 1960; Erasmus Darwin, 1963; Theory of Satellite Orbits in an Atmosphere, 1964; Space Research V (editor), 1965; Observing Earth Satellites, 1966, 2nd edition, 1983; Essential Writings of Erasmus Darwin (editor), 1968; The End of the Twentieth Century?, 1970; Poems and Trixies, 1972; Doctor of Revolution, 1977; Letters of Erasmus Darwin (editor), 1981; The RAE Table of Earth Satellites (editor), 1981, 4th edition, 1990; Animal Spirits, 1983; Erasmus Darwin and the Romantic Poets, 1986; Satellite Orbits in an Atmosphere: Theory and Applications, 1987; A Tapestry of Orbits, 1992; John Herschel (editor), 1992; A Concordance to the Botanic Garden (editor), 1994; Antic and Romantic (poems), 1999; Erasmus Darwin: A Life of Unequalled Achievement, 1999. Contributions to: Numerous scientific and literary journals. Honours: Eddington Medal, Royal Astronomical Society, 1971; Charles Chree Medal, Institute of Physics, 1971; Lagrange Prize, Académie Royale de Belgique, 1972; Honorary Doctorates, Universities of Aston, 1979, and Surrey, 1986; Nordberg Medal, International Committee on Space Research, 1990. Memberships: British National Committee for the History of Science, Medicine and Technology, chairman, 1985-89; Institute of Mathematics and Its Applications, fellow; Royal Astronomical Society, fellow; Royal Society, fellow; Wilkins Lecturer, Royal Society, 1997. Address: 7 Hilltops Court, 65 North Lane, Buriton, Hampshire GU31 5RS, England.

KING-SMITH Dick, b. 27 Mar 1922, Bitton, Gloucestershire, England. Writer. Education: BEd, Bristol University, 1975. Publications: The Fox Busters, 1978; Daggie Dogfoot, 1980; The Mouse Butcher, 1981; Magnus Powermouse, 1982; The Queen's Nose, 1983; The Sheep-Pig, 1985; Noah's Brother, 1986; Yob, 1986; E S P, 1986; Friends and Brothers, 1987; Dodos Are Forever, 1987; Sophie's Snail, 1988; The Trouble With Edward, 1988; Martin's Mice, 1988; The Water Horse, 1990; Paddy's Pot of Gold, 1990; Alpha Beasts, 1992; The Hodgeheg, 1992; numerous others. Literary Agent: A.P. Watt, 20 John Street, London WC1N 2DR. Address: Diamond's Cottage, Queen Charlton, Near Keynsham, Somerset, BS31 2SJ, England.

KINGDON Robert McCune, b. 29 Dec 1927, Chicago, Illinois, USA. Professor of History; Writer. Education: AB, Oberlin College, 1949; MA, 1950, PhD, 1955, Columbia University; Postgraduate Studies, University of Geneva, 1951-52. Appointments: Instructor to Assistant Professor, University of Massachusetts, 1952-57; Visiting Instructor, Amherst College, 1953-54; Assistant Professor to Professor of History, University of Iowa, 1957-65; Visiting Professor, Stanford University, 1964, 1980; Professor of History, 1965-, Hilldale Professor of History, 1988-98, University of Wisconsin at Madison; Editor, Sixteenth Century Journal, 1973-97; Member, 1974-, Director, 1975-87, Institute for Research in the Humanities. Publications: Geneva and the Coming of the Wars of Religion in France 1555-1563, 1956; Registres de la Compagnie des Pasteurs de Genévè au Temps de Calvin (editor with J-F Bergier), 2 volumes, 1962, 1964; William Cecil: Execution of Justice in England (editor), 1965; William Allen: A True, Sincere and Modest Defence of English Catholics (editor), 1965; Geneva and the Consolidation of the French Protestant Movement 1564-1572, 1967; Calvin and Calvinism: Sources of Democracy (co-editor with R D Linder), 1970; Theodore de Béze: Du Droit des magistrats (editor), 1971; Transition and Revolution: Problems and Issues of European Renaissance and Reformation History (editor), 1974; The Political Thought of Peter Martyr Vermigli, 1980; Church and Society in Reformation Europe, 1985; Myths About the St Bartholomew's Day Massacres 1572-1576, 1988; A Bibliography of the Works of Peter Martyr Vermigli (editor with J P Donnelly), 1990; Adultery and Divorce in Calvin's Geneva, 1995; Registres du Consistoire de Genève au temps de Calvin, co-editor with T-A Lambert, J-R Watt, Vol I, 1996.Contributions to: Scholarly journals. Memberships: American Society of Reformation Research, president, 1971; International Federation of Societies and Institutions for the Study of the Renaissance; Renaissance Society of America, executive board, 1972-92; American Society of Church History, president, 1980. Address: 4 Rosewood Circle, Madison, WI 53711, USA.

KINGMAN Lee, b. 1919, Reading, Massachusetts, USA. Freelance Writer and Editor. Education: AA, Colby Junior College, 1938; BA, Smith College, 1940. Publications: Pierre Pidgeon, 1943; Ilenka, 1945; The Rocky Summer, 1948; The Best Christmas, 1949; Philippe's Hill, 1950; The Quarry Adventure, 1951, UK edition as Lauri's Surprising Summer; Kathy and the Mysterious Statue, 1953; Peter's Long Walk, 1953; Mikko's Fortune, 1955; The Magic Christmas Tree, 1956;

The Village Band Mystery, 1956; Flivver, the Heroic Horse, 1958; The House of the Blue Horse, 1960; The Saturday Gang, 1961; Peter's Pony, 1963; Sheep Ahoy, 1963; Private Eyes, 1964; Newbery and Caldecott Medal Books: 1956-1965 (editor), 1965; The Year of the Raccoon, 1966; The Secret of the Silver Reindeer, 1968; Illustrators of Children's Books: 1957-1966 (editor with J Foster and R G Lontoft), 1968; The Peter Pan Bag, 1970; Georgina and the Dragon, 1971; The Meeting Post: A Story of Lapland, 1972; Escape from the Evil Prophecy, 1973; Newbery and Caldecott Medal Books: 1966-1975 (editor), 1975; Break a Leg, Betsy Maybe, 1976; The Illustrator's Notebook, 1978; Head over Wheels, 1978; Illustrators of Children's Books: 1967-1976 (editor with G Hogarth and H Quimby), 1978; The Refiner's Fire, 1981; The Luck of the Miss L, 1986; Newbery and Caldecott Medal Books: 1976-1985 (editor), 1986; Catch the Baby!, 1990. Address: 105 High Street, Gloucester, MA 01930, USA.

KINGSOLVER Barbara, b. 8 Apr 1955, Annapolis, Maryland, USA. Author; Poet. m. (1) Joseph Hoffmann, 1985, div 1993, 1 daughter, (2) Steven Hopp, 1995, 1 daughter. Education: BA, DePauw University, 1977; MS, University of Arizona, 1981. Appointments: Research Assistant, Department of Physiology, 1977-79, Technical Writer, Office of Arid Land Studies, 1981-85, University of Arizona, Tucson; Journalist, 1985-87; Author, 1987-; Founder, Bellwether Prize to recognize a first novel of social significance, 1997. Publications: The Bean Trees (novel), 1988; Homeland and Other Stories, 1989; Holding the Line: Women in the Great Arizona Mine Strike of 1983 (non-fiction), 1989; Animal Dreams (novel), 1990; Pigs in Heaven (novel), 1993; Another America (poems), 1994, new edition, 1998; High Tide in Tucson: Essays from Now or Never, 1995; The Poisonwood Bible (novel), 1998. Contributions to: Many anthologies and periodicals. Honours: Feature-Writing Award, Arizona Press Club, 1986; American Library Association Awards, 1988, 1990; United Nations National Council of women Citation of Accomplishment, 1989; PEN Fiction Prize, 1991; Edward Abbey Ecofiction Award, 1991; Los Angeles Times Book Award for Fiction, 1993. Memberships: Amnesty International; Committee for Human Rights in Latin America; International Women's Writing Guild; PEN West. Address: c/o Frances Goldin, 305 East 11th Street, New York, NY 10003, USA.

KINGSTON Maxine Hong, b. 27 Oct 1940, Stockton, California, USA. Writer; Teacher. m. 23 Nov 1962, 1 son. Education: AB, 1962, Secondary Teaching Credential, 1965, University of California, Berkeley. Appointment: Teacher, University of California, Berkeley, 1990-. Publications: The Woman Warrior, 1976; China Men, 1980; Hawaii One Summer, 1987; Tripmaster Monkey: His Fake Book, 1989. Contributions to: Many publications. Honours: National Book Critics Circle Award, 1977; Anisfield-Wolf Race Relations Book Award, 1978; National Endowment for the Arts Fellowship, 1980; National Book Award, 1981; Guggenheim Fellowship, 1981; Hawaii Award for Literature, 1982; California Council for the Humanities Award, 1985; Governor's Award for the Arts, California, 1989; PEN West Award in Fiction, 1990; American Academy and Institute of Arts and Letters Award, 1990; Brandeis University National Women's Committee Major Book Collection Award, 1992; National Humanities Medal, 1997; Fred Cody Lifetime Achievement Award, 1998; John Dos Passos Award, 1998; Honorary doctorates. Memberships: American Academy of Arts and Sciences; Authors Guild; PEN American Centre; PEN West. Literary Agent: Sandra Dijkstra. Address: c/o Department of English, University of California at Berkeley, CA 94720, USA.

KINGTON Miles (Beresford), b. 13 May 1941, Downpatrick, Northern Ireland. Writer. m. (1) Sarah Paine, 1964, div 1987, 1 son, 1 daughter, (2) Caroline Maynard, 1987, 1 son. Education: BA, Modern Languages, Trinity College, Oxford, 1963. Appointments: Jazz Reviewer, 1965, Columnist, 1980-87, The Times; Staff, 1967-73, Literary Editor, 1973-80, Columnist, 1980-87, Punch; Columnist, The Independent, 1987-. Publications: The World of Alphonse Allais, 1977,

reprinted as A Wolf in Frog's Clothing, 1983; 4 Franglais books, 1979-82; Moreover, Too..., 1985; Welcome to Kington, 1985; The Franglais Lieutenant's Woman, 1986; Steaming Through Britain, 1990; Anthology of Jazz (editor), 1992. Address: Lower Hayze, Limpley Stoke, Bath BA3 6HR, England.

KINKAID Matt. See: ADAMS Clifton.

KINLOCH David, b. 21 Nov 1959, Glasgow, Scotland. University Senior Lecturer; Poet; Editor. Education: MA, University of Glasgow, 1982; DPhil, Balliol College, Oxford, 1986. Appointments: Junior Research Fellow, St Anne's College, Oxford, 1985-87; Research Fellow, University of Wales, 1987-89; Lecturer, University of Salford, 1989-90; Lecturer, 1990-94, Senior Lecturer, 1994-, University of Strathclyde; Editor, Southfields Magazine; Founder/Co-Editor, Verse Poetry Magazine. Publications: Other Tongues (co-author), 1990; Dustie-Fute, 1992; Paris-Forfar, 1994. Contributions to: Reviews, journals and magazines. Address: c/o Department of Modern Languages, University· of Strathclyde, Glasgow, Scotland.

KINNELL Galway, b. 1 Feb 1927, Providence, Rhode Island, USA. Poet; Writer. 1 son, 1 daughter. Education: Princeton University. Publications: Poetry: What a Kingdom It Was, 1960; Flower Herding on Mount Monadnock, 1963; Body Rags, 1966; The Book of Nightmares, 1971; The Avenue Bearing the Initial of Christ into the New World, 1974; Mortal Acts, Mortal Words, 1980; Selected Poems, 1982; The Past, 1985; When One Has Lived a Long Time Alone, 1990; Imperfect Thirst, 1994. Other: The Poems of François Villon (translator), 1965; Black Light (novel), 1966; On the Motion and Immobility of Douve, 1968; The Lackawanna Elegy, 1970; Interviews: Walking Down the Stairs, 1977; How the Alligator Missed His Breakfast (children's story), 1982; The Essential Whitman (editor), 1987. Honours: National Institute of Arts and Letters Award, 1962; Cecil Hemley Poetry Prize, 1969; Medal of Merit, 1975; Pulitzer Prize in Poetry, 1983; National Book Award, 1983; John D and Catharine T MacArthur Foundation Fellowship, 1984. Memberships: PEN; Poetry Society of America; Modern Language Association. Address: RR 2 Box 138, Sheffield, VT 05866, USA.

KINNEY Arthur F(rederick), b. 6 Sept 1933, Cortland, New York, USA. Professor of Literary History; Editor. Education: AB, magna cum laude, Syracuse University, 1955; MA, Columbia University, 1956; PhD, University of Michigan, 1963. Appointments: Thomas W Copeland Professor of Literary History, University of Massachusetts, Amherst; Founder-Editor, English Literary Renaissance journal, 1971-; Editor, Massachusetts Studies in Early Modern Culture series, Twayne English Authors in the Renaissance series; Director, Massachusetts Center for Renaissance Studies, 1996-. Publications: Humanist Poetics, 1986; John Skelton: Priest as Poet, 1987; Continental Humanist Poetics, 1989; Renaissance Historicism, 1989; Elizabethan Backgrounds, 1990; Rogues, Vagabonds, and Sturdy Beggars, 1990; Classical, Renaissance, and Postmodern Acts of the Imagination: Essays in Honor of O B Hardison Jr (editor), 1994; Poetics and Praxis, Understanding and Imagination: The Collected Essays of O B Hardison Jr (editor), 1995; Go Down, Moses: The Miscegenation of Time, 1997; Dorothy Parker Revisited, 1998; The Witch of Edmonton by Thomas Dekker, John Ford, and William Rowley (editor), 1998; The Cambridge Companion to English Literature 1500-1600, forthcoming; Shakespeare, Text and Theatre, forthcoming; Renaissance Drama: An Anthology of Plays and Performances edited from manuscript and early quartos, forthcoming. Contributions to: Scholarly books and journals. Honours: Various fellowships, scholarships, and awards. Memberships: Conference of Editors of Learned Journals, president, 1971-73, 1980-82; Renaissance English Text Society, president, 1985-; Renaissance Society of America, executive council; Shakespeare Association of America, trustee. Address: Massachusetts Center for Renaissance Studies, PO Box 2300, Amherst, MA 01004, USA.

KINNEY Harrison Burton, b. 16 Aug 1921, Mars Hill, Maine, USA. Writer. m. Doris Getsinger, Feb 1952, 1 son, 3 daughters. Education: Bachelor Degree, Washington Anlee University; Master Degree, Columbia University. Publications: The Lonesome Bear (juvenile), 1949; The Supper of Leonardo Da Vinci (non-fiction), 1953; Has Anybody Seen My Father? (novel), 1960; The Kangaroo In the Attic (juvenile), 1960; James Thurber: His Life and Times (biography), 1993. Contributions to: Colliers; Saturday Evening Post; American Heritage; Readers Digest. Membership: Authors Guild. Literary Agent: Peter Lampack. Address: 551 Fifth Avenue, New York, NY 10176-0187, USA.

KINSELLA Thomas, b. 4 May 1928, Dublin, Ireland. Poet; Translator; Editor; Retired Professor of English. m. Eleanor Walsh, 27 Dec 1955, 1 son, 2 daughters. Appointments: Irish Civil Service, 1946-65; Artist-in-Residence, 1965-67, Professor of English, 1967-70, Southern Illinois University; Professor of English, Temple University, Philadelphia, 1970-90. Publications: Poetry: Poems, 1956; Another September, 1958; Downstream, 1962; Nightwalker and Other Poems, 1968; Notes From the Land of the Dead, 1972; Butcher's Dozen, 1972, 2nd edition, 1992; A Selected Life, 1972; Finistere, 1972; New Poems, 1973; Selected Poems, 1956-68, 1973; Song of the Night and Other Poems, 1978; The Messenger, 1978; Fifteen Dead, 1979; One and Other Poems, 1979; Poems, 1956-73, 1980; Peppercanister Poems, 1972-78, 1980; One Fond Embrace, 1981, new edition, 1988; Songs of the Psyche, 1985; Her Vertical Smile, 1985; St Catherine's Clock, 1987; Out of Ireland, 1987; Blood and Family, 1988; Personal Places, 1990; Poems From Centre City, 1990; Madonna, 1991; Open Court, 1991; From Centre City, 1994; Collected Poems, 1956-94, 1996; The Pen Shop, 1997. Other: The Tain, translated from Old Irish, 1970; Selected Poems of Austin Clarke (editor), 1976; An Duanaire: Poems of the Dispossessed (translator), 1981; The New Oxford Book of Irish Verse (editor and translator), 1986; The Dual Tradition: An Essay on Poetry and Politics in Ireland, 1995. Honours: Guiness Poetry Award, 1958; Denis Devlin Memorial Awards, 1966, 1969; Guggenheim Fellowships, 1968-69, 1971-72; Honorary PhD, National University of Ireland, 1984. Membership: Irish Academy of Letters. Address: Killalane, Laragh, County Wicklow, Ireland.

KINZIE Mary, b. 30 Sept 1944, Montgomery, Alabama, USA. Professor of English; Poet; Critic; Editor. Education: BA, Northwestern University, 1967; Graduate Studies, Free University of Berlin, 1967-68; MA, 1970, MA, 1972, PhD, 1980, Johns Hopkins University. Appointments: Executive Editor, TriQuarterly magazine, 1975-78; Instructor, 1975-78, Lecturer, 1978-85, Associate Professor, 1985-90, Martin J and Patricia Koldyke Outstanding Teaching Professor, 1990-92, Professor of English, 1990-, Northwestern University. Publications: Poetry: The Threshold of the Year, 1982; Summers of Vietnam, 1990; Masked Women, 1990; Autumn Eros and Other Poems, 1991; Ghost Ship, 1996. Non-Fiction: The Cure of Poetry in Age of Prose: Moral Essays on the Poet's Calling, 1993; The Judge is Fury: Dislocation and Form in Poetry, 1994; A Poet's Guide to Poetry, 1999. Contributions to: Various books, anthologies, reviews, quarterlies, journals, and magazines. Honours: Illinois Arts Council Awards, 1977, 1978, 1980, 1982, 1984, 1988, 1990, 1993, and Artist Grant, 1983; DeWitt Wallace Fellow, MacDowell Colony, 1979; Devins Award for a First Volume of Verse, 1982; Guggenheim Fellowship, 1986; Elizabeth Matchett Stover Memorial Award in Poetry, Southwest Review, 1987; Celia B Wagner Award, Poetry Society of America, 1988; President's Fund for the Humanities Research Grant, 1990-91. Memberships: PEN; Poetry Society of America; Society of Midland Authors. Address: c/o College of Arts and Sciences, Department of English, Northwestern University, University Hall 215, Evanston, IL 60208, USA.

KIRBY Marilyn. See: SISSON Marilyn.

KIRK Geoffrey Stephen, b. 3 Dec 1921, Nottingham, England. Regius Professor of Greek Emeritus; Writer.

Education: BA, 1946, MA, 1948, DLitt, 1965, Clare College, Cambridge. Appointments: Fellow, Trinity Hall, 1947-73, Trinity College, 1973-82; Lecturer, 1950-61, Reader, 1961-65, Regius Professor of Greek, 1973-82, Cambridge University; Professor of Classics, Yale University, 1965-71, Bristol University, 1971-73. Publications: Heraclitus: The Cosmic Fragments (editor), 1952; The Presocratic Philosophers (with J E Raven), 1956; The Songs of Homer, 1962; The Language and Background of Homer (editor), 1964; Euripides: Bacchae (editor and translator), 1970; Myth, 1970; The Nature of Greek Myths, 1974; Homer and the Oral Tradition, 1977; The Iliad: A Commentary, 2 volumes, 1985, 1990; Towards the Aegean Sea, 1997. Contributions to: Professional journals. Honour: British Academy, fellow, 1959; Academy of Athens, corresponding fellow, 1993-. Address: 12 Sion Hill, Bath, Somerset BA1 2UH, England.

KIRK Michael. See: **KNOX William.**

KIRK Pauline Marguerite, b. 14 Apr 1942, Birmingham, England. Writer; Poet. m. Peter Kirk, 4 Apr 1964, 1 son, 1 daughter. Education: Nottingham University, 1960-63; Sheffield University, 1963-64; Monash University, 1966-70. Appointments: Teacher, Methodist Ladies College, 1965-66; Teaching Fellow, Monash University, 1965-69. Publications: Fiction: Waters of Time, 1988; The Keepers, 1996. Poetry: Scorpion Days, 1982; Red Marl and Brick, 1985; Rights of Way, 1990; Travelling Solo, 1995; Return to Dreamtime, 1996. Contributions to: Anthologies and other publications. Honour: Yorkshire and Humberside Arts New Beginnings Award, 1994. Memberships: Aireings, editorial board; Fighting Cock Press; Pennine Poets; Society of Authors. Address: 20 Lee Lane East, Horsforth, Leeds LS18 5RE, England.

KIRK Philip. See: **LEVINSON Leonard.**

KIRK-GREENE Anthony (Hamilton Millard), b. 16 May 1925, Tunbridge Wells, England. University Lecturer; Fellow; Writer; Editor. Education: BA, 1949, MA, 1954, Clare College, Cambridge; MA, Oxford University, 1964. Appointments: Senior Lecturer in Government, Institute of Administration, Zaria, Nigeria, 1957-62; Professor of Government, Ahmadu Bello University, Nigeria, 1962-65; University Lecturer and Fellow, St Antony's College, 1967-; Director, Foreign Service Programme, 1986-90, Oxford University; Assistant Editor, New Dictionary of National Biography, 1996-. Publications: Adamawa Past and Present, 1958; The Cattle People of Nigeria (with Caroline Sassoon), 1959; The River Niger (with Caroline Sassoon), 1961; Barth's Travels in Nigeria, 1962; Principles of Native Administration in Nigeria, 1965; The Making of Northern Nigeria (editor), 1965; The Emirates of Northern Nigeria (with S J Hogben), 1966; Hausa Proverbs, 1966; A Modern Hausa Reader (with Y Aliyu), 1967; Lugard and the Amalgamation of Nigeria, 1968; Language and People of Bornu (editor), 1968; Crisis and Conflict in Nigeria, 1971; West African Narratives (with P Newman), 1972; Gazetteers of Northern Nigeria (editor), 1972; Teach Yourself Hausa (with C H Kraft), 1973; The Concept of the Good Man in Hausa, 1974; Nigeria: Faces North (with Pauline Ryan), 1975; The Transfer of Power in Africa (editor), 1978; Stand by Your Radios: The Military in Tropical Africa, 1980; Biographical Dictionary of the British Colonial Governor, 1981; Nigeria since 1970 (with D Rimmer), 1981; The Sudan Political Service: A Profile, 1982; Margery Perham: West African Passage (editor), 1983; Pastoralists of the Western Savanna (with Mahdi Adamu), 1986; Margery Perham: Pacific Prelude (editor), 1988; The Sudan Political Service: A Preliminary Register of Second Careers (with Sir Gawain Bell), 1989; A Biographical Dictionary of the British Colonial Service, 1939-66, 1991; Diplomatic Initiative: A History of the Foreign Service Programme, 1994. Contributions to: Various reference books and scholarly journals. Honours: Member of the Order of the British Empire, 1963; Hans Wolff Memorial Lecturer, 1973; Fellow, Royal Historical Society, 1985, Festschrift, 1993. Memberships: Royal African Society; International African Institute; African

Studies Association of UK, president, 1989-91. Address: c/o St Antony's College, Oxford OX2 6JF, England.

KIRKPATRICK Sidney Dale, b. 4 Oct 1955, New York, New York, USA. Writer; Filmmaker. m. 26 Nov 1983, 2 sons. Education: BA, Hampshire College, Amherst, 1978; MFA, New York University, 1982. Appointment: Reader, Huntington Library, 1992. Publications: A Cast of Killers, 1986; Turning the Tide, 1991; Lords of Sipan, 1992. Contributions to: Los Angeles Times; American Film. Honour: Winner, American Film Festival, 1982. Membership: PEN Center West, board of directors, 1991-92. Address: c/o Tim Seldes, Russell and Volkening, 50 West 29th Street, New York, NY 10001, USA.

KIRKUP James (Falconer), b. 23 Apr 1918, South Shields, Tyne and Wear, England. Poet; Author; Dramatist; Translator. Education: BA, Durham University. Appointments: Gregory Fellow in Poetry, University of Leeds, 1950-52; Visiting Poet and Head of the Department of English, Bath Academy of Art, Corsham, 1953-56; Professor of English, University of Salamanca, 1957-58; Tohoku University of Malaya, Kuala Lumpur, 1961-62, Japan Women's University, Tokyo, 1963-70; Literary Editor, Orient/West Magazine, Tokyo, 1963-64; Professor of English Literature, Nagoya University, 1969-72; Professor of Comparative Literature, Kyoto University of Foreign Studies, 1976-88. Publications: Poetry: The Drowned Sailor and Other Poems, 1947; The Submerged Village and Other Poems, 1951; A Correct Compassion and Other Poems, 1952; The Spring Journey and Other Poems of 1952-53, 1954; the Descent Into the Cave and Other Poems, 1957; The Prodigal Son: Poems 1956-59, 1959; Refusal to Conform: Last and First Poems, 1963; Paper Windows: Poems from Japan, 1968; White Shadows, Black Shadows: Poems of Peace and War, 1970; A Bewick Bestiary, 1971; The Body Servant: Poems of Exile, 1971; Cold Mountain Poems, 1979; To the Ancestral North: Poems for an Autobiography, 1983; The Sense of the Visit: New Poems, 1984; Fellow Feelings, 1986; Throwback: Poems Towards the Autobiography, 1992; Shooting Stars, 1992; Strange Attractors, 1995; Counting to 9,999, 1995; Noems, Koans and a Navel Display, 1995; Collected Longer Poems, 2 volumes, 1995, 1997; Selected Shorter Poems, 1995; Broad Daylight, 1996; Figures in a Setting, 1997; The Patient Obituarist, 1997; One-Man Band: Poems Without Words, 1998. Novels: The Love of Others, 1962; Insect Summer, 1971; Gaijin on the Ginza, 1991; Queens Have Died Young and Fair, 1993. Non-Fiction: The Only Child: An Autobiography of Infancy, 1957; Sorrows, Passions, and Alarms: An Autobiography of Childhood, 1959; I, Of All People: An Autobiography of Youth, 1988; Object Lessons, 1990; A Poet Could Not But Be Gay: Some Legends of My Lost Youth, 1991; Me All Over: Memoirs of a Misfit, 1993; Child of the Tyne, 1997. Other: Travel books, essays, plays and translations. Contributions to: Various publications. Honours: Many awards and prizes. Memberships: Royal Society of Literature, fellow; British Haiku Society. Address: c/o British Monomarks, Box 2780, London WC1N 3XX, England.

KIRSCH Sarah, b. 16 Apr 1935, Limlingerode, Germany. Author; Poet. m. Rainer Kirsch, 1958, div 1968, 1 son. Education: Diploma, University of Halle, 1959; Johannes R Becher Institute, Leipzig, 1963-65. Publications: Landaufenthalt, 1967; Die Vögel signen im Regen am Schönsten, 1968; Zaubersprüche, 1973; Es war der merkwürdigste Sommer, 1974; Musik auf dem Wasser, 1977; Rückenwind, 1977; Drachensteigen, 1979; Sieben Häute: Ausgewählte Gedichte 1962-79, 1979; La Pagerie, 1980; Erdreich, 1982; Katzenleben, 1984; Hundert Gedichte, 1985; Landwege: Eine Auswahl 1980-85, 1985; Irrstern, 1986; Allerlei-Rauh, 1988; Schneewärme, 1989; Die Flut, 1990; Spreu, 1991; Schwingrasen, 1991; Sic! natur!, 1992; Erlkönigs Tochter, 1992; Das simple Leben, 1994; Winternachtigall, 1995; Ich Crusoe, 1995; Nachtsonnen, 1995; Bodenlos, 1996. Honours: Petrarca Prize, 1976; Austrian State Prize for Literature, 1981; Austrian Critics Prize, 1981; Gandersheim Literary Prize, 1983; Hölderlin Prize, Bad

Homburg, 1984; Art Prize, Schleswig-Holstein, 1987; Author-in-Residence, City of Mainz, 1988; Heinrich-Heine-Gesellschaft Award, Düsseldorf, 1992; Peter Huchel Prize, 1993; Konrad Adenauer Foundation Literature Prize, 1993; Büchner Prize, 1996. Address: Eiderdeich 22, D-25794 Tielenhemme. Germany.

KISS Iren, b. 25 Sept 1947, Budapest, Hungary. Writer; Poet; Dramatist; University Professor. m. Laszlo Tabori, 10 June 1988. Education: PhD, History of Literature, University of Budapest, 1992. Publications: Szelcsend (poems), 1977; Allokep (novel), 1978; Arkadiat Tatarozxzak (poems), 1979; Maganrecept (cycle), 1982; Kemopera (plays), 1988. Contributions to: Various publications. Honours: Yeats Club Award, 1987; Gold Medal, Brianza World Competition of Poetry, Italy, 1988. Memberships: Association of Hungarian Writers; Hungarian PEN. Address: Somloi ut 60/B, Budapest 1118, Hungary.

KISSANE Sharon Florence, b. 2 July 1940, Chicago, Illinois, USA. Writer; Educator. m. James Q Kissane, dec, 2 July 1966, 2 daughters. Education: BA, English and Speech, DePaul University, 1962; MA, Communications, Northwestern University, Evanston, Illinois, 1963; PhD, English Education, Loyola University's School of Education, Chicago, 1970. Appointments: Technical Writer, Editor, Commerce Clearing House, Chicago, 1962-63; Night Editor, Daily Herald newspapers, Des Plaines and Park Ridge Editions, 1964-66; Columnist, Daily Herald, Barrington and Palatine Editions, 1982-; Business and Financial Correspondent, Chicago Tribune, 1983-85; Fiction Instructor, Harper College, Palatine, Illinois, 1985-88. Publications: Career Success for People with Physical Disabilities, 1966; Polish Biographical Dictionary (co-author), 1993; What is Child Abuse?, 1994; Gang Awareness, 1995; Autobiography of Paul "Mousie" Garner: A Broadway Stooge, 1998. Contributions to: Journals and magazines. Memberships: Founding Member, Barrington Area Arts Council; Founder, Creative Writing Sub-Group. Address: 15 Turning Shores, South Barrington, IL 60010, USA.

KISSINGER Henry (Alfred), b. 27 May 1923, Furth, Germany (US citizen, 1943). Company Executive; Author. m. (1) Ann Fleischer, 6 Feb 1949, div 1964, 1 son, 1 daughter, (2) Nancy Maginnes, 30 Mar 1974. Education: AB, 1950, MA, 1952, PhD, 1954, Harvard University. Appointments: Executive Director, Harvard International Seminar, 1951-69; Faculty, Center for International Affairs, 1954-69, Associate Professor, 1959-62, Professor of Government, 1962-69, Harvard University; Assistant to the President of the US for National Security Affairs, 1969-75; US Secretary of State, 1973-77; Founder-Chairman, Kissinger Associates Inc, New York City; Consultant, Advisor, and Member of various boards and commissions. Publications: Nuclear Weapons and Foreign Policy, 1957; A World Restored: Castlereagh, Metternich and the Restoration of Peace 1812-1822, 1957; The Necessity for Choice: Prospects of American Foreign Policy, 1961; The Troubled Partnership: A Reappraisal of the Atlantic Alliance, 1965; Problems of National Strategy: A Book of Readings (editor), 1965; American Foreign Policy: Three Essays, 1969; White House Years, 1979; For the Record: Selected Statements 1977-1980, 1981; Years of Upheaval, 1982; Observations: Selected Speeches and Essays 1982-1984, 1985; Diplomacy, 1994. Contributions to: Professional journals. Honours: Woodrow Wilson Prize, 1958; Guggenheim Fellowship, 1965-66; Nobel Prize for Peace, 1973; Distinguished Public Service Award, American Institute of Public Service, 1973; Presidential Medal of Freedom, 1977; Medal of Liberty, 1986. Memberships: American Academy of Arts and Sciences; American Political Science Association; Council on Foreign Relations; Phi Beta Kappa. Address: c/o International Creative Management, 40 West 57th Street, New York, NY 10019, USA.

KITCHEN (Her)Bert (Thomas), b. 24 Apr 1940, Liverpool, England. Artist; Illustrator; Author. m. Muriel Chown, 2 Apr 1960, 2 daughters. Education: London Central School of Arts and Crafts, 1958-61. Publications:

Mythical Creatures; Tenrecs Twigs; Somewhere Today; Animal Alphabet; Animal Numbers; Gorilla/Chinchilla; Pig in a Barrow; And So They Build, 1993; When Hunger Calls, 1994. Membership: Society of Authors. Address: 5-8 Lower John Street, Golden Square, London W1R 4HA, England.

KITCHEN Martin, b. 21 Dec 1936, Nottingham, England. Professor of History; Writer. Education: Magdalen College, Oxford; BA, 1963, PhD, 1966, University of London. Appointment: Professor of History, Simon Fraser University, Burnaby, British Columbia. Appointment: Faculty, 1966-76, Professor of History, 1976-, Simon Fraser University, Burnaby, British Columbia. Publications: The German Officer Corps 1890-1914, 1968; A Military History of Germany, 1975; The Silent Dictatorship: The Politics of the German High Command Under Hindenburg and Ludendorff, 1976; Fascism, 1976; The Political Economy of Germany 1815-1914, 1978; The Coming of Austrian Fascism, 1980; Germany in the Age of Total War, 1981; British Policy Towards the Soviet Union During the Second World War, 1986; Europe Between the Wars, 1988; The Origins of the Cold War in Comparative Perspective: American, British and Canadian Relations with the Soviet Union, 1941-48, 1988; Nazi Germany at War, 1994; The British Empire and Commonwealth: A Short History, 1996; The Cambridge Illustrated History of Germany, 1996. Contributions to: Professional journals. Honour: Moncado Prize, American Military Academy, 1978. Memberships: Royal Historical Society, fellow; Royal Society of Canada, fellow. Address: c/o Department of History, Simon Fraser University, Burnaby, British Columbia V5A 1S6, Canada.

KITT Tamara. See: **DE REGNIERS Beatrice Schenk.**

KITTREDGE William Alfred, (Owen Rountree), b. 14 Aug 1932, Portland, Oregon, USA. Professor; Writer. 1 son, 1 daughter. Education: BS, Agriculture, Oregon State University, 1954; MFA, University of Iowa, 1969. Appointment: Professor Emeritus of English, University of Montana. Publications: We Are Not In This Together, 1982; Owning It All, 1984; Hole in the Sky, 1992; Who Owns the West?, 1996; Portable Western Reader (editor), 1998. Contributions to: Time; Newsweek; New York Times; Wall Street Journal; Esquire; Outside; Paris Review. Literary Agent: Amanda Urban, ICM, 40 West 57th Stree, New York, USA. Address: 143 South 5th East, Missoula, MT 59801, USA.

KITZINGER Sheila, b. Taunton, Somerset, England. Writer; Lecturer; Birth Activist. m. Uwe Kitzinger, 5 daughters. Education: MLitt, Oxford. Publications include: Some Mothers' Experience of Induced Labour, 1978; Good Birth Guide, 1979; Women as Mothers, 1980; Birth at Home, 1980; Birth Over Thirty, 1982; Women's Experience of Sex, 1983; Being Born, 1986; A Celebration of Birth, 1986; Pregnancy and Childbirth, 1986, new edition, 1998; Some Women's Experience of Epidurals, 1987; Giving Birth: How it Really Feels, 1987; The Crying Baby, 1989; Homebirth and Other Alternatives to Hospital, 1991; Ourselves as Mothers, 1992; The Year After Childbirth, 1994; Birth Over Thirty-Five, 1994; Talking with Children About Things That Matter, 1995; Becoming a Grandmother, 1997; Breastfeeding Your Baby, 2nd edition, 1998; Breastfeeding Your Baby, 2nd edition, 1998; The Midwife Challenge, 3rd edition, 1999; Things That Matter, 2nd edition, 1999; The Midwife Challenge, 3rd edition, 1999. Honours: MBE; Honorary Professor, Thames Valley University. Literary Agent: Mary Clemmey. Address: 6 Dunollie Road, London NW5 2XP, England.

KIZER Carolyn Ashley, b. 10 Dec 1925, Spokane, Washington, USA. Poet; Professor. Education: BA, Sarah Lawrence College, 1945; Postgraduate studies, Columbia University, 1946-47; Studied poetry with Theodore Roethke, University of Washington, 1953-54. Appointments: Founder-Editor, Poetry North West, 1959-65; Specialist in Literature, US Department of State, Pakistan, 1964-65; 1st Director, Literature Programs, National Endowment for the Arts, 1966-70; Poet-in-Residence, University of North Carolina at Chapel Hill, 1970-74; Hurst Professor of Literature, Washington University, St Louis, 1971; Lecturer, Barnard College, 1972; Acting Director, Graduate Writing Program, 1972, Professor, School of Arts, 1982, Columbia University; Poet-in-Residence, Ohio University, 1974; Visiting Poet, Iowa Writer's Workshop, 1975; Professor, University of Maryland, 1976-77; Poet-in-Residence, Distingusihed Visiting Lecturer, Centre College, Kentucky, 1979; Distinguished Visiting Poet, East Washington University, 1980; Elliston Professor of Poetry, University of Cincinnati, 1981; Bingham Distinguished Professor, University of Louisville, 1982; Distinguished Visiting Poet, Bucknell University, 1982; Visiting Poet, State University of New York at Albany, 1982; Professor, School of Arts, Columbia University, 1982; Professor of Poetry, Stanford University, 1986; Senior Fellow, Humanities Council, Princeton University, 1986. Publications; The Ungrateful Garden, 1961; Knock Upon Silence, 1965; Midnight Was My Cry, 1971; Mermaids in the Basement: Poems for Women, 1984; Yin: New Poems, 1984; Carrying Over, 1988. Proses: On Poems and Poets, 1993; The Essential John Clare (editor), 1993; 100 Great Poems by Women (editor), 1995; Picking and Choosing: Prose on Prose, 1996; Harping On: Poems, 1985-1995, 1996. Contributions to: Poems and articles in various journals including The Paris Review; Antaeus; Michigan Quarterly. Honours: Governor's Awards, State of Washington, 1965, 1985, 1995, 1998; Pulitzer Prize in Poetry, 1985; American Academy and Institute of Arts and Letters Award, 1985; San Francisco Arts Commission Award in Literature, 1986; Silver Medal Commonwealth Club, 1998. Memberships; American Civil Liberties Union; American Poets; Amnesty International; PEN; Academy of American Poets, chancellor; Poetry Society of America; Associate Writing Programs, director. Address: 19772 8th Street East, Sonoma, CA 95476, USA.

KJELDBOERG Hans Meschede, b. 9 Jan 1954, Aalborg, Denmark. Writer. Education: Archaeology, Arhus University, 1974-75, Spanish, 1978-79. Publications: Summertime Blues, 1987; Refuge, 1987; Pilgrim on the Bridge of the World, 1991. Contributions to: Amber; A Nature Diary; Fever. Membership: Danish Writers Union. Address: Sandkasvej 36, 8210 Arhus v, Denmark.

KLAPPERT Peter, b. 14 Nov 1942, Rockville Center, New York, USA. Professor; Poet; Writer. Education: BA, Cornell University, 1964; MA, Honours, Renaissance English Literature, 1967, MFA, Poetry, 1968, University of Iowa. Appointments: Instructor, Rollins College, 1968-71; Briggs-Copeland Lecturer, Harvard University, 1971-74; Visiting Lecturer, New College, 1972; Writer-in-Residence, 1976-77, Assistant Professor, 1977-78, College of William and Mary; Assistant Professor, 1978-81, Associate Professor, 1981-91, Professor, 1991-, Director, MFA Degree Program in Poetry, 1995-98, George Mason University. Publications: On a Beach in Southern Connecticut, 1966; Lugging Vegetables to Nantucket, 1971, reprint, 1998; Circular Stairs, Distress in the Mirrors, 1975, reprint, 1998; Non Sequitur O'Connor, 1977; The Idiot Princess of the Last Dynasty, 1984, reprint, 1998; '52 Pick-Up: Scenes From the Conspiracy, A Documentary, 1984. Contributions to: Many anthologies, books, journals, and magazines. Honours: Yale Series of Younger Poets Prize, 1970; Yaddo Resident Fellowships, 1972, 1973, 1975, 1981; MacDowell Colony Resident Fellowships, 1973, 1975; National Endowment for the Arts Fellowships, 1973, 1979; Lucille Medwick Award, Poetry Society of America, 1977; Virginia Center for the Creative Arts Resident Fellowships, 1978, 1979, 1981, 1983, 1984, 1987, 1993, 1995; Millay Colony for the Arts Resident Fellowship, 1981; Ingram Merrill Foundation Grant, 1983; Klappert-Ai Poetry Award established in his honour by Gwendolyn Brooks, George Mason University, 1987; Poet-Scholar, American Library Association-National Endowment for the Humanities Voices and Visions Project, 1988. Memberships: Academy of American Poets; Associated Writing Programs; Association of Literary Scholars and Critics; PEN; Poetry Society of America; Writers' Center, Bethesda, Maryland. Address: 2003 Klingle Road North West, Washington, DC 20010, USA.

KLASS Perri Elizabeth, b. 29 Apr 1958, Trinidad. Pediatrician; Writer. 2 sons, 1 daughter. Education: AB, magna cum laude, Biology, Radcliffe College, Harvard University, 1979; MD, Harvard Medical School, 1986. Publications: Recombinations (novel), 1985; I Am Having An Adventure (short stories), 1986; A Not Entirely Benign Procedure (essays), 1987; Other Women's Children (novel), 1990; Baby Doctor (essays), 1992. Contributions to: New York Times Magazine; Massachusetts Medicine; Discover; Vogue; Glamour; Esquire; Boston Globe Magazine; Mademoiselle; TriQuarterly; North American Review. Honours: O Henry Awards, 1983, 1984, 1991, 1992, 1995; Honors Award, New England chapter, American Medical Writers Association, 1995. Memberships: PEN New England, executive board; American Academy of Pediatrics; American Medical Women's Association; Massachusetts Medical Society; Tilling Society. Address: c/o Maxine Groffskiy, 853 Broadway Suite, 708, New York, NY 10003, USA.

KLEIN Joseph (Joe Klein), b. 7 Sept 1946, New York, USA. Journalist; Writer. m. Janet Eklund, 8 Feb 1967, div 1975, 2 sons. Education: AB, University of Pennsylvania, 1968. Appointments: Reporter, Beverly/Peabody Times, Beverly, Massachusetts, 1969-72, WGBH-TV, Boston, 1972; News Editor, Real Paper, Boston, 1972-74; Associate Editor, 1974-78, Washington Bureau Chief, 1976, Rolling Stone Magazine; Senior Editor, 1992-96, Contributing Editor, 1996-, Newsweek Magazine; Columnist, New Yorker Magazine, 1996-. Publications: Woody Guthrie: A Life, 1980; Payback: Five Marines After Vietnam, 1984; Primary Colors: A Novel of Politics (published anonymously), 1996. Contributions to: Newspapers and magazines. Honours: Robert Kennedy Journalism Award, 1973; Washington Monthly Journalism Award, 1989; Honorary DLit, Franklin and Marshall College, Lancaster, Pennsylvania, 1990; National Headliner Award, 1994. Address: c/o Newsweek Magazine, 251 West 57th Street, New York, NY 10019, USA.

KLEIN Rudolf Ewald, b. 26 Aug 1930, Prague, Czech Republic. Academic. m. Josephine Parfitt, 24 May 1957, dec 1996, 1 daughter. Education: MA, Merton College, Oxford, England. Appointments: Leader Writer, London Evening Standard, 1952-62; Leader Writer, The Observer, 1962-72; Senior Fellow, Centre for Studies in Social Policy, 1973-77; Professor of Social Policy, University of Bath, 1978-98; Senior Associate, King's Fund, 1998-. Publications: Complaints Against Doctors, 1973; The Politics of Consumer Representation, with Janet Lewis, 1976; Accountabilites, with Patricia Day, 1987; The New Politics of the NHS, 1995; Managing Scarcity, with Patricia Day, Sharon Redmayne, 1996; Only Dissect: Rudolf Klein on Politics and Society and Patricia Day, 1996. Contributions to: Over 200 papers' articles reviews in general, political science and health policy journals. Honour: Honorary Doctor of Arts, Oxford Brooke's University. Address: 12A Laurier Road, London NW5 1SG, England.

KLEIN Theodore Eibon Donald, b. 15 July 1947, New York, New York, USA. Writer; Editor. Education: AB, Brown University, 1969; MFA, Columbia University, 1972. Appointments: Editor-in-Chief, Brown Daily Herald, 1968, Twilight Zone magazine, 1981-85, Crime Beat magazine, 1991-93. Publications: The Ceremonies (novel), 1984; Dark Gods (story collection), 1985. Contributions to: New York Times; New York Daily News; Washington Post Book World; Film column, Night Cry Magazine; Writer's Digest. Honours: Phi Beta Kappa, 1969; Award for Best Novel, British Fantasy Society, 1985; Award for Best Novella, World Fantasy, 1986. Membership: Arthur Machen Society. Address: 210 West 89th Street, New York, NY 10024, USA.

KLEIN Zachary, b. 6 July 1948, New Brunswick, New Jersey, USA. Writer. 2 sons. Education: Hillel Academy, Jewish Educational Centre, Mirrer Yeshia; University of Wisconsin. Publications: Still Among the Living, 1990; Two Way Toll, 1991; No Saving Grace, 1994. Honours: Notable Book of 1990, New York Times; Editor's Choice,

Drood Review. Address: 5 Oakview Terace, Boston, MA 02130, USA.

KLEMP Harold, b. USA. Ministry Writer; Lecturer. Education: Colleges in Milwaukee, Fort Wayne, Indiana. Appointments: US Air Force; Radio Intercept Operator, Goodfellow AFB, Texas. Publications: The Wind of Change; Soul Travelers of the Far Country; Child in the Wilderness; The Living Word, Books 1 and 2; The Book of ECK Parables, vols 1-4; The Spiritual Exercises of ECK; Ask the Master, Books 1 and 2; The Dream Master; We Come as Eagles; The Drumbeat of Time; The Slow Burning Love of God; The Secret Love; Our Spiritual Wake-Up Calls; A Modern Prophet Answers Your Questions About Life. Address: c/o Eckankar, PO Box 27300, Minneapolis, MN 55427, USA.

KLIKOVAC Igor, b. 16 May 1970, Bosnia. Poet. Education: General Literture and Librarianship, University of Sarajevo, 1989-92. Appointments: Editor, Literary Review, Sarajevo, 1991-92; Editor, Stone Soup Magazine, London, 1995-. Publications: Last Days of Peking (collection of poetry), 1996. Contributions to: Literary Review; Echo; Bridge; Transitions; Stone Soup; New Iowa Review. Address: 37 Chesterfield Road, London W4 3HQ, England.

KLIMA Ivan, b. 14 Sept 1931, Prague, Czechoslovakia. Dramatist; Writer. m. Helena Mala-Klimova, 24 Sept 1958, 1 son, 1 daughter. Education: MA, Charles University, Prague, 1956. Appointments: Editor, publishing, 1958-63, literary weeklies, 1963-69; Visiting Professor, University of Michigan, 1969-70; Visiting Professor, Berkeley, California, 1998. Publications: Plays: The Castle, 1964; The Jury, 1968 Bridegroom for Marcela, 1969; The President and the Angel, 1975; The Games, 1985; Kafka and Felice, 1986; Novels: A Ship Named Hope, 1969; A Summer Affair, 1972; The Judge on Trial, 1987; Love and Garbage, 1990; Waiting for the Dark, Waiting for the Light, 1996; The Ultimate Intimacy, 1997; Short Stories: My Merry Mornings, 1985; My First Loves, 1986; My Golden Trades, 1990; Waiting for the Dark, Waiting for the Light, 1995; The Ultimate Intimacy, 1998. Contributions to: Publications worldwide. Honour: Hostovsky Award, New York, 1985. Memberships: Czech PEN Centre; Czech Writers. Address: c/o Adam Bromberg Literary Agency, Stockholm, Sweden.

KLINE Suzy Weaver, b. 27 Aug 1943, Berkeley, California, USA. Teacher; Children's Author. m. Rufus Kline, 12 Oct 1968, 2 daughters. Education: BA, University of California, Berkeley; Standard Teachers Credential, California State University. Publications: Shhhh!, 1984; Don't Touch, 1985; Herbie Jones, 1985; What's the Matter with Herbie Jones?, 1986; Herbie Jones and the Monster Ball, 1988; Horrible Harry in Room 2B, 1988; Ooops, 1988; The Hole Book, 1989; Horrible Harry and the Green Slime, 1989; Horrible Harry and the Ant Invasion, 1989; Herbie Jones and the Hamburger Head, 1989; Orp, 1989; Orp and the Chop Suey Burgers, 1990; Horrible Harry's Secret, 1990; Horrible Harry's Christmas Surprise, 1991; Orp Goes to the Hoop, 1991; Herbie Jones and the Dark Attic, 1992; Herbie Jones Reader's Theater, 1992; Horrible Harry and the Kickball Wedding, 1992; Mary Marony and the Snake, 1992; Mary Marony Hides Out, 1993; Herbie Jones and the Birthday Showdown, 1993; Song Lee in Room 2B, 1993; Who's Orp's Girlfriend?, 1993; Mary Marony, Mummy Girl, 1994. Address: 124 Hoffman Street, Torrington, CT 06790, USA.

KLINKOWITZ Jerome, b. 24 Dec 1943, Milwaukee, Wisconsin, USA. Author; Professor of English. m. (1) Elaine Plaszynski, 29 Jan 1966, (2) Julie Huffman, 27 May 1978, 1 son, 1 daughter. Education: BA, 1966, MA, 1967, Marquette University; University Fellow, 1968-69, PhD, 1970, University of Wisconsin. Appointments: Assistant Professor, Northern Illinois University, 1969-70; Associate Professor, 1972-75, Professor of English, 1975-, University Distinguished Scholar, 1985-, University of Northern Iowa. Publications: Literary Disruptions, 1975; The Life of Fiction, 1977; The American 1960s, 1980; The Practice of Fiction in America, 1980; Kurt Vonnegut, 1982; Peter Handke and the Postmodern Transformation, 1983; The Self Apparent Word, 1984; Literary Subversions, 1985; The New American Novel of Manners, 1986; Rosenberg/Barthes/Hassan: The Postmodern Habit of Thought, 1988; Short Season and Other Stories, 1988; Their Finest Hours: Narratives of the RAF and Luftwaffe in World War II, 1989; Slaughterhouse-Five: Reinventing the Novel and the World, 1990; Listen: Gerry Mulligan/An Aural Narrative in Jazz, 1991; Donald Barthelme: An Exhibition, 1991; Writing Baseball, 1991; Structuring the Void, 1992; Basepaths, 1995; Yanks Over Europe, 1996; Here at Ogallala State U..,1997; Keeping Literary Company, 1997; Vonnegut in Fact, 1997; Owning a Piece of the Minors, forthcoming. Contributions to: Over 250 essays to Partisan Review, New Republic, Nation, American Literature; Short stories to North American Review, Chicago Tribune, San Francisco Chronicle. Honours: PEN Syndicated Fiction Prizes, 1984, 1985. Memberships: PEN American Center; Modern Language Association. Address: Department of English, University of Northern Iowa, Cedar Falls, IA 50614-0502.

KLOPFENSTEIN Eduard, b. 14 June 1938, Frutigen, Switzerland. Researcher; Translator (Japanese). m. Tomoko Arii, 1969, 1 daughter. Education: DPhil, University Bern, Switzerland, 1968; Habiliation, University Zürich, 1979. Appointments: Literary Critic, Swiss Broadcasting Corporation, 1966; University Assistant, 1969; Full Professor, Japanology University Zürich, 1989; Member, Selection Committee, The Noma Award, 1993; Editor, Japan Edition, 1994-; President, Swiss Asia Society, 1996. Publications: Tausend Kirschbäume - Yoshitsune, 1982; Poetsiche Perlen, Ein Funf-Tagekettengedicht, 1986; Lob des Schattens, 1987; Picknick auf der Erdkugel, 1990; Zürcher Reihe Japanische Literatur, 1990-93; Mondscheintropfen - Japanische Erzählungen 1940-1990, 1993; Ooka Makoto: Botschaft an die Wasser meiner Heimat Gedichte 1951-1996, 1997. Contributions to: A Dialogue Between Modern Poetry and Haiku, 1980; Asiatische Studien; Hefte für Ostasiatische Literatur. Membership: Gruppe Olten (Swiss Writers Association. Address: Ostasiatisches Seminar, University Zürich, Zürichbergstr 4, 8032 Zürich, Switzerland.

KLUBACK William, b. 6 Nov 1927, Brooklyn, New York, USA. Professor of Philosophy. Education: AB, George Washington University; AM, Columbia University; PhD, Hebrew University, Jerusalem. Publications: Paul Valéry, 6 volumes, 1987-97; Juan Ramon Jiménez, 1995; Benjamin Fondane, 1996; Emil Cioran, 1997; Léopold Sédar Senghor, 1997. Contributions to: Midstream; Shofar; Archives de Philosophie. Address: 65 Oriental Boulevard, Apt 8D, Brooklyn, NY 11235, USA.

KLUGER Steve, b. 24 June 1952, Baltimore, Maryland, USA. Writer; Dramatist. Education: University of Southern California, 1971. Publications: Changing Pitches, 1984, 2nd edition, 1990; Lawyers Say the Darndest Things, 1990; Last Days of Summer, 1998. Stage Plays: Cafe 50's, 1988-89; James Dean Slept Here, 1989; Pilots of the Purple Twilight, 1989; Jukebox Saturday Night, 1990; Yank: World War II From The Guys Who Brought You Victory, 1990; Bullpen, 1990; Bye Bye Brooklyn, 1997. Films: Once Upon a Crime, 1992; Yankee Doodle Boys, 1996; Bye Bye Brooklyn, 1997; Almost Like Being in Love, 1997. Contributions to: Chicago Tribune; Los Angeles Times; Sports Illustrated; Inside Sports; Diversion; Playboy; Science Digest. Address: c/o Gail Hochman, Brandt & Brandt, 1501 Broadway, Suite 2310, New York, NY 10036, USA.

KNAAK Richard Allen, b. 28 May 1961, Chicago, Illinois, USA. Author. Education: BA, Rhetoric, University of Illinois. Publications: The Legend of Huma, 1988; Firedrake, 1989; Ice Dragon, 1989; Kaz the Minotaur, 1990; Wolfhelm, 1990; Shadow Steed, 1990; The Shrouded Realm, 1991; Children of the Drake, 1991; Dragon Tome, 1992; The Crystal Dragon, 1993; King of the Grey, 1993; The Dragon Crown, 1994; Frostwing, 1995. Membership: Science Fiction and Fantasy Writers of America. Address: PO Box 8158, Bartlett, IL 60103, USA.

KNASTER Mirka, b. 11 May 1947, Bari, Italy. Writer. Publications: Women in Spanish America From Pre-Conquest to Contemporary Times, 1976; Discovering the Body's Wisdom, 1996. Publications: Women's Health Care: A Guide to Alternatives (contributor), 1984; Encyclopedia of Complementary Health Practices (contributor), 1998. Contributions to: Washington Post; Ladies' Home Journal; East West; Natural Health; Yoga Journal; Massage Therapy Journal; Better Health and Living; Shape; D & B Reports; Honolulu; The Maui News; Pleasant Hawaii; Maui Inc; America West; Mothering; Marriage Encounter; Journal of Traditional Acupuncture. Honours: Phi Beta Kappa, 1968; NDEA Title IV Fellowship, 1968-69; Ford Foundation Fellow, 1973-76; 1st Place, Non-Fiction, Hawaii National Writers Group, 1991. Box 7464, Asheville, NC 28802, USA.

KNECHT Robert Jean, b. 20 Sept 1926, London, England. Professor of French History Emeritus. m. (1) Sonia Hodge, 8 Aug 1956, (2) Maureen White, 28 July 1986. Education: BA, 1948, MA, 1953, DLitt, 1984, King's College, London. Publications: The Voyage of Sir Nicholas Carewe, 1959; Francis I and Absolute Monarchy, 1969; The Fronde, 1975; Francis I, 1982; French Renaissance Monarchy, 1984; The French Wars of Religion, 1989; Richelieu, 1991; Renaissance Warrior and Patron, 1994; The Rise and Fall of Renaissance France, 1996; Catherine de'Medici, 1998; Un Prince de la Renaissance: François Ier et son royaume, 1998. Contributions to: Professional journals and to periodicals. Memberships: Royal Historical Society, fellow; Society of Renaissance Studies, chairman, 1989-92; Society for the Study of French History, 1995-98; Société de l'Histoire de France. Address: 79 Reddings Road, Moseley, Birmingham B13 8LP, England.

KNEVITT Charles (Philip Paul), b. 10 Aug 1952, Dayton, Ohio, USA (British citizen). Journalist. m. Lucy Joan Isaacs, 4 June 1981, 1 daughter. Education: BA, Honours, School of Architecture, University of Manchester. Appointments: Editor, What's New in Building, 1978-80; Architecture Correspondent, Sunday Telegraph, 1980-84, The Times, 1984-; Architecture and Planning Consultant, Thames News, Thames Television, 1983-86. Publications: Manikata, 1980; Connections, 1984; Monstrous Carbuncles (editor), 1985; Space on Earth, 1985; Perspectives, 1986; Community Architecture (with Nick Wates), 1987; Architectural Anecdotes (editor), 1988. Contributions to: Journals and newspapers. Honours: Commendation, Young Writer of the Year, 1978, Architectural Journalist of the Year, International Building Press, 1984. Memberships: Architecture Club; International Building Press; Royal Society of Arts, fellow. Address: Crest House, 102-104 Church Road, Teddington, Middlesex TW11 8PY, England.

KNIGHT Alanna, b. South Shields, Tyne and Wear, England. Novelist; Biographer. m. Alexander Harrow Knight, 2 sons. Appointments: Founder, Chairman, Aberdeen Writers Workshop, 1967; Lecturer, Creative Writing, Workers Educational Association, and Andrews' University Summer School, 1971-75; Tutor, Arvon Foundation, 1982; Secretary, Society of Authors in Scotland, 1991-98. Publications: Legend of the Loch, 1969; This Outward Angel, 1971; October Witch, 1971; Castle Clodha, 1972; Lament for Lost Lovers, 1972; White Rose, 1974; A Stranger Came By, 1974; Passionate Kindness, 1974; A Drink for the Bridge, 1976; Black Duchess, 1980; Castle of Foxes, 1981; Colla's Children, 1982; Robert Louis Stevenson Treasury, 1985; The Clan, 1985; Robert Louis Stevenson in the South Seas, 1986; Estella, 1986; Deadly Beloved, 1989; Killing Cousins, 1990; A Quiet Death, 1991; Sweet Cheat Gone, 1993; Bright Ring of Words (with E S Warfel), 1994; The Outward Angel, 1994; Inspector Faro and the Edinburgh Mysteries, 1994; The Bull Slayers, 1995; Inspector Faro's Casebook, 1996; Murder by Appointment, 1996. Contributions to: Various publications. Honour: 1st Novel Award, Romantic Novelists Association, 1969; Honorary President Edinburgh Writers Club, 1996-. Memberships:

Scottish PEN; Crime Writers Association, 1992-95; Mystery Writers of America; Radiowriters Association; Romantic Novelists Association; Royal Society of Antiquaries, Scotland. Literary Agent: Giles Gordon, Curtis Brown, Haymarket House, 28/29 Haymarket, London SW1Y 4SP, England. Address: 24 March Hall Crescent, Edinburgh EH16 5HL, Scotland.

KNIGHT Arthur Winfield, b. 29 Dec 1937, San Francisco, California, USA. Professor of English; Writer; Poet; Film Critic. m. Kit Duell, 25 Aug 1976, 1 daughter. Education: AA, Santa Rosa Junior College, 1958; BA, English, 1960, MA, Creative Writing, 1962, San Francisco State University. Appointments: Professor of English, California University of Pennsylvania, 1966-93; Film Critic, Russian River News, Guerneville, California, 1991-92, Anderson Valley Advertiser, Boonville, California, 1992-, Potpourri, Prairie Village, Kansas, 1993-; Part-time Professor, University of San Francisco, 1995. Publications: A Marriage of Poets (with Kit Knight), 1984; King of the Beatniks, 1986; The Beat Vision (co-editor), 1987; Wanted!, 1988; Basically Tender, 1991; Cowboy Poems, 1993, retitled Outlaws, Lawmen and Bad Women; Tell Me An Erotic Story, 1993; The Darkness Starts Up Where You Stand, 1996; The Secret Life of Jesse James, 1996; The Cruelest Month, 1997; Johnnie D. (novel), 1999. Contributions to: Reviews, quarterlies, and journals. Honour: 1st Place, Joycean Lively Arts Guild Poetry Competition, 1982. Membership: Western Writers of America. Literary Agent: Nat Sobel, Sobel Weber Associates, Inc. 146 East 19 St, New York, NY 10003-2404. Address: PO Box 2580, Petaluma, CA 94953, USA.

KNIGHT Bernard, b. 3 May 1931, Cardiff, Wales. Emeritus Professor of Forensic Pathology; Writer. Education: Diploma in Medical Jurisprudence, 1966, MD, 1966, FRC, Pathology, 1976, University of Wales; (Hon)DSc, 1996;(Hon) LLD, 1998. Appointments: Lecturer in Forensic Medicine, University of London, 1959-62; Medical Editor, Medicine, Science and the Law, 1960-63; Lecturer, 1962-65, Senior Lecturer, 1965-76, Reader to Professor and Consultant in Forensic Pathology, College of Medicine, University of Wales, 1976-96; Senior Lecturer in Forensic Pathology, University of Newcastle, 1965-68; Managing Editor, 1992-96, Pathology Editor, 1980-92, Forensic Science International. Publications: The Lately Deceased, 1963; Thread of Evidence, 1965; Mistress Murder, 1968; Policeman's Progress, 1969; Tiger at Bay, 1970; Murder, Suicide or Accident, 1971; Deg Y Dragwyddoldeb, 1972; The Sanctuary Seeker, 1998; The Poisoned Chalice, 1998; Crowners Quest, 1998; Legal Aspects of Medical Practice, 1972, 4th edition, 1987; Discovering the Human Body, 1980; Forensic Radiology, 1981; Lawyer's Guide to Forensic Medicine, 1982, 2nd edition 1998; Sudden Death in Infancy, 1983; Post-Modern Technicians Handbook, 1984; Pocket Guide to Forensic Medicine, 1985; Simpson's Forensic Medicine, 10th edition, 1991, 11th edition, 1996; Forensic Pathology, 1991, new edition, 1996; The Estimation of the Time Since Death (editor), 1995. Honour: Commander of the Order of the British Empire, 1993. Memberships: Academi Gymraeg; Crime Writers Association; Welsh Union of Writers. Address: 26 Millwood, Cardiff CF4 5TL, Wales.

KNIGHT Cranston Sedrick, b. 10 Sept 1950, Chicago, Illinois, USA. Historian; Poet; Writer; Dramatist. m. Joyce Anderson, 5 Aug 1977, 2 sons, 1 daughter. Education: BA, History, Southern Illinois University, 1977; MA, History, Northeastern Illinois University, 1990; Doctoral Studies, History, Loyola University, Chicago. Appointments: Literary Consultant, BOLT (Black Open Lab Theater, Southern Illinois University, 1975-77, Mystic Voyage theatre group, Carbondale, Illinois, 1977-80; Columnist, Chicago Daily Defender newspaper, 1987-; Dramatis (Historian), National Passtime Theatre, Chicago, 1996; Poet-in-Residence, Loyola University, Chicago, 1996. Publications: Poetry: Freedom Song, 1988; In the Garden of the Beast, 1989, 2nd edition as In the Garden of the Beast: Vietnam Cries a Love Song, 1996; I, 1996; On the Borders of Hiroshima: I Heard a Rumor of War, 1998. Play: When Silence Cries, 1998.

Other: Tour of Duty: Vietnam in the Words of Those Who Were There (editor), 1986. Contributions to: Anthologies, journals and magazines. Honours: Benjamin Henry Matchett Foundation Grant, 1989; Illinois Arts Council Writers Grants, 1996, 1998; Illinois Humanities Plaque, 1998. Memberships: Associated Writing Programs; Association for Asian Studies; Illinois Writers Inc; Japan Society of America; Joint Center for Political Studies; Midwest Asian Association; National Association for Development Educators; Phi Alpha Theta; West Side Writers Guild. Address: 5935 North Magnolia, No 1, Chicago, IL 60660, USA.

KNIGHT David. See: PRATHER Richard Scott.

KNIGHT David Marcus, b. 30 Nov 1936, Exeter, England. Professor of History and Philosophy of Science; Author. m. Sarah Prideaux, 21 July 1962, 2 sons, 4 daughters. Education: BA, Chemistry, 1960, Diploma, History and Philosophy of Science, 1962, DPhil, 1964, University of Oxford. Appointments: Lecturer, 1964-75, Senior Lecturer, 1975-88, Reader, 1988-91, Professor of History and Philosophy of Science, 1982-88; General Editor, Cambridge Science Biographies, 1996-. Publications: Atoms and Elements: A Study of Theories of Matter in England in the 19th Century, 1967, 2nd edition, 1970; Natural Science Books in English 1600-1900, 1972, 2nd edition, 1989; Sources for the History of Science 1660-1914, 1975; The Nature of Science: The History of Science in Western Culture since 1600, 1977; Zoological Illustration: An Essay Towards a History of Printed Zoological Pictures, 1977; The Transcendental Part of Chemistry, 1978; Ordering the World: A History of Classifying Man, 1981; The Age of Science: The Scientific World View in the 19th Century, 1986, 2nd edition, 1988; A Companion to the Physical Sciences, 1989; Ideas in Chemistry: A History of the Science, 1992, 2nd edition, 1995; Humphry Davy: Science and Power, 1992, 2nd edition, 1998; Science in the Romantic Era, 1998; The Making of the Chemist 1789-1914, 1998. Contributions to: Scholarly books and journals. Memberships: British Association; British Society for the History of Science, president, 1995-96; Royal Society. Address: c/o Department of Philosophy, University of Durham, 50 Old Elvet, Durham DH1 3HN, England.

KNIGHT Gareth. See: WILBY Basil Leslie.

KNIGHT Kit, b. 21 Sept 1952, North Kingston, Rhode Island, USA. Writer; Poet. m. Arthur Winfield Knight, 25 Aug 1976, 1 daughter. Education: BA, Communications, California University of Pennsylvania, 1975. Appointments: Co-Editor, Unspeakable Views of the Individual, 1976-88; Poet and Columnist, Russian River News, Guerneville, California, 1988-92; Poet/columnist, movie critic, Russian River Times, Monte Rio, California, 1997-. Publications: A Marriage of Poets (with Arthur Winfield Knight), 1984; Women of Wanted Men, 1994. Contributions to: Periodicals. Honour: Perry Award for Best Achievement in Poetry, 1994. Address: PO Box 2580, Petaluma, CA 94953, USA.

KNIGHT Stephen Edward, b. 10 June 1960, Swansea, Wales. Theatre Director; Poet. Education: BA, Honours, Jesus College, Oxford, 1981; Old Vic Theatre School, 1985-86. Publication: Flowering Limbs, 1993. Contributions to: Anthologies, reviews, journals, and magazines. Honours: Prizes, 1984, 1987, 1st Prize, 1992, National Poetry Competition; Eric Gregory Award, 1987; 2nd Prize, Cardiff Poetry Competition, 1989.

KNIGHT William Edwards, b. 1 Feb 1922, Tarrytown, New York, USA. Retired Foreign Service Officer; Publisher; Writer. m. Ruth L Lee, 14 Aug 1946, 2 sons. Education: BA, Yale College, 1942; Pilot Training, US Army Air Force, 1943-44; MA, Yale University, 1946; Industrial College of the Armed Forces, 1961-62; State Department Senior Seminar in Foreign Policy, 1971-72. Appointments:B-24 Co-Pilot, 1944-45; Foreign Service Officer, US Department of State, 1946-75; President and Chief Executive Officer, Araluen Press, 1982-. Publications: The Tiger Game, 1986; The Bamboo Game,

1993; Footprints in the Sand (light verse), 1995; Letter to the Twenty- Second Century: An American Family's Odyssey, 1998. Contributions to: Journals. Memberships: Yale Club; Washington Independent Writers; Diplomatic and Consular Officers Retired; American Foreign Service Association; Army/Navy Country Club. Address: Araluen Press, 5000 Park Place, Suite 300, Bethesda, MD 20816, USA.

KNIGHTLEY Phillip (George), b. 23 Jan 1929, Sydney, New South Wales, Australia. Journalist; Writer. m. Yvonne Fernandes, 13 July 1964, 1 son, 2 daughters. Appointments: Reporter, Northern Star, Lismore, 1948-49, Herald, Melbourne, 1952-54; Reporter, 1954-56, Foreign Correspondent, 1956-60, Daily Mirror, Sydney; Editor, Imprint, Bombay, 1960-62; Special Correspondent, Sunday Times, 1965-85. Publications: Philby: The Spy Who Betrayed a Generation (with Bruce Page and David Leitch), 1968; The Games (with Hugh Atkinson), 1968; The Secret Lives of Lawrence of Arabia (with Colin Simpson), 1969; The First Casualty: The War Correspondent as Hero Propagandist and Myth-Maker, Crimea to Vietnam, 1975; Lawrence of Arabia, 1976; The Death of Venice (with Stephen Fay), 1976; Suffer the Children (editor), 1979; The Vestey Affair, 1981; The Second Oldest Profession: The Spy as Bureaucrat, Patriot, Fantasist, and Whore, 1986; An Affair of State: The Profumo Case and the Framing of Stephen Ward (with Caroline Kennedy), 1987; Philby: KGB Masterspy, 1988; A Hack's Progress, 1997. Honours: British Journalist of the Year Awards, 1980, 1988. Memberships: Society of Authors; Royal Overseas League; The Queen's Club. Address: 4 Northumberland Place, London W2 5BS, England.

KNODT Reinhard Helmut Rudolf, b. 13 Oct 1951, Dinkelsbuehl, Germany. Author. m. Kerstin Schmidt, 2 daughters. Education: PhD in Philosophy. Appointments: Teacher, Universitat Bayreuth, Maynooth College, Dublin, Ireland, Universitat Erlangen-Nuremberg, Hochschule Kassel, Kunstakademie, Nurenberg. Publications: Die Ewige Wiederkehr des Leidens, 1987; Aesthetische Korrespondenzen, 1994. Contributions to: Magazines. Honours: Wolfram V Eschenbach Award; IHK Literary Award. Membership: German Writers Association. Address: Schnackenhof 16, D 90552 Roethenbach, Germany.

KNOTT Will(iam) C(ecil), (Bill Knott), b. 7 Aug 1927, Boston, Massachusetts, USA. Writer. Education: AA, 1949, BA, 1951, Boston University; MA, State University of New York, Oswego, 1966. Publications: Circus Catch, 1963; Scatback, 1964; Long Pass, 1966; Night Pursuit, 1966; Junk Pitcher, 1967; Lefty's Long Throw, 1967; High Fly to Center, 1972; Fullback Fury, 1974; The Craft of Fiction, 1974; Taste of Vengeance, 1975; Lyncher's Moon, 1980; Longarm and the Railroaders, 1980; Longarm on the Yellowstone, 1980; Mission Code: King's Pawn, 1981; The Trailsman Series, 15 volumes, 1984-86; The Golden Hawk Series, 9 volumes, 1986-88; The Texan, 1987; Longarm and the Outlaws of Skull Canyon, 1990; Longarm and the Tattoed Lady, 1990. Membership: Western Writers of America, president, 1980-81. Address: 216 Falls of Venice, South Venice, FL 34292, USA.

KNOWLES John, b. 26 Sept 1926, Fairmount, West Virginia, USA. Author. Education: BA, Yale University, 1949. Appointments: Reporter, hartford Courant, 1950-52; Associate Editor, Holiday magazine, 1956-60; Writer-in-Residence, University of North Carolina at Chapel Hill, 1963-64, Princeton University, 1968-69. Publications: A Separate Peace, 1959; Morning in Antibes, 1962; Double Vision: American Thoughts Abroad, 1964; Indian Summer, 1966; Phineas: Six Stories, 1968; The Paragon, 1971; Spreading Fires, 1974; A Vein of Riches, 1978; Peace Breaks Out, 1980; A Stolen Past, 1983; The Private Life of Axie Reed, 1986; Backcasts, 1993. Honours: Richard and Hinda Rosenthal Foundation Award, American Academy and Institute of Arts and Letters, 1960; William Faulkner Foundation Award, 1960; National Association of Independent Scholars Award, 1961. Address: c/o E P Dutton and

Company, PO Box 120, Bergenfield, NJ 07621, USA.

KNOWLING Michael John, b. 26 Apr 1953, Edinburgh, Scotland. College Principal; Journalist; Editor. Education: MA, Honours, University of Glasgow, 1975; Master of Letters, University of New England, 1987. Appointments: Editor, Northern Newspapers Ltd, New South Wales, 1981-88; College Principal. Publications: Collins Concise Encyclopaedia, 1977; Race Relations in Australia: A History, 1982; University of New England Gazette, 1990-92. Honour: Association of Rhodes Scholars in Australia Scholarship, England-Australia, 1977. Memberships: Media, Entertainment and Arts Alliance; International Federation of Journalists; Australian and New Zealand Communication Association; Australian Rhodes Scholars Association. Address: PO Box 503, Armidale, New South Wales 2350, Australia.

KNOX Elizabeth, b. 15 Feb 1959, Wellington, New Zealand. Novelist. m. Fergus Barrowman, 1989. Education: BA, Victoria University, Wellington, 1986. Appointment: Lecturer, Film Studies, Victoria University, 1989; Writer-in-residence, Victoria University of Wellington. Publications: After Z Hour, 1987; Paremata, 1989; Treasure, 1992; Pomare, 1994; Glamour and the Sea, 1996; Tawa, 1998; The Vinter's Luck, 1998. Short Stories: The Sword, 1990; After Images, 1990; Post Mortem, 1990; Afraid, 1991; Take as Prescribed, 1991; The Black Disc, 1992; Heat, 1993; Where We Stopped, 1995; Depth Charge, 1995; Reuben Avenue, 1996; Getting Over It, 1997; The Dig (short film script), 1994. Honours: ICI Bursary, 1988; Pen Award, 1988, Fellowship, 1991; New Zealand Book Council Lecture Award, 1998; Katherine Mansfield Memorial Fellowship, 1999. Address: PO Box 11-806 Wellington, New Zealand.

KNOX William, (Michael Kirk, Bill Knox, Robert MacLeod, Noah Webster), b. 20 Feb 1928, Glasgow, Scotland. Author; Journalist. m. Myra Ann Mackill, 31 Mar 1950, 1 son, 2 daughters. Appointments: Deputy News Editor, Evening News, 1957; Scottish Editor, Kemsley Newspapers, 1957-60; News Editor, Scottish Television, 1960-62; Freelance author and broadcaster 1962-; Presenter, STV Crimedesk, 1977-89; Editor, RNLI Scottish Lifeboat, 1984-97. Publications: Over 60 novels of crime, sea and adventure, including Death Bytes, 1998; also radio and TV adaptations of own work. Honours: William Knox Collection established, Boston University, 1969; Police Review Award, 1986; Paul Harris Fellow, Rotary International, 1989. Memberships: Association of Scottish Motoring Writers; Society of Authors; Crime Writers Association; Mystery Writers Association. Literary Agent: Heather Jeeves, Kingsfield, Witney, Oxon, OX8 6JB, England. Address: 55 Newtonlea Avenue, Newton Mearns, Glasgow G77 5QF, Scotland.

KNOX-JOHNSTON, Sir Robin, b. 17 Mar 1939, Putney, London, England. Master Mariner; Author. m. 6 Jan 1962, 1 daughter. Education: Master's Certificate, 1965. Publications: A World of My Own, 1969; Sailing, 1974; Twilight of Sail, 1978; Last But Not Least, 1978; Seamanship, 1986; The BOC Challenge 1986-87, 1987; The Cape of Good Hope, 1989; The History of Yachting, 1990; The Columbus Venture, 1991; Sea Ice Rock (with Chris Bonington), 1992; Cape Horn, 1994; Beyond Jules Verne, 1995. Contributions to: Yachting Monthly; Cruising World; Guardian. Honours: Knight Bachelor, 1995; Commander of the Order of the British Empire 1969; Honorary DSc, Maine Maritime Academy; Honorary Doctor of Technology, Nottingham Trent University, 1993. Memberships: Younger Brother, Trinity House; Honourable Company of Master Mariners; Royal Institute of Navigation; National Maritime Museum, Greenwich; Sail Training Association. Literary Agent: Curtis Brown. Address: St Francis Cottage, Torbryan, Newton Abbot, Devon TQ12 5UR.

KNOX-MAWER June Ellis, b. 10 May 1930, Wrexham, North Wales. Writer; Broadcaster. m. Ronald Knox-Mawer, 30 June 1951, 1 son, 1 daughter. Appointments: Trained as Journalist, Chester Chronicle, 1948-50; Aden Correspondent, Daily Express, 1952-56;

Presenter and Author, various literary and feature programmes, Womans Hour, BBC Radio 4, 1970-. Publications: The Sultans Came to Tea, 1961; A Gift of Islands, 1965; A World of Islands, 1968; Marama, 1972; A South Sea Spell, 1975; Tales from Paradise, 1986; Marama of the Islands, 1986; Sandstorm, 1991; The Shadow of Wings, 1995. Contributions to: Guardian; Various women's magazines. Honour: Romantic Novel of the Year Award, 1992. Memberships: Royal Commonwealth Society; Commonwealth Trust. Address: c/o David Higham Associates, 5-8 Lower John Street, Golden Square, London W1, England.

KNUDSON R(ozanne) R, b. 1 June 1932, Washington, District of Columbia, USA. Writer. Education: BA, Brigham Young University, 1954; MA, University of Georgia, 1958; PhD, Stanford University, 1967. Publications: Selected Objectives in the English Language Arts (with Arnold Lazarus), 1967; Sports Poems (editor with P K Ebert), 1971; Zanballer, 1972; Jesus Song, 1973; You Are the Rain, 1974; Fox Running, 1974; Zanbanger, 1977; Zanboomer, 1978; Weight Training for the Young Athlete (with F Colombo), 1978; Starbodies (with F Colombo), 1978; Rinehart Lifts, 1980; Just Another Love Story, 1982; Speed, 1982; Muscles, 1982; Punch, 1982; Zan Hagen's Marathon, 1984; Babe Didrikson, 1985; Frankenstein's 10 K, 1985; Martina Navratilova, 1986; Rinehart Shouts, 1986; Julie Brown, 1987; American Sports Poems (editor with May Swenson), 1987; The Wonderful Pen of May Swenson, 1993. Address: 73 Boulevard, Sea Cliff, NY 11579, USA.

KOBER Peter. See: PFEIFER Tadeus.

KOCH Christopher John, b. 16 July 1932, Hobart, Tasmania, Australia. Author. m. Irene Vilnonis, 23 Apr 1960, 1 son. Education: BA Honours; DLitt, University of Tasmania. Publications: The Boys in the Island, 1958; Across the Sea Wall, 1965; The Doubleman, 1965; The Year of Living Dangerously, 1978; Crossing the Gap (essays), 1987; Highways to War, 1995. Honours: National Book Council Award for Australian Literature, 1979; Miles Franklin Prize, 1985. Address: PO Box 19, Paddington, New South Wales 2021, Australia.

KOCH Dolores M, Havana, Cuba. Translator. m. Gerard R Koch 4 June 1949, 1 son, 1 daughter. Education includes: PhD, Spanish-American Literature, City University of New York, 1986. Appointments: Editor, Music Department, Saturday Review, 1972; Director, Spanish Programmes, Regents Publishing, 1980-84; Adjunct Lecturer, Assistant Professor, Spanish American Literature; Textbook Author, Harcourt Brace Jovanovich EMC; Translator of children's books into Spanish, Viking/Penguin; Translator, novels and memoirs. Publications: Translations: Before Night Falls, memoir by Reinaldo Arenas, 1993, 1994; The Doorman, novel by Reinaldo Arenas, 1991, 1995; Where Light and Shadow Meet, memoir by Emilie Schindler, 1997; The Angel of Galilea, novel by Laura Restrepo, 1998; Castro's Daughter, An Exile's Memoir of Cuba, by Alina Fernández, 1998. Publications: Book reviews mainly in Revista Internacional de Literatura Iberoamericana; Essays on Spanish American literature in academic journals. Honour: Before Night Falls 1 of 13 Best Booksof 1993, New York Times Book Review. Memberships: Instituto Internacional de Literatura Iberoamericana; American of Literary Translators Association; SpanSIG. Address: 160 West End Avenue (2M), New York, NY 10023, USA.

KOCH Joanne (Barbara), (Joanna Z Adams), b. 28 Mar 1941, Chicago, Illinois, USA. Author; Dramatist. m. Lewis Z Koch, 30 May 1964, 1 son, 2 daughters. Education: BA, Honours, Cornell University; MA, Columbia University. Appointments: Guest Lecturer, Loyola University, DePaul University; Writer-in-Residence, Lake Forest College, Southern Illinois University; Syndicated Columnist, Newspaper Enterprise Association. Publications: The Marriage Savers (with Lewis Z Koch), 1976; Makeovers (novel), 1987; Rushes (novel), 1988. Other: Various plays. Contributions to: Newspapers and magazines. Honours:

Various awards. Memberships: Dramatists Guild; Phi Beta Kappa; Phi Kappa Phi; Society of Midland Authors; Women in Film; Women in Theatre. Address: 343 Dodge Avenue, Evanston, IL 60202, USA.

KOCH Kenneth (Jay), b. 27 Feb 1925, Cincinnati, Ohio, USA. Professor of English; Poet; Dramatist; Writer. m. (1) Mary Janice Elwood, 1955, 1 daughter, (2) Karen Steinbrink, 1994. Education: AB, Harvard University, 1948; MA, 1953, PhD, 1959, Columbia University. Appointments: Lecturer, Rutgers University, 1953-54, 1955-56, 1957-58, Brooklyn College, 1957-59; Director, Poetry Workshop, New School for Social Research, New York City, 1958-66; Lecturer, 1959-61, Assistant Professor, 1962-66, Associate Professor, 1966-71, Professor of English, 1971-, Columbia University; Associated with Locus Solus magazine, Lansen-Vercours, France, 1960-62. Publications: Poetry: Poems, 1953; Ko, or, A Season on Earth, 1960; Permanently, 1960; Thank You and Other Poems, 1962; Poems from 1952 and 1953, 1968; When the Sun Tries to Go On, 1969; Sleeping with Women, 1969; The Pleasures of Peace and Other Poems, 1969; Penguin Modern Poets 24 (with Kenward Elmslie and James Schuyler), 1973; The Art of Love, 1975; The Duplications, 1977; The Burning Mystery of Anna in 1951, 1979; From the Air, 1979; Days and Nights, 1982; Selected Poems 1950-1982, 1985; On the Edge, 1986; Seasons on Earth, 1987; One Train, 1994; On the Great Atlantic Rainway: Selected Poems 1950-1988, 1994; Straits, 1998; Plays: Bertha and Other Plays, 1966; A Change of Hearts: Plays, Films, and Other Dramatic Works 1951-1971, 1973; One Thousand Avant-Garde Plays, 1988; The Gold Standard, 1996; Fiction: Interlocking Lives (with Alex Katz), 1970; The Red Robins, 1975; Hotel Lambosa, 1993. Editor: Sleeping on the Wing: An Anthology of Modern Poetry, with Essays on Reading and Writing (with Kate Farrell), 1981; Talking to the Sun: An Illustrated Anthology of Poems for Young People (with Kate Farrell), 1985; Other: The Art of Poetry (criticism), 1997; Making Your Own Days - The Pleasures of Reading and Writing Poetry, 1998. Contributions to: Poetry; New York Review of Books; Paris review. Honours: Fulbright Fellowships, 1950, 1978; Guggenheim Fellowship, 1961; National Endowment for the Arts Grant, 1966; Ingram Merrill Foundation Fellowship, 1969; Harbison Award for Teaching, 1970; Frank O'Hara Prize, 1973; National Institute of Arts and Letters Award, 1976; Award of Merit for Poetry, American Academy of Arts and Letters, 1986; Bollingen Prize for Poetry, 1995; Rebekah Johnson Bobbitt National Prize for Poetry, 1996. Membership: American Academy of Arts and letters. Address: 25 Claremont Avenue, Apt 2-B, New York, NY 10027, USA.

KOCH Klaus, b. 4 Oct 1926, Sulzbach, Thüringen, Germany. Professor Emeritus; Writer. m. Eva-Maria Koch, 28 Mar 1978. Education: Universities of Heidelberg, Mainz and Tübingen, 1945-50; Dr theol, University of Heidelberg, 1953; Habilitation, University of Erlangen, 1956. Appointments: Assistant, University of Heidelberg, 1950; Pastor, Lutheran Church, Jena, 1954; Dozent, Old Testament, University of Erlangen, 1956; Dozent, University of Hamburg, 1957; Professor, Old Testament, Kirchliche Hochschule, Wuppertal, 1960; Professor, Old Testament, History of Ancient Near Eastern Religions, University of Hamburg, 1962-91, Professor Emeritus, 1991-. Publications: Was ist Formgeschichte?, 1964, 5th edition, 1989; Ratlos vor der Apokalyptik, 1970, English translation as The Rediscovery of Apocalyptic, 1972; Die Profeten I, Assyrische Zeit, 1978, 3rd edition, 1995, English translation as The Prophets I, 1982; Die Profeten II, Babylonisch-Persische Zeit, 1980, 2nd edition 1988, English translation as The Prophets II, 1984; Spuren des hebraeischen Denkens, Gesammelte Aufsaetze I, 1991; Geschichte der aegyptischen Religion, 1993; Studien zum Danielbuch, Gesammelte Aufsätze 2, 1995; Beitraege zur apokalyptischen Literatur, Gesammelte Aufsaetze 2, 1996; Europa, Rom und der Kaiser vor dem Hintergrund von zwei Jahrtausenden Rezeption des Buches Daniel, 1997. Contributions to: 80 scholarly journals. Honour: Honorary DTheol, University of

Rostock, 1996. Memberships: Joachim-Jurgius Gesellschaft der Wissenchaften, Hamburg; Wissenschaftliche Gesellschaft für Theologie; Bayerische Akademie der Wissenschaften. Address: Diekbarg 13 A, D-22397 Hamburg, Germany.

KOEGLER Hans Herbert, b. 13 Jan 1960, Darmstadt, Germany. Professor of Philosophy. Education: MA, 1986, PhD, 1991, J W Goethe University, Frankfurt. Appointments: Dissertation Fellow, German Fellowship Foundation, 1987-91; Research Fellow, Visiting Scholar, Northwestern University, New School for Social Research, University of California at Berkeley, 1989-90; Assistant Professor of Philosophy, Department of Philosophy, 1991, Assistant Professor, Unit for Criticism and Interpretive Theory, 1994, University of Illinois at Urbana-Champaign; Honorary Faculty Associate, University of Catamarca, Argentina, 1996; Visiting Professor as NEH Fellow, University of Boston, 1997; Assistant Professor of Philosophy, Department of History and Philosophy, 1997, Associate Professor, 1999, University of North Florida, Jacksonville. Publications: Die Macht des Dialogs: Kritische Hermeneutik nach Gadamer, 1992; Michel Foucault: Ein antihumanistischer Aufklarer, 1994; The Power of Dialogue: Critical Hermeneutics After Gadamer and Foucault, 1996; Empathy and Agency: The Problem of Understanding in the Human Sciences, 1999. Contributions to: Journals, periodicals, reviews and magazines. Address: c/o Department of Philosophy, University of North Florida, 4567 St Johns Bluff Road South, Jacksonville, FL 32224-2645, USA.

KOELB Clayton, b. 12 Nov 1942, New York, New York, USA. Educator. m. Susan J Noakes, 1 Jan 1979, 1 son, 1 daughter. Education: BA, 1964, MA, 1966, PhD, 1970, Harvard University. Appointments: Assistant Professor, Associate Professor, Professor of German and Comparative Literature, 1969-91, Chairman, Department of Germanic Languages, 1978-82, University of Chicago; Visiting Professor, Purdue University, 1984-85, Princeton University, 1985-86; Visiting Eugene Falk Professor, 1990, Guy B Johnson Professor, 1991-, Chairman, Department of Germanic Languages, 1997-, University of North Carolina, Chapel Hill. Publications: The Incredulous Reader, 1984; Thomas Mann's Goethe and Tolstoy, 1984; The Current in Criticism, 1987; Inventions of Reading, 1988; The Comparative Perspective on Literature, 1988; Kafka's Rhetoric, 1989; Nietzsche as Postmodernist, 1990; Thomas Mann's Death in Venice: A Critical Edition, 1994. Contributions to: Professional journals. Honours: Germanistic Society of America Fellow, 1964-65; Woodrow Wilson Foundation Fellow, 1965; Danforth Foundation Fellow, 1965-69; Susan Anthony Potter Prize, Harvard University, 1970; Guggenheim Fellowship, 1993-94. Memberships: Modern Language Association of America; International Association for Philosophy and Literature; Semiotics Society of America; Kafka Society of America. Address: University of North Carolina, 414 Dey Hall, Chapel Hill, NC 27599, USA.

KOEMEDA Adolf Jens, b. 18 Apr 1937, Prague, Czech Republic. Psychiatrist; Psychotherapist; Author. m. Margit Koemeda-Lutz, 17 Aug 1984, 3 daughters. Education: Dr.Med, Karls-Universität, Prague, 1962. Publications: Uberfordertes Dasein, 1977; Noran, 1988; Breitenstein, 1989; Die Grenzgängerin, 1997. Contributions to: Tages-Auzeiger; NZZ. Membership: Schweizer Schriftsteller Verband. Address: Breitenstein, CH-8272 Ermatingen, Switzerland.

KOEMEDA Margit, b. 29 Sept 1954, Nuremberg, Germany. Psychologist; Psychotherapist; Author. m. Adolf Jens Koemeda, 17 Aug 1984, 2 daughters. Education: Dr Soc, Universität Konstanz, 1985. Publications: Struktur und Abruf von semantischem Wissen bei Aphasikern, 1985; Eine Frau ist eine Frau ist eine Frau, 1997; Suchbild Liebe, 1998. Contributions to: Scientific journals and literary magazines. Membership: Netzwerk schreibender Frauen; Zürcher Schriftseller, Verband. Address: Breitenstein, CH 8272 Ermatingen, Switzerland.

KOESTENBAUM Wayne, b. 20 Sept 1958, San Jose, California, USA. Professor of English; Poet; Writer; Critic. Education: BA, magna cum laude, English, Harvard College, 1980; MA, Creative Writing, Hopkins University, 1981; PhD, English, Princeton University, 1988. Appointments: Associate Professor of English, Yale University, 1988-97; Co-Editor, The Yale Journal of Criticism, 1991-96; Professor of English, City University of New York, 1997-. Publications: Double Talk: The Erotics of Male Literary Collaboration, 1989; Ode to Anna Moffo and Other Poems, 1990; The Queen's Throat: Opera, Homosexuality, and the Mystery of Desire, 1993; Rhapsodies of a Repeat Offender, 1994; Jackie Under My Skin: Interpreting an Icon, 1995. Other: Jackie O (libretto for the opera by Michael Daugherty), 1997. Contributions to: Anthologies, books, newspapers, reviews, quarterlies, and journals. Honours: Whiting Fellowship in the Humanities, 1987-88; Twentieth Century Literature Prize in Literary Criticism, 1988; Co-Winner, Discovery/The Nation Poetry Contest, 1989; Morse Fellowship, Yale University, 1990-91; New York Times Book Review Notable Book, 1993; Whiting Writer's Award, 1994. Address: c/o English Department, CUNY Graduate School, 33 W. 42nd St. New York, NY 10036-8099, USA

KOGAN Norman, b. 15 June 1919, Chicago, Illinois, USA. Professor Emeritus of Political Science. m. Meryl Reich, 18 May 1946, 2 sons. Education: BA, 1940, PhD, 1949, University of Chicago. Appointments: Faculty, University of Connecticut, 1949-88; Visiting Professor, University of Rome, 1973, 1979, 1987. Publications: Italy and the Allies, 1956; The Government of Italy, 1962; The Politics of Italian Foreign Policy, 1963; A Political History of Postwar Italy, 1966; Storia Politica dell' Italia Repubblicana, 1982, 2nd edition, revised and expanded, 1990; A Political History of Italy: The Postwar Years, 1983. Contributions to: Yale Law Journal; Il Ponte; Western Political Quarterly; Journal of Politics; Comparative Politics; Indiana Law Journal. Address: 13 Westwood Road, Storrs, CT 06268, USA.

KOGAWA Joy (Nozomi), b. 6 June 1935, Vancouver, British Columbia, Canada. Writer; Poet. m. David Kogawa, 2 May 1957, div 1968, 1 son, 1 daughter. Education: University of Alberta, 1954; Anglican Women's Training College, 1956; University of Saskatchewan, 1968. Appointment: Writer-in-Residence, University of Ottawa, 1978. Publications: Poetry: The Splintered Moon, 1967; A Choice of Dreams, 1974; Jericho Road, 1977; Woman in the Woods, 1985; Fiction: Obasan, 1981; Naomi's Road, 1986; Itsuka (novel), 1992; The Rain Ascends, 1995. Contributions to: Canadian Forum; Chicago Review; Prism International; Quarry; Queen's Quarterly; West Coast Review; Others. Honours: 1st Novel Award, Books in Canada, 1982; Book of the Year Award, Canadian Authors Association, 1982; American Book Award, Before Columbus Foundation, 1983; Best Paperback Award, Periodical Distributors, 1983; Notable Book Citation, American Library Association, 1982; Member of the Order of Canada; Honorary doctorates. Memberships: Canadian Civil Liberties Association, director; Canadian Tribute to Human Rights, patron; PEN International; Writers Union of Canada. Address: c/o Writers Union of Canada, 24 Ryerson, Toronto, Ontario M5T 2P3, Canada.

KOHUT Thomas A(ugust), b. 11 Mar 1950, Chicago, Illinois, USA. Professor of History; Writer. m. Susan Neeld Kohut, 21 June 1975, 1 son, 1 daughter. Education: BA, Oberlin College, 1972; MA, History, 1975, PhD, History, 1983, University of Minnesota; Graduate, Cincinnati Psychoanalytic Institute, 1984. Appointments: Assistant Clinical Professor of Psychiatry, University of Psychiatry, University of Cincinnati, 1982-84; Assistant Professor, 1984-90, Associate Professor, 1990-95, Sue and Edgar Wachenheim III Professor of History, Williams College; Guest Professor, University of Munich, 1988, University of Siegen, 1991-92, 1995-96. Publication: Wilhelm II and the Germans: A Study in Leadership, 1991. Contributions to: Scholarly books, journals and anthologies. Honours: Deutscher Akademischer Austauschdienst Grant, 1978-79; International Research and Exchanges Board Grant, 1979; Fulbright Scholarship, 1987-88; Köhler Foundation Grant, 1996. Memberships: American Historical Association; German Studies Association. Address: c/o Department of History, Williams College, Williamstown, MA 01267, USA.

KOLAKOWSKI Leszek, b. 23 October 1927, Radom, Poland. Philosopher; Retired Senior Research Fellow. m. Tamara Dynenson, 19 Nov 1949, 1 daughter. Education: MA, University of Lodz, 1950; PhD, University of Warsaw, 1953. Appointments: Assistant in Philosophy, University of Lodz, 1947-49; Assistant in Philosophy, 1950-59, Professor and Chairman of the Section on Philosophy, 1959-68, University of Warsaw; Visiting Professor, McGill University, 1968-69, University of California at Berkeley, 1969-70, Yale University, 1975, University of Chicago, 1981-; Senior Research Fellow, All Souls College, Oxford, 1970-95. Publications (in English): Marxism and Beyond, 1968; Conversations with the Devil, 1972; Positivist Philosophy, 1972; Husserl and the Search for Certitude, 1975; Main Currents of Marxism, 3 volumes, 1978; Religion, 1982; Bergson, 1985; Metaphysical Horror, 1988. Contributions to: Various publications. Honours: Jurzykowski Foundation Award, 1968; Friedenpreis des Deutschen Buchhandels, 1977; Fellow, British Academy, 1980; Charles Veillou Prix Européen d'Essai, 1980; John D and Catharine T MacArthur Foundation Fellowship, 1983; Co-Winner, Erasmus Prize, 1984; Jefferson Award, 1986; Prix Tocqueville, 1993; Honorary doctorates. Memberships: American Academy of Arts and Letters, foreign member; Bayerische Akademie des Künste, corresponding member; International Institute of Philosophy. Address: 77 Hamilton Road, Oxford OX2 7QA, England.

KOLLER James, b. 30 May 1936, Oak Park, Illinois, USA. Writer; Poet; Artist. Div, 2 sons, 4 daughters. Education: BA, North Central College, Naperville, Illinois, 1958. Publications: Poetry: Two Hands, 1965; Brainard and Washington Street Poems, 1965; The Dogs and Other Dark Woods, 1966; Some Cows, 1966; I Went To See My True Love, 1967; California Poems, 1971; Bureau Creek, 1975; Poems for the Blue Sky, 1976; Messages-Botschaften, 1977; Andiamo, 1978; O Didn't He Ramble-O ware er nicht unhergezogen, 1981; Back River, 1981; One Day at a Time, 1981; Great Things Are Happening-Grossartoge Dige passieren, 1984; Give the Dog a Bone, 1986; Graffiti Lyriques (with Franco Beltrametti), graphics and texts, 1987; Openings, 1987; Fortune, 1987; Roses Love Sunshine, 1989; This Is What He Said, graphics and texts, 1991. Prose: Messages, 1972; Working Notes 1960-82, 1985; Gebt dem alten Hund'nen Knochen (Essays, Gedichte and Prosa 1959-85), 1986; The Natural Order, essay and graphics, 1990. Fiction: If You Don't Like Me You Can Leave Me Alone, UK edition, 1974, US edition, 1976; Shannon Who Was Lost Before, 1975. Address: PO Box 629, Brunswick, ME 04011, USA.

KOLM Ronald Akerson, b. 21 May 1947, Pittsburgh, Pennsylvania, USA. Writer; Editor; Publisher. m. Donna Sterling, 5 Sept 1984, 2 sons. Education: BA, Albright College, 1970. Publications: Plastic Factory, 1989; Welcome to the Barbecue, 1990; Suburban Ambush, 1991; Rank Cologne, 1991. Contributions to: Cover Magazine; Appearances Magazine; New Observations; Semiotext(e); Red Tape. Address: 30-73 47th Street, Long Island City, NY 11103, USA.

KOMUNYAKAA Yusef, (James Willie Brown Jr), b. 29 Apr 1947, Bogalusa, Louisiana, USA. Professor of Creative Writing; Poet. m. Mandy Sayer, 1985. Education: BA, University of Colorado, 1975; MA, Colorado State University, 1979; MFA, University of California at Irvine, 1980. Appointments: Visiting Professor, 1985, Associate Professor of Afro-American Studies, 1987-96, Indiana University; Professor of Creative Writing, Princeton University, 1997-; Many poetry readings. Publications: Dedications and Other Darkhorses, 1977; Lost in the Bonewheel Factory, 1979; Copacetic, 1984; I Apologize for the Eyes in My Head, 1986; Dien Cai Dau, 1988; The Jazz Poetry Anthology (editor with Sascha Feinstein), 1991; Magic City, 1992;

Neon Vernacular: New and Selected Poems, 1993. Contributions to: Anthologies and periodicals. Honours: Pulitzer Prize in Poetry, 1994; Kingsley Tufts Poetry Award, 1994; Union League Civic Arts and Poetry Prize, Chicago, 1998. Address: c/o Department of English, Princeton University, Princeton, NJ 08544, USA.

KONER Pauline, b. 26 June 1912, New York, New York, USA. Choreographer; Writer; Lecturer; Teacher. m. 23 May 1939. Education: Columbia University, 1928; Professional Training with Michel Fokine, Michio Ito and Angel Cansino. Publications: Solitary Song: An Autobiography, 1989; Elements of Performance, 1993. Essays: The Truth about the Moor's Pavane, 1966; Intrinsic Dance, 1966; Pauline Koner Speaking, 1966. Contributions to: Dance Magazine; Ballet Review; Dance Chronicle. Honours: Dance Magazine Award, 1963; Honorary Doctorate of Fine Arts, Rhode Island College, 1985; Special Citation, De La Torre Bueno Award, 1989. Membership: American Dance Guild. Address: 263 West End Avenue, 9F, New York, NY 10023, USA.

KÖNIG Hans, b. 30 Sept 1925, Erlangen, Germany. Writer. m. 1 Jan 1949, 1 son. Publications: Der Pelzermärtl kummt, 1977; Woss wissd denn ihr, 1981; Anekdoten Erzählungen Originale aus Erlangen, 1981-84; Burschen, Knoten und Philister - Erlanger Studentenleben von 1843-1983, 1984; Erlangen vorwiegend heiter - ein unterhaltsamer Streifzug dürch die Stadt und ihre Geschichte, 1988; Wie es Lem so is, 1994. Contributions to: Anthologies, journals and periodicals. Honours include: Verdienstmedaille u Verdienstkreuz der BRD, 1985-91; Kultureller Ehrenbrief der Stadt Erlangen, 1989. Memberships: Verband Fränkischer Schriftstelle; Pegnesischer Blumenorden. Address: Tenneloher Str 26, D 91058 Erlangen, Germany.

KONOPINSKI Lech Kazimierz, (Wiktor Leliwa, Wlodzimierz Sciskowski), b. 16 Mar 1931, Poznan, Poland. Writer; Journalist. m. Hanna Zapytowska, 26 July 1956, 1 son, 1 daughter. Education: MA, Higher School of Economics, 1955; PhD, University of Lodz, 1973. Publications: 53 books including: Actions and Reactions, 1960; Devil's Dodges, 1968; Paradise Apples, 1971; Eyes of Peacock's Tail, 1975; The Amor Alphabet, 1977; Jocular Leaflets, 1980; Funny Resentments, 1981; Ridiculous Aphorisms, 1994; Sneers and Tears, epigrams, 1998; Many children's books; 6 plays, 600 songs; Research works including History of the Polish Satirical Press; Many articles. Contributions to: Numerous publications. Honours: Golden Book Award, 1971; Golden Ring Award, 1973, 1980. Membership: Qualifying Board, Polish Writers Association. Literary Agent: WAL, Poznan. Address: WAL, Wielkopolska Agencja Literacka, ul Michalowska 18, PL 60-645 Poznan, Poland.

KOONTZ Dean R(ay), (David Axton, Brian Coffey, Deanna Dwyer, K R Dwyer, John Hill, Leigh Nichols, Anthony North, Richard Paige, Owen West), b. 9 July 1945, Everett, Pennsylvania, USA. Writer. m. Gerda Ann Cerra, 15 Oct 1966. Education: BS, Shippensburg University, 1966. Publications: Star Quest, 1968; The Fall of the Dream Machine, 1969; Fear That Man, 1969; Anti-Man, 1970; Beastchild, 1970; Dark of the Woods, 1970; The Dark Symphony, 1970; Hell's Gate, 1970; The Crimson Witch, 1971; A Darkness in My Soul, 1972; The Flesh in the Furnace, 1972; Starblood, 1972; Time Thieves, 1972; Warlock, 1972; A Werewolf Among Us, 1973; Hanging On, 1973; The Haunted Earth, 1973; Demon Seed, 1973; Strike Deep, 1974; After the Last Race, 1974; Nightmare Journey, 1975; The Long Sleep, 1975; Night Chills, 1976; Prison of Ice, 1976, revised edition as Icebound, 1995; The Vision, 1977; Whispers, 1980; Phantoms, 1983; Darkfall, 1984; Twilight Eyes, 1985; The Door to December, 1985; Strangers, 1986; Watchers, 1987; Lightning, 1988; Midnight, 1989; The Bad Place, 1990; Cold Fire, 1991; Hideaway, 1992; Dragon Tears, 1992; Mr Murder, 1993; Winter Moon, 1993; Dark Rivers of the Heart, 1994; Strange Hideways, 1995; Intensity, 1995; Tick-Tock, 1996; Fear Nothing, 1988. Contributions to: Books, journals, and magazines. Honours: Daedalus Award, 1988; Honorary DLitt, Shippensburg University, 1989. Address: PO Box 9529, Newport Beach, CA 92658, USA.

KOOSER Ted, (Theodore Kooser), b. 25 Apr 1939, Ames, Iowa, USA. Poet; Teacher; Company Vice-President. m. (1) Diana Tresslar, 1962, div 1969, 1 son, (2) Kathleen Rutledge, 1977. Education: BS, Iowa State University, 1962; MA, University of Nebraska, 1968. Appointments: Underwriter, Bankers Life Nebraska, 1965-73; Part-Time Instructor in Creative Writing, University of Nebraska, 1970-; Senior Underwriter, 1973-84, Vice-President, 1984-, Lincoln Benefit Life. Publications: Poetry: Official Entry Blank, 1969; Grass County, 1971; Twenty Poems, 1973; A Local Habitation, and a Name, 1974; Shooting a Farmhouse: So This is Nebraska, 1975; Not Coming to be Barked At, 1976; Hatcher, 1978; Old Marriage and New, 1978; Cottonwood County (with William Kloefkorn), 1979; Sure Signs: New and Selected Poems, 1980; One World at a Time, 1985; The Blizzard Voices, 1986; Weather Central, 1994. Editor: The Windflower Home Almanac of Poetry, 1980; As Far as I Can See: Contemporary Writers of the Middle Plains, 1989. Honours: Prairie Schooner Prizes, 1975, 1978; National Endowment for the Arts Fellowships, 1976, 1984; Poetry Award, Society of Midland Authors, 1980; Stanley Kunitz Prize, 1984; Governor's Art Award, Nebraska, 1988; Richard Hugo Prize, 1994. Address: Route 1, Box 10, Garland, NE 68360, USA.

KOPIT Arthur, b. 10 May 1937, New York, New York, USA. Dramatist; Screenwriter. m. Leslie Ann Garis, 2 sons, 1 daughter. Education: AB, Harvard University, 1959. Appointments: Fellow, 1974-75, Playwright-in-Residence, 1975-76, Wesleyan University; CBS Fellow, 1976-77, Adjunct Professor of Playwriting, 1977-80, Yale University; Adjunct Professor of Playwriting, City Colleg of the City University of New York, 1981-. Publications: Plays: Questioning of Nick, 1957; Gemini, 1957; Don Juan in Texas, 1957; On the Runway of Life You Never Know What's Coming Off Next, 1957; Across the River and Into the Jungle, 1958; Sing to Me Through Open Windows, 1959; To Dwell in a Place of Strangers, 1959; Aubade, 1959; Oh Dad, Poor Dad, Mamma's Hung You in the Closet and I'm Fellin' So Sad, 1960;Asylum, or What the Gentlemen Are Up To, and As For the Ladies, 1963; Mhil'daim, 1963; Chamber Music, 1965; Sing to Me Through Open Windows, 1965; The Day the Whores Came Out to Play Tennis, 1965; Indians, 1968; What's Happened to the Thorne's House, 1972; The Conquest of Everest, 1973; The Hero, 1973; Louisiana Territory, or Lewis and Clark Lost and Found, 1975; Secrets of the Rice, 1976; Wings, 1978; End of the World, 1984; Road to Nirvana, 1991. Contributions to: Films and television. Honours: Vernon Rice Award, 1960; Outer Critics Circle Award, 1960; Guggenheim Fellowship, 1967; Rockefeller Foundation Grant, 1968; American Institute of Arts and Letters Award, 1971; National Endowment for the Humanities Grant, 1974; Prix Italia, 1978; Tony Award, 1982. Memberships: Dramatists Guild; Hasty Pudding Society; PEN; Phi Beta Kappa; Signet Society; Writers Guild of America. Address: c/o The Tartleff Office, 375 Greenwich Street, Suite 700, New York, NY 10013, USA.

KOPPANY Zsolt, b. 20 Aug 1955, Budapest, Hungary. Writer; Poet; Dramatist. m. Aranka Hegyesi, 15 Aug 1981. Education: Qualification as Locksmith. Publications: 10 books, including fiction, poems, and non-fiction, 1988-98. Contributions to: Various publications. Honour: Josef Lengyel Grant, 1985. Membership: Hungarian Writers Association. Address: Fadrusz utca 2 IV/7, 1114 Budapest, Hungary.

KOPS Bernard, b. 28 Nov 1926, London, England. Poet; Writer; Dramatist. m. Erica Gordon, 1956, 4 children. Appointments: Lecturer, Spiro Institute, 1985-86, Surrey Education Authority, Ealing Education Authority, Inner London Education Authority, Arts Educational School/Acting Co, 1989-90, Cith Literary Institute, 1990-93. Publications: Poetry: Poems, 1955; Poems and Songs, 1958; Anemone for Antigone, 1959;Erica, I Want to Read You Something, 1967; For the Record, 1971; Barricades in West Hampstead, 1988. Other: Awake for Mourning, 1958; Motorbike, 1962; Yes From No Man's land, 1965; By the Waters of Whitechapel, 1970; The Passionate Past of Gloria Gaye, 1971; Settle Down Simon Katz, 1973; Partners, 1975; On Margate Sands, 1978; Collected Plays Volume I, 1998. Plays: The Hamlet of Stepney Green, 1958; Goodbye World, 1959; Change for the Angel, 1960; Stray Cats and Empty Bottles, 1961; Enter Solly Gold, 1962; The Boy Who Wouldn't Play Jesus, 1965; More Out Than In, 1980; Ezra, 1981; Simon at Midnight, 1982; Some of These Days, 1990; Sophie: Last of the Red Hot Mamas, 1990; Playing Sinatra, 1991; Androcles and the Lion, 1992; Dreams of Anne Frank, 1992; Who Shall I Be Tomorrow?, 1992; Call in the Night, 1995; Green Rabbi, 1997; Cafe Zeitgeist, 1998; Houdini Escapes, 1999. Honours: Arts Council Bursaries, 1957, 1979, 1985, and Award, 1991; C Day-Lewis Fellowship, 1981-83; London Fringe Award, 1993; Writer's Guild of Great Britain Best Radio Play Award, 1995. Literary Agent: John Rush, Sheil Land Associates, 43 Doughty Street, London. Address: 41B Canfield Gardens London NW6 3JL, England.

KORAB. See: **HEN Jozef.**

KORDA Michael (Vincent), b. 8 Oct 1933, London, England. Writer; Editor. m. (1) Carolyn Keese, 16 Apr 1958, div, 1 son, (2) Margaret Mogford. Education: BA, Magdalene College, Cambridge, 1958. Appointments: Editorial Assistant to Editor-in-Chief, Simon & Schuster Inc, New York City, 1958-. Publications: Male Chauvinism! How it Works, 1973; Power! How to Get It, How to Use It, 1975; Success!, 1977; Charmed Lives: A Family Romance, 1979; Worldly Goods, 1982; Queenie, 1985; The Fortune, 1988; Curtain, 1991. Contributions to: Periodicals. Address: c/o Simon & Schuster Inc, 1230 Avenue of the Americas, New York, NY 10020, USA.

KORFIS Tasos. See: **ROMBOTIS Anastasios.**

KORG Jacob, b. 21 Nov 1922, New York, New York, USA. Professor of English Emeritus; Writer. Education: BA, City College of New York, 1943; MA, 1947, PhD, 1952, Columbia University. Appointments: Bard College, 1948-50; City College, 1950-55; Assistant to Associate Professor, 1955-65, Professor of English, 1965-91, Professor Emeritus, 1991-, University of Washington, Seattle. Publications: Westward to Oregon (editor with S F Anderson), 1958; Thought in Prose (editor with R S Beal), 1958, 3rd edition, 1966; An Introduction to Poetry, 1959; London in Dickens's Day (editor), 1960; The Complete Reader (editor with R S Beal), 1961; George Gissing's Commonplace Book (editor), 1962; George Gissing: A Critical Biography, 1963; Dylan Thomas, 1965, updated edition, 1991; The Force of Few Words, 1966; Twentieth Century Interpretations of Bleak House (editor), 1968; The Poetry of Robert Browning (editor), 1971; George Gissing: Thyrza (editor), 1974; George Gissing: The Unclassed (editor), 1978; Language in Modern Literature, 1979, updated edition, 1992; Browning and Italy, 1983; Ritual and Experiment in Modern Poetry, 1995. Contributions to: Professional journals. Memberships: International Association of University Professors of English; Modern Language Association; Association of Literary Scholars and Critics. Address: 6530 51st Avenue North East, Seattle, WA 98115, USA.

KÖRMENDI Lajos, b. 6 June 1946, Karcag, Hungary. Writer; Poet; Journalist. m. Julianna Varga, 19 Apr 1984, 1 son, 1 daughter. Education: Journalist, Journalists School, Budapest, 1976; Secondary School Teacher, Hungarian Language and Literature, Adult Education, Eötvös University, Budapest, 1985. Appointments: Civil Engineering Technician, 1964-74; Journalist, 1974-; Arts Lecturer, Official in charge of Arts, 1981-83; Librarian, Arts Historian, 1983-85, 1987-89; Secondary School Teacher, 1985-87; Chief Editor, Jászkunság, county journal, 1989-95; Vice Mayor, Karcag, 1990-92; Freelance Writer, Journalist, 1995-. Publications: Barbaricum, poems, 1981; Boldog emberek, prose, 1985; Művész Pista huszonegye, novel, 1987; A gyökeres állat, poems, 1992; Vad játékok, short stories, 1994; Édesem, ma oly fanyar vagyok, poems, 1994; Telefax a Megváltónak, avagy IV, Louis Bejgliumban, diary, 1995;

A puszta fiai, literary translations from Kazakh poetry, 1996; Magánkrónikák, short stories, 1996; Kurgán, poems, 1997; Öt perc az élet, prose, 1997. Contributions to: Numerous to newspapers and journals. Honours: Prize for Adult Education, 1993; Kölcsey Prize, 1994; József Darvas Prize, 1995; Attila József Prize, 1995; Sándor Petőfi Free Press Prize, 1996. Memberships: Hungarian Journalists Society, 1976-; Hungarian Writers Association, 1984-; Hungarian Artists Society, 1984-; Hungarian Literary Historians Society, 1993-. Address: Kossuth tér 15, 5300 Karcag, Hungary.

KORMONDY Edward (John), b. 10 June 1926, Beacon, New York, USA. Professor of Biology (retired); Writer. Education: BA, Tusculum College, 1950; MS, 1951, PhD, 1955, University of Michigan. Appointments: Assistant Professor to Professor of Biology, Oberlin College, 1957-68; Director, Commission on Undergraduate Education in the Biological Sciences and the Office of Biological Education, American Institute of Biological Sciences, 1968-71; Faculty, 1971-79, Interim Acting Dean, 1972-73, Vice-President and Provost, 1973-78, Evergreen State College, Olympia, Washington; Senior Professional Associate, National Science Foundation, 1979; Provost and Professor of Biology, University of Southern Maine, Portland, 1979-82; Vice-President for Academic Affairs and Professor of Biology, California State University, Los Angeles, 1982-86; Senior Vice-President, Chancellor, and Professor of Biology, University of Hawaii at Hilo and at West Oahu, 1986-93; President, University of West Los Angeles, 1995-97; Honorarr Doctor of Science, Tuscuham College, 1997. Publications: Introduction to Genetics, 1964; Readings in Ecology (editor), 1965; Readings in General Biology (editor), 2 volumes, 1966; Concepts of Ecology, 1969, 4th edition, 1996; Population and Food (editor with Robert Leisner), 1971; Pollution (editor with Robert Leisner), 1971; Ecology (editor with Robert Leisner), 1971; General Biology: The Natural History and Integrity of Organisms (with others), 1977; Handbook of Contemporary Developments in World Ecology (with F McCormick), 1981; Environmental Sciences: The Way the World Works (with B Nebell), 1981, 2nd edition, 1987; Biology (with B Essenfield), 1984, 2nd edition, 1988; International Handbook of Pollution Control, 1989; Environmental Education: Academia's Response (with P Corcoran), 1997; Fundamentals of Human Ecology (with D Brown), 1998. Contributions to: Professional journals. Address: 1388 Lucile Avenue, Los Angeles, CA 90026-1520, USA.

KORNFELD Robert Jonathan, b. 3 Mar 1919, Newtonville, Massachusetts, USA. Dramatist; Writer; Poet. m. Celia Seiferth, 23 Aug 1945, 1 son. Education: AB, Harvard University, 1941; Attended, Columbia University, Tulane University, New York University, New School for Social Research, Circle-in-the-Square School of Theatre, and Playwrights Horizons Theatre School and Laboratory. Publications: Plays: Great Southern Mansions, 1977; A Dream Within a Dream, 1987; Landmarks of the Bronx, 1990; Music For Saint Nicholas, 1992; Hot Wind From the South, 1995; The Hanged Man, 1996. Plays produced: Father New Orleans, 1997; The Queen of Carnival, 1997; The Celestials, 1998. Other: Fiction and poetry. Contributions to: Various publications. Honours: Numerous awards and prizes; Visiting Artist, American Academy, Rome, 1996. Memberships: Authors League; Dramatists Guild; National Arts Club; New York Drama League; PEN. Address: 5286 Sycamore Avenue, Riverdale, NY 10471, USA.

KORZENIK Diana, b. 15 Mar 1941, New York, New York, USA. Professor Emerita; Writer. Education: Oberlin College; BA, Vassar College; Master's Programme, Columbia University; EdD, Graduate School of Education, Harvard University. Appointments: Professor Emerita, Massachusetts College of Art, Boston. Publications: Art and Cognition (editor with Leonard Perkins), 1977; Drawn to Art, 1986; Art Making and Education (with Maurice Brown), 1993; The Cultivation of American Artists (co-editor with Sloat and Barnhill), 1997. Contributions to: Professional journals and to magazines. Honour: National Art Education Association Lowenfeld Award, 1998.

Memberships: Friends of Longfellow House, founder, board member; Archives of American Art. Address: 7 Norman Road, Newton Highlands, MA 02161, USA.

KOSTASH Myrna Ann, b. 2 Sept 1944, Edmonton, Canada. Writer. Education: BA, University of Alberta, 1965; MA, University of Toronto, 1968. Publications: All of Baba's Children, 1977; Long Way From Home, 1980; No Kidding, 1988; Bloodlines, 1993; The Doomed Bridgeroom: A Memoir, 1998. Contributions to: Saturday Night; Canadian Forum; Brick; Border Crossings; Prairie Fire. Honours: Canada Council Senior Artist Grants; National Magazine Silver Prize; National Magazine Award Finalist, 1997. Memberships: Writer's Union of Canada Chairman, 1993-94; Writer's Guild of Alberta, President, 1989-90. Literary Agent: Westwood Creative Artists, Toronto. Address: 10415-87 Avenue Edmonton, AB T6E 2P4, Canada.

KOSTELANETZ Richard (Cory), b. 14 May 1940, New York, New York, USA. Writer; Poet; Critic; Artist; Composer. Education: AB, Honours, Brown University, 1962; Graduate Studies, King's College, London, 1964-65; MA, Columbia University, 1966; Study in music and theatre, Morley College, London, and New School for Social Research, New York. Appointments: Co-Founder-President, Assembling Press, New York, 1970-82; Literary Director, Future Press, New York, 1976-; Co-Editor-Publisher, Precisely: A Critical Magazine, 1977-84; Sole Proprietor, R K Editions, New York, 1978-; Coordinator-Interviewer, American Writing Today: Voice of America Forum Series, 1979-81; Contributing Editor to various journals; Guest lecturer and reader at many colleges and universities; Numerous exhibitions as an artist. Publications: Poetry: Visual Language, 1970; I Articulations/Short Fictions, 1974; Portraits From Memory, 1975; Numbers: Poems and Stories, 1976; Rain Rains Rain, 1976; Illuminations, 1977; Numbers Two, 1977; Richard Kostelanetz, 1980; Turfs/Arenas/Fields/Pitches, 1980; Arenas/Fields/Pitches/Turfs, 1982; Fields/Pitches/Turfs/Arenas, 1990; Solos, Duets, Trios, and Choruses, 1991; Wordworks: Poems Selected and New, 1993; Paritions, 1993; Repartitions, 1994. Fiction: In the Beginning (novel), 1971; Constructs, 5 volumes, 1975-91; One Night Stood (novel), 1977; Tabula Rasa: A Constructivist Novel, 1978; Exhaustive Parallel Intervals (novel), 1979; Fifty Untitled Constructivist Fictions, 1991; Many others. Non-Fiction: Recyclings: A Literary Autobiogrphy, 2 volumes, 1974, 1984; The End of Intelligent Writing: Literary Politics in America, 1974; Metamorphosis in the Arts, 1980; The Old Poetries and the New, 1981; The Grants-Fix: Publicly Funded Literary Granting in America, 1987; The Old Fictions and the New, 1987; On Innovative Music(ian)s, 1989; Unfinished Business: An Intellectual Nonhistory, 1990; The New Poetries and Some Old, 1991; Published Encomia, 1967-91, 1991; On Innovative Art(ist)s, 1992; On Innovative Performance(s), 1994; Fillmore East: 25 Years After: Recollections of Rock Theatre, 1995; An ABC of Contemporary Reading, 1995; Crimes of Culture, 1995; John Cage (Ex)plain(ed), 1996; One Million Words of Booknotes, 1958-1993, 1996; Many others. Editor: American Writing Today, 2 volumes, 1981, revised edition, 1991; The Avant-Garde Tradition in Literature, 1982; Gertrude Stein Advanced: An Anthology of Criticism, 1990; Writing About John Cage, 1993; Nicholas Slonimsky: The First 1000 Years, 1994; A Portable Baker's Biographical Dictionary of Musicians, 1994; Classic Essays on 20th Century Music, 1996; Writing on Glass, 1996; A Frank Zappa Companion, 1996; A B B King Companion, 1996; Another e e cummings, 1997; Many others. Other: Films; Videotapes; Radio Scripts; Recordings. Contributions to: Many anthologies; Numerous poems, articles, essays, reviews, in journals and other publications. Honours: Woodrow Wilson Fellowship, 1962-63; Fulbright Fellowship, 1964-65; Pulitzer Fellowship, 1965-66; Guggenheim Fellowship, 1967; 1 of Best Books, American Institute of Graphic Arts, 1976; Many grants from National Endowment for the Arts ; Pushcart Prize, 1977; Deutscher Akademischer Austauschdienst Stipend, Berlin, 1981-83; American Society of Composers, Authors, and Publishers Awards,

1983-91; Phi Beta Kappa; Many others. Memberships: American PEN; American Society of Composers, Authors, and Publishers; Artist Equity; International Association of Art Critics; National Writers Union; Others. Address: PO Box 444, Prince Street Station, New York, NY 10012-0008 USA.

KOTKER (Mary) Zane, (Maggie Strong), b. 2 Jan 1934, Waterbury, USA. Writer. m. Norman Kotker, 7 June 1965, 1 son, 1 daughter. Education: MA, Columbia University, 1959-60. Publications: Bodies in Motion (novel), 1972; A Certain Man (novel), 1976; White Rising (novel), 1981; Mainstay (as Maggie Strong), 1988; Try to Remember (novel), 1997; Mainstay (as Maggie Strong), 1997. Honour: National Endowment for the Arts, 1972. Literary Agent: Molly Friedrich. Address: 160 Main Street, Northampton, MA 01060, USA.

KOTZWINKLE William, b. 22 Nov 1938, Scranton, Pennsylvania, USA. Writer. m. Elizabeth Gundy, 1970. Education: Rider College; Pennsylvania State University. Publications: Elephant Bangs Train, 1971; Hermes 3000, 1971; The Fat Man, 1974; Night-Book, 1974; Swimmer in the Secret Sea, 1975; Doctor Rat, 1976; Fata Morgana, 1977; Herr Nightingale and the Satin Woman, 1978; Jack in the Box, 1980; Christmas at Fontaine's, 1982; E T, the Extra-Terrestrial: A Novel, 1982; Superman III, 1983; Queen of Swords, 1983; E T, the Book of the Green Planet: A New Novel, 1985; Seduction in Berlin, 1985; Jewell of the Moon, 1985; The Exile, 1987; The Midnight Examiner, 1989; Hot Jazz Trio, 1989; The Game of Thirty, 1994. Other: Many children's books. Honours: National Magazine Awards for Fiction, 1972, 1975; O Henry Prize, 1975; World Fantasy Award for Best Novel, 1977; North Dakota Children's Choice Award, 1983, and Buckeye Award, 1984. Address: c/o Houghton Mifflin Co, 1 Beacon Street, Boston, MA 02108, USA.

KOUNS Alan Terry, b. 31 December 1941, Long Beach, California, USA. Medical Writer; Consultant; Publicist. Education: MAC, University of Pennsylvania. Appointments: Journalist in print and broadcast media, 1961-70; Public Relations Writer, University of Southern California, 1965; Health Sciences Writer, 1970-72; Associate Producer in educational television, 1973; Consultant and Writer for health care multimedia, D'Antoni and Associates, 1974; Correspondent, US Information Agency, 1975-81, 1982-93; Fundraising Consultant for educational film, One World Foundation, 1978; Medical Filmstrip Scriptwriter, Trainex Corporation, 1980-81; Lecturer in Communication Arts, California State Polytechnic University, Pomona, 1981; Writer-Publicist, City of Hope National Medical Center, 1981-82; Associate Editor, Creative Age Publications, 1982-88; Consultant in medical communications and media relations, 1984-; Los Angeles Correspondent, Physicians Radio Network, 1987. Contributions to periodicals including: Contemporary Dialysis and Nephrology; Dialysis and Transplantation; Dreamworks; Emergency Medical Services; Los Angeles Times; Nutritional Support Services; Ocular Surgery News; The Progressive; Radiology Today; Rehab Management; The Russian. Honours: Journalism Scholarship, Ford Motor Co; Communications Scholarship, University of Pennsylvania; Director of Continuing Education, Ivy League Association of Southern California, 1986-; Distinguished Service Award, 1990. Memberships: National Association of Science Writers; American Medical Writers Association. Address: 9936 Ramona Street, No 5, Bellflower, CA 90706-6951, USA.

KOURVETARIS George A, b. 21 Nov 1933, Eleochorion, Arcadia, Greece. Professor of Sociology; Writer; Editor. m. (1) Toula Savas, 22 Nov 1966, div 1987, 2 sons, 1 daughter, (2) Vassia Dumas Siapkaris, 1998. Education: Associate Degree, Teacher's College, Tripolis, Greece, 1955; BS, Loyola University, Chicago, 1963; MA, Honours, Roosevelt University, Chicago, 1965; PhD, Northwestern University, Evanston, Illinois, 1969. Appointments: Assistant Professor, Chicago City College, 1967; Fellow and Lecturer, Northwestern University, 1967-68; Assistant Professor, 1969-73, Associate Professor, 1973-78, Professor of Sociology, 1978-,

Northern Illinois University, DeKalb; Founder-Editor, The Journal of Political and Military Sociology, 1973-. Publications: First and Second Generation Greeks in Chicago: An Inquiry Into Their Stratification and Mobility Patterns, 1971; Social Origins and Political Orientations of Officer Corps in a World Perspective (co-author), 1973; World Perspectives in the Sociology of the Military (co-editor), 1977; Political Sociology: Readings in Research and Theory (co-editor), 1980; Society and Politics: An Overview and Reappraisal of Political Sociology (co-author), 1980; A Profile of Modern Greece: In Search of Identity (co-author), 1987; Social Thought, 1994, reprinted 1997; The Impact of European Integration: Political, Sociological, and Economic Changes (co-editor), 1996; Political Sociology: Structure and Process, 1997; Studies on Greek Americans, 1997; Studies on Moden Greek Society and Politics, 1999. Contributions to: Various scholarly books and journals, over 60 articles and over 35 book reviews. Honours: Various academic grants and awards; Heritage Award, Greek American Community Services, Chicago, 1987; Recognition Award, Hellenic Council on Education, Chicago, 1991; Department Recognition Award for the Silver Anniversary of the Founding of the Journal of Political and Military Sociology. Memberships: American Sociological Association; European Community Studies Association; Modern Greek Studies Association; Southeast European Association. Address: 109 Andresen Court, DeKalb, IL 60115, USA.

KOVAL Leonid Ben Josif, b. 5 Feb 1926, Bobruisk. Writer. 1 son, 2 daughters. Education: Higher, State University, Belorussia, Faculty of Journalism. Appointments: Journalist, Editor of Newspapers in Belorussia & Latvia. Publications: Leap Through The Night, 1973; Wild Pear Roots, novel, 1988; Moan, novel, 1990; The Book of Salvation, 2 volumes, historical documentary research of the holocaust, 1993; Hours of Love, poetry & prose, 1997; Eyes of the Earth, poetry, 1999. Contributions to: Hundreds of articles in Latvian, Israels, Belorus and others. Honours: Winner, many literary prizes in Belorussia & Latvia. Membership: Union of Writers, Latvia. Address: Leonid Koval, Turaidas St 98/2, Jurmala, LV-2015, Latvia.

KOVEL Ralph, b. USA. Author; Company President. m. 1 son, 1 daughter. Appointment: Editor-Publisher, Kovels on Antiques and Collectibles Newsletter, 1974-. Publications: Kovels' Dictionary of Marks, Pottery and Porcelain, 1953, updated edition, 1995; A Directory of American Silver, Pewter and Silver Plate, 1958; American Country Furniture 1780-1875, 1963; Kovels' Know Your Antiques, 1967, 4th edition, 1990; Kovels' Antiques and Collectibles Price List, annually since 1968-; Kovels' Bottles Price List, biennially, 1971-; Kovels' Collector's Guide for Collector Plates, Figurines, Paperweights and Other Limited Edition Items, 1978; Kovels' Collectors' Guide to Limited Editions, 1974; Kovels' Collector's Guide to American Art Pottery, 1974; Kovels' Organizer for Collectors, 1978, 2nd edition, 1983; Kovels' Illustrated Price Guide to Royal Doulton, 1980, 2nd edition, 1984; Kovels' Depression, Glass and American Dinnerware, Price List, 1981, 5th edition, 1995; Kovels' Know Your Collectibles, 1981; Kovels' Book of Antique Labels, 1982; Kovels' Collectors Source Book, 1983; Kovels' New Dictionary of Marks, Pottery and Porcelain, 1850-Present, 1985; Kovel's Advertising Collectibles Price List, 1986; Kovels' Guide to Selling Your Antiques and Collectibles, 1987, updated edition, 1990; Kovels' American Silver Marks, 1650 to the Present, 1989; Kovels' Quick Tios: 799 Helpful Hints on How to Care for Your Collectibles, 1995. Contributions to: Periodicals. Honours: Recipient of numerous honours and awards. Address: 9090 Bank Street, Valley View, OH 44125, USA.

KOWALCZYK David Theodore, b. 22 Nov 1952, New York, USA. Teacher; Writer. Education: BA, 1974, MA, English and Creative Writing, 1988, State University of New York. Appointments: English Instructor, Arizona State University, 1983-84, Genesee Community College, 1987-93. Publication: A Gentle Metamorphosis, 1993. Contributions to: Albany Review; Maryland Review; Oxalis; Entelechy. Honours: 1st Prize, Poetry

Competition, City Magazine, 1984; First Prize, Fiction, Chatauqua Council on Arts Awards, 1990. Membership: Phi Beta Kappa. Address: 73-72 Yong-Ho Dong, Changwon City, Kylingnam-Do, 641-041, South Korea.

KOWALSKI Kazimierz (Maria), b. 18 Aug 1926, Chelmno, Poland. Writer. m. Stanislawa Novak, 12 June 1948, 1 son, 1 daughter. Education: University of Wroclaw. Appointment: Polish Radio, Opole, 1954-92. Publications: Some 30 books; Many radio plays; Various translations. Contributions to: Many publications. Honours: Voivodship Literary Awards, 1959, 1984, 1991; Jan Langowski Award, 1981; Main Award, President of Polish Radio and Television, 1982; Opole City Manager's Literary Award, 1996. Memberships: National Council of Culture; Society of Polish Writers. Address: ul Strzelcow Bytomskich 5 m 6, 45 084 Opole, Poland.

KOWALSKI Marian, b. 8 Sept 1936, Szymonki, Poland. Writer. m. Jadwiga Abrahamow, 13 Jan 1961, 1 daughter. Education: MA, University of Wroclaw. Publications: Many novels, short stories, plays and screenplays. Contributions to: Various publications. Honours: Several awards. Memberships: Polish Marine Writers Association; Polish Writers Union. Address: ul Szafera 130 m 12, 71-245 Szczecin, Poland.

KOZAK Henryk (Jozef), b. 15 July 1945, Krasna, Poland. Writer; Poet. m. Maria Tomasiewicz, 1 July 1967, 2 sons. Education: MA, History, University of Marie Curie-Sklodowskiej, 1969. Publications: Various novels and books of poetry. Contributions to: Numerous journals and magazines. Honours: Josef Czechowicz Literary Awards, 1980, 1987. Membership: Society of Polish Writers. Address: ul Paryska 7 m 6, 20 854 Lublin, Poland.

KOZBELT Laurie, b. 11 Nov 1963, Greensburg, Pennsylvania, USA. Writer; Editor; Designer. Education: BA magna cum laude, Journalism, Indiana University of Pennsylvania, 1985; MA summa cum laude, Journalism, Communications, Point Park College, Pittsburgh, 1991. Appointments: Editor, Designer, Allegheny Ludlum Corp, 1988-; Contributing Editor, Out Publishing Co, Pittsburgh, Pennsylvania, 1991. Contributions to: Hundreds of news and feature articles in various publications, 1983-; News and features articles, Out monthly magazine, 1988-. Honours: Winner's Circle Award for Best Newsletter, International Association of Business Communicators, 1985; Best in the East Award for Best Internal Publication, Virginia Society for Hospital Public Relations and Marketing, 1985; Gold Quill, International Association of Business Communicators, 1986; 3 Effie Awards, 1986, 4 Effie Awards, 1987, Editors Forum; Honourable Mention, 1987, Award of Excellence, 1991, Matrix Award, Women in Communications; Design Finalist, International Mercury Award, MerComm Inc, 1990; Honourable Mentions, 1992, 1993, Printing Industry of Western Pennsylvania. Memberships: International Association of Business Communicators; Women in Communications Inc. Address: 3004 Greenridge Drive, Verona, PA 15147, USA.

KOZER José, b. 28 Mar 1940, Havana, Cuba. Retired Professor of Spanish Literature and Language; Poet; Writer. m. Guadalupe Kozer, 15 Dec 1974, 2 daughters. Education: BA, New York University, 1965; MA, PhD Equivalent, 1983, Queens College of the City University of New York. Appointment: Professor of Spanish Literature and Language, Queens College of the City University of New York, 1960-97. Publications: Poetry: 13 chapbooks, 1974-96. Other: 15 books, 1972-97. Contributions to: Numerous poetry magazines, literary journals, and newspapers in North and South America, and Spain. Honours: CINTAS Foundation Award, 1973; Julio Tovar Poetry Prize, 1974; City University of New York/PSC Foundation Award, 1991. Address: 6937 Bay Drive, No 511, Miami Beach, FL 33141, USA.

KOZOL Jonathan, b. 5 Sept 1936, Boston, Massachusetts, USA. Author. Education: Harvard College; Magdalen College, Oxford, England. Appointments: Teacher and Education Director, Boston

area, 1964-74; Lecturer, numerous universities, 1973-97. Publications: Death At An Early Age, 1967; Free Schools, 1972; The Night is Dark, 1975; Children of the Revolution, 1978; On Being a Teacher, 1979; Prisoners of Silence, 1980; Illiterate America, 1985; Rachel and Her Children, 1988; Savage Inequalities, 1991; Amazing Grace, 1995. Honours: Rhodes Scholar, 1958; National Book Award, 1968; Guggenheim Fellowships, 1972, 1984, 1985; Field Foundation Fellow, 1973, 1974; Rockefeller Fellow, 1978; Robert F Kennedy Memorial Book Award, 1989; Lannan Book Award, 1994; Anisfield-Wolf Book Award, 1996. Address: PO Box 145, Byfield, MA 01922, USA.

KRAEUTER David Warren, b. 21 Apr 1941, Homestead, Pennsylvania, USA. Librarian; Writer; Editor. Education: BA, Geneva College, 1963; MLS, University of Pittsburgh, 1968. Appointment: Editor, Pittsburgh Oscillator, 1986-95. Publications: Radio and Television Pioneers, 1992; British Radio and Television Pioneers, 1993; Radio and Electronics Pioneers, 1994; Index to Radio and Electronics Patents, 1995; Numerical Index to Radio and Electronic Patents, 1997. Other: Editor, 7 radio monographs, Pittsburgh Antique Radio Society, 1990-95. Honour: Antique Wireless Association, Ace Author Award, 1992. Address: 506 East Wheeling Street, Washington, PA 15301, USA.

KRAMER Aaron, b. 13 Dec 1921, Brooklyn, New York, USA. Professor of English Emeritus; Author; Poet; Translator. m. Katherine Kolodny, 10 Mar 1942, 2 daughters. Education: BA, 1941, MA, 1951, Brooklyn College; PhD, New York University, 1966. Appointments: Instructor, 1961-63, Assistant Professor, 1963-66, Adelphi University; Lecturer, Queens College, Flushing, New York, 1966-68; Associate Professor, 1966-70, Professor of English, 1970-91, Professor Emeritus, 1991-, Dowling College, Oakdale, New York. Publications: The Glass Mountain, 1946; Poetry and Prose of Heine, 1948; Denmark Vesey, 1952; The Tinderbox, 1954; Serenade, 1957; Tune of the Calliope, 1958; Moses, 1962; Rumshinsky's Hat, 1964; Rilke: Visions of Christ, 1967; The Prophetic Tradition in American Poetry, 1968; Poetry Therapy (co-author), 1969; Melville's Poetry, 1972; On the Way to Palermo, 1973; Poetry the Healer (co-author), 1973; The Emperor of Atlantis, 1975; O Golden Land, 1976; Death Takes a Holiday, 1979; Carousel Parkway, 1980; The Burning Bush, 1983; In the Suburbs, 1986; A Century of Yiddish Poetry, 1989; Indigo, 1991; Life Guidance Through Literature (co-author), 1991; Dora Teitelboim: Selected Poems (editor and translator), 1995. Contributions to: Professional journals. Honours: Hart Crane Memorial Award, 1969; Eugene O'Neill Theatre Center Prize, 1983; National Endowment for the Humanities Grant, 1993; Festschrift published in his honour, 1995. Memberships: American Society of Composers, Authors and Publishers; Association for Poetry Therapy; Edna St Vincent Millay Society; E E Cummings Society; International Academy of Poets; PEN; Walt Whitman Birthplace Association, executive board, 1969-85. Address: 96 Van Bomel Boulevard, Oakdale, NY 11769, USA.

KRAMER Dale (Vernon), b. 13 July 1936, Mitchell, South Dakota, USA. Professor Emeritus of English; Writer. m. Cheris Gamble Kramarae, 21 Dec 1960, 2 children. Education: BS, South Dakota State University, 1958; MA, 1960, PhD, 1963, Case Western Reserve University. Appointments: Instructor, 1962-63, Assistant Professor, 1963-65, Ohio University; Assistant Professor, 1965-67, Associate Professor, 1967-71, Professor of English, 1971-96, Acting Head, Department of English, 1982, 1986-87, Associate Dean, College of Arts and Sciences, 1992-95, University of Illinois; Associate Member, Center for Advanced Study, Urbana, Illinois, 1971; Associate Vice-Provost, University of Oregon, 1990. Publications: Charles Robert Maturin, 1973; Thomas Hardy: The Forms of Tragedy, 1975; Critical Approaches to the Fiction of Thomas Hardy (editor), 1979; Thomas Hardy: The Woodlanders (editor), 1981, 2nd edition, 1985; Thomas Hardy: The Mayor of Casterbridge (editor), 1987; Critical Essays on Thomas Hardy: The Novels (editor), 1990; Thomas Hardy: Tess of the d'Urbervilles, 1991; The Cambridge Companian to Thomas Hardy, 1999. Contributions to: Professional journals. Honours: American Philosophical Society Grants, 1969, 1986; National Endowment for the Humanities Grant, 1986; Boydston Prize, Association for Documentary editing, 1997. Memberships: Association of American University Professors; Association for Documentary Editing; Modern Language Association; Society for Textual Scholarship; Victorian Periodicals Society. Address: c/o Department of English, University of Illinois at Urbana-Champaign, Champaign, IL 61820, USA.

KRAMER Leonie Judith (Dame), b. 1 Oct 1924, Melbourne, Victoria, Australia. University Professor and Chancellor; Writer. m. Harold Kramer, 2 Apr 1952, dec, 2 daughters. Education: BA, University of Melbourne, 1946; DPhil, University of Oxford, 1953. Appointments: University Professor; Chair, Board of Directors, National Institute of Dramatic Art, 1987-92; Deputy Chairman and Senior Fellow, Institute of Public Affairs, 1988-96; Deputy Chancellor, 1989-91, Chancellor, 1991-, University of Sydney. Publications: Henry Handel Richardson and Some of Her Sources, 1954; Companion to Australia Felix, 1962; Coast to Coast, 1963-64, 1965; Myself When Laura: Fact and Fiction in Henry Handel Richardson's School Career, 1966; Henry Handel Richardson, 1967; Language and Literature: A Synthesis (with R D Eagleson), 1976; A D Hope (co-editor), 1979; Oxford History of Australian Literature, 1981; Oxford Anthology of Australian Literature, 1985; My Country: Australian Poetry and Short Stories, 2 volumes, 1985; James McAuley: Poetry, Essays and Personal Commentary (editor), 1988; David Campbell: Collected Poems (editor), 1989; Collected Poems of James McAuley (editor), 1995. Contributions to: Numerous journals. Honours: Dame of the Order of the British Empire, 1982; Companion of the Order of Australia, 1993; Honorary doctorates. Membership: Australian Academy of Humanities, fellow. Address: 12 Vaucluse Road, Vaucluse, New South Wales 2030, Australia.

KRAMER Lotte Karoline, b. 22 Oct 1923, Mainz, Germany. Poet; Painter. m. Frederic Kramer, 20 Feb 1943, 1 son. Education: Art; History of Art. Publications: Poetry: Scrolls, 1979; Ice Break, 1980; Family Arrivals, 1981; A Lifelong House, 1983; The Shoemaker's Wife, 1987; The Desecration of Trees, 1994; Earthquake and Other Poems, 1994; Selected and New Poems, 1980-1997. Contributions to: Anthologies, newspapers, reviews, quarterlies and journals. Honour: 2nd Prize, York Poetry Competition, 1972. Memberships: Decorative and Fine Arts Society; PEN; Peterborough Museum Society; Poetry Society; Ver Poets; Writers in Schools. Address: 4 Apsley Way, Longthorpe, Peterborough PE3 9NE, England.

KRANTZ Judith (Tarcher), b. 9 Jan 1928, New York, New York, USA. Writer. m. Stephen Falk Krantz, 19 Feb 1954, 2 sons. Education: BA, Wellesley College, 1948. Appointments: Fashion Editor, Good Housekeeping, 1949-56; Contributor, McCalls, 1956-59, Ladies Home Journal, 1959-71; Contributing West Coast Editor, Cosmopolitan, 1971-79. Publications: Scruples, 1978; Princess Daisy, 1980; Mistral's Daughter, 1982; I'll Take Manhattan, 1986; Till We Meet Again, 1989; Dazzle, 1990; Scruples Two, 1992; Lovers, 1994; Spring Collection, 1996; The Jewels of Tessa Kent, 1998. Membership: PEN. Address: c/o Morton Janklow, Lyn Nesbitt Associates, 598 Madison Avenue, New York, NY 10022, USA.

KRAPF Norbert, b. 14 Nov 1943, Jasper, Indiana, USA. Professor of English; Writer. m. 13 June 1970, 1 son, 1 daughter. Education: BA,English, St Joseph's College, Indiana, 1965; MA, English, 1966, PhD, English and American Literature, 1971, University of Notre Dame. Appointments: Faculty, 1970-84, Professor of English, 1984-, Long Island University. Publications: Arriving on Paumanok, 1979; Lines Drawn from Durer, 1981; Circus Songs, 1983; A Dream of Plum Blossoms, 1985; Under Open Sky: Poets on William Cullen Bryant (editor), 1986; Beneath the Cherry Sapling: Legends from Franconia (editor and translator), 1988; Shadows on the Sundial: Selected Early Poems of Rainer Maria Rilke (editor and translator), 1990; Somewhere in Southern Indiana: Poems of Midwestern Origins, 1993; Finding the Grain: Pioneer Journals and Letters from Dubois County, Indiana, 1996; Blue-eyed Grass: Poems of Germany, 1997. Contributions to: Professional journals. Address: c/o Department of English, Long Island University, Brookville, NY 11548, USA.

KRATT Mary, b. 7 June 1936, Beckley, West Virginia, USA. Writer; Poet. m. Emil F Kratt, 29 Aug 1959, 1 son, 2 daughters. Education: BA, Agnes Scott College, 1958; MA, University of North Carolina at Charlotte, 1992. Publications: Southern Is, 1985; Legacy: The Myers Park Story, 1986; The Imaginative Spirit: Literary Heritage of Charlotte and Mecklenburg County, 1988; A Little Charlotte Scrapbook, 1990; A Bird in the House, 1991; The Only Thing I Fear is a Cow and a Drunken Man (poems and prose), 1991; Charlotte: Spirit of the New South, 1992; On the Steep Side (poems), 1993. Contributions to: Newspapers, reviews, and magazines. Honours: Lyricist Prize, 1982; Oscar Arnold Young Award for Best Original Poetry Book by a North Carolinian, 1983; Sidney Lanier Award, North Carolina Poetry Society, 1985; St Andrews Writer and Community Award, 1994; Distinguished Alumnae Writer Award, Agnes Scott College, 1994; MacDowell Colony Residency, 1996. Memberships: North Carolina Writers Conference, chairman, vice president, secretary, 1989-92; North Carolina Writers Network, board member; Poets and Writers. Address: 7001 Sardis Road, Charlotte, NC 28270, USA.

KRAUSS Bruno. See: **BULMER Henry Kenneth.**

KRAUSS Clifford, b. 30 July 1953, New York, New York, USA. Journalist. Education: BA, Vassar College, 1975; MA, History, University of Chicago, 1976; MS, Journalism, Columbia University, 1977. Publication: Inside Central America: Its People, Politics and History, 1991. Contributions to: Nation; Foreign Affairs; Wilson Quarterly; Times Literary Supplement. Address: 1305 Corcoran Street North West, Washington DC 20009, USA.

KRAUSS Rosalind, b. 30 Nov 1940, Washington, District of Columbia, USA. Art Historian; Writer. m. Richard I Krauss, 17 Sept 1962, div. Education: AB, Wellesley College; MA, PhD, Harvard University. Appointments: Professor of Art History, Columbia University; Guest Curator. Publications: Terminal Iron Works: The Sculpture of David Smith, 1971; Joan Miro: Magnetic Fields, 1972; Line as Language, 1974; Passages in Modern Sculpture, 1977; Cindy Sherman: 1975-1993, 1993. Contributions to: Art in America; October; Partisan Review; Artforum (editor). Honour: Mather Award for Criticism, College Art Association, 1973. Address: Department of Art History, Columbia University, 2960 Columbia University, New York, NY 10027, USA.

KRAUZER Steven M(ark), (Terry Nelson Bonner), b. 9 June 1948, Jersey City, New Jersey, USA. Writer. m. Dorri T Karasek, 2 Nov 1992, 2 daughters. Education: BA, Yale University, 1970; MA, English Literature, University of New Hampshire, 1974. Publications: The Cord Series, 1982-86; The Executioner Series, 1982-83; Blaze, 1983; The Diggers, 1983; The Dennison's War Series, 1984-86; Framework, 1989; Brainstorm, 1991; Rojak's Rule, 1992. Anthologies: Great Action Stories, 1977; The Great American Detective, 1978; Stories into Film, 1979; Triquarterly 48: Western Stories, 1980. Contributions to: Magazines. Memberships: Writers Guild of America West; Authors Guild; Authors League; Mystery Writers of America. Address: c/o Virginia Barber Literary Agency, 101 5th Avenue, New York, NY 10003, USA.

KRESS Nancy, b. 20 Jan 1948, Buffalo, New York, USA. Teacher; Writer. m. (1) Michael Kress, div, 2 sons, (2) Mark P Donnelly, 19 Aug 1988. Education: BS, State University of New York College, Plattsburgh, 1969; MS, Education, 1978, MA, English, 1979, State University of New York College, Brockport. Appointments: Elementary School Teacher, Penn Yan, 1970-73; Adjunct Instructor, State University of New York College, Brockport, 1980-; Senior Copywriter, Stanton and Hucko, Rochester, 1984-. Publications: The Prince of Morning Bells, 1981; The Golden Grove, 1984; The White Pipes, 1985; Trinity and Other Stories, 1985; An Alien Light, 1988; Brain Rose, 1990; Maximum Light, 1998. Contributions to: Anthologies and periodicals. Honour: Nebula Award, Science Fiction Writers of America, 1985. Membership: Science Fiction Writers of America. Address: 50 Sweden Hill Road, Brockport, NY 14420, USA.

KRESSEL Neil Jeffrey, b. 28 Aug 1957, Newark, New Jersey, USA. Writer; College Professor; Psychologist. m. Dorit Fuchs Kressel JD, 11 Aug 1991, 1 son, 1 daughter. Education: BA, Magna Cum Laude, 1978, MA, 1978, Brandeis University; MA, 1981, PhD, 1983, Harvard University. Appointment: Associate Professor of Psychology, William Paterson University of New Jersey, Wayne, 1984-99; Full Professor 1999-. Publications: Political Psychology, 1993; Mass Hate: The Global Rise of Genocide and Terror, 1996. Contributions to: American Journal of Sociology; Political Psychology; Contemporary Psychology; Midstream; Judaism; New York Daily News; Boston Globe; Boston Herald; Aggressive Behaviour; Journal of Psychohistory; The Forward; Teaching of Psychology. Honour: Mass Hate, selected as an Outstanding book for 1996 by Choice Magazine. Literary Agent: Susan Ann Protter, New York. Address: Department of Psychology, William Paterson College of New Jersey, Wayne, NJ 07470, USA.

KREUZENAU. See: **LAW Michael.**

KRIEGER Murray, b. 27 Nov 1923, Newark, New Jersey, USA. University Research Professor; Writer. m. Joan Alice Stone, 15 June 1947, 1 son, 1 daughter. Education: Rutgers University, 1940-42; MA, University of Chicago, 1948; PhD, Ohio State University, 1952. Appointments: Instructor in English, Kenyon College, 1948-49, Ohio State University, 1951-52; Assistant Professor, then Associate Professor, University of Minnesota, 1952-58; Professor of English, 1958-63, Associate Member, Center for Advanced Study, 1961-62, University of Illinois; M F Carpenter Professor of Literary Criticism, University of Iowa, 1963-66; Professor of English and Director of the Program in Criticism, University of California at Irvine, 1966-85; Professor of English, UCLA, 1972-83; University Professor, 1974-94, Co-Director, 1975-77, Director, 1977-81, School of Criticism and Theory, Honorary Senior Fellow, 1981-; Director, Humanities Research Institute, 1987-89, University Research Professor, 1994-, University of California. Publications: The Problems of Aesthetics (editor with Eliseo Vivas), 1953; The New Apologists for Poetry, 1956; The Tragic Vision, 1960; A Window to Criticism: Shakespeare's Sonnets and Modern Poetics, 1964; Northrop Frye in Modern Criticism (editor), 1966; The Play and Place of Criticism, 1967; the Classic Vision, 1971; Theory of Criticism: A Tradition and Its System, 1976; Directions for Criticism: Structuralism and Its Alternatives (editor with L S Dembo), 1977; Poetic Presence and Illusion, 1979; Arts on the Level, 1981; The Aims of Representation: Subject/Text/History (editor), 1987; Words About Words About Words: Theory, Criticism and the Literary Text, 1988; A Reopening of Closure: Organicism Against Itself, 1989; Ekphrasis: The Illusion of the Natural Sign, 1992; The Ideological Imperative: Repression and Resistance in Recent American Theory, 1993; The Institution of Theory, 1994. Contributions to: Scholarly publications. Honours: Guggenheim Fellowships, 1956-57, 1961-62; American Council of Learned Societies Postdoctoral Fellowship, 1966-67; National Endowment for the Humanities Grant, 1971-72; Rockefeller Foundation Fellowship, 1978, and Resident Scholar, Bellagio, Italy, 1990; Humboldt Foundation Research Prize, Federal Republic of Germany, 1986-87; Medal, University of California at Irvine, 1990. Memberships: Academy of Literary Studies; American Academy of Arts and Sciences, fellow; International Association of University Professors of

English; Modern Language Association. Address: 407 Pinecrest Drive, Laguna Beach, CA 92651, USA.

KRIEGLER-ELLIOTT Carolyn Patricia, b. 14 Apr 1949, Niagara Falls, New York, USA. Author and Illustrator of Children's Books. m. Tom Elliott, 8 Apr 1983. Education: BFA Honours, Illustration, Virginia Commonwealth University; Early Childhood Education, St Petersburg Junior College, Tarpon Springs, Florida, 1987. Publications: Rosie Moonshine (with Anthony Holcroft), 1989; A Lollipop, Please, 1989; Good Night, Little Brother, 1989; Pins and Needles, 1989; Rain, 1990; Chen Li and the River Spirit (with Anthony Holcroft), 1990; Lulu, 1990; Lucky for Some, 1990; Cat Concert, 1990; A Present for Anna, 1990; Higgledy Piggledy Hobbledy Hoy, 1991; Woodsmoke, 1991; The Cave, 1991; Googer in Space, 1991; Night Cat, 1991; By Jingo!, 1992; What Peculiar People, 1992; Good Night, Alice, 1992; Island in the Lagoon (with Anthony Holcroft), 1992; A Dog for Keeps (with Pauline Cartwright), 1992. Contributions to: Magazines. Memberships: New Zealand Book Council; PEN; Sathya Sai Organization of New Zealand. Address: c/o Richards Literary Agency, PO Box 31240, Milford, Auckland 9, New Zealand.

KRIST Gary Michael, b. 23 May 1957, New Jersey, USA. Writer. m. Elizabeth Cheng, 2 Oct 1983, 1 daughter. Education: AB, Comparative Literature, Princeton University, 1979; Fulbright Scholar, Universität Konstanz, 1980. Publications: The Garden State (short stories), 1988; Bone by Bone (short stories), 1994; Bad Chemistry (novel), 1998; Chaos Theory (novel), 1999. Contributions to: New York Times Book Review; Salon Internet; Washington Post; Hudson Review; New Republic. Honour: Sue Kaufman Prize, American Academy of Arts and Letters, 1989. Memberships: PEN; National Book Critics Circle. Literary Agent: Irene Skolnick Agency. Address: 22 West 23rd Street, New York, NY 10010, USA.

KRISTENSEN Lise Lotte, b. 13 May 1961, Frederiksberg, Denmark. Writer; Poet. Education: University of Copenhagen. Publications: Immediately But Flowing, 1989; The Time it Takes Being God, 1991; Southern Balm, 1994. Contributions to: Various publications. Memberships: Buddhist Forum; Committee for World Peace; Danish Writers Union. Address: Toldbodgade 14B Tv, 1253 Copenhagen, Denmark.

KRISTEVA Julia, b. 24 June 1941, Silven, Bulgaria. Professor of Linguistics; Psychoanalyst; Writer. m. 1 son. Education: Diploma, Philology, University of Sofia, 1963; Preparation for Doctorate, Academy of Sciences and Comparative Literature, Sofia; Ecole pratique des Hautes-Etudes, Paris; Doctorate, French Literature, 1968; Doctorat d'Etat es Lettres, University of Paris VII, 1973. Appointments: Research in Linguistics and French Literature, Laboratory of Social Anthropology, l'École des Hautes Études en Sciences Sociales, 1967-73; Professor of Linguistics, 1973-, University of Paris VII; Permanent Visiting Professor, Department of French Literature, Columbia University, New York, 1974; Private Psychoanalytic Practice, Paris, 1978-; Director of Research Diplomas in Psychopathology and Semiology, University of Paris VI, 1988; Director of Doctoral School, University of Paris 7, 1992; Permanent Visiting Professor, Department of Comparative Literature, University of Toronto, Canada, 1992. Publications: Non-Fiction: Séméiotike: Recherches pour une sémanalyse, 1969, English translation as Desire in Language: A Semiotic Approach to Literature and Art, 1980; Le Langage, cet inconnu, Une initiation a la linguistique, 1969, English translation as Language: The Unknown: An Initiation into Linguistics, 1989; Le Texte du roman, 1970; La Révolution du langage poétique, 1974, English translation as Revolution in Poetic Language, 1984; Des Chinoises, 1974, English translation as About Chinese Women, 1977; La Traversée des signes (with others), 1975; Polylogue, 1977, English translation, 1980; Folle Vérité (with Jean Michel Ribettes), 1979; Pouvoirs de l'horreur, Essai sur l'abjection, 1980, English translation as Powers of Horror: An Essay on Abjection, 1982; Histoires d'amour, 1983, English translation as Tales of Love,

1987; Au commencement était l'amour: Psychanalyse et foi, 1985, English translation as In the Beginning Was Love: Psychoanalysis and Faith, 1987; Soleil noir: Depression et melancolie, 1987, English translation as Black Sun: Depression and Melancholia, 1989; Etrangers à nous-mêmes, 1988, English translation as Strangers to Ourselves, 1991; Lettre ouverte à harlem Désir, 1990, English translation as Nations Without Nationalism, 1993; Les Nouvelles Maladies de l'âmé, 1993, English translation as New Maladies of the Soul, 1995; Le Temps sensible: Proust et l'Expérience littéraire, 1994, English translation as Time and Sense: Proust and the Experience of Literature, 1996. Fiction: Les Samouraïs, 1990, English translation as The Samurai, 1992; Le Vieil Homme et les loups, 1991, English translation as The Old Man and the Wolves, 1994; Le Temps sensible: Proust et l'Expérience littéraire, 1994; Possessions (novel), 1996; La révolte intime: Pouvoirs et limites de la psychanalyse II, 1997; Contre la dépression nationale: Conversation avec Philippe Petit, 1997; L'avenir d'une révolte, 1998. Contributions to: Books, professional journals, and periodicals. Honours: Chevalier des Arts et des Lettres, 1987; Prix Henri Hertz, Chancellerie des universités de Paris, 1989; Chevalier de l'Ordre du Merite, 1991; Chevalier de la Légion d'Honneur, 1997. Memberships: Editorial Board, Tel quel, 1970-82; Société psychanalytique de Paris. Address: c/o University of Paris VII-Denis Diderot, UFR de Sciences des Textes et Documents, 34-44, 2e étage, 2 place Jussieu, 75005 Paris, France.

KRISTO Odi. See: GRILLO Odhise.

KRISTOF Nicholas D(onabet), b. 27 Apr 1959, Chicago, Illinois, USA. Journalist; Writer. m. Sheryl WuDunn, 1988, 2 sons. Education: BA, Harvard University, 1981; BA and MA, Law, University of Oxford, 1983; Diploma, Arabic, American University, Cairo, 1984; Taipei Language Institute, 1987-88. Appointments: Economics Reporter, 1984-85, Financial Correspondent, Los Angeles Bureau, 1985-86, Chief, Hong Kong Bureau, 1986-87, Beijing Bureau, 1988-93, Tokyo Bureau, 1995-, New York Times; Visiting Fellow, East-West Center, 1993; Visiting Scholar, Linfield College, 1994. Publications: China Wakes: The Struggle For the Soul of a Rising Power (with Sheryl WuDunn), 1994. Contributions to: Periodicals. Honours: Rhodes Scholar, 1981-83; Pulitzer Prize for International Reporting, 1990; George Polk Award for Foreign Reporting, Long Island University, 1990; Hal Boyle Award, Overseas Press Club, 1990; Citations for Excellence in Journalism, 1994, 1996. Address: c/o Foreign Desk, New York Times, 229 West 43rd Street, New York, NY 10036, USA.

KRISTOL Irving, b. 22 Jan 1920, New York, New York, USA. Editor; Writer; Professor of Social Thought (retired). m. Gertrude Himmelfarb, 18 June 1942, 1 son, 1 daughter. Education: City College, New York City, 1940. Appointments: Managing Editor, Commentary Magazine, 1947-52; Co-Founder and Co-Editor, Encounter magazine, 1953-58; Editor, The Reporter magazine, 1959-60; Executive Vice-President, Basic Books Inc, 1961-69; Co-Editor, The Public Interest magazine, 1965-; Faculty, New York University, 1969-88; John M Olin Senior Fellow, American Enterprise Institute, 1987-. Publications: On the Democratic Idea in America, 1972; Two Cheers for Capitalism, 1978; Reflections of a Neoconservative, 1983; Neoconservatism: The Autobiography of an Idea, 1995. Editor: Encounters (with Stephen Spender and Melvin Lasky), 1963; Confrontation: The Student Rebellion and the University (with Daniel Bell), 1969; Capitalism Today, 1971; The American Commonwealth (with Nathan Glazer), 1976; The Americans (with Paul Weaver), 1976; The Crisis in Economic Theory, 1981; Third World Instability (with others), 1985. Contributions to: Various publications. Memberships: American Academy of Arts and Sciences, fellow; Council on Foreign Relations. Address: c/o The Public Interest, 1112 16th Street North West, Suite 530, Washington, DC 20036, USA.

KROETSCH Robert, b. 26 June 1927, Heisler, Alberta, Canada. Professor of English; Writer. Education: BA,

University of Alberta, 1948; MA, Middlebury College, Vermont, 1956; PhD, University of Iowa, 1961. Appointments: Assistant Professor, 1961-65, Associate Professor, 1965-68, Professor of English, 1968-78, State University of New York at Binghamton; Professor of English, 1978-85, Distinguished Professor, 1985-, University of Manitoba. Publications: The Studhorse Man, 1969; Badlands, 1975; What the Cow Said, 1978; Alibi, 1983; Completed Field Notes (poems), 1989; The Lovely Treachery of Words, 1989; The Puppeteer, 1992. Address: 4081 Cedar Hill Road, Victoria, British Columbia V8N 3C2, Canada.

KROETZ Franz Xaver, b. 25 Feb 1946, Munich, Germany. Dramatist; Author; Theatre Director; Publisher. m. Marie-Theres Relin, 4 children. Education: Max Reinhardt Seminar, Vienna. Appointments: Various appearannces as an actor; Co-Founder, Franz Xaver Kroetz Dramatik publishing house; Director, Münchener Kammerspiele. Publications: Gesammelte Stücke, 1975; Der Mondscheinknecht, 1981; Nicht Fisch nicht Fleisch, 1981; Frühe Stucke/Frühe Prosa, 1983; Furcht und Hoffnung der BRD: Das Stück, Das Stück, das Material, das Tagebuch, 1984; Bauern sterben, 1986; Nicaragua Tagebuch, 1986; Der Leibwächter, 1987; Stücke I-IV, 1988; Brasilian-Peru-Aufzeichnungen, 1986. Honours: Ludwig Thoma Medal, 1970; Fontane Prize, Berlin, 1972; Berlin Critics Prize for Literature, 1973; Hannoverian Drama Prize, 1974; Wilhelmine Lübke Prize, 1975; Mühlheim Drama Prize, 1976; Adolf Grimme Prize, 1987; Brecht PRize, Augsburg, 1995. Address: c/o Münchener Kammerspiele, Maximilianstrasse 26-28, D-80539 Munich, Germany.

KROHN Tim, b. 9 Feb 1965, Germany. Writer. Publications: De Siliwan in Stücken, 1994; Die apokalyptishe Show von den vie Flücher, 1996; Dreigroschenkabineh, 1997; La chaine et la chevre, 1997; Polly, 1998; Revolution mit Hund, 1998; Quatenbukinder, 1998. Honours: C F Meyer Prize, 1994. Membership: Swiss Writers Assocition, president. Address: Röntgenstr 75, CH-8005 Zurich, Switzerland.

KRONENFELD Judy Z, b. 17 July 1943, New York, New York, USA. University Lecturer; Poet; Writer. m. David Brian Kronenfeld, 21 June 1964, 1 son, 1 daughter. Education: BA, summa cum laude, Smith College, 1964; MA, 1966; PhD, 1971, Stanford University; University of Oxford, 1968-69. Appointments: Lecturer, 1971, 1984-, Visiting Scholar, 1977-78, 1981-83, Instructor, 1978, Visiting Assistant Professor, 1980-81, 1988-89, University of California at Riverside; Lecturer, 1972-73, 1978-79, Visiting Lecturer, 1984, 1985-86, Visiting Associate Professor, 1987, University of California at Irvine; Assistant Professor, Purdue University, 1976-77. Publications: Shadow of Wings (poems), 1991; King Lear and the Naked Truth: Rethinking the Language of Religion and Resistance, 1998. Contributions to: Articles in scholarly books and journals; Poems in anthologies, reviews, quarterlies, and magazines. Honours: Leverhulme Trust Fund Fellowship, 1968-69; Squaw Valley Community of Writers Scholarship, 1983; Non-Senate Academic Distinguished Researcher Award, University of California at Riverside, 1996-97. Address: c/o Department of Creative Writing, University of California at Riverside, Riverside, CA 92521, USA.

KROTZ Joseph Larry, b. 6 Apr 1948, Palmerston, Canada. Writer; Documentary Film Maker. 1 d. Education: BA, History, Glendon College, York University, Toronto, Canada, 1972. Publications: Urban Indians, 1980; Shutter Speed, novel, 1988; Indian Country, Inside Another Canada, 1990; Tourists, How Our Fastest Growing Industry is Changing the World, 1996. Membership: Writers Union of Canada. Literary Agent: New England Publishing Associates. Address: c/o PO Box 5, Chester, CT 06412, USA.

KRUGER Arnd, b. 1 July 1944, Mühlhausen. Professor of Sport Science. m. Barbara Weber, 11 Nov 1972, 2 sons, 1 daughter. Education: BA, UCLA, 1967; Dr Phil, University Cologne, Germany, 1971. Appointments: Managing Editor, 1971-74, University Assistant, 1974-78,

Associate Professor, 1978-80, Professor and Chair, University Göttingen, 1980-. Publications: Die Olympischen Spiele und Weltmeinung, 1972; Sport und Politik, 1975; Das Berufs Bild Des Trainers, 1980; Ritual and Record, 1990; Sport Tourismus, 1995; The Story of Workers Sport, 1996; Die Anfänge des Modernen Sports, 1984; Sport und Gesellschaft, 1981; Wie Die Medien Den Sport Aufbereiten, 1993; La Comune Eredità dello Sport in Europe, 1997. Contributions to: Journal of Sport History; International Journal of the History of Sport; Leistungssport; Sportreport. Honour: Semi-Final Olympic Games (1500m), 1968. Memberships: Arete; President of CESH, 1995-97. Address: Im Hacketal 3, 37136 Waake, Germany.

KRUKOWSKI Lucian Wladyslaw, b. 22 Nov 1929, New York, New York, USA. Professor of Philosophy; Artist; Writer. m. Marilyn Denmark, 17 Jan 1955, 1 daughter. Education: BA, Brooklyn College, 1952; BFA, Yale University, 1955; MS, Pratt Institute, 1958; PhD, Washington University, St Louis, 1977. Appointments: Faculty, Pratt Institute, 1955-69; Dean, School of Fine Arts, 1969-77, Professor of Philosophy, 1977-, Chairman, Department of Philosophy, 1986-89, Washington University, St Louis. Publications: Art and Concept, 1987; Aesthetic Legacies, 1992. Anthologies: The Arts, Society, and Literature, 1984; The Reasons of Art, 1985; Cultural Literacy and Arts Education, 1990; Ethics and Architecture, 1990; The Future of Art, 1990; Schopenhauer, Philosophy and the Arts, 1996. Contributions to: Professional journals. Memberships: American Philosophical Association; Society for Aesthetics. Address: PO Box 497, East Hampton, NY 11937, USA.

KRUMINS Anita Ilze, b. 15 Nov 1946, Flensburg, Germany. Educator; Writer. m. George Swede, 23 July 1974, 2 sons. Education: BA summa cum laude, 1973, MA, 1974, York University. Appointments: Instructor, Ryerson Polytechnic University, 1975-81; Chair, Business and Technical Communication, 1981-86; Appeals Chair, 1990-94, President, 1994-97, Ryerson Faculty Association; Nominating Chair, The Writers Union of Canada, 1996-97. Publications: Children's fiction: Quillby, The Porcupine Who Lost His Quills, co-author, 1979; Who's Going To Clean Up The Mess?, 1980, 1985; Mr Wurtzel And The Hallowe'en Bunny, 1982; Poetry: This Day's New Face, 1993. Contributions to: Brussels Sprout; Frogpond; Haiku Canada Newsletter; Inkstone; Lynx; Modern Haiku; Others. Honours: Canada Council Doctoral Fellowship, 1974; Ontario Arts Council Writers' Grants, 1980-83; Brady Award, Haiku Society of America, 1990. Memberships: The Writers' Union of Canada; Haiku Canada; Haiku Society of America. Address: 70 London Street, Toronto, Ontario, Canada M5S 2S8.

KRUMMACHER Jo(hann Henrich Karl Daniel), (Carl Danielson), b. 27 Dec 1946, Heidelberg, Germany. Writer; Minister. m. Ingrid Elisabeth Weng, 17 July 1986, 6 sons. Education: University of Heidelberg; University of Tübingen, 1972; Ordained to Ministry, Lutheran Church, 1972. Publications: Frieden im Klartext, 1980; Motivationen, 1982; Ratgeber für Kriegsdienstverweigerer, 1987; Übergänge, 1987; Wachzweige, 1991; Für jeden Sonn-und Feiertag, 1996. Contributions to: Deutsches Allgemeines Sonntagsblatt; Junge Kirche; Das Plateau; Sonntag Arkuell. Memberships: Verein für Kirche und Kunst, president, 1993; Protestant Academy, executive director, Bad Boll, 1996; vice-president, Foundation Church and Art, 1998-. Address: Akademieweg 11, D-73087 Bad Boll, Germany.

KRUPAT Arnold, b. 22 Oct 1941, New York, New York, USA. Professor; Writer; Editor. 1 son, 1 daughter. Education: BA, New York University, 1962; MA, 1965, PhD, 1967, Columbia University. Appointment: Professor, Sarah Lawrence College. Publications: For Those Who Come After, 1985; I Tell You Now (editor with Brian Swann), 1987; Recovering the Word (editor with Brian Swann), 1987; The Voice in the Margin, 1989; Ethnocriticism: Ethnography, History, Literature, 1992; New Voices: Essays on Native American Literature (editor), 1993; Native American Autobiography (editor), 1993; The Turn to the Native: Studies in Culture and Criticism, 1996; Everything Matters: Autobiographical Essays by Native American Writers (editor with Brian Swann), 1997. Contributions to: Numerous critical journals. Address: Sarah Lawrence College, Bronxville, NY 10708, USA.

KUCHKINA-PAVLOVA Olga Andreyevna, b. 9 Apr 1936, Moscow, Russia. Journalist; Playwright; Poet; Novelist. m. Valery Nikolayev, 24 Nov 1987, 1 daughter. Education: MA summa cum laude, Journalism, Moscow State University, 1958. Appointments: Correspondent, 1958-80, Columnist, 1980-, Komsomolskaya Pravda, 1958-80; Programme Host, Theater Hall, monthly TV Review, Central TV, Moscow, 1977-80. Publications: Farewell in April, Travel Diary; Passions by Barbara, play; The Face and the Landscape, book of essays; White Summer, book of plays; Communicating Vessel, book of poetry; Faces Dear to Russia, 2 volumes; Cadre, novel; Joseph and Nadezhda, play; Bes Gluzdy, story; Suvorov Atoll, Or Crossing to Pushkin Square, story; Krandievsky's Love to Alisa, story; The Philosopher and the Maid, novel. Contributions to: Arion; Noviy Mir; Druzhba Narodov; Zvezda; Oktyabr; Others. Address: 1-370 Kudrinskaya Square, Moscow 123242, Russia.

KUEI-HSIANG HWANG Hu-Yen, b. 13 Jan 1951, Taipei, Taiwan. Journalist; Columnist. m. 3 Jan 1974, 2 sons, 1 daughter. Education: MD, United Nations Open International University, 1993; PhD, Natural Medicine, American Pacific Coast University, 1994. Contributions to: Newspapers and other publications. Honours: Deputy Director General, International Biographical Centre, Cambridge, England; Deputy Governor, American Biographical Institute Research Association. Memberships: Society of Urban Planning, China; Society of Public Policy, China; Society of Surpass Psychology, China; Society of Land Economics, China; American Association of Parapsychology; World Association of Women Journalists and Writers. Address: 6F, No 26, Lane 50, I-Hsien Road, Taipei, Taiwan.

KUEPPER Philip Watson, b. 14 Aug 1948, Burlington, Iowa, USA. Poet; Short Story Writer. Education: BA, St Francis College, 1982. Contributions to: The Washingtonian, 1975; Currents, 1997. Honours: Golden Poet Award, World of Poetry, 1987-91. Memberships: Poets and Writers; Amherst Society. Address: 233 Bouton Street West, Stamford, CT 06907, USA.

KUHN Laura (Diane), b. 19 Jan 1953, San Francisco, California, USA. Musicologist; Former Assistant Professor. Education: Vocal and piano training, San Francisco, 1975-82; BA, Dominican College, San Rafael, California, 1981; MA, 1986, PhD, 1992, University of California at Los Angeles. Apointments: Member, San Francisco Symphony Chorus, 1980, Oakland Symphony Chorus, 1980-82; Music Critic, Independent Journal, Marin County, California, 1980-82; Reviewer, Los Angeles Times, 1982-87, New York Times, 1986-89; Vocalist, Daniel Lentz Group, 1983-85; Editorial Associate, Nicolas Slonimsky, 1984-95; Associate, John Cage, 1986-92; Assistant Professor, Arizona State University West, Phoenix, 1991-96; Founder-Director, John Cage Trust, New York City, 1993-; Secretary, American Music Center, New York City, 1995-. Publications: Baker's Biographical Dictionary of Musicians (contributing editor), 7th edition, 1984, 8th edition, 1992; A Pronouncing Pocket Manual of Musical Terms (editor), 5th edition, 1995; Baker's Biographical Dictionary of 20th Century Classical Musicians (editor), 1997. Contributions to: Supplement to Music Since 1900, 1986; Music Since 1900, 5th edition, 1994; Music Today; Musical Quarterly; Perspectives of New Music. Membership: American Musicological Society. Honour: Outstanding Reference Source Citation, American Library Association, 1998. Address: 2 West St, CH3, Cold Spring, NY 10516, USA

KUKAINIS Margers, (Hermanis Margers Majevskis), b. 25 Apr 1951, Riga, Latvia. Writer. m. Henrika, 7 Mar 1987, 1 daughter. Education: National Institute of Theatre Art, Moscow, 1971-77. Publications: Farewell to River (poetry), 1979; The Birth of Solitude, 1987; Several translations of poetry. Membership: Latvian Writers Society. Literary Agent: Diana Kukainyte. Address: K Valdemara iela 159 dz 51, Riga, LV-1013, Latvia.

KULTERMANN Udo, b. 14 Oct 1927, Stettin, Germany (US citizen, 1981). Professor of Architecture Emeritus; Writer. Education: University of Greifswald, 1946-50; PhD, University of Münster, 1953. Appointments: Curatorial Assistant, Kunsthalle, Bremen, 1954-55; Art Editor, Bertelsmann Publishers, 1955-56; Programme Director, America House, Bremen, 1956-59; Director, City Art Museum, Leverkusen, 1959-64; Professor of Architecture 1967-94, Professor Emeritus, 1994-, Washington University, St Louis; International Correspondent, MIMAR, Singapore/London, 1981-92. Publications: Architecture of Today, 1958; Hans und Wassili Luckhardt: Bauten und Projekte, 1958; Dynamische Architektur, 1959; New Japanese Architecture, 1960; Junge deutsche Bildhauer, 1963; Der Schlüssel zur Architektur von heute, 1963; New Architecture in Africa, 1963; New Architecture in the World, 1965, 2nd edition, 1976; Geschichte der Kunstgeschichte: Der Weg einer Wissenschaft, 1966, 3rd edition, revised, 1996; Architektur der Gegenwart, 1967; The New Sculpture, 1967, 2nd edition, 1972; The New Painting, 1969, revised edition, 1978; New Directions in African Architecture, 1969; Kenzo Tange: Architecture and Urban Design, 1970; Modern Architecture in Color (with Werner Hofmann), 1970; Art and Life: The Function of Intermedia, 1970; New Realism, 1972; Ernest Trova, 1977; Die Architektur im 20. Jahrhundert, 1977, 5th edition, 1987; I Contemporanei: Storia della scultura nel mondo, 1979; Architecture in the Seventies, 1980; Architekten der Dritten Welt, 1980; Contemporary Architecture in Eastern Europe, 1985; Kleine Geschichte der Kunsttheorie, 1987, revised second edition, 1998; Visible Cities-Invisible Cities: Urban Symbolism and Historical Continuity, 1988; Art and Reality: From Fiedler to Derrida: Ten Approaches, 1991; Architecture in the 20th Century, 1993; History of Art History, 1993; Die Maxentius Basilika: Ein Schlüsselwerk spätantiker Architektur, 1996; Contemporary Architecture in the Arab States: Renaissance of a Region, 1999. Contributions to: Books, encyclopedias, and periodicals. Honour: Distinguished Faculty Award, Washington University, St Louis, 1985. Memberships: National Faculty of Humanities, Arts, and Sciences, Atlanta, 1986-; Croatian Academy of Sciences and Arts, Zagreb, corresponding member, 1997-. Address: 300 Mercer Street, 17B, New York, NY 10003, USA.

KUMAR Shiv K(umar), b. 16 Aug 1921, Lahore, Punjab, India. Retired Professor of English; Poet. Education: PhD, Fitzwilliam College, Cambridge, 1956. Appointment: Professor of English, Osmania University, 1959-86. Publications: Articulate Silences, 1970; Cobwebs in the Sun, 1974; Subterfuges, 1976; Woodpeckers, 1979; Trapfalls in the Sky, 1986. Editor: British Romantic Poets: Recent Revelations, 1966; Indian Verse in English, 1970, 1971. Honour: Fellow, Royal Society of Literature, 1978. Address: 2-F/Kakatiya Nagar, PO Jamia Osmania, Hyderabad 500 007, India.

KUMIN Maxine, b. 6 June 1925, Philadelphia, Pennsylvania, USA. Poet; Writer; Teacher. m. Victor M Kumin, 29 June 1946, 1 son, 2 daughters. Education: AB, 1946, MA, 1948, Radcliffe College. Appointments: Instructor, 1958-61, Lecturer in English, 1965-68, Tufts University; Staff, Bread Loaf Writers Conference, 1969-71, 1973, 1975, 1977, Sewanee Writers Conference, 1993; Lecturer, Newton College of the Sacred Heart, Massachusetts, 1971; Visiting Lecturer, Professor, and Writer, University of Massachusetts, Amherst, 1972, Columbia University, 1975, Brandeis University, 1975, Washington University, St Louis, 1977, Princeton University, 1977, 1979, 1982, Randolph-Macon Women's College, Lynchburg, Virginia, 1978, Bucknell University, 1983, Atlantic Center for the Arts, New Smyrna Beach, Florida, 1984, University of Miami, 1995. Publications: Poetry: Halfway, 1961; The Privilege, 1965; The Nightmare Factory, 1970; Up Country: Poems of New England, New and Selected, 1972; House, Bridge, Fountain, Gate, 1975; The Retrieval System, 1978; Our

Ground Time Here Will Be Brief, 1982; Closing the Ring, 1984; The Long Approach, 1985; Nurture, 1989; Looking for Luck, 1992; Connecting the Dots, 1996; Selected poems 1960-1990, 1997. Fiction: Through Dooms of Love, 1965; The Passions of Uxport, 1968; The Abduction, 1971; The Designated Heir, 1974; Why Can't We Live Together Like Civilized Human Beings?, 1982. Other: In Deep: Country Essays, 1987; To Make a Prairie: Essays on Poets, Poetry, and Country Living, 1989; Women, Animals, and Vegetables: Essays and Stories, 1994. For Children: Various books. Contributions to: Numerous magazines and journals. Honours: Lowell Mason Palmer Award, 1960; National Endowment for the Arts Grant, 1966; National Council on the Arts Fellowship, 1967; William Marion Reedy Award, 1968; Eunice Tietjens Memorial Prize, 1972; Pulitzer Prize in Poetry, 1973; American Academy of Arts and Letters Award, 1980; Academy of American Poets Fellowship, 1985; Levinson Award, 1987; Poet Laureate, State of New Hampshire, 1989; Sarah Josepha Hale Award, 1992; Poet's Prize, 1994; Aiken Taylor Poetry Award, 1995; Centennial Award, Harvard Graduate School, 1996; Various honorary doctorates. Memberships: PEN; Poetry Society of America; Writers Union. Address: Joppa Road, Warner, NH 03278, USA.

KUMMINGS Donald D, b. 28 July 1940, Lafayette, Indiana, USA. Professor of English; Poet; Writer. m. 21 Mar 1987, 2 sons. Education: BA, 1962, MA, 1964, Purdue University; PhD, English and American Studies, Indiana University, 1971. Appointments: Instructor, Adrian College, Michigan, 1964-66; Associate Instructor, Indiana University, 1966-70; Assistant Professor, 1970-75, Chair, Department of English, 1974-76, 1991-94, Associate Professor, 1975-85, Professor of English, 1985-, University of Wisconsin, Parkside; Book Review Editor, The Mickle Street Review, 1983-90. Publications: Walt Whitman, 1940-1975: A Reference Guide, 1982; The Open Road Trip: Poems, 1989; Approaches to Teaching Whitman's Leaves of Grass, 1990; The Walt Whitman Encyclopedia (editor with J R LeMaster), 1998. Contributions to: Anthologies, reviews, quarterlies, and journals. Honours: Academy of American Poets Prize, 1969; Posner Poetry Prize, Council for Wisconsin Writers, 1990; Wisconsin Professor of the Year, Carnegie Foundation for the Advancement of Teaching, 1997. Address: c/o Department of English, University of Wisconsin, Parkside, Kenosha, WI 53141, USA.

KUNDERA Milan, b. 1 Apr 1929, Brno, Czechoslovakia. Professor; Writer; Dramatist. m. Vera Hrabankova, 1967. Education: Film Faculty, Academy of Music and Dramatic Arts, Prague. Appointments: Assistant to Assistant Professor, Film Faculty, Academy of Music and Dramatic Arts, Prague, 1958-69; Professor, University of Rennes, 1975-80, Ecole des hautes études en sciences sociales, Paris, 1980-. Publications: Plays: The Owners of the Keys, 1962; Jacques and his Master, 1971-81. Short Stories: Laughable Loves, 1970. Fiction: The Joke, 1967; Life is Elsewhere, 1973; The Farewell Party, 1976; The Book of Laughter and Forgetting, 1979; The Unbearable Lightness of Being, 1984; Identity, 1998. Other: The Art of the Novel, 1987; Immortality, 1990; Slowness (Essay on the Right to Privacy), 1995; Testaments Betrayed: Essay in 9 Parts, 1995; Slowness, 1996. Honours: Union of Czechoslovak Writer's Prize, 1968; Czechoslovak Writers' Publishing House Prize, 1969; Prix Medicis, 1973; Premio Letterario Mondello, 1978; Commonwealth Award, 1981; Prix Europa-Litterature, 1982; Los Angeles Times Prize, 1984; Jerusalem Prize, 1985; Prix de la critique de l'Academie Française, 1987; Prix Nelly Sachs, 1987; Österreichischere staatspreis für europäische litterateur, 1987; Officier, Légion d'honneur, 1990; Prize, The Independent, 1991; Prize, Aujourd'hui, France, 1993; Medal of Merit, Czech Republic, 1995. Address: c/o École des hautes études en sciences sociales, 54 boulevard Raspail, Paris 75006, France.

KUNERT Günter, b. 6 Mar 1929, Berlin, Germany. Poet; Author; Dramatist. m. Marianne Todten. Education: Hochschule für angewandte Kunst, Berlin-Weissensee. Publications: Poetry: Wegschilder und Mauerinschriften, 1950; Erinnerung an einen Planeten: Gedichte aus Fünfzehn Jahren, 1963; Der ungebetene Gast, 1965; Verkündigung des Wetters, 1966; Warnung vor Spiegeln, 1970; Im weiteren Fortgang, 1974; ; Unterwegs nach Utopia, 1977; Abtötungsverfahren, 1980; Stilleben, 1983; Berlin beizeiten, 1987; Fremd daheim, 1990; Mein Golem, 1996; Nachtvorstellung, 1999. Novel: Im Namen der Hüte, 1967. Other: Der ewige Detektiv und andere Geschichten, 1954; Kramen in Fächen: Geschichten, Parabeln, Merkmale, 1968; Die Beerdigung findet in aller Stille statt, 1968; Tagträume in Berlin und andernorts, 1972; Gast aus England, 1973; Der andere Planet: Ansichten von Amerika, 1974; Warum schreiben?: Notizen ins Paradies, 1978; Ziellose Umtriebe: Nachrichten von Reisen und Daheimsein, 1979; Verspätete Monologe, 1981; Leben und Schreiben, 1983; Vor der Sintflut: Das Gedicht als Arche Noah, 1985; Die letzten Indianer Europas, 1991. Honours: Heinrich Mann Prize, 1962; Heinrich Mann Prize, 1962; Heinrich Heine Prize, Düsseldorf, 1985; Hölderlin Prize, 1991. Memberships: Deutsche Akademie für Sprache und Dichtung e.v., Darmstadt. Address: Schulstrasse 7, D-25560 Kaisborstel, Germany.

KÜNG Hans, b. 19 Mar 1928, Lucerne, Switzerland. Professor of Ecumenical Theology Emeritus; Author. Education: Gregorian University, Rome; Institut Catholique, Paris; Sorbonne, University of Paris. Appointments: Ordained Roman Catholic Priest, 1954; Practical Ministry, Lucerne Cathedral, 1957-59; Scientific Assistant for Dogmatic Catholic Theology, University of Münster/Westfalen, 1959-60; Professor of Fundamental Theology, 1960-63, Professor of Dogmatic and Ecumenical Theology, 1963-80, Director, Institute of Ecumenical Research, 1963-96, Professor of Ecumenical Theology, 1980-96, Professor Emeritus, 1996- University of Tübingen; President, Foundation Global Ethic, Germany, 1995, Switzerland, 1997; Various guest professorships and lectureships throughout the world. Publications: The Council: Reform and Reunion, 1961; That the World May Believe, 1963; The Council in Action, 1963; Justification: The Doctrine of Karl Barth and a Catholic Reflection, 1964, new edition, 1981; Structures of the Church, 1964, new edition, 1982; Freedom Today, 1966; The Church, 1967; Truthfulness, 1968; Infallible?: An Inquiry, 1971; Why Priests?, 1972; On Being a Christian, 1976; Signposts for the Future, 1978; The Christian Challenge, 1979; Freud and the Problem of God, 1979; Does God Exist?, 1980; The Church: Maintained in Truth, 1980; Eternal Life?, 1984; Christianity and the World Religions: Paths to Dialogue with Islam, Hindus and Buddhism (with others), 1986; The Incarnation of God, 1986; Church and Change: The Irish Experience, 1986; Why I Am Still A Christian, 1987; Theology for a Third Millennium: An Ecumenical View, 1988; Christianity and Chinese Religions (with Julia Ching), 1989; Paradigm Change in Theology: A Symposium for the Future, 1989; Reforming the Church Today, 1990; Global Responsibility: In Search of a New World Ethic, 1991; Judaism, 1992; Credo: The Apostles' Creed Explained for Today, 1993; Great Christian Thinkers, 1994; Christianity, 1995; Islam, 1995; A Global Ethic for Global Politics and Economics, 1997. Honours: Oskar Pfister Award, American Psychiatric Association, 1986; Many honorary doctorates. Address: Waldhäuserstrasse 23, 72076 Tübingen, Germany.

KUNITZ Stanley J(asspon), b. 29 July 1905, Worcester, Massachusetts, USA. Poet; Editor; Essayist; Educator. m. (1) Helen Pearce, 1930, div 1937, (2) Eleanor Evans, 21 Nov 1939, div 1958, 1 daughter, (3) Elise Asher, 21 June 1958. Education: AB, summa cum laude, 1926, MA, 1927, Harvard University. Appointments: Editor, Wilson Library Bulletin, 1928-43; Teacher, Bennington College, 1946-49; Professor of English, Potsdam State Teachers College, New York, 1949-50; Director, Potsdam Summer Workshop in Creative Arts, 1949-53; Lecturer, New School for Social Research, New York City, 1950-57; Visiting Professor of Poetry, University of Washington, Seattle, 1955-56, Yale University, 1970, Rutgers University at Camden, New Jersey, 1974; Visiting Professor of English, Queens College, New York City, 1956-57, Brandeis University, 1958-59; Director, Poetry Workshop, Poetry Center, Young Men's Hebrew Association, New York City, 1958-62; Lecturer, 1963-66, Adjunct Professor in Writing, Graduate School of the Arts, 1967-85, Columbia University; Consultant on Poetry, 1974-76, Honorary Consultant in American Letters, 1979-83, Library of Congress, Washington, DC; Visiting Professor and Senior Fellow in Humanities, Princeton University, 1978, Vassar College, 1981; Numerous poetry readings and lectures. Publications: Poetry: Intellectual Things, 1930; Passport to the War: A Selection of Poems, 1944; Selected Poems, 1928-1958, 1958; The Testing Tree: Poems, 1971; The Terrible Threshold: Selected Poems, 1940-70, 1974; The Coat Without a Seam: Sixty Poems, 1930-72, 1974; The Lincoln Relics, 1978; Poems of Stanley Kunitz: 1928-78, 1979; The Wellfleet Whale and Companion Poems, 1983; Next-to-Last Things: New Poems and Essays, 1985; Passing Through: The Later Poems, 1995. Non-Fiction: Robert Lowell: Poet of Terribilita, 1974; A Kind of Order, a Kind of Folly: Essays and Conversations, 1975; Interviews and Encounters, 1993. Editor: Living Authors: A Book of Biographies, 1931; Authors Today and Yesterday: A Companion Volume to "Living Authors" (with Howard Haycraft), 1933; The Junior Book of Authors: An Introduction to the Lives of Writers and Illustrators for Younger Readers (with Howard Haycraft), 1934, 2nd edition, revised, 1951; British Authors of the Nineteenth Century (with Howard Haycraft), 1936; American Authors, 1600-1900: A Biographical Dictionary of American Literature (with Howard Haycraft), 1938, 8th edition, 1971; Twentieth Century Authors: A Bographical Dictionary (with Howard Haycraft), 1942, first supplement, 1955; British Authors before 1800: A Biographical Dictionary (with Howard Haycraft), 1952; Poems of John Keats, 1964; European Authors, 1000-1900: A Biographical Dictionary of European Literature (with Vineta Colby), 1967; Selections: University and College Poetry Prizes, 1973-78, 1980. Translator: Poems of Anna Akhmatova (with Max Hayward), 1973; Andrei Voznesensky: Story Under Full Sail, 1974. Contributions to: Many anthologies, books and periodicals. Honours: Garrison Medal for Poetry, Harvard University, 1926; Oscar Blumenthal Prize, 1941; Guggenheim Fellowship, 1945-46; Amy Lowell Travelling Fellow for Poetry, 1953-54; Levinson Prize for Poetry, 1956; Harriet Monroe Award, University of Chicago, 1958; Ford Foundation Grant, 1958-59; National Institute of Arts and Letters Grant, 1959; Pulitzer Prize in Poetry, 1959; Brandeis University Creative Arts Award, 1964; Lenore Marshall Award for Poetry, 1980; National Endowment for the Arts Senior Fellow, 1984; Bollingen Prize, 1987; Walt Whitman Award, 1987; State Poet of New York, 1987-88; Montgomery Fellow, Dartmouth College, 1991; Centennial Medal, Harvard University, 1992; National Medal of Arts, 1993; National Book Award for Poetry, 1995; Phi Beta Kappa. Memberships: Academy of American Poets, chancellor, 1970-; American Academy and Institute of Arts and Letters, secretary, 1985-88; Poets House, New York, founding president, 1985-90. Address: 37 West 12th Street, New York, New York 1011, USA.

KUNSTLER James Howard, b. 19 Oct 1948, New York, New York, USA. Author. m. 15 June 1996. Education: BS, Brockport State College, 1971. Publications: The Wampanaki Tales, 1979; A Clown in the Moonlight, 1981; The Life of Byron Jaynes, 1983; An Embarrassment of Riches, 1985; Blood Solstice, 1986; The Halloween Ball, 1987; The Geography of Nowhere, 1993; Home From Nowhere, 1996. Contributions to: Atlantic Monthly; New York Times Sunday Magazine. Honour: Humanities Prize, 1995. Address: PO Box 193, Saratoga Springs, NY 12866, USA.

KUNZE Reiner, b. 16 Aug 1933, Oelsnitz, Germany. Poet; Author. m. Elisabeth Mifka, 1 son, 1 daughter. Education: University of Leipzig, 1951-55. Publications: Poetry: Vögel über dem Tau: Liebesgedichte und Lieder, 1959; Widmungen, 1963; Sensible Wege, 1969; Zimmerlautstärke, 1972; Das Kätzchen, 1979; auf die eigene hoffnung, 1981; Gespräch mit der Amsel, 1984; eines jeden einziges leben, 1986; wohin der schlaf sich schlafen legt, 1991. Other: Der Löwe Leopold: Fast ein

Märchen, fast Geschichten, 1970; Die wunderbaren Jahre, 1976; In Deutschland zuhaus, 1984; Das weisse Gedicht, 1989; Zurückgeworfen auf sich selbst, 1989; Menschen ohne Macht, 1991; Am Sonnenhang, 1992; Bindewort deutsch, 1997; Ein Tag aut dieser Erde, 1998. Honours: German Children's Book Prize, 1971; Literary Prize, Bavarian Academy of Fine Arts, Munich, 1973; Georg Trakt Prize, Salzburg, 1977; Georg Büchner Prize, 1977; Bavarian Film Prize, 1978; Eichendorff Literature Prize, 1984; Federal Cross of Merit, 1st Class, Germany, 1984; Upper Bavarian Cultural Prize, 1988; Freemasons'Prize for Culture, Chemnitz, 1993; Europapreis für Poesie, Serbien, 1998; Friedrick-Hölderlin-Preis, 1999. Memberships: Bavarian Academy of Fine Arts, Munich; Deutsche Akademie für Sprache für Dichtung e.v., Darmstadt. Address: Am Sonnenhang 19, D-94130 Obernzell, Germany.

KUO Gloria Liang-Hui, b. 10 July 1926, Kaifeng, Henan, China. Author. m. 1949, 2 sons. Education: BA, National Szechuan University, Chengtu, 1948. Publications: 34 novels, 20 novelettes, 2 non-fiction books, some in English including: Debt of Emotion, 1959; The Lock of a Heart, 1962; Far Far Way to Go, 1962; Stranger in Calcutta, 1973; Taipei Women, 1980; Appreciating Chinese Art, 1985; Untold Tales of Chinese Art, 1987. Contributions to: Newspapers and magazines. Membership: Chinese Literature Association, Taiwan. Address: 11F, 126-23 Chung Hsiao East Road, Sec 4, Taipei, China.

KUPFERBERG Herbert, b. 20 Jan 1918, New York, New York, USA. Journalist; Music Critic. Education: BA, Cornell University, 1939; MA, 1940, MS, 1941, Columbia University. Appointments: Staff, New York Herald Tribune, 1942-66; Music Critic, Atlantic Monthly, 1962-69, National Observer, 1967-77; Senior Editor, Parade magazine, 1967-. Publications: Those Fabulous Philadelphians: The Life and Times of a Great Orchestra, 1969; The Mendelssohns: Three Generations of Genius, 1972; Opera, 1975; Tanglewood, 1976; The Book of Classical Music Lists, 1985; Basically Bach, 1986; Amadeus: A Mozart Mosaic, 1986. For Young People: Felix Mendelssohn: His Life, His Family, His Music, 1972; A Rainbow of Sound: The Instruments of the Orchestra and Their Music, 1973. Contributions to: Newspapers and magazines. Address: 113-114 72 Road, Forest Hills, NY 11375, USA.

KUPPNER Frank, b. 1951, Glasgow, Scotland. Writer; Poet. Education: University of Glasgow. Publications: Novels: Ridiculous! Disgusting!, 1989; A Very Quiet Street, 1989; A Concussed History of Scotland, 1990; Something Very Like Murder, 1994. Poetry: A Bad Day For the Sung Dynasty, 1984; The Intelligent Observation of Naked Women, 1987; Everything is Strange, 1994. Address: c/o Polygon, 22 George Square, Edinburgh EH8 9LF, Scotland.

KURAPEL Alberto, b. 5 Feb 1946, Santiago, Chile. Playwright; Poet; Essayist; Performer. m. Susana Cáceres, 5 Jan 1968. Education: Graduate, School of Theatre, University of Chile, 1969. Appointment: Artistic Director, Compagnie des Arts Exilio, 1981-94. Publications: Correo de Exilio/Courrier de'exil, 1986; Promethée Enchainé selon Alberto Kurapel, 1988; Carta de Ajuste ou Nous N'avons Plus Besoin de Calendrier, 1991; Pasarelas/Passerelles, 1991; Berri-UQAM, 1992; Des marches sur le dos de la neige/Peldaños en la espalda de la nieve, 1993. Contributions to: Canadian Theatre Review; Revue Possibles; La Escena Latinoamericana; Revue Humanitas; Ellipse. Honours: Gold Medal, International Competition, Verso il Futuro, Italy, 1976; Special Prize, F de Santis per la Poesia, Italy, 1976; Honorary Mention, contribution for knowledge and diffussion of Latin American Theatre, University of Santiago and Instituto Internacional de Teoría y Crítica de Teatro Latinoamericano, 1992. Memberships: PEN Club; Playwrights Union of Canada; Union des écrivains et écrivaines québécois; Association des poètes du Québec. Address: La Compagnie des Arts Exilio, 6865 Christophe Colomb 313, Montréal, Québec H2S 2H3, Canada.

KURCZYNSKI Antoni, b. 15 Mar 1935, Czerwona Wola, Poland. Teacher. m. Teresa Srodkowska, 6 Feb 1960, 1 son, 1 daughter. Education: Engineer, Institute of Technology, Lodz, 1957; Master of Administration, Academy of Interior Affairs, Warsaw, 1976. Appointments: Engineer of Investment, Electromontage , Lodz, 1957-67; Analyst, City Police Headquarters, Lodz, 1967-73; Teacher, Police School of Traffic, Piaseczno, 1973-90; Teacher, Police Education Centre, Legionowo, 1990-96. Publications: For Better Development of Thematic Philately, 1984; How to Pass an Examination for Driving Licence of B and T Category, 1991; Thematic Philately, 1992; Traffic Regulations - Guide-Book for Drivers, 1992; Traffic Regulations in the Questions and Answers, 1993; Handbook for Drivers, 1994; History of the Posts in Warsaw, typescript, 1998. Contributions to: About 80 articles to Filatelista, Polish philatelic journal. Honours: Medal, Services to Philatelic Publications, 1992, 1994. Literary Agent: Kram Publishing House, Grenadierow 67-69 m 18, 04-007 Warsaw, Poland. Address: Janowskiego 52 m 2, 02-784 Warsaw, Poland.

KUREISHI Hanif, b. 5 Dec 1954, London, England. Author; Dramatist; Screenwriter. Education: BA, Philosophy, King's College, University of London. Appointment: Writer-in-Residence, Royal Court Theatre, London, 1981, 1985-86. Publications: Fiction: The Buddha of Suburbia, 1990; The Black Album, 1995; Love in a Blue Time, 1997. Other: Plays: Soaking the Heat, 1976; The Mother Country, 1980; The King and Me, 1980; Outskirts, 1981; Cinders (after a play by Janusz Glowacki), 1981; Borderline, 1981; Artists and Admirers (after a play by Ostrovsky, with David Leveaux), 1981; Birds of Passage, 1983; Mother Courage (adaptation of a play by Brecht, 1984. Screenplays: My Beautiful Launderette, 1986; Sammy and Rosie Get Laid, 1988; London Kills Me, 1991. Honours: George Devine Award, 1981; Evening Standard Award for Screenplay, 1985; New York Critics Best Screenplay Award, 1986; Whitbread Award for Best First Novel, 1990. Address: c/o Stephen Durbridge, The Agency, 24 Pottery Lane, Holland Park, London W11 41Z, England.

KURTZ Katherine Irene, b. 18 Oct 1944, Coral Gables, Florida, USA. Author. m. Scott Roderick MacMillan, 9 Apr 1983, 1 son. Education: BS, University of Miami, 1966; MA, University of California, Los Angeles, 1971. Publications: Deryni Rising, 1970; Deryni Checkmate, 1972; High Deryni, 1973; Camber of Culdi, 1976; Saint Camber, 1978; Camber the Heretic, 1981; Lammas Night, 1983; The Bishop's Heir, 1984; The King's Justice, 1985; The Quest for Saint Camber, 1986; The Legacy of Lehr, 1986; The Deryni Archives, 1986; The Harrowing of Gwynedd, 1989; Deryni Magic: A Grimoire, 1990; King Javan's Year, 1992; The Bastard Prince, 1994; Two Crowns for America, 1996; King Kelson's Bride, forthcoming. With Deborah Turner Harris: The Adept, 1991; Lodge of the Lynx, 1992; The Templar Treasure, 1993; Dagger Magic, 1994; Death of an Adept, 1996; The Temple and the Stone, 1998. With Robert Reginald: Codex Derynianus, 1998. Editor: Tales of the Knights Templar, 1995; On Crusade, 1998. Various short stories. Honours: Edmund Hamilton Memorial Award, 1977; Balrog Award, 1982. Memberships: Authors Guild; Science Fiction Writers of America. Literary Agent: Russell Galen, Scovil-Chichak-Galen. Address: Holybrooke Hall, Kilmacanogue, Bray, County Wicklow, Ireland.

KURZMAN Dan, b. 27 Mar 1929, San Francisco, California, USA. Writer. m. Florence Knopf. Education: BA, University of California at Berkeley, 1946; Certificate, Sorbonne, University of Paris, 1947. Appointments: Correspondent, International News Service, 1948; Feature Writer, Marshall Plan Information Office, Paris, 1948-49; Correspondent, National Broadcasting Company, Middle East, 1950-53, Washington Post, 1962-69; Bureau Chief, McGraw Hill World News Service, Tokyo, 1954-59; Contributor, Washington Star, 1975-80, Independent News Alliance, 1979-84, San Francisco Chronicle, 1991-92. Publications: Kishi and Japan: The Search for the Sun, 1960; Subversion of the Innocents, 1963; Santo Domingo: Revolt of the Damned, 1965; Genesis 1948: The First Arab-Israeli War, 1970; The Race for Rome, 1975; The Bravest Battle: The Twenty-Eight Days of the Warsaw Ghetto Uprising, 1976; Miracle of November: Madrid's Epic Stand 1936, 1980; Ben-Gurion: Prophet of Fire, 1983; Day of the Bomb: Countdown to Hiroshima, 1985; A Killing Wind: Inside Union Carbide and the Bhopal Catastrophe, 1987; Fatal Voyage: The Sinking of the USS Indianapolis, 1990; Left to Die: The Tragedy of the USS Juneau, 1994; Blood and Water: Sabotaging Hitler's Bomb, 1995; Soldier of Peace: The Life of Yitzhak Rabin, 1922-1995, 1998. Contributions to: New York Times Op-Ed Page, 1988-; Washington Post, book reviewer, 1988-; Los Angeles Times, book reviewer, 1988-. Address: The Parker Imperial, 7855 Boulevard East, North Bergen, NJ 07047, USA.

KUSHNER Aleksandr Semyonovich, b. 14 Sep 1936, Leningrad, Russia. Poet. m. Elena Vsevolodovna Nevzgliadova, 21 July 1984, 1 son. Education: Graduate, Leningrad Pedagogical Institute, 1959. Appointment: Editor-in- Chief, Biblioteka Poeta, publishing house. Publications: First Impression, 1962; Omens, 1969; Letter, 1974; Voice, 1978; The Tavrichesky Garden, 1984; The Hedgerow, 1988; A Night Melody, 1991; Apollo in the Snow (essays and memoirs), 1991; On a Clouded Star, 1994. Contributions to: Novii Mir; Znamya; Zvezda; Unost; Voprosi Literaturi. Honours: Severnaya Palmira Award, 1995; Russia's State Award, 1996. Memberships: Union of Writers; PEN Club. Address: Kaluzhsky Pereulok 9, Apt 48, St Petersburg 193015, Russia.

KUSHNER Donn Jean, b. 29 Mar 1927, Lake Charles, Louisiana, USA. Professor Emeritus; Writer. m. Eva Milada Dubska, 15 Sept 1949, 3 sons. Education: BSc, Chemistry, Harvard University, 1948; MSc, Biochemistry, 1950, PhD, Biochemistry, 1952, McGill University. Appointments: Editor, Canadian Journal of Microbiology, 1980-84, Archives of Microbiology, 1986-94. Publications: Books for children and young adults: The Violin Maker's Gift, 1980; The Witnesses and Other Stories, 1980; Uncle Jacob's Ghost Story, 1984; A Book Dragon, 1987; The House of the Good Spirits, 1990; The Dinosaur Duster, 1992; A Thief Among Statues, 1993; The Night Voyagers, 1995; Life on Mars, 1998. Editor: Microbial Life in Extreme Environments, 1978. Contributions to: Scientific books and journals. Honours: Book of the Year Award for Children, Canadian Library Association, 1981; Ottawa Biological and Biochemical Society Award, 1986; IODE Canada Chapter Award, 1988; Canadian Society of Microbiologists Award, 1992. Memberships: Writers' Union of Canada; Children's Authors, Illustrators and Performers; Canadian Society of Microbiologists, president 1980-81; American Society for Microbiology; American Society for Biological Chemistry and Molecular Biology; Fellow, American Academy of Microbiology, 1997-. Literary Agent: Transatlantic Literary Agency, 72 Glengowan Road, Toronto, Ontario M4N 1G4, Canada. Address: 63 Albany Avenue, Toronto, Ontario M5R 3C2, Canada.

KUSHNER Tony, b. 16 July 1956, New York, New York, USA. Dramatist. Education: BA, Columbia University, 1978; MFA, New York University, 1984. Appointment: Playwright-in-Residence, Juilliard School, New York City, 1990-92. Publications: Yes, Yes, No, No, 1985; Stella, 1987; A Bright Room Called Day, 1987; Hydriotaphia, 1987; The Illusion, 1988, revised version, 1990; Widows (with Ariel Dorfman), 1991; Angels in America: A Gay Fantasia on National Themes, Part One: Millenium Approaches, 1991, and Part Two: Perestroika, 1992. Honours: National Endowment for the Arts Grants, 1985, 1987, 1993; Princess Grace Award, 1986; New York State Council for the Arts Fellowship, 1987; John Whiting Award, Arts Council of Great Britain, 1990; Kennedy Center/American Express Fund for New American Plays Awards, 1990, 1992; Kesserling Award, National Arts Club, 1992; Will Glickman Prize, 1992; Evening Standard Award, 1992; Pulitzer Prize in Drama, 1993; Antoinette Perry Award, 1993; American Academy of Arts and Letters Award, 1994. Address: c/o Joyce Ket, 334 West 89th Street, New York, NY 10024, USA.

KUSKIN Karla (Seidman), (Nicholas J Charles), b. 17 July 1932, New York, New York, USA. Writer and Illustrator of Children's Fiction and Verse. m. (1) Charles M Kuskin, 4 Dec 1955, div Aug 1987, 1 son, 1 daughter, (2) William L Bell, 24 July 1989. Education: Antioch College, 1950-53; BFA, Yale University, 1955. Appointments: Illustrator for several publishers; Conductor of poetry and writing workshops. Publications: Roar and More, 1956, revised edition, 1990; James and the Rain, 1957, new edition, 1995; In the Middle of the Trees, 1958; The Animals and the Ark, 1958; Just Like Everyone Else, 1959; Which Horse is William?, 1959, new edition, 1992; Square As a House, 1960; The Bear Who Saw the Spring, 1961; All Sizes of Noises, 1962; Alexander Soames: His Poems, 1962; How Do You Get From Here to There?, 1962; ABCDEFGHIJKLMNOPQRSTUVWXYZ, 1963; The Rose on My Cake, 1964; Sand and Snow, 1965; Jane Anne June Spoon and Her Very Adventurous Search for the Moon, 1966; The Walk the Mouse Girls Took, 1967; Watson, the Smartest Dog in the USA, 1968; In the Flaky Frosty Morning, 1969; Any Me I Want To Be: Poems, 1972; What Did You Bring Me?, 1973; Near the Window Tree: Poems and Notes, 1975; A Boy Had a Mother Who Brought Him a Hat, 1976; A Space Story, 1978; Herbert Hated Being Small, 1979; Dogs and Dragons, Trees and Dreams: A Collection of Poems, 1980; Night Again, 1981; The Philharmonic Gets Dressed, 1982; Something Sleeping in the Hall, 1985; The Dallas Titans Get Ready for Bed, 1986; Jerusalem, Shining Still, 1987; Soap Soup, 1992; A Great Miracle Happened Here: A Chanukah Story, 1993; Patchwork Island, 1994; The City Dog, 1994; City Noise, 1994; Paul (watercolours by Milton Avery, 1994; James and the Rain, 1995; The Upstairs Cat, 1997; The Sky is Always in the Sky (Poems), 1998. Contributions to: Choice; House and Garden; New York Magazine; New York Times; Parents; Saturday Review; Village Voice; Wilson Library Bulletin. Honours: Book Show Awards, American Institute of Graphic Arts, 1955-60; Children's Book Award, International Reading Association, 1976; Children's Book Council Showcase Selections, 1976-77; National Council of Teachers of English Award, 1979; Children's Science Book Award, New York Academy of Sciences, 1980; American Library Association Awards, 1980, 1982, 1993; School Library Journal Best Book, 1987. Address: 96 Joralemon Street, Brooklyn, NY 11201, USA.

KUSTOW Michael (David), b. 18 Nov 1939, London, England. Writer. Appointments: Director, Institute of Contemporary Arts, 1967-71; Associate Director, National Theatre of Great Britain, 1973-81; Lecturer in Dramatic Arts, Harvard University, Cambridge, Massachusetts, 1980-82; Commissioning Editor, Channel 4 TV, 1981-. Publications: Night of the Assassins (translator), 1968; Tank, Roger Planchon and People's Theatre, 1975; Stravinsky: The Soldier's Story, 1980; Charles Wood's Has Washington Legs, Harold Pinter's Family Voices, 1981; The Manhabbaraten, 1989; The War That Never Ends, 1991. Address: c/o Tom Corrie, Peters Fraser and Dunlop Group Ltd, The Chambers, Chelsea Harbour, Lots Road, London SW10 0XF, England.

KUTTNER Paul, b. 20 Sept 1922, Germany. Publicity Director; Author. m. Ursula Timmermann, 1963, div 1972, 1 son. Education: Bryanston College, 1939-40. Appointments: US Publicity Director for the Guinness Book of World Records, 1964-89; Publicity Director, Sterling Publishing Co Inc, 1989-96. Publications: The Man Who Lost Everything, 1976; Condemned, 1983; Absolute Proof, 1984; The Iron Virgin, 1985; History's Trickiest Questions, 1990; Arts & Entertainment's Trickiest Questions, 1993; Science's Trickiest Questions, 1994; The Holocaust: Hoax or History? - The Book of Answers to Those Who Would Deny the Holocaust, 1997. Contributions to: Der Weg; London Week. Address: Apt 5C, 37-26 87th Street, Jackson Heights, NY 11372, USA.

KVASNOSKY Laura McGee, b. 27 Jan 1951, Sacramento, California, USA. Author; Illustrator. m. John Kvasnosky, 16 Dec 1972, 1 son, 1 daughter. Education: BA, Occidental College, 1973. Publications: See You Later Alligator, 1995; What Shall I Dream ?, 1996; Red

Wagon Year, 1996; Mr Chips, 1996; If Somebody Lived Next Door, 1997; Zelda and Ivy, 1998; Zelda and Ivy and the Boy Next Door. Honours: Best Book of 1995; ARWY, ABA Booksellers Pick of the Lists, 1996; School Library Journal Best Books of 1998 List; Bulletin for the Centre of Children's Books Notable Books of 1998 List. Membership: Society of Children's Book Writers and Illustrators Board, 1992-95; Authors Guild.

KWONG Daniel W, b. 1 Aug 1958, Hong Kong. Professor of Law and International Business; Business Owner. Div., 1 daughter. Education: BA, California State University, 1982; JD, Thomas Jefferson College of Law, 1993. Publications: A Hidden Tool, 1990; Tales of Marshlands (translation Chinese to English), 1990. Contributions to: New Asia Review; Law books. Membership: American Society of Composers, Authors and Publishers. Address: 601 S Cecil Street, Monterey Park, CA 91755, USA.

KYLE Duncan. See: BROXHOLME John Franklin.

KYLE Susan (Eloise Spaeth), (Diana Blayne, Diana Palmer), b. 12 Dec 1946, Cuthbert, Georgia, USA. Author. m. James Edward Kyle, 9 Oct 1972, 1 son. Education: BA, Piedmont College, 1995. Publications: Heather's Song, 1982; Diamond Spur, 1988; Amelia, 1993; Nora, 1994; All That Glitters, 1995; many other books. Contributions to: Journals and magazines. Honours: Many awards. Membership: Authors Guild.Address: PO Box 844, Cornelia, GA 30531, USA.

L

L'HEUREUX John (Clarke), b. 26 Oct 1934, South Hadley, Massachusetts, USA. Professor of English; Writer. m. Joan Ann Polston, 26 June 1971. Education: AB, 1959, Licentiate in Philosophy, 1960, Weston College; MA, Boston College, 1963; Licentiate in Sacred Theology, Woodstock College, 1967; Postgraduate Studies, Harvard University, 1967-68. Appointments: Writer-in-Residence, Georgetown University, 1964-65, Regis College, 1968-69; Ordained Roman Catholic Priest, 1966, laicized, 1971; Staff Editor, 1968-69, Contributing Editor, 1969-83, The Atlantic; Visiting Professor, Hamline University, 1971, Tufts College, 1971-72; Visiting Assistant Professor, Harvard University, 1973; Assistant Professor, 1973-79, Director, Creative Writing Programme, 1976-89, Associate Professor, 1979-81, Professor, 1981-, Lane Professor of the Humanities, 1985-90, Stanford University. Publications: Quick as Dandelions, 1964; Rubrics for a Revolution, 1967; Picnic in Babylon, 1967; One Eye and a Measuring Rod, 1968; No Place for Hiding, 1971; Tight White Collar, 1972; The Clang Birds, 1972; Family Affairs, 1974; Jessica Fayer, 1976; Desires, 1981; A Woman Run Mad, 1988; Comedians, 1990; An Honorable Profession, 1991; The Shrine at Altamira, 1992; The Handmaid of Desire, 1996. Address: c/o Department of English, Stanford University, Stanford, CA 94305, USA.

LA ROCQUE Cheryl Dawn, b. 4 Jan 1959, Lac Megantic, Québec, Canada. Freelance Health Columnist; Writer. m. Peter Kapyrka, 14 Nov 1987, 2 stepdaughters. Education: Nursing Studies, Vanier College, Montreal, Quebec, Canada, 1976-78; Diploma, Social Studies, Champlain College, 1978-79; BA, Classical Studies Major Program, Biology Minor, Bishop's University, 1979-82; Pre Masters, Qualifying, Anthropology, Trent University, Peterborough, Ontario, Canada. Publications: Newspapers: Health: Your Choice published in: The Cape Breton Post; Sydney; Nova Scotia, 1991-97; Western Star; Corner Brook, Newfoundland, 1991; Prince Albert Daily Herald; Prince Albert, Saskatchewan, 1991; The Daily Courier Kelowna, British Columbia, 1997; The Trail Times; Trail, British Columbia, 1997-98; Lifestyles Review, Okanagan Falls, British Columbia, 1998-99; Articles: Canadian Chiropractic Newsletter, 1995; Chiropractic Business Magazine, 1998; BioInform, a science newsletter, 1998. Honours: Academic Award, Grey Trust Company Bursary Fund, Peterborough, Ontario, 1984; Beaver Food Service, London, Ontario, 1984. Address: 1913 Horizon Drive, Kelowna, BC V1Z 3L3, Canada.

LA TOURETTE Jacqueline, b. 5 May 1926, Denver, Colorado, USA. Writer. Education: San Jose State College, 1948-51. Publications: The Joseph Stone, 1971; A Matter of Sixpence, 1972; The Madonna Creek Witch, 1973; The Previous Lady, 1974; The Pompeii Scroll, 1975; Shadows in Umbria, 1979; The Wild Harp, 1981; Patarran, 1983; The House on Octavia Street, 1984; The Incense Tree, 1986. Address: c/o Raines and Raines, 71 Park Avenue, New York, NY 10016, USA.

LABAND John Paul Clow, b. 18 Mar 1947, Johannesburg, South Africa. University Professor of History. m. Fenella Robbins, 15 Dec 1973, 1 son, 1 daughter. Education: MA, Sidney Sussex College, Cambridge, 1977; MA, University of Natal, Pietermaritzbur, 1981; PhD, University of Natal, Pietermaritzburg, 1991. Appointments: From Temporary Lecturer to Full Professor, University of Natal, Pietermaritzburg, 1972-96. Publications: Field Guide to the War in Zululand and the Defence of Natal, 1983, reprinted, 1987; Kingdom and Colony at War: Sixteen Studies on the Anglo-Zulu War of 1879, 1982; Kingdom in Crisis: The Zulu Response to the British Invasion of 1879, 1992; Lord Chelmsford's Zululand Campaign 1878-1879, 1994; Rope of Sand: The Rise and Fall of the Zulu Kingdom, 1995, 1997. Contributions to: South African Historical Journal; Journal of Natal and Zulu History; Natalia; Theoria; Military History Journal; Soldiers of the Queen; Journal of the Victorian Military Society. Honours: Runner-up, Alan Paton Literary Awards; Honourable Mention, Noma Award for Publishing in Africa; Special Mention, CNA Literary Award; Winner, University of Natal Book Prize. Memberships: International PEN; South African Historical Society. Literary Agent: University of Natal Press, University of Natal, Pietermaritzburg, South Africa.

LABRUSSE Hughes (Henri), b. 21 June 1938, Melun, France. Professor; Philosopher. m. Paris, 1966, 4 sons, 1 daughter. Education: Licence de Philosophie, 1963; Diplome d'Etudes Supérieures de Philosophie, 1965; Agrégation de Philosophie, 1967. Publications: Equerre embarcation, 1976; Rome, ou quand on a un coeur et une chemise, 1978; La Dame du Désert, 1986; Terrena l'arbre excessif, 1986; Le donateur, 1991; Michel Mousseau, le temps de peindre, 1993. Contributions to: Magazines and journals. Honour: Prix Louis Guillaume du poème en prose, 1980. Memberships: Membre de la commission du Livre au Centre Régional des Lettres de Basse-Normandie, France; Conseil de Rédaction de la revue SUD. Address: Le Bourg, 14260 Saint Georges d'Aunay, France.

LACEY Robert, b. 3 Jan 1944, Guildford, Surrey, England. Author. Education: BA, 1966, Diploma in Education, 1967, MA, 1970, Selwyn College, Cambridge. Appointments: Assistant Editor, Sunday Times Magazine, 1969-73; Editor, Look! pages, Sunday Times, 1973-74. Publications: The French Revolution, 2 volumes, 1968; The Rise of Napoleon, 1969; The Peninsular War, 1969; 1812: The Retreat From Moscow, 1969; Robert, Earl of Essex: An Elizabethan Icarus, 1971; The Life and Times of Henry VIII, 1972; The Queens of the North Atlantic, 1973; Sir Walter Raleigh, 1973; Sir Francis Drake and the Golden Hinde, 1975; Heritage of Britain (editor, contributor), 1975; Majesty: Elizabeth II and the House of Windsor, 1977; The Kingdom: Arabia and the House of Saud, 1981; Princess, 1982; Aristocrats, 1983; Ford: The Men and the Machine, 1986; God Bless Her: Her Majesty Queen Elizabeth the Queen Mother, 1987; Little Man: Meyer Lansky and the Gangster Life, 1991; Grace, 1994. Address: 12783 East West Forest Hill Boulevard, Suite 105, West Palm Beach, FL 33414, USA.

LACKEY Mercedes, b. 1950, South Bend, Indiana, USA. Writer. m. 14 Dec 1990. Education: BSci Biology, Purdue University, 1972. Publications: Arrows of the Queen, 1987; Arrow's Flight, 1987; Arrow's Fall, 1988; Oathbound, 1988; Oathbreakers, 1989; Reap the Whirlwind, 1989; Magic's Pawn, 1989; Burning Water, 1989; Magic's Promise, 1990; The Magic-Winds Books: Winds of Change, 1992; Winds of Fury, 1993; The Bard's Tale Series: Fortress of Frost and Fire, 1993; Prison of Souls, 1993; Lyrics for and recorded nearly 50 songs for Off-Centaur. Honour: Best Books, American Library Association, 1987. Membership: Science Fiction and Fantasy Writers of America. Address: PO Box 8309, Tulsa, OK 74101 8309, USA.

LADD Veronica. See: **MINER Jane Claypool.**

LADERO QUESADA Miguel-Angel, b. 14 Jan 1943, Valladolid, Spain. Professor of Mediaeval History. m. Isabel Galan Parra, 22 June 1968, 2 sons, 1 daughter. Education: PhD, History, University of Valladolid, 1967. Appointments: Professor of Mediaeval History, La Laguna University, Canary Islands, 1970, University of Seville, 1974; Professor of Mediaeval History, 1978-, Director, Mediaeval History Department, 1980-99, University Vice-Rector, 1986-87, Complutensian University, Madrid. Publications: Castilla y la conquista del reino de Granada, 1967, 3rd edition, 1993; Granada: Historia de un pais islamico, 1969, 3rd edition, 1988; La Hacienda Real de Castilla en el siglo XV, 1973; Historia de Sevilla La ciudad Medieval, 1976, 3rd edition 1988; Historia Universal Edad Media, 1987, 2nd edition 1992; Los mudejares de Castilla y otros estudios, 1988; Los Reyes Catolicos, La Corona y la unidad de Espana, 1988; Andalusia en torno a 1492, 1992; Fiscalidad y Poder Real en Castilla (1252-1369), Madrid, 1993; Historia de España IX 1035-1217, 1998;Los Señores de Andalucia, 1998; Lecturas sobre la España histórica, 1998. Contributions to: Scholarly journals. Honours: Officer, Ordre des Palmes Academiques, 1987; National Prize for History, 1994. Memberships: Full Member, Royal Historical Academy of Spain; International Commission of Urban History; International Commission of Representative and Parliamentary Institutions; Society for Spanish and Portuguese Historical Studies, USA. Address: Departamento de Historia Medieval, Facultad de Geografia e Historia, Universidad Complutense, 28040 Madrid, Spain.

LADIA Eleni, b. 13 Aug 1945, Athens, Greece. Writer. Education: Graduated, Archaeology, University of Athens, 1970. Publications: Figures on a Krater (short stories), 1973; The Fragmentary Relationship (novel), 1974, 3rd edition, 1983; The Black Hermes (short stories), 1977; The Copper Sleep (short stories), 1980; The Schizophrenic God (short stories), 1983; X, The Lion-Faced (novel), 1986; Horography (short stories), 1990; Frederic and John (narrative), 1991; Physiognomies of Places (travelling texts), 1992; Theteia (novel), 1994; Saints of Copts (biographies of saints), 1995. Contributions to: Short stories, essays and archaeological articles to various journals and magazines, Athens and abroad. Honours: 2nd State Prize, 1981; Prize, Academy of Athens-Uranis Foundation, 1991. Memberships: National Greek Literary Society; PEN Club. Address: 44 Kavatha Street, 157 73 Athens, Greece.

LAFFIN John (Alfred Charles), b. 21 Sept 1922, Sydney, New South Wales, Australia. Author; Journalist; Lecturer. m. Hazelle Stonham, 6 Oct 1943, dec 13 Mar 1997, 1 son, 2 daughters. Education: MA; DLitt. Appointments: Battlefield Archaeologist; Advisor/Consultant, War, Military History and Islam; Founder, John Laffin Australian Battlefield Museum, 1988. Publications include: Return to Glory, 1953; Digger: Story of the Australian Soldier, 1959 (several editions); Codes and Ciphers, 1964; Anzacs at War, 1965; Jackboot: Story of the German Soldier, 1965 (several editions);The Hunger to Come, 1966; Women in Battle, 1967; Devil's Goad, 1970; Americans in Battle, 1972; The Arab Mind, 1974; Dagger of Islam, 1979; Damn the Dardanelles!, 1980, 2nd edition, 1985; Fight for the Falklands, 1982; The PLO Connections, 1982; Australian Army at War 1899-1975, 1982; The Man the Nazis Couldn't Catch, 1984; On the Western Front, 1985; Know the Middle East, 1985; Brassey's Battles, 1986; War Annual 1, 1986; War Annual 2, 1987; Battlefield Archaeology, 1987; War Annual 3, 1987; Western Front, 1916-17: The Price of Honour, 1988; Western Front, 1917-18: The Cost of Victory, 1988; Holy War - Islam Fights, 1988; War Annual 4, 1988; British Butchers and Bunglers of World War I, 1989; War Annual 5, 1991; The Western Front Illustrated, 1991; Dictionary of Africa Since 1960, 1991; Guidebook to Australian Battlefields of France and Flanders 1916-18, 1992; Digging up the Diggers, War, 1993; Panorama of the Western Front, 1993; A Western Front Companion, 1994; Forever Forward, 1994; War Annual 6, 1994; Aussie Guide to Britain, 1995; Hitler Warned Us, 1995; War Annual 7, 1995; Brassey's Book of Espionage 1996; War Annual 8, 1997; British VCs of World War II, 1997; The Spirit and the Source (poetry), 1997; Brassey's Battles (new updated edition), 1997; Forthcoming publications: Gallipoli; The Somme; Raiders; Hamel: The Australians' Greatest Victory; A Kind of Immortality (autobiography), vol 1. Contributions to: Newspapers, magazines and journals. Memberships: Society of Authors, UK; Australian Society of Authors. Address: 37 Horizon Avenue, Sundown Village, Narrabundah, ACT 2604, Australia.

LAGZDINS Viktors, b. 28 Aug 1926, Riga, Latvia. Writer. m. Dzidra Reita, 6 June 1952, 1 daughter. Education: Pedagogic School, Liepaja, 1947; Diploma of Education, Faculty of Philology, Riga Pedagogic Institute, 1958. Appointments: Teacher, 1947-58; Writer, 1955-; Journalist on the Editorial Staff of a Daily Newspaper, Liepaja, 1958-63, and Monthly magazine, Riga, 1963-82. Publications: Parbaude, English translation as The Test,

1959; Indianu Virsaitis Drossirdigais Kikakis, 1963; Kedes Loks, 1972; Nakts Mezazos, English translation as A Night at Elk Farm, 1976; Zili Zala, English translation as The Blue and The Green, 1986. Membership: Writers' Union of Lativia, chairman of the prose section, 1979-80. Address: Agenskalna iela 22-48, Riga, LV-1046, Latvia.

LAI Larissa, b. 13 Sept 1967, La Jolla, California, USA. Writer. Education: BA, Honours, Sociology, University of British Columbia, 1990. Appointments: Assistant Curator, Yellow Peril: Reconsidered, 1990; Coordinator, Saw Video Co-op, 1991; Television and Video Associate, Banff Centre for the Arts, 1994; Editor, Front Magazine, 1994-95; Gallery Animateur, Vancouver Art Gallery, 1996-97; Writer-in-Residence, University of Calgary, 1997-98. Publications: Fiction: New Reeboks, 1994; The Home Body, 1994; Water, and Other Measures of Distance, 1996; The Voice of the Blind Concubine, 1996; The Peacock Hen, 1996. Poetry: The Birdwoman, 1990; Lullabye for the Insect Catcher, 1990; Eighty Years Bathing, 1991; Where, 1991; Trap I, 1991; Trap II, 1991; Bone China, 1991; Nora, 1991; Glory, 1991; Arrangements, 1991; Shade, 1991; Nostalgia, 1992; Calling Home, 1992; The Escape, 1992; Tell: Longing and Belonging, 1994. Honours: Astraea Foundation Emerging Writers Award, 1995; Finalist, Books in Canada First Novel Award, 1996. Memberships: Writers Union of Canada; Asian Canadian Writers Workshop. Address: 78 Albany Avenue, Toronto, Ontario M5R 3C3, Canada.

LAIRD Elizabeth Mary Risk, b. 21 Oct 1943, Wellington, New Zealand. Writer. m. David Buchanan McDowall, 19 Apr 1975, 2 sons. Education: BA, Bristol University, 1966; MLitt, Edinburgh University, 1972. Publications: The Miracle Child, 1985; The Road to Bethlehem, 1987; Red Sky in the Morning, 1988; Arcadia, 1990; Kiss the Dust, 1991; Hiding Out, 1993; Secret Friends, 1996; Jay, 1997; Forbidden Ground, 1997. Honours: Children's Book Award, 1992; Smarties Young Judges Award, 1994. Membership: Society of Authors. Literary Agent: Rosemary Sandberg. Address: 31 Cambrian Road, Richmond, Surrey TW10 6JQ, England.

LAKE David John, b. 26 Mar 1929, Bangalore, India. University Professor; Writer. m. Marguerite Ivy Ferris, 30 Dec 1964, 1 daughter, 3 stepchildren. Education: BA, MA, DipEd, Trinity College, Cambridge, 1949-53; Diploma of Linguistics, University of Wales, Bangor, 1964-65; PhD, University of Queensland, Australia, 1974. Publications: Hornpipes and Funerals (poems), 1973; The Canon of Thomas Middleton's Plays, 1975; Walkers on the Sky, 1976; The Right Hand of Dextra, 1977; The Wildings of Westron, 1977; The Gods of Xuma, 1978; The Man who Loved Morlocks, 1981; The Changelings of Chaan, 1985. Contributions to: Extrapolation; Science Fiction Studies; Foundation; Notes and Queries; Explicator; Ring Bearer. Honours: Ditmar Awards for best Australian Science Fiction Novel, 1977, 1982. Address: 7 8th Avenue, St Lucia, Queensland 4067, Australia.

LAKER Rosalind. See: OVSTEDAL Barbara Kathleen.

LAMANTIA Philip, b. 23 Oct 1927, San Francisco, California, USA. Poet. Education: University of California, Berkeley, 1947-49. Publications: Erotic Poems, 1946; Narcotica: I Demand Extinction of Laws Prohibiting Narcotic Drugs, 1959; Ekstasis, 1959; Destroyed Works, 1962; Touch of the Marvelous, 1966; Selected Poems 1943-1966, 1967; Penguin Modern Poets 13 (with Charles Bukowski and Harold Norse), 1969; The Blood of the Air, 1970; Becoming Visible, 1981; Meadowland West, 1986. Address: c/o City Lights Books, 261 Columbus Avenue, San Francisco, CA 94133, USA.

LAMB Andrew (Martin), b. 23 Sept 1942, Oldham, Lancashire, England. Writer on Music. m. Wendy Ann Davies, 1 Apr 1970, 1 son, 2 daughters. Education: Corpus Christi College, Oxford, 1960-63; MA, Honours, Oxford University. Publications: Jerome Kern in Edwardian London, 1985; Ganzl's Book of the Musical Theatre (with Kurt Ganzl), 1988; Skaters' Waltz: The

Story of the Waldteufels, 1995. Editor: The Moulin Rouge, 1990; Light Music from Austria, 1992; An Offenbach Family Album, 1997. Contributions to: The New Grove Dictionary of Music and Musicians; The New Grove Dictionary of American Music; The New Grove Dictionary of Opera; Gramophone; Musical Times; Classic CD; American Music; Music and Letters; Wisden Cricket Monthly; Cricketer; Listener; Notes. Memberships: Fellow, Institute of Actuaries; Associate Member, Institute of Investment Management and Research; Lancashire County Cricket Club. Address: 12 Fullers Wood, Croydon CR0 8HZ, England.

LAMB Elizabeth Searle, b. 22 Jan 1917, Topeka, Kansas, USA. Poet; Writer; Editor. m. F Bruce Lamb, 11 Dec 1941, dec 1992, 1 daughter. Education: BA, 1939, BMus, 1940, University of Kansas. Appointments: Editor, Frogpond, 1984-90, 1994; Co-Editor, Haiku Southwest, 1993-94. Publications: Pelican Tree and Other Panama Adventures, 1953; Today and Every Day, 1970; Inside Me, Outside Me, 1974; In This Blaze of Sun, 1975; Picasso's Bust of Sylvette, 1977; 39 Blossoms, 1982; Casting Into a Cloud, 1985; Lines for My Mother, Dying, 1988; The Light of Elizabeth Lamb: 100 American Haiku, 1993; Ripples Spreading Out, 1997; Platek Irysa (Petals of Iris), 1998; Across the Windharp, 1999. Contributions to: Many anthologies, journals, and magazines. Honours: Numerous, including: Cicada Awards, Canada, 1977, 1980; Henderson Awards, 1978, 1981, 1982, 1991, 1993; Dellbrook Poetry Award, 1979; HSA Merit Book Awards, 1979, 1983, 1987; Yuki Teikei, 1981, 1982, 1989, 1994; Certificate of Achievement, Haiku Society of America, 1995; Honorary Curator, American Haiku Archive, California State Library, Sacramento, 1996-97. Memberships: Haiku Society of America; Haiku International, Japan; Association of International Renku, Japan; Haiku Canada; Haiku International League of American Pen Women; New York Women Poets; Poetry Society of America. Address: 970 Acequia Madre, Sante Fe, NM 87501, USA.

LAMB Sir Larry, b. 15 July 1929, Fitzwilliam, Yorkshire, England. Editor. m. Joan Mary Denise Grogan, 2 sons, 1 daughter. Appointments: Journalist, Brighouse Echo, Shields Gazette, Newcastle Journal, London Evening Standard; Sub-Editor, Daily Mirror; Editor, Daily Mail, Manchester, 1968-69; The Sun, 1969-72, 1975-81; Director, 1970-81, Editorial Director, 1971-81, News International Ltd; Deputy Chairman, News Group, 1979-81; Director, News Corporation Ltd, Australia, 1980-81; Deputy Chairman, Editor-in-Chief, Western Mail Ltd, Perth, Australia, 1981-82; Editor-in-Chief, Australian, 1982-83; Editor, Daily Express, 1983-86; Chairman, Larry Lamb Associates, 1986-. Publication: Sunrise, 1989. Address: 42 Malvern Court, Onslow Square, London SW7 3HY, England.

LAMBDIN Dewey Whitley II, b. 21 Jan 1945, San Diego, California, USA. Writer. m. (1) Melinda Alice Phillips, 17 July 1971, (2) Julie Dawn Pascoe, 27 Oct 1984. Education: BS, Film and Television, Montana State University, 1969. Publications: The King's Coat, 1989; The French Admiral, 1990; King's Commission, 1991; King's Privateer, 1992, 2nd edition, 1996; The Gun Ketch, 1993, 2nd edition, 1996; For King and Country, 1994; HMS Cockerel, 1995, 2nd edition, 1997; King's Commander, 1997. Contributions to: Newspapers and periodicals. Honour: Theme Vault, University of Tennessee, 1963. Membership: Sisters in Crime. Address: c/o Wieser & Wieser Inc, 118 East 25th Street, New York, NY 10010, USA.

LAMBERT Angela Maria, b. 14 Apr 1940, Beckenham, Kent, England. Writer; Journalist. m. Martin Lambert, 10 Dec 1962, div. Aug 1966, 1 son, 2 daughters. Education: St Hilda's College, Oxford, 1959-61; Honours degree in Philosophy, Politics and Economics. Appointments: Publishing, 1961-62; Journalism, 1962-63; Politics, 1964-67; Newspaper Journalism, 1967-72; Television Reporter, 1972-88; Newspaper Feature Writer and Columnist, The Independent, 1988-95, Daily Mail, 1995-. Publications: Non-fiction: Unquiet Souls, 1984; 1939: The Last Season

of Peace, 1989; Fiction: Love among the Single Classes, 1986; No Talking after Lights, 1989; A Rather English Marriage, 1991; The Constant Mistress, 1994; Kiss and Kin, 1997. Contributions to: Several, 1965-. Honours: Runner-up, Whitbread Prize for Biography, 1984; Winner, Romantic Novel of the Year, 1988. Membership: Executive Committee, English PEN, 1991-96. Literary Agent: A P Watt, Caradoc King, London, England. Address: c/o A P Watt, Caradoc King, 20 John Street, London WC1N 2DR, England.

LAMBERT Derek (William), (Richard Falkirk), b. 10 Oct 1929, London, England. Journalist; Author. Appointments: Journalist, Devon, Norfolk, Yorkshire and National newspapers, 1950-68. Publications: Novels: For Infamous Conduct, 1970; Grans Slam, 1971; The Great Land, 1977; The Lottery, 1983. Mystery Novels: Angels in the Snow, 1969; The Kites of War, 1970; The Red House, 1972; The Yermakov Transfer, 1974; Touch the Lion's Paw, 1975; The Saint Peter's Plot, 1978; The Memory Man, 1979; I, Said the Spy. 1980; Trance, 1981; The Red Dove, 1982; The Judas Code, 1983; The Golden Express, 1984; The Man Who Was Saturday, 1985; Chase, 1987; Triad, 1988. Mystery Novels as Richard Falkirk: The Chill Factor, 1971; The Twisted Wire, 1971; Blackstone, 1972; Beau Blackstone, 1973; Blackstone's Fancy, 1973; Blackstone and the Scourge of Europe, 1974; Blackstone Underground, 1976; Blackstone on Broadway, 1977. Other: The Sheltered Days: Growing Up in the War, 1965; Don't Quote Me - But, 1979; And I Quote, 1980; Unquote, 1981; Just Like the Blitz: A Reporter's Notebook, 1987; The Night and the City, 1989; The Gate of the Sun, 1990. Address: 350 Hudson Street, New York, NY 10014, USA.

LAMBOT Isobel Mary, (Daniel Ingham, Mary Turner), b. 21 July 1926, Birmingham, England. Novelist. m. Maurice Edouard Lambot, 19 Dec 1959, dec. Education: BA, Liverpool University; Teaching Certificate, Birmingham University. Appointment: Tutor in Creative Writing, Lichfield Evening Institute, 1973-80. Publications: As Isobel Lambot: Taste of Murder, 1966; Deadly Return, 1966; Shroud of Canvas, 1967; Dangerous Refuge, 1967; Danger Merchant, 1968; The Queen Dies First, 1968; Killer's Laughter, 1968; Let the Witness Die, 1969; Point of Death, 1969; Watcher on the Shore, 1971; Come Back and Die, 1972; Grip of Fear, 1974; The Identity Trap, 1978; Past Tense, 1979; Rooney's Gold, 1984; Still Waters Run Deadly, 1987; Blood Ties, 1987; Bloody Festival, 1991; The Flower of Violence, 1992; The Craft of Writing Crime Novels, 1992. As Daniel Ingham: Contract for Death, 1972. As Mary Turner: The Justice Hunt, 1975; So Bright a Lady, 1977; Runaway Lady, 1980. Contributions to: Women's journals. Memberships: Crime Writers' Association; Society of Authors; Writers' Guild of Great Britain; Mystery Writers of America. Address: 45 Bridge Street, Kington, Herefordshire HR5 3DW, England.

LAMBOVSKI Boyko Panov, b. 13 Mar 1960, Sofia, Bulgaria. Poet; Writer. m. Liudmila Kirilova Koteva, 13 May 1992. Education: Maxim Gorky Literary Institute, Moscow, 1982-87. Publications: Poetry and Prose in Bulgarian. Contributions to: Anthologies, reviews, and journals. Honours: Vladimir Bashev National Prize for Poetry, 1987; Achievement in the Arts Prize, Svoboden Narod, 1992. Memberships: Union of Bulgarian Writers; Friday the 13th, co-founder. Address: Shipchenski Prokhod 7-11, Bl 228-A, Ap 65, Sofia 1111, Bulgaria.

LAMM Barbara H, b. 28 May 1920, USA. Writer; Former Educator. Div, 1 son. Education: BA, Stanford University; MEd, University of North Crolina. Appointments: Counselor, Social Studies, North Carolina; Child Welfare, General and Rehabilitation Counseling, California; Freelance Writer. Publications: Hands and Hearts, 1975; World War One Flyer's Album, 1979; Dad and His Flying Machines, 1979. Honours: Certificate of Appreciation, National Steering Committee, 1996. Address: 20 Irwin Way, Apt 731, Orinda, CA 94563, USA.

LAMMING George (Eric), b. 8 June 1927, Carrington Village, Barbados. Novelist. Appointments:

Writer-in-Residence, University of the West Indies, Kingston, 1967-68. Publications: In the Castle of My Skin, 1953; The Emigrants, 1955; Of Age and Innocence, 1958; Water with Berries, 1971; Natives of My Person, 1972. Short Stories: David's Walk, 1948; A Wedding in Spring, 1960; Birthday Weather, 1966; Birds of a Feather, 1970. Honours: Guggenheim Fellowship, 1954; Maugham Award, 1957; Canada Council Fellowship, 1962; D Litt, University of West Indies, 1980. Address: 14a Highbury Place, London N5, England.

LAMONT-BROWN Raymond, b. 20 Sept 1939, Horsforth, England. Author; Broadcaster. m. (2) Dr Elizabeth Moira McGregor, 6 Sept 1985. Education: MA; AMIET. Appointment: Managing Editor, Writers Monthly, 1984-86. Publications: Over 50 books including: Discovering Fife, 1988; The Life and Times of Berwick-upon-Tweed, 1988; The Life and Times of St Andrews, 1989; Royal Murder Mysteries, 1990; Scottish Epitaphs, 1990; Scottish Superstitions, 1990; Scottish Witchcraft, 1994; Scottish Folklore, 1996; St Andrews, 1996; Kamikaze: Japan's Suicide Samurai, 1997; Scotland of One Hundred Years Ago, 1998; Kempeitai: Japan's Dreaded Military Police, 1998; Edward VII's Last Loves, 1998; Tutor to the Dragon Emperor, forthcoming. Contributions to: Magazines and newspapers. Memberships: Society of Authors, Scotland, fellow; Rotary International, president, St Andrews Branch, 1984-85. Address: 11 Seabourne Gardens, Broughty Ferry, Dundee DD5 2RT, Scotland.

LAMPARD Dulcie Irene, b. 30 May 1923, Albany, Western Australia. Writer. Publications: Ride!, 1985, Saddle Up!, 1994. Honours: Bookshop of the Year Awards, 1980, 1984, 1988. Address: 1045 Mayo Road, Wooroloo, Western Australia 6558, Australia.

LAMPITT Dinah, b. 6 Mar 1937, Essex, England. Author. m. L F Lampitt, 28 Nov 1959, dec, 1 son, 1 daughter. Education: Regent Street Polytechnic, London. Publications: Sutton Place Trilogy: Sutton Place, 1983; The Silver Swan, 1984; Fortune's Soldier, 1985; To Sleep No More, 1987; Pour the Dark Wine, 1989; The King's Women, 1992; As Shadows Haunting, 1993; Banishment, 1994; Writing as Deryn Lake: Death in the Dark Walk, 1995; Death at the Beggar's Opera, 1996; Death at the Devil's Tavern, 1997; Death on the Romney Marsh, 1998. Serials: The Moonlit Door; The Gemini Syndrome; The Staircase; The Anklets; The Wardrobe. Contributions to: Numerous short stories to women's magazines. Memberships: Society of Authors; Crime Writers Association. Address: c/o Darley Anderson, Estelle House, 11 Eustace Road, London SW6 1JB, England.

LAMPLUGH Lois Violet, b. 9 June 1921, Barnstaple, Devon, England. Author. m. Lawrence Carlile Davis, 24 Sep 1955, 1 son, 1 daughter. Education: BA, Honours, Open University, 1980. Appointment: Editorial Staff, Jonathan Cape Publishers, 1946-56. Publications: The Pigeongram Puzzle, 1955; Nine Bright Shiners, 1955; Vagabond's Castle, 1957; Rockets in the Dunes, 1958; Sixpenny Runner, 1960; Midsummer Mountains, 1961; Rifle House Friends, 1965; Linhay on Hunter's Hill, 1966; Fur Princess and Fir Prince, 1969; Mandog, 1972; Sean's Leap, 1979; Winter Donkey, 1980; Falcon's Tor, 1984; Barnstaple: Town on the Taw, 1983; History of Ilfracombe, 1984; Minehead and Dunster, 1987; A Shadowed Man: Henry Williamson, 1990; Take Off From Chivenor, 1990; Sandrabbit, 1991; Lundy: Island Without Equal, 1993; A Book of Georgeham and the North West Corner of Devon, 1995; Ilfracombe in Old Photographs, 1996; Two Rivers Meeting, 1998; Four Centuries of Devon Dialect, forthcomming. Contributions to: Western Morning News. Memberships: West Country Writers Association. Address: Springside, Bydown, Swimbridge, Devon EX32 0QB, England.

LAN David Mark, b. 1 June 1952, Cape Town, South Africa. Writer; Dramatist; Social Anthropologist. Education: BA, University of Cape Town, 1972; BSc, 1976, PhD, 1983, London School of Economics; Writer in Residence, Royal Court Theatre, 1996-97. Publications: Guns and Rain, Guerrillas and Spirit Mediums in Zimbabwe, 1985. Plays: Painting a Wall, 1974; Bird Child, 1974; Homage to Been Soup, 1975; Paradise, 1975; The Winter Dancers, 1977; Not in Norwich, 1977; Red Earth, 1978; Sergeant Ola and His Followers, 1979; Flight, 1986; A Mouthful of Birds (with Caryl Churchill), 1986; Desire, 1990; The Ends of the Earth, 1996. Television Films: The Sunday Judge, 1985; The Crossing, 1988; Welcome Home Comrades, 1990; Dark City, 1990. Radio Plays: Charley Tango, 1995; Artist Unknown (writer, director), 1996; Royal Court Diaries (writer, director), 1997. Adaptations: Ghetto, 1989; Hippolytos, 1991; Ion, 1993; The She Wolf, 1996; Uncle Vanya, 1998. Honours: John Whiting Award, 1977; George Orwell Memorial Award, 1983; Zürich International Television Prize, 1990. Address: c/o Judy Daish Associates, 2 St Charles Mews, London W10 6EG, England.

LANCASTER David. See: **HEALD Tim(othy Villiers).**

LANCASTER-BROWN Peter, b. 13 Apr 1927, Cue, Western Australia. Author. m. Johanne Nyrerod, 15 Aug 1953, 1 son. Education: Astronomy; Surveying; Mining Engineering; Civil Engineering. Publications: Twelve Came Back, 1957; Call of the Outback, 1970; What Star is That?, 1971; Astronomy in Colour, 1972; Australia's Coast of Coral and Pearl, 1972; Comets, Meteorites, and Men, 1973; Megaliths, Myths, and Men, 1976; Planet Earth in Colour, 1976; Megaliths and Masterminds, 1979; Fjord of Silent Men, 1983; Astronomy, 1984; Halley and His Comet, 1985; Halley's Comet and the Principia, 1986; Skywatch, 1993. Contributions to: Blackwood's Nature; New Scientist; Sky and Telescope. Membership: Society of Authors. Address: 10A St Peter's Road, Aldeburgh, Suffolk IP1 5BG, England.

LANCEFIELD Albert John, (Wandering Minstrel), b. 15 Sept 1920, Willesborough, Ashford, Kent, England. Engineer. Appointments: Poet; Classical Musician; Campanologist; Naturalist; World Traveller. Publications: By Wandering Tempest, book of poems written in New Zealand, 1955; The Windmill and Fifty Other Sonnets, 1995; On Younger Soil - A Working Tour of New Zealand in Verse, 1995; An Album of Thirty Christmas Carols, Words and Music, 1996; Footfalls - A Working Tour of Australia in Verse, 1997; I Remember, I Remember - Poems and Verses of Childhood, 1998; The Complete History of a Downland Church; Saint Mary the Blessed Virgin, 1999. Membership: The Cinque Ports Poets, New Romney, Kent. Address: Coulsdon, 35 Bentley Road, Willesborough, Ashford, Kent TN24 0HP, England.

LANDERT Walter, b. 3 Jan 1929, Zürich, Switzerland. Writer; Poet. m. Elsu Weber, 15 Apr 1954, 3 sons, 1 daughter. Education: Neuchâtel; London. Publications: Manager auf Zeit (novel), 1968; Selbstbefragung (poems), 1969; Entwurf Schweiz (literary essay), 1970; Koitzsch (novel), 1971; Traum einer besseren Welt (short stories and poems), 1980; Unkraut im helvetischen Kulturgartchen (literary essays), 1981; Meine Frau baut einen Bahnhof (short stories), 1982; Klemms Memorabilien: Ein Vorspiel (novel), 1989; Umwerfende Zeiten: Ein Prozess (novel), 1990; Treffpunkt: Fondue Bourguignonne (novel), 1993. Contributions to: Various newspapers. Honours: Artemis Jubilee Prize, 1969; Poetry Prize, Literary Union, Saarbrücken, 1977. Memberships: Swiss Authors Group, Olten. Address: Lendikonerstrasse 54, CH 8484 Weisslingen/ZH, Switzerland.

LANDESMAN Jay (Irving), b. 15 July 1919, St Louis, Missouri, USA. Author; Dramatist; Producer; Publisher. m. Frances Deitsch, 15 July 1950, 2 sons. Education: University of Missouri, 1938-40; Rice Institute, Houston, 1940-42. Publications: The Nervous Set (novel), 1954, as a musical, 1959; A Walk on the Wild Side (musical), 1960; Molly Darling (musical), 1963; The Babies (play), 1969; Bad Nipple (novel), 1970; Rebel Without Applause (memoir), 1987; Small Day Tomorrow (screenplay), 1990; Jaywalking (memoirs vol 2), 1992. Memberships: American Federation of Television and Radio Artists; Dramatists Guild. Address: 8 Duncan Terrace, London N1 8BZ, England.

LANDIS J(ames) D(avid), b. 30 June, 1942, Springfield, Massachusetts, USA. Publisher; Author. m. (1) Patricia Lawrence Straus, 15 Aug 1964, div, 1 daughter, (2) Denise Evelyn Tillar, 20 July 1982, 2 sons. Education: BA, magna cum laude, Yale College, 1964. Appointments: Assitant Editor, Abelard Schuman, 1966-67; Editor to Senior Editor, 1967-80, Senior Vice-President, 1985-91, Publisher and Editor-in-Chief, 1988-91, William Morrow & Co; Editorial Director, senior Vice-President and Publisher, Quill Trade paperbacks, 1980-85. Publications: The Sisters Impossible, 1979; Love's Detective, 1984; Daddy's Girl, 1984; Joey and the Girls, 1987; The Band Never Dances, 1989; Looks Aren't Everything, 1990; Lying in Bed, 1995. Contibutions to: Periodicals. Honours: Roger Klein Award for Editing, 1973; Advocate Humanitarian Award, 1977; Morton Dauwen Zabel Award for Fiction, American Academy of Arts and Letters, 1996. Memberships: PEN; Phi Beta Kappa. Address: c/o Henry Dunow Literary Agency, New York, NY 10010, USA.

LANDON H(oward) C(handler) Robbins, b. 6 Mar 1926, Boston, Massachusetts, USA. Musicologist; Writer. m. (1) Christa Landon, (2) Else Radant. Education: Swarthmore College; BMus, Boston University, 1947. Appointments: Guest Lecturer, various US and European colleges and universities; Many radio and television talks. Publications: The Symphonies of Joseph Haydn, 1955; The Mozart Companion (editor with Donald Mitchell), 1956, 2nd edition, revised, 1965; The Collected Correspondence and London Notebooks of Joseph Haydn, 1959; Beethoven: A Documentary Study, 1970; Essays on the Viennese Classical Style: Gluck, Haydn, Mozart, Beethoven, 1970; Haydn: Chronicle and Works, 5 volumes, 1976-80; Haydn: A Documentary Study, 1981; Mozart and the Masons, 1983; Handel and His World, 1984; 1791: Mozart's Last Year, 1988; Haydn: His Life and Music (with D Jones), 1988; Mozart: The Golden Years, 1989; The Mozart Compendium (editor), 1990; Mozart and Vienna, 1991; Five Centuries of Music in Venice, 1991; Une Journée Particulière de Mozart, 1993; Vivaldi: Voice of the Baroque, 1993; The Mozart Essays, 1995. Other: Editor of complete editions of Haydn's symphonies, 1965-68, string quartets (co-editor), 1968-83, and piano trios, 1970-78. Contributions to: Scholarly books and professional journals. Honours: Various. Memberships: Musicological societies. Address: Chateau de Foncoussières, 81800 Rabastens, Tarn, France.

LANDRY Yves, b. 23 Dec 1952, St Jean sur Richelieu, Quebec, Canada. Historian; Demographer. m. Manon Pomerleau, 17 Aug 1974, 2 sons. Education: BA, History, 1974, MA, History, Université de Montreal, 1977; Doctorate, Historical Demography, École des hautes études en sciences sociales, Paris, 1990. Appointment: Professor of History, Université de Montréal. Publications: Inventaire des registres paroissiaux catholiques du Quebec 1621-1876 (co-author), 1990; Pour le Christ et le Roi La vie au temps des premiers Montréalais (editor), 1992; Orphelines en France, pionnières au Canada: Les Filles du roi au XVII siècle, 1992; The First French Canadians: Pioneers in the St Lawrence Valley (co-author), 1993. Contributions to: Revue d'histoire de l'Amérique française; Histoire sociale-Social History; Annales de Démographie Historique; Journal of Family History; Social Science History; Cahiers Québécois de Démographie; Histoire, Economie et Société. Honours: Queen's Fellowship, Canada Council, 1975; Jean Charles Falardeau Prize, 1993; Percy W Foy Prize, 1993. Memberships: International Union for the Scientific Study of Population, 1985-; Institut d'histoire de l'Amérique Française, treasurer, 1993-95; Société de Démographie Historique. Address: Départment d'Histoire, Université de Montréal, CP 6128, Succursale Centreville, Montreal, Québec H3C 3J7, Canada.

LANE Helen, (Helen Hudson), b. 31 Jan 1920, New York, New York, USA. Writer. m. Robert Lane, 15 Nov 1944, 2 sons. Education: BA, Bryn Mawr College, 1941; MA, 1943, PhD, 1950, Columbia University. Publications: Tell the Time to None, 1966; Meyer Meyer, 1967; The Listener, 1968; Farnsbee South, 1971; Criminal

Trespass, 1986; A Temporary Residence, 1987. Contributions to: Antioch Review; Sewannee Review; Virginia Quarterly; Northwest Review; Mademoiselle; Quarterly Review of Literature; Red Book; Ellery Queen; Mid-Stream; Best American Short Stories; O Henry Prize Stories. Honour: Virginia Quarterly Prize Story, 1963. Memberships: Authors Guild; Authors League; American PEN. Address: 558 Chapel Street, New Haven, CT 06511, USA.

LANE M(illicent Elizabeth) Travis, (Millicent Elizabeth Travis), b. 23 Sept 1934, San Antonio, Texas, USA (Canadian citizen, 1973). Poet; Writer. m. Lauriat Lane, 26 Aug 1957, 1 son, 1 daughter. Education: BA, Vassar College, 1956; MA, 1957, PhD, 1967, Cornell University. Appointments: Assistantships, Cornell University, University of New Brunswick; Poetry Reviewer, Fiddlehead Magazine. Publications: Five Poets: Cornell, 1960; An Inch or So of Garden, 1969; Poems 1969-72, 1973; Homecomings, 1977; Divinations and Shorter Poems, 1973-78, 1980; Walking Under the Nebulae, 1981; Reckonings: Poems 1979-83, 1988; Solid Things: Poems New and Selected, 1993; Temporary Shelter, 1993; Night Physics, 1994. Contributions to: Reviews, quarterlies, and reviews. Honours: Honorary Research Associate, University of New Brunswick; Pat Lowther Prize, League of Canadian Poets, 1980. Memberships: Canadian Poetry Association; League of Canadian Poets; Writers Federation of New Brunswick. Address: 807 Windsor Street, Fredericton, New Brunswick E3B 4G7, Canada.

LANE Patrick, b. 26 Mar 1939, Nelson, Canada. Writer; Poet. 4 sons, 1 daughter. Education: University of British Columbia. Appointments: Editor, Very Stone House, Publishers, Vancouver, 1966-72; Writer-in-Residence, University of Manitoba, Winnepeg, 1978-79, University of Ottawa, 1980, University of Alberta, Edmonton, 1981-82, Saskatoon Public Library, 1982-83, Concordia University, 1985, Globe Theatre Co, Regina, Saskatchewan, 1985-. Publications: Letters From the Savage Mind, 1966; For Rita: In Asylum, 1969; Calgary City Jail, 1969; Separations, 1969; Sunflower Seeds, 1969; On the Street, 1970; Mountain Oysters, 1971; Hiway 401 Rhapsody, 1972; The Sun Has Begun to Eat the Mountain, 1972; Passing into Storm, 1973; Beware the Months of Fire, 1974; Certs, 1974; Unborn Things: South American Poems, 1975; For Riel in That Gawdam Prison, 1975; Albino Pheasants, 1977; If, 1977; Poems, New and Selected, 1978; No Longer Two People (with Lorna Uher), 1979; The Measure, 1980; Old Mother, 1982; Woman in the Dust, 1983; A Linen Crow, a Caftan Magpie, 1985; Milford and Me, 1989; Winter, 1990; Mortal Remains, 1992; Too Spare, Too Fierce, 1995; Selected Poems, 1978-1997, 1997. Contributions to: Most major Canadian magazines, American and English journals. Honour: Governor-General's Award for Poetry, 1979; CAA Award, 1985; B C Book Award, 1997. Memberships: League of Canadian Poets; Writer's Union of Canada; PEN, Canada. Address: c/o Writer's Union of Canada, 24 Ryerson Avenue, Toronto, Ontario M5T 2P3, Canada.

LANE Roumelia, b. 31 Dec 1927, Bradford, West Yorkshire, England. Writer. m. Gavin Green, 1 Oct 1949, 1 son, 1 daughter. Publications: Numerous books, including: Sea of Zanj; Rose of the Desert; Cafe Mimosa; Harbour of Deceit; Desert Haven; Bamboo Wedding; Night of the Beguine; The Chasm; The Nawindi Flier. Television and film scripts: Stardust; The Chasm; Tender Saboteur; Chantico; Turn of the Tide; Gilligan's Last Gamble; Where Are the Clowns?; Death From the Past. Contributions to: Various journals and magazines. Memberships: Society of Authors of Great Britain; Writers Guild of Great Britain; Writers Guild of America (East and West). Address: Casa Mimosa, Santa Eugenia, Majorca, Beleares, Spain.

LANG Grace. See: FLOREN Lee.

LANG King. See: TUBB E(dwin) C(harles).

LANG Serge, b. 6 June 1920, France. Writer. m. 1 son, 1 daughter. Education: Bachelor Degree, University

of Basle. Publications: Cinema D;au Jourd Hui, 1946; Trait Geneva Portrait Eines Menschheits-Verbrechers/Rosenberg Memory (with Ernst von Schenk), 1948; Notre Victgoire Olympique, 1961. Contributions to: Journals, periodicals, quarterlies and reviews. Honour: Legion D'Honneur. Address: Rheintalwe 6, 106 CH 4125 Riehen, Switzerland.

LANG-DILLENBURGER Elmy, (Elmy Lang), b. 13 Aug 1921, Pirmasens, Germany. Author. m. Franz Dillenburger, 1947, 1 son. Education: Interpreter's Diploma. Publications: Mitternachtsspritzer, poetry, 1970; Frühstück auf französisch, novel, 1971; Die Verfolgung, radio play, 1974; Dani und Heseki reisen zur Erde, radio story, 1975; Kleine Maus auf großer Reise, Dackel Strolch und der Schnupfer. and others, children's books, 1976; Die Bodenguckkinder, tale, 1977; Pingpong Pinguin, English-German poems, 1978, 1980; Das Wort, Blick ins Paradies, poetry, 1980; Limericks, 1984; Der Rabenwald, novel, 1985; Stufen zum Selbst, poetry, 1986; Der Schäfer von Madrid, tales, 1986; Lebenszeichen, poetry, 1988; ICH-Vincent van Gogh, novel, 1990; Verdammt geliebtes Leben - Vie maudite bien aimée, French-German poetry, 1992; Paradies mit Streifen, short stories, 1994; Bis der Adler stürzt, novel, 1997. Contributions to: Lady International; Der Literat; Many other newspapers and magazines. Honours: Diplomas di Merito, Università di Salsomaggiore, 1982; Landgrafmedaille Stadt Pirmasens, 1986; Gran Premio d'Europa, La Musa dell' Arte; Elk-Feder, Munich; Selected, Woman of the Year, American Biographical Institute, 1998. Memberships: Europäische Autorenvereinigung Die Kogge; German Authors Association; Regensburg International; Artists for Peace Assocation; Association Européen François Mauriac. Address: Strobelallee 62, 66953 Pirmasens, Germany.

LANGBACKA Ralf Runar, b. 20 Nov 1932, Narpes, Finland. Theatre Director; Professor. m. Birgitta Danielsson, 5 Nov 1961, 2 sons, 1 daughter. Education: MA, Abo Akademi, Turku, Finland, 1956. Appointments: Artistic Director, Swedish Theatre, Turku, Finland, 1960-63; Director, Finnish National Theatre, Helsinki, 1963-65; Artistic Director, Swedish Theatre, Helsinki, 1965-67; Director, Gothenburg City Theatre, Sweden, 1967-71; Artistic Director, Turku City Theatre, 1971-77; Professor of Arts, Helsinki, , 1975-83, 1988-93; Managing Director, Helsinki City Theatre, 1983-87; Visiting Professor, Theatre Science, ABO Akademi, 1994-97. Publications: Bland annat om Brecht (On Brecht and Others), 1982, revised edition in Finnish, 1983; Möten med Tjechov (Meetings with Chekhov), 1986; Denna langa dag, detta korta liv (This Long Day, this Short Life), poems, 1988; Krocketspelaren (The Croquetplayer), play, 1990; Olga, Irina och jag (Olga, Irina and I), play, 1991; Brecht og det realisticke teater, De første 100 ar (Brecht and the Realistic Theatre) in Danish, 1998. Contributions to: About 800 articles on film, literature, theatre and politics. Honours: The Critics Spurs, 1963; The Henrik Steffen Award, 1997. Address: Hopeasalmenranta 1B, 00570 Helsinki, Finland.

LANGDALE Cecily, b. 27 July 1939, New York, New York, USA. Art Dealer; Art Historian. m. Roy Davis, 24 July 1972. Education: BA, Swarthmore College, 1961. Publications: Gwen John: Paintings and Drawings from the Collection of John Quinn and Others (with Betsy G Fryberger), 1982; Monotypes by Maurice Prendergast in the Terra Museum of Art, 1984; Gwen John: An Interior Life (with David Fraser Jenkins), 1985; Gwen John: With a Catalogue of the Paintings and a Selection of the Drawings, 1987; Maurice Brazil Prendergast, Charles Prendergast: A Catalogue Raisonné, 1990. Contributions to: Books and journals. Address: 231 East 60th Street, New York, NY 10022, USA.

LANGE John. See: CRICHTON Michael.

LANGER Lawrence L(ee), b. 20 June 1929, New York, New York, USA. Professor Emeritus; Author. m. Sondra Weinstein, 21 Feb 1951, 1 son, 1 daughter. Education: BA, City College, New York City, 1951; MA, 1952, PhD, 1961, Harvard University. Appointments:

Instructor, 1956-61, Assistant Professor, 1961-66, Associate Professor, 1966-72, Professor, 1972-76, Alumnae Chair Professor, 1976-92, Professor Emeritus, 1992-, Simmons College. Publications: The Holocaust and the Literary Imagination, 1975; The Age of Artocity: Death in Modern Literature, 1978; Versions of Survival: The Holocaust and the Human Spirit, 1982; Holocaust Testimonies: The Ruins of Memory, 1991; Admitting the Holocaust: Collected Essays, 1994; Art from the Ashes: A Holocaust Anthology, 1994. Contributions to: Journals. Honour: National Book Critics Circle Award, 1991. Membership: PEN. Address: 249 Adams Avenue, West Newton, MA 02165, USA.

LANGFORD Gary (Raymond), b. 21 Aug 1947, Christchuch, New Zealand. Writer; Dramatist; Poet; Senior Lecturer. 1 daughter. Education: BA, 1969, MA, Honours, History, 1971, MA, Honours, English, 1973, University of Canterbury; Diploma of Teaching Drama, Christchurch Secondary Teachers College, 1973. Appointments: Senior Lecturer in Creative Writing, University of Western Sydney, 1986; Writer-in-Residence, University of Canterbury, 1989. Publications: Over 20 books, including novels and poetry. Other: Plays and scripts for stage, radio, and television. Contributions to: Anthologies and other publications. Honours: Australia Council Young Writers Fellowship, 1976; Alan Marshall Award, 1983. Address: c/o Curtis Brown Pty Ltd, Box 19, Paddington, New South Wales, 2021, Australia.

LANGFORD GINIBI Ruby, b. 26 Jan 1934, Box Ridge Mission, Coraki, New South Wales, Australia. Author; Poet. Div., 4 sons, 5 daughters, 3 dec. Publications: Don't take your love to town, 1988; Real Deadly, 1992; My Bundjalung People, 1994; Haunted By The Past, 1998. Contributions to: Women's Weekly; HQ; Sun Herald; Meanjin; Best of Independent, monthly, 1990; A to Z Authorship by Ken Methold; Aboriginal English, 1996; Australian Literary Studies; Canonozities by Southerlys, 1997. Honours: Human Rights Literature, 1988; Honorary Fellowship, 1995. Membership: Australian Society of Authors. Literary Agent: Rose Crestwell, Cameron & Crestwell Agency, Suite 5, Edgecliff Court, 2 New McLean Street, NSW 2027, Australia. Address: 18 Hewlett Street, Granville, NSW 2142, Australia.

LANGHOLM Neil. See: BULMER Henry Kenneth.

LANGLAND Joseph Thomas, b. 16 Feb 1917, Spring Grove, Minnesota, USA. Professor Emeritus; Writer. m. Judith Gail Wood, 26 June 1943, 2 sons, 1 daughter. Education: AA, Santa Ana College, 1936; BA, 1940, MA, 1941, Graduate Studies, 1946-48, University of Iowa; Harvard University, Columbia University, 1953-54. Appointments: Instructor, Dana College, 1941-42, University of Iowa, 1946-48; Assistant, then Associate Professor, University of Wyoming, 1948-49; Associate Professor to Professor, 1959-80, Professor Emeritus, 1980-, University of Massachusetts. Publications: A Dream of Love, 1986; Twelve Poems, 1991; Selected Poems, 1992. Contributions to: Reviews, quarterlies, journals, and magazines. Honours: Ford Foundation Faculty Fellowship; Amy Lowell Poetry Fellowship; New England Living Legend; Chancellor's Prize. Address: 18 Morgan Circle, Amherst, MA 01002, USA.

LANGTON Jane (Gillson), b. 30 Dec 1922, Boston, Massachusetts, USA. Writer. m. William Langton, 10 June 1943, 3 sons. Education: BA, 1944, MA, 1945, University of Michigan; MA, Radcliffe College, 1948. Publications: For Adults: The Transcendental Murder, 1964; Dark Nantucket Noon, 1975; The Memorial Hall Murder, 1978; Natural Enemy, 1982; Emily Dickinson is Dead, 1984; Good and Dead, 1986; Murder at the Gardner, 1988; The Dante Game, 1991; God in Concord, 1992; Divine Inspiration, 1993; The Shortest Day, 1995; Dead as a Dodo, 1996; The Face on the Wall, 1998; The Thief of Venice, 1999. For Children: Her Majesty, Grace Jones, 1961; Diamond in the Window, 1962; The Swing in the Summerhouse, 1967; The Astonishing Stereoscope, 1971; The Boyhood of Grace Jones, 1972; Paper Chains, 1977; The Fledgling, 1980; The Fragile Flag, 1984. Honours: Newbery Honor Book, 1981; Nero

Wolfe Award, 1984. Literary Agent: Meg Ruley, Jane Rotrosen Agency, New York. Address: Baker Farm Road, Lincoln, MA 01773, USA.

LANIER Sterling E(dmund), b. 18 Dec 1927, New York, New York, USA. Writer; Sculptor. Appointments: Research Historian, Winterthur Museum, Switzerland, 1958-60; Editor, John C Winston Co, 1961, Chilton Books, 1961-62, 1965-67, Macrae-Smith Co, 1963-64; Full-time Writer and Sculptor, 1967-. Publications: The War for the Lot (juvenile), 1969; The Peculiar Exploits of Brigadier Ffellowes (short stories), 1972; Hiero's Journey, 1973; The Unforsaken Hiero, 1983; Menace Under Marwood, 1983; The Curious Quest of Brig Ffellowes, 1986. Address: c/o Curtis Brown Ltd, 10 Astor Place, New York, NY 10003, USA.

LANSIDE Luke. See: **CRAGGS Robert S.**

LANTRY Mike. See: **TUBB E(dwin) C(harles).**

LAPHAM Lewis H, b. 8 Jan 1935, San Francisco, California, USA. Writer. m. 3 children. Education: BA, Yale University, 1956; Cambridge University. Appointments: Reporter, San Francisco Examiner, 1957-59, New York Herald Tribune, 1960-62; Managing Editor, Harper's Magazine, 1976-81, 1983-; Syndicated newspaper columnist, 1981-87; Lecturer in universities including Yale, Stanford, Michigan, Virginia and Oregon; Appearances on American and British television, National Public Radio and Canadian Public Radio. Publications: Fortune's Child (essays), 1980; Money and Class in America, 1988; Imperial Masquerade, 1990; Hotel America: Scenes in the Lobby of the Fin-de-Siècle, 1995; Waiting for the Barbarians, 1997; The Agony of Mammon, 1999. Contributions to: Monthly essay for Harper's magazine as "Notebook"; Commentary; National Review; Yale Literary Magazine; Elle; Fortune; Forbes; American Spectator; Vanity Fair; Parade; Channels; Maclean's; London Observer; New York Times; Wall Street Journal. Honour: National Magazine Award, 1995. Address: c/o Harper's Magazine, 666 Broadway, New York, NY 10012, USA.

LAPIN Leonhard, (Albert Trapeezh), b. 29 Dec 1947, Räpina, Estonia. Architect; Artist; Poet. 1 son, 1 daughter. Education: Tallinn Art University, 1966-71. Appointments: Editor, Estonian Architecture Review, Ehituskunst, 1991-; Professor, Helsinki Art School, 1992-, Tallinn Art Academy, 1995-. Publications: As Albert Trapeezh: Sitased Seitsmekimrendad, English translation as The Dirty 70s, 1993; Hääcitsusi Ja Sonu, English translation as Sounds and Words, 1995; Void and Space, 1994; Pimeydesta Valoon, 1996; Kontseptsioonid Protjessid, English translation as Conceptions, Processes, 1997; Tuhjus sa Ruum Void and Sapce, 1998. Address: Liivalaia 7-41, Tallinn 10118, Estonia.

LAPINE James (Elliot), b. 10 Jan 1949, Mansfield, Ohio, USA. Dramatist; Director. m. Sarah Marshall Kernochan, 24 Feb 1985, 1 daughter. Education: BA, Franklin and Marshall College; MFA, California Institute of the Arts. Appointments: Director of several plays and films; Lecturer on drama. Publications: Photographs, 1977; Table Settings, 1980; Twelve Dreams, 1983; Sunday in the Park with George, 1984; Into the Woods, 1987; Falsettoland, 1990; Luck, Pluck and Virtue, 1993; Passion, 1994. Honours: Obie Award, 1977; George Oppenheimer/Newsday Award, 1983; Pulitzer Prize for Drama, 1984; New York Critic's Circle Awards, 1984, 1988; Tony Awards, 1988, 1992, 1994. Membership: Dramatists Guild. Address: c/o International Creative Management, 40 West 57th Street, New York, NY 10019, USA.

LAPPE Frances Moore, b. 10 Feb 1944, Pendleton, Oregon, USA. Author, nonprofit Executive. 1 son, 1 daughter. Education: BA, Earlham College, Richmond, Indiana. Publications: Diet for a Small Planet, 1971; Food First: Beyond the Myth of Scarcity (co-author), 1977; World Hunger, Ten Myths (co-author), 1979; Aid as Obstacle, 1980; Mozambique and Tanzania: Asking the Big Questions and Casting New Molds: First Steps

Toward Worker Control in a Mozambique Factory (co-author), 1980; What to Do After You Turn Off the TV: Fresh Ideas for Enjoying Family Time, 1985; World Hunger: Twelve Myths, 1986; Betraying the National Interest (co-author), 1987; Rediscovering America's Values, 1989; Taking Population Seriously (co-author), 1989; The Quickening of America (co-author), 1994. Contributions to: New York Times; Harper's; Reader's Digest; Journal of Nutrition Education; War on Hunger. Honours: Right Livelihood Award; World Hunger Media Award; Henry George Award. Address: 289 Fox Farm Road, Box 8187, Brattleboro, VT 05304, USA.

LAPPING Brian (Michael), b. 13 Sept 1937, London, England. Television Producer; Journalist; Editor. Education: BA, Pembroke College, Cambridge, 1959. Appointments: Reporter, Daily Mirror, London, 1959-61; Reporter and Deputy Commonwealth Correspondent, The Guardian, London, 1961-67; Editor, Venture, Fabian Society monthly journal, 1965-69; Feature Writer, Financial Times, London, 1967-68; Deputy Editor, New Society, London, 1968-70; Television Producer, Granada Television Ltd, 1970-88; Executive Producer, World in Action 1976-78, The State of the Nation 1978-80, End of Empire 1980-85; Chief Executive, Brian Lapping Associates, 1988-; Executive Producer, Countdown to War, 1989; Hypotheticals (three programmes annually for BBC2); The Second Russian Revolution (8 programmes for BBC2), 1991; Question Time (weekly for BBC1), 1991-94; The Washington Version (for BBC2), 1992; Watergate (for BBC2), 1994; Fall of the Wall (for BBC2), 1994; The Death of Yugoslavia, 1995. Publications: More Power to the People (co-editor), 1968; The Labour Government 1964-70, 1970; The State of the Nation: Parliament (editor), 1973; The State of the Nation: The Bounds of Freedom, 1980; End of Empire, 1985; Apartheid: A History, 1986; The 50 Years War: Israel and the Arabs, 1998; Hostage, 1999. Honours: Royal Television Society Award, Broadcasting Press Guild Award, 1991; Emmy Award, DuPont Award; 12 international awards, 1995. Address: 61 Eton Avenue, London NW3, England.

LAQUEUR Walter (Ze'ev), b. 26 May 1921, Breslau, Germany. History Educator. m. (1) Barbara Koch, 29 May 1941, dec, 2 daughters, (2) Susi Wichmann, 1995. Appointments: Journalist, Freelance Author, 1944-55; Editor, Survey, 1955-65; Co-Editor, Journal of Contemporary History, 1966-; Member, Center for Strategic and International Studies, Washington, DC. Publications: Communism and Nationalism in the Middle East, 1956; Young Germany, 1961; Russia and Germany, 1965; The Road to War, 1968; Europe since Hitler, 1970; Out of the Ruins of Europe, 1971; Zionism, a History, 1972; A Reader's Guide to Contemporary History (co-editor), 1972; Confrontation: The Middle East and World Politics, 1974; Weimar: A Cultural History 1918-1933, 1974; Guerrilla, 1976; Terrorism, 1977; Fascism: A Reader's Guide (editor), 1978; The Missing Years, 1980; The Terrible Secret, 1980; Farewell to Europe, 1981; Germany Today: A Personal Report, 1985; World of Secrets: The Uses and Limits of Intelligence, 1986; The Long Road to Freedom: Russia and Glasnost, 1989; Thursday's Child Has Far to Go, 1993. Honours: 1st Distinguished Writer's Award, Center for Strategic and International Studies, 1969; Inter Nations Award, 1985. Address: Center for Strategic and International Studies, 1800 K Street North West, Washington, DC 20006, USA.

LARDNER Ring(gold Wilmer), Jr, b. 19 Aug 1915, Chicago, Illinois, USA. Screenwriter; Author. m. Frances Chaney, 28 Sept 1946. Education: Phillips Academy, Andover, Massachusetts; Princeton University. Publications: The Ectasy of Owen Muir, 1954; The Lardners: My Family Remembered, 1976; All for Love, 1985. Other: Various screenplays. Honours: Best Original Screenplay, 1942, Best Screenplay Based on Material from Another Medium, 1970, Academy of Motion Picture Arts and Sciences; Best Comedy Award, 1970; Laurel Award for Lifetime Achievement in Screenwriting, 1989, Writers Guild of America. Memberships: PEN; Screen Writers Guild; Writers Guild of America. Address: c/o Jim

Preminger Agency, 1650 Westwood Boulevard, Los Angeles, CA 90024, USA.

LARKIN Rochelle, b. 6 May 1935, New York, New York, USA. Writer. Appointments: Editor, Countrywide Publications, 1963; Kanrom Inc, 1964-70, Pinnacle Books, 1970, Walman Publishing, 1992-; Editor-in-Chief, Lancer Books, 1973-74, Female Bodybuilding Magazine, 1986-89, Bodybuilding Lifestyles Magazine, 1990-91. Publications: Soul Music, 1970; Supermarket Superman, 1970; Teen Scene (with Milburn Smith), 1971; The Godmother, 1971; Honour Thy Godmother, 1972; For Godmother and Country, 1972; 365 Ways to Say I Want To Be Your Friend (with Milburn Smith), 1973; Black Magic, 1974; The Beatles: Yesterday, Today, Tomorrow, 1974; The Greek Goddess, 1975; Call Me Anytime, 1975; International Joke Book, 1975; The Raging Flood, 1976; Hail Columbia, 1976; The First One, 1976; Valency Girl (with Robin Moore), 1976; Pusher, 1976; Sexual Superstars, 1976; Harvest of Desire, 1976; Kitty, 1977; Mafia Wife (with Robin Moore), 1977; Mistress of Desire, 1978; Instant Beauty (with Pablo Manzoni), 1978; Tri (with Robin Moore), 1978; Torches of Desire, 1979; Glitterball, 1980; Beverly Johnson's Guide to a Life of Health and Beauty (with Julie Davis), 1981; Only Perfect, 1981; Golden Days, Silver Nights, 1982; Amber series (as Darrell Fairfield), 6 volumes, 1982; The Crystal Heart, 1983; Angels Never Sleep, 1984. Address: 351 East 84th Street, New York, NY 10028, USA.

LARSEN Eric Everett, b. 29 Nov 1941, Northfield, Minnesota, USA. Professor of English; Writer. m. Anne Schnare, 5 June 1965, 2 daughters. Education: BA, Carleton College, 1963; MA, 1964, PhD, 1971, University of Iowa. Appointment: Professor of English, John Jay College of Criminal Justice, City University of New York, 1971-. Publications: Novels: An American Memory, 1988; I Am Zoe Handke, 1992. Contributions to: Harper's; New Republic; Nation; Los Angeles Times Book Review; North American Review; New England Review. Honour: Heartland Prize, Chicago Tribune, 1988. Address: c/o Brandt and Brandt, Literary Agents Inc, 1501 Broadway, New York, NY 10036, USA.

LARSEN Jeanne (Louise), b. 9 Aug 1950, Washington, District of Columbia, USA. Professor of English; Writer; Poet; Translator. m. Thomas Hugh Mesner, 13 Aug 1977, 1 stepson, 1 stepdaughter. Education: BA, Oberlin College, 1971; MA, Hollins College, 1972; Graduate Research Certificate, Nagasaki University, 1980; PhD, University of Iowa, 1983. Appointments: Lecturer, Tunghai University, 1972-74; Assistant Professor, 1975, 1980-86, Associate Professor, 1986-92, Professor of English, 1992-98, Hollins College; Professor of English, Hollins University, 1998-. Publications: Novels: Silk Road, 1989; Bronze Mirror, 1991; Manchu Palaces, 1996. Poetry: James Cook in Search of Terra Incognita: A Book of Poems, 1979. Other: Brocade River Poems: Selected Works of the Tang Dynasty Courtesan Xue Tao (translator and editor), 1987; Engendering the Word: Feminist Essays in Psychosexual Poetics (editor with others), 1989. Contributions to: Scholarly books, anthologies, learned journals and periodicals. Honours: 1st Selection, Associated Writing Programs' Annual Poetry Book Competition, 1979; Resident Fellowships, Virginia Center for the Creative Arts, 1982, 1986, 1987, 1989, 1990, 1995; John Gardner Fellowship in Fiction, Bread Loaf Writers' Conference, 1990; William L Crawford Award for Year's Best New Novelist, International Association for the Fantastic in the Arts, 1990; National Endowment for the Arts Fellowship in Translation, 1995. Memberships: Association for Asian Studies; Authors Guild; International Association for the Fantastic in the Arts; PEN; Poets and Writers. Address: c/o Department of English, Hollins University, Roanoke, VA 24020, USA.

LARSON Ingrid Dana, b. 30 Sept 1965, Manchester, Connecticut, USA. Administrative Assistant; Author. Education: Bachelor of Arts Communication, Stonehill College, North Easton, Massachusetts, 1997. Publications: The Adventures of Herman and Hurby, 1995, 1997; Poems in anthologies: Spring, 1995; Streets of Emptiness, 1996; Have a Nice Day, 1997; Broken Down Fishing House, 1997; It Is Spring, 1997; Wings, 1997; Their Home, 1997; Gorse, 1998; Was It You, 1998; Loch Lomond, 1998; York, 1998; Ode to the Words of Worth, 1998. Honours: 5th Place for Was It You, Poetic Voices of America, 1998; Several Certificates of Merit for poems. Address: 486 West Union Street, East Bridgewater, MA 02333, USA.

LARUE Monique, b. 1948, Montreal, Quebec, Canada. Author; College Teacher. Education: BPh, University of Montreal, 1970; MA, Philosophy, 1971, Doctorat de 3éme cycle en lettres, 1976, Sorbonne, University of Paris. Appointment: Teacher, Department of French, Collège Edouard Montpetit, Montreal, 1974-. Publications: La cohorte fictive, 1979; Les faux fuyants, 1982; Copies conformes, 1989, English translation as True Copies, 1996; Promenades littéraires dans Montréal (with Jean-Francois Chassay), 1989; La démarche du crabe, 1995. Honour: Grand Prix du livre de Montreal, 1990. Address: c/o Union des écrivaines et écrivains québécois, La Maison des écrivains, 3492 Avenue Laval, Montreal, Quebec H2X 3C8, Canada.

LASKA Vera, b. 21 July 1928, Kosice, Czechoslovakia. Professor of History; Lecturer; Columnist; Author. m. Andrew J Laska, 5 Nov 1949, 2 sons. Education: MA, History, 1946, MA, Philosophy, 1946, Charles University, Prague; PhD, History, University of Chicago, 1959. Appointments: Professor of History, Regis College, Weston, Massachusetts, 1966-; Fulbright Professor, Charles University, Prague, 1993. Publications: Remember the Ladies; Outstanding Women of the American Revolution, 1976; Franklin and Women, 1978; Czechs in America 1633-1977, 1978; Benjamin Franklin the Diplomat, 1982; Women in the Resistance and in the Holocaust, 1983, 2nd edition, 1988; Nazism, Resistance and Holocaust: A Bibliography, 1985; Two Loves of Benjamin Franklin (in Czech), 1994. Contributions to: Over 300 articles and book reviews in newspapers and professional journals. Honours: Kidger Award for Excellence in History, 1984; George Washington Honor Medal in Communication, 1990. Address: 50 Woodchester Drive, Weston, MA 02193, USA.

LASKOWSKI Jacek Andrzej, b. 4 June 1946, Edinburgh, Scotland. Dramatist; Translator. m. Anne Grant Howieson, 8 July 1978, 2 daughters. Education: MagPhil, Jagiellonian Universiy, Kraków, Poland, 1973. Appointment: Literary Manager, Haymarket Theatre, Leicester, 1984-87. Publications: Plays produced: Dreams to Damnation, BBC Radio 3, 1977; Pawn Takes Pawn, BBC Radio 4, 1978; The Secret Agent, BBC Radio 4, 1980; Nostromo, BBC Radio 4, 1985; Phoney Physician (after Molière), 1986; Orestes/Electra (with Nancy Meckler), 1987; Wiseguy Scapino (after Molière), 1993. Memberships: Society of Authors, vice-chairman, Broadcasting Committee, 1983-83; Writers' Guild of Great Britain. Address: c/o Alan Brodie Representation, 211 Piccadilly, London W1V 9LD, England.

LATHAM Mavis. See: **CLARK Mavis Thorpe.**

LAU Evelyn, b. 1970, Canada. Poet; Writer. Publications: Poetry: You Are Not Who You Claim, 1990; Oedipal Dreams, 1993; In the House of the Slaves, 1993. Fiction: Fresh Girls, and Other Stories, 1993; Other Women, 1995. Non-Fiction: Runaway: Diary of a Street Kid, 1989. Contributions to: Periodicals. Honour: Air Canada Award, 1989. Address: c/o Coach House Press, 50 Prince Arthur Avenue, Suite 107, Toronto, Ontario M5R 1B5, Canada.

LAUER Bernhard, b. 2 Jan 1954, Britten, Saar. Director; Museum Curator. Education: PhD, Department of Slavic and Romanic Languages, University of Marburg, Lahn, 1983. Publications: On poetom rozden... (A Study of the Lyrical Poetry of Fedor Sologub, 1983; The Brothers Grimm, Documents of Life and Work, 1985; Rapunzel, European Traditions of a Fairy Tale, 1993. Contributions to: Yearbook of Association of Brothers Grimm. Membership: Association of Brothers Grimm,

Geneneral Secretary. Address: Brüder Grimm-Museum Kassel, Brüder Grimm-Platz 4A, 34117, Kassel, Germany.

LAURENTS Arthur, b. 14 July 1917, New York, New York, USA. Dramatist; Writer; Director. Education: BA, Cornell University, 1937. Publications: Plays: Home of the Brave, 1946; The Bird Cage, 1950; The Time of the Cuckoo, 1952; A Clearing in the Woods, 1956; Invitation to a March, 1960; The Enclave, 1973; Scream, Houston, 1978; The Hunting Season, 1995; The Radical Mystique, 1995. Musical Plays: West Side Story, 1957; Gypsy, 1959; Do I Hear a Waltz?, 1964; Hallelujah Baby, 1967; Nick and Nora, 1991. Screenplays: The Snake Pit, 1948; Rope, 1948; Caught, 1948; Anna Lucasta, 1949; Anastasia, 1956; Bonjour Tristesse, 1958; The Way We Were, 1973; The Turning Point, 1977. Novels: The Way We Were, 1972; The Turning Point, 1977. Honours: Tony Awards, 1967, 1984; Drama Desk Awards, 1974, 1978; Golden Glove Award, 1977; Writers Guild of America, 1977; Best Director Award, 1985. Memberships: Academy of Motion Picture Arts and Sciences; Authors League; Dramatists Guild; PEN; Screenwriters Guild; Theatre Hall of Fame. Address: c/o William Morris Agency, 1325 Avenue of the Americas, New York, NY 10019, USA.

LAURIDSEN Soren K, b. 12 May 1945, Esbjerg, Denmark. Writer; Director. m. Liselotte, 26 Sept 1992, 2 daughters. Education: MA, Royal Academy of Educational Studies, Copenhagen, 1985. Publications: A Place in the Reservate, 1974; Landscape with Windmill, 1982; Against a Sinking Globe, 1988; The Dream of Boca del Cielo, 1993. Membership: Danish Writers Union. Address: Brombaervej 10, 8410 Ronde, Denmark.

LAURIE Rona, b. 16 Sept 1916, Derby, England. Actress; Writer; Drama Lecturer; Professor of Speech and Drama. m. Edward James Neilson, 1961. Education: Penrhos College; University of Birmingham; Royal Academy of Dramatic Art. Appointment: Professor of Speech and Drama, Guildhall School of Music. Publications: A Hundred Speeches from the Theatre, 1966; Speaking Together I & II, 1966; Scenes and Ideas, 1967; Festivals and Ajudication, 1975; Children's Plays from Beatrix Potter, 1980; Auditioning, 1985; Mrs Tiggywinkle and Friends, 1986; The Actors' Art and Craft, 1994. Contributions to: Speaking Shakespeare Today (Speech and Drama); Speaking the Sonnet (Speech and Drama). Memberships: British Federation of Music, Dance and Speech Festivals; Honorary Member, Guild of Drama Adjudicators; Society of Teachers of Speech and Drama; Scottish Association of Speech and Drama Adjudicators; Royal Society of Arts, fellow. Address: 21 New Quebec Street, London W1H 7DE, England.

LAURO Shirley (Shapiro), b. 18 Nov 1933, Des Moines, Iowa, USA. Actress; Playwright; Teacher. m. (1) Norton Mezvinsky, div, (2) Louis Paul Lauro, 18 Aug 1973. Education: BS, Northwestern University, 1955; MS, University of Wisconsin at Madison, 1957. Appointments: Actress, stage, films and television; Instructor, City College of the City University of New York, 1967-71; Yeshiva University, 1971-76, Manhattan Community College, 1978, Marymount Manhattan College, 1978-79; Literary Consultant, 1975-80, Resident Playwright, 1976-, Ensemble Studio Theatre, New York City; Resident Playwright, Alley Theatre, Houston, 1987; Adjunct Professor of Playwrighting, Tisch School of the Arts, New York University, 1989-. Publications: The Edge, 1965; The Contest, 1975; Open Admissions, Nothing Immediate, I Don't Know Where You're Coming From At All!, The Coal Diamond, Margaret and Kit, 1979; In the Garden of Eden, 1982; Sunday Go to Meetin', 1986; Pearls on the Moon, 1987; A Piece of My Heart, 1992; A Moment in Time, 1994; The Last Trial of Clarence Darrow, 1997; Railing it Uptown, 1997. Contributions to: Periodicals. Honours: Numerous. Memberships: Authors Guild; Authors League; Dramatists Guild; League of Professional Theatre Women; PEN; Writers Guild of America. Address: 275 Central Park West, New York, NY 10024, USA.

LAVERS Norman, b. 21 Apr 1935, Berkeley, California, USA. Teacher; Writer. m. Cheryl Dicks, 20 July 1967, 1 son. Education: BA, 1960, MA, 1963, San Francisco State University; PhD, University of Iowa, 1969. Publications: Mark Harris (criticism) 1978; Selected Short Stories, 1979; Jerzy Kosinski (criticism) 1982; The Northwest Passage (novel), 1984; Pop Culture Into Art: The Novels of Manuel Puig (criticism), 1988; Growing up in Berkeley with the Bomb (autobiography), 1998. Contributions to: Editor, Arkansas Review; Contributing Editor, Bird Watcher's Digest. Honours: National Endowment for the Arts Fellowships, 1982, 1991; Editor's Choice Award, 1986; Hohenberg Award, 1986; O Henry Award, 1987; Pushcart Award, 1992; William Peden Prize, 1992; Porter Fund Award, 1995. Address: 3968 CR 901, Jonesboro, AR 72401, USA.

LAVIN S R, b. 2 Apr 1945, Springfield, Massachusetts, USA. Professor of English; Poet; Writer. 2 sons, 4 daughters. Education: AIC, BA, 1967; MA, Literature, Trinity College, 1970. Appointments: Poet-in-Residence, Clark University, Worcester, Massachusetts, 1972; Professor of English, Castleton State College, Vermont, 1987-. Publications: Poetry: The Stonecutters at War with the Cliff Dwellers, 1972; Cambodian Spring, 1973; Let Myself Shine, 1979. Novels: Metacomet; Opal; Feingold's Loop. Translation: I and You, by Martin Buber. Contributions to: Broadway Boogie; Cold Drill; Hiram; I.P.R.; Mandrake; Stand; Vermont Literary Magazine. Address: c/o Department of English, Castleton State College, Castleton, VT 05735, USA.

LAW Michael, (Kreuzenau), b. 17 Apr 1925, Kerman, Iran. Retired University Lecturer. m. Dorothea V Schön, 15 Aug 1954, 4 sons. Education: Peterhouse, Cambridge, 1948-51; BA, Modern Languages Tripos, 1951, Cambridge. Appointments: Teacher, St Paul's School, 1956-65, Nuffield Modern Languages Project, 1965-68; Lecturer in Education, Leeds University, 1969-83. Publications: The Vienna Opera House (translation), 1955; Caricature from Leonard to Picasso (translation), 1957; 7 German Readers for Schools, 1960-75; How to Read German (textbook), 1963; Brecht's Man is Man (translation), 1983; Tankred Dorst's The Great Denunciation Outside the City Wall (translation), 1998; Published plays: Two or Three Ghosts, 1997; Come and Get Me, 1997, A Companion for Claire, 1997; Helen of Rhodes, 1997; Aquarium, 1997; The Magic Man, 1997; Just Us, 1998; The Nurse's Tale, 1998; The Wench is Dead, 1998. Contributions to: Numerous educational journals. Honours: Numerous prizes for plays from The Drama Association of Wales, Understanding, other organisations. Memberships: Society of Authors; Writers' Guild. Address: 90A Upper Tollington Park, London N4 4NB, England.

LAWRENCE Clifford Hugh, b. 28 Dec 1921, London, England. Professor of Medieval History Emeritus; Writer. m. Helen Maud Curran, 11 July 1953, 1 son, 5 daughters. Education: BA, 1st Class Honours, 1948; MA, 1953, DPhil, 1956, University of Oxford. Appointments: Assistant Lecturer, 1951, Lecturer, 1953-63, Reader in Medieval History, 1963-70, Bedford College, London; External Examiner, University of Newcastle upon Tyne, 1972-74, University of Bristol, 1975-77, University of Reading, 1977-79; Professor of Medieval History, 1970-87, Professor Emeritus, 1987-, University of London. Publications: St Edmund of Abingdon: A Study in Hagiography and History, 1960; The English Church and the Papacy in the Middle Ages, 1965; 2nd Edition, 1999; The University in State and Church, Vol 1 of The History of the University of Oxford, 1984; Medieval Monasticism: Forms of Religious Life in Western Europe in the Middle Ages, 1984, 2nd edition, 1989; The Friars: The Impact of the Early Mendicant Movement on Western Society, 1994; The Life of St Edmund, by Matthew Prior (translator and biographer), 1996. Contributions to: Reference works, and scholarly books and journals. Memberships: Royal Historical Society, fellow; Society of Antiquaries. Address: 11 Durham Road, London SW20 0QH, England.

LAWRENCE Jerome, b. 14 July 1915, Cleveland, Ohio, USA. Playwright; Lyricist; Biographer. Education: BA, Ohio State University, 1937; Graduate Studies, University of California at Los Angeles, 1939-40. Appointments: Partner, 1942-, President, 1955, Lawrence and Lee Inc, New York City and Los Angeles; Professor of Playwriting, University of Southern California, New York University, Baylor University, Ohio State University. Publications: Look, Ma, I'm Dancin' (co-author), musical, 1948; Inherit the Wind (with Robert E Lee), 1955; Auntie Mame (with Lee), 1957; The Gang's All Here (with Lee), 1960; Only in America (with Lee), 1960; Checkmate (with Lee), 1961; Mame (co-author), musical, 1967; Dear World, musical, 1969; Sparks Fly Upward (co-author), 1969; The Night Thoreau Spent in Jail (with Lee), 1970; Live Spelled Backwards, 1970; The Incomparable Max (with Lee), 1972; The Crocodile Smile (with Lee), 1972; Actor: The Life and Times of Paul Muni, 1974; Jabberwock (with Lee), 1974; First Monday in October (with Lee), 1975; Whisper in the Mind (with Lee and Norman Cousins), 1987. Memberships: Dramatists Guild; Authors League. Address: 21056 Las Flores Mesa Drive, Malibu, CA 90265, USA.

LAWRENCE Karen Ann, b. 5 Feb 1951, Windsor, Ontario, Canada. Writer. m. Robert Gabhart, 18 Dec 1982, 1 son. Education: BA, Honours, University of Windsor, 1973; MA, University of Alberta, 1977. Publications: Nekuia: The Inanna Poems, 1980; The Life of Helen Alone, 1986; Springs of Living Water, 1990. Honours: W H Smith/Books in Canada First Novel Award, 1987; Best First Novel Award, PEN, Los Angeles Center, 1987. Memberships: Writers' Union of Canada; Association of Canadian Radio and Television Artists. Address: 2153 Pine Street, San Diego, CA 92103, USA.

LAWRENCE Louise, b. 5 June 1943, Surrey, England. Novelist. m. Graham Mace, 28 Aug 1987, 1 son, 2 daughters. Publications: Andra, 1971; Power of Stars, 1972; Wyndcliffe, 1974; Sing and Scatter Daisies, 1977; Star Lord, 1978; Cat Call, 1980; Earth Witch, 1981; Calling B for Butterfly, 1982; Dram Road, 1983; Children of the Dust, 1985; Moonwind, 1986; Warriors of Taan, 1986; Extinction is Forever, 1990; Ben-Harran's Castle, 1992; The Disinherited, 1994. Address: 22 Church Road, Cinderford, Gloucestershire GL14 2EA, England.

LAWRENCE P. See: **TUBB E(dwin) C(harles)**.

LAWRENCE Steven C. See: **MURPHY Lawrence Agustus**.

LAWSON Chet. See: **TUBB E(dwin) C(harles)**.

LAWSON Greg, b. 8 Aug 1944, Pittsburgh, Pennsylvania, USA. Author; Photographer; Lecturer; Naturalist. m. Fortunata Antonuccio, 12 May 1979, 2 daughters. Education: Varied. Appointments: Broadcast Journalist, KDB Radio, Santa Barbara, California, 1979-81; Author, Photographer, First Choice Publishers, Santa Barbara, California, 1981-95; Creative Director, Blue Pacific Publishers, San Diego, California, 1995-97; Author, Photographer, LandAlone Publishing Co, Santa Ysabel, California, 1998-99. Publications: Beauty Spot - Santa Barbara, 1981; San Diego International 1983; California International, 1984; Hawaii International, 1985; Los Angeles International, 1985; San Diego County, 1986; Palm Springs Oasis, 1989; Oh California, 1990; Savoring San Diego, 1995; Colorado - Pretty in its Time, 1998; Sketches of Earth, 1998; America's Wonderful Corner, 1998; California in the Beginning, 1998. Contributions to: Numerous North American magazines. Literary Agent: Erick Hale Agency. Address: PO Box 120, Santa Ysabel, CA 92070, USA.

LAWSON James, b. 8 Dec 1938, New York, New York, USA. Author; Company Executive. Education: Sorbonne, University of Paris, 1959-60; BA, Boston University, 1961. Appointments: Copywriter, McCann-Marschalk Advertising, 1961-62; Thompson Advertising, 1963-64; Al Paul Lefton Advertising, 1964-66; Reporter, Aspen Times, Colorado, 1962; Vice-President, Copy Supervisor, Doyle Bernbach

Advertising, 1966-78; Senior Vice-President, Director, Creative Services, Doremus and Co, 1978-80, Senior Vice-President, Creative Director, DDB Needham Worldwide, 1982-93. Publications: XXX, 1963; Disconnections, 1968; The American Book of the Dead, 1972; Crimes of the Unconscious, 1974; The Girl Watcher, 1976; The Copley Chronicles, 1980; The Fanatic, 1980; Forgeries of the Heart, 1982; The Madman's Kiss, 1988; Frederick Law Olmsted (teleplay), 1990; The Reluctant God, 1993; Andris in Isolation (play), 1993. Address: 756 Greenwich Street, New York, NY 10014, USA.

LAYTON Andrea. See: **BANCROFT Iris**.

LAYTON Irving (Peter), b. 12 Mar 1912, Neamt, Romania. Poet; Author. m. (1) Faye Lynch, 13 Sept 1938, div 1946, (2) Betty Frances Sutherland, 1 son, 1 daughter, (3) Aviva Cantor, 1 son, (4) Harriet Bernstein, div 1983, 1 daughter, (5) Anna Pottier. Education: BSc, Macdonald College, 1939; MA, McGill University, 1946. Appointments: Poet-in-Residence, University of Guelph, 1969; Visiting Professor, 1978, Adjunct Professor, 1988, 1989, Writer-in-Residence, 1989, Concordia University; Writer-in-Residence, University of Toronto, 1981. Publications: Poetry: Numerous volumes, including: The Collected Poems of Irving Layton, 1971; The Darkening Fire: Selected Poems, 1945-68, 1975; The Unwavering Eye: Selected Poems, 1969-75; Uncollected Poems, 1935-59, 1976; A Wild Peculiar Joy: Selected Poems, 1945-82, 1982; Final Reckoning: Poems 1982-86, 1987; Fornalux: Selected Poems, 1928-90, 1992. Other: Engagements: The Prose of Irving Layton, 1972; Taking Sides: The Collected Social and Political Writings, 1977; Waiting for the Messiah: A Memoir, 1985; Wild Gooseberries: The Selected Letters of Irving Layton, 1989; Irving Layton and Robert Creeley: The Complete Correspondence, 1953-78, 1990. Editor: Various anthologies. Contributions to: Many publications. Honours: Governor-General's Award for Poetry, 1959; 1st Prize, Prix Litteraire de Quebec, 1963; Centennial Medal, 1967; Doctor of Civil Laws, Bishop's University, 1970; Officer of the Order of Canada, 1976; DLitt, Concordia University, 1976, York University, Toronto, 1976; Canada Council Arts Award, 1979-81; Petrarch Award for Poetry, Italy, 1993. Address: c/o McClelland & Stewart, 481 University Avenue, Toronto, Ontario M5G 2E9, Canada.

LAZARUS Arnold (Leslie), b. 20 Feb 1914, Revere, Massachusetts, USA. Writer; Poet. m. Keo Felker, 24 July 1938, 2 sons, 2 daughters. Education: BA, University of Michigan, 1935; BS, Middlesex Medical School, 1937; MA, 1939, PhD, 1957, University of California, Los Angeles. Publications: Entertainments and Valedictions, 1970; Harbrace Adventures in Literature (editor with R Lowell and E Hardwick), 1970; Modern English (editor with others), 1970; A Suit of Four, 1973; The Indiana Experience, 1977; Beyond Graustark (with Victor H Jones), 1981; Glossary of Literature and Composition (editor with H Wendell Smith), 1983; Best of George Ade (editor), 1985; Some Light: New and Selected Verse, 1988; A George Jean Nathan Reader (editor), 1990. Contributions to: Numerous periodicals. Honours: Ford Foundation Fellow, 1954; Kemper McComb Award, 1976. Memberships: Academy of American Poets; American Society for Theatre Research; Comparative Literature Association; Modern Language Association; Poetry Society of America. Address: 709 Chopin Drive, Sunnyvale, CA 94087, USA.

LAZARUS Henry. See: **SLAVITT David Rytman**.

LAZARUS Marguerite, (Marguerite Gascoigne, Anna Gilbert), b. 1 May 1916, Durham, England. Author. m. Jack Lazarus, 3 Apr 1956. Education: BA, Honours, English Language and Literature, 1937, MA, 1945, Durham University. Publications: Images of Rose, 1973; The Look of Innocence, 1975; A Family Likeness, 1977; Remembering Louise, 1978; The Leavetaking, 1979; Flowers for Lilian, 1980; Miss Bede is Staying, 1982; The Long Shadow, 1984; A Walk in the Wood, 1989; The Wedding Guest, 1993; The Treachery of Time, 1995. Contributions to: Magazines and BBC. Honour: Romantic

Novelists' Major Award, 1976; Catherine Cookson Award, 1994. Address: c/o Watson Little Ltd, Capo di Monte, Windmill Hill, London NW3 6RJ, England.

LAZENBY John Francis, b. 14 Apr 1934, Tiruchirapalli, Tamil Nadu, India. University Professor. m. Elizabeth Mary Leithead, 24 July 1967, 1 son, 1 daughter. Education: MA (Oxon); Scholar of Keble College, Oxford, 1952-56; Senior Demy, Magdalen College, Oxford, 1957-9. Appointments: Lecturer in Ancient History, King's College, Newcastle upon Tyne, University of Durham, 1959-62; Lecturer in Ancient History, University of Newcastle upon Tyne, 1962-71; Senior Lecturer in Ancient History, University of Newcastle upon Tyne, 1971-79; Reader, Ancient History, University of Newcastle upon Tyne, 1979-94; Professor of Ancient History, University of Newcastle upon Tyne, 1994-. Publications: The Catalogue of the Ships in Homer's Iliad, 1970; Hannibal's War, 1978; The Spartan Army, 1985; The Defence of Greece, 490-479 BC, 1993; The First Punic War, 1996. Contributions to: Annual of the British School at Athens; Antiquity; Hermes; The Classical Quarterly; The British Army Magazine; War in History; Athenaeum. Address: 15 Rectory Terrace, Gosforth, Newcastle upon Tyne, NE3 1YB, England.

LE CARRÉ John. See: **CORNWELL David John Moore**.

LE GUIN Ursula K(roeber), b. 21 Oct 1929, Berkeley, California, USA. Writer; Poet. m. Charles A Le Guin, 1953, 3 children. Education: BA, Radcliffe College, 1951; MA, Columbia University, 1952. Publications: Novels: Rocannon's World, 1966; Planet of Exile, 1966; City of Illusion, 1967; A Wizards of Earthsea, 1968; The Left Hand of Darkness, 1969; The Tombs of Atuan, 1970; The Lathe of Heaven, 1971; The Farthest Shore, 1972; The Dispossessed: An Ambiguous Utopia, 1974; The Word for World is Forest, 1976; Very Far Away From Anywhere Else, 1976; Malafrena, 1979; The Beginning Place, 1980; The Eye of the Heron, 1983; Always Coming Home, 1985; Tehanu: The Last Book of Earthsea, 1990. Story Collections: The Wind's Twelve Quarters, 1975; Orsinian Tales, 1976; The Compass Rose, 1982; Buffalo Gals, 1987; Searoad, 1991; A Fisherman of the Inland Sea, 1994; Four Ways to Forgiveness, 1995; Unlocking the Air, 1996. Poetry: Wild Angels, 1974; Walking in Cornwall, 1976; Tillai and Tylissos (with Theodora Kroeber), 1979; Hard Words, 1981; In the Red Zone, 1983; Wild Oats and Fireweed, 1988; No Boats, 1992; Blue Moon Over Thurman Street, 1993; Going Out with Peacocks, 1994; The Twins, The Dream/Las Gemelas, El Sueno (with Diana Bellessi), 1997. Non-Fiction: Dancing at the Edge of the World, 1989; The Language of the Night, revised edition, 1992; Steering the Craft, 1998. Editor: Nebula Award Stories XI, 1977; Interfaces (with Virginia Kidd), 1980; Edges (with Virginia Kidd), 1980; The Norton Book of Science Fiction (with Brian Attebery and Karen Fowler), 1993. Other: 12 children's books, 1979-98. Honours: Boston Globe-Horn Book Award, 1968; Hugo Awards, 1969, 1973, 1974, 1975, 1988; Nebula Awards, 1969, 1975, 1975, 1988, 1996; Newbery Silver Medal, 1972; National Book Award, 1972; Pushcart Prize, 1991; Harold Versell Award, American Academy and Institute of Arts and Letters, 1991; James Triptree Jr Awards, 1995, 1996, 1997. Address: PO Box 10541, Portlandl, OR 97296, USA.

LE PLASTRIER Robert. See: **WARNER Francis**.

LEA Katherine Rachael, b. 27 July 1944, London, England. Career Writer; Editor. m. Professor Michael Lea, 31 Dec 1966. Education: BA, University of Lancaster, 1967. Appointments: Career Advisor Officer, Lancashire County Council; Careers Advisory Officer, London Borough of Hillingdon; Senior Careers Information Officer, Hampshire County Council; Full-time Freelance Careers Writer & Editor, 1990. Publications: Careers Encyclopedia, 13th editor; Getting into Vocational Qualifications; Careers Encyclopedia, 14th editor; How to Choose Your MBA; Working in Manufacturing. Contributions to: You Can; Springboard; Careerscope; FE Now; Education and Training in Britain; Study UK;

Graduate Casebooks. Membership: Careers Writers Association, Treas, 1994-96. Address: Manor Farm Lodge, Upper Wield, Alresford, Hampshire SO24 9RU, England.

LEA-JONES Julian, b. 2 Dec 1940, Bristol, England. Avionics Researcher; Writer; Presenter. m. Diane Susan Parsons, 22 Dec 1962, 1 son, 1 daughter. Education: College Certificates; Diplomas for Telecommunications and Business Management Studies. Appointments: Contributing Author, Editor, The Templar, 1980-; Past Joint Editor, Alha Journal, Avon Past, 1986. Publications: St John's Conduit: An Account of Bristol's Medieval Water Supply, 1985; Survey of Parish Boundary Markers and Stones for Eleven of the Ancient Bristol Parishes, 1986; Yesterday's Temple, 1987; Bristol Past Revisited, 1989; Bristol Faces and Places, 1992. Contributions to: Newspapers, journals, radio and television. Memberships: West of England Writers Association; Temple Local History Group, founder, life member; Bristol History Research Exchange, archivist. Address: 33 Springfield Grove, Henleaze, Bristol BS6 7XE, England.

LEACH Penelope (Jane), b. 19 Nov 1937, London, England. Psychologist. m. Gerald Leach, 23 Mar 1963, 1 son, 1 daughter. Education: BA, Cantab, 1959; Graduate Diploma in Social Sciences, London School of Economics and Political Science, 1961; PhD, Psychology, London University, 1964. Publications: Your Baby and Child, 1977, 2nd edition, 1989, revised edition, 1997; Babyhood, revised edition, 1983; The Parents' A-Z (in US as Your Growing Child), 1985; The First Six Months: Coming to Terms With Your Baby, 1986; Children First: what society must do - and is not doing - for children today, 1994; Your Baby and Child, new version, 1997. Contributions to: Numerous magazines and journals. Honours: Fellow, British Psychological Society, 1989; Cable Ace Award, Best Informational Television Presentation, 1993; Honorary Doctorate of Education, 1996. Membership: Society of Authors. Address: 3 Tanza Road, London NW3 2UA, England.

LEAKEY Richard (Erskine Frere), b. 19 Dec 1944, Nairobi, Kenya. Paleontologist; Wildlife Consultant; Writer. m. Maeve Gillian Epps, 1970, 3 daughters. Education: Duke of York School, Nairobi. Appointments: Administrative Director, 1968-74, Director, 1974-89, National Museums of Kenya; Leader, East Rudolf, later East Turkana Research Project, Rift Valley, Kenya, 1968-; Director, Wildlife and Conservation Management Service, Kenya, 1989-90; Chairman, 1989-93, Director, 1993-94, Kenya Wildlife Service; Managing Director, Richard Leakey and Associates, wildlife consultancy, 1994-; Secretary General, SAFINA, 1995-. Publications: General History of Africa (contributor), Vol I, 1976; Origins (with R Lewin), 1978; People of the Lake (with R Lewin), 1979; Koobi Fora Research Project, Vol I (with M G Leakey), 1979; The Making of Mankind, 1981; Human Origins of Humankind (with R Lewin), 1995; The Sixth Extinction: Biodiversity and its Survival (with R Lewin), 1996. Contributions to: Scientific journals. Honours: Various honorary doctorates; Golden Ark Medal for Conservation, 1989. Memberships: East African Wild Life Society, chairman, 1984-89; Foundation for Research into the Origin of Man, chairman, 1974-81; Kenya Wildlife Service, board of trustees; National Museums of Kenya, board of governors; Wildlife Clubs of Kenya, trustee, 1980-. Address: PO Box 24926, Nairobi, Kenya.

LEALE B(arry) C(avendish), b. 1 Sept 1930, Ashford, Middlesex, England. Poet. Publications: Under a Glass Sky, 1975; Preludes, 1977; Leviathan and Other Poems, 1984; The Colours of Ancient Dreams, 1984. Contributions to: Anthologies and periodicals. Address: Flat E10, Peabody Estate, Wild Street, London WC2B 4AH, England.

LEAN-VERCOE Roger, b. 4 Oct 1942, Weymouth, England. Writer; Journalist; Yachting. m. June Elizabeth Adams, 30 Nov 1984, 3 daughters. Appointments: Freelance Writer; Editor, The Superyachts. Publictions: The Superyachts, volumes 1-12. Contributions to: Boat International Boat International USA; Meer und Yachten;

Mer et Bateaux. Membership: Yachting Journalists Association. Address: Paradise, Church Lane, Yealmpton, Devon, Plymouth PL8 2HG, England.

LEAPMAN Michael Henry, b. 24 Apr 1938, London, England. Writer; Journalist. m. Olga Mason, 15 July 1965, 1 son. Appointment: Journalist, The Times, 1969-81. Publications: One Man and His Plot, 1976; Yankee Doodles, 1982; Companion Guide to New York, 1983; Barefaced Cheek, 1983; Treachery, 1984; The Last Days of the Beeb, 1986; Kinnock, 1987; The Book of London (editor), 1989; London's River, 1991; Treacherous Estate, 1992; Eyewitness Guide to London, 1993; Master Race (with Catrine Clay), 1995; Witnesses to War, 1998. Contributions to: Numerous magazines and journals. Honours: Campaigning Journalist of the Year, British Press Award, 1968; Thomas Cook Travel Book Award, Best Guide Book of 1983; Garden Writers Guild Award, 1995. Memberships: Society of Authors; National Union of Journalists; Garden Writers' Guild. Address: 13 Aldebert Terrace, London SW8 1BH, England.

LEAR Peter. See: **LOVESEY Peter.**

LEASOR (Thomas) James (Andrew MacAllan), b. 20 Dec 1923, Erith, Kent, England. Author. m. Joan Margaret Bevan, 1 Dec 1951, 3 sons. Education: City of London School; BA, 1948, MA, 1952, Oriel College, Oxford. Appointments: Feature Writer, Foreign Correspondent, Daily Express, London, 1948-55; Editorial Advisor, Newness and Pearson, later IPC, publishing, 1955-69; Director, Elm Tree Books, 1970-73. Publications: Novels and non-fiction books. Honours: Order of St John; Fellow, Royal Society of Arts. Address: Swallowcliffe Manor, Salisbury, Wiltshire SP3 5PB, England.

LEAVITT David, b. 23 June 1961, Pittsburgh, Pennsylvania, USA. Writer. Education: BA, Yale University, 1983. Publications: Family Dancing, 1984; The Lost Language of Cranes, 1986; Equal Affections, 1989; A Place I've Never Been, 1990; While England Sleeps, 1993, new edition, 1995; The Penguin Book of Gay Short Stories (editor with Mark Mitchell), 1994. Contributions to: Periodicals. Honours: O Henry Award, 1984; National Endowment for the Arts Grant, 1985; Guggenheim Fellowship, 1990. Address: c/o Wylie, Aitken and Stone Inc, 250 West 57th Street, New York, NY 10107, USA.

LEBOW Jeanne, b. 29 Jan 1951, Richmond, Virginia, USA. Writer; Poet; Teacher. m. (1) Howard Lebow, 1975, div 1981, (2) Steve Shepard, 1985. Education: AB, English, College of William and Mary, 1973; MA, Liberal Arts, Hollins College, 1982; PhD, English, University of Southern Mississippi, 1989. Appointments: Instructor, Memphis State University, 1982-84; Teaching Assistant, University of Southern Mississippi, 1984-87; Fulbright Lecturer in American Studies, University of Ouagadougou, Burkina Faso, 1987-88; Assistant Professor, Northeast Missouri State University, 1988-92; Freelance Nature Columnist, 1991-; Adjunct Professor, 1992-93, 1994-95, Visiting Professor, 1993-94, University of Southern Mississippi. Publication: The Outlaw James Copeland and the Champion-Belted Empress (poems), 1991. Contributions to: Anthologies, books, reviews, and journals. Honours: National Award, Georgia State Poetry Society, 1983; Runner-up, Norma Farber First Book Award, 1991; Mississippi Humanities Council Grants, 1994, 1995. Memberships: Associated Writing Programs; Mid-America Studies Association; Mississippi Humanities Council; Mississippi Philological Association; Southern Central Modern Language Association. Address: PO Box 1295, Gautier, MS 39553, USA.

LEBRECHT Norman, b. 11 July 1948, London, England. Writer. m. Elbie Spivack, 1977, 3 daughters. Publications: Discord, 1982; Book of Musical Anecdotes, 1985; Mahler Remembered, 1987; Music in London, 1991; The Maestro Myth, 1991; The Companion to 20th Century Music, 1992; Who Killed Classical Music?, 1997. Membership: Society of Authors. Address: c/o The Daily

Telegraph, 1 Canada Square, Canary Wharf, London E14 5DT, England.

LEBRECHT Susan Frances, b. 23 July 1962, Toronto, Ontario, Canada. Freelance Writer. Publications: Toronto Parks, 1997; Adventuring Around Vancouver Island, 1997; 52 Weekend Activities Around Vancouver, 1995; 52 Weekend Activities for the Toronto Adventurer, 1990. Contributions to: Columnist with the Toronto Star Newspaper, regular contributor to Ski Canada and Ski magazines. Memberships: Society of American Travel Writers; North American Snowsports Journalists Association. Address: 1123 Dufferin Street, Toronto, Ontario M6H 4B7, Canada.

LEBRUN HOLMES Sandra, b. 24 Apr 1924, Bulcoomatta Station, New South Wales, Australia. Writer; Filmmaker; Researcher. m. Cecil William Holmes, 1956, 2 sons, 1 daughter. Education: Anthropology, Sydney University, 2 years. Publications: Yirawala: Artist and Man, 1972; Yirawala: Painter of the Dreaming, 1992. Contributions to: Various publications. Memberships: Australian Society of Authors; Film Directors Guild. Address: Box 439 PO, Potts Pt, New South Wales 2011, Australia.

LECHTMAN Pamela Joy, (Pamela Price), b. 29 Apr 1943, St Paul, Minnesota, USA. Travel Editor; Writer. m. 16 June 1967, 2 sons. Education: BS, University of Minnesota, 1965; CTC Certified Travel Counselor, University of Massachusetts, 1978; Travel Editor, Malibu Times, California, 1989-. Publication: Fun With the Family in Southern California, 1998. Contributions to: Host and Producer, Tea and Travel, KNWZ Radio, Palm Desert, CA; Host and Producer, Traveltalk, KWNK Radio, 1990-93; Travel Editor, Shape Magazine, 1981-89; Dutchess of Parma Award, Parma, Italy, 1988. Memberships: International, Food, Wine and Travel Writer's Association, President, 1995-96; Society of American Travel Writers, 1983-. Address: 2471 Caliente Drive, Palm Springs, CA 92264, USA.

LEDINA Rute, b. 19 May 1929, Riga, Latvia. Translator. m. 21 Marc 1953, dec Sept 1994, 1 son. Education: Diploma, cum laude, Latvian University, 1953. Appointments: Latvian Society for Cultural Relations with Foreign Countries, 1956-87; Translator and Teacher of Swedish, 1987-. Publications: Translations of fiction into Latvian from Scandinavian languages: Swedish Short Stories, 1968; Danish Short Stories, 1977; Peter Seeberg-Herdsmen, 1977; Turborg Nedreaas - In the Next New Moon, 1980; Suzanne Pordgger - Creme Fraiche, 1993; Maerta Tikkaheu - Love Story of the Century, 1997; Peter Hoeg - Borderliners, 1998. Membership: Latvian Writers' Union, 1993-. Address: Vecumnieku 3, LV-1067, Riga, Latvia.

LEDOUX Denis, b. 18 Jan 1947, Lewiston, USA. Writer; Publisher; Teacher. m. Martha Blowen, 1 son, 1 daughter. Education: BA, English Literature, MAEd, Catholic University, Washington, DC. Honours: Maine Fiction Award, 1989; Maine Individual Writing Fellowship, 1991, 1996. Memberships: MWPA; APH. Address: 95 Gould Road, Lisbon Falls, ME 04252, USA.

LEDOUX Paul Martin, b. 4 Nov 1949, Halifax, Nova Scotia, Canada. Dramatist. m. Ferne Downey. Education: BA, Dalhousie University, Halifax; Postgraduate work, Nova Scotia Academy of Drama, Halifax. Publications: Love is Strange, 1985; Children of the Night, 1986; Fire, 1987; The Secret Garden, 1993; Radio dramas. Honours: Best Play, Quebec Drama Festival, 1975; Outstanding Drama, Chalmer Award, 1989; Dora Manor Moore Award, Best Canadian Drama, Toronto, 1990. Memberships: Association of Canadian Television and Radio Artists; Dramatists Cooperative of Nova Scotia; Playwrights Union of Canada, chairman, 1985-87; Society of Composers, Authors, and Music Publishers of Canada. Address: 41 Cowan Avenue, Toronto, Ontario M6K 2N1, Canada.

LEE Brian Robert Leonard, b. 12 July 1935, Ealing, London, England. Retired; Former Lecturer. m. Christina

Mary Thompson, 21 Apr 1979, 3 sons, 1 daughter. Education: BA Honours, University College London, 1962; Dip Ed, Leeds University, 1963; MLitt, Edinburgh University, 1976. Appointments: Newspaper Reporter, Uxbridge Gazette, 1955-59; Lecturer, Letchworth College of Technology, 1963-66; Senior Lecturer, Newcastle Polytechnic/University of Northumbria, 1966-90. Publications: Late Home: Poems for children, 1977; Theory and Personality: T S Eliot's Criticism, 1979; Six of the Best: Selected poems for children (with others). Contributions to: Numerous in Encounter, English, Human World, The Gadfly, others. Address: Wydon Burn House, Causey Hill, Hexham, Northumberland NE46 2JG, England.

LEE Dennis Beynon, b. 31 Aug 1939, Toronto, Ontario, Canada. Poet; Writer. m. (1), 1 son, 1 daughter, (2) Susan Perly, 1985. Education: BA, 1962, MA, 1965, University of Toronto. Appointments: Lecturer, University of Toronto, 1963-67; Editor, House of Anasi Press, 1967-72; Consulting Editor, Macmillan of Canada, 1972-78; Poetry Editor, McClelland and Stewart, 1981-84. Publications: Poetry: Kingdom of Absence, 1967; Civil Elegies, 1972; The Gods, 1979; The Difficulty of Living on Other Planets, 1998; Riffs, 1993; Nightwatch: New and Selected Poems, 1968-96, 1996. Children's Poetry: Wiggle to the Laundromat, 1970; Alligator Pie, 1974; Nicholas Knock, 1974; Garbage Delight, 1977; Jelly Belly, 1983; Lizzy's Lion, 1984; The Ice Cream Store, 1991. Non-Fiction: Savage Fields, 1977. Contributions to: Journals and magazines. Honours: Governor-General's Award for Poetry, 1972; Member of the Order of Canada, 1994. Memberships: PEN, Canada; Writers' Union of Canada. Address: c/o Westwood Creative Artists, 10 St Mary Street, No 510, Toronto, Ontario M4Y 1P9, Canada.

LEE Don Yoon, b. 7 Apr 1936, Seoul, Korea. Education: BA, University of Washington, 1963; MA, St Johns University, 1967; MS, Georgetown University, 1971; MA, Indiana University, 1975. Appointments: Publisher, Academic Researcher, Writer, Founder, Eastern Press Inc, Bloomington, 1981-. Publications: History of Early Relations Between China and Tibet, 1981; An Annotated Bibliography of Selected Works on China, 1981; An Introduction to East Asian and Tibetan Linguistics and Culture, 1981; Light Literature and Philosophy of East Asia, 1982; An Annotated Biography on Inner Asia, 1983; An Annotated Archaeological Biography of Selected Works in Northern and Central Asia, 1983; Learning Standard Arabic, 1988; Traditional Chinese Thoughts, 1990; Arab Verb Frequency, 1991. Address: PO Box 881, Bloomington, IN 47402, USA.

LEE Hamilton, b. 10 Oct 1921, Zhouxian, Shandong, China. Professor Emeritus; Poet; Writer. m. Jean C Chang, 24 Aug 1945, 1 son, 3 daughters. Education: BS, Beijing Normal University, 1948; MA, University of Minnesota, 1958; EdD, Wayne State University, Detroit, 1964. Appointments: Teacher of English, High Schools, Taiwan, 1948-56; Research Associate, Wayne State University, Detroit, 1958-64; Visiting Professor of Chinese Literature, Seton Hall University, summer, 1964; Assistant Professor, Moorhead State University, 1964-65; Visiting Scholar, Harvard University, 1965-66; Associate Professor, University of Wisconsin at La Crosse, 1965-66; Professor, 1966-84, Professor Emeritus, 1984-, East Stroudsburg University, Pennsylvania; Visiting Fellow, Princeton University, 1976-78. Publications: Readings in Instructional Technology, 1970; Relection (poems), 1989; Revelation (poems), 1991. Contributions to: Numerous anthologies, journals, and literary magazines. Honours: Many poetry contest awards; Editor's Choice, National Library of Poetry, 1994. Memberships: Academy of American Poets; International Society of Poets; Poetry Society of America; World Literary Academy, fellow. Address: PO Box 980, Los Alles, CA 94023, USA.

LEE (Nelle) Harper, b. 28 Apr 1926, Monroeville, Alabama, USA. Writer. Education: Huntington College, 1944-45; University of Alabama, 1945-49; University of Oxford. Publication: To Kill a Mockingbird, 1960. Contributions to: Magazines. Honours: Alabama Library Association Award, 1961; Brotherhood Award, National Conference of Christians and Jews, 1961; Pulitzer Prize for Fiction, 1961; Best Sellers' Paperback of the Year Award, 1962. Membership: National Council on the Arts, 1966-71. Address: c/o J B Lippincott Co, 227 East Washington Square, Philadelphia, PA 19106, USA.

LEE John (Darrell), b. 12 Mar 1931, Indiahoma, Oklahoma, USA. Writer; Former Professor. Education: BA, Texas Technological College, 1952; MSJ, West Virginia University, 1965. Appointment: Former Professor of Journalism. Publications: Caught in the Act, 1968; Diplomatic Persuaders, 1968; Assignation in Algeria, 1971; The Ninth Man, 1976; The Thirteenth Hour, 1978; Lago, 1980; Stalag Texas, 1990. Address: c/o Don Congdon Associates Inc, 156 Fifth Avenue, Suite 625, New York, NY 10010, USA.

LEE Joyce Isabel, b. 19 June 1913, Murtoa, Australia. Lecturer; Poet. m. Norman Edward, 18 Dec 1937, 2 sons. Education: Methodist Ladies' College; Registered Pharmacist, Victorian College of Pharmacy, Melbourne. Appointment: Lecturer-Tutor in Poetry, Victoria College of Advanced Education, Toorak Campus, 1981-. Publications: Sisters Poets 1, 1979; Abruptly from the Flatlands, 1984; Plain Dreaming, 1991. Contributions to: Anthologies and journals. Address: 13/205 Burke Road, Glen Iris, Victoria 3146, Australia.

LEE Kuei-shien, b. 19 June 1937, Taipei, Taiwan. Patent Agent; Chemical Engineer; Corporation President; Poet; Essayist; Translator. m. Huei-uei Wang, 1965, 1 son, 1 daughter. Education: Chemical Engineering, Taipei Institute of Technology, 1958; German Literature, European Language Center, Ministry of Education, 1964. Publications (in Chinese): Poetry: 10 works, 1963-93. Essays: 8 works, 1971-94. Translations: 8 works, 1969-95. Contributions to: Anthologies and other publications. Honours: Honorary PhD, Chemical Engineering, Marquis Giuseppe Scicluna International Academy Foundation Alfred Nobel Medal for Peace, 1991; Poetic Creation Award, Le Poetry Society, 1994; Secretary General, Asian Poets Conference, 1995. Memberships: International Academy of Poets, founder-fellow, Li Poetry Society; Rilke Gesellschaft; Taiwan PEN, president, 1995. Address: c/o Asia Enterprise Center, No 142 Minchuan East Road, Sec 3, Taipei, Taiwan.

LEE Lance (Wilds), b. 25 Aug 1942, New York, New York, USA., Dramatist; Poet; Writer; Editor. m. Jeanne Barbara Hutchings, 30 Aug 1962, 2 daughters. Education: Boston University; BA, Brandeis University, 1964; MFA, Playwriting and Dramatic Literature, Yale School of Drama, 1967. Appointments: Lecturer, University of Bridgeport, 1967-68, University of California at Los Angeles, 1971-73, California State University at Northridge, 1981-; Instructor, Southern Connecticut State College, 1968; Assistant Professor, Senior Lecturer, University of Southern California at Los Angeles, 1968-71. Publications: Fox, Hound and Huntress (play), 1973; Time's Up (play), 1979; The Understructure of Screenwriting (with Ben Brady), 1988; Wrestling with the Angel (poems), 1990; A Poetics for Screenwriters, 1999. Contributions to: Reviews, quarterlies, journals, and periodicals, in England and the US. Honours: Arts of the Theatre Foundation Fellowship, 1967; University of Southern California Research and Publication Grants, 1970, 1971; Rockefeller Foundation Grant, 1971; Theatre Development Fund Grant, 1976; National Endowment for the Arts Fellowship, 1976; Squaw Valley Scholarships in Poetry, 1982, 1983; Port Townsend Writers Conference Scholarship in Poetry, 1985. Memberships: Academy of American Poets; Poetry Society of America. Address: 1127 Galloway Street, Pacific Palisades, CA 90272, USA.

LEE Li-Young, b. 19 Aug 1957, Jakarta, Indonesia. Poet. m. Donna Lee, 25 Nov 1978, 2 children. Education: University of Pittsburgh, 1975-79; University of Arizona, 1979-80; State University of New York at Brockport, 1980-81. Publications: Rose, 1986; The City in Which I Love You, 1990; The Winged Seed: A Remembrance, 1995. Honours: Delmore Schwartz Memorial Poetry Award, New York University, 1986; Ludwig Vogelstein Foundation Fellowship, 1987; Mrs Giles Whiting Foundation Writer's Award, 1988; Lamont Poetry Selection, Academy of American Poets, 1990. Address: c/o Simon and Schuster, 1230 Avenue of the Americas, New York, NY 10020, USA.

LEE Marie. See: **JACOBSEN Rich Shirley Marie.**

LEE Tanith, b. 19 Sept 1947, London, England. Writer; Playwright. Publications: The Betrothed (short stories), 1968; The Dragon Hoard (juvenile), 1971; Princess Hynchatti and Some Other Surprises (juvenile), 1972; Animal Castle (juvenile), 1972; Companions on the Road (juvenile), 1975; The Birthgrave, 1975; Don't Bite the Sun, 1976; The Storm Lord, 1976; The Winter Players (juvenile), 1976; East of Midnight (juvenile), 1977; Drinking Sapphire Wine, 1977; Volkhavaar, 1977; Vazkor, Son of Vazkor, 1978; Quest for the White Witch, 1978; Night's Master, 1978; The Castle of Dark (juvenile), 1978; Shon the Taken (juvenile), 1979; Death's Master, 1979; Electric Forest, 1979; Sabella, or, The Blood Stone, 1980; Kill the Dead, 1980; Day by Night, 1980; Delusion's Master, 1981; The Silver Metal Lover, 1982; Cyrion (short stories), 1982; Prince on a White Horse (juvenile), 1982; Sung in Shadow, 1983; Anackire, 1983; Red as Blood, or, Tales from the Sisters Grimmer, 1983; The Dragon Hoard, 1984; The Beautiful Biting Machine (short stories), 1984; Tamastara, or, the Indian Nights (short stories), 1984; Days of Grass, 1985; The Gorgon and Other Beastly Tales, 1985; Dreams of Dark and Light, 1986. Address: c/o Macmillan London Ltd, 4 Little Essex Street, London WC2R 3LF, England.

LEE Warner. See: **BATTIN B W.**

LEE Wayne C, (Lee Sheldon), b. 2 July 1917, Lamar, Nebraska, USA. Author. Publications: Prairie Vengeance, 1954; Broken Wheel Ranch, 1956; Slugging Backstop, 1957; His Brother's Guns, 1958; Killer's Range, 1958; Bat Masterson, 1960; Gun Brand, 1961; Blood on the Prairie, 1962; Thunder in the Backfield, 1962; Stranger in Stirrup, 1962; The Gun Tamer, 1963; Devil Wire, 1963; The Hostile Land, 1964; Gun in His Hand, 1964; Warpath West, 1965; Fast Gun, 1965; Brand of a Man, 1966; Mystery of Scorpion Creek, 1966; Trail of the Skulls, 1966; Showdown at Julesburg Station, 1967; Return to Gunpoint, 1967; Only the Brave, 1967; Doomed Planet (as Lee Sheldon), 1967; Sudden Guns, 1968; Trouble at Flying H, 1969; Stage to Lonesome Butte, 1969; Showdown at Sunrise, 1971; The Buffalo Hunters, 1972; Suicide Trail, 1972; Wind Over Rimfire, 1973; Son of a Gunman, 1973; Scotty Philip: The Man Who Saved the Buffalo (non-fiction), 1975; Law of the Prairie, 1975; Die Hard, 1975; Law of the Lawless, 1977; Skirmish at Fort Phil Kearney, 1977; Gun Country, 1978; Petticoat Wagon Train, 1978; The Violent Man, 1978; Ghost of a Gunfighter, 1980; McQuaid's Gun, 1980; Trails of the Smoky Hill (non-fiction), 1980; Shadow of the Gun, 1981; Guns at Genesis, 1981; Putnam's Ranch War, 1982; Barbed Wire War, 1983; The Violent Trail, 1984; White Butte Guns, 1984; War at Nugget Creek, 1985; Massacre Creek, 1985; The Waiting Gun, 1986; Hawks of Autumn, 1986; Wild Towns of Nebraska (non-fiction), 1988; Arikaree War Cry, 1992; Bad Men and Bad Towns (non-fiction), 1993; Deadly Days in Kansas (non-fiction), 1997. Memberships: Western Writers of America, president, 1970-71; Nebraska Writers Guild, president, 1974-76. Address: PO Box 906, Imperial, NE 69033, USA.

LEE (William) David, b. 13 Aug 1944, Matador, Texas, USA. Poet; Professor of English. m. Jan M Lee, 13 Aug 1971, 1 son, 1 daughter. Education: BA, Colorado State University, 1967; Idaho State University, 1970; PhD, University of Utah, 1973. Appointments: Professor of English, 1971-, Chair, 1973-82, Acting Chair, 1984-85, Department of English, Head, 1987-, Department of Language and Literature, Southern Utah University; Poetry Editor, Weber Studies, 1986-; John Neihardt Distinguished Lectureships, State of Nebraska, 1990, 1996; First Poet Laureate, State of Utah, 1997.

Publications: The Porcine Legacy, 1978; Driving and Drinking, 1979, 2nd edition, 1982; Shadow Weaver, 1984; The Porcine Canticles, 1984, 2nd edition, 1989; Paragonah Canyon, Autumn, 1990; Day's Work, 1990; My Town, 1995; Covenants, 1996; The Fish, 1997; The Wayburne Pig, 1998; A Legacy of Shadows: Poems 1979-1999, 1999. Contributions to: Many anthologies, reviews, quarterlies, journals, and magazines. Honours: National Endowment for the Arts Fellowship, 1985; 1st Place, Poetry, Creative Writing Competition, 1988, Publication Prize, 1989, Utah Arts Council; Outstanding Utah Writer, Utah Endowment for the Humanities and National Council of Teachers of English, 1990; Governor's Award for Lifetime Achievement, Utah, 1994; Western States Book Award, 1995; Mountain and Plain Booksellers Award, 1995. Memberships: National Foundation for Advancement of the Arts, board of directors, 1996-; Western States Foundation; Writers at Work, board of advisors, 1993-. Address: c/o Department of Language and Literature, Southern Utah University, Cedar City, UT 84720, USA.

LEECH Geoffrey Neil, b. 16 Jan 1936, Gloucester, England. Professor of Linguistics and Modern English Language; Writer. m. Frances Anne Berman, 29 July 1961, 1 son, 1 daughter. Education: BA, English Language and Literature, 1959, MA, 1963, PhD, 1968, University College London. Appointments: Assistant Lecturer, 1962-64, Lecturer, 1965-69, University College, London; Reader, 1969-74, Professor of Linguistics and Modern English, 1974-, University of Lancaster; Visiting Professor, Brown University, 1972, Kobe University, 1984, Kyoto University, 1991. Publications: English in Advertising, 1966; A Linguistic Guide to English Poetry, 1969; Towards a Semantic Description of English, 1969; Meaning and the English Verb, 1971, 2nd edition, 1987; A Grammar of Contemporary English (with R Quirk, S Greenbaum, and J Svartvik), 1972; Semantics, 1974, 2nd edition, 1981; A Communicative Grammar of English (with J Svartvik), 1975, 2nd edition, 1994; Explorations in Semantics and Pragmatics, 1980; Style in Fiction (with Michael H Short), 1981; English Grammar for Today (with R Hoogenraad and M Deuchar), 1982; Principles of Pragmatics, 1983; A Comprehensive Grammar of the English Language (with R Quirk, S Greenbaum, and J Svartvik), 1985; Computers in English Language Teaching and Research (editor with C N Candlin), 1986; The Computational Analysis of English (editor with R Garside and G Sampson), 1987; An A-Z of English Grammar and Usage, 1989; Introducing English Grammar, 1992; Statistically-driven Computer Grammars in English (editor with E Black and R Garside), 1993; Spoken English on Computer (editor with G Myers and J Thomas), 1995; Corpus Annotation (editor with R. Garside and T. McEnery), 1997. Contributions to: A Review of English Literature; Lingua; New Society; Linguistics; Dutch Quarterly Review of Anglo-American Letters; Times Literary Supplement; Prose Studies; The Rising Generation; Transactions of the Philological Society. Honours: FilDr, University of Lund, 1987; British Academy, fellow, 1987. Membership: Academia Europea. Address: Department of Linguistics and Modern English Language, Lancaster University, Lancaster, LA1 4YT, England.

LEEDOM-ACKERMAN Joanne, b. 7 Feb 1947, Dallas, Texas, USA. Writer; Novelist. m. Peter Ackerman, 3 June 1972, 2 sons. Education: BA, Principia College, 1968; MA, Johns Hopkins University, 1969; MA, Brown University, 1974. Publications: No Marble Angels, 1985; The Dark Path to the River, 1988; Women for All Seasons (editor), 1989. Contributions to: Anthologies, newspapers, and magazines. Membership: International PEN, chair, Writers in Prison Committee, 1993-97; International PEN, vice-president. Address: 3229 R Street NW, Washington, DC 20007, USA.

LEEDY Paul Dellinger, b. 4 Mar 1908, Harrisburg, Pennsylvania, USA. Retired University Professor; Author; Consultant on Format and Readability. m. Irene Brandt Force, 30 Nov 1933, 1 son. Education: AB, Dickinson College, 1930; LLB, American School of Law (Extension), 1933; MA, University of Pennsylvania, 1938; PhD, New

York University, 1958. Appointments: Book Reviewer, David C Cook, Publishers, 1935-38; Newark College, Rutgers University, 1938-42; School of Education, New York University, 1943-45; Assistant Editor, Abingdon-Cokesbury Press, New York, 1945-47; Chief Consultant and Senior Specialist in College and Adult Reading, The Reading Institute, New York University, 1950-61; School of Education, The American University, 1961-76; Editorial Consultant, Chilton Publishing Company, 1955-56; James Henry Morgan Lecturer, Dickinson College, 1958; Adjunct Professor, Fairleigh Dickinson University, George Mason Universityand University of Colorado; Abstractor, Psychological Abstracts, Washington, DC, 1959-66. Publications: The Wonderful World of Books (co-author), 1952; Reading Improvement for Adults, 1956; A History of the Origin and Development of Instruction in Reading Improvement at the College Level (microfilm), 1959; Improve Your Reading, 1962; Read with Speed and Precision, 1963; Perspectives in Reading: Adult Reading Instruction (editor), 1963; A Key to Better Reading, 1967; How to Read and Understand Research, 1980; Practical Research: Planning and Design, 1974, 6th edition, 1997. Contributions to: Various journals. Honours: New York University Founder's Day Award, 1958; Outstanding Educators of America Citation, 1972; Men of Achievement Award for Distinguished Achievement in Education and Authorship. Memberships: International Reading Association; College Reading Association, board of directors, 1965-68; American Association of University Professors. Address: La Maison des Gros Piliers, 239 North 25th Street, Camp Hill, PA 17011, USA.

LEES-MILNE James, b. 6 Aug 1908, Worcestershire, England. Author. Education: Eton College, 1921-26; Grenoble University, 1927-28; MA, Magdalen College, Oxford, 1931. Appointments: Private Secretary to Baron Lloyd, 1931-35; Staff Member, Reuters, 1935-36. Publications: The National Trust (editor), 1945; The Age of Adam, 1947; National Trust Guide: Buildings, 1948; Tudor Renaissance, 1951; The Age of Inigo Jones, 1953; Roman Mornings, 1956; Baroque in Italy, 1959; Baroque in Spain and Portugal, 1960; Earls of Creation, 1962; Worcestershire: A Shell Guide, 1964; St Peter's, 1967; English Country Houses: Baroque, 1970; Another Self, 1970; Heretics in Love (novel), 1973; Ancestral Voices, 1975; William Beckford, 1976; Prophesying Peace, 1977; Round the Clock (novel), 1978; Harold Nicolson, 2 volumes, 1980-81; The Country House (anthology), 1982; The Last Stuarts, 1983; Enigmatic Edwardian, 1986; Some Cotswold Country Houses, 1987; The Fool of Love, 1987; Venetian Evenings, 1988; Bachelor Duke, 1991; People and Places, 1992; A Mingled Measure, 1994; Fourteen Friends, 1996. Honours: Royal Society of Literature, fellow; Society of Arts, fellow. Address: Essex House, Badminton, Avon GL9 1DD, England.

LEESON Robert (Arthur), b. 31 Mar 1928, Barnton, Cheshire, England. Journalist; Writer. m. Gunvor Hagen, 25 May 1954, 1 son, 1 daughter. Education: External Degree, Honours, English, London University, 1972. Appointment: Literary Editor, Morning Star, London, 1960-80. Publications: Third Class Genie, 1975; Silver's Revenge, 1978; Travelling Brothers, 1979; It's My Life, 1980; Candy for King, 1983; Reading and Righting, 1985; Slambash Wangs of a Compo Gorner, 1987; Coming Home, 1991; Zarnia Experiment 1-6, 1993; Robin Hood, 1994; Red, White and Blue, 1996; Liar, 1999. Contributions to: Newspapers and journals. Honour: Eleanor Farjeon Award for Services to Children and Literature, 1985. Memberships: International Board of Books for Young People, British Section, treasurer, 1972-91; Writers' Guild of Great Britain, chairman, 1985-86. Address: 18 McKenzie Road, Broxbourne, Hertfordshire EN10 7JH, England.

LEFEBURE Leo Dennis, b. 20 Nov 1952, Chicago, Illinois, USA. Professor of Theology. Education: BA, Loyola University of Chicago, 1973; STB, 1976, MDiv, 1978, STL, 1978, St Mary of the Lake Seminary; PhD, Christian Theology, University of Chicago, 1987. Appointments: Professor, Systematic Theology, Mundelein Seminary, 1987-98; Dean, Ecclesiastical

Faculty of Theology, University of St Mary of the Lake, 1992-98; Distinguished Visiting Professor, Fordham University, 1999-2001. Publications: Toward a Contemporary Wisdom Christology, 1988; Life Transformed, 1989; The Buddha and the Christ, 1993. Contributions to: Christian Century; Jrnl of Religion; Chicago Studies; Cross Currents; Centagion. Address: Forham University, Department of Theology, 441 East Fordham Road, Bronx, NY 10458, USA.

LEFEBURE Molly, b. England. Author. Publications: Evidence for the Crown, 1955; Murder with a Difference, 1958; The Lake District, 1963; Scratch and Co, 1968; The Hunting of Wilberforce Pike, 1970; Cumberland Heritage, 1971; The Loona Balloona, 1974; Samuel Taylor Coleridge: A Bondage of Opium, 1974; Cumbrian Discovery, 1977; The Bondage of Love: A Life of Mrs Samuel Taylor Coleridge, 1986; The Illustrated Lake Poets, 1987; Blitz: A Novel of Love and War, 1988; The Coleridge Connection (editor with Richard Gravil), 1990; Thunder in the Sky, 1991; Thomas Hardy's World, 1997. Address: c/o Watson Little Ltd, Capo di Monte, Windmill Hill, London NW3 6RJ, England.

LEFF Leonard J, b. 23 Jan 1942, Houston, Texas, USA. Professor of English. m. Linda Ringer, 26 Jan 1969, 1 son. Education: BBA, University of Texas, Austin, 1963; MA, University of Houston, 1965; PhD, Northern Illinois University, 1971. Appointments: Instructor, English, McNeese State University, 1965-68, University of Illinois, Urbana-Champaign, 1971-72, Northern Illinois University, 1972-73; Assistant Professor, Associate Professor, Head of English, Bellevue College, 1973-79; Assistant Professor, 1979-82, Associate Professor, 1983-91, Interim Head of English, 1989-90, Professor, 1991-, Oklahoma State University, Stillwater. Publications: Film Plots, 2 volumes, 1983, 1988; Hitchcock and Selznick: The Rich and Strange Collaboration of Alfred Hitchcock and David O Selznick in Hollywood, 1987; The Dame in the Kimono: Hollywood, Censorship, and the Production Code from the 1920s to the 1960s (with Jerold Simmons). 1990; Hemingway and His Conspirators: Hollywood. Scribners and the making of American Celebrity Culture (Rowman and Littlefield), 1997. Address: 3002 Loma Verde Lane, Stillwater, OK 74074, USA.

LEFFLAND Ella Julia, b. 25 Nov 1931, Martinez, California, USA. Writer. Education: BA, Fine Arts, San Jose State College, 1953. Publications: Mrs Munck, 1970; Love out of Season, 1974; Last Courtesies, 1979; Rumors of Peace, 1980; The Knight, Death and the Devil, 1990. Contributions to: New Yorker; Harper's; Atlantic Monthly; Mademoiselle; New York Magazine; New York Times. Honours: Gold Medals for Fiction, 1974, 1979, Silver Medal, 1991, Commonwealth Club of California; O Henry First Prize, 1977; Bay Area Book Reviewers Award for Fiction, 1990. Address: Wallace Literary Agency, 177 East 70th Street, New York, NY 10021, USA.

LEGAGNEUR Serge, b. 10 Jan 1937, Jérémie, Haiti. Professor; Writer; Poet. Appointments: Professor of French Literature; Reader and Re-Writer in publishing houses. Publications: Textes Muets; Glyphes; Textes Interdits; Textes en Croix; Le Crabe; Inaltérable. Contributions to: Semences; Rond-Pond; Conjunction; Lettres et écritures; Passe-Partout; Estuaire; Nouvelle Optique; Possibles; Mot pour Mot; Nouvelliste; Panorama; Haiti Littéraire; Le Matin. Memberships: Founder, Haiti Littéraire; Quebec Writers Union; PEN. Address: 3320 Boulevard Gouin E app 401, Montreal, Quebec H1H 5P3, Canada.

LEGAT Michael Ronald, b. 24 Mar 1923, London, England. Writer. m. Rosetta Clark, 20 Aug 1949, 2 sons. Appointments: Editorial Director, Transworld Publishers Ltd, 1956-73; Editorial Director, Cassell Ltd, 1973-78. Publications: Dear Author..., 1972, revised edition, 1989; Mario's Vineyard, 1980; The Silver Fountain, 1982; An Author's Guide to Publishing, 1983, revised edition, 1998; Putting on a Play, 1984; The Shapiro Diamond, 1984; The Silk Maker, 1985; Writing for Pleasure and Profit, 1986, revised edition, 1993; The Cast Iron Man, 1987;

The Illustrated Dictionary of Western Literature, 1987; We Beheld His Glory, 1988; The Nuts and Bolts of Writing, 1989; How to Write Historical Novels, 1990; Plotting the Novel, 1992; Understanding Publishers' Contracts, 1992; Non-Fiction: A Writer's Guide, 1993; The Writer's Rights, 1995; An Author's Guide to Literary Agents, 1995; Revision: An Author's Guide, 1998; Writing your Life Story, 1999. Contributions to: Author; Writers News; Writers' Monthly; Writers' Forum. Memberships: Weald of Sussex Writers; Society of Authors; Society of Sussex Authors; Uckfield & District Writers Club. Literary Agent: Campbell Thomson & McLaughlin. Address: Bookends, Lewes Road, Horsted Keynes, Haywards Heath, West Sussex RH17 7DP, England.

LEGGATT Alexander Maxwell, b. 18 Aug 1940, Oakville, Ontario, Canada. Professor of English; Writer. m. Anna Thomas, 31 Mar 1964, 4 daughters. Education: BA, University of Toronto, 1962; MA, 1963, PhD, 1965, Shakespeare Institute, Stratford-on-Avon, affiliated with University of Birmingham. Appointments: Lecturer, 1965-67, Assistant Professor, 1967-71, Associate Professor, 1971-75, Professor of English, 1975-, University College, University of Toronto; Associate Editor, Modern Drama, 1972-75; Editorial Board, English Studies in Canada, 1984-91, University of Toronto Quarterly, 1996-. Publications: Citizen Comedy in the Age of Shakespeare, 1973; Shakespeare's Comedy of Love, 1974; Ben Jonson: His Vision and His Art, 1981; English Drama: Shakespeare to the Restoration, 1988; Shakespeare's Political Drama, 1988; Harvester-Twayne New Critical Introductions to Shakespeare: King Lear, 1988; Coriolanus: An Annotated Bibliography (co-author), 1989; Craft and Tradition: Essays in Honour of William Blissett (co-editor), 1990; Shakespeare in Performance: King Lear, 1991; Jacobean Public Theatre, 1992; English Stage Comedy 1490-1990, 1998. Contributions to: Many scholarly journals. Honours: Guggenheim Fellowship, 1985-86; Killam Research Fellowship, 1995; Outstanding Teaching Award, University of Toronto, 1995. Memberships: Amnesty International; Anglican Church of Canada, lay reader, 1979-; Association of Canadian College and University Teachers of English; International Association of University Professors of English; International Shakespeare Association, executive committee, 1987-96; PEN Canada; Shakespeare Association of America, trustee, 1986-89. Address: c/o University College, University of Toronto, Toronto, Ontario, M5S 3H7, Canada.

LEGUEY-FEILLEUX Jean-Robert, b. 28 Mar 1928, Marseilles, France. Associate Professor of Political Science; Writer. m. Virginia Louise Hartwell, 19 Sept 1953, 4 daughters. Education: Diplome Supérieur, Ecole Supérieure de Commerce, Marseilles, 1949; Diplome Supérieur d'Enseignement Coloniales, Université d'Aix-Marseille, 1959; MA, University of Florida, 1951; Certificate, English Life and Institutions, Cambridge, 1952; PhD, Georgetown University, 1965. Appointments: Lecturer, School of Foreign Service, 1957-66, Director, Research Institute of World Politics, 1960-66, Georgetown University; Assistant Professor, 1966-70, Associate Professor, 1970-, Chairman, Department of Political Science, 1983-96, St Louis University; Visiting Scholar, Harvard Law School, 1974-75; Visiting Researcher, United Nations, New York City, 1981. Publication: The Law of Limited International Conflict (with others), 1965. Contributions to: Various books and professional journals. Honours: Fulbright Award, US Department of State, 1950; Certificate of Distinguished Service, Institute of International Education, 1976; Outstanding Educator, Nutshell Magazine, 1988. Memberships: Academic Council on the UN System; UN Association. Address: 6139 Kingsbury Avenue, St Louis, MO 63112, USA.

LEHMAN David (Cary), b. 11 June 1948, New York, New York, USA. Writer; Poet; Editor. m. Stefanie Green, 2 Dec 1978, 1 son. Education: BA, 1970, PhD, 1978, Columbia University; BA, MA, 1972, University of Cambridge. Appointments: Instructor, Brooklyn College of the City University of New York, 1975-76; Assistant Professor, Hamilton College, Clinton, New York, 1976-80;

Fellow, Society for the Humanities, Cornell University, 1980-81; Lecturer, Wells College, Aurora, New York, 1981-82; Book Critic and Writer, Newsweek, 1983-89; Series Editor, The Best American Poetry, 1988-, Poets on Poetry, 1994-; Editorial Adviser in Poetry, W W Norton & Co, 1990-93. Publications: Some Nerve, 1973; Day One, 1979; Beyond Amazement: New Essays on John Ashbery (editor), 1980; James Merrill: Essays in Criticism (editor), 1983; An Alternative to Speech, 1986; Ecstatic Occasions, Expedient Forms: 65 Leading Contemporary Poets Select and Comment on Their Poems (editor), 1987; Twenty Questions, 1988; The Perfect Murder: A Study in Detection, 1989; Operation Memory, 1990; The Line Forms Here, 1992; Signs of the Times: Deconstruction and the Fall of Paul de Man, 1992; The Best American Poetry (editor with Charles Simic), 1992; The Best American Poetry (editor with Louise Glück), 1993; The Big Question, 1995; Valentine Place, 1996. Contributions to: Anthologies, newspapers, reviews and journals. Honours: Academy of American Poets Prize, 1974; Ingram Merrill Foundation Grants, 1976, 1982, 1984; National Endowment for the Humanities Grant, 1979; National Endowment for the Arts Fellowship, 1987; American Academy of Arts and Letters Fellowship, 1990; Lila Wallace-Reader's Digest Fund Writers Award, 1991-94. Address: 900 West End Avenue, No 14E, New York, NY 10025, USA.

LEHMAN Geoffrey (John), b. 20 June 1940, Sydney, New South Walese, Australia. Lawyer; Poet. m. 1981, 3 sons, 2 daughters. Education: BA, LLM, University of Sydney. Appointments: Partner, Price Waterhouse; Lecturer in Law, University of New South Wales. Publications: The Ilex Tree (with Les Murray), 1967; A Voyage of Lions and Other Poems, 1970; Conversation with a Rider, 1972; Selected Poems, 1975; Ross' Poems, 1978; Children's Games, 1990; Spring Forest, 1992. Other: Editor or Co-Editor, anthologies. Contributions to: Various publications. Honours: Grace Levin Prizes, 1967, 1981. Membership: Australia Council Literature Board, 1982-85. Address: c/o Curtis Brown Pty Ltd, 27 Union Street, Paddington, New South Wales, 2021, Australia.

LEHRER Keith (Edward), b. 10 Jan 1936, Minneapolis, Minnesota, USA. Philosopher; Professor; Writer. Education: BA, University of Minnesota, 1957; AM, 1959, PhD, 1960, Brown University. Appointments: Instructor and Assistant Professor, Wayne State University, 1960-63; Assistant Professor to Professor, University of Rochester, 1963-73; Visiting Associate Professor, University of Calgary, 1966; Visiting Professor, Vanderbilt University, 1970, University of Illinois at Chicago Circle, 1979, University of the Witwatersrand, 1994; Professor, 1974-90, Regents Professor, 1990-, University of Arizona; Director, Summer Seminars, Center for Advanced Study in the Behavioral Sciences, Stanford, 1977; Guest Professor, University of Salzburg, 1982; Honorary Professor, Karl-Franzens-University, Graz, 1985-; Associate, CREA, École Polytechnique, Paris, 1993-94. Publications: Philosophical Problems and Arguments: An Introduction (with James Cornman), 1968, 4th edition, 1992; Knowledge, 1978; Rational Consensus in Science and Society: A Philosophical and Mathematical Study (with Carl Wagner), 1981; Thomas Reid, 1989; Metamind, 1990; Theory of Knowledge, 1990; Self-Trust: A Study of Reason, Knowledge and Autonomy, 1997. Editor: Freedom and Determinism, 1966; Theories of Meaning (with Adrienne Lehrer), 1970; New Readings in Philosophical Analysis (with Herbert Feigl and Wilfrid Sellars), 1972; Reid's Inquiry and Essays (with Ronald Beanblossom), 1975, new edition, 1984; Analysis and Metaphysics: Essays in Honor of R M Chisholm, 1975; Science and Morality, 1988; Knowledge and Skepticism (with M Clay), 1989; The Opened Curtain: A US-Soviet Philosophy Summit (with Ernest Sosa), 1991; Knowledge, Teaching and Wisdom (with Jeannie Lum, Beverly Slichta, and Nicholas Smith), 1996. Contributions to: Numerous books and journals. Honours: American Council of Learned Societies Fellowship, 1973-74; National Endowment for the Humanities Fellowship, 1980; Guggenheim Fellowship, 1983-84; Visiting Fellow, University of London, 1996, and Australian National University, 1997. Memberships:

American Philosophical Association, president, 1989, chair, national board of officers, 1992-95; Council for Philosophical Studies; Institute International de Philosophie, Paris and Lund; Philosophy of Science Association; Vereinigung für Wissenschaftliche Grundlagen-forschung, Austria, honorary member. Address: 65 Sierra Vista Drive, Tucson, Arizona 85719, USA.

LEICHUK Alan, b. 15 Sept 1938, Brooklyn, New York, USA; Writer; Teacher. m. Barbara, Oct 1981, 2 sons. Education: BA, Brooklyn College, 1960; MA, 1963, PhD, 1965, Stanford University. Appointments: Brandeis University, 1966-81; Amherst College, 1982-84; Dartmouth College, 1985-; Visiting Writer, Professor, Haifa University, 1986-87, CUNY, 1993. Publications: Novels: American Mischief, 1973; Shrinking, 1978; Miriam in Her Forties, 1985; Brooklyn Roy, 1990; Playing the Game, 1995; For Young Adults: On Home Ground, 1987; 8 Great Hebrew Short Novels, 1982. Contributions to: New York Times Book Review; New Republic; Dissent; Atlantic Monthly; New York Review of Books. Honours: Guggenheim Fellow, 1976-77; Fulbright Award, 1986-87. Address: RFD 2, Box 67, Canaan, NH 03741, USA.

LEIGH Meredith. See: KENYON Bruce Guy.

LEIGH Mike, b. 20 Feb 1943, Salford, Lancashire, England. Dramatist; Film and Theatre Director. m. Alison Steadman, 1973, 2 sons. Education: Royal Academy of Dramatic Arts; Camberwell School of Arts and Crafts; Central School of Art and Design; London Film School. Publications: Plays: The Box Play, 1965; My Parents Have Gone to Carlisle, 1966; The Last Crusade of the Five Little Nuns, 1966; Nenaa, 1967; Individual Fruit Pies, 1968; Down Here and Up There, 1968; Big Basil, 1968; Epilogue, 1969; Glum Victoria and the Lad with Specs, 1969; Bleak Moments, 1970; A Rancid Pong, 1971; Wholesome Glory, The Jaws of Death, 1973; Dick Whittington and His Cat, 1973; Babies Grow Old, 1974; The Silent Majority, 1974; Abigail's Party, 1977 (also TV play); Ecstasy, 1979; Goose-Pimples, 1981; Smelling a Rat, 1988; Greek Tragedy, 1989; It's a Great Big Shame!, 1993. TV Films: A Mug's Game, 1973; Hard Labour, 1973; The Permissive Society, The Bath of the 2001 F A Cup, Final Goalie, Old Chums, Probation, A Light Snack, Afternoon, all 1975; Nuts in May, 1976; Knock for Knock, 1976; The Kiss of Death, 1977; Who's Who, 1978; Grown Ups, 1980; Home Sweet Home, 1981; Meantime, 1983; Four Days in July, 1984. Feature Films: Bleak Moments, 1971; The Short and Curlies, 1987; High Hopes, 1988; Life is Sweet, 1990; Naked, 1993. Radio Play: Too Much of a Good Thing, 1979. Honours: Golden Leopard, Locarno Film Festival, 1972; Golden Hugo, Chicago Film Festival, 1972; George Devine Award, 1973; Evening Standard Award, 1981; Drama Critics Choice, London, 1981; Critics Prize, Venice Film Festival, 1988; Honorary MA, Salford University, 1991; Officer of the Order of the British Empire, 1993; Best Director Award, Cannes Film Festival, 1993; Palme D'Or, Cannes Film Festival, 1996. Address: Peters, Fraser and Dunlop Group Ltd, 503/4 The Chambers, Chelsea Harbour, London SW10 0XF, England.

LEIGH Richard Harris, b. 16 Aug 1943, New Jersey, USA. Writer. Education: BA, Tufts University, 1965; MA, University of Chicago, 1967; PhD, State University of New York at Stony Brook, 1970. Publications: The Holy Blood and the Holy Grail (with Michael Baigent and Henry Lincoln), 1982; The Messianic Legacy (with Michael Baigent and Henry Lincoln), 1986; The Temple and the Lodge (with Michael Baigent), 1989; The Dead Sea Scrolls Deception (with Michael Baigent), 1991. Contributions to: Anthologies and journals. Address: 21 Kelly Street, London NW1 8PG, England.

LEIGH FERMOR Patrick (Michael), b. 11 Feb 1915, London, England. Author. Education: King's School, Canterbury. Publications: The Traveller's Tree, 1950; Julie de Carneilhan and Chance Acquaintances, by Colette (translator), 1951; A Time to Keep Silence, 1953; The Violins of Saint-Jacques, 1953; Mani, 1958; Roumeli,

1966; A Time of Gifts, 1977; Between the Woods and the Water, 1986; Three Letters from the Andes, 1991. Honours: DSO; Officer of the Order of the British Empire; CLitt; DLitt; Chevalier des Arts et des Lettres. Membership: Athens Academy, visiting member. Address: Messrs John Murray Ltd, 50 Albemarle Street, London W1, England.

LEITH Linda, b. 13 Dec 1949, Belfast, Northern Ireland. Writer; Editor. m. András Barnabás Göllner, 19 July 1974, 3 sons. Education: BA, 1st Class Honours, Philosophy, McGill University, 1970; PhD, Queen Mary College, London, 1976. Publications: Telling Differences: New English Fiction From Quebec (anthology), 1989; Introducing Hugh MacLennan's "Two Solitudes" (essay), 1990; Birds of Passage (novel), 1993; The Tragedy Queen (novel), 1995. Contributions to: Many magazines and journals. Address: Department of English, PO Box 2000, Ste Anne de Bellevue, Quebec H9X 3L9, Canada.

LEITHAUSER Brad, b. 27 Feb 1953, Detroit, Michigan, USA. Poet; Writer. m Mary Jo Salter, 1980, 1 daughter. Education: BA, 1975, JD, 1980, Harvard University. Appointments: Research Fellow, Kyoto Comparative Law Center, 1980-83; Visiting Writer, Amherst College, 1984-85; Lecturer, Mount Holyoke College, 1987-88. Publications: Poetry: Hundreds of Fireflies, 1982; A Seaside Mountain: Eight Poems from Japan, 1985; Cats of the Temple, 1986; Between Leaps: Poems 1972-1985, 1987; The Mail from Anywhere: Poems, 1990. Fiction: The Line of Ladies, 1975; Equal Distance, 1985; Hence, 1989; Seaward, 1993. Non-Fiction: Penchants & Places: Essays and Criticism, 1995. Editor: The Norton Book of Ghost Stories, 1994. Honours: Harvard University-Academy of American Poets Prizes, 1973, 1975; Harvard University McKim Garrison Prizes, 1974, 1975; Amy Lowell Traveling Scholarship, 1981-82; Guggenheim Fellowship, 1982-83; Lavan Younger Poets Award, 1983; John D and Catharine T MacArthur Foundation Fellowship, 1983-87. Address: c/o Alfred A Knopf Inc, 201 East 50th Street, New York, NY 10022, USA.

LELAND Christopher Towne, b. 17 Oct 1951. Writer; Professor. Education: BA, English, Pomona College, 1973; MA, Spanish, 1980, PhD, Comparative Literature, University of California, San Diego, 1982. Appointment: Professor of English, Wayne State University, 1990-. Publications: Mean Time, 1982; Fiction and the Argentine Reality, 1986; Mrs Randall, 1987; The Book of Marvels, 1990; The Last Happy Men: The Generation of 1922, 1992; The Professor of Aesthetics, 1994; Letting Loose, 1996; The Art of Compelling Fiction, 1998; How to Be Your Own Best Critic, 1998Contributions to: Principal Translator, Open Door by Luise Valengnela, 1988. Honours: Finalist, PEN Hemingway Award, 1982; Fellow, Massachusetts Artists Foundation, 1985. Memberships: Poets and Writers; Modern Language Association. Address: c/o Department of English, Wayne State University, Detroit, MI 48202, USA.

LELCHUK Alan, b. 15 Sept 1938, New York, New York, USA. Writer. m. Barbara Kreiger, 7 Oct 1979, 2 sons. Education: BA, Brooklyn College, 1960; MA, 1963, PhD, English Literature, 1965, Stanford University. Appointments: Brandeis University, 1966-81; Associate Editor, Modern Occasions, 1980-82; Amherst College, 1982-84; Dartmouth College, 1985-; Fulbright Writer-in-Residence, Haifa University, Israel, 1986-87; Visiting Writer, City College of New York, 1991; Editor, Publisher, Steerforth Press, South Royalton, Vermont, 1993-. Publications: American Mischief, 1973; Miriam at Thirty-Four, 1974; Shrinking: The Beginning of My Own Ending, 1978; 8 Great Hebrew Short Novels (co-editor), 1983; Miriam in Her Forties, 1985; On Home Ground, 1987; Brooklyn Boy, 1989; Playing the Game, 1995. Contributions to: New York Times Book Review; Sewanee Review; Atlantic; New Republic; Dissent; New York Review of Books. Honours: Guggenheim Fellowship, 1976-77; Mishkenot Sha'Ananim Resident Fellow, 1976-77; Fulbright Award, 1986-87; Manuscript Collection, Mugar Memorial Library, Boston University.

Memberships: PEN; Authors Guild. Address: RFD 2, Canaan, NH 03741, USA.

LELIWA Wiktor. See: KONOPINSKI Lech Kazimierz.

LELYVELD Joseph (Salem), b. 5 Apr 1937, Cincinnati, Ohio, USA. Journalist; Editor. m. Carolyn Fox, 14 June 1958, 2 daughters. Education: BA, 1958, MA, 1959, Harvard University; MS, Columbia University, 1960. Appointments: Staff, 1963-, Foreign Correspondent, 1965-86, Foreign Editor, 1987-89, Managing Editor, 1990-94, Executive Editor, 1994-, New York Times. Publication: Move Your Shadow: South Africa Black and White, 1985. Contributions to: Periodicals. Honours: George Polk Memorial Awards, 1972, 1984; Guggenheim Fellowship, 1984; Pulitzer Prize in General Non-Fiction, 1986; Los Angeles Times Book Prize, 1986; Sidney Hillman Award, 1986; Cornelius P Ryan Award, 1986. Membership: Century Association. Address: c/o The New York Times, 229 West 43rd Street, New York, NY 10036, USA.

LEM Stanislaw, b. 12 Sept 1921, Lvov, Russia. Author. m. Barbara Lesnik, 11 Aug 1953, 1 son. Education: Studied Medicine in Lvov, 1939-41, and Kraków, Poland, 1944-45. Appointments: Lecturer, University of Kraków, part-time, 1973-. Publications: 40 books translated into 35 languages including: The Star Diaries, 1957; Eden, 1959; Solaris, 1961; Memoirs Found in a Bathtub, 1961; The Invincible, 1964; The Cyberiad, 1965; His Master's Voice, 1968; Tales of Pirx the Pilot, 1968; A Perfect Vacuum, 1971; The Futurological Congress, 1971; The Chain of Chance, 1976; Fiasco, 1986. Contributions to: New Yorker; Encounter; Penthouse; Omni. Honours: Polish Ministry of Culture Awards, 1965, 1973; Polish State Prize for Literature, 1976; Austrian State Award for European Literature, 1985; Alfred Jurzykowski Foundation for Literature Prize, 1987; Honorary PhD, University of Wroclaw. Membership: International Association of Poets, Playwrights, Editors, Essayists and Authors. Address: c/o Franz Rottensteiner, Marchettigasse 9 17, A 1060 Vienna, Austria.

LEMAIRE Michael, b. 6 Aug 1936, Bordeaux, France. Writer. Education: BS, Civil Engineering, 1957; Minors, Literature and Journalism, 1958. Publications: Love Me or at Least Let Me Love You, 1986; A Romantic Interlude, 1990; Poems Published, 1990-91; Vindicated Episode at Salton Sea (novel), 1993; Tracks Through Time and Space (fantasy novel), 1993. Contributions to: Newspapers and journals. Memberships: International Writers and Artists Association, honorary member; Jazz Journalists Association; National Writers Club; Writers Guild. Address: 6030 Shady Creek Road, Agoura, CA 92549, USA.

LEMANN Nancy Elise, b. 4 Feb 1956, New Orleans, Louisiana, USA. Writer. m. Mark Paul Clein, 5 Oct 1991. Education: BA, Brown University, 1978; MFA, Columbia University, 1984. Publications: Lives of the Saints; The Ritz of the Bayou; Sportsmans Paradise. Contributions to: Chicago Tribune; Los Angeles Times; New Republic; New York Review of Books; New York Times; People; Washington Post. Memberships: PEN; Authors Guild. Address: 254 West 73rd Street, No 5, New York, NY 10023, USA.

LEMASTER J(immie) R(ay), b. 29 Mar 1934, Pike County, Ohio, USA. Professor of English; Poet; Writer; Editor. m. Wanda May Ohnesorge, 21 May 1966, 1 son, 2 daughters. Education: BS, English, Defiance College, 1959; MA, English, 1962, PhD, English, 1970, Bowling Green State University, Ohio. Appointments: Faculty, Defiance College, 1962-77; Professor of English and Director of American Studies, Baylor University, 1977-; Associate Editor, 1988-90, Editor, 1992-96, JASAT (Journal of the American Studies Association of Texas). Publications: Poetry: The Heart is a Gypsy, 1967; Children of Adam, 1971; Weeds and Wildflowers, 1975; First Person, Second, 1983; Purple Bamboo, 1986; Journey to Beijing, 1992. Other: Jesse Stuart: A Reference Guide, 1979; Jesse Stuart: Kentucky's

Chronicler-Poet, 1980; The New Mark Twain Handbook (with E Hudson Long), 1985. Editor: Poets of the Midwest, 1966; The World of Jesse Stuart: Selected Poems, 1975; Jesse Stuart: Essays on His Work (with Mary Washington Clarke), 1977; Jesse Stuart: Selected Criticism, 1978; Jesse Stuart on Education, 1992; The Mark Twain Encyclopedia (with James D Wilson), 1993. Honours: South and West Inc Publishers Award, 1970; Ohio Poet of the Year, 1976; Honorary Doctor of Letters, Defiance College, 1988; Outstanding Reference Source Citation, American Library Association, 1993. Memberships: American Studies Association; Conference of College Teachers of English; Jesse Stuart Foundation, board of directors, 1989-; Mark Twain Circle of America; Modern Language Association; Texas Association of Creative Writing Teachers. Address: 201 Harrington Avenue, Waco, TX 76706, USA.

LENGYEL Balazs, b. 21 Aug 1918, Budapest, Hungary. Writer. m. (1) Agnes Nemes Nagy, 1944, (2) Veronika Kerek. Education: Doctor of Law. Appointments: Editor-in-Chief, Ujhold literary journal, Budapest, 1946-48, 1986-91; Editor, Corvina Publishing Company, Budapest, 1961-63; Editor, Ferenc Mora Publishing Company, Budapest, 1963-88. Publications: The New Hungarian Poetry, 1948; Tradition and Attempt, 1972; The Turks in Hungary, 1972; Various novels for young people, 1951-64; Collections of essays: Contemporary Hungarian Poetry, 1948; Tradition and Experiment, 1972; From Anthology to Anthology, 1977; Close Pictures, 1980; The Story of Behaviour, 1986; Green and Gold, 1988; Returning, 1990; Rome Revisited, 1995; Two Changes of Fortune, 1998. Editor: Ujhold (New Moon), Literary yearbook. Honours: Attila Jozsef Award, Hungarian Writers' Union, 1981; Youth Award, Hungarian Writers' Union, 1982; Tibor Déry Award, Hungarian Writers' Union, 1988; Dezsö Kosztolányi Award, Soros Foundation, 1990; Bölöni Oeuvre Award, Hungarian Writers' Union, 1991; National Széchenyi Award, 1995; Yad Vashem, La Médaille des justes parmi les nations, Israel, 1997. Memberships: Hungarian Writers' Union, presidium, 1989; Széchenyi Academy of Arts, founding member, 1992; Hungarian PEN, deputy chairman, 1995. Address: 5/B Királyhagó utca, Budapest H-1126, Hungary.

LENTRICCHIA Frank, b. 23 May 1940, Utica, New York, USA. Professor; Writer. m. (1) Karen Young, 24 June 1967, div 1973, 2 children, (2) Melissa Christensen, 1973, div 1992, (3) Johanna McAuliffe, 1994, 1 child. Education: BA, Utica College of Syracuse University, 1962; MA, 1963, PhD, 1966, Duke University. Appointments: Assistant Professor, University of California at Los Angeles, 1966-68; Assistant Professor, 1968-70, Associate Professor, 1970-76, Professor, 1976-82, University of California at Irvine; Autrey Professor of Humanities, Rice University, 1982-84; Gilbert Professor of Literature, Duke University, 1984-. Publications: The Gaeity of Language: An Essay on the Radical Poetics of W B Yeats and Wallace Stevens, 1968; Robert Frost: Modern Poetics and the Landscapes of Self, 1975; Robert Frost: A Bibliography, 1913-1974 (editor with Melissa Christensen Lentricchia), 1976; After the New Criticism, 1980; Criticism and Social Change, 1983; Ariel and the Police, 1988; Critical Terms for Literary Study, 1990, 2nd edition, 1995; New Essays on White Noise, 1991; Introducing Don DeLillo, 1991; The Edge of Night: A Confession, 1994; Johnny Critelli and The Knifemen: Two Novels, 1996; The Music of the Inferno: A Novel, forthcoming. Contributions to: Professional journals. Memberships: Modern Language Association; PEN. Literary Agent: Watkins/Loomis. Address: c/o Department of English, Duke University, Durham, NC 27708, USA.

LENZ Siegfried, b. 17 Mar 1926, Lyck, Germany. Author; Dramatist. m. Liselotte Lenz. Education: Philosophy, English Philology, and History of Literature, Hamburg. Publications: Es waren Habichte in der Luft, 1951; Duell mit dem Schatten, 1953; So zärtlich war Suleyken, 1955; Der Mann im Strom, 1957; Der Jäger des spotts, 1958; Brot und Spiele, 1959; Das Feuerschiff, 1960; Der Zeit der Schuldlosen, 1961; Stimmungen der

See, 1962; Lehmanns Erzählungen oder so schön war mein Markt, 1964; Der Spielverderber, 1965; Haussuchung, 1967; Deutschstunde, 1968; Das Vorbild, 1973; Der Geist der Mirabella: Geschichten aus Bollerup, 1974; Einstein überquert die Elbe bei Hamburg, 1975; Heimatmuseum, 1978; Ein Kriegsende, 1984; Exerzierplatz, 1985; Das serbische Mädchen, 1987; Die Klangprobe, 1990; Die Auflehnung, 1994; Ludmilla, 1996. Honours: Lessing Prize, Hamburg, 1953; Gerhart Hauptmann Prize, 1961; Honorary Doctorates, University of Hamburg, 1976, Ben Gurion University, Beer Sheva, 1993; Literary Prize, Freemasons of Germany, 1979; Thomas Mann Prize, 1984; Peace Prize, Federal Book Trade Association, 1988; Bavarian Literature Prize, 1995. Memberships: Berlin Academy of Arts; Deutsche Akademie für Sprache und Dichtung e.v., Darmstadt; Free Academy of Arts, Hamburg; PEN. Address: Preusserstrasse 4, D-22605, Hamburg, Germany.

LEONARD Elmore (John, Jr), b. 11 Oct 1925, New Orleans, Louisiana, USA. Novelist. m. (1) Beverly Cline, 30 Aug 1949, 3 sons, 2 daughters, div 7 Oct 1977, (2) Joan Shepard, 15 Sep 1979, dec. 13 Jan 1993, (3) Christine Kent, 15 Aug 1993. Education: BA, University of Detroit, 1950. Publications: 33 novels including: Hombre, 1961; City Primeval, 1980; Split Images, 1981; Cat Chaser, 1982; Stick, 1983; Labrava, 1983; Glitz, 1985; Bandits, 1986; Touch, 1987; Freaky Deaky, 1988; Killshot, 1989; Get Shorty, 1990; Maximum Bob, 1991; Rum Punch, 1992; Pronto, 1993; Riding the Rap, 1995; Out of Sight, 1996. Other: The Tonto Woman and Other Western Stories, 1998. Honours: Edgar Allan Poe Award, 1984, and Grand Master Award, 1992, Mystery Writers of America; Michigan Foundation for the Arts Award for Literature, 1985; Honorary degrees in Letters from Florida Atlantic University, 1995, University of Detroit Mercy, 1997. Memberships: Writers Guild of America; PEN; Authors Guild; Western Writers of America; Mystery Writers of America. Address: c/o Michael Siegel, Brillstein-Grey Entertainment, 9150 Wilshire Boulevard, Beverly Hills, CA 90212, USA.

LEONARD Hugh (John, Jr), (John Keyes Byrne), b. 9 Nov 1926, Dublin, Ireland. Playwright. m. Paule Jacquet, 1955, 1 daughter. Publications: Plays: The Big Birthday, 1957; A Leap in the Dark, 1957; Madigan's Lock, 1958; A Walk on the Water, 1960; The Passion of Peter Ginty, 1961; Stephen D, 1962; The Poker Session, 1963; Dublin 1, 1963; The Saints Go Cycling In, 1965; Mick and Mick, 1966; The Quick and the Dead, 1967; The Au Pair Man, 1968; The Barracks, 1969; The Patrick Pearse Motel, 1971; Da, 1973; Thieves, 1973; Summer, 1974; Times of Wolves and Tigers, 1974; Irishmen, 1975; Time Was, 1976; A Life, 1977; Moving Days, 1981; The Mask of Moriarty, 1984. Television: Silent Song, 1967; Nicholas Nickleby, 1977; London Belongs to Me, 1977; The Last Campaign, 1978; The Ring and the Rose, 1978; Strumpet City, 1979; The Little World of Don Camillo, 1980; Kill, 1982; Good Behaviour, 1982; O'Neill, 1983; Beyond the Pale, 1984; The Irish RM, 1985; A Life, 1986; Troubles, 1987. Films: Herself Surprised, 1977; Da, 1984; Widows' Peak, 1984; Troubles, 1984. Autobiography: Home Before Night, 1979; Out After Dark, 1988. Honours: Honorary DHL (RI); Writers Guild Award, 1966; Tony Award; Critics Circle Award; Drama Desk Award; Outer Critics Award, 1978; Doctor of Literature, Trinity College, Dublin, 1988. Address: 6 Rossaun Pilot View, Dalkey, County Dublin, Ireland.

LEONARD Richard (Lawrence), (Dick Leonard), b. 12 Dec 1930, Ealing, Middlesex, England. Journalist; Editor; Broadcaster; Writer. m. Irene Heidelberger, 29 Mar 1963, 1 son, 1 daughter. Education: Institute of Education, London University; MA, Essex University, 1969. Appointments: Senior Research Fellow, Essex University, 1968-70; Member of Parliament, Labour Party, Romford, 1970-74; Assistant Editor, The Economist, 1974-85; Visiting Professor, Free University of Brussels, 1988-96; Brussels and European Union Correspondent, The Observer, 1989-96; Senior Advisor, Center for European Policy Studies, 1994-. Publications: Elections in Britain, 1968, 4th edition, 1997; The Backbencher and Parliament (co-editor), 1972; Paying for Party Politics, 1975; The Socialist Agenda (co-editor), 1981; World Atlas of Elections (co-author), 1986; Pocket Guide to the EEC, 1988; Elections in Britain Today, 1991; The Economist Guide to the European Community, 1992, 6th edition as The Economist Guide to the European Union, 1998; Replacing the Lords, 1995; Eminent Europeans (co-author), 1996; Crosland and New Labour (editor), 1998. Contributions to: Newspapers and periodicals worldwide. Memberships: Fabian Society, chairman, 1977-78; Reform Club. Address: 32 rue des Bégonias, 1170 Brussels, Belgium.

LEONARD Tom, (Thomas Anthony Leonard), b. 22 Aug 1944, Glasgow, Scotland. Writer. m. Sonya Maria O'Brien, 24 Dec 1971, 2 sons. Education: MA, Glasgow University, 1976. Appointments: Writer-in-Residence, Renfrew District Libraries, 1986-89, Glasgow University/Strathclyde University, 1991-92, Bell College of Technology, 1993-94. Publications: Intimate Voices (writing), 1965-83, 1984; Situations Theoretical and Contemporary, 1986; Radical Renfrew (editor), 1990; Nora's Place, 1990; Places of the Mind: The Life and Work of James Thomson 'BV' Cafe, 1993; Reports From the Present: Selected Works 1982-94, 1995. Contributions to: Edinburgh Review. Honour: Joint Winner, Saltire Scottish Book of the Year Award, 1984. Address: 56 Eldon Street, Glasgow G3 6NJ, Scotland.

LEOPOLD Peter. See: **HAMBURGER Michael.**

LEOTTA Guido, b. 2 May 1957, Faenza, Italy. Writer; Poet; Publisher. Education: Accountant's Diploma. Appointments: President, Tratti/Mobydick Cultural Cooperative and Publishing House, 1987; Author and Coordinator, Tratti Folk Festival, 1989-95. Publications: Sacsaphone (collected novels), 1981; Anatre (short stories), 1989; Strategie di Viaggio Nel Non Amore (poems), 1992; Il Bambino Ulisse (children's stories), 1995. Contributions to: Magazines. Honours: Premio Leonforte for Children's Stories, 1991; Laoghaire Poetry Prize, Ireland, 1994. Address: Via Bubani 4, I 48018 Faenza, Italy.

LEPAGE Robert, b. 12 Dec 1957, Quebec, Canada. Education: Arts and Literature, Laval University, Quebec, 1994; Faculty of Arts, McGill University, Montreal, 1997; Theatre Department, Toronto University, 1997. Appointments: Scriptwriter, Director, Le Confessionnal, 1994; Scriptwriter, Director, Le Polygraphe, 1996; Scriptwriter, Artistic Director, Les Sept branches de la rivière Ota, directed by Francis Leclerc, 1997; Scriptwriter, Director, Nô, 1998. Honours include: Creation Award, Conseil de la culture de Québec, 1986; Chevalier de l'Ordre des Arts et des Lettres, 1990; Ottawa National Arts Centre Award, 1994; Order of Canada, 1995; Award for Best Director, 1995; Dora Mavor Moore Awards, Best Achievement in Direction 1995, Best Production, 1996; City TV Award, Best Canadian Feature Film, Toronto International Film Festival, 1998. Address: 103 Dalhousie St, Quebec, G1K 4B9, Canada.

LEPAN Douglas (Valentine), b. 25 May 1914, Toronto, Ontario, Canada. Professor Emeritus; Poet; Writer. 2 sons. Education: BA, University of Toronto, 1935; BA, 1937, MA, 1948, Oxford University. Appointments: Counsellor, later Minister Counsellor, Canadian Embassy, Washington, DC, 1951-55; Secretary and Director of Research, Royal Commission on Canada's Economic Prospects, 1955-58; Assistant Under Secretary of State for External Affairs, 1958-59; Professor of English Literature, Queen's University, Kingston, 1959-64; Principal, 1964-70, Principal Emeritus, 1970-, University College, University of Toronto; University Professor, 1970-79, University Professor Emeritus, 1979-, University of Toronto; Senior Fellow, 1970-75, Senior Fellow Emeritus, 1985-, Massey College. Publications: The Wounded Prince and Other Poems, 1948; The Net and the Sword, 1953; The Deserter, 1964; Bright Glass of Memory, 1979; Something Still to Find: New Poems, 1982; Weathering It: Complete Poems 1948-87, 1987; Far Voyages: Poems, 1990; Macalister, or Dying in the Work, 1995. Honours: Guggenheim Fellowship, 1948-49; Governor-General's Award for Poetry, 1953, and for Fiction, 1964; Lorne Pierce Medal, Royal Society of Canada, 1976. Address: c/o Massey College, 4 Devonshire Place, Toronto, Ontario M5S 2E1, Canada.

LEPSCHY Anna Laura, b. 30 Nov 1933, Turin, Italy. Professor of Italian; Writer. m. 20 Dec 1962. Education: BLitt, MA, Somerville College, Oxford, 1952-57. Appointment: Professor of Italian, University College, London. Publications: Viaggio in Terrasanta 1480, 1966; The Italian Language Today (co-author), 1977, new edition, 1991; Tintoretto Observed, 1983; Narrativa e Teatro fra due Secoli, 1984; Varietà linguistiche e pluralità di codici nel Rinascimento, 1996; Davanti a Tintozetto, 1998. Contributions to: Italian Studies; Romance Studies; Studi Francesi; Studi sul Boccaccio; Studi Novecenteschi; Yearbook of the Pirandello Society; Modern Languages Notes; Lettere Italiane. Memberships: Pirandello Society, president, 1988-92; Society for Italian Studies, chair, 1988-95; Association for the Study of Modern Italy; Associazione Internazionale di Lingua e Letteratura Italiana, Vice-President, 1998-. Address: Department of Italian, University College, Gower Street, London WC1E 6BT, England.

LERMAN Rhoda, b. 18 Jan 1936, New York, USA. Writer. m. Robert Lerman, 15 Sept 1957, 1 son, 2 daughters. Education: BA, University of Miami, 1957. Appointments: National Endowment for the Arts Distinguished Professor of Creative Writing, Hartwick College, Oneonta, New York, 1985; Visiting Professor of Creative Writing, 1988, 1990, Chair, English Literature, 1990, State University of New York at Buffalo. Publications: Call Me Ishtar, 1973; Girl That He Marries, 1976; Eleanor, a Novel, 1979; Book of the Night, 1984; God's Ear, 1989; Animal Acts, 1994. Address: c/o Henry Holt & Co, 115 West 18th Street, New York, NY 10011, USA.

LERNER Laurence (David), b. 12 Dec 1925, Cape Town, South Africa (British citizen). Retired Professor; Poet; Writer. m. Natalie Winch, 15 June 1948, 4 sons. Education: MA, University of Cape Town, 1945; BA, Pembroke College, Cambridge, 1949. Appointments: Lecturer, University College of the Gold Coast, 1949-53, Queen's University, 1953-62; Lecturer to Professor, University of Sussex, 1962-84; Kenan Professor, Vanderbilt University, Nashville, Tennessee, 1985-89; Several visiting professorships. Publications: Poems, 1955; Domestic Interior and Other Poems, 1959; The Directions of Memory: Poems 1958-63, 1964; Selves, 1969; A.R.T.H.U.R.: The Life and Opinions of a Digital Computer, 1974; The Man I Killed, 1980; A.R.T.H.U.R. and M.A.R.T.H.A., or, The Loves of the Computer, 1980; Chapter and Verse: Bible Poems, 1984; Selected Poems, 1984; Rembrandt's Mirror, 1987. Novels: The Englishmen, 1959; A Free Man, 1968; My Grandfather's Grandfather, 1985. Play: The Experiment, 1980. Non-Fiction: The Truest Poetry, 1960; The Truthtellers: Jane Austen, George Eliot, Lawrence, 1967; The Uses of Nostalgia, 1973; An Introduction to English Poetry, 1975; Love and Marriage: Literature in its Social Context, 1979; The Frontiers of Literature, 1988; Angels and Absences, 1997. Contributions to: Newspapers, reviews, journals, and magazines. Honours: South-East Arts Literature Prize, 1979; Fellow, Royal Society of Literature, 1986. Address: Abinger, 1-B Gundreda Road, Lewes, East Sussex BN7 1PT, England.

LERNER Michael P(hillip), b. 7 Feb 1943, Newark, New Jersey, USA. Writer. Education: AB, Columbia University, 1964; MA, 1968, PhD, 1972, University of California at Berkeley. Publications: Surplus Powerlessness, 1986; Jewish Renewal, 1994; Blacks and Jews, 1995; The Politics of Meaning, 1995. Contributions to: Newspapers and magazines. Address: c/o Tikkun Magazine, 26 Fell Street, San Francisco, CA 94102, USA.

LERNER Robert E(arl), b. 8 Feb 1940, New York , New York, USA. Professor of History; Writer. m. Erdmut Krumnack, 25 Oct 1963, 2 daughters. Education: BA,

University of Chicago, 1960; MA, 1962, PhD, 1964, Princeton University; University of Münster, 1962-63. Appointments: Instructor, Princeton University, 1963-64; Assistant Professor, Western Reserve University, 1964-67; Assistant Professor, 1967-71, Associate Professor, 1971-76, Professor, 1976-, Peter B Ritzma Professor in the Humanities, 1993-, Northwestern University. Publications: The Age of Adversity: The Fourteenth Century, 1968; The Heresy of the Free Spirit in the Later Middle Ages, 1972, revised edition, 1991; The Powers of Prophecy: The Cedar of Lebanon Vision from the Mongol Onslaught to the Dawn of the Enlightenment, 1983; Weissagungen über die Päpste (with Robert Moynihan), 1985; World Civilizations (with P Ralph, S Meacham and E Burns), 9th edition, 1997; Western Civilizations (with Standish Meacham and E M Burns), 13th edition, 1998; Johannes de Rupescissa, Liber secretorum eventuum: Edition critique, traduction et introduction historique (with C Morerod-Fattebert), 1994; Propaganda Miniata: Le origini delle profezie papali 'Ascende Calve' (with Orit Schwartz), 1994; Neue Richtungen in der hoch - und spätmittelalterlichen Bibelexegese (editor), 1995. Contributions to: Professional journals. Honours: Fulbright Senior Fellowship, 1967-68; National Endowment for the Humanities Research Grant, 1972-73; American Academy in Rome Fellowship, 1983-84; Guggenheim Fellowship, 1984-85; Rockefeller Foundation Study Center Residency, Bellagio, Italy, 1989; Historisches Kolleg, Munich, Forschungspreis, 1992, Stipendiat, 1992-93; Woodrow Wilson Center for Scholars Fellow, 1996-97. Address: c/o Department of History, Northwestern University, Evanston, IL 60208, USA.

LESCHAK Peter, b. 11 May 1951, Chisholm, Minnesota, USA. Writer. m. Pamela Cope, May 1974. Appointments: Contributing Editor, Twin Cities magazine, 1984-86, Minnesota Monthly, 1984-. Publications: Letters from Side Lake, 1987; The Bear Guardian, 1990; Bumming with the Furies, 1993; Seeing the Raven, 1994; Hellroaring, 1994; The Snow Lotus, 1996. Honour: Minnesota Book Award, 1991. Membership: Authors Guild. Address: Box 51, Side Lake, MN 55781, USA.

LESSARD Suzannah, b. 12 Jan 1944, Islip, New York, USA. Writer. 1 son. Education: BA, Columbia School of General Studies, 1969. Appointments: Editor, Contributor, Washington Monthly, 1969-73; Staff Writer, New Yorker, 1975-95. Publications: The Architect of Desire: Beauty and Danger in the Stanford White Family. Honour: Whiting Award, 1995. Membership: PEN. Literary Agency: Wylie Agency. Address: c/o The Dial Press, 1540 Broadway, NY 10036, USA.

LESSER Milton. See: **MARLOWE Stephen.**

LESSING Charlotte, b. 14 May 1924, London, England. Journalist; Wine Writer. m. Walter Lessing, 25 May 1948, 3 daughters. Education: Diploma English Literature, Henrietta Barnet School (Matric) Evening Classes City Literary Institute. Appointments: Editorial Assistant, Lilliput Magazine; Dpty Editor, 1964-73, Editor, 1973-88, Good Housekeeping; Wine Editor, The Lady, 1992-. Contributions to: Lilliput; Punch; The New Statesman; Woman & Home; Ideal Home; Good Housekeeping; Sainsbury Magazine; Food and Wiine. Honours: Editor of the Year, Good Housekeeping, 1982; Wine Guild/Taittinger Wine Writer (National Press), 1995; Ordre du Merit Mericole, Republique Francaise, 1996.

LESTER Andrew D(ouglas), b. 8 Aug 1939, Coral Gables, Florida, USA. Professor of Pastoral Theology and Pastoral Counselling; Writer. m. Judith L Laesser, 8 Sept 1960, 1 son, 1 daughter. Education: BA, Mississippi College, Clinton, 1961; BD, 1964, PhD, 1968, Southern Baptist Theological Seminary, Louisville, Kentucky; Clinical Pastoral Education, Central State, Louisville General, Jewish and Children's Hospitals, Louisville, 1964-68; Clinical Training in Pastoral Counselling Service, Clarksville, Indiana, 1964-69; Diplomate, Association of Pastoral Counselors, 1979. Appointments: Professor of Pastoral Theology and Pastoral Counselling, Brite Divinity School, Texas Christian University; General Editor, Resources for Living series, 1989-90; Editor, series on Pastoral Counselling, Westminster-John Knox Press, 1992-. Publications: Pastoral Care in Crucial Human Situations (editor with Wayne Oates), 1969; Sex Is More Than a Word, 1973; It Hurts So Bad, Lord!: The Christian Encounters Crisis, 1976; Coping with Your Anger: A Christian Guide, 1983; Pastoral Care with Children in Crisis, 1985; Spiritual Dimensions of Pastoral Care: Witness to the Ministry of Wayne E Oates (editor with Gerald L Borchert), 1985; Hope in Pastoral Care and Counselling, 1995; It Takes Two: The Joy of Intimate Marriage(co-authored with Judith L. Lester), 1998. Address: Brite Divinity School, Texas Christian University, Fort Worth, TX 76129, USA.

LESTER Geoffrey, b. 18 Mar 1948, Isleworth, Middleworth, England. Racing Journalist. m. Geraldine Lester, 2 Sept 1978, 1 son, 1 daughter. Appointments: Reporter, 1964-98, Sub-Editor, Reporter, Chief Race Reporter, 1985-98, Sporting Life; Freelance, 1998-. Contributions to: Ruffs Guide; Irish Racing Annual; Racing Post; Weekender; Official festival magazines, Cheltenham, Aintree, Epsom, Royal Ascot, Longchamp, Dubai. Honour: Lord Derby's Horserace Writers, Journalist of the Year, 1988. Membership: Committee Member, Horserace Writers Association. Address: 65 Penwood Heights, Burghclere, Nr Newbury, Berks RG20 9EZ, England.

LESTER Julius, b. 27 Jan 1939, St Louis, Missouri, USA. Professor of Judaic Studies; Writer; Musician; Singer. 2 sons, 2 daughters. Education: BA, Fisk University, 1960. Appointment: Professor of Judiac Studies, University of Massachusetts, 1971-. Publications: The 12-String Guitar as Played by Leadbelly: An Instructional Manual (with Pete Seeger), 1965; To Praise Our Bridges: An Autobiography by Fanny Lou Hamer (editor with Mary Varela), 1967; Our Folk Tales: High John, The Conqueror, and Other Afro-American Tales (editor with Mary Varela), 1967; The Mud of Vietnam: Photographs and Poems, 1967; Revolutionary Notes, 1969; Ain't No Ambulances for No Nigguhs Tonight, by Stanley Couch (editor), 1969; Look Out Whitey, Black Power's Gon' Get Your Mama, 1968; To Be a Slave, 1968; Black Folktales, 1969; Search for the New Land: History as Subjective Experience, 1969; The Seventh Son: The Thought and Writings of W E B Du Bois (editor), 2 volumes, 1971; The Knee-High Man and Other Tales, 1972; Long Journey Home: Stories from Black History, 1972; Two Love Stories, 1972; Who I Am?, 1974; All Is Well (autobiography), 1976; This Strange New Feeling (short stories), 1982; Do Lord Remember Me, 1984; The Tales of Uncle Remus: The Adventures of Brer Rabbit, 1987; More Tales of Uncle Remus: Further Adventures of Brer Rabbit, His Friends, Enemies and Others, 1988; How Many Spots Does a Leopard Have? and Other Tales, 1989; Further Tales of Uncle Remus: The Misadventure of Brer Rabbit, Brer Fox, Brer Wolf, The Dooding and Other Creatures, 1990; Falling Pieces of the Broken Sky, 1990; Last Tales of Uncle Remus, 1994; And All Our Wounds Forgiven, 1994; The Man Who Knew Too Much, 1994; John Henry, 1994; Othello: A Novel, 1995. Address: PO Box 9634, North Amherst, MA 01059, USA.

LETRIA José Jorge, b. 8 June 1951, Cascais, Portugal. Writer; Poet; Songwriter; Dramatist. m. Isabel Letria, 9 July 1973, 3 sons. Education: Law and History, University of Lisbon. Appointments: Journalist, Editor, Portuguese newspapers, 1970-94; Director, National Radio, 1974-75; City Councillor for Culture, Cascais, 1994. Publications: Poetry: Capela Dos Ocios: Odes Mediterranicas, 1993; Actas Da Desordem Do Dia, 1993; La Tentation Du Bonheur, 1993; O Fantasma Da Obra, 1994; Os Achados Da Noite, 1994; Lisboa, Capital Do Coraca, 1994; A Duvida Melodica, 1994; O Dom Intranquilo, 1995. Other: 30 children's books; songs; plays. Contributions to: Many publications in Portugal, Spain, Mexico and Germany. Honours: ECA de Queiroz, Lisbon, 1989; Cidade de Ourense, Spain, 1989, 1994; Plural, Mexico, 1990; Gulbenkian Prize, 1992; International UNESCO Prize, 1993. Memberships: Collège de L'Europe, correspondent; International Association of Critics; PEN Club; Portuguese Author's Society; Portuguese Writer's Association; World Literary Academy. Address: Avenue General Humberto Delgado, No 5-7-B, 2745 Queluz, Portugal.

LETTE Kathy, b. 11 Nov 1958, Sydney, New South Wales, Australia. Writer; Screenwriter; Playwright. m. Geoffrey Robertson, 1 May 1990, 1 son, 1 daughter. Publications: Plays: Wet Dreams, 1985; Perfect Mismatch, 1985; Grommitts, 1986; I'm So Happy for You, I Really Am, 1991. Books: Puberty Blues, 1979; Hits and Ms, 1984; Girls' Night Out, 1988; The Llama Parlour, 1991; Foetal Attraction, 1993; Mad Cows, 1996; Altar Ego, 1998. Contributions to: Satirical columnist for the Sydney Morning Herald; The Bulletin; Cleo Magazine; Irregular contributor to the Guardian; She magazine; Women's Journal; New Woman. Honour: Australian Literature Board Grant, 1982. Address: c/o Ed Victor, 6 Bayley Street, Bedford Square, London WC1B 3HB, England.

LEVANT Victor Avrom, b. 26 Nov 1947, Winnipeg, Manitoba, Canada. Professor; Film Consultant; Practising Gestalt Therapist; Writer. Education: BA, Honours, Economics, Political Science, 1968, MA, Political Science 1975, PhD, Political Philosophy and International Relations, 1981, McGill University; Institut des Sciences Politiques, Sorbonne, University of Paris, 1968-69. Publications: How to Make a Killing: Canadian Military Involvement in the Indo-China War, 1972; How to Buy a Country: Monograph on Global Pentagon Contracts (co-editor), 1973; Capital and Labor: Partners?, 1976; Capital et Travail, 1977; Quiet Complicity: Canada and the Vietnam War, 1987; The Neighborhood Gourmet, 1989; Secrète Alliance, 1990. Address: 2243 Oxford, Montreal, H4A 2X7, Canada.

LEVENDOSKY Charles (Leonard), b. 4 July 1936, New York, New York, USA. Journalist; Poet. Education: BS, Physics, 1958, BA, Mathematics, 1960, University of Oklahoma; MA, Secondary Education, New York University, 1963. Appointments: Assistant Professor of English, New York University, 1967-71; Visiting Poet, Poetry-in-the-Schools Program, New York State, Georgia, New Jersey, 1971-72; Poet-in-Residence, Wyoming Council on the Arts, 1972-82; Editorial Page Editor, Casper Star-Tribune, Wyoming; Columnist, New York Times; Poet Laureate of Wyoming, 1988-96. Publications: Perimeters, 1970; Small Town America, 1974; Words and Fonts, 1975; Aspects of the Vertical, 1978; Distances, 1980; Wyoming Fragments, 1981; Nocturnes, 1982; Hands and Other Poems, 1986; Circle of Light, 1995. Contributions to: Numerous magazines and journals. Honours: National Endowment for the Arts Fellowship, 1974; Wyoming Governor's Award for the Arts, 1983. Membership: Wyoming Centre for the Book, advisory board, 1995-98. Address: PO Box 3033, Casper, WY 82602, USA.

LEVENSON Christopher, b. 13 Feb 1934, London, England (Canadian citizen, 1973). Poet; Editor; Translator; Educator. Education: University of Cambridge; University of Bristol; MA, University of Iowa, 1970. Appointments: Teacher, University of Münster, 1958-61, Carleton University, Ottawa, 1968-; Editor-in-Chief, ARC magazine, 1978-88; Founder-Director, ARC Reading Series, Ottawa, 1981-91; Series Editor, Harbinger Poetry Series, 1995-; Poetry Editor, Literary Review of Canada. Publications: Poetry: In Transit, 1959; Cairns, 1969; Stills, 1972; Into the Open, 1977; The Journey Back, 1978; Arriving at Night, 1986; The Return, 1986; Half Truths, 1990; Duplicities: New and Selected Poems, 1993. Other: Seeking Heart's Solace (translator), 1981; Light of the World (translator), 1982; Reconcilable Differences: The Changing Face of Poetry by Canadian Men Since 1970 (editor), 1994. Contributions to: Various anthologies, reviews, quarterlies, and journals. Honours: Eric Gregory Award, 1960; Archibald Lampman Award, 1987. Membership: League of Canadian Poets. Address: c/o Department of English, Carleton, 1812 Dunton Tower, 1125 Colonel by Drive, Ottawa, Ontario K1S 5B6, Canada.

LEVER Tresham Christopher Arthur Lindsay (Sir) (3rd Baronet), b. 9 Jan 1932, London, England. Naturalist; Writer. m. Linda Weightman McDowell Goulden, 6 Nov 1975. Education: Eton College, 1945-49; BA, 1954, MA, 1957, Trinity College, Cambridge. Publications: Goldsmiths and Silversmiths of England, 1975; The Naturalized Animals of the British Isles, 1977; Naturalized Mammals of the World, 1985; Naturalized Birds of the World, 1987; The Mandarin Duck, 1990; They Dined on Eland: The Story of the Acclimatisation Societies, 1992; Naturalized Animals: The Ecology of Successfully Introduced Species, 1994; Naturalized Fishes of the World, 1996. Contributions to: Books, Art, Scientific and general publications. Memberships: Fellow, Linnean Society of London; World Conservation Union Species' Survival Commission; Honarary Life member Brontë Society, 1988. Address: Newell House, Winkfield, Berkshire SL4 4SE, England.

LEVESQUE Anne-Michèle, b. 29 May 1939, Val d'Or, Québec, Canada. Writer. Div, 2 daughters. Education: BS, University of Montreal, 1957; Outremont Business College, 1958. Publications: Persil Frisé, 1992; A La Recherche d'un Salaud, 1994; Fleurs de Corail, 1994; La Maison du Puits Sacré, 1997; Quartiers divers, 1997. Contributions to: Lumière d'Encre magazine. Honour: First Prize, Concours Litteraire, 1991. Memberships: Regroupement des Ecrivains de l'Abitibi-TemisCamingue; Union des Ecrivains; Oonseil de la Culture de l'Abitibi-Térniscamingue. Address: 184 Williston Street, Val d'Or, Quebec J9P 4S7, Canada.

LEVEY Sir Michael (Vincent), b. 8 June 1927, London, England. Writer. m. Brigid Brophy, dec 1995, 1 daughter. Education: Exeter College, Oxford. Appointments: Assistant Keeper, 1951-66, Deputy Keeper, 1966-68, Keeper, 1968-73, Deputy Director, 1970-73, Director, 1973-87, National Gallery, London; Slade Professor of Fine Art, Cambridge, 1963-64, Oxford, 1994-95. Publications: Six Great Painters, 1956; National Gallery Catalogues: 18th Century Italian Schools, 1956; The German School, 1959; Painting in 18th Century Venice, 1959, 3rd edition, 1994; From Giotto to Cézanne, 1962; Dürer, 1964; The Later Italian Paintings in the Collection of HM The Queen, 1964, revised edition, 1991; Canaletto Paintings in the Royal Collection, 1964; Tiepolo's Banquet of Cleopatra, 1966; Rococo to Revolution, 1966; Bronzino, 1967; Early Renaissance, 1967; Fifty Works of English Literature We Could Do Without (co-author), 1967; Holbein's Christina of Denmark, Duchess of Milan, 1968; A History of Western Art, 1968; Painting at Court, 1971; The Life and Death of Mozart, 1971, 2nd edition, 1988; The Nude: Themes and Painters in the National Gallery, 1972; Art and Architecture in 18th Century France (co-author), 1972; The Venetian Scene, 1973; Botticelli, 1974; High Renaissance, 1975; The World of the Ottoman Art, 1976; Jacob van Ruisdael, 1977; The Case of Walter Pater, 1978; The Painter Depicted, 1981; Tempting Fate, 1982; An Affair on the Appian Way, 1984; Pater's Marius the Epicurean (editor), 1985; Giambattista Tiepolo, 1986; The National Gallery Collection: A Selection, 1987; Men at Work, 1989; The Soul of the Eye: Anthology of Painters and Painting (editor), 1990; Painting and Sculpture in France 1700-1789, 1992; Florence: A Portrait, 1996. Contributions to: Periodicals. Honours: Hawthornden Prize, 1968; Knighted, 1981; Honorary Fellow, Royal Academy, 1986; Banister Fletcher Prize, 1987; Lieutenant, Royal Victoria Order, 1965. Memberships: Ateneo Veneto, foreign member; British Academy, fellow; Royal Society of Literature, fellow. Address: 36 Little Lane, Louth, Lincolnshire LN11 9DU, England.

LEVI Makeda. See: BLAKE-HANNAH Barbara Makeda.

LEVI Peter, (Chad Tigar), b. 16 May 1931, Ruislip, Middlesex, England. Poet; Writer; Translator; Professor. m. Deirdre Connolly, 1977, 1 stepson. Education: Beaumont College, 1946-48; Pass Degree, Campion Hall, Oxford, 1958; British School of Archaeology, Athens, 1965-68. Appointments: Member, Society of Jesus, 1948-77; Roman Catholic Priest, 1964-77; Tutor

and Lecturer in Classics, Campion Hall, Oxford, 1965-77; Fellow, 1977-91, Emeritus Fellow, 1993-, St Catherine's College, Oxford; Lecturer in Classics, Christ Church, Oxford, 1979-82; Professor of Poetry, Oxford University, 1984-89. Publications: Poetry: Earthly Paradise, 1958; The Gravel Ponds, 1958; Beaumont, 1981-1961, 1961; Orpheus Head, 1962; Water, Rock, and Sand, 1962; The Shearwaters, 1965; Fresh Water, Sea Water, 1966; Pancakes for the Queen of Babylon: Ten Poems for Nikos Gatsos, 1968; Ruined Abbeys, 1968; Life is a Platform, 1971; Death is a Pulpit, 1971; Penguin Modern Poets 22 (with John Fuller and Adrian Mitchell), 1973; Collected Poems, 1955-1975, 1976; Five Ages, 1977; Private Ground, 1981; The Echoing Green: Three Elegies, 1983; Shakespeare's Birthday, 1985; Shadow and Bone: Poems 1981-1988, 1989; Goodbye to the Art of Poetry, 1989; The Marches (with Alan Powers), 1989; Rags of Time, 1994; Read Music, 1997. Fiction: The Head in the Soup, novel, 1979; Grave Witness (mystery), 1985; Knit One, Drop One (mystery), 1986; To the Goat (novella), 1988; Shade Those Laurels (with Cyril Connolly), mystery, 1990. Non-Fiction: The Light Garden of the Angel King: Journeys in Afghanistan, 1972; The Noise Made by Poems, 1977; The Hill of Kronos, 1980; The Flutes of Autumn, 1983; The Lamentation of the Dead, 1984; A History of Greek Literature, 1985; The Frontiers of Paradise: A Study of Monks and Monasteries, 1987; The Life and Times of William Shakespeare, 1988; The Art of Poetry, 1990; Boris Pasternak, 1990; Life of Lord Tennyson, 1993; Edward Lear, 1994; A Bottle in the Shade, 1996; Eden Renewed: The Public and Private Life of John Milton, 1996; Horace: A Life, 1997. Editor: Richard Selig: Poems, 1963; The English Bible, 1534-1859, 1974; Pope, 1974; Atlas of the Greek World, 1980; The Penguin Book of English Christian Verse, 1984; New Verses by Shakespeare, 1988. Translator: Yevgeny Yevtushenko: Selected Poems (with Robin Milner-Gulland), 1962; Pausanias: Guide to Greece, 2 volumes, 1971, revised edition, 1984; The Psalms, 1977; George Pavlopoulos: The Cellar, 1977; Alexandros Papadiamantis: The Murderess, 1982; Marco the Prince: Serbo-Croat Heroic Songs (with Anne Pennington), 1983; The Holy Gospel of John, 1985; Revelation, 1992. Memberships: Society of Greek Writers, corresponding member; Kingman Committee on English, 1987-88; Virgil Society, president, 1993-95. Address: Prospect Cottage, The Green, Frampton on Severn, Glos GL2 7DY, England.

LEVIN (Henry) Bernard, b. 19 Aug 1928, England. Journalist; Broadcaster; Writer. Education: BSc, Economics, London School of Economics and Political Science, University of London. Appointments: Writer, Broadcaster, radio and television, 1952-; Writer, numerous domestic and foreign newspapers and journals, 1953-. Publications: The Pendulum Years, 1971; Taking Sides, 1979; Conducted Tour, 1981; Speaking Up, 1982; Enthusiasms, 1983; The Way We Live Now, 1984; A Shakespeare Mystery, 1985; Hannibal's Footsteps, 1985; In These Times, 1986; To the End of the Rhine, 1987; All Things Considered, 1988; A Walk Up Fifth Avenue, 1989; Now Read On, 1990; If You Want My Opinion, 1992; A World Elsewhere, 1994; I Should Say So, 1995; Enough Said, 1998. Honours: Various journalistic awards; Order of Polonia Restituta, 1976; Honorary Fellow, London School of Economics and Political Science, 1977; Commander of the Order of the British Empire, 1990. Membership: English Association, president, 1984-85. Address: c/o The Times, 1 Pennington Street, London E1 9XN, England.

LEVIN Ira, b. 27 Aug 1929, New York, New York, USA. Novelist; Dramatist. m. (1) Gabrielle Aronsohn, 20 Aug 1960, div Jan 1968, 3 sons, (2) Phyllis Finkel, 1979, div 1981. Education: Drake University, 1946-48; AB, New York University, 1950. Publications: Novels: A Kiss Before Dying, 1953; Rosemary's Baby, 1967; This Perfect Day, 1970; The Stepford Wives, 1972; The Boys From Brazil, 1976; Silver, 1991; Son of Rosemary, 1997. Plays: No Time for Sergeants, 1956; Interlock, 1958; Critic's Choice, 1961; General Seeger, 1962; Drat!, The Cat!, 1965; Dr Cook's Garden, 1968; Veronica's Room, 1974; Deathtrap, 1979; Break a Leg, 1981; Cantorial, 1990.

Contributions to: Television and films. Honours: Edgar Allan Poe Awards, Mystery Writers of America, 1953, 1980. Memberships: American Society of Composers, Authors and Publishers; Authors Guild; Authors League of America; Dramatists Guild. Address: c/o Harold Ober Associates, 425 Madison Avenue, New York, NY 10017, USA.

LEVIN Michael Graubart, b. 8 Aug 1958, New York, New York, USA. Novelist. Education: BA, Amherst College, 1980; JD, Columbia University Law School, 1985. Appointments: Writers Programme, University of California, Los Angeles, 1990-; Visiting Professor of English, Stonehill College, 1993-94. Publications: Journey to Tradition, 1986; The Socratic Method, 1987; Settling the Score, 1989; Alive and Kicking, 1993; What Every Jew Needs To Know About. Contributions to: New York Times; Jerusalem Post. Honours: John Woodruff Simpson Fellowships, 1982, 1983. Memberships: PEN; Authors Guild; Writers Guild of America. Address: Box 181, Boston, MA 02101, USA.

LEVIN Torres, (Tereska Torres), b. 3 Sept 1920, Paris, France. Writer. m. Meyer Levin, 25 Mar 1948, 3 sons, 1 daughter. Education: French Baccalaureat. Publications: Le Sable et l'ecume, 1945; Women's Barracks, 1951; Not Yet, 1952; The Dangerous Games, 1953; The Golden Cage, 1954; By Colette, 1955; The Only Reason, 1961; The Open Doors, 1968; The Converts, 1971; Les Annees Anglaises, 1980; Le Pays des Chuchotements, 1983; Les Poupees de Cendre, 1978; Les Maisons Hantees de Meyer Levin, 1990. Address: 65 Boulevard Arago, Studio 13, Paris 75013, France.

LEVINE Norman, b. 22 Oct 1923, Ottawa, Ontario, Canada. Writer. m. (1) Margaret Emily Payne, 2 Jan 1952, dec 1978, 3 daughters, (2) Anne Sarginson, 10 Aug 1983. Education: BA, 1948, MA, 1949, McGill University, Montreal; Trinity College, Cambridge, England, 1945; King's College, London, 1949-50. Publications: Canada Made Me (travel), 1958; From a Seaside Town (novel), 1970; I Don't Want to Know Anyone Too Well (stories), 1971; Champagne Barn, 1984; Something Happened Here (stories), 1991-92; Pourquoi habitez-vous si loin?, 1997. Contributions to: Atlantic Monthly; Sunday Times; New Statesman; Spectator; Vogue; Harper's Bazaar; Encounter; Times Literary Supplement; Saturday Night. Address: c/o Liepman AG, Maienburgweg, CH-8044, Zürich, Switzerland.

LEVINE Paul, b. 9 Jan 1948, Williamsport, Pennsylvania, USA. Writer; Lawyer. m. Alice Holmstrom, 22 Aug 1975, div, 27 July 1992, 1 son, 1 daughter. Education: BA, Pennsylvania State University, 1969; JD, University of Miami, 1973. Appointments: Admitted to the Bar, State of Florida, 1973, US Supreme Court, 1977, District of Columbia, 1978, Commonwealth of Pennsylvania, 1989; Attorney and/or Partner, various law firms, 1973-91. Publications: What's Your Verdict?, 1980; To Speak for the Dead, 1990; Night Vision, 1992; False Dawn, 1994; Mortal Sin, 1994; Slashback, 1995; Fool Me Twice, 1996. Memberships: American Bar Association; American Trial Lawyers Association; Authors Guild; Kappa Tau Alpha; Omicron Delta Kappa; Phi Eta Sigma; Phi Kappa Phi; Sigma Delta Chi Journalism Society. Address: c/o International Creative Management, 40 West 57th Street, New York, NY 10019, USA.

LEVINE Philip, b. 10 Jan 1928, Detroit, Michigan, USA. Poet; Writer; Retired Professor of English. m. Frances Artley, 12 July 1954, 3 sons. Education: BA, 1950, AM, 1955, Wayne University; MFA, University of Iowa, 1957; Studies with John Berryman, 1954. Appointments: Instructor, University of Iowa, 1955-57; Instructor, 1958-69, Professor of English, 1969-92, California State University at Fresno; Elliston Professor of Poetry, University of Cincinnati, 1976; Poet-in-Residence, National University of Australia, Canberra, 1978; Visiting Professor of Poetry, Columbia University, 1978, 1981, 1984, New York University, 1984, 1991; Brown University, 1985; Chairman, Literature Panel, National

Endowment for the Arts, 1985; Various poetry readings. Publications: Poetry: On the Edge, 1961, 2nd edition, 1963; Silent in America: Vivas for Those Who Failed, 1965; Not This Pig, 1968; 5 Detroits, 1970; Thistles: A Poem of Sequence, 1970; Pili's Wall, 1971, revised edition, 1980; Red Dust, 1971; They Feed, They Lion, 1972; 1933, 1974; New Season, 1975; On the Edge and Over: Poems Old, Lost, and New, 1976; The Names of the Lost, 1976; 7 Years from Somewhere, 1979; Ashes: Poems New and Old, 1979; One for the Rose, 1981; Selected Poems, 1984; Sweet Will, 1985; A Walk with Tom Jefferson, 1988; New Selected Poems, 1991; What Work Is, 1991; The Simple Truth: Poems, 1994. Non-Fiction: Don't Ask (interviews), 1979; Earth, Stars, and Writers (with others), lectures, 1992; The Bread of Time: Toward an Autobiography, 1994. Editor: Character and Crisis: A Contemporary Reader (with Henri Coulette), 1966; Tarumba: The Selected Poems of Jaime Sabines (with Ernesto Trejo), 1979; Gloria Fuertes: Off the Map: Selected Poems (with Ada Long), 1984; The Pushcart Prize XI (with D Wojahn and B Henderson), 1986; The Essential Keats, 1987. Contributions to: Many anthologies; Atlantic; Harper's; Hudson Review; New York Review of Books; New Yorker; Paris Review; Poetry. Honours: Joseph Henry Jackson Award, San Francisco Foundation, 1961; National Endowment for the Arts Grants, 1969, 1976, 1981, 1987; Frank O'Hara Prizes, 1973, 1974; Award of Merit, American Academy of Arts and Letters, 1974; Levinson Prize, 1974; Guggenheim Fellowships, 1974, 1981; Harriet Monroe Memorial Prizefor Poetry, University of Chicago, 1976; Leonore Marshall Award for Best American Book of Poems, 1976; American Book Award for Poetry, 1979; National Book Critics Circle Prize, 1979; Notable Book Award, American Library Association, 1979; Golden Rose Award, New England Poetry Society, 1985; Ruth Lilly Award, 1987; Elmer Holmes Bobst Award, New York University, 1990; National Book Award for Poetry, 1991; Pulitzer Prize in Poetry, 1995. Address: 4549 North Van Ness Boulevard, Fresno, CA 93704, USA.

LEVINE Stuart (George), b. 25 May 1932, New York, New York, USA. Professor Emeritus; Writer; Musician. m. Susan Fleming Matthews, 6 June 1963, 2 sons, 1 daughter. Education: AB, magna cum laude, Harvard University; MA, 1956, PhD, 1958, Brown University. Appointments: Instructor, 1958-61, Assistant Professor, 1961-65, Associate Professor, 1965-69, Chairman, Department of American Studies, 1965-70, Professor, 1969-92, Professor Emeritus, 1992-, University of Kansas; Visiting Professor, Kansas State University, 1964, University of Missouri at Kansas City, 1966, 1974, California State University at Los Angeles, 1969, 1971; Fulbright Distinguished Lecturer, Naples, Italy, 1995; Many engagements as a professional horn player. Publications: Materials for Technical Writing, 1963; The American Indian Today (with Nancy O Lurie), 1968, revised edition, 1970; Edgar Poe, Seer and Craftsman, 1972; The Short Fiction of Edgar Allan Poe: An Annotated Edition (with Susan Levine), 1990; The Monday-Wednesday-Friday Girl and Other Stories, 1994; The Collected Writings of Edgar Allan Poet (editor with Susan Levine), forthcoming. Contributions to: Various scholarly reviews, quarterlies, and journals. Honours: Anisfield-Wolf Award in Race Relations, 1968; Theodore Blegen Award, 1975; Citation for 30-year editorship of American Studies, 1989; Gross Award for Short Fiction, 1994. Address: 1644 University Drive, Lawrence, KS 66044, USA.

LEVINSON Harry, b. 16 Jan 1922, Port Jervis, New York, USA. Clinical Psychologist; Management Consultant; Writer. m. Roberta Freiman, 11 Jan 1946, div June 1972, 2 sons, 2 daughters. Education: BSEd, 1943, MSEd, 1947, Psychology, Emporia State University; PhD, Clinical Psychology, University of Kansas, 1952. Publications: Men, Management, and Mental Health, 1962; Organizational Diagnosis, 1972; The Great Jackass Fallacy, 1973; Executive Stress, 1975; Psychological Man, 1976; Emotional Health in the World of Work, 1980; Executive, 1981; Ready, Fire, Aim: Avoiding Management by Impulse, 1986; Designing and Managing Your Career (editor), 1989; Career Mastery, 1992. Contributions to: Numerous professional journals and magazines. Address: Levinson Institute, 404 Wyman Street, Suite 400, Waltham, MA 02154, USA.

LEVINSON Leonard, (Nicholas Brady, Lee Chang, Glen Chase, Richard Hale Curtis, Gordon Davis, Clay Dawson, Nelson De Mille, Josh Edwards, Richard Gallagher, March Hastings, J Farragut Jones, Leonard Jordan, Philip Kirk, John Mackie, Robert Novak, Philip Rawls, Bruno Rossi, Jonathon Scofield, Jonathon Trask, Cynthia Wilkerson), b. 1935, New Bedford, Massachussets, USA. Writer. m. (1) Div, 1 daughter, (2) Dec. Education: BA, Michigan State University, 1961. Publications: (as Bruno Rossi) Worst Way To Die, 1974; Headcrusher, 1974; (as Nicholas Brady) Shark Fighter, 1975; (as Leonard Jordan) Operation Perfida, 1975; Without Mercy, 1981; (as Cynthia Wilkerson) Sweeter Than Candy, 1978; The Fast Life, 1979; (as Philip King) Hydra Conspiracy, 1979; (as Gordon Davis) The Battle of the Bulge, 1981; (as John Mackie) Hit the Beach, 1983; Nightmare Alley, 1985; (as Clay Dawson) Gold Town, 1989; (as J Farragut Jones) 40 Fathoms Down, 1990; (as Josh Edwards) Searcher, 1990; Warpath, 1991; (as Nelson De Mille) The General's Daughter, 1993; Spencerville, 1994. Address: c/o Lowenstein Associates Inc, Suite I6, 121 West 27th Street, New York NY 10001, USA.

LEVY Alan, b. 10 Feb 1932, New York, New York, USA. Journalist; Editor; Author. Education: AB, Brown University, 1952; MS, Columbia University, 1953. Appointments: Reporter, Courier-Journal, Louisville, 1953-60; Foreign Correspondent, Life Magazine and Good Housekeeping Magazine, Prague, 1967-71, New York Times and International Herald Tribune, Vienna, 1971-91; Dramaturg, English Theatre Ltd, Vienna, 1977-82; Founding Editor-in-Chief, Prague Post, 1991-. Publications: Draftee Confidential Guide (with B Krisher and J Cox), 1957, revised edition (with R Flaste), 1966; Operation Elvis, 1960; The Elizabeth Taylor Story, 1961; Wanted: Nazi Criminals at Large, 1962; Interpret Your Dreams, 1962, 2nd edition, 1975; Kind-Hearted Tiger (with G Stuart), 1964; The Culture Vultures, 1968; God Bless You Real Good: My Crusade with Billy Graham, 1969; Rowboat to Prague, 1972; Good Men Still Live, 1974; The Bluebird of Happiness, 1976; Forever, Sophia, 1979, 2nd edition, 1986; So Many Heroes, 1980; The World of Ruth Draper (play), 1982; Just an Accident (libretto for requiem), 1983; Ezra Pound: The Voice of Silence, 1983; W H Auden: In the Autumn of the Age of Anxiety, 1983; Treasures of the Vatican Collections, 1983; Vladimir Nabokov: The Velvet Butterfly, 1984; Ezra Pound: A Jewish View, 1988; The Wiesenthal File, 1993. Contributions to: Newspapers and magazines. Honours: Bernard De Voto Fellowship, 1963; Golden Johann Strauss Medal, Vienna, 1981; Ernst Krenek Prize, Vienna, 1986. Memberships: American PEN; American Society of Journalists and Authors; Authors Guild; Czech Union of Journalists; Dramatists Guild; Foreign Correspondents Association of Prague; Foreign Press Association of Vienna; Overseas Press Club. Address: c/o Serafina Clarke, 96 Tunis Road, London W12 7EY, England.

LEVY Faye, b. 23 May 1951, Washington, District of Columbia, USA. Syndicated Columnist; Cooking Teacher. m. Yakir Levy, 28 Sept 1970. Education: BA, Sociology, Anthropology, Tel Aviv University, 1973; Grand Diplome, École de Cuisine la Varenne, Paris, 1979. Appointments: Cookery Editor, La Varenne, Paris, 1977-81; Columnist, Bon Appetit Magazine, 1982-88, At Magazine, Israel, 1988-, Jerusalem Post, 1990-; Syndicated Columnist, Los Angeles Times, 1990-. Publications: La Cuisine du Poisson, 1984; Faye Levy's Chocolate Sensations, 1986; Fresh from France: Vegetable Creations, 1987; Fresh from France: Dinner Inspirations, 1989; Sensational Pasta, 1989; Fresh from France: Dessert Sensations, 1990; Faye Levy's International Jewish Cookbook, 1991; Faye Levy's International Chicken Cookbook, 1992; Faye Levy's International Vegetable Cookbook, 1993. Address: 5116 Marmol Drive, Woodland Hills, CA 91364, USA.

LEVY Owen, b. 16 Aug 1946, New York City, USA. Writer. Education: BA, English Literature, Hunter College. Publication: A Brother's Touch, 1982. Contributions to: Variety; Billboard. Honours: Fellowships, MacDowell Colony and Wurlitzer Foundation. Membership: Authors Guild. Address: 217 Central Park North, New York, NY 10026, USA.

LEWIN Michael Zinn, b. 21 July 1942, Cambridge, Massachusetts, USA. Writer; Dramatist. 1 son, 1 daughter. Education: AB, Harvard University, 1964; Churchill College, Cambridge, England. Appointment: Co-Editor, Crime Writers Association Annual Anthology, 1992-94. Publications: Author of 15 novels including: Called by a Panther, 1991; Underdog, 1993; Family Business, 1995; Rover's Tales, 1998. Other: Various radio plays, stage plays and short stories. Honours: Maltese Falcon Society Best Novel, 1987; Raymond Chandler Society of Germany Best Novel, 1992; Mystery Masters Award, 1994. Memberships: Detection Club; Crime Writers Association; Mystery Writers of America; Private Eye Writers Association; Authors Guild. Address: 5 Welshmill Road, Frome, Somerset BA11 2LA, England.

LEWING Anthony Charles, (Mark Bannerman), b. 12 July 1933, Colchester, England. Author. m. Françoise Faury, 2 Aug 1966, 1 son, 1 daughter. Appointments: Royal Army Pay Corps, 1951-89; Civil Service, 1989-95. Publications: Grand Valley Feud, 1995; The Beckoning Noose, 1996; Escape To Purgatory, 1996; The Early Lynching, 1997; Renegade Rose, 1997; Ride Into Destiny, 1997; Goose Pimples, 1997; Man Without A Yesterday, 1998; Trail To Redemption, 1998; Bridges To Cross, 1998. Contributions to: Over 300 short stories in magazines, newspapers and anthologies. Address: Greenmantle, Horseshoe Lane, Ash Vale, Surrey, GU12 5LJ, England.

LEWINS Frank William, b. 18 July 1941, Melbourne, Victoria, Australia. Writer. m. Margaret Houghton, 6 Feb 1964, 2 daughters. Education: Diploma in Physiotherapy, 1961; BA, Honours, 1972; PhD, 1976. Publications: The Myth of the Universal Church, 1978; Why Ethnic Schools, 1981; The First Wave, 1985; Writing a Thesis, 1987; Recasting the Concept of Ideology, 1989; Social Science Methodology, 1992; Transexualism in Society, 1995; Bioethics for Health Professionals, 1996. Address: 12 Granville Close, Queanbeyan, New South Wales 2620, Australia.

LEWIS Anthony, b. 27 Mar 1927, New York, New York, USA. Journalist; Visiting Professor. m. (1) Linda Rannells, 8 July 1951, div, 1 son, 2 daughters, (2) Margaret H Marshall, 23 Sept 1984. Education: AB, Harvard University, 1948. Appointments: Deskman, Sunday Department, 1948-52, Reporter, Washington Bureau, 1955-64, Chief, London Bureau, 1965-72, Editorial Columnist, 1969-, New York Times; Reporter, Washington Daily News, 1952-55; Lecturer on Law, Harvard University, 1974-89; James Madison Visiting Professor, Columbia University, 1983-. Publications: Gideon's Trumpet, 1964; Portrait of a Decade: The Second American Revolution, 1964; Make No Law: The Sullivan Case and the First Admendment, 1991. Contributions to: Professional journals. Honours: Heywood Broun Award, 1955; Pulitzer Prizes for National Reporting, 1955, 1963; Nieman Fellow, 1956-57; Best Fact-Crime Book Award, Mystery Writers of America, 1964; Honorary DLitt, Adelphi University, 1964, Rutgers University, 1973, Williams College, 1978, Clark University, 1982; Honorary LLD, Syracuse University, 1979, Colby College, 1983, Northeastern University, 1987. Membership: American Academy of Arts and Sciences. Address: c/o New York Times, 2 Faneuil Hall Marketplace, Boston, MA 02109, USA.

LEWIS Arnold, b. 13 Jan 1930, New Castle, Pennsylvania, USA. Architectural Historian; Art Historian; Professor. m. Beth Irwin, 24 June 1958, 2 sons, 1 daughter. Education: BA, Allegheny College, 1952; MA, 1954, PhD, 1962, University of Wisconsin; University of Bonn, 1959-60; University of Munich, 1960. Appointments: Wells College, Aurora, New York,

1962-64; College of Wooster, Ohio, 1964-96. Publications: American Victorian Architecture, 1975; Wooster in 1876, 1976; American Country Houses of the Gilded Age, 1983; American Interiors of the Gilded Age (with James Turner and Steven McQuillin), 1987; An Early Encounter with Tomorrow: Europeans, Chicago's Loop, and the World's Columbian Exposition, 1997. Contributions to: Journal of the Society of Architectural Historians. Honours: Founder's Award, JSAH, 1974; SAH Western Reserve Book Award, 1977; Barzun Prize in Cultural History, American Philosophical Society, 1998. Memberships: College Art Association; Society of Architectural Historians, director, 1979-82. Address: c/o Department of Art, College of Wooster, Wooster, OH 44691, USA.

LEWIS Bernard, b. 31 May 1916, London, England (US citizen, 1982). Professor of Near Eastern Studies Emeritus; Writer. m. Ruth Helene Oppenhejm, 1947, div 1974, 1 son, 1 daughter. Education: BA, 1936, PhD, 1939, University of London; Diplome des études semitiques, University of Paris, 1937. Appointments: Professor of History of the Near and Middle East, University of London, 1949-74; Visiting Professor, University of California at Los Angeles, 1955-56, Columbia University, 1960, Indiana University, 1963, University of California at Berkeley, 1965, Collège de France, 1980, École des Hautes Études en Sciences Sociales, Paris, 1983, University of Chicago, 1985; Class of 1932 Lecturer, 1964, Cleveland E Dodge Professor of Near Eastern Studies, 1974-86, Professor Emeritus, 1986-, Princeton University; Visiting Member, 1969, Member, 1974-86, Institute for Advanced Study, Princeton, New Jersey; Gottesman Lecturer, Yeshiva University, 1974; Douglas Robb Foundation Lecturer, University of Auckland, 1982; Director, Annenberg Research Institute, Philadelphia, 1986-90; Tanner Lecturer, Brasenose College, Oxford, 1990; Merle Curti Lecturer, University of Wisconsin, 1993. Publications: The Origins of Ismailism: A Study of the Historical Background of the Fatimid Caliphate, 1940; A Handbook of Diplomatic and Political Arabic, 1947; Land of Enchanters: Egyptian Short Stories from the Earliest Times to the Present Day (editor), 1948; The Arabs in History, 1950, revised edition, 1993; Notes and Documents from the Turkish Archives: A Contribution to the History of the Jews in the Ottoman Empire, 1952; Encyclopedia of Islam (co-editor), 1956-86; The Emergence of Modern Turkey, 1961, revised edition, 1968; Historians of the Middle East (editor with P M Holt), 1962; Istanbul and the Civilization of the Ottoman Empire, 1963; The Assassins: A Radical Sect in Islam, 1967; The Cambridge History of Islam (editor with P M Holt and Ann K S Lambton), 2 volumes, 1970; Islam in History: Ideas, Men and Events in the Middle East, 1973, revised edition, 1993; Islam, from the Prophet Muhammad to the Capture of Constantinople (editor and translator), 2 volumes, 1974; History: Remembered, Recovered, Invented, 1975; Studies in Classical and Ottoman Islam: Seventh to Sixteenth Centuries, 1976; The World of Islam, 1976; Population and Revenue in the Towns of Palestine in the Sixteenth Century (with Amnon Cohen), 1978; The Muslim Discovery of Europe, 1982; Christians and Jews in the Ottoman Empire, 2 volumes, 1982; The Jews of Islam, 1985; The Political Language of Islam, 1988; Race and Slavery in the Middle East: A Historical Enquiry, 1990; Islam and the West, 1993; The Shaping of the Modern Middle East, 1994; Cultures in Conflict: Christians, Muslims, and Jews in the Age of Discovery, 1995; The Middle East: Two Thousand Years of History from the Rise of Christianity to the Present Day, 1995; The Future of the Middle East, 1997; Semites and Anti-Semites: An Inquiry into Conflict and Prejudice, 1997. Contributions to: Professional journals. Honours: Citation of Honour, Turkish Ministry of Culture, 1973; Fellow, University College, London, 1976; Harvey Prize, Technion-Israel Institute of Technology, 1978; 11 honorary doctorates. Memberships: American Academy of Arts and Sciences; American Historical Society; American Oriental Society; American Philosophical Society; British Academy, fellow; Council on Foreign Relations; Royal Asiatic Society; Royal Historical Society; Royal Institute of International Affairs. Address: c/o Department of Near Eastern Studies, 110 Jones Hall, Princeton University, Princeton, NJ 08544, USA.

LEWIS Charles. See: **DIXON Roger.**

LEWIS David K(ellogg), b. 28 Sept 1941, Oberlin, Ohio, USA. Professor of Philosophy; Writer. m. Stephanie Robinson, 5 Sept 1965. Education: BA, Swarthmore College, 1962; MA, 1964, PhD, 1967, Harvard University. Appointments: Assistant Professor of Philosophy, University of California, Los Angeles, 1966-70; Faculty, 1970-73, Professor of Philosophy, 1973-, Princeton University; Fulbright Lecturer, Australia, 1971; John Locke Lecturer, Oxford University, 1984; Kant Lecturer, Stanford University, 1988. Publications: Convention: A Philosophical Study, 1969; Counterfactuals, 1973; Philosophical Papers, 2 volumes, 1983, 1986; On the Plurality of Worlds, 1986; Parts of Classes, 1991; Papers in Philosophical Logic, 1998; Papers in Metaphysics and Epistemology, 1999. Honours: Matchette Prize for Philosophical Writing, 1972; Fulbright Research Fellow, New Zealand, 1976; Santayana Fellow, Harvard University, 1988; Doctor of Letters, University of Melbourne, 1995. Memberships: American Association of University Professors; Australian Academy of the Humanities; British Academy; National Association of Scholars; American Academy of Arts and Sciences. Address: c/o Department of Philosophy, Princeton University, Princeton, NJ 08544, USA.

LEWIS David L(evering), b. 25 May 1936, Little Rock, Arkansas, USA. Professor of History; Writer. m. (1) Sharon Siskind, 15 Apr 1966, div Oct 1988, 2 sons, 1 daughter, (2) Ruth Ann Stewart, 15 Apr 1994, 1 daughter. Education: BA, Fisk University, 1956; MA, Columbia University, 1958; PhD, London School of Economics and Political Science, 1962. Appointments: Lecturer, University of Ghana, 1963-64, Howard University, Washington, DC, 1964-65; Assistant Professor, University of Notre Dame, 1965-66; Associate Professor, Morgan State College, Baltimore, 1966-70, Federal City College, Washington, DC, 1970-74; Professor of History, University of the District of Columbia, 1974-80, University of California at San Diego, La Jolla, 1981-85; Martin Luther King Jr Professor of History, Rutgers University, 1985-. Publications: Martin Luther King: A Critical Biography, 1971, 2nd edition, 1978; Prisoners of Honor: The Dreyfus Affair, 1973; District of Columbia: A Bicentennial History, 1977; When Harlem Was in Vogue: The Politics of the Arts in the Twenties and the Thirties, 1981; Harlem Renaissance: Art of Black America (with others), 1987; The Race to Fashoda: European Colonialism and African Resistance in the Scramble for Africa, 1988; W E B Du Bois: Biography of a Race, 1868-1919, 1994; The Portable Harlem Renaissance Reader (editor), 1994; W E B Du Bois: A Reader (editor), 1995. Honours: American Philosophical Society Grant, 1967; Social Science Research Council Grant, 1971; National Endowment for the Humanities Grant, 1975; Woodrow Wilson International Center for Scholars Fellow, 1977-78; Guggenheim Fellowship, 1986; Bancroft Prize, 1994; Ralph Waldo Emerson Prize, 1994; Pulitzer Prize for Biography, 1994; Francis Parkman Prize, 1994. Memberships: African Studies Association; American Association of University Professors; American Historical Association; Authors Guild; Organization of American Historians; Phi Beta Kappa; Society for French Historical Studies; Southern Historical Association. Address: c/o Department of History, Van Dyck Hall, Rutgers University, New Brunswick, NJ 08903, USA.

LEWIS D(esmond) F(rancis), b. 18 Jan 1948, Colchester, Essex, England. Poet; Writer. m. Denise Jean Woolgar, 23 May 1970, 1 son, 1 daughter. Education: BA, Honours, English, Lancaster University, 1969. Contributions to: Hundreds of prose poems and stories in various UK and USA publications. Address: 7 Lloyd Avenue, Coulsdon, Surrey CR5 2QS, England.

LEWIS Edith Grace Mize, (Edith Mize), b. Gary, Indiana, USA. Freelance Writer. m. (1) Frederick Mize, dec 1990, 1 son, dec 1973, 1 daughter, (2) Harry J Lewis, 25 May 1983. Education: Registered Nurse; BS, State University of New York. Appointments: 1st Lieutenant, Flight Nurse, World War II, Europe, 1943-45; Freelance Writer, 1974-. Publications: A Mother Mourns, essay, 1975, reprinted, 1986; Haiku is...a Feeling, children's book, 1990; Grief Hurts, chapbook. Contributions to: Life Magazine; Journal of Practical Nursing; Home Life; Grit; Sunshine Magazine; Woman's Day; Children's and travel magazines; Others. Honours: 6 medals, World War II; Cancer Society Award, Service to the Cause of Cancer, 1974; 1st Place, Juvenile Article, 1974, 1st Place, Inspirational Article, 1983, National League of American Pen Women; Poetry Awards, 1987, 1989, 2nd Place, Instructional Juvenile Book, Florida State Association, National League of American Pen Women, 1991; Other poetry awards. Memberships: National League of American Pen Women, Boca Raton Branch President, 1986-88; Florida Freelance Writer's Association; Society of Children's Book Writers; Haiku Society of America; Poets of the Palm Beaches. Address: 8919 Old Pine Road, Boca Raton, FL 33433, USA.

LEWIS F(rances) R, b. 30 Apr 1939, USA. Writer. m. Howard D Lewis, 16 Apr 1961, 2 sons, 1 daughter. Education: BA, State University of New York at Albany, 1960. Publications: Various short stories. Contributions to: Anthologies and periodicals. Honours: PEN-National Endowment for the Arts Syndicated Fiction Project Awards, 1986, 1988; Millay Colony Fellow, 1991; MacDowell Colony Fellow, 1993. Memberships: Associated Writing Programs; International Women's Writing Guild; Poets and Writers. Address: PO Box 12093, Albany, NY 12212, USA.

LEWIS Jeremy Morley, b. 15 Mar 1942, Salisbury, Wiltshire, England. Writer. m. Petra Lewis, 28 July 1968, 2 daughters. Education: BA, Trinity College, Dublin, 1965; MA, Sussex University, 1967. Appointments: Editor, Andre Deutsch Ltd, 1969-70, Oxford University Press, 1977-79; Literary Agent, A P Watt Ltd, 1970-76; Director, Chatto and Windus, 1979-89; Deputy Editor, London Magazine, 1991-94; Editorial Consultant, Peters, Fraser and Dunlop Group Ltd. Publications: Playing for Time, 1987; Chatto Book of Office Life, 1992; Kindred Spirits, 1995; Cyril Connolly: A Life, forthcoming. Memberships: Royal Society of Literature fellow; R S Surtees Society, secretary. Address: c/o Gillon Aitken, Aitken and Stone Ltd, London, England.

LEWIS Linda Joy, b. 20 June 1946, New York, New York, USA. Writer. m. 31 Mar 1965, 1 son, 1 daughter. Education: BA, City College of New York, 1972; MEd, Florida Atlantic University, 1976. Publications: We Hate Everything But Boys, 1985; Is There Life After Boys?, 1987; We Love Only Older Boys, 1988; 2 Young 2 Go 4 Boys, 1988; My Heart Belongs to That Boy, 1989; All for the Love of That Boy, 1989; Want to Trade 2 Brothers for a Cat?, 1989; Dedicated to That Boy I Love, 1991; Preteen Means in Between, 1992. Membership: Authors Guild. Address: 2872 North East 26 Place, Ft Lauderdale, FL 33306, USA.

LEWIS Mervyn. See: **FREWER Glyn Mervyn Louis.**

LEWIS William Edward, (Bill Lewis), b. 1 Aug 1953, Maidstone, Kent, England. Poet; Writer; Editor; Storyteller; Mythographer. m. Ann Frances Morris, 17 Oct 1981. Appointment: Writer-in-Residence, Brighton Festival, 1985. Publications: Poems, 1975-83, 1983; Night Clinic, 1984; Communion, 1986; Rage Without Anger, 1987; Skyclad Christ, 1992; Paradigm Shift (editor), 1992; Coyote Cosmos (short stories), 1994; Translation Women, 1996; The Book of North Kent Writers (co-editor), 1996; The Wine of Connecting (poems), 1996; Intellect of the Heart, 1997; Shattered English: Complete North Kent Poems, 1998. Contributions to: Anthologies, review, and journals. Membership: Medway Poets, founder-member. Address: 66 Glencoe Road, Chatham, Kent ME4 5QE, England.

LEWIS-SMITH Anne Elizabeth, (Emily Devereaux, A McCormich, Quilla Slade), b. 14 Apr 1925, London, England. Poet; Writer; Editor; Publisher. m. Peter Lewis-Smith, 17 May 1944, 1 son, 2 daughters.

Appointments: Assistant Editor, 1967-83, Editor, 1983-91, Envoi; Editor, Aerostat, 1973-78, British Association of Friends of Museums Yearbook, 1985-91; Publisher, Envoi Poets Publications, 1986-. Publications: Seventh Bridge, 1963; The Beginning, 1964; Flesh and Flowers, 1967; Dandelion Flavour, 1971; Dina's Head, 1980; Places and Passions, 1986; In The Dawn, 1987; Circling Sound, 1996. Contributions to: Newspapers and magazines. Honours: Tissadier Diploma for Services to International Aviation; Debbie Warley Award for Services to International Aviation; Dorothy Tutin Award for Services to Poetry. Membership: PEN. Address: Pen Ffordd, Newport, Pembrokeshire, Dyfed SA42 0QT, Wales.

LEWISOHN Leonard C, b. 28 Aug 1953, New York, USA. Translator; Editor. m. Jane Ferril, 1973. Education: BA, International Relations, Pahlavi University, 1978; PhD, Persian Literature, University of London, 1988. Publications: Beyond Faith and Infidelity: The Sufi Poetry and Teachings of Mahmud Shabistari, 1995. Editor: The Legacy of Mediaeval Persian Sufism, 1992; Classical Persian Sufism from its Origins to Rumi, 1993; A Critical Edition of the Divan of Maghribi, 1993; Late Classical Persionate Sufism: The Safavid and Mughal Period. Translator: Several books. Address: The Old Chapel, High Street, Eydon, Daventry, Northamptonshire NN11 3PP, England.

LEY Alice Chetwynd, b. 12 Oct 1913, Halifax, Yorkshire, England. Novelist; Teacher. m. Kenneth James Ley, 3 Feb 1945, 2 sons. Education: Diploma in Sociology, London University; Gilchrist Award of 1962 for work in connection with Diploma in Sociology. Appointments: Tutor in Creative Writing, 1962-84, Lecturer in Sociology and Social History, 1968-71, Harrow College of Further Education. Publications: 19 novels. Contributions to: Numerous journals. Memberships: Jane Austen Society; Romantic Novelists Association, chairman, 1970, honorary life member, 1987-; Society of Women Writers and Journalists. Address: 42 Cannonbury Avenue, Pinner, Middlesex HA5 1TS, England.

LEYS Simon. See: **RYCKMANS Pierre.**

LEYTON Sophie. See: **WALSH Sheila.**

LEZENSKI Cezary Jerzy, b. 6 Jan 1930, Poznan, Poland. Journalist; Writer. m. Antonina Czebatul, 1958, 1 son, 1 daughter. Education: Journalism, 1951, MA, Polish Philology, 1952, Jagiellonian University, Krakow. Appointments: Editor-in-Chief, Kurier Polski, 1969-81, Epoka Literacke, 1981-90, Poland Today, 1991-93, Micro-Way Computer Press Agency, 1994-. Publications: 28 books, including adult and children's novels, stories, biographies, and essays, 1963-98. Contributions to: Magazines. Honours: Polish Military Cross, 1944; Commander, Polonia Restituta, 1978; Order of Smile for Young People's Novels, 1979; Honarary citizen of New Orleans. Memberships: Society of Polish Writers; Mazurek Dabrowski Society; Order of Smile, chapter chancellor; UNICEF. Address: al Jana Pawtce II, 70 m 15, 00-175 Warsaw, Poland.

LI Leslie, b. 21 November 1945, New York, USA. Author; Writer; Playwright. Education: BA, University of Michigan, 1967; Alliance Française, 5ème dégré, 1970. Publications: Bittersweet, 1992; The Magic Whip (children's play), 1995; Contributions to: American Identitities: Contemporary Multicultural Voices, 1994; New York Times; International Herald Tribune; Health; Gourmet; Modern Maturity; Condé Nast's Traveler. Honour: Leo Maitland Fellowship, 1992. Literary Agent: Kimberly Witherspoon. Address: Witherspoon Associates, 157 West 57 Street, New York, NY 10019, USA.

LI Lilia Huiying, b. 14 June 1932, Hunan, China. Writer; Journalist; Speaker; Lecturer. m. (1) Ma Luk Son, dec, (2) George Oakley Totten III, 1 July 1976, 1 daughter. Education: BA, Yenching University, China, 1946; MA, Hong Kong University, Hong Kong, 1955. Appointments: Leader of Delegation of Hong Kong Business Women to Conference on Commerce in Beijing, introduced to Chairman Mao Zedong, 1956; Managing Director, Church Guest House, Hong Kong, 1962-68; Special Correspondent to the United Nations, New York City, 1975; Speaker with Betty Friedan, at First International Women's Conference in Mexico City, 1975; An Organizer of International Women's Year Arts Festival, NYC, 1975-76; Visiting Lecturer, 1976 and Fellow, 1976-, East Asian Studies Center, University of Southern California, Los Angeles; Founder and President, China Seminar; Invited as Participant to conferences on cross-straits relations in Beijing, 1985-, Taipei, 1990-. Publications: Unforgettable Journey, 1957; Nine Women and Other Writings, 1959; Li Huiyang's Writings, 1979; Sidelights on World Affairs, 1985; Expanded Edition of Collected Writings, 1988. Contributions to: Magazines and journals; Written articles for magazines, especially in Hong Kong (in Chinese) such as Mirror Monthly, Overseas Chinese, Horizon, etc and articles for Chinese newspapers in Los Angeles, New York and Hong Kong. Honours: Chosen as Outstanding Hong Kong Author, South China Morning Post, 1962; Honored as First Life Time Member, US China Peoples Friendship Association, New York City Chapter; Award for Outstanding Effort by US-China Peoples Friendship Association, Los Angeles Chapter; Awarded as Outstanding Member, Los Angeles-Guangzhou Sister City Association; Awarded for Outstanding Contribution to Center of Pacific Asia Studies, University of Stockholm, Sweden; Promoting Across-Straits Relations, Association for Relations Across the Taiwan (ARATS), Beijing, China. Memberships: The Asia American Journalists Association; Association for Asian Studies. Address: 5129 Village Green, Los Angeles, CA 90016-5205, USA.

LIAKOS Kostas, b. 6 Nov 1952, Athens, Greece. Employee. m. Katerina Zabella-Liakos, 14 Jan 1989, 1 son. Education: Accountancy School, 1977. Appointments: Newspapers: Ta Nea; To Bima Tis Kipiakis, 1971. Publication: Ena chamogelo, 1996. Contributions to: Aiolika grammata; Pnevmatiki Zoi; Nea Skepsi; Filalogiki Protochronia; Logotechnica kimena; Logotechnes tu keru mas. Membership: Greek Literary Association. Address: Antigonis 201, 10443 Athens, Greece.

LIBBY Ronald T(heodore), b. 20 Nov 1941, Los Angeles, California, USA. Professor of Political Science; Writer. 2 daughters. Education: BA, Washington State University, Pullman, 1965; MA, 1966, PhD, 1975, University of Washington, Seattle. Appointments: Lecturer, University of Botswana, Lesotho, and Swaziland, 1973-75, Malawi, 1975-76, and Zambia, 1976-79; Visiting Assistant Professor, University of Notre Dame, 1981-83; Senior Lecturer, University of the West Indies, Jamaica, 1983-85, Victoria University of Wellington, New Zealand, 1987-89; Visiting Associate Professor, Northwestern University, 1985-86; Senior Research Fellow, Australian National University, 1986-87; Professor and Chair, Department of Political Science, Southwest State University, Marshall, Minnesota, 1989-96, Saint Joseph's University, Philadelphia, 1996-. Publications: Towards an Africanized US Policy for Southern Africa, 1980; The Politics of Economic Power in Southern Africa, 1987; Hawke's Law: The Politics of Mining and Aboriginal Land Rights in Australia, 1989; Protecting Markets: US Policy and the World Grain Trade, 1992; Eco-Wars: Political Campaigns and Social Movements, 1999. Contributions to: Scholarly books and journals. Honours: Grants; Visiting Research Scholar, University of California at Irvine, 1972; Outstanding Academic Book, Choice magazine, 1990. Address: c/o Department of Political Science, Saint Joseph's University, 5600 City Avenue, Philadelphia, PA 19131, USA.

LIBOV Charlotte, b. 5 May 1950, New Haven, Connecticut, USA. Author; Speaker. Education: BA, Honours, University of Connecticut, 1973; MS, University of Oregon, 1979. Appointments: Reporter, Milford Citizen, 1974-76, Journal Inquirer, Connecticut, 1980-81; Bureau Chief, Springfield Daily News, Massachusetts, 1981-85. Publications: the Woman's Heart Book: The Complete Guide to Keeping Your Heart Healthy and What to Do if Things Go Wrong, 1994; 50 Essential Things To Do When the Doctor Says Its Heart Disease, 1995. Contributions to: Cardiovascular Disease Management. Honours: Will Solimene Award for Excellence, American Medical Writers Association, 1994; National Mature Media Bronze Award, 1996. Memberships: Authors Guild; American Society of Journalists and Authors. Literary Agent: Carole Abel. Address: 160 West 87th Street, New York, USA.

LICHTENBERT Robert Henry, b. 26 Dec 1945, Chicago, Illinois, USA. Professor of Philosophy. m. 8 Jan 1973, 2 sons. Education: BA with high honors, DePaul University; MA, PhD, Tulane University. Appointments: Teaching, 15 colleges; Former Editor and Reviewer, Illinois Entertainer, Cares For To Sing; Senior Reviewer, The Streak. Contributions to: 36 articles on philosophy, 3 book reviews, in The Meaning of Life Quarterly, 1988-, and Journal for the Development of Philosophy Teaching, 1991-. Address: 1823 W Barry, Chicago, IL 60657, USA.

LICHTENSTEIN Rosa See: **SCHAAD Isolde G.**

LICKONA Thomas (Edward), b. 4 Apr 1943, Poughkeepsie, New York, USA. Developmental Psychologist; Professor of Education; Writer; Consultant; Lecturer. m. Judith Barker, 10 Sept 1966, 2 sons. Education: BA, English, Siena College, 1964; MA, English, Ohio University, 1965; PhD, Psychology, State University of New York at Albany, 1971. Appointments: Instructor, State University of New York at Albany, 1968-70; Assistant Professor, 1970-75, Associate Professor, 1975-82, Professor of Education, 1982-, State University of New York College at Cortland; Visiting Professor, Harvard University, 1978-79, Boston University, 1979-80; Numerous radio and television talk show appearances. Publications: Open Education: Increasing Alternatives for Teachers and Children (editor with Jessie Adams, Ruth Nickse, and David Young), 1973; Moral Development and Behavior: Theory, Research, and Social Issues (editor), 1976; Raising Good Children: Helping Your Child Through the Stages of Moral Development, 1983; Educating for Character: How Our Schools Can Teach Respect and Responsibility, 1991; Sex, Love and You (with Judith Lickona and William Boudreau), 1994. Contributions to: Journals and magazines. Honours: Distinguished Alumni Award, State University of New York at Albany; Christopher Award, 1992. Memberships: Association for Moral Education, past president; Character Counts Coalition, advisory board; Character Education Partnership, board of directors; Medical Institute for Sexual Health, advisory board. Address: c/o State University of New York College at Cortland, PO Box 2000, Cortland, NY 13045, USA.

LIDDLE Peter (Hammond), b. 26 Dec 1934, Sunderland, England. Senior Lecturer in History; Writer. Education: BA, University of Sheffield, 1956; Teacher's Certificate, University of Nottingham, 1957; Diploma in Physical Education, Loughborough University of Technology, 1958. Appointments: History Teacher, Havelock School, Sunderland, 1957; Head, History Department, Gateacre Comprehensive School, Liverpool, 1958-67; Lecturer, Notre Dame College of Education, 1967; Lecturer, 1967-70, Senior Lecturer in History, 1970-, Sunderland Polytechnic; Keeper of the Liddle Collection, University of Leeds, 1988-; Founder and Editor, The Poppy and the Owl, 1990. Publications: Men of Gallipoli, 1976; World War One: Personal Experience Material for Use in Schools, 1977; Testimony of War 1914-18, 1979; The Sailor's War 1914-18, 1985; Gallipoli: Pens, Pencils and Cameras at War, 1985; 1916: Aspects of Conflict, (editor and contributor), 1985; Home Fires and Foreign Fields, 1985; The Airman's War 1914-18, 1987; The Soldier's War 1914-18, 1988; Voices of War, 1988; The Battle of the Somme, 1992; The Worst Ordeal: Britons at Home and Abroad 1914-18, 1994; Facing Armageddon: The First World War Experienced (co-editor and contributor), 1996; Passchendaele in Perspective: The Third Battle of Ypres (editor and contributor), 1997; At the Eleventh Hour (co-editor and contributor), 1998. Contributions to: Journals and other books. Honours:

MLitt, University of Newcastle, 1975; PhD, University of Leeds, 1997. Memberships: British Audio Visual Trust; Royal Historical Society, fellow. Address: Prospect House, 39 Leeds Road, Rawdon, Leeds LS19 6NW, England.

LIDDY James (Daniel Reeves), b. 1 July 1934, Dublin, Ireland. Professor of English; Poet; Writer. Education: BA, 1956, MA, 1959, English Language and Literature, National University of Ireland; Barrister-at-Law, King's Inns, Dublin, 1961. Appointments: Visiting Lecturer, San Francisco State College, 1967-68; Visiting Assistant Professor, State University of New York at Binghamton, 1969, University of Wisconsin at Parkside, 1972-73; Visiting Lecturer, Lewis and Clark College, Portland, Oregon, 1970, University College, Galway, 1973-74; Assistant Professor, Denison University, Ohio, 1970-71; Lecturer, Delgado Community College, New Orleans, 1975; Visiting Assistant Professor, 1976, Lecturer and Poet-in-Residence, 1976-80, Assistant Professor, 1981-82, Associate Professor, 1982-88, Professor of English, 1988-, University of Wisconsin at Milwaukee. Publications: Poetry: In a Blue Smoke, 1964; Blue Mountain, 1968; A Life of Stephen Dedalus, 1968; A Munster Song of Love and War, 1969; Orpheus in the Ice Cream Parlour, 1975; Corca Bascin, 1977; Comyn's Lay, 1979; Moon and Starr Moments, 1982; At the Grave of Fr Sweetman, 1984; A White Thought in a White Shade, 1987; In the Slovak Bowling Alley, 1990; Art is Not for Grownups, 1990; Trees Warmer Than Green: Notes Towards a Video of Avondale House, 1991; Collected POems, 1994; Epitaphery, 1997. Other: Esau My Kingdom for a Drink, 1962; Patrick Kavanagh: An Introduction to his Work, 1971; Baudelaire's Bar Flowers (translator), 1975; You Can't Jog for Jesus: Jack Kerouac as a Religious Writer, 1985; Young Men Go Walking (novella), 1986. Contributions to: Books and journals. Honours: University of Wisconsin at Parkside Teaching Award, 1973; Council of Wisconsin Writers Prize for Poetry, 1995. Membership: Aosdána, Irish Academy of Arts and Letters. Address: c/o Department of English and Comparative Literature, University of Wisconsin at Milwaukee, PO Box 413, Milwaukee, WI 53201, USA.

LIDE Mary Ruth, (Mary Clayton, Mary Lomer), b. Cornwall, England. Writer. 3 sons, 1 daughter. Education: MA, History, St Hugh's College, Oxford. Publications: As Mary Lide: The Bait, 1961; Ann of Cambray (Trilogy), 1985, 1986, 1987; Gifts of the Queen, 1985; Diary of Isobelle, 1985; Hawks of Sedgemont, 1987; Tregaran, 1989; Command of the King, 1990; The Legacy, 1991; The Homecoming, 1992; Polmena Cove, 1994. As Mary Lomer: Robert of Normandy, 1991; Fortune's Knave, 1993. As Mary Clayton: Pearls Before Swine, 1995; Deadmen's Bones, 1996; The Prodigal's Return, 1997. Contributions to: Short stories; Poetry; Book reviews. Honours: Avery Hopwood Award for Poetry, 1955; Best Historical Novel, 1984. Address: c/o Goodman Associates, 500 West End Avenue, New York, NY 10024, USA.

LIDSTONE John Barrie Joseph, b. 21 July 1929. m. Primrose Vivien, 1957, daughter. Education: Presentation College Reading, University of Manchester, RAF Education Officers' Course. Appointments: National Service RAF, 1947-48; English Master Repton, 1949-52; Shell-Mex and BP and Assoc cos, 1952-62, Deputy Md Vicon Agricultural Machinery Ltd, 1962-63; Director and General Manager, Marketing Selections Ltd, 1969-72; Marketing Improvements Group plc, joined 1965, Director, 1968-, Director and General Manager, 1972-74, Dep Md, 1974-88, Dep Chairman, 1988-89, Non-Executive Director, 1989-93; Non-Executive Director, Kalamazoo plc, 1986-91, North Hampshire Trust Co Ltd, 1986-93, St Nicholas' School Fleet Educational Trust Ltd, 1982-90 and 1995-96; Member, UK Management Consultancies Association, 1978-88 (Chairman 1986-87); Senior Visiting Lecturer, University of Surrey, 1990-96; Member, Chemical and Allied Products Indust Trg Board, 1975-79, National Inter-Active Video Centre, 1988-90; Editor, Lidstorian, 1985-88, Marketing Editor, Pharmaceutical Times, 1994-; Voted Top Speaker on Marketing in Europe, 1974; Dartnell

lecture tours USA, 1978-82; Member, National Executive Committee Chartered Institute of Marketing, 1985-90; Freeman, City of London, Liveryman Worshipful Co of Marketers, Member Ct of Assistants Guild of Management Consultants, 1993; Member, BAFTA, FIMC, FIMgt, FInstD, FCIM; Films and Video Technical Advisor and Scriptwriter: The Persuaders (EMI 1975), Negotiating Profitable Sales, 1979; Training Salesman Salesmen on the Job, 1981, won highest award for creative excellence at US Industrial Film Festival, 1982; Marketing for Managers, 1985; Marketing Today, 1985; Reaching Agreement and Interviewing, 1987, 1988; Books Training Salesmen on the Job, 1975, 2nd edition, 1986; Recruiting and Selecting Successful Salesmen, 1976, 2nd edition, 1983; Negotiating Profitable Sales, 1977, made into two part film by Video Arts, 1979; Motivating Your Sales Force, 1978, 2nd edition, 1995; Making Effective Presentations, 1985; The Sales Presentation, jointly, 1985; Profitable Selling, 1986; Marketing Planning for the Pharmaceutical Industry, 1987; Manual of Sales Negotiation, 1991; Manual of Marketing for University of Surrey, 1991; Beyond the Pay-Packet, 1992; Face the Press, 1992; Contributing chapters to: The Best of Dilemma and Decision, 1985; Marketing in the Service Industries, 1985; Marketing Handbook, 3rd edition, 1989; Gower Book of Management Skills, 2nd edition, 1992; the Director's Manual, 1992, 1995; The Marketing Book, 3rd edition, 1992; The Director's Manual, 1992, 1995; The Marketing Book, 3rd edition, 1994; Ivanhoe Guide to Management Consultants, 1994; International Encyclopedia of Business and Management, 1996; Author of articles contributed to: The Times and Sunday Times, Daily and Sunday Telegraph, Financial Times, Observer, Long Range Planning, International Management, Management Today, Marketing, Marketing Week. Hobbies: Writing; Cricket; Golf (Capt N Hants Golf Club, 1992-93). Address: c/o Reform Club, Pall Mall, London SW1Y 5EW, England.

LIEBER Robert J(ames), b. 29 Sept 1941, Chicago, Illinois, USA. Professor of Government; Writer. m. Nancy Lee Isaksen, 2 sons. Education: BA, University of Wisconsin, 1963; University of Chicago, 1963-64; PhD, Harvard University, 1968; Postdoctoral Studies, Oxford University, 1969-70. Appointments: Assistant Professor, 1968-72, Associate Professor, 1972-77, Professor, 1977-81, University of California at Davis; Visiting Fellow, 1969-70, Senior Associate Member, 1972-73, St Antony's College, Oxford; Research Associate, Center for International Affairs, Harvard University, 1974-75; Visiting Fellow, Atlantic Institute for International Affairs, Paris, 1978-79; Fellow, Wilson Center, Smithsonian Institution, 1980-81; Guest Scholar, Brookings Institution, 1981; Professor of Government, 1982-, Chairman, Department of Government, 1990-96, Georgetown University; Visiting Professor, Fudan University, Shanghai, 1988. Publications: British Politics and European Unity: Parties, Elites and Pressure Groups, 1970; Theory and World Politics, 1972; Contemporary Politics: Europe (with Alexander Groth and Nancy I Lieber), 1976; Oil and the Middle East War: Europe in the Energy Crisis, 1976; Eagle Entangled: US Foreign Policy in a Complex World (editor with Kenneth Oye and Donald Rothchild), 1979; The Oil Decade: Conflict and Cooperation in the West, 1983; Will Europe Fight for Oil?: Energy Relations in the Atlantic Area (editor), 1983; Eagle Defiant: US Foreign Policy in the 1980s (editor with Kenneth Oye and Donald Rothchild), 1983; Eagle Resurgent?: The Reagan Era in American Foreign Policy (editor with Kenneth Oye and Donald Rothchild), 1987; No Common Power: Understanding International Relations, 1988, 3rd edition, 1995; Eagle in a New World: American Grand Strategy in the Post-Cold War Era (editor with Kenneth Oye and Donald Rothchild), 1992; Eagle Adrift: American Foreign Policy at the End of the Century (editor), 1997. Contributions to: Books and professional journals. Honours: Woodrow Wilson Fellowship, 1963; Council on Foreign Relations International Affairs Fellowship, 1972-73; Guggenheim Fellowship, 1973-74; Rockefeller Foundation Fellowship, 1978-79; Ford Foundation Grant, 1981. Memberships: Council on Foreign Relations; International Institute for Strategic Studies. Address: c/o

Department of Government, Georgetown University, Washington DC 20057, USA.

LIEBERMAN Herbert Henry, b. 22 Sept 1933, New Rochelle, New York, USA. Novelist; Playwright; Editor. m. Judith Barsky, 9 June 1963, 1 daughter. Education: AB, City College of New York, 1955; AM, Columbia University, 1957. Publications: The Adventures of Dolphin Green, 1967; Crawlspace, 1971; The Eighth Square. 1973; Brilliant Kids, 1975; City of the Dead, 1976; The Climate of Hell, 1978; Nightcall from a Distant Time Zone, 1982; Night Bloom, 1984; The Green Train, 1986; Shadow Dancers, 1989; Sandman Sleep, 1993; The Girl with the Botticelli Eyes, 1996. Honours: 1st Prize for Playwriting, University of Chicago, 1963; Guggenheim Fellowship, 1964; Grand Prix de Litterature Policiere, Paris, 1978. Memberships: Mystery Writers of America; International Association of Crime Writers. Address: c/o Georges Borchardt, 136 East 57th Street, New York, NY 10022, USA.

LIEBERMAN Laurence, b. 16 Feb 1935, Detroit, Michigan, USA. Professor of English and Creative Writing; Poet; Writer; Editor. m. Bernice Braun, 17 June 1956, 1 son, 2 daughters. Education: BA, 1956, MA, 1958, University of Michigan; Doctoral Program, University of California, 1958-60. Appointments: Associate Professor of English, College of the Virgin Islands, 1964-68; Associate Professor of English, 1968-70, Professor of English and Creative Writing, 1970-, University of Illinois at Urbana-Champaign; Poetry Editor, University of Illinois Press, 1971-. Publications: The Unblinding (poems), 1968; The Achievement of James Dickey, 1968; The Osprey Suicides (poems), 1973; Unassigned Frequencies: American Poetry in Review, 1964-77, 1977; God's Measurements, 1980; Eros at the World Kite Pageant: Poems, 1979-83, 1983; The Mural of Wakeful Sleep (poems), 1985; The Creole Mephistopheles (poems), 1990; New and Selected Poems: 1962-92, 1993; The St Kitts Monkey Feuds (poem), 1995; Beyond the Muse of Memory: Essays on Contemporary American Poets, 1995; Dark Songs: Slave House and Synagogue, 1996; Compass of the Dying (poems), 1998; The Regatta in the Skies: Selected Long Poems, 1998. Contributions to: Anthologies, reviews, journals, and magazines. Honours: Yaddo Foundation Fellowship, 1964; Illinois Arts Council Fellowship, 1981; National Endowment for the Arts Fellowship, 1986-87; Jerome J Shestack Poetry Prize, American Poetry Review, 1986-87 Runner-up, William Carlos Williams Award, Poetry Society of America, 1997. Memberships: Academy of American Poets; Associated Writing Program; Poetry Society of America. Address: 1304 Eliot Drive, Urbana, IL 61801, USA.

LIEBERMAN Shari, b. 24 June 1958, New York, USA. Nutrition Scientist. Education: MS, Clinical Nutrition, New York University, 1982; PhD, Clinical Nutrition and Exercise Physiology, 1993. Appointments: Professor, University of Bridgeport, School of Human Nutrition; Nutrition Consultant to various companies; Private Practice Clinical Nutritionist. Publication: The Real Vitamin and Mineral Book, 1992, 2nd edition, 1997. Contributions to: Better Nutrition for Today's Living; New Life. Address: 60 East 8th St, New York, NY 10003, USA.

LIEBERTHAL Kenneth Guy, b. 9 Sept 1943, Asheville, North Carolina, USA. Professor of Political Science; Writer. m. Jane Lindsay, 15 June 1968, 2 sons. Education: BA, With Distinction, Dartmouth College, 1965; MA, 1968, Certificate for East Asian Institute, 1968, PhD, Political Science, 1972, Columbia University. Appointments: Instructor, 1972, Assistant Professor, 1972-75, Associate Professor, 1976-82, Professor, 1982-83, Political Science Department, Swarthmore College; Visiting Professor, 1983, Professor, 1983-, University of Michigan, Ann Arbor; Editorial Boards, China Economic Review, China Quarterly, Journal of Contemporary China. Publications: Policy Making in China: Leaders, Structures and Processes (with Michel Oksenberg), 1988; Research Guide to Central Party and Government Meetings in China 1949-86 (with Bruce Dixon), 1989; Perspectives on Modern China: Four

Anniversaries (co-editor), 1991; Bureaucracy, Politics and Policy Making in Post-Mao China (co-editor), 1991; Governing China, 1995. Contributions to: Foreign Affairs, China Quarterly; Book reviews to American Political Science Review; China Economic Review; China Quarterly. Address: 202 South Thayer, Ann Arbor, Michigan, MI 48104-1608, USA.

LIEBESCHUETZ John Hugo Wolfgang Gideon, b. 22 June 1927, Hamburg, Germany. Retired Professor of Classical and Archaeological Studies; Writer. m. Margaret Rosa Taylor, 9 Apr 1955, 1 son, 3 daughters. Education: BA, 1951, PhD, 1957, University of London. Appointments: Professor and Head of Department of Classical and Archaeological Studies, University of Nottingham, 1979-92. Publications: Antioch, 1972; Continuity and Change in Roman Religion, 1979; Barbarians and Bishops, 1992; From Diocletian to the Arab Conquest, 1992. Honours: Fellow, British Academy, 1992; Corresponding Fellow, German Archaeological Institute, 1994; Fellow, University College, London, 1997. Address: 1 Clare Valley, The Park, Nottingham NG7 1BU, England.

LIEBICH Andre, b. 5 Jan 1948, London, England. Academic. m. Hayat Salam, 28 Jan 1972, 2 daughters. Education: BA Hons, McGill, 1968; AM, Harvard, 1970; PhD, Harvard, 1974. Appointments: Assistant Professor to Professor, Universite Du Quebec A Montreal, 1973-89; Professor of International History & Politics, Graduate of International Studies Geneva. Publications: Between Ideology & Utopia: The Politics & Philosophy of August Cieszkowski, 1979; From the Other Shore: Russian Social Democracy After 1921, 1997; Les Minorities Nationales en Europe Centrale Et Orientale, 1997; Editor: Citizenship, East and West, 1995; Le Liberalisme Classique, 1985; L'Avenir Du Socialisme En Europe, 1979. Contributions to: Dissent, Behind the Headlines, Slavic Review International Journal; Political Theory, Politics and Society. Honour: Frankel Prize, 1995.

LIEBLER M(ichael) L(ynn), b. 24 Aug 1953, Detroit, Michigan, USA. University Senior Lecturer; Poet. m. Pamela Mary Liebler, 5 Nov 1976, 1 son, 1 daughter. Education: BA, 1976, MAT, 1980, Oakland University, Rochester, Michigan. Appointments: Part-time Instructor, Henry Ford Community College, 1980-86; Lecturer, 1981-92, Senior Lecturer, 1992-, Wayne State University; Detroit Director, National Writers' Voice Project, 1995-; Arts and Humanities Director, YMCA of Metro Detroit. Publications: Measuring Darkness, 1980; Breaking the Voodoo: Selected Poems, 1990; Deliver Me, 1991; Stripping the Adult Century Bare, 1995; Brooding the Heartlands, 1998. Contributions to: Rattle; Exquisite Corpse; Cottonwood Review; Relix Magazine; Christian Science Monitor; Detroit Sunday Journal; Review of Contemporary Fiction; American Book Review. Memberships: American Association of University Professors; Associate Writing Programs; Modern Language Association; National Council of Teachers of English; National Writers Voice Project; National Writers Corp Program; Poetry Resource Center of Michigan, president, 1987-93; Popular Culture Association. Address: PO Box 120, Roseville, MI 48066, USA.

LIFSHIN Lyn (Diane), b. 12 July 1944, Burlington, Vermont, USA. Poet; Teacher. Education: BA, Syracuse University, 1960; MA, University of Vermont, 1963. Appointments: Instructor, State University of New York at Cobleskill, 1968, 1970; Writing Consultant, New York State Mental Health Department, Albany, 1969, Empire State College of the State University of New York at Saratoga Springs, 1973; Poet-in-Residence, Mansfield State College, Pennsylvania, 1974, University of Rochester, New York, 1986, Antioch's Writers' Conference, Ohio, 1987. Publications: Poetry: Over 75 collections, including: Upstate Madonna: Poems, 1970-74, 1975; Shaker House Poems, 1976; Some Madonna Poems, 1976; Leaning South, 1977; Madonna Who Shifts for Herself, 1983; Kiss the Skin Off, 1985; Many Madonnas, 1988; The Doctor Poems, 1990; Apple Blossoms, 1993; Blue Tattoo, 1995; The Mad Girl Drives in a Daze, 1995. Editor: Tangled Vines: A Collection of Mother and Daughter Poems, 1978; Ariadne's Thread: A Collection of Contemporary Women's Journals, 1982; Unsealed Lips, 1988. Contributions to: Many books and numerous other publications, including journals. Honours: Hart Crane Award; Bread Loaf Scholarship; Yaddo Fellowships, 1970, 1971, 1975, 1979, 1980; MacDowell Fellowship, 1973; Millay Colony Fellowships, 1975, 1979; Jack Kerouac Award, 1984; Centennial Review Poetry Prize, 1985; Madeline Sadin Award, New York Quarterly, 1986; Footwork Award, 1987; Esterscefler Award, 1987. Address: 2142 Appletree Lane, Niskayuna, NY 12309, USA.

LIFTON Betty Jean, b. USA. Writer. Education: PhD, UMM Institute, 1992. Publications: Joji and the Dragon, 1957; Mogo the Mynah, 1958; Joji and the Fog, 1959; Kap the Kappa (play), 1960; The Dwarf Pine Tree, 1963; Joji and the Amanojaku, 1965; The Cock and the Ghost Cat, 1965; The Rice-Cake Rabbit, 1966; The Many Lives of Chio and Goro, 1966; Taka-Chan and I: A Dog's Journey to Japan, 1967; Kap and the Wicked Monkey, 1968; The Secret Seller, 1968; The One-Legged Ghost, 1968; A Dog's Guide to Tokyo, 1969; Return to Hiroshima, 1970; The Silver Crane, 1971; The Mud Snail Son, 1971; Good Night, Orange Monster, 1972; Children of Vietnam (with Thomas C Fox), 1972; Contemporary Children's Theater (editor), 1974; Jaguar, My Twin, 1976; Lost and Found: The Adoption Experience, 1979; I'm Still Me, 1981; A Place Called Hiroshima, 1985; The King of Children: A Biography of Janusz Korczak, 1988; Tell Me a Real Adoption Story, 1991; Journey of the Adopted Self: A Quest for Wholeness, 1994. Address: 300 Central Park West, New York, NY 10024, USA.

LIFTON Robert Jay, b. 16 May 1926, New York, New York, USA. Psychiatrist; Professor; Writer. m. Betty Kirschner, 1 Mar 1952, 2 daughters. Education: Cornell University, 1942-44; MD, New York Medical College, 1948. Appointments: Intern, Jewish Hospital, Brooklyn, 1948-49; Resident, State University of New York Downstate Medical Center, 1949-51; Faculty, Washington School of Psychiatry, 1954-55; Research Associate in Psychiatry, Harvard University, 1955-61; Foundation's Fund for Research Psychiatry Associate Professor of Psychiatry and Psychology, 1961-67, Research Professor, 1967-, Yale Medical School; Distinguished Professor of Psychiatry and Psychology, Director, Center on Violence and Human Survival, John Jay College of Criminal Justice, the Graduate School and University Center, and Mount Sinai School of Medicine, City University of New York, 1985-; Several guest lectureships. Publications: Thought Reform and the Psychology of Totalism: A Study of Brainwashing in China, 1961, new edition, 1989; Revolutionary Immorality: Mao Tse-Tung and the Chinese Cultural Revolution, 1968; Death in Life: Survivors of Hiroshima, 1969, new edition, 1991; History and Human Survival, 1970; Boundaries: Psychological Man in Revolution, 1970; Home from the War: Vietnam Veterans--Neither Victims Nor Executioners, 1973; Living and Dying (with Eric Olson), 1974; The Life of the Self, 1976; Six Lives, Six Deaths: Portraits from Modern Japan (with Shuichi Kato and Michael Reich), 1979; The Broken Connection: On Death and the Continuity of Life, 1979; Indefensible Weapons: The Political and Psychological Case Against Nuclearism (with Richard A Falk), 1982, new edition, 1991; In a Dark Time, 1984; The Nazi Doctors: Medical Killing and Psychology of Genocide, 1986; The Future of Immortality and Other Essays for a Nuclear Age, 1987; The Genocidal Mentality: Nazi Holocaust and Nuclear Threat (with Eric Markusen), 1990; The Protean Self: Human Resilience in an Age of Fragmentation, 1993; Hiroshima in America: Fifty Years of Denial, 1995. Editor: Woman in America, 1965; America and the Asian Revolutions, 1970; Crimes of War (with Richard A Falk and G Kolko), 1971; Explorations in Psychohistory: The Wellfleet Papers (with Eric Olson), 1975; Last Aid: Medical Dimensions of Nuclear War (with Eric Chivian, Suzanna Chivian, and John E Mack), 1982; The Genocidal Mentality: Nazi Doctor and Nuclear Threat, 1990. Contributions to: Professional journals. Honours: National Book Award, 1970; Van Wyck Brooks Award, 1971; Hiroshima Gold Medal, 1975; Gandhi Peace Award, 1984; Bertrand Russell Society Award, 1985; Holocaust Memorial Award, 1986; National Jewish Book Award, 1987; Los Angeles Times Book Prize for History, 1987; Lisl and Leo Eitinger Award, Oslo, 1988; Max A Hayman Award, American Orthopsychiatrists Association, 1992; National Living Treasure Award, Psychiatric Institute, 1994; Outstanding Achievement Award, Armenian-American Society for Studies on Stress and Genocide, 1996. Memberships: American Academy of Arts and Sciences, fellow; American Psychiatric Association; Association of Asian Studies; Federation of American Scientists; Society for Psychological Study of Social Issues. Address: c/o John Jay College of Criminal Justice, 899 10th Avenue, New York, NY 10019, USA.

LIGHTMAN Alan (Paige), b. 28 Nov 1948, Memphis, Tennessee, USA. Physicist; Professor; Author. m. Jean Greenblatt, 28 Nov 1976, 2 daughters. Education: AB, Princeton University, 1970; PhD, Physics, California Institute of Technology, 1974. Appointments: Postdoctoral Fellow, Cornell University, 1974-76; Assistant Professor, Harvard University, 1976-79; Staff Scientist, Smithsonian Astrophysical Observatory, Cambridge, 1979-88; Professor of Science and Writing, 1988-, John E Burchard Chair, 1995-, Massachusetts Institute of Technology. Publications: Problem Book in Relativity and Gravitation, 1974; Radiative Processes in Astrophysics, 1976; Time Travel and Papa Joe's Pipe, 1984; A Modern Day Yankee in a Connecticut Court, 1986; Origins: The Lives and Worlds of Modern Cosmologists, 1990; Ancient Light, 1992; Great Ideas in Physics, 1992; Time for the Stars, 1992; Einstein's Dreams, 1993; Good Benito, 1995; Dance for Two, 1996. Contributions to: Professional journals and to general publications. Honours: Most Outstanding Science Book in the Physical Sciences Award, Association of American Publishers, 1990; Boston Globe Winship Book Prize, 1993; Andrew Gemant Prize, 1996. Memberships: American Academy of Arts and Sciences, fellow; American Astronomical Society; American Physical Society, fellow. Address: Massachusetts Institute of Technology, 77 Massachusetts Avenue, Cambridge, MA 02139, USA.

LILIENTHAL Alfred M(orton), b. 25 Dec 1913, New York, New York, USA. Author; Historian; Attorney; Lecturer. Education: BA, Cornell University, 1934; LLD, Columbia University School of Law, 1938. Appointment: Editor, Middle East Perspective, 1968-85. Publications: What Price Israel?, 1953; There Goes the Middle East, 1958; The Other Side of the Coin, 1965; The Zionist Connection I, 1978; The Zionist Connection II, 1982. Contributions to: Numerous journals. Honour: National Press Club Book Honours, 1982. Memberships: University Club; Cornell Club; National Press Club; Capital Hill Club. Address: 800 25 North West, Washington, DC 20037, USA.

LILLEY Stephen R, b. 13 Sept 1957, Louisiana, MO, USA. Teacher; Musician; Writer. m. Rebecca Jean Schuster, 10 June 1972, 1 son, 1 daughter. Education: Bachelor Science Education, University of Missouri, Columbia, 1972; MA, History, Northeast Missouri State University, Kirksville, 1976. Appointments: Teacher, Lincoln County R-IV Schools, 1972-74; Teacher, Lincoln County R-II Schools, 1974-; Adjunct Faculty, Northeast Missouri State University, 1977; Hannibal La Grange College. Publications: The Importance of Hernando Cortez, 1996; The Conquest of Mexico, 1997; Fighters Against Slavery, 1998. Contributions to: Missouri Historical Review, A Minuteman for Years, 1980; Highlights for Children, Alexander's First Conquest, 1986; To Reach the Promised Land, 1990; Missouri Lite, 1984; And In this Corner, 1984. Honour: Highlights for Children History Feature of the Year, 1990. Address: 274 Lilley Lane, Elsberry, MO 63343, USA.

LILLINGTON Kenneth (James), b. 7 Sept 1916, London, England. Author; Dramatist; Lecturer in English Literature (retired). Education: St Dunstan's College; Wandsworth Training College. Appointment: Lecturer in English Literature, Brooklands Technical College, Weybridge, Surrey (retired). Publications: The Devil's

Grandson, 1954; Soapy and the Pharoah's Curse, 1957; Conjuror's Alibi, 1960; The Secret Arrow, 1960; Blue Murder, 1960; A Man Called Hughes, 1962; My Proud Beauty, 1963; First (and Second) Book of Classroom Plays. 1967-68; Fourth (and Seventh) Windmill Book of One-Act Plays. 1967-72; Cantaloup Crescent, 1970; Olaf and the Ogre, 1972; Nine Lives (editor), 1977; For Better for Worse, 1979; Young Map of Morning, 1979; What Beckoning Ghost, 1983; Selkie, 1985; Full Moon, 1986. Address: 90 Wodeland Avenue, Guildford, Surrey GU2 5LD, England.

LIM Shirley Geok-Lin, b. 27 Dec 1944, Malacca, Malaya. Professor of English and Women's Studies; Author; Poet. m. Dr Charles Bazerman, 27 Nov 1972, 1 son. Education: BA, 1st Class Honours, English Literature, 1967, MA Studies, 1967-69, University of Malaya; MA, 1971, PhD, 1973, English and American Literature, Brandeis University. Appointments: Lecturer and Teaching Assistant, University of Malaya, 1967-69; Teaching Fellow, Queens College, City University of New York, 1972-73; Assistant Professor, Hostos Community College, City University of New York, 1973-76; Lecturer, Universiti Sains, Penang, Malaysia, 1974; Associate Professor, State University of New York College at Westchester, 1976-90; Writer-in-Residence, University of Singapore, 1985, East West Center, Honolulu, 1988; Chair, Asian American Studies, 1990-93, Women's Studies, 1997-, Professor of English and Women's Studies, 1993-, University of California at Santa Barbara; Fulbright Distinguished Lecturer, Nanyang Technological University. 1996. Publications: Crossing the Peninsula and Other Poems, 1980; Another Country and Other Stories, 1982; No Man's Grove and Other Poems, 1985; Modern Secrets: New and Selected Poems, 1989; Nationalism and Literature: Literature in English from the Philippines and Singapore, 1993; Monsoon History: Selected Poems, 1994; Writing Southeast/Asia in English: Against the Grain, 1994; Life's Mysteries: The Best of Shirley Lim, 1995; Among the White Moon Faces: An Asian-American Memoir of Homelands, 1996; Two Dreams: Short Stories, 1997; What the Fortune Teller Didn't Say, 1998. Editor: The Forbidden Stitch: An Asian American Women's Anthology, 1989; Reading the Literatures of Asian America, 1992; One World of Literature, 1993; Asian American Literature: An Anthology, forthcoming. Contributions to: Anthologies. books, reviews, quarterlies, and journals. Honours: Numerous grants and fellowships; Fulbright Scholarship, 1969-72; Commonwealth Poetry Prize, 1980; American Book Awards, 1990, 1997. Memberships: American Studies; Association for Asian American Studies; Association for Commonwealth Languages and Literatures; Modern Language Association; Multi-Ethnic Literatures of the United States; National Women's Studies Association; PEN; Popular Culture Association. Address: c/o Women's Studies Program, University of California at Santa Barbara, Santa Barbara, CA 93106, USA.

LIMA Robert, b. 7 Nov 1935, Havana, Cuba. Professor of Spanish and Comparative Literature; Writer; Poet; Dramatist; Editor; Translator. m. Sally Murphy, 27 June 1964, 2 sons, 2 daughters. Education: BA, English, Philosophy, and History, 1957, MA, Theatre and Drama, 1961, Villanova University; PhD, Romance Languages and Literatures, New York University, 1968. Appointments: Lecturer, Hunter College, New York City, 1962-65; Assistant Professor, 1965-69, Associate Professor, 1969-73, Professor of Spanish and Comparative Literature, 1973-, Pennsylvania State University. Publications: Readers Encyclopedia of American Literature (co-editor), revised edition, 1962; The Theatre of Garcia Lorca, 1963; Borges the Labyrinth Maker (editor and translator), 1965; Ramón del Valle-Inclán, 1972; An Annotated Bibliography of Ramón del Valle-Inclán, 1972; Dos ensayos sobre teatro espanol de los veinte (co-author), 1984; Valle-Inclán: The Theatre of His Life, 1988; Savage Acts: Four Plays (editor and translator), 1993; Borges and the Esoteric (editor and contributor), 1993; Valle-Inclán: El teatro de su vida, 1995; Dark Prisms: Occultism in Hispanic Drama, 1995; Homenaje a/Tribute to Martha T Halsey (co-editor and

contributor), 1995; The International Annotated Bibliography of Ramón del Valle-Inclán, 2 volumes, 1999. Contributions to: Many books. reference works, anthologies. newspapers, reviews, quarterlies, and journals. Honours: Fellowships and awards. Memberships: Poetry Society of America; International PEN, American Center; Institute for the Arts and Humanistic Studies, fellow; Academia Norteamericana de la Lengua Española, academician; Real Academia Española, corresponding member. Address: c/o Department of Spanish, Italian, and Portuguese, Pennsylvania State University, 352 North Burrowes Building, University Park, PA 16802, USA.

LIMAN Horia, b. 12 Oct 1912, Bucharest, Romania. Critic; Editor; Writer. m. Isabelle Fallet-Liman, 27 Jan 1994. Education: License es Letters, University of Bucharest, 1924. Appointments: Editor, Contemporanul, 1947-57; Literary Correspondent, Prague, 1959-65, Switzerland, 1965-70. Publications: La Foire aux Jeunes Filles, 1987; L'Echeance, 1992; Les Bottes. Honour: Prix Schiller, 1993. Address: Port-Roulant, 30-2003 Neuchatel, Switzerland.

LIMBAUGH Rush (Hudson), b. 12 Jan 1951, Cape Girardeau, Missouri, USA. Radio and Television Personality. m. Marta Fitzgerald, 27 May 1994. Appointments: Various radio disc jockey posts, 1960-88; Host, The Rush Limbaugh Show, radio, 1988-, television, 1992-96; Editor-Publisher, The Limbaugh Letter, 1995-. Publications: The Way Things Ought to Be, 1992; See, I Told You So, 1993. Address: c/o WABC, 125 West End Avenue, No 6, New York, NY 10023, USA.

LIMBURG Peter R(ichard), b. 14 Nov 1929, New York, New York, USA. Writer; Editor. Education: BA, Yale University, 1950; BSFA, Georgetown University, 1951; MA, Columbia University, 1957. Appointments: Special Editor, Harper Encyclopaedia of Science, 1960-61; Senior Technology Editor, The New Book of Knowledge, 1961-66; Editor, School Department, Harcourt, Brace and World, publishers, 1966-69; Coordinating Editor, Collier's Encyclopaedia, 1969-70; President, Forum Writers for Young People, 1975-76, 1980-81. Publications: The First Book of Engines, 1969; The Story of Corn, 1971; What's in the Names of Fruit, 1972; What's in the Names of Antique Weapons, 1973; Vessels for Underwater Exploration: A Pictorial History (with James B Sweeney), 1973; Watch Out, It's Poison Ivy!, 1973; What's in the Names of Flowers, 1974; 102 Questions and Answers about the Sea (with James B Sweeney), 1975; What's in the Names of Birds, 1975; Chickens, Chickens, Chickens, 1975; What's in the Names of Stars and Constellations, 1976; Poisonous Plants, 1976; What's in the Names of Wild Animals, 1977; Oceanographic Institutions, 1979; The Story of Your Heart, 1979; Farming the Waters, 1980; Stories Behind Words, 1986. Memberships: American Society of Journalists and Authors; National Association of Science Writers. Address: RR 4, Banksville Road, Bedford, NY 10506, USA.

LINCOLN Bruce (Kenneth), b. 5 Mar 1948, Philadelphia, Pennsylvania, USA. Professor; Writer. m. Louise Gibson Hassett, 17 Apr 1971, 2 daughters. Education: BA, Haverford College, 1970; PhD, University of Chicago, 1976. Appointments: Assistant Professor, 1976-79, Associate Professor, 1979-84, Professor of Humanities, Religious Studies and South Asian Studies, and Chair, Religious Studies Programme, 1979-86, Professor of Comparative Studies in Discourse and Society, 1986-93, University of Minnesota; Visiting Professor, Università degli Studi di Siena, 1984-85, University of Uppsala, 1985, Novosibirsk State Pedagogical Institute, 1991; University of Copenhagen 1998; Professor of History of Religions Anthropology, Classics and Middle Eastern Studies, University of Chicago, 1993-. Publications: Priests, Warriors, and Cattle: A Study in the Ecology of Religions, 1981; Emerging from the Chrysalis: Studies in Rituals of Women's Initiation, 1981, revised edition, 1991; Religion, Rebellion, Revolution: An Interdisciplinary and Crosscultural Collection of Essays (editor), 1985; Myth, Cosmos. and Society: Indo-European Themes of

Creation and Destruction, 1986; Discourse and the Construction of Society: Comparative Studies of Myth, Ritual, and Classification, 1989; Death, War, and Sacrifice: Studies in Ideology and Practice, 1991; Authority: Construction and Corrosion, 1994. Contributions to: Professional journals. Honours: American Council of Learned Societies Grant, 1979; Rockefeller Foundation Grant, 1981; Best New Book in History of Religion Citation, American Council of Learned Societies, 1981; Guggenheim Fellowship, 1982-83; National Endowment for the Humanities Grant, 1986; Outstanding Academic Book Citation, Choice, 1989; Scholar of the College, University of Minnesota, 1990-93. Address: 5735 S Dorchester Avenue, Chicago, IL 60637. USA.

LINCOLN Geoffrey. See: **MORTIMER John Clifford.**

LINCOLN W(illiam) Bruce, b. 6 Sept 1938, Stafford Springs, Connecticut, USA. Professor; Historian. m. Mary Eagle Lincoln, 27 Mar 1984, 2 daughters. Education: AB, Honours, College of William and Mary, 1960; MA, 1962, PhD, 1966, University of Chicago. Appointments: Assistant Professor, Memphis State University, 1966-67; Assistant Professor, 1967-70, Associate Professor, 1970-78, Professor, 1978-, Northern Illinois University, DeKalb; Visiting Fellow, St Antony's College, Oxford, 1983. Publications: Nikolai Miliutin: An Enlightened Russian Bureaucrat, 1977; Nicholas I: Emperor and Autocrat of All the Russias, 1978; Petr Petrovich Semenov-Tian-Shanskii: The Life of a Russian Geographer, 1980; The Romanovs: Autocrats of All the Russias, 1981; In the Vanguard of Reform: Russia's Enlightened Bureaucrats, 1825-1961, 1982; In War's Dark Shadow: Russians Before the Great War, 1983; Passage through Armageddon: The Russians in War and Revolution, 1986; Red Victory: A History of the Russian Civil War, 1989; The Great Reforms: Autocracy, Bureaucracy, and the Politics of Change in Imperial Russia, 1990; Moscow: Treasures and Traditions (co-editor), 1990; The Conquest of a Continent: Siberia and the Russians, 1994; Between Heaven and Hell: A History of the Russian Artistic Experience, 1998. Contributions to: Numerous professional journals. Honours: Various grants; Guggenheim Fellowship, 1982-83; New York Times Notable Book of the Year, 1990; Publishers Weekly Best Book of the Year, 1994. Memberships: American Association for the Advancement of Slavic Studies; Phi Beta Kappa. Address: 1 Timber Trail, DeKalb, IL 60115, USA.

LIND William Sturgiss, b. 9 July 1947, Lakewood, Ohio, USA. Writer. Education: AB, Dartmouth College, 1969; MA, Princeton University, 1971. Publications: Maneuver Warfare Handbook, 1985; America Can Win: The Case for Military Reform (with Gary Hart), 1986; Cultural Conservatism: Toward a New National Agenda (with William H Marshner), 1987; Cultural Conservatism: Theory and Practice (editor with William H Marshner), 1991. Contributions to: Marine Corps Gazette; US Naval Institute Proceedings; Military Review; Parameters; Washington Post; Harper's. Address: Free Congress Foundation, 717 2nd Street North East, Washington, DC 20002, USA.

LINDBLOM Charles Edward, b. 21 Mar 1917, Turlock, California, USA. Professor; Writer. m. Rose K Winther, 4 June 1942, 2 sons, 1 daughter. Education: BA, Stanford University, 1937; PhD, University of Chicago, 1945. Appointments: Instructor, University of Minnesota, 1939-46; Assistant Professor to Professor, Yale University, 1946-. Publications: Unions and Capitalism, 1949; Politics, Economics and Welfare, 1953; The Intelligence of Democracy, 1965; The Policy Making Process, 1968; Politics and Markets, 1977; Usable Knowledge, 1979; Democracy and the Market System, 1988; Inquiry and Change, 1990. Contributions to: Professional journals. Honours: Various. Membership: American Political Science Association. Address: 9 Cooper Road, North Haven, CT 06473, USA.

LINDEMAN Jack, b. 31 Dec 1924, Philadelphia, Pennsylvania, USA. Professor Emeritus; Poet; Writer.

Education: West Chester State College, Pennsylvania, 1949; University of Pennsylvania, 1949; University of Mississippi, 1949-50; Villanova University, 1973. Appointments: Faculty, Lincoln University, Pennsylvania, 1963-64, Temple University, 1964-65; Faculty, 1969-85, Professor Emeritus, 1985-, Kutztown University, Pennsylvania. Publications: Twenty-One Poems; The Conflict of Convictions. Contributions to: Anthologies; Apocalypse; Bellowing Ark; Beloit Poetry Journal; Blueline; Blue Unicorn; California Poetry Quarterly; California Quarterly; Christian Science Monitor; Colorado Quarterly; Commonweal; Dickinson Review; Eureka Literary Magazine; Harper's Bazaar; High Plains Review; Hollins Critic; Kansas Quarterly; Massachusetts Review; Nation; New World Writing; Oregon East; Poetry; Prairie Schooner; Rocky Mountain Review; Slant; South Carolina Review; Southern Poetry Review; Southwest Review. Membership: Poets and Writers. Address: 133 South Franklin Street, Fleetwood, PA 19522, USA.

LINDEY Christine, b. 26 Aug 1947. Art Historian. Education: BA, Honours, History of European Art, Courtauld Institute, University of London. Publications: Superrealist Painting and Sculpture, 1980; 20th Century Painting: Bonnard to Rothko, 1981; Art in the Cold War, 1990. Address: c/o West Herts College, The Art School, Ridge Street, Watford, Herts WD2 5BY, England.

LINDGREN Gustav Torgny, b. 16 June 1938, Raggsjo, Sweden. Author. m. Stina Andersson, 19 June 1959, 1 son, 2 daughters. Education: DPhil. Publications: Ovriga tragor, 1973; Brannvinsfursten, 1979; Skrammer dig minuten, 1981; Merabs skonhet, 1983; Ormens vag pa halleberget, 1983; Batseba, 1984; Legender, 1986; Ljuset, 1987; Karleksguden Fro, 1988; Till Sanningens lov, 1991; Hummelhonung, 1995. Honours: Prix Fomina, 1986; Guralid Prize, 1990. Memberships: PEN; Swedish Academy. Address: Tjärstad prästgård, S-59041, Rimforsa, Sweden.

LINDMAN-STRAFFORD Kerstin Margareta, b. 30 May 1939, Abo, Finland. Writer; Critic. 2 children. Education: BA, Hum Kand, 1961; MA, 1962. Appointments: Critic, UK Editor, Hufvudstadsbladet, Helsinki, 1964-; Cultural Presenter, OBS Kulturkvarten, Swedish Radio, 1975-. Publications: Sandhogen and Other Essays, 1974; Tancred Borenius, 1976; Landet med manga ansikten, 1979; English Writers in Literaturhandboken, 1984; Faeder och Dottrar, 1986; Moedrar och soener, 1990; Foeraendringen, 1994. Contributions to: Numerous journals and magazines. Honour: Finland's Swedish Literary Society Prize, 1976. Memberships: PEN; Finlands Svenska Litteraturforening. Address: 16 Church Path, Merton Park, London SW19 3HJ, England.

LINDNER Carl Martin, b. 31 Aug 1940, New York, New York, USA. Professor of English; Poet. 1 son, 1 daughter. Education: BS, 1962, MA, 1965, City College of the City University of New York; PhD, University of Wisconsin at Madison, 1970. Appointments: Assistant Professor, 1969-74, Associate Professor, 1974-87, Professor of English, 1987-, University of Wisconsin at Parkside. Publications: Vampire, 1977; The Only Game, 1981; Shooting Baskets in a Dark Gymnasium, 1984; Angling into Light, forthcoming. Contributions to: Reviews, journals and periodicals. Honours: Wisconsin Arts Board Creative Writing Fellowship for Poetry, 1981; University of Wisconsin at Parkside Award for Excellence in Research and Creative Activity, 1996. Address: c/o Department of English, University of Wisconsin at Parkside, Box 2000, Wood Road, Kenosha, WI 53141, USA.

LINDOP Grevel (Charles Garrett), b. 6 Oct 1948, Liverpool, England. Professor of Romantic and Early Victorian Studies; Poet; Writer; Editor. m. Amanda Therese Marian, 4 July 1981, 1 son, 2 daughters. Education: Liverpool College; MA, BLitt, Wadham College, Oxford. Appointments: Lecturer, 1971-84, Senior Lecturer, 1984-93, Reader in English Literature, 1993-96, Professor of Romantic and Early Victorian Studies, 1996-, University of Manchester; Assistant Editor, Temenos

Academy Review. Publications: Poetry: Against the Sea, 1970; Fools' Paradise, 1977; Moon's Palette, 1984; Tourists, 1987; A Prismatic Toy, 1991. Prose: British Poetry Since 1960 (with Michael Schmidt), 1971; The Opium-Eater: A Life of Thomas De Quincey, 1981; A Literary Guide to the Lake District, 1993; The Path and the Palace: Reflections on the Nature of Poetry, 1996. Editor: Selected Poems, by Thomas Chatterton, 1971; Confessions of an English Opium-Eater and Other Writings, by Thomas De Quincey, 1985; The White Goddess, by Robert Graves, 1997; Complete Works, of Thomas De Quincey, 21 volumes, 1999-2001. Contributions to: Poetry Nation Review, Times Literary Supplement, and other publications. Honour: Lake District Book of the Year Award, 1993. Memberships: Temenos Academy, fellow; Theravada Buddhist; Wordsworth Museum and Library, Dove Cottage, Grasmere, trustee. Address: c/o Department of English and American Studies, University of Manchester, Oxford Road, Manchester M13 9PL, England.

LINDSAY Hilarie Elizabeth, b. 18 Apr 1922, Sydney, New South Wales, Australia. Writer; Company Director. m. Philip Singleton Lindsay, 19 Feb 1944, 1 son, 2 daughters. Education: Graduate, William's Business College, 1938; BA, Deakin University, 1991; PhD, Sydney, 1998. Publications: 101 Toys to Make, 1972; So You Want to Be a Writer, 1977; You're On Your Own - Teenage Survival Kit, 1977; One for the Road (short stories), 1978; Midget Mouse Finds a House, 1978; Culinary Capers, 1978; The Short Story, 1979; Learn to Write, 1979; The Naked Gourmet, 1979; The Society of Women Writers Handbook, 1980; The Withered Tree, 1980; One Woman's World, 1980; Echoes of Henry Lawson, 1981; The Gravy Train, 1981; Mr Poppleberry and the Dog's Own Daily, 1983; Mr Poppleberry and the Milk Thieves, 1983; Murder at the Belle Vue, 1983; Mr Poppleberry's Birthday Pie, 1989; Midget Mouse Goes to Sea, 1989; Beyond the Black Stump of My Pencil, 1993; When I Was Ten (with Len Fox), 1993; Sydney Life (with P McGowan), 1994; Mrs Poppleberry's Cuckoo-Clock, 1995. Address: 19-25 Beeson Street, Leichhardt, New South Wales 2020, Australia.

LINDSAY (John) Maurice, b. 21 July 1918, Glasgow, Scotland. Poet; Writer; Editor. m. 3 Aug 1946, 1 son, 3 daughters. Education: Glasgow Academy, 1928-36; Scottish National Academy of Music, 1936-39. Appointments: Programme Controller, Border Television, 1959-62; Editor, Scottish Review, 1975-85; Honorary Secretary General, Europea Nostra, 1983-90; President, Association for Scottish Literary Studies, 1982-83. Publications: The Advancing Day, 1940; Predicament, 1942; No Crown for Laughter, 1943; The Enemies of Love: Poems, 1941-45, 1946; Selected Poems, 1947; At the Wood's Edge, 1950; Ode for St Andrew's Night and Other Poems, 1951; The Exiled Heart: Poems, 1941-56, 1957; Snow Warning and Other Poems, 1962; One Later Day and Other Poems, 1964; This Business of Living, 1971; Comings and Goings, 1971; Selected Poems, 1942-72, 1973; The Run from Life: More Poems, 1942-72, 1975; Walking Without an Overcoat: Poems, 1972-76, 1977; Collected Poems, 2 volumes, 1979, 1993; A Net to Catch the Wind and Other Poems, 1981; The French Mosquitoe's Woman and Other Diversions, 1985; Requiem for a Sexual Athlete and Other Poems and Diversions, 1988; The Scottish Dog (with Joyce Lindsay), 1989; The Theatre and Opera Lover's Quotation Book (with Joyce Lindsay), 1993; News of the World: Last Poems, 1995; Spaeking likenesses, 1997. Other: Editions of poetry, plays, etc. Honours: Commander of the Order of the British Empire, 1979; DLitt, University of Glasgow, 1982; Address: 7 Milton Hill, Milton, Dumbarton, Dumbartonshire, GB2 2TS, Scotland.

LINE David. See: DAVIDSON Lionel.

LINEHAN Fergus Patrick, b. 4 June 1934, Kuala Lumpur, Malaysia. Journalist; Novelist; Playwright. m. Rosaleen McMenamin, 26 Aug 1960, 3 sons, 1 daughter. Education: BA, University College, Dublin. Appointments: Film Critic, Irish Times; Arts Editor, Irish Times. Publications: Under the Durian Tree (novel); The Safest

Place (novel); Irelande. Contributions to: Irish Times. Literary Agent: Martin Pick. Address: c/o Charles Pick Consultancy, 3 Bryanston Place, London W1H 7FN, England.

LINETT Deena, b. 30 Aug 1938, Boston, Massachusetts, USA. Professor of English; Writer. 2 sons, 1 daughter. Education: EdD, Rutgers University, 1982. Appointment: Professor of English, Montclair State University. Publications: On Common Ground, 1983; The Translator's Wife, 1986; Visit, 1990. Contributions to: Journals. Honours: Yaddo Fellowships, 1981, 1985; PEN-Syndicated Fiction Project, 1990. Memberships: Modern Language Association; National Council of Teachers of English; PEN; Poets and Writers. Address: c/o Department of English, Montclair State University, Upper Montclair, NJ 07043, USA.

LINGARD Joan Amelia, b. 8 Apr 1932, Edinburgh, Scotland. Author. 3 daughters. Education: General Teaching Diploma, Moray House Training College, Edinburgh. Publications: Children's Books: The Twelfth Day of July, 1970; Frying as Usual, 1971; Across the Barricades, 1972; Into Exile, 1973; The Clearance, 1974; A Proper Place, 1975; The Resettling, 1975; Hostages to Fortune, 1976; The Pilgrimage, 1976; The Reunion, 1977; The Gooseberry, 1978; The File on Fraulein Berg, 1980; Strangers in the House, 1981; The Winter Visitor, 1983; The Freedom Machine, 1986; The Guilty Party, 1987; Rags and Riches, 1988; Tug of War, 1989; Glad Rags, 1990; Between Two Worlds, 1991; Hands Off Our School!, 1992; Night Fires, 1993; Dark Shadows, 1998; A Secret Place, 1998; Tom and the Tree House, 1998. Novels: Liam's Daughter, 1963; The Prevailing Wind, 1964; The Tide Comes In, 1966; The Headmaster, 1967; A Sort of Freedom, 1968; The Lord on Our Side, 1970; The Second Flowering of Emily Mountjoy, 1979; Greenyards, 1981; Sisters by Rite, 1984; Reasonable Doubts, 1986; The Women's House, 1989; After Colette, 1993; Lizzie's Leaving, 1995; Dreams of Love and Modest Glory, 1995; Dark Shadows, 1998; A Secret Place, 1998; Tom and the Tree House, 1998. Honours: Scottish Arts Council Bursary, 1967-68; Preis der Leseratten ZDF, Germany, 1986; Buxtehuder Bulle, Germany, 1987; Scottish Arts Council Award, 1994; MBE, 1998. Memberships: Society of Authors in Scotland, chairman, 1982-86; Scottish PEN; Director, Edinburgh Book Festival. Address: David Higham Associates Ltd, 5-8 Lower John Street, Golden Square, London W1R 4HA, England.

LINGEMAN Richard (Roberts), b. 2 Jan 1931, Crawfordsville, Indiana, USA. Editor; Writer. m. Anthea Judy Nicholson, 3 Apr 1965, 1 daughter. Education: BA, Haverford College, 1953; Postgraduate Studies, Yale Law School, 1956-58, Columbia University Graduate School, 1958-60. Appointments: Executive Editor, Monocle magazine, 1960-69; The Nation, 1978-; Associate Editor, Columnist, The New York Times Book Review, 1969-78. Publications: Drugs from A to Z, 1969; Don't You Know There's a War On?, 1971; Small Town America, 1980; Theodore Dreiser: At the Gates of the City, 1871-1907, 1986; Theodore Dreiser: An American Journey, 1908-1945, 1990. Honour: Chicago Sun-Times Book of the Year Award, 1990. Memberships: Authors Guild; National Book Critics Circle; New York Historical Society; PEN; Phi Beta Kappa; Society of American Historians. Address: c/o The Nation, 72 Fifth Avenue, New York, NY 10011, USA.

LINKLATER Magnus (Duncan), b. 21 Feb 1942, Orkney, Scotland. Journalist; Broadcaster; Writer. m. Veronica Lyle, 1967, 2 sons, 1 daughter. Education: University of Freiburg; Sorbonne, University of Paris; BA, 2nd Class Honours, Modern Languages, Trinity Hall, Cambridge. Appointments: Reporter, Daily Express, Manchester, 1965-66; London Evening Standard, 1966-67; Editorial positions, Evening Standard, 1967-69; Sunday Times, 1969-72, 1975-83, Sunday Times Colour Magazine, 1972-75; Managing Editor, News, The Observer, 1983-86; Editor, London Daily News, 1987; The Scotsman, 1988-94; Columnist, The Times, 1994-; Broadcaster, Radio Scotland, 1994-; Chairman, Scottish

Arts Council, 1996-. Publications: Hoax: The Inside Story of the Howard Hughes/Clifford Irving Affair (with Stephen Fay and Lewis Chester), 1972; Jeremy Thorpe: A Secret Life (with Lewis Chester and David May), 1979; Massacre: The Story of Glencoe, 1982; The Falklands War (with others), 1982; The Fourth Reich: Klaus Barbie and the Neo-Fascist Connection (with Isabel Hilton and Neal Ascherson), 1984; Not With Honour: Inside Story of the Westland Scandal (with David Leigh), 1986; For King and Conscience: The Life of John Graham of Claverhouse, Viscount Dundee (with Christian Hesketh), 1989; Anatomy of Scotland (co-editor), 1992; Highland Wilderness (with Colin Prior), 1993; People in a Landscape, 1997. Honours: Honorary DArts, Napier University, 1994; Honorary LLD, University of Aberdeen, 1997. Address: 5 Drummond Place, Edinburgh, EH3 6PH, Scotland.

LINKLETTER Art(hur Gordon), b. 17 July 1912, Moose Jaw, Saskatchewan, Canada. Radio and Television Broadcaster; Businessman; Writer. m. Lois Foerster, 25 Nov 1935, 2 sons, 3 daughters. Education: AB, San Diego State College, 1934. Appointments: Former Host and Writer, People Are Funny, NBC Radio and TV, Art Linkletter's House Party, CBS Radio and TV; President, Linkletter Productions; Chairman of the Board, Linkletter Enterprises; Owner, Art Linkletter Oil Enterprises. Publications: People Are Funny, 1953; Kids Say the Darndest Things, 1957; The Secret World of Kids, 1959; Confessions of a Happy Man, 1961; Kids Still Say the Darndest Things, 1961; A Child's Garden of Misinformation, 1965; I Wish I'd Said That, 1968; Linkletter Down Under, 1969; Oops, 1969; Drugs at My Door Step, 1973; Women Are My Favorite People, 1974; How to be a Super Salesman, 1974; Yes, You Can!, 1979; I Didn't Do It Alone, 1979; Public Speaking for Private People, 1980; Linkletter on Dynamic Selling, 1982; Old Age is Not for Sissies, 1988. Honours: Many awards. Address: 8484 Wilshire Boulevard, Suite 205, Beverly Hills, CA 90211, USA.

LINNEY Romulus, b. 21 Sept 1930, Philadelphia, Pennsylvania, USA. Dramatist; Writer. m. (1) Ann Leggett Sims, 14 Apr 1963, div 1966, 1 daughter, (2) Jane Andrews, 14 Sept 1967, 1 daughter. Education: AB, Oberlin College, 1953; MFA, Yale School of Drama, 1958; New School for Social Research, New York City, 1960. Appointments: Visiting Associate Professor of Dramatic Arts, University of North Carolina at Chapel Hill, 1961; Director of Fine Arts, North Carolina State College, Raleigh, 1962-64; Faculty, Manhattan School of Music, New York City, 1964-72; Visiting Professor, Columbia University, 1972-74, Connecticut College, 1979, University of Pennsylvania, 1979-86, Princeton University, 1982-85. Publications: Plays: The Sorrows of Frederick, 1966; Democracy and Esther, 1973; The Love Suicide at Schofield Barracks, 1973; Holy Ghosts, 1977; Old Man Joseph and His Family, 1978; El Hermano, 1981; The Captivity of Pixie Shedman, 1981; Childe Byron, 1981; F.M., 1984; The Death of King Philip, 1984; Sand Mountain, 1985; A Woman Without a Name, 1986; Pops, 1987; Heathen Valley, 1990; Three Poets, 1990; Unchanging Love, 1990; Juliet--Yancey--April Snow, 1990; Spain, 1993. Novels: Heathen Valley, 1962; Slowly, by Thy Hand Unfurled, 1965; Jesus Tales, 1980. Honours: National Endowment for the Arts Grant, 1974; Guggenheim Fellowship, 1980; Obie Awards, 1980, 1990; Mishma Prize, 1981; American Academy and Institute of Arts and Letters Award, 1984; Rockefeller Foundation Fellowship, 1986. Memberships: Actor's Equity Association; Authors Guild; Authors League of America; Directors Guild; PEN. Address: 35 Claremont Avenue, 9N, New York, NY 10027, USA.

LINSCOTT Gillian, b. 27 Sept 1944, Windsor, England. Journalist; Writer. m. Tony Geraghty, 18 June 1988. Education: Somerville College, Oxford, 1963-66; Honours Degree, English Language and Literature, Oxford University, 1966. Publications: A Healthy Body, 1984; Murder Makes Tracks, 1985; Knightfall, 1986; A Whiff of Sulphur, 1987; Unknown Hand, 1988; Murder, I Presume, 1990; Sister Beneath the Sheet, 1991; Hanging on the Wire, 1992; Stage Fright, 1993; Widow's Peak,

1994; Crown Witness, 1995; Dead Man's Music, 1996; Dance on Blood, 1998; Absent Friends, 1999. Memberships: Society of Authors; Crime Writers Association; Mystery Writers of America. Address: Wood View, Hope Under Dinmore, Leominster, Herefordshire HR6 0PP, England.

LINTON Martin, b. 11 Aug 1944, Stockholm, Sweden. 2 daughters. Education: MA, PPE, Christ's Hospital, Universite de Lyon, Pembroke College, Oxford, England, 1944. Appointments: Journalist, Daily Mail, 1966-71, The Financial Times, 1971; Labour Weekly, 1971-79; The Daily Star, 1980-81; The Guardian, 1981-97; MP, elected to London constituency of Battersea, 1997; Member, House of Commons Home Affairs Committee. Publications: Get Me Out of Here, 1980; The Swedish Road to Socialism, 1984; Labour Can Still Win, 1988; The Guardian Guide to the House of Commons, 1992; What's Wrong With First-Past-The-Post?, 1993; Money and Votes, 1994; Was It The Sun Wot Won It, 1995; The Guardian Election Guide, 1997; Making Votes Count, 1998. Memberships: Chairman, Battersea Arts Centre; Chairman, Governors of Somerset Primary School. Address: House of Commons, London SW1A 0AA, England.

LIOGARIS Basil, b. 9 Jan 1933, Athens, Greece. Author. Education: Graduate, Athens Dramatic School; Certified Accountant. Appointments: Theatre Actor, 1960-67; Accountant, several Greek manufacturing companies, 1967-93. Publications: Novels: Charocopou neighbourhood, 1985, improved re-edition; The mother of summer, 1987, 3 editions; A usual event, 1990; What is going to happen with mother eventually?, 1994; The great dilemma, 1997; Looking for the lost cat, forthcoming. Contributions to: Eolika Letters; Ellispodes. Honours: Peace and Friendship Award for novel, 1985; Greek Author's Society Award for novel, 1990, 1994. Membership: Greek Author's Society. Address: Evagelistrias 39, 17671 Kallithea, Athens, Greece.

LIOTTA P H, b. 16 Sept 1956, Burlington, Vermont, USA. Poet; Essayist; Novelist; Professor. Education: MFA, Writing, Cornell University, 1987; PhD, Salve Regina, 2000. Appointment: Professor of National Security Affairs, Newport, RI, USA. Publications: The Ruins of Athens: A Balkan Memoir, 1999; The Wreckage Reconsidered: Five Oxymorons from Balkan Deconstruction, 1999; Diamond's Compass, a novel, 1993; Rules of Engagement: Poems 1974-1991, 1991; Learning to Fly: A Season with the Peregrine Falcon, 1989. Contributions to: Hudson Review; New England Review; Poetry; Yankee; Antioch Review; The Prose Poem: An International Journal. Honours: Daniel Varoujan Prize, 1997; Pushcart Prize, 1998; International Quarterly Crossing Boundaries Award, 1995; NEA Fellow, 1993-95. Literary Agent: Jennifer Lyons. Address: 686 Cushing Road, Newport, Rhode Island 02841-1207, USA.

LIPMAN Elinor, b. 16 Oct 1950, Lowell, Massachusetts, USA. Writer. m. Robert M Austin, 29 July 1975, 1 son. Education: AB, Simmons College, Boston, 1972. Appointments: Lecturer, Smith College, 1997-. Publications: Into Love and Out Again (stories), 1987; Then She Found Me, 1990; The Way Men Act, 1992; Isabel's Bed, 1995; The Inn at Lake Devine (novel), forthcoming. Contributions to: Yankee; Playgirl; Ascent; Ladies Home Journal; Cosmopolitan; Self; New England; Living; Redstart; Wigwag. Honours: Distinguished Story Citations, Best American Short Stories, 1984, 1985. Membership: Author's Guild. Address: 67 Winterberry Lane, Northampton, MA 01060, USA.

LIPSET Seymour Martin, b. 18 Mar 1922, New York, New York, USA. Sociologist; Political Scientist; Professor; Writer; Editor. m. (1) Elsie Braun, 26 Dec 1944, dec Feb 1987, 2 sons, 1 daughter, (2) Sydnee Guyer, 29 July 1990. Education: BS, City College of New York, 1943; PhD, Columbia University, 1949. Appointments: Lecturer, University of Toronto, 1946-48; Assistant Professor, 1948-50, Professor of Sociology, 1956-66, Director, Institute of International Studies, 1962-66, University of

California at Berkeley; Henry Ford Visiting Research Professor, Yale University, 1960-61; Visiting Professor of Social Relations and Government, 1965-66, Professor of Government and Sociology, 1966-75, Harvard University; Paley Lecturer, Hebrew University, 1973; Senior Fellow, Hoover Institution, 1975-, Professor of Political Science and Sociology, 1975-92, Caroline S G Munro Professor, 1981-92, Stanford University; Co-Editor, Public Opinion magazine, 1977-89, International Journal of Public Opinion Research, 1989-; Fulbright 40th Anniversary Distinguished Lecturer, 1987; Visiting Scholar, Russell Sage Foundation, 1988-89; Hazel Professor of Public Policy, George Mason University, 1990-. Publications: Agrarian Socialism, 1950; Union democracy (with others), 1956; Social Mobility in Industrial Society (with R Bendix), 1959, new edition, 1991; Political Man, 1960, new edition, 1981; The First New Nation, 1963, new edition, 1979; Revolution and Counter Revolution, 1968, new edition, 1988; The Politics of Unreason (with Earl Raab), 1970, new edition, 1978; Rebellion in the University, 1972; Academics and the 1972 Election (with Everett Ladd), 1973; Professors, Unions and American Higher Education, 1973; The Divided Academy, 1975; Education and Politics at Harvard (with David Riesman), 1975; Dialogues on American Politics (with I L Horowitz), 1978; The Confidence Gap (with William Schneider), 1983, new edition, 1987; Consensus and Confilct, 1987; Continental Divide: The Institutions and Values of the United States and Canada, 1990; The Educational Background of American Jews, 1994; Jews and the New American Scene (with Earl Raab), 1995; American exceptionalism: A Double-Edged Sword, 1996. Editor or Co-Editor: Failure of a Dream?: Essays in the History of American Socialism, 1974, revised edition, 1984; Democracy in Developing Countries, 3 volumes, 1988-89; Politics in Developing Countries, 1990, 1995; American Pluralism and the Jewish Community, 1990; The Encyclopedia of Democracy, 4 volumes, 1995. Contributions to: Many scholarly books and journals. Honours: 125th Anniversary Alumni Medal, City College of New York, 1963; Gunnar Myrdal Prize, 1970; Tod Harris Medal, 1971; Center for Advanced Study in Behavioral Sciences Fellow, 1971-72; M B Rawson Award, 1986; Leon Epstein Prize, American Political Science Association, 1989; Marshall Sklare Award, 1993; Woodrow Wilson Center for International Scholars Fellow, 1995-96; Various honorary doctorates. Memberships: American Academy of Arts and Sciences; American Philosophical Society; American Political Science Association, president, 1981-82; American Sociological Association, president, 1992-93; International Political Science Association; International Sociological Association; National Academy of Sciences; Sociological Research Association, president, 1985; World Association of Public Opinion Research, president, 1984-86. Address: c/o Hoover Institution, Stanford University, Stanford, CA 94305, USA.

LIPSEY David Lawrence, b. 21 Apr 1948, Cheltenham, Gloucestershire, England. Journalist; Writer. m. Margaret Robson, 1982, 1 daughter. Education: Magdalen College, Oxford. Appointments: Research Assistant, General and Municipal Workers' Union, 1970-72; Special Advisor to Anthony Crossland, Member of Parliament, 1972-77; Staff, Prime Minister, 1977-79; Journalist, 1979-80, Editor, 1986-88, New Society; Political Staff, 1980-82, Economics Editor, 1982-86, The Sunday Times; Co-Founder and Deputy Editor, The Sunday Correspondent, 1988-90; Associate Editor, The Times, 1990-92; Journalist, 1992-, Political Editor, 1994-, The Economist. Publications: Labour and Land, 1972; The Socialist Agenda: Crosland's Legacy (editor with Dick Leonard), 1981; Making Government Work, 1982; The Name of the Rose, 1992. Membership: Fabian Society, chairman, 1981-82. Address: 44 Drakefield Road, London SW17 8RP, England.

LIS Ketty Alejandrina de, b. 15 Oct 1946, Sante Fe, Argentina. Poet; Writer. m. Dr Abraham Lis, 13 Aug 1971. Education: Advanced Studies in Psychology, National University, Rosario. Publications: Poetry: Imaginaciones, 1987; Cartas para Adriana, 1992; Piedra Filosofal, 1997. Other: Un Genio llamado Wolfgang Amadeus Mozart, 1991; Quiénes leen poesia hoy?, 1994; Alejandra

Pizarnik, una muneca de huesos de pájaro, 1994; Juan L Ortiz, Localismo y Universalidad, 1995; Poetry: Piedra Filosofal, 1997; Poetry and essays in internet magazines. Contributions to: Various publications. Honours: Several literary awards. Memberships: Argentine Mozarteum, executive committee, Rosario branch; Argentine Writers Society. Address: Italia 873, 2000 Rosario, Argentina.

LIST Anneliese, (Alice Pervin), b. 6 Jan 1922, Heroldsberg, Germany. Operetta-Soubrette; Author; Poet. m. Huldreich List, 28 Feb 1947, dec. Education: Opera-House Nuremberg Ballet School, 1926-38; Ballet School, Munich, 1939; State Examination as Dancer. Appointments: Dancer, Municipal Theatre Guben; Dance Soubrette, Municipal Theatre of Landsberg/Warthe, Thorn and Elbing; Clerk, US European Exchange System; Secretary, Refugee and Migration Section, Nuremberg Field Office, American Consulate General US Embassy's Escapee Programme; Clerk in Charge at Foreign Office, City of Nuremberg. Publications: The Tree, 1973; The Work was in Vain, 1974; Miracles Happen Always Again, 1974; Over and Over Again I Saw the Cross, 1975; What I'll Never Be Able to Forget in All My Life, 1975; My Long Way From the War Until Today, 1975; Not Before Today I Understood Why Mother Left Me, 1975; How I Earned My First Money, 1977; The First Dance, 1977; The Little Witch, 1977; The Luck Behind the Mountains, 1978; A Fairy Tale, 1986; Ten Promises, 1987; First Love, 1987; Realization, 1988; Prayer in the Sunshine and Our Lumpi, 1989; Dedicated to My Little Cat, 1990; Jubilate, 1991; The Heroine, 1992; The Rainbow and the Window, 1992; Thank You, 1993; The Fireplace, 1993; The Revenge is Mine Says Our Lord, 1994; Just a Poor Devil, 1994; Unbelievable Stories, 1995. Contributions to: Stories, poems and articles in various publications including: Main-Echo; Frau Aktuell; 7 Tage; Welt am Sonnabend; True Stories; Zenit. Honours: 2nd Prize, Contest for Best Story in True Stories magazine, 1975; Cultural Doctorate in Literature, Certificate of Merit, World Literary Academy; Woman of the Year, IBC, 1990; International Order of Merit, IBC, 1991; Most Admired Woman of the Decade, 1992; 20th Century Award for Achievement, IBC, 1993; 20th Millennium Medal of Honour, 20th Millennium Hall of Fame, 1997. Memberships: World Literary Academy; IBA; Schoenbuch-Verlag, present editor. Address: Ritter-von-Schuh-Platz 15, Nuremberg 90459, Germany.

LISTER Raymond George, b. 28 Mar 1919, Cambridge, England. Writer. Appointments: Managing Director and Editor, Golden Head Press, Cambridge, 1952-72; Senior Research Fellow, 1975-85, Fellow, 1985-86, Fellow Emeritus, 1986-, Wolfson College, Cambridge. Publications: The British Miniature, 1951; Silhouettes, 1953; Thomas Gosse, 1953; The Muscovite Peacock: A Study of the Art of Léon Bakst, 1954; Decorated Porcelains of Simon Lissim, 1955; Decorative Wrought Ironwork in Great Britain, 1957; The Loyal Blacksmith, 1957; Decorative Cast Ironwork in Great Britain, 1960; The Craftsman Engineer, 1960; Edward Calvert, 1962; Great Craftsmen, 1962; The Miniature Defined, 1963; Beulah to Byzantium, 1965; How to Identify Old Maps and Globes, 1965; Victorian Narrative Paintings, 1966; The Craftsman in Metal, 1966; Great Works of Craftmanship, 1967; William Blake, 1968; Samuel Palmer and His Etchings, 1969; Hammer and Hand: An Essay on the Ironwork of Cambridge, 1969; British Romantic Art, 1973; Samuel Palmer, 1974; The Letters of Samuel Palmer (editor), 2 volumes, 1974; Infernal Methods: A Study of William Blake's Art Techniques, 1975; Apollo's Bird, 1975; For Love of Leda, 1977; Great Images of British Printmaking, 1978; Samuel Palmer: A Vision Recaptured, 1978; Samuel Palmer in Palmer Country, 1980; George Richmond, 1981; Bergomask, 1982; There Was a Star Danced, 1983; Prints and Printmaking, 1984; Samuel Palmer and the Ancients, 1984; The Paintings of Samuel Palmer, 1985; The Paintings of William Blake, 1986; Catalogue Raisonné of the Works of Samuel Palmer, 1988; British Romantic Painting, 1989; A M St Léon's Stenochoreography (translator), 1992; With My Own Wings (memoirs), 1994. Address: 9 Sylvester Road, Cambridge CB3 9AF, England.

LISTER Richard Percival, b. 23 Nov 1914, Nottingham, England. Author; Poet; Painter. m. Ione Mary Wynniatt-Husey, 24 June 1985. Education: BSc, Manchester University. Publications: Novels: The Way Backwards, 1950; The Oyster and the Torpedo, 1951; Rebecca Redfern, 1953; The Rhyme and the Reason, 1963; The Questing Beast, 1965; One Short Summer, 1974. Poetry: The Idle Demon, 1958; The Albatross, 1986. Travel: A Journey in Lapland, 1965; Turkey Observed, 1967; Glimpses of a Planet, 1997. Biography: The Secret History of Genghis Khan, 1969; Marco Polo's Travels, 1976; The Travels of Herodotus, 1979. Short Stories: Nine Legends, 1991; Two Northern Stories, 1996. Contributions to: Punch; New Yorker; Atlantic Monthly. Honour: Royal Society of Literature, fellow, 1970. Membership: International PEN. Address: Flat H, 81 Ledbury Road, London W11 2AG, England.

LITOBARSKI Stuart Laurence Henry, b. 29 Mar 1952, Lichfield, Staffordshire, England. Consulting Chartered Engineer. m. Rachel Mary Hudson, 5 May 1984, 2 sons. Education: BSc, EE, 1982; MSc, Acoustic, 1985; BBC C Cert, 1984; CEng, 1996; European Engineer, 1996. Appointments: Research Associate, University of Bristol; Consulting Chartered Engineer, Acoustical, Henry T Wright Associates, 1992-; Research Fellow, Curtin University, Western Australia, 1989-90; Systems Engineer, Baesema, Bristol, 1988-89; Research Officer, Bath University, 1985-89; Recording Engineer, BBC TV, London, 1982-84. Publications: Series of 11 technical articles published by Home & Studio Recording; The Mix; Studio Sound mags, 1993-95; New Developments in Cad Acoustical Design of Recording Control Rooms, 1997. Contributions to: Electronic Letters; Freelance Writer, The Mix Magazine; Covering technical reviews of audio products, Total Marketing Circles, IEE Management Journal, 1997. Membership: Bath Royal Literary and Scientific Institute. Literary Agent: Henry T Wright Assocs. Address: PO Box 489, Bristol BS99 7AP, England.

LITOWINSKY Olga Jean, b. 9 Feb 1936, Newark, New Jersey, USA. Writer; Editor. Education: BS, Honours, History, Columbia University, 1965. Publications: The High Voyage, 1977; The New York Kids Book, 1978; Writing and Publishing Books for Children in the 1990s, 1992. Contributions to: Atlas; Publishers Weekly; The Writer; Writers' Digest; Society of Children's Book Writers and Illustrators Bulletin. Honour: Christopher Award, 1979. Membership: Society of Children's Book Writers and Illustrators. Address: c/o Simon and Schuster, 12 30 Sixth Avenue, New York, NY 10023, USA.

LITTELL Robert, b. 1935, USA. Writer. Publications: If Israel Lost the War (with Richard Z Cheznoff and Edward Klein), 1969; The Czech Black Book, 1969; The Defection of A J Lewinter, 1973; Sweet Reason, 1974; The October Circle, 1976; Mother Russia, 1978; The Debriefing, 1979; The Amateur, 1981; The Sisters, 1985; The Revolutionist; The Visiting Professor, 1994. Address: c/o Simon and Schuster, 1230 Sixth Avenue, New York, NY 10020, USA.

LITTLE Charles Eugene, b. 1 Mar 1931, Los Angeles, California, USA. Writer. m. Ila Dawson. Education: BA, Distinction, Creative Writing, Wesleyan University, 1955. Appointments: Editorial Director, Open Space Action Magazine, 1968-69; Editor-in-Chief, American Land Forum, 1980-86; Books Editor, Wilderness Magazine, 1987-97; Consulting Editor, Johns Hopkins University Press, 1989-. Publications: Challenge of the Land, 1969; Space for Survival (with J G Mitchell), 1971; A Town is Saved ... (with photos by M Mort), 1973; The American Cropland Crisis (with W Fletcher), 1980; Green Fields Forever, 1987; Louis Bromfield at Malabar (editor), 1988; Greenways for America, 1990; Hope for the Land, 1992; Discover America: The Smithsonian Book of the National Parks, 1995; The Dying of the Trees, 1995. Contributions to: Magazines and journals. Address: 33 Calle del Norte, Placitas, NM 87043, USA.

LITTLE Geraldine Clinton, b. 20 Sept 1925, Portstewart, Ireland. Poet; Writer. m. Robert Knox Little, 26 Sept 1953, 3 sons. Education: BA, Goddard College, 1971; MA, Trenton State College, 1976. Appointment: Adjunct Professor of English. Publications: Hakugai: Poem from a Concentration Camp, 1983; Seasons in Space, 1983; A Well-Tuned Harp, 1988; Beyond the Boxwood Comb, 1988; Heloise and Abelard: A Verse Play, 1989; Star-Mapped, 1989. Contributions to: Journals. Honours: Associated Writing Program Anniversary Award, 1986; Pablo Neruda Award, 1989; Grants. Memberships: Haiku Society of America; PEN; Poetry Society of America. Address: 1200 Campus Drive, Mt Holly, NJ 08060, USA.

LITTLE (Flora) Jean, b. 2 Jan 1932, T'ai-nan, Formosa. Children's Writer. Education: BA, Victoria College, University of Toronto, 1955. Publications: Mine for Keeps, 1962; Home From Far, 1965; Spring Begins in March, 1966; When the Pie was Opened, 1968; Take Wing, 1968; One to Grow On, 1969; Look Through My Window, 1970; Kate, 1971; From Anna, 1972; Stand In the Wind, 1975; Listen for the Singing, 1977; Mama's Going to Buy You a Mockingbird, 1984; Lost and Found, 1985; Different Dragons, 1986; Hey, World, Here I Am, 1986; Little By Little, 1987; Stars Came Out Within, 1990; Jess was the Brave One, 1991; Revenge of the Small Small, 1992. Honours: Little, Brown Canadian Children's Book Award, 1961; Vicky Metcalf Award, 1974; Canada Council Children's Book Award, 1977; Canadian Library Association Children's Book of the Year Award, 1984; Ruth Schwartz Award, 1984; Boston Globe Horn Book Honor Book, 1988; Shortlisted, Governor General's Children's Literature Award, 1989. Memberships: Writers' Union of Canada; Canadian Society for Children's Authors, Illustrators and Performers; Canadian Authors' Association; PEN; IBBY. Address: 198 Glasgow North, Guelph, Ontario N1H 4X2, Canada.

LITVINOFF Emanuel, b. 30 June 1915, London, England. Writer; Dramatist. Appointments: Director, Contemporary Jewish Library, London, 1958-88; Founder, Jews in Eastern Europe, journal, London. Publications: Conscripts: A Symphonic Declaration, 1941; The Untried Soldier, 1942; A Crown for Cain, 1948; The Lost Europeans, 1959; The Man Next Door, 1968; Journey Through a Small Planet, 1972; Notes for a Survivor, 1973; A Death Out of Season, 1974; Soviet Anti-Semitism: The Paris Trial (editor), 1974; Blood on the Snow, 1975; The Face of Terror, 1978; The Penguin Book of Jewish Short Stories (editor), 1979; Falls the Shadow, 1983. Address: c/o David Higham Associates, 5-8 Lower John Street, London W1R 4HA, England.

LIVAS Harriet (Haris) Parker, b. 1 Apr 1936, USA. Journalist; Author; Professor. m. John Livas, 18 June 1962, dec 1976, 3 sons, 3 daughters. Education: BS, Syracuse University, 1958; MLitt, University of Pittsburgh, 1960; PhD, Pacific Western University, 1990. Appointments: English Department, University of Maryland Overseas Faculty, 1966-78; Foreign Correspondent, 1978-82; Director, Feature Service, Athens News Agency, Greece, 1982-88; Director, Hellenic Features International, Ministry of the National Economy, Greece, 1988-90; Humberside Council, UK, 1991; Beverley College, 1991-94; University of Hull, 1993-95; University of Lincolnshire and Humberside, 1995-96. Publication: Contemporary Greek Artists, 1992. Contributions to: Periodicals; Book Reviewer, International PEN. Address: 19 Thurlow Avenue, Beverley HU17 7QJ, England.

LIVELY Penelope Margaret, b. 17 Mar 1933, Cairo, Egypt. Writer. m. 27 June 1957, 1 son, 1 daughter. Education: Honours Degree, Modern History, Oxford University, England. Publications: Fiction: The Road to Lichfield, 1977; Nothing Missing But the Samovar, and Other Stories, 1978; Treasures of Time, 1979; Judgement Day, 1980; Next to Nature, Art, 1982; Perfect Happiness, 1983; Corruption and Other Stories, 1984; According to Mark, 1984; Moon Tiger, 1986; Pack of Cards: Stories 1978-86, 1987; Passing On, 1989; City of the Mind, 1991; Cleopatra's Sister, 1993. Non-Fiction:

The Presence of the Past: An Introduction to Landscape History, 1976. Children's Books: Astercote, 1970; The Whispering Knights, 1971; The Driftway, 1972; Going Back, 1973; The Ghost of Thomas Kempe, 1974; Boy Without a Name, 1975; Fanny's Sister, 1976; The Stained Glass Window, 1976; A Stitch in Time, 1976; Fanny and the Monsters, 1978; The Voyage of QV66, 1978; Fanny and the Battle of Potter's Piece, 1980; The Revenge of Samuel Stokes, 1981; Uninvited Ghosts and Other Stories, 1984; Dragon Trouble, Debbie and the Little Devil, 1984; A House Inside Out, 1987; Heat Wave, 1996; Beyond the Blue Mountains: Stories, 1997; Spiderweb, 1998. Contributions to: Numerous journals and magazines. Honours: Officer of the Order of the British Empire, 1989; Several literary awards. Address: c/o David Higham Associates, 5-8 Lower John Street, Golden Square, London W1R 4HA, England.

LIVERSAGE Toni, b. 31 Jan 1935, Hellerup, Denmark. Writer. m. 19 May 1962, 1 son, 1 daughter. Education: MA, Slavonic Languages, University of Copenhagen, 1965. Publications: 14 books on womens' history and social movements. Contributions to: Various newspapers and magazines. Honour: Thit Jensen Award for Women's Literature, 1989. Membership: Danish Writers Union. Address: Morlenesvej 26, 2840 Holte, Denmark.

LIVERSIDGE (Henry) Douglas, b. 12 Mar 1913, Swinton, Yorkshire, England. Journalist; Author. m. Cosmina Pistola, 25 Sept 1954, 1 daughter. Publications: White Horizon, 1951; The Last Continent, 1958; The Third Front, 1960; The Whale Killers, 1963; Saint Francis of Assisi, 1968; Peter the Great, 1968; Lenin, 1969; Joseph Stalin, 1969; Saint Ignatius of Loyola, 1970; The White World, 1972; Queen Elizabeth II, 1974; Prince Charles, 1975; Prince Phillip, 1976; Queen Elizabeth the Queen Mother, 1977; The Mountbattens, 1978. Contributions to: Numerous journals and newspapers. Address: 56 Love Lane, Pinner, Middlesex HA5 3EX, England.

LIVESEY Anthony John, b. 11 Jan 1964, Burnley, Lancashire, England. Journalist. m. Barbara Livesey, 3 Apr 1995, 1 son, 1 daughter. Appointments: Editor, Sunday Sport, London, 1993-95; Editor-in-Chief, 1995-98, Managing Director, 1998-, Sport Newspapers. Publication: Booze, Bireds, Orgies and Aliens, 1998. Address: Sport Newspapers, 19 Great Ancoats Street, Manchester M60 4BT, England.

LIVINGS Henry, b. 20 Sept 1929, Prestwich, Lancashire, England. Writer; Playwright. Education: Liverpool University, 1945-47. Publications: Stop it Whoever You Are, 1961; Nil Caborundum, 1963; Kelly's Eye and Other Plays, 1965; Eh?, 1965; The Little Mrs Foster Show, 1967; Good Grief!, 1968; Honour and Offer, 1969; The Ffinest Ffamily in the Land, 1970; Pongo Plays 1-6, 1971; The Jockey Drives Late Nights, 1972; Six More Pongo Plays, 1974; Jonah, 1975; That the Medals and the Baton Be Put in View: The Story of a Village Band 1875-1975, 1975; Cinderella, 1976; Pennine Tales, 1983; Flying Eggs and Things: More Pennine Tales, 1986; The Rough Side of the Boards, 1994. Address: 49 Grains Road, Delph, Oldham OL3 5DS, England.

LLEWELLYN Roderic Victor, b. 9 Oct 1947, Crickhowell, Wales. Gardening Journalist; Author; Lecturer; Presenter. m. Tatiana Soskin, 11 July 1981, 3 daughters. Education: Shrewsbury, 1961-66; Aix-en-Provence University, 1967-68; Merrist Wood Agricultural College, 1976-77. Appointments: Gardening Correspondent, Mail on Sunday, 1987-; Own series, Roddy Llewellyn's Indoor Gardens, 1997-; Regular gardening presenter, This Morning, 1998-. Publications: Town Gardens, 1981; Beautiful Backyards, 1985; Water Gardens - The Connoisseur's Choice, 1987; Elegance and Eccentricity, 1989; Roddy Llewellyn's Gardening Year, 1997; others. Contributions to: Country Life; Gardens Illustrated; Homes and Gardens. Literary Agent: Limelight Management. Address: 33 Newman Street, London W1P 3PD, England.

LLEWELLYN Sam, b. 2 Aug 1948, Isles of Scilly. Author. m. Karen Wallace, 15 Feb 1975, 2 sons. Education: St Catherine's College, Oxford; BA, Honours, Oxford University. Appointments: Editor, Picador, 1973-76; Senior Editor, McClelland and Stewart, 1976-79; President, Publisher, Arch Books, 1982-; Captain, SY Lucille, 1993-. Publications: Hell Bay, 1980; The Worst Journey in the Midlands, 1983; Dead Reckoning, 1987; Blood Orange, 1988; Death Roll, 1989; Pig in the Middle, 1989; Deadeye, 1990; Blood Knot, 1991; Riptide, 1992; Clawhammer, 1993; Maelstrom, 1994; The Rope School, 1994; The Magic Boathouse, 1994; The Iron Hotel, 1996; Storm Force from Navarone, 1996; The Polecat Cafe, 1998; The Shadow in the Sands, 1998; Thunderbolt from Navarone, 1998. Contributions to: Periodicals. Memberships: Society of Authors; CPRE; The Academy. Literary Agent: Curtis Brown. Address: c/o Curtis Brown, 28-29 Haymarket, London SW1Y 4SP, England.

LLOYD Geoffrey (Ernest Richard) (Sir), b. 25 Jan 1933, London, England. Professor of Ancient Philosophy and Science; Writer. m. Janet Elizabeth Lloyd, 1956, 3 sons. Education: BA, 1954, MA, 1958, PhD, 1958, King's College, Cambridge. Appointments: Fellow, 1957, Senior Tutor, 1969-73, King's College, Cambridge; Assistant Lecturer in Classics, 1965-67, Lecturer in Classics, 1967-74, Reader in Ancient Philosophy and Science, 1974-83, Professor of Ancient Philosophy and Science, 1983-, Cambridge University; Bonsall Professor, Stanford University, 1981; Sather Professor, University of California at Berkeley, 1984; Visiting Professor, Beijing University and Academy of Sciences, 1987; Master, Darwin College, 1989-; Professor at Large, Cornell University, 1990. Publications: Polarity and Analogy, 1966; Early Greek Science: Thales to Aristotle, 1970; Greek Science After Aristotle, 1973; Magic, Reason and Experience, 1979; Science, Folklore and Ideology, 1983; Science and Morality in Greco-Roman Antiquity, 1985; The Revolution of Wisdom, 1987; Demystifying Mentalities, 1990; Methods and Problems in Greek Science, 1991; Adversaries and Authorities, 1996; Aristotelian Explorations, 1996; Editor: Hippocratic Writings, 1978; Aristotle on Mind and Senses (with G E L Owen), 1978; Le Savoir Grec (with Jacques Brunschwig), 1996. Contributions to: Books and journals. Honours: Sarton Medal, 1987; Honorary Fellow, King's College, Cambridge, 1990; Honorary Foreign Member, American Academy of Arts and Sciences, 1995; Knighted, 1997. Memberships: British Academy, fellow; East Asian History of Science Trust, chairman, 1992-; International Academy of the History of Science, 1997. Address: 2 Prospect Row, Cambridge CB1 1DU, England.

LLOYD Kathleen Annie, (Kathleen Conlon, Kate North), b. 4 Jan 1943, Southport, England. Writer. m. Frank Lloyd, 3 Aug 1962, div, 1 son. Education: BA, Honours, King's College, Durham University. Publications: Apollo's Summer Look, 1968; Tomorrow's Fortune, 1971; My Father's House, 1972; A Twisted Skein, 1975; A Move in the Game, 1979; A Forgotten Season, 1980; Consequences, 1981; The Best of Friends, 1984; Face Values, 1985; Distant Relations, 1989; Unfinished Business, 1990; As Kate North: Land of My Dreams, 1997; Gollancz, 1997. Contributions to: Atlantic Review; Cosmopolitan; Woman's Journal; Woman; Woman's Own. Membership: Society of Authors. Literary Agent: Lavinia Trevor. Address: 26A Brighton Road, Birkdale, Southport PR8 4DD, England.

LLOYD Levannah. See: PETERS Maureen.

LLOYD Linda Mary Teressa, (L M T Edwards), b. 3 July 1951, Southport, England. Assistant Verger. m. David A Lloyd, 14 Sept 1998, 3 sons, 1 daughter. Publications: Poetry: Words of Wisdom; The Cracked Mirror; Valley of Thought; Light of the World. Contributions to: Christian Viewpoint. Address: Church Institute House, Church Lane, Bromborough, Wirral L62 7AB, England.

LLOYD Trevor Owen, b. 30 July 1934, London, England. Professor of History; Writer. Education: BA,

Merton College, Oxford, 1956; MA, DPhil, Nuffield College, Oxford, 1959. Appointments: Lecturer, 1959-73, Professor, 1973-97, Department of History, University of Toronto. Publications: Canada in World Affairs 1957-59, 1968; The General Election of 1880, 1968; Suffragettes International, 1971; The Growth of Parliamentary Democracy in Britain, 1973; Empire, Welfare State, Europe: English History 1906-1992, 1993; The British Empire 1558-1995, 1996. Contributions to: Various journals. Honour: Guggenheim Fellowship, 1978-79. Memberships: William Morris Society; Victorian Studies Association of Ontario. Address: Department of History, University of Toronto, Toronto M5S 1A1, Canada.

LLOYD-JONES Sir (Peter) Hugh (Jefferd), b. 21 Sept 1922, St Peter Port, Jersey, Channel Islands. Classical Scholar. m. (1) Frances Hedley, 1953, div 1981, 2 sons, 1 daughter, (2) Mary R Lefkowitz, 1982. Education: Christ Church, Oxford; MA (Oxon), 1947. Publications: The Justice of Zeus, 1971, 2nd edition, 1983; Blood for the Ghosts, 1982; Supplementum Hellenisticum (with P J Parsons), 1983; Sophoclis Fabulae (with N G Wilson), 1990; Sophoclea (with N G Wilson), 1990; Academic Papers, 2 volumes, 1990; Greek in a Cold Climate, 1991; Sophocles (editor and translator), 3 volumes, 1994-96; Sophocles: Second Thoughts (with N G Wilson), 1997. Contributions to: Numerous periodicals. Honours: Honorary DHL, University of Chicago, 1970; Honorary PhD, University of Tel Aviv, 1984; Knighted, 1989. Memberships: British Academy, fellow; Academy of Athens, corresponding member; American Academy of Arts and Sciences; American Philosophical Society; Rheinisch-Westfälische Akademie; Bayerische Akademie der Wissenschaften; Accademia di Lettere, Archeologia e Belle Arti, Naples. Address: 15 West Riding, Wellesley, MA 02482, USA.

LOADES David Michael, b. 19 Jan 1934, Cambridge, England. Retired Professor of History; Writer. m. Judith Anne Atkins, 18 Apr 1987. Education: Emmanuel College, Cambridge, 1955-61, BA, 1958, MA, PhD, 1961, LittD, 1981. Appointments: Lecturer in Political Science, University of St Andrews, 1961-63; Lecturer in History, University of Durham, 1963-70; Senior Lecturer, 1970-77, Reader, 1977-80, Professor of History, 1980-96, University College of North Wales, Bangor; Director, British Academy John Foxe Project, 1993. Publications: Two Tudor Conspiracies, 1965; The Oxford Martyrs, 1970; The Reign of Mary Tudor, 1979; The Tudor Court, 1986; Mary Tudor: A Life, 1989; The Tudor Navy, 1992; John Dudley: Duke of Northumberland, 1996; Tudor Government, 1997. Editor: The Papers of George Wyatt, 1968; The End of Strife, 1984; Faith and Identity, 1990; John Foxe and the English Reformation, 1997. Contributions to: Journals. Memberships: Royal Historical Society, fellow; Society of Antiquaries of London, fellow. Address: The Cottage, Priory Lane, Burford, Oxon OX18 4SG, England.

LOCHHEAD Douglas (Grant), b. 25 Mar 1922, Guelph, Ontario, Canada. Poet; Writer; Professor of Canadian Studies Emeritus. m. Jean St Clair, 17 Sept 1949, dec, 2 daughters. Education: BA, 1943, BLS, 1951, McGill University; MA, University of Toronto, 1947. Appointments: Librarian, Victoria College, British Columbia, 1951-52, Cornell University, Ithaca, New York, 1952-53, Dalhousie University, Halifax, Nova Scotia, 1953-60, York University, Toronto, 1960-63; Librarian and Fellow, Massey College, 1963-75; Professor of English, University College, University of Toronto, 1963-75; Davidson Professor of Canadian Studies and Director of the Centre for Canadian Studies, 1975-87, Professor Emeritus, 1987-, Mount Allison University, Sackville, New Brunswick. Publications: The Heart is Fire, 1959; It is all Around, 1960; Millwood Road Poems, 1970; The Full Furnace: Collected Poems, 1975; A & E, 1980; Battle Sequence, 1980; High Marsh Road, 1980; The Panic Field, 1984; Tiger in the Skull: New and Selected Poems, 1959-85, 1986; Dykelands, 1989; Upper Cape Poems, 1989; Black Festival: A Long Poem, 1991; Homage to Henry Alline & Other Poems, 1992; Breakfast at Mel's and Other Poems of Love and Places, 1997; All things do continue, poems, 1997. Contributions to: Various publications. Honours: Golden Dog Award, 1974; Fellow, Royal Society of Canada, 1976; Honorary DLitt, St Mary's University, 1987; Honorary LLD, Dalhousie University, 1987. Memberships: League of Canadian Poets, life member; Bibliographical Society of Canada. Address: 9 Quarry Lane, Sackville, New Brunswick, E4L 4G3, Canada.

LOCHHEAD Liz, b. 26 Dec 1947, Motherwell, Scotland. Poet; Playwright; Screenwriter; Teacher. Education: Dilpoma, Glasgow School of Art, 1970. Appointments: Art teacher in Glasgow and Bristol schools; Lecturer, University of Glasgow. Publications: Poetry: Memo for Spring, 1972; The Grimm Sisters, 1981; Dreaming Frankenstein and Collected Poems, 1984; True Confessions and New Clichés, 1985. Screenplay: Now and Then, 1972. Plays: Blood and Ice, 1982; Silver Service, 1984; Dracula, and Mary Queen of Scots Got Her Head Chopped Off, 1989. Honours: BBC Scotland Prize, 1971; Scottish Arts Council Award, 1972. Address: 11 Kersland Street, Glasgow G12 8BW, Scotland.

LOCKE Elsie Violet, b. 17 Aug 1912, Hamilton, New Zealand. Writer. m. John Gibson Locke, 7 Nov 1941, 2 sons, 2 daughters. Education: BA, Auckland University, 1933. Publications: The Runaway Settlers, 1965; The End of the Harbour, 1968; The Boy with the Snowgrass Hair, 1976; Student at the Gates, 1981; The Kauri and the Willow, 1984; Journey under Warning, 1984; A Canoe in the Mist, 1984; Two Peoples One Land, 1988; Peace People, 1992; Joe's Ruby, 1995. Contributions to: Journals. Honours: Katherine Mansfield Award for Non-Fiction, 1959; Honorary DLitt, University of Canterbury, Christchurch, New Zealand, 1987; Children's Literature Association of New Zealand award for distinguished services to children's literature, 1992; Joe's Ruby, 1995. Memberships: Childrens Literature Association; Children's Book Foundation; New Zealand Society of Authors (incorporating PEN). Address: 392 Oxford Tce, Christchurch 1, New Zealand.

LOCKE Hubert G(aylord), b. 30 Apr 1934, Detroit, Michigan, USA. Professor of Public Service; Writer. 2 daughters. Education: BA, Latin and Greek, Wayne State University, 1955; BD, New Testament Studies, University of Chicago, 1959; MA, Comparative Literature, University of Michigan, 1961. Appointments: Assistant Director, 1957-62, Director, 1967-70, Office of Religious Affairs, Adjunct Assistant Professor of Urban Education, 1970-72, Wayne State University; Associate Professor of Urban Studies and Dean, College of Public Affairs and Community Service, University of Nebraska, 1972-75; Professor, 1976-, Associate Dean, College of Arts and Sciences, 1976-77, Vice Provost for Academic Affairs, 1977-82, Dean, Graduate School of Public Affairs, 1982-87, John and Marguerite Corbally Professor of Public Service, 1996-, University of Washington, Seattle. Publications: The Detroit Riot of 1967, 1969; The Care and Feeding of White Liberals, 1970; The German Church Struggle and the Holocaust (editor with Franklin H Littell), 1974; The Church Confronts the Nazis (editor), 1984; Exile in the Fatherland: The Prison Letters of Martin Niemöller (editor), 1986; The Barmen Confession: Papers from the Seattle Assembly (editor), 1986; The Black Antisemitism Controversy: Views of Black Protestants (editor), 1992. Contributions to: Books and professional journals. Honours: Michigan Bar Association Liberty Bell Award, 1967; Honorary Doctor of Divinity, Payne Theological Seminary, 1968, Chicago Theological Seminary, 1971; Honorary Doctor of Humane Letters, University of Akron, 1971, University of Nebraska, 1992; Distinguished Alumni Award, Wayne State University, 1979. Memberships: Commission on State Trial Courts, State of Washington; Institute of European/Asian Studies, board of governors; Interfaith Housing Inc, board of directors; National Academy of Public Administration, board of trustees. Address: c/o Graduate School of Public Affairs, University of Washington, Box 353055, Seattle, WA 98195, USA.

LOCKE Ralph P(aul), b. 9 Mar 1949, Boston, Massachusetts, USA. Musicologist; Teacher; Writer. m. Lona M Farhi, 26 May 1979, 2 daughters. Education: BA,

cum laude, Music, Harvard University, 1970; MA, 1974, PhD, 1980, History and Theory of Music, University of Chicago. Appointments: Faculty, Eastman School of Music, Rochester, New York, 1975-; Senior Editor, Eastman Studies in Music; Editorial Board Member, Journal of Musicological Research; H-mus TXT; AMS-L. Publications: Music, Musicians, and the Saint-Simonians, 1986; Cultivating Music in America: Women Patrons and Activists since 1860, 1997. Contributions to: Reference books and professional journals. Honours: Best Article Citation, Music Library Association, 1980; Galler Dissertation Prize, 1981; ASCAP-Deems Taylor Awards, 1992, 1996. Memberships: American Musicological Society; International Musicological Society; Sonneck Society for American Music. Address: c/o Department of Musicology, Eastman School of Music, 26 Gibbs Street, Rochester, NY 14604, USA.

LOCKE Robert Howard, (Clayton Bess), b. 30 Dec 1944, Vallejo, California, USA. Librarian; Playwright; Author. Education: BA, Speech Arts, California State University, Chico, 1965; MA, Drama, San Francisco State University, 1967; MS, Library Science, Simmons College, Boston, 1973. Publications: As Clayton Bess: Story for a Black Night, 1982; The Truth About the Moon, 1984; Big Man and the Burn-Out, 1985; Tracks, 1986; The Mayday Rampage, 1993. Plays: The Dolly; Play; Rose Jewel and Harmony; On Daddy's Birthday; Murder and Edna Redrum; Premiere. Honours: Best First Novel, Commonwealth Club of California, 1982; Best Book for Young Adults, American Library Association, 1987. Address: c/o Lookout Press, PO Box 19131, Sacramento, CA 95819, USA.

LOCKERBIE D(onald) Bruce, b. 25 Aug 1935, Capreol, Ontario, Canada. Scholar; Writer. Education: AB, 1956, MA, 1963, New York University. Appointments: Scholar-in-Residence, Stony Brook School, New York, 1957-91; Visiting Consultant at American Schools in Asia and Africa, 1974; Visiting Lecturer/Consultant to American universities. Publications: Billy Sunday, 1965; Patriarchs and Prophets, 1969; Hawthorne, 1970; Melville, 1970; Twain, 1970; Major American Authors, 1970; Success in Writing (with L Westdahl), 1970; Purposeful Writing, 1972; The Way They Should Go, 1972; The Liberating Word, 1974; The Cosmic Center: The Apostles' Creed, 1977; A Man under Orders: Lt Gen William K Harrison, 1979; Who Educates Your Child?, 1980; The Timeless Moment, 1980; Asking Questions, 1980; Fatherlove, 1981; In Peril on the Sea, 1984; The Christian, the Arts and Truth, 1985; Thinking and Acting Like a Christian, 1989; Take Heart (with L Lockerbie), 1990; College: Getting In and Staying In (with D Fonseca), 1990. Address: PO Box 26, Stony Brook, NY 11790, USA.

LOCKLEY John, b. 10 Feb 1948, Sale, Cheshire, England. General Practitioner. m. Mavis June Watt, 5 Aug 1972, 2 sons, 1 daughter. Education: Gonville and Caius College, Cambridge, England, 1966-69; MA, 1975; MB BChir (Cantab), 1973. Appointments: House Surgeon, Royal London Hospital, 1972; Vocational Training Course for General Practice, Colchester, 1973; General Practitioner, Ampthill, Bedfordshire, England, 1976-. Publications: The Complete BBC Computer User Handbook, 1988; Acorn to PC: Changing from DFS and ADFS to DOS, 1990; A Practical Workbook for the Depressed Christian, 1991; Headaches - A Comprehensive Guide to Relieving Headaches and Migraine, 1993; After the Fire, 1994; After the Fire II - A Still Small Voice, 1996; After the Fire III - Chronicles, 1998. Contributions to: Many articles to General Practitioner, Daily Telegraph, Daily Mail and Guardian. Honour: Medeconomics GP Writer of Year, 1989. Membership: Society of Authors. Literary Agent: William Neill-Hall. Address: 107 Flitwick Road, Ampthill, Bedfordshire MK45 2NT, England.

LOCKLIN Gerald (Ivan), b. 17 Feb 1941, Rochester, New York, USA. Poet; Writer; Professor. m. (1) Mary Alice Keefe, 3 children, (2) Maureen McNicholas, 2 children, (3) Barbara Curry, 2 children. Education: BA, St John Fisher College, 1961; MA, 1963, PhD, 1964,

University of Arizona. Appointments: Instructor, California State College at Los Angeles, 1964-65; Associate Professor, Professor of English, California State University at Long Beach, 1965-. Publications: Poetry: The Toad Poems, 1970; Poop, and Other Poems, 1973; Tarzan and Shane Meet the Toad (with Ronald Koertge and Charles Stetler), 1975; The Criminal Mentality, 1976; Toad's Sabbatical, 1978; The Last of Toad, 1980; By Land, Sea, and Air, 1982; The Ensenada Poems (with Ray Zepada), 1984; Gringo and Other Poems, 1987; The Death of Jean-Paul Satre and Other Poems, 1988; Lost and Found, 1989; The Firebird Poems, 1992; Big Men on Canvas, 1994; The Old Mongoose and Other Poems, 1994; Fiction: Locked In, short stories, 1973; The Chase, novel, 1976; The Four-Day Work Week and Other Stories, 1977; The Cure, novel, 1979; A Weekend in Canada, short stories, 1979; The Case of the Missing Blue Volkswagen, novella, 1984; The Gold Rush and Other Stories, 1989; The First Time He Saw Paris, novella, 1998; Go West, Young Toad, stories and poems, 1998; Down and Out, novel, 1998; Charles Bukowski: A Sure Bet (biography), 1996. Contributions to: Many periodicals including Wormwood Review. Membership: Phi Beta Kappa. Address: Department of English, California State University at Long Beach, Long Beach, CA 90840, USA.

LOCKRIDGE Ernest Hugh, b. 28 Nov 1938, Bloomington, Indiana, USA. Professor; Novelist. m. Laurel Richardson, 12 Dec 1981, 2 sons, 3 daughters. Education: BA, Indiana University, 1960; MA, 1961, PhD, 1964, Yale University. Appointments: Professor, Yale University, 1963-71, Ohio State University, 1971-. Publications: Novels: Hartspring Blows His Mind, 1968; Prince Elmo's Fire, 1974; Flying Elbows, 1975. Non-Fiction: 20th Century Studies of the Great Gatsby, 1968. Contributions to: Professional journals. Honours: Book-of-the-Month Club Selection, 1974; Distinguished Teaching Award, Ohio State University, 1985. Membership: Phi Beta Kappa. Address: 143 West South Street, Washington, OH 43085, USA.

LODGE David John, b. 28 Jan 1935. Honorary Professor of Modern English Literature; Author. m. Mary Frances Jacob, 1959, 2 sons, 1 daughter. Education: BA, Honours, MA, Univeristy of London ; PhD, University of Birmingham. Appointments: British Council, London, 1959-60; Assistant Lecturer, 1960-62, Lecturer, 1963-71, Senior Lecturer, 1971-73, Reader of English, 1973-76, University of Birmingham; Harkness Commonwealth Fellow, 1964-65; Visiting Associate Professor, University of California, Berkeley, 1969; Henfield Writing Fellow, University of East Anglia, 1977. Publications: Novels: The Picturegoers, 1960; Ginger, You're Barmy, 1962; The British Museum is Falling Down, 1965; Out of the Shelter, 1970, revised edition, 1985; Changing Places, 1975; How Far Can You Go?, 1980; Small World, 1984; Nice Work, 1988; Paradise News, 1991; Therapy, 1995. Criticism: Language of Fiction, 1966; The Novelist at the Crossroads, 1971; The Modes of Modern Writing, 1977; Working with Structuralism, 1981; Write On, 1986; After Bakhtin (essays), 1990; The Art of Fiction, 1992; The Practice of Writing, 1996. Honours: Yorkshire Post Fiction Prize, 1975; Hawthornden Prize, 1976; Whitbread Book of the Year Award, 1980; Sunday Express Book of the Year Award, 1988; Chevalier de l'Ordre des Arts et des Lettres, 1997; Commander of the Order of the British Empire, 1998. Address: Department of English, University of Birmingham, Birmingham B15 2TT, England.

LOEWE Michael (Arthur Nathan), b. 2 Nov 1922, Oxford, England. Retired Lecturer in Chinese Studies; Writer. Education: Magdalen College, Oxford, 1941; BA, Honours, 1951, PhD, 1962, University of London; MA, University of Cambridge, 1963. Appointments: Lecturer in History of the Far East, University of London, 1956-63; Lecturer in Chinese Studies, University of Cambridge, 1963-90. Publications: Imperial China: The Historical Background to the Modern Age, 1966; Records of Han Administration, 2 volumes, 1967; Everyday Life in Early Imperial China during the Han Period, 202 B.C.- A.D. 220, 1968, 2nd edition, 1988; Crisis and Conflict in Han China, 104 B.C. to A.D. 9, 1974; Ancient Cosmologies (editor with Carmen Blacker), 1975; Ways to Paradise: The Chinese Quest for Immortality, 1979; Divination and Oracles (editor with Carmen Blacker), 1981; Chinese Ideas of Life and Death: Faith, Myth, and Reason in the Han Period (202 B.C.-A.D. 220), 1982; The Ch'in and Han Empires, 221 B.C.-A.D. 220, Vol 1 of The Cambridge History of China (editor with Denis Twichett), 1986; The Pride That Was China, 1990; Early Chinese Texts: A Bibliographical Guide, 1993; Divination, Mythology and Monarchy in Han China, 1994. Contributions to: Scholarly publications. Honours: Fellow, Society of Antiquaries, 1972; Fellow, Clare Hall, 1968-90. Address: Willow House, Grantchester, Cambridge CB3 9NF, England.

LOGAN Mark. See: **NICOLE Christopher Robin.**

LOGUE Christopher (John), b. 23 Nov 1926, Portsmouth, Hampshire, England. Poet; Writer; Dramatist. m. Rosemary Hill, 1985. Education: Prior College, Bath. Publications: Poetry: Wand and Quadrant, 1953; Devil, Maggot and Son, 1954; The Weakdream Sonnets, 1955; The Man Who Told His Love: 20 Poems Based on P Neruda's "Los Cantos d'amores", 1958, 2nd edition, 1959; Songs, 1960; Songs from "The Lily-White Boys", 1960; The Establishment Songs, 1966; The Girls, 1969; New Numbers, 1970; Abecedary, 1977; Ode to the Dodo, 1981; War Music: An Account of Books 16 to 19 of Homer's Iliad, 1981; Fluff, 1984; Kings: An Account of Books 1 and 2 of Homer's Iliad, 1991, revised edition, 1992; The Husbands: An Account of Books 3 and 4 of Homer's Iliad, 1994; Selected Poems (edited by Christopher Reid), 1996. Plays: The Lily-White Boys (with Harry Cookson), 1959; The Trial of Cob and Leach, 1959; Antigone, 1961; War Music, 1978; Kings, 1993. Screenplays: Savage Messiah, 1972; The End of Arthur's Marriage, 1965; Crusoe (with Walter Green), 1986. Other: Lust, by Count Plamiro Vicarion, 1955; The Arrival of the Poet in the City: A Treatment for a Film, 1964; True Stories, 1966; The Bumper Book of True Stories, 1980. Editor: Count Palmiro Vicarion's Book of Limericks, 1959; The Children's Book of Comic Verse, 1979; London in Verse, 1982; Sweet & Sour: An Anthology of Comic Verse, 1983; The Children's Book of Children's Rhymes, 1986. Literary Agent: David Godwin. Address: 41 Camberwell Grove, London SE5 8JA, England.

LOIDL Peter Christian, b. 17 Sept 1957, Linz, Austria. Poet; Performer. Education: Doctorate, University of Vienna. Publications: Weisse Rede, poems, 1990; Friction of Things and Magic Formulas, audiotape, 1990; Falsche Prophezeiungen, poems, 1994; Wiener Mysterien, prose, 1995; Farnblüte, poems, 1996; CD: Christi Austern: Mortu Tombu Miyi and Falsche Prophezeiungen. Contributions to: Numerous literary journals and magazines in Austria, Netherlands and USA. Honours: Staatsstipendium für Literature, 1996-97. Membership: Grazer Autorenversammlung. Address: Vereinsgasse 3/12, A-1020 Vienna, Austria.

LOM Herbert, b. 11 Sept 1917, Prague. Actor; Writer. m. Dina Scheu, 10 Jan 1948, div, 2 sons, 1 daughter. Education: Prague University; Cambridge University. Publications: Enter A Spy (The Double Life of Christopher Marlowe), 1978; Dr Guillotine, 1992. Address: London Management, 2-4 Noel Street, London W1V 3RB, England.

LOMAS Herbert, b. 7 Feb 1924, Yorkshire, England. Poet; Critic; Translator. m. Mary Marshall Phelps, 27 June 1968, 1 son, 1 daughter. Education: BA, 1949, MA, 1952, University of Liverpool. Appointments: Teacher, Spetsai, Greece, 1950-51; Lecturer, Senior Lecturer, University of Helsinki, 1952-65; Senior Lecturer, 1966-72, Principal Lecturer, 1972-82, Borough Road College. Publications: Chimpanzees are Blameless Creatures, 1969; Who Needs Money?, 1972; Private and Confidential, 1974; Public Footpath, 1981; Fire in the Garden, 1984; Letters in the Dark, 1986; Trouble, 1992; Selected Poems, 1995; A Useless Passion, 1998. Translations: Contemporary Finnish Poetry, 1991; Wings of Hope and Daring, 1992; Black and Red, 1993; Narcissus in Winter, 1994; The Year of the Hare, 1994; Selected Poems, Eeva-Lisa Manner, 1997. Contributions to: Reviews, journals, and magazines. Honours: Prize, Guinness Poetry Competition; Runner Up, Arvon Foundation Poetry Competition; Chlmondeley Award; Poetry Book Society Biennial Translation Award; Knight First Class, Order of the White Rose of Finland, 1991. Memberships: Society of Authors. Address: North Gable, 30 Crag Path, Aldeburgh, Suffolk IP15 5BS, England.

LOMAX Alan, b. 31 Jan 1915, Austin, Texas, USA. Ethnomusicologist; Writer. m. E Harold, 1937, 1 daughter. Education: Harvard University, 1932-33; BA, University of Texas at Austin, 1936; Graduate Studies in Anthropology, Columbia University, 1939. Appointments: Folk Song Collector, US and Europe; Director, Bureau of Applied Social Research, 1963, Cantometrics Project, Columbia University, 1963. Publications: American Folk Song and Folk Lore: A Regional Bibliography (with S Cowell), 1942; Mr Jelly Roll, 1950, 2nd edition, 1973; Harriett and Her Harmonium, 1955; The Rainbow Sign, 1959; Cantometrics: A Handbook and Training Method, 1976; Index of World Song, 1977; The Land Where the Blues Began, 1993. Editor: American Ballads and Folksongs (with John Lomax), 1934; Negro Folk Songs as Sung by Leadbelly (with John Lomax), 1936; Our Singing Country (with John Lomax), 1941; Folk Song: USA (with John Lomax), 1947, 4th edition, 1954; Leadbelly: A Collection of World Famous Songs (with John Lomax), 1959, 2nd edition, 1965; The Folk Songs of North America in the English Language, 1960; The Penguin Book of American Folk Songs, 1966; Hard-Hitting Songs for Hard-Hit People, 1967; Folk Song Style and Culture, 1968. Honours: National Medal of Arts, 1986; National Book Critics Circle Award, 1993. Memberships: American Association for the Advancement of Science; American Folklore Society, fellow; American Anthropological Association. Address: c/o Association for Cultural Equity, 450 West 41st Street, 6th Floor, New York, NY 10036, USA.

LOMAX Marion, b. 20 Oct 1953, Newcastle upon Tyne, England. Professor of Literature; Poet; Editor. m. Michael Lomax, 29 Aug 1974. Education: BA, Librarianship, 1974, BA, Honours, English and American Studies, 1979, University of Kent; DPhil, University of York, 1983. Appointments: Part-time Lecturer, King Alfred's College, 1983-86; Creative Writing Fellow, University of Reading, 1987-88; Lecturer, Senior Lecturer in English, 1988-95, Professor of Literature, 1995-98, St Mary's University College, Strawberry Hill, Middlesex; Writer-in-residence, University og Stockholm, 1998-. Publications: Poetry: The Peepshow Girl, 1989; Raiding the Borders, 1996. Non-Fiction: Stage Images and Traditions: Shakespeare to Ford, 1987. Editor: Time Present and Time Past: Poets at the University of Kent 1965-1985, 1985; Four Plays by John Ford, 1995; The Rover, by Alpha Behn, 1995. Contributions to: Collections of essays, anthologies and periodicals. Honours: E C Gregory Award, Society of Authors, 1981; 1st Prize, Cheltenham Festival Poetry Competition, 1981; Hawthornden Fellowship, 1993. Memberships: National Association for Writers in Education; Poetry Society. Address: c/o Bloodaxe Books, PO Box 1SN, Newcastle upon Tyne, NE99 1SN, England.

LOMBINO Salvatore A, (Curt Cannon, Hunt Collins, Ezra Hannon, Evan Hunter, Richard Marsten, Ed McBain), b. 15 Oct 1916, New York, USA. Writer. m. (1) Anita Melnick, 1949, 3 sons, (2) Mary Vann Finley, 1973, 1 stepdaughter. Education: Cooper Union; Hunter College. Publications: The Blackboard Jungle, 1954; Second Ending,1956; Strangers When We Meet, 1958 (screenplay 1959); A Matter of Conviction, 1959; Mother and Daughters, 1961; The Birds (screenplay), 1962; Happy New Year Herbie, 1963; Buddwing, 1964; The Easter Man (play), 1964; The Paper Dragon, 1966; A Horse's Head, 1967; Last Summer, 1968; Sons, 1969; The Conjurer (play), 1969; Nobody Knew They Were There, 1971; Every Little Crook and Nanny, 1972; The Easter Man, 1972; Come Winter, 1973; Streets of Gold, 1974; The Chisholms, 1976; Me and Mr Stenner, 1976; Love, Dad, 1981; 87th Precinct Mysteries, Far From the Sea, 1983; Lizzie, 1984. As Ed McBain: Cop Hater, 1956; The Mugger, 1956; The Pusher, 1956; The Con Man, 1957; Killer's Choice, 1957; Killer's Payoff, 1958; Lady Killer, 1958; Killer's Wedge, 1959; 'Til Death, 1959; King's Ransom, 1959; Give the Boys a Great Big Hand, 1960; The Heckler, 1960; See Them Die, 1960; Lady, Lady, I Did It, 1961; Like Love, 1962; The Empty Hours (3 novelettes), 1962; Ten Plus One, 1963; Ax, 1964; He Who Hesitates, 1965; Doll,1965; The Sentries, 1965; Eighty Million Eyes, 1966; Fuzz, 1968 (screenplay 1972); Shotgun, 1969; Jigsaw, 1970; Hail, Hail, the Gang's All Here, 1971; Sadie When She Died, 1972; Let's Hear It for the Deaf Man, 1972; Hail to the Chief, 1973; Bread, 1974; Where There's Smoke, 1975; Blood Relatives, 1975; So Long as You Both Shall Live, 1976; Long Time No See, 1977; Goldilocks, 1977; Calypso, 1979; Ghosts, 1980; Rumpelstiltskin, 1981; Heat, 1981; Ice, 1983; Beauty and the Beast, 1983; Jack and the Beanstalk, 1984; Lightening, 1984; Snow White and Rose Red, 1985; Eight Black Horses, 1985; Cinderella, 1986; Another Part of the City, 1986; Poison, 1987; Puss in Boots, 1987; Tricks, 1987; McBain's Ladies, 1988; The House That Jack Built, 1988; Lullaby, 1989; McBain's Ladies Too, 1989; Downtown, 1989; Vespers, 1990; Three Blind Mice, 1990; The Last Best Hope, 1998. Address: c/o John Farquharson Ltd, 250 West 57th Street, New York, NY 10019, USA.

LOMER Mary. See: **LIDE Mary Ruth.**

LOMPERIS Timothy J(ohn), b. 6 Mar 1947, Guntur, India (US citizen). Professor of Political Science. m. Ana Maria Turner, 15 May 1976, 1 son, 1 daughter. Education: AB, magna cum laude, History and Political Science, Augustana College, 1969; MA, School of Advanced International Studies, Johns Hopkins University, 1975; MA, Political Science, 1978, PhD, Political Science, 1981, Duke University. Appointments: Instructor and Assistant Professor, Louisiana State University, 1980-84; Visiting Assistant Professor, 1983-84, Assistant Professor of Political Science, 1984-94, Duke University; John M Olin Postdoctoral Fellow, Harvard University, 1985-88; Fellow, Woodrow Wilson International Center for Scholars, Washington, DC, 1988; Associate Professor of Political Science, United States Military Academy, West Point, New York, 1994-96; Professor of Political Science and Chairman, Department of Political Science, St Louis University, 1996-. Publications: The War Everyone Lost--and Won: America's Intervention in Viet Nam's Twin Struggles, 1984, revised edition, 1993; Hindu Influence on Greek Philosophy: The Odyssey of the Soul from the Upanishads to Plato, 1984; "Reading the Wind": The Literature of the Vietnam War, 1987; From People's War to People's Rule: Insurgency, Intervention, and the Lessons of Vietnam, 1996. Contributions to: Scholarly books and journals. Honours: United States Army Bronze Star, 1973; Vietnamese Army Staff Medal First Class, 1973; Presidential Outstanding Community Achievement Award for Vietnam Era Veterans, Chapel Hill, North Carolina, 1979; Helen Dwight Reid Award, American Political Science Association, 1982; Finalist, Furniss Award, 1984; Civilian Superior Service Award, United States Military Academy, West Point, New York, 1996; Winner, Alpha Sigma Nu National Jesuit Book Award, 1997; Winner, St Louis University Phi Beta Kappa Book Award, 1998. Address: c/o Department of Political Science, St Louis University, St Louis, MO 63103, USA.

LONDON Herbert Ira, b. 6 Mar 1939, New York, New York, USA. Professor; Writer. m. (1) Joy Weinman, 13 Oct 1962, div 1974, 2 daughters, (2) Vicki Pops, 18 Nov 1980, 1 daughter. Education: BA, 1960, MA, 1961, Columbia University; PhD, New York University, 1966. Appointments: Instructor, New School for Social Research, New York City, 1964-65; Instructor, 1964-65, Assistant Professor, 1967-68, University Ombudsman, 1968-69, Associate Professor, 1969-73, Professor, 1973-, Dean, Gallatin Division, 1972-92, John M Olin University Professor of Humanities, 1992-, New York University; Research Scholar, Australian National University, Canberra, 1966-67; Research Fellow, 1974-, Trustee, 1979-, Hudson Institute, Indianapolis. Publications: Education in the Twenty-First Century (editor), 1969; Non-White Immigration and the White Australia Policy,

1970; Fitting In: Crosswise at Generation Gap, 1974; Social Science Theory, Structure and Applications (editor), 1975; The Overheated Decade, 1976; The Seventies: Counterfeit Decade, 1979; Myths That Rule America, 1981; Closing the Circle: A Cultural History of the Rock Revolution, 1984; Why Are They Lying to Our Children?, 1984; Military Doctrine and the American Character, 1984; Armageddon in the Classroom, 1986; A Strategy for Victory Without War, 1989; The Broken Apple: Notes on New York in the 1980s, 1989; From the Empire State to the Vampire State: New York in a Downtown Transition, 1994. Contributions to: Professional journals. Honours: Fulbright Award, 1966-67; Defence Science Journal Award, 1985; Honarary Degrees: U.Aix-Marseille, 1977; Grove City College, 1991; Peter Shaw Award for Distinguished Writing on Higher Education, 1996; Martin Luther King Award for Humanitarian Service. Memberships: American Historical Association; Education Excellence Center; Ethics and Public Policy Center; Freedom House; Heritage Foundation; President, Hudson Institute, 1997-. Address: 2 Washington Square Village, New York, NY 10012, USA.

LONG Robert, b. New York City, USA. Writer; Editor. Education: BA, Long Island University; MFA, Vermont College. Appointments: Writer-in-Residence, La Salle University, 1990-92; Professor of English, Long Island University, Suffolk College, Orange County College, 1977-97; Senior Editor, East Hampton Star, 1997-. Publications: Getting Out of Town (poems), 1977; What Is It (poems), 1980; Long Island Poets (editor, anthology), 1986; What Happens (poems), 1988; For David Igratow (anthology, editor), 1994; Blue (poem), 1999. Contributions to: New Yorker; Poetry; Partisan Review. Honours: Yeats Fellowship, 1976; New York Foundation for the Arts Fellowship, 1993. Address: 313A Three Mile Harbor, Hog Creek Road, East Hampton, NY 11937, USA.

LONG Robert Emmet, b. 7 June 1934, Oswego, New York, USA. Literary Critic; Freelance Writer. Education: BA, 1956, PhD, 1968, Columbia University; MA, Syracuse University, 1964. Appointments: Instructor, State University of New York, 1962-64; Assistant Professor, Queens College, City University of New York, 1968-71. Publications: The Achieving of the Great Gatsby: F Scott Fitgerald 1920-25, 1979; The Great Succession: Henry James and the Legacy of Hawthorne, 1979; Henry James: The Early Novels, 1983; John O'Hara, 1983; Nathanael West, 1985; Barbara Pym, 1986; James Thurber, 1988; James Fenimore Cooper, 1990; The Films of Merchant Ivory, 1991, (newly updated edition), 1997; Ingmar Bergman: Film and Stage, 1994. Editor: American Education, 1985; Drugs and American Society, 1985; Vietnam, Ten Years After, 1986; Mexico, 1986; The Farm Crisis, 1987; The Problem of Waste Disposal, 1988; AIDS, 1989; The Welfare Debate, 1989; Energy and Conservation, 1989; Japan and the USA, 1990; Censorship, 1990; The Crisis in Health Care, 1991; The State of US Education, 1991; The Reunification of Germany, 1992; Immigration to the United States, 1992; Drugs in America, 1993; Banking Scandals: The S&L and BCCI, 1993; Religious Cults in America, 1994; Criminal Sentencing, 1995; Suicide, 1995; Immigration, 1996; Affirmative Action, 1996; Multiculturalism, 1997; Right to Privacy, 1997. Contributions to: Several hundred articles in magazines, journals and newspapers. Address: 254 South Third Street, Fulton, NY 13069, USA.

LONG Robert Hill, b. 23 Nov 1952, Raleigh, North Carolina, USA. Senior Lecturer in Creative Writing; Poet; Writer. m. Sandra Morgen, 22 Mar 1980, 1 son, 1 daughter. Education: BA, Honours Studies, Comparative Literature, Davidson College, 1975; MFA, Program for Writers, Warren Wilson College, 1983. Appointments: Visiting Lecturer, Clark University, University of Hartford, Smith College, University of Connecticut at Torrington, 1987-91; Senior Lecturer in Creative Writing, University of Oregon, 1991-. Publications: The Power to Die (poems), 1987; The Work of the Bow (poems), 1997; The Effigies (fiction), 1998. Contributions to: Various anthologies and journals. Honours: Aspen Writers' Conference Poetry Fellowship, 1981; 1st Prize, North Carolina Poetry Award, 1986; Grand Prize, A Living Culture in Durham Anthology, 1986; North Carolina Arts Council Literary Fellowship, 1986; National Endowment for the Arts Fellowship, 1988; Cleveland State University Poetry Center Prize, 1995; Oregon Arts Commission Literary Fellowship, 1997. Membership: Associated Writing Programs. Address: c/o Program in Creative Writing, University of Oregon, Eugene, OR 97403, USA.

LONGFORD Countess of, (Elizabeth Pakenham), b. 30 Aug 1906, London, England. Author. m. F A Pakenham, 1931, 4 sons, 3 daughters. Education: MA, Lady Margaret Hall, Oxford. Publications: Points for Parents, 1956; Catholic Approaches (editor), 1959; Jameson's raid, 1960, new edition, 1982; Victoria RI, 1964; Wellington: Years of the Sword, 1969; Wellington: Pillar of State, 1972; The Royal House of Windsor, 1974; Churchill, 1974; Byron's Greece, 1975; Life of Byron, 1976; A Pilgrimage of Passion: The Life of Wilfrid Scawen Blunt, 1979; Louisa: Lady in Waiting (editor), 1979; Images of Chelsea, 1980; The Queen Mother: A Biography, 1981; Eminent Victorian Women, 1981; Elizabeth R, 1983; The Pebbled Shore (autobiography), 1986; The Oxford Book of Royal Anecdotes (editor), 1989; Darling Loosy: Letters to Princess Louise 1856-1939 (editor), 1991; Poet's Corner: An Anthology (editor), 1992; Royal Throne: The Future of the Monarchy, 1993. Honours: James Tait Black Memorial Prize for Non-Fiction, 1964; Yorkshire Post Prize, 1969; Honorary DLitt, Sussex University, 1970; Commander of the Order of the British Empire, 1974. Membership: Women Writers and Journalists, honorary life president, 1979-. Address: 18 Chesil Court, Chelsea Manor Street, London SW3 5QP, England.

LONGLEY Clifford, b. Middlesex, England. Journalist. m. Elizabeth Holzer, 26 Aug 1980, 1 son. Education: BSC, Southampton University, England, 1961. Appointments: Reporter, Essex and Thurrock Gazette, 1961-64; Reporter, Portsmouth Evening News, 1964-67; The Times, 1967-92; Reporter, 1967-69; Assistant News Editor, 1969-71; Religious Affairs Correspondent, Religious Affairs Editor, 1986-, Columnist, 1972-92; British Press Awards Commendation, 1986; Specialist Writer of the Year, 1986; Leader Writer, 1984-90; Assistant Editor (Leaders) and Chief Leader Writer, 1990-92; Father of The Times, NUJ Chapel, 1972-74, 1986-89; Chairman, Docklands Branch, NUJ, 1989-90; The Daily Telegraph, 1992-; Leader Writer, Feature Writer, 1992-95; Religious Affairs Editor, 1995; Sacred and Profane Columnist, 1992-; The Tablet, 1994-; Contributing Editor and Columnist, 1994-96; Acting Editor, 1996; Chief Columnist and Leader Writer, 1996-. Publication: The Times Book of Clifford Longley, 1990. Honour: Hon Fellow, St Mary's University College, University of Surrey. Literary Agent: Sheila Watson, 24 Broughton Road, Orpington, Kent BR6 8EQ, England.

LONGLEY Michael, b. 27 July 1939, Belfast, Northern Ireland. Poet; Arts Administrator. m. Edna Broderick, 1964, 1 son, 2 daughters. Education: BA, Trinity College, Dublin, 1963. Appointments: Assistant Master, Avoca School, Blackrock, 1962-63, Belfast High School and Erith Secondary School, 1963-64, Royal Belfast Academical Institution, 1964-69; Director, Literature and the Traditional Arts, Arts Council of Northern Ireland, Belfast, 1970-. Publications: Poetry: Ten Poems, 1965; Room To Rhyme (with Seamus Heaney and David Hammond), 1968; Secret Marriages: Nine Short Poems, 1968; Three Regional Voices (with Barry Tebb and Ian Chrichton Smith), 1968; No Continuing City: Poems, 1963-1968, 1969; Lares, 1972; An Exploded View: Poems, 1968-72, 1973; Fishing in the Sky, 1975; Man Lying on a Wall, 1976; The Echo Gate: Poems 1975-1978, 1979; Selected Poems, 1963-1980, 1980; Patchwork, 1981; Poems 1963-1983, 1985; Gorse Fires, 1991. Editor: Causeway: The Arts in Ulster, 1971; Under the Moon, Over the Stars: Young People's Writing from Ulster, 1971; Selected Poems by Louis MacNeice, 1988; The Ghost Orcid, 1995; Selected Poems, 1998. Contributions to: Periodicals. Honours: Eric Gregory Award, Society of Authors, 1965; Commonwealth Poetry Prize, 1985; Honarary DLitt, Queens University, Belfast, 1995. Address: 32 Osborne Gardens, Malone, Belfast 9, Northern Ireland.

LONGMATE Norman Richard, b. 15 Dec 1925, Newbury, Berkshire, England. Freelance Writer. Education: BA, Modern History, 1950, MA 1952, Worcester College, Oxford. Appointments: Leader Writer, Evening Standard, 1952; Feature Writer, Daily Mirror, 1953-56; Administrative Officer, Electricity Council, 1957-63; Schools Radio Producer, 1963-65, Senior, subsequently Chief Assistant, BBC Secretariat, 1965-83, BBC; Freelance Writer, 1983-. Publications: A Socialist Anthology (editor), 1953; Oxford Triumphant, 1955; King Cholera, 1966; The Waterdrinkers, 1968; Alive and Well, 1970; How We Lived Then, 1971; If Britain had Fallen, 1972; The Workhouse, 1974; The Real Dad's Army, 1974; The GI's, 1975; Milestones in Working Class History, 1975; Air Raid, 1976; When We Won the War, 1977; The Hungry Mills, 1978; The Doodlebugs, 1981; The Bombers, 1982; The Breadstealers, 1984; Hitler's Rockets, 1985; Defending the Island from Caeser to the Armada, 1989. Memberships: Oxford Society; Society of Authors; Fortress Study Group; United Kingdom Fortification Club; Historical Association; Ramblers Association; Society of Sussex Downsmen; Prayer Book Society; Royal Historical Society, fellow. Address: c/o Century Hutchison, 62-65 Chandos Place, London WC2 4NW, England.

LONGWORTH Phillip, b. 17 Feb 1933, London, England. Professor of History; Writer. Education: BA, 1956, MA, 1960, Balliol College, Oxford. Appointment: Professor of History, McGill University, Montreal, 1984-. Publications: A Hero of Our Time, by Lermontov (translator), 1962; The Art of Victory, 1965; The Unending Vigil, 1967, new edition, 1985; The Cossacks, 1969; The Three Empresses, 1971; The Rise and Fall of Venice, 1974; Alexis, Tsar of All the Russias, 1984; The Making of Eastern Europe, 1992, new edition, 1997. Contributions to: Periodicals. Address: c/o Heath and Co, 79 St Martin's Lane, London WC2N 4AA, England.

LONGYEAR Barry (Brookes), b. 12 May 1942, Harrisburg, Pennsylvania, USA. Writer. Appointment: Publisher, Sol III Publications, Philadelphia, 1968-72, and Farmington, Maine, 1972-77. Publications: City of Baraboo, 1980; Manifest Destiny (stories), 1980; Circus World (stories), 1980; Elephant Song, 1981; The Tomorrow Testament, 1983; It Came from Schenectady, 1984; Sea of Glass, 1986; Enemy Mine, 1988; Saint MaryBlue, 1988; Naked Came the Robot, 1988; The God Box, 1989; Infinity Hold, 1989; The Homecoming, 1989; Slag Like Me, 1994. Address: PO Box 100, Vienna Road, Rt 41, New Shanon, ME 04955, USA.

LOOMIE Albert (Joseph), b. 29 July 1922, New York, New York, USA. Professor of History Emeritus; Writer. Education: BA, Loyola University, 1944; PhL, West Baden College, 1946; MA, Fordham University, 1949; STL, Woodstock College, 1953; PhD, University of London, 1957. Appointments: Member, Jesuit Order, 1939-; Faculty, 1958-68, Professor of History, 1968-93, Professor Emeritus, 1993-, Fordham University. Publications: The Spanish Jesuit Mission in Virginia 1570-72 (with C M Lewis), 1953; Toleration and Diplomacy: The Religious Issue in Anglo-Spanish Relations 1603-05, 1963; The Spanish Elizabethans: The English Exiles at the Court of Philip II, 1964; Guy Fawkes in Spain, 1971; Spain and the Jacobean Catholics, 2 volumes, 1973, 1978; Ceremonies of Charles I: The Notebooks of John Finet 1628-41, 1987; English Polemics at the Spanish Court: Joseph Creswell's Letter to the Ambassador from England, the English and Spanish Texts of 1606, 1993; Spain and the Early Stuarts 1585-1655: Collected Studies. Contributions to: Professional journals. Address: c/o Loyola-Faber Hall, Fordham University, New York, NY 10458, USA.

LOPATE Phillip, b. 16 Nov 1943, Brooklyn, New York, USA. Professor of English; Writer; Poet; Editor. m. Cheryl Cipriani, 31 Dec 1990, 1 child. Education: BA, Columbia College, 1964; PhD, Union Institute, 1979. Appointments:

Associate Professor of English, University of Houston, 1980-88; Associate Professor of Creative Writing, Columbia University, 1988-90; Professor of English, Bennington College, 1990, Hofstra University, 1991-; Editor, The Anchor Essay Annual, 1997-. Publications: Novels: Confessions of Summer, 1979; The Rug Merchant, 1987. Poetry: The Eyes Don't Always Want to Stay Open, 1972; The Daily Round, 1976. Other: Being with Children (memoir), 1975; Bachelorhood (essays), 1981; Against Joie de Vivre (essays), 1989; Portrait of My Body (essays), 1996; Totally, Tenderly, Tragically (film criticism), 1998. Editor: Journal of a Living Experiment, 1979; The Art of the Personal Essay, 1994; Writing New York, 1998. Contributions to: Anthologies, newspapers, reviews, quarterlies, journals, and magazines. Honours: Guggenheim Fellowship; National Endowment for the Arts Grants; New York Foundation for the Arts Grants; Christopher Medallion; Texas Institute of Letters Award. Address: 402 Sackett Street, Brooklyn, NY 11231, USA.

LOPES Dominic M McIver, b. 3 July 1964, Aberdeen, Scotland. Scholar. Education: BA, Philosophy, McGill University, 1983-86; DPhil, Philosophy, Oxford University, 1986-92. Appointments: Visiting Assistant Professor, Philosophy, Purdue University, Calumet, 1991-92; Assistant Professor of Philosophy, Indiana University, Kokomo, 1992-97; Associate Professor of Philosophy, Indiana University, Kokomo, 1997-. Publications: A Handful of Grams, 1996; Understanding Pictures, 1996. Contributions to: British Journal of Aesthetics; Journal of Aesthetics and Art Criticism; Philosophical Quarterly; Philosophical Studies; Encyclopedia of Aesthetics. Honour: Philosophical Quarterly Essay Prize, 1997. Address: Indiana University, Kokomo, Kokomo, IN 46904-9003, USA.

LOPES Henri (Marie-Joseph), b. 12 Sept 1937, Leopoldville, Belgian Congo. Novelist. m. Nirva Pasbeau, 13 May 1961, 1 son, 3 daughters. Education: Licence es Lettres, 1962, Diplome d'Etudes Superieures, History, 1963, Sorbonne, University of Paris. Publications: Tribaliques, 1971, English translation as Tribaliks, 1989; La Nouvelle Romance, 1976; Sans Tam-Tam, 1977; The Laughing Cry, 1988; Le Chercheur d'Afriques, 1990; Sur L'Autre Rive, 1992; Le Lys et le Flamboyant, 1997. Honours: Grand Prix de la Litterature d'Afrique Noire, 1972; Prix Jules Verne, 1990; Doctor Honoris Causa, University Paris-Val de Marne, France; Grand Prix de Littérature de La Francophonie de L'Académie Française, 1993; Homme de Lettres 1993, 1994. Address: UNESCO, 7 Place de Fontenoy, 75352 Paris, France.

LOPEZ Barry (Holstun), b. 6 Jan 1945, Port Chester, New York, USA. Author. m. Sandra Jean Landers, 10 June 1967. Education: BA, 1966, MA, 1968, University of Notre Dame. Publications: Desert Notes, 1976; Giving Birth to Thunder, 1978; Rivert Notes, 1978; Of Wolves and Men, 1978; Winter Count, 1981; Arctic Dreams, 1986; Crossing Open Ground, 1988; The Rediscovery of North America, 1991; Field Notes, 1994. Contributions to: Periodicals. Honours: John Burroughs Medal, 1979; Christopher Medals, 1979, 1987; American Academy of Arts and Letters Award, 1986; Guggenheim Fellowship, 1987; National Book Award, 1987; Honorary LDH, Whittier College, 1988; Lannan Foundation Award, 1990. Membership: PEN American Center. Address: c/o Sterling Lord Listeristic, 1 Madison Avenue, New York, NY 10010, USA.

LOPEZ Tony, b. 5 Nov 1950, London, England. Poet; Lecturer. m. Sara Louise Banham, 19 Oct 1985, 1 s, 1 d. Education: BA Literature (US & English), Essex University, 1980; PhD, English, Gonville & Caius College, Cambridge. Appointments: Lecturer in English, University of Leicester, 1986-87; Lectuer in English, University of Edinburgh, 1987-89; Lecturer & Senior Lecturer, Now Reader in Poetry, University of Plymouth, 1989-. Publications: Snapshots, 1976; Change, 1978; The English Disease, 1979; A Handbook of British Birds, 1982; Abstract and Delicious, 1983; A Theory of Surplus Labour, 1990; Stress Management, 1994; Negative Equity, 1995; False Memory, 1996; Critical writings include: The Poetry of W S Graham, 1989. Contributions to: Conductors of Chaos, anthology, editor Iian Sinclair, 1996; Picador. Honours: Blundel Award, 1990; Wingate Scholarship, 1996. Literary Agent: John Parker, MBA Literary Agents Ltd, 45 Fitzroy Street, London W1P 5HR, England.

LOPEZ SAAVEDRA Josefina Del C, b. 21 Oct 1964, Caracas, Venezuela. Poet; Writer; Editor; Translator. m. Mauricio Machuca, 7 Apr 1990. Education: Medicine, Universidad Central de Venezuela, 1991; Poetry, School of Continuing Studies, Rice University, Houston, Texas, 1993; Licentiate Degree, Letters, Universidad Catolica Andres Bello. Appointment: Founder, President, Director, Editor, La Casa del Poeta literary magazine. Publication: Poems and Friendship, 1991; En el fondo del mar, forthcoming. Contributions to: Periodicals and journals. Memberships: Iberoamericans Academy of Poetry; Instituto Internacional de Literatura Iberoamericans; Instituto Literario y Cultural Hispanico. Address: Apartado Postal No 66908, Caracas 1061-A, Venezuela.

LORD Graham John, b. 16 Feb 1943, Mutare, Southern Rhodesia. Journalist; Author. m. Jane Carruthers, 12 Sept 1962, 2 daughters. Education: BA, Honours, University of Cambridge, 1965. Appointments: Literary Editor, Sunday Express, London, 1969-92; Originator, 1987, Judge, 1987-89, Sunday Express Book of the Year Award; Editor, Raconteur, short story magazine, 1994-95. Publications: Marshmallow Pie, 1970; A Roof Under Your Feet, 1973; The Spider and the Fly, 1974; God and All His Angels, 1976; The Nostradamus Horoscope, 1981; Time Out of Mind, 1986; Ghosts of King Solomon's Mines, 1991; Just the One: The Wives and Times of Jeffrey Bernard, 1992; A Party to Die For, 1997; James Herriot: The Life of a Country Vet, 1997; Sorry, We're Going to have to Let You Go, 1999. Contributions to: Journals. Address: c/o Giles Gordon, Curtis Brown & Co, 6 Ann Street, Edinburgh EH4 1PJ, Scotland.

LORD Walter, b. 8 Oct 1917, Baltimore, Maryland, USA. Author. Education: BA, Princeton University, 1939; LLB, Yale University, 1946. Publications: The Fremantle Diary, 1954; A Night to Remember, 1955, illustrated edition, 1976; Day of Infamy, 1957; The Good Years, 1960; A Time to Stand, 1961; Peary to the Pole, 1963; The Past That Would Not Die, 1965; Incredible Victory, 1967; Dawn's Early Light, 1972; Lonely Vigil, 1977; Miracle of Dunkirk, 1982; The Night Lives On, 1986. Contributions to: Periodicals. Honour: Special Achievement Award, Society of American Historians, 1996. Literary Agent: Sterling Lord. Address: 116 East 68th Street, New York, NY 10021, USA.

LORENC Kito, b. 4 Mar 1938, Schleife, Germany. Poet; Writer; Editor. Education: Serbian/Russian Pedagogical Exam, University of Leipzig, 1961. Appointment: Editor, Serbska poezija (Serbian poetry series), 1973-. Publications: Poetry: Struga, 1967; Flurberinigung, 1973; Die Rasselbande im Schlamassellande (children's poems), 1983; Wortland, 1984; Rymarej a drydomej (children's poems), 1985; Gegen den grossen Popanz, 1990. Other: Die wendische schiffahrt, 1994; Kim Broiler, 1996. Honours: Heinrich Heine Prize, 1974; Heinrich Mann Prize, 1991. Membership: Sächsische Akademie der Künste. Address: D-02627 Wuischke bei Hochirch 4, Germany.

LORENZ Sarah E. See: **WINSTON Sarah.**

LORRIMER Claire. See: **CLARK Patricia Denise.**

LOTT Bret, b. 8 Oct 1958, Los Angeles, California, USA. Assistant Professor of English; Writer. m. Melanie Kai Swank, 28 June 1980, 2 sons. Education: BA, California State University at Long Beach, 1981; MFA, University of Massachusetts, 1984. Appointments: Reporter, Daily Commercial News, Los Angeles, 1980-81; Instructor in Remedial English, Ohio State University, Columbus, 1984-86; Assistant Professor of English, College of Charleston, 1986-. Publications: The Man Who Owned Vermont, 1987; A Stranger's House, 1988; A Dream of Old Leaves, 1989; The Hunt Club, 1997. Contributions to: Anthologies and periodicals. Honours: Awards and fellowships. Memberships: Associated Writing Programs; Poets and Writers. Address: c/o Department of English, College of Charleston, Charleston, SC 29424, USA.

LOVAT Terence John, b. 29 Mar 1949, Sydney, New South Wales, Australia. Professor of Education; Writer. m. Tracey Majella Dennis, 4 Jan 1986, 1 son, 2 daughters. Education: BEd, 1982, MTh, 1983, MA, Honours, 1984, PhD, 1988, Sydney University. Appointment: Professor of Education, University of Newcastle, New South Wales, Australia. Publications: Understanding Religion, 1987; What Is This Thing Called Religious Education?, 1989; Studies in Australian Society, 1989; Curriculum: Action on Reflection (with D Smith), 1990, 2nd edition, 1995; Bioethics for Medical and Health Professionals (with K Mitchell and I Kerridge), 1991, 2nd edition, 1996; Teaching and Learning Religion, 1995. Editor: Sociology for Teachers, 1992; Studies in Religion, 1993. Contributions to: Professional journals. Memberships: Australian College of Education; European Association for Research on Learning and Instruction. Address: Faculty of Education, University of Newcastle, New South Wales 2308, Australia.

LOVE William F, b. 20 Dec 1932, Oklahoma City, Oklahoma, USA. Writer. m. Joyce Mary Athman, 30 May 1970, 2 daughters. Education: BA, St John's University, Collegeville, Minnesota, 1955; MBA, University of Chicago, 1972. Publications: The Chartreuse Clue, 1990; The Fundamentals of Murder, 1991; Bloody Ten, 1992. Memberships: Authors Guild; International Association of Crime Writers; Mystery Writers of America; PEN Midwest; Private Eye Writers of America; Society of Midland Authors. Address: 940 Cleveland, Hinsdale, IL 60521, USA.

LOVELL (Alfred Charles) Bernard (Sir), b. 31 Aug 1913, Oldland Common, Gloucestershire, England. Professor of Radio Astronomy Emeritus; Writer. m. Mary Joyce Chesterman, 1937, dec 1993, 2 sons, 3 daughters. Education: University of Bristol. Appointments: Professor of Radio Astronomy, 1951-80, Professor Emeritus, 1980-, University of Manchester; Director, Jodrell Bank Experimental Station, later Nuffield Radio Astronomy Laboratories, 1951-81; Various visiting lectureships. Publications: Science and Civilisation, 1939; World Power Resources and Social Development, 1945; Radio Astronomy, 1951; Meteor Astronomy, 1954; The Exploration of Space by Radio, 1957; The Individual and the Universe, 1958; The Exploration of Outer Space, 1961; Discovering the Universe, 1963; Our Present Knowledge of the Universe, 1967; The Explosion of Science: The Physical Universe (editor with T Margerison), 1967; The Story of Jodrell Bank, 1968; The Origins and International Economics of Space Exploration, 1973; Out of the Zenith, 1973; Man's Relation to the Universe, 1975; P M S Blackett: A Biographical Memoir, 1976; In the Centre of Immensities, 1978; Emerging Cosmology, 1981; The Jodrell Bank Telescopes, 1985; Voice of the Universe, 1987; Pathways to the Universe (with Sir Francis Graham Smith), 1988; Astronomer By Chance (autobiography), 1990; Echoes of War, 1991. Contributions to: Professional journals. Honours: Officer of the Order of the British Empire, 1946; Duddell Medal, 1954; Royal Medal, 1960; Knighted, 1961; Ordre du Mérite pour la Recherche et l'Invention, 1962; Churchill Gold Medal, 1964; Gold Medal, Royal Astronomical Society, 1981; Many honorary doctorates. Memberships: American Academy of Arts and Sciences, honorary foreign member; American Philosophical Society; International Astronomical Union, vice-president, 1970-76; New York Academy; Royal Astronomical Society, president, 1969-71; Royal Society, fellow; Royal Swedish Academy, honorary member. Address: The Quinta, Swettenham, Cheshire CW12 2LD, England.

LOVELL Mary Sybilla, b. 23 Oct 1941, Prestatyn, North Wales. Writer. m. (2) Geoffrey A H Watts, 11 July 1991, 1 son, 2 stepsons, 2 stepdaughters. Publications: Hunting Pageant, 1980; Cats as Pets, 1982; Boys Book of Boats, 1983; Straight on till Morning, 1987; The Splendid Outcast, 1988; The Sound of Wings, 1989; Cast No Shadow, 1991; A Scandalous Life, 1995; The Rebel Heart, 1996; A Rage to Live, 1998. Contributions to: Many technical articles on the subjects of accounting and software. Memberships: Society of Authors; New Forest Hunt Club; R S Surtees Society, vice president, 1980-; Fellow, Royal Geographical Society. Literary Agent: Robert Ducas. Address: Stroat House, Stroat, Gloucestershire NP6 7LR, England.

LOVELOCK Yann Rufus, b. 11 Feb 1939, Birmingham, England. Writer; Poet; Translator. m. Ann Riddell, 28 Sept 1961. Education: BA, English Literature, St Edmund Hall, Oxford, 1963. Appointments: Various Writer-in-Residencies. Publications: The Vegetable Book, 1972; The Colour of the Weather (editor and translator), 1980; The Line Forward, 1984; A Vanishing Emptiness (editor and part translator), 1989; A Townscape of Flanders, Versions of Grace by Anton von Wilderode (translator), 1990; Landscape with Voices, Poems 1980-95, 1995; In the Pupil's Mirror (editor and translator), 1997; Some 25 other books of poems, experimental prose, anthologies and translations. Contributions to: Periodicals and anthologies. Honour: Silver Medal, Haute Académie d'Art et de Littérature de France, 1986. Memberships: Freundkreis Poesie Europe, assistant director; La Société de Langue et de la Littérature Wallonnes, corresponding member. Address: 80 Doris Road, Birmingham, West Midlands B11 4NF, England.

LOVESEY Peter, (Peter Lear), b. 10 Sept 1936, Whitton, Middlesex, England. Writer. m. Jacqueline Ruth Lewis, 30 May 1959, 1 son, 1 daughter. Education: BA, Honours, English, University of Reading, 1958. Publications: The Kings of Distance, 1968; Wobble to Death, 1970; The Detective Wore Silk Drawers, 1971; Abracadaver, 1972; Mad Hatters Holiday, 1973; Invitation to a Dynamite Party, 1974; A Case of Spirits, 1975; Swing, Swing Together, 1976; Goldengirl, 1977; Waxwork, 1978; Official Centenary History of the Amateur Athletic Association, 1979; Spider Girl, 1980; The False Inspector Dew, 1982; Keystone, 1983; Butchers (short stories), 1985; The Secret of Spandau, 1986; Rough Cider, 1986; Bertie and the Tinman, 1987; On the Edge, 1989; Bertie and the Seven Bodies, 1990; The Last Detective, 1991; Diamond Solitaire, 1992; Bertie and the Crime of Passion, 1993; The Crime of Miss Oyster Brown (short stories), 1994; The Summons, 1995; Bloodhounds, 1996; Upon a Dark Night, 1997; Do Not Exceed the Stated Dose (short stories), 1998; The Vault, 1999. Honours: Macmillan/Panther 1st Crime Novel Award, 1970; Crime Writers Association Silver Dagger, 1978, 1995, 1996 and Gold Dagger, 1982; Grand Prix de Littérature Policière, 1985; Prix du Roman D'Aventures, 1987; Anthony Award, 1992; Macavity Award 1997. Memberships: Crime Writers Association, chairman, 1991-92; Detection Club; Society of Authors. Literary Agent: Vanessa Holt. Address: 59 Crescent Road, Leigh-on-Sea, Essex SS9 2PF, England.

LOVETT A(lbert) W(inston), b. 16 Dec 1944, Abingdon, England. Associate Professor; Historian. Education: BA, 1965, PhD, 1969, University of Cambridge. Appointments: Jean Monnet Associate Professor in the History of the European Union, 1970-, University College, Dublin. Publications: Philip II and Mateo Vázquez de Leca: The Government of Spain (1572-1592), 1977; Europe, 1453-1610, 1978; Spain Under the Early Habsburgs, 1986, revised edition, 1989; European Integration, 1945-1957: An Insider's View, 1997. Contributions to: Scholarly books and journals. Membership: Royal Historical Society, fellow. Address: c/o Department of History, University College, Dublin 4, Ireland.

LOW Denise, (Denise Low-Weso), b. 9 May 1949, Emporia, Kansas, USA. Poet; Writer; University Instructor of Humanities. m. Thomas F Weso, 2 sons. Education: BA, English, 1971, MA, English, 1974, PhD, English, 1997, University of Kansas; MFA, Creative Writing, Wichita State University, 1984. Appointments: Assistant Instructor, 1970-72, Lecturer, 1977-84, Visiting Lecturer, 1988, University of Kansas; Temporary Instructor, Kansas State University, 1975-77; Part-time Instructor, Washburn University, Topeka, 1982-84; Instructor of Humanities, Haskell Indian Nations University, Lawrence, Kansas, 1984-. Publications: Dragon Kite, 1981; Quilting, 1984; Spring Geese and Other Poems, 1984; Learning the Language of Rivers, 1987; Starwater, 1988; Selective Amnesia: Stiletto I, 1988; Vanishing Point, 1991; Tulip Elegies: An Alchemy of Writing, 1993; Touching the Sky: Essays, 1994; A Daybook of Interiors: Essays, 1998. Contributions to: Anthologies, books, reviews, quarterlies, journals, and magazines. Honours: Several grants and fellowships. Memberships: Associated Writing Programs; Modern Language Association; Poets and Writers. Address: c/o Haskell Indian Nations University, Lawrence, KS 66046, USA.

LOW Lois Dorothea, (Zoe Cass, Dorothy Mackie Low, Lois Paxton), b. 15 July 1916, Edinburgh, Scotland. Writer. Education: Edinburgh Ladies' College. Publications: Isle for a Stranger, 1962; Dear Liar, 1963; A Ripple on the Water, 1964; The Intruder, 1965; A House in the Country, 1968; The Man Who Died Twice, 1969; To Burgundy and Back, 1970; The Quiet Sound of Fear, 1971; Who Goes There?, 1972; Island of the Seven Hills, 1974; The Silver Leopard, 1976; A Twist in the Silk, 1980; The Man in the Shadows, 1983. Memberships: Crime Writers Association; Romantic Novelists Association, chairman, 1969-71; Society of Authors. Address: 6 Belmont Mews, Abbey Hill, Kenilworth, Warwickshire CV8 1LU, England.

LOW Rachael, b. 6 July 1923, London, England. Film Historian. Education: BSc, 1944, PhD, 1950, London School of Economics and Political Science. Appointments: Researcher, British Film Institute, London, 1945-48; Gulbenkian Research Fellow, 1968-71, Fellow Commoner, 1983, Lucy Cavendish College, Cambridge. Publications: History of the British Film 1896-1906, 1948; with Roger Manvell: History of the British Film, 1906-1914, 1949, 1914-1918, 1950, 1918-1929, 1971, 1929-1939, Vols I and II, 1979, Vol III, 1985. Address: c/o Allen & Unwin Ltd, 40 Museum Street, London WC1, England.

LOW Robert Nicholas, b. 15 Aug 1948, Addlestone, Surrey, England. Journalist. m. Angela Levin, 6 Oct 1983, 1 son. Education: BA Hons, Fitzwilliam College, Cambridge, England. Appointments: Teacher, Universidad De Chile, La Serena, Chile, 1970-72; Journalist, Birmingham Post & Mail, Birmingham, England, 1973-77; The Observer, London, 1977-93; Senior Editor/Deputy Editor, Reader's Digest, British Edition, 1994-98; European Bureau Chief, Reader's Digest, 1998-. Publications: (with Mark Bles): The Kidnap Business, 1987; Editor, The Observer Book of Profiles, 1991; La Pasionaria, The Spanish Firebrand, 1992; WG: A Life of W G Grace, 1997. Honour: Shortlist, William Hill Sports Book of the Year, 1997. Literary Agent: Jonathan LLoyd, Curtis Brown, London, England. Address: 33 Canfield Gardens, London NW6 3JP, England.

LOW-WESO Denise. See: **LOW Denise.**

LOWBURY Edward (Joseph Lister), b. 6 Dec 1913, London, England. Physician; Poet; Writer on Medical, Scientific and Literary Subjects. m. Alison Young, 12 June 1954, 3 daughters. Education: BA, 1936, BM and BCh, 1939, University College, Oxford; MA; London Hospital Medical College, 1940; DM, Oxford University, 1957. Appointments: Bacteriologist, Medical Research Council Burns Research Unit, Birmingham Accident Hospital, 1949-79; Founder-Honorary Director, Hospital Infection Research Laboratory, Birmingham, 1966-79. Publications: Poetry: Over 20 collections, including: Time for Sale, 1961; Daylight Astronomy, 1968; The Night Watchman, 1974; Poetry and Paradox: Poems and an Essay, 1976; Selected Poems, 1978; Selected and New Poems, 1990; Collected Poems, 1993; Mystic Bridge, 1997. Non-Fiction: Thomas Campion: Poet, Composer, Physician (with Alison Young and Timothy Salter), 1970; Drug Resistance in Antimicrobial Therapy (with G A Ayliffe), 1974; Hallmarks of Poetry (essays), 1994; To Shirk No Idleness: A Critical Biography of the Poet Andrew Young (with Alison Young), 1998. Editor: Control of Hospital Infection: A Practical Handbook (with others), 1975, 3rd edition, 1992; The Poetical Works of Andrew Young (with Alison Young), 1985. Contributions to: Numerous medical, scientific, and literary publications, including reference works and journals. Honours: Newdigate Prize, 1934; Honorary Research Fellow, Birmingham University; John Keats Memorial Lecturer Award, 1973; Everett Evans Memorial Lecturer Award, 1977; DSc, Aston University, 1977; A B Wallace Memorial Lecturer and Medal, 1978; Honorary Professor of Medical Microbiology, Aston University, 1979; LL D, Birmingham University, 1980; Officer of the Order of the British Empire, 1980. Memberships: British Medical Association; Fellow, Royal College of Pathologists, Royal College of Surgeons, Royal Society of Literature; Honorary Fellow, Royal College of Physicians; Society for Applied Bacteriology; Society for General Microbiology; Others. Address: 79 Vernon Road, Birmingham B16 9SQ, England.

LOWDEN Desmond Scott, b. 27 Sept 1937, Winchester, Hampshire, England. Writer. m. 14 July 1962, 1 son, 1 daughter. Publications: Bandersnatch, 1969; The Boondocks, 1972; Bellman and True, 1975; Boudapesti 3, 1979; Sunspot, 1981; Cry Havoc, 1984; The Shadow Run, 1989; Chain, 1990. Honour: Silver Dagger Award, Crime Writers' Association, 1989. Membership: Crime Writers' Association. Address: c/o Deborah Rogers, Rogers, Coleridge and White Ltd, 20 Powys Mews, London W11 1JN, England.

LOWE Barry, b. 16 May 1947, Sydney, New South Wales, Australia. Playwright; Writer; Scriptwriter. Partner: Walter Figallo, 24 Dec 1972. Publications: Plays: Writers Camp, first performed, 1982; Tokyo Rose, 1989; The Death of Peter Pan, 1989; Seeing Things, 1994; Relative Merits, 1994; The Extraordinary Annual General Meeting of the Size-Queen Club, 1996. Contributions to: Various publications. Memberships: Australian Writers Guild; Australian Society of Authors. Literary Agent: Kevin Palmer, 258 Bulwara Road, Ultimo, New South Wales 2007, Australia. Address: GPO Box 635, Sydney, New South Wales 1034, Australia.

LOWE John Evelyn, b. 23 Apr 1928, London, England. Writer. m. (1) Susan Sanderson, 1956, 2 sons, 1 daughter, (2) Yuki Nomura, 1989, 1 daughter. Education: English Literature, New College, Oxford, 1950-52. Appointments: Associate Editor, Collins Crime Club, 1953-54; Editor, Faber Furniture Series, 1954-56; Deputy Story Editor, Pinewood Studios, 1956-57; Literary Editor, Kansai Time Out Magazine, 1985-89. Publications: Thomas Chippendale, 1955; Cream Coloured Earthenware, 1958; Japanese Crafts, 1983; Into Japan, 1985; Into China, 1986; Corsica - A Traveller's Guide, 1988; A Surrealist Life - Edward James, 1991; A Short Guide to the Kyoto Museum of Archaeology, 1991; Glimpses of Kyoto Life, 1996; The Warden - A Portrait of John Sparrow, 1998; Olakyoto, forthcomming. Contributions to: Encyclopaedia Britannica; Oxford Junior Enecyclopaedia; American Scholar; Country Life; Listener; Connoisseur; Apollo; Others. Honour: Honorary Fellow, Royal College of Art. Memberships: Society of Antiquaries, fellow; Royal Society of Arts, fellow. Address: Paillole Basse, 47360 Prayssas, France.

LOWE Robson, b. 7 Jan 1905, London, England. Editor; Author; Auctioneer. m. Winifred Marie Deane, 7 Mar 1928, 2 daughters. Education: Fulham Central School. Publications: Regent Catalogue of Empire Postage Stamps, 1933; The Encyclopaedia of Empire Postage Stamps, 1935; Handstruck Postage Stamps of the Empire, 1937; The Birth of the Adhesive Postage Stamp, 1939; Masterpieces of Engraving on Postage Stamps, 1943; The Encyclopaedia of Empire Postage Stamps, 7 volumes, 1950-90; Sperati and His Work, 1956; The British Postage Stamp, 1968; Leeward Islands, 1990; The House of Stamps, Imitations, 1993. Contributions to: Many philatelic and postal journals.

Address: c/o East India Club, 16 St James' Square, London SW1, England.

LOWE Stephen, b. 1 Dec 1947, Nottingham, England. Playwright. m. (1) Tina Barclay, (2) Tany Myers, 1 son, 1 daughter. Education: BA, Honours, English and Drama, 1969; Postgraduate Research, 1969-70. Appointments: Senior Tutor in Writing for Performance, Dartington College of Arts Performance, 1978-82; Resident Playwright, Riverside Studios, London, 1982-84; Senior Tutor, Birmingham University, 1987-88; Nottingham Trent University Advisory Board to Theatre Design Degree, 1987-. Publications: Touched, 1981; Cards, 1983; Moving Pictures and Other Plays, 1985; Body and Soul in Peace Plays, 2 volumes, 1985, 1990; Divine Gossip/Tibetan Inroads, 1988; Ragged Trousered Philanthropists, 1991. Contributions to: Books and journals. Honour: George Devine Award for Playwriting, 1977. Memberships: Theatre Writers Union; Writers Guild; PEN. Literary Agent: Judy Daish Associates. Address: S Stroud, Judy Daish Associates, 83 Eastbourn Mews, London W2 6LQ, England.

LOWELL Susan Deborah, b. 27 Oct 1950, Chihuahua, Mexico. Writer. m. William Ross Humphreys, 21 Mar 1975, 2 daughters. Education: BA, 1972, MA, 1974, Stanford University, USA; MA, PhD, 1979, Princeton University Appointments: University of Arizona, 1974-76, 1981; University of Texas, Dallas, 1979-80. Publications: Ganado Red: A Novella and Stories, 1988; I am Lavinia Cumming, 1993. Honours: Milkweed Editions National Fiction Prize, 1988; Mountain and Plains Booksellers Association Regional Book Award, Children's Writing, 1994. Membership: Southern Arizona Society of Authors. Address: c/o Milkweed Editions, PO Box 3226, Minneapolis, MN 55403, USA.

LOWERY Joanne, b. 30 July 1945, Cleveland, Ohio, USA. English Educator; Writer; Editor. m. Stephen Paul Lowery, 15 June 1968, div 1988, 1 son, 1 daughter. Education: AB, Distinction, University of Michigan, 1967; MA, University of Wisconsin, 1968. Appointments: Part-time Instructor of English, Elgin College, 1986-91, College of DuPage, Glen Ellyn, 1991-96, St Mary's College, Notre Dame, 1997-98; Poetry Editor, Black Dirt, literary magazine, 1994-. Publications: Coming to This, 1990; Corinth, 1990; Heroics, 1996. Contributions to: Magazines. Honour: New Letters Literary Award, 1993. Address: 62095 Pine Road, North Liberty, IN 46554, USA.

LOWNIE Andrew (James Hamilton), b. 11 Nov 1961, Kenya. Literary Agent; Writer; Editor. m. Angela Doyle, 2 May 1998. Education: Magdalene College, Cambridge, 1981-84; BA, Cantab; MA, Cantab; MSc, University of Edinburgh, 1989. Appointments: Member, 1985-86, Director, 1986-88, John Farquharson Literary Agents; Director, Andrew Lownie Associates, 1988-; Partner, Denniston and Lownie, 1991-93; Director, Thistle Publishing, 1996-. Publications: North American Spies, 1992; Edinburgh Literary Guide, 1992; John Buchan: The Presbyterian Cavalier, 1995; John Buchan's Collected Poems (editor), 1996; The Complete Short Stories of John Buchan, Vols 1 - 3 (editor), 1997-98. Contributions to: Books and periodicals. Honour: English Speaking Union Scholarship, 1979-80. Memberships: Association of Authors' Agents; Royal Geographical Society, fellow; Royal Society of Arts, fellow; Society of Authors. Address: 17 Sutherland St, London, SW1V 4JU.

LOWRY Beverly (Fey), b. 10 Aug 1938, Memphis, Tennessee, USA. Writer. m. Glenn Lowry, 3 June 1960, 2 sons. Education: University of Mississippi, 1956-58; BA, Memphis State University, 1960. Publications: Come Back, Lolly Ray, 1977; Emma Blue, 1978; Daddy's Girl, 1981; The Perfect Sonya, 1987; Breaking Gentle, 1988; Crossed Over: The True Story of the Houston Pickax Murders, 1992; The Track of Real Desire, 1994. Contributions to: Newspapers and magazines. Address: c/o Penguin Books, 375 Hudson Street, New York, NY 10014, USA.

LOWRY Lois, b. 20 Mar 1937, Honolulu, Hawaii. Writer. m. Donald Grey Lowry, 11 June 1956, div 1977, 2 sons, 2 daughters. Education: Brown University, 1954-56; BA, University of Southern Maine, 1972. Publications: Children's Books: A Summer to Die, 1977; Find a Stranger, Say Goodbye, 1978; Anastasia Krupnik, 1979; Autumn Street, 1979; Anastasia Again!, 1981; Anastasia at Your Service, 1982; Taking Care of Terrific, 1983; Anastasia Ask Your Analyst, 1984; Us and Uncle Fraud, 1984; One Hundredth Thing About Caroline, 1985; Anastasia on Her Own, 1985; Switcharound, 1985; Anastasia Has the Answers, 1986; Rabble Starkey, 1987; Anastasia's Chosen Career, 1987; All About Sam, 1988; Number the Stars, 1989; Your Move J P!, 1990; Anastasia at This Address, 1991; Attaboy Sam!. 1992; The Giver, 1993. Other: Black American Literature, 1973; Literature of the American Revolution, 1974; Values and the Family, 1977. Honours: Children's Literature Award, International Reading Association, 1978; American Library Association Notable Book Citation, 1980; Boston Globe-Horn Book Award, 1987; National Jewish Book Award, 1990; Newbery Medals, 1990, 1994. Literary Agent: Wendy Schmalz, Harold Ober Associates. Address: 205 Brattle Street, Cambridge, MA 02138, USA.

LTAIF Nadine. Publications: Les Métamorphoses d'Ishtar, 1987; Entre les Fleuves, 1991; Élégies du Levant, 1995; Vestige d'un Jardin, livre d'artiste. Contributions to: Tessera; Arcade; Estuaire. Address: 2004 St Laurent, 303, Montreal, Quebec H2X 2T2, Canada.

LUARD Nicholas, (James McVean), b. 26 June 1937, London, England. Writer. Education: Winchester College, 1951-54; Sorbonne, University of Paris, 1954-55; MA, Cambridge University, 1960; MA, University of Pennsylvania, 1961. Publications: Fiction: The Warm and Golden War, 1967; The Robespierre Serial, 1975; Traveling Horseman, 1975; The Orion Line, 1976; Bloodspoor, 1977; The Dirty Area, 1979; Seabird Nine, 1981; Titan, 1984. Non-Fiction: Refer to Drawer (with Dominick Elwes), 1964; The Last Wilderness: A Journey Across the Great Kalahari Desert, 1981; The Wildlife Parks of Africa, 1985. Address: 227 South Lambeth Road, London SW8, England.

LUBEJA Ludmila, b. 1 Apr 1929, Minsk, Byelorussia. Editor. m. Ints Lubejs, 25 June 1959, 1 son. Education: Graduate, Editorial Publishing Faculty, Moscow Polygraphic Institute, 1951. Appointments: Editor of Fiction, Latvian State Publishing House, 1951-65; Deputy Editor, Scientific Editor, Magazine Proceedings, Latvian Academy of Sciences, 1965-84. Publications: Several Translations into Russian. Honour: Award, Translation Competition, 1956. Memberships: Latvian Union of Journalists; Writers Union of Latvia. Address: K. Valdemara iela 145, 1 K, dz 23, Riga, LV-1013, Latvia.

LUBEJS Ints, b. 19 June 1931, Riga, Latvia. Writer. m. Lyudmila Beilina, 25 June 1959, 1 son. Education: Graduate, Latvian State University, Riga. Appointments: Prose Fiction Editor, Senior Editor, Latvian State Publishing House, 1957-64; Executive Secretary, Literary magazine, Karogs, 1964-79. Publications: Satiksanas (short stories), 1959; Makoni virs pilsetas (short stories), 1961; Salta rasa (story), 1968; Dvinu zvaigznajs, 1977; Attalinadamies un tuvodamies (selected prose), 1981; Naivas speles (trilogy), 1994. Contributions to: Berniba; Zvaigzne; Liesma; Dadzis; Karogs; Daugava; Rizhskiy Almanach. Honours: Literary Award, Karogs magazine, 1993. Membership: Writers Union of Latvia, 1961. Address: K. Valdemara iela 145, 1 K, dz 23, Riga, LV-1013, Latvia.

LUBINGER Eva, b. 3 Feb 1930, Steyr, Austria. Writer. m. Dr Walter Myss, 7 Oct 1952, 2 sons. Publications: Paradies mit Kleinen Fehlein, 1976; Gespenster in Sir Edwards Haus, 1978; Pflucke den Wind, 1982; Verlieb Dich nicht in Mark Aurell, 1985; Zeig mir Lamorna, 1985; Flieg mit Nach Samarkand, 1987; Annas Fest (novel), 1991; Eine Handvoll Lebenstage (novel), 1995. Contributions to: Prasent, weekly newspaper. Honours: Literature Prize for Lyrics, Innsbruck, 1963; Literature

Prize for Drama, Innsbruck, 1969. Membership: PEN, Austria. Address: Lindenbuhelweg 16, 6020 Innsbruck, Austria.

LUCAS Celia, b. 23 Oct 1938, Bristol, England. Writer. m. Ian Skidmore, 20 Oct 1971. Education: BA, Honours, Modern History, St Hilda's College, Oxford, 1961. Publications: Prisoners of Santo Tomas, 1975, 3rd edition, 1996; Steel Town Cats, 1987; Glyndwr Country (with Ian Skidmore), 1988; Anglesey Rambles (with Ian Skidmore), 1989; The Adventures of Marmaduke Purr Cat, 1990; The Terrible Tale of Tiggy Two, 1995. Contributions to: Numerous journals and magazines. Honours: TIR NA N-OG Award for Junior Fiction, 1988; Irma Chilton Award for Junior Fiction, 1995. Membership: Welsh Academy, 1989-. Address: Aberbraint, Llanfairpwll, Isle of Anglesey, North Wales LL61 6PB, Wales.

LUCAS John, b. 26 June 1937, Exeter, Devon, England. Professor of English; Poet; Writer; Publisher. m. 30 Sept 1961, 1 son, 1 daughter. Education: 1st Class Honours, Philosophy and English Literature, 1959, PhD, 1965, University of Reading. Appointments: Assistant Lecturer, University of Reading, 1961-64; Lecturer, Senior Lecturer, Reader, University of Nottingham, 1964-77; Visiting Professor, University of Maryland and Indiana University, 1967-68; Professor of English, Loughborough University, 1977-; Lord Byron Visiting Professor, University of Athens, 1984-85; Publisher, Shoestring Press, 1994-. Publications: About Nottingham, 1971; A Brief Bestiary, 1972; Egils Saga: Versions of the Poems, 1975; The Days of the Week, 1983; Studying Grosz on the Bus, 1989; Flying to Romania, 1992; One for the Piano, 1997. Contributions to: Anthologies, newspapers, reviews, and BBC Radio 3 and 4. Honour: Poetry Prize for Best 1st Full Volume of Poetry, Aldeburgh Festival, 1990. Memberships: John Clare Society; Poetry Book Society, chairman, 1988-92; Royal Society of Arts, fellow; William Morris Society. Address: 19 Devonshire Avenue, Beeston, Nottingham NG9 1BS, England.

LUCAS John (Randolph), b. 18 June 1929, England. Retired Reader in Philosophy; Writer. m. Morar Portal, 1961, 2 sons, 2 daughters. Education: St Mary's College, Winchester; MA, Balliol College, Oxford, 1952. Appointments: Junior Research Fellow, 1953-56, Fellow and Tutor, 1960-96, Merton College, Oxford; Fellow and Assistant Tutor, Corpus Christi College, Cambridge, 1956-59; Jane Eliza Procter Visiting Fellow, Princeton University, 1957-58; Leverhulme Research Fellow, Leeds University, 1959-60; Gifford Lecturer, University of Edinburgh, 1971-73; Margaret Harris Lecturer, University of Dundee, 1981; Harry Jelema Lecturer, Calvin College, Grand Rapids, 1987; Reader in Philosophy, Oxford University, 1990-96. Publications: Principles of Politics, 1966, 2nd edition, 1985; The Concept of Probability, 1970; The Freedom of the Will, 1970; The Nature of Mind, 1972; The Development of Mind, 1973; A Treatise on Time and Space, 1973; Essays on Freedom and Grace, 1976; Democracy and Participation, 1976; On Justice, 1980; Space, Time and Causality, 1985; The Future, 1989; Spacetime and Electromagnetism, 1990; Responsibility, 1993; Ethical Economics, 1996; The Conceptual Roots of Mathematics, forthcoming. Contributions to: Scholarly journals. Memberships: British Academy, fellow; British Society for the Philosophy of Science, president, 1991-93. Address: Lambrook House, East Lambrook, Somerset TA13 5HW, England.

LUCAS Stephen E, b. 5 Oct 1946, White Plains, New York, USA. Professor; Writer. m. Patricia Vore, 14 June 1969, 2 sons. Education: BA, University of California at Santa Barbara, 1968; MA, 1971, PhD, 1973, Pennsylvania State University. Appointments: Assistant Professor, 1972-76, Associate Professor, 1976-82, Professor, 1982-, University of Wisconsin at Madison; Visiting Associate Professor, University of Virginia, 1979. Publications: Portents of Rebellion: Rhetoric and Revolution in Philadelphia, 1765-1776, 1976; The Art of Public Speaking, 1983, 6th edition, 1998; George Washington: The Wisdom of an American Patriot, 1998. Contributions to: Scholarly books and journals. Honours:

National Communication Association Golden Anniversary Award, 1977; J Jeffrey Auer Lecturer, Indiana University, 1988; Wisconsin Teaching Academy, 1997. Memberships: International Society for the History of Rhetoric; Organization of American Historians; Society for Eighteenth-Century Studies; National Communication Association. Address: c/o Department of Communication Arts, University of Wisconsin at Madison, Madison, WI 53706, USA.

LUCHETTI Cathy, b. 6 Oct 1945, Phoenix, Arizona, USA. Author; Historian. m. Larry Luchetti, 25 July 1972, 3 sons. Education: BA, English, University of Utah. Publications: Women of the West; Under God's Spell: Frontier Evangelists, 1772-1915; Home on the Range: A Culinary History of the American West; I Do! Courtship, Love and Marriage in the American West; The Hot Flash Cook Book; Medicine Women: The Story of Early - American Women Doctors. Honours: Pacific Northwest Bookseller's Award for Literary Excellence, 1984; James Beard Award for Best Writing on American Food, 1994. Memberships: Women Writing the West; Authors Guild. Literary Agent: Anne Edelstein, 404 Riverside Drive, New York, NY 10025, USA. Address: Anne Edelstein, 404 Riverside Drive, New York, NY 10025, USA.

LUCIE-SMITH (John) Edward (McKenzie), (Peter Kershaw), b. 27 Feb 1933, Kingston, Jamaica. Art Critic; Poet; Journalist; Broadcaster. Education: MA, Honours, Modern History, Merton College, Oxford. Publications: A Tropical Childhood, 1961; Confessions and Histories, 1964; Penguin Modern Poets 6 (with Jack Clemo and George MacBeth), 1964; Penguin Book of Elizabethan Verse (editor), 1965; What is a Painting?, 1966; The Liverpool Scene (editor), 1967; A Choice of Browning's Verse (editor), 1967; Penguin Book of Satirical Verse (editor), 1967; Thinking About Art, 1968; Towards Silence, 1968; Movements in Art Since 1945, 1969; British Poetry Since 1945 (editor), 1970; A Primer of Experimental Verse (editor), 1971; French Poetry: The Last Fifteen Years (editor with S W Taylor), 1971; A Concise History of French Painting, 1971; Symbolist Art, 1972; Eroticism in Western Art, 1972; The First London Catalogue, 1974; The Well Wishers, 1974; The Burnt Child (autobiography), 1975; The Invented Eye, 1975; World of the Makers, 1975; How the Rich Lived (with Celestine Dars), 1976; Joan of Arc, 1976; Work and Struggle (with Celestine Dars), 1977; Fantin-Latour, 1977; The Dark Pageant (novel), 1977; Art Today, 1977; A Concise History of Furniture, 1979; Super Realism, 1979; Cultural Calendar of the Twentieth Century, 1979; Art in the Seventies, 1980; The Story of Craft, 1981; The Body, 1981; A History of Industrial Design, 1983; Art Terms: An Illustrated Dictionary, 1984; Art in the Thirties, 1985; American Art Now, 1985; Lives of the Great Twentieth Century Artists, 1986; Sculpture Since 1945, 1987; The New British Painting (with Carolyn Cohen and Judith Higgins), 1988; Art in the Eighties, 1990; Art Deco Painting, 1990; Fletcher Benton, 1990; Jean Rustin, 1991; Harry Holland, 1992; Art and Civilization, 1992; The Faber Book of Art Anecdotes (editor), 1992; Andres Nagel, 1992; Wendy Taylor, 1992; Alexander, 1992; British Art Now, 1993; Race, Sex and Gender: Issues in Contemporary Art, 1994; Elisabeth Frink: A Portrait (with Elisabeth Frink), 1994; American Realism, 1994; Art Today, 1995; Visual Arts in the Twentieth Century, 1996; As Erotica, 1997; Lyn Chadwick, 1997; Adam, 1998; Zoe, 1998. Contributions to: Many newspapers and journals. Membership: Royal Society of Literature, fellow. Address: c/o Rogers, Coleridge and White, 20 Powis Mews, London W11 1JN, England.

LUCKLESS John. See: IRVING Clifford.

LUDLUM Robert, (Jonathan Ryder, Michael Shepherd), b. 25 May 1927, New York, New York, USA. Author. m. Mary Ryducha, 31 Mar 1951, 2 sons, 1 daughter. Education: BA, Wesleyan University, 1951. Publications: The Scarlatti Inheritance, 1971; The Osterman Weekend, 1972; The Matlock Paper, 1973; Trevayne, 1973; The Cry of the Halidon, 1974; The Rhinemann Exchange, 1974; The Road to Gandolfo, 1975; The Gemini Contenders, 1976; The Chancellor

Manuscript, 1977; The Holcroft Covenant, 1978; The Maltarese Circle, 1979; The Bourne Identity, 1980; The Parsifal Mosaic, 1982; The Aquitaine Progression, 1984; The Bourne Supremacy, 1986; The Icarus Agenda, 1988; The Bourne Ultimatum, 1990; The Road to Omaha, 1992; The Scorpio Illusion, 1993; The Apocalypse Watch, 1995; The Maltarese Countdown, 1997. Honours: Several awards and grants. Memberships: American Federation of Television and Radio Artists; Authors Guild; Authors League of America; Screen Actors Guild. Address: c/o Henry Morrison, Box 235, Bedford Hills, NY 10507, USA.

LUDWIKOWSKI Rett R(yszard), b. 6 Nov 1943, Skawina-Kraków, Poland. Professor of Law; Writer. m. Anna Ludwikowski, 19 Jan 1995, 1 son. Education: LLM, Law, 1966, PhD Law, 1971, Habilitation, Law, 1976, Jagiellonian University, Kraków. Appointments: Senior Lecturer, 1967-71, Adjunct Professor, 1971-76, Assistant Professor, 1976-81, Associate Professor of Law, 1981, Senior Fulbright Scholar, 1997, Jagiellonian University, Kraków; Visiting Professor, Elizabethtown College, Pennsylvania, 1982-83, Alfred University, 1983; Visiting Scholar, Hoover Institution, Stanford University, 1983, Max Planck Institute, Hamburg, 1990; Visiting Professor of Politics, 1984, Visiting Professor of Law, 1985, Professor of Law, 1986-, Director, Comparative and International Law Institute, 1987-, Catholic University of America, Washington, DC. Publications: The Crisis of Communism: Its Meaning, Origins and Phases, 1986; Continuity and Change in Poland, 1991; Constitutionalism and Human Rights (editor with Kenneth Thompson), 1991; The Beginning of the Constitutional Era: A Comparative Study of the First American and European Constitution (with William Fox Jr), 1993; Constitution Making in the Countries of Former Soviet Dominance, 1996; Regulations of International Trade and Business, 2 volumes, 1996, 1998. Contributions to: Scholarly books and journals. Honours: Various grants. Address: 7712 Grolnick Place, Springfield, VA 22153, USA.

LUEBKE Frederick (Carl), b. 26 Jan 1927, Reedsburg, Wisconsin, USA. Professor of History Emeritus. Education: BS, Concordia University, River Forest, Illinois, 1950; MA, Claremont Graduate University, 1958; PhD, University of Nebraska, 1966. Appointments: Associate Professor, 1968-72, Professor, 1972-87, Charles Mach Distinguished Professor of History, 1987-94, Professor Emeritus, 1994-, University of Nebraska; Editor, Great Plains Quarterly, 1980-84; Director, Center for Great Plains Studies, 1983-88. Publications: Immigrants and Politics, 1969; Ethnic Voters and the Election of Lincoln (editor), 1971; Bonds of Loyalty: German-Americans and World War I, 1974; The Great Plains: Environment and Culture (editor), 1979; Ethnicity on the Great Plains (editor), 1980; Vision and Refuge: Essays on the Literature of the Great Plains (co-editor), 1981; Mapping the North American Plains (co-editor), 1987; Germans in Brazil: A Comparative History of Cultural Conflict During World War I, 1987; Germans in the New World: Essays in the History of Immigration, 1990; A Harmony of the Arts: The Nebraska State Capital (editor), 1990; Nebraska: An Illustrated History, 1995; European Immigration in the American West: Community Histories (editor), 1998. Contributions to: Professional journals. Address: 3117 Woodsdale Boulevard, Lincoln, NE 68502, USA.

LUELLEN Valentina. See: POLLEY Judith Anne.

LUHRMANN Tanya Marie, b. 24 Feb 1959, Dayton, Ohio, USA. Professor of Anthropology. Education: BA summa cum laude, Harvard University, 1981; MPhil, Social Anthropology, 1982, PhD, Social Anthropology, 1986, University of Cambridge. Appointments: Research Fellow, Christ's College, Cambridge, England, 1985-89; Associate Professor of Anthropology, University of California at San Diego, 1989-. Publications: Persuasions of the Witch's Craft, 1989; The Good Parsi, 1996. Contributions to: Professional journals. Honours: Bowdoin Prize, 1981; National Science Foundation Graduate Fellow, 1982-85; Emanuel Miller Prize, 1983; Partingdon Prize, 1985; Stirling Prize, 1986; Fulbright Award, 1990. Memberships: American Anthropology Association;

Society for Psychological Anthropology; Royal Anthropological Institute. Address: c/o Department of Anthropology, University of California at San Diego, 0532, La Jolla, CA 92093, USA.

LUKACS John (Adalbert), b. 31 Jan 1924, Budapest, Hungary (US citizen, 1953). Professor of History (Retired); Writer. m. (1) Helen Schofield, 29 May 1953, dec 1970, 1 son, 1 daughter, (2) Stephanie Harvey, 18 May 1974. Education: PhD, Palatine Joseph University, Budapest, 1946. Appointments: Professor of History, 1947-94, Chairman, Department of History, 1947-74, Chestnut Hill College, Philadelphia; Visiting Professor, La Salle College, 1949-82, Columbia University, 1954-55, University of Toulouse, 1964-65, University of Pennsylvania, 1964, 1967, 1968, 1995-97, Johns Hopkins University, 1970-71, Fletcher School of Law and Diplomacy, 1971-72, Princeton University, 1988, University of Budapest, 1991. Publications: The Great Powers and Eastern Europe, 1953; A History of the Cold War, 1961; The Decline and Rise of Europe, 1965; Historical Consciousness, 1968, 3rd edition, 1994; The Passing of the Modern Age, 1970; The Last European War, 1939-41, 1976; 1945: Year Zero, 1978; Philadelphia: Patricians and Philistines, 1900-1950, 1981; Outgrowing Democracy: A Historical Interpretation of the US in the 20th Century, 1984; Budapest 1900, 1988; Confessions of an Original Sinner, 1990; The Duel: Hitler vs. Churchill, 10 May-31 August 1940, 1991; The End of the 20th Century and the End of the Modern Age, 1993; Destinations Past, 1994; George P Kennan and the Origins of Containment: The Kennan/Lukacs Correspondence, 1997; The Hitler of History, 1997. Contributions to: Many scholarly journals. Honours: Ingersoll Prize, 1991; Order of Merit, Republic of Hungary, 1994. Memberships: American Catholic History Association, president, 1977; Society of American Historians, fellow. Address: Valley Park Road, Phoenixville, PA 19460, USA.

LUKAS Richard Conrad, b. 29 Aug 1937, Lynn, Massachusetts, USA. Historian; Professor. Education: BA, 1957, MA, 1960, PhD, 1963, Florida State University. Appointments: Research Consultant, US Air Force Historical Archives, 1957-58; Assistant Professor, 1963-66, Associate Professor, 1966-69, Professor, 1969-83, University Professor of History, 1983-89, Tennessee Technological University, Cookeville; Professor, Wright State University, Lake Campus, 1989-92; Adjunct Professor, University of South Florida, Fort Myers, 1993-96; Consultant, Documentary Films, Zegota: A Time to Remember, 1997, Burning Questions, 1998. Publications: Eagles East: The Army Air Forces and the Soviet Union, 1941-45, 1970; From Metternich to the Beatles (editor), 1973; The Strange Allies: The United States and Poland 1941-45, 1978; Bitter Legacy: Polish-American Relations in the Wake of World War II, 1982; Forgotten Holocaust: The Poles under German Occupation, 1986; Out of the Inferno: Poles Remember the Holocaust, 1989; Did the Children Cry?: Hitler's War Against Jewish and Polish Children, 1994. Honours: Doctor of Humane Letters, 1987; Polonia Restituta, 1988; Janusz Korczak Literary Award, 1996. Address: 1344 Rock Dove Court, D-104, Punta Gorda, FL 33950, USA.

LUKE Thomas. See: MASTERTON Graham.

LUKER Nicholas (John Lydgate), b. 26 Jan 1945, Leeds, England. University Senior Lecturer in Russian; Writer; Editor; Translator. 1 son. Education: MA, French, Russian, Hertford College, Oxford, 1968; Lecteur d'Anglais, University of Grenoble, 1967; Postgraduate Scholar, Slavonic Studies, 1968-70, PhD, 1971, University of Nottingham. Appointments: Lecturer, 1970-88, Senior Lecturer in Russian, 1988-, University of Nottingham; Various visiting lectureships and fellowships. Publications: Alexander Grin, 1973; The Seeker of Adventure, by Alexander Grin (translator with B Scherr), 1978; A I Kuprin, 1978; The Forgotten Visionary, 1982; An Anthology of Russian Neo-Realism: The "Znanie" School of Maxim Gorky (editor and translator), 1982; Fifty Years On: Gorky and His Time (editor), 1987; Alexander Grin: Selected Short Stories (editor and translator), 1987;

From Furmanov to Sholokhov: An Anthology of the Classics of Socialist Realism (editor and translator), 1988; In Defence of a Reputation: Essays on the Early Prose of Mikhail Artsybashev, 1990; The Russian Short Story, 1900-1917 (editor), 1991; Urban Romances, by Yuri Miloslavsky (editor and co-translator), 1994; After the Watershed: Russian Prose, 1917-1927 (editor), 1996. Contributions to: Numerous scholarly journals. Memberships: British Association of Slavists. Address: c/o Department of Slavonic Studies, University of Nottingham, Nottingham NG7 2RD, England.

LULUA Abdul-Wahid, b. 16 July 1931, Mowsil, Iraq. Professor of English Literature. m. Mariam Abdul-Bagi, 22 July 1962, 1 son, 1 daughter. Education: Licence-es-Lettres, English, University of Baghdad, 1952; EdM, English, Harvard University, 1957; PhD, English, Western Reserve University, Cleveland, 1962. Appointments: Lecturer, Assistant Professor, Head, Department of European Languages, Ecole Normale Superieure, Baghdad, 1962-67; Assistant Professor, 1967-70, Associate Professor, 1970-71, 1972-73, University of Kuwait; Visiting Scholar, University of Cambridge, 1971-72; Associate Professor, 1983, Chairman, Department of English Language and Literature, 1983-84, Professor of English Literature, 1983-89, Yarmouk University, Jordan; Professor of English Literature, United Arab Emirates University, 1989-. Publications: Critical Studies: In Search of Meaning, 1973, 2nd edition, 1983; T S Eliot, The Wase Land: The Poet and the Poem, 1980, 2nd edition, 1986; Blowing into Ashes, 1982, 2nd edition, 1989; Aspect of the Moon, 1990; Arabic Poetry and the Rise of European Love Lyrics. Contributions to: Major Arabic magazines. Memberships: Association Internationale de Litterature Comparative; Modern Humanities Research Association, Cambridge. Address: c/o Riad El-Rayyes Books, 56 Knightsbridge, London SW1X 7NJ, England.

LUNARI Luigi, b. 3 Jan 1934, Milan, Italy. Writer. m. Laura Pollaroli, 8 July 1961, 1 son, 1 daughter. Education: Degree in Law, University of Milan, 1956; Diploma in Common Law, City of London College, 1958; Composition and Orchestra Conducting, Academy Chigiana, Siena, 1978. Appointments: Director, Study Office of Piccolo Teatro, 1961-82; Professor, History of Dramatic Art, University of Modern Languages, 1984-. Publications: L'Old Vic di Londra, 1959; Laurence Olivier, 1959; Il movimento drammatico irlandese, 1960; Il teatro irlandese: storia e antologia, 1961; Henry Irving e il teatro inglese dell'800, 1962; Il senatore Fox, 1908; Maria di Nazareth, 1986; La Bella e la Bestia, 1988; La stagione del garofane rosso, 1989; Tre sull'altalena, 1990; Nel nome del padre, 1996. Contributions to: Il giornale nuovo, 1991. Memberships: International Society of Authors; International Society of Dramatists; PEN Club. Address: 20047 Brugherio, Via Volturno 80, Milan, Italy.

LUND Gerald Niels, b. 12 Sept 1939, Fountain Green, Utah, USA. Educator; Writer. m. Lynn Stanard, 5 June 1963, 3 sons, 4 daughters. Education: BA, Sociology, 1965, MS, Sociology, 1969, Brigham Young University; Further graduate studies, Pepperdine University. Appointment: Faculty, Brigham Young University. Publications: The Coming of the Lord, 1971; This is Your World, 1973; One in Thine Hand, 1981; The Alliance, 1983; Leverage Point, 1986; Freedom Factor, 1987; The Work and the Glory: Vol I, Pillar of Light, 1990, Vol II, Like a Fire is Burning, 1991, Vol III, Truth Will Prevail, 1992, Vol IV, Thy Gold to Refine, 1993, Vol V, A Season of Joy, 1994, Vol VI, Praise to the Man, 1995, Vol VII, No Unhallowed Hand, 1996, Vol VIII, So Great A Cause, 1998, Vol IX All is Well. Contributions to: Monographs and magazines. Honours: Outstanding Teacher in Continuing Education, Brigham Young University, 1985; Best Novel Awards, Association of Mormon Letters, 1991, 1993; Independent Booksellers Book of the Year Award, 1994; Orton Award for Literature, 1994; Independent Booksellers, Outstanding Book, Fiction. Membership: Association of Mormons Letters, honorary lifetime membership, 1997. Address: 50 E North Temple Street, 9th Floor, Salt Lake City, UT 84150, USA.

LUNDBERG Ulla-Lena, b. 14 July 1947, Kökar, Åland Islands, Finland. Education: MA, University of Åbo Akademi, 1985. Appointments: Artist Professor, Finland, 1994-99. Publications: Documentation: Gaijin, 1970; Kökar, 1976; Öar i Afrikas inre, 1981; Sibirien, 1993; Novels: Kungens Anna, 1982; Ingens Anna, 1984; Sand, 1986; Sjöfarartrilogin, 1989-95; Regn, 1997. Honours: Finland Prize, Swedish Academy, 1990; PhD hc, University of Åbo Akademi, 1993; Runeberg Prize, Finland, 1998. Memberships: Finnish PEN; Society of Swedish Authors in Finland. Literary Agent: Marianne Bargum, Söderström and Co, Box 97, 00211 Helsinki, Finland. Address: Borgå, Finland.

LUNN Janet Louise, b. 28 Dec 1928, Dallas, Texas, USA. Writer. m. Richard Lunn, 1 Mar 1950, 4 sons, 1 daughter. Education: Queen's University, Kingston, Ontario. Appointments: Writer-in-Residence, Regina Public Library, Saskatchewan, 1982-83, Kitchener Public Library, Ontario, 1987, Ottawa University, Ontario, 1993. Publications: The Country, 1967; Double Spell, 1968; Larger Than Life, 1979; The Twelve Dancing Princesses, 1979; The Root Cellar, 1981; Shadow in Hawthorn Bay, 1986; Amos's Sweater, 1988; Duck Cakes for Sale, 1989; One Hundred Shining Candles, 1990; The Story of Canada, 1992; Ghost Stories for Children (editor), 1994; The Hollow Tree, 1997; The Umbrella Party, 1998; Charlotte, 1998. Contributions to: Periodicals. Honours: Honorary LLD, Queen's University, 1992; Order of Ontario, 1996; Order of Canada, 1997. Memberships: Writers' Union of Canada, chair, 1984-85; Canadian Children's Book Center; PEN Canada. Literary Agent: Lee Davis. Address: RR No 2, Hillier, Ontario K0K 2J0, Canada.

LUNSFORD M Rosser, b. 1 Mar 1922, Hogansville, Georgia, USA. Author; Poet. m. Vera Jenkins, 22 Feb 1955, 2 sons, 1 daughter. Education: Student; South Georgia College, 1939-40. Publications: Folkway, 1962; I Am, 1962; Eye of Memory, 1986; After Thoughts, 1986. Contributions to: Over 400 poems to numerous literary magazines and periodicals. Honours: Freedom Award, 1982; Little Brothers Award, Inky Trails magazine, 1983; Poet of Year Award, Rhyme Time Magazine, 1993; 2 Best of Issue Awards, Tiotis magazine, 1983; Certificate of Merit, Georgia Poetry Society, 1983; 1st Place Award, Explorer magazine, 1984, 1985; Numerous others. Memberships: Poets and Writers; Poets Council; Heritage Society; Authors and Writers of America; Honorary Member, Dr Stella Woodall Poets International. Address: 456 Rockville Springs Drive, Eatonton, GA 31024, USA.

LUPOFF Richard Allen, b. 21 Feb 1935, New York, New York, USA. Author. m. Patricia Enid Loring, 27 Aug 1958, 2 sons, 1 daughter. Education: BA, University of Miami at Coral Gables, 1956. Appointments: Editor, Canaveral Press, 1963-70; Contributing Editor, Crawdaddy Magazine, 1968-71, Science Fiction Eye, 1988-90; Editor, Canyon Press, 1986-. Publications: Edgar Rice Burroughs: Master of Adventure, 1965; All in Color for a Dime, 1971; Sword of the Demon, 1977; Space War Blues, 1978; Sun's End, 1984; Circumpolar!, 1984; Lovecrafts Book, 1985; The Forever City, 1987; The Comic Book Killer, 1988; The Classic Car Killer, 1992; The Bessie Blue Killer, 1994; The Sepia Siren Killer, 1994; The Cover Girl Killer, 1995. Contributions to: Ramparts; Los Angeles Times; Washington Post; San Francisco Chronicle; New York Times; Magazine of Fantasy and Science Fiction. Honour: Hugo Award, 1963. Address: 3208 Claremont Avenue, Berkeley, CA 94705, USA.

LURAGHI Raimondo, b. 16 Aug 1921, Milan, Italy. Professor Emeritus. m. 24 June 1950, 1 son, 1 daughter. Education: MD, University of Turin, 1946; PhD, University of Rome, 1958. Appointments: Professor of History, Junior College, 1954-64; Professor of American History, 1964-, Emeritus Professor, 1995-, University of Genoa. Publications: Storia della Guerra Civile Americana, 1966; Gli Stati Uniti, 1972; The Rise and Fall of the Plantation South, 1975; Marinai del Sud, 1993; A History of the Confederate Navy 1861-1865, 1995. Contributions to: Italian, French, American and Chinese historical magazines. Membership: Italian Association for Military History, president. Address: Corso Regina Margherita 155, 10122 Torino, Italy.

LURIE Alison, b. 3 Sept 1926, Chicago, Illinois, USA. Professor of English; Author. 3 sons. Education: AB, magna cum laude, Radcliffe College, 1947. Appointments: Lecturer, 1969-73, Adjunct Associate Professor, 1973-76, Associate Professor, 1976-79, Professor of English, 1979-, Cornell University. Publications: Love and Friendship, 1962; The Nowhere City, 1965; Imaginary Friends, 1967; Real People, 1969; The War Between the Tates, 1974; V R Lang: Poems and Plays, With a memoir by Alison Lurie, 1975; Only Children, 1979; Clever Gretchen and Other Forgotten Folktales (juvenile), 1980; The Heavenly Zoo (juvenile), 1980; The Language of Clothes (non-fiction), 1981; Fabulous Beasts (juvenile), 1981; Foreign Affairs, 1984; The Truth About Lorin Jones, 1988; Don't Tell the Grownups: Subversive Children's Literature, 1990; Women and Ghosts, 1994; The Last Resort, 1998. Contributions to: Many publications. Honours: Guggenheim Fellowship, 1966-67; Rockefeller Foundation Grant, 1968-69; New York State Cultural Council Foundation Grant, 1972-73; American Academy of Arts and Letters Award, 1984; Pulitzer Prize in Fiction, 1985; Radcliffe College Alumnae Recognition Award, 1987; Prix Femina Etranger, 1989; Parents' Choice Foundation Award, 1996. Address: c/o Department of English, Cornell University, Ithaca, NY 14853, USA.

LURIE Morris, b. 30 Oct 1938, Melbourne, Victoria, Australia. Writer; Dramatist. Education: Architecture studies, Royal Melbourne Institute of Technology, 1957-60, no degree. Appointments: Writer-in-Residence, Latrobe University, 1984, Holmesglen Tafe, 1992. Publications: Rappaport, 1966; The Twenty-Seventh Annual African Hippopotamus Race, 1969; Flying Home, 1978; Outrageous Behaviour, 1984; Whole Life, 1987. Novels: Seven books for Grossmar, 1983; Madness, 1991. Contributions to: Virginia Quarterly Review; Times; Punch; Telegraph Magazine; Age; National Times; New Yorker; Stories broadcast on BBC, and plays on ABC. Honours: State of Victoria Short Story Award, 1973; National Book Council Selection, 1980; Children's Book Council, 1983; Bicentennial Banjo Award, 1988. Address: 2/3 Finchley Court, Hawthorn, Victoria 3122, Australia.

LUSTBADER Eric Van, b. 24 Dec 1946, New York, New York, USA. Writer. m. Victoria Lustbader. Education: BA, Columbia University, 1968. Publications: The Sunset Warrior, 1977; Shallows of Night, 1978; Dai-San, 1978; Beneath an Opal Moon, 1980; The Ninja, 1980; Sirens, 1981; Black Heart, 1982; The Miko, 1984; Jian, 1985; Shan, 1987; Zero, 1988; French Kiss, 1988; White Ninja, 1989; Angel Eyes, 1991; Black Blade, 1993; The Keishe, 1993; Batman: The Last Angel, 1994; The Floating City, 1994. Contributions to: Magazines. Address: c/o Henry Morrison Inc, Box 235, Bedford Hills, NY 10507, USA.

LUSTGARTEN Celia Sophie, b. 24 Oct 1941, New York, New York, USA. Consultant; Writer. Contributions to: Various publications. Honour: 1st Prize, Short Story, Alternate Realities Society and Imaginative Fiction Society, Victoria, British Columbia, 1986. Membership: Poets and Writers; International Women's Writing Guild. Address: 317 Third Avenue, San Francisco, CA 94118, USA.

LUSTIG Arnost, b. 21 Dec 1926, Prague, Czechoslovakia. Writer; Screenwriter; Educator. m. Vera Weislitz, 24 July 1949, 1 son, 1 daughter. Education: MA, College of Political and Social Science, Prague, 1951. Appointments: Arab-Israeli War Correspondent, Radio Prague, 1948-49; Correspondent, Czechoslovak Radio, 1950-68; Screenwriter, Barrandov Film Studies, Prague, 1960-68; Jury Member, Karlsbad Film Festival, 1995, 1996; Writer, Kibutz Hachotrim, Israel, 1968-69; Screenwriter, Jadran Film Studio, Zagreb, 1969-70; Visiting Lecturer, English, 1971-72, Visiting Professor, English, 1972-73, Drake University; Professor, Literature and Film, American University, Washington, DC, 1973-. Publications: Night and Hope, 1958; Diamonds of the

Night, 1958; Street of Lost Brothers, 1959; Dita Saxova, 1962; My Acquaintance Vili Feld, 1962; A Prayer for Katarina Horovitzova, 1964; Nobody Will be Humiliated, 1964; Bitter Smells of Almonds, 1968; Darling, 1969; The Unloved (From the Diary of a Seventeen Year Old), 1986; Indecent Dreams, 1988. Films/Screenplays: Transport from Paradise, 1963; Diamonds of the Night, 1964; Dita Saxova, 1968; The Triumph of Memory, 1989; Precious Legacy, 1995; Prayers for Katerina Hordvitzova. Honours: State Prize, 1965; National Jewish Book Award, 1980, 1986; Doctor of Hebrew Letters, Spertus College, 1986; Karel Capek Prize, 1996. Membership: Franz Kafka Society, Prague, honorary president. Address: 4000 Tunlaw Road North West, Apt 825, Washington, DC 20007, USA.

LUTTWAK Edward N(icholae), b. 4 Nov 1942, Arad, Romania (US citizen, 1981). Political Scientist; Author. m. Dalya Iaari, 14 Dec 1970, 1 son, 1 daughter. Education: Carmel College, England; BSc, London School of Economics and Political Science, 1964; PhD, Johns Hopkins University, 1975. Appointments: Associate Director, Washington Center of Foreign Policy Research, District of Columbia, 1972-75; Visiting Professor of Political Science, Johns Hopkins University, 1973-78; Senior Fellow, 1976-87, Research Professor in International Security Affairs, 1978-82, Arleigh Burke Chair in Strategy, 1987-, Director, Geo-Economics, 1991-, Center for Strategic and International Studies, Washington, DC; Nimitz Lecturer, University of California, Berkeley, 1987; Tanner Lecturer, Yale University, 1989. Publications: A Dictionary of Modern War, 1971, new edition with Stuart Koehl, 1991; The Grand Strategy of the Roman Empire: From the First Century A.D. to the Third, 1976; The Economic and Military Balance Between East and West 1951-1978 (editor with Herbert Block), 1978; Sea Power in the Mediterranean (with R G Weinland), 1979; Strategy and Politics: Collected Essays, 1980; The Grand Strategy of the Soviet Union, 1983; The Pentagon and the Art of War: The Question of Military Reform, 1985; Strategy and History, 1985; On the Meaning of Victory: Essays on Strategy, 1986; Global Security: A Review of Strategic and Economic Issues (editor with Barry M Blechman), 1987; Strategy: The Logic of War and Peace, 1987; The Endangered American Dream: How to Stop the United States from Becoming a Third World Country and How to Win the Geo-Economic Struggle for Industrial Supremacy, 1993. Contributions to: Numerous books and periodicals. Address: c/o Center for Strategic and International Studies, Georgetown University, 1800 K Street North West, Washington, DC 20006, USA.

LUTZ John Thomas, b. 11 Sept 1939, Dallas, Texas, USA. Writer. m. Barbara Jean Bradley, 15 Mar 1958, 1 son, 2 daughters. Education: Meramac Community College. Publications: The Truth of the Matter, 1971; Buyer Beware, 1976; Bonegrinder, 1977; Lazarus Man, 1979; Jericho Man, 1980; The Shadow Man, 1981; Exiled with Steven Greene, 1982; Nightlines, 1985; The Right to Sing the Blues, 1986; Tropical Heat, 1986; Ride the Lightning, 1987; Scorcher, 1987; Kiss, 1988; Shadowtown, 1988; Time Exposure, 1989; Flame, 1990; Diamond Eyes, 1990; SWF Seeks Same, 1990; Bloodfire, 1991; Hot, 1992; Dancing with the Dead, 1992; Spark, 1993; Shadows Everywhere (short stories), 1994; Torch, 1994; Thicker Than Blood, 1994. Contributions to: Anthologies and magazines. Honours: Scroll, 1981, Edgar Award, 1983, Mystery Writers of America; Shamus Awards, 1982, 1988. Memberships: Mystery Writers of America; Private Eye Writers of America, board of directors. Address: 880 Providence Avenue, Webster Groves, MO 63119, USA.

LUX Thomas, b. 10 Dec 1946, Northampton, Massachusetts, USA. Poet; Teacher. m. Jean Kilbourne, 1983, 1 daughter. Education: BA, Emerson College, Boston, 1970; University of Iowa, 1971. Appointments: Managing Editor, Iowa Review, 1971-72, Ploughshares, 1973; Poet-in-Residence, Emerson College, 1972-75; Faculty, Sarah Lawrence College, 1975, Warren Wilson College, 1980-, Columbia University, 1980-. Publications: The Land Sighted, 1970; Memory's Handgrenade, 1972; The Glassblower's Breath, 1976; Sunday, 1979; Like a Wide Anvil From the Moon the Light, 1980; Massachusetts, 1981; Tarantulas on the Lifebuoy, 1983; Half Promised Land, 1986; Sunday: Poems, 1989; The Drowned River, 1990; A Boat in the Forest, 1992; Pecked to Death by Swans, 1993; Split Horizon, 1994; The Sanity of Earth and Grass (editor with Jane Cooper and Sylvia Winner), 1994. Honours: Bread Loaf Scholarship, 1970; MacDowell Colony Fellowships, 1973, 1974, 1976, 1978, 1980, 1982; National Endowment for the Arts Grants, 1976, 1981, 1988; Guggenheim Fellowship, 1988; Kingsley Tufts Poetry Award, 1995. Address: 67 Temple Street, West Newton, MA 02164, USA.

LYALL Gavin Tudor, b. 9 May 1932, Birmingham, England. Author; Journalist. m. Katharine Whitehorn, 4 Jan 1958, 2 sons. Education: MA, Pembroke College, Cambridge, 1956; MA, 1986. Appointments: Staff, Picture Post, 1956-57, Sunday Times, 1959-63. Publications: The Wrong Side of the Sky, 1961; The Most Dangerous Game, 1964; Midnight Plus One, 1965; Shooting Script, 1966; Freedom's Battle, Vol II, 1968; Venus with Pistol, 1969; Blame the Dead, 1972; Judas Country, 1975; Operation Warboard, 1976; The Secret Servant, 1980; The Conduct of Major Maxim, 1982; The Crocus List, 1985; Uncle Target, 1989; Spy's Honour, 1993; Flight from Honour, 1996; All Honourable Men, 1997. Contributions to: Observer; Sunday Telegraph; Punch; London Illustrated News. Honours: Silver Dagger, Crime Writer's Association, 1964, 1965. Memberships: Crime Writers' Association, chairman, 1966-67; Detection Club; Society of Authors. Address: 14 Provost Road, London NW3 4ST, England.

LYKIARD Alexis (Constantine), b. 2 Jan 1940, Athens, Greece. Poet; Writer; Translator. m. Erica Bowen, 20 Sept 1985, div, 1 son. Education: BA, 1962, MA, 1966, King's College, Cambridge. Appointments: Creative Writing Tutor, Arvon Foundation, 1974-; Writer-in-Residence, Sutton Central Library, 1976-77, Loughborough Art College, 1982-83, Tavistock, Devon Libraries, 1983-85, HMP Channings Wood, 1988-89, HMP Haslar, 1992. Publications: Lobsters, 1961; Journey of the Alchemist, 1963; The Summer Ghosts, 1964; Wholly Communion (editor), 1965; Zones, 1966; Paros Poems, 1967; A Sleeping Partner, 1967; Robe of Skin, 1969; Strange Alphabet, 1970; Best Horror Stories of J Sheridan Le Fanu (editor), 1970; Eight Lovesongs, 1972; The Stump, 1973; Greek Images, 1973; Lifelines, 1973; Instrument of Pleasure, 1974; Last Throes, 1976; Milesian Fables, 1976; A Morden Tower Reading, 1976; The Drive North, 1977; New Stories 2 (editor), 1977; Scrubbers, 1983; Cat Kin, 1985; Out of Exile, 1986; Safe Levels, 1990; Living Jazz, 1991; Beautiful is Enough, 1992; Selected Poems, 1956-96, 1997. Other: Many French translations. Address: 77 Latimer Road, Exeter, Devon EX4 7JP, England.

LYNCH Audry Louise, b. 18 July 1933, Cambridge, Massachusetts, USA. Guidance Counsellor; Community College English Instructor. m. Gregory Lynch, 8 Sept 1956, 1 son, 2 daughters. Education: BA, Harvard University, 1955; EdM, Boston University, 1968; EdD, University of San Francisco, 1983. Publications: With Steinbeck in the Sea of Cortez, 1991; Father Joe Young: A Priest and His People, 1993. Contributions to: Yankee Magazine; West Magazine; Parade Magazine; Writer; International Herald Tribune. Memberships: California Writers Club; Writers Connection. Address: 20774 Meadow Oak Road, Saratoga, CA 95070, USA.

LYNCH Frances. See: **COMPTON D(avid) G(uy).**

LYNCH John, b. 11 Jan 1927, Boldon, England. Professor Emeritus; Historian. Education: MA, University of Edinburgh, 1952; PhD, University of London, 1955. Appointments: Lecturer in History, University of Liverpool, 1954-61; Lecturer, Reader and Professor of Latin American History, University College, London, 1961-74; Professor of Latin American History and Director of Institute of Latin American Studies, University of London, 1974-87. Publications: Spanish Colonial Administration 1782-1810: The Intendant System in the Viceroyalty of the Rio de la Plata, 1958; Spain Under the Habsburgs, 2 volumes, 1964, 1967, 2nd edition, revised, 1981; The Origins of the Latin American Revolutions 1808-1826 (with R A Humphreys), 1965; The Spanish American Revolutions 1808-1826, 1973, 2nd edition, revised, 1986; Argentine Dictator: Juan Manuel de Rosas 1829-1852, 1981; The Cambridge History of Latin America (with others), Vol 3, 1985, Vol 4, 1986; Bourbon Spain 1700-1808, 1989; Caudillos in Spanish America 1800-1850, 1992; Latin American Revolutions 1808-1826: Old and New World Origins, 1994; Massacre in the Pampas, 1872: Britain and Argentina in the Age of Migration, 1998. Honours: Encomienda Isabel La Católica, Spain, 1988; Doctor, Honoris Causa, University of Seville, 1990; Order of Andres Bello, 1st Class, Venezuela, 1995. Membership: Royal Historical Society, fellow. Address: 8 Templars Crescent, London N3 3QS, England.

LYNCH Timothy Jeremy Mahoney, b. 10 June 1952, San Francisco, California, USA. Lawyer; Classical Scholar; Author; Business Executive. Education: MS, JD, Civil Law, Taxation Law, Golden Gate University; MA, PhD, University of San Francisco, 1983; PhD, Classics, Divinity, Harvard University, 1988; JSD, Constitutional Law, Hastings Law Center, San Francisco; Postdoctoral research, Writing in Classics. Appointments: Chairman, Patristic, Biblical, Latin and Greek Literary Publications Group, Institute of Classical Studies; Chairman, Postdoctoral Research and Writing in Humanities Group, National Association of Scholars; Fellow, Harvard University Center for Hellenic Studies, 1991, 1993; Senior Research and Writing Fellow, Medieval Theological Philosophy manuscripts of St Gallen Monks, Medieval Academy of America; Research Professor, University of California at Berkeley, 1996-99; Graduate Theological Union, 1998-; Senior Fellow, History of Religion Project, Harvard University, 1998. Publications: History of Europe, 5 volumes, 1987; Essays and Papers on US-Soviet Relations, Iran-British Relations, 1988; Legal Essays, 1990-94; Musical Papers, 1994; History of Classical Tradition, 20 volumes, 1995; Poems for children; Textbooks; Co-editor, co-author: Commentary on Classical Philology; Greek Hellenic Philosophy, Literary Translations and Commentary on Philodemus Project, 1995; 50 volumes on classical philology, literary styles and analysis of Old Testament Exegesis, history of mediaeval and modern moral and ecumenical theological institutes; Love Duchess; Odyssey of Clotilda; Composer of Operas, Symphonies; Plays; Books; Cello Percussion Pieces. Contributions to: Journals. Honour: Member, International Platform Association; Eminent Scholar of the Year, National Association of Scholars, 1993; Academy Award, American Academy of Achievement, 1998; Royal Society Special Citation for Exceptional Performance in Literatary Performing Arts; Elected, American Academy of Poets; Presidential Seal of Honor. Memberships: American Philological Association, president, 1996-97; American Historical Association; Law Society of America; Society of Biblical Literature; American Institute of Archaeology. Address: 540 Jones Street, Suite 201, San Francisco, CA 94102-2022, USA.

LYNDS Dennis, (William Arden, Nick Carter, Michael Collins, John Crowe, Carl Dekker, Maxwell Grant, Mark Sadler), b. St Louis, Missouri, USA. Writer. m. (1) Doris Flood, 1949, div 1956, (2) Sheila McErlean, 1961, div 1985, 2 daughters, (3) Gayle Hallenbeck Stone, 1986. Education: BA, Hofstra College, 1949; MA, Syracuse University, 1951. Publications: Combat Soldier, 1962; Uptown Downtown, 1963; Why Girls Ride Sidesaddle (short stories), 1980; Freak, 1983; Minnesota Strip, 1987; Red Rosa, 1988; Castrato, 1989; Chasing Eights, 1990; The Irishman's Horse, 1991; Cassandra in Red, 1992; Crime, Punishment and Resurrection, 1992; Talking to the World, 1995; The Cadillac Cowboy, 1995. Address: 12 St Anne Drive, Santa Barbara, CA 93109, USA.

LYNN Jonathan, b. 3 Apr 1943, Bath, England. Theatre and Film Director; Actor; Writer; Dramatist. Education: MA, Pembroke College, Cambridge, 1964. Appointments: Artistic Director, Cambridge Theatre Co,

1976-81; Company Director, National Theatre, 1987. Publications: A Proper Man, 1976; The Complete Yes Minister, 1984; Yes Prime Minister, Vol I, 1986; Yes Prime Minister, Vol II, 1987; Mayday, 1993. Other: Various screenplays and television series. Address: c/o Peters, Fraser and Dunlop Group Ltd, The Chambers, Chelsea House, Lots Road, London SW10, England.

LYNTON Ann. See: **RAYNER Claire Berenice.**

LYNTON Harriet Ronken, b. 22 May 1920, Rochester, Minnesota, USA. Writer. m. Rolf P Lynton, 16 Apr 1955, 1 son, 2 daughters. Education: AB, Radcliffe. Appointments: Food Administrator, USDA, 1941-44; Admissions Office, Bryn Mawr College, 1944-45; Faculty, Harvard Business School, 1945-54; Freelance Writer, 1954-. Publications: Administrating Changes, 1952; Training for Human Relations, 1954; The Days of the Beloved, 1974; Born to Dance, 1995. Membership: North Carolina Writers Network. Address: 4558 Fearrington Post, Fearrington Village, NC 27312, USA.

LYON Bryce Dale, b. 22 Apr 1920, Bellevue, Ohio, USA. Professor of History. m. Mary Elizabeth Lewis, 3 June 1944, 1 son, 1 daughter. Education: AB, Baldwin-Wallace College, 1942; PhD, Cornell University, 1949. Appointments: Assistant Professor of History, University of Colorado, Boulder, 1949-51, Harvard University, 1951-56; Professor of History, University of California, Berkeley, 1959-65; Barnaby and Mary Critchfield Keeney Professor of History, 1965-, Chairman, Department of History, 1968-, Brown University. Publications: Medieval Institutions: Selected Essays, 1954; A Constitutional and Legal History of Medieval England, 1960, 2nd edition, 1980; A History of the World (with others), 1960; The High Middle Ages 1000-1300, 1964; Frankish Institutions Under Charlemagne (with M Lyon), 1968; A History of the Western World, 1969, 2nd edition, 1974; The Origins of the Middle Ages: Pirenne's Challenge to Gibbon, 1972; Studies of West European and Medieval Institutions, 1978; The Wardrobe Book of William de Norwell: 12 July 1338 to 27 May 1340 (with H S Lucas and M Lyon), 1983; The Firth of Annales History: The Letters of Lucien Febvre and Marc Bloch to Henri Pirenne 1921-1935 (with Mary Lyon), 1991. Address: Department of History, Brown University, Brown Station, Providence, RI 02912, USA.

LYONS Arthur, b. 5 Jan 1946, Los Angeles, California, USA. Writer. m. Marie Lyons. Education: BA, University of California, Santa Barbara, 1967. Publications: The Second Coming: Satanism in America, 1970; The Dead Are Discreet, 1974; All God's Children, 1975; The Killing Floor, 1976; Dead Ringer, 1977; Castles Burning, 1979; Hard Trade, 1981; At the Hands of Another, 1983; Three With a Bullet, 1985; Fast Fade, 1987; Unnatural Causes (with Thomas Noguchi), 1988; Satan Wants You, 1988; Other Poeple's Money, 1989; Physical Evidence (with Thomas Noguchi), 1990; The Blue Sense (with Marcello Truzzi), 1991; False Pretences, 1993. Address: c/o Putnam Publishing Group, 200 Madison Avenue, New York, NY 10016, USA.

LYONS Elena. See: **FAIRBURN Eleanor M.**

LYONS Esther Mary, b. 27 Nov 1940, Calcutta, India. Teacher. m. N K Chaudhry, 28 May 1972, 2 sons. Education: BA, Agra University, India; BEd, DipTech, Sydney University, Australia; MEd, Pastoral Care, Catholic University, Sydney; Graduate Diploma, Special Education, Bathurst University. Appointments: Teaching: Convent schools, India, 1963-66; La Martiniere Girls School, Lucknow, 1967-68; Frank Anthony School, Delhi, 1969-70; Department of School Education, Perth, Western Australia, 1971-72; Department of School Education, Sydney, New South Wales, 1991-99. Publications: Unwanted; Woman and Philosopher. Contributions to: Old La Martiniere Association; Ambitious Friends. Address: 63 Melford Street, Hurlstone Park, NSW 2193, Australia.

LYONS Garry Fairfax, b. 5 July 1956, Kingston-upon-Thames, England. Dramatist. m. Ruth Caroline Willis, 6 Apr 1985, 1 son, 1 daughter. Education: BA, English Literature, University of York, 1978; MA, Drama and Theatre Arts, University of Leeds, 1982. Appointments: Playwright-in-Residence, Major Road Theatre Co, 1983; Fellow in Theatre, University of Bradford, 1984-88. Major Productions: Echoes from the Valley, 1983; Mohicans, 1984; St Vitus' Boogie, 1985; Urban Jungle, 1985; The Green Violinist, 1986; Irish Night, 1987; Divided Kingdoms, 1989; The People Museum, 1989; Dream Kitchen, 1992; Frankie and Tommy, 1992; Wicked Year, 1994. Membership: Theatre Writers' Union. Address: c/o International Creative Management, Oxford House, 76 Oxford Street, London W1N 0AX, England.

M

MA Fei. See: **MARR William Wei-Yi.**

MA Zhuorong, b. 1 Aug 1929, Xiangtan City, Hunan, China. Research Fellow of Literature and Art; Writer; Poet; Translator. m. Chen Huixun, 15 Oct 1962, 1 son, 1 daughter. Education: Self-taught. Publications: Various scholarly works, translations, and poems. Contributions to: Numerous journals and magazines. Honours: Hunan Literature and Art Award, 1981; Hunan Social Science Awards, 1991, 1994. Memberships: Chinese Comparative Literature Association; Chinese Writer's Association. Address: No 8, Mingxingli, Wuyi Road, Changsha, China.

MAALOUF Amin, b. 25 Feb 1949, Beirut, Lebanon. Writer. m. Andrée Abouchdid, 24 Apr 1971, 3 children. Education: Université Saint-Joseph, Beirut; Université de Lyon. Appointments: Journalist, An-Nahar, 1971-76, Economia, 1976-77; Editor, Jeune Afrique, 1978-79, 1982-84. Publications: Les Croisades vues par les Arabes, 1983; Léon l'Africain, 1986; Samarcande, 1988; Les Jardins de lumière, 1991; Le Premier siècle après Béatrice, 1992; Le Rocher de Tanios, 1993; Les Echelles du Levant, 1996. Honours: Grand prix de la Méditerranée; Prix France-Liban; Grand prix de l'Unicef; Prix Paul Flat, l'Académie francaise; Prix Goncourt, 1993. Address: c/o Editions Grasset, 61 rue des Saints-Pères, 75006 Paris, France.

MABBETT Ian William, b. 27 Apr 1939, London, England. Historian; University Lecturer. m. Jacqueline Diana June Towns, 11 Dec 1971, 2 daughters. Education: BA, 1960, DPhil, 1963, MA, 1964, University of Oxford. Appointment: Faculty, Monash University. Publications: A Short History of India, 1968, 2nd edition, 1983; Modern China, The Mirage of Modernity, 1985; Kings and Emperors of Asia, 1985; Patterns of Kingship and Authority in Traditional Asia (editor), 1985; The Khmers (co-author), 1995. Contributions to: Hemisphere, Canberra; Asian Pacific Quarterly, Seoul; The Cambridge History of Southeast Asia. Honour: President, IXth World Sanskrit Conference, 1994. Memberships: Federation of Australian Writers; Australian Society of Authors. Address: c/o School of Historical and Gender Studies, Monash University, Clayton, Victoria 3168, Australia.

MABEY Richard Thomas, b. 20 Feb 1941, Berkhamsted, Hertfordshire, England, Writer; Broadcaster. Education: BA Honours, 1966, MA, 1971, St Catherine's College, Oxford. Appointment: Senior Editor, Penguin Books, 1966-73. Publications: The Pop Process, 1969; Food for Free, 1972; Unofficial Countryside, 1973; Street Flowers, 1976; Plants with a Purpose, 1977; The Common Ground, 1980; The Flowering of Britain, 1980; In a Green Shade, 1983; Oak and Company, 1983; Frampton Flora, 1985; Gilbert White, 1986; The Flowering of Kew, 1988; Home Country, 1990; Whistling in the Dark, 1993; Oxford Book of Nature Writing (editor), 1995; Flora Britannica, 1996. Contributions to: Times; Telegraph; Sunday Times; Observer; The Guardian; Nature; Modern Painters; Independent. Honours: Information Book Award, Times Educational Supplement, 1977; Children's Book Award, New York Academy of Sciences, 1984; Whitbread Biography Award, 1986; National Book Awards, 1997; Honorary DSc, University of St Andrews, 1997. Memberships: Botanical Society of British Isles, council, 1981-83; Nature Conservancy, council, 1982-86; London Wildlife Trust, president, 1982-92; Plantlife, advisory council, 1990-; Open Spaces Society, advisory council, 1992-; Richard Jefferies Society, president, 1996-98. Address: c/o Sheil Land Associates, 43 Doughty Street, London, England.

MAC AVOY Roberta Ann, b. 13 Dec 1949, Cleveland, Ohio, USA. Writer. Education: BA, Case Western Reserve University, 1971. Publications: Tea with the Black Dragon, Damiano, 1983; Damiano's Lute, Raphael, 1984; The Book of Kells (co-author), 1985; Twisting the Rope, 1986; The Grey Horse, 1987; The Third Eagle,

1989; Lens of the World, 1990. Address: Underhill at Nelson Farm, 1669 Nelson Road, Scotts Valley, CA 95066, USA.

MACADAMS William, b. 3 Dec 1944, Richmond, Indiana, USA. Writer. m. 2 sons. Appointment: Editor, Zygote Magazine, 1972. Publications: As Rob Morreale: Anxious to Please (novel), 1972; As William MacAdams: The Book: A Story, 1982; Ben Hecht: The Man Behind the Legend, 1990; Ben Hecht: A Biography, 1995; 701 Toughest Movie Trivia Questions of All Time, 1995. Contributions to: New York Times; Film Comment; Oui; New York Observer; Rolling Stone; Penthouse; Changes; Crawdaddy. Address: c/o Doris Ashbrook, 625 South 8th Street, Richmond, IN 47374, USA.

MACALLAN Andrew. See: **LEASOR (Thomas) James.**

MACAULAY David (Alexander), b. 2 Dec 1946, Burton-on-Trent, England. Writer; Illustrator. m. (1) Janice Elizabeth Michel, 1970, div, 1 daughter, (2) Ruth Marris, 1978, div, (3) Charlotte Valerie. Education: Bachelor in Architecture, Rhode Island School of Design, 1969. Publications: Cathedral: The Story of Its Construction, 1973; City: A Story of Roman Planning and Construction, 1974; Pyramid, 1975; Underground, 1976; Castle, 1977; Great Movements in Architecture, 1978; Motel of the Mysteries, 1979; Unbuilding, 1980; Electricity, 1983; Mill, 1983; BAAA, 1985; Why the Chicken Crossed the Road, 1987; The Way Things Work, 1988; Black and White, 1990; Ship, 1993; Shortcut, 1995. Honours: Caldecott Honor Books, 1973, 1977; Christopher Medal, 1991. Address: c/o Houghton Mifflin Co, 222 Berkeley Street, Boston, MA 02116, USA.

MacCARTHY Fiona, b. 23 Jan 1940, London, England. Biographer; Cultural Historian. m. David Mellor, 1966, 1 son, 1 daughter. Education: MA, English Language and Literature, Oxford University, 1961. Appointments: Reviewer, The Times, 1981-91, The Observer, 1991-. Publications: The Simple Life: C R Ashbee in the Cotswolds, 1981; The Omega Workshops: Decorative Arts of Bloomsbury, 1984; Eric Gill, 1989; William Morris: A Life for our Time, 1994; Stanley Spencer, 1997 Contributions to: Times Literary Supplement; New York Review of Books. Honours: Royal Society of Arts Bicentenary Medal, 1987; Honorary Fellowship, Royal College of Art, 1989; Honorary D Litt, University of Sheffield, 1996; Senior Fellowship, Royal College of Art, 1997; Fellow, Royal Society of Literature, 1997. Memberships: PEN Club; Royal Society of Literature. Address: The Round Building, Hathersage, Sheffield S32 1BA, England.

MACCOBY Michael, b. 5 Mar 1933, Mt Vernon, New York, USA. Consultant; Writer. m. Sandylee Weille, 19 Dec 1959, 1 son, 3 daughters. Education: BA, 1954, PhD, 1960, Harvard University; New College, Oxford, 1954-55; University of Chicago, 1955-56; Diploma, Mexican Institute of Psychoanalysis, 1964. Publications: Social Change and Character in Mexico and the United States, 1970; Social Character in a Mexican Village (with E Fromm), 1970, 2nd edition, 1996; The Gamesman, 1977; The Leader, 1981; Why Work, 1988, 2nd edition, 1995; Sweden at the Edge, 1991; A Prophetic Analyst (with M Cortina), 1996. Memberships: PEN; Signet Society; Cosmos; American Psychological Association; American Anthropological Association; National Academy of Public Administration. Address: 4825 Linnean Avenue North West, Washington, DC 20008, USA.

MacCREIGH James. See: **POHL Frederik.**

MACDONALD Alastair A, b. 24 Oct 1920, Aberlour, Scotland. Professor of English Emeritus; Poet; Writer. Education: MA, 1st Class Honours, University of Aberdeen, 1948; BLitt, Christ Church, Oxford, 1953; Senior Studentship in Arts, 1953-55, PhD, 1956, University of Manchester. Appointments: Temporary Senior English Master, King William's College, Isle of Man, 1953; Professor of English, 1955-87, Professor Emeritus, 1992-, Memorial University, Newfoundland,

Canada; Various poetry readings. Publications: Poetry: Between Something and Something, 1970; Shape Enduring Mind, 1974; A Different Lens, 1981; Towards the Mystery, 1985; A Figure on the Move, 1991; Landscapes of Time: New, Uncollected, and Selected Poems, 1994. Other: Prose and criticism. Contributions to: Various anthologies, reviews, journals, and magazines. Honours: Best Poem, Canadian Author and Bookman, 1972; New Voices in American Poetry, 1973; 1st Prize for Poetry, 1976, Honorable Mention, 1978, 2nd Prize for Poetry, 1982, Newfoundland Government Arts and Letters Competition. Memberships: League of Canadian Poets; Scottish Poetry Library Association; Writers' Alliance of Newfoundland and Labrador. Address: c/o Department of English, Arts and Administration Building, Memorial University, St John's, Newfoundland, AC1 5S7, Canada.

MACDONALD (Alexa Eleanor) Fiona, b. 25 Apr 1945, India. Writer. Publications: The Duke Who Had Too Many Giraffes; Little Bird I Have Heard. Contributions to: International Construction; Construction News; Underground Engineering. Membership: PEN. Address: 41 Donne Place, London SW3 2NH, England.

MACDONALD Cynthia, b. 2 Feb 1928, New York, New York, USA. Poet; Lecturer. m. E C Macdonald, 1954, div 1975, 1 son, 1 daughter. Education: BA, Bennington College, Vermont, 1950; Graduate Studies, Mannes College of Music, New York City, 1951-52; MA, Sarah Lawrence College, 1970. Appointments: Assistant Professor, 1970-74, Associate Professor and Acting Dean of Studies, 1974-75, Sarah Lawrence College; Professor, Johns Hopkins University, 1975-79; Consultant, 1977-78, Co-Director, Writing Program, 1979-, University of Houston; Guest Lecturer at various universities, colleges, seminars, etc. Publications: Amputations, 1972; Transplants, 1976; Pruning the Annuals, 1976; (W)holes, 1980; Alternate Means of Transport, 1985; Living Wills: New and Selected Poems, 1991; I Can't Remember, 1997. Contributions to: Anthologies and other publications. Honours: MacDowell Colony Grant, 1970; National Endowment for the Arts Grants, 1973, 1979; Yaddo Foundation Grants, 1974, 1976, 1979; CAPS Grant, 1976; American Academy and Institute of Arts and Letters Award, 1977; Rockefeller Foundation Fellow, 1978. Memberships: American Society of Composers, Authors, and Publishers; Associated Writing Programs. Address: c/o Alfred A Knopf Inc, 201 East 50th Street, New York, NY 10022, USA.

MACDONALD Hugh (John), b. 31 Jan 1940, Newbury, Berkshire, England. Musicologist; Professor. m. (1) Naomi Butterworth, 14 Sept 1963, 1 son, 3 daughters, (2) Elizabeth Babb, 15 Sept 1979, 1 son. Education: BA, 1961, MA, 1966, PhD, 1969, University of Cambridge. Appointments: Lecturer in Music, University of Cambridge, 1966-71, University of Oxford, 1971-80; Gardiner Professor of Music, University of Glasgow, 1980-87; Avis Blewett Professor of Music, Washington University, St Louis, 1987-. Publications: Berlioz Orchestral Music, 1969; Skryabin, 1978; Berlioz, 1982; Berlioz: Correspondence générale, Vol 4, 1984, 5, 1989, 6, 1995; Selected Letters of Berlioz, 1995. Contributions to: The New Grove Dictionary of Music and Musicians; The New Grove Dictionary of Opera; Many journals. Honours: Grand Prix de Littérature Musicale Charles Cros, 1985, 1996. Address: c/o Department of Music, Washington University, St Louis, MO 63130, USA.

MACDONALD Malcolm. See: **ROSS-MACDONALD Malcolm John.**

MACDONOGH Giles Malachy Maximilian, b. 6 Apr 1955, London, England. Author; Journalist. Education: Balliol College, Oxford, 1975-78; BA, Honours, Modern History, Oxford University, 1978; École des Hautes Études Pratiques, France, 1980-83; MA, Oxon, 1992. Appointments: Freelance Journalist, 1983-; Editor, Made in France, 1984; Columnist, Financial Times, 1989-. Publications: A Palate in Revolution: Grimod de La Reynière and the Almanach des Gourmands, 1987; A

Good German: Adam von Trott zu Solz, 1990; The Wine and Food of Austria, 1992; Brillat Savarin: The Judge and his Stomach, 1992; Syrah Grenache, Mourvèdre, 1992; Prussia, the Perversion of an Idea, 1994; Berlin, 1997. Contributions to: Reference works, books, and periodicals. Honours: Shortlisted, Andre Simon Award, 1987; Glenfiddich Special Award, 1988. Memberships: International PEN; Octagon of Wine Writers. Address: c/o Curtis Brown, 162 Regent Street, London W1, England.

MACDOUGALL Ruth Doan, b. 19 Mar 1939, Laconia, New Hampshire, USA. Writer. m. Donald K MacDougall, 9 Oct 1957. Education: Bennington College, 1957-59; BEd, Keene State College, 1961. Publications: The Lilting House, 1965; The Cost of Living, 1971; One Minus One, 1971; The Cheerleader, 1973; Wife and Mother, 1976; Aunt Pleasantine, 1978; The Flowers of the Forest, 1981; A Lovely Time Was Had By All, 1982; Snowy, 1993; Fifty Hikes in the White Mountains, 1997; Fifty More Hikes in New Hampshire, 1998; The Cheerleader: 25th Anniversary Edition, 1998. Contributions to: Book Reviewer: New York Times Book Review; Newsday; Others. Honours: Winner, PEN Syndicated Fiction Project, 1983, 1984, 1985. Membership: National Writers Union. Literary Agent: Henry Morrison Inc. Address: 285 Range Road, Center Sandwich, NH 03227, USA.

MACDOWELL Douglas Maurice, b. 8 Mar 1931, London, England. Professor of Greek; Writer. Education: BA, 1954, MA, 1958, DLitt, 1992, Balliol College, Oxford. Appointments: Assistant Lecturer, Lecturer, Senior Lecturer, Reader in Greek and Latin, University of Manchester, 1958-71; Professor of Greek, University of Glasgow, 1971-. Publications: Andokides: On the Mysteries (editor), 1962; Athenian Homicide Law, 1963; Aristophanes: Wasps (editor), 1971; The Law in Classical Athens, 1978; Spartan Law, 1986; Demosthenes: Against Meidias (editor), 1990; Aristophanes and Athens, 1995; Antiphon and Andocides (with M Gagarin), 1998. Honours: Fellow, Royal Society of Edinburgh, 1991; Fellow, British Academy, 1993. Address: Department of Classics, University of Glasgow, Glasgow G12 8QQ, Scotland.

MACDOWELL John. See: **PARKS T(imothy) Harold.**

MACER-STORY Eugenia, b. 20 Jan 1945, Minneapolis, Minnesota, USA. Writer; Dramatist. m. Leon A Story, 1970, div 1975, 1 son. Education: BS, Speech, Northwestern University, 1965; MFA, Playwriting, Columbia University, 1968. Appointments: Fond du Lac Commonwealth Reporter, 1970; Polyarts, Boston, 1970-72; Joy of Movement, Boston, 1972-75; Magik Mirror, Salem, 1975-76; Magick Mirror Communications, Woodstock and New York City, 1977-. Publications: Congratulations: The UFO Reality, 1978; Angels of Time: Astrological Magic, 1981; Du Fu Man Chu Meets the Lonesome Cowboy: Sorcery and the UFO Experience, 1991, 2nd edition, 1992; Legacy of Daedalus, 1995; Cattle Bones and Coke Machines (anthology), 1995; The Dark Frontier, 1997; Crossing Jungle River (poetry), 1998. Plays include: Meister Hemmelin, 1994; Double or Nothing, 1994; Radish, 1995; Conquest of the Asteroids, 1996; Mister Shooting Star, 1997; Wild Dog Casino, 1998; Holy Dragonet, 1998-99. Contributions to: Numerous publications, including Sensations magazine, 1996-97, Rift Magazine, Magonia Magazine; Poetry chapbooks. Honour: Shubert Fellowship, 1968. Memberships: Dramatists Guild; US Psychotronics Association; Poet's House, New York City; American Society for Psychical Research. Address: Magick Mirror Communications, Box 741, JAF Building, New York, NY 10116, USA.

MACFARLANE Alan Donald James, b. 20 Dec 1941, Shillone, India. Academic. m. Sarah Harrison, 24 July 1980, 1 daughters. Education: MA, 1963; DPhil, 1967, Oxford; MPhil, 1968; PhD, University of London, 1972. Appointments: University Lecturer, Cambridge, 1975; University Reader, Cambridge, 1981; University Profession, Cambridge, 1991. Literary Agent: John Davey, Oxford. Address: King's College, Cambridge CB2 1ST, England.

MACGOWAN Christopher John, b. 6 Aug 1948, London, England. Professor of English; Writer; Editor. m. Catherine Levesque, 10 July 1988. Education: BA, King's College, Cambridge, 1976; MA, 1979, PhD, 1983, Princeton University, USA. Appointments: Research Assistant, The Writings of Henry D Thoreau, 1981-83; Assistant Professor, 1984-90, Associate Professor, 1990-96, Professor, 1996-, College of William and Mary, Williamsburg, Virginia. Publications: William Carlos Williams' Early Poetry: The Visual Arts Background, 1984; The Collected Poems of William Carlos Williams, Vol I, 1909-1939 (co-editor), 1986, vol II, 1939-1962 (editor), 1988; William Carlos Williams' Paterson (editor), 1992; The Letters of Denise Leverton and William Carlos Williams, 1998. Contributions to: Reference works and journals. Honours: James Prize, King's College, Cambridge, England, 1976, 1977; Teaching Assistantship, Pennsylvania State University, 1976-77; Graduate Fellowship, Princeton University, 1977-81; Summer Grants, College of William and Mary, 1985, 1987, 1989; Summer Stipend, 1986, Fellowship 1990-91, National Endowment for the Humanities. Memberships: Modern Lanaguage Association; William Carlos Williams Society, president, 1989-91. Address: Department of English, College of William and Mary, Williamsburg, VA 23187, USA.

MACGREGOR David Roy, b. 26 Aug 1925, London, England. Author. m. Patricia Margaret Aline Purcell-Gilpin, 26 Oct 1962. Education: BA, 1948, MA, 1950, Trinity College, Cambridge; Hammersmith School of Building, 1954-55; Associate, Royal Institute of British Architects, 1957. Publications: The Tea Clippers, 1952, revised edition, 1983; The China Bird, 1961; Fast Sailing Ships 1775-1875, 1973; Clipper Ships, 1977; Merchant Sailing Ships 1775-1815, 1980; Merchant Sailing Ships 1815-1850, 1984; Merchant Sailing Ships 1858-1875, 1984. Contributions to: Mariner's Mirror; Journal of Nautical Archaeology. Honour: Gold Medal, Daily Express, 1973. Memberships: Royal Historical Society, fellow; Society of Nautical Research, council member, 1959-63, 1965-69, 1974-77, 1980-85, honorary vice president, 1985; Maritime Trust. Address: 99 Lonsdale Road, London SW13 9DA, England.

MACGREGOR-HASTIE Roy Alasdhair Niall, b. 28 Mar 1929, Rusholme, England. Author; Poet; University Professor. m. Maria Grazia, 25 Dec 1977, 1 son. Education: New College, Royal Military Academy, Sandhurst, 1947-48; BA, University of Manchester; MFA, University of Iowa, USA; MEd, PhD, University of Hull. Appointments: Editor, The New Nation, 1955-56, Prospice, 1967-77; Joint Editor, Miorita, 1977-; Professoe, Osaka Gakuin University, Japan. Publications: The Man from Nowhere, 1960; The Red Barbarians, 1961; Pope John XXIII, 1962; The Day of the Lion: A History of Fascism, 1964; Pope Paul VI, 1966; The Throne of Peter, 1967; Never to Be Taken Alive, 1985; Nell Gwyn, 1987; History of Western Civilisation, 1989; Getting it Right, 1990. Travel: The Compleat Migrant, 1962; Don't Send Me to Omsk, 1964; Signor Roy, 1967; Africa, 1968. Art History: Picasso, 1988. Poetry and Criticism: A Case for Poetry, 1960; Interim Statement, 1962; Eleven Elegies, 1969; Frames, 1972; The Great Transition, 1975; Poems of Our Lord and Lady, 1976; Poeme, 1980. Contributions to: Anthologies and periodicals. Honours: Victoria Poetry Prize, 1986; UNESCO Author, 1989. Memberships: PEN; Society of Authors; British Association for Romanian Studies, secretary, 1966-77, president, 1977-; International Association of Translators, president, 1978-80; Asian History Association; Scottish Record Society. Address: c/o Osaka Gakuin University, Kishibe, Suita, Osaka 564, Japan.

MACHUNG Anne, b. 30 Jan 1947, Long Beach, California, USA. Sociologist. m. Ron Rothbart, 27 Sept 1986. Education: BA summa cum laude, University of Seattle, 1968; MA 1972, PhD 1983, University of Wisconsin. Publication: The Second Shift (with Arlie Hochschild), 1989. Contributions to: Journals and periodicals. Honour: Distinguished Achievement for Bay Area Women Writers', National Women's Political Caucus, 1991. Memberships: American Sociological Association; National Women's Studies Association. Address: 1003 Keith Avenue, Berkeley, CA 94708, USA.

MACINNES Patricia, b. 7 Apr 1954, Quantico, Virginia, USA. Writer. Education: BA, San Diego State University, 1977; MFA, Writing, University of Montana, Missoula, 1981. Publication: The Last Night on Bikini, 1995. Contributions to: Journals. Honours: Wallace Stegner Writing Fellowship, Stanford University, 1984; Nelson Algren Award for Short Fiction, 1987; Writing Fellowship, Provincetown Fine Arts Work Center, 1988-89; Ludwig Vogelstein Grant, 1989. Address: c/o Mary Jack Wald Associates, Suite 113, Zeckendorf Towers, 111 East 14th Street, New York, NY 10003, USA.

MACINTYRE Alasdair, b. 12 Jan 1929, Glasgow, Scotland. Philosopher; Professor; Writer. Education: BA, Queen Mary College, University of London, 1949; MA, Manchester University, 1951; MA, Oxford University, 1961. Appointments: Lecturer, Manchester University, 1951-57, Leeds University, 1957-61; Research Fellow, Nuffield College, Oxford, 1961-62; Senior Fellow, Princeton University, 1962-63; Fellow, University College, Oxford, 1963-66; Riddell Lecturer, University of Newcastle upon Tyne, 1964; Bampton Lecturer, Columbia University, 1966; Professor of the History of Ideas, Brandeis University, 1969-72; Dean, College of Liberal Arts, 1972-73, Professor of Philosophy and Political Science, 1972-80, Boston University; Henry Luce Professor, Wellesley College, 1980-82; W Alton Jones Professor, Vanderbilt University, 1982-88; Gifford Lecturer, University of Edinburgh, 1988; Henry Luce Scholar, Yale University, 1988-89; McMahon/Hank Professor, University of Notre Dame, Indiana, 1988-94; Professor of Arts and Sciences, Duke University, 1995-. Publications: Marxism and Christianity, 1953; The Unconscious, 1957; Difficulties in Christian Belief, 1960; Short History of Ethics, 1966; The Religious Significance of Atheism, 1969; Against the Self-Images of the Age, 1971; After Virtue: A Study in Moral Theory, 1981; Is Patriotism a Virtue?, 1984; Education and Values, 1987; Whose Justice? Which Rationality?, 1988; Three Rival Versions of Moral Enquiry, 1990; First Principles, Final Ends and Contemporary Philosophy, 1990. Memberships: American Academy of Arts and Sciences; British Academy, corresponding member; Honorary, Phi Beta Kappa. Address: c/o Department of Philosophy, Duke University, Durham, NC 27708, USA.

MACINTYRE Stuart (Forbes), b. 21 Apr 1947, Melbourne, Victoria, Australia. Professor of History; Author. m. (1) Margaret Joan Geddes, Dec 1970, (2) Martha Adele Bruton, 26 Aug 1976, 2 daughters. Education: BA, University of Melbourne, 1968; MA, Monash University, 1969; PhD, Cambridge University, 1975. Appointments: Tutor in History, 1976, Lecturer in History, 1979, Murdoch University, Perth; Research Fellow, St John's College, Cambridge, 1977-78; Lecturer, 1980-84, Senior Lecturer, 1984-86, Reader in History, 1987-90, Ernest Scott Professor, 1990-, University of Melbourne. Publications: A Proletarian Science: Marxism in Britain 1917-1933, 1980; Little Moscows, 1980; Militant: The Life and Times of Paddy Troy, 1983; Ormond College Centenary Essays (editor), 1983; Making History (editor), 1984; Winners and Losers: The Pursuit of Social Justice in Australian History, 1985; The Oxford History of Australia, Vol IV, 1986; The Labour Experiment, 1989; A Colonial Liberalism: The Lost World of Three Victorian Visionaries, 1990; A History for a Nation, 1995; The Reds: The Communist Party of Australia, from Origins to Illegality, 1998. Contributions to: Professional journals. Honours: Prizes and awards. Membership: Academy of the Social Sciences in Australia. Address: c/o Department of History, University of Melbourne, Parkville, Victoria 3052, Australia.

MACK William P, b. 6 Aug 1915, Hillsboro, Illinois, USA. Naval Officer (retired); Writer. m. Ruth McMillian, 11 Nov 1939, 1 son, 1 daughter. Education: BS, US Naval Academy; Naval War College; George Washington University. Appointments: US Naval Officer, 1935-75; Deputy Assistant Secretary of Defense, 1968-71.

Publications: Non-Fiction: Naval Officers Guide, 1958; Naval Customs, Traditions and Usage, 1978; Command at Sea, 1980. Fiction: South to Java, 1988; Pursuit of the Sea Wolf, 1991; Checkfire, 1992; New Guinea, 1993; Straits of Messina, 1994. Contributions to: Various publications. Honour: Alfred Thayer Mahan Award for Literary Excellence, Navy League, 1982. Address: 3607 Rundelac Road, Annapolis, MD 21403, USA.

MACKAY Claire Lorraine, b. 21 Dec 1930, Toronto, Ontario, Canada. Writer. m. Jackson F Mackay, 12 Sept 1952, 3 sons. Education: BA, Political Science, University of Toronto, 1952; Postgraduate Study in Social Work, University of British Columbia, 1968-69; Certificate, Rehabilitation Counseling, University of Manitoba, 1971. Appointment: Writer-in-Residence, Metropolitan Toronto Library, 1987. Publications: Mini-Bike Hero, 1974; Mini-Bike Racer, 1976; Exit Barney McGee, 1979; One Proud Summer, 1981; Mini-Bike Rescue, 1982; Minerva Program, 1984; Pay Cheques and Picket Lines, 1987; The Toronto Story, 1990; Touching All the Bases, 1994; Bats About Baseball, 1995; Laughs: Funny Stories, Selected by Claire Mackay, 1997. Contributions to: Newspapers and magazines. Honours: Toronto Star Short Story Prize, 1980; Ruth Schwartz Children's Book Award, 1982; Vicky Metcalf Award for Body of Work, 1983; Vicky Metcalf Short Story Award, 1988; Award of Excellence, Humour, Parenting Publications of America, 1989, 1990; City of Toronto Award of Merit, 1993. Memberships: Writers' Union of Canada; Canadian Society of Children's Authors, Illustrators and Performers, founding member, 1977, president, 1979-81, secretary, 1997-99; International Board on Books for Young People, councillor, 1991-93; Canadian Children's Book Centre, director, 1985-89; Canadian National Institute for the Blind, Children's Book Selection Committee, 1993-. Address: 6 Frank Crescent, Toronto, Ontario M6G 3K5, Canada.

MACKAY James Alexander, (Ian Angus, William Finlay, Bruce Garden, Peter Whittington), b. 21 Nov 1936, Inverness, Scotland. Author; Journalist. m. (1) Mary Patricia Jackson, 24 Sept 1960, diss 1972, 1 son, 1 daughter, (2) Renate Finlay-Freundlich, 11 Dec 1992. Education: MA, Honours, History, 1958, DLitt, 1993, Glasgow University. Appointments: Philatelic Columnist, The New Daily, 1962-67; Collecting Wisely in Financial Times, 1967-85; Editor-in-Chief, IPC Stamp Encyclopaedia, 1968-72; Antiques Advisory Editor, Ward Lock, 1972-79; Editor, The Burns Chronicle, 1977-91, The Postal Annual, 1978-90, The Burnsian, 1986-89, Seaby Coin and Medal Bulletin, 1990-92; Consultant Editor, Antiques Today, 1992-94, Stamp and Coin Mart, 1993-, Coin News, 1994-, International Stamp and Exhibition News, 1996-. Publications: The Tapling Collection, 1964; Glass Paperweights, 1973, 3rd edition, 1988; The Dictionary of Stamps in Colour, 1973; The Dictionary of Western Sculptors in Bronze, 1977, 2nd edition, 1992; The Guinness Book of Stamps Facts and Feats, 1982, 2nd edition, 1988; Complete Works of Robert Burns, 1986; Complete Letters of Burns, 1987; Burns A-Z: The Complete Word Finder, 1990; Burns: A Biography, 1992; Vagabond of Verse: A Life of Robert W Service, 1993; William Wallace: Brave Heart, 1994; The Eye Who Never Slept: A Life of Allan Pinkerton, 1995; Michael Collins: A Life, 1996; Sounds Out of Silence: A Life of Alexander Graham Bell, 1997; Biographies of Thomas Lipton and John Paul Jones, 1998. Contributions to: Numerous publications. Honours: Silver Medal Amphilex, Amsterdam, 1965; Vermeil Medals, Spellman Foundation, USA, 1982, 1987, 1990; Thomas Field Award for Services to Irish Philatelic Literature, 1983; Saltire Book of the Year, 1993; Gold Medal of American Philatelic Society, 1998. Membership: Burns Federation, executive council, 1977-95. Address: 67 Braidpark Drive, Glasgow G46 6LY, Scotland.

MACKAY Simon. See: **NICOLE Christopher Robin.**

MacKENZIE Andrew Carr, b. 30 May 1911, Oamaru, New Zealand. Journalist; Author. m. Kaarina Sisko Sihvonen, 1 Mar 1952, 1 son, 2 daughters. Education: Victoria University College, New Zealand, 1930-32. Appointment: London News Editor, Sheffield Morning Telegraph, England, 1963-76. Publications: The Unexplained, 1966; Frontiers of the Unknown, 1968; Apparitions and Ghosts, 1971; A Gallery of Ghosts (editor), 1972; Riddle of the Future, 1974; Dracula Country, 1977; Hauntings and Apparitions, 1982; Romanian Journey, 1983; A Concise History of Romania (editor), 1985; Archaeology in Romania, 1986; The Seen and the Unseen, 1987; A Journey into the Past of Transylvania, 1990; Adventures in Time: A Study of Retrocognition, 1997. Contributions to: Journal of the Society of Psychical Research. Membership: Society for Psychical Research, council member, 1970-91, vice president, 1991. Literary Agent: A M Heath, 79 St Martin's Lane, London WC2N 4AA, England. Address: 67 Woodland Drive, Hove, East Sussex BN3 6DF, England.

MACKENZIE David, b. 10 June 1927, Rochester, New York, USA. Professor of History. m. Patricia Williams, 8 Aug 1953, 3 sons. Education: AB, University of Rochester, 1951; MA and Certificate of Russian Institute, 1953, PhD, Columbia University, 1962. Appointments: US Merchant Marine Academy, 1953-58; Princeton University, 1959-61; Wells College, 1961-68; University of North Carolina, Greensboro, 1969-. Publications: The Serbs and Russian Pan-Slavism 1875-1878, 1967; The Lion of Tashkent: The Career of General M G Cherniaev, 1974; A History of Russia and the Soviet Union, 1977; Ilija Garašanin: The Balkan Bismarck, 1985; A History of the Soviet Union, 1986, 2nd edition, revised, 1991; Ilija Garasanin Državnik i Diplomata, 1987; Apis: The Congenial Conspirator, 1989; Imperial Dreams/Harsh Realities: Tsarist Russian Foreign Policy, 1815-1917, 1993; A History of Russia, the Soviet Union and Beyond, 5th edition revised, 1998; From Messianism to Collapse: Soviet Foreign Policy 1917-1991, 1994; The Black Hand on Trial: Salonika 1917, 1995; Violent Solutions: Revolutions, Nationalism, and Secret Societies in Europe to 1918, 1996; Serbs and Russians, 1996; Russia and the USSR in the Twentieth Century, 3rd edition, 1997; Solunski proces, 1997; Exonerating the Black Hand 1917-1953, 1999. Contributions to: Books and professional journals. Address: 1000 Fairmont Street, Greensboro, NC 27401, USA.

MACKENZIE Norman Hugh, b. 8 Mar 1915, Salisbury, Rhodesia. Professor of English Emeritus; Writer. m. Rita Mavis Hofmann, 14 Aug 1948, 1 son, 1 daughter. Education: BA, 1934, MA, 1935, Diploma in Education, 1936, Rhodes University, South Africa; PhD, University of London, 1940. Appointments: Professor of English, 1966-80, Emeritus Professor, 1980-, Queen's University, Kingston, Ontario, Canada. Publications: South African Travel Literature in the 17th Century, 1955; The Outlook for English in Central Africa, 1960; Hopkins, 1968; A Reader's Guide to G M Hopkins, 1981. Editor: The Poems of Gerard Manley Hopkins (with W H Gardner), 1967, revised edition, 1970; Poems by Hopkins, 1974; The Early Poetic Manuscripts and Notebooks of Gerard Manley Hopkins in Facsimile, 1989; The Poetical Works of Gerard Manley Hopkins, 1990; The Later Poetic Manuscripts of Gerard Manley Hopkins in Facsimile, 1991; Various book chapters. Contributions to: International Review of Education; Bulletin of the Institute for Historical Research; Times Literary Supplement; Modern Language Quarterly; Queen's Quarterly; Others. Honours: Fellow, Royal Society of Canada, 1979; Honorary DLitt, 1989. Address: 416 Windward Place, Kingston, Ontario K7M 4E4, Canada.

MACKENZIE Suzanne (Dale), b. 22 Mar 1950, Vancouver, British Columbia, Canada. Professor of Geography; Writer. m. Alan Eric Nash, 29 May 1984. Education: BA, Honours, Simon Fraser University, 1976; MA, University of Toronto, 1978; DPhil, Geography, University of Sussex, 1983. Appointments: Assistant Professor of Geography, Queen's University, 1982-85; Professor of Geography, Carleton University, 1985-. Publications: Gender Sensitive Theory and the Housing Needs of Mother Led Families (co-author), 1987; Visible Histories: Gender and Environment in a Post-War British City, 1989; Remaking Human Geography (co-editor), 1989. Contributions to: Various publications. Memberships: Canadian Association of Geographers; Institute of British Geographers; International Geographic Union. Address: c/o Department of Geography, Carleton University, Ottawa, Ontario K1S 5B6, Canada.

MACKERRAS Colin Patrick, b. 26 Aug 1939, Sydney, New South Wales, Australia. Professor; Writer; Editor. m. Alyce Barbara Brazier, 29 June 1963, 2 sons, 3 daughters. Education: BA, University of Melbourne, 1961; BA, Honours, 1962, PhD, 1970, Australian National University; MLitt, University of Cambridge, 1964. Appointments: Foreign Expert, Beijing Institute of Foreign Languages, 1964-66, 1986; Research Scholar, 1966-69, Research Fellow, 1969-73, Senior Research Fellow, 1973, Australian National University; Professor, 1974-, Chairman, 1979-85, Head, 1988-89, 1996-, School of Modern Asian Studies, Griffith University. Publications: China Observed 1964/1967 (with Neale Hunter), 1967; The Rise of the Peking Opera, 1770-1970: Social Aspects of the Theatre in Manchu China, 1972; The Chinese Theatre in Modern Times from 1840 to the Present Day, 1975; The Performing Arts in Contemporary China, 1981; Modern China: A Chronology from 1842 to the Present (with Robert Chan), 1982; From Fear to Friendship: Australia's Policies Towards the People's Republic of China 1966-1982 (with Edmund S K Fung), 1985; Western Images of China, 1989; Portaits of China, 1989; Dragon's Tongue: Communicating in Chinese (with Peter Chang, Yu Hsiu-ching, and Alyce Mackerras), 2 volumes, 1990-91; Chinese Drama: A Historical Survey, 1990; The Cambridge Handbook of Contemporary China (with Amanda Yorke), 1991; Unlocking Australia's Language Potential: Profiles of 9 Key Languages in Australia, Vol 2--Chinese (with Doug Smith, Ng Bee Chin, and Kam Louie), 1993; China Since 1978: Reform, Modernisation, and 'Socialism with Chinese Characteristics' (with Pradeep Taneja and Graham Young), 1994; China's Minorities: Integration and Modernization in the Twentieth Century, 1994; China's Minority Cultures: Identities and Integration Since 1912, 1995; Peking Opera, 1997; China in Transformation, 1900-1949, 1998. Editor: Essays on the Sources for Chinese History (with Donald Leslie and Wang Gungwu), 1973; China: The Impact of Revolution, A Survey of Twentieth Century, China, 1976; Chinese Theater from Its Origins to the present Day, 1983; Marxism in Asia (with Nick Knight), 1985; Drama in the People's Republic of China (with Constantine Tung), 1987; Chinese Language Teaching and Its Application (with Hugh Dunn), 1987; Contemporary Vietnam: Perspectives from Australia (with Robert Cribb and Allan Healy), 1988; Eastern Asia: An Introductory History, 1992, 2nd editon, revised, 1995; Asia Since 1945: History Through Documents, 1992; China in Revolution: History Through Documents, 1993; Imperialism, Colonialism and Nationalism in East Asia: History Through Documents, 1994; Australia and China: Partners in Asia, 1996; Dictionary of the Politics of the People's Republic of China (with Donald H McMillen and Andrew Watson), 1998; Culture and Society in the Asia-Pacific (with Ricahrd Maidment), 1998. Contributions to: Various scholarly books and journals. Honours: Co-Recipient, Gold Citation for the Media Peace Prize, United Nations Association of Australia, 1981; Twentieth Century Award for Achievement, International Biographical Centre, Cambridge, England, 1993; Albert Einstein International Academy Foundation Cross of Merit Award, 1993. Memberships: Asian Studies Association of Australia, president, 1992-95; Chinese Studies Association, president, 1991-93; Queensland History Teachers Association. Address: c/o School of Modern Asian Studies, Faculty of International Business and Politics, Griffith University, Nathan, Queensland, 4111, Australia.

MACKESY Piers Gerald, b. 15 Sept 1924, Cults, Aberdeenshire, Scotland. Historian; Writer. Education: BA, Christ Church, Oxford, 1950; DPhil, Oriel College, Oxford, 1953; DLitt, Oxford, 1978. Appointments: War Service: Lieutenant, The Royal Scots Greys, N.W. Europe, 1943-7; Harkness Fellow, Harvard University, 1953-54; Fellow, 1954-87, Emeritus, 1988-, Pembroke College, Oxford; Visiting Fellow, Institute for Advanced Study, Princeton, New Jersey, 1961-62; Visiting

Professor, California Institute of Technology, 1966. Publications: The War in the Mediterranean 1803-1810, 1957; The War for America 1775-1783, 1964; Statesmen at War: The Strategy of Overthrow 1798-1799, 1974; The Coward of Minden: The Affair of Lord George Sackville, 1979; War without Victory: The Downfall of Pitt 1799-1802, 1984; British Victory in Egypt, 1801: The End of Napoleon's Conquest, 1995. Memberships: National Army Museum, council member, 1983-92; Society for Army Historical Research, council member, 1985-94; British Academy, fellow, 1988. Address: Westerton Farmhouse, Dess, by Aboyne, Aberdeenshire AB34 5AY, Scotland.

MACKEY Mary, b. 21 Jan 1945, Indianapolis, Indiana, USA. Author; Poet; Professor of English. Education: BA, magna cum laude, Radcliffe College, 1966; MA, 1967, PhD, Comparative Literature, 1970, University of Michigan. Appointments: Assistant Professor, 1972-76, Associate Professor, 1976-80, Professor of English, 1980-, California State University, Sacramento. Publications: Fiction: Immersion, 1972; McCarthy's List, 1979; The Last Warrior Queen, 1983; A Grand Passion, 1986; The Kindness of Strangers, 1988; Season of Shadows, 1991; The Year the Horses Came, 1993; The Horses at the Gate, 1996; The Fires of Spring, 1998. Poetry: Split Ends, 1974; One Night Stand, 1977; Skin Deep, 1978; The Dear Dance of Eros, 1987. Other: Screenplays. Contributions to: Various publications. Memberships:Authors Guild; Bay Area Book Reviewers Association; PEN American Center, West, chair, 1989-92; Writers Guild of America. Address: c/o Department of English, California State University, 6000 J Street, Sacramento, CA 95819, USA.

MACKEY Nathaniel, b. 25 Oct 1947, Miami, Florida, USA. Professor; Poet; Writer; Editor. m. Pascale Gaitet, 1991, 1 daughter, 1 stepson. Education: AB in English, Princeton University, 1969; PhD in English and American Literature, Stanford University, 1975. Appointments: Assistant Professor, University of Wisconsin at Madison, 1974-76; Editor, Hambone, literary magazine, 1974-; Assistant Professor and Director of Black Studies, University of Southern California at Los Angeles, 1976-79; Visiting Professor, Occidental College, 1979; Assistant Professor, 1979-81, Associate Professor, 1981-87, Professor, 1987-, Board of Studies in Literature and American Studies Program, University of California at Santa Cruz; Writer-in-Residence, Washington, DC, Project for the Arts, 1986, Institute of American Indian Arts, Santa Fe, New Mexico, 1987, 1988, Brown University, 1990, Intersection for the Arts San Francisco, 1991; Faculty, Naropa Institute, Boulder, summers 1991, 1993; Visiting Foreign Artist, Kootenay School of Writing, Vancouver, British Columbia, 1994. Publications: Poetry: Four for Trane, 1978; Septet for the End of Time, 1983; Eroding Witness, 1985; Outlandish, 1992; School of Udhra, 1993; Song of the Andoumboulou: 18-20, 1994. Fiction: From a Broken Bottle Traces of Perfume Still Emanate, Vol I, Bedouin Hornbook, 1986, Vol II, Djbot Baghostus's Run, 1993. Non-Fiction: Discrepant Engagement: Dissonance, Cross-Culturality and Experimental Writing, 1993. Other: Moment's Notice: Jazz in Poetry and Prose (editor with Art Lange), 1993. Compact Disc: Strick: Song of the Andoumboulon 16-25 (poetry read by the author with musical accompaniment), 1995. Contributions to: Anthologies, scholarly journals and magazines. Honours: Coordinating Council of Literary Magazines Editor's Grant, 1985; Whiting Writer's Award, 1993. Address: c/o Kresge College, University of California at Santa Cruz, Santa Cruz, CA 95064, USA.

MACKIE John. See: **LEVINSON Leonard.**

MACKINNON Catharine, b. 1946, USA. Professor of Law; Writer. Education: BA, Smith College, 1969; JD, 1977, PhD, 1987, Yale University. Appointments: Professor of Law, University of Michigan, 1990-; Several visiting professorships. Publications: Sexual Harrassment of Working Women, 1979; Feminism Unmodified, 1987; Toward a Feminist Theory of the State, 1989; Only Words, 1993; In Harm's Way (with Andrea Dworkin),

1998. Contributions to: Journals. Address: c/o School of Law, University of Michigan, Ann Arbor, MI 48109, USA.

MACKLIN Elizabeth, b. 28 Oct 1952, Poughkeepsie, New York, USA. Poet. Education: BA in Spanish, State University of New York at Potsdam, 1973; Graduate School of Arts and Sciences, New York University, 1975-78. Appointment: Poetry Editor, Wigwag Magazine, 1989-91. Publication: A Woman Kneeling in the Big City, 1992. Contributions to: Nation; New Republic; New York Times; New Yorker; Paris Review; Threepenny Review. Honours: Ingram Merrill Foundation Award in Poetry, 1990; Guggenheim Fellowship, 1994. Memberships: Authors Guild; PEN American Center, executive board, 1995-96. Address: 207 West 14th Street, 5F, New York, NY 10011, USA.

MACKSEY K(enneth) J(ohn), b. 1 July 1923, Epsom, Surrey, England. Army Officer (retired); Historian. Education: Royal Military College, Sandhurst, 1943-44; British Army Staff College,1956. Appointments: Officer, Royal Tank Regiment, British Army, 1941-68, until retirement with rank of Major, 1968; Deputy Editor, History of the Second World War, History of the First World War, 1968-70. Publications: The Shadow of Vimy Ridge, 1965; To the Green Fields Beyond, 1965; Armoured Crusader: General Sir Percy Hobart, 1967; Africa Korps, Panzer Division, 1968; Crucible of Power: The Fight for Tunisia, 1969; Tank Force, 1970; Tank: A History of AFVs, 1970; Tank Warfare, Beda Fomm, 1971; The Guinness History of Land (Sea, Air) Warfare, 3 volumes, 1973-76; Battle (in US as Anatomy of a Battle), 1974; The Partisans of Europe in the Second World War, 1975; The Guinness Guide to Feminine Achievements, 1975; Guderian: Panzer General, 1975; The Guinness Book 1952 (1953, 1954), 3 volumes, 1977-79; Kesselring, 1978; Rommel's Campaigns and Battles, 1979; The Tanks, Vol III of the History of the Royal Tank Regiment, 1979; Invasion: The German Invasion of England, July 1940, 1980; The Tank Pioneers, 1981; History of the Royal Armoured Corps 1914-1975, 1983; Commando Strike, 1985; First Clash, 1985; Technology in War, 1986; Godwin's Saga, 1987; Military Errors of World War II, 1987; Tank Versus Tank, 1988; For Want of a Nail, 1989; The Penguin Encyclopedia of Modern Warfare, 1991; Penguin Encyclopedia and Technology, 1993; The Hitler Options, 1994; From Triumph to Disaster, 1996; Turning Points (memoirs), 1997. Address: Whatley Mill, Beaminster, Dorset DT8 3EN, England.

MACKWORTH Cecily, b, Llantillio Pertholey, Gwent, Wales. Writer. 1 daughter. m. Marquis de Chabannes la Palice, 1956. Publications: I Came Out of France, 1942; A Mirror for French Poetry, 1942; François Villon: A Study, 1947; The Mouth of the Sword, 1949; The Destiny of Isobella Eberhardt, 1952; Spring's Green Shadow (novel), 1953; Guillaume Apollinaire and the Cubist Life, 1961; English Interludes, 1974; Ends of the World (memoirs), 1987; Lucy's Nose (novel), 1992. Contributions to: Horizon; Life and Letters Today; Poetry Quarterly; Cornhill; Twentieth Century; Cultures for all Peoples (UNESCO); Critique; Les Lettres Nouvelles. Honour: Darmstadt Award, 1965. Memberships: PEN, France; Association Internationale des Critiques Litteraires; Society of Authors of Great Britain. Literary Agent: L Pollinger, 18 Madox Street, London W1R 0EG, England. Address: 6 Rue des Countures-St-Gervais, Paris 75003, France.

MACLAVERTY Bernard, b. 14 Sept 1942, Belfast, Northern Ireland. Novelist; Dramatist. m. Madeline McGuckin, 1967, 1 son, 3 daughters. Education: BA, Honours, Queen's University, Belfast, 1974. Publications: Bibliography: Secrets and Other Stories, 1977; Lamb (novel), 1980; A Time to Dance and Other Stories, 1982; Cal (novel), 1983; The Great Profundo and Other Stories, 1987; Walking the Dog and Other Stories, 1994; Grace Notes (novel), 1997. For Young Children: A Man in Search of a Pet, 1978; Andrew McAndrew, 1988, US edition, 1993. Radio Plays: My Dear Palestrina, 1980; Secrets, 1981; No Joke, 1983; The Break, 1988; Some Surrender, 1988; Lamb, 1992. Television Plays: My Dear Palestrina, 1980; Phonefun Limited, 1982; The Daily

Woman, 1986; Sometime in August, 1989. Screenplays: Cal, 1984; Lamb, 1985. Drama Documentary: Hostages, 1992, US edition, 1993; Television Adaptation: The Real Charlotte by Somerville and Ross, 1989. Honours: Northern Ireland and Scottish Arts Councils Awards; Irish Sunday Independent Award, 1983; London Evening Standard Award for Screenplay, 1984; Joint Winner, Scottish Writer of the Year, 1988; Society of Authors Travelling Scholarship, 1994; Shortlisted, Saltire Society Scottish Book of the Year, 1994; Grace Notes awarded The Saltire Scottish Book of the Year Award, 1997; A Scottish Arts Council Book Award; Shortlisted for: The Booker Prize; the Writers Guild Best Fiction Book; The Stakis Scottish Writer of the Year; The Whitbread Novel of the Year.

MACLEAN Arthur. See: **TUBB E(dwin) C(harles).**

MACLEOD Alison, b, 12 Apr 1920, Hendon, Middlesex, England. Writer. Publications: Dear Augustine, 1958; The Heretics (in US as The Heretic), 1965; The Hireling (in UK as The Trusted Servant), 1968; City of Light (in UK as No Need of the Sun), 1969; The Muscovite, 1971; The Jesuit (in US as Prisoner of the Queen), 1972; The Portingale, 1976; The Death of Uncle Joe, 1997. Address: 63 Muswell Hill Place, London N10 3RP, England.

MacLEOD Charlotte, (Alisa Craig, Matilda Hughes), b. 12 Nov 1922, Bath, England (US citizen, 1952). Writer. Publications: As Charlotte MacLeod: Mystery of the White Knight, 1964; Next Door to Danger, 1965; The Fat Lady's Ghost, 1968; Mouse's Vineyard (juvenile), 1968; Ask Me No Questions, 1971; Brass Pounder (juvenile), 1971; Astrology for Sceptics (non-fiction), 1972; King Devil, 1978; Rest You Merry, 1978; The Family Vault, 1979; The Luck Runs Out, 1979; The Withdrawing Room, 1980; We Dare Not Go a Hunting, 1980; The Palace Guard, 1981; Wrack and Rune, 1982; Cirak's Daughter (juvenile), 1982; The Bilbao Looking Glass, 1983; Something the Cat Dragged In, 1983; Maid of Honour (juvenile), 1984; The Convival Codfish, 1984; The Curse of the Giant Hogweed, 1985; The Plain Old Man, 1985; Grab Bag, 1987; The Corpse in Oozak's Pond, 1987; The Recycled Citizen, 1988; The Silver Ghost, 1988; Vane Pursuit, 1989; The Gladstone Bag, 1990. As Matilda Hughes: The Food of Love, 1965; Headlines for Caroline, 1967. As Alisa Craig: A Pint of Murder, 1980; The Grubland Stakers Move a Mountain, 1981; Murder Goes Mumming, 1981; The Terrible Tide, 1983; The Grub and Stakers Quilt a Bee, 1985; The Grub-and-Stakers Pinch a Poke, 1988; Trouble in the Brasses, 1989; The Grub-and-Stakers Spin and Yarn, 1990; An Owl Too Many; Something in the Water. Address: c/o Jed Mattes, 175 West 73rd Street, New York, NY 10023, USA.

MACLEOD Robert. See: **KNOX William.**

MACLURE John Stuart, b. 8 Aug 1926, London, England. Journalist. m. Constance Mary Butler, 8 Sept 1951, 1 son, 2 daughters. Education: Hon D, University (Open University); MA, Christ's College, Cambridge, 1951. Appointments: The Times, 1950; The Times Educational Supplement, 1951; Editor, Education, 1954; Editor, The Times Educational Supplement, 1969-89. Publications: Documents on Modern Political Thought, with T E Utley, 1959; Educational Documents 1816 - Present Day, editor, 1965; A Hundred Years of London Education, 1970; Politics of Curriculum Change, with Tony Becher, 1978; Education Re-Formed, 1988. Honour: CBE, 1981. Address: 109 College Road, London SE21 7HN, England.

MACMILLAN James. See: **BROWN Hamish Macmillan.**

MACMULLEN Ramsay, b. 3 Mar 1928, New York, New York, USA. Retired Professor of History and Classics; Writer; Publisher. m. (1) Edith Merriman Nye, 7 Aug 1954, div 1991, 2 sons, 2 daughters, (2) Margaret McNeill, 1 Aug 1992. Education: AB, 1950, AM, 1953, PhD, 1957, Harvard University. Appointments: Instructor to Assistant Professor, University of Oregon, 1956-61;

Associate Professor to Professor, 1961-67, Chairman, Department of Classics, 1965-66, Brandeis University; Fellow, Institute for Advanced Study, Princeton, New Jersey, 1964-65; Professor, 1967-93, Chairman, Department of History, 1970-72, Dunham Professor of History and Classics, 1979-93, Master, Calhoun College, 1984-90, Yale University. Publications: Soldier and Civilian in the Later Roman Empire, 1963; Enemies of the Roman Order, 1966; Constantine, 1969; Roman Social Relations, 1974; Roman Government's Response to Crisis, 1976; Paganism in the Roman Empire, 1981; Christianizing the Roman Empire, 1984; Corruption and the Decline of Rome, 1988; Changes in the Roman Empire, 1990; Paganism and Christianity (with E N Lane), 1992; Christianity and Paganism, 1997; Sisters of the Brush, 1997. Contributions to: Professional journals. Honours: Fulbright Fellowship, 1960-61; Porter Prize, College Art Association, 1964; Guggenheim Fellowship, 1964; Senior Fellow, National Endowment for the Humanities, 1974-75. Memberships: Association of Ancient Historians, president, 1978-81; Friends of Ancient History; Society for the Promotion of Roman Studies. Address: 25 Temple Court, New Haven, CT 06511, USA.

MACNAB Roy Martin, b. 17 Sept 1923, Durban, South Africa. Retired Diplomat. m. Rachel Heron-Maxwell, 6 Dec 1947, 1 son, 1 daughter. Education: Hilton College, Natal, South Africa; MA, Jesus College, Oxford, 1955; DLitt et Phil, University of South Africa, 1981. Publications: The Man of Grass and Other Poems, 1960; The French Colonel, 1975; Gold Their Touchstone, 1987; For Honour Alone, 1988. Co-Editor: Oxford Poetry, 1947; Poets in South Africa, 1958; Journey Into Yesterday, 1962. Editor: George Seferis: South African Diary, 1990; The Cherbourg Circles, 1994. Contributions to: Times Literary Supplement; Spectator; Poetry Review; History, Today. Honour: Silver Medal, Royal Society of Arts, 1958. Address: c/o Barclays Private Bank, 59 Grosvenor Street, London W1X 9DA, England.

MacNEACAIL Aonghas, b, 7 June 1942, Uig, Isle of Skye, Scotland. Writer; Poet. m. Gerda Stevenson, 21 June 1980, 1 son. Education: University of Glasgow. Appointments: Writing Fellowships, The Gaelic College, Isle of Skye, 1977-79, An Comunn Gaidhealachm Oban, 1979-81, Ross-Cromarty District Council, 1988-90. Publications: Poetry Quintet, 1976; Imaginary Wounds, 1980; Sireadh Bradain Sicir/Seeking Wise Salmon, 1983; An Cathadh Mor/The Great Snowbattle, 1984; An Seachnadh/The Avoiding, 1986; Rocker and Water, 1990. Contributions to: Many publications. Honours: Grampian TV Gaelic Poetry Award; Diamond Jubilee Award, Scottish Association for the Speaking of Verse, 1985; An Comunn Gaidhealach Literary Award, 1985. Membership: Scottish Poetry Library Association, council member, 1984-. Address: 1 Roseneath Terrace, Marchmont, Edinburgh EH9 1JS, Scotland.

MACNEIL Duncan. See: **McCUTCHAN Philip Donald.**

MACSOVSZKY Peter, b. 4 Nov 1966, Slovakia. Teacher. Education: Graduate, Teachers Training College, Mitra; Master Degree, University of Constantine the Philosopher. Publications: Strach z Utopie, English translation as Fear of Utopia, 1994; Ambit, 1995; Somrak Cudnosti, English translation as The Dusk of Chastity, 1996; Cvicna Pitva, English translation as Training Autopsy, 1997; A'lbonctan, English translation as False Pathology, 1998. Membership: Obec Slovensky Spisovatelov. Address: Holubicia 7, 91001 Nove Zamky, Slovakia.

MACTHOMAIS Ruaraidh. See: **THOMSON Derick S(mith).**

MACVEAN Jean Elizabeth, b. Bradford, England. Poet; Writer. m. James Bernard Wright, 10 Oct 1952, 1 son, 1 daughter. Education: Collège d'Hulst, Versailles; Sorbonne, University of Paris. Publications: Poetry and prose, including: Eros Reflected, 1981; The Dolorous Death of King Arthur, 1992; The True and Holy Story of the Sangrail, 1995. Contributions to: Anthologies,

reviews, and magazines. Memberships: PEN International, fellow; Poetry Society. Address: 21 Peel Street, London W8 7PA, England.

MACVEY John Wishart, b. 19 Jan 1923, Kelso, Scotland. Technical Information Officer (retired); Writer. Education: Diploma, Applied Chemistry, University of Strathclyde, 1951; BA, Open University, Milton Keynes, 1978. Appointments: Research Chemist, 1956-61, Plant Manager, 1961-62, Assistant Technical Information Officer, 1962-71, Technical Information Officer, Nobel's Explosives Ltd. Publications: Speaking of Space (with C P Snow, B Lovell and P Moore), 1962; Alone in the Universe?, 1963; Journey to Alpha Centauri, 1965; How We Will Reach the Stars, 1969; Whispers from Space, 1973; Interstellar Travel: Past, Present and Future, 1977; Space Weapons/Space War, 1979; Where We Will Go When the Sun Dies?, 1980; Colonizing Other Worlds, 1984; Time Travel, 1987. Address: Mellendean, 15 Adair Avenue, Saltcoats, Ayrshire KA21 5QS, Scotland.

MADDEN David, b. 25 July 1933, Knoxville, Tennessee, USA. Educator; Writer; Critic; Editor; Poet; Dramatist. m. Roberta Margaret Young, 6 Sept 1956, 1 son. Education: BS, University of Tennessee, 1957; MA, San Francisco State College, 1958; Postgraduate Studies, Yale Drama School, 1959-60. Appointments: Faculty, Appalachian State Teachers College, Boone, North Carolina, 1957-58, Centre College, 1964-66, Ohio University, 1966-68; Assistant Editor, Kenyon Review, 1964-66; Writer-in-Residence, 1968-92, Director, Creative Writing Program, 1992-94, and US Civil War Center, 1992-, Alumni Professor, 1994, Louisiana State University. Publications: Fiction: The Beautiful Greed, 1961; Cassandra Singing, 1969; The Shadow Knows, 1970; Brothers in Confidence, 1972; Bijou, 1974; The Suicide's Wife, 1978; Pleasure-Dome, 1979; On the Big Wind, 1980; The New Orleans of Possibilities, 1982; Sharpshooter, 1995. Non-Fiction: Wright Morris, 1964; The Poetic Image in 6 Genres, 1969; James M Cain, 1970; Creative Choices: A Spectrum of Quality and Technique in Fiction, 1975; Harlequin's Stick: Charlie's Cane: A Comparative Study of Commedia dell' arte and Silent Slapstick Comedy, 1975; A Primer of the Novel: For Readers & Writers, 1980; Writer's Revisions (with Richard Powers), 1981; Cain's Craft, 1986; Revising Fiction, 1988; The World of Fiction, 1990; The Fiction Tutor, 1990; Eight Classic American Novels, 1990; A Pocketful of Prose: Vintage, 1992; A Pocketful of Prose: Contemporary, 1992. Editor: Proletarian Writers of the Thirties, 1968; Tough Guy Writers of the Thirties, 1968; American Dreams, American Nightmares, 1970; Rediscoveries, 1971; the Popular Culture Explosion (with Ray B Browne), 1972; The Contemporary Literary Scene (associate editor), 1973; Nathanael West: The Cheaters and the Cheated, 1973; Remembering James Agee, 1974; Studies in the Short Story, 4th, 1975, 5th, 1980, and 6th, 1984, editions; Rediscoveries II (with Peggy Bach), 1988; Classics of Civil War Fiction, 1991. Contributions to: Poems, essays and short stories in various publications. Honours: John Golden Fellow in Playwriting, 1959; Rockefeller Foundation Grant in Fiction, 1969; National Council on the Arts Award, 1970. Memberships: Associated Writing Programs; Authors League. Address: c/o United States Civil War Center, Raphael Semmes Drive, Louisiana State University, Baton Rouge, LA 70803, USA.

MADDISON Tyler. See: **SMITH Moe Gerard.**

MADDOX Carl. See: **TUBB E(dwin) C(harles).**

MADELEY John, b. 14 July 1934, Salford, England. Writer; Broadcaster. m. Alison Madeley, 10 Mar 1962, 1 son, 1 daughter. Education: BA, Honours, Economics, 1972. Appointments: Broadcaster, BBC and Deutsche Welle. Publications: Human Rights Begin with Breakfast, 1981; Diego Garcia: Contrast to the Falklands, 1982; When Aid is No Help, 1991; Trade and the Poor, 1992, 2nd edition, 1996. Contributions to: Newspapers and magazines. Address: 19 Woodford Close, Caversham, Reading, Berkshire RG4 7HN, England.

MADGETT Naomi Long, b. 5 July 1923, Norfolk, Virginia, USA. Poet; Publisher; Professor of English Emeritus. m. Leonard P Andrews Sr. Education: BA, Virginia State College, 1945; MEd, English, Wayne State University; PhD, International Institute for Advanced Studies, 1980. Appointments: Research Associate, Oakland University; Lecturer in English, University of Michigan; Associate Professor to Professor of English Emeritus, Eastern Michigan University; Publisher; Editor, Lotus Press. Publications: Songs to a Phantom Nightingale, 1941; One and the Many, 1956; Star by Star, 1965; Pink Ladies in the Afternoon, 1972; Exits and Entrances, 1978; Phantom Nightingale, 1981; A Student's Guide to Creative Writing, 1990. Contributions to: Numerous anthologies and journals. Address: 16886 Inverness Avenue, Detroit, MI 48221, USA.

MADOUESSE Ti-Pique Le. See: **PARATTE Henri-Dominique.**

MADSEN Richard Paul, b. 2 Apr 1941, Alameda, California, USA. Professor of Sociology; Writer. m. Judith Rosselli, 12 Jan 1974. Education: BA, Maryknoll College, Glen Ellyn, Illinois, 1963; BD, 1967, MTh, 1968, Maryknoll Seminary, Ossining, New York; MA, 1972, PhD, 1977, Harvard University. Appointments: Ordained, Roman Catholic Priest, 1968; Maryknoll missioner, Taiwan, 1968-71; Left priesthood, 1974; Lecturer in Sociology, Harvard University, 1977-78; Assistant Professor, 1978-83, Associate Professor, 1983-85, Professor of Sociology, 1985-, University of California at San Diego, La Jolla. Publications: Chen Village: The Recent History of a Peasant Community in Mao's China (with Anita Chan and Jonathan Unger), 1984, revised edition as Chen Village Under Mao and Deng, 1992; Morality and Power in a Chinese Village, 1984; Habits of the Heart: Individualism in American Life (with Robert N Bellah, William M Sullivan, Ann Swidler and Steven M Tipton), 1985; Individualism and Commitment in American Life: A Habits of the Heart Reader (with Robert N Bellah, William M Sullivan, Ann Swidler and Steven M Tipton), 1987; Unofficial China (editor with Perry Link and Paul Pickowicz), 1989; The Good Society (with Robert N Bellah, William M Sullivan, Ann Swidler and Steven M Tipton), 1991; China and the American Dream: A Moral Inquiry, 1995; China's Catholics: Tragedy and Hope in a Emerging Civil Society, 1998. Contributions to: Journals. Honours: C Wright Mills Award, Society for the Study of Social Problems, 1985; Current Interest Book Award, Los Angeles Times, 1985; Book Award, Association of Logos Bookstores, 1986. Memberships: American Sociological Association; Association of Asian Studies, governing council for China and Inner Asia, 1989-91. Address: c/o Department of Sociology, University of California at San Diego, La Jolla, CA 92093, USA.

MADSEN Viggo, b. 6 Jan 1943, Esbjerg, Denmark. Poet; Librarian. Education: Royal School of Librarianship, Copenhagen, 1966. Publications: Brandmand På to Hjul (Fireman on Two Wheels), 1966; Kroppen Er En Genvej (The Body is A Short-Cut), 1989; Forlang Mirakler På Den sidste Dag (Demand Miracles on the Last Day), 1991; Händtegn Uden Händ (Handsigns Without a Hand), 1994; Vär Folk Som Gä Forbi (Be Passerby), 1998. Contributions to: Almost all literary magazines. Honours: Fellow, Cambridge Seminar, 1996. Membership: Danish Writers Union. Address: Naesbygaardsvej 23, DK 5270 Odense N, Denmark.

MAFFI Mario, b. 23 May 1947, Milan, Italy. University Professor. m. Maria Matilde Merli, 7 May 1973, 1 daughter. Education: Degree in Humanities, magna cum laude, University of Milan, 1971. Publications: La cultura underground, 1972; La giungla e il grattacielo: Gli scrittori e il "sogno americano" 1865-1920, 1982; Nel mosaico della citta: Differenze etniche e nuove culture in un quartiere di New York, 1992; Gateway to the Promised Land: Ethnic Cultures in New York's Lower East Side, 1994; New York: L'isola delle colline, 1995; Sotto le Torri di Manhattan, 1998. Honour: Premio Libro Giovane, 1975. Address: Istituto di Anglistica, Piazza S Alessandro 1, 20123 Milan, Italy.

MAGEE Bryan, b. 12 Apr 1930, London, England. Writer. m. Ingrid Söderlund, 1954, dec 1986, 1 daughter. Education: MA, Oxford University, 1956; Yale University, 1955-56. Appointments: Theatre Critic, The Listener, 1966-67; Regular Columnist, The Times, 1974-76. Publications: Go West Young Man, 1958; To Live in Danger, 1960; The New Radicalism, 1962; The Democratic Revolution, 1964; Towards 2000, 1965; One in Twenty, 1966; The Television Interviewer, 1966; Aspects of Wagner, 1968; Modern British Philosophy, 1971; Popper, 1973; Facing Death, 1977; Men of Ideas, 1978; The Philosophy of Schopenhauer, 1983; The Great Philosophers, 1987; On Blindness, 1995, reissued as Sight Unseen, 1998; Confessions of a Philosopher, 1997; The Story of Philosophy, 1998. Contributions to: Numerous journals. Honour: Silver Medal, Royal Television Society, 1978. Memberships: Critics Circle; Society of Authors. Address: 12 Falkland House, Marloes Road, London W8 5LF, England.

MAGEE Wes(ley Leonard Johnston), b. 20 July 1939, Greenock, Scotland. Poet; Writer. m. Janet Elizabeth Parkhouse, 10 Aug 1967, 1 son, 1 daughter. Education: Teaching Certificate, Goldsmith's College, University of London, 1967; Advanced Certificate in Education, University of Bristol, 1972. Publications: Over 40 books for children, 1972-98. Contributions to: Reviews and journals. Honours: New Poets Award, 1972; Poetry Book Society Recommendation, 1978; Cole Scholar, Florida, 1985. Memberships: Poetry Society of Great Britain; Philip Larkin Society. Address: Crag View Cottage, Thorgill, Rosedale, North Yorkshire YO18 8SG, England.

MAGER Donald Northrop, b. 24 Aug 1942, Santa Rita, New Mexico, USA. Associate Professor; Poet; Writer; Translator. m. Barbara Feldman, div, 2 sons. companion William McDowell. Education: BA, Drake University, 1964; MA, Creative Writing, Syracuse University, 1966; PhD, English Literature, Wayne State University, 1986. Appointments: Instructor, Syracuse University; Associate Professor, Johnson C Smith University. Publications: Poetry: To Track the Wounded One: A Journal, 1988; Glosses: Twenty-four Preludes and Etudes, 1995; That Which is Owed to Death, 1998; Borderings, 1998. Contributions to: Anthologies, books, reviews, quarterlies, journals, and magazines. Honours: 1st Prize, Hallmark Competition, 1965; Approach Magazines Award, 1978; Tompkings Award 1st Prize for Poetry, Wayne State University, 1986; 1st Prize, The Lyricist Statewide Poetry Competition, Campbell University, 1992; Associate Artist Residency, Atlantic Center for the Arts, New Smyrna Beach, Florida, 1994; Winner, Union County Writers Club Chapbook Contest, 1998. Membership: Modern Language Association. Address: c/o Johnson C Smith University, UPO 2441, Charlotte, NC 28216, USA.

MAGNUS Jirgen-Ulv Joram, b. 13 Nov 1922, Berlin, Germany. m. Irene Gitta Mollu, 5 June 1998, 2 sons, 2 daughters. Education: Stockholm Universitate Officers Akademie. Appointments: Chairman, political party in Forum CPU; Judge, Hillerod Catle Courd. Publications: Cabala for Freemasons; Loftet der gih i oplyldese. Contributions to: Hjemmet; Juleneget. Literary Agent: Dansk Lulhersk Forlag.

MAGNUSSON Haraldur Sigfus, b. 25 June 1931, Iceland. m. Erla Gudbjörg Sigurdar, 7 Nov 1959, 2 sons, 2 daughters. Publications: The Raggi Series, 5 booksd for children; Ospin Og Ylustraia, short stories; Gegnum Einghyrnja, poets. Membership: Rithofunda Samband Islands. Address: Huerfisgata 23c, Hafnarfjordur, Iceland.

MAGNUSSON Magnus, b. 12 Oct 1929, Reykjavík, Iceland. Writer; Translator; Broadcaster. m. Mamie Baird, 1954, 1 son, 3 daughters, 1 son dec. Education: MA, Jesus College, Oxford, 1951. Publications: Introducing Archaeology, 1972; Viking Expansion Westwards, 1973; The Clacken and the Slate, 1974; Hammer of the North, 1976, 2nd edition as Viking Hammer of the North, 1980; BC: The Archaeology of the Bible Lands, 1977; Landlord or Tenant?: A View of Irish History, 1978; Iceland, 1979;

Vikings!, 1980; Magnus on the Move, 1980; Treasures of Scotland, 1981; Lindisfarne: The Cradle Island, 1984; Iceland Saga, 1987. Translations (all with Hermann Palsson): Njal's Saga, 1960; The Vinland Sagas, 1965; King Herald's Saga, 1966; Laxaela Saga, 1969; (all by Halldor Laxness): The Atom Station, 1961; Paradise Reclaimed, 1962; The Fish Can Sing, 1966; World Light, 1969; Christianity under Glacier, 1973; (by Samivel) Golden Iceland, 1967. Editor: Echoes in Stone, 1983; Reader's Digest Book of Facts, 1985; Chambers Biographical Dictionary, 1990; The Nature of Scotland, 1994. Contributions to: Many books. Honours: Knight of the Order of the Falcon, 1975, Knight Commander, 1986, Iceland; Silver Jubilee Medal, 1977; Iceland Media Award, 1985; Honorary Knighthood, Great Britain, 1989; Honorary Fellow, Jesus College, Oxford, 1990; Honorary Degrees, and many other honours and awards. Memberships: Society of Antiquaries of London, fellow, 1991; Royal Scottish Geographical Society, fellow, 1991. Literary Agent: Deborah Rogers, Rogers, Coleridge & White, 20 Powis Mews, London W11 1JN, England. Address: Blairskaith House, Balmore-Torrance, Glasgow G64 4AX, Scotland.

MAGNUSSON Sigurdur A, b. 31 Mar 1928, Reykjavík, Iceland. Writer; Poet. m. (1), div, (2), div, 2 sons, 3 daughters. Education: University of Iceland, 1948-50; University of Copenhagen, 1950-51; University of Athens, 1951-52; University of Stockholm, 1952-53; BA, New School for Social Research, New York City, 1955. Appointments: Literary and Drama Critic, Morgunbladid, 1956-67; Editor-in-Chief, Samvinnan, 1967-74; Member, International Writing Programme, University of Iowa, 1976, 1977, International Artists' Programme, West Berlin, 1979-80, Jury, Nordic Council Prize for Literature, 1990-98. Publications: In English: Northern Sphinx: Iceland and the Icelanders from the Settlement to the Present, 1977, 2nd edition, 1984; Iceland: Country and People, 1978, 2nd edition, 1987; The Iceland Horse, 1978; The Postwar Poetry of Iceland, 1982; Icelandic Writing Today, 1982; Iceland Crucible: A Modern Artistic Renaissance, 1985; The Icelanders, 1990; Iceland: Isle of Light, 1995. Other: 28 books in Icelandic. Contributions to: Professional journals. Honours: Golden Cross of Phoenix, Greece, 1955; Cultural Council Prize for Best Play, 1961, and Best Novel, 1980; European Jean Monnet Prize for Literature, 1995. Memberships: Amnesty International, chairman, 1988-89, 1993-95; Greek-Icelandic Society, chairman, 1985-88; Society of Icelandic Drama Critics, chairman, 1963-71; Writers Union of Iceland, chairman, 1971-78. Address: Barónsstig 49, 101 Reykjavík, Iceland.

MAGORIAN James, b. 24 Apr 1942, Palisade, Nebraska, USA. Poet; Writer. Education: BS, University of Nebraska, 1965; MS, Illinois State University, 1969; Graduate Studies, Oxford University, 1972, Harvard University, 1973. Publications: Poetry: Hitchhiker in Hall County, 1968; The Garden of Epicurus, 1971; Safe Passage, 1977; Phases of the Moon, 1978; Tap Dancing on a Tightrope, 1981; Taxidermy Lessons, 1982; The Walden Pond Caper, 1983; The Emily Dickinson Jogging Book, 1984; Weighing the Sun's Light, 1985; The Hideout of the Sigmund Freud Gang, 1987; Borderlands, 1992; The Yellowstone Meditations, 1996; Haymarket Square, 1998. Novels: America First, 1992; The Man Who Wore Layers of Clothing in the Winter, 1994; Hearts of Gold, 1996; Souvenir Pillows From Mars, 1996. Other: Children's books. Contributions to: Reviews, quarterlies, and journals. Address: 1224 North 46th Street, Lincoln, NE 68503, USA.

MAGORIAN Michelle Jane, b. 6 Nov 1947, Southsea, Portsmouth, Hampshire, England. Writer; Actress. m. Peter Keith Venner, Aug 1987, div 1998, 2 sons. Education: Diploma, Speech and Drama, Rose Bruford College of Speech and Drama, Kent, 1969; École Internationale de Mime Marcel Marceau, Paris, 1969-70. Publications: Novels: Goodnight Mister Tom, 1981, US edition, 1982, also book and lyrics as musical; Back Home, 1984; A Little Love Song, 1991; Cuckoo in the Nest, 1994. Poetry: Waiting for My Shorts to Dry, 1989; Orange Paw Marks, 1991. Short Story Collection: In

Deep Water, 1992; A Spoonful of Jam, 1998. Contributions to: Puffin Post. Honours: Guardian Award for Children's Fiction, UK, 1981; Commended for Carnegie Medal, UK, 1981; Children's Award, International Reading Association, USA, 1982; Notable Children's Books, 1982, Best Book of Young Adults, 1982, Young Adult Reviewers Choice, 1982, American Library Association; Western Australia Young Readers Book Award, 1983; Teachers Choice, NCTE, 1983; Best Books for Adults, American Library Association, 1984; Western Australia Young Readers Book Award, 1987. Memberships: Society of Authors; PEN; British Actors Equity. Address: 2 Harbour Mount, Church Road, Bembridge, Isle of Wight, PO35 5NA, England.

MAHAPATRA Jayanta, b. 22 Oct 1928, Cuttack, Orissa, India. Poet; Writer; Editor. Translator. m. Jyotsna Rani Das, 16 Jan 1951, 1 son. Education: University of Cambridge, 1941; BSc, Utkal University, 1946; MSc, Patna University, 1949. Appointments: Lecturer, Reader, 1950-86; Poet-in-Residence, Rockefeller Foundation Conference Center, Bellagio, Italy, 1986; Poetry Editor, The Telegraph, Calcutta, 1994-; Editor, Lipi, 1998. Publications: Close the Sky, 1971; Svayamvara and Other Poems, 1971; A Rain of Rites, 1976; Waiting, 1979; The False Start, 1980; Life Signs, 1983; Dispossessed Nests, 1984; Selected Poems, 1987; Burden of Waves and Fruit, 1988; A Whiteness of Bone, 1992; The Best of Jayanta Mahapatra, 1995; Shadow Space, 1997; The Green Gardner, 1997. Other: Various children's stories and translations. Contributions to: Reviews, quarterlies, and journals. Honours: Various awards, including National Academy of Letters Award, New Delhi, 1981; El Consejo Nacional Para la Cultura y las Artes, Mexico, 1994; Gangadhar National Award for Poetry, 1994; Jaidayal Harmony Award, 1994. Address: Tinkonia, Bagicha, Cuttack 753 001, Orissa, India.

MAHARIDGE Dale (Dimitro), b. 24 Oct 1956, Cleveland, Ohio, USA. University Lecturer; Writer. Education: Cleveland State University, 1974-76; Cuyahoga Community College, 1976. Appointments: Staff, Gazette, Medina, Ohio, 1977-78; Journalist, Sacramento Bee, California, 1980-91; Assistant Professor, Columbia University, 1991-92; Lecturer, Stanford University, 1992-. Publications: Journey to Nowhere: The Saga of the New Underclass, 1985; And Their Children After Them: The Legacy of "Let Us Now Praise Famous Men", James Agee, Walker Evans, and the Rise and Fall of Cotton in the South, 1989; Yosemite: A Landscape of Life, 1990; The Last Great American Hobo, 1993. Contributions to: Periodicals. Honours: World Hunger Award, New York City, 1987; Lucius W Nieman Fellowship, Harvard University, 1988; Pulitzer Prize for General Non-Fiction, 1990; Pope Foundation Award, 1994; Freedom Forum Professors' Publishing Program Grant, 1995. Membership: Sierra Club. Address: c/o Department of Communications, Stanford University, Stanford, CA 94305, USA.

MAHESHWARI Shriram, b. 27 Nov 1931, Kanpur, India. Professor; Writer. m. Bimla, 30 May 1955, 3 sons, 2 daughters. Education: BA, 1951, MA, Economics, 1953, MA, Political Science, 1955, Agra University; MGA, Wharton School, University of Pennsylvania, 1964; PhD, University of Delhi, 1965. Appointments: Professor of Political Science and Public Administration, Indian Institute of Public Administration, 1973-91; Guest faculty, Jawaharla Nehru University, New Delhi, 1979-83; Director, Centre for Political and Administrative Studies, 1991-; Visiting Professor, Department of Political Studies, University of Guelph, Ontario, Canada; National Fellow, Indian Council of Social Science Research, 1998. Publications: Rural Development in India: A Public Policy Approach, 1986, revised edition, 1996; The Higher Civil Service in Japan, 1986; The Higher Civil Service in France, 1991; Problems and Issues in Administrative Federalism, 1991; Administrative Reform in India, 1991; Indian Administration: An Historical Account, 1994; Major Civil Service Systems in the World, 1997; The Census Administration in India Under the Raj and After; Administrative Theories, 1997; Administrative Thinkers, 1998. Contributions to: Philippines Journal of Public

Administration; Indian Express; Hindustan Times. Honour: Sardar Patel Prize for Best Work in Hindi, 1988. Memberships: Indian Public Administration Association, president, 1988-89; Indian Political Science Association; Indian Institute of Public Administration; Indian Public Administration Association; Indian Political Science Association. Address: 156 Golf Links, New Delhi 110003, India.

MAHFOUZ Naguib (Abdel Aziz Al-Sabilgi), b. 11 Dec 1911, Cairo, Egypt. Writer; Journalist; Civil Servant. m., 2 daughters. Education: Degree in Philosophy, University of Cairo, 1934. Appointments: Journalist, Ar-Risala; Ministry of Islamic Affairs, Department of Art; Head, State Cinema Organisation; Advisor to Minister of Culture. Publications: 16 collections of short stories including (in translation), The Time and the Place, 1991; 34 novels including (in translation), Midaq Alley, 1975; Mirrors, 1977; Miramar, 1978; Al-Karnak, 1979; Children of Gebelawi (translated by Philip Stewart) 1981, new translation, 1995; The Thief and the Dogs, 1984; Wedding Song, 1984; The Beginning and the End, 1985; The Beggar, 1986; Respected Sir, 1986; The Search, 1987, Fountain and Tomb, 1988; (The Cairo Trilogy) Palace Walk, 1990, Palace of Desire, 1991, Sugar Street, 1992; The Journey of Ibn Fattouma, 1992; Adrift on the Nile, 1993; Al-Harafish, 1994; Arabian Nights and Days, 1995; Echoes of an Autobiography, 1997. Honours: Nobel Prize for Literature, 1988; Honorary Member, American Academy and Institute of Arts and Letters, 1992. Address: 113 Sharia Kasr El Aini, Cairo, Egypt.

MAHON Derek, b. 23 Nov 1941, Belfast, Northern Ireland. Critic; Editor; Poet. Education: BA, Belfast Institute; BA, Trinity College, Dublin, 1965. Appointments: Drama Critic, Editor, Poetry Editor, New Statesman, 1981-; Poet-in-Residencies. Publications: Twelve Poems, 1965; Night-Crossing, 1968; Lives, 1972; The Man Who Built His City in Snow, 1972; The Snow Party, 1975; Light Music, 1977; The Sea in Winter, 1979; Poems 1962-1978, 1979; Courtyards in Delft, 1981; The Hunt by Night, 1982; A Kensington Notebook, 1984; Antarctica, 1986; Selected Poems, 1991. Editor: Modern Irish Poetry, 1972; The Penquin Book of Contemporary Irish Poetry, 1990. Address: c/o Rogers, Coleridge & White Ltd, 20 Powis Mews, London W11 1JN, England.

MAHONEY Rosemary, b. 28 Jan 1961, Boston, Massachusetts, USA. Writer. Education: BA, Harvard College, 1983; MA, Johns Hopkins University, 1985. Publications: The Early Arrival of Dreams; A Year in China; Whoredom in Kimmage; Irish Women Coming of Age, 1993. Honours: C E Horman Prize for Fiction, Harvard College, 1982; Henfield-Transatlantics Review Award for Fiction, 1985. Contributions to: Newspapers and journals. Address: c/o Houghton Mifflin Company, 215 Park Avenue South, New York, NY 10003, USA.

MAHY Margaret, b. 21 Mar 1936, Whakatane, New Zealand. Writer; Poet. Education: BA, University of New Zealand, 1958. Appointments: Writer-in-Residence, Canterbury University, 1984, College of Advanced Education, Western Australia, 1985. Publications: Some 50 books for children, 1969-95. Honours: Several. Address: RD No 1, Lyttelton, New Zealand.

MAI Gottfried Erhard Willy, b. 11 May 1940, Finsterwalde, Germany. Theologian; Freelance Writer. m. Gunhild Flemming, 1 Sept 1962, 2 sons, 2 daughters. Education: Navigation Certificate, Nautical School, Bremen; Studied Theology and History, Universities of Bonn, Göttingen, Hamburg and Copenhagen; Dr Theol; Dr Phil. Publications: The Protestant Church and the German Emigration to North America (1815-1914), 1972; The German Federal Armed Forces 1815-1864, 1977; Die niederdeutsche Reformbewegung, 1979; Geschichte der stadt Finsterwalde, 1979; Der Uberfall des Tigers, 1982; Chronicle of the 4th Minesweeper Squadron Wilhelmshaven, 1985; Buddha, 1985; Napoleon: Temptation of Power, 1986; Zwischen Polor und Wonderkreis, 1987; Lenin: The Perverted Moral, 1987. Contributions to: Books and journals. Honour: Book Prize for History, AWMM, 1983. Address: Harlinger Weg 2, D-2948 Grafschaft, Germany.

MAIDEN Jennifer (Margaret), b. 7 Apr 1949, Penrith, New South Wales, Australia. Poet; Writer. m. David Toohey, 14 July 1984, 1 daughter. Education: BA, Macquarie University, 1974; The Occupying Forces, 1975; The Problem of Evil, 1975; Birthstones, 1978; The Border Loss, 1979; For the Left Hand, 1981; The Terms, 1982; The Trust, 1988; Play with Knives, 1990; Selected Poems of Jennifer Maiden, 1990; Acoustic Shadow, 1993. Contributions to: Many newspapers and magazines. Honours: Several Australia Council Fellowships and Grants; Grenfell Henry Lawson Award, 1979; New South Wales Premier's Prize, 1991; Victorian Premier's Prize, 1991. Membership: Australian Society of Authors. Address: PO Box 4, Penrith, New South Wales, 2751, Australia.

MAIER Paul Luther, b. 31 May 1930, St Louis, Missouri, USA. Professor of Ancient History; Chaplain. m. Joah M Ludtke, 1967, 4 daughters. Education: MA, Harvard University, 1954; BD, Concordia Seminary, St Louis, 1955; Postgraduate Studies, Heidelberg; PhD, University of Basel, 1957. Appointments: Campus Chaplain, 1958-, Professor of Ancient History, 1961-, Western Michigan University; Lecturer. Publications: A Man Spoke, A World Listened: The Story of Walter A Maier, 1963; Pontius Pilate, 1968; First Christmas, 1971; First Easter, 1973; First Christians, 1976; The Flames of Rome, 1981; In the Fullness of Time, 1991; A Skeleton in God's Closet, 1994. Editor: The Best of Walter A Maier, 1980; Josephus: The Jewish War, 1982. Editor and Translator: Josephus: The Essential Writings, 1988; Josephus: The Essential Works, 1995; Eusebius: Eusebius: The Church History, 1999. Contributions to: Many professional journals. Honours: Alumni Award for Teaching Excellence, 1974, Distinguished Faculty Scholar, 1981, Western Michigan University; Outstanding Educator in America, 1974-75; Professor of the Year, Council for the Advancement and Support of Education, 1984; Citation, Michigan Academy of Sciences, Arts and Letters, 1985; Gold Medallion Book Award, ECPA, 1989; Phi Beta Kappa, 1998. Address: c/o Department of History, Western Michigan University, Kalamazoo, MI 49008, USA.

MAILER Norman (Kingsley), b. 31 Jan 1923, Long Beach, California, USA. Writer. m. (1) Beatrice Silverman, 1944, div 1951, 1 daughter, (2) Adele Morales, 1954, div 1962, 2 daughters, (3) Lady Jeanne Campbell, 1962, div 1963, 1 daughter, (4) Beverly Rentz Bentley, 1963, div 1980, 2 sons, 1 daughter, (5) Carol Stevens, div, 1 daughter, (6) Norris Church, 1980, 1 son. Education: BS, Harvard University. Publications: The Naked and the Dead, 1948; Barbary Shore, 1951; The Deer Park, 1955 (dramatised 1967); Advertisements for Myself, 1959; Deaths for the Ladies (poems), 1962; The Presidential Papers, 1963; An American Dream, 1964; Cannibals and Christians, 1966; Why are We in Vietnam?, 1967; The Armies of the Night, 1968; Miami and the Siege of Chicago, 1968; Moonshot, 1969; A Fire on the Moon, 1970; The Prisoner of Sex, 1971; Existential Errands, 1972; St George and the Godfather, 1972; Marilyn, 1973; The Faith of Graffiti, 1974; The Fight, 1975; Some Honourable Men, 1976; Genius and Lust: A Journey Through the Writings of Henry Miller, 1976; A Transit to Narcissus, 1978; The Executioner's Song, 1979; Of Women and Their Elegance, 1980; The Essential Mailer, 1982; Pieces and Pontifications, 1982; Ancient Evenings, 1983; Tough Guys Don't Dance, 1983; Harlot's Ghost, 1991; How the Wimp Won the War, 1991; Oswald's Tale, 1995; Portrait of Picasso as a Young Man, 1995; The Gospel According to the Son, 1997; The Time of Our Time, 1998. Contributions to: Numerous journals and magazines. Honours: National Book Award for Arts and Letters, 1969; Pulitzer Prize for Non-Fiction, 1969; Award for Outstanding Service to the Arts, McDowell Colony, 1973. Memberships: PEN, president, 1984-86; American Academy of Arts and Letters. Address: c/o Rembar, 19th West 44th Street, New York, NY 10036, USA.

MAILLET Antonine, b. 10 May 1929, Bouctouche, New Brunswick, Canada. Author; Dramatist. Education: Collège de Notre-Dame d'Acadie, Moncton, 1950; MA, University of Moncton, 1959; Licence es Lettres, University of Montreal, 1962; Doctorat ès Lettres, Université Laval, 1970. Appointments: Teacher, University of Moncton, 1965-67, Collège des Jesuites, Quebec, 1968-69, Université Laval, 1971-74, University of Montreal, 1974-75; Visiting Professor, University of California at Berkeley, 1983, State University of New York at Albany, 1985. Publications: Pointe-aux-Coques, 1958; On a mangé la dune, 1962; La Sagouine, 1971, English translation, 1979; Don l'Original, 1972, English translation as The Tale of Don l'Original, 1978; Par derrière chez mon père, 1972; Mariaagélas, 1973, English translation, 1986; Emmanuel a Joseph a Davit, 1975; La Cordes-de-bois, 1977; Pélagie-la-Charrette, 1979, English translation as Pélagie: The Return to a Homeland, 1982; Cent ans dans les bois, 1981; La Gribouille, 1982; Crache-a-Pic, 1984, English translation as The Devil is Loose, 1986; Le huitième jour, 1986, English translation as On the Eighth Day, 1989; L'Oursiade, 1990; Les Confessions de Jeanne de Valois, 1992. Other: Many plays. Honours: Governor-General's Award for Fiction, 1972; Prix France-Canada, 1975; Prix Goncourt, France, 1979; Officer des Palmes académiques francaises, 1980; Companion of the Order of Canada, 1982; Officer des Arts et des Lettres de France, 1985; Officer de l'ordre National du Québec, 1990; Commandeur de l'ordre du mérite culturel de Monaco, 1993; Several honorary doctorates. Memberships: Académie canadienne-francaise; Association des Ecrivains de Langue francaise; PEN; Queen's Privy Council for Canada; Royal Society of Canada; Société des Gens de Lettres de France. Address: 735 Antonine Maillet Avenue, Montreal, Quebec H2V 2Y4, Canada.

MAINE David. See: **AVICE Claude (Pierre Marie).**

MAIR (Alexander) Craig, b. 3 May 1948, Glasgow, Scotland. Schoolteacher; Writer. m. Anne Olizar, 1 Aug 1970, 2 sons, 1 daughter. Education: BA, Stirling University, 1971. Publications: A Time in Turkey, 1973; A Star for Seamen, 1978; The Lighthouse Boy, 1981; Britain at War 1914-18, 1982; Mercat Cross and Tolbooth, 1988; David Angus, 1989; Stirling, The Royal Burgh, 1990; The Incorporation of Glasgow Maltmen: A History, 1990. Memberships: Scottish Society of Antiquaries, fellow; Educational Institute of Scotland; Various local history groups. Address: 21 Keir Street, Bridge of Allan, Stirling, Scotland.

MAIRS Nancy Pedrick, b. 23 July 1943, Long Beach, California, USA. Writer. m. George Anthony Mairs, 18 May 1963, 1 son, 1 daughter. Education: AB cum laude, Wheaton College, Massachusetts, 1964; MFA, 1975, PhD, 1984, University of Arizona. Publications: Instead It is Winter, 1977; In All the Rooms of the Yellow House, 1984; Plaintext, 1986; Remembering the Bone House, 1989; Carnal Acts, 1990; Ordinary Time, 1993; Voice Lessons, 1994. Contributions to: American Voice; MSS; Tri Quarterly. Honours: Western States Book Award, 1984; National Endowment for the Arts Fellowship, 1991. Memberships: Authors Guild; Poets and Writers; National Women's Studies Association. Address: 1527 East Mabel Street, Tucson, AZ 85719, USA.

MAJA-PEARCE Adewale, b. 3 June 1953, London, England. Researcher; Consultant; Writer. Education: BA, University of Wales, University College of Swansea, 1975; MA, School of Oriental and African Studies, London, 1986. Appointments: Researcher, Index on Censorship, London, 1986-; Consultant, Heinemann International, Oxford, 1986-94. Publications: Christopher Okigbo: Collected Poems (editor), 1986; In My Father's Country: A Nigerian Journey (non-fiction), 1987; Loyalties (stories), 1987; How Many Miles to Babylon? (non-fiction), 1990; The Heinemann Book of African Poetry in English (editor), 1990; Who's Afraid of Wole Soyinka?: Essays on Censorship, 1991; A Mask Dancing: Nigerian Novelists of the Eighties, 1992. Contributions to: Various periodicals. Memberships: PEN; Society of

Authors. Literary Agent: David Grossman Address: 33 St George's Road, Hastings, East Sussex TN34 3NH, England.

MAJEVSKIS Hermanis Margers. See: **KUKAINIS Margers.**

MAJOR André, b. 22 Apr 1942, Montreal, Quebec, Canada. Author; Poet; Critic; Dramatist; Radio Producer. m. Ginette Lepage, June 1970, 1 son, 1 daughter. Publications: Fiction: La cabochon, 1964; Le chair de poule, 1965; Levent du diable, 1968; Histoire des déserteurs, Vol 1, L'épouvantail, 1974, English translation as The Scarecrows of Saint-Emmanuel, 1977, Vol 2, L'épidémie, 1975, English translation as Inspector Therrien, 1980, Vol 3, Les rescapés, 1976; La folle d'Elvis, 1981, English translation as Hooked on Elvis, 1983; L'hiver au coeur, 1987, English translation as Winter of the Heart, 1989; La vie provisoire, 1995. Poetry: Le froid se meurt, 1961; Holocauste a 2 voix, 1961; Poèmes pour durer, 1969. Non-Fiction: Félix-Antoine Savard, 1968. Other: Stage and radio plays. Honours: Governor-General's Award for Fiction, 1977; Prix Belgique-Canada, 1991; Prix David, 1992. Membership: Union des écrivaines et écrivains québécois. Address: 10595 Tanguay, Montreal, Quebec H3L 3G9, Canada.

MAJOR Clarence, b. 31 Dec 1936, Atlanta, Georgia, USA. Poet; Writer; Artist; Professor. m. (1) Joyce Sparrow, 1958, div 1964, (2) Pamela Ritter. Education: BS, State University of New York at Albany, 1976; PhD, Union Graduate School, 1978. Appointments: Editor, Coercion Review, 1958-66, Writer-in-Residence, Center for Urban Education, New York, 1967-68, Teachers and Writers Collaborative-Teachers College, Columbia University, 1967-71, Aurora College, Illinois, 1974, Albany State College, Georgia, 1984, Clayton College, Denver, 1986, 1987; Associate Editor, Caw, 1967-70, Journal of Black Poetry, 1967-70; Lecturer, Brooklyn College of the City University of New York, 1968-69, 1973, 1974-75, Cazenovia Collge, New York, 1969, Wisconsin State University, 1969, Queens College of the City University of New York, 1972, 1973, 1975, Sarah Lawrence College, 1972-75, School of Continuing Education, New York University, 1975; Columnist, 1973-76, Contributing Editor, 1976-86, American Poetry Review; Assistant Professor, Howard University, 1974-76, University of Washington, 1976-77; Visiting Assistant Professor, University of Maryland at College Park, 1976, State University of New York at Buffalo, 1976; Associate Professor, 1977-81, Professor, 1981-89, University of Colorado at Boulder; Editor, 1977-78, Associate Editor, 1978-, American Book Review; Professor, 1989-, Director, Creative Writing, 1991-, University of California at Davis. Publications: Poetry: The Fires That Burn in Heaven, 1954; Love Poems of a Black Man, 1965; Human Juices, 1965; Swallow the Lake, 1970; Symptons and Madness, 1971; Private Line, 1971; The Cotton Club: New Poems, 1972; The Syncopated Cakewalk, 1974; Inside Diameter: The France Poems, 1985; Surfaces and Masks, 1988; Some Observations of a Stranger in the Latter Part of the Century, 1989; Parking Lots, 1992; Configurations: New and Selected Poems 1958-1998, 1998. Fiction: All-Night Visitors, 1969; new version, 1998; NO, 1973; Reflex and Bone Structure, 1975; Emergency Exit, 1979; My Amputations, 1986; Such Was the Season, 1987; Painted Turtle: Woman with Guitar, 1988; Fun and Games, 1990; Dirty Bird Blues, 1996. Other: Dictionary of Afro-American Slang, 1970; The Dark and Feeling: Black American Writers and Their Work, 1974; Juba to Jive: A Dictionary of African-American Slang, 1994. Editor: Writers Workshop Anthology, 1967; Man is Like a Child: An Anthology of Creative Writing by Students, 1968; The New Black Poetry, 1969; Calling the Wind: Twentieth Century African-American Short Stories, 1993; The Garden Thrives: Twentieth Century African-American Poetry, 1995. Honours: Fulbright-Hays Exchange Award, 1981-83; Western States Book Award, 1986; Pushcart Prize, 1989. Address: c/o Department of English, University of California at Davis, Davis, CA 95616, USA.

MAJOR Kevin (Gerald), b. 12 Sept 1949, Stephenville, Newfoundland, Canada. Writer. m. Anne Crawford, 3 July 1982, 2 sons. Education: BSc, Memorial University, St John's, Newfoundland, 1972. Publications: Far from Shore, 1980; Thirty-Six Exposures, 1984; Dear Bruce Springsteen, 1987; Blood Red Ochre, 1989; Eating Between the Lines, 1991; Diana: My Autobiography, 1993; No Man's Land, 1995; Gaffer: A Novel of Newfoundland, 1997. Honours: Book of the Year Award, Canadian Association of Children's Librarians, 1978; Canada Council Award for Children's Literature, 1978; Canadian Young Adult Book Award, 1980; Book of the Year Award for Children, Canadian Library Association, 1991; Vicky Metcalf Award, 1992. Membership: Writers' Union of Canada. Address: 27 Poplar Avenue, St John's, Newfoundland, A1B 1C7, Canada.

MAKARENKO Alexander Borisovich, b. 23 June 1954, Kherson, Ukraine. Physician; Psychotherapist. Education: Graduated, Crimea Medical Institute, 1978; Doctor of Medicine, 1990. Appointments: Therapeutist, 1978-82; Physiologist, 1983-86; Head of Diagnostic Laboratory, 1987-90; Director, Research Psychotherapy Centre. Publications: Several medical books. Membership: International Psychotherapy Association, Moscow. Address: 32A Donetskaya Str, Kherson 325033, Ukraine.

MAKARSKI Henryk, b. 17 Aug 1946, Biala, Podlaska, Poland. Writer; Poet. m. Maria Anna Koziolkiewicz, 24 July 1971, 1 son, 1 daughter. Education: MA, Polish Philology, Marie-Curie-Slowdoska University of Lublin, 1969. Publications: 7 volumes of fiction; 5 volumes of poetry; various essays of literary criticism. Honours: Numerous awards. Membership: Polish Writers Association, Lublin. Address: ul Radzynska 18 m 23, 20-850 Lublin, Poland.

MAKINSON Robert Bruce, b. 7 Dec 1929, New York City, USA. Writer. Eduction: New York University; Juilliard School of Music. Appointments: Clerk, Belgian-American Banking Corporation, New York City, 1948; Music Copyist, Pro-Art Publishing Company, New York City, 1952; Office Manager, Comet Messenger Service, New York City, 1955; Music Teacher, New York Schools of Music, New York City, 1957; Nightclub Pianist, New York City, 1960; Comedy Writer, 1970-; Editor, Latest Jokes (newsletter), 1974-. Publications: How to Write Jokes; Latest Jokes; Songwriters and Lyricists Handbook. Memberships: American Society of Composers, Authors and Publishers; Comedy Writers Association; Songwriters and Lyricists Club; Carnegians; Toastmasters Interational; Platform Association. Address: PO Box 23304, Brooklyn, NY 11202-0066, USA.

MAKOWIECKI Andrzej, b. 5 Aug 1938, Warsaw, Poland. Reporter; Editor; Writer. Education: State School of Music, Lodz, 1962; MA, Polish Philology, University of Lodz, 1968. Appointments: Reporter-Editor, Odgiosy, literary weekly, 1965-87; Correspondent, Polityka, weekly, 1970-72; Reporter, Zwierciadlo, weekly, 1973-75. Publications: 6 novels, 1972-87; Short stories. Contributions to: Periodicals. Honours: Various awards and prizes. Memberships: Association of Polish Authors; Association of Polish Journalists; Union of Polish Writers. Address: ul Pietrkowska 147 m 1, 90-440 Lodz, Poland.

MALIK Farzana, (Farzana Moon), b. 29 Aug 1950, Lahore, Pakistan. Teacher. m. Shonil Datta, 24 Nov 1972, 1 daughter. Education: BSc, Lahore College for Women; MEd, Punjab University; CIS, Clark State. Publications: Short stories and plays. Contributions to: Nexus; Ebbing Tide; Poetic Expressions; Orbis. Honour: 1st Prize in Poetry. Membership: Antioch Writers Conference. Address: 2441 Garland Avenue, Springfield, OH 45503-2365, USA.

MALINS Penelope. See: **HOBHOUSE Penelope.**

MALLET-JONES Françoise, b. 6 July 1930, Antwerp, Belgium (French citizen). Novelist. Education: Bryn Mawr College, Pennsylvania, Sorbonne, University of Paris, 1947-49. Appointments: Reader, Grasset Publishers, 1965-. Publications: Into the Labyrinth, 1951; The Red Room, 1955; Cordelia and Other Stories, 1956; House of Lies, 1956; Café Celeste, 1958; The Favourite, 1961; Signs and Wonders, 1966; The Witches: Three Tales of Sorcery, 1968; The Underground Game, 1973; Allegra, 1976; Le Rire de Laura, 1985; La Tristesse du cerf-volant, 1988; Adriana Sposa, 1989; Divine, 1991. Other: French version of Shelagh Delaney's play A Taste of Honey, 1960; A Letter to Myself, 1964; The Paper House, 1970; Juliette Greco, 1975; Marie-Paule Belle, 1987. Honours: Ordre National du Mérite, 1986. Address: c/o Flammarion et Cie, 26 rue Racine, 75278 Paris, France.

MALLINSON Jeremy John Crosby, b. 16 Mar 1937, Ilkley, Yorkshire, England. Director; Writer. m. Odette Louise Guiton, 26 Oct 1963, 1 son, 1 daughter. Appointments: Director, Jersey Wildlife Preservation Trust; Chairman, Editorial Board, International Zoo Yearbook. Publications: Okavango Adventure, 1973; Earning Your Living With Animals, 1975; Modern Classic Animal Stories (editor), 1977, US edition as Such Agreeable Friends, 1978; The Shadow of Extinction, 1978; The Facts About a Zoo, 1980; Travels in Search of Endangered Species, 1989. Contributions to: Numerous journals and magazines; Over 180 papers and articles for over 40 different publications. Honours: Senior Biology and Conservation Award, American Society of Primatologists, 1997; Officer of the Order of the British Empire. Memberships: International Union for the Conservation of Nature and Natural Resources; International Union of Zoo Directors; Wildlife Preservation Trust International, Philadelphia; Wildlife Preservation Trust of Canada; Council of Wildfowl and Wetlands Trust. Literary Agent: Curtis Brown Ltd. Address: c/o Jersey Wildlife Preservation trust, Les Augrès Manor, Trinity, Jersey, Channel Islands.

MALLON Maurus Edward, b. 10 July 1932, Greenock, Scotland. Teacher; Writer; Dramatist. Education: MA, Honours, University of Glasgow, 1956; BEd, University of Manitoba, Winnipeg, 1966. Publications: Basileus, 1971; The Opal, 1973; Pegaso, 1975; Way of the Magus, 1978; Anogia, 1980; Bammer McPhie, 1984; Treasure Mountain, 1986; Postcards, 1991; Ex Novo Mundo (short stories), 1992; Compendulum, 1993; A Matter of Conscience (play), 1994. Honours: Gold Records of Excellence, 1994, 1995, Lifetime Achievement Award, 1996, Platinum Records for Exceptional Performance, 1997, 1998, ABI. Memberships: Living Authors' Society; National Writers' Association, USA; PEN, Canada. Address: Box 331, Deep River, Ontario K0J 1P0, Canada.

MALLOY Ruth Gwendolyn Lor, (Ruth Lor Malloy), b. 4 Aug 1932, Brockville, Ontario, Canada. Author; Travel Writer; Lecturer; Photographer. m. Michael Malloy, 5 June 1965, 2 sons, 1 daughter. Education: BA, Victoria College, University of Toronto, Canada, 1954; BSW, School of Social Work, University of Toronto, 1960. Appointments: Cashier and Hostess, New York Restaurant; Organizer, WMS, Presbyterian Church of Canada; Secretary, Canadian Broadcasting Corporation, Canadian Friends Service Committee, Canadian Mental Health Association, Student Christian Movement; Social Worker, YWCA, St Christopher's House, Children's Aid Society; Information Officer, Taiwan Church World Service, Department of External Affairs of Government of Canada, Overseas Institute of Canada, American Friends Service Committee. Publications: 13 editions of a guidebook on travel in China, 1973-99; Beyond the Heights, Chinese-Canadian novel, 1980; Post Guide Hong Kong, South China Morning Post, 1983; Gems and Jewellery in Hong Kong, A Buyer's Guide and Hong Kong Gems and Jewelry, 1984, 1986; On Leaving Bai Di Cheng, The Cultures of the Yangzi Gorges, 1993; Hong Kong and Macau Guide (with Linda Jo Malloy), 1994; Hijras: Who We Are, by Meena Balaji and other Eunuchs, 1997. Contributions to: Weekend Magazine; Star Weekly; Globe and Mail; CFTO-Toronto; Canadian Broadcasting Corporation; Copley News Service; Hotelier; Asian Wall St Journal; Columnist, Asia Mail, monthly, 1976-78; Founder, 1987, Editor, until 1995, Travel China Newsletter. Memberships: Literary Societies, Vice President, Secretary; Canadian Chapter, Society of

American Travel Writers. Address: c/o Open Road Publishing, 32 Turkey Lane, Cold Spring Harbor, NY 11724, USA.

MALONE Joseph L(awrence), b. 2 July 1937, New York, New York, USA. Professor of Linguistics; Writer; Poet; Translator. m. 31 Jan 1964, 2 sons. Education: AB, 1963, PhD, 1967, University of California at Berkeley. Appointments: Instructor, University of California Extension, San Francisco, 1965; Instructor, 1967-68, Chairman, Department of Linguistics, 1967-, Assistant Professor, 1968-71, Associate Professor, 1971-75, Professor of Linguistics, 1975-, Barnard College and Columbia University; Consultant in Linguistics Continuity Author, Academic American Encyclopedia, 1977-, Grolier Multimedia Encyclopedia; Editorial Board, Hellas, 1990-. Publications: The Science of Linguistics in the Art of Translation: Some Tools from Linguistics for the Analysis and Practice of Translation, 1988; Tiberian Hebrew Phonology, 1993; Carmina Gaiana, 1998. Contributions to: Numerous publications. Memberships: American Oriental Society; Linguistic Society of America; North American Conference on Afro-Asiatic Linguistics. Address: 169 Prospect Street, Leonia, NJ 07605, USA.

MALOUF (George Joseph) David, b. 20 Mar 1934, Brisbane, Queensland, Australia. Poet; Novelist. Education: BA, University of Queensland, 1954. Appointments: Assistant Lecturer in English, University of Queensland, 1955-57; Supply Teacher, London, 1959-61; Teacher of Latin and English, Holland Park Comprehensive, 1962; Teacher, St Anselm's Grammar School, 1962-68; Senior Tutor and Lecturer in English, University of Sydney, 1968-77. Publications: Poetry: Bicycle and Other Poems, 1970; Neighbours in a Thicket: Poems, 1974; Poems, 1975-1976, 1976; Wild Lemons, 1980; First Things Last, 1981; Selected Poems, 1981; Selected Poems, 1959-1989, 1994. Fiction: Johnno (novel), 1975; An Imaginary Life (novel), 1978; Child's Play (novella), 1981; The Bread of Time to Come (novella), 1981, republished as Fly Away Peter, 1982; Eustace (short story), 1982; The Prowler (short story), 1982; Harland's Half Acre (novel), 1984; Antipodes (short stories), 1985; The Great World (novel), 1990; Remembering Babylon (novel), 1993: The Conversations at Curlow Creek (novel), 1996. Play: Blood Relations, 1988. Opera Libretti: Voss, 1986; Mer de Glace; Baa Baa Black Sheep, 1993. Memoir: Twelve Edmondstone Street, 1985. Editor: We Took Their Orders and Are Dead: An Anti-War Anthology, 1971; Gesture of a Hand (anthology), 1975. Contributions to: Four Poets: David Malouf, Don Maynard, Judith Green, Rodney Hall, 1962; Australian; New York Review of Books; Poetry Australia; Southerly; Sydney Morning Herald. Honours: Grace Leven Prize for Poetry, 1974; Gold Medals, Australian Literature Society, 1975, 1982; Australian Council Fellowship, 1978; New South Wales Premier's Award for Fiction, 1979; Victorian Premier's Award for Fiction, 1985; New South Wales Premier's Award for Drama, 1987; Commonwealth Writer's Prize, 1991; Miles Franklin Award, 1991; Prix Femina Etranger, 1991; Inaugural International IMPAC Dublin Literary Award, 1996. Address: 53 Myrtle Street, Chippendale, New South Wales 2008, Australia.

MALZBERG Barry, (Mike Barry, Claudine Dumas, Mel Johnson, Lew W Mason, Francine de Natale, K M O'Donnell, Gerrold Watkins), b. 24 July 1939, New York, New York, USA. Writer. Education: AB, 1960, Graduate Studies, 1964-65, Syracuse University. Publications: Author or editor of over 30 books under various pseudonyns. Address: Box 61, Teaneck, NJ 07666, USA.

MAMET David (Alan), b. 30 Nov 1947, Chicago, Illinois, USA. Dramatist; Director; Writer. m. (1) Lindsay Crouse, Dec 1977, div, (2) Rebecca Pidgeon, 22 Sept 1991. Education: BA, Goddard College, Plainfield, Vermont, 1969. Appointment: Artist-in-Residence, Goddard College, 1971-73; Artistic Director, St Nicholas Theatre Co, Chicago, 1973-75; Guest Lecturer, University of Chicago, 1975, 1979, New York University, 1981; Associate Artistic Director, Goodman Theater, Chicago,

1978; Associate Professor of Film, Columbia University, 1988; Chairman of the Board, Atlantic Theater Co. Publications: Plays: The Duck Variations, 1971; Sexual Perversity in Chicago, 1973; Reunion, 1973; Squirrels, 1974; American Buffalo, 1976; A Life in the Theatre, 1976; The Water Engine, 1976; The Woods, 1977; Lone Canoe, 1978; Praire du Chien, 1978; Lakeboat, 1980; Donny March, 1981; Edmond, 1982; The Disappearance of the Jews, 1983; Glengarry Glen Ross, 1984; The Shawl, 1985; Speed-the-Plow, 1987; Bobby Gould in Hell, 1989; The Old Neighborhood, 1991; Oleanna, 1992; The Cryptogram, 1994; Death Defying Acts, 1995. Screenplays: The Postman Always Rings Twice, 1979; The Verdict, 1980; The Untouchables, 1986; House of Games, 1986; Things Change (with Shel Silverstein), 1987; We're No Angels, 1987; Homicide, 1991; Hoffa, 1991; Oleanna, 1994; The Edge, 1997; Wag the Dog, 1997; Spanish Prisoner, 1998; The Winslow Boy, 1999. Novels: The Village, 1994; The Old Religion, 1997. Poetry: The Hero Pony, 1990. Essays: Writing in Restaurants, 1986; Some Freaks, 1989; On Directing Film, 1990; The Cabin, 1992; True and False: Heresy and Common Sense for the Actor, 1997. Honours: CBS Creative Writing Fellowship, Yale University Drama School, 1976-77; Obie Awards, 1976, 1983; New York Drama Critics Circle Awards, 1976, 1987; Rockefeller Foundation Grant, 1977; Outer Critics Circle Award, 1978; Pulitzer Prize for Drama, 1987. Address: c/o Howard Rosenstone/Wender, 3 East 48th Street, 4th Floor, New York, NY 10017, USA.

MAMLEYEV Yuri, b. 11 Dec 1931, Moscow, Russia. Writer. m. Farida Mamleyev, 14 Apr 1973. Education: Forestry Institute, Moscow, 1955. Publications: The Sky Above Hell, 1980; Iznanka Gogena, 1982; Chatouny, 1986; Zivaja Smert, 1986; Dernier Comedie, 1988; Golos iz Nichto, 1990; Ytopi Moyu Golovu, 1990; Vechnyi dom, 1991; Der Murder aus dem Nichts, 1992; Izbzannoe, 1993; Die Letzte Komödie, 1994; Shatuny, 1996; Union Mistice, 1997; Charnoe zerkalo, 1998; J M Chatouny, 1998. Contributions to: Periodicals. Membership: French PEN Centre; Russian PEN Centre, 1994. Address: 142 rue Legendre, 75017 Paris, France.

MANA Samira Al, b. 25 Dec 1935, Basra, Iraq. Librarian. m. Salah Niazi, July 1959, 2 daughters. Education: BA, Honours, University of Baghdad, 1958; Postgraduate Diploma in Librarianship, Ealing Technical College, 1976. Appointment: Assistant Editor, Alightrab Al-Adabi (Literature of the Exiled), 1985-. Publications: The Forerunners and the Newcomers, 1972; The Song, 1976; A London Sequel, 1979; Only a Half, 1979; The Umbilical Cord, 1990. Contributions to: Alightrab Al-Adabi; Many short stories in Arabic magazines; Translations in Dutch and English periodicals. Membership: PEN Club. Address: 46 Tudor Drive, Kingston-Upon-Thames, Surrey KT2 5PZ, UK.

MANCHEL Frank, b. 22 July 1935, Detroit, Michigan, USA. Writer; Editor. m. Seila Wachtel, 30 Mar 1958, 2 sons. Education: BA, Ohio State University, 1957; MA, Hunter College, 1960; EdD, Columbia University, 1966. Appointments: Editor, Journal of Popular Film and TV, 1977-, Film and History, 1996-. Publications: Terrors of the Screen, 1970; Cameras West, 1972; An Album of Great Science Fiction Films, 1976; Great Sports Movies, 1980; An Album of Modern Horror Films, 1983; Film Study: An Analytical Bibliography, 4 volumes, 1990. Contributions to: Periodicals. Memberships: American Federation of Film Societies, chairman, 1974-76; Society for Cinema Studies, treasurer, 1971-76. Address: RR 1, Box 1373, Shelburne, VT 05482, USA.

MANCHESTER Seán (The Right Reverend), b. 15 July 1944, Nottingham, England. Author; Catholic Prelate. Education: Doctor of Pastoral Ministry, St David's College, 1990; Ordained Priest, 15 July 1990; Consecrated Bishop, 4 October 1991. Appointments: President, Vampire Research Society, 1970; Superior General, Ordo Sancti Graal, 1973; Chairman, British Grail Society, 1988; Chairman, Society of St George, 1990; Bishop of Glastonbury, 1993. Publications: From Satan to Christ: A Story of Salvation, 1988; The Highgate Vampire:

The Infernal World of the Undead Unearthed at London's Highgate Cemetery, 1991; Mad, Bad and Dangerous to Know: The Life of Lady Caroline Lamb, 1992; The Grail Church: Its Ancient Tradition and Renewed Flowering, 1995. Honour: Knight Commander, Order of St George. Memberships: Life Member, The Ghost Club Society; The Gothic Revival Society. Address: 5 John Street, Penmachno, Gwynedd LL24 0UH, North Wales.

MANCHESTER William, b. 1 Apr 1922, Attleboro, Massachusetts, USA. Professor of History Emeritus; Author. m. Julia Brown Marshall, 27 Mar 1948, 1 son, 2 daughters. Education: BA, University of Massachusetts, 1946; AM, University of Missouri, 1947. Appointments: Reporter, Daily Oklahoman, 1945-46; Reporter, Foreign Correspondent, War Correspondent, Baltimore Sun, 1947-55; Managing Editor, Publications, 1955-64, Fellow, Center for Advanced Studies, 1959-60, Writer-in-Residence, 1975-, Adjunct Professor of History, 1979-92, Professor of History Emeritus, 1992-, Wesleyan University; Fellow, Pierson College, Yale University, 1991-. Publications: Disturber of the Peace, 1951; The City of Anger, 1953; Shadow of the Monsoon, 1956; Beard the Lion, 1958; A Rockefeller Family Portrait, 1959; The Long Gainer, 1961; Portrait of a President, 1962; The Death of a President, 1967; The Arms of Krupp, 1968; The Glory and the Dream, 1974; Controversy and Other Essays in Journalism, 1976; American Caesar: Douglas MacArthur, 1880-1964, 1978; Goodbye, Darkness, 1980; The Last Lion: Winston Spencer Churchill, Visions of Glory, 1874-1932, 1983; One Brief Shining Moment: Remembering Kennedy, 1983; The Last Lion: Winston Spencer Churchill, Alone 1932-1940, 1988; In Our Time, 1989; A World Lit Only by Fire: The Medieval Mind and the Renaissance, Portrait of an Age, 1992. Contributions to: Numerous publications. Honours: Guggenheim Fellowship, 1959-60; Honorary LHD, University of Massachusetts, 1965, University of New Haven, 1979, Russell Sage College, 1990; Dag Hammarskjöld Prize, Association Internationale Correspondents Diplomatiques, Rome, 1967; Best Book on Foreign Affairs Citation, Overseas Press Club, 1968; Honor Award for Distinguished Service to Journalism, University of Missouri, 1969; Connecticut Book Award, 1975; Literary Lion, New York Public Library, 1983; Blenheim Award, International Churchill Society, 1986; Honorary LittD, Skidmore College, 1987, University of Richmond, 1988; Washington Irving Award, 1988; Sarah Josepha Hale Award, 1993. Memberships: American Historical Association; Authors Guild; PEN; Society of American Historians. Address: c/o Department of History, Wesleyan University, Middletown, CT 06459, USA.

MANDEL Oscar, b. 24 Aug 1926, Antwerp, Belgium (US citizen). Professor of Humanities; Writer; Dramatist; Poet. m. Adriana Schizzano, 1960. Education: BA, New York University, 1947; MA, Columbia University, 1948; PhD, Ohio State University, 1951. Appointments: Faculty, University of Nebraska, 1955-60; Fulbright Lecturer, University of Amsterdam, 1960-61; Associate Professor, 1961-65, Professor of Humanities, 1965-, California Institute of Technology, Pasadena. Publications: Fiction: Chi Po and the Sorcerer: A Chinese Tale for Children and Philosophers, 1964; Gobble-Up Stories, 1966; The Kukkurrik Fables, 1987; Blossoms and Incantations, 1998. Poetry: Simplicities, 1974; Collected Lyrics and Epigrams, 1981; Collected Plays, 2 volumes, 1970, 1972; Sigismund, Prince of Poland: A Baroque Entertainment, 1988; The Virgin and the Unicorn: Four Plays by Oscar Mandel, 1993; Two Romantic Plays, 1996; Prince Poupon Needs a Wife, 1998; Blossoms and Incantations, 1998; A Definition of Tragedy, 1961; The Theatre of Don Juan: A Collection of Plays and Views 1630-1963 (editor), 1963; Seven Comedies by Marivaux (editor and translator), 1968; Five Comedies of Medieval France (editor and translator), 1970; Three Classic Don Juan Plays (editor and translator), 1971; Philoctetes and the Fall of Troy: Plays, Documents, Iconography, Interpretations, 1981; Annotations to "Vanity Fair", 1981; The Book of Elaborations: Essays, 1985; August von Kotzebue: The Comedy, The Man, 1988; The Art of Alessandro Magnasco: An Essay in the Recovery of Meaning, 1994; The Cheerfulness of Dutch Art: A Rescue

Operation, 1996; Fundamentals of the Art of Poetry, 1998. Contributions to: Professional journals. Memberships: College Art Association; Dramatists Guild; Modern Language Association; Société des Auteurs et Compositeurs Dramatiques. Address: c/o Division of Humanities and Social Sciences, California Institute of Technology, Pasadena, CA 91125, USA.

MANDELA Nelson (Rolihlahla), b. 18 July 1918, Transkei, South Africa. President of South Africa. m. (1) Evelyn, 1944, div 1957, 4 children, (2) Winnie, 1958, div 1996, (3) Graca Machel, 18 July 1998. Education: University College, Fort Hare; University of the Witwatersrand. Appointments: Lawyer; Imprisoned for anti-apartheid activities, 1964-90; Deputy President, 1990-91, President, 1991-97, African National Congress; President of South Africa, 1994-. Publications: No Easy Walk to Freedom, 1965; Long Walk to Freedom, 1994. Honours: Various honorary doctorates; Jawaharlal Nehru Award, 1979; Simon Bolivar Prize, 1983; Sakharov Prize, 1988; Co-Winner, Novel Prize for Peace, 1993; Honorary Order of Merit, 1995; Congressional Gold Medal, 1998. Address: c/o Office of the President, Private Bag X 1000, Cape Town 8000, South Africa.

MANDLER Peter, b. 29 Jan 1958, Boston, Massachusetts, USA. Historian. m. Ruth Enrlich, 21 Dec 1987, 1 son, 1 daughter. Education: BA, Honours 1st Class, Magdalen College, Oxford, 1978; PhD, Harvard University, 1984. Appointments: Assistant Professor, Princeton University, 1984-91; Senior Lecturer, 1991-95, Reader, 1995-97, Professor, 1997-, London Guildhall University. Publications: Aristocratic Government in the Age of Reform, 1990; The Uses of Charity (editor), 1990; After the Victorians (co-editor), 1994; The Fall and Rise of the Stately Home, 1997. Contributions to: Journals, magazines and newspapers. Memberships: Royal Historical Society, honorary secretary, 1998-. Address: c/o Dept of Politics and Modern History, London Guildhall University, London E1 7NT, England.

MANEA Norman, b. 19 July 1936, Suceava, Romania. Writer. m. Cella Boiangiu, 28 June 1969. Education: MS, Engineering, Institute of Construction, Bucharest, 1959. Publications: In English: October, eight o'clock, 1992, On Clowns 1992-; The Black Envelope, 1995. Others: Captivi, 1970; Atrium, 1974; Anii de ucenicie ai lui August Prostul, 1979. Contributions to: New Republic; Partisan Review; Paris Review; Lettre Internationale; Vuelta; Akzente; Neue Rundschau; Sinn und Form. Honours: Guggenheim Fellowship, 1992; John D and Catharine T MacArthur Foundation Fellowship, 1992. Membership: American PEN. Literary Agent: Wylie, Aitken & Stone. Address: 201 West 70th Street, Apt 10-I, New York, NY 10023, USA.

MANES Christopher, b. 24 May 1957, Chicago, Illinois, USA. Writer. 1 daughter. Education: BA, 1979 JD, 1992, University of California; MA, University of Wisconsin, 1981. Publications: Place of the Wild, 1994; Post Modernism and Environmental Philosophy, 1994. Contributions to: Reference works, books, journals and magazines. Memberships: California State Bar Association; Phi Beta Kappa; Writers Guild. Address: 34542 Paseo Real, Cathedral City, CA 92234, USA.

MANGUEL Alberto (Adrian), b. 13 Mar 1948, Buenos Aires, Argentina. Div, 1 son, 2 daughters. Education: Colegio Nacional de Buenos Airs, 1961-67; Universidad de Buenos Aires, 1967-68; London University, 1976. Appointments: Theatre Critic, CBLT Morning, 1984-86; Head of Contemporary Reading Group, McGill Club, 1986-89; Contributing Editor, Saturday Night, 1988, Grand Street, 1991. Publications: The Oxford Book of Canadian Ghost Stories; Black Water; Dark Arrows; The Dictionary of Imaginary Places; News from a Foreign Country Came; Other Fires; The Gates of Paradise. Contributions to: Saturday Night; Washington Post; New York Times; Village Voice; Rubicon; Whig Standard. Honours: Juan Angel Fraboschi Gold Medal; Ricardo Monner Sans Gold Medal; McKitterick Prize, 1992; Canadian Authors Association Prize, 1992; Harbourfront Prize, 1992. Memberships: Writers Union of Canada; PEN Canada. Address: c/o Lucinda Vardey Agency, Toronto, Ontario M5A 2T6, Canada.

MANN Anthony Philip, b. 7 Aug 1942, North Allerton, Yorkshire, England. Writer; Theatre Director. Education; BA, Honours, English and Drama, Manchester University, 1966; MA, Design and Directing, Humboldt State University, California, 1969. Appointments: Trustee, New Zealand Players, 1992; Advisory Board, New Zealand Books, 1993. Publications: Eye of the Queen, 1982; Master of Paxwax, 1986; Fall of the Families, 1987; Pioneers, 1988; Wulfsyarn - A Mosaic, 1990; A Land Fit For Heroes, Vol 1, Into the Wild Wood, 1993, Vol 2, Stand Alone Stan, 1994, Vol 3, The Dragon Wakes, 1995, Vol 4, The Burning Forest, 1996. Contributions to: Books. Honour: Personal Chair in Drama, Victoria University of Wellington, 1997. Memberships: PEN, New Zealand; British Society of Dowsers; NZADIE (New Zealand Association for Drama in Education). Address: 22 Bruce Avenue, Brooklyn, Wellington, New Zealand.

MANN Christopher Michael, (Zithulele), b. 6 Apr 1948, Port Elizabeth, South Africa. Poet; Writer; Dramatist. m. Julia Georgina Skeen 10 Dec 1981, 1 son, 1 daughter. Education: BA, University of the Witwatersrand, 1969; MA, University of Oxford, 1973; MA, University of London, 1974. Publications: First Poems, 1977; A New Book of South African Verse (editor with Guy Butler), 1979; New Shades, 1982; Kites, 1990; Mann Alive (video and book), 1992; South Africans: A Series of Portrait Poems, 1995. Plays: The Sand Labyrinth, 1980; Mahoon's Testimony, 1995; The Horn of Plenty: A Series of Painting-Poems, with Jullia Skeen (artist), 1997; Frail Care: A Play in Verse, 1997. Contributions to: Numerous journals and magazines. Honours: Newdigate Prize; Olive Schreiner Award; South African Performing Arts Council Playwright Award; Honorary DLitt, University of Durban-Westville, 1993. Address: 19 Frances Street, Grahamstown, 6140, South Africa.

MANN Jessica, b. England. Writer. Publications: A Charitable End, 1971; Mrs Knox's Profession, 1972; The Only Security, 1973; The Sticking Place, 1974; Captive Audience, 1975; The Eighth Deadly Sin, 1976; The Sting of Death, 1978; Funeral Sites, 1981; Deadlier Than the Male, 1981; No Man's Island, 1983; Grave Goods, 1984; A Kind of Healthy Grave, 1986; Death Beyond the Nile, 1988; Faith, Hope and Homicide, 1991; Telling Only Lies, 1992; A Private Inquiry, 1996; Hanging Fire, 1997; The Survivor's Revenge, 1998. Contributions to: Daily Telegraph; Sunday Telegraph; Various magazines and journals. Memberships: Detection Club; Society of Authors: PEN; Crime Writers Association. Literary Agent: Lavinia Trevor, 49A Goldhawk Road, London, W12 8QP, England. Address: Lambessow, St Clement, Cornwall, England.

MANNING Paul, b. 22 Nov 1912, Pasadena, California, USA. Author. m. Louise Margaret Windels, 22 Mar 1947, 4 sons. Education: Occidental College, Los Angeles. Appointments: Editor, Time-Life, New York City, 1937-38, Everyweek, 1939; Chief European Correspondent in London, Newspaper Enterprise Association and Scripps Howard Newspaper Group, 1939-42; Joined Edward R Murrow as CBS News Commentator from London, England, 1942; Only journalist to witness and broadcast both German surrender ceremonies, Reims, France, and Japanese surrender aboard USS Missouri, Tokyo Bay. Publications: Mr England: Biography of Winston Churchill, 1941; Martin Bormann: Nazi in Exile, 1986; Hirohito: The War Years, 1986; The Silent War: KGB Against the West, 1987; Years of War, 1988. Contributions to: New York Times; Reader's Digest; Saturday Evening Post; Articles to numerous journals including 8th Air Force News. Honours: Nominated for Pulitzer Prize, 1943, 1971, 1986; Special Citations, Secretary of War Robert Patterson and Secretary of Navy James Forrestal; Nominated for Congressional Medal for War Coverage, 1947. Membership: Eighth Air Force Historical Society. Address: PO Box 3129, Jersey City, NJ 07302, USA.

MANNING Phillip, b. 8 July 1936, Atlanta, Georgia, USA. Science Writer. m. Diane Karraker, 26 Nov 1960, 1 son, 1 daughter. Education: BS, The Citadel, 1958; PhD, University of North Carolina at Chapel Hill, 1963. Appointments: Research Chemist, E I du Pont de Nemours, 1963-65; Research Supervisor, du Pont, 1965-68; Senior Supervisor, du Pont, 1968-71; President, NMF Inc, Charlotte, NC, USA, 1971-83; Chairman, Sunguard Shareholder Systems, San Mateo, California, 1985-89; Freelance Writer, Chapel Hill, NC, 1989-. Publications: Afoot in the South, 1993; Palmetto Journal, 1995; Orange Blossom Trails, 1997. Contributions to: Over 70 articles published in Backpacker, Field & Stream. Memberships: NC Writer's Network; Outdoor Writer's Association of America; Southeastern Outdoor Press Association. Address: 315 E Rosemary St, Chapel Hill, NC 27514, USA.

MANO D Keith, b. 12 Feb 1942, New York, New York, USA. Writer; Screenwriter. m. Laurie Kennedy, 18 July 1980, 2 sons. Education: BA, Columbia University, 1963; Clare College, Cambridge. Appointments: Contributing Editor, National Review, 1975-, Playboy, 1980; Book Editor, Esquire, 1979-80. Publications: Bishop's Progress, 1968; Horn, 1969; War is Heaven, 1970; The Death and Life of Harry Goth, 1971; The Proselytizer, 1972; The Bridge, 1973; Take Five, 1982; Resistance, 1984; Topless, 1991. Contributions to: Newspapers and magazines. Honours: Modern Language Association Award, 1968; Playboy Award, 1975; Literary Lion, New York Public Library, 1987. Address: c/o National Review, 150 East 35th Street, New York, NY 10016, USA.

MANOR Jason. See: **HALL Oakley Maxwell.**

MANSEL Philip Robert Rhys, b. 19 Oct 1951, London, England. Writer. Education: MA, Balliol College, Oxford, 1974; PhD, University College, London, 1978. Appointments: Editor, The Court Historian, Newsletter of the Society for Court Studies, 1995. Publications: Louis XVIII, 1981; Pillars of Monarchy, 1984; Sultans in Splendour: The Last Years of the Ottoman World, 1988; The Court of France 1789-1830, 1989; Charles Joseph de Ligne, 1992; Constantinople, 1995. Contributions to: Apollo; History Today; International Herald Tribune; Spectator. Membership: Society for Court Studies. Address: 13 Prince of Wales Terrace, London W8 5PG, England.

MANSELL Chris, b. 1 Mar 1953, Sydney, New South Wales, Australia. Poet; Writer. m. Steven G Sturgess, Dec 1986, 1 son, 1 daughter. Education: BSc, University of Sydney. Appointments: Residencies, Curtin University, 1985, University of Southern Queensland, 1990, K S Prichard Centre, 1992, Bundanon, 1996; Lecturer, University of Wollongong, 1987-89, University of Western Sydney, 1989-91. Publications: Delta, 1978; Head, Heart and Stone, 1982; Redshift/Blueshift, 1988; Shining Like a Jinx, 1992; Day Easy Sunlight Fine, 1995. Contributions to: Many reviews, quarterlies, and magazines. Honours: Amelia Chapbook Award, 1987; Queensland Premier's Prize for Poetry, 1993. Memberships: Australian Society of Authors; Poets Union; Women in Publishing. Address: PO Box 94, Berry, New South Wales 2535, Australia.

MANSER Martin Hugh, b. 11 Jan 1952, Bromley, England. Reference Book Editor. m. Yusandra Tun, 1979, 1 son, 1 daughter. Education: BA, Honours, University of York, 1974; MPhil, C.N.A.A., 1977. Publications: Concise Book of Bible Quotations, 1982; A Dictionary of Everyday Idioms, 1983, 2nd edition, 1997; Listening to God, 1984; Pocket Thesaurus of English Words, 1984; Children's Dictionary, 1984; Macmillan Student's Dictionary, 1985, 2nd edition, 1996; Penguin Wordmaster Dictionary, 1987; Guinness Book of Words, 1988; Dictionary of Eponyms, 1988; Visual Dictionary, Bloomsbury Good Word Guide, 1988; Printing and Publishing Terms, 1988; Marketing Terms, 1988; Guinness Book of Words, 1988, 2nd edition, 1991; Bible Promises: Outlines for Christian Living, 1989; Oxford Learner's Pocket Dictionary, 2nd edition, 1991; Get To the Roots: A Dictionary of Words and Phrase Origins, 1992; The Lion Book of Bible Quotations, 1992; Oxford Learner's Pocket Dictionary with Illustrations, 1992; Guide to Better English, 1994; Chambers Compact Thesaurus, 1994; Bloomsbury Key to English Usage, 1994; Collins Gem Daily Guidance, 1995; NIV Thematic Study Bible, 1996; Chambers English Thesaurus, 1997; Dictionary of Bible Themes, 1997; NIV Shorter Concordance, 1997; Guide to English Grammar, 1998; Crash Course in Christian Teaching, 1998; Dictionary of the Bible, 1998; Christian Prayer (large print), 1998. Address: 102 Northern Road, Aylesbury, Bucks HP19 3QY, England.

MANSFIELD. See: **BROMIGE David.**

MANSFIELD Kathy, b. 17 Sept 1949, White Plains, NY, USA. Writer; Photographer. m. Peter Turquand Mansfield, 30 Dec 1988, 1 daughter. Education: Cambridge University, England, 1970; BA, Connecticut College, 1971. Appointments: Sales/Marketing Manager, Frank Cass & Co Publishers, 1977-79; Sales/Marketing Manager, Chas Griffins & Co, 1978-84; Freelance Book Importer, 1984-93; Freelance Writer & Photographer, 1993 (regular Correspondent for Water Craft, The Boatman). Publication: History: The Traditional Boats of Shetland, 1999. Contributions to: Magazines & journals: Wooden Boat Magazine: The Shetland Sixaveen, 1993; John Cabot's Matthew, 1996; McGruer & Co, 1996; The Luggers of Scotland, 1999; Classic Boat Magazine: On the Trail of the Trenail, 1996; Cruising World: A Scottish Overture, 1995; The Boatman Magazine: In the Viking's Wake, 1995; The Shetland Sixaveen, 1996; An Electric Experience, 1996; Motorboat & Yachting: 3 part Cruising the West Coast of Scotland, 1997; Chasse Marée: The Shetland Sixaveen, 1999; Water Craft: Numerous articles. Address: White Cottage, 34 Wood Street, Wallingford, Oxon OX10 0AX, England.

MANSOOR Menahem, b. 4 Aug 1911, Port Said, Egypt. Retired University Educator; Writer. m. Claire D Kramer, 29 Nov 1951, 1 son, 1 daughter. Education: University of London School of Oriental Studies, London, 1936-39; BA with Honours, 1941, MA, 1942, PhD, 1944, Trinity College, Dublin. Appointments: Chief Interpreter and Assistant Press Attache, British Embassy, Tel Aviv, 1949-54; Chairman, Department of Semitic Languages, University of Wisconsin, Madison, 1955-77; Editor, Hebrew Studies, Annual of National Association of Professors of Hebrew, 1979-81. Publications: The Thanksgiving Hymns Scrolls (translator), 1961; The Dead Sea Scrolls, 1964; Political and Diplomatic History of the Arab World: 1900-1967, Chronological, 1972, Biographical, 1975, Documentary, 1978 (16 volumes); The Book of Direction to the Duties of the Heart (translator), 1973; Jewish History and Thought: An Introduction, 1992. Other: Over 12 textbooks in Hebrew and Arabic including 2 courses for Linguaphone, London. Contributions to: Journal of Biblical Literature; Studies in the History of Religions; Biblical Research; Revue de Qumran; Hebrew Studies; Wisconsin Academy of Arts, Sciences and Letters. Honours: Fulbright Grant, 1954; Honorary doctorates, Edgewood College, Madison, 1986, Hebrew Union College, Cincinnati, Ohio, 1993. Memberships: Society of Biblical Literature; Middle East Studies; Society of Biblical Literature, Midwest president, 1969-70; American Oriental Society, Midwest president, 1970-71; Wisconsin Academy of Arts, Sciences and Letters, vice president, 1983. Address: 5015 Sheboygan Avenue 206, Madison, WI 53705, USA.

MANTEL Hilary (Mary), b. 6 July 1952, Derbyshire, England. Author. m. Gerald McEwen, 23 Sept 1972. Education: London School of Economics; Sheffield University; Bachelor of Jurisprudence, 1973. Publications: Every Day is Mother's Day, 1985; Vacant Possession, 1986; Eight Months on Ghazzah Street, 1988; Fludd, 1989; A Place of Greater Safety, 1992; A Change of Climate, 1994; An Experiment in Love, 1995; The Giant, O'Brien, 1998. Contributions to: Film column, Spectator, 1987-91; Book reviews to range of papers. Honours: Shiva Naipaul Prize, 1987; Winifred Holtby Prize, 1990; Cheltenham Festival Prize, 1990; Southern Arts Literature Prize, 1990; Sunday Express Book of the Year Award, 1992; Hawthornden Prize, 1996. Memberships: Royal Society of Literature, fellow; Society of Authors.

Address: c/o A M Heath & Co, 79 St Martin's Lane, London WC2, England.

MANWARING Randle (Gilbert), b. 3 May 1912, London, England. Poet; Writer. m. Betty Violet Rout, 9 Aug 1941, 3 sons, 1 daughter. Education: Private schools; MA, University of Keele, 1982. Publications: The Heart of This People, 1954; Satires and Salvation, 1960; Christian Guide to Daily Work, 1963; Under the Magnolia Tree, 1965; In a Time of Unbelief, 1977; The Swifts of Maggiore, 1981; The Run of the Downs, 1984; Collected Poems, 1986; The Singing Church, 1990; Some Late Lark Singing, 1992; The Swallows, The Fox and the Cuckoo, forthcoming. Contributions to: Reviews, quarterlies, and magazines. Memberships: Downland Poets, chairman, 1981-83; Kent and Sussex Poetry Society; Society of Authors; Society of Sussex Authors. Address: Marbles Barn, Newick, East Sussex BN8 4LG, England.

MAPLE Gordon Extra, b. 6 Aug 1932, Jersey, Channel Islands. Writer; Dramatist. m. Mabel Atkinson-Frayn, 29 Jan 1953, 1 son, 1 daughter. Publications: Limeade, 1963; Here's a Funny Thing, 1964; Dog, 1967; Elephant, 1968; Tortoise, 1974; Singo, 1975; Napoleon Has Feet, 1977; Pink Circle, 1984; Chateau Schloss, 1985; Popeye, 1985; Keeping in Front (memoirs), 1986; Sour Grapes (with Miles Whittier), 1986; Yet Another Falklands Film, 1987. Honours: Oscar Nomination, 1964; Evening Standard Awards, 1964, 1973; SWEAT Award, 1986. Memberships: BPM, Oxford Yec; Royal Society of Literature, fellow. Address: The Manor, Milton, nr Banbury, Oxfordshire, England.

MAPLES Evelyn Lucille Palmer, b. 7 Feb 1919, Ponce de Leon, Missouri, USA. Editor; Author. m. William Eugene Maples, 23 Dec 1938, 2 sons, 1 daughter. Education: Southwest Missouri State University, 1936-38. Appointments: Proof Reader, Contributing Author, 1953, Copy Editor, Editor, 1963-81, Herald House. Publications: Norman Learns About the Sacraments, 1961; That Ye Love, 1971; The Many Selves of Ann-Elizabeth, 1973; Endnotes, 1989. Contributions to: Various journals; 3 Poems to Sisters in Christ, 1994. Honours: Midwestern Books Competition, 1983; Poetry Awards, 1984, 1985. Memberships: American Association of Retired Persons; Scroll Club; Missouri Writers Guild. Address: 11336 Maples Road, Niangua, MO 65713, USA.

MARAS Karl. See: **BULMER Henry Kenneth.**

MARBER Patrick, b. 19 Sept 1964, London, England. Playwright. Education: BA, English Langage and Literature, Wadham College, Oxford Univerity, 1983-86. Publications: Dealer's Choice; After Miss Julie; Closer. Honours: Writer's Guild, Evening Standard Award, 1995; Evening Standard, Critic's Circle, Olivier Awards, 1997. Literary Agent: Judy Daish. Address: 2 St Charles Place, London W10 6EG, England.

MARCEAU Felicien, b. 16 Sept 1913, Cortenberg, Belgium. Author; Playwright. Publications: Plays: L'Oeuf, 1956; La Bonne Soupe, 1958; La Preuve par Quatre, 1964; Madame Princesse, 1965; La Babour, 1968; L'Homme en Question, 1973; A Nous de Jouer, 1979. Novels: Bergere Legere, 1953; Les Elans du Coeur, 1955; Creezy, 1969; Le Corps de Mon Ennemi, 1975; Appelez-moi Mademoiselle, 1984; La Carriole du Pere Juniet, 1985; Les Passions Partagees, 1987; Un Oiseau Dans Le Ciel, 1989; La Terrasse de Lucrezia, 1993; La Grande Fille, 1997. Memoirs: Les Années Courtes, 1968; Une insolente Liberte ou Les Aventures de Casanova, 1983; Les Ingenus, 1992; Le Voyage de Noce de Figaro, 1994. Honours: Prix Pellman du Théâtre, 1954; Prix Interallie, 1955; Prix Goncourt, 1969; Grand Prix Prince Pierre de Monaco, 1974; Grand Prix de Théâtre, 1975; Prix Jean Giono, 1993; Prix Jacques Audibezzti, 1994. Membership: Académie Française. Address: c/o Editions Gallimard, 5 Rue Sebastien-Bottin, Paris 75007, France.

MARCH Jessica. See: **AFRICANO Lillian.**

MARCHAND Philip Edward, b. 18 Dec 1946, Pittsfield, Mass, USA. Books Columnist for Toronto Star. m. Patricia Thorvaldson, 6 Dec 1981. Education: BA, English Literature, University of Toronto, 1969; MA, English Literature, University of Toronto, 1970. Publications: Just Looking Thank You, 1976; Marshall McLuhan: The Medium and the Messenger, 1989, 1998; Deadly Spirits, novel, 1994; Ripostes Reflections on Canadian Literature, 1998. Literary Agent: Westwood Creative Artists. Address: 94 Harbord Street, Toronto, Ontario M5S 1G6, Canada.

MARCHANT Anyda, (Sarah Aldridge), b. 27 Jan 1911, Rio de Janeiro, Brazil. Writer. Education: AB, Distinction, 1931, MA, 1933, LLB, 1936, National University, Washington, DC. Appointments: Admitted to the bars, Virginia, District of Columbia, and US Supreme Court; Staff, Law Library, Library of Congress, Washington, DC, 1940-45, Bureau of Foreign and Domestic Commerce, US Department of Commerce, Washington, DC, 1951-53, International Bank for Reconstruction and Development, Washington, DC, 1954-73; Co-Founder, Naiad Press, 1974, and A & M Books, 1995. Publications: The Latecomer, 1974; Tottie: The Tale of the Sixties, 1975; Cytherea's Breath, 1976; All True Lovers, 1978; The Nesting Place, 1982; Madame Aurora, 1983; Misfortune's Friend, 1985; Magdalena, 1987; Keep to Me Stranger, 1989; A Flight of Angels, 1992; Michaela, 1994; Amantha, 1995. Contributions to: Books and journals. Honour: Jeanine Rae Award, National Women's Music Festival, Bloomington, Indiana, 1992. Address: 212 Laurel Street, Rehoboth Beach, DE 19971, USA.

MARCUS Jeffrey Scott, b. 4 Oct 1962, Wisconsin, USA. Novelist. Education: BA, University of Wisconsin at Madison, 1984. Publications: The Art of Cartography, 1991; The Captain's Fire. Contributins to: Newspapers and magazines. Honours: Whiting Writers Award, 1992. Address: 4735 North Woodruff Avenue, Milwaukee, WI 53211, USA.

MARCUS Joanna. See: **ANDREWS Lucilla Matthew.**

MARCUS Ruth (Barcan), b. 2 Aug 1921, New York, New York, USA. Professor of Philosophy; Writer. Div, 2 sons, 2 daughters. Education: BA, New York University, 1941; MA, 1942, PhD 1946, Yale University. Appointments: Research Associate Institute for Human Relations, 1945-47, Reuben Post Halleck Professor of Philosophy, 1973-, Yale University; Visiting Professor, 1950-57, Professor of Philosophy, 1970-73, Northwestern University; Assistant Professor to Associate Professor, Roosevelt University, Chicago, 1957-63; Professor of Philosophy, Head, Department of Philosophy, University of Illinois, Chicago, 1964-70; Fellow, Center for Advanced Study, University of Illinois, 1968-69, Center for Advanced Study in the Behavioral Sciences, Stanford, California, 1979; Visiting Fellow, Institute for Advanced Study, University of Edinburgh, 1983, Wolfson College, Oxford, 1985, 1986, Clare Hall, Cambridge, 1988; Mellon Senior Fellow, National Humanities Center, 1992-93; Visiting Distinguished Professor, University of California, Irvine, 1994-. Publications: The Logical Enterprise (editor), 1975; Logic, Methodology, and Philosophy of Science, VII (editor), 1986; Modalities: Philosophical Essays, 1993. Contributions to: Scholarly books and journals. Honours: Guggenheim Fellowship, 1953-54; Medal, Collège de France, 1986; Honorary LHD, University of Illinois, 1995. Memberships: American Academy of Arts and Sciences; Board of Officers, Chairman, 1977-83, American Philosophical Association; Association for Symbolic Logic, president, 1981-83; Council on Philosophical Studies, president, 1985-; Institut International de Philosophie, president, 1990-93; 1994-, Phi Beta Kappa, honorary president; Philosophy of Science Association. Address: c/o Department of Philosophy, Yale University, PO Box 208306, New Haven, CT 06525, USA.

MARCUS Steven, b. 13 Dec 1928, New York, New York, USA. Professor of English; College Dean; Writer. m. Gertrud Lenzer, 20 Jan 1966, 1 son. Education: AB,

1948, PhD, 1961, Columbia University. Appointments: Professor of English, 1966-, George Delacorte Professor of Humanities, 1976-, Chairman, Department of English and Comparative Literature, 1977-80, 1985-90, Vice-President, School of Arts and Sciences, 1993-95, Dean, Columbia College, 1993-95, Columbia University; Fellow, Center for Advanced Studies in the Behavioural Sciences, 1972-73; Director of Planning, 1974-76, Chairman of the Executive Committee, Board of Directors, 1976-80, National Humanities Center; Chairman, Lionel Trilling Seminars, 1976-80. Publications: Dickens: From Pickwick to Dombey, 1965; Other Victorians, 1966; Engels, Manchester and the Working Class, 1974; Representations: Essays on Literature and Society, 1976; Doing Good (with others), 1978; Freud and the Culture of Psychoanalysis, 1984. Editor: The Life and Work of Sigmund Freud (with Lionel Trilling), 1960; The World of Modern Fiction, 2 volumes, 1968; The Continental Op, 1974; Medicine and Western Civilization (with David Rothman), 1995. Contributions to: Professional journals and to general periodicals. Honours: Guggenheim Fellowship, 1967-68; Rockefeller Foundation Fellowship, 1980-81; National Humanities Center Fellowship, 1980-82; Fulbright Fellowship, 1982-84; Honorary DHL, Clark University, 1985; Fellow, Centre for Advanced Study in the Behavioural Science, Stanford, California, 1972-73. Memberships: Academy of Literary Studies, fellow; American Academy of Arts and Sciences, fellow; American Academy of Psychoanalysis; American Psychoanalytic Association, honorary; Institute for Psychoanalytic Teaching and Research, honorary. Address: c/o Department of English and Comparative Literature, Columbia University, New York, NY 10027, USA.

MARFEY Anne, b. 19 Feb 1927, Copenhagen, Denmark. Writer; Adjunct Lecturer in Danish. m. Dr Peter Marfey, 6 Jan 1964, dec, 1 son, 1 daughter. Education: Teachers' Certificate, Danish Teachers' College, Copenhagen, 1950; Postgraduate studies, Columbia University, 1961-62; PhD, Pacific Western University, Hawaii, 1998. Appointment: Adjunct Lecturer in Danish, State University of New York at Albany. Publications: Learning to Write, 1961; Vejen til hurtigere Laesning, 1962; Svante, 1965; Las Bedre, 1966; Amerikanere, 1967; Telefontraden, 1968; Skal Skal ikke, 1969; How Parents Can Help Their Child with Reading, 1976; Rose's Adventure, 1989; Moderne Dansk, 1989; The Duckboat, The Pump, The Pine Tree, 1994; The Chipmunk, 1994; The Miracle of Learning, 1997. Membership: Danish Writers Guild; Board Member, UN Albany; US-China Friendship Association, Albany; New York Academy of Sciences, 1997; American Association of University Women, 1998. Address: 9 Tudor Road, Albany, NY 12203, USA.

MARGOSHES Dave, b. 8 July 1941, New Brunswick, New Jersey, USA. Writer; Poet. m. Ilya Silbar, 29 Apr 1963. Education: BA, 1963, MFA, 1969, University of Iowa. Appointments: Director, numerous writers' workshops and creative writing courses; Writer-in-Residence, University of Winnipeg, 1995-96. Publications: Third Impressions (short stories with Barry Dempster and Don Dickinson), 1982; Small Regrets (short stories), 1986; Walking at Brighton (poems), 1988; Northwest Passage (poems), 1990; Nine Lives (short stories), 1991; Saskatchewan, 1992; Long Distance Calls (short stories), 1996; Fables of Creation (short stories), 1997. Contributions to: Numerous anthologies, journals, and magazines. Honours: Canadian Author and Bookman Poem of the Year Award, 1980; Saskatchewan Writers Guild Long Manuscript Award, 1990; 2nd Prize, League of Canadian Poets' National Poetry Contest, 1991; Stephen Leacock Award for Poetry, 1996. Address: 2922 19th Avenue, Regina, Saskatchewan S4T 1X5, Canada.

MARIANANDA. See: **JANSEN Garfield.**

MARIANI Paul (Louis), b. 29 Feb 1940, New York, New York, USA. Professor; Writer; Poet. m. Eileen Spinosa, 24 Aug 1963, 3 sons. Education: BA, Manhattan College, 1962; MA, Colgate University, 1964; PhD, Graduate Center, City University of New York, 1968. Appointments: Assistant Professor, John Jay College of Criminal Justice, 1967-68; Assistant Professor, 1968-71, Associate Professor, 1971-75, Professor, 1975-, Distinguished University Professor, 1985, University of Massachusetts, Amherst; Robert Frost Fellow, 1980, Faculty, 1982, 1983, 1984, Robert Frost Professor, 1983, Visiting Lecturer, 1986, School of English, Poetry Staff, 1985-96, Bread Loaf Writers' Conference; Director, The Glen, Colorado Springs, 1995, 1996, 1998. Publications: Poetry: Timing Devices, 1979; Crossing Cocytus, 1982; Prime Mover, 1985; Salvage Operations: New and Selected Poems, 1990; The Great Wheel, 1996. Other: William Carlos Williams: A New World Naked, 1981; Dream Song: The Life of John Berryman, 1990, new edition, 1996; Lost Puritan: A Life of Robert Lowell, 1994; The Broken Tower: A Life of Hart Crane, 1999. Contributions to: Books and journals. Honours: National Endowment for the Humanities Fellowships, 1972-73, 1981-82; New Jersey Writers' Award, 1982; New York Times Notable Books, 1982, 1994; Nominated, American Book Award in Biography, 1983; Chancellor's Medal, University of Massachusetts, 1984; National Endowment for the Arts Fellowship, 1984; Choice Awards, Prairie Schooner, 1989, 1995; Honorary Doctor of Humane Letters, Manhattan College, 1998. Memberships: Academy of American Poets; Poetry Society of America. Address: Box M, Montague, MA 01351, USA.

MARINEAU Michele, b. 12 Aug 1955, Montreal, Quebec, Canada. Writer; Translator. Div, 1 son, 1 daughter. Education: BA, Traduction et Histoire de l'art, University of Montreal, 1988. Publications: Cassiopée ou L'été Polonais, 1988; L'été des Baleines, 1989; L'Homme du Cheshire, 1990; Pourquoi pas Istambul?, 1991; La Route de Chlifa, 1992. Honours: Prix du Gouverneur Général, 1988, 1993; Prix, Brive-Montreal, 1993; Prix, Alvine-Bélisle, 1993. Memberships: Union des Écrivaines et Écrivains, Quebec; Corporation Professionnelle des Traducteurs et Interprétes Agréés du Quebec; Association des Traducteurs Litteraires du Canada; Communication-Jeunesse. Literary Agent: Editions Quebec/Amérique, 425 St Jean Baptiste, Montreal, Quebec, Canada. Address: 4405 rue de Brebeuf, Montreal, Quebec H2J 3K8, Canada.

MARIZ Linda Catherine French, (Linda French), b. 27 Nov 1948, New Orleans, Louisiana, USA. Mystery Novelist. m. George Eric Mariz, 22 Aug 1970, 1 son, 1 daughter. Education: BA, History, University of Missouri, Columbia, 1970; MA, History, Western Washington University, 1973. Appointment: Creative Writing Instructor, Western Washington University, 1994. Publications: As Linda Mariz: Body English, 1992; Snake Dance, 1992. As Linda French: Talking Rain, 1998; Coffee to Die For, 1998; Intro to Murder, forthcoming. Contributions to: Cash Buyer (story) in Reader, I Murdered Him Too (anthology), 1995. Memberships: Sisters in Crime; International Association of Crime Writers; Washington Commission for the Humanities. Literary Agent: Jane Chelius, 548 Second Street, Brooklyn, NY, USA. Address: 708 17th Street, Bellingham, WA 98225, USA.

MARK Jan(et Marjorie), b. 22 June 1943, Welwyn, Hertfordshire, England. Writer; Dramatist. m. Neil Mark, 1 Mar 1969, div 1989, 1 son, 1 daughter. Education: NDD, Canterbury College of Art, 1965. Appointments: Teacher, Southfields School, Gravesend, Kent, 1965-71; Arts Council Writer-Fellow, Oxford Polytechnic, 1982-84. Publications: Fiction: Two Stories, 1984; Zeno was Here (novel), 1987; God's Story, 1997. Plays: Izzy, 1985; Interference, 1987; Captain Courage and the Rose Street Gang (with Stephen Cockett), 1987; Time and the Hour, and, Nothing to Be Afraid Of, 1990. Other: Over 20 juvenile novels, 1976-99; Over 10 juvenile story collections, 1980-99, including The Oxford Book of Children's Stories (editor), 1993; 9 picture books, 1986-95. Contributions to: Anthologies, periodicals, radio and television. Honours: Penguin/Guardian Award, 1975; Carnegie Medals, 1976, 1983; Rank Observer Prize, 1982; Angel Literary Awards, 1983, 1988. Literary Agent: David Higham Associates. Address: 98 Howard Street, Oxford Ox4 3BG, England.

MARKER Beverly Brydon, b. 3 Mar 1938, Umatilla, Florida, USA. Poet; Retired English Teacher. m. Paul Marker, 23 June 1962, 2 sons. Education: BA, Fresno State University, Fresno, California, 1960; MA, State University of Iowa, Iowa City, 1961. Appointments: English Teacher: Port Hueneme High School, Oxnard, California, 1961-62; Carrier High School, Enid, Oklahoma, 1962-63; Robinson High School, Tampa, Florida, 1963-66; University of Tampa, 1963-64; Macarthur High School, Levittown, New York, 1968-71; H B Plant High School, Tampa, 1971-75; Western Connecticut State University, Danbury, 1976-77; Henry Abbott Technical High School, Danbury, 1981-82. Contributions to: Poems: Feelings, 1996; Poet's Fantasy, 1997-; Creative With Words, 1997; Eclectics!, Good and Bad of Nature Anthology, 1977; Christian Poet's Pen, 1997-; Fireside Anthology, 1998; Folklore, 1998-. Address: PO Box 3326, Dunnellon, FL 34430, USA.

MARKERT Joy, b. 8 May 1942, Tuttlingen, Germany. Author; Dramatist; Screenwriter. Publications: Asyl, 1985; Malta, 1986. Film scripts: Harlis, 1973; Der letzte Schrei, 1975; Belcanto, 1977; Das andere Lacheln (with R van Ackeren), 1978; Ich fühle was, was du nicht fühlst, 1982. Theatre: Asyl, 1984; Erichs Tag, 1985. 30 radio plays, 1976-. Contributions to: German and Austrian radio stations; Various literary publications. Honours: German Film Prize, 1972; German Film Awards, 1977, 1980; Berlin Literary Awards, 1982, 1984. Memberships: German Authors Association; Berlin Film Makers. Address: Bredowstrasse 33, D-1000 Berlin, Germany.

MARKFIELD Wallace (Arthur), b. 12 Aug 1926, New York, New York. USA. Writer. Appointment: Film Critic, New Leader, New York City, 1954-55. Publications: To an Early Grave, 1964; Teitelbaum's Window, 1970; You Could Live If They Let You, 1974; Multiple Orgasms, 1977; Radical Surgery, 1991. Address: c/o Alfred A Knopf Inc, 201 East 50th Street, New York, NY 10022, USA.

MARKHAM E(dward) A(rchibald), b. 1 Oct 1939, Montserrat, West Indies (British citizen). Editor; Poet; Writer; Dramatist; Professor. Education: University of Wales; University of East Anglia; University of London. Appointments: Lecturer, Abraham Moss Centre, Manchester, 1976-78; Assistant Editor, Ambit Magazine, London, 1980-; Editor, Artage, 1985-87, Sheffield Thursday, 1992-; Writer-in-Residence, University of Ulster, Coleraine, 1988-91; Professor, Sheffield Hallam University, 1991-. Publications: Poetry: Crossfire, 1972; Mad and Other Poems, 1973; Lambchops, 1976; Philpot in the City, 1976; Love Poems, 1978; Games and Penalities, 1980; Love, Politics and Food, 1982; Human Rites: Selected Poems, 1970-82, 1983; Lambchops in Papua New Guinea, 1985; Living in Disguise, 1986; Towards the End of the Century, 1989; Letter from Ulster and the Hugo Poems, 1993; Misapprehensions, 1995. Plays: The Masterpiece, 1964; The Private Life of the Public Man, 1970; Dropping Out is Violence, 1971; The Windrush Review, 1998. Short Stories: Something Unusual, 1981; Ten Stories, 1994; A Papua New Guinea Sojourn: More Pleasures of Exile (memoir), 1998; Marking Time (novel) 1999. Editor: Hinterland, 1989; The Penguin Book of Caribbean Short Stories, 1995. Honours: C Day-Lewis Fellowship, 1980-81; Certificate of Honour, Government of Montserrat, 1997. Address: c/o Bloodaxe Books Ltd, PO Box 1SN, Newcastle-upon-Tyne NE99 1SN, England.

MARKHAM Marion Margaret, b. 12 June 1929, Chicago, Illinois, USA. Writer. m. Robert Bailey Markham, 30 Dec 1955, 2 daughters. Education: BS, Northwestern University. Publications: Escape from Velos, 1981; The Halloween Candy Mystery, 1982; The Christmas Present Mystery, 1984; The Thanksgiving Day Parade Mystery, 1986; The Birthday Party Mystery, 1989; The April Fool's Day Mystery, 1991; The Valentine's Day Mystery, 1992. Memberships: Society of Midland Authors; Mystery Writers of America; Authors Guild of America; Society of

Children's Book Writers. Address: 2415 Newport Road, Northbrook, IL 60062, USA.

MARKO Katherine Dolores, b. 26 Nov 1913, Allentown, Pennsylvania, USA. Writer. m. Alex Marko, 20 Oct 1945, 2 sons, 1 daughter. Publications: The Sod Turners, 1970; God, When Will I Ever Belong?, 1979; Whales, Giants of the Sea, 1980; How the Wind Blows, 1981; God, Why Did Dad Lose His Job?, 1982; Away to Fundy Bay, 1985; Animals in Orbit, 1991; Hang Out the Flag, 1992; Pocket Babies, 1995. Contributions to: Children's Encyclopaedia Britannica; Jack and Jill; Highlights for Children; Children's Playmate; Straight; Alive; The Friend; On the Line; Childlife; Christian Science Monitor; Young Catholic Messenger; Wow. Honours: Prizes for Short Stories, 1967; Child Study Association List, 1970; Honorable Mention, Manuscript at Conference, 1973. Memberships: Childrens Reading Round Table, Chicago; Society of Childrens Book Writers; Off Campus Writers Workshop. Address: 471 Franklin Boulevard, Elgin, IL 60120, USA.

MARKOWITZ Harry M(ax), b. 24 Aug 1927, Chicago, Illinois, USA. Economist; Professor; Writer. m. Barbara Gay. Education: PhB, 1947, MA, 1950, PhD, 1954, University of Chicago. Appointments: Research Staff, Rand Corp, Santa Monica, California, 1952-60, 1961-63; Vice-President, Institute of Management Science, 1960-62; Technical Director, Consolidated Analysis Centers Inc, Santa Monica, California, 1963-68; Professor, University of California at Los Angeles, 1968-69; President, Arbitrage Management Co, New York City, 1969-72; Private Consultant, New York City, 1972-74; Staff, T J Watson Research Center, IBM, Yorktown Hills, New York, 1974-83; Speiser Professor of Finance, Baruch College of the City University of New York, 1982-93; Director of Research, Daiwa Securities Trust Co, Jersey City, New Jersey, 1990-. Publications: Portfolio Selection: Journal of Finance, 1952; Portfolio Selection: Efficient Diversification of Investments, 1959; Simscript: A Simulation Programming Language (co-author), 1963; Studies in Process Analysis of Economic Capabilities (co-editor), 1963; Mean-Variance Analysis in Portfolio Choice, 1987. Contributions to: Professional journals and other publications. Honours: John von Neumann Theory Prize, 1989; Nobel Prize for Economics, 1990. Memberships: American Academy of Arts and Sciences; American Finance Association, president, 1982-; Econometric Society, fellow. Address: Harry Markowitz Company, 1010 Turquoise Street, Suite 245, San Diego, CA 92109, USA.

MARKS Paula Mitchell, b. 29 Mar 1951, El Dorado, Arkansas, USA. Professor; Writer. m. Alan Ned Marks, 2 Apr 1971, 1 daughter. Education: BA, St Edwards University, Texas, 1978; MA, 1980, PhD, 1987, University of Texas. Publications: And Die in the West, 1989; Turn Your Eyes Toward Texas, 1989; Precious Dust: The American Gold Rush Era 1848-1900, 1994. Contributions to: American History Illustrated; Civil War Times; True West; Old West. Honours: T R Fehrenbach Texas History Award, 1990; Finalist, Western Writers of America, Non-Fiction Book Award, 1990; Certificate of Commendation, 1990; Kate Broocks Bates Texas History Research Award, 1991. Memberships: Authors Guild; Western Writers of America; Western History Association; Texas State Historical Association. Address: St Edwards University, 3001 South Congress, Austin, TX 78704, USA.

MARKS Stanley, b. 1929, London, England. Writer; Dramatist. m. Eve Mass, 1 son, 1 daughter dec. Education: University of Melbourne. Appointments: Journalist and Foreign Correspondent, Australia, UK, USA, Canada; Originator-Writer, MS cartoon series, Australian and New Zealand newspapers, 1975-80. Publications: God Gave You One Face, 1964; Graham is an Aboriginal Boy, 1968; Fifty Years of Achievement, 1972; Animal Olympics, 1972; Rarua Lives in Papua New Guinea, 1974; Ketut Lives in Bali, 1976; St Kilda Sketchbook, 1980; Malvern Sketchbook, 1981; Welcome to Australia, 1981; Out and About in Melbourne, 1988; St Kilda Heritage Sketchbook, 1995. Contributions to:

Newspapers and journals. Memberships: Australian Journalists Association; Australian Society of Authors; Society of Australian Travel Writers. Address: 348 Bambra Road, South Caulfield, Melbourne, Victoria 3162, Australia.

MARLATT Daphne (Shirley), b. 11 July 1942, Melbourne, Victoria, Australia. Poet; Writer. m. Gordon Alan Marlatt, 24 Aug 1963, div 1970, 1 son. Education: BA, English and Creative Writing, University of British Columbia, 1964; MA, Comparative Literature, Indiana University, 1968. Appointments: Co-Editor, Tessera (Journal), 1983-91. Various writer-in-residence; Special Lecturer in Creative Writing, University of Saskatchewan, 1998-99. Publications: Frames of a Story, 1968; Leaf/Leaf/s, 1969; Rings, 1971; Vancouver Poems, 1972; Steveston, 1974; Our Lives, 1975; Steveston Recollected: A Japanese-Canadian History (with M Koizumi), 1975; Zócalo, 1977; Opening Doors: Vancouver's East End (with Carole Itter), 1979; What Matters, 1980; Selected Writing: Net Work, 1980; How Hug a Stone, 1983; Touch to My Tongue, 1984; Double Negative (with Betsy Warland), 1988; Ana Historic, 1988; Salvage, 1991; Ghost Works, 1993; Taken, 1996; Readings from the Labyrinth, 1998. Honours: Awards and grants. Membership: Writers' Union of Canada. Address: c/o Writers' Union of Canada, 24 Ryerson Avenue, Toronto, Ontario M5T 2P3, Canada.

MARLIN Brigid, b. 16 Jan 1936, Washington, District of Columbia, USA. Artist; Writer. Div., 2 sons. Education: National College of Art, Dublin; Centre d'Art Sacré, Paris; Studio André L'Hôte, Paris; Beaux-Arts Académie, Montreal; Art Students League, New York; Atelier of Ernest Fuchs, Vienna. Publications: From East to West, 1989; Paintings in the Mische Technique, 1990. Illustrator: King Oberon's Forest (Hilda von Stockern); Celebration of Love (Mary O'Hara); Bright Sun, Dark Sun (Nickolas Fisk); The Leap from the Chess-Board (Charles Sprague). Contributions to: Journals and magazines. Honours: Special Children's Book Award, USA, 1958; 1st Prize, America Art Appreciation Award, 1987; 1st Prize, Visions of the Future, New English Library. Memberships: PEN Club; Authors Club; Free Painters Society; Inscape Group; WIAC; PEN Club; Society for Art of the Imagination, founder member and president, 1998. Literary Agent: Fiona Spencer Thomas. Address: PO Box 240, Berkhamsted, Herts HP4 1HE, England.

MARLIN Henry. See: **GIGGAL Kenneth.**

MARLOW Joyce, b. 27 Dec 1929, Manchester, England. Writer. Appointment: Professional Actress, 1950-65. Publications: The Man with the Glove, 1964; A Time to Die, 1966; Billy Goes to War, 1967; The House on the Cliffs, 1968; The Peterloo Massacre, 1969; The Tolpuddle Martyrs, 1971; Captain Boycott and the Irish, 1973; The Life and Times of George I, 1973; The Uncrowned Queen of Ireland, 1975; Mr and Mrs Gladstone, 1977; Kings and Queens of Britain, 1977; Kessie, 1985; Sarah, 1987; Tribunals and Appeals, 1991. Address: 3 Spring Bank, New Mills, High Peak SK22 4AS, England.

MARLOWE Hugh. See: **PATTERSON Harry.**

MARLOWE Stephen, (Andrew Frazer, Milton Lesser, Jason Ridgway, C H Thames), b. 7 Aug 1928, New York, New York, USA. Author. m. (1) Leigh Lang, 1950, (2) Ann Humbert, 1964, 2 daughters. Education: AB, College of William and Mary, 1949. Appointment: Writer-in-Residence, College of William and Mary, 1974-75, 1980-81. Publications: Over 50 novels, including: The Shining, 1963; Colossus, 1972; The Valkyrie Encounter, 1978; The Memoirs of Christopher Columbus, 1987; The Death and Life of Miguel de Cervantes, 1991; The Lighthouse at the End of the World, 1995. Honours: Prix Gutenberg du Livre, 1988; Life Achievement Award, Private Eye Writers of America, 1997. Address: c/o Mildred Marmur Associates, 2005 Palmer Avenue, Suite 127, Larchmont, NY 10538, USA.

MARNY Dominique Antoinette Nicole, b. 21 Feb 1948, Neuilly, France. Novelist; Screenwriter; Journalist. m. Michel Marny, 5 Oct 1970, div, 1 daughter. Appointment: Director for J C Lattès, Mille et une femmes collection, 1993-. Publications: Crystal Palace, 1985; Les orages desirés, 1988; Les fous de lumière, 1991; Les desirs et les jours, 1993; Les courtisanes, 1994; Les belles de Cocteau, 1995. Contributions to: Madame Figaro; Vogue; Marie France. Honour: Prix Madame Europe, 1993. Membership: PEN Club. Address: 4 Avenue de New York, 75016 Paris, France.

MARON Margaret, b. Greensboro, North Carolina, USA. Writer. m. Joseph J Maron, 20 June 1959, 1 son. Education: University of North Carolina. Publications: One Coffee With, 1981; Death of a Butterfly, 1984; Bloody Kin, 1985; Death in Blue Folders, 1985; Bootlegger's Daughter, 1992; Shooting at Loons, 1994. Contributions to: Redbook; McCall's; Alfred Hitchcock. Honour: Edgar Allan Poe Award, 1993. Memberships: Mystery Writers of America; North Carolina Writers Conference. Address: c/o Vicky Bijur Literary Agency, 333 West End Avenue, Suite 5B, New York, NY 10023, USA.

MAROWITZ Charles, b. 26 Jan 1934, New York, USA. Writer. m. Jane Elizabeth Allsop, 14 Dec 1980. Appointments: Artistic Director, Malibu Stage Co, Texas Stage Co; West Coast Correspondent, Theatre Week Magazine; Senior Editor, Matzoh Ball Gazette; Theatre Critic, Los Angeles Village View; Guest Artist in Residence, California State University, Long Beach, California, 1997. Publications: The Method as Means, 1961; The Marowitz Hamlet, 1966; The Shrew, 1972; Artaud at Rodez, 1975; Confessions of a Counterfeit Critic, 1976; The Marowitz Shakespeare, 1980; Act of Being, 1980; Sex Wars, 1983; Sherlock's Last Case, 1984; Prospero's Staff, 1986; Potboilers, 1986; Recycling Shakespeare, 1990; Burnt Bridges, 1991; Directing the Action, 1992; Cyrano de Bergerac (translation), 1995; Alarums and Excursions, 1996; The Otherway: An Alternative Approach to Acting and Directing, 1998. Contributions to: Drama Critic, The Jewish Journal; Columnist, In-Theater magazine; Newspapers, journals and magazines. Honours: Order of Purple Sash, 1965; Whitbread Award, 1967; 1st Prize, Louis B Mayer Award, 1984. Memberships: Dramatists Guild; Writers Guild. Address: 3058 Sequit Drive, Malibu, CA 90265, USA.

MARQUIS Max, (Edward Frank Marquis), b. Ilford, Essex, England. Author. m. (1), 1 son, (2) Yvonne Cavenne, 1953. Appointments: News Writer and Reader, RDF French Radio, 1952; Sub Editor, Columnist, Continental Daily Mail, 1952; Evening News, London, 1955; Chief British Correspondent, L'Equipe, Paris, 1970; Football Commentator, Broadcaster, Télévision Suisse-Romande, 1972. Publications: Sir Alf Ramsey: Anatomy of a Football Manager, 1970; The Caretakers, 1975; A Matter of Life, 1976; The Shadowed Heart, 1978; The Traitor Machine, 1980; Body Guard to Charles, 1989; Vengeance, 1990; The Twelfth Man, 1991; Deadly Doctors, 1992; Elimination, 1993; Undignified Death, 1994; Written in Blood, 1995; Death of a Good Woman, 1998. Address: c/o Rupert Crew Ltd, 1A Kings Mews, London WC1N 2JA, England.

MARR William Wei-Yi, (Fei Ma), b. 3 Sept 1936, China. Retired Engineer; Poet; Editor. m. Jane Jy Chyun Liu, 22 Sept 1962, 2 sons. Education: Taipei Institute of Technology, 1957; MS, Marquette University, 1963; PhD, University of Wisconsin, 1969. Appointments: Editorial Advisor, The Chinese Poetry International, New World Poetry; Advisor, Chinese Writers Association of Greater Chicago, Association of Modern Chinese Literature and Arts of North America. Publications: In the Windy City, 1975; Selected Poems, 1983; White Horse, 1984; Selected Poems of Fei Ma, 1985; The Galloping Hoofs, 1986; Road, 1987; Selected Short Poems, 1991; Fly Spirit, 1992; Selected Poems, 1994; Autumn Windows, 1995. Contributions to: Periodicals and magazines. Honours: Wu Cho Liu Poetry Award, 1982; Li Poetry Translation Award, 1982, and Poetry Award, 1984. Memberships: Chinese Artists Association of North

America; First Line Poetry Society; Illinois State Poetry Society, president, 1993-95; Li Poetry Society; New Poetry, Beijing, vice president, 1994-; Poets Club of Chicago. Address: 737 Ridgeview Street, Downers Grove, IL 60516, USA.

MARRECO Anne. See: WIGNALL Anne.

MARRIOTT-BURTON Elsie Gwendoline, b. 15 Feb 1901, Auckland, New Zealand. Journalist; Radio Broadcaster; Poet; Writer. m. Harry Marriott-Burton. Education: Commercial Art Studies, partially completed 1919-20. Appointment: Community Creative Writing Tutor, Noosa Community Queensland, 1984-98. Publications: Private Diary of HRH Prince Chula, 1991; Fate Is My Journey, 1995. Contributions to: South African Newspapers, 1937-43, 1950-54; Regular contributions, Magazines, Africa, Australia and New Zealand, 1937-77. Memberships: Australian Society of Authors; FAW, Queensland Branch. Address: 269 Studio, Buderim Garden Village, Hooloolaba Road, Buderim, Queensland 4556, Australia.

MARRODAN Mario Angel, b. 7 June 1932, Portugalete, Vizcaya, Spain. Lawyer; Critic; Writer; Poet; Editor. m. Mercedes Gómez Estibaliz, 31 May 1961, 2 sons. Education: Bachillerato Superior; Licentiate in Law; Philosophy; Letters. Publications: Over 250 books, including essays, art criticism, and poetry. Contributions to: About 2000 journals and magazines. Honours: Several literary awards and prizes. Memberships: Asociación Española de Críticos de Arte; Asociación Española de Críticos Literarios; Asociación Colegial de Escritores de España; International Association of Art Critics. Address: Cristobal Mello 7, 2o izqda, Apartado Postal 16, 48920 Portugalete, Vizcaya, Spain.

MARS-JONES Adam, b. 26 Oct 1954, London, England. Education: BA, Cambridge University, 1976. Appointments: Film Critic, Reviewer, The Independent, London. Publications: Lantern Lecture and Other Stories, 1981; The Darker Proof: Stories from a Crisis (with Edmund White), 1987; Venus Envy, 1990; Monopolies of Loss, 1992; The Waters of Thirst, 1993; Blind Bitter Happiness, 1997. Editor: Mae West is Dead: Recent Lesbian and Gay Fiction. Honour: Maugham Award, 1982. Literary Agent: Peters, Fraser and Dunlop Group Ltd, 503-4 The Chambers, Chelsea Harbour, Lots Road, London SW10 0XF. Address: 3 Gray's Inn Square, London WC1R 5AH, England.

MARSDEN Christopher, b. 26 July 1964, Burnley, Lancashire, England. Contributions to: Anchor Books; Poetry Now; Triumph House; Arrival Press; International Library of Poets; Pulp Poetry; Poetry Guild; Poetry Today. Honours: Runner-Up, 2 Poetry Competitions. Address: 26 Westgate, Burnley, Lancashire BB11 1RT, England.

MARSDEN David Lawrence Francis, b. 17 May 1954, Dayton, Ohio, USA. Writer; Psychiatrist Aid; Nurses Aid. Div, 4 sons. Education: Alcohol Counseling, University of Evansville, St Mary's Medical Center; Institute for Alcohol and Drug Studies, University of Evansville. Appointments: Nursing Assistant, Integrated Health System, Cambridge, Indianapolis, Indiana, Caretenders Home Health Care Inc, Carmel, Indiana. Publications: Songs: Wasn't It Yesterday; You Were There; You Got the Wrong Man; Where You Ever Mine. Poems: Witches In the Night; The River of Light. Contributions to: Sparrowgrass; National Library of Poetry. Address: 6510 Covington Road, Apt E237, Fort Wayne, IN 46804-7350, USA.

MARSDEN George M, b. 25 Feb 1939, Harrisburg, Pennsylvania, USA. Professor of History; Writer. m. Lucie Commeret, 30 Mar 1969, 1 son, 1 daughter. Education: BA, Haverford College, 1959; BD, Westminster Theological Seminary, 1963; MA, 1961, PhD, 1965, Yale University. Appointments: Instructor, Assistant, and Associate Professor, 1965-74, Professor, 1974-86, Calvin College, Grand Rapids; Associate Editor, Christian Scholar's Review, 1970-77; Visiting Professor of Church History, Trinity Evangelical Divinty School, Deerfield, Illinois, 1976-77; Editor, The Reformed Journal, 1980-90;

Visiting Professor of History, University of Californiat at Berkeley, 1986, 1990; Professor of the History of Christianity in America, Divinity School, Duke University, 1986-92; Francis A McAnaney Professor of History, University of Notre Dame, 1992-. Publications: The Evangelical Mind and the New School Presbyterian Experience, 1970; A Christian View of History? (editor with Frank Roberts), 1975; Fundamentalism and American Culture: The Shaping of Twentieth-Century Evangelicalism, 1870-1925, 1980; Eerdman's Handbook to the History of Christianity in America (editor with others), 1983; The Search for Christian America (with Mark A Noll and Nathan O Hatch), 1983, revised edition, 1989; Evangelicalism and Modern America (editor), 1984; Reforming Fundamentalism: Fuller Seminary and the New Evangelicalism, 1987; Religion and American Culture, 1990; Understanding Fundamentalism and Evangelicalism, 1991; The Secularization of the Academy (editor with Bradley J Longfield), 1992; The Soul of the American University, 1994; The Outrageous Idea of Christian Scholarship, 1997. Contributions to: Many scholarly books and journals. Honours: Younger Humanists Fellowship, National Endowment for the Humanities, 1971-72; Fellow, Calvin Center for Christian Scholarship, 1979-80; Book of the Year Citations, Eternity magazine, 1981, 1988; Calvin Research Fellowship, 1982-83; J Howard Pew Freedom Trust Grant, 1988-92; Guggenheim Fellowship, 1995. Memberships: American Society of Church History, president, 1992; Institute for the Study of American Evangelicals, advisory council. Address: c/o Department of History, University of Notre Dame, Notre Dame, IN 46556, USA.

MARSDEN Peter Richard Valentine, b. 29 Apr 1940, Twickenham, Middlesex, England. Archaeologist. m. Frances Elizabeth Mager, 7 Apr 1979, 2 sons, 1 daughter. Education: Kilburn Polytechnic; Oxford University. Publications: Londinium, 1971; The Wreck of the Amsterdam, 1974 revised edition, 1985; Roman London, 1980; The Marsden Family of Paythorne and Nelson, 1981; The Roman Forum Site in London, 1987; The Historic Shipwrecks of South-East England, 1987. Contributions to: Geographical Magazine; Independent; Times Literary Supplement; Illustrated London News; Telegraph Colour Magazine; Various academic journals. Memberships: Society of Antiquaries, fellow; Institute of Field Archaeologists. Address: 21 Meadow Lane, Lindfield, West Sussex RH16 2RJ, Sussex.

MARSDEN Simon Neville Llewelyn, b. 1 Dec 1948, Lincoln, England. Photographer; Author. m. Caroline Stanton, 30 Aug 1984, 1 son, 1 daughter. Education: Ampleforth College, Yorkshire, England; Sorbonne University, Paris, France. Publications: In Ruins, 1980, 1981, 1997; The Haunted Realm, 1986, 1987, 1996, 1998; Visions of Poe, 1988, 1993; Phantoms of the Isles, 1990, 1991; The Journal of a Ghost Hunter, 1994, 1995, 1996; Beyond the Wall: The Lost World of East Germany, 1999. Honours: Arts Council of Great Britain Award, 1975, 1976. Membership: Arthur Machen Society. Literary Agent: Giles Gordon, Curtis Brown Ltd, England. Address: The Presbytery, Hainton, Market Rasen, Lincolnshire LN8 6LR, England.

MARSHAL Nell. See: TAZE Nell.

MARSHALL Jack, b. 25 Feb 1937, New York, New York, USA. Writer; Poet. Education: Brooklyn Public Schools. Publications: The Darkest Continent, 1967; Bearings, 1970; Floats, 1972; Bits of Thirst, 1974; Bits of Thirst and Other Poems and Translations, 1976; Arriving on the Playing Fields of Paradise, 1983; Arabian Nights, 1986; Sesame, 1993. Address: 1056 Treat Avenue, San Francisco, CA 94110, USA.

MARSHALL James Vance. See: PAYNE Donald Gordon.

MARSHALL Owen. See: JONES Owen Marshall.

MARSHALL Paule, b. 9 Apr 1929, Brooklyn, New York, USA. Writer. m. (1) Kenneth E Marshall, 1957, div 1963, 1 son, (2) Nourry Menard, 1970. Education: BA in

English Literature, Brooklyn College, 1953. Appointment: Staff, Our World magazine, 1953-56. Publications: Brown Girl, Brownstones, 1959; Soul Clap Hands and Sing, 1962; The Chosen Place, The Timeless People, 1969; Praisesong for the Widows, 1983; Reena and Other Stories, 1983; Daughters, 1991. Contributions to: Anthologies and periodicals. Honours: Guggenheim Fellowship, 1961; John D and Catharine T MacArthur Foundation Fellowship, 1992. Membership: Phi Beta Kappa. Address: 407 Central Park West, New York, NY 10025, USA.

MARSHALL Rosalind Kay, b. Dysart, Scotland. Historian. Education: MA, Dip Ed, PhD, University of Edinburgh. Appointment: Assistant Keeper, Scottish National Portrait Gallery, 1973-99. Publications: The Days of Duchess Anne, 1973; Mary of Guise, 1977; Virgins and Viragos: A History of Women in Scotland, 1983; Queen of Scots, 1986; Bonnie Prince Charlie, 1988; Henrietta Maria, 1990; Elizabeth I, 1992; Mary I, 1993; The Winter Queen, 1998. Contributions to: Various publications on social history. Honours: Hume Brown Senior Prize for PhD Thesis, 1970; Jeremiah Dalziel Prize, 1970; Scottish Arts Council New Writing Award, 1973; R B K Stevenson Prize, 1998. Memberships: Royal Society of Literature, fellow; Scottish Record Society 1993-, council member; Scots Ancestry Research Society, council member, 1993-; Royal Society of Arts, fellow; Society of Antiquaries of Scotland, fellow. Address: Scottish National Portrait Gallery, Scotland.

MARSTEN Richard. See: LOMBINO Salvatore A.

MARTER Joan M, b. 13 Aug 1946, Philadelphia, Pennsylvania, USA. Professor of Art History; Writer. m. Walter Marter, Nov 1967, 1 daughter. Education: BA, magna cum laude, Temple University, Philadelphia, 1968; MA, 1970, PhD, 1974, University of Delaware. Appointments: Instructor, Pennsylvania State University, 1970-73, Temple University, 1974; Assistant Professor, Sweet Briar College, 1974-77; Assistant Professor, 1977-80, Associate Professor, 1980-89, Professor of Art History, 1990-, Rutgers, the State University of New Jersey at New Brunswick. Publications: Vanguard American Sculpture 1913-1939 (with Roberta K Tarbell and Jeffrey Wechsler), 1979; Jose de Rivera, 1980; Alexander Calder, 1991, revised edition, 1997; Theodore Roszak: The Drawings, 1992; Off Limits: Rutgers and the Avant-Garde, 1998; American Sculpture: The Collection of the Metropolitan Museum of Art (co-author), 1999; Off Limits: Rutgers University and the Avant-Garde, 1999. Contributions to: Scholarly books and journals. Honours: Chester Dale Fellowship, National Gallery of Art, Washington, DC, 1973-74; Charles F Montgomery Prize, Decorative Arts Society of the Society of Architectural Historians, 1984; George Wittenborn Award Art Libraries Society of North America, 1985; John Sloan Memorial Foundation Grant, 1989-90; National Endowment for the Arts Grant, 1992; Diamond Achievement Award in the Humanities, Temple University, 1993; Betty Parsons Foundation Grant, 1997; Judith Rothschild Foundation Grants, 1997, 1998; Jane and Morgan Whitney Senior Fellowship, Metropolitan Museum of Art, New York City, 1997-98. Memberships: American Association of Museums; College Art Association of America; International Association of Art Critics, executive board 1987-89; Women's Caucus for Art, national advisory board, 1984-87. Address: Department of Art History, Voorhees Hall, 71 Hamilton Street, Rutgers University, New Brunswick, NJ 08901, USA.

MARTI René, b. 7 Nov 1926, Frauenfeld, Switzerland. Education: Diplomas in French and English; Further Education in Zurich. Publications: Das unquslöschliche Licht, 1954; Dom des Herzens, 1967; Die füng Unbekannten, 1970; Der unsichtbare Kreis, 1975; Weg an Weg (poetry), 1979; Besuche dich in der Natur, 1983; Stationen, 1986; Gedichte zum Verschenken (with Lili Keller), 1984; Die verbrannten Schreie (poetry), 1989; Gib allem ein bisschen Zeit, 1993; Rückblicke, 1996. Contributions to: Periodicals, reviews, journals, quarterlies, magazines and newspapers. Address: Haldenstr 5, Haus am Herterberg, 8500 Fruenfeld,

Switzerland.

MARTIN Alexander George, b. 8 Nov 1953, Baltimore, Maryland, USA. Writer. m. 28 July 1979, 2 sons. Education: MA, English, University of Cambridge, 1975; Diploma, Theatre, University College, Cardiff, 1976. Publications: Boris the Tomato, 1984; Snow on the Stinker, 1988; The General Interruptor, 1989; Modern Poetry, 1990; Modern Short Stories, 1991. Honour: Betty Trask Award, 1988. Membership: Society of Authors. Address: c/o David Higham Associates, 5-8 Lower John Street, London W1R 4HA, England.

MARTIN Barry John, b. 20 Feb 1943, Amersham, Buckinghamshire, England. Artist; Writer; Lecturer; Inventor. m. Sarah Gillespie, 18 Nov 1977, 1 daughter. Education: NDD and Post-Diploma, Goldsmiths College, University of London; Post-Diploma, St Martin's School of Art, London. Appointments: Lecturer, Goldsmiths College, University of London, 1967-78; Lecturer, Croydon College of Art, 1972-85; Has lectured in many colleges including The Royal College of Art, London, The Royal Academy Schools, London, The Slade School of Fine Art, London; Recent lectures and symposium papers including Art and Chess, 1991, 1993, Mondrian Revealed, 1997, The Tate Gallery, London. Publications: Queen's Silver Jubilee of British Sculpture, 1977; Composition with Red - A Perceptual Study, 1984; Light and Movement, Painting and Sculpture 1960-1974, 1985; Chess for Absolute Beginners (with Keene), 1994; Chapters on Chiswick House, in Lord Burlington: The Man and his Politics, 1998; Inventor, Moving Light, 1960s, patented, 1969, prototype in Science Museum, London. Contributions to: Studio International; Art Monthly; Arts Review; One; Chess Monthly. Memberships: International Association of Art Critics; Royal Society of British Sculptors. Address: 98 Cole Park Road, Twickenham TW1 1JA, England.

MARTIN David (Alfred), b. 30 June 1929, London, England. Professor of Sociology Emeritus; Priest; International Fellow; Writer. m. (1) Daphne Sylvia Treherne, 1953, 1 son, (2) Bernice Thompson, 30 June 1962, 2 sons, 1 daughter. Education: DipEd, Westminster College, 1952; External BSc, 1st Class Honours, 1959, PhD, 1964, University of London; Postgraduate Scholar, London School of Economics and Political Science, 1959-61. Appointments: Assistant Lecturer, Sheffield University, 1961-62; Lecturer, 1962-67, Reader, 1967-71, Professor of Sociology, 1971-89, Professor Emeritus, 1989-, London School of Economics and Political Science; Ordained Deacon, 1983, Priest, 1984; Scurlock Professor of Human Values, Southern Methodist University, Dallas, 1986-90; Senior Professorial Fellow, later International Fellow, Institute for the Study of Economic Culture, Boston University, 1990-; Various visiting lectureships. Publications: Pacifism, 1965; A Sociology of English Religion, 1967; The Religious and the Secular, 1969; Tracts Against the Times, 1973; A General Theory of Secularisation, 1978; Dilemmas of Contemporary Religion, 1978; Crisis for Cranmer and King James (editor), 1978; The Breaking of the Image, 1980; Theology and Sociology (co-editor), 1980; No Alternative (co-editor), 1981; Unholy Warfare (co-editor), 1983; Divinity in a Grain of Bread, 1989; Tongues of Fire, 1990; The Forbidden Revolution, 1996; Reflections on Sociology and Theology, 1997; Does Christianity Cause Wars?, 1997. Contributions to: Journals. Honours: Honorary Assistant Priest, Guildford Cathedral, 1983-; Honorary Professor, Lancaster University, 1993-. Membership: International Conference of the Sociology of Religion, president, 1975-83. Address: Cripplegate Cottage, 174 St John's Road, Woking, Surrey GU21 1PQ, England.

MARTIN F(rancis) X(avier), b. 2 Oct 1922, County Kerry, Ireland. Professor of Medieval History; Writer. Education: LPh, Augustinian College, Dublin, 1944; BA, 1949, MA, 1952, University College, Dublin; National University of Ireland; BD, Ponfifical Gregorian University, Rome, 1951; PhD, Peterhouse College, Cambridge, 1959. Appointments: Assistant Lecturer, 1959-62, Professor of Medieval History, 1962-87, University College, National University of Ireland, Dublin; Chairman, Council of Trustees, National Library of Ireland, 1977-. Publications: The Problem of Giles of Viterbo 1469-1532, 1960; Medieval Studies Presented to Aubrey Gwynn (editor with J A Wyatt and J B Morrall), 1961; Friar Nugent: A Study of Francis Lavalin Nugent 1569-1635, 1962; The Irish Volunteers 1913-15 (editor), 1963; The Howth Gun-Running 1914: Recollections and Documents (editor), 1966; The Course of Irish History (editor with T W Moody), 1967, 2nd edition, 1984; Leaders and Men of the Easter Rising, Dublin 1916 (editor), 1967; The Easter Rising, Myth, Fact and Mystery, 1967; The Scholar Revolutionary: Eoin MacNeil 1867-1945 and the Making of the New Ireland (editor with F J Byrne), 1973; A New History of Ireland (editor with T W Moody and J F Byrne), Vols: III, 1974, VIII, 1982, IX, 1984, IV, 1986, II, 1987, V 1989; No Hero in the House: The Coming of the Normans to Ireland, 1977; The Conquest of Ireland by Giraldus Cambrensis (editor with A B Scott), 1978; Lambert Simnel: The Crowning of a King at Dublin, 24th May 1487, 1988; The Irish Augustinians in Rome: With Foreign Missions in 5 Continents - Europe (England and Scotland), India, Australia, North America, Africa (Nigeria and Kenya) 1656-1994 (editor with Clare O'Reilly), 1994. Address: Augustinian House of Studies, Taylor's Lane, Ballyboden, Dublin 16, Ireland.

MARTIN Gerald Michael, b. 22 Feb 1944, Writer; Translator; Professor of Literature. m. Gail Shannon, 21 Aug 1965, 2 daughters. Education: BA, Spanish, University of Bristol, 1965; PhD, University of Edinburgh, 1970; Visiting Scholar, Stanford University, 1971. Appointments: Teacher, Cochabamba, Bolivia, 1965-66; Lecturer, 1969, Professor, 1984, University of Portsmouth, England; Andrew Mellon Professor of Modern Languages, University of Pittsburgh, USA, 1992-. Publications: M A Asturias' Men of Maize, translation, 1975, in critical edition, 1981; Journeys through the Labyrinth: Latin American Fiction in the 20th Century, 1989. Contributions to: Articles and reviews in The Guardian and The New Statesman, 1988-. Honour: Order of Miguel Angel Asturias, Guatemala, 1996. Address: Woodside, 2 Mill Lane, Sheet, Petersfield, Hampshire GU32 3AJ, England.

MARTIN Sir Laurence (Woodward), b. 30 July 1928, Saint Austell, England. Emeritus Professor; Research Associate; Writer. m. Betty Parnall, 19 Aug 1951, 1 son, 1 daughter. Education: BA, History, 1948, MA, 1952, Christ's College, Cambridge; MA, International Politics, 1951, PhD, Distinction, 1955, Yale University. Appointments: Instructor, Yale University, 1955-56; Assistant Professor, Massachusetts Institute of Technology, 1956-61; Associate Professor, Johns Hopkins University 1961-64; Wilson Professor of International Politics, 1964-68, Visiting Professor, 1985-, University of Wales; Research Associate, Washington Center of Foreign Policy Research, 1964-76, 1979-; Professor of War Studies, 1968-77, Fellow, 1983-, King's College, University of London; Vice Chancellor, 1978-90, Emeritus Professor, 1991, University of Newcastle-upon-Tyne; Director, Royal Institute of International Affairs, 1991-96; Burhe Chair in Strategy, Center for Strategic and International Studies, Washington, DC, 1998-. Publications: The Anglo-American Tradition in Foreign Affairs (with Arnold Wolfers), 1956; Peace without Victory, 1958; Neutralism and Non-Alignment, 1962; The Sea in Modern Strategy, 1967; America in World Affairs (co-authors), 1970; Arms and Strategy, 1973; Retreat from Empire? (co-author), 1973; Strategic Thought in the Nuclear Age (co-author), 1979; The Two-Edged Sword, 1982; Before the Day After, 1985; The Changing Face of Nuclear Warfare, 1987; British Foreign Policy (co-author), 1997. Honours: Honorary DCL, University of Newcastle-upon-Tyne, 1991; Knighted, 1994. Memberships: Center of International and Strategic Studies; Royal Institute of International Affairs. Address: CSIS, 1800 K St NW, Washington, DC 20007, USA.

MARTIN Mircea Aurelian, b. 12 Apr 1940, Resita, Romania. Literary Critic; Educator. m. Angela Teodorescu, 1 son, 1 daughter. Education: BA, 1961, MA, 1962, PhD, 1980, Faculty of Letters, University of Bucharest, Romania. Appointments: Assistant Professor, 1962-67, Associate Professor, 1967-90, Professor, 1990-, Division of Literary Theory & Comparative Literature, Faculty of Letters, University of Bucharest; Chair of the Division, 1990-, Director, 1990-, Univeristy Publishing House, Bucharest. Publications: The Sole Criticism, 1986; Introduction to Benjamin Fundoianu's Work, 1984; G Calinescu and the Complexes of Romanian Literature, 1981; The Diction of Ideas, 1977; Identifications, 1977; Criticism and Profoundity, 1974; Generation and Creation, 1969. Contributions to: Over 500 articles in Romanian literary journals and magazines including: Romania Literara, Contemporanul, Euresia. Honours: Romanian Writers' Union Prize, 1969, 1974, 1981. Membership: Board of Directors, Romanian Writers' Union, 1990-95. Address: University Publishing House, 1 Piata Presei Libere, 79739, Bucharest, Romania.

MARTIN Philip (John Talbot), b. 28 Mar 1931, Melbourne, Victoria, Australia. Retired Senior Lecturer; Poet. Education: BA, University of Melbourne, 1958. Appointments: Tutor to Senior Tutor in English, University of Melbourne, 1960-62; Lecturer in English, Australian National University, 1963; Lecturer to Senior Lecturer, Monash University, 1964-88. Publications: Poetry: Voice Unaccompanied, 1970; A Bone Flute, 1974; From Sweden, 1979; A Flag for the Wind, 1982; New and Selected Poems, 1988. Other: Shakespeare's Sonnets: Self Love and Art (criticism), 1972; Lars Gustafsson: The Stillness of the World Before Bach (translator), 1988. Contributions to: 7 anthologies, 1986-98; Age; Australian; Carleton Miscellany; Helix; Meanjin; New Hungarian Quarterly; Poetry USA; Quadrant; Southerly; Times Literary Supplement. Address: 25/9 Nicholson Street, Balmain 2041, New South Wales, Australia.

MARTIN Ralph G(uy), b. 4 Mar 1920, Chicgo, Illinois, USA. Writer. m. Marjorie Jean Pastel, 17 June 1944, 1 son, 2 daughters. Education: BJ, University of Missouri, 1941. Appointments: Managing Editor, Box Elder News Journal, Brigham, Utah, 1941; Associate Editor, The New Republic, New York City, 1945-48, Newsweek magazine, New York City, 1953-55; Executive Editor, House Beautiful, New York City, 1955-57. Publications: Boy from Nebraska, 1946; The Best is None too Good, 1948; Eleanor Roosevelt: Her Life in Pictures (with Richard Harrity), 1958; The Human Side of FDR (with Richard Harrity), 1959; Front Runner, Dark Horse (with Ed Plaut), 1960; Money, Money, Money (with Morton Stone), 1961; Man of Destiny: Charles de Gaulle (with Richard Harrity), 1962; World War II: From D-Day to VE-Day (with Richard Harrity), 1962; The Three Lives of Helen Keller (with Richard Harrity), 1962; Ballots and Bandwagons, 1964; The Bosses, 1964; President from Missouri, 1964; Skin Deep, 1964; World War II: Pearl Harbor to VJ-Day, 1965; Wizard of Wall Street, 1965; The GI War: 1941-1945, 1967; A Man for All People: Hubert H Humphrey, 1968; Jennie: The Life of Lady Randolph Churchill, 2 volumes, 1969, 1971; Lincoln Center for the Performing Arts, 1971; The Woman He Loved: The Story of the Duke and Duchess of Windsor, 1973; Cissy: The Life of Elenor Medill Patterson, 1979; A Hero of Our Time: An Intimate Study of the Kennedy Years, 1983; Charles and Diana, 1985; Golda: Golda Meir, the Romantic Years, 1988; Henry and Clare: An Intimate Portrait of the Luces, 1991; Seeds of Destruction: Joe Kennedy and His Sons, 1995. Contributions to: Books and periodicals. Memberships: Authors Guild; Century Association; Dramatists Guild; Overseas Press Club. Address: 235 Harbor Road, Westport, CT 06880, USA.

MARTIN Reginald, b. 15 May 1956, Memphis, Tennessee, USA. Editor; Director of Professional Writing Programmes; Writer. Apppointments: Feature Editor, Reporter, News, Boston, Massachusetts, 1974-77; Instructor in English, Memphis State University, 1979-80; Research Fellow, Tulsa Center for the Study of Women's Literature, 1980-81; Editor, Continental Heritage Press, 1981; Instructor in English, Tulsa Junior College; Assistant Instructor in English, University of Tulsa, 1982-83; Assistant Professor, 1983-87, Associate Professor of Composition, 1988-, Memphis State University; Visiting Lecturer, Mary Washington College,

1984; Lecturer in Literary Criticism, University of Wisconsin, Eau Claire, 1988; Director of Professional Writing Programmes, 1987-. Publications: Ntozake Shange's First Novel: In the Beginning Was the Word, 1984; Ishmael Reed and the New Black Aesthetic Critics, 1988; An Annotated Bibliography of New Black Aesthetic Criticism, 1992. Contributions to: Stories, poems, articles and reviews to various anthologies and periodicals. Honours: Winner, Mark Allen Everell Poetry Contest, 1981; Winner in Fiction, 1982, Winner in Poetry, 1983, Friends of the Library Contest; Award in Service for Education, Alpha Kappa, 1984; Award for Best Novel, Deep South Writers Competition, 1987; Award for Best Critical Article, South Atlantic Modern Language Association, 1987; Award for Best Critical Article, College English Association, 1988. Memberships: Numerous professional associations. Address: PO Box 111306, Memphis, TN 38111, USA.

MARTIN Rhona (Madeline), b. 3 June 1922, London, England. Writer; Artist. m. (1) Peter Wilfrid Alcock, 9 May 1941, div, 2 daughters, (2) Thomas Edward Neighbour. Appointment: Part-time Tutor, Creative Writing, University of Sussex, 1986-91. Publications: Gallows Wedding, 1978; Mango Walk, 1981; The Unicorn Summer, 1984; Goodbye Sally, 1987; Writing Historical Fiction, 1988. Contributions to: London Evening News; South East Arts Review; Cosmopolitan; Prima. Honour: Georgette Heyer Historical Novel Award, 1978. Memberships: Romantic Novelists Association; Society of Authors; PEN; Friends of the Arvon Foundation; Society of Limners. Address: 25 Henwood Crescent, Pembury, Kent TN2 4LJ, England.

MARTIN Robert Bernard, (Robert Bernard), b. 11 Sept 1918, La Harpe, Illinois, USA. Writer. Education: AB, University of Iowa, 1943; AM, Harvard University, 1947; BLitt, Oxford University, 1950. Appointments: Professor of English, Princeton University, 1950-75; Emeritus Professor, 1975; Citizens Professor of English, 1980-81, 1984-88, Emeritus Citizens Professor, 1988-, University of Hawaii. Publications: The Dust of Combat: A Life of Charles Kingsley, 1959; Enter Rumour: Four Early Victorian Scandals, 1962; The Accents of Persuasion: Charlotte Brontë's Novels, 1966; The Triumph of Wit: Victorian Comic Theory, 1974; Tennyson: The Unquiet Heart, 1980; With Friends Possessed: A Life of Edward FitzGerald, 1985; Gerard Manley Hopkins: A Very Private Life, 1991; 3 other critical books and 4 novels. Contributions to: Numerous magazines and journals. Honours: Guggenheim Fellowships, 1971-72, 1983-84; Senior Fellow, National Endowment for the Humanities, 1976-77; Fellow, Rockefeller Research Center, 1979; Duff Cooper Award, 1981; James Tait Black Award, 1981; Christian Gauss Award, 1981; DLitt, Oxford University, 1987; Fellow, National Humanities Center, 1988-89. Memberships: Royal Society of Literature, fellow; Tennyson Society, honorary vice-president. Address: Apt 901, Capitol Centre, 344 West Dayton St, Madison, WI 53703, USA.

MARTIN Ronald. See: DELIUS Anthony.

MARTIN (Roy) Peter, (James Melville), b. 5 Jan 1931, London, England. Author. 2 sons. Education: BA, Philosophy, 1953, MA, 1956, Birkbeck College, London University; Tübingen University, Germany, 1958-59. Appointments: Crime Fiction Reviewer, Hampstead and Highgate Express, 1983-; Occasional Reviewer, Times Literary Supplement. Publications: The Superintendent Otani mysteries, 13 in all; The Imperial Way, 1986; A Tarnished Phoenix, 1990; The Chrysanthemum Throne, 1997. Honour: Member of the Order of the British Empire, 1970. Memberships: Crime Writers Association; Mystery Writers of America; Detection Club. Address: c/o Curtis Brown, Haymarket House, London SW1Y 4SP, England.

MARTIN Ruth. See: RAYNER Claire Berenice.

MARTIN Victoria Carolyn, b. 22 May 1945, Windsor, Berkshire, England. Writer. m. Tom Storey, 28 July 1969, 4 daughters. Education: Winkfield Place, Berks, 1961-62; Byam Shaw School of Art, 1963-66. Publications: September Song, 1970; Windmill Years, 1975; Seeds of the Sun, 1980; Opposite House, 1984; Tigers of the Night, 1985; Obey the Moon, 1987. Contributions to: Woman; Woman's Own; Woman's Realm; Woman's Journal; Good Housekeeping; Woman's Weekly; Redbook; Honey, 1967-87. Address: Newells Farm House, Lower Beeding, Horsham, Sussex RH13 6LN, England.

MARTIN-JENKINS Christopher Dennis Alexander, b. 20 Jan 1945, England. Editor; Correspondent; Writer. m. Judith Oswald Hayman, 1971, 2 sons, 1 daughter. Education: BA, Modern History, MA, Fitzwilliam College, Cambridge. Appointments: Deputy Editor, 1967-70, Editor, 1981-87, Editorial Director, 1988-, The Cricketer; Sports Broadcaster, 1970-72, Cricket Correspondent, 1973-80, 1984-90, BBC; Cricket Correspondent, Daily Telegraph, 1991-. Publications: Testing Time, 1974; Assault on the Ashes, 1975; MCC in India, 1977; The Jubilee Tests and the Packer Revolution, 1977; In Defence of the Ashes, 1979; Cricket Contest, 1980; The Complete Who's Who of Test Cricketers, 1980; The Wisden Book of County Cricket, 1981; Bedside Cricket, 1981; Sketches of a Season, 1981, 1989; Twenty Years On: Cricket's Years of Change, 1984; Cricket: A Way of Life, 1984; Cricketer Book of Cricket Eccentrics (editor), 1985; Seasons Past (editor), 1986; Quick Singles (co-editor), 1986; Grand Slam, 1987; Cricket Characters, 1987; Ball by Ball, 1990; The Spirit of Cricket, 1994; World Cricketers, 1996. Address: Daily Telegraph, Canada Square, Canary Wharf, London E14 9DT, England.

MARTINET Gilles, b. 8 Aug 1916, Paris, France. Retired Journalist, Politician and Diplomat; Writer. m. Iole Buozzi, 1938, 2 daughters. Appointments: Editor in Chief, Agence France Presse, 1944-49, Observateur, 1950-61; Director, Observateur, 1960-64; Board of Directors, Nouvel Observateur, 1964-87, Matin, 1973-81; Member, European Parliament, 1979-81; Ambassador to Italy, 1981-85; Ambassadeur de France (dignity), 1984. Publications: Le Marxisme de notre temps, 1961; La conquete des pouvoirs, 1968; Les cinq communismes, 1971; Le systeme Pompidou, 1973; L'avenir depuis vingt ans, 1975; Les sept syndicalismes, 1977; Cassandre et les tueurs, 1986; Les Italiens, 1990; Le reveil du nationalisme français, 1994; Une certaine idée de la gauche, 1997. Address: 12 rue Las Cases, 75007 Paris, France.

MARTINUS Eivor Ruth, b. 30 Apr 1943, Göteborg, Sweden. Writer; Translator. m. Derek Martinus, 27 Apr 1963, 2 daughters. Education: Double Honours Degree, English and Swedish Literature, Universities of Lund and Göteborg, 1981. Publications: 5 novels in Swedish; Strindberg translations: Thunder in the Air, 1989; The Great Highway, 1990; Chamber Plays, 1991; Strindberg and Women (biography), 1999; The Father; Lady Julie; Playing with Fire. Contributions to: Swedish Book Review; Swedish Books; Scandinavica. Honours: Literary Prizes, Swedish Society of Authors, Swedish Academy. Memberships: Society of Authors; Swedish Writers Union; Swedish Playwrights Union; Swedish English Translators Association. Literary Agent: Tony Peake, Peake Associates, 14 Grafton Crescent, London NW1 8SL, England. Address: 16 Grantham Road, London W4 2RS, England.

MARTONE Michael, b. 22 Aug 1955, Fort Wayne, Indiana, USA. Professor; Writer; Poet. m. Theresa Pappas, 3 Apr 1984. Education: Butler University, Indianapolis, 1973-76; AB, English, Indiana University, 1977; MA, Fiction Writing, Johns Hopkins University, 1979. Appointments: Assistant Professor, 1980-83, Associate Professor, 1983-87, Iowa State University; Editor, Poet and Critic magazine, 1981-86; Contributing Editor, North American Review, 1984-; Briggs-Copeland Lecturer on Fiction, 1987-89, Briggs-Copeland Assistant Professor on Fiction, 1989-91, Harvard University; Associate Professor of English, 1991-96, Director, Program for Creative Writing, 1998-, University of Alabama. Publications: Fiction: Alive and Dead in Indiana, 1984; Safety Patrol, 1988; Fort Wayne is Seventh on Hitler's List, 1990, revised edition, 1992; Pensees: The Thoughts of Dan Quayle, 1994; Seeing Eye, 1995. Prose Poems: At a Loss, 1977; Return to Powers, 1985. Editor: A Place of Sense: Essays in Search of the Midwest, 1988; Townships: Pieces of the Midwest, 1992. Contributions to: Various books and journals. Honours: National Endowment for the Arts Fellowships, 1983, 1988; Margaret Jones Fiction Prize, Black Ice magazine, 1987; Ingram Merrill Foundation Award, 1989; Pushcart Prize, 1990; 2nd Place, Thin Air Fiction Contest, 1998; Honorable Mention, 32 Pages Chapbook Contest, 1998; Associated Writing Programs Award for Non-Fiction, 1998. Memberships: Associated Writing Programs; National Writers Union; PEN. Address: PO Box 21179, Tuscaloosa, AL 35402, USA.

MARTUZA Eva, b. 15 Dec 1954, Rezekne, Latvia. Novelist. m. Peteris Martuzs, 20 June 1975, 2 sons, 1 daughter. Education: Latvian University, 1978; Moscow Literature Institute, 1989. Appointments: Project Manager, ISC; Culture Department Manager, Newsppr Neatkariga CTNA, 1973-94; Editor Latvian TV, 1978-98. Publications: Acis (Eyes), 1978; No Mana Kodiena Nemirst, 1993; Tendite, 1993; Vina (She), 1995; Sniegs Apsedz Valeju Bruci, 1996; Neatsaki Vtrietim, novel, 1996. Contributions to: Karogs, magazine, 1976-90. Memberships: Latvian Union of Writers, 1988. Address: Zemes 8-24, Riga, LV1082, Latvia.

MARTUZEVA Bronislava, b. 8 Apr 1924, Latvia. Poet. Education: Rezekne Teacher Training college, 1944. Publications: Poetry: White Flower in the Lake, 1981; The Embroiderer of Nations Fate, 1987; Roads Crosses, 1990; Drop of the Light, 1994; Waybread Ears Are in Blossom, 1996. Honours: Three Stars Order, 1994. Membership: Writers Union of Latvia. Address: Darzini, Lubana P.K. 118, Madonas Raj, LV 4830, Latvia.

MARTY Martin E(mil), b. 5 Feb 1928, West Point, Nebraska, USA. Professor; Writer on Religion; Editor. m. (1) Elsa Schumacher, 21 June 1952, dec, 4 sons, (2) Harriet Lindeman, 23 Aug 1982. Education: Concordia University; Concordia Seminary; AB, 1949, MDiv, 1952, Concordia Seminary; STM, Lutheran School of Theology, Chicago, 1954; PhD, University of Chicago, 1956. Appointments: Ordained Lutheran Minister; Minister, 1950-63; Senior Editor, Christian Century magazine, 1956-98; Faculty, 1963-98, Associate Dean, Divinity School, 1970-75, University of Chicago; Founding President and George B Caldwell Senior Scholar-in-Residence, Park Ridge Center for the Study of Health, Faith and Ethics; Fairfax M Cone Distinguished Service Professor, 1978-98, University of Chicago; Director, The Public Religion Project, 1996-. Publications: A Short History of Christianity, 1959, 2nd edition, revised, 1987; The New Shape of American Religion, 1959; The Improper Opinion, 1961; The Infidel: Freethought and American Religion, 1961; Baptism, 1962; The Hidden Discipline, 1963; Second Chance for American Protestants, 1963; The Outbursts That Await Us (co-author), 1963; The Religious Press in America (co-author), 1963; Pen-Ultimates (co-author), 1963; Babylon by Choice, 1964; Church Unity and Church Mission, 1964; Varieties of Unbelief, 1964; Youth Considers "Do-It-Yourself" Religion, 1965; What Do We Believe?: The Stance of Religion in America (with Stuart E Rosenberg and Andrew Greeley), 1968; The Search for a Usable Future, 1969; The Modern Schism: Three Paths to the Secular, 1969; Righteous Empire: The Protestant Experience in America, 1970, 2nd edition, revised, as Protestantism in the United States, 1986; Protestantism, 1972; The Fire We Can Light: The Role of Religion in a Suddenly Different World, 1973; The Lutheran People, 1973; You Are Promise, 1974; What a Catholic Believes as Seen by a Non-Catholic, 1974; The Pro and Con Book of Religious America: A Bicentennial Argument, 1975; Lutheranism: A Restatement in Question and Answer Form, 1975; A Nation of Behavers, 1976; Good News in the Early Church, 1976; Religion, Awakening and Revolution, 1977; Religion in America, 1950 to the Present (with Douglas W Johnson and Jackson W Carrol), 1979; The Lord's Supper, 1980; Religious Crises in Modern America, 1980; Friendship, 1980; By Way of Response, 1981; The Public Church: Mainline,

Evangelical, Catholic, 1981; Health/Medicine and the Faith Traditions: An Inquiry into Religion and Medicine (with Kenneth L Vaux), 1982; A Cry of Absence: Reflections for the Winter of the Heart, 1983, revised edition, 1993; Health and Medicine in the Lutheran Tradition: Being Well, 1983; Faith and Ferment: An Interdisciplinary Study of Christian Beliefs and Practices (with Joan D Chittister), 1983; Being Good and Doing Good, 1984; Christian Churches in the United States, 1800-1983, 1984, 2nd edition, 1987; Christianity in the New World, 1984; Pilgrims in Their Own Land: Five Hundred Years of Religion in America, 1984; The Word: People Participating in Preaching, 1984; Modern American Religion, 3 volumes, 1986, 1990, 1996; Invitation to Discipleship, 1986; Religion and Republic: The American Circumstance, 1987; The Glory and the Power: The Fundamentalist Challenge to the Modern World (with R Scott Appleby), 1992; Places Along the Way: Meditations on the Journey of Faith (with Micah Marty), 1994; A Short History of American Catholicism, 1995; Our Hope for Years to Come (with Micah Marty), 1995; The One and the Many, 1997; A Cry of Absence: Reflections for the Winter of the Heart, 1983, new edition, 1997; The Promise of Winter: Quickening the Spirit on Ordinary Days and in Fallow Seasons (with Micah Marty), 1997; When True Simplicity is Gained: Finding Spiritual Clarity in a Complex World (with Micah Marty), 1998. Editor: New Directions in Biblical Thought, 1960; The Place of Bonhoeffer: Problems and Responsibilities of His Thought (with Peter Berger), 1962; Religion and Social Conflict (with Robert Lee), 1964; Our Faiths, 1975; Where the Spirit Leads: American Denominations Today, 1980; Pushing the Faith: Proselytism and Civility in a Pluralistic World (with Frederick E Greenspahn), 1988; The Fundamentalism Project (with R Scott Appleby), 5 volumes, 1991-95; Civil Religion, Church and State, 1992; Missions and Ecumenical Expressions, 1992; Protestantism and Regionalism, 1992; Varieties of Protestantism, 1992; The Writing of American Religious History, 1992; Protestantism and Social Christianity, 1992; New and Intense Movements, 1992; Theological Themes in the American Protestant World, 1992; Trends in American Religion and the Protestant World, 1992; Ethnic and Non-Protestant Themes, 1993; Fundamentalism and Evangelicalism, 1993; Varieties of Religious Expression, 1993; Women and Women's Issues, 1993; Native American Religion and Black Protestantism, 1993. Contributions to: Numerous publications. Honours: Brotherhood Award, 1960; National Book Award, 1971; Christopher Award, 1985; 60 honorary doctorates; Medal of the American Academy of Arts and Sciences; National Humanities Medal. Memberships: American Academy of Arts and Sciences, fellow; American Academy of Religion, president, 1987; American Catholic Historical Association, president, 1981; American Philosophical Society, elected member; American Society of Church History, president, 1971; American Antiquarian Association; Society of Historians. Address: 239 Scottswood, Riverside, IL 60546, USA.

MARTZ Louis Lohr, b. 27 Sept 1913, Berwick, Pennsylvania, USA. Professor; Writer. Education: AB, Lafayette College, 1935; PhD, Yale University, 1939. Appointments: Instructor, 1938-44, Assistant Professor, 1944-48, Associate Professor, 1948-54, Professor, 1954-57, Chairman of Department, 1956-62, Douglas Tracy Smith Professor, 1957-71, Sterling Professor, 1971-, Director, Beinecke Library, 1972-77, Yale University; Editorial Chairman, Yale Edition of the Works of Thomas More. Publications: The Later Career of Tobias Smollett, 1942; Pilgrim's Progress, 1949; The Poetry of Meditation, 1954; The Meditative Poem, 1963; The Paradise Within, 1964; The Poem of the Mind, 1966; The Wit of Love, 1969; Hero and Leander, 1972; Thomas More's Dialogue of Comfort, 1976; The Author in His Work, 1978; Poet of Exile (Milton), 1980; H D: Collected Poems 1912-1944, 1983; George Herbert and Henry Vaughan, 1986; H D: Selected Poems, 1988; Thomas More: The Search for the Inner Man, 1990; From Renaissance to Baroque Essays on Literature and Art, 1991; George Herbert, Selected Poems, 1994; D H Lawrence, Quetzalcoatl, 1995; Many Gods and Many Voices: The Role of the Prophet in English and American

Modernism, 1998. Memberships: American Academy of Arts and Sciences; British Academy of Arts and Sciences. Address: 994 Yale Station, New Haven, CT 06520, USA.

MARUTA Leszek, b. 8 Nov 1930, Torun, Poland. Journalist; Writer. Div, 1 son, 1 daughter. Education: Jagellonian University, 1949-52. Appointments: Staff, Art Director, Scenarist, Estrada Krakówska, 1962-69; Staff, later Editor, Gazeta Krakówska, 1969-71, Lektura magazine, 1991-93; Director, WOK, Culture Centre, Tarnow, 1975-77. Publications: 8 books, 1958-93. Contributions to: Numerous journals and magazines. Honours: Karuzela Literary Award, 1958; Medal of the Millennium, 1968; Polish Radio Award, 1973; Governor's Award, Tarnow, 1976; Golden Cross of Merit, 1988; Golden Badge of the City of Kraków, 1988. Memberships: Polish Journalistic Association; Polish Writers Union; Society of Authors. Address: ul Kolbertga 10/4, PL-160 Kraków, Poland.

MARVIN Blanche, b. 17 Jan 1926, New York, New York, USA. Actress; Writer; Dramatist; Critic; Publisher. m. Mark Marvin, 31 Oct 1950, 1 son, 1 daughter. Education: BA, Antioch College. Appointment: Editor and Artistic Director, Merri-Mimes; Editor, Drama Critic and publisher of London Theatre Reviews. Publications: Over 30 plays, including 15 for children. Contributions to: Periodicals. Honours: Children's Theatre Association Award; Emmy Award; Silver Hugo Award, American Video Conference Award. Memberships: British Association of Film and Television Artists; Equity; PMA; Royal Academy of Art; Screen Actors Guild; Theatre Writers Union; Writers Guild; Empty Space/Peter Brook Award, initiator; The Academy of Arts and Sciences; A.C.E. Address: 21a St John's Wood High Street, London NW8 7NG, England.

MARWICK Arthur, b. 29 Feb 1936, Edinburgh, Scotland. Professor of History; Writer. Education: MA, University of Edinburgh, 1957; BLitt, Balliol College, Oxford, 1960. Appointments: Assistant Lecturer, University of Aberdeen, 1959-60; Lecturer, University of Edinburgh, 1960-69; Visiting Professor of History, State University of New York at Buffalo, 1966-67, Rhodes College, Memphis, 1991, University of Perugia, 1991; Professor of History, 1969-, Dean of Arts, 1978-84, The Open University; Visiting Scholar, Hoover Institution, and Visiting Professor, Stanford University, 1984-85; Directeur d'études invité, L'École des hautes études en sciences sociales, Paris, 1985. Publications: The Explosion of British Society 1914-1962, 1963; Clifford Allen: The Open Conspirator, 1964; The Deluge: British Society and the First World War, 1965; Britain in the Century of Total War, Peace and Social Change 1900-1967, 1968; The Nature of History, 1970, 3rd edition, 1989; War and Social Change in the Twentieth Century, 1974; The Home Front: The British and the Second World War, 1976; Women at War 1914-1918, 1977; Class: Image and Reality in Britain, France and the USA Since 1930, 1980, 2nd edition, 1990; The Thames and Hudson Illustrated Dictionary of British History (editor), 1980; British Society Since 1945, 1982, 3rd edition, 1996; Britain in Our Century: Images and Controversies, 1984; Class in the Twentieth Century (editor), 1986; Beauty in History: Society, Politics and Personal Appearance, c1500 to the Present, 1988; The Arts, Literature and Society (editor), 1990; Culture in Britain Since 1945, 1991; The Sixties: Cultural Revolution in Britain, France, Italy and the United States 1958-74, 1998. Contributions to: Professional journals. Address: 67 Fitzjohn's Avenue, Flat 5, Hampstead, London NW3 6PE, England.

MARX Arthur, b. 21 July 1921, New York, New York, USA. Film Writer; Television Writer; Playwright; Director; Author. Education: University of Southern California, Los Angeles, 1939-40. Publications: The Ordeal of Willie Brown, 1951; Life with Groucho, biography, 1954; Not as a Crocodile (short stories), 1958; The Impossible Years (play), 1965; Minnie's Boys (play), 1970; Son of Groucho (autobiography), 1972; Everybody Loves Somebody Sometime, Especially Himself (biography), 1974; Sugar and Spice (play), 1974; My Daughter's Rated X (play),

1975; Goldwyn, 1976; Red Skelton (biography), 1979; Groucho: A Life in Revue (play), 1986; The Nine Lives of Mickey Rooney (biography), 1986; The Ghost and Mrs Muir (play), 1987; My Life with Groucho (biography), 1988; Set to Kill (mystery novel), 1993; The Secret Life of Bob Hope (biography), 1993. Contributions to: Los Angeles Magazine; Cigar Aficionado. Honour: Laurence Olivier Award Nomination, 1987. Memberships: Authors Guild; Dramatists Guild; International Association of Crime Writers; Writers Guild of America. Address: c/o Scovil, Chichak & Galen, 381 Park Avenue South, New York, NY 10016, USA.

MASATSUGU Mitsuyuki, b. 25 Jan 1924, Taiwan. Writer. m. Kiyoko Takeda, 3 Nov 1951, 1 son, 1 daughter. Education: BS, Osaka University of Foreign Studies, Japan, 1945; Course in Industrial Management, Tokyo, 1952. Publications: How to Run a Successful Business, 1969; The Turning Point of Japanese Enterprises Overseas, 1972; The Modern Samurai Society, 1982; Zigzags to the Meiji Restoration: The Divine Puppet Dazzled the Blue-Eyed Imperialists, 1994. Contributions to: Newspapers. Address: 3-35-16 Tomioka-nishi, Kanazawa-ku, Yokohama 236, Japan.

MASCHLER Thomas Michael, b. 16 Aug 1933. Publisher. m. (1) Fay Coventry, 1970, 1 son, 2 daughters, (2) Regina Kulinicz , 1987. Appointments: Production Assistant, André Deutsch, 1955-56; Editor, MacGibbon and Kee, 1956-58; Fiction Editor, Penguin Books, 1958-60; Editorial Director, 1960-70, Chairman, 1970-, Publisher, Children's Books, 1991-, Jonathan Cape; Director, Random House, 1987-. Publications: Editor: Declarations, 1957; New English Dramatists Series, 1959-63. Address: 20 Vauxhall Bridge Road, London SW1V 2SA, England.

MASINI Eleonora Barbieri, b. 19 Nov 1928, Guatemala. Sociologist. m. Francesco Maria Masini, 31 Jan 1953, 3 sons. Education: BA, 1948, Law Degree, 1952; Comparative Law Specialisation, 1953, Sociology Specialisation, 1969, Rome. Publications: Visions of Desirable Societies, 1983; Women - Households and Change (with Susan Stratigos), 1991; Why Future Studies?, 1992. Contributions to: Futures; Technological Forecasting and Social Change; Futurist. Memberships: World Futures Studies Federation; World Academy of Art and Sciences. Address: Via A Bertoloni 23, 00197 Rome, Italy.

MASLOW Jonathan Evan, b. 4 Aug 1948, Long Branch, New Jersey, USA. Writer. Education: BA, High Honours, American Literature, Marlboro College, Vermont; MS, Columbia University Graduate School of Journalism. Publications: The Owl Papers, 1983; Bird of Life, Bird of Death: A Political Ornithology of Central America, 1986; Sacred Horses: Memoirs of a Turkmen Cowboy, 1994. Other: A Tramp in the Darien, film for BBC-WGBH-TV, 1990. Contributions to: Over 200 magazine articles to Atlantic Monthly, Saturday Review, GEO. Honours: George Varsell Award, American Academy of Arts and Letters, 1988; Guggenheim Fellowship, 1989-90. Memberships: Authors Guild; National Writers Union. Address: Cutter's Way, Rd 3, Woodbine, NJ 08270, USA.

MASON Bobbie Ann, b. 1 May 1940, Mayfield, Kentucky, USA. Writer. m. Roger B Rawlings, 12 Apr 1969. Education: BA, University of Kentucky, 1962; MA, State University of New York at Binghamton, 1966; PhD, University of Connecticut, 1972. Appointment: Assistant Professor of English, Mansfield State College, Pennsylvania, 1972-79. Publications: Nabokov's Garden, 1974; The Girl Sleuth: A Feminist Guide to the Bobbsey Twins, Nancy Drew and Their Sisters, 1976, 2nd edition, 1995; Shiloh and Other Stories, 1982; In Country, 1985; Spence and Lila, 1988; Love Life, 1989; Feather Crowns, 1993; Clear Springs, 1999. Contributions to: Anthologies and magazines. Honours: Ernest Hemingway Award, 1982; National Endowment for the Arts Grant, 1983; Pennsylvania Arts Council Grants, 1983, 1989; American Academy and Institute of Arts and Letters Award, 1984; Guggenheim Fellowship, 1984; O Henry Anthology

Awards, 1986, 1988; Southern Book Award, 1993. Memberships: Authors Guild; PEN. Address: c/o Amanda Urban, International Creative Management, 40 West 57th Street, New York, NY 10019, USA.

MASON Connie, b. 22 Apr 1930, Niles, Michigan, USA. Author. m. Lewis G Mason, 1 July 1950, 1 son, 2 daughters. Publications: Tender Fury, 1984; Caress and Conquer, 1985; For Honor's Sake, 1985, 1998; Promised Splendour, 1986; My Lady Vixen, 1986; Desert Ecstasy, 1987; Wild Is My Heart, 1987; Bold Land, Bold Love, 1988, 1998; Tempt The Devil, 1988; Beyond The Horizon, 1989; Love Me With Fury, 1989, 1997; Wild Love, Wild Land, 1989, 1998; Promise Me Forever, 1990, 1998; Brave Land, Brave Love, 1990, 1998; Surrender To the Fury, 1990, 1998; The Greatest Gift Of All, novella, 1990; Ice and Rapture, 1991; A Promise Of Thunder, 1991; Lord Of The Night, 1991, 1998; Treasures Of The Heart, 1992; Christmas Star, novella, 1992; Tears Like Rain, 1993; Wind Rider, 1993; A Child Is Born, novella, 1993; Sierra, 1994; A Christmas Miracle, novella, 1994; The Lion's Bride, 1994; Taken By You, 1996; Pure Temptation, 1996; A Love To Cherish, 1996; Flame, 1997; Shadow Walker, 1997; To Love A Stranger, 1997; Sheik, 1997; Viking!, 1998; Promise Me Passion, novella, 1998; To Tame A Renegade, 1998; Pirate, 1998. Honours: Storyteller of the Year, Career, 1992; Achievement Award, Romantic Times, 1994. Membership: RWA Novelists Inc. Literary Agent: Natasha Kern. Address: PO Box 2908. Portland, OR 97208-2908, USA.

MASON David (James), b. 11 Dec 1954, Bellingham, Washington, USA. Assistant Professor; Poet; Critic; Writer; Translator. m. Anne Lennox, 16 Oct 1988, 1 stepdaughter. Education: BA, magna cum laude, English, Colorado College, 1978; MA, English, 1986, PhD, English, 1989, University of Rochester. Appointments: Visiting Instructor, 1983, 1987, Visiting Professor, 1986, 1987, 1988, 1994, Assistant Professor, 1998-, Colorado College; Instructor, University of Rochester, 1986-88; Assistant Professor, 1989-93, Associate Professor, 1993-98, Moorhead State University. Publications: Blackened Peaches, 1989; Small Elegies, 1990; The Buried Houses, 1991; Questions at Christmas, 1994; Three Characters from a Lost Home, 1995; The Country I Remember, 1996; Land Without Grief, 1996; Rebel Angeles: 25 Poets of the New Formalism (editor with Mark Jarman), 1996; Kalamitsi, 1997; The Poetry of Life and the Life of Poetry (essays), 1999. Contributions to: Books, reviews, quarterlies, and journals. Honours: Nicholas Roerich Poetry Prize, 1991; Alice Fay Di Castagnola Award, Poetry Society of America, 1993; Minnesota Professor of the Year, Carnegie Foundation for the Advancement of Teaching and Council for Advancement and Support of Education, 1994; Honorary Doctor of Humane Letters, Colorado College, 1996; Fulbright Artist-in-Residence Fellowship, Greece, 1997. Address: 1131 Paradise Valley Drive, Woodland Park, CO 80863, USA.

MASON Francis K(enneth), b. 4 Sept 1928, London, England. Editor; Writer; Archivist; Researcher. Education: Graduate, Royal Air Force College, Cranwell, 1951. Appointments: Editor, Flying Review International, 1963-64; Managing Director, Profile Publications Ltd, 1964-67, Alban Book Services Ltd, Watton, Norfolk; Managing Editor, Guiness Superlatives Ltd, Enfield, Middlesex, 1968-71. Publications: Author and/or Editor of some 90 books, 1961-96. Contributions to: Radio and television. Honours: International History Diploma, Aero Club of France, Paris, 1973; Founder Fellowship, Canadian Guild of Authors, 1988. Membership: Royal Historical Society, fellow. Address: Beechwood, Watton, Thetford, Norfolk IP15 6AB, England.

MASON Haydn Trevor, b. 12 Jan 1929, Saundersfoot, Pembrokeshire, Wales. Professor Emeritus of French; Writer. Education: BA, University College of Wales, 1949; AM, Middlebury College, Vermont, 1951; DPhil, Jesus College, Oxford, 1960. Appointments: Instructor, Princeton University, 1954-57; Lecturer, 1964-65, Reader, 1965-67, University of Reading; Professor of European Literature, University of East Anglia, 1967-79; Editor, Studies on Voltaire and the Eighteenth Century, 1977-95; Professor of French Literature, University of Paris III, 1979-81; Professor of French, 1981-94, Professor Emeritus and Senior Research Fellow, 1994-, University of Bristol; Scholar-in-Residence, University of Maryland, 1986; General Editor, Complete Works of Voltaire, 1998- President, Modern Humanities Research Association, 1999. Publications: Pierre Bayle and Voltaire, 1963; Marivaux: Les Fausses Confidences (editor), 1964; Leibniz-Arnauld Correspondence (translator and editor), 1967; Voltaire: Zadig and Other Stories (editor), 1971; Voltaire, 1974; Voltaire: A Life, 1981; French Writers and Their Society 1715-1800, 1982; Cyrano de Bergerac: L'Autre Monde, 1984; Voltaire: Discours en vers sur l'homme (editor), 1991; Candide: Optimism Demolished, 1992; Candide (editor), 1995. Honours: Officier dans l'Ordre des Palmes Académiques, 1985; Medaille d'Argent de la Ville de Paris, 1989; Prize Winner (with A Mason), Philosphical Dialogue Competition, European Humanities Research Centre, 1998. Memberships: Association of University Professors of French, chairman, 1981-82; Society for French Studies, president, 1982-84; British Society for Eighteenth-Century Studies, president, 1984-86; International Society for Eighteenth-Century Studies, president, 1991-95; Voltaire Foundation, director, 1977-97, chairman, board of directors, 1989-93. Address: c/o Department of French, University of Bristol, Bristol BS8 1TE, England.

MASON Lee W. See: **MALZBERG Barry.**

MASON Stanley (Allen), b. 16 Apr 1917, Blairmore, Alberta, Canada. Editor; Translator; Poet; Dramatist. m. Cloris Ielmini, 29 July 1944, 1 daughter. Education: MA, English Literature, Oriel College, Oxford, 1938. Appointments: Technical Translator, 1943-63; Literary Editor, Graphis Magazine, 1963-83; Editor, Elements, Dow Chemical Europe house organ, 1969-75. Publications: Modern English Structures (with Ronald Ridout), 4 volumes, 1968-72; A Necklace of Words (poems), 1975; A Reef of Honours (poems), 1983; Send Out the Dove (play), 1986; The Alps, by Albrecht von Haller (translator), 1987; The Everlasting Snow (poems), 1993; Collected Poems, 1993; A German Treasury (anthology, translator), 1993-95. Contributions to: Many publications. Honours: Borestone Mountain Poetry Award; Living Playwright Award. Address: Im Zelgli 5, 8307 Effretikon, Switzerland.

MASSIE Allan (Johnstone), b. 19 Oct 1938, Singapore. Author. m. Alison Agnes Graham Langlands, 1973, 2 sons, 1 daughter. Education: Trinity College, Glenalmond; BA, Trinity College, Cambridge. Appointments: Fiction Reviewer, The Scotsman, 1976-; Creative Writing Fellow, University of Edinburgh, 1982-84, University of Glasgow and University of Strathclyde, 1985-86; Columnist, Glasgow Herald, 1985-88, Sunday Times Scotland, 1987-, Daily Telegraph, 1991-. Publications: Novels: Change and Decay in All Around I See, 1978; The Last Peacock, 1980; The Death of Men, 1981; One Night in Winter, 1984; Augustus: The Memoirs of the Emperor, 1986; A Question of Loyalties, 1989; The Hanging Tree, 1990; Tiberius: The Memoirs of an Emperor, 1991; The Sins of the Father, 1991; These Enchanted Woods, 1993; Caesar, 1993; The Ragged Lion, 1994; King David, 1995. Other: Muriel Spark, 1979; Ill Met by Gaslight: Five Edinburgh Murders, 1980; The Caesars, 1983; Edinburgh and the Borders: In Verse (editor), 1983; A Portrait of Scottish Rugby, 1984; Eisenstadt: Aberdeen, Portrait of a City, 1984; Colette: The Woman, the Writer and the Myth, 1986; 101 Great Scots, 1987; PEN New Fiction: Thirty-Two Short Stories (editor), 1987; How Should Health Services be Financed? A Patient's View, 1988; The Novelist's View of the Market Economy, 1988; Byron's Travels, 1988; Glasgow: Portraits of a City, 1989; The Novel Today: A Critical Guide to the British Novel, 1970-1989, 1990; Edinburgh, 1994. Contributions to: Periodicals. Honours: Niven Award, 1981; Scottish Arts Council Award, 1982. Memberships: Royal Society of Literature, fellow; Scottish Arts Council. Address: Thirladean House, Selkirk TD7 5LU, Scotland.

MASSIE Robert K(inloch), b. 5 Jan 1929, Lexington, Kentucky, USA. Writer. m. (1) Suzanne L Rohrbach, 1954, div 1990, 1 son, 2 daughters, (2) Deborah L Karl, 1992, 1 son. Education: BA, Yale University, 1950; BA, Oxford University, 1952. Appointments: Reporter, Collier's magazine, New York City, 1955-56; Writer, Newsweek magazine, New York City, 1956-62; Writer, USA-1 magazine, New York City, 1962, Saturday Evening Post, New York City, 1962-65; Ferris Professor of Journalism, Princeton University, 1977, 1985; Mellon Professor in the Humanities, Tulane University, 1981. Publications: Nicholas and Alexandra, 1967; Journey, 1976; Peter the Great: His Life and World, 1980; Dreadnought: Britain, Germany and the Coming of the Great War, 1991. Contributions to: Periodicals. Honours: Christopher Award, 1976; Pulitzer Prize for Biography, 1981. Memberships: Authors Guild of America; PEN; Society of American Historians. Address: 60 West Clinton Avenue, Irvington, NY 10533, USA.

MASSON Jeffrey Moussaieff, b. 28 Mar 1941, Chicago, Illinois, USA (as Jeffrey Lloyd Masson). Writer; Editor; Translator. Appointments: Former Professor of Sanskrit; Project Director, Sigmund Freud Archives, New York City, 1980-81; Co-Director, Freud Copyrights. Publications: The Oceanic Feeling: The Origins of Religious Sentiment in Ancient India, 1980; The Assault on Truth: Freud's Suppression of the Seduction Theory, 1984; Complete Letters of Sigmund Freud to Wilhelm Fuess, 1887-1904 (editor and translator), 1985; A Dark Science: Women, Sexuality and Psychiatry in the Nineteenth Century (editor and translator), 1987; My Father's Guru: A Journey Through Spirituality and Disillusion, 1992. Contributions to: Atlantic Monthly; International Journal of Psycho-Analysis; New York Times; New York Review of Books. Address: c/o Elaine Markson Literary Agency, 44 Greenwich Avenue, New York, NY 10011, USA.

MASTERS Hilary (Thomas), b. 3 Feb 1928, Kansas City, Missouri, USA. Professor of English and Creative Writing; Author. Div, 1 son, 2 daughters. Education: AB, Brown University, 1952. Appointments: Writer-in-Residence, Drake University, 1975-77, Clark University, 1978, Ohio University, 1979, 1982, University of North Carolina at Greensboro, 1980-81, University of Denver, 1982; Fulbright Lecturer on American Literature, University of Jyvaskyla, Finland, 1983; Professor of English and Creative Writing, Carnegie Mellon University, 1983-. Publications: Novels: The Common Pasture, 1967; An American Marriage, 1969; Palace of Strangers, 1971; Clemmons, 1985; Cooper, 1987; Manuscript for Murder, 1987; Strickland, 1990; Home is the Exile, 1996. Short Stories: Hammertown Tales, 1986; Success: New and Selected Stories, 1992. Non-Fiction: Last Stands: Notes from Memory, 1982. Contributions to: Anthologies, books, reviews, quarterlies, journals, and magazines. Honours: Yaddo Fellowships, 1980, 1982; Editor's Choice, Time magazine, 1984; Los Angeles Times Notable Novel, 1990; Notable Novels of the Year, Dictionary of Literary Biography, 1995, 1997; Monroe Spears Prize, Sewanee Review, 1997; Best Essay 1998. Memberships: Associated Writing Programs; Authors Guild; PEN Center, New York. Address: c/o Department of English, Carnegie Mellon University, Pittsburgh, PA 15213, USA.

MASTERTON Graham, (Thomas Luke, Angel Smith), b. 16 Jan 1946, Edinburgh, Scotland. Writer. m. Wiescka Walach, 11 Nov 1975, 3 sons. Appointments: Deputy Editor, Mayfair magazine, London, 1967-70; Executive Editor, Penthouse magazine, London, 1970-74. Publications: Fiction: Over 30 books, including: Fireflash Five, 1976; The Sphinx, 1977; The Devils of D-Day, 1978; Rich, 1979; The Wells of Hell, 1982; Maiden Voyage, 1984; Family Portrait, US edition as Picture of Evil, 1986; Night Warriors, 1988; Lords of the Airs, 1989; Night Plague, 1990; The Burning, 1991. Non-Fiction: How to Drive Your Man Wild in Bed, 1976; 1001 Erotic Dreams Interpreted, 1977; How to Drive Your Women Wild in

Bed, 1988. Address: c/o Mandarin Books, Michelin House, 81 Fulham Road, London SW3 6RB, England.

MATAS Carol, b. 14 Nov 1949, Winnipeg, Manitoba, Canada. Writer. m. Per K Brask, 19 Feb 1977, 1 son, 1 daughter. Education: BA, English, University of Western Ontario, 1969; Graduate, Actors' Lab, London England, 1972. Publications: The D.N.A Dimension, 1982; The Fusion Factor, 1986; Zanu, 1986; Me, Myself and I, 1987; Lisa, 1987, US edition as Lisa's War, 1989; Jesper, 1989, US edition as Code Name Kris, 1990; Adventure in Legoland, 1991; The Race, 1991; Sworn Enemies, 1993; Safari Adventure in Legoland, 1993; Daniel's Story, 1993; The Lost Locket, 1994; The Burning Tree, 1994; Of Two Minds (with Perry Nodelman), 1994; The Primrose Path, 1995; After the War, 1996; More Minds (with Perry Nodelman), 1996; The Freak, 1997; The Garden, 1997; Greater Than Angels, 1998; Telling, 1998. Honours: Many awards and citations for young people's literature. Memberships: International PEN; Manitoba Writers Guild; Society of Children's Book Writers and Illustrators; Writers Guild of Canada; Writer's Union of Canada. Address: c/o Ashley Grayson Literary Agency, 1342 18th Street, San Pedro, CA 90732, USA.

MATEI Nicolae, b. 22 Nov 1960, Cluj, Romania. Publisher. m. Liana Ancuta Matei, 5 Mar 1993. Education: Higher Commercial Examination, Aarhus Commercial School, 1990. Appointments: Publisher, Eksperimental Forlag, Aarhus. Publications: Crawling to the west (Târâs spre vest), 1995; Rumanian conversation guide (Rumænsk Parlor), 1996; George Bacovia, Poems (George Bacovia, Digte), translation from Romanian to Danish, 1997; Copenhagen dream of ice (Copenhaga vis de gheata), 1998; The lost generation (Generatia pierduta), 1999. Membership: The Danish Writers Union. Address: Holmkærvej 68, 8380, Denmark.

MATHERS Peter, b. 1931, Fulham, London. Novelist. Education: Sydney Technical College. Appointments: Researcher, Theatre Adviser, University of Pittsburgh, 1968. Publications: Trap, 1970; The Wort Papers, 1972; Story, A Change for the Better, 1984. Honours: Miles Franklin Award, 1967. Address: c/o Wav Publications, 499 The Parade, Magill, South Australia 5072, Australia.

MATHESON Richard (Burton), b. 20 Feb 1926, Allendale, New Jersey, USA. Writer. Education: BA, University of Missouri, 1949. Publications: Someone is Bleeding, 1953; Fury on Sunday, 1954; I Am Legend, 1954; Born of Man and Woman, 1954; Third from the Sun, 1955; The Shrinking Man, 1956; The Shores of Space, 1957; A Stir of Echoes, 1958; Ride the Nightmare, 1959; The Beardless Warriors, 1960; Shock! I, 1961; Shock! II, 1964; Shock! III, 1966; Shock Waves, 1970; Hell House, 1971; Bid Time Return, 1975; What Dreams May Come, 1978; Shock! IV, 1980; Earthbound, 1989; Collected Stories, 1989; Journal of the Gun Years, 1991; By the Gun, 1994. Address: PO Box 81, Woodland Hills, CA 91365, USA.

MATHEWS Nieves Hayat (Nieves de Madariaga), b. 3 Dec 1917, Glasgow, Scotland. Writer; Poet; Retired International Civil Servant. m. Paul William Mathews, 23 Apr 1939, 1 son, 1 daughter. Education: BA, 1st Class Honours, Spanish, French, Kings College, University of London. Appointments: Functional Officer, The British Council, Mexico City, 1954-57; International Civil Servant, Food and Agriculture Organisation, United Nations, Rome, Italy, 1957-74. Publications: She Died without Light, detective story, 1956; Francis Bacon, the History of a Character Assassination, 1996. Contributions to: Poetry; Encounter, Botteghe Oscure, Rome; The Literary Review, Fairleigh Dickinson University; Elsinore, Rome; Essays on Patrick White and Francis Bacon, in Cambridge Review, Baconiana; Salvador de Madariaga in Cuenta y Razón, Madrid. Honour: Prize for children's story, The White Marble House and the Hungry Drain, Mexico. Address: Tecognano, 52040, Montanare di Cortona, Arezzo, Italy.

MATHIAS Roland Glyn, b. 4 Sept 1915, Talybont-on-Usk, Breconshire, Wales. Schoolmaster;

Poet; Writer. m. Mary (Molly) Hawes, 4 Apr 1944, 1 son, 2 daughters. Education: BA, Modern History, 1936, BLitt (by thesis), 1939, MA, 1944, Jesus College, Oxford. Appointments: Schoolmaster; Editor, The Anglo-Welsh Review, 1961-76; Extra-Mural Lecturer, University College, Cardiff, 1970-77; Visiting Professor, University of Alabama at Birmingham, 1971. Publications: Poetry: Break in Harvest, 1946; The Roses of Tretower, 1952; The Flooded Valley, 1960; Absalom in the Tree, 1971; Snipe's Castle, 1979; Burning Brambles, 1983; A Field at Vallorcines, 1996. Short Stories: The Eleven Men of Eppynt, 1956. Non-Fiction: Whitsun Riot, 1963; Vernon Watkins, 1974; John Cowper Powys as Poet, 1979; A Ride Through the Wood, 1985; Anglo-Welsh Literature: An Illustrated History, 1987. Contributions to: Many literary journals and periodicals. Honour: Honorary DHL, Georgetown University, Washington, DC, 1985. Membership: Welsh Arts Council, chairman, literature committee, 1976-79. Address: Deffrobani, 5 Maescelyn, Brecon, Powys LD3 7NL, Wales.

MATHIEU André, (Andrew Matthew, Andrew Matthews), b. 10 Apr 1942, Beauce, France. Novelist. m. B Perron, 20 July 1963, 1 daughter. Education: BA, Laval University. Publications: Nathalie, 1982; La Sauvage, 1985; Aurore, 1990; Donald and Marion, 1990; Arnold's Treasure, 1994; 20 Others. Address: CP 55, Victoriaville, Quebec G6P 6S4, Canada.

MATHIS EDDY Darlene, b. 19 Mar 1937, Indiana, USA. Poet; Professor; Editor. m. Spencer Livingston Eddy, 23 May 1964, dec. Education: BA, Goshen College, 1959; MA, 1961, PhD, 1967, Rutgers University. Appointments: Poetry Editor, Forum, 1985-89; Poet-in-Residence, Ball State University, 1989-93; Consulting Editor, Blue Unicorn: A Tri-Quarterly of Poetry, 1995-; Founding Editor, The Hedgerow Press, Tennessee. Publications: The Worlds of King Lear, 1968; Leaf Threads Wind Rhymes, 1985; Weathering, 1991. Contributions to: Books and journals. Honours: Woodrow Wilson National Fellow, 1959-62; Rutgers University Graduate Honours Fellowship and Dissertation Award, 1964-65, 1966; Numerous Research, Creative Arts Awards; Notable Woodrow Wilson Fellow, 1991. Memberships: Associated Writing Programs; American Association of University Professors; National Council of Teachers of English; American League of PEN Women. Address: Department of English, RB 248, Ball State University, Muncie, IN 47306, USA.

MATRAY James Irving, b. 6 Dec 1948, Chicago, Illinois, USA. Professor of History; Writer. m. Mary Karin Heine, 14 Aug 1971, 1 son, 1 daughter. Education: BA, European and American History, Lake Forest College, 1970; MA, 1973, PhD, 1977, American History, University of Virginia. Appointments: Visiting Assistant Professor, 1980-82, Assistant Professor, 1982-87, Associate Professor, 1987-92, Professor of History, 1992-, New Mexico State University; Visiting Associate Professor of History, University of Southern California, 1988-89; Distinguished Visiting Scholar, Hyung Hee University, Seoul, 1990. Publications: The Reluctant Crusade: American Foreign Policy in Korea, 1941-1950, 1985; Historical Dictionary of the Korean War, 1991; Korea and the Cold War: Division, Destruction, and Disarmament (editor with Kim Chull-Baum), 1993; Japan's Emergence as a Global Power, 1999. Contributions to: Many scholarly books and journals. Honours: Several research grants; Co-Recipient, Stuart L Bernath Article Award, Society for Historians of American Relations, 1980; Best Book Prize, Phi Alpha Theta, 1986; Best Reference Book Award, Library Journal, 1992; Outstanding Academic Book Award, Choice, 1992. Memberships: American Historical Association; Association for Asian Studies; Society for Historians of American Foreign Relations. Address: 4426 Echo Canyon Road, Las Cruces, NM 88011, USA.

MATSON Clive, b. 13 Mar 1941, Los Angeles, California, USA. Poet; Playwright; Teacher. Education: Undergraduate work, University of Chicago, 1958-59; MFA, Poetry, School of the Arts, Columbia University. Publications: Mainline to the Heart, 1966; Space Age,

1969; Heroin, 1972; On the Inside, 1982; Equal in Desire, 1983; Hourglass, 1987; Breath of Inspiration (essay), 1987; Let the Crazy Child Write, 1998. Contributions to: Anthologies and journals. Honour: Graduate Writing Fellowship, Columbia University, 1987-88. Address: 472 44th Street, Oakland, CA 94609, USA.

MATTHEW Andrew. See: MATHIEU André.

MATTHEW Christopher Charles Forrest, b. 8 May 1939, London, England. Novelist; Journalist; Broadcaster. m. Wendy Mary Matthew, 19 Oct 1979, 2 sons, 1 daughter. Education: BA, Honours, MA, Honours, St Peter's College, Oxford. Appointment: Editor, Times Travel Guide, 1972-73. Publications: A Different World; Stories of Great Hotels, 1976; Diary of a Somebody, 1978; Loosely Engaged, 1980; The Long Haired Boy, 1980; The Crisp Report, 1981; Three Men in a Boat, annotated edition, with Benny Green, 1982; The Junket Man, 1983; How to Survive Middle Age, 1983; Family Matters, 1987; The Amber Room, 1995; A Nightingale Sang in Fernhurst Road, 1998. Contributions to: Many leading newspapers; Columnist for Punch, 1983-88; Restaurant Critic for English Vogue, 1983-86; Book reviewer for Daily Mail, 1996-. Membership: Society of Authors. Literary Agent: Sheil Land Associates. Address: 43 Doughty Street, London WC1N 2LF, England.

MATTHEWS Andrew. See: MATHIEU André.

MATTHEWS Patricia Anne, (P A Brisco, Patty Brisco, Laura Wylie), b. 1 July 1927, San Fernando, California, USA. Author. m. (1) Marvin Owen Brisco, 1946, div 1961, 2 sons, (2) Clayton Hartly Matthews, 1971. Education: California State University, Los Angeles. Appointments: Secretary, Administrator, California State University, 1959-77. Publications: Merry's Treasure, 1969; The Other People, 1970; The House of Candles, 1973; Mist of Evil, 1976; Love, Forever More, 1977; Raging Rapids, 1978; Love's Daring Dream, 1978; Love's Golden Destiny, 1979; Love's Many Faces (poetry), 1979; The Night Visitor, 1979; Love's Raging Tide, 1980; Love's Sweet Agony, 1980; Love's Bold Journey, 1980; Tides of Love, 1981; Embers of Dawn, 1982; Flames of Glory, 1983; Dancer of Dreams, 1984; Gambler in Love, 1985; Tame the Restless Heart, 1986; Destruction at Dawn, 1986; Twister, 1986; Enchanted, 1987; Thursday and the Lady, 1987; Mirrors, 1988; The Dreaming Tree, 1989; Sapphire, 1989; Oasis, 1989; The Death of Love, 1990; The Unquiet, 1991. With Clayton Matthews: Midnight Whispers, 1981; Empire, 1982; Midnight Lavender, 1985; The Scent of Fear, 1992; Taste of Evil, 1993; Vision of Death, 1993; The Sound of Murder, 1994. Contributions to: Anthologies and magazines. Honours: Porgie Award, 1979, Silver Medal, 1983, Bronze Medal, 1983, West Coast Review of Books; Team Writing Award (with husband), 1983, Reviewers Choice Awards for Best Historical Gothic, 1986-87, Affaire de Coeur Silver Pen Readers Award, 1989, Romantic Times. Memberships: Romantic Writers Association; Mystery Writers of America; Sisters in Crime; Novelists Ink. Address: c/o Jay Garon, 415 Central Park West, New York, NY 10025, USA.

MATTHEWS Peter John, b. 6 Jan 1945, Fareham, Hampshire, England. Editor; Writer; Television Commentator. m. Diana Randall, 1969, 2 sons. Appointments: Director, Guinness Publishing, 1981-84, 1989-96; Sports Editor, 1982-91, Editor, 1991-95, Guinness Book of Records; Co-Editor, Athletics Internationa, 1993-; Athletics Commentator, IAAF. Publications: Guinness Book of Athletics Facts and Feats, 1982; International Athletics Annual, 1985-; Track and Field Athletics: The Records, 1986; Guinness Encyclopaedia of Sports Records and Results, 1987-95; Cricket Firsts (with Robert Brooke), 1988; Guinness International Who's Who of Sport, 1993; Whitaker's Almanac of International Sports Records and Results, 1998. Contributions to: Athletics and general sports publications. Address: 10 Madgeways Close, Great Amwell, Ware, Hertfordshire SG12 9RU, England.

MATTHEWS Victoria, b. 28 Jan 1941, Brighton, Sussex, England. Botanist; Editor. m. Brinsley Burbidge, 3 Jan 1969. Education: BSc Hons, Botany, University of Liverpool, England, 1965; Diploma in Plant Taxonomy, University of Edinburgh, England, 1966. Appointments: Research Associate, University of Edinburgh, 1966-74; Scientific Staff, Royal Botanic Garden, Edinburgh, 1974-86; Editor, The Kew Magazine and associated monographs, Royal Botanic Gardens, Kew, 1986-93; Editor, The New Plantsman, 1993-94; International Clematis Registrar, employed by Royal Horticultural Society, 1994-. Publications: Gardening on Walls, with C Grey-Wilson, 1983; Kew Gardening Guide - Lilies, 1989; Editor of Contemporary Botanical Artists by S Sherwood, 1996; Gardening with Climbers, with C Grey-Wilson, 1997. Contributions to: Flora of Turkey; Flora Europaea; European Garden Flora; Manual of Alpine Plants; RHS Encyclopedia of Plants and Flowers; New RHS Dictionary of Gardening; Many articles in Notes from RBG Edinburgh, Kew Magazine, The New Plantsman, The Clematis, Clematis International. Honour: Fellow of Linnean Society of London, 1966. Address: 7350 SW 173rd Street, Miami, FL 33157-4835, USA.

MATTHIAS John (Edward), b. 5 Sept 1941, Columbus, Ohio, USA. Professor; Poet; Writer; Translator. m. Diana Clare Jocelyn, 27 Dec 1967, 2 children. Education: BA, Ohio State University, 1963; MA, Stanford University, 1966; Postgraduate Studies, University of London, 1966-67. Appointments: Assistant Professor, 1967-73, Associate Professor, 1973-80, Professor, 1980-, University of Notre Dame; Visiting Fellow in Poetry, 1976-77, Associate, 1977-, Clare Hall, Cambridge; Visiting Professor, Skidmore College, 1978, University of Chicago, 1980. Publications: Bucyrus, 1971; 23 Modern Poets (editor), 1971; Turns, 1975; Crossing, 1979; Five American Poets (editor), 1979; Contemporary Swedish Poetry (translator with Goran Printz-Pahlson), 1979; Barthory and Lermontov, 1980; Northern Summer: New and Selected Poems, 1984; David Jones: Man and Poet, 1989; Tva Dikter, 1989; A Gathering of Ways, 1991; Reading Old Friends, 1992; Selected Works of David Jones, 1993; Swimming at Midnight: Selected Shorter Poems, 1995; Beltane at Aphelion: Collected Longer Poems, 1995. Contributions to: Numerous anthologies, reviews, quarterlies, and journals. Honours: Fulbright Grant, 1966; Swedish Institute Translation Award, 1977-78; Columbia University Translation Award, 1978; Ingram Merrill Foundation Awards, 1984, 1990; Society of Midland Authors Poetry Award, 1986; Society for the Study of Midwestern Literature Poetry Prize, 1986; Slobodan Janovic Literary Prize, 1989; George Bogin Memorial Award, Poetry Society of America, 1990; Lilly Endowment Grant, 1991-92; Ohio Library Association Poetry Award, 1996. Memberships: American Literary Translators Association; PEN American Center; Poetry Society of America. Address: c/o Department of English, University of Notre Dame, Notre Dame, IN 46556, USA.

MATTHIESSEN Peter, b. 22 May 1927, New York, New York, USA. Writer. m. (1) Patricia Southgate, 8 Feb 1951, div, 1 son, 1 daughter, (2) Deborah Love, 16 May 1963, dec Jan 1972, 1 son, 1 daughter, (3) Maria Eckhart, 28 Nov 1980. Education: Sorbonne, University of Paris, 1948-49; BA, Yale University, 1950. Appointment: Co-Founder and Editor, Paris Review, 1951-. Publications: Race Rock, 1954; Partisans, 1955; Wildlife in America, 1959; Raditzer, 1960; The Cloud Forest, 1961; Under the Mountain Wall, 1963; At Play in the Fields of the Lord, 1965; The Shorebirds of North America, 1967; Oomingmak: The Expedition to the Musk Ox Island in the Bering Sea, 1967; Sal Si Puedes, 1969; Blue Meridian, 1971; The Tree Where Man Was Born, 1972; Far Tortuga, 1975; The Snow Leopard, 1978; Sand Rivers, 1981; In the Spirit of Crazy Horse, 1983; Indian Country, 1984; Nine-Headed Dragon River, 1986; Men's Lives, 1986; On the River Styx and Other Stories, 1989; Killing Mister Watson, 1990; African Silences, 1991; Baikal, 1992; Shadows of Africa, 1992; East of Lo Monthang, 1995; Lost Man's River, 1997; Bone by Bone, 1999. Honours: Atlantic Prize, 1950; National Book Award, 1978; John Burroughs Medal, 1981; African Wildlife Leadership Foundation Award, 1982; Gold Medal for Distinction in Natural History, 1985. Membership: American Academy of Arts and Letters, 1974-; National Institute of Arts and Science, 1986-. Address: PO Box 392, Bridge Lane, Sagaponack, NY 11962, USA.

MATTINGLEY Christobel Rosemary, 26 Oct 1931, Adelaide, South Australia, Australia. Writer. m. Cecil David Mattingley, 17 Dec 1953, 2 sons, 1 daughter. Education: BA, 1st Class Honours, German, 1951; Registration Certificate and Associate of the Library Association of Australia, 1971. Publications: Numerous including: Windmill at Magpie Creek, 1971; The Great Ballagundi Damper Bake, 1975; Rummage, 1981; The Angel with a Mouth Organ, 1984; The Miracle Tree, 1985; Survival in Our Own Land: Aboriginal Experiences in South Australia since 1836, 1988; The Butcher, the Beagle and the Dog Catcher, 1990; Tucker's Mob, 1992; The Sack, 1993; No Gun for Asmir, 1993; The Race, 1995; Asmir in Vienna, 1995; Escape from Sarajevo, 1996; Ginger, 1997; Daniel's Secret, 1997; Work Wanted, 1998; Hurry up Alice, 1998. Contributions to: Australian Library Journal; New Zealand Libraries; Landfall; Reading Time; Classroom; Magpies; Something About the Author Autobiography Series. Honours: Advance Australia Award, 1990; Honorary Doctorate, University of South Australia, 1995; Member of the Order of Australia, 1996; Patron, Society of Women Writers, 1998-. Literary Agent: Hickson Associates, 128 Queen Street, Woollahra, NSW 2025, Australia. Address: 10 Rosebank Terrace, Stonyfell, South Australia 5066, Australia.

MATURA Thaddee, b. 24 Oct 1922, Zalesie Wielkie, Poland. Franciscan Monk; Theologian; Scholar. Education: LicTh, Pontificio Ateneo Antoniano, Rome, 1953; LicBiblical Studies, Studio Biblico Francescano, Jerusalem, 1955. Appointments: Entered Franciscan Order, 1940; Member, Tantur Ecumenical Institute, Jerusalem, 1973-75; Religious Counselor, all cloistered monasteries, France, 1981-90. Publications: Célibat et communauté: Les Fondements évangéliques de la vie religieuse, 1967, English translation as Celibacy and Community: The Gospel Foundation for Religous Life, 1968; La Vie religieuse au tournant, 1971, English translation as The Crisis of Religious Life, 1973; Readings in Franciscanism (editor with Dacian Francis Bluma), 1972; La Naissance d'un charisme, 1973, English translation as The Birth of a Movement, 1975; Le Projet évangélique de Francois d'Assise aujourd-hui, 1977, English translation as The Gospel Life of Francis of Assisi Today, 1980; Le Radicalisme évangélique, 1978, English translation as Gospel Radicalism, 1984; Franz von Assisi (with Anton Rotzetter), 1981; Francois d'Assise, Ecrits (with Theophile Desbonnets), 1981; Suivre Jésus, 1983; Claire d'Assise, Ecrits (with Marie-France Becker), 1985; Une absence ardente, 1988; Dieu le Père trés saint, 1990; Chants de terre étrangere, 1991; Prier 15 jours avec Francois d'Assise, 1994; Francois d'Assise "auteur spirituel," 1996, English translation as Francis of Assisi: The Message in his Writings, 1997. Address: 33 rue de la Porte-Evèque, 84000 Avignon, France.

MAULINS Janis, b. 16 June 1933, Latvia. Lawyer. m. Anna Brūvere, 24 Feb 1968, 2 sons, 2 daughters. Education: Lawyer, University of Latvia, 1959; Investigator, Head of Department, Ministry of Social Maintenance, 1960-61. Appointments: Instructor, Trade Union, 1961-62; Economist, Lawyer, Legal Adviser, 1962-72; Professional writer, 1972-95; Member of Parliament, 1994-98. Publications: Pēdas (Footsteps), 1980; Ragana (The Witch), 1981; Kājāmājējs (The Walker); Pelēkie zimejumi (The Grey Drawings), Milesubas infraskinas (The Inner Sounds of Love), 1982; Malēniesi (The Outsiders), 1983; Ezera salu vilinajurns (The Seduction of Islands in the Lake), 1988; Apakszemes straumes (Underground Streams), 1989; Tālava (Tālava), 1990; Austrumi sārtojas (The East Reddens), 1994; Garīgā pagride (The Intellectual Underground), 1994; Dēmonu spēles (Devilish Games), 1998. Memberships: Writers Association of Latvia, 1971-. Address: Brivibas gatve 398, 74, Riga, LV 1025, Latvia.

MAUMELA Titus Ntsieni, b. 25 Dec 1924, Sibasa, Venda, South Africa. Author; Dramatist. m. Rose Maumela, 27 June 1949, 2 sons, 1 daughter. Education: BA, University of South Africa, 1961. Publications: Novels: Elelwani, 1954; Mafangambiti, 1956; Vhavenda Vho-Matshivha, 1958; Vhuhosi Whu tou Bebelwa, 1962; Zwa Mulovha Zwi a Fhela, 1963; Maela wa Vho-Mathavha, 1967; Ndi Vho-Muthukhuthukhu, 1977; Vho-Rammbebo, 1981; Tshiphiri Tsho Bvela Khagala, 1986; Vhulahani, 1995; Dyambila La Manoni, 1997; Vho-Thathani Na Nwana Wavho Ramalata, 1997. Plays: Tshililo, 1957; A Hu Bebiwi Mbilu, 1975; Vhuhosi A Vhu Thetshelwi, 1975; Edzani, 1985; Tomolambilu, 1989. Essay: Maanea A Pfadzaho, 1992; Lufu Lwa Thivhulawi (drama), 1997; Dzinwe Ngano Dzavhudi (folklore), 1993; Mithetshelo (Short-story), 1981. Other: Short stories, folktalkes, and language manuals. Honour: Honorary Doctor of Philosophy in Literature, University of Venda, 1998. Address: PO Box 2, Vhufuli, Venda, South Africa.

MAUPIN Armistead, b. 13 May 1944, Washington, District of Columbia, USA. Writer. Education: BA, University of North Carolina at Chapel Hill, 1966. Appointments: Reporter, News and Courier, Charleston, 1970-71, Associated Press, 1971-72; Columnist, Pacific Sun, San Francisco, 1974, San Francisco Chronicle, 1976-77. Publications: Tales of the City, 1978; More Tales of the City, 1980; Further Tales of the City, 1982; Babycakes, 1984; Significant Others, 1987; Sure of You, 1989; Maybe the Moon, 1992. Other: Libretto for the musical Heart's Desire, 1990. Television Programme: Armistead Maupin's Tales of the City, 1993. Contributions to: Periodicals. Honours: Best Dramatic Serial Award, Royal TV Society, 1994; George Foster Peabody Award, 1994. Address: c/o International Creative Management, 40 West 57th Street, New York, NY10019, USA.

MAVOR Elizabeth (Osborne), b. 17 Dec 1927, Glasgow, Scotland. Author. Education: St Andrews, 1940-45; St Leonard's and St Anne's College, Oxford, England, 1947-50. Publications: Summer in the Greenhouse, 1959; The Temple of Flora, 1961; The Virgin Mistress: A Biography of the Duchess of Kingston (US edition as The Virgin Mistress: A Study in Survival: The Life of the Duchess of Kingston), 1964; The Redoubt, 1967; The Ladies of Llangollen: A Study in Romantic Friendship, 1971; A Green Equinox, 1973; Life with the Ladies of Llangollen, 1984; The Grand Tour of William Beckford, 1986; The White Solitaire, 1988; The American Journals of Fanny Kemble, 1990; The Grand Tours of Katherine Wilmot, France 1801-3 and Russia 1805-7, 1992; The Captain's Wife, The South American Journals of Maria Graham 1821-23, 1993. Address: Curtis Brown Ltd, 28-29 Haymarket, London SW1Y 4SP, England.

MAW. See: **WILLIAMS Michael Arnold.**

MAXWELL Doris June, b. 13 May 1922, Birmingham, Warwickshire, England. Telegraphist. m. Harry Maxwell, 18 Sept 1945, dec, 1 son. Education: RAF Cranwell College, Lincoln, 1943; Dip Merit, Lit, 1978, Cumbria College of Art; Hilton Publishers Special Commendation, 1996. Appointments: Dressmaker (cert); Furrier; GPO Telegraphist. Publication: The Travels of Nelson James Broughton, script for pantomime, 1982. Contributions to: Troubador Art Poetry Music, London; Horse and Pony; Wild Horse Back in Time, 1984; News and Views 37, 1984; History of Carlisle in the Year 2000; Lakescene Poem About Loch Ness: Small Write Up of Monster Mentioned. Honours: Diploma of Merit, 1978; Certificate of Merit, 1980; Certificate of Merit, Lyric Writing, 1982. Address: Silloth on Solway, Cumbria.

MAXWELL Glyn (Meurig), b. 7 Nov 1962, Welwyn Garden City, Hertfordshire, England. Poet; Writer; Reviewer; Editor. Education: BA, 1st Class Honours, English, Worcester College, Oxford, 1985; MA, Creative Writing, Boston University, Massachusetts, 1988. Publications: Tale of the Mayor's Son (poems), 1990; Out of the Rain (poems), 1992; Gnyss the Magnificent: Three Verse Plays, 1993; Blue Burneau (novel), 1994; Rest for the Wicked (poems), 1955. Contributions to: Reviews, journals, and magazines. Honours: Poetry Book Society

Choice, 1990, and Recommendation, 1992; Shortlisted, John Llewellyn Rhys Memorial Prize, 1991; Eric Gregory Award, 1991; Somerset Maugham Award, 1993. Memberships: PEN; Poetry Society. Address: c/o Bloodaxe Books, PO Box 1SN, Newcastle-upon-Tyne NE99 1SN, England.

MAXWELL Gordon Stirling, b. 21 Mar 1938, Edinburgh, Scotland. Archaeologist. m. Kathleen Mary King, 29 July 1961, 2 daughters. Education: MA (Hons), St Andrews. Appointments: Curatorial Officer, Royal Commission for Ancient and Historical Monuments, Scotland, 1964-. Publications: The Impact of Aerial Reconnaissance on Archaeology (editor), 1983; Rome's Northwest Frontier: The Antonine Wall, 1983; The Romans in Scotland, 1989; A Battle Lost: Romans and Caledonians at Mons Graupius, 1990. Contributions to: Britannia; Proceedings of the Society of Antiquaries of Scotland; Glasgow Archaeological Journal. Memberships: Royal Society of Arts, fellow; Society of Antiquaries of London, fellow; Society of Antiquaries of Scotland, fellow. Address: Micklegarth, 72a High Street, Aberdour, Fife KY3 0SW, Scotland.

MAXWELL Jane. See: **SMITH Jane (Marilyn) Davis.**

MAXWELL John. See: **FREEMANTLE Brian.**

MAXWELL Patricia Anne, (Jennifer Blake, Maxine Patrick, Patricia Ponder, Elizabeth Trehearne), b. 9 Mar 1942, Winn Parish, Louisiana, USA. Writer; Poet. m. Jerry R Maxwell, 1 Aug 1957, 2 sons, 2 daughters. Appointment: Writer-in-Residence, University of Northeastern Louisiana. Publications: Over 40 novels, including: Love's Wild Desire, 1977; Tender Betrayal, 1979; The Storm and the Splendor, 1979; Golden Fancy, 1980; Embrace and Conquer, 1981; Royal Seduction, 1983; Surrender in Moonlight, 1984; Midnight Waltz, 1985; Fierce Eden, 1985; Royal Passion, 1986; Prisoner of Desire, 1986; Southern Rapture, 1987; Louisiana Dawn, 1987; Perfume of Paradise, 1988; Love and Smoke, 1989; Spanish Serenade, 1990; Joy and Anger, 1991; Wildest Dreams, 1992; Arrow to the Heart, 1993; Shameless, 1994; Silver-Tongued Devil, 1996; Tigress, 1996; Garden of Scandal, 1997. Contributions to: Anthologies and periodicals. Honours: Best Historical Romance Novelist of the Year, 1985; Reviewer's Choices, 1984, 1995, Romantic Rimes; Golden Treasure Award, Romance Writers of America, 1987; Romance Hall of Fame, Affaire de Coeur, 1995; Frank Waters Award for Writing Excellence, 1997. Memberships: National League of American Pen Women; Romance Writers of America. Literary Agent: Richard Curtis Associates Inc. Address: PO Box 9218, Quitman, LA 71268, USA.

MAXWELL William, b. 16 Aug 1908, Lincoln, Illinois, USA. Author. m. Emily Gilman Noyes, 17 May 1945, 2 daughters. Education: University of Illinois, 1926-30, 1931-33; Harvard University, 1930-31. Appointments: Faculty, University of Illinois, 1931-33; Editorial Staff, New York magazine, 1936-76. Publications: Bright Center of Heaven, 1934; They Came Like Swallows, 1937; The Folded Leaf, 1945; The Heavenly Tenants, 1946; Time Will Darken It, 1948; Stories (with John Cheever, Daniel Fuchs and Jean Stafford), 1956; The Chateau, 1961; The Old Man at the Railroad Crossing, 1966; Ancestors, 1971; Over by the River, 1977. Editor: So Long, See You Tomorrow, 1979; Letters of Sylvia Townsend Warner, 1982; The Outermost Dream, 1989; Billie Dyer, 1992; Collected Stories: All the Days and Nights, 1996; The Happiness of Getting It Down Right, Correspondence with Frank O'Connor, 1996. Contributions to: Periodicals. Honours: Honorary DLitt, University of Illinois, 1973; William Dean Howells Medal, American Academy of Arts and Letters, 1980; American Book Award, 1982; Brandeis University Creative Arts Award, 1984; Ivan Sandorf Award, National Book Critics Circle, 1994; American Academy of Arts and Letters Gold Medal for Fiction, 1995. Memberships: American Academy of Arts and Letters; National Institute of Arts and Letters, president, 1969-72. Address: 544 East 86th Street, New York NY 10028, USA.

MAY Beatrice. See: **ASTLEY Thea.**

MAY Derwent James, b. 29 Apr 1930, Eastbourne, Sussex, England. Author; Journalist. m. Yolanta Izabella Sypniewska, 1 son, 1 daughter. Education: MA, Lincoln College, Oxford, 1952. Appointments: Theatre and Film Critic, Continental Daily Mail, Paris, 1952-53; Lecturer in English, University of Indonesia, 1955-58; Senior Lecturer in English, Universities of Lodz and Warsaw, 1959-63; Chief Leader Writer, Times Literary Supplement, 1963-65; Literary Editor, The Listener, 1965-86; Literary and Arts Editor, Sunday Telegraph, 1986-90; The European, 1990-91; European Arts Editor, The Times, 1992-. Publications: Novels: The Professionals, 1964; Dear Parson, 1969; The Laughter in Djakarta, 1973; A Revenger's Comedy, 1979. Non-Fiction: Proust, 1983; The Times Nature Diary, 1983; Hannah Arendt, 1986; The New Times Nature Diary, 1993; Feather Reports, 1996. Contributions to: Encounter; Hudson Review. Honours: Member, Booker Prize Jury, 1978; Hawthornden Prize Committee, 1987-. Membership: Beefsteak Club; Garrick Club. Address: 201 Albany Street, London NW1 4AB, England.

MAY Gita, b. 16 Sept 1929, Brussels, Belgium. Professor of French; Writer. m. Irving May, 21 Dec 1947. Education: Hunter College, 1953; MA, 1954, PhD, 1957, Columbia University. Appointments: Professor of French and Chairman, Department of French, Columbia University. Publications: Diderot Studies III (editor with O Fellows), 1961; Madame Roland and the Age of Revolution, 1970; Stendhal and the Age of Napoleon, 1977; Diderot: Essais sur la peinture, Vol XIV of his complete works (editor), 1984; Pensées détachées sur la peinture, 1995; Rebecca West, 1996, Anita Brookner, 1997. Contributions to: Books and professional journals. Honours: Guggenheim Fellowship, 1964; Chevalier, 1968, Officier, 1981, Ordre des Palmes Académiques; National Endowment for the Humanities Senior Fellow, 1971; Van Amringe Distinguished Book Award, Columbia University, 1971. Memberships American Society of 18th Century Studies, president, 1985-86; Modern Language Association, executive council, 1980-83; European Writers series, Diderot, 1984, George Sand, 1985; The Age of Revolution and Romanticism, general editor, 1990-. Memberships: Société Française d'Étude du 18e Siècle; Société Diderot; North American Society for the Study of Rousseau. Address: c/o Department of French, Columbia University, 516 Philosophy Hall, New York, NY 10027, USA.

MAY Julian, b. 10 July 1931, Chicago, Illinois, USA. Writer. m. Thaddeus E Dikty, 1953, 2 sons, 1 daughter. Publications: Over 250 books including: The Many Colored Land, 1981; The Golden Torc, 1982; The Nonborn King, 1983; The Adversary, 1984; Intervention, 1987; Black Trillium, 1990; Jack the Bodiless, 1991; Blood Trillium, 1992; Diamond Mask, 1994; Magnificat, 1996; Sky Trillium, 1997; Perseus Spur, 1998. Address: Box 851 Mercer Island, WA 98040, USA.

MAY Naomi Young, b. 27 Mar 1934, Glasgow, Scotland. Novelist; Journalist; Painter. m. Nigel May, 3 Oct 1964, 2 sons, 1 daughter. Education: Slade School of Fine Art, London, 1953-56; Diploma, Fine Art, University of London. Publications: At Home, 1969, radio adaptation, 1987; The Adventurer, 1970; Troubles, 1976. Contributions to: Anthologies, newspapers, and magazines. Honour: History of Art Prize, Slade School of Fine Art. Membership: PEN. Address: 6 Lion Gate Gardens, Richmond, Surrey TW9 2DF, England.

MAY Stephen James, (Julian Poole), b. 10 Sept 1946, Toronto, Ontario, Canada. College Professor and Advisor; Educator; Novelist; Essayist; Historian; Critic. m. Caroline C May, 13 Oct 1972. Education: BA, 1975, MA, 1977, California State University, Los Angeles; DLitt, International University, Bombay, 1992. Publications: Pilgrimage, 1987; Fire from the Skies, 1990; Footloose on the Santa Fe Trail, 1992; A Land Observed, 1993; Zane Grey: Romancing the West, 1997. Contributions to: Denver Post; Frontier Rocky Mountain News; Southwest Art; Artists of the Rockies; National Geographic.

Memberships: Colorado Authors League; World Literary Academy; Western Writers of America; Society of Southwestern Authors; Zane Grey Society. Address: 5546 Escondido Drive, Colorado Springs, CO 80918, USA.

MAYER Bernadette, b. 12 May 1945, Brooklyn, New York, USA. Poet; Writer. 1 son, 2 daughters. Education: New School for Social Research, New York City. Appointments: Resident Director, St Mark's Poetry Project, Greenwich Village, 1980-84; Various workshops. Publications: Ceremony Latin, 1964; Story, 1968; Moving, 1971; The Basketball Article (with Anne Waldman), 1975; Memory, 1975; Studying Hunger, 1975; Poetry, 1976; Eruditio Ex Memoria, 1977; The Golden Book of Words, 1978; Midwinter Day, 1982; Incidents Reports Sonnets, 1984; Utopia, 1984; Mutual Aid, 1985; the Art of Science Writing (with Dales Worsley), 1989; Sonnets, 1989; The Formal Field of Kissing, 1990; A Bernadette Mayer Reader, 1992; The Desires of Mothers to Please Others in Letters, 1994. Contributions to: Anthologies. Address: c/o Hard Press Inc, PO Box 184, West Stockbridge, MA 01266, USA.

MAYER Gerda (Kamilla), b. 9 June 1927, Karlovy Vary, Czechoslovakia (British citizen). Poet. m. Adolf Mayer, 3 Sept 1949. Education: BA, Bedford College, London, 1963. Publications: Oddments, 1970; Gerda Mayer's Library Folder, 1972; Poet Tree Centaur: A Walthamstow Group Anthology (editor), 1973; Treble Poets 2, 1975; The Knockabout Show, 1978; Monkey on the Analyst's Couch, 1980; The Candy Floss Tree, 1984; March Postman, 1985; A Heartache of Grass, 1988; Time Watching, 1995; Bernini's Cat, 1999. Contributions to: Anthologies and other publications. Memberships: Poetry Society; Society of Authors. Address: 12 Margaret Avenue, Chingford, London E4 7NP, England.

MAYER Robert, b. 24 Feb 1939, Bronx, New York, USA. Writer. m. La Donna Cocilovo, 24 Feb 1989, 1 stepdaughter. Education: BA, City College of New York, 1959; MS, Journalism, Columbia University, 1960. Appointments: Reporter, Columnist, Newsday, 1961-71; Managing Editor, Santa Fe Reporter, 1988-90. Publications: Superfolks, 1977; The Execution, 1979; Midge and Decker, 1982; Sweet Salt, 1984; The Grace of Shortstops, 1984; The Search, 1986; The Dreams of Ada, 1987; I, JFK, 1989. Contributions to: Vanity Fair; New York Magazine; Travel and Leisure; Rocky Mountain Magazine; New Mexico Magazine; Santa Fe Reporter; Newsday. Honours: National Headliner Award, 1968; Mike Berger Awards, 1969, 1971; Nominee, Edgar Allan Poe Award, 1988. Address: 135 Cedar Street, Santa Fe, NM 87501, USA.

MAYER Wolf, b. 23 June 1934, Stuttgart, Germany. Visiting Fellow in Geology. m. Veronica Mayer, 22 Aug 1959, 2 daughters. Education: BSc, University of New Zealand, 1962; MSc, University of Auckland, 1964; PhD, University of New England, 1972. Appointments: Senior Lecturer in Geology, retired; Visiting Scholar, University of Canberra, 1994-95; Visiting Fellow, Australian National University, Canberra, 1996-. Publications: Gemstone Identification, in Australian and New Zealand Gemstones, 1972; Gemstone Identification, in Australian Gemstones, 1974; Field Guide to Australian Rocks, Minerals and Gemstones, 1976, 3rd edition, 1992; Images in Stone: A Guide to the Building Stones of Parliament House, 1996. Contributions to: Numerous to professional journals on a variety of geological subjects. Memberships: Geological Society of Australia; History of Earth Science Society. Literary Agent: Curtis Brown, PO Box 19, Paddington, New South Wales 2021, Australia. Address: 22 Bennet Street, Spence, Australian Capital Territory 2615, Australia.

MAYER-KOENIG Wolfgang, b. 28 Mar 1946, Vienna, Austria. Poet; Writer; Editor; University Professor. Education: Universities of Vienna, Saarbrücken, and Los Angeles. Appointments: Editor, LOG poetry magazine, 1983-; University Professor, 1986-. Publications: Sichtbare Pavillons, 1968; Texte und Bilder, 1972; Sprache-Politik-Aggression, 1975; In den Armen unseres

Waerters, 1979; Chagrin non dechiffré, 1986; A Hatalom bonyolult Angyala, 1988; Coloquios nel cuarto, 1990; Verzogerung des Vertrauens, 1995; Verkannte Tiefe, 1996; Grammatik der Modernen Poesie, 1996. Contributions to: Various publications. Honours: Theodor Körner Prize for Poetry, 1974; Cross of Honour for Science and Arts for Literature, Republic of Austria, 1974; Chevalier des Arts et des Lettres, France, 1987. Membership: Austrian Poets and Writers Association. Address: Hemalser Guertel 41, A-1170 Vienna, Austria.

MAYHAR Ardath, (Frank Cannon, Frances Hurst, John Killdeer), b. 20 Feb 1930, Timpson, Texas, USA. Writer; Poet. m. Joe E Mayhar, June 1958. Education: Self-educated. Publications: Over 35 books, including: How the Gods Wove in Kyrannon, 1979; Soul Singer of Tyrnos, 1981; Runes of the Lyre, 1982; Lords of the Triple Moons, 1983; The World Ends in Hickory Hollow, 1985; A Place of Silver Silence, 1987; Texas Gunsmoke, 1988; Island in the Swamp, 1994; Hunters of the Plains, 1995; High Mountain Winter, 1996. Contributions to: Quarterlies and magazines. Honours: Awards and prizes for fiction and poetry. Memberships: Science Fiction Writers of America; Western Writers of America. Address: PO Box 180, Chireno, TX 75937, USA.

MAYNARD Fredelle Bruser, b. 9 July 1922, Foam Lake, Canada. Writer; Lecturer; Television Host. Div., 2 daughters. Education: BA Honours, University of Manitoba, 1942; MA, University of Toronto, 1943; PhD, Harvard University, Cambridge, Massachusetts, 1947. Appointments: Radcliffe Institute Scholar, 1967-69; Writer-in-Residence, University of Illinois, 1974. Publications: Raisins and Almonds, 1972; Guiding Your Child to a More Creative Life, 1973; The Child Care Crisis, 1985; The Tree of Life, 1988. Contributions to: Numerous journals in USA, Canada, England, Australia, South Africa. Honours: Governor-General's Medal; Fellowship, Canadian Federation of University Women; Flavelle Fellowship, Harvard University; Award for Excellence in Women's Journalism, University of Missouri; Senior Arts Award, Canada Council. Memberships: Phi Beta Kappa; Periodical Writers Association of Canada; Ontario Association of Marriage and Family Therapy; International Association for Promotion of Humanistic Studies in Gynaecology, honorary member. Address: 25 Metcalfe Street, Toronto, Ontario M4X 1R5, Canada.

MAYNE Richard (John), b. 2 Apr 1926, London, England. Writer; Broadcaster. m. Jocelyn Mudie Ferguson, 2 daughters. Education: MA, PhD, Trinity College, Cambridge, 1947-53. Appointments: Rome Correspondent, New Statesman, 1953-54; Official of the European Community, Luxembourg and Brussels, 1956-63; Personal Assistant to Jean Monnet, Paris, 1963-66; Paris Correspondent, 1963-73, Co-Editor, 1990-94, Encounter; Visiting Professor, University of Chicago, 1970; Director, Federal Trust, London, 1971-73; Head, UK Offices of the European Commission, London, 1973-79; Film Critic, Sunday Telegraph, London, 1987-89, The European, 1990-98. Publications: The Community of Europe, 1962; The Institutions of the European Community, 1968; The Recovery of Europe, 1970; The Europeans, 1972; Europe Tomorrow (editor), 1972; The New Atlantic Challenge (editor), 1975; The Memoirs of Jean Monnet (translator), 1978; Postwar: The Dawn of Today's Europe, 1983; Western Europe: A Handbook (editor), 1987; Federal Union: The Pioneers (with John Pinder), 1990; Europe: A History of its Peoples (translator), 1990; History of Europe (translator), 1993; A History of Civilizations (translator), 1994. Contributions to: Numerous in UK, USA, France and Germany. Honour: Scott-Moncrieff Prize for Translation from French, 1978. Memberships: Society of Authors; Royal Institute of International Affairs; Federal Trust for Education and Research. Address: Albany Cottage, 24 Park Village East, Regent's Park, London NW1 7PZ, England.

MAYNE Seymour, b. 18 May 1944, Montreal, Quebec, Canada. Professor of English; Poet; Writer; Editor; Translator. Education: BA, Honours, English, McGill University, 1965; MA, English and Creative Writing, 1966, PhD, 1972, University of British Columbia. Appointments: Lecturer, University of British Columbia, 1972; Lecturer, 1973, Assistant Professor, 1973-78, Associate Professor, 1978-85, Professor of English, 1985-, University of Ottawa; Visiting Professor, 1979-80, Visiting Professor and Scholar, 1983-84, 1992, Writer-in-Residence, 1987-88, Hebrew University of Jerusalem; Visiting Professor, Concordia University, Montreal, 1982-83, University of La Laguna, Spain, 1993; Contributing Editor, 1982-90, Poetry Editor, 1990-95, Viewpoints; Contributing Editor, Tel Aviv Review, 1989-96, Poet Lore, 1992-, Jerusalem Review, 1997-; Founder-Consulting Editor, Bywords, 1990-, Graffito, 1994-. Publications: That Monocycle the Moon, 1964; Tiptoeing on the Mount, 1965; From the Portals of Mouseholes, 1966; Manimals, 1969; Mouth, 1970; For Stems of Light, 1971, 2nd edition, revised, 1974; Face, 1971; Name, 1975, 2nd edition, revised, 1976; Diasporas, 1977; The Impossible Promised Land: Poems New and Selected, 1981; Children of Abel, 1986; Diversions, 1987; Six Ottawa Poets (with others), 1990; Killing Time, 1992; The Song of Moses and Other Poems, 1995; Five-O'Clock Shadows (with others), 1996; Dragon Trees, 1997; City of the Hidden, 1998; Carbon Filter, forthcoming. Editor or Co-Editor: 13 books, 1968-97. Translator or Co-Translator: 8 books, 1974-98. Contributions to: Anthologies, books, journals, reviews, and quarterlies. Honours: Numerous grants and fellowships; Chester Macnaghten First Prize in Creative Writing, 1962; J I Segal Prize in English-French Literature, 1974; York Poetry Workshop Award, 1975; American Literary Translators Association Poetry Translation Award, 1990; Jewish Book Committee Prize, 1994; Louis L Lockshin Memorial Award, 1997. Address: c/o Department of English, Faculty of Arts, University of Ottawa, PO Box 450, Station A, Ottawa, Ontario K1N 6N5, Canada.

MAYNE William (James Carter), b. 16 Mar 1928, Kingston-upon-Hull, Yorkshire, England. Writer. Appointments: Lecturer, Creative Writing, Deakin University, Geelong, Australia, 1976, 1977. Publications: About 100 stories for children and young people, 1953-. Honours: Library Association's Carnegie Medal for Best Children's Book of the Year, 1957; Guardian Award for Children's Fiction, 1993; Kurt Maschler Award, 1997. Memberships: Fellow, Creative Writing, Rolle College, Exmouth, 1979-80. Address: c/o David Higham Associates, 5-8 Lower John Street, Golden Square, London W1R 4HA, England.

MAYOTTE Judith A (Moberly), b. 25 Jan 1937, Wichita, Kansas, USA. Writer; Television Producer; Refugee Advocate; Adviser. m. Jack Parnell Mayotte, 6 Oct 1972, dec 9 Sept 1975. Education: BA, Mundelein College, Chicago; MA, PhD, Marquette University, Milwaukee, 1976. Appointments: Special Adviser, US Department of State, Washington, DC; Producer, Writer, many television programmes. Publication: Disposable People: The Plight of Refugees, 1992. Contributions to: Journal of International Affairs; Numerous popular journals and newspapers; Maryknoll Magazine. Honours: Emmy, 1985; Mickey Leland Award, Refugee Voices, 1994; All University Alumni Merit Award for Professional Achievement, Marquette University, 1994; Honorary Doctor of Humanities, 1994; Annual Award, Refugees International, 1994. Memberships: Women's Commission for Refugee Women and Children; International Rescue Committee; Refugees International; Senior Fellow, Policy Group; International Women's Media Foundation. Address: 1275 25th Street North West, Washington, DC 20037, USA.

MAYROCKER Friederike, b. 20 Dec 1924, Vienna, Austria. Writer; Poet; Dramatist. Publications: Over 70 books, including: Magische Blätter I-IV, 1983-87; Reise durch die Nacht, 1984; Das Herzzerreiszende der Dinge, 1985; Winterglück, 1986; Lection, 1994; Notizen auf einem Kamel, 1996; Das zu Sehende, das zu Hörende, 1997; brütt Oder die Seufzenden Gärten (prose), 1998; Benachbarte Metalle, 1998; Magishe Blätter V, 1999. Contributions to: Journals and magazines. Honours: Grosser Österreichischer Staatspreis, 1982; Friedrich-Hölderlin-Preis, 1993; Grosser Literatur Preis, Bavarian Academy of Fine Arts, Munich, 1996; Else-Lasker-Schüler-Preis, 1996; Meersburger Droste-Preis, 1997. Memberships: Several Austrian and German literary associations. Address: Zentagasse 16/40, A-1050 Vienna, Austria.

MAYSON Marina. See: **ROGERS Rosemary.**

MAYUMI Inaba, b. 1950, Aichi Prefecture, Japan. Writer. Publications: Wakai Kage no Itami wo; Hotel Zambia; Endless Waltz; Kohaku no Machi; Dakareru. Short story collection: Koe no Shôfu (The Voice Prostitute). Honours: Prize for Young Female Authors, 1973; Sakuhin shô, 1980; Womens' Literary Award, 1992. Address: c/o Japan PEN Club, 265 Akasaka Residential Hotel, 9-1-7 Akasaka, Minato-ku, Tokyo 107, Japan.

MAZER Norma Fox, b. 15 May 1931, New York, New York, USA. Writer. m. Harry Mazer, 12 Feb 1950, 1 son, 3 daughters. Education: Antioch College; Syracuse University. Publications: I Trissy, 1971; A Figure of Speech, 1973; Saturday, The Twelfth of October, 1975; Dear Bill, Remember Me, 1976; The Solid Gold Kid, 1977; Up in Seth's Room, 1979; Mrs Fish, Ape and Me and the Dump Queen, 1980; Taking Terri Mueller, 1981; When We First Met, 1982; Summer Girls, Love Boys, and Other Stories, 1982; Someone To Love, 1983; Supergirl, 1984; Downtown, 1984; A, My Name is Ami, 1986; Three Sisters, 1986; B, My Name is Bunny, 1987; After the Rain, 1987; Silver, 1988; Heartbeat, 1989; Babyface, 1989; C, My Name is Cal, 1990; D, My Name is Danita, 1991; Bright Days, Stupid Nights, 1992; E, My Name is Emily, 1991; Out of Control, 1993. *Contributions to:* English Journal; Alan Review; The Writer; Signal; Writing; Redbook; Playgirl; Voice; Ingenue. Literary Agent: Elaine Markson literary Agency, 44 Greenwich Avenue, New York, NY 10011, USA. Address: Brown Gulf Road, Jamesville, NY 13078, USA.

MAZLISH Bruce, b. 15 Sept 1923, New York, New York, USA. Professor of History; Writer. m. (1), 3 sons, 1 daughter, (2) Neva Goodwin, 22 Nov 1988. Education: BA, 1944, MA, 1947, PhD, 1955, Columbia University. Appointments: Instructor, University of Maine, 1946-48, Columbia University, 1949-50; Instructor, 1950-53, Faculty, 1955-, Professor of History, 1965-, Chairman, History Section, 1965-70, Head, Department of Humanities, 1974-79, Massachusetts Institute of Technology; Director, American School, Madrid, 1953-55. Publications: The Western Intellectual Tradition (with J Bronowski), 1960; The Riddle of History, 1966; In Search of Nixon, 1972; James and John Stuart Mill: Father and Son in the 19th Century, 1975, 2nd edition, 1988; The Revolutionary Ascetic, 1976; Kissinger: The European Mind in American Policy, 1976; The Meaning of Karl Marx, 1984; A New Science: The Breakdown of Connections and the Birth of Sociology, 1989; The Leader, the Led and the Psyche, 1990; The Fourth Discontinuity: The Co-Evolution of Humans and Machines, 1993; Progress: Fact or Illusion? (with Les Marx), 1996. Editor: Psychoanalysis and History, 1963, revised edition, 1971; The Railroad and the Space Program: An Exploration in Historical Analogy, 1965; Conceptualizing Global History (with Ralph Bultjens), 1993. Contributions to: Professional journals. Honours: Clement Staff Essay Award, 1968; Toynbee Prize, 1986-87. Memberships: American Academy of Arts and Sciences, fellow; Rockefeller Family Fund, board of directors; Toynbee Prize Foundation, board of directors. Address: 11 Lowell Street, Cambridge, MA 02138, USA.

MAZUR Grace Dane, b. 22 Apr 1944, Boston, USA. Literary Writer. m. Barry C Mazur, 1 son. Education: BA, Harvard College, 1971; PhD, Harvard University, 1981; MFA, Warren Wilson, 1993. Appointments: Harvard University Extension School, 1996-. Publications: Silk, stories, 1996; Trespass, novel, 1998. Contributions to: Harvard Review; New England Review; Southern Review; Story. Honour: Breadloaf Literary Fellowship. Literary Agent: Michele Rubin. Address: Writers House, (Michele Rubin), 21 West 26th St, New York, NY 10010, USA.

MAZZARO Jerome (Louis), b. 25 Nov 1934, Detroit, Michigan, USA. Retired Professor of English and Comparative Literature; Poet; Writer; Editor. Education: AB, Wayne University, 1954; MA, University of Iowa, 1956; PhD, Wayne State University, 1963. Appointments: Instructor, University of Detroit, 1958-61; Editor, Fresco, 1960-61, Modern Poetry Studies, 1970-79; Assistant Professor, State University of New York College at Cortland, 1962-64; Assistant Editor, North American Review, 1963-65, Noetics, 1964-65; Professor of English and Comparative Literature, State University of New York at Buffalo, 1964-96; Contributing Editor, Salmagundi, 1967-, American Poetry Review, 1972-, Italian-American, 1974-88; Poetry Editor, Helios, 1977-79. Publications: The Achievement of Robert Lowell, 1939-1959, 1960; Juvenal: Satires (translator), 1965; The Poetic Themes of Robert Lowell, 1965; Changing the Windows (poems), 1966; Modern American Poetry (editor), 1970; Transformation in the Renaissance English Lyric, 1970; Profile of Robert Lowell (editor), 1971; Profile of William Carlos Williams (editor), 1971; William Carlos Williams: The Later Poetry, 1973; Postmodern American Poetry, 1980; The Figure of Dante: An Essay on the "Vita Nuova", 1981; The Caves of Love (poems), 1985; Rubbings (poems), 1985; John Logan: The Collected Poems (editor with Al Poulin), 1989; John Logan: The Collected Fiction (editor), 1991. Contributions to: Reference works, books and journals. Honours: Guggenheim Fellowship, 1964-65; Hadley Fellowship, 1979-80. Memberships: Dante Society of America; Mark Twain Society. Address: 147 Capen Boulevard, Buffalo, NY 14226, USA.

MCADAM Doug(las John), b. 31 Aug 1951, Pasadena, California, USA. Professor of Sociology; Writer. m. Tracy Lynn Stevens, 20 Feb 1988. Education: BA, Sociology, Occidental College, Los Angeles, 1973; MA, Sociology, 1977, PhD, Sociology, 1979, State University of New York at Stony Brook. Appointments: Instructor, Occidental College, Los Angeles, 1975, State University of New York at Stony Brook, 1977-79; Assistant Professor, George Mason University, Fairfax, Virginia, 1979-82; Assistant Professor, 1983-86, Associate Professor, 1986-90, Professor of Sociology, 1990-98, University of Arizona; Fellow, Center for Advanced Study in the Behavioral Sciences, 1991-92, 1997-98, Udall Center for Studies in Public Policy, 1994-95; Hollingshead Lecturer, Yale University, 1997; Professor of Sociology, Stanford University, 1998-. Publications: The Politics of Privacy (with James Rule, Linda Stearns, and David Uglow), 1980; Political Process and the Development of Black Insurgency, 1930-1970, 1982; Freedom Summer, 1988; Collective Behavior and Social Movements (with Gary Marx), 1994; Comparative Perspectives on Social Movements: Political Opportunities, Mobilizing Structures, and Cultural Framings (editor with John McCarthy and Mayer Zald), 1996; Social Movements: Readings on Their Emergence, Mobilization and Dynamics (with David Snow), 1996; How Movements Matter: Theoretical and Comparative Studies on the Consequences of Social Movements (editor with Marco Giugni and Charles Tilly), 1998; From Contention to Democracy (editor with Marco Guigni and Charles Tilly), 1999. Contributions to: Scholarly books and professional journals. Honours: Guggenheim Fellowship, 1984-85; Gustavus Myers Center Outstanding Book, 1988; C Wright Mills Award, 1990. Memberships: American Sociological Association; Sociological Research Association. Address: c/o Department of Sociology, Stanford University, Stanford, CA 94305, USA.

MCALLISTER Casey. See: **BATTIN B W.**

MCAULEY James J(ohn), b. 8 Jan 1936, Dublin, Ireland. Professor; Poet. m. Deirdre O'Sullivan, 1982. Education: University College Dublin; University of Arkansas, Fayetteville. Appointments: Editor, Dolmen Press, Dublin, 1960-66; Professor, Eastern Washington University, Cheney, 1978-; Director, Eastern Washington University Press, 1993. Publication: Observations, 1960; A New Address, 1965; Draft Balance Sheet, 1970; Home and Away, 1974; After the Blizzard, 1975; The Exile's Recurring Nightmare, 1975; Recital, Poems, 1975-80, 1982; The Exile's Book of Hours, 1982; Coming and Going: New and Selected Poems, 1968-88, 1989. Play: The Revolution, 1966. Libretto: Praise, 1981. Honours: National Endowment for the Arts Grant, 1972; Washington Governor's Award, 1976. Address: Eastern Washington University Press, MS#14, Eastern Washington University, Cheney, WA 99004, USA.

MCBAIN Ed. See: **LOMBINO Salvatore A.**

MCCAFFREY Anne (Inez), b. 1 Apr 1926, Cambridge, Massachusetts, USA. Author. m. Wright Johnson, 14 Jan 1950, div Aug 1970, 2 sons, 1 daughter. Education: BA, Radcliffe College, 1947; University of Dublin, 1970-71. Publications: Restoree, 1967; Dragonflight, 1968; Decision at Doona, 1969; Ship Who Sang, 1969; Mark of Merlin, 1971; Dragonquest: Being the Further Adventures of the Dragonriders of Pern, 1971; Ring of Fear, 1971; To Ride Pegasus, 1973; Cooking Out of This World, 1973; A Time When, 1975; Dragonsong, 1976; Kilteran Legacy, 1975; Dragonsinger, 1977; Dinosaur Planet, 1977; Get Off the Unicorn, 1977; White Dragon, 1978; Dragondrums, 1979; Crystal Singer, 1981; The Worlds of Anne McCaffrey, 1981; The Coelura, 1983; Moreta: Dragonlady of Peru, 1983; Dinosuar Planet Survivors, 1984; Stitch in Snow, 1984; Killashandra, 1985; The Girl Who Heard Dragons, 1985; The Year of the Lucy, 1986; Nerilka's Story, 1986; The Lady, 1987; People of Pern, 1988; Dragonsdown, 1988; Renegades of Pern, 1989; The Dragonlover's Guide to Pern (with Jody-Lynn Nye), 1989; The Rowan, 1990; Pegasus in Flight, 1990; Sassinak (with Elizabeth Moon), 1990; The Death of Sleep (with Jody-Lynn Nye), 1990; All the Weyrs of Pern, 1991; Generation Warriors, 1991; Damia, 1991; The Partnership (with Margaret Ball), 1991; Crisis at Doona (with Jody Lynn Nye), 1991; Damia, 1992; The City Who Fought (with Mercedes Lackey), 1993; Powers That Be (with Elizabeth Ann Scarborough), 1993; Chronicles of Pern: First Fall, 1993; Lyon's Pride, 1994; The Ship Who Won (with Jody-Lynn Nye), 1994; Power Lines (with Elizabeth Ann Scarborough), 1994; Dolphins of Pern, 1994; Power Play (with Elizabeth Ann Scarborough), 1995; Freedom's Landing, 1995; Black Horses for the King, 1996; Red Star Rising, 1996. Honours: Hugo Award, 1967; Nebula Award, 1968; E E Smith Award, 1975; Ditmar Award, 1979; Eurocon/Streso Award, 1979; Gandalf Award, 1979; Barlog Award, 1980; Golden PEN Award, 1981; Science Fiction Book Club Awards, 1986, 1989, 1991, 1992, 1993. Memberships: Authors Guild; PEN, Ireland; Science Fiction Writers of America. Address: Dragonhold Underhill, Timmore Lane, Newcastle, County Wicklow, Ireland

MCCALL Christina, b. 29 Jan 1935, Toronto, Ontario, Canada. Writer; Editor. m. (1) Peter Charles Newman, 1959, div 1977, (2) Stephen Clarkson, 1 Sept 1978, 3 daughters. Education: Jarvis College Institute, Toronto, 1952; BA, English Language and Literature, Victoria College, University of Toronto, 1956. Appointments: Staff, 1956-58, Associate Editor, 1971-74, Maclean's; Associate Editor, then Ottawa Editor, Chatelaine, 1958-62; Ottawa Editor, 1967-70, Executive Editor, 1976, Contributing Editor, 1980-88, 1994-, Saturday Night; National Reporter, Globe and Mail, 1974-76. Publications: The Man from Oxbow, 1967; Grits: An Intimate Portrait of the Liberal Party, 1982; Trudeau and Our Times (co-author), Vol 1, The Magnificent Obsession, 1990, Vol 2, The Heroic Delusion, 1994. Honours: Southam Fellowship in Journalism, University of Toronto, 1977; National Magazine Award Gold Medal, 1981; Canadian Authors' Association Book of the Year Award, 1983; Governor-General's Award for Non-Fiction, 1990; John W Dafoe Prize, 1995. Address: 59 Lowther Avenue, Toronto, Ontario M5R 1C5, Canada.

MCCARRY Charles, b. 14 June 1930, Pittsfield, Massachusetts, USA. Journalist; Editor; Writer. m. Nancy Neill, 12 Sept 1953, 4 sons. Appointments: Reporter and Editor, Lisbon Evening Journal, Ohio, 1952-55; Reporter and Columnist, Youngstown Vindicator, Ohio, 1955-56; Assistant to US Secretary of Labor, Washington, DC, 1956-57; Employee, Central Intelligence Agency, 1958-67; Editor-at-Large, National Geographic magazine, 1983-90. Publications: The Miernik Dossier, 1973; The Tears of Autumn, 1975; The Secret Lovers, 1977; The Better Angels, 1979; The Last Supper, 1983; The Bride of the Wilderness, 1988; Second Sight, 1991. Non-Fiction: Citizen Nader, 1972; Double Eagle (with Ben Abruzzo, Maxie Anderson and Larry Newman), 1979; Isles of the Caribbean (co-author), 1979; The Great Southwest, 1980; Caveat, 1983; For the Record (with Donald Y Regan), 1988; Inner Circles: How America Changed the World (with Alexander M Haig Jr), 1992; Shelley's Heart, 1995; Lucky Bastard, 1998. Contributions to: Periodicals. Address: c/o William Morris Agency, 1350 Avenue of the Americas, New York, NY 10019, USA.

MCCARTHY Cormac, (Charles McCarthy Jr), b. 20 July 1933, Providence, Rhode Island, USA. Author; Dramatist. m. Lee Holleman, 1961, div 1 child, (2) Anne deLisle, 1967, div. Publications: Novels: The Orchard Keeper, 1965; Outer Dark, 1968; Child of God, 1974; Suttree, 1979; Blood Meridian, or The Evening Redness in the West, 1985; All the Pretty Horses, 1992; The Crossing, 1994; Cities of the Plain, 1998. Plays: The Gardner's Son, 1977; The Stonemason, 1994. Honours: Ingram Merrill Foundation Grant, 1960; William Faulkner Foundation Award, 1965; American Academy of Arts and Letters Travelling Fellowship, 1965-66; Rockefeller Foundation Grant, 1966; Guggenheim Fellowship, 1976; John D and Catharine T MacArthur Foundation Fellowship, 1981; National Book Award, 1992; National Book Critics Circle Award, 1993. Address: c/o Alfred A Knopf Inc, 201 East 50th Street, New York, NY 10022, USA.

MCCARTHY Gary, b. 23 Jan 1943, South Gate, California, USA. Writer. m. Virginia Kurzwell, 14 June 1969, 1 son, 3 daughters. Education: BS, Agriculture, California State University, 1968; MS, Economics, University of Nevada, 1970. Appointments: Labour Economist, State of Nevada, Carson City, 1970-77; Economist, Copley International Corp, La Jolla, California, 1977-79. Publications: The Derby Man, 1976; Showdown at Snakegrass Junction, 1978; The First Sheriff, 1979; Mustang Fever, 1980; The Pony Express War, 1980; Winds of Gold, 1980; Silver Shot, 1981; Explosion at Donner Pass, 1981; The Legend of the Lone Ranger, 1981; North Chase, 1982; Rebel of Bodie, 1982; The Rail Warriors, 1983; Silver Winds, 1983; Wind River, 1984; Powder River, 1985; The Last Buffalo Hunt, 1985; Mando, 1986; The Mustangers, 1987; Transcontinental, 1987; Sodbuster, 1988; Blood Brothers, 1989; Gringo Amigo, 1990; Whiskey Creek, 1992; The American River, 1992; Comstock Camels, 1993; The Gila River, 1993; Yosemite, 1995; Grand Canyon, 1996; Mesa Verde, 1997. Address: PO Box 2057, Lake Havasu City, AZ 86405, USA.

MCCARTHY Patrick A, b. 12 July 1945, Charlottesville, Virginia, USA. Professor of English; Writer; Educator. m. Catherine Anne Leatherbury, 31 Aug 1968, 3 children. Education: BA, 1967, MA, 1968, University of Virginia; PhD, University of Wisconsin at Milwaukee, 1973. Appointments: Instructor in English, Murray State University, Kentucky, 1968-69, William Paterson College of New Jersey, 1973-74, Broome Community College, Binghamton, New York, 1975-76; Visiting Professor of English, State University of New York at Binghamton, 1974-75; Assistant Professor, 1976-81, Associate Professor, 1981-84, Professor of English, 1984-, University of Miami at Coral Gables. Publications: The Riddles of "Finnegans Wake", 1980; Olaf Stapledon, 1982; Critical Essays on Samuel Beckett (editor), 1986; The Legacy of Olaf Stapledon: Critical Essays and an Unpublished Manuscript (editor with Charles Elkins and Martin H Greenberg), 1989; "Ulysses": Portrals of Discovery, 1990; Critical Essays on James Joyce's "Finnegans Wake" (editor), 1992; Forests of Symbols: World, Text and Self in Malcolm Lowry's Fiction, 1994; Malcolm Lawry's La Mordida: A Scholarly Edition (editor), 1996. Address: c/o Department of English, University of Miami at Coral Gables, Coral Gables, FL 33124, USA.

MCCARTHY Rosemary P, b. 21 Oct 1928, Newark, New Jersey, USA. Genealogist; Editor; Poet; Artist. Education: BSN, St John's University, 1963; MEd, Teachers College, Columbia University, 1973; Institute of Adult Education, Catholic University of America, 1980-81; Long Island University, Southampton Campus, 1986. Appointments: Editor, International Family Tree Newsletter, 1979-, International Family Director, 1983-. Publications: Family Tree of the Connors-Walsh Family of Kiltimagh, County Mayo, Eire and the USA, with Branches in Great Britain and Throughout the World, 1979; Gradma, 1986; Life of Margaret Walsh Connors. Contributions to: Journals. Memberships: Civic and historical societies. Address: 814A Jefferson Street, Alexandria, VA 22314, USA.

MCCARTHY William E(dward) J(ohn), b. 30 July 1925, London, England. College Fellow; Writer. Education: Ruskin College, 1953-55; BA, Merton College, Oxford, 1957; PhD, Nuffield College, Oxford, 1959. Appointments: Research Fellow, Nuffield College, 1959-63; Staff Lecturer, Tutor, Industrial Relations, 1964-65, Fellow, Nuffield College and Centre for Management Studies, 1968-, Oxford University; Director of Research, Royal Commission on Trade and Unions and Employers Association, London, 1965-68; Senior Economic Adviser, Department of Employment, 1968-70; Special Adviser, European Economic Commission, 1974-75. Publications: The Future of the Unions, 1962; The Closed Shop in Britain, 1964; The Role of Shop Stewards in British Industrial Relations: A Survey of Existing Information and Research, 1966; Disputes Procedures in Britain (with Arthur Ivor Marsh), 1966; Employers' Associations: The Results of Two Studies (with V G Munns), 1967; The Role of Government in Industrial Relations, Shop Stewards and Workshop Relations: The Results of a Study, 1968; Industrial Relations in Britain: A Guide for Management and Unions (editor), 1969; The Reform of Collective Bargaining: A Series of Case Studies, 1971; Trade Unions, 1972, new edition, 1985; Coming to Terms with Trade Unions (with A J Collier), 1972; Management by Agreement (with N D Ellis), 1973; Wage Inflation and Wage Leadership (with J F O'Brien and V C Dowd), 1975; Making Whitley Work, 1977; Change in Trade Unions (co-author), 1981; Strikes in Post War Britain (with J W Durcun), 1985; Freedom at Work, 1985; The Future of Industrial Democracy, 1988; Employee Relations Audits (co-author), 1992; Legal Intervention in Industrial Relations (editor), 1992; New Labour at Work, 1997; Fairness at Work and Trade Union Recognition, 1998. Address: 4 William Orchard Close, Old Headington, Oxford, England.

MCCARTY Clifford, b. 13 June 1929, Los Angeles, California, USA. Writer; Bookseller. m. Maxine Reich, 21 July 1955, 1 son, 2 daughters. Education: BA, California State University, Los Angeles, 1952. Publications: Bogey: The Films of Humphrey Bogart, 1965; The Films of Errol Flynn (in collaboration), 1969; Published Screenplays: A Checklist, 1971; The Films of Frank Sinatra (in collaboration), 1971; Film Music 1 (editor), 1989. Contributions to: Films in Review; Film and TV Music; Notes; Pro Musica Sana; Gissing Journal; Cue Sheet. Address: PO Box 89, Topanga, California 90290, USA.

MCCAUGHREAN Geraldine Margaret, (Felix Culper), b. 6 June 1951, Enfield, England. Writer. m. John McCaughrean, 26 Nov 1988, 1 daughter. Education: BEd Hons Degree, Christchurch College, Canterbury, England. Appointments: Secretary, Thames TV, 1969-72; Sub Editor, Marshall Cavendish Partworks Ltd, 1976-86. Publications: Childrens: A Little Lower Than the Angels; A Pack of Lies; Gold Dust; Plundering Paradise; Forever X; World Myths and Legends (4 volumes); Canterbury Tales; Moby Dick; Adult: The Maypole; Fires' Astonishment; Vainglory; Lovesong; The Ideal Wife. Honours: Whitbread; Carnegie; Guardian; Beefeater; Finalist Smarties; Carnegie; Whitbread. Literary Agent: David Higham Assoc. Address: 5-8 Lower John Street, Golden Square, London W1R 4HA, England.

MCCAULEY Martin, b. 18 Oct 1934, Omagh, Northern Ireland. Senior Lecturer in Politics; Writer. Education: BA, 1966, PhD, 1973, University of London. Appointments: Senior Lecturer in Soviet and East European Studies, 1968-91, Senior Lecturer in Politics, 1991-98, Chairman, Department of Social Sciences, 1993-96, School of Slavonic and East European Studies, University of London. Publications: The Russian Revolution and the Soviet State 1917-1921 (editor), 1975, 2nd edition, 1980; Khruschev and the Development of Soviet Agriculture: The Virgin Land Programme, 1953-64, 1976; Communist Power in Europe 1944-1949 (editor and contributor), 1977, 2nd edition, 1980; Marxism-Leninism in the German Democratic Republic: The Socialist Unity Party (SED), 1978; The Stalin File, 1979; The Soviet Union Since 1917, 1981; Stalin and Stalinism, 1983, 2nd edition, 1995; Origins of the Cold War, 1983, 2nd edition, 1995; The Soviet Union Since Brezhnev (editor and contributor), 1983; The German Democratic Republic Since 1945, 1984; Octobrists to Bolsheviks: Imperial Russia 1905-1917, 1984; Leadership and Succession in the Soviet Union, East Europe and China (editor and contributor), 1985; The Origins of the Modern Russian State 1855-1881 (with Peter Waldron), 1986; The Soviet Union under Gorbachev (editor), 1987; Gorbachev and Perestroika (editor), 1990; Khrushchev, 1991; The Soviet Union 1917-1991, 1991, 2nd edition, 1993; Directory of Russian MPs (editor), 1993; Longman Biographical Directory of Decision Makers in Russia and the Successor States (editor), 1994; Who's Who in Russia and the Soviet Union, 1997; Russia 1917-1941, 1997; Longman Companion to Russia since 1914, 1997; Gorbachev, 1998; America, Russia and the Cold War 1949-1991, 1998. Contributions to: Professional journals. Memberships: Economic and Social Research Council; Politics and Society Group. Address: c/o School of Slavonic and East European Studies, University of London, Senate House, Malet Street, London WC1E 7HU, England.

MCCLAIN Michael H, (Carlos Estuardo de Borbon), b. 30 Aug 1940, Middletown, Ohio, USA. Writer; Researcher. Education: BA, Miami University of Ohio, 1962; University of Granada, Spain, 19667-73. Appointment: Staff Columnist, El Correo Gallego, newspaper, Santiago de Compostela, Spain, 1974-84. Publication: Spain & Persia: Aryium & Iran, 1999. Contributions to: Grial; Actes du IV Symposium International d'Etudes Morisques; Al-Noor; Mélanges Louis Cardaillac; Mé;anges Maria Soledad Carrasco Urgoiti. Honours: Congratulations from Vatican for Research on St John of the Cross, 1993. Membership: Association of Literary Scholars and Critics, 1998-; Mensa, 1997-; National Association of Scholars, 1998-. Address: 4518 Bonita Drive, Unit 130, Middletown, OH 45044, USA.

MCCLANE Kenneth (Anderson Jr), b. 19 Feb 1951, New York, New York, USA. Professor; Poet; Writer. m. Rochelle Evette Woods, 22 Oct 1983. Education: AB, 1973, MA, 1974, MFA, 1976, Cornell University. Appointments: Instructor, Colby College, 1974-75; Luce Visiting Professor, Williams College, 1983; Associate Professor, 1983-89, Professor, 1989-93, W E B DuBois Professor, 1993-, Cornell University; Visiting Professor, Wayne State University, 1987, University of Michigan, 1989, Washington University, 1991. Publications: Take Five: Collected Poems, 1988; Walls: Essays 1985-90, 1991. Contributions to: Journals. Honours: George Harmon Coxe Award, 1973; Corson Morrison Poetry Prize, 1973. Memberships: Associated Writing Programs; Phi Beta Kappa; Poets and Writers. Address: c/o Department of English, Cornell University, Rockefeller Hall, Ithaca, NY 14853, USA.

MCCLATCHY J(oseph) D(onald Jr), b. 12 Aug 1945, Bryn Mawr, Pennsylvania, USA. Poet; Writer; Editor. Education: AB, Georgetown University, 1967; PhD, Yale University, 1974. Appointments: Instructor, LaSalle College, Philadelphia, 1968-71; Associate Editor, Four Quarters, 1968-72; Assistant Professor, Yale University, 1974-81; Poetry Editor, 1980-91, Editor, 1991-, The Yale Review; Lecturer in Creative Writing, Princeton University, 1981-93. Publications: Anne Sexton: The Artist and Her Critics, 1978; Scenes from Another Life (poems), 1981; Stars Principal (poems), 1986; James Merrill: Recitative: Prose (editor), 1986; Kilim (poems), 1987; Poets on Painters: Essays on the Art of Painting by Twentieth-Century Poets (editor), 1988; White Paper: On Contemporary American Poetry, 1989; The Rest of the Way (poems), 1990; The Vintage Book of Contemporary American Poetry (editor), 1990; Woman in White: Selected Poems of Emily Dickinson (editor), 1991; The Vintage Book of Contemporary World Poetry (editor), 1996; Ten Commandments (poems), 1998; Questions (essays), 1998. Contributions to: Anthologies and magazines. Honours: Woodrow Wilson Fellowship, 1967-68; O Henry Award, 1972; Ingram Merrill Foundation Grant, 1979; Michener Award, 1982; Gordon Barber Memorial Award, 1984, Melville Cane Award, 1991, Poetry Society of America; Eunice Tietjens Memorial Prize, 1985, Oscar Blumenthal Prize, 1988, Levinson Prize, 1990, Poetry Magazine; Witter Bynner Poetry Prize, 1985, Award in Literature, 1991, American Academy of Arts and Letters; National Endowment for the Arts Fellowship, 1986; Guggenheim Fellowship, 1988; Academy of American Poets Fellowship, 1991. Memberships: Alpha Sigma Nu; International PEN; Phi Beta Kappa; Academy of American Poets, chancellor, 1996-. Address: 15 Grand Street, Stonington, CT 06378, USA.

MCCLELLAND Herbert Lee, b. 22 Nov 1938, Dayton, Ohio, USA. Freelance Writer. Publications: The Ranatan Stories, 1984; The Souvenirs Book of Dayton Cinemas, 1989; The Gem City Treasure Chest, 1991; Daytonians - Their Story, 1992. Address: 4083 Poston Drive, Bellbrook, OH 45305, USA.

MCCLINTOCK David, b. 4 July 1913, Newcastle upon Tyne, England. Writer. m. Elizabeth Anne Dawson, 6 July 1940, dec 1993, 2 sons, 2 daughters. Education: BA, 1934, MA, 1940, Trinity College, Cambridge. Publications: Pocket Guide to Wild Flowers (with R S R Fitter), 1956; Supplement to Pocket Guide to Wild Flowers, 1957; Natural History of the Garden of Buckingham Palace (co-author), 1964; Companion to Flowers, 1966; Guide to the Naming of Plants, 1969, 2nd edition, 1980; Wild Flowers of Guernsey, 1975, Supplement, 1987; Wild Flowers of the Channel Islands (with J Bichard), 1975; Joshua Gosselin of Guernsey, 1976; The Heather Garden by H van de Laar (editor and rewriter), 1978; Guernsey's Earliest Flora, 1982; Heathers of the Lizard, 1998. Contributions to: Many books and other publications. Memberships: Kent Wildlife Trust, vice president, 1963-; Ray Society, president, 1970-73; Botanical Society of the British Isles, president, 1971-73; Linnean Society, vice president, 1971-74; Royal Horticultural Society, scientific committee, 1978-95, vice chairman, 1983-93; Kent Field Club, president, 1978-80; Heather Society, president, 1990-; Wild Flower Society, president, 1997-. Address: Bracken Hill, Platt, Sevenoaks, Kent TN15 8JH, England.

MCCLURE Gillian Mary, b. 29 Oct 1948, Bradford, England. Author; Illustrator. m. 26 Sept 1971, 3 sons. Education: BA, Combined Honours in French, English and History of Art, Bristol University; Teaching Diploma, Moray House. Publications: 14 children's books, 1974-99. Honours: Smarties Award, 1985; Kate Greenaway Award, 1985. Membership: CWIG Society of Authors, committee member, 1989-; PLR Advisory Committee, 1992. Address: 9 Trafalgar Street, Cambridge CB4 1ET, England.

MCCLURE James (Howe), b. 9 Oct 1939, Johannesburg, South Africa. Managing Director; Writer. Appointments: Journalist, Natal, Edinburgh, Oxford, 1963-69; Deputy Editor, Oxford Times Group, 1971-74; Managing Director, Sabensa Gakula Ltd, Oxford, 1975-. Publications: The Steam Pig, 1971; The Caterpillar Cop, 1972; Four and Twenty Virgins, 1973; The Gooseberry Fool, 1974; Snake, 1975; Killers, 1976; Rogue Eagle, 1976; The Sunday Hangman, 1977; The Blood of an Englishman, 1980; Spike Island: Portrait of a British Police Division, 1980; The Artful Egg, 1984; Copworld, 1985; Imago: A Modern Comedy of Manners, 1988; The Song Dog, 1991. Honours: Gold Dagger Award, 1971,

Silver Dagger Award, 1976, Crime Writers Association. Address: 14 York Road, Headington, Oxford OX3 8NW, England.

MCCLURE Michael (Thomas), b. 20 Oct 1932, Marysville, Kansas, USA. Professor; Poet; Dramatist; Writer. m. Joanna Kinnison, 1954, 1 daughter. Education: University of Wichita, 1951-53; University of Arizona, 1953-54; BA, San Francisco State College, 1955. Education: Assistant Professor, 1962-77, Associate Professor, 1977-78, Professor, 1978-, California College of Arts and Crafts, Oakland; Playwright-in-Residence, American Conservatory Theatre, San Francisco, 1975; Associate Fellow, Pierson College, Yale University, 1982. Publications: Poetry: Passage, 1956; For Artaud, 1959; Hymns to St Geryon and Other Poems, 1959; The New Book: A Book of Torture, 1961; Dark Brown, 1961; Ghost Tantras, 1964; 13 Mad Sonnets, 1964; Hail Thee Who Play, 1968, revised edition 1974; The Sermons of Jean Harlow and the Curses of Billy the Kid, 1969; Star, 1971; The Book of Joanna, 1973; Rare Angel (writ with raven's blood), 1974; September Blackberries, 1974; Jaguar Skies, 1975; Antechamber and Other Poems, 1978; The Book of Benjamin, 1982; Fragments of Perseus, 1983; Selected Poems, 1986; Rebel Lions, 1991; Simple Eyes and Other Poems, 1994. Plays: The Growl, in Four in Hand, 1964; The Blossom, or, Billy the Kid, 1967; The Beard, 1967; The Shell, 1968; The Cherub, 1970; Gargoyle Cartoons (11 plays), 1971; The Mammals, 1972; The Grabbing of the Fairy, 1973; Gorf, 1976; General Gorgeous, 1975; Goethe: Ein Fragment, 1978; The Velvet Edge, 1982; The Beard and VKTMs: Two Plays, 1985. Novels: The Mad Club, 1970; The Adept, 1971. Other: Meat Science Essays, 1963, revised edition, 1967; Freewheelin' Frank, Secretary of the Angels, as Told to Michael McClure by Frank Reynolds, 1967; Scratching the Beat Surface, 1982; Specks, 1985; Lighting the Corners: On Art, Nature, and the Visionary: Essays and Interviews, 1993. Honours: National Endowment for the Arts Grants, 1967, 1974; Guggenheim Fellowship, 1971; Magic Theatre Alfred Jarry Award, 1974; Rockefeller Foundation Fellowship, 1975; Obie Award, 1978. Address: 264 Downey Street, San Francisco, CA 94117, USA.

MCCOLLEY Diane Kelsey, b. 9 Feb 1934, Riverside, California, USA. Professor of English; Writer. m. Robert M McColley, 30 Aug 1958, 1 son, 5 daughters. Education: AB, University of California at Berkeley, 1957; PhD, University of Illinois at Urbana-Champaign, 1974. Appointments: Teaching Assistant, 1966-74, Visiting Lecturer, 1975-78, University of Illinois at Urbana-Champaign; Assistant Professor, 1979-84, Associate Professor, 1984-93, Professor of English, 1993-, Camden College of Arts and Sciences, Rutgers University; Visiting Fellow, Lucy Cavendish College, University of Cambridge, 1990. Publications: Milton's Eve, 1983; A Gust for Paradise: Milton's Eden and the Visual Arts, 1993; Poetry and Music in Seventeenth-Century England, 1997. Contributions to: Scholarly books and journals. Honours: National Endowment for the Humanities Fellowship, 1989-90; American Philosophical Society Research Grant, 1990; James Holly Hanford Award, Milton Society of America, 1993. Memberships: Association for the Study of Literature and the Environment; Association of Literary Scholars and Critics; Milton Society of America, president, 1990; Modern Language Association; Renaissance Society of America. Address: c/o Camden College of Arts and Sciences, Rutgers University, Camden, NJ 08102, USA.

MCCONCHIE Lyn, (Elizabeth Underwood, Jan Bishop), b. 3 Apr 1946, Auckland, New Zealand. Writer. Appointments: Justice Department, Agriculture and Fisheries Department, Probation Department. Publications: Farming Daze (as Elizabeth Underwood), 1993; The Key of the Kelian, 1995; The Lonely Troll (also as) The Troll's New Jersey, 1997; Tales From the Marrigan Trade House, 1998; Ciara's Song, 1998; The Troll and the Taniwha, 1998. Contributions to: New Zealand Cat Fancy Yearbook; Disinformation. Honours: Australasion Medal, 1992; New York Public Library Best Books for Teenagers Listing, 1995; Music Medallion, 1996, 1997. Memberships: SFWA; CWA; FAW; NZSA. Literary Agent: Sternig and Bryne, USA. Address: Farside Farm, R D Norsewood 5491, New Zealand.

MCCONICA James Kelsey, b. 24 Apr 1930, Luseland, Saskatchewan, Canada. Professor of History Emeritus; Author. Education: BA, University of Saskatchewan, 1951; BA, 1954, MA, 1957, DPhil, 1963, Oxford University; MA, University of Toronto, 1964. Appointments: Instructor, 1956-57, Assistant Professor, 1957-62, University of Saskatchewan; Associate Professor, 1967-70, Professor of History, 1971-, later Professor Emeritus, Pontifical Institute of Medieval Studies, Toronto; Ordained Roman Catholic Priest, 1968; Visiting Fellow, 1969-71, 1977, Special Ford Lecturer, 1977, Research Fellow, 1978-84, Academic Dean, 1990-92, All Souls College, Oxford; Fellow, Davis Center for Historical Studies, Princeton University, 1971; Professor, University of Toronto, 1972-; President, University of St Michael's College, Toronto, 1984-90. Publications: English Humanists and Reformation Politics under Henry VIII and Edward VI, 1965; The Correspondence of Erasmus (editor), Vol III, 1976, Vol IV, 1977; Thomas More: A Short Biography, 1977; The History of the University of Oxford (editor), Vol III, 1986; Erasmus, 1991. Contributions to: Books and professional journals. Honours: Rhodes Scholar, 1951; Guggenheim Fellowship, 1969-70; Killiam Senior Research Scholar, 1976-77; Honorary LLD, University of Saskatchewan, 1986; Honorary DLitt, University of Windsor, 1989. Memberships: American Society for Reformation Research; Canadian Society for Renaissance Studies; Oxfrod Historical Society; Renaissance Society of America; Royal Historical Society, fellow; Royal Society of Canada, fellow; British Academy, Corresponding Fellow; Royal Belgian Academy, Foreign Member. Address: c/o Department of History, University of Toronto, Toronto, Ontario M5S 1A1, Canada.

MCCONKEY James (Rodney), b. 2 Sept 1921, Lakewood, Ohio, USA. Professor of English Literature Emeritus; Writer. m. Gladys Jean Voorhees, 6 May 1944, 3 sons. Education: BA, Cleveland College, 1943; MA, Western Reserve University, 1946; PhD, University of Iowa, 1953. Appointments: Assistant Professor to Associate Professor, Morehead State College, Kentucky, 1950-56; Director, Morehead Writer's Workshop, 1951-56, Antioch Seminar in Writing and Publishing, Yellow Springs, Ohio, 1957-60; Assistant Professor to Associate Professor, 1956-62, Professor of English, 1962-87; Goldwin Smith Professor of English Literature, 1987-92, Professor Emeritus, 1992-. Publications: The Novels of E M Forster, 1957; The Structure of Prose (editor), 1963; Night Stand, 1965; Crossroads: An Autobiographical Novel, 1968; A Journal to Sahalin (novel), 1971; The Tree House Confessions (novel), 1979; Court of Memory, 1983; To a Distant Island (novel), 1984; Chekhov and Our Age: Responses to Chekhov by American Writers and Scholars (editor), 1984; Kayo: The Authentic and Annotated Autobiographical Novel from Outer Space, 1987; Rowan's Progress, 1992; Stories from My Life with the Other Animals, 1993; The Anatomy of Memory (editor), 1996. Contributions to: Magazines. Honours: Eugene Saxton Literary Fellow, 1962-63; National Endowment for the Arts Essay Award, 1967; Ohioana Book Award, 1969; Guggenheim Fellowship, 1969-70; American Academy of Arts and Letters Award, 1979. Membership: PEN. Address: 402 Aiken Road, Trumansburg, NY 14886, USA.

MCCONNELL Will. See: SNODGRASS W D.

MCCONVILLE Michael Anthony, b. 3 Jan 1925, Crowsborough, England. Writer. m. Beryl Anne Jerrett, 15 May 1952, 2 sons, 4 daughters. Education: Mayfield College, 1940-42; Trinity College, Dublin, 1947-50, BA (Mod); MA. Publications: Leap in the Dark, 1980; More Tales from the Mess, 1983; The Burke Foundation, 1985; A Small War in the Balkans, 1986; Ascendancy to Oblivion, 1986. Contributions to: Blackwoods; Rusi Journal; Malayan Monthly. Membership: Writers' Guild. Address: 72 Friarn Street, Bridgewater, Somerset, TA6 3ES, England.

MCCORMICH A. See: **LEWIS-SMITH Anne Elizabeth.**

MCCORMICK John Owen, b. 20 Sept 1918, Thief River Falls, Minnesota, USA. Professor of Comparative Literature Emeritus; Writer. m. Mairi MacInnes, 4 Feb 1954, 3 sons, 1 daughter. Education: BA, 1941, MA, 1947, University of Minnesota; PhD, Harvard University, 1951. Appointments: Senior Tutor and Teaching Assistant, Harvard University, 1946-51; Lecturer, Salzburg Seminar in American Studies, Austria, 1951-52; Professor of American Studies, Free University of Berlin, 1952-53, 1954-59; Professor of Comparative Literature, 1959-, now Emeritus, Rutgers University, New Brunswick, New Jersey. Publications: Catastrophe and Imagination, 1957, 1998; Versions of Censorship (with Mairi MacInnes), 1962; The Complete Aficionado, 1967, 2nd edition, 1998; The Middle Distance: A Comparative History of American Imaginative Literature, 1919-1932, 1971; Fiction as Knowledge: The Modern Post-Romantic Novel, 1975, 1998; George Santayana: A Biography, 1987; Sallies of the Mind: Essays of Francis Fergusson (editor with G Core), 1997. Contributions to: Numerous magazines and journals. Honours: Longview Award for Non-Fiction, 1960; Guggenheim Fellowships, 1964-65, 1980-81; National Endowments for the Humanities Senior Fellow, 1983-84; American Academy and Institute of Arts and Letters Prize, 1988. Address: Hovingham Lodge, Hovingham, York YO6 4NA, England.

MCCOURT James, b. 4 July 1941, New York, New York, USA. Author. Education: BA, Manhattan College, 1962; Graduate Studies, New York University, 1962-64; Yale University, 1964-65. Publications: Maurdrew Czgowdiwz, 1975; Kaye Wayfaring, 1984; Time Remaining, 1993. Contributions to: Anthologies and magazines. Address: c/o Vincent Virga, 145 East 22nd Street, New York, NY 10003, USA.

MCCRACKEN Amanda Jane, b. 15 Mar 1958, Nottingham, England. Editor. m. Ian McCracken, 13 May 1989. Appointments: Features Assistant, Nottingham Evening Post, 1977; Deputy Editor, Life and Countryside, 1981; Assistant Editor, The Lady, 1989; Editor, Boat International, 1997. Contributions to: Under the Gavel; The Lady. Address: c/o Boat International, Edisea Limited, Ward House, Kingston Hill, Kingston Upon Thames, Surrey KT2 7PW, England.

MCCRAW Thomas K(incaid), b. 11 Sept 1940, Corinth, Mississippi, USA. Professor of Business History; Writer; Editor. m. Susan Morehead, 22 Sept 1962, 1 son, 1 daughter. Education: BA, University of Mississippi, 1962; MA, 1968, PhD, 1970, University of Wisconsin. Appointments: Newcomen Research Fellow, 1973-74, Visiting Associate Professor, 1976-78, Professor, 1978-89, Isidor Straus Professor Business History, 1989-, Harvard University; Assistant Professor, 1970-74, Associate Professor, 1974-78, University of Texas at Austin; Editor, Business History Review, 1994-. Publications: Morgan Versus Lilienthal: The Feud Within the TVA, 1970; TVA and the Power Fight, 1933-39, 1971; Regulation in Perspective: Historical Essays (editor), 1981; Prophets of Regulation, 1984; America Versus Japan (editor), 1986; The Essential Alfred Chandler (editor), 1988; Management Past and Present (co-author), 1996; Creating Modern Capitalism (editor), 1997; The Intellectual Venture Capitalist: John H. McArthur and the Work of the Harvard Business School, 1980-1995 (co-editor), forthcoming. Contributions to: Scholarly books and journals. Honours: Woodrow Wilson Fellow, 1966-67; William P Lyons Master's Essays Award, Loyola University, Chicago, 1969; Younger Humanist Award, National Endowment for the Humanities, 1975; Pulitzer Prize in History, 1985; Thomas Newcomen Book Award, 1986; Inducted, Alumni Hall of Fame, University of Mississippi, 1986. Memberships: American Economic Association; Business History Conference, trustee, 1986-95, president, 1989; Economic History Association; Massachusetts Historical Society; Organization of American Historians. Address: c/o Harvard University Business School, Soldiers Field, Boston, MA 02163, USA.

MCCREADY Jack. See: POWELL Talmage.

MCCRORIE Edward Pollitt, b. 19 Nov 1936, Central Falls, Rhode Island, USA. Professor of English. m. 27 May 1995. Education: PhD, Brown University, 1970. Publications: After a Cremation, poems, 1974; The Aeneid of Virgil, translation, 1995. Contributions to: Poems in USA journals. Address: English Department, Providence College, Providence, RI 02918, USA.

MCCRUMB Sharyn Elaine Atwood, b. 26 Feb 1948, Wilmington, North Carolina, USA. Writer. m. David McCrumb, 9 Jan 1982, 1 son, 2 daughters. Education: BA, University of North Carolina, 1970; MA, Virginia Polytechnic Institute and State University, 1987. Publications: The Hangman's Beautiful Daughter; If Ever I Return Pretty Peggy O; Bimbos of the Death Sun; Missing Susan; Highland Laddie Gone; Sick of Shadows; Lovely in Her Bones; Paying the Piper; The Windsor Knot; Zombies of the Gene Pool; MacPherson's Lament. Contributions to: Magazines. Honours: Notable Book, New York Times; Best Appalachian Novel Award; Edgar Award; Macavity Award; Agatha Award. Memberships: Mystery Writers of America; Sisters in Crime; Appalachian Writers Association; Whimsey Foundation. Address: Rowan Mountain Inc, PO Box 10111, Blacksburg, VA 24062, USA.

MCCRYSTAL Cahal, (Cal McCrystal), b. 20 Dec 1935, Belfast, Northern Ireland. Journalist; Author. m. Stella Doyle, 15 Oct 1958, 3 sons. Education: St Mary's College, Dundalk; St Malachy's College, Belfast. Appointments: Reporter, Northern Herald; Labour Correspondent, Belfast Telegraph; Crime Reporter, Chief Reporter, Foreign Correspondent, New York Bureau Chief, News Editor, Foreign Features Editor, Sunday Times, London; Senior Writer, Independent-on-Sunday; Senior Writer, The Observer. Publications: Watergate: The Full Inside Story (co-author), 1973; Reflections on A Quiet Rebel, 1997. Contributions to: Vanity Fair, British Magazines, and British Journalism Review. Honours: Various journalism awards; Belfast Arts Council Literary Award, 1998. Membership: Editorial Board, British Journalism Review. Literary Agent: Greene and Heaton Ltd. Address: 37 Goldhawk Road, London W12 8QQ, England.

MCCULLAGH Sheila Kathleen, b. 3 Dec 1920, Surrey, England. Writer. Education: Bedford Froebel College, 1939-42; MA, University of Leeds, 1949. Publications: Pirate Books, 1957-64; Tales and Adventures, 1961; Dragon Books, 1963-70; One, Two, Three and Away, 1964-92; Tim Books, 1974-83; Into New Worlds, 1974; Hummingbirds, 1976-92; Whizzbang Adventures, 1980; Buccaneers, 1980-84; Where Wild Geese Fly, 1981; Puddle Lane, 1985-88; The Sea Shore, 1992. Honour: Member of the Order of the British Empire, 1987. Membership: Society of Authors. Literary Agent: A P Watt. Address: 27 Royal Crescent, Bath, Avon BA1 2CT, England.

MCCULLOUGH Colleen, b. 1 June 1937, Wellington, New South Wales, Australia. Writer. m. Ric Robinson, 1984. Education: Holy Cross College, Woollahra, Sydney University; Institute of Child Health, London University. Appointments: Neurophysiologist, Sydney, London and Yale University Medical School, New Haven, Connecticut, USA, 1967-77; Relocated to Norfolk Island, South Pacific, 1980. Publications: Tim, 1974; The Thorn Birds, 1977; An Indecent Obsession, 1981; Cooking with Colleen McCullough and Jean Easthope, 1982; A Creed for the Third Millennium, 1985; The Ladies of Missalonghi, 1987; The First Man in Rome, 1990; The Grass Crown, 1991; Fortune's Favorites, 1993; Caesar's Women, 1996; Hail Caesar, 1997; The Song of Troy, 1998. Honour: Doctor of Letters (honoris causa), Macquarie University, Sydney, 1993. Address: Out Yenna, Norfolk Island, Oceania (via Australia).

MCCULLOUGH David (Gaub), b. 7 July 1933, Pittsburgh, Pennsylvania, USA. Historian; Author. m. Rosalee Ingram Barnes, 18 Dec 1954, 3 sons, 2 daughters. Education: BA, Yale University, 1955. Appointments: Editor, Time Inc, New York City, 1956-61; United States Information Agency, Washington, DC, 1961-64; American Heritage Publishing Co, New York City, 1964-70; Scholar-in-Residence, University of New Mexico, 1979; Wesleyan University, 1982, 1983; Host, Smithsonian World, 1984-88, The American Experience, 1988-, PBS-TV; Visiting Professor, Cornell University, 1989. Publications: The Great Bridge, 1972; The Path Between the Seas, 1977; The Johnstown Flood, 1978; Mornings on Horseback, 1981; Brave Companions, 1991; Truman, 1992. Honours: National Book Award for History, 1978; Samuel Eliot Morison Award, 1978; Cornelius Ryan Award, 1978; Francis Parkman Prizes, 1978, 1993; Los Angeles Times Prize for Biography, 1981; American Book Award for Biography, 1982; Pulitzer Prize for Biography, 1993; Harry S Truman Public Service Award, 1993; Pennsylvania Governor's Award for Excellence, 1993; St Louis Literary Award, 1993; Pennsylvania Society Gold Medal Award, 1994; National Book Foundation Medal for Distinguished Contributions to American Letters, 1995; Various honorary doctorates. Memberships: Jefferson Legacy Foundation; National Trust for Historic Preservation; Society of American Historians, president, 1991-; Harry S Truman Library Institute. Address: c/o Janklow & Nesbit Associates, 598 Madison Avenue, New York, NY 10022, USA.

MCCULLOUGH Ken(neth), b. 18 July 1943, Staten Island, New York, USA. Poet; Writer; Teacher. Education: BA, University of Delaware, 1966; MFA, University of Iowa, 1968. Appointments: Teacher, Montana State University, 1970-75, University of Iowa, 1983-95; Kirkwood Community College, Cedar Rapids, 1987, St Mary's University, Winona, Minnesota, 1996; Writer-in-Residence, South Carolina ETV Network, 1975-78; Participant, Artist-in-the-Schools Program, Iowa Arts Council, 1981-96. Publications: Poetry: The Easy Wreckage, 1971; Migrations, 1972; Creosote, 1976; Elegy for Old Anna, 1985; Travelling Light, 1987; Sycamore Oriole, 1991; Walking Backwards, 1997. Contributions to: Numerous publications. Honours: Academy of American Poets Award, 1966; 2nd Place, Ark River Awards, 1972; Helene Wurlitzer Foundation of New Mexico Residencies, 1973, 1994; National Endowment for the Arts Fellowship, 1974; 2nd Prize, Sri Chinmoy Poetry Awards, 1980; Writers' Voice Capricorn Book Award, 1985; 2nd Place, Pablo Neruda Award, Nimrod magazine 1990; 3rd Prize, Kudzu Poetry Contest, 1990; Ucross Foundation Residency, Wyoming, 1991; Witter Bynner Foundation for Poetry Grant, 1993; Iowa Arts Council Grants, 1994, 1996. Memberships: Associated Writing Programs; Association of American University Professors; National Association of College Academic Advisers; Renaissance Artists and Writers Association and Renaissance International; Rocky Mountain Modern Language Association; Science Fiction Writers of America. Address: 372 Center Street, Winona, MN 55987, USA.

MCCULLY Emily Arnold, (Emily Arnold), b. 7 Jan 1939, Galesburg, Illinois, USA. Author; Illustrator. 2 sons. Education: BA, Brown University, 1961; MA, Columbia University, 1964. Publications: A Craving, 1982; Picnic, 1985; Life Drawing, 1986; Mirette on the High Wire, 1992; The Amazing Felix, 1993; Little Kit, or, the Industrious Flea Circus Girl, 1995; The Pirate Queen, 1995. Honours: O Henry Award Collection, 1977; Caldecott Award, 1993. Memberships: PEN Society; Authors Guild. Address: c/o Harriet Wasserman, 137 East 36th Street, New York, NY 10026, USA.

MCCUNN Ruthanne Lum, b. 21 Feb 1946, San Francisco, California, USA. Writer. m. Donald H McCunn, 15 June 1965. Education: BA, 1968. Publications: Illustrated History of the Chinese in America, 1979; Thousand Pieces of Gold, 1981; Pie Biter, 1983; Sole Survivor, 1985; Chinese American Portraits, 1988; Chinese Proverbs, 1991; Wooden Fish Songs, 1995. Contributions to: Yihai and Chinese America: History and Perspectives. Honour: Before Columbus Foundation American Book Award, 1983; Jeanne Fair McDonnell Award, Best Fiction, Women's Heritage Museums, 1997. Memberships: Chinese Historical Society of America; Asian Women United; American Civil Liberties Union; Chinese for Affirmative Action; Amnesty International. Address: 1007 Castro Street, San Francisco, CA 94114, USA.

MCCUTCHEON Elsie Mary Jackson, b. 6 Apr 1937, Glasgow, Scotland. Writer. m. James McCutcheon, 14 July 1962, dec, 1 daughter. Education: BA, University of Glasgow, 1960; Jordanhill College of Education, 1961. Appointments: English Teacher, Glasgow, 1961-63; Publicity Officer, Norfolk Archaeological Rescue Group, 1976-78; Editor, Newsletter, Friends of the Suffolk Record Office, 1984-91. Publications: Summer of the Zeppelin; The Rat War; Smokescreen; Storm Bird; Twisted Truth. Contributions to: She; Good Housekeeping; Ideal Home; Scotland's Magazine; Scottish Field; Suffolk Fair; Eastern Daily Press. Honour: Runner-up, Guardian Award for Children's Fiction. Memberships: Bury St Edmunds Library Users Group; Writers Guild of Great Britain; Suffolk Local History Council; Suffolk Institute of Archaeology. Address: Wendover, Sharpers Lane, Horringer, Bury St Edmunds, Suffolk IP29 5PS, England.

MCCUTCHEON Hugh, (Hugh Davie-Martin, Griselda Wilding), b. 24 July 1909, Glasgow, Scotland. Author. Education: University of Glasgow, 1928-33; Qualified as Solicitor, 1933. Appointment: Town Clerk, Renfrew, Scotland, 1945-74. Publications: Alamein to Tunis, 1946; The Angel of Light, US edition as Murder at the Angel, 1951; None Shall Sleep Tonight, 1954; Prey for the Nightingale, 1954; Cover Her Face, 1955; The Long Night Through, 1956; Comes the Blind Fury, 1957; To Dusty Death, 1960; Yet She Must Die, 1961; The Deadly One, 1962; Suddenly in Vienna, 1963; Treasure of the Sun, 1964; The Black Attendant, 1966; Killer's Moon, US edition as The Moon Was Full, 1967; The Scorpion's Nest, 1968; A Hot Wind from Hell, 1969; Brand for the Burning, 1970; Something Wicked, 1970; Red Sky at Night, 1972; Instrument of Vengeance, 1975; Night Watch, 1978; The Cargo of Death, 1980. As Hugh Davie-Martin: The Girl in My Grave, 1976; The Pearl of Oyster Island, 1977; Spaniard's Leap, 1979; Death's Bright Angel, 1982. As Griselda Wilding: Promise of Delight, 1988; Beloved Wolf, 1991. Address: 19 Bentinck Drive, Troon, Ayrshire, Scotland.

MCDERMOTT Alice, b. 27 June 1953, Brooklyn, New York, USA. Writer. m. David M Armstrong. Education: BA, State University of New York, 1975; MA, University of New Hampshire, 1978. Publications: A Bigamist's Daughter, 1982; That Night, 1987; At Weddings and Wakes, 1991; Charming Billy, 1998. Contributions to: Magazines. Honours: Whiting Writers Award, 1987; National Book Award, 1998. Memberships: Associated Writing Programs; PEN; Poets and Writers; Writer's Guild. Address: 8674-3 Villa La Jolla Drive, La Jolla, CA 92037, USA.

MCDEVITT Jack, b. 14 Apr 1935, Philadelphia, Pennsylvania, USA. Writer. m. Maureen McAdams, 16 Dec 1967, 2 sons, 1 daughter. Education: BA, La Salle College, 1953-57; MA, Wesleyan University, 1967-71. Publications: The Hercules Text, 1986; A Talent for War, 1989; The Engines of God, 1984; Ancient Shores, 1996; Standard Candles, 1996; Eternity Road, 1997; Moonfall, 1998. Contributions to: approx 50 short stories. Honours: Nebula and Hugo Finalist, Winner UPC Grand Prize, 1992; Philip K Dick Special Award, 1986; Runner-Up, UPA Award, 1994. Membership: SFWA. Literary Agent: Ralph Vioinanza. Address: 57 Sunset Boulevard, Brunswick, GA 31525, USA.

MCDONALD Catherine Donna, b. 20 Dec 1942, Vancouver, British Columbia, Canada. Writer; Arts Administrator. m. Robert Francis McDonald, 28 Aug 1965. Education: BA, 1964. Publications: Illustrated News: Juliana Horatia Ewing's Canadian Pictures 1867-1869; The Odyssey of the Philip Jones Brass Ensemble; Lord Strathcona; A Biography of Donald Alexander Smith. Contributions to: Periodicals and journals. Address: 10 Chelwood Gardens, Richmond, Surrey TW9 4JQ, England.

MCDONALD Forrest, b. 7 Jan 1927, Orange, Texas, USA. Distinguished University Research Professor; Historian; Writer. m. (1), 3 sons, 2 daughters, (2) Ellen Shapiro, 1 Aug 1963. Education: BA, MA, 1949, PhD, 1955, University of Texas. Appointments: Executive Secretary, American History Research Centre, Madison, Wisconsin, 1953-58; Associate Professor, 1959-63, Professor of History, 1963-67, Brown University; Professor, Wayne State University, 1967-76; Professor, 1976-87, Distinguished University Research Professor, 1987-, University of Alabama, Tuscaloosa; Presidential Appointee, Board of Foreign Scholarships, Washington, DC, 1985-87; Advisor, Centre of Judicial Studies, Cumberland, Virginia, 1985-92; James Pinckney Harrison Professor, College of William and Mary, 1986-87; Jefferson Lecturer, National Endowment for the Humanities, 1987. Publications: We the People: The Economic Origins of the Constitution, 1958; Insull, 1962; E Pluribus Unum, 1965; The Presidency of George Washington, 1974; The Phaeton Ride, 1974; The Presdiency of Thomas Jefferson, 1976; Alexander Hamilton: A Biography, 1979; Novus Ordo Seclorum, 1985; Requiem, 1988; The American Presidency: An Intellectual History, 1994. Contributions to: Professional journals. Honours: Guggenheim Fellowship, 1962-63; George Washington Medal, Freedom's Foundation, 1980; Frances Tavern Book Award, 1980; Best Book Award, American Revolution Round Table, 1986; Richard M Weaver Award, Ingersoll Foundation, 1990; First Salvatori Award, Heritage Foundation, 1992; Salvatori Book Award, Intercollegiate Studio International, 1994; Mount Vernon Society Choice, One of the Ten Great Books on George Washington, 1998. Memberships: American Antiquarian Society; Philadelphia Society; The Historical Society. Address: PO Box 155, Coker, AL 35452, USA.

MCDONALD Gregory (Christopher), b. 15 Feb 1937, Shrewsbury, Massachusetts, USA. Writer. m. Susan Aiken, 12 Jan 1963, div 1990, 2 sons. Education: BA, Harvard University, 1958. Appointment: Critic, Boston Globe, 1966-73. Publications: Fiction: Running Scared, 1964; Fletch, 1974; Confess, Fletch, 1976; Flynn, 1977; Love Among the Mashed Potatoes, 1978; Fletch's Fortune, 1978; Fletch Forever, 1978; Who Took Tony Rinaldi?, 1980; Fletch and the Widow Bradley, 1981; The Buck Passes Flynn, 1981; Fletch's Moxie, 1982; Fletch and the Man Who, 1983; Carioca Fletch, 1984; Flynn's In, 1984; Fletch Won, 1985; Safekeeping, 1985; Fletch, Too, 1986; Fletch Chronicle, 3 volumes, 1986-88; A World Too Wide, 1987; Exits and Entrances, 1988; Merely Players, 1988; The Brave, 1991; Son of Fletch, 1993; Fletch Reflected, 1994; Skylar, 1995; Skylar in Yankeeland, 1997. Non-Fiction: The Education of Gregory McDonald, 1985. Editor: Last Laughs, 1986. Honours: Edgar Allan Poe Awards, Mystery Writers of America, 1975, 1977; Humanitarian of the Year Award, Tennessee Association of Federal Executives, 1989; Citizen of the Year Award, National Association of Social Workers, 1990; Roger William Straus Award, 1990; Alex Haley Award, 1992. Memberships: Authors Guild; Crime Writers Association, England; Dramatists Guild; Mystery Writers of America, president, 1985-86; Writers Guild of America. Address: c/o Arthur Greene Esquire, 101 Park Avenue, New York, NY 10178, USA.

MCDONALD Ian (A), b. 18 Apr 1933, St Augustine, Trinidad. Poet; Writer; Dramatist; Editor. m. Mary Angela Callender, 1984, 3 sons. Education: Queen's Royal College, Trinidad; University of Cambridge, 1951-55. Appointments: Director, Theatre Co of Guyana, Georgetown, 1981-; Editor, Kyk-Over-Al, West Indian literary journal, 1984-; Chairman, Demerana Publishers, 1988-. Publications: The Tramping Man (play), 1969; The Humming Bird Tree (novel), 1969; Selected Poems, 1983; Mercy World, 1988; Essequibo, 1992; Jaffo the Calypsonian (poems), 1994; The Heinemann Book of Caribbean Poetry (co-editor), 1994. Honours: Fellow, Royal Society of Literature, 1970; Guyana National Award, 1987; Honorary DLitt, University of the West Indies, 1997. Address: c/o Guyana Sugar Corp, 22 Church Street, Georgetown, Guyana.

MCDONALD J O. See: **HIBBERD Jean.**

MCDONALD Walter R(obert), b. 18 July 1934, Lubbock, Texas, USA. Horn Professor of English; Poet; Writer. m. Carol Ham, 28 Aug 1959, 2 sons, 1 daughter. Education: BA, 1956, MA, 1957, Texas Technological College; PhD, University of Iowa, 1966. Appointments: Faculties, US Air Force Academy, University of Colorado, Texas Tech University; Paul W Horn Professor of English and Poet-in-Residence, Texas Tech University, Lubbock. Publications: Poetry: Caliban in Blue, 1976; One Thing Leads to Another, 1978; Anything, Anything, 1980; Working Against Time, 1981; Burning the Fence, 1981; Witching on Hardscrabble, 1985; Flying Dutchman, 1987; After the Noise of Saigon, 1988; Rafting the Brazos, 1988. Fiction: A Band of Brothers: Stories of Vietnam, 1989; Night Landings, 1989; The Digs in Escondido Canyon, 1991; All That Matters: The Texas Plains in Photographs and Poems, 1992; Where Skies Are Not Cloudy, 1993; Counting Survivors, 1995. Contributions to: Numerous journals and magazines. Honours: Poetry Awards, Texas Institute of Letters, 1976, 1985, 1987; George Elliston Poetry Prize, 1987; Juniper Prize, 1988; Western Heritage Awards for Poetry, National Cowboy Hall of Fame, 1990, 1992; 1993. Memberships: Texas Association of Creative Writing Teachers; PEN; Poetry Society of America; Associated Writing Programs; Texas Institute of Letters, councillor; Past President Conference of College Teachers of English of Texas. Address: Department of English, Texas Tech University, Lubbock, TX 79409, USA.

MCDOUGALL Bonnie Suzanne, b. 12 Mar 1941, Sydney, Australia. Professor. m. H Anders Hansson, 1980, 1 son. Education: BA, 1965, MA, 1967, PhD, 1970, University of Sydney. Publications: Introduction of Western Literary Theories into China; Mao Zedong's Talks at the Yanan Conference; Popular Chinese Literature and Performing Arts; The Yellow Earth: A Film by Chen Kaige; The August Sleepwalker; Old Snow; Brocade Valley. Contributions to: Journal of the Oriental Society of Australia; Modern Chinese Literature; Renditions; Contemporary China; Stand; Grand Street; New Directions. Memberships: British Association of Chinese Studies; Universities' China Committee in London; Amnesty International. Address: Department of East Asian Studies, University of Edinburgh, 8 Buccleuch Place, Edinburgh EH8 9LW, Scotland.

MCDOUGALL Walter A(llan), b. 3 Dec 1946, Washington, District of Columbia, USA. Professor of History; Writer. m. Elizabeth Swoope, 8 Aug 1970, div 1979. Education: BA cum laude, Amherst College, 1968; MA, 1971, PhD, 1974, University of Chicago. Appointments: Assistant Professor, 1975-83, Associate Professor, 1983-87, Professor of History, 1987-, University of California, Berkeley; Vestryman, St Peter's Episcopal Church. Publications: France's Rhineland Diplomacy 1914-1924: The Last Bid for a Balance of Power in Europe, 1978; The Grenada Papers (editor with Paul Seabury), 1984; Social Sciences and Space Exploration: New Directions for University Instruction (contributor), 1984; ...The Heavens and the Earth: A Political History of the Space Age, 1985; Let the Sea Make a Noise, 1993. Contributions to: Numerous articles and reviews to periodicals. Honours: Pulitzer Prize for History, 1986; Visiting Scholar, Hoover Institution, 1986; One of America's Ten Best College Professors, Insight, 1987; Dexter Prize for Best Book, Society for the History of Technology, 1987. Memberships: American Church Union; Pumpkin Papers Irregulars; Delta Kappa Epsilon. Address: Department of History, University of California, Berkeley, CA 94720, USA.

MCDOWALL David Buchanan, b. 14 Apr 1945, London, England. Writer. m. 19 Apr 1975, 2 sons. Education: MA, St John's College, Oxford. Publications: Palestine and Israel: The Uprising and Beyond; The Kurds: A Nation Denied; An Illustrated History of Britain; Britain in Close Up; The Spanish Armada; Europe and the Arabs: Discord or Symbiosis?; Lebanon: A Conflict of Minorities; A Modern History of the Kurds, 1996; Richmond Park: The Walkers Historical Guide, 1996;

Hampstead Heath: The Walker's Guide (co-author Bedorah Wolten), 1998. Contributions to: World Directory of Minorities, middle east section, 1997. Honour: The Other Award. Address: 31 Cambrian Road, Richmond, Surrey TW10 6JQ, England.

MCDOWELL Edwin (Stewart), b. 13 May 1935, Somers Point, New Jersey, USA. Journalist; Writer. m. Sathie Akimoto, 7 July 1973, 1 son, 2 daughters. Education: BS, Temple University, 1959. Appointment: Staff, New York Times. Publications: Three Cheers and a Tiger, 1966; To Keep Our Honor Clean, 1980; The Lost World, 1988. Membership: Authors Guild. Address: c/o New York Times, 229 West 43rd Street, New York, NY 10036, USA.

MCDOWELL Michael, (Nathan Aldyne, Axel Young), b. 1 June 1950, Enterprise, Alabama, USA. Author. Education: BA, Harvard University, 1972; PhD, Brandeis University, 1978. Publications: Over 20 novels, 1979-88. Address: c/o The Otte Company, 6 Golden Street, Belmont, MA 01278, USA.

MCELROY Colleen J(ohnson), b. 30 Oct 1935, St Louis, Missouri, USA. Professor; Poet; Writer. Div, 1 son, 1 daughter. Education: BS, 1958, MS, 1963, Kansas State University; PhD, University of Washington, Seattle, 1973. Appointments: Editor, Dark Waters, 1973-79; Professor, University of Washington, Seattle, 1973-. Publications: Music From Home, 1976; The Halls of Montezuma, 1979; The New Voice, 1979; Winters Without Snow, 1979; Lie and Say You Love Me, 1981; Queen of the Ebony Isles, 1984; Jesus and Fat Tuesday, 1987; What Madness Brought Me Here, 1990. Contributions to: Various journals. Address: c/o Creative Writing Program, Department of English, University of Washington, Seattle, WA 98195, USA.

MCELROY Joseph (Prince), b. 21 Aug 1930, New York, New York, USA. Author. Education: BA, Williams College, 1951; MA, 1952, PhD, 1961, Columbia University. Publications: A Smuggler's Bible, 1966; Hind's Kidnap, 1969; Ancient History, 1971; Lookout Cartridge, 1974; Plus, 1977; Ship Rock, 1980; Women and Men, 1987. Address: c/o Georges Borchardt, 136 East 57th Street, New York, NY 10022, USA.

MCELROY Lee. See: **KELTON Elmer Stephen.**

MCEVEDY Colin (Peter), b. 6 June 1930, Stratford, England. Writer. Education: BA, 1948, BM, BCH, 1955, DM, 1970, Magdalen College, Oxford; DPM, University of London, 1963. Publications: The Penguin Atlas of Medieval History, 1961; The Penguin Atlas of Ancient History, 1967; The Atlas World History (with Sarah McEvedy), 3 volumes, 1970-73; The Penguin Atlas of Modern History, 1972; Atlas of World Population History (with Richard Jones), 1980; The Penguin Atlas of African History, 1980; The Penguin Atlas of Recent History (Europe since 1815), 1982; The Century World History FactFinder, 1984; The Penguin Atlas of North American History, 1988; The New Penguin Atlas of Medieval History, 1992. Contributions to: Bubonic Plague; Scientific American. Address: 7 Caithness Road, London W14, England.

MCEVOY Marjorie, (Gillian Bond, Marjorie Harte), b. York, England. Novelist. m. William Noel McEvoy, 1 son, 1 daughter. Publications: Doctors in Conflict, 1962; The Grenfell Legacy, 1967; Dusky Cactus, 1969; Echoes from the Past, 1978; Calabrian Summer, 1980; Sleeping Tiger, 1982; Star of Randevi, 1984; Temple Bells, 1985; Camelot Country, 1986; The Black Pearl, 1988. Contributions to: Newspapers and magazines. Membership: Romantic Novelists Association. Address: 54 Miriam Avenue, Chesterfield, Derbyshire, England.

MCEWAN Ian (Russell), b. 21 June 1948, Aldershot, Hampshire, England. Writer. m. (1) Penny Allen, 1982, div 1995, 2 sons, 2 daughters, (2) Annalena McAfee. Education: BA, Honours, English Literature, University of Sussex, 1970; MA, English Literature, University of East Anglia, 1971. Publications: First Love, Last Rites, 1975;

In Between the Sheets, 1978; The Cement Garden, 1978; The Imitation Game, 1981; The Comfort of Strangers, 1981; The Child in Time, 1987; The Innocent, 1990; Black Dogs, 1992; The Daydreamer, 1994; The Short Stories, 1995; Enduring Love, 1997; Amsterdam, 1998. Other: Or Shall We Die? (libretto for the oratorio by Michael Berkeley), 1982; film scripts. Honours: Somerset Maugham Award, 1975; Fellow, Royal Society of Literature, 1982; Whitbread Awards, 1987; Honorary DLitt, University of Sussex, 1989; Prix Fémina, 1993; Honorary LittD, University of East Anglia, 1993; Fellow, American Academy of Arts and Sciences, 1995. Address: c/o Jonathon Cape, Random Century House, 20 Vauxhall Bridge Road, London SW1V 2SA, England.

MCEWEN Christian, b. 21 Apr 1956, London, England. Writer. Education: BA, Cambridge University; MA, University of California at Berkeley. Appointments: Teacher, Goldsmiths College, London, Eugene Lang and Parsons School of the Arts, New York City, Lesley College, Cambridge, Massachusetts, Williams College, Williamstown, Massachusetts. Publications: Naming the Waves: Contemporary Lesbian Poetry; Out The Other Side: Contemporary Lesbian Writing; Jo's Girls: Tomboy Tales of High Adventure, True Grit and Real Life. Contributions to: American Voice; Orion; Nation; Village Voice; Voice Literary Supplement. Honours: Fulbright Scholarship; Lambda Literary Award. Membership: Writers Union. Literary Agent: Jennie Dunham. Address: 28 Clesson Brook Road RR1, Charlemont, MA 01339, USA.

MCFARLAND Ronald E(arl), (Ron McFarland), b. 22 Sept 1942, Bellaire, Ohio, USA. Professor of English; Poet; Writer. m. Elsie Roseland Watson, 29 Jan 1966, 1 son, 2 daughters. Education: AA, Brevard Junior College, 1962; BA, 1963, MA, 1965, Florida State University; PhD, University of Illinois, 1970. Appointments: Teaching Assistant, Florida State University, 1964-65, University of Illinois, 1967-70; Instructor, Sam Houston State College, 1965-67; Assistant Professor, Associate Professor, 1970-79, Professor of English, 1979-, University of Idaho; Idaho State Writer-in-Residence, 1984-85; Exchange Professor, Ohio University, 1985-86. Publications: Poetry: Certain Women, 1977; Composting at Forty, 1984; The Haunting Familiarity of Things, 1993. Non-Fiction: The Villanelle: Evolution of a Poetic Form, 1988; David Wagoner, 1989; Norman Maclean, 1993; Tess Gallagher, 1995; The World of David Wagoner, 1997. Editor: Eight Idaho Poets, 1979; James Welch, 1987; Norman Maclean (with Hugh Nichols), 1988; Idaho's Poetry: A Centennial Anthology (with William Studebaker), 1988; Deep Down Things: Poems of the Inland Pacific Northwest (with Franz Schneider and Kornel Skovajsa), 1990. Contributions to: Scholarly books and journals, poetry anthologies, reviews, quarterlies, and periodicals. Honours: National Endowment for the Arts Grant, 1978; Association for the Humanities in Idaho Grant, 1983; Burlington-Northern Faculty Achievement Award, 1990; Alumni Award for Faculty Excellence, 1991; Distinguished Alumnus, Brevard Community College, 1996. Memberships: Academy of American Poets; Inland Northwest Council of Teachers of English; Pacific Northwest American Studies Association; Popular Culture Association; Western Literature Association. Address: 857 East Street, Moscow, ID 83843, USA.

MCFARLANE James Walter, b. 12 Dec 1920, Sunderland, England. Professor of European Literature Emeritus; Writer. m. Lillie Kathleen Crouch, 1944, 2 sons, 1 daughter. Education: MA, BLitt, 1948, Oxford University. Appointments: Lecturer to Senior Lecturer in German and Scandinavian Studies, King's College, University of Durham, later University of Newcastle upon Tyne, 1947-63; Professor of European Literature, 1964-82, Professor Emeritus, 1982-, Founding Dean, European Studies, 1964-68, Public Orator, 1964-68, 1974-75, 1978-79, Pro-Vice Chancellor, 1968-71, Professorial Fellow, 1982-86, University of East Anglia; Editor, 1975-90, Editor-at-Large, 1991-, Scandinavica: An International Journal of Scandinavian Studies; Managing Editor, Norvik Press, 1985-. Publications: Ibsen and the Temper of Norwegian Literature, 1960; Discussions of Ibsen, 1962; Henrik Ibsen, 1970; Modernism: European Literature 1890-1930 (with Malcolm Bradbury), 1976; Ibsen and Meaning, 1989. Editor and Translator: The Oxford Ibsen, 8 volumes, 1960-77; Slaves of Love and Other Norwegian Short Stories (with Janet Garton), 1982; Knut Hamsun's Letters (with Harald Naess), Vol 1, 1990, Vol 2, 1998. Editor: The Cambridge Companion to Henrik Ibsen, 1994. Translator: Hamsun: Pan, 1955; Hamsun: Wayfarers, 1980; Obstfelder: A Priest's Diary, 1988. Contributions to: Professional journals. Honours: Commander's Cross, Royal Norwegian Order of St Olav, 1975; Det Norske Videnskaps-Akademie Fellow, Oslo, 1977; Festschrift published in his honour, 1985; Honorary DLitt, Loughborough University, 1990; Honorary D Litt, University of Sunderland, 1995. Memberships: Danish Academy of Science and Letters, foreign member; Royal Norwegian Society of Sciences and Letters, foreign member; Svenska Litteratursällskapet i Finland, corresponding member. Address: The Croft, Stody, Melton Constable, Norfolk NR24 2EE, England.

MCFARLANE Sheryl Patricia, b. 20 Jan 1954, Pembroke, Ontario, Canada. Author. m. John Hewitt, Sept 1978 to 1979, 3 daughters. Education: UBC graduated with a BEd in Science, Canadian Studies. Publications: Going to the Fair, Victoria, 1996; Tides of Change, 1995; Eagle Dreams, 1994; Moonsnail Song, 1994; Jessie's Island, 1992; Waiting for the Whales, 1991. Honours: Canadian Children's Book Centre, Our Choice Award, 1992, 1993, 1995, 1997; IODE National Book Award, 1992. Membership: Canadian Writer's Union. Address: c/o Orca Book Publishers, PO Box 5626, Station B, Victoria, V8R 6S4, Canada.

MCFEE Oonah, b. 11 Sept 1919, New Brunswick, Canada. Author. m. Allan McFee, 16 Aug 1941. Education: Lisgar Collegiate; Instituto Allende, San Miguel, Mexico. Publications: Sandbars, 1977; Short stories published in University of Texas Quarterly, Redbook, Chatelaine. Honour: Books in Canada First Novel Award, 1978. Address: 312-54 Foxbar Road, Toronto, Ont M4V 2G6, Canada.

MCFEELY William S(hield), b. 25 Sept 1930, New York, New York, USA. Professor of History; Author. m. Mary Drake, 13 Sept 1952, 1 son, 2 daughters. Education: BA, Amherst College, 1952; MA, 1962, PhD, 1966, Yale University. Appointments: Assistant Professor, 1966-69, Associate Professor, 1969-70, Yale University; Professor of History, 1970-80, Rodman Professor of History, 1980-82, Andrew W Mellon Professor in the Humanities, 1982-86, Mount Holyoke College; Visiting Professor, University College London, 1978-79, Amherst College, 1980-81; Visiting Professor, 1984-85, John J McCloy Professor, 1988-89, University of Massachusetts; Richard B Russell Professor of American History, 1986-94, Abraham Baldwin Professor of the Humanities, 1994-, University of Georgia. Publications: Yankee Stepfather: General O O Howard and the Freedmen, 1968; The Black Man in the Land of Equality (with Thomas J Ladenburg), 1969; Grant: A Biography, 1981; Ulysses S Grant: Memoirs and Selected Letters 1839-1865 (editor with Mary Drake McFeely), 1990; Frederick Douglass, 1991; Sapelo's People: A Long Walk into Freedom, 1994. Honours: Morse Fellow, 1968-69; Fellow, American Council of Learned Societies, 1974-75; Pulitzer Prize in Biography, 1982; Francis Parkman Prize, 1982; Guggenheim Fellowship, 1982-83; National Endowment for the Humanities Grant, 1986-87; Avery O Craven Award, 1992; Lincoln Prize, 1992. Memberships: American Historical Association; Authors Guild; Century Association; Organization of American Historians; PEN; Southern Historical Association. Address: 445 Franklin Street, No 25, Athens, GA 30606, USA.

MCGAHERN John, b. 12 Nov 1934, Leitrim, Ireland. Author. m. Madeline Green, 1973. Education: University College, Dublin. Appointments: Research Fellow, University of Reading, 1968-71; O'Connor Professor, Colgate University, 1969, 1972, 1977, 1979, 1983, 1992; Visiting Fellow, Trinity College, 1988. Publications: The Barracks, 1963; The Dark, 1965; Nightlines, 1970; The Leavetaking, 1975; Getting Through, 1978; The Pornographer, 1979; High Ground, 1985; The Rockingham Shoot, BBC 2, 1987; Amongst Women, 1990; The Collected Stories, 1992. Address: c/o Faber & Faber, 3 Queen Square, London WC1N 3AU, England.

MCGARRITY Mark, (Bartholomew Gill), b. 22 July 1943, Holyoke, Massachusetts, USA. Author. Education: BA, Brown University, 1966; MLitt, Trinity College, Dublin, 1971. Publications: As Mark McGarrity: Little Augie's Lament, 1973; A Passing Advantage, 1980; Neon Caesar, 1989. As Bartholomew Gill: McGarr and the Politician's Wife, 1977; McGarr on the Cliffs of Moher, 1978; McGarr and the P M of Belgrave Square, 1983; The Death of a Joyce Scholar, 1989; The Death of Love, 1992; Death on a Cold Wild River, 1993; Death of an Ardent Bibliophile, 1995; Death of an Irish Sea Wolf, 1996. Contributions to: Newspapers. Honours: Fellow, New Jersey Council of the Arts, 1981-82; 1st Place, New Jersey Press Association Critical Writing. Membership: PEN. Address: 159 North Shore Road, Andover, NJ 07821, USA.

MCGARRY Jean, b. 18 June 1952, Providence, Rhode Island, USA. Writer; Teacher. Education: BA, Harvard University, 1970; MA, Johns Hopkins University, 1983. Appointment: Teacher, Johns Hopkins University. Publications: Airs of Providence, 1985; The Very Rich Hours, 1987; The Courage of Girls, 1992. Contributions to: Antioch Review; Southern Review; Southwest Review; Sulfur; New Orleans Review. Honour: Short Fiction Prize, Southern Review-Louisiana State University, 1985. Membership: Associated Writing Programs. Address: 100 West University Parkway, Baltimore, MD 21210, USA.

MCGINN Bernard (John), b. 19 Aug 1937, Yonkers, New York, USA. Professor of Historical Theology and the History of Christianity; Author; Translator; Editor. m. Patricia Ferris, 12 July 1971, 2 sons. Education: BA, St Joseph's Seminary and College, Yonkers, New York, 1959; STL, Pontifical Gregorian University, Rome, 1963; Graduate Studies, Columbia University, 1963-66; Studies, University of Munich, 1967-68; PhD, Brandeis University, 1970. Appointments: Lecturer, Regis College, Weston, Massachusetts, 1966-67; Instructor, Catholic University of America, Washington, DC, 1968-69; Instructor, 1969-70, Assistant Professor, 1970-75, Associate Professor, 1975-78, Professor of Historical Theology and the History of Christianity, 1978-, Naomi Shenstone Donnelley Professor, 1992-, Divinity School, University of Chicago. Publications: The Golden Chain: A Study in the Theological Anthropology of Isaac of Stella, 1972; The Crusades, 1973; Visions of the End: Apocalyptic Traditions in the Middle Ages, 1979; The Calabrian Abbot: Joachim of Fiore in the History of Western Thought, 1985; The Presence of God: A History of Christian Mysticism, 2 volumes, 1991, 1996; Apocalypticism in the Western Tradition, 1994; Antichrist: Two Thousand Years of the Human Fascination with Evil, 1994; The Growth of Mysticism: Gregory the Great through the 12th Century, 1994; The Flowering of Mysticism: Men and Women in the New Myst icism 1200-1350, 1998. Translator: Apocalyptic Spirituality, 1979; Meister Eckhart: The Essential Sermons, Commentaries, Treatises and Defense (with Edmund Colledge), 1981; Meister Eckhart: Teacher and Preacher (with Frank Tobin and Elvira Borgstadt), 1986. Editor: Three Treatises on Man: A Cistercian Anthropology, 1977; Christian Spirituality: Origins to the Twelfth Century (with John Meyendorff and Jean Leclercq), 1985; Christian Spirituality: High Middle Ages and Reformation (with Jill Raitt and John Meyendorff), 1987; Mystical Union and Monotheistic Faith: An Ecumenical Doctrine (with Moshe Idel), 1989, 2nd edition, 1996; God and Creation: An Ecumenical Symposium (with David B Burrell), 1990; The Apocalypse in the Middle Ages (with Richard K Emmerson), 1992; Meister Eckhart and the Beguine Mystics: Hadewijch of Brabant, Mechthild of Magdeburg, and Marguerite Porete, 1994; Eriugena: East and West: Papers of the Eighth International Colloquium of the Society for the Promotion of Eriugenean Studies: Chicago and Notre Dame, 18-20 October 1991 (with Willemiem Otten), 1994; The Encyclopedia of Apocalypticism, volume 2: Apocalypticism in Western

History and Cultures, 1998. Contributions to: Articles in many books and journals. Honours: Fulbright-Hays Research Fellowship, 1967-68; AATS Research Award, 1971; Research Fellow, Institute for Advanced Studies, Hebrew University, Jerusalem, 1988-89, and Institute for Ecumenical and Cultural Research, St John's University, 1992. Memberships: American Society of Church History, president, 1995-; Eckhart Society; International Society for the Promotion of Eriugenean Studies, president; Medieval Academy of America, fellow, 1994-. Address: 5701 South Kenwood, Chicago, IL 60637, USA.

MCGINNISS Joe, b. 9 Dec 1942, New York, New York, USA. Writer. Education: BS, Holy Cross College, 1964. Appointment: Newspaper Reporter, 1964-68. Publications: The Selling of the President, 1968; The Dream Team, 1972; Heroes, 1976; Going to Extremes, 1980; Fatal Vision, 1983; Blind Faith, 1989; Cruel Doubt, 1991; Last Brother, 1993; The Miracle of Castel di Sangro, 1999. Address: c/o Elaine Koster, 55 Central Park, West Suite 6, New York, NY 10023, USA.

MCGIVERN Maureen Daly. See: DALY Maureen.

MCGONIGAL James, b. 20 May 1947, Dumfries, Scotland. Educator; Poet. m. Mary Alexander, 1 Aug 1970, 1 son, 3 daughters. Education: MA, 1970, MPhil, 1974, PhD, 1978, University of Glasgow. Appointments: High School English Teacher, 1971-84; College Lecturer, 1985-91; Head, Department of English, 1991-92, Department of Language and Literature, 1992-, St Andrew's College of Education, Glasgow. Publications: A Sort of Hot Scotland: New Writing Scotland 12 (with A L Kennedy), 1994; Last Things First: New Writing Scotland 13 (with A L Kennedy), 1995; Sons of Ezra: British Poets and Ezra Pound (with M Alexander), 1995; Full Strength Angels: New Writing Scotland 14 (with K Jamie), 1996; Driven Home: Selected Poems, 1998. Contributions to: Poems in Aquarius; The Dark Horse; New Blackfriars; New Edinburgh Review; Temenos; various others. Address: c/o Department of Curriculum Studies, Faculty of Education, University of Glasgow, Duntocher Road, Bearsden, Glasgow G61 4QA, Scotland.

MCGOUGH Roger, b. 9 Nov 1937, Liverpool, England. Poet. m. 20 Dec 1986, 3 sons, 1 daughter. Education: St Mary's College, Crosby; BA and Graduate Certificate of Education, Hull University. Appointments: Fellow of Poetry, University of Loughborough, 1973-75; Writer-in-Residence, West Australian College of Advanced Education, Perth, 1986. Publications: The Mersey Sound (with Brian Patten and Adrian Henri), 1967; Strictly Private (editor), 1982; An Imaginary Menagerie, 1989; Blazing Fruit (selected poems 1967-87), 1990; Pillow Talk, 1990; The Lighthouse That Ran Away, 1991; You at the Back (selected poems 1967-87, Vol 2), 1991; My Dad's a Fire Eater, 1992; Defying Gravity, 1992; The Elements, 1993; Lucky, 1993; Stinkers Ahoy!, 1994; The Magic Fountain, 1995; The Kite and Caitlin, 1996; Sporting Relations, 1996; Bad, Bad Cats, 1997; Until I Met Dudley, 1997; The Spotted Unicorn, 1998; The Ring of Words (editor), 1998. Honours: Honorary Professor, Thames Valley University, 1993; Officer of the Order of the British Empire, 1997; Honorary MA, 1998. Address: c/o The Peters, Fraser and Dunlop Group Ltd, 5th Floor, The Chambers, Chelsea Harbour, Lots Road, London SW10 0XF, England.

MCGOVERN Ann, b. 25 May 1930, New York, New York, USA. Author. m. Martin L Scheiner, 6 June 1970, 3 sons, 1 daughter. Education: BA, University of New Mexico. Appointment: Publisher, The Privileged Traveler, 1986-90. Publications: Over 50 books including: If You Lived in Colonial Times, 1964; Too Much Noise, 1967; Stone Soup, 1968; The Secret Soldier, 1975; Sharks, 1976; Shark Lady, The Adventures of Eugenie Clark, 1978; Swimming with Sea Lions and Other Adventures in the Galapagos Islands, 1992; Playing with Penguins amd Other Adventures in Antarctica, 1994; Lady in the Box, 1997; Adventures of the Shark Led Eugenie Clark Around the World, 1998. Contributions to: Signature; Saturday Review. Honours: Outstanding Science Books, National Science Teachers Association, 1976, 1979, 1984, 1993;

Author of the Year, Scholastic Publishing Inc, 1978; Cuffie Award, 1998. Memberships: Explorers Club; PEN; Authors Guild; Society of Children's Book Writers; Society of Journalists and Authors. Address: 30 East 62nd Street, New York, NY 10021, USA.

MCGOWAN Frankie, b. London, England. Novelist; Columnist; Editor. m. Peter Glossop, 27 Mar 1971, 1 son, 1 daughter. Education: Central London Polytechnic. Appointments: Feature Writer for national magazines and newspapers; Evening News, London, 1969-73; Coordinating Editor, Journal, 1986; Assistant Editor, Sunday Mirror, 1987; Editor, New Woman, 1988; Editor, People Magazine, 1990; Editor, Top Sante, 1992-; Columnist, Good Housekeeping Magazine. Publications: Non-Fiction: Women Going Back to Work, 1993; The things we do for love (with John McGowan), 1993; Fiction: Ellie, 1993; Out There, 1994; Unfinished Business, 1996; A Kept Woman, 1998. Literary Agent: A M Heath and Co, 79 St Martin's Lane, London WC2N 4AA, England.

MCGRATH John (Peter), b. 1 June 1935, Birkenhead, Cheshire, England. Dramatist; Director. m. Elizabeth MacLennan, Mar 1962, 2 sons, 1 daughter. Education: MA, DipEd, St John's College, Oxford. Appointments: Founder-Director, 7:84 Theatre Co, 1971-88; Lecturer, Cambridge University, 1979, 1989; Founding Director, Freeway Films, 1983-. Publications: Plays: Tell Me Tell Me, 1960; Events While Guarding the Bofors Gun, 1966; Random Happenings in the Hebrides, or, The Social Democrat and the Stormy Sea, 1972; Bakke's Night of Fame, 1973; The Cheviot, the Stag, and the Black, Black Oil, 1973, revised version, 1981; The Game's a Bogey, 1975; Fish in the Sea, 1977; Little Red Hen, 1977; Yobbo Nowt, 1978; Joe's Drum, 1979; Swings and Roundabouts, 1981; Blood Red Roses, 1981; Six Pack, Six Plays for Scotland, 1999; Many other non-published plays, 1958-90. Other: A Good Night Out: Popular Theatre: Audience, Class, and Form, 1981; The Bone Won't Break: On Theatre and Hope in Hard Times, 1990; Also 6 screenplays, 1967-89, and 15 television plays or series, 1961-87. Honours: Honorary Doctorate, University of Stirling, 1993; British Association of Film and Television Arts Writers Award, 1994. Address: c/o Freeway Films, 67 George Street, Edinburgh EH2 2JG, Scotland.

MCGRATH Patrick, b. 7 Feb 1950, London, England. Author. Education: BA, University of London, 1971; Simon Fraser University, Burnaby, British Columbia. Appointment: Managing Editor, Speech Technology magazine, 1982-87. Publications: The Lewis and Clark Expedition, 1985; Blood and Water and Other Tales, 1988; The Grotesque, 1989; New York Life, or, Friends and Others, 1990; Spider, 1990; Dr Haggard's Disease, 1993. Contributions to: Periodicals. Address: 21 East Second Street, No 10, New York, NY 10003, USA.

MCGRAW Eloise Jarvis, b. 9 Dec 1915, USA. Writer. m. William Corbin McGraw, 29 Jan 1940, 1 son, 1 daughter. Education: BA, Principia College, 1937. Publications: Sawdust in His Shoes, 1950; Moccasin Trail, 1952; Mara, Daughter of the Nile, 1953; Techniques of Fiction Writing, 1959; The Golden Goblet, 1961; Steady Stephanie, 1962; Merry Go Round in Oz, 1963; Master Cornhill, 1973; A Really Weird Summer, 1977; The Forbidden Fountain of Oz, 1980; The Money Room, 1981; Hideaway, 1983; The Seventeenth Swap, 1986; The Trouble with Jacob, 1988; The Striped Ships, 1991; Tangled Webb, 1993; The Moorchild, 1996. Contributions to: Magazines. Honours: Newbery Honours, Moccasin Trail, 1952; Golden Goblet, 1961, The Moorchild, 1997. Membership: Authors Guild. Address: 2545 Terwilliger Boulevard, #805, Portland, OR 97201, USA.

MCGREEVY Susan Brown, b. 28 Jan 1934, Chicago, Illinois, USA. Lecturer; Writer. m. Thomas J McGreevy, 16 June 1973, 3 children. Education: BA, Honours, Roosevelt University, 1969; MA, Northwestern University, 1971. Appointments: Staff Consultant, Heart of America Indian Center, Kansas City, Missouri, 1973-75; Curator of North American Ethnology, Kansas City Museum of

History and Science, 1975-77; Adjunct Professor, Ottowa University, Kansas City Campus, 1976-77; Director, 1978-82, Research Associate, 1983-, Member, Board of Trustees, 1987-, Wheelwright Museum of the American Indian, Santa Fe, New Mexico; Guest Lecturer, colleges and museums, 1978-; Faculty, Northwestern University, Gallina, New Mexico, 1980-; Member, various Boards of Directors. Publications: Woven Holy People: Navajo Sandpainting Textiles (editor), 1983; Translating Tradition: Basketry Arts of the San Juan Paiutes (with Andrew Hunter Whiteford), catalogue, 1985; Guide to Microfilm Edition of the Washington N Matthews Papers (with Katherine Spencer Halpern), 1985. Contributions to: Various art journals. Honours: National Historic Publications and Records Commission Grant, 1980; National Endowment for the Humanities Grant, 1981; National Endowment for the Arts Grant, 1985. Memberships: American Anthropological Association; American Association of Museums; American Ethnological Society. Address: Route 7, Box 129-E, Santa Fe, NM 87505, USA.

MCGREGOR Iona, b. 7 Feb 1929, Aldershot, England. Writer. Education: BA, Honours, University of Bristol, 1950. Publications: Novels: Death Wore a Diadem, 1989; Alice in Shadowtime, 1992. Historical fiction for children: An Edinburgh Reel, 1968, 4th edition, 1986; The Popinjay, 1969, 2nd edition, 1979; The Burning Hill, 1970; The Tree of Liberty, 1972; The Snake and the Olive, 1974, 2nd edition, 1978. Non-Fiction: Edinburgh and Eastern Lowlands, 1979; Wallace and Bruce, 1986; Importance of Being Earnest, 1987; Huckleberry Finn, 1988. Honour: Writer's Bursary, Scottish Arts Council, 1989. Membership: Scottish PEN. Address: 9 Saxe Coburg Street, Edinburgh EH3 5BN, Scotland.

MCGRORY Edward, b. 6 Nov 1921, Stevenston, Ayrshire, Scotland. Retired Sales Consultant; Poet. m. Mary McDonald, 20 Nov 1948, 1 son, 1 daughter. Education: BA, Open University, 1985. Publications: Selected Poems, 1984; Plain and Coloured, 1985; Pied Beauty, 1986; Orchids and Daisies, 1987; Light Reflections - Mirror Images, 1988; Chosen Poems by Celebrities: Eddie McGrory's Poems, 1988; Masks and Faces, 1989; Illuminations, 1990; Letters from Flora, 1991; Candles and Lasers, 1992. Memberships: Various literary societies. Address: 41 Sythrum Crescent, Glenrothes, Fife KY7 5DG, Scotland.

MCGUANE Thomas (Francis III), b. 11 Dec 1939, Wyandotte, Michigan, USA. Writer. m. (1) Portia Rebecca Crockett, 8 Sept 1962, div 1975, 1 son, (2) Margot Kidder, Aug 1976, div 1977, 1 daughter, (3) Laurie Buffett, 19 Sept 1977, 1 stepdaughter, 1 daughter. Education: University of Michigan; Olivet College; BA, Michigan State University, 1962; MFA, Yale University, 1965; Stanford University, 1966-67. Publications: The Sporting Club, 1969; The Bushwacked Piano, 1971; Ninety-Two in the Shade, 1973; Panama, 1977; An Outside Chance: Essays on Sport, 1980, new edition as An Outside Chance: Classic and New Essays on Sports, 1990; Nobody's Angel, 1982; In the Crazies: Book and Portfolio, 1984; Something to Be Desired, 1984; To Skin a Cat, 1986; Silent Seasons: Twenty-One Fishing Stories, 1988; Keep the Change, 1989; Nothing But Blue Skies, 1992. Honours: Wallace Stegner Fellowship, Stanford University, 1966-67; Richard and Hinda Rosenthal Foundation Award, American Academy of Arts and Letters, 1971; Honorary Doctorates, Montana State University, 1993, Rocky Mountain College, 1995. Address: Box 25, McLeod, MT 59052, USA.

MCGUCKIAN Medbh, b. 12 Aug 1950, Belfast, Northern Ireland. Poet; Teacher. m. John McGuckian, 1977, 3 sons, 1 daughter. Education: BA, 1972, MA, 1974, Queen's University, Belfast. Appointments: Teacher, Dominican Convent, Fortwilliam Park, Belfast, 1974; Instructor, St Patrick's College, Knock, Belfast, 1975-; Writer-in-Residence, Queen's University, Belfast, 1986-88. Publications: Poetry: Single Ladies: Sixteen Poems, 1980; Portrait of Joanna, 1980; Trio Poetry (with Damian Gorman and Douglas Marshall), 1981; The Flower Master, 1982; The Greenhouse, 1983; Venus and the Rain, 1984, revised edition, 1994; On Ballycastle Beach, 1988; Two Women, Two Shores, 1989; Marconi's Cottage, 1991; The Flower Master and Other Poems, 1993; Captain Lavender, 1994. Editor: The Big Striped Golfing Umbrella: Poems by Young People from Northern Ireland, 1985. Honours: National Poetry Competition Prize, 1979; Eric Gregory Award, 1980; Rooney Prize, 1982; Ireland Arts Council Award, 1982; Alice Hunt Bartlett Award, 1983; Cheltenham Literature Festival Poetry Competition Prize, 1989. Address: c/o Gallery Press, Oldcastle, County Meath, Ireland.

MCGURN Barrett, b. 6 Aug 1914, New York, New York, USA. Author. m. Janice Ann McLaughlin, 19 June 1962, 5 sons, 1 daughter. Education: AB, Fordham University, New York, 1935. Appointments: Reporter, New York and Paris Herald Tribune, 1935-66; Bureau Chief, Herald Tribune, Rome, Paris, Moscow, 1946-62. Publications: Decade in Europe, 1958; A Reporter Looks at the Vatican, 1960; A Reporter Looks at American Catholicism, 1966; America's Court, The Supreme Court and the People, 1997. Pilgrim's Guide to Rome, 1998. Co-author: Best From Yank, 1945; Heroes For Our Times '68; 10 others. Contributions to: Reader's Digest; Catholic Digest; Commonweal; Colliers; Yank. Honours: Long Island Polk Award, 1956; Overseas Press Club Award, 1957; Honorary DLitt, Fordham University, 1958. Memberships: Overseas Press Club of America, president, 1963-65; Foreign Press Association in Italy, president, 1961, 1962; National Press Club, Washington. Address: 5229 Duvall Drive, Bethesda, MD 20816-1875, USA.

MCCGWIRE Michael Kane, b. 9 Dec 1924, Madras, India. Retired Commander of the Royal Navy and Professor; Writer. m. Helen Jean Scott, 22 Nov 1952, 2 sons, 3 daughters. Education: Royal Naval College, Dartmouth, 1938-42; BSc, University of Wales, 1970. Appointments: Commander, Royal Navy, 1942-67; Professor, Dalhousie University, 1971-79; Senior Fellow, Brookings Institution, Washington, DC, 1979-90; Visiting Professor, Global Security Programme, Cambridge University, 1990-93; Honorary appointments: Fellow, Social and Political Sciences, Cambridge University, 1993-; Senior Fellow, Foreign Policy Studies, Dalhousie University, 1996-; Professor of International Politics, University of Wales, 1997-. Publications: Military Objectives and Soviet Foreign Policy, 1987; Perestroika and Soviet National Security, 1991; NATO Expansion and European Security, 1997. Editor: Soviet Naval Developments, 1973; Soviet Naval Policy, 1975; Soviet Naval Influence, 1977. Contribrutions to: 40 books; numerous journals.. Honour: Officer of the Order of the British Empire. Address: Hayes, Durlston, Swanage, Dorset BH19 2JF, England.

MCHUGH Heather, b. 20 Aug 1948, San Diego, California, USA. Professor of English; Poet; Writer; Translator. m. Nikolai Popov. Education: BA, Harvard University, 1969-70; MA in English Literature, University of Denver, 1972. Appointments: Associate Professor, State University of New York at Binghamton, 1974-83; Core Faculty, MFA Program for Writers, Goddard College, later Warren Wilson College, 1976-; Milliman Distinguished Writer-in-Residence and Professor of English, University of Washington, 1984-; Holloway Lecturer in Poetry, University of California at Berkeley, 1987; Visiting Professor, University of Iowa, 1991-92, 1995, University of California at Los Angeles, 1994, University of California at Irvine, 1994; Coal-Royalty Chair in Poetry, University of Alabama, Tuscaloosa, 1992; Elliston Professor of Poetry, University of Cincinnati, 1993; Visiting Lecturer, University of Bergen, Norway, 1994. Publications: Poetry: Dangers, 1977; A World of Difference, 1981; To the Quick, 1987; Shades, 1988; Hinge & Sign: Poems 1968-1993, 1994; The Father of the Predicaments (Poems 1993-1998), 1999. Essays: Broken English: Poetry and Partiality, 1993. Translations: D'Apres Tout: Poems by Jean Follain, 1981; Because the Sea is Black: Poems by Blaga Dimitrova (with Niko Boris), 1989. Other: Where Are They Now? (with Tom Phillips), 1990. Contributions to: Many anthologies and journals. Honours: National Endowment for the Arts

Grants, 1974, 1979, 1981; Pushcart Prizes, 1978 et seq; Guggenheim Fellowship, 1989; Woodrow Wilson National Poetry Fellow, 1992-93; Daniel A Pollack Prize, Harvard University and Harvard College Library, 1995; Bingham Prize, Boston Book Review, 1995; Times Literary Supplement International Book of the Year List, 1995; Lila Wallace/Reader's Digest Writing Award, 1996-99; O D Hardison Award, 1998. Address: c/o Department of English, Box 354330, University of Washington, Seattle, WA 98195, USA.

MCILVANNEY William, b. 25 Nov 1936, Kilmarnock, Ayrshire, Scotland. Author; Poet. Education: MA, University of Glasgow, 1959. Publications: Fiction: Remedy is None, 1966; A Gift from Nessus, 1968; Docherty, 1975; Laidlaw, 1977; The Papers of Tony Veitch, 1983; The Big Man, 1985; Walking Wounded (short stories), 1989. Poetry: The Long Ships in Harbour, 1970; Landscapes and Figures, 1973; Weddings and After, 1984. Address: c/o John Farquharson Ltd, 162-168 Regent Street, London W1R 5TB, England.

MCINERNEY Jay, b. 13 Jan 1955, Hartford, Connecticut, USA. Author. m. (1) Mary Reymond, 2 June 1984, (2) Helen Bransford, 27 Dec 1991. Education: BA, Williams College, 1976; Postgraduate Studies, Syracuse University. Publications: Bright Lights, 1984; Ransom, 1985; Story of My Life, 1988; Brightness Falls, 1992; Savage and Son, 1995; The Last of the Savages, 1996. Contributions to: Anthologies and magazines. Memberships: Authors Guild; Authors League of America; PEN; Writers Guild. Address: c/o International Creative Management, 40 West 57th Street, New York, NY 10019, USA.

MCINNIS (Harry) Don(ald), b. 18 Apr 1916, Worcester, Massachusetts, USA. Public Administrator; International Developer; Writer; Dramatist. m. Marjorie E Graber, 7 Aug 1948, 2 sons, 2 daughters. Education: AB, Clark University, 1938; Graduate Studies, Clark University, 1938-39, American University, 1939-40, Johns Hopkins University, 1968-69. Publications: The Running Years, 1986; Cobwebs and Twigs, 1990; Will - Man from Stratford (play), 1992; New Work No Lines (play), 1994. Contributions to: Regularly to US personnel management journals, 1940's, 1950's. Honours: Special awards, US Government, Government of Guatemala, Republic of Korea. Memberships: Australian Writers Guild; US Dramatists Guild. Address: 22 Chauvel Circle, Chapman, ACT 2611, Australia.

MCINTIRE Dennis K(eith), b. 25 June 1944, Indianapolis, Indiana, USA. Historian (Music and Literature); Lexicographer. Education: Indiana University. Appointments: Research Editor, various general reference works, 1965-79; Editorial Associate, Nicolas Slonimsky, 1979-95; Advisor, The Oxford Dictionary of Music, 1985, 2nd edition, 1994; The New Grove Dictionary of American Music, 1986, The New Everyman Dictionary of Music, 1988, Brockhaus Riemann Musik Lexikon: Ergänzungsband, 1989, 2nd edition, 1995, Dictionnaire biographique des musiciens, 1995, The Hutchinson Encyclopedia of Music, 1995. Publications: Baker's Biographical Dictionary of Musicians (contributing editor), 7th edition, 1984, (associate editor), 8th edition, 1992; International Who's Who in Music and Musicians' Directory (consultant editor), 12th edition, 1990, (appendices editor), 13th to 15th editions, 1992-96; Baker's Biographical Dictionary of 20th Century Classical Musicians (associate editor), 1997; International Authors and Writers Who's Who (consultant editor), 15th edition, 1997, 16th edition, 1999; International Who's Who in Poetry and Poets' Encyclopaedia (consultant editor), 8th edition, 1997, 9th edition, 1999. Contributions to: The New Grove Dictionary of American Music, 1986; Supplement to Music Since 1900, 1986; The New Grove Dictionary of Opera, 1992; Music Since 1900, 5th edition, 1994. Forthcoming: The New Grove Dictionary of Music and Musicians, revised edition. Honours: Advisor, Encyclopaedia Britannica, 1996-; Outstanding Reference Source Citation, American Library Association, 1998. Memberships: High Churchman (Conservative); Freemason; Ancient Accepted Scottish Rite; American

Musicological Society; Music Library Association; Sir Thomas Beecham Society, USA; Fine Arts Society of Indianapolis. Address: 9170 Melrose Court, Indianapolis, IN 46239, USA.

MCINTYRE Ian James, b. 9 Dec 1931, Banchory, Scotland. Writer; Broadcaster. m. Leik Sommerfelt Vogt, 24 July 1954, 2 sons, 2 daughters. Education: BA, MA, St John's College, Cambridge, 1950-53; College of Europe, Bruges, 1953-54. Appointments: National Service, Intelligence Corps, 1955-57; Producer, Editor, BBC Radio, 1957-61; Programme Executive, ITA, 1961-62; Director of Information Research, Scottish Conservative Central Office, 1962-69; Freelance Broadcaster, BBC, 1970-76; Controller, Radio 4, BBC, 1978-87; Associate Editor, The Times, 1989-90. Publications: The Proud Doers: Israel After Twenty Years, 1968; Words: Reflections on the Use of Language (editor, contributor), 1975; Dogfight: The Transatlantic Battle over Airbus, 1992; The Expense of Glory: A Life of John Reith, 1993; Dirt and Deity: A Life of Robert Burns, 1995; Garrick, 1999. Contributions to: Articles and book reviews in The Listener, The Independent, The Times. Address: Spylaw House, Newlands Avenue, Radlett, Hertfordshire WD7 8EL, England.

MCINTYRE Lee Cameron, b. 2 Jan 1962, Portland, OR, USA. Philsophy Professor. m. Josephine Hernandez, 26 July 1986, 1 son, 1 daughter. Education: BA, Wesleyan University, 1984; MA, University of Michigan, 1987; PhD, University of Michigan, 1991. Appointments: Research Associate, Center for the Philosophy and History of Science, Boston University, 1991-93; Assistant Professor of Philsophy, Colgate University, 1993-. Publications: Readings in the Philosophy of Social Science, editor with Michael Martin, 1994; Laws and Explanation in the Social Sciences: Defending a Science of Human Behavior, 1996. Contributions to: Complexity and Social Scientific Laws, 1993; The Case for the Philosophy of Chemistry, 1997. Honour: Phi Beta Kappa, 1984. Literary Agent: Christina Ward. Address: Department of Philsophy and Religion, Colgate University, Hamilton, NY 13346, USA.

MCKAY Don(ald Fleming), b. 25 June 1942, Owen Sound, Ontario, Canada. Poet; Writer; Editor. div, 1 son, 1 daughter. Education: Bishop's University; BA, 1965, MA, 1966, University of Ontario; PhD, University College, Swansea, Wales, 1971. Appointments: Teacher, University of New Brunswick, 1990-96; Editor, The Fiddlehead. Publications: Air Occupies Space, 1973; Long Sault, 1975; Lependu, 1978; Lightning Ball Bait, 1980; Birding, or Desire, 1983; Sanding Down This Rocking Chair on a Windy Night, 1987; Night Field, 1991; Apparatus, 1997. Contributions to: Periodicals. Honours: Canadian Authors' Association Award for Poetry, 1983; Governor-General's Award for Poetry, 1991; National Magazine Award for Poetry, 1991. Memberships: League of Canadian Poets; PEN; Writers' Union of Canada. Address: 434 Richmond Avenue, Victoria, British Columbia V8S 3Y4, Canada.

MCKEAN John Maule Laurie, (Laurie Melville), b. 7 Nov 1943, Glasgow, Scotland. Professor of Architecture; Writer. m. 2 sons, 1 daughter. Education: B.Arch University of Strathclyde, 1968; MA, History and Theory of Architecture, University of Essex, 1971. Appointments: Architect in practice, 1966-67, 1969-71; Teacher of Architectural Design, University of Ceylon, 1968-69, University of East London, 1976-80, University of North London, 1980-90; Teacher of Design and Archit ecture History, UNL, 1983-88; Middlesex University 1984-88;Editorial Staff, The Architects' Journal, 1971-75; Director of Interior Architecture, 1990-95, Professor of Architecture, 1995-, University of Brighton. Publications: Architecture of the Western World (co-author), 1980; Learning from Segal, 1989; Royal Festival Hall, 1991; Crystal Palace, 1994; Leicester Engineering Building, 1994; Alexander Thomson (co-author), 1995; The Parthenon, 1996; C R Mackintosh (co-author), 1996; Charles Rennie Mackintosh, 1998; Giancarlo de Carlo, 1999. Regular contributions to: Architects' Journal; Building Design; Spazio e Societa, Milan, 1970-98.

Honours: 2 AIA International Book Awards; Elected member, Critics Circle of International Association of Architects, 1990. Address: c/o University of Brighton, Brighton BN2 4AT, England.

MCKENNA Virginia Anne, b. 7 June 1931, London, England. Actress; Conservationist. m. Bill Travers, 19 Sept 1957, 3 sons, 1 daughter. Education: Herschel, Capetown, South Africa, 1940-45; Herons Ghyll, 1945-47; Central School of Speech and Drama, London, 1947-49. Publications: On Playing with Lions, co-authored with Bill Travers; Some of My Friends Have Tails; Beyond the Bars (contributor and co-editor with Will Travers and Jonathon Wray); Headlines From the Jungle: Anthology of Verse (co-compiler with Anne Harvey); Into the Blue; Back to the Blue; Journey to Freedom. Honour: International Society for Animal Rights Inc, USA. Literary Agent: Michael Shaw. Address: c/o The Born Free Foundation, 3 Grove House, Foundry Lane, Horsham, West Sussex RH13 5PL, England.

MCKEOWN Tom S, b. 29 Sept 1937, Evanston, Illinois, USA. Poet; Writing Consultant. m. Patricia Haebig, 22 Apr 1989, 1 son, 1 daughter. Education: BA, 1961, MA, 1962, University of Michigan; MFA, Vermont College, 1989. Appointments: Writer-in-Residence, Stephens College, 1968-74; Poet-in-Residence, Savannah College of Art and Design, 1982-83, University of Wisconsin, Oshkosh, 1983-87, University of Wisconsin at Madison, 1989-94. Publications: The Luminous Revolver, 1973; The House of Water, 1974; Driving to New Mexico, 1974; Certain Minutes, 1978; Circle of the Eye, 1982; Three Hundred Tigers, 1994. Contributions to: Newspapers, reviews, and magazines. Honours: Avery Hopwood Award, 1968; Wisconsin Arts Fellowship, 1980. Address: 1220 North Gammon Road, Middleton, WI 53562, USA.

MCKERNAN Llewellyn McKinnie, b. 12 July 1941, Hampton, Arkansas, USA. Poet; Children's Writer. m. John Joseph McKernan, 3 Sept 1967, 1 daughter. Education: BA, English, summa cum laude, Hendrix College, 1963; MA, English, University of Arkansas, 1966; MA, Creative Writing, Brown University, 1976. Appointments: Instructor of English, Georgia Southern College, 1966-67; Adjunct Professor of English, Marshall University, 1980-86, 1991; Professor of English, St Mary's College, 1989. Publications: Short and Simple Annals, 1979, 2nd edition, 1983; More Songs of Gladness, 1987; Bird Alphabet, 1988; Many Waters, 1993; This is the Day and This is the Night, 1994. Contributions to: Reviews and journals. Honours: 3rd Prize, Chester H Jones National Poetry Competition, 1982; West Virginia Humanities Artist Grant, 1983; 2nd Prize, National Founders Award Contest, National Federation of State Poetry Societies, 1994. Memberships: West Virginia Writers; Poetry Society of West Virginia; Society of Children's Book Writers and Illustrators. Address: Route 10, Box 4639B, Barboursville, WV 25504, USA.

MCKINLEY Hugh, b. 18 Feb 1924, Oxford, England. Poet. m. Deborah Waterfield, 15 Sept 1979. Appointments: Literary Editor, Athens Daily Post, 1966-77; European Editor, Poet, India, 1967-91; Editorial Panel, Bitterroot, USA, 1980-89. Publications: Poetry: Starmusic, 1976; Transformation of Faust, 1977; Poet in Transit, 1979; Exulting for the Light, 1983; Skylarking, 1994; Countries of the Soul, forthcomming; The Volume of Ireland, forthcomming. Contributions to: Numerous publications worldwide. Honours: President Marcos Medal, Philippines, 1967; Honorary DLitt, International Academy of Leadership, 1967, Free University of Asia, Karachi, 1973; Directorate, Academia Pax Mundi, Israel, 1978.Memberships: Suffolk Poetry Society; Baha'i World Faith, life member. Address: Owls Hoot, 10 The Glebe, Lawshall, Bury St Edmunds, Suffolk, IP29 4PW, England.

MCKISSACK Frederick L(emuel), b. 12 Aug 1939, Nashville, Tennessee, USA. Children's Writer. m. Patricia McKissack, 12 Dec 1964, 3 sons. Education: BS, Tennessee Agricultural and Industrial State University, 1964. Publications: About 70 books, 1984-97. Honours: Jane Addams Children's Book Award, 1990; Boston Globe/Horn Book Award, 1993. Address: 5900 Pershing Avenue, St Louis, MO 63112, USA.

MCKISSACK Patricia (L'Ann) C(arwell), b. 9 Aug 1944, Nashville, Tennessee, USA. Children's Writer. m. Frederick L McKissack, 12 Dec 1964, 3 sons. Education: BA, Tennessee Agricultural and Industrial State University, 1964; MA, Webster University, 1975. Publications: About 90 books, 1978-97. Honours: Jane Addams Children's Book Award, 1990; Boston Globe/Horn Book Award, 1993. Address: 5900 Pershing Avenue, St Louis, MO 63112, USA.

MCKNIGHT Natalie Joy Brown, b. 18 Apr 1962, McKeesport, Pennsylvania, USA. Professor. m. Christopher James McKnight, 3 Oct 1987, 2 daughters. Education: BA, Washington University, 1984; MA, Johns Hopkins University, 1985; PhD, University of Delaware, 1990. Appointments: Lecturer in Rhetoric, College of General Studies, Boston University, 1990; Assistant Professor, 1991, Associate Professor in Humanities and Rhetoric, 1997, Acting Char in Humanities and Rhetoric. Publictions: Idiots, Madmen and Other Prisoners in Dickens, 1993; Suffering Mothers in Mid-Victorian Novels, 1996. Contributions to: Dickens Quarterly; Culture Review; Poet Lore. Honours: Scholar, Teacher of the Year, Boston University, 1998-99. Memberships: Dickens Society, trustee; Modern Language Association. Address: 871 Commonwealth Avenue, Boston, MA 02215, USA.

MCKNIGHT Reginald, b. 26 Feb 1956, Germany. Professor of English. 2 daughters. Education: BA, African Studies, Colorado College; MA, English, University of Denver. Appointments: University of Pittsburgh, 1988-91; Carnegie Mellon University, 1991-94; University of Maryland, 1994-. Publications: Moustapha's Eclipse, 1988; I Get on the Bus, 1990; The Kind of Light That Shines on Texas, 1992; White Boys, 1998. Contributions to: Story; African-American Review; Kenyon Review; Callaloo. Honours: NEA Fellowship, 1991. Membership: PEN America. Literary Agent: Christina L Ward. Address: c/o Department of English, University of Maryland, 3101 Susquehanna Hall, College Park, MD 20742, USA.

MCKUEN Rod, b. 29 Apr 1933, Oakland, California, USA. Poet; Composer; Writer. Appointments: Many concert, film, and television appearances. Publications: Poetry: And Autumn Came, 1954; Stanyan Street and Other Sorrows, 1966; Listen to the Warm, 1967; Lonesome Cities, 1968; Twelve Years of Christmas, 1968; In Someone's Shadow, 1969; A Man Alone, 1969; With Love, 1970; Caught in the Quiet, 1970; New Ballads, 1970; Fields of Wonder, 1971; The Carols of Christmas, 1971; And to Each Season, 1972; Pastorale, 1972; Grand Tour, 1972; Come to Me in Silence, 1973; America: An Affirmation, 1974; Seasons in the Sun, 1974; Moment to Moment, 1974; Beyond the Boardwalk, 1975; The Rod McKuen Omnibus, 1975; Alone, 1975; Celebrations of the Heart, 1975; The Sea Around Me, 1977; Hand in Hand, 1977; Coming Close to Earth, 1978; We Touch the Sky, 1979; Love's Been Good To Me, 1979; Looking for a Friend, 1980; The Power Bright and Shining, 1980; Too Many Midnights, 1981; Rod McKuen's Book of Days, 1981; The Beautiful Strangers, 1981; The Works of Rod McKuen, Vol 1, Poetry, 1950-82, 1982; Watch for the Wind ..., 1982; Rod McKuen: 1984 Book of Days, 1983; The Sound of Solitude, 1986; Intervals, 1987. Prose: Finding My Father: One Man's Search for Identity, 1976; An Outstretched Hand, 1980. Other: Various classical, film, and television scores. Honours: 41 Gold and Platinum Records Awards; Grand Prix du Disque, Paris, 1966, 1974, 1975, 1982; Grammy Award, 1969. Address: PO Box 2783, Los Angeles, CA 90078, USA.

MCLANATHAN Richard, b. 12 Mar 1916, Methuen, Massachusetts, USA. Author; Art Historian. m. Jane Fuller, 3 Jan 1942, Education: AB, 1938, PhD, 1951, Harvard University. Appointments: Visiting Professor, US and European Universities; Museum Curator, Director, Trustee. Publications: Images of the Universe, 1966; The Pageant of Medieval Art and Life, 1966; The American Tradition in the Arts, 1968; The Brandywine Heritage, 1971; Art in America, 1973; The Art of Marguerite Stix, 1977; East Building, A Profile, National Gallery of Art, 1978; World Art in American Museums, 1983; Gilbert Stuart, 1986; Michelangelo, 1993. Contributions to: Numerous journals and magazines. Honours: Prix de Rome, 1948; Distinguished Service Award, United States Information Agency, 1959; Rockefeller Senior Fellowship, 1975. Address: The Stone School House, Phippsburg, ME 04562, USA.

MCLAREN Colin Andrew, b. 14 Dec 1940, Middlesex, England. University Librarian; Writer. 1 son, 1 daughter. Education: BA, MPhil, Dip Arch Administration, University of London. Publications: Rattus Rex, 1978; Crows in a Winter Landscape, 1979; Mother of the Free, 1980; A Twister over the Thames, 1981; The Warriors under the Stone, 1983; Crown and Gown: An Illustrated History of the University of Aberdeen (with J J Carter), 1994; Rare and Fair: A Visitor's History of Aberdeen University Library, 1995. Contributions to: BBC Radio 3 and 4. Honour: Society of Authors Award for Best Adaptation, 1986. Membership: Society of Authors. Address: c/o The Library, University of Aberdeen, Aberdeen, Scotland.

MCLAREN John (David), b. 7 Nov 1932, Melbourne, Victoria, Australia. Professor; Writer; Editor. Education: BA, Honours, 1954, BEd, 1959, PhD, 1982, University of Melbourne; MA, Monash University, 1972. Appointments: Associate Editor, 1966-93, Editor, 1993-97, Consulting Editor, 1997-, Overland; Head, Department of General Studies, 1972-75, and Humanities, 1975-76, Foundation Chairman, School of the Arts, 1973-76, Darling Downs Institute of Advanced Education; Head, Department of Humanities, Footscray Institute of Technology, 1976-89; Editor, Australian Book Review, 1978-86; Principal Lecturer, Footscray Institute of Technology/Victoria University of Technology, 1989-91; Professor of Humanities, 1991-97, Honorary Professor, 1997-, Victoria University of Technology. Publications: Our Troubled Schools, 1968; Dictionary of Australian Education, 1974; Australian Literature: An Historical Introduction, 1989; The New Pacific Literatures: Culture and Environment in the European Pacific, 1993; Prophet from the Desert: Critical Essays on Patrick White (editor), 1995; Writing in Hope and in Fear: Postwar Australian Literature as Politics, 1945-72, 1996. Contributions to: Scholarly books and journals. Honours: Fulbright Senior Scholar, 1990; Australian Research Council Research Grants, 1991, 1993, 1996; Humanities Research Centre Scholar, Australian National University, 1994. Memberships: Association for the Study of Australian Literature; Australian Studies Association for South Asia, vice president, 1997-; International Australian Studies Association, honorary life member; South Pacific Association for Commonwealth Language and Literature Studies. Address: c/o Victoria University of Technology, PO Box 14428, MCMC, Melbourne, Victoria 8001, Australia.

MCLELLAN David Thorburn, b. 10 Feb 1940, Hertford, England. Professor of Political Theory; Writer. m. Annie Brassart, 1 July 1967, 2 daughters. Education: MA, 1962, DPhil, 1968, St John's College, Oxford. Appointment: Professor of Political Theory, Eliot College, University of Kent. Publications: The Young Hegelians and Karl Marx, 1969; Karl Marx: His Life and Thought, 1974; Engels, 1977; Marxism After Marx, 1980; Ideology, 1986; Marxism and Religion, 1987; Simone Weil: Utopian Pessimist, 1989; Unto Caesar: The Political Importance of Christianity, 1993; Political Christianity, 1997. Contributions to: Professional journals. Address: c/o Eliot College, University of Kent, Canterbury CT2 7NS, England.

MCLELLAN Gamon Paul Averre, b. 30 Oct 1949, Brighton, England. Journalist. m. Dr Bengisu Rona, 26 Nov 1983. Education: BA, 1971, MA, 1976, Keble College, Oxford, England; Postgraduate Research, Patriarchal Institute for Patristic Studies, Thessaloniki, Greece, 1971-76. Appointments: Freelance Translator, (Greek and Turkish), 1975-79; Editor, Political & Economic Weekly, Ankara, 1976-78; Assistant Editor, Arab Month Magazine, 1978; Head, BBC Turkish Service and Commentator on Eastern Mediterranean Affairs,

1979-88; Deputy Head, BBC Central European Services, 1988-92; Head of BBC Arabic Service, 1992-. Publications: The Oecumenical Patriarchate in the Orthodox Church by Maximos of Sardes, translated, 1973. Address: BBC, Bush House, Strand, London WC2B 4PH, England.

MCLEOD Wallace (Edmond), b. 30 May 1931, East York, Ontario, Canada. Professor of Classics Emeritus; Author. m. Elizabeth Marion Staples, 24 July 1957, 3 sons, 1 daughter. Education: BA, University of Toronto, 1953; AM, 1954, PhD, 1966, Harvard University. Appointments: Instructor, Trinity College, Hartford, Connecticut, 1955-56, University of British Columbia, 1959-61; Lecturer, University of Western Ontario, 1961-62; Special Lecturer, 1962-63, Assistant Professor, 1963-66, Associate Professor, 1966-74, Anson Jones Lecturer, 1984; Professor of Classics, 1974-96, Professor Emeritus, 1996-, ANZMRC Lecturer, 1997; Victoria College, University of Toronto; Inaugural Sam Houston Lecturer, 1998. Publications: Composite Bows from the Tomb of Tut'ankhamun, 1970; Beyond the Pillars: More Light on Freemasony (editor and contributor), 1973; Meeting the Challenge: The Lodge Officer at Work (editor and contributor), 1976; The Sufferings of John Coustos (editor), 1979; Whence Come We?: Freemasonry in Ontario 1764-1980 (editor and contributor), 1980; Self Bows and Other Archery Tackle from the Tomb of Tut'ankhamun, 1982; The Old Gothic Constitutions (editor), 1985; The Old Charges, 1986; A Candid Disquisition (editor), 1989; For the Cause of Good, 1990; The Grand Design: Selected Masonic Addresses and Papers, 1991; The Quest for Light: Selected Masonic Addresses, 1997. Contributions to: Numerous books and journals. Honour: Philalethes Certificate of Literature, 1984. Memberships: Freemason; Philalethes Society, president, 1992; Society of Blue Friars, Grand Abbot, 1991. Address: c/o Victoria College, University of Toronto, 73 Queen's Park, Toronto, Ontario M5S 1K7, Canada.

MCLERRAN Alice, b. 24 June 1933, West Point, New York, USA. Writer. m. Larry Dean McLerran, 8 May 1976, 2 sons, 1 daughter. Education: BA, 1965, PhD, 1969, University of California; MS, 1973, MPH, 1974, Harvard School of Public Health. Publications: The Mountain that Loved a Bird, 1985; Secrets, 1990; Roxaboxen, 1991; I Want to go Home, 1992; Dreamsong, 1992; Hugs, 1993; Kisses, 1993; The Ghost Dance, 1995; The Year of the Ranch, 1996; The Legacy of Roxaboxen: A Collection of Voices, 1998. Honours: Southwest Book Award, 1991; Notable Children's Trade Book in Field of Social Studies, 1996, 1997. Memberships: Authors Guild; Society of Childrens Book Writers and Illustrators. Address: 121 Washington Ave South #417, Minneapolis, MN 55401, USA.

MCMAHON Barrie, b. 2 June 1939, Perth, Australia. Educator; Writer. m. Jan Murphy, 7 May 1960, 2 sons. Education: Teachers Certificate; Teachers Higher Certificate; BA; MA; Graduate Diploma, Design Education and Film. Publications: (all with Robyn Quin) Exploring Images, 1984; Real Images, 1986; Stories and Stereotypes, 1987; Meet the Media, 1988; Australian Images, 1990; Understanding Soaps, 1993. Contributions to: Australian Journal of Education; Canadian Journal of Education Communication; Education Para la Reception, Mexico; Tijdschrift voor Theaterwetenschap, Netherlands. Honour: Curtin University, School of English Prize. Membership: Australian Teachers of Media. Address: PO Box 8064, Perth Business Centre, Pier Street, Perth 6849, Western Australia.

MCMANUS James, b. 22 Mar 1951, New York, New York, USA. Poet; Writer; Teacher. m. Jennifer Arra, 9 July 1992, 1 son, 1 daughter. Education: BA, 1974, MA, 1977, University of Illinois at Chicago. Appointment: Faculty School of the Art Institute, Chicago, 1981-. Publications: Several works. Contributions to: Many publications. Honour: Guggenheim Fellowship, 1994-95. Memberships: Associated Writing Programs; PEN. Address: c/o School of the Art Institute, 37 South Wabash, Chicago, IL 60603, USA.

MCMASTER Juliet Sylvia, b. 2 Aug 1937, Kisumu, Kenya. University Professor. m. Rowland McMaster, 10 May 1968, 1 son, 1 daughter. Education: BA, 1959, MA, 1962, St Anne's College, Oxford; MA, 1963, PhD, 1965, University of Alberta. Appointments: Assistant Professor, 1965-70, Associate Professor, 1970-76, Professor, 1976-86, University Professor, 1986-, University of Alberta. Publications: Thackeray: The Major Novels, 1971; Jane Austen's Achievement, 1976; Trollope's Palliser Novels, 1978; Jane Austen on Love, 1978; The Novel from Sterne to James, 1981; Dickens the Designer, 1987; The Beautiful Cassandra, 1993; Jane Austen the Novelist, 1995. Contributions to: 19th-Century Fiction; Victorian Studies; Modern Language Quarterly; English Studies in Canada. Honours: Canada Council Post-Doctoral Fellowship, 1969-70; Guggenheim Fellowship, 1976-77; McCalla Professorship, 1982-83; University of Alberta Research Prize, 1986; Killam Research Fellowship, 1987-88; Molson Prize Winner, 1994. Memberships: Jane Austen Society of North America; Association of Canadian University Teachers of English. Address: Department of English, University of Alberta, Alberta T6G 2E5, Canada.

MCMASTER Susan, (S M Page), b. 11 Aug 1950, Toronto, Canada. Poet; Editor. m. Ian McMaster, 5 July 1969, 2 daughters. Education: BA, English, Carleton University, 1970; Teaching Certificate, Ottawa Teachers' College, 1971; Graduate Studies, Journalism, Carleton University, 1975-80. Appointments: Founding Editor, Branching Out Magazine, Edmonton, 1973-75; Freelance Writer and Editor, Ottawa, 1975-89; Senior Book Editor, National Gallery of Canada, 1989-. Publications: Pass This Way Again, co-auth, 1983; Dark Galaxies, 1986; North/South, co-author, 1987; audio tape with Sugarbeat; Wordmusic, with First Draft, 1987; Dangerous Graces, editor, 1987; Women and Language, editor, 1990; Two Women Talking, Erin Mouré and Bronwen Wallace, 1991; Illegitimate Positions, editor, 1991; The Hummingbird, 1992; Learning to Ride, 1994; Dangerous Times, 1996; Uncommon Prayer, 1997; Siolence: Poets on Violence and Silence, editor, 1998. Contributions to: Branching Out Magazine, Founding Editor; editor/contributor, various magazines and journals. Memberships: PEN; League of Canadian Poets; Chair, Freedom of Expression; Feminist Caucus. Address: 43 Belmont Avenue, Ottawa, Ontario K15 0T9, Canada.

MCMILLAN James (Coriolanus), b. 30 Oct 1925. Journalist. m. Doreen Smith, 7 Apr 1953, 3 sons, 1 daughter. Education: MA, Economics, University of Glasgow University. Publications: The Glass Lie, 1964; American Take-Over, 1967; Anatomy of Scotland, 1969; The Honours Game, 1970; Roots of Corruption, 1971; British Genius (with Peter Grosvenor), 1972; The Way We Were 1900-1950 (trilogy), 1977-80; Five Men at Nuremberg, 1984; The Dunlop Story, 1989; From Finchley to the World - Margaret Thatcher, 1990. Address: Thurleston, Fairmile Park Road, Cobham, Surrey KT11 2PL, England.

MCMILLAN Terry, b. 18 Oct 1951, Port Huron, Michigan, USA. Writer. 1 son. Education: BS, University of California, 1979; MFA, Columbia University, 1979. Appointments: Instructor, University of Wyoming, 1987-90; Professor, University of Arizona, 1990-92. Publications: Mama, 1987; Disappearing Acts, 1989; Breaking Ice, 1990; Waiting to Exhale, 1992; A Day Late and a Dollar Short, 1995; How Stella Got Her Groove Back, 1996. Contributions to: Periodicals. Honours: National Book Award; National Endowment for the Arts Fellowship; New York Foundation for the Arts Fellowship; Doubleday-Columbia University Literary Fellowship.

MCMILLEN Neil Raymond, b. 2 Jan 1939, Lake Odessa, Michigan. Professor of History; Writer. Education: BA, 1961, MA, 1963, University of Southern Mississippi; PhD, Vanderbilt University, 1969. Appointments: Assistant Professor of History, Ball State University, Muncie, 1967-69; Assistant Professor, 1969-70, Associate Professor, 1970-78, Professor of History, 1978-, University of Southern Mississippi, Hattiesburg. Publications: The Citizens' Council: Organized Resistance to the Second Reconstruction, 1971; Thomas Jefferson: Philosopher of Freedom, 1973; A Synopsis of American History (with C Sellers and H May), 1984, 7th edition, 1992; Dark Journey: Black Mississippians in the Age of Jim Crow, 1989. Honour: Bancroft Prize, 1990. Address: Department of History, University of Southern Mississippi, Hattiesburg, MS 39401, USA.

MCMONIGAL Glenne M, b. 28 Jan 1938, Berlin, Wisconsin, USA. Publisher; Editor; Author. m. James, 13 June 1959, 2 sons, 1 daughter. Education: Marquette University; Beloit College. Appointments: Charter Member, Barrington Chamber Ambassador's Club; PCC Publicity Club, Chicago; Board Member, Barrington Chapter, Chicago Lyric Opera. Publications: Numerous news articles and stories for Lifestyles Magazines. Address: 559 Tamarisk Lane, Crystal Lake, IL 60014, USA.

MCMONIGAL Valwyn Christina, b. 6 June 1938, Sydney, New South Wales, Australia. Retired Home Economics Teacher; Writer. m. Geoffrey G McMonigal, 28 Sept 1957, 2 sons, 2 daughter. Education: School Leaving Certificate, 1954. Publications: Cookbooks: Popular Potato, 1989; Pumpkin and Other Squash, 1994; Australia Wide Cookbook (with panavisions by Ken Duncan), 1994. Contributions to: Magazines. Honours: Short Story Awards, Fellowship of Australian Writers, 1983, 1985. Memberships: Australian Society of Authors; Girl Guide Association; Wine and Food Appreciation Society, vice-president. Address: 23 Grevillea Crs, Berkeley Vale, New South Wales 2261, Australia.

MCMURTRY Larry (Jeff), b. 3 June 1936, Wichita Falls, Texas, USA. Author. m. Josephine Ballard, 15 July 1959, div 1966, 1 sons. Education: BA, North Texas State College, 1958; MA, Rice University, 1960. Appointments: Instructor, Texas Christian University, Ft Worth, 1961-62; Lecturer in English and Creative Writing, Rice University, 1963-69; Visiting Professor, George Mason College, 1970, American University, 1970-71. Publications: Novels: Horseman, Pass By, 1961; Leaving Cheyenne, 1963; The Last Picture Show, 1966; Moving On, 1970; All My Friends Are Going to be Strangers, 1972; Terms of Endearment, 1975; Somebody's Darling, 1978; Cadillac Jack, 1982; The Desert Rose, 1983; Lonesome Dove, 1985; Texasville, 1987; Anything for Billy, 1988; Some Can Whistle, 1989; Buffalo Girls, 1990; The Evening Star, 1992; Streets of Laredo, 1993; Pretty Boy Floyd (with Diana Ossana), 1994; The Late Child, 1995; Dead Man's Walk, 1995; Zeke and Ned (with Diana Ossana), 1997; Comanche Moon, 1997. Non-Fiction: In a Narrow Grave: Essays on Texas, 1968; It's AlwaysWe Rambled: An Essay on Rodeo, 1974; Film Flam: Essays on Hollywood, 1987. Screenplays: The Last Picture Show (with Peter Bogdanovich), 1971; Texasville, 1990; Montana, 1990; Falling From Grace, 1992; Memphis (with Cybill Shepherd), 1992. Contributions to: Newspapers and periodicals. Honours: Wallace Stegner Fellow, 1960; Jesse H Jones Award, 1962, Barbara McCombs/Lon Tinkle Award, 1986, Texas Institute of Letters; Guggenheim Fellowship, 1964; Pulitzer Prize for Fiction, 1986. Membership: Texas Institute of Letters. Address: c/o Saria Co Inc, 2509 North Campbell, No 95, Tucson, AZ 85719, USA.

MCNAIR Wesley, b. 19 June 1941, Newport, New Hampshire, USA. Professor; Poet. m. Diane Reed McNair, 24 Dec 1962, 3 sons, 1 daughter. Education: BA, English, Keene State College, 1963; MA, English, 1968, MLitt, American Literature, 1975, Middlebury College. Appointments: Associate Professor, Colby Sawyer College, 1968-87; Senior Fulbright Professor, Catholic University of Chile, 1977-78; Visiting Professor Dartmouth College, 1984; Associate Professor to Professor, University of Maine at Farmington, 1987-98. Publications: The Town of No, 1989; Twelve Journeys in Maine, 1992; My Brother Running, 1993; Talking in the Dark, 1998. Contributions to: Anthologies, reviews, quarterlies, and journals. Honours: National Endowment for the Arts Fellowships, 1980, 1990; Devins Award, 1984; Eunice Tietjens Prize, 1984; Guggenheim Fellowship, 1986;

Pushcart Prize, 1986; New England Emmy Award, 1991; Rockefeller Residency, Bellagio, Italy, 1993; Theodore Roethke Prize, 1993; Yankee Magazine Poetry Prize, 1995; Sarah Josepha Hale Medal, 1997. Address: c/o Department Humanities, University of Maine at Farmington, Farmington, ME 04938, USA.

MCNALLY Terrence, b. 3 Nov 1939, St Petersburg, Florida, USA. Playwright. Appointments: Stage Manager, Actors Studio, New York City, 1961; Tutor, 1961-62; Film Critic, The Seventh Art, 1963-65; Assistant Editor, Columbia College Today, 1965-66. Publications: Apple Pie, Sweet Eros Next and Other Plays, 1969; Three Plays: Cuba Si!, Bringing It All Back Home, Last Gasps, 1970; Where Has Tommy Flowers Gone?, 1972; Bad Habits: Ravenswood and Dunelawn, 1974; The Ritz and Other Plays,1976; The Rink, 1985; And Things That Go Bump in the Night, 1990; Frankie and Jonny in the Clair de Lune, 1990; Lips Together, Teeth Apart, 1992; Until Your Heart Stops, 1993; Corpus Christi, 1998. Honours: Stanley Award, 1962; Obie Award, 1974; American Academy of Arts and Letters Citation; National Institute of Arts and Letters Citation. Address: 218 West 10th Street, New York, NY 10014, USA.

MCNAMARA Eugene Joseph, b. 18 Mar 1930, Oak Park, Illinois, USA. Professor; Editor; Poet; Writer. m. Margaret Lindstrom, 19 July 1952, 4 sons, 1 daughter. Education: BA, MA, DePaul University; PhD, Northwestern University, 1964. Appointments: Editor, University of Windsor Review, 1965-, Mainline, 1967-72, Sesame Press, 1973-80; Professor of English, University of Windsor. Publications: Poetry: For the Mean Time, 1965; Outerings, 1970; Dillinger Poems, 1970; Love Scenes, 1971; Passages, 1972; Screens, 1977; Forcing the Field, 1980; Call it a Day, 1984. Short Stories: Salt, 1977; Search for Sarah Grace, 1978; Spectral Evidence, 1985; The Moving Light, 1986. Contributions to: Queens Quarterly; Saturday Night; Chicago; Quarry; Denver Quarterly. Address: 166 Randolph Place, Windsor, Ontario N9B 2T3, Canada.

MCNAMARA Robert (James), b. 28 Mar 1950, New York, New York, USA. University Lecturer in English; Poet. 1 daughter. Education: BA, Amherst College, 1971; MA, Colorado State University, 1975; PhD, University of Washington, Seattle, 1985. Appointments: Founder-Editor, L'Epervier Press, 1977; Senior Lecturer in English, University of Washington, Seattle, 1985-. Publication: Second Messengers, 1990. Contributions to: Anthologies, reviews, quarterlies, and journals. Honours: National Endowment for the Arts Fellowship, 1987-88; Fulbright Grant, Jadavpur University, Calcutta, 1993. Memberships: Academy of American Poets; Associated Writing Programs. Address: c/o Department of English, Box 354330, University of Washington, Seattle, WA 98195, USA.

MCNEIL Florence (Ann), b. 8 May 1940, Vancouver, British Columbia, Canada. Poet; Children's Author. m. David McNeal, 3 Jan 1973. Education: BA, 1960, MA, 1965, University of British Columbia. Appointments: Instructor, Western Washington University, 1965-68; Professor, University of Calgary, 1968-73; Professor, 1973-76, Visiting Lecturer, 1989-90, University of British Columbia. Publications: The Rim of the Park, 1972; Walhachin, 1972; Emily, 1975; Ghost Towns, 1975; A Balancing Act, 1979; When is a Poem: Creative Ideas for Teaching Poetry Collected from Canadian Poets, 1980; Miss P and Me, 1982; The Overlanders, 1982; Here is a Poem (editor), 1983; Barkerville, 1984; Catriona's Island, 1988; Do Whales Jump at Night?: Poems for Kids (editor), 1990; Swimming Out of History, 1991; Breathing Each Others Air, 1994. Contributions to: Anthologies, journals, and magazines. Honours: Many Canada Council Grants; Thea Koetner Award, 1963; MacMillan Prize, 1963; National Magazine Award for Poetry, 1980; Sheila A Egoff Prize for Children's Literature, 1989. Memberships: British Columbia Writers Federation; Canadian Society of Children's Authors, Illustrators, and Performers; Canadian Writers Union; League of Canadian Poets. Address: 20 Georgia Wynd, Delta, British Columbia V4M 1A5, Canada.

MCNEIL William Francis, b. 26 Feb 1932, No Attleboro, MA, USA. Engineer; Business Executive; Writer. m. Janet Kathleen Hill, 14 Nov 1953, 2 sons, 2 daughters. Education: Northeastern University, Boston, MA, USA; BS, Chemical Engineering, Emerson College, Boston, Philadelphia Business College. Publications: Dodger Diary, 1986; The King of Swat, 1997; The Dodgers Encyclopedia, 1997; Ruth, Maris, McGwire & Sosa, 1999; Baseball's Forgotten All-Stars, 2000. Honour: Sabr Robert Peterson Award, 1998. Address: PO Box 4227, Pittsfield, MA 01201, USA.

MCNEILL Christine, b. 4 Apr 1953, Vienna, Austria. Poet. m. Ralph McNeill, 24 May 1975, div 21 Oct 1992. Education: English as a Foreign Language Teaching Certificate, London, 1976; German Teaching Certificate, London, 1976; English as a Second Language Teaching Certificate, London, 1977. Appointment: Language Tutor. Publication: Kissing the Night, 1993. Contributions to: Reviews, quarterlies, and journals. Honour: Co-Winner, Richard Ellmann Award, 1993. Membership: National Poetry Society. Address: 31 Burnt Hills, Cromer, Norfolk NR27 9LW, England.

MCNEILL Daniel Richard, b. 1 June 1947, San Francisco, California, USA. Writer. m. Rosalind Gold, 20 Dec 1984. Education: AB, University of California at Berkeley, 1975; JD, Harvard Law School, 1982. Publications: Fuzzy Logic, 1993; The Face, 1998. Honour: Los Angeles Times Book Prize in Science and Technology, 1993. Membership: Author's Guild. Address: 9848 Tabor Street #214, Los Angeles, CA 90034, USA.

MCNEISH James, b. 23 Oct 1931, Auckland, New Zealand. Writer. Education: BA, University of Auckland, 1952. Appointment: Writer-in-Residence, Berlin Kunstler-program, 1983. Publications: Tavern in the Town, 1957; Fire Under the Ashes, 1965; Mackenzie, 1970; The Mackenzie Affair, 1972; Larks in a Paradise (co-author), 1974; The Glass Zoo, 1976; As for the Godwits, 1977; Art of the Pacific (with Brian Brake), 1980; Belonging: Conversations in Israel, 1980; Joy, 1982; Walking on My Feet, 1983; The Man from Nowhere: A Berlin Diary, 1985; Lovelock, 1986; Penelope's Island, 1990; The Man from Nowhere and Other Prose, 1991; My Name is Paradiso, 1995. Address: c/o James Hale, 47 Peckham Rye, London SE15 3NX, England.

MCPHEE John (Angus), b. 8 Mar 1931, Princeton, New Jersey, USA. Professor of Journalism; Author. m. (1) Pryde Brown, 16 Mar 1957, 4 daughters, (2) Yolanda Whitman, 8 Mar 1972, 2 stepsons, 2 stepdaughters. Education: AB, Princeton University, 1953; Graduate studies, Cambridge University, 1953-54. Appointments: Dramatist, Robert Montgomery Presents Television Programme, 1955-57; Associate Editor, Time magazine, New York City, 1957-64; Staff Writer, The New Yorker magazine, 1965-; Ferris Professor of Journalism, Princeton University, 1975-. Publications: A Sense of Where You Are, 1965; The Headmaster, 1966; Oranges, 1967; The Pine Barrens, 1968; A Roomful of Hovings and Other Profiles, 1969; The Crofter and the Laird, 1969; Levels of the Game, 1970; Encounters with the Archdruid, 1972; Wimbledon: A Celebration, 1972; The Deltoid Pumpkin Seed, 1973; The Curve of Binding Energy, 1974; Pieces of the Frame, 1975; The Survival of the Bark Canoe, 1975; The John McPhee Reader, 1977; Coming into the Country, 1977; Giving Good Weight, 1979; Alaska: Images of the Country (with Galen Rowell), 1981; Basin and Range, 1981; In Suspect Terrain, 1983; La Place de la Concorde Suisse, 1984; Table of Contents, 1985; Rising from the Plains, 1986; Outcroppings, 1988; The Control of Nature, 1989; Looking for a Ship, 1990; Assembling California, 1993; The Ransom of Russian Art, 1994; Irons in the Fire, 1997. Honours: American Academy and Institute of Arts and Letters Award, 1977; Woodrow Wilson Award, Princeton University, 1982; American Association of Petroleum Geologists Journalism Awards, 1982, 1986; John Wesley Powell Award, United States Geological Survey, 1988; Walter Sullivan Award, American Geophysical Union, 1993; Various honorary doctorates. Memberships: American Academy of Arts and Letters;

Geological Society of America, fellow. Address: 475 Drake's Corner Road, Princeton, NJ 08540, USA.

MCPHERSON James A, b. 16 Sept 1943, Savannah, Georgia, USA. Professor. div, 1 daughter. Education: BA, Morris Brown College, 1965; MA, LLB, Harvard Law School, 1968; MFA, University of Iowa, 1972; Visiting Scholar, Yale Law School, New Haven, 1978. Appointments: Rhetoric Program and Law School, University of Iowa, 1968-69; Lecturer, University of California at Santa Cruz, 1969-72; Assistant Professor, Morgan State University, 1975-76; Associate Professor, University of Virginia, Charlottesville, 1976-81; Professor of English, Writers' Workshop, University of Iowa, 1981-; Lecturer, Meiji University, Tsuda College, Chiba University, 1989-90. Publications: Hue and Cry, 1969; Railroad, 1976; Elbow Room, 1977; Crabcakes, 1998. Contributions to: Atlantic; Harvard Advocate; Ploughshares; Nimrod; New York Times; Esquire; Readers Digest; Washington Post; World Literature Today. Honours: Guggenheim Fellowship, 1973; Pulitzer Prize for Fiction, 1978; MacArthur Prize Fellows Award, 1981; Award for Excellence in Teaching, University of Iowa, 1990; Green Eyeshades Award for Excellence in Print Commentary, Society of Southern Journalists, 1994; Fellow, Center for Advanced Studies, Stanford University, 1997-98. Memberships: American Civil Liberties Union; PEN; Writers Guild; National Association for the Advancement of Colored People; American Academy of Arts and Sciences. Address: 711 Rundell Street, Iowa City, IA 52240, USA.

MCPHERSON James Munro, b. 11 Oct 1936, Valley City, North Dakota, USA. Professor of History; Writer. m. Patricia Rasche, 28 Dec 1957, 1 daughter. Education: BA, Gustavus Adolphus College, St Peter, Minnesota, 1958; PhD, Johns Hopkins University, 1963. Appointments: Instructor, 1962-65, Assistant Professor, 1965-66, Associate Professor, 1966-72, Professor of History, 1972-82, Edwards Professor of American History, 1982-91, George Henry Davis '86 Professor of American History, 1991-, Princeton University; Commonwealth Fund Lecturer, University College, London, 1982. Publications: Struggle for Equality, 1964; The Negro's Civil War, 1965; Marching Toward Freedom: The Negro in the Civil War, 1968; Blacks in America: Bibliographical Essays, 1971; The Abolitionist Legacy: From Reconstruction to the NAACP, 1975; Ordeal by Fire: The Civil War and Reconstruction, 1981, 2nd edition, 1992; Battle Cry of Freedom: The Civil War Era, 1988; Abraham Lincoln and the Second American Revolution, 1991; Images of the Civil War, 1992; Gettysburg, 1993; What They Fought For, 1861-1865, 1994; The Atlas of the Civil War, 1994; Drawn with the Sword: Reflections on the American Civil War, 1996; For Cause and Comrades: Why Men Fought in the Civil War, 1997; Lamson of the Gettysburg: The Civil War Letters of Lieutenant Roswell H Lamson, US Navy, 1997; Is Blood Thicker Than Water?: Crises of Nationalism in the Modern World, 1998. Contributions to: Professional journals. Honours: Danforth Fellow, 1958-62; Anisfield-Wolf Award, 1965; Guggenheim Fellowship, 1967-68; National Emdowment for the Humanities Fellowship, 1977-78; Pulitzer Prize in History, 1989; Several honorary doctorates; Lincoln Prize, 1998. Memberships: American Historical Association; American Philosophical Society; Organization of American Historians; Phi Beta Kappa; Society of American Historians; Southern Historical Association. Address: 15 Randall Road, Princeton, NJ 08540, USA.

MCPHERSON Sandra Jean, b. 2 Aug 1943, San Jose, California, USA. Professor of English; Poet. m. (1) Henry D Carlile, 24 July 1966, div 1985, 1 daughter, (2) Walter D Pavlich, 3 Jan 1995. Education: BA, San Jose State University, 1965; Postgraduate Studies, University of Washington, 1965-66. Appointments: Visiting Lecturer, University of Iowa, 1974-76, 1978-80; Holloway Lecturer, University of California, Berkeley, 1981; Teacher, Oregon Writers Workshop, Portland, 1981-85; Professor of English, University of California, Davis, 1985-. Publications: Elegies for the Hot Season, 1970; Radiation, 1973; The Year of Our Birth, 1978; Patron

Happiness, 1983; Streamers, 1988; The God of Indeterminacy, 1993. Contributions to: Periodicals. Honours: Ingram Merrill Foundation Grants, 1972, 1984; National Endowment for the Arts Grants, 1974, 1980, 1985; Guggenheim Fellowship, 1976; Oregon Arts Commission Fellowship, 1984; American Academy and Institute of Art and Letters Award, 1987. Address: c/o Department of English, University of California at Davis, CA 95616, USA.

MCQUAIN Jeffrey Hunter, b. 23 Nov 1955, Frederick, Maryland, USA. Writer; Researcher. Education: AA in General Education, Montgomery College, 1974; BA, 1976, MA, 1977, in English, University of Maryland; PhD in Literary Studies, American University, 1983. Appointment: Researcher to William Safire, New York Times, 1983-. Publications: Books: The Elements of English. 1986; Guide to Good Word Usage, 1989; Power Language, 1996; Coined by Shakespeare, 1998; Never Enough Words, 1999. Contributions to: New York Times Magazine. Honours: Words From Home Award to Power Language, 1996. Membership: Modern Language Association. Literary Agent, David Hendin. Address: Box 4008, Rockville, MD 20849, USA.

MCQUEEN Cilla, b. 22 Jan 1949, Birmingham England. Teacher; Artist; Poet. m. Ralph Hotere, 1974, 1 daughter. Education: MA, Dunedin University, Otago, 1970. Publications: Homing in, 1982; Anti Gravity, 1984; Wild Sweets, 1986; Benzina, 1988; Berlin Diary, 1990; Crikey, 1994. Play: Harlequin and Colombine, 1987. Radio Play: Spacy Calcutta's Travelling Truth Show, 1986. Honours: Robert Burns Fellowships, 1985, 1986; Goethe Institute Scholarship, 1988. Address: PO Box 69, Portobello, Dunedin, New Zealand.

MCRAE Hamish Malcolm Donald, b. 20 Oct 1943, Barnstaple, Devon, England. Journalist; Author. m. Frances Annes Cairncross, 10 Sept 1971, 2 daughters. Education: Fettes College, Edinburgh, 1957-62; Honours Degree, Economics and Political Science, Trinity College, Dublin, 1966. Appointments: Editor, Euromoney, 1972, Business and City, The Independent, 1989; Financial Editor, The Guardian, 1975; Associate Editor, The Independent, 1991. Publications: Capital City - London as a Financial Centre (with Frances Cairncross), 1973, 5th edition, 1991; The Second Great Crash (with Frances Cairncross), 1975; Japan's Role in the Emerging Global Securities Market, 1985; The World in 2020, 1994. Contributions to: Numerous magazines and journals. Honours: Financial Journalist of the Year, Wincott Foundation, 1979; Special Merit Award, Amex Bank Review Essays, 1987; Times Columnist of the Year, Periodical Publishers Association Awards, 1996. Address: 6 Canonbury Lane, London N1 2AP, England.

MCTRUSTRY Chris(tifor John), b. 29 Oct 1960, Wellington, New South Wales, Australia. Screenwriter; Novelist. m. Patricia Rose Dravine, 1 Nov 1986, 1 son, 1 daughter. Education: Bachelor of Creative Arts, 1989, Master of Creative Arts, 1990, University of Wollongong. Publications: Television: Neighbours, 1989, 1990, 1991, 1992, 1993; A Country Practice, 1991; Home and Away, 1992, 1993. Radio: Alien Evangelist, 4x30 minute comedy series, 1992. Novels: The Cat Burglar, 1995; The Card Shark, 1996; Axeman!, 1997; Frankenkid, 1997; George and the Dragon, 1997; Susie Smelly-Feet, 1997. Memberships: Australian Writers Guild; Australian National Playwrights Centre; Australian Society of Authors; Mystery Writers of America; Crime Writers Association of Australia. Address: 22 Stanleigh Crescent, West Wollongong, New South Wales 2500, Australia.

MCVEAN James. See: LUARD Nicholas.

MCWHIRTER George, b. 26 Sept 1939, Belfast, Northern Ireland. Writer; Poet; Translator; Professor. m. Angela Mairead Cold, 26 Dec 1963, 1 son, 1 daughter. Education: BA, Queen's Univerity; MA, University of British Columbia. Appointments: Co-Editor-in-Chief, 1977, Advisory Editor, 1978-, Prism International Magzine; Professor, University of British Columbia, 1982-. Publications: Catalan Poems, 1971; Bodyworks, 1974;

Queen of the Sea, 1976; Gods Eye, 1981; Coming to Grips with Lucy, 1982; Fire Before Dark, 1983; Paula Lake, 1984; Cage, 1987; The Selected Poems of José Emilio Pacheco (editor and translator), 1987; The Listeners, 1991; A Bad Day to be Winning, 1992; A Staircase for All Souls, 1993; Incubus: The Dark Side of the Light, 1995; Musical Dogs, 1996; Fab, 1997; Where Words Like Monarchs Fly (editor and translator), 1998; Ovid in Saskatchewan, 1998. Contributions to: Numerous magazines and journals. Honours: McMillan Prize, 1969; Commonwealth Poetry Prize, 1972; F R Scott Prize, 1988; Ethel Wilson Fiction Prize, 1988; Killan Prize for Teaching, UBC, 1998; League of Canadian Poets' National Chapbook Competition, for Ovid in Saskatchewan, 1998. Memberships: League of Canadian Poets; Writers' Union of Canada; PEN; Literary Translators Association of Canada. Address: 4637 West 13th Avenue, Vancouver, British Columbia V6R 2V6, Canada.

MCWHIRTER Norris Dewar, b. 12 Aug 1925, London, England. Author; Editor; Broadcaster. m. (1) Carole Eckert, 28 Dec 1957, dec 1987, 1 son, 1 daughter, (2) Tessa Mary Pocock, 26 Mar 1991. Education: BA, 1947, MA, 1948, Trinity College, Oxford. Appointments: Athletics Correspondent, Star, 1951-60, Observer, 1951-67; Editor, Athletics World, 1952-56; Founder-Editor, Guinness Book of Records, 1955. Publications: Get To Your Marks, 1951; Guinness Book of Records, 1955-86 (36 languages); Dunlop Book of Facts, 1964-73; Guinness Book of Answers, 1976-86; Ross, Story of a Shared Life, 1976; Treason of Maastricht, 1995. Contributions to: Encyclopaedia Britannica; Whitakers Almanack. Honour: Commander of the Order of the British Empire, 1980. Membership: Royal Institution. Address: c/o Guinness Publishing Co, 338 Easton Road, London NW1 3BD, England.

MCWILLIAM Candia Frances Juliet, b. 1 July 1955, Edinburgh, Scotland. Writer. m. (1) Earl of Portsmouth, 10 Feb 1981, (2) F E Dinshaw, 27 Sept 1986, 2 sons, 1 daughter. Education: Sherborne School for Girls, 1968-73; BA, Girton College, Cambridge, 1976. Publications: A Case of Knives, 1988; A Little Stranger, 1989; Debatable Land, 1994; Wait Till I Tell You, 1997. Honours: Betty Trask Prize; Scottish Arts Council Prize; Guardian Fiction Prize; Pumio Grinzane Cavour, Italy; Forderpreis, Germany. Memberships: Society of Authors; PEN; Royal Society of Literature, fellow. Address: c/o Bloomsbury Publishing, 38 Soho Square, London W1V 5DE, England.

MCWILLIAMS Peter, b. 5 Aug 1949, Detroit, Michigan, USA. Publisher; Writer. Education: Eastern Michigan University; Maharishi International University. Publications: Come Live With Me and Be My Life, 1967; Surviving the Loss of a Love, 1971; Portraits, 1992; Life 101 and 102 series. Contributions to: Playboy. Address: c/o Prelude Press, 8159 Santa Monica Boulevard, Los Angeles, CA 90046, USA.

MEAD Matthew, b. 12 Sept 1924, Buckinghamshire, England. Poet. Appointment: Editor, Satis Magazine, Edinburgh, 1960-62. Publications: A Poem in Nine Parts, 1960; Identities, 1964; Kleinigkeiten, 1966; Identities and Other Poems, 1967; Penguin Modern Poets 16 (with Harry Guest and J Beeching), 1970; In the Eyes of the People, 1973; Minusland, 1977; The Midday Muse, 1979; A Roman in Cologne, 1986. Address: c/o Anvil Press, 69 King George Street, London SE10 8PX, England.

MEADES Jonathan Turner, b. 21 Jan 1947, Salisbury, Wiltshire, England. Journalist; Writer; Broadcaster. m. (1) Sally Browne, (2) Frances Bentley, 4 daughters. Education: King's College, Taunton, 1960-64; Royal Academy of Dramatic Art, 1967-69. Publications: Filthy English; Peter Knows What Dick Likes; Pompey. TV: The Victorian House; Abroad in Britain; Further Abroad; Jerry Building; Even Further Abroad. Contributions to: Times; Sunday Times; Observer; Independent. Honours: Essay Prize, Paris International Art Film Festival, 1994; Glewfiddich Awards, 1986, 1990,

1996. Address: David Godwin Associates, 14 Goodwin's Court, London, WC2N 4LL, England.

MEASHAM Donald Charles, b. 19 Jan 1932, Birmingham, England. Retired Teacher of Higher Education; Writer; Editor. m. Joan Doreen Barry, 15 Dec 1954, 1 son, 1 daughter. Education: BA. Honours, Birmingham University, 1953; MPhil, Nottingham University, 1971. Appointments: Founding Editor 1983, Company Secretary, Continuing Co-Editor, 1988-, Staple New Writing. Publications: Leaving, 1965; Fourteen, 1965; English Now and Then, 1965; Larger Than Life, 1967; Quattordicenni, 1967; The Personal Element, 1967; Lawrence and the Real England, 1985; Ruskin: The Last Chapter, 1989. Contributions to: Periodicals. Address: Tor Cottage, 81 Cavendish Road, Matlock, Derbyshire DE4 3HD, England.

MECKEL Christoph, b. 12 June 1935, Berlin, Germany. Author; Poet; Graphic Artist. Education: Studied Graphic Art, Freiburg, Paris, Munich. Publications: Manifest der Toten, 1960, revised edition, 1971; Im Land der Umbramauten, 1961; Wildnisse, 1962; Die Drummheit liefert uns ans Messer: Zeitgespräch in zehn Sonetten (with Volker von Törne), 1967; Bockshorn, 1973; Wen es angeht, 1974; Komödie der Hölle. 3 volumes, 1979, 1984, 1987; Suchbild: Über meinen Vater, 1980; Ein roter Faden, 1983; Das Buch Jubal, 1987; Das Buch Shiralee, 1989; Von den Luftgeschäften der Poesie, 1989; Die Messingstadt, 1991; Gesang vom unterbrochenen Satz, 1995. Honours: Rainer Maria Rilke Prize, 1979; Georg Trakl Prize, 1982; Literature Prize, Kassel, 1993. Memberships: Academy of Science and Literature, Mainz; Akademie für Sprache und Dichtung e. V., Darmstadt; PEN. Address: Kulmbacher Strasse 3. D-10777 Berlin, Germany.

MEDOFF Mark (Howard), b. 18 Mar 1940, Mount Carmel, Illinois, USA. Dramatist; Screenwriter. m. Stephanie Thorne, 3 daughters. Education: BA, University of Miami, Coral Gables, 1962; MA, Stanford University, 1966. Publications: Plays: When You Comin' Back, Red Ryder?, 1973; Children of a Lesser God, 1979; The Majestic Kid, 1981, revised edition, 1989; The Hands of Its Enemy, 1984; The Heart Outright, 1986; Big Mary, 1989; Stumps, 1989; Stephanie Hero, 1990; Kringle's Window, 1991. Film Scripts: Good Guys Wear Black, 1977; When You Comin' Back, Red Ryder?, 1978; Off Beat, 1985; Apology, 1986; Children of a Lesser God, 1987; Clara's Heart, 1988; City of Joy, 1992. Contributions to: Periodicals. Honours: Obie Award, 1974; Drama Desk Awards, 1974, 1980; New York Outer Critics Circle Awards, 1974, 1980; Guggenheim Fellowship, 1974-75; Antoinette Perry Award, 1980; Governor's Award for Excellence in the Arts, State of New Mexico, 1980; Distinguished Alumnus, University of Miami, 1987; California Media Access Award, 1988. Memberships: Actors Equity Association; Screen Actors Guild; Writers Guild of America. Address: Box 3585, Las Cruces, NM 88003, USA.

MEDVED Michael, b. 3 Oct 1948, Philadelphia, Pennsylvania, USA. Film Critic; Writer. m. (1) Nancy Harris Herman, 5 Aug 1972, div 1983, (2) Diane Elvenstar, 27 Jan 1985, 1 son, 2 daughters. Education: BA, Yale University, 1969; MFA, California State University at San Francisco, 1974. Appointments: Political Speech Writer, 1970-73; Creative Director, Advertising, Anrick Inc, Oakland, California, 1973-74; Co-Founder and President, Pacific Jewish Center, Venice, California, 1977-94; On-Air Film Critic, People Now, Cable News Network, 1980-83; President, Emanuel Streisand School, Venice, California, 1980-85; On-Air Film Critic and Co-Host, Sneak Previews, PBS-TV, 1985-; Chief Film Critic, New York Post, 1993-; Lecturer; Radio Talk Show Host, Seattle, Washington, 1996-; Nationally Syndicated Radio Host, SRN Radio Network, 1998-. Publications: What Really Happened to the Class of '65?, 1976; The 50 Worst Films of All Time (with Harry Medved), 1978; The Shadow Presidents, 1979; The Golden Turkey Awards (with Harry Medved), 1980; Hospital, 1983; The Hollywood Hall of Shame (with Harry Medved), 1984; Son of Golden Turkey Awards (with

Harry Medved), 1986; Hollywood vs America, 1992; Saving Childhood (with Dr Diane Medved), 1998. Contributions to: Periodicals. Memberships: American Federation of Television and Radio Artists; Writers Guild of America. Address: c/o KV1, 1809 7th Avenue, Suite 200, Seattle, WA 98101, USA.

MEDVEDEV Roy (Alexandrovich), b. 14 Nov 1925, Tbilisi, USSR. Historian; Sociologist; Author. m. Galina A Gaidina, 1956, 1 son. Education: University of Leningrad; Russian Academy of Pedagogical Sciences. Appointments: Teacher of History, Ural Secondary School, 1951-53; Director, Secondary School, Leningrad Region, 1954-56; Deputy to Editor-in-Chief, Publishing House of Pedagogical Literature, Moscow, 1957-59; Head of Department, Research Institute of Vocational Education, 1960-70, Senior Scientist, 1970-71, Russian Academy of Pedagogical Sciences; People's Deputy, Supreme Soviet of the USSR, 1989-91; Member, Central Committee, Communist Party of Russia, 1990-91; Co-Chairman, Socialist Party of Labour, 1991-. Publications: A Question of Madness (with Zhores Medvedev), 1971; Let History Judge, 1972; On Socialist Democracy, 1975; Khrushchev: The Years in Power (with Zhores Medvedev), 1976; Political Essays, 1976; Problems in the Literary Biography of Mikhail Sholokhov, 1977; Samizdat Register, 2 volumes (editor), 1977, 1980; Philip Mironov and the Russian Civil War (with S Starikov), 1978; The October Revolution, 1979; On Stalin and Stalinism, 1979; On Soviet Dissent, 1980; Nikolai Bukharin: The Last Years, 1980; Leninism and Western Socialism, 1981; An End to Silence, 1982; Khrushchev, 1983; All Stalin's Men, 1984; China and the Superpowers, 1986; Time of Change (with G Chiesa), 1990; Brezhnev: A Political Biography, 1991; Gensek s Lybianki (political biography of Andropov), 1994; Capitalism in Russia?, 1998. Contributions to: Professional journals and general publications. Address: Abonement Post Box 258, Moscow A-475, 125475, Russia.

MEDVEDEV Zhores (Alexandrovich), b. 14 Nov 1925, Tbilisi, USSR. Biologist; Writer. m. Margarita Nikolayevna Buzina, 1951, 2 sons. Education: Timiriazev Academy of Agricultural Sciences, Moscow; Institute of Plant Physiology, Russian Academy of Sciences. Appointments: Scientist to Senior Scientist, Department of Agrochemistry and Biochemistry, Timiriazev Academy of Agricultural Sciences, Moscow, 1951-62; Head of Laboratory, Molecular Radiobiology, Institute of Medical Radiology, Obninsk, 1963-69; Senior Scientist, All-Union Scientific Research Institute of Physiology and Biochemistry of Farm Animals, Borovsk, 1970-72, National Institute for Medical Research, London, 1973-92. Publications: Protein Biosynthesis and Problems of Heredity, Development, and Ageing, 1963; Molecular-Genetic Mechanisms of Development, 1968; The Rise and Fall of T D Lysenko, 1969; The Medvedev Papers, 1970; A Question of Madness (with Roy Medvedev), 1971; Ten Years After, 1973; Khrushchev: The Years in Power (with Roy Medvedev), 1976; Soviet Science, 1978; The Nuclear Disaster in the Urals, 1979; Andropov, 1983; Gorbachev, 1986; Soviet Agriculture, 1987; The Legacy of Chernobyl, 1990. Contributions to: Many professional journals. Honour: René Schubert Prize in Gerontology, 1985. Address: 4 Osborn Gardens, London NW7 1DY, England.

MEDVEI Victor Cornelius, (C Monk), b. 6 June 1905, Budapest, Hungary. Consultant Physician; Writer. m. Sheila Mary Wiggins, 9 May 1946, dec 1989, 1 son, 2 daughters. Education: Prince Eszterhazy Gymnasium, Vienna, 1916-24; MD, University of Vienna, 1930; MRCS LRCP, St Bartholomew's Hospital, London, 1941; MRCP, 1943, FRCP, 1965. Publications: The Mental and Physical Effects of Pain, 1949; The Royal Hospital of St Bartholomew's 1923-1973 (co-editor), 1974; A History of Endocrinology, 1982, 2nd edition, 1993. Contributions to: About 80 papers to medical scientific journals, 1931-92. Honours: Buckston Browne Prize, Harveian Society of London, 1948; Commander of the Order of the British Empire, 1965; Chevalier de l'ordre National du Merite, 1981; Golden MD, Diploma of the University of Vienna, 1991. Memberships: London PEN; Harveian Society,

president, 1970; Osler Club of London, president, 1983; Garrick Club. Address: 38 Westmoreland Terrace, London SW1V 3HL, England.

MEEK Jay, b. 23 Aug 1937, Grand Rapids, Michigan, USA. Professor; Poet. m. Martha George, 29 Aug 1966, 1 daughter. Education: BA, University of Michigan, 1959; MA, Syracuse University, 1965. Appointments: Faculty, Wake Forest University, 1977-80, Sarah Lawrence College, 1980-82; Associate Professor, Massachusetts Institute of Technology, 1982-83; Writer-in-Residence, Memphis State University, 1984; Professor, University of North Dakota, 1985-. Publications: The Week the Dirigible Came, 1976; Drawing on the Walls, 1980; Earthly Purposes, 1984; Stations, 1989; Windows, 1994; Headlands: New and Selected Poems, 1997. Contributions to: Journals and magazines. Honours: National Endowment for the Arts Award, 1972-73; Guggenheim Fellowship, 1985-86; Bush Artist Fellowship, 1989. Address: c/o Department of English, University of North Dakota, Box 7209, University Station, Grand Forks, ND 58202, USA.

MEEKER Eunice Juckett, Writer; Photographer; Broadcaster. m. (1) Charles Juckett, 1940, (2) John Meeker, 1985, 1 child. Education: BS, Russell Sage College; BEd, University of Southern California. Publication: Cooking Wisdom, 1996. Contributions to: Journals, reviews and quarterlies. Address: 66 Davids Lane, East Hampton, NY 11937, USA.

MEGGED Aharon, b. 10 Aug 1920, Wloclawek, Poland. Writer. m. Eda Zoritte, 11 May 1944, 2 sons. Appointments: Editor, MASSA, 1953-55; Literary Editor, Lamerchav Daily, 1955-68; Cultural Attaché, Israel Embassy, London, England, 1968-71; Columnist, Davar Daily, 1971-85. Publications: Hedva and I, 1953; Fortunes of a Fool, 1960; Living on the Dead, 1965; The Short Life, 1971; The Bat, 1975; Asahel, 1978; Heinz, His Son and the Evil Spirit, 1979; Journey in the Month of Av, 1980; The Flying Camel and the Golden Hump, 1982; The Turbulent Zone (essays), 1985; Foiglmann, 1987; The Writing Desk (literary essays), 1988; The Selvino Children (documentary), 1984; Anat's Day of Illumination, 1992; Longing for Olga, 1994; Iniquity, 1996; Love-Flowers from the Holy Land, 1998. Plays: Hedva and I, 1955; Hannah Senesh, 1963; Genesis, 1965; The High Season, 1968. Contributions to: Atlantic Monthly; Encounter; Midstream; Listener; Moment; Present-Tense; Partisan Review; Ariel. Honours: Brennen Prize, 1960; Bialik Prize, 1973; Agnon Prize, 1997; Wizt-Paris Prize, 1998. Memberships: Israel PEN Centre, president, 1980-87; Hebrew Academy, 1982-. Address: 8 Pa'amoni St., Tel-Aviv 6218, Israel.

MEHROTRA Arvind Krishna, b. 16 Apr 1947, Lahore, Pakistan. Lecturer; Poet. Education: MA, University of Bombay, 1968. Appointment: Lecturer, University of Hyderbad, 1977-78. Publications: Bharatmata: A Prayer, 1966; Woodcuts on Paper, 1967; Poems, Poemes, Poemas, 1971; Nine Enclosures, 1976; Distance in Statute Miles, 1982; Middle Earth, 1984. Editor: Twenty Indian Poems, 1990; Twelve Modern Indian Poets, 1991. Honour: Homi Bhabha Fellowship, 1981. Address: Department of English Studies, University of Allahabad, Allabahad 211002, Uttar Pradesh, India.

MEHROTRA Sri Ram, b. 23 June 1931, Anantram, Etawah, Uttar Pradesh, India. Author; Educator. m. Eva Mehrotra, 24 July 1957. Education: MA, History, University of Allahabad, 1950; PhD, History, University of London, 1960. Appointments: Lecturer, University of London, 1962; Professor, Himachal Pradesh University, 1972; Visiting Professor, University of Wisconsin, 1974; Visiting Fellow, St John's College, Cambridge, 1983-84; Nehru Professor, MD University, 1992-96. Publications: India and the Commonwealth, 1885-1929, 1965; The Emergence of the Indian National Congress, 1971; The Commonwealth and the Nation, 1978; Towards India's Freedom and Partition, 1979; A History of the Indian National Congress, Vol 1, 1885-1918, 1995. Contributions to: Scholarly journals. Address: Seva,

Kenfield Estate, Ambedkar Chowk, Shimla, HP 171004, India.

MEHTA Ved (Parkash), b. 21 Mar 1934, Lahore, India. Writer; Teacher. m. Linn Fenimore Cooper Cary, 1983, 2 daughters. Education: Pomona College, 1956; BA, 1959, MA, 1962, Oxford University; MA, Harvard University, 1961. Appointments: Residential Fellow, Eliot House, Harvard University, 1959-61; Staff Writer, The New Yorker magazine, 1961-94; Visiting Scholar, Case Western Reserve University, 1974; Beatty Lecturer, McGill University, 1979; Visiting Professor, Bard College, 1985, 1986, Sarah Lawrence College, 1988, New York University, 1989-90; Visiting Fellow, Balliol College, Oxford, 1988-89; Visiting Professor, Yale University, 1990-93, Williams College, 1994, Vasser College, 1994-96; Senior fellow, Freedom Forum, Media Studies Center, Visiting Scholar, Columbia University, 1996-97; Fellow, Center for Advanced Studies in the Behavioural Sciences, 1997-98. Publications: Face to Face, 1957; Walking the Indian Streets, 1960, revised edition, 1971; Fly and the Fly-Bottle, 1963, 2nd edition, 1983; The New Theologian, 1966; Delinquent Chacha, 1967; Portrait of India, 1970, 2nd edition, 1993; John is Easy to Please, 1971; Mahatma Gandhi and His Apostles, 1977; The New India, 1978; Photographs of Chachaji, 1980; A Family Affair: India Under Three Prime Ministers, 1982; Three Stories of the Raj, 1986; Rajiv Gandhi and Rama's Kingdom, 1994; A Ved Mehta Reader: The Craft of the Essay, 1998. Autobiographical series: Daddyji, 1972; Mamaji, 1979; Vedi, 1982; The Ledge Between the Streams, 1984; Sound-Shadows of the New World, 1986; The Stolen Light, 1989; Up At Oxford, 1993; Remembering Mr Shawn's New Yorker, 1998. Contributions to: PBS-TV and BBC-TV. Honours: Guggenheim Fellowships, 1971-72, 1977-78; Ford Foundation Grant, 1971-76; Association of Indians in America Award, 1978; John D and Catharine T MacArthur Foundation Fellowship, 1982-87; Distinguished Service Award, Asian/Pacific American Library Association, 1986; New York City Mayor's Liberty Medal, 1986; New York Institute for the Humanities Fellowship, 1988-92; Literary Lion Medal, New York Public Library, 1990; Literary Lion Centennial Medal, 1996; Honorary doctorates. Memberships: Council on Foreign Relations; Phi Beta Kappa. Address: 139 East 79th St, New York, NY 10021, USA.

MEIDINGER-GEISE Ingeborg Lucie, b. 16 Mar 1923, Berlin, Germany. Writer; Poet; Dramatist. Education: DPhil. Publications: Over 60 works, including novels, stories, poems, essays, criticism, and radio plays. Contributions to: Various publications. Honours: Hans Sachs Drama Prize, 1976; International Mölle Literary Prize, Sweden, 1979. Honours: Over 13 literary honours. Memberships: Die Kogge, chairman, 1967-88; PEN. Address: Schobertweg 1 a, D-91056 Erlangen, Germany.

MEIER Herbert, b. 29 Aug 1928, Solothurn, Switzerland. Writer. m. Yvonne Haas, 23 Sept 1954, 2 sons, 1 daughter. Education: Doctor Phil I, Universities: Basle, Paris, Vienne, Fribourg. Appointments: Chief Dramaturge: Schauspielhaus, Zurich, 1977-82; Writer-in-Residence, University of S California, Los Angeles, 1986. Publications: Novels: Ende September, 1959; Verwandtschaften, 1962; Stiefelchen Fallein, 1970; Winterball, 1996; Plays: Theater I-III, 1993; Poems: Siebengestirn, 1956; Sequenzen, 1969; Aufbrüche Reisen von Dorther, 1998. Honours: Bremer Literatur-Preis, 1955; Schiller-Preis, 1997. Membership: PEN. Address: Appenzeller Str 73, CH-8049 Zurich, Switzerland.

MEIGHAN Roland, b. 29 May 1937, Sutton Coldfield, England. Writer; Publisher; Consultant. m. Janet Meighan, 1 son, 2 stepsons. Education: DSocSc; PhD; BSc; LCP. Appointments: Various school teacher positions; Lecturer, Senior Lecturer in Education, University of Birmingham; Special Professor of Education, University of Nottingham; Independent Writer and Consultant. Publications: A Sociology of Educating, 1981; Flexischooling, 1988; Theory and Practice of Regressive Education, 1993; The Freethinkers' Guide to the Educational Universe, 1994; John Holt: Personalised Education and the Reconstruction of Schooling, 1995; The Next Learning System, 1997. Contributions to: Natural Parent Magazine; Observer; Yorkshire Post; Times Educational Supplement. Address: 113 Arundel Drive, Bramcote Hills, Nottingham NG9 3FO, England.

MEINKE Peter, b. 29 Dec 1932, Brooklyn, New York, USA. Retired Professor of Literature; Poet; Writer. m. Jeanne Clark, 14 Dec 1957, 2 sons, 2 daughters. Education: AB, Hamilton College, 1955; MA, University of Michigan, 1961; PhD, University of Minnesota, 1965. Appointments: Assistant Professor, Hamline University, St Paul, Minnesota, 1961-66; Professor of Literature and Director of the Writing Workshop, Eckerd College, St Petersburg, Florida, 1966-93; Fulbright Senior Lecturer, University of Warsaw, 1978-79; Visiting Distinguished Writer, University of Hawaii, 1993, University of North Carolina, Greensboro, 1996; Fellow, Le Château de Lavigny, Switzerland, 1998; Several Writer-in-residencies. Publications: Lines from Neuchâtel, 1974; The Night Train and the Golden Bird, 1977; The Rat Poems, 1978; Trying to Surprise God, 1981; The Piano Tuner, 1986; Underneath the Lantern, 1987; Night Watch on the Chesapeake, 1987; Far from Home, 1988; Liquid Paper: New and Selected Poems, 1991; Scars, 1996; Campocorto, 1996; The Shape of Poetry, 1999. Contributions to: Periodicals. Honours: 1st Prize, Olivet Sonnet Competition, 1966; National Endowment for the Arts Fellowships, 1974, 1989; Gustav Davidson Memorial Award, 1976, Lucille Medwick Memorial Award, 1984, Emily Dickinson Award, 1992, Poetry Society of America; Flannery O'Connor Award, 1986; Paumanok Poetry Award, 1993; Master Artist's Fellowship, Fine Arts Work Center, Provincetown, 1995. Memberships: Academy of American Poets; Poetry Society of America. Address: 147 Wildwood Lane South East, St Petersburg, FL 33705, USA.

MELBYE Iben, b. 28 Feb 1943, Copenhagen, Denmark. Author; Producer of Radio Programs. Div, 1 son. Appointments: Librarian, Oslo, Copenhagen; Editor, 1975-; Freelance Writer, 1975-. Publications: Elskede Anne, 1982; Fange nr 198, 1985; Det Begydte Pa Havnen, 1985; Moonie, 1988; Ramt, 1997. Honours: Several. Memberships: Danish Writers Union. Literary Agent: ICBS, Copenhagen. Address: Vennemindevej 2, 2100 Copenhagen O, Denmark.

MELCHETT Sonia. See: SINCLAIR Sonia Elizabeth.

MELCHIOR Ib (Jorgen), b. 17 Sept 1917, Copenhagen, Denmark. Author; Dramatist; Director. Education: Graduate, Stenhus College, 1936; Candidatus Philosophiae, University of Copenhagen, 1937. Appointments: Writer, Director, over 500 live and filmed TV episodes, 12 feature films, 60 documentary films, 1959-76. Publications: Order of Battle, 1972; Sleeper Agent, 1975; The Haigerloch Project, 1977; The Watchdogs of Abaddon, 1979; The Marcus Device, 1980; Hour of Vengeance, 1982; Eva, 1984; V-3, 1985; Code Name: Grand Guignol, 1987; Steps and Stairways, 1989; Quest, 1990; Hitler's Werewolves, 1991; Case by Case, 1993; Reflections on the Pool, 1997. Honours: Golden Scroll, 1976; Hamlet Award, 1982; Outstanding American-Scandinavian, 1995. Memberships: Authors Guild; Directors Guild of America; Manuscript Society; Writers Guild of America. Address: 8228 Marmont Lane, Los Angeles, CA 90069, USA.

MELDRUM James. See: BROXHOLME John Franklin.

MELEAGROU Evie, b. 28 May 1930, Nicosia, Cyprus. Author. m. Dr John Meleagrou, MD, 26 Nov 1952, 1 son, 2 daughters. Education: Diplome de la Literature Française, Athenaeum Institute, Athens; BA, University of London. Appointments: Producer, Literary Programmes, CBC, 1952-55; Editor, Cyprus Chronicles, 1960-72; Secretary, Cyprus Chronicles Cultural Centre, 1960-74; Cyprus Representative, World Writers Conference, 1965. Publications: Solomon's Family, 1957; Anonymous City, 1963; Eastern Mediterranean, 1969; Conversations with Che, 1970; Penultimate Era, 1981; Persona is the Unknown Cypriot Woman (literary essays and poetry), 1993; The Virgin Plunge in the Ocean Depths (short stories and novels), 1993; Cyprus Chronaca (historical essays), 1974-1992, 1993; Translations. Honours: Severian Literary Prize, 1945; 1st Pancyprian Prize Short Story Competition, 1952; Pancyprian Novella Competition, 1957; Cyprus National Novel Awards, 1970, 1982; Panhellenic National Novel Award, 1982. Memberships: Cyprus Chronicles Cultural Centre, general secretary; Cyprus Cultural Association of Women, general secretary; First Cypriot Writers Association, secretary, 1961-70; Association of Greek Writers, Athens; Cyprus State Literary Awards Committee, 1969-79. Literary Agent: Dodoni Publishing House, 3 Asklipios Street, Athens, 10679, Greece. Address: 22 Messolongi Street, Nicosia, Cyprus.

MELFI Mary, b. 10 June 1951, Italy. Writer. m. George Nemeth, 17 May 1975, 2 sons. Education: BA, Loyola College, Concordia University, 1973; MLS, McGill University, Montreal, 1977. Publications: The Dance, the Cage and the Horse (poetry), 1976; A Queen Is Holding a Mummified Cat (poetry), 1982; A Bride in Three Acts (poetry), 1983; A Dialogue with Masks (novella), 1985; The O Canada Poems, 1986; A Season in Beware (poetry), 1989; Infertility Rites (novel), 1991, French translation, 1999; Ubu, The Witch Who Would Be Rich (children's novel), 1994; Sex Therapy (play), 1996; Painting Moments, Art, AIDS and Nick Palazzo (editor), 1998; Stages: Selected Poems, 1998. Contributions to: Toronto Life; Quarry; The Canadian Forum; Exile; Descant; Poetry Canada Review; The Antigonish Review; Event; Ariel; Room of One's Own; Canadian Literature; Vice Versa; Zymergy; Canadian Women's Study; Prism International; Waves; Poetry WLU; Northern Light; Simcoe Review; Prairie Fire. Honours: Canada Council Arts Grants, 1981-82, 1982-83; Quebec Arts Council Grant, 1993-94, 1996-97; Canadian Heritage Grant (Nick Palazzo), 1995. Address: 5040 Grand Blvd, Montreal, Quebec, Canada H3X 3S2.

MELLERS Wilfrid (Howard), b. 26 Apr 1914, Leamington, Warwickshire, England. Author; Professor of Music (retired); Composer. m. (1) Vera M Hobbs, (2) Pauline P Lewis, 3 daughters, (3) Robin S Hildyard. Education: Leamington College, 1933; BA, 1936, MA, 1938, Cambridge University; DMus, University of Birmingham, 1960. Appointments: Staff Tutor in Music, University of Birmingham, 1948-60; Andrew Mellon Professor of Music, University of Pittsburgh, 1960-63; Professor of Music, University of York, 1964-81; Visiting Professor, City University, 1984-. Publications: Music and Society: England and the European Tradition, 1946; Studies in Contemporary Music, 1947; François Couperin and the French Classical Tradition, 1950, 2nd edition, revised, 1987; Music in the Making, 1952; Romanticism and the 20th Century, 1957, 2nd edition, revised, 1988; The Sonata Principle, 1957, 2nd edition, revised, 1988; Music in a New Found Land: Themes and Developments in the History of American Music, 1964, 2nd edition, revised, 1987; Harmonius Meeting: A Study of the Relationship between English Music, Poetry, and Theatre, c.1600-1900, 1965; Caliban Reborn: Renewal in Twentieth-Century Music, 1967; Twilight of the Gods: The Music of the Beatles, 1973; Bach and the Dance of God, 1980; Beethoven and the Voice of God, 1983; A Darker Shade of Pale: A Backdrop to Bob Dylan, 1984; Angels of the Night: Popular Female Singers of Our Time, 1986; The Masks of Orpheus: Seven Stages in the Story of European Music, 1987; Le Jardin Parfumé: Homage to Federico Mompou, 1989; Vaughan Williams and the Vision of Albion, 1989, new enlarged edition, 1997; The Music of Percy Grainger, 1992; Francis Poulenc, 1994; Between Old Worlds and New: Occasional Writings on Music by Wilfrid Mellers, 1998; Singing in the Wilderness, 1999. Contributions to: Reference works and journals. Honours: Honorary DPhil, City University, 1981; Officer of the Order of the British Empire, 1982. Membership: Sonneck Society, honorary member. Address: Oliver Sheldon House, 17 Aldwark, York, YO1 7BX, England.

MELLING John Kennedy, b. 11 Jan 1927, Westcliff-on-Sea, Essex, England. Drama Critic; Editor; Writer; Lecturer; Broadcaster; Chartered Accountant. Education: Thirsk School, 1932-38; Westcliff High School for Boys, 1938-42. Appointments: Drama Critic, The Stage, 1957-90; Drama Critic, Fur Weekly News, 1968-73; Editor, The Liveryman Magazine, 1970-75, Chivers Black Dagger Series of Crime Classics, 1986-91; Radio Crime Book Critic, BBC London, 1984-85, BBC Essex, 1987. Publications: Discovering Lost Theatres, 1969; Southend Playhouses from 1793, 1969; Discovering Theatre Ephemera, 1973; Discovering London's Guilds and Liveries, 5 editions, 1973-95; Crime Writers' Handbook of Practical Information (editor), 1989; Gwendoline Butler: Inventor of the Women's Police Procedural, 1993; Murder Done to Death, 1996; Scaling the High C's (with John L Brecknock), 1996. Contributions to: Newspapers and journals; Regular columnist, Crime Time. Honours: Knight Grand Cross; Order of St Michael; Police Medal of Honour, USA, 1984; Knight, Order of St Basil, 1984; Crime Writers Association Award for Outstanding Services, 1989; Master of the Worshipful Company of Poulters, 1980-81; Memberships: British Academy of Film and Television Arts; Institute of Taxation, fellow; Faculty of Building, Royal Society of Arts, fellow; Crime Writers' Association, committee member; Governor of the Corporation of the Sons of the Clergy, 1981-. Address: 44 A Tranquil Vale, Blackheath, London SE3 0BD, England.

MELLOR D(avid) H(ugh), b. 10 July 1938, England. Professor of Philosophy; Writer. Education: BA, Natural Sciences and Chemical Engineering, 1960, PhD, 1968, ScD, 1990, M in English, 1992, Pembroke College, Cambridge; MSc, Chemical Engineering, University of Minnesota, 1962. Appointments: Research Student in Philosophy, Pembroke College, 1963-68, Fellow, Pembroke College, 1965-70, University Assistant Lecturer in Philosophy, 1965-70, University Lecturer in Philosophy, 1970-83, Fellow, 1971-, and Vice-Master, 1983-87, Darwin College, University Reader in Metaphysics, 1983-85, Professor of Philosophy, 1986-, Cambridge University; Visiting Fellow in Philosophy, Australian National University, Canberra, 1975; Honorary Professor of Philosophy, University of Keele, 1989-92. Publications: The Matter of Chance, 1971; Real Time, 1981; Cambridge Studies in Philosophy, (editor), 1978-82; Matters of Metaphysics, 1991; The Facts of Causation, 1995. Contributions to: Scholarly journals. Memberships: Aristotelian Society, president, 1992-93; British Academy, fellow; British Society for the Philosophy of Science, president, 1985-87. Address: 25 Orchard Street, Cambridge CB1 1JS, England.

MELLY (Alan) George (Heywood), b. 17 Aug 1926, Liverpool, England. Writer; Jazz Singer. Appointments: Jazz Singer, Mick Mulligan's Band, 1949-61; Writer, Flook Strip Cartoon, 1956-71; Pop Music Critic, 1965-67; Critic, 1967-71, Film Critic, 1971-73, Observer, London; Compere, George, Granada TV Show, 1974. Publications: I Flook, 1962; Owning Up, 1965; Revolt into Style, 1970; Flook by Trog, 1970; Rum, Bum and Concertina, 1977; Media Mob (with B Fantoni), 1980; Great Lovers, 1981; Tribe of One, 1981; Mellymobile, 1982; Swans Reflecting Elephants, 1982; Scouse Mouse, 1984; It's All Writ Out For You, The Life and Works of Scottie Wilson, 1986; Paris and the Surealists (with Michael Woods), 1991; Don't Tell Sybil, 1997. Address: 81 Frithville Gardens, London W12 7JQ, England.

MELNIKOFF Pamela Rita, b. London, England. Journalist; Author; Poet. m. Edward Harris, 29 Mar 1970. Education: North London Collegiate School. Appointments: Reporter, Feature Writer, 1960-70, Film Critic, 1970-96, The Jewish Chronicle. Publications: The Star and the Sword; Plots and Players; Prisoner in Time; The Ransomed Menorah. Libretto: Cantata Heritage, 1993. Contributions to: Jewish Quarterly; Poetry Review. Honours: Golden Pen Award; Greenwood Prize, Poetry Society. Memberships: PEN; Society of Authors; Guild of Jewish Journalists; Critics Circle. Address: 25 Furnival Street, London EC4A 1JT, England.

MELNYCZUK Askold, b. 12 Dec 1954, Irvington, New Jersey, USA. Writer; Editor. m. Alexandra Johnson, 30 July 1995. Education: BA, Rutgers University, 1976; MA, Boston University, 1978. Appointments: Preceptor, Harvard University, 1990-92; Preceptor, Editor, Boston University, 1982-; Lecturer, Bennington Graduate Writing Seminars, 1995-. Publications: What Is Told (novel), 1994; Take Three New Poets Series (editor), 1996; From Three Worlds (co-editor), 1997. Contributions to: Poetry; New York Times; Antioch Review; Boston Globe; Southwest Review. Honours: McDonough Fiction Prize, 1995; Lila Wallace-Reedin's Digest Writers Award, 1997. Membership: PEN New England, vice chair, 1997-99. Address: c/o Boston University, 236 Bay State Road, Boston, MA 02215-1402, USA.

MELOSH Barbara, b. 19 July 1950, Salt Lake City, Utah, USA. Associate Professor of English and American Studies; Writer. m. Gary Kulik, 19 Nov 1981, 1 son. Education: AB, Middlebury College, Vermont, 1972; AM, 1975, PhD, 1979, Brown University. Appointments: Visiting Lecturer, Brown University, 1978-79; Assistant Professor, University of Wisconsin, Madison, 1979-83; Associate Curator of Medical Sciences, National Museum of American History, 1983-90; Assistant Professor, 1983-86, Associate Professor of English and American Studies, 1986-92, Professor of English, American Studies and History, 1992-, George Mason University; Professor, English and History, 1992-. Publications: The Physician's Hand: Work Culture and Conflict in American Nursing, 1983; American Nurses in Fiction (editor), 1984; Engendering Culture: Manhood and Womanhood in New Deal Public Art and Theatre, 1991; Gender and American History Since 1890 (editor), 1993. Contributions to: Books and journals. Honours: Ellen H Richards Fellow, American Association of University Women, 1976-77; Smithsonian Institution Fellow, 1980-81; George Mason-Smithsonian Fellow in New Deal Culture, 1982-83; Regents Publication Program Fellow, 1987-89; National Endowment for the Humanities Fellowship, 1998-99; Woodrow Wilson Center Fellow, 1998-99. Memberships: American Historical Association; American Studies Association; Berkshire Conference on the History of Women; National Women's Studies Association; Organization of American Historians. Address: c/o Department of English, George Mason University, Fairfax, VA 22030, USA.

MELTZER David, b. 17 Feb 1937, Rochester, New York, USA. Poet; Writer; Teacher; Editor; Musician. m. Christina Meyer, 1958, 1 son, 3 daughters. Education: Los Angeles City College, 1955-56; University of California at Los Angeles, 1956-57. Appointments: Editor, Maya, 1966-71, Tree magazine and Tree Books, 1970-; Faculty, Graduate Poetics Program, 1980-, Chair, Undergraduate Writing and Literature Program, Humanities, 1988-, New College of California, San Francisco. Publications: Poetry: Poems (with Donald Schenker), 1957; Ragas, 1959; The Clown, 1960; Station, 1964; The Blackest Rose, 1964; Oyez!, 1965; The Process, 1965; In Hope I Offer a Fire Wheel, 1965; The Dark Continent, 1967; Nature Poem, 1967; Santamaya (with Jack Shoemaker), 1968; Round the Poem Box: Rustic and Domestic Home Movies for Stan and Jane Brakhage, 1969; Yesod, 1969; From Eden Book, 1969; Abulafia Song, 1969; Greenspeech, 1970; Luna, 1970; Letters and Numbers, 1970; Bronx Lil/Head of Lilian S A C, 1970; 32 Beams of Light, 1970; Knots, 1971; Bark: A Polemic, 1973; Hero/Lil, 1973; Tens: Selected Poems 1961-1971, 1973; The Eyes, the Blood, 1973; French Broom, 1973; Blue Rags, 1974; Harps, 1975; Six, 1976; Bolero, 1976; The Art, the Veil, 1981; The Name: Selected Poetry 1973-1983, 1984; Arrows: Selected Poetry 1957-1992, 1994. Novels: Orf, 1968; The Agency, 1968; The Agent, 1968; How Many Blocks in the Pile?, 1968; Lovely, 1969; Healer, 1969; Out, 1969; Glue Factory, 1969; The Martyr, 1969; Star, 1970; The Agency Trilogy, 1994. Other: We All Have Something to Say to Each Other: Being an Essay Entitled "Patchen" and Four Poems, 1962; Introduction to the Outsiders, 1962; Bazascope Mother, 1964; Journal of the Birth, 1967; Isla Vista Notes: Fragmentary, Apocalyptic, Didactic Contradictions, 1970; Two-way Mirror: A Poetry

Note-Book, 1977. Editor: Journal for the Protection of All Beings 1 and 3 (with Lawrence Ferlinghetti and Michael McClure), 2 volumes, 1961, 1969; The San Francisco Poets, 1971, revised as Golden Gate, 1976; Birth: An Anthology, 1973; The Secret Garden: An Anthology in the Kabbalah, 1976; Death, 1984; Reading Jazz: The White Invention of Jazz, 1993; Writing Jazz, 1997. Honours: Council of Literary Magazine Grants, 1972, 1981; National Endowment for the Arts Grants, 1974, 1975; Tombstone Award for Poetry, James Ryan Morris Memorial Foundation, 1992. Address: Box 9005, Berkeley, CA 94709, USA.

MELVILLE James. See: **MARTIN (Roy) Peter.**

MELVILLE Jennie. See: **BUTLER Gwendoline (Williams).**

MENASHE Samuel, b. 16 Sept 1925, New York, New York, USA. Poet. Education: BA, Queen's College, Flushing, New York, 1947; Doctoral d'Université, Sorbonne, University of Paris, 1950. Publications: The Many Named Beloved, 1961; No Jerusalem But This, 1971; Fringe of Fire, 1973; To Open, 1974; Collected Poems, 1986; Penguin Modern Poets 7, 1996. Contributions to: Periodicals. Honour: Longview Foundation Award, 1957. Membership: PEN. Address: 75 Thompson Street, Apt 15, New York, NY 10012, USA.

MENDELSOHN Heather Leigh, b. 20 Feb 1946, Bradford, Yorkshire, England. PR Consultant; Journalist. Education: Darlington Technical College. Appointments: R Ackrill Group; Western Mail; Daily Record; Reveille; The Sun; Market-Link PR; Phoenix PR. Publications: Various business booklets; First Parliamentary Advisors Code. Address: 105-107 Farringdon Road, London EC1R 3BU, England.

MENDELSON Paul Anthony, b. 6 Apr 1951, Newcastle Upon Tyne. m. Michael Zipora Safier, 31 Mar 1974, 2 d. Education: MA Law, Cambridge Univ, 1969-72; Deputy Creative Director, Wasey Campbell-Ewald, 1980-82. Appointments: Creative Group Head, Dorland Advertising, 1982-88; Creative Director, The Capper Cranker Agency, 1988-90; Senior Partner, The Mendelson Partnership, 1990-. Publications: May to December; Pigsty; So Haunt Me; Under the Moon; My Hero; I Can't Be Ill, I'm A Hypochondriac. Honour: Finalist, BAFTA, 1990. Membership: Writers Guild. Address: c/o Alan Brodie Representation, 211 Piccadilly, London W1V 9LD, England.

MENDES David, (Bob Mendes), b. 15 May 1928, Antwerp, Belgium. Accountant. Education: Graduate in Accountancy, 1953. Publications: 2 Collections of Poetry, 11 Novels and 14 Short-stories including: Day of Shame, 1988; The Chunnel Syndrome, 1989; The Fourth Sura, 1990; The Fraud Hunters, 1991; The Bunco Hunters, 1991; Vengeance, 1992; Races/Riots, 1993; Link, 1994; Merciless, 1995; Power of Fire, 1996; The Power of Ice, 1998; Taste of Freedom, 1999. Translations into English, German, Spanish, Chech and Japanese. Honours: The Golden Halter, 1993; Dutch Award for the Best Thriller, 1993; The Golden Noose, 1997. Memberships: Flemish Writers Guild; PEN Club. Literary Agent: Dan Wright, Ann Wright Literary Agency, 136 East 56th Street, New York, NY 10022, USA. Address: Wezelsebaan 191, B 2900 Schoten, Belgium.

MÉNDEZ LUENGO Ernesto, b. 22 Feb 1922, La Bañeza, León, Spain. Historian; Writer. m. Nela Méndez, 13 Feb 1956, 1 son, 1 daughter. Publications: Tempestad al Amanecer, Spanish Civil War, 1977; El Ultimo Templario, Novel from 14th century, 1983; Llanto Por un Lobo Muerto, Novel from 19th century, 1988; Los Guerreros de Bronce, Novel from 3rd century BC, 1995. Contributions to: Many articles and short historical stories. Honours: Larra Award, Tempestad Al Amanecer, 1977; First Hispano-Americanism Novel Award, Llanto Por Un Lobo Muerto, 1988. Membership: Spanish ACE (Writers Collegiate Association). Address: c/Majuelo 1, p 3, 8 c, 28005 Madrid, Spain.

MERCHANT Carolyn, b. 12 July 1936, Rochester, New York, USA. Professor; Environmental Historian. Education: AB, Vassar College, 1958; MA, History of Science, 1962, PhD, History of Science, 1967, University of Wisconsin. Appointments: Professor of Environmental History, Philosophy, and Ethics, University of California at Berkeley; Fellowships; Consultantships; Lectureships. Publications: The Death of Nature: Women, Ecology and the Scientific Revolution, 1980, 2nd edition, 1990; Ecological Revolutions: Nature, Gender, and Science in New England, 1989; Radical Ecology: The Search for a Livable World, 1992; Major Problems in American Environmental History: Documents and Essays (editor), 1993; Key Concepts in Critical Theory: Ecology (editor), 1994; Earthcare: Women and the Environment, 1996; Green Versus Gold: Sources in California's Environmental History (editor), 1998. Contributions to: Scholarly journals. Honours: National Science Foundation Grants, 1976-78; National Endowment for the Humanities Grants, 1977, 1981-83; Center for Advanced Study in the Behavioural Sciences, fellow, 1978; American Council of Learned Societies Fellowship, 1978; Fulbright Senior Scholar, Umeå, Sweden, 1984; John Simon Guggenheim Fellow, 1995; Honorary Doctorate, Umeå University, Sweden, 1995. Address: c/o Department of Environmental Science Policy and Management, University of California, 207 Giannini Hall, Berkeley, CA 94720, USA.

MEREDITH Christopher (Laurence), b. 15 Dec 1954, Tredegar, Wales. Writer; Poet; Senior Lecturer. m. V Smythe, 1 Aug 1981, 2 sons. Education: BA, Joint Honours, Philosophy and English, University College Wales, Aberystwyth, 1976. Appointment: Senior Lecturer, University of Glamorgan. Publications: Poetry: This, 1984; Snaring Heaven, 1990. Novels: Shifts, 1988; Griffri, 1991. Contributions to: Literary magazines in Wales, England and USA. Honours: Eric Gregory Award, 1984; Welsh Arts Council Young Writer's Prize, 1985 and Fiction Prize, 1989; Shortlisted, Book of the Year Award, 1992. Membership: Yr Academi Gymreig (English language Section). Address: c/o Seren Books, Wyndham Street, Bridgend, Mid Glamorgan, Wales.

MEREDITH William (Morris), b. 9 Jan 1919, New York, New York, USA. Poet; Retired Professor of English. Education: AB, Princeton University, 1940. Appointments: Instructor in English and Woodrow Wilson Fellow in Writing, Princeton University, 1946-50; Associate Professor in English, University of Hawaii, 1950-51; Associate Professor, 1955-65, Professor in English, 1965-83, Connecticut College, New London; Instructor, Bread Loaf School of English, Middlebury College, Vermont, 1958-62; Consultant in Poetry, Library of Congress, Washington, DC, 1978-80. Publications: Poetry: Love Letters from an Impossible Land, 1944; Ships and Other Figures, 1948; The Open Sea and Other Poems, 1958; The Wreck of the Thresher and Other Poems, 1964; Winter Verse, 1964; Year End Accounts, 1965; Two Pages from a Colorado Journal, 1967; Earth Walk: New and Selected Poems, 1970; Hazard, the Painter, 1975; The Cheer, 1980; Partial Accounts: New and Selected Poems, 1987. Non-Fiction: Reasons for Poetry and the Reason for Criticism, 1982; Poems Are Hard to Read, 1991. Editor: Shelley: Poems, 1962; University and College Poetry Prizes, 1960-66, 1966; Eighteenth-Century Minor Poets (with Mackie L Jarrell), 1968; Poets of Bulgaria (with others), 1985. Translator: Guillaume Apollinaire: Alcools: Poems, 1898-1913, 1964. Honours: Yale Series of Younger Poets Award, 1943; Harriet Monroe Memorial Prize, 1944; Rockefeller Foundation Grants, 1948, 1968; Oscar Blumenthal Prize, 1953; National Institute of Arts and Letters Grant, 1958, and Loines Prize, 1966; Ford Foundation Fellowship, 1959-60; Van Wyck Brooks Award, 1971; National Endowment for the Arts Grant, 1972, and Fellowship, 1984; Guggenheim Fellowship, 1975-76; International Vaptsarov Prize for Literature, Bulgaria, 1979; Los Angeles Times Prize, 1987; Pulitzer Prize in Poetry, 1988. Memberships: Academy of American Poets, chancellor; National Institute of Arts and Letters. Address: 6300 Bradley Avenue, Bethseda, MD 20817, USA.

MERRILL Christopher (Lyall), b. 24 Feb 1957, Northampton, Massachusetts, USA. Poet; Writer; Editor; Teacher. m. Lisa Ellen Gowdy, 4 June 1983, 1 daughter. Education: BA, Middlebury College, Vermont, 1979; MA, University of Washington, 1982. Appointments: Director, Santa Fe Writer's Conference, 1987-90; Founder-Director, Taos Conference on Writing and the Natural World, 1987-92, Santa Fe Literary Center, 1988-92; General Editor, Peregrine Smith Poetry Series, 1987-; Adjunct Professor, Santa Fe Community College, 1988-90; Contributing Editor, Tyuonyi, 1989-, The Paris Review, 1991-; Adjunct Faculty, Lewis and Clark College, 1993-95; Poetry Editor, Orion Magazine, 1993-; Faculty, Open Society Institute/University of Sarajevo, 1995; William H Jenks Chair in Contemporary Letters, College of the Holy Cross, 1995-. Publications: Workbook (poems), 1988; Fevers & Tides (poems), 1989; The Forgotten Language: Contemporary Poets and Nature (editor), 1991; From the Faraway Nearby: Georgia O'Keefe as Icon (with Ellen Bradbury), 1992; The Grass of Another Country: A Journey Through the World of Soccer, 1993; Watch Fire (poems), 1994; The Old Bridge: The Third Balkan War and the Age of the Refugee, 1995; What Will Suffice: Contemporary American Poets on the Art of Poetry (editor with Christopher Buckley), 1995; Only the Nails Remain: A Balkan Triptych, 1999; The Cauldron: Fifty American Poets (editor with Catherine Bowman), 1999. Contributions to: Books, journals, and periodicals. Honours: John Ciardi Fellow in Poetry, Bread Loaf Writers' Conference, 1989; Pushcart Prize in Poetry, 1990; Ingram Merrill Foundation Award in Poetry, 1991; Peter I B Lavan Younger Poets Award, Academy of American Poets, 1993. Membership: Academy of American Poets. Address: PO Box 172, East Woodstock, CT 06244, USA.

MERSSERLI Douglas John, b. 30 May 1947, Waterloo, Iowa, USA. Publisher; Poet; Writer. Education: BA, University of Wisconsin; MA, 1974, PhD, 1979, University of Maryland. Appointments: Publisher, Sun & Moon Press, 1976-; Assistant Professor, Literature, Temple University, 1979-85; Director, Contemporary Arts Education Project Inc, 1982-. Publications: Djuna Barnes: A Bibliography, 1976; Dinner on the Lawn, 1979; Some Distance, 1982; River to Rivet: A Poetic Manifesto, 1984; Language, Poetries (editor), 1987; Maxims from My Mother's Milk/Hymns to Him: A Dialogue, 1988; Silence All Round Marked: An Historical Play in Hysteria Writ, 1992; Along Without: A Film for Poetry, 1992. Contributions to: Roof; Mississippi Review; Paris Review; Boundry 2; Art Quarterly; Los Angeles Times. Membership: Modern Language Association. Address: c/o Sun & Moon Press, PO Box 481170, Los Angeles, CA 90048, USA.

MERTZ Barbara Louise Gross, (Barbara Michaels, Elizabeth Peters), b. 29 Sept 1927, Canton, Illinois, USA. Writer. Div, 1 son, 1 daughter. Education: PhD, University of Chicago, 1952. Publications: Temples, Tombs & Hieroglyphs, 1964; Red Land, Black Land: The World of Ancient Egyptians, 1966; Sons of the Wolf, 1967; The Dark on the Other Side, 1970; Greygallows, 1972; The Crying Child, 1973; Wait For What Will Come, 1978; Street of the Five Moons, 1978; Summer of the Dragon, 1979; The Love Talker, 1980; The Curse of the Pharaohs, 1981; The Copenhagen Connection, 1982; Silhouette in Scarlet, 1982; Die for Love, 1984; The Mummy Case, 1985; Lion in the Valley, 1986; Trojan Gold, 1987; Deeds of the Disturber, 1988; Naked Once More, 1989; The Last Camel Died at Noon, 1991; Vanish with the Rose, 1991; Houses of Stone, 1993; The Snake, the Crocodile and the Dog, 1992; Night Train to Memphis, 1994; Stitches in Time, 1995; The Hippopotamus Pool, 1996; The Danding Floor, 1997; Seeing a Large Cat, 1997; The Ape Who Guards the Balance, 1998; Other Worlds, 1999; The Falcon at the Portal, 1999. Contributions to: Reference works and periodicals. Honour: Doctor of Humane Letters, Hood College, 1992; Grandmaster Award, Mystery Writers of America, 1998. Memberships: Authors Guild; Mystery Writers of America. Address: c/o Dominick Abel, 498 West End Avenue, New York, NY 10024, USA.

MERVILLON Pol-Jean. See: NADAUS Roland.

MERWIN W(illiam) S(tanley), b. 30 Sept 1927, New York, New York, USA. Poet; Dramatist; Writer; Translator. m. Diane Whalley, 1954. Education: AB, Princeton University, 1947. Appointments: Playwright-in-Residence, Poet's Theatre, Cambridge, Massachusetts, 1956-57; Poetry Editor, The Nation, 1962; Associate, Theatre de la Citié, Lyons, 1964-65. Publications: Poetry: A Mask for Janus, 1952; The Dancing Bears, 1954; Green with Beasts, 1956; The Drunk in the Furnace, 1960; The Moving Target, 1963; The Lice, 1967; Three Poems, 1968; Animae, 1969; The Carrier of Ladders, 1970; Signs, 1971; Writings to an Unfinished Accompaniment, 1973; The First Four Books of Poems, 1975; Three Poems, 1975; The Compass Flower, 1977; Feathers from the Hill, 1978; Finding the Islands, 1982; Opening the Hand, 1983; The Rain in the Trees, 1988; Selected Poems, 1988; Travels, 1993. Plays: Darkling Child (with Dido Milroy), 1956; Favor Island, 1957; The Gilded West, 1961; adaptations of 5 other plays. Other: A New Right Arm, n.d.; Selected Translations 1948-1968, 1968; The Miner's Pale Children, 1970; Houses and Travellers, 1977; Selected Translations 1968-1978, 1979; Unframed Originals: Recollections, 1982; Regions of Memory: Uncollected Prose 1949-1982, 1987; The Lost Upland, 1993. Editor: West Wind: Supplement of American Poetry, 1961; The Essential Wyatt, 1989. Translator: 19 books, 1959-89. Honours: Yale Series of Younger Poets Award, 1952; Bess Hokin Prize, 1962; Ford Foundation Grant, 1964; Harriet Monroe Memorial Prize, 1967; PEN Translation Prize, 1969; Rockefeller Foundation Grant, 1969; Pulitzer Prize in Poetry, 1971; Academy of American Poets Fellowship, 1973; Shelley Memorial Award, 1974; National Endowment for the Arts Grant, 1978; Bollingen Prize, 1979; Aiken Taylor Award, 1990; Maurice English Award, 1990; Dorothea Tanning Prize, 1994; Lenore Marshall Award, 1994; Ruth Lilly Poetry Prize, 1998. Memberships: Academy of American Poets; American Academy of Arts and Letters. Address: c/o Georges Borchardt Inc, 136 East 57th Street, New York, NY 10022, USA.

MESERVE Walter Joseph, b. 10 Mar 1923, Portland, Maine, USA. Distinguished Professor Emeritus; Editor; Writer. m. (1), 2 sons, 2 daughters, (2) Mollie Ann Lacey, 18 June 1981. Education: Portland Junior College, 1941-42; AB, Bates College, Lewiston, Maine, 1947; MA, Boston University, 1948; PhD, University of Washington, 1952. Appointments: Instructor to Professor, University of Kansas, 1951-68; Professor of Dramatic Literature and Theory, 1968-88, Director, Institute for American Theatre Studies, 1983-88, Indiana University; Vice President, Feedback Services, New York City, Brooklin, Maine, 1983-; Editor-in-Chief, Feedback Theatrebooks, 1985-; Distinguished Professor, 1988-93, Distinguished Professor Emeritus, 1993-, Graduate Center, PhD Programs in Theatre and English, City University of New York; Co-Editor, American Drama and Theatre journal, 1989-93. Publications: The Complete Plays of W D Howells (editor), 1960; Outline History of American Drama, 1965, revised edition, 1994; American Satiric Comedies (co-editor), 1969; Robert E Sherwood, 1970; Modern Drama from Communist China (co-editor), 1970; Studies in Death of a Salesman (editor), 1972; Modern Literature from China (co-editor), 1974; An Emerging Entertainment: The Drama of the American People to 1828, 1977; The Revels History of Drama in English, Vol VIII: American Drama (co-author), 1977; Cry Woolf (co-author), 1982; Heralds of Promise: The Drama of the American People During the Age of Jackson 1829-1849, 1986; Who's Where in the American Theatre (co-editor), 1990, 3rd edition, 1993; A Chronological Outline of World Theatre (co-author), 1992; The Theatre Lover's Cookbook (co-editor), 1992; Musical Theatre Cookbook (co-editor), 1993. Honours: National Endowment for the Humanities Fellowships, 1974-75, 1983-84, 1988-89; Rockefeller Foundation Fellowship, 1979; Guggenheim Fellowship, 1984-85. Membership: Cosmos Club. Address: PO Box 174, Brooklin, ME 04616, USA.

MESSENT Peter Browning, b. 24 Oct 1946, Wimbledon, England. Reader in Modern American

Literature. m. (1) Brenda, 10 July 1972, div, 1 son, 1 daughter, (2) Carin, 9 July 1994. Education: BA, Honours, American Studies, 1969, MA, 1972, University of Manchester; PhD, University of Nottingham, 1991. Appointments: Temporary Lecturer, University of Manchester, 1972-73; Lecturer, 1973-94, Senior Lecturer in American and Canadian Studies, 1994-95, Reader in Modern American Literature, 1995-, University of Nottingham. Publications: Twentieth Century Views: Literature of the Occult (editor), 1981; New Readings of the American Novel, 1990, 2nd edition with new preface, 1998; Ernest Hemingway, 1992; Henry James: Selected Tales (editor), 1992; Mark Twain, 1997; Criminal Proceedings (editor), 1997. Contributions to: Books, journals, and magazines. Memberships: British Association for American Studies; Mark Twain Circle. Address: c/o School of American and Canadian Studies, University of Nottingham, Nottingham NG7 2RD, England.

MESSER Thomas M(aria), b. 9 Feb 1920, Bratislava, Czechoslovakia (US citizen, 1944). Museum Director; Writer. m. Remedios Garcia Villa, 10 Jan 1948. Education: Institute of International Education, 1939; Thiel College, Greenville, Pennsylvania, 1939-41; BA, Boston University, 1942; Degree, Sorbonne, University of Paris, 1947; MA, Harvard University, 1951. Appointments: Director, Roswell Museum, New Mexico, 1949-52, Institute of Contemporary Art, Boston, 1957-61; Assistant Director, 1952-53, Director of Exhibitions, 1953-55, Director, 1955-56, American Federation of Arts, New York City; Adjunct Professor, Harvard University, 1960, Barnard College, 1966, 1971; Director, 1961-88, Director Emeritus, 1988-, Solomon R Guggenheim Museum, New York City; President, MacDowell Colony, 1977-78, 1993-94; Professor, Hochschule für Angewandte Kunst, Vienna, 1984, Goethe University, Frankfurt am Main, 1991-92, 1993-; Chief Curator, Schinn Kunsthalle, Frankfurt am Main, 1994-. Publication: Edvard Munch, 1973. Contributions to: Various museum catalogues and art journals. Honours: Chevalier, 1980, Officier, 1989, Legion d'Honneur, France. Memberships: Trustee, Fontana Foundation, Milan, 1988-; Trustee, Institute of International Education, 1991-. Address: 35 Sutton Place, New York, NY 10022, USA.

MESTAS Jean-Paul, b. 15 Nov 1925, Paris, France. Poet; Writer; Translator. m. Christiane Schoubrenner, 23 Dec 1977, 2 sons, 1 daughter. Education: BA, 1947, LLB, 1947, Institute of Political Studies, Paris. Publications: Various poems, essays, and translations, 1965-95. Contributions to: Many anthologies and periodicals. Honours: Excellence in Poetry, International Poet, New York, 1982; Premio de la Cultura, Palermo, 1991; Prix Marcel Beguey, Bergerac, 1992. Memberships: International Academy, Madras, fellow; International Poetry, Korea; International Writers and Artists, board of research. Address: B401, 43 Quai Magellan, 44000 Nantes, France.

METCALF John Wesley, b. 12 Nov 1938, Carlisle, England. Writer. m. Myrna Teitelbaum, 3 sons, 2 daughters. Education: BA, Bristol University, 1960. Appointments: Writer-in-Residence, University of New Brunswick, 1972-73, Loyola of Montreal, 1976, University of Ottawa, 1977, Concordia University, 1980-81, University of Bologna, 1985. Publications: The Lady Who Sold Furniture, 1970; The Teeth of My Father, 1975; Girl in Gingham, 1978; Kicking Against the Pricks, 1982; Adult Entertainment, 1986; How Stories Mean, 1993; Shooting the Stars, 1993; Freedom from Culture, 1994. Contributions to: Many publications in Canada and USA. Honour: Canada Council Arts Awards, 1968-69, 1971, 1974, 1976, 1978, 1980, 1983, 1985. Address: 128 Lewis Street, Ottawa, Ontario K2P 0S7, Canada.

METCALF Paul, b. 7 Nov 1917, E Milton, MA, USA. Writer. m. Nancy Blackford, 30 May 1942, 2 daughters. Publications: The Collected Works of Paul Metcalf, 3 volumes, 1997-98. Address: PO Box 386, Chester, MA 01011-0386, USA.

METTLER Clemens, b. 1 Sept 1936, Ibach, Switzerland. Writer. Education: A-Matura, Schwyz, 1956; Diploma of Drawing Teacher, Lucerne, 1960. Appointments: Drawing Teacher, Schwyz, 1960-61, Altdorf, 1964; Part-time, Swiss Post, Zurich, 1962-65. Publications: Der Glasberg, (novel), 1968; Greller frisher Mittagsbrand (short stories), 1971; Kehrdruck und andere Geschichten (short stories), 1974; Gleich einem Standbild, so unbewegt (short stories), 1982; Findelbuch, Literary Collage, 1993; Symmetrie oder wiech zu zwei Kommuniongespanen Kam (short story), 1998. Contributions to: Der Sprachspiegel. Honours: Förderpreis der Stadt Bremen, 1983; Luzerner Gastpreis, 1983; Anerkennungspreis des kantons Schwyz, 1986; Werkjahr der Stadt Zurich, 1998. Memberships: Schweizer Autorinnen und Autoren Gruppe Olten; Innerschweizer Schriftstellerinnen und Schriftstellerverein. Address: Stettbachstr 43/6, CH-8051 Zurich, Switzerland.

METZ Jerred, b. 5 May 1943, Lakewood, New Jersey, USA. Writer; Poet; Editor; Social Service Administrator. m. Sarah Barker, 14 May 1978, 1 son, 1 daughter. Education: BA, 1965, MA, 1967, University of Rhode Island; PhD, University of Minnesota, 1972. Appointment: Poetry Editor, Webster Review, 1973-. Publications: Speak Like Rain, 1975; The Temperate Voluptuary, 1976; Three Legs Up, 1977; Angels in the House, 1979; Drinking the Dipper Dry: Nine Plain-Spoken Lives, 1980; Halley's Comet: Fire in the Sky, 1985. Contributions to: Magazines and journals. Address: 56200 Jackson Street, Pittsburgh, PA 15206, USA.

METZGER Deena, b. 17 Sept 1936, Brooklyn, New York, USA. Writer; Poet; Playwright; Teacher; Healer. m. (1) H Reed Metzger, 26 Oct 1957, (2) Michael Ortiz Hill, 20 Dec 1987, 2 sons. Education: BA, Brooklyn College; MA, University of California; PhD, International College, Los Angeles. Appointments: Professor, Los Angeles Valley College, 1966-69, 1973-74, 1975-79; Faculty, California Institute of the Arts, 1970-75; International Lecturer, Teacher of Writing, Supervision and Training of Healers in the Ethical, Creative and Spiritual Aspects of Healing, 1997-. Publications: Skin Shadows/Silence, 1976; Dark Milk, 1978; The Book of Hags, 1978; The Axis Mundi Poems, 1981; What Dinah Thought, 1989; Looking for the Face of God, 1989; A Sabbath Among the Ruins, 1992; Writing for Your Life: A Guide and Companion to the Inner Worlds, 1992; Tree: Essays and Pieces (co-editor), 1997; Intimate Nature: Women's Bond with Animals (co-editor), 1998. Address: PO Box 186, Topanga, CA 90290, USA.

MEWSHAW Michael, b. 19 Feb 1943, Washington, District of Columbia, USA. Author; Poet. m. Linda Kirby, 17 June 1967, 2 sons. Education: MA, 1966, PhD, 1970, University of Virginia. Appointments: Instructor, 1970, Visiting Writer, 1989-91, University of Virginia; Assistant Professor of English, University of Massachusetts, 1970-71; Assistant Professor to Associate Professor of English, University of Texas, Austin, 1973-83; Visiting Artist, 1975-76, Writer-in-Residence, 1977-78, American Academy, Rome. Publications: Fiction: Man in Motion, 1970; Waking Slow, 1972; The Troll, 1974; Earthly Bread, 1976; Land Without Shadow, 1979; Year of the Gun, 1984; Blackballed, 1986; True Crime, 1991; Non-fiction: Life for Death, 1980; Short Circuit, 1983; Money to Burn: The True Story of the Benson Family Murders, 1987; Playing Away: Roman Holidays and Other Mediterranean Encounters, 1988; Ladies of the Court: Grace and Disgrace on the Women's Tennis Tour, 1993. Contributions to: Newspapers and magazines. Honours: Fulbright Fellowship, 1968-69; William Rainey Fellowship, 1970; National Endowment for the Arts Fellowship, 1974-75; Carr Collins Awards for Best Book of Non-Fiction, 1980, 1983; Guggenheim Fellowship, 1981-82; Book of the Year Award, Tennis Week, 1993. Memberships: PEN; Phi Beta Kappa; Society of Fellows of the American Academy in Rome; Texas Institute of Letters; US Tennis Writers Association. Address: c/o William Morris Agency, 1350 Sixth Avenue, New York, NY 10019, USA.

MEYER Ben F(ranklin), b. 5 Nov 1927, Chicago, Illinois, USA. Professor of Religious Studies; Writer. m. Denise Oppliger, 27 Mar 1969. Education: BA, 1952, MA, 1953; STM, University of Santa Clara, 1958; SSL, Biblical Institute, Rome, 1961; STD, Gregorian University, Rome, 1965. Appointments: Assistant Professor of Religion, Graduate Theological Union, Berkeley, 1965-68; Associate Professor, 1969-74, Professor of Religious Studies, 1974-, McMaster University, Hamilton, Ontario. Publications: The Man for Others, 1970; The Church in Three Tenses, 1971; The Aims of Jesus, 1979; The Early Christians, 1986; Critical Realism and the New Testament, 1989; Lonergan's Hermenuetics (editor with S E McEvenue), 1989; Christus Faber: The Master Builder and the House of God, 1992; One Loaf, One Cup, 1993; Five Speeches That Changed the World, 1994; Reality and Illusion in New Testament Scholarship, 1995. Contributions to: Professional journals. Memberships: Canadian Society of Biblical Studies, president, 1988-89; Society of Biblical Literature; Studiorum Novi Testament Societas. Address: c/o Department of Religious Studies, McMaster University, Hamilton, Ontario L8S 4K1, Canada.

MEYER E Y, b. 11 Oct 1946, Liestal, Switzerland. Novelist; Essayist; Dramatist. m. Florica Malureanu. Publications: Ein Reisender in Sachen Umsturz, 1972; In Trubschachen, 1973; Eine entfernte Aehnlichkeit, 1975; Die Ruckfahrt, 1977; Die Halfte der Erfahrung, 1980; Plädoyer, 1982; Sundaymorning, 1984; Das System des Doktor Maillard oder Die Welt der Maschinen, 1994; Wintergeschichten, 1995; Venezianisches Zwischenspiel, 1997; Der Trubschachen-Komplex, 1998. Contributions to: Numerous periodicals. Honours: Literature Prize, Province of Basel, 1976; Gerhart Hauptmann Prize, 1983; Prize, Swiss Schiller Foundation, 1984; Welti Prize for Drama, 1985. Memberships: Swiss Writers Association; Swiss-German PEN Centre. Address: Brunnen-Gut, CH-3027 Bern, Switzerland.

MEYER Lynn. See: **SLAVITT David Rytman.**

MEYER Michael (Leverson), b. 11 June 1921, London, England. Writer; Dramatist; Translator. 1 daughter. Education: MA, Christ Church, Oxford. Appointments: Lecturer in English Literature, Uppsala University, 1947-50; Visiting Professor of Drama, Dartmouth College, 1978, University of Colorado, 1986, Colorado College, 1988, Hofstra University, 1989, University of California, Los Angeles, 1991. Publications: Eight Oxford Poets (editor with Sidney Keyes), 1941; Collected Poems of Sidney Keyes (editor), 1945; Sidney Keyes: The Minos of Crete (editor), 1948; The End of the Corridor (novel), 1951; The Ortolan (play), 1967; Henrik Ibsen: The Making of a Dramatist, 1967; Henrik Ibsen: The Farewell to Poetry, 1971; Henrik Ibsen: The Top of a Cold Mountain, 1971; Lunatic and Lover (play), 1981; Summer Days (editor), 1981; Ibsen on File, 1985; Strindberg: A Biography, 1985; File on Strindberg, 1986; Not Prince Hamlet (memoirs), US edition as Words Through a Windowpane, 1989; The Odd Women (play), 1993. Other: Numerous translations, including sixteen plays by Ibsen (1960-86) and eighteen by Strindberg (1964-91). Honours: Gold Medal, Swedish Academy, 1964; Whitbread Biography Prize, 1971; Knight Commander of the Order of the Polar Star, Sweden, 1977; Royal Norwegian Order of Merit, 1995. Membership: Royal Society of Literature, fellow. Address: 3 Highbury Place, London, N5 1QZ, England.

MEYERS Carol, b. 26 Nov 1942, Wilkes-Barre, Pennsylvania, USA. Professor; Archaeologist; Writer. m. Eric Meyers, 25 June 1964, 2 daughters. Education: AB, Honours, Biblical History, Literature, and Interpretation, Wellesley College, 1964; Hebrew Union College Biblical and Archaeological School, Jerusalem, 1964; Hebrew University, Jerusalem, 1964-65; MA, 1966, PhD, 1975, Near Eastern and Judaic Studies, Brandeis University. Appointments: Instructor, Academy of Jewish Studies Without Walls, 1974-78; Lecturer, 1975, Part-time Lecturer, 1976-77, Visiting Assistant Professor, 1979, University of North Carolina at Chapel Hill; Assistant Professor, 1977-84, Associate Professor, 1984-90,

Professor, 1990-, Duke University; Associate Director, Meiron Excavation Project, Israel, 1978-; Co-Director, Joint Sepphoris Project, 1984-, Sepphoris Regional Project, 1992-; Associate Editor, Semeia, 1990-96; Bulletin of the American Schools of Oriental Research, 1997-; Member, Center of Theological Inquiry, Princeton, 1991-; Visiting Faculty, MA Program in Judaic Studies, University of Connecticut, 1994-. Publications: The Tabernacle Menorah: A Synthetic Study of a Symbol from the Biblical Cult, 1976; Excavations at Ancient Meiron: Upper Galilee, Israel, 1971-72, 1974-75, 1977 (with E M Meyers and J F Strange), 1981; The Word of the Lord Shall Go Forth (editor with M O'Connor), 1983; Haggai, Zechariah 1-8 (with E Meyers), 1987; Discovering Eve: Ancient Israelite Women in Context, 1988; Excavations at the Ancient Synagogue of Gush Halav (with E Meyers), 1990; Sepphoris (with E Netzer and E Meyers), 1992; Zechariah 9-14 (with E Meyers), 1993; Ethics and Politics in the Hebrew Bible (editor with D A Knight), 1995; Community, Identity, and Ideology: Social Science Approaches to the Hebrew Bible (editor with C W Carter), 1996; Sepphoris in Galilee: Cross-Currents of Culture (editor with R Nagy, E M Meyers, and Z Weiss), 1996; Families in Ancient Israel (with L G Perdue, J Blenkinsopp, and J J Collins), 1997. Contributions to: Scholarly books and professional journals. Honours: Various grants; National Endowment for the Humanities Fellowships, 1982-83, 1990-91; Howard Foundation Fellowship, 1985-86; Severinghaus Award, Wellesley College, 1991; International Corresponding Fellow, Ingeborg Rennert Center for Jerusalem Studies, Bar Ilan University, Israel, 1998-. Memberships: American Academy of Religion; American Schools of Oriental Research; Archaeological Institute of America; Archaeology Society of Jordan; Association for Jewish Studies; British School of Archaeology in Jerusalem; Catholic Biblical Association; Center for Cross-Cultural Research on Women, Oxford; Israel Exploration Society; Palestine Exploration Society; Society for Values in Higher Education; Society of Biblical Literature; Wellesley College Center for Research on Women; Women's Association of Ancient Near Eastern Studies. Address: c/o Department of Religion, Duke University, Box 909864, Durham, NC 27708, USA.

MEYERS Jeffrey, b. 1 Apr 1939, New York, New York, USA. Writer. Education: BA, University of Michigan, 1959; MA, 1961, PhD, 1967, University of California at Berkeley. Publications: Fiction and the Colonial Experience, 1973; The Wounded Spirit: A Study of Seven Pillars of Wisdom, 1973; T E Lawrence: A Bibliography, 1975; A Reader's Guide to George Orwell, 1975; George Orwell: The Critical Heritage, 1975; Painting and the Novel, 1975; A Fever at the Core, 1976; George Orwell: An Annotated Bibliography of Criticism, 1977; Married to Genius, 1977; Homosexuality and Literature, 1890-1930, 1977; Katherine Mansfield: A Biography, 1978; The Enemy: A Biography of Wyndham Lewis, 1980; Wyndham Lewis: A Revolution, 1980; D H Lawrence and the Experience of Italy, 1982; Hemingway: The Critical Heritage, 1982; Disease and the Novel, 1860-1960, 1984; Hemingway: A Biography, 1985; D H Lawrence and Tradition, 1985; The Craft of Literary Biography, 1985; The Legacy of D H Lawrence, 1987; Manic Power: Robert Lowell and His Circle, 1987; Robert Lowell: Interviews and Memoirs, 1988; The Biographer's Art, 1989; The Spirit of Biography, 1989; T E Lawrence: Soldier, Writer, Legend, 1989; Graham Greene: A Revaluation, 1989; D H Lawrence: A Biography, 1990; Joseph Conrad: A Biography, 1991; Edgar Allan Poe: His Life and Legacy, 1992; Scott Fitzgerald: A Biography, 1994; Edmund Wilson: A Biography, 1995; Robert Frost: A Biography, 1996; Bogart: A Life in Hollywood, 1997. Membership: Royal Society of Literature. Address: 84 Stratford Road, Kensington, CA 94707, USA.

MEYNELL Hugo Anthony, b. 23 Mar 1936, Derbyshire, England. Professor of Religious Studies; Writer. m. Jennifer Routledge, 24 Feb 1969, 1 adopted son, 3 daughters. Education: BA, 1959, PhD, 1963, King's College, Cambridge. Appointments: Lecturer, University of Leeds, 1961-81; Visiting Professor, Emory University, 1978; Professor of Religious Studies,

University of Calgary, 1981-. Publications: Sense, Nonsense and Christianity, 1964; Grace versus Nature, 1966; The New Theology and Modern Theologians, 1967; God and the World, 1971; An Introduction to the Philosophy of Bernard Lonergan, 1976; Freud, Marx and Morals, 1981; The Intelligible Universe: A Cosmological Argument, 1982; The Nature of Aesthetic Value, 1986; The Theology of Bernard Lonergan, 1986; The Art of Handel's Operas, 1986; Is Christianity True?, 1994. Contributions to: Scholarly journals. Memberships: Canadian Philosophical Association; Canadian Society for Religious Studies; Royal Society of Canada. Address: c/o Department of Religious Studies, University of Calgary, Calgary, Alberta T2N 1N4, Canada.

MEZEY Katalin, b. 30 May 1943, Budapest, Hungary. Poet; Writer; Journalist; Translator. m. Janos Olah, 1 Mar 1971, 2 sons, 1 daughter. Education: Philology, German Literature, University of Zurich, 1964; Philology, Hungarian Literature, Adult Education, Eötvös University, Budapest. Appointments: Secretary, 1987-92, General Secretary, 1992-, Trade Union of Hungarian Writers; Founder-Editor, Szephalorn Konyvmuhely, publishers. Publications: 11 books, 1970-94. Address: Pesthidegkut 2 pf 5, Budapest 1286, Hungary.

MIALL Robert. See: **BURKE John Frederick.**

MICHAEL Donnelly. See: **CARROLL Paul.**

MICHAEL John. See: **CRICHTON Michael.**

MICHAEL John A, b. 5 Jan 1921, West Chester, Ohio, USA. Professor Emeritus; Writer. m. Betty J Shewalter, 14 June 1958, 1 son, 1 daughter. Education: BS, Education, Ohio State University, 1942; MEd, University of Cinncinnati, 1948; DEd, Pennsylvania State University, 1959. Appointments: Teacher, Cinncinnati Public Schools, Fairview, Hoffman and Hughes High School, 1942-59; Art Supervisor, Finneytown Schools, 1959-61; Professor, 1961-85, Professor Emeritus, 1985-, Miami University of Ohio. Publications: Art Education in the Junior High School (editor), 1964; A Handbook for Art Instructors and Students Based Upon Concepts and Behaviours, 1970; The Lowenfeld Lectures (editor), 1982; Art and Adolescence: Teaching Art at the Secondary Level, 1983; Visual Arts Resource Handbook (editor), 1993; The National Art Education Association: Our History Celebrating 50 Years (editor/archivist), 1947-97, 1997. Contributions to: Art Teacher; Art Education; NAEA Newsletter; OAEA Journal; Ohio Artline; School Arts; Studies in Art Education: Arts and Activities; Arts at Miami; Issues in Art Education; Proceedings - Lifelong Learning; The Working Craftsman; Women's Caucus Report. Honours: Ohio Art Educator of the Year, 1980, 1984; Lowenfeld Memorial Lecture Award, 1984; Marion Quin Dix Award, 1986; Distinguished Fellow, National Art Education Association, 1988; June King McFee Award, 1989; National Art Educator of the Year, 1990; Miami University Achievement Award, 1991; Distinguished Fellow, Ohio Art Education Association, 1991; National Retired Art Educator of the Year, 1993; Penn State Leadership and Service Award, 1995; SRAE Marilyn Zurmuehlen Research Award, 1997; Award of Excellence, Distinguished Alumni, Alumni Association College of Education, University of Cincinnati, 1997. Memberships: Cincinnati McDowell Society; National Art Education Association; Ohio Art Education Association. Address: 5300 Hamilton Avenue, No 203, Cincinnati, Ohio 45224, USA.

MICHAEL Judith (pseudonym of husband and wife, Judith Barnard and Michael Fain). Publications: Deceptions; Possessions; Private Affairs; A Ruling Passion; Inheritance; Sleeping Beauty; Pot of Gold, 1993; A Tangled Web, 1994. Address: c/o Ann Patty, Editor-in-Chief, Crown Books, 201 East 50th Street, New York, NY 10022, USA.

MICHAELS Anne, b. 15 Apr 1958, Toronto, Ontario, Canada. Poet; Writer; Teacher of Creative Writing. Education: BA, Honours, University of Toronto, 1980. Appointments: Many workshops and poetry readings;

Teacher of Creative Writing, University of Toronto, 1988-. Publications: Poetry: The Weight of Oranges, 1986; Miner's Pond, 1991. Fiction: Fugitive Pieces, 1996. Contributions to: Numerous anthologies, reviews, and magazines. Honours: Epstein Award for Poetry, 1980; Commonwealth Poetry Prize for the Americas, 1986; Canadian Authors' Association Award for Poetry, 1991; National Magazine Award for Poetry, 1991; Chapter/Books in Canada First Novel Award, 1997; Trillium Award, 1997; Lannan Prize, 1997; Guardian Fiction Award, 1997; H H Wingate Award, 1997; Orange Prize for Fiction, 1997; Harry Rubalow Award, 1998. Memberships: League of Canadian Poets; Writers' Union of Canada. Address: c/o McClelland and Stewart Inc, 481 University Avenue, Suite 900, Toronto, Ontario M5G 2E9, Canada.

MICHAELS Barbara. See: **MERTZ Barbara Louise Gross.**

MICHAELS Kristin. See: **WILLIAMS Jeanne.**

MICHAELS Leonard, b. 2 Jan 1933, New York, New York, USA. Professor of English Emeritus; Writer. m. Katharine Ogden, 1996. Education: BA, New York University, 1953; MA, 1956, PhD, 1967, University of Michigan; University of California at Berkeley, 1958-60. Appointments: Assistant Professor, Paterson State College, New Jersey, 1961-62, University of California at Davis, 1966-68; Assistant Professor, 1969-71, Associate Professor, 1971-76, Professor of English, 1976-94, Professor Emeritus, 1994-, University of California at Berkeley. Publications: Going Places, 1969; I Would Have Saved Them It I Could, 1975; The State of the Language (editor with Christopher Ricks), 1980, new edition, 1990; The Men's Club, 1981; Shuffle, 1990; West of the West (editor with David Reid and Raquel Scherr), 1990; Sylvia, 1992; To Feel These Things, 1993; A Cat, 1995. Contributions to: Anthologies, books, newspapers and journals. Honours: National American Academy of Arts and Letters Award, 1972; Notable Book of the Year, New York Times Book Review, 1992; Various other awards and nominations.

MICHEL Sandra Seaton, b. 30 Jan 1935, Hancock, MI, USA. Writer; Poet; Teacher. m. Philip R Michel, 28 July 1956, 3 sons, 1 daughter. Education: BA, Leland Stanford Junior University, 1980. Appointments: Editor, Highland Publishing House, 1996-; Delaware State Arts Council, National Endowment for the Arts Residency Artist, Creative Writing, Arts in Education, 1974-79, 1984-; Editor, Lenape Publishing, 1972-78; Teacher, Coast Episcopal Schools, Pass Christian, Mississippi, USA, 1984-84. Publications: My Name is Jaybird, 1972; No More Someday, 1973; From the Peninsula South, 1980; Thomas, My Brother, 1981; Visions to Keep, 1990. Honours: Distinguished Service Award, Lutheran Community Services Board, Wilm, Delaware, 1994-95; 1st Place, 1976; 1st State Writers Poetry Award, 1998; American PEN Women Children's Short Story Award, 1st Place. Memberships: Children's Book Writers & Illustrators, Delaware Literary Connection; National League of American PEN Women, State President, 1996-98; Diamond State Branch, 1994-96. Address: 3 Lanark Drive, Wilmington, DE 19803, USA.

MICHIE Jonathan, b. 25 Mar 1957, London, England. Economist. m. Carolyn Downs, 5 Nov 1988, 2 sons. Education: Balliol College, Oxford, 1976-79, 1980-85; Queen Mary College, London University, 1979-80. Publications: Unemployment in Europe, 1994; Managing the Global Economy, 1995; Creating Industrial Capacity, 1996; Firms, Organizations and Contracts, 1997; Employment and Economic Performance, 1997; Technology, Globalisation and Economic Performance, 1997; The Political Economy of South Africa's Transition, 1997; Technology, Innovation and Competitiveness, 1997; Contracts, Co-operation and Competition, 1997; Trade, Growth and Technical Change, 1998. Address: Birkbeck College, University of London, Malet Street, London WC1E 7HX, England.

MIDDLEBROOK Diane Wood, b. 16 Apr 1939, Pocatello, Idaho, USA. Professor of English; Writer; Poet. m. (1) Jonathan Middlebrook, 15 June 1963, div 1972, 1 daughter, (2) Carl Djerassi, 21 June 1985. Education: Whitman College, Walla Walla, Washington, 1957-58; AB, University of Washington, 1961; MA, 1962, PhD, 1968, Yale University. Appointments: Assistant Professor, 1966-73, Associate Professor, 1974-83, Director, Center for Research on Women, 1977-79, Associate Dean, Undergraduate Studies, 1979-82, Professor of English, 1983-, Chair, Program in Feminist Studies, 1985-88, Howard H and Jessie T Watkins University Professor, 1985-90, Stanford University; Visiting Associate Professor, Rutgers University, 1973. Publications: Walt Whitman and Wallace Stevens, 1974; Worlds Into Words: Understanding Modern Poets, 1980; Gin Considered as a Demon (poems), 1983; Coming to Light: American Women Poets (editor with Marilyn yalom), 1985; Selected Poems of Anne Sexton (editor with Diana Hume George), 1988; Anne Sexton: A Biography, 1991; Suits Me: The Double Life of Billy Tipton, 1998. Contributions to: Books, anthologies and journals, including poems, articles and reviews. Honours: Woodrow Wilson Fellowship, 1961; Albert S Cook Memorial Prize for Poetry, 1962, Theron Rockwell Field Prize for Doctoral Dissertation, 1968, Yale University; Academy of American Poets Prize, 1965; Dean's Award for Distinguished Teaching, 1977, Walter J Gores Award for Excellence in Teaching, 1987, Stanford University; National Endowment for the Humanities Fellowship, 1982-83; Fellow, Bunting Institute, Radcliffe College, 1982-83, Stanford Humanities Center, 1983-84, Rockefeller Study Center, Bellagio, Italy, 1990; Guggenheim Fellowship, 1988-89; Finalist, Bay Area Book Reviewers Award, 1992; Commonwealth Club of California Gold Medal for Non-Fiction, 1992. Memberships: Chawyck-Healey LION (Literature Online), editorial board, 1997-; Djerassi Resident Artists Program, trustee, 1980-96, chair, board, 1994; Humanities West, advisory board, 1997-; Investigative Reporters and Editors, 1995-; Modern Language Association, 1966-. Address: 1101 Green Street, No 1501, San Francisco, CA 94109, USA.

MIDDLETON (John) Christopher, b. 10 June 1926, Truro, Cornwall, England. Professor of Germanic Languages and Literatures Emeritus; Poet; Writer; Translator. 1 son, 2 daughters. Education: BA, Merton College, Oxford, 1951; MA, DPhil, 1954, University of Oxford. Appointments: Lecturer, University of Zürich, 1952-55; Lecturer, 1955-65, Senior Lecturer, 1965-66, King's College, University of London; Visiting Associate Professor, 1961-62, Professor of Germanic Languages and Literatures, 1966-98, Professor Emeritus, 1998-, University of Texas at Austin; Judith E Wilson Lecturer, University of Cambridge, 1992; Poet-in-Residence, W B Yeats Poetry Summer School, Sligo, Ireland, 1993; Various poetry readings. Publications: Poetry: Torse 3: Poems 1949-61, 1962; Nonsequences/Selfpoems, 1965; Our Flowers and Nice Bones, 1969; The Lonely Suppers of W V Balloon, 1975; Carminalenis, 1980; 111 Poems, 1983; Two Horse Wagon Going By, 1986; The Balcony Tree, 1992; Some Dogs, 1993; Intimate Chronicles, 1996; The Swallow Diver, 1997. Prose: Pataxanadu and Other Prose, 1977; Serpentine, 1985; In the Mirror of the Eighth King, 1999. Other: 'Bolshevism in Art' and Other Expository Writings, 1978; The Pursuit of the Kingfisher, 1983; Jackdaw Jiving: Selected Essays on Poetry and Translation, 1998. Translations: Ohne Hass und Fahne (with W Deppe and H Schönherr), 1958; Modern German Poetry, 1910-60 (with Michael Hamburger), 1962; German Writing Today, 1967; Selected Poems, by Georg Trakl, 1968; Selected Letters, by Friedrich Nietzsche, 1969; Selected Poems, by Friedrich Hölderlin and Eduard Mörike, 1972; Andalusian Poems (with Leticia Garza-Falcón), 1993; Faint Harps and Silver Voices: Selected Translations, 1999. Honours: Sir Geoffrey Faber Poetry Prize, 1964; Guggenheim Fellowship, 1974-75; Deutscher Akademischer Austauschdienst Fellowships, 1975, 1978; National Endowment for the Arts Fellowship, 1980; Schlegel-Tieck Translation Prize, 1985; Max Geilinger-Stiftung Prize in Anglo-Swiss Cultural Relations, 1987; Soeurette Diehl Fraser Award for Translation,

Texas Institute of Letters, 1993. Address: 1112 West 11th Street, No 201, Austin, TX 78703, USA.

MIDDLETON Osman Edward, b. 25 Mar 1925, Christchurch, New Zealand. Author. m. 1949, div, 1 son, 1 daughter. Education: Auckland University College, 1946, 1948; University of Paris, 1955-56. Appointments: Robert Burns Fellow, University of Otago, 1970-71; Visiting Lecturer, Universities of Canterbury, 1971, Zürich, Frankfurt, Giessen, Kiel, Erlangen, Regensburg, Turin, Bologna, Pisa, Venice, Rome, 1983; Writer-in-Residence, Michael Karolyi Memorial Foundation, Vence, France, 1983. Publications: 10 Stories, 1953; The Stone and Other Stories, 1959; From the River to the Tide (juvenile), 1962; A Walk on the Beach, 1964; The Loners, 1972; Selected Stories, 1976; Confessions of an Ocelot, 1979; The Big Room and Other Stories, 1998. Contributions to: Anthologies worldwide; Numerous magazines and journals. Honours: Achievement Award, 1959, Scholarship in Letters, 1965, New Zealand Literary Fund; Hubert Church Prose Award, 1964; Joint Winner, New Zealand Prose Fiction Award, 1976. Membership: New Zealand Association of the Blind and Partially Blind, committee, 1970-95. Address: 20 Clifford Street, Dalmore, Dunedin, New Zealand.

MIDDLETON Roger, b. 19 May 1955, England. Senior Lecturer in Economic History; Writer. Education: BA, First Class Honours, Victoria University of Manchester, 1976; PhD, Cambridge University, 1981. Appointments: Lecturer in Economic History, University of Durham, 1979-87; Senior Lecturer in Economic History, University of Bristol, 1987-90; Reader in the History of Political Economy, 1997-. Publications: Towards the Managed Economy, 1985; Government Versus the Market, 1996; Charlatans or Saviours?, 1998. Contributions to: Economic, history and computing journals. Honours: T S Ashton Prize, Economic History Society, 1980; Choice of Outstanding Academic Book, 1996; Royal Historical Society, fellow. Memberships: Royal Economic Society; Economic History Society; Conference of Socialist Economists; Association of History and Computing; Institute of Fiscal Studies. Address: Department of Economic and Social History, University of Bristol, Bristol BS1 1TB, England.

MIDDLETON Stanley, b. 1 Aug 1919, Bulwell, Nottingham, England. Novelist. m. Margaret Shirley Charnley, 22 Dec 1951, 2 daughters. Education: University College, Nottingham; BA, London University; Cert Ed, Cambridge University; MEd, Nottingham University. Appointments: Head of English, High Pavement College, Nottingham; Judith E Wilson Visiting Fellow, Emmanuel College, Cambridge. Publications: A Short Answer, 1958; Harris's Requiem, 1960; A Serious Woman, 1961; The Just Exchange, 1962; Two's Company, 1963; Him They Compelled, 1964; The Golden Evening, 1968; Wages of Virtue, 1969; Brazen Prison, 1971; Holiday, 1974; Still Waters, 1976; Two Brothers, 1978; In a Strange Land, 1979; The Other Side, 1980; Blind Understanding, 1982; Entry into Jerusalem, 1983; Daysman, 1984; Valley of Decision, 1985; An After Dinner's Sleep, 1986; After a Fashion, 1987; Recovery, 1988; Vacant Places, 1989; Changes 2 Chances, 1990; Beginning to End, 1991; A Place to Stand, 1992; Married Past Redemption, 1993; Catalysts, 1994; Toward the Sea, 1995; Live and Learn, 1996; Brief Hours, 1997; Against the Dark, 1997; Necessary Ends, 1999. Contributions to: Various. Honours: Co-Recipient, Booker Prize, 1974; Honorary MA, Nottingham University; Honorary MUniv, Open University; Honorary DLitt, De Montfort University; FRSL. Membership: PEN. Literary Agent: Hutchinson. Address: 42 Caledon Road, Sherwood, Nottingham NG5 2NG, England.

MIDWINTER Eric (Clare), b. 11 Feb 1932, Sale, England. Educator. m. 2 sons, 1 daughter. Education: BA, Honours, History, St Catharine's College, Cambridge; MA, Cambridge; MA, Education, University of Liverpool; DPhil, University of York. Appointments: Director, Liverpool Education Priority Area Project, 1968-72; Head of the Public Affairs Unit, National Consumer Council, London, 1975-80; Chair, London Regional Passengers'

Committee, 1978-96; Director, Centre for Policy on Ageing, London, 1980-91; Visiting Professor of Education, Exeter University, 1993-; Chair, Community Education Development Centre, 1995-. Publications: Victorian Social Reform, 1968; Nineteenth Century Education, 1970; Old Liverpool, 1971; Social Environment and the Urban School, 1972; Priority Education, 1972; Patterns of Community Education, 1973; Education and the Community, 1975; Education for Sale, 1977; Schools in Society, 1980; W G Grace: His Life and Times, 1981; Age is Opportunity: Education and Older People, 1982; Fair Game: Myth and Reality in Sport, 1986; The Lost Seasons, 1987; The Old Order: Crime and Older People, 1990; Out of Focus: Old Age, Press and Broadcasting, 1991; Brylcreem Summer: The 1947 Summer, 1991; Illustrated History of County Cricket, 1992; Lifelines, 1994; The Development of Social Welfare in Britain, 1994; First Knock: Cricket's Opening Pairs, 1994; State Educator: The Life and Enduring Influence of W E Forster, 1995; Darling Old Oval: History of Surrey County Cricket Club, 1995; Pensioned Off: Retirement and Income Examined, 1997; The Billy Bunter Syndrome: Or Why Britain Failed to Create a Relevant Secondary School System, 1998; Yesterdays: The Way We Were, 1998. Honours: Officer of the Order of the British Empire, 1992; Honorary Doctorate, Open University. Address: Savage Club, 6 Whitehall Place, London SW14 2HD, England.

MIGNOT Dorine Madeleine Marie Ghislaine, b. 16 June 1944, Eindhoven. Curator; Writer. Education: DRS, History of Art, University of Amsterdam; Appointment: Curator, Stedelyk Museum, Amsterdam. Address: 96 De Lairessestraat, NL 1071 PJ Amsterdam, The Netherlands.

MIHAILOVICH Vasa D, b. 12 Aug 1926, Prokuplje, Yugoslavia (US citizen, 1956). Retired Professor of Slavic Languages and Literatures; Writer; Poet. m. Branka, 28 Dec 1957, 2 sons. Education: BA, 1956, MA, 1957, Wayne State University; PhD, University of California at Berkeley, 1966. Appointments: Instructor, 1961-63, Assistant Professor, 1963-68, Associate Professor, 1968-75, Professor of Slavic Languages and Literatures, 1975-95, University of North Carolina at Chapel Hill. Publications: Library of Literary Criticism: Modern Slavic Literatures, 2 volumes, 1972, 1976; Introduction to Yugoslav Literature, 1973; A Comprehensive Bibliography of Yugoslav Literature in English, 1976, 5th edition, revised, 1998; Contemporary Yugoslav Poetry, 1977; Stari i Novi Vilajet, 1977; Bdenja, 1980; Emigranti i Druge Price, 1980; Krugovi na Vodi, 1982; U Tudjem Pristanistu, 1988; Serbian Poetry From the Beginnings to the Present, 1988; Litija Malih Praznika, 1990; Na Brisanom Prostoru, 1994; Bozic u Starom Kraju, 1994; Dictionary of Literary Biography: South Slavic Writers, 2 volumes, 1994, 1997; Songs of the Serbian People: From the Collections of Vuk St Karadzic, 1997; Rasejano Slovo/The Scattered World, 1997; Braca i Druge Price, 1997. Contributions to: Books Abroad/World Literature Today; Saturday Review; Serbian Studies; Slavic and East European Journal; Slavic Review. Honours: Serbian PEN Center, 1988; Zlatni Prsten, 1994; Vukova Zaduzbina, 1997; Povelja Rastko Petrovic, 1998. Membership: Association of Writers of Serbia. Address: 821 Emory Drive, Chapel Hill, NC 27514, USA.

MIKHAIL Edward H(alim), b. 29 June 1926, Cairo, Egypt. Professor of English Literature; Writer. Education: BA, 1947, BEd, 1949, University of Cairo; DES, Trinity College, Dublin, 1959; PhD, University of Sheffield, 1966. Appointments: Lecturer to Assistant Professor, University of Cairo, 1949-66; Associate Professor, 1966-72; Professor of English Literature, 1972-, University of Lethbridge. Publications: The Social and Cultural Setting of the 1890's, 1969; John Galsworthy the Dramatist, 1971; Comedy and Tragedy: A Bibliography of Criticism, 1972; Sean O'Casey: A Bibliography of Criticism, 1972; A Bibliography of Modern Irish Drama 1899-1970, 1972; Dissertations on Anglo-Irish Drama, 1973; The Sting and the Twinkle: Conversations with Sean O'Casey (co-editor), 1974; J M Synge: A Bibliography of Criticism, 1975; Contemporary British Drama 1950-1976: An

Annotated Critical Bibliography, 1976; W B Yeats: Interviews and Recollections, 1977; J M Synge: Interviews and Recollections, 1977; English Drama 1900-1950, 1977; Lady Gregory: Interviews and Recollections, 1977; Oscar Wilde: An Annotated Bibliography of Criticism, 1978; A Research Guide to Modern Irish Dramatists, 1979; Oscar Wilde: Interviews and Recollections, 1979; The Art of Brendan Behan, 1979; Brendan Behan: An Annotated Bibliography of Criticism, 1980; An Annotated Bibliography of Modern Anglo-Irish Drama, 1982; Brendan Behan: Interviews and Recollections, 1982; Lady Gregory: An Annotated Bibliography of Criticism, 1982; Sean O'Casey and His Critics, 1985; The Abbey Theatre, 1987; Sheridan: Interviews and Recollections, 1989; James Joyce: Interviews and Recollections, 1990; The Letters of Brendan Behan, 1991; Goldsmith: Interviews and Recollections, 1993; Dictionary of Appropriate Adjectives, 1994. Contributions to: Journals. Address: 6 Coachwood Point West, Lethbridge, Alberta T1J 4B3, Canada.

MIKKELSEN Nina Elizabeth Markowitz, b. 3 Dec 1942, Mullens, West Virginia, USA. Writer. m. Vincent P Mikkelsen, 16 Aug 1965, 2 sons. Education: Concord College, 1964; MA, 1966, PhD, 1971, Florida State University. Appointments: Department of English, Florida State University, 1964-71; Department of English, Indiana University of Pennsylvania, 1986-. Publications: Virginia Hamilton, 1994; Susan Cooper, 1998; Words and Pictures, 1999. Contributions to: Cambridge Guide to Childrens Literature; Canadian Childrens Literature; African-American Review; Scribner's Writers for Young Adults; Childrens Literature Association Quarterly; Language Arts. Memberships: PMLA; MELUS. Address: 503 South 7th Street, Indiana, PA 15701, USA.

MIKLOWITZ Gloria, b. 18 May 1927, New York, New York, USA. Writer. m. Julius Miklowitz, 28 Aug 1948, 2 sons. Education: Hunter College, New York City, 1944-45; BA, University of Michigan, 1948; New York University, 1948. Appointment: Instructor, Pasadena City College, 1970-80. Publications: Some 47 books for children, 1964-98. Contributions to: Newspapers, journals and magazines. Honours: Western Australia Young Book Award, 1984; Bucks Herald for Teens Publishers Award, 1990; Wyoming Soaring Eagle Award, 1993. Memberships: PEN; Society of Children's Book Writers. Address: 5255 Vista Miguel Drive, La Canada, CA 91011, USA.

MILCINSKI Jana, (Katarina Jarc), b. 5 Dec 1920, Ljubljana, Slovenia. Editor. m. Frane Milcinski, 19 Aug 1944, 2 sons. Appointment: Editor, Otrok in Druzina magazine 1993-. Publications: Maticek in Maja vceraj, danes, jutri in vsak dan, 1968; Pisane zgodbe, 1976; Lukec dobi sestrico, 1986; To si ti, Nina, 1988; Lutkovne igrice - Boj v omari, 1989. Contributions to: Otrok in Druzina; Rodna Gruda; Ciciban; Kurircek; Other magazines. Honour: Levstikova Nagrada, 1986. Address: Dolenjska, 1000 Ljubljana, Slovenia.

MILES Betty, b. 16 May 1928, Chicago, Illinois, USA. Writer. m. Matthew B Miles, 27 Sept 1949, 1 son, 1 daughter. Education: BA, Antioch College, 1950. Publications: 14 picture books for children, 1958-95; 10 books for young adults, 1974-91. Address: 94 Sparkhill Avenue, Tappan, NY 10983, USA.

MILES Jack (John Russiano Miles), b. 30 July 1942, Chicago, Illinois, USA. Journalist; Critic; Educational Administrator. m. Jacqueline Russiano, 23 Aug 1980, 1 daughter. Education: LittB, Xavier University, Cincinnati, 1964; PhB, Pontifical Gregorian University, Rome, 1966; Hebrew University, Jerusalem, 1966-67; PhD, Harvard University, 1971. Appointments: Assistant Professor, Loyola University, Chicago, 1970-74; Assistant Director, Scholars Press, Missoula, Montana, 1974-75; Postdoctoral Fellow, University of Chicago, 1975-76; Editor, Doubleday & Co, New York City, 1976-78; Executive Editor, University of California Press at Berkeley, 1978-85; Book Editor, 1985-91, Member, Editorial Board, 1991-95, Los Angeles Times; Director, Humanities Center, Claremont Graduate School,

California, 1995-. Publications: Retroversion and Text Criticism, 1984; God: A Biography, 1995. Contributions to: Many periodicals. Honours: Guggenheim Fellowship, 1990-91; Pulitzer Prize in Biography, 1996. Memberships: American Academy of Religion; Amnesty International; National Books Critics Circle, president, 1990-92; PEN. Address: Graduate Center, Claremont Graduate School, Claremont, CA 91711, USA.

MILES Steen, b. 20 Aug 1946, South Bend, Indiana, USA. Broadcast Journalist. m. LeRoy King, 12 Feb 1966, 2 daughters. Education: Ball State University; Indiana University. Appointments: Reporter, Talk Show Hostess, WNDU-TV, South Bend, Indiana, 1970-74; Reporter, NBC Chicago, 1974-78; News Director, WGCI Radio Chicago, 1978-80; Georgia Broadcast Editor, United Press International, 1980-84; Assignment Editor, 1984-85, Managing Editor, 1985-89, News Reporter and Anchor, 1989, WXIA-TV Atlanta, Georgia. Honours: 1 Emmy; 3 Emmy Nominations; Associated Press; United Press International; Best of Gannett. Memberships: National Academy of Television Arts and Sciences; Association of Black Journalists. Address: 1611 W Peachtree Street NE, Atlanta, GA 30309, USA.

MILIONIS Christoforos, b. 4 Nov 1932, Greece. Writer. m. Tatiana Tsaliki, 28 Dec 1969, 1 daughter. Education: Diploma, Classical Greek Literature. Publications: Novels: Acrokeraunia, 1976; Dytiki Synicia, 1980; Silvestros, 1987. Short stories: The Short Stories of Trial, 1978; The Shirt of Centaur, 1982; Kalamas ke Acherontas, 1985; Chiristis Anelkystiros, 1993. Contributions to: Various publications. Honour: 1st State Award for Short Stories, 1986. Memberships: Society of Greek Writers; Union of Greek Philologists. Address: 1 Agathiou Street, Athens 11472, Greece.

MILLAR Sir Ronald (Graeme), b. 12 Nov 1919, Reading, England. Dramatist; Screenwriter; Author. Education: King's College, Cambridge. Appointments: Actor; Screenwriter, Hollywood, 1948-54. Publications: Plays: Frieda, 1946; Champagne for Delilah, 1948; Waiting for Gillian, 1954; The Bride and the Bachelor, 1956; The More the Merrier, 1960; The Bride Comes Back, 1960; The Affair (after C P Snow), 1961; The New Men (after C P Snow), 1962; The Masters (after C P Snow), 1963; Number 10, 1967; Abelard and Heloise, 1970; The Case in Question (after C P Snow), 1975; A Coat of Varnish (after C P Snow), 1982. Musicals: Robert and Elizabeth, 1964; On The Level, 1966. Autobiography: A View from the Wings, 1993. Honour: Knighted, 1980. Address: 7 Sheffield Terrace, London W8 7NG, England.

MILLARD Hamilton. See: KIRK-GREENE Anthony.

MILLER Alex, (Alexander McPhee Miller), b. 27 Dec 1936, London, England. Author. m. (1) Anne Roslyn Neil, 1962, div 1983, 1 son, 1 daughter, (2) Stephanie Ann Pullin, 13 Dec 1983. Education: BA, University of Melbourne; DipEd, Hawthorn Institute. Appointment: Visiting Fellow, La Trobe University, 1994-. Publications: Watching the Climbers on the Mountain, 1988; The Tivington Nott, 1989; The Ancestor Game, 1992; The Sitters, 1995. Plays: Kitty Howard, 1978; The Exiles, 1981. Contributions to: Newspapers, journals and periodicals. Honours: Braille Book of the Year Award, 1990; Commonwealth Writers Prize, 1993; Miles Franklin Literary Award, 1993; Barbara Ramsden Award, Fellowship of Australian Writers, 1993. Memberships: Australian Society of Authors; Fellowship of Australian Writers. Address: c/o Department of English, La Trobe University, Bundoora, Victoria 3083, Australia.

MILLER Arthur, b. 17 Oct 1915, New York, New York, USA. Dramatist; Writer. m. (1) Mary G Slattery, 5 Aug 1940, div 1956, 1 son, 1 daughter, (2) Marilyn Monroe, June 1956, div 1961, (3) Ingeborg Morath, Feb 1962, 1 son, 1 daughter. Education: AB, University of Michigan, 1938. Publications: Plays: Honors at Dawn, 1936; No Villain: They Too Arise, 1937; The Man Who Had All the Luck, 1944; That They May Win, 1944; All My Sons, 1947; Death of a Salesman, 1949; The Crucible, 1953; A View from the Bridge, 1955; A Memory of Two Mondays,

1955; After the Fall, 1964; Incident at Vichy, 1964; The Price, 1968; Fame, 1970; The Reason Why, 1970; The Creation of the World and Other Business, 1972; Up From Paradise, 1974; The Archbishop's Ceiling, 1976; The American Clock, 1983; Some Kind of Love Story, 1983; Elegy for a Lady, 1983; Playing for Time, 1986; Danger Memory!, 1986; The Last Yankee, 1990; The Ride Down Mt Morgan, 1991; Broken Glass, 1994. Screenplays: The Story of G I Joe, 1945; The Witches of Salem, 1958; The Misfits, 1961; The Hook, 1975; Everybody Wins, 1990. Other: Situation Normal, 1944; Focus, 1945; Jane's Blanket, 1963; I Don't Need You Anymore, 1967; In Russia, 1969; In the Country, 1977; The Theatre Essays of Arthur Miller, 1978; Chinese Encounters, 1979; Salesman in Beijing, 1987; Timebends: A Life, 1987; The Misfits and Other Stories, 1987; Homely Girl, 1994. Honours: New York Drama Critics Circle Awards, 1947, 1949; Tony Awards, 1947, 1949, 1953; Donaldson Awards, 1947, 1949, 1953; Pulitzer Prize in Drama, 1949; Obie Award, 1958; National Institute of Arts and Letters Gold Medal, 1959; Brandeis University Creative Arts Award, 1970; George Foster Peabody Award, 1981; Emmy Awards, 1981, 1985; Literary Lion Award, New York Public Library, 1983; John F Kennedy Lifetime Achievement Award, 1984; Algur Meadows Award, Southern Methodist University, 1991; Berlin Prize Fellowship, 1998; PEN/Laura Pels Foundation Award, 1998. Memberships: American Academy of Arts and Letters; International PEN, president, 1965-69. Address: Tophet Road, Roxbury, CT 06783, USA.

MILLER Edmund, b. 18 July 1943, Queens, New York, USA. Professor; Poet; Writer. Education: BA, summa cum laude, C W Post Campus, Long Island University, 1965; MA, Ohio State University, 1969; PhD, State University of New York at Stony Brook, 1975. Appointments: Lecturer, Ohio State University, 1968-69; Instructor, Rockhurst College, 1969-71; Assistant Professor, Temple University, 1977-78, Illinois State University, 1979-80; Associate Professor, Hofstra University, 1980-81; Assistant Professor, 1981-86, Associate Professor, 1986-90, Professor, 1990-, Chairman, Department of English, 1993, C W Post Campus, Long Island University. Publications: Poetry: Fucking Animals: A Book of Poems, 1973; The Nadine Poems, 1973; Winter, 1975; A Rider of Currents, 1986; The Happiness Cure, and Other Poems, 1993; Leavings, 1995. Non-Fiction: Drudgerie Divine: The Rhetoric of God and Man in George Herbert, 1979; Exercises in Style, 1980, 6th edition, 1990; Like Season'd Timber: New Essays on George Herbert (editor with Robert DiYanni), 1987; George Herbert's Kinships: An Ahnentafel with Annotations, 1993. Contributions to: Books and journals. Memberships: Conference on Christianity and Literature; Lewis Carroll Society of North America; Milton Society of America, life member; Modern Language Association, life member; New York Seventeenth-Century Seminar, founding member. Address: c/o Department of English, C W Post Campus, Long Island University, Brookville, NY 11548, USA.

MILLER E(ugene) Ethelbert, b. 20 Nov 1950, New York, New York, USA. University Administrator; Poet. m. Denise King, 25 Sept 1982, 1 son, 1 daughter. Education: BA, Howard University. Appointments: Director, African American Resource Center, Howard University, 1974-; Jessie Ball duPont Scholar, Emory and Henry College, 1996. Publications: Andromeda, 1974; The Land of Smiles and the Land of No Smiles, 1974; Migrant Worker, 1978; Season of Hunger/Cry of Rain, 1982; Where are the Love Poems for Dictators?, 1986; First Light, 1994. Editor: Synergy: An Anthology of Washington, D.C. Black Poetry, 1975; Women Surviving Massacres and Men, 1977; In Search of Color Everywhere, 1994. Contributions to: Anthologies and National Public Radio. Honours: Mayor's Art Award for Literature, Washington, DC, 1982; Public Humanities Award, DC Humanities Council, 1988; Columbia Merit Award, 1993; PEN Oakland Josephine Miles Award, 1994; O B Hardison Jr Poetry Prize, 1995; Honorary Doctor of Literature, Emory and Henry College, 1996; Stephen Henderson Poetry Award, African American Literature and Culture Society,

1997. Memberships: Associated Writing Programs; DC Commission on the Arts and Humanities; Institute for Policy Studies; PEN American Center; PEN/Faulkner Foundation. Address: c/o Department of Afro-American Studies, College of Arts and Sciences, Howard University, Washington, DC 20059, USA.

MILLER Hugh, b. 27 Apr 1937, Wishaw, Lanarkshire, Scotland. Writer. Education: University of Glasgow; Stow College; London Polytechnic. Publications: A Pocketful of Miracles, 1969; Secrets of Gambling, 1970; Professional Presentations, 1971; The Open City, 1973; Levels, 1973; Drop Out, 1973; Short Circuit, 1973; Koran's Legacy, 1973; Kingpin, 1974; Double Deal, 1974; Feedback, 1974; Ambulance, 1975; The Dissector, 1976; A Soft Breeze from Hell, 1976; The Saviour, 1977; The Rejuvenators, Terminal 3, 1978; Olympic Bronze, 1979; Head of State, 1979; District Nurse, 1984; Honour a Physician, 1985; Eastenders, 1986; Teen Eastenders, 1986; Snow on the Wind, 1987; Silent Witnesses, 1988; The Paradise Club, 1989; An Echo of Justice, 1990; Home Ground, 1990; Skin Deep 1992; Scotland Yard (co-author), 1993; Unquiet Minds, 1994; Proclaimed in Blood, 1995; Prime Target, 1996; Ballykissangel, 1997; Borrowed Time, 1997; Forensic Fingerprints, 1998. Literary Agent: Lucas Alexander Whitley Ltd, Elsinore House, 77 Fulham Palace Road, London, W6 8JA, England.

MILLER Ian. See: MILNE John Frederich.

MILLER Jason, b. 22 Apr 1939, Scranton, Pennsylvania, USA. Dramatist; Screenwriter; Actor; Director. m. Linda Gleason, 1963, div 1973, 3 sons, 1 daughter. Education: Catholic University of America; BA, University of Scranton, 1961. Appointments: Actor in theatre, films and television, 1969-. Publications: Plays: Lou Gehrig Did Not Die of Cancer, 1967; Perfect Son, 1967; The Circle Lady, 1967; Nobody Hears a Broken Drum, 1970; It's a Sin to Tell a Lie, 1970; The Championship Season, 1971. Screenplay: that Championship Season, 1982. Television Plays: The Reward, 1980; Marilyn: The Untold Story, 1980. Honours: New York Drama Critics Circle Award, 1972; Pulitzer Prize for Drama, 1973; Tony Award, 1973. Address: c/o The Artists Agency, 10000 Santa Monica Boulevard, Suite 305, Los Angeles, CA 90067, USA.

MILLER Jonathan (Wolfe), b. 21 July 1934, London, England. Theatre, Film, and Television Director; Writer. m. Helen Rachel Collet, 1956, 2 sons, 1 daughter. Education: MB, BCh, St John's College, Cambridge, 1959. Appointments: Theatre, film, and television director; Resident Fellow in the History of Medicine, 1970-73, Fellow, 1981-, University College, London; Associate Director, National Theatre, 1973-75; Visiting Professor in Drama, Westfield College, London, 1977-; Artistic Director, Old Vic, 1988-90; Research Fellow in Neuropsychology, University of Sussex. Publications: McLuhan, 1971; Freud: The Man, His World, His Influence (editor), 1972; The Body in Question, 1978; Subsequent Performances, 1986; The Don Giovanni Book: Myths of Seduction and Betrayal (editor), 1990. Honours: Silver Medal, Royal Television Society, 1981; Commander of the Order of the British Empire, 1983; Albert Medal, Royal Society of Arts, 1990; Honorary Doctor of Letters, University of Cambridge. Memberships: Royal Academy, fellow; American Academy of Arts and Sciences. Address: c/o IMG Artists, Media House, 3 Burlington Lane, London W4 2TH, England.

MILLER Karl (Fergus Connor), b. 2 Aug 1931, England. Retired Professor of Modern English Literature; Writer; Editor. m. Jane Elisabeth Collet, 2 sons, 1 daughter. Education: Downing College, Cambridge. Appointments: Assistant Principal, HM Treasury, 1956-57; Producer, BBC TV, 1957-58; Literary Editor, The Spectator, 1958-61, The New Statesman, 1961-67; Editor, The Listener, 1967-73; Lord Northcliffe Professor of Modern Literature, University College, London, 1974-92; Editor, 1979-89, Co-Editor, 1989-92, London Review of Books. Publications: Poetry from Cambridge, 1952-54 (editor), 1955; Writing in England Today: The

Last Fifteen Years (editor), 1968; Memoirs of a Modern Scotland (editor), 1970; A Listener Anthology, August 1967-June 1970 (editor), 1970; A Second Listener Anthology (editor), 1973; Cockburn's Millenium, 1975; Robert Burns (editor), 1981; Doubles: Studies in Literary History, 1985; Authors, 1989; Rebecca's Vest (autobiography), 1993; Boswell and Hyde, 1995; Dark Horses, 1998. Honours: James Tait Black Award; Scottish Arts Council Book Award. Memberships: Royal Society of Literature, fellow. Address: 26 Limerston Street, London SW10 0HH, England.

MILLER Leslie Adrienne, b. 22 Oct 1956, Medina, Ohio, USA. Poet; Associate Professor of English. Education: BA, English, Stephens College, 1978; MA, English, University of Missouri, 1980; MFA, Creative Writing, Poetry, University of Iowa, 1982; PhD, Literature, Creative Writing, University of Houston, 1991. Appointments: Director, Creative Writing Program, Stephens College, 1983-87; Visiting Writer, University of Oregon, 1990; Associate Professor of English, University of St Thomas, 1991-. Publications: Hanging on the Sunburned Arm of Some Homeboy (with Matthew Graham), 1982; No River, 1987; Staying Up for Love, 1990 Ungodliness, 1994; Yesterday Had a Man In It, 1998. Contributions to: Anthologies, reviews, quarterlies, and journals. Honours: National Endowment for the Arts Fellowship, 1989; John and Becky Moores Fellowship, University of Houston, 1990; Goethe-Institut Cultural Exchange Fellowship, Berlin, 1992; Loft-McKnight Award in Poetry, 1993, and Award of Distinction, 1998. Memberships: Associated Writing Programs; Modern Language Association; Poetry Society of America; Poets and Writers. Address: 168 College Avenue South, No 2, St Paul, MN 55102, USA.

MILLER Marc William, b. 29 Aug 1947, Annapolis, Maryland, USA. Writer. m. Darlene File, 24 Sept 1981, 1 son, 1 daughter. Education: BS, Sociology, University of Illinois, 1969. Appointments: Contributing Editor, Fire and Movement Magazine, 1977-84; Staff, Grenadier Magazine, 1977-79, Journal of the Traveller's Aid Society, 1979-85, Challenge Magazine, 1986-92. Publications: Traveller, 1977; Imperium, 1977; 2300 AD, 1986; Mega Traveller, 1988; Mega Traveller II, Quest for the Ancients, 1991; Spellbound, 1992. Contributions to: Journals. Honours: Several awards. Memberships: Academy of Adventure Gaming Arts and Sciences; Game Designer's Guild; Science Fiction Writers of America. Address: PO Box 193, Normal, IL 61761, USA.

MILLER Margaret J. See: **DALE Margaret Jessy.**

MILLER Merton H(oward), b. 16 May 1923, Boston, Massachusetts, USA. Professor of Banking and Finance; Writer. Education: AB, Harvard University, 1943; PhD, Johns Hopkins University, 1952. Appointments: Employee, US Treasury Department, 1944-47, Federal Reserve Board, 1947-49; Assistant Lecturer, London School of Economics and Political Science, 1952; Assistant Professor to Associate Professor, Graduate School of Industrial Administration, Carnegie Institute of Technology, Pittsburgh, 1958-61; Professor of Banking and Finance, Graduate School of Business, University of Chicago, 1961-. Publications: The Theory of Finance (with Eugene F Fama), 1972; Macroeconomics: A Neoclassical Introduction, 1974; Financial Innovation and Market Volatility, 1991. Honour: Nobel Prize for Economic Science, 1990. Memberships: American Economic Association; American Finance Association, president, 1976; American Statistical Association; Econometric Society, fellow. Address: c/o Graduate School of Business, University of Chicago, 1101 East 58th Street, Chicago, IL 60637, USA.

MILLER Olga Eunice, b. 27 Mar 1920, Maryborough, Queensland, Australia. Aboriginal Historian; Consultant; Artist. Separated, 3 sons, 2 daughters. Education: Junior Public Examination Status, Maryborough Girls Grammar Schools, 1935. Publications: Legends of Moonie Jarl (co-author), 1964; Fraser Island Legends, 1993 new edition, 1994. Televisin programmes: Legends of Our Land, 1965; Across Australia, 1988. Radio Programmes:

This Was Our Town, 1965; Fraser Island Legends, 1983. Contributions to: Facts about Artefacts, 1965, First 200 Years, 1983, Maryborough Chronicle. Honour: Advance Australia Foundation Award, 1992. Address: 4/227 Ellena Street, Maryborough, Queensland 4650, Australia.

MILLER Seumas Roderick Macdonald, b. 11 Mar 1953, Edinburgh, Scotland, England. University Professor. Education: BA, Australia National University, 1976; MA, University of Oxford, 1978; Diploma in Education, State College of Victoria, Australia, 1979; Higher Diploma in Journalism, Rhodes University, 1984; Doctorate in Philosophy, University of Melbourne, Australia, 1985. Publication: Re-thinking Theory, 1992. Contributions to: Numerous articles in internationally distributed professional philosophy journals and other academic journals. Address: 21 Lochbury Street, Macquarie, ACT 2614, Australia.

MILLER Sue, b. 29 Nov 1943, USA. Writer. m. (1) div, 1 son, (2) Doug Bauer. Education: BA, Radcliffe College, 1964; MA, Harvard University, Boston University, Wesleyan University. Publications: The Good Mother, 1986; Inventing the Abbotts and other Stories, 1987; Family Pictures: A Novel, 1990; For Love, 1993; The Distinguished Guest, 1995. Honours: MacDowell Colony Fellowship; Guggenheim Fellowship. Address: c/o Maxine Groffsky Literary Agency, 2 Fifth Avenue, New York, NY 10011, USA.

MILLER Yolanda, b. 8 May 1957, Chicago Heights, Illinois, USA. Writer; Publisher. m. Andrew Miller, 4 Feb 1982. Education: BSc, University of Wisconsin, Stout, Vocational Rehabilitation, 1978; MSc, Rehabilitation Counseling, University of Wisconsin, Milwaukee, 1984. Publications: Ode to Precious; Priceless and Irreplaceable African-American Men A Collection of Poems, 1996. Address: 2526 Delaware Avenue, Racine, WI 53403, USA.

MILLETT Kate, (Katherine Murray Millett), b. 14 Sept 1934, St Paul, Minnesota, USA. Feminist; Writer; Sculptor; Painter; Photographer. m. Fumio Yoshimura, 1965, div 1985. Education: BA, University of Minnesota, 1956; MA, St Hilda's College, Oxford, 1958; PhD, Columbia University, 1970. Appointments: Instructor of English, University of North Carolina, Greensboro, 1958; Teacher of English, Waseda University, Tokyo, 1961-63; Instructor of English and Philosophy, Barnard College, 1964-69; Instructor of Sociology, Bryn Mawr College, 1971; Distinguished Visiting Professor, State College of Sacramento, 1972-73. Publications: Sexual Politics, 1970; Prostitution Papers, 1971; Flying, 1974; Sita, 1977; The Basement, 1980; Going to Iran, 1981; The Loony-Bin Trip, 1990; The Politics of Cruelty, 1994; A.D., 1996. Contributions to: Periodicals. Memberships: Congress of Racial Equality; National Organization of Women; Phi Beta Kappa. Address: c/o Georges Borchardt Inc, 136 East 57th Street, New York, NY 10022, USA.

MILLHAUSER Steven, b. 3 Aug 1943, New York, New York, USA. Author. m. Cathy Allis, 16 June 1986, 1 son, 1 daughter. Education: BA, Columbia College, 1965; Brown University, 1968-71. Publications: Edwin Mullhouse: The Life and Death of an American Writer, 1972; Portrait of a Romantic, 1976; In the Penny Arcade, 1986; From the Realm of Morpheus, 1986; The Barnum Museum, 1990; Little Kingdoms, 1993; The Knife Thrower and Other Stories, 1998. Honours: Prix Medicis Etranger, 1975; Award in Literature, 1987. Address: Saratoga Springs, NY, USA.

MILLHISER Marlys (Joy), b. 27 May 1938, Charles City, Iowa, USA. Writer. m. David Millhiser, 25 June 1960, 1 son, 1 daughter. Education: BA, University of Iowa, 1960; MA, University of Colorado, 1963. Publications: Michael's Wife, 1972; Nella Waits, 1974; Willing Hostage, 1976; The Mirror, 1978; Nightmare Country, 1981; The Threshold, 1984; Murder at Moot Point, 1992; Death of the Office Witch, 1993; Murder in a Hot Flash, 1995. Contributions to: Magazines. Honours: Top Hand Awards, 1975, 1985. Memberships: Authors Guild; Colorado Authors League; Mystery Writers of America; Sisters in

Crime; Western Writers of America. Address: 1843 Orchard Avenue, Boulder, CO 80304, USA.

MILLIEX Tatiana Gritsi, b. 20 Oct 1920, Athens, Greece. Writer. m. Roger Milliex, 1 June 1939, 1 son, 1 daughter. Education: Diploma, French Institute, Athens. 1938. Publications: Platia Thisiou, 1947; Sto Dromo Ton Anghelon, 1950; Kopiontes Ke Pefortismeni, 1951; Imeroloyio, 1951; Se Proto Prosopo, 1958; Allazoume?, 1958, French translation, 1985; Kai Idou Ippos Chloros, 1963; Sparagmata, 1973; H Tripoli Tou Pontou, 1977; Anadromes, 1983; Chroniko Eivos Efialti, 1986; Apo Tin Alli Oyhti Tuu Chronou, 1988, (French translation: De la part de la malade), 1992; Onirika, 1991; To Aloni Tis Ekatis, 1993; Odiporiko Stin India, 1996. Contributions to: Variety of Greek and Cypriot magazines and journals. Honours: State Prizes for short story, 1958, 1985, Novel, 1964, 1974; Prize, Athens Academy, 1973; Prize Nikiphoros Vrettakos, 1995; Gold Medal of the Athens Municipality, 1998. Membership: Greek Writers Society. Literary Agent: Castaniotis, odos Zalongou, 16078, Athens, Greece. Address: 20 Odos Metsovou, BP 26180 Exarchia, Athens, Greece.

MILLIGAN Terence Alan, (Spike Milligan), b. 1918, India. Playwright; Screenwriter; Humourist. Appointments: Radio and TV Personality: The Goon Show, BBC Radio; Show Called Fred, ITV; World of Beachcomber, Q5-Q10, BBC-2 Television; Curry and Chips, BBC; Oh in Colour, BBC; A Milligan for All Seasons, BBC. Publications: The Bed Sitting Room (play with J Antrobus); Oblommov (play); Son of Oblommov (play); Silly Verse for Kids, 1959; A Dustbin of Milligan, 1961; Puckoon, 1963; The Little Pot Boiler, 1963; A Book of Bits, 1965; The Bedside Milligan, 1968; Milliganimals, 1968; The Bald Twit Lion, 1970; Milligan's Ark, 1971; Adolf Hitler: My Part in His Downfall, 1971; The Goon Show Scripts, 1972; Small Dreams of a Scorpion, 1972; Rommel? Gunner Who? 1973; Badjelly the Witch, 1973; More Goon Show Scripts, 1974; Spike Milligan's Transport of Delights, 1974; Dip the Puppy, 1974; The Great McGonagal Scrapbook, 1975; The Milligan Book of Records, Games, Cartoons and Commercials (with Jack Hobbs), 1975; Monty: His Part in My Victory, 1976; Mussolini: His Part in My Downfall, 1978; A Book of Goblins, 1978; Open Heart University (verse), 1979; Indefinite Articles and Slunthorpe, 1981; The 101 Best and Only Limericks of Spike Milligan, 1982; The Goon Cartoons, 1982; Sir Nobonk and the Terrible Dragon, 1982; The Melting Pot, 1983; More Goon Cartoons, 1983; There's a Lot About, 1983; Further Transports of Delight, 1985; Floored Masterpieces and Worse Verse, 1985; Where Have All the Bullets Gone, 1985; Goodbye Soldier, 1986; The Mirror Running, 1987; Startling Verse for All the Family, 1987; The Looney, 1987; William McGonall Meets George Gershwin, 1988; It Ends with Magic..., 1990; Peacework, 1991; Condensed Animals, 1991; Dear Robert, Dear Spike, 1991; Depression and How to Survive It (with Anthony Clare), 1993; Hidden Words, 1993; The Bible - Old Testament According to Spike Milligan, 1993; Lady Chatterley's Lover According to Spike Milligan, 1994; Wuthering Heights According to Spike Milligan 1994; Spike Milligan: A Celebration, 1995; John Thomas and Lady Jane According to Spike Milligan, 1995; Black Beauty According to Spike Milligan, 1996; Frankenstein: According to Spike Milligan, 1997; The Hound of Baskervilles: According to Spike Milligan, 1998; Robin Hood: According to Spike Milligan, 1998. Honours: TV Writer of the Year Award, 1956; Golden Rose and Special Comedy Award, Montreux, 1972; Commander of the Order of the British Empire, 1992; Lifetime Achievement Award, British Comedy Awards, 1994. Address: Spike Milligan Productions, 9 Orme Court, London W2, England.

MILLINGTON Barry (John), b. 1 Nov 1951, Essex, England. Music Journalist; Writer. Education: BA, Cambridge University, 1974. Appointments: Chief Music Critic, Times; Reviews Editor, BBC Music Magazine. Publications: Wagner, 1984, revised edition, 1998; Selected Letters of Richard Wagner (translator and editor with S Spencer), 1987; The Wagner Compendium: A Guide to Wagner's Life and Music (editor), 1992; Wagner in Performance (editor with S Spencer), 1992; Wagner's Ring of the Nibelung: A Companion (editor with S Spencer), 1993. Contributions to: Articles on Wagner to New Grove Dictionary of Opera, 1992, New Grove Dictionary of Music and Musicians, 7th edition forthcoming; Newspapers and magazines. Membership: Critics' Circle. Address: 50 Denman Drive South, London NW11 6RH, England.

MILLS Claudia, b. 21 Aug 1954, New York, New York, USA. Writer. m. Richard W Wahl, 19 Oct 1985, 2 sons. Education: BA, Wellesley College, 1976; MA, 1979, PhD, 1991, Princeton University. Publications: Luisa's American Dream, 1981; At the Back of the Woods, 1982; The Secret Carousel, 1983; All the Living, 1983; Boardwalk with Hotel, 1985; The One and Only Cynthia Jane Thornton, 1986; Melanie Magpie, 1987; Cally's Enterprise, 1988; Dynamite Dinah, 1990; Hannah on her Way, 1991; Dinah in Love, 1993; Phoebe's Parade, 1994; The Secret Life of Bethany Barrett, 1994; Dinah Forever, 1995; Losers, Inc, 1997; Gus and Grandpa, 1997; Gus and Grandpa and the Christmas Cookies, 1997; One Small Lost Sheep, 1997; Gus and Grandpa Ride the Train, 1998; Gus and Grandpa at the Hospital, 1998; Standing Up to Mr O, 1998. Memberships: Authors Guild; Society of Children's Book Writers. Address: 2575 Briarwood Drive, Boulder, CO 80303, USA.

MILLS Derek Henry, b. 19 Mar 1928, Bristol, England. University Fellow; Consultant. m. Florence Cameron, 26 May 1956, 1 son, 1 daughter. Education: BSc, Honours, University of London, 1953; MSc, University of London, 1957; PhD, University of London, 1963. Appointments: Editor, Fisheries Management, 1974-84, John Buchan Journal, 1979-83, Edinburgh, Walter Scott Club Bulletins, 1996-; Co-Editor, Aquaculture and Fisheries Management, 1985-93, Fisheries Management and Ecology, 1994-95. Publications: Salmon and Trout: A Resource, its Ecology, Conservation and Management, 1971; Introduction to Freshwater Ecology, 1972; Scotland's King of Fish, 1980; The Salmon Rivers of Scotland, 1981, 1992; The Fishing Here Is Great!, 1985; The Ecology and Management of Atlantic Salmon, 1989; Freshwater Ecology: Principles and Applications, 1990. Contributions to: Blackwood Magazine; Field; Fly Fishers'Journal; John Buchan Journal; Salmon and Trout Magazine; Fisheries Research; The Scots Magazine.Memberships: John Buchan Society; Trollope Society; Institute of Fisheries Management, fellow; Linnean Society of London, fellow; Walter Scott Club, Edinburgh; Atlantic Salmon Trust; Fly Fishers' Club; Tweed Foundation, trustee. Address: Valerna, Aldie Crescent, Darnick, Melrose TD6 9AY, Scotland.

MILLS Ralph J(oseph) Jr, b. 16 Dec 1931, Chicago, Illinois, USA. Professor of English; Poet; Writer. m. Helen Daggett Harvey, 25 Nov 1959, 2 sons, 1 daughter. Education: BA, Lake Forest College, 1954; MA, 1956, PhD, 1963, Northwestern University; Oxford University, 1956-57. Appointments: Instructor, 1959-61, Assistant Professor, 1962-65, University of Chicago; Associate Professor, 1965-67, Professor of English, 1967-, University of Illinois at Chicago; Emeritus Professor, 1997-. Publications: Poetry: Door to the Sun, 1974; A Man to His Shadow, 1975; Night Road, 1978; Living with Distance, 1979; With No Answer, 1980; March Light, 1983; For a Day, 1985; Each Branch: Poems 1976-1985, 1986; A While, 1989; A Window in Air, 1993; In Wind's Edge, 1997. Other: Contemporary American Poetry, 1965; On the Poet and His Craft: Selected Prose of Theodore Roethke (editor), 1965; Edith Sitwell: A Critical Essay, 1966; Kathleen Raine: A Critical Essay, 1967; Creation's Very Self: On the Personal Element in Recent American Poetry, 1969; Cry of the Human: Essays on Contemporary American Poetry, 1975. Contributions to: Books and journals. Honours: English-Speaking Union Fellowship, 1956-57; Illinois Arts Council Awards for Poetry, 1979, 1983, 1984; Society of Midland Authors Prize for Poetry, 1980; Carl Sandburg Prize for Poetry, 1984. Memberships: Phi Beta Kappa; Phi Kappa Phi. Address: 1451 North Astor Street, Chicago, IL 60610, USA.

MILLWARD Eric (Geoffrey William), b. 12 Mar 1935, Longnor, Staffordshire, England. Poet. m. Rosemary Wood, 1975. Education: Buxton College, Derbyshire, 1946-54. Publications: A Child in the Park, 1969; Dead Letters, 1978; Appropriate Noises, 1987. Honour: Arts Council Writers Award, 1979. Address: 2 Victoria Row, Knypersley, Stoke on Trent, Staffordshire ST8 7PU, England.

MILNE John Frederich, (Ian Miller), b. 20 Sept 1952, Bermondsey. Novelist; Scriptwriter. m. Sarah Laetotia Beresford Verity, 1983, 2 sons. Education: St Joseph's Academy Blackheath; Chelsea School of Art; Ravensborne School of Art, BA Fine Art, 1979. Publications: Novels: Tyro, 1981; London Fields, 1982; Wet Wickets and Dusty Balls, as Ian Miller, 1982; Dead Birds, 1984; Out of the Blue, 1985; Shadow Play, 1986; Daddy's Girl, 1988; Alive and Kicking, 1998; TV Contributor to Bergerac; Lovejoy; Taggart; Pie in the Sky; Wycliffe; Silent Witness; Maisie Raine. Contributions to: Time Out; Daily Telegraph. Honour: John Lleweheryh Rhys Prize, 1986; Writer's Guild Award, 1991; MWA Edgar, 1998. Memberships: Writer's Guild; CWA. Literary Agent: Bethan Evans, The Agency, 24 Pottery Lane, London W11 4LZ, England. Address: c/o Bethan Evans, The Agency, 24 Pottery Lane, London W11 4LZ, England.

MILNE Larry. See: **HOYLE Trevor.**

MILOSZ Czeslaw, b. 30 June 1911, Szetejnie, Lithuania. (US citizen, 1970). Poet; Novelist; Critic; Essayist; Translator; Professor of Slavic Languages and Literatures Emeritus. Education: M Juris, University of Wilno, 1934. Appointments: Programmer, Polish National Radio, Warsaw, 1934-39; Diplomatic Service, Polish Ministry of Foreign Affairs, 1945-50; Visiting Lecturer, 1960-61, Professor of Slavic Languages and Literatures, 1961-78, Professor Emeritus, 1978-, University of California at Berkeley. Publications: Poetry: Poems, 1940; Poems, 1969; Selected Poems, 1973, revised edition, 1981; Selected Poems, 1976; The Bells in Winter, 1978; The Separate Notebooks, 1984; Collected Poems, 1990; Provinces: Poems 1987-1991, 1991; Facing the River: New Poems, 1995; Roadside Dog, 1998. Novels: The Seizure of Power, 1955; The Issa Valley, 1981. Non-Fiction: The Captive Mind (essays), 1953; Native Realm: A Search for Self-Definition (essays), 1968; The History of Polish Literature, 1969, revised edition, 1983; Emperor of the Earth: Modes of Eccentric Vision, 1977; Nobel Lecture, 1981; Visions From San Francisco Bay, 1982; The Witness of Poetry (lectures), 1983; The Land of Ulro, 1984; The Rising of the Sun, 1985; Unattainable Earth, 1986; Beginning With My Streets: Essays and Recollections, 1992; Striving Towards Being (correspondence), 1997. Editor and Translator: Postwar Polish Poetry: An Anthology, 1965, revised edition, 1983. Honours: Prix Littéraire Européen, Les Guildes du Livre, Geneva, 1953; Marian Kister Literary Award, 1967; Guggenheim Fellowship, 1976; Neustadt International Literary Prize, 1978; Nobel Prize for Literature, 1980; National Medal of Arts, 1990; Several honorary doctorates. Memberships: American Academy and Institute of Arts and Letters; American Academy of Arts and Sciences; American Association for the Advancement of Slavic Studies; Polish Institute of Letters and Sciences in America. Address: c/o Department of Slavic Languages and Literatures, University of California at Berkeley, Berkeley, CA 94720, USA.

MINARIK John Paul, b. 6 Nov 1947, McKeesport, Pennsylvania, USA. Poet; Writer; Engineer. m. Susan Kay Minarik, 15 Oct 1988, 1 son. Education: BS, Mechanical Engineering, Carnegie Mellon University, 1970; BA, magna cum laude, English and Psychology, University of Pittsburgh, 1978. Appointments: Engineer, United Steel Corp, 1966-71; Instructor, Community College of Allegheny County, 1977-83; Teaching Consultant, University of Pittsburgh, 1978-96; Poet-in-the-Schools, Pennsylvania Council on the Arts, 1979-83; Project Engineer-Consultant, Economy Industrial Corp, 1981-82; Chief Engineer, New Directions, 1989-96; Founder-Editor, Academy of Prison Arts;

Advisory Editor, Greenfield Review Press; Poetry readings. Publications: a book, 1974; Patterns in the Dusk, 1978; Past the Unknown, Remembered Gate, 1981; Kicking Their Heels with Freedom (editor), 1982; Working Knowledge, forthcoming. Contributions to: Over 100 newspapers in the USA; American Ethnic; Backspace; Caprice; Carnegie Mellon Magazine; Confrontation; Gravida; Greenfield Review; Happiness Holding Tank; Hyacinths and Biscuits; Interstate; Joint Conference; Journal of Popular Culture; Mill Hunk Herald; New Orleans Review; Nitty-Gritty; Old Main; Painted Bride Quarterly; Pittsburgh and Tri-State Area Poets; Prison Writing Review; Poetry Society of America Bulletin; Small Pond; Sunday Clothes; Poems read via Monitoradio, Voice of America, WQED-FM, and WYEP, and at Three Rivers Arts Festival and American Wind Symphony. Honours: Honorable Mention, PEN Writing Award, 1976-77; Carnegie Magazine Best Book of the Year Citation, 1982; Pushcart Prize Nomination, 1984; Winner, Poetry and Prose Writing Contests, Pennsylvania Department of Corrections, 1985, 1988. Membership: American Society of Mechanical Engineers, full member. Address: 1600 Walters Mill Road, Somerset, PA 15510, USA.

MINATOYA Lydia, b. 8 Nov 1950, New York, New York, USA. Writer. 1 son. Education: BA, Lawrence University, 1972; MA, George Washington University, 1976; PhD, University of Maryland, 1981. Publication: Talking to High Monks in the Snow, 1992. Honours: PEN Jerard Fund Award, 1991; American Library Association Notable Book, 1992; New York Public Library Notable Book, 1992; Pacific Nova West Booksellers Award, 1993. Address: Harper Collins, 10 East 53rd Street, New York, NY 10022 5299, USA.

MINCHIN Devon George, b. 28 May 1919, Sydney, New South Wales, Australia. Farmer; Writer. m. Margo Slater, 2 sons, 2 daughters. Education: BA, MacQuarie University, Sydney. Publications: The Potato Man, 1944; The Money Movers, 1975; Isabel's Mine, 1989. Other: The 13th Diamond (short stories). Address: Wappa Falls Farm Yandina, Queensland 4561, Australia.

MINEAR Richard H(offman), b. 31 Dec 1938, Evanston, Illinois, USA. Professor of History; Writer. m. Edith Christian, 1962, 2 sons. Education: BA, Yale University, 1960; MA, 1962, PhD, 1968, Harvard University. Appointments: Assistant Professor, Ohio State University, 1967-70; Associate Professor, 1970-75, Professor of History, 1975-, University of Massachusetts. Publications: Japanese Tradition and Western Law, 1970; Victors' Justice, 1971; Through Japanese Eyes, 1974; Requiem for Battleship Yamato, 1985; Hiroshima: Three Witnesses, 1990; Black Eggs, 1994; When we say 'Hiroshima', 1999; Dr Seuss goes to War, 1999. Contributions to: Professional journals and general magazines. Membership: Association for Asian Studies. Address: c/o Department of History, University of Massachusetts, Amherst, MA 01003, USA.

MINER Earl (Roy), b. 21 Feb 1927, Marshfield, Wisconsin, USA. Professor; Writer. m. Virginia Lane, 15 July 1950, 1 son, 1 daughter. Education: BA, 1949, MA, 1955, PhD, University of Minnesota. Appointment: Professor, Princeton University. Publications: The Japanese Tradition in British and American Literature, 1958; Japanese Court Poetry, 1961; Dryden's Poetry, 1967; Comparative Poetics, 1992; Naming Properties, 1996. Contributions to: Professional journals. Honours: Fulbright Lectureships, 1960-61, 1966-67, 1985; American Council of Learned Societies Fellowship, 1963; Guggenheim Fellowship, 1977-78; Yamagato Banto Prize, 1988; Koizumi Yakumo Prize, 1991; Howard T Behrman Prize, 1993; Order of the Rising Sun with Gold Rays and Neck Ribbon, Government of Japan, 1994. Memberships: American Comparative Literature Association; American Society for 18th Century Studies; Association for Asian Studies; International Comparative Literature Association; Milton Society of America; Renaissance Society of America. Address: Princeton University, Princeton, NJ 08544, USA.

MINER Jane Claypool, (Jane Claypool, Veronica Ladd), b. 22 Apr 1933, McAllen, Texas, USA. Writer. m. (1) Dennis A Shelley, 1952, dec, 1 daughter, (2) Richard Yale Miner, 1962, dec. Education: BA, California State University, Long Beach, 1956. Publications: Over 60 books for teenagers. Contributions to: Numerous periodicals. Memberships: American Society of Authors and Journalists; Society of Children's Book Writers. Address: 2883 Lone Jack Road, Olivenhain, CA 92024, USA.

MINGAY G(ordon) E(dmund), b. 20 June 1923, Long Eaton, Derbyshire, England. Professor of Agrarian History Emeritus; Writer. m. Mavis Tippen, 20 Jan 1945. Education: BA, 1952, PhD, 1958, University of Nottingham. Appointments: Lecturer, Woolwich Polytechnic, London, 1953-56, London School of Economics and Political Science, 1957-65; Reader in Economic History, 1965-68, Professor of Agrarian History, 1968-85, Professor Emeritus, 1985-, University of Kent, Canterbury; Editor, Agricultural History Review, 1972-84. Publications: English Landed Society in the Eighteenth Century, 1963; The Agricultural Revolution 1750-1880 (with J D Chambers), 1966; Land, Labour, and Population in the Industrial Revolution (editor with E L Jones), 1967; Enclosure and the Small Farmer in the Age of the Industrial Revolution, 1968; Britain and America: A Study of Economic Change 1850-1939 (with Philip S Bagwell), 1970, revised edition, 1987; Fifteen Years On: The B E T Group 1956-1971, 1973; The Gentry, 1975; Arthur Young and His Times, 1975; Georgian London, 1975; Rural Life in Victorian England, 1976; The Agricultural Revolution, 1977; Mrs Hurst Dancing, 1981; The Victorian Countryside (editor), 1981; An Epic of Progress: A History of British Friesian Cattle, 1982; The Transformation of Britain 1830-1939, 1986; The Agrarian History of England and Wales, Vol VI, 1750-1850 (editor), 1989; The Rural Idyll, 1989; The Unquiet Countryside (editor), 1989; A Social History of the English Countryside, 1990; Land and Society in England 1750-1980, 1994; Parliamentary Enclosure in England 1750-1850, 1997. Contributions to: Professional journals. Honour: Fellow, Royal Historical Society. Membership: British Agricultural History Society, president, 1987-89. Address: Mill Field House, Selling Court, Selling, Faversham, Kent ME13 9RJ, England.

MINOGUE Valerie Pearson, b. 26 Apr 1931, Llanelli, South Wales. Professor Emeritus. m. Kenneth Robert Minogue, 16 June 1954, 1 son, 1 daughter. Education: BA, 1952, MLitt, 1956, Girton College, Cambridge. Appointments: Assistant Lecturer, University College, Cardiff, Wales, 1952-53; Contributor, Cambridge Italian Dictionary, 1956-61; Lecturer, 1963-74, Senior Lecturer, 1975-81, Queen Mary College, London, England; Professor, 1981-88, Research Professor, 1988-96, Professor Emeritus, 1996, University of Wales, Swansea. Publications: Proust: Du Côte de chez Swann, 1973; Nathalie Sarraute: The War of the Words, 1981; Zola: L'Assommoir, 1991; Eight texts, Pléiade Oeuvres complètes of Nathalie Sarraute (editor, with notes and critical essays), 1996. Contributions to: Romance Studies (editor), 1982-; Quadrant; Literary Review; Modern Language Review; French Studies; Romance Studies; Forum for Modern Language Studies; New Novel Review; Revue des Sciences Humaines; Numerous chapters in books. Memberships: Association of University Professors of French; Modern Humanities Research Association; Society for French Studies; Romance Studies Institute. Address: 23 Richford Street, London, W6 7HJ.

MINOT Susan Anderson, b. 7 Dec 1956, Boston, Massachusetts, USA. Writer. m. Davis McHenry, 30 Apr 1988, div. Education: BA, Brown University, 1978; MFA, Columbia University, 1983. Publications: Monkeys, 1986; Lost & Other Stories, 1989; Folly, 1992. Contributions to: New Yorker; Grand Street; Paris Review; Mademoiselle; Harper's; GQ; New England Monthly; Conde Nasts Traveler; Esquire; New York Times Magazine; Atlantic Monthly. Honour: Priz Femina Etranger, 1987. Address: c/o Houghton Mifflin Co, 222 Berkeley Street, Boston, MA 02116, USA.

MINTER David (Lee), b. 20 Mar 1935, Midland, Texas, USA. Professor of English; Writer. Education: BA, 1957, MA, 1959, North Texas State University; BD, 1961, PhD, 1965, Yale University. Appointments: Lecturer, University of Hamburg, 1965-66, Yale University, 1966-67; Assistant Professor, 1967-69, Associate Professor 1969-74, Professor, 1974-80, 1991-, Rice University; Professor, Dean of Emory College, Vice-President for Arts and Sciences, Emory University, 1981-90. Publications: The Interpreted Design as a Structural Principle in American Prose, 1969; William Faulkner: His Life and Work, 1980; The Harper American Literature, 1986; The Norton Critical Edition of The Sound and the Fury, 1987; A Cultural History of the American Novel: Henry James to William Faulkner, 1994. Contributions to: Professional journals. Address: 6100 Main Street, Houston, TX 77005, USA.

MIRABELLI Eugene, b. 3 Feb 1931, Arlington, Massachusetts, USA. Writer; Professor Emeritus. m. Margaret Anne Black, 18 July 1959, 1 son, 2 daughters. Education: BA, 1952, PhD, 1964, Harvard University; MA, Johns Hopkins University, 1955. Appointments: Faculty, Williams College, 1960-64, State University of New York at Albany, 1965-95. Publications: The Burning Air, 1959; The Way In, 1968; No Resting Place, 1972; The World at Noon, 1994; The Language Nobody Speaks, 1999. Contributions to: Numerous fiction and non-fiction book reviews in various publications. Memberships: Authors Guild; PEN American Center. Address: 29 Bennett Terrace, Delmar, NY 12054, USA.

MIRANDA DA MOTA José Manuel, b. 16 June 1944, Esposende, Portugal. Teacher. m. Delfina R Vieira da Silva Miranda da Mota, 1 Sept 1993. Education: Licentiate, Chemical Engineering, Faculty of Engineering, Oporto University, 1969; Postgraduate, Science Education, University of Aveiro, 1994. Publications: Periodic Table of the Elements, 1991; Portugal Ceres - Variedades de Cliché, 1992. Contributions to: Portu-Info, International Society for Portuguese Philately; A Filatelia Portuguesa; Jornal de Filatelia; Correio do Alentejo. Honours: Associado do Ano, Clube Nacional de Filatelia, 1990; A Guedes de Magalhaes, 1991, Medalha de Merito Filatelico, 1993, Federaçao Portuguesa de Filatelia; ISPP Research and Writing Award, International Society for Portuguese Philately, USA, 1994. Membership: Association Internationale des Journalistes Philatéliques, 1995-. Address: Rua Pierre Durand 94, 4490 Povoa de Varzim, Portugal.

MISTRAY Rohinton, b. 1952, Bombay, India (Canadian citizen). Author. m. Freny Elavia. Education: BSc, St Xavier's College, University of Bombay; BA, University of Toronto, 1982. Publications: Tales from Firozsha Bagga, 1987; Such a Long Journey, 1991; A Fine Balance, 1995. Contributions to: Anthologies and periodicals. Honours: Hart House Prizes for Fiction, 1983, 1984; Governor-General's Award for Fiction, 1991; Commonwealth Writer's Prizes, 1992, 1996; Giller Prize, 1995. Address: c/o Westwood Creative Artists, 94 Harbord Street, Toronto, Ontario M5S 1G6, Canada.

MITCHELL Adrian, (Volcano Jones, Apeman Mudgeon, Gerald Stimpson), b. 24 Oct 1932, London, England. Poet; Writer; Dramatist; Lyricist. 2 sons, 3 daughters. Education: Christ Church, Oxford, 1953-55. Appointments: Granada Fellow, University of Lancaster, 1968-70; Fellow, Wesleyan University, 1972; Resident Writer, Sherman Theatre, 1974-75, Unicorn Theatre for Children, 1982-83; Judith Wilson Fellow, University of Cambridge, 1980-81; Fellow in Drama, Nanyang University, Singapore, 1995; Dylan Thomas Fellow, UK Festival of Literature, Swansea, 1995. Publications: Various poems and plays including, Plays with Songs, 1995; The Siege, 1996; The Lion, The Witch and the Wardrobe, 1998; Who Killed Dylan Thomas, 1998. Contributions to: Newspapers, magazines, and television. Honours: Eric Gregory Award; PEN Translation Prize; Tokyo Festival Television Film Award; Honarary Doctorate, North London University, 1997. Memberships: Royal Society of Literature; Society of Authors; Writers Guild. Address: c/o Peters, Fraser and Dunlop Group Ltd, 5th Floor, The Chambers, Chelsea Harbour, Lots Road, London SW10 0XF, England.

MITCHELL David John, b. 24 Jan 1924, London, England. Writer. m. 1955, 1 son. Education: Bradfield College, Berkshire; MA, Honours, Modern History, Trinity College, Oxford, 1947. Appointment: Staff Writer, Picture Post, 1947-52. Publications: Women on the Warpath, 1966; The Fighting Pankhursts, 1967; 1919 Red Mirage, 1970; Pirates, 1976; Queen Christabel, 1977; The Jesuits: A History, 1980; The Spanish Civil War, 1982; Travellers in Spain, 1990. Contributions to: Newspapers and magazines. Membership: Society of Authors. Address: 20 Mountacre Close, Sydenham Hill, London SE26 6SX, England.

MITCHELL (Sibyl) Elyne Keith, b. 30 Dec 1913, Melbourne, Victoria, Australia. Author; Grazier. m. Thomas Waller Mitchell, 2 sons (1 dec.), 2 daughters. Education: St Catherine's, Melbourne; Radcliffe College, Cambridge, Massachusetts, USA. Publications: Australia's Alps, 1942; Speak to the Earth, 1943; Soil and Civilization, 1946; Flow River Blow Wind, 1951; Silver Brumby, series for children, 1968-; Light Horse: The Story of Australia's Mounted Troops, 1978; Discoverers of the Snowy Mountains, 1985; Channel Country, 1988; The Colt from Snowy River (series for children). Contributions to: Canberra Times; The Age, Melbourne; Walk About; Wild. Honour: Honorary Doctorate, Sturt University. Membership: Australian Society of Authors. Address: Towong Hill, via Corryong, Victoria 3707, Australia.

MITCHELL G(eoffrey) Duncan, b. 5 June 1921, England. Professor of Sociology Emeritus. Education: BSc, University of London, 1949. Appointments: Senior Research Worker, University of Liverpool, 1950-52; Lecturer in Sociology, University of Birmingham, 1952-54; Lecturer to Senior Lecturer, 1954-67, Professor of Sociology, 1967-86, Professor Emeritus and Research Fellow, 1986-, Institute of Population Studies, University of Exeter. Publications: Neighbourhood and Community (with T Lupton, M W Hodges and C S Smith), 1954; Sociology: The Study of Social Systems, 1959, new edition, 1972; A Dictionary of Sociology (editor); A Hundred Years of Sociology, 1968; A New Dictionary of Sociology (editor), 1979; The Artificial Family (with R Snowden), 1981; Artificial Reproduction (with R and E Snowden), 1983. Contributions to: Professional journals. Honours: Member of the Order of the British Empire, 1946; Officer of the Order of the British Empire, 1964. Address: 26 West Avenue, Exeter, Devon, England.

MITCHELL James, (James Munro), b. 12 Mar 1926, South Shields, England. m. 16 May 1998, 2 sons, 1 daughter. Education: BA, MA, St Edmund Hall, Oxford. Appointment: Freelance Writer. Publications include: Here's A Villan, 1957; Dancing For Yoy, 1997. Contributions to: Sunday Express; Telegraph. Honours: Crime Writers Critics Award, 1960; BAFTA Award, 1970; Sun Award; Television Industries Awards; Writers Guild Award. Membership: Writers Guild, committee, 2 years. Literary Agent: Carole Blake, Blake Friedmann. Address: 7 Abigail Court, Sandringham Road, South Gosforth, Newcastle upon Tyne NE3 1PP, England.

MITCHELL Jerome, b. 7 Oct 1935, Chattanooga, Tennessee, USA. Retired Professor; Writer. Education: BA, Emory University, 1957; MA, 1959, PhD, 1965, Duke University. Appointments: Assistant Professor, University of Illinois, 1965-67; Associate Professor, 1967-72, Professor, 1972-97, University of Georgia; Fulbright Guest Professor, University of Bonn, 1972-73; Visiting Exchange Professor, University of Erlangen, 1975; Richard Merton Guest Professor, University of Regensburg, 1978-79. Publications: Thomas Hoccleve: A Study in Early 15th Century English Poetic, 1968; Hoccleve's Works: The Minor Poems, 1970; Chaucer: The Love Poet, 1973; The Walter Scott Operas, 1977; Scott, Chaucer and Medieval Romance, 1987; Old and Middle English Literature, 1994; More Scott Operas, 1996. Contributions to: Various scholarly journals. Address: PO Box 1268, Athens, GA 30603, USA.

MITCHELL Julian, b. 1 May 1935, Epping, Essex, England. Author; Dramatist. Education: BA, Wadham College, Oxford, 1958. Appointment: Midshipman, Royal Naval Volunteer Reserve, 1953-55. Publications: Imaginary Toys, 1961; A Disturbing Influence, 1962; As Far as You Can Go, 1963; The White Father, 1964; A Heritage and Its History (play), 1965; A Family and a Fortune (play), 1966; A Circle of Friends, 1966; The Undiscovered Country, 1968; Jennie Lady Randolph Churchill: A Portrait with Letters (with Peregrine Churchill), 1974; Half-Life (play), 1977; Another Country (play), 1982, (film), 1984; Francis (play), 1983; After Aida (play), 1985; Falling Over England (play), 1994; August (adaptation of Uncle Vanya) (play), 1994, (film), 1995; Wilde (film script), 1997. Contributions to: Welsh History Review; Monmouthshire Antiquary. Address: 47 Draycott Place, London SW3 3DB, England.

MITCHELL Juliet (Constance Wyatt), b. 4 Oct 1940, Christchurch, New Zealand. Professor; Psychoanalyst; Writer; Broadcaster. Education: MA, St Anne's College, Oxford. Appointments: Lecturer in English, University of Leeds, 1962-63, University of Reading, 1965-70; Luce Lecturer, Yale University, 1984-85; A D White Professor-at-Large, Cornell University, 1994-2000; Lecturer in Gender, SPS, University of Cambridge, 1996-; Fellow, Jesus College, Cambridge. Publications: Women: The Longest Revolution, 1966; Woman's Estate, 1972; Psycho-Analysis and Feminism, 1974; Rights and Wrongs of Women (co-editor), 1977; Feminine Sexuality (co-editor), 1982; Women: The Longest Revolution, 1983; What is Feminism? (co-editor), 1986; The Selected Writings of Melanie Klein (editor), 1986; Before I was I (co-editor), 1991; Who's Afraid of Feminism (co-editor), 1997. Address: Jesus College, Cambridge CB5 8BC, England.

MITCHELL Kenneth (Ronald), b. 13 Dec 1940, Moose Jaw, Saskatchewan, Canada. Professor; Writer; Dramatist. m. Jeanne Shami, 23 Aug 1983, 4 sons, 1 daughter. Education: BA, 1965, MA, 1867, University of Saskatchewan. Appointments: Instructor, 1967-70, Professor, 1984-, University of Regina; Visiting Professor, University of Beijing, 1980-81, Foreign Affairs College, Beijing, 1986-87. Publications: Wandering Rafferty, 1972; The Meadowlark Connection, 1975; Everybody Gets Something Here, 1977; Cruel Tears (co-author), 1977; Horizon: Writings of the Canadian Prairie (editor), 1977; The Con Man, 1979; Davin, 1979; Sinclair Ross, 1981; Ken Mitchell Country, 1984; Gone the Burning Sun, 1985; Through the Nan Da Gate, 1986; Witches and Idiots, 1990; The Plainsman, 1992; Stones of the Dalai Lama, 1993. Honours: Ottawa Little Theatre Prize, 1971; Canadian Authors Association Award for Best Canadian Play, 1985. Memberships: Canadian Association of University Teachers; Playwrights Union of Canada. Address: c/o Department of English, University of Regina, Regina, Saskatchewan, Canada S4S 0A2.

MITCHELL Margaretta Meyer Kuhlthau, b. 27 May 1935, Brooklyn, New York, USA. Photographer; Author. m. 23 May 1959, 3 daughters. Education: BA, Smith College, 1957; MA, University of California, 1985. Appointments: University of California Extension Program, 1976-78; City College, 1980; Civic Arts, 1980-84; Visiting Professor, Carleton College, 1988; Teacher, Academy of Art, San Francisco, 1990-94; Academy of Art, 1990-95; U C Extension, 1995-98. Publications: Recollections: Gift of Place, 1969; To a Cabin, 1973; Recollections: Ten Women of Photography, 1979; Dance for Life, 1985; Flowers, 1991; English Gardens (limited edition), 1996. Contributions to: Ramparts; Vermont Life; Camera Art. Honour: Phi Beta Kappa, 1957. Membership: American Society of Media Photographers, vice president. Address: 280 Hillcrest Road, Berkeley, CA 94705, USA.

MITCHELL Michael Robin, b. 10 Apr 1941, Rochdale, Lancashire, England. Former University Lecturer; Translator; Writer. m. Jane Speakman, 3 Jan 1970, 3 sons. Education: MA, 1964, BLitt, 1968, Lincoln College, Oxford. Publications: Harrap's German Grammar (co-author), 1989; Peter Hacks: Theatre for a Socialist

Society, 1991; The Dedalus Book of Austrian Fantasy (editor and translator), 1992 Other: 15 translations of authors. Contributions to: Short translations in magazines and anthologies. Address: Kirkokerry, Millhouse, Tighnabruaich, Argyll, Scotland.

MITCHELL Roger (Sherman), b. 8 Feb 1935, Boston, Massachusetts, USA. Poet; Teacher. 2 daughters. Education: AB, Harvard College, 1957; MA, University of Colorado, 1961; PhD, Manchester University, 1963. Appointments: Editor, Minnesota Review, 1973-81; Director, Writers Conferences, 1975-85, Creative Writing Program, 1978-96, Indiana University. Publications: Letters from Siberia, 1971; Moving, 1976; A Clear Space on a Cold Day, 1986; Adirondack, 1988; Clear Pond, 1991; The Word for Everything, 1996; Braid, 1997. Contributions to: Periodicals. Honours: Abby M Copps Award, 1971; Midland Poetry Award, 1972; Borestone Mountain Award, 1973; PEN Award, 1977; Arvon Foundation Awards, 1985, 1987; National Endowment for the Arts Fellowship, 1986; Chester H Jones Award, 1987. Membership: Associated Writing Programs. Address: 1010 East First Street, Bloomington, IN 47401, USA.

MITCHELL William John Thomas, b. 24 Mar 1942, Anaheim, California, USA. Professor; Editor; Writer. m. Janice Misurell, 11 Aug 1968, 1 son, 1 daughter. Education: BA, Michigan State University, 1963; MA, PhD, 1968, Johns Hopkins University. Appointments: Editor, Critical Inquiry, 1979-; Professor of English and Art History, Chair, Department of English, 1989-92, University of Chicago. Publications: Blake's Composite Art, 1977; The Language of Images, 1980; The Politics of Interpretation, 1983; Against Theory, 1983; Iconology, 1986; Art and the Public Sphere, 1993; Landscape and Power, 1993; Picture Theory, 1994; The Last Dinosaur Book: The Life and Times of a Cultural Icon, 1998. Contributions to: Professional journals and general periodicals. Honours: American Philosophical Society Essay Prize, 1968; National Endowment for the Humanities Fellowships, 1978, 1986; Guggenheim Fellowship, 1983; Gaylord Donnelley Distinguished Service Professorship, 1989; College Art Association's Charles Rufus Morey Prize for Distinguished Book in Art History, 1996; Laing Prize for Picture Theory, University of Chicago Press, 1997. Memberships: Academy of Literary Studies; Modern Language Association; PEN. Address: c/o Department of English and Art History, University of Chicago, 1050 East 59th Street, Chicago, IL 60637, USA.

MITCHISON Naomi Margaret (Haldane), b. 1 Nov 1897, Edinburgh, Scotland. Author. m. Gilbert Richard Mitchison, 1916, 3 sons, 2 daughters. Publications: The Conquered, 1923; When the Bough Breaks, 1924; Cloud Cuckoo Land, 1925; Black Sparta, 1928; Anna Comnena, 1928; Nix-Nought-Nothing, 1928; Barbarian Stories, 1929; The Corn King and the Spring Queen, 1931; The Delicate Fire, 1932; We Have Been Warned, 1935; The Fourth Pig, 1936; Socrates (with R H S Crossman), 1937; Moral Basis of Politics, 1938; The Kingdom of Heaven, 1939; As It Was in the Beginning (with L E Gielgud), 1939; The Blood of the Martyrs, 1939; Re-Educating Scotland, 1945; The Bull Calves, 1947; Men and Herring (with D Macintosh), 1949; The Big House, 1950; Lobsters on the Agenda, 1952; Travel Light, 1952; Swan's Road, 1954; Graeme and the Dragon, 1954; Land the Ravens Found, 1955; To the Chapel Perilous, 1955; Little Boxes, 1956; Behold Your King, 1957; The Far Harbour, 1957; Other People's Worlds, 1958; Five Men and a Swan, 1958; Judy and Lakshmi, 1959; Rib of the Green Umbrella, 1960; The Young Alexander, 1960; Karensgaard, 1961; Memoirs of a Spacewoman, 1962; The Fairy Who Couldn't Tell a Lie, 1963; When We Became Men, 1964; Return to the Fairy Hill, 1966; Friends and Enemies, 1966; African Heroes, 1968; The Family at Ditlabeng, 1969; The Africans: A History, 1970; Sun and Moon, 1970; Cleopatra's People, 1972; A Danish Teapot, 1973; A Life for Africa, 1973; Sunrise Tomorrow, 1973; Small Talk (autobiography), 1973; All Change Here (autobiography), 1975; Solution Three, 1975; Snake!, 1976; The Two Magicians, 1979; The Cleansing of the Knife and Other Poems, 1979; You May

Well Ask: A Memoir 1920-40, 1979; Images of Africa, 1980; The Vegetable War, 1980; Mucking Around (autobiography) 1981; What Do You Think Yourself?, 1982; Not by Bread Alone, 1983; Among You Taking Notes, 1985; Early in Orcadia, 1987; A Girl Must Live, 1990; Sea-Green Ribbons, 1991; The Oathtakers, 1991. Honours: Commander of the Order of the British Empire, 1985; Honorary doctorates. Address: Carradale House, Carradale, Campbeltown, Scotland.

MITSON Eileen Nora, b. 22 Sept 1930, Langley, Essex, England. Author. m. Arthur Samuel Mitson, 22 Sept 1951, 2 daughters, 1 dec. Education: Cambridge Technical College and School of Art, 1946-47. Appointment: Columnist, Christian Woman magazine, later Woman Alive Magazine, 1982-94. Publications: Beyond the Shadows, 1968; Amazon Adventure, 1969; The Inside Room, 1973; A Kind of Freedom, 1976; Reaching for God, 1978; Creativity (co-author), 1985. Address: 39 Oaklands, Hamilton Road, Reading, Berkshire RG1 5RN, England.

MITSUMOTO Minoru, b. 20 July 1942, Tokyo, Japan. Journalist. m. Education: Agriculture, Tokyo Agriculture University, 1964. Appointment: Director, Magic Motion International Ltd. Publication: Flom, 1982. Contributions to: Motor Cyclist; Kazi; New Cycling; Biker's Station. Address: 39 Highlands Road, Camberley, Surrey GU15 4ET, England.

MIURA Hiroshi, b. 27 May 1944, Tokushima, Japan. University Lecturer. Education: BA, Shikoku Gakuin University, Japan, 1967; MLA, Pacific University, Alaska, 1982; MLA, University of Aberdeen, 1988; MPhil, University of Edinburgh, 1997. Appointments: Tutor, Centre for Japanese Studies, Edinburgh, 1989, 1996-97; Lecturer, Shikoku University, 1998-. Publication: The Life and Thought of Kanzo Uchimura 1860-1930, 1996. Contributions to: Dictionary of Scottish Church History and Theology, 1993. Address: 1-48-2-302 Nakamaegawa-cho, Tokushima-shi, Tokushima-ken, 770-0807, Japan.

MIZE Edith. See: LEWIS Edith Grace Mize.

MO Timothy (Peter), b. 30 Dec 1950, Hong Kong. Writer. Education: Convent of the Precious Blood, Hong Kong; Mill Hill School, London; BA, St John's College, Oxford. Publications: The Monkey King, 1978; Sour Sweet, 1982; An Insular Possession, 1986; The Redundancy of Courage, 1991; Brownout on Breadfruit Boulevard, 1995. Contributions to: Periodicals. Honours: Gibbs Prize, 1971; Geoffrey Faber Memorial Prize, 1979; Hawthornden Prize, 1983; E M Forster Award, American Academy of Arts and Letters, 1992. Address: c/o Chatto & Windus, 20 Vauxhall Bridge Road, London SW1V 2SA, England.

MOAT John, b. 11 Sept 1936, India. Author; Poet. m. 1962, 1 son, 1 daughter. Education: MA, Oxford University, 1960. Publications: 6d per Annum, 1966; Heorot (novel), 1968; A Standard of Verse, 1969; Thunder of Grass, 1970; The Tugen and the Toot (novel), 1973; The Ballad of the Leat, 1974; Bartonwood (juvenile), 1978; Fiesta and the Fox Reviews and His Prophecy, 1979; The Way to Write (with John Fairfax), 1981; Skeleton Key, 1982, complete edition, 1997; Mai's Wedding (novel), 1983; Welcombe Overtunes, 1987; The Missing Moon, 1988; Firewater and the Miraculous Mandarin, 1990; Practice, 1994; The Valley (poems and drawings), 1998; 100 Poems, 1998. Address: Crenham Mill, Hartland, North Devon EX39 6HN, England.

MOCK Michele L, b. 5 July 1962, Bloomington, California, USA. Assistant Professor of English. 2 sons. Education: BA in English and Secondary Education, University of Pittsburgh, 1991; MA in English Literature and Criticism, 1993, PhD in English Literature and Criticism, 1996, Indiana University of Pennsylvania. Appointments: Assistant Professor of English, University of Pittsburgh, Johnstown, 1996-. Publication: An Ardor That Was Human, and a Power That Was Art. Contributions to: NWSA Journal; Emily Dickinson Journal;

College Literature; Willa. Honours: Scholarship Grant, University of Pittsburgh, Johnstown, 1996-97; Phi Eta Sigma's Professor of the Year, University of Pittsburgh, Johnstown, 1998. Membership: 19th Century American Women Writers Study Group. Address: Stone Hollow Farm, PO Box 249, Jerome, PA 15937, USA.

MODIANO Patrick (Jean), b. 30 July 1945, Boulogne-Billancourt, France. Author. m. Dominique Zehrfuss, 1970, 2 daughters. Publications: La Place de l'Etoile, 1968; La Ronde de nuit, 1969; Les Boulevards de ceinture, 1972; Lacombe Lucien (screenplay), 1974; Villa triste, 1975; Livret de famille, 1977; Rue des boutiques obscures, 1978; Une jeunesse, 1981; De si braves garcons, 1982; Quartier perdu, 1984; Voyage de Noces, 1990; Chien de Printemps, 1993; Du plus loin de l'oublie, 1996; Dora Bruder, 1997; Des inconnues, 1999. Honours: Prix Roger Nimier, 1968; Prix Goncourt, 1978; Chevalier des Arts des Lettres. Address: c/o Editions Gallimard, 5 rue Sebatien Bottin, 75007 Paris, France.

MOE Christian Hollis, b. 6 July 1929, New York, New York, USA. Retired Educator. Playwright. m. Carolyn Forman, 7 May 1952, 2 sons. Education: AB, College of William and Mary, 1951; MA, University of North Carolina at Chapel Hill, 1955; PhD, Cornell University, 1958. Appointments: Assistant Professor, Professor, 1958-96, Chair, 1988-96, Theatre Department, Southern Illinois University. Publications: Creating Historical Drama, 1965; The Strolling Players (play), 1965; Six New Plays for Children, 1971; Three Rabbits White (play), 1975; Tom Sawyer (play adaptation), 1977; Eight Plays for Youth, 1992. Contributions to: Journals. Honours: 7 playwriting awards; Fulbright Scholarship, 1975; American College Theatrical Festival Amoco Award, 1976; Illinois Theatre Association Award of Excellence, 1988, 1992. Memberships: Dramatists Guild; Southern Illinois Writers. Address: 603 South Curtis Place, Carbondale, IL 62901, USA.

MOENICH David Richard, b. 16 July 1952, Pittsburgh, PA, USA. Writer; Songwriter. m. Margaret Joan Siddle, 6 Oct 1973. Publications: Lizards, 1990; Unpublished works: Screenplay, short story, cartoons, advanced snare drum study book. Contributions to: 9 published magazine articles; 19 published magazine articles. Address: 715 Greenleaf Drive, Monroeville, PA 15146-1133, USA.

MOFFAT Gwen, b. 3 July 1924, Brighton, Sussex, England. Author. m. Gordon Moffat, 1948, 1 daughter. Publications: Space Below My Feet, 1961; Two Star Red, 1964; On My Home Ground, 1968; Survival Count, 1972; Lady With a Cool Eye, 1973; Deviant Death, 1973; The Corpse Road, 1974; Hard Option, 1975; Miss Pink at the Edge of the World, 1975; Over the Sea to Death, 1976; A Short Time to Live, 1976; Persons Unknown, 1978; Hard Road West, 1981; The Buckskin Girl, 1982; Die Like a Dog, 1982; Last Chance Country, 1983; Grizzly Tail, 1984; Snare, 1987; The Stone Hawk, 1989; The Storm Seekers, 1989; Rage, 1990; The Raptor Zone, 1990; Pit Bull, 1991; Veronica's Sisters, 1992; The Outside Edge, 1993; Cue the Battered Wife, 1994; The Lost Girls, 1998; A Wreath of Dead Moths, 1998. Contributions to: Newspapers and magazines. Memberships: Crime Writers Association; Mystery Writers of America; Society of Authors. Address: c/o Laurence Pollinger Ltd, 18 Maddox Street, Mayfair, London W1R 0EU, England.

MOFFEIT Tony A, b. 14 Mar 1942, Claremont, Oklahoma, USA. Librarian; Poet. Education: BSc, Psychology, Oklahoma State University, 1964; MLS, University of Oklahoma, 1965. Appointments: Assistant Director, Library, 1980-, Poet-in-Residence, 1986-95, University of Southern Colorado; Director, Pueblo Poetry Project, 1980-. Publications: La Nortenita, 1983; Outlaw Blues, 1983; Shooting Chant, 1984; Coyote Blues, 1985; Hank Williams Blues, 1985; The Spider Who Walked Underground, 1985; Black Cat Bone, 1986; Dancing With the Ghosts of the Dead, 1986; Pueblo Blues, 1986; Boogie Alley, 1989; Luminous Animal, 1989; Poetry is Dangerous, the Poet is an Outlaw, 1995. Contributions to: Journals and magazines. Honours: Jack Kerouac Award, 1986; National Endowment for the Arts Fellowship, 1992. Membership: American Library Association. Address: 1501 East 7th, Pueblo, CO 81001, USA.

MOFFETT Judith, b. 30 Aug 1942, Louisville, Kentucky, USA. Poet; Writer; Teacher. m. Edward B Irving, 1983. Education: BA, Hanover College, Indiana, 1964; MA, Colorado State University, 1966; University of Wisconsin at Madison, 1966-67; MA, 1970, PhD, 1971, University of Pennsylvania. Appointments: Fulbright Lecturer, University of Lund, Sweden, 1967-68; Assistant Professor, Behrend College, Pennsylvania State University, 1971-75; Visiting Lecturer, University of Iowa, 1977-78; Visiting Lecturer, 1978-79, Assistant Professor, 1979-86, Adjunct Assistant Professor, 1986-88, Adjunct Associate Professor, 1988-93, Adjunct Professor of English, 1993-94, University of Pennsylvania. Publications: Poetry: Keeping Time, 1976; Whinny Moor Crossing, 1984. Fiction: Pennterra, 1987; The Ragged World, 1991; Time, Like an Ever-Rolling Stream, 1992; Two That Came True, 1992. Other: James Merrill: An Introduction to the Poetry, 1984; Homestead Year: Back to the Land in Suburbia, 1995. Honours: Fulbright Grants, 1967, 1973; American Philosophical Society Grant, 1973; Eunice Tiejens Memorial Prize, 1973; Borestone Mountain Poetry Prize, 1976; Levinson Prize, 1976; Ingram Merrill Foundation Grants, 1977, 1980, 1989; Columbia University Translation Prize, 1978; Bread Loaf Writers Conference Tennessee Williams Fellowship, 1978; Swedish Academy Translation Prize, 1982; National Endowment for the Humanities Translation Fellowship, 1983; National Endowment for the Arts Fellowship, 1984; Swedish Academy Translation Grant, 1993. Address: 951 East Laird Avenue, Salt Lake City, UT 84105, USA.

MOGGACH Deborah, b. 28 June 1948, London, England. Novelist; Screenwriter. m. Anthony Moggach, Nov 1972, 1 son, 1 daughter. Education: BA Hons, English, Bristol University, England; Diploma Education, University of London, England. Publications: Novels: You Must Re Sisters; Close to Home: A Quiet Drink; Hot Water Man; Porky; To Have and To Hold; Driving in the Dark; Stolen; The Stand In; The Ex-Wives; Seesaw; Close Relations; Tulip Fever. Short stories; Smile and Other Stories; Changing Babies. Stage play: Double Take. TV dramas: To Have and To Hold; Stolen; Goggle Eyes; Seesaw; Close Relations. Contributions to: Many newspapers and magazines including The Sunday Times; The Guardian; The Independent; The Daily Mail. Honours: Writers Guild Award for Best Adapted TV Drama (Goggle Eyes), 1993. Memberships: Committee Member, PEN; Society of Authors. Literary Agent: Curtis Brown. Address: c/o Curtis Brown, 28/9 Haymarket, London SW14 4SP, England.

MOHAMED N P, b. 1 July 1929, Calicut, India. Author. m. 27 Nov 1954, 4 sons, 3 daughters. Education: Intermediate, Madras University. Appointments: Assistant Editor, Kerala Kaumundi, 1987. Publications: Thopplyum Thattavum, 1952; Maram, 1959; Hiranya Kashipu, 1976; Abudabi-Dubai, 1978; Ennapadem, 1981; Avar Nalupaer, 1987. Contributions to: Journals and peridocials. Honours: Madras Government Award, Short Stories, 1959; Kerala Sahitya Academy Awards, 1969, 1981. Memberships: Kerala Sahitya Academy, executive committee; Central Academy of Letters, advisory member in Malayasian. Address; Suthalam, Calicut-Pin 6730007, Kerala, India.

MOHLER James A(ylward), b. 22 July 1923, Toledo, Ohio, USA. Roman Catholic Priest; Professor of Religious Studies Emeritus; Writer. Education: LittB, Xavier University, 1946; PhL, 1949, STL, 1956, Bellarmine School of Theology; MSIR Loyola University, 1960; PhD, University of Ottawa, 1964; STD, University of St Paul, 1965. Appointments: Entered Society of Jesuits, 1942; Ordained Roman Catholic Priest, 1955; Instructor, 1960-65, Assistant Professor, 1965-69, Associate Professor, 1969-74, Professor of Religious Studies, 1974-94, Professor Emeritus, 1994-, John Carroll University, Cleveland; Visiting Scholar, Union Theological Seminary, New York City, 1966; Various research fellowships in colleges and universities in the US and overseas. Publications: Man Needs God: An Interpretation of Biblical Faith, 1966; The Beginning of Eternal Life: The Dynamic Faith of Thomas Aquinas, Origins and Interpretation, 1968; Dimensions of Faith, Yesterday and Today, 1969; The Origin and Evolution of the Priesthood, 1970; The Heresy of Monasticism: The Christian Monks, Types and Anti-Types, 1971; The School of Jesus: An Overview of Christian Education, Yesterday and Today, 1973; Cosmos, Man, God, Messiah: An Introduction to Religion, 1973; Dimensions of Love, East and West, 1975; Sexual Sublimation and the Sacred, 1978; The Sacrament of Suffering, 1979; Dimensions of Prayer, 1981; Love, Marriage and the Family, Yesterday and Today, 1982; Paradise: Gardens of the Gods, 1984; Health, Healing and Holiness: Medicine and Religion, 1986; Late Have I Loved You: Augustine on Human and Divine Relationships, 1991; A Speechless Child is the Word of God: Augustine on the Trinity, Christ, Mary, Church and Sacraments, Prayer, Hope and the Two Cities, 1992. Contributions to: Religious journals. Memberships: American Academy of Religion; American Association of University Professors; Association for Asian Studies; Catholic Theological Society of America; College Theology Society. Address: John Carroll University, University Heights, Cleveland, OH 44118, USA.

MOHR Steffen, b. 24 July 1942, Leipzig, Germany. Author. 3 sons, 4 daughters. Education: Diplomas in Theatre, University of Leipzig and Institute of Literature, Leipzig. Publications: 8 books, 1975-89; Screenplays; Television films; Radio plays. Memberships: Free Society of Literature; Union of Crime Writers. Address: Liechtensteinstrasse 35, Leipzig, Germany.

MOHRT Michel, b. 28 Apr 1914, Morlaix, France. Writer; Editor. m. Françoise Jarrier, 1955, 1 son. Education: Law School, Rennes. Appointments: Lawyer, Marseilles Bar until 1942; Professor, Yale University, 1947-52; Editor, Head of English Translations, Les Editions Gallimard, 1952-. Publications: Novels: Le repit: Mon royaume pour un cheval, 1949; La prison martitime, 1961; La campagne d'Italie, 1965; L'ours des Adirondacks, 1969; Deux Americaines a Paris, 1974; Les moyens du bord, 1975; La guerre civile, 1986; Le Telesieje, 1989. Essays: Montherlant, homme libre, 1943; Le nouveus Roman American, 1956; L'air du large,1969; Vers l'Ouest, 1988; Benjamin ou Lettes sur l'Inconstance, 1989. Plays: Une jeu d'enfer, 1970; La maison du père, 1979; Vers l'Ouest, 1988; On Liquide et on s'en Va, 1992. Honours: Officier, Legion d'honneur, Croix de guerre; Grand Prix du roman de l'Académie Française, 1962; Grand Prix de la Critique Litteraire, 1970; Grand prix du Litteraure de l'Académie Française, 1983. Memberships: Académie Française, 1985; Garrick Club. Address: Editions Gallimard, 5 rue Sebastien-Bottin, Paris 75007, France.

MOJTABAI Ann Grace, b. 8 June 1937, New York, New York, USA. Author; Educator. m. Fathollah Motabai, 27 Apr 1960, div 1966, 1 son, 1 daughter. Education: BA, Philosophy, Antioch College, 1958; MA, Philosophy, 1968, MS, Library Science, 1970, Columbia University. Appointments: Lecturer in Philosophy, Hunter College, 1966-68; Briggs-Copeland Lecturer on English, Harvard University, 1978-83; Writer in Residence, University of Tulsa, 1983-. Publications: Mundome, 1974; The 400 Eels of Sigmund Freud, 1976; A Stopping Place, 1979; Autumn, 1982; Blessed Assurance, 1986; Ordinary Time, 1989; Called Out, 1994; Soon, 1998 Contributions to: New York Times Book Review; New Republic; Philosophy Today; Philosophical Journal. Honours: Radcliffe Institute Fellow, 1976-78; Guggenheim Fellowship, 1981-82; Richard and Hinda Rosenthal Award, American Academy and Institute of Arts and Letters, 1983; Lillian Smith Award, Southern Regional Council, 1986; Award in Literature, American Academy of Arts and Letters, 1993. Memberships: Mark Twain Society; PEN; Texas Institute of Letters; Phi Beta Kappa. Address: 2102 South Hughes, Amarillo, TX 79109, USA.

MOKYR Joel, b. 26 July 1946, Leyden, the Netherlands. Professor of Art and Science and

Economics and History. m. Margalit B Mokyr PhD, 29 Sept 1969, 2 daughters. Education: BA, Hebrew University, 1968; PhD, Yale University, 1974. Publications: Industrialization in the Low Countries, 1976; Why Ireland Starved, 1983; The Lever of Riches, 1990; The British Industrial Revolution, 1993; 2nd edition, 1998. Memberships: Fellow, American Academy of Arts and Sciences, 1996. Address: Department of Economics, Northwestern University, Evanston, IL 60208, USA.

MOLBJERG Lis Guri Nostahl, b. 26 July 1920, Copenhagen, Denmark. Retired Government Official; Writer; Poet. m. Hans Molbjerg, 1944, 1 daughter. Education: BA, Public Administration, 1974. Publications: Member of the Party (non-fiction), 1995; Two Minutes Silence (poems), 1995. Contributions to: Periodicals. Memberships: Society of Danish Authors. Address: Krogerrupgade 593, 2200 Copenhagen, Denmark.

MOLDON Peter Leonard, b. 31 Mar 1937, London, England. Writer; Freelance Designer. Publications: Your Book of Ballet (illustrated and designed by author), 1974, revised, 1980; Nureyev, 1976; The Joy of Knowledge Encyclopaedia (ballet articles), 1976. Contributions to: Dancing Times. Honours: Your Book of Ballet, selected as one of the Children's Books of the Year, National Book League, 1974. Address: 11 Oxlip Road, Witham, Essex CM8 2XY, England.

MOLE John Douglas, b. 12 Oct 1941, Taunton, Somerset, England. Poet; Critic. m. Mary Norman, 22 Aug 1968, 2 sons. Education: MA, Magdalene College, Cambridge, 1964. Appointments: Teacher, Haberdashers' School, Elstree, 1964-73; Exchange Teacher, Riverdale School, New York, 1969-70; Head, Department of English, Verulam School, 1973-81, St Albans School, 1981-98; Poet-in-Residence, Magdalene College, Cambridge, 1996; Visiting Poet, University of Hertfordshire, 1998-. Publications: Poetry: Feeding the Lake, 1981; In and Out of the Apple, 1984; Homing, 1987; Boo to a Goose, 1987; The Mad Parrot's Countdown, 1989; Catching the Spider, 1990; The Conjuror's Rabbit, 1992; Depending on the Light, 1993; Selected Poems, 1995; Hot Air, 1996; Copy Cat (for children), 1997. Other: Passing Judgements: Poetry in the Eighties, 1989; The Dummy's Dilemma, 1999. Contributions to: Newspapers, reviews, and magazines. Honours: Eric Gregory Award, 1970; Signal Award for Outstanding Contribution to Children's Poetry, 1988; Cholmondeley Award, 1994. Memberships: Society of Authors; Ver Poets, vice president. Address: 11 Hill Street, St Albans, Hertfordshire AL3 4QS, England.

MOLINARI María Angélica, (Kato Molinari), b. 9 July 1943, Altagracia, Córdoba Province, Argentina. University Professor. div. Education: MA, Universidad Nacional de Córdoba, 1965. Appointments: Professor, French Literature, Universidad Nacional de Córdoba; Journalist and Translator, several Argentinian journals including Confirmado, Panorama, Clarín. Publications: Poetry books: Por Boca de Quién, 1972; Miradas y Peregrinaciones, 1982; Noche de las Cosas, Mitad del Mundo, 1986; Las Simias, 1989; Umbral, 1993; Un Jerónimo de Duda, 1996. Contributions to: La Prensa, Buenos Aires; La Gaceta, Tucumán; Textures, Spain. Honours: Third Award for Poetry, Municipality of Buenos Aires; Ribbon of Honour, Argentine Society of Writers. Membership: Argentine Society of Writers. Address: Pacheco de Melo 2523, 1425 Buenos Aires, Argentina.

MOLLENKOTT Virginia (Ramey), b. 28 Jan 1932, Philadelphia, Pennsylvania, USA. Professor of English Emeritus; Writer; Lecturer. m. Friedrich H Mollenkott, 17 June 1954, div 1973, 1 son. Education: BA, Bob Jones University, 1953; MA, Temple University, 1955; PhD, New York University, 1964. Appointments: Chair, Department of English, Shelton College, 1955-63, Nyack College, 1963-67; Associate Professor, 1967-74, Professor of English, 1974-97, Chair, Department of English, 1972-76, Professor Emeritus, 1997-, William Paterson University, New Jersey, Wayne. Publications: Adamant and Stone Chips: A Christian Humanist Approach to Knowledge, 1967; In Search of Balance,

1969; Adam Among the Television Trees: An Anthology of Verse by Contemporary Christian Poets (editor), 1971; Women, Men and the Bible, 1976, revised edition, 1988; Speech, Silence, Action, 1977; Is the Homosexual My Neighbor? (with L D Scanzoni), 1978, revised and expanded edition, 1994; The Divine Feminine: Biblical Imagery of God as Female, 1983; Views from the Intersection (with Catherine Barry), 1984; Women of Faith in Dialogue (editor), 1987; Sensuous Spirituality: Out from Fundamentalism, 1992. Contributions to: Numerous journals and reviews; The Witness, contributing editor, 1994. Honours: Penfield Fellow, 1973, Andiron Award, 1964, Founders Day Award, 1964, New York University; Honorary DMin, Samaritan College, 1989; New Jersey Lesbian and Gay Coalition Achievement Award, 1992. Memberships: Milton Society of America, life member; Modern Language Association, life member. Address: 11 Yearling Trail, Hewitt, NJ 07421, USA.

MOLLOY Michael (John), b. 22 Dec 1940, England. Journalist; Editor; Writer. m. Sandra June Foley, 1964, 3 daughters. Education: Ealing School of Art. Appointments: Staff, 1962-70, Assistant Editor, 1970-75, Deputy Editor, 1975, Editor, 1975-85, Daily Mirror; Director, 1976-90, Editor-in-Chief, 1985-90, Mirror Group Newspapers; Editor, Sunday Mirror, 1986-88. Publications: The Black Dwarf, 1985; The Kid from Riga, 1987; The Harlot of Jericho, 1989; The Century, 1990; The Gallery, 1991; Sweet Sixteen, 1992; Cat's Paw, 1993; Home Before Dark, 1994; Dogsbody, 1995. Address: 62 Culmington Road, London W13 9NH, England.

MOMADAY Navarre Scott, b. 27 Feb 1934, Lawton, Oklahoma, USA. Writer; Painter; Professor. m. Regina Heitzer, 21 July 1978, 4 daughters. Education: BA, University of New Mexico, 1958; MA, 1960, PhD, 1963, Stanford University. Appointments: Visiting Professor, Columbia University, Princeton University, 1979; Writer-in-Residence, Southeastern University, 1985, Aspen Writers Conference, 1986. Publications: House Made of Dawn, 1968; The Way to Rainy Mountain, 1969; The Names, 1976; The Gourd Dancer, 1976; The Ancient Child, 1989; In the Presence of the Sun, 1992; Enchanted Circle, 1993; The Native Americans (with Linda Hozan), 1993; The Man Made of Words, 1997. Honours: Pulitzer Prize in Fiction, 1969; Premio Mondello, Italy, 1979; Honorary Degrees, various universities. Membership: PEN. Address: c/o Julian Bach Literary Agency, New York, USA.

MOMI Balbir Singh, b. 20 Nov 1935, Amagarh, India. Retired Teacher and Education Officer; Writer; Translator. m. Baldev Kaur, 28 Oct 1954, 4 daughters. Education: Honours in Punjabi, 1953, MA, 1970, in Punjabi, Honours in Persian, 1974, PhD registration, 1977, Panjab University, Chandigarh. Appointments: School Teacher, 1954-71; Education Officer, 1976-93; Lecturer and Research Assistant, GND University, Amritsar, 1974-76; Literary Editor, Perdesi Canafi Ajit Punjab, Toronto, Ontario, Canada, 1982-97. Publications: Short stories, novels, plays and translations. Contributions to: Many publications. Honours: Vrious literary awards. Memberships: International Cultural Forum, India and Canada, senior international vice president, 1993-; International Perdesi Punjab, Sahit Sabha, Toronto, and Ajit Sahit Sa, 1982-97. Address: 17 Donaldson Drive, Brampton, Ontario L6Y 3H1, Canada.

MOMMSEN Katharina Zimmer, b. 18 Sept 1925, Berlin, Germany. Retired Professor of German Literature; Writer. m. Momme H Mommsen, 23 Dec 1948. Education: Abitur, 1943, DrPhilHabil, 1962, University of Berlin; DPhil, University of Tübingen, 1956. Appointments: Researcher, German Academy of Sciences, Berlin, 1949-61; Docent, Professor, Free University of Berlin, 1962-70; Professor of German Literature, Carleton University, Ottawa, 1970-74, Stanford University, 1974-93. Publications: Goethe und 1001 Nacht, 1960; Goethe und Diez, 1961; Goethe und der Islam, 1964; Natur und Fabelreich in Faust II, 1968; Schillers Anthologie, 1973; Kleists Kampf mit Goethe, 1974; Gesellschaftkritik bei Fontane und Thomas Mann,

1974; Herders Journal Meiner Reise, 1976; Hofmannsthal und Fontane, 1978; Who is Goethe?, 1983; Goethe - Warum?, 1984; Goethes Marchen, 1984; Goethe und die arabische Welt, 1988; Facsimile edition, 1996; Goethes Kunst des Lebens, 1999. Contributions to: Numerous journals and magazines. Honours: Guggenheim Fellowship, 1976; Alexander von Humboldt Forschungspreis, 1980; Bundesverdienskreuz 1 Klasse, 1985; Endowed Chair as Albert Guerard Professor of Literature, Stanford University; Gold Medaille of the International Goethe Society, 1999. Memberships: Various professional organisations. Address: 980 Palo Alto Avenue, Palo Alto, CA 94301, USA.

MONACO James Frederick, b. 15 Nov 1942, New York, New York, USA. Writer; Publisher. m. Susan R Schenker, 24 Oct 1976, 2 sons, 1 daughter. Education: BA, Muhlenberg College, 1963; MA, Columbia University, 1964. Publications: How to Read a Film, 1977, 3rd edition, 1995; American Film Now, 1979, 2nd edition, 1984; The New Wave, 1976; Media Culture, 1977; Celebrity, 1977; Connoisseurs Guide to the Movies, 1985; The International Encyclopedia of Film, 1991; The Movie Guide, 1992; Cinemania: Interactive Movie Guide, 1992; How to Read a Film (CD-Rom), 1998; Dictionary of Film and New Media, 1999. Contributions to: Numerous publications. Memberships: Authors Guild; Writers Guild. Address: UNET 2 Corporation, 80 East 11th Street, New York, NY 10003, USA.

MONAHOF Ania, b. 12 June 1929, St Petersburg, Russia. Author; Poet. m. Allan Frankel, 3 sons, 1 daughter. Education: Folk High School, Sweden, 1981-84. Appointments: President, LIRA Honour Foundation, St Petersburg. Publications: Epic of Refuge; Through the Granite, 1987; Refuge, 1988; Towards the Star, 1989; Black Cottage, 1992; Grandmother's Chicken (anthology), 1997; Cathrina, daughter of Simo, 1997; The Holy Tears of Anguish, 1997. Honours: Alva Myrdal Award, Sweden, twice; Recipient, The Nine, literature award. Memberships: Literature of Russia; Poets and Authors of Ingermanland. Literary gent: Bonniers, Stockholm. Address: Bruksvägen 5, S-696 73 Aspa Bruk, Sweden.

MONCURE Jane Belk, b. 16 Dec 1926, Orlando, Florida, USA. Teacher; Author; Consultant. m. James Ashby Moncure, 14 June 1952, 1 son. Education: BS, Virginia Commonwealth University, 1952; MA, Columbia University, 1954. Appointments: Instructor, Early Childhood Education, University of Richmond, Virginia, 1972-73, Burlington Day School, North Carolina, 1974-78. Publications: First Steps to Reading - Sound Box Books/The Child's World (24 books), 1970's; Magic Castle Books/ The Child's World (27 books), 1980's; First Steps to Math (10 books), 1980's; Word Bird (27 books), 1980's and 1990's; Discovery World (15 books), 1990's. Honours: Outstanding Service to Young Children, 1979; C S Lewis Gold Medal Award, Best Children's Book of the Year, 1984; The Five Senses (series of 5 books), 1997; My First Steps to Reading Treasury, 1997; Toymaker's Tales, 1999. Address: Cove Cottage, Seven Lakes Box 3336, West End, NC 27376, USA.

MONETTE Madeleine, b. 3 Oct 1951, Montreal, Quebec, Canada. Author. m. William R Leggio, 27 Dec 1979. Education: MA, Literature, University of Quebec. Publications: Le Double Suspect, 1980; Petites Violences, 1982; Fuites et Poursuites, 1982; Plages, 1986; L'Aventure, la Mesaventure, 1987; Amandes et melon, 1991; Nouvelles de Montreal, 1992; La Femme furieuse, 1997; Nouvelles d'Amérique, 1998. Contributions to: Periodicals. Honours: Robert-Cliche Award, 1980; Grants, Canadian Council of Arts, the Conseil des Arts et des Lettres du Quebec, Fonds Gabrielle-Roy. Memberships: Quebec Writers Union; PEN. Address: 2 Charlton Street, 11K, New York, NY 10014, USA.

MONEY David Charles, b. 5 Oct 1918, Oxford, England. Retired Schoolmaster; Writer. m. Madge Matthews, 30 Nov 1945, 1 son. Education: Honours Degree, Chemistry, 1940, Honours Degree, Geography,

1947, St John's College, Oxford University. Publications: Human Geography, 1954; Climate, Soils and Vegetation, 1965; The Earth's Surface, 1970; Patterns of Settlement, 1972; Environmental Systems (series), 1978-82; Foundations of Geography, 1987; Climate and Environmental Systems, 1988; China - The Land and the People, 1984, revised edition, 1989; China Today, 1987; Australia Today, 1988; Environmental Issues - The Global Consequences, 1994; China in Change, 1996; The Vocation of Bachan Singh, 1997. Honour: Geographical Association, honorary member. Memberships: Farmer's Club; Royal Geographical Society, fellow. Address: 52 Park Avenue, Bedford MK40 2NE, England.

MONEY Keith, b. 1934, Auckland, New Zealand. Author; Artist; Photographer. Publications: Salute the Horse, 1960; The Horseman in Our Midst, 1963; The Equestrian World, 1963; The Art of the Royal Ballet, 1964; The Art of Margot Fonteyn, 1965; The Royal Ballet Today, 1968; Fonteyn: The Making of a Legend, 1973; John Curry, 1978; Anna Pavlova: Her Life and Art, 1982; The Bedside Book of Old Fashioned Roses, 1985; Some Other Sea: The Life of Rupert Brooke, 1988-89; Margot, assoluta, 1993; Fonteyn and Nureyev: The Great Years, 1994. Other: Screenplays. Contributions to: Anthologies, journals, and magazines. Address: Carbrooke Hall Farm, Thetford, Norfolk, England.

MONGRAIN Serg, b. 15 Jan 1948, Trois Rivieres, Quebec, Canada. Writer; Photographer. Education: Mathematical Université du Quebec a Trois Rivieres, 1972. Publications: L'Oeil du l'idée, 1988, 2nd edition, 1991; Le calcul des heures, 1993. As Photographer: Lis: écris, 1981; L'image titre, 1981; Agrestes, 1988; Many exhibition catalogues in art. Contributions to: Periodicals. Membership: Union des écrivains du Quebec. Address: 994 rue Sainte Cecile, Trois Rivieres, Quebec G9A 1L3, Canada.

MONK C. See: **MEDVEI Victor Cornelius.**

MONOD Jean, b. 19 Oct 1941, Paris, France. Writer; Ethnologist; Filmmaker; Editor. m. (1) Marie Laure Chaude, 1962, (2) Kagumi Onodera, 1989, 3 sons, 2 daughters. Education: University of Paris, 1974. Appointments: Lecturer, 1970-; Editor-in-Chief, Aiou, 1987-. Publications: Several books. Contributions to: Journals and periodicals. Honours: Prix Georges Sadoul; Prix Louis Marinde l'Académie des Sciences; d'Ortre-Mer. Address: L'Espinassounel, 48330 Saint Etienne Valle Française, France.

MUNRO James. See: **MITCHELL James.**

MONSARRAT Ann Whitelaw, b. 8 Apr 1937, Walsall, England. Journalist; Writer. m. Nicholas Monsarrat, 22 Dec 1961. Appointments: Journalist, West Kent Mercury, 1954-58, Daily Mail, London, 1958-61, Tatler, 1993-, UNESCO Courier, 1994; Assistant Editor, Stationery Trade Review, 1961. Publications: And the Bride Wore ... The Story of the White Wedding, 1973; An Uneasy Victorian: Thackeray the Man, 1980. Address: 15 Triq Il-Wileg, San Lawrenz, Gozo GRB 104, Malta.

MONTAG Tom, b. 31 Aug 1947, Fort Dodge, Iowa, USA. Poet; Writer; Editor; Publisher. Education: BA, Dominican College of Racine, 1972. Appointments: Editor, Publisher, Monday Morning Press, Milwaukee, 1971-, Margins Books, 1974-. Publications: Wooden Nickel, 1972; Twelve Poems, 1972; Measurers, 1972; To Leave This Place, 1972; Making Hay, 1973; The Urban Ecosystem: A Holistic Approcah (editor with F Steams), 1974; Making Hay and Other Poems, 1975; Ninety Notes Toward Partial Images and Lover Prints, 1976; Concerns: Essays and Reviews: 1977; Letters Home, 1978: The Essential Ben Zen, 1992. Address: c/o Sparrow Press, 193 Waldron Street, West Lafayette, IN 47906, USA.

MONTAGU OF BEAULIEU Edward John Barrington Douglas-Scott-Montagu, 3rd Baron, b. 20 Oct 1926, London, England. Museum Administrator; Author. m. (1) Elizabeth Belinda, 1959, div 1974, 1 son, 1 daughter, (2) Fiona Herbert, 1974, 1 son. Education: St Peter's Court, Broadstairs; Ridley College, St Catharines, Ontario; New College, Oxford. Appointments: Founder, Montagu Motor Car Museum, 1952, world's first Motor Cycle Museum, 1956, National Motor Museum, Beaulieu, 1972; Founder-Editor, Veteran and Vintage magazine, 1956-79; Chairman, Historic Buildings and Monuments Commission, 1983-92; Free-lance motoring journalist. Publications: The Motoring Montagus, 1959; Lost Causes of Motoring, 1960; Jaguar: A Biography, 1961, revised edition, 1986; The Gordon Bennett Races, 1963; Rolls of Rolls-Royce, 1966; The Gilt and the Gingerbread, 1967; Lost Causes of Motoring: Europe, 2 volumes, 1969, 1971; More Equal Than Others, 1970; History of the Steam Car, 1971; The Horseless Carriage, 1975; Early Days on the Road, 1976; Behind the Wheel, 1977; Royalty on the Road, 1980; Home James, 1982; The British Motorist, 1987; English Heritage, 1987; The Daimler Century, 1995. Memberships: Federation of British Historic Vehicle Clubs, president, 1989-; British Salvage Vehicle Federation, 1998-; Federation Internationale des Voitures Anciennces, president, 1980-83; Historic Houses Association, president, 1973-78; Museums Association, president, 1982-84; Union of European Historic Houses, president, 1978-81; Guild of Motoring Writers. Address: Palace House, Beaulieu, Brockenhurst, Hants SO42 7ZN, England.

MONTAGUE John (Patrick), b. 28 Feb 1929, New York, New York, USA. Poet; Writer; Lecturer. Education: BA, 1949, MA, 1953, University College, Dublin; Postgraduate Studies, Yale University, 1953-54; MFA, University of Iowa, 1955. Appointment: Lecturer in Poetry, University College, Cork. Publications: Forms of Exile, 1958; The Old People, 1960; Poisoned Lands and Other Poems, 1961; The Dolmen Miscellany of Irish Writing (editor), 1962; Death of a Chieftain and Other Stories, 1964; All Legendary Obstacles, 1966; Patriotic Suite, 1966; A Tribute to Austin Clarke on His Seventieth Birthday, 9th May 1966 (editor with Liam Miller), 1966; Home Again, 1967; A Chosen Light, 1967; Hymn to the New Omagh Road, 1968; The Bread God: A Lecture, with illustrations in Verse, 1968; A New Siege, 1969; The Planter and the Gael (with J Hewitt), 1970; Tides, 1970; Small Secrets, 1972; The Rough Field (play), 1972; The Cave of Night, 1974; O'Riada's Farewell,1974; The Faber Book of Irish Verse (editor), 1974; A Slow Dance, 1975; The Great Cloak, 1978; Selected Poems, 1982; The Dead Kingdom, 1984; Mount Eagle, 1989. Address: Department of English, University College, Cork, Ireland.

MONTELEONE Thomas Francis, b. 14 Apr 1946, Baltimore, Maryland, USA. Writer; Dramatist. m. Elizabeth, 2 sons, 1 daughter. Education: BS, Psychology, 1964, MA, English Literature, 1973, University of Maryland. Publications: The Time Swept City, 1977; The Secret Sea, 1979; Night Things, 1980; Dark Stars and Other Illuminations, 1981; Guardian, 1981; Night Train, 1984; Lyrica, 1987; The Magnificent Gallery, 1987; Crooked House, 1988; Fantasma, 1989; Borderlands, 1990; Borderlands 2, 1991; Borderlands 3, 1992; The Blood of the Lamb, 1992; Borderlands 4, 1993. Contributions to: Anthologies and magazines. Honours: Nebula Awards, 1976, 1977; Gabriel Award, 1984; Bronze Award, International Film and TV Festival, New York, 1984; Bram Stoker Award for Superior Achievement in the Novel, 1993. Memberships: Science Fiction Writers of America; Horror Writers of America. Address: c/o Howard Morhaim, 175 Fifth Avenue, New York, NY 10010, USA.

MONTGOMERY Marion H Jr, b. 16 Apr 1925, Thomaston, Georgia, USA. Professor of English; Writer; Poet. m. Dorothy Carlisle, 20 Jan 1952, 1 son, 4 daughters. Education: AB, 1950, MA, 1953, University of Georgia; Creative Writing Workshop, University of Iowa, 1956-58. Appointments: Assistant Director, University of Georgia Press, 1950-52; Business Manager, Georgia Review, 1951-53; Instructor, Darlington School for Boys, 1953-54; Instructor, 1954-60, Assistant Professor, 1960-67, Associate Professor, 1967-70, Professor of English, 1970-, University of Georgia; Writer-in-Residence, Converse College, 1963. Publications: Fiction: The Wandering of Desire, 1962; Darrell, 1964; Ye Olde Bluebird, 1967; Fugitive, 1974. Poetry: Dry Lightening, 1960; Stones from the Rubble, 1965; The Gull and Other Georgia Scenes, 1969. Non-Fiction: Ezra Pound: A Critical Essay, 1970; T S Eliot: An Essay on the American Magus, 1970; The Reflective Journey Toward Order: Essays on Dante, Wordsworth, Eliot and Others, 1973; Eliot's Reflective Journey to the Garden, 1978; The Prophetic Poet and the Spirit of the Age, Vol 1, Why Flannery O'Connor Stayed Home, 1980, Vol II, Why Poe Drank Liquor, 1983, Vol III, Why Hawthorne Was Melancholy, 1984; Possum, and Other Receipts for the Recovery of "Southern" Being, 1987; The Trouble with You Innerleckchuls, 1988; The Men I Have Chosen for Fathers: Literary and Philosophical Passages, 1990; Liberal Arts and Community: The Feeding of the Larger Body, 1990; Virtue and Modern Shadows of Turning: Preliminary Agitations, 1990; Romantic Confusions of the Good: Beauty as Truth, Truth Beauty, 1997; Practical Liberal Arts and the Decline of Higher Education, 1997; Concerning Intellectual Philandering: Poets and Philosophers, Priests and Politicians, 1998; Making: The Proper Habit of Our Being, 1999. Contributions to: Anthologies and magazines. Honours: Eugene Saxton Memorial Award, 1960; Georgia Writers Association Award for Fiction; Earhart Foundation Fellowship, 1973-74. Address: Box 115, Crawford, GA 30630, USA.

MONTI Nicolas, b. 8 Jan 1956, Milan, Italy. Architect; Writer. Education: Liceo Gonzaga, Milan, 1974; Paris VI University, 1976; Polytechnic School of Architecture, Milan, 1984. Publications: Mediterranean Houses; Cunha Moraes, Viagens en Angola; Italian Modern: A Design Heritage; Africa Then; Emilio Sommariva; Luca Comerio, Fotografo e Cineasta; Design Ethno, 1994; Il Gioco della Seduzione, 1996; Novelle Napoleoniche, forthcoming. Contributions to: Various publications. Honour: Study Tour of Japan essay contest. Memberships: Ordine degli Architetti; Collegio degli Ingegneri; Società degli Architetti; Studio Professionnale Associati; American Institute of Architects (AIA). Literary Agent: Melanie Jackson Agency, 250 West 57th Street, New York, New York, USA. Address: Via Borghetto 5, 20122 Milan, Italy.

MONTPETIT Charles, b. 3 Jan 1958, Montreal, Quebec, Canada. Novelist; Scriptwriter; Cartoonist. Education: BA, Communications, Concordia University, 1979. Publications: Moi ou la planète, 1973; Une Conquête de plus, 1981; Temps perdu, 1984; Temps mort, 1989; La Première Fois, 1991; Copie carbone, 1993; The First Time, 1995; The First Time, Australian version, 1996. Contributions to: Numerous magazines and journals. Honours: Actuelle-Jeunesse Prize, 1973; Radio-Canada Scriptwriting Competitions, 1978, 1979, 1991, 1995; Governor-General's Award, 1989; White Raven, 1992; Signet d'or, 1993. Memberships: Communication jeunesse; Canadian Society of Children's Authors, Illustrators and Performers; Canadian Children's Book Centre; Union des écrivaines et écrivains du Québec. Address: 4282C Fullum Street, Montreal, Quebec H2H 2J5, Canada.

MOODY A David, b. 21 Jan 1932, New Zealand. University Teacher; Writer. m. Joanna S Moody. Education: BA, 1951, MA, 1952, Canterbury College, University of New Zealand; BA, Oxford University, 1955. Appointments: Assistant Information Officer, UNHCR, Geneva; Senior Lecturer in English, University of Melbourne; Professor of English and American Literature, University of York. Publications: Virginia Woolf, 1963; Shakespeare: The Merchant of Venice, 1964; The Waste land in Different Voices (editor), 1974; Thomas Stearns Eliot: Poet, 1979; At the Antipodes: Homage to Paul Valéry, 1982; News Odes: The El Salvador Sequence, 1984; Cambridge Companion to T S Eliot (editor), 1994; Tracing T S Eliot's Spirit, 1996. Address: Church Green House, Old Church Lane, Pateley Bridge HG3 5LZ, England.

MOODY Rick, (Hiram F Moody III), b. 18 Oct 1961, New York, New York, USA. Writer; Editor. Education: BA, Brown University, 1983; MFA, Columbia University, 1986.

Publications: Garden State: A Novel, 1991; The Ice Storm, 1994; the Ring of Brightest Angels Around Heaven (short stories), 1995. Contributions to: Various periodicals. Honour: Editor's Book Award, Pushcart Press, 1991. Address: c/o Little, Brown & Co, 1271 Avenue of the Americas, New York, NY 10020, USA.

MOODY III, Hiram F. See: **MOODY Rick.**

MOON Farzana. See: **MALIK Farzana.**

MOONEY Bel, b. 8 Oct 1946, Liverpool, England. Writer; Broadcaster. m. Jonathan Dimbleby, 23 Feb 1968, 1 son, 1 daughter. Education: BA, 1st Class Honours, English Language and Literature, University College, London, 1969. Appointments: Columnist, Daily Mirror, 1979-80, Sunday Times, 1982-83, The Listener, 1984-86; Television interview series, television films and radio programmes; Governor, Bristol Polytechnic, 1989-91. Publications: Novels: The Windsurf Boy, 1983; The Anderson Question, 1985; The Fourth of July, 1988; Lost Footsteps, 1993; Intimate Letters, 1997. Children's Books: Liza's Yellow Boat, 1980; I Don't Want To!, 1985; The Stove Haunting, 1986; I Can't Find It!, 1988; It's Not Fair!, 1989; A Flower of Jet, 1990; But You Promised!, 1990; Why Not?, 1990; I Know!, 1991; The Voices of Silence, 1994; I'm Scared!, 1994; I Wish!, 1995; The Mouse with Many Rooms, 1995; Why Me?, 1996; I'm Bored!, 1997; Joining the Rainbow, 1997; The Green Man, 1997; It's not my Fault, 1999. Other: The Year of the Child, 1979; Differences of Opinion, 1984; Father Kissmass and Mother Claws (with Gerald Scarfe), 1985; Bel Mooney's Somerset, 1989; From this Day Forward, 1989; Perspectives for Living, 1992. Honour: Fellow, University College, London, 1994. Address: c/o David Higham Associates, 5 Lower John Street, London W1R 3PE, England.

MOONMAN Eric, b. 29 Apr 1929, Liverpool, England. Visiting Professor in Marketing. m. Jane Moonman, 10 Sept 1962, div 1991, 2 sons, 1 daughter. Education: Christ Church, Southport; Diploma, Social Sciences, University of Liverpool, 1955; University of Manchester. Appointments: Senior Lecturer in Industrial Relations, South Western Essex Technical College, 1962-64; Senior Research Fellow in Management Sciences, University of Manchester, 1964-66; Member of Parliament, Labour Party, Billericay, 1966-70, Basildon, 1974-79; Director, Centre for Contemporary Studies, 1979-90; Consultant, International Red Cross, 1991-94; Chairman, Essex Radio, 1991-; Visiting Professor, City University, 1992-; Chairman, Academic Response to Anti-Semitism and Racism, 1994-. Publications: The Manager and the Organization, 1961; Employee Security, 1962; European Science and Technology, 1968; Communication in an Expanding Organization, 1970; Reluctant Partnership, 1970; Alternative Government, 1984; The Violent Society (editor), 1987. Contributions to: Newspapers and periodicals. Honour: Order of the British Empire, 1991. Memberships: Institute of Management, fellow; Royal Society of Arts, fellow. Address: 1 Beacon Hill, London N7 9LY, England.

MOORCOCK Michael (John), (Edward P Bradbury, Desmond Read), b. 18 Dec 1939, Mitcham, Surrey, England. Writer. Appointments: Editor, Tarzan Adventures, 1956-58, Sexton Blake Library, 1959-61, New Worlds, London, 1964-79. Publications: The Stealer of Souls and Other Stories (with James Cawthorn), 1961; Caribbean Crisis, 1962; The Fireclown, 1965, as The Winds of Limbo, 1969; The Sundered World, 1965, as The Blood Red Game, 1970; Stormbringer, 1965; Michael Kane series: Warriors of Mars, 1965, as The City of the Beast, 1970; The Distant Suns (with Philip James), 1975; The Quest for Tanelorn, 1975; The Adventures of Una Persson and Catherine Cornelius in the Twentieth Century, 1976; The End of All Songs, 1976; Moorcock's Book of Martyrs, 1976; The Lives and Times of Jerry Cornelius, 1976; Legends from the End of Time, 1976; The Sailor on the Seas of Fate, 1976; The Transformation of Miss Mavis Ming, 1977, as Messiah at the End of Time, 1978; The Weird of the White Wolf, 1977; The Bane of the Black Sword, 1977; Sojan (for

children), 1977; Condition of Muzak, 1977; Glorianna, 1978; Dying for Tomorrow, 1978; The Golden Barge, 1979; My Experiences in the Third World War, 1980; The Russian Intelligence, 1980; The Great Rock'n'Roll Swindle, 1980; Byzantium Endures, 1981; The Entropy Tanga, 1981; The Warhound and the World's Pain, 1981; The Brothel in Rosenstrasse, 1982; The Dancers at the End of Time (omnibus), 1983; The Retreat from Liberty, 1983; The Language of Carthage, 1984; The Opium General and Other Stories, 1984; The Chronicles of Castle Brass, 1985; Letters from Hollywood, 1986; The City in the Autumn Stars, 1986; The Dragon in the Sword, 1986; Death is No Obstacle, 1992. Editor: The Best of New Worlds, 1965; England Invaded, 1977; New Worlds: An Anthology, 1983. Address: c/o Anthony Sheil Associates, 43 Doughty Street, London WC1N 2LF, England.

MOORE Charles. See: **COFFEY Charles M.**

MOORE Charles Hilary, b. 31 Oct 1956, England. Journalist; Editor; Writer. m. Caroline Mary Baxter, 1981, 1 son, 1 daughter. Education: BA, Trinity College, Cambridge. Appointments: Joined Editorial Staff, 1979, Leader Writer, 1981-83, Deputy Editor, 1990-92, The Daily Telegraph; Assistant Editor, Political Columnist, 1983-84, Editor, 1984-90, Fortnightly Columnist, 1990-95, The Spectator; Weekly Columnist, The Daily Express, 1987-90; Editor, The Sunday Telegraph, 1992-95; The Daily Telegraph, 1995-. The Daily Telegraph, No 1 Canada Square, London E14 5DT, England.

MOORE Christine. See: **PALAMIDESSI Christine Maria.**

MOORE Christopher Hugh, b. 9 June 1950, Stoke-on-Trent, England. Historian; Writer. m. Louise Brophy, 7 May 1977. Education: BA, Honours, University of British Columbia, 1971; MA, University of Ottawa, 1977. Publications: Louisbourg Portraits, 1982; The Loyalists, 1984; The Illustrated History of Canada (co-author), 1987. Other: School texts, historical guidebooks, educational software programmes, and radio documentaries. Contributions to: Numerous scholarly journals and magazines. Honours: Governor-General's Award for Non-Fiction, 1982; Canadian Historical Association Award of Merit, 1984; Secretary of State's Prize for Excellence in Canadian Studies, 1985. Memberships: Writers Union of Canada; Canadian Historical Association; Ontario Historical Society; Heritage Canada Foundation. Address: 620 Runnymede Road, Toronto, Ontario M6S 3A2, Canada.

MOORE Eric. See: **BRUTON Eric.**

MOORE John Evelyn, b. 1 Nov 1921, Sant Illario, Italy. Retired Naval Officer; Editor; Writer. m. (1) Joan Pardoe, 1945, 1 son, 2 daughters, (2) Barbara Kerry. Education: Scherborne School, Dorset. Appointments: Royal Navy, 1939-72; Editor, Jane's Fighting Ships, 1972-87, Jane's Naval Review, 1982-87; Honorary Professor, University of Aberdeen, 1987-90, St Andrews University, 1990-92. Publications: Jane's Major Warships, 1973; The Soviet Navy Today, 1975; Submarine Development, 1976; Soviet War Machine (co-author), 1976; Encyclopaedia of World's Warships (co-editor), 1978; World War 3 (co-author), 1978; Seapower and Politics, 1979; Warships of the Royal Navy, 1979; Warships of the Soviet Navy, 1981; Submarine Warfare: Today and Tomorrow (co-author), 1986. Membership: Royal Geographical Society, fellow. Address: 1 Ridgelands Close, Eastbourne, East Sussex BN20 8EP, England.

MOORE Lorrie, (Marie Lorena Moore), b. 13 Jan 1957, Glen Falls, New York, USA. Professor of English; Writer. Education: BA, St Lawrence University, 1978; MFA, Cornell University, 1982. Appointments: Lecturer in English, Cornell University, 1982-84; Assistant Professor, 1984-87, Associate Professor, 1987-91, Professor of English, 1991-, University of Wisconsin at Madison. Publications: Self-Help, 1985; Anagrams, 1986; The Forgotten Helper, 1987; Like Life, 1990; I Know Some

Things: Stories About Childhood by Contemporary Writers (editor), 1992; Birds of America, 1998. Contributions to: Periodicals. Honours: Several fiction prizes; Various fellowships. Memberships: Associated Writing Programs; Authors Guild; Authors League. Address: c/o Department of English, University of Wisconsin at Madison, Madison, WI 53706, USA.

MOORE Patrick Alfred Caldwell, b. 4 Mar 1923, Pinner, Middlesex, England. Astronomer; Writer; Editor. Education: Private. Appointments: The Sky at Night, BBC TV series, 1957-; Editor, Year Book of Astronomy, 1962-; Director, Armagh Planetarium, 1965-68. Publications: Over 60 books, including: The Amateur Astronomer, 1970, revised edition, 1990; Atlas of the Universe, 1970, revised edition, 1995; Guide to the Planets, 1976; Guide to the Moon, 1976; Guide to the Stars, 1977; Guide to Mars, 1977; Out of the Darkness: The Planet Pluto (co-author), 1980; The Unfolding Universe, 1982; Travellers in Space and time, 1983; The Return of Halley's Comet (co-author), 1984; Stargazing, 1985; Exploring the Night Sky with Binoculars, 1986; The A-Z of Astronomy, 1986; TV Astronomer, 1987; The Planet Uranos (co-author), 1988; The Planet Neptune, 1989; Mission to the Planets, 1990; A Passion for Astronomy, 1991; Fireside Astronomy, 1992; The Starry Sky, 1994; The Great Astronomical Revolution, 1994; Stars of the Southern Skies, 1994; Guinness Book of Astronomy, 1995; Teach Yourself Astronomy, 1995; Eyes on the Universe, 1997. Honours: Lorimer Gold Medal, 1962; Goodacre Gold Medal, 1968; Officer, 1968; Commander, 1988, of the Order of the British Empire; Honorary DSc, University of Lancaster, 1974; Hatfield Polytechnic, 1989, University of Birmingham, 1990; Jackson-Gwilt Medal, Royal Astronomical Society, 1977; Roberts-Klumpke Medal, Astronomical Society of the Pacific, 1979; Minor Planet No 2602 named "Moore" in his honour. Memberships: British Astronomical Association, president, 1982-84; Royal Astronomical Society of Canada; Royal Astronomical Society of New Zealand. Address: Farthings, 39 West Street, Selsey, West Sussex PO19 1RP, England.

MOORE Peter Dale, b. 20 June 1942, Nantyglo, Wales. University Lecturer. m. Eunice P Jervis, 18 Dec 1966, 2 daughters. Education: BSc, 1963, PhD, 1966, University of Wales. Publications: Peatlands; Geography; Pollen Analysis; Atlas of Living World; Encyclopedia of Animal Ecology; Mitchell Beazeley Guide to Wild Flowers; European Mires; Methods in Plant Ecology; Global Environmental Change; Encyclopedia of Ecology and Environmental Mangagement. Contributions to: New Scientist; Nature; Plants Today; Journal of Ecology. Memberships: British Ecological Society; Botanical Society of British Isles. Address: Division of Life Sciences, Kings College, Campden Hill Road, London W8 7AH, England.

MOORE Sally, b. 12 Feb 1936, Buffalo, New York, USA. Writer; Photographer. m. Richard E Moore, 10 Dec 1960, 1 son, 2 daughters. Education: Mount Holyoke College, 1954-56. Publications: Country Roads of Pennsylvania, 1st edition 1993, 2nd edition, 1998; Pennsylvania Outdoor Activity Guide, 1995; Country Roads of New Mexico, 1999. Contributions to: Newspapers and magazines. Memberships: American Society of Journalists & Authors; Society of American Travel Writers; Southwest Writers Association; American Society of Media Photographers. Address: PO Box 45060, Rio Rancho, NM 87174, USA.

MOORE Susanna, b. 9 Dec 1948, Bryn Mawr, Pennsylvania, USA. Writer. m., 1 daughter. Publications: My Old Sweetheart, 1982; The Whiteness of Bones, 1990; Sleeping Beauties, 1994; In the Cut, 1995. Honours: PEN/Ernest Hemingway Citation; Sue Kaufman Prize, American Academy of Arts and Letters, 1983. Address: c/o International Creative Management, 40 West 57th Street, New York, NY 10019, USA.

MOOREHEAD Caroline, b. 28 Oct 1944, London, England. Journalist; Writer. Education: BA, University of London, 1965. Appointments: Reporter, Time magazine,

Rome, 1968-69; Feature Writer, Telegraph Magazine, London, 1969-70, The Times, London, 1973-88; Features Editor, Times Educational Supplement, 1970-73; Human Rights Columnist, The Independent, 1988-93. Publications: Myths and Legends of Britain (editor and translator), 1968; Helping: A Guide to Voluntary Work, 1975; Fortune's Hostages, 1980; Sidney Bernstein: A Biography, 1983; Freya Stark: A Biography, 1985; Troublesome People: Enemies of War 1916-1986, 1987; Over the Rim of the World: The Letters of Freya Stark (editor), 1988; Betrayed: Children in the Modern World, 1988; Bertrand Russell: A Life, 1992; The Lost Treasures of Troy, 1996; 6 Dunant's Dream: War, Switzerland and the Red Crown, 1998. Contributions to: Newspapers and magazines. Address: 89 Gloucester Avenue, London NW1, England.

MOORHOUSE Frank, b. 21 Dec 1938, Nowra, Queensland, Australia. Writer. Education: University of Queensland; WEA. Appointments: President, Australian Society of Authors, 1979-82; Chairman, Copyright Council of Australia, 1985. Publications: Futility and Other Animals, 1969; The Americans, Baby, 1972; The Electrical Experience, 1974; Conference-Ville, 1976; Tales of Mystery and Romance, 1977; Days of Wine and Rage, 1980; Room Service, 1986; Forty-Seventeen, 1988; Lateshows, 1990. Contributions to: Bulletin. Honours: Henry Lawson Short Story Prize, 1970; National Award for Fiction, 1975; Awgie Award, 1976; Gold Medal for Literature, Australian Literary, 1989. Memberships: Australian Royal Automobile Club, Sydney; Crouchos Club, London; Member, Order of Australia. Address: c/o Rosemary Cresswell, Private Bag 5, PO Balmain, New South Wales 2041, Australia.

MOORHOUSE Geoffrey, b. 29 Nov 1931, Bolton, Lancashire, England. Author. m. (1) Janet Marion Murray, 1956, 2 sons, 2 daughters, 1 dec, (2) Barbara Jane Woodward, 1974, div 1978, (3) Marilyn Isobel Edwards, 1983, div 1996. Education: Bury Grammar School. Appointments: Editorial Staff, Bolton Evening News, 1952-54, Grey River Argus, New Zealand, Auckland Star, and Christchurch Star-Sun, 1954-56, New Chronicle, 1957, Guardian, Manchester, 1958-70. Publications: The Other England, 1964; The Press, 1964; Against All Reason, 1969; Calcutta, 1971; The Missionaries, 1973; The Fearful Void, 1974; The Diplomats, 1977; The Boat and the Town, 1979; The Best-Loved Game, 1979; India Britannica, 1983; Lord's, 1983; To the Frontier, 1984; Imperial City: The Rise and Rise of New York, 1988; At the George, 1989; Apples in the Snow, 1990; Hell's Foundations: A Town, Its Myths and Gallipoli, 1992; Om: An Indian Pilgrimage, 1993; A People's Game: The Centenary History of Rugby League Football 1895-1995, 1995; Sun Dancing: A Medieval Vision, 1997. Contributions to: Newspapers and magazines. Honours: Cricket Society Award, 1979; Thomas Cook Award, 1984. Membership: Royal Society of Literature, fellow. Address: Park House, Gayle, near Hawes, North Yorkshire DL8 3RT, England.

MORA Sonia Marta, b. 1 July 1953, San José, Costa Rica. University Researcher; Writer. m. Heian Mora Corrales, 13 July 1974, 3 daughters. Education: DEA, 1988, PhD, 1990, Université Paul Valéry, France, 1988; MA, Universidad de Costa Rica, San José, 1989. Publications: La enseñanza del Español en aristo (co-author), 1986; Las poetas del buen amor, 1991; Indomitas voces: las poetas de Costa Rica (co-author), 1994; El Perigvillo Sarniento y los origenes de la novela hispanoamericana, 1995; Cultura y desarrollo (essay), 1996. Contributions to: Journals. Honours: Fulbright Visiting Scholarship, 1987; International Visitor's Programme, US Government, 1996. Memberships: Instituto Internacional de Literatura, 1988; International Institute of Sociocriticism, France, 1990; National Committee, UNESCO, 1994. Address: PO Box 511-2350, San José, Costa Rica.

MORAES Dominic, b. 19 July 1938, Bombay, India. Writer; Poet. Education: Jesus College, Oxford. Appointments: Managing Editor, Asia Magazine, 1972-; Consultant, United Nations Fund for Population Activities, 1973-. Publications: A Beginning, 1957; Gone Away, 1960; My Son's Father (autobiography), 1968; The Tempest Within, 1972; The People Time Forgot, 1972; A Matter of People, 1974; Voices for Life (essays), 1975; Mrs Gandhi, 1980; Bombay, 1980; Ragasthan: Splendour in the Wilderness, 1988. Other: Poetry and travel books. Honour: Hawthornden Prize, 1957. Address 521 Fifth Avenue, New York, NY 10017, USA.

MORAN John Charles, b. 4 Oct 1942, Nashville, Tennessee, USA. Librarian; Editor; Foundation Director; Researcher. Education: BA, 1967, MLS, 1968, George Peabody College for Teachers. Appointments: Director, F Marion Crawford Memorial Society, 1975-; Editor, The Romantist, 1977-, The Worthis LIbrary, 1980-. Publications: In Memoriam: Gabriel Garcia Moren 1875-1975, 1975; Seeking Refuge in Torre San Nicola, 1980; An F Marion Crawford Companion, 1981; Anne Crawford von Rabe: A Shadow on a Wave (editor), 1981, 2nd edition, 1997; Bibliography of Marketing of Fruits and Vegetables in Honduras 1975-1985 (author, compiler), 1985. Contributions to: Professional journals and to general magazines. Honours: Special Guest, Il Magnifico Crawford - Conference on Francis Marion Crawford, Sant' Agnelio Di Sorrento. Address: c/o F Marion Crawford Society, Sarascinesca House, 3610 Meadowbrook Avenue, Nashville, TN 37205, USA.

MORAN NEIL Janet, b. 21 July 1954, Croydon, Surrey, England. Writer; Editor; Lecturer. m. Sydney Neil, 7 Sept 1985, 1 daughter. Education: BEd, Hons, Central School of Speech & Drama. Appointments: Voice Lecturer, Dome Theatre Montreal, 1976-77; Artistic Director, Ruddles Theatre Co, A-One Theatre Co, 1977-81; Repertory Theatre, 1981-86; Creative Writing Lecturer, Beaconsfield Adult Continuing Education Centre, 1988-99; Editor, Rhyme & Reason, 1994-2000. Contributions to: School Leaver; Company; Limited Edition; Mother; Third Degree; Readers Digest; Commended Finalist, Aural Images; Poetry Prize Winner - Worldwide Writers. Honours: Winner, BBC Writers Weekly Competition, 1995; Editor of Rhyme & Reason, Winner of Writers News National Anthology Cup, 1998. Membership: Society of Authors. Literary Agent: Mandy Little, Watson Little Ltd. Address: 11 Pitch Pond Closes, Knotty Green, Beaconsfield, Bucks HP9 1XY, England.

MORAY WILLIAMS Ursula, b. 19 Apr 1911, Petersfield, Hampshire, England. Children's Author. m. Conrad Southey John, 28 Sept 1935, 4 sons. Education: Winchester Art College. Publications: Approximately 70 titles, 1931-, including: Jean-Pierre; Adventures of the Little Wooden Horse; Gobbolino the Witch's Cat; Further Adventures of Gobbolino and the Little Wooden Horse; Nine Lives of Island Mackenzie; The Noble Hawks; Bogwoppit; Jeffy the Burglar's Cat; Good Little Christmas Tree; Cruise of the Happy-Go-Gay; Bellabelinda and the No-Good Angel; The Moonball. Contributions to: Magazines. Membership: West of England Writers Guild. Address: Pearcroft, Conderton, Tewkesbury, Gloucestershire GL20 7PU, England.

MOREHEAD James Bruce, b. 16 Aug 1916, Paoli, Oklahoma, USA. USAF Retired. m. Betty Bob Angerman, 1 Aug 1961, 2 daughters. Education: University of Oklahoma ug, UCLA ug, 1938-1939, 1939 respectively; USAF Senior Officer Cs, USAF Command & Staff, USAF Air War College, 1946-1966.Publications: Chapter I, Top Guns, 1991; In My Sights, 1998. Contributions to: Pacific Sweep Wm Hess Aces Over Japan; Eric Hammel. Honour: Amazon COM best seller, In My Sights, 1998. Address: 485 Sonoma Mt Road, Petaluma, CA 94954, USA.

MORELL Virginia Louise, b. 3 Aug 1949, Inglewood, California, USA. Writer; Science; Biography. m. Michael James McRae, 7 Nov 1981. Education: BA, Pomona College, Claremont, California, 1971; MA, McGill University, Montreal, 1993; MSc, California State University, Dominguez Hills, 1979. Appointments: English Lecturer, Haile Selassie I University, Addis Ababa, Ethiopia, 1973-75; Technical Writer in Computer Industry, 1976-80; Self Employed Writer. Publication: Ancestral Passions: The Leakey Family and The Quest for Humankind's Beginnings, 1995. Contributions to: Contributing Correspondent for Science; Contributing Editor for Discover; National Geographic; Audubon and International Wildlife. Honour: Finalist, AAAS Science Writing Award, 1997. Membership: National Association of Science Writers. Literary Agent: Michael J Hamilburg. Address: 292 La Cienega Boulevard #312, Beverely, Hills, CA 90211, USA.

MORENCY Pierre, b. 8 May 1942, Lauzon, Quebec, Canada. Poet; Writer; Dramatist; Broadcaster. Education: BA, Collège de Lévis, 1963; Licence ès Lettres, Université Laval, Quebec, 1966. Appointments: Broadcaster; Co-Founder, Estuaire poetry journal. Publications: L'ossature, 1972; Lieu de naissance, 1973; Le temps des oiseaux, 1975; Torrentiel, 1978; Effets personnels, 1987; L'oeil américain: Histories naturelles du Nouveau Monde, 1989; Lumière des oiseaux: Histoires naturelles du Nouveau Monde, 1992; Les paroles qui marchent dans la nuit, 1994; La vie entière, 1996. Honours: Prix Alain Grandbois, 1987; Prix Québec-Paris, 1988; Prix Ludger Duvernay, 1991; Prix France Québec, 1992; Chevalier Ordre des Arts et des Lettres de France. Memberships: PEN Club; Union des écrivaines et écrivains québécois. Address: 155 Avenue Laurier, Quebec G1R 2K8, Canada.

MORENO Armando, b. 19 Dec 1932, Porto, Portugal. Professor; Physician; Writer; Poet; Dramatist. m. Maria Guinot Moreno, 3 Oct 1987. Education: Licentiate in Medicine, 1960; MD, 1972; Aggregation in Medicine, 1984; Licentiate in Literature, 1986. Publications: A Chamada (short stories), 1982; As Carreiras, 1982; O Bojador, 1982; Historias Quase Clinicas (short stories), 3 volumes, 1982, 1984, 1988; Cais do Sodre (short stories), 1988; O Animal Que deupla Mente, 1993; Contos Oeirenses (short stories), 1994; A Governacao pela Competencia, 1995. Other: Medical books, poetry, plays, and television series. Contributions to: Periodicals. Honours: Drama and fiction awards. Memberships: Many professional and literary organizations. Address: Rua Almirante Matos Moreira 7, 2775 Carcavelos, Portugal.

MORETON John. See: **COHEN Morton Norton.**

MORFEA Nicola, b. 30 Nov 1942, Italy. Poet; Teacher (retired). m. Lorraine, 10 Aug 1968, 1 son, 1 daughter. Publications: Books of Poetry: Liriche Stanche; Rime Gentili E Barbare; L'Estro Di Una Musa Querula; Years 1987 1990 1994; Unpublished novels: La Novella Di Un Novellista; L'Indomita Domata; Stage works: Saint Maria Goretti; Saint Francis of Assisi; Saint Caterina de Siena; Paolo Di Tarso; Un Miracolo Di Natale; Lo Sciagurato Della Maremma. Honours: Accadenia Ferdinandea Attestato Di Merito, Catania, Italia First Awards in Poetry, 1992. Memberships: Sociata Letteraria, 1996.

MORGAN David Henry, b. 28 Sept 1928, Invercargill, New Zealand. Retired Technical Writer. m. Patricia Margaret Taylor, 30 Dec 1961, 2 sons, 1 daughter. Education: MA, University of New Zealand, 1961. Publications: Thinking and Writing, 1966; Effective Business Letters, 1970; Working with Words, 1989; Online learning packages on writing and communications. Contributions to: Professional journals. Membership: Council for Programs in Technical and Scientific Communication. Address: PO Box 687, Civic Square Australian Capital Territory 2608, Australia.

MORGAN Edwin (George), b. 27 Apr 1920, Glasgow, Scotland. Titular Professor of English Emeritus; Poet; Writer; Translator. Education: MA, University of Glasgow, 1947. Appointments: Assistant Lecturer, 1947-50, Lecturer, 1960-65, Senior Lecturer, 1965-71, Reader, 1971-75, Titular Professor of English, 1975-80, Professor Emeritus, 1980-, University of Glasgow; Visiting Professor, University of Strathclyde, 1987-90; Honorary Professor, University College, Wales, 1991-95. Publications: Poetry: The Vision of Cathkin Braes, 1952; The Cape of Good Hope, 1955; Starryveldt, 1965; Scotch Mist, 1965; Sealwear, 1966; Emergent Poems, 1967; The Second Life, 1968; Gnomes, 1968; Proverbfolder, 1969;

Penguin Modern Poets 15 (with Alan Bold and Edward Brathwaite), 1969; The Horseman's Word: A Sequence of Concrete Poems, 1970; Twelve Songs, 1970; The Dolphin's Song, 1971; Glasgow Sonnets, 1972; Instamatic Poems, 1972; The Whittrick: A Poem in Eight Dialogues, 1973; From Glasgow to Saturn, 1973; The New Divan, 1977; Colour Poems, 1978; Star Gate: Science Fiction Poems, 1979; Poems of Thirty Years, 1982; Grafts/Takes, 1983; Sonnets from Scotland, 1984; Selected Poems, 1985; From the Video Box, 1986; Newspoems, 1987; Themes on a Variation, 1988; Tales from Limerick Zoo, 1988; Collected Poems, 1990; Hold Hands Among the Atoms, 1991; Sweeping Out the Dark, 1994; Virtual and Other Realities, 1997. Other: Essays, 1974; East European Poets, 1976; Hugh MacDiarmid, 1976; Twentieth Century Scottish Classics, 1987; Nothing Not Giving Messages (interviews), 1990; Crossing the Border: Essays in Scottish Literature, 1990; Language, Poetry and Language Poetry, 1990; Evening Will Come They Will Sew the Blue Sail, 1991. Editor: Collins Albatross Book of Longer Poems: English and American Poetry from the Fourteenth Century to the Present Day, 1963; Scottish Poetry 1-6 (co-editor), 1966-72; New English Dramatists 14, 1970; Scottish Satirical Verse, 1980; James Thomson: The City of Dreadful Night, 1993. Translator. Honours: Cholmondeley Award for Poetry, 1968; Scottish Arts Council Book Awards, 1968, 1973, 1975, 1977, 1978, 1983, 1984, 1991, 1992; Hungarian PEN Memorial Medal, 1972; Soros Translation Award, 1985. Address: 19 Whittingehame Court, Glasgow G12 0BG, Scotland.

MORGAN (George) Frederick, b. 25 Apr 1922, New York, New York, USA. Poet; Writer; Editor. m. (1) Constance Canfield, 1942, div 1957, 6 children, (2) Rose Fillmore, 1957, div 1969, (3) Paula Deitz, 1969. Appointments: Co-Founder, 1947-98, Editor, 1947-98, The Hudson Review; Chair, Advisory Council, Department of Romance Languages and Literatures, Princeton University, 1973-90. Publications: Poetry: A Book of Change, 1972; Poems of the Two Worlds, 1977; Death Mother and Other Poems, 1979; The River, 1980; Northbook, 1982; Eleven Poems, 1983; Poems, New and Selected, 1987; Poems for Paula, 1996. Other: The Tarot of Cornelius Agrippa, 1978; The Fountain and Other Fables, 1985; Poems for Paula, 1995. Editor: The Hudson Review Anthology, 1961; The Modern Image: Outstanding Stories from "The Hudson Review", 1965. Honour: Chevalier de l'Ordre des Arts et des Lettres, France, 1984. Address: c/o The Hudson Review, 684 Park Avenue, New York, NY 10021, USA.

MORGAN Michaela, b. 7 Apr 1951, Manchester, England. Writer; Teacher. m. Colin Holden, 1 son. Education: BA, University of Warwick, 1973; PGCE, University of Leicester, 1975. Appointment: Writer-in-Residence, HM Prisons, Ashwell and Stocken, Leicester, 1992. Publications: The Monster is Coming; The Edward Stories; Dinostory; The Helpful Betty Stories;. Harraps Junior and Longmans Project. Contributions to: Poetry anthologies for children. Honours: Children's Book of the Year; Children's Choice, International Reading Association and United Kingdom Reading Association Award. Memberships: Society of Authors; NAWE. Address: 9 Main Street, Bisbrooke, Oakham, Rutland, Leics LE15 9EP, England.

MORGAN Mihangel. See: **MORGAN-FINCH Mihangel Ioan.**

MORGAN (Colin) Pete(r), b. 7 June 1939, Leigh, Lancashire, England. Poet; Dramatist. Education: Normanton School, Buxton, 1950-57. Appointments: Creative Writing for Northern Arts, Loughborough University, 1975-77. Publications: A Big Hat or Waht, 1968; Loss of Two Anchors, 1970; Poems for Shortie, 1973; The Grey Mare Being the Better Steed, 1973; I See You on My Arm, 1975; Ring Song, 1977; The Poet's Deaths, 1977; Alpha Beta, 1979; The Spring Collection, 1979; One Greek Alphabet, 1980; Reporting Back, 1983; A Winter Visitor, 1984; The Pete Morgan Poetry Pack, 1984. Plays: Still the Same Old Harry, 1972; All the Voices Going Away, 1979. Television Documentaries.

Honour: Arts Council of Great Britain Award, 1973. Address: c/o Fordon Fraser Publications, Eastcotts Road, Bedford MK4Z 0JX, England.

MORGAN Robert, b. 3 Oct 1944, Hendersonville, North Carolina, USA. Professor of English; Poet; Writer. m. Nancy K Bullock, 1965, 1 son, 2 daughters. Education: Emory College, Oxford, 1961-62; North Carolina State University, Raleigh, 1962-63; BA, University of North Carolina at Chapel Hill, 1965; MFA, University of North Carolina at Greensboro, 1968. Appointments: Instructor, Salem College, Winston-Salem, North Carolina, 1968-69; Lecturer, 1971-73, Assistant Professor, 1973-78, Associate Professor, 1978-84, Professor, 1984-92, Kappa Alpha Professor of English, 1992-, Cornell University. Publications: Poetry: Zirconia Poems, 1969; The Voice in the Crosshairs, 1971; Red Owl, 1972; Land Diving, 1976; Trunk & Thicket, 1978; Groundwork, 1979; Bronze Age, 1981; At the Edge of the Orchard Country, 1987; Sigodlin, 1990; Green River: New and Selected Poems, 1991. Fiction: The Blue Valleys: A Collection of Stories, 1989; The Mountains Won't Remember Us and Other Stories, 1992; The Hinterlands: A Mountain Tale in Three Parts, 1994; The Truest Pleasure, 1995. Non-Fiction: Good Measure: Essays, Interviews and Notes on Poetry, 1993. Honours: National Endowment for the Arts Fellowships, 1968, 1974, 1981, 1987; Southern Poetry Review Prize, 1975; Eunice Tietjins Award, 1979; Jacaranda Review Fiction Prize, 1988; Guggenheim Fellowship, 1988-89; Amon Liner Prize, 1989; James G Hanes Poetry Prize, 1991; North Carolina Award in Literature, 1991. Address: c/o Department of English, Goldwin Smith Hall, Cornell University, Ithaca, NY 14853, USA.

MORGAN Robin (Evonne), b. 29 Jan 1941, Lake Worth, Florida, USA. Journalist; Editor; Writer; Poet. 1 child. Education: Columbia University. Appointments: Editor, Grove Press, 1967-70; Visiting Chair and Guest Professor, New College, Sarasota, Florida, 1973; Editor and Columnist, 1974-87, Editor-in-Chief, 1989-93, Ms Magazine; Distinguished Visiting Scholar and Lecturer, Rutgers University, 1987. Publications: Sisterhood is Powerful: An Anthology of Writings from the Women's Liberation Movement (editor), 1970; Going Too Far: The Personal Chronicle of a Feminist, 1978; The Anatomy of Freedom: Feminism, Physics and Global Politics, 1982, 2nd edition, 1994; Sisterhood is Global: The International Women's Movement Anthology (editor), 1984; The Demon Lover: On the Sexuality of Terrorism, 1989; The Word of a Woman: Feminist Dispatches 1968-91, 1992, 2nd edition, 1994. Fiction: Dry Your Smile: A Novel, 1987; The Mer-Child: A New Legend, 1991. Poetry: Monster, 1972; Lady of the Beasts, 1976; Death Benefits, 1981; Depth Perception: New Poems and a Masque, 1982; Upstairs in the Garden: Selected and New Poems, 1968-88, 1990. Plays: In Another Country, 1960; The Duel, 1979. Contributions to: Magazines and periodicals. Honours: National Endowment for the Arts Grant, 1979-80; Yaddo Grant, 1980; Ford Foundation Grants, 1982, 1983, 1984; Feminist of the Year Award, Fund for a Feminist Majority, 1990. Memberships: Feminist Writers' Guild; Media Women; North American Feminist Coalition; Sisterhood is Global Institute, co-founder. Address: 230 Park Avenue, New York, NY 10169, USA.

MORGAN Robin Richard, b. 16 Sept 1953, Stourbridge, England. Editor; Journalist; Author. 2 sons, 1 daughter. Appointments: Insight Editor, Sunday Times; Features Editor, Sunday Times; Editor, Sunday Express; Editor, Sunday Times Magazine; Editorial Director Designate, Readers Digest; Editor, Sunday Times Magazine, 1995-. Publications: The Falklands War, co-author, 1982; Bullion, co-author, 1983; Rainbow Warrior, co-author, editor, 1986; Manpower, editor, 1986; Ambush, co-author, 1988; Book of Movie Biographies, co-editor, 1997. Honours: Campaigning Journalist of the Year, 1982, 1983. Literary Agent: Jonathon Lloyd. Address: Sunday Times Magazine, 1 Pennington Street, London E1 9XW, England.

MORGAN-FINCH Mihangel Ioan, (Mihangel Morgan), b. 7 Dec 1959, Aberdare, Wales. University

Lecturer; Writer; Poet. Education: BA, 1990, PhD, 1995, University of Wales. Publications: Diflaniad Fy Fi, 1988; Beth Yw Rhif Ffon Duw, 1991; Hen Lwybr A Storiau Eraill, 1992; Saith Pechod Marwol, 1993; Dirgel Ddyn, 1993; Te Gyda'r Frenhines, 1994; Tair Ochr Geiniog, 1996. Contributions to: Several publications. Honours: Prose Medal, Eisteddfod, 1993; Runner-Up, BBC Wales Arts Award, 1993; Welsh Arts Council Book of the Year Short List, 1993-94. Memberships: Gorsedd Beirdd; Ynys Prydain. Address: Porth Ceri, Talybont, Aberystwyth, Dyfed, Wales.

MORIARTY J. See: **KELLY Tim.**

MORITZ A(lbert) F(rank), b. 15 Apr 1947, Niles, Ohio, USA. Poet; Writer. m. Theresa Carrothers, 1 son. Education: BA, 1969, MA, 1971, PhD, 1975, Marquette University. Appointment: Northrop Frye Visiting Lecturer in Poetry, University of Toronto, 1993-94. Publications: Here, 1975; Signs and Certainties, 1979; Music and Exile, 1980; Black Orchid, 1981; The Pocket Canada (with Theresa Moritz), 1982; Canada Illustrated: The Art of Nineteenth-Century Engraving, 1982; Between the Root and the Flower, 1982; The Visitation, 1983; America the Picturesque: The Art of Nineteenth-Century Engraving, 1983; Stephen Leacock: A Biography (with Theresa Moritz), 1987; Song of Fear, 1992; The Ruined Cottage, 1993; Mahoning, 1994; Phantoms in the Ark, 1994. Contributions to: Periodicals. Honours: American Academy of Arts and Letters Award, 1991; Guggenheim Fellowship, 1993; Ingram Merrill Foundation Fellowship, 1993-94. Address: 31 Portland Street, Toronto, Ontario, Canada M5V 2V9.

MORLAND Dick. See: **HILL Reginald (Charles).**

MORLEY Don, b. 28 Jan 1937, Derbyshire, England. Photographer; Journalist. m. Josephine Mary Munro, 17 Sept 1961, 2 sons. Education: National Certificates, Electrical Engineering, Photography. Appointments: Former Picture Editor, The Guardian; Former Chief Photographer, Sports World Magazine, British Olympic Association; Chief Photographer, Moto Course; Founder Member/Director All Sport Photographic Ltd, 1975. Publications: Action Photography, 1975; Motorcycling, 1977; Everyone's Book of Photography, 1977; Everyone's Book of Motorcycling, 1981; The Story of the Motorcycle, 1983; Motorbikes, 1983; Classic British Trial Bikes, 1984; Classic British Moto Cross Machines, 1985; The Classic British Two Stroke Trials Bikes, 1987; The Spanish Trials Bikes, 1987; Trials: A Rider's Guide, 1990; BSA (History in Colour), 1990; Triumph (History in Colour), 1990; Norton (History in Colour), 1990; BMW (History in Colour), 1993. Contributions to: Magazines and journals worldwide. Honours: 17 national and international photography awards. Memberships: Professional Sports Photographers Association, founder, chairman, and honorary life member; Guild of Motoring Writers; Sports Writers Association of Great Britain. Address: 132 Carlton Road, Reigate, Surrey RH2 0JF, England.

MORLEY Patricia Marlow, b. 25 May 1929, Toronto, Ontario, Canada. Writer; Educator. m. Lawrence W Morley, div, 3 sons, 1 daughter. Education: BA, Honours, English Language and Literature, University of Toronto, 1951; MA, English, Carleton University, 1967; PhD, English Literature, University of Ottawa, 1970. Appointments: Assistant Professor, 1972-75, Associate Professor, 1975-80, Fellow, 1979-89, Professor of English and Canadian Studies, 1980-89, Lifetime Honorary Fellow, 1989-, Simone de Beauvoir Institute, Concordia University. Publications: The Mystery of Unity: Theme and Technique in the Novels of Patrick White, 1972; The Immoral Moralists: Hugh MacLennan and Leonard Cohen, 1972; Robertson Davies: Profiles in Canadian Drama, 1977; The Comedians: Hugh Hood and Rudy Wiebe, 1977; Morley Callaghan, 1978; Kurelek: A Biography, 1986; Margaret Laurence: The Long Journey Home, 1991; As Though Life Mattered: Leo Kennedy's Story, 1994; The Mountain is Moving: Japanese Women's Lives, 1999. Contributions to: Professional and mainstream journals. Honours: Award for Non-fiction, 1987; Ottawa-Carleton Literary Award, 1988; D S Litt

(Doctor of Sacred Letters), Thorneloe College, Laurentian University, 1992. Membership: Writer's Union of Canada. Address: Box 137, Manotick, Ontario K4M 1A2, Canada.

MORLEY Sheridan Robert, b. 5 Dec 1941, Ascot, Berkshire, England. Journalist; Broadcaster; Writer. m. (1) Margaret Gudekjo, 18 July 1965, div 1990, 1 son, 2 daughters. (2) Ruth Leon, 1995. Education: MA, Honours, Merton College, Oxford, 1964. Appointments: Staff, ITN, 1964-67; Interviewer, Late Night Up, BBC2, 1967-71; Deputy Features Editor, 1973-75, Arts Diarist and Television Critic, 1989-90, The Times; Arts Editor, 1975-88, Drama Critic, 1975-89, Punch; London Drama Critic, International Herald Tribune, 1979-; Drama Critic, Spectator, 1990-; Film Critic, Sunday Express, 1992-95. Publications: A Talent to Amuse: The Life of Noel Coward, 1969; Review Copies, 1975; Oscar Wilde, 1976; Sybil Thorndike, 1977; Marlene Dietrich, 1977; Gladys Cooper, 1979; Noel Coward and His Friends (with Cole Lesley and Graham Payn), 1979; The Stephen Sondheim Songbook, 1979; Gertrude Lawrence, 1981; The Noel Coward Diaries (editor with Graham Payn), 1982; Tales from the Hollywood Raj, 1983; Shooting Stars, 1983; The Theatregoers' Quiz Book, 1983; Katharine Hepburn, 1984; The Other Side of the Moon, 1985; Bull's Eyes (editor), 1985; Ingrid Bergman, 1985; The Great Stage Stars, 1986; Spread a Little Happiness, 1986; Out in the Midday Sun, 1988; Elizabeth Taylor, 1988; Odd Man Out: The Life of James Mason, 1989; Our Theatres in the Eighties, 1990; Methuen Book of Theatrical Short Stories (editor), 1992; Robert My Father, 1993; Methuen Book of Movie Stories (editor), 1993; Audrey Hepburn, 1993; Ginger Rogers, 1995; Faces of the 90s, 1995; Dirk Bogarde: Rank Outsider, 1996; Gene Kelly (with Ruth Leon), 1996; Marilyn Monroe (with Ruth Leon), 1997; Hey Mr Producer, The Musicals of Cameron Mackintosh (with Ruth Leon), 1998; Stage: Spread a Little Happiness, London, 1996; Noel and Gertie, USA, 1998. Contributions to: Newspapers and journals. Honour: BP Arts Journalist of the Year, 1989. Membership: Critics Circle. Address: 5 Admiral Square, Chelsea Harbour, London SW10 0UU, England.

MORPURGO Jack Eric, b. 26 Apr 1918, London, England. Author; Literary Agent; University Professor. m. Catherine Noel Kippe Cammaerts, 16 July 1947, dec 1993, 3 sons, 1 daughter. Education: Christ's Hospital, England; University of New Brunswick, Canada; BA, College of William and Mary, USA, 1938; Durham University, 1939; Institute of Historical Research, 1946. Appointments: Editor, Penguin Books, 1945-69, Penguin Parade, 1949-50; General Editor, Penguin History of England and Penguin History of the World, 1949-69; Assistant Director, Nuffield Foundation, 1951-54; Director General, National Book League, 1954-69; Professor of American and Canadian Studies, University of Geneva, 1968-70; Professor of American Literature, University of Leeds, 1969-83. Publications: American Excursion, 1949; Leigh Hunt: Autobiography (editor), 1949; Charles Lamb and Elia, 1949; The Christ's Hospital Book (with Edmund Blunden), 1952; History of the United States (co-author), 2 volumes, 1955; The Road to Athens, 1963; Barnes Wallis: A Biography, 1972; Their Majesties: Royall Colledge, 1976; Allen Lane: King Penguin, 1979; Christ's Hospital (with G A T Allan), 1986; Master of None: An Autobiography, 1990; Christ's Hospital: An Introductory History, 1990; Editions of Trelawny, Keats, Cobbett, Fenimore Cooper, Lewis Carroll, Marlowe and others. Contributions to: Times Literary Supplement; Daily Telegraph; Yorkshire Post; Quadrant, Australia; Mayfair, Canada. Honours: 5 honorary doctorates, USA institutions; Special Literary Award, Yorkshire Post, 1980. Memberships: Army and Navy Club; Pilgrims. Address: 12 Laurence Mews, Askew Road, London W12 9AT, England.

MORRELL David, b. 24 Apr 1943, Kitchener, Ontario, Canada. Author. m. Donna Maziarz, 10 Oct 1965, 1 son, dec, 1 daughter. Education: BA, University of Waterloo, 1966; MA, 1967, PhD, 1970, Pennsylvania State University. Appointments: Assistant Professor, 1970-74, Associate Professor, 1974-77, Professor of American Literature, 1977-86, University of Iowa. Publications: Fiction: First Blood, 1972; Testament, 1975; Last Reveille, 1977; The Totem, 1979; Blood Oath, 1982; The Hundred-Year Christmas, 1983; The Brotherhood of the Rose, 1984; Rambo: First Blood, Part II, 1985; The Fraternity of the Stone, 1985; The League of Night and Fog, 1987; Rambo III, 1988; The Fifth Profession, 1990; The Covenant of the Flame, 1991; Assumed Identity, 1993; Desperate Measures, 1994; Extreme Denial, 1996; Double Image, 1998. Non-Fiction: John Barth: An Introduction, 1976; Fireflies, 1988. Contributions to: Journals and magazines. Honours: Distingusihed Recognition Award, Friends of American Writers, 1972; Best Novella Awards, Horror Writers of America, 1989, 1991. Memberships: Horror Writers of America; Writers Guild of America. Address: c/o Henry Morrison, PO Box 235, Beford Hills, NY 10507, USA.

MORRIS Christopher Crosby, (Daniel Stryker, Casey Prescott), b. 15 Mar 1946, New York, New York, USA. Defense Policy Analyst. m. Janet Ellen Freeman, 31 Oct 1970. Education: Rockford College, Rockford, Illinois, USA. Appointments: Senior Fellow, US Global Strategy Council, 1989, 1990, 1991, 1992; Adjunct Fellow, Center for Strategic & International Studies, 1992, 1993, 1994. Publications: The Forty Minute, 1985; Medusa, 1986; Assetin Black, 1986, 1987; Hawkeye, 1988; Cobra, 1989; Threshold, 1990; The Little Helliad, 1990; Tempus Unbound, 1990; City of the Edge of Time, 1991; American Warrior, 1992; Trust Territory, 1992; Outpassage, 1993; The Stalk, 1994; Storm Seed, 1995. Contributions to: Op Ed, Defense News, 1995, 1997; Weapons of Mass Protection; Air Force Journal, 1994; Sea Change; The Yacht Magazine. Honours: Helva Award, Best Novel of the Year, Science Fiction Writers of America, 1985. Membership: Pseunomously, Mystery Writers Guild. Literary Agent: Curtis Brown Ltd, Perry Knowlton. Address: PO Box 312, West Hyonnisport, MA 02672, USA.

MORRIS Desmond John, b. 24 Jan 1928, Purton, Wiltshire, England. Zoologist. m. Ramona Baulch, 30 July 1952, 1 son. Education: BSc, Birmingham University, 1951; DPhil, Oxford University, 1954. Publications include: The Biology of Art, 1962; The Big Cats, 1965; Zootime, 1966; The Naked Ape, 1967; The Human Zoo, 1969; Patterns of Reproductive Behaviour, 1970; Intimate Behaviour, 1971; Manwatching, 1977; Animal Days, 1979; The Soccer Tribe, 1981; Bodywatching: A Field Guide to the Human Species, 1985; Catwatching, 1986; Dogwatching, 1986; Catlore, 1987; The Human Nestbuilders, 1988; The Animal Contract, 1990; Animal-Watching, 1990; Babywatching, 1991; Christmas Watching, 1992; The World of Animals, 1993; The Naked Ape Trilogy, 1994; The Human Animal, 1994; The World Guide to Gestures, 1994; Bodytalk: A World Guide to Gestures, 1994; Catworld: A Feline Encyclopedia, 1996; The Human Sexes: A Natural History of Man and Woman, 1997; Illustrated Horsewatching, 1998. Contributions to: Many journals and magazines. Membership: Scientific Fellow, Zoological Society of London. Address: c/o Jonathan Cape, Random Century House, 20 Vauxhall Bridge Road, London SW1V 2SA, England.

MORRIS Jan, b. 2 Oct 1926, Clevedon, Somerset, England. Writer. Education: BA, 2nd Class Honours, 1951, MA, 1961, Christ Church College, Oxford. Publications: As James Morris: Coast to Coast, 1956, 2nd edition, 1962, US edition as I Saw the USA, 1956; The Market of Seleukia, 1957, US edition as Islam Inflamed: A Middle East Picture, 1957; Sultan in Oman, 1957; Coronation Everest, 1958; South African Winter, 1958; The Hashemite Kings, 1959; Venice, 1960, 3rd edition, revised, 1995; South America, 1961; The World Bank: A Prospect, 1963, US edition as The Road to Huddersfield: A Journey to Five Continents, 1963; Cities, 1963; The Outriders: A Liberal View of Britain, 1963; The Presence of Spain, 1964; Oxford, 1965, 3rd edition, 1988; Pax Britannica: The Climax of an Empire, 1968; The Great Port: A Passage through New York, 1969; Places, 1972; Heaven's Command: An Imperial Progress, 1973; Farewell the Trumpets: An Imperial Retreat, 1978. As Jan Morris: Conundrum (autobiography), 1974; Travels, 1976; The Oxford Book of Oxford (editor), 1978; Destinations: Essays from "Rolling Stone", 1980; The Venetian Empire: A Sea Voyage, 1980; The Spectacle of Empire, 1982; A Venetian Bestiary, 1982; Stones of Empire: The Buildings of the Raj, 1984; Among the Cities, 1985; Journeys, 1985; Last Letters from Hav: Notes from a Lost City, 1985; The Matter of Wales: Epic Views of a Small Country, 1985; Scotland: The Place of Visions, 1986; Manhattan, '45, 1987; Hong Kong: Xianggang, 1988; Pleasures of a Tangled Life (autobiography), 1989; Ireland: Your Only Place, 1990; City to City, 1990; Sydney, 1992; Locations, 1993; A Machynlleth Triad, 1994; Fisher's Face, 1995; 50 Years of Europe, 1997; The Princeship of Wales, 1995; The World of Venice, 1995; 50 Years of Europe, 1997. Honours: Commonwealth Fund Fellow, 1953; Cafe Royal Prize, 1957; George Polk Memorial Award, 1960; Heinemann Award, Royal Society of Literature, 1961; Honorary Fellow, Royal Institute of British Architects, 1998; Honorary doctorates, University of Wales, University of Glamorgan. Memberships: Royal Society of Literature, fellow; Yr Academi Gymreig. Address: Trefan Morys, Llanystumdwy, Cricieth, Gwynedd LL52 0LP, Wales.

MORRIS Janet Ellen, (Casey Prescott, Daniel Stryker), b. 25 May 1946, Boston, Massachusetts, USA. Writer. m. 31 Oct 1970. Publications: Silistra Quartet, 1976-78, 1983-84; Dream Dance Trilogy, 1980-83; I the Sun, 1984; Heroes in Hell, 10 volumes, 1984-88; Beyond Sanctuary, 3 volumes, 1985-86; Warlord, 1986; The Little Helliad, 1986; Outpassage, 1987; Kill Ratio, 1987; City at the Edge of Time, 1988; Tempus Vabound, 1989; Target (with David Drake), 1989; Warrior's Edge, 1990; Threshold, 1991; Trust Territory, 1992; American Warrior, 1992; The Stalk, 1994. Contributions to: Various publications. Honour: Hellva Award for Best Novel, 1985. Memberships: Science Fiction Writers of America; Mystery Writers of America; New York Academy of Science; National Intelligence Study Center; Association of Old Crows. Address: c/o Curtis Brown Ltd, 10 Astor Place, New York, NY 10003, USA.

MORRIS Julian. See: **WEST Morris.**

MORRIS Mark, b. 15 June 1963, Bolsover, Derbyshire, England. Full Time Writer. m. Nel Whatmore, 19 May 1990, 1 son, 1 daughter. Education: Trinity and All Saints College, Horsforth, Leeds, England; BA, History and Public Media, 1984. Appointment: Full Time Writer, 1988-. Publications: Novels: Toady, 1989; Stitch, 1991; The Immaculate, 1992; The Secret of Anatomy, 1994; Mr Bad Face, 1996; Longbarrow, 1997; Doctor Who: The Bodysnatchers, 1997; Genesis, 1999; Doctor Who: Deep Blue, 1999; Short Story Collection: Close to the Bone, 1995. Contributions to: Fear; Interzone; Million; SFX; The Third Alternative; The Dark Side; Me; Skeleton Crew; Beyond. Membership: British Fantasy Society. Literary Agent: Caroline Dawnay. Address: Peters, Fraser and Dunlop, 503/4 The Chambers, Chelsea Harbour, London SW10 0XF, England.

MORRIS Mary, b. 14 May 1947, Chicago, Illinois, USA. Writer. m. Larry O'Connor, 20 Aug 1989, 1 daughter. Education: BA, Tufts College, 1969; MA, 1973, MPhil, 1977, Columbia University. Appointments: Teacher, Princeton University, 1980-87, 1991-94, New York University, 1988-94, Sarah Lawrence College, 1994. Publications: Nothing to Declare: Memoirs of a Woman Travelling Alone, 1989; Wall to Wall: From Beijing to Berlin by Rail, 1992; A Mother's Love, 1993; Maiden Voyages, 1993; House Arrest, 1996; The Lifeguard, 1997. Contributions to: Periodicals. Honours: Rome Prize; Guggenheim Fellowship. Memberships: American PEN; Authors Guild; Friends of the American Academy in Rome. Address: Ellen Levine Literary Agency, 15 East 26th Street, New York, NY 10010, USA.

MORRIS Sara. See: **BURKE John Frederick.**

MORRIS Stephen, b. 14 Aug 1935, Smethwick, England. Artist; Poet; Writer. m. 31 Aug 1963, div 1 Jan 1989, 1 son, 2 daughters. Education: Moseley Art School, 1950-53; Fircroft College, 1958-59; Marie Borgs Folk

High School, 1959-60; Cardiff University, 1960-63; Leicester University, 1965-66. Appointments: Assistant Lecturer, 1967-69, Lecturer, 1969-72, Senior Lecturer, 1972-86, Wolverhampton Polytechnic; 40 one-man painting exhibitions. Publications: Poetry: The Revolutionary, 1972; The Kingfisher Catcher, 1974; Death of an Clown, 1976; The Moment of Truth, 1978; Too Long at the Circus, 1980; Rolling Dice, 1986; To Forgive the Unforgivable, 1997; Twelve, 1998. Other; Lord of Death (play), 1963. Contributions to: Guardian; Observer; Peace News; Rolling Stone; Sunday Times; Tribune. Address: 4 Rue Las Cours, Aspiran, L'Herault, 34800, France.

MORRIS Vera. See: **KELLY Tim.**

MORRISON Anthony James (Tony Morrison), b. 5 July 1936, Gosport, England. Television Producer; Writer. m. Elizabeth Marion Davies, 30 July 1965, 1 son, 1 daughter. Education: BSc, University of Bristol, 1959. Appointments: Partner, South American Pictures; Director, Nonesuch Expeditions Ltd. Publications: Steps to a Fortune (co-author), 1967; Animal Migration, 1973; Land Above the Clouds, 1974; The Andes, 1976; Pathways to the Gods, 1978; Lizzie: A Victorian Lady's Amazon Adventure (co-editor), 1985; The Mystery of the Nasca Lines, 1987; Margaret Mee: In Search of Flowers of the Amazon (editor), 1988; QOSQO: Navel of the World, 1995. Address: 48 Station Road, Woodbridge, Suffolk IP12 4AT, England.

MORRISON Bill, b. 22 Jan 1940, Ballymoney, Northern Ireland. Playwright; Theatre Director. Div, 1 son, 1 daughter. Education: LLB, Honours, Queen's University, Belfast, 1962. Appointments: Resident Playwright, Victoria Theatre, Stoke-on-Trent, 1968-71, Everyman Theatre, Liverpool, 1976-79; Associate Director, 1981-83, Artistic Director, 1983-85, Liverpool Playhouse. Publications: Stage Plays: Patrick's Day, 1971; Flying Blind, 1979; Scrap, 1982; Cavern of Dreams (with Carol Ann Duffy), 1984; Be Bop a Lula, 1988; A Love Song for Ulster, 1993; Drive On, 1996. Radio and Stage Plays: Sam Slade is Missing, 1971; The Love of Lady Margaret, 1972; Ellen Cassidy, 1975; The Emperor of Ice Cream, 1977; Blues in a Flat, 1989; The Little Sister, 1990. Radio Plays: The Great Gun-Running Episode, 1973; Simpson and Son, 1977; Maguire, 1978; The Spring of Memory, 1981; Affair, 1991; Three Steps to Heaven, 1992; Waiting for Lefty, 1994; Murder at the Cameo, 1996. Television Plays: McKinley and Sarah, 1974; Joggers, 1979; Potatohead Blues, 1980; Shergar, 1986; A Safe House, 1990; Force of Duty, 1992; C'mon Everybody, 1996; A Love Song for Ulster (French edition), 1999. Honour: Best Programme, Rye Radio Awards, 1981. Address: c/o Alan Brodie Presentations, 211 Piccadilly, London W1V 9LD, England.

MORRISON (Philip) Blake, b. 8 Oct 1950, Burnley, Lancashire, England. Literary Editor; Poet; Writer. m. Katherine Ann Drake, 1976, 2 sons, 1 daughter. Education: BA, University of Nottingham, 1972; PhD, University College, London, 1978. Appointments: Literary Editor, The Observer, 1987-89, The Independent on Sunday, 1990-. Publications: The Movement: English Poetry and Fiction of the 1950's, 1980; Seamus Heaney, 1982; The Penguin Book of Contemporary British Poetry (co-editor), 1982; Dark Glasses, 1984-89; The Ballad of the Yorkshire Ripper and Other Poems, 1987; The Yellow House, 1987; And When Did You Last See Your Father?, 1994. Honours: Somerset Maugham Award, 1984; Dylan Thomas Prize, 1985; J R Ackerley Prize, 1994. Membership: Royal Society of Literature, fellow. Address: c/o The Independent on Sunday, 40 City Road, London EC1Y 2DB, England.

MORRISON Dorothy Jean Allison, b. 17 Feb 1933, Glasgow, Scotland. Author; Lecturer. m. James F T Morrison, 12 Apr 1955, 1 son, 1 daughter. Education: MA, Honours, University of Glasgow. Appointments: Principal Teacher of History, Montrose Academy, 1968-73; Lecturer in History, Dundee College of Education, 1973-83; Advisor to Scottish History series, History at Hand series, Scotland's War series, Scottish TV.

Publications: Old Age, 1972; Young People, 1973; Health and Hospitals, 1973; The Civilian War (with M Cuthbert), 1975; Travelling in China, 1977; The Romans in Britain, 1978, 2nd edition, 1980; Billy Leaves Home, 1979; Story of Scotland (with J Halliday), I, 1979, 1980, II, 1982; The Great War, 1914-18, 1981; Historical Sources for Schools, I Agriculture, 1982; History Around You, 1983; People of Scotland, I, 1983, II, 1985; Ancient Greeks (with John Morrison), 1984; Handbook on Money Management, 1985; Modern China, 1987; The Rise of Modern China, 1988; Montrose Old Church - A History, 1991; Scotland's War, 1992; A Sense of History - Castles, 1994; Ancient Scotland, 1996; The Wars of Independence, 1996. Address: Craigview House, Usan, Montrose, Angus DD10 9SD, Scotland.

MORRISON Robert Hay, b. 11 May 1915, South Yarra, Melbourne, Australia. Poet; Writer; Translator. m. Anna Dorothea Booth, 20 Sept 1939, 1 son, 1 daughter. Publications: Lyrics from Pushkin, 1951; Lyric Images, 1954; A Book of South Australian Verse, 1957; Opus 4, 1971; Australia's Russian Poets, 1971; Some Poems of Verlaine, 1972; Australia's Ukrainian Poets, 1973; Leaf-fall, 1974; America's Russian Poets, 1975; Australia's Italian Poets, 1976; In the Ear of Dusk, 1977; The Secret Greenness and Other Poems, 1978; One Hundred Russian Poems, 1979; Ancient Chinese Odes, 1979; Sonnets from the Spanish, 1980; For the Weeks of the Year, 1981; Poems for an Exhibition, 1985; Poems from My Eight Lives, 1989; Poems from Mandelstam, 1990; All I Have is a Fountain, 1995; The Voice of the Hands, 1996. Contributions to: Newspapers, reviews, and journals. Honours: Prize, International Haiku Contest, 1990; Roberts Memorial Prize, USA, 1994. Address: 6 Bradfield Street, Burnside, South Australia 5066, Australia.

MORRISON Sally, b. 29 June 1946, Sydney, New South Wales, Australia. Writer. 1 son. Education: BSc, Honours, Australian National University, 1970. Publications: Who's Taking You to the Dance? (novel), 1979; I Am a Boat (short stories), 1989; Mad Meg (novel), 1994. Contributions to: Bulletin; Australian Literary Supplement; Overland; Quadrant; Island; Sydney Morning Herald; Age Monthly Review. Honours: Project Assistance Grants, Victorian Ministry of the Arts, 1988, 1993, 1994; Writer's Grants, Australia Council Literary Board, 1990, 1991, 1992; National Book Council Banjo Award for Fiction, 1995. Memberships: Fellowship of Australian Writers; Australian Society of Authors; Victorian Writers Centre. Address: c/o Margaret Connolly and Associates, PO Box 495, Wahroonga, New South Wales 2021, Australia.

MORRISON Toni, b. 18 Feb 1931, Lorain, Ohio, USA. Professor; Author. m. Harold Morrison, 1958, div 1964, 2 sons. Education: BA, Howard University, 1953; MA, Cornell University, 1955. Appointments: Instructor, Texas Southern University, Houston, 1955-57; Howard University, 1957-64; Senior Editor, Random House Inc, New York City, 1965-85; Associate Professor, State Unversity of New York at Purchase, 1971-72; Visiting Lecturer, Yale University, 1976-77; Bard College, 1986-88; Albert Schweitzer Chair in Humanities, State University of New York at Albany, 1984-89; Robert F Goheen Professor in the Council of Humanities, Princeton University 1989-; Clark Lecturer, Trinity College, Cambridge, 1990; Massey Lecturer, Harvard University, 1990. Publications: Fiction: The Bluest Eye, 1969; Sula, 1973; Song of Solomon, 1977; Tar Baby, 1981; Beloved, 1987; Jazz, 1992; Paradise, 1998. Play: Dreaming Emmett, 1986. Other: The Black Book (editor), 1974; Playing in the Dark: Whiteness and the Literary Imagination (lectures), 1992; Race-ing Justice, En-Gendering Power: Essays on Anita Hill, Clarence Thomas, and the Construction of Social Reality (editor), 1992; Nobel Prize Speech, 1994. Honours: Ohioana Book Award, 1975; American Academy and Institute of Arts and Letters Award, 1977; National Book Critics Circle Awards, 1977, 1997; New York State Governor's Arts Award, 1987; Pulitzer Prize in Fiction, 1988; Nobel Prize for Literature, 1993; National Book Foundation Medal, 1995. Memberships: American Academy of Arts

and Letters; American Academy of Arts and Sciences; Authors Guild; Authors League of America; National Council on the Arts. Address: c/o Department of Creative Writing, Princeton University, Princeton, NJ 08544, USA.

MORRISON Wilbur Howard, b. 21 June 1915, Plattsburgh, New York, USA. Freelance Writer. Education: Plattsburgh State Normal School, 1922-30; Plattsburgh High School, 1930-34. Publications: Hellbirds, the Story of the B-29s in Combat, 1960; The Incredible 305th: The Can Do Bombers of World War II, 1962; Wings Over the Seven Seas: US Naval Aviation's Fight for Survival, 1974; Point of No Return: The Story of the Twentieth Air Force, 1979; Fortress Without a Roof: The Allied Bombing of the Third Reich, 1982; Above and Beyond, 1941-45, 1983; Baja Adventure Guide, 1990; The Elephant and the Tiger: The Full Story of the Vietnam War, 1990; Donald W Douglas: A Heart With Wings, 1991; Twentieth Century American Wars, 1993; The Adventure Guide to the Adirondacks and Catskills, 1995; The Adventure Guide to the Sierra Nevada, 1999; Pilots, Man Your Planes: The Story of Naval Aviation, 1999. Honour: Papers, manuscripts, memorabilia, housed in American Heritage Center, University of Wyoming. Address: 2036 East Alvarado Street, Fallbrook, CA 92028, USA.

MORRISS Frank, b. 28 Mar 1923, Pasadena, California, USA. Writer; Teacher. m. Mary Rita Moynihan, 11 Feb 1950, 1 son, 3 daughters. Education: BS, Regis College, Denver, 1943; JD, Georgetown University School of Law, Washington, DC, 1948; Doctor of Letters, Register College of Journalism, Denver, 1953. Appointments: News Editor, Denver Catholic Register, 1960, National Register, 1963; Associate Editor, Vermont Catholic Tribune, 1961; Founding Editor, Twin Circle, 1967; Contributing Editor, Wanderer, St Paul, Minnesota, 1968-. Publications: The Divine Epic, 1973; The Catholic as Citizen, 1976; A Neglected Glory, 1976; Abortion (co-author), 1979; The Forgotten Revelation: A Christmas Celebration (editor and contributor), 1985; A Little Life of Our Lord, 1993. Membership: Fellowship of Catholic Scholars (USA). Address: 3505 Owens Street, Wheat Ridge, CO 80033, USA.

MORRISS Peter, b. 7 Jan 1940, Chesterfield, England. Technical Instructor, NHS. m. Joan Margaret, 7 Sept 1963, 1 son, 1 daughter. Education: Melton Further Education Secondary. Publications: Poetry Anthologies: Poets England, 1992; Fury-United Reformed Church Anthology, 1994; Poetry Club, 1995; Forward Press Anthologies: Arrival Press, 1992, 1993, 1994, 1995, 1996; Poetry Now, 1995, 1996, 1997, 1998; Anchor Books, 1995, 1996, 1997; Triumph House, 1996, 1997, 1998; Poetry Guild, 1997, 1998; Paper Doll, 1999. Contributions to: Fosse Focus; Fosse Health Trust Magazine. Honours: Commendation Poetry Club, 1996, Triumph House, 1997; Editors Choice Award, International Society of Poets, 1996; Editors Choice Award International Library of Poetry, 1998. Address: 16 Solway Close, Melton Mowbray, Leicestershire, LE13 0EF, England.

MORT Graham Robert, b. 11 Aug 1955, Middleton, England. Poet. m. Maggie Mort, 12 Feb 1979, 3 sons. Education: BA, University of Liverpool, 1977; St Martin's College, Lancaster, 1980. Appointment: Creative Writing Course Leader, Open College of the Arts, 1989-. Publications: A Country on Fire; Into the Ashes; A Halifax Cider Jar; Sky Burial; Snow from the North; Starting to Write; The Experience of Poetry, Storylines; Circular Breathing. Contributions to: Numerous literary magazines and journals. Honours: 1st Prizes, Cheltenham Poetry Competition, 1979, 1982; Duncan Lawrie Prizes, Arvon Poetry Competition, 1982, 1992, 1994; Major Eric Gregory Award, 1985; Authors Foundation Award, 1994. Memberships: Society of Authors; National Association of Writers in Education. Address: The Beeches, Riverside, Clapham, Lancaster LA2 8DT, England.

MORTIMER John Clifford (Geoffrey Lincoln) (Sir), b. 21 Apr 1923, London, England. Barrister; Playwright; Novelist. m. (1) Penelope Ruth Fletcher, 1 son, 1 daughter, (2) Penelope Gollop, 2 daughters. Education: Brasenose College, Oxford. Appointments: Called to the Bar, 1948; Queen's Council, 1966; Master of the Bench, Inner Temple, 1975. Publications: Charade, 1947; Rumming Park, 1948; Answer Yes or No, 1950; Like Men Betrayed, 1953; Three Winters, 1956; The Narrowing Stream, 1958; Will Shakespeare, 1977; Rumpole of the Bailey, 1978; The Trials of Rumpole, 1979; Rumpole's Return, 1981; Clinging to the Wreckage (autobiography), 1982; In Character, 1983; Rumpole and the Golden Thread, 1983; Rumpole's Last Case, 1986; Paradise Postponed, 1986; Character Parts (interviews), 1986; Summer's Lease, 1988; Rumpole and the Age of Miracles, 1988; Titmuss Regained, 1989; Rumpole à la Carte, 1990; Rumpole on Trial, 1992; Dunster, 1992; Rumpole and the Angel of Death, 1996; Felix in the Underworld, 1997; The Sound of Trumpets, 1998; Murderers and Other Friends (autobiography), forthcoming. Plays: The Dock Brief and Other Plays, 1959; The Wrong Side of the Park, 1960; Two Stars for Comfort, 1962; The Judge, 1967; Come As You Are, 1970; A Voyage Round My Father, 1972; The Bells of Hell; Villians, 1992. Film Scripts: John and Mary, 1970; Edwin, 1984. Television Series: Rumpole of the Bailey, 9 series; Brideshead Revisited, 1981; Unity Mitford, 1981; The Ebony Tower, 1984; Paradise Postponed, 1986; Summer Lease, 1989; Titmus Regained, 1991; Under the Hammer, 1993; The Sound of Trumpets, 1998. Contributions to: Various periodicals. Honours: Italia Prize, Short Play, 1958; British Academy Writers Award, 1979; Writer of the Year, British Academy of Film and Television Arts, 1980; Book of the Year, Yorkshire Post, 1982; Susquehanna University, 1985; Commander of the Order of the British Empire, 1986; BANF Television Festival Lifetime Achievement Award; Knighted, 1998; Honorary doctorates. Memberships: Howard League for Penal Reform, president, 1991-; Royal Court Theatre, chairman, 1990-; Royal Society of Literature, chairman, 1989-97. Address: c/o The Peter, Fraser and Dunlop Group Ltd, 5th Floor, The Chambers, Chelsea Harbour, Lofts Road, London SW10, England.

MORTIMER Penelope (Ruth), (Penelope Dimont, Ann Temple), b. 19 Sept 1918, Rhyl, Flint, Wales. Author. Education: University College, London. Appointment: Film Critic, The Observer, London, 1967-70. Publications: Johanna, 1947; A Villa in Summer, 1954; The Bright Prison, 1956; With Love and Lizards (with John Mortimer), 1957; Daddy's Gone A-Hunting, US edition as Cave of Ice, 1958; Saturday Lunch with the Brownings, 1960; The Pumpkin Eater, 1962; My Friend Says It's Bullet-Proof, 1967; The Home, 1971; Long Distance, 1974; About Time: An Aspect of Autobiography, 1979; The Handyman, 1983; Queen Elizabeth: A Life of the Queen Mother, 1986; Portrait of a Marriage (screenplay), 1990; About Time Too (autobiography), 1993. Honour: Whitbread Prize, 1979; Literary Agent: Anthony Sheil, 43 Doughty Street, London WC1N 2LF, England. Address: 19 St Gabriel's Road, London NW2 4DS, England.

MORTIMER-DUNN Gloria (Smythe), b. 22 July 1928, Sydney, New South Wales, Australia. Designer; Teacher; Artist. m. Bernard Mortimer-Dunn, 24 Dec 1954. Education: Honours Diploma in Art (Design and Crafts), Sydney Institute of Technology, East Sydney campus. Publications: Pattern Design, 1960, 2nd revised edition, 1980; Fashion Making, 1964; Fashion Design, 1972, 2nd revised edition, 1980; UK Edition as ABC of Fashion, 1975; Pattern Design for Children, 1993, UK Edition as Pattern Design for Children's Clothes, 1996. Address: 15 Roberts Street, Rose Bay, NSW 2029, Australia.

MORTON Colin Todd, b. 26 July 1948, Toronto, Ontario, Canada. Writer; Poet; Editor. m. Mary Lee Bragg, 30 Aug 1969, 1 son. Education: BA, University of Calgary, 1970; MA, University of Alberta, 1979. Appointments: Creative Writing Instructor, Algonquin College, 1993-94; Writer-in-Residence, Concordia College, 1995-96, Connecticut College, 1997. Publications: Oceans Apart (novel), 1995; Various poems. Contributions to: Anthologies, reviews, and journals. Honours: Several poetry and film awards.

Membership: League of Canadian Poets. Address: 40 Grove Avenue, Ottawa, Ontario K1S 3A6, Canada.

MORTON Frederic, b. 5 Oct 1924, Vienna, Austria. Author. m. Marcia Colman, 28 Mar 1957, 1 daughter. Education: BS, College of the City of New York, 1947; MA, New School for Social Research, New York City. Publications: The Rothschilds, 1962; A Nervous Splendour, 1978; The Forever Street, 1987; Thunder at Twilight, 1991. Contributions to: Newspapers and journals. Memberships: Authors Guild; PEN Club. Address: c/o Lantz Office Ltd, 888 Seventh Avenue, New York, NY 10019, USA.

MORTON G L. See: **FRYER Jonathan.**

MORTON Harry Edwin Clive, (Pindar Pete), b. 24 Mar 1931, Gordonvale, Queensland, Australia. Sugar Cane Grower; Writer. m. Desma Baird, 18 Jan 1958, 1 son, 2 daughters. Education: Cairns High School. Publications: The Cane Cutters (with G Burrows), 1986; Smoko the Farm Dog, 1989; By Strong Arms, 1995. Contributions to: Australian, UK and Canadian magazines; Australian, Italian and US anthologies; Short stories and features, Australian Cane Grower, 1960-. Honours: Fellowship of Australian Writers Regional History, 1986; Vaccari Historical Trust, 1987. Address: PO Box 166, Gordonvale, North Queensland 4865, Australia.

MORTON Henry Albert, (Harry Morton), b. 20 July 1925, Gladstone, Manitoba, Canada. Retired Associate Professor of History; Writer. Education: BA, BEd, University of Manitoba; MA, University of Cambridge, England; PhD, University of Otago, New Zealand. Appointment: Pilot, RCAF, 1942-45. Publications: And Now New Zealand, 1969; The Wind Commands, 1975; Which Way New Zealand, 1975; Why Not Together?, 1978; The Whale's Wake, 1982; The Farthest Corner, 1988. Honour: Sir James Wattie Award, Book of the Year, 1976. Memberships: Blenheim Club; New Zealand Society of Authors; Royal New Zealand Airforce Association. Address: 55B Brooklyn Drive, Blenheim, Marlborough, New Zealand.

MOSBY Aline, b. 27 July 1922, Missoula, Montana, USA. Journalist. Education: BA, University of Montana School of Journalism, 1943; Postgraduate studies, Columbia University, 1965. Appointments: Journalist, Time magazine, 1943; Journalist, Foreign Correspondent, United Press International, 1943-85; Freelance Writer, Paris, France, 1985-; Lecturer, Guest Instructor, University of Montana. Publication: The View from Number 13 People's Street. Address: 1 Rue Maître Albert, Paris 75005, France.

MOSCA Julius. See: **HEDMAN Dag Sven Gustav.**

MOSER Paul Kenneth, b. 29 Oct 1957, Bismarck, North Dakota, USA. Philosophy Professor; Chairperson. m. Denise Bilbrey, 20 June 1980, 2 daughters. Education: MA, Western Kentucky University, 1979; MA, PhD, Vanderbilt University, 1982. Appointments: Professor of Philosophy, Loyola University of Chicago, 1983-. Publications: Empirical Justification, 1985; Knowledge & Evidence, 1989; Philosophy after Objectivity, 1998; Ed: A Priori Knowledge, 1987; Ed: Rationality in Action, 1990. Contributions to: American Philosophical Quarterly; Nous; Synthese; Philosophical Studies; Analysis; Canadian Journal of Philosophy. Honours: Critics Choice Award, American Educational Association. Membership: American Philosophical Association. Address: Philosophy Department, Loyola University, 6525 N Sheridan Road, Chicago, IL 60626, USA.

MOSES Daniel (David), b. 18 Feb 1952, Ohsweken, Ontario, Canada. Writer; Dramatist; Poet. Education: BA, Honours, York University, 1975; MFA, University of British Columbia, 1977. Appointments: Instructor in Creative Writing, University of British Columbia, 1990; Instructor in Playwriting, Graduate Drama Centre, University of Toronto, 1992; Resident Artist, Banff Centre for the Arts, 1993; Writer-in-Residence, University of

Western Ontario, 1994, University of Windsor, 1995-96. Publications: Plays: The Dreaming Beauty, 1989; Coyote City, 1991; Almighty Voice and His Wife, 1992; The Indian Medicine Shows, 1995. Poetry: Delicate Bodies, 1980; The White Line. Other: An Anthology of Canadian Native Literature in English (co-editor), 1992. Honours: 1st Prize, Theatre Canada National Playwrighting Competition, 1990; Winner, New Play Centre Playwrighting Competition, 1994. Memberships: League of Canadian Poets; Playwrights Union of Canada; Writers' Guild of Canada; Writers' Union of Canada. Address: 1 Browning Avenue, No 4, Toronto, Ontario, Canada M4K 1V6.

MOSES Elbert Raymond Jr, b. 31 Mar 1908, New Concord, Ohio, USA. Professor Emeritus. m. (1) Mary M Sterrett, 21 Sept 1933, dec 1984, 1 son, (2) Caroline M Chambers, 19 June 1985. Education: AB, University of Pittsburgh; MSc, PhD, University of Michigan. Publications: A Guide to Effective Speaking, 1956, 1957; Phonetics: History and Interpretation, 1964; Three Attributes of God, 1983; Adventure in Reasoning, 1988; Beating the Odds, 1992; The Range, 1993; Where Is Virtue, 1993; Reflections Within, 1993. Contributions to: American Speech and Hearing Magazine; Journal of American Speech; Speech Monographs; Veterans Voices. Honours: Paul Harris Fellow, Rotary, 1971; Certificate, Humanitarian Services, Nicaraguan Government, 1974; Phi Delta Kappa Service Key, 1978; Certificate, Services to Education, 1981; Life Patron, 1985, Grand Ambassador, 1985, American Biographical Institute; World Literary Academy, life fellow, 1987. Membership: International Society of Poets, 1993. Address: 2001 Rocky Dells Drive, Prescott, AZ 86303, USA.

MOSKOWITZ Faye Stollman, b. 31 July 1930, Detroit, Michigan, USA. Professor of English; Writer. m. Jack Moskowitz, 29 Aug 1948, 2 sons, 2 daughters. Education: BA, George Washington University, 1970; MA, 1979; PhD (abd), 1974. Publications: A Leak in the Heart; Whoever Finds This; I Love You; And the Bridge is Love; Her Face in the Mirror: Jewish Women Write about Mothers and Daughters (editor), 1994. Contributions to: New York Times; Washington Post; Chronicle of Higher Education; Womans Day; Feminist Studies; Calyx; Christian Science Monitor; Wigwag Magazine. Honours: Michael Karolyi Foundation: Bread Loaf Scholar; EdPress Merit Award; PEN Syndicated Fiction Award. Membership: Jenny McKean Moore Fund for Writers. Address: 3306 Highland Place, North West, Washington, DC 20008, USA.

MOSLEY Nicholas (Lord Ravensdale), b. 25 June 1923, London, England. Author. Education: Balliol College, Oxford, 1946-47. Publications: Spaces of the Dark, 1951; The Rainbearers, 1955; Corruption, 1957; African Switchback, 1958; The Life of Raymond Raynes, 1961; Meeting Place, 1962; Accident, 1965; Experience and Religion: A Lay Essay in Theology, 1965; Assassins, 1966; Impossible Object, 1968, screenplay, 1975; Natalie, Natalia, 1971; The Assassination of Trotsky, 1972, screenplay, 1973; Julian Grenfell: His Life and the Times of His Death 1888-1915, 1976; Catastrophe Practice, 1979; Imago Bird, 1980; Serpent, 1981; Rules of the Game: Sir Oswald and Lady Cynthia Mosley 1896-1933, 1982; Beyond the Pale: Sir Oswald Mosley and Family 1933-1980, 1983; Judith, 1986; Hopeful Monsters, 1990; Efforts at Truth, 1994; Children of Darkness and Light, 1996. Honour: Whitbread Prize, 1990. Address: 2 Gloucester Crescent, London NW1 7DS, England.

MOSLEY Walter, b. 1952, Los Angeles, California, USA. Writer. m. Joy Kellman. Education: Goddard College; Johnson State College; City College of the City University of New York. Publications: Devil in a Blue Dress, 1990; A Red Death, 1991; White Butterfly, 1992; Black Betty, 1994; R L's Dream, 1995; Gone Fishin', 1996; Always Outnumbered, Always Outgunned: The Socrates Fortlow Stories, 1997. Honour: Shamus Award, Private Eye Writers of America, 1990. Address: c/o W W Norton, 500 Fifth Avenue, New York, NY 10110, USA.

MOSS Norman Bernard, b. 30 Sept 1928, London, England. Journalist; Writer. m. Hilary Sesta, 21 July 1963, 2 sons. Education: Hamilton College, New York City, 1946-47. Appointments: Staff Journalist with newspapers, news agencies and radio networks. Publications: Men Who Play God - The Story of the Hydrogen Bomb, 1968; A British-American Dictionary, 1972, 5th edition, revised, 1994; The Pleasures of Deception, 1976; The Politics of Uranium, 1982; Klaus Fuchs: The Man Who Stole the Atom Bomb, 1987; The Politics of Global Warming, 1992. Honour: Magazine Writer of the Year, Periodical Publishers Association, 1982. Memberships: International Institute of Strategic Studies; Society of Authors. Address: 21 Rylett Crescent, London W12 9RP, England.

MOTION Andrew (Peter), b. 26 Oct 1952, London, England. Poet; Author; Professor of Creative Writing. m. (1) Joanna Jane Powell, 1973, div 1983, (2) Janet Elisabeth Dalley, 1985, 2 sons, 1 daughter. Education: Radley College; BA, 1st Class Honours, 1974, MLitt, 1976, University Oxford College, Oxford. Appointments: Lecturer in English, University of Hull, 1977-81; Editor, Poetry Review, 1981-83; Poetry Editor, 1983-89, Editorial Director, 1985-87, Chatto and Windus; Professor of Creative Writing, University of East Anglia, 1995-. Publications: Poetry: The Pleasure Steamers, 1978, 3rd edition, 1983; Independence, 1981; Secret Narratives, 1983; Dangerous Play, 1984; Natural Causes, 1987; Live in a Life, 1991; The Price of Everything, 1994; Salt Water, 1997. Fiction: The Pale Companion, 1989; Famous for the Creatures, 1991. Other: The Poetry of Edward Thomas, 1981; Philip Larkin, 1982; The Lamberts, 1986; Philip Larkin: A Writer's Life, 1993; William Barnes: Selected Poems (editor), 1994; Keats, 1997. Contributions to: Various publications. Honours: Arvon/Observer Prize, 1982; Rhys Memorial Prize, 1984; Somerset Maugham Award, 1987; Dylan Thomas Award, 1987; Whitbread Award, 1993; Honorary DLitt, University of Hull, 1996. Memberships: Arts Council, chairman, literature advisory panel, 1996-; Royal Society of Literature, fellow. Address: 64 Anson Road, London N7 0AA, England.

MOTT Michael, (Charles Alston), b. 8 Dec 1930, London, England. Professor of English Emeritus; Writer; Poet. m. (1) Margaret Ann Watt, 6 May 1961, dec 1990, 2 daughters, (2) Emma Lou Powers, 16 Nov 1992. Education: Diploma, Central School of Arts and Crafts, London; Intermediate Law Degree, Law Society, London; BA, History of Art, Courtauld and Warburg Institutes, London. Appointments: Editor, Air Freight, 1954-59, Thames and Hudson publishers, 1961-64; Assistant Editor, Adam International Review, 1956-66, The Geographical Magazine, 1964-66; Poetry Editor, The Kenyon Review, 1966-70; Visiting Professor and Writer-in-Residence, Kenyon College, 1966-70, State University of New York at Buffalo, 1968, Concordia University, Montreal, Quebec, 1970, 1974, Emory University, 1970-77, College of William and Mary, 1978-79, 1985-86; Professor of English, 1980-92, Professor Emeritus, 1992-, Bowling Green State University. Publications: Fiction: The Notebooks of Susan Berry, 1962; Master Entrick, 1964; Helmet and Wasps, 1964; The Blind Cross, 1968. Poetry: Absence of Unicorns, Presence of Lions, 1977; Counting the Grasses, 1980; Corday, 1986, 1995; Piero di Cosimo: The World of Infinite Possibility, 1990; Taino, 1992; The Woman and the Sea: Selected Poems, 1999. Non-Fiction: The Seven Mountains of Thomas Merton, 1984. Contributions to: Journals and newspapers. Honours: Governor's Award in Fine Arts, State of Georgia, 1974; Guggenheim Fellowship, 1979-80; Honorary DLitt, St Mary's College, Notre Dame, 1983; Christopher Award, 1984; Ohioana Book Award, 1985; Olscamp Research Award, 1985; Nancy Dasher Book Award, 1985; Phi Beta Kappa, Alpha Chapter, 1994. Memberships: Amnesty International; British Lichen Society; Royal Geographical Society. Address: 122 The Colony, Williamsburg, VA 23185, USA.

MOTTRAM Eric, b. 1920, England. Professor; Poet. Education: University of Cambridge. Appointments: Professor, King's College, University of London, 1983; Other University Appointments in USA, India, Europe. Publications: Inside the Whale, 1970; The He Expression, 1973; Local Movement, 1973; Two Elegies, 1974; Against Tyranny, 1975; 1922 Earth Raids and Other Poems, 1973-75, 1976; Homage to Braque, 1976; Spring Ford, 1977; Tunis, 1977; Elegy 15: Neruda, 1978; Precipe of Fishes, 1979; 1980 Mediate; Elegies, 1981; A Book of Herne, 1975-81; Interrogation Rooms: Poems, 1980-81; Address, 1983; Three Letters, 1984; The Legal Poems, 1984; Selected Poems, 1989; Peace Projects and Brief Novels, 1989; Studies and Editions of American Literature. Address: Department of English, King's College, University of London, The Strand, London WC2R 2LS, England.

MOUFFE Chantal, b. 17 June 1943, Baulet, Belgium. Political Philosopher. m. Ernesto Laclau, 1 May. Education: Licence en Philosophy, University of Louvain, 1965; MA, Politics, Essex, 1975. Appointments: Lecturer in Philosophy, National University of Colombia, 1967-73, Collège International de Philosophie, Paris, 1969-95, Centre for the Study of Democracy, University of Westminster, London, 1995-. Publications: Routledge and Kegan Paul, 1974; Hegemony and Socialist Strategy, 1985; Dimensions F Radical Democracy (editor), 1992; The Return of the Political Deconstruction and Pragmatism, 1996; The Challenge of Carl Schmitt, 1999. Address: 116 Fordwych Road, London NW2 3NL, England.

MOULD Daphne Desiree Charlotte Pochin, b. 15 Nov 1920, Salisbury, England. Author. Education: BSc, 1st Class Honours, Geology, 1943, PhD, Geology, 1946, University of Edinburgh. Publications: The Celtic Saints, 1956; The Irish Saints (critical biographies), 1963; The Aran Islands, 1972; Ireland from the Air, 1972; Irish Monasteries, 1976; Captain Roberts of the Sirius, 1988; Discovering Cork, 1991. Contributions to: Numerous publications; Broadcaster on Radio Telefis Eireann. Honour: LLD, National University of Ireland, 1993. Membership: Aircraft Owners and Pilots Association. Address: Aherla House, Aherla, County Cork, Ireland.

MOUNT William Robert Ferdinand, b. 2 July 1939, London, England. Novelist; Journalist; Editor. m. Julia Lucas, 20 July 1968, 2 sons, 1 daughter. Education: BA, Christ Church, Oxford, 1961. Appointments: Political Correspondent, 1977-82, Literary Editor, 1984-85, Spectator; Head of Prime Minister's Policy Unit, 1982-84; Columnist, Daily Telegraph, 1985-90; Editor, Times Literary Supplement, 1991-. Publications: Very Like a Whale, 1967; The Theatre of Politics, 1972; The Man Who Rode Ampersand, 1975; The Clique, 1978; The Subversive Family, 1982; The Selkirk Strip, 1987; Of Love and Asthma, 1991; The British Constitution Now, 1992; Umbrella, 1994; The Liquidator, 1995; Jem and Sam, 1998. Contributions to: Spectator; Encounter; National Interest; Politique Internationale. Honour: Hawthornden Prize, 1992. Address: 17 Ripplevale Grove, London N1, England.

MOUNTFIELD David. See: **GRANT Neil.**

MOUNTROSE Phillip, b. 21 Nov 1950, Buffalo, New York, USA. Teacher; Writer. m. Jane Mountrose, 21 June 1981. Education: BA, SUNY at Stony Brook, 1972; MFA, TV Production, UCLA, 1976; MEd, Boston State College, 1980; Special Education, Credential Sacramento State College, 1994. Publications: Getting Thru to Kids: Problem Solving with Children Ages 6 to 18, 1997; Audiobook, 2 tapes, Getting Thru to Kids, 1998; Tips and Tools for Getting Thru to Kids, 1999. Contributions to: Concepts, Health, Wealthy & Wise; many parenting publications including Family News, Space Coast Parent, Washington Families, Our Kids Atlanta, Boston Parents' Paper, Brooklyn & Staten Island Parent Baton Rouge Parents' Magazine. Honours: Parent Council Selection, 1997; Best Book Award Sacramento Publishers Association, 1998. Membership: Sacramento Publishers Association. Address: PO Box 41152, Sacramento, CA 95841-0152, USA.

MOURE Erin, b. 17 Apr 1955, Calgary, Alberta, Canada. Poet. Education: University of Calgary; University of British Columbia. Publications: Empire, York Street, 1979; The Whisky Vigil, 1981; Wanted Alive, 1983; Domestic Fuel, 1985; Furious, 1988; WSW (West South West), 1989; Sheepish Beauty, Civilian Love, 1992; The Green World: Selected Poems, 1994; Search Procedures, 1996. Contributions to: Various publications. Honour: Governor-General's Award for Poetry, 1988. Memberships: League of Canadian Poets; Writers' Union of Canada. Address: c/o League of Canadian Poets, 54 Wolseley Street, 3rd Floor, Toronto, Ontario M5T 1A5, Canada.

MOWAT David, b. 16 Mar 1943, Cairo, Egypt (British citizen). Playwright. Education: BA, New College, Oxford, 1964. Publications: Jens, 1965; Pearl, 1966; Anna Luse, 1968; Dracula, 1969; Purity, 1969; The Normal Woman, and Tyypi, 1970; Adrift, 1970; The Others, 1970; Most Recent Least Recent, 1970; Inuit, 1970; The Diabolist, 1971; John, 1971; Amalfi (after Webster), 1972; Phoenix-and-Turtle, 1972; Morituri, 1972; My Relationship with Jayne, 1973; Come, 1973; Main Sequence, 1974; The Collected Works, 1974; The Memory Man, 1974; The Love Maker, 1974; X to C, 1975; Kim, 1977; Winter, 1978; The Guise, 1979; Hiroshima Nights, 1981; The Midnight Sun, 1983; Carmen, 1984; The Almas, 1989; Jane, or The End of the World, 1992. Radio Plays. Honour: Arts Council Bursaries. Address: 7 Mount Street, Oxford OX2 6DH, England.

MOXHAM Gwenyth Constance, b. 3 Sept 1943, Adelaide, South Australia, Australia. Teacher; Writer. m. Kenneth Ewing Moxham, 14 May 1966, 1 son, 1 daughter. Education: Associate in Arts and Education, 1965, BA, 1966, University of Adelaide; Diploma of Teaching, Adelaide Teachers College, 1966. Publication: They Built South Australia: Engineers, Technicians, Manufacturers, Contractors and their Work (with D A Cumming), 1986. Contribution to: Australian Dictionary of Biography, Vol 4, 1940-1980, Sir Claude Gibb, 1996. Memberships: Australian Reading Association; Australian College of Education. Address: 6 Barr Smith Drive, Urrbrae, South Australia 5064, Australia.

MOYERS Bill, b. 5 June 1934, Hugo, Oklahoma, USA. Journalist; Broadcaster. m. Judith Davidson, 18 Dec 1954, 2 sons, 1 daughter. Education: BJ, University of Texas, 1956; Graduate Studies, University of Edinburgh, 1956-57; MTh, Southwestern Baptist Theological Seminary, 1959. Appointments: Personal Assistant, Senator Lyndon B Johnson, 1960; Associate Director, 1961-62, Deputy Director, 1963, Peace Corps; Special Assistant, 1963-67, Press Secretary, 1965-67, President Lyndon B Johnson; Publisher, Newsday, Garden City, New York, 1967-70; Editor-in-Chief, Bill Moyers Journal, Public-TV, 1971-76, 1978-81; Chief Correspsondent, CBS Reports, CBS-TV, 1976-78; Senior News Analyst, CBS News, CBS-TV, 1981-86; Founder and Executive Director, Public Affairs TV Inc, 1987-; Various special series, PBS-TV. Publications: Listening to America, 1971; Report from Philadelphia, 1987; The Secret Government, 1988; Joseph Campbell and the Power of the Myth, 1988; A World of Ideas, 1989, 2nd edition, 1990; Healing and the Mind, 1993; Genesis, 1996. Honours: George Foster Peabody Awards, 1976, 1980, 1985, 1986, 1988, 1989, 1990; DuPont-Columbia University; George Polk Awards, 1981, 1986; Communicator of the Decade Award, Religious Communications Congress, 1990; TV Hall of Fame, 1995; Religious Liberty Award, American Jewish Committee, 1995; Charles Frankel Prize on the Humanities, 1995; Career Achievement Award, International Documentary Association; Nelson Mandela Award for Health and Human Rights, 1996; Numerous Emmy Awards. Membership: American Academy of Arts and Sciences, fellow; Society of American Historians; American Philosophical Society, fellow. Address: c/o Public Affairs TV Inc, 356 West 58th Street, New York, NY 10019, USA.

MOYES Gertrude Patricia, b. 19 Jan 1923, Bray, Ireland. Author. m. (1) John Moyes, 29 Mar 1952, (2) John Haszard, 13 Oct 1962. Publications: Henry Tibbett mystery series, 1959-89; Several other books, 1989-95. Contributions to: Magazines. Honour: Edgar Special Scroll, Mystery Writers of America. Memberships: Authors Guild; Crime Writers Association; Detection Club. Address: Po Box 1, Virgin Gorda, British Virgin Islands.

MOYNIHAN Daniel Patrick, b. 16 Mar 1927, Tulsa, Oklahoma, USA. United States Senator; Writer. m. Elizabeth Therese Brennan, 29 May 1955, 2 sons, 1 daughter. Education: City College of New York, 1943; BA, Tufts University, 1948; MA, 1949, PhD, 1961, Fletcher School of Law and Diplomacy. Appointments: Special Assistant, 1961-62, Executive Assistant, 1962-63, to the US Secretary of Labor; Assistant Secretary of Labor, 1963-65; Fellow, Center for Advanced Studies, Wesleyan University, 1965-66; Professor of Education and Urban Politics, 1966-73, Senior Member, 1966-77, Professor of Government, 1973-77, Kennedy School of Government, Harvard University; Assistant for Urban Affairs, 1969-70, Counsellor, 1969-70, Consultant, 1971-73, to the President of the US; US Ambassador to India, 1973-75; US Permanent Representative to the United Nations, 1975-76; US Senator (Democrat) from the State of New York, 1977-. Publications: Beyond the Melting Pot (with Nathan Glazer), 1963; The Defenses of Freedom: The Public Papers of Arthur J Goldberg (editor), 1966; Equal Educational Opportunity (co-author), 1969; On Understanding Poverty: Perspectives for the Social Sciences (editor), 1969; The Politics of a Guaranteed Income, 1973; Coping: On the Practice of Government, 1974; Ethnicity: Theory and Experience (editor with Nathan Glazer), 1975; A Dangerous Place (with S Weaver), 1978; Counting Our Blessings: Reflections on the Future of America, 1980; Loyalties, 1984; Family and Nation, 1986; Came the Revolution: Argument in the Reagan Era, 1988; On the Law of Nations, 1990; Pandaemonium: Ethnicity in International Politics, 1993. Contributions to: Professional journals. Honours: Meritorious Service Award, US Department of Labor, 1965; Centennial Medal, Syracuse University, 1969; International League for Human Rights Award, 1975; John LaFarge Award for Interracial Justice, 1980; Medallion, State University of New York at Albany, 1984; Henry Medal, Smithsonian Institution, 1985; SEAL Medallion, Central Intelligence Agency, 1986; Laetare Medal, University of Notre Dame, 1992; Thomas Jefferson Award, 1993; Numerous honorary doctorates. Address: c/o United State Senate, Washington DC 20510, USA.

MOYNIHAN John Dominic, b. 31 July 1932, London, England. Journalist; Author. 1 son, 2 daughters. Education: Felsted School, Essex; Chelsea School of Art. Appointments: Bromley Mercury, 1953-54; Evening Standard, 1954-63; Daily Express, 1963-64; The Sun, 1964-65; Assistant Literary Editor, Sports Correspondent, Sunday Telegraph, 1965-89; Freelance, The Sunday Telegraph, The Sunday Times, The Independent on Sunday, The Daily Express, 1989-. Publications: The Soccer Syndrome, 1966, 2nd edition, 1987; Not All a Ball (autobiography), 1970; Park Football, 1970; Football Fever, 1974; Soccer, 1974; The Chelsea Story, 1982; The West Ham Story, 1984; Soccer Focus, 1989; Kevin Keegan: Black and White, 1993. Contributions to: Newspapers and magazines. Memberships: Society of Authors; Sports Writers Association; Football Writers Association; Lawn Tennis Writers Association; Chelsea Arts Club; Badminton Writers Association. Address: 102 Ifield Road, London SW10, England.

MPHAHLELE Ezekiel, (Es'kia Mphahlele), b. 17 Dec 1919, Pretoria, South Africa. Author; Professor of African Literature. Education: MA, University of South Africa, Pretoria, 1956. Appointments: Teacher of English and Afrikaans, Orlando High School, Johannesburg, 1942-52; Fiction Editor, Drum magazine, Johannesburg, 1955-57; Lecturer in English Literature, University of Ibadan, Nigeria, 1957-61; Director of African Programmes, International Association for Cultural Freedom, Paris, 1961-63; Director, Chem-chemi Creative Centre, Nairobi, Kenya, 1963-65; Lecturer, University College, Nairobi, 1965-66, University of Denver, 1966-74, University of Pennsylvania, 1974-77; Professor of African Literature,

University of the Witwatersrand, Johannesburg, 1979-. Publications: Man Must Live and Other Stories, 1947; Down Second Avenue (autobiography), 1959; The Living Dead and Other Stories, 1961; The African Image (essays), 1962, 2nd edition, 1974; Modern African Stories (editor with E Komey), 1964; African Writing Today (editor), 1967; In Corner B and Other Stories, 1967; The Wanderers (novel), 1971; Voices in the Whirlwind and Other Essays, 1972; Chirundu (novel), 1979; The Unbroken Song, 1981; Bury Me at the Marketplace, 1984; Father Come Home, 1984; Afrika My Music: An Autobiography 1957-1983, 1986. Honours: Honarary Doctorate of Literature and Philosophy, Universities of Pennsylvania and Colorada; Natal Rhodes, Witwatersrand, South Africa, The North, Venda, 1986-1987. Address: African Studies Institute, University of the Witwatersrand, Johannesburg 2001, South Africa.

MUAMBA Muepu, b. 23 Nov 1946, Tshilundu, Belgian Congo. Journalist; Writer; Poet. Education: Institut St Ferdinand, Jernappes, Belgium. Appointments: Literary Director, Editions Les Presses Africaines, Kinshasa; Literary Critic, Salongo and Elima. Publications: Ventre Creux (short stories); Afrika in eigener Sache (essays with Jochen Klicker and Klaus Paysan), 1980; Devoir d'ingérence, nouvelles et poèmes, 1988; Ma Terre d'O (poems), forthcoming. Contributions to: Anthologies and other publications. Memberships: Maison Africaine de la Poésie Internationale, Dakar; Royal African Society, London; Société Francaise des Gens de Lettres, Paris; Union Internationale des Journalistes et de la Presse de la Langue Francaise, Paris. Address: c/o M Kohlert-Neméth, Schaumainkai 99, 6000 Frankfurt am Main 70, Germany.

MUDGEON Apeman. See: MITCHELL Adrian.

MUEHL Lois Baker, b. 29 Apr 1920, Oak Park, Illinois, USA. Retired Associate Professor of Rhetoric; Writer; Poet. m. Siegmar Muehl, 15 Apr 1944, 2 sons, 2 daughters. Education: BA, English, Oberlin College, 1941; MA, English, Education, University of Iowa, 1965. Publications: My Name is ..., 1959; Worst Room in the School, 1961; The Hidden Year of Devlin Bates, 1967; Winter Holiday Brainteasers, 1979; A Reading Approach to Rhetoric, 1983; Trading Cultures in the Classroom (with Siegmar Muehl), 1993; Talktables Tales, 1993. Other: Poems. Contributions to: Scholarly journals and to general magazines. Honours: Phi Beta Kappa, 1941; Old Gold Creative Fellowship, 1970; Community Service Commendation, Merced, California, 1984; Grand Prize, Poetry Guild Contest, 1997. Memberships: Iowa Poetry Association; National League of American Pen Women; University Women's Writers Group. Address: 430 Crestview Avenue, Iowa City, IA 52245, USA.

MUELLER Lisel, b. 8 Feb 1924, Hamburg, Germany (US citizen, 1945). Poet; Writer; Translator. m. Paul E Mueller, 15 June 1943, 2 daughters. Education: BA, University of Evansville, 1944; Graduate Studies, Indiana University, 1950-53. Appointments: Instructor in Poetry, Elmhurst College, 1969-72; Associated with Poets in the Schools Programme, 1972-77; Visiting Professor, Goddard College and Warren Wilson College, 1977-86. Publications: Poetry: Dependencies, 1965; Life of a Queen, 1970; The Private Life, 1976; Voices From the Forest, 1977; The Need to Hold Still, 1980; Second Language, 1986; Waving From Shore, 1989; Alive Together, 1996. Other: Learning to Play by Ear (essays and poetry), 1990. Contributions to: Anthologies and journals. Honours: Robert M Ferguson Memorial Award, Friends of Literature, 1966; Helen Bullis Awards, 1974, 1977; Lamont Poetry Selection, 1975; Emily Clark Balch Award, 1976; National Book Award, 1981; Honorary Doctorate, Lake Forest College, 1985; National Endowment for the Arts Fellowship, 1990; Carl Sandburg Award, 1990; Pulitzer Prize for Poetry, 1997. Address: 27240 North Longwood Road, Lake Forest, IL 60045, USA.

MUGGESON Margaret Elizabeth, (Margaret Dickinson, Everatt Jackson), b. 30 Apr 1942, Gainsborough, Lincolnshire, England. Writer; Partner in

Retail Store. m. Dennis Muggeson, 19 Sept 1964, 2 daughters. Education: Lincoln College of Technology, 1960-61. Publications: Pride of the Courtneys, 1968; Brackenbeck, 1969; Portrait of Jonathan, 1970; The Road to Hell (as Everatt Jackson), 1975; Abbeyford Trilogy, 1981; Lifeboat!, 1983; Beloved Enemy, 1984; Plough the Furrow, 1994; Sow the Seed, 1995; Reap the Harvest, 1996; The Miller's Daughter, 1997; Chaff Upon the Wind, 1998; The Fisher Lass, forthcoming. Membership: Romantic Novelists Association. Address: 17 Seacroft Drive, Skegness, Lincolnshire PE 25 3AP, England.

MUHRINGER Doris Agathe Annemarie, b. 18 Sept 1920, Graz, Austria. Poet; Writer. Publications: Gedichte I, 1957, II, 1969, III, 1976, IV, 1984, Tag, mein Jahr (with H Valencak), 1983; Das hatten die Ratten vom Schatten: Ein Lachbuch, 1989, 2nd edition, 1992; Reisen wir (selected poems), 1995; Späte Gedichte, 1999. Contributions to: Numerous literary magazines, domestic and foreign. Honours: Georg Trakl Prize, 1954; Award of Achievement, Vienna, 1961; Lyric Prize of Steiermark, 1973; Austrian State Scholarship, 1976; Award of Achievement, Board of Austrian Litera-Mechana, 1984; Grosser Literturpreis des Landes Steiermark, 1985. Memberships: Association of Austrian Writers; Kogge; PEN; Poium. Address: Goldeggasse 1, A-1040 Vienna, Austria.

MUIR Richard, b. 18 June 1943, Yorkshire, England. Author; Photographer. Education: 1st Class Honours, Geography, 1967, PhD, 1970, University of Aberdeen. Appointment: Editor, National Trust Regional Histories and Countryside Commission National Park Series. Publications: Over 25 books, including: Modern Political Geography, 1975; Hedgerows: Their History and Wildlife (with N Muir), 1987; Old Yorkshire, 1987; The Countryside Encyclopaedia, 1988; Fields (with Nina Muir), 1989; Portraits of the Past, 1989; Barleycorn (fiction), 1989; The Dales of Yorkshire, 1991; The Villages of England, 1992; The Coastlines of Britain, 1993; Political Geography: A New Introduction, 1997; The Yorkshire Countryside: A Landscape History, 1997; Approaches to Landscape, forthcoming. Contributions to: Academic journals and general periodicals. Honour: Yorkshire Arts Literary Prize, 1982-83. Address: Waterfall Close, Station Road, Birstwith, Harrogate, Yorkshire, England.

MUJICA Barbara, b. 25 Dec 1943, Los Angeles, California, USA. Professor of Spanish; Author; Poet. m. Mauro E Mujica, 26 Dec 1966, 1 son, 2 daughters. Education: AB, University of California at Los Angeles, 1964; MA, Middlebury Graduate School, Paris, 1965; PhD, Honours, New York University, 1974. Appointments: Teacher of French, University of California at Los Angeles Extension Division, 1963-64; Associate Editor of Modern Languages, Harcourt Brace Jovanovich, New York City, 1966-73; Instructor, 1973-74, Assistant Professor of Romance Languages, 1974, Bernard Baruch College of the City University of New York; Assistant Professor, 1974-79, Associate Professor, 1979-91, Professor of Spanish, 1991-, Georgetown University. Publications: Scholarly: Readings in Spanish Literature (editor with Anthony Zahareas), 1975; Calderón's Characters: An Existential Point of View, 1983; Expanding the Curriculum in Foreign Language Classes: Spanish and Contemporary Affairs (with William Cressey and Mark Goldin), 1983; Iberian Pastoral Characters, 1986; Texto y espectáculo: Selected Proceedings of the Symposium on Spanish Golden Age Theater, March, 1987, 1989; Texto y vida: Introducción a la literatura española, 1990; Antología de literatura española, Vol I, La Edad Media (with Amanda Curry), 1991, Vol II, Renacimiento y Siglo de Oro, 1991, Vol III, Siglos XVIII y XIX (with Eva Florensa), 1999; Et in Arcadia Ego: Essays on Death in the Pastoral Novel (with Bruno Damiani), 1990; Texto y vida: Introducción a la literatura hispanoamericana, 1992; Looking at the Comedia in the Year of the Quincentennial (editor with Sharon Voros), 1993; Premio Nóbel: Once grandes escritores del mundo hispánico (editor), 1997; Books of the Americas: Reviews and Interviews from Americas Magazine, 1990-1991, 1997; El texto puesto en escena (editor with Anita Stoll),

1999. Other: The Deaths of Don Bernardo (novel), 1990; Sanchez across the Street (short stories), 1997; Far from My Mother's Home (short stories), 1999; Affirmative Actions (novel), 1999. Contributions to: Anthologies and other publications; Short stories; Articles and reviews in scholarly publications; Articles in the popular press. Honours: Poets and Writers Reognition for Fiction, New York, 1984; Pushcart Prize Nomination for Fiction, 1989; One of Best Fifty Op Ed Pieces of the Decade, New York Times, 1990; Winner, E L Doctorow International Fiction Contest, 1992; Pangolin Prize for Best Short Story of 1998. Memberships: American Association of Teachers of Spanish and Portuguese; American Association of University Professors; American Council on the Teaching of Foreign Languages; Association for Hispanic Classical Theater, board of directors; Feministas Unidas; Modern Language Association; Washington Independent Writers; Writer's Center; South Atlantic Modern Language Association; Golden Age Division, secretary, 1999, president, 2000. Address: c/o Department of Spanish and Portuguese, Georgetown University, Box 571039, Washington, DC 20057, USA.

MUKHERJEE Bharati, b. 27 July 1940, Calcutta, India (Canadian citizen, 1972). Associate Professor; Author. m. Clarke Blaise, 19 Sept 1963, 2 sons. Education: BA, University of Calcutta, 1959; MA, University of Baroda; MA, PhD, University of Iowa. Appointment: Associate Professor, McGill University, Montreal, Canada, 1966-. Publications: Tiger's Daughter, 1972; Wife, 1975; Kautilya's Concept of Diplomacy, 1976; Days and Nights in Calcutta (with Clark Blaise), 1977; The Middleman, 1989. Honour: National Book Critics Circle Award, 1988. Address: Department of English, McGill University, Montreal, Quebec, Canada.

MULDOON Paul, b. 20 June 1951, Portadown, County Armagh, Northern Ireland. Poet; Writer; Dramatist; Professor in the Humanities. Education: BA, English Language and Literature, Queen's University, Belfast, 1973. Appointments: Producer, 1973-78, Senior Producer, 1978-85, Radio Arts Programmes, Television Producer, 1985-86, BBC Northern Ireland; Judith E Wilson Visiting Fellow, University of Cambridge, 1986-87; Creative Writing Fellow, University of East Anglia, 1987; Lecturer, Columbia University, 1987-88; Lecturer, 1987-88, 1990-95, Director, Creative Writing Programme, 1993-, Howard G B Clark Professor in the Humanities, 1998-, Princeton University; Writer-in-Residence, 92nd Street Y, New York City, 1988; Roberta Holloway Lecturer, University of California at Berkeley, 1989; Visiting Professor, University of Massachusetts, Amberst, 1989-90, Bread Loaf School of English, 1997-. Publications: Poetry: Knowing My Place, 1971; New Weather, 1973; Spirit of Dawn, 1975; Mules, 1977; Names and Addresses, 1978; Immram, 1980; Why Brownlee Left, 1980; Out of Siberia, 1982; Quoof, 1983; The Wishbone, 1984; Meeting the British, 1987; Madoc: A Mystery, 1990; Incantata, 1994; The Prince of the Quotidian, 1994; The Annals of Chile, 1994; Kerry Slides, 1996; New Selected Poems, 1968-94, 1996; Hopewell Haiku, 1997; The Bangle (Slight Return), 1998; Hay, 1998. Theatre: Monkeys (television play), 1989; Shining Brow (opera libretto), 1993; Six Honest Serving Men (play), 1995; Bandanna (opera libretto), 1999. Essays: To Ireland, I, 1999. Translator: The Astrakhan Cloak, by Nuala Ni Dhomhnaill, 1993; The Birds, by Aristophanes (with Richard Martin), 1999. Editor: The Scrake of Dawn, 1979; The Faber Book of Contemporary Irish Poetry, 1986; The Essential Byron, 1989; The Faber Book of Beasts, 1997. Children's Books: The O-O's Party, 1981; The Last Thesaurus, 1995; The Noctuary of Narcissus Batt, 1997. Contributions to: Anthologies and other publications. Honours: Eric Gregory Award, 1972; Sir Geoffrey Faber Memorial Awards, 1980, 1991; Guggenheim Fellowship, 1990; T S Eliot Prize for Poetry, 1994; American Academy of Arts and Letters Award, 1996; Irish Times Poetry Prize, 1997. Memberships: Aosdana; Poetry Society of Great Britain, president, 1996-; Royal Society of Literature, fellow. Address: c/o Faber and Faber, 3 Queen Square, London WC1N, England.

MULISCH Harry, b. 29 July 1927, Haarlem, Netherlands. Novelist; Poet; Dramatist. Education: Haarlem Lyceum. Publications: 22 books of fiction, 1952-92, poetry collections and plays. Honour: Knight, Order of Orange Nassau, 1977. Address: Van Miereveldstraat 1, 1071 DW Amsterdam, Netherlands.

MULLIGAN Barbara Laird Welch, b. 29 Jan 1935, Orangeburg, South Carolina, USA. Artist; Writer; Editor. m. George Richard, 15 June 1957, 2 sons, 2 daughters. Education: BS, Home Economics and Nutrition, Florida State University, 1957; MS, Political Science, Troy State University, 1979; Registered Dietitian of Florida. Appointments: Teacher, Bridgewater (NJ) School Board, 1966-70; Teacher, Administrator, Bay County (FL) School Board, 1970-92; Artist, Art Zone, Panama City, Florida, 1992-. Publications: Editor, Illustrator, Manatee, 1992, Black's Island, 1992, Manatee Christmas, 1992. Contributions to: Journals, magazines, quarterlies, reviews and newspapers. Membership: Panhandle Writers Guild, co-founder, 1984-99. Address: 1016 Buena Vista Boulevard, Panama City, FL 32401, USA.

MULLIN Chris(topher John), b. 12 Dec 1947, Chelmsford, England. Member of Parliament; Writer. m. Nguyen Thi Ngoc, 14 Apr 1987, 1 daughter. Education: LLB, University of Hull. Appointments: Subeditor, BBC World Service, 1974-78; Editor, Tribune, 1982-84; Member of Parliament, Labour Party, Sunderland South, 1987-. Publications: Novels: A Very British Coup, 1982; The Last Man Out of Saigon, 1986; The Year of the Fire Monkey, 1991. Non-Fiction: Error of Judgement: The Truth About the Birmingham Bombings, 1986, revised edition, 1996. Address: c/o House of Commons, London SW1A 0AA, England.

MULVIHILL Maureen Esther, b Detroit, Michigan, USA. Writer; Scholar; Teacher. m. Daniel R Harris, 18 June 1983. Education: BPHil, Monteith College, 1966; MA, Wayne State University, 1968; PhD, University of Wisconsin at Madison, 1983; Postdoctoral Studies, Yale Centre for British Art, 1986, Columbia University Rare Book School, 1986. Appointments: Corporate Communications Director, Gruntal & Co Inc, New York City, 1983-85; Communications Consultant, New York City, 1985-; Visiting Scholar and Lecturer, various colleges and universities. Publications: Essays in Restoration, 1987; British Women Writers, 1989; Scriblerian, 1989; Encyclopedia of Continental Women Writers, 1991; Curtain Calls, 1991; Poems by Ephelia, 1992; Studies in 18th-Century Culture, 1992; Encyclopedia of British Women Writers, 1998. Honours: National Endowment for the Humanities Fellowship; Hutner Foundation Awards, Princeton, 1992, 1995, 1997; Awards and scholarships. Memberships: American Society for 18th-Century Studies; Bibliographical Society of America; Institute for Research in History; Modern Language Associaton; Princeton Research Forum; Society for Textual Scholarship; SHARP Joyce Society. Address: 45 Plaza Street West, Park Slope, Brooklyn, NY 11217, USA.

MUNONYE John (Okechukwu), b. 22 Apr 1929, Akokwa, Nigeria. Novelist. m. Regina Nwokeji, 1957, 1 son, 1 daughter. Education: Cert Ed, University of London, 1953. Appointments: Chief Inspector of Education, East Central State, 1973-76, Imo State, 1976-77. Publications: The Only Son, 1966; Obi, 1969; Oil Man of Obange, 1971; A Wreath for Maidens, 1973; A Dancer of Fortune, 1974; Bridge to a Wedding, 1978. Short Stories: Silent Child, 1973; Pack Pack Pack, 1977; Man of Wealth, 1981; On a Sunday Morning, 1982; Rogues, 1985. Honour: Member, Order of the Niger, 1980. Address: PO Box 436 Orlu, Imo State, Nigeria.

MUÑOZ Willy O, b. 6 Apr 1949, Cochabamba, Bolivia. University Professor. Education: BA, Spanish, Loras College, 1972; MA, Spanish, 1974, PhD, Spanish, 1979, University of Iowa. Appointments: Teaching Assistant, Spanish, University of Iowa, USA, 1972-76, 1978; Instructor in Spanish, Saint Ambrose College, Iowa, 1976-77, Clarke College, Iowa, 1978-79; Assistant Professor of Spanish, 1984-88, Associate Professor of Spanish, 1988-94, Professor of Spanish, 1994-, Kent State University, Ohio. Publications: Teatro boliviano contemporáneo, 1981; El personaje femenino en la narrativa de escritores hispanoamericanas, 1992. Contributions to: 60 articles on contemporary Spanish-American writers and on Bolivian theatre and film in literary journals. Honour: 1st Prize in Essay, XIV Franz Tamayo Annual Literary Contest, Bolivia, 1980. Memberships: American Association of Teachers of Spanish and Portuguese; Asociación de Hispanistas; Instituto Internacional de Teoría y Crítica de Teatro Latinoamericano; Instituto International de Literature Iberoamericana. Address: Modern and Classical Language Studies, Kent State University, Kent, OH 44242, USA.

MUNRO Alice, b. 10 July 1931, Wingham, Ontario, Canada. Author. m. (1) James Armstrong Munro, 29 Dec 1951, div 1976, 3 daughters, (2) Gerald Fremlin, 1976. Education: BA, University of Western Ontario, 1952. Publications: Dance of the Happy Shades, 1968; A Place for Everything, 1970; Lives of Girls and Women, 1971; Something I've Been Meaning to Tell You, 1974; Who Do You Think You Are?, 1978, US and British editions as The Beggar Maid: Stories of Flo and Rose, 1984; The Moons of Jupiter, 1982; The Progress of Love, 1986; Friend of My Youth, 1990; Open Secrets, 1994; Selected Stories, 1996. Honours: Governor-General's Awards for Fiction, 1968, 1978, 1986; Guardian Booksellers Award, 1971; Honorary DLitt, University of Western Ontario, 1976; Marian Engel Award, 1986; Canada-Australia Literary Prize, 1994; Lannan Literary Award, 1995; W H Smith Literary Award, 1996. Address: PO Box 1133, Clinton, Ontario N0M 1L0, Canada.

MUNRO David Mackenzie, b. 28 May 1950, Glasgow, Scotland. Geographer. Education: BSc, 1973, PhD, 1983, University of Edinburgh. Appointments: Research Associate, then Research Fellow, University of Edinburgh, 1979-96; Director and Secretary, Royal Scottish Geographical Society, 1996-. Publications: Chambers World Gazetteer (editor), 1988; Ecology and Environment in Belize (editor), 1989; A World Record of Major Conflict Areas (with Alan J Day), 1990; The Hutchinson Guide to the World (associate editor), 1990; Loch Leven and the River Leven: A Landscape Transformed, 1994; The Oxford Dictionary of the World (editor), 1995. Contributions to: Reference works and journals. Memberships: Michael Bruce Trust, chairman; National Trust for Scotland, council member; Permanent Committee on Geographical Names for British Official Use, chairman; Royal Geographical Society, fellow; Royal Society of Arts, fellow; Society of Antiquaries, Scotland, fellow. Address: c/o Royal Scottish Geographical society, 40 George Street, Glasgow G1 1QE, Scotland.

MUNRO John Murchison, b. 29 Aug 1932, Wallasey, Cheshire, England. University Administrator; Writer. m. Hertha Ingrid Bertha Lipp, 12 Aug 1956, 2 sons, 2 daughters. Education: BA, English Literature, University of Durham, 1955; PhD, English Literature, Washington University, St Louis, 1960. Appointments: Part-time Instructor of English, Washington University, St Louis, 1956-60; Instructor, University of North Carolina, 1960-63; Assistant Professor, University of Toronto, Canada, 1963-65; Professor, American University of Beirut, Lebanon, 1965-87; Director, Outreach Services, Professor of Mass Communications, 1987-, Associate Dean for External Affairs, 1990-97, American University, Cairo, Egypt; Media Consultant, NSCE, Cairo, 1998-. Publications: English Poetry in Transition, 1968; Arthur Symons, 1969; The Decadent Poets of the 1890's, 1970; Selected Poems of Theo Marzials, 1974; James Elroy Flecker, 1976; A Mutual Concern: The Story of the American University of Beirut, 1977; Cyprus: Between Venus and Mars (with Z Khuri), 1984; Selected Letters of Arthur Symons (with Karl Beckson), 1988; Theatre of the Absurd: Lebanon, 1982-88, 1989; Middle East Times (senior editor). Contributions to: Contributing Editor, Cairo Times, 1997-; Scholarly journals and general periodicals. Honour: Fulbright Research Award, University of California, Los Angeles, 1987. Address: MEDA Team,

Egypt, 29 Ismail Mohammed Street, Zamalek, Cairo, Egypt.

MUNRO Rona, b. 7 Sept 1959, Aberdeen, Scotland. Playwright. Education: MA, University of Edinburgh, 1980. Appointment: Literary Associate, Hampstead Theatre, Lodndon, 1996-. Publications: Fugue, 1983; Piper's Cave, 1985; Saturday at the Commodore, 1989; Bold Girls, 1990; Your Turn to Clear the Stair, 1992; The Maiden Stone, 1995. Other: Plays for Stage, Radio and Film. Honour: Evening Standard Award, 1991. Address: Casarotto Ramsay Ltd, National House, 60-66 Wardour Street, London W1V 3HP, England.

MUNRO Ronald Eadie. See: **GLEN Duncan Munro.**

MUNSCH Robert N(orman), b. 11 June 1945, Pittsburgh, Pennsylvania, USA. Writer. m. Ann D Metta, 20 Jan 1973, 1 son, 2 daughters. Education: BA, History, Fordham University, 1969; MA, Anthropology, Boston University, 1971; MEd, Child Studies, Tufts University, 1973. Appointments: Lecturer, 1975-80, Assistant Professor, 1980-84, University of Guelph; Full-time writer, 1984-. Publications: 31 books, including: The Paper Bag Princess, 1980; Love You Forever (best selling Children's Picture Book), 1986; Stephanie's Ponytail, 1996; Andrew's Loose Tooth, 1998; Get Out of Bed, 1998. Honour: Canadian Bookseller's Association Author of the Year, 1991. Memberships: Writer's Union of Canada; Canadian Association of Children's Authors, Illustrators and Performers; Canadian Author's Association. Address: c/o Writers' Union of Canada, 24 Ryerson Avenue, Toronto, Ontario M5T 2P3, Canada.

MURA David (Alan), b. 17 June 1952, Great Lakes, Illinois, USA. Poet; Writer; Teacher. m. Susan Sencer, 18 June 1983, 1 daughter. Education: BA, Grinnell College, 1974; Graduate Studies, University of Minnesota, 1974-79; MFA, Vermont College, 1991. Appointments: Instructor, 1979-85, Associate Director of the Literature Program, 1982-84, Writers and Artists-in-the-Schools, St Paul, Minnesota; Faculty, The Loft, St Paul, Minnesota, 1984-; Instructor, St Olaf College, 1990-91; Visiting Professor, University of Oregon, 1991; Various poetry readings. Publications: A Male Grief: Notes on Pornography and Addiction, 1987; After We Lost Our Way (poems), 1989; Turning Japanese, 1991; The Colors of Desire (poems), 1995; Where the Body Meets Memory, 1996. Contributions to: Anthologies and magazines. Honours: Fanny Fay Wood Memorial Prize, American Academy of Poets, 1977; US/Japan Creative Artist Fellow, 1984; National Endowment for the Arts Fellowship, 1985; Discovery/Nation Award, 1987; National Poetry Series Contest, 1988; Pushcast Prize, 1990; Minnesota State Arts Board Grant and Fellowship, 1991; New York Times Notable Book of the Year, 1991; Loft McKnight Award of Distinction, 1992; NEA Fellowship, 1993; Lila Wallace Reader's Digest Writers' Award, 1995; Doctor of Humane Letters, Cornell College, 1997. Memberships: Asian-American Renaissance Conference; Center for Arts Criticism, president, 1991-92; Jerome Foundation; The Playwright's Center; Phi Beta Kappa. Address: 1920 East River Terrace, Minneapolis, MN 55414, USA.

MURATA Kiyoaki, b. 19 Nov 1922, Ono, Hyogo, Japan. Educator; Author. m. (1) Minako Iesaka, 1960, div 1981, 2 sons, 1 daughter, (2) Kayoko Matsukura, 1987. Education: MA, University of Chicago, USA. Appointments: Editorial Writer, 1957-66, Managing Editor, 1971-76, Executive Editor, 1976-77, Managing Director, 1976-83, Editor-in-Chief, 1977-83, The Japan Times; Director, Japan Graphic Inc, 1977-82; Professor, International Communications, Yachiyo International University, 1988. Publications: Japan's New Buddhism - An Objective Account of Soka Gakkai, 1969; Japan - The State of the Nation, 1979; Kokuren Nikki-Suppon Wan no Kaiso (UN Diary - Recollections of Turtle Bay), 1985; An Enemy Among Friends, 1991. Honours: Honorary LLD, Carleton College; Vaughn Prize, Japan Newspaper Editors and Publishers Association. Address: 19-12 Hiroo 2 chome, Shibuya-ku, Tokyo 150, Japan.

MURMA V, See: **BAAL Voldemar.**

MURNANE Gerald, b. 1939, Melbourne, Victoria, Australia. Author. m. 3 sons. Education: BA, University of Melbourne, 1969. Appointments: Lecturer, Victoria College, Melbourne; Senior Lecturer, Deakin University, Melbourne. Publications: Tamarisk Row, 1974; A Lifetime on Clouds, 1976; The Plains, 1982; Landscape with Landscape, 1985; Inland, 1988; Velvet Waters (stories), 1990; Emerald Blue (stories), 1995. Address: 2 Falcon Street, Macleod, Victoria 3085, Australia.

MURPHEY Rhoads, b. 13 Aug 1919, Philadelphia, Pennsylvania, USA. Professor of Asian Studies and History; Writer. m. (1) Katherine Elizabeth Quinn, 26 Nov 1942, dec July 1950, 1 son, 1 daughter, (2) Eleanor Taylor Albertson, 12 Jan 1952, 1 son, 1 daughter. Education: AB, 1941, MA, 1942, PhD, 1950, Harvard University. Appointments: Assistant Professor of Geography, Ohio State University, 1950-51; Assistant Professor to Professor of Geography, University of Washington, 1952-64; Professor of Asian Studies and History, University of Michigan, Ann Arbor, 1964-. Publications: Shanghai: Key to Modern China, 1953; A New China Policy (with others), 1967; An Introduction to Geography, 1969, 4th edition, 1978; The Scope of Geography, 1969, 4th edition, 1987; The Treaty Ports and China's Modernization, 1970; China Meets the West, 1975; The Mozartian Historian (with others), 1976; The Outsiders, 1977; The Fading of the Maoist Vision, 1980; Civilizations of the World (with others), 1990, 3rd edition, 1996; A History of Asia, 1992, 2nd edition, 1996; East Asia: A New History, 1996. Contributions to: Scholarly books and journals. Honours: Ford Foundation Fellowship, 1955-56; Guggenheim Fellowship, 1966-67; National Endowment for the Humanities Fellowship, 1972-73; Honours Award, Association of American Geographers, 1980. Memberships: Association of American Geographers; Association for Asian Studies, president, 1987-88. Address: 2012 Washtenaw Avenue, Ann Arbor, MI 48104, USA.

MURPHY C L. See: **MURPHY Lawrence Agustus.**

MURPHY Clive, b. 28 Nov 1935, Liverpool, England. Writer; Compiler; Editor. Education: BA, LLB, Trinity College, Dublin, 1958; Incorporated Law Society of Ireland, 1958. Publications: Novels: Summer Overtures, 1972, new edition, 1976; Freedom for Mr Mildew, 1975; Nigel Someone, 1975; Compiler and Editor of 10 autobiographies, 1978-94. Contributions to: Anthologies and magazines. Honour: Co-Winner, Adam International Review Competition, 1968. Memberships: PEN; Royal Society of Literature, associate; Society of Authors. Address: 132 Brick Lane, London E1 6RU, England.

MURPHY Dervla Mary, b. 28 Nov 1931, Ireland. Author; Critic. Publications: Full Tilt, 1965; Tibetan Foothold, 1966; The Waiting Land, 1967; In Ethiopia With a Mule, 1968; On a Shoestring to Coorg, 1976; Where the Indus is Young, 1977; A Place Apart, 1978; Wheels Within Wheels, 1979; Race to the Finish?, 1981; Eight Feet in the Andes, 1983; Muddling Through in Madagascar, 1985; Ireland, 1985; Tales From Two Cities, 1987; Cameroon with Egbert, 1989; Transylvania and Beyond, 1992; The Ukimwi Road, 1993; South From the Limpopo, 1997; Visiting Rwanda, 1998; One Foot in Laos, 1999. Honours: Ewart-Biggs Memorial Prize, 1978; Irish American Cultural Institute Literary Award, 1985. Address: Lismore, County Waterford, Ireland.

MURPHY Jim, b. 25 Sept 1947, Newark, New Jersey, USA. Writer; Children's Book Editor. m. Elaine Kelso, 12 Dec 1970. Education: BA, Rutgers University; Radcliffe College. Publications: Weird and Wacky Inventions, 1978; Rat's Christmas Party, 1979; Harold Thinks Big, 1980; Death Run, 1982; Two Hundred Years of Bicycles, 1983; The Indy 500, 1983; Trackers, 1984; Baseball's All-Time Stars, 1984; Guess Again: More Weird and Wacky Inventions, 1985; The Long Road to Gettysburg, 1992. Contributions to: Cricket. Honour: Golden Kite Award, Society of Children's Book Writers and Illustrators,

1993. Address: 138 Wildwood Avenue, Upper Montclair, NJ 07043, USA.

MURPHY Lawrence Agustus, (Steven C Lawrence, C L Murphy), b. 17 May 1924, Brockton, Massachusetts, USA. Retired Educator; Writer. Education: BS, Massachusetts Maritime Academy, 1944; BS, Journalism, 1950, MA, English and American Literature, 1951, Boston University. Appointments: English Teacher/Department Chairman, South Junior High School, Brockton, Massachusets, 1951-87; Instructor in Creative Writing, Stonehill College, North Easton, Massachusets, 1967. Publications: The Naked Range, 1956; Saddle Justice, 1957; Brand of a Texan, 1958; The Iron Marshal, 1960; Night of the Gunmen, 1960; Gun Fury, 1961; With Blood in their Eyes, 1961; Slattery, 1961; Bullet Welcome for Slattery, 1961; Walk a Narrow Trail, 1962; A Noose for Slattery, 1962; Longhorns North, 1962; Slattery's Gun Says No, 1962; A Texan Comes Riding, 1966; Buffalo Grass (with C L Murphy), 1966; That Man From Texas, 1972; Edge of the Land, 1974; Six-Gun Junction, 1974; North to Montana, 1975; Slattery Stands Alone, 1976; Trial for Tennihan, 1976; A Northern Saga, 1976; Day of the Commancheros, 1977; Gun Blast, 1977; Through Which We Serve, 1985; The Green Concord Stagecoach, 1988. Memberships: Navy League of the United States; US Naval Institute; Battle of Nomandy Foundation; US Navy Memorial Foundation; Christian Coalition; American Air Museum in Britain; Massachussetts Maritime Academy Alumni Association; Boston University Alumni Association; Liberty Ship - John W Brown Memorial; Merchant Marine Veterans of World War II. Address: MA, USA.

MURPHY Paddy, b. 7 June 1951, Belfast, Northern Ireland. Journalist; Research Writer. m. Marie Murphy, 29 Oct 1982, 1 son, 1 daughter. Education: BA Honours, Queen's University, Belfast, 1974. Appointments: Manager, Maysfield Local Council, Belfast; Publication Officer, Sport Council, Northern Ireland; Public Relations Officer, Eastern Health and Social Services Board, Northern Ireland; Vice-Chairman, Northern Ireland Healthcare Association; President, Northern Ireland Volleyball Association; Secretary, Council for Ethnic Equality; Deputy Editor, SCAN; Presenter, Blarney, BBC Northern Ireland. Publications: Volleyball Section, International Olympic Committee Official Atlanta 1996 Guide; Poems in anthologies Northern Ireland Poetry Today and Rhythms of Northern Ireland; Designed and published Yellow Birds and Other Poems (D McDonnell). Contributions to: The Belfast Review; Fortnight magazine; SCAN, journal of Northern Ireland Health Association; The Belfast Telegraph; The Irish News, Belfast; Irish Times, Dublin; Ulster Medicine; ON journal of Ethnic Equality Council. Address: 21 Broughton Park, Ravenhill, Belfast BT6 0BD, Northern Ireland.

MURPHY Walter Francis, b. 21 Nov 1929, Charleston, South Carolina, USA. McCormick Professor of Jurisprudence Emeritus; Writer. m. Mary Therese Dolan, 28 June 1952, 2 daughters. Education: AB, University of Notre Dame, 1950; AM, George Washington University, 1954; PhD, University of Chicago, 1957. Appointments: Research Fellow, Brookings Institution, Washington, DC, 1957-58; Assistant Professor, 1958-61, Associate Professor, 1961-65, Professor of Politics, 1965-95, McCormick Professor of Jurisprudence, 1968-95, Emeritus, 1995-, Princeton University. Publications: Courts, Judges and Politics (editor with C Herman Pritchett), 1961, 4th edition, 1986; Congress and the Court, 1962; American Democracy (co-author), 4th edition, 1963, to 10th edition, 1983; Elements of Judicial Strategy, 1964; Wiretapping on Trial, 1965; Modern American Democracy (with M N Danielson), 1969; The Study of Public Law (with Joseph Tanehaus), 1972; Public Evaluations of Constitutional Courts (co-author), 1974; Comparative Constitutional Law (co-author), 1977; The Vicar of Christ (fiction), 1979; Basic Cases in Constitutional Law (editor with W D Lockard), 1980, 3rd edition, 1991; The Roman Enigma (fiction), 1981; Upon This Rock (fiction), 1986; American Constitutional Interpretation (with J Fleming and S A Barber), 2nd edition, 1995. Contributions to: Professional journals.

Honours: Distinguished Service Cross; Purple Heart; Birkhead Award, 1958; Merriam-Cobb-Hughes Award, 1963; Guggenheim Fellowship, 1973-74; National Endowment for the Humanities Fellowship, 1978-79; Chicago Foundation for Literature Award, 1980; Lifetime Achievement Award, Law and Courts Section, American Political Science Association, 1995. Memberships: American Academy of Arts and Sciences, fellow; American Political Science Association. Address: 1533 Eagle Ridge Drive North East, Albuquerque, NM 87122, USA.

MURRAY Albert, b. 12 May 1916, Nokomis, Alabama, USA. Writer. m. 31 May 1941, 1 daughter. Education: BS, Tuskegee University, 1939; MA, New York University, 1948. Publications: The Omni-Americans, 1970; South to a Very Old Place, 1971; The Hero and the Blues, 1973; Train Whistle Guitar (novel), 1974; Stomping the Blues, 1976; Good Morning Blues, 1985; The Spyglass Tree (novel), 1991; The Blue Devils of Nada, 1996. Honours: Honorary DLitt, Colgate University, 1975; Lillian Smith Award for Fiction, 1977; ASCAP-Deems Taylor Award, 1977; Lincoln Center Alumni Emeirto Award, 1991; Honorary Doctor of Humane Letters, Spring Hill College, 1996; Honorary DLitt, Hamerton College, 1997. Memberships: American PEN; Authors Guild. Address: 45 West 132nd Street, New York, NY 10037, USA.

MURRAY Frances. See: **BOOTH Rosemary Sutherland.**

MURRAY Les(lie Allan), b. 17 Oct 1938, Nabiac, New South Wales, Australia. Poet; Writer; Translator. m. 29 Sept 1962, 3 sons, 2 daughters. Education: BA, University of Sydney, 1969. Appointments: Co-Editor, Poetry Australia, 1973-80; Poetry Reader, Angus and Robertson Publishers, 1976-91; Literary Editor, Quadrant, 1990-. Publications: Poetry: The Ilex Tree (with Geoffrey Lehmann), 1965; The Weatherboard Cathedral, 1969; Poems Against Economics, 1972; Lunch and Counter Lunch, 1974; Selected Poems: The Vernacular Republic, 1976, 2nd edition, 1982; Ethnic Radio, 1978; The Boys Who Stole the Funeral, 1980; Equanimities, 1982; The People's Otherworld, 1983; Persistence in Folly, 1984; The Australian Year (with Peter Solness), 1986; The Daylight Moon, 1986; Dog Fox Field, 1990; Collected Poems, 1991; The Rabbiter's Bounty, 1992; Translations from the Natural World, 1991; Subhuman Redneck Poems, 1997. Prose: The Peasant Mandarin, 1978; Blocks and Tackles, 1991; The Paperbark Tree: Selected Prose, 1992; A Working Forest, 1997. Editor: The New Oxford Book of Australian Verse, 1986; Collins Dove Anthology of Australian Religious Verse, 1986; Fivefathers: Five Australian Poets of the Pre-Academic Era, 1994. Contributions to: Many publications. Honours: Grace Leven Prizes, 1965, 1980, 1990; Cook Bicentennial Prize, 1970; National Book Awards, 1974, 1984, 1985, 1991, 1993; C J Dennis Memorial Prize, 1976; Gold Medal, Australian Literary Society, 1984; New South Wales Premier's Prizes, 1984, 1993; Canada-Australia Award, 1985; Australian Broadcasting Corporation Bicentennial Prize, 1988; National Poetry Award, 1988; Order of Australia, 1989; Victorian Premier's Prize, 1993; Petrarca Preis, Germany, 1995; T S Eliot Prize, UK, 1997; Honorary doctorates. Membership: Poetry Society of Great Britain, honorary vice-president. Address: c/o Margaret Connolly and Associates, 16 Winton Street, Warrawee, New South Wales 2074, Australia.

MURRAY Rona Jean, b. 10 Feb 1924, London, England. Retired University Lecturer; Poet; Dramatist; Writer. m. (1) Gerry Haddon, 10 Feb 1944, 2 sons, 1 daughter, (2) Walter Dexter, 28 Jan 1972. Education: Mills College, Oakland, California, 1941-44; BA, 1961, MA, 1968, University of British Columbia; PhD, University of Kent, Canterbury, 1972. Appointments: Lecturer, University of British Columbia, 1963-66, Selkirk College, 1968-74, Douglas College, 1974-76, University of Victoria, 1977-84. Publications: Poetry: The Enchanted Adder, 1965; The Power of the Dog and Other Poems, 1968; Ootischenie, 1974; Selected Poems, 1974; An Autumn Journal, 1980; Journey, 1981; Adam and Eve in Middle Age, 1984. Other: Blue Ducks Feather and Eagledown (verse play), 1958; One, Two, Three, Alary (play), 1970; The Art of Earth: An Anthology (co-editor), 1979; Creatures (play), 1980; The Indigo Dress and Other Stories, 1986; Journey Back to Peshawar (memoirs/travel), 1992; Threshold, 1999. Contributions to: Anthologies, reviews, journals, and radio. Honours: Blue Ducks Feather Award, 1958; Macmillan of Canada Creative Writing Award, 1964; Norma Epstein National Award for Creative Writing, 1965; Canada Council Grants, 1976, 1979; Pat Lowther Award, 1982; Commemorative Medal for the 125th Anniversary of the Confederation of Canada; Annual Award Arts and Letters, Hawthorne Society, 1998. Address: 3825 Duke Road, Victoria, British Columbia V9C 4B2, Canada.

MURRELL John, b. 15 Oct 1945, Lubbock, Texas, USA (Canadian citizen). Dramatist; Translator. Education: BFA, Southwestern University, Georgetown, Texas, 1966; BEd, University of Calgary, 1969. Appointments: Playwright-in-Residence, Alberta Theatre Project, 1975-76; Associate Director, Stratford Festival, 1977-78; Dramaturg, Theatre Calgary, 1981-82; Head, Playwright's Colony, Banff Centre School of Fine Art, 1986; Head, Theatre Section, Canada Council, 1988-92. Publications: Haydn's Head, 1973; Power in the Blood, 1975; Teaser (with Kenneth Dyba), 1975; Arena, 1975; A Great Noise, a Great Light, 1976; Memoir, 1977; Waiting for the Parade, 1980; Farther West, 1986; New World, 1986; October, 1988; Democracy, 1992; Faraway Nearby, 1995. Honour: Clifford E Lee Playwrighting Award, 1975. Address: c/o Talonbooks, #104-3100 Production Way, Burnaby, British Columbia V5A 4R4, Canada.

MURTI Kotikalapudi Venkata Suryanarayana, (K V S Murti), b. 9 May 1925, Parlakhemundi, Orissa, India. Retired Professor of English; Writer; Poet; Critic. Education: MA, English Language and Literature, 1963, PhD, English, 1972, Andhra University, Visakhapatnam; Intensive Course in Linguistics and Phonetics, Central Institute of English and Foreign Languages, Hyderabad, 1969. Appointments: Lecturer up to 1980, Assistant Professor, 1980-85, Professor of English, 1986-87, MMA Law College, Madras; Many international seminars and lectures; Various poetry readings. Publications: Poetry in Telugu: Ihamlo Param, 1979; Liilaahela, 1981; Pranavamtho Pranayam, 1994. Poetry in English: Allegory of Eternity, 1975; Triple-Light, 1975; Sparks of the Absolute, 1976; Spectrum, 1976; Symphony of Discords, 1977; Araku, 1982; Comic and Absolute, 1995; Convex-Image and Concave-Mirror, 1995; Glimpses and Grandeur, 1998. Criticism: Waves of Illumination, 1978; Sword and Sickle: Critical Study of Mulk Raj Anand's Novels, 1983; Kohinoor in the Crown: Critical Studies in Indian English Literature, 1987; Old Myth and New Myth: Letters From MRA to KVS, 1993. Contributions to: Many national and international publications. Honours: Fellow, International Academy of Poets, England, 1976; Honorary DLitt, Free University of Asia, Manila, Philippines 1976, World University, Tucson, Arizona, 1977; Several merit certificates and honours. Memberships: Authors Guild of India; Indian PEN; World University Round Table. Address: 43-21-9A Venkataraju Nagar, Visakhapatnam 530 016 AP, India.

MURUA CONTRERAS Dámaso, (Pablo Huarache), b. 13 Aug 1933, Escuinapa, Sin Mexico. Public Accountant and Auditor. m. Elia Enriquez Aguilar, 19 Dec 1959, 3 sons. Education: National Polytechnic Institute; High School of Commerce and Administration; Vocational qualifications, 1953; Professional qualifications, 1967. Publications: El Mineral de los Cauques, 1966; La Ronda, 1969; El Güilo Mentiras, 1971; Tiempo Regiomontano, 1972; Colachi, 1973; Vacum Totoliboque, 1975; Las Playas de las Cabras, 1976; En Brasil Crece un Almendro, 1979; Amor en el Yanqui Stadium, 1978; Palabras Sudadas, 1986; La Muerte de Marcos Cachano, 1986; Para Mis Amigos, 1987; Club Escarlata, 1988; El Detective Tropical, 1992; Exodo en la Perla, 1994; Others. Contributions to: Reports, essays and general narratives in cultural magazines, City of Mexico and Mexico Province. Honours: 2 National Prizes for Stories; Represented in 3 anthologies published in Germany, Poland and Chile. Membership: Asociación de Escritores de México. Address: Pilastra 15, CP 14390, Mexico DF, Mexico.

MURUA-BELTRAN CONTRERAS Damaso, (Damaso Murua), b. 13 Aug 1933, Escuinapa, Sinaloa, Mexico. Accountant; Fiction Writer; Essayist. m. Elia Enriquez Aguilar, 19 Dec 1959, 3 sons. Education: Accountant's degree, National Polytechnic Institute, Mexico, DF Mexico. Publications: More than 20 works including: El Mineral de los Cauques, 1966; La Ronda, 1969; Tiempo Regiomontano, 1971; El Gui lo mentiras, 1971, 1976, 1991; Las Playas de las Cabras, 1975, 1976; Amor en el Yanqui Stadium, 1976; En Brasil crece un Almendro, 1977; Club Escarlata, 1986; Exodo en la Perla, 1996. Contributor to: Anthologies in Germany, Poland, Chile and Mexico; Newspapers and magazines, Mexico City, Sinaloa, Monterrey, NL, and South America. Honour: Puerto Vallarta National Award for Literature. Membership: Mexican Writers Association. Address: Pilastra 15, Tlalpan, Mexico 14390, DF Mexico.

MUSCHG Adolf, b. 13 May 1934, Zollikon, Switzerland. Author; Dramatist; Professor. Education: Zürich; Cambridge, England; PhD, 1959. Appointment: Professor, Eidgenössische Tecnische Hochschule, Zürich, 1970-. Publications: Im Sommer des Hasen, 1965; Fremdkörper, 1968; Das Kerbelgericht, 1969; Die Aufgeregten von Goethe, 1971; Liebesgeschichten, 1972; Albissers Grund, 1974; Kellers Abend, 1975; Gottfried Keller, 1977; Baiyun oder dieFreundschaftsgesellschaft, 1980; Literatur als Therapie?, 1981; Das Licht und der Schlüssel, 1984; Der rote Ritter, 1993; Nur ausziehen wollte sie sich nicht, 1995. Honours: Hermann Hesse Prize, 1974; Literature Prize, Zürich, 1984; Carl Zuckmayer Medal, 1990; Georg Büchner Prize, 1994. Address: Hasenackerstrasse 24, 8708 Männedorf, Switzerland.

MUSGRAVE Susan, b. 12 Mar 1951, Santa Cruz, California, USA (Canadian citizen).Poet; Author. m. (3) Stephen Reid, 1986, 2 daughters. Appointments: Instructor and Writer-in-Residence, University of Waterloo, Ontario, 1983-85; Instructor, Kootenay School of Writing, British Columbia, 1986, Camosun College, Victoria, 1988-; Writer-in-Residence, University of New Brunswick, 1985, University of Western Ontario, 1992-93, University of Toronto, 1995, Victoria School of Writing, 1996, 1998; Writer-in-Electronic-Residence, York University and Writers' Development Trust, 1991-. Publications: Poetry: Songs of the Sea-Witch, 1970; Entrance of the Celebrant, 1972; Grave-Dirt and Selected Strawberries, 1973, revised edition as Selected Strawberries and Other Poems, 1977; The Impstone, 1976; Becky Swan's Book, 1978; A Man to Marry, A Man to Bury, 1979; Tarts and Muggers: Poems New and Selected, 1982; Cocktails at the Mausoleum, 1985, revised edition, 1992; The Embalmer's Art: Poems New and Selected, 1991; In the Small Hours of the Rain, 1991; Forcing the Narcissus, 1994; Things That Keep and Do Not Change, 1999. Fiction: The Charcoal Burners, 1980; The Dancing Chicken, 1987; Other: Great Musgrave, 1989; Clear Cut Words: Writers for Clayoquot (editor), 1993; Musgrave Landing: Musings on the Writing Life, 1994; Because You Loved Being a Stranger: 55 Poets Celebrate Patrick Lane (editor), 1994. Children's Books: Gullband (poems), 1974; Hag Head (fiction), 1980; Kestrel and Leonardo (poems), 1990; Dreams Are More Real than Bathtubs (fiction), 1998. Contributions to: Many anthologies, reviews, quarterlies, and journals. Honours: Many grants; 2nd Prize, National Magazine Award, 1981; 1st Prize, b p nichol Poetry Chapbook Award, 1991; Readers' Choice Award, Prairie Schooner, 1993; Vicky Metcalf Short Story Editor's Award, 1996. Memberships: British Columbia Federation of Writers; Writer's Union of Canada, chair, 1997-98. Address: PO Box 2421, Station Main, Sidney, British Columbia V8L 3Y3, Canada.

MUSGROVE Frank, b. 16 Dec 1922, Nottingham, England. Professor of Education Emeritus; Writer. m. Dorothy Ellen Nicholls, 1 daughter. Education: BA, Magdalen College, Oxford, 1947; PhD, University of

Nottingham, 1958. Appointments: Lecturer, University of Leicester, 1957-62; Senior Lecturer, University of Leeds, 1963-65; Professor of Research in Education, University of Bradford, 1965-70; Sarah Fielden Professor of Education, 1970-82, Professor Emeritus, 1982-, University of Manchester; Co-Editor, Research in Education, 1971-76; Honorary Professor, University of Hull, 1985-88; Various guest lectureships. Publications: The Migratory Elite, 1963; Youth and the Social Order, 1964; The Family, Education and Society, 1966; Society and the Teacher's Role (with P H Taylor), 1969; Patterns of Power and Authority in English Education, 1971; Ectasy and Holiness, 1974, new edition, 1994; Margins of the Mind, 1977; School and the Social Order, 1979; Education and Anthropology, 1982; The North of England: A History from Roman Times to the Present, 1990. Contributions to: Professional journals. Honour: Doctor of Letters, Open University, 1982. Memberships: Royal Anthropological Institute; Royal Society of Arts, fellow. Address: Dib Scar, the Cedar Grove, Beverley, East Yorkshire HU17 7EP, England.

MUSICANT Ivan Martin, b. 18 Dec 1943, New York City, USA. Naval Historian. m. Gretchen Granlund Musicant, 17 July 1982, 1 son. Education: Bachelor Degree, History, Bemidji State University. Publications: United States Armored Cruisers: A Design and Operational History, 1985; Battleship At War: The Epic Story of the USS Washington, 1986; The Banana Wars: United States Military Intervention in Latin America, 1990; Divided Waters: The Naval History of the Civil War, 1995; Empire by Default: The Spanish-American War, 1998. Contributions to: Journals, reviews, periodicals and quarterlies. Honours: Samuel Eliot Morison Award for Naval Literature, 1987, 1998. Address: 3701 Glendale Terrace, Minneapolis, MN 55410, USA.

MUSKE Carol (Anne), (Carol Muske Dukes), b. 17 Dec 1945, St Paul, Minnesota, USA. Poet; Author; Professor. m. David Dukes, 31 Jan 1983, 1 stepson, 1 daughter. Education: BA, English, Creighton University, Omaha, 1967; MA, English, California State University, San Francisco, 1970. Appointments: Founder-Writing Program Director, Art Without Walls, New York, 1971-84; Lecturer, New School for Social Research, New York City, 1975; Assistant Professor, University of New Hampshire, 1978-79; Visiting Writer, 1978, Visiting Poet, 1983, 1993, University of California at Irvine; Adjunct Professor, Columbia University, 1979-81; Visiting Poet, Iowa Writers' Workshop, 1980; Jenny McKean Moore Lecturer, George Washington University, 1980-81; Writer-in-Residence, University of Virginia, 1981; Lecturer, 1984-88, Assistant Professor, 1989-91, Associate Professor, 1991-93, Professor, 1993-, University of Southern California, Los Angeles; Visiting Fiction Writer, University of California, Los Angeles, 1989. Publications: Poetry: Camouflage, 1975; Skylight, 1981; Wyndmere, 1985; Applause, 1989; Red Trousseau, 1993; An Octave Above Thunder: Selected and New Poems, 1997. Fiction: Dear Digby, 1989; Saving St Germ, 1993; Epitaph, 1998. Contributions to: Numerous anthologies and journals. Honours: Dylan Thomas Poetry Award, 1973; Pushcart Prizes, 1978, 1988-89, 1992-93, 1998; Alice Fay di Castagnola Award, Poetry Society of America, 1979; Guggenheim Fellowship, 1981; National Endowment for the Arts Grant, 1984; Ingram Merrill Foundation Fellowship, 1988; New York Times Most Notable Book Citation, 1993; Alumni Achievement Award, Creighton University, 1996; Witter Bynner Award, Library of Congress, Washington, DC, 1997-98; Finalist, Los Angeles Times Book Prize, 1998. Memberships: Poetry Society of America, West, program director and president, 1992-94. Address: c/o Department of English, University of California at Los Angeles, Los Angeles, CA 90095, USA.

MUSSON Cecile Norma. See: **SMITH Cecile Norma Musson**.

MYCROFT. See: **OLSEN David Leslie**.

MYERS Jack (Elliot), b. 29 Nov 1941, Lynn, Massachusetts, USA. Professor of English; Poet; Writer.

m. (1) Nancy, 1967, (2) Willa, 1981, (3) Thea, 1993, 3 sons, 1 daughter. Education: BA, English Literature, University of Massachusetts, Boston, 1970; MFA, Poetry Writing, University of Iowa, 1972. Appointments: Assistant Professor, 1975-81, Associate Professor, 1982-88, Professor of English, 1988-, Director, Creative Writing Program, 1990-94, Southern Methodist University, Dallas; Poetry Editor, Fiction International, 1978-80, Cimarron Review, 1989-91; Faculty, MFA Program in Writing, Vermont College, 1981-; Distinguished Poet-in-Residence, Wichita State University, 1992; Distinguished Visiting Writer, University of Idaho, 1993; Distinguished Writer-in-Residence, Northeast Louisiana University, 1995. Publications: Poetry: Black Sun Abraxas, 1970; Will It Burn, 1974; The Family War, 1977; I'm Amazed That You're Still Singing, 1981; Coming to the Surface, 1984; As Long as You're Happy, 1986; Blindsided, 1993; Human Being, 1997. Other: A Trout in the Milk: A Composite Portrait of Richard Hugo, 1980; New American Poets of the 80s (editor with Roger Weingarten), 1984; The Longman Dictionary of Poetic Terms, 1985, revised edition, 1997; A Profile of Twentieth-Century American Poetry (editor with David Wojahn), 1991; New American Poets of the 90s (editor with Roger Weingarten), 1991; Leaning House Poets, Vol 1 (editor with Mark Elliott), 1996; One On One, 1999. Contributions to: Anthologies, reviews, quarterlies, journals, and magazines. Honours: Academy of American Poets Award, 1972; Texas Institute of Letters Poetry Awards, 1978, 1993; Yaddo Fellowship, 1978; National Endowment for the Arts Fellowships, 1982-83, 1986-87; Winner, National Poetry Series Open Competition, 1985; Southern Methodist University Author's Award, 1987. Memberships: Associated Writing Programs; PEN; Texas Association of Creative Writing Teachers; Texas Institute of Letters. Address: 6402 Abrams Road, Dallas, TX 75231, USA.

N

NADAUS Roland, (Pol-Jean Mervillon), b. 28 Nov 1945, Paris, France. Writer; Poet. m. Simone Moris, 9 Sept 1967, 1 daughter. Publications: Maison de Paroles, 1969; Journal: Vrac, 1981; Je ne Tutoie que Dieu et ma femme (poems), 1992; Dictionnaire initiatique de l'orant, 1993; L'homme que tuèrent les mouches, 1996. Contributions to: Journals. Honour: Prix Gustave Gasser, 1993. Membership: PEN Club of France. Address: 20 route de Troux, 78280 Guyancourt, France.

NADICH Judah, b. 13 May 1912, Baltimore, Maryland, USA. Rabbi; Writer. m. Martha Hadassah Ribalow, 26 Jan 1947, 3 daughters. Education: AB, College of New York, 1932; Jewish Theological Seminary of America, 1932-36; MA, Columbia University, 1936; Rabbi, Master of Arts, Doctor of Hebrew Literature, 1953. Publications: Eisenhower and the Jews, 1953; Menachem Ribalow: The Flowering of Modern Hebrew Literature (translator), 1957; Louis Ginzberg: Al Halakhah Ve-Aggadah (editor), 1960; Jewish Legends of the Second Commonwealth, 1983; Legends of the Rabbis, 1994; Rabbi Akiba and His Contemporaries, 1998. Contributions to: Reference works, books, and journals. Honours: OBE, 1944; Croix de Guerre, 1945; Doctor of Divinity, honoris causa, 1966; Aleh, Israel, 1985. Memberships: Jewish Book Council of America, president, 1970-72; Rabbinical Assembly, president, 1972-74. Address: Park Avenue Synagogue, 50 East 87th Street, New York, NY 10028, USA.

NADOLNY Sten, b. 29 July 1942, Zehdenick/Havel, Germany. Author. Education: Abitur, 1961; Dr phil, Modern History, 1977. Publications: Netzkarte, 1981; Die Entdeckung der Langsamkeit, 1983; Selim oder die Gabe der Rede, 1990; Das Erzählen und die guten Absichten, 1990; Ein Gott der Frechheit, 1994. Honours: Ingeborg Bachmann Prize, 1980; Hans Fallada Prize, 1985; Vallombrosa Prize, Florence, 1986; Ernst Hoferichter Prize, 1995. Literary Agent: Agence Hoffman, Bechsteinstrasse 2, D-80804 Munich, Germany. Address: Kollatzstrasse 19, D-14059 Berlin, Germany.

NAFTALI Ben. See: **OFFEN Yehuda.**

NAGARAJA RAO C K, (Haida, Haritas, Rajanna), b. 12 June 1915, Chellakere, India. Author; Journalist. m. Rajamani Nagarajo Rao, 18 May 1934, 2 sons, 6 daughters. Education: Intermediate Engineering Exam, Mysore University, 1933; Hindi Preaveshika Exam, 1937. Publications: Wild Jasmine, 1937; Mushrooms, 1942; Shoodramuni, 1943; Dayadadavanala, 1944; Sangama, 1944; Place and Date of Mahakavi Lakshmeesha, 1969; Pattamahadevi Shantaladevi, 1978; Sankole Basava, 1979; Sampanna Samaja, 1979; Savilladavaru, 1982; Kuranganayani, 1983; Ekalavya, 1988; Veeranganga Vishnuvardhana, 1992. Contributions to: Various publications. Honours: Award for Research and Criticism, 1969-70, Best Creative Literature of the Year, 1978, Karnataka State Sahitya Akademi; Moorthidevi Sahitya Puraskar of Bharatiya Jnanpith, 1983. Memberships: Kannada Sahitya Parishat; Karnataka Lekhakar Sangha; PEN All India Centre; Mythic Society; Authors Guild of India. Address: 7/61/2 Mandaara, 1 Main Road, Padmanabhanagar, Bangalore 560 070, India.

NAGATSUKA Ryuji, b. 20 Apr 1924, Nagoya, Japan. Professor; Writer. m. 20 July 1949. Education: Graduated, French Literature, University of Tokyo, 1948. Appointments: Professor, Nihon University, 1968-. Publications: Napoleon tel qu'il était, 1969; J'étais un kamikaze, 1972; George Sand, sa vie et ses oeuvres, 1977; Napoleon, 2 volumes, 1986; Talleyrand, 1990. Contributions to: Yomiuri Shimbun. Honours: Prix Pierre Mille, 1972; Prix Senghor, 1973. Membership: Association Internationale des Critiques Littéraires, Paris. Address: 7-6-37 Oizumigakuen-cho, Nerima-ku, Tokyo, Japan.

NAGEL Paul C(hester), b. 14 Aug 1926, Independence, Missouri, USA. Historian; Writer. m. Joan Peterson, 19 Mar 1948, 3 sons. Education: BA, 1948, MA, 1949, PhD, 1952, University of Minnesota. Appointments: Historian, Strategic Air Command, US Air Force, Omaha, 1951-53; Assistant Professor, Augustana College, Sioux Falls, South Dakota, 1953-54; Assistant Professor to Associate Professor, Eastern Kentucky University, Richmond, 1954-61; Visiting Professor, Amherst College, 1957-58, Vanderbilt University, 1959, University of Minnesota, 1964; Faculty, 1961-65, Professor of History, 1965-69, Dean, College of Arts and Sciences, 1965-69, University of Kentucky; Special Assistant to the President for Academic Affairs, 1969-71, Professor of History, 1969-78, Vice-President for Academic Affairs, 1971-74, University of Missouri; Professor of History and Head, Department of History, University of Georgia, 1978-80; Director, Virginia Heritage Society, Richmond, 1981-85; Distinguished Lee Scholar, Lee Memorial Foundation, 1986-90; Visiting Scholar, Duke University, 1991-92, University of Minnesota, 1992-, Carleton College, 1993-. Publications: One Nation Indivisible: The Union in American Thought 1776-1861, 1964, 2nd edition, 1980; This Sacred Trust: American Nationality 1798-1898, 1971, 2nd edition, 1980; Missouri: A History, 1977, 2nd edition, 1988; Descent from Glory: Four Generations of the John Adams Family, 1983; Extraordinary Lives: The Art and Craft of American Biography (co-author), 1986; The Adams Women: Abigail and Louisa Adams, Their Sisters and Daughters, 1987; George Caleb Bingham (co-author), 1989; The Lees of Virginia: Seven Generations of an American Family, 1990; Massachusetts and the New Nation (co-author), 1992; John Quincy Adams: A Public Life, A Private Life, 1997. Contributions to: Professional journals and general publications. Honours: Best Book Award, 1977; Book of the Month Club Main Selection, 1983; Laureate of Virginia, 1988; American Society of Colonial Dames Book Award, 1998. Memberships: Massachusetts Historical Society; Pilgrim Society; Society of American Historians; Southern Historical Association, president, 1984-85. Address: 1314 Marquette Avenue, Apt 2206, Minneapolis, MN 55403, USA.

NAGEL Thomas, b. 4 July 1937, Belgrade, Yugoslavia (US citizen, 1944). Professor of Philosophy and Law; Writer. m. (1) Doris Blum, 18 June 1958, div 1973, (2) Anne Hollander, 26 June 1979. Education: BA, Cornell University, 1958; BPhil, Corpus Christi College, Oxford, 1960; PhD, Harvard University, 1963. Appointments: Assistant Professor of Philosophy, University of California at Berkeley, 1963-66; Assistant Professor, 1966-69, Associate Professor, 1969-72, Professor, 1972-80, Princeton University; Tanner Lecturer, Stanford University, 1977; Tanner Lecturer, 1979, John Locke Lecturer, 1990, University of Oxford; Professor of Philosophy, 1980-, Chairman, Department of Philosophy, 1981-86, Professor of Philosophy and Law, 1986-, New York University; Howison Lecturer, University of California at Berkeley, 1987; Thalheimer Lecturer, Johns Hopkins University, 1989; Hempel Lecturer, Princeton University, 1995; Whitehead Lecturer, Harvard University, 1995; Immanuel Kant Lecturer, Stanford University, 1995. Publications: The Possibility of Altruism, 1970; Mortal Questions, 1979; The View from Nowhere, 1986; What Does It All Mean?, 1987; Equality and Partiality, 1991; Other Minds: Critical Essays, 1969-94, 1995; The Last Word, 1997. Contributions to: Scholarly journals. Honours: Guggenheim Fellowship, 1966-67; National Endowment for the Humanities Fellowships, 1978-79, 1984-85; Honorary Fellow, Corpus Christi College, Oxford, 1992-. Memberships: American Academy of Arts and Sciences, fellow; British Academy, fellow. Address: c/o School of Law, New York University, 40 Washington Square South, New York, NY 10012, USA.

NAGY Paul, b. 23 Aug 1934, Hungary. Writer. Education: BA, Hungary, 1953; Diploma, French Language and Literature, Sorbonne, University of Paris, 1962. Appointments: Co-Founder, Atelier Hongrois, 1962, p'ART video review, 1987. Publications: Les faineants de Hampstead, 1969; Sadisfaction IS, 1977; Journal in-time, I, 1984, II, 1994; Points de Repères "Postmodernes": Lyotard, Habermas, Derrida, 1993. Contributions to: Several publications. Membership: Union des écrivains francais. Address: 141 Avenue Jean Jaures, 92120 Montrouge, France.

NAGY-ZEKMI Silvia, b. 15 May 1953, Budapest, Hungry. Writer; University Professor. m. Nadir Zekmi, 9 May 1995. Education: PhD, Latin American Studies, Eötvös Lorand University. Appointments: Assistant Professor of Spanish, Loyola University, 1987-90; Assistant Professor of Latin American Literature, Catholic University, Washington, DC, 1990-97; Associate Professor of Latin American Literature, State University of New York at Albany, 1998-. Publications: De Texto a Contexto: Practicas Discursivas en Lit Hisp am Ana Yespanola; Identidades en Transformacion: El Discurso Neoindigenista de los Paises Andinos; Paralelismos Transatlanticos: Postcolonialismo y Narrativa Femenina en America Latina y Africa del Norte; Historia de la Cancion Folklorica de los Andes. Contributions to: Poetry and Poetics; Princeton Encyclopedia; Solar: Signo; Chasqui. Memberships: Modern Language Association; LASA; Third World Studies; American Association of Women. Address: Hispanic Studies, HU 215 SUNY at Albany, Albany, NY 12222, USA.

NAHAL Chaman, b. 2 Aug 1927, Sialkot, India. Writer. Education: MA, Delhi University, 1948; PhD, University of Nottingham, 1961. Appointments: Member, Department of English, Delhi University, 1963-; Columnist, Talking About Books, The Indian Express newspaper, 1966-73; Associate Professor of English, Long Island University, New York, USA, 1968-70. Publications: The Weird Dances (short stories), 1965; A Conversation with J Kristnamurti, 1965; D H Lawrence: An Eastern View, 1970; Drugs and the Other Self (editor), 1971; The Narrative Pattern in Ernest Hemingway's Fiction, 1971; The New Literatures in English, 1985; The Bhagavad-Gita: A New Rendering, 1987. Novels: My True Faces, 1973; Azadi, 1975; Into Another Dawn, 1977; The English Queens, 1979; The Crown and the Loincloth, 1982; Sunrise in Fiji, 1988; The Salt of Life, 1990. Address: 2/1 Kalkaji Extension, New Delhi 110019, India.

NAIDU Prabmakar, b. 23 Aug 1937, Kurudu, India. Professor. m. Madmumati, 27 July 1967, 3 sons. Education: BSc, Honours, MTech, PhD, University of British Columbia, Canada. Appointments: Assistant Professor, 1971, Associate Professor, 1976, Professor, 1982, Indian Institute of Science, Bangalore. Publications: Modern Spectrum Analysis of Time Science, 1996; Analysis of Geophysical Potential Fields: A Digital Signal Processing Approach, 1998. Contributions to: International journals. Honours: Humboldt Fellow; Research Associate, Stiftung Bonn, Germany. Address: c/o Indian Institute of Science, Bangalore 560 012, India.

NAIFEH Steven (Woodward), b. 19 June 1952, Tehran, Iran. Writer. Education: AB, Princeton University, 1974; JD, 1977, MA, 1978, Harvard University. Appointments: Lecturer, National Gallery of Art, Washington, DC, 1976; Associate, Milbank, Tweed, Haldey and McCloy, New York City, 1976; Vice President, Sabbagh, Naifeh, and Associates, Washington, DC, 1980-. Publications: Culture Making: Money, Success, and the New York Art World, 1976; Moving Up in Style (with Gregory White Smith), 1980; Gene Davis, 1981; How to Make Love to a Woman, 1982; What Every Client Needs to Know About Using a Lawyer, 1982; The Bargain Hunter's Guide to Art Collecting, 1982; Why Can't Men Open Up?: Overcoming Men's Fear of Intimacy, 1984; The Mormon Murders: A True Story of Greed, Forgery, Deceit, and Death, 1988; Jackson Pollack: An American Saga, 1989; The Best Lawyers in America (editor with Gregory White Smith), 1990; The Best Doctors in America (editor with Gregory White Smith), 1992; Final Justice: The True Story of the Richest Man Ever Tried for Murder, 1993; A Stranger in the Family: A True Story of Murder, Madness, and Unconditional Love, 1995. Honour: Pulitzer Prize for Biography, 1991. Address: 129 First Avenue South West, SC 29801, USA.

NAIMAN Anatoly G, b. 23 Apr 1936, Leningrad, Russia. Poet; Writer; Translator. m. Galina Narinskaia, 1 son, 1 daughter. Education: Degree, Organic Chemistry, Leningrad Technological Institute, 1958; Postgraduate Diploma, Screenwriting, Moscow, 1964. Appointments: Visiting Professor, Bryn Mawr College, Pennsylvania, 1991; Visiting Fellow, All Souls College, Oxford, 1991-92. Publications: Remembering Anna Akhmatova, 1992. Other: Various translations into Russian. Contributions to: Newspapers and journals. Honour: Latvian Union of Writers Translators Prize, 1981. Memberships: PEN Club, France; Writers Committee, Moscow. Address: Dmitrovskoye Schosse 29, fl 56, Moscow, Russia.

NAIPAUL V(idiadhar) S(urajprasad) (Sir), b. 17 Aug 1932, Chaguanas, Trinidad. Author. m. (1) Patricia Ann Hale, 1955, dec 1996, (2) Nadira Khannum Alvi, 1996. Education: Queen's Royal College, Trinidad; BA, Honours, English, University College, Oxford, 1953. Publications: Novels: The Mystic Masseur, 1957; The Suffrage of Elvira, 1958; Miguel Street, 1959; A House for Mr Biswas, 1961; Mr Stone and the Knights Companion, 1963; The Mimic Men, 1967; A Flag on the Island, 1967; In a Free State, 1971; Guerrillas, 1975; A Bend in the River, 1979; The Enigma of Arrival, 1987; A Way in the World, 1994. Other: The Middle Passage, 1962; An Area of Darkness, 1964; The Loss of El Dorado, 1969; The Overcrowded Barracoon, and Other Articles, 1972; India: A Wounded Civilization, 1977; The Return of Eva Perón, 1980; Among the Believers, 1981; Finding the Centre, 1984; A Turn in the South, 1989; India: A Million Mutinies Now, 1990; Beyond Belief: Islamic Excursions Among the Converted Peoples, 1998. Contributions to: Journals and magazines. Honours: John Llewelyn Rhys Memorial Prize, 1958; Somerset Maugham Award, 1961; Hawthornden Prize, 1964; W H Smith Award, 1968; Booker Prize, 1971; Honorary Doctor of Letters, Columbia University, New York City, 1981; Honorary Fellow, University College, Oxford, 1983; Honorary DLitt, University of Cambridge, 1983, University of Oxford, 1992; Knighted, 1990; British Literature Prize, 1993. Memberships: Royal Society of Literature, fellow; Society of Authors. Address: c/o Gillon Aitken Associates, 29 Fernshaw Road, London SW10 0TG, England.

NAJNAGORET. See: **TER-OGANIAN Leon.**

NAMBOOTHIRI K Sankaran, b. 29 Mar 1922, Mavelikara, Alappuzha District, Kerala State, India. Retired Professor; Freelance Writer. m. S Choodamani Devi, 2 July 1930, 2 sons, 4 daughters. Education: BSc, 1947, MA, 1956, BT, 1952, University of Kerala. Appointments: Assistant Lecturer in Chemistry; High School Assistant; Lecturer in English; Professor of English; Assistant Editor, Encyclopaedia of Indian Literature; Assistant Editor, Modern Indian Literature. Publications: Teaching English in India; An Outline of English Grammar and Composition; Kilippattu Prasthaanam; Samskara Dalangal (collection of essays); Light and Might (biographical sketches); Sooranattu Kuryan Pillai (biography); Mahakavi Pandalam Kerala Varma (biography); English-English-Malayalam Dictionary (chief editor); Thulasi Dalangal (collection of poems); Commentary on Ullor Parameswara Iyer's collection of poems entitled Manimanjusha. Contributions to: Essays in Malayalam and English, book reviews, critical articles and poems in Malayalam, in magazines and journals. Honours: Thunchan Award, Kerala Sahitya Akademi; Kerala Sastra Sahitya Parishat Award; Silver Jubilee of Independence Award, Government of Kerala. Memberships include: Ulloor Memorial; Jayashree Balavedi Yogakshema Sabha; Sahitya Akademi. Address: Aradhana, LIC Colony, Thirumala PO, Thiruvananthapuram 6, Kerala State, India.

NANDA Bal Ram, b. 11 Oct 1917, Rawalpindi, India. Historian; Writer. m. Janak Khosla, 24 May 1946, 2 sons. Education: MA, History, 1st Class, University of Punjab, Lahore, 1939. Appointment: Director, Nehru Memorial Museum and Library, New Delhi, 1965-79. Publications: Mahatma Gandhi: A Biography, 1958; The Nehrus, Motilal and Jawaharlal, 1962; Gandhi: A Pictorial Biography, 1972; Gokhale: The Indian Moderates and the British Raj, 1977; Jawaharlal Nehru: A Pictorial Biography, 1980; Gandhi and His Critics, 1986; Gandhi, Pan-Islamism, Imperialisn and Nationalism in India, 1989; In Gandhi's Footsteps: Life and Times of Jamnalal Bajaj, 1990; Jawaharal Nehru: Rebel and Statesman, 1996; The Making of a Nation: India's Road to Independence, 1998. Editor: Socialism in India, 1972; Indian Foreign Policy: The Nehru Years, 1975; Science and Technology in India, 1977; Essays in Modern Indian History, 1980; Mahatma Gandhi: 125 Years, 1995; The Making of a Nation: Indi;a Road to Independence, 1998; Selected Works of Govind Ballabh Pant, Volume 1 to 11 (1993-1999). Contributions to: Numerous newspapers, magazines and journals. Honours: Rockefeller Fellowship, 1964; National Fellowship, Indian Council of Social Science Research, New Delhi, 1979; Dadabhai Naoroji Memorial Prize, 1981; Padma Bhushan, 1988. Memberships: Institute for Defence Studies and Analyses, New Delhi; Authors Guild of India; Indian International Centre. Address: S-174 Panchshila Park, New Delhi 110017, India.

NAOMI French Wallace, b. 17 Aug 1960, USA. Dramatist; Poet. Education: BA, Hampshire College, 1982; MFA, University of Iowa, 1986. Appointments: Teacher of Playwriting, University of Iowa, 1990-93; Playwrite-in-Residence, Illinois State University, 1994. Publications: Slaughter City (play); In the Heart of America (play); To Dance a Stony Field (poems). Contributions to: Reviews, journals, and magazines. Honours: The Nation/Discovery Award; Kentucky Arts Council Fellowship; Mobil Playwriting Award; Susan Smith Blackburn Playwriting Award. Address: 4575 Highway 6 South East, Iowa City, IA 52240, USA.

NAPIER William McDonald, (Bill Napier), b. 29 June 1940, Perth, Scotland. Astronomer. m. Nancy Miller Baillie, 7 July 1965, 1 son, 1 daughter. Education: BSc, 1963; PhD, 1966. Publications: The Cosmic Serpent, 1982; The Cosmic Winter, 1990; The Origin of Comets, 1990; Nemesis (novel), 1998. Contributions to: New Scientist; Astronomy Today. Honour: Joint recipient, Arthur Beer Memorial Prize, 1986-87. Membership: Royal Astronomical Society, fellow; International Astronomical Union; Spaceguard UK. Literary Agent: Peter Robinson at Curtis Brown. Address: Armagh Observatory, College Hill, Armagh BT61 9DG, Northern Ireland.

NARAIN Vineet, b. 18 Apr 1956, Khurja, Uttar Pradesh, India. Journalist. m. Dr Meeta Narain, 4 Aug 1982, 2 sons. Education: PhD, Agra University, 1983. Publication: My Hawala Kurushetra, 1997. Contributions to: Newspapers and magazines. Address: C 6/28 Safdarjung Dev Area, New Delhi 110016, India.

NARANG Gopi Chand, b. 1 Jan 1931, Dukki, Baluchistan, India. Professor. m. Manorama Narang, 9 Dec 1973, 2 sons. Education: Honours, 1st in 1st Class, Urdu, 1948, Honours, 1st in 1st Class, Persian 1958, Punjab University; MA, 1st in 1st Class, Urdu, 1954, PhD, 1958, Diploma in Linguistics, 1st Division, 1961, University of Delhi; Postdoctoral courses in Acoustic Phonetics and Transformational Grammar, Indiana University, USA, 1964. Appointment: Professor of Urdu Language and Literature, Delhi University; Acting Vice Chancellor, Jamia Millia University, 1981-82; Vice-Chairman, Urdu Academy, Delhi, 1996-; Vice-President, Sahitya Akademi, National Academy of Letters, 1998-; Visiting Professor Norway University, Oslo, 1998. Publications: Karkhandari Dialect of Delhi Urdu, 1961; Puranon Ki Kahaniyan, 1976; Anthology of Modern Urdu Poetry, 1981; Urdu Afsana, Riwayat aur Masail, 1982; Safar Ashna, 1982; Usloobiyat-e-Mir, 1985; Saniha-e-Karbala bataur Sheri Istiara, 1987; Amir Khusrau ka Hindavi Kalaam, 1988; Adabi Tanqeed aur Usloobiyat, 1989; Rajinder Singh Bedi (anthology), 1990; Urdu Language and Literature: Critical Perspectives, 1991; Sakhtiyat, Pas-Sakhtiyat, Mashriqi Sheriyat, 1993; Balwant Singh (anthology), 1995; Hindustan ke Urdu Musannifin aur Shoara, 1996; Urdu Postmodernism, a Dialogue, 1998. Honours: Padma Shri, Highest Civilian Award by the President of India, 1991; Sahita Akademi Award, 1995; Rockefeller Foundation Fellowship for Residency at Belagio, Italy, 1997. Address: D-252 Sarvodaya Enclave, New Delhi 110017, India.

NARAYAMA Fujio, b. 13 June 1948, Iwate, Japan. Writer; Poet. Education: Graduate in Drama, Toho Gakuen Junior College, Tokyo, 1970. Publications: Manhattan Ballad, 1977; Sanctuary of Evil, 1979; Lay Traps in the Winter, 1981; The Scarred Bullet, 1989; Neverending Night, 1992. Honours: Iwate Arts Festival Awards, 1967, 1969; All Yomimono New Writer's Award, 1975. Memberships: Japan Writers Association; Mystery Writers of America; Mystery Writers of Japan; Sino-Japanese Cultural Exchange Society. Address: 2-1-11 Veruzone 2-B, Nukui, Nerima-ku, Tokyo, Japan.

NARDON Anita Lucia, b. 2 Apr 1931, Belgium. Multi-Lingual Secretary; Art Critic. div., 3 sons. Appointments: Staff, Peau de Serpent, 1962-78, Le Drapeau Rouge, 1980-91, IDEART, 1989, Saison, 1989. Publications: Poetry: 18 Booklets; La Chanson d'Isis; Tale: Contes pour Yannick; Art Books: more than 20 artist's monographs; 50 Artistes de Belgique, Vol IV, V, VI. Contributions: Various monthly art magazines. Honours: Médaille d'argent Arthur Rimbaud; Prix Ville de Toulon, France; Prix Silarus Francia; Médaille de Bronze, Poésiades de Paris. Memberships: PEN; Association International des Critiques d'Art. Address: Rue Jourdan 57, 1060 Brussels, Belgium.

NASH Gary Baring, b. 27 July 1933, Philadelphia, Pennsylvania, USA. Professor of History; Writer. m. (1) Mary Workum, 20 Dec 1955, div, 1 son, 3 daughters, (2) Cynthia Shelton, 24 Oct 1981. Education: BA, 1955, PhD, 1964, Princeton University. Appointments: Assistant to the Dean, Graduate School, 1959-61, Instructor, 1964-65, Assistant Professor, 1965-66, Princeton University: Assistant Professor, 1966-68, Associate Professor, 1969-72, Professor of History, 1972-, Dean, Undergraduate Curriculum Development, 1984-91, University of California at Los Angeles; Associate Director, 1988-94, Director, 1994-, National Center for History in the Schools; Co-Chairman, National History Studies Project, 1992-95. Publications: Quakers and Politics: Pennsylvania, 1681-1726, 1968, revised edition, 1993; Class and Society in Early America, 1970; The Great Fear: Race in the Mind of America (editor with Richard Weiss), 1970; Red, White, and Black; The Peoples of Early America, 1974, 3rd edition, 1991; The Urban Crucible: Social Change, Political Consciousness, and the Origins of the American Revolution, 1979; Struggle and Survival in Colonial America (editor with David Sweet), 1980; The Private Side of American History (co-editor), 2 volumes, 1983, 1987; The American People: Creating a Nation and a Society (with J R Jeffrey), 2 volumes, 1985, 1989, 4th edition, 1997; Retracing the Past, 2 volumes, 1985, 1989, 1993, 1997; Race, Class and Politics: Essays on American Colonial and Revolutionary Society, 1986; Forging Freedom: The Formation of Philadelphia's Black Community, 1720-1840, 1988; Race and Revolution, 1990; Freedom by Degrees: Emancipation and Its Aftermath in Pennsylvania (with Jean R Soderlund), 1991; American Odyssey: The United States in the 20th Century, 1991, revised edition, 1993; History on Trial: Culture Wars and the Teaching of the Past (with Charlotte Crabtree and Ross Dunn), 1997. Contributions to: Professional journals. Honours: Guggenheim Fellowship, 1969-70; American Council of Learned Societies Fellowship, 1973-74. Memberships: American Antiquarian Society; American Historical Association; Institute of Early American History and Culture; Organization of American Historians, president, 1994-95; Society of American Historians. Address: 16174 Alcima Avenue, Pacific Palisades, CA 90272, USA.

NASH Gerald David, b. 16 July 1928, Berlin, Germany (US citizen, 1944). Historian; Distinguished Porfessor. m. Marie L Norris, 19 Aug 1967, 1 daughter. Education: BA, New York University, 1950; MA, Columbia Universty, 1952; PhD, University of California at Berkeley, 1957. Appointments: Instructor, 1957-58, Visiting Assistant Professor, 1959-60, Stanford University; Assistant Professor, Northern Illinois University, DeKalb, 1958-59; Postdoctoral Fellow, Harvard University, 1960-61; Faculty, 1961-68, Professor of History, 1968-85, Chairman, Department of History, 1974-80, Presidential

Professor, 1985-90, Distinguished Professor, 1990-, University of New Mexico: Visiting Associate Professor, New York University, 1965-66; Editor, The Historian, 1974-84; George Bancroft Professor of American History, University of Göttingen, 1990-91. Publications: State Government and Economic Development, 1964; Issues in American Economic History (editor), 1964, 3rd edition, 1984; F D Roosevelt (editor), 1967; US Oil Policy, 1968; Perspectives on Administration, 1969; The Great Transition, 1971; The American West in the 20th Century, 1973; The Great Depression and World War II, 1979; Urban West (editor), 1979; The American West Transformed: The Impact of World War II, 1985; Social Security in the US: The First Half Century (editor with Noel Pugach and Richard Tomasson), 1988; Perspectives on the 20th Century West (editor with Richard Etulain), 1989; World War II and the West: Reshaping the Economy, 1990; Creating the West: Historical Interpretations, 1991; A P Giannini and the Bank of America, 1992; The Crucial Era, 1992; Research Opportunities in 20th Century Western History (editor with Richard Etulain), 1996. Contributions to: Professional journals. Honours: Newberry Library Fellow, 1959; Huntington Library Grant, 1979; National Endowment for the Humanities Senior Fellow, 1981; Project 87 Fellow, 1982-83; Phi Beta Kappa. Memberships: Agricultural History Society; American Historical Association; Business History Society; Organization of American Historians; Western History Association. Address: c/o Department of History, University of New Mexico, Albuquerque, NM 87131, USA.

NASSAR Eugene Paul, b. 20 June 1935, Utica, New York, USA. Professor of English; Writer; Poet. m. Karen Nocian, 30 Dec 1969, 1 son, 2 daughters. Education: BA, Kenyon College, 1957; MA, Worcester College, Oxford, 1960; PhD, Cornell University, 1962. Appointments: Instructor in English, Hamilton College, 1962-64; Assistant Professor, 1964-66, Associate Professor, 1966-71, Professor of English, 1971-, Utica College, Syracuse University; Director, Ethnic Heritage Studies Center. Publications: Wallace Stevens: An Anatomy of Figuration, 1965, 2nd edition, 1968; The Rape of Cinderella: Essays in Literary Continuity, 1970; Selections from a Prose Poem: East Utica, 1971; The Cantos of Ezra Pound: The Lyric Mode, 1975; Wind of the Land: Two Prose Poems, 1979; Essays: Critical and Metacritical, 1983; Illustrations to Dante's Inferno, 1994; Editor of several books. Contributions to: Various publications. Address: 704 Lansing Street, Utica, NY 13501, USA.

NASSAUER Rudolf, b. 8 Nov 1924, Frankfurt am Main, Germany. Writer; Poet. Education: University of Reading, 1943-45. Publications: Poems, 1947; The Holigan, 1959; The Cuckoo, 1962; The Examination, 1973; The Unveiling, 1975; The Agents of Love, 1976; Midlife Feasts, 1977; Reparations, 1981; Kramer's Goats, 1986. Address: 51 St James' Gardens, London W11, England.

NATALE Francine de. See: **MALZBERG Barry.**

NATHAN David, b. 9 Dec 1926, Manchester, England. Journalist; Writer; Dramatist. m. Norma Ellis, 31 Mar 1957, 2 sons. Appointments: Copy Boy, Copy Taker, News Chronicle, Manchester, 1942-44, 1947; Reporter, St Helen's Reporter, 1947-49; Reporter, Feature Writer, Theatre Critic, London Editor, Nottingham Guardian, 1949-52; Daily Mail, 1952-54; Associated Press, 1954-55; Reporter, Feature Writer, Theatre Critic, Daily Herald/Sun, 1955-69; Theatre Critic, 1970-, Deputy Editor, 1978-91, Jewish Chronicle. Publications: Hancock (with Freddie Hancock), 1969; A Good Human Story (television play), 1978; The Freeloader (novel), 1970; The Laughtermakers, 1971; The Story So Far (novel), 1986. Radio Plays: The Belman of London, 1982; The Bohemians, 1983; Glenda Jackson, a critical profile, 1984; John Hurt, An Actor's Progress, 1986. Contributions to: Prospect; Times Saturday Review; Daily Telegraph; Sunday Telegraph; Independent; Harper's and Queens; TV Times; Observer Colour Magazine. Honour: Highly Commended, Writer's Award, Royal Television

Society, 1978. Membership: Critics Circle, president, 1986-88. Address: 16 Augustus Close, Brentford Dock, Brentford, Middlesex, England.

NATHAN Leonard (Edward), b. 8 Nov 1924, Los Angeles, California, USA. Professor Emeritus; Poet; Writer; Translator. m. Carol G Nash, 27 June 1949, 1 son, 2 daughters. Education: BA, Highest Honours, 1950, MA, 1951, PhD, 1961, University of California at Berkeley. Appointments: Instructor, Modesto Junior College, California, 1954-60; Professor, 1961-91, Chairman, Department of Rhetoric, 1968-72, Professor Emeritus, 1991-, University of California at Berkeley. Publications: Poetry: Glad and Sorry Seasons, 1963; The Matchmaker's Lament, 1967; The Day the Perfect Speakers Left, 1969; Flight Plan, 1971; Without Wishing, 1973; Coup and Other Poems, 1975; The Likeness: Poems Out of India, 1975; Returning Your Call, 1975; Teachings of Grandfather Fox, 1976; Lost Distance, 1978; Dear Blood, 1980; Holding Patterns, 1982; Carrying On: New and Selected Poems, 1985; The Potato Eaters, 1999. Prose: The Tragic Drama of W B Yeats: Figures in Dance, 1963; The Poet's Work: An Introduction to Czeslaw Milosz (with Arthur Quinn), 1991; Diary of a Left-Handed Bird Watcher, 1996. Translator: First Person, Second Person, by "Agyeya", 1971; The Transport of Love; Kalidasa "The Cloud Messenger", 1976; Grace and Mercy in Her Wild Hair, by Ramprasad sen (with Clinton Seely), 1982; Songs of Something Else, by Gunnar Ekelof (with James Larson), 1985; Happy as a Dog's Tail, by Anna Swir (with Czeslaw Milosz, 1985; With the Skin, by Aleksander Wat (with Czeslaw Milosz), 1989; Talking to My Body, by Anna Swir (with Czeslaw Milosz), 1996. Contributions to: Reviews, journals, and magazines. Honours: Phalen Award for Narrative Poetry, 1955; Longview Foundation Award for Poetry, 1962; Creative Arts Fellowships, University of California, 1963-64, 1973-74; American Institute of Indian Studies Fellowship, 1967-68; National Institute of Arts and Letters Award, 1971; Guggenheim Fellowship, 1976-77; Commonwealth Club Silver Medals for Poetry, 1976, 1980. Address: 40 Beverly Road, Kensington, CA 94707, USA.

NATHAN Robert S(tuart), b. 13 Aug 1948, Johnstown, Pennsylvania, USA. Writer. Education: BA, Amherst College, 1970. Appointment: Producer, Law and Order series, NBC-TV. Publications: Amusement Park, 1977; Rising Higher, 1981; The Religion, 1982; The Legend, 1986; The White Tiger, 1988; In the Deep Woods, 1989. Other: In the Deep Woods (television film), 1992. Contributions to: Periodicals and National Public Radio. Address: c/o William Morris Agency, 1350 Avenue of the Americas, New York, NY 10019, USA.

NATHAN-DAVIS Sarah. See: **WHYTE Sally C.**

NATO Le Peintre, b. 6 Feb 1944, Bruxelles, Belgium. Artist. m. 15 Apr 1963, 1 son, 3 daughters. Appointments: Organizer, International Meetings of Artists. Publications: Books: Mundial Master Class in Universities and Art Schools; Poetry of the Obscene; Be Art; Knowledge of the Body and of its Eloquence. Contributions to: Journals, anthologies, quarterlies and reviews. Address: 16 rue Eugene Sue, 75018 Paris, France.

NATUSCH Sheila (Ellen), b. 14 Feb 1926, Invercargill, New Zealand. Writer; Illustrator. m. Gilbert G Natusch, 28 Nov 1950. Education: MA, Otago University, 1948. Publications: Stewart Island (with N S Seaward), 1951; Native Plants, 1956; Native Rock, 1959; Animals of New Zealand, 1967; new edtion, 1999; A Bunch of Wild Orchids, 1968, 2nd edition, 1977; New Zealand Mosses, 1969; 2nd edition, 1998; Brother Wohlers: A Biography, 1969, 2nd edition, 1992; On the Edge of the Bush: Women in Early Southland, 1976; Hell and High Water: A German Occupation of the Chatham Islands 1843-1910, 1977, 2nd edition, 1992; The Cruise of the Acheron: Her Majesty's Steam Vessel on Survey in New Zealand Waters 1848-1851, 1978, 2nd edition 1998; The Roaring Forties, 1978; Fortnight in Ireland, 1979; Wild Fare for Wilderness Foragers, 1979; A Pocket Full of Pebbles, 1983; South Ho!: The Search for a Southern

Edinburgh, 1844, 1985; Granny Gurton's Garden (with Lois Chambers), 1987; William Swainson: The Anatomy of a Nineteenth-Century Naturalist, 1987, 2nd edition, 1998; Roy Traill of Stewart Island, 1991; An Island Called Home, 1992; The Natural World of the Traills: An Investigation into Some of the 19th Century Naturalists of a Particular Family in Scotland and the Colonies, 1996; Ruapuke Visited, 1998; My Dear Friend Tuckett, Volume I, 1998. Contributions to: Books and periodicals. Honour: Hubert Church Award, PEN New Zealand, 1969. Address: 46 Owhiro Bay Parade, Wellington 6002, New Zealand.

NAUMOFF Lawrence Jay, b. 23 Jul 1946, Charlotte, North Carolina, USA. Author. Div, 1 son. Education: BA, University of North Carolina, Chapel Hill, 1969. Publications: The Night of the Weeping Women, 1988; Rootie Kazootie, 1990; Taller Women, 1992; Silk Hope, NC, 1994; A Plan for Women, 1997. Contributions to: Various literary magazines, short stories. Honours: Thomas Wolfe Memorial Award, 1969; National Endowment for the Arts Grant, 1970; Whiting Foundation Writers Award, 1990. Membership: PEN. Address: 1240 Epps Clark Rd, Siler City, NC 27344.

NAVARRO Gilles, b. 11 June 1958, Perpignan. Reporter. 1 daughter. Appointment: L'Equipe Newspapers. Publications: L'Année des Rallyes-Raids, 1986, 1987; Hubert Auriol; Les Records du Monde en Athlétisme. Contributions to: L'Equipe. Address: 4 rue Rouget de Lisle 92137 Issy, France.

NAVASKY Victor S, b. 5 July 1932, New York, New York, USA. Editor; Writer. m. Anne Dandy Strongin, 27 Mar 1966, 1 son, 2 daughters. Education: AB, Swarthmore College, 1954; JD, Yale Law School, 1959. Publications: Kennedy Justice, 1971; Naming Names, 1980. Contributions to: Many magazines and journals. Honour: American Book Award, 1981. Memberships: American PEN; Authors Guild; Committee to Protect Journalists. Address: 33 West 67th Street, New York, NY 10023, USA.

NAVON Robert, b. 18 May 1954, New York, New York, USA. Editor; Philosopher. Education: BA, Lehman College, City University of New York, 1975; MS, State University of New York, Geneseo, 1978; MA studies, New School for Social Research, New York City, 1982-86; PhD candidate, University of New Mexico, 1991-. Publications: Patterns of the Universe, 1977; Autumn Songs: Poems, 1983; The Pythagorean Writings, 1986; Healing of Man and Woman, 1989; Harmony of the Spheres, 1991; Cosmic Patterns, Vol I, 1993; Great Works of Philosophy, 7 volumes (editor). Honours: New York State Regents Scholar, 1971; Phi Beta Kappa, 1975; Intern, Platform Association, 1980. Memberships: Society of Ancient Greek Philosophy; American Philosophical Association. Address: PO Box 81702, Albuquerque, NM 87198, USA.

NAYAK Harogadde Manappa, b. 5 Feb 1931, Hosamane, India. Writer. m. Yashodharamma, 11 May 1955, 1 son, 1 daughter. Education: BA, Honours, University of Mysore, 1955; MA, University of Calcutta, 1959; PhD, Indiana University, USA, 1964. Appointment: Editor, Prabuddha Karnataka, 1967-84. Publications: Over 60 books. Contributions to: Various publications. Honours: Gold Medal, University of Calcutta, 1959; Jubilee Award, University of Mysore, 1978; Karnataka State Award, 1982; Karnataka Sahitya Akademy Award, 1985. Memberships: Indian National Academy of Letters; Indian PEN; National Book Trust. Address: Godhuli, Jayalakshmi Puram, Mysore 570-021, Karnataka, India.

NAYLOR Gloria, b. 25 Jan 1950, New York, New York, USA. Author; President of Film Production Company. Education: BA, Brooklyn College of the City University of New York, 1981; MA, Yale University, 1983. Appointments: Writer-in-Residence, Cummington Community of the Arts, 1983; Visiting Professor, George Washington University, 1983-84, Princeton University, 1986-87, Boston University, 1987; United States Information Agency Cultural Exchange Lecturer, India,

1985; Visiting Writer, New York University, 1986; Fannie Hurst Visiting Professor, Brandeis University, 1988; Senior Fellow, Society for the Humanities, Cornell University, 1988; President, One Way Productions films, New York City, 1990-. Publications: The Women of Brewster Place: A Novel in Seven Stories, 1982; Lindin Hills, 1985; Mama Day, 1988; Bailey's Cafe, 1992; Children of the Night: The Best Short Stories by Black Writers, 1967 to the Present (editor), 1995; The Men of Brewster Place, 1998. Contributions to: Magazines. Honours: National Book Award for Best First Novel, 1983; Distinguished Writer Award, Mid-Atlantic Writers Association, 1983; National Endowment for the Arts Fellowship, 1985; Candace Award, National Coalition of 100 Black Women, 1986; Guggenheiim Fellowship, 1988; Lillian Smith Award, 1989. Address: c/o One Way Productions, 638 2nd Street, Brooklyn, NY 11215, USA.

NAYLOR Phyllis, b. 4 Jan 1933, Anderson, Indiana, USA. Writer. Education: Diploma, Joliet Junior College, 1953; BA, American University, 1963. Publications: Over 90 books for adults or children, 1965-96. Honour: Newbery Medal, American Library Association, 1992. Address: 9910 Holmhurst Road, Bethesda, MD 20817, USA.

NAYLOR Thomas (Herbert), b. 30 May 1936, Jackson, Mississippi, USA. Professor of Economics Emeritus; Writer. m. Magdalena Raczkowska, 14 Dec 1985, 1 son, 1 daughter. Education: BS, Mathematics, Millsaps College, 1958; BS, Industrial Engineering, Columbia University, 1959; MBA, Quantitative Business Analysis, Indiana University, 1961; PhD, Economics, Tulane University, 1964. Appointments: Instructor, Tulane University, 1961-63; Assistant Professor, 1964-66, Associate Professor, 1966-68, Professor of Economics, 1968-93, Professor Emeritus, 1994-, Duke University; Visiting Professor, University of Wisconsin, 1969-70; Middlebury College, 1993-94, University of Vermont, 1994-96; President, Social Systems Inc, 1971-80; Managing Director, Naylor Group, 1980. Publications: Numerous books, including: Linear Programming (with Eugene Byrne), 1963; Computer Simulation Techniques (with Joseph L Balintfy, Donald S Burdick and King Chu), 1966; Microeconomics and Decision Models of the Firm (with John Vernon), 1969; Computer Simulation Experiments with Models of Economic Systems, 1971; Corporate Planning Models, 1979; Strategic Planning Management, 1980; Managerial Economics: Corporate Economics and Strategy (with John M Vernon and Kenneth Wertz), 1983; The Corporate Strategy Matrix, 1986; The Gorbachev Strategy, 1988; The Cold War Legacy, 1991; The Search for Meaning, 1994; The Abandoned Generation: Rethinking Higher Education (with William H Willimon), 1995; The Search for Meaning in the Workplace (with Rolf Osterberg and William H Willimon), 1996; Downsizing the USA, 1997. Contributions to: Various scholarly books and journals. Address: c/o Department of Economics, Duke University, Durham, NC 27708, USA.

NEAL Patricia. See: FLAGG Fannie.

NEEDLE Jan, b. 8 Feb 1943, Holybourne, England. Writer. Education: Drama Degree, Victoria University of Manchester, 1971. Publications: Albeson and the Germans, 1977; My Mate Shofiq, 1978; A Fine Boy for Killing, 1979; The Size Spies, 1979; Rottenteeth, 1980; The Bee Rustlers, 1980; A Sense of Shame, 1980; Wild Wood, 1981; Losers Weepers, 1981; Another Fine Mess, 1981; Brecht (with Peter Thomson), 1981; Piggy in the Middle, 1982; Going Out, 1983; A Pitiful Place, 1984; Great Days at Grange Hill, 1984; Tucker's Luck, 1984; Behind the Bike Sheds, 1985; A Game of Soldiers, 1985; Tucker in Control, 1985, 1985; Wagstaffe, The Wind-Up Boy, 1987; Uncle in the Attic, 1987; Skeleton at School, 1987; In the Doghouse, 1988; The Sleeping Party, 1988; Mad Scramble, 1989; As Seen on TV, 1989; The Thief, 1990; The Bully, 1992. Television Plays and Serials: A Game of Soldiers, 1985; Trucking, 1987; Soft Soap, 1987; The Thief, 1989; The Bill, 1992. Address: c/o Rochell Stevens and Co, 2 Terretts Place, Upper Street, London N1 1QZ, England.

NEELY Mark Edward Jr, b. 10 Nov 1944, Amarillo, Texas, USA. Writer; Editor; Professor. m. Sylvia Eakes, 15 June 1966. Education: BA, 1966, PhD, 1973, Yale University. Appointments: Director, Louis A Warren Lincoln Library and Museum, Fort Wayne, Indiana; Visiting Instructor, Iowa State University, 1971-72; Editor, Lincoln Lore, 1973-; Professor, St Louis University. Publications: The Abraham Lincoln Encyclopedia, 1981; The Lincoln Image: Abraham Lincoln and the Popular Print (with Harold Holzer and Gabor S Boritt), 1984; The Insanity File: The Case of Mary Todd Lincoln (with R Gerald McMurty), 1986; The Confederate Image: Prints of the Large Cause, 1987; The Lincoln Family Album: Photographs from the Personal Collection of a Historic American Family, 1990; The Fate of Liberty: Abraham Lincoln and Civil Libertires, 1991; The Last Best Hope on Earth: Abraham Lincoln and the Promise of America, 1993; Mine Eyes Have Seen the Glory: The Civil War in American Art (with Harold Holzer), 1993. Honour: Pulitzer Prize for History, 1992. Memberships: Abraham Lincoln Association; Indiana Association of Historians, president, 1987-88; Society of Indiana Archivists, president, 1980-81. Address: c/o Department of History, St Louis University, 221 North Grand Avenue, St Louis, MO 63103, USA.

NEELY William Robert Nicholas, b. 21 May 1959, Belfast, Ireland. TV Correspondent. m. Marion Kerr, 5 June 1988, 2 daughters. Education: BA, Honours, Queens University, Belfast. Appointments: BBC News Reporter, 1981-89; Sky TV News Reporter & Presenter, 1989; ITN Reporter, 1989-90; ITN Washington Correspondent, 1991-97; ITN Europe Correspondent, 1997-. Address: Bvd Charlemagne 1/18, 1041 Brussels, Belgium.

NEESER Andreas, b. 25 Jan 1964, Schlossrued, Switzerland. Teacher; Writer; Poet. Education: Graduated, University of Zürich, 1990; Teacher's Diploma, 1994. Publications: Schattensprünge (novel), 1995; Treibholz (poems), 1997. Honours: Grants, Canton of Aargau, 1991,1992, 1998. Memberships: PEN Switzerland; Swiss Writers Union, Zürich. Address: Neugutstrasse 4, CH-5000 Aarau, Switzerland.

NEHAMAS Alexander, b. 22 Mar 1946, Athens, Greece (Spanish citizen). Professor in the Humanities, Philosophy, and Comparative Literature; Author. m. Susan Glimcher, 22 June 1983, 1 son. Education: BA, Swarthmore College, 1967; PhD, Princeton University, 1971. Appointments: Assistant Professor, 1971-76, Associate Professor, 1976-81, Professor of Philosophy, 1981-86, University of Pittsburgh; Visiting Fellow, 1978-79, Professor of Philosophy, 1988, 1990-, Edmund N Carpenter II Class of 1943 Professor in the Humanities, 1989-, Professor of Comparative Literature, 1990-, Princeton University; Mills Professor of Philosophy, 1983; Sather Professor of Classical Literature, 1993, University of California at Berkeley; Visiting Scholar, 1983-84, Professor of Philosophy, 1986-90, University of Pennsylvania. Publications: Nietzsche: Life as Literature, 1985; Plato's "Symposium" (translator and editor with Paul Woodruff), 1989; Aristotle's "Rhetoric": Philosophical Essays (co-editor with D J Furley), 1994; Plato's "Phaedrus" (translator and editor with Paul Woodruff), 1995; Virtues of Authenticity: Essays on Plato and Socrates, 1999; The Art of Living: Socratic Reflections from Plato to Foucault, 1998. Contributions to: Books and professional journals. Honours: National Endowment for the Humanities Fellowship, 1978-79; Guggenheim Fellowship, 1983-84; Romanell-Phi Beta Kappa Professor in Philosophy, 1990-91; D Phil (Hon) University of Athens, 1993; Phi Beta Kappa Visiting Scholar, 1995. Memberships: American Academy of Arts and Sciences, Membership Committee, 1998-2000; American Society for Aesthetics; Modern Greek Studies Association; North American Nietzsche Society. Address: 692 Pretty Brook Road, Princeton, NJ 08540, USA.

NEIL Andrew, b. 21 May 1949, Paisley, Scotland. Newspaper Editor; Broadcaster; Columnist; Media Consultant. Education: MA, University of Glasgow. Appointments: Reporter and Correspondent, Economist,

1973-82; London Editor, 1982-83, Editor, 1983-94, Sunday Times; Executive Editor and Chief Correspondent, Fox News Network, 1994; Contributing Editor, Vanity Fair, New York, 1995; Editor-in-Chief, Scotsman, Edinburgh, The European, London, 1997; Sunday Business, London, 1998; Anchorman, BBC TV's Midnight Hour, ITV's Thursday Night Live. Publications: The Cable Revolution, 1982; Britain's Free Press: Does It Have One?, 1988; Full Disclosure (autobiography), 1996. Address: Glenburn Enterprises Ltd, PO Box 584, London SW7 3QY, England.

NEILAN Sarah, b. Newcastle-upon-Tyne, England. 4 children. Education: MA, Oxon. Publications: The Braganza Pursuit; An Air of Glory; Paradise; The Old Enchantment. Contributions to: Observer; Evening Standard; Times Educational Supplement; Reader's Digest; several women's magazines; The Bookseller, educational journals. Honour: Mary Elgin Prize. Memberships: PEN; Society of Authors. Literary Agent: Peters Fraser Dunlop. Address: c/o Peters Fraser Dunlop, 5 The Chambers, Chelsea Harbour, London SW10, England.

NEILL William, (Uilleam Neill), b. 22 Feb 1922, Prestwick, Ayrshire, Scotland. Retired Teacher; Poet; Writer. m. (1), 2 daughters, (2) Doris Marie Walker, 2 Apr 1970. Education: MA, Honours, University of Edinburgh, 1971; Teacher's Certificate, 1972. Publications: Scotland's Castle, 1970; Poems, 1970; Four Points of a Saltire (co-author), 1970; Despatches Home, 1972; Galloway Landscape, 1981; Cnù a Mogail, 1983; Wild Places, 1985; Blossom, Berry, Fall, 1986; Making Tracks, 1991; Straight Lines, 1922; Tales from the Odyssey, 1992; Selected Poems 1969-92, 1994. Contributions to: Various publications, BBC Scotland, and BBC Radio 4. Honours: Bardic Crown, National Gaelic MOD, 1969; Sloan Verse Prize, 1970; Grierson Prize, 1970; Scottish Arts Council Book Award, 1985. Membership: PEN International, Scottish Branch. Address: Burnside, Crossmichael, Castle Douglas, Kirkcudbrightshire DG7 3AP, Scotland.

NELSON Marguerite. See: FLOREN Lee.

NELSON Marilyn, (Marilyn Nelson Waniek), b. 26 Apr 1946, Cleveland, Ohio, USA. Professor of English; Poet; Translator. 1 son, 1 daughter. Education: BA, University of California at Davis, 1968; MA, University of Pennsylvania, 1970; PhD, University of Minnesota, 1979. Appointments: Visiting Assistant Professor, Reed College, Portland, Oregon, 1971-72; Assistant Professor, St Olaf College, Northfield, Minnesota, 1973-78; Instructor, University of Hamburg, 1977; Assistant Professor to Professor of English, University of Connecticut at Storrs, 1978-; Faculty, MFA Program, New York University, 1988, 1994, Vermont College, 1991; Elliston Poet-in-Residence, University of Cincinnati, 1994. Publications: For the Body, 1978; The Cat Walked Through the Casserole (with Pamela Espeland), 1984; Mama's Promises, 1985; The Homeplace, 1990; Partial Truth, 1992; Magnificat, 1995; The Fields of Praise: New and Selected Poems, 1997. Contributions to: Books and journals. Honours: Kent Fellowship, 1976; National Endowment for the Arts Fellowships, 1981, 1990; Danish Ministry of Culture Grant, 1984; Connecticut Arts Award, 1990; Individual Artist Grant, Connecticut Commission for the Arts, 1990; Finalist in Poetry, National Book Award, 1991, 1997; Annisfield-Wolf Award, 1992; Fulbright Teaching Fellow, 1995. Memberships: Associated Writing Programs; Poetry Society of America; Society for the Study of Multi-Ethnic Literature of the USA; Society for Values in Higher Education. Address: c/o Department of English, U-25, University of Connecticut, Storrs, CT 06268, USA.

NELSON Nigel David, b. 16 Apr 1954, London, England. Journalist; Writer; Broadcaster. 3 sons, 2 daughters. Education: Sutton Valence School, Kent, England; Department of Journalism, Harlow College. Appointments: Crime Reporter, Kent Evening Post; Reporter, Daily Mail; Royal Correspondent; Daily Mail; New York Correspondent; Daily Mail; Feature Writer, TV

Critic, Sunday Mirror; Political Editor, Sunday People. Publications: If I Should Die, film biography of Rupert Brooke For Burfield-Bastable Productions, 1986; The Porton Phial, a political thriller, 1991; The Honeytrap, short story, 1991. Honour: Commended, Young Journalist of the Year, 1974. Literary Agent: Michael Shaw, Curtis Brown. Address: Sunday People, 1 Canada Square, Canary Wharf, London E14 5AP, England.

NELSON Richard, b. 17 Oct 1950, Chicago, Illinois, USA. Dramatist; Screenwriter. Education: BA, Hamilton College, 1972. Appointments: Literary Manager, BAM Theatre Co, Brooklyn, 1979-81; Associate Director, Goodman Theatre, Chicago, 1980-83; Dramaturg, Guthrie Theatre, Minneapolis, 1981-82. Publications: The Vienna Notes (in Word Plays I), 1980; Il Campiello (adaptation), 1981; An American Comedy and Other Plays, 1984; Between East and West (in New Plays USA 3), 1986; Principia Scriptoriae, 1986; Strictly Dishonorable and Other Lost American Plays (editor), 1986; Rip Van Winkle, 1986; Jungle Coup (in Plays from Playwrights Horizons), 1987; Accidental Death of an Anarchist (adaptation), 1987. Address: 32 South Street, Rhinebeck, NY 12572, USA.

NELSON-HUMPHRIES Luisa-Teresa, (Tessa Nelson-Humphries), b. Yorkshire, England. Professor; Writer; Poet. m. (1) Kenneth Nelson Brown, 1 June 1957, dec 1962, (2) Cecil H Unthank, 26 Sept 1963, dec 1979. Education: BA, English, MA, English, University of North Carolina; PhD, English, University of Liverpool, 1974. Appointments: Director of English, Windsor College, Buenos Aires; Professor of English, Cumberland College, Williamsburg, Kentucky, 1964-90; Part-time Faculty, New Mexico State University, Las Cruces, 1990-92. Contributions to: Anthologies, reviews, and journals. Honours: Numerous honourable mentions; 1st Prize, 1978, 3rd Prizes, 1988, 1995, 2nd Prize, 1989, Julia Cairns Competition; Clemence Dane Trophy, 1995; Tessa Nelson-Humphries Scholarship for Excellence in English, established 1997. Memberships: American Association of University Women; Mesilla Valley Writers, New Mexico, vice president; MENSA; Society of Children's Book Writers; Society of Women Writers and Journalists. Address: 3228 Jupiter Road, 4 Hills, Las Cruces, NM 88012, USA.

NEMCHIN V. See: **BAAL Voldemar.**

NEUBERGER Julia Babette Sarah, b. 27 Feb 1950, London, England. Rabbi; Author; Broadcaster. m. Anthony John Neuberger, 17 Sept 1973, 1 son, 1 daughter. Education: Newnham College, Cambridge, 1969-73; BA, Assyriology, Hebrew, MA, 1975, University of Cambridge; Rabbinic Ordination, Leo Baeck College, 1977. Appointments: Chief Executive, The King's Fund, London; Judge, Irish Times International Fiction Prize, 1997. Publications: Judaism, 1986; Caring for Dying People of Different Faiths, 1987; Days of Decision, 4 volumes (editor), 1987; Whatever's Happening to Women?, 1991; A Necessary End (editor with John White), 1991; Ethics and Healthcare: Research Ethics Committees in the UK, 1992; The Things that Matter, 1993; On Being Jewish, 1995. Contributions to: Jewish Chronicle; Times; Irish Times; Irish Sunday Tribune; Vogue; Cosmopolitan; Sunday Times; Telegraph; Sunday Express; Mail on Sunday; Evening Standard. Honours: Honorary Fellow, Mansfield College, Oxford; Honorary Fellow City and Guilds Institute; Honorary Doctorates from the Universities of: Humberside, Ulster, City, Nottingham, Open, Stirling, Oxford Brookes, Teesside. Membership: Royal Society of Arts, fellow. Address: The King's Fund, 11-13 Cavendish Square, London W1M 0AN, England.

NEUGEBOREN Jay (Michael), b. 30 May 1938, New York, New York, USA. Writer. Education: BA, Columbia University, 1959; MA, Indiana University, 1963. Appointments: Visiting Writer, Stanford University, 1966-67; Writer-in-Residence, University of Massachusetts, 1971-. Publications: Big Man, 1966; Corky's Brother, 1969; Sam's Legacy, 1974; The Stolen Jew, 1981; Before My Life Began, 1985; Imagining Robert: M y Brother, Madness, and Survival (memoir), 1997; Don't Worry About the Kids, 1997. Contributions to: Magazines. Honours: Transatlantic Review Novella Award, 1967; National Endowment for the Arts Fellowships, 1967; Guggenheim Fellowship, 1978; Present Tense Award for Best Novel, 1981; PEN Syndicated Fiction Prizes, 1982-88; Wallant Memorial Prize for Best Novel, 1985. Memberships: Authors Guild; PEN. Literary Agent: Richard Parks, 138 E 16th St, New York City 10003. Address: 35 Harrison Avenue, Northampton, MA 01060, USA.

NEUMEYER Peter F(lorian), b. 4 Aug 1929, Munich, Germany. Professor; Writer. m. Helen Wight Snell, 28 Dec 1952, 3 sons. Education: BA, 1951, MA, 1955, PhD, 1963, University of California at Berkeley. Appointments: Assistant Professor, Harvard University, 1963-69; Associate Professor, State University of New York at Stony Brook, 1969-75; Professor and Chairman, Department of English, West Virginia University, 1975-78; Professor, San Diego State University, 1978-. Publications: Kafka's The Castle, 1969; Donald and the ..., 1969; Donald Has a Difficulty, 1970; The Faithful Fish, 1971; Elements of Fiction (co-editor), 1974; Homage to John Clare, 1980; Image and Makers (co-editor), 1984; The Phantom of the Opera (adaptation), 1988; The Annotated Charlotte's Web, 1994. Contributions to: Journals. Address: 45 Marguerita Road, Kensington, CA 94707, USA.

NEUSTADT Richard E(lliott), b. 26 June 1919, Philadelphia, Pennsylvania, USA. Professor Emeritus; Writer. m. (1) Bertha Frances Cummings, 21 Dec 1945, dec 1984, 1 son, 1 daughter, (2) Shirley Williams, 19 Dec 1987. Education: AB, University of California at Berkeley, 1939; MA, 1941, PhD, 1951, Harvard University. Appointments: Economist, US Office of Price Administration, 1942, US Bureau of the Budget, 1946-50, White House, Washington, DC, 1950-53; Professor of Public Administration, Cornell University, 1953-54; Professor of Government, Columbia University, 1954-64; Visiting Professor, Princeton University, 1957, University of California at Berkeley, 1986, Cornell University, 1992, University of Essex, 1994-95; Visiting Lecturer, 1961-62, Associate Member, 1965-67, 1990-92, Nuffield College, Oxford; Consultant to President John F Kennedy, 1961-63, President Lyndon B Johnson, 1964-66; Professor of Government, 1965-78, Lucius N Littauer Professor of Public Administration, 1978-87, Douglas Dillon Professor, 1987-89, Professor Emeritus, 1989-, Harvard University; Fellow, Center for Advanced Study in the Behavioral Sciences, 1978-79. Publications: Presidential Power, 1960, revised edition, 1990; Alliance Politics, 1970; The Swine Flu Affair (with Harvey V Fineberg), 1978, republished as The Epidemic That Never Was, 1982; Thinking in Time (with Ernest R May), 1986. Contributions to: Professional journals. Memberships: American Academy of Arts and Sciences, fellow; American Philosophical Society; American Political Science Association; Council on Foreign Relations; Institute for Strategic Studies; National Academy of Public Administration. Address: 79 JFK Street, Cambridge, MA 02138, USA.

NEUSTATTER Angela Lindsay, b. 24 Sept 1943, Buckinghamshire, England. Journalist. Author. 2 sons. Education: Regent Street Polytechnic, London; Diploma in Journalism. Publications: Twiggy - Health and Beauty, 1985; Mixed Feelings, 1986; Hyenas in Petticoats: A Look at 20 Years of Feminism, 1989; Look the Demon in the Eye, 1996, revised edition as This is Our Time, 1998. Contributions to: Guardian; Times; Observer; Sunday Telegraph; Daily Telegraph. Honours: Feminist Top Twenty List, 1986; Institute for the Study of Drug Dependency Award, 1994. Address: 32 Highbury Place, London N5, England.

NEVES Augusto. See: **CARDOSO PIRES Joao.**

NEVEU Angéline, b. 2 Sept 1946, France. Writer; Poet. Publications: Synthèse, 1976; Lyrisme télévisé, 1982; Rêve, 1982; Désir, 1985; Le vent se fieau vent, 1994; Contributions to: Journals. Honour: Bursary, Centre National des Lettres, Paris, 1986. Membership: Union des écrivaines et écrivains québecois. Address: 1020 St-Mathieu, App 1020, Montréal, Québec H3H 2J1, Canada.

NEVILLE Robert Cummings, b. 1 May 1939, St Louis, Missouri, USA. Professor of Philosophy and Religion; Author. m. Elizabeth E Neville, 1963, 3 daughters. Education: BA, 1960, MA, 1962, PhD, 1963, Yale University. Appointments: Instructor, Yale University, 1963-65; Visiting Lecturer and Instructor, Wesleyan University, 1964-65; Assistant Professor, 1965-68, Associate Professor, 1968-73, Fordham University; Associate for the Behavioral Sciences, Institute of Society, Ethics, and the Life Sciences, Hastings-on-Hudson, New York, 1971-73; Associate Professor, 1971-74, Professor of Philosophy, 1974-77, State University of New York College at Purchase; Adjunct Professor of Religious Studies and Research Professor, 1977-78, Professor of Philosophy and Professor of Religious Studies, 1978-87, State University of New York at Stony Brook; Professor, Departments of Religion and Philosophy, and School of Theology, 1987-, Dean, School of Theology, 1988-, Boston University. Publications: God the Creator: On the Transendence and Prescence of God, 1968, new edition, 1992; The Cosmology of Freedom, 1974, new edition, 1995; Soldier, Sage, Saint, 1978; Creativity and God: A Challenge to Process Theology, 1980, new edition, 1995; Reconstruction of Thinking, 1981; The Tao and the Daimon: Segments of a Religious Enquiry, 1982; The Puritan Smile, 1987; Recovery of the Measure, 1989; Behind the Masks of God, 1991; A Theology Primer, 1991; The Highroad Around Modernism, 1992; Eternity's and Time's Flow, 1993; Normative Cultures, 1995; The Truth of Broken Symbols, 1996. Editor: Operating on the Mind: The Psychosurgery Conflict (with Willard Gaylin and Joel Meister), 1975. Encyclopedia of Bioethics (associate editor), 1978; New Essays in Metaphysics, 1987; The Recovery of Philosophy in America (with Thomas Rasulis), 1997. Contributions to: Books, professional journals, and periodicals. Memberships: American Academy of Religion, president, 1992; American Philosophical Association; American Theological Society; Boston Theological Society; Institute of Society, Ethics, and the Life Sciences; Society for Studies of Process Philosophies; Society of Philosophers in America; International Society for Chinese Philosophy, president, 1993; Metaphysical Society of America, president, 1989. Address: 5 Cliff Road, Milton, MA 02186, USA.

NEVINS Francis M(ichael) (Jr), b. 6 Jan 1943, Bayonne, New Jersey, USA. Professor of Law; Writer. m. (1) Muriel Walter, 6 June 1966, div 1978, (2) Patricia Brooks, 24 Feb 1982. Education: AB, St Peter's College, 1964; JD, New York University, 1967. Appointments: Admitted to the New Jersey Bar, 1967; Assistant Professor, 1971-75, Associate Professor, 1975-78, Professor, 1978-, St Louis University School of Law. Publications: Novels: Publish and Perish, 1975; Corrupt and Ensnare, 1978; The 120 - Hour Clock, 1986; The Ninety Million Dollar Mouse, 1987; Into the Same River Twice, 1996. Non-Fiction: Detectionary (with 4 co-authors), 1971; Royal Bloodline: Elley Queen, Author and Detective, 1974; Missouri Probate: Intestacy, Wills and Basic Administration, 1983; The Films of Hopalong Cassidy, 1988; Cornell Woolrich: First You Dream , Then You Die, 1988; Bar-20: The Life of Clarence E Mulford, Creator of Hopalong Cassidy, 1993; Joseph H Lewis: Overview, Interview and Filmography, 1998; Joseph H Lewis: Overview, Interwiew and Filmography, 1998; The Films of the Cisco Kid, 1998. Fiction edited or co-edited: Nightwebs, 1971; The Good Old Stuff, 1983; Exeunt Murderers, 1983; Buffet for Unwelcome Guests, 1983; More Good Old Stuff, 1985; Carnival of Crime, 1985; Hitchcock in Prime Time, 1985; The Best of Ellery Queen, 1985; Leopold's Way, 1985; The Adventures of Henry Turnbuckle, 1987; Better Mousetraps, 1988; Mr President- Private Eye, 1988; Death on Television, 1989; Little Boxes of Bewilderment, 1989; The Night My Friend, 1991. Non-fiction edited or co-edited: The Mystery Writer's Art, 1970; Mutiplying Villainies, 1973. Honours:

Edgar Awards, Mystery Writers of America, 1975, 1988. Address: 7045 Cornell, University City, MO 63130, USA.

NEVZGLIADOVA Elena Vsevologovna, (Elena Ushakova), b. 2 June 1939, Leningrad, Russia. Poet; Literary Critic. m. Aleksandr Semyonovich Kushner, 1 son, Education: Graduate, 1962, PhD, 1974, Unversity of Leningrad. Publication: Nochnoe Solntse (A Night Sun), 1991. Contributions to: Various publications. Membership: Writers' Union. Address: Kaluzhskii per 9, Apt 48, St Petersburg 193015, Russia.

NEW Anthony Sherwood Brooks, b. 14 Aug 1924, London, England. Architect; Writer. m. Elizabeth Pegge, 11 Apr 1970, 1 son, 1 daughter. Education: Northern Polytechnic School of Architecture, 1941-43, 1947-51. Publications: Observer's Book of Postage Stamps, 1967; Observer's Book of Cathedrals, 1972; A Guide to the Cathedrals of Britain, 1980; Property Services Agency Historic Buildings Register, Vol II (London), 1983; A Guide to the Abbeys of England and Wales, 1985; New Observer's Book of Stamp Collecting, 1986; A Guide to the Abbeys of Scotland, 1988. Memberships: Society of Antiquaries, fellow; Royal Institute of British Architects, fellow; Institution of Structural Engineers. Address: 45A Woodbury Avenue, Petersfield, Hants, GU32 2ED, England

NEWBY (George) Eric, b. 6 Dec 1919, England. Writer. m. Wanda Skof, 1946, 1 son, 1 daughter. Education: St Paul's School. Appointments: Travel Editor, The Observer, and General Editor, Time Off Books, 1964-73. Publications: The Last Grain Race, 1956; A Short Walk in the Hindu Kush, 1958; Something Wholesale, 1962; Slowly Down the Ganges, 1966; Time Off in Southern Italy, 1966; Grain Race: Pictures of Life Before the Mast in a Windjammer, 1968; The Wonders of Britain (co-author), 1968; The Wonders of Ireland (co-author), 1969; Love and War in the Apennines, 1971; The World of Evelyn Waugh (co-author), 1973; Ganga, 1973; World Atlas of Exploration, 1975; Great Ascents, 1977; The Big Red Train Ride, 1978; A Traveller's Life, 1982; On the Shores of the Mediterranean, 1984; A Book of Travellers' Tales, 1985; Round Ireland in Low Gear, 1987; What the Traveller Saw, 1989; A Small Place in Italy, 1994; A Merry Dance Around the World, 1995. Honours: Military Cross, 1945; Commander of the Order of the British Empire, 1994; Honorary DLitt, University of Bournemouth, 1994; Honorary Doctorate, Open University, 1997. Memberships: Association of Cape Horners; Royal Geographical Society, fellow; Royal Society of Literature, fellow; Garrick Club. Address: Pine View House, 4 Pine View Close, Chilworth, Surrey GU4 8RS, England.

NEWCOMER James William, b. 14 Mar 1912, Gibsonburg, Ohio, USA. Retired College Professor; Vice Chancellor Emeritus; Writer; Poet. m. 17 Aug 1946, 1 son, 2 daughters. Education: PhB, Kenyon College; MA, University of Michigan; PhD, University of Iowa. Publications: Non-Fiction: Maria Edgeworth the Novelist, 1967; Maria Edgeworth, 1973; The Grand Duchy of Luxembourg, 1984; Lady Morgan the Novelist, 1990; Luxembourg, 1995; The Nationhood of Luxembourg, 1996. Poetry: The Merton Barn Poems, 1979; The Resonance of Grace, 1984. Contributions to: Journals and periodicals. Honours: Phi Beta Kappa; Commander, Order of Merit, Honorary Member, L'Institut Grand-Ducal, Grand Duchy of Luxembourg. Address: 1100 Elizabeth Boulevard, Fort Worth, TX 76110, USA.

NEWLANDS Willy, (William Newlands of Lauriston), b. 5 Nov 1934, Perth, Scotland. Travel Writer. m. (1), 1 son, 2 daughters, (2) Dorothy Straton Walker, 1985. Appointments: Scriptwriter, Presenter, TV travel series, Grampian/STV, 1993-94. Contributions to: Daily Telegraph; Observer; Mail on Sunday; Guardian; Times; Daily Express; Field. Honours: Churchill Fellow, 1968; Travel Writer of the Year, 1983-84, 1987-88. Address: Lauriston Castle, by Montrose, Angus DD10 0DJ, Scotland.

NEWLOVE John (Herbert), b. 13 June 1938, Regina, Saskatchewan, Canada. Poet. m. Susan Mary Philips, 1966. Appointments: Writer-in-Residence, various Canadian institutions, 1974-83; English Editor, Office of the Commissioner of Official Languages, Ottawa, 1986-95. Publications: Grave Sirs, 1962; Elephants, Mothers and Others, 1963; Moving in Alone, 1965; Notebook Pages, 1966; Four Poems, 1967; What They Say, 1967; Black Night Window, 1968; The Cave, 1970; Lies, 1972; The Fat Man: Selected Poems 1962-72, 1977; Dreams Surround Us: Fiction and Poetry (with John Metcalf), 1977; The Green Plain, 1981; Three Poems, 1985; The Night the Dog Smiled, 1986; Apology for Absence: Poems Selected and New, 1993. Other: Editor of various poetry volumes. Honours: Governor-General's Award for Poetry, 1972; Literary Press Group Award, 1983; Saskatchewan Writers' Guild Founders' Award, 1986; Archibald Lampern Award, 1993. Address: Box 71041, RPO L'Esplanade, Ottawa, Ontario K2P 2L9, Canada.

NEWMAN Andrea, b. 7 Feb 1938, Dover, England. Writer. Div. Education: BA, Honours, English, 1960, MA, 1972, London University. Publications: A Share of the World, 1964; Mirage, 1965; The Cage, 1966; Three Into Two Won't Go, 1967; Alexa, 1968; A Bouquet of Barbed Wire, 1969; Another Bouquet, 1977; An Evil Streak, 1977, 1999; Mackenzie, 1980; A Sense of Guilt, 1988; Triangles, 1990; A Gift of Poison, 1991; Imogens Face (TV scripts), 1998. Contributions to: Magazines and television Memberships: PEN; Writers' Guild. Address: c/o Rod Hall, 7 Goodge Place, London W1, England.

NEWMAN Arnold Clifford, b. 10 Apr 1941, New York, New York, USA. Naturalist; Author. m. Arlene Ruth Newman (Ash), 7 Dec 1963, 1 son, 1 daughter. Education: BBA, 1962; PhD, 1996. Publications: The Tropical Rainforest: The Lungs of the Planet, 1987; Tropical Deforestation: Global Consequences and Alternatives, (with Dr Brent Blackwelder), 1989; Tropical Rainforest - A World Survey of Our Most Valuable and Endangered Habitat with a Blueprint for it's Survival, 1990. Honours: Decorated by USSR Academy of Sciences for Service to Earth's Species, Congressional Acclamation for Conservation, 1987; Humanitarian Award, Southern California Motion Picture Council, 1994; National Humanity Award, Honoring America's Best Role Models, 1995. Address: 3931 Camino de la Cumbre, Sherman Oaks, CA 91423, USA.

NEWMAN Aubrey N(orris), b. 14 Dec 1927, London, England. Professor of History; Writer. Education: MA, University of Glasgow, 1949; BA, 1953, MA, DPhil, 1957, Wadham College, Oxford. Appointments: Research Fellow, Bedford College, University of London, 1954-55; Professor of History, University of Leicester. Publications: The Parliamentary Diary of Sir Edward Knatchbull, 1722-1730, 1963; The Stanhopes of Chevening: A Family Biography, 1969; A Bibliography of English History, 1485-1760; The United Synagogue, 1870-1970, 1977; The Jewish East End, 1840-1939, 1981; The Board of Deputin, 1760-1985: A Brief Survey, 1987; The World Turned Inside Out: New Views on George II, 1988. Membership: Jewish Historical Society of England, president, 1977-79. Address: c/o Department of History, University of Leicester, Leicester LE1 7RH, England.

NEWMAN G(ordon) F, b. 22 May 1942, England. Writer; Dramatist. 1 son, 1 daughter. Publications: Sir, You Bastard, 1970; You Nice Bastard, 1972; The Abduction, 1972; The Player and the Guest, 1972; Billy: A Family Tragedy, 1972; The Split, 1973; Three Professional Ladies, 1973; The Price, 1974; The Streetfighter, 1975; A Prisoner's Tale, 1977; The Guvnor, 1977; The Detective's Tale, 1977; A Villain's Tale, 1978; The List, 1980; The Obsession, 1980; Charlie and Joanna, 1981; The Men With the Guns, 1982; Law and Order, 1983; Set a Thief, 1986; The Testing Ground, 1987; Trading the Future, 1992; Circle of Poison, 1995. Plays: Operation Bad Apple, 1982; An Honourable Trade, 1986; The Testing Ground, 1989. Screenplay: Number One, 1984. Television Plays: Law and Order, 1978; Billy, 1979; The Nation's Health, 1983; Here Is the News, 1989;

Black and Blue, 1992; The Healer, 1994. Honours: Writer's Awards, British Association of Film and Television Arts, 1992, Best Drama, 1995. Address: Kempley House, Kempley, Gloucestershire GL18 2BS, England.

NEWMAN Jay, b. 28 Feb 1948, Brooklyn, New York, USA. Philosophy Professor. Education: BA, Brooklyn College, 1968; MA, Brown University, 1969; PhD, York University, 1971. Appointments: Lecturer, 1971-72, Assistant Professor, 1972-77, Associate Professor, 1977-82, Professor of Philosophy, 1982-, University of Guelph. Publications: Non-Fiction: Foundations of Religious Tolerance, 1982; The Mental Philosophy of John Henry Newman, 1986; Fanatics and Hypocrites, 1986; The Journalist in Plato's Cave, 1989; Competition in Religious Life, 1989; On Religious Freedom, 1991; Religion vs Television: Competitors in Cultural Context, 1996; Religion and Technology: A Study in the Philosophy of Culture, 1997; Inauthentic Culture and Its Philosophical Critics, 1997. Honours: Several grants; Distinguished Alumnus Award, Brooklyn College, 1988. Memberships: Royal Society of Canada, fellow; Canadian Theological Society, president, 1990-91. Address: 313-19 Woodlawn Road East, Guelph, Ontario N1H 7B1, Canada.

NEWMAN John Kevin, b. 17 Aug 1928, Bradford, Yorkshire, England. Classics Educator. m. Frances M Stickney, 8 Sept 1970, 1 son, 2 daughters. Education: BA, Lit Humaniores, 1950, BA, Russian, 1952, MA, 1953, University of Oxford; PhD, University of Bristol, 1967. Appointments: Classics Master, St Francis Xavier College, Liverpool, 1952-54; Downside School, Somerset, 1955-69; Faculty, 1969-, Professor of Classics, 1980-, University of Illinois, Urbana; Editor, Illinois Classical Studies, 1982-87. Publications: Augustus and the New Poetry, 1967; The Concept of Vates in Augustan Poetry, 1967; Latin Compositions, 1976; Golden Violence, 1976; Dislocated: An American Carnival, 1977; Pindar's Art, 1984; The Classical Epic Tradition, 1986; Roman Catullus, 1990; Lelio Guidiccioni, Latin Poems, 1992; Augustan Propertius, 1997. Honours: Silver Medals, Vatican, Rome, for original Latin Poems 1960, 1962, 1965, 1997. Membership: Senior Common Room, Corpus Christi College Oxford, 1985-86. Address: 703 West Delaware Avenue, Urbana, IL 61801, USA.

NEWMAN Leslea, b. 5 Nov 1955, Brooklyn, New York, USA. Writer; Poet; Teacher. Education: BS, Education, University of Vermont, 1977; Certificate in Poetics, Naropa Institute, 1980. Appointment: Teacher, women's writing workshops. Publications: Good Enough to Eat, 1986; Love Me Like You Mean It, 1987; A Letter to Harvey Milk, 1988; Heather Has Two Mommies, 1989; Bubbe Meisehs by Shayneh Maidelehs, 1989; Secrets, 1990; In Every Laugh a Tear, 1992; Writing from the Heart, 1992; Every Woman's Dream, 1994; Fat Chance, 1994; Too Far Away to Touch, 1995; A Loving Testimony: Remembering Loved Ones Lost to AIDS, 1995; The Feminine Mystique, 1995; Remember That, 1996; My Lover is a Woman: Contemporary Lesbian Love Poems, 1996; Out of the Closet and Nothing to Wear, 1997. Contributions to: Magazines. Honour: 2nd Place Finalist, Raymond Carver Short Story Competition, 1987; Massachusetts Artists Fellowship in Poetry, 1989; National Endowment for the Arts Fellowship, 1997. Memberships: Authors Guild; Authors League of America; Poets and Writers. Address: PO Box 815, Northampton, MA 01061, USA.

NEWMAN Peter C(harles), b. 10 May 1929, Vienna, Austria. Journalist; Writer. m. (1) Christina McCall, div, (2) Camilla Jane Turner, div, (3) Alvie Björklund, 2 daughters. Education: Upper Canada College, Toronto; BA, 1950, MCom, 1954, University of Toronto. Appointments: Assistant Editor, 1951-54, Montreal Editor, 1954-55, Production Editor, 1955-56, Financial Post; Assistant Editor, 1956-60, Ottawa Editor, 1960-63, National Affairs Editor, 1963-64, Editor, 1971-82, Maclean's magazine; Ottawa Editor, 1964-69, Editor-in-Chief, 1969-71; Toronto Daily Star; Visiting Professor of Political Science, McMaster University,

1969-71, York University, 1979-80; Professor of Creative Writing, University of Victoria, 1985-90. Publications: Flame of Power: Intimate Profiles of Canada's Greatest Businessmen, 1959; Renegade in Power: The Diefenbaker Years, 1963; The Distemper of Our Times, 1968; Home Country: People, Places and Power Politics, 1973; The Canadian Establishment, Vol 1, The Great Business Dynasties, 1975; Bronfman Dynasty: The Rothschilds of the New World, 1978; The Acquistors: The Canadian Establishment, Vol 2, 1981; The Establishment Man: Portrait of Power, 1982; True North, Not Strong and Free: Defending the Peaceable Kingdom in the Nuclear Age, 1983; Debrett's Illustrated Guide to the Canadian Establishment (general editor), 1983; Company of Adventurers: An Unauthorized History of the Hudson's Bay Company, 1985; Caesars of the Wilderness, 1985; Sometimes a Great Nation: Will Canada Belong to the 21st Century?, 1988; Empire of Bay, 1989; Merchant Princes, 1991; Canada 1892: Portraits of a Promised Land, 1992; The Canadian Revolution From Deference to Defiance, 1995. Contributions to: Newspapers, journals, and television. Honours: National Newspaper Award for Journalism, 1971; Quill Award for Excellence in Canadian Journalism, 1977; Officer, 1979, Companion, 1990, Order of Canada; Knight Commander, Order of St Lazarus, 1980; Canadian Authors Association Literary Award for Non-Fiction, 1986. Address: 777 Bay Street, Toronto, Ontario M5W 1A7, Canada.

NEWPORT Cris, b. 14 July 1960, Melrose Park, Illinois, USA. Senior Editor. Education: BA, English and Creative Writing, University of Massachusetts, Boston, 1990; MAT, Tufts University, 1991. Appointments: Assistant Professor of English, New Hampshire Techincal Institute, 1991, Associate Professor of English, 1994; Senior Editor, Pride and Imprints, 1997-. Publications: Sparks Might Fly, 1994; The White Bones of Truth, 1994; Queen's Champion: The Legend of Lancelot Retoud, 1997; Exotica: A Collection of Erotic Stories, 1999. Contributions to: Bay Windows; Book Reviewer; Midwest Book Review; Online. Honour: Outstanding Achievement in Creative Writing Award, 1990. Address: 7419 Ebbert Drive South East, Port Orchard, WA 98367, USA.

NEWTON David Edward, b. 18 June 1933, Grand Rapids, Michigan, USA. University Educator; Science Writer. Education: AS, Grand Rapids Junior College, 1953; BS, High Distinction, Chemistry, 1955, MA, Education, 1961, University of Michigan; DEd, Science Education, Harvard University, 1971. Publications: Chemistry Problems, 1962, 3rd edition, 1984; Understanding Venereal Disease, 1973, 2nd edition, 1978; Math in Everyday Life, 1975, 2nd edition, 1991; Scott Foresman Biology (with Irwin Slesnick, A LaVon Blazar, Alan McCormack and Fred Rasmussen), 1980, 2nd edition, 1985; Science and Social Issues, 1983, 3rd edition, 1992; Biology Updated, 1984, 2nd edition, 1987; Chemistry Updated, 1985, 2nd edition, 1989; An Introduction to Molecular Biology, 1986; Science Ethics, 1987; Particle Accelerators, 1989; Taking a Stand Against Environmental Pollution, 1990; Land Use, 1991; James Watson and Francis Crick: A Search for DNA and Beyond, 1992; Contributions to: Books and journals. Honours: Sloane Scholarship, University of Michigan, 1958; Star '60 Award, National Science Teachers Association, 1960; William Payne Scholar, Horace Rackham Graduate School, University of Michigan, 1961-62; Shell Merit Fellow, 1964; Outstanding Young Science Educator of the Year, AETS, 1968. Memberships: Phi Beta Kappa; Phi Kappa Phi; Phi Lambda Upsilon; Delta Pi Alpha; National Science Teachers Association; Association for the Education of Teachers in Science; American Association for the Advancement of Science; National Association of Science Writers; Children's Science Book Review Committee. Address: Instructional Horizons Inc, 297 Addison Street, San Francisco, CA 94131, USA.

NEWTON Suzanne, b. 8 Oct 1936, Bunnlevel, North Carolina, USA. Children's Writer. Education: AB, Duke Unversity, 1957. Appointments: Consultant in Creative Writing, North Carolina Public Schools, 1972; Writer-in-Residence, Meredith College, Raleigh, North Carolina. Publications: 10 books, 1971-95. Address: 829-A Barringer Drive, Raleigh, NC 27606, USA.

NEY James W(alter Edward Colby), b. 28 July 1932, Nakaru, Kenya. Professor of English; Writer. m. Joan Marie Allen, 12 June 1954, 2 sons, 1 daughter. Education: AB, 1955, AM, 1957, Wheaton College; EdD, University of Michigan, 1963. Appointments: Visiting Professor, University of Montreal, 1962, George Peabody College for Teachers, Nashville, Tennessee, 1965, University of Hawaii, 1967, Western New Mexico University, 1971; Faculty, University of Ryukyus, Okinawa, 1962-64; Assistant Professor, Michigan State University at Hunt Valley, 1964-69; Professor of English, Arizona State University, Tempe, 1969-. Publications: Readings on American Society, 1969; Exploring in English, 1972; Discovery in English, 1972; American English for Japanese Students, 1973; Linguistics, Language, Teaching and Composition in the Grades, 1975; Semantic Structures for the Syntax of the Modal Auxiliaries and Complements in English, 1982; Transformational Grammar: Essays for the Left Hand, 1988; American College Life in English Communication, 1991; American English in a Situational Context, 1991; GMAT Study Guide and Time Saver, 1993; English Proficiency through American Culture, 1994. Contributions to: Books and professional journals. Memberships: American Linguistic Association; Canadian Linguistic Association; National Council of Teachers of English. Address: 13375 North 96th Place, Scottsdale, AZ 85260, USA.

NEYREY Jerome H(enry), b. 5 Jan 1940, New Orleans, Louisiana, USA. Professor. Education: BA, 1963; MA, 1964; MDiv, 1970; MTh, 1972; PhD, 1977; STL, 1987. Appointments: Weston School of Theology, 1977-92; University of Notre Dame, Indiana, 1992-. Publications: The Passion According to Luke, 1983; Christ is Community, 1983; An Ideology of Revolt, 1988; Calling Jesus Names, 1988; The Resurrection Stories, 1988; Paul, In Other Words, 1990; The Social World of Luke - Acts, 1991. Contributions to: Catholic Biblical Quarterly; Journal of Biblical Literature; Biblica; Novum Testamentum; New Testament Studies. Honours: Bannan Fellowship, Santa Clara University, 1984-85; Young Scholars Grant, 1984; ATS Grant, 1989; Visiting Professor, Pontifical Biblical Institute, Rome, 1989; Lilly Foundation, 1989; Plowshares, 1990. Memberships: Catholic Biblical Association; Society of Biblical Literature, New England Region President 1990; Context Group, executive secretary. Address: Department of Theology, University of Notre Dame, Notre Dame, IN 46556, USA.

NEZZLE. See: **SAUNDERS Nezzle Methelda.**

NGUGI WA THIONG'O, b. 5 Jan 1938, Limuru, Kenya. Writer; Dramatist; Critic. m. (1) Nyambura, 1961, div 1982, (2) Njeeri, 1992, 4 sons, 2 daughters. Education: BA, Makerere University, Kampala, 1963; BA, University of Leeds, 1964. Appointments: Lecturer, 1967-69, Senior Lecturer, Associate Professor, and Chair, Department of Literature, 1972-77, University of Nairobi; Creative Writing Fellow, Makerere University, 1969-70; Visiting Associate Professor, Northwestern University, Evanston, Illinois, 1970-71. Publications: The Black Hermit (play), 1963; Weep Not, Child (novel), 1964; The River Between (novel), 1965; A Grain of Wheat (novel), 1967; This Time Tomorrow: Three Plays, 1970; Homecoming: Essays on African and Caribbean Literature, Culture, and Politics, 1972; Secret Lives, and Other Stories, 1975; The Trial of Dedan Kimathi (with Micere Githae-Mugo), 1976; Petals of Blood (novel), 1977; Mtawa Mweusi, 1978; Caitaani mutharaba-ini, 1980, English translation as Devil on the Cross, 1982; Writers in Politics: Essays, 1981; Detained: A Writer's Prison Diary, 1981; Njamba Nene na mbaathi i mathagu, 1982, English translation as Njamba Nene and the Flying Bus, 1986; Ngaahika Ndeena: Ithaako ria Ngerekano (play with Ngugi wa Mirii), 1982, English translation as I Will Marry When I Want, 1982; Barrel of a Pen: Resistance to Repression in Neo-Colonial Kenya, 1983; Bathitoora va Njamba Nene, 1984, English translation as Njamba Nene's Pistol, 1986; Decolonizing the Mind: The Politics of Language in African Literature, 1986; Writing Against Neocolonialism, 1986; Matigari ma Njiruungi, 1986, English translation as Matigari, 1989; Njambas Nene no Chiubu King'ang'i, 1986; Moving the Centre: The Struggle for Cultural Freedoms, 1993. Contributions to: Books, newspapers, and magazines. Honour: Fonlon-Nicholas Award, 1996. Address: c/o Heinemann International, Halley Court, Jordan Hill, Oxford OX2 8EJ, England.

NGUYEN Nhu Y, b. 14 June 1942, Hung Son, Ha Tinh, Vietnam. Scientific Researcher; Editor. m. Nguyen Thi Nhi, 1975, 1 son. Education: BA, Hanoi University, 1966; PhD, USSR Academic Institute, 1983; Professor, 1996. Appointments: Deputy Director, Linguistics Institute, 1985; Deputy Director, 1994-, Editor-in-Chief, 1996-, Educational Publishing House. Publications: Over 60 works including: The principle of comparison in a dictionary of terminology, 1977; An important stage in the development of Vietnamese scientific terminology, 1979; Researching on Chinese original and French original terms in the Vietnamese language, 1983; Language policy: the policy for ethnic languages in Vietnam, 1986; Socio-linguistic aspects of literacy, 1988; The internationalization of terminology - a new tendency in the development of the languages of the world, 1989; Social role and linguistic behaviour in communication, 1990; On the teaching of Vietnamese to adults in the literacy program for adults in regions of ethnic minorities, 1991; Language policy for ethnic languages, 1991; The liquidation of illiteracy - an important point in the national policy for social development, 1992; Dictionary of International Abbreviations (chief author), 1994; Dictionary of Vietnamese orthography (co-author), 1996; Vietnamese dictionary in common use, 1996; Monolingual dictionary of linguistic terminology (chief author), 1996; Vietnamese great dictionary (chief author), 1998. Memberships: Linguistics Association; Vietnamese Folklore Association; Chairman, Association for Teaching Vietnamese Language; Deputy Director, Research Centre for Self-Education. Address: Trích Sai Village, Buoi Quarter, Tây Hô District, Hanoi, Vietnam.

NÍ CHUILLEANÁIN Eiléan, b. 28 Nov 1942. Lecturer; Writer; Poet. m. Macdara Woods, 27 June 1978, 1 son. Education: BA, 1962, MA, 1964, University College, Cork; BLitt, Lady Margaret Hall, Oxford, 1969. Appointments: Lecturer in Mediaeval and Renaissance English, Trinity College, Dublin, 1966-; Professor of American History and Institutions, University of Oxford, 1969-78. Publications: Acts and Monuments, 1972; Site of Ambush, 1975; Cork, 1977; The Second Voyage, 1977; The Rose-Geranium, 1981; Irish Women: Image and Achievement (editor), 1985; The Magdalene Sermon, 1989; The Brazen Serpent, 1994. Contributions to: Cyphers Literary Magazine; Journal of Ecclesiastical History; Poems in many magazines. Honours: Irish Times Poetry Prize, 1966; Patrick Kavanagh Pize, 1972; O'Shaughnessy Poetry Award, 1992. Memberships: Aosdana; Irish Writers Union. Address: 2 Quarry Hollow, Headington, Oxford OX3 8JR, England.

NI DHOMHNAILL Nuala Maire, b. 16 Feb 1952, St Helens, Lancashire, England. Poet. m. 16 Dec 1973, 1 son, 3 daughters. Education: BA, Honours, English and Irish, 1972, HDipEd, 1973, University College, Cork. Appointments: Instructor, METU, Ankara, 1975-80; Writer-in-Residence, University College, Cork, 1992-93. Publications: An Dealg Droighinn, 1981; Fear Suaithinseach, 1984; Rogla Danta: Selected Poems, 1986, 4th edition, 1991; Pharoah's Daughter, 1990; The Astrachan Cloak, 1991; Feis, 1991. Contributions to: Many anthologies and magazines. Honours: Oireachtas Poetry Awards, 1982, 1989, 1990; Irish Arts Council Awards, 1985, 1988; O'Shaughnessy Poetry Award, Irish-American Cultural Institute, 1988; Ireland Fund Literature Prize, 1991. Memberships: Aosdána; Irish Writers Union; Poetry Ireland. Address: 2 Little Meadow, Pottery Road, Cabinteely, County Dublin, Ireland.

NICHOLAS Julia. See: **JAMES Mary.**

NICHOLLS Christine Stephanie, b. 23 Jan 1943, Bury, Lancashire, England. Editor; Writer. m. Anthony James Nicholls, 12 Mar 1966, 1 son, 2 daughters. Education: BA, Lady Margaret Hall, Oxford, 1964; MA, DPhil, 1968, St Antony's College, Oxford. Appointments: Henry Charles Chapman Research Fellow, Institute of Commonwealth Studies, University of London, 1968-69; Joint Editor, 1977-89, Editor, 1989-95, Dictionary of National Biography; Editor, Sutton Pocket Biographies, 1996-. Publications: The Swahili Coast, 1971; Cataract (with Philip Awdry), 1985; Power: A Political History of the 20th Century, 1990; Missing Persons, 1993; 1986-90, 1996; The Hutchinson Encyclopedia of Biography, 1996; David Livingstone, 1998. Address: 27 Davenant Road, Oxford OX2 8BU, England.

NICHOLS (Joanna) Ruth, b. 4 Mar 1948, Toronto, Ontario, Canada. Theologian; Author. m. W N Houston, 21 Sept 1974. Education: BA, University of British Columbia; MA, Religious Studies, 1972, PhD, Theology, 1977, McMaster University. Publications: Ceremony of Innocence, 1969; A Walk Out of the World, 1969; The Marrow of the World, 1972; Song of the Pearl, 1976; The Left-handed Spirit, 1978; The Burning of the Rose, 1989; What Dangers Deep: A Story of Philip Sidney, 1992. Honours: Shankar International Literay Contest Awards, 1963, 1965; Woodrow Wilson Fellowship, 1968; Fellow, 1971-72, Research Fellow, 1978, Canada Council; Gold Medal, Canadian Association of Children's Librarians, 1972. Address: 276 Laird Drive, Toronto, Ontario MY6 3XY, Canada.

NICHOLS Grace, b. 18 Jan 1950, Guyana. Writer; Poet. Education: University of Guyana, Georgetown. Publications: Trust You, Wriggly, 1980; I Is a Long-Memoried Woman, 1983; Leslyn in London, 1984; The Fat Black Woman's Poems, 1984; The Discovery, 1986; Whole of a Morning Sky, 1986; Come On Into My Tropical Garden, 1988; Black Poetry (editor), 1988; Lazy Thoughts of a Lazy Woman and Other Poems, 1989; Can I Buy a Slice of Sky? (editor), 1991; No Hickory Dickory Dock (co-author with John Agard), 1991; Give Yourself a Hug, 1994; A Caribbean Dozen (editor), 1994; SUNRIS, 1996; Asana and the Animals, 1997. Honours: Commonwealth Poetry Prize, 1983; Arts Council Bursary, 1988; Guyana Prize for Poetry, 1996. Address: c/o Curtis Brown Ltd, Haymarket House, 28/29 Haymarket, London SW1Y 4SP, England.

NICHOLS John (Treadwell), b. 23 July 1940, Berkeley, California, USA. Writer; Photographer. 1 son, 1 daughter. Education: BA, Hamilton College, New York, 1962. Publications: The Sterile Cuckoo, 1965; The Wizard of Loneliness, 1966; The Milagro Beanfield War, 1974; The Magic Journey, 1978; A Ghost in the Music, 1979; If Mountains Die, 1979; The Nirvana Blues, 1981; The Last Beautiful Days of Autumn, 1982; On the Mesa, 1986; American Blood, 1987; A Fragile Beauty, 1987; The Sky's the Limit, 1990; An Elegy for September, 1992; Keep It Simple, 1993; Conjugal Bliss, 1994; Dancing on the Stones, 1999. Address: Box 1165, Taos, NM 87571, USA.

NICHOLS Leigh. See: **KOONTZ Dean R(ay).**

NICHOLS Peter Richard, b. 31 July 1927, Bristol, England. Playwright. m. Thelma Reed, 1960, 1 son, 3 daughters (1 dec). Appointments: Actor, 1950-55; Teacher, Primary and Secondary Schools, 1958-60; Arts Council Drama Panel, 1973-75; Playwright-in-Residence, Guthrie Theater, Minneapolis, 1976. Publications: Television Plays: Walk on the Grass, 1959; Promenade, 1960; Ben Spray, 1961; The Reception, 1961; The Big Boys, 1961; Continuity Man, 1963; Ben Again, 1963; The Heart of the Country, 1963; The Hooded Terror, 1963; When the Wind Blows, 1964, later adapted for radio; The Brick Umbrella, 1968; Daddy Kiss It Better, 1968; The Gorge, 1968; Hearts and Flowers, 1971; The Common, 1973. Films: Catch Us If You Can, 1965; Georgy Girl, 1967; Joe Egg, 1971; The National Health, 1973; Privates on Parade, 1983. Stage Plays: A Day in the Death of Joe Egg, 1967; The National Health, 1969; Forget-me-not Lane, 1971; Chez Nous, 1973; The Freeway, 1974;

Privates on Parade, 1977; Born in the Gardens, 1979, televised, 1986; Passion Play, 1980; Poppy (musical), 1982; A Piece of My Mind, 1986; Blue Murder, 1995. Autobiography: Feeling You're Behind, 1984. Honours: Standard Best Play Awards, 1967, 1969, 1983; Evening Standard Best Comedy, Society of West End Theatre Best Comedy, Ivor Novello Best Musical Awards, 1977; Society of West End Theatre Best Musical, 1982; Tony Award, 1985. Membership: Royal Society of Literature, fellow. Literary Agent: Alan Brodie Representation, 211 Piccadilly, London, W1V 9LD, England. Address: 22 Belsize Park Gardens, London NW3 4LH, England.

NICHOLS Roger (David Edward), b. 6 Apr 1939, Ely, Cambridgeshire, England. Writer; Broadcaster. m. Sarah Edwards, 11 Apr 1964, 2 sons, 1 daughter. Education: MA, Worcester College, Oxford. Appointments: Master, St Michael's College, Tenbury, 1966-73; Lecturer, Open University, 1974-80, University of Birmingham, 1974-80. Publications: Debussy, 1973; Through Greek Eyes (with Kenneth McLeish), 1974; Messiaen, 1975; Through Roman Eyes, 1976; Ravel, 1977; Greek Everyday Life (with Sarah Nichols), 1978; Ravel Remembered, 1987; Debussy: Letters (editor and translator), 1987; Claude Debussy: Pelléas and Mélisande (with Richard Langham Smith), 1989; Debussy Remembered, 1992; The Life of Debussy, 1998. Address: The School House, The Square, Kington, Herefordshire HR5 3BA, England.

NICHOLSON Christina. See: **NICOLE Christopher Robin.**

NICHOLSON Geoffrey Joseph, b. 4 Mar 1953, Sheffield, England. Writer. Education: MA, English, Gonville and Caius College, Cambridge, 1975; MA, Drama, University of Essex, Colchester, 1978. Publications: Street Sleeper, 1987; The Knot Garden, 1989; What We Did On Our Holidays, 1990; Hunters and Gatherers, 1991; Big Noises, 1991; The Food Chain, 1992; Day Trips to the Desert, 1992; The Errol Flynn Novel, 1993; Still Life with Volkswagens, 1994; Everything and More, 1994; Footsucker, 1995; Bleeding London, 1997; Flesh Guitar, 1998; Female Ruins, 1999. Contributions to: Ambit magazine; Grand Street; Tiger Dreams; Night; Twenty Under 35; A Book of Two Halves; The Guardian, Independent; Village Voice. Honour: Shortlisted, Yorkshire Post 1st Work Award, 1987; Shortlisted, The Whitbread Prize, 1998. Address: c/o A P Watt, 20 John Street, London EC1N 2DR, England.

NICHOLSON Margaret Beda. See: **YORKE Margaret.**

NICHOLSON Michael Thomas, b. 9 Jan 1937, Romford, Essex, England. Foreign Correspondent. m. Diana Margaret Slater, 16 Dec 1968, 2 sons, 1 daughter (adopted). Education: Leicestor University MA. Appointments: Publications: Partridge Kite, 1978; Red Joker, 1979; December Ultimatum, 1981; Across the Limpoto, 1985; Pilgrims Rest, 1987; Measure of Danger, 1991; Natasha's Story, 1993. Contributions to: Daily Mail; Express; Spectator. Honour: OBE, 1991. Literary Agent: Michael Sissons PFD. Address: Grayswood House, Grayswood, Surrey GU27 2DM, England.

NICHOLSON Robin. See: **NICOLE Christopher Robin.**

NICK Dagmar, b. 30 May 1926, Breslau, Germany. Writer; Poet. Education: Psychology and Graphology studies, Munich, 1947-50. Publications: Poetry: Martyrer, 1947; Das Buch Holofernes, 1955; In den Ellipsen des Mondes, 1959; Zeugnis und Zeichen, 1969; Fluchtlinien, 1978; Gezählte Tage, 1986; Im Stillstand der Stunden, 1991; Gewendete Masken, 1996; Trauer ohne Tabu, 1999. Prose: Einladung nach Israel, 1963; Rhodos, 1967; Israel gestern und heute, 1969; Sizilien, 1976; Götterinseln der Ägäis, 1981; Medea, ein Monolog, 1988; Lilith, eine Metamorphose, 1992; Jüdisches Wirken in Breslau, 1998. Contributions to: Zeit; Frankfurter Allgemeine Zeitung; Akzente; Merian; Westermanns Monatshefte; Horen; Chicago Review; International Poetry Review; Chariton Review. Honours: Liliencron Prize, Hamburg, 1948; Eichendorff Prize, 1966; Honorary

Award, Gryphius Prize, 1970; Roswitha Medal, 1977; Kulturpreis Schlesien des Landes Niedersachsen, 1986; Gryphius Prize, 1993. Memberships: PEN Club; Association of German Writers. Address: Kuglmüllerstrasse 22, D 80638 Munich, Germany.

NICOL Donald MacGillivray, b. 4 Feb 1923, Portsmouth, England. Historian; Professor Emeritus. m. Joan Mary Campbell, 1950, 3 sons. Education: MA, 1948, PhD, 1952, Pembroke College, Cambridge. Appointments: Scholar, British School of Archaeology, Athens, 1949-50; Lecturer in Classics, University College, Dublin, 1952-64; Visiting Fellow, Dumbarton Oaks, Washington, DC, 1964-65; Visiting Professor of Byzantine History, Indiana University, 1965-66; Senior Lecturer and Reader in Byzantine History, University of Edinburgh, 1969-70; Koraës Professor of Modern Greek and Byzantine History, Language and Literature, 1970-88, Assistant Principal, 1977-80, Vice Principal, 1980-81, Professor Emeritus, 1988-, King's College, University of London; Editor, Byzantine and Modern Greek Studies, 1973-83; Birbeck Lecturer, University of Cambridge, 1976-77; Director, Gennadius Library, Athens, 1989-92. Publications: The Despotate of Epiros, 1957; Meterora: The Rock Monasteries of Thessaly, 1963, revised edition, 1975; The Byzantine Family of Kantakouzenos (Cantacuzenus) ca 1100-1460: A Genealogical and Prosopographical Study, 1968; Byzantium: Its Ecclesiastical History and Relations with the Western World, 1972; The Last Centuries of Byzantium 1261-1453, 1972, 2nd edition, 1993; Church and Society in the Last Centuries of Byzantium, 1979; The End of the Byzantine Empire, 1979; The Despotate of Epiros 1267-1479: A Contribution to the History of Greece in the Middle Ages, 1984; Studies in Late Byzantine History and Prosopography, 1986; Byzantium and Venice: A Study in Diplomatic and Cultural Relations, 1988; Joannes Gennadios - The Man: A Biographical Sketch, 1990; A Biographical Dictionary of the Byzantine Empire, 1991; The Immortal Emperor: The Life and Legend of Constantine Palaiologos, Last Emperor of the Romans, 1992; The Byzantine Lady: Ten Portraits 1250-1500, 1994; The Reluctant Emperor: A Biography of John Cantacuzene, Byzantine Emperor and Monk c. 1295-1383, 1996; Theodore Spandounes: On the Origin of the Ottoman Emperors (translator and editor), 1997. Contributions to: Professional journals. Membership: British Academy, fellow. Address: 4 Westberry Court, Pinehurst, Grange Road, Cambridge, CB3 9BG, England.

NICOL Michael George, b. 17 Nov 1951, Cape Town, South Africa. Writer; Journalist. 1 daughter. Education: BA, Honours, University of South Africa, 1993. Appointments: Reporter, To The Point, Johannesburg, 1974-76, The Star, Johannesburg, 1976-79; Editor, African Wildlife, Johannesburg, 1979-81; Freelance Journalist, 1981-85; Assistant to the Editor, Leadership, Cape Town, 1986-88; Writer, Journalist, 1989-. Publications: Among the Souvenirs (poetry), 1979; The Powers That Be (novel), 1989; A Good-Looking Corpse (history), 1991; This Day and Age (novel), 1992; This Sad Place (poetry), 1993; Horseman (novel), 1994; The Waiting Country (memoir), 1995; The Ibis Tapestry (novel), 1998; Bra Henry (novella for young adults), 1998; The Invisible Line: The Life and Photography of Ken Oosterbroek (biography), 1998. Contributions to: The Guardian; New Statesman; London Magazine. Honour: Ingrid Jonker Award, 1980. Literary Agent: Derek Johns, A P Watt. Address: 20 John Street, London WC1N 2DR, England.

NICOLE Christopher (Robin), (**Daniel Adams, Leslie Arlen, Robin Cade, Peter Grange, Nicholas Grant, Caroline Gray, Mark Logan, Simon Mackay, Christina Nicholson, Robin Nicholson, Alan Savage, Alison York, Andrew York**), b. 7 Dec 1930, Georgetown, Guyana. Novelist. m. Diana Bachmann, 8 May 1982, 4 sons, 3 daughters. Education: Harrison College, Barbados; Queen's College, Guyana; Fellow, Canadian Bankers Association. Publications: As Christopher Nicole: Ratoon, 1962; Caribee Series, 1974-78; Byron, 1979; The Haggard Series, 1980-82; The China Series, 1984-86; The Japan Series, 1984-86; Black Majesty, 2 volumes, 1984-85; The Old Glory series, 1986-88; Ship with No Name, 1987; The High Country, 1988; The Regiment, 1988; The Pearl of the Orient, 1988. As Andrew York: The Eliminator Series, 1966-75; The Operation Series, 1969-71; Where the Cavern Ends, 1971; Dark Passage, 1976; The Tallant Series, 1977-78; The Combination, 1984. As Peter Grange: King Creole, 1966; The Devil's Emissary, 1968. As Robin Cade: The Fear Dealers, 1974. As Mark Logan: The Tricolour Series, 1976-78. As Christina Nicholson: The Power and the Passion, 1977; The Savage Sands, 1978; The Queen of Paris, 1983. As Alison York: The Fire and the Rape, 1979; The Scented Sword, 1980. As Robin Nicholson: The Friday Spy, 1981. As Leslie Arlen: The Borodin Series, 1980-85. As Daniel Adams: The Brazilian Series, 1982-83. As Simon Mackay: The Anderson Series, 1984-85. As Caroline Gray: First Class, 1984; Hotel de Luxe, 1985; White Rani, 1986; Victoria's Walk, 1986; The Third Life, 1988; Shadow of Dealth, 1989; Blue Water, Black Depths, 1990; The Daughter, 1992; Golden Girl, 1992; Spares, 1993; Spawn of the Devil, 1993. As Christopher Nicole: The Happy Valley, 1989; The Triumph, 1989; The Command, 1989; Dragon'd Blood, 1989; Dark Sun, 1990; Sword of Fortune, 1990; Sword of Empire, 1990; Days of Wine & Roses, 1991; The Titans, 1992; Resumption, 1992; The Last Battle, 1993. As Alan Savage: Ottoman, 1990; Mughal, 1991; The Eight Banners, 1992; Queen of Night, 1993; The Last Bannerman, 1993. As Nicholas Grant: Khan, 1993. Also several books written jointly with wife, Diana Bachmann. Contributions to: Numerous journals and magazines. Memberships: Society of Authors; Literary Guild of America; Mark Twain Society. Address: Curtis Brown & John Farquharson Ltd, 162-168 Regent Street, London W1R 5TB, England.

NICOLSON Nigel, b. 19 Jan 1917, London, England. Writer. m. Philippa Tennyson d'Eyncourt, July 1953, 1 son, 2 daughters. Education: Eton College, England, 1930-35; Balliol College, Oxford, 1935-38. Appointments: Member of Parliament, 1952-59; Co-Founder/Director, Weidenfield & Nicolson, Publishers, 1949. Publications: People and Parliament, 1958; Lord of the Isles, 1960; Alex, biography of Field Marshal Alexander, 1973; Portrait of a Marriage, 1973; Mary Curzon, 1977; Napoleon 1812, 1985; The World of Jane Austen, 1991; Long Life (Memoirs), 1997; Edited Letters and Diaries of Harold Nicolson (3 vols); Letters of Virginia Woolf, 6 vols. Honour: Whitbread Prize for Mary Curzon. Memberships: RSL; Jane Austen Society; Trollope Society. Literary Agent: Ed Victor. Address: Sissinghurst Castle, Cranbrook, Kent TN17 2AB, England.

NIEDZIELSKI Henryk Zygmunt, b. 30 Mar 1931, Troyes, France. Educator. m. 26 July 1977, 3 sons, 1 daughter. Education: BA, 1959, MA, 1963, PhD, 1964, Romance Philology, University of Connecticut, USA. Appointments: Editor-in-Chief, Language and Literature in Hawaii, 1967-72; Correspondent, France Amerique, 1969-72; Editorial Board, Conradiana, 1971-76, Science et Francophonie, 1985-91; Associate Editor, The Phonetician, 1994-. Publications: Le Roman de Helcanus, 1966; The Silent Language of France, 1975; Studies on the Seven Sages of Rome, 1978; Jean Misrahi Memorial Volume, 1978; The Silent Language of Poland, 1989. Contributions to: Professional journals. Honours: Distinguished Fellow, University of Auckland, New Zealand, Foundation, 1989; Silver Cross of Merit, Polish People's Republic, 1989. Memberships: Medieval Academy of America; International Arthurian Society; American Association of Teachers of French, 1981-83; Hawaii Association of Translators, founding president, 1982; International Association of Teachers of English as a Foreign Language; Chopin Society of Hawaii, founding director, 1990; VP Membership Toastmasters International, 1997. Address: 2425 West Orange Avenue, Anaheim, CA 92804, USA.

NIELSEN Kjeld Osterling, b. 12 July 1924, Copenhagen, Denmark. Journalist; Writer. m. Vera Vegetti, 7 Dec 1965, 1 son, 3 daughters. Education: MA, Slavonic Languages, Copenhagen; Law and Economics, Copenhagen. Appointments: Foreign Correspondent,

Eastern Europe, 1959-65, Mediterranean Area, 1965-74; Secretary, Group General Secretary, European Parliament, 1974-83; Correspondent, Rome, 1983-90; Freelance Writer, 1990-. Publictions: Antonio Gramsci: Kultur og Politik, 1972; Marx-Engels: Litteratur og Samfund, 1974. Contributions to: Journals and periodicals. Membership: Danish Writers Union. Address: c/o Den Danske Bank, Holmens kauol 2, Copenhagen, Denmark.

NIELSEN Lars, b. 18 Jan 1968, Kerteminde, Denmark. Illustrator. Education: Design School, Kolding, Denmark, 1991-96, Diploma, 1996. Publication: Gudindens Lover (Lions of the Goddess). Contributions to: Illustrator, Danish newspaper, Berlingske Tidende. Honours: Award of Excellence, Society of Newspaper Design, Snd Providence, USA. Address: Dybbolsgade 47, 4th 1721 Copenhagen V, Denmark.

NIEMANN Linda Grant, b. 22 Sep 1946, Pasadena, California, USA. Railroad Brakeman. Education: BA, University of California, Santa Cruz, 1968; PhD, University of California, Berkeley, 1975. Publication: Boomer: Railroad Memoirs, 1990, Retitled, On the Rails, 1997; Railroad Voices (Lina Bertucci, Photographer), 1998. Honour: Non-Fiction Award, Bay Area Book Reviewers Association, 1991. Memberships: PEN West; National Writers Union. Address: PO Box 7409, Santa Cruz, CA 95061, USA.

NIEMINEN Kai Tapani, b. 11 May 1950, Helsinki, Finland. Poet; Translator. m. 1991, 1 daughter. Education: Philosophy and Musicology, 1970-72; Private studies in Japanese, 1971. Publications: 14 books of poetry, 1971-97; Several translations from Japanese poetry and drama. Contributions to: Various publications. Honour: National Literary Awards, Ministry of Culture, 1986, 1990. Memberships: Authors Society; Finnish PEN, president, 1991-94. Address: Baggböle 99A, 07740 Gammelby, Finland.

NIGG Joseph Eugene, b. 27 Oct 1938, Davenport, Iowa, USA. Editor; Writer. m. (1) Gayle Madsen, 20 Aug 1960, div 1979, 2 sons, (2) Esther Muzzillo, 27 Oct 1989. Education: BA, Kent State University, 1960; MFA, Writers Workshop, University of Iowa, 1963; PhD, University of Denver, 1975. Appointments: Assistant Editor, Essays in Literature, 1974-75; Associate Editor, Liniger's Real Estate, 1979-85; Fiction Editor, Wayland Press, 1985-92. Publications: The Book of Gryphons, 1982; The Strength of Lions and the Flight of Eagles, 1982; A Guide to the Imaginary Birds of the World, 1984; Winegold, 1985; The Great Balloon Festival, 1989; Wonder Beasts, 1995; The Book of Fabulous Beasts, 1998. Contributions to: Various journals and magazines. Honours: Non-Fiction Book of the Year Awards, Colorado Authors League, 1983, 1985, 1989, 1996; Mary Chase Author of the Year, Rocky Mountain Writers Guild, 1984. Memberships: Colorado Authors League; Rocky Mountain Writers Guild. Address: 1114 Clayton Street, Denver, CO 80206, USA.

NIGHBERT David, b. 26 July 1948, Knoxville, TN, USA. Writer; Video Store Manager. m. Sheila Mayhew York, 1 Mar 1996. Education: Maryville College & University of Tennessee. Publications: Timelapse, 1988; Strikezone, 1989; Clouds of Magellan, 1991; Squeezeplay, 1992; Shutout, 1995. Honour: Finalist, 1993 Nero Award for Best American Detective Novel. Address: 501 E 87 St, Apt 9-D, New York, NY 10128, USA.

NIKOSI Lewis, b. 5 Dec 1936, Natal, South Africa. Writer; Dramatist. Education: M C Sultan Technical College, 1954-55; Harvard University, 1961-62; Diploma in Literature, University of London, 1974; University of Sussex, 1977. Appointments: Staff, Ilange Lae Natal (Zulu newspaper), Durban, 1955-56, Drum magazine and Golden City Post, Johannesburg, 1956-60, South African Information Bulletin, Paris, 1962-68; Radio Producer, BBC Transcription Centre, London, 1962-64; Literary Editor, New African magazine, London, 1965-68. Publications: The Rhythm of Violence, 1964; Home and Exile (essays), 1965; The Transplanted Heart: Essays on

South Africa, 1975; Tasks and Masks: Themes and Styles of African Literature, 1981; Mating Birds (novel), 1986. Address: Flat 4, Burgess Park Mansions, Fortune Green Road, London NW6, England.

NILAUS Henrik, b. 19 Aug 1952, Denmark. Writer. m. Maj-Britt Nordmaj, 6 July 1985, 3 daughters. Publications: De sà det ikke Ku ske, 1984; Kys eller bomber, 1984; Tak for sidst, 1986; Den fantastiske Stoutur, 1993. Membership: Dansk Forfatter Forcning. Literary Agent: Gyldendal. Address: ALMA, Kaalundsvej 13, 3400 Hillerod, Denmark.

NIMMO Ian Alister, b. 14 Oct 1934, Lahore, Pakistan. Journalist. m. Grace, 11 July 1959, 2 sons, 1 daughter. Education: Royal School of Dunkeld; Breadalbane Academy. Appointments: Lieutenant, Royal Scots Fusiliers, 1956; Editor, Weekly Scotsman, 1962; Editor, Evening Gazette, 1970; Editor, Evening News, Edinburgh, 1976. Publications: Robert Burns, 1964; Portrait of Edinburgh, 1970; The Bold Adventure, 1970; Scotland at War, 1989; The Commonwealth Games, 1986; Edinburgh The New Town, 1991; Edinburgh's Green Heritage, 1996; Rhythms of the Celts, stage musical, 1997. Membership: Vice President, Scottish Arts Club, 1998-. Address: The Yett, Lamancha, By West Linton, Peebleshire EH46 7BD, Scotland.

NINES. See: **ALVAREZ FERRERAS Felix**.

NIOSI Jorge Eduardo, b. 8 Dec 1945, Buenos Aires, Argentina. Professor of Economics. m. Graciela Ducatenzeiler, 25 Nov 1971, 2 daughters. Education: Licence, Sociology, National University of Buenos Aires, 1967; Advanced Degree, Economics, IEDES, Paris, 1970; Doctorate, Sociology, École Pratique, Paris, 1973. Appointments: Professor of Economics, Université du Québec à Montréal. Publications: Les entrepeneurs dans la politique argentine, 1976; The Economy of Canada, 1978; Canadian Capitalism, 1981; Firmes Multinationales et autonomie nationale, 1983; Canadian Multinationals, 1985; La montee de l'ingenierie canadienne, 1990; Technology and National Competitiveness, 1991; New Technology Policy and Social Innovation in the Firm (editor), 1994; Flexible Innovation, 1995. Contributions to: Journals and magazines. Honours: John Porter Award, Canadian Sociology and Anthropology Association, 1983; Fellow, Statistics Canada, 1989-92; Fellow, Fulbright Programme. Memberships: International Sociological Association; European Association of Evolutionary Political Economy; International Management of Technology Association; Royal Society of Canada. Address: Department of Administrative Science, Université du Québec à Montréal, Box 8888, Station Centre Ville, Montreal, Quebec H3C 3P8, Canada.

NISBET Jim, b. 20 Jan 1947, USA. Writer; Poet. Publications: Poems for a Lady, 1978; Gnachos for Bishop Berkeley, 1980; The Gourmet (novel), 1980; Morpho (with Alaistair Johnston), 1982; The Visitor, 1984; Lethal Injection (novel), 1987; Death Puppet (novel), 1989; Laminating the Conic Frustum, 1991; Small Apt, 1992; Ulysses' Dog, 1993; Sous le Signe de la Razoir, 1994. Address: c/o William Morris Agency, 1350 Avenue of the Americas, New York, NY 10019, USA.

NISH Ian Hill, b. 3 June 1926, Edinburgh, Scotland. Retired Professor. m. Rona Margaret Speirs, 29 Dec 1965, 2 daughters. Education: University of Edinburgh, 1943-51; University of London, 1951-56. Appointments: University of Sydney, New South Wales, Australia, 1957-62; London School of Economics and Political Science, England, 1962-91. Publications: Anglo-Japanese Alliance, 1966; The Story of Japan, 1968; Alliance in Decline, 1972; Japanese Foreign Policy, 1978; Anglo-Japanese Alienation 1919-52, 1982; Origins of the Russo-Japanese War, 1986; Contemporary European Writing on Japan, 1988; Japan's Struggle with Internationalism, 1931-33, 1993; The Iwakura Mission in America and Europe, 1998. Honours: Commander of the Order of the British Empire, 1990; Order of the Rising Sun, Japan, 1991. Memberships: European Association of Japanese Studies, president, 1985-88; British

Association of Japanese Studies, president, 1978. Address: Oakdene, 33 Charlwood Drive, Oxshott, Surrey KT22 0HB, England.

NISIPEANU Constantin, b. 10 Oct 1907, Craiova, Romania. Author. m. Maria Scuratoschi, 18 Sept 1945, 2 sons. Education: Licentiate, Academy of Higher Commercial and Industrial Studies, Bucharest. Appointments: Director, Radical magazine, 1929-31; Senior Official, Vacuum-Oil company; Editor, UNV, Bucharest; Director, Sinaia-Peles Museum of Art; Treasurer, Union of Romanian Writers. Publications: Cartea cu grimase, 1933; Metamorfoze, 1934; Spre tara închisa în diamant, 1937; Femeia de aer, 1943; Sa ne iubim visele, 1967; Stapâna viselor, anthology, 1968; Pastorul de umbre, 1971; O lautâ de Frunze, 1977; Pasari de fum, 1982; Arbori cu aripi de harfa, 1986; Fata Pescarusului, 1988; Paduri ae oglinzi, 1998. Contributions to: Bilete de Papagal magazine, 1928-29; Radical magazine; România Literara; Literatorul. Honour: Prize, Union of Writers, 1997. Memberships: Society of Romanian Writers, 1945-49; Union of Writers, 1949-98. Address: Bulevardi 1 Mai No 321, Sc C, Etaj IV, ap 84, Sector 1, cod 78322 Bucharest, Romania.

NISTOR Ioan Silviu, b. 24 May 1941, Lunca, Romania. Professor of History. m. Nastasia Nistor, 21 Aug 1975, 2 sons. Education: University of History and Philosophy, Cluj-Napoca, 1973, Master in History, 1987. Appointments: Scientific Researcher, Romanian Academy, 1973-82; Lecturer and Professor, University Technical, Cluj-Napoca, Department of History and Theory, 1982-98. Publications: The Contributions of the People from the Mures Valley to the Great Union in 1918, 1981; The Place of Monarchism in History; Issues Regarding the Monarchic Institution in Romania, 1994; The History of the Transnistrian Romanians, 1995; The Romanian People in the Second World War, 1996; The Romanian Modern Culture and the Nationale Ideal, 1997; The History of the Technical Education in the City of Cluj-Napoca. Contributions to: 51 research works in scientific magazines; 96 articles in art magazines; 178 articles in newspapers. Honour: 4 scientific awards. Membership: Romanian Society of Historical Sciences. Address: Aleea Peana, nr 3, Bloc R 16, Scara 4, Ap 71, 3400 Cluj-Napoca, Romania.

NITA. See: **BRATCHER Juanita.**

NITCHIE George Wilson, b. 19 May 1921, Chicago, Illinois, USA. Professor of English Emeritus; Writer; Poet. m. Laura Margaret Woodard, 19 Jan 1947, 3 daughters. Education: BA, Middlebury College, 1953; MA, 1947, PhD, 1958, Columbia University. Appointments: Instructor, 1947-50, Assistant Professor, 1950-59, Associate Professor, 1959-66, Professor of English, 1966-86, Chairman, Department of English, 1972-79, Professor Emeritus, 1986-, Simmons College. Publications: Human Values in the Poetry of Robert Frost, 1960; Marianne Moore: An Introduction to the Poetry, 1969. Contributions to: Various critical essays in scholarly journals and poems in many publications. Membership: American Association of University Professors. Address: 50 Pleansantview Avenue, Weymouth, MA 02188, USA.

NIVEN Alastair Neil Robertson, b. 25 Feb 1944, Edinburgh, Scotland. Director of Literature of the British Council; Writer. m. Helen Margaret Trow, 22 Aug 1970, 1 son, 1 daughter. Education: BA, 1966, MA, 1968, University of Cambridge; MA, University of Ghana, 1968; PhD, University of Leeds, 1972. Appointments: Lecturer, English, University of Ghana, 1968-69, University of Leeds, England, 1969-70; Lecturer, English Studies, University of Stirling, Scotland, 1970-78; Visiting Professor, Ârhus University, Denmark, 1975-76; Honorary Lecturer, University of London, 1979-84; Editor, Journal of Commonwealth Literature, 1979-92; Chapman Fellow, Institute of Commonwealth Studies, 1984-85; Visiting Fellow, Australian Studies Centre, London, 1985; Director of Literature, Arts Council of Great Britain, 1987-94, Arts Council of England, 1994-97; Director of Literature, The British Council, 1997-. Publications: D H

Lawrence: The Novels, 1978; The Yoke of Pity: The Fictional Writings of Mulk Raj Anand, 1978; The Commonwealth of Universities (with Hugh W Springer), 1987; Truth into Fiction, Raja Rao's The Serpent and the Rope, 1988. Editor: The Commonwealth Writer Overseas, 1976; Under Another Sky, 1987. Study guides on William Golding, R K Narayan, Elechi Amadi; Enigmas and Arrivals, 1997; Enigmas and Arrivals: An Anthology of Commonwealth Writing (co-editor with Michael Schmidt). Contributions to: Times; Ariel; Literary Criterion; Commonwealth Essais et Études. Honours: Commonwealth Scholar, 1966-68; Laurence Olivier Awards Panel, 1989-91; Judge, Booker Prize, 1994; Chairman, Stakis prize, 1998. Memberships: Greater London Arts Association Literature Advisory Panel, chairman, 1980-84; Association for Commonwealth Literature and Language Studies, secretary, 1986-89; UK Council for Overseas Student Affairs, executive committee, chairman, 1987-92; Commonwealth Trust; Garrick Club; Chairman, Southern African Book Development Trust, 1997-. Address: Eden House, 28 Weathercock Lane, Woburn Sands, Buckinghamshire MK17 8NY, England.

NIVEN Larry, (Laurence Van Cott Niven), b. 30 Apr 1938, Los Angeles, California, USA. Writer. m. Marilyn Joyce Wisowaty, 6 Sept 1969. Education: California Institute of Technology, 1956-58; BA, Mathematics, Washburn University, Kansas, 1962. Publications: Neutron Star, 1966; Ringworld, 1970; Inconstant Moon, 1971; The Hole Man, 1974; Protector, 1974; The Borderland of Sol, 1975; Dream Park (with Steven Barnes), 1981; Football (with Jerry Pournelle), 1985; Playgrounds, 1991; The Gripping Hand (with Jerry Pournelle), 1993. Contributions to: Books and magazines. Honours: Honorary Doctor of Letters, Washburn University, 1984; Science Fiction Achievement Awards, 1966, 1970, 1971, 1974, 1975; Nebula Best Novel, 1970; Australian Best International Science Fiction, 1972, 1974; Inkpot Award, San Diego Comic Convention, 1979. Address: c/o Spectrum Literary Agency, 111 8th Vanalden Avenue, Tarzana, CA 91356, USA.

NIXON Colin Harry, b. 9 Mar 1939, Putney, London. Civil Servant. m. Betty Morgan, 2 Sept 1967, 3 daughters. Education: Diploma in Sociology, London University, 1968. Appointments: Civil Servant, 1960-99; Disablement Resettlement Officer, 1974-83; ACAS Conciliation Officer, 1983-99. Publications: Roads, 1975; Geography of Love, 1977; With All Angles Equal, 1980; The Bright Idea, 1983; Included in anthologies: Spongers, 1984; Affirming Flame, 1989; Poetry Street 3, 1991; Red Candle Treasury, 1948-1998, 1998. Contributions to: Outposts; Tribune; Countryman; Cricketer. Honours: George Camp Memorial Poetry Prize, 1975, 1983; 1st Prize, Civil Service Poetry, 1979; Runner-up in Voting for Small Press Poet, 1986. Address: 72 Barmouth Road, Wandsworth Common, London SW18 2DS, England.

NJEMOGA-KOLAR Ana, b. 5 July 1951, Padina, Yugoslavia. Writer; Dramatist. m. Samo Kolar, 5 Apr 1980. Education: Faculty of Philosophy, Novi Sad University; Qualified Secondary School Teacher of Slovak Language and Literature. Appointments: Junior Journalist, Radio Novi Sad, 1976-81; Senior Journalist, Editor, TV Novi Sad, 1981-82; Co-Founder, Editorial Board Member, IGROPIS magazine (on children's theatre), 1990. Contributions to: Magazines, radio and television. Honours: 2nd Prize, Yugoslav Competition for Best Children's Play, Radio Sarajevo, 1988; 2nd and 3rd Prizes, Competition for Best Children's Radio Story, Radio Novi Sad, 1988-89; 2nd Prize, Competition for Best Children's Story, Pioneers magazine, 1990; 1st Prizes, Republic Competition for Best Children's Story, 1990, 1991; 1st Prize, Competition for Best Theatre Play for Adults, New Life literary magazine, 1991. Membership: Vojvodina Journalists Association. Address: PO Box 11, 07 801 Secovce, Slovakia.

NNADOZIE Emmanuel Uzoma Arthur, b. 2 July 1956, Nsu, Imo, Nigeria. Economist; Professor. 2 daughters. Education: BS, MS, University of Nigeria, Nsukka; PhD, Sorbonne. Appointments: Associate Professor of

Economics, Truman State University, 1989-; Chief Planning Officer, World Bank Rural Development Program, Nigeria. Publications: Oil and Socioeconomic Crisis in Nigeria; Chad: A Nation in Search of Its Future, 1997; African Culture & American Business in Africa, 1998; Trade and Regional Integration Strategy for African Economic Development; Casuality Tests of Export-Led Growth: The Case of Mexico, 1995. Honours: William O'Donnell Award; Oxford Fellow.

NOAKES Vivien, b. 16 Feb 1937, Twickenham, England. Writer. m. Michael Noakes, 9 July 1960, 2 sons, 1 daughter. Education: MA, D Phil, English, Senior Scholar, Somerville College, Oxford. Publications: Edward Lear: The Life of a Wanderer, 1968, 3rd edition, 1985; For Lovers of Edward Lear, 1978; Scenes from Victorian Life, 1979; Edward Lear 1812-1888, The Catalogue of the Royal Academy Exhibition, 1985; The Selected Letters of Edward Lear, 1988; The Painter Edward Lear, 1991. Contributions to: Times; Times Literary Supplement; Daily Telegraph; New Scientist; Punch; Harvard Magazine; Tennyson Research Bulletin; Memberships: Fellow, Royal Society of Literature; Member, Society of Authors; PEN. Address: 146 Hamilton Terrace, London NW8 9UX, England.

NOBBS David Gordon, b. 13 Mar 1935, Orpington, Kent, England. Writer. m. (1) Mary Jane Goddard, 18 Nov 1968, 2 stepsons, 1 stepdaughter, div 1998, (2) Susan Sutcliffe, 4 Aug 1998, 1 stepdaughter. Education: Marlborough College, 1948-59; BA, English, St John's College, Cambridge, 1955-58. Publications: Novels: The Itinerant Lodger, 1965; Ostrich Country, 1967; A Piece of the Sky is Missing, 1968; The Fall and Rise of Reginald Perrin, 1975; The Return of Reginald Perrin, 1977; The Better World of Reginald Perrin, 1978; Second From Last in the Sack Race, 1983; A Bit of a Do, 1986; Pratt of the Argus, 1988; Fair Dos, 1990; The Cucumber Man, 1994; The Legacy of Reginald Perrin, 1995; TV: The Fall and Rise of Reginald Perrin; Fairly Secret Army; A Bit of a Do; The Life and Times of Henry Pratt; Love On a Branch Line. Literary Agent: Jonathon Clowes. Address: 10 Iron Bridge House, Bridge Approach, London NW1 8BD, England.

NOBLE Jayne. See: **DOWNES Mary Raby.**

NOBLE William, b. 25 Jan 1932, New York, New York, USA. Writer; Lecturer; Consultant. m. Angela Elizabeth Warner Whitehill, 27 Dec 1998, 2 sons. Education: JD, University of Pennsylvania, Philadelphia, PA, 1961; BA, Lehigh University, Bethlehem, PA, 1954. Appointments: Attorney, Philadelphia, Lancaster, PA, USA, 1962-68; Director, Model Cities Program, Lancaster, PA, 1968-69; Humanities Scholar, Vermont Council on the Humanities, 1991-. Publications: The Custody Trap, with June Nobel, 1975; How to Live With Other People's Children, with June Noble, 1978; The Private Me, with June Nobel, 1980; The Psychiatric Fix, with June Nobel, 1981; Steal, 1981 This Plot, with June Noble, 1985; "Shut Up!" He Explained, 1987; Parents Book of Ballet, with Angela Whithill, 1987; Make That Scene, 1988; Young Professionals Book of Ballet, with Angela Whitehill, 1990; Bookbanning in America, 1990; Show Don't Tell, 1991; Twenty-Eight Most Common Writing Blunders, 1992; Conflict, Action and Suspence, 1994; The Complete Guide to Writer's Conferences and Workshops, 1995; Show Three Rules for Writing a Novel, 1997. Contributions to: Magazines and journals, more than 50 articles and short fiction on politics, sports, history and the arts. Membership: Author's Guild. Address: PO Box 187, Island Heights, NJ 08732, USA.

NOEL. See: **ADAMS Douglas.**

NOEL Arthur. See: **RAVEN Simon.**

NOEL Lise, b. 19 Apr 1944, Montreal, Quebec, Canada. Writer; Former Professor; Columnist. Education: BA, 1965, Licence in Letters, 1970, MA, History, 1975, PhD, History, 1982, University of Montreal; University of Aix-en-Provence, France. Publication: Intolerance: The Parameters of Oppression, 1994. Contributions to:

Critère; Liberté; Possibles; Service Social; Le Devoir. Honours: Hachette-Larousse, 1967; Governor-General's Award for Non Fiction, 1989; Myers Centre Award for the Study of Human Rights in North America, 1994. Address: 2608 Chemin Cote Sainte Catherine, Montreal, Quebec H3T 1B4, Canada.

NOEL-HUME Ivor, b. 1927, London, England. Archaeologist; Writer. Education: St Lawrence College, Kent, 1942-44. Appointments: Archaeologist, Guildhall Museum Corp, London, 1949-57; Chief Archaeologist, 1957-64, Director, Department of Archaeology, 1964-72, Resident Archaeologist, 1972-87, Colonial Williamsburg; Research Associate, Smithsonian Institution, Washington, DC, 1959-; Guest Curator, Steuben Glass Co, 1990; Director, Roanoke Project, 1991-93; Chairman, Jamestown Rediscovery Advisory Board, 1994-95. Publications: Archaeology in Britain, 1953; Tortoises, Terrapins and Turtles (with Audrey Noël-Hume), 1954; Treasure in the Thames, 1956; Great Moments in Archaeology, 1957; Here Lies Virginia, 1963, new edition, 1994; 1775: Another Part of the Field, 1966; Historical Archaeology, 1969; Artifacts of Early America, 1970; All the Best Rubbish, 1974; Early English Delftware, 1977; Martin's Hundred, 1982; The Virginia Adventure, 1994; Shipwreck: History from the Bermuda Reeds, 1995; In Search of This and That, 1995. Films: Doorway to the Past, 1968; The Williamsburg File, 1976; Search for a Century, 1981. Contributions to: Professional journals. Honours: Award for Historical Archaeology, University of South Carolina, 1975; Doctorate of Humane Letters, University of Pennsylvania, 1976; Doctorate of Humane Letters College of William and Mary, Williamsberg, VA, 1983; Achievement Award, National Society of the Daughters of the Founders and Patriots of America, 1989, National Society of the Daughters of the American Colonists, 1990; Officer of the Order of the British Empire, 1992. Memberships: American Antiquarian Society; Society of Antiquaries, London, fellow; Society of Historical Archaeology; Society for Post-Medieval Archaeology; Virginia Archaeological Society. Literary Agent: Curtis Brown, NY. Address: 2 West Circle, Williamsburg, VA 23185, USA.

NOLAN Patrick, b. 2 Jan 1933, Bronx, New York, USA. Professor; Writer; Dramatist. 3 sons. Education: MA, University of Detroit; PhD, English Literature, Bryn Mawr College. Appointments: Instructor, University of Detroit; Professor, Villanova University. Publications: Films: Hourglass Moment, 1969; Jericho Mile, 1978. Plays: Chameleons, 1981; Midnight Rainbows, 1991. Honours: Emmy Award, 1979; Citation, Teaching Excellence, Philadelphia Magazine, 1980. Membership: Writers Guild of America, West; Dramatists Guild. Address: c/o Department of English, Villanova University, Villanova, PA 19085, USA.

NOLAN William F(rancis), (Frank Anmar, Mike Cahill, F E Edwards, Michael Phillips), b. 6 Mar 1928, Kansas City, Missouri, USA. Writer; Poet. Education: Kansas City Art Institute, 1946-47; San Diego State College, 1947-48; Los Angeles City College, 1953. Publications: Numerous books, including: Barney Oldfield, 1961; Phil Hall: Yankee Champion, 1962; Impact 20 (stories), 1963; John Huston: King Rebel, 1965; Sinners and Superman, 1965; Death is for Losers, 1968; Dashiell Hammett: A Casebook, 1969; Alien Horizons (stories), 1974; Hemingway: Last Days of the Lion, 1974; Wonderworlds (stories), 1977; Hammett: A Life on the Edge, 1983; Things Beyond Midnight (stories), 1984; Dark Encounters (poems), 1986; Logan: A Trilogy, 1986; How to Write Horror Fiction, 1990; Six in Darkness (stories), 1993; Night Shapes (stories), 1993. Address: c/o Loni Perkins Associates Literary Agency, 301 West 53rd Street, New York, NY 10019, USA.

NONHEBEL Clare, b. 7 Nov 1953, London, England. Writer. m. Robin Nonhebel, 30 Aug 1975. Education: BA, Honours, French Studies, University of Warwick. Publications: Cold Showers, 1985; The Partisan, 1986; Incentives, 1988; Healed and Souled, 1988; Child's Play, 1991; Eldred Jones, Lulubelle and the Most High (novel), 1998; Don't Ask Me to Believe (non-fiction), 1998. Contributions to: Newspapers, journals, and magazines. Honour: Joint Winner, Betty Trask Award, 1984. Membership: MENSA. Address: c/o Curtis Brown Ltd, Haymarket House, 28/29 Haymarket, London SW1Y 4SP, England.

NORDBRANDT Henrik, b. 21 Mar 1945, Copenhagen, Denmark. Poet; Writer. Education: Oriental, Chinese, Persian, Turkish, and Arabic studies. Publications: 18 books of poetry, including several in English translation. Contributions to: Journals and magazines. Honours: Many literary awards, including: Danish Academy Prize; Danish Critics' Prize for Best Book of the Year; Life Grant of Honour, Danish State. Address: Plaza Santa Cruz 9, 29700 Velez-Malaga, Spain.

NORLING Bernard, b. 23 Feb 1924, Hunters, Washington, USA. Retired Professor of History; Writer. m. Mary Pupo, 30 Jan 1948. Education: BA, Gonzaga University, 1948; MA, 1949, PhD, 1955, Notre Dame University. Appointments: Instructor, 1952-55, Assistant Professor, 1955-61, Associate Professor, 1961-71, Professor of History, 1971-86, University of Notre Dame. Publications: Towards a Better Understanding of History, 1960; Timeless Problems in History, 1970; Understanding History Through the American Experience, 1976; Return to Freedom, 1983; Behind Japanese Lines, 1986; The Nazi Impact on a German Village, 1993; Lapham's Raiders, 1996; The Intrepid Guerrillas of North Luzon, forthcomming. Contributions to: Magazines and journals. Honour: Best Teacher of Freshman, University of Notre Dame, 1968. Memberships: Indiana Association of Historians; Michiana Historians, president, 1972. Address: 504 East Pokagon, South Bend, IN 46617, USA.

NORMAN Barry Leslie, b. 21 Aug 1933, London, England. Writer; Broadcaster. m. Diana Narracott, 1957, 2 daughters. Appointments: Entertainments Editor, Daily Mail, London, 1969-71; Weekly Columnist, The Guardian, 1971-80; Writer and Presenter, BBC 1 Film, 1973-81, 1983-88, The Hollywood Greats, 1977-79, 1984, The British Greats 1980, Omnibus, 1982, Film Greats, 1985, Talking Pictures, 1988; Radio 4 Today, 1974-76, Going Places, 1977-81, Breakaway, 1979-80. Publications: Novels: The Matter of Mandrake, 1967; The Hounds of Sparta, 1968; End Product, 1975; A Series of Defeats, 1977; To Nick a Good Body, 1978; Have a Nice Day, 1981; Sticky Wicket, 1984. Non-Fiction: Tales of the Redundance Kid, 1975; The Hollywood Greats, 1979; The Movie Greats, 1981; Talking Pictures, 1987; 100 Best Films of the Century, 1992, 1998; Thriller: The Birddog Tape, 1992; The Mickey Mouse Affair, 1995; Death on Sunset, 1998. Honours: British Association of Film and Television Arts Richard Dimbleby Award, 1981; Magazine Columnist of the Year, 1991; Honorary DLitt, University of East Anglia, 1991, University of Hertfordshire, 1996; Magazine Columnist of the Year, 1991; Commander of the Order of the British Empire, 1998. Address: c/o Curtis Brown Ltd, Haymarket House, 28-29 Haymarket, London SW1Y 4SP, England.

NORMAN Geraldine (Lucia), (Geraldine Keen, Florence Place), b. 13 May 1940, Wales. Journalist. m. Frank Norman, July 1971. Education: MA, Honours, Mathematics, St Anne's College, Oxford, 1961; University of California at Los Angeles, USA, 1961-62. Publications: The Sale of Works of Art (as Geraldine Keen), 1971; 19th Century Painters and Paintings: A Dictionary, 1977; The Fake's Progress (co-author), 1977; The Tom Keating Catalogue (editor), 1977; Mrs Harper's Niece (as Florence Place), 1982; Biedermeier Painting, 1987; Top Collectors of the World (co-author), 1993; The Hermitage: The Biography of a Great Museum, 1997. Contributions to: The Daily Telegraph and other Newspapers. Honour: News Reporter of the Year, 1976. Address: 5 Seaford Court, 220 Great Portland Street, London W1, England.

NORMAN Hilary, (Alexandra Henry), b. London, England. Writer. Education: Queen's College, London. Appointments: Director, Henry Norman textile manufacturing and retail firm, London, 1971-79; Production Assistant, Capital Radio, London, 1980-82, British Broadcasting Corporation, 1982-85; Writer, 1985-. Publications: Novels: In Love and Friendship, 1986; Château Ella, 1988; Shattered Stars, 1991; Fascination, 1992; Spellbound, 1993; Laura, 1994; Susanna, 1996; The Pact, 1997. As Alexandra Henry: If I Should Die, 1995; Too Close, 1998. Contributions to: Woman's Own. Address: c/o A M Heath Co Ltd, 79 St Martins Lane, London WC2N 4AA, England.

NORMAN Howard, b. 4 Mar 1949, Toledo, Ohio, USA. Writer; Translator. m. Jane Shore, 1 daughter. Education: Indiana University. Publications: The Wishing Bone Cycle: Narrative Poems from the Swampy Cree Indians (editor and translator), 1976, augmented edition, 1982; Where the Chill Came From: Cree Windigo Tales and Journeys (editor and translator), 1982; The Owl Scatterer, 1986; The Northern Lights, 1987; Who Paddled-Backward-with-Trout, 1987; Kiss i the Hotel Joseph Conrad, and Other Stories, 1989; The Bird Artist, 1994; The Museum Guard, 1998. Contributions to: Various publications. Honour: Lannan Prize, 1996. Address: c/o Melanie Jackson Agency, 250 West 57th Street, Suite 1119, New York, NY 10107, USA.

NORMAN John, b. 20 July 1912, Syracuse, New York, USA. Professor Emeritus; Writer; Poet. m. Mary Lynott, 28 Dec 1948, 4 daughters. Education: BA, 1935, MA, 1938, Syracuse University; PhD, Clark University, 1942. Publications: Edward Gibbon Wakefield: A Political Reappraisal, 1963; Labor and Politics in Libya and Arab Africa, 1965; Life Lines: A Volume of Verse, 1997. Contributions to: Anthologies, reference books, and journals. Honour: World Poetry Prize, 1991. Address: 94 Cooper Road, John's Pond, Ridgefield, CT 06877, USA.

NORMAN Marsha, b. 21 Sept 1947, Louisville, Kentucky, USA. Dramatist; Writer. m. (1) Michael Norman, div 1974, (2) Dann C Byck Jr, Nov 1978, div, (3) Timothy Dykman, 1 son, 1 daughter. Education: BA, Agnes Scott College, 1969; MAT, University of Louisville, 1971. Appointments: Teacher, Kentucky Arts Commission, 1972-76; Book Reviewer and Editor, Louisville Times, 1974-79. Publications: Plays: Getting Out, 1977; Third and Oak: The Laundromat (and) The Pool Hall, 1978; 'Night, Mother, 1982; Four Plays by Marsha Norman, 1988. Novel: The Fortune Teller, 1987. Musical: The Secret Garden, 1991. Honours: National Endowment for the Arts Grant, 1978-79; John Gassner New Playwrights Medallion, Outer Critics Circle, 1979; George Oppenheimer-Newsday Award, 1979; Rockefeller Foundation Playwright-in-Residence Grant, 1979-80; Susan Smith Blackburn Prize, 1982; Pulitzer Prize in Drama, 1983; Tony Award for Best Book of a Musical, 1991. Address: c/o The Tantleff Office, 375 Greenwich Street, No 700, New York, NY 10013, USA.

NORRIE Philip Anthony, b. 5 Feb 1953, Sydney, New South Wales, Australia. Medical Practitioner. m. Belinda Jill Vivian, 6 June 1974, 2 sons. Education: MB BS, University of New South Wales, 1977; Certificate, Family Planning Association, 1980; MSc, University of Sydney, 1993; MSocSc honours, Charles Sturt University, 1998; PhD University of Western Sydney, in progress. Appointments: Wine Writer for various publications; Editorial Board, Alcohol in Moderation, 1992; Lecturer, Research Fellow, Member Academic Advisory Board on Wine and Health, University of Western Sydney. Publications: Vineyards of Sydney, Cradle of Australian Wine Industry, 1990; Lindeman - Australia's Classic Winemaker, 1993; Penfold - Time Honoured, 1994; Australia's Wine Doctors, 1994; Wine and Health, 1995; Leo Buring - Australia's Wine Authority, 1996; Dr Philip Norrie's Wine and Health Diary, 1998-; Wine and Health: A New Look at an Old Medicine, 1999; Wine and Health Quotes - Thinking and Drinking Health, 1998; Dr Philip Norrie's advice on Wine and Health - Thinking and Drinking Health, 1999. Contributions to: Australasian Journal of Psychopharmacology; Australian Doctor; Australian Medical Observer; Journal of Medical Biography; Australian; Alcohol in Moderation; Hunter Valley Wine Society Journal. Memberships: Australian Medical Association; Australian National Trust; Royal Australian Historical Society; Australian Society of the

History of Medicine; New South Wales Medical History Society; Australian Medical Friends of Wine Society, founder-president; FIBA; Wine Press Club of New South Wales. Literary Agent: Charles Pierson, PO Box 87, Mosman 2088, Australia. Address: 22 Ralston Road, Palm Beach, New South Wales 2108, Australia.

NORRIS Ken, b. 3 Apr 1951, Bronx, New York, USA. Professor of Canadian Literature; Poet. 2 daughters. Education: BA, State University of New York at Stony Brook, 1972; MA, Concordia University, 1975; PhD, McGill University, 1980. Appointment: Professor of Canadian Literature, University of Maine, 1985-. Publications: Vegetables, 1975; The Perfect Accident, 1978; Autokinesis, 1980; Whirlwinds, 1983; The Better Part of Heaven, 1984; Islands, 1986; Report: Books 1-4, 1988, 8-11, 1993; In the House of No, 1991; Full Sun: Selected Poems, 1992; The Music, 1995; Odes, 1997; Limbo Road, 1998. Contributions to: Various reviews, journals, and periodicals. Honours: 3rd Prize, CBC Literary Competition, 1986. Memberships: League of Canadian Poets; Writers' Union of Canada. Address: c/o Department of English, University of Maine, 5752 Neville Hall, Room 304, Orono, ME 04469, USA.

NORRIS Leslie, b. 21 May 1921, Merthyr Tydfil, Wales. Professor; Poet; Writer. m. Catherine Mary Morgan, 1948. Education: MPhil, University of Southampton, 1958. Appointments: Principal Lecturer, West Sussex Institute of Education, 1956-74; Professor, Brigham Young University, Provo, Utah, 1981-. Publications: Tongue of Beauty, 1941; Poems, 1944; The Loud Winter, 1960; Finding Gold, 1964; Ransoms, 1970; Mountains, Polecats, Pheasants and Other Hegies, 1973; Selected Poems, 1986; Collected Poems, 1996. Contributions to: Various publications. Honours: British Arts Council Award, 1964; Alice Hunt Bartlett Prize, 1969; Chomondeley Poetry Prize, 1979; Katherine Mansfield Award, 1981. Memberships: Royal Society of Literature, fellow; Welsh Academy, fellow. Address: 849 South Carterville Road, Orem, UT 84058, USA.

NORSE Harold George, b. 6 July 1916, New York, New York, USA. Professor; Writer; Poet. Education: BA, Brooklyn College, 1938; MA, New York University, 1951. Appointments: Instructor, Cooper Union College, New York, 1949-52, Lion School of English, Rome, Italy, 1956-57, United States Information Service School, Naples, Italy, 1958-59; Instructor in Creative Writing, San Jose State University, California, 1973-75; Professor in Creative Writing, New College of California, 1994-95. Publications: The Roman Sonnets of Giuseppe Gioacchino Belli (translator), 1960, 2nd edition, 1974; Karma Circuit (poems), 1967; Hotel Nirvana (poems), 1974; Carnivorous Saint (poems), 1977; Mysteries of Magritte (poems), 1984; Love Poems, 1986; Memoirs of a Bastard Angel (autobiography), 1989; Seismic Events (poems), 1993. Contributions to: Journals and magazines. Honours: National Endowment for the Arts Fellowship, 1974; R H de Young Museum Grant, 1974; Lifetime Achievement Award in Poetry, National Poetry Association, 1991. Membership: PEN. Address: 157 Albion Street, San Francisco, CA 94110, USA.

NORTH Andrew. See: NORTON André.

NORTH Anthony. See: KOONTZ Dean R(ay).

NORTH Elizabeth (Stewart), b. 20 Aug 1932, Hampshire, England. Author; Teacher of Creative Writing. Education: BA, University of Leeds, 1973. Appointment: Writer-in-Residence, Bretton Hall College of Higher Education, 1984-85. Publications: Make Thee an Ark (radio play), 1969; Wife Swopping (radio play), 1969; The Least and Vilest Things (novel), 1971; Pelican Rising (novel), 1975; Enough Blue Sky (novel), 1977; Everything in the Garden (novel), 1978; Florence Avenue (novel), 1980; Dames (novel), 1981; Ancient Enemies (novel), 1982; The Real Tess (radio feature), 1984; Jude the Obscure (adaptation for radio), 1985. Address: 8 Huby Park, Huby, Leeds, England.

NORTH Kate. See: LLOYD Kathleen Annie.

NORTHCUTT Wayne, b. 5 July 1944, New Orleans, Louisiana, USA. Professor of History; Writer. Education: BA, History, 1966, MA, History, 1968, California State University, Long Beach; PhD, Modern European History, University of California, Irvine, 1974. Appointments: Teaching Assistant, 1969-72, Teaching Associate, 1973-74, 1979-80, University of California, Irvine; Lecturer, 1972-73, Assistant Professor, 1975-78, Monterey Institute of International Studies, California; Lecturer, Schiller College, Paris, 1978; Assistant Professor, 1980-83, Associate Professor, 1983-88, Professor of History, 1988-, Niagara University; Foreign Expert, Chinese People's University, Beijing, 1983; Adjunct Professor of History, State University of New York at Buffalo, 1993-. Publications: The French Socialist and Communist Party Under the Fifth Republic, 1958-1981: From Opposition to Power, 1985; Historical Dictionary of the French Fourth and Fifth Republics, 1946-1991 (editor-in-chief), 1992; Mitterrand: A Political Biography, 1992; The Regions of France: A Reference Guide to History and Culture, 1997. Contributions to: Scholarly books and journals. Honours: Numerous research grants and fellowships. Address: c/o Department of History, Niagara University, PO Box 1932, Niagara University, NY 14109, USA.

NORTON André, (Andrew North), b. 17 Feb 1912, Cleveland, Ohio, USA. Author. Education: Western Reserve University, 1930-32. Appointment: Children's Librarian, Cleveland Public Library. Publications: Over 150 books, 1934-97. Address: High Hallack, 4911 Celtkiller Highway, Monterey, TN 38574, USA.

NORTON Augustus Richard, b. 2 Sept 1946, New York, USA. Professor of International Relations and Anthropology. m. Deanna J Lampros, 27 Dec 1969, 1 son. Education: BA, magna cum laude 1974, MA, Political Science, 1974, University of Miami; PhD, Political Science, University of Chicago, 1984. Appointment: Professor, United States Military Academy, West Point, New York. Publications: Studies in Nuclear Terrorism, 1979; International Terrorism, 1980; NATO, 1985; Touring Nam: The Vietnam War Reader, 1985; Amal and the Shia: Struggle for the Soul of Lebanon, 1987; The International Relations of the Palestine Liberation Organization, 1989; UN Peacekeepers: Soldiers with a Difference, 1990; Political Tides in the Arab World, 1992; Civil Society in the Middle East, 2 Volumes, 1995, 1996. Contributions to: Survival & Foreign Policy; Current History; New Outlook; New Leader; Middle East Journal. Membership: Council on Foreign Relations. Address: Department of International Relations, 152 Bay State Road, Boston, MA 02215, USA.

NORWICH John Julius, b. 15 Sept 1929, London, England. Writer; Broadcaster. m. (1) Anne Clifford, 5 Aug 1952, 1 son, 1 daughter, (2) Mollie Philipps, 14 June 1989. Education: University of Strasbourg, 1947; New College, Oxford, 1949-52. Publications: Mount Athos, 1966; Sahara, 1968; The Normans in the South, 1967; The Kingdom in the Sun, 1970; A History of Venice, 1977; Christmas Crackers 1970-79, 1980; Glyndebourne, 1985; The Architecture of Southern England, 1985; A Taste for Travel, 1985; Byzantium: The Early Centuries, 1988; More Christmas Crackers 1980-89, 1990; Venice: A Traveller's Companion (editor), 1990; The Oxford Illustrated Encyclopaedia of the Arts (editor), 1990; Byzantium, the Apogee, 1991; Byzantium: The Decline and Fall, 1995; A Short History of Byzantium, 1997. Contributions to: Numerous magazines and journals. Honours: Commander, Royal Victorian Order; Commendatore, Ordine al Merito della Repubblica Italiana. Memberships: Royal Society of Literature, fellow; Royal Geographical Society, fellow; Club: Beefsteak. Literary Agent: Felicity Bryan, 2A North Parade, Oxford, England. Address: 24 Blomfield Road, London W9 1AD, England.

NOSKOWICZ-BIERON Helena, b. 5 July 1931, Sobolow, Poland. Journalist. m. Wladystaw Bieron, 27 Dec 1956, 2 sons. Education: BA, Journalism, Jangiellonian University, Kraków, 1964; MA, Journalism, University of Warsaw, 1964. Appointments: Reporter,

Polish Radio, 1953-63; Columnist, Echo Krakowa, daily, 1964-81, Gazeta Krakowska and Dziennik Polski, 1989- ; Editor, Underground Press, 1981-89. Publications: Ciagle czekaja z obiadem, 1978; Kto Ukradl Zloty Fon, 1991. Contributions to: Periodicals. Honours: Book of the Year, 1978; Association of Polish Journalists prizes and awards. Membership: Association of Polish Journalists. Address: ul Batorego 19/16, 31-135 Kraków, Poland.

NOTLEY Alice, b. 8 Nov 1945, Bisbee, Arizona, USA. Poet; Writer. m. (1) Ted Berrigan, 1972, dec 1983, 2 sons, (2) Douglas Oliver, 10 Feb 1988. Education: BA, Barnard College, 1967; MFA, University of Iowa, 1969. Publications: Poetry: 165 Meeting House Lane, 1971; Phoebe Light, 1973; Incidentals in the Days World, 1973; For Frank O'Hara's Birthday, 1976; Alice Ordered Me to be Made: Poems 1975, 1976; A Diamond Necklace, 1977; Songs for the Unborn Second Baby, 1979; When I Was Alive, 1980; Waltzing Matilda, 1981; How Spring Comes, 1981; Three Zero, Turning Thirty (with Andrei Codrescu), 1982; Sorrento, 1984; Margaret and Dusty, 1985; Parts of a Wedding, 1986; At Night the States, 1988; Selected Poems of Alice Notely, 1993. Other: Doctor Williams' Heiresses: A Lecture, 1980; Tell Me Again, 1981; Homer's "Art", 1990; The Scarlet Cabinet: A Compendium of Books (with Douglas Oliver), 1992. Contributions to: Various publications. Honours: National Endowment for the Arts Grant, 1979; Poetry Center Award, 1981; General Electric Foundation Award, 1983; Fund for Poetry Awards, 1987, 1989. Address: 101 St Mark's Place, No 12A, New York, NY 10009, USA.

NOVA Craig, b. 5 July 1945, Los Angeles, California, USA. Writer. m. Christina Barnes, 2 July 1977, 2 children. Education: BA, University of California at Berkeley, 1967; MFA, Columbia University, 1969. Publications: Turkey Hash, 1972; The Geek, 1975; Incandescence, 1978; The Good Son, 1982; The Congressman's Daughter, 1986; Tornado Alley, 1989; Trombone, 1992; The Book of Dreams, 1994; The Universal Door, 1997. Honours: National Endowment for the Arts Fellowships, 1973, 1975, 1985; Guggenheim Fellowship, 1977. Address: c/o Stanford J Greenburger Associates Inc, 825 Third Avenue, New York, NY 10022, USA.

NOVAK Maximillian Erwin, b. 26 Mar 1930, New York, New York, USA. University Professor. m. Estelle Gershgoren, 21 Aug 1966, 2 sons, 1 daughter. Education: PhD, University of California, 1958; DPhil, St John's University, Oxford, 1961. Appointments: Assistant Professor, University of Michigan, 1958-62; Assistant Professor to Professor, University of California, Los Angeles, 1962-. Publications: Economics and the Fiction of Daniel Defoe, 1962; Defoe and the Nature of Man, 1963; Congreve, 1970; Realism Myth and History in the Fiction of Daniel Defoe, 1983; Eighteenth Century English Literature, 1983; Stoke Newington Defoe. Volume 1, 1998. Editor: The Wild Man Within, 1970; English Literature in the Age of Disguise, 1977; California Dryden, Vols X and X111, 1971, 1984. Contributions to: Professional journals. Address: Deparment of English, University of California, Los Angeles, CA 90095, USA.

NOVAK Michael (John), b. 9 Sept 1933, Johnstown, Pennsylvania, USA. Professor; Author; Editor. m. Karen Ruth Laub, 29 June 1963, 1 son, 2 daughters. Education: AB, Stonehill College, North Easton, Massachusetts, 1956; BT, Gregorian University, Rome, 1958; MA, Harvard University, 1966. Appointments: Assistant Professor, Stanford University, 1965-68; Associate Editor, Commonweal magazine, 1966-69; Associate Professor of Philosophy and Religious Studies, State University of New York at Old Westbury, 1968-71; Provost, Disciplines College, State University of New York at Old Westbury, 1969-71; Associate Director for Humanities, Rockefeller Foundation, New York City, 1973-75; Writer-in-Residence, Washington Star, 1976; Syndicated Columnist, 1976-80, 1984-89; Resident Scholar in Religion and Public Policy, 1978-, George Frederick Jewett Chair in Public Policy Research, 1983-, Director, Social and Political Studies, 1987-, American Enterprise Institute, Washington, DC; Head (with rank of Ambassador), US Delegation, United Nations Human

Rights Commission, Geneva, 1981, 1982, Conference on Security and Cooperation in Europe, 1986; Founder-Publisher, 1982-96, Editor-in-Chief, 1993-96, Crisis; Faculty, University of Notre Dame, 1986-87; Columnist, Forbes magazine, 1989-94; Various lectureships. Publications: The Tiber was Silver (novel), 1961; A New Generation, 1964; The Experience of Marriage, 1964; The Open Church, 1964; Belief and Unbelief, 1965, 3rd edition, 1994; A Time to Build, 1967; Vietnam: Crisis of Conscience (with Brown and Herschel), 1967; American Philosophy and the Future, 1968; A Theology for Radical Politics, 1969; Naked I Leave (novel), 1970; The Experience of Nothingness, 1970; Story in Politics, 1970; All the Catholic People, 1971; Ascent of the Mountain, Flight of the Dove, 1971; Politics: Realism and Imagination, 1971; A Book of Elements, 1972; The Rise of the Unmeltable Ethnics, 1972; Choosing Our King, 1974; The Joy of Sports, 1976, revised edition, 1994; The Guns of Littimer, 1978; The American Vision, 1978; Rethinking Human Rights I, 1981, II, 1982; The Spirit of Democratic Capitalism, 1982; Confession of a Catholic, 1983; Moral Clarity in the Nuclear Age, 1983; Freedom with Justice, 1984; Human Rights and the New Realism, 1986; Will It Liberate?: Questions About Liberation Theology, 1986; Character and Crime, 1986; The New Consensus on Family and Welfare, 1987; Taking Glasnost Seriously: Toward an Open Soviet Union, 1988; Free Persons and the Common Good, 1989; This Hemisphere of Liberty, 1990; The Spirit of Democratic Capitalism, 1991; Choosing Presidents, 1992; The Catholic Ethic and the Spirit of Capitalism, 1993; To Empower People: From State to Civil Society, 1996; Business as a Calling, 1996; Fire of Invention, 1997; Tell Me Why, 1998. Contributions to: Numerous publications. Honours: Freedom Award, Coalition for a Democratic Majority, 1979; George Washington Honor Medal, Freedom Foundation, 1984; Award of Excellence, Religion in Media, 1985; Ellis Island Medal of Honor, 1986; Anthony Fisher Prize, 1992; Templeton Prize for Progress in Religion, 1994; International Award, Institution for World Capitalism, Jacksonville University, Florida, 1994; Many honorary doctorates. Memberships: American Academy of Religion; Catholic Theological Society; Council on Foreign Relations; Institute for Religion and Democracy, director, 1981-; National Center of Urban and Ethnic Affairs, director, 1982-86; Society of Christian Ethics; Society of Religion in Higher Education. Literary Agent: Loretta Barrett, Barrett Inc. Address: c/o American Enterprise Institute, 1150 17th Street North West, Washington, DC 20036, USA.

NOVAK Robert. See: **LEVINSON Leonard.**

NOWRA Louis, b. 1950, Melbourne, Victoria, Australia. Playwright; Author. Education: La Trobe University, Victoria. Appointment: Co-Artistic Director, Lighthouse Co, Sydney, 1983. Publications: Albert Names Edward, 1975; Inner Voices, 1977; Visions, 1978; Inside the Island, 1980; The Precious Woman, 1980; The Song Room, 1981; Royal Show, 1982; The Golden Age, 1985; Whitsunday Opera Libretto, 1988; Byzantine Flowers, 1989; Summer of the Aliens, 1989; Cosi, 1992; Radiance, 1993; Crow, 1994. Novels: The Misery of Beauty, 1976; Palu, 1987; Red Nights, 1997. Other: Radio, television and screenplays. Honours: Australian Literature Board Fellowships. Address: Hilary Linstead & Associates, Level 18, Plaza 11, 500 Oxford Street, Bondi Junction, New South Wales 2022, Australia.

NOYES Stanley Tinning, b. 7 Apr 1924, San Francisco, California, USA. Writer; Poet. m. Nancy Black, 12 Mar 1949, 2 sons, 1 daughter. Education: BA, English, 1950, MA, English, 1951, University of California, Berkeley. Publications: No Flowers for a Clown (novel), 1961; Shadowbox (novel), 1970; Faces and Spirits (poems), 1974; Beyond the Mountains (poems), 1979; The Commander of Dead Leaves (poems), 1984; Los Comanches: The Horse People, 1751-1845, 1993; Comanches in the New West: Historic Photographs, 1895-1908, 1999. Contributions to: Reviews and quarterlies. Honour: MacDowell Fellow, 1967. Membership: PEN American Center. Address: 634 East Garcia, Santa Fe, NM 87501, USA.

NOZICK Robert, b. 16 Nov 1938, Brooklyn, New York, USA. Professor of Philosophy; Writer. m. Gjertrud Schnackenberg, 5 Oct 1987, 1 son, 1 daughter. Education: AB, Columbia College, 1959; PhD, Princeton University, 1963. Appointments: Assistant Professor, Princeton University, 1964-65; Assistant Professor, 1965-67, Professor, 1969-, Arthur Kingsley Professor of Philosophy, 1985-98, Pellegrino University Professor, 1998-, Harvard University; Associate Professor, Rockefeller University, 1967-69. Publications: Anarchy, State and Utopia, 1974; Philosophical Explanations, 1981; The Examined Life, 1989; The Nature of Rationality, 1993; Socratic Puzzles, 1997. Honours: National Book Award, 1975; Ralph Waldo Emerson Award, 1982. Memberships: PEN; American Academy of Arts and Sciences; American Philosophical Association; British Academy. Address: Emerson Hall, Harvard University, Cambridge, MA 02138, USA.

NUDELSTEJER Sergio, b. 24 Feb 1924, Warsaw, Poland. Journalist; Writer. m. Tosia Malamud. Education: National University of Mexico. Publications: Theodor Herzl: Prophet of Our Times, 1961; The Rebellion of Silence, 1971; Albert Einstein: A Man in His Time, 1980; Franz Kafka: Conscience of an Era, 1983; Rosario Castellanos: The Voice, the Word, the Memory (anthology), 1984; Borges: Getting Near to His Literary Work, 1987; Elias Canetti: The Language of Passion, 1990; Spies of God: Authors at the End of the Century, 1992; Stefan Zweig: The Conscience of Man, 1992; Everlasting Voices: Latin American Writers, 1996; Jerusalem: 3000 Years of History, 1997. Contributions to: Periodicals. Address: Heraclito 331, Apt 601, Polanco 11560, Mexico City.

NUGENT Neill, b. 22 Mar 1947, Newcastle upon Tyne, England. Professor. m. Maureen Nugent, 12 Sept 1969, 2 daughters. Education: BA, Politics, Social Administration, University of Newcastle, 1969; MA, Government, University of Kent, 1970; London School of Economics, 1970-71. Publications: The British Right (with R King); Respectable Rebels (with R King); The Left in France (with D Lowe); The European Union: Annual Review of Activities, 1992-96; The Government and Politics of the European Union, 1994; The European Business Environment (with R O'Donnell), 1994; At the Heart of the Union: Studies of the European Commission, 1997. Contributions to: Professional journals and edited books. Memberships: Political Studies Association; University Association for Contemporary European Studies; European Community Studies Association, USA. Address: Department of Politics and Philosophy, Manchester Metropolitan University, Geoffrey Manton Building, Rosamond Street West, Manchester M15 6LA, England.

NULAND Sherwin, b. 8 Dec 1930, New York, New York, USA. Surgeon; Professor; Author. m. Sarah Peterson, 29 May 1977, 2 sons, 2 daughters. Education: BA, New York University, 1951; MD, Yale University, 1955. Appointments: Surgeon, Yale-New Haven Hospital, Connecticut, 1962-91; Clinical Professor of Surgery, Yale School of Medicine, 1962-; Literary Editor, Connecticut Medicine, 1977-; Contibuting Editor, The American Scholar, 1998. Publications: The Origins of Anesthesia, 1983; Doctors: The Biography of Medicine, 1988; Medicine: The Art of Healing, 1991; The Face of Mercy, 1993; How We Die: Reflections on Life's Final Chapter, 1994; The Wisdom of the Body: How We live, 1997. Contibutions: Numerous to professional journals. Honours: National Book Award for Non-Fiction, 1994; Finalist Book Critics Circle Award, 1994; Finalist Pulitzer Prize, 1995. Memberships: American College of Surgeons, fellow; Associates of the Yale Medical School Library, chairman, 1982-94; New England Surgical Society; Yale-China Association, medical chairman, 1988-93; PEN; Authors' Guild. Literary Agent: Writers' Representatives Inc., 116 W 14th St, New York, NY 10011. Address: 29 Hartford Turnpike, Hamden, CT 06517, USA.

NUNIS Doyce Blackman Jr, b. 30 May 1924, Cedartown, Georgia, USA. Professor of History Emeritus; Writer; Editor. Education: BA, University of California at Los Angeles, 1947; MS, 1950, MEd, 1952, PhD, 1958, University of Southern California at Los Angeles. Appointments: Lecturer, 1951-56, Associate Professor, 1965-68, Professor of History, 1968-89, Professor Emeritus, 1989-, University of Southern California at Los Angeles; Instructor, El Camino College, 1956-59; Assistant Professor, University of California at Los Angeles, 1959-65; Editor, Southern California Quarterly, 1962-. Publications: Andrew Sublette: Rocky Mountain Prince, 1960; Josiah Belden: 1841 California Overland Pioneer, 1962; The Golden Frontier: The Recollections of Herman Francis Rinehart, 1851-69 (editor), 1962; The California Diary of Faxon Dean Atherton, 1836-39 (editor), 1964; Letters of a Young Miner (editor), 1964; The Journal of James H Bull (editor), 1965; The Trials of Isaac Graham, 1967; The Medical Journey of Pierre Garnier in California, 1851, 1967; Past is Prologue: Centennial Profile of Pacific Mutual Life Insurance Company, 1968; Hudson's Bay Company's First Fur Brigade to the Sacramento Valley: Alexander McLeod's 1829 Hunt, 1968; Sketches of a Journey on Two Oceans by Abbe Henri - J A Alric, 1850-1867 (editor), 1971; San Francisco 1856 Vigilance Committee: Three Views (editor), 1971; The Drawings of Ignatio Tirsh, S J (editor), 1972; Los Angeles and Its Environs in the Twentieth Century: A Bibliography of a Metropolis, 1973; A History of American Political Thought, 2 volumes, 1975; The Mexican War in Baja, California, 1977; Henry F Hoyt's A Frontier Doctor (editor), 1979; Los Angeles From the Days of the Old Pueblo (editor), 1981; The Letters of Jacob Baegart, 1749-1761: Jesuit Missionary in Baja, California (editor), 1982; Transit of Venus: The First Planned Scientific Expedition in Baja, California, 1982; Men, Medicine and Water: The Building of the Los Angeles Acqueduct, 1908-1913, 1982; Frontier Fighter by George W Coe (editor), 1984; Southern California Historical Anthology (editor), 1984; The Life of Tom Horn (editor), 1987; A Guide to the History of California (co-editor), 1988; Great Doctors of Medicine, 1990; The Bidwell- Bartleson Party, 1991; The Life of Tom Horn Revisited, 1992; Southern California's Spanish Heritage, 1992; Southern California Local History: A Gathering of W W Robinson's Writings (editor), 1993; From Mexican Days to the Gold Rush, 1993; Tales of Mexican California (editor), 1994; Women in the Life of Southern California, 1995; Mission San Fernando, Rez de España: A Bicentennial Tribute, 1997; Mission San Fernando, Rey de Espana 1797-1997: A Bicentennial Tribute (editor), 1997; A Parochial and Institutional History of the Diocese of Oakland (editor), 1999. Contributions: Over 100 to professional journals. Honours: Henry E Huntington Library Grant, 1960; Guggenheim Fellowship, 1963-64; American Philosophical Society Grant, 1969; Papal Medal, 1984; Franciscan History Award, 1990; Distinguished Emeritus Award, Univeristy of Southern California at Los Angeles, 1993; Knight Commander of St Gregory, 1993; Order of Isabel the Catholic, Spain, 1995. Memberships: American Antiquarian Society; American Historical Association; California Historical Society, vice-president, 1989-93; Historical Society of Southern California; Organization of American Historians; Western Historical Association; Zamorano Club, Los Angeles, Secretary. Address: 4426 Cromwell Avenue, Los Angeles, CA 90027, USA.

NUNN Frederick McKinley, b. 29 Oct 1937, Portland, Oregon, USA. Professor of History; Writer. m. (1) Tey Diana Rebolledo, 10 Sept 1960, div 1973, 1 daughter, (2) Susan Karant Boles, 8 Feb 1974, 1 daughter. Education: BA, University of Oregon, 1959; MA, 1963, PhD, 1963, University of New Mexico. Appointments: Assistant Professor, 1965-67, Associate Professor, 1967-72, Professor of History, 1972-, Portland State University, Oregon. Publications: Chilean Politics, 1920-31: The Honorable Mission of the Armed Forces, 1970; The Miltary in Chilean History: Essays on Civil-Military Relations, 1810-1973, 1976; Yesterday's Soldiers: European Military Professionalism in South America, 1890-1940, 1983; The Time of the Generals: Latin American Professional Militarism in World Perspective,

1992. Contributions to: Professional journals. Address: c/o Department of History, Portland State University, PO Box 751, Portland, OR 92707, USA.

NUSSBAUM Martha (Craven), b. 6 May 1947, New York, New York, USA. Philosopher; Classicist; Professor; Writer. m. Alan Jeffrey Nussbaum, Aug 1968, div 1987, 1 daughter. Education: BA, New York University, 1969; MA, 1971, PhD, 1973, Harvard University. Appointments: Assistant Professor of Philosophy and Classics, 1975-80, Associate Professor, 1980-83, Harvard University; Visiting Professor, Wellesley College, 1983-84; Associate Professor of Philosophy and Classics, 1984-85, Professor of Philosophy, Classics, and Comparative Literature, 1985-87, David Benedict Professor of Philosophy, Classics, and Comparative Literature, 1987-89, Professor, 1989-95, Brown University; Visiting Fellow, All Souls College, Oxford, 1986-87; Gifford Lecturer, University of Edinburgh, 1993; Visiting Professor of Law, 1994, Professor of Law and Ethics, 1995-96, Ernst Freund Professor of Law and Ethics, 1996-, University of Chicago. Publications: Aristotle's De Motu Animalium, 1978; Language and Logic (editor), 1983; The Fragility of Goodness, 1986; Love's Knowledge, 1990; Essays on Aristotle's De Anima (editor with A Rorty), 1992; The Quality of Life (editor with A Sen), 1993; Passions and Perceptions (editor with J Brunschwig), 1993; The Therapy of Desire, 1994; Women, Culture, and Development (editor), 1995. Honours: Guggenheim Fellowship, 1983; Creative Arts Award, Brandeis University, 1990; Spielvogel-Diamondstein Award, 1991. Memberships: American Academy of Arts and Sciences, fellow; American Philological Association; American Philosophical Association; American Philosophical Society; PEN. Address: c/o Law School, University of Chicago, 1111 East 60th Street, Chicago, IL 60637, USA.

NUTTALL Jeffrey, b. 8 July 1933, Clitheroe, Lancashire, England. Artist; Writer; Poet; Teacher. Div, 5 sons, 1 daughter. Education: Intermediate Examination, Arts and Crafts, Hereford School of Art, 1951; NDD, Painting, Special Level, Bath Academy of Art, Corsham, 1953; ATD, Institute of Education, University of London, 1954. Appointments: Lecturer, Bradford College of Art, 1968-70; Senior Lecturer, Leeds Polytechnic, 1970-81; Head, Department of Fine Arts, Liverpool Polytechnic, 1981-84; Numerous painting exhibitions; Occasional radio and television broadcasts. Publications: Poetry: Objects, 1973; Sun Barbs, 1974; Grape Notes/Apple Music, 1979; Scenes and Dubs, 1987; Mad with Music, 1987. Fiction: The Gold Hole, 1968; Snipe's Spinster, 1973; The Patriarchs, 1975; Anatomy of My Father's Corpse, 1976; What Happened to Jackson, 1977; Muscle, 1980; Teeth, 1994. Non-Fiction: King Twist: A Portrait of Frank Randle, 1978; Performance Art, Vol I, Memoirs, 1979, Vol II, Scripts, 1979; The Pleasures of Necessity, 1989; The Bald Soprano, 1989. Contributions to: Newspapers and journals. Honour: No 3 Winner, Novel in a Day Competition, Grovcho Club, 1994. Address: 71 White Hart lane, Barnes, London SW13 0PP, England.

NUWER Henry (Joseph), (Hank Nuwer), b. 19 Aug 1946, Buffalo, New York, USA. Author. m. (1) Alice Cerniglia, 28 Dec 1968, div 1980, 1 son, (2) Jenine Howard, 9 Apr 1982, 1 son. Education: BS, State University College of New York, Buffalo, 1968; MA, New Mexico Highlands University, 1971; PhD Equivalency, Ball State University, 1988. Appointments: Assistant Professor of English, Clemson University, 1982-83; Associate Professor of Journalism, Ball State University, 1985-89; Senior Writer, Rodale Press Book Division, Emmaus, Pennsylvania, 1990-91; Historian, Cedar Crest College, 1991-93; Editor, Arts Indiana Magazine, 1993-95; Visiting Associate Professor of Journalism, University of Richmond, Virginia 1995-97. Publications: Non-Fiction: Come Out, Come Out Wherever You Are (with Carole Shaw), 1982; Strategies of the Great Football Coaches, 1987; Strategies of the Great Baseball Managers, 1988; Rendezvous with Contemporary Authors, 1988; Recruiting in Sports, 1989; Steroids, 1990; Broken Pledges: The Deadly Rite of Hazing, 1990; Sports Scandals, 1994; How To Write Like an Expert, 1995; The

Lesson of Jesse Owens, 1998; Wrongs of Passage, 1999; High School Hazing, 1999; To The Young Writer, 1999. Fiction: The Bounty Hunter series (with William Boyles), 4 volumes, 1980-82. Editor: Rendezvous at the Ezra Pound Centennial Conference, 1982.

NYE Simon Beresford, b. 29 July 1958, Burgess Hill, Sussex, England. Writer. Education: BA, French, German, Bedford College, University of London, 1980; Diploma, Technical Translation, Polytechnic of Central London, 1985. Publications: Men Behaving Badly, 1990; Wideboy, 1991, as television series, I, 1993, 2, 1994; Frank Stubbs Promotes, television series, 2 1993-94; Is It Legal?, television series, 1995, 1996; Men Behaving Badly, 7 television series, 1992-1998; How Do You Want Me?, 2 television series 1998, 1999; My Wonderful Life, 3 television series, 1997-1999. Contributions to: Periodicals. Honours: Best ITV Sitcom, ITV Comedy Awards, 1993; Best Sitcom, 1995; Best Comedy Series, Writers Guild of Great Britain, 1995, and Royal Television Society, 1996; Nomination, International Emmy Award for Best Comedy, 1996. Address: 55 South Hill Park, London NW3 2SS, England.

NYLUND Anna Kristina, b. 1 Dec 1911, Petalax, Finland. Retired Teacher; Writer. m. Gunnar Nylund, 25 Aug 1947, 2 daughters. Education: Elementary School Teacher's Examination, 1933. Publications: Sanna, 1978; Sommarens Fotspar, 1981; Ur Bikiston, 1981; Dold Visdom Och Gömd Skatt, Petalax Historia I, 1982; Blommis Maj, Petalax Historia II, 19831; Aronstaven, 1997. Contributions to: Anthologies. Memberships: Svenska Österbottens Litteraturförening; Finlands Svenska Författareförening RF. Address: Strandgatan 7B, Fin 65100 Vasa, Finland.

NYLUND Gunnar Isak Georg, b. 2 June 1916, Nykarleby Ytterjeppo, Finland. Retired Teacher; Writer. m. Anna Nordman Holm, 25 Aug 1947, 2 daughters. Education: Elementary School Teacher's Examination, 1944. Publications: Alla de Dagar, 1978; Såsom Blommor På Röd Jord, 1981; Solvarv, 1982; Oändlighetens Eftermiddag, 1984; Vår by Vid Älven - Ytterjeppo, 1985; Gnistor av Liv, 1987; Sällsamma Samtal, 1994; Ringen, 1999. Contributions to: Anthologies. Memberships: Svenska Österbottens Litteraturförening; Finlands Svenska Författareförening RF. Address: Strandgatan 7B, Fin 65100 Vasa, Finland.

NYSTROM Debra, b. 12 July 1954, Pierre, South Dakota, USA. Poet; Writer; University Lecturer. Education: BA, English, University of South Dakota, 1976; Boston University, 1978-79; MFA, Creative Writing, Goddard College, 1980; Postgraduate Fellowship in Poetry, University of Virginia, 1982-83. Appointments: Lecturer in Creative Writing, University Virginia, 1984-; Guest Instructor, Aspen Writers' Conference, 1986. Publication: A Quarter Turn, 1991. Contributions to: Various anthologies, reviews, quarterlies, and journals. Honours: Yaddo Fellowship, 1983; Pushcart Prize Nominations, 1984, 1985, 1988, 1990; Virginia Commission for the Arts Prizes for Poetry, 1987, 1997; Balch Prize for Poetry, Virginia Quarterly Review, 1991; James Boatwright Prize for Poetry, Shenandoah, 1994. Memberships: Associated Writing Programs; Poetry Society of America. Address: c/o Department of English, 430 Bryan Hall, University of Virginia, Charlottesville, VA 22903, USA.

O

O'BALANCE Edgar, b. 17 July 1918, Dalkey, County Dublin, Ireland. Writer. m. (1) Mary Edington-Gee, 1949, dec 1969, 2 sons, 1 daughter, (2) Kathleen Barbara Tanner, 1972. Education: Private studies, Ireland. Publications: The Arab-Israeli War, 1956; The Sinai Campaign, 1956; The Story of the French Foreign Legion, 1961; The Red Army of China, 1962; The Indo-China War 1945-1954, 1964; The Red Army of Russia, 1964; The Greek Civil War 1948-1960, 1966; The Algerian Insurrection 1954-1962, 1967; The Third Arab-Israeli War 1967, 1972; The Kurdish Revolt 1961-1970, 1973; Arab Guerilla Power, 1974; The Electronic War in the Middle East 1968-1970, 1974; The Wars in Vietnam 1954-1972, 1975; The Secret War in the Sudan 1955-1972, 1977; No Victor, No Vanquished, 1978; The Language of Violence, 1979; Terror in Ireland, 1979; The Tracks of the Bear, 1982; The Gulf War, 1988; The Cyanide War, 1989; Terrorism in the 1980s, 1989; Wars in Afghanistan: 1839-1990, 1991; The Second Gulf War; The Civil War in Yugoslavia; Civil War in Bosnia: 1992-1994; The Kurdish Struggle: 1920-94, 1995; Islamic Fundamentalist Terrorism, 1996; Wars in the Caucasus: 1990-95, 1996; The Palestinian Intifada, forthcoming. Membership: Military Commentators Circle. Address: Wakebridge Cottage, Wakebridge, Matlock, Derbyshire, England.

O'BRIEN (William) Tim(othy), b. 1 Oct 1946, Austin, Minnesota, USA. Writer. m. Anne O'Brien. Education: BA, Macalester College, 1968; Graduate Studies, Harvard University. Publications: If I Die in a Combat Zone, Box Me Up and Ship Me Home, 1973; Northern Lights, 1975; Going After Cacciato, 1978; The Nuclear Age, 1981; The Things They Carried: A Work of Fiction, 1990; In the Lake of Woods, 1994; Tomcat in Love, 1998. Contributions to: Magazines. Honours: O Henry Memorial Awards, 1976, 1978; National Book Award, 1979; Vietnam Veterans of America Award, 1987; Heartland Prize, Chicago Tribune, 1990; Phi Beta Kappa. Address: c/o International Creative Managment, 40 West 57th Street, New York, NY 10019, USA,

O'BRIEN Conor Cruise, (Donat O'Donnell), b. 3 Nov 1917, Dublin, Ireland. Writer; Editor. m. (1) Christine Foster, 1939, div 1962, 1 son, 1 daughter, (2) Máire MacEntee, 1962, 1 adopted son, 1 adopted daughter. Education: BA, 1940, PhD, 1953, Trinity College, Dublin. Appointments: Member, Irish diplomatic service, 1944-61; Vice-Chancellor, University of Ghana, 1962-65; Albert Schweitzer Professor of Humanities, New York University, 1965-69; Member, Labour Party, Dublin North-east, Dail, 1969-77, Senate, Republic of Ireland, 1977-79; Visiting Fellow, Nuffield College, Oxford, 1973-75; Minister for Posts and Telegraphs, 1973-77; Pro-Chancellor, University of Dublin, 1973-; Fellow, St Catherine's College, Oxford, 1978-81; Editor-in-Chief, The Observer, 1979-81; Visiting Professor and Montgomery Fellow, Dartmouth College, New Hampshire, 1984-85; Senior Resident Fellow, National Humanities Center, North Carolina, 1993-94. Publications: Maria Cross, 1952; Parnell and His Party, 1957; The Shaping of Modern Ireland (editor), 1959; To Katanga and Back, 1962; Conflicting Concepts of the UN, 1964; Writers and Politics, 1965; The United Nations: Sacred Drama, 1967; Murderous Angels (play), 1968; Power and Consciousness, 1969; Conor Cruise O'Brien Introduces Ireland, 1969; Albert Camus, 1969; The Suspecting Glance (with Máire Cruise O'Brien), 1970; A Concise History of Ireland, 1971; States of Ireland, 1972; King Herod Advises (play), 1973; Neighbours: The Ewart-Biggs Memorial Lectures 1978-79, 1980; The Siege: The Saga of Israel and Zionism, 1986; Passion and Cunning, 1988; God Land: Reflections on Religion and Nationalism, 1988; The Great Melody: A Thematic Biography and Commented Anthology of Edmund Burke, 1992; Ancestral Voices, 1994; On the Eve of the Millennium, 1996; The Long Affair: Thomas Jefferson and the French Revolution, 1996. Honours: Valiant for Truth Media Award, 1979; Honorary doctorates. Memberships:

Royal Irish Academy; Royal Society of Literature. Address: Whitewater, Howth Summit, Dublin, Ireland.

O'BRIEN Denis Patrick, b. 24 May 1939, Knebworth, Hertfordshire, England. Retired University Teacher. m. (1) Eileen Patricia O'Brien, 1961, dec 1985, (2) Julia Stapleton, 1993, 1 son, 3 daughters. Education: BSc, University College, London, 1960; PhD, Queens University, Belfast, 1969. Appointments: Assistant Lecturer, Queens University, Belfast, 1963-64; Lecturer, 1965-69, Reader, 1970-72, Professor of Economics, 1972-97, Emeritus Professor, 1998-, University of Durham. Publications: Information Agreements (co-author), 1969; J R McCulloch, 1970; the Correspondence of Lord Overstone (3 volumes), 1971; Competition in British Industry, 1974; The Classical Economist, 1975; J R McCulloch Treatise on Taxation, 1975; Competition Policy, Profitability and Growth, 1979; Pioneers of Modern Economics in Britain, 1981; Authorship Puzzles in the History of Economics (co-author), 1982; Lionel Robbins, 1988; Thomas Joplin, 1993; Methodology, Money and the Firm, 1994. Contributions to: Economic Journal; Economica; History of Political Economy; Scottish Journal of Political Economy. Honour: Fellow, British Academy, 1988. Address: c/o Department of Economics, University of Durham, 23-26 Old Elvet, Durham DH1 3HY, England.

O'BRIEN Edna, b. 15 Dec 1936, Tuamgraney, County Clare, Ireland. Author; Dramatist. m. 1954, div 1964, 2 sons. Education: Convents; Pharmaceutical College of Ireland. Publications: The Country Girls, 1960; The Lonely Girl, 1962; Girls in Their Married Bliss, 1963; August is a Wicked Month, 1964; Casualties of Peace, 1966; The Love Object, 1968; A Pagan Place, 1970; Night, 1972; A Scandalous Woman, 1974; Mother Ireland, 1976; Johnnie I Hardly Knew You, 1977; Mrs Reinhardt and Other Stories, 1978; Virginia (play), 1979; The Dazzle, 1981; Returning, 1982; A Christmas Treat, 1982; A Fanatic Heart, 1985; Tales for Telling, 1986; Flesh and Blood (play), 1987; Madame Bovary (play), 1987; The High Road, 1988; Lantern Slides, 1990; Time and Tide, 1992; House of Splendid Isolation, 1994; Down by the River, 1997; James Joyce: A Biography, 1999. Honours: Yorkshire Post Novel Award, 1971; Los Angeles Times Award, 1990; Writers' Guild Award, 1993. Address: David Godwin Associates, 14 Goodwin Court, Covent Garden, London WC2N 4LL, England.

O'BRIEN Sean Patrick, b. 19 Dec 1952, London, England. Writer; Poet. Education: BA, Honours, English, Selwyn College, Cambridge, 1974; MA, University of Birmingham, 1977; University of Hull, 1976-79; PGCE, University of Leeds, 1981. Appointments: Fellow in Creative Writing, University of Dundee, 1989-91; Northern Arts Literary Fellow, 1992-94. Publications: The Indoor Park, 1983; The Frighteners, 1987; Boundary Beach, 1989; HMS Glasshouse, 1991. Contributions to: Anthologies, newspapers, reviews, and radio. Honours: Eric Gregory Award, 1979; Somerset Maugham Award, 1984; Cholmondeley Award, 1988; Arts Council Writer's Bursary, 1992. Address: 15 Connaught Gardens, Forest Hall, Newcastle-upon-Tyne NE12 8AT, England.

O'BRIEN Shannon Catherine, b. 11 Mar 1973, Melbourne, Australia. Education: BA, Hons, Writing, Middlesex University, England, 1995-98. Publications: Black and White Snow, 1995; I Am a Doughnut, 1995; Strategic Moves, 1994. Contributions to: Loaded; 3-D. Honour: Mike Brown Prize, 1998. Address: 2 Sunningdale Court, Southgate, Crawley, West Sussex RH10 6EB, England.

O'CASEY Brenda. See. **HAYCRAFT Anna (Margaret).**

O'CONNELL Richard (James), b. 25 Oct 1928, New York, New York, USA. Professor Emeritus; Poet; Translator. Education: BS, Temple University, 1956; MA, Johns Hopkins University, 1957. Appointments: Instructor, 1957-61, Assistant Professor, 1961-69, Associate Professor, 1969-86, Senior Associate Professor, 1986-93, Professor Emeritus, 1993-, Temple

University; Fulbright Lecturer, University of Brazil, Rio de Janeiro, 1960, University of Navarre, Pamplona, Spain, 1962-63; Guest Lecturer, Johns Hopkins University, 1961-74; Poet-in-the-Schools, Pennsylvania Council for the Arts, 1971-73. Publications: From an Interior Silence, 1961; Cries of Flesh and Stone, 1962; New Poems and Translations, 1963; Brazilian Happenings, 1966; Terrane, 1967; Thirty Epigrams, 1971; Hudson's Fourth Voyage, 1978; Temple Poems, 1985; Hanging Tough, 1986; Battle Poems, 1987; Selected Epigrams, 1990; Lives of the Poets, 1990; The Caliban Poems, 1992; RetroWorlds, 1993; Simulations, 1993; Voyages, 1995; The Bright Tower, 1997. Translator: Various works, including: Irish Monastic Poems, 1975; Middle English Poems, 1976; More Irish Poems, 1976; Epigrams from Martial, 1976; The Epigrams of Luxorius, 1984; New Epigrams from Martial, 1991. Honour: Contemporary Poetry Press Prize, 1972. Memberships: Associated Writing Programs; Modern Language Association; PEN. Address: 1147 Hillsboro Mile, Apt 907, Hillsboro Beach, FL 33062, USA.

O'CONNOR Patrick, b. 8 Sept 1949, London, England. Writer; Editor. Appointments: Deputy Editor, Harpers and Queen, 1981-86; Contributing Editor, F M R, 1986; Editor-in-Chief, Publications, Metropolitan Opera Guild, 1987-89; Consulting Editor, The New Grove Dictionary of Opera, 1989-91. Publications: Josephine Baker (with B Hammond), 1988; Toulouse-Lautrec: The Nightlife of Paris, 1991; The Amazing Blonde Woman, 1991; Sickert and the Theatre, Sickert Paintings, 1992; Music for the Stage in the Twentieth Century, 1995. Contributions to: Times Literary Supplement; Literary Review; Daily Telegraph; Gramophone; Opera; House and Garden; Music and Letters; Guardian. Memberships: National Union of Journalists; PEN. Address: c/o Rodgers, Coleridge and White, 20 Powis Mews, London W11 1JN, England.

O'DONNELL Donat. See: **O'BRIEN Conor Cruise.**

O' DONNELL K M. See: **MALZBERG Barry.**

O'DONNELL M R. See: **ROSS-MACDONALD Malcolm John.**

O'DONNELL Mary (Elizabeth Eugenie), b. 3 Apr 1954, Monaghan, Ireland. Writer; Poet; Critic. m. Martin Nugent, 18 June 1977. Education: BA, Honours, German and Philosophy, 1977, 1st Class Honours Diploma, Higher Education, 1983, Maynooth College. Appointments: Writer-in-Residence, University College, Dublin, and County Laois, 1995. Publications: Reading the Sunflowers in September, 1990; Strong Pagans and Other Stories, 1991; The Light-Makers, 1992; Spiderwoman's Third Avenue Rhapsody, 1993. Contributions to: Anthologies, reviews, quarterlies, and periodicals. Honours: 2nd Prize, Patrick Kavanagh Poetry Award, 1986; 3rd Prize Runner-Up, Bloodaxe National Poetry Competition, 1987; Allingham Poetry Award, 1988. Memberships: Irish Council for Civil Liberties; Poetry Ireland; Poetry Society. Address: Rook Hollow, Newtown Macabe, Maynooth, County Kildare, Ireland.

O'DONNELL Michael, b. 20 Oct 1928, England. Author; Dramatist; Broadcaster. m. Catherine Dorrington Ward, 1953, 1 son, 2 daughters. Education: MBBChir, St Thomas' Hospital Medical School, London, England. Appointments: Editor, Cambridge Writing, 1948, World Medicine, 1966-82; Scriptwriter, BBC Radio, 1949-52; General Medical Practitioner, 1954-64. Publications: O Lucky Man, 1972; Inside Cambridge Anthology, 1952; The Europe We Want, 1971; My Medical School, 1978; The Devil's Prison, 1982; Doctor! Doctor! An Insider's Guide to the Games Doctors Play, 1986; The Long Walk Home, 1988; Dr Michael O'Donnell's Executive Health Guide, 1988. Other: Television plays and documentaries; Radio scripts. Contributions to: Punch; New Scientist; Vogue; Times; Sunday Times; Daily Telegraph; Daily Mail; Listener. Address: Handon Cottage, Markwick Lane, Loxhill, Godalming, Surrey GU8 4BD, England.

O'DONNELL Peter, (Madeleine Brent), b. 11 Apr 1920, London, England. Author. Education: Catford

Central School, London. Appointments: Writer of Strip Cartoons, Garth, 1953-66, Tug Transom, 1954-66, Romeo Brown, 1956-62, Modesty Blaise, 1963-. Publications: Modesty Blaise, 1965; Sabre-Tooth, 1966; I, Lucifer, 1967; A Taste for Death, 1969; The Impossible Virgin, 1971; Pieces of Modesty (short stories), 1972; The Silver Mistress, 1973; Murder Most Logical (play), 1974; Last Day in Limbo, 1976; Dragon's Claw, 1978; The Xanadu Talisman, 1981; The Night of Morningstar, 1982; Dead Man's Handle, 1985; Cobra Trap, 1996 (under Peter O'Donnell). As Madeleine Brent: Tregaron's Daughter, 1971; Moonraker's Bride, 1973; Kirkby's Changeling, 1975; Merlin's Keep, 1977; The Capricorn Stone, 1979; The Long Masquerade, 1981; A Heritage of Shadows, 1983; Stormswift, 1984; Golden Urchin, 1986. Address: 49 Sussex Square, Brighton BN2 1GE, England.

O'DONOGHUE (James) Bernard, b. 14 Dec 1945, Cullen, County Cork, Ireland. University Teacher of English; Poet. m. Heather MacKinnon, 23 July 1977, 1 son, 2 daughters. Education: MA in English, 1968, BPhil in Medieval English, 1971, Lincoln College, Oxford. Appointments: Lecturer and Tutor in English, Magdalen College, Oxford, 1971-75; Fellow in English Wadham College, Oxford, 1995-. Publications: Razorblades and Pencils, 1984; Poaching Rights, 1987; The Weakness, 1991; Gunpowder, 1995; Here Nor There, 1999. Contributions to: Norton Anthology of Poetry; Poetry Ireland Review; Poetry Review; Times Literary Supplement. Honours: Southern Arts Literature Prize, 1991; Whitbread Poetry Award, 1995. Membership: Poetry Society, London, 1984-; Fellow, Royal Society of Literature, 1999. Address: Wadham College, Oxford OX1 3PN, England.

O'DONOVAN Joan Mary, b. 31 Dec 1914, Mansfield, England. Writer. Publications: Dangerous Worlds, 1958; The Visited, 1959; Shadows on the Wall, 1960; The Middle Tree, 1961; The Niceties of Life, 1964; She, Alas, 1965; Little Brown Jesus, 1970; Argument with an East Wind, 1986. Contributions to: Times Educational Supplement; Guardian; Punch; Vogue; Harper's and Queen. Memberships: Society of Authors; International PEN. Address: 14 Rue du Four, 24600 Ribérac, France.

O'DRISCOLL Dennis, b. 1 Jan 1954, Thurles, County Tipperary, Ireland. Editor; Poet. m. Julie O'Callaghan, 1985. Education: University College, Dublin, 1972-75. Appointments: Literary Organiser, Dublin Arts Festival, 1977-79; Editor, Poetry Ireland Review, 1986-87. Publications: Kist, 1982; Hidden Extras, 1987. Co-Editor: The First Ten Years: Dublin Arts Festival Poetry, 1979. Honour: Irish Arts Council Bursary. Address: Ketu, Breffni Gate, Church Road, Dalkey, County Dublin, Ireland.

O'FAOLAIN Julia, b. 6 June 1932, London, England. Writer. m. Lauro Rene Martines, 14 Dec 1957, 1 son. Education: BA, 1952, MA, 1953, University College, Dublin; University of Rome, 1952-53; Sorbonne, University of Paris, 1953-55. Publications: We Might See Sights! and Other Stories, 1968; Godded and Codded, 1970; Not in God's Image: Women in History from the Greeks to the Victorians (editor with Lauro Rene Martines), 1973; Man in the Cellar, 1974; Women in the Wall, 1975; No Country for Young Men, 1980; Daughters of Passion, 1982; The Obedient Wife, 1982; The Irish Signorina, 1984; The Judas Cloth, 1992. Contributions to: Newspapers and magazines. Membership: Society of Authors; Fellow, Royal Society of Literature. Address: c/o Deborah Rogers Ltd, 20 Powis Mews, London W11 1JN, England.

O'FARRELL Patrick James, b. 17 Sept 1933, Greymouth, New Zealand. Professor of History. m. Deirdre Genevieve MacShane, 29 Dec 1956, 3 sons, 2 daughters. Education: MA, University of New Zealand, 1956; PhD, Australian National University, 1961. Appointments: Professor, School of History, University of New South Wales, Australia. Publications: The Catholic Church in Australia: A Short History, 1968; Documents in Australian Catholic History, 2 volumes, 1969; Harry Holland: Militant Socialist, 1969; Ireland's English Question, 1971; England and Ireland since 1800, 1975; Letters from Irish Australia, 1984; The Catholic Church and Community: An Australian History, 1985; The Irish in Australia, 1986; Vanished Kingdoms: Irish in Australia and New Zealand, 1990; Through Irish Eyes: Australian and New Zealand Images of the Irish, 1788-1948, 1994; UNSW: A Portrait, 1999. Contributions to: Historical, literary and religious journals. Honour: New South Wales Premier's Literary Award, 1987. Memberships: Australian Society of Authors; Australian Academy of the Humanities, fellow. Address: School of History, University of New South Wales, Sydney 2052, New South Wales, Australia.

O'FIANNACHTA Padraig, b. 20 Feb 1927, County Kerry, Ireland. Retired Professor; Poet; Writer; Editor. Education: St Patrick's College, Maynooth, 1944-48; BA, 1947, MA, 1955, National University of Ireland; University College, Cork, 1949-50; D Ph Pontifical University, Maynooth. Appointments: Lecturer, 1959-60, Professor of Early Irish and Lecturer in Welsh, 1960-81, Professor of Modern Irish, 1981-92, St Patrick's College, Maynooth. Publications: Ponc, 1966; Ruin, 1969; Feoirlingi Fileata, 1972; Donn Bo, 1976; An Bíobla Naofa (editor, translator), 1981; Spaisteoireacht, 1982; Deora De, 1987. Contributions to: Various publications. Honour: Douglas Hyde Prize for Literature, 1969. Memberships: Cumann na Sagart; Oireachtas, president, 1985; Poetry Ireland; Royal Irish Academy. Address: Dingle, Tralee, County Kerry, Ireland.

O'FLAHERTY Patrick Augustine, b. 6 Oct 1939, Long Beach, Newfoundland, Canada. Professor Emeritus; Writer. Education: BA, Honours, 1959; MA, 1960, Memorial University, St John's, Newfoundland; PhD, University of London, 1963. Appointments: Professor, 1965-95, Head, Department of English, 1981-86, Professor Emeritus, 1997-, Memorial University. Publications: The Rock Observed, 1979; Part of the Main: An Illustrated History of Newfoundland and Labrador (with Peter Neary), 1983; Summer of the Greater Yellowlags, 1987; Priest of God, 1989; A Small Place in the Sun, 1989; Come Near at Your Peril: A Visitor's Guide to the Island of Newfoundland, 1992; Benny's Island, 1994; Reminiscences of J P Howley: Selected Years (co-editor), 1997. Contributions to: Numerous publications. Membership: Writers' Union of Canada. Address: PO Box 2676, St John's, Newfoundland, A1C 6K1, Canada.

O'GRADY Desmond James Bernard, b. 27 Aug 1935, Limerick, Ireland. Poet; Writer; Translator. 1 son, 2 daughters. Education: MA, 1964, PhD, 1982, Harvard University. Appointments: Secondary School Teacher, University Professor, 1955-82. Publications: Chords and Orchestrations, 1956; Reilly, 1961; Professor Kelleher and the Charles River, 1964; Separazioni, 1965; The Dark Edge of Europe, 1967; The Dying Gaul, 1968; Off Licence (translator), 1968; Hellas, 1971; Separations, 1973; Stations, 1976; Sing Me Creation, 1977; The Gododdin (translator), 1977; A Limerick Rake (translator), 1978; The Headgear of the Tribe, 1979; His Skaldcrane's Nest, 1979; Grecian Glances (translator), 1981; Alexandria Notebook, 1989; The Seven Arab Odes (translator), 1990; Tipperary, 1991; Ten Modern Arab Poets (translator), 1992; My Fields This Springtime, 1993; Alternative Manners (translator), 1993; Trawling Tradition: Collected Translations, 1954-1994, 1994; Il Galata Morente, 1996; The Road Taken: Poems, 1956-1996, 1996; C P Cavafy: Selected Poems (translator), 1998. Prose Memoirs: Ezra Pound, Patrick Kavanagh, Samuel Beckett, Olga Rudge, Anna Akhmatova. Essays: On poetry, poets, translating poetry. Contributions to: Anthologies and magazines. Membership: Aosdána. Address: Ardback, Kinsdale, County Cork, Ireland.

O'GRADY Irenia, (Aineri Yoargo), b. 18 Jan, South Australia. Freelance Writer. m. Michael O'Grady, 27 Jan 1975, 1 daughter. Appointments: Storyteller, various primary schools; Journalist; Critic; Radio Presenter. Publications include: Love Has Many Faces; Moods and Fantasies, Love Trust and Other Things. Contributions to: Peoples Friend; Womans Weekly; Truth; Parnassus of World Poetry. Address: Elphin Cottage, Blackhill Road, c/o Houghton, South Australia, 5131 Australia.

O'GRADY Tom, b. 26 Aug 1943, Baltimore, Maryland, USA. Poet; Writer; Dramatist; Translator; Editor; Vintner. m. Bronwyn Southworth, 2 sons. Education: BA, English, University of Baltimore, 1966; MA, English, Johns Hopkins University, 1967; Graduate Studies, English and American Literature, University of Delaware, 1972-74. Appointments: Teacher of writing and literature, various colleges and universities, 1966-96; Founder-Editor, The Hampden-Sydney Poetry Review, 1975-; Numerous lectures and poetry readings. Publications: Poetry: Unicorn Evils, 1973; Establishing a Vineyard, 1977; Photo-Graphs, 1980; The Farmville Elegies, 1981; In the Room of the Just Born, 1989; Carvings of the Moon, 1992; Sun, Moon, and Stars, 1996. Prose: Shaking the Tree: A Book of Works and Days, 1993. Editor: The Hampden-Sydney Poetry Anthology, 1990. Other: Translations; Stage and television plays. Contributions to: Anthologies, newspapers, journals, and magazines. Honours: Leache Prize for Poetry, 1975; Editor's Award, Coordinating Council of Literary Magazine, 1977; Merit Award, 1977; Mettauer Research Award, 1984; Trustees Award, 1986, Hampden-Sydney College; Virginia Prize for Poetry, 1989; Teacher of the Arts Award, National Foundation for Advancement in the Arts, 1989-90; Virginia Center for the Arts Fellowship Residency, 1995; Henrico Theater Co Prize, 1997. Address: c/o Rose Bower Vineyard and Winery, PO Box 126, Hampden-Sydney, VA 23943, USA.

O'KEEFE BAZZONI Jana, b. 15 Oct 1941, Boston, Massachusetts, USA. Associate Professor. m. Enrico A Bazzoni, 28 June 1969, 3 sons. Education: Graduated, Speech, Drama, St Mary of the Woods College, 1963; MA, Theatre, Hunter College, 1974; PhD, Theatre, Graduate Center, City University of New York, 1983. Appointments: Assistant Professor, 1985-95, Associate Professor, 1995-, Baruch College, New York City. Publications: Alter Egos: Clowning and Enactment in Pirandello and Fo; Reluctant Pilgrim: Pirandello's Journey Toward the Modern Stage; A Production History of Pirandello's Six Characters in Search of an Author and Henry IV, 1991; Entries on Luigi Pirandello, F T Marinetti, Luca Ronconi and Giuseppe Patroni-Griffi, in Theatrical Directors: A Biographical Dictionary, 1994; Pirandello and Film (with Nina DaVinci Nichols), 1995; Pirandello e I collaboratori per un film dei Sei personaggi, 1997. Contributions to: Articles and translations in Performing Arts Journal, Review of National Literature, Modern Drama, Theater Three, Western European Stages, Rivista di studi pirandelliani, Offstage Perspectives, Forum Italicum. Memberships: American Society for Theatre Research; Modern Language Association; National Communication Association; Association for Business Communication. Address: Baruch College, 17 Lexington Avenue, New York City, NY 10010, USA.

O'LEARY Rosemary, b. 26 Jan 1955, Kansas City, Missouri, USA. Professor; Writer. m. Larry Schroeder, 8 July 1989, 1 daughter. Education: BA, Honours, English Literature, 1978, JD, 1981, MPA, 1982, University of Kansas; PhD, Syracuse University, 1988. Appointments: Admitted to Kansas and Federal Bars, 1981; Assistant General Counsel, Kansas Corporation Commission, 1982-83; Director, division of Policy and Planning, Kansas Department of Health and Environment, 1983-85; Assistant Professor, 1988-90, Associate Professor, 1994-97, Professor, 1997-98, Indiana University; Assistant Professor, 1990-93, Associate Professor, 1993-94, Syracuse University; Senior Fulbright Research Fellow, Indonesia, 1998-99. Publications: Emergency Planning: Local Government and the Community Right-to-Know Act, 1993; Environmental Change: Federal Courts and the EPA, 1993; Public Administration and Law (with David Rosenbloom), 2nd edition, 1997; Managing for the Environment (with Robert Durant and Daniel Fiorino), 1999. Contributions to: Many professional books and journals. Honours: American Bar Association Award for Excellence, 1981; Lilly Foundation Award for Outstanding Research, 1992; Distinguished Service Award, American Society for Public Administration, 1996;

President's Award for Distinguished Teaching, Indiana University, 1998. Memberships: Academy of Management; American Bar Association; American Political Science Association; American Society for Public Administration; Association for Public Policy Analysis and Management; Law and Society Association. Address: 8150 East Fleener Road, Bloomington, IN 47408, USA.

O'MALLEY Mary, b. 19 Mar 1941, Bushey, Hertfordshire, England. Playwright. Appointments: Resident Writer, Royal Court Theatre, 1977. Publications: Superscum, 1972; A 'Nevolent Society, 1974; Oh If Ever a Man Suffered, 1975; Once a Catholic, 1977; Look out, Here Comes Trouble, 1978; Talk of the Devil, 1986. Honour: Evening Standard Award, 1978. Address: Knockeven, Cliffs of Moher, County Clare, Ireland.

O'NEILL Joseph, b. 23 Feb 1964, Cork, Republic of Ireland. Novelist; Non-Fiction Writer. m. Sally Singer, 30 Dec 1994. Education: Girton College, Cambridge, 1982-85; BA Law, Cambridge, 1985. Appointment: Barrister, 1990-. Publications: This Is The Life, 1990; The Breezes, 1994. Contributions to: Reviews and articles in: Times Literary Supplement; Spectator; Literary Review, New York. Literary Agent: Rogers, Coleridge and White. Address: c/o Rogers, Coleridge and White, 11 Powys Mews, London W11, England.

O'NEILL Michael (Stephen Charles), b. 2 Sept 1953, Aldershot, Hampshire, England. Professor of English; Writer; Poet; Editor. m. Rosemary Ann McKendrick, 16 July 1977, 1 son, 1 daughter. Education: BA, Honours, 1st Class, English, 1975, DPhil, 1981, Exeter College, Oxford. Appointments: Faculty, 1979-91, Senior Lecturer, 1991-93, Reader, 1993-95, Professor of English, 1995-, University of Durham; Co-Founder and Editor, Poetry Durham, 1982-94. Publications: The Human Mind's Imaginings: Conflict and Achievement in Shelley's Poetry, 1989; Percy Bysshe Shelley: A Literary Life, 1989; The Stripped Bed (poems), 1990; Auden, MacNeice, Spender: The Thirties Poetry (with Gareth Reeves), 1992; Percy Bysshe Shelley (editor), 1993; The 'Defence of Poetry' Fair Copies (editor), 1994; Keats: Bicentenary Readings (editor), 1997; Fair Copies of Shelley's Poems in American and European Libraries (editor with Donald H Reiman), 1997; Romanticism and the Self-Conscious Poem, 1997; Literature of the Romantic Period: A Bibliographical Guide (editor), 1998. Contributions to: Books and journals. Honours: Eric Gregory Award, 1983; Cholmondeley Award, 1990. Address: c/o Department of English Studies, University of Durham, Elvet Riverside 1, New Elvet, Durham DH1 3JT, England.

O'NEILL Patrick Geoffrey, b. 9 Aug 1924, London, England. Professor of Japanese Emeritus; Writer. m. Diana Howard, 1951, 1 daughter. Education: BA, 1949, PhD, 1957, School of Oriental and African Studies, University of London. Appointments: Lecturer in Japanese, 1949-68, Professor of Japanese, 1968-86, Professor Emeritus, 1986-, School of Oriental and African Studies, University of London. Publications: A Guide to No, 1954; Early No Drama, 1958; Introduction to Written Japanese (with S Yanada), 1963; A Programmed Course on Respect Language in Modern Japanese, 1966; Japanese Kana Workbook, 1967; A Programmed Introduction to Literary-style Japanese, 1968; Japanese Names, 1972; Essential Kanji: 2000 Japanese Characters, 1973; Tradition and Modern Japan (editor), 1982; A Dictionary of Japanese Buddhist Terms (editor with H Inagaki), 1984; A Reader of Handwritten Japanese, 1984; T Kawatake: Japan on Stage (translator), 1990; Annotated plate supplement in H Plutschow: Matsuri - The Festivals of Japan, 1996. Address: 44 Vine Road, East Molesey, Surrey KT8 9LF, England.

O'NEILL Paul, b. 26 Oct 1928, St John's, Newfoundland, Canada. Author. Education: National Academy of Theatre Arts, New York. Publications: Spindrift and Morning Light, 1968; The City in Your Pocket, 1974; The Oldest City, 1975; Seaport Legacy, 1976; Legends of a Lost Tribe, 1976; Breakers, 1982; The Seat Imperial, 1983; A Sound of Seagulls, 1984;

Upon This Rock, 1984. Other: Radio and stage plays; Television and film scripts. Contributions to: Many periodicals. Honours: Literary Heritage Award, Newfoundland Historical Society; Robert Weaver Award, National Radio Producers Association of Canada, 1986; Honorary Doctor of Laws, Memorial University of Newfoundland, 1988; Order of Canada, 1990; Newfoundland and Labrador Arts Hall of Honour, 1991; Canada Commemorative Medal, 1992. Memberships: Canadian Authors Association; Canadian Radio Producers Association; Newfoundland and Labrador Arts Council, chairman, 1988-89; Newfoundland Writers Guild; Writers Union of Canada. Address: 115 Rennies Mill Road, St John's, Newfoundland, A18 2P2, Canada.

O'REILLY Kaite, b. 26 Sept 1963. Playwright; Fiction Writer. Education: BA, Honours, Sheffield University. Appointments: Writer-in-Residence, Essex University, 1990-91; Visiting Writer, Birmingham Polytechnic, 1992; Lecturer in Theatre and Media Drama, University of Glamorgan, 1992-97. Publications: Mouth, Extract From Novel in Minerva's New Writing 3; Sight (short story); A Slow Motion Life; Yard (play). Contributions to: Disability Arts Magazine; New Welsh Review. Honour: Peggy Ramsay Award, 1998. Literary Agent: Sebastian Born, The Agency, 24 Pottery Lane, London W11 4LZ. Address: 25 Durham Street, Grangetown, Cardiff, Wales.

O'ROURKE Andrew Patrick, b. 26 Oct 1933, Plainfield, New Jersey, USA. County Executive; Writer. Separated, 1988, 1 son, 2 daughters. Education: BA, Fordham College, 1954; JD, Fordham Law School, 1962; LLM, New York University Graduate Law School, 1965. Publications: Red Banner Mutiny, 1986; Hawkwood, 1989. Contributions to: Bar journals and digests; The Proceedings of the Naval Institute; Journal of Ancient and Medieval Studies. Honours: Honorary DHL, Mercy College, 1984; Honorary LLD, Manhattanville College, 1986; Honorary JD, Pace University, 1988. Address: 148 Martine Avenue, White Plains, NY 10601, USA.

O'SHAUGHNESSY Bernadette Bay. See: **GRIFFIN RESS Patricia.**

O'SIADHAIL Micheal, b. 12 January 1947, Dublin, Ireland. Poet. m. 2 July 1970. Education: Trinity College, University of Dublin; BA (Mod), University of Oslo, Norway, 1968; MLitt, University of Dublin, 1971. Appointments: Lecturer, Trinity College, Dublin, 1969-73; Professor, Dublin Institute for Advanced Studies, 1974-87. Publications: Springnight, 1983; The Image Wheel, 1985; The Chosen Garden, 1985; Hail! Madam Jazz: New and Selected Poems, 1992; A Fragile City, 1995; Our Double Time, 1995; Poems 1975-1995, 1999. Contributions to: numerous. Honours include: Irish American Cultural Institute Prize for Poetry, 1987; Marten Toonder Award for Literature, 1998. Literary Agent: Bloodaxe Books, PO Box 1SN, Newcastle upon Tyne, NE99 1SN, England.

O'SULLIVAN Vincent (Gerard), b. 28 Sept 1937, Auckland, New Zealand. Poet; Writer; Dramatist. Education: MA, University of Auckland, 1959; BLitt, Lincoln College, Oxford, 1962. Appointments: Visiting Fellow, Yale University, New Haven; Writer-in-Residence, University of Virginia. Publications: Poetry: Our Burning Time, 1965; Revenants, 1969; Bearings, 1973; From the Indian Funeral, 1976; Brother Jonathan, Brother Kafka, 1980; The Rose Ballroom and Other Poems, 1982; The Butcher Papers, 1982; The Pilate Tapes, 1986. Plays: Shuriken, 1985; Jones and Jones, 1989. Fiction: Miracle: A Romance, 1976; The Boy, the Bridge, the River, 1978; Dandy Edison for Lunch and Other Stories, 1981. Non-Fiction: New Zealand Poetry in the Sixties, 1973; Katherine Mansfield's New Zealand, 1974. Editor:Various books. Honour: New Zealand Book Award, 1981. Address: c/o John McIndoe Ltd, 51 Crawford Street, PO Box 694, Dunedin, New Zealand.

O'TOOLE James (Joseph), b. 15 Apr 1945, San Francisco, California, USA. Business Educator; Writer. m. Marilyn Louise Burrill, 17 June 1967, 2 children. Education: BA, University of Southern California 1966;

DPhil, University of Oxford, 1970. Appointments: Director, Twenty Year Forecast Project, Center for Futures Research, 1973-81; University Professor of Management, 1980-; The Leadership Institute, 1991; Senior Fellow, Aspen Institute, Colorado, 1994. Publications: Work, Learning and the American Future, 1977; Making America Work, 1981; Vanguard Management: Redesigning the Corporate Future, 1985; The Executive's Compass: Business and the Good Society, 1993; Leading Change, 1995; Leadership A to Z, 1999. Address: 19912 Pacific Coast Highway, Malibu, CA 90265, USA.

O'TOOLE Joanne Rose, b. 27 Jan 1939, Cleveland, OH, USA. Travel Journalist. m. Thomas Joseph O'Toole, 31 July 1965. Education: St Agnes Elementary School, Cleveland, OH, USA, 1952; Graduate Diploma, St Joseph Academy, Rocky River, OH, USA, 1956; BA, Ursuline College, Cleveland, OH; John Carroll University, University Heights, OH, USA, 1960. Appointments: Elementary School Teacher, followed by Journalist, 1965-. Honours: SATW Lowell Thomas Journalism Award Winner; SATW Central States Chapter Awards; Midwest Travel Writers Association Awards. Memberships: Society of American Travel Writers; Travel Journalists Guild; Midwest Travel Writers Association; Press Club of Cleveland. Address: 4603 Wood Street, Willoughby, OH 44094-5821, USA.

O'TOOLE Peter James, b. 2 Aug 1932, Eire, Ireland. Actor. 1 son, 2 daughters. Education: RADA (Diploma), Assoicate, RADA. Publications: The Child, 1992; The Apprentice, 1996. Honour: Commander of the Order of Arts and Letters, France. Address: c/o Charles Opick Consultancy, 3 Byanston Place, London W1H 7FN, England.

O'TOOLE Thomas Robert, b. 14 May 1935, Cleveland, OH, USA. Travel Journalist; Photographer. m. Joanne Rose O'Toole, 31 July 1965. Education: James A Garfield, Willoughby Hills, OH, USA, 1949; Graduate Diploma, Cathedral Latin, Cleveland, OH, 1953; BA, Honors, John Carroll University, University Heights, OH, USA, 1959. Appointment: Journalist. Honours: SATW Lowell Thomas Journalism Award Winner; SATW Central States Chapter Awards; Multiple Midwest Travel Writers Association Awards. Memberships: Society of American Travel Writers; Travel Journalists Guild; Midwest Travel Writers Association; National Press Photographers Association; Ohio News Photographers Association; National Press Club; Press Club of Cleveland; Active Member, Outdoor Writers Association of America; Association of Great Lakes Outdoor Writers; Outdoor Writers of Ohio. Address: 4603 Wood Street, Willoughby, OH 44094 5821, USA.

OAKES Philip, b. 31 Jan 1928, Burslem, Staffordshire, England. Author; Poet. Appointments: Scriptwriter, Granada TV and BBC, London, 1958-62; Film Critic, The Sunday Telegraph, London, 1963-65; Assistant Editor, Sunday Times Magazine, 1965-67; Arts Columnist, Sunday Times, London, 1969-80; Columnist, Independent on Sunday, London, 1990, Guardian Weekend, London, 1991-. Publications: Unlucky Jonah: Twenty Poems, 1954; The Punch and Judy Man (with Tony Hancock), screenplay, 1962; Exactly What We Want (novel), 1962; In the Affirmative (poems), 1968; The God Botherers, US edition as Miracles: Genuine Cases Contact Box 340 (novel), 1969; Married/Singular (poems), 1973; Experiment at Proto (novel), 1973; Tony Hancock: A Biography, 1975; The Entertainers (editor), 1975; A Cast of Thousands (novel), 1976; The Film Addict's Archive, 1977; From Middle England (memoirs), 1980; Dwellers All in Time and Space (memoirs), 1982; Selected Poems, 1982; At the Jazz Band Ball: A Memory of the 1950's, 1983; Shopping for Women (novel), 1994. Address: Fairfax Cottage, North Owersby, Lincolnshire LN8 3PX, England.

OAKLEY Ann (Rosamund), b. 17 Jan 1944, London, England. Professor of Sociology and Social Policy; Writer. 1 son, 2 daughters. Education: MA, Somerville College, Oxford, 1965; PhD, Bedford College, London,

1974. Appointments: Research Officer, Social Research Unit, Bedford College, London, 1974-79; Wellcome Research Fellow, Radcliffe Infirmary, National Perinatal Epidemiology Unit, Oxford, 1980-83; Deputy Director, Thomas Coram Research Unit, 1985-90, Director, Social Science Research Unit, 1990-, Professor of Sociology and Social Policy, 1991-, University of London. Publications: Sex, Gender and Society, 1972; The Sociology of Housework, 1974; Housewife, 1974, US edition as Women's Work: A History of the Housewife, 1975; The Rights and Wrongs of Women (editor with Juliet Mitchell), 1976; Becoming a Mother, 1980; Women Confined, 1980; Subject Women, 1981; Miscarriage (with A McPherson and H Roberts), 1984; Taking It Like a Woman, 1984; The Captured Womb: A History of the Medical Care of Pregnant Women, 1984; Telling the Truth about Jerusalem, 1986; What Is Feminism (editor with Juliet Mitchell), 1986; The Men's Room, 1988; Only Angels Forget, 1990; Matilda's Mistake, 1990; Helpers in Childbirth: Midwifery Today (with S Houd), 1990; The Secret Lives of Eleanor Jenkinson, 1992; Social Support and Motherhood: The Natural History of a Research Project, 1992; Essays on Women, Medicine and Health, 1992; Scenes Originating in the Garden of Eden, 1993; Young People, Health and Family Life (with J Brannen, K Dodd and P Storey), 1994; The Politics of the Welfare State (editor with S Williams), 1994; Man and Wife, 1996; The Gift Relationship by Richard Titmuss (with John Ashton), 1997. Contributions to: Professional journals; Many chapters in academic books. Address: c/o Tessa Sayle Ltd, 11 Jubilee Place, London SW3, England.

OAKLEY Graham, b. 27 Aug 1929, Shrewsbury, England. Children's Writer. Education: Warrington Art School, 1950. Appointments: Scenic artist, theatres and Royal Opera House, London; Designer, BBC-TV, 1962-77. Publications: Church Mice series, 1972-87; Graham Oakley's Magical Changes, 1980; Once Upon a Time: A Prince's Fantastic Journey, 1990. Address: c/o Macmillan Children's Books, 4 Little Essex Street, London WC2R 3LF, England.

OAKLEY Robin (Robert Francis Leigh), b. 20 Aug 1941, Kidderminster, England. Journalist. m. Carolyn Rumball, 4 June 1966, 1 son, 1 daughter. Education: Brasenose College, Oxford; MA, Oxford. Appointments: Liverpool Daily Post, 1964-70; Crossbencher Columnist, then Assistant Editor, Sunday Express, 1971-79; Assistant Editor, Now! magazine, 1979-81; Assistant Editor, Daily Mail, 1981-86; Political Editor, Times, 1986-92; Presenter, Week in Westminster, BBC Radio, 1987-92; Political Editor, BBC, 1992-; Turf Columnist, Spectator, 1995-; Racing Post, 1998-. Contributions to: Various horse-racing books. Literary Agent: Roger Houghton. Address: 46 Cleaver Square, Kennington, London SE11 4EA, England.

OANDASAN William Cortes, b. 17 Jan 1947, Santa Rosa, California, USA. Poet; Educator. m. 28 Oct 1973, 2 daughters. Education: BA, 1974; MA, 1981; MFA, 1984; Instructor Credential, 1989. Appointments: Editor, A Publications, 1976-; Senior Editor, American Indian Culture and Research Journal, University of California, Los Angeles, 1981-86; Instructor, English Department, University of Orleans, Louisiana State University, 1988-90. Publications: Moving Inland, 1983; Round Valley Songs, 1984; Summer Night, 1989; The Way to Rainy Mountain: Internal and External Structures, in Approaches to Teaching World Literature, 1988; Poetry in Harper's Anthology of 20th Century Native American Poetry, 1988. Contributions to: Colorado Review; Southern California Anthology; California Courier; American Indian Culture and Research Journal. Honours: Publishing Grant, National Endowment for the Arts, 1977; American Book Award, 1985; Summer Scholar Award for Writers, 1989; Research Council Grant, 1989. Memberships: Associated Writing Programs; A Writers Circle; Modern Language Association; Society for the Study of Multi-Ethnic Literatures; Association for the Study of American Indian Literatures; National Association on Ethnic Studies; Philological Society of the Pacific Coast. Address: 3832 West Avenue 43, No 13, Los Angeles, CA 90041, USA.

OATES Joyce Carol, b. 16 June 1938, Millersport, New York, USA. Author; Dramatist; Poet; Professor; Publisher. m. Raymond Joseph Smith, 23 Jan 1961. Education: BA, Syracuse University, 1960; MA, University of Wisconsin at Madison, 1961. Appointments: Instructor, 1961-65, Assistant Professor, 1965-67, University of Detroit; Faculty, Department of English, University of Windsor, Ontario, Canada, 1967-78; Co-Publisher (with Raymond Joseph Smith), Ontario Review, 1974-; Writer-in-Residence, 1978-81, Professor, 1987-, Princeton University. Publications: Fiction: With Shuddering Fall, 1964; A Garden of Earthly Delights, 1967; Expensive People, 1968; Them, 1969; Wonderland, 1971; Do With Me What You Will, 1973; The Assassins: A Book of Hours, 1975; Childworld, 1976; Son of the Morning, 1978; Unholy Loves, 1979; Cybele, 1979; Angel of Light, 1981; Bellefleur, 1980; A Bloodsmoor Romance, 1982; Mysteries of Winterthurn, 1984; Solstice, 1985; Marya: A Life, 1986; You Must Remember This, 1987; Lives of the Twins, 1987; Soul-Mate, 1989; American Appetites, 1989; Because It Is Bitter, and Because It Is My Heart, 1990; Snake Eyes, 1992; Black Water, 1992; Foxfire, 1993; What I Lived For, 1994; Zombie, 1995; You Can't Catch Me, 1995; First Love: A Gothic Tale, 1996; We Were the Mulvaneys, 1996; Man Crazy, 1997; My Heart Laid Bare, 1998; Come Meet Muffin, 1998. Stories: By the North Gate, 1963; Upon the Sweeping Flood and Other Stories, 1966; The Wheel of Love, 1970; Cupid and Psyche, 1970; Marriages and Infidelities, 1972; A Posthumous Sketch, 1973; The Girl, 1974; Plagiarized Material, 1974; The Goddess and Other Women, 1974; Where Are You Going, Where Have You Been?: Stories of Young America, 1974; The Hungry Ghosts: Seven Allusive Comedies, 1974; The Seduction and Other Stories, 1975; The Poisoned Kiss and Other Stories from the Portuguese, 1975; The Triumph of the Spider Monkey, 1976; Crossing the Border, 1976; Night-Side, 1977; The Step-Father, 1978; All the Good People I've Left Behind, 1979; Queen of the Night, 1979; The Lamb of Abyssalia, 1979; A Middle-Class Education, 1980; A Sentimental Education, 1980; Last Day, 1984; Wild Saturday and Other Stories, 1984; Wild Nights, 1985; Raven's Wing, 1986; The Assignation, 1988; Heat and Other Stories, 1991; Where Is Here?, 1992; Haunted Tales of the Grotesque, 1994. Plays: Three Plays: Ontological Proof of My Existence, Miracle Play, The Triumph of the Spider Monkey, 1980; Twelve Plays, 1991; The Perfectionist and Other Plays, 1995. Poetry: Women in Love and Other Poems, 1968; Anonymous Sins and Other Poems, 1969; Love and Its Derangements, 1970; Wooded Forms, 1972; Angel Fire, 1973; Dreaming America and Other Poems, 1973; The Fabulous Beasts, 1975; Seasons of Peril, 1977; Women Whose Lives Are Food, Men Whose Lives Are Money, 1978; Celestial Timepiece, 1980; Nightless Nights: Nine Poems, 1981; Invisible Women: New and Selected Poems 1970-1982, 1982; Luxury of Sin, 1984; The Time Traveller: Poems 1983-1989, 1989. Other: The Edge of Impossibility: Tragic Forms in Literature, 1972; The Hostile Sun: The Poetry of D H Lawrence, 1973; New Heaven, New Earth: The Visionary Experience in Literature, 1974; The Stone Orchard, 1980; Contraries: Essays, 1981; The Profane Art: Essays and Reviews, 1983; Funland, 1983; On Boxing, 1987, expanded edition, 1994; (Woman) Writer: Occasions and Opportunities, 1988. Editor: Scenes from American Life: Contemporary Short Fiction, 1973; The Best American Short Stories 1979 (with Shannon Ravenel), 1979; Night Walks: A Bedside Companion, 1982; First Person Singular: Writers on Their Craft, 1983; Story: Fictions Past and Present (with Boyd Litzinger), 1985; Reading the Fights (with Daniel Halpern), 1988. Honours: National Endowment for the Arts Grants, 1966, 1968; Guggenheim Fellowship, 1967; O Henry Awards, 1967, 1973, and Special Awards for Continuing Achievement, 1970, 1986; Rosenthal Award, 1968; National Book Award, 1970; Rea Award, 1990; Heideman Award, 1990; Bobst Lifetime Achievement Award, 1990; Walt Whitman Award, 1995. Membership: American Academy of Arts and Letters. Address: 185 Nassau Street, Princeton, NJ 08540, USA.

OATES Stephen B(aery), b. 5 Jan 1936, Pampa, Texas, USA. Professor; Writer. m. (1), 1 son, 1 daughter, (2) Marie Philips. Education: BA, 1958, MA, 1960, PhD, 1969, University of Texas at Austin. Appointments: Instructor, 1964-67, Assistant Professor, 1967-68, Arlington State College; Assistant Professor, 1968-70, Associate Professor, 1970-71, Professor of History, 1971-80, Adjunct Professor of English, 1980-85, Paul Murray Kendall Professor of Biography, 1985-, University of Massachusetts at Amherst; Various guest lectureships. Publications: Confederate Cavalry West of the River, 1961; John Salmon Ford: Rip Ford's Texas (editor), 1963; The Republic of Texas (general editor), 1968; Visions of Glory, Texas on the Southwestern Frontier, 1970; To Purge This Land with Blood: A Biography of John Brown, 1970, 2nd edition, revised, 1984; Portrait of America (editor): Vol I, From the European Discovery to the End of Reconstruction, Vol II, From Reconstruction to the Present, 1973, 6th edition, 1994; The Fires of Jubilee: Nat Turner's Fierce Rebellion, 1975; With Malice Toward None: The Life of Abraham Lincoln, 1977; Our Fiery Trial: Abraham Lincoln, John Brown, and the Civil War Era, 1979; Let the Trumpet Sound: The Life of Martin Luther King, Jr, 1982; Abraham Lincoln: The Man Behind the Myths, 1984; Biography as High Adventure: Life-Writers Speak on Their Art (editor), 1986; William Faulkner: The Man and the Artist, a Biography, 1987; A Woman of Valor: Clara Barton and the Civil War, 1994; The Approaching Fury: Voices of the Storm, 1820-1861, 1997; The Whirlwind of War: Voices of the Storm, 1861-1865, 1998. Contributions to: Professional journals. Honours: Texas State Historical Association Fellow, 1968; Texas Institute of Letters Fellow, 1969; Guggenheim Fellowship, 1972; Christopher Awards, 1977, 1982; Barondess/Lincoln Award, New York Civil War Round Table, 1978; National Endowment for the Humanities Fellow, 1978; Robert F Kennedy Memorial Book Award, 1983; Institute for Advanced Studies in the Humanities Fellow, 1984; Kidger Award, New England History Teachers Association, 1992; Nevins-Freeman Award, Chicago Civil War Round Table, 1993; Phi Beta Kappa. Memberships: American Antiquarian Society; Society of American Historians; Texas Institute of Letters. Address: 10 Bridle Path, Amherst, MA 01002, USA.

OBARSKI Marek, b. 2 July 1947, Poznań, Poland. Writer; Poet; Critic; Editor; Translator. m. Aleksandra Zaworska, 27 Mar 1982, 2 sons, 2 daughters. Appointments: Director, Flowering Grass Theatre, 1974-79, Literary Department, Nurt magazine, 1985-90; Critic, Art for Child magazine, 1989-90; Editor, 1991-93, Translator, 1993-, Rebis Publishing House; Editor, Europe, 1992-94. Publications: 10 volumes, 1969-97. Contributions to: Journals and magazines. Honours: Medal of Young Artists, 1984; Stanislaw Pietak Award, 1985. Memberships: Ecologic Association of Creators; Union de Gens de Lettres Polonaises. Address: os Wl Lokietka 13 F m 58, 61-616 Poznań, Poland.

OBERG Leon Erik, b. 5 Jan 1944, Goulborn, New South Wales, Australia. Newspaper Editor; Writer. m. Tricia Noakes, 14 Oct 1967, 2 sons, 2 daughters. Publications: Locomotives of Australia, 1975, 3rd edition, 1996; Diesel Locomotives of Australia, 1980; Trains, 1984; Motive Power, 1995; Australian Rail at Work, 1995. Contributions to: Magazines.Memberships: Australian Media Arts; Australian Entertainment Alliance. Address: 102 Taralga Road, Bradfordville, New South Wales, Australia.

OBERMAN Sheldon Arnold, b. 20 May 1949, Winnipeg, Canada. Writer; Educator. m. (1) Lee Anne Block, 8 Sept 1973, div 1990, 1 son, 1 daughter, (2) Lisa Ann Dveris, 2 Sept 1990, 1 child. Education: BA in English, University of Winnipeg, 1972; BA in English with Honours, University of Jerusalem, Israel, 1973; Teaching Certificate, University of Manitoba, 1974. Appointments: Teacher, W C Miller Collegiate, Altona, 1975-76, Joseph Wolinsky Collegiate, Winnipeg, 1976-95. Publications: The Folk Festival Book, 1983; Lion in the Lake: A French-English Alphabet Book, 1988; Julie Gerond and the Polka Dot Pony, 1988; TV Sal and the Game Show From Outer Space, 1993; This Business with Elijah, 1993; The Always Prayer Shawl, 1994; The White Stone in the Castle Wall, 1995; By the Hannukah Light, 1997.

Honours include: National Jewish Book Award, Jewish Book Council, 1995; Sydney Taylor Award, 1995; Best Book of the Year, Childrens magazine, 1995. Address: c/o Joseph Wolinsky Collegiate, 123 Doncaster Avenue, Winnipeg, MB R2W 0E1, Canada.

OBSTFELD Raymond, (Pike Bishop, Jason Frost, Don Pendleton, Carl Stevens), b. 22 Jan 1952, Williamsport, Pennsylvania, USA. Assistant Professor of English; Wrier; Poet; Dramatist; Screenwriter. Education: BA, Johnston College, University of Redlands, 1972; MA, University of California at Davis, 1976. Appointments: Lecturer to Assistant Professor of English, Orange Coast College, 1976-. Publications: Fiction: The Golden Fleece, 1979; Dead-End Option, 1980; Dead Heat, 1981; Dead Bolt, 1982; The Remington Factor, 1985; Masked Dog, 1986; Redtooth, 1987; Brainchild, 1987; The Whippin Boy, 1988. As Pike Bishop: Diamondback, 1983; Judgement at Poisoned Well, 1983. As Jason Frost: Warlord series, 1983-85; Invasion USA, 1985. As Don Pendleton: Bloodsport, 1982; Flesh Wounds, 1983; Savannah Swingsaw, 1985; The Fire Eaters, 1986. As Carl Stevens: The Centaur Conspiracy, 1983; Ride of the Razorback, 1984. Poetry: The Cat With Half a Face, 1978. Contributions to: Anthologies and other publications. Membership: Mystery Writers of America. Address: 190 Greenmoor, Irvine, CA 92714, USA.

ODA Makoto, b. 2 June 1932, Osaka, Japan. Novelist; Writer. m. Hyon Sune, Dec 1982, 1 daughter. Education: University of Tokyo, Japan, 1957; Harvard University, 1958-59. Publications: Japanese Intellectuals (essay), 1964; Hiroshima (novel), 1981; Far From Vietnam (novel), 1992; Thought on the Earthquake and War (critical essay), 1996; Demokratia (critical essay), 1997; Osaka Symphony (novel), 1997; Stomping on Aboji (short story), 1998; Gyokusai (novel), 1998. Honours: Lotus Prize, Afro-Asian Writers Association, 1987; Kawabata Yasunari Literary Prize, 1997. Membership: Japanese PEN. Address: 1-41-801 Ohama-cho, Nishinomiya, Japan.

ODAGA Asenath (Bole), b. 5 July 1937, Rarieda, Kenya. Author. Education: Kikuyu Teacher Training College, 1955-56; BA, 1974, Diploma in Education, 1974, MA, 1981, University of Nairobi. Appointments: Tutor, Church Missionary Society Teacher Training College, Ngiya, 1957-58; Teacher, Butere Girls School, 1959-60; Headmistress, Nyakach Girls School 1961-63; Assistant Secretary, Kenya Dairy Board, Nairobi, 1965-67; Secretary, Kenya Library Services, Nairobi, 1968; Advertising Assistant, East African Standard Newspaper and Kerr Downey and Selby Safaris, both Nairobi, 1969-70; Assistant Director, Curriculum Development Programme, Christian Churches Educational Association, Nairobi, 1974-75; Research Fellow, Institute of African Studies, University of Nairobi, 1976-81. Publications: God, Myself and Others (editor with David Kirui and David Crippen), 1976; Kip Goes to the City (children's fiction), 1977; Poko Nyar Mugumba (Poko Mugumba's Daughter, children's folktale), 1978; Thu Tinda: Stories from Kenya (folktales), 1980; The Two Friends (folktales), 1981; Miaha (in Luo: The Bride, play), 1981; Simbi Nyaima (The Sunken Village, play), 1982; Oral Literature: A School Certificate Course (school text book), 1982; Ange ok Tel (Regret Never Comes First, children's fiction), 1982; Kenyan Folk Tales, 1982; Sigendini gi Timbe Luo Moko (Stories and Some Customs of the Luo), 1982; A Reed on the Roof, Block Ten, With Other Stories (fiction), 1982; Mouth and Pen: Literature for Children and Young People in Kenya, 1983; My Home (reader), 1983; The Shade Changes (fiction), 1984; Yesterday's Today: The Story of Oral Literature, 1984; The Storm (fiction), 1986; Nyamgondho the Son of Ombare and Other Luo Stories, 1986; Between the Years (fiction), 1987; A Bridge in Time (fiction), 1987; Munde and his Friends (children's fiction), 1987; Munde Goes to the Market (children's fiction), 1987; The Rag Ball (children's fiction), 1987; The Silver Cup (children's fiction), 1988; The Storm (adolescent's fiction), 1988; Rianan (fiction), 1990; A Night on a Tree (fiction), 1991; Luo Sayings, 1992. Address: PO Box, 1743 Kisumu, Kenya, Africa.

ODEGARD Knut, b. 6 Nov 1945, Molde, Norway. Poet; Writer; Critic. m. Thorgerdur Ingolfsdottir, 2 Aug 1981, 2 daughters. Education: Theology and Philosophy, University of Oslo. Appointments: Poetry Critic, Aftenposten newspaper, 1968-; Managing Director, Scandinavian Centre, Nordens Hus, Reykjavik, 1984-89; President, Norwegian Festival of International Literature, 1992-; Consul, Republic of Slovakia, 1995-97; Consul General, Republic of Macedonia, 1997-. Publications: 10 poetry books, 1967-98; prose; fiction; non-fiction. Honours: Knighted by President of Iceland, 1987; Norwegian State Scholar for Life, 1989-; Grand Knight Commander, Order of the Icelandic Falcon, 1993; International Order of Merit, 1993; Knight, Norwegian Order of Literature, 1995. Memberships: Academy of Norwegian Language; Icelandic Society of Authors; Literary Academy of Romania; Norwegian Literary Council; Norwegian Society of Authors. Address: Chateau Parkv 42, 6400 Molde, Norway.

ODELL Peter Randon, b. 1 July 1930, Coalville, England. Professor of International Energy Studies Emeritus; Writer. m. Jean Mary McKintosh, 1957, 2 sons, 2 daughters. Education: BA, 1951, PhD, 1954, University of Birmingham; AM, Fletcher School of Law and Diplomacy, Cambridge, Massachusetts, 1958. Appointments: Economist, Shell International Petroleum Co, 1958-61; Lecturer, 1961-65, Senior Lecturer, 1965-68, Visiting Professor, 1983-, London School of Economics and Political Science; Professor of Economic Geography, 1968-81, Director, Centre for International Energy Studies, 1981-90, Professor Emeritus, 1991-, Erasmus University, Rotterdam; Stamp Memorial Lecturer, University of london, 1975; Professor, College of Europe, Bruges, 1983-90; Scholar-in-Residence, Rockefeller Centre, Bellagio, Italy, 1984; European Editor, Energy Journal, 1988-90; Killam Visiting Scholar, University of Calgary, 1989; Visiting Scholar, University of Cambridge, 1996-. Publications: An Economic Geography of Oil, 1963; Oil: The New Commanding Height, 1966; Natural Gas in Western Europe: A Case Study in the Economic Geography of Energy Resources, 1969; Oil and World Power: A Geographical Interpretation, 1970, 8th edition, 1986; Economies and Societies in Latin America (with D A Preston), 1973, 2nd edition, 1978; Energy: Needs and Resources, 1974, 2nd edition, 1977; The North Sea Oil Province (with K E Rosing), 1975; The West European Energy Economy: The Case for Self-Sufficiency, 1976; The Optimal Development of the North Sea Oilfields (with K E Rosing), 1976; The Pressures of Oil: A Strategy for Economic Revival (with L Vallenilla), 1978; British Offshore Oil Policy: A Radical Alternative, 1980; The Future of Oil, 1980-2080 (with K E Rosing), 1980, 2nd edition, 1983; Energie: Geen Probleem? (with J A van Reiyn), 1981; The International Oil Industry: An Interdisciplinary Perspective (editor with J Rees), 1986; Global and Regional Energy Supplies: Recent Fictions and Fallacies Revisited, 1991; Energy in Europe: Resources and Choices, 1998; Fossil Fuel Reserves in the 21st Century, 1998; The Evolution of the European Energy Economy, 1945-1995, 1998; The New Europe: Energy Resources and Voices, 1998. Honours: Canadian Council Fellow, 1978; International Association for Energy Economics Prize, 1991; Royal Scottish Geographical Society Centenary Medal, 1993. Memberships: F.R.G.S.; F. Inst. Pet. Address: 7 Constitution Hill, Ipswich IPI 3RG, England.

ODELL Robin Ian, b. 19 Dec 1935, Totton, Hampshire, England. Writer. m. Joan Bartholomew, 19 Sept 1959. Publications: Jack the Ripper in Fact and Fiction, 1965; Exhumation of a Murder, 1975; Jack the Ripper: Summing-up and Verdict (with Colin Wilson), 1977; The Murderers' Who's Who (with J H H Gaute), 1979; Lady Killers, 1980; Murder Whatdunit, 1982; Murder Whereabouts, 1986; Dad Help Me Please (with Christopher Berry-Dee), 1990; A Question of Evidence, 1992; Lady Killer, 1992; The Long Drop, 1993; Landmarks in Twentieth Century Murder, 1995; The International Murderer's Who's Who, 1996. Contributions to: Crimes and Punishment; The Criminologist. Honours: FCC Watts Memorial Prize, 1957; International Humanist and Ethical Union, 1960; Edgar Award, Mystery Writers of America, 1980. Memberships: Paternosters; Our Society; Crime Writers Association. Address: 11 Red House Drive, Sonning Common, Reading RG4 9NT, England.

ODEN Fay (Giles), b. 17 Nov 1929, Nashville, Tennessee, USA. Retired Teacher; Author; Poet; Illustrator. m. Edward A Oden, 16 Apr 1961. Education: AB, Tennessee State University, 1951; Reading Specialist, Howard University, 1957. Appointments: Teacher, Cincinnati Public Schools, 1954-88; Author, 1985-; Storyteller, 1993-; Volunteer, several schools, 1993-; Publisher, 1994-. Publications: Calvin in His Video Camera, 1992; Where Is Calvin, 1993; The Flying School, 1994; Believe, 1995; I Dream a Journey, 1996; Discover, 1998; Calvin's Curtain Call, 1999. Contributions to: Cincinnati Enquiry; Cincinnati Herald; Recorder. Memberships: Zeta's Society of Published Authors; Librarian League of Greater Cincinnati. Address: 6315 Elwynne Drive, Cincinnati, OH 45236-4013, USA.

ODGERS Darrel Allan, b. 7 Mar 1957, Smithton, Tasmania, Australia. Secretary; Manager; Writer. m. Sally P Farrell, 26 May 1979, 1 son, 1 daughter. Education: School Board Certificate. Publications: Timedetector (with S Odgers), 1995; Dad's New Path, 1995; Maria's Diary, 1996; Theft in Time, forthcoming; Timedetectors II (with S Odgers), forthcoming; The Giant Cat (with S Odgers), forthcoming. Membership: Australian Society of Authors. Address: PO Box 41, Latrobe, Tasmania 7307, Australia.

ODGERS Sally Farrell, (Tegan James), b. 26 Nov 1957, Latrobe, Tasmania, Australia. Freelance Writer and Lecturer. m. Darrel Allan Odgers, 26 May 1979, 1 son, 1 daughter. Publications: Dreadful David, 1984; Five Easy Lessons, 1989; Kayak, 1991; Shadowdancers, 1994; Timedetector (with D Odgers), 1995; Timedetectors II (with D Odgers), forthcoming; The Giant Cat (with D Odgers), forthcoming. Contributions to: Lucky; Organic Growing; Australian Women's Weekly; Good House Keeping; Australian Author; Writer's News. Honour: Journalism Award, Circular Head Festival, 1993. Memberships: Australian Society of Authors; Society of Women Writers. Address: PO Box 41, Latrobe, Tasmania 7307, Australia.

OÉ Kenzaburó, b. 31 Jan 1935, Ehime, Shikoku, Japan. Author. m. Yukari Kenzaburó, 2 children. Education: Degree in French Literature, University of Tokyo, 1959. Publications: Fiction: Shiiku, 1958, English translation as The Catch, 1966; Memushiri kouchi, 1958, English translation as Nip the Buds, Shoot the Kids, 1995; The Perverts, 1963; Adventures in Daily Life, 1964; Kojinteki na taiken, 1964, English translation as A Personal Matter, 1968; Man'en gannen no futtoburu, 1967, English translation as The Silent Cry, 1974; Pinchi ranna chosho, 1976, English translation as The Pinch Runner Memorandum, 1995; Teach Us to Outgrow Our Madness (also includes Aghwee the Sky Monster, The Day He Himself Shall Wipe My Tears Away, and Prize Stock), 1977; The Crazy Iris and Other Stories of the Atomic Aftermath, 1984. Non-Fiction: Hiroshima Notes, 1963; Japan, the Ambiguous, and Myself: The Nobel Prize Speech and Other Lectures, 1995. Other: Many fiction and non-fiction books in Japanese. Honours: Akutagawa Prize, Japanese Society for the Promotion of Literature, 1958; Shinchosha Literary Prize, 1964; Tanizaki Prize, 1967; Europelia Arts Festival Literary Prize, 1989; Nobel Prize for Literature, 1994. Address: 585 Seijo-machi, Setagaya-Ku, Tokyo, Japan.

OFFEN Yehuda, (Huri Halim, Ben Naftali), b. 4 Apr 1922, Altona, Germany. Writer; Poet. m. Tova Arbisser, 28 Mar 1946, 1 daughter. Education: BA, University of London, 1975; MA, Comparative Literature, Hebrew University of Jerusalem, 1978. Appointments: Senior Editor, Al Hamishmar, Daily Guardian, 1960-80. Publications: L'Lo L'An, 1961; Har Vakhol, 1963; Lo Agadat Khoref, 1969; Nofim P'nima, 1979; B'Magal Sagur (short stories), 1979; N'Vilat Vered, 1983; Shirim Bir'hov Ayaif, 1984; P'Gishot Me'ever Lazman, 1986; Massekhet Av, 1986; Stoning on the Cross Road (short stories),

1988; Who Once Begot a Star, 1990; Silly Soil, 1992; Back to Germany, 1994. Contributions to: Various publications. Honours: ACUM Prizes for Literature, 1961, 1979, 1984; Talpir Prize for Literature, 1979; Efrat Prize for Poetry, 1989. Memberships: ACUM (Society of Authors, Composers and Editors in Israel); Hebrew Writers Association, Israel; International Academy of Poets, USA; International Federation of Journalists, Brussels; National Federation of Israeli Journalists; PEN Centre, Israel. Address: 8 Gazit Street, Tel Aviv 69417, Israel.

OFFERMANN Bill, b. 15 Sept 1935, Düren, Germany. Writer. m. 6 Sept 1966, 2 sons, 1 daughter. Publications: Tötliche Liebe (autobiography), 1993; Soiree brut, 1994; Fund-orte 3: Im Falle eines Falles, 1996. Contributions to: Journals. Membership: Swiss Writers' Union. Address: Rest Fernsichet, 9427 Zelg-Wolfhalden, Switzerland.

OGADA Asenath (Bole), b. 5 July 1937, Rarieda, Kenya. Writer. Education: Kikuyu Teacher Training College, 1955-56; BA, 1974, Diploma, Education, 1974, MA, 1981, University of Nairobi. Appointments: Assistant Director, Curriculum Development Programme, Christian Churches Educational Association, Nairobi, 1974-75; Research Fellow, Institute of African Studies, University of Nairobi, 1976-81. Publications: God, Myself and Others (editor with David Kirui and David Crippen), 1976; Kip Goes to the City, 1977; Poko Mugumba, 1978; Thu Tinda: Stories From Kenya, 1980; The Two Friends, 1981; Miaha (play), 1981; Simbi Nyaima (play), 1982; Oral Literature: A School Certificate Course (textbook), 1982; Ange ok Tel, 1982; Kenyan Folk Tales, 1982; Sigendini gi Timbe Luo, 1982; A Reed on the Roof, Block Ten, with Other Stories, 1982; Mouth and Pen: Literature for Children and Young People in Kenya, 1983; My Home (reader), 1983; The Shade Changes, 1984; Yesterday's Today: The Story of Oral Literature, 1984; The Storm, 1986; Nyamgondho, the Son of Ombare and Other Stories, 1986; Between the Years, 1987; A Bridge in Time, 1987; Munde and his Friends, 1987; Munde Goes to the Market, 1987; The Rag Ball, 1987; The Silver Cup, 1988; The Storm, 1988; Rianan, 1990; A Night on a Tree, 1991; Luo Sayings, 1992.

OGDEN Hugh, b. 11 Mar 1937, Erie, Pennsylvania, USA. Professor; Poet; Writer. m. Ruth Simpson, 3 Mar 1960, 1 son, 2 daughters. Education: BA, Haverford College, 1959; MA, New York University, 1961; PhD, University of Michigan, 1967. Appointments: Teaching Assistant, 1961-65, Instructor, 1965-67, University of Michigan; Assistant Professor, 1967-75, Associate Professor, 1975-91, Professor, 1991-, Trinity College, Hartford, Connecticut. Publications: Looking for History, 1991; Two Road and this Spring, 1993; Windfalls, 1996; Gift, 1998; Natural Things, 1998. Contributions to: Reviews, quarterlies, and journals. Honours: Connecticut Commission on the Arts Poetry Project Grant, 1990; National Endowment for the Arts Grant, 1993. Memberships: Associated Writing Programs; Poetry Society of America; Poets and Writers. Address: c/o Department of English, Trinity College, Hartford, CT 06106, USA.

OGILVY George. See: **AYERST David.**

OGRAJA. See: **GRILLO Odhise.**

OJALA Ossi Arne Atos, b. 22 Mar 1933, Savonlinna, Finland. Author; Playwright. Education: BA, University of Helsinki. Publications: 7 novels, 1966-85; Over 30 plays broadcast. Contributions to: Several publications. Honours: Otava Prize, 1964; 1st Prize, Novel Competition, 1966; Best Finnish Novel for Young People, 1967. Memberships: Several literary organizations. Address: Keskustie 39, 19600 Hartola, Finland.

OKARA Gabriel (Imomotimi Gbaingbain), b. 21 Apr 1921, Burmodi, Ijaw District, Rivers State, Western Nigeria. Writer; Poet; Publishing Director. Education: Government College, Umuahia. Appointment: Director, Rivers State Publishing House, Port Harcourt, 1972-. Publications: The Voice (novel), 1964; Poetry from Africa,

1968; The Fisherman's Invocation, 1978. Honour: Commonwealth Poetry Prize, 1979. Address: PO Box 219, Port Harcourt, Nigeria.

OKON Zbigniew Waldemar, b. 21 July 1945, Chelm, Poland. Poet; Writer. m. Halina Pioro Maciejewska, 6 Oct 1969, 2 sons, 1 daughter. Education: Marie Curie-Sklodowska University, Lublin. Publications: Outlooks and Reflections, 1968; The Soldiers of the Chalk Hills, 1970; Impatience of the Tree, 1979; Intimidation by Twilight, 1986; Calling Up the Darkness, 1987; Taste of Childhood, 1990; In a Halfway, 1996; Grandpa Tudrey's Cavalry, 1997. Contributions to: Journals and magazines. Honours: 1st Prizes, Poetry Competitions, 1964, 1966, 1968, 1974; Czechowicz Literary Prize, 1987; National Scholarship, Ministry of Culture and Art, 1991. Memberships: Union of Polish Literary Men. Address: ul Kolejowa 86-19, 22-100 Chelm, Poland.

OKRI Ben, b. 15 Mar 1959, Minna, Nigeria. Author; Poet. Education: Urohobo College, Warri, Nigeria; University of Essex, Colchester. Appointments: Broadcaster and Presenter, BBC, 1983-85; Poetry Editor, West Africa, 1983-86; Fellow Commoner in Creative Arts, Trinity College, Cambridge, 1991-93. Publications: Flowers and Shadows, 1980; The Landscapes Within, 1982; Incidents at the Shrine, 1986; Stars of the New Curfew, 1988; The Famished Road, 1991; An African Elegy, 1992; Songs of Enchantment, 1993; Astonishing the Gods, 1995; Birds of Heaven, 1995; Dangerous Love, 1996; A Way of Being Free, 1997; Mental Fight, 1999. Contributions to: Many newspapers and journals. Honours: Commonwealth Prize for Africa, 1987; Paris Review/Aga Khan Prize for Fiction, 1987; Booker Prize, 1991; Premio Letterario Internazionale Chianti-Ruffino-Antico-Fattore, 1993; Premio Grinzane Cavour, 1994; Crystal Award, 1995. Membership: Society of Authors; Royal Society of Literature; Vice-president, English Centre, International PEN, 1997-. Address: c/o Vintage, Random House, 20 Vauxhall Bridge Road, London SW1 2SA, England.

OLBIK Aleksandr Stepanovich, b. 28 Apr 1939, Dubrovka, Pskov, Latvia. Journalist; Writer. m. Eleonora, 3 Nov 1963. Education: Faculty of Journalism, Latvian University. Appointments: Soviet Youth, newspaper, 1974, 1980-81; Quite Frankly, newspaper, 1990-96. Publications: A Book of Interviews, 1989; Bees on a Sunny Beach; Agents Case; Killers; Trotyl Terror. Honour: Merited Journalist of Latvia. Address: Jasminu Street 3, Apt 3, Jurmala, LV-2010, Latvia.

OLDHAM Andrew Jeffrey, b. 1 Jan 1975, Bolton, England. Writer. Education: BA, Honours, English, Fine Art, Performing Arts De Montfort University, 1996; Certificate Education, Manchester University, 1998. Appointments: Journalist, Critic, Big Issue in the North, 1996-97; Freelance Researcher, BBC, 1997; Staff Writer, Flux Magazine, 1997-98; Writer, 1997-. Publications: Poetry: Technical Support, 1997; Columns of Frozen Light, 1997; Poetry 8 short stories: Breathing Slowly?, 1998; Internet: Neuter, 1998; Plays: Dossers, 1998. Contributions to: Big Issue in the North, 1996-97; Flux Magazine, 1997-98. Honours: North West Arts Board Young Writers Bursary, 1997-98; Dramarama 2, 1998. Address: 28 Longworth Road, Horwich, Bolton, Lancashire BL6 7BE, England.

OLDKNOW Antony, b. 15 Aug 1939, Peterborough, England. Poet; Literary Translator; Professor. Education: BA, University of Leeds, 1961; Postgraduate Diploma, Phonetics, University of Edinburgh, 1962; PhD, University of North Dakota, USA, 1983. Appointments: Editor, Publisher, Scopcraeft Press Inc, 1966-; Travelling Writer, The Great Plains Book Bus, 1979-81; Writer-in-Residence, Wisconsin Arts Board, 1980-83; Poetry Staff, Cottonwood, 1984-87; Professor of Literature, Eastern New Mexico University, 1987-; Associate Editor, Blackwater Quarterly, 1993. Publications: Lost Allegory, 1967; Tomcats and Tigertails, 1968; The Road of the Lord, 1969; Anthem for Rusty Saw and Blue Sky, 1975; Consolations for Beggars, 1978;

Miniature Clouds, 1982; Ten Small Songs, 1985; Clara d'Ellébeuse (translated novel), 1992; The Villages and Other Poems (translated book), 1993. Contributions to: Anthologies, reviews, journals, and magazines. Address: Department of Languages and Literature, Eastern New Mexico University, Portales, NM 88130, USA.

OLDS Sharon, b. 19 Nov 1942, San Francisco, California, USA. Poet; Associate Professor. Education: BA, Stanford University, 1964; PhD, Columbia University, 1972. Appointments: Lecturer-in-Residence on Poetry, Theodor Herzl Institute, New York, 1976-80; Adjunct Professor, 1983-90, Director, 1988-91, Associate Professor, 1990-, Graduate Program in Creative Writing, New York University; Fanny Hurst Chair in Literature, Brandeis University, 1986-87. Publications: Satan Says, 1980; The Dead and the Living, 1984; The Gold Cell, 1987; The Matter of This World: New and Selected Poems, 1987; The Sign of Saturn, 1991; The Father, 1992; The Wellspring, 1996. Honours: Creative Arts Public Service Award, 1978; Madeline Sadin Award, 1978; Guggenheim Fellowship, 1981-82; National Endowment for the Arts Fellowship, 1982-83; Lamont Prize, 1984; National Book Critics Circle Award, 1985; T S Eliot Prize Shortlist, 1993; Lila Wallace-Reader's Digest Fellowship, 1993-96. Address: c/o Department of English, New York University, 19 University Place, New York, NY 10003, USA.

OLDSEY Bernard, b. 18 Feb 1923, Wilkes-Barre, Pennsylvania, USA. Professor; Editor; Writer. m. Ann Marie Re, 21 Sep 1946, 1 son, 1 daughter. Education: BA, 1948, MA, 1949, PhD, 1955, Pennsylvania State University. Appointments: Instructor to Associate Professor, English, Pennsylvania State University, 1951-69; Senior Fulbright Professor, American Literature, Universidad de Zaragoza, Spain, 1964-65; Professor, English, West Chester University of Pennsylvania, 1969-90; Editor, College Literature, 1974-90; University Professor, University of Innsbruck, Austria, 1986. Publications: From Fact to Judgment, 1957; The Art of William Golding, 1967; The Spanish Season (novel), 1970; Hemingway's Hidden Craft, 1979; Ernest Hemingway: Papers of a Writer, 1981; British Novelists, 1930-1960, 1983; Critical Essays on George Orwell, 1985; The Snows of Yesteryear, novel. Address: 520 William Ebbs Lane, West Chester, PA 19380, USA.

OLIVER (Symmes) Chad(wick), b. 30 Mar 1928, Cincinnati, Ohio, USA. Writer. m. Betty Jane Jenkins, 1 Nov 1952, 1 son, 1 daughter. Publications: Shadows in the Sun, 1954; Another Kind (short stories), 1955; The Winds of Time, 1957; Unearthly Neighbors, 1960; Ecology and Cultural Continuity as Contributing Factors in the Social Organization of the Plains Indians, 1962; The Wolf is My Brother (western novel), 1967; The Shores of Another Sea, 1971; The Edge of Forever (short stories), 1971; Giants in the Dust, 1976; Cultural Anthropology: The Discovery of Humanity, 1980; Broken Eagle, 1989. Honour: Western Heritage Award for Best Novel, 1989. Address: 301 Eanes Road, Austin, TX 78746, USA.

OLIVER Douglas Dunlop, b. 14 Sept 1937, Southampton, England. Poet; Novelist; Prosodist. m. (1) Janet Hughes, July 1962, (2) Alice Notley, Feb 1988, 2 stepsons, 2 daughters. Education: BA, Literature, 1975, MA, Applied Linguistics, 1982, University of Essex. Appointments: Journalist, newspapers in England, Agence France-Presse, Paris, 1959-72; University Lecturer, Literature, English, various, 1975-; Editorial Board, Franco-British Studies; Co-Editor, Gare du Nord Magazine. Publications: Oppo Hectic, 1969; The Harmless Building, 1973; In the Cave of Succession, 1974; The Diagram Poems, 1979; The Infant and the Pearl, 1985; Kind, 1987; Poetry and Narrative in Performance, 1989; Three Variations on the Theme of Harm, 1990; Penniless Politics, 1991; The Scarlet Cabinet (with Alice Notley), 1992; Selected Poems, 1996; Penguin Modern Poets 10, 1996. Contributions to: Anthologies including: A Various Art, 1987; The New British Poetry 1968-1988, 1988; Numerous poems, articles, fiction, to magazines and journals. Honours:

Eastern Arts Grant, 1977; South-East Arts Grant, 1987; Fund for Poetry Grants, 1990, 1991; Judith E. Wilson Lecturer, University of Cambridge, 1995. Address: c/o British Institute in Paris, 11 Rue de Constantine, 75007 Paris, France.

OLIVER Mary, b. 10 Sept 1935, Cleveland, Ohio, USA. Poet; Educator. Education: Ohio State University; Vassar College. Appointments: Mather Visiting Professor, Case Western Reserve University, 1980, 1982; Poet-in-Residence, Bucknell University, 1986; Elliston Visiting Professor, University of Cincinnati, 1986; Margaret Banister Writer-in-Residence, Sweet Briar College, 1991-95; William Blackburn Visiting Professor of Creative Writing, Duke University, 1995; Catharine Osgood Foster Professor, Bennington College, 1996-. Publications: No Voyage, and Other Poems, 1963, augmented edition, 1965; The River Styx, Ohio, and Other Poems, 1972; The Night Traveler, 1978; Twelve Moons, 1978; Sleeping in the Forest, 1979; American Primitive, 1983; Dream Work, 1986; Provincetown, 1987; House of Light, 1990; New and Selected Poems, 1992; A Poetry Handbook, 1994; White Pine: Poems and Prose Poems, 1994; Blue Pastures, 1995; West Wind, 1997; Rules for the Dance, 1998. Contributions to: Periodicals in the US and England. Honours: Poetry Society of America 1st Prize, 1962; Devil's Advocate Award, 1968; Shelley Memorial Award, 1972; National Endowment for the Arts Fellowship, 1972-73; Alice Fay di Castagnola Award, 1973; Guggenheim Fellowship, 1980-81; American Academy and Institute of Arts and Letters Award, 1983; Pulitzer Prize in Poetry, 1984; Christopher Award, 1991; L L Winship Award, 1991; National Book Award for Poetry, 1992. Memberships: PEN; Poetry Society of America. Address: c/o Molly Malone Cook Literary Agency, Box 338, Provincetown, MA 02657, USA.

OLIVER Paul H(ereford), b. 25 May 1927, Nottingham, England. Author; Lecturer in Architecture and Popular Music. m. Valerie Grace Coxon, 19 Aug 1950. Education: Drawing Exam Distinction, 1945; Painting Exam, National Diploma in Design, 1947; Art Teachers' Diploma, 1948, Diploma in Humanities, History of Art, Distinction, 1955, University of London. Appointments: Editor, Architectural Association Journal, 1961-63; Reviewer, Arts Review, 1965-70; Member, Cambridge University Press Popular Music Editorial Board, 1980-. Publications: Bessie Smith, 1959; Blues Fell This Morning, 1960, revised edition, 1990; Conversation with the Blues, 1965, revised edition, 1997; Screening the Blues, 1968; The Story of the Blues, 1969, revised edition, 1997; Shelter and Society (editor), 1970; Savannah Syncopators: African Retentions in the Blues, 1970; Shelter in Africa, 1971; Shelter in Greece (editor with Orestis Doumanis), 1994; Shelter, Sign and Symbol, 1975; Dunroamin: The Suburban Semi and Its Enemies (with Ian Davis and Ian Bentley), 1981; Early Blues Songbook, 1984; Songsters and Saints: Vocal Traditions on Race Records, 1984; Blues Off the Record: Thirty Years of Blues Commentary, 1984; Dwellings: The House Across the World, 1987; Black Music in Britain (editor), 1990; Blackwell's Guide to Blues Records (editor), 1990; Architecture - An Invitation (with Richard Hayward), 1990; The New Blackwell Guide to Recorded Blues (editor with John Cowley), 1996; The Encyclopedia of Vernacular Architecture of the World (editor), 1997. Contributions to: Journals and magazines. Honours: Prix d'Etrangers, Paris, 1962; Prix du Disque, Paris, 1962; Honorary Fellow, AmCAS University of Exeter, 1986; Honorary Fellow, Oxford Polytechnic, 1988; Sony Radio Award Best Special Music Programme, 1988; Katherine Briggs Folklore Award, 1990; Honorary Doctor of Arts, Oxford Brookes University, 1995; Sir Banister Fletcher Award, 1998. Memberships: Royal Anthropological Institute, fellow; Architectural Association; International Association for the Study of Popular Music; International Association for the Study of Traditional Environments; Vernacular Architecture Group, UK. Address: Wootton-by-Woodstock, Oxon, England.

OLIVER Reginald Rene St John, b. 7 July 1952, London, England. Actor; Dramatist. Education: BA Honours, University College, Oxford, 1975. Appointments: Literary Consultant to Drama Panel, Arts Council of Great Britain, 1983-86; Director of Publications, Seeds Ltd, 1986-. Publications: Zuleika, 1975; Interruption to the Dance, 1977; You Might as Well Live, 1978; The Shewstone, 1981; Passing Over, 1982; Absolution, 1984; Back Payments, 1985; Rochester, 1986; A Portrait of Two Artists, 1986; Imaginary Lines, 1987. Contributions to: Numerous magazines and journals. Honours: Time Out Award Best Fringe Play; International Theatre Award, 1985. Memberships: Dramatist's Club; British Actors Equity; Theatre Writers Union. Address: The Bothy, Wormington Grange, Broadway, Worcestershire, England.

OLIVER Roland Anthony, b. 30 Mar 1923, Srinagar, Kashmir. Professor of the History of Africa; Author. m. (1) Caroline Florence, 1947, dec 1983, 1 daughter, (2) Suzanne Doyle, 1990. Education: MA, PhD, King's College, Cambridge. Appointments: Foreign Office, 1942-45; R J Smith Research Studentship, King's College, Cambridge, 1946-48; Lecturer, School of Oriental and African Studies, 1948-58; Reader in African History, 1958-63, Professor of the History of Africa, 1963-86, University of London; Editor (with J D Fage), Journal of African History, 1960-73; Francqui Professor, University of Brussels, 1961; Visiting Professor, Northwestern University, 1962, Harvard University, 1967. Publications: The Missionary Factor in East Africa, 1952; Sir Harry Johnston and the Scramble for Africa, 1957; The Dawn of African History (editor), 1961; A Short History of Africa (with J D Fage), 1962; A History of East Africa (editor with Gervase Mathew), 1963; Africa since 1800 (with A E Atmore), 1967; The Middle Age of African History (editor), 1967; Papers in African Prehistory (with J D Fage), 1970; Africa in the Iron Age (with B M Fagen), 1975; The Cambridge History of Africa (general editor with J D Fage), 8 volumes, 1975-86; The African Middle Ages, 1400-1800 (with A E Atmore), 1981; The African Experience, 1991; In the Realms of the Gold: Pioneering in African History, 1997. Contributions to: Scholarly journals. Honours: Haile Selassie Prize Trust Award, 1966; Distinguished Africanist Award, American African Studies Association, 1989; Honorary Fellow, School of Oriental and African Studies, 1992. Memberships: Académie Royale des Sciences d'Outremer, Brussels, corresponding member; African Studies Association, president, 1967-68; British Academy, fellow; British Institute in Eastern Africa, president, 1981-93; International Congress of Africanists; Royal African Society, vice-president, 1965-. Address: Frilsham Woodhouse, Thatcham, Berkshire RG18 9XB, England.

OLLARD Richard (Laurence), b. 9 Nov 1923, Bainton, Yorkshire, England. Historian; Writer. Education: MA, New College, Oxford, 1952. Appointments: Lecturer, 1948-52, Senior Lecturer in History and English, 1952-59, Royal Naval College, Greenwich; Senior Editor, William Collins and Sons, London, 1960-83. Publications: Historical Essays 1600-1750 (editor wth H E Bell), 1963; The Escape of Charles II, 1967; Man of War: Sir Robert Holmes and the Restoration Navy, 1969; Pepys, 1974, new illustrated edition, 1991; War Without an Enemy: A History of the English Civil Wars, 1976; The Image of the King: Charles I and Charles II, 1979; An English Education: A Perspective of Eton, 1982; For Veronica Wedgwood These: Studies on 17th Century History (editor with Pamela Tudor Craig), 1986; Clarendon and His Friends, 1987; Fisher and Cunningham: A Study in the Personalities of the Churchill Era, 1991; Cromwell's Earl: A Life of Edward Montagu, 1st Earl of Sandwich, 1994; Dorset: A Pimlico County History Guide, 1995; The Sayings of Samuel Pepys, 1996. Memberships: Royal Society of Literature, fellow; Society of Antiquaries, fellow. Address: c/o Curtis Brown Ltd, 162-168 Regent Street, London W1, England.

OLMSTEAD Andrea Louise, b. 5 Sep 1948, Dayton, Ohio, USA. Musicologist. m. Larry Thomas Bell, 2 Jan 1982. Education: BM, Hartt College of Music, 1972; MA, New York University, 1974. Appointments: Faculty, The Juilliard School, 1972-80; Boston Conservatory, 1981-. Publications: Roger Sessions and His Music, 1985; Conversations With Roger Sessions, 1987; The New Grove 20th Century American Masters, 1987; The Correspondence of Roger Sessions, 1992; Juilliard: A History, 1999. Contributions to: Journal of the Arnold Schoenberg Institute; American Music; Musical Quarterly; Tempo; Musical America; Perspectives of New Music; Music Library Association Notes. Honours: National Endowment for the Humanities Grants; Outstanding Academic Book Choice, 1986. Memberships: Sonneck Society; Pi Kappa Lambda. Address: 73 Hemenway Street, Apt 501, Boston, MA 02115, USA.

OLSEN David Leslie, (Mycroft), b. 13 Dec 1943, Berkeley, California, USA. Writer; Consultant. m. Barbara Gail Schonborn, 17 Mar 1985, 1 son, 1 daughter. Education: BA, University of California at Berkeley, 1965; MBA, Golden Gate University, 1983; MA, San Francisco State University, 1987. Appointments: Marketing, Shell Oil, 1965-76; Manager, Energy Markets, SRI International, Menlo Park, California, 1976-83; Project Manager, Pacific Gas and Electric Company, San Francisco, 1983-86; Senior Staff Writer, Editor, LSI Logic Corporation, Milpitas, California, 1987-89; Consulting Director, Schonborn Associates, Westford Massachusetts, 1989-; Editorial Page Columnist, Community Newspaper Company, Boston Area, 1998-; Internet Economic Analyst, Stockhouse, Raging Bull and Yahoo Websites, 1998-. Publications: 27 technical reports; 9 software manuals; Stage Plays: Captives, 1987; Shall We Begin Again?, 1987; Two Roses, 1990; Third Person Singular, 1990. Contributions to: Newspapers, magazines, anthologies and online publications. Honours: Daly City Arts Commission Trophy for Excellence in Poetry, 1990; Over 24 literary prizes. Memberships: Dramatists Guild; Academy of American Poets; Poetry Center of San Francisco State University. Address: 14 Vine Brook Road, Westford, MA 01886, USA.

OLSEN Jonna Raagevang, b. 16 Apr 1955, Sanderum, Denmark. Social Worker. m. Kristian Poulsen, 21 Apr 1994. Education: Odense Socialpaedagagishe, Gogiske Seminarium, 1982. Appointments: Social Worker, Minibo Hojby, Fyns Amt, 1984-89; Social Worker, Odense Kommune, 1989-98; Writer, 1996-. Publications: Novels for mentally retarded people: Gerda Far En Kaereste, 1996; The Life Story of Ole Jensen: Jeg Stammer Fra Frorup, 1998; Armlaenken, 1999. Contributions to: A number of novels about animals for Hjemmet, Denmark. Membership: Dansk Forfatterforening, 1996. Address: Dyrehavelund 8, 5462 Morud, Denmark.

OLSEN Lance, b. 14 Oct 1956, USA. Writer; Poet; Critic; Professor. m. Andrea Hirsch, 3 Jan 1981. Education: BA, Honours, University of Wisconsin, 1978; MFA, University of Iowa, 1980; MA, 1982, PhD, 1985, University of Virginia. Appointments: Professor of Creative Writing and Contemporary Fiction, University of Idaho, 1996-; Writer-in-Residence, State of Idaho, 1996-98. Publications: Ellipse of Uncertainty, 1987; Circus of the Mind in Motion, 1990; Live From Earth, 1991; William Gibson, 1992; My Dates With Franz, 1993; Natural Selections (poems with Jeff Worley), 1993; Scherzi, I Believe, 1994; Tonguing the Zeitgeist, 1994; Lolita, 1995; Burnt, 1996; Time Famine, 1996; Rebel Yell: A Short Guide to Fiction Writing, 1998. Contributions to: Journals and magazines. Address: Bear Creek Cabin, 1490 Ailor Road, Deary, ID 83823, USA.

OLSEN Theodore Victor, (Joshua Stark, Christopher Storm, Cass Willoughby), b. 25 Apr 1932, Rhinelander, Wisconsin, USA. Writer. m. Beverly Butler, 25 Sept 1976. Education: BSc, English, University of Wisconsin, 1955. Publications: Haven of the Hunted, 1956; The Rhinelander Story, 1957; The Man from Nowhere, 1959; McGivern, 1960; High Lawless, 1960; Gunswift, 1960; Ramrod Rider, 1960; Brand of the Star, 1961; Brothers of the Sword, 1962; Savage Sierra, 1962; The Young Duke, 1963; Break the Young Land, 1964; The Sex Rebels, 1964; A Man Called Brazos, 1964; Canyon of the Gun, 1965; Campus Motel, 1965; The Stalking Moon, 1965; The Hard Men, 1966; Autumn

Passion, 1966; Bitter Grass, 1967; The Lockhart Breed, 1967; Blizzard Pass, 1968; Arrow in the Sun, 1969; Keno, 1970; A Man Named Yuma, 1971; Eye of the Wolf, 1971; There Was a Season, 1973; Mission to the West, 1973; Run to the Mountain, 1974; Track the Man Down, 1975; Day of the Buzzard, 1976; Westward They Rode, 1976; Bonner's Stallion, 1977; Rattlesnake, 1979; Roots of the North, 1979; Allegories for One Man's Moods, 1979; Our First Hundred Years, 1981; Blood of the Breed, 1982; Birth of a City, 1983; Red is the River, 1983; Lazlo's Strike, 1983; Lonesome Gun, 1985; Blood Rage, 1987; A Killer is Waiting, 1988; Under the Gun, 1989; The Burning Sky, 1991; The Golden Chance, 1992. Contributions to: 20 short stories in Ranch Romances, 1956-57. Honour: Award of Merit, State Historical Society of Wisconsin, 1983; Western Writers of America Spur Award for Best Western Paperback Novel, 1992. Membership: Western Writers of America. Address: PO Box 856, Rhinelander, WI 54501, USA.

OLSON Lynn, b. 23 Mar 1952, Chicago, Illinois, USA. Sculptor; Painter; Writer. Publication: Sculpting With Cement (book). Contributions to: Raven. Address: 4607 Claussen Lane, Valparaiso, IN 46383, USA.

OLSON Toby, (Merle Theodore Olson), b. 17 Aug 1937, Berwyn, Illinois, USA. Professor of English; Writer; Poet. Education: BA, English and Philosophy, Occidental College, Los Angeles, 1965; MA, English, Long Island University, 1968. Appointments: Associate Director, Aspen Writers' Workshop, 1964-67; Assistant Professor, Long Island University, 1966-74; Faculty, New School for Social Research, New York City, 1967-75; Professor of English, Temple University, Philadelphia, 1975-. Publications: Fiction: The Life of Jesus, 1976; Seaview, 1982; The Woman Who Escaped From Shame, 1986; Utah, 1987; Dorit in Lesbos, 1990; The Pool, 1991; Reading, 1992; At Sea, 1993. Poetry: Maps, 1969; Worms Into Nails, 1969; The Hawk-Foot Poems, 1969; The Brand, 1969; Pig's Book, 1970; Vectors, 1972; Fishing, 1973; The Wrestler and Other Poems, 1974; City, 1974; Changing Appearances: Poems 1965-1975, 1975; Home, 1976; Three and One, 1976; Doctor Miriam, 1977; Aesthetics, 1978; The Florence Poems, 1978; Birdsongs, 1980; Two Standards, 1982; Still/Quiet, 1982; Sitting in Gusevik, 1983; We Are the Fire, 1984; Unfinished Building, 1993; Human Nature, 1999. Editor: Writing Talks: Views on Teaching Writing from Across the Professions (with Muffy E A Siegel), 1983. Other: Dorit (opera libretto), 1994. Contributions to: Numerous anthologies, newspapers, and magazines. Honours: CAPS Award in Poetry, New York State, 1974; Pennsylvania Council on the Arts Fellowship, 1983; PEN/Faulkner Award for Fiction, 1983; Guggenheim Fellowship, 1985; National Endowment for the Arts Fellowship, 1985; Yaddo Fellowships, 1985, 1986; Rockefeller Foundation Fellowship, Bellagio, Italy, 1987; Creative Achievement Award, Temple University, 1990; PENN/Book Philadelphia Award for Fiction, 1990. Address: 275 South 19th Street, Philadelphia, PA 19103, USA.

OLSON Walter Karl, b. 20 Aug 1954, Detroit, Michigan, USA. Writer; Editor. Education: BA, Yale University, 1975. Publications: New Directions in Liability Law (editor), 1988; The Litigation Explosion, 1991. Address: Manhattan Institute, 52 Vanderbilt Avenue, New York, NY 10017, USA.

OLUDHE-MACGOYE Marjorie Phyllis, b. 21 Oct 1928, Southampton, England (Kenyan Citizen). Writer; Poet; Bookseller. m. D G W Oludhe-Macgoye, 4 June 1960, dec 1990, 3 sons, 1 daughter. Education: BA, English, 1948, MA, 1953, University of London. Publications: Growing Up at Lina School (juvenile), 1971, 2nd edition, 1988; Murder in Majengo (novel), 1972; Song of Nyarloka and Other Poems, 1977; Coming to Birth (novel), 1986; The Story of Kenya (history), 1986; The Present Moment (novel), 1987; Street Life (novella), 1988; Victoria and Murder in Majengo, 1993; Homing In (novel), 1994; Moral Issues in Kenya, 1996; Chira (novel), 1997; The Black Hand Gang (juvenile), 1997; Make It Sing and Other Poems, 1998. Contributions to:

Anthologies, reviews, and journals. Honours: BBC Arts in Africa Poetry Award, 1982; Sinclair Prize for Fiction, 1986. Address: PO Box 70344, Nairobi, Kenya.

OMAN Julia Trevelyan, b. 11 July 1930, Kensington, England. Designer; Writer. m. Sir Roy Colin Strong, 10 Sept 1971. Education: Royal Scholar, 1953, Silver Medal, 1955, Royal College of Art, London. Appointments: Designer, BBC TV, 1955-67, operas, 1957-96, films, 1966-82, plays, 1967-96, ballets, 1968-98. Publications: All with Sir Roy Colin Strong: Elizabeth R, 1971; Mary Queen of Scots, 1972; The English Year, 1982; A Celebration of Gardens, 1991; A Country Life, 1994; Vanitas, 1994; On Happiness, 1997. Contributions to: Periodicals. Honours: Royal Designer for Industry, Royal Society of Arts, 1977; Commander of the Order of the British Empire, 1986. Membership: Chartered Society of Designers, fellow. Address: c/o Oman Productions Ltd, The Laskett, Much Birch, Hereford HR2 8HZ, England.

OMOLEYE Mike, b. 26 Jan 1940, Oyo Ekiti, Ondo State, Nigeria. Journalist; Publisher. m. M A Omoleye, 1970, 4 sons, 3 daughters. Education: Diploma in Journalism. Appointments: Freelance Journalist, 1960-63; Reporter, Morning Post and Sunday Post, 1964-69; Special Roving Features Writer, 1969-71, News Editor, 1972-73, Assistant Editor, 1974-76, Daily Sketch and Sunday Sketch; Managing Director, Omoleye Publishing Co Ltd, 1976-; Publisher, Sunday Glory, 1986-. Publications: You Can Control Your Destiny, 1974; Fascinating Folktales, 1976; Great Tales of the Yorubas, 1977; Mystery World Under the Sea, 1979; Awo As I Know Him, 1982; The Book of Life, 1982; Self Spiritual Healing, 1982; Issues at Stake, 1983; Make the Psalms Perform Wonders for You, 1990; Awo Speaks of Revolution, 1991. Contributions to: Newspapers. Address: GPO 1265, Ibadan, Oyo State, Nigeria.

ONDAATJE (Philip) Michael, b. 12 Sept 1943, Colombo, Sri Lanka. Poet; Novelist; Dramatist; Teacher; Film Director. Education: St Thomas' College, Colombo; Dulwich College, London; Bishop's University, Lennoxville, Quebec, 1962-64; BA, University of Toronto, 1965; MA, Queen's University, Kingston, Ontario, 1967. Appointments: Teacher, University of Western Ontario, 1969-71; Glendon College, York University, Toronto, 1971-; Visting Professor, University of Hawaii, 1979, Brown University, Providence, Rhode Island, 1990; Film Director. Publications: Poetry: The Dainty Monsters, 1967; The Man With Seven Toes, 1969; Left Handed Poems, 1970; Rat Jelly, 1973; Elimination Dance, 1978, revised edition, 1980; There's a Trick with a Knife I'm Learning to Do: Poems, 1963-1978, 1979; Claude Glass, 1979; Tin Roof, 1982; Secular Love, 1984; All Along the Mazinaw: Two Poems, 1986; The Cinnamon Peeler: Selected Poems, 1989. Novels: The Collected Works of Billy the Kid, 1970; Coming Through Slaughter, 1976; In the Skin of a Lion, 1987; The English Patient, 1992. Criticism: Leonard Cohen, 1970. Non-Fiction: Running in the Family, 1982. Editor: The Broken Ark, verse, 1971, revised edition as A Book of Beasts, 1979; Personal Fictions: Stories by Monroe, Wiebe, Thomas, and Blaise, 1977; The Long Poem Anthology, 1979; Brushes With Greatness: An Anthology of Chance Encounters with Greatness (with Russell Banks and David Young), 1989; The Brick Anthology (with Linda Spalding), 1989; From Ink Lake: An Anthology of Canadian Short Stories, 1990; The Faber Book of Contemporary Canadian Short Stories, 1990. Honours: Ralph Gustafson Award, 1965; Epstein Award, 1966; E J Pratt Medal, 1966; Canadian Governor-General's Awards for Literature, 1971, 1980, 1992; W H Smith/Books in Canada First Novel Award, 1977; Canada-Australia Prize, 1980; City of Toronto Arts Award, 1987; Ritz-Hemingway Prize Nomination, 1997; Trillium Book Awards, 1987, 1992; Booker McConnell Prize, British Book Council, 1992; Canadian Authors Association Author of the Year Award, 1993; Commonwealth Prize (regional), international nomination, 1993; Chianti Ruffino-Antonio Fattore International Literary Prize, 1994; Nelly Sachs Award, 1995; Premio Grinzane Cavour, 1996. Address: c/o Ellen Levine Literary Agency, 15 East 26th Street, Suite 1801, New York, NY 10010, USA.

ONG Walter Jackson, b. 30 Nov 1912, Kansas City, Missouri, USA. Roman Catholic Priest; Professor Emeritus; Writer. Education: BA, Rockhurst College, 1933; PhL, 1940, MA, 1941, STL, 1948, St Louis University; PhD, Harvard University, 1955. Appointments: Roman Catholic Priest, Society of Jesus; Professor, 1959-70, Professor of Humanities in Psychiatry, 1970-81, University Professor of Humanities, 1981-84, Professor Emeritus, 1984-, St Louis University; Many visiting lectureships in the USA and abroad. Publications: Rhetoric, Romance and Technology, 1971; Interfaces of the Word, 1977; Fighting for Life: Contest, Sexuality and Consciousness, 1981; Orality and Literacy, 1982; Hopkins, The Self and God, 1986; Faith and Contexts, 3 volumes, 1995. Contributions to: Numerous publications worldwide. Honours: Many honorary doctorates. Address: c/o Department of Humanities, St Louis University, St Louis, MO 63103, USA.

ONWUEME Tess Osonye, (Osonye Tess Akaeke), b. 8 Sept 1955, Nigeria. Playwright; Novelist; Professor. m. Obika Gray, 21 June 1998, 2 sons, 3 daughters. Education: BA, Education, 1979, MA, Literature, 1982, University of Ife, Nigeria; PhD, African Drama, University of Benin, Nigeria, 1988. Appointments: Lecturer, University of Ife, 1980-82; Assistant Professor, Federal University of Technology, Owerri, Nigeria, 1982-87; Associate Professor, Imo State University, Nigeria, 1986-88; Distinguished Writer, Associate Professor, Wayne State University, Detroit, 1990-98; Associate Professor, Montclair State University, 1990-92; Professor, Vassar College, 1992-93; Distinguished Professor of Cultural Diversity, Professor of English, University of Wisconsin-Eau Claire, 1994-. Publications: A Hen Too Soon, 1983; The Broken Calabash, 1985; The Desert Encroaches, 1986; Ban Empty Barn, 1986; Mirror for Campus, 1987; The Reign of Wazobia, 1988; Legacies, 1989; The Missing Face, 1996; Riot in Heaven, 1997; Tell it to Women, 1997; Why the Elephant Has No Butt, 1997; The President's Bag of Luck, 1999. Contributions to: Magazines and journals. Honours include: Distinguished Writer-in-Residence Award, Eugene B Redmond's Writers Foundation, Southern Illinois University, 1993; Award of Excellence, University of Wisconsin, 1995; Drama Prize, Association of Nigerian Authors, 1995. Memberships: Association of Nigerian Authors; Organization of Women Writers of African Descent; PEN International; African Studies Association; African Literature Association; International Women Playwrights Association. Literary Agent: Stanley Ogunedo, 808 Lexington Avenue, Brooklyn, New York, USA. Address: c/o English Department, University of Wisconsin, Eau Claire, WI 54701, USA.

ONWY. See: EVANS Donald.

ONYEAMA Charles Dillibe Ejiofor, b. 6 Jan 1951, Enugu, Nigeria. Publisher; Author; Journalist. m. Ethel Ekwueme, 15 Dec 1984, 4 sons. Education: Premier School of Journalism, Fleet Street, London, England. Appointments: Board of Directors, Star Printing and Publishing Co Ltd, 1992-94; Managing Director, Delta Publications (Nigeria) Ltd. Publications: Nigger at Eton, 1972; John Bull's Nigger, 1974; Sex is a Nigger's Game, 1975; The Book of Black Man's Humour, 1975; I'm the Greatest, 1975; Juju, 1976; Secret Society, 1977; Revenge of the Medicine Man, 1978; The Return, 1978; Night Demon, 1979; Female Target, 1980; The Rules of the Game, 1980; The Story of an African God, 1982; Modern Messiah, 1983; Godfathers of Voodoo, 1985; African Legend, 1985; Correct English, 1986; Notes of a So-Called Afro-Saxon, 1988. Contributions to: Books and Bookmen; Spectator; Times; Daily Express; Sunday Express; Drum; West Africa; Roots; Guardian; Evening News. Membership: Udi Local Government Council, Enugu State, caretaker committee, councillor, 1994-. Literary Agent: Elspeth Cochrane Agency, London, England. Address: 8B Byron Onyeama Close, New Haven, PO Box 1171, Enugu, Enugu State, Nigeria.

OPATRNY Josef, b. 19 Nov 1945, Skryje, Czechoslovakia. Historian; Professor; Teacher; Writer. m. Olga Titerová-Opatrná, 20 Feb 1970, 1 son, 2 daughters.

Education: MA, 1968, PhD, 1969. Appointment: Professor of History, Charles University, Prague, 1995-. Publications: Válka Severu proti Jihu (American Civil War), 1986, 1998; Objevitelé, dobyvatelé, osadníci (Discoverers, Conquerors, Colonists), 1992; US Expansionism and Cuban Annexationism in the 1850s, 1993; Amerika presidenta Granta (President Grant's America), 1994; Historical Pre-Conditions of the Origin of the Cuban Nation, 1994; Cuba - Algunes Problemas de su Historia (editor), 1995; Amerika v promenách staletí (America: Centuries of Change), 1998. Contributions to: Revista de Indias; Cuban Studies; Ibero-Americana Pragensia; Estudios Migratorios Latinoamericanos. Honour: Czechoslovakian Literary Fund Award, 1987. Memberships: European Latinoamericanists Association, vice-president, 1996-; New York Academy of Sciences. Address: Bulharská 12, 101 00 Prague 10, Czech Republic.

OPIE Iona, b. 13 Oct 1923. Colchester, England. Writer. m. Peter Opie, 2 Sept 1943, dec, 2 sons, 1 daughter. Publications: A Dictionary of Superstitions (with Moira Tatem), 1989; The People in the Playground, 1993; With Peter Opie: The Oxford Dictionary of Nursery Rhymes, 1951, new edition, 1997; The Oxford Nursery Rhyme Book, 1955; The Lore and Language of Schoolchildren, 1959; Puffin Book of Nursery Rhymes, 1963; A Family Book of Nursery Rhymes, 1964; Children's Games in Street and Playground, 1969; The Oxford Book of Children's Verse, 1973; Three Centuries of Nursery Rhymes and Poetry for Children, 1973; The Classic Fairy Tales, 1974; A Nursery Companion, 1980; The Oxford Book of Narrative Verse, 1983; The Singing Game, 1985; Babies: an unsentimental anthology, 1990; Children's Games with Things, 1997. Honours: Honorary MA, Oxon, 1962, Open University, 1987, DLitt, University of Southampton, 1987, University of Nottingham, 1991, Doctorate, University of Surrey, 1997. Address: Mells House, Liss, Hampshire GU33 6JQ, England.

OPITZ May, (May Ayim), b. 3 May 1960, Hamburg, Germany. Poet; Educator; Speech Therapist. Education: MA, Adult Education, 1986; Diploma, Speech Therapy, 1990. Publications: Showing Our Colors, 1992; Daughters of Africa, 1992; Entfernte Verbindungen, 1993; Schwarze Frauen der Welt, 1994. Contributions to: Books and journals. Memberships: Deutscher Schriftstellerverband; Initiative of Black Germans, co-founder, 1986; Literatur frauen, co-founder, 1989. Address: Hohenstaufenstrasse 63, 1000 Berlin 30, Germany.

ORBAN Otto, b. 20 May 1936, Budapest, Hungary. Poet; Essayist; Translator; Editor. m. 23 May 1962, 2 sons. Education: Unfinished university studies. Appointments: Senior Editor, Kortars literary magazine, 1981-; Fulbright Poet, Hamline University, St Paul, Minnesota, University of Minnesota, 1987. Publications: Poetry: Szegenynek lenni, 1974; Osszegyujott versek, 1986; Egyik oldalarol a masikra fordulel, 1992. Other: Essays and translations. Honours: Jozef Attila Prizes, 1973, 1985; Robert Graves Prize, 1974; Dery Prize, 1986; Radnoti Prize, 1987; Weores Sandor Prize, 1990; Kossuth Prize, 1992. Memberships: Hungarian PEN Club, vice president, 1989-; Hungarian Writers' Union; Union of Hungarian Journalists. Address: Becsi ut 88-90, H-1034 Budapest, Hungary.

ORFALEA Gregory Michael, b. 9 Aug 1949, Los Angeles, California, USA. Writer; Editor. m. Eileen Rogers, 4 Aug 1984, 3 sons. Education: AB, Honours, English, Georgetown University; MFA, Creative Writing, University of Alaska. Appointments: Reporter, Northern Virginia Sun, 1971-72; Professor, Santa Barbara City College, California,1974-76; Editor, Political Focus, 1979-81, Small Business Administration, 1985-91, Resolution Trust Corporation, 1991-95, Federal Deposit Insurance Corporation, 1995-96, Comptroller of the Currency, 1996-97; Freddie Mac, 1997-. Publications: Before the Flames, 1988; The Capital of Solitude, 1988; Grape Leaves, 1988; Imagining America: Stories of the Promised Land, 1991; Messengers of the Lost Battalion, 1997. Contributions to: Washington Post; TriQuarterly;

Cleveland Plain-Dealer; Christian Science Monitor. Honours: California Arts Council Award, 1976; American Middle East Peace Research Award, 1983; District of Columbia Commission on the Arts and Humanities Awards, 1991, 1993. Membership: American PEN. Address: 3220 Patterson St N.W. Washington, DC 20015, USA.

ORGEL Doris, (Doris Adelberg), b. 15 Feb 1929, Vienna, Austria. Writer. m. Shelley Orgel, 25 June 1949, 2 sons, 1 daughter. Education: BA, Barnard College, 1960. Appointments: Senior Staff Writer,Editor, Publications and Media Group, Bank Sheer College of Education, 1961-. Publications: Sarah's Room, 1963; The Devil in Vienna, 1978; My War with Mrs Galloway, 1985; Whiskers Once and Always, 1986; Midnight Soup and a Witch's Hat, 1987; Starring Becky Suslow, 1989; Nobodies and Somebodies, 1991; Next Time I Will, 1993; The Mouse Who Wanted To Marry, 1993; Ariadne, Awake, 1994. Young Adult Novels: Risking Love, 1985; Crack in the Heart, 1989. Other: Some 30 works. Contributions to: Cricket magazine. Address: c/o Writers House, 21 West 26th Street, New York, NY 10010, USA.

ORIOL Jacques, (Jacques F G Vandievoet), b. 1 Oct 1923, Brussels, Belgium. Retired Geography Teacher; Poet; Essayist, Critic. 1 son. Education: Agregation, secondary school teaching, 1951. Publications: Quarantaine, 1983; Dédicaces, 1984; Midi, déjè Minuit, 1985; Voyage, 1986; Etat critique, 1987; Poète aujourd'hui, comment dire?, 1989; Demi-deuil, 1990; Dilecta, 1993. Contributions to: Books and journals. Honours: Francois Villon Prize, National Association of French Writers, 1986; 1st Prize, Classical Poetry, Ecole de la Loire, Blois, 1989. Memberships: Association of Belgian Authors; PEN Club, Belgian Section; Union of Walloon Writers and Artists. Address: 210 Avenue Molière, boite 10, B-1060 Brussels, Belgium.

ORLEDGE Robert Francis Nicholas, b. 5 Jan 1948, Bath, Somerset, England. Professor of Music; Author. Education: Associate, Royal College of Organists, 1964; Clare College, Cambridge; BA (Hons), Music, 1968, MA, 1972, PhD, 1973, University of Cambridge. Appointment: Professor of Music, University of Liverpool. Publications: Gabriel Fauré, 1979, revised edition, 1983; Debussy and the Theatre, 1982; Charles Koechlin (1867-1950): His Life and Works, 1989, revised edition, 1995; Satie the Composer, 1990; Satie Remembered, 1995. Contributions to: Music and Letters; Musical Quarterly; Musical Times; Music Review; Current Musicology; Journal of the Royal Musical Association. Memberships: Royal Musical Association; Centre de Documentation Claude Debussy; Association des Amis de Charles Koechlin; Fondation Erik Satie. Address: Windermere House, Windermere Terrace, Liverpool L8 3SB, England.

ORMEROD Roger, b. 17 Apr 1920, Wolverhampton, Staffordshire, England. Author. Publications: Time to Kill, 1974; The Silence of the Night, 1974; Full Fury, 1975; A Spoonful of Luger, 1975; Sealed with a Loving Kill, 1976; The Colour of Fear, 1976; A Glimpse of Death, 1976; Too Late for the Funeral, 1977; The Murder Come to Mind, 1977; A Dip into Murder, 1978; The Weight of Evidence, 1978; The Bright Face of Danger, 1979; The Amnesia Trap, 1979; Cart Before the Hearse, 1979; More Dead than Alive, 1980; Double Take, 1980; One Breathless Hour, 1981; Face Value, 1983; Seeing Red, 1984; The Hanging Doll Murder, 1984; Dead Ringer, 1985; Still Life with Pistol, 1986; A Death to Remember, 1986; An Alibi Too Soon, 1987; The Second Jeopardy, 1987; An Open Window, 1988; By Death Possessed, 1988; Guilt on the Lily, 1989; Death of an Innocent, 1989; No Sign of Life, 1990; Hung in the Blance, 1990; Farewell Gesture, 1990. Address: c/o Constable, 10 Orange Street, London WC2H 7EG, England.

ORMONDE Paul Fraser, b. 7 Feb 1931, Sydney, New South Wales, Australia. Journalist; Public Relations Consultant. m. Marie Therese Kilmartin, 27 Aug 1955, 2 sons, 2 daughters. Education: St Patricks' College, Strathfield, Sydney. Appointments: Editorial Board, Catholic Worker, Melbourne, 1959-76; Feature

writer/leader writer, Melbourne Herald, 1970-81; Vice Chairman, Victorian Writers Centre, 1993-. Publications: The Movement, 1972; A Foolish Passionate Man, 1981; Catholics in Revolution, 1988. Contributions to: Meanjin; Overland; Eureka Street; Sydney Morning Herald; The Age, Sunday Age (Melbourne); Catholic Worker (Melbourne). Memberships: Fellowship of Australian Writers; National Book Council Committee. Address: 23/2A Robe Street, St Kilda, Victoria, 3182 Australia.

ORMSBY Frank, b. 30 Oct 1947, Enniskillen County, Fermanagh, Northern Ireland. Poet; Writer; Editor. Education: BA, English, 1970, MA, 1971, Queen's University, Belfast. Appointment: Editor, The Honest Ulsterman, 1969-89. Publications: A Store of Candles, 1977; Poets from the North of Ireland (editor), 1979, new edition, 1990; A Northern Spring, 1986; Northern Windows: An Anthology of Ulster Autobiography (editor), 1987; The Long Embrace: Twentieth Century Irish Love Poems (editor), 1987; Thine in Storm and Calm: An Amanda McKittrick Ros Reader (editor), 1988; The Collected Poems of John Hewitt (editor), 1991; A Rage for Order: Poetry of the Northern Ireland Troubles (editor), 1992; The Ghost Train, 1995. Address: 36 Strathmore Park North, Belfast BT15 5HR, Northern Ireland.

ORNSTEIN Robert E, b. 17 Feb 1942, New York, New York, USA. Psychologist; Writer. Education: BA, Queens College, City of New York; PhD, Stanford University. Appointment: President, Langley Porter Institute, San Fancisco. Publications: On the Experience of Time, 1968; On the Psychology of Meditation, 1971; Psychology of Consciousness, 1974; The Healing Brain (co-author), 1987; New World, New Mind: Moving Towards Conscious Evolution (co-author), 1989; The Roots of the Self, 1993. Contributions to: Psychonomic Science; Psychophysiology; Psychology Today. Honours: Creative Talent Award, American Institute for Research, 1968; UNESCO Award, Best Contribution to Psychology, 1972; Media Award, American Psychological Foundation, 1973. Memberships: International Society for the Study of Time; Institute for the Study of Human Consciousness; Biofeedback Society. Address: Langley Porter Institute, 401 Parnassus, San Francisco, CA 94143, USA.

ORR Gregory (Simpson), b. 3 Feb 1947, Albany, New York, USA. Professor of English; Poet; Writer. m. Trisha Winer, 1973, 2 daughters. Education: BA, Antioch College, 1969; MFA, Columbia University, 1972. Appointments: Assistant Professor, 1975-80, Associate Professor, 1980-88, Professor of English, 1988-, University of Virginia; Poetry Consultant, Virginia Quarterly Review, 1976-; Visting Writer, University of Hawaii at Manoa, 1982. Publications: Poetry: Burning the Empty Nests, 1973; Gathering the Bones Together, 1975; Salt Wings, 1980; The Red House, 1980; We Must Make A Kingdom of It, 1986; New and Selected Poems, 1988; City of Salt, 1995. Non-Fiction: Stanley Kunitz: An Introduction to the Poetry, 1985; Richer Entanglements: Essays and Notes on Poetry and Poems, 1993. Honours: Academy of American Poets Prize, 1970; YM-YWHA Discovery Award, 1970; Bread Loaf Writers Conference Transatlantic Review Award, 1976; Guggenheim Fellowship, 1977; National Endowment for the Arts Fellowships, 1978, 1989; Fulbright Grant, 1983. Address: c/o Department of English, University of Virginia, Charlottesville, VA 22903, USA.

ORR Wendy Ann, b. 19 Nov 1953, Edmonton, Alberta, Canada. Children's and Young Adult Writer. m. Thomas Orr, 11 Jan 1975, 1 son, 1 daughter. Education: Diploma of Occupational Therapy, 1975; BSc, 1982. Publications: Amanda's Dinosaur, 1988; The Tin Can Puppy, 1990; Bad Martha, 1991; Leaving It To You, 1992; Aa-Choo!, 1992; Micki Moon & Daniel Day, 1993; Ark in the Park, 1994; Mind-Blowing, Australian edition, 1994, Canadian edition as A Light in Space, 1994; The Great Yackandandah Billy Cart Race, 1994; Yasou Nikki, 1995; The Bully Biscuit Gang, 1995; Jessica Joan, 1995; Dirtbikes, 1995; Grandfather Martin, 1995; Peeling the Onion, 1996; Alroy's Very Nearly Clean Bedroom, 1996; Arabella. 1998. Honours: Australian Children's Book

Council Book of the Year, Winner 1995; Australian C.B.C. Book of the Year, Honour Book, 1997; American Library Association Best Book for Young Adults; New York Public Library Book for the Teenager. Memberships: Australian Society of Authors; Australian Children's Book Council. Literary Agent: Debbie Golvan, Golvan Arts Management, PO Box 766, Kew 3101, Australia. Address: RMB 1257, Cobram, Victoria 3644, Australia.

ORSZAG-LAND Thomas, b. 12 Jan 1938, Budapest, Hungary. Writer; Poet; Translator. 2 sons. Publications: Berlin Proposal, 1990; Free Women, 1991; Tales of Matriarchy, 1998. Translations: Bluebeard's Castle, 1988; Splendid Stags, 1992; 33 Poems by Radnoti, 1992; Poems by Mezei, 1995. Contributions to: Newspapers and reviews. Memberships: Foreign Press Association; International PEN, fellow; Royal Institute of International Affairs; Society of Authors. Address: PO Box 1213, London, N6 6HZ, England.

ORTIZ Federico, b. 11 June 1935, Mexico DF. Medical Doctor. m. Mónica Alvarado, 1 son, 2 daughters. Education: MD, Medical Faculty, Universidad Nacional Autónoma de Mexico, 1959; Intern, 1959, Urology Resident, 1959-61, General Hospital, Health Ministry, Mexico; Urology Resident, New York Hospital, Cornell Medical Center, USA, 1962-63; Certified, Mexican Urological Council, 1968. Appointments include: Urologist, 1963-67, Chief, Urology Department, 1967-74, General Hospital, National Medical Center, Instituto Mexicano del Seguro Social; Adjunct Professor, 1967-74, Professor of Urology, 1974-88, Professor of Epistemology, 1988-, Universidad Nacional Autónoma de Mexico; General Director of Medicine, Occupational Safety and Health, Labour Ministry, 1973-76; Chief of Staff, Humana Hospital of Mexico, 1985-87; Expert Consultant, Health and Social Security, UN Development Programme, 1988-89; Chief of Staff, 1994-96, General Director of International Affairs, 1996-, Health Ministry of Mexico. Publications: Fasciculos de Urologia (editor), 1970; Adenocarcinoma de Riñón en el Adulto (editor), 1973; Vida y Meurte del Mexicano (editor), 1982; Salud en la pobreza, 1983, 2nd edition, 1985; El Acto de Morir, 1987, 2nd edition, 1987; Diagnóstico: La Medicina y el Hombre en el Mundo Moderno, 1987; El Adivinador de lo Cierto, 1988, 1997; Cartas a Un Joven Médico, 1990, 2nd edition, 1991; La Medicina está enferma, 1991; Ser e Identidad Nacional, 1992; Reflexiones: Ciencia Médica y Derechos Humanos, 1993; Manos de Dioses, 1995; Memoria de la Muerte, 1996; AMORICIDA, 1996; El Trabajo del Médico, 1997. Contributions to: Numerous scientific journals; Newspapers. Membership: Mexican Writers Association, 1984-. Address: PO Box 22-477, 14090 Mexico, DF Mexico.

ORTIZ Simon J(oseph), b. 27 May 1941, Albuquerque, New Mexico, USA. Poet; Writer. m. Marlene Foster, Dec 1981, div Sept 1984, 3 children. Education: Fort Lewis College, 1961-62; University of New Mexico, 1966-68; University of Iowa, 1968-69. Appointments: Instructor, San Diego State University, 1974; Institute of American Arts, Santa Fe, New Mexico, 1974; Navajo Community College, Tsaile, Arizona, 1975-77; College of Marin, Kentfield, California, 1976-79; University of New Mexico, Albuquerque, 1979-81, Sinte Gleska College, Mission, South Dakota, 1985-86; Lewis and Clark College, Portland, Oregon, 1990; Consulting Editor, Navajo Comunity College Press, Tsaile, 1982-83; Pueblo of Acoma Press, Acoma, New Mexico, 1982-84; Arts Coordinator, Metropolitan Arts Commission, Portland, Oregon, 1990. Publications: Naked in the Wind (poems), 1971; Going for the Rain (poems), 1976; A Good Journey, poetry, 1977; Howbah Indians (short stories), 1978; Song, Poetry, Language (essays), 1978; Fight Back: For the Sake of the People, For the Sake of the Land (poems and prose), 1980; From Sand Creek: Rising in This Heart Which is Our America (poems), 1981; A Poem is a Journey, 1981; The Importance of Childhood, 1982; Fightin': New and Collected Stories, 1983; Woven Stone: A 3-in-1 Volume of Poetry and Prose, 1991; After and Before the Lightning (poems), 1994. Editor: Califa: The California Poetry (co-editor), 1978; A Ceremony of Brotherhood (co-editor), 1980;

Earth Power Coming (anthology of Native American short fiction), 1983. Contributions to: Various anthologies and textbooks. Honours: National Endowment for the Arts Discovery Award, 1969, and Fellowship, 1981; Honored Poet, White House Salute to Poetry and American Poets, 1980; New Mexico Humanities Council Humanitarian Award for Literary Achievement, 1989. Address: 3535 North 1st Avenue, No R-10, Tucson, AZ 85719, USA.

OSBORN Betty Olive, b. 15 July 1934, Melbourne, Victoria, Australia. Writer; Historian. m. Bruce Jamieson Osborn, 23 Apr 1962, 1 son, 3 daughters. Education: BA, University of Melbourne, 1959. Appointments: Journalist, Argus, 1952-57; Book Editor, Melbourne University Press, 1958-62. Publications: History of Holy Trinity Bacchus Marsh, 1971; The Bacchus Story, 1973; Pieces of Glass (play), 1977; Maryborough, A Social History 1854-1904 (with Trenear DuBourg), 1985; Against the Odds: Maryborough, 1905-1961, 1995. Contributions to: Argus Weekend Magazine; Age Literary Supplement; Wimmera-Mallee Country Bulletin. Honour: Montague Grover Prize, 1955. Memberships: Fellowship of Australian Writers (Victoria) Inc; Graduate Union, Melbourne University; Committee Member, Midlands Historical Society; Life Member, Bacchus Marsh and District Historical Society. Address: 18 Douglass Street, Maryborough, Victoria 3465, Australia.

OSBORN W(illiam) P(almer), b. 6 Oct 1946, Hastings, Michigan, USA. Professor of English. m. Sylvia Watanabe, 26 Mar 1991. Education: PhD, SUNY Bingamton; MFA, Bowling Green; BA, University of California at South Dakota. Appointment: Grand Valley State University, 1988-. Contributions to: Mississippi Review; Gettysburg Review; Carolina Quarterly; Southern Humanities Review; Chicago Review. Memberships: Associated Writing Programs. Address: 145 Crestwood North West, Grand Rapids, MI 49504, USA.

OSBORNE Charles (Thomas), b. 24 Nov 1927, Brisbane, Queensland, Australia. Writer; Critic; Poet. Education: Griffith University, 1944. Appointments: Assistant Editor, London Magazine, 1958-66; Assistant Literary Director, 1966-71, Director, 1971-86, Arts Council of Great Britain; Opera Critic, Jewish Chronicle, 1985-; Chief Theatre Critic, Daily Telegraph, 1986-92. Publications: The Gentle Planet, 1957; Swansong, 1968; The Complete Operas of Verdi, 1969; W H Auden: The Life of a Poet, 1980; Letter to W H Auden and Other Poems, 1984; Giving It Away, 1986; The Bel Canto Operas, 1994; The Pink Danube, 1998. Contributions to: Anthologies, newspapers, and journals. Honour: Gold Medal, 1993; . Memberships: Critics' Circle; PEN; Royal Society of Literature. Address: 125 St George's Road, London SE1 6HY, England.

OSBORNE Maggie, (Margaret Ellen, b. 10 June 1941, Los Angeles, California, USA. Writer. m. George M Osborne II, 27 Apr 1972, 1 son. Publications: Alexa, 1980; Salem's Daughter, 1981; Portrait in Passion, 1981; Yankee Princess, 1982; Rage to Love, 1983; Flight of Fancy, 1984; Castles and Fairy Tales, 1986; Winter Magic, 1986; The Heart Club, 1987; Where There's Smoke, 1987; Chase the Heart, 1987; Heart's Desire, 1988; Dear Santa, 1989; Partners (with Carolyn Bransford), 1989; Jigsaw, 1990; American Pie, 1990; Lady Reluctant, 1991; Emeral Rain, 1991; Happy New Year Darling, 1992; Murder By the Book, 1992; The Pirate and His Lady, 1992; Cache Poor, 1993; A Wish and a Kiss, 1993; The Accidental Princess, 1994; The Drop in Bride, 1994; The Wives of Bowie Stone, 1994. Address: Box E, Dillon, CO 80435, USA.

OSBORNE Mary Pope, b. 20 May 1949, Fort Sill, Oklahoma, USA. Writer. m. Will Osborne, 16 May 1976. Education: BA, University of North Carolina. Publications: Run, Run, As Fast As You Can, 1982; Love Always, Blue, 1983; Best Wishes, Joe Brady, 1984; Mo to the Rescue, 1985; Last One Home, 1986; Beauty and the Beast, 1987; Christopher Columbus, Admiral of the Ocean Sea, 1987; Pandora's Box, 1987; Jason and the Argonauts, 1988; The Deadly Power of Medusa (with Will Osborne), 1988; Favorite Greek Myths, 1989; A Visit to Sleep's

House, 1989; Mo and His Friends, 1989; American Tall Tales, 1990; Moonhorse, 1991; Spider Kane Series, 1992; Magic Treehouse Series, 1993; Mermaid Tales, 1993; Molly and the Prince, 1994; Haunted Waters, 1994; Favourite Norse Myths, 1996; One World, Many Religions, 1996; Rockinghorse Christmas, 1997; Favourite Medieval Tales, 1998; Standing in the Light, 1998; The Life of Jesus, 1998. Honour: Distinguished Alumnus Award, University of North Carolina, 1994. Membership: President, Authors' Guild Inc., 1993-997. Address: Brandt & Brandt Agancy, 1501 Broadway, No 2310, New York, NY 10036, USA.

OSBOURNE Ivor Livingstone, b. 6 Nov 1951, Porus, Jamaica. Author; Publisher. Partner, Charline Mertens, 2 daughters. Publications: The Mercenary, 1976; The Mango Season, 1979, 2nd edition, 1987; Prodigal, 1987; The Rasta Cookbook, 1990; The Exotic Cookbook of Optima, 1990. Contributions to: Various journals and magazines. Address: 27c Chippenham Road, Maida Vale, London W9 2AH, England.

OSERS Ewald, b. 13 May 1917, Prague, Czechoslovakia. Poet; Writer; Translator. m. Mary Harman, 3 June 1942, 1 son, 1 daughter. Education: University of Prague; BA, Honours, University of London. Appointment: Editorial Director, Babel, 1979-87. Publications: Poetry: Wish You Were Here, 1976; Arrive Where We Started, 1995. Translations: Over 120 books, including 35 volumes of poetry. Contributions to: Magazines. Cyril and Methodius Order, 1st Class, Bulgaria, 1987; European Poetry Translation Prize, 1987; Vitezlaw Nezval Medal, Czechoslovakia, 1987; Golden Pen, Macedonia, 1988; Officer's Cross of Merit, Germany, 1991; Order of Merit, Czech Republic, 1997. Memberships: International PEN, English Centre, fellow; Poetry Society; Royal Society of Literature, fellow; Society of Authors. Address: 33 Reades Lane, Sonning Common, Reading, Berkshire, RG4 9LL, England.

OSOFISAN Femi, (Babafemi Adeyemi Osofisan), b. 16 June 1946, Erunwon, Nigeria. Dramatist; Writer; Poet; University Teacher. Education: BA, 1969, PhD, 1974, University of Ibadan. Appointment: Faculty, University of Ibadan, 1973-. Publications: Many plays, including: You Have Lost Your Fine Face, 1969; Red is the Freedom Road, 1974; A Restless Run of Locusts, 1975; Once Upon Four Robbers, 1978; Farewell to a Cannibal Rage, 1978; Birthdays Are Not for Dying, 1981; The Oriki of a Grasshopper, 1981; No More the Wasted Breed, 1982; Midnight Hotel, 1982; Aringindin and the Nightwatchman, 1989. Fiction: Kolera Kolej, 1975; Cordelia, 1990. Poetry: Minted Coins, 1986; Dreamseeker On Divining Chain, 1993. Honour: Fulbright Fellowship, 1986. Address: c/o Department of Theatre Arts, University of Ibadan, Ibadan, Nigeria.

OSTRIKER Alicia Suskin, b. 11 Nov 1937, New York, New York, USA. Professor of English; Poet; Writer. m. 2 Dec 1958, 1 son, 2 daughters. Education: BA, Brandeis University, 1959; MA, 1960, PhD, 1964, University of Wisconsin. Appointments: Assistant Professor to Professor of English, Rutgers University, 1965-. Publications: Poetry: Songs, 1969; Once More Out of Darkness and Other Poems, 1974; A Dream of Springtime: Poems, 1970-77, 1978; The Mother-Child Papers, 1980; A Woman Under the Surface, 1983; The Imaginary Lover, 1986; Green Age, 1989; The Nakedness of the Fathers, 1994; The Crack in Everything, 1996; The Little Space: Poems Selected and New 1968-1998, 1998. Criticism: Vision and Verse in William Blake, 1965; Writing Like a Woman, 1982; Stealing the Language, 1986; Feminist Revision and the Bible, 1993. Contributions to: Professional journals and general publications. Honours: National Endowment for the Arts Fellowship, 1977; Guggenheim Fellowship, 1984-85; William Carlos Williams Prize, Poetry Society of America, 1986; Strousse Poetry Prize, Prairie Schooner, 1987; Anna Rosenberg Poetry Award, 1994; Nominee, National Book Award, 1996. Memberships: Modern Languages Association; PEN; Poetry Society of America, board of governors, 1988-91. Address: 33 Philip Drive, Princeton, NJ 08540, USA.

OSTROM Hans (Ansgar), b. 29 Jan 1954, Grass Valley, California, USA. Professor of English; Writer; Poet. m. Jacquelyn Bacon, 18 July 1983, 1 son. Education: BA, English, 1975, MA, English, 1979, PhD, English, 1982, University of California at Davis. Appointments: Faculty, University of California at Davis, 1977-80, 1981-83; Visiting Lecturer in American Studies, Johannes Gutenberg University, Mainz, 1980-81; Professor of English, University of Puget Sound, Tacoma, Washington, 1983-; Fulbright Senior Lecturer, University of Uppsala, 1994. Publications: The Living Language: A Reader (co-editor), 1984; Leigh Hunt: A Reference Guide (with Tim Lulofs), 1985; Spectrum: A Reader (co-editor), 1987; Lives and Moments: An Introduction to Short Fiction, 1991; Three to Get Ready (novel), 1991; Langston Hughes: A Study of the Short Fiction, 1993; Colors of a Different Horse (editor with Wendy Bishop), 1994; Water's Night (poems with Wendy Bishop), 1994; Genres of Writing: Mapping the Territories of Discourse (editor with Wendy Bishop), 1997; The Coast Starlight (poems), 1998. Contributions to: Books, journals, reviews, and magazines. Honours: 1st Prize, Harvest Awards, University of Houston, 1978; Grand Prize, Ina Coolbrith Memorial Award, 1979; 1st Prize, Warren Eyster Competition, New Delta Review, 1985; 2nd Prize, Redbook Magazine Annual Fiction Contest, 1985; John Lantz Fellowship, University of Puget Sound, 1996-97. Memberships: American Association of University Professors; Conference on College Composition and Communication; Modern Language Association; National Book Critics Circle; National Council of Teachers of English. Address: c/o Department of English, University of Puget Sound, Tacoma, WA 98416, USA.

OTTEN Charlotte F(lennema), b. 1 Mar 1926, Chicago, Illinois, USA. Retired Professor of English; Poet; Writer. m. Robert T Otten, 21 Dec 1948, 2 sons. Education: AB, English and American Language and Literature, Calvin College, Grand Rapids, 1949; MA, English and American Language and Literature, 1969, PhD, English Literature and Language, 1971, Michigan State University. Appointments: Associate Professor of English, Grand Valley State University, Allendale, Michigan, 1971-77; Lecturer on Women and Literature, University of Michigan Extension Center, 1972; Professor of English, Calvin College, Grand Rapids, 1977-91. Publications: Environ'd with Eternity: God, Poems, and Plants in Sixteenth and Seventeenth Century England, 1985; A Lycanthropy Reader: Werewolves in Western Culture, 1986; The Voice of the Narrator in Children's Literature (editor with Gary D Schmidt), 1989; English Women's Voices, 1540-1700, 1992; The Virago Book of Birth Poetry, 1993; The Book of Birth Poetry, 1995; January Rides the Wind, 1997. Contributions to: Scholarly books and journals and poetry journals. Honours: Several grants and fellowships; Roland H Bainton Book Prize in Early Modern Studies Nomination, 1992; Editors' Choice, Booklist, 1997. Memberships: Milton Society of America; Modern Language Association; Shakespeare Association of America; Society for Literature and Science; Society for Textual Scholarship; Society of Children's Book Writers and Illustrators. Address: c/o Department of English, Calvin College, 3201 Burton Street South East, Grand Rapids, MI 49546, USA.

OUELLETTE (Marie Léonne) Francine, b. 11 Mar 1947, Montreal, Quebec, Canada. Writer. 1 daughter. Education: Fine Arts Diploma in Sculpture, 1968; Pilot Licence, 1973. Publications: Au Nom du Père et du Fils, 1984; Le Sorcier, 1985; Sire Gaby du Lac, 1989; Les Ailes du Destin, 1992; Le Grand Blanc, 1993; L'Oiseau Invisible, 1994; BIP, 1995. Honours: France-Québec, Jean Hamelin, 1986; Prix, Du Grand Public, 1993. Memberships: Union des écrivaines et écrivains québécois. Address: CP 30, 1044 ch Presquîle, Lac Des Iles, Québec J0W 1J0, Canada.

OUSMANE Sembene, b. 1 Jan 1923, Ziguinchor, Casamance Region, Senegal. Writer; Filmmaker. Education: Studied Film Production under Marc Donski, USSR. Appointment: Founder, Editor, 1st Wolof Language Monthly, Kaddu. Publications: Novels: Le docker noir, 1956; O Pays mon beau peuple, 1957; Les bouts de bois de Dieu, 1960; Voltaïque, 1962; L'harmattan, 1964; Vehi-Ciosane suivi du mandat, 1966; Xala, 1974; Fat ndiay Diop, 1976; Dernier de l'empire, 1979. Honours: 1st Prize for Novelists, World Festival of Negro Arts, Dakar, 1966; Grand Prix pour les lettres, President of Republic of Senegal, 1993; Numerous international awards. Memberships: Association des Ecrivain du Sénégal; Societé des Gens de Lettres, France; Société Africaine de Culture; German Academy of Letters, corresponding member; International PEN Club, Senegal Section, president. Address: PO Box 8087, Yoff, Dakar, Senegal.

OUTRAM Richard (Daley), b. 9 Apr 1930, Oshawa, Ontario, Canada. Poet; Publisher. m. Barbara Howard, 13 Apr 1957. Education: BA, Victoria College, University of Toronto, 1953. Appointments: Co-Founder (with Barbara Howard), The Gauntlet Press, 1959. Publications: Eight Poems, 1959; Exsulate, Jubilate, 1966; Creatures, 1972; Seer, 1973; Thresholds, 1974; Locus, 1974; Turns and Other Poems, 1975; Arbor, 1976; The Promise of Light, 1979; Selected Poems 1960-1980, 1984; Man in Love, 1985; Hiram and Jenny, 1989; Mogul Recollected, 1993; Around and About the Toronto Islands, 1993; Peripatetics, 1994; Tradecraft, 1994; Eros Descending, 1995. Honour: Reading and exibition of his published work, National Library of Canada, 1986. Membership: PEN Canada. Address: 226 Roslin Avenue, Toronto, Ontario M4N 1Z6, Canada.

OVERY Paul (Vivian), b. 14 Feb 1940, Dorchester, England. Art Critic; Writer. Education: BA, 1962, MA, 1966, King's College, Cambridge. Appointments: Art Critic, The Listener, London, 1966-68, The Financial Times, London, 1968-70; Literary Editor, New Society, London, 1970-71; Chief Art Critic, The Times, London, 1973-78; Freelance critic and writer, 1978-; Reader in the History and Theory of Moderism, Middlesex University, 1997-; Publications: Edouard Manet, 1967; De Stijl, 1969; Kandinsky: The Language of the Eye, 1969; Paul Neagu: A Generative Context, 1981; The Rietveld Schroder House (co-author), 1988; The Complete Rietveld Furniture (with Peter Vöge), 1993; A Recognition of Restrictions (essay), in Josef Albers, 1994; Designing for the Modern World, De Stijl: The Red Blue Chair and the Schröder House (essay), in Investigating Modern Art, 1996; The Cell in the City: Cubism and Architecture (essay), 1997; Norman Foster: 30 Colours (co-author), 1998. Contributions to: Books and journals. Honour: Leverhulme Research Fellowship, 1984-85. Memberships: National Union of Journalists; Society of Authors; International Association of Art Critics. Literary Agent: Andrew Hewson, John Johnson Author's Agents, Clerkenwell House, 47 Clerkenwell Green, London, EC1. Address: 92 South Hill Park, London NW3 2SN, England.

OVESEN Ellis, b. 18 July 1923, New Effington, South Dakota, USA. Poet; Writer; Artist; Composer. m. Thor Lowe Smith, 27 Aug 1949, 2 sons. Education: MA, cum laude, University of Wisconsin, 1948; California Teachers Credential, San Jose State University, 1962; Extra classes in poetry writing. Appointments: Teacher of English, University of Wisconsin, 1946-48, San Jose State University, 1962-63; Teaching Poetry, 1963-90. Publications: Gloried Grass, 1970; Haloed Paths, 1973; To Those Who Love, 1974; The Last Hour: Lives Touch, 1975; A Time for Singing, 1977; A Book of Praises, 1977; Beloved I, 1980, II, 1990; The Green Madonna, 1984; The Flowers of God, 1985; The Keeper of the Word, 1985; The Wing Brush, 1986; The Year of the Snake, 1989; The Year of the Horse, 1990. Contributions to: Poet India; Los Altos Town Crier; Paisley Moon; Fresh Hot Bread; Samvedana; Plowman. Honours: Los Altos Hills Poet, 1976-90; Honorary Doctorate, World Academy of Arts and Culture, 1986; Dame of Merit, Knights of Malta, 1988; Golden Poet Awards, 1988, 1989, 1991; Research Fellow, 1992. Memberships: National Writers Club; California Writers Club; Poetry Society of America; California State Poetry Society. Address: Box 482, Los Altos, CA 94023, USA.

OVNI. See: **TÔRRES Luiz Rebouças.**

OVSTEDAL Barbara Kathleen, (Rosalind Laker), b. England. Writer. m. Inge Ovstedal, 1945, 1 son, 1 daughter. Education: West Sussex College of Art. Publications: As Rosalind Laker: The Smuggler's Bride, 1976; Ride the Blue Ribbon, 1977; The Warwyck Trilogy, 1979-80; Banners of Silk, 1981; Gilded Splendour, 1982; Jewelled Path, 1983; What the Heart Keeps, 1984; This Shining Land, 1985; Tree of Gold, 1986; The Silver Touch, 1987; To Dance With Kings, 1988; Circle of Pearls, 1990; The Golden Tulip, 1991; The Venetian Mask, 1992; The Sugar Pavilion, 1993; The Fortuny Gown, 1995; The Fragile Hour, 1996. Contributions to: Good Housekeeping; Country Life; Woman; Woman's Own; Woman's Weekly. Memberships: Society of Authors; Romantic Novelists Association. Address: c/o Laurence Pollinger Ltd, 18 Maddox Street, London W1R 0EU, England.

OWEN Charles, b. 14 Nov 1915, England. Retired Royal Navy Officr; Writer; Consultant. m. Felicity, 14 Feb 1950, 1 son, 1 daughter. Education: Royal Navy Colleges, Dartmouth and Greenwich, England. Publications: Independent Traveller, 1966; Britons Abroad, 1968; The Opaque Society, 1970; No More Heroes, 1975; The Grand Days of Travel, 1979; Just Across the Channel, 1983; Plain Yarns from the Fleet, 1997. Contributions to: Various magazines and journals. Honour: Distinguished Service Cross, 1943. Memberships: Society of Authors; Writers Guild of Great Britain; PEN. Address: Flat 31, 15 Portman Square, London W1H 9HD, England.

OWEN Douglas David Roy, b. 17 Nov 1922, Norton, Suffolk, England. Retired University Professor; Writer; Translator. m. Berit Mariann Person, 31 July 1954, 2 sons. Education: University College, Nottingham, 1942-43; BA, 1948, MA, 1953, PhD, 1955, University of Cambridge; Sorbonne and Collège de France, Paris, 1950-51. Appointment: Founder, General Editor, Forum for Modern Language Studies, 1965-. Publications: The Evolution of the Grail Legend, 1968; The Vision of Hell, 1970; The Song of Roland (translator), 1972, new expanded edition, 1990; The Legend of Roland: A Pageant of the Middle Ages, 1973; Noble Lovers, 1975; Chrétien de Troyes: Arthurian Romances (translator), 1987; Guillaume le Clerc: Fergus of Galloway (translator), 1989; A Chat Round the Old Course, 1990; Eleanor of Aquitaine: Queen and Legend, 1993; The Romance of Reynard the Fox (translator), 1994; William the Lion, 1143-1214: Kingship and Culture, 1997. Editor with R C Johnston: Fabliaux, 1957; Two Old French Gauvain Romances, 1972. Contributions to: Books and journals. Memberships: International Arthurian Society; Société Rencesvals; International Courtly Literature Society; Modern Humanities Research Association. Address: 7 West Acres, St Andrews, Fife KY16 9UD, Scotland.

OWEN Eileen, b. 27 Feb 1949, Concord, New Hampshire, USA. Poet; Writer. m. John D Owen, 19 June 1971. Education: BA, Spanish, University of New Hampshire, 1971; BA, English, 1979, MA, Creative Writing, 1981, University of Washington. Appointment: Artist-in-Residence, Ucross Foundation, Wyoming, 1984. Publication: Facing the Weather Side, 1985. Contributions to: Reviews and journals. Honour: Honourable Mention, Washington Poets Association. Address: 18508 90th Avenue West, Edmonds, WA 98020, USA.

OWEN Jan Jarrold, b. 18 Aug 1940, Adelaide, South Australia, Australia. Poet; Writer. 2 sons, 1 daughter. Education: BA, 1963, University of Adelaide; ALAA, 1970. Appointments: Writer-in-Residence, Venice Studio of the Literature Board of the Australian Council, 1989, Tasmanian State Institute of Technology, 1990, Brisbane Grammar School, 1993, Tasmanian Writers Union, 1993, B R Whiting Library, Rome, 1994; Rimbun Dahan, Kuala Lumpur, 1997-98. Publications: Boy With a Telescope, 1986; Fingerprints on Light, 1990; Blackberry Season, 1993; Night Rainbows, 1994. Contributions to: Newspapers and magazines. Honours: Ian Mudie Prize, 1982; Jessie Litchfield Prize, 1984; Grenfell Henry Lawson Prize, 1985; Harri Jones Memorial Prize, 1986;

Anne Elder Award, 1987; Mary Gilmore Prize, 1987; Wesley Michel Wright Poetry Prize, 1992. Memberships: South Australian Writers Centre. Address: 14 Fern Road, Crafers, South Australia 5152, Australia.

OWEN Maureen, b. 6 July 1943, Graceville, Minnesota, USA. Poet. 3 sons. Education: University of Seattle, 1961-62; San Francisco State College, 1962-64. Publications: Country Rush, 1973; No Travels Journal, 1975; A Brass Choir Approaches the Burial Ground/Big Deal, 1977; Hearts in Space, 1980; Amelia Earhart, 1984; Zombie Notes, 1986; Imaginary Income, 1992; Untapped Maps, 1993. Contributions to: Many anthologies and other publications. Honours: National Endowment for the Arts Fellowship, 1979-80; American Book Award, Before Columbus Foundation, 1985; Fund for Poetry Awards, 1987, 1990, 1995. Memberships: Before Columbus Foundation; Coordinating Council of Literary Magazines, vice chairperson, board; St Mark's Poetry Project, advisory board. Address: 109 Dunk rock Road, Guildford, CT 06437, USA.

OWENS Agnes, b. 24 May 1926, Milngavie. Fiction Writer. m. Patrick Owens, 30 Aug 1964, 3 sons, 4 daughters. Publications: Gentlemen of the West, 1985; Lean Tales, 1985; Like Birds in the Wildnerness, 1986; A Working Mother, 1994; People Like That, 1996; For the Love of Willie, 1998. Honour: Short Leet for Scottish Writer of the Year Award (Stakis Prize), 1998. Membership: Scottish Pen Centre. Address: 21 Roy Young Avenue, Balloch, Dunbartonshire, G83 8ER, Scotland.

OWENS John Edwin, b. 13 June 1948, Widnes, Cheshire, England. Political Scientist. m. Margaret Owens, 1 Oct 1971, 1 son, 1 daughters. Education: BA Honours, University of Reading, 1973; University of Warwick, 1973-75; PhD, University of Essex, 1982. Appointments: Lecturer, Central London Polytechnic, 1978-85; Lecturer, University of Essex, 1985-86; Senior Lecturer, 1986-98, Reader, 1998-, University of Westminster, London. Publications: After Full Employment, with John Kearne, 1986; Congress and the Presidency: Institutional Politics in a Separated System, with Michael Foley, 1996; The Republican Takeover of Congress, with Dean McSweeney, 1998. Contributions to: British Journal of Political Science; Political Studies; American Review of Politics; Roll Call; Times Higher Educational Supplement. Memberships: Political Studies Association, UK; Legislative Studies Section, American Political Science Association; International Political Science Association. Address: The Centre for the Study of Democracy, The University of Westminster, 100 Park Village East, London NW1 3SR, England.

OWENS Rochelle, b. 2 Apr 1936, Brooklyn, New York, USA. Poet; Dramatist; Critic; Professor; Translator. m. (1) David Owens, 30 Mar 1956, diss 1959, (2) George Economou, 17 June 1962. Education: Theatre Arts, New School for Social Research, New York City; University of Montreal, Alliance Française, Paris, New York City. Appointments: Visiting Lecturer, University of California at San Diego, 1982; Writer-in-Residence, Brown University, Providence, Rhode Island, 1989; Adjunct Professor, University of Oklahoma, at Norman, 1993-; Poet and Playwright-in Residence, Deep South Writers Conference, University of Southwestern Louisiana, 1997. Publications: Poetry: Not Be Essence That Cannot Be, 1961; Four Young Lady Poets (with others), 1962; Salt and Core, 1968; I Am the Babe of Joseph Stalin's Daughter: Poems 1961-1971, 1972; Poems From Joe's Garage, 1973; The Joe 82 Creation Poems, 1974; The Joe Chronicles, Part 2, 1979; Shemuel, 1979; French Light, 1984; Constructs, 1985; W C Fields in French Light, 1986; How Much Paint Does the Painting Need, 1988; Black Chalk, 1992; Rubbed Stones and Other Poems, 1994; New and Selected Poems, 1961-1996, 1997; Luca: Discourse on Life and Death, forthcoming. Plays: Futz and What Came After, 1968; The Karl Marx Play and Others, 1974; Emma Instigated Me, 1976; The Widow and the Colonel, 1977; Mountain Rites, 1978; Chucky's Hunch, 1982. Editor: Spontaneous Combustion: Eight New American Plays, 1972. Contributions to:

Poems in many anthologies, including: Poems for the Millennium Volume 2 and periodicals; Critical articles and essays in various journals. Honours: Rockefeller Grants, 1965, 1976; Obie Awards, 1965, 1967, 1982; Yale School of Drama Fellowship, 1968; American Broadcasting Corporation Fellowship, 1968; Guggenheim Fellowship, 1971; National Endowment for the Arts Award, 1976; Villager Award, 1982; Franco-Anglais Festival de Poésie, Paris, 1991; Rockefeller Foundation Resident Scholar, Bellagio, Italy, 1993; Oklahoma Centre for the Book Award, 1998. Memberships: American Society of Composers, Authors, and Publishers; Authors League; Dramatists Guild. Address: 1401 Magnolia, Norman, OK 73072, USA.

OXLEY William, b. 29 Apr 1939, Manchester, England. Poet; Writer; Translator. m. Patricia Holmes, 13 Apr 1963, 2 daughters. Education: Manchester College of Commerce, 1953-55. Publications: The Dark Structures, 1967; New Workings, 1969; Passages from Time: Poems from a Life, 1971; The Icon Poems, 1972; Sixteen Days in Autumn (travel), 1972; Opera Vetera, 1973; Mirrors of the Sea, 1973; Eve Free, 1974; Mundane Shell, 1975; Superficies, 1976; The Exile, 1979; The Notebook of Hephaestus and Other Poems, 1981; Poems of a Black Orpheus, 1981; The Synopthegms of a Prophet, 1981; The Idea and Its Imminence, 1982; Of Human Consciousness, 1982; The Cauldron of Inspiration, 1983; A Map of Time, 1984; The Triviad and Other Satires, 1984; The Inner Tapestry, 1985; Vitalism and Celebration, 1987; The Mansands Trilogy, 1988; Mad Tom on Tower Hill, 1988; The Patient Reconstruction of Paradise, 1991; Forest Sequence, 1991; In the Drift of Words, 1992; The Playboy, 1992; Cardboard Troy, 1993; The Hallsands Tragedy, 1993; Collected Longer Poems, 1994; Completing the Picture (editor), 1995; The Green Crayon Man, 1997; No Accounting for Paradise (autobiography), forthcoming. Contributions to: Anthologies and periodicals. Address: 6 The Mount, Furzeham, Brixham, South Devon TQ5 8QY, England.

OZ Amos, b. 4 May 1939, Jerusalem, Israel. Author; Professor of Hebrew Literature. m. Nily Zuckerman, 5 Apr 1960, 1 son, 2 daughters. Education: BA cum laude, Hebrew Literature, Philosophy, Hebrew University, Jerusalem, 1965. Appointments: Teacher, Literature, Philosophy, Hulda High School and Givat Brenner Regional High School, 1963-86; Visiting Fellow, St Cross College, Oxford, England, 1969-70; Writer-in-Residence, Hebrew University, Jerusalem, 1975, 1990; Visiting Professor, University of California, Berkeley, USA, 1980; Writer-in-Residence, Professor of Literature, The Colorado College, Colorado Springs, 1984-85; Writer in Residence, Visiting Professor of Literature, Boston University, Massachusetts, 1987; Full Professor of Hebrew Literature, Ben Gurion University, Beer Sheva, Israel, 1987-; Writer-in-Residence, Tel Aviv University, 1996; Writer in Residence, Visiting Professor of Literature, Princeton University, (Old Dominion Fellowship), 1997; Weidenfeld Visiting Professor of European Comparative Literature, St Anne's College, Oxford, 1998. Publications include: Where the Jackals Howl (stories), 1965, My Michael (novel), 1968; Under This Blazing Light (essays), 1978; Black Box (novel), 1987; Don't Call It Night (novel), 1994; All Our Hopes (essays) 1998. Honours include: Holon Prize, 1965; Wingate Prize, London, 1988; Honorary Doctorate, Tel Aviv University, 1992; Cross of the Knight of the Legion D'Honneur, 1997; Honorary Doctorate, Brandeis University, USA, 1998; Israel Prize for Literature, 1998. Address: c/o Deborah Owen Ltd, 78 Narrow Street, London E14, England.

OZICK Cynthia, b. 17 Apr 1928, New York, New York, USA. Author; Poet; Dramatist; Critic; Translator. m. Bernard Hallote, 7 Sept 1952, 1 daughter. Education: BA, cum laude, English, New York University, 1949; MA, Ohio State University, 1950. Appointment: Phi Beta Kappa Orator, Harvard University, 1985. Publications: Trust, 1966; The Pagan Rabbi and Other Stories, 1971; Bloodshed and Three Novellas, 1976; Leviation: Five Fictions, 1982; Art and Ardor: Essays, 1983; The Cannibal Galaxy, 1983; The Messiah of Stockholm, 1987;

Metaphor and Memory: Essays, 1989; The Shawl, 1989; Epodes: First Poems, 1992; What Henry James Knew, and Other Essays on Writers, 1994; Portrait of the Artist as a Bad Character, 1996; The Cynthia Ozick Reader, 1996; Fame and Folly, 1996; The Puttermesser Papers, 1997. Contributions to: Many anthologies, reviews, quarterlies, journals, and periodicals. Honours: Guggenheim Fellowship, 1982; Mildred and Harold Strauss Living Award, American Academy of Arts and Letters, 1983; Lucy Martin Donnelly Fellow, Bryn Mawr College, 1992; PEN/Spiegel-Diamonstein Award for the Art of the Essay, 1997; Harold Washington Literary Award, City of Chicago, 1997; Mony honorary doctorates. Memberships: American Academy of Arts and Letters; American Academy of Arts and Sciences; Authors League; Dramatists Guild; PEN; Phi Beta Kappa. Address: c/o Alfred A Knopf Inc, 201 East 50th Street, New York, NY 10022, USA.

P

PAANANEN Eloise (Katherine), b. 12 Apr 1923, Seattle, Washington, USA. Author. m. (1) P R Engle, 1 son, 1 daughter, (2) Lauri A Paananen, 26 Oct 1973. Education: BA, George Washington University, 1947. Publications: Some 30 books on military history, culture, travel, etc. Contributions to: Newspapers and magazines. Honours: Several awards. Memberships: American Society of Journalists and Authors; Society of Women Geographers. Address: 6348 Crosswoods Drive, Falls Church, VA 22044, USA.

PACK Robert, b. 29 May 1929, New York, New York, USA. Professor; Poet; Writer. m. (1) Isabelle Miller, 1950, (2) Patricia Powell, 1961, 2 sons, 1 daughter. Education: BA, Dartmouth College, 1951; MA, Columbia University, 1953. Appointments: Teacher, Barnard College, 1957-64; Abernathy Professor, Middlebury College, Vermont, 1970-; Director, Bread Loaf Writers Conferences, 1973-. Publications: Poetry: The Irony of Joy, 1955; A Stranger's Privilege, 1959; Guarded by Women, 1963; Selected Poems, 1964; Home from the Cemetery, 1969; Nothing But Light, 1972; Keeping Watch, 1976; Waking to My Name: New and Selected Poems, 1980; Faces in a Single Tree: A Cycle of Monologues, 1984; Clayfield Rejoices, Clayfield Laments: A Sequence of Poems, 1987; Before It Vanishes: A Packet for Professor Pagels, 1989; Fathering the Map: New and Selected Later Poems, 1993. Other: Wallace Stevens: An Approach to His Poetry and Thought, 1958; Affirming Limits: Essays on Morality, Choice and Poetic Form, 1985; The Long View: Essays on the Discipline of Hope and Poetic Craft, 1991. Editor: The New Poets of England and America (with Donald Hall and Louis Simpson), 1957, 2nd edition, 1962; Poems of Doubt and Belief: An Anthology of Modern Religious Poetry (with Tom Driver), 1964; Literature for Composition on the Theme of Innocence and Experience (with Marcus Klein), 1966; Short Stories: Classic, Modern, Contemporary (with Marcus Klein), 1967; Keats: Selected Letters, 1974; The Bread Loaf Anthology of Contemporary American Poetry (with Sydney Lea and Jay Parini), 1985; The Bread Loaf Anthology of Contemporary American Short Stories (with Jay Parini), 2 volumes, 1987, 1989; Poems for a Small Planet: An Anthology of Nature Poetry (with Jay Parini), 1993. Honours: Fulbright Fellowship, 1956; American Academy of Arts and Letters Grant, 1957; Borestone Mountain Poetry Awardf, 1964; National Endowment for the Arts Grant, 1968. Address: c/o Middlebury College, Middlebury, VT 05742, USA.

PACNER Karel, b. 29 Mar 1936, Janovice-n-Uhl, Czechoslovakia. Science Journalist; Writer. Education: MA, Economics University, Prague, 1959. Appointment: Staff, Mlada fronta, later Mlada fronta Dnes, newspaper, 1959-. Publications: 15 books in Czech, 1968-97. Contributions to: Periodicals. Honours: Publishing house literary awards. Memberships: Czech Society of Arts and Sciences in the USA, Czech Branch; Community of Writers in the Czech Republic. Address: K Vidouli 216, 15500 Prague 5, Czech Republic.

PADEL Ruth, b. 8 May 1946, London, England. Poet; Writer; Journalist. 1 daughter. Education: BA, 1969, PhD, 1976, University of Oxford. Publications: Poetry: Alibi, 1985; Summer Snow, 1990; Angel, 1993; Fusewire, 1996; Rembrandt Would Have Loved You, 1998. Non-Fiction: In and Out of the Mind, 1992; Whom Gods Destroy, 1995, Heroes, 2000. Honours: Prizes, 1985, 1992, 1994, First Prize, 1996, National Poetry Competition; Poetry Book Society Recommendation, 1993, Choice, 1998, Arts Council Bursary, 1996. Poetry Book Society Choice, 1998; Shortlisted for T.S. Eliot Prize, 1998. Memberships: PEN; Royal Zoological Society; Poetry Society; Society of Authors; Royal Society of Literature, fellow. Literary Agent: A.P. Watt.

PADFIELD Peter Lawrence Notton, b. 3 Apr 1932, Calcutta, India. Author. m. Dorothy Jean Yarwood, 23 Apr 1960, 1 son, 2 daughters. Publications: The Titanic and the Californian, 1965; An Agony of Collisions, 1966; Aim Straight: A Biography of Admiral Sir Percy Scott, 1966; Broke and the Shannon: A Biography of Admiral Sir Philip Broke, 1968; The Battleship Era, 1972; Guns at Sea: A History of Naval Gunnery, 1973; The Great Naval Race: Anglo-German Naval Rivalry 1900-1914, 1974; Nelson's War, 1978; Tide of Empires: Decisive Naval Campaigns in the Rise of the West, Vol I 1481-1654, 1979, Vol II 1654-1763, 1982; Rule Britannia: The Victorian and Edwardian Navy, 1981; Beneath the Houseflag of the P & O, 1982; Dönitz, The Last Führer, 1984; Armada, 1988; Himmler, Reichsführer - SS, 1990; Hess: Flight for the Führer, 1991, revised, updated edition, 1993; War Beneath the Sea: Submarine Conflict 1939-1945, 1995; Maritime Supremacy and the Opening of the Western Mind: Naval Campaigns that Shaped the Modern World 1588-1782, 1999. Novels: The Lion's Claw, 1978; The Unquiet Gods, 1980; Gold Chains of Empire, 1982; Salt and Steel, 1986. Membership: Society for Nautical Research. Address: Westmoreland Cottage, Woodbridge, Suffolk, England.

PADHY Pravat Kumar, b. 27 Dec 1954, India. Geologist; Poet. m. Namita Padhy, 6 Mar 1983, 2 daughters. Education: MSc, 1979; MTech, Mineral Exploration, 1980; PhD, Applied Geology, 1992. Appointment: Geologist, ONGC, Baroda, Gujarat. Publication: Silence of the Seas, 1992. Contributions to: Anthologies and periodicals. Honour: Certificate of Honour, Writer's Life Line, Canada, 1986. Address: 166 HIG Complex, Sailashri Vihar, Bhubaneshwar 751016, Orissa, India.

PADOVANO Anthony Thomas, b. 18 Sept 1934, Harrison, New Jersey, USA. Professor of American Literature; Writer. m. Theresa P Lackamp, 1 Sept 1974, 3 sons, 1 daughter. Education: BA, magna cum laude, Seton Hall University, 1956; STB, magna cum laude, 1958, STL, magna cum laude, 1960, STD, magna cum laude, 1962, Pontifical Gregorian University, Rome; PhL, St Thomas Pontifical International University, Rome, 1962; MA, New York University, 1971; PhD, Fordham University, 1980. Appointments: Professor of Systematic Theology, Darlington School of Theology, Mahwah, New Jersey, 1962-74; Professor of American Literature, Ramapo College of New Jersey, 1971-; Various visiting professorships. Publications: The Cross of Christ, The Measure of the World, 1962; The Estranged God, 1966; Who Is Christ?, 1967; Belief in Human Life, 1969; American Culture and the Quest for Christ, 1970; Dawn Without Darkness, 1971; Free to Be Faithful, 1972; Eden and Easter, 1974; A Case for Worship, 1975; Presence and Structure, 1975; America: Its People, Its Promise, 1975; The Human Journey: Thomas Merton, Symbol of a Century, 1982; Contemplation and Compassion, 1984; Winter Rain: A Play in One Act and Six Scenes, 1985; His Name is John: A Play in Four Acts, 1986; Christmas to Calvary, 1987; Love and Destiny, 1987; Summer Lightening: A Play in Four Acts and Four Seasons, 1988; Conscience and Conflict, 1989; Reform and Renewal: Essays on Authority, Ministry and Social Justice, 1990; A Celebration of Life, 1990; The Church Today: Belonging and Believing, 1990; Scripture in the Street, 1992; A Retreat with Thomas Merton: Biography as Spiritual Journey, 1995; Hope is a Dialogue, 1998. Contributions to: Books and periodicals. Honours: Awards and citations; All professional and personal papers retained in the archives of the University of Notre Dame, Indiana, USA, under Padovano Papers listing. Memberships: Catholic Theological Society of America; International Federation of Married Priests; International Thomas Merton Society; Priests for Equality; Sigma Tau Delta, honorary member; Theta Alpha Kappa, National Honour Society for Religious Studies and Theology. Address: c/o School of American and International Studies, Ramapo College of New Jersey, Mahwah, NJ 07430, USA.

PAGAC Karl Heinz, b. 29 June 1936, Graz, Austria. Freelance Writer and Broadcaster; Consultant; Corporate Business Executive. m. Yolanda Levitus, 22 Dec 1987, 1 son. Education: PhD, Law, Graz University; Bachelor in International Diplomacy, Wesleyan University, Connecticut, USA. Appointments: Junior Diplomat; Senior corporate business positions, Europe, Africa, Middle East, North America; International Consultant; Current Affairs Analyst and Broadcaster, Riviera Radio, Monaco; Programme Coordinator, TV talk show, NBC Europe, London; Contributor on special documentaries, ITN, Monaco; Columnist, Swiss Review of World Affairs, monthly, Zurich. Contributions to: Finance Magazine, UK quarterly; International Herald Tribune; Newsweek; The European; Others. Honour: Finalist, Philip Morris Policy Research Europa Prize, 1997. Memberships: United Nations Society of Writers, New York; Institute of Directors, London, Monaco. Address: 12 Allée des Courdoules, Les Hauts de Vaugrenier, F-06270 Villeneuve-Loubet, France.

PAGE S M. See: MCMASTER Susan.

PAGE Clarence, b. 2 June 1947, Dayton, Ohio, USA. Journalist; Columnist. m. Lisa Johnson Cole, 3 May 1987. Education: BS in Journalism, Ohio University, 1969. Appointments: Reporter and Assistant City Editor, 1969-80, Columnist and Editorial Board Member, 1984-, Chicago Tribune; Director, Department of Community Affairs, WBBM-TV, 1980-82; Syndicated Columnist; Many television appearances. Contributions to: Various periodicals. Honours: James P McGuire Award, 1987; Pulitzer Prize for Commentary, 1989. Address: c/o Tribune Media Services, 435 North Michigan Avenue, Suite 600, Chicago, IL 60611, USA.

PAGE Eleanor. See: COERR Eleanor (Beatrice).

PAGE Emma. See: TIRBUTT Honoris.

PAGE Geoff(rey Donald), b. 7 July 1940, Grafton, New South Wales, Australia. Poet; Writer; Educator. m. Carolyn Mau, 4 Jan 1972, 1 son. Education: BA, Honours, DipEd, University of New England, Armidale, New South Wales. Appointments: Head, Department of English, Narrabundah College, Canberra, 1974-; Writer-in-Residence, University of Wollongong, New South Wales, 1982. Publications: The Question, 1971; Smalltown Memorials, 1975; Collecting the Weather, 1978; Cassandra Paddocks, 1980; Clairvoyance in Autumn, 1983; Shadows from Wire: Poems and Photographs of Australians in the Great War Australian War Memorial (editor), 1983; Benton's Conviction, 1985; Century of Clouds: Selected Poems of Guillaume Apollinaire (translator with Wendy Coutts), 1985; Collected Lives, 1986; Smiling in English, Smoking in French, 1987; Footwork, 1988; Winter Vision, 1989; Invisible Histories, 1990; Selected Poems, 1991; Gravel Corners, 1992; On the Move (editor), 1992; Human Interest, 1994; Reader's Guide to Contemporary Australian Poetry, 1995; The Great Forgetting, 1996; The Secret, 1997. Contributions to: Newspapers and magazines. Honours: Australia Council Literature Board Grants, 1974, 1983, 1987, 1989, 1992, 1997; Queensland Premier's Prize, 1990. Memberships: Australian Society of Authors; Australian Teachers Union. Address: 8 The Crescent, Leahy Close, Narrabundah, ACT 2604, Australia.

PAGE Jeremy Neil, b. 23 Feb 1958, Folkestone, Kent, England. Educator; Poet; Editor. Education: BA, Honours, French and Theatre Studies, University of Warwick, 1980; French Drama and Theatre History, University of Bristol, 1983; DipRSA, Teaching English as a Foreign Language; Certificates in Counselling. Appointments: Teacher and Trainer, 1984-, Director of Studies, 1995-, International House, London; Editor, The Frogmore Papers, 1983-; Founder, Frogmore Poetry Prize, 1987; Teacher, Academia Britannica, Arezzo, Italy, 1987-88; Series Editor, Crabflower Pamphlets, 1990-. Publications: Bliss, 1989; Frogmore Poetry (co-editor), 1989; Secret Dormitories, 1993. Contributions to: Various anthologies and journals. Honours: 4th Prize, Kent and Sussex Poetry Open Competition, 1989; Grand Transcendent Knight Salamander, Academy of Paraphysical Science, 1992. Address: 6 Vernon Road, Hornsey, London N8 0QD, England.

PAGE Katherine Hall, b. 9 July 1947, New Jersey, USA. Writer. m. Alan Hein, 5 Dec 1975, 1 son. Education: AB, Wellesley College, 1969; EdM, Tufts University, 1974; EdD, Harvard University, 1985. Publications: The Body in the Belfry, 1990; The Body in the Bouillon, 1991; The Body in the Kelp, 1991; The Body in the Vestibule, 1992; The Body in the Cast, 1993; The Body in the Basement, 1994; The Body in the Bog, 1996; The Body in the Fjord, 1997; The Body in the Bookcase, 1998; Christie & Company, (juvenile), 1996; Christie & Company Down East, (juvenile), 1997; Christie and Company in the Year of the Dragon (juvenile), 1998. Honours: Agatha for Best First Domestic Mystery, 1991; Edgar Nominee, Best Juvenile Mystery, Mystery Writers of America. Memberships: Mystery Readers International; Mystery Writers of America; Authors Guild; Sisters in Crime; American Crime Writers League; Society of Children's Bookwriters and Illustrators; International Association of Crime Writers; Boston Author's Club, Member of the Board of Directors. Address: c/o Faith Hamlin, Sanford J Greenburger Associates Inc, 55 Fifth Avenue, New York, NY 10003, USA.

PAGE Louise, b. 7 Mar 1955, London, England. Playwright. Education: BA, University of Birmingham, 1976. Appointment: Resident Playwright, Royal Court Theatre, 1982-83. Publications: Want Ad, 1977; Glasshouse, 1977; Tissue, 1978; Lucy, 1979; Hearing, 1979; Flaws, 1980; House Wives, 1981; Salonika, 1982; Real Estate, 1984; Golden Girls, 1984; Beauty and the Beast, 1985; Diplomatic Wives, 1989; Adam Wasxa Gardener, 1991; Like to Live, 1992; Hawks and Doves, 1992; Radio and TV plays. Honour: George Devine Award, 1982. Address: 6J Oxford & Cambridge Mansions, Old Marylebone Road, London NW1 5EC, England.

PAGE Norman, b. 8 May 1930, Kettering, Northamptonshire, England. Professor of Modern English Literature; Author. m. Jean Hampton, 29 Mar 1958, 3 sons, 1 daughter. Education: BA, 1951, MA, 1955, Emmanuel College, Cambridge; PhD, University of Leeds, 1968. Appointments: Principal Lecturer in English, Ripon College of Education, Yorkshire, 1960-69; Assistant Professor, 1969-70, Associate Professor, 1970-75, Professor of English, 1975-85, University of Alberta; Professor of Modern English Literature, University of Nottingham, 1985-. Publications: The Language of Jane Austen, 1972; Speech in the English Novel, 1973, 2nd edition, 1988; Thomas Hardy, 1977; A E Housman: A Critical Biography, 1983; A Kipling Companion, 1984; E M Forster, 1988; Tennyson: An Illustrated Life, 1992. Contributions to: Professional journals. Honours: Guggenheim Fellowship, 1979; University of Alberta Research Prize, 1983. Membership: Royal Society of Canada, fellow; Thomas Hardy Society; Newstead Abbey Byron Society; Tennyson Society. Address: 23 Braunston Road, Oakham, Rutland LE15 6LD, England.

PAGE P(atricia) K(athleen), b. 23 Nov 1916, Swanage, Dorset, England. Writer; Poet; Painter. m. W Arthur Irwin, 16 Dec 1950, 1 stepson, 2 stepdaughters. Education: Studied art with Frank Schaeffer, Brazil, Charles Seliger, New York; Art Students League, New York; Pratt Graphics, New York. Appointments: Scriptwriter, National Film Board, Canada, 1946-50; Conducted writing workshops, Toronto, 1974-77; Teacher, University of Victoria, British Columbia, 1977-78. Publications: The Sun and the Moon (novel), 1944; As Ten as Twenty, 1946; The Metal and the Flower, 1954; Cry Ararati: Poems New and Selected, 1967; The Sun and the Moon and Other Fictions, 1973; Poems Selected and New, 1974; To Say the Least (editor), 1979; Evening Dance of the Grey Flies, 1981; The Glass Air (poems, essays, and drawings), 1985; Brazilian Journal (prose), 1988; I-Sphinx: A Poem for Two Voices, 1988; A Flask of Sea Water (fairy story), 1989; The Glass Air: Poems Selected and New, 1991; The Travelling Musicians (children's book), 1991; Unless the Eye Catch Fire (short story), 1994; The Goat That Flew (fairy story), 1994; Hologram: A Book of Glosas, 1994; A Children's Hymn for the United Nations, 1995; The

Hidden Room, Collected Poems, 2 volumes, 1997; Alphabetical (a poem), 1998; Compass Rose (Italian translations of selected poems), 1998. Contributions to: Journals and magazines. Honours: Oscar Blumenthal Award for Poetry, 1974; Governor-General's Award for Poetry, 1954; Officer of the Order of Canada, 1977; National Magazines Gold Award, 1986, and Silver Award, 1990, for Poetry; BC Book Awards, Hubert Swans Prize, 1988; Banff Centre School of Fine Arts National Award, 1989; Subject of National Film Board film Still Waters, 1991; Readers' Choice Award, Prairie Schooner, 1994; Subject of 2-part sound feature The White Glass, CBC, 1996; Subject of special issue of Malahat Review, 1997; Honorary doctorates including: DLitt. University of Toronto, 1998. Membership: PEN International. Address: 3260 Exeter Road, Victoria, British Columbia V8R 6A6, Canada.

PAGE Robin, b. 3 May 1943, Cambridgeshire, England. Writer. Publications: Down with the Poor, 1971; The Benefits Racket, 1972; Down Among the Dossers, 1973; The Decline of an English Village, 1974; The Hunter and the Hunted, 1977; Weather Forecasting: The Country Way, 1977; Cures and Remedies: The Country, 1978; Weeds: The Country Way, 1979; Animal Cures: The Country Way, 1979; The Journal of a Country Parish, 1980; Journeys into Britain, 1982; The Country Way of Love, 1983; The Wildlife of the Royal Estates, 1984; Count One to Ten, 1986; The Fox's Tale, 1986; The Duchy of Cornwall, 1987; The Fox and the Orchid, 1987; The Twitcher's Guide to British Birds, 1989. Address: Bird's Farm, Barton, Cambridgeshire, England.

PAGELS Elaine (Hiesey), b. 13 Feb 1943, Palo Alto, California, USA. Professor of Religion; Writer. m. (1) Heinz R Pagels, 7 June 1969, dec 24 July 1988, 2 sons, 1 dec, 1 daughter, (2) Kent Greenawalt, June 1995. Education: BA, 1964, MA, 1965, Stanford University; PhD, Harvard University, 1970. Appointments: Assistant Professor, 1970-74, Associate Professor, Professor of Religion, and Head, Department of Religion, 1974-82, Barnard College; Harrington Spear Paine Professor of Religion, Princeton University, 1982-. Publications: The Johannine Gospel in Gnostic Exegesis: Heracleon's Commentary on John, 1973; The Gnostic Paul: Gnostic Exegesis of the Pauline Letters, 1975; The Gnostic Gospels, 1979; The Gnostic Jesus and Early Christian Politics, 1981; Adam, Eve and the Serpent, 1988; The Origin of Satan: The New Testament Origins of Christianity's Demonization of Jews, Pagans and Heretics, 1995. Contributions to: Various scholarly books and journals. Honours: National Endowment for the Humanities Grant, 1972-73; Mellon Fellow, Aspen Institute of Humanistic Studies, 1974; Hazen Fellow, 1975; Rockefeller Foundation Fellowship, 1978-79; National Book Critics Circle Award, 1979; Guggenheim Fellowship, 1979-80; National Book Award, 1980; John D and Catharine T MacArthur Foundation Fellowship, 1981-87. Memberships: American Academy of Religion; Biblical Theologians Club; Society of Biblical Literature. Address: c/o Department of Religion, Princeton University, Princeton, NJ 08544, USA.

PAGLIA Camille (Anna), b. 2 Apr 1947, Endicott, New York, USA. Professor of Humanities; Writer. Education: BA, State University of New York at Binghamton, 1968; MPhil, 1971, PhD, 1974, Yale University. Appointments: Faculty, Bennington College, Vermont, 1972-80; Visiting Lecturer, Wesleyan University, 1980; Visiting Lecturer, Yale University, 1980-84; Assistant Professor, 1984-87, Associate Professor, 1987-91, Professor of Humanities, 1991-, Philadelphia College of the Performing Arts, later the University of the Arts, Philadelphia. Publications: Sexual Personae: Art and Decadence from Nefertiti to Emily Dickinson, 1990; Sex, Art, and American Culture: Essays, 1992; Vamps and Tramps: New Essays, 1994; Alfred Hitchcock's "The Birds", 1998. Contributions to: Journals and periodicals and Internet communications. Address: c/o Department of Liberal Arts, University of the Arts, 320 South Broad Street, Philadelphia, PA 19102, USA.

PAIGE Richard, See: **KOONTZ Dean R(ay)**.

PAIN Margaret, b. 27 Mar 1922, Woking, Surrey, England. Poet; Editor. Education: Business college. Appointment: Co-Editor, Weyfarers Magazine, 1978-97. Publications: Walking to Eleusis, 1967; No Dark Legend, 1977; A Fox in the Garden, 1979; Shadow Swordsman, 1988. Contributions to: Various anthologies, 1972-98, and other publications. Honours: 3rd Prize, 1977, Eleanor B North Award, 1st Prize, 1981, Surrey Poetry Centre Open Competition; Joint 3rd Prize, Lake Aske Memorial Award, 1977; 1st Prize, New Poetry Competition, 1978; Special Commendation, South East Arts Group Literary Prize, 1985. Membership: Surrey Poetry Society and Wey Poets, chairman, 1987-94. Address: Hilltop Cottage, 9 White Rose Lane, Woking, Surrey GU22 7JA, England.

PAINE Lauran Bosworth, b. 25 Feb 1916, Duluth, Minnesota, USA. Author. m. Mona Margarette Lewellyn, 26 June 1982, 1 son, 4 daughters. Education: Pacific Military Academy, 1930-32; St Alban's Episcopal School, 1932-34. Publications: Over 700 westerns, 1950-92, 79 mysteries, 1958-75, 119 romances, and non-fiction books. Address: 9413 North Highway 3, Fort Jones, CA 96032, USA.

PAINTER John, b. 22 Sept 1935, Bellingen, New South Wales, Australia. University Professor. m. Gillian Gray, 18 Jan 1963, 2 daughters. Education: ThL, Australian College of Theology; BD, University of London; PhD, Durham University. Appointments: Tutor, St John's College, Durham, 1965-68; Associate Professor, University of Cape Town, South Africa, 1971-76; Associate Professor, Reader, Latrobe University, Melbourne, Australia, 1977-97; Professor of Theology, Charles Sturt University, Canberra, Australia, 1998-. Publications: John Witness and Theologian, 1975; Theology and Hermeneutics: Rudolf Bultmann's Interpretation of the History of Jesus, 1987; The Quest for the Messiah, 1991, 2nd edition, 1993; Worlds in Conflict, 1997; Just James, The Brother of Jesus in History and Tradition, 1997. Contributions to: New Testament Studies; Journal for the Study of the New Testament; Scottish Journal of Theology. Honour: Fellow, Australian Academy of the Humanities, 1991. Memberships: SNTS, SBL, CBA. Address: PO Box 321, Jamison Centre, Macquarie, Australian Capital Territory 2614, Australia.

PAJOR Johnjoseph, b. 5 Feb 1948, South Bend, Indiana, USA. Poet. m. Cass Peters-Pajor, 18 Nov 1989, 3 sons, 1 daughter. Education: Technical colleges; Some university education. Appointments: Poetry readings, radio and cable TV broadcasts, 1965-98. Publications: Dies Faustus, revised edition, 1976; In Transit, 1978; A Collection of 3, 1979; Auditions, 1979; Traveler, 1979; African Violets, 1989; Challenger, 1990; Sacred Fire, 1990; Chiaroscuro, 1991; Wilderness: Land of the Raining Moon, 1991; A Brave Boy's Journeying, 1994; The Ten Books, 1997. Contributions to: Various journals and anthologies. Honour: Literary Honorarium, National Poetry Awards, 1978. Address: 848 51st Street, Port Townsend, WA 98368, USA.

PALAMIDESSI Christine Maria, (Christine Moore), b. 4 June 1954. m. Matthew Bagedonow, 8 Mar 1987, 1 daughter. Education: BA, University of Pittsburgh, 1973; Radcliffe College, 1987; MA, Boston University, 1990. Appointments: Cambridge Lieder and Opera Society, 1991-99; Peabody School, 1998. Publications: The Virgin Knows; Pineapple. Contributions to: New Video; Andy Warhol's Interview; New Woman; Italian-Americana. Honours: Urban Arts Award, 1988; Dante Alighieri Award, 1995. Membership: PEN America. Literary Agent: Anne Edelstein. Address: 310 Riverside Drive #181, New York, NY 10025, USA.

PALEY Grace, b. 11 Dec 1922, New York, New York, USA. Author; Poet; Retired University teacher. m. (1) Jess Paley, 20 June 1942, div, 1 son, 1 daughter, (2) Robert Nichols, 1972. Education: Hunter College, New York City, 1938-39; New York University. Appointments: Teacher, Columbia University, Syracuse University, Sarah Lawrence College, City College of the City University of New York. Publications: Fiction: The Little Disturbances of Man: Stories of Women and Men at

Love, 1968; Enormous Changes at the Last Minute, 1974; Later the Same Day, 1985; The Collected Stories, 1994. Poetry: Long Walks and Intimate Talks (includes stories), 1991; New and Collected Poems, 1992. Other: Leaning Forward, 1985; Three Hundred Sixty-Five Reasons Not to Have Another War: 1989 Peace Calender (with Vera B Williams), 1988; Just as I Thought, 1998. Contributions to: Books, anthologies and magazines. Honours: Guggenheim Fellowship, 1961; National Institute of Arts and Letters Award, 1970; Edith Wharton Citation of Merit as the first State Author of New York, New York State Writers Institute, 1986; National Endowment for the Arts Senior Fellowship, 1987; Vermont Governor's Award for Excellence in the Arts, 1993. Membership: American Academy of Arts and Letters. Address: Box 620, Thetford Hill, VT 05074, USA.

PALIN Michael (Edward), b. 5 May 1943, Sheffield, Yorkshire, England. Writer; Actor. m. Helen M Gibbins, 1966, 2 sons, 1 daughter. Education: BA, Brasenose College, Oxford, 1965. Appointments: Actor and Writer, Monty Python's Flying Circus, 1969-74, Ripping Yarns, 1976-80, BBC TV; Film Actor and Co-Screenwriter, And Now for Something Completely Different, 1970, Monty Python and the Holy Grail, 1974, Monty Python's Life of Brian, 1978, Time Bandits, 1980, Monty Python's "The Meaning of Life", 1982, Brazil, 1984, A Private Function, 1984, A Fish Called Wanda, 1988, American Friends, 1991, Fierce Creatures, 1997. Publications: Monty Python's Big Red Book, 1970; Monty Python's Brand New Book, 1973; Small Harry and the Toothache Pills, 1981; Dr Fegg's Encyclopaedia of All World Knowledge, 1984; Limericks, 1985; The Mirrorstone, 1986; The Cyril Stories, 1986; Around the World in Eighty Days, 1989; Pole to Pole, 1992; Pole to Pole: The Photographs, 1994; Hemingway's Chair, 1995; Full Circle, 1997; Full Circle: The Photographs, 1997. Honours: Best Supporting Film Actor, British Association of Film and Television Arts, 1988; Travel Writer of the Year, British Book Awards, 1993. Address: 34 Tavistock Street, London WC2E 7PB, England.

PALING Chris, b. 7 Dec 1956, Derby, England. Writer; Radio Producer. m. Julie Fiona, 18 Aug 1979, 1 son, 1 daughter. Education: Honours Degree, Economic History, Sussex University, 1975-78. Publications: After the Raid; Deserters; Morning All Day; The Silent Sentry. Contributions to: Literary Review; Punch; Independent Magazine; Spectator. Address: Deborah Rogers, Rogers, Coleridge & White, 20 Powis Mews, London, W11 1JN, England.

PALLEY Julian, b. 16 Sept 1925, Atlantic City, New Jersey, USA. Professor of Spanish Literature; Poet; Translator. m. Shirley Wilson, 17 Sept 1950, 4 sons. Education: BA, Mexico City College, 1950; MA, Spanish, University of Arizona, 1952; PhD, Romance Languages, University of New Mexico, 1958. Appointments: Instructor, Rutgers University, 1956-59; Associate Professor, Arizona State University, 1959-62, University of Oregon, 1962-66; Professor of Spanish Literature, University of California at Irvine, 1966-. Publications: Spinoza's Stone, 1976; Bestiary, 1987; Pictures at an Exhibition, 1989; Family Portraits, 1994. Other: Several translations. Contributions to: Reviews, quarterlies, and journals. Honours: Arizona Quarterly Poetry Prize, 1956; Jefferson Poetry Prize, 1976. Membership: California State Poetry Society. Address: c/o Department of Spanish and Portuguese, University of California at Irvine, Irvine, CA 92697, USA.

PALMER (George) Michael, b. 11 May 1943, New York, New York, USA. Poet; Writer; Translator. Education: MA in Comparative Literature, Harvard University, 1968; University of Florence. Appointments: Various visiting lectureships at colleges and universities. Publications: Blake's Newton, 1972; The Circular Gates, 1974; Without Music, 1977; Notes for Echo Lake, 1981; Code of Signals: Recent Writings in Poetics (editor), 1983; First Figure, 1984; SUN, 1988; The Surrealists Look at Art (translator with Norma Cole), 1990; Palmer/Davidson: Poets and Critics Respond to the Poetry of Michael Palmer and Michael Davidson (P Michael Campbell, editor), 1992; An Alphabet Underground/Underjordisk Alfabet, 1993; At Passages, 1995. Contributions to: Many anthologies, books and journals. Address: c/o New Directions Publishing Corp, 80 Eighth Avenue, New York, NY 10011, USA.

PALMER Alan Warwick, b. 28 Sept 1926, Ilford, Essex, England. Retired Schoolmaster; Writer. m. Veronica Mary Cordell, 1 Sept 1951. Education: MA, 1950, MLitt, 1954, Oriel College, Oxford. Publications: Alexander I, Tsar of War and Peace, 1974; The Chancelleries of Europe, 1982; Crowned Cousins: The Anglo-German Royal Connection, 1986; The East End, 1989; Bernadotte: Napoleon's Marshal, Sweden's King, 1990; The Penguin Dictionary of Twentieth Century History, 4th edition, 1990; The Decline and Fall of the Ottoman Empire, 1992; Twilight of the Hapsburgs, 1994; Dictionary of the British Empire and Commonwealth, 1996. Contributions to: Journals. Memberships: International PEN; Royal Society of Literature, fellow. Address: 4 Farm End, Woodstock, Oxford OX20 1XN, England.

PALMER Diana. See: **KYLE Susan (Eloise Spaeth).**

PALMER Frank Robert, b. 9 Apr 1922, Westerleigh, Gloucestershire, England. Retired Professor; Linguist; Writer. m. Jean Elisabeth Moore, 1948, 3 sons, 2 daughters. Education: MA, New College, Oxford, 1948; Graduate Studies, Merton College, Oxford, 1948-49. Appointments: Lecturer in Linguistics, School of Oriental and African Studies, University of London, 1950-52, 1953-60; Professor of Linguistics, University College of North Wales, Bangor, 1960-65; Professor and Head, Department of Linguistic Science, 1965-87, Dean, Faculty of Letters and Social Sciences, 1969-72, University of Reading. Publications: The Morphology of the Tigre Noun, 1962; A Linguistic Study of the English Verb, 1965; Selected Papers of J R Firth, 1951-1958 (editor), 1968; Prosodic Analysis (editor), 1970; Grammar, 1971, 2nd edition, 1984; The English Verb, 1974, 2nd edition, 1987; Semantics, 1976, 2nd edition, 1981; Modality and the English Modals, 1979, 2nd edition, 1990; Mood and Modality, 1986; Grammatical Roles and Relations, 1994. Contributions to: Professional journals. Memberships: Academia Europaea; British Academy, fellow; Linguistic Society of America; Philological Society. Address: Whitethorns, Roundabout Lane, Winnersh, Wokingham, Berkshire RG41 5AD, England.

PALMER John, b. 13 May 1943, Sydney, Nova Scotia, Canada. Playwright; Director. Education: BA, English, Carleton University, Ottawa, Canada, 1965. Appointments: Dramaturge, Associate, Factory Theatre Lab, Toronto, 1970-73; Co-Founder, Co-Artistic Director, Literary Manager, Toronto Free Theatre, 1972-76; Resident Playwright, Canadian Repertory Theatre, Toronto, 1983-87, National Theatre School of Canada, 1993-94; Course Director, Final Year Playwrighting, York University, Toronto, 1991-93. Publications: 2 Plays: The End, and A Day at the Beach, 1991; Before the Guns, Memories for my Brother, Part I, Dangerous Traditions: Four Passe-Muraille Plays, 1992; Henrik Ibsen On the Necessity of Producing Norwegian Drama, 1992-93; Selected Plays. Contributions to: Various publications. Address: 32 Monteith Street, Toronto, Ontario M4Y 1K7, Canada.

PALMER Leslie (Howard), b. 25 Jan 1941, Memphis, Tennessee, USA. Professor of Literature; Poet; Writer. m. 27 Aug 1965, 1 son, 1 daughter. Education: BA, University of Memphis, 1962; MA, 1963, PhD, 1966, University of Tennessee, Knoxville. Appointments: Instructor, University of Tennessee, 1966-67; Professor of Literature, University of North Texas, Denton, 1967-. Publications: Ten Poems, 1980; A Red Sox Flag, 1983; Ode to a Frozen Dog, and Other Poems, 1992; Artemis' Bow, 1993; The Devil Sells Ice Cream, 1994; The Jim Tom Poems, 1996. Contributions to: Numerous anthologies, reviews, quarterlies, journals, and magazines. Honours: Beaudoin Gemstone Awards, 1962, 1963; Midsouth Poetry Award, 1963; Pushcart Prize Nomination, 1984; Cape Rock Poetry Award, 1990. Memberships: Coda; Modern Humanities Research Association; Modern Language Association; PEN. Address: 1905 West Oak, Denton, TX 76201, USA.

PALMER Peter John, b. 20 Sept 1932, Melbourne, Victoria, Australia. Writer. m. Elizabeth Fischer, 22 Dec 1955, 1 son, 1 daughter. Education: BA, 1953, BEd, 1966, University of Melbourne. Publications: The Past and Us, 1957; The Twentieth Century, 1964; Earth and Man, 1980; Man on the Land, 1981; Man and Machines, 1983; Macmillan Australian Atlas (executive editor), 1983, 4th edition, 1993; Challenge, 1985; Geography 10 (author, illustrator), 1992. Editor, contributor, illustrator: Confrontation, 1971; Interaction, 1974; Expansion, 1975; Survival, 1976; Three Worlds, 1978. Address: 34 Ardgower Court, Lower Templestowe, Victoria 3107, Australia.

PALMER Tony, b. 29 Aug 1941, London, England. Film, Theatre, Opera, and Television Director; Writer. Education: Lowestoft Grammar School. Appointments: Director, 1968-; Presenter, Night Waves, R3, 1994-. Publications: Born Under a Bad Sign, 1970; Trials of Oz, 1971; Electric Revolution, 1972; Biography of Liberace, 1976; All You Need is Love, 1976; Charles II, 1979; A Life on the Road, 1982; Menuhin: A Family Portrait, 1991. Honours: Numerous awards as a director. Address: Nanjizal, St Levan, Cornwall TR19 6JH, England.

PALMOVA Violeta. See: **SEMYONOVA Violeta.**

PALOMINO JIMENEZ Angel, b. 2 Aug 1929, Toledo, Spain. Writer; Poet. Education: Linguistics, Science, and Chemistry, Central University, Madrid. Publications: Numerous novels, short stories, essays, and poems, 1957-98. Contributions to: Journals. Honours: International Prize, Press Club, 1966; Miguel de Cervantes National Literary Prize, 1971; Finalist, Planeta Prize, 1977. Memberships: International Association of Literary Critics; International Federation of Tourism Writers; National Academy of Astronomy; Royal Academy of Fine Arts and Historical Sciences; Spanish Association of Book Writers. Address: Conde de Penalver 17, 28006, Madrid, Spain.

PALSSON Sigurdur, b. 30 July 1948, Skinnastadur, Iceland. Theatre and Television Director; Writer; Poet; Translator. m. Kristin Johannesdottir, 26 June 1987, 1 son. Education: BA, 1967, DUEL Libre, 1972, Maîtrise libre, 1980, DEA, 1982, Institut d'Études Théâtrales, Sorbonne, University of Paris; Diploma, Film Direction, CLCF, Paris, 1978. Publications: Ljod vega salt, 1975; Ljod vega menn, 1980; Ljod vega gerd; Ljod namu land, 1985; Ljod namu menn, 1988; Ljod namu vold, 1990; Ljodlinudans, 1993; Ljodlinuskip, 1995; Ljodlinuspil, 1997; Võlundarhus, 1997; Parisarhjol, 1998. Contributions to: Various publications. Honour: Chevalier de l'Ordre des Arts et des Lettres, Ministre de la Culture, France, 1989. Memberships: Alliance Française of Iceland, president, 1976-77; PEN Club of Iceland, board of directors, 1983-; Union of Icelandic Theatre Directors; Writers Union of Iceland, chairman, 1984-88. Address: Mavahlid 38, 105 Reykjavík, Iceland

PANICHAS George Andrew, b. 21 May 1930, Springfield, Massachusetts, USA. Educator; Literary Critic; Scholar. Education: BA, American International College, 1951; MA, Trinity College, Hartford, Connecticut, 1952; PhD, University of Nottingham, 1962. Appointments: Instructor, Assistant/Associate Professor, Professor of English, University of Maryland, 1962-. Editor, Modern Age, quarterly review; Advisory editor, Continuity, history journal. Publications: Adventure in Consciousness: The Meaning of D H Lawrence's Religious Quest, 1964; Renaissance and Modern Essays (co-editor), 1966; Epicurus, 1967; The Reverent Discipline: Essays in Literary Criticism and Culture, 1974; The Burden of Vision: Dostoevsky's Spiritual Art, 1977; The Courage of Judgement: Essays in Literary Criticism, Culture and Society, 1983; Editor of numerous books. Contributions to: Books and journals. Honours: Royal Society of Arts, UK, fellow, 1971-; Grant, Earhart Foundation, 1982. Address: Department of English,

University of Maryland, College Park, MD 20742, USA.

PANIKER Ayyappa, b. 12 Sept 1930, Kavalam, India. Retired Professor of English; Poet; Writer; Editor; Translator. m. Sreeparvathy Paniker, 1961, 2 daughters. Education: BA, Honours, Travancore University, 1951; MA, Kerala University, 1959; CTE, Hyderabad, 1966; MA, PhD, 1971, Indiana University. Appointments: Lecturer, 1951-73, Reader, 1973-80, Professor of English and Head, Department of English, 1980-90, University of Kerala; Chief Editor, Medieval Indian Literature, 1990-94; Birla Fellowship, 1994-96; UNESCO Subcommission for Culture. Publications: Numerous books, including: Ayyappa Panikerude Kritikal I, 1974, II, 1982, III, 1990; Ayyappa Panikerude Lekhanangal I, 1982, II, 1990; Selected Poems, 1985; Mayakovskiyude Kavitakal, 1987; Gotrayanam, 1989; Avatarikakal, 1993; Medieval Indian Literature (editor), 1998; Madhyakala Malayala Karuta, 1998. Contributions to: Many anthologies, books, reviews, quarterlies, journals, and magazines. Honours: Kerala Sahitya Akademi Award, 1975; Kalyani Krishna Menon Prize, 1977; Central Sahitya Akademi Award, 1984; Asan Prize, 1991; Muscat Award, Kerala Cultural Centre, 1992; Sahitya Parishad Award, 1993; Indira Gandhi Fellowship, 1997-99; Kabir Prize, 1997; Gandadhar Meher Award, 1998. Memberships: National Book Trust; National Literacy Mission; Sahitya Akademi. Address: 111 Gandhi Nagar, Trivandrum 695014, India.

PANIKER Salvador, b. 1 Mar 1927, Barcelona, Spain. Publisher; Writer. Education: Lic Philos; Doctor of Industrial Engineering. Publications: Conversaciones en Cataluna, 1966; Los Signos y las Cosas, 1968; Conversaciones en Madrid, 1969; La Dificultad de Ser Español, 1979; Aproximacion al Origen, 1982; Primer Testamento, 1985; Ensayos retroprogresivos, 1987; Segunda Memoria, 1988; Lectura de los Griegos, 1992. Contributions to: La Vanguardia; El País; Revista de Occidente. Honour: International Press Prize, 1969. Address: Numancia 117-121, Barcelona 08029, Spain.

PANNENBERG Wolfhart (Ulrich), b. 2 Oct 1928, Stettin, Germany. Professor of Systematic Theology (Retired); Author. m. Hilke Sabine Schütte, 3 May 1954. Education: ThD, University of Heidelberg, 1953. Appointments: Ordained Lutheran Minister, 1955; Privatdozent, University of Heidelberg, 1955-58; Professor of Systematic Theology, University of Wuppertal, 1958-61, University of Mainz, 1961-67; Professor of Systematic Theology and Head of the Institute of Ecumenical Theology, University of Munich, 1967-94; Several visiting professorships. Publications: Offenbarung als Geschichte, 1961, English translation as Revelation as History, 1969; Was ist der Mensch?: Die Anthropologie der Gegenwart im Lichte der Theologie, 1962, English translation as What is Man?, 1970; Grundzüge der Christologie, 1964, English translation as Jesus: God and Man, 1968; Grundfragen systematischer Theologie, 2 volumes, 1967, 1980, English translation as Basic Questions in Theology, 2 volumes, 1970-71; Theology and the Kingdom of God, 1969; Spirit, Faith and Church (with Carl E Braaten and Avery Dulles), 1970; Thesen zur Theologie der Kirche, 1970;Das Glaubensbekenntnis, 1972, English translation as The Apostles' Creed in the Light of Today's Questions, 1972; Gottesgedanke und menschliche Freiheit, 1972, English translation as The Idea of God and Human Freedom, 1973; Wissenschaftstheorie und Theologie, 1973, English translation as Theology and the Philosophy of Science, 1976; Glaube und Wirklichkeit, 1975, English translation as Faith and Reality, 1977; Ethik und Ekklesiologie, 1977, English translation, 1983; Human Nature, Election and History, 1977; Anthropologie in Theologischer Perspektive, 1983, English translation as Anthropology in Theological Perspective, 1985; Christian Spirituality, 1983; Lehvererurteilungen-kirchentrennend? (with Karl Lehmann), I-III, 1986-90; Christenum in Einer Säkularisierten Welt, 1988, English translation as Christianity in a Secularized World, 1989; Systematische Theologie, 3 volumes, 1988-93, English translation as Systematic Theology, 3 volumes, 1991-97; Metaphysik und Gottesgedanke, 1988, English translation as Metaphysics and the Idea of God, 1990; An Introduction to Systematic Theology, 1991; Toward a Theology of Nature: Essays on Science and Faith, 1993; Grundlagen der Ethik, 1996; Theologie und Philosophie, 1996; Problemgeschichte der neureren Evangelischen Theologie in Deutschland, 1997. Contributions to: Scholarly books and journals. Honours: Honorary doctorates, University of Glasgow, 1972, University of Manchester, 1977, Trinity College, Dublin, 1979, University of St Andrews, Scotland, 1993; University of Cambridge, 1997. Memberships: Bavarian Academy of Sciences; British Academy, fellow. Address: Sudetenstrasse 8, 82166 Gräfelfing, Germany.

PANYCH Morris (Stephen), b. 30 June 1952, Calgary, Alberta, Canada. Dramatist; Writer; Actor; Director. Education: Radio and Television Arts, NAIT, Edmonton, 1971-73; BFA, University of British Columbia, 1977. Publications: Last Call, 1983; 7 Stories, 1990; The Ends of the Earth, 1993; Other Schools of Thought, 1994; Vigil, 1995. Honours: 6 Jessie Awards, Vancouver Theatre; Governor-General's Award for English Drama, 1994. Address: c/o Christopher Banks and Associates, 6 Adelaide Street East, Suite 610, Toronto, Ontario, Canada M5C 1H6.

PAOLUCCI Anne (Attura), b. Rome, Italy. Retired Professor of English; Poet; Writer; Dramatist; Editor. m. Henry Paolucci. Education: BA, English Literature and Creative Writing, Barnard College, 1947; MA, Italian Literature, 1950, PhD, English and Comparative Literature, 1963, Columbia University. Appointments: Instructor, 1959-61, Assistant Professor, 1961-69, City College of the City University of New York; Fulbright Lecturer, University of Naples, 1965-67; Research Professor, 1969-75, Professor of English, 1969-97, Chair, Department of English, 1974-75, 1982-91, Director, Doctor of Arts Degree Program in English, 1982-96, St John's University, Jamaica, New York; Founder, Publisher, and Editor-in-Chief, Review of National Literatures, 1970-; Founder-President, Council on National Literatures, 1974-. Publications: Poetry: Poems Written for Sbek's Mummies, Marie Menken, and Other Important People, Places, and Things, 1977; Riding the Mast Where It Swings, 1980; Gorbachev in Concert (and Other Poems), 1991; Queensboro Bridge (and Other Poems), 1995. Fiction: Eight Short Stories, 1977; Sepia Tones: Seven Short Stories, 1985; Terminal Degrees, 1997. Non-Fiction: Hegel on Tragedy (with Henry Paolucci), 1962; A Short History of American Drama, 1966; Eugene O'Neills, Arthur Miller, Edward Albee, 1967; From Tension to Tonic: The Plays of Edward Albee, 1972; Pirandello's Theater: The Recovery of the Stage for Dramatic Art, 1974; Dante and the 'Quest for Eloquence' in the Vernacular Languages of India (with Henry Paolucci), 1984. Plays: Minions of the Race, 1978; Cipango!, 1986. Editor: Dante's Influence on American Writers, 1977. Contributions to: Numerous books, reviews, and journals. Honours: Fulbright Scholarship, Italy, 1951-52; Woodbridge Honorary Fellowship, Columbia University, 1961-62; Writer-in-Residence, Yaddo, 1965; American Council of Learned Societies Grant, 1978; Cavaliere, 1986, Commendatore, 1992, Order of Merit, Italy; Gold Medal, Canada, 1991; Honorary Degree in Humane Letters, Lehman College of the City University of New York, 1995. Memberships: American Comparative Literature Association; City University of New York, board of trustees, 1996-, chairwoman, 1997-; Dante Society of America; Dramatists Guild; Hegel Society of America; International Comparative Literature Association; Modern Language Association; PEN American Center; Pirandello Society of America, president, 1972-95; Renaissance Association of America; Renaissance Institute of America; Shakespeare Association of America; World Centre for Shakespeare Studies. Address: 166 25 Powells Cove Boulevard, Beechhurst, NY 11357, USA.

PAPAGEORGIOU Kostas, b. 4 July 1945, Athens, Greece. Poet; Writer; Editor. Education: Law Diploma, 1968; Literature, Philology, University of Athens, 1969-72. Appointment: Editor, Grammata ke Technes. Publications: Several poetry and prose volumes, 1966-. Contributions to: Various publications. Membership: Greek Authors Union. Address: Kerasountos 8, 11528 Athens, Greece.

PAPAKOU-LAGOU Avgi, b. 1923, Phthiotida, Greece. Writer; Poet; Dramatist. Education: Pedagogical Academy, Lamia. Publications: Novels: The Father's Secret, 1980; The Forest and its World, 1986; Don't Cry My Little One, 1988; Theodora, the Princess from Trebizond, 1994; The Kiss of Life, 1998. Other: Various short stories, fairy tales, poems, and plays, 1962-98. Honours: Penelope Delta Award, Children's Book Circle of Greece; Evgenia Kleidara Prize, Aeolian Letters. Memberships: Children's Book Circle of Greece; Greek Folklore Society; Society of Greek Authors; Union of Authors and Illustrators of Greek Children's Books. Address: 121 Pandossias Street, North Ionia, GR-14232 Athens, Greece.

PAPALEO Joseph, b. 13 Jan 1926, New York, New York, USA. Professor of Literature and Writing; Writer. m. 4 sons. Education: BA, Sarah Lawrence College, 1949; Diploma di Profitto, University of Florence, Italy, 1951; MA, Columbia University, 1952. Appointments: Teacher, Fieldston Prep School, 1952-60; Professor, Literature and Writing, Sarah Lawrence College, 1960-68, 1969-92; Guest Professor, Laboratorio de Cibernetica, Naples, Italy, 1968-69. Publications: All the Comforts (novel), 1968; Out of Place (novel), 1971; Picasso at Ninety One, 1988; Other: Several short stories. Contributions to: Journals and magazines. Honours: Guggenheim Fellowship, 1974; Ramapo College Poetry Prize, 1986. Memberships: Authors Guild; Italian American Writers Association; American Association of University Professors. Address: 60 Puritan Avenue, Yonkers, NY 10710, USA.

PAPANIKOLAOU Miltiades, b. 8 Jan 1947, Grevena, Greece. Professor of History of Art. m. Sophia Halkidou, 10 Oct 1980, 1 daughter. Education: Modern Greek Literature and Archaeology, Univeristy of Thessaloniki, 1972; History of Art, University of Munich. Appointments: Professor, History of Art, 1987, Director, Archaeological Section, 1995, Head, Department of History and Archaeology, 1997, University of Thessaloniki. Publications: Greek Genre Painting in the 19th Century, 1978; German Painters in Greece in the 19th Century, 1981; The Portrait Collection of the University of Thessaloniki, 1985; The Blue Horse: Essays on Art History and Criticism, 1995; Loukas Venetoulias: A Monograph, 1998; Giorgos Lasongas: A Monograph, 1998. Contributions to: Kathimerini; Zygos; Arti; Eikastika. Honour: Stiftung Alexander von Humboldt. Membership: AICA. Address: 9 Ziaka Str, Thessaloniki, 55134, Greece.

PAPAS William, b. 1927, South Africa. Author. Education: South Africa; Beckham, England. Appointments: Formerly Cartoonist, The Guardian, The Sunday Times Newspapers, Punch Magazine; Book Illustrator, Painter, Print Maker. Publications: The Press, 1964; The Story of Mr Nero, 1965; The Church, 1965; Parliament, 1966; Freddy the Fell-Engine, 1966; The Law, 1967; Tasso, 1967; No Mules, 1967; Taresh, the Tea Planter, 1968; A Letter from India, 1968; A Letter from Israel, 1968; Theodore, or, The Mouse Who Wanted to Fly, 1969; Elias the Fisherman, 1970; The Monk and the Goat, 1971; The Long-Haired Donkey, 1972; The Most Beautiful Child, 1973; The Zoo, 1974; People of Old Jerusalem, 1980; Papas' America, 1986; Papas' Portland, 1994. Membership: Savage Club, London. Address: 422 North West 8th Avenue, Portland, OR 97209, USA.

PAPASTRATU Danae, b. 20 Mar 1936, Patras, Greece. Author; Journalist. Education: Diploma, Law, University of Athens, 1959; Greek-American Institute, 1965; Sorbonne, University of Paris, 1969. Appointments: Protevoussa Journal; News of Municipalitis; Collector Magazine; Nautical Greece; Editor, Perigramma Magazine. Publications: Travels with the Polar Book, 1978; A vol d'oiseau, 1979; We Will See in Philippi, 1981; Without Periphrasis (poems), 1981; An Essay about Poetry, 1983; Diadromes sto Horo and Hrono (travel book), 1989; Anichnefsis (essays), 1992; A Little Odyssey - Translation; Human Orizons, 1996; The Trial of

Pythagoras, translation from the poem by William Davey, 1998. Contributions to: Many publications. Honour: Literary Doctorate from the W. Academy of Arts and Culture. Memberships: Society of Greek Writers. Address: Bouboulinas 1a, Hilioupolis 16345, Athens, Greece.

PAPINEAU David Calder, b. 30 Sept 1947, Como, Italy. Philosopher. m. Rose Wild, 6 July 1986, 1 son, 1 daughter. Education: BSc, Honours, University of Natal, 1967; BA, Honours, 1970, PhD, University of Cambridge. Appointment: Professor, King's College, London, 1990-. Publications: For Science in the Social Sciences, 1978; Theory and Meaning, 1979; Reality and Representation, 1987; Philosophical Naturalism, 1993. Membership: British Society for the Philosophy of Science, president, 1993-95. Address: Department of Philosophy, King's College, London WC2R 2LS, England.

PARATODOS Vyday Akrasiap. See: **ALVAREZ FERRERAS Felix.**

PARATTE Henri-Dominique, (Ti-Pique le Madouesse), b. 19 Mar 1950, Berne, Switzerland. Professor; Writer; Translator; Journalist. m. Genevieve Houet, 1974; Partner, Martine L Jacquet, 1981; 2 sons, 1 daughter. Education: Licence ès lettres, 1969; Maîtrise, Strasbourg, 1970; Doctorat IIIe cycle, Lille, 1974; Certified Translator, ATINS, 1992; Certified Literary Translator, Canada Council, 1986. Appointments: Jury, Prix Suisse-Canada, 1980-85; Editor, Swiss-French Studies, 1980-86; Literary Editor, Les Editions du Grand-Pré, 1984-97; Editorial board of various journals; Juries, Canada Council; Chair, Canadian Status of the Artist Federal Commission, 1986-92; President, Société de la Presse Acadienne, 1996-97; Board Member, cultural organizations. Publications: Virgée Tantra Non Arpadar, 1972; La Mer Ecartelée, 1979; Jura-Acadie, 1980; Dis-Moi la Nuit, 1982; Cheval des Iles, 1984; Alexandre Voisard, 1985; Anne: la maison aux pignons verts, 1987; Acadians, 1991, reprinted, 1997; Confluences, 1996. Contributions to: Eloizes; Ecriture; Ven'd'Est; Rivière; Feux Chalins; Poésie-USA; Littèréalite; Envols; Mensuel 25; Etudes Irlandaises; Cahiers Ramu; Various anthologies. Honours: Literary Awards, Canton de Berne, Switzerland, 1972, 1979; Honorable Mention, John Glassco Award, 1985. Memberships: Writers' Federation of Nova Scotia, executive member, 1979-82; Association des Ecrivains Acadiens, executive, 1980-85, president, 1985-87; Conseil Culturel Acadien de la Nouvelle-Ecosse, president, 1993-95; Association des Artistes Acadiens de la Nouvelle-Ecosse, president, 1992-96. Address: 298 Acadia University, Wolfville, Nova Scotia B0P 1X0, Canada.

PARES Marion, (Judith Campbell, Anthony Grant), b. 7 Nov 1914, West Farleigh, Kent, England. Writer. m. Humphrey Pares, 5 June 1937, 4 daughters. Publications: Family Pony, 1962; The Queen Rides, 1965; Horses in the Sun, 1966; Police Horse, 1967; World of Horses, 1969; World of Ponies, 1970; Anne: Portrait of a Princess, 1970; Family on Horseback (with N Toyne), 1971; Princess Anne and Her Horses, 1971; Elizabeth and Philip, 1972; The Campions, 1973; Royalty on Horseback, 1974; The World of Horses, 1975; Anne and Mark, 1976; Queen Elizabeth II, 1979; The Mutant, 1980; Charles: A Prince of His Time, 1980; The Royal Partners, 1982; Royal Horses, 1983; Address: c/o A M Heath Ltd, 79 St Martin's Lane, London WC2N 4AA, England.

PARFITT Joanna Elizabeth, b. 25 Mar 1961, Peterborough, England. Writer. m. 19 Dec 1987, 2 sons. Education: BA, Honours, French Studies, Hull University, 1983. Appointments: Freelance Writer, 1985-; Proprietor, Owner, Computer Training Company, 1986-91. Publications: French Tarts, 1985; Wordstar 2000, 1986; Word Perfect, 1986; Mastering Word Processing Easily into Desktop Publishing, 1987; Master Pagemaker, 1988; Master Ventura, 1988; Easily into WordStar 2000, 1989; Easily into WordStar 1512, 1989; Easily into Multimate, 1989; Easily into DisplayWrite 4 1989; Dates, 1996; A Career in Your Suitcase, 1998; Forced to Fly, 1998. Contributions to: Rsident Abroad; The Independent on Sunday; Smart Moves, Shoreline; Oman Today; Emitates Woman, What's On; The European, Golden Falcon; Ceramics Monthly; SilverKris. Address: Longacre, 16 Main Road, Collyweston, Stamford, Lincolnshire, PE9 3PF, England.

PARINI Jay (Lee), b. 2 Apr 1948, Pittston, Pennsylvania, USA. Professor of English; Author; Poet; Literary Critic. m. Devon Stacey Jersild, 21 June 1981, 3 sons. Education: AB, Lafayette College, 1970; PhD, University of St Andrews, Scotland, 1975. Appointments: Faculty, Dartmouth College, 1975-82; Co-Founder, New England Review, 1976; Professor of English, Middlebury College, 1982-. Publications: Novels: The Love Run, 1980; The Patch Boys, 1986; The Last Station, 1990; Bay of Arrows, 1992; Benjamin's Crossing, 1997. Poetry: Singing in Time, 1972; Anthracite Country, 1982; Town Life, 1988; House of Days, 1988. Other: Theodore Roothke: An American Romantic, 1979; An Invitation to Poetry, 1988; John Steinbeck: A Biography, 1995; Some Necessary Angels (essays), 1998. Editor: Gore Vidal: Writer Against the Grain, 1992; The Columbia History of American Poetry, 1993; The Columbia Anthology of American Poetry, 1995; The Norton Book of American Autobiography, 1999. Address: Route 1, Box 195, Middlebury, VT 05753, USA.

PARIS Bernard Jay, b. 19 Aug 1931, Baltimore, Maryland, USA. Retired Professor of English; Writer. m. Shirley Helen Freedman, 1 Apr 1949, 1 son, 1 daughter. Education: AB, 1952, PhD, 1959, Johns Hopkins University. Appointments: Instructor, Lehigh University, 1956-60; Assistant Professor, 1960-64, Associate Professor, 1964-67, Professor, 1967-81, Michigan State University; Professor of English, University of Florida, 1981-96; Director, Institute for Psychological Study of the Arts, 1985-92, International Karen Horney Society, 1991-. Publications: Experiments in Life: George Eliot's Quest for Values, 1965; A Psychological Approach to Fiction: Studies in Thackeray, Stendhal, George Eliot, Dostoevsky and Conrad, 1974; Character and Conflict in Jane Austen's Novels, 1978; Third Force Psychology and the Study of Literature (editor), 1986; Shakespeare's Personality (co-editor), 1989; Bargains with Fate: Psychological Crises and Conflicts in Shakespeare and His Plays, 1991; Character as a Subversive Force in Shakespeare: The History and the Roman Plays, 1991; Karen Horney: A Psychoanalyst's Search for Self-Understanding, 1994; Imagined Human Beings: A Psychological Approach to Character and Conflict in Literature, 1997; The Therapeutic Process by Karen Horney (editor), 1999. Contributions to: Numerous scholarly and literary journals. Honours: Phi Beta Kappa, 1952; National Endowment for the Humanities Fellow, 1969; Guggenheim Fellowship, 1974.Memberships: Modern Language Association of America; Association for the Advancement of Psychoanalysis, honorary member; American Academy of Psychoanalysis, scientific associate. Address: 1430 North West 94th Street, Gainesville, FL 32606, USA.

PARISI Joseph (Anthony), b. 18 Nov 1944, Duluth, Minnesota, USA. Editor; Writer; Administrator; Consultant. Education: BA, Honours, English, College of St Thomas, St Paul, Minnesota, 1966; MA, English, 1967, PhD, Honours, English, 1973, University of Chicago. Appointments: Instructor to Assistant Professor of English, Roosevelt University, Chicago, 1969-78; Associate Editor, 1976-83, Acting Editor, 1983-85, Editor, 1985-, Poetry Magazine, Chicago; Visiting and Adjunct Assistant Professor of English, University of Illinois at Chicago, 1978-87; Consultant, American Library Association, 1980-; Chair, Ruth Lilly Poetry Prize, 1986-, and Fellowships, 1989-; Producer, Writer, and Host, Poets in Person, National Public Radio, 1991; Executive Director, Modern Poetry Association, 1996-. Publications: The Poetry Anthology, 1912-1977: Sixty-five Years of America's Most Distinguished Verse Magazine (editor with Daryl Hine), 1978; Voices & Visions: Viewer's Guide, 1987; Marianne Moore: The Art of a Modernist (editor), 1989; Poets in Person: Listener's Guide, 1992, 2nd edition, revised and expanded, 1997. Contributions to: Reference books, scholarly journals, and literary publications. Address: 3440 North Lake Shore Drive, Chicago, IL 60657, USA.

PARK (Rosina) Ruth (Lucia), b. Australia. Author; Playwright. Publications: The Uninvited Guest (play), 1948; The Harp in the South, 1948; Poor Man's Orange, US edition as 12 and a Half Plymouth Street), 1949; The Witch's Thorn, 1951; A Power of Roses, 1953; Pink Flannel, 1955; The Drums Go Bang (autobiographical with D'Arcy Niland), 1956; *One-a-Pecker, Two-a-Pecker*, US edition as The Frost and the Fire, 1961; The Good Looking Women, 1961; The Ship's Cat, 1961, US edition as Serpent's Delight, 1962; Uncle Matt's Mountain, 1962; The Road to Christmas, 1962; The Road Under the Sea, 1962; The Muddle-Headed Wombat series, 11 volumes, 1962-76; The Hole in the Hill, US edition as The Secret of the Maori Cave, 1964; Shaky Island, 1962; Airlift for Grandee, 1964; Ring for the Sorcerer, 1967; The Sixpenny Island, US edition as Ten-Cent Island, 1968; Nuki and the Sea Serpent, 1969; The Companion Guide to Sydney, 1973; Callie's Castle, 1974; The Gigantic Balloon, 1975; Swords and Crowns and Rings, 1977; Come Danger, Come Darkness, 1978; Playing Beatie Bow, 1980; When the Wind Changed, 1980; The Big Brass Key, 1983; The Syndey We Love, 1983; Missus, 1985; My Sister Sif, 1986; The Tasmania We Love, 1987; Callie's Family: James, 1991; A Fence Around the Cuckoo, 1992; Fishing in the Styx, 1993; Home Before Dark, 1995. Address: c/o Curtis Brown Pty Ltd, PO Box 19, Paddington, New South Wales 2021, Australia.

PARKER Franklin, b. 2 June 1921, New York, New York, USA. Professor of Education Emeritus; Writer. m. Betty Parker, 12 June 1950. Education: BA, Berea College, 1949; MS, University of Illinois, 1950; EdD, Peabody College of Vanderbilt University, 1956. Appointments: Librarian, Ferrum College, Virginia, 1950-52, Belmont College, Nashville, 1952-54, George Peabody College for Teachers, Vanderbilt University, 1955-56; Associate Professor of Education, State University of New York at New Paltz, 1956-57, University of Texas at Austin, 1957-64; Professor of Education, University of Oklahoma, 1964-68; Benedum Professor of Education, 1968-86, Professor Emeritus, 1986-, West Virginia University, Morgantown; Distinguished Visiting Professor, Northern Arizona University, 1986-89, Western Carolina University, 1989-94. Publications: African Development and Education in Southern Rhodesia, 1960, 2nd edition, 1974; Africa South of the Sahara, 1966; George Peabody: A Biography, 1971, revised edition, 1995; The Battle of the Books: Kanawha Country, 1975; What Can We Learn from the Schools of China?, 1977; British Schools and Ours, 1979. Co-Author: John Dewey: Master Educator, 2nd edition, revised, 1961; Government Policy and International Education, 1965; Church and State in Education, 1966; Strategies for Curriculum Change: Cases from 13 Nations, 1968; Dimensions of Physical Education, 1969; International Education: Understandings and Misunderstandings, 1969; *Understanding the American Public High School*, 1969; Education in Southern Africa, 1970; Curriculum for Man in an International World, 1971; Administrative Dimensions of Health and Physical Education Programs, Including Athletics, 1971; Education and the Many Faces of the Disadvantaged, 1972; The Saber-Tooth Curriculum, 1972; Accelerated Development in Southern Africa, 1974; Myth and Reality: A Reader in Education, 1975; Six Questions: Controversy and Conflict in Education, 1975; Crucial Issues in Education, 6th edition, revised, 1977; Censorship and Education, 1981; Academic Profiles in Higher Education, 1993. Editor: American Dissertations on Foreign Education: A Bibliography with Abstracts, 20 volumes, 1971-90; Education in Puerto Rico and of Puerto Ricans in the USA (with Betty June Parker), 2 volumes, 1978, 1984; Women's Education: A World View: Annotated Bibliography of Doctoral Dissertations, 2 volumes, 1979, 1981; US Higher Education: A Guide to Information Sources, 1980; Education in the People's Republic of China, Past and Present: Annotated Bibliography, 1986; Education in England and Wales: An Annotated

Bibliography. Contributions to: Reference works, books and professional journals, three articles in Tennessee Encyclopaedia, Tennessee Historical Society, 1998; Six biographical articles on prominent educators in American National Biography, forthcoming. Honours: Fulbright Senior Research Fellow, 1961-62; Distinguished Alumnus Award, Peabody College of Vanderbilt University, 1970, Berea College, 1989. Memberships: African Studies Association; American Academy of Political and Social Sciences; American Educational Research Association; Comparative and International Education Society; History Education Society. Address: PO Box 100, Pleasant Hill, TN 38578, USA.

PARKER Gordon, b. 28 Feb 1940, Newcastle upon Tyne, England. Author; Playwright. Education: Newcastle Polytechnic, 1965-68. Appointment: Book Reviewer, BBC Radio and ITV. Publications: The Darkness of the Morning, 1975; Lightning in May, 1976; The Pool, 1978; Action of the Tiger, 1981. Radio plays: The Seance, 1978; God Protect the Lonely Widow, 1982. Address: 14 Thornhill Close, Seaton Delaval, Northumberland, England.

PARKER Jean. See: **SHARAT CHANDRA Gubbi Shankara Chetty.**

PARKER Peter Robert Nevill, b. 2 June 1954, Hereford, England. Education: BA, Honours, University College, London, 1977. Appointments: Executive Committee, English PEN, 1994-97; Trustee, 1994-, Chair, 1998-, PEN Literary Foundation; Associate Editor, New D.N.B., 1996-; Committee, London Library, 1998-. Publications: The Old Lie, 1987; Ackerley, 1989; The Reader's Companion to the Twentieth-Century Novel (editor), 1994; The Reader's Companion to Twentieth-Century Writers (editor), 1995. Contributions to: Daily Telegraph; Independent; Sunday Times; Hortus. Honour: FRSL, 1997. Literary Agent: David Higham Associates Ltd. Address: c/o David Higham Associates Ltd, 5-8 Lower John Street, Golden Square, London W1R 4HA, England.

PARKER Robert B(rown), b. 17 Sept 1932, Springfield, Massachusetts, USA. Author. m. Joan Hall, 26 Aug 1956, 2 sons. Education: BA, Colby College, 1954; MA, 1957, PhD, 1971, Boston University. Appointments: Lecturer, Boston University, 1962-64; Faculty, Lowell State College, 1964-66; Bridgwater State College, 1966-68; Assistant Professor 1968-73, Associate Professor 1973-76, Professor of English 1976-79, Northeastern University. Publications: Fiction: The Godwulf Manuscript, 1973; God Save the Child, 1974; Mortal Stakes, 1975; Promised Land, 1976; The Judas Goat, 1978; Wilderness, 1979; Looking for Rachel Wallace, 1980; Early Autumn, 1981; A Savage Place, 1981; Surrogate, 1982; Ceremony, 1982; The Widening Gyre, 1983; Love and Glory, 1983; Valediction, 1984; A Catskill Eagle, 1985; Taming a Sea Horse, 1986; Pale Kings and Princes, 1987; Crimson Joy, 1988; Playmates, 1989; Poodle Springs (completion of unfinished novel by R Chandler), 1989; Stardust, 1990; Perchance to Dream, 1991; Pastime, 1991; Double Deuce, 1992; All Our Yesterdays, 1994; Walking Shadow, 1994; Sudden Mischief, 1998; Trouble in Paradise, 1998. Other: The Personal Response to Literature, 1971; Order and Diversity, 1973; Three Weeks in Spring (with Joan Parker), 1973. Address: c/o Helen Brann Agency, 94 Curtis Road, Bridgewater, CT 06752, USA.

PARKES Joyce Evelyne, (J E Dubois), b. 30 June 1930, Serang, West Java, Indonesia. Writer; Retired Archivist. 1 son, 2 daughters. Education: Archivist's course, Java, 1948-49. Publications: The Land of Sand and Stone, 1977; Silver and Gold, 1977; Changes, 1977. Contributions to: Numerous including: Westerly; Pen International, UK; Fremantle Arts Review; Overland; Sydney Morning Herald. Memberships: Peter Cowan Writers Centre; PEN; W B Yeats Society; KSP Foundation of Western Australia. Address: 10 Desault Cove, Ballajura, Western Australia 6066, Australia.

PARKES Roger Graham, b. 15 Oct 1933, Chingford, Essex, England. Novelist; Scriptwriter. m. Tessa Isabella McLean, 5 Feb 1964, 1 son, 1 daughter. Education: National Diploma of Agriculture. Appointments: Staff Writer, Farming Express and Scottish Daily Express, 1959-63; Editor, Farming Express, 1963; Staff Script Editor, Drama, BBC-TV, London, 1964-70. Publications: Death Mask, 1970; Line of Fire, 1971; The Guardians, 1973; The Dark Number, 1973; The Fourth Monkey, 1978; Alice Ray Morton's Cookham, 1981; Them and Us, 1985; Riot, 1986; Y-E-S, 1986; An Abuse of Justice, 1988; Troublemakers, 1990; Gamelord, 1991; The Wages of Sin, 1992. Contributions to: Daily Express; Sunday Express. Honour: Grand Prix de Littérature, Paris, 1974. Memberships: Writers Guild of Great Britain; Magistrates Association. Address: Cartlands Cottage, Kings Lane, Cookham Dean, Berkshire SL6 9AY, England.

PARKIN Andrew Terence Leonard, (Jiang An Dao), b. 30 June 1937, Birmingham, England. Poet; Critic. m. (1) Christine George, 14 June 1950, 1 son, (2) Françoise Lentsch, 28 Apr 1990. Education: BA, 1961, MA, 1965, Pembroke College, Cambridge; PhD, Bristol. Appointments: Part-time Lecturer in Adult Education; School Teacher; Part-time Lecturer in Education; Professor of English, University of British Columbia, Canada; Professor of English, Chinese University of Hong Kong. Publications: Stage One: A Canadian Scenebook, 1973; The Dramatic Imagination of W B Yeats, 1978; Shaw's Caesar and Cleopatra, 1980; Dion Boucicault: Selected Plays, 1987; Dancers in a Web, 1987, reprinted 1990; Yeats's Herne's Egg, 1991; Yokohama Days, Kyoto Nights, 1991; File on Nichols, 1993; Hong Kong Poems, 1997; Editor, Canadian Journal of Irish Studies, twice yearly 1974-89. Contributions to: Over 100 essays and reviews in scholarly journals; Over 30 radio broadcasts; 2 TV interviews; 200 poems. Honours: Open Exhibition in English, Pembroke College, Cambridge; Honorary Life Member, Canadian Association for Irish Studies; Most Distinguished Editor of a Learned Journal, 1989. Memberships: Canadian Association for Irish Studies; Canadian Writers' Union; League of Canadian Poets; Modern Language Association; IAUPE. Address: Department of English, Chinese University of Hong Kong, Shatin, New Territories, Hong Kong.

PARKINSON Michael, b. 28 Mar 1935, Yorkshire, England. Journalist; Television Producer, Interviewer, and Presenter; Writer. m. Mary Heneghan, 3 sons. Appointments: Producer, Interviewer, and Presenter, many television programmes; Founder-Director, Pavilion Books, 1980-97; Columnist, Daily Mirror, 1986-90, Daily Telegraph, 1991-; Editor, Catalyst, 1988-. Publications: Football Draft, 1968; Cricket Mad, 1969; Pictorial History of Westerns (with Clyde Jeavons), 1972; Sporting Fever, 1974; Football Classified (with Willis Hall), 1974; George Best: An Intimate Biography, 1975; A-Z of Soccer (with Willis Hall), 1975; Bats in the Pavilion, 1977; The Woofits, 1980; Parkinson's Lore, 1981; The Best of Parkinson, 1982; Sporting Lives, 1992; Sporting Profiles, 1995. Honour: Sports Feature Writer of the Year, British Sports Journalism Awards, 1995; Sports Writer of the Year, British Press Awards, 1998; Variety Club's Media Personality of the Year, 1998; Sony Radio Award, 1998; Comic Heritage Gold Award for Special Contribution to the World of Entertainment, 1998; Yorkshire Man of the Year, 1998; BASCA Gold Award, 1998; National Television Awards Most Popular Talk Show, 1998. Address: c/o Parkinson Partnership, 48 Gray's Inn Road, London WC1X 8LT, England.

PARKS Suzan-Lori, b. 1964, USA. Dramatist; Instructor in Playwrighting. Education: Mt Holybrooke College; Drama Studios, London, England. Publications: Plays: Imperceptible Mutabilities in the Third Kingdom, 1989; Betting on the Dust Commander, 1990; Death of the Last Black Man in the Whole World, 1990; Devotees of the Garden of Love, 1992. Other: Video, film, and radio items. Honours: Obie Award, 1990; Whiting Writer's Award, 1992; Numerous grants and fellowships. Address:

c/o Giles Whiting Foundation, 30 Rockefeller Plaza, New York, NY 10112, USA.

PARKS T(imothy) Harold, (John MacDowell), b. 19 Dec 1954, Manchester, England. Educator; Translator; Author. Education: BA, University of Cambridge, 1977; MA, Harvard University, 1979. Publications: Tongues of Flame, 1985; Loving Roger, 1986; Home Thoughts, 1987; Family Planning, 1989; Cara Massimina (as John MacDowell), 1990; Goodness, 1991; Italian Neighbours, 1992; Shear, 1993. Short stories: Keeping Distance, 1988; The Room, 1992. Translations: La Cosa (short stories), 1985; Notturno indiano (novel), 1988; L'uomo che guarda (novel), 1989; Viaggio a Romas, 1989; Il filo dell'orrizonto (novel), 1989; La donna di Porto Pim, I volatili del Beato Angelico (short story collections), 1991; C'un punto della terra, 1991; I beati anni del castigo (novel), 1991; Le nozze di Cadmo e Armonia, 1993; La strada di San Giovanni (stories), 1993. Contributions to: Numerous articles, reviews and talks for BBC Radio 3. Honours: Somerset Maugham Award 1986; Betty Trask Prize, 1986; Rhys Prize, 1986; John Floria Prize for Best Translation from Italian. Membership: Authors Society. Literary Agent: Curtis Brown. Address: Via delle Primule 6, Montorio, 37033 Verona, Italy.

PARLAKIAN Nishan, b. 11 July 1925, New York, New York, USA. Professor Emeritus of Drama; Playwright. m. Florence B Mechtel, 1 son, 1 daughter. Education: BA, Syracuse University, 1948; MA, 1950, MA, 1952, PhD, 1967, Columbia University. Appointments: Editorial Board, Ararat, 1970-, MELUS, 1977-80; Editor, Pirandello Society Newsletter, Armenian Church Magazine; Associate Editor, Pirandello Society Annual. Publications: Original plays: The Last Mohigian, 1959; Plagiarized, 1962; What Does Greta Garbo Mean to You?, 1973; Grandma, Pray for Me, 1988. Translated plays: For the Sake of Honor, 1976; Evil Spirit, 1980; The Bride, 1987; Be Nice, I'm Dead, 1990. Contributions to: Armenian Literature Between East and West; Review of National Literature, 1984. Honours: Prizewinner, Stanley Awards, 1961; International Arts Award for Playwriting, Columbus Countdown, 1992. Memberships: Modern Language Association; Pirandello Society of America, president, 1995. Address: 415 West 115th Street, New York, NY 10025, USA.

PARMELEE David Freeland, b. 20 June 1924, Oshkosh, Wisconsin, USA. Research Curator; Former Professor. m. Jean Marie Peterson, 4 Dec 1943, 1 daughter. Education: BA, Lawrence University, Appleton, Wisconsin, 1950; MSc, University of Michigan, Ann Arbor, 1952; PhD, University of Oklahoma, Norman, 1957. Appointments: Professor, University of Minnesota, 1970-92; Research Curator of Ornithology, University of Nevada, Las Vegas, 1992-. Publications: The Birds of West-Central Ellesmere Island and Adjacent Areas, 1960; The Birds of Southeastern Victoria Island and Adjacent Small Islands, 1967; Bird Island in Antarctic Waters, 1980; Antarctic Birds, 1992. Contributions to: Arctic; Antarctic Journal US; Auk; Beaver; Bird-Banding; Condor; Ibis; Living Bird; Loon; Wilson Bulletin. Honours: Antarctic Place Name 'Parmelee Massif' at 70°58' S, 62°10'W, Geographic Names Division, Defense Mapping Agency, Topographic Center, Washington, DC, 1977; Native Son Award, Michigan Rotary International, 1982. Memberships: Organization of Biological Field Stations; British Ornithological Society; Cooper's Ornithological Society; Wilson Ornithological Society; Explorers Club, fellow; British Ornithologists' Club. Address: Marjorie Barrick Museum of Natural History, 4505 Maryland Parkway, Box 454012, Las Vegas, NV 89154, USA.

PARMET Herbert Samuel, b. 28 Sept 1929, New York, New York, USA. Professor of History Emeritus; Writer. m. Joan Kronish, 12 Sept 1948, 1 daughter. Education: BS, State University of New York at Oswego, 1951; MA, Queens College, New York City, 1957; Postgraduate Studies, Columbia University, 1958-62. Appointments: Professor of History, 1968-83, Distinguished Professor of History, 1983-95, Professor Emeritus, 1995-, Graduate School, City University of New York; Consultant, ABC-TV, New York City, 1983,

KERA-TV, Dallas, 1986-91, WGBH-TV, Boston, 1988-91. Publications: Aaron Burr: Portrait of an Ambitious Man, 1967; Never Again: A President Runs for a Third Term, 1968; Eisenhower and the American Crusades, 1972; The Democrats: The Years after FDR, 1976; Jack: The Struggles of John F Kennedy, 1980; JFK: The Presidency of John F Kennedy, 1983; Richard Nixon and His America, 1990; George Bush: The Life of a Lone Star Yankee, 1997. Contributions to: Professional journals. Honour: National Endowment for the Humanities Grant, 1987. Memberships: American Historical Association; Authors Guild; Authors League; Organization of American Historians; Society of American Historians, fellow. Address: 36 Marsten Lane, Hillsdale, NY 12529, USA.

PARQUE Richard (Anthony), b. 8 Oct 1935, Los Angeles, California, USA. Writer; Poet; Teacher. m. Vo Thi Lan, 1 May 1975, 3 sons. Education: BA, 1958, MA, 1961, California State University, Los Angeles; California State Teaching Credential, 1961; Postgraduate studies, University of Redlands. Publications: Sweet Vietnam, 1984; Hellbound, 1986; Firefight, 1987; Flight of the Phantom, 1988; A Distant Thunder, 1989. Contributions to: Journals, magazines and newspapers. Honours: Bay Area Poets Award, 1989; Vietnam novels have been placed in the Colorado State University Vietnam War Collection. Memberships: Authors Guild; Academy of American Poets. Address: PO Box 327, Verdugo City, CA 91046, USA.

PARRINDER (John) Patrick, b. 11 Oct 1944, Wadebridge, Cornwall, England. Professor of English; Literary Critic. 2 daughters. Education: Christ's College, 1962-65, Darwin College, 1965-67, Cambridge; MA, PhD, Cambridge University. Appointments: Fellow, King's College, Cambridge, 1967-74; Lecturer, 1974-80, Reader, 1980-86, Professor of English, 1986-, University of Reading. Publications: H G Wells, 1970; Authors and Authority, 1977, 2nd edition, enlarged, 1991; Science Fiction: Its Criticism and Teaching, 1980; James Joyce, 1984; The Failure of Theory, 1987; Shadows of the Future, 1995. Editor: H G Wells: The Critical Heritage, 1972; Science Fiction: A Critical Guide, 1979. Contributions to: London Review of Books; Many academic journals. Honour: President's Award, World Science Fiction, 1987. Memberships: H G Wells Society; Science Fiction Foundation. Address: Department of English, University of Reading, PO Box 218, Reading, Berkshire RG6 6AA, England.

PARTLETT Launa, (Launa Gillis), b. 19 May 1918, Miles, Queensland, Australia. Writer; Poet. m. Charles Henry Partlett, 19 June 1943, dec, 1 son, 1 daughter. Education: Art classes; Writing courses. Publications: Guluguba Pioneers: Stories from Queensland Rural Community, 1986; John Jones and Family: Rocky River Gold (co-author), 1987; Contributions to: Anthologies, newspapers, and magazines. Honours: Newshound Certificate, Leader Newspaper, 1984; Gold Medal, ABI, 1995; Certificate, IBC. Memberships: British Bible Society; National Parks and Wildlife Service, honorary ranger. Address: 3/11 Parry Avenue, Narwee, New South Wales, 2209, Australia.

PARTRIDGE Derek, b. 24 Oct 1945, London, England. Professor of Computer Science. m. 27 Aug 1971, 2 daughters. Education: BSc, Chemistry, University College, London, 1968; PhD, Computer Science, Imperial College, London, 1972. Appointments: Professor, University of Exeter; Editor, Computational Science, book series, Ablex Publishing Corporation, Norwood, New Jersey, USA. Publications: Artificial Intelligence: Applications in the Future of Software Engineering, 1965; A New Guide to Artificial Intelligence, 1991; Engineering Artificial Intelligence Software, 1992. Contributions to: More than 100 articles to professional magazines and journals. Memberships: American Association for Artificial Intelligence; Society for Artificial Intelligence and Simulation of Behaviour. Address: Department of Computer Science, University of Exeter, Exeter EX4 4PT, England.

PARTRIDGE Frances Catherine, b. 15 Mar 1900, London, England. Writer. m. Ralph Partridge, 2 Mar 1933, 1 son. Education BA, Honours, English, Moral Sciences, Newnham College, Cambridge, 1921. Appointment: Editor, The Greville Memoirs (with Ralph Partridge), 1928-38; Translator, 20 books from French and Spanish. Publications: A Pacifist's War, 1978; Memories, 1981; Julia, 1983; Everything to Lose, 1985; Friends in Focus, 1987; The Pasque Flower, 1990; Hanging On, 1990; Other People, 1993; Good Company, 1994; Life Regained. Contributions to: Many book reviews and obituaries to various publications. Memberships: Royal Society of Literature, fellow; International PEN. Address: 15 West Halkin Street, London SW1X 8JL, England.

PASCALIS Stratis, b. 4 Mar 1958, Athens, Greece. Poet; Translator. m. Sophia Phocas, 28 Feb 1982, 2 daughters. Education: Graduated, Political Science, University of Athens, 1983. Publications: 4 volumes of poetry, 1977, 1984, 1989, 1991; Several translations. Contributions to: Newspapers and magazines. Honour: Maris P Ralli Prize, 1977. Membership: Society of Greek Writers. Address: Diamandidou 36, Palio Psychiko, Athens 15452, Greece.

PASCHE Jean-Robert, b. 15 Aug 1950, Lausanne, Switzerland. Writer. m. 26 Apr 1977, 2 daughters. Education: Higher education, Switzerland. Publications: Les rêves ou la Connaissance Intérieure, 1987; Etre selon ses Rêves, 1992. Contributions to: Newspapers and magazines. Memberships: Pro Litteris, Switzerland; Société Genevoise des Écrivains; Société Suisse des Écrivains. Address: c/o Centre International d'études et de recherche sur les Rêves, Casa postale 473, 1211 Geneva, Switzerland.

PASCHEN Elise Maria, b. 4 Jan 1959, Chicago, Illinois, USA. Arts Administrator; Poet. Education: BA, Honours, Harvard University, 1982; MPhil, 1984, DPhil, 1988, University of Oxford. Appointment: Executive Director, Poetry Society of America. Publications: Houses: Coasts, 1985; Infidelities, 1996. Contributions to: Reviews, journals, and magazines. Honours: Lloyd McKim Garrison Medal for Poetry, Harvard University, 1982; Joan Grey Untermyer Poetry Prize, Harvard University/Radcliffe College, 1982; Richard Selig Prize for Poetry, Magdalen College, Oxford, 1984; Nicholas Roerich Poetry Prize, 1996. Membership: National Arts Club. Address: c/o Poetry Society of America, 15 Gramercy Park, New York, NY 10003, USA.

PASHMAN Susan Ellen, b. 17 Dec 1942, New York City, USA. Writer. divorced, 2 sons. Education: BA, New York University, 1963; ABD, Philosophy, Columbia University, 1967; JD, Brooklyn Law School, 1982. Appointments: Instructor in Philosophy, Adelphi University, 1966-79; new Associate Proskauer, Rose, Goetz & Mendelsohn, 1982-84; Lawyer, Moses Singer, 1984-86; Lawyer, Cravath, Swaine & Moore, 1986-91; Director, Public Access Continuing Education, Sag Harbor, 1991-. Publications: The Speed of Light, 1997. Contribution: Dozens of Features - The East Hampton Star, 1991-98. Memberships: Ashawagh Hall Writer's Group. Literary Agent: International Management Group, Julian Bach Literary Agency. Address: PO Box 2580, Sag Harbor, NY 11963, USA.

PASKANDI Géza, b. 18 May 1933, Szatmarhegy-Viile Satumare, Romania. Writer; Poet; Dramatist; Screenwriter. m. Anna-Maria Sebök, 24 Apr 1970, 1 daughter. Education: University Bolyai-Kolozsvar-Cluj, 1953-57. Publications: Novels, poems, plays, Screenplays, and essays. Contributions to: Journals and magazines. Honours: Romanian Writers Association Award, 1970; József Attila Award, Hungary, 1977; Award for Hungarian Art, 1991; Kossuth Prize, Hungary, 1992. Memberships: Hungarian Academy of Arts; Hungarian Writers Association; Moricz Zsigmond Literary Society; PEN Club. Address: Nagyszalonta utca 50, 1112 Budapest, Hungary.

PASSMORE Jacki, b. 2 July 1947, Queensland, Australia. Food Writer; Cookbook Author. 1 daughter.

Appointments: Food Writer: Queensland Newpapers, Sunday Mail, Courier Mail, 1993. Publications: Asia: The Beautiful Cookbook, 1987; The Encyclopedia of Asian Food and Cooking, 1990; The Complete Spanish Cookbook, 1992; Festival Foods of Thailand, 1992; The Noodle Shop Cookbook, 1994; 15 others. Memberships: Queensland Wine Writers Club; International Association of Culinary Professionals, USA. Address: 50 Turin Street, West End, Brisbane, Queensland 4101, Australia.

PATCHETT Ann, b. 2 Dec 1963, Los Angeles, California, USA. Writer. Education: BA. Sarah Lawrence College, 1984; MFA, University of Iowa, 1987. Appointments: Writer-in-Residence, Allegheny College, 1989-90; Visiting Assistant Professor, Murray State University, 1992. Publications: The Patron Saint of Liars, 1992; Taft, 1994. Contributions to: Anthologies and periodicals. Honours: James A Michener/Copernicus Award, University of Iowa, 1989; Yaddo Fellow, 1990; Millay Fellow, 1990; Resident Fellow, Fine Arts Work Center, Provincetown, Massachusetts, 1990-91; Notable Book, American Library Association, 1992. Address: c/o Carol Fass Ivy Publishing, 201 East 50th Street, New York, NY 10022, USA.

PATEL Gieve, b. 18 Aug 1940, Bombay, India. Physician; Poet; Dramatist; Painter. m. Toni Diniz, 1969, 1 daughter. Education: BSc, St Xavier's College, Bombay; MBBS, Grant Medical Collee, Bombay. Publications: Poetry: Poems, 1966; How Do You Withstand, Body, 1976; Mirrored, Mirroring, 1991. Plays: Princes, 1971; Savaksa, 1982; Mister Behram, 1987. Honours: Woodrow Wilson Fellowship, 1984; Rockefeller Foundation Fellowship, 1992. Address: SE Malabar Apartments, Nepean Road, Bombay 400 036, India.

PATERAKIS Yolanda, b. 27 Oct 1934, Greece. Writer. m. Andreas Paterakis, 14 Sept 1963, 1 son, 1 daughter. Education: Greek Literary Certificate, 1954; University of Cambridge, England, 1958. Publications: Some 25 books, 1976-96, including: Once in Macedonia, Novel, 1994; The Moonman, Tale, 1995; With a Stretched Ear: Short Stories, 1996. Contributions to: Many publications in NEA ESTIA. Memberships: Children's Book Circle of Greece; National Society of Greek Authors, general secretary, 1979-. Address: 17 Kritonis Street, 11634 Athens, Greece.

PATERSON Aileen (Francis), b. 30 Nov 1934, Burntisland, Fife, Scotland. Author; Illustrator of Children's Books. m. Hamish Paterson, 5 Apr 1963, div, 2 sons, 4 daughters. Education: DA, Edinburgh, 1955; Moray House Teaching Qualification, 1961. Publications: Maisie Comes to Morningside, 1984; Maisie Goes to School, 1988; Maisie in the Rainforest, 1992; Maisie and the Puffer, 1992; Maisie Goes to Hollywood, 1994; Maisie Digs Up the Past, 1994; Maisie's Merry Christmas, 1996; Maisie and the Pirates, 1998. Contributions to: Scotsman; Scotland on Sunday; Scotland's Languages Magazine; Insider; Short Story on Wonderous Christmas Stories, 1997. Membership: Society of Authors in Scotland. Address: c/o Mile Sharland, 9 Marlborough Crescent, Bedford Park, London, W4 1HE, England.

PATERSON Alistair Ian, (Ian Hughes). b. 28 Feb 1929, Nelson, New Zealand. Poet; Writer; Educational Consultant. m. Dec 1984, 2 sons, 3 daughters. Education: BA, University of New Zealand, 1961; Diploma in Education, University of Auckland, 1972. Appointments: Royal New Zealand Navy, 1954-74; Dean of General Studies, New Zealand Police, 1974-78; Tertiary Inspector, New Zealand Department of Education, 1979-89; Educational Consultant, 1990-. Publications: Caves in the Hills, 1965; Birds Flying, 1973; Cities and Strangers, 1976; The Toledo Room: A Poem for Voices, 1978; 15 Contemporary New Zealand Poets (editor), 1980; Qu'appelle, 1982; The New Poetry, 1982; Incantations for Warriors, 1982; Oedipus Rex, 1986; Short Stories from New Zealand (editor), 1988; How to be a Millionaire by Next Wednesday (novel), 1994. Contributions to: Various publications. Honours: Fulbright Fellowship, 1977; John Cowie Reid Award, University of Auckland, 1982; Katherine Mansfield Award for Fiction,

1993; New Zealand Creative Writing Grant, 1995. Memberships: PEN; Wellington Poetry Society. Address: PO Box 9612, Newmarket, Auckland, New Zealand.

PATERSON Don(ald), b. 30 Oct 1963, Dundee, Scotland. Musician; Editor; Poet. Appointment: Writer-in-Residence, Dundee University, 1993-95. Publications: Nil Nil, 1993; God's Gift to Women, 1997; The Eyes, 1999. Honours: Eric Gregory Award, 1990; Arvon/Observer International Poetry Competition, 1993; Forward Poetry Prize, 1993; Scottish Arts Council Book Award, 1993; Geoffrey Faber Memorial Prize, 1998; T S Eliot Prize, 1998. Address: c/o Faber and Faber, 3 Queen Square, London WC1N 3AU, England.

PATERSON Katherine (Womeldorf), b. 31 Oct 1932, Qing Jiang, China. Writer. m. John Barstow Paterson, 2 sons, 2 adopted daughters. Education: AB, King College; MA, Presbyterian School of Christian Education; MRS, Kobe University School of Japanese Language, Union Theological Seminary. Publications: Sign of the Chrysanthemum, 1973; The Great Gilly Hopkins, 1978; Jacob Have I Loved, 1980; Consider the Lilies: Plants of the Bible, 1986; Park's Quest, 1988; The Spying Heart, 1989; Tale of the Mandarin Ducks, 1990; The King's Equal, 1992; Flip-Flop Girl, 1994; Angel and the Donkey, 1996. Honours: American Library Association Awards, 1974, 1976, 1977, 1978; Newbery Medals, 1978, 1981; National Book Award, 1979; Christopher Award, 1979; Parent's Choice Award, 1983; Laura Ingalls Wilder Award, 1986; Regina Medal Award, Catholic Library Association, 1988; Boston Globe/Horn Book Award, 1991. Address: c/o Dutton Children's Books, 375 Hudson Street, New York, NY 10014, USA.

PATERSON Stuart A, b. 31 Jan 1966, Truro, Cornwall, England. Writer; Poet; Editor. Education: Stirling University, 1988-92. Appointments: Founder-Editor, Spectrum review, 1990-96; Scottish Arts Council Writer-in-Residence, Dumfries and Galloway Region, 1996-98. Publications: Mulaney of Larne and Other Poems, 1991; Saving Graces, 1997. Contributions to: Anthologies, reviews, newspapers and journals. Honour: Eric Gregory Award, 1992; Scottish Arts Council Writer's Bursary, 1993. Memberships: Kilmarnock North West Writers Group, founder; Artists for Independence; Scottish Poetry Library; Scottish National Party. Address: c/o 2A Leslie Road, New Farm Loch, Kilmarnock, Ayrshire KA3 7RR, Scotland.

PATERSON-HOWE R. See: FLEMING Robert Paterson Howe.

PATILIS Yannis, b. 21 Feb 1947, Athens, Greece. Teacher of Literature; Poet; Editor; Publisher. m. Elsa Liaropoulou, 2 sons. Education: Degree, Law School, 1971, Byzantine and Neo-Hellenic Studies, 1977, University of Athens. Appointments: Co-Founder and Co-Editor, Nesus, journal, 1983-85; Editor and Publisher, Planodion, 1986-. Publications: Volumes of poetry, 1970-97, including collected poems, 1993; Camel of Darkness: Selected Poems of Yannis Patilis 1970-1990, 1997. Contributions to: Various publications. Membership: Society of Greek Writers. Address: 23 G Mistriotou Street, 112 55 Athens, Greece.

PATON WALSH Jill, b. 29 Apr 1937, London, England. Children's Author. 1 son, 2 daughters . Education: Diploma in Education, 1959, MA, St Anne's College, Oxford. Publications: Over 30 books for children and adults including Fireweed, 1970; The Emperor's Winding Sheet, 1974; A Parcel of Patterns, 1984; Knowledge of Angels, 1994. Honours: Book World Festival Award, 1970; Whitbread Prize (childrens'novel), 1974; Boston Globe-Horn Book Award, 1976; The Universe Prize, 1984; Smarties Grand Prix, 1984; Booker Prize, Short-List, 1994; Commader of the Order of the British Empire, 1996. Address: c/o David Higham Associates, 5/8 Lower John Street, London W1R 3PE.

PATRICK Maxine. See: MAXWELL Patricia Anne.

PATRICK Susan. See: CLARK Patricia Denise.

PATRICK William. See: HAINING Peter Alexander.

PATTEN Brian, b. 7 Feb 1946, Liverpool, England. Poet; Writer. Appointment: Regents Lecturer, University of California at San Diego. Publications: Poetry: The Mersey Sound: Penguin Modern Poets 10, 1967; Little Johnny's Confession, 1967; The Home Coming, 1969; Notes to the Hurrying Man: Poems, Winter '66-Summer '68, 1969; The Irrelevant Song, 1970; At Four O'Clock in the Morning, 1971; Walking Out: The Early Poems of Brian Patten, 1971; The Eminent Professors and the Nature of Poetry as Enacted Out by Members of the Poetry Seminar One Rainy Evening, 1972; The Unreliable Nightingale, 1973; Vanishing Trick, 1976; Grave Gossip, 1979; Love Poems, 1981; New Volume, 1983; Storm Damage, 1988; Grinning Jack: Selected Poems, 1990; Armada, 1996; The Utterly Brilliant Book of Poetry (editor), 1998. Editor: Clare's Countryside: A Book of John Clare, 1981. Children's Books: Prose: The Jumping Mouse, 1972; Mr Moon's Last Case, 1975; Emma's Doll, 1987; Jimmy Tag-along, 1988; Grizzelda Frizzle, 1992; Impossible Parents, 1994. Poetry: Gargling With Jelly, 1985; Thawing Frozen Frogs, 1990; The Puffin Book of 20th Century Children's Verse, 1991; The Magic Bicycle, 1993; The Utter Nutters, 1994. Contributions to: Journals and newspapers. Honour: Special Award, Mystery Writers of America, 1977. Membership: Chelsea Arts Club. Literary Agent: Rogers, Coleridge and White. Address: c/o Puffin Penguin Books, 27 Wrights Lane, London W8 5TZ, England.

PATTERSON Glenn, b. 9 Aug 1961, Belfast, Ireland. Writer; Broadcaster. m. Ali Fitzgibbon, 12 May 1995. Education: BA Honours, English and American Literature, MA, Creative Writing, University of East Anglia, 1982-86. Appointments: Arts Council Northern Ireland, Writer-in-the-Community, 1989-91; University of East Anglia Creative Writing Fellow, 1992; University College, Cork, Writer-in-Residence, 1993-94; Queen's University, Belfast, Writer-in-Residence, 1994-97; Arts Council Northern Ireland (Board), 1996-. Publications: Novels: Burning Your Own, 1988; Fat Lad, 1992; Black Night at Big Thunder Mountain, 1995; The International, 1999. Honours: Betty Trask Prize, 1988; Rooney Prize for Irish Literature, 1988. Memberships: Society of Authors. Literary Agent: Antony Harwood. Address: c/o Gillon Aitken Associates, 29 Fernshaw Road, London SW10 0TG, England.

PATTERSON Henry (Harry), (Martin Fallon, James Graham, Jack Higgins, Hugh Marlowe), b. 27 July 1929, Newcastle upon Tyne, England. Author. m. (1) Amy Margaret Hewitt, 1958, div, 1984, 1 son, 3 daughters, (2) Denise Lesley Anne Palmer, 1985. Education: Certificate in Education, Carnegie College, 1958; BSc, London School of Economics and Political Science, 1962. Appointments: NCO, The Blues, 1947-50, 1950-58. Publications: As Jack Higgins: Prayer for the Dying, 1973, filmed, 1985; The Eagle Has Landed, 1975, filmed, 1976; Storm Warning, 1976; Day of Judgement, 1978; Solo, 1980; Luciano's Luck, 1981; Touch the Devil, 1982; Exocet, 1983; Confessional, 1985, filmed, 1985; Night of the Fox, 1986, filmed, 1990; Season in Hell, 1989; Coldharbour, 1990; The Eagle Has Flown, 1991. As Harry Patterson: The Valhalla Exchange, 1978; To Catch a King, 1979, filmed, 1983; Dillinger, 1983. Many others under pseudonyms, including: The Violent Enemy, filmed, 1969; The Wrath of God, filmed, 1972; Some books translated into 42 languages. Address: c/o Ed Victor, 162 Wardour Street, London W1V 3AT, England.

PATTERSON James, b. 22 Mar 1947, Newburgh, New York, USA. Author. Education: BA, Manhattan College, 1969; MA, Vanderbilt University, 1970. Publications: The Thomas Berryman Number, 1976; The Season of the Machete, 1977; The Jericho Commandment, 1979; Virgin, 1980; Black Market, 1986; The Midnight Club, 1989; The Day America Told the Truth, 1991; Along Came the Spider, 1993; The Second American Revolution, 1994; Kiss the Girls, 1995; Miracle on the 17th Green, 1996; Jack & Jill, 1996; Cat & Mouse, 1997; When the Wind Blows, 1998. Address: c/o Warner Books, 1271 Avenue of the Americas, New York, NY 10020, USA.

PATTERSON Michael (Wyndham), (formerly Michael Wyndham Richards), b. 7 Sept 1939, London, England. Professor of Theatre; Writer. m. (1) Ellinor von Einsiedel, (2) Diana (Dixi) Patterson, (3) Jane Prentice, 3 sons, 5 daughters. Education: BA, Medieval and Modern Languages, 1962, DPhil, 1968, University of Oxford. Appointments: Lecturer in German, Queen's University, Belfast, 1965-70; Lecturer in Drama, University College of North Wales, Bangor, 1970-74; Senior Lecturer in Drama and Theatre Arts, University of Leeds, 1974-87; Reader in Theatre Studies, University of Ulster, Coleraine, 1987-94; Professor of Theatre, De Montfort University, Leicester, 1994-. Publications: German Theatre Today, 1976; The Revolution in German Theatre 1900-1933, 1981; Peter Stein, 1981; Georg Büchner: The Complete Plays (editor), 1987; The First German Theatre, 1990; German Theatre: A Bibliography, 1996. Contributions to: Professional journals. Address: c/o Department of Performing Arts, De Montfort University, Leicester LE1 9BH, England.

PATTERSON Neil Michael, b. 22 Mar 1951, Aberdeen, Scotland. Copywriter. m. Doris Karen Boll, 22 July 1984, 1 son. Appointments: Copywriter, Halls, Edinburgh, 1972; Saatchi Saatchi, 1973-75; TBWA, 1975-82; Creative Director, TBWA, 1982-85; Executive Creative Director, Young & Rubicam, 1985-90; Creative Partner, Mitchell Patterson Grime Mitchell, 1990-. Publications: The Complete Flyfisher, 1989; The One That Got Away, 1992; Contributer, The Art of The Day Fly, 1993; Distant Waters, 1996; Novel: Chalkstream Chronicle, 1996. Contributions to: Trout and Salmon; International Fly Fisher; Trout Fisherman; Fly Fishers Club Journal. Memberships: Campaign Press; Clio; ILR Radio; Cannes Angling Writer's Association. Address: Wilderness Lodge, Newbury, Berks RG20 8NH, England.

PATTERSON (Horace) Orlando (Lloyd), b. 5 June 1940, Jamaica, West Indies. Professor of Sociology; Writer. Education: BSc, University of West Indies, 1962; PhD, London School of Economics and Political Science, 1965. Appointments: Professor of Sociology 1971-, John Cowles Professor of Sociology 1993, Harvard University; Associate Editor, American Sociological Review, 1989-92. Publications: Fiction: The Children of Sisyphus, 1964; An Absence of Ruins, 1967; Die the Long Day, 1972. Non-Fiction: The Sociology of Slavery: Jamaica 1655-1838, 1967; Ethnic Chauvinism: The Reactionary Impulse, 1977; Slavery and Social Death: A Comparative Study, 1982; Freedom, 1991; The Ordeal of Integration: Progress and Resentment in America's "Racial" Crisis, 1997; Rituals of Blood: The Consequences of Slavery Across Two American Centuries, 1999. Contributions to: Books and professional journals. Honours: Best Novel in English Award, Dakar Festival of Negro Arts, 1965; Walter Channing Cabot Faculty Prize, Harvard University, 1983; Co-Winner, Ralph Bunche Award, American Political Science Association, 1983; Distinguished Contribution to Scholarship Award, American Sociological Association, 1983; National Book Award for Non-Fiction, 1991; University of California at Los Angeles Medal, 1992; Walter Channing Cabot Faculty Prize, Harvard, 1997. Memberships: American Academy of Arts and Sciences, fellow; American Sociological Association. Address: c/o Department of Sociology, Harvard University, Cambridge, MA 02138, USA.

PATTERSON Richard North, b. 22 Feb 1947, Berkeley, California, USA. Novelist. m. Laurie Anderson Patterson, 13 Apr 1993, 4 sons, 2 daughters. Education: BA, History, Ohio Wesleyan Universty, 1968; JD, Case Western Reserve Law School. Publications: The Lasko Tangent, 1979; The Outside Man, 1981; Escape the Night, 1983; Private Screening, 1985; Degree of Guilt, 1993; Eyes of a Child, 1995; The Final Judgement, 1995; Silent Witness, 1997; When the Wind Blows, 1998. Contributions to: Magazines, journals and newspapers. Honours: Edgar Allan Poe Award, 1979; French Grand Prix de Litterateur Policiere, 1995; President's Award to Distinguished Alumni, Case Western Reserve University,

1997. Membership: PEN, board of directors. Address: c/o PEN American, American Center, 568 Broadway, New York, NY 10012, USA.

PATTIS S William, b. 3 July 1925. Author; Publisher. m. Bette Zoe Levin, 16 July 1950, 1 son, 1 daughter. Education: BSc, University of Illinois. Appointments: Various directorships. Publications: Careers in Advertising; Opportunities in Advertising; Opportunities in Magazine Publishing; Opportunities in Publishing; VGM Career Planning - Advertising. Honours: Chicago Book Clinic Distinguished Service Award; Senator Paul Simon Award for International Studies. Address: 195 Elder Lane, Highland Park, IL 60035-5368, USA.

PATTISON Robert, b. 28 Oct 1945, Orange, New Jersey, USA. Professor of English; Writer. Education: AB, Yale University; MA, University of Sussex, 1968; PhD, Columbia University, 1974. Appointments: Adjunct Lecturer, Richmond College, City University of New York, 1974; Adjunct Instructor, Queensborough Community College, City University of New York, 1974-75; Instructor, English, St Vincent's College, St John's University, New York, 1975-77; Professor of English, Southampton College, Long Island University, New York, 1978-. Publications: The Child Figure in English Literature, 1978; Tennyson and Tradition, 1980; On Literacy, 1982; The Triumph of Vulgarity, 1987; The Great Dissent: John Henry Newman and the Liberal Heresey, 1991. Contributions to: Nation; ADE Bulletin; University of Toronto Quarterly; Mosaic; New York Times; Dickens Studies Newsletter; Various edited volumes. Honours: Long Island University Trustees Awards for Scholarship, 1979, 1985; Rockefeller Foundation Fellowship, 1980-81; Guggenheim Fellowship, 1988-87. Address: PO Box 2106, Southampton, NY 11969, USA.

PATTRICK William. See: **HAINING Peter.**

PAUL Barbara Jeanne, b. 5 June 1931, Maysville, Kentucky, USA. Writer. Div, 1 son. Education: AB, Bowling Green State University, 1955; MA, University of Redlands, 1957; PhD, University of Pittsburgh, 1969. Appointment: Mellon Fellow, University of Pittsburgh, 1967-69. Publications: An Exercise for Madmen, 1978; The Fourth Wall, 1979; Pillars of Salt, 1979; Bibblings, 1979; First Gravedigger, 1980; Under the Canopy, 1980; Your Eyelids Are Growing Heavy, 1981; Liars and Tyrants and People Who Turn Blue, 1982; A Cadenza for Caruso, 1984; The Renewable Virgin, 1984; Prima Donna at Large, 1985; Kill Fee, 1985; But He Was Already Dead When I Got There, 1986; A Chorus of Detectives, 1987; The Three-Minute Universe, 1988; He Huffed and He Puffed, 1989; Good King Sauerkraut, 1989; In-Laws and Out Laws, 1990; You Have the Right to Remain Silent, 1992; The Apostrophe Thief, 1993; Fare Play, 1995; Full Frontal Murder, 1997. Contributions to: Magazines and journals. Memberships: Science Fiction and Fantasy Writers of America; Sisters in Crime; President, Internet Chapter Sisters in Crime. Address: c/o William Morris Agency, 1350 Ave of the Americas, New York, NY 10019, USA.

PAUL Jeremy, b. 29 July 1939, Bexhill, Sussex, England. Writer. m. Patricia Garwood, 26 Nov 1960, 4 daughters. Education: King's, Canterbury and St Edmund Hall, Oxford. Publications: Numerous TV plays, series and adaptations, 1960-, including: Upstairs, Downstairs, 1971-75; Country Matters, 1972; The Duchess of Duke Street, 1976; Danger, UXB, 1977; A Walk in the Forest, 1980; The Flipside of Dominick Hide (with Alan Gibson), 1980; Sorrell and Son, 1983; The Adventures, Return and Memoirs of Sherlock Holmes, 1984-94; Lovejoy, 1991-94; Hetty Waintropp Investigates, 1996-98. Theatre: David Going Out, 1971; Manoeuvres, 1971; Visitors (with Carey Harrison), 1980; The Secret of Sherlock Holmes, 1988; The Watcher, 1989. Film: Countess Dracula, 1970. Membership: Writers Guild of Great Britain. Address: c/o London Management, 2-4 Noel Street, London W1V 3RB, England.

PAULIN Tom, (Thomas Neilson Paulin), b. 25 Jan 1949, Leeds, Yorkshire, England. Poet; Critic; Lecturer in English Literature. m. Munjiet Kaut Khosa, 1973, 2 sons. Education: BA, University of Hull; BLitt, Lincoln College, Oxford. Appointments: Lecturer, 1972-89, Reader in Poetry, 1989-94, University of Nottingham; G M Young Lecturer in English Literature, University of Oxford, 1994-; Fellow, Hertford College, Oxford, 1994-. Publications: Poetry: Theoretical Locations, 1975; A State of Justice, 1977; Personal Column, 1978; The Strange Museum, 1980; The Book of Juniper, 1981; Liberty Tree, 1983; The Argument at Great Tew, 1985; Fivemiletown, 1987; Selected Poems 1972-90, 1993; Walking a Line, 1994. Other: Thomas Hardy: The Poetry of Perception, 1975; Ireland and the English Crisis, 1984; The Faber Book of Political Verse (editor), 1986; Hard Lines 3 (co-editor), 1987; Minotaur: Poetry and the Nation State, 1992; Writing to the Moment: Selected Critical Essays, 1996. Honours: Eric Gregory Award, 1978; Somerset Maugham Award, 1978; Faber Memorial Prize, 1982; Fulbright Scholarship, 1983-84. Address: c/o Faber and Faber, 3 Queen Square, London WC1N 3AU, England.

PAULSON Ronald (Howard), b. 27 May 1930, Bottineau, North Dakota, USA. Professor of Humanities; Writer. m. Barbara Lee Appleton, 25 May 1957, div 1982, 1 son, 1 daughter. Education: BA, 1952, PhD, 1958, Yale University. Appointments: Instructor, 1958-59, Assistant Professor, 1959-62, Associate Professor, 1962-63, University of Illinois; Professor of English, 1967-75, Chairman, Department of English, 1968-75, Andrew W Mellon Professor of Humanities, 1973-75, Mayer Professor of Humanities, 1984-, Chairman, Department of Humanities, 1985-91, Johns Hopkins University; Professor of English, Yale University, 1975-84. Publications: Theme and Structure in Swift's Tale of a Tub, 1960; Fielding: The Critical Heritage (editor with Thomas Lockwood), 1962; Fielding: 20 Century Views (editor), 1962; Hogarth's Graphic Works, 1965, 3rd edition, revised, 1989; The Fictions of Satire, 1967; Satire and the Novel, 1967; Satire: Modern Essays in Criticism, 1971; Hogart: His Life, Art and Times, 1971; Rowlandson: A New Interpretation, 1972; Emblem and Expression: Meaning in Eighteenth Century English Art, 1975; The Art of Hogarth, 1975; Popular and Polite Art in the Age of Hogarth and Fielding, 1979; Literary Landscape: Turner and Constable, 1982; Book and Painting: Shakespeare, Milton and the Bible, 1983; Representations of Revolution, 1983; Breaking and Remaking, 1989; Figure and Abstraction in Contemporary Painting, 1990; Hogarth: Vol I, The Modern Moral Subject, 1991, Vol II, High Art and Low, 1992, Vol III, Art and Politics, 1993; The Beautiful, Novel and Strange: Aesthetics and Heterodoxy, 1996; William Hogarth: The Analysis of Beauty (editor), 1997; Don Quixote in England: The Aesthetics of Laughter (editor), 1997; Hogarth: The Analysis of Beauty, 1997. Contributions to: Professional journals. Honours: Guggenheim Fellowships, 1965-66, 1986-87; National Endowment for the Humanities Fellow, 1977-78. Memberships: American Academy of Arts and Sciences, fellow; American Society of 18th Century Studies, president, 1986-87. Address: 2722 St Paul Street, Baltimore, MD 21218, USA.

PAUWELS Rony, (Claude Van De Berge), b. 30 Apr 1945, Assenede, Belgium. Docent; Writer; Poet. m. Drongen Pauwels, 30 Jan 1973. Education: Royal Conservatory, Ghent. Appointments: Docent, Academy of Arts, Ecklo, Universities of Brussels, Ghent, Louvain, and Bonn. Publications: De koude wind du over het zand waeut, 1977; Het bewegen van her hoge gras op de top van de hevvel, 1981; Hiiumaa, 1987; Attu, 1988; Aztlan, 1990. Poetry: De zang van de maskers, 1988; De Mens in der ster, 1991; Het Silhouet, 1993. Contributions to: Journals and magazines. Honours: Several literary prizes. Membership: Flemish Writers Union. Address: Oude Molenstraat 2, 9960 Assenede, Belgium.

PAVEY Don, (Jack Adair), b. 25 July 1922, London, England. Retired Senior Lecturer of Art and Design; Writer. Education: Associate Royal College of Art, 1946; University of London, 1956-59. Appointments: Senior Lecturer of Art and Design, Kingston Polytechnic; Editor, Athene, Journal of the Society for Education Through Art, 1972-80; Director, Migro Academy, London, 1986-. Publications: Methuen Handbook of Colour and Colour Dictionary (editor), 1963, 3rd edition, 1978; Art-Based Games, 1979; Genius, 1980; Colour, 1981; The Artist's Colourmen's Story, 1985; Virtual Genius, 1986. Contributions to: Journals. Honours: Freedom of the City of London, Guild of Painter Stainers, 1987; Newton Medal, Colour Group (Great Britain), City University, London. Memberships: Colour Group, Great Britain; Design Research Society; Junior Arts and Science Centres, founder-chairman, 1970-80; National Art Education Archives, Bretton Hall, Wakefield, founder-trustee, 1985-86; Royal Society of Arts, life fellow; Society for Education Through Art, council member, 1972-83. Address: 30 Wayside, Sheen, London SW14 7LN, England.

PAVLOVICH. See: **AKSENOV Vasilii.**

PAXTON Lois. See: **LOW Lois Dorothea.**

PAYNE Donald Gordon, (Ian Cameron, Donald Gordon, James Vance Marshall), b. 3 Jan 1924, London, England. Author. m. Barbara Back, 20 Aug 1947, 4 sons, 1 daughter. Education: MA, History, Oxford. Publications: Over 30 books, 1958-91. Contributions to: Reader's Digest; National Geographic. Address: Pippacre, Westcott Heath, Dorking, Surrey RH4 3JZ, England.

PAYNE Laurence, b. 5 June 1919, London, England. Author; Actor. Education: London Schools. Appointments: Numerous stage, film, television and radio roles; Drama Teacher, Royal College of Music, London, St Catherine's School, Guildford, Surrey. Publications: The Nose of My Face, 1962; Too Small for His Shoes, 1962; Deep and Crisp and Even, 1964; Birds in the Belfry, 1966; Spy for Sale, 1969; Even My Foot's Asleep, 1971; Take the Money and Run, 1982; Malice in Camera, 1983; Vienna Blood, 1984; Dead for a Ducat, 1985; Late Knight, 1987. Address: c/o Hodder and Stoughton, 47 Bedford Square, London WC1B 3DP, England.

PAYNE Peggy, b. 8 Jan 1949, Wilmington, North Carolina, USA. Writer. m. Dr Bob Dick, 8 Dec 1983. Education: AB, English, Duke University. Publications: Revelation, 1988; The Healing Power of Doing Good (co-author), 1992. Contributions to: Cosmopolitan; Ms; Family Circle; Travel & Leisure; New York Times; Washington Post; McCall's. Honours: Annual Fiction Award, Crucible, 1978; National Endowment for the Humanities Fellowship, 1979; Indo-American Fellowship, 1991-92. Memberships: American Society of Journalists and Authors; Authors Guild. Address: 512 St Mary's Street, Raleigh, NC 27605, USA.

PEACOCK Molly, b. 30 June 1947, Buffalo, New York, USA. Writer; Poet. m. Michael Groden, 19 Aug 1992. Education: BA, magna cum laude, Harpur College, State University of New York at Binghamton, 1969; MA, Honours, Johns Hopkins University, 1977. Appointments: Lecturer, State University of New York at Binghamton, 1975-76, University of Delaware, 1978-79; Writer-in-Residence, Delaware State Arts Council, 1978-81, University of Western Ontario, 1995-96; English Faculty, Friends Seminary, New York City, 1981-87; Visiting Poet, Hofstra University, 1986, Columbia University, 1986, 1992, Carlow College, 1993; Poet-in-Residence, Bucknell University, 1993; Contributing Writer, Conde Nast House & Garden, 1996-; Regents Lecturer, University of California at Riverside, 1998. Publications: Poetry: And Live Apart, 1980; Raw Heaven, 1984; Take Heart, 1989; Original Love, 1995. Other: Paradise, Piece by Piece (literary memoir), 1998; How to Read a Poem...and start a poetry circle, 1999 Editor: Poetry in Motion: 100 Poems from the Subways and Busses (with Elise Paschen and Neil Neches), 1996. Contributions to: Anthologies, reviews, quarterlies, journals, and magazines. Honours: MacDowell Colony Fellowships, 1975-76, 1979, 1982, 1985, 1989; Danforth Foundation Fellowships, 1976-77; Yaddo Fellowships, 1980, 1982; Ingram Merrill Foundation Awards, 1981, 1986; New Virginia Review Fellowship, 1983; PEN/National Endowment for the Arts Fiction Award,

1984; New York Foundation for the Arts Grant, 1985, 1989; National Endowment for the Arts Grant, 1990; Lila Wallace/Woodrow Wilson Foundation Grant, 1994; Woodrow Wilson Grants, 1995, 1996, 1997, 1999. Memberships: Academy of American Poets; Associate Writing Programs; PEN; Poet Society of America, president, 1989-95. Address: 505 East 14th Street, No 3G, New York, NY 10009, USA.

PEARCE Ann Philippa, b. Great Shelford, Cambridgeshire, England. Children's Writer. m. Martin James Christie, 9 May 1963, 1 daughter. Education: MA, University of Cambridge. Appointments: Script Writer, Producer, School Broadcasting, Radio, 1945-58; Children's Editor, André Deutsch Ltd, 1960-67. Publications: Minnow on the Say, 1954; Tom's Midnight Garden, 1958; Mrs Cockle's Cat, 1961; A Dog So Small, 1962; The Children of the House (with Sir Brian Fairfax-Lucy), 1968, reissued as The Children of Charlecote, 1989; The Squirrel Wife, 1971; What the Neighbours Did and Other Stories, 1972; The Shadow Cage and Other Stories of the Supernatural, 1977; The Battle of Bubble and Squeak, 1978; The Elm Street Lot, 1979; The Way to Sattin Shore, 1983; Lion at School and Other Stories, 1985; Who's Afraid? and Other Strange Stories, 1986; Emily's Own Elephant, 1987; The Toothball, 1987; Freddy, 1988; Old Belle's Summer Holiday, 1989; Here Comes Tod, 1992; Dread and Delight: A Century of Children's Ghost Stories (editor), 1995. Contributions to: Times Literary Supplement; Guardian. Honours: Carnegie Medal, 1959; New York Herald Tribune Spring Festival Prize, 1962; Whitbread Prize, 1979; Honorary Doctor of Letters, University of Hull, 1995; Officer of the Order of the British Empire, 1997. Membership: Society of Authors; Fellow, Royal Society of Literature, 1994. Address: c/o Laura Cecil, 17 Alwyne Villas, London N1 2HG, England.

PEARCE Brian Leonard, (Joseph Redman), b. 8 May 1915, Weymouth, Dorset, England. Translator. m. (1) Lilla Fox, 1940, 1 son, 2 daughters, (2) Fanny Greenspan, 1954, (3) Margaret Mills, 1966. Education: University College, London, 1934-37; BA, Honours, History, University of London, 1937. Appointments: Honorary Visiting Fellow, University of Aberdee, University of Glasgow; School of Slavonic and East European Studies, University of London, 1992. Publications: The Starolesky Problem, 1984; How Haig Saved Lenin, 1987. Translations: The New Economics (E Preobrazhensky), 1965; Islam and Capitalism (M Rodinson), 1974; The Communist Movement, Part 1 (F Claudin), 1975; How the Revolution Armed (L D Trotsky), 1979-81; The Thinking Reed (Boris Kagarlitsky), 1988; Bread and Circuses (Paul Veyne), 1990; The Staroselsky Problem, 1994; Others. Contributions to: Sbornik and its successor Revolutionary Russia. Honours: Scott-Moncrieff Prizes, 1975, 1979, 1990. Membership: Translators Association. Address: 8 Chester House, Prospect Road, New Barnet, Hertfordshire EN5 5BW, England.

PEARCE Brian Louis, b. 4 June 1933, London, England. Poet; Author; Lecturer. m. Margaret Wood, 2 Aug 1969, 1 daughter. Education: University College, London. Appointments: Examiner in English, Library Association, 1964-70; College Librarian-Senior Lecturer, Richmond upon Thames College, 1977-88; Occasional Lecturer, National Portrait Gallery, London, 1990-; Honorary Librarian, Theological College of Zimbabwe, Bulawayo, 1997-1998. Publications: Poetry: Selected Poems 1951-1973, 1978; Dutch Comfort, 1985; Gwen John Talking, 1985, 2nd edition, 1996; Jack O'Lent, 1991; Leaving the Corner: Selected Poems 1973-1985, 1992; Coeli at terra, 1993; Thames Listener: poems 1949-89, 1993; The Proper Fuss, 1996. Fiction: Victoria Hammersmith, 1988; London Clay, 1991; The Bust of Minerva, 1992; A Man in his Room, 1992; Battersea Pete, 1994; The Servant of his Country, 1994; The Tufnell Triptych, 1997; Tribal Customs, 1997; The Goldhawk Variations, 1999. Other: Palgrave: Selected Poems (editor), 1985; Thomas Twining of Twickenham, 1988; The Fashioned Reed: The Poets of Twickenham from 1500, 1992; Varieties of Fervour: Portraits of Victorian

and Edwardian Poets, 1996; Dame Ethel Walker: An Essay in Reassessment, 1997; The Palgraves and John Murray: Letters (editor), 1997. Contributions to: Various publications. Honours: 5th-6th Place, 1-Act Verse Play Competition, Poetry Society, 1964; 1st Place, Christian Poetry Competition, 1989. Memberships: Browning Society; Hopkins Society; Library Association, fellow; Masefield Society; Palgrave Society; PEN; Royal Society of Arts, fellow; Royal Society of Literature. Address: 72 Heathfield South, Twickenham, Middlesex TW2 7SS, England.

PEARCE Leslie Dennis, b. 20 Apr 1945, Bow, East London, England. Factory Worker; Road Worker; Security Officer; Local Government Officer; Retired. m. Anne Black, 21 Dec 1990. Education: Upton House Central School, 1956-60. Appointments: J Compton Sons & Webb, Uniform Clothing, Cap Cutter; R M Turner and Hunter, Timber Merchants, Trainee Sales; Poplar Borough Council, Road Labourer; United Dairies, Milk Roundsman; Securicor, Brinks Mat, Security Express, Cash In Transit Security Guard; London Borough of Hackney, Cashier, 1975-95, early retired. Publications include: Making Matters Verse; Pre-Conception, poem, 1997; Travelling Moon, 1997; Mirrors of the Soul, 1996; Voices in the Heart, 1997; Expressions, 1997; Tibby, 1998; Winter Warmer, 1998; What Love, 1998; Science, 1998; A Moving Sonnet, 1998, 1999. Honour: Editors Choice Award, 1996. Membership: International Society of Poets, Distinguished Member. Address: 29 Eastwood Road, Bexhill-on-Sea, East Sussex, TN39 3PR, England.

PEARCE Mary Emily, b. 7 Dec 1932, London, England. Writer. Publications: Apple Tree Lean Down, 1973; Jack Mercybright, 1974; The Sorrowing Wind, 1975; Cast a Long Shadow, 1977; The Land Endures, 1978; Seedtime and Harvest, 1980; Polsinney Harbour, 1983; The Two Farms, 1985; The Old House at Railes, 1993. Membership: Society of Authors. Address: Owls End, Shuthonger, Tewkesbury, Gloucestershire, England.

PEARCY Lee Theron, b. 20 Aug 1947, Little Rock, Arkansas, USA. Teacher; Scholar. m. Kathryn Eyre, 15 Aug 1970, 2 sons, 1 daughter. Education: BA, Columbia University, 1969; MA, Columbia University, 1971; PhD, Bryn Mawr College, 1974. Appointments: Master Englewood School for Boys, 1969-71; Assistant Professor, St Olaf College, 1973-77; Assistant Professor, The University of Texas, 1977-84; Lounsbery Chair in Classics, The Episcopal Academy, 1985-. Publications: Mediated Muse: English Translations of Oyid, 1560-1700, 1984; The Shorter Homeric Hymns, 1989; Ancient Medicine/Medicina Antiqua, 1996; Editor, Articulating the Curriculum From School to College = Classical World 92.1, 1998. Contributions to: Articles and reviews in American Journal of Philology, Bryn Mawr Classical Review and Elsewhere. Honours: Fellow, American Council of Learned Societies, 1979; National Endowment for the Humanities Teacher, Scholar Award, 1991. Memberships: American Philological Association; Classical Association of the Atlantic States, President, 1995-96; Society for the Promotion of Roman Studies. Address: The Episcopal Academy, Merion, PA 19066, USA.

PEARSALL Derek Albert, b. 28 Aug 1931, Birmingham, England. Professor of English. m. Rosemary Elvidge, 30 Aug 1952, 2 sons, 3 daughters. Education: BA, 1951, MA, 1952, University of Birmingham. Appointments: Assistant Lecturer, Lecturer, King's College, University of London, 1959-65; Lecturer, Senior Lecturer, Reader, 1965-76, Professor, 1976-87, University of York; Visiting Professor, 1985-87, Gurney Professor of English, 1987-, Harvard University, Cambridge, Massachusetts, USA. Publications: John Lydgate, 1970; Landscapes and Seasons of the Medieval World (with Elizabeth Salter), 1973; Old English and Middle English Poetry, 1977; Langland's Piers Plowman: An Edition of the C-Text, 1978; The Canterbury Tales: A Critical Study, 1985; The Life of Geoffrey Chaucer: A Critical Biography, 1992; John Lydgate (1371-1449): A Bio-bibliography, 1997; Chaucer to Spenser: An Anthology of Writings in English 1375-1575, 1999.

Memberships: Early English Text Society, council member; Medieval Academy of America, fellow; New Chaucer Society, president, 1988-90; American Academy of Arts and Sciences, fellow. Address: Harvard University, Department of English, Barker Centre, 12 Quincy Street, Cambridge, MA 02138, USA.

PEARSALL Ronald, b. 20 Oct 1927, Birmingham, England. Author. Education: Birmingham College of Art, 1952-54. Publications: Is That My Hook in Your Ear?, 1966; Worm in the Bud, 1969; The Table-Rappers, 1972; The Possessed, 1972; The Exorcism, 1972; Diary of Vicar Veitch, 1972; A Day at the Big Top, 1973; The Wizard and Elidog, 1973; Victorian Sheet Music Covers, 1973; Victorian Popular Music, 1973; Edwardian Life and Leisure, 1973; Collecting Mechanical Antiques, 1973; Collecting Scientific Instruments, 1974; Inside the Antique Trade (with Graham Webb), 1974; Edwardian Popular Music, 1975; Night's Black Angels, 1975; Collapse of Stout Party, 1975; Popular Music of the 1920s, 1976; Public Purity Private Shame, 1976; The Alchemists, 1976; The Belvedere, 1976; Conan Doyle, 1977; Antique Hunter's Handbook, 1978; Tides of War, 1978; Thomas en Olihond, 1979; The Iron Sleep, 1979; Making and Managing an Antique Shop, 1979, revised edition, 1986; Tell Me Pretty Maiden, 1981; Practical Painting, 1983, 4 volumes, 1990; Joy of Antiques, 1988; The Murder in Euston Square, 1989; Antique Furniture for Pleasure and Profit, 1990; Lifesaving, 1991; Painting Abstract Pictures, 1991; Encyclopedia of Everyday Antiques, 1992; Antique Furniture Almanac, 1992. Address: Sherwell, St Teath, Bodmin, Cornwall PL30 3JB, England.

PEARSE Lesley Margaret, b. 24 Feb 1945, Rochester, Kent, England. Novelist. 3 daughters. Education: Northbrook School Lee, London. Publications: Georgia, 1992; Tara, 1993; Clarity, 1994. Contributions to: Periodicals. Membership: Romantic Writers Association; RNA, West Country Writers Association. Address: 16 Withleigh Road, Knowle, Bristol BS4 2LQ, England.

PEARSON Ridley, b. 13 Mar 1953, Glen Cove, New York, USA. Author. Education: University of Kansas, 1972; Brown University, 1974. Publications: Never Look Back, 1985; Blood of the Albatross, 1986; The Seizing of Yankee Green Mall, 1987; Undercurrents, 1988; Probable Cause, 1990; Hard Fall, 1992; The Angel Maker, 1993; No Witnesses, 1994; Chain of Evidence, 1995; Beyond Recognition, 1997; The Pied Piper, 1998. Honour: Fulbright Fellow, 1990-91. Memberships: Writers Guild of America; Mystery Writers of America; Authors Guild; International Crime Writers Association. Address: PO Box 670, Hailey, ID 83333, USA.

PEARSON William Harrison, (Bill Pearson), b. 18 Jan 1922, Greymouth, New Zealand. Writer; Retired University Teacher. Education: Greymouth Technical High School, 1934-38; MA, Canterbury University College, Christchurch, 1948; PhD, King's College, University of London, England, 1952. Publications: Coal Flat, 1963, 5th edition, 1985; Henry Lawson Among Maoris, 1968; Fretful Sleepers and Other Essays, 1974; Rifled Sanctuaries, 1984; Six Stories, 1991. Honours: Co-Recipient, Landfall Readers Award, 1960; New Zealand Book Award for Non-Fiction, 1975. Address: 49 Lawrence Street, Herne Bay, Auckland, New Zealand.

PECK John (Frederick), b. 13 Jan 1941, Pittsburgh, Pennsylvania, USA. Poet. m. Ellen Margaret McKee, 1963, div, 1 daughter. Education: AB, Allegheny College, Meadville, Pennsylvania, 1962; PhD, Stanford University, 1973. Appointments: Instructor, 1968-70, Visiting Lecturer, 1972-75, Princeton University; Assistant Professor, 1977-79, Professor of English, 1980-82, Mount Holyoke College, South Hadley, Massachusetts. Publications: Poetry: Shagbark, 1972; The Broken Blockhouse Wall, 1978; Argura, 1993. Other: The Poems and Translations of Hi-Lo, 1991. Honours: American Academy of Arts and Letters Award, 1975, and Rome Fellowship, 1978; Guggenheim Fellowship, 1981. Address: c/o Englisches Seminar, Plattenstrasse 47, 8032 Zürich, Switzerland.

PECK M(organ) Scott, b. 22 May 1936, New York, New York, USA. Psychiatrist; Writer. m. Lily Ho, 27 Dec 1959, 1 son, 2 daughters. Education: Middlebury College, 1954-56; AB, Harvard University, 1958; MD, Case Western Reserve University, 1963. Appointments: US Army, 1963-72; Psychiatric practice, New Preston, Connecticut, 1972-84; Medical Director, New Milford Hospital Mental Health Clinic, 1973-81; Co-Founder and Board Member, Foundation for Community Encouragement, Ridgefield, Connecticut, 1984-93. Publications: The Road Less Traveled: A New Psychology of Love, Traditional Values and Spiritual Growth, 1978; People of the Lie: The Hope for Healing Human Evil, 1983; What Return Can I Make?: The Dimensions of the Christian Experience (with Marilyn von Waldener and Patricia Kay), 1985; The Different Drum: Community Making and Peace, 1985; A Bed by the Window: A Novel of Mystery and Redemption, 1990; The Friendly Snowflake: A Fable of Faith, Love and Family, 1992; Further Along the Road Less Traveled: The Unending Journey toward Spiritual Growth, 1993; A World Waiting to Be Born: Civility Rediscovered, 1993; Meditations from the Road: Daily Reflections from the Road Less Traveled and the Different Dru, 1993. Address: Bliss Road, New Preston, CT 06777, USA.

PECK Richard (Wayne), b. 5 Apr 1934, Decatur, Illinois, USA. Writer. Education: BA, DePauw University, 1956; MA, Southern Illinois University, 1959. Publications: Don't Look and It Won't Hurt, 1972; The Ghost Belonged to Me, 1975; Are You in the House Alone?, 1976; Secrets of the Shopping Mall, 1979; Amanda/Miranda, 1980; New York Time, 1981; Close Enough To Touch, 1981; This Family of Women, 1983; Remembering the Good Times, 1985; Blossom Culp and the Sleep of Death, 1986; Princess Ashley, 1987; Those Summer Girls I Never Met, 1988; Unfinished Portrait of Jessica, 1991. Contributions to: New York Times; School Library Journal. Honours: Edgar Allan Poe Award, American Society of Mystery Writers, 1977; American Library Association Margaret Edwards Young Adult Author Award, 1990. Memberships: Authors Guild; Authors League. Address: 155 East 72nd St, New York, NY 10021, USA.

PECK Robert Newton, b. 17 Feb 1928, Vermont, USA. Author. Education: AB, Rollins College, 1953; Cornell University. Appointment: Director, Rollins College Writers Conference, 1978-. Publications: A Day No Pigs Would Die, 1972; Millie's Boy, 1973; Path of Hunters: Animal Struggle in a Meadow, 1973; Soup, 1974; Soup for Me, 1975; Wild Cat, 1975; Bee Tree and Other Stuff (verse), 1975; Fawn, 1975; I Am the King of Kazoo, 1976; Rabbits and Redcoats, 1976; Hamilton, 1976; Hang for Treason, 1976; King of Kazoo (music and lyrics), play, 1976; Last Sunday, 1977; Trig, 1977; Patooie, 1977; The King's Iron, 1977; Soup for President, 1978; Eagle Fur, 1978; Trig Sees Red, 1978; Basket Case, 1979; Hub, 1979; Mr Little, 1979; Clunie, 1979; Soup's Drum, 1980; Secrets of Successful Fiction, 1980; Trig Goes Ape, 1980; Soup of Wheels, 1981; Justice Lion, 1981; Trig or Treat, 1982; Banjo, 1982; Soup in the Saddle, 1983; Soup's Goat, 1984; Spanish Hoof, 1985; Soup on Ice, 1985; Jo Silver, 1985; Soup on Fire, 1987; My Vermont, 1987; Hallapoosa, 1988; Arly, 1989; Soup's Hoop, 1990; Higbee's Halloween, 1990; Little Soup's Hayride, 1991; Little Soup's Birthday, 1991; Arly II, 1991; Soup in Love, 1994; Soup Ahoy, 1994; A Part of the Sky, 1994; Soup 1776, 1995. Honour: Mark Twain Award, Missouri, 1981. Address: 500 Sweetwater Club Circle, Longwood, FL 32779, USA.

PECKHAM Morse, b. 17 Aug 1914, Yonkers, New York, USA. Distinguished Professor Emeritus of English and Comparative Literature. Education: BA, University of Rochester, 1935; MA, 1938, PhD, 1947, Princeton University. Appointments: Instructor, 1946-47, Assistant Professor 1948-49, Rutgers University; Assistant Professor, 1949-52, Associate Professor, 1952-61, Director, Institute for Humanistic Education for Business Executives, 1953-54, University Press, 1953-55, Professor, 1961-67, University of Pennsylvania, Philadelphia; Distinguished Professor of English and Comparative Literature, 1967-80, Distinguished Professor Emeritus, 1980-, University of South Carolina, Columbia. Publications: On the Origin of Species: A Variorum Text, by Charles Darwin (editor), 1959; Humanistic Education for Business Executives: An Essay in General Education, 1960; Word, Meaning, Poem: An Anthology of Poetry (editor with Seymour Chapman), 1961; Beyond the Tragic Vision: The Quest for Identity in the Nineteenth Century, 1962; Man's Rage for Chaos: Biology, Behaviour and the Arts, 1965; Romanticism: The Culture of the Nineteenth Century (editor), 1965; Paracelsus, by Robert Browning (editor), 1969; Art and Pornography: An Experiment in Explanation, 1969; The Triumph of Romanticism; Speculation on Some Heroes of a Culture Crisis, 1970; Pippa Passes, by Robert Browning (editor), 1971; Luria, by Robert Browning (editor), 1973; Romanticism and Behaviour: Collected Essays II, 1976; Sordello, by Robert Browning (editor), 1977; Explanation and Power: The Control of Human Behavior, 1979; Romanticism and Ideology, 1985; The Birth of Romanticism, 1986. Address: 6478 Bridgewood Road, Columbia, SC 29206, USA.

PEDEN W(illiam) Creighton, b. 25 July 1935, Concord, North Carolina, USA. Fuller E Callaway Professor Emeritus of Philosophy; Writer; Editor. m. (2) Harriet McKnight Peden, 6 Oct 1978, 1 stepson, 2 daughters. Education: BA, Davidson College, North Carolina, 1957; MA, 1960, BD, 1962, University of Chicago; PhD, St Andrews University, Scotland, 1965. Appointments: Founding Faculty, Florida Presbyterian College, 1960-61; Assistant Professor, St Andrews College, 1964-65; Professor, Radford College, Virginia, 1965-68; Chair, Department of Philosophy, Millikin University, Decatur, Illinois, 1968-69; Visiting Professor, Iliff School of Theology, 1969, 1973, 1978, University of Glasgow, 1982-83, Vrije University, Amsterdam, 1991; Fuller E Callaway Professor of Philosophy, 1969-93, Professor Emeritus, 1993-, Augusta College, later Augusta State University, Georgia; Founding Editor, Journal of Social Philosophy, 1970-83; Founding Co-Editor, American Journal of Theology and Philosophy, 1980-91; Executive Director, 1987-92, President, 1992-98, Highlands Institute for American Religious Thought; Scholar-in-Residence, University of Copenhagen, 1988; President, Highlands Institute for American Religious and Philosophical Thought, 1998-. Publications: Wieman's Empirical Process Philosophy, 1977; Whitehead's View of Reality (with Charles Hartshorne), 1981; The Chicago School: Voices of Liberal Religious Thought, 1987; The Philosopher of Free Religion: Francis Ellingwood Abbot, 1836-1903, 1992; Civil War Pulpit to World's Parliament of Religion: The Thought of William James Potter, 1829-1893, 1996. Editor: Philosophical Reflections on Education and Society (with Donald Chapman), 1978; Critical Issues in Philosophy of Education (with Donald Chapman), 1979; Philosophy for a Changing Society, 1983; Philosophical Essays on Ideas of a Good Society, 1988; Freedom, Equality and Social Change, 1989; God, Values and Empiricism, 1989; Revolution, Violence, and Equality, 1990; Terrorism, Justice and Social Values, 1990; The American Constitutional Experiment, 1991; ; Communitarianism, Liberalism, and Social Responsibility, 1991; Rights, Justice, and Community, 1992; The Bill of Rights: Biocentennial Reflections, 1993; Freedom, Dharma, and Rights, 1993; New Essays in Religious Naturalism (with Larry E Axel), 1993; The Chicago School of Theology: Pioneers in Religious Inquiry, (with J Stone), 2 volumes, 1996; The Collected Essays of Francis Ellingwood Abbot (1836-1903): American Philosopher and Free Religionist (with Everett J Tarbox Jr), 4 volumes, 1996. Contributions to: Scholarly Books and journals. Honours: Awards; Grants; Phi Kappa Phi; Fellow, Society of Philosophers in America. Memberships: American Academy of Religion; American Philosophical Association; North American Society for Social Philosophy; Social Philosophy Research Institute; Society for the Advancement of American Philosophy; Society of Religious Humanism. Address: PO Box 2009, Bonnie Drive, Highlands, NC 28741, USA.

PEDERSEN Else Henneberg, b. 3 Aug 1937, Brørup, Denmark. Translator. m. Herluf Henneberg Pedersen, 19 Apr 1962, div 1986, 2 daughters. Education: MA, French, English, Language and Literature, University of Copenhagen. Publications: Translations from French and English into Danish including: Michel de Montaigne: Essays, 1992; Colette: Den gryende dag, 1992; Anne-Marie Garat: Mørkekammer, 1993; Henri Bergson: Latteren, 1993; Anthony Giddens: Intimitetens forandring, 1994; André Malraux: Kongevejen, 1994; Fr Sahebjam: En kvinde stenes, 1994; Anne-Marie Garat: Aden, 1995; Saint-Exupéry: Forord til Den lille prins, 1995; L Fronty og Y Duronsoy: Blomster og farver, 1995; A Borrel et al: Til bords med Proust, 1995; Judith L. Herman: I voldens kølvand, 1995; Jean Giono: Husaren på taget, 1996; Prins Henrik: Skæbne forpligter, 1996; Marcel Proust: På sporet af den tabte tid, forthcoming. Honours: The Translators' Award of The Danish Academy, 1993; Nomination for the European Aristeion Prize for Translators, 1994; Grant from His Royal Highness Prince Henrik's Foundation, 1995; The Danish Arts Foundation Working Scholarship for 3 years, 1996. Address: Amagerbrogade 133, 4.tv., DK - 2300 Copenhagen S, Denmark.

PEIRCE Neal R, b. 5 Jan 1932, Philadelphia, Pennsylvania, USA. Writer; Editor. Education: AB, Princeton University, 1954; Graduate Studies, Harvard University, 1957-58. Appointments: Political Editor, Congressional Quarterly, 1960-69; Co-Founder, Contributing Editor, The National Journal, Washington, DC, 1969-; Fellow, Woodrow Wilson Center for Scholars, 1971-74; Syndicated Columnist, Washington Post Writers Group. Publications: The People's President, 1968, 2nd edition, 1981; The Megastates of America, 1972; The Pacific States of America, 1972; The Great Plains States of America, 1973; The Deep South States of America, 1974; The Border South States, 1975; The New England States, 1976; The Mid-Atlantic States of America, 1977; The Great Lakes States of America, 1980; The Book of America, 1983; Corrective Capitalism, 1987; Enterprising Communities, 1989; Citisates, 1993; Breakthroughs, 1994. Address: 610 G Street South West, Washington, DC 20024, USA.

PEK Pal, (Annotator), b. 26 July 1939, Nagykanizsa, Hungary. Teacher. Education: Graduated, Pecs College, 1965; Elte University, Budapest, 1984. Appointments: Chief Editor, Kanizsa, local journal, 1989-91; Chief Editor, Pannon Tükör, cultural periodical, 1996-. Publications: Books of poems: Rapszodia a remenyröl, 1976; Nyar füstje, 1984; Holtag, 1990; Az idö metszetei, 1994; Havak tanca, 1997. Contributions to: Kortars; Hitel; Elet es Irodalom; Mühely; Argus; Tiszataj; Eletünk; Jelenkor; Somogy. Honour: Zala County Literary Award, 1997. Memberships: Chairman, Writers' Association, Zala County, 1995-; Association of Hungarian Writers. Address: Ady Endre utca 12/B II/4, 8800 Nagykanizsa, Hungary.

PELIKAN Jaroslav Jan, b. 17 Dec 1923, Akron, Ohio, USA. Professor of History; Writer. m. Sylvia Burica, 9 June 1946, 2 sons, 1 daughter. Education: Graduated, Concordia Junior College, Ft Wayne, Indiana, 1942; BD, Concordia Theological Seminary, St Louis, 1946; PhD, University of Chicago, 1946. Appointments: Faculty, Valparaiso University, 1946-49, Concordia Seminary, St Louis, 1949-53, University of Chicago, 1953-62; Titus Street Professor of Ecclesiastical History, 1967-72, Sterling Professor of History, 1972-, Dean, Graduate School, 1973-78, Director, Division of Humanities, 1974-75, Chairman, Medieval Studies, 1974-75, 1978-80, William Clyde DeVane Lecturer, 1984-86, Yale University; Various guest lectureships. Publications: From Luther to Kierkegaard, 1950; Fools for Christ, 1955; The Riddle of Roman Catholicism, 1959; Luther the Expositor, 1959; The Shape of Death, 1961; The Light of the World, 1962; Obedient Rebels, 1964; The Finality of Jesus Christ in an Age of Universal History, 1965; The Christian Intellectual, 1966; Spirit Versus Structure, 1968; Development of Doctrine, 1969; Historical Theology, 1971; The Christian Tradition, 5 volumes, 1971-89; Scholarship and Its Survival, 1983; The Vindication of

Tradition, 1984; Jesus Through the Centuries, 1985; The Mystery of Continuity, 1986; Bach Among the Theologians, 1986; The Excellent Empire, 1987; The Melody of Theology, 1988; Confessor Between East and West, 1990; Imago Dei, 1990; Eternal Feminines, 1990; The Idea of the University: A Reexamination, 1992; Christianity and Classical Culture, 1993; Faust the Theologian, 1995; The Reformation of the Bible/The Bible of the Reformation, 1996; Mary Through the Centuries, 1996. Editor: Makers of Modern Theology, 5 volumes, 1966-68; The Preaching of Chrysostom, 1967; Interpreters of Luther, 1968; Twentieth-Century Theology in the Making, 3 volumes, 1969-70; The Preaching of Augustine, 1973; The World Treasury of Modern Religious Thought, 1991; Sacred Writings, 7 volumes, 1992. Contributions to: Many books and professional journals. Honours: Abingdon Award, 1959; John Gilmary Shea Prize, American Catholic Historical Association, 1971; National Award, Slovak World Congress, 1973; Religious Book Award, Catholic Press Association, 1974; Christian Unity Award, Atonement Friars, 1975; Senior Fellow, Carnegie Foundation for the Advancement of Teaching, 1982-83; Festschrifts published in his honour, 1984, 1996; Haskins Medal, Medieval Academy of America, 1985; Award for Excellence, American Academy of Religion, 1989; Umanita Award, Newbery Library, 1990; Joseph A Sittler Award, 1993; Various honorary doctorates and other honours. Memberships: American Academy of Arts and Sciences, president, 1994-97; American Historical Association; American Philosophical Society; American Society of Church History, president, 1965; International Congress of Luther Research, president, 1971; Medieval Academy of America, fellow; Phi Beta Kappa. Address: 156 Chestnut Lane, Hamden, CT 06518, USA.

PELLATON Jean-Paul, b. 10 Aug 1920. Teacher. m. Jeanne Boinay, 24 May 1947, 2 sons, 1 daughter. Education: BA. Appointments: Teacher, Porrentruy, Bienne; Master, Training School Delémont; Lecturer, Berne University. Publications: Cent fleurs et un adjudant, 1953; Les prisons et leurs clés, 1973; Ces miroirs jumaux, 1975; Coplas, 1979; Quelques oiseaux étourdis, 1981; Poissons d'or, 1984; Dans la nuit une rose, 1985; Une ombre sur la terrasse, 1988; Septembre mouillé, 1990; Le Mège, 1993; Georges au vélo, 1994; Un habit chasse l'autre, 1996; D'Ici-bas, 1998. Contributions to: Coopération; Service de presse suisse. Honours: Prix Schiller, 1984, 1993; Prix Bibl. p. tous. Memberships: Institut Jurassien des Arts des Lettres des Sciences; Ecrivains Suisses; Association des ecrivains neuchâtelois et jurassiens. Address: Rue du 24 Septembre 9, CH 2800 Delémont, Switzerland.

PELLICER Juan, b. 24 Jan 1944, Mexico City. Lawyer; Philologist. m. Holly Kristoffersen, 6 Sept 1969, 2 sons, 1 daughter. Education: Law (Licentciatura), Universidad Nacional Autonoma of Mexico, 1962-67; Public Administration, London School of Economics & Political Science, 1968-69; Spanish Literature, University of Oslo, Masters Degree, 1987, Doctorate, 1995. Appointments: Foreign Service, Mexico, 1970-81; Ambassador to Norway & Iceland, 1977-81; Associate Professor, University of Oslo, 1996-. Publications: Ausencia De Principios Universales En El Derecho Internacional Privado, 1968; Mexico, Mexico, 1982; La Intertextualidad En De Anima, 1987. Contributions to: Bulletin of Hispanic Studies, Liverpool University; Revista Iberoamericana, University of Pittsburgh. Address: Klassisk og Romasnk Institute, PB 1007, University of Oslo, Norway.

PELUFFO Luisa, b. 20 Aug 1941, Buenos Aires, Argentina. Writer. m. Pablo Masllorens, 2 sons. Appointments: Producer, Channel 7 Television, Buenos Aires, 1970-71; Freelance Newspaper Journalist, Editorial Abril, Buenos Aires, 1968-70, La Nacián, Buenos Aires, 1971-79, Río Negro, San Carlos de Bariloche, 1977-82; Creative Writing Coach, San Carlos de Bariloche Municipal Art School, 1985-99. Publications: Materia Viva (poems), 1976; Conspiraciones (short stories), 1982, 2nd edition, 1989; Materia de Revelaciones (poems), 1983; Todo Eso Oyes (novel), 1989; La Otra Orilla (poems), 1991; La Doble Vida, (novel), 1993. Contributions to: Anthologies and newspapers. Honours: 1st Prize, Victoria Ocampo Literary Contest, Buenos Aires, 1980; Emecé Ediciones Prize, Buenos Aires, 1989; Regional Poetry Prize, National Arts Foundation, Buenos Aires, 1991; Finalist, Latin American Pegaso Prize for Literature, Colombia, 1993; Culture Bureau Regional Contest, Buenos Aires, 1999. Address: Palacios 465 (8400) Bariloche, Provincia de Rio Negro, Argentina.

PEMBERTON Margaret, b. 10 Apr 1943, Bradford, England. Writer. m. 1 son, 4 daughters. Publications: Harlot, 1981; Lion of Languedoc, 1981; The Flower Garden, 1982; Silver Shadows, Golden Dreams, 1985; Never Leave Me, 1986; Multitude of Sins, 1988; White Christmas in Saigon, 1990; An Embarrassment of Riches, 1992; Zadruga, 1993; Moonflower Madness, 1993; Tapestry of Fear, 1994; The Londoners, 1995; Magnolia Square, 1996; Yorkshire Rose, 1996; *Coronation* Summer, 1997. Memberships: Crime Writers Association; Romantic Novelists Association; PEN; Society of Authors. Address: 13 Manor Lane, London SE13, England.

PENA MUNOZ Margarita, b. 21 Aug 1937, Mexico. Writer; Scholar. m. B Lima, 6 Nov 1971, 1 son. Education: BD, Hispanic Literature, 1963, MD, Hispanic Literature, 1965, University of Mexico; PhD, El Colegio de Mexico, 1968. Appointments: Researcher, Literary Researching Centre, 1969-75, Professor, 1975-87, University of Mexico. Publications: Living Again, 1980; Flores de varia poesia, 1980; America's Discovery and Conquest, An Anthology of Chronicles, 1982; To Pass Over in Silence, 1983; Mofarandel, 1986. Contributions to: Journals and magazines. Memberships: International Hispanists Association; PEN; International Institute of Latin-American Literature; Latin-American Linguistics Association, University of Mexico. Address: Cerrada del Convento 45, Casa 2, Tlalpan, Mexico DF 14420, Mexico.

PENDLETON Don. See: **OBSTFELD Raymond.**

PENN John. See: **TROTMAN Jack.**

PENNANT-REA Rupert Lascelles, b. 23 Jan 1948, Southern Rhodesia. Economist; Writer. m. (1) Elizabeth Louise Greer, 1970, div 1975, (2) Jane Trevelyan Hamilton, 1979, div 1986, 1 son, 1 daughter, (3) Helen Jay, 1986, 1 son, 2 stepdaughters. Education: BA, Economics, Trinity College, Dublin, 1970; MA, University of Manchester, 1972. Appointments: Staff, 1977-86, Editor, 1986-93, The Economist; Deputy Governor, Bank of England, 1993-95; Chairman, The Stationery Office, 1996-. Publications: Gold Foil, 1979; Who Runs the Economy? (co-author), 1980; The Pocket Economist (co-author), 1983; The Economist Economics (co-author), 1986. Address: c/o The Stationery Office, 51 Nine Elms Lane, London SW8 5DR, England.

PEPPE Rodney Darrell, b. 24 June 1934, Eastbourne, East Sussex, England. Author; Artist. m. Tatjana Tekkel, 16 July 1960, 2 sons. Education: Eastbourne School of Art, 1951-53, 1955-57; London County Council Central School of Art, 1957-59; NDD, Illustration (special subject) and Central School Diploma. Publications: The Alphabet Book, 1968; The House That Jack Built, 1970; Odd One Out, 1974; Henry series, 1975-84; The Mice Who Lived in a Shoe, 1981; The Kettleship Pirates, 1983; The Mice and the Clockwork Bus, 1986; Huxley Pig series, 1989; The Mice on the Moon, 1992; The Mice and the Travel Machine, 1993; The Magic Toybox, 1996; Gus and Nipper, 1996; Hippo Plays Hide and Seek, 1997. Contributions to: Periodicals. Membership: Society of Authors. Address: Park House, Wellington Square, Cheltenham, Gloucestershire, GL50 4JZ, England.

PEPPERCORN Lisa Margot, b. 2 Oct 1913, Frankfurt am Main, Germany (Brazilian citizen). Musicologist. m. Lothar Bauer, 9 Apr 1938. Education: Degree, History of Music, Royal Conservatory, Brussels. Appointments: Music Correspondent, New York Times, 1939-46, Musical America, 1940-47; Musicological research, 1961-. Publications: Villa-Lobos in Paris, 1985; Villa-Lobos: Collected Studies, 1992; Letters, 1994; The World of Villa-Lobos in Pictures and Documents, 1996. Contributions to: Numerous publications. Honours: Outstanding Academic Book Citation, Choice Magazine, 1992. Address: Schulhaus Strasse 53, 8002 Zürich, Switzerland.

PEREIRA Teresinka, b. Brazil. Writer; Poet; Professor. m. (1) Heitor Martins, 1968, (2) Pedro Melendez, 1978, (3) Dennis Kann, 1993, 2 sons, 2 daughters. Education: Instituto de Educacao, 1958; BA, Universidade de Minas Gerais, 1960; PhD, University of New Mexico, 1973. Appointments: Faculty, Tulane University, 1962-67, Stanford University, 1968, University of Colorado, 1975-88, Moorhead State University, 1988-91, Bluffton College, 1991-. Publications: Over 30 books, including fiction and poetry. Contributions to: Numerous journals and magazines. Honours: Over 200. Memberships: International Writers and Artists Association, president; Royal Spanish Academy, corresponding member. Address: c/o Bluffton College, Bluffton, OH 45817, USA.

PERERA Victor Haim, b. 12 Apr 1934, Guatemala City, Guatemala. Writer. m. Padma Hejmadi, 8 Aug 1960, div 1974. Education: BA, Brooklyn College, 1956; MA, University of Michigan, 1958. Appointments: Editorial Staff, The New Yorker, 1963-66; Reporter, The New York Times Magazine, 1971-75; Contributing Editor, Present Tense, 1974-89; Editorial Board, Tikkun, 1990-. Publications: The Conversion, 1970; The Loch-Ness Monster Watchers, 1974; The Last Lords of Palenque (with Robert D Bruce), 1982; Rites: A Guatemalan Boyhood, 1986; Testimony: Death of a Guatemalan Village, by Victor Montejo (translator), 1987; Unfinished Conquest: The Guatemalan Tragedy, 1993; The Cross and the Pear Tree: A Sephardic Journey, 1995. Contributions to: New Yorker; Atlantic Monthly; Nation; New York Review; Partisan Review. Honours: Avery Hopwood Major Award in the Essay, 1962; National Endowment of the Arts Writing Award, 1980; PEN Fiction (Short Story) Award, 1984; Present Tense/Joel Cavior Award in Biography, 1987; Lila Wallace, Reader's Digest Writing Award, 1992-94. Membership: PEN American Centre. Address: c/o Watkins-Loomis Agency, 133 East 35th Street, New York, NY 10016, USA.

PEREZ Alberto Julián, b. 15 Sept 1948, Rosario, Argentina. University Professor. 1 daughter. Education: Instituto Nacional Profesorado, Rosario, Argentina, Master Education, 1975; MPh, New York University, 1984; PhD, New York University, 1986. Appointments: Fordham University, 1986-87; Dartmouth College, 1987-94; Michigan State University, 1994-95; Associate Professor of Spanish American Literature, Texas Tech University, 1995-. Publications: Poética de la prosa de J L Borges-Madrid, Gredos, 1986; La Poética de Rubén Darío, Orígenes, Madrid, 1992; Modernismo, Vanguardias, Postmodernidad, Buenos Aires, Corregidor, 1995. Contributions to: Revista Hispanoamericana, Hispania, Hispanofila. Membership: LASA; SCOLAS; IILH. Address: Texas Tech University, Box 42071, Lubbock, TX 79409, USA.

PERKINS George Burton, b. 16 Aug 1930, Lowell, Massachusetts, USA. Professor; Writer. m. Barbara Miller, 9 May 1964, 3 daughters. Education: AB, Tufts College, 1953; MA, Duke University, 1954; PhD, Cornell University, 1960. Appointments: Teaching Assistant, Cornell University, 1957-60; Assistant Professor, Farleigh Dickinson University, 1963-66; Lecturer, American Literature, University of Edinburgh, 1966-67; Professor, Eastern Michigan University, 1967-; General Editor, Journal of Narrative Technique, 1970-92. Publications: Writing Clear Prose, 1964; The Theory of the American Novel, 1970; Realistic American Short Fiction, 1972; American Poetic Theory, 1972; The American Tradition in Literature (with Bradley, Beatty, Long and Perkins), 4th to 9th editions, 1974-99; The Practical Imagination (with Frye and Baker), 1985; Contemporary American Literature (with B Perkins), 1991; Kaleidoscope (with B Perkins), 1993; Women's Work (with Perkins and Warhol), 1994; The Harper Handbook to Literature (with Frye, Baker and Perkins), 1997; A Season in New South Wales, 1998. Contributions to: Professional journals.

Honours: Duke University Fellow, 1953-54; Cornell University Fellow, 1954-55; Phi Kappa Phi, 1956; Distinguished Faculty Award, Eastern Michigan University, 1978; Fellow, Institute for Advanced Studies in the Humanities, University of Edinburgh, 1981; Senior Fulbright Scholar, University of Newcastle, Australia, 1989. Memberships: Various professional organisations. Address: 1316 King George Boulevard, Ann Arbor, MI 48108, USA.

PERKINS Michael, b. 3 Nov 1942, Lansing, Michigan, USA. Writer; Editor. m. Renie (Shoemaker) McCune, 20 June 1960, 1 son, 2 daughters. Education: New School for Social Research, New York City, 1962; Ohio University, Athens, 1963; City College, New York City, 1966. Appointments: Editor, Tompkins Square Press, 1966-68, Croton Press Ltd, 1969-72; Ulster Arts Magazine, 1978-79; Program Director, Woodstock Guild, 1985-95; Program Director, Woodstock Library, 1985-; Senior Editor, Masquerade Books, New York City, 1992-98. Publications: Evil Companions, 1968; Down Here, 1969; The Secret Record, 1977; The Persistence of Desire, 1977; The Good Parts, 1994; Gift of Choice, 1994; Dark Matter, 1996; Coming Up (editor), 1996. Contributions to: Reviews and periodicals. Memberships: Authors Guild; National Book Critics Circle. Address: 750 Ohayo Mt Road, Glenford, NY 12433, USA.

PERKINS-COOPER Barbie, b. 22 Aug 1950, Columbus, Georgia, USA. Business Writer. m. Phil Cooper, 18 Feb 1968, 1 son. Appointment: Business Writer, 1998. Publications include: We Need to Reach for the Stars, 1986; South Carolina Doing Well, 1990; Freelance Screenwriter's Forum, 1992; Let Us Decide, 1993; Mays Needs, 1993; Parking Problem, 1994; Faulkner and the Citadel, Why Wasn't She Ready, 1995. Honours include: Deans List Award, 1989-90; Graduate, Trident Technical College, 1991; Honourable Mention, National Writers Association, 1995; 2nd Place, Honourable Mention, Sandhills Writers Conference, Georgia, USA, 1996; Editors Choice Award, 1996. Memberships: The Dramatists Guild, 1997S Carolina Writers Workshop; North Carolina Writers Network; Scriptwriters of South Carolina; NAFE; Writers Workshop, Los Angeles; Writers Connection, Script Consultant; Scriptwriters Network. Address: 641 Palmetto St, Mt Pleasant, SC 29464, USA.

PERRETT Bryan, b. 9 July 1934, Liverpool, England. Author; Military Historian. m. Anne Catherine Trench, 13 Aug 1966. Education: Liverpool College. Appointment: Defence Correspondent to Liverpool Echo, during Falklands War and Gulf War. Publications: The Czar's British Squadron (with A Lord), 1981; A History of Blitzkrieg, 1983; Knights of the Black Cross: Hitler's Panzerwaffe and its Leaders, 1986; Desert Warfare, 1988; Encyclopaedia of the Second World War (with Ian Hogg), 1989; Canopy of War, 1990; Liverpool: A City at War, 1990; Last Stand: Famous Battles Against the Odds, 1991; The Battle Book: Crucial Conflicts in History from 1469 BC to the Present, 1992; At All Costs: Stories of Impossible Victories, 1993; Seize and Hold: Master Strokes of the Battlefield, 1994; Iron Fist: Crucial Armoured Engagements, 1995; Against All Odds! More Dramatic Last Stand Actions, 1995; Impossible Victories: Ten Unlikely Battlefield Successes, 1996; The Real Hornblower: The Life and Times of Admiral Sir James Gordon, GCB, 1998. Contributions to: War Monthly; Military History; World War Investigator; War in Peace (partwork); The Elite (partwork). Memberships: Rotary Club of Ormskirk; Royal United Services Institute; Army Records Society; Society for Army Historical Research. Address: 7 Maple Avenue, Burscough, Nr Ormskirk, Lancashire L40 5SL, England.

PERRIAM Wendy Angela, b. 23 Feb 1940, London, England. Writer. m. (1) 22 Aug 1964, 1 daughter, (2) John Alan Perriam, 29 July 1974. Education: St Anne's College, Oxford, 1958-61; BA, Honours, History, 1961, MA, 1972, University of Oxford; London School of Economics and Political Science, 1963-64. Publications: Absinthe for Elevenses, 1980; Cuckoo, 1981; After Purple, 1982; Born of Woman, 1983; The Stillness, The

Dancing, 1985; Sin City, 1987; Devils, for a Change, 1989; Fifty-Minute Hour, 1990; Bird Inside, 1992; Best Short-Stories, 1992; Michael, Michael, 1993; Breaking and Entering, 1994; Coupling, 1996; Second Anthology of Women's Short-Stories, 1997; Second Skin, 1998. Contributions to: Anthologies, newspapers, and magazines. Memberships: British Actors Equity Association; PEN; Society of Authors. Address: c/o Curtis Brown Ltd, 4th Floor, Haymarket House, 28/29 Haymarket, London SW1Y 4SP, England.

PERRICK Penny, b. 30 June 1941, London, England. Novelist; Critic. m. Clive Labovitch, 26 June 1962, div 1973, 1 son, 1 daughter. Education: Alliance Francaise, Paris, France, 1959-62. Appointments: Feature Writer, Vogue magazine; Columnist, The Sun, 1974-79; Columnist, The Times, 1983-89; Fiction Editor, Sunday Times, 1989-95. Publications: Malina, 1993; Impossible Things, 1995; Evermore, 1997. Contributions to: Times; Sunday Times; Country Homes and Interiors; You Magazine; The Irish Times; The Irish Tatler; Gardens Illustrated. Memberships: Society of Authors; Royal Society of Literature. Address: c/o Caradoc King, A P Watt, 20 John St, London WC1N 2DR, England.

PERRIE Walter, b. 5 June 1949, Lanarkshire, Scotland. Poet; Author; Critic. Education: MA, Honours, Mental Philosophy, University of Edinburgh, 1975; MPhil, English Studies, University of Stirling, 1989. Appointments: Editor, Chapman, 1970-75; Scottish-Canadian Exchange Fellow, University of British Columbia, Canada, 1984-85; Managing Editor, Margin: International Arts Quarterly, 1985-90; Stirling Writing Fellow, University of Stirling, 1991. Publications: Metaphysics and Poetry (with Hugh MacDiarmid), 1974; Poem on a Winter Night, 1976; A Lamentation for the Children, 1977; By Moon and Sun, 1980; Out of Conflict, 1982; Concerning the Dragon, 1984; Roads that Move: A Journey Through Eastern Europe, 1991; Thirteen Lucky Poems, 1991; From Milady's Wood and Other Poems, 1997. Contributions to: Journals and periodicals. Honours: Scottish Arts Council Bursaries, 1976, 1983, 1994, and Book Awards, 1976, 1983; Eric Gregory Award, 1978; Ingram Merrill Foundation Award, 1987. Memberships: PEN, Scotland; Society of Authors. Address: 10 Croft Place, Dunning, Perthshire PH2 0SB, Scotland.

PERROTT David, b. 25 Aug 1946, London, England. Writer; Cartographer. m. Morag Elizabeth Mary Wemyss, 3 July 1976, 3 sons, 1 daughter. Education: London College of Printing, 1st Martins School of Art. Appointments: Graphic Designer, Nicholson Publications; Visiting Lecturer, London University; Self-employed at present. Publications: Shell Guide to the Islands of Britain, 1984; Ordnance Survey Guide to the Broads and Fens, 1986; The Edinburgh Guide, 1988; Western Islands Handbook, 1988; Nicholson and Ordnance Survey Guides to the Waterways, 7 volumes, 1996; Ordnance Survey Map of the Waterways, 1997; Camra Best Pubs for Families, 1988; Numerous walking guides. Contributions to: Regular Contributor to Walking Wales. Membership: Outdoor Writers Guild. Address: Cysgod-Y-Fron, Darowen, Machynlleta, Monts SY20 8NS.

PERRY George (Cox), b. 7 Jan 1935, London, England. Writer. m. 1 July 1976, 1 son. Education: BA, 1957, MA, 1961, Trinity College, Cambridge. Appointments: Staff, Sunday Times Magazine, 1963-; Film Critic, Illustrated London News, 1982-88. Publications: The Films of Alfred Hitchcock, 1965; A Competitive Cinema (with Terence Kelly and Graham Norton), 1966; The Penguin Book of Comics (with Alan Aldridge), 1967; The Book of the Great Western, 1970; King Steam, 1971; Wheels of London, 1972; Rule Britannia: The Victorian World (with Nicholas Mason), 1974; The Great British Picture Show, 1974; The Movie-Makers: Hitchcock, 1975; Movies from the Mansion, 1976; The Great British, 1979; Forever Ealing, 1981; Diana: A Celebration, 1982; Life of Python, 1983; Give My Regards to Broad Street, 1984; Frank Sinatra (with Derek Jewell), 1985; Rupert, 1985; Bluebell, 1985;

The Complete Phantom of the Opera, 1987; The Golden Screen, 1989. Contributions to: Periodicals. Address: 7 Roehampton Lane, London SW15 5LS, England.

PERRY Margaret, b. 15 Nov 1933, Cincinnati, Ohio, USA. Retired Librarian; Writer. Education: AB, Western Michigan University, 1954; Certificate d'etudes Francaises, University of Paris, 1956; MSLS, Catholic University, 1959. Appointments: Young Adult and Reference Librarian, New York Public Library, 1954-55, 1957-58; Librarian, US Army, France and Germany, 1959-63, 1964-67; Chief of Circulation, US Military Library, West Point, New York, 1967-70; Head of Education Library, University of Rochester, 1970-75; Assistant professor, 1973-75, Associate Professor, 1975-82, Assistant Director of Libraries for Reader Services, 1975-82, Acting Director of Libraries, 1976-77, 1980; University Librarian, Valparaiso University, 1982-93, Retired, 1993. Publications: A Bio-bibliography of Countee P Cullen 1903-1946, 1971; Silence to the Drums: A Survey of the Literature of the Harlem Renaissance, 1976; The Harlem Renaissance, 1982; The Short Fiction of Rudolph Fisher, 1987. Contributions to: Arts Alive; Panache. Honours: 1st Prize, Short Story Contest, Armed Forces Writers League, 1966; 2nd Prize, Frances Steloff Fiction Prize, 1968; 1st prize, Short Story, Arts Alive, 1990; 2nd Prize, Short Story, Willow Rev, 1990; 3rd Prize, Short Story, West Shore C.C. Scottville, 1995. Membership: Academy of American Poets. Address: 15050 Roaring Brook Road, Thompsonville, MI 49683, USA.

PERRY Ritchie, (John Allen), b. 7 Jan 1942, King's Lynn, Norfolk, England. Teacher; Author. Education: BA, St John's College, Oxford, 1964. Publications: The Fall Guy, 1972; Nowhere Man, US edition as A Hard Man to Kill, 1973; Ticket to Ride, 1973; Holiday with a Vengeance, 1974; Your Money and Your Wife, 1975; One Good Death Deserves Another, 1976; Dead End, 1977; Brazil: The Land and Its People, 1977; Copacabana Stud (as John Allen), 1977; Dutch Courage, 1978; Bishop's Pawn, 1979; Up Tight (as John Allen), 1979; Grand Slam, 1980; Fool's Mate, 1981; Foul Up, 1982; MacAllister, 1984; Kolwezi, 1985; Presumed Dead, 1988; Comeback, 1991. Children's Books: George H Ghastly, 1982; George H Ghastly to the Rescue, 1982; George H Ghastly and the Little Horror, 1985; Fenella Fang, 1986; Fenella Fang and the Great Escape, 1987; Fenella Fang and the Wicked Witch, 1989; The Creepy Tale, 1989; Fenalla Fang and the Time Machine, 1991; The Runton Werewolf, 1994. Address: The Linhay, Water Lane, West Runton, Norfolk NR27 9QP, England.

PERUTZ Kathrin, b. 1 July 1939, New York, New York, USA. Author; Executive. Education: BA, Barnard College, 1960; MA, New York University, 1966. Appointment: Executive Director, Contact Program Inc. Publications: The Garden, 1962; A House on the Sound, 1964; The Ghosts, 1966; Mother is a Country: A Popular Fantasy, 1968; Beyond the Looking Glass: America's Beauty Culture, 1970; Marriage is Hell: The Marriage Fallacy, 1972; Reigning Passions, 1978; Writing for Love and Money, 1991. Also as Johanna Kingsley: Scents, 1985; Faces, 1987. Memberships: PEN; Authors Guild. Address: 16 Avalon Road, Great Neck, NY 10021, USA.

PERVIN Alice. See: LIST Anneliese.

PESETSKY Bette, b. 16 Nov 1932, Milwaukee, Wisconsin, USA. Writer. m. Irwin Pesetsky, 25 Feb 1956, 1 son. Education: BA, Washington University, 1954; MFA, University of Iowa, 1959. Publications: Stories Up to a Point, 1982; Author from a Savage People, 1983; Midnight Sweets, 1988; Digs, 1988; Confessions of a Bad Girl, 1989; Late Night Muse, 1991; Cast a Spell, 1993. Contributions to: New Yorker; Vanity Fair; Ms; Vogue; Paris Review; Ontario Review; Stand. Honours: Creative Writing Fellowship, National Endowment for the Arts, 1979-80; Creative Writing Public Service Award, New York Council for the Arts, 1980-81. Membership: PEN. Address: Hilltop Park, Dobbs Ferry, NY 10522, USA.

PETE Pindar. See: MORTON Harry Edwin Clive.

PETERFREUND Stuart (Samuel), b. 30 June 1945, Brooklyn, New York, USA. Professor of English; Poet. m. Carol Jean Litzler, 12 Sept 1981, div 17 December 1997, 1 daughter. Education: BA, English, Cornell University, 1966; MFA, Creative Writing, University of California at Irvine, 1968; English Literature and German Language, Columbia University, 1970-71; PhD, English, University of Washington, 1974. Appointments: Lecturer, University of Puget Sound, 1975; Assistant Professor, University of Arkansas at Little Rock, 1975-78; Assistant Professor, 1978-82, Associate Professor, 1982-91, Professor of English and Chair, Department of English, Northeastern University, 1991-. Publications: Poetry: The Hanged Knife and Other Poems, 1970; Harder than Rain, 1977; Interstatements, 1986. Other: William Blake in the Age of Newton: Essays on Literature as Art and Science, 1998. Editor: Critical Theory and the Teaching of Literature, 1985; Culture/Criticism/Ideology, 1986; Literature and Science: Theory and Practice, 1990. Contributions to: Scholarly books, professional journals, poetry anthologies, and reviews. Honours: Grants; Fellowships; 1st Prize in Poetry, Writers' Digest Competition, 1970; Poet-in-Residence, Southern Literary Festival, 1977; 1st Prize, Worcester County Poetry Association Contest, 1989; 3rd Prize, Abiko Journal Poetry Contest, 1994; 3rd Prize, Anna Davidson Rosenberg Award for Poems on the Jewish Experience, 1996. Memberships: American Society for Eighteenth-Century Studies; British Society for History of Science; Byron Society; History of Science Society; Interdisciplinary Nineteenth-Century Studies; International Association for Philosophy and Literature; Keats-Shelley Association of America; Modern Language Association; Poets and Writers; Society for Literature and Science, president, 1995-; Wordsworth-Coleridge Association. Address: c/o Department of English, Northeastern University, 406 Holmes Hall, 360 Huntington Avenue, Boston, MA 02115, USA.

PETERKIEWICZ Jerzy, b. 29 Sept 1916, Fabianki, Poland. Retired Professor of Polish Language and Literature; Poet; Writer; Dramatist. Education: University of Warsaw; MA, University of St Andrews, Scotland, 1944; PhD, King's College, London, 1947. Appointments: Lecturer, then Reader, 1952-72, Head, Department of East European Languages and Literature, 1972-77, Professor of Polish Language and Literature, 1972-79, University of London. Publications: Prowincja, 1936; Wiersze i poematy, 1938; Pogrzeb Europy, 1946; The Knotted Cord, 1953; Loot and Loyalty, 1955; Polish Prose and Verse, 1956; Antologia liryki angielskiej, 1958; Future to Let, 1958; Isolation, 1959; Five Centuries of Polish Poetry (with Burns Singer), 1960, enlarged edition, 1970; The Quick and the Dead, 1961; That Angel Burning at My Left Side, 1963; Poematy Londynskie, 1965; Inner Circle, 1966; Green Flows the Bile, 1969; The Other Side of Silence: The Poet at the Limits of Language, 1970; The Third Adam, 1975; Easter Vigil and Other Poems, by Karol Wojtyla (Pope John Paul II) (editor and translator), 1979; Kula magiczna, 1980; Collected Poems, by Karol Wojtyla (Pope John Paul II) (editor and translator), 1982; Poezje Wybrane, 1986; Literatura polska w perspektywie europejskiej, 1986; Modlitwy intelektu, 1988; Messianic Prophecy, 1991; In the Scales of Fate, 1993; Wiersze dobrzynskie, 1994; The Place Within: The Poetry of Pope John Paul II (editor and translator), 1994; Slowa sa bez Poreczy (Poems 1935-56), 1998. Contributions to: Numerous periodicals and BBC3. Address: 7 Lyndhurst Terrace, London NW3 5QA, England.

PETERS Catherine Lisette, b. 30 Sept 1930, London, England. Lecturer; Writer. m. (1) John Glyn Barton, 14 Jan 1952, 3 sons, (2) Anthony Storr, 9 Oct 1970. Education: BA, 1st Class Honours, 1980, MA, 1984, University of Oxford. Appointments: Editor, Jonathan Cape, 1960-74; Lecturer in English, Somerville College, Oxford, 1981-92. Publications: Thackeray's Universe, 1987; The King of Inventors: A Life of Wilkie Collins, 1991; Charles Dickens, 1998. Contributions to: Books and journals. Memberships: Wilkie Collins Society; Society of Authors; Royal Society of Literature, fellow; International PEN. Literary Agent: Michael Sissons, Peters, Fraser and Dunlop. Address: 45 Chalfont Road, Oxford OX2 6TJ, England.

PETERS Elizabeth. See: MERTZ Barbara Louise Gross.

PETERS Lance, b. 8 May 1934, Auckland, New Zealand. Author; Dramatist; Screenwriter. m. Laura Chiang, 25 Feb 1981, 2 sons, 2 daughters. Publications: Carry On Emmannuelle, 1978; The Dirty Half Mile, 1981; Cut-Throat Alley, 1982; Enemy Territory, 1988; God's Executioner, 1988; The Civilian War Zone, 1989; The Red Collar Gang, 1989; The Dirty Half Mile (Again), 1989; Gross Misconduct, 1993; Savior in the Grave, 1994. Other: Assault with a Deadly Weapon (play); 5 screenplays; Many television comedies, documentaries. Contributions to: Numerous popular magazines. Memberships: Honorary Life Member, Australian Writers Guild, president, 1970-72; Australian Society of Authors; Writers Guild of Great Britain; British Academy of Film and Television Arts. Address: 291 Fitzwilliam Road, Vaucluse, Sydney, New South Wales 2030, Australia.

PETERS Margot McCullough, b. 13 May 1933, Wausau, Wisconsin, USA. Professor of English Emerita; Author. m. Peter Ridgway Jordan, 5 Nov 1981, 1 son, 1 daughter. Education: BA, 1961, MA, 1965, PhD, 1969, University of Wisconsin at Madison. Appointments: Assistant Professor of English, Northland College, Ashland, Wisconsin, 1963-66; Assistant Professor, 1969-74, Associate Professor, 1974-77, Professor of English, 1977-91, Professor Emerita, 1991-, University of Wisconsin at Whitewater; Kathe Tappe Vernon Professor of Biography, Dartmouth College, 1978. Publications: Charlotte Brontë: Style in the Novel, 1973; Unquiet Soul: A Biography of Charlotte Brontë, 1975; Bernard Shaw and the Actresses, 1980; Mrs Pat: The Life of Mrs Patrick Campbell, 1984; The House of Barrymore, 1990; Wild Justice (as Margret Pierce), 1995; May Sarton: A Biography, 1997. Contributions to: Professional journals, newspapers, reviews, and periodicals. Honours: Friends of American Writers Award for Best Prose Work, 1975; American Council of Learned Society Fellow, 1976-77; George R Freedley Memorial Awards, 1980, 1984; Banta Awards, 1981, 1985; Guggenheim Fellowship, 1988-89; Wisconsin Institute for Research in the Humanities Grant, 1988-89; English-Speaking Union Ambassador Award, 1991; Wisconsin Library Association Distinguished Achievement Awards, 1991. 1998; Triangle Book Publishers Judy Gran Award, 1998. Memberships: Authors Guild; Brontë Society; Mark Twain Society; Bernard Shaw Society. Address: 511 College Street, Lake Mills, WI 53551, USA.

PETERS Mark. See: TAYLOR Peter Mark.

PETERS Maureen, (Victoria Black, Catherine Darby, Belinda Grey, Levannah Lloyd, Judith Rothman, Sharon Whitby), b. 3 Mar 1935, Caernarvon, North Wales. Writer. Education: BA and Diploma in Education, University College of North Wales, 1956. Publications: Over 40 books, fiction and non-fiction, 1980-90. Address: 45-47 Clerkenwell Green, London EC1R 0HT, England.

PETERS Michael Adrian, b. 4 Sept 1948, Wellington, New Zealand. Professor. m. Christine Athlone Besley, 23 Nov 1996, 2 sons. Education: BA, Honours, Geography, Victoria University of Wellington, 1971; Diploma of Teaching, Christchurch College of Education, 1972; MA, Philosophy, PhD, Education, University of Auckland, 1979-84. Appointments: Secondary Teacher, Linwood High School, 1973-78; Head of Geography, Longbay High School, 1979-80; Private Consultant, 1981-89; Lecturer in Education, University of Canterbury, 1990-92; Senior Lecturer, University of Auckland, 1993-95; Associate Professor, University of Auckland, 1996-. Publications: Education and the Postmodern Conditon, 1995; Poststructuralism, Politics and Education, 1996; Critical Theory, Poststructuralism and the Social Context, 1996; Cultural Politics and the University, 1997; Virtual Technologies and Teriary Education, 1998; Naming the Multiple: Poststructuralism and Education, 1998; Witgenstein: Philosophy, Postmodernism, Pedagogy (with James Marshall), 1999; Individualism and Community: Education and Social Policy in the Postmodern Condition (with James Marshall), 1999;

University Futures and the Politics of Reform (with Peter Roberts), 1999. Contributions to: Journals. Membership: Council Member, Humanities Society of New Zealand, 1997-98. Address: c/o School of Education, University of Auckland, Private Bag 92019, Auckland, New Zealand.

PETERS Richard. See: HAINING Peter.

PETERS Richard Stanley, b. 31 Oct 1919, Missouri, India. Professor of the Philosophy of Education Emeritus; Writer. m. Margaret Lee Duncan, 16 July 1943, 1 son, 2 daughters. Education: Clifton College, Bristol; Queen's College, Oxford; Birkbeck College, London; BA, Oxon; BA, London; PhD, London, 1949. Appointments: Part-time Lecturer, 1946-49, Full-time Lecturer, 1949-58, Reader in Philosophy, 1958-62, Birkbeck College, London; Visiting Professor, Harvard University, 1961. University of Auckland, 1975; Professor of the Philosophy of Education, 1962-82, Professor Emeritus, 1982-, University of London; Part-time Lecturer, Bedford College, London, and London School of Economics and Political Science, 1966; Visiting Fellow, Australian National University, Canberra, 1969. Publications: Ethics and Education, 1945; Brett's History of Psychology, revised edition, 1953; Hobbes, 1956; The Concept of Motivation, 1958; Social Principles and the Democratic State (with S I Benn), 1959; Authority, Responsibility and Education, 1960; Ethics and Education, 1966; The Concept of Education (editor), 1967; Perspectives on Plowden (editor), 1969; The Logic of Education (with P H Hirst), 1970; Hobbes and Rousseau (editor with M Cranston), 1971; Education and the Development of Reason (editor with R F Dearden and P H Hirst), 1972; Reason and Compassion, 1973; The Philosophy of Education (editor), 1973; Psychology and Ethical Development, 1974; Nature and Conduct (editor), 1975; The Role of the Head (editor), 1976; Education and the Education of Teachers, 1977; John Dewey Reconsidered (editor), 1977; Essays on Education, 1981; Moral Development and Moral Education, 1981. Address: Flat 3, 16 Shepherd's Hill, Highgate, London N6 5AQ, England.

PETERS Robert Louis, b. 20 Oct 1924, Eagle River, Wisconsin, USA. Professor of English; Poet; Writer. Div, 3 sons, 1 daughter. Education: BA, 1948, MA, 1949, PhD, 1952, University of Wisconsin at Madison. Appointments: Instructor, University of Idaho, 1952-53, Boston University, 1953-55; Assistant Professor, Ohio Wesleyan University, 1955-58; Associate Professor, Wayne State University, 1958-63; Professor of English, University of California at Riverside, 1963-68, and Irvine, 1968-. Publications: The Drowned Man to the Fish, 1978; Picnic in the Snow: Ludwig of Bavaria, 1982; What Dillinger Meant to Me, 1983; Hawker, 1984; Kane, 1985; Ludwig of Bavaria: Poems and a Play, 1986; The Blood Countess: Poems and a Play, 1987; Haydon, 1988; Brueghel's Pigs, 1989; Poems: Selected and New, 1992; Goodnight Paul: Poems, 1992; Snapshots for a Serial Killer: A Fiction and Play, 1992; Zapped: 3 Novellas, 1993; Nell: A Woman from Eagle River, 1994; Lili Marlene: A Memoir of World War II, 1995. Other: Victorians in Literature and Art, 1961; The Crowns of Apollo: Swinburne's Principles of Literature and Art, 1965; The Letters of John Addington Symonds (co-editor), 3 volumes, 1967-69; Gabriel: A Poem by John Addington Symonds, 1974; The Collected Poems of Amnesia Glassclock: John Steinbeck (editor), 1977; Letter to a Tutor: The Tennyson Family Letters to Henry Graham Dakyns (editor), 1988. Contributions to: Professional journals. Honours: Guggenheim Fellowship, 1966-67; Yaddo, MacDowell Colony, and Ossabaw Island Project Fellowships, 1973-74; National Endowment for the Arts Grant, 1974. Memberships: American Society for Aesthetics; PEN; Writer's Guild. Address: 9431 Krepp Drive, Huntington Beach, CA 92646, USA.

PETERSEN Peter James, b. 23 Oct 1941, Santa Rosa, California, USA. Writer; Teacher. m. Marian Braun, 6 July 1964, 2 daughters. Education: AB, Stanford University; MA, San Francisco State University; PhD, University of New Mexico. Appointments: English Instructor, Shasta College. Publications: Would You

Settle for Improbable, 1981; Nobody Else Can Walk It for You, 1982; The Boll Weevil Express, 1983; Here's to the Sophomores, 1984; Corky & the Brothers Cool, 1985; Going for the Big One, 1986; Good-bye to Good O'Charlie, 1987; The Freshman Detective Blues, 1987; I Hate Camping, 1991; Liars, 1992; The Sub, 1993; I Want Answers and a Parachute, 1993; Some Days, Other Days, 1994. Honour: National Endowment for the Humanities Fellowship, 1976-77. Membership: Society of Children's Book Writers. Address: 1243 Pueblo Court, Redding, CA 96001, USA.

PETERSON Donald Macandrew, b. 23 June 1956, Dumfries, Scotland. Lecturer in Cognitive Science. Education: MA, Philosophy and Psychology, Edinburgh University, 1978; PhD, Philosophy, University College London, 1985, MSc, DIc, in Foundations of Advanced Information Technology, Imperial College, London, 1986. Publication: Wittgenstein's Early Philosophy - Three Sides of the Mirror, 1990. Contributions to: Professional journals and magazines. Membership: Society of Artificial Intelligence and the Simulation of Behaviour. Address: Department of Computer Science, University of Birmingham, Birmingham B15 2TT, England.

PETERSON Robert, b. 2 June 1924, Denver, Colorado, USA. Writer; Poet. 1 daughter. Education: BA, University of California, Berkeley, 1947; MA, San Francisco State College, 1956. Appointment: Writer-in-Residence, Reed College, Portland, Oregon, 1969-71. Publications: Home for the Night, 1962; The Binnacle, 1967; Wondering Where You Are, 1969; Lone Rider, 1976; Under Sealed Orders, 1976; Leaving Taos, 1981; The Only Piano Player in La Paz, 1985; Waiting for Garbo: 44 Ghazals, 1987; All The Time in the World, 1996. Honours: National Endowment for the Arts Grant, 1967; Amy Lowell Travelling Fellowship, 1972-73. Memberships: Marin Poetry Society. Address: PO Box 417, Fairfax, CA 94978, USA.

PETERZEN (Anna Karin) Elisabet, b. 15 Apr 1938, Stockholm, Sweden. Author, 1 daughter. Education: London School of Foreign Trade, 1960; University of Stockholm, 1980-83. Appointment: Women's Committee, Swedish Union of Authorss, 1985-88. Publications: Marmor och Ebenholts, 1964; Njutning, 1967; Trygghet, 1968; Aktenskaps Brott, 1969; Den konstgjorda mannen, 1973; En mans liv (Mustafa Said), 1974; Roman, 1976; Ljusnatten, 1981; Lura Livet, 1981; Sista Sticket, 1983; Mamsell Caroline, 1986; Djursager, 1987; Nubiens Hjarta, 1989; Sista Ordet, 1993. Honours: 1st Prize, Best 2nd World Novel, 1976; 1st Prize, Best Book Club Novel, 1986. Memberships: Swedish Union of Authors, 1970-; Sisters in Crime, USA/Germany, 1996-. Address: S-14832 Osmo, Sweden.

PETOCZ Andras, b. 27 Aug 1959, Budapest, Hungary. Editor; Writer; Poet. 2 daughters. Education: Graduated, Lorand Eötvös University, Budapest, 1986. Appointments: Chief Editor, Jelenlet, literary periodical, 1981-83; Editor and Publisher, Medium Art, underground literary periodical during the Communist regime, 1983-89; Editor, Magyar Muhley, literary periodical, 1989-91; Chief editor, Budapesti Jelenlet, Literary Magazine. Publications: Poems, essays, and children's poems. Contributions to: Periodicals. Honour: Several literary prizes. Memberships: Art Association of the Hungarian Republic; Hungarian Writers Association. Address: Studio of Medium Art, Donati u 6, H-1015 Budapest, Hungary.

PETRAKIS Harry Mark, b. 5 June 1923, St Louis, Missouri, USA. Writer. m. Diane Perparos, 30 Sept 1945, 3 sons. Education: University of Illinois, 1940-41. Appointments: Teacher, writing workshops; McGuffey Visiting Lecturer, Ohio University, 1971; Writer-in-Residence, Chicago Public Library, 1976-77, Chicago Board of Education, 1978-79; Kazantzakis Professor, San Francisco State University, 1992. Publications: Lion at My Heart, 1959; The Odyssey of Kostas Volakis, 1963; Pericles on 31st Street, 1965; The Founder's Touch, 1965; A Dream of Kings, 1966; The Waves of Night, 1969; Stelmark: A Family Recollection, 1970; In the Land of Morning, 1973; The Hour of the Bell, 1976; A Petrakis Reader: 28 Stories, 1978; Nick the Greek, 1979; Days of Vengence, 1983; Reflections on a Writer's Life and Work, 1983; Collected Stories, 1986; Ghost of the Sun, 1990. Contributions to: Various magazines. Honours: Several awards, including Carl Sandburg Award; Ellis Island Medal of Honour, 1995. Memberships: Authors Guild; PEN; Writers Guild of America, West. Address: 80 East Road, Dune Acres, Chesterton, IN 46304, USA.

PETRIE Paul James, b. 1 July 1928, Detroit, Michigan, USA. Retired Professor of English; Poet. m. Sylvia Spencer, 21 Aug 1954, 1 son, 2 daughters. Education: BA, 1950, MA, 1951, Wayne State University; PhD, University of Iowa, 1957. Appointments: Associate Professor, Peru State University, 1958-59; Instructor to Professor of English, University of Rhode Island, 1959-90. Publications: Confessions of a Non-Conformist, 1963; The Race With Time and the Devil, 1965; From Under the Hill of Night, 1969; The Academy of Goodbye, 1974; Light From the Furnace Rising, 1978; Not Seeing is Believing, 1983; Strange Gravity, 1985; The Runners, 1988. Contributions to: Newspapers, reviews, quarterlies, journals, and magazines. Honours: Phi Beta Kappa Poet, Brown University, 1968; Scholarly Achievement Award, University of Rhode Island, 1983; Capricorn Award, Writers Voice, West Side YMCA, 1984; Catholic Press Award, 1985; Arts Achievement Award, Wayne State University, 1990. Address: 200 Dendron Road, Peace Dale, RI 02879, USA.

PETROSKI Catherine (Ann), b. 7 Sept 1939, St Louis, Missouri, USA. Writer. m. Henry Petroski, 15 July 1966, 1 son, 1 daughter. Education: BA, MacMurray College, 1961; MA, University of Illinois, 1962. Publications: Gravity and Other Stories, 1981; Beautiful My Mane is the Wind, 1983; The Summer That Lasted Forever, 1984; A Bride's Passage: Susan Hathorn's Year Under Sail, 1997. Contributions to: Reviews, quarterlies, and periodicals. Honours: Berlin Prize, 1960; Texas Institute of Letters Prize, 1976; National Endowment for the Arts Fellowships, 1978-79, 1983-84; PEN Syndicated Fiction Prizes, 1983-85, 1988; Honorary DLitt, MacMurray College, 1984; O Henry Award, 1989; John Lyman Book Award, 1997. Memberships: Author's Guild; National Book Critics Circle. Address: 2528 Wrightwood Avenue, Durham, NC 27705, USA.

PETROSKI Henry, b. 6 Feb 1942, New York, USA. Engineer; Teacher; Writer. m. Catherine Ann Groom, 15 July 1966, 1 son, 1 daughter. Education: BME, Manhattan College, 1963; MS, 1964, PhD, 1968, University of Illinois. Appointment: Faculty, School of Engineering, Duke University. Publications: To Engineer is Human, 1985; Beyond Engineering, 1986; The Pencil, 1990; The Evolution of Useful Things, 1992; Design Paradigms, 1994; Engineers of Dreams, 1995; Invention by Design, 1996; Remaking the World, 1997; The Book on the Bookshelf, 1999. Contributions to: American Scientist (Engineering Columnist). Honours: Honorary degrees: Clarkson University, 1990; Trinity College, Hartford, Connecticut, 1997. Memberships: American Society of Civil Engineers; American Society of Mechanical Engineers; National Academy of Engineering. Address: School of Engineering, Duke University, Durham, NC 27708, USA.

PETROVITS Loty, b. 12 Aug 1937, Athens, Greece. Author. m. Andreas Andrutsopoulos, 23 July 1966, 1 son, 1 daughter. Education: University of Michigan; Istituto Italiano di Cultura in Atene, 1960. Appointments: Editorial Correspondent, Phaedrus, 1980-88; Associate Editor, Bookbird, 1982-; Co-Editor, Diadromes, 1986-. Publications: O Mikros Adelfos, 1976, Japanese translation, 1988; Tris Fores Ki Enan Kero, 1977; Gia Tin Alli Patrida, 1978; Sto Tsimentenio Dasos, 1981; Zetete Mikros, 1982; Istories pou kanenas den xerei, 1984; Spiti Gia Pente, 1987, Japanese translation, 1990; Istories me tous dodeca mines, 4 volumes, 1988; Lathos Kyrie Noyger!, 1989; Tragoudi yia Treis, 1992; Yousouri stin Tsepi, 1994; Kanarini kai Menta, 1996; Ta tessera Tango, 1996; 15 more books for children and 6 for adults; Translations from English into Greek include: Blowfish Live in the Sea, by Paula Fox, 1979; The Camelthorn Papers, by Ann Thwaite, 1987. Contributions to: Phaedrus; Bookbird; Diadromes; Efthini; Diavazo; Kypriaki Martyria; Helidonia; Gia Hara. Honours: Women's Literary Club Annual Awards, 1976, 1979, 1981, 1987; Academy of Athens Award for Children's Literature, 1984; Pier Paolo Vergerio Honour List Diploma, 1988; Society of Christian Letters Award and IBBY Honour List Diploma, 1992; Greek IBBY Annual Awards, 1977, 1994; Nominee for H.C. Andersen Award, 1994. Address: 129 Aristotelous Street, GR 11251 Athens, Greece.

PETTIFER James Milward, b. 6 Apr 1949, Hereford, England. Writer; Teacher. m. 7 June 1974, 1 son, 1 daughter. Education: Hertford College, Oxford, MA, 1971. Appointments: Co-Editor, "Albania Life" magazine; Member, Royal Institute of International Affairs, London; Senior Associate Member, St Antony's College, Oxford; Visiting Professor, Institute of Balkan Studies, Aristotle University of Thessalonika, Greece. Publications: Blue Guide/Guide Bleu to Albania, 1991; The Greeks - Land and People Since the War, 1993; Blue Guide to Bulgaria, 1996; Albania: From Anarchy to a Balkan Identity (with M Vickers). Contributions to: The Times (London), Wall Street Journal; The Economist, others. Memberships: Institute of Balkan Studies, Greece; Institute of Balkan History, Sofia, Bulgaria. Address: c/o Curtis Brown Ltd, 28 Haymarket, London SW1, England.

PETTIFER Julian, b. 21 July 1935, Malmesbury, England. Freelance Writer; Broadcaster. Education: St John's College, Cambridge, 1955-58. Appointments: TV Reporter, Writer, Presenter: Southern TV, 1958-62; Tonight, 1962-64, 24 Hours, 1964-69, Panorama, 1969-75, BBC; Presenter, Cuba - 25 Years of Revolution, series, 1984, Host, Busman's Holiday, 1985-86, ITV; Numerous TV documentaries including: Vietnam War Without End, 1970; The World About Us, 1976; The Spirit of 76, 1976; Diamonds in the Sky, 1979; Nature Watch, 5 series, 1981-90; Automania, 1984; The Living Isles, 1986; Africawatch, 1989; Missionaries, 1990; BBC Assignment, 1993-94; BBC Correspondent, 1994-95. Publications: Diamonds in the Sky: A Social History of Air Travel (co-author), 1979; Nature Watch, 1981; Automania, 1984; The Nature Watchers, 1985; Missionaries, 1990; Nature Watch, 1994. Honour: Reporter of the Year Award, Guild of Television Directors and Producers, 1968. Memberships: Royal Society for Nature Conservation, vice-president, 1992-; Royal Society for the Protection of Birds, president, 1994. Address: c/o Curtis Brown, 28/29 Haymarket, London SW1Y 4SP, England.

PETTY William Henry, b. 7 Sept 1921, Bradford, Yorkshire, England. Retired Educator; Poet. m. Margaret Elaine Bastow, 31 May 1948, 1 son, 2 daughters. Education: Peterhouse, Cambridge, 1940-41, 1945; MA, Cantab, 1950; BSc, London, 1953; D Litt, Kent, 1983. Appointments: Administrative, Teaching, and Lecturing posts, London, Doncaster, North and West Ridings of Yorkshire, Kent, 1945-73; Chief Education Officer, Kent, 1973-84; Chairman of Governors, Christ Church College, Canterbury, 1992-94. Publications: No Bold Comfort, 1957; Conquest, 1967; Springfield: Pieces of the Past, 1994; Genius Loci (with Robert Roberts), 1995; The Louvre Imperial, 1997. Contributions to: Various anthologies, 1954-96, reviews, quarterlies, and journals. Honours: Cheltenham Festival of Literature Prize, 1968; Camden Festival of Music and the Arts Prize, 1969; Greenwood Prize, Poetry Society, 1978; Lake Aske Memorial Award, 1980; Commander of the Order of the British Empire, 1981; Swanage Festival of Literature Prize, 1995; Ali Competition Prize, 1995; Kent Federation of Writers Prize, 1995. Membership: Poetry Society. Address: Willow Bank, Moat Road, Headcorn, Kent TN27 9NT, England.

PEYREFITTE (Pierre) Roger, b. 17 Aug 1907, Castres, Taran, France. Author. Education: BA, École des Sciences Politiques, Paris. Publications: Les amitiés particulières, 1944-45; Mademoiselle de Murville, 1946; Le prince des neiges, 1947; L'oracle, 1948; Les amours singulières, 1949; La Mort d'une mère, 1950; Les ambassades, 1951; Du Vesuve a l'Etna, 1952; Les clés de St Pierre, 1955; Jeunes Proies, 1956; Chevaliers de Malte, 1957; L'exile de Capri, 1959; Le Spectateur nocturne, 1960; Les fils de la lumière, 1961; La nature du prince, 1963; Les Juifs, 1965; Notre Amour, 1967; Les Americains, 1968; Des Francais, 1970; La Coloquinte, 1971; Manouche, 1972; La muse garçonnière, 1973; Tableaux de chasse ou la vie extraordinaire de Fernand Legros, 1976; Propos secrets, 1977; La Jeunesses d'Alexandre, 1977; L'enfant de coeur, 1978; Roy, 1979; Les conquêtes d'Alexandre, 1979; Propos Secrets II, 1980; Alexandre Le Grand, 1981; L'illustre ecrivain, 1982; La soutane rouge, 1983; Henry de Montherlent- Roger Peyrefitte correspondence, 1983; Voltaire, sa Jeunesse et son Temps, 1985; L'Innominato, nouveaux propos secrets, 1989; Reflexion sur De Gaulle, 1992. Honour: Prix Theophaste Renaudot. Address: 9 Avenue du Marechal Manoury, 75016, Paris, France.

PEYTON Kathleen Wendy, (Kathleen Herald, K M Peyton), b. 2 Aug 1929, Birmingham, England. Writer. m. Michael Peyton, 1950, 2 daughters. Education: ATD, Manchester School of Art. Publications: As Kathleen Herald: Sabre, the Horse from the Sea, 1947; The Mandrake, 1949; Crab the Roan, 1953. As K M Peyton: North to Adventure, 1959; Stormcock Meets Trouble, 1961; The Hard Way Home, 1962; Windfall, 1963; Brownsea Silver, 1964; The Maplin Bird, 1964; The Plan for Birdsmarsh, 1965; Thunder in the Sky, 1966; Flambards Trilogy, 1969-71; The Beethoven Medal, 1971; The Pattern of Roses, 1972; Pennington's Heir, 1973; The Team, 1975; The Right-Hand Man, 1977; Prove Yourself a Hero, 1977; A Midsummer Night's Death, 1978; Marion's Angels, 1979; Flambards Divided, 1981; Dear Fred, 1981; Going Home, 1983; The Last Ditch, 1984; Froggett's Revenge, 1985; The Sound of Distant Cheering, 1986; Downhill All the Way, 1988; Darkling, 1989; Skylark, 1989; No Roses Round the Door, 1990; Poor Badger, 1991; Late to Smile, 1992; The Boy Who Wasn't There, 1992; The Wild Boy and Queen Moon, 1993; Snowfall, 1994; The Swallow Tale, 1995; Swallow Summer, 1995; Unquiet Spirits, 1997; Firehead, 1998; Swallow the Star, 1998. Honours: New York Herald Tribune Award, 1965; Carnegie Medal, 1969; Guardian Award, 1970. Address: Rookery Cottage, North Fambridge, Chelmsford, Essex CM3 6LP, England.

PEYTON Richard. See: **HAINING Peter Alexander.**

PFANNER (Anne) Louise, b. 6 Mar 1955, Sydney, New South Wales, Australia. Illustrator; Writer. m. (1) Glenn Woodley, 24 Dec 1976, (2) Tim Maddox, 12 Jan 1987, 4 sons. Education: Diploma, Graphic Design, 1977; BA, Visual Communication, 1986; MA, Children's Literature and Literacy, 1997. Appointment: Regular exhibits of illustrations. Publications: Louise Builds a Boat, 1986; Louise Builds a House, 1987; The Little Red Hen, 1997; The Country Mouse, 1997. Illustrator: Your Book of Magic Secrets (R Deutch), 1991; I'm a Little Teapot, 1995; First Book of Gardening, 1995; Mean Charlotte the Good Idea, 1996; Sing Book, infants section, 1996. Contributing Illustrator: Under the Clock, 1996. Contributions to: Illustrations in various publications. Memberships: Society of Book Illustrators, Sydney; Australian Society of Authors; Australian Society of Authors. Address: 4 Catalpa Avenue, Avalon, New South Wales 2107, Australia

PFEFFER Susan Beth, b. 17 Feb 1948, New York, New York, USA. Children's Writer. Education: BA, New York University, 1969. Publications: Some 40 books, 1970-96. Address: 14 South Railroad Avenue, Middletown, NJ 10940, USA.

PFEIFER Tadeus, (Peter Kober), b. 5 Apr 1949, Freiburg. Writer. Publications: Häxebanner, 1971; Trauer, 1974; Buddenbrooks, Schauspiel nach dem Roman von Thomas Mann, 1976; Das Feuer des Steins, 1981; Ich ahne was ich weiss, 1982; Die schönen Seiten des Lebens, 1984; Die sieben Farben des Lichts, 1986; Im Gras kreischt freundlich der Affe, 1989; Das Echo von Bois-Rateau, 1992; Nicht Fisch, Nicht Vogel, 1994; Die

Architektur der Liebe, 1997; Rebenzeilen, 1998. Honours: Pro Helvetia, Div. Memberships: Gruppe Olten; PEN. Literary Agent: Liepman Ltd, Zurich. Address: Leonhardsstrasse 12, CH-4051 Basel, Switzerland.

PHELAN Thomas Joseph, b. 5 Nov 1940, Mountmellick, Ireland. Novelist. m. Patricia Mansfield, 14 Sept 1991, 2 sons. Education: BA, Philosophy, St Patricks Seminary, Carlow, 1965; Master Degree, Seattle University, 1977. Appointments: Priest; Assistant Professor of English, Harriman College, New York; Insurance Arbitrator; Carpenter, Garden City Public Schools, New York. Publications: In the Season of the Saisies, 1993; Iscariot, 1995; Saying Goodbye, 1995; In the Vatican Museum, 1998; Derry Clooney, 1999. Memberships: Authors Guild; Poets and Contemporary Authors; Poets and Writers. Address: 237 Church Street, Freeport, NY 11520, USA.

PHILANDERSON Flavian Titus, (Johnny Goad, Flavian P Stimulus, John Stimulus), b. 3 Mar 1933, Penang, British Malaya. Freelance Journalist; Writer. m. Martha Bernadette Pillai, 29 Dec 1956, 2 sons, 2 daughters. Education: Overseas School Certificate A, University of Cambridge, 1951; Teacher Training, Ministry of Education, British Administration, Malaya; Fiction Writing, Premier School of Journalism, Fleet Street, London. Publications: A Course in Primary English (co-author), 1969; Window in the Sky (novel), 1982; Diary of a Sydney Girl, 1992; All Flesh Is Grass, 1995. Contributions to: Various publications. Memberships: Australian Society of Authors; Royal Australian Historical Society; Fellowship of Australian Writers. Address: "San Antone", 32 Hillcrest Avenue, Winston Hills, Sydney, New South Wales 2153, Australia.

PHILIP Marlene Nourbese, b. 3 Feb 1947, Tobago. Poet; Writer; Lawyer. m. Paul Chamberlain, 1978, 3 children. Education: BSc, University of the West Indies, 1968; MA, 1970, LLB, 1973, University of Western Ontario. Publications: Thorns, 1980; Salmon Courage, 1983; Harriet's Daughter, 1988; She Tries Her Tongue, 1989; Her Silence Softly Breaks, 1989; Looking for Livingstone: An Odyssey of Silence, 1991; Frontiers: Essays and Writings on Racism and Culture, 1992; Showing Grit: Showboating North of the 44th Parallel, 1993. Honours: Casa de las Americas Prize for Poetry,, 1988; Toronto Book Award for Fiction, 1990; Max and Greta Abel Award for Multicultural Literature, 1990; Guggenheim Fellowship, 1990; Toronto Arts Award, 1995. Address: c/o Women's Press, 517 College Street, Suite 233, Toronto, Ontario, Canada M6G 4A2.

PHILLIPS Caryl, b. 13 Mar 1958, St Kitts, West Indies (British citizen) Playwright; Novelist. Education: BA, University of Oxford, 1979. Appointments: Visiting Writer, 1990-92, Writer-in-Residence, Co-Director, Creative Writing Center, 1992-94, Professor of English, Writer-in-Residence, 1994-97, Amherst College; Professor of English and Henry R Luce Professor of Migration and Social Order, Barnard College, Columbia University, New York City, 1998-. Publications: Strange Fruit, 1980; Where There is Darkness, 1982; The Shelter, 1983; The Wasted Years, 1984; The Final Passage, 1985; A State of Independence, 1986; Higher Ground, 1989; Cambridge, 1991; Crossing the River, 1993; The Nature of Blood, 1997. Non-Fiction: The European Tribe, 1987; Extravavant Strangers: A Literature of Belonging (editor of anthology), 1997. Other: Playing Away (screenplay), 1987; Extravagant Strangers, Anthology (editor), 1997; Radio and television plays. Honours: Martin Luther King Memorial Prize, 1987; Guggenheim Fellowship, 1992; James Tait Black Memorial Prize, 1993; Lannan Foundation Fiction Award, 1994; Honorary AM, Amherst College, Massachusetts, 1995; DUniv, Leeds Metropolitan University, 1997. Memberships: English PEN, 1997; Writers' Guild (UK), 1997; American PEN, council member, 1998. Address: c/o Gillon Aitken Associates, 29 Fernshaw Road, London SW10 0TG, England.

PHILLIPS Edward O, b. 26 Nov 1931, Montreal, Quebec, Canada. Teacher; Writer. Education: BA, McGill

University, 1953; LL.L, University of Montreal, 1956; AMT, Harvard University, 1957; MA, Boston University, 1962. Publications: Sunday's Child, 1981; Where There's a Will, 1984; Buried on Sunday, 1986; Hope Springs Eternal, 1988; Sunday Best, 1990; The Landlady's Niece, 1992; The Mice Will Play, 1996; Working on Sunday, 1998. Contributions to: Short stories to various Canadian journals. Honour: Arthur Ellis Award, 1986. Memberships: Canadian Writers Union; PEN. Address: 425 Wood Avenue, Westmount, Quebec H3Y 3J3, Canada.

PHILLIPS H(erbert) I(vor Leason), b. 18 Mar 1913, London, England. Poet; Novelist; Dramatist. m. 28 Sept 1940, 1 son, 1 daughter. Education: Diploma, Dental Surgery, 1940. Appointments: Dentist, 1941-74. Publications: Poems, novels, and plays. Contributions to: Daily Mail; Envoi; Observer; Outposts; Poetry Review. Membership: Poetry Society. Address: 15 Sandy Lane, Cheam, Sutton, Surrey SM2 7NU, England.

PHILLIPS Jayne Anne, b. 19 July 1952, Buckhannon, West Virginia, USA. Writer. m. Mark Brian Stockman, 26 May 1985, 1 son, 2 stepsons. Education: BA, West Virginia University, 1974; MFA, University of Iowa, 1978. Appointments: Adjunct Associate Professor of English, Boston University, 1982-; Fanny Howe Chair of Letters, Brandeis University, 1986-87. Publications: Sweethearts, 1976; Counting, 1978; Black Tickets, 1979; How Mickey Made It, 1981; Machine Dreams, 1984; Fast Lanes, 1984; Shelter, 1994. Honours: Pushcart Prizes, 1977, 1979, 1983; Fels Award in Fiction, Coordinating Council of Literary Magazines, 1978; National Endowment for the Arts Fellowships, 1978, 1985; St Lawrence Award for Fiction, 1979; Sue Kaufman Award for Fiction, American Academy and Institute of Arts and Letters, 1980; O Henry Award, 1980; Bunting Institute Fellowship, Radcliffe College, 1981; Notable Book Citation, American Library Association, 1984; Best Book Citation, New York Times, 1984. Memberships: Authors Guild; Authors League of America; PEN. Address: c/o International Creative Management, 40 West 57th Street, New York, NY 10019, USA.

PHILLIPS Louis, b. 15 June 1942, Lowell, Massachusetts, USA. Poet; Playwright. m. Patricia L Ranard, 26 Aug 1971, 2 sons. Education: BA, Stetson University, DeLand, FL, USA, 1964; MA, University of North Carolina, Chapel Hill, NC, USA, 1965. Appointment: Professor of Humanities, School of Visual Arts, New York City, 1977-. Publications: The Man Who Stole the Atlantic Ocean, 1971; Theodore Jonathon Wainwright is Going to Bomb the Pentagon, 1973; The Time, The Hour, The Solitariness of the Place, poetry, 1986; A Dream of Countries Where No One Dare Live, 1994; Plays; The Envoi Messages; The Hot Corner, 1997. Contributions to: The Georgia Review; Massachusetts Review; Chicago Review; Regular Columnist for The Armchair Detective; Shakespeare Bulletin. Literary Agent: Ivy Fischer-Stone, Fifi Oscard Agency. Address: 375 Riverside Drive, Apt 14C, New York, NY 10025, USA.

PHILLIPS Michael. See: **NOLAN William.**

PHILLIPS Michael (Joseph), b. 2 Mar 1937, Indianapolis, Indiana, USA. Poet. Education: Purdue University, 1955-56; University of Edinburgh, 1957-58, 1959-60; Alliance Francaise, 1958; BA, cum laude, Wabash College, 1959; MA, 1964, PhD, Indiana University. Appointments: Lecturer in English, University of Wisconsin, 1970, 1971, Indiana University-Purdue University at Indianapolis, 1973-78; Instructor in English, Free University of Indianapolis, 1973, 1977-79; Visiting Fellow, Harvard University, 1976-77. Publications: Poetry: Libretto for 23 poems, 1968; Kinetics and Concretes, 1971; The Concrete Book, 1971; 8 Page Poems, 1971; Love, Love, Love, 1975; Visual Sequences, 1975; Abstract Poems, 1978; Underworld Love Poems, 1979; Erotic Concrete Sonnets for Samantha, 1979; Selected Love Poems, 1980; Indy Dolls, 1982; Superbeuts, 1983; Selected Concrete Poems, 1986; Dreamgirls, 1989; 11 Poems, 1992. Other: Edwin Muir, 1979; The Poet as Mythmaker, 1990. Contributions to: Numerous anthologies and periodicals. Memberships: Academy of American Poets; American Comparative Literature Association; Mensa; Modern Language Association; Phi Beta Kappa; Society for the Study of Midwestern Literature. Address: 238 North Smith Road, Apt 25, Bloomington, IN 47408, USA.

PHILLIPS Robert (Schaeffer), b. 2 Feb 1938, Milford, Delaware, USA. Professor of English; Poet; Writer. m. Judith Anne Bloomingdale, 16 June 1962, 1 son. Education: BA, English, 1960, BA, Communications, 1960, MA, American Literature, 1962, Syracuse University. Appointments: Instructor, New School for Social Research, New York City, 1966-68, Belle Levine Arts Center, 1968-69; Poetry Review Editor, Modern Poetry Studies, 1969-73; Professor of English, 1991-, Director, Creative Writing Program, 1991-96, John and Rebecca Moores University Scholar, 1998-2003, University of Houston; Poetry Reviewer, Houston Post, 1992-95, Houston Chronicle, 1995-. Publications: Poetry: Inner Weather, 1966; The Pregnant Man, 1978; Running on Empty, 1981; Personal Accounts: New and Selected Poems, 1966-1986, 1986; The Wounded Angel, 1987; Face to Face, 1993; Breakdown Lane, 1994. Fiction: The Land of the Lost Content, 1970; Public Landing Revisited, 1992. Criticism: Aspects of Alice (editor), 1971; The Confessional Poets, 1973; Denton Welch, 1974; William Gogen, 1978. Contributions to: Many anthologies, reviews, quarterlies, and journals. Honours: American Academy and Institute of Arts and Letters Award, 1987; Arents Pioneer Medal, Syracuse University, 1988; Greenwood Award, 1993; New York Times Notable Book of the Year Citation, 1994; Fort Concho Literary Festival Fiction Prize, 1994; Semi-finalist, The Poets' Prize, 1996. Memberships: Academy of American Poets; American PEN Center, board of directors; Association of Literary Scholars and Critics; English-Speaking Union; Friends of Poets and Writers; National Book Critics' Circle; Poetry Society of America; South Central Modern Language Association; Texas Institute of Letters, councilor. Address: c/o Creative Writing Program, Department of English, University of Houston, Houston, TX 77204, USA.

PHILLIPS Shelley, b. 18 Mar 1934, Melbourne, Victoria, Australia. Psychological Consultant; Writer. 2 daughters. Education: BA, Honours, English, History, University of Melbourne; BA, Psychology, University of Western Australia; PhD, University of Sydney, 1972. Appointment: Visiting Scientist, Programme Associate, Tavistock Clinic, London, 1975-76, 1978-79, 1982-83. Publications: Young Australian: The Attitudes of Our Children, 1979; Relations With Children: The Psychology of Human Development in a Changing World, 1986; Beyond the Myths: Mother-Daughter Relations in Psychology, History, Literature and Everyday Life, 1991. Contributions to: Books and professional journals. Honours: Prox Accesit Arts Convocation Prize, University of Western Australia, 1959; Honorary appointments: University of Birmingham, England, 1975, Georgia State University, USA, 1975, University of Alberta, Canada, 1976, London University Institute of Education, 1979, Institute of Early Childhood Studies, Melbourne, 1982, University College, London, 1983; Research grants. Memberships: Australian Society of Authors; Society of Women Writers; Jane Austen Society; National Trust; Australian Psychological Society; College of Educational and Developmental Psychologists. Address: Sydney, New South Wales, Australia.

PHILLIPSON (Charles) Michael, b. 16 June 1940, Gatley, Cheshire, England. Freelance Painter; Writer. m. Julia Hauxwell, 1 Sept 1971, 1 son, 2 daughters. Education: BA, 1961, MA, 1964, Nottingham University. Publications: Making Fuller Use of Survey Data, 1968; Sociological Aspects of Crime and Delinquency, 1971; New Directions in Sociological Theory (co-author), 1972; Understanding Crime and Delinquency, 1974; Problems of Reflexivity and Dialectics in Sociological Inquiry (co-author), 1975; Painting, Language and Modernity, 1985; In Modernity's Wake, 1989. Contributions to: Numerous journals and other periodicals. Address: Derlwyn, Glandwr, Hebron, Whitland, Pembrokshire SA34 OYD, Wales.

PHILP Peter, b. 10 Nov 1920, Cardiff, Wales. Writer. m. 25 Sept 1940, 2 sons. Publications: Beyond Tomorrow, 1947; The Castle of Deception, 1952; Love and Lunacy, 1955; Antiques Today, 1960; Antique Furniture for the Smaller Home, 1962; Furniture of the World, 1974; The Real Sir John (play), 1995. Contributions to: Times; Antique Dealer and Collectors Guide; Antique Collecting; Antique Furniture Expert (with Gillian Walkling), 1991; Antiques Trade Gazette, monthly feature, 1992-. Honours: Arts Council Award, 1951; C H Foyle Award, 1951. Membership: Society of Authors. Address: 77 Kimberley Road, Cardiff CF2 5DP, Wales.

PHIPPS Christine, b. 5 Dec 1945, Bristol, England. University Lecturer; Counsellor. Div. Education: BA, 1st Class Honours, Hull University, 1968; MLitt, St Hugh's College, Oxford, 1971; Advanced Diploma in Linguistics, Lancaster University, 1986; Advanced Diploma in Counselling, Wigan College of Technology, 1989. Publication: Buckingham: Public and Private Man (George Villiers 1628-1687), 1985. Contributions to: Notes and Queries Journal. Address: 21 Hurstway, Fulwood, Preston, Lancashire PR2 9TT, England.

PHIPPS Constantine Edmund (Marquis of Normanby), (Constantine Phipps), b. 24 Feb 1954, Whitby, N Yorkshire, England. Company Director; Author. m. Mrs Nicola St Aubyn, 21 July 1990, 2 sons, 1 daughter. Education: MA, Politics, Philosophy, Economics, Worcester College, Oxford, England. Publications: Careful With the Sharks; Among the Thin Ghosts. Address: Mulgrave Castle, Whitby YO21 3RJ, England.

PHIPSON Joan. See: **FITZHARDINGE Joan Margaret.**

PICANO Felice, b. 22 Feb 1944, New York, New York, USA. Writer; Poet. Education: BA, cum laude, Queens College, City University of New York, 1960. Publications: Smart as the Devil, 1975; Eyes, 1976; Deformity Lover and Other Poems, 1977; The Lure, 1979; Late in the Season, 1980; An Asian Minor, 1981; Slashed to Ribbons in Defense of Love and Other Stories, 1982; House of Cards, 1984; Ambidextrous, 1985; Men Who Loved Me, 1989; To the Seventh Power, 1989; The New Joy of Gay Sex, 1992; Dryland's End, 1995; Like People in History, 1995. Contributions to: Men on Men; Violet Quill Reader; Numerous magazines and journals. Honours: Finalist, Ernest Hemingway Award; PEN Syndicated Short Fiction Award; Chapbook Award, Poetry Society of America. Memberships: PEN Club; Writers Guild of America; Authors Guild; Publishing Triangle. Address: 95 Horatio Street, No 423, New York, NY 10014, USA.

PICARD Barbara Leonie, b. 4 Dec 1917, Richmond, Surrey, England. Author. Publications: Ransom for a Knight, 1956; Lost John, 1962; One is One, 1965; The Young Pretenders, 1966; Twice Seven Tales, 1968; Three Ancient Kings, 1972; Tales of Ancient Persia, reprinted, 1993; The Iliad, 1991; The Odyssey, 1991; French Legends, Tales and Fairy Stories, 1992; German Hero-sagas and Folk-tales, 1993; Tales of the Norse Gods, 1994; Selected Fairy Tales, 1994; The Deceivers, 1996; The Midsummer Bride, 1999. Address: Oxford University Press, Walton Street, Oxford, England.

PICARD Robert George, b. 15 July 1951, Pasadena, California, USA. Professor; Author. m. Elizabeth Carpelan, 15 Sept 1979, 2 daughters, 1 son. Education: BA, Loma Linda University, 1974; MA, California State University, Fullerton, 1980; PhD, University of Missouri, 1983. Appointments: Editor, Journal of Media Economics, 1988-97; Associate Editor, Political Communication and Persuasion, 1989-91. Publications: The Press and the Decline of Democracy, 1985; Press Concentration and Monopoly, 1988; The Ravens of Odin: The Press in the Nordic Nations, 1988; In the Camera's Eye: News Coverage of Terrorist Events, 1991; Media Portrayals of Terrorism: Functions and Meaning of News Coverage, 1993; The Cable Networks Handbook, 1993; Joint Operating Agreements: The Newspaper Preservation Act and its Application, 1993; The Newspaper Publishing Industry, 1997. Address: 2806 Gertrude Street, Riverside, CA 92506, USA.

PICK Frederick Michael, b. 21 June 1949, Leicestershire, England. Antique Dealer; Designer/Director; Author; Lecturer. Education: MA, History and Law, Gonville and Caius College, Cambridge. Publications: The English Room, 1985; The National Trust Pocket Guide to Furniture, 1985; The English Country Room, 1988. Contributions to: Periodicals. Honour: Exhibitioner in History, Gonville and Caius, Cambridge, 1969. Memberships: Society of Authors; Twentieth Century Society; Royal Society for Asian Affairs; British Antique Dealer Association; Lansdowne Club; Costume Society. Literary Agent: Curtis Brown. Address: 14 Mount Street, London W1Y 5RA, England.

PICKARD Tom, (Thomas Marriner Pickard), b. 7 Jan 1946, Newcastle upon Tyne, England. Writer; Poet; Dramatist. m. Joanna Voit, 22 July 1978, 2 sons, 1 daughter. Appointment: Arts Council Writer-in-Residence, University of Warwick, 1979-80. Publications: Arts Council Writer-in-Residence, University of Warwick, 1979-80. Publications: High on the Walls, 1967; New Human Unisphere, 1969; The Order of Chance, 1971; Guttersnipe, 1972; Dancing Under Fire, 1973; Hero Dust: New and Selected Poems, 1979; OK Tree, 1980; The Jarrow March, 1982; Custom and Exile, 1985; We Make Ships, 1989; Tiepin Eros: New and Selected Poems, 1994. Other: Television plays and documentaries. Address: c/o Judy Daish Associates, 83 Eastbourne Mews, London W2 6LQ, England.

PICKERING Sir Edward (Davies), b. 4 May 1912, England. Journalist; Publishing Executive. m. (1) Margaret Soutter, 1936, div 1947, 1 daughter, (2) Rosemary Whitton, 1955, 2 sons, 1 daughter. Education: Middlesborough High School. Appointments: Chief Sub-Editor, 1939, Managing Editor, 1947-49, Daily Mail; Managing Editor, 1951-57, Editor, 1957-62, Daily Express; Director, Beaverbrook Newspapers, 1956-64, Scottish Daily Record and Sunday Mail Ltd, 1966-69, Times Newspapers Holdings Ltd, 1981-, William Collins Sons & Co Ltd, 1981-89, Harper Collins Publishers Ltd, 1989-; Editorial Director, Daily Mirror Newspapers Ltd, 1964-68; Director, 1966-75, Chairman, Newspaper Division, 1968-70, and Magazines, 1970-74, International Publishing Corporation; Chairman, Mirror Group Newspapers, 1975-77, Times Supplements Ltd, 1989-; Executive Vice-Chairman, Times Newspapers Ltd, 1982-. Honours: Knighted, 1977; Honorary Freeman, Stationers' and Newspaper Makers' Company, 1985; Astor Award for Distinguished Service to the Commonwealth Press, 1986; Honorary DLitt, City University of London, 1986. Memberships: Commonwealth Press Union, chairman, council, 1977-86; Fédèration Internationale de la Presse Periodique, treasurer, 1971-75; Press Council, vice chairman, 1976-82. Address: Chatley House, Norton St Philip, Somerset, England.

PICKERING Paul Granville, b. 9 May 1952, Rotherham, England. Novelist; Playwright. m. Alison Beckett, 11 Dec 1983, 1 daughter. Education: BA, Honours, Psychology, Leicester University. Publications: Wild About Harry, 1985; Perfect English, 1986; The Blue Gate of Babylon, 1989; Charlie Peace, 1991. Anthologies: Winters Tales (contributed short story), 1989; Play: After Hamlet, New Grove Theatre, London, 1994. Contributions to: Times; Sunday Times; Indepedent. Honours: Included in Best of Young British Novelists, W.H. Smith Top 10, 1989. Membership: Society of Authors. Literary Agent: Sheil Land Associates Ltd., 43 Doughty Street, London WC1N 2LF. Address: 20 Brackenbury Gardens, London W6 0BP, England.

PICKTHALL Barry, b. 2 Mar 1949, Cheam, England. Photo; Journalist. m. 6 Oct 1973, 4 sons. Education: Wellington Grammar School; Brooklands Technical College Weybridge. Appointments: Editorial Assistant, Yachts & Yachting magazine, 1971-73; Yachting Correspondent to The Times newspaper, 1986-96. Publications: the Key Facts Book of Sailing; Flyes - The Quest to Win the Round the World Race; Blue Water

Racing; The Ultimate Challenge - The Story of the 1982-3 BOC Solo Round the World Race; The BOC Challenge 1986-87; No Suts-No Story. Contributions to: The Times; Sunday Times; Yachting (US); Sailing Today; Yachts & Yachting. Memberships: Yachting Journalists' Association, Committee Member, 1990-95, 1997-. Address: 68 East Ham Road, Littlehampton, Sussex, BN17 7BE, England.

PIDDINGTON Jean Frances, b. 8 Jan 1932. Homemaker; Artist. m. Peter Piddington, 3 Jan 1955, 2 daughters. Education: Art College; Teacher's Diploma, England. Publications: Poetry: The Path Not Taken, revised, 1996; Apple Trees, 1997, on tape, 1997. Contributions to: Review for West Coast, Paradise Publishing, 1998. Membership: West Coast Paradise Publishing. Address: 97 Briscoe Street East, London, Ontario, Canada N6C 1X1.

PIECHOCKI Stanislaw Ryszard, b. 8 Feb 1955, Olsztyn, Poland. Lawyer; Writer. m. Elzbieta Piechocki, 27 Oct 1979, 1 daughter. Education: MSc, Department of Law, University of Torun, 1978. Publications: Na krancu drogi (On the End of Way), story, 1975; Przedostatni przystanek (The Last But One Stop), novel, 1980; Tekturowe czolgi (The Cardboard Tanks), novel, 1983; Przysposobienie dziecka (Adoption of Child), science material, 1983; Przyladek burz (Cape of Storm), novel, 1989; Czysciec zwany Kortau (Purgatory called Kortau), report, 1993; Dzieje olsztynskich ulic (History of Streets in Olsztyn), 1994, 3rd edition, 1998. Contributions to: Various publications. Honours: Ignacy Krasicki Memorial Medal for Best First Novel, 1980; Award, Minister of Culture and Art, 1984. Memberships: Polish Writers Association; Polish Lawyers Association; Society of the Friends of Warmia and Masuriás Literature. Address: ul Pszenna 8, 10-833 Olsztyn, Poland.

PIELMEIER John, b. 3 Feb 1949, Altoona, Pennsylvania, USA. Dramatist; Actor. m. Irene O'Brian, 9 Oct 1982. Education: BA, Catholic University of America; MFA, Pennsylvania State University. Publications: Agnes of God, 1983; Haunted Lives (A Witches Brew, A Ghost Story, A Gothic Tale), 1984. Honours: Christopher Award, 1984; Humanitas Award, 1984. Memberships: Writers Guild of America; Dramatists Guild; American Federation of Television and Radio Artists; Actors Equity Association. Address: c/o Artists Agency, 230 West 55th Street, New York, NY 10019, USA.

PIERARD Richard V(ictor), b. 29 May 1934, Chicago, Illinois, USA. Professor of History; Writer. m. Charlene Burdett, 15 June 1957, 1 son, 1 daughter. Education: BA, 1958, MA, 1959, California State University, Los Angeles; University of Hamburg, 1962-63; PhD, University of Iowa, 1964. Appointments: Instructor, University of Iowa, 1964; Assistant Professor, 1964-67, Associate Professor, 1967-72, Professor of History, 1972-, Indiana State University, Terre Haute; Research Fellow, University of Aberdeen, 1978; Fulbright Professor, University of Frankfurt, 1984-85, University of Halle 1989-90. Publications: Protest and Politics: Christianity and Contemporary Affairs (with Robert G Clouse and Robert D Linder), 1968; The Unequal Yoke: Evangelical Christianity and Political Conservatism, 1970; The Cross and the Flag (editor with Robert G Clouse and Robert D Linder), 1972; Politics: A Case for Christian Action (with Robert D Linder), 1973; The Twilight of the Saints: Christianity and Civil Religion in Modern America (with Robert D Linder), 1977; Streams of Civilization, Vol II (with Robert G Clouse), 1980; Bibliography on the Religious Right in America, 1986; Civil Religion and the Presidency (with Robert D Linder), 1988; Two Kingdoms: The Church and Culture Through the Ages (with Robert G Clouse and E M Yamauchi), 1993; The Revolution of the Candles (with Joerg Swoboda), 1996; The New Millennium Manual (with Robert G Clouse and Robert N Hosdck), 1999. Contributions to: Many books, reference works, and professional journals. Honour: Research and Creativity Award, Indiana State University, 1994. Memberships: American Historical Society; American Society of Church History; American Society of Missiology; Baptist World Alliance, Baptist Heritage Study Committee, 1990-2000; Evangelical Theological Society, president, 1985; Greater Terre Haute Church Federation, president, 1987-88; International Association of Mission Studies; American Baptist Historical Society, board of managers. Address: c/o Department of History, Indiana State University, Terre Haute, IN 47809, USA.

PIERCE Meredith Ann, b. 5 July 1958, Seattle, Washington, USA. Writer. Education: AA, Liberal Arts, 1976, BA, English, 1978, MA, English, 1980, University of Florida. Publications: The Darkangel, 1982; A Gathering of Gargoyles, 1984; The Woman Who Loved Reindeer, 1985; Birth of the Firebringer, 1985; Where the Wild Geese Go, 1988; Rampion, 1989; The Pearl of the Soul of the World, 1990. Contributions to: Magazines. Honours: Several citations and awards for children's and young adult's literature. Memberships: Author's Guild; Phi Beta Kappa; Science Fiction Writers of America. Address: 703 North West 19th Street, Gainesville, FL 32603, USA.

PIERCY Marge, b. 31 Mar 1936, Detroit, Michigan, USA. Poet; Writer. m. (3) Ira Wood, 2 June 1982. Education: AB, University of Michigan, 1957; MA, Northwestern University, 1958. Appointments: Poet-in-Residence, University of Kansas, 1971; Distinguished Visiting Lecturer, Thomas Jefferson College and Grand Valley State College, Allendale, Michigan, 1975-76, 1978, 1980; Staff, Fine Arts Work Center, Provincetown, Massachusetts, 1976-77; Writer-in-Residence, College of the Holy Cross, Worcester, Massachusetts, 1976; Butler Professor of Letters, State University of New York at Buffalo, 1977; Fiction Writer-in-Residence, Ohio State University, 1985; Elliston Poetry Fellow, University of Cincinnati, 1986; Poetry Editor, Tikkun Magazine, 1988-; DeRoy Distinguished Visiting Professor, University of Michigan, 1992; Guest, University of North Dakota Writers Conference, 1995, Florida Suncoast Writers Conference, 1996. Publications: Poetry: Breaking Camp, 1968; Hard Loving, 1969; To Be of Use, 1973; Living in the Open, 1976; The Twelve-Spoke Wheel Flashing, 1978; The Moon is Always Female, 1980; Circles on the Water: Selected Poems of Marge Piercy, 1982; Stone, Paper, Knife, 1983; My Mother's Body, 1985; Available Light, 1988; Mars and Her Children, 1992; The Eight Chambers of the Heart: Selected Poems, 1995; What Are Big Girls Made Of?, 1997. Fiction: Going Down Fast, 1969; Dance the Eagle to Sleep, 1970; Small Changes, 1973; Woman on the Edge of Time, 1976; The High Cost of Living, 1978; Vida, 1980; Braided Lives, 1982; Fly Away Home, 1984; Gone to Soldiers, 1987; Summer People, 1989; He, She and It, 1991; The Longings of Women, 1994; City of Darkness, City of Light, 1996. Editor: Parti-Colored Blocks for a Quilt: Poets on Poetry, 1982; Early Ripening: American Women Poets Now, 1988. Contributions to: Anthologies and periodicals. Honours: Borestone Mountain Poetry Awards, 1968, 1974; National Endowment for the Arts Award, 1978; Carolyn Kizer Poetry Prizes, 1986, 1990; Sheaffer Eaton-PEN New England Award, 1989; Brit ha-Darot Award, Shalom Center, 1992; Arthur C Clarke Award, 1992. Memberships: Authors Guild; Authors League; National Organization for Women; National Writers Union; New England Poetry Club; Poetry Society of America. Address: Box 1473, Wellfeet, MA 02667, USA.

PIERPOINT Katherine Mary, b. 16 Aug 1961, Northampton, England. Writer; Poet. Education: BA, Honours, Modern Languages, University of Exeter, 1984. Publication: Truffle Beds, 1995. Contributions to: Independent; New Yorker; Sunday Times. Honours include: Hawthornden International Creative Writing Fellowship, 1993; John Downes/Oppenheim Award, 1994; Somerset Maugham Award, 1996; Sunday Times Young Writer of the Year, 1996. Memberships: Poetry Society; Society of Authors. Address: c/o Left Bank, 17 North Street, Mears Ashby, Northampton NN6 0DW, England.

PIERRE José, b. 24 Nov 1927, Bénesse-Maremne, France. Writer; Dramatist. m. Nicole Pierre, 5 Sept 1953. Education: Docteur ès-Lettres, Sorbonne, University of Paris, 1979. Appointment: Director of Research, Centre National de la Recherche Scientifique. Publications: Qu'est-ce que Thérèse? -C'est les marronniers en fleurs (novel), 1974; Gauguin aux Marquises (novel), 1982; L'Univers Surréaliste (history of art), 1983; André Breton et la peinture, 1987; L'Univers Symboliste (history of art and literature), 1991. Plays: Magdeleine LeClerc, le dernier amour du Marquis de Sade, 1993. Contributions to: La Quinzaine Littéraire, 1969-76. Memberships: Société des Gens de Lettres; Association Internationale des Critiques d'Art. Address: 2 rue Cournot, 75015 Paris, France.

PIETRASS Richard Georg, b. 11 June 1946, Lichtenstein, Sachsen, Germany. Poet; Writer; Translator; Psychologist. m. Erika Schulze, 26 Aug 1982, dec 22 Dec 1993, 2 sons, 1 daughter. Eduction: Diploma, Psychology, Humboldt University, Berlin, 1975. Publications: Poesiealbum 82, 1974; Notausgang, 1980; Freiheitsmuseum, 1982; Spielball, 1987; Was mir zum Glück fehlt, 1989; Weltkind, 1990; Letzte Gestalt, 1994; Randlage, 1996; Grenzfriedhof, 1998. Honours: Several. Memberships: Association of German Writers; PEN Germany. Address: Schleusinger Strasse 13, D-12687 Berlin, Germany.

PIGUET Marie-José, b. 21 Apr 1941, Lausanne, Switzerland. m. Lionel Knight, 16 Dec 1972. Education: Postgraduate, Faculty of Arts, Exeter University. Appointments: Literary Research on Catherine Colomb and Monique St Helier. Publications: Une Demoiselle Eblouissante, 1987; Petits Contes D'Outre-Manche, 1990. Contributions to: Writer, 700th Anniversary of Swiss Confederation, 1991; Five Short Stories, tales, 1991; Le Parcours de Katherine Mansfield, 1995; Anniversaires, Anniversaires, 1997; Ricichets (studies on the theme of 'le cycle', 1998. Honours: Prix G Nicole, Alpes Jura, Schiller. Address: 2 Chudleigh Road, Caroline Place, Exeter, Devon EX2 8TU, England.

PIGUET-CUENDET Suzanne. See: **DERIEX Suzanne.**

PIKE Charles R. See: **BULMER Henry Kenneth.**

PIKE Charles R. See: **HARKNETT Terry.**

PIKE Roderick Douglas, (Dag Pike), b. 26 Jan 1933, Surrey, England. Writer; Consultant. m. Catherine B C Bennett, 24 Aug 1978, 1 son, 3 daughters. Education: Master's Certificate of Competency, Sutton Grammar School. Appointments: International Editor, Work Boat World, 1984; Power Editor, Boat International, 1993; Editor, World of Power, 1993; International Editor, RIB International, 1995. Publications: Electronics Afloat, 1986; Practical Motor Cruising, 1988; Fast Boats and Rough Seas, 1989; Fast Boat Navigation, 1990; Electronic Afloat, 1991; Boat Electrical Systems, 1992; Motor Sailers, 1993; RORC Manual of Safety and Survival, 1993; RORC Manual of the Weather, 1993; Inflatables, 1994; The Sextant Simplified, 1995. Contributions to: Many periodicals. Honours: Royal Institute of Navigation, fellow; Royal Geographical Society, fellow. Membership: Yachting Journalists Association. Address: 8 Lower Street, Stroud, Gloucester GL5 2HT, England.

PIKE Roderick Douglas, b. 28 Jan 1933, Surrey, England. Writer; Consultant. 1 son, 3 daughters. Education: Sutton Grammer School. Appointments: Merchant Navy Apprentice, Nourse Line, 1950-53; Deck Officer, New Zealand Shipping Company, 1953-54; Deck Officer rising to Captain, Trinity House Lightvessel Service, 1954-63; Inspector of Lifeboats, Royal National Lifeboat Institution, 1963-73; Director Cormorant Fisheries Ltd, 1973-74; Marine Surveyor, Consultant, Writer and Author, 1973-; European Agent for Offshore Surveys (Overseas) Ltd, Consultancy, 1983-95; European Editor, Work Boat World (freelance position), 1983-95. Publications include: Fast Boat Navigation, 1990; Electronic Charts, 1991; Boat Electrical Systems, 1992; Motor Sailers, 1993; RORC Manual of Safety and Survival, 1993; RORC Manual of The Weather, 1993; Inflatables, 1994; The Sextant Simplified, 1995; Electronic Charts, 1997. Address: 8 Lower Street, Stroud,

Glos GL5 2HT, England.

PILCHER Rosamunde, b. 22 Sept 1924, Lelant, Cornwall, England. Writer. m. Graham Pilcher, 4 children. Publications: April, 1957; On My Own, 1965; Sleeping Tiger, 1967; Another View, 1969; The End of the Summer, 1971; Snow in April, 1972; The Empty House, 1973; The Day of the Storm, 1975; Under Gemini, 1977; Wild Mountain Thyme, 1978; The Carousel, 1981; Voices in Summer, 1984; The Blue Bedroom and Other Stories, 1985; The Shell Seekers, 1988; September, 1989; Flowers in the Rain, 1991; Coming Home, 1996. Contributions to: Woman and Home; Good Housekeeping. Honour: Romantic Novelists Association Award, 1996. Literary Agent: Felicity Bryan. Address: Penrowan, Longforgan, by Dundee DD2 5ET, Scotland.

PILGER John Richard, b. 9 Oct 1939, Sydney, Australia. Journalist; Author; Film Maker. divorced, 1 son, 1 daughter. Education: AJA, Journalism. Publications: The Last Day, 1975; Aftermath: The Struggle of Cambodia and Vietnam, 1983; Heroes, 1986; A Secret Country, 1989; Distant Voices, 1992; Hidden Agendas, 1998; Films: 51 documentary films from The Quiet Muting, 1970; Cambodia Year Zero, 1979; The Last Dream, 1988; Death of a Nation, 1994; Inside Burma, 1996; Apatheid Did Not Die, 1998. Contributions to: Independent; New Statesman (England); New York Times; The Age. Honours: Descriptive Writer of the Year, 1966; Journalist of the Year, 1967, 1979; International Reporter of the Year, 1970; Reporter of the Year, 1974; Reported Sans Frontiers, France; US Television Academy Award, Emmy, 1991; UK Television Academy Award, 1991; Honorary Doctorates: DLitt, Staffordshire University, DPhil, Dublin City University, Ireland, DArts, Oxford Brookes University. Address: 57 Hambalt Road, London SWX 9EQ, England.

PILGRIM Anne. See: ALLAN Mabel Esther.

PILKINGTON Roger Windle, b. 17 Jan 1915, St Helens, England. Author. m. (1) Miriam Jaboor, 27 July 1937, (2) Ingrid Geijer, 11 Oct 1972. Education: Magdalene College, Cambridge, 1933-37; MA, Cantab; PhD. Publications: 20 volumes in Small Boat series, including: Small Boat Down the Years, 1988; Small Boat in the Midi, 1989; Scientific philosophy and Christianity, notably: World Without End, 1960; Heavens Alive, 1962; Children's books, including: The Ormering Tide, 1974; I Sailed on the Mayflower, 1990; One Foot in France, 1992; View from the Shore, 1995; History and Legends of the European Waterways, 1998. Contributions to: Sunday Telegraph; Guardian. Honours: Chevalier, Compagnons du Minervois. Membership: Master, Glass Sellers Company, 1968. Address: Les Cactus, Moutouliers 34 310, France.

PILLING Christopher (Robert), b. 20 Apr 1936, Birmingham, England. Writer; Poet. m. Sylvia Hill, 6 Aug 1960, 1 son, 2 daughters. Education: Diplome d'Etudes Francaises, University of Leeds, 1957; Certificate of Education, Loughborough College, 1959. Appointments: Reviewer, Times Literary Supplement, 1973-74; Head of Modern Languages and Housemaster, Knottingley High School, West Yorkshire, 1973-78; Tutor, Department of Adult Education, University upon Tyne, 1978-80; Language Teacher, Keswick School, Cumbria, 1980-88. Publications: Snakes and Girls, 1970; In All the Spaces on All the Lines, 1971; Foreign Bodies, 1992; Cross Your Legs and Wish, 1994; These Jaundiced Loves (translation of Les Amours Jaunes by Tristan Corbière), 1995. Contributions to: Various books and anthologies, 1971-98, and to newspapers, reviews, quarterlies, and journals. Address: 25 High Hill, Keswick, Cumbria CA12 5NY, England.

PILON Jean-Guy, b. 12 Nov 1930, St Polycarpe, Quebec, Canada. Poet; Writer. m. Denise Viens, 2 sons. Education: BA, 1951, LLL, 1954, University of Montreal. Appointments: Co-Founder and Director, Liberté, 1959-79. Publications: Poetry: La Fiancée du Matin, 1953; Les Cloitres de l'Eté, 1955; L'Homme et le Jour, 1957; La Mouette et le Large, 1960; Recours au pays,

1961; Pour saluer une ville, 1963; Comme eau retenue, 1969, augmented edition, 1986; Saisons pour la Continuelle, 1969; Silences pour une souveraine, 1972. Novel: Solange, 1966. Contributions to: Various publications. Honours: David Prize, 1957; Louise Labé Prize, 1969; France-Canada Prize, 1969; Governor-General's Award for Poetry, 1970; Athanase David Prize, 1984; Officer of the Order of Canada, 1987; Chevalier de l'Ordre national du Québec, 1987; Officier dans l'Ordre des Arts et Lettres, France, 1992. Memberships: Académie des lettres du Québec; Royal Society of Canada. Address: 5724 Cote St-Antoine, Montreal, Quebec H4A 1R9, Canada.

PINCHER (Henry) Chapman, b. 29 Mar 1914, Ambala, India. Author. m. (1), 1 daughter, 1 son, (2) Constance Wolstenholme, 1965. Education: BSc Honours, Botany, Zoology, 1935. Appointments: Staff, Liverpool Institute, 1936-40; Royal Armoured Corps, 1940; Defence, Science and Medical Editor, Daily Express, 1946-73; Assistant Editor, Daily Express, Chief Defence Correspondent, Beaverbrook Newspapers, 1972-79. Publications: Breeding of Farm Animals, 1946; A Study of Fishes, 1947; Into the Atomic Age, 1947; Spotlight on Animals, 1950; Evolution, 1950; It's Fun Finding Out (with Bernard Wicksteed), 1950; Sleep and How to Get More of It, 1954; Sex in Our Time, 1973; Inside Story, 1978; Their Trade is Treachery, 1981; Too Secret Too Long, 1984; The Secret Offensive, 1985; Traitors - the Labyrinth of Treason, 1987; A Web of Deception, 1987; The Truth about Dirty Tricks, 1991; One Dog and Her Man, 1991; Pastoral Symphony, 1993; A Box of Chocolates, 1993; Life's a Bitch!, 1996; Tight Lines!, 1997. Novels: Not with a Bang, 1965; The Giantkiller, 1967; The Penthouse Conspirators, 1970; The Skeleton at the Villa Wolkonsky, 1975; The Eye of the Tornado, 1976; The Four Horses, 1978; Dirty Tricks, 1980; The Private World of St John Terrapin, 1982; Contamination, 1989. Honours: Granada Award, Journalist of the Year, 1964; Reporter of the Decade, 1966; Honorary DLitt, University of Newcastle upon Tyne, 1979; King's College, London, fellow, 1979. Address: The Church House, 16 Church Street, Kintbury, Near Hungerford, Berkshire RG15 0TR. England.

PINKUS Lydia Tolchinsky de, b. 9 May 1941, Buenos Aires, Argentina. Psychologist; Writer. m. Carlos Pinkus, 9 July 1965, 2 sons. Education: Architect, Faculty of Architecture and Town Planning, University of Buenos Aires; Psychologist, Faculty of Philosophy and Literature, University of Buenos Aires. Publications: Natalia no era, short stories, 1991; Ser Vienésa en tiempos de Freud, essays, 194; Un día con Neruda, 1996. Memberships: Amnesty International; Alba de America; La Prensa; Psicologias de Buenos Aires; Vivir. Honours: 1st Prize, 1982, 2nd Prize, 1983, School of Psychoanalysis; Literary Lecture, Oklahoma, 1986; 2nd Prize, Faja Honor Sade, Municipality of Buenos Aires. Memberships: Modern Language Association; Sociedad Argentina de Escritores. Address: 11 de Septiembre 1061, Buenos Aires, cód 1426, Argentina.

PINNER David John, b. 6 Oct 1940, Peterborough, England. Writer; Dramatist. m. Catherine, 23 Oct 1965, 1 son, 1 daughter. Education: Royal Academy of Dramatic Art, 1959-60. Publications: Stage Plays: Dickon, 1965; Fanghorn, 1966; The Drums of Snow, 1969; The Potsdam Quartet, 1973; An Evening with the GLC, 1974; The Last Englishman, 1975; Lucifer's Fair, 1979; Screwball, 1985; The Teddy Bears' Picnic, 1988. Television plays: Juliet and Romeo, 1975; 2 Crown Courts, 1978; The Potsdam Quartet, 1980; The Sea Horse. Novels: Ritual, 1967; With My Body, 1968; Corgi, 1969; There'll Always Be an England, 1984. Address: Barnes, London, England.

PINNEY Lucy Catherine, b. 25 July 1952, London, England. Author; Journalist. m. Charles Pinney, 14 June 1975, 2 sons, 1 daughter. Education: BA, Honours, English, Education, York University, 1973. Publications: The Pink Stallion, 1988; Tender Moth, 1994. Contributions to: Sunday Times; Observer; Daily Mail; Telegraph; Company; Cosmopolitan; Country Living;

Country Homes and Interiors; She; The Times, columnist. Honour: Runner-up, Betty Trask Prize, 1987. Membership: West Country Authors Association. Address: Egremont Farm, Payhembury, Honiton, Devon EX14 0JA, England.

PINNOCK Winsome, b. 1961, London. Playwright. Education: BA, Goldsmith's College, London, 1982; MA, Birkbeck Coll, London. Appointments: Playwright-in-Residence, Tricycle Theatre, Kilburn, 1990, Royal Court Theatre, London, 1991, Clean Break Theatre Company, 1994. Publications: The Wind of Change, 1987; Leave Taking, 1988; Picture Palace, 1988; A Rock in Water, 1989; A Hero's Welcome, 1989; Talking in Tongues, 1991. Television Plays: Episodes in South of the Border and Chalkface Series. Screenplay: Bitter Harvest. Honours: Thames TV Award, 1991; George Devine Award, 1991. Address: c/o Lemon, Unna and Durbridge, 24 Pottery Lane, Holland Park, London W11 4LZ, England.

PINSDORF Marion Katheryn, b. 22 June 1932, Teaneck, New Jersey, USA. Corporate Officer; Journalist; Senior Fellow in Communications. Div. Education: BA, cum laude, Drew University, 1954; MA, 1967, PhD, 1976, New York University. Appointments: Vice President, 1971-77, Senior Consultant, 1988-90, Hill and Knowlton Inc; Vice President for Corporate Communications, Textron Inc, 1977-80, INA Corporation, 1980-82; Adjunct Assistant Professor in Brazilian Studies, Brown University, 1979-; Senior Fellow in Communications, Graduate School of Business, Fordham University, 1987-. Publications: Communicating When Your Company is Under Seige: Surviving Public Crises, 1987, 3rd edition, 1998; German-Speaking Entrepreneurs: Builders of Business in Brazil South, 1990. Contributions to: Academic journals and general publications. Memberships: Americas Society; Arthur Page Society; Authors Guild; Northeast Brazilianists; Western Front Association. Address: 114 Leonia Avenue, Leonia, NJ 07605, USA.

PINSKER Sanford, b. 28 Sept 1941, Washington, Pennsylvania, USA. Professor of Humanities; Writer; Poet. m. Ann Getson, 28 Jan 1968, 1 son, 1 daughter. Education: BA, Washington and Jefferson College, 1963; PhD, University of Washington, 1967. Appointments: Assistant Professor, 1967-74, Associate Professor, 1974-84, Professor, 1984-88, Shadek Professor of Humanities, 1988-, Franklin and Marshall College; Visiting Professor, University of California at Riverside, 1973, 1975; Editor, Academic Questions, 1995-. Publications: The Schlemiel as Metaphor: Studies in the Yiddish and American-Jewish Novel, 1971, revised and expanded edition, 1991; The Comedy That "Hoits": An Essay on the Fiction of Philip Roth, 1975; Still Life and Other Poems, 1975; The Languages of Joseph Conrad, 1978; Between Two Worlds: The American Novel in the 1960s, 1978; Philip Roth: Critical Essays, 1982; Memory Breaks Off and Other Poems, 1984; Conversations with Contemporary American Writers, 1985; Whales at Play and Other Poems of Travel, 1986; Three Pacific Northwest Poets: Stafford, Hugo, and Wagoner, 1987; The Uncompromising Fictions of Cynthia Ozick, 1987; Bearing the Bad News: Contemporary American Literature and Culture, 1990; Understanding Joseph Heller, 1991; Jewish-American Literature and Culture: An Encyclopedia (editor with Jack Fischel), 1992; Jewish-American Fiction, 1917-1987, 1992; Sketches of Spain (poems), 1992; The Catcher in the Rye: Innocence Under Pressure, 1993; Oedipus Meets the Press and Other Tragi-Comedies of Our Time, 1996. Contributions to: Artifcles, stories, poems, and reviews in numerous publications. Honours: Fulbright Senior Lecturer, Belgium, 1984-85, Spain, 1990-91; Pennsylvania Humanist, 1985-87, 1990-91, 1996-97. Membership: National Book Critics Circle, 1995-. Address: 700 North Pine Street, Lancaster, PA 17603, USA.

PINSKY Robert (Neal), b. 20 Oct 1940, Long Branch, New Jersey, USA. Professor of English; Poet; Writer; Editor; Translator. m. Ellen Jane Bailey, 30 Dec 1961, 3 daughters. Education: BA, Rutgers University, 1962; MA,

1965, PhD, 1966, Stanford University. Appointments: Assistant Professor of English, University of Chicago, 1966-67; Professor of English, Wellesley College, 1967-80, University of California at Berkeley, 1980-89, Boston University, 1988-; Poetry Editor, The New Republic, 1978-87, Slate, 1996-; Visiting Lecturer in English, Harvard University, 1980; Poet Laureate of the US, 1997-. Publications: Landor's Poetry, 1968; Sadness and Happiness, 1975; The Situation of Poetry, 1977; An Explanation of America, 1980; The Separate Notebooks, by Czeslaw Milosz (co-translator), 1984; History of My Heart, 1984; Poetry and the World, 1988; The Want Bone, 1990; The Inferno of Dante, 1995; The Figured Wheel: New and Collected Poems 1966-1996, 1995. Contributions to: Anthologies and journals. Honours: Fulbright Fellowship, 1965; Stegner Fellowship in Creative Writing, 1965; National Endowment for the Humanities Fellowship, 1974; Massachusetts Council for the Arts Award, 1976; Oscar Blumenthal Prize, 1979; American Academy and Institute of Arts and Letters Award, 1980; Saxifrage Prize, 1980; Guggenheim Fellowship, 1980; Eunice B Tietjens Prize, 1983; National Endowment for the Arts Fellowship, 1984; William Carlos Williams Prize, 1985; Landon Prize in Translation, 1995; Los Angeles Times Book Award, 1995; Shelley Memorial Award, 1996; Ambassador Book Award in Poetry, 1997. Membership: American Academy of Arts and Sciences. Address: c/o Creative Writing Program, Boston University, 236 Bay State Road, Boston, MA 02215, USA.

PINTER Harold, b. 10 Oct 1930, London, England. Dramatist; Writer; Poet. m. (1) Vivien Merchant, 1956, div 1980, 1 son, (2) Lady Antonia Fraser, 1980. Appointments: Actor, 1949-57; Associate Director, National Theatre, 1973-83. Publications: The Caretaker, 1960; The Birthday Party, and Other Plays, 1960; A Slight Ache, 1961; The Collection, 1963; The Lover, 1963; The Homecoming, 1965; Tea Party, and The Basement, 1967; PEN Anthology of New Poems (co-editor), 1967; Mac, 1968; Landscape, and Silence, 1969; Five Screenplays, 1971; Old Times, 1971; Poems, 1971; No Man's Land, 1975; The Proust Screenplay: A la Recherche du Temps Perdu, 1978; Betrayal, 1978; Poems and Prose, 1949-1977, 1978; I Know the Place, 1979; Family Voices, 1981; Other Places, 1982; The French Lieutenant's Woman and Other Screenplays, 1982; One for the Road, 1984; Collected Poems and Prose, 1986; 100 Poems by 100 Poets (co-editor), 1986; Mountain Language, 1988; The Heat of the Day, 1989; The Dwarfs, 1990; Party Time, 1991; Moonlight, 1993; 99 Poems in Translation (co-editor), 1994; Ashes to Ashes, 1995. Other: Many nonpublished stage, film, radio, and television plays. Honours: Commander of the Order of the British Empire, 1966; Shakespeare Prize, Hamburg, 1970; Austrian State Prize for European Literature, 1973; Pirandello Prize, 1980; Donatello Prize, 1982; Giles Cooper Award, 1982; Elmer Holmes Bobst Award, 1984; David Cohen British Literary Prize, 1975; Laurence Olivier Special Award, 1996. Membership: Royal Society of Literature, fellow. Address: c/o Judy Daish Associates Ltd, 2 St Charles Place, London W10 6EG, England.

PIONTEK Heinz, b. 15 Nov 1925, Kreuzberg, Silesia, Germany. Poet; Author. m. Gisela Dallman, 1951. Education: Theologisch-Philosophische Hochschule, Dillingen. Publications: Poetry: Die Furt, 1952; Die Rauchfahne, 1953; Wassermarken, 1957; Mit einer Kranichfeder, 1962; Klartext, 1966; Tot oder lebendig, 1971; Die Zeit der anderen Auslegung, 1976; Früh im September, 1982; Helldunkel, 1987. Novels: Dichterleben, 1976; Juttas Neffe, 1979; Zeit meines Lebens, 1984; Stunde der Uberlebenden, 1989; Goethe unterwegs in Schlesien: Fast ein Roman, 1993. Collections: Die Erzählungen 1950-1970, 1971; Das Schweigen Uberbrucken: Meditationen, Geditchte, Szenen, Erzählungen, 1977; Träumen, Wachen, Widerstehen: Aufzeichnungen aus diesen Jahren, 1978; Das Handwerk des Lesens: Erfahrungen mit Buchern und Autoren, 1979; Farbige Schatten, Die Aufzeichnungen, Die Reiseprosa, 1984; Feuer im Wind, Die Erzählungen, Die Hörspiele, Eine Komödie, 1985; Werkauswahl: Indianersommer (selected poems), 1990, and Anhalten um eine Hand (selected stories), 1990. Honours: Many, including: Tukan Prize, 1971; Georg Büchner Prize, 1976; Werner Egk Prize, 1981. Memberships: Bavarian Academy of Fine Arts, Munich. Address: Duffer Strasse 97, 8000 Munich 50, Germany.

PIOTRKOWSKI Aleksander. See: **RUDZINSKI Cezary Aleksander.**

PIRIE David Tarbat, b. 4 Dec 1946, Dundee, Scotland. Dramatist; Writer. m. Judith Harris, 21 June 1983, 1 son, 1 daughter. Education: University of York; University of London. Appointments: Tutor; Film Critic, Editor, Time Out Magazine, 1980-84. Publications: Heritage of Horror, 1974; Mystery Story, 1980; Anatomy of the Movies, 1981. Films: Rainy Day Women, 1984; Wild Things, 1988; Black Easter, 1993; Wildest Dreams, 1995; Element of Doubt, 1996; The Woman in White, 1997. Television: Never Come Back, BBC serial, 1989; Ashenden, BBC serial, 1990; Natural Lies, serial, 1991. Contributions to: Various journals. Honours: Drama Prize, New York Festival, 1985; Best TV Network Series Prize, 1990, Best TV Feature Film Prize, 1996, Chicago Film Festival. Membership: Screenwriters Studio, Dartington Hall, 1990. Address: c/o Lemon Unna and Durbridge, 24 Pottery Lane, London W11, England.

PIRSIG Robert Maynard, b. 6 Sept 1928, Minneapolis, Minnesota, USA. Author. m. (1) Nancy Ann James, 10 May 1954, div Aug 1978, 2 sons, (2) Wendy Kimball, 28 Dec 1978, 1 daughter. Education: BA, 1950, MA, 1958, University of Minnesota. Publications: Zen and the Art of Motorcycle Maintenance, 1974; Lila, 1991. Honours: Guggeneheim Fellowship, 1974; AAAL Award, 1979. Address: c/o Bantam Books, 1540 Broadway, New York, NY 10036, USA.

PITCHER Harvey John, b. 26 Aug 1936, London, England. Writer. Education: BA, 1st Class Honours, Russian, University of Oxford. Publications: Understanding the Russians, 1964; The Chekhov Play: A New Interpretation, 1973; When Miss Emmie was in Russia, 1977; Chekhov's Leading Lady, 1979; Chekhov: The Early Stories, 1883-1888 (with Patrick Miles), 1982; The Smiths of Moscow, 1984; Lily: An Anglo-Russian Romance, 1987; Muir and Mirrielees: The Scottish Partnership that became a Household Name in Russia, 1994; Witnesses of the Russian Revolution, 1994; Chekhov: The Comic Stories, 1998. Contributions to: Times Literary Supplement. Address: 37 Bernard Road, Cromer, Norfolk NR27 9AW, England.

PITT Barrie William Edward, b. 7 July 1918, Galway, Ireland. Historian. m. (1) Phyllis Kate Edwards, 1 son, dec, (2) Sonia Deidre Hoskins, 1953, div 1971, (3) Frances Mary Moore, 1983. Appointments: Historical Consultant to the BBC series, The Great War, 1963. Publications: The Edge of Battle, 1958; Zeebrugge, St George's Day, 1918, 1958; Coronel and Falkland, 1960; The Last Act, 1962; Purnell's History of the Second World War (editor), 1964; Ballantine's Illustrated History of World War I (editor-in-chief), 1967; Purnell's History of the First World War (editor), 1969; Ballantine's Illustrated History of the Violent Century (editor-in-chief), 1971; British History Illustrated (editor), 1974-78; The Battle of the Atlantic, 1977; The Crucible of War: Western Desert, 1941, 1980; The Crucible of War: Year of Alamein, 1942, 1982; Special Boat Squadron, 1983. Contributions to: Encyclopaedia Britannica; Sunday Times. Address: 10 Wellington Road, Taunton, Somerset TA1 4EG, England.

PITT David C(harles), b. 15 Aug 1938, Wellington, New Zealand. Sociologist; Writer. m. Carol Haigh, 13 Feb 1959, 3 sons, 4 daughters. Education: BA, University of New Zealand, 1961; BLitt, 1963, DPhil, 1965, MLitt, 1980, University of Oxford. Appointments: Assistant Professor of Anthropology and Sociology, University of Victoria, British Columbia, 1966-67; Professor of Sociology and Head, Department of Sociology, University of Waikato, Hamilton, New Zealand, 1968-71; Professor of Sociology, Head, Department of Sociology, Chairman, European Studies Committee, University of Auckland, 1971-79; Charge de Recherches and Member of the Executive Council, Institut International de Recherches pour la Paix, Geneva, 1982-; Consultant to various world organizations. Publications: Tradition and Economic Progress in Samoa: A Case Study in the Role of Traditional Social Institutions in Economic Development, 1970; Historical Documents in Anthropology and Sociology, 1972; Emerging Pluralism (with C Macpherson), 1975; Social Dynamics of Development, 1976; Development from Below: Anthropologists and Development Situations (editor), 1976; Social Class in New Zealand (editor), 1977; Child Labour: A Threat to Health and Development (editor), 1981; Children and War (editor), 1983; Culture and Conservation, 1984; The Nature of United Nations Bureaucracies (editor), 1984; Rethinking Population, Environment and Development, 1986; Nuclear Free Zones (editor), 1987; New Ideas in Environmental Education (editor), 1988; Deforestation: Social Dynamics in Watersheds and Mountain Ecosystems (editor), 1988; The Future of the Environment (editor), 1988; The Anthropology of War and Peace (editor), 1989; Mountain Worlds in Danger (with Sten Nilsson), 1991. Contributions to: Professional journals. Memberships: International Sociological Association; International Union of Anthropological and Ethnological Sciences; Royal Anthropological Institute. Address: c/o Institut International de Recherches pour la Paix, 34 Boulevard du Pont d'Arve, Geneva 1205, Switzerland.

PITT David George, b. 12 Dec 1921, Musgravetown, Newfoundland, Canada. Retired Professor of English Literature; Writer. m. Marion Woolfrey, 5 June 1946, 1 son, 1 daughter. Education: BA, Honours, English, Mt Allison University, 1946; MA, 1948, PhD, 1960, University of Toronto. Appointment: Professor of English Literature, Memorial University of Newfoundland, 1949-83. Publications: Elements of Literacy, 1964; Windows of Agates, 1966; Critcal Views on Canadian Writers: E J Pratt, 1969; Toward the First Spike: The Evolution of a Poet, 1982; Goodly Heritage, 1984; E J Pratt: The Truant Years, 1984; E J Pratt: The Master Years, 1987; Tales From the Outer Fringe, 1990. Honours: Medal for Biography, University of British Columbia, 1984; Artist of the Year, Newfoundland Arts Council, 1988; Honorary LLD, Mt Allison University, 1989. Memberships: Association of Canadian University Teachers of English; Humanities Association of Canada. Address: 7 Chestnut Place, St John's, Newfoundland A1B 2T1, Canada.

PITT-KETHLEY (Helen) Fiona, b. 21 Nov 1954, Edgware, Middlesex, England. Writer; Poet. m. James Plaskett, 1 son. Education: BA, Honours, Chelsea School of Art, 1976. Publications: London, 1984; Rome, 1985; The Tower of Glass, 1985; Gesta, 1986; Sky Ray Lolly, 1986; Private Parts, 1987; Journeys to the Underworld, 1988; The Perfect Man, 1989; The Misfortunes of Nigel, 1991; The Literary Companion to Sex, 1992; The Maiden's Progress, 1992; Too Hot to Handle, 1992; Dogs, 1993; The Pan Principle, 1994; The Literary Companion to Low Life, 1995; Double Act, 1996. Contributions to: Numerous newspapers and magazines. Honour: Calouste Gulbenkian Award, 1995. Address: 7 Ebenezer Road, Hastings, East Sussex TN34 3BS, England.

PITTOCK Murray G(eorge) H(ornby), b. 5 Jan 1962, Nantwich, England. Professor in Literature; Writer; Editor. m. Anne Grace Thornton Martin, 15 Apr 1989, 2 daughters. Education: MA 1st Class Honours, English Language and Literature, University of Glasgow, Scotland, 1983; DPhil, University of Oxford, England, 1986. Appointments: Lecturer, Pembroke College, Oxford, 1986-87; British Academy Postdoctoral Fellow, 1988-89, Visiting Fellow, 1994, University of Aberdeen; Reader, Department of English Literature, 1994-96, University of Edinburgh; Editor, Scottish Literary Journal, 1995-; Professor in Literature, 1996-, Head, Department of Literature, 1997-, University of Strathclyde. Publications: The Invention of Scotland: The Stuart Myth and the Scottish Identity, 1638 to the Present, 1991; Spectrum of Decadence: The Literature of the 1890s, 1993; Poetry and Jacobite Politics in Eighteenth-Century Britain and Ireland, 1994; The Myth of the Jacobite Clans, 1995; Inventing and Resisting Britain, 1997. Contributions to: Scholarly books and journals. Honours: Various research grants; Royal Society of Edinburgh BP Humanities Research Prize, 1992-93; Fellow, Society of Antiquaries, Scotland, 1995; Royal Historical Society. Address: c/o Department of English Studies, University of Strathclyde, Livingstone Tower, Richmond Street, Glasgow G1 1XH, Scotland.

PIWOWARSKI Claire Rhiannon, b. 14 July 1980, Huddersfield, England. 1 daughter. Publications: Nowhere Man, 1996; Misery Man, 1997; Friends, 1997; Lifes Doubts, 1997; Forever in My Heart, 1997; Literature Left to Rot, 1997; Poetic Mind Games, 1997; Diary of Death, 1998; Sweet Insanity, 1998; Winter Song, 1999. Honour: Editors Choice Awards, both 1997. Address: 30 Oakes Lane, Brockholes, Huddersfield, HD7 7AR, England.

PLACE Florence. See: **NORMAN Geraldine.**

PLAICE Stephen James, b. 9 Sept 1951, Watford, Hertfordshire, England. Writer; Poet; Editor. Education: BA, Honours, German, 1973, MPhil, Comparative Literature, 1979, University of Sussex; University of Marburg, 1972; University of Zürich, 1975. Appointments: Writer-in-Residence, H M Prison, Lewes, 1987-94; Artistic Director, Alarmist Theatre, 1987-; Editor, Printer's Devil, 1990-. Publications: Rumours of Cousins, 1983; Over the Rollers, 1992. Contributions to: Guardian; Cumberland Poetry Review; Honest Ulsterman; London Magazine; Orbis; Poetry Durham; Poetry Nottingham. Address: 83 Stanford Road, Brighton, East Sussex BN2 2GL, England.

PLAIN Belva, b. 9 Oct 1919, New York, New York, USA. Writer. m. Irving Plain, 14 June 1941, dec 1982, 3 children. Education: Barnard College. Publications: Evergreen, 1978; Random Winds, 1980; Eden Burning, 1982; Crescent City, 1984; The Golden Cup, 1987; Tapestry, 1988; Blessings, 1989; Harvest, 1990; Treasures, 1992; Whispers, 1993; Daybreak, 1994; The Carousel, 1995; Promises, 1996; Secrecy, 1997; Homecoming, 1997; Legacy of Silence, 1998. Literary Agent: Janklow & Nesbit Associates, 598 Madison Avenue, New York, NY 10022. Address: c/o Delacourte Press, 1540 Broadway, New York, NY 10036, USA.

PLANO Jack Charles, b. 25 Nov 1921, Merrill, Wisconsin, USA. Professor of Political Science Emeritus; Writer. m. Ellen L Ruehlow, 25 June 1954, 2 sons, 1 daughter. Education: AA, Merrill Commercial College, 1940; AB, Ripon College, 1949; MA, 1950, PhD, 1954, University of Wisconsin. Appointments: Assistant Professor, 1952-57, Associate Professor, 1957-63, Professor of Political Science, 1963-87, Chairman, Department of Political Science, 1979-84, Professor Emeritus, 1987-, Western Michigan University, Kalamazoo; Assistant State Director, Michigan Citizenship Clearing House, 1957-60; Co-Director, Associated Educators, Troy, Alabama, 1961-69; Visiting Fellow, Institute for the Study of International Organizations, University of Sussex, 1971-72; Managing Editor, Personality Press, 1990-. Publications: The Content of the Introductory International Politics Course: Basic Framework and Concepts, 1958; The American Political Dictionary (with Milton Greenberg), 1962, 10th edition 1997; The United Nations and the Indian-Pakistan Dispute, 1966; Forging World Order: The Politics of International Organization (with Robert E Riggs), 1967, 2nd edition, 1971; The International Relations Dictionary (with Roy Olton), 1969, 5th edition (with Roy Olton and Lawrence Irving), 1996; Political Science Dictionary (with Milton Greenberg, Roy Olton, and Robert E Riggs), 1973; Dictionary of Political Analysis (with Robert E Riggs), 1973, 2nd edition (with Robert E Riggs and H S Robin), 1982; United Nations Capital Development Fund: Poor and Rich Worlds in Collision (with Marjon Vashti Kamara), 1974; Experiments in Undergraduate Teaching (co-author), 1976; The Latin American Political Dictionary (with Ernest E Rossi), 1980, 2nd edition 1993; The Public Administration Dictionary (with Ralph C Chandler), 1982, 2nd edition, 1988; The Soviet and East European Political Dictionary (with Barbara McCrea and George Klein), 1984; The United Nations: International Organization and World Politics (with Robert E Riggs), 1988, 2nd edition, 1993; Memoirs: Vol I, Fishhooks, Apples and Outhouses: Memories of the 1920's, 1930's and 1940's, 1991, Vol II, Life in the Educational Trenches: Memories of College and University Days (1946-1952), 1991, Vol III, Pulling the Weeds and Watering the Flowers (1952-1993), 1993. Honours: Hubert Herring Award for Best Reference Book on Latin America, 1981; Phi Beta Kappa, Ripon College Chapter, 1981; Charter Member, Phi Beta Kappa, Western Michigan University Chapter, 1997; First Outstanding Emeritus Scholar Award, Western Michigan University, 1997. Memberships: Academy of Political Science; American Academy of Political and Social Science; American Association for the United Nations; International Studies Association. Address: 705 Weaver Circle, Kalamazoo, MI 49006, USA.

PLANTA Maxie V. See: **SCHAAD Isolde G.**

PLANTE David (Robert), b. 4 Mar 1940, Providence, Rhode Island, USA. Writer. Education: University of Louvain, Belgium, 1959-60; BA, Boston College, 1961. Appointments: Writer-in-Residence, University of Tulsa, 1979-82; Visiting Fellow, University of Cambridge, 1984-85; L'Université de Québec à Montreal, 1990; Gorky Institute of Literature, Moscow, Russia, 1991; Professor, Columbia University, New York, 1998-. Publications: Fiction: The Ghost of Henry James, 1970; Slides, 1971; Relatives, 1974; The Darkness of the Body, 1974; Figures in Bright Air, 1976; The Family, 1978; The Country, 1981; The Woods, 1982; The Foreigner, 1984; The Catholic, 1986; The Native, 1988; The Accident, 1991; Annunciation, 1994; The Age of Terror, forthcoming. Non-Fiction: Difficult Women: A Memoir of Three, 1983. Contributions to: Anthologies and magazines. Honours: Henfield Fellow, University of East Anglia, 1975; British Arts Council Grant, 1977; Guggenheim Fellowship, 1983; American Academy and Institute of Arts and Letters Award, 1983; Senior Member, King's College, Cambridge. Address: 38 Montagu Square, London W1, England.

PLANTEY Alain, b. 19 July 1924, Mulhouse, France. Diplomat; Writer. m. Christiane Wioland, 4 daughters. Education: University of Bordeaux; LLD, University of Paris, 1949; Diploma, National School of Public Administration, Paris, 1949. Appointments: Diplomat; Councillor of State; Chairman, International Court of Arbitration, International Chamber of Commerce. Publications: Traite Pratique de la Fonction Publique, 1953, 3rd edition, 1971; Prospective de l'Etat Paris, 1974; La Fonction Publique Internationale Paris, 1977; Le Negociation Internationale, 1980, 2nd edition, 1994; International Civil Service, 1981; La Funcion Publica Internacional y Europea, 1982; De la Politique les Etats, 1987, 2nd edition, 1992; Tratado de Derecho Diplomatico, 1991; La Fonctioin Publique, Traite Général, 1992. Contributions to: Journals and magazines. Honours: Award, Academy of Moral and Political Sciences, 1979; Award, Académie Francaise, 1982; Commander, Légion d' Honneur, Palmes Académiques. Memberships: Academy of Moral and Political Sciences; Various professional organizations. Address: 6 Avenue Sully Prudhomme, Paris 75007, France.

PLANTINGA Alvin, b. 15 Nov 1932, Ann Arbor, Michigan, USA. Professor of Philosophy; Writer. m. Kathleen Ann DeBoer, 16 June 1955, 2 sons, 2 daughters. Education: AB, Calvin College, Grand Rapids, 1954; MA, University of Michigan, 1955; PhD, Yale University, 1958. Appointments: Instructor, Yale University, 1957-58; Associate Professor, Wayne State University, 1958-63; Professor, Calvin College, 1963-82; Fellow, Center for Advanced Study in the Behavioral Sciences, 1968-69; Visiting Fellow, Balliol College, Oxford, 1975-76; John A O'Brien Professor of Philosophy, 1982-, Director, Center for Philosophy of Religion, 1983-, University of Notre Dame, Indiana; Gifford Lecturer, Aberdeen University, 1987. Publications: God and Other Minds, 1967; The Nature of Necessity, 1974; God, Freedom, and Evil, 1974; Does God Have a Nature?, 1980; Faith and Rationality, 1983; Warrant: The Current Debate, 1993; Warrant and Proper Function, 1993. Honours: Guggenheim Fellowship, 1971-72; National Endowment for the Humanities Fellowships, 1975-76, 1987, 1995-96; Honorary doctorates. Memberships: American Philosophical Association; Society of Christian Philosophers, president, 1983-86. Address: c/o Department of Philosophy, University of Notre Dame, Notre Dame, IN 46556, USA.

PLATE Andrea, (Andrea Darvi), b. 29 July 1952, Los Angeles, California, USA. Teacher; Writer. m. Thomas Plate, 22 Sept 1979, 1 daughter. Education: MA, Journalism, University of Southern California, Los Angeles; BA, English, University of California, Berkeley. Appointments: Assistant Professor, Communications Department, Fordham University, 1988-90; Senior Lecturer, Journalism, University of Southern California, 1990-92, Santa Monica College, 1993-; English Teacher, Oakwood School, 1994-. Publication: Secret Police, 1981. Contributions to: Periodicals. Address: 812 16th Street, No 2, Santa Monica, CA 90403, USA.

PLATER Alan Frederick, b. 15 Apr 1935, Jarrow on Tyne, County Durham, England. Writer; Dramatist. m. (1) Shirley Johnson, 1958, div 1985, 2 sons, 1 daughter, (2) Shirley Rubinstein, 1986, 3 sons. Education: King's College, Durham, 1953-57; University of Newcastle. Contributions to: Stage, screen, radio, television, anthologies and periodicals. Honours: Various stage, radio and television drama awards. Memberships: Royal Society of Literature, fellow; Royal Society of Arts, fellow; Writer's Guild of Great Britain, president, 1991-95. Address: c/o 200 Fulham Road, London SW10 9PN, England.

PLATH James Walter, b. 29 Oct 1950, Chicago, Illinois, USA. Writer; Editor; Educator. 5 sons. Education: BA, English, California University at Chicago, 1980; MA, English, 1982, PhD, English, 1988, University of Wisconsin-Milwaukee. Appointments: Editor, Publisher, Clockwatch Review, 1983-; Associate Professor of English, Illinois-Wesleyan University. Publications: Conversations With John Updike, 1994; Courbet, On The Rocks, 1994; Remembering Ernest Hemingway, 1999. Contributions to: Anthologies, reviews, periodicals, journals, quarterlies, magazines and newspapers. Honours include: Fulbright Scholar; Editors Award, Council of Literary Magazines and Presses, 1990. Memberships: Academy of American Poets; Council of Literary Magazines and Presses; Democratic National Committee; Fitzgerald Society; Fulbright Association; Hemingway Society; Illinois College Press Association; Society of Midland Authors. Address: c/o Department of English, Illinois-Wesleyan University, Bloomington, IL 61702-2900, USA.

PLATT Charles, b. 26 Apr 1945, London, England. Writer; Poet. 1 daughter. Education: University of Cambridge; London College of Printing. Publications: Fiction: The Garbage World, 1967; The City Dwellers, 1970, US edition as Twilight of the City, 1977; Planet of the Voles, 1971; New Worlds 6 (editor with M Moorcock), 1973, US edition as New Worlds 5, 1974; New Worlds 7 (editor with H Bailey), 1974; US edition as New Worlds 6, 1975; Sweet Evil, 1977; Free Zone, 1989; Soma, 1989; The Silicon Man, 1991. Non-Fiction: Dream Makers: The Uncommon People Who Write Science Fiction, 1980; When You Can Live Twice as Long, What Will You Do?, 1989. Poetry: Highway Sandwiches (with T M Disch and M Hacker), 1970; The Gas, 1970. Address: c/o Gollancz, 14 Henrietta Street, London WC2E 8QJ, England.

PLATTHY Jeno, b. 13 Aug 1920, Hungary. Poet; Writer; Editor; Publisher. m. Carol Louise Abell, 25 Sept 1976. Education: Peter Pazmany University, Budapest, 1939-42; Jozsef Ferencz University, 1943-44; Catholic University of America, 1963-65. Appointments: Editor-in-Chief, Monumenta Classical Perennia, 1967-84; Executive Director, Federation of International Poetry Associations of UNESCO, 1976-96; Publisher, New Muses, 1976-. Publications: Poetry: 58 volumes, 1976-96, including: Odes Europénnes, 1986; Asian Elegies, 1987; Nova Comoedia, 3 parts, 1988, 1990,

1991; Elegies Asiatiques, 1991; Paeans, 1993; Prosodia, 1994; Songs of the Soul, 1996; Ultimacy, 1999. Other: Sources on the Earliest Greek Libraries with the Testimonia, 1968; Ch'u Yuan, 1975; The Mythical Poets of Greece, 1985; Bartók: A Critical Biography, 1988; Plato: A Critical Biography, 1990; Near-Death Experiences in Antiquity, 1992; The Duino Elegies of Rilke (translation and commentary), 1999. Contributions to: Various publications. Honours: Poet Laureate, World Congress of Poets, 1973; Confucius Award, 1974; Poet Laureate and President, International Congress of Poets, 1976; Officier, Ordre des Arts et des Lettres, France, 1992. Memberships: Academy of American Poets; American Society of Composers, Authors and Publishers; Association of Literary Critics and Scholars; International PEN Club; International Poetry Society; Literarische Union, Germany. Address: 961 W Sled Circle, Santa Claus, IN 47579, USA.

PLAYER Corrie Lynne (Oborn), b. 14 Oct 1942, Ogden, Utah, USA. Journalist; Writer; Teacher. m. Gary Farnsworth Player, 5 sons, 3 daughters. Education: AA, Weber College; BA, 1964, MA, 1965, Stanford University. Publication: Anchorage Altogether, 1972, revised edition, 1977. Contributions to: Magazines and newspapers. Honours: Non-Fiction Book Awards, Oklahoma Writers Federation, 1986, 1988. Memberships: Oklahoma Writers Federation; League of Utah Writers; National Writers Club; National Foster Parents Association. Address: 429 400th South, Cedar City, UT 84720, USA.

PLAYER Trezevant. See: **YEATMAN Ted P.**

PLEIJEL Agneta, b. 26 Feb 1940, Stockholm, Sweden. Writer; Poet; Dramatist. m. Maciej Zaremba, 27 Nov 1982, 1 daughter. Education: MA, 1970. Publications: Novels, poems, and plays. Contributions to: Various publications. Membership: Swedish PEN Club. Address: Tantogatan 45, 117 42 Stockholm, Sweden.

PLIMPTON George (Ames), b. 18 Mar 1927, New York, New York, USA. Writer; Editor. m. (1) Freddy Medora Espy, 1968, div 1988, 1 son, 1 daughter, (2) Sarah Whitehead Dudley, 1991, 2 daughters. Education: AB, Harvard University, 1948; MA, University of Cambridge, 1952. Appointments: Editor-in-Chief, Paris Review, 1953-, Paris Review Editions, 1965-72, 1987-; Instructor, Barnard College, 1956-58; Associate Editor, Horizon magazine, 1959-61, Harper's magazine, 1972-81; Director, American Literary Anthology program, 1967-71; Host, various television specials. Publications: Rabbit's Umbrella, 1956; Out of My League, 1961; Paper Lion, 1966; The Bogey Man, 1968; Mad Ducks and Bears, 1973; One for the Record, 1974; Shadow-Box, 1976; One More July, 1976; Sports! (with Neil Leifer), 1978; A Sports Bestiary (with Arnold Roth), 1987; The X-Factor, 1990; The Best of Plimpton, 1990. Editor: Writers at Work, 9 volumes, 1957-92; American Journey: The Times of Robert Kennedy (with Jean Stein), 1970; Pierre's Book, 1971; The Fancy, 1973; Edie: An American Biography (with Jean Stein), 1982; D V (with Christopher Hemphill), 1984; The Paris Review Anthology, 1989; The Writer's Chapbook, 1989; Women Writers at Work, 1989; Poets at Work, 1989; The Norton Book of Sports, 1992; Chronicles of Courage (with Jean Kennedy Smith), 1992. Contributions to: Numerous publications. Honours: Distinguished Achievement Award, University of Southern California, 1967; Blue Pencil Award, Columbia Spectator, 1981; Mark Twain Award, International Platform Association, 1982; Chancellor's Award, Long Island University, 1986; L'Ordre des Arts et des Lettres, France, 1994. Memberships: American Pyrotechnics Association; Explorers Club; Linnean Society; Mayflower Descendants Society; PEN; National Football League Alumni Association; Pyrotechnics Guild International. Address: c/o Paris Review Inc, 541 East 72nd Street, New York, NY 10021, USA.

PLINGE Walter. See: **THURGOOD Nevil.**

PLOWDEN Alison, b. 18 Dec 1931, Simla, India. Writer. Publications: Over 16 books, 1971-96. Contributions to: Radio and television. Honours: Writers

Guild of Great Britain Award; Best British Educational TV Script, 1972. Address: c/o John Johnson, Clerkenwell House, 45-47 Clerkenwell Green, London EC1R 0HT, England.

PLUCKROSE Henry Arthur, (Richard Cobbett), b. 23 Oct 1931, London, England. Teacher; Children's Writer. Education: St Mark and St John College, London, 1952-54; Institute of Education, London, 1958-60; FCP, College of Preceptors, 1976. Appointments: Teacher, Elementary School, Inner London, 1954-68; Head, Education, Prior Weston School, London, 1968-; Editor, Let's Go Series. Publications: Over 50 books, 1965-90. Address: 3 Butts Lane, Danbury, Essex, England.

PLUMB Sir John (Harold), b. 20 Aug 1911, Leicester, England. Professor of Modern English History Emeritus; Writer. Education: University College, Leicester; Christ's College, Cambridge; BA, University of London, 1933; PhD, University of Cambridge, 1936. Appointments: Ehrman Research Fellow, King's College, Cambridge, 1939-46; Fellow, 1946-, Steward, 1948-50, Tutor, 1950-59, Vice-Master, 1964-68, Master, 1978-82, Christ's College, Cambridge; University Lecturer in History, 1946-62, Reader in Modern English History, 1962-65, Professor of Modern English History, 1966-74, Professor Emeritus, 1974-, University of Cambridge; Various visiting professorships; Editor, History of Human Society, 1959-; Pelican Social History of Britain, 1982-; Historical Advisor, Penguin Books, 1960-92. Publications: English in the Eighteenth Century, 1950; West African Explorers (with C Howard), 1952; Chatham, 1953; Studies in Social History (editor), 1955; Sir Robert Walpole, 2 volumes, 1956, 1960; The First Four Georges, 1956; The Renaissance, 1961; Men and Places, 1962; Crisis in the Humanities, 1964; The Growth of Political Stability in England, 1675-1725, 1967; Death of the Past, 1969; In the Light of History, 1972; The Commercialisation of Leisure, 1974; Royal Heritage, 1977; New Light on the Tyrant, George III, 1978; Georgian Delights, 1980; Royal Heritage: The Reign of Elizabeth II, 1980; The Birth of a Consumer Society (with Neil McKendrick and John Brewer), 1982; Collected Essays: Vol I, The Making of a Historian, 1988, Vol II: The American Experience, 1989. Contributions to: Books and journals. Honours: Festschrift published in his honour, 1974; Knighted, 1982; Honorary doctorates. Memberships: British Academy, fellow; Royal Historical Society, fellow. Address: c/o Christ's College, Cambridge CB2 3BU, England.

PLUMLY Stanley (Ross), b. 23 May 1939, Barnesville, Ohio, USA. Poet; Professor of English. Education: BA, Wilmington College, 1961; MA, Ohio University, 1968. Appointments: Instructor in Creative Writing, Louisiana State University, 1968-70; Editor, Ohio Review, 1970-75, Iowa Review, 1976-78; Professor of English, Ohio University, 1970-74, University of Houston, 1979-; Visiting lecturer at several universities. Publications: In the Outer Dark, 1970; How the Plains Indians Got Horses, 1973; Giraffe, 1973; Out-of-the-Body Travel, 1977; Summer Celestial, 1983; Boy on the Step, 1989; The Bridge in the Trees, 1997. Contributions to: Periodicals. Honours: Delmore Schwartz Memorial Award, 1973; Guggenheim Fellowhip, 1973; National Endowment for the Arts Grant, 1977. Address: c/o Department of English and Creative Writing, University of Houston, 4800 Calhoun, Houston, TX 77004, USA.

PLUNKETT James, b. 21 May 1920, Dublin, Ireland. Writer; Dramatist. Education: Dublin College of Music. Appointments: Senior Producer, Radio Telefis Eireann, 1974-85. Publications: Strumpet City, 1969; The Gems She Wore: A Book of Irish Places, 1972; Farewell Companions, 1977; The Circus Animals, 1990. Short Stories: The Trusting and the Maimed, Other Irish Stories, 1959; Collected Short Stories, 1977. Plays: Homecoming, 1954; Big Jim, 1954; The Risen People, 1958; Radio Plays; TV Plays and Programmes. Other: Boy on the Back Wall and Other Essays, 1987. Honours: Jacob's Awards, 1963, 1969; Yorkshire Post Award, 1969; Sunday Independent Irish Life Award, 1990; Irish Butler Award, Irish-American Cultural Institute, 1993. Memberships: Irish Academy of letters, president,

1980-81; Society of Irish Playwrights; Aosdana. Address: 29 Parnell Road, Bray, County Wicklow, Ireland.

POAGUE Leland Allen, b. 15 Dec 1948, San Francisco, California, USA. Professor of English; Writer. m. Susan Aileen Jensen, 24 Aug 1969, 2 daughters. Education: BA, San Jose State College, 1970; PhD, University of Oregon, 1973. Appointments: Instructor, 1973-74, Assistant Professor, 1974-78, State University of New York at Geneseo; Visiting Assistant Professor, University of Rochester, 1977; Assistant Professor, 1978-81, Associate Professor, 1981-86, Professor of English, 1986-, Iowa State University. Publications: The Cinema of Frank Capra: An Approach to Film Comedy, 1975; The Cinema of Earnest Lubitsch: The Hollywood Films, 1978; Billy Wilder and Leo McCarey, 1980; Howard Hawks, 1982; Film Criticism: A Counter Theory (with William Cadbury), 1982; A Hitchcock Reader (editor with Marshall Deutelbaum), 1986; Another Frank Capra, 1994; Conversations with Susan Sontag (editor), 1995. Contributions to: Various journals. Address: c/o Department of English, Iowa State University, Ames, IA 50011, USA.

POCOCK Tom, (Thomas Allcot Guy Pocock), b. 18 Aug 1925, London, England. Author; Journalist. m. Penelope Casson, 26 Apr 1969, 2 daughters. Publications: Nelson and His World, 1968; Chelsea Reach, 1970; Fighting General, 1973; Remember Nelson, 1977; The Young Nelson in the Americas, 1980; 1945: The Dawn Came Up Like Thunder, 1983; East and West of Suez, 1986; Horatio Nelson, 1987; Alan Moorehead, 1990; The Essential Venice, 1990; Sailor King, 1991; Rider Haggard and the Lost Empire, 1993; Norfolk, 1995; A Thirst for Glory, 1996; Battle for Empire, 1998. Contributions to: Numerous newspapers and magazines. Address: 22 Lawrence Street, London SW3 5NF, England.

PODHORETZ Norman, b. 16 Jan 1930, Brooklyn, New York, USA. Editor; Writer. m. Midge Rosenthal Decter, 21 Oct 1956, 1 son, 3 daughters. Education: AB, Columbia University, 1950; BHL, Jewish Theological Seminary, 1950; BA, 1952, MA, 1957, University of Cambridge. Appointments: Associate Editor, 1956-58, Editor-in-Chief, 1960-95, Editor-at-Large, 1995-, Commentary Magazine; Member, University Seminar on American Civilization, Columbia University, 1958; Editor-in-Chief, Looking Glass Library, 1959-60; Chairman, New Directions Advisory Committee, United States Information Agency, 1981-87; Senior Fellow, Hudson Institute, 1995-. Publications: Doings and Undoings: The Fifties and After in American Writing, 1964; The Commentary Reader (editor), 1966; Making It, 1968; Breaking Ranks, 1979; The Present Danger, 1980; Why We Were in Vietnam, 1982; The Bloody Crossroads, 1986. Contributions to: Periodicals. Honours: Fulbright Fellowship, 1950-51; Kellet Fellow, University of Cambridge, 1952; Honorary LHD, Hamilton College, 1969, Yeshiva University, 1991, Boston University, 1995, Adelphi University, 1996; Honorary LLD, Jewish Theological Seminary, 1980. Membership: Council on Foreign Relations. Address: c/o Commentary Magazine, American Jewish Committee, 165 East 56th Street, New York, NY 10022, USA.

POGACNIK Bogdan, b. 12th July 1921, Maribor. Retired Journalist. m. Miljana Peternel, 2nd Feb 1945, 2 sons, 1 dec. Education: Classical College, Maribor, 1940; Faculty of Law, Ljubljana, 1947; Doctorate in Journalism, Paris. Appointments: Correspondent, Tanjuc Press Agency; Editor, Delo, daily newspaper, Ljubljana. Publications: Everything Are the Human People; The People of My Time; He Sang for All; In Fire was Born our Liberty (poetry). Contributions to: Delo Daily; Nasi Razgedi (fortnightly); Slovenian PEN Review. Honour: Tonsic Award for Journalism. Memberships: Slovenian PEN Centre; Slovenian Writers Association. Address: Trubarjeva 61, 1000 Ljubljana, Slovenia.

POGREBIN Letty Cottin, b. 9 June 1939, New York, New York, USA. Writer; Editor. m. Bertrand Pogrebin, 1963, 1 son, 2 daughters. Education: BA, Brandeis University, 1959. Appointments: Columnist for various periodicals, 1970-; Editor, MS magazine, 1971- . Publications: How to Make it in a Man's World, 1970; Getting Yours, 1975; Growing Up Free, 1980; Stories for Free Children (editor), 1982; Family Politics, 1983; Among Friends, 1986; Free to be...A Family (editor), 1987. Contributions to: Anthologies and periodicals. Honours: Emmy Award, 1974; Matrix Award, 1981. Memberships: Author's Guild; National Women's Political Caucus; Jewish Fund for Justice; Women's Action Alliance. Address: c/o Ms Magazine, 1 Times Square, New York, NY 10036, USA.

POHL Frederik (James MacCreigh), b. 26 Nov 1919, New York, New York, USA. Writer; Editor. Appointments: Book Editor and Associate Circulation Manager, Popular Science Co, New York City, 1946-49; Literary Agent, New York City, 1949-53; Editor, Galaxy Publishing Co, New York City, 1960-69; Executive Editor, Ace Books, New York City, 1971-72; Science Fiction Editor, Bantam Books, New York City, 1973-79. Publications: Author or editor of over 45 books, 1953-98. Memberships: Author's Guild; Science Fiction Writers of America, president, 1974-76; World Science Fiction, president, 1980-82. Address: c/o World, 855 South Harvard Drive, Palatine, IL 60067, USA.

POIRIER Richard, b. 9 Sept 1925, Gloucester, Massachusetts, USA. Literary Critic. Education: University of Paris, 1946; BA, Amherst College, 1949; MA, Yale University, 1950; Fulbright Scholar, University of Cambridge, England, 1952; PhD, Harvard University, 1960. Appointments: Williams College, 1950-52; Harvard University, 1955-62; Rutgers University, 1962-; Editor, Partisan Review, 1963-71, Raritan Quarterly, 1980-; Vice-President, Founder, Library of America, 1980-. Publications: Comic Sense of Henry James, 1960; In Defense of Reading (co-editor), 1962; A World Elsewhere, 1966; The Performing Self, 1971; Norman Mailer, 1976; Robert Frost: The Work of Knowing, 1977; The Renewal of Literature, 1987; Poetry and Pragmatism, 1992. Contributions to: Daedalus; New Republic; Partisan Review; New York Review; London Review of Books; Times Literary Supplement. Honours: Phi Beta Kappa, 1949; Fulbright Fellow, 1952; Bollingen Fellow, 1963; Guggenheim Fellowship, 1967; National Endowment for the Humanities Fellow, 1972; HHD, Amherst College, 1978; Award, American Academy of Arts and Letters, 1980; Literary Lion of New York, 1992. Memberships: Poets, Playwrights, Editors, Essayists and Novelists; American Academy of Arts and Sciences; Century Club. Address: 104 West 70th Street, 9B, New York, NY 10023, USA.

POLAND Dorothy Elizabeth Hayward, (Alison Farely, Jane Hammond), b. 3 May 1937, Barry, Wales. Author. Publications: As Alison Farely: The Shadows of Evil, 1963; Plunder Island, 1964; High Treason, 1966; Throne of Wrath, 1967; Crown of Splendour, 1968; The Lion and the Wolf, 1969; Last Roar of the Lion, 1969; Leopard From Anjou, 1970; King Wolf, 1974; Kingdom under Tyranny, 1974; Last Howl of the Wolf, 1975; The Cardinal's Nieces, 1976; The Tempestuous Countess, 1976; Archduchess Arrogance, 1980; Scheming Spanish Queen, 1981; Spain for Mariana, 1982. As Jane Hammond: The Hell Raisers of Wycombe, 1970; Fire and the Sword, 1971; The Golden Courtesan, 1975; Shadow of the Headsman, 1975; The Doomtower, 1975; Witch of the White House, 1976; Gunpowder Treason, 1976; The Red Queen, 1976; The Queen's Assassin, 1977; The Silver Madonna, 1977; Conspirator's Moonlight, 1977; Woman of Vengeance, 1977; The Admiral's Lady, 1978; The Secret of Petherick, 1982; The Massingham Topaz, 1983; Beware the King's Enchantress, 1983; Moon in Aries, 1984; Eagle's Talon, 1984; Death in the New Forest, 1984. Address: Horizons, 99 Dock View Road, Barry, Glamorgan, Wales.

POLE J(ack) R(ichon), b. 14 Mar 1922, London, England. Historian; Writer. m. Marilyn Louise Mitchell, 31 May 1952, div 1988, 1 son, 2 daughters. Education: BA, University of Oxford, 1949; PhD, Princeton University, 1953; MA, Cantab, 1963. Appointments: Instructor, Princeton University, 1952-53; Assistant Lecturer to Lecturer in American History, University College, London, 1953-63; Reader in American History and Government, University of Cambridge, Fellow, Churchill College, 1963-79, Vice Master, 1975-78; Fellow, Center for Advanced Study in the Behavioral Sciences, USA, 1969-70; Guest Scholar, Woodrow Wilson International Center, Washington, DC, 1978-79; Rhodes Professor of American History and Institutions, Oxford University, 1979-89; Fellow, St Catherine's College, Oxford, 1979-; Senior Research Fellow, College of William and Mary, Virginia, 1991; Leverhulme Trust Emeritus Fellow, 1991-93. Publications: Abraham Lincoln and the Working Classes of Britain, 1959; Abraham Lincoln, 1964; Political Representation in England and the Origins of the American Republic, 1966; The Advance of Democracy (editor), 1967; The Seventeenth Century: The Origins of Legislative Power, 1969; The Revolution in America: Documents of the Internal Development of America in the Revolutionary Era (editor), 1971; The Meanings of American History (co-editor), 1971; Foundations of American Independence, 1763-1815, 1972; American Historical Documents (general editor), 1975; The Decision for American Independence, 1975; The Idea of Union, 1977; The Pursuit of Equality in American History, 1978, 2nd edition, revised, 1993; Paths to the American Past, 1979; The Gift of Government: Political Responsibility from the English Restoration to American Independence, 1983; Colonial British America: Essays in the New History of the Early Modern Era (co-editor), 1983; The American Constitution: For and Against: The Federalist and Anti-Federalist Papers (editor), 1987; The Blackwell Encyclopedia of the American Revolution (co-editor), 1991, revised as The Blackwell Companion to the American Revolution, 1999; Freedom of Speech: Right or Privilege, 1998. Contributions to: Reference works and professional journals. Memberships: British Academy, fellow; Royal Historical Society, fellow; Selden Society; International Commission for the History of Representative and Parliamentary Institutions, vice president, 1990-. Address: 20 Divinity Road, Oxford OX4 1LJ, England.

POLIAKOFF Stephen, b. 1952, London, England. Dramatist; Director. m. Sandy Welch, 1983, 1 son, 1 daughter. Education: Westminster School; University of Cambridge. Publications: Plays: Clever Soldiers, 1974; The Carnation Gang, 1974; Hitting Town, 1975; City Sugar, 1976; Strawberry Fields, 1978; Shout Across the River, 1978; The Summer Party, 1980; Favourite Nights, 1981; Breaking the Silence, 1984; Coming into Land, 1987; Playing with Trains, 1989; Sienna Red, 1992. Other: Films and television plays. Honours: Several awards and prizes. Address: 33 Donia Devonia Road, London N1 8JQ, England.

POLING-KEMPES Lesley Ann, b. 9 Mar 1954, Batavia, New York, USA. Writer. m. James Kempes, 31 May 1976, 1 son, 1 daughter. Education: BA, cum laude, University of New Mexico, 1976. Publications: Harvey Girls: Women Who Opened the West, 1989; Canyon of Remembering, 1996; Valley of Shining Stone: The Story of Abiquiu, 1997. Contributions to: Puerta del Sol; Writer's Forum 16; Best of the West 3; Higher Elevations; New Mexico Magazine. Honour: Zia Award for Excellence, New Mexico Press Women, 1991. Address: PO Box 36, Abiquiu, NM 87510, USA.

POLITO Robert, b. 27 Oct 1951, Boston, Massachusetts, USA. Writer; Poet. m. Kristine M Harris, 27 June 1987. Education: BA, Boston College, 1973; PhD, Harvard University, 1981. Appointments: Faculty, Harvard University, 1976-81, Wellesley College, 1981-89, New York University, 1990-92, New School for Social Research, New York City, 1992-. Publications: Fireworks: The Lost Writings of Jim Thompson (editor), 1988; A Reader's Guide to James Morrill's The Changing Light at Sandover, 1994; Doubles (poems), 1995; Savage Art: A Biography of Jim Thompson, 1995. Contributions to: Newspapers and magazines. Honour: National Book Critics Circle Award, 1995. Address: c/o Writing Program, New School for Social Research, 66 West 12th Street, No 507, New York, NY 10021, USA.

POLLAND Madelaine Angela, (Frances Adrian), b. 31 May 1918, Kinsale, County Cork, Ireland. Writer. Publications: Children of the Red King, 1961; Beorn the Proud, 1962; The White Twilight, 1962; Chuiraquimba and the Black Robes, 1962; City of the Golden House, 1963; The Queen's Blessing, 1963; Flame over Tara, 1964; Thicker Than Water, 1964; Mission to Cathay, 1965; Queen Without Crown, 1965; Deirdre, 1967; The Little Spot of Bother (US edition as Minutes of a Murder), 1967; To Tell My People, 1968; Stranger in the Hills, 1968; Random Army (US edition as Shattered Summer), 1969; To Kill a King, 1970; Alhambra, 1970; A Family Affair, 1971; Package to Spain, 1971; Daughter to Poseidon (US edition as Daughter of the Sea), 1972; Prince of the Double Axe, 1976; Double Shadow (as Francis Adrian), 1977; Sabrina, 1979; All Their Kingdoms, 1981; The Heart Speaks Many Ways, 1982; No Price Too High, 1984; As It Was in the Beginning, 1987; Rich Man's Flowers, 1990; The Pomegranate House, 1992. Address: Edificio Hercules 634, Avenida Gamonal, Arroyo de La Miel, Malaga, Spain.

POLLARD Jane, (Jane Jackson, Dana James), b. 22 Nov 1944, Goole, Yorkshire, England. Author. m. (3) Michael Pollard, 2 June 1992, 2 sons, 1 daughter. Publications: Historical Romances: Harlyn Tremayne, 1984; The Consul's Daughter, 1986; Contemporary Romance: Doctor in The Andes, 1984; Desert Flower, 1986; Doctor in New Guinea, 1986; Rough Waters, 1986; The Marati Legacy, 1986; The Eagle and the Sun, 1986; Heart of Glass, 1987; Tarik's Mountain, 1988; Snowfire, 1988; Pool of Dreaming, 1988; Dark Moon Rising, 1989; Love's Ransom, 1989; A Tempting Shore, 1992; Bay of Rainbows, 1993; Mystery: Deadly Feast, 1997; Historical Romance: A Place of Birds, 1997; The Iron Road, 1999. Contributions to: Falmouth Packet; West Briton; Western Morning News; Woman's Way; Radio Cornwall; BFBS Gibraltar, GIB TV. Memberships: Romantic Novelists Association; Society of Authors. Address: 32 Cogos Park, Comfort Road, Mylor, Falmouth, Cornwall TR11 5SF, England.

POLLARD John (Richard Thornhill), b. 5 Apr 1914, Exeter, Devon, England. Retired Senior Lecturer in Classics. Writer. m. Shirley Holt, 12 July 1952, 1 son, 3 daughters. Education: BA, 1936, MA, 1939, University College, Exeter; MLitt, University of Oxford, 1947. Appointment: Senior Lecturer in Classics, University College of North Wales, Bangor. Publications: Journey to the Styx, 1955; Adventure Begins in Kenya, 1957; Africa for Adventure, 1961; African Zoo Man, 1963; Wolves and Werewolves, 1964, 2nd edition, 1991; Helen of Troy, 1965; Seers, Shrines and Sirens, 1965; The Long Safari, 1967; Virgil: The Aeneid Appreciation (with C Day-Lewis), 1969; Birds in Greek Life and Myth, 1977; Divination and Oracles: Greece, Civilization of the Ancient Mediterranean, 1986; No County to Compare, 1994. Address: The Yard, Red Wharf Bay, Angelesey LL75 8RX, Wales.

POLLEY Judith Anne, (Helen Kent, Valentina Luellen, Judith Stewart), b. 15 Sept 1938, London, England. Author. m. Roy Edward Polley, 28 Mar 1959, 1 son. Education: High School, Belgravia and Maida Vale, London. Publications: About 50 Modern and Historical Romance novels, including: To Touch the Stars, 1980; Beloved Enemy, 1980; Don't Run From Love, 1981; Moonshadow, 1981; Prince of Deception, 1981; Beloved Adversary, 1981; Shadow of the Eagle, 1982; Silver Salamander, 1982; The Wind of Change, 1982; The Measure of Love, 1983; The Peaceful Homecoming, 1983; The Valley of Tears, 1984; Moonflower, 1984; Elusive Flame of Love, 1984; Mistress of Tanglewood, 1984; Black Ravenswood, 1985; The Lord of Darkness, 1985; Devil of Talland, 1985; Passionate Pirate, 1986; Where the Heart Leads, 1986; Love the Avenger, 1986; The Devil's Touch, 1987; My Lady Melisande, 1987; Dark Star, 1988; Love and Pride (Book 1), 1988; The Web of Love (Book 2), 1989; Winter Embers, Summer Fire, 1991; To Please a Lady, 1992; One Love, 1993; Hostage of Love, 1994; many foreign editions and translations. Contributions to: Woman's Weekly Library; Woman's Realm; Woman's Weekly Fiction series; Museum of

Peace and Solidarity, Samarkand, Uzbekistan. Membership: Founding Member, English Romantic Novelists Association. Address: Calcada, 8150 Sao Braz de Alportel, Algarve, Portugal.

POLLITT Katha, b. 14 Oct 1949, New York, New York, USA. Writer; Poet; Editor. Div, 1 child. Education: BA, Harvard University, 1972; MFA, Columbia University, 1975. Appointments: Literary Editor, 1982-84, Contributing Editor, 1986-92, Associate Editor, 1992-, The Nation; Junior Fellow, Council of Humanities, Princeton University, 1984; Lecturer, New School for Social Research, New York City, 1986-90, Poetry Center, 92nd Street YMHA and WYHA, New York City, 1986-95. Publications: Antarctic Traveller, 1982; Reasonable Creatures: Essays on Women and Feminism, 1994. Contributions to: Journals and periodicals. Honours: National Book Critics Circle Award, 1983; I B Lavan Younger Poet's Award, Academy of American Poets, 1984; National Endowment for the Arts Grant, 1984; Guggenheim Fellowship, 1987; Whiting Fellowship, 1993. Address: 317 West 93rd Street, New York, NY 10025, USA.

POLLOCK John (Charles), b. 9 Oct 1923, London, England. Clergyman; Writer. m. Anne Barrett-Lennard, 4 May 1949. Education: Trinity College, Cambridge, BA 1946, MA 1948; Ridley Hall, Cambridge. Appointments: Captain, Coldstream Guards 1943-45; Assistant Master (History and Divinity), Wellington College, Berkshire, 1947-49; Ordained Anglican Deacon, 1951, Priest, 1952; Curate, St Paul's Church, Portman Square, London, 1951-53; Rector, Horsington, Somerset, 1953-58; Editor, The Churchman (quarterly), 1953-58. Publications: Candidate for Truth, 1950; A Cambridge Movement, 1953; The Cambridge Seven, 1955, new editions, 1985, 1996; Way to Glory: The Life of Havelock of Lucknow, 1957, revised edition, 1996; Shadows Fall Apart, 1958; The Good Seed, 1959; Earth's Remotest End, 1960; Hudson Taylor and Maria, 1962, new edition, 1996; Moody Without Sankey, 1963, new edition, 1995; The Keswick Story, 1964; The Christians from Siberia, 1964; Billy Graham, 1966, revised edition, 1969; The Apostle: A Life of Paul, 1969, revised edition, 1985, new edition as Paul the Apostle, 1999; Victims of the Long March, 1970; A Foreign Devil in China: The Life of Nelson Bell, 1971, new edition, 1988; George Whitefield and the Great Awakening, 1972; Wilberforce, 1977, new edition, 1988; Billy Graham: Evangelist to the World, 1979; The Siberian Seven, 1979; Amazing Grace: John Newton's Story, 1981; The Master: A Life of Jesus, 1984, new edition, 1999; Billy Graham: Highlights of the Story, 1984; Shaftesbury: The Poor Man's Earl, 1985, new edition, 1990; A Fistful of Heroes: Great Reformers and Evangelists, 1988, new combined edition with On Fire for God, 1998; John Wesley 1989; On Fire for God: Great Missionary Pioneers, 1990; Fear No Foe: A Brother's Story, 1992; Gordon: The Man Behind the Legend, 1993; Kitchener: The Road to Omdurman, 1998. Contributions to: Reference works and religious periodicals. Membership: English Speaking Union Club. Address: Rose Ash House, South Molton, Devonshire EX36 4RB, England.

POLOMÉ Edgar (Ghislain) C(harles), b. 31 July 1920, Brussels, Belgium (US citizen, 1966). Retired Professor of Liberal Arts; Author. m. (1) Julia Joséphine Schwindt, 22 June 1944, dec 29 May 1975, 1 son, 1 daughter, (2) Barbara Baker Harris, 11 July 1980, div Jan 1991, (3) Sharon Looper Rankin, 8 Feb 1991. Education: BA, 1940, PhD, 1949, Free University of Brussels; MA, Catholic University of Louvain, 1943. Appointments: Professor of Germanic Languages, Athénée Adolphe Max, Brussels, 1942-56; Professor of Dutch, Belgian Broadcasting Corp, Brussels, 1954-56; Professor of Linguistics, University of the Belgian Congo, 1956-61; Visiting Associate Professor, 1961-62, Professor of Germanic, Oriental and African Languages and Literatures, 1961-90, Director, Center for Asian Studies, 1962-72, Christie and Stanley Adams Jr Centennial Professor of Liberal Arts, 1984-98, University of Texas at Austin; Co-Editor, 1973-, Managing Editor, 1987-, Journal of Indo-European Studies; Co-Editor, Mankind Quarterly, 1980-; Emeritus Professor, 1998. Publications: Swahili Language Handbook, 1967; Language Surveys in the Developing Nations (editor with Sirarpi Ohannessian and Charles Ferguson), 1974; Linguistics and Literary Studies in Honor of Archibald A Hill (editor with M A Jazayery and Werner Winter), 1976; Language in Tanzania (editor with C P Hill), 1980; Man and the Ultimate: A Symposium (editor), 1980; The Indo-Europeans in the Fourth and Third Millennia (editor), 1982; Language, Society and Paleoculture, 1982; Essays on Germanic Religion, 1989; Guide to Language Change (editor), 1990; Reconstructing Languages and Cultures (editor), 1992; Indo-European Religion after Dumézil (co-editor), 1996; Festschrift J Puhvel (co-editor). 1997. Contributions to: Scholarly books and professional journals; Review editor, Mankind Quarterly, 1997-. Honours: Fulbright-Hays Scholar, University of Kiel, 1968; First Sociolinguistic Prize, University of Umeå, Sweden, 1988. Memberships: American Anthropological Association; American Institute of Indian Studies; American Oriental Society; Indogermanische Gesellschaft; Linguistics Society of America; Modern Language Association; Societas Linguistica Europea; Société de Linguistique de Paris; Honorary Member, Belgian Association for Celtic Studies. Address: 2701 Rock Terrace Drive, Austin, TX 78704, USA.

POLONSKY Antony (Barry), b. 23 Sept 1940, Johannesburg, South Africa. Lecturer in International History; Writer. Education: BA, University of the Witwatersrand, 1960; MA, DPhil, University of Oxford, 1967. Appointments: Lecturer in East European History, University of Glasgow, 1968-70; Lecturer in International History, London School of Economics and Political Science, 1970-, London University, 1981-. Publications: Politics in Independent Poland, 1972; The Little Dictator, 1975; The Great Powers and the Polish Question, 1976; The Beginnings of Communist Rule in Poland (with B Druckier), 1978; The History of Poland since 1863 (co-author), 1981; My Brother's Keeper?: Recent Polish Debates on the Holocaust, 1990; Jews in Eastern Poland and the USSR (editor with Norman Davies), 1991; From Shtetl to Socialism: Studies from Polin, 1994. Contributions to: Professional journals. Address: 27 Dartmouth Park Road, London NW5, England.

PONDER Patricia. See: **MAXWELL Patricia Anne.**

POOLE Josephine. See: **HELYAR Jane Penelope Josephine.**

POOLE Julian. See: **MAY Stephen James.**

POOLE Margaret Barbara, (Peggy Poole, Terry Roche, Margaret Thornton), b. 8 Mar 1925, Petham, Kent, England. Broadcaster; Poet; Writer. m. Reginald Poole, 10 Aug 1949, 3 daughters. Appointments: Co-Organiser, Jabberwocky; Producer-Presenter, First Heard poetry programme, BBC Radio Merseyside, 1976-88; Poetry Consultant, BBC Network Northwest, 1988-96. Publications: Never a Put-up Job, 1970; Cherry Stones and Other Poems, 1983; No Wilderness in Them, 1984; Midnight Walk, 1986; Hesitations, 1990; Trusting the Rainbow, 1994. Editor: Windfall, 1994; Poet's England, Cumbria, 1995; Marigolds Grow Wild on Platforms, 1996. Contributions to: Various anthologies and other publications. Honours: Runner-Up, Edmund Blunden Memorial Competition, 1979; 1st Prize, Waltham Forest Competition, 1987; Prizewinner, Lancaster Literature Festival, 1987, 1991; 1st Prize, Southport Competition, 1989; Prizewinner, LACE Competition, 1992; Commended or Highly Commended in various other competitions. Memberships: London Writers' Circle; Poetry Society; Society of Women Writers and Journalists. Address: 36 Hilbre Court, West Kirby, Wirral, Merseyside L48 3JU, England.

POOLE Richard Arthur, b. 1 Jan 1945, Yorkshire, England. Tutor in English Literature; Poet. m. Sandra Pauline Smart, 18 July 1970, 1 son. Education: BA, 1966, MA, 1968, University College of North Wales. Appointments: Tutor in English Literature, Coleg Harlech, 1970-; Editor, Poetry Wales, 1992-96. Publications: Goings and Other Poems, 1978; Words Before Midnight, 1981; Natural Histories, 1989; Autobiographies and Explorations, 1994. Contributions to: Many reviews and journals. Membership: Welsh Academy. Address: Glan-y-Werydd, Llandanwg, Gwynedd LL46 2SD, Wales.

POPE Pamela Mary Alison, b. 26 Apr 1931, Lowestoft, Suffolk, England. Novelist. m. Ronald Pope, 3 Apr 1954, 2 daughters. Publications: The Magnolia Seige, 1982; The Candleberry Tree, 1982; Eden's Law, 1983; The Wind in the East, 1989; The Rich Pass By, 1990; Neither Angels Nor Demons, 1992; A Collar of Jewels, 1994. Contributions to: Good Housekeeping; Woman; Woman's Realm; Vanity Fair; True; Loving; Hampshire Magazine; Hampshire Life; London Evening News. Memberships: Romantic Novelists Association; Society of Women Writers and Journalists. Address: 1 Rhiners Close, Sway, Lymington, Hampshire, SO41 6BZ.

POPESCU Christine, (Christine Pullein-Thompson), b. 30 Oct 1930, London, England. Children's Writer. m. Julian Popescu, 6 Oct 1954, 2 sons, 2 daughters. Publications: 103 children's books, 1956-93. Contributions to: Magazines. Memberships: Book Trust; PEN; Society of Authors. Address: The Old Parsonage, Mellis, Eye, Suffolk IP23 8EE, England.

PORAD Francine Joy, b. 3 Sept 1929, Seattle, Washington, USA. Poet; Painter. m. Bernard L Porad, 12 June 1949, 3 sons, 3 daughters. Education: BFA, University of Washington, 1976. Appointments: Editor, Brussels Sprout haiku journal, 1988-95, Red Moon Anthologies, 1996-. Publications: Many poetry books, including: Pen and Inklings, 1986; After Human Rain, 1987; Free of Clouds, 1989; Round Renga Round, 1990; A Mural of Leaves, 1991; Joy is My Middle Name, 1993; Waterways, 1995; Extended Wings, 1996; Fog Lifting, 1997; Let's Count the Trees (edited by Le Roy Gorman), 1998; Linked Haiku, 1998. Contributions to: Haiku journals worldwide. Honours: Cicada Chapbook Award, 1990; International Tanka Awards, 1991, 1992, 1993; 1st Prize, Poetry Society of Japan International Tanka Competition, 1993; Haiku Society of America Merit Book Award, 1994; Haiku Oregon PEN Women Award, 1995. Memberships: Association of International Renku; Haiku Society of American, President, 1993-95; National League of American Pen Women. Address: 6944 South East 33rd, Mercer Island, WA 98040, USA.

PORÉE-KURRER Philippe Lucien-Marie, b. 30 Apr 1954, Fécamp, France. Writer. m. Marylis DuFour, 14 Feb 1976, 4 sons, 2 daughters. Publications: Les Portes du Paradis, 1986; Le Retour de l'Orchidée, 1990; La Promise du Lac, 1992; La Quête de Nathan Barker, 1994; Shalôm, 1996. Contributions to: Jerusalem Post; DeVoir. Honour: Prix du Public, Québec, 1993. Membership: Union des écrivaines at écrivains québécois. Address: 17 Avenue Garry, Blenheim, Ontario N0P 1A0, Canada.

PORTER Bern(ard Harden), b. 14 Feb 1911, Porter Settlement, Maine, USA. Writer. Education: BS, Colby College, 1932; ScM, Brown University, 1933. Publications: 86 books, including: Dieresis, 1976; The Wastemaker, 1980; I've Left, 1982; The Book of Do's, 1984; Here Comes Everybody's Don't Book, 1984; Sweet End, 1984; Last Acts, 1985; Dear Me, 1985; Gee-Whizzels, 1986; H L Mencken: A Bibliography, 1987; First Publications of F Scott Fitgerald, 1987; Sounds That Arouse, 1992. Contributions to: Various magazines, 1932-89. Honours: Carnegie Authors Award, 1976; PEN Award, 1976; National Endowment for the Arts Award, 1981. Memberships: Society of Programmed Instruction, fellow; Maine Writers and Publishers Alliance. Address: 50 Salmond Street, Belfast, ME 04915, USA.

PORTER Bernard (John), b. 5 June 1941, Essex, England. Professor of Modern History; Writer. m. Deidre O'Hara, 29 July 1972, 1 son, 2 daughters. Education: BA, 1963, MA, PhD, 1967, Corpus Christi College, Cambridge. Appointments: Fellow, Corpus Christi College, Cambridge, 1966-68; Lecturer, 1968-78, Senior Lecturer, 1978-87, Reader, 1987-92, University of Hull; Professor of Modern History, University of Newcastle,

1992-. Publications: Critics of Empire: British Radical Attitudes to Colonialism in Africa 1896-1914, 1968; The Lion's Share: A Short History of British Imperialism 1850-1970, 1976, 2nd edition, revised, 1984; The Refugee Question in Mid-Victorian Politics, 1979; Britain, Europe and the World 1850-1982: Delusions of Grandeur, 1983, 2nd edition, 1987; The Origins of the Vigilant State: The London Metropolitan Police Special Branch Before the First World War, 1987; Plots and Paranoia: A History of Political Espionage in Britain 1790-1988, 1989; Britannia's Burden: The Political Development of Britain 1857-1990, 1994. Contributions to: Professional journals. Address: c/o Department of History, University of Newcastle, Newcastle upon Tyne, NE 7RU, England.

PORTER Brian (Ernest), b. 5 Feb 1928, Seasalter, Kent, England. Lecturer; Writer. Education: BSc, 1954, PhD, 1962, London School of Economics and Political Science. Appointments: Lecturer in Political Science, University of Khartoum, 1963-65; Lecturer, 1965-71, Senior Lecturer in International Politics, 1971-85, University College, Aberystwyth; Acting Vice-Counsel, Muscat, 1967; Honorary Lecturer in International Relations, University of Kent, Canterbury, 1984-. Publications: Britain and the Rise of Communist China, 1967; The Aberystwyth Papers: International Politics 1919-1969 (editor), 1972; The Reason of States (co-author), 1982; Home Fires and Foreign Fields: British Social and Military Experience in the First World War (co-author), 1985; The Condition of States (co-author), 1991; Martin Wight's International Theory: The Three Traditions (co-editor), 1991. Honours: Gladstone Memorial Essay Prize, 1956; Mrs Foster Watson Memorial Prize, 1962-67. Memberships: Royal Historical Society, fellow; Royal Institute of International Affairs. Address: Rutherford College, University of Kent, Canterbury, Kent, England.

PORTER Burton (Frederick), b. 22 June 1936, New York, New York, USA. Professor of Philosophy; Academic Dean; Writer. m. (1) Susan Jane Porter, 10 May 1966, div 1974, 1 daughter, (2) Barbara Taylor Metcalf, 31 Dec 1980, 1 son, 1 stepdaughter. Education: BA, University of Maryland, 1959; Postgraduate Studies, University of Oxford, 1962; PhD, St Andrews University, Scotland, 1969. Appointments: Assistant Professor, University of Maryland Overseas Division, London, 1966-69; Associate Professor, King's College, Wilkes-Barre, Pennsylvania, 1969-71; Professor of Philosophy, Russell Sage College, Troy, New York, 1971-87, Drexel University, 1987-91; Dean of Arts and Sciences, Western New England College, Springfield, Massachusetts, 1991-. Publications: Deity and Morality, 1968; Philosophy: A Literary and Conceptual Approach, 1974, 3rd edition, 1995; Personal Philosophy: Perspectives on Living, 1976; The Good Life: Alternatives in Ethics, 1980, 3rd edition, 1994; Reasons for Living: A Basic Ethics, 1988; Religion and Reason, 1993. Contributions to: Professional journals. Honour: Outstanding Educator of America, 1973. Memberships: American Philosophical Association; Modern Language Association. Address: c/o Office of the Dean of Arts and Sciences, Western New England College, Springfield, MA 01119, USA.

PORTER Catherine Marjorie, b. 27 June 1947, Oxford, England. Writer: Translator. 1 son, 1 daughter. Education: BA, Honours, Russian, Czech, School of Slavonic Studies, University of London, 1970. Publications: Fathers and Daughters, 1976; Alexandra Kollontai: A Biography, 1980; Blood and Laughter: Images of the 1905 Revolution, 1983; Moscow in World War 2, 1987; Women in Revolutionary Russia, 1987; Larissa Reisner: A Biography, 1988. Translations: Love of Worker Bees, 1977; A Great Love, 1981; Ship of Widows, 1985; Sofia Tolstoya's Diary, 1985; Arise and Walk, 1990; The Best of Ogonoyok, 1990; Little Vera, 1990. Contributions to: Independent; Guardian; New Statesman and Society; Independent on Sunday. Honours: Various translation awards. Membership: Society of Authors. Address: c/o Curtis Brown Ltd, Haymarket House, 28-29 Haymarket, London SW1Y 4SP, England.

PORTER Joshua Roy, b. 1921, England. Theologian; Writer. Appointments: Fellow, Chaplain and Tutor, Oriel College, Oxford and University Lecturer in Theology, Oxford University, 1949-62; Canon and Prebendary of Wightring, Chichester Cathedral and Theological Lecturer, 1965-88; Dean, Faculty of the Arts 1968-71, Department Head and Professor of Theology 1972-86, University of Exeter. Publications: Eight Oxford Poets (with J Heath-Stubbs and S Keyes), 1941; Poetry from Oxford in War-Time (with W Bell) 1944; World in the Heart, 1944; Promise and Fulfilment (with F F Bruce), 1963; Moses and Monarchy, 1963; The Extended Family in the Old Testament, 1967; A Source Book of the Bible for Teachers (with R C Walton), 1970; Proclamation and Presence (editor with J I Durham), 1970; The Non-Juring Bishops, 1973; The Journey to the Other World (with H R E Davidson), 1975; The Book of Leviticus, 1976; Animals in Folklore (editor with W D M Russell), 1978; The Monarchy, the Crown and the Church, 1978; Tradition and Interpretation (with G W Anderson), 1979; A Basic Introduction to the Old Testament (with R C Walton), 1980; Folklore Studies in the Twentieth Century (co-editor), 1980; Divination and Oracles (with M Loewe and C Blacker), 1981; The Folklore of Ghosts (with H R E Davidson), 1981; Israel's Prophetic Tradition (co-author), 1982; Tracts for Our Times (co-author), 1983; The Hero in Tradition and Folklore (with C Blacker), 1984; Arabia and the Gulf: From Traditional Society to Modern States (with I Netton), 1986; Schöpfung und Befreiung, co-author, 1989; Synodical Government in the Church of England, 1990; Christianity and Conservatism, co-author, 1990; Oil of Gladness, 1993; Boundaries and Thresholds (with H R E Davidson), 1993; World Mythology, 1993; The Illustrated Guide to the Bible, 1995; The Jesus of History: The Christ of Faith, forthcoming. Memberships: Wiccamical Canon and Prebendary of Exceit, Chichester Cathedral, 1988-; Society for Old Testament Study, President, 1983; Society of Biblical Literature; Folklore Society, President, 1976-79; Prayer Book Society, Vice-Chairman, 1987-96. Address: 36 Theberton Street, Barnsbury, London N1 OQX, England.

PORTER Michael E, b. 23 May 1947, Ann Arbor, Michigan, USA. Professor of Business Administration; Writer. m. Deborah Zylberberg, 26 Oct 1985, 2 daughters. Education: BSE, Princeton University, 1969; MBA,1971, PhD, 1973, Harvard University. Appointments: Assistant Professor, 1973-77, Associate Professor, 1977-82, Professor of Business Administration, 1982-90, C Roland Christensen Professor of Business Administration, 1990-, Harvard University; Consultant to various businesses and governments. Publications: Interbrand Choice, Strategy, and Bilateral Market Power, 1976; Studies in Canadian Industrial Organization (with A M Spence, R E Caves and J M Scott), 1977; Competitive Strategy: Techniques for Analyzing Industries and Competitors, 1980; Competition in the Open Economy (with A M Spence and R E Caves), 1980; Cases in Competitive Strategy, 1982; Competitive Advantage: Creating and Sustaining Superior Performance, 1985; Business Policy: Text and Cases (with C R Christensen, K R Andrews, R L Hammermesch, and J L Bower), 6th edition, 1986; Competition in Global Industries (editor), 1986; The Competitive Advantage of Nations, 1990; Upgrading New Zealand's Competitive Advantage (with Graham T Crocombe and Michael J Enright), 1991; Strategy: Seeking and Securing Competitive Advantage (editor with Cynthia A Montgomery), 1991; Advantage Sweden (with Orjan Solbell and Ivo Zander), 1991; International Wettbewerbsvorteile: Ein Strategisches Konzept für die Schweiz (with Silvio Borner, Rolf Weder, and Michael J Enright), 1991; Capital Choices: Changing the Way America Invests in Industry (editor), 1992. Contributions to: Professional journals and general publications. Honours: McKinsey Foundation Awards, 1979, 1987; Graham and Dodd Award, Financial Analysts Federation, 1980; International Academy of Management Fellow, 1985; George F Terry Award, 1985, Fellow, 1988, Academy of Management; Distinguished Professional Award, Society of Competitor Intelligence Professionals, 1989; Charles Coolidge Parlin Award, American Marketing Association, 1991; Honorary doctorates. Memberships: American Economic Association; American Marketing Association; Phi Beta Kappa; Royal Academy of Engineering Sciences; Sigma Xi; Tau Beta Pi. Address: c/o School of Business, Harvard University, Aldrich 200, Boston, MA 02163, USA.

PORTER Peter Neville Frederick, b. 16 Feb 1929, Brisbane, Queensland, Australia. Writer; Poet. m. Jannice Henry, 1961, dec 1974, 2 daughters. Publications: Once Bitten, Twice Bitten, 1961; Penguin Modern Poets 2, 1962; Poems, Ancient and Modern, 1967; A Porter Folio, 1969; The Last of England, 1970; Preaching to the Converted, 1972; After Martial (translator), 1972; Jonah (with Arthur Boyd), 1973; The Lady and the Unicorn, 1975; Living in a Calm Country, 1975; New Poetry I (co-editor), 1975; The Cost of Seriousness, 1978; English Subtitles, 1981; Collected Poems, 1983; Fast Forward, 1984; Narcissus (with Arthur Boyd), 1985; Possible Worlds, 1989; The Chain of Babel, 1992. Honour: Duff Cooper Prize, 1983. Address: 42 Cleveland Square, London W2, England.

PORTER Spence, b. 17 Dec 1948, Scranton, Pennsylvania, USA. Playwright. Education: AB, Harvard College, 1970; MFA, Ohio University, 1974. Publications: Plays: Hippolytus; Francesca; The Mouse Prince; Sick Minds; Aguments With Myself. Membership: Dramatists Guild. Address: 3435 Giles Place, Apt 5F, Bronx, NY 10463, USA.

PORTER William Sydney, b. 2 Feb 1944, Liverpool, England. Retired Electrical Engineer. m. Christine Leadbeater, 6 Sept 1969. Education: BSc, Electrical Engineering, University of Salford, 1968. Appointment: British Aerospace: Apprenticeship, 1963; Junior Test Engineer, 1968, Senior Test Engineer, Senior Project Test Engineer, Performance Engineer, Team Leader, Test Systems Manager, 1987. Publication: Cover Up, poem, 1994; Northern Lights - NW94 Anthology. Address: 27 Mendip Avenue, Winstanley, Wigan WN3 6EB, England.

PORTIS Charles McColl, b. 28 Dec 1933, El Dorado, Arkansas, USA. Writer. Education: BA, University of Arkansas, 1958. Publications: Novels: Norwood, 1966; True Grit, 1968; The Dog of the South, 1979; Masters of Atlantis, 1985; Gringos, 1991. Address: 7417 Kingwood, Little Rock, AR 72207, USA.

PORTOCALA Radu, b. 27 Mar 1951, Bucharest, Romania. Writer; Journalist. m. Delphine Beaugonin, 21 Dec 1987, 2 daughters. Education: Master of International Relations, Paris, 1986; BA, Romanian, Paris, 1986. Publications: Autopsie Du Coup D'Etat Roumain, 1990; Călătorie in Cusca Hidrelor, 1994; La Chute Dans L'Enthousiasme, 1995; Several volumes of poetry in Romanian. Contributions to: Le Point; Est & Ouest; Cuvintul, Bucharest; Voice of America; Radio France International. Address: 7 Rue Du Docteur Roux, 75015 Paris, France.

PORTWAY Christopher (John), b. 30 Oct 1923, Halstead, Essex, England. Writer. m. Jaroslava Krupickova, 4 Apr 1957, 1 son, 1 daughter. Publications: Journey to Dana, 1955; The Pregnant Unicorn, 1969; All Exits Barred, 1971; Corner Seat, 1972; Lost Vengeance, 1973; Double Circuit, 1974; The Tirana Assignment, 1974; The Anarchy Pedlars, 1976; The Great Railway Adventure, 1983; Journey Along the Spine of the Andes, 1984; The Great Travelling Adventure, 1985; Czechmate, 1987; Indian Odyssey, 1993; A Kenyan Adventure, 1993; Pedal for Your Life, 1996. Contributions to: Daily Telegraph; Country Life; Lady; Railway Magazine; In-Flight Magazines; Glasgow Herald; Scotsman; Liverpool Daily Post; Morning and Leisure Magazine; Holiday Magazine; Motoring and Leisure. Honour: Winston Churchill Fellow, 1993. Membership: Royal Geographical Society, fellow. Address: 22 Tower Road, Brighton BN2 2GF, England.

POSNER Gerald, b. 20 May 1954, San Francisco, California, USA. Attorney; Writer. m. Trisha D Levene, Apr 1984. Education: BA, University of California, 1975; JD, Hastings College of Law, 1978. Publications: Mengele: The Complete Story, 1986; Warlords of Crime, 1988; Bio-Assassins, 1989; Hitler's Children, 1991; Case Closed, 1993; Citizen Perot, 1996; Killing the Dream, 1998. Contributions to: New York Times; New Yorker; Chicago Tribune; US News & World Report. Honour: Pulitzer Finalist, 1993. Memberships: National Writers Union; Authors Guild; PEN. Address: 250 West 57th Street, Suite 2114, New York, NY 10019, USA.

POSTER Mark, b. 6 July 1941, New York, New York, USA. Professor of History; Writer. Education: BS, University of Pennsylvania, 1962; MA, 1965, PhD, 1968, New York University. Appointments: Assistant Professor, 1969-74, Associate Professor, 1974-78, Professor of History, 1978-, University of California at Irvine; Member, Editorial Board, The 18th Century: A Journal of Interpretation. Publications: The Utopian Thought of Restif de la Bretonne, Harmonian Man: Selected Writings of Charles Fourier (editor), 1971; Existential Marxism in Postwar France, 1976; Critical Theory of the Family, 1978; Satre's Marxism, 1979; Foucalt, Marxism and History, 1984; Baudrillard: Selected Writings (editor), 1988; Critical Theory and Poststructuralism, 1989; The Mode of Information, 1990; Postsuburban California: The Social Transformation of Orange County Since 1945 (editor with Rob King and Spencer Olin), 1991. Address: c/o Department of History, University of California at Irvine, Irvine, CA 92717, USA.

POSTMA Johannes, b. 14 Jan 1935, Friesland, Netherlands (US citizen, 1966). Professor; Historian. Education: BA, Liberal Arts, Graceland College, Iowa, 1962; MA, History of Germany, Russia, and England, University of Kansas, 1964; PhD, History of Modern Europe and Africa, Michigan State University, 1970; Rijksuniversiteit at Leiden, 1967-68; University of Michigan, 1973. Appointments: Assistant Instructor, University of Kansas, 1962-64, Michigan State University, 1966-67; Instructor, Western Michigan University, 1964-66, 1968; Assistant Professor, 1969-73, Associate Professor, 1973-76, Professor, 1976-, Chairperson, Department of History, 1989-95, Minnesota State University at Mankato; Visiting Professor, Rijsuniversiteit at Leiden, 1986-87. Publication: The Dutch in the Atlantic Slave Trade, 1600-1815, 1990. Contributions to: Book chapters and journal articles, 1972-98. Honours: American Council of Learned Societies Fellowship, 1972-73; Dutch Government Grant, 1986-87; Research Fellowship-in-Residence, Royal Dutch Academy for Advanced Studies, 1995-96. Memberships: American Historical Association; Royal Institute of Linguistics and Anthropology; Social Science History Association. Address: 50 Woodview Drive, Mankato, MN 56001, USA.

POTOK Chaim, b. 17 Feb 1929, New York, New York, USA. Writer. m. Adena Sara Mosevitsky, 8 June 1958, 1 son, 2 daughters. Education: BA, Yeshiva University, 1950; MHL, Rabbinic Ordination, Jewish Theological Seminary, 1954; PhD, University of Pennsylvania, 1965. Appointments: Visiting Professor, University of Pennsylvania, 1983-92, 1995-98, John Hopkins University, 1994, 1996. Publications: The Chosen, 1967; The Promise, 1969; My Name is Asher Lev, 1972; In the Beginning, 1975; Wanderings, 1978; The Book of Lights, 1981; Davita's Harp, 1985; The Gift of Asher Lev, 1990; I am the Clay, 1992; The Tree of Here, 1993; The Sky of Now, 1995; The Gates of November, 1996; Zebra and Other Stories, 1998 Contributions to: New York Times Sunday Book Review; Esquire; Commentary; TriQuarterly; Philadelphia Enquirer Book Review; Forward; Moment; The Kenyon Review. Honours: Wallant Prize, 1967; Athenaeum Award, 1970; National Jewish Book Award, 1991; National Foundation for Jewish Culture Award, 1997. Memberships: PEN; Drama Guild; Writers Guild. Address: 20 Berwick Road, Merion, PA 19066, USA.

POTTER Beverly Ann, b. 3 Mar 1944, Summit, New Jersey, USA. Psychologist; Publisher; Business Executive. Education: BA, 1966, MS, 1968, San Francisco State University; PhD, Stanford University, 1974. Publications: Chlorella: The Amazing Alchemist; Turning Around: Keys to Motivation and Productivity, 1980; Beating Job Burnout: How to Transform Work Pressure into Productivity, 1980, 2nd edition, 1993; The Way of the Ronin: Riding the Waves of Change at Work, 1985; Preventing Job Burnout: A Work Book, 1987, 2nd edition, 1995; Drug Testing at Work: A Guide for Employers and Employees, 1990; Brain Boosters: Foods & Drinks That Make You Smarter, 1993; Finding a Path With a Heart, 1994; From Conflict to Cooperation: How to Mediate a Dispute, 1996; The Worry Wart's Companion: Twenty-One Ways to Soothe Yourself and Worry Smart, 1997. Contributions to: Journals and magazines. Memberships: North California Booksellers Association; Bay Area Organisation Development Network. Address: PO Box 1035, Berkeley, CA 94701, USA.

POTTER Jeremy (Ronald), b. 25 Apr 1922, London, England. Writer; Publisher. m. 11 Feb 1950, 1 son, 1 daughter. Education: MA, Queen's College, Oxford. Publications: Good King Richard?, 1983; Pretenders, 1986; Independent Television in Britain, Vol 3: Politics and Control 1968-80, 1989 and Vol 4: Companies and Programmes 1968-80, 1990; Tennis and Oxford, 1994. Novels: Hazard Chase, 1964; Death in Office, 1965; Foul Play, 1967; The Dance of Death, 1968; A Trail of Blood, 1970; Going West, 1972; Disgrace and Favour, 1975; Death in the Forest, 1977; The Primrose Hill Murder, 1992; The Mystery of the Campden Wonder, 1995. Address: The Old Pottery, Larkins Lane, Headington, Oxford OX3 9DW, England.

POULIN Gabrielle, b. 21 June 1929, St Prosper, Québec, Canada. Writer; Poet. Education: MA, University of Montreal; DLitt, University of Sherbrooke. Appointment: Writer-in-Residence, Ottawa Public Library, 1988. Publications: Les Miroirs d'un poète: Image et reflets de Paul Eluard, 1969; Cogne la caboche, 1979, English translation as All the Way Home, 1984; L'Âge de l'interrogation, 1937-52, 1980; Un Cri trop grand (novel), 1980; Les Mensonges d'Isabelle (novel), 1983; La Couronne d'oubli (novel), 1990; Petites Fugues pour une saison sèche (poems), 1991; Le Livre de déraison (novel), 1994; Mon père aussi était horloger (poems), 1996; Qu'est-ce qui passe ici si tard? (novel), 1998. Contributions to: Periodicals. Honours: Swiss Embassy Prize, 1967; II Arts Council of Canada Grants, 1968-83, 1985; Champlain Literary Prize, 1979; Carleton Literary Prize, Ottawa, 1983; Alliance Française Literary Prize, 1984; Salon du Livre de Toronto Literary Prize, 1994. Literary Agent: René Dionne, 1997 Avenue Quincy, Ottawa, Canada, K1J 6B4. Memberships: Union des écrivaines at écrivains québécois. Address: 1997 Avenue Quincy, Ottawa, Ontario K1J 6B4, Canada.

POULSEN Morten. See: **VIZKI Morti.**

POULSON Joan, (Joan Gregory), b. Manchester, England. Writer; Poet. m. Lewis S Poulson, 1 son, 2 daughters. Appointments: Writer in Residence, Winwick Hospital, 1991-93; Warrington (European Year of the Elderly); Ladywell Hospital, Salford, 1994-96; with Scherzo Dance Company, and at Durham Art Gallery, 1997. Publications: Yorkshire Cookery, 1979; Celebration, 1993; Girls Are Like Diamonds, 1996. Contributions to: International PEN; Resurgence; Stride; The Frogmore Papers; O Correo Galego; Slow Dancer; Envoi. Memberships: The Society of Authors; The Poetry Society; International PEN. Literary Agent: Marilyn Malin. Address: c/o Marilyn Malin, Consultancy & Reprentation, 5/33 Ferncroft Avenue, London NW3 7PG, England.

POUPLIER Erik, b. 16 June 1926, Svendborg, Denmark. Writer. m. Annalise Hansen, 28 Sept 1947, 1 daughter. Education: Trained as journalist. Publications: In Danish: Lend Me Your Wife, 1957; My Castle in Ardèche, 1968; The Gentle Revolt, 1970; The Discreet Servant of the Death, 1972; The Adhesive Pursuer, 1973; Murder, Mafia and Pastis'er, 1974; My Castle in Provence, 1979; The Old Man in Provence, 1980; The Clumsy Kidnappers, 1981; The World of Annesisse, 1982; The Galic Cock, 1984; My Own Provence, 1984; The Cuisine of Provence, 1985; Panic in Provence, 1986; All Year Round in Provence, 1987; Machiavelli, 1987; The Anaconda-Coup in Provence, 1988; Long Live the Grandparents, 1988; Barbaroux and the Flood, 1989; Always Around the Next Corner (memoirs), 1990; Pearls of Provence, 1991; Barbaroux and the Nuns, 1992; Merry-Go-Round, 1993; The 4 Seasons of Provence, 1995; The Hangman, 1996. Contributions to: Jyllands Posten, Denmark. Honour: Prix France,1997. Memberships: Danish Author's Society; Danish Press Association; Danish PEN. Address: Les Charmettes, Chemin de Plateau, 83550 Vidauban, France.

POURNELLE Jerry Eugene, (Wade Curtis), b. 7 Aug 1933, Shreveport, Louisiana, USA. Writer; Lecturer; Consultant. Education: University of Iowa, 1953-54; BS, 1955, MS, 1957, PhD, Psychology, 1960, PhD, Political Science, 1964, University of Washington. Publications: Red Heroin (as Wade Curtis), 1969; The Strategy of Technology: Winning the Decisive War (with Stefan Possony), 1970; Red Dragon (as Wade Curtis), 1971; A Spaceship for the King, 1973; Escape From the Planet of the Apes (novelization of screenplay), 1973; The Mote in God's Eye (with Larry Niven), 1974; 20/20 Vision (editor), 1974; Birth of Fire, 1976; Inferno (with Larry Niven), 1976; West of Honor, 1976; High Justice (short stories), 1977; The Mercenary, 1977; Lucifer's Hammer (with Larry Niven), 1977; Exiles to Glory, 1978; Black Holes (editor), 1979; A Step Further Out (non-fiction), 1980; Janisseries, 1980; Oath of Fealty (with Larry Niven), 1981; Clan and Crown (with Roland Green), 1982; There Will Be War (co-editor), 1983; Mutual Assured Survival (with Dean Ing), 1984; Men of War (co-editor), 1984; Blood and Iron (co-editor), 1984; Day of the Tyrant (co-editor), 1985; Footfall (with Larry Niven), 1985; Warriors (co-editor), 1986; Imperial Stars: The Stars at War, Republic and Empire (co-editor), 2 volumes, 1986-87; Guns of Darkness (co-editor), 1987; Storms of Victory (with Roland Green), 1987; Legacy of Hereot (with Larry Niven), 1987; Prince of Mercenaries, 1989; The Gripping Hand (with Larry Niven), 1993. Contributions to: Magazines. Memberships: Operations Research Society of America, fellow; American Association for the Advancement of Science, fellow; Science Fiction Writers of America, president, 1974. Address: 121901 1/2 Ventura Boulevard, Box 372, Studio City, CA 91604, USA.

POWE Bruce William, b. 23 Mar 1955, Ottawa, Ontario, Canada. Author; Teacher. m. Robin Leslie Mackenzie, 7 Sept 1991, sep Dec 1996, 1 son, 1 daughter. Education: BA, Special Honours, York University, Toronto; MA, University of Toronto. Appointment: Academic Advisor, York University, Toronto, 1994-. Publications: A Climate Charged, 1984; The Solitary Outlaw, 1987, reprint 1996; Noise of Time, text for Glenn Gould Profile, 1989; A Tremendous Canada of Light, 1993, reprint 1997; Outage: A Journey into Electric City, 1995. Contributions to: Globe and Mail; Toronto Star; Grail; Antigonish Review; Bennington Review; Exile; Modern Drama. Honours: York University Book Award, 1977; Special MA Scholarship to University of Toronto, 1979; Explorations Grant, Canada Council, 1980; Maclean-Hunter Fellowship, 1989; Ontario Arts Council Awards, 1990, 1991, 1992, 1994, 1996, 1997. Membership: Fellow of McLuhan Program, Centre for Culture and Technology, University of Toronto. Literary Agent: Michael Levine. Address: 18 Alderwood Street, Stouffville, Ontario, Canada, L4A 5C9.

POWELL Anthony (Dymoke), b. 21 Dec 1905, London, England. Writer. m. Lady Violet Pakenham, 1934, 2 sons. Education: Balliol College, Oxford. Appointments: Duckworth Publishers, 1926-35; Literary Editor, Punch, 1953-59; Trustee, National Portrait Gallery, 1962-76. Publications: A Dance to the Music of Time (sequence of 12 novels), from A Question of Upbringing, 1959, to Hearing Secret Harmonies, 1975; The Soldier's Art, 1966; The Military Philosophers, 1968; The Garden God and the Rest I'll Whistle: The Text of Two Plays, Books Do Furnish a Room, 1971; Temporary Kings, 1973; Infants of the Spring, 1976; Messengers of

Day, 1978; Faces in My Time, 1980; The Strangers All Are Gone, 1982; O, How the Wheel Becomes It!, 1983; To Keep the Ball Rolling (abridged memoirs), 1983; The Fisher King, 1986; Miscellaneous Verdicts (criticism), 1990; Under Review (criticism), 1992; Journals 1982-1986, 1996; Journals 1987-1989, 1996; Journals 1990-1992, 1997. Honours: Commander of the Order of the British Empire, 1956; James Tait Black Prize; Honorary Fellow, Balliol College, Oxford, 1974; W H Smith Award, 1974; Hudson Review Bennett Award, 1984; Companion of Honour, 1988; Ingersoll Foundation; Many honorary doctorates and foreign orders. Address: The Chantry, Near Frome, Somerset BA11 3LJ, England.

POWELL Geoffrey Stewart, (Tom Angus), b. 25 Dec 1914, Scarborough, Yorkshire, England. Soldier; Bookseller; Writer. m. Felicity Wadsworth, 15 July 1944, 1 son, 1 daughter. Education: Scarborough College, 1923-31; Army Staff College, 1945-46; United States Command and General Staff College, 1950-51; Joint Services Staff College, 1953-54; BA, Open University, 1981. Publications: The Green Howards, 1968; The Kandyan Wars, 1973; Men at Arnhem, 1978; Suez: The Double War (with Roy Fullick), 1979; The Book of Campden, 1982; The Devil's Birthday: The Bridges to Arnhem, 1984; Plumer: The Soldier's General, 1990; The Green Howards: 300 Years of Service, 1992; Buller: A Scapegoat: A Life of General Sir Redvers Buller, VC, 1994. Contributions to: Journals and magazines. Honour: Fellow, Royal Historical Society, 1989. Address: Chipping Campden, Goucestershire GL55 6AE, England.

POWELL Joseph M(ichael), b. 27 Dec 1938, Bootle, Lancashire, England (Australian citizen). Professor of Historical Geography; Writer. m. Suzanne Margaret Geehman, 28 Dec 1967, 1 son, 1 daughter. Education: BA, Honours, 1960, MA, 1962, University of Liverpool; PhD, 1969, DLitt, 1983, Monash University. Appointments: Assistant Lecturer in Geography, St Mary's College of Education, London, 1962-63; Senior Teaching Fellow, 1964-65, Lecturer, 1965-69, Senior Lecturer, 1970-77, Reader in Geography, 1977-92, Professor of Historical Geography, 1992-, Monash University; Editor, Monash Publications in Geography, 1972-74, 1975-78, Australian Geographical Studies, 1978-81. Publications: Western Victoria, 1967; The Public Lands of Australia Felix, 1970; Yeomen and Bureaucrats: The Victorian Commission on Crown Lands 1878-79 (editor), 1973; The Making of Rural Australia: Environment, Society, Economy (editor), 1974; Urban and Industrial Australia: Readings in Human Geography (editor), 1974; Australian Space, Australian Time: Geographical Perspectives (editor with M Williams), 1975; Environmental Management in Australia, 1788-1914: Guardians, Improvers, Profit, 1976; Mirrors of the New World: Images and Image-Makers in the Settlement Process, 1977; Approaches to Resource Management, 1980; An Historical Geography of Modern Australia: The Restive Fringe, 1988, new edition, 1991; Watering the Garden State: Water, Land and Community in Victoria, 1834-1988, 1989; Plains of Promise, Rivers of Destiny: Water Resources and the Development of Queensland, 1824-1990, 1991; Griffith Taylor and 'Australia Unlimited', 1993; 'MDB': The Emergence of Bioregionalism in the Murray-Darling Basin, 1993; Watering the Western Third: Water, Land and Community in Western Australia, 1826-1998, 1998. Contributions to: Professional journals. Honours: 1st Prize, Cook Biocentenary Literary Competition, 1970; Fellow, Academy of the Social Sciences in Australia, 1985; Research Medal, Royal Society of Victoria, 1988; Thomson Medal, Royal Geographical Society of Queensland, 1998. Memberships: American Agricultural History Society; Australian Conservation Foundation, life member; Institute of Australian Geographers, president, 1984-85; National Trust of Australia, life member; Royal Australian Historical Society, life member; Royal Victorian Historical Society, life member. Address: c/o Department of Geography and Environmental Science, Monash University, Clayton, Victoria 3168, Australia.

POWELL Neil (Ashton), b. 11 Feb 1948, London, England. Writer; Poet. Education: BA, English and American Literature, 1969, MPhil, English Literature, 1971, University of Warwick. Publications: Suffolk Poems, 1975; At the Edge, 1977; Carpenters of Light, 1979; Out of Time, 1979; A Season of Calm Weather, 1982; Selected Poems of Fulke Greville (editor), 1990; True Colours: New and Selected Poems, 1991; Unreal City, 1992; The Stones on Thorpeness Beach, 1994; Roy Fuller: Writer and Society, 1995; Gay Love Poetry (editor), 1997; The Language of Jazz, 1997; Selected Poems, 1998. Contributions to: Anthologies, newspapers, reviews, and journals. Honours: Eric Gregory Award, 1969; Authors' Foundation Award, 1992. Memberships: Poetry Society; Society of Authors. Address: c/o Carcanet Press Ltd, 4th Floor, Conavon Court, 12-16 Blackfriars Street, Manchester M3 5BQ, England.

POWELL Padgett, b. 25 Apr 1952, Gainesville, Florida, USA. Professor of Creative Writing; Writer. m. Sidney Wade, 22 May 1984, 2 daughters. Education: BA, College of Charleston 1975; MA, University of Houston, 1982. Appointment: Professor of Creative Writing, University of Florida, Gainesville, 1984-. Publications: Edisto (novel), 1984; A Woman Named Drown (novel), 1987; Typical (stories), 1991; Edisto Revisited (novel), 1996; Aliens of Affection (stories), 1998. Contributions to: Periodicals; Harper's Magazine. Honours: Best Book Citation, Time Magazine, 1984; Whiting Foundation Writers' Award, 1986; American Academy and Institute of Arts and Letters Rome Fellowship in Literature 1987. Memberships: PEN; Authors Guild; Writers Guild of America, East. Literary Agent: Cynthia Cannell, Janklow & Nesbit, 598 Madison Avenue, NY 10022, USA. Address: Department of English, University of Florida, Gainesville, FL 32611, USA.

POWELL Talmage, (Jack McCready, Anne Talmage), b. 4 Oct 1920, Hendersonville, North Carolina, USA. Writer. Education: University of North Carolina. Publications: Cabins & Castles, 1981; Western Ghosts, 1990; New England Ghosts, 1990; Murder for Halloween, 1994; Encyclopedia Mysteriosa, 1994; Wild Game, 1994; Six-Gun Ladies, Stories of Women on the American Western Frontier, 1996. Contributions to: Anthologies, films, and television. Address: 33 Caledonia Road, Kenilworth, Asheville, NC 28803, USA.

POWELL Violet Georgiana, b. 13 Mar 1912, London, England. Writer. Publications: Five out of Six, 1960; A Substantial Ghost, 1967; The Irish Cousins, 1970; A Compton-Burnett Compendium, 1973; Within the Family Circle, 1976; Margaret, Countess of Jersey, 1978; Flora Annie Steel, Novelist of India, 1981; The Constant Novelist, 1983; The Album of Anthony Powell's Dance to the Music of Time (editor), 1987; The Life of a Provincial Lady: A Study of E M Delafield and Her Works, 1988; A Jane Austen Compendium, 1993; The Departure Platform, 1998. Address: The Chantry, Nr Frome, Somerset BA11 3LJ, England.

POWELL-SMITH Vincent, (Elphinstone Francis, Judiciar, Santa Maria), b. 28 Apr 1939, Kent, England. Arbitrator; Advocate. m. Martha Marilyn Du Barry, 4 Apr 1989, 1 daughter. Education: LLB; LLM; MCL; PhD; DLitt. Appointments: Editor, Construction Law Reports, 52 volumes, 1959, Asia-Pacific Law Reports, 1992; Consultant, Malayan Law Journal. Publications: Law of Boundaries and Fences, 1966, 2nd edition, 1972; Building Contract Claims, 2nd edition, 1988; Malaysian Standard Form of Building Contract, 1990; Building Contract Dictionary, 2nd edition, 1990; Building Regulations Explained and Illustrated, 10th edition, 1995. Contributions to: Contract Journal; Times; Field, Building, Architect's Journal; Malaysian Law Journal; Construction Law Journal; International Journal of Construction Law; Islamic Studies. Address: No B1 Menara Impian, 68000 Ampang, Selangor, Malaysia.

POWERS M L. See: **TUBB E(dwin) C(harles).**

POWERS Richard, b. 1957, USA. Author. Publications: Three Farmers on Their Way to a Dance, 1985; Prisoner's Dilemma, 1988; The Gold Bug Variations, 1991; Operation Wandering Soul, 1993; Galatea 2.2, 1995. Contributions to: Journals and magazines. Honours: Richard and Hinda Rosenthal Foundation Award, American Academy and Institute of Arts and Letters, 1986; Special Citation, PEN/Hemingway Foundation, 1986; John D and Catherine T MacArthur Foundation Grant, 1989. Address: c/o Gunther Stuhlmann, Box 276, Beckett, MA 01223, USA.

POWERS Thomas (Moore), b. 12 Dec 1940, New York, New York, USA. Writer; Editor. m. Candace Molloy, 21 Aug 1965, 3 daughters. Education: BA, Yale University, 1964. Appointments: Reporter, Rome Daily American, 1965-67, United Press International, 1967-70; Editor-Founding Printer, Steerforth Press, South Royalton, Vermont, 1993-. Publications: Diana: The Making of a Terrorist, 1971; The War at Home, 1973; The Man Who Kept the Secrets: Richard Helms and the CIA, 1979; Thinking About the Next War, 1982; Total War: What It Is, How It Got That Way, 1988; Heisenberg's War: The Secret History of the German Bomb, 1993. Honour: Pulitzer Prize for National Reporting, 1971. Memberships: Council on Foreign Relations; PEN American Center. Address: c/o Susan P Urstadt, PO Box 1676, New Canaan, CT 06840, USA.

POWNALL David, b. 19 May 1938, Liverpool, England. Author; Dramatist. m. (1) Glenys Elsie Jones, 1961, div, 1 son, (2) Mary Ellen Ray, 1981, 1 son (3) Alex Sutton, 1993, 1 son. Education: BA, University of Keele, 1960. Appointments: Resident Writer, Century Theatre, 1970-72; Resident Playwright, Duke's Playhouse, Lancaster, 1972-75; Founder-Resident Writer, Paines Plough Theatre, London, 1975-80. Publications: Fiction: The Raining Tree War, 1974; African Horse, 1975; The Dream of Chief Crazy Horse, 1975; God Perkins, 1977; Light on a Honeycomb, 1978; Beloved Latitudes, 1981; The White Cutter, 1989; The Gardener, 1990; Stagg and His Mother, 1991; The Sphinx and the Sybarites, 1994; The Catalogue of Men. Plays: Over 40 stage plays, 1969-98; Radio and television plays. Honours: Edinburgh Festival Fringe Awards, 1976, 1977; Giles Cooper Awards, 1981, 1985; John Whiting Award, Arts Council of Great Britain, 1982; Sony Gold and Silver Awards for Original Radio Drama, 1994, 1995, 1996. Membership: Royal Society of Literature, fellow. Address: c/o John Johnson Ltd, 45-47 Clerkenwell Green, London EC1R 0HT, England.

POYER Joe, (Joseph John Poyer), b. 30 Nov 1939, Battle Creek, Michigan, USA. Writer; Editor; Publisher. m. Bonnie Prichard, Oct 1987. Education: BA, Michigan State University, 1961. Appointments: Publisher/Editor, Safe and Secure Living, International Military Review, International Naval Review. Publications: Fiction: North Cape, 1968; Balkan Assignment, 1971; Chinese Agenda, 1972; Shooting of the Green, 1973; The Contract, 1978; Tunnel War, 1979; Vengeance 10, 1980; Devoted Friends, 1982; Time of War, 2 volumes, 1983, 1985. Non-Fiction: The 45-70 Springfield, 1991; US Winchester Trench and Riot Guns, 1993; Pocket Guide 45-70 Springfield, 1994; The M1 Garand, 1936 to 1957, 1995; The SKS Carbine, 1997. Contributions to: Journals. Address: PO Box 1027, Tustin, CA 92681, USA.

POYNDER Edward. See: **GRIGG John.**

PRABHU Avatar. See: **CRASTA Richard.**

PRALL Stuart Edward, b. 2 June 1929, Saginaw, Michigan, USA. Professor of History; Author. m. Naomi Shafer, 20 Jan 1958, 1 son, 1 daughter. Education: BA, Michigan State University, 1951; MA, University of Rhode Island, 1953; University of Manchester, England, 1953-54; PhD, Columbia University, 1960. Appointments: Queens College and Graduate School, University Center, City University of New York, 1955-58, 1960-; Newark State College, New Jersey, 1958-60; Executive Officer, PhD Program in History, Graduate School, City University of New York, 1988-94. Publications: The Agitation for Law Reform during the Puritan Revolution, 1640-1660, 1966; The Puritan Revolution: A Documentary History, 1968; The Bloodless Revolution: England, 1688, 1972; A History of England, 1984; Church and State in Tudor and

Stuart England, 1993. Contributions to: The Development of Equity in Tudor England; American Journal of Legal History. Honours: Fulbright Scholar, University of Manchester, 1953-54; Fellow, Royal Historical Society, 1978. Memberships: American Historical Association; North American Conference on British Studies. Address: 1479 Court Place, Hewlett, NY 11557, USA.

PRANTERA Amanda, b. 23 Apr 1942, England. Author. Publications: Strange Loop, 1984; The Cabalist, 1985; Conversations with Lord Byron on Perversion, 163 Years After His Lordship's Death, 1987; The Side of the Moon, 1991; Pronto-Zoe, 1992; The Young Italians, 1993. Address: Jane Conway Gordon, 1 Old Compton Street, London, W1V 5PH, England.

PRATCHETT Terry, b. 28 Apr 1948, Beaconsfield, England. Author. m. Lyn Pratchett, 1 daughter. Publications: Adult Fiction: The Dark Side of the Sun, 1976; Strata, 1981; The Colour of Magic, 1983; The Light Fantastic, 1986; Equal Rites, 1987; Mort, 1987; Sourcery, 1989; Wyrd Sisters, 1988; Pyramids, 1989; Eric, 1989; Guards! Guards!, 1989; Moving Pictures, 1990; Reaper Man, 1991; Witches Abroad, 1991; Small Gods, 1992; Lords and Ladies, 1993; Men at Arms, 1993; Soul Music, 1994; Interesting Times, 1994; The Discworld Companion (with Stephen Briggs), 1994; Maskerade, 1995; Discworld Mapp (with Stephen Briggs), 1995; Feet of Clay, 1996; Hogfather, 1996; The Pratchett Portfolio, 1996. Juvenile Fiction: The Carpet People, 1971, revised edition, 1992; Truckers, 1989; Diggers, 1990; Wings, 1990; Only You Can Save Mankind, 1992; Johnny and the Dead, 1993. Other: The Unadulterated Cat, 1989; Good Omens: The Nice and Accurate Predictions of Agnes Nutter, Witch (with Neil Gaiman), 1990. Honours: British Science Fiction Awards, 1989, 1990. Address: c/o Colin Smythe Ltd, PO Box 6, Gerrards Cross, Buckinghamshire SL9 8XA, England.

PRATHER Richard S(cott), (David Knight, Douglas Ring), b. 9 Sept 1921, Santa Ana, California, USA. Writer. Education: Riverside Junior College, California, 1940-41. Publications: Over 50 books, 1950-88. Address: c/o Tor Books, 175, Fifth Avenue, New York, NY 10010, USA.

PRATT John Clark, b. 19 Aug 1932, St Albans, Vermont, USA. Writer; Educator. m. (2) Doreen Goodman, 28 June 1968, 1 son, 5 daughters. Education: BA, University of California, 1954; MA, Columbia University, 1960; PhD, Princeton University, 1965. Appointments: Instructor, 1960-65, Assistant Professor, 1965-69, Associate Professor, 1969-73, Professor, 1973-75, United States Air Force Academy; Professor, Colorado State University, 1975-; President, Pratt Publishing Company, 1989-. Publications: The Meaning of Modern Poetry, 1962; John Steinbeck, 1970; One Flew Over the Cuckoo's Nest (editor), 1973, revised edition, 1996; Middlemarch Notebooks (co-editor), 1978; Vietnam Voices, 1984, revised edition, 1998; The Laotian Fragments, 1985; Reading the Wind: The Literature of the Vietnam War (co-author), 1986; Writing from Scratch: The Essay, 1987; The Quiet American (editor), 1996. Contributions to: Vietnam War Literature; Vietnam-Perkasie; Fourteen Landing Zones; Unaccustomed Mercy; Encyclopedia of the Vietnam War; John Steinbeck Encyclopedia; War, Literature and the Arts. Honours: Fulbright Lecturer, University of Lisbon, 1974-75, anf Leningrad State University, 1980; Honours Professor, Colorado State University, 1989; Award for Excellence in the Arts, Vietnam Veterans of America, 1995. Address: Department of English, Colorado State University, Ft Collins, CO 80523, USA.

PRAWER Siegbert Salomon, b. 15 Feb 1925, Cologne, Germany. Professor of German Language and Literature Emeritus; Writer. m. Helga Alice Schaefer, 1949, 2 sons, 1 dec, 2 daughters. Education: Jesus College, Cambridge; Christ's College, Cambridge; Charles Oldham Shakespeare Scholar, 1945, MA, 1950, LittD, 1962, Cantab; PhD, University of Birmingham, 1953; MA, 1969, DLitt, 1969, Oxon. Appointments: Assistant Lecturer to Senior Lecturer, University of Birmingham, 1948-63; Professor of German, Westfield College, University of London, 1964-69; Taylor Professor of German, Westfield College, University of London, 1964-69; Taylor Professor of German Language and Literature, 1969-86, Professor Emeritus, University of Oxford; Professorial Fellow, 1969-86, Dean of Degrees, 1978-93, Supernumerary Fellow, 1986-90, Honorary Fellow, 1990, Queen's College, Oxford; Various visiting professorships and fellowships. Publications: German Lyric Poetry, 1952; Mörike und seine Leser, 1960; Heine's Buch der Lieder: A Critical Study, 1960; Heine: The Tragic Satirist, 1962; The Penguin Book of Lieder (editor), 1964; Essays in Germany Language, Culture and Society (editor with L W Forster), 1969; The Romantic Period in Germany (editor), 1970; Seventeen Modern German Poets (editor), 1971; Comparative Literary Studies: An Introduction, 1973; Karl Marx and World Literature, 1976; Caligari's Children: The Film as Tale of Terror, 1980; Heine's Jewish Comedy: A Study of His Portraits of Jews and Judaism, 1983; Frankenstein's Island: England and the English in the Writings of Heinrich Heine, 1986; Israel at Vanity Fair: Jews and Judaism in the Writings of W M Thackeray, 1992; The Cabinet of Dr Caligari (co-editor of German Screenplay), 1996; Breeches and Metaphysics: Thackeray's German Discourse, 1997. Contributions to: Scholarly publications. Honours: Goethe Medal, 1973; Isaac Deutscher Memorial Prize, 1977; Honorary Drphil, University of Cologne, 1984; Friendrich Gundolf Prize, 1986; Honorary DLitt, University of Birmingham, 1988; Gold Medal, German Goethe Society, 1995. Memberships: British Academy, fellow; British Comparative Literature Association, president, 1984-87, honorary fellow, 1989; Deutsche Akademie für Sprache und Dichtung, fellow; English Goethe Society, president, 1990-94; Modern Language Association of America, honorary member. Address: 9 Hawkswell Gardens, Oxford OX2 7EX, England.

PREBBLE John (Edward Curtis), b. 23 June 1915, Edmonton, Middlesex, England. Author. Publications: Where the Sea Breaks, 1944; The Edge of Darkness (US edition as, The Edge of the Night), 1948; Age Without Pity, 1950; The Mather Story, 1954; The Brute Streets, 1954; The High Girders (US edition as Disaster at Dundee), 1956; My Great-Aunt Appearing Day, 1958, reissued with additions as Spanish Stirrup, 1973; Mongaso (with John A Jordan) (US edition as Elephants and Ivory), 1959; The Buffalo Soldiers, 1959; Culloden, 1961; The Highland Clearances, 1963; Glencoe, 1966; The Darien Disaster, 1968; The Lion in the North, 1971; Mutiny, 1975; John Prebble's Scotland, 1984; The King's Jaunt: George IV in Edinburgh, 1988; Landscapes and Memories, 1993. Honours: McVitie Award, Scottish Writer of the Year, 1993; Honorary DLitt, Glasgow, 1997; O.B.E., 1998. Memberships: Royal Society of Literature, fellow; Royal Society of Arts, fellow; Society of Authors; International PEN; Writer's Guild. Literary Agent: Curtis Brown. Address: 905 Nelson House, Dolphin Square, London SW1V 3PA, England.

PRELUTSKY Jack, b. 8 Sept 1940, Brooklyn, New York, USA. Writer; Poet. m. Carolynn Prelutsky, 1979. Education: Hunter College, New York City. Publications: Over 40 books for young readers, 1967-96. Honours: Many citations and awards. Address: c/o Greenwillow Books, 1350 Avenue of the Americas, New York, NY 10019, USA.

PRENTIS Malcolm David, b. 27 June 1948, Auchenflower, Queensland, Australia. Senior Lecturer in History; Writer. m. Marion Anne Bird, 7 Jan 1978, 2 sons, 1 daughter. Education: BA, Honours, University of Sydney, 1970; MA, Honours, 1973, PhD, 1980, Macquarie University; Dip Tertiary Ed, University of New England, 1982. Appointments: Tutor in History, Macquarie University, 1971-74; Lecturer in History, Catholic College of Education, Sydney, 1975-90; Senior Lecturer in History, Australian Catholic University, 1991-. Publications: A Study in Black and White: The Aborigines in Australian History, 1975, 2nd edition, 1988; Fellowship: A History of the Presbyterian Fellowship Movement in New South Wales, 1874-1977, 1977; St David's Kirk: A History of the Presbyterian Church in Dee Why, 1927-1977, 1977; Continuity and Change: A History of Manly Girls High School, 1959-1982 (with M A Prentis), 1982; The Scots in Australia: A Study of New South Wales, Victoria, Queensland, 1788-1900, 1983; The Scottish in Australia, 1987; Warringah History (editor), 1989; The Forest Kirk: A History, 1948-1993, 1993; Scots to the Fore: A History of The Scots College, Sydney, 1893-1993, 1993; Science, Race and Faith: A Life of John Mathew, 1849-1929, 1998. Contributions to: Journals. Address: c/o Australian Catholic University, Mount Saint Mary Campus, 179 Albert Road, Strathfield, New South Wales 2135, Australia.

PRESCOTT Casey. See: **MORRIS Janet Ellen.**

PRESCOTT J(ohn) R(obert) V(ictor), b. 1931, Newcastle upon Tyne, England. Professor of Geography Emeritus. Education: BSc, 1952, Diploma in Education, 1955, MA, 1957, University of Durham; PhD, Birkbeck College, London, 1961. Appointments: Lecturer, University College, Ibadan, 1956-61; Lecturer to Reader, 1961-85, Professor of Geography, 1985-, Professor Emeritus, 1997-, University of Melbourne. Publications: The Geography of Frontiers and Boundaries, 1965, revised edition as Frontiers and Boundaries, 1978; The Geography of State Policies, 1968; The Evolution of Nigeria's International and Regional Boundaries 1861-1971, 1971; Political Geography, 1972; The Political Geography of the Oceans, 1975; The Map of Mainland Asia by Treaty, 1975; Our Fragmented World: An Introduction to Political Geography (with W G East), 1975; The Frontiers of Asia and Southwest Asia (with H J Collier and D F Prescott), 1976; The Last of Lands: Antartica (with J Lovering), 1979; Australia's Continental Shelf (with other), 1979; Maritime Jurisdiction in Southeast Asia, 1981; Australia's Maritime Boundaries, 1985; The Maritime Political Boundaries of the World, 1985; Political Frontiers and Boundaries, 1987; Aboriginal Frontiers and Boundaries in Australia (with S Davis), 1992; A Geographical Description of the Spratly Islands and an Account of Hydrographic Surveys Amongst Those Islands (with David Hancox), 1995; Secret Hydrographic Surveys of the South China Sea (with David Hancox), 1997; Gulf of Thailand, 1998. Address: Department of Geography, University of Melbourne, Parkville, Victoria 3052, Australia.

PRESS John Bryant, b. 11 Jan 1920, Norwich, England. Retired Officer of the British Council; Writer. m. Janet Crompton, 20 Dec 1947, 1 son, 1 daughter. Education: Corpus Christi College, Cambridge, England. Publications: The Fire and the Fountain, 1955; The Chequer'd Shade, 1958; A Map of Modern English Verse, 1969; The Lengthening Shadows, 1971; John Betjeman, 1974; Poets of World War II, 1984; A Girl with Beehive Hair, 1986. Contributions to: Encounter; Southern Review; Art International. Honours: Royal Society of Literature Heinemann Award, 1959; 1st Prize, Cheltenham Poetry Festival, 1959. Membership: Royal Society of Literature, Fellow. Address: 5 South Parade, Frome, Somerset BA11 1EJ, England.

PRESTON Bruce Edward, b. 10 May 1935, London, England. Writer; Photographer. m. Brenda Alwyn Preston, 29 May 1965, 2 sons, 1 daughter. Education: West Kensington Central London School of Printing. Appointments: Freelance, 1966-; Editor, Motorcycle Rider, 1966-73; Production Manager, London Daily Mail, left 1989; Touring Editor, Motorcycle Sport and Leisure, 1992-. Publications: Better Motorcycling; Motorcycle Maintenance; BMW - The Complete Story. Contributions to: Motorcycle Sport and Leisure; Classic and Motorcycle Mechanics; American Motorcyclist; Bike SA; Motor Caravan; Motorhome Monthly. Honour: Motorcycle Journalist of the Year, Guild of Motoring Writers, 1981. Memberships: Guild of Motoring Writers; Caravan Writers Guild. Address: 14 Ivydene, West Molesey, Surrey KT8 2HG.

PRESTON Ivy Alice Kinross, b. 11 Nov 1913, Timaru, Canterbury, New Zealand. Writer. m. Percival Edward James Preston, 14 Oct 1937, 2 sons, 2 daughters. Publications: The Silver Stream (autobiography), 1958;

Hospital on the Hill, 1967; Voyage of Destiny, 1974; The House Above the Bay, 1976; Fair Accuser, 1985; Stranger From the Sea, 1987; 40 romance novels, reprinted in 9 languages and 130 editions. Contributions to: Many publications. Memberships: South Canterbury Writers Guild; New Zealand Women Writers Society; South Island Writers Association. Romance Writers of America; Romantic Novelists Association, London. Address: 95 Church Street, Timaru, Southe Canterbury, New Zealand.

PRESTON Peter John, b. 23 May 1938, England. Journalist; Editor; Newspaper Executive. m. Jean Mary Burrell, 1962, 2 sons, 2 daughters. Education: MA, English Literature, St John's College, Oxford. Appointments: Political Reporter, 1963-64, Education Correspondent, 1965-66, Diary Editor, 1966-68, Features Editor, 1968-72, Production Editor, 1972-75, Editor, 1975-95, The Guardian; British Executive Chairman, International Press Institute, 1988-; Editor-in-Chief and Chairman, The Guardian and The Observer, 1995-96; Non-Executive Director, Guardian Media Group, 1996-98; Director, Guardian Foundation, 1997-. Publication: 51st State (novel) 1998. Contributions to: Newspapers and journals. Honours: Honorary DLitt, Loughborough University, 1982; Honorary Doctorate, University of Essex, 1994. Address: c/o The Guardian and The Observer, 119 Farringdon Road, London EC1R 3ER, England.

PRESTON Richard McCann, b. 5 Aug 1954, Cambridge, Massachusetts, USA. Writer. m. 11 May 1985. Education: BA, summa cum laude, Pomona College, 1977; PhD, English and American Literature, Princeton University, 1983. Appointments: Lecturer in English, Princeton University, 1983; Visiting Fellow, Princeton University Council of the Humanities, 1994-95. Publications: First Light, 1987; American Steel, 1991; The Hot Zone, 1994; Cobra's Eye, 1997. Contributions to: Newspapers and magazines. Honours: American Institute of Physics Science Writing Award, 1988; Asteroid 3686 named 'Preston', 1989; AAAS, Westinghouse Award, 1992; MIT McDermott Award, 1993. Membership: Authors Guild. Address: c/o Nesbit & Nesbit Associates, 598 Madison Avenue, New York, NY 10022, USA.

PRESTON-MAFHAM Rodney Arthur, b. 14 June 1942, Harrow, England. Author; Photographer. m. Jean Brown, 31 July 1969, 1 son, 2 daughters. Education: University College, London, 1960-63; BSc, Zoology, Wye College, University of London, 1963-68; MSc, PhD. Publications: Spiders of the World, 1984; Spiders: An Illustrated Guide, 1991; Cacti: The Illustrated Dictionary, 1991; The Encyclopedia of Land Invertebrate Behaviour, 1993; The Natural History of Insects, 1996; The Natural History of Spiders, 1996. Address: Amberstone, 1 Kirland Road, Bodmin, Cornwall PL30 5JQ, England.

PREUSS Paul F, b. 7 Mar 1942, Albany, Georgia, USA. Writer. m. (1) Marsha May Pettit, 1963, 1 daughter, (2) Karen Reiser, 1973, (3) Debra Turner, 1993. Education: BA, cum laude, Yale University, 1966. Publications: The Gates of Heaven, 1980; Re-entry, 1981; Broken Symmetries, 1983; Human Error, 1985; Venus Prime series (with Arthur C Clarke), 1987-91; Starfire, 1988; The Ultimate Dinosaur, 1992; Core, 1993; Secret Passages, 1997. Contributions to: Books and newspapers; New York Review of Science Fiction. Memberships: Northern California Science Writers Association; Science Fiction and Fantasy Writers of America; Bay Area Book Reviewers' Association. Address: 304 Donahue Street, Sausalito, CA 94965, USA.

PRICE A(lice) Lindsay, b. 21 Oct 1927, Augusta, Georgia, USA. Writer; Artist; Publisher. Education: BA, Oklahoma State University, 1949; MA, University of Tulsa, 1970. Appointment: Scholar-in-Residence, Voices and Visions, 1990, 1992. Publications: Faces of the Waterworld, 1976; Our Dismembered Shadow, 1982; Swans of the World in Nature, History, Myth and Art, 1994. Contributions to: Enwright House; Rhino; Commonweal; Gryphon; Phoenix; Nimrod; Greenfield

Review; Suncatcher. Honours: Fist Award, Nimrod, 1970; Pegasus Award, 1981; Arts and Humanities Literary Award, 1992. Membership: Poets and Writers. Address: 3113 South Florence Avenue, Tulsa, OK 74015, USA.

PRICE (Alan) Anthony, b. 16 Aug 1928, Hertfordshire, England. Author; Journalist; Editor. m. (Yvonne) Ann Stone, 1953, 2 sons, 1 daughter. Education: Exhibitioner, MA, Merton College, Oxford, 1952. Appointment: Editor, The Oxford Times, 1972-88. Publications: The Labryinth Makers, 1970; The Alamut Ambush, 1971; Colonel Butler's Wolf, 1972; October Men, 1973; Other Paths to Glory, 1974; Our Man in Camelot, 1975; War Game, 1976; The '44 Vintage, 1978; Tomorrow's Ghost, 1979; The Hour of the Donkey, 1980; Soldier No More, 1981; The Old Vengeful, 1982; Gunner Kelly, 1983; Sion Crossing, 1984; Here Be Monsters, 1985; For the Good of the State, 1986; A New Kind of War, 1987; A Prospect of Vengeance, 1988; The Memory Trap, 1989; The Eyes of the Fleet, 1990. Honours: Silver Dagger, 1970, Gold Dagger, 1974, Crime Writers' Association; Swedish Academy of Detection Prize, 1978. Address: Wayside Cottage, Horton cum Studley, Oxford OX33 1AW, England.

PRICE Glanville, b. 16 June 1928, Rhaeadr, Wales. Professor Emeritus; Writer. m. Christine Winifred Thurston, 18 Aug 1954, 3 sons, 1 daughter. Education: BA, 1949, MA, 1952, University of Wales, Bangor; University of Paris, 1956. Appointments: Professor of French, University of Stirling, 1967-72; Professor of French, 1972-92, Research Professor, 1992-95, Professor Emeritus, 1995-, University of Wales, Aberystwyth. Publications: The Present Position of Minority Languages in Western Europe, 1969; The French Language, Present and Past, 1971; The Year's Work in Modern Language Studies, co-editor, 1972-92; William, Count of Orange: Four Old French Epics (editor), 1975; Romance Linguistics and the Romance Languages (with Kathryn F Bach), 1977; The Languages of Britain, 1984; Ireland and the Celtic Connection, 1987; An Introduction to French Pronunciation, 1991; A Comprehensive French Grammar, 1992; The Celtic Connection (editor), 1992; Hommages offerts à Maria Manoliu (editor with Coman Lupu), 1994; Encyclopedia of the Languages of Europe (editor), 1998. Contributions to: Professional journals. Memberships: Modern Humanities Research Association, chairman, 1979-90; Philological Society; Society for French Studies. Address: c/o Department of European Languages, University of Wales, Aberystwyth, Ceredigion SY23 3DY, Wales.

PRICE Jennifer. See: HOOVER Helen Mary.

PRICE Pamela. See: LECHTMAN Pamela Joy.

PRICE (Edward) Reynolds, b. 1 Feb 1933, Macon, North Carolina, USA. Professor; Author; Poet; Dramatist. Education: AB, Duke University, 1955; BLitt, Merton College, Oxford, 1958. Appointments: Faculty, 1958-61, Assistant Professor, 1961-68, Associate Professor, 1968-72, Professor, 1972-77, James B Duke Professor, 1977-, Duke University; Writer-in-Residence, University of North Carolina at Chapel Hill, 1965, University of Kansas, 1967, 1969, 1980, University of North Carolina at Greensboro, 1971, Glasgow Professor, Washington and Lee University, 1971; Faculty, Salzburg Seminar, 1977. Publications: A Long and Happy Life, 1962; The Names and Faces of Heroes, 1963; A Generous Man, 1966; Love and Work, 1968; Permanent Errors, 1970; Things Themselves, 1972; The Surface of Earth, 1975; Early Dark, 1977; A Palpable God, 1978; The Source of Light, 1981; Vital Provisions, 1982; Private Contentment, 1984; Kate Vaiden, 1986; The Laws of Ice, 1986; A Common Room, 1987; Good Hearts, 1988; Clear Pictures, 1989; The Tongues of Angels, 1990; The Use of Fire, 1990; New Music, 1990; The Foreseeable Future, 1991; Conversations with Reynolds Price, 1991; Blue Calhoun, 1993; Full Moon, 1993; The Collected Stories, 1993; A Whole New Life, 1994; The Promise of Rest, 1995; Three Gospels, 1996; Roxanne Slade, 1998. Honours: William Faulkner Foundation Award for Notable First Novel, 1962; Sir Walter Raleigh Awards, 1962,

1976, 1981, 1984, 1986; Guggenheim Fellowship, 1964-65; National Endowment for the Arts Fellowship, 1967-68; National Institute of Arts and Letters Award, 1971; Bellamann Foundation Award, 1972; North Carolina Award, 1977; National Book Critics Circle Award, 1986; Elmer H Bobst Award, 1988; R Hunt Parker Award, North Carolina Literary and Historical Society, 1991. Memberships: American Academy of Arts and Letters; Phi Beta Kappa; Phi Delta Theta. Address: PO Box 99014, Durham, NC 27708, USA.

PRICE Richard, b. 15 Aug 1966, Reading, England. Poet; Librarian. m. Jacqueline Canning, 6 Dec 1990, 1 daughter. Education: BA, Honours, English and Librarianship, PhD, Modern Scottish Fiction, University of Strathclyde, Glasgow. Appointments: Curator, Modern British Collections, The British Library, London, 1992-. Publications: The Fabulous Matter of Fact: The Poetics of Neil M Gunn, 1991; Poetry Collections: Sense and a Minor Fever, 1993; Tube Shelter Perspective, 1993; Marks & Sparks, 1995; Hand Held, 1997; Perfume and Petrol Fumes, 1999. Contributions to: Comparative Criticism; Independent; Glasgow Herald; New Writing Scotland. Address: c/o Modern British Collections, The British Library, 96 Euston Road, London NW1 2DB, England.

PRICE Roger (David), b. 7 Jan 1944, Port Talbot, Wales. Professor of Modern History; Writer. Education: BA, University of Wales, University College of Swansea, 1965. Appointments: Lecturer, 1968-82, Senior Lecturer, 1982-83, Reader in Social History, 1984-91, Professor, European History, 1991-94, University of East Anglia; Professor of Modern History, University of Wales, Aberystwyth, 1993-. Publications: The French Second Republic: A Social History, 1972; The Economic Modernization of France, 1975; Revolution and Reaction: 1848 and The Second French Republic (editor and contributor), 1975; 1848 in France, 1975; An Economic History of Modern France, 1981; The Modernization of Rural France: Communications Networks and Agricultural Market Structures in 19th Century France, 1983; A Social History of 19th Century France, 1987; The Revolutions of 1848, 1989; A Concise History of France, 1993; Documents on the French Revolution of 1848, 1996; Napoleon III and the French Second Empire, 1997. Contributions to: Numerous Magazines and journals. Honour: DLitt, University of East Anglia, 1985. Membership: Fellow, Royal Historical Society, 1983. Address: Department of History and Welsh History, University of Wales, Aberystwyth, Ceredigion SY23 3DY, Wales.

PRICE Stanley, b. 12 Aug 1931, London, England. Writer; Dramatist. m. Judy Fenton, 5 July 1957, 1 son. Education: MA, University of Cambridge. Publications: Novels: Crusading for Kronk, 1960; A World of Difference, 1961; Just for the Record, 1962; The Biggest Picture, 1964. Stage Plays: Horizontal Hold, 1967; The Starving Rich, 1972; The Two of Me, 1975; Moving, 1980; Why Me?, 1985. Screenplays: Arabesque, 1968; Gold, 1974; Shout at the Devil, 1975. Television Plays: All Things Being Equal, 1970; Exit Laughing, 1971; Minder, 1980; The Kindness of Mrs Radcliffe, 1981; Moving, 1985; Star Quality, series, 1986; Close Relations, 1986-87; The Bretts, 1990. Contributions to: Observer; Sunday Telegraph; New York Times; Los Angeles Times; Punch; Plays and Players; New Statesman; Independent; Town. Memberships: Writer's Guild; Dramatists Club. Address: Douglas Rae, 28 Charing Cross Road, London WC2, England.

PRICE Susan, b. 8 July 1955, Brades Row, England. Children's Fiction Writer. Education: Tividale, England. Publications: Devil's Piper, 1973; Twopence a Tub, 1975; Sticks and Stones, 1976; Home from Home, 1977; Christopher Uptake, 1981; The Carpenter (stories), 1981; In a Nutshell, 1983; From Where I Stand, 1984; Ghosts at Large, 1984; Odin's Monster, 1986; The Ghost Drum, 1987; The Bone Dog, 1989; Forbidden Doors, 1990. Honours: The Other Award, 1975; Carnegie Medal, 1987. Membership: Society of Authors. Address: c/o Faber &

Faber Ltd, 3 Queen Square, London WC 1N 3AU, England.

PRICE Victor, b. 10 Apr 1930, Newcastle, County Down, Northern Ireland. Writer; Poet. Education: BA, Honours, Modern Languages (French and German), Queen's University, Belfast, 1947-51. Appointments: With the BBC, 1956-90, ending as Head of German Language Service. Publications: Novels: The Death of Achilles, 1963; The Other Kingdom, 1964; Caliban's Wooing, 1966; The Plays of Georg Büchner, 1971; Two Parts Water (poems), 1980. Contributions to: Financial Times; Scotsman; BBC World Service; Deutschland Funk; Channel Four. Address: 22 Oxford Gardens, London W4 3BW, England.

PRIESNITZ Wendy, b. 30 May 1950, Hamilton, Ontario, Canada. Writer; Journalist; Editor. m. Rolf Priesnitz, 11 Apr 1970, 2 daughters. Education: Hamilton Teachers College, 1968-69; University of Waterloo, 1987-89. Publications: Summer Love Winter Fires; School Free; Bringing It Home; Markam - A Contemporary Portrait; A Child's Guide to Starting a Business; The House Where I Grew Up. Contributions to: Natural Life; York Region Business Journal; Globe and Mail; Childs Play Magazine. Address: RR1, St George, Ontario N0E 1N0, Canada.

PRIEST Christopher (McKenzie), b. 1943. Writer. Publications: Indoctrinaire, 1970; Fugue for a Darkening Island, US edition as Darkening Island, 1972; Inverted World, 1974; Your Book of Film-Making, 1974; Real-Time World, 1974; The Space Machine, 1976; A Dream of Wessex, US edition as The Perfect Lover, 1977; Anticipations (editor), 1978; An Infinite Summer, 1979; Stars of Albion (co-editor), 1979; The Affirmation, 1981; The Glamour, 1984; The Quiet Woman, 1990; The Book on the Edge of Forever, 1994; The Prestige, 1995; The Extremes, 1998; The Dream Archipelago, 1999. Honours: James Tait Black Memorial Prize for Fiction, 1995; World Fantasy Award, 1996. Memberships: Society of Authors, management committee, 1985-88. Address: c/o Peters, Fraser & Dunlop, 503/4 The Chambers, Chelsea Harbour, London SW10 0XF, England.

PRIEST Christopher, b. 14 July 1943, Cheadle, Cheshire, England. Author. m. Leigh Kennedy, 20 Oct 1988, 1 son, 1 daughter. Publications: Novels: Indoctrinaire, 1970; Fugue for a Darkening Island, 1972; Inverted World, 1974; The Space Machine, 1976; A Dream of Wessex, 1977; The Affirmation, 1981; The Glamour, 1984; The Quiet Woman, 1990; The Prestige, 1995; The Extremes, 1998; Short Story Collections: Real Time World, 1974; An Infinite Summer, 1979; The Dream Archipelago, 1999; Essays, Criticism, Journalism: published in: The Guardian; The Times; The Independent on Sunday; The Scotsman; Washington Post; New Scientist; Times Educational Supplement; New Statesman; Time Out; Foundation; The Wellsian; Radio Times; The Bookseller; Publishing News; The Author. Honours: Kurd Lasswitz Award, 1988; James Tait Black Memorial Prize, 1995; World Fantasy Award, 1996; Best of Young British Novelists, 1983. Membership: Society of Authors. Literary Agent: Peters, Fraser and Dunlop. Address: c/o Peters Fraser and Dunlop, 503 The Chambers, Chelsea Harbour, London SW10 0XF, England.

PRIESTLEY Brian, b. 10 July 1946, Manchester, England. Writer; Musician. Education: BA, Honours, French; Diploma of Education, University of Leeds. Publications: Mingus, A Critical Biography, 1982; Jazz Piano, 6 volumes, 1983-90; Charlie Parker, 1984; John Coltrane, 1987; Jazz: The Essential Companion (with Ian Carr and Digby Fairweather), 1987; Jazz on Record, A History, 1988; Jazz - The Rough Guide (with Ian Carr and Digby Fairweather), 1995. Contributions to: Books and journals. Address: 120A Farningham Road, Caterham, Surrey CR3 6LJ, England.

PRINCE Alison (Mary), b. 26 Mar 1931, Kent, England. Writer. m. Goronwy Siriol Parry, 26 Dec 1957, 2 sons, 1 daughter. Education: Beckenham Grammar School; Slade School Diploma, London University; Art Teacher's Diploma, Goldsmith's College. Appointment: Fellow in Creative Writing, Jordanhill College, Glasgow, 1988-90. Publications: The Doubting Kind (young adults), 1974; How's Business (children's book), 1985; The Ghost Within (supernatural stories), 1987; The Blue Moon Day (children's book), 1989; The Necessary Goat (essays on creativity), 1992; Kenneth Grahame: An Innocent in the Wild Wood (biography), 1994; Having Been in the City (poetry), 1994; The Witching Tree (novel), 1996; The Sherwood Hero (children's book), 1996; Hans Christian Andersen: The Fan Dancer (biography), 1998. Contributions to: Various educational and other journals. Honours: Runner-Up for Smarties Prize, 1986; Guardian Children's Fiction Award, 1996; Literary Review Grand Poetry Prize. Memberships: Scottish PEN; Society of Authors. Literary Agent: Jennifer Luithlen. Address: Burnfoot, Whiting Bay, Isle of Arran KA27 8QL, Scotland.

PRINCE F(rank) T(empleton), b. 13 Sept 1912, Kimberley, Cape Province, South Africa. Retired Professor of English; Poet. m. Pauline Elizabeth Bush, 10 Mar 1943, 2 daughters. Education: BA, Balliol College, Oxford, 1934. Appointments: Visiting Fellow, Princeton University, USA, 1935-36, All Souls College, Oxford, 1968-69; Lecturer, 1945-55, Reader, 1955-56, Professor of English, 1957-74, University of Southampton; Clark Lecturer, University of Cambridge, 1972-73; Professor of English, University of the West Indies, Mona, Kingston, Jamaica, 1975-78; Fannie Hurst Visiting Professor, Brandeis University, Waltham, Massachusetts, 1978-80; Visiting Professor, Washington University, St Louis, 1980-81, Sana'a University, North Yemen, 1981-83; Writer-in-Residence, Hollins College, Virginia, 1984. Publications: Poetry: Poems, 1938; Soldiers Bathing and Other Poems, 1954; The Stolen Heart, 1957; The Doors of Stone: Poems, 1938-1962, 1963; Memoirs of Oxford, 1970; Penguin Modern Poets 20 (with John Heath-Stubbs and Stephen Spender), 1971; Drypoints of the Hasidim, 1975; Afterword on Rupert Brooke, 1976; Collected Poems, 1979; The Yuan Chen Variations, 1981; Later On, 1983; Fragment Poetry, 1986; Walks in Rome, 1987; Collected Poems, 1935-92, 1993. Other: The Italian Element in Milton's Verse, 1954. Editor: John Milton: Samson Agonistes, 1957; William Shakespeare: The Poems, 1960; John Milton: Paradise Lost, Books I and II, 1962; John Milton: Comus and Other Poems, 1968. Contributions to: Keats Country (poem), PN Review 106, 1995. Honours: DLitt, University of Southampton, 1981, University of York, 1982; American Academy and Institute of Arts and Letters Award, 1982. Address: 32 Brookvale Road, Southampton, Hampshire S017 1QR, England.

PRINCE Peter Derek V, b. 14 Aug 1915, Bangalore, India. Bible Teacher; Author. m. (1) Lydia Christensen, 16 Feb 1946, 9 adopted daughters, (2) Ruth Hemmingson Baker, 17 Oct 1978. Education: BA, Classics, King's College, Cambridge, England, 1938; MA, Classics, Philosophy, 1949; Studies, Hebrew University, Jerusalem, 1945, 1946. Appointments: Fellow, Philosophy, King's College, Cambridge, England, 1940-49; Director, Swedish Children's Home, Jerusalem, Israel, 1946-48; Principal, Nyang'ori Teacher Training College, Kisumu, Kenya, 1957-61; Bible Teacher, Author, Founder and President, Derek Prince Ministries, International, 1967-; Radio Bible Teacher, Radio Programme, Today With Derek Prince in 14 languages, 1978-. Publications: More than 30 books including: Self Study Bible Course, 1969; Shaping History Through Prayer and Fasting, 1973; Appointment in Jerusalem, 1975; Faith to Live By, 1977; The Grace of Yielding, 1977; The Marriage Covenant, 1978; The Last Word on the Middle East, 1982; God is a Matchmaker, 1986; Blessing or Curse: You Can Choose!, 1990; The Destiny of Israel and the Church, 1992; The Spirit-Filled Believer's Handbook, 1993; They Shall Expel Demons, 1998; Over 450 audio and 150 video cassette teachings. Honours: King's Scholar, Eton College, England, 1929-34; King's Scholar, King's College, Cambridge University, England, 1934-38; Craven Research Student, 1939-40; World Missionary Broadcast Award, High Adventure Ministries Inc, 1994. Address: Derek Prince Ministries International, PO Box 19501, Charlotte, North Carolina, 28219-9501, USA.

PRINGLE Heather Anne, b. 8 Dec 1952, Edmonton, Alberta, Canada. Science Writer; Author. m. 11 Mar 1978. Education: BA, University of Alberta, 1973; MA, University of British Columbia, 1976. Publication: In Search of Ancient North America, 1996. Contributions to: Science; Discover; Stern; Geo; New Scientist; National Geographic Traveler; Islands; Saturday Night; Canadian Geographic. Honours: National Magazine Award, 1988; Authors Award, 1992; Finalist, National Magazine Award, 1998. Literary Agent: Anne McDermid, Anne McDermid and Associates, 78 Albany Avenue, Toronto, Ontario, Canada M5R 3C3. Address: Suite 24, Third Floor, 712 Robson Street, Vancouver, British Columbia, Canada, V6Z 1A2.

PRINGLE Margaret Douglas (Maggie). Journalist. Education: History, Oxford University. Appointments: Standard; Pendennis Assistant; Observer; Fiction Editor, Nova; Senior Editor, John Murray, 1981-82; Contributing Editor, Michael Joseph, 1983-97; Books Editor, Today, 1987-92; Books Editor, Express, 1996-98; Literary Editor, Express, 1998. Publication: Dance Little Ladies, 1979. Contributions to: Woman's Journal. Membership: PEN. Address: Express, 245 Blackfriars Road, London SE1 9UX, England.

PRIOR Allan, b. 13 Jan 1922, Newcastle upon Tyne, England. Author. Education: Newcastle upon Tyne; Blackpool. Publications: A Flame in the Air, 1951; The Joy Ride, 1952; The One-Eyed Monster, 1958; One Away, 1961; The Interrogators, 1965; The Operators, 1966; The Loving Cup, 1968; The Contract, 1970; Paradiso, 1972; Affair, 1976; Never Been Kissed in the Same Place Twice, 1978; Theatre, 1981; A Cast of Stars, 1983; The Big March, 1983; Her Majesty's Hit Man, 1986; Führer - the Novel, 1991; The Old Man and Me, 1994; The Old Man and Me Again, 1996. Address: Summerhill, 24 Waverley Road, St Albans, Herts, England.

PRITCHARD Margaret (Marged) Jones, b. 29 Aug 1919, Tregaron, Dyfed, Wales, England. Modern Languages Teacher; Lecturer for Welsh Learners. m. Robert Gwilym Pritchard, 5 Apr 1949, 1 son. Education: Honours Degree in French, 1940; 1st Class Teaching Diploma, Bangor, 1941. Appointments: Literary Adjudicator, Welsh Arts Council, 1991; Adjudicator for the main Novel Competition, National Eisteddfod, 1996. Publications: Cregyn Ar y Traeth, 1974; Gwylanod yn y Mynydd, 1975; Clymau and Disgwyl, 1976; Mid Mudan Mo'r Môr, 1976; Enfys y Bore, 1980; Nhw Oedd Yno, 1986; Adar Brith; Unwaith Eto (short stories), 1994. Contributions to: Taliesin; Traethodydd; Barn; y Genhinen; y Faner. Honour: Welsh Arts Council Prize, 1975. Membership: Welsh Academy, adjudicator of prose, 1993. Address: Glaslyn, Minffordd, Penrhyndeudraeth, Gwynedd LL48 6HL, Wales.

PRITCHARD R(obert) John, b. 30 Nov 1945, Los Angeles, California, USA. Freelance Writer and Broadcaster. m. (1) Sonia Magbanna Zaide, 15 Aug 1969, div 1984, 1 son, 1 daughter, (2) Lady Elayne Antonia Lodge, 20 Dec 1989. Education: AB, University of California, 1967; MA, 1968, PhD, 1980, London School of Economics; LLB, University of Kent at Canterbury, 1996; Bar Vocational Course, Inns of Court School of Law, 1996-97, London. Appointments: Managing Editor, Millennium: Journal of International Studies, 1974-78; Consultant Editor/Compiler, Tokyo War Trial Project, London School of Economics, 1981-87; Director/Company Secretary, Integrated Dictionary Systems Ltd, 1988-90; Lecturer in History, University of Kent, 1990-93; Fellow in War Studies, King's College, London, 1990-93; Simon Senior Research Fellow in History, University of Manchester, 1993-94; Director, Historical Enterprises, 1993-; Director, Robert M Kempner Collegium, 1996-. Publications: Reichstag Fire and Ashes of Democracy, 1972; Cry Sabotage, 1972; Tokyo War Crimes Trial Complete Transcripts, Proceedings of International Military Tribunal for Far East (with S M Zaide), 22 volumes, 1981; Tokyo War Crimes Trial, Index and Guide (with S M Zaide), 5 volumes, 1981-87; General History of the Philippines (co-author), vol 1, American Half Century 1898-1946, 1984; The

Tokyo War Crimes Trial: An International Symposium (co-author), 1984, 2nd edition, 1986; Far Eastern Influences on British Strategy Towards the Great Powers 1937-39, 1987; Overview of the Historical Importance of the Tokyo War Trial, 1987; Total War (co-author), 1989, 2nd edition, 1995; Japan and the Second World War (with Lady Toskiko Marks), 1989; Unit 731: World War II in Asia and the Pacific and the War's Aftermath, with General Themes: A Handbook of Literature and Research; The Japanese Army's Secret of Secrets (co-author), 1989; From Pearl Harbour to Hiroshima (co-author), 1993; La Déportation: La Système Concentrationnaire Nazi (co-author), 1995; Wada umi no Koe wo Kiku: senso sekinin to Ningen no Tsumi; to no Ma (Harken to the Cries at Our Birth: The Intervals Separating War Responsibility and Crimes of Humanity (co-author), 1996; Handbook of the Literature and Research of World War Two (co-author), 1998; The Tokyo Major War Crimes Trial: The Records of the International Military Tribunal for the Far East with an Authoritative Commentary and Comprehensive Guide, 124 Volumes, 1998-99. Contributions to: Cambridge Encyclopedia of Japan, 1993; International Criminal Law, 3 volumes, 1999. Address: 11 Charlotte Square, Margate, Kent, CT9 1LR, England.

PRITCHARD William H(arrison), b. 12 Nov 1932, Binghampton, New York, USA. Professor of English; Author. m. Marietta Pritchard, 24 Aug 1957, 3 sons. Education: BA, Amherst College, 1953; Columbia University, 1953-54; MA, English, 1956, PhD, English, 1960, Harvard University. Appointments: Teacher, 1958-, later Henry Clay Folger Professor of English, Amherst College; Member, Editorial Board, Hudson Review. Publications: Wyndham Lewis, 1972; Wyndham Lewis: Profiles in Literature, 1972; W B Yeats (editor), 1972; Seeing Through Everything: English Writers 1918-1940, 1977; Lives of the Modern Poets, 1980, 2nd edition, 1996; Frost: A Literary Life Reconsidered, 1984, 2nd edition, 1993; Randall Jarrell: A Literary Life, 1990; Selected Poems of Randall Jarrell (editor), 1990; Playing It By Ear: Literary Essays and Reviews, 1994; Talking Back to Emily Dickinson and Other Essays, 1998. Contributions to: American Scholar; Boston Sunday Globe; Hudson Review; New Republic; New York Times Book Review; Numerous others. Honours: Phi Beta Kappa, 1953; American Council of Learned Societies Junior Fellowship, 1963-64, and Fellowship, 1977-78; Guggenheim Fellowship, 1973-74; National Endowment for the Humanities Fellowships, 1977-78, 1986; Book of essays published in his honour, 1998. Membership: Association of Literary Scholars and Critics. Address: 62 Orchard Street, Amherst, MA 01002, USA.

PRITZKER Andreas E M, b. 4 Dec 1945, Baden, Switzerland. Physicist. m. Marthi Ehrlich, 4 Dec 1970, dec 1998. Education: PhD, Physics, Swiss Federal Institute of Technology, Zürich. Publications: Filberts Verhaengnis, 1990; Das Ende der Taeuschung, 1993. Memberships: Swiss Writers Association; Swiss-German PEN Centre. Address: Rebmoosweg 55, CH-5200 Brugg, Switzerland.

PROCTOR Patrick. See: **STREETEN Paul Patrick.**

PROKES Mary Timothy, b. 5 June 1931, Jackson, Minnesota, USA. Professor of Theology and Spirituality. Member of Franciscan Sisters of the Eucharist. Education: BA, Journalism, Marquette University, Milwaukee, Wisconsin, USA, 1962; MA, Theology, Marquette University, Milwaukee, 1967; PhD, Theology, Institute of Christian Thought, St Michael's University College in University of Toronto, Ontario, Canada, 1976. Appointments: Faculty of Religious Studies, College of Notre Dame, Baltimore, Maryland, USA, 1976-81; Visiting Lecturer, Kroger Intern University, 1982-83; Distinguished Visiting Scholar, Lonergan University College in Concordia University, Montreal, Quebec, 1983-84; Department of Religious Studies, St Thomas More College, University of Saskatchewan, Saskatoon, Sask, Canada, 1984, tenured, 1988; Professor of Theology and Spirituality, Notre Dame Graduate School of Theology, Alexandria, Virginia, USA, 1995-. Publications: Women's Challenge: Ministry in the Flesh, 1977; The Challenge of

HIV/AIDs: Caring in Faith, 1991; Transcendence: An Interdisciplinary Issue (editor), 1992; Mutuality: The Human Image of Trinitarian Love, 1993; Toward a Theology of the Body, 1997; The Nuptial Meaning of Body in Light of Mary's Assumption, Communio, Vol II, No 2, Summer 1984. Honour: Distinguished Visiting Scholar, Lonergan College, 1983-84. Address: La Verna Center, 14 Kingshouse Court, Silver Spring, MD 20905, USA.

PROKOPIUK Jerzy Stepan, b. 5 June 1931. Translator; Author Education: Oriental and English Philology, Philosophy, University of Warsaw. Publications: Translations of 106 books. Honours: Awards, Deutsches Polen Institut, Darmstadt, Polish Society of Translators. Memberships: Polish Society of Writers; Polish Society of Translators. Address: Nowolipie 20/23, 01 005 Warsaw, Poland.

PROSSER Harold Lee, b. 31 Dec 1944, Springfield, Missouri, USA. Author; Composer; Interfaith Minister. m. (1), div 1988, 2 daughters, (2) Debra Cunningham Phipps, 6 Dec 1994. Education: AA, Santa Monica College, 1968; BS, 1974, MSED, 1982, Southwest Missouri State University; Ordained Interfaith Minister, New Mexico Theological Seminary, 1994. Publications: Dandelion Seeds: 18 Stories, 1974; Goodbye Lon Chaney Jr, Goodbye, 1977; Desert Woman Visions: 100 Poems, 1987; Jack Bimbo's Touring Circus Poems, 1988; Charles Beaumont (biography), 1994; Numerous musical compositions for publication. Honours: Manuscripts permanently housed at Eastern New Mexico University, Portales, University of Wyoming, Laramie, and New Mexico Highlands University, Las Vegas. Memberships: American Society of Composers, Authors, and Publishers; Vedanta Society. Address: 1313 South Jefferson Avenue, Springfield, MO 65807, USA.

PROUD Linda Helena, b. 9 July 1949, Broxbourne, England. Writer. Education: Diploma, Design and Exhibition, College of Distributive Trades, London. Appointments: Picture Researcher, Marshall Cavendish, 1971-75; Freelance Picture Researcher, 1975-83; Picture Manager, Equinox/Phaidon, 1983-87; Freelance Picture Researcher, Writer, Teacher, 1987-. Publications: Consider England, 1994; Knights of the Grail, 1995; Tabernacle for the Sun, 1997; 2000 Years, 1999. Honours: Southern Arts Bursary Fund, 1995; Hawthornden Fellowship, 1998. Membership: Writers in Oxford, newsletter editor, 1996-98. Address: c/o John Johnson Ltd, 45/47 Clerkenwell Green, London EC1R 0HT, England.

PROULX E(dna) Annie, b. 22 Aug 1935, Norwich, Connecticut, USA. Writer. m. James Hamilton Lang, 22 June 1969, div 1990, 3 sons. Education: BA, University of Vermont, 1969; MA, Sir George Williams University, Montreal, 1973. Publications: Heart Songs and Other Stories, 1988; Postcards, 1992; The Shipping News, 1993; Accordion Crimes, 1996. Contributions to: Periodicals. Honours: Guggenheim Fellowship, 1992; PEN/Faulkner Award, 1993; National Book Award for Fiction, 1993; Chicago Tribune Heartland Award, 1993; Irish Times International Fiction Award, 1993; Pulitzer Prize in Fiction, 1994. Memberships: Phi Alpha Theta; Phi Beta Kappa; PEN American Centre. Address: c/o Simon and Schuster Inc, 1230 Avenue of the Americas, New York, NY 10020, USA.

PRUTER Robert, b. 1 July 1944, Philadelphia, Pennsylvania, USA. Editor. m. 22 July 1972, 1 daughter. Education: BA, 1967, MA, 1976, Roosevelt University. Publications: Chicago Soul, 1991; Blackwell Guide to Soul Recordings (editor and contributor), 1993; Doowop: The Chicago Scene, 1996. Contributions to: Chicago History; Living Blues; Goldmine; Juke Blues; Record Collectors' Monthly; Journal of Sport History. Membership: Society of Midland Authors. Address: 576 Stratford Avenue, Elmhurst, IL 60126, USA.

PRUTKOV Kozma. See: **SNODGRASS W D.**

PRVULOVICH Zika Rad, (Dr Peters), b. 4 Dec 1920, Vlahovo, Serbia, Yugoslavia. Retired University Senior Lecturer. m. Janet Mary Atkins, 11 Aug 1959, 1 son, 1 daughter. Education: BA, Mod, Trinity College, Dublin, 1951; BA, Oxon, 1952; DPhil, Oxon, 1956; MA, Oxon, 1957. Publications: Njegoseva Teorija Saznauja i Sistem, 1981; Prince-Bishop Hjegosh's Religious Philosophy, 1984; Serbia between the Swastika and the Red Star, 1986; Tajna Boga i Tajna Sveta, 1991; The Ray of the Microcosm, translation of Prince-Bishop Njegosh's poem Luca Mikrokozma (bilingual edition with critical commentary and introduction in English), 1992. Contributions to: Many literary, political, religious and philosophical journals and magazines. Honour: Wray Prize in Philosophy, University of Dublin, 1951. Memberships: Dublin University Philosophical Society, honorary librarian; PEN, English Section; Serbian Writers Club, honorary member; Society of Serbian Writers and Artist, England; Philosophy of Education Society of Great Britain; Oriel Society; University of Birmingham Common Room. Address: 26 Wheeler's Lane, King's Heath, Birmingham B13 0SA, England.

PRYCE-JONES David, b. 15 Feb 1936, Vienna, Austria. Writer. m. 29 July 1959, 1 son, 2 daughters. Education: BA, MA, Magdalen College, Oxford, 1956-59. Appointments: Literary Editor, Time & Tide, 1961; Spectator, 1964. Publications: Owls & Satyrs, 1961; The Sands of Summer, 1963; Next Generation, 1964; Quondam, 1965; The Stranger's View, 1967; The Hungarian Revolution, 1969; Running Away, 1969; The Face of Defeat, 1971; The England Commune, 1973; Unity Mitford, 1976; Vienna, 1978; Shirley's Guild, 1981; Paris in the Third Reich, 1983; Cyril Connolly, 1984; The Afternoon Sun, 1986; The Closed Circle, 1989; Inheritance, 1992; You Can't Be Too Careful, 1993; The War That Never Was, 1995. Contributions to: Numerous journals and magazines. Honours: Wingate Prize, 1986; Sunlight Literary Prize, 1989. Membership: Royal Society of Literature. Address: Lower Pentwyn, Gwenddwr, Powys LD2 3LQ, Wales.

PRYNNE J(eremy) H(alvard), b. 24 June 1936, England. Poet. Education: Graduate, Jesus College, Cambridge, 1960. Appointments: Frank Knox Fellow, Harvard University, 1960-61; Fellow, University Lecturer, and Librarian, Gonville and Caius College, Cambridge, 1962-. Publications: Kitchen Poems, 1968; Day Light Songs, 1968; The White Stones, 1969; Brass, 1971; Into the Day, 1972; Wound Response, 1974; High Pink on Chrome, 1975; News of Warring Clans, 1977; Down where changed, 1979; Poems, 1982; The Oval Window, 1983; Bands Around the Throat, 1987; Word Order, 1989; Not-You, 1993; Her Weasles Wild Returning, 1994; For the Monogram, 1997; Red D Gypsum, 1998; Pearls That Were, 1999; Poems, 1999. Address: Gonville and Caius College, Cambridge CB2 1TA, England.

PRYOR Adel. See: **WASSERFALL Adel.**

PRYOR Bonnie Helen, b. 22 Dec 1942, Los Angeles, California, USA. Author. m. Robert E Pryor, 2 sons, 4 daughters. Publications: Grandpa Bear, 1985; Rats, Spiders and Love, 1986; Amanda and April, 1986; Grandpa Bear's Christmas, 1986; Mr Z and the Time Clock, 1986; Vinegar Pancakes and Vanishing Cream, 1987; House on Maple Street, 1987; Mr Munday and Rustlers, 1988; Seth of Lion People, 1989; Plumtree War, 1989; Porcupine Mouse, 1989; Perfect Percy, 1989; Mr Munday and Space Creatures, 1989; Merry Christmas Amanda and April, 1990; 24 Hour Lipstick Mystery, 1990; Greenbrook Farm, 1991; Jumping Jenny, 1992; Beaver Boys, 1992; Lottie's Dream, 1992; Poison Ivy and Eyebrow Wigs, 1993; Horses in the Garage, 1993; Birthday Blizzard, 1993; Marvelous Marvin and the Werewolf Mystery, 1994; Marvelous Marvin and the Pioneer Ghost, 1995; Dream Jar, 1996; Toenails, Tonsils and Tornadoes, 1997; Thomas, 1998, Joseph, 1999, (American Adventure Series). Contributions to: Magazines. Honours: Children's Choice, 1986; Outstanding Book List, National Society of Science Teachers and National Society of Social Studies, 1987; Irma Simonton Black Award, Bank Street College, 1989;

National Society of Science Teachers Award, 1990; Ohioana Alice Louise Wood Award for Contributions to Children's Literature; Maryland State Intermediate Award for Poison Ivy and Eyebrow Wigs. Memberships: Society of Children's Book Writers; Ohioana; Midland Authors. Address: 19600 Baker Road, Gambier, OH 43022, USA.

PRZYBYSZ Janusz Anastazy, b. 31 May 1926, Poznan, Poland. Journalist; Writer. m. Danuta Maria Magolewska, 10 Sept 1951, 1 daughter. Education: University of Poznań, 1950. Publications: Several books and short-story collections, 1962-90. Contributions to: Periodicals. Honours: Reymont Literary Prize, 1987; City of Poznan Prize, 1988. Memberships: Association of Authors and Composers; Polish Journalists Association. Address: ul Galileusza 6A m.6, 60-159 Poznań, Poland.

PRZYMANOWSKI Janusz, b. 20 Jan 1922, Warsaw, Poland. Author; Journalist. m. Aleksandra Nowinska, 2 June 1984, 1 daughter. Education: University of Warsaw, 1964. Publications: Over 15 books and 200 songs. Contributions to: Various publications and television. Honours: Literary Prizes, Ministry of National Defence, 1959, 1961, 1966, 1967, 1987, Ministry of Culture and Art, 1967, and the Prime Minister, 1977. Membership: Union of Polish Authors. Address: ul Deuga, 30/34m 00-238 Warsaw, Poland.

PUGLISI Angela Aurora, b. 28 Jan 1949, Messina, Italy. Professorial University Lecturer; Writer. Education: BA, Dunbarton College, 1972; MFA, Painting, 1974, MA, Art History, MA, Language and Literature, 1977, PhD, Comparative Literature, 1983. Appointments: Education Consultant, US Government, 1983-86; Faculty, Georgetown University, Washington, DC, 1986-; Education Specialist, US Government 1993-. Publications: Towards Excellence in Education Through Liberal Arts, 1984; Homage, 1985; Nature's Canvas, 1985; Sonnet, 1985; Primavera, 1986; Sand Dunes, 1986; Sun's Journey, 1986; Jet d'Eau, 1986; Ocean Waves, 1986; Prelude, 1987; Woodland Revisited, 1988; Ethics in Journalism, 1989; Ethics in Higher Education, 1995; Homage II, in Voce Italiana, 1996. Other: Artistic publications, 1989-90. Honour: Certificate for Outstanding Service to Education and Education Reform. Memberships: Catholic Academy of Sciences; Corcoran College of Art Association; Italian Cultural Center, Casa Italiana, founding member; SEE; Lady of the Holy Sepulchre of Jerusalem; Board of Directors, Casa Italiana Language School, Washington DC, 1998; Editorial Board, Voce Italiana, Washington DC, 1998. Address: 2843 Cedar Lane, Vienna, VA 22180, USA.

PULLEIN-THOMPSON Christine. See: **POPESCU Christine.**

PULLEIN-THOMPSON Diana. See: **FARR Diana.**

PULLMAN Philip, b. 19 Oct 1946, Norwich, England. Author. m. Jude Speller, 15 Aug 1970, 2 sons. Education: BA, Oxford University, 1968. Appointments: Teacher, Middle School, 1972-86; Lecturer, Westminster College, Oxford, England, 1986-96. Publications: The Ruby in the Smoke, 1986; The White Mercedes, 1992; The Golden Compass, 1996; The Subtle Knife, 1997; Clockwork, 1998. Contributions to: Reviews in Times Educational Supplement; The Guardian. Honours: Carnegie Medal, 1996; Guardian Children's Fiction Award, 1996. Literary Agent: Caradoc King, A P Watt, 20 John St, London WC1N 2DR, England. Address: 24 Templar Road, Oxford OX2 2DR, England.

PULSFORD Petronella, b. 4 Feb 1946, Leeds, Yorkshire, England. Actress; Writer. Education: BA, Honours, English, St Hilda's College, Oxford. Publication: Lee's Ghost (novel), 1990. Honour: Constable Trophy for Fiction, 1989. Memberships: Society of Authors; Equity. Address: 8 Thomas Street West, Savile Park, Halifax, West Yorkshire HX1 3HF, England.

PUNNOOSE Kunnuparambil P, b. 26 Mar 1942, Kottayam, India. Editor. m. Santhamma, 9 Jan 1967, 1 son, 2 daughters. Education: College Graduate, 1962.

Appointments: Managing Editor, Concept Publishing Company, 1974-75, Asian Literary Market Review, 1975-; Director, Darsan Books Ltd, 1983-; General Convener, Kottayam International Book Fair, 1984-. Publications: Directory of American University Presses, 1979; American Book Trade in India, 1981; Bookdealers in India and the Orient, 1992; Studying in India, 1994; Studying in America, 1999. Contributions to: Over 100 articles on the art and craft of writing and the business of book and magazine publishing. Honours: Kottayam International Book Fair Awards, 1989, 1994. Memberships: Authors Guild of India; Kerala Book Society; Afro-Asian Book Council, New Delhi. Address: Kunnuparambil Buildings, Kurichy, Kottayam 686549, India.

PUNTER David Godfrey, b. 19 Nov 1949, London, England. Professor of English; Writer; Poet. m. Caroline Case, 5 Dec 1988, 1 son, 2 daughters. Education: BA, 1970, MA, 1974, PhD, 1984, University of Cambridge. Appointments: Lecturer in English, University of East Anglia, 1973-86; Professor and Head of Department, Chinese University of Hong Kong, 1986-88; Professor of English, University of Stirling, 1988-; Romanticism and Ideology, 1982; China and Class, 1985; The Hidden Script, 1985; Introduction to Contemporary Cultural Studies (editor), 1986; Lost in the Supermarket, 1987; Blake: Selected Poetry and Prose (editor), 1988; The Romantic Unconscious, 1989; Selected Poems of Philip Larkin (editor), 1991; Asleep at the Wheel, 1997; Gothic Pathologies, 1998. Contributions to: Hundreds of articles, essays, and poems in various publications. Honours: Fellow, Royal Society of Authors; Scottish Arts Council Award. Address: 11 Castlehill Loan, Kippen, Stirling, FK8 3DZ, Scotland.

PURDY Al(fred Wellington), b. 30 Dec 1918, Wooler, Ontario, Canada. Poet; Author; Editor. m. Eurithe Mary Jane Parkhurst, 1941, 1 son. Education: Albert College, Belleville, Ontario; Trenton Collegiate Institute. Appointments: Visiting Associate Professor, Simon Fraser University, 1970; Writer-in-Residence, Loyola College, 1973-74, University of Western Ontario, 1977-78, University of Toronto, 1987-88. Publications: Poetry: The Enchanted Echo, 1944; Pressed on Sand, 1956; The Crafte so Longer to Lerne, 1959; Poems for All the Annettes, 1962; The Blur in Between, 1963; The Cariboo Horses, 1965; North of a Summer, 1967; Wild Grape Wine, 1968; Love in a Burning Building, 1970; Hiroshima Poems, 1972; Selected Poems, 1972; On the Bearpath Sea, 1973; In Search of Owen Roblin, 1974; Sex and Death, 1973; The Poems of Al Purdy, 1976; Sun Dance at Dusk, 1976; At Marsport Drugstore, 1977; No Other Country, 1977; A Handful of Earth, 1977; Being Alive: Poems, 1958-78, 1978; No Second Spring, 1978; Moths in the Iron Curtain, 1979; The Stone Bird, 1981; Bursting into Song: An Al Purdy Omnibus, 1982; Birdwatching at the Equator, 1983; Piling Blood, 1984; Collected Poems, 1986; The Woman on the Shore, 1990; Naked with Summer in Your Mouth, 1994; Rooms for Rent in the Outer Planets: Selected Poems, 1962-94, 1996; The Gods of Nimrud Dag, 1997. Other: A Splinter in the Heart (novel), 1990; Margaret Laurence--Al Purdy: A Friendship in Letters, 1993; Starting from Ameliasburgh: Collected Prose, 1995. Honours: Governor-General's Awards, 1966, 1987; Order of Canada, 1982; Order of Ontario, 1987. Address: RR No 1, Ameliasburgh, Ontario K0K 1A0, Canada.

PURDY Carol Ann, b. 5 Jan 1943, Long Beach, California, USA. Writer; Psychotherapist. m. John Purdy, 8 June 1963, 1 son, 2 daughters. Education: BA, California State University, Long Beach, 1964; MSW, California State University, Sacramento, 1990. Publications: Iva Dunnit and the Big Wind, 1985; Least of All, 1987; The Kid Power Program, Groups for High Risk Children, 1989; Mrs Merriwether's Musical Cat, 1994; Nesuya's Basket, 1997. Memberships: Society of Children's Book Writers; National Association of Social Workers; Association for Play Therapy. Address: Kid Power, 645 Antelope Boulevard No 22, Red Bluff, CA 96080, USA.

PURDY James (Amos), b. 17 July 1923, Ohio, USA. Author; Poet; Dramatist. Education: University of Chicago; University of Puebla, Mexico. Publications: Fiction: Dream Palace, 1956; Malcolm, 1959; The Nephew, 1961; Cabot Wright Begins, 1964; Eustace Chisholm and the Works, 1967; Jeremy's Version, 1970; I Am Elijah Thrush, 1972; The House of the Solitary Maggot, 1974; Color of Darkness, 1974; In a Shallow Grave, 1976; Narrow Rooms, 1978; Mourners Below, 1981; On Glory's Course, 1984; In the Hollow of His Hand, 1986; Candles of Your Eyes, 1986; Garments the Living Wear, 1989; Collected Stories, 1956-1986, 1991; Out with the Stars, 1992; Gertrude of Stony Island Avenue, 1998. Poetry: The Running Sun, 1971; Sunshine Is an Only Child, 1973; Lessons and Complaints, 1978; Sleep Tight, 1979; The Brooklyn Branding Parlors, 1985; Collected Poems, 1990. Plays: Cracks, 1963; Wedding Finger, 1974; Two Plays, 1979; Scrap of Paper, 1981; The Berrypicker, 1981; Proud Flesh, 1981; Gertrude of Stony Island Avenue (novel), 1997. Honours: National Institute of Arts and Letters Grant, 1958; Guggenheim Fellowships, 1958, 1962; Ford Foundation Grant, 1961; Morton Dauwen Zabel Fiction Award, American Academy of Arts and Letters, 1993; Oscar Williams and Gene Durwood Poetry Award, 1995. Address: 236 Henry Street, Brooklyn, NY 11201, USA.

PURSER Philip John, b. 28 Aug 1925, Letchworth, England. Journalist; Author. m. Ann Elizabeth Goodman, 18 May 1957, 1 son, 2 daughters. Education: MA, St Andrews University, 1950. Appointments: Staff, Daily Mail, 1951-57; Television Critic, Sunday Telegraph, 1961-87. Publications: Peregrination 22, 1962; Four Days to the Fireworks, 1964; The Twentymen, 1967; Night of Glass, 1968; The Holy Father's Navy, 1971; The Last Great Tram Race, 1974; Where is He Now?, 1978; A Small Explosion, 1979; The One and Only Phyllis Dixey, 1978; Halliwell's Television Companion (with Leslie Halliwell), 1982, 2nd edition, 1986; Shooting the Hero, 1990; Poeted: The Final Quest of Edward James, 1991; Done Viewing, 1992. Contributions to: Numerous magazines and journals. Memberships: Writers Guild of Great Britain; British Academy of Film and Television Arts. Address: 10 The Green, Blakesley, Towcester, Northamptonshire NN12 8RD, England.

PURVES Libby, (Elizabeth Mary Purves), b. 2 Feb 1950, London, England. Journalist; Broadcaster; Writer. m. Paul Heiney, 2 Feb 1980, 1 son, 1 daughter. Education: BA, 1st Class Honours, University of Oxford, 1971. Appointments: Presenter-Writer, BBC, 1975-; Editor, Tatler, 1983. Publications: Adventures Under Sail (editor), 1982; Britain at Play, 1982; The Sailing Weekend Book, 1984; How Not to Be a Perfect Mother, 1987; One Summer's Grace, 1989; How Not to Raise a Perfect Child, 1991; Casting Off, 1995; A Long Walk in Wintertime, 1996; Home Leave, 1997; More Lives Than One, 1998; Holy Smoke, 1998; Regatta, 1999. Contributions to: Newspapers and magazines. Honour: Best Book of the Sea, 1984. Address: Vale Farm, Middleton, Saxmundham, Suffolk IP17 3LT, England.

PUTNAM Hilary, b. 31 July 1926, Chicago, Illinois, USA. Philosopher; Professor; Writer. m. (1) Erna Diesendruck, 1 Nov 1948, div 1962, (2) Ruth Anna Hall, 11 Aug 1962, 2 sons, 2 daughters. Education: BA in Philosophy, University of Pennsylvania, 1948; PhD in Philosophy, University of California at Los Angeles, 1951. Appointments: Instructor in Philosophy, Northwestern University, 1952-53; Assistant Professor, 1953-60, Associate Professor, 1960-61, of Philosophy, Princeton University; Professor of the Philosophy of Science, Massachusetts Institute of Technology, 1961-65; Professor of Philosophy, 1965-, Walter Beverly Pearson Professor of Modern Mathematics and Mathematical Logic, 1976-95, Cogan University Professor, 1995-, Harvard University. Publications: Philosophy of Logic, 1971; Philosophical Papers: Vol 1, Mathematics, Matter and Method, 1975, Vol 2, Mind, Language and Reality, 1975, Vol 3, Realism and Reason, 1983; Meaning and the Moral Sciences, 1978; Reason, Truth and History, 1981; Philosophy of Mathematics (editor with Paul Benacerraf), revised edition, 1983; Epistemology,

Methodology and Philosophy of Science: Essays in Honor of Carl G Hempel on the Occasion of his 80yh Birthday (editor with W K Essler and W Stegmüller), 1985; The Many Faces of Realism, 1987; Realism with a Human Face, 1990; Renewing Philosophy, 1992; Pursuits of Reason: Essays Presented to Stanley Cavell (editor with T Cohen and P Guyer), 1992; Definitions, 1993; Pragmatism: An Open Question, 1994; Words and Life, 1994. Honours: Guggenheim Fellowship: National Endowment for the Humanities Fellowship; National Science Foundation Fellowship; Rockefeller Foundation Fellowship. Memberships: American Academy of Arts and Sciences, fellow; American Philosophical Association; Association for Symbolic Logic; British Academy, corresponding fellow; Philosophy of Science Association. Address: 116 Winchester Road, Arlington, MA 02174, USA.

PUTNINS Alfreds, b. 4 Feb 1919, Perm, Latvia. m. Faunsems Senta, 27 Oct 1957, 2 sons. Education: University, 1938-1944. Appointments: Officer, 1944-45; Prisoner of War, 1945-48; Deported 1948-55; Workman, Master Builder, 1956-91; Retired. Publications: The Book of BP Chapter: Songs, 1956; Boston Immortal Flags, 1994; Selected Songs and Poems: Under the Rainbow, 1953; Sonata, 1955; The Reliance, 1986; In the Rainstorm, 1993; The Reverance, 1995; The Emotions, 1996; Disenchanted Words, 1996; The Visions of Night, 1997; Miniatures, 1998. Contributions to: Songs published at home and abroad. Honours: Literary Prizes, Toronto, 1992, Riga, 1997. Membership: Society of Latvian Writers, 1996. Address: Volguntes iela 5, dz 28, Riga, LV-1046, Latvia.

PUTNINS Pauls, b. 12 Nov 1937, Latvia. Playwright; Director; Publicist. m. Liga Liepina, 13 Mar 1969, 1 son, 1 daughter. Education: Latvian State Conservatory, 1963. Appointments: Director, Latvian Television, 1962-63; Director, Latvian Dailes (Art) Theatre, 1963-67; Director, Liepaja's Theatre, 1969-70; Chairman, Latvian Theatre Union, 1992-97; Member of Parliament, Deputy, Latvian Parliament, 1993-98. Publications: Plays: Put the Heads Together to Given Way, 1965; How to Share the Golden Goddess, 1965; Themselves Blew. Themselves Burnt, 1967; The Fool and the Ironers, 1971; The Cattle Counting, 1971; Yoo-Hoo, 1973; This Divine Knock-Knock, 1973; Invitation to Thrashing, 1974; Oh, My God! Janka Just Started Thinking..., 1975; Oh, World, You Peoples House!, 1977; Night Watchman and a Laundress, 1978; Joy to Wait, 1978; Half and Half, 1979; The Sweet Burden of Trustiness, 1980; Wedding Within Wedding, 1982; Our Sons, 1983; By the Flowers - Where the Family Gathers, 1984; I In My Boots, 1985; To Church With the Hut, 1986; When Tighten by Strange Ropes, 1991. Contributions to: Magazines. Honours: A Upisa Literary Award, 1970; A Pumpura Literary Award, 1980. Membership: Writers Union of Latvia. Address: Vesetas iela 8 dz 32, Riga, LV-1013, Lativa.

PUZO Mario, b. 15 Oct 1920, New York, New York, USA. Author; Screenwriter. m. Erika Lina Broske, 1946, 3 sons, 2 daughters. Education: New School for Social Research, New York City; Columbia University. Publications: The Dark Arena, 1955, revised edition, 1985; The Fortunate Pilgrim, 1964; The Godfather, 1969; Fools Die, 1978; The Sicilian, 1984; The Fourth K, 1991; The Last Don, 1996. Screenplays: The Godfather (with Francis Ford Coppola), 1972; The Godfather, Part II (with Francis Ford Coppola), 1974; Earthquake (with George Fox), 1974; Superman (with Robert Benton, David Newman and Leslie Newman), 1978; Superman II (with David Newman and Leslie Newman), 1981; The Godfather, Part III (with Francis Ford Coppola), 1990; Christopher Columbus: The Discovery (with Cary Bates and John Briley), 1992. Other: The Godfather Papers and Other Confessions, 1972; Inside Las Vegas, 1977. Contributions to: Many magazines. Honours: Academy Awards, 1972, 1974; Golden Globe Awards, 1973, 1990. Address: c/o Random House Inc, 201 East 50th Street, New York, NY 10022, USA.

PYBUS Rodney, b. 5 June 1938, Newcastle upon Tyne, England. Writer; Poet. m. Ellen Johnson, 24 June 1961, 2 sons. Education: BA, Honours, Classics, English, MA, 1965, Gonville and Caius College, Cambridge. Appointments: Lecturer, Macquarie University, Australia, 1976-79; Literature Officer, Cumbria, 1979-81. Publications: In Memoriam Milena, 1973; Bridging Loans, 1976; At the Stone Junction, 1978; The Loveless Letters, 1981; Talitha Cumi, 1985; Cicadas in Their Summers: New and Selected Poems, 1988; Flying Blues, 1994. Contributions to: Numerous publications. Honours: Alice Hunt Bartlett Award, Poetry Society, 1974; Arts Council Writer's Fellowships, 1982-85; National Poetry Competition Awards, 1984, 1985, 1988; 1st Prize, Peterloo Poetry Competition, 1989; Hawthornden Fellowship, 1988. Memberships: Poetry Society; Society of Authors. Address: 21 Plough Lane, Suffolk CO10 2AU, England.

PYENSON Lewis Robert, b. 26 Sept 1947, Pt Pleasant Beach, New Jersey, USA. Professor of History and Mathematics; Writer. m. Susan Ruth Sheets, 18 Aug 1973, dec 18 Aug 1998, 2 sons, 1 daughter. Education: BA, Honors, Physics, Swarthmore College, 1969; MSc Physics, University of Wyoming, 1970; PhD, History of Science, Johns Hopkins University, 1974. Appointments: Lecturer, 1973-86; Professor of History, 1986-95, University of Montreal; Professor of History and Mathematics and Dean of the Graduate School, University of Southwestern Louisiana, 1995-; Servants of Nature (with Susan Sheets-Pyenson), 1999. Publications: Neohumanism and the Persistence of Pure Mathematics in Wilhelmian Germany, 1983; The Young Einstein, 1985; Cultural Imperialism and Exact Sciences, 1985; Empire of Reason, 1989; Civilizing Mission, 1993. Contributions to: Professional journals. Honours: Sigma Xi, 1985; Royal Society of Canada, fellow, 1994. Memberships: History of Science Society. Address: Graduate School, University of Southwestern Louisiana, Lafayette, LA 70504, USA.

PYNCHON Thomas (Ruggles Jr), b. 8 May 1937, Glen Cove, Long Island, New York, USA. Author. Education: BA, Cornell University, 1958. Publications: V, 1963; The Crying of Lot 49, 1965; Gravity's Rainbow, 1973; Mortality and Mercy in Vienna, 1976; Low-lands, 1978; Slow Learner (short stories), 1984; In the Rocket's Red Glare, 1986; Vineland, 1990; Mason and Dixon, 1997. Contributions to: Periodicals. Honours: Rosenthal Foundation Award, National Institute of Arts and Letters, 1967; Howells Medal, American Academy of Arts and Letters, 1975; John D and Catharine T MacArthur Foundation Fellowship, 1988. Address: c/o Melanie Jackson Agency, 250 West 57th Street, Suite 1119, New York, NY 10107, USA.

Q

QAZI Moin, b. 4 Apr 1956, Nagpur, India. Bank Executive; Writer; Poet. m. Nahid Qazi, 30 Dec 1984, 2 sons. Education: BA, 1977, LLB, 1980, MA, 1989, Nagpur University; PhD, International University, Los Altos, 1992; DLitt, World Academy of Arts and Culture, 1993. Publications: A Wakeful Heart, 1989; The Real Face, 1992; Songs of Innocence, 1994; Voices From a Tinctured Heart, 1996; Empowerment of Women Through Microcredit, 1997. Contributions to: Numerous articles and poems in publications worldwide. Honours: Poetry commendations and prizes; International Eminent Poet, 1991; World Bank Fellow, University of Manchester, 1996; Michael Madhusudan Poetry Award, 1996. Address: Sadar, Nagpur 440 001, India.

QI FANG. See: **WANG Zhechang.**

QUANDT William B(auer), b. 23 Nov 1941, Los Angeles, California, USA. Professor of Government and Foreign Affairs; Writer. m. (1) Anna Spitzer, 21 June 1964, div 1980, (2) Helena Cobban, 21 Apr 1984, 1 daughter. Education: BA, Stanford University, 1963; PhD, Massachusetts Institute of Technology, 1968. Appointments: Researcher, Rand Corporation, Santa Monica, California, 1967-72; Staff Member, 1972-74, Senior Staff Member, 1977-79, National Security Council, Washington, DC; Associate Professor, University of Pennsylvania, 1974-76; Senior Fellow, Brookings Institution, Washington, DC, 1979-94; Senior Associate, Cambridge Energy Research Associates, Massachusetts, 1983-90; Professor of Government and Foreign Affairs, University of Virginia, 1994-. Publications: Revolution and Political Leadership: Algeria 1954-68, 1969; The Politics of Palestinian Nationalism, 1973; Decade of Decisions, 1977; Saudi Arabia in the 1980's, 1981; Camp David: Peacemaking and Politics, 1986; The Middle East: Ten Years After Camp David, 1988; The United States and Egypt, 1990; Peace Process: American Diplomacy and the Arab-Israeli Conflict Since 1967, 1994; The Algerian Crisis, with Andrew Preire, 1996; Between Ballots and Bullets: Algeria's Transition from Authoritarianism, 1998. Contributions to: Professional journals. Honours: Phi Beta Kappa, 1963; NDEA Fellow, 1963; Social Science Research Council Fellow, 1966; Council on Foreign Relations Fellow, 1972. Memberships: Council on Foreign Relations; Middle East Institute; Middle East Studies Association, president, 1987-88. Address: c/o Department of Government and Foreign Affairs, University of Virginia, Cabell Hall 255, Charlottesville, VA 22901, USA.

QUARTUS Appleton. See: **CREGAN David.**

QUERRY Ronald Burns, (Ron Querry), b. 22 Mar 1943, Washington, DC, USA. Novelist. m. Elaine Stribling Querry, 1 daughter. Education: BA, Central State University, Oklahoma, 1969; MA, New Mexico Highlands University, 1970; PhD, University of New Mexico, 1975. Appointments: Assistant Professor, New Mexico Highlands University, 1975-77; Associate Professor, Lake Erie College, 1979-83; Instructor, University of Oklahoma, 1979-83; Visiting Associate Professor, Writer-in-Residence, University of Oklahoma, Writer, 1993-. Publications: Growing Old at Willie Nelson's Picnic, 1983; I See By My Get-Up, 1987; Native Americans Struggle for Equality, 1992; The Death of Bernadette Lefthand, 1993; Bad Medicine, 1998. Contributions to: Journals, anthologies, periodicals and quarterlies. Honour: Literary Award, 1994. Membership: PEN. Literary Agent: Ralph Vicinanza Ltd. Address: 111 Eighth Avenue, New York, NY 10011, USA.

QUICK Barbara, b. 28 May 1954, Los Angeles, California, USA. Writer. m. John Quick, 1 Aug 1988. Education: BA, Honours, Literature, University of California, Santa Cruz. Publication: Northern Edge (novel), 1990, revised edition, 1995; The Stolen Child (novel), 1997. Contributions to: New York Times Book Review. Honours: 2nd Place, Ina Coolbrith Poetry Prize,

1977; Citation, B Dalton Bookseller, 1990. Address: c/o Elizabeth Wales, 108 Hayes Street, Seattle, WA 98109, USA.

QUILLER Andrew. See: **BULMER Henry Kenneth.**

QUILTER Deborah, b. 24 June 1950, San Diego, California, USA. Writer. Education: San Francisco State University, USA. Appointments: Columnist, Computer Currents; Senior Editor, Dance Spirit; Contributing Editor, Stage Directions. Publications: Repetitive Strain Injury: A Computer User's Guide, with Emil Pascarelli, 1994; The Repetitive Strain Injury Recovery Book, 1998. Contributions to: New York Times; Good Housekeeping; Columbia Journalism Review; San Francisco Chronicle and Mag. Honour: Honorary Mention, Best News Story in Non-Daily, San Francisco Press Club. Membership: Auths Guild. Literary Agent: Jonathan Dolger. Address: PO Box 1502, New York, NY 10023, USA.

QUINE Willard Van Orman, b. 25 June 1908, Akron, Ohio, USA. Professor of Philosophy; Writer. m. (1) Naomi Ann Clayton, 19 Sept 1930, 2 daughters, (2) Marjorie Boynton, 2 Sept 1948, 1 son, 1 daughter. Education: AB, Mathematics, summa cum laude, Oberlin College, 1930; AM, 1931, PhD, 1932, Philosophy, Harvard University; MA, University of Oxford, 1953. Appointments: Instructor, Tutor, 1936-41, Associate Professor, 1941-48, Professor of Philosophy, 1948-, Chairman, Department of Philosophy, 1952-53, Edgar Pierce Professor of Philosophy, 1955-78, Harvard University; Visiting Professor, University of Sao Paulo, 1942, Rockefeller University, 1968, Collège de France, 1969; George Eastman Visiting Professor, University of Oxford, 1953-54, University of Tokyo, 1959; Member, Institute for Advanced Study, Princeton University, 1956-57; Fellow, Center for Advanced Study in the Behavioral Sciences, 1958-59, Center for Advanced Studies, Wesleyan University, 1965; Gavin David Young Lecturer in Philosophy, University of Adelaide, 1959; Paul Carus Lecturer, American Philosophical Association, 1971; Hagerstrom Lecturer, University of Uppsala, 1973; Sir Henry Savile Fellow, Merton College, Oxford, 1973-74; Ferrater Mora Lecturer, Gerona, Spain, 1990. Publications: A System of Logistics, 1934; Mathematical Logic, 1940; Elementary Logic, 1941; O Sentido da Nova Logica, 1944; Methods of Logic, 1950; From a Logical Point of View, 1953; Word and Object, 1960; Set Theory and Its Logic, 1963; The Ways of Paradox, 1966; Selected Logic Papers, 1966; Ontological Relativity, 1969; Philosophy of Logic, 1970; The Web of Belief (with J S Ullian), 1970; The Roots of Reference, 1974; Theories and Things, 1981; The Time of My Life, 1985; Quiddities, 1987; La Scienza e i Dati di Senso, 1987; Pursuit of Truth, 1989; The Logic of Sequences, 1990; From Stimulus to Science, 1995. Contributions to: Scholarly books and journals. Honours: Nicholas Murray Butler Gold Medal, Columbia University, 1970; Rockefeller Fellow, Bellagio, Italy, 1975; Frantisek Polacky Gold Medal, Czech Republic, 1991; Silver Medal, Charles University, Prague, 1993; Rolf Schock Prize in Philosophy, Sweden, 1993; Kyoto Prize, 1996; Many honorary doctorates. Memberships: Academie Internationale de la Philosophie de Science; American Academy of Arts and Sciences; American Philosophical Association; Association of Symbolic Logic, president, 1953-56; British Academy, fellow; Institut de France, corresponding member; Institut Internationale de Philosophie; National Academy of Sciences; Phi Beta Kappa. Address: c/o Department of Philosophy, Emerson Hall, Harvard University, Cambridge, MA 02138, USA.

QUINN Sunny, b. 10 May 1949, Rockville Center, New York, USA. Radio Broadcaster; Broadcast Instructor. m. Don Brewer, 20 Sept 1997, 1 daughter. Education: Registered Nurse, Community College of Denver, Colorado, 1980; Connecticut School of Broadcasting, 1986. Appointments: Morning Radio Personality, WNGS 92.1 FM, West Palm Beach, Florida, 1986-93; Radio Personality, WEAT 104.3 FM, West Palm Beach, 1993-96; Morning Radio Personality, WZZR 92.7 FM, Stuart, Florida, 1996-97; Broadcast Instructor, Connecticut School of Broadcasting, West Palm Beach,

1997-99; Midday Air Personality, WEAT 104.3 FM, West Palm Beach, Florida, 1999. Publications: Put Your Mouth Where The Money Is; Radio and TV Voiceovers, 1998; Morning Mosh; Radio Games and Show Prep, 1998; Tales of the American Band; Grand Funk Railroad, 1999. Honours: Addy Awards for Radio Excellence, 1989-96; Public Radio Affairs Radio Programming, Associated Press, 1992, 1993; Radio Newsmaker Award, Florida Teacher's Association, 1992, 1993; Public Affairs Radio Programming, American Cancer Society, 1992, 1993, 1994; Radio Personality of the Year, 1992, 1993; Programming Excellence, 1994, Morning Radio Show Personality, 1996, American Women in Radio and Television. Literary Agent: Airwave Publications. Address: Airwave Publications, PO Box 753, Jupiter, FL 33468-0753, USA.

QUINNEY Richard, b. 16 May 1934, Elkhorn, Wisconsin, USA. Professor of Sociology Emeritus; Writer. Education: BS, Carroll College, 1956; MA, Sociology, Northwestern University, 1957; PhD, Sociology, University of Wisconsin, 1962. Appointments: Instructor, St Lawrence University, 1960-62; Assistant Professor, University of Kentucky, 1962-65; Associate Professor, 1965-70, Professor, 1970-73, New York University; Visiting Professor, City University of New York, 1974-75; Boston Univrsity, 1975; Visiting Professor, 1975-78, Adjunct Professor, 1978-83, Brown University; Associate Editor, Victimology, 1976-82, Contemporary Crises, 1977-90, California Sociologist, 1977-, Critical Sociology, 1978-, Western Sociological Review, 1982-, Journal of Political and Military Sociology, 1984-, Visual Sociology, 1991-, Contemporary Justice Review, 1997-; Distinguished Visiting Professor, 1978-79, Adjunct Professor, 1980-83, Boston College; Professor, University of Wisconsin at Milwaukee, 1980; Professor of Sociology, 1983-97, Professor Emeritus, 1998-, Northern Illinois University. Publications: Criminal Behavior Systems: A Typology (with Marshall B Clinard), 1967, 3rd edition (with Marshall B Clinard and John Wildeman), 1994; The Problem of Crime, 1970, 3rd edition (with John Wildeman), 1991; The Social Reality of Crime, 1970; Criminal Justice in America: A Critical Understanding (editor), 1974; Critique of Legal Order: Crime Control in Capitalist Society, 1974; Criminology: Analysis and Critique of Crime in America, 1975, 2nd edition, 1979; Class, State, and Crime: On the Theory and Practice of Criminal Justice, 1977, 2nd edition, 1980; Capitalist Society: Readings for a Critical Sociology (editor), 1979; Providence: The Reconstruction of Social and Moral Order, 1980; Marxism and Law (editor with Piers Beirne), 1982; Social Existence: Metaphysics, Marxism and the Social Sciences, 1982; Criminology as Peacemaking (editor with Harold E Pepinsky), 1991; Journey to a Far Place: Autobiographical Reflections, 1991; For the Time Being: Ethnography of Everyday Life, 1998. Contributions to: Professional journals. Honours: Edwin Sutherland Award, American Society of Criminology, 1984; Fulbright Lecture and Research Award, University College, Galway, Ireland, 1986; President's Award, Western Society of Criminology, 1992; Canterbury Visiting Fellowship, University of Canterbury, New Zealand, 1993; Fellow, American Society of Criminology, 1995. Memberships: American Society of Criminology; American Sociological Association. Address: 345 Rolfe Road, DeKalb, IL 60115, USA.

QUINTAVALLE Uberto Paolo, b. 1 Nov 1926, Milan, Italy. Writer. m. Josephine Hawke, 1970, 5 sons. Education: D Litt, University of Milan, 1949; Playwriting, Yale Drama School, 1950. Publications: La festa, 1953; Segnati a dito, 1956; Capitale Mancata, 1959; Tutti compromessi, 1961; Rito Romano, rito ambrosiano, 1964; Carolinda, 1974; Il Dio riciclato, 1989; Le Diecimila Canzoni di Putai, 1992; Fastoso Degrado, 1993; Il Memoriale di Pinocchio, 1993; Filottete, 1994; Milano Perduta, 1994; Incerca di Upamanyu, 1995; Le Erinni, 1996. Contributions to: Il Corriere Della Sera; Il Ciornale. Membership: PEN Club, Italy, secretary general. Address: Via Mangili 2, 20121 Milan, Italy.

QUIRK Sir Charles Randolph (Baron Quirk of Bloomsbury), b. 12 July 1920, Isle of Man, England.

Retired Professor of English Language and Literature; Writer. m. (1) Jean Williams, 1946, div 1979, 2 sons, (2) Gabriele Stein, 1984. Education: BA, 1947, MA, 1949, PhD, 1951, DLitt, 1961, University College, London. Appointments: Lecturer in English, 1947-54, Quain Professor of English Language and Literature, 1968-81, University College, London; Commonwealth Fund Fellow, Yale University and University of Michigan, 1951-52; Reader in English Language and Literature, 1954-58, Professor of English Language, 1958-60, University of Durham; Professor of English Language, 1960-68, Vice Chancellor, 1981-85, University of London. Publications: The Concessive Relation in Old English Poetry, 1954; Studies in Communication (with A J Ayer and others), 1955; An Old English Grammar (with C L Wrenn), 1955, enlarged edition (with S E Deskis), 1994; Charles Dickens and Appropriate Language, 1959; The Teaching of English (with A H Smith), 1959, revised edition, 1964; The Study of the Mother-Tongue, 1961; The Use of English, 1962, enlarged edition, 1968; Prosodic and Paralinguistic Features in English (with D Crystal), 1964; A Common Language (with A H Marckwardt), 1964; Investigating Linguistic Acceptability (with J Svartvik), 1966; Essays on the English Language: Mediaeval and Modern, 1968; Elicitation Experiments in English (with S Greenbaum), 1970; A Grammar of Contemporary English (with S Greenbaum, G Leech, and J Svartvik), 1972; The English Language and Images of Matter, 1972; A University Grammar in English (with S Greenbaum), 1973; The Linguist and the English Language, 1974; Old English Literature: A Practical Introduction (with V Adams and D Davy), 1975; A Corpus of English Conversation (with J Svartvik), 1980; Style and Communication in the English Language, 1982; A Comprehensive Grammar of the English Language (with S Greenbaum, G Leech and J Svartvik), 1985; English in the World (with H Widdowson), 1985; Words at Work: Lectures on Textual Structure, 1986; English in Use (with G Stein), 1990; A Student's Grammar of the English Language (with S Greenbaum), 1990; An Introduction to Standard English (with G Stein), 1993; Grammatical and Lexical Variance in English, 1995. Contributions to: Scholarly books and journals. Honours: Commander of the Order of the British Empire, 1976; Knighted, 1985; Life Peerage, 1994; Numerous honorary doctorates; Various fellowships. Memberships: Academia Europaea; British Academy, president, 1985-89. Address: c/o University College London, Gower Street, London WC1E 6BT, England.

R

RAAB Lawrence (Edward), b. 8 May 1946, Pittsfield, Massachusetts, USA. Professor of English; Poet; Writer. m. Judith Ann Michaels, 29 Dec 1968, 1 daughter. Education: BA, Middlebury College, 1968; MA, Syracuse University, 1972. Appointments: Instructor, American University, 1970-71; Lecturer, University of Michigan, 1974; Professor of English, Williams College, 1976-; Staff, Bread Loaf School of English, 1979-81, Bennington Writer's Conference, 1988, Bread Loaf Writer's Conference, 1994. Publications: Poetry: Mysteries of the Horizon, 1972; The Collector of Cold Weather, 1976; Other Children, 1986; What We Don't Know About Each Other, 1993. Contributions to: Many anthologies, scholarly journals, and periodicals. Honours: Academy of American Poets Prize, 1972; National Endowment for the Arts Fellowships, 1972, 1984; Robert Frost Fellowship, Bread Loaf Writer's Conference, 1973; Yaddo Residencies, 1979-80, 1982, 1984, 1986-90, 1994, 1996; Bess Hokin Prize, Poetry Magazine, 1983; National Poetry Series Winner, 1992; National Book Award Finalist, 1993; MacDowell Colony Residencies, 1993, 1995, 1997. Address: 139 Bulkley Street, Williamstown, MA 01267, USA.

RABAN Jonathan, b. 14 June 1942, Fakenham, Norfolk, England. Writer; Dramatist. Education: BA, University of Hull, 1963. Publications: The Technique of Modern Fiction: Essays in Practical Criticism, 1968; Mark Twain: Huckleberry Finn, 1969; Technique of Modern Fiction, 1969; The Society of the Poem, 1971; Soft City, 1974; Robert Lowell's Poems: A Selection (editor), 1974; Arabia: A Journey Through the Labyrinth, 1979; Old Glory: An American Voyage, 1981; Foreign Land (novel), 1985; Coasting, 1986; For Love and Money: A Writing Life, 1987; God, Man and Mrs Thatcher, 1989; Hunting Mr Heartbreak, 1991; The Oxford Book of the Sea (editor), 1992; Bad Land: An American Romance, 1996. Other: Plays for radio and television. Contributions to: Harper's; Esquire; New Republic; New York Review of Books; Outside; Granta; New York Times Book Review; Vogue. Honours: Heinemann Award, Royal Society of Literature, 1982; Thomas Cook Awards, 1982, 1992; National Book Critics Circle Award, 1997. Memberships: Royal Society of Literature, fellow; Society of Authors. Address: c/o Aitken Stone and Wylie, 29 Fernshaw Road, London SW10 0TG, England.

RABE Berniece, b. 11 Jan 1928, Parma, Missouri, USA. Author. m. 30 July 1946, 3 sons, 1 daughter. Education: BSEd, National College; Graduate work in Psychology and Administration, Northern Illinois University and Roosevelt University; MA, Columbia College, Chicago. Appointments: Writing Instructor, Columbia College, Chicago; Consultant, Missouri Council of the Arts. Publications: Rass, 1973; Naomi, 1975; The Girl Who Had No Name, 1977; The Orphans, 1978; Who's Afraid, 1980; Margaret's Moves, 1987; A Smooth Move, 1987; Rehearsal for the Bigtime, 1988; Where's Chimpy, 1988; Tall Enough to Own the World, 1988; Magic Comes In It's Time, 1993; The Legend of the First Candy Cares, 1994. Picture Books: The Balancing Girl, 1982; Can They See Me; Two Peas in a Pod. Other: 2 film scripts. Contributions to: Short stories and articles. Honours: Honor Book, 1975; Golden Kite Award, 1977, National Society of Children's Book Writers; Midland Author's Award, 1978; Notable Book of the Year, American Library Association, 1982; National Children's Choice Award, 1987. Memberships: Society of Midland Authors; Off Campus Writers; Fox Valley Writers. Address: Denton, TX 76205, USA.

RABE David (William), b. 10 Mar 1940, Dubuque, Iowa, USA. Dramatist; Screenwriter; Author. m. (1) Elizabeth Pan, 1969, div, 1 child, (2) Jill Clayburgh, Mar 1979. Education: BA in English, Loras College, 1962; MA, Villanova University, 1968. Appointments: Feature Writer, Register, New Haven, 1969-70; Assistant Professor, Villanova University, 1970-72. Publications: Plays: The Basic Training of Pavlo Hummel, 1971; Sticks and Bones,

1971; The Orphan, 1973; In the Boom Boom Room, 1973; Burning, 1974; Streamers, 1976; Goose and Tomtom, 1976; Hurlyburly, 1984; Those the River Keeps, 1990; Crossing Guard, 1994. Screenplays: I'm Dancing as Fast as I Can, 1982; Streamers, 1983; Casualties of War, 1989; State of Grace, 1990; The Firm, 1993. Novel: Recital of the Dog, 1992. Honours: Rockefeller Foundation Grant, 1969; Associated Press Award, 1970; Drama Desk Award, 1971; Drama Guild Award, 1971; Elizabeth Hull-Kate Warriner Award, Dramatists Guild, 1971; Obie Award, 1971; Outer Critics' Circle Award, 1972; Tony Award, 1972; American Academy of Arts and Letters Awards, 1974, 1976; Guggenheim Fellowship, 1976; New York Drama Critics' Circle Award, 1976. Address: c/o Grove-Atlantic, 841 Broadway, 4th Floor, New York, NY 10003, USA.

RABIE Mohamed, b. 5 June 1940, Yazour, Palestine. Professor; Author. m. Maha El-Halabie, 23 June 1969, 1 son, 2 daughters. Education: BSc, Agricultural Economics, 1962; MA, Rural Sociology, 1965; MA, Economics, 1968; PhD, Economics, 1970; Studies in Jordan, Egypt, Germany and USA. Appointments: Assistant Professor, Texas Southern University, Houston, 1968; Associate Professor, Kuwait University, 1973; Adjunct Professor, Georgetown University, Johns Hopkins University, 1982, 1984, 1986. Publications: 16 books including: Economics and Society (Arabic), 1973; The Politics of Foreign Aid (English), 1987; The Other Side of Arab Defeat (Arabic), 1987; The Making of US Foreign Policy (Arabic), 1990; The New World Order (English), 1992; Conflict Resolution and Ethnicity (English), 1994; US-PLO Dialogue (English and Arabic), 1995. Contributions to: Several articles to journals in the USA, Germany, Austria and Arab countries. Honours: Kuwait's Council and Higher Art and Literature; Von Humboldt, Stiftung, Germany. Memberships: Arab Thought Forum; Contemporary Authors; Palestinian Writers and Journalists Association. Address: 7416 Helmsdale Road, Bethesda, MD 20817, USA.

RACHLIN Nahid, b. 6 June 1944, Abadan, Iran. Writer; Instructor. m. Howard Rachlin, 1 daughter. Education: BA, Psychology, Lindenwood College, St Charles, Missouri; Creative Writing, Columbia University. Appointments: New York University, School of Continuing Education, 1978-90; Marymount Manhattan College, 1986-87; Hofstra University, 1988-90; Yale University, 1989-90; Hunter College, 1990; Barnard College, 1991-. Publications: Foreigner, 1978; John Murray, 1978; Married to a Stranger, 1983; Veils, 1992. Contributions to: Reviews, journals and magazines. Honours: Doubleday-Columbia Fellowship; Stegner Fellowship, Stanford University; National Endowment for the Arts Grant; Bennet Certificate Award; PEN Syndicated Fiction Project. Membership: PEN. Address: 501 East 87th Street, Apt PHC, New York, NY 10128, USA.

RADLEY Sheila. See: ROBINSON Sheila (Mary).

RAE Hugh Crauford, (James Albany, Robert Crawford, R B Houston, Stuart Stern, Jessica Stirling), b. 22 Nov 1935, Glasgow, Scotland. Novelist. m. Elizabeth Dunn, 3 Sept 1960, 1 daughter. Publications: Skinner, 1965; Night Pillow, 1966; A Few Small Bones, 1968; The Saturday Epic, 1970; Harkfast, 1976; Sullivan, 1978; Haunting at Waverley Falls, 1980; Privileged Strangers, 1982. As Jessica Stirling: The Spoiled Earth, 1974; The Hiring Fair, 1976; The Dark Pasture, 1978; The Deep Well at Noon, 1980; The Blue Evening Gone, 1982; The Gates at Midnight, 1983; Treasures on Earth, 1985; Creature Comforts, 1986; Hearts of Gold, 1987; The Good Provider, 1988; The Asking Price, 1989; The Wise Child, 1990; The Welcome Light, 1991; Lantern for the Dark, 1992; Shadows on the Shore, 1993; The Penny Wedding, 1994; The Marrying Kind, 1995; The Workhouse Girl, 1996; The Island Wife, 1997. As James Albany: Warrior Caste, 1982; Mailed Fist, 1982; Deacon's Dagger, 1982; Close Combat, 1983; Matching Fire, 1983; Last Bastion, 1984 Borneo Story, 1984. Membership: Scottish Association of Writers. Address: Drumore Farm Cottage, Balfron Station, Stirlingshire, Scotland.

RAE John Malcolm, b. 20 Mar 1931, London, England. Writer. Education: MA, Sidney Sussex College, Cambridge, 1955; PhD, King's College, London. Publications: The Custard Boys, 1960; Conscience and Politics, 1970; The Golden Crucifix, 1974; The Treasure of Westminster Abbey, 1975; Christmas is Coming, 1976; Return to the Winter Place, 1979; The Third Twin: A Ghost Story, 1980; The Public School Revolution, 1981; Letters from School, 1987; Too Little, Too Late?, 1989; Delusions of Grandeur, 1993; Letters to Parents, 1998. Contributions to: Encounter; Times Literary Supplement; Times Educational Supplement; Times; Sunday Telegraph. Honour: United Nations Award for Film Script, 1962. Address: 25 Cedar Lodge, Lythe Hill Park, Haslemere, Surrey GU27 3TD, England.

RAFFEL Burton (Nathan), b. 27 Apr 1928, New York, New York, USA. Distinguished Professor of Humanities and Professor of English; Lawyer; Writer; Poet; Editor; Translator. m. Elizabeth Clare Wilson, 16 Apr 1974, 3 sons, 3 daughters. Education: BA, Brooklyn College, 1948; MA, Ohio State University, 1949; JD, Yale University, 1958. Appointments: Lecturer, Brooklyn College, 1950-51; Editor, Foundation News, 1960-63; Instructor, 1964-65, Assistant Professor, 1965-66, State University of New York at Stony Brook; Associate Professor, State University of New York at Buffalo, 1966-68; Visiting Professor, Haifa University, 1968-69; York University, Toronto, 1972-75; Emory University, 1974; Professor of English and Classics, University of Texas at Austin, 1969-71; Senior Tutor (Dean), Ontario College of Art, Toronto, 1971-72; Professor of English, 1975-87, Lecturer in Law, 1986-87, University of Denver; Editor-in-Chief, Denver Quarterly, 1976-77; Contributing Editor, Humanities Education, 1983-87; Director, Adirondack Mountain Foundation, 1987-89; Advisory Editor, The Literary Review, 1987-; Distinguished Professor of Humanities and Professor of English, University of Southwestern Louisiana, 1989-. Publications: Non-Fiction: The Development of Modern Indonesian Poetry, 1967; The Forked Tongue: A Study of the Translation Process, 1971; Introduction to Poetry, 1971; Why Re-Create?, 1973; Robert Lowell, 1981; T S Eliot, 1982; American Victorians: Explorations in Emotional History, 1984; How to Read a Poem, 1984; Ezra Pound: The Prime Minister of Poetry, 1985; Politicians, Poets and Con Men, 1986; The Art of Translating Poetry, 1988; Artists All: Creativity, the University, and the World, 1991; From Stress to Stress: An Autobiography of English Prosody, 1992; The Art of Translating Prose, 1994. Fiction: After Such Ignorance, 1986; Founder's Fury (with Elizabeth Raffel), 1988; Founder's Fortune (with Elizabeth Raffel), 1989. Poetry: Mia Poems, 1968; Four Humours, 1979; Changing the Angle of the Sun-Dial, 1984; Grice, 1985; Evenly Distributed Rubble, 1985; Man as a Social Animal, 1986. Other: Numerous translations. Contributions to: Professional journals. Honours: Frances Steloff Prize for Fiction, 1978; American-French Foundation Translation Prize, 1991; Several grants. Memberships: National Faculty; Phi Kappa Phi. Address: 203 South Mannering Avenue, Lafayette, LA 70508, USA.

RAGAN James, b. 19 Dec 1944, Pennsylvania, USA. Poet; Dramatist; Director; Professor. m. Debora Ann Skovranko, 29 May 1982, 1 son, 2 daughters. Education: BA, Vincent College, 1966; PhD, Ohio University, 1971. Appointments: Professor and Director, Professional Writing Program, University of Southern California at Los Angeles, 1981-; Visiting Professor, CALTECH, 1989-; Poet-in-Residence, Charles University, Prague, 1993-. Publications: In the Talking Hours, 1979; Womb-Weary, 1990; Yevgeny Yevtushenko: The Collected Poems (editor), 1991; The Hunger Wall, 1995; Lusions, 1996; The World Shouldering I, 1999; The Last Story of the Century (screenwriter), 1999. Contributions to: Anthologies, reviews, quarterlies, journals, and magazines. Honours: Humanitarian Award, Swan Foundation, Pittsburgh, 1972; NEA, 1972; Fulbright Fellow, 1985, 1988; Co-Winner, Gertrude Claytor Award, Poetry Society of America, 1987; Honorary Doctorate of Humane Letters, St Vincent College, 1990; Medal of Merit for Poetry, Ohio University, 1990; Telly Award, Poet's

Corner, BHTV, 1996; Honorary Member, Russian Academy of Arts and Sciences, 1997. Memberships: Associated Writing Programs; Modern Language Association; Modern Poetry Association; PEN; Phi Kappa Phi; Poetry Society of America; Writers Guild of America, West. Address: 1516 Beverwil Drive, Los Angeles, CA 90035, USA.

RAIJADA Rajendrasinh, b. 1 July 1943, Sondarda, India. Educator; Writer; Poet. m. Gulabkumari Raijada, 21 Feb 1969, 2 sons, 1 daughter. Education: BEd, 1973, MA, 1975, Saurashtra University, Rajkot; PhD, Sardar Patel University, Vallabhvidyanagar, 1979. Appointments: Language Expert, 1975-82, Central Committee Member, 1997-2000, Gujarat State Textbook Board, Gandhinagar. Publications: Radha Madhav (translation from Hindi), 1970; Farva avyo chhun (poems), 1976; Gulmahor ni niche (short stories), 1977; Rahasyavad (essays), 1980; Hun, Kali chhokari ane Suraj (poems), 1982; Darsdhan ane Itishas (collection of articles), 1983; Sant Parampara Vimarsh (criticism), 1989; Tantra Sadhana, Maha Panth Ane Anya Lekho (collection of articles), 1993. Address: Sondarda, via Kevadra 362227, Gujarat, India.

RAINE Craig (Anthony), b. 3 Dec 1944, Shildon, County Durham, England. Poet; Writer. m. Ann Pasternak Slater, 27 Apr 1972, 3 sons, 1 daughter. Education: Honours Degree in English Language and Literature, 1966, BPhil, 1968, Exeter College, Oxford. Appointments: Lecturer, Exeter College, Oxford, 1971-72, Lincoln College, Oxford, 1974-75; Christ's Church, Oxford, 1976-79; Books Editor, New Review, London, 1977-78; Editor, Quarto, London, 1979-80; Poetry Editor, New Statesman, London, 1981, Faber & Faber, London, 1981-91; Fellow, New College, Oxford, 1991-. Publications: Poetry: The Onion, Memory, 1978; A Journey to Greece, 1979; A Martian Sends a Postcard Home, 1979; A Free Translation, 1981; Rich, 1984, 1953: A Version of Racine's Andromaque, 1990; History: The Home Movie, 1994; Clay: Whereabouts Unknown, 1996. Other: The Electrification of the Soviet Union (libretto), 1986; A Choice of Kipling's Prose (editor), 1987; Haydn and the Valve Trumpet (essays), 1990. Contributions to: Periodicals. Honours: 1st Prizes, Cheltenham Festival Poetry Competition, 1977, 1978; 2nd Prize, National Poetry Competition, 1978; Prudence Farmer Awards, New Statesman, 1979, 1980; Cholmondeley Award, 1983. Memberships: PEN; Royal Society of Literature. Address: c/o New College, Oxford OX1 3BN, England.

RAINE Kathleen (Jessie), b. 14 June 1908, London, England. Poet; Critic; Editor; Translator. m. (1) Hugh Skyes Davies, div, (2) Charles Madge, div, 1 son, 1 daughter. Education: MA, Girton College, Cambridge, 1929. Appointment: Founder, Temenos Academy, 1990. Publications: Poetry: Stone and Flower: Poems, 1935-1943, 1943; Living in Time, 1946; The Pythoness and Other Poems, 1948; Selected Poems, 1952, revised edition, 1989; The Year One, 1953; Collected Poems of Kathleen Raine, 1956; The Hollow Hill and Other Poems, 1960-64, 1965; Ninfa Revisited, 1968; Six Dreams and Other Poems, 1968; A Question of Poetry, 1969; The Lost Country, 1971; Three Poems Written in Ireland, 1973; On a Deserted Shore, 1973; The Oracle in the Heart and Other Poems, 1975-1978, 1980; Collected Poems, 1935-1980, 1981; The Presence: Poems, 1984-87, 1988; Living with Mystery: Poems, 1987-1991, 1992. Non-Fiction: Poetry in Relation to Traditional Wisdom, 1958; Blake and England, 1960; Defending Ancient Springs, 1967; The Written Word, 1967; Blake and Tradition, 2 volumes, 1968; William Blake, 1970; Faces of Day and Night (autobiography), 1972; Yeats, the Tarot, and the Golden Dawn, 1972, revised edition, 1976; Farewell Happy Fields: Memories of Childhood, 1973; Death-in-Life and Life-in-Death: Cuchulain Comforted and News for the Delphic Oracle, 1974; A Place, a State, 1974; David Jones, Solitary Perfectionist, 1974, enlarged edition, 1975; The Land Unknown (autobiography), 1975; The Lion's Mouth: Concluding Chapters of Autobiography, 1977; From Blake to a Vision, 1978; David Jones and the Actually Loved and Known, 1978; Blake and the New Age, 1979; Cecil Collins, Painter of Paradise, 1979; What is Man?, 1980; The Human Face

of God: William Blake and the Book of Job, 1982; The Inner Journey of the Poet and Other Papers, 1982; Yeats the Initiate: Essays on Certain Themes in the Writings of W B Yeats, 1984; Poetry and the Frontiers of Consciousness, 1985; The English Language and the Indian Spirit: Correspondence between Kathleen Raine and K D Sethna, 1986; India Seen Afar, 1991; Golgonooza, City of Imagination: Last Studies in William Blake, 1991. Editor: Aspects de la litterature anglaise (with Max-Pol Fouchet), 1947; The Letters of Samuel Taylor Coleridge, 1952; Selected Poems and Prose of Coleridge, 1957; Coleridge: Letters, 1969; Selected Writings of Thomas Taylor the Platonist (with George Mills Harper), 1969; A Choice of Blake's Verse, 1974; Shelley, 1974. Contributions to: Books and journals. Honours: Harriet Monroe Memorial Prize, 1952; Arts Council Award, 1953; Oscar Blumenthal Prize, 1961; Cholmondeley Award, 1970; W H Smith & Son Literary Award, 1972; Foreign Book Prize, France, 1979; Queen's Gold Medal for Poetry, 1993. Address: 47 Paultons Square, London SW3, England.

RAJA P, b. 7 Oct 1952, Pondicherry, India. Writer; Poet; Lecturer in English. m. Periyanayaki, 6 May 1976, 2 sons, 1 daughter. Education: BA, English, 1973; MA, English Language and Literature, 1975; PhD, Indian Writing in English, 1992. Appointments: Literary Editor, Pondicherry Today; Editorial Associate, Indian Book Chronicle. Publications: From Zero to Infinity (poems), 1987; Folktales of Pondicherry, 1987; A Concise History of Pondicherry, 1987; Tales of Mulla Nasruddin, 1989; The Blood and Other Stories, 1991; M P Pandit: A Peep Into His Past, 1993; Many Worlds of Manoj Das, 1993; The Best Woman in My Life and Other Stories, 1994; Sudden Tales the Folks Told, 1995; For Your Ears Only (essays), 1997; Kozhi Grandpa's Chickens (Short-stories, 1997; To the Lonely Grey Hair (poem), 1997. Contributions to: Numerous journals. Honours: Literary Award, Pondicherry University, 1987; International Eminent Poet Award, Madras, 1988; Michael Madhusudan Academy Award, Calcutta, 1991. Address: 74 Poincare Street, Olandai-Keerapalayam, Pondicherry 605004, India.

RAJAN Tilottama, b. 1 Feb 1951, New York, New York, USA. Professor; Writer; Poet. Education: BA, Honours, Trinity College, Toronto, 1972; MA, 1973, PhD, 1977, University of Toronto. Appointments: Assistant Professor, Huron College, University of Western Ontario, 1977-80, Queen's University, 1980-83; Associate Professor, Queen's University, 1983-85; Professor, University of Wisconsin at Madison, 1985-90; Professor, 1990-, Director, Centre for the Study of Theory and Criticism, 1995-, University of Western Ontario. Publications: Myth in a Metal Mirror, 1967; Dark Interpreter: The Discourse of Romanticism, 1980; The Supplement of Reading, 1990; Intersections: Nineteenth Century Philosophy and Contemporary Theory, 1995. Contributions to: Professional journals. Honours: Guggenheim Fellowship, 1987-88; Fellow, Royal Society of Canada, 1994-. Memberships: Canadian Comparative Literature Association; University of Teachers of English; Keats-Shelley Association; Modern Language Association of America; North American Society for the Study of Romanticism; Wordsworth-Coleridge Association. Address: 870 Wellington Street, London, Ontario N6A 5S7, Canada.

RAJANNA. See: NAGARAJA RAO C K.

RAJIC Negovan, b. 24 June 1923, Belgrade, Yugoslavia (Canadian citizen). Writer. m. Mirjana Knezevic, 28 Mar 1970, 1 son, 1 daughter. Education: University of Belgrade, 1945-46; Diplome d'étudese techniques superieures, 1962; Diploma in Electrical Engineering, 1968, Conservatoire des Arts et Metiers, France. Appointments: Fought with Resistance during World War II; Research Engineer, Physical Laboratory, Ecole Polytechnique de Paris, 1956-63; Researcher in Electronics, France, 1963-69; Settled in Canada, 1969; Professor of Mathematics, Cegep Trois Rivieres, to 1987. Publications: Les Hommes-taupes, 1978, English translation as The Mole Men, 1980; Propos d'un vieux

radoteur, 1982, English translation as The Master of Strappado, 1984; Sept Roses pour une boulangere, 1987, English translation as Seven Roses for a Baker, 1988; Service penitentiarire national, 1988, English translation as Shady Business, 1989. Contributions to: Numerous publications. Honours: Prix Esso du Cercle du Livre de France, 1978; Prix Air Canada for Best Short Story, 1980; Prix Slobodan Yovanovitch Association des ecrivains et artistes serbes en exile, 1984; Prix litteraire de Trois-Rivières, 1988. Memberships: Association of Serbian Writers, Belgrade, honorary member; Association of Writers of Quebec; PEN International. Address: 300 Dunnant, Trois-Rivières, Quebec, G8Y 2W9, Canada.

RAJU Chethput, b. 28 Jan 1916, Vellore, North Arcot District, Tamil Nadu, India. Retired Commercial Executive and Manager; Poet. m. Eashwari Raju, 14 Nov 1947, 2 sons. Education: BA, English, 1957. Publications: This Modern Age and Other Poems, 1954; No Exit, 1970. Contributions to: Anthologies and reviews. Honours: Prizewinner, All India Poetry Contests, 1991, 1992. Membership: PWN India. Address: 3 Ganga Vihar, 318 Bhalchandra Road, Matunga, CR, Bombay 400 019, India.

RAKOFF Alvin Abraham, b. 6 Feb 1927, Toronto, Canada. Director (Film, TV, Theatre). m. Jacqueline Hill, 4 June, dec, 1 son, 1 daughter. Education: BA, University of Toronto; Graduated, Class of 1949, 1948. Appointments: Reporter, Northern Daily News, 1949; News Editor, New Toronto Advertiser, 1950-52; Producer, Director, BBC London, 1953-57; Freelance Producer; Director, Screen Writer. Publications: & Gillian, novel, 1996; TV Plays: A Flight of Fancy, 1952; The Troubled Air, 1953; Thunder in the Realm, 1955; TV Adaptations: Waiting for Gillian, 1954; The Lover, 1954; Our Town, 1957; Summer and Smoke, 1971; Shadow of a Gunman, 1973; Harleyquinade, 1973; In Praise of Love, 1975; The Promise, 1976; The Dance of Spark, 1976; Romeo & Juliet, 1978; Feature Films: Say Hello to Yesterday, 1970; City on Fire, 1978. Literary Agent: Christopher Little. Address: 1 The Orchard, Chiswick, London W4 1J2, England.

RAKUSA Ilma, b. 2 Jan 1946, Rimavská Sobota, Slovakia. Writer; Translator; Literary Critic. 1 son. Education: PhD, Slavic Languages and Literatures, University of Zurich, 1971. Publications: Die Insel, 1982; Miramar, 1986; Steppe, 1990; Jim, 1993; Farbband und Randfigur, 1994; Ein Strich durch alles, 1997; Anthology: Einsamkeiten, 1996; Translations of Marguerite Duras, Marina Tsvetaeva, Danilo Kiš and others. Honours: Petrarca Award Translation, 1991; Schiller Award, 1998; Deutsche Akademie für Sprache und Dichtung, Darmstadt; Leipziger Buchpreis zur Europäischen Verständigung, Anerkennungs, 1998; Schiller Award, 1998. Address: Richard Kissling-Weg 3, CH-8044 Zürich, Switzerland.

RAMA RAO Vadapalli Vijaya Bhaskara, b. 1 Jan 1938, Srikakulam District, A P, India. Educator. m. Ramani Rama Rao, 15 Apr 1959, 1 son, 3 daughters. Education: BA, Economics, 1957; BA, English, 1958; MA, English, 1961; Diploma in Teaching English, 1966; Diploma in French, 1979; PhD, 1980. Publications: In English: Poosapati Ananda Gajapati Raju (biography), 1985; Tapaswi (novel), 1989; Graham Greene's Comic Vision (criticism), 1990; Into That Heaven of Freedom (novel), 1991; Warm Days Will Never Cease. Translation: Trapped (novel, from English to Telugu), 1991; 6 novels in Telugu: Sparasarekhalu, 1977; Neetikireetalu, 1977; Maguvalu - Manasulu, 1980; Gaalipadagalu - Deepakalikalu, 1981; Tapaswi, 1985; The Joy of the Divine, 1994; The Drunken Boat, 1994; Malapalli (English translation), 1994; Unnava, Sahitya Akademi (monograph), 1994. Contributions to: 15 literary reviews in English and about 125 short fiction in Telugu to magazines and journals; About 400 English and about 20 Telugu feature and newspaper articles. Address: 19-5-13 Kanukurti Street, Vizianagaram 535 002, India.

RAMA RAU Santha, (Rama Rau Wattles), b. 24 Jan 1923, Madras, India. Freelance Writer. m. (1) Faubion

Bowers, 24 Oct 1951, div 1966, 1 son, (2) Gurdon W Wattles, 1970. Education: BA, Honours, Wellesley College, USA, 1945. Publications: Home to India, 1945; East of Home, 1950; This India, 1953; Remember the House, 1955; View to the South-East, 1957; My Russian Journey, 1959; A Passage to India (dramatisation of E M Forster's novel), 1962; Gifts of Passage, 1962; The Cooking of India, 1970; The Adventuress, 1970; A Princess Remembers, 1976; An Inheritance, 1977. Contributions to: Numerous journals and magazines. Honours: Honorary Degrees, Bates College, 1960; Roosevelt University, 1962, Brandeis University, 1962, Russell Sage College, 1965; Mlle Mag Merit Award, 1965; Association of Indians in America Award, 1977. Address: c/o William Morris Agency, 1350 6th Avenue, New York, NY 10019, USA.

RAMAMURTI Krishnamurthy Sitaraman, (Madhuram Ramamurti), b. 4 Nov 1930, Madras, India. Professor of English; Dean. m. Rajesnari Ramamurti, 4 July 1958, 2 daughters. Education: BSc, Physics, 1950, MA, English Language and Literature, 1954, University of Madras; MA, English Literature, Muslim University, Aligarh, 1963; Diploma, Teaching of English, Central Institute of English, Hyderabad; PhD, Madurai University, 1975. Appointments: Lecturer, English, St Aloysius College, Mangalore, 1954-65; Professor, Head, Department of English, Sri Palaniasndowar Arts College, Palmi, 1965-76; Lecturer, 1976-78, Reader, 1978-84, Professor, 1984-91, Dean, College Development Council, 1991-, Bharathidasan University, Tiruchirapalli. Publications: Thomas Kyd: The Spanish Tragedy (editor), 1978; Vazhithunai (novel), 1980; Perspectives on Modern English Prose, 1985; Rise of the Indian Novel, 1986; Variety in Short Stories, 1988. Contributions to: Newspapers, reviews and journals. Honour: Prize for novel, 1980. Memberships: Indian Association of English Teachers; Comparative Literature Association of India; Indian Association of Canadian Studies, executive committee. Address: Bharatidasan University, Tiruchirapalli 620024, India.

RAMDIN Ronald Andrew, b. 20 June 1942, Marabella, Trinidad. Historian; Writer; Lecturer. m. Irma de Freitas, 20 Dec 1969, 1 son. Education: Diploma in Speech and Drama, New Era Academy of Drama and Music, 1963; Diploma in Industrial Relations and Trade Union Studies, University of Middlesex, 1977; BSc, Economics, London School of Ecnomics and Political Science, 1982; DLitt, University of London, 1995. Publications: From Chattel Slave to Wage Earner, 1982; Introductory Text: The Black Triangle, 1984; The Making of the Black Working Class in Britain, 1987; Paul Robeson: The Man and His Mission, 1987; World in View: West Indies, 1990; Arising From Bondage: A History of East Indians in the Caribbean 1838-1991; The Other Middle Passage, 1995. Contributions to: Anglo-British Review; City Limits; Dragon's Teeth; Race Today; Caribbean Times; West Indian Digest; History Workshop Journal. Honours: Scarlet Ibis Medal, Gold Award, Trinidad and Tobago High Commission, London, 1990; Hansib, Caribbean Times, Community Award, Britain, 1990. Memberships: Society of Authors; Royal Historical Society. Address: The British Library, Humanities and Social Science Section, Great Russell Street, London WC1B 3DG, England.

RAMKE Bin, b. 19 Feb 1947, Port Neches, Texas, USA. Professor of English; Editor; Poet. m. 31 May 1967, 1 son. Education: Louisiana State University, 1970; MA, University of New Orleans, 1971; PhD, Ohio University, 1975. Appointments: Professor of English, Columbus University, Georgia, 1976-85, University of Denver, 1985-; Editor, Contemporary Poetry Series, University of Georgia Press, 1984-; Poetry Editor, 1985-, Editor, 1994-, The Denver Quarterly. Publications: The Difference Between Night and Day, 1978; White Monkeys, 1981; The Language Student, 1987; The Erotic Light of Gardens, 1989; Massacre of the Innocents, 1995. Contributions to: Reviews, quarterlies, and journals. Honours: Yale Younger Poets Award, 1977; Texas Institute of Arts and Letters Award for Poetry, 1978; Iowa Poetry Award, 1995. Memberships: Associated Writing

Programs; National Book Critics' Circle; PEN, American Centre. Address: c/o Department of English, University of Denver, Denver, CO 80208, USA.

RAMNEFALK (Sylvia) Marie Louise, b. 21 Mar 1941, Stockholm Sweden. Poet; Literary Critic. Education: FK, 1964, FL, 1968, FD, 1974 (Equivalent to PhD, Literature), University of Stockholm. Appointment: Literary Critic, several newspapers and magazines. Publications: 14 volumes in Swedish, 1971-97. Contributions to: Various periodicals. Honours: Several scholarships. Memberships: Several, including Swedish PEN. Address: Vastra Valhallavagen 25A, S-182 66 Djursholm, Sweden.

RAMPERSAD Arnold, b. 13 Nov 1941, Trinidad, West Indies. Professor of English; Writer. m. 1985, 1 child. Education: BA, MA, Bowling Green State University; MA, PhD, Harvard University. Publications: Melville's Israel Potter: A Pilgrimage and Progress, 1969; The Art and Imagination of W E B Dubois, 1976; Life of Langston Hughes, Vol I, 1902-1941: I Too Sing America, 1986, Vol II, 1941-1967: I Dream a World, 1988; Slavery and the Literary Imagination (co-editor), 1989; Days of Grace: A Memoir (with Arthur Ashe), 1993. Honours: Ansfield Wolf Book Award in Race Relations, Cleveland Foundation, 1987; Clarence L Hotte Prize, Phelps Stoke Fund, 1988; Pulitzer Prize Finalist, 1989; American Book Award, 1990. Address: Department of English, Princeton University, Princeton, NJ 08544, USA.

RAMPLING Anne. See: RICE Anne.

RAMSAY Jay. See: RAMSAY-BROWN John Andrew.

RAMSAY-BROWN John Andrew, (Jay Ramsay), b. 20 Apr 1958, Guildford, Surrey, England. Poet; Writer; Editor; Translator. Education: BA, Honours, English Language and Literature, Pembroke College, Oxford, 1980; Foundation Year Diploma in Psycho-synthesis, London Institute, 1987. Publications: Psychic Poetry: A Manifesto, 1985; Angels of Fire (co-editor), 1986; New Spiritual: Selected Poems, 1986; Trwyn Meditations, 1987; The White Poem, 1988; Transformation: The Poetry of Spiritual Consciousness (editor), 1988; The Great Return, books 1 to 5, 2 volumes, 1988; Transmissions, 1989; Strange Days, 1990; Journey to Eden (with Jenny Davis), 1991; For Now (with Geoffrey Godbert), 1991; The Rain, the Rain, 1992; St Patrick's Breastplate, 1992; Tao Te Ching: A New Translation, 1993; I Ching, 1995; Kuan Yin, 1995; Chuang Tzu (with Martin Palmer), 1996; Alchemy: The Art of Transformation, 1996; Earth Ascending: An Anthology of New and Living Poetry (editor), 1996; Kingdom of the Edge: New and Selected poems 1980-1998. Contributions to: Periodicals. Memberships: College of Psychic Studies, London; Poetry Society; Psychosynthesis Education and Trust, London. Address: c/o Susan Mears, The Old Church, Monkton Deverill, near Warminster, Wiltshire BA12 7EX, England.

RAMSEY Jarold (William), b. 1 Sept 1937, Bend, Oregon, USA. Professor Emeritus; Poet; Writer; Dramatist. m. Dorothy Ann Quinn, 16 Aug 1959, 1 son, 2 daughters. Education: BA, Honours, English, University of Oregon, 1959; PhD, English Literature, University of Washington, 1966. Appointments: Acting Instructor, University of Washington, 1962-65; Assistant Professor, 1965-70, Associate Professor, 1970-80, Professor, 1980-97, Professor Emeritus, 1997-, University of Rochester; Visiting Professor of English, University of Victoria, British Columbia, 1974, 1975-76. Publications: Poetry: The Space Between Us, 1970; Love in an Earthquake, 1973; Dermographia, 1983; Hand-Shadows, 1989. Non-Fiction: Coyote Was Going There: Indian Literature of the Oregon Country, 1977; Reading the Fire: Essays in the Traditional Indian Literatures of the Far East, 1983, new and expanded edition, 1999. Editor: The Stories We Tell: An Anthology of Oregon Folk Literature (with Suzi Jones), 1994. Contributions to: Anthologies, reviews, quarterlies, and journals. Honours: National Endowment for the Arts Grant, 1974, and Fellowship, 1975; Ingram Merrill Foundation Grant, 1975; Don Walker

Award for Best Essay on Western Literature, 1978; Helen Bullis Award for Poetry, 1984; Quarterly Review International Poetry Prize, 1989. Membership: Modern Language Association. Address: c/o Department of English, University of Rochester, Rochester, NY 14627, USA.

RANCE Joseph. See: HOYLE Trevor.

RAND Peter, b. 23 Feb 1942, San Francisco, California, USA. Writer. m. Bliss Inui, 19 Dec 1976, 1 son. Education: MA, Johns Hopkins University, 1975. Appointments: Fiction Editor, Antaeus, 1970-72; Editor, Washington Monthly, 1973-74; Teaching Fellow, Johns Hopkins University, 1975; Lecturer in English, Columbia University, 1976-91. Publications: Firestorm, 1969; The Time of the Emergency, 1977; The Private Rich, 1984; Gold From Heaven, 1988; Deng Xiaoping: Chronicle of an Empire, by Ruth Ming (editor and translator with Nancy Liu and Lawrence R Sullivan), 1994; China Hands, 1995. Contributions to: Periodicals. Honour: CAPS, 1977. Memberships: PEN; Authors Guild; Poets and Writers; East Asian Institute, Columbia University; Research Associate, Fairbank Center, Harvard University. Address: 24 Winslow Road, Belmont, MA 02178, USA.

RANDALL Clay. See: ADAMS Clifton.

RANDALL Margaret, b. 6 Dec 1936, New York, New York, USA. Writer; Poet; Photographer; Teacher; Activist. 1 son, 3 daughters. Appointments: Managing Editor, Frontiers: A Journal of Women's Studies, 1990-91; Distinguished Visiting Professor, University of Delaware, 1991; Visiting Professor, Trinity College, Hartford, Connecticut, 1992. Publications: Giant of Tears, 1959; Ecstasy is a Number, 1961; Poems of the Glass, 1964; Small Sounds from the Brass Fiddle, 1964; October, 1965; Twenty-Five Stages of My Spine, 1967; Getting Rid of Blue Plastic, 1967; So Many Rooms Has a House But One Roof, 1967; Part of the Solution, 1972; Day's Coming, 1973; With These Hands, 1973; All My Used Parts, Shackles, Fuel, Tenderness and Stars, 1977; Carlota: Poems and Prose from Havana, 1978; We, 1978; A Poetry of Resistance, 1983; The Coming Home Poems, 1986; Albuquerque: Coming Back to the USA, 1986; This is About Incest, 1987; Memory Says Yes, 1988; The Old Cedar Bar, 1992; Dancing with the Doe, 1992; Hunger's Table: The Recipe Poems, 1997; Oral History: Cuban Women Now, 1974; Sandino's Daughters, 1981; Photography: Women Brave in the Face of Danger, 1985; Nicaragua Libre!, 1985. Contributions to: Anthologies, reviews, journals, and magazines. Honours: 1st Prizes, Photography, Nicaraguan Children's Association, 1983; Creating Ourselves National Art Exhibition, 1992. Address: 50 Cedar Hill Road North East, Albuquerque, NM 87122, USA.

RANDALL Rona, b. Birkenhead, Cheshire, England. Author. m. 1 son. Publications: 60 published novels, including: Dragonmede, 1974; The Watchman's Stone, 1976; The Eagle at the Gate, 1978; The Mating Dance, 1979; The Ladies of Hanover Square, 1981; Curtain Call, 1982; The Drayton Trilogy: The Drayton Legacy, 1985; The Potter's Niece, 1987; The Rival Potters, 1990. Non-Fiction: Jordan and the Holy Land, 1968; The Model Wife, 19th Century Style, 1989; Writing Popular Fiction, 1992; 2nd edition, 1998. Honours: Romantic Novelists Association Award, 1969; US Literay Guild Exclusive Selection, 1975. Memberships: Society of Authors; International PEN; Society of Women Writers and Journalists; Society of Sussex Authors. Address: c/o Lawrence Pollinjer Ltd, 18 Maddox Street, Mayfair, London, W1R OEU, England.

RANSFORD Tessa, b. 8 July 1938, Bombay, India. Poet; Writer; Editor. m. (1) Iain Kay Stiven, 29 Aug 1959, div 1986, 1 son, 3 daughters, (2) Callum Macdonald, 7 Dec 1989. Education: MA, University of Edinburgh, 1958; Teacher Training, Craiglockhart College of Education, 1980. Appointments: Founder, School of Poets, Edinburgh, 1981-; Director, Scottish Poetry Library, 1984-; Editor, Lines Review, 1988-98. Publications: Light of the Mind, 1980; Fools and Angels, 1984; Shadows from the Greater Hill, 1987; A Dancing Innocence, 1988; Seven Valleys, 1991; Medusa Dozen and Other Poems, 1994; Scottish Selection, 1998; When it Works it Feels Like Play, 1998. Contributions to: Anthologies, reviews, and journals. Honours: Scottish Arts Council Book Award, 1980; Howard Sergeant Award for Services to Poetry, 1989; Heritage Society of Scotland Annual Award, 1996. Memberships: Royal Society of Arts; Saltire Society, honorary member; Scottish International PEN. Address: c/o Scottish Poetry Library, 5 Crichton's Close, Canongate, Edinburgh EH8 8DT, Scotland.

RANSLEY Peter, b. Leeds, England. Writer; Dramatist. m. Cynthia Harris, 14 Dec 1974, 1 son, 1 daughter. Education: Queen Mary College, London, 1950-52. Publications: The Price, 1988; Bright Hair About the Bone, 1989. Theatre: Ellen and Disabled, 1972; Runaway, 1974. Other: Numerous television plays and series, including Bread or Blood, 1982; The Price, 1985; Underbelly, 1991; Seaforth, 1994. Film: The Hawk, 1992. Honours: Gold Medal, 1st Commonwealth TV Film Festival, 1980; Royal Television Society Writer's Award, 1981; Golden Gate Award, San Francisco International Film Festival, 1995. Address: The Chambers, Chelsea Harbour, Lots Road, London SW10, England.

RANSOM Bill, b. 6 June 1945, Puyallup, Washington, USA. Writer; Poet. 1 daughter. Education: BA, University of Washington, 1970. Appointment: Poetry-in-the-Schools Master Poet, National Endowment for the Arts, 1974-77. Publications: Novels: The Jesus Incident, 1979; The Lazarus Effect, 1983; The Ascension Factor, 1988; Jaguar, 1990; Viravax, 1993; Burn, 1995. Poetry: Finding True North, 1974; Waving Arms at the Blind, 1975; Last Rites, 1979; The Single Man Looks at Winter, 1983; Last Call, 1984; Semaphore, 1993. Other: Learning the Ropes (poems, essays, and short fiction), 1995. Contributions to: Numerous publications. Honour: National Endowment for the Arts Discovery Award, 1977. Memberships: International Assocation of Machinists and Aerospace Workers; Poetry Society of America; Poets and Writers; Poets, Essayists, and Novelists; Science Fiction and Fantasy Writers of America. Address: PO Box 284, Grayland, WA 98547, USA.

RANZ-HORMAZABAL Maria de las Candelas, b. 23 Aug 1950, Spain. Poet; Writer. m. Agustin Garcia Alonso, 2 sons, 1 daughter. Education: Colegio de Religiosas de Duenas, Palencia. Publications: Poetry: Al principio del camino, 1962; Como la luz de la aurora, 1982; Petalos de mis rosas, 1983; Mis poemas, 1983; De verso en verso de flor en flor, 1984; Armor incompleto, 1984, 5th edition, 1985; Caprichosas protuberancias poeticas, 1986; Alondra-10, 1986; Sonetos, 1994. Other: Pequenas biografias de grandes personajes, 1982; Desde mi butaca: Critica de cine, 1982; Conoce usted a..., 1983; Les presento, a..., 1983. Contributions to: Periodicals. Honour: Poetry Prize, Concurso El Paisaje de Dibujo del Centro Cultural Aga, Vizcaya, 1974. Memberships: Academia O jornal de Felgueiras; Association Cultural La Marcilla, Léon, founder-secretary; Centro Cultural Literario y Artistico AGA. Address: Entre los Rios, 10, 24760 Castrocalbon, Léon, Spain.

RAO Raja, b. 21 Nov 1909, Hassan, Mysore, India. Author. m. (1) Camille Mouly 1931, (2) Katherine Jones, Apr 1966, 1 son, (3) Susan Vaught, 1986. Education: Aligarh Muslim University, 1926-27; BA, Nizam College, Hyderabad, University of Madras, 1929; University of Montpellier, 1929-30; Sorbonne, University of Paris, 1930-33. Appointment: Professor of Philosophy, University of Texas at Austin, 1966-80. Publications: Kanthapura, 1938; The Cow of the Barricades and Other Stories, 1947; The Serpent and the Rope, 1960; The Cat and Shakespeare: A Tale of India, 1965; Comrade Kirillov, 1976; The Chessmaster and His Moves, 1978; The Policeman and the Rose, 1978; On Ganga Ghat, 1989. Honours: Sahitya Academy Award, 1964; Padma Bhushan, Government of India, 1970; Neustadt International Prize for Literature, 1988. Address: 1806 Pearl, Austin, TX 78701, USA.

RAPHAEL Adam E G, b. 22 Apr 1938, London, England. m. Caroline Ellis, 1970, 1 son, 1 daughter. Education: BA, Honours, Oriel College, Oxford. Appointments: 2nd Lieutenant, Royal Artillery, 1956-58. Appointments: Washington Correspondent, The Guardian, 1968-73; Political Correspondent, The Guardian, 1973-76; Political Editor, The Observer, 1976-87; TV Presenter, BBC TV, 1987-88; Author, My Learned Friends, 1990, 1993; Executive Editor, The Observer, 1988-93; Writer on Home Affairs, The Economist, 1994-. Hobbies: Tennis; Skiing; Reading. Address: 50 Addison Avenue, London W11 4QP, England.

RAPHAEL Frederic Michael, b. 14 Aug 1931, Chicago, Illinois, USA. Writer. m. 17 Jan 1955, 2 sons, 1 daughter. Education: St John's College, Cambridge, England. Publications: Obbligato, 1956; The Earlsdon Way, 1958; The Limits of Love, 1960; The Trouble With England, 1962; The Graduate Wife, 1962; Lindmann, 1963; Darling, 1965; Orchestra and Beginners, 1967; Two for the Road (film script with preface), 1968; Like Men Betrayed, 1970; Who Were You With Last Night?, 1971; April, June and November, 1972; Richard's Things, 1973; California Time, 1975; The Glittering Prizes, 1976; Somerset Maugham (biography), 1977; Sleeps Six (short stories), 1979; Cracks in the Ice: Views and Reviews, 1979; Oxbridge Blues (short stories), 1980; Byron (biography), 1982; Heaven and Earth, 1985; Think of England I, 1990; A Double Life, 1993; Of Gods and Men (Greek mythology revisited), 1993; The Latin Lover (short stories), 1994; Old Scores, 1995. Translations (with Kenneth McLeish): The Poems of Catullus, 1978; The Plays of Aeschylus, 2 volumes, 1991; Coast to Coast, 1998; All his SOns (short stories), 1999. Contributions to: Sunday Times; Times Literary Supplement; Prospect. Honours: Lippincott Prize, 1961; Writers' Guild, 1965, 1966; USA Academy Award, 1966; British Academy Award, 1966; Royal TV Society Award, 1976; ACE (US Cable TV) Awards, 1985, 1991. Membership: Royal Society of Literature, fellow. Address: c/o Deborah Rogers, Rogers, Coleridge and White, 20 Powis Mews, London W11 1JN, England.

RAPOPORT Janis, b. 22 June 1946, Toronto, Ontario, Canada. Poet; Writer; Dramatist. m. (1) 1 son, 2 daughters, (2) Douglas Donegani, 20 May 1980, 1 daughter. Education: BA, University of Toronto, 1967. Appointments: Associate Editor, Tamarack Review, 1970-82; Playwright-in-Residence, Tarragon Theatre, 1974-75; Director, Ethos Cultural Development Foundation, 1981-; Editor, Ethos magazine, 1983-87; Part-time Instructor, Sheridan College, 1984-86; Writer-in-Residence, St Thomas Public Library, 1987, Beeton Public Library, 1988, Dundas Public Library, 1990, North York Public Library, 1991; Instructor, School of Continuing Studies, University of Toronto, 1988-. Publications: Within the Whirling Moment, 1967; Foothills, 1973; Jeremy's Dream, 1974; Landscape (co-editor), 1977; Dreamgirls, 1979; Imaginings (co-author), 1982; Upon Her Fluent Route, 1992; After Paradise, 1996. Contributions to: Anthologies, newspapers, magazines, and radio. Honours: Canadian Council Arts Award, 1981-82; AIGA Certificate of Excellence, 1983; New York Directors Club Award, 1983; Outstanding Achievement Award, American Poetry Association, 1986; Toronto Arts Council Research and Development Awards, 1990, 1992; Excellence in Teaching Award for Creative Writing, School of Continuing Studies, University of Toronto, 1998. Memberships: League of Canadian Poets; Playwrights' Union of Canada; Writers' Guild of Canada; Writers' Union of Canada. Address: c/o Writers' Union of Canada, 24 Ryerson Avenue, Toronto, Ontario M5T 2P3, Canada.

RASKY Harry, b. 9 May 1928, Toronto, Ontario, Canada. Film and Television Producer; Director; Writer. m. Ruth Arlene Werkhoven, 21 Mar 1965, 1 son, 1 daughter. Education: BA, 1949; LLD, 1982, University of Toronto. Appointments: President, Harry Rasky Productions Inc, 1967-; Producer, Director, and Writer of numerous film and television productions. Publications: Nobody Swings on Sunday (memoirs), 1980; Stratas: An Affectionate Tribute, 1988. Contributions to: Many newspapers and magazines. Honours: Over 200 awards. Memberships: Academy of TV Arts and Sciences; Directors Guild of America; Writers Guild of America. Address: c/o CBC, Box 500, Station A, Toronto, Ontario M5W 1E6, Canada.

RATCLIFFE Eric Hallam, b. 8 Aug 1918, Teddington, Middlesex, England. Retired Physicist and Information Scientist; Writer; Poet; Editor. Appointments: Staff, National Physical Laboratory, Teddington, Water Pollution Research Laboratory, Stevenage; Founder-Editor, Ore, 1955-95. Publications: Over 30, including: The Visitation, 1952; The Chronicle of the Green Man, 1960; Gleanings for a Daughter of Aeolus, 1968; Leo Poems, 1972; Commius, 1976; Nightguard of the Quaternary, 1979; Ballet Class, 1986; The Runner of the Seven Valleys, 1990; The Ballad of Polly McPoo, 1991; Advent, 1992; The Golden Heart Man, 1993; Fire in the Bush: POems, 1955-1992, 1993; William Ernest Henley (1849-1903): An Introduction, 1993; The Caxton of Her Age: The Career and Family Background of Emily Faithful (1835-1895), 1993; Winstanley's Walton, 1649: Events in the Civil War at Walton-on-Thames, 1994; Ratcliffe's Megathesaurus, 1995; Anthropos, 1995; Odette, 1995; Sholen, 1996; The Millennium of the Magician, 1996; The Brussels Griffon, 1996; Strange Furlongs, 1996; Wellington- A Broad Front, 1998; Capabilities of the Alchemical Mind, forthcoming. Contributions to: Anthologies and journals. Address: 7 The Towers, Stevenage, Hertfordshire SG1 1HE, England.

RATHBONE Julian, b. 10 Feb 1935, London, England. Writer. Education: BA Hons, Magdalene College, Cambridge, 1958. Publications: Diamonds Bid; Hand Out; Trip-Trap; Kingfisher Lives; Joseph; The Euro-Killers; The Last Resort; Watching the Detectives; A Spy of the Old School; Wellington's War; Nasty Very; Lying In State; The Crystal Contract; Dangerous Games, novel and film script; Intimacy; Blame Hitler; The Last English King, also as film script; Trajectories. Contributions to: Short stories for various anthologies; The Times; The Independent; The Guardian; The New Statesman; Occasional poetry. Honours: Deutschekrimi Preis; Swanage Poetry Prize; CWA Short Story Silver Dagger; Two Booker Prize Nominations. Membership: Crime Writers' Association. Address: Sea View, School Road, Thorney Hill, Christchurch, BH23 8DS, England.

RATHER Dan, b. 31 Oct 1931, Wharton, Texas, USA. Broadcast Journalist. m. Jean Goebel, 1 son, 1 daughter. Education: BA, Journalism, Sam Houston State College, Huntsville, Texas, 1953; University of Houston; South Texas School of Law. Appointments: Staff, United Press International, Houston Chronicle, KTRH Radio, Houston, KHOU-TV, Houston; White House Correspondent, 1964-65, 1966-74, Chief, London Bureau, 1965-66, CBS-TV; Anchorman-Correspondent, CBS Reports, 1974-75; Co-Editor, 60 Minutes, CBS-TV, 1975-81; Anchorman, Dan Rather Reporting, CBS Radio, 1977-; Anchorman and Managing Editor, CBS Evening News with Dan Rather, 1981-; CBS News special programmes. Publications: The Palace Guard (with Gary Gates), 1974; The Camera Never Blinks (with Mickey Herskowitz), 1977; Memoirs: I Remember (with Peter Wyden), 1991; The Camera Never Blinks Twice: The Further Adventures of a Television Journalist, 1994. Honours: Many Emmy Awards; Dan Rather Communications Building named in his honour, Sam Houston State University, Huntsville, Texas. Address: c/o CBS News, 524 West 57th Street, New York, NY 10019, USA.

RATNER Rochelle, b. 2 Dec 1948, Atlantic City, New Jersey, USA. Poet; Writer; Editor. m. Kenneth Thorp, 30 Mar 1990. Appointments: Poetry Columnist, Soho Weekly News, 1975-82; Co-Editor, Hand Book, 1976-82; Executive Editor, American Book Review, 1978-; Small Press Columnist, Library Journey, 1985; Poetry Consultant, Israel Horizons, 1988-97; Editor, New Jersey Online: Reading Room, 1995-96; NBCC Board of Directors, 1995-. Publications: Poetry: A Birthday of Waters, 1971; False Trees, 1973; The Mysteries, 1976;

Pirate's Song, 1976; The Tightrope Walker, 1977; Quarry, 1978; Combing the Waves, 1979; Sea Air in a Grave Ground Hog Turns Toward, 1980; Hide and Seek, 1980; Practicing to be a Woman: New and Selected Poems, 1982; Someday Songs, 1992; Zodiac Arrest, 1995. Fiction: Bobby's Girl, 1986; The Lion's Share, 1991. Other: Trying to Understand What It Means to be a Feminist: Essays on Women Writers, 1984; Without Child: Women Writing on Childlessness (editor), 1999. Memberships: Authors Guild; Hudson Valley Writers Guild; National Book Critics Circle; National Writers Union; PEN; Poetry Society of America; Poets and Writers. Address: 609 Columbus Avenue, Apt 16F, New York, NY 10024, USA.

RATUSHINSKAYA Irina, b. 4 Mar 1954, Odessa, Russia. Poet; Writer. m. Igor Geraschenko, 17 Nov 1979, 2 sons. Education: Diploma in Physics, University of Odessa. Appointment: Visiting Scholar, Northwestern University, Evanston, Illinois, 1987-88. Publications: No I'm Not Afraid, 1986; A Tale of Three Heads, 1986; Beyond the Limit, 1987; Grey is the Colour of Hope, 1988; Pencil Letter, 1988; In the Beginning, 1990; The Odessans, 1996. Contributions to: Various anthologies, 1989-95. Honours: Poetry International Rotterdam Award, 1986; Ross McWhirter Foundation, 1987; Christopher Award, USA, 1988; Individual Templeton Award, UK, 1993. Membership: PEN International, London. Address: 15 Crothall Close, London N13 4BN, England.

RAUHVARGERS Eizens, (Davis Galvins), b. 23 July 1923, Latvia. Translator of Art Literature; Professor of Educational Studies. m. Gaida Adamsons, 3 June 1998, 2 sons. Education: Graduated, College of Ancient Classical Languages, Riga, 1943; Pedagogical Institute of Latvia, Riga, 1950-54. Appointments: Associate Director, Professor, French College, Riga, 1954-68; Director, Translators Section, Latvian Literary Society, Riga, 1974-83; Director, Library, Literary Society of Riga, 1974-83. Publications: Translations of Russian authors: A Pushkin, M Lermontov, A Pisemski, J Tinianov, M Bulgakov, M Zoschenco, L Leonov, B Pasternak, I Jefremov, S Zaligin, J Bogat, D Granin, M Zagoskin; Own works as Davis Galvins: Drumalinas, aphorisms; My friends, essays; Synonyms in the Latvian language, dictionary; Latvian fables; Latvian Ballads; Others. Contributions to: Magazines: The Star, School and Family, The Flag; Journals: Literature and Art, North Latvia. Membership: Latvian Literary Society, Riga, 1971-. Address: P/K 635, Riga LV-1050, Latvia.

RAVEN Simon (Arthur Noël), b. 28 Dec 1927, London, England. Author. m. Susan Kilner, Oct 1951, 1 son. Education: King's College, Cambridge, 1948-52; BA Hons, MA. Appointments: Captain, King's Shropshire Light Infantry; Resigned, 1957. Publications: Novels: The Feathers of Death, 1959; Alms for Oblivion, 10 vols, 1964-1976; The First-Born of Egypt, 7 vols, 1984-92; Memoirs: Shadows on the Grass, 1982; Bird of Ill Omen, 1989; Is There Anybody There? Said the Traveller, 1990; General: The English Gentleman, 1961; TV Series: The Pallisers, 26th ed, 1974; Edward and Mrs Simpson, 7th ed, 1978. Contributions to: New Statesman; Spectator; Listener; Encounter; Punch. Honour: Royal Society of Literature, fellow, 1993-. Address: c/o Curtis Brown Ltd, 28/29 Haymarket, London SW1Y 4SP, England.

RAVIV Dan, b. 27 Sept 1954, New York, New York, USA. News Correspondent. m. Dori Phaff, 27 June 1982, 1 son, 1 daughter. Education: BA, cum laude, Harvard University, 1976. Publications: Behind the Uprising: Israelis, Jordanians, Palestinians, 1988; The Imperfect Spies, 1989; Every Spy a Prince: Complete History of Israel's Intelligence Community, 1990; Friends in Deed: Inside the US-Israel Alliance, 1994. Honour: Overseas Press Club of America Award, 1987. Address: CBS News, 4770 Biscayne Boulevard, Miami, FL 33137, USA.

RAVVIN Norman, b. 26 Aug 1963, Calgary, Alberta, Canada. Novelist; University Instructor. Education: BA, Honours, 1986, MA, English, 1988, University of British Columbia; PhD, University of Toronto, 1994. Publication: Café des Westens (novel), 1991. Contributions to: Various publications. Honours: Alberta Culture and Multiculturalism New Fiction Award, 1990; PhD Fellowship, Social Sciences and Humanities Research Council of Canada. Memberships: Writers Guild of Alberta; Association of Canadian College and University Teachers of English; Modern Language Society of America. Address: c/o Red Deer College Press, 56 Avenue and 32nd Street, Box 5005, Red Deer, Alberta, T4N 5H5, Canada.

RAWLS John (Bordley), b. 21 Feb 1921, Baltimore, Maryland, USA. Professor of Philosophy; Writer. m. Margaret Warfield Fox, 28 June 1949, 2 sons, 2 daughters. Education: AB, 1943, PhD, 1950, Princeton University; Cornell University, 1947-48. Appointments: Instructor in Philosophy, Princeton University, 1950-52; Assistant Professor to Associate Professor of Philosophy, Cornell University, 1953-59; Visiting Professor, 1959-60, Professor of Philosophy, 1962-, Harvard University; Professor of Philosophy, Massachusetts Institute of Technology, 1960-62. Publications: A Theory of Justice, 1971; Justice as Fairness, 1991; Two Concepts of Rules, 1991; Political Liberalism, 1993. Contributions to: Books and philosophical journals. Honours: Fulbright Fellow, University of Oxford, 1952-53; Phi Beta Kappa Ralph Waldo Emerson Award, 1972. Memberships: American Academy of Arts and Sciences; American Association of Political and Legal Philosophy, president, 1970-72; American Philosophical Association; American Philosophical Society. Address: c/o Department of Philosophy, Harvard University, Cambridge, MA 02138, USA.

RAWLS Philip. See: **LEVINSON Leonard.**

RAWNSLEY Andrew Nicholas James, b. 5 Jan 1962, Leeds, England. Journalist; Broadcaster. m. Jane Hall, 1990, 3 sons. Education: Sidney Sussex College, Cambridge; MA, History, Cambridge. Appointments: BBC, 1983-85; Reporter, Feature Writer, 1985-87, Political Columnist, 1987-93, The Guardian; Writer, Presenter, A Week in Politics, 1989-97, Bye Bye Blues, 1997, Blair's Year, 1998, Channel 4 series; Associate Editor, Chief Political Commentator, The Observer, 1993-; Writer, Presenter, The Agenda, ITV series, 1996, The Westminster Hour, Radio 4 series, 1998-. Honours: Student Journalist of the Year, 1983; Young Journalist of the Year, 1987; Commended, What The Papers Say, 1991. Literary Agent: Gill Coleridge, Rogers, Coleridge and White. Address: c/o Rogers, Coleridge and White, 20 Powis Mews, London W11 1JN, England.

RAWORTH Thomas Moore, b. 19 July 1938, London, England. Poet; Writer. m. Valerie Murphy, 4 sons, 1 daughter. Education: MA, University of Essex, 1970. Appointments: Poet-in-Residence, University of Essex, 1969, Northeastern University, Chicago, 1973-74, King's College, Cambridge, 1977-78; Lecturer, Bowling Green State University, Ohio, 1972-73; Visiting Lecturer, University of Texas, 1974-75, University of Cape Town, 1991, University of San Diego, 1996. Publications: The Relation Ship, 1967; The Big Green Day, 1968; A Serial Biography, 1969; Lion, Lion, 1970; Moving, 1971; Act, 1973; Ace, 1974; Common Sense, 1976; Logbook, 1977; Sky Tails, 1978; Nicht Wahr, Rosie?, 1979; Writing, 1982; Levre de Poche, 1983; Heavy Light, 1984; Tottering State: Selected Poems, 1963-83, 1984, UK edition, 1987; Lazy Left Hand, 1986; Visible Shivers, 1987; All Fours, 1991; Catacoustics, 1991; Eternal Sections, 1991; Survival, 1991; Clean and Well Lit: Selected Poems 1987-1995, 1996. Contributions to: Periodicals. Honours: Alice Hunt Bartlett Prize, 1969; Cholmondeley Award, 1971; International Committee on Poetry Award, New York, 1988. Membership: PEN. Address: 3 St Philip's Road, Cambridge CB1 3AQ, England.

RAWSON Claude Julien, b. 8 Feb 1935, Shanghai, China. Professor of English; Writer. m. Judith Ann Hammond, 14 July 1959, 3 sons, 2 daughters. Education: Magdalen College, Oxford, England, 1952-57; BA, 1955; MA, BLitt, 1959. Appointments: George M Bodman Professor of English, Yale University, 1986-; Editor, Modern Language Review, and Yearbook of English Studies, 1974-88; General Editor, Unwin Critical Library, 1975-; Executive Editor, Cambridge History of Literary Criticism, 1983-; General Editor, Blackwell Critical Biographies, 1986-; Chairman and General Editor, Yale Editions of the Private Papers of James Boswell, 1990-. Publications: Henry Fielding, 1968; Focus Swift, 1971; Henry Fielding and the Augustan Ideal under Stress, 1972, 2nd edition, 1991; Gulliver and the Gentle Reader, 1973, 2nd edition, 1991; Fielding: A Critical Anthology, 1973; The Character of Swift's Satire, 1983; English Satire and the Satiric Tradition, 1984; Order from Confusion Sprung: Studies in 18th Century Literature, 1985, 2nd edition, 1994; Thomas Parnell's Collected Poems (editor with F P Lock), 1989; Satire and Sentiment 1660-1800, 1994; Jonathan Swift: A Collection of Critical Essays (editor), 1995. Memberships: British Society for 18th Century Studies, president, 1974-75; American Society for 18th Century Studies, 1992; Modern Humanities Research Association, Committee member, 1974-88. Address: 50 Malthouse Lane, Kenilworth, Warwickshire CV8 1AD, England.

RAY David Eugene, b. 20 May 1932, Sapulpa, Oklahoma, USA. Professor of English Emeritus; Poet; Writer. m. Suzanne Judy Morrish, 21 Feb 1970, 1 son, 3 daughters. Education: BA, 1952, MA, 1957, University of Chicago. Appointments: Instructor, Wright Junior College, 1957-58, Northern Illinois University, 1958-60; Assistant Professor, Reed College, Portland, Oregon, 1964-66; Lecturer, University of Iowa, 1969-70; Visiting Associate Professor, Bowling Green State University, 1970-71; Professor of English, 1971-95, Professor Emeritus, 1995-, University of Missouri, Kansas City; Visiting Professor, Syracuse University, 1978-79, University of Rajasthan, India, 1981-82; Exchange Professor, University of Otago, New Zealand, 1987; Visiting Fellow, University of Western Australia, 1991; Senior Academy Professor, University of Arizona, 1996-. Publications: X-Rays, 1965; Dragging the Main and Other Poems, 1968; A Hill in Oklahoma, 1972; Gathering Firewood: New Poems and Selected, 1974; Enough of Flying: Poems Inspired by the Ghazals of Ghalib, 1977; The Tramp's Cup, 1978; The Farm in Calabria and Other Poems, 1979; The Touched Life, 1982; Not Far From the River, 1983; On Wednesday I Cleaned Out My Wallet, 1985; Elysium in the Halls of Hell, 1986; Sam's Book, 1987; The Maharani's New Wall, 1989; Wool Highways, 1993; Kangaroo Paws, 1994; Heart Stones: New and Selected poems, 1998; Demons in the Diner, 1999. Short Stories: The Mulberries of Mingo, 1978. Contributions to: Journals and newspapers. Honours: William Carlos Williams Awards, Daniel Varoujan Award, New England Poetry Club, 1979, 1993, Emily Dickinson Award, 1988, Poetry Society of America; PEN Syndicated Fiction Awards, 1982-86; Bernice Jennings Award for Traditional Poetry, Amelia Magazine, 1987; Emily Dickinson Award, Poetry Society of America, 1988; Maurice English Poetry Award, 1988; National Poetry Award, Passaic Community College, 1989; 1st Prize, Stanley Hanks Memorial Contest, St Louis Poetry Centre, 1990; New England Poetry Club Daniel Varoujan Award, 1996; New Millennium Poetry Award, 1997; Allen Ginsberg Poetry Award form Poetry Centre, Patesson, 1997; Explorations magazine Poetry Award, 1997; Amelia Magazine Long Poem Award, 1998; Richard Snyder Memorial Prize, 1999. Memberships: Academy of American Poets; PEN; Phi Kappa Phi; Poetry Society of America. Address: 2033 East 10th Street, Tucson, AZ 85719, USA.

RAY Robert Henry, b. 29 Apr 1940, San Saba, Texas, USA. Professor of English. m. Lynette Elizabeth Dittmar, 1 Sept 1962, 2 daughters. Education: BA, 1963, PhD, 1967, University of Texas at Austin. Appointments: Assistant Professor of English, 1967-75, Associate Professor of English, 1975-85, Professor of English, 1985-, Baylor University. Publications: The Herbert Allusion Book, 1986; Approaches to Teaching Shakespeare's King Lear, 1986; A John Donne Companion, 1990; A George Herbert Companion, 1995. Contributions to: Various publications. Honour: Phi Beta Kappa, 1962. Memberships: Modern Language Association of America; John Donne Society. Address:

Department of English, PO Box 97406, Baylor University, Waco, TX 76798, USA.

RAY Robert J, b. 15 May 1935, Amarillo, Texas, USA. Teacher; Writer. m. (1) Ann Allen, div, (2) Margot M Waale, July 1983. Education: BA, 1957, MA, 1959, PhD, 1962, University of Texas, Austin. Appointments: Instructor, 1963-65, Assistant Professor, 1965-68, Associate Professor, 1968-75, Professor, 1976, Beloit College, Beloit, Wisconsin; Writing Teacher, Valley College, 1984-88, University of California, Irvine, 1985-88; Adjunct Professor, Chapman College, 1988-. Publications: The Art of Reading: A Handbook on Writing (with Ann Ray), 1968; The Heart of the Game (novel), 1975; Cage of Mirrors (novel), 1980; Small Business: An Entrepreneur's Plan (with L A Eckert and J D Ryan), 1985; Bloody Murdock (novel), 1987; Murdock for Hire (novel), 1987; The Hitman Cometh (novel), 1988; Dial M for Murder (novel), 1988; Murdock in Xanadu (novel), 1989. Membership: Mystery Writers of America. Address: c/o Ben Kamsler, H N Swanson Inc, 8523 Sunset Boulevard, Los Angeles, CA 90069, USA.

RAYBAN Chlöe. See: **BEAR Carolyn Ann.**

RAYMOND Diana Joan, b. 25 Apr 1916, London, England. Novelist. m. Ernest Raymond, Aug 1940, 1 son. Education: Cheltenham Ladies' College. Publications: The Small Rain, 1954; Guest of Honour, 1960; The Climb, 1962; People in the House, 1964; Incident on a Summer's Day, 1974; Emma Pride, 1981; Lily's Daughter, 1974; Roundabout, 1994; The Sea Family, 1997. Membership: Society of Authors. Address: 22 The Pryors, East Heath Road, London NW3 1BS, England.

RAYMOND Laurie Watson, b. 20 June 1951, San Francisco, USA. Psychiatrist. Education: BA, Princeton University, 1973; MD, Harvard Medical School, 1977. Appointment: Clinical Instructor in Psychiatry, Harvard Medical School, 1983-. Publication: The Inward Eye, 1997.

RAYMOND Mary. See: **KEEGAN Mary Constance.**

RAYMOND Patrick Ernest, b. 25 Sept 1924, Cuckfield, Sussex, England. Retired Royal Air Force Officer; Writer. m. Lola Pilpel, 27 May 1950, 1 son. Education: Art School, Cape Town, South Africa. Appointments: Royal Air Force, rising to Group Captain, 1942-77. Publications: A City of Scarlet and Gold, 1963; The Lordly Ones, 1965; The Sea Garden, 1970; The Last Soldier, 1974; A Matter of Assassination, 1977; The White War, 1978; The Grand Admiral, 1980; Daniel and Esther, 1989. Address: 24 Chilton Road, Chesham, Buckinghamshire HP5 2AU, England.

RAYNER Claire Berenice, (Sheila Brandon, Ann Lynton, Ruth Martin), b. 22 Jan 1931, London, England. Writer; Broadcaster. m. Desmond Rayner, 23 June 1957, 2 sons, 1 daughter. Education: State Registered Nurse, Gold Medal, Royal Northern Hospital, London, 1954; Midwifery, Guy's Hospital. Publications: Over 90 books, ranging from medical to fiction, 1965-96. Contributions to: Professional journals, newspapers, radio, and television. Honours: Freeman, City of London, 1981; Medical Journalists Association Award, 1987; Honorary Fellow, University of North London, 1988; Best Specialist Consumer Columnist Award, 1988; Order of the British Empire, 1996. Memberships: Royal Society of Medicine, fellow; Society of Authors. Address: Holly Wood House, Roxborough Avenue, Harrow-on-the-Hill, Middlesex HA1 3BU, England.

RAYNER Mary Yoma, b. 30 Dec 1933, Mandalay, Burma. Author. m. (1) Eric Rayner, 6 Aug 1960, 2 sons, 1 daughter, (2) Adrian Hawksley, 9 Mar 1985. Education: Honours Degree, English, University of St Andrews, Scotland. Publications: Witch-Finder, 1975; Mr and Mrs Pig's Evening Out, 1976; Garth Pig and the Icecream Lady, 1977; The Rain Cloud, 1980; Mrs Pig's Bulk Buy, 1981; Crocodarling, 1985; Mrs Pig Gets Cross, 1986;2nd edition (picture book), 1996; Reilly, 1987; Oh Paul!, 1988; Rug, 1989; Marathon and Steve (USA), 1989; Bathtime

for Garth Pig, 1989; 2nd edition (picture book), 1999; Open Wide, 1990; The Echoing Green, 1992; Garth Pig Steals the Show, 1993; One by One, Ten Pink Piglets, 1994; Wicked William, 1996; The Small Good Wolf, 1997; Dark Sunday, 1997; Benjamins Pig's Bad day, 1999. Memberships: Society of Authors; Public Lending Right, advisory committee, 1989-93. Literary Agent: Laura Cecil. Address: c/o Laura Cecil, 17 Alwyne Villas, London N1 2HG, England.

RAYSON Hannie, b. 31 Mar 1957, Brighton, Melbourne, Australia. Playwright. Education: BA, University of Melbourne, 1977; Dip Art in Dramatic Arts, Victoria College of Arts, 1980. Appointments: Writer-in-Residence, various institutions; Literature Board, Australia Council, 1992-95. Publications: Please Return to Sender, 1980; Mary, 1981; Leave it Till Monday, 1984; Room to Move, 1985; Hotel Sorrento, 1990; SLOTH (television play), 1992; Falling From Grace, 1994. Honours: Australian Writers Guild Awards, 1986, 1991; New South Wales Premier's Literary Award; Sidney Myer Performing Arts Award, 1996. Address: Hilary Linstead & Associates, Level 18, Plaza 2, 500 Oxford Street, Bondi Junction, New South Wales 2022, Australia.

RAZ Joseph, b. 21 Mar 1939, Haifa, Palestine. Professor of the Philosophy of Law; Writer. Education: Magister Juris, Hebrew University, Jerusalem, 1963; DPhil, University of Oxford, 1967. Appointments: Lecturer, Hebrew University, Jerusalem, 1967-70; Research Fellow, Nuffield College, Oxford, 1970-72; Tutorial Fellow, 1972-85, Professor of the Philosophy of Law, 1985-, Balliol College, Oxford. Publications: The Concept of a Legal System, 1970, 2nd edition, 1980; Practical Reason and Norms, 1975, 2nd edition, 1990; The Authority of Law, 1979; The Morality of Freedom, 1986; Ethics in the Public Domain, 1994. Contributions to: Professional journals and other publications. Honours: W J M Mackenzie Book Prize, Political Studies Association, UK, 1987; Elaine and David Spitz Book Prize, Conference for the Study of Political Thought, New York, 1987; Honorary Doctorate, Katolieke University, Brussels, 1993. Memberships: American Academy of Arts and Sciences, honorary foreign member; British Academy, fellow. Address: c/o Balliol College, Oxford OX1 3BJ, England.

READ Miss. See: **SAINT Dora Jessie.**

READ Anthony, b. 21 Apr 1935, Staffordshire, England. Writer; Dramatist. m. Rosemary E Kirby, 29 Mar 1958, 2 daughters. Education: Central School of Speech and Drama, London, 1952-54. Publications: The Theatre, 1964; Operation Lucy (with David Fisher), 1980; Colonel Z (with David Fisher), 1984; The Deadly Embrace (with David Fisher), 1988; Kristallnacht (with David Fisher), 1989; Conspirator (with Ray Bearse), 1991; The Fall of Berlin (with David Fisher), 1992; Berlin: The Biography of a City (with David Fisher), 1994; The Proudest Day: India's Long Road to Indendence (with David Fisher), 1997. Other: Over 100 television films, plays and serials. Honours: Pye Colour TV Award, 1983; Wingate Literary Prize, 1989. Membership: Writers Guild of Great Britain; Authors' Licensing and Collecting Society, vice-chairman. Literary Agent: Books: Sara Menguc, David Higham Assosiates Ltd. TV & Film: Bethan Evans, The Agency Ltd. Address: 7 Cedar Chase, Taplow, Buckinghamshire, England.

READ Desmond. See: **MOORCOCK Michael (John).**

READ Piers Paul, b. 7 Mar 1941, Beaconsfield, England. Writer. m. Emily Albertine Boothby, 29 July 1967, 2 sons, 2 daughters. Education: MA, St John's College, Cambridge. Publications: Game in Heaven (with Tussy Marx), 1966; The Junkers, 1968; Monk Dawson, 1969; The Upstart, 1973; The Professor's Daughter, 1975; Polonaise, 1976; A Married Man, 1979; The Villa Golitsyn, 1981; A Season in the West, 1988; On the Third Day, 1990. Non-Fiction: Alive, 1974; The Train Robbers, 1978; Quo Vadis?: The Free Frenchman, 1986; The Subversion of the Catholic Church, 1991; Ablaze, 1993; A Patriot in Berlin, 1995; Knights of the Cross, 1997.

Contributions to: Spectator; Tablet. Honours: Sir Geoffrey Faber Memorial Prize, 1968; Hawthornden Prize, 1969; Somerset Maugham Award, 1969; Thomas More Award, 1976; James Tait Black Memorial Prize, 1988. Memberships: Society of Authors; Royal Society of Literature, fellow. Address: 50 Portland Road, London W11 4LG, England.

READE Hamish. See: **GRAY Simon (James Holliday).**

READING Peter, b. 27 July 1946, Liverpool, England. Poet. m. (1) Diana Gilbert, 1968, div, 1 daughter, (2) Deborah Jackson, 1996. Education: BA, Liverpool College of Art, 1967. Appointments: Lecturer, Department of Art History, Liverpool College of Art, 1968-70; Fellowship, Sunderland Polytechnic, 1981-83. Publications: Water and Waste, 1970; For the Municipality's Elderly, 1974; The Prison Cell and Barrel Mystery, 1976; Nothing for Anyone, 1977; Fiction, 1979; Tom O'Bedlam's Beauties, 1981; Diplopic, 1983; 5 x 5 x 5 x 5 x 5, 1983; C, 1984; Ukulele Music, 1985; Stet, 1986; Essential Reading, 1986; Final Demands, 1988; Perduta Gente, 1989; Shitheads, 1989; Evagatory, 1992; 3 in 1, 1992; Last Poems, 1993; Eschatological, 1996; Collected Poems 1970-96, 1996; Work in Regress, 1997; Chinoiserie, 1997; O B, 1999; Marfan, 1999. Honours: Cholmondeley Award for Poetry, 1978; First Dylan Thomas Award, 1983; Whitbread Award for Poetry, 1986; Lannan Foundation, Literary Fellowship Award, USA, 1990; Arts Council of Great Britain Literary Bursary, 1997. Membership: Royal Society of Literature, fellow. Address: c/o Bloodaxe Books, P O Box 1SN, Newcastle Upon Tyne, Ne99 1SN, England.

READSHAW Grahame George Cochrane, b. 23 Feb 1933, Toowoomba, Queensland, Australia. Medical Practitioner. m. Laurel Gray, 27 Oct 1956, 2 sons, 2 daughters. Education: MB, BS, 1955; Diploma of Ophthalmology, 1964; Fellow, Royal Australian College of Ophthalmology, 1978. Publications: Looking Up, Looking Back at Old Brisbane (with R Wood), 1987; Keep It Simple System for Watercolour Painting, 1992. Contributions to: Medical Journal of Australia; Australian Journal of Ophthalmology; Australian Artist Magazine; International Artist Magazine.Honour: Grumbacher Gold Medallion for Painting, 1983. Memberships: Royal Queensland Art Society; Watercolour Society of Queensland; Australian Medical Association; Royal Australian College of Ophthalmologists; Aviation Medical Society of Australia and New Zealand. Address: 44 Victoria Avenue, Chelmer, Queensland 4068, Australia.

REAKES Janet Elizabeth, b. 26 Jan 1952, Bristol, England. Genealogist. Education: Diploma of Family History Studies; Accredited Genealogist (GSU). Publications: How To Trace Your Convict Ancestors, 1986; A to Z of Genealogy: A Handbook, 1987, 3rd edition, 1993; How to Trace Your Family Tree and Not Get Stuck on a Branch, 1987; How to Trace Your English Ancestors, 1987; How to Trace Your Irish Ancestors, reprinted, 1993; How to Write the Family Story, 1993. Contributions to: Newspapers and magazines. Membership: Australian Authors. Address: PO Box 937, Hervey Bay, Queensland, Australia.

REANEY James Crear, b. 1 Sept 1926, South Easthope, Ontario, Canada. Professor; Poet; Dramatist. m. 29 Dec 1951, 2 sons, 1 daughter. Education: BA, 1948, MA, 1949, University of Toronto. Appointments: Faculty, University of Manitoba, Winnipeg, 1948-60; Professor, Middlesex College, University of Western Ontario, 1960-. Publications: Poetry: The Red Heart, 1949; A Suit of Nettles, 1958; Twelve Letters to a Small Town, 1962; The Dance of Death at London, 1963; Poems, 1972; Selected Shorter and Longer Poems, 1975-76; Performance Poems, 1990. Plays: Night Blooming Cereus, 1959; The Killdeer, 1960; One Masque, 1960; The Sun and the Moon, 1965; Listen to the Wind, 1966; The Canada Tree, 1967; Genesis, 1968; Masque, 1972; The Donnellys: A Trilogy, 1973-75; Baldoon, 1976; King Whistle, 1979; Antler River, 1980; Gyroscope, 1981; I, the Parade, 1982; The Canadian

Brothers, 1983; Alice Through the Looking Glass (adaptation of Lewis Carroll's book), 1994. Opera Libretto: The Shivaree (music by John Beckwith), 1982. Other: The Box Social and Other Stories, 1996. Contributions to: Books, journals and periodicals. Honours: Governor-General's Awards, 1949, 1958, 1963; University of Alberta Award for Letters, 1974; Order of Canada, 1975. Memberships: Association of Canadian University Teachers, president, 1959-60; Playwright's Union of Canada; League of Canadian Poets. Literary Agent: John Miller, Cultural Support Services, 14 Earl Street, 1st Floor, Toronto, Ontario M4Y 1M3, Canada. Address: Department of English, University of Western Ontario, London, Ontario N6A 3K7, Canada.

REBOUÇAS. See: TÔRRES Luiz Rebouças.

RECHEIS Kathe, b. 11 Mar 1928, Engelhartszell, Austria. Freelance Writer of Children's and Young People's Literature. Publications: Geh heim und vergiss Alles, 1964; Fallensteller am Bibersee, 1972; London 13 Juli, 1974; Der weite Weg des Nataiyu, 1978; Wo die Wolfe glücklich sind, 1980; Der Weisse Wolf, 1982; Weisst du dass die Baume reden, 1983; Lena - Unser Dorf und der Krieg, 1987; Tomasita, 1989; Wolfsaga, 1994. Honours: Austrian State Prizes for Children's and Young People's Literature, 1961, 1963, 1964, 1967, 1971, 1972, 1975, 1976, 1979, 1980, 1984, 1987, 1992, 1995; Österreichischer Würdigungspreis für Kinder-und Jugendliteratur for Complete Works, 1986; IBBY Certificate of Honour, 1978, 1982, 1987, 1994; Grober Preis der Deutschen Akademie für Kinder und Jugendliteratur e.v. Volkach für Gesamtwerk. Memberships: Austrian Writers Association; PEN Club. Address: Rembrandtstrasse 1/28, A 1020 Vienna, Austria.

REDDY T Vasudeva, b. 21 Dec 1943, Mittapalem, India. Lecturer in English; Writer; Poet. m. 5 Nov 1970, 2 sons, 1 daughter. Education: BSc, 1963; MA English, 1966; PhD Engliah, 1985; PGDTE, 1983. Appointment: Lecturer in English, 1966-. Publications: When Grief Rains (poems), 1982; The Vultures (novel), 1983; The Broken Rhythms (poems), 1987; Jane Austen, 1987; Jane Austen: Matrix of Matrimony, 1987; The Fleeting Bubbles (poems), 1989. Contributions to: Poems, critical articles and reviews to various journals and magazines. Honours: Award of International Eminent Poet, 1987; Honorary DLitt, World Academy of Arts and Culture, California, 1988; State Award for Best Teacher, University College Teachers, Andhra Pradesh, India, 1991. Memberships: International Poets Academy, Madras; World Poetry Society, California; American Biographical Institute, USA; Government College Teachers Association, Andhra Pradesh, India. Address: Narasingapuram Post, Via Chandragiri, Pin 517 102, AP, India.

REDGROVE Peter, b. 2 Jan 1932, Kingston-on-Thames, Surrey, England. Analytical Psychologist; Poet; Writer. m. (1) 1 daughter, (2) Penelope Shuttle, 2 sons, 1 daughter. Education: Queens' College, Cambridge. Appointments: Visiting Poet, University of Buffalo, 1961-62; Gregory Fellow in Poetry, University of Leeds, 1962-65; O'Connor Professor of Literature, Colgate University, 1974-75; Writer-at-Large, North Cornwall Arts, 1988. Publications: Poetry: The Collector, 1960; The Nature of Cold Weather, 1961; At the White Monument, 1963; The Force, 1966; Penguin Modern Poets 11, 1968; Work in Progress, 1969; Dr Faust's Sea-Spiral Spirit, 1972; Three Pieces for Voices, 1972; The Hermaphrodite Album (with Penelope Shuttle), 1973; Sons of My Skin: Selected Poems, 1975; From Every Chink of the Art, 1977; Ten Poems, 1977; The Weddings at Nether Powers, 1979; The Apple Broadcast, 1981; The Working of Water, 1984; The Man Named East, 1985; The Mudlark Poems and Grand Buveur, 1986; In the Hall of the Saurians, 1987; The Moon Disposes: Poems 1954-1987, 1987; The First Earthquake, 1989; Dressed as for a Tarot Pack, 1990; Under the Reservoir, 1992; The Laborators, 1993; The Cyclopean Mistress, 1993; My Father's Trapdoors, 1994; Abyssophone, 1995; Assembling a Ghost, 1996; The

Best of Redgrove, 1996; Orchard End, 1997; What the Black Mirror Saw, 1997. Novels: In the Country of the Skin, 1973; The Terrors of Dr Treviles (with Penelope Shuttle), 1974; The Glass Cottage, 1976; The Sleep of the Great Hypnotist, 1979; The God of Glass, 1979; The Beekeepers, 1980; The Facilitators, 1982; Tales from Grimm, 1989. Other: Plays for stage, radio and television. Non-Fiction: The Wise Wound (with Penelope Shuttle), 1978, 2nd edition, 1986; The Black Goddess and the Sixth Sense, 1987; Alchemy for Women (with Penelope Shuttle), 1995. Honours: George Rylands' Verse-Speaking Prize, 1954; Poetry Book Society Choices, 1961, 1966, 1979, 1981; 5 Arts Council Awards, 1969-82; Guardian Fiction Prize, 1973; Prudence Farmer Poetry Award, 1977; Cholmondeley Award, 1985; Queen's Gold Medal for Poetry, 1996. Membership: Royal Society of Literature, fellow. Address: c/o David Higham Associates, 5-8 Lower John Street, Golden Square, London W1R 4HA, England.

REDMAN Joseph. See: PEARCE Brian Leonard.

REED Ishmael (Scott), b. 22 Feb 1938, Chattanooga, Tennessee, USA. Writer; Poet; Publisher; Editor; Teacher. m. (1) Priscilla Rose, 1960, div 1970, 1 daughter, (2) Carla Blank-Reed, 1970, 1 daughter. Education: University of Buffalo, 1956-60. Appointments: Lecturer, University of California at Berkeley, 1967-, University of Washington, 1969-70, State University of New York at Buffalo, 1975, 1979, University of Arkansas, 1982, Columbia University, 1983, Harvard University, 1987, University of California at Santa Barbara, 1988; Chairman and President, Yardbird Publishing Company, 1971-; Director, Reed Cannon and Johnson Communications, 1973-; Visiting Professor, 1979, Associate Fellow, 1983-, Calhoun House, Yale University; Visiting Professor, Dartmouth College, 1980; Co-Founder (with Al Young) and Editor, Quilt Magazine, 1981-; Associate Fellow, Harvard University Signet Society, 1987-. Publications: Fiction: The Free-Lance Pallbearers, 1967; Yellow Black Radio Broke-Down, 1969; Mumbo-Jumbo, 1972; The Last Days of Louisiana Red, 1974; Flight to Canada, 1976; The Terrible Twos, 1982; Reckless Eyeballing, 1986; The Terrible Threes, 1989; Japanese by Spring, 1993. Poetry: Catechism of a Neoamerican Hoodoo Church, 1970; Conjure: Selected Poems 1963-1970, 1972; Chattanooga, 1973; A Secretary to the Spirits, 1978; New and Collected Poems, 1988. Other: The Rise, Fall and ...? of Adam Clayton Powell (with others), 1967; Shrovetide in Old New Orleans, 1978; God Made Alaska for the Indians, 1982; Cab Calloway Stands in for the Moon, 1986; Ishmael Reed: An Interview, 1990; Airin' Dirty Laundry, 1993. Editor: 19 Necromancers from Now, 1970; Yardbird Reader, 5 volumes, 1971-77; Yardbird Lives! (with Al Young), 1978; Calafia: The California Poetry, 1979; Quilt 2-3 (with Al Young), 2 volumes, 1981-82; Writin' is Fightin': Thirty-Seven Years of Boxing on Paper, 1988; The Before Columbus Foundation Fiction Anthology: Selections from the American Books Awards, 1980-1990 (with Kathryn Trueblood and Shawn Wong), 1992. Honours: National Endowment for the Arts Grant, 1974; Rosenthal Foundation Award, 1975; Guggenheim Fellowship, 1975; American Academy of Arts and Letters Award, 1975; Michaux Award, 1978. Membership: Before Columbus Foundation, president, 1976-. Address: c/o Ellis J Freedman, 415 Madison Avenue, New York, NY 10017, USA.

REED Jeremy, b. 1951, Jersey, Channel Islands. Poet; Writer. Education: BA, University of Essex, Colchester. Publications: Target, 1972; Saints and Psychotics: Poems 1973-74, 1974; Vicissitudes, 1974; Diseased Near Deceased, 1975; Emerald Cat, 1975; Ruby Onocentaur, 1975; Blue Talaria, 1976; Count Bluebeard, 1976; Jacks in His Corset, 1978; Walk on Through, 1980; Bleecker Street, 1980; No Refuge Here, 1981; A Long Shot to Heaven, 1982; A Man Afraid, 1982; By the Fisheries, 1984; Elegy for Senta, 1985; Skies, 1985; Border Pass, 1986; Selected Poems, 1987; Engaging Form, 1988; The Escaped Image, 1988; Nineties, 1990; Dicing for Pearls, 1990; Red-Haired Android, 1992. Novels: The Lipstick Boys, 1984; Blue

Rock, 1987; Madness: The Price of Poetry, 1990. Honour: Somerset Maugham Award, 1985. Address: c/o Jonathan Cape Ltd, 20 Vauxhall Bridge Road, London SW1V 2SA, England

REED John (Reginald), b. 30 May 1909, Aldershot, Hants, England. Retired Schoolmaster; Music Critic. m. Edith Marion Hampton, 30 Oct 1936, 2 sons, 2 daughters. Education: Diploma of Education, 1930, BA, Honours, English Language and Literature, University of London, 1935. Appointment: Music Critic, The Guardian, 1974-81. Publications: Schubert: The Final Years, 1972; Schubert, 1978; The Schubert Song Companion, 1985; Schubert, 1986. Contributions to: Newspapers and journals. Honours: Duckles Award, Music Library Association of America, 1987; Honorary Member, International Franz Schubert Institute of Vienna, 1989. Membership: Schubert Institute UK, chairman, 1991-94. Address: c/o Jane Ayers, 30 Furze View, Chorleywood, Herts, WD3 5HU, England.

REED Michael Arthur, b. 25 Apr 1930, Aylesbury, Bucks, England. University Professor. m. Gwynneth Vaughan, 1 Oct 1955, 1 son. Education: BA, 1954, MA, 1958, University of Birmingham; LLB, University of London, 1966; PhD, University of Leicester, 1973. Appointment: Professor, Loughborough University. Publications: The Buckinghamshire Landscape, 1979; The Georgian Triumph, 1983; The Age of Exuberance, 1986; The Landscape of Britain, 1990; A History of Buckinghamshire, 1993. Contributions to: Journals. Memberships: Fellow, Royal Historical Society, 1985; Fellow, Society of Antiquaries of London, 1985. Address: Department of Information and Library Studies, Loughborough University, Loughborough, Leicestershire, England.

REEDER Carolyn, b. 16 Nov 1937, Washington, District of Columbia, USA. Writer. m. Jack Reeder, 15 Aug 1959, 1 son, 1 daughter. Education: BA, 1959, MEd, 1971, American University. Publications: Historical fiction for children: Shades of Grey, 1989; Grandpa's Mountain, 1991; Moonshiner's Son, 1993. Adult fiction (with Jack Reeder): Shenandoah Heritage, 1978; Shenandoah Vestiges, 1980; Shenandoah Secrets, 1991; Across the Lines, 1997; Foster's War, 1998; Captain Kate, 1999. Honours: Scott O'Dell Award for Historical Fiction, 1989; Child Study Association Award, 1989; American Library Association Notable Book, 1989; Honour Book for the Jane Addam's Children's Book Award, 1989; Notable Trade Book in the Language Arts, 1989; Jefferson Cup Award, 1990; International Reading Association Young Adult Choice, 1991; Joan G Sugarman Children's Book Award, 1992-93; Hedda Seisler Mason Honor Award, 1995. Membership: Children's Book Guild of Washington, DC, former treasurer. Address: 7314 University Avenue, Glen Echo, MD 20812, USA.

REEMAN Douglas Edward, (Alexander Kent), b. 15 Oct 1924, Thames Ditton, Surrey, England. Author. m. Kimberley June Jordan, 5 Oct 1985. Publications: A Prayer for the Ship, 1958; High Water, 1959; Send a Gunboat, 1960; Dive in the Sun, 1961; The Hostile Shore, 1962; The Last Raider, 1963; With Blood and Iron, 1964; HMS Saracen, 1965; Path of the Storm, 1966; The Deep Silence, 1967; The Pride and the Anguish, 1968; To Risks Unknown, 1969; The Greatest Enemy, 1970; Against the Sea, 1971; Rendezvous - South Atlantic, 1972; Go In and Sink!, 1973; The Destroyers, 1974; Winged Escort, 1975; Surface with Daring, 1976; Strike from the Sea, 1978; A Ship Must Die, 1979; Torpedo Run, 1981; Badge of Glory, 1982; The First to Land, 1984; D-Day: A Personal Reminiscence, 1984; The Volunteers, 1985; The Iron Pirate, 1986; In Danger's Hour, 1988; The White Guns, 1989; Killing Ground, 1990; The Horizon, 1993; Sunset, 1994; The Douglas Reeman Omnibus, 1994; A Dawn Like Thunder, 1996; Battlecruiser, 1997; Dust on the Sea, 1999. As Alexander Kent: To Glory We Steer, 1968; Form Line of Battle, 1969; Enemy in Sight!, 1970; The Flag Captain, 1971; Sloop of War, 1972; Command a King's Ship, 1974; Signal - Close Action!, 1974; Richard Bolitho - Midshipman, 1975; Passage to Mutiny, 1976; In Gallant Company, 1977;

Midshipman Bolitho and the 'Avenger', 1978; Captain Richard Bolitho, RN, 1978; The Inshore Squadron, 1978; Stand Into Danger, 1980; A Tradition of Victory, 1981; Success to the Brave, 1983; Colours Aloft!, 1986; Honour This Day, 1987; With All Despatch, 1988; The Only Victor, 1990; The Bolitho Omnibus, 1991; Beyond the Reef, 1992; The Darkening Sea, 1993; For My Country's Freedom, 1995; Cross of St. George, 1996; Sword of Honour, 1998; Second to None, 1999. Contributions to: Various journals and magazines. Address: Peters, Fraser and Dunlop, The Chambers, Chelsea Harbour, London SW10 0XF, England.

REES Barbara Elizabeth, b. 9 Jan 1934, Worcester, England. Writer. m. Larry Herman, 1 Sept 1967, div 1978, 1 daughter. Education: BA, Honours, English Language and Literature, University of Oxford; MA. Appointment: Arts Council of Great Britain Creative Writer-in-Residence, North London Polytechnic, 1976-78. Publications: Try Another Country (3 short novels), 1969; Diminishing Circles, 1970; Prophet of the Wind, 1973; George and Anna, 1976; The Victorian Lady, 1977; Harriet Dark, 1978. Contributions to: Good Housekeeping; Melbourne Herald; Annabella; Det Nye; Woman's Own. Honour: Arts Council Award, 1974. Address: 102 Savernake Road, London NW3 2JR, England.

REES Brian, b. 20 Aug 1929, Strathfield, Sydney, Australia. Writer. m. (1) Julia Birley, 17 Dec 1959, dec, (2) Juliet Akehurst, 3 Jan 1987, 2 sons, 3 daughters. Education: 1st Class Historical Tripos, Parts I and II, Trinity College, Cambridge. Appointments: Assistant Master, Eton College, 1952-65; Headmaster, Merchant Taylor's School, 1965-73; Charterhouse, 1973-81; Rugby School, 1981-84. Publications: A Musical Peacemaker (biography of Sir Edward German), 1987; History and Idealism (editor), 1990. Address: 52 Spring Lane, Flore, Northamptonshire NN7 4LS, England.

REES David Benjamin, b. 1 Aug 1937, Wales. Minister of Religion. m. 31 July 1963, 2 sons. Education: BA, BD, MSc, University of Wales; MA, University of Liverpool; PhD, University of Salford. Appointments: Minister, Presbyterian Church of Wales, Cynon Valley, 1962-68, Heathfield Road, Liverpool, 1968-; Part-time Lecturer, University of Liverpool, 1970-. Publications: Wales: A Cultural History, 1980; Preparation for a Crisis: Adult Education in England and Wales 1945-1980, 1981; Liverpool, Welsh and Their Religions, 1984; Owen Thomas: A Welsh Preacher in Liverpool, 1991; The Welsh of Merseyside, 1997; Violence and Virtue in the Life and Politics of Liverpool 1800-1911, 1999. Contributions to: Magazines and newspapers such as Independent and Guardian. Honour: Ellis Griffith Prize, 1979. Membershipo: Welsh Union of Authors; Cummrodorion Society. Address: 32 Garth Drive, Liverpool L18 6HW, England.

REES-MOGG Lord William, Baron Rees-Mogg of Hinton Blewitt, b. 14 July 1928, Bristol, England. Journalist; Writer. m. Gillian Shakespeare Morris, 1962, 2 sons, 3 daughters. Education: Balliol College, Oxford. Appointments: Staff, The Financial Times, 1952-60; City Editor, 1960-61, Political and Economic Editor, 1961-63, Deputy Editor, 1964-67, The Sunday Times; Editor, 1967-81, Columnist, 1992-, The Times; Director, The Times Ltd, 1968-81, GEC, 1981-97, Private Bank and Trust Co, 1993-, Value Realisation Trust plc, 1996-; Vice-Chairman, Board of Governors, BBC, 1981-86; Chairman, Arts Council of Great Britain, 1982-89, Pickering and Chatto Ltd, 1983-, Sidgwick and Jackson, 1985-89, Broadcasting Standards Council, 1988-93, International Business Communications plc, 1994-. Publications: The Reigning Error: The Crisis of World Inflation, 1974; An Humbler Heaven, 1977; How to Buy Rare Books, 1985; Blood in the Streets (with James Dale Davidson), 1988; The Great Reckoning (with James Dale Davidson), 1991; Picnics on Vesuvius: Steps Toward the Millennium, 1992; The Sovereign Individual: How to Survive and Thrive During the Collapse of the Welfare State (with James Dale Davidson), 1997. Contributions to: Periodicals. Honours: Honorary LLD, University of

Bath, 1977; Knighted, 1981; Life Peerage, 1988. Address: 17 Pall Mall, London SW1Y 5NB, England.

REEVE F(ranklin) D(olier), b. 18 Sept 1928, Philadelphia, Pennsylvania, USA. Professor of Letters; Writer; Poet. Education: PhD, Columbia University, 1958. Appointments: Professor of Letters, Wesleyan University, 1970; Visiting Professor, Oxford University, 1964; Visiting Lecturer, Yale University, 1972-86; Editor, Poetry Review, 1982-84; Visiting Professor, Columbia University, 1988. Publications: Five Short Novels by Turgenev (translator), 1961; Anthology of Russian Plays (translator), 1961, 1963; Aleksandr Blok: Between Image and Idea, 1962; Robert Frost in Russia, 1964; The Russian Novel, 1966; In the Silent Stones, 1968; The Red Machines, 1968; Just Over the Border, 1969; The Brother, 1971; The Blue Cat, 1972; White Colors, 1973; Nightway, 1987; The White Monk, 1989; The Garden (translator), 1990; Concrete Music, 1992; The Trouble with Reason (translator), 1993; A Few Rounds of Old Maid and Other Stories, 1995; The Blue Boat on the St, Anne, 1999; The Moon and Other Failures, 1999. Contributions to: Journals and periodicals. Honours: American Academy of Arts and Letters Award, 1970; PEN Syndicated Fiction Awards, 1985, 1986; Golden Rose, New England Poetry Society, 1994. Memberships: Poets House, secretary, board director. Address: PO 14, Wilmington, VT 05363, USA.

REGAN Dian Curtis, b. 17 May 1950, Colorado Springs, Colorado, USA. Children's Book Author. m. John Regan, 25 Aug 1979. Education: BS, Honours, Education, University of Colorado, Boulder, 1980. Appointments: Speaker, numerous writers' conferences, USA. Publications: I've Got Your Number, 1986; The Perfect Age, 1987; Game of Survival, 1989; The Kissing Contest, 1990; Jilly's Ghost, 1990; Liver Cookies, 1991; The Class With the Summer Birthdays, 1991; The Curse of the Trouble Dolls, 1992; My Zombie Valentine, 1993; Princess, 1993; Cripple Creek Ghost Mine, 1993; Thirteen Days of Halloween, 1993. Contributions to: Magazines and children's publications. Honours: Children's Choice Award, 1987; Pick of the List, American Library Association, 1989; Oklahoma Cherubim Awards, 1990, 1991, 1992. Memberships: Authors Guild; Society of Children's Book Writers; Oklahoma Writers Federation. Address: c/o Curtis Brown Ltd, 10 Astor Place, 3rd Floor, New York, NY 10003, USA.

REGISTER Cheri, (Cheryl Lynn Register), b. 30 Apr 1945, Albert Lea, Minnesota, USA. Writer; Freelance Teacher. m. 1966-85, 2 daughters. Education: BA, Honours, 1967, MA Honours, 1968, PhD Honours, 1973, University of Chicago. Appointments: Co-Founder, organizer and workshop leader, Emma Willard Task Force on Education, Minnesota, 1970-73; Coordinator, Women's Center, University of Idaho, Moscow, 1973-74; Assistant Professor of Women's Studies and Scandinavian Languages and Literatures, University of Minnesota - Twin Cities, Minneapolis, 1974-80; Writer and Freelance Teacher, 1980-. Publications: As Cheri Register: Sexism in Education (co-author), 1971; Kvinnokamp och litteratur i USA och Sverige (Women's Liberation and Literature in the United States and Sweden), 1977; A Telling Presence: Westminster Presbyterian Church 1857-1982 (editor), 1982; Mothers, Saviours, Peacemakers: Swedish Women Writers in the Twentieth Century, 1983; Living With Chronic Illness: Days of Patience and Passion, 1987; Are Those Kids Yours?: American Families With Children Adopted from Other Countries, 1990. Contributions to: Various edited volumes and to magazines. Honours: Jerome Foundation Travel and Study Grant, 1991; Minnesota Historical Society Research Grant, 1996. Address: 4226 Washburn Avenue South, Minneapolis, MN 55410, USA.

REICH Asher, b. 5 Sept 1937, Jerusalem, Palestine. Poet; Writer; Editor. Education: Literature, University of Jerusalem. Appointments: Consulting Editor, Proza Magazine, 1977-79; Editor, The Literary Magazine, Israel, 1979-90. Publications: Poetry: 10 volumes, 1963-92. Other: Reminiscences of an Amnesiac, 1993. Contributions to: Anthologies and journals worldwide. Honours: Anna Frank Prize, 1961; 5 Writer's Guild Prizes,

1972-85; Tel Aviv Prizes, 1973, 1980, 1988; Chounsky Prize, 1977; Iowa International Writing Program Grant, 1985; Israeli Publishers Organization Poetry Prize, 1987; Deutscher Akademischer Austauschdienst Grant, Berlin, 1990. Memberships: Hebrew Writer's Association; PEN Club, Israel; Writer's Guild. Address: 14 Nechemya Street, Tel Aviv 65604, Israel.

REID Alastair, b. 22 Mar 1926, Whithorn, Wigtonshire, Scotland. Writer; Translator; Poet. Education: MA, University of St Andrews, Scotland, 1949. Appointments: Visiting Lecturer at universities in the UK and USA; Staff Writer, Correspondent, New Yorker, 1959-. Publications: To Lighten my House, 1953; Oddments, Inklings, Omens Moments, 1959; Passwords: Places, Poems, Preoccupations, 1963; Mother Goose in Spanish, 1967; Corgi Modern Poets in Focus 3, 1971; Weathering: Poems and Translations, 1978; Whereabouts: Notes on Being a Foreigner, 1987; An Alastair Reid Reader, 1995. Other: Stories for children and translations from Spanish of Pablo Neruda, Jorge Luis Borges and other writers. Honour: Scottish Arts Council Award, 1979. Address: c/o New Yorker, 20 West 43rd Street, NY 10036, USA.

REID Christina, b. 12 Mar 1942, Belfast, Northern Ireland. Playwright. Education: Queen's University, Belfast, 1982-83. Appointments: Writer-in-Residence, Lyric Theatre, Belfast, 1983-84, Young Vic Theatre, London, 1988-89. Publications: Did You Hear the One About the Irishman?, 1980; Tea in a China Cup, 1983; Joyriders, 1986; The Last of a Dyin' Race, 1986; The Belle of The Belfast City, 1986; My Name? Shall I Tell You My Name?, 1987; Les Miserables (after Hugo), 1992; Clowns, 1996; Christina Reid: Plays One, 1997. Plays produced in England, Ireland, Europe (in translation) and USA. Honours: Ulster TV Drama Award, 1980; Giles Cooper Award, 1986; George Devine Award, 1986. Address: c/o Alan Brodie Representation, 211 Piccadilly, London W1V 9LD, England.

REID Loren, b. 26 Aug 1905, Gilman City, Missouri, USA. Professor Emeritus of Communication. m. Augusta Towner, 28 Aug 1930, 3 sons, 1 daughter. Education: BA, Grinnell College, 1927; MA, 1930, PhD, 1932, University of Iowa. Appointments: Professor of Communication, 1935-39, 1944-75, Professor Emeritus, 1975-, University of Missouri. Publications: Teaching Speech, 4 editions, 1960-71; Speaking Well, 4 editions, 1962-82; Hurry Home Wednesday, 1978; Finally It's Friday, 1981; Professor on the Loose, 1992; Reflections, 1995. Contributions to: School and Society; History Today; Kansas City Star; Quarterly Journal of Speech; Parliamentary History. Honours: Distinguished Research/Service Awards, Grinnell College, University of Missouri. Memberships: Missouri Writers Guild; Missouri Library Association; Central States Speech Association; National Communication Association. Address: 200 East Brandon Road, Columbia, MO 65203, USA.

REID Lady Michaela Ann, b. 14 Dec 1933, Tean Staffordshire, England. Author. m. Alexander James Reid, 15 Oct 1955, 1 son, 3 daughters. Education: Law Tripos, Part 1, Girton College, Cambridge. Publications: Ask Sir James: Sir James Reid, Personal Physician to Queen Victoria and Physician-in-Ordinary to Three Monarchs, 1987, 4th edition, 1996. Address: Lanton Tower, Jedburgh, Roxburghshire, Scotland.

REID Philip. See: **INGRAMS Richard Reid.**

REIF Stefan Clive, b. 21 Jan 1944, Edinburgh, Scotland. Library Researcher; Writer. m. Shulamit Stekel, 19 Sept 1967, 1 son, 1 daughter. Education: BA, Honours, 1964, PhD, 1969, University of London; MA, University of Cambridge, England, 1976. Appointment: Editor, Cambridge University Library's Genizah Series, 1978-. Publications: Shabbethai Sofer and his Prayer-book, 1979; Interpreting the Hebrew Bible, 1981; Published Material from the Cambridge Genizah Collections, 1988; Genizah Research after Ninety Years, 1992; Judaism and Hebrew Prayer, 1993; Hebrew Manuscipts at Cambridge University Library, 1997. Contributions to: Over 200 articles in Hebrew and Jewish studies. Memberships: Fellow, Royal Asistic Society; Councli, Jewish Historical Society of England; British Association for Jewish Studies; Society for Old Testament Study. Address: Taylor-Schechter Genizah Research Unit, Cambridge University Library, West Road, Cambridge CB3 9DR, England.

REIN Evgeny Borisovich, b. 29 Dec 1935, Leningrad, Russia. Poet; Writer. m. Nadejda Rein, 21 Jan 1989, 1 son. Education: Graduated, Mechanical Engineer, Leningrad Technological Institute, 1959. Publications: Poetry: The Names of Bridges, 1984; Shore Line, 1989; The Darkness of Mirrors, 1989; Irretrievable Day, 1991; Counter-Clockwise, 1992. Contributions to: Russian, European and US magazines. Honours: Smena Magazine Award, 1970; Tallinn Magazine Award, 1982. Memberships: Russian Writers Union; Russian PEN Centre. Address: ulitza Kuusinena 7, Apt 164, 123308 Moscow, Russia.

REINER Annie, b. 11 May 1949, New York, New York, USA. Writer; Psychotherapist. Education: BA, University of California at Los Angeles, 1973; MSW, University of Southern California, Los Angeles, 1975. Publications: A Visit to the Art Galaxy, 1991; The Naked I, 1994; Dancing in the Park, 1995; This Nervous Breakdown is Driving Me Crazy, 1996; The Long Journey of the Little Seed, 1996; Infancy and the Essential Nature of Work, 1996. Contributions to: Journals. Honours: Various awards. Literary Agent: Jim Preminger Literary Agency. Address: 10553 Almayo Avenue, Los Angeles, CA 90064, USA.

REITER David Philip, b. 30 Jan 1947, Cleveland, Ohio, USA. Publisher; Writer. m. Cherie Lorraine Reiter, 26 Apr 1992. Education: BA, Independent Study, University of Oregon; MA, American Literature, University of Alberta, Canada; PhD, Creative Writing, University of Denver, 1982. Appointments: Lecturer, Cariboo University College, Canada, 1975-84, University of British Columbia, 1984, British Columbia Institute of Technology, 1984, University of Canberra, Australia, 1986-90. Publications: The Snow in Us, 1989; Changing House, 1991; The Cave After Saltwater Tide, 1992. Contributions to: Australian, Canadian, US and UK journals. Honours: Queensland Premier's Poetry Award, 1989; Imago-QUT Short Story Competition, 1990. Address: 15 Gavan Street, Ashgrove, Queensland 4060, Australia.

REKAI Kati, b. 20 Oct 1921, Budapest, Hungary. Journalist; Broadcaster. m. John Rekai, 15 Aug 1941, 2 daughters. Education: High School, Budapest. Publications: 22 travel books for children. Contributions to: Magazines and radio. Honours: Award for Canadian Unity, 1979; Knighthood of St Ladislaus, 1980; Prix Saint-Exupéry-Valeur Jeunesse, 1988; Rakoczi Foundation Award, 1991; Cross of the Order of Merit, Republic of Hungary, 1993; Order of Canada, 1993. Memberships: Canadian Scene; Ethnic Journalists and Writers Club; Writers Union of Canada; Arts and Letters Club; Toronto Historical Board. Address: 623-21 Dale Avenue, Toronto, Ontario M4W 1K3, Canada.

REMEC Miha, b. 10 Aug 1928, Pluj, Yugoslavia. Journalist; Writer; Dramatist; Poet. m. Mira Iskra, 1 July 1970, 3 sons. Appointment: Editorial Staff, Delo Newspaper, Delo, 1953-. Publications: Novels: Solstice, 1969; Recognition, 1980; Iksion, 1981; Mana, 1985; The Big Carriage, 1986; Two Short Novels: The Hunter and The Unchaste Daughter, 1987. Dramas: The Dead Kurent, 1959; The Happy Dragons, 1963; Workshop of Clouds, 1966; The Plastionic Plague, 1982. Other: Stories; Poems. Contributions to: Articles in numerous professional magazines and journals. Honours: Literary Awards for Drama, 1950, 1976; SFera Awards, 1981, 1987. Memberships: Slovene Writers Association; World Science Fiction Organization; SFera Science Fiction Club. Address: Pod lipami 58, Ljubljana 61000, Slovenia.

REMNICK David J, b. 29 Oct 1958, Hackensack, New Jersey, USA. Journalist; Writer. m. Esther B Fein, 2 sons. Education: AB, Princeton University, 1981. Appointments: Reporter, Washington Post, 1982-91; Staff, The New Yorker, 1992-. Publications: Lenin's Tomb: The Last Days

of the Soviet Empire, 1993; The Devil Problem (and Other True Stories), 1996; Resurrection: The Struggle for a New Russia, 1997; King of the World: Muhammad Ali and the Rise of an American Hero, 1998. Contributions to: Newspapers and periodicals. Honours: Livingston Award, 1991; Pulitzer Prize for General Non-Fiction, 1993; Helen Bernstein Award, New York Public Library, 1994; George Polk Award, 1994. Address: 233 West 72nd Street, New York, NY 10023, USA.

REMY Pierre-Jean. See: ANGREMY Jean-Pierre.

RENAS Y. See: ELBERG Yehuda.

RENAUD (Ernest) Hamilton Jacques, b. 10 Nov 1943, Montreal, Quebec, Canada. Author; Poet; Translator; Speaker. 2 sons, 1 daughter. Appointments: Critic and Researcher, Radio Canada, 1965-67; Reporter, Metro-Express, Montreal, 1966; Critic, Le Devoir, Montreal, 1975-78; Teacher, Creative Writing Workshop, University of Quebec, 1980-89; Spokesman, Equality Party, 1989; Researcher, Senator Jacques Hebert, 1990. Publications: 20 books, including: Electrodes (poems), 1962; Le Casse (stories), 1964; Clandestines (novel), 1980; L'espace du Diable (stories), 1989; Les Cycles du Scorpion (poems), 1989; La Constellation du Bouc Emissaire (non-fiction), 1993. Contributions to: Various publications. Address: 205 Ivy Crescent 3, Ottawa, Ontario K1M 1X9, Canada.

RENDELL Ruth Barbara (Baroness Rendell of Babergh), (Barbara Vine), b. 17 Feb 1930, England. Writer. m. Donald Rendell, 1950, div 1975, 1 son, remarried Donald Rendell, 1977. Publications: From Doon with Death, 1964; To Fear a Painted Devil, 1965; Vanity Dies Hard, 1966; A New Lease of Death, 1967; Wolf to the Slaughter, 1967 (televised 1987); The Secret House of Death, 1968; The Best Man to Die, 1969; A Guilty Thing Surprised, 1970; One Across Two Down, 1971; No More Dying Then, 1971; Murder Being Once Done, 1972; Some Lie and Some Die, 1973; The Face of Trespass, 1974 (televised as An Affair in Mind, 1988); Shake Hands for Ever, 1975; A Demon in My View, 1976 (film 1991); A Judgement in Stone, 1977; A Sleeping Life, 1978; Make Death Love Me, 1979; The Lake of Darkness, 1980 (televised as Dead Lucky, 1988); Put on by Cunning, 1981; Master of the Moor, 1982 (televised 1994); The Speaker of Mandarin, 1983; The Killing Doll, 1984; The Tree of Hands, 1984 (film 1989); An Unkindness of Ravens, 1985; Live Flesh, 1986; Heartstones, 1987; Talking to Strange Men, 1987; A Warning to the Curious: The Ghost Stories of M R James (editor), 1987; The Veiled One, 1988 (televised 1989); The Bridesmaid, 1989; Ruth Rendell's Suffolk, 1989; Undermining the Central Line (with Colin Ward), 1989; Going Wrong, 1990; Kissing the Gunner's Daughter, 1992; The Crocodile Bird, 1993; Simisola, 1994; The Reason Why (editor), 1995; The Keys to the Street, 1997; Road Rage, 1997; The Chimney Sweeper's Boy, 1998; As Barbara Vine: A Dark-Adapted Eye, 1986 (televised 1994); A Fatal Inversion, 1987 (televised 1992; The House of Stairs, 1988; Gallowglass, 1990; King Solomon's Carpet, 1981; Asta's Book, 1993; No Night is Too Long, 1994; The Brimstone Wedding, 1996; Short Stories: The Fallen Curtain, 1976; Means of Evil, 1979; The Fever Tree, 1982; The New Girl Friend, 1985; Collected Short Stories, 1987; The Copper Peacock, 1991; Blood Linen, 1995. Honours: Arts Council National Book Award for Genre Fiction, 1981; Royal Society of Literature, Fellow, 1988; Sunday Times Award for Literary Exellence, 1990; Cartier Diamond Dagger Award, Crime Writers Assocation, 1991; Commander of the Order of the British Empire, 1996; Life Peerage, 1997. Memberships: Royal Society of Literature, Fellow. Address: 11 Maida Avenue, London W2 1SR, England.

RENDELL-SMOCK Shara (Sharon), b. 22 Nov 1954, Chicago, Illinois, USA. Non-fiction Writer. m. Larry Rendell, 1988, div. 1996, 1 son. Education: BSW, 1978, Postgraduate work, early 1980s, University of Illinois, Urbana-Champaign. Appointments: Newspaper Reporter, Fort Myers Beach Bulletin, Fort Myers Beach, Florida, 1974; Reporter, The Urban Courier, Urbana, Illinois,

1975-76; Freelance Writer, Editor, 1978-; Technical Writer, Gould Computer Systems, 1980-85; Research Information Specialist, University of Illinois at Urbana-Champaign, 1987-88; Technical Writer, Kuck & Associates, Champaign, 1988-89; Columnist, The Sarasota Herald-Tribune, 1996-97; Consultant to software companies, 1997-. Publications: 20 computer user manuals, 1980-89; Living with Big Cats: The Story of Jungle Larry, Safari Jane, and David Tetzlaff, 1995; Getting Hooked: Fiction's Opening Sentences 1950s-1990s, 1997. Contributions to: Co-author, many articles in technical journals. Honour: Award of Excellence, Cat Writers Association, 1995. Memberships: National Writers Association; Small Publishers, Artists and Writers Network; HTML Writers Guild. Address: PO Box 34012, Indialantic, FL 32903-0912, USA.

RENÉE, (Renée Gertrude Taylor), b. 19 July 1929, Napier, New Zealand. Playwright; Writer. Education: BA, University of Auckland, 1979. Appointments: Member of women's writers collective groups, 1979-84; Director and actress, Napier Repertory Players; Robert Burns Fellowship, University of Otago, 1989; Writers Fellowship, University of Waikato and Creative, New Zealand, 1995. Publications: Secrets: Two One-Woman Plays, 1982; Breaking Out, 1982; Setting the Table, 1982; What Did You Do in the War, Mummy?, 1982; Asking For It, 1983; Dancing, 1984; Wednesday to Come, 1984; Groundwork, 1985; Pass It On, 1986; Born to Clean, 1987; Jeannie Once, 1990; Touch of the Sun, 1991; Missionary Position, 1991; The Glass Box, 1992; Tiggy Tiggy Touchwood, 1992; Willy Nilly (novel), 1990; Daisy and Lily, 1993; Does This Make Sense To You?, 1995. Other: Television plays and short stories. Honours: Queen Elizabeth II Arts Council Grant and Award; Project Grant, 1991; Queen Elizabeth II Arts Council Scholarship in Letters, 1993; Others. Literary Agent: (Plays) Playmarket, PO Box 9767, Wellington, New Zealand. Address: 3/45 Whites Line West, Woburn, Lower Hutt, New Zealand.

RENIER Elizabeth. See: BAKER Betty (Lou).

RENO Dawn Elaine, b. 15 Apr 1953, Waltham, Massachusetts, USA. Writer. m. Robert G Reno, 25 Feb 1978, 1 daughter, 3 stepsons, 1 stepdaughter. Education: AA, cum laude, Liberal Arts, Bunker Hill Community College, Boston, 1976; BA, summa cum laude, Liberal Studies, Johnson State College, Vermont, 1990; MFA, Vermont College, 1996. Appointments: Reporter, New England County Antiques, 1979-86; Assistant Editor, Vermont Woman, 1988-91; Columnist, Daytona Beach News Journal, 1992-93. Publications: Jenny Moves, 1984; Jenny's First Friend, 1984; Collecting Black Americana, 1986; American Indian Collectibles, 1989; American Country Collectibles, 1991; All That Glitters, 1992; Collecting Advertising, 1993; Native American Collectibles, 1994; The Silver Dolphin, 1994; Collecting Romance Novels, 1995; Contemporary Native American Artists, 1996; Encyclopaedia of Black Collectibles, 1996. Contributions to: Journals. Honours: Semi-finalist, Writer's Digest Non-Fiction Contest, 1986; Fiction Award, Johnson State College, 1990; Virginia Centre for the Creative Arts Fellowship, 1990; Vermont Studio Colony Fellowship, 1993. Memberships: League of Vermont Writers; National Writers Union; Society of Children's Book Writers; Romance Writers of America; Novelists Inc. Address: 3280 Shingler Terrace, Deltona, FL 32738, USA.

RENRICK D F. See: KERNER Fred.

REPLANSKY Naomi, b. 23 May 1918, Bronx, New York, USA. Poet. Education: BA, University of California, Los Angeles, 1956. Appointment: Poet-in-Residence, Pitzer College, Claremont, California, 1981. Publications: Ring Song, 1952; Twenty-One Poems, Old and New, 1988; The Dangerous World, New and Selected Poems, 1994. Contributions to: Ploughshares; Missouri Review; Nation; Feminist Studies. Honour: Nominated for National Book Award, 1952. Memberships: PEN American Center; Poetry Society of America. Address: 711 Amsterdam Avenue, No 8E, New York, NY 10025, USA.

RESCHER Nicholas, b. 15 July 1928, Hagen, Westphalia, Germany (US citizen, 1944). Professor of Philosophy; Writer. m. (1) Frances Short, 5 Sept 1951, 1 daughter, (2) Dorothy Henle, 10 Feb 1968, 2 sons, 1 daughter. Education: BS, Queens College, New York City, 1949; PhD, Princeton University, 1951. Appointments: Instructor in Philosophy, Princeton University, 1951-52; Associate Professor of Philosophy, Lehigh University, Bethlehem, Pennsylvania, 1957-61; University Professor of Philosophy, 1961-, Vice Chairman, Center for the Philosophy of Science, 1985-, University of Pittsburgh; Secretary General, International Union of the History and Philosophy of Science, United Nations Educational, Scientific, and Cultural Organization, 1969-75; Honorary Member, Corpus Christi College, Oxford, 1977-; Founder-Editor, American Philosophical Quarterly, History of Philosophy Quarterly, and Public Affairs Quarterly. Publications: The Coherence Theory of Truth, 1973; Scientific Progress, 1978; The Limits of Science, 1985; A System of Pragmatic Idealism, 3 volumes, 1992-93; Predicting the Future, 1997. Contributions to: Various scholarly journals. Honours: Honorary doctorates, Loyola University, Chicago, 1970, University of Córdoba, Argentina, 1992, Lehigh University, 1993, University of Konstanz, Germany, 1995; Alexander von Humboldt Prize, Germany, 1983. Memberships: Academia Europea; Académie Internationale de Philosophie des Sciences; American Philosophical Association; G W Leibnitz Society of America; Institut International de Philosphie; Royal Asiatic Society. Address: c/o Department of Philosophy, University of Pittsburgh, 1012 Cathedral, Pittsburgh, PA 15260, USA.

RESTAK Richard Martin, b. 4 Feb 1942, Wilmington, Delaware, USA. Physician; Author. m. Carolyn Serbent, 18 Oct 1968, 3 daughters. Education: MD, Georgetown Medical School, 1966; Trained in Neurology and Psychiatry. Appointments: Consultant, Encyclopedia of Bioethics, 1978; Special Contributing Editor, Science Digest, 1981-85; Editorial Board, Integrative Psychiatry: An International Journal for the Synthesis of Medicine and Psychiatry, 1986. Publications: Premeditated Man: Bioethics and the Control of Future Human Life, 1975; The Brain: The Last Frontier: Explorations of the Human Mind and Our Future, 1979; The Self Seekers, 1982; The Brain, 1984; The Infant Mind, 1986; The Mind, 1988; The Brain Has a Mind of Its Own, 1991; Receptors, 1994; Modular Brain, 1994. Contributions to: Anthologies, journals, and periodicals. Honours: Summer Fellowship, National Endowment for the Humanities Fellowship, 1976; Claude Bernard Science Journalism Award, National Society for Medical Research, 1976; Distinguished Alumni Award, Gettysburg College, 1985. Memberships: American Academy of Neurology; American Academy of Psychiatry and the Law; American Psychiatric Association; Behavioral Neurology Society; New York Academy of Sciences; International Neuropsychological Society; National Book Critics Circle; International Brotherhood of Magicians; Philosophical Society of Washington; International Platform Association. Address: 1800 R Street North West, Suite C-3, Washington, DC 20009, USA.

RESTON James B(arrett) Jr, b. 8 Mar 1941, New York, New York, USA. Writer. m. Denise Brender Leary, 12 June 1971. Education: Oxford University, 1961-62; BA, University of North Carolina at Chapel Hill, 1963. Appointments: Reporter, Chicago Daily News, 1964-65; Lecturer in Creative Writing, University of North Carolina at Chapel Hill, 1971-81. Publications: Fiction: To Defend, To Destroy, 1971; The Knock at Midnight, 1975. Non-Fiction: The Amnesty of John David Herndon, 1973; Perfectly Clear: Nixon from Whittier to Watergate (with Frank Mankiewicz), 1973; The Innocence of Joan Little: A Southern Mystery, 1977; Our Father Who Art in Hell: The Life and Death of Jim Jones, 1981; Sherman's March and Vietnam, 1985; The Lone Star: The Life of John Connally, 1989; Collision at Home Plate: The Lives of Peter Rose and Bart Giamatti, 1991; Galileo: A Life, 1994; The Last Apocalypse: Europe at the Year 1000 AD, 1998; Other: Radio and television documentaries, and plays. Contributions to: Various periodicals. Honours:

Dupont-Columbia Award, 1982; Prix Italia, Venice, 1982; National Endowment for the Arts Grant, 1982; Valley Forge Award, 1985. Memberships: Authors Guild; Dramatists Guild; PEN. Address: 4714 Hunt Avenue, Chevy Chase, MD 20815, USA.

RETEZAN Sever. See: **VERZEA Ernest-George.**

REUTHER David Louis, b. 2 Nov 1946, Detroit, Michigan, USA. Children's Book Publisher; Writer. m. Margaret Alexander Miller, 21 July 1973, 1 son, 1 daughter. Education: BA, Honours, University of Michigan, Ann Arbor, 1968. Publications: The Hidden Game of Baseball (co-author), 1984; Total Baseball, 1989, revised edition, 1991; The Whole Baseball Catalog, 1990. Co-Editor: The Armchair Quarterback, 1982; The Armchair Aviator, 1983; The Armchair Mountaineer, 1984; The Armchair Book of Baseball, 1985; The Armchair Angler, 1986; The Armchair Traveler, 1989. Children's Books: Fun to Go, 1982; Save-the-Animals Activity Book, 1982. Contributions to: The Horn Book, 1984. Memberships: American Booksellers Asociation-CBC Joint Committee, 1990-93; American Library Association; Authors Guild; Children's Book Council, board of directors, 1985-88, 1991-94, chairman, 1993; Society of Children's Book Writers. Address: 271 Central Park West, New York, NY 10024, USA.

REYES Carlos, b. 2 June 1935, Marshfield, Missouri, USA. Poet; Teacher. m. (1) Barbara Ann Hollingsworth, 13 Sept 1958, div 1973, 1 son, 3 daughters, (2) Karen Ann Stoner, 21 May 1979, div 1992, (3) Elizabeth Atly, 27 Dec 1993. Education: BA, University of Oregon, 1961; MA, ABD, University of Arizona, 1965. Appointments: Governor's Advisory Committee on the Arts, Oregon, 1973; Poet to the City of Portland, 1978; Poet-in-Residence, various public schools in Oregon and Washington; Editor, Hubbub, 1982-90; Editor Ar Mhuin Na Muicea (journal of Irish Literature, music, current events), 1995. Publications: The Prisoner, 1973; The Shingle Weaver's Journal, 1980; At Doolin Quay, 1982; Nightmarks, 1990; A Suitcase Full of Crows, 1995. Contributions to: Various journals and magazines. Honours: Oregon Arts Commission Individual Artist Fellowship, 1982; Yaddo Fellowship, 1984; Fundación Valparaíso, Mojácar, Spain, fellow, 1998. Memberships: Portland Poetry Festival Inc, board, 1974-84; PEN Northwest, co-chair, 1992-93; Buard, Mountain Writers Series, 1996-. Address: 3222 North East Schuyler, Portland, OR 97212, USA.

REYNOLDS Arlene V, b. 26 Feb 1947, Pittsfield, Massachusetts, USA. Actress; Author. m. (1) 27 Aug 1964, div 18 Oct 1993, 1 son, 1 daughter, (2) R W King, 2 Mar 1997. Education: AA, Cypress College, California, 1979. Appointments: Member, Company A Productions, specializing in Elizabeth Custer, wife of General Custer, and other nineteenth century women; Various first-person shows. Publication: The Civil War Memories of Elizabeth Bacon Custer, 1994. Honour: John M Carroll Literary Award, 1994. Address: PO Box 2762, Everett, WA 98203, USA.

REYNOLDS Graham (Arthur), b. 10 Jan 1914, Highgate, London, England. Writer; Art Historian. Education: BA, Honours, Queen's College, Cambridge. Publications: Nicholas Hilliard and Isaac Oliver, 1947, 2nd edition, 1971; English Portrait Miniatures, 1952, revised edition, 1988; Painters of the Victorian Scene, 1953; Catalogue of the Constable Collection, Victoria and Albert Museum, 1960, revised edition, 1973; Constable, The Natural Painter, 1965; Victorian Painting, 1966, revised edition, 1987; Turner, 1969; Concise History of Watercolour Painting, 1972; Catalogue of Portrait Miniatures, Wallace Collection, 1980; The Later Paintings and Drawings of John Constable, 2 volumes, 1984; English Watercolours, 1988; The Earlier Paintings of John Constable, 2 volumes, 1996; Catalogue of European Portrait Minatures, Metropolitan Museum of Art, New York, 1996; The Miniatures in the Collection of H.M. the Queen, The Sixteenth and Seventeenth Centuries, 1999. Contributions to: Times Literary Supplement; Burlington Magazine; Apollo; New

Departures. Honours: Mitchell Prize, 1984; Officer of the Order of the British Empire, 1984; British Academy, fellow, 1993; Honorary Keeper of Minatures, Fitzwilliam Museum, Cambridge, 1994. Address: The Old Manse, Bradfield St George, Bury St Edmunds, Suffolk IP30 0AZ, England.

REYNOLDS Keith Reynolds, (Kev Reynolds), b. 7 Dec 1943, Ingatestone, Essex, England. Author; Photojournalist; Lecturer. m. Linda Sylvia Dodsworth, 23 Sept 1967, 2 daughters. Publications: Walks and Climbs in the Pyrenees, 1978, 3rd edition, 1993; Mountains of the Pyrenees, 1982; The Weald Way and Vanguard Way, 1987; Walks in the Engadine, 1988; The Valais, 1988; Walking in Kent, 1988; Classic Walks in the Pyrenees, 1989; Classic Walks in Southern England, 1989; The Jura, 1989; South Downs Way, 1989; Eye on the Hurricane, 1989; The Mountains of Europe, 1990; Visitors Guide to Kent, 1990; The Cotswold Way, 1990; Alpine Pass Route, 1990; Classic Walks in the Alps, 1991; Chamonix to Zermatt, 1991; The Bernese Alps, 1992; Walking in Ticino, 1992; Central Switzerland, 1993; Annapurna, A Trekkers' Guide, 1993; Walking in Kent, Vol II, 1994; Everest, A Trekkers' Guide, 1995; Langtang: A Trekkers Guide, 1996; Tour of the Vanoise, 1996; Walking in the Alps, 1998. Contributions to: The Great Outdoors; Climber and Hill Walker; Environment Now; Trail Walker; Country Walking; High. Membership: Outdoor Writers' Guild. Address: Little Court Cottage, Froghowe, Crockham Hill, Edenbridge, Kent TN8 6TD, England.

REYNOLDS Sheri, b. 29 Aug 1967, Conway, South Carolina, USA. Writer. Education: AB, Davidson College, 1989; MFA, Virginia Commonwealth University, 1992. Appointment: Part-time Instructor of English, Virginia Commonwealth University. Publications: Bitterroot Landing, 1994; A Gracious Plenty, 1997. Membership: Authors Guild. Address: 700 Albermarle Street, Richmond, VA 23220, USA.

REYNOLDS Vernon, b. 14 Dec 1935, Berlin, Germany. University Teacher. m. Frances Glover, 5 Nov 1960, 1 son, 1 daughter. Education: BA, PhD, London University; MA, Oxford University. Publications: Budongo: A Forest and its Chimpanzees, 1965; The Apes, 1967; The Biology of Human Action, 1976, 2nd edition, 1980; The Biology of Religion (with R Tanner), 1983; Primate Behaviour: Information, Social Knowledge and the Evolution of Culture (with D Quiatt), 1993. Memberships: Fellow, Royal Anthropological Institute; Chairman, Biosocial Society; Primate Society of Great Britain; Society for the Study of Human Biology. Address: Institute of Biological Anthropology, Oxford University, 58 Banbury Road, Oxford OX2 6QS, England.

RHODES Anthony (Richard Edward), b. 24 Sept 1916, Plymouth, Devon, England. Writer; Translator. m. Rosaleen Forbes, 9 Apr 1956. Education: Royal Military Academy, Woolwich; MA, Trinity College, Cambridge; Licence et Lettres, University of Geneva, Switzerland. Publications: Sword of Bone, 1942; The Uniform, 1949; A Sabine Journey, 1952; A Ball in Venice, 1953; The General's Summer House, 1954; The Dalmation Coast, 1955; Where the Turk Trod, 1956; The Poet as Superman: A Life of Gabriele D'Annunzio, 1959; Rise and Fall of Louis Renault, 1966; The Prophet's Carpet, 1969; Princes of the Grape, 1970; Art Treasures of Eastern Europe, 1971; The Vatican in the Age of the Dictator, 1922-45, 1973; Propaganda in the Second World War, 1976; The Vatican in the Age of the Liberal Democracies, 1983; The Vatican in the Age of the Cold War, 1992. Other: 15 book-length translations from French, Italian and German. Contributions to: Encounter; Sunday Telegraph. Honour: Cavaliere Commendatore del'Ordine di San Gregorio Magno (Papal Title). Memberships: Society of Authors; PEN; Bucks Club; Beefsteak Club. Literary Agent: Anthony Sheil. Address: 46 Fitzjames Avenue, London W14, England.

RHODES Elvi Yvonne, b. Bradford, England. Writer. m. Harry Rhodes, dec, 2 sons. Appointments: Owner, small restaurant; Supervisor, Unilever Limited;

Administrator, 2 London Advertising Agencies; Administrator, Science Research Unit, University of Sussex, England. Publications: Opal, 1984; Doctor Rose, 1985; Ruth Appleby, 1987; The Golden Girls, 1988; Madeleine, 1989; House of Bonneau, 1990; Summer Promise, 1990; Cara's Land, 1991; The Bright One, 1994; The Mountain, 1995; Rainbow Through The Rain, 1997; Merry Month of May, 1997; Portrait of Chloe, 1997; Spring Music, 1998. Contributions to: short stories; articles to magazines. Literary Agent: Mary Irvine. Address: 11 Upland Park Road, Oxford OX2 7RU, England.

RHODES Philip, b. 2 May 1922, Sheffield, England. Medical Practitioner; Retired Professor of Postgraduate Medical Education. m. Elizabeth Worley, 26 Oct 1946, 3 sons, 2 daughters. Education: Clare College, Cambridge, 1940-43; St Thomas's Hospital, London, 1943-46, MA, 1946, MB, Chir, 1946, Cantab; FRCS, 1953; FRCOG, 1964; FRACMA, 1976; FFOM, 1990; FRSA, 1990. Publications: Fluid Balance in Obstetrics, 1960; Introduction to Gynaecology and Obstetrics, 1967; Woman: A Biological Study, 1969; Reproductive Physiology, 1969; The Value of Medicine, 1976; Dr John Leake's Hospital, 1978; Letters to a Young Doctor, 1983; Outline History of Medicine, 1985; The Oxford Companion to Medicine (associate editor), 1986; Wakerley, A Village in Northamptonshire, 1994; A Short Story of Clinical Midwifery, 1995; Gynaecology for Everywoman, 1996; Barrowden: A Village in Rutland, 1998. Contributions to: Lancet; British Medical Journal; British Journal of Obstetrics and Gynaecology; Practitioner; Encyclopaedia Britannia; New Dictionary of National Biography (forthcomming). Honour: Annual Prize, Brontë Society, 1972. Memberships: Society of Authors, medical committee; British Medical Association. Address: 1 Wakerley Court, Wakerley, Oakham, Leicester LE15 8PA, England.

RHODES Richard (Lee), b. 4 July 1937, Kansas City, Kansas, USA. Writer. Education: BA, cum laude, Yale University, 1959. Publications: Non-Fiction: The Inland Ground, 1970; The Ozarks, 1974; Looking for America, 1979; The Making of the Atomic Bomb, 1988; A Hole in the World, 1990; Making Love, 1992; Dark Sun, 1995; How to Write, 1995;Deadly Feasts, 1997; Trying to get some Dignity (with Ginger Rhodes), 1996. Fiction: The Ungodly, 1973; Holy Secrets, 1978; The Last Safari, 1980; Sons of Earth, 1981. Contributions to: Numerous journals and magazines. Honours: National Book Award in Non-Fiction, 1987; National Book Critics Circle Award in Non-Fiction, 1987; Pulitzer Prize in Non-Fiction, 1988. Membership: Authors Guild. Address: c/o Janklow and Nesbit Associates, 598 Madison Avenue, New York, NY 10022, USA.

RHONE Trevor Dave, b. 24 Mar 1940, Kingston, Jamaica, West Indies. Playwright; Director; Screenwriter. m. Camella King, 5 Mar 1974, 2 sons, 1 daughter. Education: Diploma, Speech and Drama, Rose Bruford College of Speech and Drama, 1963. Appointment: Resident Playwright, Barn Theatre, Kingston, 1968-75. Publications: Old Time Story, 1981; Two Can Play, 1984. Honours: Silver Musgrave Medal, 1972, Gold Musgrave Medal, 1988, Institute of Jamaica; Commander of the Order of Distinction, National Honour, Jamaica, 1980; Gold Musgrave Medal, 1988; Academy Award, Film Canada, 1989. Address: 1 Haining Mews, Kingston 5, Jamaica, West Indies.

RHOTEN Kenneth, b. 28 Dec 1950, Hammond, Indiana, USA. Author; Composer; Inventor; Artist. m. (1) Virginia Haynie, June 1974, (2) Robin Damron, Dec 1984, div 1985, (3) Josephine Meese, 1986. Appointments: Various, including Draftsman, Graphic Artist, Designer, Inventor; Patentholder; Winemaker. Publications include: Flying Saucer Man, album, 1977; A Brief Essay On The History Of Creativity; Your Tree; The Diamond; The Price of Paradise; Dark Twist Of Fate (epic novel), forthcoming. Songs include: A Voice From Beyond; Mornin' Daytime Dreamin'; All Night Long; Stretch Me A Road; Reflection In Your Eyes; Make A Dream Come True; Pages in a Book of Love; Fade Away; Let It Rain On Me. Honours:

Winner, local Writer's Contest, 1984. Membership: American Society of Composers, Authors and Publishers, 1975-93. Address: Box 225, 9981 Firebaugh, Stoy, IL 62464, USA.

RIBMAN Ronald (Burt), b. 28 May 1932, New York, New York, USA. Dramatist. m. Alice Rosen, 27 Aug 1967, 1 son, 1 daughter. Education: Brooklyn College, 1950-51; BBA, 1954, MLitt, 1958, PhD, 1962, University of Pittsburgh. Appointments: Assistant Professor of English, Otterbein College, 1962-63; Rockefeller Playwright-in-Residence, Public Theater, 1975. Publications: Harry, Noon and Night, 1965; The Journey of the Fifth Horse, 1966; The Ceremony of Innocence, 1967; Passing Through from Exotic Places, 1969; Fingernails Blue as Flowers, 1971; A Break in the Skin, 1972; The Poison Tree, 1976; Cold Storage, 1977; Buck, 1982; Seize the Day, 1985; The Cannibal Masque, 1988; The Rug Merchants of Chaos, 1991; Dream of the Red Spider, 1993. Contributions to: Films and television. Honours: Obie Award, 1966; Rockefeller Foundation Grants, 1966, 1968; Guggenheim Fellowship, 1970; National Endowment for the Arts Fellowship, 1973; Straw Hat Award, 1973; Elizabeth Hull-Kate Warriner Award, 1977; Drama Critics Award, 1977; Playwrights USA Award, 1984. Membership: Dramatists Guild. Address: c/o Dramatists Guild, 234 West 44th Street, New York, NY 10036, USA.

RICARD Charles, b. 9 Jan 1922, Gap, France. Author; Poet. m. J Balmens, 28 July 1951. Education: Professeur de Lettres. Publications: Novels: Le puits, 1967; La derniere des revolutions, 1968; A propos d'un piano casse, 1977; Le Pot-a-Chien, 1979; Alerte rouge aux cités soleils, 1985; Le mercredi des Cendres, 1986; Le Chemin des Oiseaux, 1991; Rédé, 1992; Les Mysteres du Villaret, 1993. Poetry: Si j'avais su, 1960; Je Voudrais, 1963; Les ombres du chemin, 1964. Contributions to: Various magazines and journals. Honours: Gold Medal, International Competition of Clubs of Cote d'Azur; Gold Medal, International Competition, Lutece, 1976; Prix Diamant, 1985; Prix du Vimeu, 1986. Memberships: Academy of the French Provinces; Society of French Poets, associate; Gens de Lettres de France, associate. Address: 20 rue du Super-Gap, 05000 Gap, France.

RICCHIUTI Paul B(urton), b. 4 July 1925, Redford Township, Michigan, USA. Writer. Education: Andrews University, 1949-52; Loma Linda University, 1953. Appointment: Layout and Design Artist, Pacific Press Publishing Association, 1955-. Publications: For Children: I Found a Feather, 1967; Whose House is It?, 1967; Up in the Air, 1967; When You Open Your Bible, 1967; Jeff, 1973; Amy, 1975; Five Little Girls, 1975; Let's Play Make Believe, 1975; My Very Best Friend, 1975; Elijah Jeremiah Phillip's Great Journey, 1975; Yankee Dan, 1976; General Lee, 1978; Mandy, 1978; Mike, 1978; Jimmy and the Great Balloon, 1978; Charlie Horse, 1992; Mrs White's Secret Sock, 1992. Other: Ellen (adult biography of Ellen G White), 1977; End of the World Man and Other Stories, 1989; Rocky and Me, 1989; New Dog in Town, 1991. Contributions to: Anthologies, newspapers, and magazines. Address: 5702 East Powerline, Nampa, ID 83687, USA.

RICCI Nino (Pio), b. 23 Aug 1959, Leamington, Ontario, Canada. Author. Education: BA, English, York University, 1981; MA, Creative Writing, Concordia University, 1987; Italian Literature, University of Florence. Appointments: Teacher of Creative Writing and Canadian Literature, Concordia University, 1987-88; Board of Directors, Canadian Centre, International PEN, 1990-97, president, 1995-96. Publications: Lives of the Saints, 1990; In a Glass House, 1993; Where She Has Gone, 1997. Honours: F G Bressani Prize for Fiction, 1990; Governor-General's Award for Fiction, 1990; W H Smith/Books in Canada First Novel Award, 1990; Betty Trask Award, 1991; Winifred Holtby Prize for Best Regional Novel, 1991; Giller Prize Shortlisted, 1997. Address: c/o Writers' Union of Canada, 24 Ryerson Avenue, Toronto, Ontario M5P 2P3, Canada.

RICE Anne, (Anne Rampling, A N Roquelaure), b. 4 Oct 1941, New Orleans, Louisiana, USA. Writer. m. Stan Rice, 14 Oct 1961, 1 son, 1 daughter, dec. Education: Texas Women's University, 1959-60; BA, 1964, MA, 1971, San Francisco State College; Graduate Studies, University of California, Berkeley, 1969-70. Publications: Interview with the Vampire, 1976; The Feast of All Saints, 1980; Cry to Heaven, 1982; The Claiming of Sleeping Beauty, 1983; Beauty's Punishment, 1984; Beauty's Release: The Continued Erotic Adventures of Sleeping Beauty, 1985; Exit to Eden, 1985; The Vampire Lestat, 1985; Belinda, 1986; The Queen of the Damned, 1988; The Mummy: Or Ramses the Damned, 1989; The Witching Hour, 1990; Tale of the Body Thief, 1992; Lasher, 1993; Taltos, 1994; Memnoch the Devil, 1995; Servant of the Bones, 1996; Violin, 1997; Pandora, 1998; Vampire Armand, 1998. Membership: Authors Guild. Address: c/o Alfred A Knopf Inc, 201 East 50th Street, New York, NY 10022,USA.

RICE Earle Wilmont Jr, (Earle Rice Jr), b. 21 Oct 1928, Lynn, Massachusetts, USA. Author; Freelance Writer. m. Georgia Joy Black Wood, 1 Nov 1958, 1 son, 1 daughter. Education: San Jose City College, 1958-60; Foothill College, Los Altos, 1970-71. Appointments: US Marine Corps, 1948-57; Letter Carrier, USPO, 1957-59; Draftsman, Designer, Checker, Technical Writer, Senior Designer, Senior Design Engineer, Electronics, Atomic and Aerospace Industries, 1960-93; Author, Freelance Writer, 1993-. Publications: Fiction: Tiger, Lion, Hawk, 1977; The Animals, 1979; Fear on Ice, 1981; More Than Macho, 1981; Death Angel, 1981; The Gringo Dies at Dawn, 1993; Non-fiction: The Cuban Revolution, 1995; The Battle of Britain, 1996; The Battle of Midway, 1996; The Inchon Invasion, 1996; The Battle of Belleau Wood, 1996; The Attack on Pearl Harbor, 1996; The Tet Offensive, 1996; The Nuremberg Trials, 1996; The Salem Witch Trials, 1996; The O J Simpson Trial, 1996; The Final Solution, 1997; Nazi War Criminals, 1997; The Battle of the Little Bighorn, 1997; Life Among the Great Plains Indians, 1997; Life During the Crusades, 1997; Life During the Middle Ages, 1997; The Kamikazes, 1999; Escape from Paradise: The South Sea Adventures of Herman Melville, forthcoming; Adaptations: Dracula, 1995; All Quiet on the Western Front, 1995; The Grapes of Wrath, 1996; Eleven Miles Too Far: The Journals of Robert Falcon Scott, forthcoming; In Arduous Service: The Lewis and Clark Chronicles, forthcoming. Contributions to: California Today; PSA Magazine; Pro/Am Hockey Review. Honours: 2nd Place, Children's Book Chapters Category, for The Secret of Barking Dog Bayou, 1993, 3rd Place, Children's Book Chapters Category, for White Sun and Blue Sky, 1994, 9th Honorable Mention, Novel Chapter, for So Long, Slimeball!, 1994, Florida State Writing Competition, Florida Freelance Writers Association. Memberships: Society of Children's Book Writers and Illustrators; League of World War I Aviation Historians; Cross and Cockade International; US Naval Institute. Address: PO Box 2131, Julian, CA 92036-2131, USA.

RICH Adrienne (Cecile), b. 16 May 1929, Baltimore, Maryland, USA. Professor of English and Feminist Studies; Poet; Writer. m. Alfred H Conrad, 1953, dec 1970, 3 sons. Education: AB, Radcliffe College, 1951. Appointments: Visiting Poet, Swarthmore College, 1966-68; Adjunct Professor, Columbia University, 1967-69; Lecturer, 1968-70, Instructor, 1970-71, Assistant Professor, 1971-72, Professor, 1974-75, City College of New York; Fannie Hurst Visiting Professor, Brandeis University, 1972-73; Professor of English, Douglass College, New Brunswick, New Jersey, 1976-78; A D White Professor-at-Large, Cornell University, 1981-85; Clark Lecturer and Distinguished Visiting Professor, Scripps College, Claremont, California, 1983; Visiting Professor, San Jose State University, California, 1985-86; Burgess Lecturer, Pacific Oaks College, Pasadena, California, 1986; Professor of English and Feminist Studies, Stanford University, 1986-. Publications: Poetry: A Change of World, 1951; (Poems), 1952; The Diamond Cutters and Other Poems, 1955; Snapshots of a Daughter-in-Law: Poems 1954-1962, 1963; Necessities of Life: Poems 1962-1965, 1966;

Selected Poems, 1967; Leaflets: Poems 1965-1968, 1969; The Will to Change: Poems 1968-1970, 1971; Diving into the Wreck: Poems 1971-1972, 1973; Poems Selected and New, 1975; Twenty-One Love Poems, 1976; The Dream of a Common Language: Poems 1974-1977, 1978; A Wild Patience Has Taken Me This Far: Poems 1978-1981, 1981; Sources, 1983; The Fact of a Doorframe: Poems Selected and New 1950-1984, 1984; Your Native Land, Your Life, 1986; Time's Power: Poems 1985-1988, 1989; An Atlas of the Difficult World: Poems 1988-1991, 1991; Collected Early Poems 1950-1970, 1993; Dark Fields of the Republic, 1995. Other: Of Woman Born: Motherhood as Experience and Institution, 1976; Women and Honor: Some Notes on Lying, 1977; On Lies, Secrets and Silence: Selected Prose 1966-1978, 1979; Compulsory Heterosexuality and Lesbian Existence, 1980; Blood, Bread and Poetry: Selected Prose 1979-1985, 1986; What Is Found There: Notebooks on Poetry and Politics, 1993. Honours: Yale Series of Younger Poets Award, 1951; Guggenheim Fellowships, 1952, 1961; American Academy of Arts and Letters Award, 1961; Bess Hokin Prize, 1963; Eunice Tietjens Memorial Prize, 1968; National Endowment for the Arts Grant, 1970; Shelley Memorial Award, 1971; Ingram Merrill Foundation Grant, 1973; National Book Award, 1974; Fund for Human Dignity Award, 1981; Ruth Lilly Prize, 1986; Brandeis University Creative Arts Award, 1987; Elmer Holmes Bobst Award, 1989; Commonwealth Award in Literature, 1991; Frost Silver Medal, Poetry Society of America, 1992; Los Angeles Times Book Award, 1992; Lenore Marshall/Nation Award, 1992; William Whitehead Award, 1992; Lambda Book Award, 1992; Harriet Monroe Prize, 1994; John D and Catharine T MacArthur Foundation Fellowship, 1994; Tanning Prize, 1996; Honorary doctorates. Address: c/o W W Norton & Co, 500 Fifth Avenue, New York, NY 10110, USA.

RICH Elaine Sommers, b. 8 Feb 1926, Plevna, Indiana, USA. Writer; Poet. m. Ronald L Rich, 14 June 1953, 3 sons, 1 daughter. Education: BA, Goshen College, 1947; MA, Michigan State University, 1950. Appointments: Instructor, Goshen College, 1947-49, 1950-53, Bethel College, North Newton, Kansas, 1953-66; Lecturer, International Christian University, Tokyo, 1971-78; Columnist, Mennonite Weekly Review, 1973-; Advisor to International Students, Bluffton College, Ohio, 1979-89; Adjunct Professor of English, University of Findlay, Ohio, 1990-. Publications: Breaking Bread Together (editor), 1958; Hannah Elizabeth, 1964; Tomorrow, Tomorrow, Tomorrow, 1966; Am I This Countryside?, 1981; Mennonite Women, 1683-1983: A Story of God's Faithfulness, 1983; Spritual Elegance: A Biography of Pauline Krehbiel Raid, 1987; Prayers for Everyday, 1990; Walking Together in Faith (editor), 1993; Pondered in Her Heart, 1998. Contributions to: Books and journals. Memberships: International League for Peace and Freedom. Address: 112 South Spring Street, Bluffton, OH 45817, USA.

RICH Frank Hart, b. 2 June 1949, Washington, District of Columbia, USA. Critic. m. (1) Gail Winston, 1976, 2 sons, (2) Alexandra Rachelle Witchel, 1991. Education: BA, Harvard University, 1971. Appointments: Co-Editor, Richmond Mercury, Virginia, 1972-73; Senior Editor and Film Critic, New York Times Magazine, 1973-75; Film Critic, New York Post, 1975-77; Film and Television Critic, Time Magazine, 1977-80; Chief Drama Critic, 1980-93, Op-Ed Columnist, 1994-, New York Times; Columnist, New York Times Sunday Magazine, 1993. Publication: The Theatre Art of Boris Aronson (with others), 1987. Contributions to: Newspapers and periodicals. Address: c/o The New York Times, 229 West 43rd Street, New York, NY 10036, USA.

RICHARD Mark, b. 1955, Lousiana, USA. Writer. Education: BA, Washington and Lee University. Publications: The Ice at the Bottom of the World: Stories, 1989; Fishboy: A Ghost's Story, 1993. Contributions to: Anthologies and periodicals. Honours: Whiting Writer's Award, 1990; Ernest Hemingway Foundation Award, 1990. Address: c/o Doubleday & Co Inc, 1540 Broadway, New York, NY 10036, USA.

RICHARDS Alun, b. 27 Oct 1929, Pontypridd, Wales. Author. m. Helen Howden, 8 July 1956, 3 sons, 1 daughter. Education: Diploma, Social Science and Education, University of Wales. Appointment: Editor, Penguin Book of Welsh Short Stories and Penguin Book of Sea Stories, Vols 1-11. Publications: The Elephant You Gave Me, 1963; The Home Patch, 1966; A Woman of Experience, 1969; Home to An Empty House, 1974; Ennal's Point, 1979; Dai Country, 1979; The Former Miss Merthyr Tydfil and Other Stories, 1980; Barque Whisper, 1982; Days of Absence (autobiography), 1987. Contributions to: Guardian; Planet; Western Mail. Honours: Arts Council Prize, 1974; Royal National Lifeboat Institution Public Relations Award, 1983; Japan Foundation Fellowship, 1984. Membership: Writers Guild of Great Britain. Address: 326 Mumbles Road, Swansea SA3 5AA, Wales.

RICHARDS David Adams, b. 17 Oct 1950, Newcastle, New Brunswick, Canada. Writer. Education: St Thomas University, New Brunswick, Canada. Publications: The Coming of Winter, 1974; Blood Ties, 1976; Dancers at Night, 1978; Lives of Short Duration, 1981; Road to the Stilt House, 1985; Nights Below Station Street, 1988; Evening Snow Will Bring Such Peace, 1990; For Those Who Hunt the Wounded Down, 1993. Honours: Governor-General's Award, 1988; Canada Authors Association Literary Award, 1991; Canada-Australian Literary Award, 1992. Address: c/o Canada Council, 350 Albert Street, PO Box 1047, Ottawa, Ontario K1P 5V8, Canada.

RICHARDS Denis George, b. 10 Sept 1910, London, England. Writer. m. Barbara Smethurst, 6 Jan 1940, 4 daughters. Education: BA, 1st Class Honours, 1931, MA, 1935, Trinity Hall, Cambridge. Publications: An Illustrated History of Modern Europe, 1938; An Illustrated History of Modern Britain, 1951; Royal Air Force, 1939-45 (with H St G Saunders), 3 volumes, 1953, 1954; Offspring of the Vic: A History of Morley College, 1958; Britain Under the Tudors and Stuarts, 1958; The Battle of Britain: The Jubilee History (with Richard Hough), 1989; The Few and the Many, 1990; The Hardest Victory: RAF Bomber Command in the Second World War, 1994; Recalling the Favour: Reflections 1910-1941, 1999; It Might Have Been Worse: Reflections 1941-1996, 1999. Contributions to: Books and Bookmen; Daily Telegraph Supplement; Financial Times; Dictionary of National Biography. Honours: C P Robertson Memorial Trophy, 1956; Officer of the Order of the British Empire, 1990. Memberships: PEN, honorary treasurer; Arts Club; Society of Authors; Garrick Club; RAF Club. Address: 4 Sussex gate, Sussex Gardens, London, N6 4LS, England.

RICHARDS Hubert John, b. 25 Dec 1921, Weilderstadt, Germany. Lecturer; Writer. m. 22 Dec 1975, 1 son, 1 daughter. Education: STL (Licence in Theology), Gregorian University, Rome; LSS (Licence in Scripture), Biblical Institute, Rome. Publications: The First Christmas: What Really Happened?, 1973; The Miracles of Jesus: What Really Happened?, 1975; The First Easter: What Really Happened?, 1977; Death and After: What Will Really Happen?, 1979; What Happens When You Pray?, 1980; Pilgrim to the Holy Land, 1985; Focus on the Bible, 1990; The Gospel According to St Paul, 1990; God's Diary, 1991; Pilgrim to Rome, 1993. Contributions to: Regular articles and reviews in various publications. Membership: Norfolk Theological Society, chairman. Address: 59 Park Lane, Norwich, Norfolk NR2 3EF, England.

RICHARDS Leonard L, b. 13 Aug 1934, Oakland, California, USA. Professor. m. Theresa Guerin, 30 Sept 1960, 2 sons, 2 daughters. Education: BA, 1958, MA, 1961, University of California at Berkeley; PhD, University of California at Davis, 1968. Appointments: Assistant Professor, San Francisco State College, 1968-69; Assistant Professor, Associate Professor, Professor, University of Massachusetts, Amherst, 1969-. Publications: Gentlemen of Property and Standing: Anti-Abolition Mobs in Jacksonian America, 1970; Advent of Democracy, 1979; Life and Times of Congressman John Quincy Adams, 1986. Honour: Beveridge Prize,

American Historical Association, 1970. Address: Department of History, University of Massachusetts, Amherst, MA 01003, USA.

RICHARDS Matt, b. 13 Mar 1968, Woodland, California, USA. Craftsman; Author; Publisher. Education: University of California at Berkeley. Appointments: Instructor, River Spirit School of Natural Living, Mad River, California, 1989-95; Instructor, Survival School's Primitive Skills Conferences, Rexburg, Idaho, and Phoenix, Arizona, 1990-; Instructor, Karok Tribal Education Program, Forks of Salmon, Colorado, 1992; Instructor, Wilderness Awakenings School, Slocan, British Columbia, Canada, 1995, 1996; Instructor, Earth Circle School of Wilderness Survival, Grangeville, Idaho, 1998-. Publication: Deerskins into Buckskins: How to Tan with Natural Materials, 1997. Contributions to: 3 feature articles in Bulletin of Primitive Technology. Address: PO Box 343, Rexford, MT 59930, USA.

RICHARDS Ronald Charles William, (Allen Saddler), b. 15 Apr 1923, London, England. Writer; Dramatist; Critic. Publications: Novels: The Great Brain Robbery, 1965; Gilt Edge, 1966; Talking Turkey, 1968; Betty, 1974. Other: Children's books, radio and television dramas. Contributions to: Newspapers, magazines, and journals. Memberships: South West Arts; Writers Guild. Address: 5 St John's Hall, Station Road, Totnes, Devon TQ9 5HW, England.

RICHARDS Sean. See: HAINING Peter.

RICHARDSON Joanna, b. London, England. Biographer. Education: MA, St Anne's College, Oxford. Publications: Fanny Brawne, 1952; Théophile Gautier: His Life and Times, 1958; The Pre-Eminent Victorian: A Study of Tennyson, 1962; The Everlasting Spell: A Study of Keats and His Friends, 1963; Essays by Divers Hands (editor), 1963; Introduction to Victor Hugo: Choses Vues, 1964; Edward Lear, 1965; George IV: A Portrait, 1966; Creevey and Greville, 1967; Princess Mathilde, 1969; Verlaine, 1971; Enid Starkie, 1973; Verlaine (translator, poems), 1974; Baudelaire (translator, poems), 1975; Victor Hugo, 1976; Zola, 1978; Keats and His Circle: An Album of Portraits, 1980; Paris Under Siege, 1982; Colette, 1983; The Brownings, 1986; Judith Gautier, 1987; Portrait of a Bonaparte, 1987; Baudelaire, 1994. Honours: Chevalier de l'Ordre des Arts et des Lettres, 1987; Prix Goncourt de la biographie, 1989. Membership: Royal Society of Literature, fellow. Address: c/o Curtis Brown Ltd, Haymarket House, 28-29 Haymarket, London SW1Y 4SP, England.

RICHARDSON Robert D(ale) Jr, b. 14 June 1934, Milwaukee, Wisconsin, USA. Former Professor of English; Independent Scholar; Writer. m. (1) Elizabeth Hall, 7 Nov 1959, div 1987, (2) Annie Dillard, 10 Dec 1988, 3 daughters. Education: AB, 1956, PhD in English and American Literature, 1961, Harvard University. Appointments: Instructor, Harvard University, 1961-63; Assistant Professor, 1963-68, Associate Professor, 1968-72, Chairman, Department of English, 1968-73, Professor of English, 1972-87, Associate Dean for Graduate Studies, 1975-76, University of Denver; Associate Editor, 1967-76, 1983-87, Book Review Editor, 1976-83, Denver Quarterly; Visiting Fellow, Huntington Library, 1973-74; Visiting Professor, Queen's College and the Graduate Center of the City University of New York, 1978, Sichuan University, China, 1983; Professor of English, University of Colorado, 1987; Visiting Lecturer, Yale University, 1989; Visiting Professor of Letters, 1990, Adjunct Professor of Letters, 1993-94, Wesleyan University; Associate Fellow, Calhoun College, Yale University, 1997-. Publications: Literature and Film, 1969; The Rise of Modern Mythology, 1680-1860 (with B Feldman), 1972; Myth and Literature in the American Renaissance, 1978; Henry Thoreau: A Life of the Mind, 1986; Ralph Waldo Emerson: Selected Essays, Lectures and Poems (editor), 1990; Emerson: The Mind on Fire, 1995. Contributions to: Scholarly books and journals. Honours: Melcher Prizes, 1986, 1995; Guggenheim Fellowship, 1990; Francis Parkman Prize, 1995; Washington Irving Award for Literary Excellence, 1995;

Dictionary of Literary Biography Award for a Distinguished Literary Biography, 1995; New York Times Book Review Notable Book Citation, 1995. Memberships: American Studies Association; Association of Literary Scholars and Critics; Author's Guild; Emerson Society; Melville Society; Society of American Historians; Society for Eighteenth Century Studies; Thoreau Society. Address: 158 Mt Vernon Street, Middletown, CT 06457, USA.

RICHARDSON Ruth, b. 19 Dec 1951, London, England. Historian. Education: BA, Honours, English Literature, 1977; MA, History, 1978; DPhil, History, 1985. Appointments: Research Officer, Institute of Historical Research, University of London, 1985-; Wellcome Research Fellow, Department of Anatomy, University College, London. Publications: Death, Dissection and the Destitute, 1988; The Builder Illustrations Index, 1843-83 (with Robert Thorne), 1994. Contributions to: Books and journals. Honours: Leverhulme Research Fellowship, 1992-93; Monkton Copeman Medal, Society of Apothecaries, London, 1993. Memberships: Folklore Society; Museum of Soho, trustee; Royal Historical Society, fellow; Society of Authors. Address: c/o Institute of Historical Research, University of London, London WC1E 7HU, England.

RICHÉ Pierre, b. 4 Oct 1921, Paris, France. Professor Emeritus; Writer. m. Suzanne Grenier, 20 Dec 1953. Education: Agregé, History, 1948; Docteur es lettres, 1962. Appointment: Professor, later Professor Emeritus, University of Paris X. Publications: Education et Culture dans l'Occident Barbare, 1962; Écoles et Enseignement dans le Haut Moyen Age, 1970; La Vie Quotidienne dans l'Empire Carolingien, 1973; Dhuoda Manuel pour Mon Fils (editor and translator), 1975; Les Carolingiens une Famille Qui fit l'Europe, 1983; Gerbert d'Aurillac Pape de l'an Mil, 1987; Petite Vie de Saint Bernard, 1989; Japanese L'Europe Barbare de 476 a 774, 1989; L'enfance au Moyen Age, 1994; Petite vie de Saint Gregoire le Grand, 1995; Dictionnaire des Francs, Les Temps Merovingiens, 1996Les Carolingiens, 1997; Grandeurs de l'an Mille, 1999. Contributions to: Professional journals. Honours: Officier des Palmes Académiques; Prix Gobert, 1963; Prix de Courcel, 1969, 1988; Prix George Goyau, 1974. Memberships: Centre International de Recherche et de Documentation sur le monachisme Celtique, honorary president; Comité des Travaux Historiques et Scientifiques, Section d'Histoire Medievale et de Philologie; Société d'Histoire de France; Société Nationale des Antiquaries de France. Address: 99 Rue Bobillot, Paris 75013, France.

RICHESON C(ena) G(older), (Velma Chamberlain, Jessica Jains, Cyndi Richards), b. 11 Apr 1941, Oregon, USA. Author; Poet. m. Jerry Dale Richeson, 3 June 1961, 2 sons. Education: AA, Diablo Valley College, 1962; BA, California State University, 1972. Appointments: Instructor, Shasta College, California, 1974-76, Liberty Union High School, Brentwood, California, 1984-85; Columnist, Anderson Press Weekly Newspaper, California, 1976-78; Frontier Correspondent, National Tombstone Epitaph, Tucson, 1986-; Book Reviewer, Publishers Weekly, 1994-95. Contributions to: Anthologies and periodicals. Honours: Several awards. Memberships: California Writers Club, president, 1991-92; Society of Children's Book Writers; Zane Grey's West Society. Address: PO Box 268, Knightsen, CA 94548, USA.

RICHIE Donald (Steiner), b. 17 Apr 1924, Lima, Ohio, USA. Critic; Writer. m. Mary Evans, Nov 1961, div 1965. Education: Antioch College, 1942; US Maritime Academy, 1943; BS, Columbia University, 1953. Appointments: Film Critic, Pacific Stars and Stripes, Tokyo, 1947-49; Arts Critic, Saturday Review of Literature, New York City, 1950-51; Film Critic, 1953-69, Literary Critic, 1972-99, Japan Times, Tokyo; Lecturer in American Literature, Waseda University, Tokyo, 1954-59; Arts Critic, The Nation, New York City, 1959-61, Newsweek Magazine, New York City, 1973-76, Time Magazine, 1997; Curator of Film, Museum of Modern Art, New York City, 1968-73; Toyoda Chair, University of Michigan, 1993; Lecturer, Film, Temple University, 1996-97. Publications: Where Are the Victors? (novel), 1956, new edition, 1986; The Japanese Film: Art and Industry (with Joseph L Anderson), 1959, expanded edition, 1982; The Japanese Movie: An Illustrated History, 1965, revised edition, 1982; The Films of Akira Kurosawa, 1965, revised edition, 1999; Companions of the Holiday (novel), 1968, new edition, 1977; George Stevens: An American Romantic, 1970; The Inland Sea, 1971, new edition, 1993; Japanese Cinema, 1971; Three Modern Kyogen, 1972; Ozu: The Man and His Films, 1974; Ji: Signs and Symbols of Japan (with Mana Maeda), 1975; The Japanese Tatoo, 1980; Zen Inklings: Some Stories, Fables, Parables, Sermons and Prints with Notes and Commentaries, 1982; A Taste of Japan: Food Fact and Fable, What the People Eat, Customs and Etiquette, 1985; Viewing Film, 1986; Introducing Tokyo, 1987; A Lateral View, 1987, new edition, 1992; Different People: Pictures of Some Japanese, 1987; Tokyo Nights, 1988, new edition, 1994; Japanese Cinema: An Introduction, 1990; The Honorable Visitors, 1994; Partial Views, 1995; The Temples of Kyoto, 1995; Lafcadio Hearn's Japan: An Anthology of His Writings on the Country and its people (editor), 1997; The Memoirs of the Warrior Kumagai, 1999; Tokyo: A View of the City, 1999. Honours: Citations, Government of Japan, 1963, 1970, 1983; Citation, US National Society of Film Critics, 1970; Kawakita Memorial Foundation Award, 1983; Presidential Citation, New York University, 1989; Novikoff Award, San Francisco Film Festival, 1990; Tokyo Metropolitan Government Cultural Award, 1993; John D Rockefeller III Award, 1994; Japan Foundation Prize, 1995. Address: Ueno 2, 12.18 (801), Taito-ku, Tokyo 110, Japan.

RICHLER Mordecai, b. 27 Jan 1931, Montreal, Quebec, Canada. Writer; Dramatist. m. Florence Wood, 1960, 3 sons, 2 daughters. Education: Sir George Williams University. Appointments: Writer-in-Residence, Sir George Williams University, 1968-69; Visiting Professor, Carleton University, 1972-74. Publications: Novels: The Acrobats, 1954; Son of a Smaller Hero, 1955; A Choice of Enemies, 1957; The Apprenticeship of Duddy Kravitz, 1959; The Incomparable Atuk, 1963; Cocksure, 1968; St Urbain's Horseman, 1971; Images of Spain, 1978; Joshua Then and Now, 1980; Solomon Grusky Was Here, 1989; Broadsides, 1991; Jacob Two-Two's First Spy Case, 1995; Barney's Version, 1997. Stories: The Street, 1972. Other: Essays, film scripts, television plays, and children's books. Honours: Canada Council Junior Arts Fellowships, 1959, 1960, Senior Arts Fellowship, 1967; Guggenheim Fellowship, 1967; Governor-General's Award for Fiction, 1969; Golden Bear, Berlin Film Festival, 1974; Giller Prize, 1997. Address: 1321 Sherbrooke Street West, Apt 80C, Montreal, Quebec H3G 1J4, Canada.

RICHTER Anne, b. 25 June 1939, Brussels, Belgium. Writer; Teacher of French. Widow, 1 daughter. Education: Licence of Philosophy and Letters, Free University of Brussels, 1963. Publications: Short Stories: La Fourmi a Fait le Coup, 1954, English translation, 1956; Les Locataires, 1967; La Grande Pitié de la Famille Zintram, 1986. Essays: Georges Simenon et l'Homme Désintégré, 1964; Milosz, 1965; Le Fantastique Féminin, Un Art Sauvage, 1984; Simenon Malgré Lui, 1993. Anthologies: L'Allemagne Fantastique, 1973; Les Contes Fantastiques de Guy de Maupassant, 1974; Le Fantastique Féminin, 1977; Histoires de Doubles et de Miroirs, 1981; Roger Bodart: La Route du Sel, 1993. Contributions to: Journals. Honours: Prizes, Belgian Academy of French Literature and Language. Memberships: PEN International; Association of Belgian Authors; International Association of Literary Critics. Address: 93 Boulevard Louis Schmidt, bte 13, 1040 Brussels, Belgium.

RICHTER Harvena, b. 13 Mar 1919, Reading, Pennsylvania, USA. Retired University Lecturer; Writer; Poet. Education: BA, University of New Mexico, 1938; MA, 1955, PhD, 1966, New York University. Appointments: Lecturer, New York University, 1955-66, University of New Mexico, 1969-89. Publications: The Human Shore, 1959; Virginia Woolf: The Inward Voyage, 1970; Writing to Survive: The Private Notebooks of Conrad Richter, 1988; The Yaddo Elegies and Other Poems, 1995; Green Girls: Poems Early and Late, 1996. Contributions to: Magazines and newspapers. Honours: Grants and fellowships. Memberships: Authors Guild; Kappa Kappa Gamma. Address: 1932 Candelaria Road North West, Albuquerque, NM 87107, USA.

RICHTER Milan, b. 25 July 1948, Bratislava, Slovakia. Writer; Diplomat. m. (1) 1 son, (2) Andriena Richteroua, 1 Oct 1980, 2 daughters. Education: German and English Linguistics and Literature, Comenius University, 1967-72; PhD, German Literature, 1985. Appointments: Editor, Publishing Houses, 1973-80; Freelance Writer and Translator, 1981-92; Diplomat, Embassy in Norway, Iceland and Oslo, 1993-95; Head, Department of Slovak Literature Abroad, National Center for Slovak Literature, Bratislava, 1995-. Publictions: Poetry: Evening Mirrors, 1973; Whips, 1975; Pollen, 1976; The Secure Place, 1987; Roots in the Air, 1992; From Behind the Velvet Curtains, 1997. Honours: Honorary LittD, Haifa, Israel, 1992; Several translation awards. Memberships: Clob of Slovak Independent Writers; Austrian Writers' Union. Address: Sidlisko 714, SK-90042 Dunajska Luzna, Slovakia.

RICKS Christopher (Bruce), b. 18 Sept 1933, London, England. Professor of English; Writer; Editor. m. (1) Kirsten Jensen, 1956, div 1975, 2 sons, 2 daughters, (2) Judith Aronson, 1977, 1 son, 2 daughters. Education: BA, 1956, BLitt, 1958, MA, 1960, Balliol College, Oxford. Appointments: Lecturer, University of Oxford, 1958-68; Visiting Professor, Stanford University, 1965, University of California at Berkeley, 1965, Smith College, 1967, Harvard University, 1971, Wesleyan University, 1974, Brandeis University, 1977, 1981, 1984; Professor of English, University of Bristol, 1968-75, University of Cambridge, 1975-86, Boston University, 1986-. Publications: Milton's Grand Style, 1963; Tennyson, 1972, revised edition, 1987; Keats and Embarrassment, 1974; The Force of Poetry, 1984; Eliot and Prejudice, 1988; Beckett's Dying Words, 1993; Essays in Appreciation, 1996. Editor: Poems and Critics: An Anthology of Poetry and Criticism from Shakespeare to Hardy, 1966; A E Housman: A Collection of Critical Essays, 1968; Alfred Tennyson: Poems, 1842, 1968; John Milton: Paradise Lost and Paradise Regained, 1968; The Poems of Tennyson, 1969, revised edition, 1987; The Brownings: Letters and Poetry, 1970; English Poetry and Prose, 1540-1674, 1970; English Drama to 1710, 1971; Selected Criticism of Matthew Arnold, 1972; The State of the Language (with Leonard Michaels), 1980, new edition, 1990; The New Oxford Book of Victorian Verse, 1987; Inventions of the March Hare: Poems 1909-1917 by T S Eliot, 1996. Contributions to: Professional journals. Honour: Honarary DLitt, oxford, 1998. Memberships: American Academy of Arts and Sciences, fellow; British Academy, fellow; Tennyson Society, vice-president. Address: 39 Martin Street, Cambridge, MA 02138, USA.

RIDGWAY Jason. See: **MARLOWE Stephen.**

RIDGWAY Judith Anne, b. 10 Nov 1939, Stalybridge, England. Writer. Education: BA, Class II, Division 1, University of Keele, 1962. Publications: Home Cooking for Money, 1983; Making the Most of Rice, 1983; Making the Most of Pasta, 1983; Making the Most of Potatoes, 1983; Making the Most of Bread, 1983; Making the Most of Eggs, 1983; Making the Most of Cheese, 1983; The Little Lemon Book, 1983; Barbecues, 1983; Cooking Round the World, 1983; Cooking with German Food, 1983; The Little Bean Book, 1983; Frying Tonight, 1984; Running Your Own Wine Bar, 1984; Sprouting Beans and Seeds, 1984; Man in the Kitchen, 1984; The Little Rice Book, 1984; Successful Media Relations, 1984; Running Your Own Catering Company, 1984; Festive Occasions, 1986; The Vegetable Year, 1985; Nuts and Cereals, 1985; Cooking Without Gluten, 1986; Vegetarian Wok Cookery, 1986; Wining and Dining at Home, 1985; Cheese and Cheese Cookery, 1986; 101 Ways With Chicken Pieces, 1987; The Wine Lovers Record Book, 1988; Pocket Book of Oils, Vinegars and Seasoning,

1989; The Little Red Wine Book, 1989; The Vitamin and Mineral Diet Cookbook, 1990; Catering for a Wedding, 1991; Vegetarian Delights, 1992; Quick After Work Pasta Cookbook, 1993; Best Wine Buys in the High Street, 1991, 5th edition, 1995; Food for Sport, 1994; Quick After Work Vegetarian Cookbook, 1994; The Noodle Cookbook, 1994; The Catering Management Handbook, 1994; Best Wine Buys in the High Street, 1996; 2nd edition, 1998; Practical Media Relations, 1996; The Wine Tasting Class, 1997; The Olive Oil Companian, 1997; The Cheese Companian, 1999. Memberships: Society of Authors; Guild of Food Writers; Circle of Wine Writers. Address: 46 Gloucester Square, London W2 2TQ, England.

RIDLER Anne (Barbara), b. 30 July 1912, Rugby, Warwickshire, England. Author; Poet; Dramatist; Translator. m. Vivian Ridler, 1938, 2 sons, 2 daughters. Education: Diploma in Journalism, King's College, University of London, 1932. Publications: Poetry: Selected Poems, 1961; Some Time After, 1972; Ten Oxford Poets (with others), 1978; New and Selected Poems, 1988; Collected Poems, 1994. Plays: The Jesse Tree (libretto), 1972; The King of the Golden River (libretto), 1975; The Lambton Worm (libretto), 1978. Other: A Measure of English Poetry (criticism), 1991. Translations:Orfeo, 1975; Così fan Tutte, 1986; Gluck's Orpheus, 1988; Don Giovanni, 1990; Figaro, 1991; Coronation of Poppea, 1992; Operas of Monteverdi (contributor), 1992; Tancredi, 1993; A Magic Flute, 1996. Biography: A Victorian Family Postbag, 1988. Editor: A Little Book of Modern Verse, 1941; Best Ghost Stories, 1945; Supplement to Faber Book of Modern Verse, 1951; The Image of the City and Other Essays by Charles Williams, 1958; Shakespeare Criticism, 1963; Poems of James Thomson, 1963; Thomas Traherne, 1966; Best Stories of Church and Clergy (with Christopher Bradby), 1966; Olive Willis and Downe House, 1967; Selected Poems of George Darley, 1979; Poems of William Austin, 1983. Honours: Cholmondely Award for Poetry, 1998; Fellow, Royal Society of Literature, 1998. Address: 14 Stanley Road, Oxford OX4 1QZ, England.

RIDLEY Jasper Godwin, b. 25 May 1920, West Hoathly, Sussex, England. Author. m. Vera Pollakova, 1 Oct 1949, 2 sons, 1 daughter. Education: Sorbonne, University of Paris, 1937; Magdalen College, Oxford University, 1938-39; Certificate of Honour, Council of Legal Education, 1945. Publications: Nicholas Ridley, 1957; Thomas Cranmer, 1962; John Knox, 1968; Lord Palmerston, 1970; Mary Tudor, 1973; Garibaldi, 1974; The Roundheads, 1976; Napolean III and Eugenie, 1979; The History of England, 1981; The Statesman and the Fanatic, 1982; Henry VIII, 1984; Elizabeth I, 1987; The Tudor Age, 1988; The Love Letters of Henry VIII, 1988; Maximillian and Juárez, 1992; Tito, 1994; History of the Carpenters' Company, 1995; Mussolini, 1997. Contributions to: Books and journals. Honour: James Tait Black Memorial Prize, 1970. Memberships: English PEN, vice-president 1985-; Royal Society of Literature, fellow; Tunbridge Wells Writers Circle, life president; Sussex Authors; Court of Assistants, Worshipful Company of Carpenters, master, 1988, 1990. Address: 6 Oakdale Road, Tunbridge Wells, Kent TN4 8DS, England.

RIDPATH Ian (William), b. 1 May 1947, Ilford, Essex, England. Writer; Broadcaster. Publications: Over 30 books, including: Worlds Beyond, 1975; Encyclopedia of Astronomy and Space (editor), 1976; Messages From the Stars, 1978; Stars and Planets, 1978; Young Astronomer's Handbook, 1981; Hamlyn Encyclopedia of Space, 1981; Life Off Earth, 1983; Collins Guide to Stars and Planets, 1984; Gem Guide to the Night Sky, 1985; Secrets of the Sky, 1985; A Comet Called Halley, 1985; Longman Illustrated Dictionary of Astronomy and Astronautics, 1987; Monthly Sky Guide, 1987; Star Tales, 1989; Norton's Star Atlas (editor), 1989; Book of the Universe, 1991; Atlas of Stars and Planets, 1992; Oxford Dictionary of Astronomy (editor), 1997; Eyewitness Handbook of Stars and Planets, 1998. Membership: Fellow, Royal Astronomical Society. Address: 48 Otho Court, Brentford Dock, Brentford, Middlesex TW8 8PY, England.

RIDPATH Michael William Gerrans, b. 7 Mar 1961, Exeter, England. Author. m. Barbara (née Nunemaker), 1 Oct 1994, 1 son, 2 daughters. Education: History, Merton College, Oxford, England, 1979-82. Appointments: Saudi International Bank, 1982-91; Apax Partners Ventures, 1991-94. Publications: Free to Trade, 1995; Trading Reality, 1996; The Market Maker, 1998. Memberships: Society of Authors, Managing Committee; Crime Writers' Association; People of Today. Literary Agent: Carole Blake, Blake Friedmann. Address: c/o Blake Friedmann, 37-41 Gower St, London WC1E 6HH, England.

RIEBS Gunnar, b. 10 Apr 1960, Leuven, Belgium. Educator. m. Ann Baert. Education: Teaching degree in Dutch, English, History, Theology, School for Higher Pedagogic Education, Leuven, 1983. Appointments: Teacher, St Jozef College, Aarschot, 1983-84; Director, Centrum Jozef Cardijn, Centre for Socio-Cultural and Religious Education, 1984-94; Assistant to President of European University, 1994. Publications: Hulde aan Componist Jan de Middeleer, 1978; Poetry: De leidende stilte - De lijdende stilte, 1984; Stranden bij de dichter, 1986. Honours: 1st Prize for Declamation, Tienen Academy of Music, 1977. Honours: Gouden Artisjokgriffel, 1981; Erkentelijkheidsmedaille, Netherlands Minister of Culture, 1985; Gold Cross, Agrupación Española de Fomento Europeo, 1995; Medaille de Vermeil des Arts, Lettres et Sciences, 1997. Membership: Vereniging Vlaamse Letterkundigen. Address: Marie-Josélaan 76, B-2600 Berchem, Belgium.

RIES Hans, b. 22 Dec 1941, Gilching, Germany. Research Scientist. m. Gitta Maikl, 24 May 1968, 1 son. Appointments: Wilhelm Busch Museum, Hannover, 1980-; Vice-President, International Youth Library, Munich, 1992-. Publications: Wilhelm Buschals Zeichner nach der Natur, 1982; Zwischen Hausse und Baisse, Börse und Geld in der Karikatur, 1987; Illustration und Illustratoren 1871-1914, 1992. Other: Allgemeines Künstlerlexikon, 1985-. Contributions to: Börsenblatt für den Deutschen Buchhandel, Aus dem Antiquariat. Address: Römerstrasse 93, D 82205 Gilching, Germany.

RIFBJERG Klaus Thorvald, b. 15 Dec 1931, Copenhagen, Denmark. Author; Dramatist; Poet. m. Inge Merete Gerner, 28 May 1955, 1 son, 2 daughters. Education: Princeton University, 1950-51; University of Copenhagen, 1951-56. Appointments: Library Critic, Information, 1955-57, Politiken, 1959-; Editor, Vindrosen, 1959-64; Literary Director, Gyldendal Publishers, 1985-92. Publications: Anna (Jeg) Anna, 1970; Marts, 1970; Leif den Lykkelige JR, 1971; Til Spanien, 1971; Lena Jorgensen, Klintevej 4, 2650, Hvidovre, 1971; Brevet til Gerda, 1972; RR, 1972; Spinatfuglene, 1973; Dilettanterne, 1973; Du skal ikke vaere ked af det Amalia, 1974; En Hugorm i solen, 1974; Vejen ad Hvilken, 1975; Tak for turen, 1975; Kiks, 1976; Tango, 1978; Dobbeltgoenger, 1978; Drengene, 1978; Joker, 1979; Voksdugshjertet, 1979; Det sorte hul, 1980. Short stories: Og Andre Historier, 1964; Rejsende, 1969; Den Syende Jomfru, 1972; Sommer, 1974. Non-Fiction: I medgang Og Modgang, 1970. Plays: Gris Pa Gaflen, 1962; Hva' Skal Vi Lave, 1963; Udviklinger, 1965; Hvad en Mand Har brug For, 1966; Voks, 1968; Ar, 1970; Narrene, 1971; Svaret Blaeser i Vinden, 1971; Det Korte af det lange, 1976; Twist, 1976; Et bortvendt ansigt, 1977; Deres majestaet!, 1977. Poetry: Livsfrisen, 1979. Honours: Danish Dramatists, 1966; Danish Academy Award, 1966; Golden Laurels, 1967; Grand Prize, Danish Academy of Arts and Letters, 1968; Soren Gyldendal Award, 1969; Nordic Council Award, 1971; Grant of Honour, Danish Writers Guild, 1973; PH Prize, 1979; Holberg Medal, 1984; H C Andersen Prize, 1987; Doctor honoris causa, Luna University, 1992. Membership: Danish Academy of Arts and Letters. Address: Kristianiagade 22, DK 2100, Copenhagen, Denmark.

RILEY James Andrew, b. 25 July 1939, Sullivan County, Tennessee, USA. Author; Feature Writer. m. Dorothy Elizabeth Taylor, 14 Oct 1960, 2 sons. Education: BS, 1961, MA, 1966, East Tennessee State University; EdS, Nova University, 1982. Publications: The All-Time All-Stars of Black Baseball, 1983; Dandy, Day, and the Devil, 1987; The Hundred Years of Chet Hoff, 1991; Biographical Encyclopedia of the Negro Baseball Leagues, 1994; Buck Leonard: The Black Lou Gehrig, 1995; Nice Guys Finish First: The Autobiography of Monte Irvin, 1996. Contributions to: Reference books and journals. Honours: Society for American Baseball Research Awards, 1990, 1994. Membership: Society for American Baseball Research. Address: PO Box 560968, Rockledge, FL 32956, USA.

RILEY Samuel Gayle III, b. 8 Oct 1939, Raleigh, North Carolina, USA. Professor of Communication Studies; Writer. m. Mary Elaine Weisner, 14 May 1966, div 1986, 1 son, 1 daughter. Education: AB, Davidson College, 1961; MBA, 1962, PhD, Mass Communication Research, 1970, University of North Carolina, Chapel Hill. Appointments: Assistant Professor of Journalism, Temple University, 1970-74; Associate Professor of Journalism, Georgia Southern University, 1971-81; Professor of Communication Studies, Virginia Polytechnic Institute and State University, 1981-. Publications: Magazines of the American South, 1986; Index to Southern Periodicals, 1986; American Magazine Journalists (Dictionary of Literary Biography), 4 volumes, 1988, 1989, 1990, 1994; Index to City and Regional Magazines of the United States, 1989; Regional Interest Magazines of the United States, 1991; GR8 PL8S, 1991; Corporate Magazines of the United States, 1992; Consumer Magazines of the British Isles, 1993; The Best of the Rest, 1993; Biographical Dictionary of American Newspaper Columnists, 1995; The American Newspaper Columist, 1998. Contributions to: Reference books, professional journals, newspapers, and magazines. Memberships: Association for Education in Journalism and Mass Communications; Research Society of American Periodicals; American Journalism Historians Association. Address: 1865 Mountainside Drive, Blacksburg, VA 24060, USA.

RINALDI Nicholas Michael, b. 2 Apr 1934, Brooklyn, New York, USA. Professor; Writer; Poet. m. Jacqueline Tellier, 29 Aug 1959, 3 sons, 1 daughter. Education: AB, Shrub Oak College, 1957; MA, 1960, PhD, 1963, Fordham University. Appointments: Instructor to Assistant Professor, St John's University, 1960-65; Lecturer, City University of New York, 1966; Associate Professor, Columbia University, 1966; Assistant Professor to Professor, Fairfield University, 1966-; Professor, University of Connecticut, 1972. Publications: The Resurrection of the Snails, 1977; We Have Lost Our Fathers, 1982; The Luftwaffe in Chaos, 1985; Bridge Fall Down, 1985. Contributions to: Virginia Quarterly Review; Periodicals. Honours: Joseph P Slomovich Memorial Award for Poetry, 1979; All Nations Poetry Awards, 1981, 1983; New York Poetry Forum Award, 1983; Eve of St Agnes Poetry Award, 1984; Charles Angoff Literary Award, 1984. Memberships: Associated Writing Programs; Poetry Society of America. Address: 190 Brookview Avenue, Fairfield, CT 06432, USA.

RING Douglas See: **PRATHER Richard Scott.**

RINGELL Susanne Gun Emilia, b. 28 Feb 1955, Helsinki, Finland. Author; Dramatist. m. Anders Larsson, 6 June 1992. Education: Theater Academy of Helsinki, 1977-81; Actress Diploma. Publications: Det Förlovade Barnet, 1993; Vestalen, The Vestal Virgin, 1994; Gall eller Våra Osynliga Väntrum, 1994; Vara Sten, 1996. Plays: Edelweiss, 1989; Pantlånekontoret, 1992; Atta Kroppar, 1998. Radio Plays: Vendettan, 1990; Vestalen, 1994; Harriets Hus, 1999. Contributions to: Fågel Fenix; Blå; Transit. Honour: Granberg Sumeliuska Priset, 1994; Prix Italia, 1995. Membership: Finlands Svenska Författareförening RF. Address: Snellmansgatan 16 B 24, 00170 Helsinki, Finland.

RINHART Marion Hutchinson, b. 20 Feb 1916, Bradley Beach, New Jersey, USA. Author; Historian. m. Lloyd, 3 Mar 1935, dec 1996, 1 son. Education: Research and study, Washington, DC. Appointments: Seminar, University of Georgia, 1977; Lecturing Professor, Ohio State University, 1985, 1986. Publications: American

Daguerrian Art, 1967; American Miniature Case Art, 1969; America's Affluent Age, 1971; Summertime, 1978; The American Daguerrotype, 1981; America's Centennial Celebration, 1976; Victorian Florida, 1986; The American Tintype (with Robert Wagner), forthcoming. Contributions to: Art in America; Antiques Journal; Modern Photography; Camera; American West; History of Photography; American History; Iowa Heritage. Honour: Fiest Daguerrian Society Award, 1990. Address: 11 Westwood Avenue, A-202, Tequesta, FL 33469, USA.

RÍO Isabel del, b. 8 Sept 1954, Madrid, Spain. Writer; Poet; United Nations Translator; Literary Translator. div 1998, 2 daughters. Education: Lic Cc Inf, Madrid Central University, 1972-77; Incorporated Linguist, Institute of Linguists, London, 1985. Appointments: Editor, Arts and Literary Programmes, Spanish Section, BBC World Service, 1978-82; Freelance journalist and writer; At present full-time Translator, International Maritime Organisation, United Nations Agency, London, England. Publications: BBC Get By In Spanish, 1992; Ciudad del interior, 1993; La duda, 1995. Translations: The Secret Garden, by F H Burnett, 1990; Poetry by Sylvia Plath and T L Beddoes. Honours: Finalist, Nuevos Narradores Competition, 1994; Finalist, Premio Icaro, 1995. Memberships: PEN; Society of Authors; Translators Association; Institute of Linguists; Institute of Translation and Interpreting; AITC, Geneva. Literary Agent: Tusquets Editores, Iradier 24, Barcelona 08017, Spain; sub-agent for the UK: The Caroline Davidson Literary Agency, 5 Queen Anne's Gardens, London W4 1TU, England. Address: PO Box 10314, London W14 0FT, England.

RIOS Juan, b. 28 Sept 1914, Lima, Peru. Poet; Dramatist; Critic. m. Rosa Saco, 16 Sept 1946, 1 daughter. Publications: Cancion de Siempre, 1941; Malstrom, 1941; La Pintura Contempranea en el Peru, 1946; Teatro, 1961; Ayar Manko, 1963; Primera Antologia Poetica, 1981. Honours: National Prizes for Drama, 1946, 1950, 1952, 1954, 1960; National Prize for Poetry, 1948, 1953. Membership: Academia Peruana de la Lengua. Address: Bajada de Banos 109, Barranco, Lima 04, Peru.

RIPLEY Alexandra (Braid), b. 8 Jan 1934, Charleston, South Carolina, USA. Author. m. (1) Leonard Ripley, 1958, div 1963, (2) John Graham, 1981, 2 daughters. Education: AB, Vassar College, 1955. Publications: Who's That Lady in the President's Bed?, 1972; Charleston, 1981; On Leaving Charleston, 1984; The Time Returns, 1985; New Orleans Legacy, 1987; Scarlett: The Sequel to Margaret Mitchell's Gone With the Wind, 1991; From the Fields of Gold, 1994; A Love Devine, 1996. Address: c/o Janklow-Nesbit Associates, 598 Madison Avenue, New York, NY 10022, USA.

RIPLEY Michael David, (Mike Ripley), b. 29 Sept 1952, Huddersfield, England. Critic; Writer. m. Alyson Jane White, 8 July 1978, 2 daughters. Education: BA, Honours, Economic History, University of East Anglia. Appointments: Crime Fiction Critic, Sunday Telegraph, 1989-91; Crime Critic, The Daily Telegraph, 1991-. Publications: Just Another Angel, 1988; Angel Touch, 1989; Angel Hunt, 1990; Angels in Arms, 1991. Short stories: The Body of the Beer, 1989; Smeltdown, 1990; Gold Sword, 1990. Contributions to: 'Britcrit' Column Mystery Scene, USA. Honours: Scholarship to public school; Runner-Up, Punch Magazine Awards for Funniest Crime Novel, 1988; Last Laugh Awards, Crime Writers Association, 1989, 1991; Angel Literary Award for Fiction, 1990. Memberships: Crime Writers Association; Sisters in Crime, USA; Dorothy L Sayers Society. Address: c/o David Higham Associates, 5-8 Lower John Street, London W1R 4HA, England.

RIPPON Angela, b. 12 Oct 1944, Plymouth, Devon, England. Television and Radio Presenter; Writer. m. Christopher Dare, 1967. Education: Grammar School, Plymouth, England. Appointments: Editor, Presenter, Producer, Westward Television, 1969-73; News Reporter, National News, 1973-76; Newsreader, Nine O'Clock News, 1976-81; Arts and Entertainment Officer, WNEV-TV, Channel 7, Boston, USA, 1984-85; Hostess, The Health Show, BBC Radio 5, 1989-90; Anchorwoman, Angela Rippon Morning Report, 1990-92, Angela Rippon's Drive Time Show, 1992-. Publications: Riding, 1980; In the Country, 1980; Mark Phillips: The Man and His Horses, 1982; Angela Rippon's West Country, 1982; Victoria Plum, 1983; Badminton: A Celebration, 1987; Many recordings. Honours: Radio and Television Industries Awards for Newsreader of the Year, 1976, 1977, 1978; Television Personality of the Year, 1977; Sony Award, 1990. Memberships: International Club for Women in Television, vice-president, 1979-; English National Ballet Association, chairman; American College, London, board member. Address: c/o International Management Group, Media House, 3 Burlington Lane, Chiswick, London W4 2TH, England.

RITCHIE David. See: **CALDER Nigel.**

RITCHIE Elisavietta, b. Kansas City, Missouri, USA. Writer; Poet. m. Clyde Farnsworth, 22 June 1991, 2 sons, 1 daughter. Education: Diplôme, Mention Très Bien, Cours de Civilisation Française, Sorbonne, University of Paris; Cornell University; BA, French, Russian, English, University of California at Berkeley; Georgetown University; MA, French Literature, minor Russian Studies, American University. Appointments: Founder, The Wineberry Press; President, Washington Writers Publishing House; Frequent Workshop Leader; Writer and Poet-in-the-Schools; Poetry readings, numerous venues, USA, Canada, Australia, Far East, Russia, Brazil, Balkans. Publications: Poetry: Timbot, novella in verse, 1970; Tightening the Circle over Eel Country, 1974; A Sheath of Dreams and Other Games, 1976; Moving to Larger Quarters, 1977; Raking the Snow, 1982; The Problem with Eden, 1985; Flying Time: Stories and Half-Stories, fiction, 1992, 1996; A Wound-Up Cat and Other Bedtime Stories, poetry, 1993; Wild Garlic: The Journal of Maria X, novella in verse, 1995; Elegy for the Other Woman: New and Selected Terribly Female Poems, 1996; The Arc of the Storm, poetry, 1998; Editor: The Dolphin's Arc: Poems on Endangered Creatures of the Sea; Finding the Name. Contributions to: Poetry; The American Scholar; New York Times; Christian Science Monitor; Washington Post; National Geographic; Other magazines and periodicals; Many anthologies. Honours: Numerous including: New Writer's Prize for Best First Book of Poetry, Great Lakes College Association, 1974; Winner, Washington Writers Publishing House 1981-82 Competition; 4 PEN Syndicated Fiction Awards; 2 Annual Awards, Poetry Society of America; 4 Grants, District of Columbia; Fellowships, Virginia Center for the Creative Arts.

RITCHIE Elisavietta Artamonoff, b. 29 June 1932, Kansas City, Missouri, USA. Writer; Poet; Translator; Teacher; Editor; Photographer. m. (1) Lyell Hale Ritchie, 11 July 1953, div 2 sons, 1 daughter, (2) Clyde Henri Farnsworth, 22 June 1991. Education: Degré Supèrieur, Mention Tres Bien, Sorbonne, University of Paris, 1951; Cornell University, 1951-53; BA, University of California at Berkeley, 1954; MA, French Literature, 1951-53; BA, University of California at Berkeley, 1954; MA, French Literature, American University, 1976; Advanced Russian courses, Georgetown University. Appointments: US Information Agency Visiting Poet, Brazil, 1972, Far East, 1977, Yugoslavia, 1979, Bulgaria, 1979; Founder-Director, The Wineberry Press, 1983-; President, Washington Writers Publishing House, 1986-89; Leader, various creative writing workshops. Publications: Timbot, 1970; Tightening the Circle Over Eel Country, 1974; A Sheath of Dreams and Other Games, 1976; Moving to Larger Quarters, 1977; Raking the Snow, 1982; The Chattanooga Cycles, 1984; The Problem with Eden, 1985; Flying Time: Stories and Half-Stories, 1992; A Wound-Up Cat and Other Bedtime Stories, 1993; Wild Garlic: The Journal of Maria X, 1995; Elegy for the Other Woman: New and Selected Terriby Female Poems, 1996; The Arc of the Storm, 1996. Contributions to: Many anthologies and periodicals. Honours: New Writer's Award for Best 1st Book of Poetry, Great Lakes Colleges Association, 1975-76; 4 PEN Syndicated Fiction Awards; 2 Awards, Poetry Society of America. Memberships: Amnesty International; PEN; Poetry Society of America; Poets and Writers; Washington Independent Writers; Writer's Center. Address: 3207 Macomb Street North West, Washington, DC 20008, USA.

RITTER Erika, b. 1948, Regina, Saskatchewan, Canada. Dramatist; Writer. Education: McGill University, Montreal, 1968; MA, University of Toronto, 1970. Appointments: Writer-in-Residence, Concordia University, 1984; Playwright-in-Residence, Smith College, 1985, Stratford Festival, 1985. Publications: Plays: A Visitor from Charleston, 1975; The Splits, 1978; Winter, 1671, 1979; Automatic Pilot, 1980; The Passing Scene, 1982; Murder at McQueen, 1986; The Road to Hell, 1992; Other: Urban Scrawl, 1984; Ritter in Residence, 1987; The Hidden Life in Humans, 1997. Honours: Chalmers Award, 1980; ACTRA Award, 1982. Address: c/o Shain Jaffe, Great North Artists, 350 Dupont Street, Toronto, Ontario M5R 1V9, Canada.

RITTERBAND Olly, b. 28 Dec 1923, Miercurea-Niraj, Romania. Artist; Author. m. Daniel Ritterband, 25 Dec 1949, 2 daughters. Education: Royal Danish Academy of Fine Arts, Copenhagen; École Nationale Supérieure des Beaux-Arts, Paris; Accademia del Mosaico, Ravenna, Italy. Appointment: Teacher, Royal Danish Academy of Fine Arts, Copenhagen. Publications: I Will Not Die, 1982; The Will to Survive, 1990. Contributions to: Publications on the Holocaust. Memberships: Danish Authors Association; Friends of Mosaic Art, president; Gentofte Society of Culture; Society of Jewish History. Address: Niels Andersensvej 65, Hellerup, DK-2900, Denmark.

RITVO Harriet, b. 19 Sept 1946, Cambridge, Massachusetts, USA. Historian. Education: AB, 1968, PhD, 1975, Harvard University. Appointment: Professor of History and Writing, Arthur J Conner Professor of History, Massachusetts Institute of Technology. Publications: The Animal Estate: The English and Other Creatures in the Victorian Age; The Macropolitics of 19th-Century Literature (co-editor with Jonathan Arac). Contributions to: Numerous essays and reviews on 18th and 19th-Century cultural history, and on the relationship between humans and other animals. Honour: Whiting Writers' Award, 1990. Memberships: PEN American Center; American Historical Association; History of Science Society; Society for the History of Natural History. Address: E51-285 Massachusetts Institute of Technology, Cambridge, MA 02139, USA.

RIVARD Ken J, b. 30 June 1947, Montreal, Quebec, Canada. Special Education Teacher; Poet; Writer. m. Micheline Rivard, 19 Sept 1972, 2 daughters. Education: BEd, University of Montreal, 1970; MEd, McGill University, 1974. Publications: Poetry: Kiss Me Down to Size, 1983; Losing His Thirst, 1985; Frankie's Desires, 1987. Fiction: Working Stiffs, 1990; If She Could Take All These Men, 1995; Mom, The School Flooded Children's Book), 1996. Contributions to: Anthologies and periodicals. Memberships: Writers Guild of Alberta; League of Canadian Poets. Address: 120 Whiteview Place North East, Calgary, Alberta T1Y 1R6, Canada.

RIZKALLA John Ramsay, b. 2 Nov 1935, Manchester, England. Writer. Education: Baccalaureat Francais, 1st and 2nd part, 1952-53; BA, Honours, University of Manchester, 1958. Publication: The Jericho Garden, 1988. Contributions to: Books, magazines and radio. Membership: Society of Authors. Address: c/o Murray Polinger, 222 Old Brompton Road, London SW5 0BZ, England.

ROBB Graham Macdonald, b. 2 June 1958, Manchester, England. Writer. m. Margaret Robb, 2 May 1986. Education: BA, 1st Class Honours, 1981; PGCE, Goldsmiths College, London, 1982; PhD, Vanderbilt University, Nashville, Tennessee, 1986. Publications: Le Corsaire - Satan en Silhouette, 1985; Baudelaire Lecteur de Balzac, 1988; Scenes de La Vie de Boheme (editor), 1988; Baudelaire, (translation), 1989; La Poésie de Baudelaire et La Poésie Française, 1993; Balzac, 1994; Unlocking Mallarmé, 1996; Victor Hugo: A Biography,

1998. Contributions to: Times Literary Supplement; Wall Street Journal; Washington Post; Revue d'Histoire Litteraire de La France; French Studies. Honours: Postdoctoral Research Fellow; British Academy Fellowship, 1987-90; Whitbread Biography of the Year Award, 1997. Memberships: Society of Authors; Société d'Histoire Litteraire de La France. Address: 139 Hollow Way, Oxford OX4 2NE, England.

ROBBE-GRILLET Alain, b. 18 Aug 1922, Brest, France. Writer; Filmmaker; Agronomist. m. Catherine Rstakian, 1957. Education: Institute Agronomique. Publications: Novels: Les Gommes, 1953; Le Voyeur, 1955; La Jalousie, 1957; Dans le Labyrinthe, 1959; La Maison de Rendez-vous, 1965; Projet pour une Revolution a New York, 1970; Topologie d'une Cite Fantome, 1976; La Belle Captive, 1977; Un Regicide, 1978; Souvenirs du Triangle d'Or, 1978; Djinn, 1981; Le Miroir qui Revient, 1984; Angélique ou l'Enchantment, 1987; Les Derniers Jours de Corinthe, 1994. Short Stories: Instantanes, 1962. Essay: Pour un Nouveau Roman, 1964. Films: L'Annee Derniere a Marienbad, 1961. Honours: Chevalier, Légion d'Honneur; Officier, Ordre National du Mérite; Prix Louis Delluc, 1963. Memberships: Various professional organisations. Address: 18 Boulevard Maillot, 92200 Neuilly-sur-Seine, France.

ROBBINS Kenneth Randall, b. 7 Jan 1944, Douglasville, Georgia, USA. Associate Professor; Writer; Dramatist. m. Dorothy Dodge, 14 May 1988, 1 son, 1 daughter. Education: AA, Young Harris College, 1964; BSEd, Georgia Southern University, 1966; MFA, University of Georgia, 1969; PhD, Southern Illinois University at Carbondale, 1982. Appointments: Assistant Professor, Jacksonville University, Florida, 1974-79; Associate Professor, Newberry College, South Carolina, 1977-85, University of South Dakota, 1985-; Presenter, Black Hills Writers Conference, 1986-90; Editor, Wayne S Knutson Dakota Playwriting Series. Publications: The Dallas File (play), 1982; Buttermilk Bottoms (novel), 1987. Contributions to: Journals and radio. Honours: Toni Morrison Prize for Fiction, 1986; Associated Writing Programs Novel Award, 1986; Festival of Southern Theatre Awards, 1987, 1990. Memberships: American College Theatre Festival; Association of Theatre in Higher Education; Dramatists Guild; The Loft, Minneapolis; Playwright's Centre, Minneapolis; Society for Humanities and Technology; Southeastern Theatre Conference. Address: 118 Willow, Vermillion, SD 57069, USA.

ROBBINS Richard H, b. 19 May 1922, New York City, USA. Sociologist; Teacher. m. Gillian Ashton, 2 daughters, 2 stepdaughters. Education: BA, Brooklyn College, New York City, 1946; MA, Washington State University, Washington, 1948; PhD, University of Illinois, 1958. Appointments: Instructor, Sociology, Anthropology, Wellesley College, MA, 1954-58; Assistant Professor to Professor, Sociology, Wheaton College, MA, 1958-67; University of Mass-Boston, Chair & Professor, Sociology, Anthropology, 1967-71; Professor, Sociology, 1971-90. Publications: International Migrations, with Donald R Taft, 1955; Desegregation and the Negro Colleges in the South, 1966; Editor, with Walter Powell; Conflict and Consensus: Essays in Honor of Lewis Coser, 1984; Sidelines Activist: Charles S Johnson and the Struggle for Civil Rights, 1996. Contributions to: New Republic; Dissent; Sociological Analysis; Contemporary Sociology; Catholic World; Phylon; Annals American Academy. Honours: Fulbright Fellow, 1949, 1963, 1967; Guggenheim Fellow, 1974-75. Address: 91 Lakeview St, Sharon, MA 02067, USA.

ROBBINS Richard (Leroy), b. 27 Aug 1953, Los Angeles, California, USA. Professor; Poet; Writer; Editor. m. Candace L Black, 8 Sept 1979, 2 sons. Education: AB, English, San Diego State University, 1975; MFA, Creative Writing, University of Montana, 1979. Appointments: Co-Editor, Cafeteria, 1971-81; CutBank and SmokeRoot Press, 1977-79, Montana Arts Council anthologies, 1979-81; Writer-in-Residence, Poet-in-the-Schools, Montana Arts Council, 1979-81; Instructor, Moorhead

State University, 1981-82, Oregon State University, 1982-84; Professor, Minnesota State University, Mankato, 1984-; Assistant Editor, Mankato Poetry Review, 1984-. Publications: Where We Are: The Montana Poets Anthology (editor with Lex Runciman), 1978; Toward New Weather, 1979; The Invisible Wedding, 1984; Famous Persons We Have Known, forthcoming. Contributions to: 9 anthologies, 1978-97, reviews, quarterlies, and journals. Honours: 1st Prize in Poetry, Branford P Millar Award, Portland Review, 1978; Frontier Award, University of Montana, 1978; Individual Artist Fellowship, Minnesota State Arts Board, 1986; Robert H Winner Memorial Award, Poetry Society of America, 1988; National Endowment for the Arts Fellowship, 1992; McKnight Individual Artist Grants, 1993, 1996, and Fellowship, 1997; Hawthornden Fellowship, 1998. Memberships: Associated Writing Programs; The Loft; Poetry Society of America; Western Literature Association. Address: c/o Department of English, Minnesota State University, PO Box 8400, Mankato, MN 56002, USA.

ROBBINS Tom, (Thomas Eugene Robbins), b. 1936, Blowing Rock, North Carolina, USA. Writer. m. (1), (2) Terrie Robbins, div, 1 son. Education: Washington and Lee University, 1954-56; Degree in Social Science, Richmond Professional Institute, Virginia, 1959; University of Washington, 1963. Publications: Guy Anderson, 1965; Another Roadside Attraction, 1971; Even Cowgirls Get the Blues, 1976; Still Life with Woodpecker, 1980; Jitterbug Perfume, 1984; Skinny Legs and All, 1990; Half Asleep in Frog Pajamas, 1994. Address: PO Box 338, La Conner, WA 98257, USA.

ROBERSON John Royster, b. 7 Mar 1930, Roanoke, Virginia, USA. Editor; Writer. m. Charlene Grace Hale, 17 Sept 1966, 1 son, 1 daughter. Education: BA, 1950, MA, 1953, University of Virginia; Certificates of French Studies, 1st and 2nd Degrees, University of Grenoble, France, 1952; Diploma in Mandarin Chinese, US Army Language School, Monterey, California, 1956. Appointments: Assistant to Senior Editor, Holiday, 1959-70; Copywriter, N W Ayer Advertising, 1971-76; Associate to Senior Staff Editor, Reader's Digest Condensed Books, 1976-95; Director of Publications, Science Education Center, Fairfield County, Connecticut. Publications: China from Manchu to Mao 1699-1976, 1980; Japan from Shogun to Sony 1543-1984, 1985; Transforming Russia 1692-1991, 1992; Japan Meets the West, 1998. Contributions to: Atlantic; Holiday; Reader's Digest; Studies in Bibliography; Virginia Magazine of History and Biography. Honours: Raven Society, University of Virginia, 1950; Rotary International Fellowship, University of Grenoble, 1951-52. Memberships: International House of Japan; US China People's Friendship Society; Board of Directors, Science Education Centre. Address: 16 Hassake Road, Old Greenwich, CT 06870, USA.

ROBERTS Andrew, b. 13 Jan 1963, London, England. Author. Education: MA, 1st Class Honours, Modern History, Gonville and Caius College, Cambridge, 1985. Publications: The Holy Fox: A Biography of Lord Halifax, 1991; Eminent Churchillians, 1994; The Aachen Memorandum, 1995. Contributions to: Spectator; Literary Review; Columnist, Sunday Times. Memberships: Beefsteak Club; University Pitt Club, Cambridge; Brooks. Address: 2 Tite Street, London SW3 4HY, England.

ROBERTS Brian, b. 19 Mar 1930, London, England. Writer. Education: Teacher's Certificate, St Mary's College, Twickenham, 1955; Diploma in Sociology, University of London, 1958. Appointments: Teacher of English and History, 1955-65. Publications: Ladies in the Veld, 1965; Cecil Rhodes and the Princess, 1969; Churchills in Africa, 1970; The Diamond Magnates, 1972; The Zulu Kings, 1974; Kimberley: Turbulent City, 1976; The Mad Bad Line: The Family of Lord Alfred Douglas, 1981; Randolph: A Study of Churchill's Son, 1984; Cecil Rhodes: Flawed Colossus, 1987; Those Bloody Women: Three Heroines of the Boer War, 1991. Literary Agent: Andrew Lownie, 17 Sutherland Street, London, SW1U

4JU. Address: North Knoll Cottage, 15 Bridge Street, Frome BA11 1BB, England.

ROBERTS Eirlys Rhiwen Cadwaladr, b. 3 Jan 1911, United Kingdom. Journalist. m. John Cullen, 1941. Education: BA, Honours, Classics, Girton College, Cambridge. Appointments: Editor, Which? magazine, 1958-73; Head of Research and Editorial Division, Consumers' Association. Publication: Consumers, 1966. Contributions to: Various journals and magazines. Honours: Officer of the Order of the British Empire, 1971; Commander of the Order of the British Empire, 1977. Membership: Royal Society of Arts. Address: 8 Lloyd Square London, WC1X 9BA, England.

ROBERTS Irene, (Roberta Carr, Elizabeth Harle, I M Roberts, Ivor Roberts, Iris Rowland, Irene Shaw), b. 27 Sept 1925, London, England. Writer. Education: London schools. Appointments: Woman's Page Editor, South Hams Review, 1977-79; Tutor, Creative Writing, Kingsbridge Community College, 1978-. Publications: Shadows on the Moon, 1968; Thunder Heights, 1969; Surgeon in Tibet, 1970; Birds Without Bars, 1970; The Shrine of Fire, 1970; Sister at Sea, 1971; Gull Haven, 1971; Moon Over the Temple, 1972; The Golden Pagoda, 1972; Desert Nurse, 1976; Nurse in Nepal, 1976; Stars Above Raffael, 1977; Hawks Burton, 1979; Symphony of Bells, 1980; Nurse Moonlight, 1980; Weave Me a Moonbeam, 1982; Jasmine for a Nurse, 1982; Sister on Leave, 1982; Nurse in the Wilderness, 1983; Moonpearl, 1986; Sea Jade, 1987; Kingdom of the Sun, 1987; Song of the Nile, 1987. Juvenile: Holiday's for Hanbury, 1964; Laughing is for Fun, 1964. As Ivor Roberts: Jump into Hell, 1960; Trial by Water, 1961; Green Hell, 1961. As Iris Rowland: Blue Feathers, 1967; Moon Over Moncrieff, 1969; Star Drift, 1970; Rainbow River, 1970; The Wild Summer, 1970; Orange Blossom for Tara, 1971; Blossoms in the Snow, 1971; Sister Julia, 1972; Golden Bubbles, 1976; Hunter's Dawn, 1977; Golden Triangle, 1978; Forgotten Dreams, 1978; Temptation, 1983; Theresa, 1985. As Roberta Carr: Sea Maiden, 1965; Fire Dragon, 1967; Golden Interlude, 1970. As Elizabeth Harle: Golden Rain, 1964; Gay Rowan, 1965; Sandy, 1967; Spray of Red Roses, 1971; The Silver Summer, 1971; The Burning Flame, 1979; Come to Me Darling, 1983. As Irene Shaw: Moonstone Manor, 1968, US edition as Murder Mansion 1976; The Olive Branch, 1968; As I M Roberts: The Throne of the Pharoahs, 1974; Hatsheput, Queeen of the Nile, 1976; Hour of the Tiger, 1985; Jezebel Street, 1994; Limehouse Lady, 1995; More Laughter Than Tears, 1996; London's Pride in Progress, 1997. Membership: Romantic Novelists Association, founder-member. Address: Alpha House, Higher Town, Marlborough, Kingsbridge, South Devon TQ7 3RL, England.

ROBERTS John Morris, b. 14 Apr 1928, Bath, England. Honorary Fellow; Writer. m. Judith Cecilia Mary Armitage, 1964, 1 son, 2 daughters. Education: BA, 1949, MA, 1952, DPhil, 1953, University of Oxford. Appointments: Member, Institute of Advanced Study, Princeton, New Jersey, 1960-61; Council, European University Institute, 1980-88; USA/UK Education Commission (Fulbright), 1981-87; Visiting Professor, University of South Carolina, 1961; Secretary, Harmsworth Trust, 1962-68; Senior Proctor, University of Oxford, 1967-68; Vice-Chancellor and Professor, Southampton University, 1979-85; Honorary Fellow, 1981-84, 1994-, Warden, 1985-94, Merton College, Oxford; Governor, BBC, 1988-93. Publications: French Revolution Documents I, 1966; Europe 1880-1945, 1967, new edition, 1990; The Mythology of the Secret Societies, 1972; The Paris Commune from the Right, 1973; Revolution and Improvement: The Western World 1775-1847, 1976; History of the World, 1976, revised edition, 1993; The French Revolution, 1978; The Triumph of the West, 1985; Shorter Illustrated History of the World, 1994. Contributions to: Professional journals. Honours: Honorary DLitt, Southampton University, 1987; Cavalier, Order of Merit, Italian Republic, 1989; Commander of the Order of the British Empire, 1996. Memberships: National Portrait Gallery, trustee, 1984-; Royal Literary Fund; Society of Authors; Royal Historical

Society. Address: c/o Merton College, Oxford OX1 4JD, England.

ROBERTS Keith (John Kingston), (Alistair Bevan), b. 10 Sept 1935, Kettering, Northamptonshire, England. Writer; Poet. Education: National Diploma in Design, Northampton School of Art, 1956; Leicester College of Art, 1956-57. Publications: Fiction: The Furies, 1966; The Inner Wheel, 1970; Anita, 1970; The Boat of Fate, 1971; Machines and Men, 1973; The Chalk Giants, 1974; The Grain Kings, 1975; Ladies from Hell, 1979; Molly Zero, 1980; Kiteworld, 1985; Kaeti and Company, 1986; The Lordly Ones, 1986; The Road to Paradise, 1988; Tears in a Glass Eye, 1989; The Event, 1989; Winterwood and Other Hauntings, 1989; Kaeti on Tour, 1992. Poetry: A Heron Caught in the Weeds, 1987. Other: Irish Encounters, 1988; The Natural History of PH, 1988. Address: c/o Carnell Literary Agency, Danes Croft, Goose Lane, Little Hallingbury, Hertfordshire CM22 7RG, England.

ROBERTS Leonard, (Len Roberts), b. 13 Mar 1947, Cohoes, New York, USA. Professor of English; Poet; Translator. m. 31 Dec 1981, 2 sons, 1 daughter. Education: BA, English, Siena College, 1970; MA, English, University of Dayton, 1972; PhD, English, Lehigh University, 1976. Appointments: Professor of English, Northampton College, 1974-83, 1986-87, 1989-93, 1995-; Visiting Assistant Professor, Lafayette College, 1983-85; Visiting Professor, University of Pittsburgh, 1984-; Fulbright cholar, Janus Pannonius University, Pécs, Hungary, 1988-89, University of Turku, Finland, 1994. Publications: Poetry: Cohoes Theater, 1980; From the Dark, 1984; Sweet Ones, 1988; Black Wings, 1989; Learning About the Heart, 1992; Dangerous Angels, 1993; The Million Branches: Selected Poems and Interview, 1993; Counting the Black Angels, 1994; The Trouble-Making Finch, 1998. Translator: The Selected Poems of Sándor Csoóri, 1992. Contributions to: Anthologies and journals. Honours: Pennsylvania Council on the Arts Writing Awards in Poetry, 1981, 1986, 1987, 1991; National Endowment for the Arts Awards, 1984, 1989; Great Lakes and Prairies Award, 1988; National Poetry Series Award, 1988; Soros Foundation Poetry Translation Awards, 1989, 1990, 1992, 1997; Guggenheim Fellowship, 1990-91; Pushcart Prize, 1991; Witter Bynner Poetry Translation Award, 1991-92; Winner, Silverfish Review Chapbook Competition, 1992; 1st Prize, Wildwood Poetry Contest, 1993. Memberships: Modern Language Association; Pennsylvania Council on the Arts, advisory board, 1990-; Poetry Society of America; Poets and Writers. Address: 2443 Wassergass Road, Hellertown, PA 18055, USA.

ROBERTS Michèle, b. 29 May 1949, Bushey, Hertfordshire, England. Poet; Writer; Dramatist. Education: BA, University of Oxford, 1970; Library Associate, University of London, 1970. Publications: Fiction: A Piece of the Night, 1978; Tales I Tell My Mother, 1978; The Wild Girl, 1984; The Book of Mrs Noah, 1986; More Tales I Tell My Mother, 1989; The Seven Deadly Sins, 1989; The Seven Cardinal Virtues, 1990; In the Red Kitchen, 1990; God, 1992; Daughters of the House, 1993. Poetry: The Mirror of the Mother, 1986; Psyche and the Hurricane, 1991. Play: The Journey Woman, 1988. Screenplay: The Heavenly Twins, 1992. Contributions to: Anthologies and other publications. Honour: W H Smith Literary Award, 1993. Address: c/o W H Smith Literary Award, Strand House, 7 Holbein Place, London SW1W 8NR, England.

ROBERTS Michele Brigitte, b. 20 May 1949, Hertfordshire, England. Novelist; Poet. m. Jim Latter, 11 Aug 1991, 2 stepsons. Education: MA (Oxon), Somerville College, Oxford, 1967-70; ALA, University College, London, 1971-72. Appointments: British Council Librarian, Bangkok, 1973-74; Writer, 1974-; Poetry Editor, Spare Rib, 1974, City Limits, 1981-83; Visiting Fellow in Creative Writing, UEA, 1992; Research Fellow in Writing, 1995-96, Visiting Professor, 1996-, Nottingham Trent University. Publications: Novels: A Piece of the Night, 1978; The Visitation, 1983; The Wild Girl, 1984; The Book of Mrs Noah, 1987; In the Red Kitchen, 1990; Daughters of the House, 1992; Flesh and Blood, 1994; Mind Readings, 1996; Impossible Saints, 1997; During Mother's Absence (stories), 1993; The Mirror of the Mother (poetry). Plays: The Journeywoman, 1988; Psyche and the Hurricane, 1991; All the Selves I Was, 1995; The Heavenly Twins (film), 1993; Child-Lover (film), 1995; Food, Sex and God (non-fiction), 1998. Contributions to: Times; Independent; Independent on Sunday. Honour: W H Smith Literary Award, 1993. Membership: Violet Needham Society. Literary Agent: Aitken and Stone. Address: c/o Aitken and Stone, 29 Fernshaw Road, London SW10 0TG, England.

ROBERTS Nora, b. 10 Oct 1950, Washington, District of Columbia, USA. Writer. m. (1) Ronald Aufdem-Brinker, 17 Aug 1968, div 1985, 2 sons, (2) Bruce Wilder, 6 July 1985. Education: Graduated, High School, 1968. Publications: Irish Thoroughbred, 1981; This Magic Moment, 1983; The MacGregors, 1985; Hot Ice, 1987; Sacred Sins, 1987; Brazen Virtue, 1988; The O'Harleys, 1988; Sweet Revenge, 1989; Public Secrets, 1990; The Calhoun Women, 1991; Genuine Lies, 1991; Carnal Innocence, 1992; Honest Illusions, 1992; Divine Evil, 1992; Private Scandals, 1993; Hidden Riches, 1994; True Betrayals, 1995; Montana Sky, 1996. As J D Robb: Glory in Death, 1995; Naked in Death, 1995; Immortal in Death, 1996. Honours: Romance Writers of America, Golden Medallions, 1982, 1983, 1984, 1986; Hall of Fame, 1986, and Rita Award, 1990, Romance Writers of America; Waldenbooks Awards, 1986, 1987, 1989, 1990, 1991; B Dalton Awards, 1990, 1991; RITA Awards, 1993, 1994, 1995. Memberships: Romance Writers of America; Mystery Writers of America; Novelists Inc; Crime Writers; Sisters-in-Crime. Address: c/o Writers House, 21 West 26th Street, New York, NY 10010, USA.

ROBERTS Willo Davis, b. 29 May 1928, Grand Rapids, Michigan, USA. Writer. m. David Roberts, 20 May 1949, 2 sons, 2 daughters. Publications: 93 books including: Murder at Grand Bay, 1955; The Girl Who Wasn't There, 1957; Nurse Kay's Conquest, 1966; The Tarot Spell, 1970; King's Pawn, 1971; White Jade, 1975-; 8 volumes in The Black Pearl Series, 1978-80; The Search for Willie, 1980; A Long Time To Hate, 1982; Keating's Landing, 1984; The Annalise Experiment, 1985; To Share a Dream, 1986; Madawaska, 1988. Books for children and young adults: The View from the Cherry Tree, 1975; Don't Hurt Laurie, 1977; The Girl with the Silver Eyes, 1980; The Pet Sitting Peril, 1983; Eddie and the Fairy God Puppy, 1984; Baby Sitting is a Dangerous Job, 1985; The Magic Book, 1986; Sugar Isn't Everything, 1987; Megan's Island, 1988; Nightmare, 1989; Scared Stiff, 1991; Dark Secrets, 1991; Twisted Summer, 1996; Secrets at Hidden Valley, 1998; The Kidnappers, 1998; Hostage, forthcomming. Honours: Mark Twain Award, 1980; Pacific Northwest Writers Achievement Award, 1986; Edgar Allan Poe Awards, 1988, 1995; Florida Sunshine State Award, 1994. Memberships: Mystery Writers of America; Society of Children's Book Writers; Seattle Freelancers; Pacific Northwest Writers Conference. Address: 12020 West Engebretsen Road, Granite Falls, WA 98252, USA.

ROBERTSON Barbara, b. 20 July 1931, Toronto, Ontario, Canada. Writer. Education: BA, University of Toronto, 1953; MA, Queen's University of Kingston, 1957. Publications: The Wind Has Wings (editor, with M A Downie), 1968, enlarged edition as The New Wind Has Wings, 1984; Wilfrid Laurier: The Great Conciliator, 1971, new edition, 1991; The Well-Filled Cupboard (with M A Downie), 1987; Doctor Dwarf and Other Poems for Children (editor with M A Downie), 1990; Ottawa at War: The Grant Dexter Memoranda 1939-1945, (editor F W Gibson), 1994. Contributions to: Periodicals. Address: 52 Florence Street, Kingston, Ontario K7M 1Y6, Canada.

ROBERTSON Charles, b. 22 Oct 1940, Glasgow, Scotland. Parish Minister; Chaplain to Her Majesty the Queen in Scotland, (Clergyman). m. 30 July 1965, 1 son, 2 daughters. Education: MA, University of Edinburgh, 1964. Publications: Editor, contributor: Common Order; Saint Margaret Queen of Scotland and her Chapel; Singing the Faith; Worshipping Together; Hymns for a Day; Songs of God's People; Common Ground. Contributions to: Record of Church Service Society; Scottish Journal of Theology (reviewer). Memberships: Joint Liturgical Group, chairman; Panel on Worship, secretary; Member of Historie Buildings Council for Scotland. Address: Manse of Canongate, Edinburgh EH8 8BR, Scotland.

ROBERTSON Denise, b. 9 June 1933, Sunderland, England. Writer; Broadcaster. m. (1) Alexander Robertson, 19 Mar 1960, (2) John Tomlin, 3 Nov 1973, 5 sons. Publications: Year of Winter, 1986; Land of Lost Content, 1987; Blue Remembered Hills, 1987; Second Wife, 1988; None to Make You Cry, 1989; Remember the Moment, 1990. Contributions to: Numerous. Honour: Constable Fiction Trophy, 1985. Address: 9 Springfield Crescent, Seaham, County Durham, England.

ROBERTSON Geoffrey Ronald, b. 30 Sept 1946, Sydney, Australia. Queen's Counsel; Barrister. m. Kathy Lette, 1990, 1 son, 1 daughter. Education: BA, 1966, LLB, 1970, University of Sydney; BCL, University College, 1972. Appointments: Barrister, 1973; Queens Counsel, 1988. Publications: Reluctant Judas, 1976; Obscenity, 1979; People Against the Press, 1983; Does Dracula Have Aids?, 1986; Freedom, The Individual and the Law, 1989; Geoffrey Robertson's Hypotheticals, 1986, 1991; The Trials of Oz, 1992; Media Law, with A Nicol, 1992; The Justice Game, 1998. Honour: BAFTA Nomination, The Trials of Oz, 1992. Address: Doughty Street Chambers, 11 Doughty Street, London WC1N 2PG, England.

ROBERTSON James (Irvin Jr), b. 18 July 1930, Danville, Virginia, USA. Professor of History. m. Elizabeth Green, 1 June 1952, 2 sons, 1 daughters. Education: BA, Randolph-Macon College, 1954; MA, 1955, PhD, 1959, Emory University; LittD, Randolph-Macon College, 1980. Appointments: Associate Professor of History, University of Montana, 1965-67; Professor of History, 1967-75, C P Miles Professor of History, 1976-92, Alumni Distinguished Professor of History, 1992-, Virginia Polytechnic Institute and State University. Publications: The Stonewall Brigade, 1963; The Civil War Letters of General Robert McAllister, 1965; Recollections of a Maryland Confederate Soldier, 1975; Four Years in the Stonewall Brigade, 1978; The 4th Virginia Infantry, 1980; Civil War Sites in Virginia: A Tour-Guide, 1982; The 18th Virginia Infantry, 1983; Tenting Tonight: The Soldiers' View, 1984; General A P Hill, 1987; Soldiers Blue and Gray, 1988; Civil War: American Becomes One Nation, 1992; Jackson and Lee: Legends in Gray (with Mort Kunstler), 1995; Stonewall Jackson: The Man, The Soldier, The Legend (winner of 8 national awards), 1997. Contributions to: More than 150 articles in historical journals and history magazines; Regular appearances in Civil War programmes on television and radio. Honours: Freeman-Nevins Award, 1981; Bruce Catton Award, 1983; William E Wine Award for Teaching Excellence, 1983; A P Andrews Memorial Award, 1985; James Robertson Award of Achievement, 1985; Jefferson Davis Medal, United Daughters of the Confederacy. Memberships: Virginia Historical Society; Organization of American Historians; Southern Historical Association; Confederate Memorial Society. Address: Department of History, Virginia Polytechnic Institute and State University, Blacksburg, VA 24061, USA.

ROBERTSON Thomas. See: **GILES Frank.**

ROBINET Harriette Gillem, b. 14 July 1931, Washington, DC, USA. Writer. m. McLouis Robinet, 6 Aug 1960, 3 sons, 3 daughters. Education: DC, College of New Rochelle, 1953; MS, 1957, PhD, 1962, Catholic University of America. Publications: Jay and the Marigold, 1976; Ride the Red Cycle, 1980; Children of the Fire, 1991; Mississippi Chariot, 1994; If You Please, President Lincoln, 1995; Washington City is Burning, 1996; The Twins, the Pirates and the Battle of New Orleans, 1997; Forty Acres and Maybe a Mule, 1998; Walking to the Bus Rider Blues, 1999. Contributions to: Mississippi Chariot; Houghton Mifflin and Scott Foresman Readers. Honours: Notable Books in Social Studies, 1991, 1994; Young

People's Literature Award, 1991; Carl Sandburg Award, 1997; Midland Author's Society Award, 1998. Memberships: Society of Childrens Book Writers and Illustrators; Mystery Writers of America; Sisters in Crime. Address: 214 South Elmwood, Oak Park, IL 60302, USA.

ROBINETTE Joseph Allen, b. 8 Feb 1939, Rockwood, Tennessee, USA. College Professor; Playwright. m. Helen M Seitz, 27 Aug 1965, 4 sons, 1 daughter. Education: BA, Carson-Newman College, 1960; MA, 1966, PhD, 1972, Southern Illinois University. Publications: The Fabulous Fable Factory, 1975; Once Upon a Shoe (play), 1979; Legend of the Sun Child (musical), 1982; Charlotte's Web (dramatization), 1983; Charlotte's Web (musical with Charles Strouse), 1989; Anne of Green Gables (dramatization), 1989; The Lion, the Witch and the Wardrobe (dramatization), 1989; The Trial of Goldilocks (operetta), 1990; Dorothy Meets Alice (musical), 1991; Stuart Little (dramatization), 1992; The Trumpet of the Swan (dramatization), 1993; The Adventures of Beatrix Potter and Her Friends (musical), 1994; The Littlest Angel (musical), 1994; The Jungle Book (dramatization), 1995. Contributions to: Children's Theatre News; Opera For Youth News. Honour: Charlotte Chorpenning Cup, National Children's Playwriting Award, 1976. Memberships: American Society of Composers, Authors and Publishers; American Association for Theatre in Education; Opera for Youth. Address: Department of Theatre and Dance, Rowan College, Glassboro, NJ 08028, USA.

ROBINS Patricia. See: CLARK Patricia Denise.

ROBINSON Bina Aitchison, (Winifred Aitchison), b. 31 Aug 1923, Schenectady, New York, USA. Editor; Writer. m. David Dunlop Robinson, 14 May 1944, 1 son, 3 daughters. Education: BA with Honors, University of Rochester, New York, 1944. Appointments: Editor, The Civil Abolitionist; previously Co-developed and Co-managed, Swain Ski Center. Contributions to: Issues in Science and Technology; Chronicle of Higher Education; mostly newspapers. Address: PO Box 26, Swain, New York 14884, USA.

ROBINSON David Bradford, b. 14 Apr 1937, Richmond, Virginia, USA. Poet; Writer. BS, 1959; MS, Honours, 1961; AA, 1970; BA, 1977; DSc, 1978; PhD, 1979; MA, 1995; JD, 1995. Publications: Characteristics of Cesium, 1978; Lyric Treasure One, 1978; Collected Poems, 1987; Praise the Wildnerness: Nineteen Original New Poems to Survival, 1990. Contributions to: Anthologies and reviews. Honours: Golden Poet Award, 1987; Pegasus Time Capsule Award, 1991; Albert Einstein Medal, 1994; World Lifetime Achivement Award, 1996. Membership: International Society of Poets. Address: PO Box 1414, Miami Shores, FL 33153, USA.

ROBINSON David Julien, b. 6 Aug 1930, England. Film Critic; Festival Director; Writer. Education: BA, Honours, King's College, Cambridge. Appointments: Associate Editor, Sight and Sound, and Editor, Monthly Film Bulletin, 1956-58; Programme Director, NFT, 1959; Film Critic, Financial Times, 1959-74, The Times, 1974-92; Director, Garrett Robinson Co, 1987-88, The Davids Film Co, 1988-, Channel 4 Young Film Maker of the Year Competition, Edinburgh Film Festival, 1992-95, Pordenone Silent Film Festival, Italy, 1997-; Guest Director, Edinburgh Film Festival, 1989-91. Publications: Hollywood in the Twenties, 1969; Buster Keaton, 1969; The Great Funnies, 1972; World Cinema, 1973, 2nd edition, 1980, US edition as The History of World Cinema, 1974, 2nd edition, 1980; Chaplin: The Mirror of Opinion, 1983; Chaplin: His Life and Art, 1985; The Illustrated History of the Cinema (co-editor), 1986; Music of the Shadows, 1990; Masterpieces of Animation 1833-1908, 1991; Richard Attenborough, 1992; Georges Méliès, 1993; Lantern Images: Iconography of the Magic Lantern 1440-1880, 1993; Sight and Sound Chronology of the Cinema, 1994-95; Musique et cinema muet, 1995; Charlot: Entre rires et larmes, 1995; Peepshow to Palace, 1995; Light and Image: Incunabula of the Motion Picture (co-author), 1996. Contributions to: Newspapers and periodicals. Honours: Several prizes. Address: 96-100

New Cavendish Street, London W1M 7FA, England, and 1 Winifreds Dale, Cavendish Road, Bath BA1 2UD, England.

ROBINSON Derek, (Dirk Robson), b. 12 Apr 1932, Bristol, England. Writer. m. Sheila Collins, 29 Apr 1968. Education: MA, Downing College, Cambridge, England. Publications: Goshawk Squadron, 1971; Rotten With Honour, 1973; Kramer's War, 1977; The Eldorado Network, 1979; Piece of Cake, 1983; War Story, 1987; Artillery of Lies, 1991; A Good Clean Fight, 1993; Hornet's Sting, 1999. Honour: Shortlisted for Booker Prize, 1971. Literary Agent: T C Wallace Ltd, Suite 1001, 425 Madison Avenue, New York, NY 10017, USA. Address: Shapland House, Somerset Street, Kingsdown, Bristol BS2 8LZ, England.

ROBINSON Ian, b. 1 July 1934, Prestwich, Manchester, England. Writer; Artist. m. Adelheid Armbrüster, 21 Dec 1959, 1 son, 2 daughters. Education: MA, Oriel College, University of Oxford, 1958. Appointments: Editor, Oasis Magazine, 1969-; Publisher, Oasis Books, 1970-. Publications: Poetry: Accidents, 1974; Three, 1978; Short Stories, 1979; Maida Vale Elegies, 1983; Journal, 1987; The Invention of Morning, 1997. Prose: Obsequies, 1979; Fugitive Aromas, 1979; Blown Footage, 1980; Dissolving Views, 1986; 26 1/2 Things, 1995. Graphic Book: The Glacier in the Cupboard, 1995. Contributions to: Prism International; London Magazine; Prospice; Poesie Europe; Osiris; Wide Skirt; Fire; Tears in the Fence; Poets Voice. Memberships: Poetry Society of Great Britain, deputy chairman, 1977-78; Association of Little Presses. Address: 12 Stevenage Road, London SW6 6ES, England.

ROBINSON Jancis Mary, b. 22 Apr 1950, Carlisle, Cumbria, England. Writer; Broadcaster. m. Nicholas Laurence Lander, 1981, 1 son, 2 daughters. Education: MA, St Anne's College, Oxford, 1971. Appointments: Editor, Wine and Spirit, 1976-80; Which Wine Guide, 1980-82; Founder-Editor, Drinker's Digest, later Which Wine? Monthly, 1977-82; Freelance Radio and Television Broadcaster, 1983-; Wine Correspondent, Sunday Times, 1987-88, Evening Standard, 1987-88; Contributor, Financial Times, 1989-. Publications: The Wine Book, 1979, revised edition, 1983; The Great Wine Book, 1981; Masterglass, 1983, revised edition, 1987; How to Choose and Enjoy Wine, 1984; Vines, Grapes and Wines, 1986; Food and Wine Adventures, 1987; The Demon Drink, 1988; Vintage Timecharts, 1989; The Oxford Companion of Wine (editor), 1994; Jancis Robinson's Wine Course, 1995; Jancis Robinson's Guide to White Grapes, 1996; Confessions of a Wine Lover, 1997. Contributions to: Periodicals. Honours: Glenfiddich Trophy, 1983, 1996; Master of Wine, 1984; Andre Simon Memorial Prizes, Wine Guild Awards, Clicquot Book of the Year, 1986, 1996; Honorary Doctorate, Open University, 1997. Address: c/o A P Watt, 20 John Street, London WC1N 2DR, England.

ROBINSON Jeffrey, b. 19 Oct 1945, New York, New York, USA. Author. m. Aline Benayoun, 27 Mar 1985, 1 son, 1 daughter. Education: BS, Temple University, Philadelphia. Publications: Bette Davis, Her Stage and Film Career, 1983; Teamwork, 1984; The Risk Takers, 1985; Pietrov and Other Games (fiction), 1985; Minus Millionaires, 1986; The Ginger Jar (fiction), 1986; Yamani: The Inside Story, 1988; Rainier and Grace, 1989; The Risk Takers: Five Years On, 1990; The End of the American Century, 1992; The Laundrymen, 1994; Bardot: Two Lives, 1994; The Margin of the Bulls (fiction), 1995. Contributions to: More than 700 articles and short stories published in major magazines and journals worldwide. Honours: Overseas Press Club, 1984; Benedictine After Dinner Speaker of the Year, 1990. Membership: PEN. Address: c/o Mildred Marmur Associates Ltd., 2005 Palmer Avenue, Larchmont, NY 10538, USA.

ROBINSON Kim Stanley, b. 23 Mar 1952, Waukegan, Illinois, USA. Author. Education: BA, 1974, PhD, 1982, University of California at San Diego; MA, Boston University, 1975. Appointments: Visiting Lecturer,

University of California at San Diego, 1982, 1985, University of California at Davis, 1982-84, 1985. Publications: The Novels of Philip K Dick, 1984; The Wild Shore, 1984; Icehenge, 1985; The Memory of Whiteness, 1985; The Planet on the Table, 1986; The Gold Coast, 1989; Green Mars, Red Mars, 1994; Antarctica, 1998. Contributions to: Periodicals. Address: 17811 Romelle Avenue, Santa Ana, CA 92705, USA.

ROBINSON Robert Henry, b. 17 Dec 1927, Liverpool, England. Writer; Broadcaster. m. Josephine Mary Richard, 1958, 1 son, 2 daughters. Education: MA, Exeter College, Oxford. Publications: Landscape With Dead Dons, 1956; Inside Robert Robinson, 1965; The Conspiracy, 1968; The Dog Chairman, 1982; Everyman Book of Light Verse (editor), 1984; Bad Dreams, 1989; Prescriptions of a Pox Doctor's Clerk, 1991; Skip All That: Memoirs, 1996. Contributions to: Newspapers, radio and television. Address: 16 Cheyne Row, London SW3, England.

ROBINSON Sheila (Mary), (Sheila Radley, Hester Rowan), b. 18 Nov 1928, Cogenhoe, Northamptonshire, England. Writer. Education: BA, University of London. Publications: Overture in Venice, 1976; The Linden Tree, 1977; Death and the Maiden, 1978; Snowfall, 1978; The Chief Inspector's Daughter, 1981; A Talent for Destruction, 1982; Blood on the Happy Highway, 1983; Fate Worse Than Death, 1985; Who Saw Him Die?, 1987; This Way Out, 1989; Cross My Heart and Hope to Die, 1992; Fair Game, 1994; New Blood from Old Bones, 1998. Address: Cyder Orchard, Church Lane, Banham, Norwich, Norfolk NR16 2HR, England.

ROBINSON Spider, b. 24 Nov 1948, New York, New York, USA. Writer. Education: BA, State University of New York at Stony Brook, 1972. Publications: Telempath, 1976; Callahan's Crossing Saloon, 1977; Stardance (with Jeanne Robinson), 1979; Antinomy, 1980; Time Travelers Strictly Cash, 1981; Mindkiller, 1982; Melancholy Elephants, 1984; Night of Power, 1985; Callahan's Secret, 1986; Time Pressure, 1987; Callahan and Company, 1987; Starseed, 1991; Lady Slings the Booze, 1993; Off the Wall at Callahan's, 1994; Starmind, 1994; Callahans Legacy, 1996. Address: c/o Ace Books, 200 Madison Avenue, New York, NY 10016, USA.

ROBINSON Stephen Julian Roper, b. 28 Sept 1961, London, England. Education: BA Hons, History, Westminster School, Oxford University. Appointments: D Tel Johannesburg Correspondent, 1977-90; D Tel Washington Correspondent, 1990-97; D Tel Foreign Editor, 1997-. Contributions to: Spectator; Times Literary Supplement. Honour: Winner, T E Utley Prize, 1990. Address: c/o Daily Telegraph, 1 Canada Square, London E14 5DT, England.

ROBLES Harold Edgar, b. 8 Oct 1948, Paramaribo, Surinam. Administrator; Writer. m. Ruth D'Agostino, 2 sons, 1 daughter. Education: BA, MBA, University of Rotterdam. Appointments: Secretary-General, International Albert Schweitzer Association, 1975-81; Founder, President, Albert Schweitzer Center, The Netherlands, 1973-81; Founder, President, Albert Schweitzer Institute for the Humanities, Wallingford, Connecticut. Publications: Bosch & Keuning (for children), 1975; J H Kok (for children), 1978; Reverence for Life: The Words of Albert Schweitzer (for adults), 1993; An Adventurer of Humanity (for children), 1994; Eerbied voor het Leven (for adults), 1994. Contributions to: Journals in USA and Holland. Honours: Medal, City of Kraków, Poland, 1978; Swedish Albert Schweitzer Award, 1980; Pro Merito Order (Gold), Austria, 1986; United Way Gold Award, 1987; Ehrenzeichen für Wissenschaft und Kunst, Austria, 1988; Knight Commander, Order of Saint Andrew, England, 1988; Cordon Bleu du Saint-Esprit, Landau, Germany, 1990; Tiffany Apple of New York, 1993; Special Citation, State of Connecticut, 1994; Commendation, US House of Representatives, 1995; DHL, Albertus Magnus College, 1996. Memberships: War and Peace Foundation; Genesis, Georgian Foundation for Health Services, Tbilisi, Georgia; Foundation of Friends for the Center of Cerebral Palsy and Child

Development, Belgrade. Address: c/o Albert Schweitzer Institute for the Humanities, PO Box 550, Wallingford, CT 06492, USA.

ROBSON Deborah Ruth, b. 6 Nov 1948, Evanston, Illinois, USA. Writer; Editor; Textile Artist. m. 1 daughter. Education: Carleton College, 1966-69; University of Iowa, 1970-71; BA, University of Washington, 1972; MFA, Goddard College, 1978. Appointments: Editor, University of Massachusetts Press; Editor, Shuttle, Spindle and Dyepot; Editor, Interweave Press; Editor, Spin-Off. Contributions to: Port Townsend Journal; Dog Soldier; Twigs; Writers Forum; New American Literature From the West; Seattle Post; Room of One's Own; Nantucket Review; Small Press Review; Frets; Ariadne's Thread; Country Journal; Spin-Off; Threads; Interweave Knits. Membership: National Writers Union. Address: c/o Interweave Press, 201 East 4th Street, Loveland, CO 80537-5655, USA.

ROBSON Dirk. See: **ROBINSON Derek.**

ROCHARD Henri. See: **CHARLIER Roger Henri.**

ROCHE Billy, (William Michael Roche), b. 11 Jan 1949, Wexford, Ireland. Playwright; Author. Appointments: Singer, the Roach Band, 1975-80; Playwright-in-Residence, Bush Theatre, London, 1988. Publications: Plays: A Handful of Stars, 1987; Amphibians, 1987; Poor Beast in the Rain, 1989; Belry, 1991; The Cavalcaders, 1993. Novel: Tumbling Down, 1986. Film Script: Trojan Eddie, 1997. Honours: London Theatre Fringe Award, 1992; Time Out Award, 1992. Address: c/o Leah Schmidt, The Agency, 24 Pottery Lane, Holland Park, London W11 4LZ, England.

ROCHE George Charles III, b. 16 May 1935, Denver, Colorado, USA. College President; Writer. m. June Bernard, 2 sons, 2 daughters. Education: BS, Regis College, Colorado, 1956; MA, 1961, PhD, 1965, University of Colorado. Appointment: President, Hillsdale College, Michigan. Publications: The Bewildered Society, 1972; Going Home, 1986; A World Without Heroes: A Modern Tragedy, 1987; A Reason for Living, 1989; One by One, 1990. Contributions to: Newspapers and magazines. Honour: Freedom Leadership Award, Freedoms Foundation, 1972. Memberships: Mont Pelerin Society; Philadelphia Society; American Association of Presidents of Independent Colleges and Universities. Address: Hillsdale College, Hillsdale, MI 49242, USA.

ROCHE Sylviane, b. 10 June 1949, Paris, France. Teacher of French Literature. m. Christophe Calame, 1 Feb 1985, 1 son, 1 daughter. Education: MA, Lausanne University, Switzerland. Appointments: Director and Editor, Ecriture literary review. Publications: Les Passantes, 1987; Le Salon Pompadour, 1990; Septembre, 1992; Maroussia va à l'école, 1993; Le Temps des cerises, 1997; L'Italienne, 1998. Contributions to: Numerous. Honours: Prix du Jubilé UBS, 1988; Prix de la commission francophone du canton de Berne, 1989; Prix des auditeurs de la RSR, 1998; Prix Franco-europeen, 1998. Membership: Société Suisse des écrivains. Address: 53 avenue de Rumine, 1005 Lausanne, Switzerland.

ROCHE Terry. See: **POOLE Margaret Barbara.**

ROCHE William Michael. See: **ROCHE Billy.**

ROCKWELL John (Sargent), b. 16 Sept 1940, Washington, District of Columbia, USA. Music Critic. Education: BA, Harvard University, 1962; Graduate Studies, University of Munich, 1962-63; MA, 1964, PhD, 1972, University of California at Berkeley. Appointments: West Coast Correspondent, Opera News, 1968-72; Music and Dance Critic, Oakland Tribune, California, 1969; Assistant Music and Dance Critic, Los Angeles Times, 1970-72; Music Critic, New York Times, 1974; Lecturer in Cultural History, Princeton University, 1977-79; Lecturer in Music, Brooklyn College of the City University of New York, 1980; Adviser, The New Grove Dictionary of American Music, 1986. Publications: Robert Wilson: A Theater of Images (with Robert Stearns), 1980; All American Music: Composition in the Late Twentieth Century, 1983; Sinatra: An American Classic, 1984. Contributions to: Books and periodicals. Honours: German Academic Exchange Fellowship, 1962-63; Woodrow Wilson Fellowship, 1963-64; National Book Critics Circle Award Nomination, 1983. Memberships: Music Critics Association, treasurer, 1977-81; Phi Beta Kappa. Address: c/o New York Times, 229 West 43rd Street, New York, NY 10036, USA.

RODDY Lee, b. 22 Aug 1921, Marion County, Illinois, USA. Writer. m. Cicely Price, 17 Oct 1947, 1 son, 1 daughter. Education: AA, Los Angeles City College, 1945. Publications: The Life and Times of Grizzly Adams, 1977; The Lincoln Conspiracy, 1977; Jesus, 1979; Ghost Dog of Stoney Ridge, 1985; Dooger, Grasshopper Hound, 1985; The City Bear's Adventures, 1985; The Hair Pulling Bear Dog, 1985; Secret of the Shark Pit, 1988; Secret of the Sunken Sub, 1989; The Overland Escape, 1989; The Desperate Search, 1989; Danger on Thunder Mountain, 1990; Secret of the Howland Cave, 1990; The Flaming Trap, 1990; Mystery of the Phantom Gold, 1991; The Gold Train Bandits, 1992. Other: Several books made into films and television programmes. Honours: Various awards and book club selections. Memberships: Authors Guild of America; Authors League; National Society of Children's Book Writers. Address: PO Box 700, Penn Valley, CA 95946, USA.

RODER Allan, b. 7 May 1958, Copenhagen, Denmark. High School Teacher. m. Ellen Bisgaard Mortensen, 7 July 1990. Education: MA, University of Copenhagen, 1983. Appointments: High School Teacher, Vordingborg Gymnasium, 1984-87; High School Teacher, Herning HF and VUC, 1988-. Publications: Historietime, in Historie og samfundsorientering, 1985; Den bortromte stadsmusikanten (with A Nesfeldt), in Norsk slektshistorisk tidsskrift, 1992; Danske talemåder, 1998. Contributions to: Poetry in Hvedekorn, 1978-94. Membership: Dansk Forfatterforening. Address: Vibevej 6, 8660 Skanderborg, Denmark.

RODGERS Carolyn Marie, b. 14 Dec 1942, Chicago, Illinois, USA. Professor; Writer; Poet; Editor. Education: BA, Roosevelt University, 1981; MA, University of Chicago, 1983. Appointments: Professor of Afro-American Literature, 1969, Lecturer in English and Coordinator of Poetry Workshop, 1970, Columbia College; Poet-in-Residence, University of Washington, 1970, Indiana University, 1974, Roosevelt University, 1983; Founder-Editor, Eden Press, 1991, Rare Form newsletter, 1994-. Publications: Paper Soul, 1968; Songs of a Blackbird, 1970; How I Got Ovah, 1976; The Heart as Evergreen, 1978; Translation, 1980; A Little Lower Than the Angels, 1984; Morning Glory, 1989; The Religious Poetry of Carolyn M Rodgers, 1993; Daughters of Africa, 1993; We're Only Human, 1994; A Train Called Judah, 1996; Chosen to Believe, 1996; Salt: The Slat of the Earth, 1999. Contributions to: Journals and magazines. Honours: National Endowment for the Arts Award, 1970; Conrad Kent Rivers Award, 1970; Society of Midland Authors Award, 1970; Carnegie Writer's Grant, 1980; Television Gospel Tribute, 1982; PEN Grant, 1987. Memberships: Gwendolyn Brooks Writing Workshop; Organization of Black American Culture. Address: PO Box 804271, Chicago, IL 60680, USA.

RODRIGUES Louis Jerome, b. 20 July 1938, Madras, India. Writer; Poet; Translator. m. (1) Malinda Weaving, dec, 1 son, (2) Josefina Bernet Soler, 6 Oct 1984, 1 son. Education: BA, Honours, English, 1960; MA, Intermediate Histories and Logic, 1962, University of Madras; MA, MPhil, Anglo-Saxon, 1965-67, University of London; MA, Law and English Tripos, 1971-73, 1977; PhD, University of Barcelona, 1990. Appointments: Assistant Director, Benedict, Mannheim, 1977; Director of Studies, Inlingua, Barcelona, 1978-82; Director, Phoenix, Barcelona, 1982-87. Publications: A Long Time Waiting, 1979; Anglo-Saxon Riddles, 1990; Seven Anglo-Saxon Elegies, 1991; Chiaroscuro, 1991; The Battles of Maldon and Brunanburh, 1991; Anglo-Saxon Verse Runes, 1992; A Choice of Salvador Espriu's Verse and Salvador Espriu's La Pell de Brau (translator), 1992; Anglo-Saxon Verse Charms, Maxims and Heroic Legends, 1993; Anglo-Saxon Elegiac Verse, 1994; Anglo-Saxon Didactic Verse, 1995; Three Anglo-Saxon Battle Poems, 1995. Contributions to: Various publications. Honour: Poetry Translation Prize, Catholic University of America, Washington, DC, 1993. Memberships: International Association of Anglo-Saxonists; Royal Society of Literature; Society of Authors, executive committee member, 1988-91; Translators Association. Address: 132 Wisbech Raod, Littleport, Ely, Cambridgeshire CB6 1JJ, England.

RODRIGUEZ Judith (Catherine), b. 13 Feb 1936, Perth, Western Australia, Australia. Poet; Dramatist; Librettist; Editor; Lecturer. m. (1) Fabio Rodriguez, 1964, div 1981, 4 children, (2) Thomas Shapcott, 1982. Education: BA, University of Queensland, Brisbane, 1957; MA, Girton College, Cambridge, 1962; Certificate of Education, University of London, 1968. Appointments: Lecturer in External Studies, University of Queensland, Brisbane, 1959-60; Lecturer in English, Philippa Fawcett College of Education, London, 1962-63, University of the West Indies, Kingston, Jamaica, 1963-65, St Mary's College of Education, Twickenham, 1966-68, Macarthur Institute of Higher Education, Milperra, Sydney, 1987-88, Royal Melbourne Institute of Technology, 1988-89, Victoria College, 1989-92; Teacher of English as a Foreign Language, St Giles School of English, London, 1965-66; Lecturer, 1969-75, Senior Lecturer in English, 1977-85, La Trobe University, Bundoora, Australia; Writer-in-Residence, Rollins College, Florida, 1986; Senior Lecturer, Deakin University, 1993-. Publications: Poetry: Four Poets, 1962; Nu-Plastik Fanfare Red, 1973 and Other Poems, 1973; Water Life, 1976; Shadow on Glass, 1978; Arapede, 1979; Mudcrab at Gambaro's, 1980; Witch Heart, 1982; Floridian Poems, 1986; The House by Water: Selected and New Poems, 1988; The Cold, 1992. Play: Poor Johanna (with Robyn Archer), 1994. Opera Libretto: Lindy, 1994. Editor: Mrs Noah and the Minoan Queen, 1982; Poems Selected from the Australian's 20th Anniversary Competition (with Andrew Taylor), 1985; Modern Swedish Poetry (with Thomas Shapcott), 1985; Collected Poems of Jennifer Rankin, 1990. Contributions to: Numerous publications. Honours: Arts Council of Australia Fellowships, 1974, 1978, 1983; Government of South Australia Biennial Prize for Literature, 1978; International PEN Peter Stuyvesant Prize for Poetry, 1981; Member of the Order of Australia, 1994; Christopher Brennan Award, Fellowship of Australian Writers, 1994. Memberships: Association for the Study of Australian Literature Programs; Australian Society of Authors; International PEN; South Pacific Association for Commonwealth Language and Literature Studies; Melbourne PEN Centre; Victorian Writer's Centre; Australian Literary Translator's Association. Address: PO Box 231, Mont Albert, Victoria 3127, Australia.

RODRIGUEZ Lazara Ana, b. 17 Apr 1938, Bejucal, Havana, Cuba. Physician; Writer. Education: University of Havana School of Medicine, 1958-61; Medical Degree, CETEC University, Dominican Republic, 1983; Medical Degree, USA, 1986. Publications: Diary of a Survivor: Nineteen Years in a Cuban Women's Prison, 1995. Other: Unpublished poems and short stories. Address: 47 Alhambra Circle, Apt 4, Coral Gables, Florida 33134, USA.

RODWAY Anne. See: **BRENNAN Patricia Winifred.**

ROEBUCK Derek, b. 22 Jan 1935, Stalybridge, England. Professor of Comparative Law; Writer. m. Susanna Leonie Hoe, 18 Aug 1981, 2 sons, 1 daughter. Education: MA, Oxon, 1960; MCom, Victoria University of Wellington, 1965. Publications: Author of 34 books on law and legal history, translated into ten languages, including: Credit and Security in Asia, 10 volumes (with D E Allan and M E Hiscock), 1973-80; Whores of War: Mercenaries Today (with Wilfred Burchett), 1976; The Background of the Common Law, 2nd edition, 1990; Hong Kong Digest of Contract, 1995; Hong Kong Digest of Criminal Law, 3 volumes, 1995-96; Hong Kong Digest of Criminal Procedure, 3 volumes, 1996-97; The Taking of Hong Kong: Charles and Clara Elliot in China Waters (with Susanna Hoe), 1999. Contributions to: Over 30 articles on law and language. Membership: Selden Society. Address: 20A Plantation Road, Oxford OX2 6JD, England.

ROECKER William Alan, b. 17 Jan 1942, Madison, Wisconsin, USA. Writer; Poet. m. Debbie Sue Huntsman, 31 Dec 1985. Education: BS, 1966, MFA, 1967, University of Oregon. Appointments: Assistant Editor, Northwest Review, 1967; Instructor, Associate Professor, English, University of Arizona, 1968-74; Editor, Windsport Magazine, 1981-82; Saltwater Editor, Today's Fishermen, 1985, Fishing and Hunting News, 1993; Associate Editor, South Coast Sportfishing, 1987; Senior Editor, South Coast Sportfishing, 1988; Senior Managing Editor, California Angler Magazine, 1992; News and Photo Editor, San Diego Sportfishing Council, 1994-. Publications: Willamette (poems), 1970; Stories that Count, 1971; You Know Me (poems), 1972; Closer to the Country (poems), 1976; Standup Fishing: Saltwater Methods, Tackle & Techniques, 1990. Contributions to: Numerous journals and magazines. Honours: Haycox Award, 1966; Neuberger Award, 1967; Runner Up, Yale Younger Poets, 1971; National Endowment for the Arts Award, 1973; Gray Prize, Hang Gliding Journalism, 1984. Address: PO Box 586071, Oceanside, CA 92058, USA.

ROGER-HENRICHSEN Gudmund, b. 16 March 1907, Copenhagen, Denmark. Literary Critic; Historian. m. Christine Marie Neergaard-Møller, 30 Nov 1934, 2 daughters. Education: Law Studies, 1925-26; Studies in Scandinavian, British, and German Literature and History, University of Copenhagen, with special studies of British Literature and History, Cambridge University; MA, 1926-32. Appointments: Literary Reader for Gyldendal, 1934-39; Lecturer, Danish Booksellers' School in Copenhagen, 1937-47; Reviewer, Paper-concern Berlingske Tidende, 1939-41; Literary Critic, Morning-paper Politiken, 1941-61; Cultural Adviser, Publisher, J H Schultz, 1941-70; Critic and Producer, Denmark's Radio, 1945-92; Editor, monthly shortwave production, The Bookeye; Lit Manager, 1967-70; Member of Literary Council, attached, Danish Ministry of Culture, 1971-95. Publications: Two Kinds of German Literature, 1937; From Highromanticism to Steelromanticism, 1939; Spiritual and Commercial Aspects of Modern Novels, 1946; They Couldn't Bear Tyranny, 1948; Greenland - A Long Passage Out and Back to Civilization, 1955; The Restoration Period of England after the War, 1961; Great Danish Writers in the Midst of Our Society, 1963; Young Was Denmark in the Sixties, 1972; A Decade of Danish Literature, 1960-1970, 1972; Ein Jahrzehnt dänische Litteratur, 1960-70, 1972; Translations of some British, American, and German Writers, amongst N Coward, Linklater and Goethe's conversations with Eckermann. Contributions to: Several essays to various magazines, periodicals and works in Scandinavia and Britain on cultural questions. Honours: The Swedish Fund Clara Lachmann, 1965; The Danish Carlsberg Fund, 1978. Memberships: Danish Society of Authors; PEN Club; Danish Union of Journalists; Young Booksellers' Union. Address: Rymarksvej 16, DK-2900 Hellerup, Denmark.

ROGERS Floyd. See: **SPENCE William (John Duncan).**

ROGERS Ingrid, b. 3 May 1951, Rinteln, Germany. Pastor; Teacher; Writer. m. H Kendall Rogers, 9 June 1972, 1 son, 1 daughter. Education: DUEL, Sorbonne Nouvelle, Paris, 1971; University of Oxford, 1972-73; Staatsexamen, 1974, PhD, 1976, Philipps University, Marburg; Doctor of Ministry Degree, Bethany Theological Seminary, 1988. Publications: Tennessee Williams: A Moralist's Answer to the Perils of Life, 1976; Peace Be Unto You, 1983; Swords into Plowshares, 1983; In Search of Refuge, 1984; Glimpses of Clima, 1989; Recollections of East Germany, 1996. Honours: Christopher Book Award, 1985; Angel Award of Excellence, 1985. Address: Manchester College, Box 131, North Manchester, IN 46962, USA.

ROGERS Jane Rosalind, b. 21 July 1952, London, England. Writer. 1 son, 1 daughter. Education: BA, Honours, English Literature, New Hall, Cambridge, 1974; Postgraduate Certificate in Education, Leicester University, 1976. Appointments: Writer-in-Residence, Northern College, Barnsley, South Yorkshire, 1985-86, Sheffield Polytechnic, 1987-88; Judith E Wilson Fellow, Cambridge, 1991. Publications: Separate Tracks, 1983; Her Living Image, 1984; The Ice is Singing, 1987; Mr Wroe's Virgins, 1991; Promised Lands, 1995. Screenplay: Dawn and the Candidate, 1989. Other: Mr Wroe's Virgins (BBC serial), 1993. Contributions to: Magazines. Honours: North West Arts Writers Bursary, 1985; Somerset Maugham Award, 1985; Samuel Beckett Award, 1990; Writers' Guild Award, Best Fiction Book, 1996. Memberships: Royal Society of Literature, Fellow; Society of Authors. Address: c/o Pat Kavanagh, Peters, Fraser and Dunlop Group Ltd, 503/4 The Chambers, Chelsea Harbour, London SW10 0XF, England.

ROGERS Linda (Hall), b. 10 Oct 1944, Port Alice, British Columbia, Canada. Poet; Writer; Lecturer. m.Rick Van Krugel, 3 sons. Education: MA, English Literature, University of British Columbia. Appointments: Lecturer, University of British Columbia, University of Victoria, Camosum College, Malaspina College. Publications: Some Breath, 1978; Queens of the Next Hot Star, 1981; I Like to Make a Mess, 1985; I Think I Am Ugly, 1985; Witness, 1985; Setting the Hook, 1986; Singing Rib, 1987; Worm Sandwich, 1989; Brown Bag Blues, 1991; Letters from the Doll Hospital, 1992; Hard Candy, 1994; The Half Life of Radium, 1994; Frank Zapper and the Disappearing Teacher, 1994; Molly Brown is Not a Clown, 1996; Love in the Rainforest (selected poetry), 1996; Heaven Cake, 1997. Contributions to: Journals, magazines, and newspapers. Honours: Aya Poetry Prize, 1983; Canada Council Arts Awards, 1987, 1990; British Columbia Writers Poetry Prize, 1989; Cultural Services Award, 1990; Governor-General's Centennial Medal for Poetry and Performance, 1993; Stephen Leacock Awards for Poetry, 1994, 1996; Dorothy Livesay Award for Poetry, 1995; Peoples Poetry Award, 1996. Memberships: Federation of British Columbia Writers, president; League of Canadian Poets; Society of Canadian Composers; Writers Union of Canada. Address: 1235 Styles Street, Victoria, British Columbia V9A 3Z6, Canada.

ROGERS Michael Alan, b. 29 Nov 1950, Santa Monica, California, USA. Novelist; Journalist. Education: BA, Creative Writing, Stanford University, 1972. Appointments: Associate Editor, Rolling Stone, 1972-76; Editor-at-Large, Outside, 1976-78; Visiting Lecturer in Fiction, University of California, 1981-82; Senior Writer, 1983-94, Contributing Editor, 1994-, Newsweek; Vice President, Post-Newsweek New Media, 1994-. Publications: Mindfogger, 1973; Do Not Worry about the Bear, 1978; Biohazard, 1979; Silicon Valley, 1983; Forbidden Sequence, 1989. Contributions to: Magazines. Honours: Distinguished Science Writing Award, American Association for the Advancement of Science, 1974; Computer Press Association, 1987; Software Publishers Association, 1991. Membership: Authors Guild. Address: c/o Newsweek, 388 Market Street, Suite 1650, San Francisco, CA 94111, USA.

ROGERS Pat, b. 17 Mar 1938, Beverley, Yorkshire, England. Professor; Writer. Education: BA, 1961, MA, 1965, PhD, 1968, Fitzwilliam College, Cambridge. Appointments: Fellow, Sidney Sussex College, Cambridge, 1964-69; Lecturer, King's College, University of London, 1969-73; Professor of English, University College of North Wales, Bangor, 1973-76, University of Bristol, 1977-86; DeBartolo Professor, Liberal Arts, University of South Florida, Tampa, 1986-. Publications: Daniel Defoe: A Tour Through Great Britain, 1971; Grub Street: Studies on a Sub-culture, 1972, revised edition as Hacks and Dunces, 1980; Daniel Defoe: The Critical Heritage (editor), 1972; The Augustan Vision: An Introduction to Pope, 1976; The Eighteenth Century (editor), 1978; Henry Fielding: A Biography, 1979; Swift: Complete Poems, Literature and Popular Culture in the Eighteenth Century (editor), 1983; Eighteenth-Century Encounters, 1985; The Oxford Illustrated History of English Literature (editor), 1987; The Economy of Arts in the 18th Century, 1989; An Outline of English Literature, 1992; Essays on Pope, 1993; Johnson and Boswell in Scotland, 1993. Address: Department of English, University of South Florida, Tampa, FL 33620, USA.

ROGERS Pete. See: **ST PIERRE Roger.**

ROGERS Robert Frederick, b. 26 May 1930, San Diego, California, USA. Writer; Consultant. 3 sons. Education: BS, US Military Academy, West Point, New York; PhD, Georgetown University. Publication: Destiny's Landfall: A History of Guam, 1995. Honour: Guam Magalahe Award, 1996. Address: PO Box 5364, UOG Station, Mangilao, Guam 96923, USA.

ROGERS Rosemary, (Marina Mayson), b. 7 Dec 1932, Sri Lanka. Writer. m. (1) Summa Navaratnam, 16 Jan 1953, div, 2 sons, 2 daughters, (2) Leroy Rogers, 1957, div 1964, (3) Christopher M Kadison, 1984. Education: BA, English, 1952. Publications: Sweet Savage Love, 1974; Wildest Heart, 1974; Dark Fires, 1975; Wicked Loving Lies, 1976; The Crowd Pleasers, 1978; The Insiders, 1979; Lost Love, Last Love, 1980; Love Play, 1981; Surrender to Love, 1982; The Wanton, 1984; Bound by Desire, 1988. Contributions to: Star Magazine; Good Housekeeping. Memberships: Writers Guild of America; Authors Guild. Address: 300 East 56th Street, Apt 27J, New York, NY 10022, USA.

ROGERS Samuel Shepard. See: **SHEPARD Sam.**

ROGGEMAN Willem Maurits, b. 9 July 1935, Brussels, Belgium. Poet; Writer. m. Jacqueline Nardi, 1975, 1 son, 1 daughter. Education: University of Ghent. Appointments: Critic, Het Laatste Nieuws newspaper, 1959-81; Editor, De Vlaamse Gids, 1970-92. Publications: Poetry: Rhapsody in Blue, 1958; Baudelaire Verliefd, 1964; Memories, 1985; Een Leegte die Verdwijnt, 1985; Al Wie Omkykt is Gezien, 1988; De Uitvinding van de Tederheid, 1994; Geschiedenis, 1998. Novels: De Centauren, 1963; De Verbeelding, 1966; De belegering van een Luchtkasteel, 1990. Essays: Cesare Pavese, 1961; Beroepsgeheim, 1975; Geschiedenis, 1998. Contributions to: Various publications. Honours: Dirk Martensprize, 1962; Prize, City of Brussels, 1975; Prize, St Truiden, 1989; Prize of Meisc, 1997. Memberships: Flemish PEN Centre, secretary, 1968-80; L P Boon Society, president, 1984-91. Address: Luchtlaan 4, 1700 Dilbeek, Belgium.

ROGOZA Yury Markovitch, b. 2 May 1962, Kiev, Ukraine. Writer. m. February 1997. Education: Kiev State Foreign Languages Institute, 1989-94. Publications: The Book of Novels, 1995. Scripts: For films American Boy, The Ransom, and The Report; Bourgois' Birthday, for 38-part TV drama, 1997, for film based on same plot, 1998. Other: Many pop-song lyrics; Chronicle of Paris, libretto for musical play; Zoya's Flat, libretto for musical play; The Fool Moon Night, play. Honours: Nomination for Best Lyrics, Song of the Year Award, 1989, 1990, 1991, 1998; American Boy, Winner, IV Moscow International Film Fair; The Ransom, Winner, International Slavutich Film Festival; The Report, Special Prize, Golden Duke Festival, Odessa; 5th Place, Russian Book Rating, for The Book of Novels. Literary Agent: 1+1 TV Channel. Address: Apt 33, 15, Lesy Ukrainky Blvd, Kiev 252133.

ROHEN Edward, (Bruton Connors), b. 10 Feb 1931, Dowlais, South Wales. Poet; Writer; Artist. m. Elizabeth Jarrett, 4 Apr 1961, 1 daughter. Education: ATD, Cardiff College of Art, 1952. Appointments: Art Teacher, Ladysmith High, British Columbia, Canada, 1956-57; Head of Art, St Bonaventures, London, 1958-73, Ilford County High for Boys, Essex, 1973-82. Publications: Nightpriest, 1965; Bruised Concourse, 1973; Old Drunk Eyes Haiku, 1974; Scorpio Broadside 15, 1975; Poems/Poemas, 1976; 109 Haiku and One Seppuku for Maria, 1987; Sonnets for Maria Marriage, 1988; Sonnets: Second Sequence for Maria, 1989. Contributions to: Anthologies and magazines. Memberships: Academician, Centro Cultural Literario e Artistico de o Jornal de

Felgeiras, Portugal; Korean War Veterans Writers and Arts Society; Welsh Academy. Address: 57 Kinfauns Road, Goodmayes, Ilford, Essex IG3 9QH, England.

ROHRBACH Peter Thomas, (James Cody), b. 27 Feb 1926, New York, New York, USA. Writer. m. Sheila Sheehan, 21 Sept 1970, 1 daughter. Education: BA, MA, Catholic University of America. Publications: 17 books, including: Conversation with Christ, 1981; Stagecoach East, 1983; American Issue, 1985; The Largest Event: World War II, 1993; National Issue, 1994. Contributions to: Encyclopedias and periodicals. Memberships: Authors Guild of America; Poets, Playwrights, Editors, Essayists and Novelists; Washington Independent Writers. Address: 9609 Barkston Court, Potomac, MD 20850, USA.

ROKKAN Elizabeth Gwenllian Clough, b. 26 May 1925, Lampeter, Wales. University Lecturer; Translator. m. Stein Rokkan, 14 Oct 1950, 1 son, 1 daughter. Education: BA, 1945, MA, 1957, University of Wales. Appointment: Associate Professor, Department of English, University of Bergen, Norway, 1986-90. Publications: Translations: Cora Sandel: Alberta & Jacob, 1962; Alberta & Freedom, 1963; Alberta Alone, 1965; Tarjei Vesaas: The Ice Palace, 1966; The Great Cycle, 1968; The House in the Dark, 1976; The Silken Thread, 1982; View from the Window (short stories), 1986; Johan Borgen: The Scapegoat, 1993; Jostein Gaarder: The Christmas Mystery, 1996. Contributions to: Various. Honour: St Olav's Medal, Norway, 1995. Membership: Translators' Association/Society of Authors. Address: 7 Maynard Court, Fairwater Road, Llandaff, Cardiff CF5 2LS, Wales.

ROLAND Alex, b. 7 Apr 1944, Providence, Rhode Island, USA. Professor of History; Writer. m. 29 June 1979, 4 children. Education: BS, Engineering, US Naval Academy, 1966; MA, American History, University of Hawaii, 1970; PhD, Military History, Duke University, 1974. Appointments: Historian, National Aeronautics and Space Administration, 1973-81; Associate Professor, 1981-87, Professor of History, 1987-, Chair, Department of History, 1996-, Duke University; Harold K Johnson Visiting Professor of Military History, US Army War College, 1988-89; Resident Fellow, Massachusetts Institute of Technology, 1994-95. Publications: Underwater Warfare in the Age of Sail, 1978; Model Research: The National Advisory Committee for Aeronautics, 1915-1958, 2 volumes, 1985; A Spacefaring People: Perspectives on Early Spaceflight (editor), 1985; Men in Arms: A History of Warfare and Its Interrelationships with Western Society (with Richard A Preston and Sydney F Wise), 5th edition, 1991; Atmospheric Flight (editor with Peter Galison), 1999; Understanding War (editor with Richard H Kohn), 1999; The Quest for Intelligent Machines: DARPA and the Strategic Computing Initiative, 1983-1993 (with Philip Shiman), 2000. Contributions to: Scholarly books and journals. Honours: Grants and fellowships. Memberships: Scientists' Institute for Public Information, consultant, 1989-; Society for Military History; Society for the History of Technology, president, 1995-96. Address: c/o Department of History, Duke University, Durham, NC 27708, USA.

ROLLS Eric Charles, b. 25 Apr 1923, Grenfell, New South Wales, Australia. Author; Farmer. m. (1) Joan Stephenson, 27 Feb 1954, dec 1985, 2 sons, 1 daughter, (2) Elaine van Kempen, 1988. Publications: Sheaf Tosser, 1967; They All Ran Wild, 1969; Running Wild, 1973; The River, 1974; The Green Mosaic, 1977; Miss Strawberry Verses, 1978; A Million Wild Acres, 1981; Celebration of the Senses, 1984; Doorways: A Year of the Cumberdeen Diaries, 1989; Selected Poetry, 1990; Sojourners, 1993; From Forest to Sea, 1993; Citizens, 1996; A Celebration of Food and Wine, vol 1, 1997; vol 2, of Flesh, of Fish, of Fowl, 1997; vol 3, of Fruit and Vegtables, of Vulger Herbs, of Sugar and Spice, 1997. Contributions to: Bulletin; Overland; National Times; Age; Sydney Morning Herald; Independent Monthly; Sun Herald; various others. Honours: David Myer Trust Award for Poetry, 1968; Captain Cook Bicentennial Award for Non-Fiction, 1970; John Franklin Award for Children's Books, 1974; Braille Book of the Year, 1975; The Age Book of the Year, 1981; Talking Book of the Year, 1982; Fellow, Australian Academy of the Humanities, 1985; Australian Creative Fellow, 1991; Order of Australia, 1991; Honorary Doctorate University of Canberra, 1995. Memberships: Australian Society of Authors; National Book Council. Address: PO Box 2038, North Haven, New South Wales 2443, Australia.

ROLOFF Michael, b. 19 Dec 1937, Berlin, Germany (US citizen, 1952). Playwright. Education: BA, Haverford College, Pennsylvania, 1958; MA, Stanford University, 1960. Publications: Screenplays: Feelings, 1982; Darlings and Monsters, 1983; Graduation Party, 1984. Plays: Wolves of Wyoming, 1985; Palombe Blue, 1985; Schizzohawk, 1986. Poetry: Headshots, 1984; It Won't Grow Back, 1985. Fiction: Darlings and Monsters Quartet, 4 titles, 1986-. Other: Numerous translations from German. Address: Box 6754, Malibu, CA 90264, USA.

ROMAINE-DAVIS Ada, b. 7 June 1929, Cumberland, Maryland, USA. Nurse Educator; Medical Historian. m. John F Davis, 1 Aug 1953, 2 sons, 1 daughter. Education: Diploma, Kings County Hospital School of Nursing, Brooklyn, New York; BS, MS, PhD, University of Maryland, Baltimore and College Park; MD, College Park; Post-doctoral Studies, History of Science and Technology/Medicine, University of Maryland; Certified Adult Nurse Practitioner, American Nurses Certification Center. Appointment: Associate Professor, Johns Hopkins University School of Nursing, Baltimore. Publications: John Gibbon and His Heart-Lung Machine, 1992; Home Health Care: An Annotated Bibliography, 1992; Home Health Care: Brief Bibliography, 1994; Encyclopedia of Home Care for the Elderly (editor), 1995; The Advanced Practice Nursing: Education, Roles and Trends, 1998; The John Hopkins Family Health Guide (editor), 1999. Contributions to: American Journal of Nursing; Health Care Trends & Transitions; Nurse Practitioner; Journal of the Academy of Nurse Practitioners. Honour: Honorable Mention, American Medical Writers Association, 1993. Memberships: American Historical Association; Society for the History of Medicine; National Organization of Nurse Practitioner Faculties; American Academy of Nurse Practitioners; Sigma Theta Tau. Address: 6400 Wilmett Road, Bethesda, MD 20817, USA.

ROMANENKO Cleopatra, b. 17 Mar 1923, Slavkovichi, Leningrad. Poet. m. Romanenko Grigory, 22 Aug 1946, 2 daughters. Education: Higher technical (without Diploma), Moscow, 1942-48; Higher courses of Literature, Moscow, 1965-67. Address: Faergestedet, Badsmandsstraede 43, 1407 Kobenhavn K, Denmark.

ROMBOTIS Anastasios, (Tasos Korfis), b. 12 Oct 1929, Corfu, Greece. Retired Vice-Admiral; Writer; Poet. m. Helen Moniakis, 5 Feb 1959, 1 son, 1 daughter. Education: Various professional schools and academies, Greece and in USA; NATO Defence College, Rome, 1971-72. Appointments: Director, Prosperos book publishers, 1973-, Anacyclisis literary magazine, 1985-90. Publications: Poetry: Diary 1, 1963; Diary 2, 1964; Diary 3, 1968; Diarios, 1971; Handiwork, 1977; Poems, 1983; Pafsilipa, 1987; 153 Graffiti, 1992. Prose: Journey without Polar Star, 1953; A Desert House, 1973; Knowledge of the Father, 1984. Essays: The Poet Romos Filyras, 1974; The Poet Nikos Kavadias, 1978; Glances at the Poets 1920-1940, 1978; Deposits in Short Terms, 1982; The Poet Napoleon Lapathiotis, 1985; Glances at the Literature 1920-1940, 1991. Translations: Lustra (Ezra Pound), 1977; Poems (William Carlos Williams), 1979; Poems (Ezra Pound), 1981. Other: Coexistences, 1982; The Writer Stratis Doukas 1895-1936 (biography), 1988. Contributions to: Diagenios, 1958-80; Numerous poems, prose pieces and essays to Greek magazines. Honours: Several awards. Membership: Society of Writers. Address: Alkiviadou 9, 10439 Athens, Greece.

ROMER Stephen Charles Mark, b. 20 Aug 1957, Bishops Stortford, Hertfordshire, England. University Lecturer; Poet. m. Bridget Stevens, 17 July 1982, 1 son. Education: Radley College, 1970-74; English Tripos, Double First, Trinity Hall, Cambridge, 1975-78; Harvard University, 1978-79; British Institute, Paris, 1980-81; PhD, Cantab, 1985. Publications: The Growing Dark, 1981; Firebird 3, 1985; Idols, 1986; Plato's Ladder, 1992. Contributions to: Anthologies, journals, and periodicals. Honour: Gregory Award for Poetry, 1985. Address: 6 rue de Verneuil, 75007 Paris, France.

ROMERIL John, b. 26 Oct 1945, Melbourne, Victoria, Australia. Playwright. Education: BA, Monash University, Clayton, 1970. Appointments: Writer-In-Residence, various Australian groups and National University, Singapore, 1974-87. Publications: A Nameless Concern, 1968; The Kitchen Table, 1968; The Man from Chicago, 1969; In a Place Like Somewhere Else, 1969; Chicago, Chicago, 1970; Marvellous Melbourne, 1970; Dr Karl's Kure, 1970; Whatever Happened to Realism, 1971; Rearguard Action, 1971; Hackett Gets Ahead, 1972; Bastardy, 1972; Waltzing Matilda, 1974; The Floating World, 1974; The Golden Holden Show, 1975; The Accidental Poke, 1977; Mickey's Moomba, 1979; Centenary Dance, 1984; The Kelly Dance, 1984; Definitely Not the Last, 1985; Koori Radio, 1987; Top End, and History of Australia (co-author), 1989; Lost Weekend, 1989; Black Cargo, 1991; The Reading Boy, 1991; Working Out, 1991; Television plays. Honour: Victorian Government Drama Fellowship, 1988. Address: Almost Managing, PO Box 1034, Carlton, Victoria 3053, Australia.

ROMERO Julia Graciela, b. 17 Feb 1961, La Plata, Buenos Aires, Argentina. Translator; Writer. Div 1992, 1 son. Education: Professor of Letters, Estoy Hacienda el Doctorado en Manuel Puig; Lugar de Trabajo, Facultad de Humanidades y Ciencias de la Educacion, Universidad Nacional de la Plata. Publications: A Notaciones en Collage; De Mologo al Estallido de la Voz; La Imaginacion Melodramatica Sentimento y Vida Nacional; Las Traiciones de Manuel Puig; Puig la Seduccion y la Historia. Membership: Instituto International de Litertura Iberoamericana. Address: 54 No 990, PA, CP 1900, La Plata, Buenos Aires, Argentina.

ROMEU Jorge Luis, (Beltran de Quiros), b. 10 Dec 1945, Havana, Cuba. Educator; Writer. m. Zoila Barreiro, 25 July 1970, 3 sons. Education: Diplomas, Language, 1964, Literature, 1966, Teaching, 1970, Alliance Française de La Havane; Licendiado en Matematicas, University of Havana, 1973; MS, 1981, MPh, 1987, PhD, 1990, Syracuse University, New York. Appointments: Editor, Club Las Palmas Newsletter; Monthly Column, Syracuse Post Standard; Radio Commentator, WAER-FM, Syracuse University Public Radio Station; Associate Professor of Statistics, State University of New York, Cortland. Publications: Los Unos, Los Otros y El Seibo, 1971; La Otra Cara de la Moneda, 1984; Thinking of Cuba (collected op-ed pieces). Contributions to: Professional journals and general periodicals. Address: PO Box 6134, Syracuse, NY 13217, USA.

ROMTVEDT David William, b. 7 June 1950, Portland, Oregon, USA. Writer. m. Margo Brown, 30 May 1987. Education: BA, Reed College, 1972. Appointment: State Literature Consultant, Wyoming, 1987. Publications: Free and Compulsory for All, 1984; Moon, 1984; Letters from Mexico, 1987; Black Beauty and Kiev the Ukraine, 1987; Crossing the River: Poets of the Western US, 1987; How Many Horses, 1988; A Flower Whose Name I Do Not Know, 1992; Crossing Wyoming, 1992. Contributions to: Paris Review; Canadian Forum; American Poetry Review; Poets and Writers Magazine. Honours: National Endowment for the Arts Residency Award, 1979, and Fellowship, 1987; Pushcart Prize, 1991; National Poetry Series Award, 1991. Address: 457 North Main, Buffalo, WY 82834, USA.

ROMVARY Susan, b. 20 Aug 1925, Miskolc, Hungary. Writer. m. John Romvary, 22 Nov 1947, 1 son. Education: Pazmany Peter University, Budapest, 1947-49; Thomas More Institute, Montreal, 1973; Concordia University, 1975. Publication: Zsuzsa not Zsazsa: Balance with a

Smile, 1992. Contributions to: Anthologies and journals. Honours: 1st Prizes, Canadian Authors Association, 1987, 1988; 1st Prize, Hungarian Literary Association, 1988. Memberships: Canadian Authors Association; Hungarian Authors Association. Address: 4000 De Maisonneuve West, Westmount, Quebec H3Z 1J9, Canada.

RONAN Frank, b. 6 May 1963, New Ross, Ireland. Novelist. Publications: The Men Who Loved Evelyn Cotton, 1989; A Picnic in Eden, 1991; The Better Angel, 1992; Dixie Chicken, 1994; Handsome Men are Slightly Sunburnt (collected stories), 1996; Lovely, 1996. Honours: Irish Times/Aerlingus Irish Literature Prize, 1989. Literary Agent: Deborah Rogers, RCW, 20 Powis Mews, London W11, England.

RONAY Egon, b. Pozsony, Hungary. Journalist. m. (1), 2 daughters, (2) Barbara Greenslade, 1967, 1 son. Education: LLD, University of Budapest; Academy of Commerce, Budapest. Appointments: General Manager, 99 Piccadilly Restaurant 1952-55; Owner, The Marquee Restaurant, London; Columnist on food, wine, eating-out and tourism, Daily Telegraph, Sunday Telegraph, 1954-60; Columnist, Evening News, 1968-74; Food Columnist, Sunday Times, 1986-91. Publications: Egon Ronay's Guide to Hotels and Restaurants (annual), 1956-87; Egon Ronay's Just a Bite (annual), 1979-85; Egon Ronay's Pub Guide (annual), 1980-85; Egon Ronay's Guide to 500 Good Restaurants in Europe's Main Cities (annual), 1983-85; The Unforgettable Dishes of My Life, 1989; Many other tourist guides. Honours: Médaille de la Ville de Paris, 1983; Chevalier de l'Ordre du Mérite Agricole, 1987. Memberships: Académie des Gastronomes, France; British Academy of Gastronomes, founder-president, 1983; International Academy of Gastronomy, founder-vice-president, 1987. Address: 37 Walton Street, London SW3 2HT, England.

ROOKE Daphne Marie, b. 6 Mar 1914, Boksburg, South Africa. Writer. m. 1 June 1937, 1 daughter. Publications: A Grove of Fever Trees, 1950, reprint, 1989; Mittee, 1951, reprint, 1987; Ratoons, 1953, reprint, 1990; Wizards Country, 1957; Beti, 1959; A Lover for Estelle, 1961; The Greyling, 1962; Diamond Jo, 1965; Boy on the Mountain, 1969; Margaretha de la Porte, 1976. Contributions to: Journals. Honours: 1st Prize, APB Novel Competition, 1946; Doctor of Literature, honoris causa, University of Natal, 1997. Address: 54 Regatta Court, Oyster Row, Cambridge CB5 8NS, England.

ROOKE Leon, b. 11 Sept 1934, Roanoke Rapids, North Carolina, USA. Author. Education: Mars Hill College, North Carolina, 1953-55; University of North Carolina at Chapel Hill, 1955-57, 1961. Appointments: Writer-in-Residence, University of North Carolina, 1965-66, University of Victoria, 1972-73, University of Southwest Minnesota, 1974-75, University of Toronto, 1984-85, University of Western Ontario, 1990-91; Visiting Professor, University of Victoria, 1980-81. Publications: Novels: Last One Home Sleeps in the Yellow Bed, 1968; Vault, 1974; The Broad Back of the Angel, 1977; The Love Parlour, 1977; Fat Woman, 1980; The Magician in Love, 1980; Death Suite, 1982; The Birth Control King of the Upper Volta, 1983; Shakespeare's Dog, 1983; Sing Me No Love Songs I'll Say You No Prayers, 1984; A Bolt of White Cloth, 1984; How I Saved the Province, 1990; The Happiness of Others, 1991; A Good Baby, 1991; Who Do You Love?, 1992; Muffins, 1995. Stage Plays: A Good Baby, 1991; The Coming, 1991; 4 others. Contributions to: About 300 short stories in leading North American journals. Honours: Canada and Australia Literary Prize, 1981; Best Paperback Novel of the Year, 1981; Governor-General's Award, 1984; North Carolina Award for Literature, 1990. Memberships: PEN; Writers' Union of Canada. Address: 209 Main Street, Eden Mills, Ontario N0B 1P0, Canada.

ROOM Adrian Richard West, b. 27 Sept 1933, Melksham, England. Writer. Education: Honours Degree, Russian, 1957, Diploma, Education, 1958, University of Oxford. Publications: Place-Names of the World, 1974; Great Britain: A Background Studies English-Russian Dictionary, 1978; Room's Dictionary of Confusibles, 1979; Place-Name Changes since 1900, 1980; Naming Names, 1981; Room's Dictionary of Distinguishables, 1981; Dictionary of Trade Name Origins, 1982; Room's Classical Dictionary, 1983; Dictionary of Cryptic Crossword Clues, 1983; A Concise Dictionary of Modern Place-Names in Great Britain and Ireland, 1983; Guide to British Place-Names, 1985; Dictionary of Changes in Meaning, 1986; Dictionary of Coin Names, 1988; Guinness Book of Numbers, 1989; Dictionary of Dedications, 1990; A Name for Your Baby, 1992; The Street Names of England, 1992; Brewer's Dictionary of Names, 1992; Corporate Eponymy, 1992; Place-Name Changes 1900-91, 1993; The Naming of Animals, 1993; African Place-Names, 1994; Cassell Dictionary of Proper Names, 1994; A Dictionary of Irish Place-Names, 1994; Cassell Dictionary of First Names, 1995; Brewer's Dictionary of Phrase and Fable, revised edition, 1995; Literally Entitled, 1996; An Alphabetical Guide to the Language of Name Studies, 1996; Placenames of Russia and the Former Soviet Union, 1996; Placenames of the World, 1997; Dictionary of Pseudonyms, 1998; Cassell's Dictionary of Word Histories, 1999. Memberships: Royal Geographical Society; English Place-Name Society; American Name Society. Address: 12 High Street, St Martin's, Stamford, Lincolnshire PE9 2LF, England.

ROONEY Lucy, b. 13 July 1926, Liverpool, England. Former Lecturer; Religious Sister of Notre Dame de Namur; Writer. Education: Teaching Certificate, Universities of Manchester and Liverpool; City and Guilds Advanced Handloom Weaver, 1965. Publications: Co-author: Mary, Queen of Peace, 1984; Medjugorje Unfolds, 1986; Medjugorje Journal, 1987; Lord Jesus Teach Me To Pray, 1988; Medjugorje Retreat, 1989; Our Lady Comes to Scottsdale, 1992; Return to God: The Scottsdale Message, 1993; Medjugorje Unfolds in Peace and in War, 1994; Finding Jesus in the World: Prayer with Teilhard de Chardin, 1996. Contributions to: Religious journals. Address: 52 Warriner Gardens, London SW11 4DU, England.

ROOSE-EVANS James, b. 11 Nov 1927, London, England. Theatre Director; Author. Education: MA, Oxon. Appointments: Founder, Hampstead Theatre, 1959; Founder, The Bleddfa Centre for Caring and the Arts, 1974. Publications: Directing a Play: Experimental Theatre; London Theatre - From the Globe to the National; One Foot on the Stage; Inner Journey: Outer Journey; revised extended new edition, 1998; Passages of the Soul-Ritual Today; The Adventures of Odd and Elsewhere; The Secret of the Seven Bright Shiners; Odd and the Great Bear; Elsewhere and The Gathering of the Clowns; The Return of the Great Bear; The Secret of Tippity-Witchit; The Lost Treasure of Wales; Darling Ma; The Time of My Life; Plays: Cider with Rosie; 84 Charing Cross Road. Membership: The Dramatists Club. Literary Agent: Sheil Land Associates Ltd. Address: c/o Sheil Land Associates, 43 Doughty Street, london, WC1, England.

ROOT William Pitt, b. 28 Dec 1941, Austin, Texas, USA. Professor; Poet. m. Pamela Uschuk, 6 Nov 1988, 1 daughter. Education: BA, University of Washington, 1964; MFA, University of North Carolina at Greensboro, 1966. Appointments: Stegman Fellow, Stanford University, 1967-68; Assistant Professor, Michigan State University, 1967-68; Visiting Writer-in-Residence, Amherst College, 1971, University of Southwest Louisiana, 1976, Wichita State University, 1976, University of Montana, 1978, 1980, 1982-85, Pacific Lutheran University, 1990; Professor, Hunter College of the City University of New York, 1986-. Publications: The Storm and Other Poems, 1969; Striking the Dark Air for Music, 1973; A Journey South, 1977; Reasons for Going It on Foot, 1981; In the World's Common Grasses, 1981; Invisible Guests, 1984; Faultdancing, 1986; Trace Elements from a Recurring Kingdom, 1994; Selected Odes of Pablo Neruda, 1997. Contributions to: Magazines and periodicals. Honours: Academy of American Poetry Prize, 1967; Rockefeller Foundation Grant, 1969-70; Guggenheim Fellowship, 1970-71; National Endowment for the Arts Grant, 1973-74; Pushcart Awards, 1977, 1980, 1985; US-UK Exchange Artist, 1978-79; Stanley Kunitz Poetry Award, 1981; Guy Owen Poetry Award, 1984. Address: c/o Department of English, Hunter College of the City University of New York, 695 Park Avenue, New York, NY 10021, USA.

ROPER David, b. 30 Nov 1954, Hessle, Yorkshire, England. Critic. Education: MA, AKC, King's College, London. Appointments: Editor, Square One, 1978; Gambit, 1978-85, Platform, 1981-82, Plays and Players, 1983-84; Drama Editor, Event, 1981-82; Theatre Critic, Daily Express, 1982-87; Arts Correspondent, BBC, 1987-90; Channel 4 TV, 1990-93; Director, Heavy Entertainment Ltd, 1993-. Publications: The Pineapple Dance Book, 1983; Bart! (biography of Lionel Bart), 1994; Scrooge's Guide to Christmas, 1997. Contributions to: Tatler; Event; Time Out; Sunday Telegraph; Daily Express; Sunday Express; Daily Mail; Harper's and Queen. Address: PO Box 5055, London W12 0ZX, England.

ROQUELAURE A N. See: **RICE Anne.**

RORTY Richard (McKay), b. 4 Oct 1931, New York, New York, USA. Philosopher; Professor; Writer. m. (1) Amelie Sarah Oksenberg, 15 June 1954, div 1972, 1 son, (2) Mary R Varney, 4 Nov 1972, 1 son, 1 daughter. Education: BA, 1949, MA, 1952, University of Chicago; PhD, Yale University, 1956. Appointments: Instructor, Yale University, 1955-57; Instructor, 1958-60, Assistant Professor, 1960-61, Wellesley College; Faculty, 1961-70, Professor of Philosophy, 1970-81, Stuart Professor of Philosophy, 1981-82, University Professor of Humanities, 1982-, University of Virginia. Publications: Philosophy and the Mirror of Nature, 1979; Consequences of Pragmatism, 1982; Contingency, Irony, and Solidarity, 1989; Objectivity, Relativism, and Truth, 1991; Essays on Heidegger and Others, 1991; Essays on Aristotle's De Anima (editor with Martha Nussbaum), 1992; Achieving Our Country: Leftist Thought in 20th-Century America, 1998. Honours: Guggenheim Fellowship, 1973-74; MacArthur Foundation Fellow, 1981-86. Memberships: American Academy of Arts and Sciences; American Philosophical Association. Address: c/o University of Virginia, 412 Cabell Hall, Charlottesville, VA 22903, USA.

ROSE Andrew Wyness, b. 11 Feb 1944, Headingley, Leeds, England. Barrister; Writer. Education: Trinity College, Cambridge, 1963-67; MA; LLM; Called to Bar, Grays Inn, London, 1968. Appointments: Barrister, 1968-88. Publications: Stinie: Murder on the Common, 1985; Scandal at the Savoy, 1991. Honour: Shortlisted, Golden Dagger Award for Non-Fiction, Crime Writers Association. Membership: Crimes Club, 1996. Address: Brock House, 26 The Street, Sutton Waldron, Blandford Forum, Dorset DT11 8N1, England.

ROSE Daniel Asa, b. 20 Nov 1949, New York, New York, USA. Writer; Poet. m. (1) Laura Love, 30 Nov 1974, div, 2 sons, (2) Shelley Roth, 5 Sept 1993. Education: AB, Honours, English, Brown University, 1971. Appointments: Travel Columnist, Esquire; Book Reviewer, Vanity Fair; Travel Editor, Madison. Publications: Flipping for it, 1987; Small Family with Rooster, 1988; Hiding Places, forthcomming. Other: Screenplays, poems, stories, reviews and literary essays. Contributions to: The New Yorker; The New York Magazine; GQ; Esquire; Playboy. Honours: O Henry Prize, 1980; PEN Literary Awards, 1987, 1988; Massachusetts Cultural Council Award, 1992. Address: 138 Bay State Road, Renoboth, MA 02769, USA.

ROSE Joel Steven, b. 1 Mar 1948, Los Angeles, California, USA. Writer. m. Catherine Texier, 2 daughters. Education: BA, Hobart College, 1970; MFA, Columbia University. Publications: Kill the Poor (novel), 1988; Between C and D (co-editor), 1988; Love is Strange (co-editor), 1993. Contributions to: Newspapers and magazines. Honours: National Endowment for the Arts Award, 1986; New York State Council on the Arts Award, 1986-87. Memberships: Coordinating Council of Literary Magazines; Poets and Writers; Writers Guild of America. Address: 255 East 7th Street, New York, NY 10009, USA.

ROSE Kenneth Vivian, b. 15 Nov 1924, Bradford, Yorkshire, England. Writer. Education: Repton School; Scholar, MA, New College, Oxford, 1948. Appointments: Assistant Master, Eton College, 1948; Editorial Staff, Daily Telegraph, 1952-60; Founder, Writer, Albany Column, Sunday Telegraph, 1961-. Publications: Superior Person: A Portrait of Curzon and his Circle in Late Victorian England, 1969; The Later Cecils, 1975; William Harvey: A Monograph, 1978; King George V, 1983; Kings, Queens and Courtiers: Intimate Portraits of the Royal House of Windsor, 1985; Harold Nicolson,1992. Contributions to: Dictionary of National Biography. Honours: Fellow, Royal Society of Literature, 1976; Wolfson Award for History, 1983; Whitbread Award for Biography, 1983; Yorkshire Post Biography of the Year Award, 1984; Commander of the Order of the British Empire, 1996. Address: 38 Brunswick Gardens, London W8 4 AL, England.

ROSE Marion. See: **HARRIS Marion Rose.**

ROSE Mark Allen, b. 4 Aug 1939, New York, New York, USA. Professor of English; Writer. Div, 1 son. Education: AB, Princeton University, 1961; BLitt, Merton College, 1963; PhD, Harvard University, 1967. Appointments: Instructor to Associate Professor of English, Yale University, 1967-74; Professor of English, University of Illinois, 1974-77, University of California at Santa Barbara, 1977-; Director, University of California Humanities Research Institute, 1989-94. Publications: Heroic Love, 1968; Golding's Tale, 1972; Shakespearean Design, 1972; Spenser's Art, 1975; Alien Encounters, 1981; Authors and Owners, 1993. Editor: Twentieth Century Views of Science Fiction, 1976; Twentieth Century Interpretations of Antony and Cleopatra, 1977; Bridges to Science Fiction (with others), 1980; Shakespeare's Early Tragedies, 1994; Norton Shakespere Workshop, 1997. Honours: Woodrow Wilson Fellow, 1961; Henry Fellow, 1961-62; Dexter Fellow, 1966; Morse Fellow, 1970-71; National Endowment for the Humanities Fellowships, 1979-80, 1990-91. Memberships: Modern Language Association; Phi Beta Kappa; Renaissance Society of America; Shakespeare Society of America. Address: 1135 Oriole Road, Montecito, CA 93108, USA.

ROSE Mitchell, b. 22 Nov 1951, Pennsylvania, USA. Literary Agent; Editor. Education: BA, Bard College, 1974; MFA, Goddard College, 1980. Appointments: Freelance Writer, 1975-80; Editor and Managing Editor for trade magazines, 1980-83; Editor, New American Library, 1983-86; Literary Agent and Editor, 1986-. Publications: The Victorian Fairy Tale Book, 1988; The Wizard of Oz: The Official Pictorial History, 1989; Gone With the Wind: The Definitive Illustrated History, 1989; The Film Encyclopaedia, 1990; Dr Deming, 1990; At Dawn We Slept, 1991; Harper Dictionary of American Government and Politics, 1992; Lawrence of Arabia, 1992; Judy Garland, 1992; Healing Through Nutrition, 1993; Kennedy as President, 1993. Contributions to: Boston Phoenix. Membership: Authors Guild. Address: Mitchell S Rose Literary Agency, 688 Avenue of the Americas, New York, NY 10010, USA.

ROSE Richard, b. 9 Apr 1933, St Louis, Missouri, USA. Professor of Public Policy; Writer. m. Rosemary J Kenny, 14 Apr 1956, 2 sons, 1 daughter. Education: BA, Double Distinction, Comparative Drama, Johns Hopkins University, 1953; London School of Economics and Political Science, 1954; DPhil, University of Oxford, 1960. Appointments: Lecturer in Government, University of Manchester, 1961-66; Professor of Politics, 1966-82, Director and Professor of Public Policy, 1976-, University of Strathclyde; Visiting Lecturer in Political Sociology, University of Cambridge, 1967; Visiting Scholar, Woodrow Wilson International Center, Washington, DC, 1974, Brookings Institution, Washington, DC, 1976, American Enterprise Institute, European University Institute, Florence, 1977, 1978, Central European University, Prague, 1992-95; Editor, Journal of Public Policy, 1985-; Hinkley Professor, Johns Hopkins University, 1987; Guest Professor, Wissenschaftsentrum, Berlin, 1988-90; Ransone Lecturer, University of Alabama, 1990; Fellow, Max Planck Transformation Process Group, Berlin, 1996. Publications: The British General Election of 1959 (with D E Butler), 1960; Must Labour Lose? (with Mark Abrams), 1960; Politics in England, 1964, 5th edition, 1989; Studies in British Politics (editor), 1966, 3rd edition, 1976; Influencing Voters, 1967; Policy Making in Britain (editor), 1969; People in Politics, 1970; European Politics (editor with M Dogan), 1971; Governing Without Consensus: An Irish Perspective, 1971; International Almanack of Electoral History (with T Mackie), 1974, 3rd edition, 1991; Electoral Behavior: A Comparative Handbook (editor), 1974; Lessons from America (editor), 1974; The Problem of Party Government, 1974; The Management of Urban Change in Britain and Germany, 1974; Northern Ireland: A Time of Choice, 1976; Managing Presidential Objectives, 1976; The Dynamics of Public Policy (editor), 1976; New Trends in British Politics (editor with D Kavanagh), 1977; Comparing Public Policies (editor with J Wiatr), 1977; What is Governing?: Purpose and Policy in Washington, 1978; Elections Without Choice (editor with G Hermet and A Rouquie), 1978; Can Government Go Bankrupt? (with B G Peters), 1978; Britain: Progress and Decline (editor with W B Gwyn), 1980; Do Parties Make a Difference?, 1980, 2nd edition, 1984; Challenge to Governance (editor), 1980; Electoral Participation (editor), 1980; Presidents and Prime Ministers (editor with E Suleiman), 1980; Understanding the United Kingdom, 1982; United Kingdom Facts (with I McAllister), 1982; The Territorial Dimension in United Kingdom Politics (editor with P Madgwick), 1982; Stress in Cities (editor with E Page), 1982; Understanding Big Government, 1984; The Nationwide Competition for Votes (with I McAllister), 1984; Public Employment in Western Nations, 1985; Voters Begin to Choose (with I McAllister), 1986; Patterns of Parliamentary Legislation (with D Van Mechelen), 1986; The Welfare State East and West (editor with R Shiratori), 1986; Ministers and Ministries, 1987; Taxation by Political Inertia (with T Karran), 1987; The Post-Modern President: The White House Meets the World, 1988, 2nd edition, 1991; Ordinary People in Public Policy, 1989; The Loyalty of Voters: A Lifetime Learning Model (with I McAllister), 1990; Lesson-Drawing in Public Policy: A Guide to Learning Across Time and Space, 1993; Inheritance in Public Policy: Change Without Choice in Britain (with P L Davies), 1994; What is Europe?, 1996; How Russia Votes (with S White and I McAllister), 1997; Democracy and its Alternatives (with W Mishler and C Haepter), 1998. Contributions to: Professional journals. Honours: Guggenheim Fellowship, 1974; Fellow, British Academy, 1992; Amex International Economics Prize, 1992. Memberships: American Academy of Arts and Sciences; Finnish Academy of Science and Letters; International Political Science Association, council member, 1976-82; Scottish Opera Ltd, council member, 1992-. Address: c/o Centre for the Study of Public Policy, University of Strathclyde, Livingstone Tower, Glasgow G1 1XH, Scotland.

ROSEN Michael Wayne, (Landgrave of Hesse), b. 7 May 1946, Harrow, England. Writer; Performer. m. 30 Nov 1987, 3 sons, 2 stepdaughters. Education: Middlesex Hospital Medical School, 1964-65; Wadham College, Oxford, 1965-69; National Film School, 1973-76. Appointments: Writer-in-Residence, Vauxhall Manor Comprehensive School, 1976-77, London Borough of Brent, 1983-84, John Scurr Primary School, 1984-87, 1988-90, Western Australia College of Advanced Education, 1987. Publications: Mind Your Own Business, 1974; Quick Let's Get Out Of Here, 1983; Don't Put the Mustard in the Custard, 1984; The Kingfisher Book of Poetry, 1984; The Hypnotiser, 1988; We're Going on a Bear Hunt, 1989; This is Our House, 1996; You Wait Till I'm Older Than You, 1996; Michael Rosen's Book of Nonsense, 1997. Contributions to: New Statesman; Guardian; Times Educational Supplement; Jewish Socialist. Honours: Signal Poetry Award, 1982; The Other Award, 1984; Smarties Award, 1989; Eleanor Fasjeon Award for contributions to Children's Literature, 1997. Membership: Equity. Address: c/o Peters, Fraser and Dunlop Group Ltd, 5th Floor, The Chambers, Chelsea Harbour, Lots Road, London SW10 0XF, England.

ROSEN Norma, b. 11 Aug 1925, New York, New York, USA. Writer; Teacher. m. Robert S Rosen, 1960, 1 son, 1 daughter. Education: BA, Mt Holyoke College, 1946; MA, Columbia University, 1953. Appointments: Teacher, Creative Writing, New School for Social Research, New York City, 1965-69, University of Pennsylvania, 1969, Harvard University, 1971, Yale University, 1984, New York University, 1987-. Publications: Joy to Levine!, 1962; Green, 1967; Touching Evil, 1969; At the Center, 1982; John and Anzia: An American Romance, 1989; Accidents of Influence: Writing as a Woman and a Jew in America (essays), 1992. Contributions to: Anthologies and other publications. Honours: Saxton, 1960; CAPS, 1976; Bunting, 1971-73. Memberships: PEN; Authors Guild; Phi Beta Kappa. Literary Agent: Gloria Loomis. Address: 133 East 35th Street, New York, NY 10016, USA.

ROSENBERG Bruce Alan, b. 27 July 1934, New York, New York, USA. Teacher; Writer. m. Ann Harleman, 20 June 1981, 3 sons. Education: BA, Hofstra University, 1955; MA, Pennsylvania State University, 1960; PhD, Ohio State University, 1965. Publications: The Art of the American Folk Preacher, 1970; Custer and the Epic of Defeat, 1975; The Code of the West, 1982; The Spy Story, 1987; Can These Bones Live?, 1988; Ian Fleming, 1989; The Neutral Ground, 1995. Contributions to: Over 60 professional journals. Honours: James Russell Lowell Prize, 1970; Chicago Folklore Prizes, 1970, 1975. Membership: Folklore Fellows International. Address: 55 Summit Avenue, Providence, RI 02906, USA.

ROSENBERG Greta. See: **GUT-RUSSENBERGER Margrit.**

ROSENBERG Liz, b. 3 Feb 1956, Glen Cove, New York, USA. Associate Professor of English; Poet; Writer. m. David Bosnick, 2 June 1996, 1 son. Education: BA, Bennington College, 1976; MA, Johns Hopkins University, 1978; PhD, Comparative Literature, State University of New York at Binghamton, 1997. Appointments: Associate Professor of English, State University of New York at Binghamton; Guest Teacher-Poet, various venues; Many poetry readings. Publications: The Fire Music (poems), 1987; A Book of Days (poems), 1992; Children of Paradise (poems), 1994; Heart and Soul (novel), 1996; The Invisible Ladder (editor), 1997; Earth-Shattering Poems (editor), 1998; These Happy Eyes (prose poems), 1999. Contributions to: Many newspapers, reviews, and journals. Honours: Kelloggs Fellow, 1980-82; Pennsylvania Council of the Arts Poetry Grant, 1982; Agnes Starrett Poetry Prize, 1987; Claudia Lewis Poetry Prize, 1997; Best Book for Teens Citation, New York Public Library, 1997; Paterson Prize for Children's Literature, 1997, 1998. Memberships: Associated Writing Programs; PEN. Address: c/o Department of English, General Literature, and Rhetoric, State University of New York at Binghamton, PO Box 6000, Binghamton, NY 13902, USA.

ROSENBERG Nancy Taylor, b. 9 July 1946, Dallas, Texas, USA. Writer. m. (1) Calvin S Kyrme, div, 2 sons, 1 daughter, (2) Jerry Rosenberg, 2 daughters. Education: Gulf Park College; University of California at Los Angeles. Publications: Mitigating Circumstances, 1993; Interest of Justice, 1993; The Eyewitness, 1994; First Offense, 1994; California Angel, 1995. Address: c/o Dytton Publicity, 375 Hudson Street, New York, NY 10014, USA.

ROSENBERG Peter Michael, b. 11 July 1958, London, England. Writer. Education: BSc, University of Sussex, 1979. Publications: The Usurper (co-author), 1988; Kissing Through a Pane of Glass, 1993; Touched By a God or Something, 1994; Because It Makes My Heart Beat Faster, 1995; Daniel's Dream, 1996. Contributions to: Journals and magazines. Honour: 2nd Prize, Betty Trask Award, 1992. Literary Agent: 48 Walham Grove, London SW6 1QR, England. Address: 430 St Ann's Road, London N15 3JJ, England.

ROSENBLATT Joe, (Joseph Rosenblatt), b. 26 Dec 1933, Toronto, Ontario, Canada. Poet; Writer; Artist. m. Faye Smith, 13 Oct 1970, 1 son. Education: Central Technical School, Toronto; George Brown College,

Toronto. Appointments: Editor, Jewish Dialog magazine, 1969-83; Writer-in-Residence, University of Western Ontario, London, 1979-80, University of Victoria, British Columbia, 1980-81, Saskatoon Public Library, Saskatchewan, 1985-86; Visiting Lecturer, University of Rome and University of Bologna, 1987. Publications: The Voyage of the Mood, 1960; The LSD Leacock, 1963; The Winter of the Luna Moth, 1968; Greenbaum, 1970; The Bumblebee Dithyramb, 1972; Blind Photographer: Poems and Sketches, 1973; Dream Craters, 1974; Virgins and Vampires, 1975; Top Soil, 1976; Doctor Anaconda's Solar Fun Club: A Book of Drawings, 1977; Loosely Tied Hands: An Experiment in Punk, 1978; Snake Oil, 1978; The Sleeping Lady, 1979; Brides of the Stream, 1984; Escape from the Glue Factory: A Memoir of a Paranormal Toronto Childhood in the Late Forties, 1985; Poetry Hotel: Selected Poems 1963-1985, 1985; The Kissing Goldfish of Siam: A Memoir of Adolescence in the Fifties, 1989; Gridi nel Buio, 1990; Beds and Consenting Dreamers, 1994; The Joe Rosenblatt Reader, 1995; The Voluptuos Gardener: The Collected Art and Writing of Jose Rosenblatt 1973-1996, 1996. Contributions to: Many publications. Honours: Canada Council Senior Arts Awards, 1973, 1976, 1980, 1987; Ontario Arts Council Poetry Award, 1970; Governor-Generals' Award for Poetry, 1976; British Columbia Book Award for Poetry, 1986. Address: 221 Elizabeth Avenue, Qualicum Beach, British Columbia V9K 1G8, Canada.

ROSENBLUM Martin Jack, b. 19 Aug 1946, Appleton, Wisconsin, USA. Poet; Writer. m. Maureen Rice, 6 Sept 1970, 2 daughters. Education: BS, 1969, MA, 1971, PhD, 1980, University of Wisconsin. Appointments: Guest Lecturer, University of East Anglia, Norwich, England, 1975; Poet-in-Residence, Wisconsin Review, University of Wisconsin at Oshkosh, 1987. Publications: Home, 1971; On, 1972; The Werewolf Sequence, 1974; Brite Shade, 1984; Conjuction, 1987; The Holy Ranger: Harley-Davidson Poems, 1989. Non-Fiction: Harley-Davidson Inc, 1903-1993: An Historical Overview, 1994. Other: Down on the Spirit Farm (CD of music and poetry), 1994. Honour: Wisconsin Award, Best Poet of 1995. Address: 2521 East Stratford Court, Shorewood, WI 53211, USA.

ROSENFELD Albert Hyman, b. 31 May 1920, Philadelphia, USA. Science Writer. m. 24 Aug 1948, 1 son, 1 daughter. Education: BA, History and Social Science, New Mexico State University. Appointments: Associate Editor, 1956-58, Senior Science Editor, 1958-60, Life; Managing Editor, Family Health, 1969-71; Senior Science Editor, Saturday Review, 1973-80; Contributing Editor, Geo, 1979-81, Science Digest, 1980-82. Publications: The Quintessence of Irving Langmuire, 1962; The Second Genesis: The Coming Control of Life, 1969; Prolongevity, 1976; Mind and Supermind (editor), 1977; Science, Invention and Social Change (editor), 1978; Responsible Parenthood (with G W Kliman), 1980; Prolongevity II, 1985. Contributions to: Magazines. Honours: Aviation Space Writers Award, 1964; Westinghouse Writing Award, 1966; Lasker Award, 1967; Claude Bernard Science Journalism Award, 1974; National Magazine Award, 1975; James P Grady Medal, American Chemical Society, 1981; Honorary DLitt, New Mexico State University; Janus Korczsak International Literary Award, 1982. Memberships: Council for the Advancement of Science Writing; National Association of Science Writers; Authors Guild. Address: 25 Davenport Avenue, New Rochelle, NY 10805, USA.

ROSENGARTEN Theodore, b. 17 Dec 1944, Brooklyn, New York, USA. Writer. m. 1974, 1 son. Education: AB, Amherst College, 1966; PhD, Harvard University, 1975. Publication: All God's Dangers: The Life of Nate Shaw, 1974. Honour: National Book Award, 1975. Address: PO Box 8, McClellanville, SC 29458, USA.

ROSENSTAND Peder Tuxen, b. 2 Nov 1935, Copenhagen, Denmark. Poet; Artist; Painter; Professor. m. Anni Rosenstand, 1960, 3 sons, 1 daughter. Education: Royal Danish Academy of Art, Copenhagen; University of Copenhagen. Publications: Osteklokken, 1974; Blik, 1988. Other: Dramatic works for Danish,

Norwegian, and Swedish TV; Painting exhibitions held in Denmark, England, Germany, Italy, New York, and Sweden, 1962-94. Contributions to: Pinqvinen. Membership: Authors Society, Copenhagen. Address: G1 Mollerup, 4673 Rodvig Stevns. Tif 53707030, Denmark.

ROSENTHAL Barbara Ann, b. 17 Aug 1948, Bronx, New York, USA. Writer; Artist; Photographer; Video Artist. 2 daughters. Education: BFA, Carnegie-Mellon University, 1970; MFA, Queens College, City University of New York, 1975. Appointments: Editor-in-Chief, Patterns, 1967-70; Adjunct Lecturer in English, College of Staten Island of the City University of New York, 1990-. Publications: Clues to Myself, 1982; Sensations, 1984; Old Address Book, 1985; Homo Futurus, 1986; In The West of Ireland, 1992; Children's Shoes, 1993; Soul and Psyche, 1999. Contributions to: Anthologies and journals. Honours: Various awards and residencies. Address: 727 Avenue of the Americas, New York, NY 10010, USA.

ROSENTHAL Jack Morris, b. 8 Sept 1931, Manchester, England. Dramatist; Writer. m. Maureen Lipman, 18 Feb 1973, 1 son, 1 daughter. Education: BA, Sheffield University. Publications: Over 300 television scripts, 1963-97; 5 stage plays; Film screenplays including: Lucky Star, 1980; Yentl (with Barbara Streisand), 1983; The Chain, 1985; The Wedding Gift, 1994; Captain Jack, 1998. Television: Eskimo Day, 1996. Honours: British Academy of Film and Television Artists Arts Award, 1976; Royal Television Society Writer's Award, 1976, and Hall of Fame, 1993; Honorary MA, University of Salford, 1994; Commander of the Order of the British Empire, 1994; Hon DLitt, University of Manchester, 1998; Associate Professor in Theatre, University of Sheffield, 1997. Address: c/o Casarotto Co Ltd, 60-66 Wardour Street, London W1, England.

ROSS Alan, b. 6 May 1922, Calcutta, India. Author; Poet; Editor; Publisher. m. Jennifer Fry, 1949, div 1985, 1 son. Education: St John's College, Oxford. Appointments: Staff, The Observer, 1950-71; Editor, London Magazine, 1961-; Managing Director, London Magazine Editions, 1965-. Publications: The Derelict Day, 1947; Time Was Away, 1948; The Forties, 1950; The Gulf of Pleasure, 1951; The Bandit on the Billiard Table, 1954; Something of the Sea, 1954; Australia 55, 1956, 2nd edition, 1983; Abroad (editor), 1957; Cape Summer and the Australians in England, 1957, 2nd edition, 1986; To Whom It May Concern, 1958; The Onion Man, 1959; Throught the Caribbean, 1960; The Cricketer's Companion (editor), 1960; Danger on Glass Island, 1960; African Negatives, 1962; Australia 63, 1963; West Indies at Lord's, 2nd edition, 1986; London Magazine Stories I-II (editor), 1964-80; North from Sicily, 1965; Poems 1942-1967, 1968; Tropical Ice, 1972; The Taj Express, 1973; Living in London (editor), 1974; Open Sea, 1975; Selected Poems of Lawrence Durell (editor), 1977; Death Valley and Other Poems, 1980; The Turf (editor), 1982; Colours of War, 1983; Ranji, 1983; Living Out of London (editor), 1984; Blindfold Games, 1986; The Emissary, 1986; Coastwise Lights, 1988; After Pusan, 1996; Winter Sea, 1998. Honours: Atlantic Award for Literature, Rockefeller Foundation, 1946; Fellow, Royal Society of Literature, 1971; Commander of the Order of the British Empire, 1982. Address: 4 Elm Park Lane, London SW3, England.

ROSS Angus. See: GIGGAL Kenneth.

ROSS Catherine. See: BEATY Betty Joan Campbell Smith.

ROSS Gary Earl, b. 12 Aug 1951, Buffalo, New York, USA. Associate Professor; Writer. m. 23 Dec 1970, div 1994, 2 sons, 1 daughter. Education: BA, 1973, MA, 1975, State University of New York at Buffalo. Appointments: Writing Educator, 1977-95, Associate Professor, 1995-, Educational Opportunity Center, State University of New York at Buffalo. Publications: Guiding the Adult Learner (editor), 1979; Developmental Perspectives (editor), 1981; Practical Considerations for Computer-Assisted Writing Instruction for Disadvantaged Learners, 1990; Teaching Creative Writing, 1990.

Contributions to: Professional journals and general periodicals; Buffalo News; ELF; Artvoice. Honours: Hearts on Fire Award, American Poetry Association, 1983; Writer-in-Residences, Just Buffalo Literary Organization, 1987, 1992; LIFT Program Fiction Fellowship, 1989. Memberships: International Society for the Exploration of Teaching Alternatives; Just Buffalo Literary Organization; Niagara-Erie Writers, board chair, 1987-89; United University Professions. Address: c/o State University of New York Educational Opportunity Center at Buffalo, 465 Washington Street, Buffalo, NY 14203, USA.

ROSS Helaine. See: DANIELS Dorothy.

ROSS John Munder, b. 20 June 1945, New York, New York, USA. Psychoanalyst; Writer. m. 1 son. Education: BA, magna cum laude, Harvard University, 1967; MA, 1973, PhD, 1974, Clinical Psychology, New York University; Certificate in Psychoanalysis, New York University Medical Centre, 1984. Publications: Father and Child, 1982; Tales of Love, Sex and Danger, 1986; The Oedipus Papers, 1988; The Male Paradox, 1992; What Men Want, 1993. Contributions to: Professional journals and general periodicals. Address: 243 West End Avenue, Suite 101, New York, NY 10023, USA.

ROSS Jonathon. See: ROSSITER John.

ROSS Malcolm. See: ROSS-MACDONALD Malcolm John.

ROSS Michael Elsohn, b. 30 June 1952, Utica, New York, USA. Writer; Naturalist. m. 20 July 1977, 1 son. Education: BS, Conservation of Natural Resources, University of California at Berkeley, 1974;Multi-Subject Teaching Credential, California State University at Fresno, 1981. Publications: Cycles, Cycles, Cycles, 1979; What Makes Everything Go?, 1979; Easy Day Hikes in Yosemite, 1985; Faces in all Kinds of Places, 1986; Yosemite Fun Book, 1987; Become a Bird and Fly, 1992; The World of Small, 1993; Sand Box Scientist, 1995; Happy Camper Handbook, 1995; Rolypolyology, 1996; Wormology, 1996; Cricketology, 1996; Snailology, 1996; Ladybugology, 1997; Caterpillarology, 1997; Bird Watching (with Margaret Morse Nice), 1997; Wildlife Watching (with Charles Eastman), 1997; Flower Watching (with Alice Eastwood, 1997; Bug Watching (with Charles Henry Turner), 1997; A Kid's Golden Gate: Adventures for Kids in Golden Gate National Parks, 1997. Honours: Awards of Excellence and Honorable Mentions, US National Park Service; Scientific American Young Readers Award, 1996; Outstanding Science Trade Books for Children, 1998; Arts Council Writers Fellowship, 1997. Membership: Society of Children's Books Writers and Illustrators; The Authors Guild. Address: PO Box 295, El Portal, CA 95318, USA.

ROSS-MACDONALD J(ohn), (Malcolm Macdonald, Malcolm Ross, M R O'Donnell), b. 29 Feb 1932, Chipping, Sodbury, Gloucestershire, England. Freelance Writer; Editor; Designer. m. Ingrid Giehr, 2 daughters. Education: Falmouth School of Art, 1950-54; Diploma, University College, London, 1958. Appointments: Lektor, Folk University, Sweden, 1959-61; Executive Editor, Aldus Books, 1962-65; Visiting Lecturer, Hornsey College of Art, 1965-69. Publications: The Big Waves, 1962; Macdonald Illustrated Encyclopaedia (executive editor), 10 volumes, 1962-65; Spare Part Surgery (co-author), 1968; Machines in Medicine, 1969; The Human Heart, 1970; World Wildlife Guide, 1971; Beyond the Horizon, 1971; Every Living Thing, 1973; World from Rough Stones, 1974; Origin of Johnny, 1975; Life in the Future, 1976; The Rich Are With You Always, 1976; Sons of Fortune, 1978; Abigail, 1979; Goldeneye, 1981; The Dukes, 1982; Tessa d'Arblay, 1983; In Love and War, 1984; Mistress of Pallas, 1986; Silver Highways, 1987; The Sky with Diamonds, 1988; A Notorious Woman, 1988; His Father's Son, 1989; An Innocent Woman, 1989; Hell Hath No Fury, 1990; A Woman Alone, 1990; The Captain's Wives, 1991; A Woman Scorned, 1991; A Woman Possessed, 1992; All Desires Known, 1993; To the End of Her Days, 1993; Dancing on Snowflakes,

1994; For I Have Sinned, 1994; Kernow and Daughter, 1994; Crissy's Family, 1995; Tomorrow's Tide, 1996; The Carringtons of Helston, 1997; Like a Diamond, 1998. Contributions to: Sunday Times; New Scientist; Science Journal; Month; Jefferson Encyclopaedia. Memberships: Authors Guild; Society of Authors. Address: c/o David Higham Ltd, 5-8 Lower John Street, London W1R 4HA, England.

ROSSI Bruno. See: **LEVINSON Leonard.**

ROSSI Maria Francesca, (Francesca Duranti), b. 2 Jan 1935, Genoa, Italy. Writer. m. (1) Enrico Magnani, 1956, (2) Massimo Duranti, 1970, 1 son, 1 daughter. Education: Studied jurisprudence, University of Pisa. Publications: La bambina, 1976; Piazza, Mia Bella Piazza, 1978; The House on Moonlake, 1984; Happy Ending, 1987; Effetti Personalia, 1988; Ultima Stesura, 1991. Contributions to: Il Secoloxx; Il Giornale; Il Messaggero. Honours: Martina Franca Citta di Milano, Bagutta, 1984; Basilicata Hemingway Campiello, 1988; Prix Lectrices d'Elle, Castiglioncello, 1991. Address: Villa Rossi, Gattaiola, Lucca, Italy.

ROSSITER John. See: **CROZIER Brian Rossiter.**

ROSSITER John, (Jonathan Ross), b. 2 Mar 1916, Devonshire, England. Writer. Education: Preparatory and military schools, Wooolwich and Bulford, 1924-32. Appointments: Detective Chief Superintendent, Wiltshire Constabulary, 1939-69; Flight Lieutenant, RAF/VR, 1943-46; Columnist, Wiltshire Courior, Swindon, 1963-64. Publications: As Jonathan Ross: The Blood Running Cold, 1968; Diminished by Death, 1968; Dead at First Hand, 1969; The Deadest Thing You Ever Saw, 1969; Death's Head, 1982; Dead Eye, 1983; Dropped Dead, 1984; Fate Accomplished, 1987; Sudden Departures, 1988; A Time for Dying, 1989; Daphne Dead and Done For, 1990; Murder be Hanged, 1992; The Body of a Woman, 1994; Murder! Murder! Burning Bright, 1996; This Too Too Sullied Flesh, 1997. As John Rossiter: The Victims, 1971; A Rope for General Dietz, 1972; The Manipulators, 1973; The Villains, 1974; The Golden Virgin, 1975; The Man Who Came Back, 1978; Dark Flight, 1981. Contributions to: Police Review. Membership: Crime Writers Association. Literary Agent: David Higham Associates Ltd. Address: 3 Leighton Home Farm Court, Wellhead Lane, Westbury, Wilts BA13 3PT, England.

ROSSNER Judith (Perelman), b. 1 Mar 1935, New York, New York, USA. Writer. m. (1) Robert Rossner, 13 June 1954, div, (2) Mort Persky, 9 Jan 1979, div, 1 son, 1 daughter. Education: City College, New York City, 1952-55. Publications: To the Precipice, 1966; Nine Months in the Life of an Old Maid, 1969; Any Minute I Can Split, 1972; Looking for Mr Goodbar, 1975; Attachments, 1977; Emmeline, 1980; August, 1983; His Little Women, 1990; Olivia or the Weight of the Past, 1994; Perfidia, 1997. Contributions to: Magazines and journals. Memberships: Authors Guild; PEN. Address: c/o Julian Bach Literary Agency, 747 Third Avenue, New York, NY 10017, USA.

ROSTON Murray, b. 10 Dec 1928, London, England. Professor of English; Writer. Education: MA, Queen's College, Cambridge, 1952; MA, 1954, PhD, 1961, Queen Mary College, London. Appointment: Professor of English, Bar-Ilan University, Ramat Gan, Israel, 1956-. Publications: Prophet and Poet: The Bible and the Growth of Romanticism, 1965; Biblical Drama in England from the Middle Ages to the Present Day, 1968; The Soul of Wit: A Study of John Donne, 1974; Milton and the Baroque, 1980; Sixteenth-Century English Literature, 1982; Renaissance Perspectives in Literature and the Visual Arts, 1987; Changing Perspectives in Literature and the Visual Arts, 1650-1820, 1990; Victorian Contexts in Literature and the Visual Arts, 1995; Modernist Patterns: In Literature and the Visual Arts, 1999. Contributions to: Professional journals. Address: 51 Katznelson Street, Kiryat Ono, Israel.

ROTBLAT Sir Joseph, b. 4 Nov 1908, Warsaw, Poland. Professor Emeritus; Writer. Education: MA, University of Warsaw; PhD, University of Liverpool. Appointments: Professor, 1950-76, Professor Emeritus, 1976-, Medical College of St Batholomew's Hospital, University of London; Editor, Physics in Medicine and Biology, 1960-73; President, Pugwash Conferences on Science and World Affairs, 1988-; Emeritus, 1997. Publications: Radioactivity and Radioactive Substances (with Sir James Chadwick), 1961; Science and World Affairs, 1962; The Uses and Effects of Nuclear Energy (co-author), 1964; Aspects of Medical Physics (editor), 1966; Pugwash: The First Ten Years, 1967; Scientists in the Quest for Peace: A History of the Pugwash Conferences, 1972; Nuclear Reactors: To Breed or Not to Breed, 1977; Nuclear Energy and Nuclear Weapon Proliferation, 1979; Nuclear Radiation in Warfare, 1981; Scientists, the Arms Race and Disarmament, 1982; The Arms Race at a Time of Decision, 1984; Nuclear Strategy and World Security, 1985; World Peace and the Developing Countries, 1986; Strategic Defence and the Future of the Arms Race, 1987; Co-existence, Co-operation and Common Security, 1988; Verification of Arms Reductions, 1989; Global Problems and Common Security, 1989; Nuclear Proliferation: Technical and Economic Aspects, 1990; Global Security Through Co-Operation, 1990; Towards a Secure World in the 21st Century, 1991; Striving for Peace, Security and Development in the World, 1992; A Nuclear-Weapon-Free World: Desirable? Feasible?, 1993; World Citizenship: Allegiance to Humanity, 1997; Nuclear Weapons: The Road to Zero, 1998. Honours: Commander of the Order of the British Empire, 1965; Albert Einstein Peace Prize, 1992; Fellow, Royal Society, 1995; Nobel Prize for Peace, 1995; Knight Commander of the Order of St. Michael and St. George, 1998. Address: 8 Asmara Road, London NW2 3ST, England.

ROTH Andrew, b. 23 Apr 1919, New York, New York, USA. Political Correspondent. m. Mathilda Anna Friederich, 1949, div 1984, 1 son, 1 daughter. Education: BSS, City College of New York, 1939; MA, Columbia University, 1940; Harvard University. Appointments: Reader, City College, 1939; Research Associate, Institute of Pacific Relations, 1940; Editorial Writer, The Nation, 1945-46; Foreign Correspondent, Toronto Star Weekly, 1946-50; London Correspondent, France Observateur, Sekai, Singapore Standard, 1950-60; Director, Parliamentary Profiles, 1955-; Political Correspondent, Manchester Evening News, 1972-84; New Statesman, 1984-96. Publications: Japan Strikes South, 1941; French Interests and Policies in the Far East, 1942; Dilemma in Japan, 1945; The Business Background of MPs, 1959, 7th edition, 1980; The MPs Chart, 1967, 6th edition, 1987; Enoch Powell: Tory Tribune, 1970; Can Parliament Decide..., 1971; Heath and the Heathmen, 1972; Lord on the Board, 1972; Sir Harold Wilson: Yorkshire Walter Mitty, 1977; Parliamentary Profiles, Vols I-IV, 1984-85, 2nd edition, 1988-90; 4th edition, 1998; New MPs of '92, 1992; Mr Nice Guy and His Chums, 1993; New MPs of '97, 1997. Address: 34 Somali Road, London NW2 3RL, England.

ROTHE-VALLBONA Rima Gretel, b. 15 Mar 1931, San José, Costa Rica. Writer; Professor Emeritus. m. Dr Carlos Vallbona, 26 Dec 1956, 1 son, 3 daughters. Education: BA, BS Colegio Superior de Senoritas, San José, Costa Rica, 1948; Diploma, Professor of French in a Foreign Country, University of Paris, Sorbonne, 1953; Diploma in Spanish Philology, University of Salamanca, Spain, 1954; MA, University of Costa Rica, 1962; DML, Doctor in Modern Languages, Middlebury College, USA, 1981. Appointments: Visiting Professor, University of St Thomas Summer Program in Argentina, 1972, Rice University Summer Program in Spain, 1974; Cullen Foundation Professor of Spanish, 1989-95, Professor Emeritus, 1995-. Publications: Noche en vela (novel), 1968; Polvo del camino (short stories), 1971; Yolanda Oreamuno (literary essay), 1972; La Salamandra Rosada (short stories), 1979; La Obra en prosa de Eunice Odio (literary essay), 1981; Mujeres y agonias (short stories), 1982; Las sombres que perseguimos (novel), 1983; Baraja de soledades (short stories), 1983; Cosecha de pecadores (short stories), 1988; El arcangel del perdon (short stories), 1990; Mundo, demonio y mujer (novel), 1991; Los infiernos de la mujer y algo mas (short stories), 1992; Vida y sucesos de la Monja Alferez (critical edition), 1992; Flowering Inferno: Tales of Sinking Hearts (short stories), 1993; Tormy, la gata Prodigiosa de Donaldito (Short story for Children), 1997. Honours: Ancora Award, 1983-84; Medal of Civil Service, 1989. Address: 3706 Lake Street, Houston, TX 77098, USA.

ROTHENBERG Jerome (Dennis), b. 11 Dec 1931, New York, New York, USA. Professor of Visual Arts and Literature; Poet; Writer. m. Diane Brodatz, 25 Dec 1952, 1 son. Education: BA, City College, New York City, 1952; MA, University of Michigan, 1953. Appointments: Professor of English and Comparative Literature, State University of New York at Binghamton, 1986-88; Professor of Visual Arts and Literature, University of California at San Diego, 1988-. Publications: New Young German Poets, 1959; White Sun, Black Sun, 1960; Technicians of the Sacred, 1968; Poems for the Game of Silence: Selected Poems, 1971; Shaking the Pumpkin, 1972, 2nd edition, 1986; America: A Prophecy, 1973; Poland/1931, 1974; Revolution of the Word, 1974; A Big Jewish Book, 1977; A Seneca Journal, 1978; Numbers and Letters, 1980; Vienna Blood, 1980; Pre-Faces, 1981; That Dada Strain, 1983; Symposium of the Whole, 1983; 15 Flower World Variations, 1984; A Merz Sonata, 1985; New Selected Poems, 1970-85, 1986; Exiled in the Word, 1989; Khurbn and Other Poems, 1989; Further Sightings and Conversations, 1989; The Lorca Variations, 1994; Gematria, 1994; Poems for the Millenium, Vol I, 1995; Vol 2, 1998; Pictures of the Crucifixion, 1996; Seedings and Other Poems, 1996; The Book: Spiritual Instrument, 1996; A Paradise of Poets, 1999. Contributions to: Various publications. Honours: National Endowment for the Arts Fellowship, 1975; Guggenheim Fellowship, 1976; American Book Award, 1982; Translation Award, PEN Center, USA West, 1994; Josephine Miles Literary Awards, PEN Oakland, 1994, 1996. Memberships: New Wilderness Foundation; PEN Internationa. Address: c/o Department of Visual Arts, University of California at San Diego, La Jolla, CA 92093, USA.

ROTHMAN Judith. See: **PETERS Maureen.**

ROTIMI (Emmanuel Gladstone) Ola(wale), b. 13 Apr 1938, Sapele, Nigeria. Playwright. Education: BFA, Boston University, 1963; MFA, Yale University, 1966. Appointment: Head, Department of Creative Arts, University of Port Harcourt, 1982-. Publications: Our Husband Has Gone Mad Again, 1966; The Gods Are Not To Blame, 1968; Kurunmi: An Historical Tragedy, 1969; Holding Talks, 1970; Ovonramwen Nogbaisi, 1971; Imitation into Madness, 1973; Grip Am, 1973; Akassi Youmi, 1977; If: A Tragedy of the Ruled, 1979; Hopes of the Living - Dead, 1985. Honour: Oxford University Press Prize, 1970. Address: Department of Creative Arts, University of Port Harcourt, PMB 5323, Port Harcourt, Rivers State, Nigeria.

ROUDINESCO Elisabeth, b. 10 Sept 1944, Paris, France. Historian; Writer. Education: State Doctor of Letters Degree, History and Human Science, University of Paris; École des Hautes Études en Sciences Sociatus, Paris. Publications: Histoire de la Psychanalyse en France, 1885-1985, 2 volumes, 1982, 1986; Madness and Revolution, 1991; Jacques Lacan Esquisse d'une vie Histoire d'une Systéme de Pensée, 1993. Contributions to: Various publications. Memberships: Société International d'histoire de la Psychiatrie et de la Psychanalyse, Paris. Address: 89 avenue Denfert-Rochereau, 75014 Paris, France.

ROUNTREE Owen. See: **KITTREDGE William Alfred.**

ROUSE Anne Barrett, b. 26 Sept 1954, Washington, DC, USA. Poet; Author. Education: BA Hons, History, University of London, England, 1977. Appointments: Nurse, Haringay and Bloomsbury Health Authorities, 1979-86; Mental Health Worker, Islington Mind, 1986-92; Director, Islington Mind, 1992-95; Writer, 1995-. Publication: Sunset Grill, 1993; Timing, 1997.

Contributions to: Times Literary Supplement; London Review of Books; Observer; The Independent; The New Statesman. Honours: Poetry Book Society Recommendation, 1993, 1997. Memberships: Society of Authors; Poetry Society. Address: c/o Bloodaxe Books, PO Box 1SN, NE99 1SN, England.

ROUSSEAU George (Sebastian), b. 23 Feb 1941, New York, New York, USA. Professor of English Literature; Writer. Education: BA, Amherst College, 1962; MA, 1964, PhD, 1966, Princeton University. Appointments: Osgood Fellow in English Literature, 1965-66, Woodrow Wilson Dissertation Fellow, 1966, Princeton University; Book Reviewer, The New York Times, 1967-; Instructor, Harvard University, 1966-68; Assistant Professor, 1968-69, Associate Professor, 1969-76, Professor of English, 1976-94, University of California at Los Angeles; Fulbright Resident Professor, West Germany, 1970; Honorary Fellow, Wolfson College, Cambridge, 1974-75; Overseas Fellow, University of Cambridge, 1979; Visiting Fellow Commoner, Trinity College, Cambridge, 1982; Senior Fulbright Resident Scholar, Sir Thomas Browne Institute, Netherlands, 1983; Visiting Exchange Professor, King's College, Cambridge, 1984; Senior Fellow, National Endowment for the Humanities, 1986-87; Visiting Fellow and Waynflete Lecturer, Magdalen College, Oxford, 1993-94; Regius Professor of English Literature, King's College, University of Aberdeen, 1994-98; Research Professor of Humanities, De Montdort University, 1999-. Publications: This Long Disease My Life: Alexander Pope and the Sciences (editor with Marjorie Hope Nicolson), 1968; John Hill's Hypochondriasis, 1969; English Poetic Satire: Wyatt to Byron (with N Rudenstine), 1969; The Augustan Milieu: Essays Presented to Louis A Landa (editor with Eric Rothstein), 1970; Tobias Smollett: Bicentennial Essays Presented to Lewis M Knapp (co-editor), 1971; Organic Form: The Life of an Idea (editor), 1972; Goldsmith: The Critical Heritage, 1974; The Renaissance Man in the 18th Century, 1978; The Ferment of Knowledge: Studies in the Historiography of Eighteenth Century Science (editor with Roy Porter), 1980; The Letters and Private Papers of Sir John Hill, 1981; Tobias Smollett: Essays of Two Decades, 1982; Literature and Science (editor), 1985; Science and the Imagination: The Berkeley Conference (editor), 1985; Sexual Underworlds of the Enlightenment (editor with Roy Porter), 1987; The Enduring Legacy: Alexander Pope Tercentenary Essays (editor with P Rogers), 1988; Exoticism in the Enlightenment (with Roy Porter), 1990; Perilous Enlightenment: Pre- and Post-Modern Discourses: Sexual, Historical, 1991; Enlightenment Crossings: Pre- and Post-Modern Discourses: Anthropological, 1991; Enlightenment Borders: Pre- and Post-Modern Discources: Medical, Scientific, 1991; Hysteria Before Freud (co-author), 1993; Gout: The Patrician Malady, 1998. Contributions to: Professional journals and general publications. Honours: Clifford Prize, 1987; Leverhulme Trust Awardee, 1999-2001. Memberships: Many professional organizations. Literary Agent: Gilian Coleridge. Address: c/o Magdalen College, Oxford, OX1 4AU, England.

ROUX Jean-Louis, b. 18 May 1923, Montreal, Quebec, Canada. Actor; Theatre Administrator; Writer; Senator. m. Monique Oligny, 28 Oct 1950, 1 son. Education: Collège Ste Marie; BA, cum laude, 1943, Medical Studies, 1943-46, University of Montreal. Appointments: Actor in numerous stage, radio and television productions; Founder, Le Théatre d'Essai de Montréal, 1950; Founder, 1951, Secretary-General, 1953-63, Artistic Director, 1966-82, Théatre du Nouveau Monde; Senator of Canada, 1993-96; Lieutenant-Governor, Province of Quebec, 1996-97; Chairman, Canada Council for the Arts, 1998-. Publications: En Grève (co-author), 1963; Bois-Brulés, 1967; La Tragédie du Roi Lear, 1996; Nous sommes tous les acteurs, 1997. Other: Various radio and television scripts. Honours: Best Actor, Congrès du Spectacle, 1960; Centenary of Confederation Medal, 1967; Société St-Jean Baptiste Victor-Morin Prize, 1969; Officer, 1971, Companion, 1987, of the Order of Canada; Molson Prize, 1977; World Theatre Award, 1985; Honorary doctorates.

Memberships: National Theatre School of Canada, life governor; Royal Society of Canada. Address: 4145 Blueridge Crescent, No 2, Montreal, Quebec, H3H 1S7, Canada.

ROVNER Arkady, b. 28 Jan 1940, Odessa, Russia. Writer; Publisher; Teacher. m. Victoria Andreyeva, 5 Aug 1969, 1 son. Education: MA, Philosophy, 1965, University of Moscow; Graduate Programme, Department of German and English, 1965-67, Moscow Pedagogical Institute; Graduate Programme, Department of Foreign Studies, American University, Washington, DC, 1974-75; Doctoral Studies, Department of Religion, Columbia University, 1976-87. Appointments: Publisher, Gnosis Press, 1978-; Instructor, New York University, 1981-85; Instructor, New School for Social Research, New York, 1981-. Publications: Gostii iz oblastii, 1975; Kalalatsy, 1980; Khod korolyom, 1989; Etagy Gadesa, 1992; Tretya Kultura, 1996. Contributions to: Various publications. Honours: Cammington Community of the Arts, USA, 1983; Mme Karolyi Foundation, Vance, France, 1984. Membership: American PEN Center; Union of Russian Writers. Address: PO Box 42, Prince Street Station, New York, NY 10012, USA.

ROWAN Deidre. See: **WILLIAMS Jeanne.**

ROWAN Hester. See: **ROBINSON Sheila (Mary).**

ROWBOTHAM David Harold, b. 27 Aug 1924, Toowoomba, Queensland, Australia. Author; Poet; Journalist. m. Ethel Jessie Matthews, 14 Jan 1952, 2 daughters. Education: BA, University of Queensland, 1965; MA (QUAL), 1969. Appointments: Australian Delegate, World Congress of Poets, 1981; Cultural Visitor, USA, Library of Congress, 1988; Commonwealth Literary Fund Lecturer in Australian Literature, 1956, 1961, 1964; National Book Reviewing Panel, Australian Broadcasting Commission, 1954-63; Arts Editor, 1970-80, Literary Editor, 1980-87, Brisbane Courier-Mail. Publications: Ploughman and Poet (poems), 1954; Town and City (stories), 1956; Inland (poems), 1958; The Man in the Jungle (novel), 1964; All the Room (poems), 1964; Bungalow and Hurricane (poems), 1967; The Makers of the Ark (poems), 1970; The Pen of Feathers (poems), 1971; Mighty Like a Harp (poems), 1974; Selected Poems, 1975; Maydays (poems), 1980; New and Selected Poems, 1945-93, 1994; The Ebony Gates: New & Wayside Poems, 1996. Contributions to: Numerous magazines and journals. Honours: Pacific Star, World War II, 1945; Emeritus Fellow of Australian Literature, Australia Council, 1989; Second Prize for Poetry, NSW Captain Cook Bi-Centennary Celebrations Literary Competition, 1970; Grace Leven Prize, 1964; Ford Memorial Medal for Poetry, University of Queensland, 1948; Order of Australia, Queen's Birthday Honours, 1991; International Order of Merit, International Biographical Centre, Cambridge, England, 1991. Memberships include: Foundation Councillor, Australian Society of Authors, 1964-; Australian Journalists Association; International Federation of Journalists; President, State Branch, Fellowship of Australian Writers, 1982. Address: 28 Percival Terrace, Holland Park, Brisbane, Queensland 4121, Australia.

ROWE Brian. See: **CRESSWELL Helen.**

ROWETT Helen Graham Quiller, b. 30 Dec 1915, London, England. Retired Lecturer; Writer. Education: Girton College, Cambridge, 1935-39; BA, Natural Science, 1938; Part II, Zoology, 1939; MA, 1942. Publications: Guides to Dissection Parts 1-5, 1950-53; Basic Anatomy, 1959, 4th edition, revised, 1999; The Rat as a Small Mammal, 1960, 3rd edition, 1974; Guide to Dissection, 1962, revised edition, 1970; Histology and Embryology, 1962; Basic Anatomy and Physiology, 1959, 3rd edition, revised, 1988; Two Moorsway Guide, 1976, 6th edition, revised, 1999; Roundabout Family Rambling, 1995. Honour: Grisedale Research Scholarship, Manchester, 1939-40. Memberships: Society of Authors; West Country Writers; Institute of Biology; Royal Society of Arts, fellow. Address: 3 Manor Park, Dousland, Yelverton, Devon PL20 6LX, England.

ROWLAND Iris. See: **ROBERTS Irene.**

ROWLAND Peter Kenneth, b. 26 July 1938, London, England. Writer. Education: Graduate, University of Bristol, 1960. Publications: The Last Liberal Governments: The Promised Land 1905-1910, 1968; The Last Liberal Governments: Unfinished Business 1911-1914, 1971; Lloyd George, 1975; Macaulay's History of English in the 18th Century (editor), 1980; Macaulay's History of England from 1485 to 1685 (editor), 1985; Autobiography of Charles Dickens (editor), 1988; The Disappearance of Edwin Drood, 1991; Thomas Day 1748-1789: Virtue Almost Personified, 1996; The Life and Times of Thomas Day 1748-1789, 1996; Just Stylish, 1998; Raffles and His Creator, 1999. Address: 18 Corbett Road, Wanstead, London E11 2LD, England.

ROWLAND Robin F, b. 17 June 1950, Tanga, Tanzania. Writer. Education: Lawrence Park Collegiate, Toronto, Canada; BA, Anthropology, York University, Toronto, 1973; Bachelor of Journalism, Carleton University, Ottawa, 1975. Appointments: Reporter, Sudbury Star, Ontario, Canada, 1975-76; Editor, CBC National Radio News, Toronto, 1977-80; Writer, Editor, CBC Teletext, Toronto, 1982-85; Freelance Writer, CTV National News, Toronto, 1988-. Publications: King of the Mob, Rocco Perri and the Women Who Ran His Rackets, 1987; Undercover: Cases of the RCMP's Most Secret Operative (with James Dubro), 1991. Radio Plays: A Truthful Witness, 1985; King of the Bootleggers, 1986; Hot Coffee, 1988. Membership: Science Fiction and Fantasy Writers of America. Address: Eridani Productions, Suite 1005, 268 Poplar Plains Road, Toronto, Ontario M4V 2P2, Canada.

ROWLAND-ENTWISTLE (Arthur) Theodore (Henry), b. 30 July 1925, Clayton-le-Moors, Lancashire, England. Writer. Education: BA, BSc Honours, Open University. Publications: Famous Composers (with J Cooke), 1974; Animal Worlds (with J Cooke), 1975; Famous Explorers (with J Cooke), 1975; Facts and Records Book of Animals, 1975; Famous Kings and Emperors (with J Cooke), 1977; The World You Never See: Insect Life, 1976; Our Earth, 1977; The Restless Earth, 1977; Exploring Animal Homes, 1978; Seashore Life (as T E Henry), 1983; Fishes (as James Hall-Clarke), 1983; Fact Book of British History (with J Cooke), 1984; Heraldry, 1984; Houses, 1985; World of Speed, 1985; Confucius, 1986; Stamps, 1986; Nebuchadnezzar, 1986; Rivers and Lakes, 1986; Focus on Rubber, 1986; Great British Architects, 1986; Great British Inventors, 1986; Great British Kings and Queens, 1986; Great British Reformers, 1986; Focus on Coal, 1987; The Royal Marines, 1987; The Secret Service, 1987; The Special Air Service, 1987; Jungles and Rainforests, 1987; Three-Dimensional Atlas of the World, 1988; Flags, 1988; Guns, 1988; Focus on Silk, 1989; Weather and Climate, 1991; Funfax History of Britain, 1993; Question and Answer Quiz Book (with A Kramer), 1995; World Events and Dates, 1995; Paras, 1997. Contributions to: Various encyclopaedias and periodicals. Memberships: Royal Geographical Society, fellow; Zoological Society, fellow. Address: West Dene, Stonestile Lane, Hastings, Sussex TN35 4PE, England.

ROWLEY Rosemary Teresa, (Rosemarie Rowley), b. Dublin, Ireland. Education: BA, Trinity College, 1974; MA, 1974; MLitt, 1984; Diploma in Psychiatry, 1996. Publications: The Broken Pledge, 1985; The Sea of Affliction, 1987; Flight into Reality, 1987; Betrayal into Origin (unathorised edition), 1996; The Wake of Wonder (unathorised edition), 1998. Contributions to: Irish Times; Sunday Tribune. Honours include: Epic Awards, Scotland, 1996, 1997; American Library of Poetry Award, 1997.

ROWSELL Terry, b. 1969. Actor; Director; Playwright. Education: Graduate, Memorial University of Newfoundland. Honours: Several. Membership: Playwrights Union of Canada. Address: 16 Massey Crescent, Mount Pearl, NF A1N 2H2, Canada.

ROXMAN (Pia) Susanna (Ellinor), b. 29 Aug 1946, Stockholm, Sweden. Writer; Poet; Critic. Education: BA,

Honours, Comparative Literature and Philosophy, University of Lund, 1973; PhD, Comparative Literature, University of Goteborg, 1984. Appointments: Critic; University Lecturer; Head, Centre for Classical Mythology, University of Lund, 1996-. Publications: Riva villor, 1978; Nymferna kommer, 1983; Glöm de döda, 1985. In English: Goodbye to the Berlin Wall, 1991; Broken Angels, 1996. Contributions to: Reviews, quarterlies, and journals worldwide. Honours: Swedish Authors' Fund Grant, 1979; Malmöhus County Council Arts Grant, Sweden, 1984; Swedish Balzac Prize, 1990; Special Mention, Open University Poetry Competition, England, 1994; Editor's Choice Prize, 1994, Marjorie Lees Linn Poetry Prize, 1995; Elk River Review, USA. Memberships: Författarcentrum Syd (Authors' Centre South); Conservatory of American Letters. Address: Ulrikedal D210, S-224 58 Lund, Sweden.

ROYLE Nicholas (John), b. 20 Mar 1963. Writer. m. Kate Ryan, 31 Aug 1996, 1 son. Education: BA combined honours, French, German, Queen Mary College, University of London, 1986. Appointments: Chief Sub-Editor, Reader's Digest, 1990-91; Chief Sub-Editor, You Magazine, 1992; Editor Guides, Time Out, 1994-. Publications: Novels: Counterparts, 1993; Saxophone Dreams, 1996; The Matter of the Heart, 1997; Editor, anthologies: Darklands, 1991; Darklands 2, 1992; A Book of Two Halves, 1996; The Tiger Garden: A Book of Writers' Dreams, 1996; The Time Out Book of New York Short Stories, 1997; The Agony and the Ecstasy, 1998; The Ex Files, 1998; Neonlit: The Time Out Book of New Writing, 1998. Contributions to: Independent; Guardian; Time Out; New Statesman; Literary Review; Others. Membership: Society of Authors. Literary Agent: Mic Cheetham, 11-12 Dover Street, London W1, England. Address: 73 Pennard Road, London W12 8DW, England.

RUAS Charles Edward, b. 14 Nov 1938, Tientsin, China. Author. m. Agneta Danielsson, 10 June 1967, div 1976, 1 son. Education: BA, 1960, MA, 1963, PhD, 1970, Princeton University; Sorbonne, University of Paris, 1964. Publications: Conversations With American Writers, 1986; Entering the Dream: Lewis Carroll, 1994. Other: Several translations. Contributions to: Newspapers and magazines. Honours: Fulbright Lecturer, 1992; Fellowships and awards. Memberships: PEN International; Writers Room. Address: c/o Curtis Brown Ltd, 10 Astor Place, 3rd Floor, New York, NY 10003, USA.

RUBENS Bernice Ruth, b. 26 July 1923, Cardiff, Wales. Author. m. Rudi Nassauer, 1947, 2 daughters. Education: BA, University of Wales, 1944. Appointments: Author, Director, documentary films on Third World subjects. Publications: Novels: Set on Edge, 1960; Madame Sontsatzka, 1962; Mate in Three, 1964; The Elected Member, 1968; Sunday Best, 1970; Go Tell the Lemming, 1972; I Sent a Letter to My Love, 1974; Ponsonby Post, 1976; A Five-year Sentence, 1978; Spring Sonata, 1979; Birds of Passage, 1980; Brothers, 1982; Mr Wakefield's Crusade, 1985; Our Father, 1987; Kingdom Come: A Solitary Grief, 1991; Mother Russia, 1992; Autobiopsy, 1993; Yesterday in the Back Lane, 1995; The Waiting Game, 1997; I, Dreyfus, 1999. Honours: Booker Prize, 1970; American Blue Ribbon, for Documentary film, 1972; Honorary DLitt, University of Wales. Membership: Fellow, University College, Cardiff. Address: Flat 3, 111 Canfield Gardens, London NW6 3DY, England.

RUBIN Diana Kwiatkowski, b. 30 Dec 1958, New York City, USA. Poet; Writer. m. Paul Rubin, 4 Jan 1986, 1 son, 2 daughters. Education: AOS, The Wood School, 1983; BA, Marymount Manhattan College, 1988; MA, New York University, 1994. Publications: Spirits in Exile, 1990; Visions of Enchantment, 1991; Dinosauria, 1995. Contributions to: Poet; Amelia; Wind; Quest; Fox Cry; Voices International. Honours: 1st Prize, 1998; Sparrowgrass Poetry Forum Awards. Membership: Academy of American Poets. Address: PO Box 398, Piscataway, NJ 08855, USA.

RUBIN Henry M, b. 21 May 1916, Portland, Oregon, USA. Writer. m. Lillian B Rubin, 4 Mar 1962, 1 daughter. Education: BS, Public Health, UCLA; MPH, UB Berkeley. Publication: Spain's Cause Was Mine. Contributions to: San Francisco Chronicle; Bon Appetit; Wine Spectator; San Jose Mercury; Vintage; Wine Enthusiast.

RUBIN Larry Jerome, b. 14 Feb 1930, Bayonne, New Jersey, USA. Professor of English; Poet. Education: BA, 1951, MA, 1952, PhD, 1956, Emory University. Appointments: Instructor, 1956-58, Assistant Professor, 1958-65, Associate Professor, 1965-73, Professor, 1973-, English, Georgia Technical University. Publications: The World's Old Way, 1963; Lanced in Light, 1967; All My Mirrors Lie, 1975; Unanswered Calls, 1997. Contributions to: New Yorker; Harpers Magazine; The Nation; Poetry; Sewanee Review; London Magazine. Honours: Reyholds Lyric Award, Poetry Society of America; Annual Award, Poetry Society of America; Smith-Mundt Award; Fulbright Awards; Several grants. Memberships: Poetry Society of America; Poetry Society of Georgia. Address: Box 15014, Druid Hills Branch, Atlanta, GA 30333, USA.

RUBIN Nancy Z, Journalist; Author; Writer-Producer. Education: BA, Jackson College, Tufts University; MAT, Brown University Graduate School; PhD (honorary), Mount Vernon College. Publications: Books: The New Suburban Woman: Beyond Myth and Motherhood, 1982; The Mother Mirror: How A Generation of Women Is Changing Motherhood in America, 1984; Isabella of Castile: The First Renaissance Queen, 1991; American Empress: The Life and Times of Marjorie Merriweather Post, 1995. Contributions to: New York Times; Stamford Advocate; AMS Press; American Imago; Working Mother; Family Circle; Travel and Leisure; Parents; Chateleine; Louisville Courier Journal. Honours: Fellow, MacDowell Colony, Peterboro, New Hampshire, 1981; Author of the Year, Excellence in Writing Award, American Society of Journalists and Authors, 1992; Washington Irving Book Award, for Non-Fiction, Westchester Library Association, 1993; Editorial Judge, Benjamin Franklin Awards, Publishers Marketing Association for American Book Association Convention, 1994; Finalist, National Magazine Awards, 1995. Memberships: American PEN; American Society of Journalists and Authors; Authors Guild. Address: 52 Sagamore Road, Apt E-5, Bronxville, NY 10708, USA.

RUBIN Rivka Leah Jacobs, b. 22 Feb 1952, Philadelphia, Pennsylvania, USA. Writer. m. Gerald E Rubin, 25 Nov 1981, 1 son. Education: BA, History, 1981, MA, Sociology, 1982, Marshall University. Publications: Experimentum Crucis, 1981; The Boy From the Moon, 1985; The Milk of Paradise, 1985; Morning on Venus, 1985. Memberships: Science Fiction Writers of America; West Virginia Sociological Association. Address: 1285 26th Street, Huntington, WV 25705, USA.

RUBINSTEIN Gillian Margaret, b. 29 Aug 1942, Berkhamsted, England. Author. m. Philip Rubinstein, 1973, 1 son, 2 daughters. Education: BA, MA, Modern Languages, University of Oxford, 1961-64; Postgraduate Certificate of Education, University of London, 1972. Publications: Space Demons, 1986; Beyond the Labyrinth, 1988; Answers to Brut, 1988; Melanie and the Night Animal, 1988; Skymaze, 1989; Flashback, 1990; At Ardilla, 1991; Dog In, Cat Out, 1991; Squawk and Screech, 1991; Galax-Arena, 1992; Keep Me Company, 1992; Mr Plunkett's Pool, 1992; The Giant's Tooth, 1993; Foxspell, 1994. Honours: Honour Books, Australian Children's Book Council, 1987, 1989; Senior Fellowships, Australia Council, 1988, 1989-92; National Children's Book Awards, 1988, 1990; New South Wales Premier's Award, 1988; Book of the Year, CBA, 1989. Membership: Australian Society of Authors. Address: c/o Australian Literary Management, 2a Armstrong Street, Middle Park, Victoria 3206, Australia.

RUBINSTEIN Hilary Harold, b. 24 Apr 1926, London, England. Literary Agent; Writer. m. Helge Kitzinger, 6 Aug 1955, 3 sons, 1 daughter. Education: Cheltenham College; MA, Merton College, Oxford. Appointments: Director, Victor Gollancz Ltd, 1953-63; Deputy Editor, The Observer Magazine, 1964-65; Managing Director, A P Watt Ltd, 1965-92, Hilary Rubinstein Books, 1992-. Publications: The Complete Insomniac, 1974; Hotels and Inns (editor), 1984; The Good Hotel Guide (founder-editor), 1978-99. Contributions to: Newspapers and magazines. Memberships: Arts Council, literature panel, 1973-79, literature financial committee, 1975-77; Open College of the Arts, trustee, 1987-93; Society of Authors. Address: 32 Ladbroke Grove, London W11 3BQ, England.

RUDKIN James David, b. 29 June 1936, London, England. Dramatist. m. Alexandra Margaret Thompson, 3 May 1967, 2 sons, 1 dec, 2 daughters. Education: MA, St Catherine's College, Oxford, 1957-61. Appointment: Judith E Wilson Fellow, University of Cambridge, 1984. Publications: Afore Night Come (stage play), 1964; Schoenberg's Moses und Aron (translation for Royal Opera), 1965; Ashes (stage play), 1974; Cries From Casement as His Bones are Brought to Dublin (radio play), 1974; Penda's Fen (TV film), 1975; Hippolytus (translation from Euripides), 1980; The Sons of Light (stage play), 1981; The Triumph of Death (stage play), 1981; Peer Gynt (translation from Ibsen), 1983; The Saxon Shore (stage play), 1986; Rosmersholm (translation from Ibsen), 1990; When We Dead Waken (translation from Ibsen), 1990. Opera Libretti: The Grace of Todd, music by Gordon Crosse, 1969; Inquest of Love, music by Jonathan Harvey, 1993; Broken Strings, 1994. Contributions to: Drama; Tempo; Encounter. Honours: Evening Standard Most Promising Dramatist Award, 1962; John Whiting Drama Award, 1974; Obie Award, New York, 1977; New York Film Festival Gold Medal for Screenplay, 1987; Sony Silver Radio Drama Award, 1994. Memberships: Hellenic Society; PEN. Address: c/o Casarotto Ramsay Ltd, National House, 60-66 Wardour Street, London W1V 3HP, England.

RUDMAN Mark, b. 11 Dec 1948, New York, New York, USA. Poet; Critic; Editor; Translator; Adjunct Professor. m. Madelaine Bates, 1 son. Education: BA, New School for Social Research, 1971; MFA, Columbia University, 1974. Appointments: Poetry and Criticism Editor, 1975-, Editor-in-Chief, 1984-, Pequod Journal; Writer-in-Residence, University of Hawaii, 1978, State University of New York at Buffalo, 1979, Wabash College, 1979; Adjunct Lecturer, Queens College of the City University of New York, 1980-81; Lecturer, Parsons School of Design, 1983; Poet-in-Residence and Associate Professor, York College, 1984-88; Assistant Director and Adjunct Professor, Graduate Creative Writing Program, New York University, 1986-; Adjunct Professor, Columbia University, 1988-91, 1992-; Poet-in-Residence, State University of New York, Purchase, 1991. Publications: In the Neighboring Cell (poems), 1982; The Mystery in the Garden (poetry chapbook), 1985; By Contraries and Other Poems: 1970-1984, Selected and New, 1986; The Ruin Revived (poetry chapbook), 1986; The Nowhere Steps (poems), 1990; Literature and the Visual Arts, 1990; Diverse Voices: Essays on Poetry, 1993; Rider, 1994; Realm of Unknowing: Meditations on Art, Suicide, Uncertainty, and Other Transformations, 1995; The Millennium Hotel (poems), 1996. Contributions to: Poems and essays in many anthologies and other publications. Honours: Academy of American Poets Award, 1971; Yaddo Residencies, 1977, 1983; Ingram Merrill Foundation Fellowship, 1983-84; New York Foundation of the Arts Fellowship, 1988; National Book Critics Circle Award in Poetry, 1994; National Endowment for the Arts Fellowship, 1995; Guggenheim Fellowship, 1996-97. Memberships: PEN; Poetry Society of America, board of governors, 1984-88. Address: 817 West End Avenue, New York, NY 10025, USA.

RUDOLF Anthony, b. 6 Sept 1942, London, England. Poet; Writer; Translator. Div, 1 son, 1 daughter. Education: BA, Trinity College, Cambridge, 1964; Diploma, British Institute, Paris, 1961. Appointments: Co-Founder and Editor, Menard Press, London, 1969; Advisory Editor, Modern Poetry in Translation, 1973-; Adam Lecturer, Kings' College, London, 1990. Publications: The Same River Twice, 1976; After the

Dream: Poems 1964-79, 1980; Primo Levi's War Against Oblivion, 1990; Mandorla, 1997; The Arithmetic of memory, 1999. Other: Translations of poetry. Contributions to: Periodicals. Address: 8 The Oaks, Woodside Avenue, London N12 8AR, England.

RUDOLPH Lee (Norman), b. 28 Mar 1948, Cleveland, Ohio, USA. Mathematician; Poet; Writer. Education: BA, Princeton University, 1969; PhD, Massachusetts Institute of Technology, 1974. Publications: Curses and Songs and Poems, 1974; The Country Changes, 1978. Contributions to: Professional journals, anthologies, and periodicals. Honours: Several awards. Memberships: Alice James Poetry Cooperative; National Writers Union. Address: PO Box 251, Adamsville, RI 02801, USA.

RUDOMIN Esther. See: HAUTZIG Esther.

RUDZINSKI Cezary Aleksander, (Aleksander Piotrkowski, Aleksander Runski, CEZ), b. 21 June 1931, Piotrkow Tryb, Poland. Journalist. m. 9 Dec 1964, 1 son. Education: Institute of Planning and Economic Administration, Lodz, 1951; Master's degree, Russian Philology, Lodz University, 1955; Institute of Journalism, Warsaw University, 1962. Appointments: Journalist, Agencja Robotnicza, Warsaw, 1963-72; Trybuna Ludu, 1972-90, Trybuna daily, 1990-; Correspondent, Polish Press, Kiev, Ukraine, 1992-97. Publications: Podbój Kosmosu w filatelistyce, 1963; Spotkania ze Zwiazkiem Radzieckim, 1967, Russian edition, 1968; Malarstwo i grafika w filatelistyce, 1970, 2nd edition, 1980; Muzyka jako temat w filatelistyce, 1971; Osiemnascie dlugich dni, 1980; Katalog Specjalizowany Znaków Pocztowych Ziem Polskich, volumes I-IV, 1981, 2nd edition, 1985; Encyklopedia Filatelistyki, 1993; Europa za 200 dolaráw, 1991; Grecja, 1998; Francja-Monaco, 1998; Hiszpania-Andorra-Gibraltar, 1998; Wlochy, San Marino, Watykan, 1998. Contributions to: Several thousand articles, reports, commentaries and other journalistic writings. Honours: Award, Minister of National Defence, 1968, 1972; Award, Minister of Home Affairs, 1979; Globetrotter Award, 1998. Memberships: Polish Journalists Association, 1965-81, 1985-; AIJP; OJA; SAP; SD-P, G. Address: Skrytka pocztowa 865, 00-950 Warsaw 1, Poland.

RUELL Patrick. See: HILL Reginald (Charles).

RUELLAND Jacques G, b. 14 Aug 1948, Spa, Belgium. Professor; Writer. m. Krystyna Brylska-Ruelland, 17 Nov 1977, 1 daughter. Education: BA, Philosophy, 1975; MA, Philosophy, 1983; MA, History, 1985; PhD, History of Science, 1994. Appointment: Professor of History and Philosophy of Science. Publications: Pierre du Calvet 1735-1786, 1986; Orwell et 1984: Trois approches, 1988; Valentin Jautard 1736-1787, 1989; De l'épistémologie à la politique, 1991; Histoire de la guerre sainte, 1993; La Moisson littéraire, 1993; Civilisation occidentale: histoire et héritages, 1995; Philosopher à Montréal, 1995; Tolérance, 1996; Lueur dans les ténèbres, 1996. Contributions to: Various publications. Honours: Honorary Member, Société de Philosophie de Montréal; Prix Percy-W-Roy, 1987, 1988; Prix du Ministre, 1995. Memberships: Fondation Aérovision, Quebec, honorary member; Musée des arts graphiques, Montreal, president, 1986-95; Société des arts et des lettres, Brossard, president, 1993-; Société des écrivains canadiens, chairman, 1993-. Address: 360 rue de Venise, Brossard, Quebec J4W 1W7, Canada.

RUETTIMANN Karin, b. 16 Oct 1942, Berlin, Germany. Writer; Painter. m. Josef Ruettimann, Sept 1966, 2 daughters. Education: Diploma, University of Freiburg, Switzerland, 1991-94. Appointments: Entrepreneur, 1971-84; Painter, 1976-; Writer, 1977-. Publications: Children, Children (theatre play), 1979; A Year As a Gift (novel), 1985; Swallow's Summer (novel), 1990; Circus Monti (prose), 1991; Waiting On L, A Winter Ballad on Sylt (novel), 1992; Quiet Paths - Magical Encounters (prose), 1993. Contributions to: Magazines, newspapers and journals. Honours: Writers Grant, 1987; Production Grant, 1991. Memberships: PEN Switzerland;

Swiss Authors Group, Olten. Address: ob Farnbuehlstr 16, CH-5610 Wohlen, Switzerland.

RUFINI Debra Claire, b. 22 Jan 1971, Hampshire, England. Hypnotherapist. m. Mr Giuseppe Rufini, 19 Sept 1998. Education: Diploma in Hypnotherapy, 1993. Appointments: 3 local television appearances, 1992, 1994, 1995. Publications: Well, Here I Am, 1992; Life Cake, 1994; The Big Bruise Show, 1996. Contributions to: The Daily Mail; The Daily Star; Poetry journals.

RUHM Gerhard, b. 12 Feb 1930, Vienna, Austria. Writer; Poet; Dramatist; Composer; Graphic Artist. Education: Academy of Music, Vienna, 1945-51. Publications: Literarisches Cabaret (with H Artmann and K Bayer), 1958-59; hosn rosn baa (with H Artmann and F Achleitner), 1959; Kinderoper (with H Artmann and K Bayer), 1964; Gesammelte Gedichte, 1970; Gesammelte Theaterstücke 1954-1971, 1972; Erste Folger Kurzer Hörstücker, 1973; Zweite Folge kurzer Hörstücke, 1975, 1975; wald: ein deutsches requiem, 1983; Allein, verlassen, verloren: 3 Kurzhörspiele zum Thema Angst (with R Hughes and Marie Luise Kaschnitz), 1986; leselieder/visuelle Musik, 1986; botschaft an die zukunft: gesammelte sprechtexte, 1988; Geschlechterdings: Chansons, Romanzen, Gedichte, 1990; Theatertexte, 1990; Mit Messer und Gabel, 1995. Honours: Association of War Blind Radio Prize, 1983; Great Austrian State Prize, 1991. Membership: Academy of Fine Arts, Hamburg. Address: Lochnerstrasse 7, D-50674 Cologne, Germany.

RUHMKORF Peter, b. 25 Oct 1929, Dortmund, Germany. Poet; Author. m. Eva-Marie Titze. Education: German Language and Literature, Psychology, Hamburg. Appointments: Writer-in-Residence, University of Texas at Austin, 1969-70; Lecturer, University of Essen, 1974, 1991-92, University of Warwick, England, 1977. Publications: Irdisches Vergnügen in g, 1959; Kunstücke: 50 Gedichte nebst einer Anleitung zum Wilderspruch, 1962; Die Jahre die Ihr kennt: Anfälle und Erinnerungen, 1972; Gesammelte Gedichte, 1976; Strömungslehre I: Poesie, 1978; Haltbar bis Ende, 199, 1979; Auf Wiedersehen in Kenilworth: Ein Märchen in dreizehn Kapiteln, 1980; agar agar: zaurzaurim: Zur Naturgeschichte dees Reims und der menschlichen Anklangsnerven, 1981; Hüter des Misthaufens, 1981; Kleine Fleckenkunde, 1981; Bleib erschütterbar und widersteh, 1984; Dintemann und Schindemann, 1987; Einmalig wie wir alle, 1989; Selbst III/88: Aus der Fassung, 1989; Tabu I: Tagebücher 1989-1991, 1995. Honours: Erich Kastner Prize, 1979; Arno Schmidt Prize, 1986; Heinrich Heine Prize, 1988; Georg Buchner Prize, 1993. Memberships: Deutsche Akademie für Sprache und Dichtung e.v., Darmstadt; Freie Akademie der Künste, Hamburg; PEN. Address: Ovelgönne 50, D-22605 Hamburg, Germany.

RUIZ Bernardo, b. 6 Oct 1953, Mexico City, Mexico. Author; Poet. m. Virginia Abrin Batule, 18 Nov 1978, 2 sons. Education: BA, Spanish and Latin American Literature, Universidad Nacional Autonoma de Mexico. Appointments: Editor, Universidad Autonoma Metropolitana, 1979, Ministry of Labour, 1985-88; Director, INBA, Centro Nacional de Informacion y Promocion de la Literatura, 1992. Publications: Fiction: Viene la Muerte, 1976; La otra orilla, 1980; Olvidar tu nombre, 1982; Vals sins fin, 1982, revised edition, 1986; Los caminos del hotel, 1991. Poetry: El Tuyo, el mismo, 1986; Juego de Cartas, 1992. Contributions to: Various publications. Memberships: Asociacion de Criticos de Mexico; Asociacion de Escritores de Mexico; Sociedad General de Escritores de Mexico. Address: Arizona 94-6, Col Napoles, CP 03810, Mexico DF.

RUKEYSER Louis (Richard), b. 30 Jan 1933, New York, New York, USA. Economic Writer and Broadcaster. m. Alexandra Gill, 3 Mar 1962, 3 daughters. Education: AB, Princeton University, 1954. Appointments: Reporter, Baltimore Sun Newspapers, 1954-65; Chief Political Correspondent, Baltimore Evening Sun, 1957-59; Chief, London Bureau, 1959-63, Chief Asian Correspondent, 1963-65, Baltimore Sun; Senior Correspondent and

Commentator, 1965-73, Paris Correspondent, 1965-66, Chief, London Bureau, 1966-68, Economic Editor and Commentator, 1968-73, ABC News; Host, Wall $treet Week With Louis Rukeyser, PBS-TV, 1970-; Syndicated Economic Columnist, McNaught Syndicate, 1976-86; Tribune Media Services, 1986-93; Editor-in-Chief, Louis Rukeyser's Wall Street, 1992-, Louis Rukeysers's Mutual Funds, 1994-. Publications: How to Make Money in Wall Street, 1974, 2nd edition, 1976; What's Ahead for the Economy: The Challenge and the Chance, 1983, 2nd edition, 1985; Louis Rukeyser's Business Almanac, 1988, 2nd edition, 1991. Honours: Overseas Press Club Award, 1963, and Citation, 1964; G M Loeb Award, University of Connecticut, 1972; George Washington Honor Medals, Freedoms Foundation, 1972, 1978; Janus Award, 1975; Literary Guild Selections, 1974, 1976, 1984; New York Financial Writers Association Award, 1980; Free Enterprise Man of the Year, Texas A & M University, 1987; Women's Economic Round Table Award, 1990; Several honorary doctorates. Address: 586 Round Hill Road, Greenwich, CT 06831, USA.

RULE Jane, b. 28 Mar 1931, Plainfield, New Jersey, USA. Writer; Teacher. Education: Mills College, Oakland, California. Appointments: Teacher of English, Concord Academy, Massachusetts, 1954-56; Assistant Director, International House, 1958-59; Intermittent Lecturer in English, 1959-70; Visiting Lecturer in Creative Writing, University of British Columbia, Vancouver, 1972-73. Publications: The Desert of the Heart, 1964; This Is Not You, 1970; Against the Season, 1971; Lesbian Images, 1975; Themes for Diverse Instruments, 1975; The Young in One Another's Arms, 1977; Contract With the World, 1980; Outlander, 1981; Inland Passage, A Hot-Eyed Moderate, 1985; Memory Board, 1987; After the Fire, 1989. Honours: Canadian Author's Association Best Novel of the Year, 1978, Best Story of the Year, 1978; US Gay Academic Union Literature Award, 1978; Fund for Human Dignity Award of Merit, 1983; Honorary Doctor of Letters, University of British Columbia, 1994; Order of British Columbia, 1998. Memberships: Writers' Union of Canada; PEN. Literary Agent: Anne Borchardt, Georges Borchardt Inc, 136 East 57th Street, New York, NY 10022, USA. Address: The Fork, Rte 1, S19 C 17, Galiano, British Columbia V0N 1P0, Canada.

RUMBAUT Helen Elizabeth, b. 8 Oct 1949, Deland, Florida, USA. Writer; Public Information Specialist. m. Carlos Alberto Rumbaut, 5 July 1970, 1 daughter. Education: BA, French, University of Kansas, 1971. Publications: Dove Dream (young adult novel), 1994. Contributions to: Quick Picks brochure; Lone Star Quarterly; Crossing Press, Women and Food. Memberships: Authors' Guild; PEN West; Society of Children's Book Writers and Illustrators; Austin Writers' League.

RUMENS Carol Ann, b. 10 Dec 1944, Forest Hill, London, England. Writer; Poet. m. David Rumens, 30 July 1965, div, 2 daughters. Education: University of London, 1964-65. Appointments: Writing Fellow, University of Kent, 1983-85; Northern Arts Writing Fellow, 1988-90; Writer-in-Residence, Queen's University, Belfast, 1991-. Publications: A Strange Girl in Bright Colours, 1973; Unplayed Music, 1981; Star Whisper, 1983; Direct Dialling, 1985; Selected Poems, 1987; Plato Park, 1988; The Greening of the Snow Beach, 1988; From Berlin to Heaven, 1990. Contributions to: Periodicals. Honours: Alice Hunt Bartlett Prize, Joint Winner, 1981; Prudence Farmer Award, 1983; Cholmondeley Award, 1984. Memberships: International PEN; Royal Society of Literature, fellow; Society of Authors. Address: 100A Tunis Road, London W12 7EY, England.

RUNCE Rute, (Rita Drava), b. 15 Nov 1926, Riga, Latvia. Linguist; Translator. m. Auseklis Runcis, 10 Nov 1949, 1 son. Education: Graduate, University of Latvia, 1952. Appointments: Publishing Houses, Liesma, Jumava, Zvaigzne; House of Press, Rija, Krauklitis, Elpa. Publications: Translations of works by W M Thackeray, Charles Dickens, W Collins, H G Wells, H Wiliamson, A Conan Doyle, R P Warren, C Barnard, J Wainwright, J

Collins. Memberships: Union of Latvian Writers; Union of Journalists. Literary Agent: Baznicas iela. Address: Baznicas iela 24, dz 3a, Riga, LV-1050, Latvia.

RUNHAM. See: **ACKROYD Peter.**

RUNSKI Aleksander. See: **RUDZINSKI Cezary Aleksander.**

RUSAN Otila Valeria. See: **BLANDIANA Ana.**

RUSCH Barbara Lynn, b. 7 July 1949, Toronto, Ontario, Canada. Ephemerist. m. Donald Zaldin, 24 May 1991, 1 son, 1 daughter, 2 stepsons, 2 stepdaughters. Education: BA, French Literature, 1971, MA, French Literature, 1976, University of Toronto. Publications: Canadian Printed Ephemera: An Historical Survey, 1988; Patterns of Alienation in 19th Century Manuscript Ephemera (editor), Ephemera Canada, 1991-; Collecting Victorian Ephemera, 1991; Blue Boxes Devour Paper Past, 1993; The Art of Persuasion: Images of Victorian Advertising Ephemera, 1994; Factory View Trade Cards: Image of a New Social Order, 1996. Honours: True Davidson Memorial Award for Excellence, 1986, Warren Carlton Memorial Awards, 1988, 1989, Bootmakers of Toronto; Maurice Rickards Award, Ephemera Society of America, 1989; Samuel Pepys Award, Ephemera Society, UK, 1992. Memberships: Ephemera Society of Canada, founder-president, 1987-; Ephemera Society of America, director, 1993-96; The Bootmakers of Toronto, Director 1987-91; 1997. Address: 36 Macauley Drive, Thornill, Ontario L3T 5S5, Canada.

RUSH Norman, b. 24 Oct 1933, San Francisco, California, USA. Writer. m. Elsa Rush, 10 July 1955, 1 son, 1 daughter. Education: BA, Swarthmore College, 1956. Appointments: Instructor in English and History and Co-Director of College A, Rockland Community College, Suffern, New York, 1973-78; Co-Director, US Peace Corps, Botswana, 1978-83. Publications: Whites (stories), 1986; Mating (novel), 1991. Contributions to: Anthologies and periodicals. Membership: PEN American Center. Address: 10 High Tor Road, New City, NY 10956, USA.

RUSHDIE (Ahmed) Salman, b. 19 June 1947, Bombay, India. Author. m. (1) Clarissa Luard, 1976, div 1987, 1 son, (2) Marianne Wiggins, 1988, div 1993, (3) Elizabeth West, 1997, 1 son. Education: MA, Honours, History, King's College, Cambridge. Appointments: Honorary Professor, Massachusetts Institute of Technology, Cambridge, 1993; Distinguished Fellow in Literature, University of East Anglia, 1995. Publications: Grimus, 1975; Midnight's Children, 1981; Shame, 1983; The Jaguar Smile: A Nicaraguan Journey, 1987; The Satanic Verses, 1988; Haroun and the Sea of Stories, 1990; Imaginary Homelands, 1991; The Wizard of Oz, 1992; East, West, 1994; The Moor's Last Sigh, 1995; The Vintage Book of Indian Writing, 1947-1997 (editor with Elizabeth West), 1997. Television Films: The Painter and the Pest, 1985; The Riddle of Midnight, 1988. Contributions to: Various publications. Honours: Booker Prize for Fiction, 1981; James Tait Black Memorial Book Prize, 1981; English-Speaking Union Literary Award, 1981; Prix du Meilleur Livre Etranger, 1984; German Author of the Year Award, 1989; Whitbread Novel Awards, 1989, 1995; Kurt Tucholsky Prize, Sweden, 1992; Booker of Bookers Prize, 1993; Prix Colette, Switzerland, 1993; Austrian State Prize for European Literature, 1994; British Book Awards Author of the Year, 1995; Honorary DLitt, Bard College, Annandale-on-Hudson, New York, 1995. Membership: Royal Society of Literature, fellow. Address: c/o Wylie Agency Ltd, 36 Parkside, 42 Knightsbridge, London SW1X 7JR, England.

RUSHTON Colin Edward, b. 21 Sept 1939, Waterloo, Liverpool, England. Metallurgist. m. Patricia Chainey, 9 Oct 1965, 1 son, 1 daughter. Education: ACT in Metallurgy, 2nd Class Hons, University of Surrey, 1961-62. Publications: Spectator in Hell, 1998; Spirit of the Trenches.

RUSS Joanna, b. 22 Feb 1937, New York, New York, USA. Educator; Writer. Education: BA in English, Cornell University, 1957; MFA in Playwriting and Dramatic Literature, Yale University School of Drama, 1960. Appointments: Instructor, 1967-70, Assistant Professor of English, 1970-72, Cornell University; Assistant Professor of English, State University of New York at Binghamton, 1972-75, University of Colorado at Boulder, 1975-77; Associate Professor of English, 1977-83, Professor of English, 1983-90, University of Washington. Publications: Novels: Picnic on Paradise, 1968; And Chaos Died, 1970; The Female Man, 1975; We Who Are About To, 1977; Kittatinny: A Tale of Magic, 1978; The Two of Them, 1978; On Strike Against God, 1980; Extra(Ordinary) People, 1984. Story Collections: The Zanibar Cat, 1983; The Adventures of Alyx, 1983; The Hidden Side of the Moon, 1987. Non-Fiction: How to Suppress Women's Writing, 1983; Magic Mommas, Trembling Sisters, Puritans and Perverts: Feminist Essays by Joanna Russ, 1985; What Are We Fighting For: Feminists Talk About Sexism, Racism, Class, 1977. Contributions to: Many books, journals, and periodicals. Honours: Nebula Award, 1972; National Endowment for the Humanities Younger Humanist Fellowship, 1974-75; Hugo Gernsback Award, World Science Fiction Convention, 1983; Pilgrim Award, Science Fiction Research Association, 1988; James Tiptree Jr Award for Science Fiction, 1991. Address: 8961 East Lester Street, Tucson, AZ 85715, USA.

RUSSELL (Irwin) Peter, b. 16 Sept 1921, Bristol, England. Poet; Writer; Translator; Editor. m. (1) Marjorie Alice Bloxam, 1 son, (2) Lana Sue Long, 1 son, 2 daughters. Education: Malvern College; Queen Mary College, London. Appointments: Owner, Pound Press, 1951-56, Grosvenor Bookship, Kent, 1951-58, Gallery Bookshop, London, 1959-63; Editor, Nine magazine, 1949-58, Marginalia newsletter, 1990-; Poet-in-Residence, University of Victoria, British Columbia, 1973-76, Purdue University, 1976-77; Teaching Fellow, Imperial Iranian Academy of Philosophy, Tehran, 1977-79. Publications: Picnic to the Moon, 1944; Omens and Elegies, 1951; Descent: A Poem Sequence, 1952; Three Elegies of Quintilius, 1954; The Spirit and the Body: An Orphic Poem, 1956; Images of Desire, 1962; Dreamland and Drunkeness, 1963; Complaints to Circe, 1963; Visions and Ruins: An Existentialist Poem, 1965; Agamemnon in Hades, 1965; The Golden Chain: Lyrical Poems 1964-1969, 1970; Paysages Légendaires, 1971; The Elegies of Quintilius, 1975, new edition, 1996; Ephimeron, 1977; Acts of Recognition: Four Visionary Poems, 1978; Theories, 1978; Africa: A Dream, 1981; Elemental Discourses, 1981; Malice Aforethought, 1981; All for the Wolves: Selected Poems 1947-1975, 1984; Teorie e Altre Liriche, 1990; The Image of Woman as a Figure of the Spirit in Christian and Islamic Medieval Poetry, 1992; The Pound Connection, 1992; Poetic Asides: Essays and Addresses on Poetry, 2 volumes, 1992-93; Dante and Islam, 1994; The Duller Olive: Poems 1942-1958, 1993; A False Start: London Poems 1959-63, 1993; Berlin Tegel 1964: Poems and Translations, 1994; Venice Poems 1965, 1996; More for the Wolves, 1997; My Wild Heart: Selected Poems 1990-1996, 1997. Contributions to: Various publications. Honours: Premio Internazionale Le Muse, City of Florence, 1990; Premio Internazionale Dante Alighieri, 1993; Festschrift for his 75th birthday, 1996; Premio Internazionale Succisa Virescit, University of Cassino, 1997; Premio Firenze, 1998. Address: "La Turbina", 52026 Pian di Scò, Arezzo, Italy.

RUSSELL James. See: **HARKNETT Terry.**

RUSSELL John, b. 22 Jan 1919, Fleet, England. Art Critic; Writer. Education: BA, Magdalen College, Oxford, 1940. Appointments: Honorary Attaché, Tate Gallery, 1940-41; Staff, Ministry of Information, 1941-43, Naval Intelligence Division, Admiralty, London, 1943-46; Contributor, 1945-49, Art Critic, 1949-74, The Sunday Times; Art Critic, 1974-82, Chief Art Critic, 1982-91, The New York Times. Publications: Shakespeare's Country, 1942; British Portrait Painters, 1944; Switzerland, 1950; Logan Pearsall Smith, 1950; Erich Kleiber, 1956; Paris, 1960, 2nd edition, 1983; Seurat, Private View (with Bryan

Robertson and Lord Snowdon), 1965; Max Ernst, 1967; Henry Moore, 1968; Ben Nicholson, 1969; Pop Art Redefined (with Suzi Gablik), 1969; The World of Matisse, 1970; Francis Bacon, 1971; Edouard Vuillard, 1971; The Meanings of Modern Art, 1981, new and enlarged edition, 1990; Reading Russell, 1989; London, 1994. Contributions to: Various publications. Honour: Member, American Academy of Arts and Letters, 1996. Address: 166 East 61st Street, New York, NY 10021, USA.

RUSSELL Martin James, b. 25 Sept 1934, Bromley, Kent, England. Writer. Publications: No Through Road, 1965; The Client, 1975; Mr T, 1977; Death Fuse, 1980; Backlash, 1981; The Search for Sara, 1983; A Domestic Affair, 1984; The Darker Side of Death, 1985; Prime Target, 1985; Dead Heat, 1986; The Second Time is Easy, 1987; House Arrest, 1988; Dummy Run, 1989; Mystery Lady, 1992; Leisure Pursuit, 1993. Memberships: Crime Writers' Association; Detection Club. Address: 15 Breckonmead, Wanstead Road, Bromley, Kent BR1 3BW, England.

RUSSELL Paul, b. 1 July 1956, Memphis, Tennessee, USA. Professor of English; Writer. Education: AB in English, Oberlin College, 1978; MA in English, 1982, MFA in Creative Writing, 1982, PhD in English, 1983, Cornell University. Appointments: Assistant Professor, 1983-90, Associate Professor, 1990-96, Professor of English, 1996-, Vassar College; Co-Founder and Editor, The Poughkeepsie Review, 1987-89. Publications: Fiction: The Salt Point, 1990; Boys of Life, 1991; Sea of Tranquillity, 1994. Non-Fiction: The Gay 100: A Ranking of the Most Influential Gay Men and Lesbians, Past and Present, 1995. Contributions to: Anthologies, journals, and periodicals. Honours: National Endowment for the Arts Creative Writers Fellowship, 1993; Regional Winner, GRANTA-Best of Young American Novelists, 1995. Address: c/o Department of English, Vassar College, Poughkeepsie, NY 12604, USA.

RUSSELL Sharman Apt, b. 23 July 1954, Edwards Air Force Base, California, USA. Assistant Professor of Writing; Author. m. Peter Russell, 24 Jan 1981, 1 son, 1 daughter. Education: BS, Conservation and Natural Resources, University of California at San Diego and Berkeley, 1976; MFA, Creative Writing, University of Montana, 1980. Appointments: Assistant Professor of Writing, Western New Mexico University, Silver City, 1981-; Faculty, MFA Program in Creative Non-Fiction, Antioch University, Los Angeles, 1997-. Publications: Built to Last: An Architectural History of Silver City, New Mexico (with Susan Berry), 1986; Frederick Douglass, 1987; Songs of the Fluteplayer: Seasons of Life in the Southwest, 1991; Kill the Cowboy: A Battle of Mythology in the New West, 1993; The Humpbacked Fluteplayer, 1994; When the Land was Young: Reflections on American Archaeology, 1996. Contributions to: Anthologies, reviews, and journals. Honours: Henry Joseph Jackson Award for Non-Fiction, San Francisco, 1989; Pushcart Prize, 1990; Mountain and Plains Booksellers Award, 1992; New Mexico Presswomen's Zia Award, 1992. Address: 1113 West Street, Silver City, NM 88061, USA.

RUSSELL Willy, (William Martin Russell), b. 23 Aug 1947, Liverpool, England. Dramatist; Writer. m. Ann Seagroatt, 1969, 1 son, 2 daughters. Education: Certificate of Education, St Katherine's College of Education, Liverpool. Appointments: Teacher, 1973-74; Fellow, Creative Writing, Manchester Polytechnic, 1977-78. Publications: Theatre: Blind Scouse, 1971-72; When the Reds (adaptation), 1972; John, Paul, George, Ringo and Bert (musical), 1974; Breezeblock Park, 1975; One for the Road, 1976; Stags and Hens, 1978; Educating Rita, 1979; Blood Brothers (musical), 1983; Our Day Out (musical), 1983; Shirley Valentine, 1986. Television Plays: King of the Castle, 1972; Death of a Young Young Man, 1972; Break In (for schools), 1974; Our Day Out, 1976; Lies (for schools), 1977; Daughter of Albion, 1978; Boy With Transistor Radio (for schools), 1979; One Summer (series), 1980. Radio Play: I Read the News Today (for schools), 1979. Screenplays: Band on the Run, 1979; Educating Rita, 1981. Honours: Honorary MA, Open University; Honorary Director, Liverpool Playhouse. Address: c/o Margaret Ramsay Ltd, 14A Goodwin's Court, St Martin's Lane, London WC2, England.

RUSSO Albert, b. 26 Feb 1943, Kamina, Belgian Congo. Writer; Poet. 1 son, 1 daughter. Education: BSc, General Business Administration, New York University. Appointments: Co-Editor, Paris Transcontinental and Plurilingual Europe; Member, Jury, Prix de l'Europe, 1982-, Neustadt International Prize for Literature, 1996. Publications: Incandescences, 1970; Eclats de malachite, 1971; La Pointe du diable, 1973; Mosaique New Yorkaise, 1975; Albert Russo: An Anthology, 1987; Sang Mêlé ou ton Fils Léopold, 1990; Le Cap des Illusions, 1991; Futureyes/Dans la nuit bleu-fauve, 1992; Kaleidoscope, 1993; Eclipse sur le Lac Tanganyika, 1994; Venetian Thresholds, 1995; Painting the Tower of Babel, 1996; Zapinette, 1996; Poetry and Peanuts (collection), 1997; Zapinette Video (novel), 1998; Mixed Blood (novel), 1999; Eclipse over Lake Taugauyika (novel), 1999. Contributions to: Professional journals and BBC World Service. Honours: Willie Lee Martin Short Story Award, 1987; Silver Medal, 1985; British Diversity Award, 1997. Memberships: Association of French Speaking Writers; Authors Guild of America; PEN. Address: BP 640, 75826 Paris Cedex 17, France.

RUTHERFORD Anne Margaret, (Meg Rutherford), b. 23 July 1932, Bathurst, Australia. Author; Illustrator. m. Amis Goldingham, 19 Mar 1966. Education: Slade School, London, , 1958-61; East Sydney Technical College, 1955-57; Diploma in Fine Art, University College, London.

RUTSALA Vern, b. 5 Feb 1934, McCall, Idaho, USA. Writer; Teacher. m. Joan Colby, 1957, 2 sons, 1 daughter. Education: BA, Reed College, 1956; MFA, University of Iowa, 1960. Publications: The Window, 1964; Small Songs, 1969; The Harmful State, 1971; Laments, 1975; The Journey Begins, 1976; Paragraphs, 1978; The New Life, 1978; Walking Home from the Icehouse, 1981; Backtracking, 1985; The Mystery of Lost Shoes, 1985; Ruined Cities, 1987; Selected Poems, 1991; Little-Known Sports, 1994. Contributions to: New Yorker; Esquire; Poetry; Hudson Review; Harper's; Atlantic; American Poetry Review; Paris Review. Honours: National Endowment for the Arts Fellowships, 1974, 1979; Northwest Poetry Prize, 1976; Guggenheim Fellowship,1982; Carolyn Kizer Poetry Prize, 1988, 1997; Masters, Fellowship, Oregon Arts Commission, 1990; Hazel Hall Award, 1992; Juniper Prize, 1993; Duncan Lawrie Prize, Arvon Foundation, 1994. Memberships: PEN; Poetry Society of America; Associated Writing Programs. Address: 2404 North East 24th Avenue, Portland, OR 97212, USA.

RUTTER Jeremy Bentham, b. 23 June 1946, Boston, Massachusetts, USA. Archaeologist. m. Sarah Robbins Herndon, 31 Jan 1970, 2 sons. Education: BA, Classics, Haverford College, 1967; PhD, Classical Archaeology, University of Pennsylvania, 1974. Appointments: Visiting Assistant Professor, University of California at Los Angeles, 1975-76; Assistant Professor, 1976-81; Associate Professor, 1981-87; Professor, 1987-, Chair of Department, 1992-98, Dartmouth College. Publications: The Transition to Mycenaean (with S H Rutter), 1976; Lerna III: The Pottery of Lerna II, 1995. Contributions to: American Journal of Archaeology; Hesperia; Journal of Mediterranean Archaeology. Address: c/o Department of Classics, Dartmouth College, Hanover, NH 03755, USA.

RUTTER Michael Llewellyn, b. 15 Aug 1933, Brummanna, Lebanon. Professor of Developmental Psychiatry; Writer. m. Marjorie Heys, 27 Dec 1958, 1 son, 2 daughters. Education: MB ChB, 1950-55, MD, 1963, University of Birmingham; DPM, University of London, 1961. Appointments: Professor of Developmental Psychopathology, University of London; Social, Genetic and Developmental Psychiatry Research Centre. Publications: Depression in Young People: Development and Clinical Perspectives (co-editor), 1986; Language

Development and Disorders (co-editor), 1987; Treatment of Autistic Children (co-editor), 1987; Parenting Breakdown: The Making and Breaking of Intergenerational Links (co-author), 1988; Assessment and Diagnosis in Child Psychopathology, 1988; Straight and Devious Pathways From Childhood to Adulthood, 1990; Biological Risk Factors for Psychosocial Disorders, 1991; Developing Minds: Challenge and Continuity Across the Lifespan, 1993; Stress, Risk and Resilience in Children and Adolescents, Processes, Mechanisms and Interventions (co-editor), 1994; Child and Adolescent Psychiatry: Modern Approaches (co-editor), 3rd edition, 1994; Development Through Life: A Handbook for Clinicians (co-editor), 1994; Psychosocial Disorders in Young People: Time Trends and their Causes (co-editor), 1995; Behavioural Genetics (co-author), 3rd edition, 1997; Antisocial Behaviour by Young People (co-author), 1998. Contributions to: Numerous professional journals. Honours: 9 honorary doctorates; Knight Baronet, 1992; American Psychological Association Distinguished Scientific Contribution Award, 1995; Castilla del Pino Prize for Achievement in Psychiatry, Cordoba, Spain, 1995; Royal Society of Medicine, honorary fellow, 1996; Royal College of Paediatrics and Child Health, honorary founding fellow, 1996; Society for Research in Child Development, president elect, 1997. Memberships: American Academy of Arts and Sciences, honorary foreign member; Royal College of Psychiatrists, fellow; Royal College of Physicians, fellow; Fellow, Royal Society, 1997-; President, Society for Research into Child Development, 1999-. Address: MRC Child Psychiatry Unit, Institute of Psychiatry, De Crespigny Park, Denmark Hill, London SE5 8AF, England.

RÜTZ Michael. See: **FALKENLÖWE Michael Sixten Joachim, Baron of Rütz.**

RUURS Margriet, b. 2 Dec 1952, The Netherlands. Children's Author. Education: Master Degree, Education, Simon Fraser University, 1998. Appointments: Conduct Teachers' in service, writing workshops, authors visits, 1986-. Publications: Fireweed, 1986; Big Little Dog, 1992; On the Write Track, 1993; Spectacular Spiders, 1994; A Mountain Alphabet, 1996; Emma's Eggs, 1996; Emma and the Coyote, 1999. Contributions to: Cricket, 1998. Honour: Storytellers World Honor Title, 1997. Memberships: Canscaip; CWILL; TWUC.

RUYS Andrew John, b. Adelaide, South Australia, Australia. Research Scientist. m. Juanita Ferros, 1 son. Education: BEng, Honours I, 1987, DPhil, 1992, University of South Wales. Appointments: Fellowship in Bioceramics, Australian Research Council, 1994; Founding Editor, International Ceramic Monographs, 1994; Contributing Editor, Phase Diagrams for Ceramists handbooks series, 1994. Contributions to: Journals and conference proceedings in Australia, UK, USA, Germany, and Singapore. Honours: Alcan Research Award, 1988; Young Achiever Finalist, 1990. Memberships: Australasian, American, and Japanese Ceramic Societies. Address: 6 Hereford Place, West Pymble, Sydney, New South Wales, 2073, Australia.

RUYSLINCK Ward. See: **DE BELSER Raymond.**

RUZICKA Penelope Susan, (Penny Kane), b. 23 Jan 1945, Kenya. Consultant; Writer. m. Ladislav Ruzicka, 21 Mar 1984. Education: MSc, Economics, University of Wales, 1986. Publications: Choice Not Chance, 1978; The Which? Guide to Birth Control, 1983; Asking Demographic Questions, 1985; China's One Child Family (editor), 1985; Tradition, Development and the Individual, 1986; The Second Billion: Population and Family Planning in China, 1987; Famine in China, 1959-61, 1988; Differential Mortality, 1989; Women's Health: From Womb to Tomb, 1991; Victorian Families in Fact and Fiction, 1994. Contributions to: Various publications. Membership: International Union for the Scientific Study of Population. Address: The Old School, Majors Creek near Braidwood, New South Wales 2622, Australia.

RYAN Francis Patrick, b. 23 July 1944, Limerick, Eire. Doctor of Medicine. m. Barbara Horrocks, 14 Sept 1968,

1 son, 1 daughter. Education: MBChB Hons, Sheffield Medical School; Fellow, Royal College of Physicians. Appointment: Consultant Physician, Sheffield Health Authority. Publications: Novels: Sweet Summer; Tiger Tiger; Goodbye Baby Blue; Non-Fiction: The Eskimo Diet; Tuberculosis: The Greatest Story Never Told; Virus X; The Sundered World. Contributions to: Many scientific articles in medical and scientific journals. Honours: 4 gold medals in medicine. Membership: Society of Authors. Literary Agent: Bill Hamilton, A M Heath, London, England.

RYAN John Gerald Christopher, b. 4 Mar 1921, Edinburgh, Scotland. Artist; Writer. m. Priscilla Ann Blomfield, 3 Jan 1950, 1 son, 2 daughters. Education: Ampleforth College, York, 1930-40; Regent Street Polytechnic Art School, 1946-47. Appointment: Cartoonist, Catholic Herald, 1965-. Publications: 14 children's picture books, Captain Pugwash, 1956-86; Tiger Pig; 12 Noah's Ark Stories; 2 Dodo books; Mabel and the Tower of Babel, 1990; Adventures of Sir Cumference, 1990; Jonah, a Whale of a Tale, 1994; Soldier Sam and Trooper Ted, 1994. Contributions to: Magazines. Membership: Society of Authors. Address: Gungarden Lodge, Rye, East Sussex TN31 7HH, England.

RYCE-MENUHIN Joel, b. 11 June 1933, USA. Analytical Psychologist; Concert Pianist. m. Yaltah Menuhin, 11 June 1960. Education: BMus, 1953; BSc, Honours, 1976; MPhil, 1982. Publications: The Self in Early Childhood, 1988; Jungian Sandplay: The Wonderful Therapy, 1992; Jung and the Monotheisms, 1993. Contributions to: Journal of Analytical Psychology; Harvest; Chiron; Free Association Journal; British Journal of Projective Psychology; Guild of Pastoral Psychology. Memberships: British and Irish Sandplay Society, founding director; PEN. Address: 85 Canfield Gardens, London NW6 3EA, England.

RYCKMANS Pierre, (Simon Leys), b. 28 Sept 1935, Brussels, Belgium. Scholar; Writer. m. Hanfang Chang, 1964, 3 sons, 1 daughter. Publications: La Vie et l'oeuvre de Su Renshan, rebelle, peintre et fou, 1970; Shitao: Les Propos sur la peinture du Moine Citrouille-amère, 1970, 1984, 1996; Chinese Shadows, 1977; The Burning Forest, 1985; The Death of Napoleon, 1991, 1992; The Analects of Confucius, 1997; Essais sur la Chine, 1998; L'Ange et le Cachalot, 1998; Illustrator, Les Deux Acrobates (Jeanne Ryckmans), 1998. Contributions to: The New York Review of Books; Commentaire; Others. Honours include: Officier, Ordre de Léopold; Prix Stanislas Julien, Institut de France; Prix Jean Walter, Académie Française; The Independent Best Foreign Fiction Award, London; Christine Stead Award, Sydney. Memberships: Académie Royale de Langue and Littérature Françaises, Brussels; Fellow, Australian Academy of the Humanities. Address: 6 Bonwick Place, Garran, ACT 2605, Australia.

RYDELL Forbes. See: **FORBES Stanton.**

RYDER Jonathan. See: **LUDLUM Robert.**

RYDER Susan Margaret, (Baroness Ryder of Warsaw, Sue Ryder), b. 3 July 1923, Leeds, England. Social Worker; Writer. m. Lord Cheshire of Woodhall, 5 Apr 1959, dec, 1 son, 1 daughter. Appointments: Co-Founder, Ryder Cheshire Foundation; Founder, Sue Ryder Foundation; President, Leonard Cheshire; Patron, The Association of Pathfinders. Publications: And the Morrow is Theirs (autobiography); Child of My Love (autobiography), 1986; Revised Edition, 1997. Honours: Member of the Order of the British Empire, 1957; Member, 1965, Commander's Cross, 1992, Order of Polonia Restituta; Companion of the Order of St Michael and St George, 1976; Created Baroness Ryder of Warsaw in Poland and of Cavendish in Suffolk, England, 1978; 9 honorary doctorates. Memberships: Special Operations Executive Club; National Memorial Arboretum, trustee. Address: Sue Ryder Home, Cavendish, Sudbury, Suffolk CO10 8AY, England.

S

S Elizabeth Von. See: FREEMAN Gillian.

SABLEMAN Mark, b. 13 Sept 1951, St Louis, Missouri, USA. Lawyer. m. Lynn Oden Melby, 26 Jan 1985, 2 sons, 1 daughter. Education: BA, Grinnell College, 1972; MS Journalism, Northwestern University, 1973; JD, Georgetown University, 1979. Appointments: Reporter, Assistant City Editor, Clearwater Sun, 1973-76; Reporter, Washington Post, 1977; Associate, Reuben and Proctor, 1979-86; Associate, Thompson and Mitchell, 1986-88; Partner, Thompson Coburn, 1989-. Publication: More Speech, Not Less: Communications Law In The Information Age, 1997. Contributions to: St Louis Journalism Review; Journal of the Missouri Bar; Communications Lawyer; The Practical Lawyer; Others. Address: One Mercantile Center, St Louis, MO 63101, USA.

SACHS Marilyn (Stickle), b. 18 Dec 1927, New York, New York, USA. Writer. m. Morris Sachs, 26 Jan 1947, 1 son, 1 daughter. Education: BA, Hunter College, New York City, 1949; MLS, Columbia University, 1953. Publications: Over 35 books, 1964-96. Honours: Many citations, prizes and awards. Address: 733 31st Avenue, San Francisco, CA 94121, USA.

SACHS Murray, b. 10 Apr 1924, Toronto, Ontario, Canada. Literary Scholar; Teacher. m. Miriam Blank, 14 Sept 1961, 1 son, 1 daughter. Eduction: BA, Modern Languges, University of Toronto, 1946; MA, French, 1947, PhD, French, 1953, Columbia University, New York, USA. Appointments: Assistant Professor of Romanic Languages, Williams College, 1954-60; Professor of French and Comparative Literature, Brandeis University, 1960-96; Professor Emeritus, 1996-. Publications: The Career of Alphonse Daudet, 1965; The French Short Story in the 19th Century, 1969; Anatole France: The Short Stories, 1974. Contributions to: Books and professional journals; Kaleidoscope. Memberships: American Comparative Literature Association; Association of Literary Scholars and Critics; Modern Language Association of America; Modern Humanities Research Association; American Association of Teachers of French; American Comparative Literature Association. Address: c/o Department of Romance and Comparative Literature, Shiffman Humanities Center, Mailstop 024, Brandeis University, Waltham, MA 02254, USA.

SACKS Oliver (Wolf), b. 9 July 1933, London, England. Neurologist; Writer. Education: BA, 1954, MA, 1958, BM, 1958, BCh, 1958, Queen's College, Oxford; University of California at Los Angeles, 1962-65. Appointments: Intern, Middlesex Hospital, London, 1958-60, Mt Zion Hospital, San Francisco, 1961-62; Resident in Neurology, University of California at Los Angeles, 1962-65; Fellow in Neurochemistry and Neuropathology, 1965-66, Instructor, 1966-75, Assistant Professor, 1975-78, Associate Professor, 1978-85, Clinical Professor of Neurology, 1985, Albert Einstein College of Medicine, Yeshiva University, New York City; Staff Neurologist, Beth Abraham Hospital, New York City, 1966-. Publications: Migraine, 1970, revised edition, 1985; Awakenings, 1973, new edition, 1990; A Leg to Stand On, 1984; The Man Who Mistook His Wife for a Hat and Other Clinical Tales, 1985; Seeing Voices: A Journey into the World of the Deaf, 1989, revised edition, 1991; An Anthropologist on Mars: Seven Paradoxical Tales, 1995; The Island of the Colour-blind, 1996. Contribdutions to: Newspapers and journals. Honours: Hawthornden Prize, 1974; Oskar Pfister Award, American Psychiatric Association, 1988; Guggenheim Fellowship, 1989; Harold D Vursell Memorial Award, American Academy and Institute of Arts and Letters, 1989; Odd Fellows Book Award, 1990; Scriptor Award, University of Southern California, 1991; Professional Support Award, National Headache Foundation, 1991; Presidential Citation, American Academy of Neurology, 1991; Honorary doctorates. Address: 2 Horatio Street No 3G, New York, NY 10014, USA.

SADDLEMYER (Eleanor) Ann, b. 28 Nov 1932, Prince Albert, Saskatchewan, Canada. Critic; Theatre Historian; Educator. Education: BA, 1953, Honours English Diploma, 1955, University of Saskatchewan; MA, Queen's University, 1956; PhD, Bedford College, University of London, England, 1961. Appointments: Faculty, University of Victoria, British Columbia, 1960-71; Faculty, Victoria College, 1971-, Director, Graduate Centre for the Study of Drama, 1972-77, 1985-88, Master, Massey College, 1988-95, Professor and Master Emeritus, 1995, University of Toronto; Berg Chair, New York University, 1975. Publications: The World of W B Yeats, 1965; In Defence of Lady Gregory, Playwright, 1966; J M Synge Plays, Books I and II, 1968; Synge and Modern Comedy, 1968; Letters to Molly: J M Synge to Maire O'Neill, 1971; Lady Gregory Plays, 4 volumes, 1971; Theatre Business, 1982; The Collected Letters of J M Synge, 2 volumes, 1983-84; Lady Gregory Fifty Years After, 1987; Early Stages: Essays on the Theatre in Ontario 1800-1914, 1990; Synge's Playboy of the Western World and other Plays, 1995; Later Stages: Essays on the Theatre in Ontario, World War I to the 1950's, 1997. Contributions to: Professional journals. Honours: Honorary Fellow, Royal Society of Canada, 1977; Honorary doctorates, Queen's, 1977, Victoria, 1989, McGill, 1989, Windsor, 1990, and Saskatchewan, 1991, universities; British Academy Rosemary Crawshay Award, 1986; Fellow, Royal Society of Arts, 1987; Alumni Award of Excellence, University of Toronto, 1991; Woman of Distinction, 1994; Officer of the Order of Canada, 1995; DLitt, University of Toronto, 1999. Memberships: International Association for Study of Anglo-Irish Literature; Association for Canadian Theatre Research, founding president; Colin Smythe Publishing, board of directors; Canadian Theatre Museums Association, board. Address: 10876 Madrona Drive, Sidney, British Columbia V8L 5N9, Canada.

SADDLER Allen. See: RICHARDS Ronald Charles William.

SADGROVE Sidney Henry, (Lee Torrance), b. 1920, England. Artist; Teacher; Writer. Publications: You've Got To Do Something, 1967; A Touch of the Rabbits, 1968; The Suitability Factor, 1968; Stanislaus and the Princess, 1969; A Few Crumbs, 1971; Stanislaus and the Frog, 1972; Paradis Enow, 1972; Stanislaus and the Witch, 1973; The Link, 1975; The Bag, 1977; Half Sick of Shadows, 1977; Bleep, 1977; All in the Mind, 1977; Icary Dicary Doc, 1978; Angel, 1978; Filling, 1979; First Night, 1980; Only on Friday, 1980; Hoodunnit, 1984; Pawn en Prise, 1985; Just for Comfort, 1986; Tiger, 1987; State of Play, 1988; Warren, 1989; Dear Mrs Comfett, 1990. Membership: Writers Guild of Great Britain. Address: Pimp Barn, Withyham, Hartfield, Sussex, TN7 4BB, England.

SADIE Stanley (John), b. 30 Oct 1930, Wembley, Middlesex, England. Musicologist; Lexicographer; Writer. m. (1) Adèle Bloom, 10 Dec 1953, dec 1978, 2 sons, 1 daughter, (2) Julie Anne McCormack, 18 July 1978, 1 son, 1 daughter. Education: BA, 1953, Mus B, 1953, MA, 1957, PhD, 1958, University of Cambridge. Appointments: Faculty, Trinity College of Music, London, 1957-65; Music Critic, The Times of London, 1964-81; Editor, The Musical Times, 1967-87. Publications: Handel, 1962; The Pan Book of Opera (with Arthur Jacobs), 1964, 3rd edition, 1984; Mozart, 1966; Beethoven, 1967, 2nd edition, 1974; Handel, 1968; Handel Concertos, 1972; The New Grove Dictionary of Music and Musicians (editor), 20 volumes, 1980, revised edition, 24 volumes, forthcoming; The New Grove Dictionary of Musical Instruments (editor), 1984; The Cambridge Music Guide (with Alison Latham), 1985; The New Grove Dictionary of American Music (editor with H Wiley Hitchcock), 4 volumes, 1986; Mozart Symphonies, 1986; The Grove Concise Dictionary of Music (editor), 1988; Handel Tercentenary Collection (editor with A Hicks), 1988; History of Opera (editor), 1989; Performance Practice (editor with Howard M Brown), 2 volumes, 1989; Man and Music (general editor), 8 volumes, 1989-93; Music Printing and Publishing (co-editor), 1990; The New Grove Dictionary of Opera (editor), 4 volumes, 1992; Wolfgang Amadè Mozart: Essays on His Life and Music (editor), 1995; New Grove Book of Operas (editor), 1996. Contributions to: Professional journals and general publications. Honours: Commander of the Order of the British Empire, 1982; Honorary LittD, 1982. Memberships: Critics Circle; International Musicological Society, president, 1992-97; Royal College of Music, fellow; Royal Academy of Music, honorary; Royal Musical Association, president, 1989-94. Address: 12 Lyndhurst Road, London NW3 5NL, England.

SADLER Mark. See: LYNDS Dennis.

SADOCK Karen, b. 12 Feb 1943. Academic Administration. m. Geoffrey J Sadock PhD, 4 Sept 1971, 1 daughter. Education: AB, University of Michigan, USA, 1965; MDiv, General Theological Seminary, 1975. Appointments: Assistant Editor, Associate Editor, Contributing Editor, Ward's Auto World, 1965-68; Technical Writer and Ms Production Supervisor, Freuhauf Corp, 1968-71; Scientific Writer and Editor, Special Projects Manager, Office of the Dean, Mt Sinai School of Medicine 1975-. Contributions to: Primary Cardiology; Ward's Auto World; Quilter's Newsletter Magazine; Christian Challenge; The Episcopalian; The Ark Foundations; The Evangelical Catholic. Honour: Hopwood Award, University of Michigan, 1964. Address: 67 West Shore Avenue, Dumont, NJ, 07628, USA.

SAETERBAKKEN Stig, b. 4 Jan 1966, Lillehammer, Norway. Author. m. Elizabeth Carlsen Sunde, 21 May 1993, 2 daughters. Appointment: Member, Norwegian Literary Council; Editor, Scandinavian essay-chronicle, Marginal, 1995-97. Publications: Flytende Paraplyer (poems), 1984; Sverdet ble til et Barn (poems), 1986; Incubus (novel), 1991; Det Nye Testamentet (novel), 1993; Estetisk Salighet (essays), 1994; Siamesisk (novel), 1997; Selvbeherskelse (novel), 1998; Sauermugg (novel), 1999. Contributions to: Morgenbladet; Passage; Res Publica; Ord & Bild. Membership: Norwegian Writers Union. Address: Anders Sandvigs GT 39, 2600 Lillehammer, Norway.

SAFIRE William, b. 17 Dec 1929, New York, New York, USA. Columnist; Writer. m. Helene Belmar Julius, 16 Dec 1962, 1 son, 1 daughter. Education: Syracuse University, 1947-49. Appointments: Reporter, New York Herald-Tribune Syndicate, 1949-51; Correspondent, Europe and the Middle East, WNBC-WNBT, 1951; Radio-TV Producer, WMBC, New York City, 1954-55; Vice-President, Tex McCrary Inc, 1955-60; President, Safire Public Relations, 1960-68; Special Assistant to President Richard M Nixon, 1969-73; Columnist, The New York Times, 1973-. Publications: The Relations Explosion, 1963; Plunging into Politics, 1964; Safire's Political Dictionary, 1968, 3rd edition, 1978, new edition as Safire's New Political Dictionary, 1993; Before the Fall, 1975; Full Disclosure, 1977; Safire's Washington, 1980; On Language, 1980; What's the Good Word?, 1982; Good Advice on Writing (with Leonard Safire), 1982, new edition, 1992; I Stand Corrected, 1984; Take My Word for It, 1986; You Could Look It Up, 1988; Language Maven Strikes Again, 1990; Leadership (with Leonard Safire), 1990; Fumblerules, 1990; The First Dissident, 1992; Lend Me Your Ears, 1992; Quoth the Maven, 1993; In Love with Norma Loquendi, 1994; Sleeper Spy, 1995. Contributions to: Newspapers and magazines. Honour: Pulitzer Prize for Distinguished Commentary, 1978. Membership: Pulitzer, board, 1995-. Address: c/o The New York Times, 1627 Eye Street North West, Washington, DC 20006, USA.

SAFRANKO Mark Peter, b. 23 Dec 1950, Trenton, New Jersey, USA. Writer; Actor. m. Lorrie Foster, 11 May 1996, 1 son. Education: BA, St Vincent College, 1968; MA, Montclair State University, 1977. Publications: Novels: The Favor, 1987; Hopler's Statement, 1998. Contributions to: South Carolina Review; North Atlantic Review; Paterson Literary Review; New Orleans Review. Membership: Dramatists Guild. Address: 205 Hudson Street, #1011, Hoboken, NJ 07030, USA.

SAGAN Françoise, b. 21 June 1935, Carjac, France. Novelist; Playwright. Education: Sorbonne, University of Paris. Publications: Bonjour Tristesse, 1954; A Certain Smile, 1956; Those Without Shadows, 1957; Aimez-vous Brahms, 1959; Wonderful Clouds, 1961; La Chamade, 1965; The Heart-Keeper, 1968; A Few Hours of Sunlight, 1969; Scars on the Soul, 1972; Lost Profile, 1974; Silken Eyes, 1976; The Unmade Bed, 1977; Le Chien Couchant, 1980; Incidental Music, 1981; The Painted Lady, 1981; The Still Storm, 1983; Engagements of the Heart, 1985; La Maison de Raquel Vega, 1985; Painting in Blood, 1987; The Leash, 1989; Les Faux-fuyants, 1991. Plays: Castle in Sweden, 1960; Les Violons parfois, 1962; Landru (screenplay for Claude Chabrol), 1963; Bonheur, impair et passe, 1964; The Dizzy Horse, 1966; Un piano dans l'herbe, 1970; Le Sang doré des Borgia (screenplay), 1977; Il fait beau jour et nuit, 1978; Opposite Extremes, 1987. Other: Mirror of Venus, 1965; Réponses 1954-74, (autobiographical conversations). 1974; Brigitte Bardot, 1975; Sand et Musset: Lettres d'amour, 1985; Dear Sarah Bernhardt, 1987; La Sentinelle de Paris, 1988; The Eiffel Tower, 1989. Address: c/o Edition Juilliard, 20 rue des Grands Augustins, 75006 Paris, France.

SAGGS Henry William Frederick, b. 2 Dec 1920, Weeley, Essex, England. Retired Professor of Semitic Languages. m. Joan Butterworth, 21 Sept 1946, 4 daughters. Education: King's College, London, 1939-42, 1946-48; School of Oriental and African Studies, London, 1949-52; BD, 1942; MTh, 1948; MA, 1950; PhD, 1953. Appointments: Lecturer, then Reader in Akkadian, School of Oriental and African Studies, London, 1953-66; Professor of Semitic Languages, University College Cardiff, University of Wales, 1966-83. Publications: The Greatness That Was Babylon, 1962, revised edition, 1987; Everyday Life in Babylon and Assyria, 1965, 2nd edition, 1987; The Encounter With the Divine in Mesopotamia and Israel, 1978; The Might That Was Assyria, 1984, 2nd edition, 1990; Civilization Before Greece and Rome, 1989; Babylonians, 1995; Au Temps de Babylone, 1998. Contributions to: Iraq; Sumer; Journal of Cuneiform Studies; Journal of Theological Studies; Archiv für Orientforschung; Revue d'Assyriologie; Journal of Semitic Studies; Bibliotheca Orientalis. Memberships: Society of Authors; Society of Antiquaries; British School of Archaeology in Iraq, council member; Savage Club; Royal Asiatic Society. Address: Eastwood, Bull Lane, Long Melford, Suffolk CO10 9EA, England.

SAHAY Akhoweri Chittaranjan, b. 2 Jan 1925, Muzaffarpur, India. Retired Associate Professor of English; Editor; Poet; Writer. m. Akhowi Priyamvada Sahay, 17 June 1945, 3 sons, 1 daughter. Education: BA, Honours, Distinction, 1945, MA, English, 1947, Patna University; MDEH, National University of Electro Homeopathy, Kanpur, 1964; PhD, English, Stanton University, New York, 1985. Appointments: Lecturer and Head, Department of English, Rajendra College, Chapra, 1948-68; Lecturer, L S College, Muzaffarpur, 1968-74; Associate Professor of English, Bihar University, Muzaffarpur, 1974-85; Chief Editor, Kavita India quarterly, 1987-. Publications: Poetry: Van Yoothi, 1939; Van Shepali, 1941; Van Geet, 1943; Ajab Desh, 1945; Roots and Branches, 1979; Emerald Foliage, 1981; Pink Blossoms, 1983; Golden Pollens, 1985; Vernal Equinox, 1987; Summer Clouds, 1989. Short stories for children: Dick Aur Ostrich, 1946; Motilal Tota, 1948; Rani Sahiba, 1964. Prose: The Rubaiyat and Other Essays, 1980; My Interest in Occultism, 1982. Contributions to: Numerous anthologies and journals. Honours: Many prizes, medals and certificates of merit. Memberships: International Writers and Artists Association, USA; PEN All-India Centre; Poetry Society, India and UK; Theosophical Society, Madras; United Writers Association, Madras; World Poetry Society; Writers Club, Madras. Address: Kavita India House, South-East Chaturbhujasthon, Muzaffarpur 842001, Bihar, India.

SAHGAL Nayantara (Pandit), b. 10 May 1927, Allahabad, Uttar Pradesh, India. Writer. m. (1), 2 Jan 1949, div, 1 son, 2 daughters, (2), 17 Sept 1979. Education: BA, History, Wellesley College, Massachusetts, 1947. Appointments: Advisory Panel for English, Sahitya Akademi, 1972-75; Writer-in-Residence, Southern Methodist University, Dallas, 1973, 1977; Research Scholar, Radcliffe (now Bunting) Institute, Cambridge, Massachusetts, 1976; Member, Indian delegation to the United Nations, 1978; Fellow, Woodrow Wilson International Center for Scholars, Washington, DC, 1981-82, National Humanities Center, North Carolina, 1983-84; Jury, Commonwealth Writers Prize, 1990, 1991. Publications: Fiction: A Time to Be Happy, 1958; This Time of Morning, 1965; Storm in Chandigarh, 1969; The Day in Shadow, 1972; A Situation in New Delhi, 1977; Rich Like Us, 1985; Plans for Departure, 1986; Mistaken Identity, 1988. Non-Fiction: Prison and Chocolate Cake, 1954, new revised edition, 1998; From Fear Set Free, 1962; The Freedom Movement in India, 1970; Indira Gandhi: Her Road to Power, 1982; Relationship: Extracts from a Correspondence (with E N Mangat Rai), 1994; Point of View, 1997. Contributions to: Newspapers and magazines. Honours: Book Society Recommendation, 1959; Sinclair Prize for Fiction, 1985; Sahitya Akademi Award, 1986; Commonwealth Writers Prize, Eurasia, 1987; Honorary Doctor of Letters, University of Leeds, 1997. Membership: American Academy of Arts and Sciences, 1990. Address: 181 B Rajpur Road, Dehra Dun 248009, Uttar Pradesh, India.

SAHU N S, b. 1 Sept 1939, India. Reader in English; Poet. m. Shanti Sahu, 17 May 1962, 3 sons. Education: MA, Linguistics, 1970; MA, English Literature, 1973; PhD, Linguistics, 1975; PhD, English, 1978. Appointments: Lecturer in English, Department of Education, Bhilai Steel Plant, Bhilainagar, 1971-79; Lecturer, 1979-92, Reader in English, 1992-, University of Gorakhpur. Publications: Aspects of Linguistics, 1982, 2nd edition, 1990; T S Eliot: The Man as a Poet, Playwright, Prophet and Critic, 1988; A Study of the Works of Matthew Arnold, 1988; Theatre of Protest and Anger, 1988; Toponymy, 1989; Christopher Marlowe and Theatre of Cruelty and Violence, 1990; An Approach to American Literature, 1991; Poems, 1996. Contributions to: Various publications. Honour: Gold Medal of Honour, American Biographical Institute. Memberships: American Studies Research Centre; International Goodwill Society of India; Linguistic Society of India. Address: 11 New Flat, Hirapuri Colony, University Campus, Gorakhpur 273009, India.

SAID Edward, b. 1 Nov 1935, Jerusalem, Palestine. Professor; Writer. m. Mariam Cortas, 14 Dec 1970, 2 children. Education: AB, Princeton University, 1957; AM, 1960, PhD, 1964, Harvard University. Appointments: Instructor, 1963-65, Assistant Professor, 1965-67, Associate Professor, 1967-70, Professor, 1970-77, Parr Professor of English and Comparative Literature, 1977-89, Old Dominion Foundation Professor of Humanities, 1989-, University Professor, 1992-, Columbia University; Visiting Professor, Harvard University, 1974; Johns Hopkins University, 1979, Yale University, 1985; Fellow, Center for Advanced Study in the Behavioural Sciences, Palo Alto, California, 1975-76; Christian Gauss Lecturer in Criticism, Princeton University, 1977; Carpenter Professor, University of Chicago, 1983; T S Eliot Lecturer, University of Kent, Canterbury, 1985; Northrop Frye Chair, University of Toronto, 1986; Messenger Lecturer, Cornell University, 1986; Wilson Lecturer, Wellesley College, 1991; Amnesty Lecturer, University of Oxford, 1992; Lord Northcliffe Lecturer, University College, London, 1993; Reith Lecturer, BBC, London, 1993. Publications: Joseph Conrad and the Fiction of Autobiography, 1966; Beginnings: Intention and Method, 1975; Orientalism, 1978; The Question of Palestine, 1979; Literature and Society, 1979; Covering Islam, 1981; The World, the Text and the Critic, 1983; After the Last Sky, 1986; Blaming the Victims, 1988; Muscial Elaborations, 1991; Culture and Imperialism, 1993; Representations of the Intellectual, 1994; The Politics of Dispossession, 1994; Ghazzah-Arihah: Salam Amriki, 1994. Contributions to: Professional journals and other publications. Honours: Guggenheim Fellowship, 1972-73; Social Science Research Fellow, 1975; Lionel Trilling Awards, Columbia University, 1976, 1994; René Wellek Award, American Comparative Literature Association, 1985. Memberships: American Academy of Arts and Sciences; American Comparative Literature Association; Association of Arab-American University Graduates; Council on Foreign Relations; Modern Language Association; PEN, executive board, 1989-. Address: c/o Department of English, Columbia University, New York, NY 10027, USA.

SAIL Lawrence Richard, b. 29 Oct 1942, London, England. Poet; Writer. m. (1) Teresa Luke, 1966, div 1981, 1 son, 1 daughter, (2) Helen Bird, 1994. Education: BA, Honours, Modern Languages, St John's College, Oxford, 1964. Appointments: Teacher of Modern Languages, Lenana School, Nairobi, 1966-71, Millfield School, 1973-74, Blundell's School, Devon, 1975-81; Exeter School, 1982-91; Editor, South West Review, 1981-85; Chairman, Arvon Foundation, 1990-94; Programme Director, Cheltenham Festival of Literature, 1991; Jury Member, European (Aristeion) Literature Prize, 1994-96. Publications: Opposite Views, 1974; The Drowned River, 1978; The Kingdom of Atlas, 1980; South West Review: A Celebration (editor), 1985; Devotions, 1987; Aquamarine, 1988; First and Always (editor), 1988; Out of Land: New and Selected Poems, 1992; Building into Air, 1995. Contributions to: Anthologies, magazines and newspapers. Honours: Hawthornden Fellowship, 1992; Arts Council Writer's Bursary, 1993; Fellow of the Royal Society of Literature. Memberships: Authors' Society; St John's College, Oxford, senior common room; Poetry Society. Address: Richmond Villa, 7 Wonford Road, Exeter, Devon EX2 4LF, England.

SAINSBURY Maurice Joseph, b. 18 Nov 1927, Sydney, New South Wales, Australia. Consultant Psychiatrist. m. Erna June Hoadley, 22 Aug 1953, 1 son, 2 daughters. Education: MB, BS, University of Sydney, 1952; DPM, Royal College of Physicians and Surgeons, 1960; MHP, University of New South Wales, 1980. Appointments: Consultant Psychiatrist, Australian Army, 1976-86, Chelmsford Royal Commission, 1988-90. Publication: Key to Psychiatry, 1973, 4th edition (with L G Lambeth), 1988. Contributions to: Professional journals. Honours: Reserve Force Decoration, 1985; Member of the Order of Australia, 1987. Memberships: After Care Association of New South Wales, past president; Guardianship Tribunal, New South Wales; Mental Health Review Tribunal, New South Wales; Royal Australian and New Zealand College of Psychiatrists, fellow, past president; Royal College of Psychiatrists, fellow. Address: 3 Bimbil Place, Killara, New South Wales 2071, Australia.

SAINT Dora Jessie, (Miss Read), b. 17 Apr 1913, Surrey, England. Novelist; Short Story and Children's Fiction Writer. Education: Homerton College, 1931-33. Publications: Village School, 1955; Village Diary, 1957; Storm in the Village, 1958; Hobby Horse Cottage, 1958; Thrush Green, 1959; Fresh From the Country, 1960; Winter in Thrush Green, 1961; Miss Clare Remembers, 1962; The Market Square, 1966; The Howards of Caxley, 1967; Country Cooking, 1969; News from Thrush Green, 1970; Tyler's Row, 1972; Christmas Mouse, 1973; Battles at Thrush Green, 1975; No Holly for Miss Quinn, 1976; Village Affairs, 1977; Return to Thrush Green, 1978; The White Robin, 1979; Village Centenary, 1980; Gossip From Thrush Green, 1981; A Fortunate Grandchild, 1982; Affairs at Thrush Green, 1983; Summer at Fairacre, 1984; At Home in Thrush Green, 1985; Time Remembered, 1986; The School at Thrush Green, 1987; The World at Thrush Green, 1988; Mrs Pringle, 1989; Friends at Thrush Green, 1990; Changes at Fairacre, 1991; Celebrations at Thrush Green, 1992; Farewell to Fairacre, 1993; Tales From a Village School, 1994; The Year at Thrush Green, 1995; A Peaceful Retirement, 1996. Honour: Member of the Order of the British Empire, 1998. Membership: Society of Authors. Address: Strouds, Shefford Woodlands, Hungerford, Berkshire RG17 7AJ, England.

SAINT-AMAND Pierre, b. 22 Feb 1957, Port-au-Prince, Haiti. Professor of French Studies and Comparative Literature. Education: BA, 1978; MA, Romance Languages, 1980; PhD, Romance Languages, 1981. Appointments: Assistant Professor, Yale University, 1981-82, Stanford University, 1982-86; Associate

Professor, 1986-90, Professor, 1990-97, Francis Wayland Professor, 1997-, Brown University. Publications: Diderot: Le Labyrinthe de la Relation, 1984; Séduire ou la Passion des Lumières, 1986; Les Lois de L'Hostilité, 1992; The Libertine's Progress, 1994; The Laws of Hostility, 1996. Editor: Diderot, 1984; Le Roman au dix-huitième siècle, 1987; Autonomy in the Age of Enlightenment, 1993. Honour: Guggenheim Foundation, 1989. Memberships: Modern Language Association; American Society for Eighteenth-Century Studies. Address: French Studies, Box 1961, Brown University, Providence, RI 02912, USA.

SAKAMOTO Yoshikazu, b. 16 Sept 1927, USA. Professor; Writer m. Kikuko Ono, 2 June 1956, 2 daughters. Education: University of Tokyo, 1948-51; Graduate Studies, University of Chicago, 1955-56. Appointments: Research Fellow, 1951-54, Associate Professor, 1954-64, Professor of International Politics, 1964-88, Professor Emeritus, 1988-, University of Tokyo; Professor of Peace and World Order Studies, Meiji Gakuin University, Tokyo, 1988-93; Senior Research Fellow, International Christian University, Tokyo, 1993-96. Publications: Elements of World Instability: Armaments, Communication, Food, International Division of Labor (editor with E Jahn), 1981; Democratizing Japan: The Allied Occupation of Japan (co-editor), 1987; Strategic Doctrines and Their Alternatives (editor), 1987; Asia: Militarization and Regional Conflict (editor), 1988; The Emperor System as a Japan Problem (editor), 1989; Global Transformation: Challenge to the State System (editor), 1994. Other: Various books in Japanese. Contributions to: Books and professional journals. Honours: Rockefeller Foundation Fellow, 1956-57; Eisenhower Fellow, 1964; Special Fellow, United Nations Institute for Training and Research, 1972-74; Mainichi Press National Book Award, 1976. Memberships: American Political Science Association; Asian Peace Research Association, secretary general, 1983-90; International Peace Research Association, secretary general, 1979-83; Japanese Political Science Association. Address: 8-29-19 Shakujii-machi, Nerima-ku, Tokyo 177-0041, Japan.

SALAMUN Tomaz, b. 4 July 1941, Zagreb, Yugoslavia. Poet; Writer. m. Metka Krasovec, 11 Apr 1979, 1 son, 1 daughter. Education: MA, Art History, University of Ljubljana; Studied Art History in Paris and Rome, 1967; International Writing Program, University of Iowa, 1971-73. Appointments: Assistant Curator, Modern Gallery, Ljubljana, 1969-70; Assistant Professor, Academy of Art, Ljubljana, 1970-72; Poetry: Pesmi (Poems), 1980; Maske (Masks), 1980; Balada za Metko Krasovec (Ballad for Metko Krasovec), 1981; Analogije svetlobe (Anthologies of Light), 1982; Glas (Voice), 1983; Sonet o mleku (Sonnet on Milk), 1984; Soy realidad (Iam Reality), 1985; Ljubljanska pomlad (Ljubljana Spring), 1986; Mera casa, 1987; Ziva rana, zivi sok (Living Wound), 1988; The Selected Poems of Tomaz Salamun, 1988; Otrok in jelen (Boy and Stag), 1990; Ambra, 1994. Contributions to: Reviews and journals. Honours: Mladost Prize, 1969; Preseren Foundation Prize, 1973; Yaddo and MacDowell Colony Residencies, USA, 1973, 1974, 1979, 1986, 1987; Zelezara Sisak Prize, 1978; Ljubisa Jocic Prize, 1981; Fulbright Grant, 1986-87; Jenko Prize, 1988; Pushcart Prize, 1994. Memberships: Slovenian PEN Centre, vice president; Slovenian Writers Assocation, board member. Address: Dalmatinova 11, 1000 Ljubljana, Slovenia.

SALAS SOMMER Dario. See: **BAINES John.**

SALE (John) Kirkpatrick, b. 27 June 1937, Ithaca, New York, USA. Editor; Writer. m. Faith Apfelbaum Sale, 21 June 1962, 2 daughters. Education: BA, Cornell University, 1958. Appointments: Editor, The New Leader, 1959-61, New York Times Magazine, 1965-68; Editor, 1981-82, Contributing Editor, 1986-, The Nations. Contributing Editor, The Nation, 1986-. Publications: SDS, 1973; Power Shift, 1975; Human Scale, 1980; Dwellers in the Land: The Bioregional Vision, 1985; The Conquest of Paradise: Christopher Columbus and the Columbian Legacy, 1990; The Green Revolution: The American Environmental Movement 1962-1992, 1993; Rebels Against the Future: The Luddites and Their War on the Industrial Revolution, 1995. Memberships: Learning Alliance; PEN American Centre, board member, 1976-97; E F Schumacher Society, secretary, 1980-86, co-director, 1986-. Address: 113 West 11th Street, New York, NY 10011, USA.

SALIH Salima, b. 1 July 1942, Mosul, Iraq. Writer; Journalist. m. Fadhil Al-Azzwi, 13 Jan 1971, 1 son. Education: Bachelor of Law, University of Baghdad, 1965; Diploma Journalist, 1981, Dr rer pol, 1986, Karl Marx University, Leipzig. Publications: Short stories: On The Caravan of Life, 1961; Because You Are a Human Being, 1963; Metamorphoses, 1975; The Tree Of Forgiveness, 1996; Novels: The Uprising, 1974; Biography of Childhood: Flower of the Prophets, 1994. Contributions to: Numerous literary and journalistic contributions to Arabic newspapers and magazines including Alif Ba, Al-Mada, Al-Katiba. Address: Weissenseer Weg 2 - 5/6, 10367, Berlin, Germany.

SALINGER J(erome) D(avid), b. 1 Jan 1919, New York, New York, USA. Author. m. Claire Douglas, 1953, div 1967, 1 son, 1 daughter. Education: Valley Forge Military Academy; Columbia University. Publications: The Catcher in the Rye, 1951; Nine Stories, 1953; Franny and Zooey, 1961; Raise High the Roof-Beam, Carpenters and Seymour: An Introduction, 1963. Contributions to: Magazines. Address: c/o Harold Ober Associates, 425 Madison Avenue, New York, NY 10017, USA.

SALISBURY Frank B(oyer), b. 3 Aug 1926, Provo, Utah, USA. Professor Emeritus of Plant Physiology; Writer. m. (1) Lois Marilyn Olson, 1 Sept 1949, 5 sons, 2 daughters, (2) Mary Thorpe Robinson, 28 June 1991. Education: BS, 1951, MA, 1952, University of Utah; PhD, California Institute of Technology. Appointments: Assistant Professor of Botany, Pomona College, Claremont, California, 1954-55; Assistant Professor, 1955-61, Professor of Plant Physiology, 1961-66, Colorado State University, Fort Collins; National Science Foundation Postdoctoral Fellow, University of Tübingen, University of Innsbruck, 1962-63; Professor of Plant Physiology, 1966-, Head, Department of Plant Science, 1966-70, Distinguished Professor of Agriculture, 1987-, Utah State University, Logan; Technical Representative in Plant Physiology, US Atomic Energy Commission, Germantown, Maryland, 1973-74; Visiting Professor, University of Innsbruck, 1983; Lady Davis Fellow, Hebrew University of Jerusalem, 1983; Member, Life Sciences Advisory Committee, 1986-88, Aerospace Medicine Advisory Committee, 1988-93, Controlled Ecological Life-Support System Discipline Working Group, 1989-, National Aeronautics and Space Administration; Editor, Americas and the Pacific Rim, Journal of Plant Physiology, 1989-97. Publications: The Flowering Process, 1963; Vascular Plants: Form and Function (with R V Parke), 1964, 2nd edition, 1970; Truth by Reason and by Revelation, 1965; Plant Physiology (with C Ross), 1969, 4th edition, 1992; The Biology of Flowering, 1971; Botany: An Ecological Approach (with W Jensen), 1972, 2nd edition, 1984; The Utah UFO Display: A Biologist's Report, 1974; The Creation, 1976; Biology (with others), 1977; Units, Symbols and Terminology for Plant Physiology (editor and contributor), 1996. Contributions to: Professional journals and general publications. Honours: Merit Award, Botanical Society of America; Founder's Award, American Society for Gravitational and Space Biology, 1994. Memberships: American Association for the Advancement of Science, fellow; American Institute of Biological Sciences, governing board, 1976-79; American Society for Gravitational and Space Biology; American Society of Plant Physiologists, editorial board, 1967-92; Botanical Society of America; Phi Kappa Phi; Sigma Xi; Utah Academy of Science, Arts and Letters. Address: 2250 Bryan Circle, Salt Lake City, UT 84108, USA.

SALISBURY John. See: **CAUTE David.**

SALISBURY Robert H(olt), b. 29 Apr 1930, Elmhurst, Illinois, USA. Professor of American Government Emeritus; Writer. Education: AB, Washington and Lee University, 1951; MA, 1952, PhD, 1955, University of Illinois. Appointments: Faculty, Washington University, 1955-97; Chairman, Department of Political Science, 1966-73, 1986-92, Souers Professor of American Government, 1982-97, Professor Emeritus, 1997-, Washington University. Publications: Functions and Policies of American Government (co-author), 1958, 3rd edition, 1967; American Government: Readings and Problems (with Eliot, Chambers and Prewitt), 1959, 2nd edition, 1965; Democracy in the Mid-Twentieth Century (editor with Chambers), 1960; State Politics and the Public Schools (with Masters and Eliot), 1964; Interest Group Politics in America, 1970; Governing America: Public Choice and Political Action, 1973; Citizen Participation in the Public Schools, 1980; Interest and Institutions: Substance and Structure in American Politics, 1992; The Hollow Core (with Heinz, Laumann and Nelson), 1993. Contributions to: Professional journals. Honours: Guggenheim Fellowship, 1990; Rockefeller Visiting Scholar, Bellagio, Italy, 1990. Address: 709 South Skinker, St Louis, MO 63105, USA.

SALOM Philip, b. 8 Aug 1950, Bunbury, Western Australia, Australia. Lecturer; Poet. Education: BA, Curtin University, Perth, 1976; Dip Ed, 1981. Appointments: Tutor and Lecturer, Curtin University, 1982-93; Writer-in-Residence, Singapore National University, 1989, B R Whiting Library/Studio, Rome, 1992; Lecturer, Murdoch University, 1994-. Publications: The Silent Piano, 1980; The Projectionist: Sequence, 1983; Sky Poems, 1987; Barbecue of the Primitives, 1989; Playback, 1991; Tremors, 1992; Feeding the Ghost, 1993; Always Then and Now, 1993. Honours: Commonwealth Poetry Prizes, 1981, 1987; Western Australian Premier's Prize, 1992; Australia/New Zealand Literary Exchange Award, 1992; Australia Council Fellowships. Address: 795 Mills Road, Glen Forest, Western Australia 6071, Australia.

SALTER Charles A, b. 12 Oct 1947, Fort Worth, Texas, USA. US Army Officer; Research Psychologist; Writer. m. 13 May 1972, 1 son, 2 daughters. Education: BS, magna cum laude, Tulane University, 1969; MA, 1970, PhD, 1973, University of Pennsylvania; MS, 1987, SD, 1989, Harvard University School of Public Health. Appointments: US Army Officer; Editor, Alternative Careers for Academics Bulletin, 1978; Syndicated Columnist, Suburban Features, 1983-85. Publications: Psychology for Living, 1977; The Professional Chef's Guide to Kitchen Management (editor), 1985; Knight's Foodservice Dictionary (editor), 1987; Foodservice Standards in Resorts, 1987; On the Frontlines, 1988; Getting it Off, Keeping it Off, 1988; Literacy and the Library, 1991; Looking Good, Eating Right, 1991; The Vegetarian Teen, 1991; Food Risks and Controversies, 1993; The Nutrition-Fitness Link, 1993. Membership: American Society of Journalists and Authors. Address: MCMR-PLC, Fort Detrick, MD 21702, USA.

SALTER James, b. 10 June 1925, New York New York, USA. Writer. m. Ann Altemus, 5 June 1951, div 1976, 2 sons, 3 daughters. Publications: The Hunters, 1957; The Arm of Flesh, 1960-; A Sport and a Pastime, 1967; Light Years, 1976; Sold Faces, 1980; Dusk and Other Stories, 1989; Burning the Days, 1997. Contributions to: Paris Review; Antaeus; Grand Street; Vogue; Esquire. Honours: American Academy of Arts and Letters, Grant, 1982; PEN-Faulkner Award, 1989. Membership: PEN USA. Address: Box 765, Bridgehampton, NY 11932, USA.

SALTER Mary Jo, b. 15 Aug 1954, Grand Rapids, Michigan, USA. Lecturer; Poet; Editor. m. Brad Leithauser, 1980, 2 daughters. Education: BA, cum laude, Harvard University, 1976; MA, Cambridge University, 1978. Appointments: Instructor, Harvard University, 1978-79; Staff Editor, Atlantic Monthly, 1978-80; Poet-in-Residence, Robert Frost Place, 1981; Lecturer in English, 1984-, Emily Dickinson Lecturer in Humanities, 1995-, Mount Holyoke College, South Hadley, Massachusetts; Poetry Editor, The New Republic, 1992-95. Publications: Henry Purcell in Japan, 1985; Unfinished Painting, 1989; The Moon Comes

Home, 1989; Sunday Skaters: Poems, 1994; A Kiss in Space: Poems, 1999. Contributions to: Periodicals. Honours: Discovery Prize, The Nation, 1983; National Endowment for the Arts Fellowship, 1983-84; Lamont Prize in Poetry, 1988; Guggenheim Fellowship, 1993; National Book Critics Circle Award Nomination, 1994; Amy Lowell Scholarship, 1995. Memberships: International PEN; Poetry Society of America, vice president, 1995-. Address: c/o Alfred A Knopf Inc, 201 East 50th Street, New York, NY 10022, USA.

SALTZMAN Arthur Michael, b. 10 Aug 1953, Chicago, Illinois, USA. Professor; Writer. 1 daughter. Education: AB, 1971, AM, 1976, PhD, 1979, University of Illinois. Appointments: Teaching Fellow, University of Illinois, 1975-80; Assistant Professor, 1981-86, Associate Professor, 1986-92, Professor, 1992-, Missouri Southern State College. Publications: The Fiction of William Gass: The Consolation of Language, 1986; Understanding Raymond Carver, 1988; Designs of Darkness in Contemporary American Fiction, 1990; The Novel in the Balance, 1993; Understanding Nicholson Baker, 1999; This Mad "Instead": Governing Metaphors in Contemporary American Fiction, forthcoming. Contributions to: Professional Journals and general periodicals. Honours: Several awards. Memberships: Modern Language Association; PEN; Phi Beta Kappa. Address: 2301 West 29th Street, Joplin, MO 64804, USA.

SALVADOR Nélida, b. 16 Dec 1925, San Rafael, Mendoza, Argentina. Professor; Poet; Essayist; Literary Critic. Education: Professor of Literature and Spanish Language, 1952; MA, Literature, 1955, University of Buenos Aires, Argentina. Appointments: Professor, Literature Introduction, 1957-85; Spanish Literature, 1975; Reading and Comments of Texts, 1962-66; Literary Theory, 1985-96; Postgraduate Seminars on Literary Theory, University of Buenos Aires, Argentina, 1988-96. Publications: Poetry: Tránsito ciego, 1958; Las fábulas insomnes, 1962; Canto de extramuros, 1963; Al acecho, 1966; Las apariencias, 1972; Tomar distancia, 1980; Los dispersos olvidos, 1989; Otras palabras, 1991; Critical Studies: Revistas Literarias Argentinas (1893-1940), 1961; Revistas argentinas de vanguardia (1920-1930), 1962; La nueva poesía argentina, 1969; Macedonio Fernández, precursor de la antinovela, 1986; Revistas literarias argentinas (1960-1990), 1997. Contributions to: Magazines: Boletín de la Academia Argentina de Letras, Filología, Ficción, Sur (Argentina); Revista Iberoamericana (USA); Journals: La Nación, La Prensa, Clarín (Argentina); Honour: Essay: National Award, 1990; CONICET, Grant, 1990-92; Award from UBA, 1993-1997; Poetry: Honorary Award, Argentine Society of Writers, 1962; Municipal Award, 1981; National Award, 1983. Membership: Instituto Internacional de Literatura Iberoamericana (USA); Instituto Literario y Cultural Hispánico (USA); PEN Club Internacional; SADE. Address: J A Cabrera 4299 (PB "A") - CP 1414 Buenos Aires, Argentina.

SAMBROOK Arthur (James), b. 5 Sept 1931, Nuneaton, Warwickshire, England. Professor of English Emeritus; Writer. m. Patience Ann Crawford, 25 Mar 1961, 4 sons. Education: BA, 1955, MA, 1959, Worcester College, Oxford; PhD, University of Nottingham, 1957. Appointments: Lecturer, St David's College, Lampeter, Wales, 1957-64; Lecturer, 1964-71, Senior Lecturer, 1971-75, Reader, 1975-81, Professor of English, 1981-92, Emeritus Professor, 1992-, University of Southampton. Publications: A Poet Hidden: The Life of R W Dixon, 1962; The Scribleriad, etc (editor), 1967; William Cobbett, 1973; James Thomson: The Seasons (editor), 1981; English Pastoral Poetry, 1983; The Eighteenth Century: The Intellectual and Cultural Context of English Literature 1700-1789, 1986, 2nd edition, 1993; Liberty, the Castle of Indolence and Other Poems, 1986; James Thomson 1700-1748: A Life: Biographical, Critical, 1992; William Cowper: The Task and Other Poems (editor), 1994; With the Rank and Pay of a Sapper, 1998. Contributions to: Reference books, professional journals and general periodicals. Address: 36 Burlesdon Road, Hedge End, Southampton SO30 0BX, England.

SAMPSON Anthony Terrell Seward, b. 3 Aug 1926, Durham, England. Writer. m. 31 May 1965, 1 son, 1 daughter. Education: Christ Church, University of Oxford, 1947-50. Appointments: Editor, Drum Magazine, South Africa, 1951-55; Staff, Observer, 1955-66; Columnist, Newsweek International, 1977-; Editorial Advisor, Brandt Commission, 1978-80. Publications: Drum, 1956; Anatomy of Britain, 1962; New Europeans, 1968; The Sovereign State of ITT, 1973; The Seven Sisters, 1975; The Arms Bazaar, 1977; The Money Lenders, 1981; Black and Gold, 1987; The Midas Touch, 1989; The Essential Anatomy of Britain: New Patterns of Power in the Nineties, 1992; Company Man: The Rise and Fall of Corporation Life, 1995; The Scholar Gypsy, 1997. Contributions to: Numerous journals. Honour: Prix International de la Presse, Nice, 1976. Membership: Society of Authors, chairman, 1992-94. Address: 27 Ladbroke Grove, London W11 3AY, England.

SAMPSON Geoffrey (Richard), b. 27 July 1944, Broxbourne, Hertfordshire, England. University Lecturer; Writer. Education: MA, PhD, St John's College, Cambridge; Yale University; University of Oxford. Appointments: Fellow, Queen's College, Oxford, 1969-72; Lecturer, London School of Economics, 1972-74; Lecturer, 1974-76, Reader, 1976-84, University of Lancaster; Professor of Linguistics, University of Leeds, 1985-90; Director, Centre for Advanced Software Applications, University of Sussex, 1991-. Publications: The Form of Language, 1975; Liberty and Language, 1979; Making Sense, School of Linguistics, 1980; An End to Allegiance, 1984; Writing Systems, 1985; The Computational Analysis of English (with Garside and Leech), 1987; English for the Computer, 1995; Evolutionary Language Understanding, 1996; Educating Eve, 1997. Contributions to: Newspapers and magazines. Membership: MBCS. Address: School of Cognitive and Computing Sciences, University of Sussex, Falmer, Brighton BN1 9QH, England.

SAMPSON Ronald Victor, b. 12 Nov 1918, St Helen's, Lancashire, England. Writer. m. 9 Jan 1943, 2 daughters. Education: Keble College, Oxford, 1936-39, 1946-47, 1948-51; Nuffield College, Oxford; MA, 1947, DPhil, 1951. Publications: Progress in the Age of Reason, 1957; Equality and Power, 1965; Tolstoy: The Discovery of Peace, 1973. Contributions to: Books, professional journals and periodicals. Membership: English PEN. Address: Beechcroft, Hinton Charterhouse, Bath, Avon, England.

SAMS Eric, b. 3 May 1926, London, England. Retired Civil Servant; Writer. m. Enid Tidmarsh, 30 June 1952, 2 sons. Education: BA, 1st Class Honours, Corpus Christi College, Cambridge, 1950; PhD, 1972. Appointments: Civil Servant, 1950-78; Visiting Professor, McMaster University, Hamilton, Ontario, Canada, 1976-77. Publications: The Songs of Hugo Wolf, 1961, 3rd edition, 1993; The Songs of Robert Schumann, 1969, 3rd edition, 1993; Brahms Songs, 1971; Shakespeare's Edmund Ironside, 1985; The Real Shakespeare, 1995, (paperback, 1996); Shakespeare's Edward III, 1996. Contributions to: Reference works and journals. Honour: Leverhulme Grant, 1984. Membership: Guildhall School of Music and Drama, honorary member, 1983-. Address: 32 Arundel Avenue, Sanderstead, Surrey CR2 8BB, England.

SAMUEL John Richard, b. 28 July 1928, Hove, England. Journalist; Writer. m. Mary Trevenen Mewton, 25 Oct 1958, 1 son, 1 daughter. Appointments: Reporter, Brighton Argus, 1944-54; Sub Editor, Reuters, 1954-55; Sports Sub Editor, Rugby Union Correspondent, Daily Herald, 1955-60; Deputy Sports Editor, Sports Editor, The Observer, 1960-62; Sports Editor, The Guardian, 1967-86; Assistant Editor, 1986-93, Motoring Editor, 1990-96. Publications: Henry Cooper, 1973; Oxford Companion Sports and Games: History of Skiing, 1974; Ski-Wise, 1975; Love of Skiing, 1978; The Olympic Games, 1980; BBC Ski Sunday Annuals, 1981-85; British Ski Federation Guide to Better Skiing, 1986; Bedside Skiing, 1987; The Lillywhites Ski Year Book, 1988. Contributions to: Times; Independent on Sunday; Radio Times; Departures; Expressions; Debretts; US Ski Racing; US Ski; US Mountain Living; Diesel Car; Saga Magazine. Honours include: Rover Industry Award; AA Safety Award. Address: Stable Barrington, Portsmouth Wood Drive, Lindfield, West Sussex RH16 2DW, England.

SAMUELS Warren Joseph, b. 14 Sept 1933, New York, New York, USA. Professor of Economics; Writer. Education: BBA, University of Miami at Coral Gables, 1954; MS, 1955, PhD, 1957, University of Wisconsin. Appointments: Assistant Professor, University of Missouri, 1957-58, Georgia State College, Atlanta, 1958-59; Assistant Professor, 1959-62, Associate Professor of Economics, 1962-68, University of Miami at Coral Gables; Professor of Economics, Michigan State University, 1968-; Editor, Journal of Economic Issues, 1971-81. Publications: The Classical Theory of Economic Policy, 1966; A Critique of Administrative Regulation of Public Utilities (editor with H M Trebing), 1972; Pareto on Policy, 1974; The Economy as a System of Power (editor), 2 volumes, 1979; Taxing and Spending Policy (co-editor), 1980; The Methodology of Economic Thought (editor), 1980; Research in the History of Economic Thought and Methodology (editor), 1983. Contributions to: Professional journals. Memberships: Association for Social Economics, president, 1988; Economics Society of Michigan, president, 1972-73; History of Economics Society, president, 1981-82. Address: 4397 Cherrywood Drive, Okemos, MI 48864, USA.

SAMUELSON Robert J(acob), b. 23 Dec 1945, New York, New York, USA. Journalist. m. Judith Herr, 10 July 1983, 2 sons, 1 daughter. Education: BA, Government, Harvard University, 1967. Appointments: Reporter, 1969-73, Columnist, 1977-, Washington Post; Economics Correspondent and Columnist, 1976-84; National Journal; Columnist, Newsweek, 1984-. Publications: The Good Life and Its Discontents: The American Dream in the Age of Entitlement, 1945-1995, 1996. Honours: National Magazine Award, 1981; Gerald Loeb Awards, 1983, 1986, 1993; National Headliner Awards, 1987, 1992, 1993, 1996; John Hancock Award, 1993; Clarion Award, 1994. Address: c/o Newsweek, 1750 Pennsylvania Avenue NW, Washington, DC 20006, USA.

SANBORN Margaret, b. 7 Dec 1915, Alameda, California, USA. Writer. Education: San Francisco Conservatory of Music, 1924-28; College of Marin, California, 1932-34; California School of Fine Arts, 1934-36. Publications: Robert E Lee: A Portrait, 1807-1861, 1966, revised edition, 1995; Robert E Lee: The Complete Man 1861-1870, 1967, revised edition, 1995; The American: River of El Dorado, 1974; The Grand Tetons, 1978; Yosemite: Its Discovery, Its Wonders and Its People, 1981; Mark Twain: The Bachelor Years, 1990. Address: 527 Northern Avenue, Mill Valley, CA 94941, USA.

SANCHEZ Sonia, b. 9 Sept 1934, Birmingham, Alabama, USA. Professor of English; Poet; Dramatist; Writer. m. Etheridge Knight, div, 2 sons, 1 daughter. Education: BA, Hunter College, 1955; New York University, 1959-60; PhD, Wilberforce University, 1972. Appointments: Instructor, San Francisco State College, 1967-69; Lecturer, University of Pittsburgh, 1969-70, Rutgers University, 1970-71, Manhattan Community College, 1971-73, City University of New York, 1972; Associate Professor, Amherst College, 1972-73, University of Pennsylvania, 1976-77; Associate Professor, 1977-79, Professor of English, 1979- Temple University. Publications: Poetry: Homecoming, 1969; WE a BaddDDD People, 1970; Liberation Poem, 1970; It's a New Day: Poems for Young Brothas and Sistuhs, 1971; Ima Talken bout the Nation of Islam, 1971; Love Poems, 1973; A Blues Book for Blue Black Magical Women, 1974; I've Been a Woman: New and Selected Poems, 1978, revised edition, 1985; Homegirls and Handgrenades, 1984; Under a Soprano Sky, 1987; Wounded in the House of a Friend, 1995. Plays: The Bronx is Next, 1968; Sister Son/ji, 1969; Dirty Hearts '72, 1973; Uh, Uh: But How Do it Free Us?, 1974. Stories: A Sound Investment, 1980. Other: Crisis in Culture, 1983.

Editor: Three Hundred Sixty Degrees of Blackness Comin' at You, 1972; We Be Word Sorcerers: 25 Stories by Black Americans, 1973. Honours: PEN Award, 1969; American Academy of Arts and Letters Award, 1970; National Endowment for the Arts Award, 1978; Smith College Tribute to Black Women Award, 1982; Lucretia Mott Award, 1984; Before Columbus Foundation Award, 1985; PEN Fellow, 1993. Address: c/o Department of English, Temple University, Philadelphia, PA 19041, USA.

SANDEN Einar, b. 8 Sept 1932, Tallinn, Estonia. Writer; Historian. m. Dr Elizabeth Gorell, 6 Sept 1994. Education: MA, 1983, PhD, 1984, USA. Appointments: Managing Director, Owner, Boreas Publishing House, 1975; Councillor, Estonian Government in Exile, 1975-90. Publications: KGB Calling Eve, 1978; The Painter From Naissaar, 1985; Ur Eldinum Til Islands, 1988; An Estonian Saga, 1995. Contributions to: Editor of various Estonian periodicals. Honours: Distinguished Freedom Writer, UPLI, Manila, the Philippines, 1968; Cultural Award, Fraternity Sakala, Toronto, 1984. Memberships: PEN Centre for Writers in Exile, 1954-80; Royal Society of Literature, London, 1960; Association of Estonian Writers Abroad, 1970; English PEN, 1976; Estonian National Council, 1959; Association for the Advancement of Baltic Studies, USA, 1980; Estonian Academic Association of War History, Tallinn, 1988. Address: Boreas House, 63 Ninian Road, Cardiff CF2 5EL, Wales.

SANDERS (James) Ed(ward), b. 17 Aug 1939, Kansas City, Missouri, USA. Poet; Writer; Singer; Lecturer. m. Miriam Kittell, 5 Oct 1961, 1 child. Education: BA, New York University, 1964. Appointments: Editor-Publisher, Fuck You/A Magazine of the Arts, 1962-65; Founder-Lead Singer, The Fugs, satiric folk-rock-theatre group, 1964-69; Owner, Peace Eye Bookstore, New York City, 1964-70; Visiting Professor of Language and Literature, Bard College, Annadale-on-Hudson, New York, 1979, 1983; Lectures, readings, performances throughout the US and Europe. Publications: Poetry: Poem from Jail, 1963; A Valorium Edition of the Entire Extant Works of Thales!, 1964; King Lord/Queen Freak, 1964; The Toe Queen Poems, 1964; The Fugs' Song Book (with Ken Weaver and Betsy Klein), 1965; Peace Eye, 1965; Egyptian Hieroglyphics, 1973; 20,000 A.D., 1976; The Cutting Prow, 1981; Hymn to Maple Syrup and Other Poems, 1985; Poems for Robin, 1987; Thirsting for Peace in a Raging Century: Selected Poems 1961-1985, 1987; Hymn to the Rebel Cafe: Poems 1987-1991, 1993; Chekov: A Biography in Verse, 1995. Editor: Poems for Marilyn, 1962. Compiler and Contributor: Bugger: An Anthology of Buttockry, 1964; Despair: poems to come down by, 1964; Fiction: Shards of God: A Novel of the Yippies, 1970; Tales of Beatnik Glory (short stories), 2 volumes, 1975, 1990; Fame and Love in New York, 1980. Non-Fiction: The Family: The Story of Charles Manson's Dune Buggy Attack Battalion, 1971; Vote! (with Abbie Hoffman and Jerry Rubin), 1972; Investigative Poetry, 1976; The Z-D Generation, 1981. Other: Musicals: Recordings with The Fugs; Solo recordings. Honours: Frank O'Hara Prize, Modern Poetry Association, 1967; National Endowment for the Arts Awards, 1966, 1970, Fellowship, 1987-88; Guggenheim Fellowship, 1983-84; American Book Award, 1988. Memberships: New York Foundation for the Arts; PEN. Address: PO Box 729, Woodstock, NY 12498, USA.

SANDERS Scott Russell, b. 26 Oct 1945, Memphis, Tennessee, USA. Distinguished Professor of English; Author. m. Ruth Ann McClure, 27 Aug 1967, 1 son, 1 daughter. Education: BA, Brown University, 1967; PhD, Cambridge University, 1971. Appointments: Literary Editor, 1969-70, Contributing Editor, 1970-71, Cambridge Reviews; Assistant Professor of English, 1996-, Indiana University; Fiction Editor, Minnesota Review, 1976-80; Fiction Columnist, Chicago Sun-Times, 1977-84; Contributing Editor, North American Review, 1982-. Publications: Fiction: Wilderness Plots: Tales About the Settlement of the American Land, 1983; Fetching the Dead (stories), 1984; Wonders Hidden: Audubon's Early Years (novella), 1984; Terrarium (novel), 1985; Hear the Wind Blow (stories), 1985; Bad Man Ballad (novel), 1986; The Engineer of Beasts (novel), 1988; The Invisible Country (novel), 1989. Other: D H Lawrence: The World of the Major Novels, 1974; Stone Country, 1985, revised edition as In Limestone Country, 1991; Audubon Reader: The Best Writings of John James Audubon, 1986; The Paradise of Bombs (essays), 1987; Secrets of the Universe (essays), 1991; Staying Put: Making a Home in a Restless World, 1993; Writing from the Center (essays), 1995; Hunting for Hope, 1998. Contributions to: Anthologies, journals, and magazines. Honours: Woodrow Wilson Fellowship, 1967-68; National Endowment for the Arts Fellowship, 1983-84; Indiana Arts Commission Master Fellowships, 1984, 1990-91; Lilly Endowment Open Fellowship, 1986-87; Associated Writing Programs Award for Non-Fiction, 1987; PEN Syndicated Fiction Award, 1988; Kenyon Review Award for Literary Excellence, 1991; Guggenheim Fellowship, 1992-93; Ohioana Book Award in Non-Fiction, 1994; Lannan Literary Award in Non-Fiction, 1995. Address: 1113 East Wylie Street, Bloomington, IN 47401, USA.

SANDERSON Anne Harvey, b. 13 Jan 1944, Brighton, England. University Lecturer (semi-retired). m. Michael Sanderson, 25 Sept 1976. Education: BA, 1966, MA, 1970, MLitt, 1978, St Anne's College, Oxford, England. Appointments: English Lectrice, Ecole Normale Supérieure De Jeunes Filles, University of Paris, 1969-71; Lecturer in European Literature, University of East Anglia, 1972-98. Publications: Poetry in small press anthologies. Contributions to: Poems in Poetry Now; Peace & Freedom; Purple Patch; Triumph Herald; Reflections; Tree Spirit; Articles in Studies on Voltaire & The (18th); Jeunesse Deracine; Norwich Papers. Honours: Prix Racine, 1969; 3rd Prize, Hilton House National Open Poetry Awards for Collections, 1998. Memberships: Norwich Writers' Circle, Open Poetry Competition Secretary, 1998-; Norwich Poetry Group. Address: Cranleigh, 20, The Street, Poringland, Norwich NR14 7JT, England.

SANDERSON John Michael, b. 23 Jan 1939, Glasgow, Scotland. University Reader. Education: MA, 1963, PhD, 1966, Queens' College, Cambridge, 1957-63. Appointments: Reader, University of East Anglia; General Editor, Cambridge University Press Economic History Society Studies in Economic and Social History Series, 1992-98; Council, Economic History Society, 1994. Publications: The Universities and British Industry, 1850-1970, 1972; The Universities in the 19th Century, 1975 (Japanese edition, 1999); Education, Economic Change and Society in England, 1780-1870, 1983, 2nd edition, 1992, Japanese edition, 1993; From Irving to Olivier, A Social History of the Acting Profession in England, 1880-1983, 1984; Educational Opportunity and Social Change in England, 1900-1980s, 1987; The Missing Stratum, Technical School Education in England, 1900-1990s, 1994; Education and Economic Decline, 1870-1990's, 1999. Contributions to: Economic History Review; Journal of Contemporary History; Contemporary Record; Business History; Northern History; Past and Present. Membership: Economic History Society. Address: School of History, University of East Anglia, Norwich NR4 7TJ, England.

SANDERSON Stewart F(orson), b. 23 Nov 1924, Blantyre, Malawi. Folklorist; Writer. Education: MA, University of Edinburgh. Appointments: Secretary-Archivist, 1952-58, Senior Research Fellow, Editor, Scottish Studies, 1957-60, University of Edinburgh; Lecturer in Folk Life Studies and Director, Folk Life Survey, 1960-64, Director, Institute of Dialect and Folk Life Studies, 1964-83, Chairman, School of English, 1980-83, Harold Orton Fellow, 1983-88, University of Leeds. Publications: Hemingway, 1961, 2nd edition, 1970; The City of Edinburgh (with others), 1963; Studies in Folk Life (with others), 1969; The Secret Common-Wealth and A Short Treatise of Charms and Spells (editor), 1976; To Illustrate the Monuments (with others), 1976; The Linguistic Atlas of England (editor with H Orton and J Widdowson), 1978; Ernest Hemingway: For Whom the Bell Tolls, 1980. Contributions to: Journals. Memberships: British Institute of Recorded Sound; Folklore Society, president, 1971-73; British Library National Sound Archive, advisory committee, 1983-97; Society of Folk Life Studies; Arvon at Moniack Mhor Management Committee, chair, 1992-93. Address: Primsidemill Farm House, Kelso, Roxburghshire TD5 8PR, Scotland.

SANDFORD Jeremy, b. England. Playwright; Author; Journalist; Musician; Performer. m. (1) Nell Dunn, 1956, div 1986, 3 sons, (2) Philippa Finnis, 1988. Education: Eton; Oxford. Appointments: Director, Hatfield Court New Age Conference Centre; Editor, Romano Drom (Gypsy Newspaper), 1970-73. Publications: Synthetic Fun, 1967; Cathy Come Home, 1967; Whelks and Chromium, 1968; Edna the Inebriate Woman, 1971; Down and Out in Britain, 1971; In Search of the Magic Mushroom, 1972; Gypsies, 1973; Tomorrow's People, 1974; Prostitutes, 1975; Smiling David, 1975; Figures and Landscapes: The Art of Lettice Sandford, 1991; Hey Days in Hay, 1992; Songs from the Roadside, 100 Years of Gypsy Music in the West Midlands, 1995; Mary Carbery's West Cork Journal (editor), 1999; Rockering to the Gorjios, 1999. Contributions to: Guardian; Sunday Times; Observer. Honours: Italia Prize, 1967; BECTU Best Television Play, 1967; Writers Guild, Best Television Plays, 1967, 1971. Memberships: Writers Guild; BECTU; Gypsy Council, executive member. Address: Hatfield Court, Near Leominster HR6 0SD, England.

SANDLER Roberta, b. 3 May 1943, New York City, New York, USA. Author; Lecturer; Freelance Writer. m. Martin Sandler, 31 Mar 1964, 3 daughters. Education: University of Miami. Appointments: Contributing Travel Writer, 50-Plus Lifestyles newspaper, 1996-. Publications: Senior Pursuits, Making the Golden Years Worth the Wait, 1993; Guide to Florida Historical Walking Tours, 1996. Contributions to: New York Times; Miami Herald; San Diego Union Tribune; Asbury Park Press; Good Housekeeping; Ladies' Home Journal; Family Circle; Others. Honours: Mature Media Award, 1994; Florida Press Women, 1994-96; Golden Quill Award, Florida Historical Society, 1997. Memberships: Society of American Travel Writers; National Federation of Press Women; Florida Press Women; Florida Freelance Writers Association. Address: 1773 Harborside Circle, Wellington, FL 33414, USA.

SANDOR András Jószef, b. 14 Nov 1932, Budapest, Hungary. Lyric Poet; Translator; Architect. m. Eva Sonja Schneebeli, 15 July 1964, 1 daughter. Education: Diploma, Architect ETH, Eidg Technische Hochschule, Zürich. Appointments: Different offices of Architecture of Zürich, 1960-88; Baudepartement of Stadt Zürich, Amt für Hochbauten, 1988-97. Publications: Wolf(e) ist noch da, Lyric Poetry, 1990; Translations: Survey of Hungarian Lyric, 1990; Spaziergang mit Hölderlin, Lyric Poetry of Agnes Rapai, 1995. Contributions to: Orte; Swiss Lyrical Magazine; Neue Zürcher Zeitung; Tages - Anzeiger; Beobachter; Zytglogge Zytig, Bern, 1976-98. Honours: Short-Story Award, Wien, 1986; Translation Award, Budapest, 1997. Membership: Schweiz Schriftstellerinnen u. Schriftsteller. Address: Drahtzugstr 21, CH-8008, Zürich, Switzerland.

SANDOZ (George) Ellis (Jr), b. 10 Feb 1931, New Orleans, Louisiana, USA. Moyse Distinguished Professor of Political Science; Writer. m. Therese Alverne Hubley, 31 May 1957, 2 sons, 2 daughters. Education: BA, 1951, MA, 1953, Louisiana State University; University of North Carolina, 1950; Georgetown University, 1952-53; University of Heidelberg, 1956-58; PhD, University of Munich, 1965. Appointments: Instructor to Professor, Louisiana Polytechnic Institute, 1959-68; Professor and Head, Department of Political Science, East Texas State University, 1968-78; Professor of Political Science, 1978-, Director, Eric Voegelin Institute for American Renaissance Studies, 1987-, Louisiana State University. Publications: Political Apocalypse: A Study of Dostoevsky's Grand Inquisitor, 1971; Conceived in Liberty: American Individual Rights Today, 1978; A Tide of Discontent: The 1980 Elections and Their Meaning, editor, 1981; The Voegelianian Revolution: A Biographical Introduction, 1981; Eric Voegelin's Thought: A Critical Appraisal (editor), 1982; Election '84: Landslade

Without a Mandate? (editor with Cecil V Crabb Jr), 1985; A Government of Laws: Political Theory, Religion and the American Founding, 1990; Political Sermons of the American Founding Era, 1730-1805 (editor), 1991, index, 1996; Eric Voegelin's Significance for the Modern Mind (editor), 1991; The Roots of Liberty: Magna Carta, Ancient Constitution, and the Anglo-American Tradition of Rule of Law (editor), 1993; The Political and Constitutional Writings of Sir John Fortescue (editor), 1997; Politics of Truth and Other Untimely Essays: The Crisis of Civic Consciousness, 1999. Contributions to: The Collected Works of Eric Voegelin (principal editor, 1986-), scholarly books and professional journals. Honours: Germanistic Society of America Fellow, 1964-65; Fulbright Scholar, 1964-65; Henry E Huntington Library Fellow, 1986-87; Fulbright 40th Anniversary Distinguished American Scholar, Italy, 1987; Distinguished Research Master and University Gold Medal, Louisiana State University, 1993; Medal and Rector's Certificate, 1994, Honorary PhD, 1995, Palacky University, Olomouc, Czech Republic. Memberships: American Historical Association; American Political Science Association; Federalist Society; Organization of American Historians; Philadelphia Society; Southern Political Science Association; Southwestern Political and Social Science Associations; Eric Voegelin Society, founder-secretary 1985-. Address: c/o Eric Voegelin Institute for American Renaissance Studies, Louisiana State University, 240 Stubbs Hall, Baton Rouge, LA 70803, USA.

SANDS Martin. See: **BURKE John Frederick.**

SANDY Stephen, b. 2 Aug 1934, Minneapolis, Minnesota, USA. Professor; Writer; Poet. m. Virginia Scoville, 1 son, 1 daughter. Education: BA, Yale University, 1955; MA, 1959, PhD, 1963, Harvard University. Appointments: Lecturer in American Literature, University of Tokyo, 1967-68; Visiting Professor, Brown University, 1968-69, Harvard University, 1986-88; Faculty, Bennington College, Vermont, 1969-; Director, Poetry Workshop, Chautauqua Institution, New York, 1975, 1977; McGee Visiting Distinguished Professor of Writing, Davidson College, North Carolina, 1994. Publications: Stresses in the Peaceable Kingdom, 1967; Roofs, 1971; Riding to Greylock, 1983; To a Mantis, 1987; Man in the Open Air, 1988; The Epoch, 1990; Thanksgiving Over the Water, 1992; A Cloak for Hercules (translation of Seneca's Hercules Oetaeus), 1995; Vale of Academe: A Prose Poem for Bernard Malamud, 1996; The Thread: New and Selected Poems, 1998; Aeschylus's Seven Against Thebes: Verse Translation (translator), 1998; Black Box: Poems, 1999. Contributions to: Journals and magazines. Honours: Yaddo Residencies, 1976, 1993, 1997, 1998; MacDowell Colony Fellowships, 1983, 1993; National Endowment for the Arts Poet-in-Residence, Poetry Center, Philadelphia, 1985; Ingram Merrill Foundation Fellowship, 1985; Vermont College on the Arts Fellowship, 1988; National Endowment for the Arts Fellowship, 1988. Membership: Academy of American Poets. Address: Box 524, North Bennington, VT 05257, USA.

SANDYS Elspeth Somerville, b. 18 Mar 1940, Timaru, New Zealand. Writer. 1 son, 1 daughter. Education: MA, University of Auckland, New Zealand; LTCL (Music); FTCL (Speech, Drama). Appointments: Frank Sargeson Fellow, Auckland, 1992; Burns Fellow, Otago University, 1995; Writer-in-Residence, Waikato University, 1998. Publications: Catch a Falling Star, 1978; The Broken Tree, 1981; Love and War, 1982; Finding Out, 1991; Best Friends (short stories), 1993; River Lines, 1995; Riding to Jerusalem, 1996; Enemy Territory, 1997. Other: Radio plays. Contribution to: Magazines. Honours: Frank Sargeson Fellow, Auckland, 1992; Burns Fellow, Otago University, 1995; Finalist, Orange Prize, 1996. Memberships: Writers Guild; Society of Authors. Address: 7/7 Rossgrove Terrace, Mt Albert, Auckland, New Zealand.

SANER Reg(inald Anthony), b. 30 Dec 1931, Jacksonville, Illinois, USA. Poet; Writer; Professor. m. Anne Costigan, 16 Aug 1958, 2 sons. Education: BA, St Norbert College, Wisconsin, 1950; MA, 1954, PhD, 1962, University of Illinois at Urbana; Università per Stranieri, Perugia, 1960-61; Università di Firenze, Florence, 1960-61. Appointments: Assistant Instructor, 1956-60, Instructor in English, 1961-62, University of Illinois at Urbana; Assistant Professor, 1962-67, Associate Professor, 1967-72, Professor of English, 1972-, University of Colorado at Boulder. Publications: Poetry: Climbing into the Roots, 1976; So This is the Map, 1981; Essay on Air, 1984; Red Letters, 1989. Non-Fiction: The Four-Cornered Falcon: Essays on the Interior West and the Natural Scene, 1993; Reaching Keet Seel: Ruin's Echo and the Anasazi, 1998. Contributions to: Poems and essays in numerous anthologies and other publications. Honours: Fulbright Scholar to Florence, Italy, 1960-61; Borestone Mountain Poetry Awards, 1971, 1973; Walt Whitman Award, 1975; National Endowment for the Arts Creative Writing Fellowship, 1976; Pushcart Prize II, 1977-78; Colorado Governor's Award for Excellence in the Arts, 1983; Quarterly Review of Literature Award, 1989; Rockefeller Foundation Resident Scholar, Bellagio, Italy, 1990; Hazel Barnes Award, University of Colorado, 1993; Wallace Stegner Award, Centre of the American West, 1997. Memberships: Dante Society; PEN; Renaissance Society; Shakespeare Association. Address: 1925 Vassar, Boulder, CO 80303, USA.

SANTA MARIA. See: **POWELL-SMITH Vincent.**

SANTIMBREANU Mircea, b. 7 Jan 1926. m. Sanda Ivanovici, 13 Feb 1948, 1 daughter. Education: Diploma, Faculty of Philosophy. Publications: Recreatia Mare, 1963; Aducatorului, Multumiri, 1970; Caramele cu Piper, 1972; Eu Eram Zana, 1974; Un Gulliver in Tara Chiticilor, 1977. Honours: Premiul Uniunii Scriitoilor, 1977, 1983. Membership: Uniunea Scriitorilor. Address: Str Hristo Botev 8, Bucharest 70335, Romania.

SANTINI Rosemarie, b. New York, New York, USA. Writer. Education: Hunter College, New York City. Appointments: Senior Editor, True Story Magazine; Lecturer, New School for Social Research. Publications: The Secret Fire, 1978; A Swell Style of Murder, 1986; The Disenchanted Diva, 1988; Blood Sisters, 1990; Private Lies, 1991. Contributions to: New Mystery Magazine; Many anthologies and magazines. Honours: New Mystery Magazine Award, 1997; McCavity Award, 1997. Memberships: Authors Guild; Dramatists Guild; International Association of Crime Writers; Mystery Writers of America; National Academy of Television Arts and Sciences; Novelists Inc; PEN; Poetry Society of America; Poets and Writers; Sisters in Crime; Society of American Journalists and Authors. Address: c/o New School, 66 West 12th Street, New York, 10011, USA.

SANTOS Helen. See: **GRIFFITHS Helen.**

SANTOS Sherod, b. 9 Sept 1948, Greenville, South Carolina, USA. Professor of English; Poet; Writer. m. Lynne Marie McMahon, 1 May 1976, 2 sons. Education: BA, 1971, MA, 1974, San Diego State University; MFA, University of California at Irvine, 1978; PhD, University of Utah, 1982. Appointments: Assistant Professor, California State University, San Bernardino, 1982-83; Contributing Editor, Pushcart Prize: The Best of the Small Presses, 1982-; Poetry Editor, Missouri Review, 1983-90; Assistant Professor, 1983-86, Associate Professor, 1986-92, University of California at Irvine, 1989-90; External Examiner and Poet-in-Residence, Poets' House, Islandmagee, Northern Ireland, summers 1991-; Various poetry readings, lectures, and seminars. Publications: Begin, Distance, 1981; Accidental Weather, 1982; The New Days, 1986; The Southern Reaches, 1989; The Unsheltering Ground, 1990; The City of Women, 1993; The Pilot Star Elegies, 1998. Contributions to: Anthologies, journals, and magazines. Honours: Discovery/The Nation Award, 1978; Pushcart Prizes in Poetry, 1980, and in the Essay, 1994; Oscar Blumenthal Prize, Poetry magazine, 1981; Ingram Merrill Foundation Grant, 1982; Delmore Schwartz Memorial Award, 1983; Robert Frost Poet and Poet-in-Residence, Robert Frost House, Franconia, New Hampshire, 1984; Guggenheim Fellowship, 1984-85; National Endowment for the Arts Grant, 1987; Yaddo Center for the Arts Fellowship, 1987; Chancellor's Award, University of Missouri, 1993; British Arts Council International Travel Grant to Northern Ireland, 1995; National Endowment for the Arts Literature Panel Member, 1995. Memberships: Academy of American Poets; Associated Writing Programs; PEN American Center; Poetry Society of America; Poets and Writers; Robinson Jeffers Society. Address: 1238 Sunset Drive, Columbia, MO 65203, USA.

SAPERSTEIN David, b. 19 Mar 1937, Brooklyn, New York, USA. Author; Screenwriter; Film Director. m. Ellen-Mae Bernard, 1 son, 1 daughter. Education: City College, New York City. Appointments: Assistant Professor of Film, Graduate Film and Television School, New York University, 1992-93; Manhattan Marymount College, 1996-99. Publications: Cocoon, 1985; Fatal Reunion, 1987; Metamorphosis: The Cocoon Story Continues, 1988; Red Devil, 1989; Fune-a-Rama, 1995; Dark Again, 1997. Other: 27 screenplays; Librettist and Lyricist, 3 shows, 70 published songs. Honour: Writers Guild of America Best Story for the Screen Nomination, 1985; New York Times Best Seller, 1985; 2 Academy Awards, 1985; Sweden Book of the Month Club, Selection, 1988; Townsend Harris Medal, City College, 1998. Memberships: Directors Guild of America; Writers Guild of America; National Honour Society BMI. Address: c/o Ebbets Field Productions, PO Box 42, Wykagyl Station, New Rochelle, NY 10804, USA.

SAPIA Yvonne, b. 10 Apr 1946, New York, New York, USA. Professor of English; Poet; Writer. Education: AA, Miami-Dade Community College, 1967; BA, English, Florida Atlantic University, 1970; MA, English, University of Florida, 1976; PhD, English, Florida State University, 1990. Appointments: Reporter and Editor, The Village Post newspaper, Miami, 1971-73; Editorial Assistant, University of Florida, 1974-76; Resident Poet and Professor of English, Lake City Community College, Florida, 1976-. Publications: The Fertile Crescent (poems), 1983; Valentino's Hair (poems), 1987; Valentino's Hair (novel), 1991. Contributions to: Anthologies, reviews, and journals. Honours: 1st Place, Anhinga Press Poetry Chapbook Award, 1983; 3rd Place, Eve of St Agnes Poetry Competition, 1983; National Endowment for the Arts Fellowship, 1986-87; 1st Place, Morse Poetry Prize, 1987; 2nd Prize, Cincinnati Poetry Review Poetry Competition, 1989; 3rd Place, Apalaches Quarterly Long Poem Contest, 1989; 1st Place, Nilon Award for Excellence in Minority Fiction, 1991. Address: 702 South Marsh Street, Lake City, FL 32025, USA.

SAPP (Eva) Jo (Barnhill), b. 4 Feb 1944, San Antonio, Texas, USA. Writer; Editor. m. David Paul Sapp, 1 son, 1 daughter. Education: BA, Honours, English and Creative Writing, 1976, MA, 1982, PhD coursework completed, 1985, University of Missouri. Appointments: Editorial Assistant, 1978-80, Senior Fiction Advisor, 1980-81, Associate Editor, Special Projects, 1981-92, and Fiction, 1986-88, Missouri Review; Editorial Consultant, Cultural Plan of Action, 1987-. Publications: Missouri Review Online (co-editor), 1986-88; The Best of the Missouri Review: Fiction 1978-90 (co-editor), 1991. Contributions to: Anthologies and magazines. Honours: McKinney Prize, 1984; Editor's Book Awards, 1988; Missouri Arts Council Grant, 1988; Elmer Holmes Bobst Award Nominations, 1992. Memberships: Associated Writing Programs; Columbia Commission on the Arts, secretary, 1986-87, vice-chair, 1987-88, chair, 1988-; Poets and Writers. Address: c/o Columbia Commission on the Arts, Columbia, MO 65211, USA.

SARAC Roger. See: **CARAS Roger (Andrew).**

SARAH Robyn (Belkin), b. 6 Oct 1949, New York, New York, USA. Poet; Writer. Education: BA, 1970, MA, 1974, McGill University; Concours Diploma in Clarinet, Conservatoire de Musique du Québec, 1972. Publications: Poetry: Shadowplay, 1978; The Space Between Sleep and Waking, 1981; Three Sestinas, 1984; Anyone Skating On That Middle Ground, 1984; Becoming

Light, 1987; The Touchstone: Poems New and Selected, 1992; Questions About the Stars, 1998. Fiction: A Nice Gazebo (stories), 1992; Promise of Shelter (stories), 1997. Address: c/o Vehicule Press, PO Box 125, Place du Parc Station, Montreal, Quebec H2W 2M9, Canada.

SARAMAGO José, b. 16 Nov 1922, Azinhaga, Portugal. Author; Poet; Dramatist. Education: Principally self-educated. Publications: Fiction: Manual de Pintura e Caligrafia, 1977, English translation as Manual of Painting and Calligraphy, 1994; Objecto Quase (short stories), 1978, English translation as Quasi Object, 1995; Levantado do Chao (Raised from the Ground), 1980; Memorial do Convento, 1982, English translation as Baltasar and Blimunda, 1987; A Jangada de Pedra, 1986, English translation as The Stone Raft, 1994; O Ano da Morte de Ricardo Reis, 1984, English translation as The Year of the Death of Ricardo Reis, 1991; Historia do Cerco de Lisboa (The History of the Siege of Lisbon), 1989; O Evangelho segundo Jesus Cristo, 1991, English translation as The Gospel According to Jesus Christ, 1994; Ensaio Sobre A Cegueira, 1996, English translation as Blindness. Other: Poems, plays, diaries, etc. Contributions to: Various publications. Honours: Several literary awards and prizes, including the Nobel Prize for Literature, 1998. Address: c/o Harcourt Brace & Co, 6277 Sea Harbor Drive, Orlando, FL 32887, USA.

SARANTI Galatia, b. 8 Nov 1920, Greece. Writer. m. Stavros Patsouris, 26 Dec 1948, 2 sons. Education: Law Faculty, University of Athens, 1947. Publications: Novels: Lilacs, 1949; The Book of Johannes and Maria, 1952; Return, 1953; Our Old House, 1959; The Limits, 1966; Cracks, 1979; The Waters of Euripoe, 1989. Stories: Bright Colours, 1962; Remember Vilna, 1972; Helen, 1982; The River, 1992. Contributions to: Nea Hestia; Helliniki Dimioyria; Epoches; Diabazo. Honours: Kostas Ouranis Prize, 1953; State Prizes, 1957, 1974; Academy of Athens Literature Prize, 1979. Memberships: National Society of Greek Writers; PEN Club; Full Member, Athens Academie, Chair of Literature, 1997. Address: Kallidromidy 87-89, 10683 Athens, Greece.

SARCA Corneliu Sebastian, b. 30 June 1946, Bucharest, Romania. Writer; Journalist. m. Gabriela Julieta, 27 Oct 1979, 1 son, 1 daughter. Education: St Sava College, Bucharest, 1960-64; Degree in Universal & Compared Literature, Faculty of Letters, University of Bucharest, 1964-69; Post University Course in Journalism, Bucharest University, Romania, 1980-82. Appointments: Reporter, Romanian Radio Television, 1971-75; Editor, 1975-80, Producer, 1980-90, Romanian Radio Television; Head of Complex Broadcasting Unit, 1990-91; Secretary General, Youth Programming, 1991-92; Deputy Editor in Chief, Youth Programming, Radio Romania, 1992-96; Director, Broadcasting Heritage & Archives, Radio Romania, 1996-. Publications: Traveling Towards My Best, 1993; Shot By Cupid's Arrow, 1996; Love and Goodmanners, 1996; Editor: A History of Romanian Radio, 1998; Hours of Culture, 1998; The Beginning of the End, 1998; Goodnight Children, 1998; Traveling Microphone, 1998; Bibliography of Romanian Radio, 1998; Memories Speaking, 1998; Happy Hour, 1998; Theatre by Radio, 1998; Broadcasts: School for the Elite, 1991; Midnight Caller, 1992; Tell Me About You, 1992-; To the Gates of Paradise, 1992-; Without Prejudice, 1990. Honour: Award, Romanian Union of Radio Producers for Tell Me About You, 1992. Memberships: UNCER; UZP; AZR. Address: c/o Radio Difuziunea Romania, Str Berthelot 60-64, Bucharest, RO 70747, Romania.

SARGENT Lyman Tower, b. 9 Feb 1940, Rehoboth, Massachusetts, USA. Professor of Political Science; Writer. m. (1) Patricia McGinnis, 27 Dec 1961, div, 1 son, (2) Mary T Weiler, 14 Aug 1985, div. Education: BA, International Relations, Macalester College, 1961; MA, American Studies, 1962, PhD, Political Science, 1965, University of Minnesota. Appointments: Faculty, University of Wyoming, 1964-65; Professor of Political Science, University of Missouri-St Louis, 1965-; Visiting Professor, University of Exeter, 1978-79, 1983-84, London School of Economics and Political Science, 1984-85, Stout Research Centre for the Study of New Zealand Society, History and Culture, Victoria University of Wellington, 1995-96; Editor, Utopian Studies, 1988-; University of East Anglia, visiting professor, 1998-99. Publications: Contemporary Political Ideologies: A Comparative Analysis, 1969, 10th edition, 1996, 11th edition, 1999; Techniques of Political Analysis: An Introduction, 1970; New Left Thought: An Introduction, 1972; British and American Utopian Literature 1516-1975: An Annotated Bibliography, 1979, revised edition, 1988; IVR NORTHAM IV Consent: Concept, Capacity, Conditions, Constraints (editor), 1979; Contemporary Political Ideologies: A Reader (editor), 1990; Extremism in America: A Reader, editor, 1995; Political Thought in the United States: A Documentary History, editor, 1997; New Zealand Utopian Literature: An Annotated Bibliography, 1997. Contributions to: Professional Journals. Address: c/o Department of Political Science, University of Missouri-St Louis, 8001 Natural Bridge Road, St Louis, MO 63121, USA.

SARGESSON Jenny. See: **DAWSON Jennifer.**

SARKAR Anil Kumar, b. 1 Aug 1912, Ranchi, India. Professor Emeritus. m. Aruna Sarkar, 1 Nov 1941 dec, 1 son, 3 daughters. Education: MA, 1st Class, 1935, PhD, 1946, DLitt, 1960, Patna University. Appointments: Professor, Rajendra College, 1940-44; Senior Lecturer, University of Ceylon, Colombo and Perdeniya, 1944-64; Visiting Professor, University of New Mexico, Albuquerque, 1964-65; Full Professor of Philosophy and West-East Philosophy, 1965-82, California State University, Hayward, USA; Research Director, Professor of Asian Studies, 1968-80, Professor Emeritus, 1980-, California Institute of Integral Studies, San Francisco. Publications: An Outline of Whitehead's Philosophy, 1940; Changing Phases of Buddhist Thought, 1968, 4th edition, 1996; Whitehead's Four Principles From West-East Perspectives, 1974, 2nd edition, enlarged, 1994; Dynamic Facets of Indian Thought, Vol 1, 1980, Vols 2-4, 1987-88; Experience in Change and Prospect: Pathways from War to Peace, 1989; Sri Aurobindo's Vision of the Super Mind - Its Indian and Non-Indian Interpreters, 1989; Buddhism and Whitehead's Process Philosopy, 1990; Zero: Its Role and Prospects in Indian Thought and its Impact on Post-Einsteinian Astrophysics, 1992; The Mysteries of Vajrayana Buddhism: From Atisha to Dalai Lama, 1993; Triadic Avenues of India's Cultural Prospects: Philosophy, Physics and Politics, 1995; Shaping of Euro-Indian Philosophy, 1995. Contributions to: Indian, US and other journals. Address: B/B/12/15-7 Kalyani, Df Nadia, West Bengal, India.

SARKAR Subhas, b. 1 Oct 1934, Mymensingh, India. Professor of English; Freelance Journalist. m. 12 Dec 1964, 1 son, 1 daughter. Education: Matriculation, 1948; BA Hons, English, Cotton College, Gauhati University, 1952; MA, English Literature, Calcutta University, 1954; PhD, Calcutta University, 1970. Appointments: Lecturer in English, Surendranath College, Calcutta, 1955; Lecturer, B E College, Shibpur, 1957; Lecturer, Rabindra Bharati University, Calcutta, 1970; Reader in English, Rabindra Bharati University, Calcutta, 1983; Professor of English, RBU, Calcutta, 1990; Head, Department of English, RBU, Calcutta, 1991. Publications: Raater Mayur, book of poems in Bengali, 1962; T S Eliot The Dramatist, book of English literary criticism, 1972; Literary Essays, Literary Criticism, 1977; Eliot and Yeats (literary criticism), 1987. Contributions to: Srinivasa Iyyengar's Indian Writing in English; Education in India, 1978; Kashmir, co-author, with Francis Brunel, 1979; The Chorus in Eliot's Plays and Other Essays, 1994; Alor Sandhane (book of poems in Bengali), 1994. Honours: Winner, Shankar's Weekly International Essay Prize, 1950. Address: The Retreat, 110/19 Kumud Ghosal Road, Ariadaha, Calcutta 700057, India.

SARNA Jonathan D(aniel), b. 10 Jan 1955, Philadelphia, Pennsylvania, USA. Professor of Jewish American History; Writer. m. Ruth Langer, 8 June 1986, 1 son, 1 daughter. Education: BHL, Honours, Hebrew College, Boston, 1974; BA, summa cum laude, Highest Honours, Judaic Studies and History, 1975, MA, Judaic Studies, 1975, Brandeis University; MA, 1976, MPhil, History, 1978, PhD, History, 1979, Yale University. Appointment: Joseph H and Belle R Braun Professor of American Jewish History, Brandeis University. Publications: Jews in New Haven (editor), 1978; Mordecai Manuel Noah: Jacksonian Politician and American Jewish Communal Leader, 1979; Jacksonian Jew: The Two Worlds of Mordecai Noah, 1981; Jews and the Founding of the Republic (co-editor), 1985; The American Jewish Experience: A Reader (editor), 1986; American Synagogue History: A Bibliography and State-of-the-Field Survey (with Alexandra S Korros), 1988; JPS: The Americanization of Jewish Culture: A History of the Jewish Publication Society 1888-1988, 1989; The Jews of Cincinnati (with Nancy H Klein), 1989; Ethnic Diversity and Civic Identity: Patterns of Conflict and Cohesion in Cincinnati Since 1820, 1992; Yuhude Artsot Ha-Berit, 1992; Jews of Boston (with Ellen Smith), 1995; Minority Faiths and the American Protestant Mainstream, editor, 1997; Religion and State in the American Jewish Experience, with David G Dalin, 1997. Contributions to: Books, professional journals and general periodicals. Address: c/o Brandeis University, Waltham, MA 02454, USA.

SARNA Nahum Mattathias, b. 27 Mar 1923, London, England. Professor of Biblical Studies Emeritus; Writer. m. Helen Horowitz, 13 Mar 1947, 2 sons. Education: BA, 1944, MA, 1946, University of London; PhD, Dropsie College, Philadelphia, 1955. Appointments: University College, London, 1946-49; Gratz College, Philadelphia, 1951-57; Jewish Theological Seminary, New York City, 1957-65; Visiting Professor, Columbia University, 1964-65, 1992, Yale University, 1992-94; Faculty, 1965-67, Dora Golding Professor of Biblical Studies, 1967-85, Professor Emeritus, 1985-, Brandeis University; Distinguished Professor, Florida Atlantic University, 1995-. Publications: Understanding Genesis, 1966; Exploring Exodus, 1985; Commentary on Genesis, 1989; Commentary on Exodus, 1991; Songs of the Heart: An Introduction to the Book of Psalms, 1993. Contributions to: Professional journals. Honours: Jewish Book Council Award, 1967; American Council of Learned Societies Senior Fellow, 1971-72; Institute for Advanced Studies, Hebrew University, fellow, 1982-83; Honorary doctorates. Memberships: American Academy for Jewish Research, fellow; American Oriental Society; Association for Jewish Studies; Dead Sea Scrolls Foundation, board of advisors; Israel Exploration Society; Palestine Exploration Society; World Union of Jewish Studies. Address: 7886 Chula Vista Crescent, Boca Raton, FL 33433, USA.

SARNOFF Irving, b. 5 May 1922, Brooklyn, New York, USA. Psychologist; Author. m. Suzanne Fischbach, 28 Nov 1946, 1 son, 1 daughter. Education: BA, Brooklyn College, 1946; MA, 1949, PhD, 1951, University of Michigan. Appointments: Mental Hygienist, University of Michigan, 1951-54; Assistant Professor, Yale University, 1955-60; Professor of Psychology and Social Work, Case Western Reserve University, 1960-62; Professor of Psychology, 1962-92, Professor Emeritus, 1992-, New York University. Publications: Personality Dynamics and Development, 1962; Society with Tears, 1966; Testing Freudian Concepts, 1971; Love-Centred Marriage in a Self-Centred World (with Suzanne Sarnoff), 1989. Sexual Excitement/Sexual Peace, 1979. Contributions to: Journals and magazines. Honours: Fulbright Advanced Research Scholar, University College, London, 1954-55; Senior Stipend, National Institute of Mental Health, 1968-69. Address: 1 Washington Square Village, Apt 14V, New York, NY 10012, USA.

SARO ALONSO María Juliana, (María Saro), b. 18 Oct 1912, Guarnizo, Cantabria, Spain. Writer. Education: Nursing Diploma, Faculty of Medicine, Valladolid. Appointments: Nursing during Spanish Civil War; Recited poems at La Casa de Granada, Madrid, Ateneo, Santander, International University of Santander, and Casa de Cervantes, Valladolid. Publications: La Braña, poetry book, 1975; Poems in anthology Brisas Poéticas. Contributions to: Literary magazines. Honours: Prize for Poetry, Friends of the Arts, Santander, 1978; Academician, Agustin García Alonso Cultural, Literary and Artistic Centre, Aranguren, Viscaya; Nominated as 1 of 5 Best Poets in Spain, UNESCO Jury; Honorary Doctorate in Literature, International Academy. Address: La Abadill de Cayón 39694, Cantabria, Spain.

SAROYAN Aram, b. 25 Sept 1943, New York, New York, USA. Writer; Poet. m. Gailyn McClanahan, 9 Oct 1968, 1 son, 2 daughters. Education: University of Chicago; New York University; Columbia University. Publications: Aram Saroyan, 1968; Pages, 1969; Words and Photographs, 1970; The Street: An Autobiographical Novel, 1974; Genesis Angels: The Saga of Lew Welch and the Beat Generation, 1979; Last Rites: The Death of William Saroyan, 1982; William Saroyan, 1983; Trio: Portrait of an Intimate Friendship, 1985; The Romantic, 1988; Friends in the World: The Education of a Writer, 1992; Rancho Mirage: An American Tragedy of Manners, Madness and Murder, 1993; Day and Night: Bolinas Poems, 1972-81, Review; Staged readings of plays. Contributions to: New York Times Book; Los Angeles Times Book Review; The Nation; Village Voice; Mother Jones; Paris Review. Honours: National Endowment for the Arts, Poetry Awards, 1967, 1968. Membership: PEN Center USA West, president, 1992-93. Address: 1107 15th Street, Santa Monica, CA 90403, USA.

SATTERTHWAIT Walter, b. 23 Mar 1946, Philadelphia, Pennsylvania, USA. Writer. 1 daughter. Education: Reed College, 1969-72. Publications: Cocain Blues, 1980; The Aegean Affair, 1981; Wall of Glass, 1987; Miss Lizzie, 1989; At Ease With the Dead, 1990; Wilde West, 1991; A Flower In the Desert, 1992; The Hanged Man, 1993, UK edition as The Death Card, 1994; Escapade, 1995; Accustomed to the Dark, 1996; Masquerade, 1998. Contributions to: Alfred Hitchcock's Mystery Magazine; Santa Fe Reporter. Honour: Prix du Roman d'Aventures, France, 1996. Memberships: Mystery Writers of America; Private Eye Writers of America. Address: PO Box 5452, Clearwater, FL 34618, USA.

SAUNDERS Ann Loreille, (Ann Cox-Johnson), b. 23 May 1930, London, England. Historian. m. Bruce Kemp Saunders, 4 June 1960, 1 son, 1 daughter. Education: Plumptre Scholar, Queen's College, London, 1946-48; BA Honours, University College, London, 1951; PhD, Leicester University,1965. Appointments: Archivist, Marylebone Public Library, London, 1956-63; Honorary Editor, Costume Society, 1967-; London Topographical Society, 1975-. Publications: London, City and Westminster, 1975; Art and Architecture of London, 1984, St Martin-in-the-Fields, 1989; The Royal Exchange, monograph, 1991; The Royal Exchange, editor and co-author, 1997. Contributions to: Magazines. Honours: Prize for Best Specialist Guide Book of the Year, British Tourist Board, 1984; Fellow, University College, London, 1992. Memberships: Society of Antiquaries, fellow; Costume Society; London Topographical Society. Address: 3 Meadway Gate, London NW11 7LA, England.

SAUNDERS James (Arthur), b. 8 Jan 1925, London, England. Playwright. m. Audrey Cross, 1951, 1 son, 2 daughters. Education: University College, Southampton, 1946-49. Publications: Plays: Moonshine, 1958; Alas, Poor Fred and The Ark, 1959; Committal, Barnstable and Return to a City, 1960; A Slight Accident, 1961; Double Double, 1962; Next Time I'll Sing To You, The Pedagogue and Who Was Hilary Maconochie?, 1963; A Scent of Flowers and Neighbours, 1964; Triangle and Opus, 1965; A Man's Best Friend and The Borage Pigeon Affair, 1969; After Liverpool, 1970; Games and Savoury Meringue, 1971; Hans Kohlhaas, 1972; Bye Bye Blues, 1973; The Island, 1975; Bodies, 1977; Birdsong, 1979; Fall, 1981; Emperor Waltz, 1983; Scandella, 1985; Making It Better, 1992; Retreat, 1995. Television: Watch Me I'm a Bird, 1964; Bloomers (series), 1979; TV adaptations of works by D H Lawrence, Henry James, H E Bates and R F Delderfield. Screenplays: Sailor's Return; The Captain's Doll. Honours: Arts Council of Great Britain Drama Bursary, 1960; Evening Standard Drama Award,1963; Writer's Guild TV Adaptation Award, 1966; Arts Council Major Bursary, 1984; BBC Radio Play Award, 1986; Molière Award, Paris, 1990. Address: c/o

Casarotto Ramsay Ltd, 60-66 Wardour Street, London W1V 3HP, England.

SAUNDERS Nezzle Methelda, (Nezzle), b. 26 May 1940, Smithville, Jamaica, West Indies. Writer. m. 27 July 1960, 3 sons, 4 daughters. Education: Diploma, Office Practice, South Nottingham College of Further Education, 1976; City and Guilds Certificate, Community Care, 1989. Appointments: Schools and Community Centres Radio Programmes, 1986-94; Channel 4 TV Programme, 1988; Lecturer, Afro-Caribbean Family and Friends, 1990-93. Publications: Divine Inspiration, 1986; Insight, 1987; Children's and Student's Anthology, 1988. Contributions to: Periodicals. Honour: Bursary Award, Nottinghamshire County Council Leisure Services. Membership: Arts Development Group, president, 1987-. Address: 48 Finsbury Avenue, Sneinton Dale, Nottingham NG2 4LL, England.

SAUVAIN Philip (Arthur), b. 28 Mar 1933, Burton on Trent, Staffordshire, England. Writer. m. June Maureen Spencley, 27 July 1963, 1 son, 1 daughter. Education: MA, University of Cambridge, 1956; Postgraduate Certificate in Education, University of London, 1957. Appointments: Senior Lecturer in Geography, James Graham College, Leeds, 1963-68; Head, Environmental Studies Department, Charlotte Mason College of Education, Ambleside, 1968-74. Publications: Looking Aroung Town and Country, 1975; A First Look at Winds, 5 volumes, 1975-78; Imagining the Past: First Series, 6 volumes, 1976, Second Series, 6 volumes, 1979; The British Isles, 1980; The Story of Britain Series, 4 volumes, 1980; Britain's Living Heritage, 1982; The History of Britain, 4 volumes, 1982; Theatre, 1983; Macmillan Junior Geography, 4 volumes, 1983; Hulton New Geographies, 5 volumes, 1983; History Map Books, 2 volumes, 1983, 1985; Hulton New Histories, 5 volumes, 1984-85; France and the French, 1985; European and World History, 1815-1919, 1985; Modern World History, 1919 Onwards, 1985; How History Began, 1985; Castles and Crusaders, 1986; What to Look For, 4 volumes, 1986; British Economic and Social History, 2 volumes, 1987; Exploring Energy, 4 volumes, 1987; GCSE History Companion Series, 3 volumes, 1988; How We Build, 3 volumes, 1989; The World of Work, 3 volumes, 1989; Skills for Geography, 1989; Skills for Standard Grade History, 1990; Exploring the Past: Old World, 1991; The Way it Works, 3 volumes, 1991; Changing World, 1992; Breakthrough: Communications, 1992; History Detectives, 3 volumes, 1992-93; Great Battles and Sieges, 4 volumes, 1992-93; Expanding World, 1993; The Era of the Second World War, 1993; Robert Scott in the Antarctic, 1993; Target Geography, 14 volumes, 1994-95; The Tudors and Stuarts, 1995; Britain Since 1930, 4 volumes, 1995; Geography Detective, 4 volumes, 1995-96; Famous Lives, 2 volumes, 1996; Key Themes of the Twentieth Century, 1996; Key Themes of the Twentieth Century: Teacher's Guide, 1996; Germany in the Twentieth Century, 1997; Vietnam, 1997. Address: 70 Finborough Road, Stowmarket, Suffolk IP14 1PU, England.

SAVAGE Alan. See: **NICOLE Christopher Robin.**

SAVAGE Jeffrey Errwood, b. 9 March 1961, Oakland, California, USA. Children's Author. m. Nancy Ann Conroy (Savage), 20 Aug 1994, 2 sons. Education: BA, Journalism and Communications, University of California, San Diego, 1988. Appointments: Sports Reporter, Features Writer, San Diego Union-Tribune, San Diego, California, 1984-92; Children's Author, 1993-. Publications include: Deion Sanders Star Athlete, 1997; Junior Seau, Star Linebacker, 1997; Julie Krone, Unstoppable Jockey, 1997; Barry Bonds, Mr Excitement, 1997; Top 10 Basketball Point Guards, 1997; Top 10 Basketball Power Forwards, 1997; Grant Hill, Humble Hotshot, 1998; Sports Great Brett Favre, 1998; Tiger Woods, King of the Course, 1998 Eric Lindros, High-Flying Center, 1998; Paul Kariya, Hockey Magician, 1998; Top 10 Professional Football Coaches, 1998; Fundamental Strength Training, 1998; Sports great Juwan Howard, 1999; Drew Bledsoe, Cool Quarterback, 1999; Julie Foudy, Soccer Superstar, 1999; Sports Great

Ken Griffey, Jr, 1999; Sports Great Stephon Marbury, 1999; Top 10 Aggressive Inline Skaters, 1999; Top 10 Heisman Trophy Winners, 1999; Mark McGwire, Home Run Hero, 1999; Home Run Kings, 1999; Olympic Kayaking, 1999; Olympic Taekwondo, 1999; Olympic Triathlon, 1999; Olympic Wrestling, 1999; Top 10 Sports Blunders, 1999; Top 10 Athletes With Disabilities, 1999; Superstar Softball Catchers, 1999; Superstar Softball Fielders, 1999; Superstar Softball Hitters, 1999; Superstar Softball Pitchers, 1999. Honours: Best Sports Writing, First Place, San Diego Press Club, 1992; Children's Choice Award, International Reading Association, Children's Book Council, 1995, (3) 1997; Honor Book, Voice of Youth Advocates, 1996. Membership: Society of Children's Book Writers and Illustrators. Address: 121 Paradise Drive, Napa, California 94558, USA.

SAVAGE Thomas, (Tom Savage), b. 14 July 1948, New York, New York, USA. Poet; Writer; Critic; Editor. Education: BA, English, Brooklyn College of the City University of New York, 1969; MLS, Columbia University School of Library Science, 1980. Appointments: Teaching Assistant, Naropa Institute School of Poetics, 1975; Editor, Roof Magazine, 1976-78, Gandhabba Magazine, 1981-93; Teacher, Words, Music, Words for Poets and Composers, St Mark's Poetry Project, 1983-85. Publications: Personalities, 1978; Filling Spaces, 1980; Slow Waltz on a Glass Harmonica, 1980; Housing Preservation and Development, 1988; Processed Words, 1990; Out of the World, 1991; Political Conditions and Physical States, 1993; Precipice, 1994; The Inheritance, 1998; Brain Surgery (poems), 1999. Contributions to: Magazines and journals. Honours: PEN Grant, 1978; Coordinating Council of Literary Magazines Grant, 1981-82. Membership: Coordinating Council of Literary Magazines. Address: 622 East 11th Street, No 14, New York, NY 10009, USA.

SAVOY Douglas Eugene, (Gene Savoy), b. 11 May 1927, Bellingham, Washington, USA. Bishop; Writer; Educator; Explorer. m. Sylvia Ontaneda, 7 July 1971, 2 sons, 1 daughter. Publications: Antisuyo: The Search for the Lost Cities of the High Amazon, 1970; The Child Christ, 1973; The Decoded New Testament, 1974; On the Trail of the Feathered Serpent, 1974; The Prophecies of Jamil, 7 volumes, 1976-83; The Secret Sayings of Jamil: The Image and the World, 7 volumes, 1976-87; The Essaei Document: Secrets of an Eternal Race, 1978; The Lost Gospel of Jesus: Hidden Teachings of Christ, 1978. Other: 39 texts, 400 audio tapes: Lectures on Religious Systems and Theology, 3 documentary videos. Contributions to: Various publications. Honours: Over 40 Flag Awards, Andean Explorers Foundation, Explorers Club, New York City, 1958-94; Silver Hummingbird Award, Ministry of Industry and Tourism of Peru, 1987; Explorer of the Century Trophy, Andean Explorers Foundation, 1988; Decorated Officer, Order of the Grand Cross, Republic of Peru, 1989; Medal of Merit Andres Reyes, 1989; Award, City of Ica, Peru, 1995. Memberships: Authors Guild; Explorers Club, New York City; Geographical Society, Lima, Peru; Andean Explorers Foundation; Ocean Sailing Club; World Council for Human Rights, Advisor for Religious Rights and Freedoms. Address: 2025 LaFond Drive, Reno, NV 89509, USA.

SAWYER Robert J(ames), b. 29 Apr 1960, Ottawa, Ontario, Canada. Writer. m. Carolyn Joan Clink, 11 Dec 1984. Education: BAA, Ryerson Polytechnical Institute, 1982. Publications: Golden Fleece, 1990; Far-Seer, 1992; Fossil Hunter, 1993; Foreigner, 1994; End of an Era, 1994; The Terminal Experiment, 1995. Honours: Aurora Award, Canadian Science Fiction and Fantasy Association, 1992; Homer Awards, 1992, 1993; Writer's Reserve Grant, Ontario Arts Council, 1993. Memberships: Crime Writers of Canada; Mystery Writers of America; Science Fiction and Fantasy Writers of America; Writers Union of Canada. Address: 7601 Bathurst Street, No 617, Thornhill, Ontario L4J 4H5, Canada.

SAWYER Roger Martyn, b. 15 Dec 1931, Stroud, England. Author. m. Diana Margaret Harte, 30 Aug 1952, 2 sons. Education: BA Honours, Diploma in Education, University of Wales, 1958; PhD, History, University of Southampton, 1979. Publications: Casement: The Flawed Hero, 1984; Slavery in the Twentieth Century, 1986; Children Enslaved, 1988; The Island from Within (editor), 1990; 'We are but Women': Women in Ireland's History, 1993; Roger Casement's Diaries 1910: The Black and The White (editor), 1997. Contributions to: Anti-Slavery Reporter Immigrants and Minorities; South. Honour: Airey Neave Award, 1985. Memberships: Anti-Slavery International, council member, 1984-98; Bembridge Sailing Club; Society of Authors. Address: Ducie House, Darts Lane, Bembridge, Isle of Wight PO35 5YH, England.

SAY Allen, b. 28 Aug 1937, USA. Children's Author and Illustrator. m. Deirdre Myles, 18 Apr 1974, 1 child. Education: Aoyama Gakuin, Tokyo; Chouinard Art Institute; Los Angeles Art Center School; University of California at Berkeley; San Francisco Art Institute. Publications: Author and Illustrator: Dr Smith's Safari, 1972; Once Under the Cherry Blossom Tree: An Old Japanese Tale, 1974; The Feast of Lanterns, 1976; The Bicycle Man, 1982; A River Dream, 1988; The Lost Lake, 1989; Tree of Cranes, 1991; Grandfather's Journey, 1993; The Stranger in the Mirror, 1995. Author: The Innkeeper's Apprentice, 1989; El Chino, 1990. Illustrator: 7 books, 1971-88. Honours: Christopher Award, 1985; Boston Globe-Horn Book Awards, 1988, 1994; Caldecott Honor Book, 1989; Caldecott Medal, 1994. Address: c/o Houghton Mifflin Children's Books, 222 Berkeley Street, Boston, MA 02116, USA.

SAYER Ian Keith Terence, b. 30 Oct 1945, Norwich, Norfolk, England. Company Director; Author. 2 sons, 3 daughters. Publications: Nazi Gold: The Story of the World's Greatest Robbery, 1984, revised edition, 1998; America's Secret Army: The Untold Story of the Counter Intelligence Corps, 1989; Hitler's Last General: The Case Against Wilhelm Mohnke, 1989. Contributions to: Freight News Express, columnist, 1984-89; The Sunday Times; The Sunday Times Magazine. Address: Westerlands, Sherbourne Drive, Sunningdale, Berkshire SL5 0LG, England.

SAYLOR Steven (Warren), b. 23 Mar 1956, Port Lavaca, Texas, USA. Writer. Registered domestic partner, Richard K Solomon, 15 Mar 1991. Education: BA, University of Texas at Austin, 1978. Publications: Roman Blood, 1991; Arms of Nemesis, 1992; Catilina's Riddle, 1993; The Venus Throw, 1995; A Murder on the Appian Way, 1996; House of the Vestals, 1997; Rubicon, 1999. Contributions to: Books and periodicals. Honours: Robert L Fish Memorial Award, Mystery Writers of America, 1993; Lambda Literary Award, 1994. Membership: Mystery Writers of America. Address: 1711 Addison Street, Berkeley, CA 94703, USA.

SCAGLIONE Aldo D(omenico), b. 10 Jan 1925, Turin, Italy. Professor of Literature; Writer. m. (1) Jeanne M Daman, 28 June 1952, dec 1986, (2) Marie M Burns, Aug 1992. Education: DLitt, University of Turin, 1948. Appointments: Faculty, University of California at Berkeley, 1952-68; W R Kenan Professor, University of North Carolina at Chapel Hill, 1969-87; Professor, 1987-91, Erich Maria Remarque Professor of Literature, 1991-, New York University. Publications: Nature and Love in the Late Middle Ages, 1963; Ars Grammatica, 1970; The Classical Theory of Composition, 1972; The Theory of German Word Order, 1981; The Liberal Arts and the Jesuit College System, 1986; Knights at Court, 1991; Essays on the Arts of Discourse, 1998. Contributions to: Professional journals. Honours: Knight of the Order of Merit, Republic of Italy; Fulbright Scholar, 1951; Guggenheim Fellowship, 1958; Newberry Fellow, 1964; Fellow, University of Wisconsin Institute for the Humanities, 1981. Memberships: American Association for Italian Studies, honorary president, 1989; Boccaccio Association of America, president, 1980-83; Medieval Academy of America. Address: 3 Reading Avenue, Frenchtown, NJ 08825, USA.

SCALAPINO Robert A(nthony), b. 19 Oct 1919, Leavenworth, Kansas, USA. Professor of Government Emeritus; Writer. m. Ida Mae Jessen, 23 Aug 1941, 3 daughters. Education: BA, Santa Barbara College, 1940; MA, 1943, PhD, 1948, Harvard University. Appointments: Lecturer, Santa Barbara College, 1940-41; Instructor, Harvard University, 1948-49; Assistant Professor, 1949-51, Associate Professor, 1951-56, Robson Research Professor of Government and Director, Institute of East Asian Studies, 1978-90, Professor Emeritus, 1990-, University of California at Berkeley; Editor, Asian Survey, 1962-96. Publications: Democracy and the Party Movement in Pre-War Japan, 1953, 2nd edition, 1967; The Chinese Anarchist Movement (with George T Yu), 1961; North Korea Today (editor), 1963; The Japanese Communist Movement, 1920-1966, 1967; The Communist Revolution in Asia (editor), 1969, 2nd edition, 1977; Communism in Korea (with Chong-Sik Lee), 1972; Elites in the People's Republic of China (editor), 1972; Asia and the Road Ahead, 1975; The Foreign Policy of Modern Japan (editor), 1977; The United States and Korea: Looking Ahead, 1979; North Korea Today: Strategic and Domestic Issues (editor with Jun-Yop Kim), 1983; The Early Japanese Labor Movement, 1984; The Politics of Development: Perspectives on Twentieth Century Asia, 1989; The Last Leninists: The Uncertain Future of Asia's Communist States. 1992. Contributions to: Many scholarly books and journals. Honours: Carnegie Foundation Grant, 1951-53; Social Science Research Council, Fellow, 1952-53; Ford Foundation Grant, 1955; Rockefeller Foundation Grants, 1956-59, 1961; Guggenheim Fellowship, 1965-66; Woodrow Wilson Award, American Political Science Association, 1973; Order of the Sacred Treasure, Japan, 1988; Presidential Order, Republic of Korea, 1990; Berkeley Fellow, 1990; Honorary Professor, Peking University, 1997; Japan Foundation Award, 1998; Honorary doctorates. Memberships: American Academy of Arts and Sciences; American Political Science Association; Association for Asian Studies; Council on Foreign Relations; Foreign Policy Association; Western Political Science Association; Member of Board, Asia Foundation, Atlantic Council, Pacific Forum, CSIS. Address: 2850 Buena Vista Way, Berkeley, CA 94708, USA.

SCAMMACCA Nat, b. 20 July 1924, Brooklyn, New York, USA. Retired Professor of English; Writer; Poet. m. Nina Scammacca, 1948, 1 son, 2 daughters. Education: BA, Literature and Philosophy, Long Island University; MA, Education, New York University; Graduated in Italian, University of Perugia. Appointments: Pilot, US Air Force, India-Burma-China theatre, World War II; Social Worker, Italian Board of Guardians; Professor of English, British College, Palermo; Editor, Third Page, Trapani Nuova newspaper. Publications: Two Worlds (novel), 1980; Schammachanat (Italian and English), 1985; Bye Bye America (short stories), 1986; Cricepeo (Italian and English), 3 volumes, 1990; Sikano L'Amerikano! (short stories), 1991; Due Poeti Americani (Italian and English, co-author), 1994; The Hump (World War II stories and poems), 1994. Other: Various books and translations. Contributions to: Anthologies and periodicals. Honours: Air Medal, Bronze Star, US Air Force; Taormina City Poetry Prize, 1978; Premio Letterario Sikania Prize, 1988; VII Premio di Poesia Petrosino Prize, 1991. Membership: Poets and Writers, New York City. Address: Villa Schammachanat, Via Argenteria KM4, Trapani, Sicily 91100, Italy.

SCAMMELL William, b. 2 Jan 1939, Hythe, Hampshire, England. Poet; Critic. m. (1) Jacqueline Webb, 15 Aug 1964, 2 sons, (2) Janet Fletcher, 1997. Education: BA, Honours, English and Philosophy, University of Bristol, 1967. Appointments: Lecturer in English, University of Newcastle, 1975-91; Chairman, Northern Arts Literature Panel, 1982-85. Publications: Yes and No, 1979; A Second Life, 1982; Time Past, 1982; Jouissance, 1985; Eldorado, 1987; Keith Douglas: A Study, 1988; Bleeding Heart Yard, 1992; The Game: Tennis Poems, 1992; Five Easy Pieces, 1993; Barnacle Bill, 1994. Editor: Between Comets: For Norman Nicholson at 70, 1984; This Green Earth: Nature Poetry 1400-1980, 1992; The New Lake Poets, 1992; The

Poetry Book Society Anthology 3, 1992; Winter Pollen: Occasional Prose of Ted Hughes, 1994. Honours: British Arts Council Award, 1985; Northern Arts Writers Awards, 1988, 1991, 1994. Address: Centre for Continuing Education, The University, Newcastle upon Tyne NE1 7RU, England.

SCANNELL Vernon, b. 23 Jan 1922, Spilsby, Lincolnshire, England. Author; Poet. m. 4 Oct 1954, 3 sons, 2 daughters. Appointments: Visiting Poet, Shrewsbury School, 1973-75; Writer-in-Residence, Berinsfield, Oxfordshire, 1975-76; Poet-in-Residence, King's School, Canterbury, 1979. Publications: Fiction: The Fight, 1952; The Wound and the Scar, 1953; The Face of the Enemy, 1960; The Big Time, 1967; Ring of Truth, 1983. Poetry: New and Collected Poems, 1980; Winterlude, 1983; Funeral Games, 1987; Soldiering On, 1989; A Time for Fires, 1991; Collected Poems 1950-1993, 1994; The Black and White Days, 1996. Non-Fiction: The Tiger and the Rose, 1971; Argument of Kings, 1987; Drums of Morning, Growing Up in the 30's, 1992. Contributions to: Newspapers, reviews, and magazines. Honours: Heinemann Award for Literature, 1960; Cholmondeley Award for Poetry, 1974. Membership: Royal Society of Literature, honorary fellow. Address: 51 North Street, Otley, West Yorkshire LS21 1AH, England.

SCARBOROUGH William Kauffman, b. 17 Jan 1933, Baltimore, Maryland, USA. Professor of History. m. Patricia Estelle Carruthers, 16 Jan 1954, 1 son, 1 daughter. Education: AB, History, 1954, PhD, US History, 1962, University of North Carolina at Chapel Hill; MA, US History, Cornell University, 1957. Appointments: Assistant Professor of History, Millsaps College, Jackson, Mississippi, 1961-63; Northeast Louisiana University, Monroe, 1963-64; Associate Professor, 1964-76, Professor of History, 1976-, Chair, Department of History, 1980-90, Charles W Moorman Distinguished Alumni Professor in the Humanities, 1996-98, University of Southern Mississippi, Hattiesburg. Publications: The Overseer: Plantation Management in the Old South, 1966; The Diary of Edmund Ruffin (editor), 3 volumes, 1972, 1977, 1989. Contributions to: Scholarly books and journals. Honours: Jules and Frances Landry Award, 1989; Willie D Halsell Prize, 1993. Memberships: Mississippi Historical Society, president, 1979-80; Organization of American Historians; Southern Historical Association; St George Tucker Society. Address: c/o Department of History, University of Southern Mississippi, Southern Station, Box 5047, Hattiesburg, MS 39406, USA.

SCARF Margaret, (Maggie Scarf), b. 13 May 1932, Philadelphia, Pennsylvania, USA. Writer. m. Herbert Eli Scarf, 28 June 1953, 3 daughters. Education: BA, South Connecticut State University, 1989. Appointments: Contributing Editor, The New Republic, 1975-; Fellow, Center for Advanced Study, Stanford, California, 1977-78, 1985-86; Writer-in-Residence, Jonathan Edwards College, Yale University, 1992-. Publications: Body, Mind, Behavior, 1976; Unfinished Business, 1980; Intimate Partners, 1987; Intimate Worlds: Life Inside the Family, 1995. Contributions to: Magazines and journals. Honours: Ford Foundation Fellow, 1973-74; Nieman Fellow, Harvard University, 1975-76; Alicia Patterson Fellow, 1978-79; Smith Richardson Foundation Grants, 1991, 1992, 1993, 1994. Memberships: Connecticut Society of Psychoanalytic Psychologists; PEN. Address: c/o Jonathan Edwards College, Yale University, 68 High Street, New Haven, CT 06517, USA.

SCARFE Allan (John), b. 30 Mar 1931, Caulfield, Victoria, Australia. Writer. m. Wendy Scarfe, 6 Jan 1955, 4 children. Education: BA; DipEd; TPTC. Appointments: Teacher, Warrnambool Secondary College, retired; Writer. Publications: With Wendy Scarfe: A Mouthful of Petals, 1967; Tiger on a Rein, 1969; People of India, 1972; The Black Australians, 1974; Victims or Bludgers?: Case Studies in Poverty in Australia, 1974; J P: His Biography, 1975, Hindustani translation, 1978, abridged and revised edition, 1997; Victims or Bludgers?: A Poverty Inquiry for Schools, 1978; Labor's Titan: The

Story of Percy Brookfield 1878-1921, 1983; All That Grief: Migrant Recollections of Greek Resistance to Facism 1941-49, 1994; Remembering Jayaprakash, 1997; No Taste for Carnage: Alex Sheppard - A Portrait 1913-1997, 1998. Contributions to: Several publications. Honours: With Wendy Scarfe: Australia Literature Boards Grants, 1980, 1988. Address: 8 Bostock Street, Warrnambool, Victoria 3280, Australia.

SCARFE Norman, b. 1 May 1923, Felixstowe, England. Writer. Education: MA, Honours, History, Oxford, 1949. Appointments: Chairman, Centre of East Anglia Studies, University of East Anglia, 1989-96; Founder, Honorary General Editor, Suffolk Records Society, 1958-92. Publications: Assault Division: The 3rd British Infantry Division from D-Day to VE Day, 1947; Suffolk, 1960, 4th edition, 1988; Essex, 1968, 2nd edition, 1982; The Suffolk Landscape, 1972, 2nd edition, 1987; Cambridgeshire, 1983; Suffolk in the Middle Ages, 1986; A Frenchman's Year in Suffolk (1784), 1988; Innocent Espionage: The La Rochefoucauld Brothers' Tour of England in 1785, 1995; Jocelin of Brakelond, 1997. Contributions to: Proceedings, Suffolk Institute of Archaeology; Aldeburgh Festival Annual Programme Book; Country Life; The Book Collector;Dictionary of National Biography. Honours: Honorary Litt D, University of East Anglia, 1989; Member of the Order of the British Empire, 1994. Memberships: International PEN; Suffolk Book League, founder chairman, 1982; Society of Antiquaries, fellow. Literary Agent: John Welch, Milton House, Milton, Cambridge, CB4 6AD, England. Address: The Garden Cottage, 3 Burkitt Road, Woodbridge, Suffolk IP12 4JJ, England.

SCARFE Wendy (Elizabeth), b. 21 Nov 1933, Adelaide, South Australia, Australia. Writer; Poet. m. Allan Scarfe, 6 Jan 1955, 4 children. Education: BA; BLitt; ATTC. Appointments: Teacher, Warrnambool Secondary College, retired; Writer; Poet. Publications: Novels: The Lotus Throne, 1976; Neither Here Nor There, 1978; Laura My Alter Ego, 1988; The Day They Shot Edward, 1991; Miranda, 1998. Poetry: Shadow and Flowers, 1964, enlarged edition, 1984. With Allan Scarfe: A Mouthful of Petals, 1967; Tiger on a Rein, 1969; People of India, 1972; The Black Australians, 1974; Victims or Bludgers?: Case Studies in Poverty in Australia, 1974; J P: His Biography, 1975, Hindustani translation, 1978, abridged and revised edition, 1997; Victims or Bludgers?: A Poverty Inquiry for Schools, 1978; Labor's Titan: The Story of Percy Brookfield, 1878-1921, 1983; All That Grief: Migrant Recollections of Greek Resistance to Fascism, 1941-1949, 1994; Remembering Jayaprakash, 1997; No Taste for Carnage: Alex Sheppard - A Portrait 1913-1997, 1998. Contributions to: Overland; Australian Short Stories; Age. Honours: With Allan Scarfe, Australia Literature Board Grants, 1980, 1988. Membership: Fellowship of Australian Writers. Address: 8 Bostock Street, Warrnambool, Victoria 3280, Australia.

SCHAAD Isolde G, (Rosa Lichtenstein, Maxie von Planta), b. 9 Oct 1944, Schaffhausen, Switzerland. Writer. Education: MA, Universities of Zurich and Geneva; Cambridge Certificate of Proficiency in English, 1966. Appointments: Former Editor, Die Weltwoche; Part-time Editor, Du; Editor, Tages Anzeiger, Zurich; Member, several jury boards. Publications: Knowhow am Kilimandscharo, 1984; Die Zürcher Constipation, 1986; Küsschentschüss, 1989; Body und Sofa, 1994; Mein Text so blau, 1997; Contributions to anthologies, including Frauen-Offensive, Luchterhand, Schweizer Lesebuch, Schanspielhaus, Zürich; Auroras Nachlass, Piece, 1994; Gruezi, Salu, Ciao, Vontobelstiftung, others. Contributions to: Essays, features and columns for: Du; Merianhefte; Kursbuch, Berlin; Die Zeit; Text und Kritik; Geo; Neue Zürcher Zeitung; Wochen Zeitung; Others. *Honours: International* H C Andersen Award List, Schillerstiftung; Awards for Journalism. Memberships: Several German and Swiss Cultural Boards. Literary Agent: Peter Fritz, Zurich, Switzerland. Address: Zähringerstr 9, 8001 Zurich, Switzerland.

SCHAEFFER Robert Allen, (Bob Schaeffer), b. 15 Aug 1947, Boston, Massachusetts, USA. Consultant; Writer. m. Elaine Christine Coughlin, 5 Sept 1971, 1 son. Education: Political Science, Massachusetts Institute of Technology, 1969. Appointments: Instructor, Education Research Center, Massachusetts Institute of Technology, 1969-71; Field Director, Citizens for Participation in Political Action, 1972-78; Research Director, Human Services Committee, Massachusetts Legislature, 1978-84; Editorial Writer, WBZ TV, 1984; President, Public Policy Communications, 1984-. Publications: Developing the Public Economy: Models from Massachusetts (editor), 1980; Winning Local and State Elections, 1986; Standing Up To The SAT, 1989; Implementing Performance Assessment, 1995. Contributions to: Giving the Media Your Message, in Community Jobs, 1983; The News Media and The Big Lie, in Peacework, 1987; Standardised Tests and Teacher Competence, in School Voices, 1996. Honour: New York Public Library Book of the Year for Teenagers, 1989. Membership: National Writer's Union. Address: 73 Trowbridge Street, Belmont, MA 02478, USA.

SCHAER Brigitte, b. 1 Feb 1958, Zürich, Switzerland. Fiction; Narration; Story Writer. Education: Studies in German Literature and European Folk, and Popular Literature, University of Zürich, Diploma, 1984. Appointments: Teacher for German Literature, 1984-88; Performances as Jazz Singer in many countries and Singing Teacher, 1984-; Writer, 1984-. Publications: Das Schubladenkind, book for children, 1988; Auf dem hohen Seil, 1991; Das geht doch nicht!, book for children, 1995; Monsterbesuch!, book for children, 1996; Liebesbriefe sind keine Rechnungen, 1998; Das Haus auf dem Hügel, book for children, 1998; Die blinde Fee/The Blind Fairy, 1998. Honours: Schweizer lugendbuchpreis, 1993; Schnabelsteher Preis, 1997; Kinderbuchpreis von Nordrhein, Westfalen, 1997; International Board on Books for Young People, 1998. Address: Badenerstrasse 531, CH-8048 Zürich, Switzerland.

SCHALLER George B(eals), b. 26 May 1933, Berlin, Germany. Researcher; Writer. m. Kay Morgan, 26 Aug 1957, 2 sons. Education: BS Zoology, BA, Anthropology, University of Alaska; MS, PhD, University of Wisconsin. Publications: The Mountain Gorilla, 1963; The Year of the Gorilla, 1964; The Deer and the Tiger, 1967; The Serengeti Lion, 1972; Golden Shadows, Flying Hooves, 1973; Mountain Monarchs: Wild Sheep and Goats of the Himalayas, 1977; Stones of Silence: Journeys in the Himalayas, 1980; The Giant Pandas of Wolong (co-author), 1985; The Last Panda, 1993; Tibet's Hidden Wilderness, 1997; Wildlife of the Tibetan Steppe, 1998. Contributions to: Zoological journals and popular periodicals. Honours: National Book Award, 1973; Cosmos Prize, Japan, 1996. Address: Wildlife Conservation Society, Bronx Park, NY 10460, USA.

SCHAU Jens Michael, b. 25 May 1948, Ronne, Bornholm, Denmark. Psychologist; Writer; Dramatist; Screenwriter. Education: BA, History, 1974, PhD, Psychology, 1978, University of Copenhagen. Publications: I Familiens Skod, 1982; Byen og Oen, 1983; Himlen begynder ved Jorden, 1984; Far, Mor og Bornf, 1988; En lille Prins, 1994. Television Films: Boksning; Naeste Sommer Maske, 1988. Radio Play: Sonner, 1984. Contributions to: Magazines and journals. Honours: Statens Kunstfond, 1983, 1984, 1985. Address: c/o Tiderne Skifter and Gyldendal Publishers, Klareboderne 3, 1115 Copenhagen K, Denmark.

SCHAUBERGER Amanda Louise, b. 11 Feb 1925. Publications: Lola's Corner, 1959; America's Swedish Nightingale, 1959; Chute Action Toy, 1960; Multiple Pocket Nut Cup, 1961; Mandy's Varieties, 1967; How to Make a Raft, 1963; How to Make a Cart, 1963. Contributions to: City Harold; Saturday Night In Town. Address: 555 5th Avenue, Apt 1011, Des Moines, IA 50309-2300, USA.

SCHEIBER Harry N(oel), b. 1935, New York, New York, USA. Professor of Law; Writer. Education: BA, Columbia University, 1955; MA, 1957, PhD, 1961, Cornell University; D Jur Hon, University of Uppsala, Sweden, 1998. Appointments: Fellow, Centre for Advanced Study in the Behavioural Sciences, 1966, 1971; Professor of Law, later Stefan Reisenfeld Professor of Law and History, University of California at Berkeley; Academic Chair for History and Civics, National Assessment of Educational Progress, 1986-88. Publications: The Wilson Administration and Civil Liberties, 1960; United States Economic History, 1964; America: Purpose and Power (co-author), 1965; The Condition of American Federalism, 1966; The Frontier in American Development (co-editor), 1969; The Old Northwest, 1969; The Ohio Canal Era 1820-1861, 1969, 2nd edition, 1987; Black Labor in American History, 1972; Agriculture in the Development of the Far West, 1975; American Economic History (co-author), 1976; American Law and the Consitutional Order, 1978, 2nd edition, 1990; Perspectives on Federalism (editor), 1987; Power Divided (co-editor), 1989; The Federalism and the Judicial Mind (editor), 1993; Legal Culture and the Legal Profession (co-author), 1995; Freedom of the Contract and the State, (editor), 1998. Contributions to: Professional journals. Honours: Guggenheim Fellowships, 1967, 1989; Distinguished Fulbright Lecturer, Australia, 1984; National Endowment for the Humanities Fellow, 1984; University of California Humanities Research Institute Fellow, 1989; Honorary Doctorate of Law, Uppsala, Sweden, 1998. Address: c/o School of Law, University of California at Berkeley, Berkeley, CA 94720-2150, USA.

SCHELL Orville (Hickok), b. 20 May 1940, New York, New York, USA. University Dean; Journalist; Writer. m. 3 sons. Education: Stanford University, 1960; National Taiwan University, 1961-62; BA, magna cum laude, Far Eastern History, Harvard University, 1964; MA, 1967, PhD, 1968, Chinese Studies, University of California at Berkeley. Appointments: Co-Director, Bay Area Institute, 1968-71; Founder and Editor-in-Chief, Pacific News Service, 1970-71; China Correspondent, The New Yorker Magazine, 1975; Research Associate, 1986, Regents' Lecturer, 1990, Dean, Graduate School of Journalism, 1996-, University of California at Berkeley; Visiting Distinguished Professor, Chico State University, 1987; Moderator, Issues and Perspectives on China, Voice of America, 1995-97. Publications: The China Reader (with Frederick Crews), 1970; Modern China: The Story of a Revolution, 1972; The Town That Fought to Save Himself, 1976; In the People's Republic, 1976; Brown, 1978; Watch Out for the Foreign Guests: China Encounters the West, 1981; Modern Meat: Antibiotics, Hormones and the Pharmaceutical Farm, 1983; To Get Rich is Glorious: China in the 1980's, 1984; Discos and Democracy: China in the Throes of Reform, 1988; Mandate of Heaven: A New Generation of Entrepreneurs, Dissidents, Technocrats, and Bohemiams Grasp for Power in China, 1994; The China Reader: The Reform Years (editor with David Shambaugh), 1999; Virtual Tibet: The West's Fascination with the Roof of the World, 1999. Contributions to: Numerous books, reviews, and journals. Honours: Alicia Patterson Foundation Journalism Fellowship, 1981; MacDowell Colony Fellowships, 1983, 1986; Guggenheim Fellowship, 1989-90; Emmy Award, 1992; Senior Fellow, Freedom Forum Media Studies Center, Columbia University, 1995; George Foster Peabody Award, 1997. Memberships: Author's Guild; Council on Foreign Relations; Global Business Network; Human Rights Watch Board, executive committee; Pacific Council; PEN; National Committee on US-China Relations; World Affairs Council of San Francisco. Address: c/o Graduate School of Journalism, University of California at Berkeley, Berkeley, CA 94720, USA.

SCHELLENBERG James Arthur, b. 7 June 1932, Vinland, Kansas, USA. Social Scientist. m. 28 Dec 1974, 3 sons, 1 daughter. Education: AB, Baker University, 1954; MA, 1955, PhD, 1959, University of Kansas. Publications: An Introduction to Social Psychology, 1970, revised edition, 1974; Masters of Social Psychology, 1978; The Science of Conflict, 1982; Conflict Between Communities, 1987; Primitive Games, 1990; An Invitation to Social Psychology, 1993; Exploring Social Behaviour, 1993. Address: 124 Madison Boulevard, Terre Haute, IN 47803, USA.

SCHEPISI Frederic Alan, b. 26 Dec 1939, Melbourne, Victoria, Australia. Film Writer; Producer; Director. m. (1) Joan Mary Ford, 2 sons, 2 daughters, (2) Rhonda Elizabeth Finlayson, 1973, 2 daughters, (3) Mary Rubin, 1984, 1 son. Appointments: Carden Advertising, 1955-61; TV Production Manager, Paton Advisory Service, Melbourne, 1961-64; Victorian Manager, Cinesound Productions, Melbourne, 1964-66; Managing Director, 1966-97, The Film House, Melbourne, 1966-97. Publications: Films: Libido, 1973; The Devil's Playground, 1975; The Chant of Jimmie Blacksmith, 1978; Barbarosa, 1981; Iceman, 1983; Plenty, 1984-85; Roxanne, 1986; Evil Angels, 1987; Russia House, 1989; Mr Baseball, 1991; Six Degrees of Separation, 1993; IQ, 1994; Fierce Creatures. 1996. Honours: Australian Film Awards, Best Film, 1975; Australian Film Awards, Best Film, Best Achievement in Direction, Best Screenplay adapted from another source and the AFI Members Prize Special Award, 1989; Chauvel Award, 1994; Honorary Doctorate, Griffith University, Queensland, Australia, 1995. Address: PO Box 743, South Yarra, Vic 3141, Australia.

SCHEVILL James (Erwin), b. 10 June 1920, Berkeley, California, USA. Writer; Poet; Dramatist; Professor of English Emeritus. m. (1) Helen Shaner, 1942, div 1966, 2 daughters, (2) Margot Blum, 1966. Education: BS, Harvard University, 1942; MA, Brown University. Appointments: Assistant Professor of Humanities, California College of Arts and Crafts, Oakland, 1951-59; Associate Professor of English, San Francisco State University, 1959-68; Professor of English, 1968-88, Professor Emeritus, 1988-, Brown University. Publications: Tensions (poems), 1947; The American Fantasies, (poems), 1951; Sherwood Anderson: His Life and Work, 1951; High Sinners, Low Angels (musical play), 1953; The Right to Greet (poems), 1956; The Roaring Market and the Silent Tomb (biography of Bern Porter), 1956; The Bloody Tenet (verse play), 1957; Selected Poems, 1945-62, 1962; Voices of Mass and Capital A (play), 1962; The Stalingrad Elegies (poems), 1964; The Black President, and Other Plays, 1965; Violence and Glory: Poems 1962-67, 1969; Lovecraft's Follies (play), 1971; Breakout! In Search of New Theatrical Environments, 1972; The Buddhist Car and Other Characters (poems), 1973; The Arena of Ants (novel), 1977; The Mayan Poems, 1978; The American Fantasies: Collected Poems 1945-1982, 1983; Oppenheimer's Chair (play), 1985; Collected Short Plays, 1986; Ambiguous Dancers of Fame: Collected Poems 1945-1986, 1987; Where to Go, What to Do, When You Are Bern Porter: A Personal Biography, 1992; 5 Plays 5, 1993; Winter Channels (poems), 1994; The Complete American Fantasies (poems), 1996. Honours: Ford Foundation Grant, 1960-61; William Carlos Williams Award, 1965; Guggenheim Fellowship, 1981; Centennial Review Poetry Prize, 1985; Honorary DHL, Rhode Island College, 1986; Pawtucket Arts Council Award for Poetry and Theatre, 1987; American Academy of Arts and Letters Award, 1991. Address: 1309 Oxford Street, Berkeley, CA 94709, USA.

SCHIFF James Andrew, b. 6 Dec 1958, Cincinnati, Ohio, USA. Teacher; Writer. m. 24 June 1989, 2 sons. Education: AB, Duke University, 1981; MA, 1985, PhD, 1990, New York University. Appointment: Visiting Instructor, 1989-96, Adjunct Assistant Professor, 1997-, Assistant Professor, 1998-, University of Cincinnati. Publications: Updike's Version: Rewriting The Scarlet Letter, 1992; Understanding Reynolds Price, 1996; John Updike Revisited, 1998; Critical Essays on Reynolds Price, 1998. Contributions to: Southern Review; American Literature; South Atlantic Review; Studies in American Fiction; Critique. Membership: Modern Language Association. Address: 2 Forest Hill Dr., Cincinnati, OH 45208, USA.

SCHLAFLY Phyllis (Stewart), b. 15 Aug 1924, St Louis, Missouri, USA. Lawyer; Columnist; Author. m. Fred Schlafly, 20 Oct 1949, 4 sons, 2 daughters. Education: BA, Washington University, St Louis, 1944; MA, Harvard University, 1945. Appointments: Conservative Political Activist; Editor, The Phyllis Schlafly Report, 1967-; Syndicated Columnist, Copley News Service, 1976-.

Publications: A Choice, Not an Echo, 1964; The Gravediggers, 1964; Strike from Space, 1965; Safe, Not Sorry, 1967; The Betrayers, 1968; Mindszenty the Man, 1972; Kissinger on the Couch, 1975; Ambush at Vladivostok, 1976; The Power of the Positive Woman, 1977; Child Abuse in the Classroom (editor), 1984; Equal Pay for Unequal Work, 1984; Pornography's Victims, 1987; Who Will Rock the Cradle?, 1989; First Reader, 1994. Contributions to: Journals, magazines, radio and television. Honours: 10 Honours Awards, Freedom Foundation. Memberships: American Bar Association; Commission on the Bicentennial of the US Constitution, 1985-91; Daughters of the American Revolution; Illinois Bar Association; Phi Beta Kappa; Pi Sigma Alpha. Address: 68 Danforth Road, Alton, IL 62002, USA.

SCHLESINGER Arthur M(eier) Jr, b. 15 Oct 1917, Columbus, Ohio, USA. Historian; Retired Professor; Author. m. (1) Marian Cannon, 1940, div 1970, 2 sons, 2 daughters, (2) Alexandra Emmet, 1971, 1 son. Education: AB, Harvard University, 1938; Postgraduate Studies, University of Cambridge, 1938-39. Appointments: Associate Professor, 1946-54, Professor of History, 1954-61, Harvard University; Special Assistant to President John F Kennedy, 1961-64; Visiting Fellow, Institute for Advanced Study, Princeton, New Jersey, 1966; Schweitzer Professor of Humanities, City University of New York, 1966-95; Chairman, Franklin Delano Roosevelt Four Freedoms Foundation, 1983-. Publications: Orestes A Brownson: A Pilgrim's Progress, 1939; The Age of Jackson, 1945; The Vital Center, 1949; The General and the President (with R H Revere), 1951; The Age of Roosevelt, Vol I, The Crisis of the Old Order 1919-1933, 1957, Vol II, The Coming of the New Deal, 1958, Vol III, The Politics of Upheaval, 1960; Kennedy or Nixon: Does It Make Any Difference?, 1960; The Politics of Hope, 1963; The National Experience (with John Blum), 1963; A Thousand Days: John F Kennedy in the White House, 1965; The Bitter Heritage: Vietnam and American Democracy 1941-66, 1967; The Crisis of Confidence, 1969; The Imperial Presidency, 1973; Robert Kennedy and His Times, 1978; The Cycles of American History, 1986; The Disuniting of America, 1991. Editor: The Harvard Guide to American History, 1954; Guide to Politics, 1954; Paths to American Thought, 1963; The Promise of American Life, 1967; The Best and Last of Edwin O'Connor, 1970; The History of American Presidential Elections (with F L Israel), 1971, new edition, 1986; The Coming to Power, 1972; The Dynamics of World Power: A Documentary History of United States Foreign Policy 1945-1972, 1973; History of US Political Parties, 1973; The American Statesman, 1982; The Almanac of American History, 1983; Running for President, 1994. Contributions to: Professional journals. Honours: Francis Parkman Prize, Society of American Historians, 1957; Bancroft Prize, Columbia University, 1958; Pulitzer Prize in Biography, 1966; National Book Awards, 1966, 1979; National Institute and American Academy of Arts and Letters Gold Medal in History and Biography, 1967; Ohio Governor's Award for History, 1973; Fregene Prize for Literature, Italy, 1983; National Humanities Medal, 1998; Grants, fellowships and honorary doctorates. Memberships: American Academy and Institute of Arts and Letters, president, 1981-84, chancellor, 1984-87; American Civil Liberties Union; American Historical Association; American Philosophical Society; Americans for Democratic Action, chairman, 1952-54; Colonial Society of Massachusetts; Council on Foreign Relations; Franklin and Eleanor Roosevelt Institute, co-chairman, 1983-; Organization of American Historians; Phi Beta Kappa. Address: 455 East 51st Street, New York, NY 10022, USA.

SCHLIEPP Shawn, b. 26 Mar 1978, Ripon, Wisconsin, USA. Radio Broadcaster. Education: Diploma, Radio Certification, Madison Media Institute. Address: 826 Congress Street, Ripon, WI 54971, USA.

SCHLIMM II, John E, b. 1 Dec 1971, St Marys, PA, USA. Writer. Education: Summa Cum Laude, BA, Communications, Marymount University, 1990-94. Appointments: Publicist, Front Page Publicity Inc, Nashville, TN, 1997-98; Executive Production Assistant,

Lone Pine Media, Washington DC, 1996-97; Adjunc Teacher, ECCHS, St Marys, PA, 1994-95; Intern Office o the Vice President, The White House, 1993-94 Publication: Corresponding With History: The Art & Benefits of Collecting Autographs, 1997. Contributions to: Contributing Editor, The Book Collection, for Autograph Collector magazine. Address: 479 Brussels St, St Marys, PA 15857, USA.

SCHLINK Bernhard, b. 6 July 1944, Bielefeld, Germany. Professor; Judge. 1 son. Publications: Selbs Justiz, 1987; Die Gordische Schleife, 1988; Selbs Betrug, 1992; Der Vorleser (The Reader), 1995. Address: Heilbronner Str 3, D-10779 Berlin, Germany.

SCHLUP Leonard, b. 22 Feb 1943, Barberton, Ohio, USA. Researcher; Scholar; Writer. Education: BA, University of Akron, 1965; MA, Kent State University, 1967; MLS, Indiana University, 1983; PhD, University of Illinois at Urbana, 1973. Appointments: Reference Librarian, Akron-Summit County Public Library, Ohio, 1985-. Publications: Historical Dictionary of the 1940's; Numerous others. Contributions to: Journals. Honours: Several fellowships. Address: 641 Polk Avenue, Akron, OH 44314, USA.

SCHMIDMAN Jo Ann, b. 18 Apr 1948, Omaha, Nebraska, USA. Theatre Director; Playwright. Education: BFA, Boston University, 1970. Appointments: Producing Artistic Director, Omaha Magic Theatre, 1968-; Team Member, Artist-in-Schools, Nebraska Arts Council, 1994. Publications: Plays: This Sleep Among Women, 1974; Running Gag, 1980; Astro Bride, 1985; Velveeta Meltdown, 1985; Right Brain (editor with M Terry and S Kimberlain), 1992; Body Leaks (with M Terry and S Kimberlain), 1995. Other: Various unpublished but produced plays, 1978-93. Address: 2309 Hanscom Boulevard, Omaha, NE 68105, USA.

SCHMIDT Grethe, b. 14 Mar 1922, Copenhagen, Denmark. Writer; Naturopath. m. Poul Blicher Schmidt, 11 Sept 1948, 2 daughters. Apointments: Bookseller; Runs health farm on basis of her books. Publications: Mit gronne kokken; Hvorfor syg - hvodan rask?; Slank, sund og glad; Gronne dage; sundhed til alle - her og nu; Health from Nature; Spis dig sund; Spis dig rask; Saftfaste og råkostkuren. Contributions to: Various ladies' journals; Newspapers. Membership: Danish Writers Society. Literary Agents: Aschelsong, Sesam, Copenhagen; Krogh, Chr Hansensvej 3, 7100 Vejle, Denmark. Address: Jægersborg Allé 45, DK-2920 Charlottenlund, Denmark.

SCHMIDT Michael (Norton), b. 2 Mar 1947, Mexico City, Mexico. Poet; Editor; Translator. m. Claire Harman, 1979, dec 1989, 2 sons, 1 daughter. Education: Harvard University, 1966; BA, Wadham College, Oxford, 1969. Appointments: Editorial Director, Carcanet Press Ltd, 1969-; Senior Lecturer in Poetry, University of Manchester, 1972-98; Editor, PN Review, 1972-; Director, Writing School, Manchester Metropolitan University, 1998-. Publications: Black Buildings, 1969; One Eye Mirror Cold, 1970; Bedlam and the Oakwood, 1970; Desert of Lions, 1972; British Poetry Since 1960 (editor with G Lindop), 1972; It Was My Tree, 1972; Flower and Song (translator with E Kissam), 1975; My Brother Gloucester, 1976; Ten British Poets (editor), 1976; A Change of Affairs, 1978; A Reader's Guide to Fifty Poets (editor), 2 volumes, 1979; The Colonist, 1980, US edition as Green Island, 1982; Eleven British Poets (editor), 1980; Choosing a Guest: New and Selected Poems, 1983; Some Contemporary Poets of Britain and Ireland (editor), 1983; The Dresden Gate, 1986; Octavio Paz: On Poets and Others (translator), 1986; The Love of Strangers, 1988; Modern Poetry, 1989; New Poetries (editor), 1994; A Calendar of Modern Poetry (editor), 1994; Selected Poems, 1997; Lives of the Poets, 1998. Address: Conavon Court, 4th Floor, 12-16 Blackfriars Street, Manchester M3 5BQ, England.

SCHMIDT-NIELSEN Knut, b. 24 Sept 1915, Trondheim, Norway (US citizen, 1950). Scientist; Writer. Education: PhD, University of Copenhagen, 1946. Appointments: Faculty, Department of Zoology, Duke

University; Editor, scientific journals. Publications: Desert Animals, 1964; How Animals Work, 1972; Animal Physiology, 1975, 5th edition, 1997; Scaling: Why is Animal Size So Important?, 1984; The Camel's Nose: Memoirs of a Curious Scientist, 1998. Contributions to: Many professional journals. Honours: Honorary MD, University of Lund, 1983; Honorary PhD, University of Trondheim, 1993. Memberships: Académie des Sciences, Paris; National Academy of Sciences, USA; Royal Society, London. Address: c/o Department of Zoology, Duke University, Durham, NC 27708-0325, USA.

SCHMITZ Dennis (Mathew), b. 11 Aug 1937, Dubuque, Iowa, USA. Professor of English; Poet. m. Loretta D'Agostino, 1960, 2 sons, 3 daughters. Education: BA, Loras College, Dubuque, Iowa, 1959; MA, University of Chicago, 1961. Appointments: Instructor, Illinois Institute of Technology, Chicago, 1961-62, University of Wisconsin at Milwaukee, 1962-66; Assistant Professor, 1966-69, Poet-in-Residence, 1966-, Associate Professor, 1969-74, Professor of English, 1974-, California State University at Sacramento. Publications: We Weep for Our Strangeness, 1969; Double Exposures, 1971; Goodwill, Inc, 1976; String, 1980; Singing, 1985; Eden, 1989; About Night: Selected and New Poems, 1993. Honours: New York Poetry Center Discovery Award, 1968; National Endowment for the Arts Fellowships, 1976, 1985, 1992; Guggenheim Fellowship, 1978; di Castagnola Award, 1986; Shelley Memorial Award, 1988. Address: c/o Department of English, California State University at Sacramento, 6000 Jay Street, Sacramento, CA 95819, USA.

SCHMOOKLER Andrew Bard, b. 19 Apr 1946, Long Branch, New Jersey, USA. Writer; Speaker; Consultant. m. 28 Sept 1986, 2 sons, 1 daughter. Education: BA, summa cum laude, Harvard College, 1967; PhD, Thelogical Union and University of California, 1977. Publications: The Parable of the Tribes, The Problem of Power in Social Evolution, 1984, 2nd edition, 1995; Out of Weakness: Healing the Wounds that Drive us to War, 1988; Sowing and Reapings: The Cycling of Good and Evil in the Human System, 1989; The Illusion of Choice: How the Market Economy Shapes Our Destiny, 1992; Fools Gold: The Fate of Values in a World of Goods, 1993; Living Posthumously: Confronting the Loss of Vital Powers, 1997; Debating the Good Society: A Quest to Bridge America's Moral Divide, 1999. Honour: Erik H Erikson Prize, International Society for Political Psychology, 1984. Address: 86 Sunset Ridge Road, Broadway, VA 22815, USA.

SCHNACKENBERG Gjertrud, b. 27 Aug 1953, Tacoma, Washington, USA. Poet; Writer. m. Robert Nozick, 5 Oct 1987. Education: BA, Mount Holyoke College, 1975. Publications: Portraits and Elegies, 1982, revised edition, 1986; The Lamplit Answer, 1985; A Gilded Lapse of Time, 1992. Contributions to: Books and journals. Honours: Glascock Awards for Poetry, 1973, 1974; Lavan Younger Poets Award, Academy of American Poets, 1983; Rome Prize, American Academy and Institute of Arts and Letters, 1983-84; Amy Lowell Traveling Prize, 1984-85; Honorary Doctorate, Mount Holyoke College, 1985; National Endowment for the Arts Grant, 1986-87; Guggenheim Fellowship, 1987-88; Academy Award in Literature, American Academy of Arts and Letters. Membership: American Academy of Arts and Sciences, fellow, 1996. Address: c/o Farrar, Straus & Giroux Inc, 19 Union Square West, New York, NY 10003, USA.

SCHNAPPER Dominique Aron, b. 9 Nov 1934, Paris, France. Educator. m. Writer. m. Antoine Schnapper, 28 Nov 1958, 1 son, 2 daughter. Education: IEP, 1957; Doctorate, Sorbonne, 1967; Doctorat d'Etat, 1979. Appointment: Director of Studies, École des Hautes Études en Sciences Sociales, Paris. Publications: L'Italie Rouge et Noire, 1971; Juifs et Israelites, 1980; L'épreuve du Chomage, 1981; La France de L'Intégration, 1991; L'Europe des Immigrés, 1992; La Communauté des Citoyens, 1994; Contra la fin du travail, 1997; La Relation à l'autre, 1998. Memberships: Société Française de

Sociologie, president; Société Française de Sciences Politiques; Society of Friends of Raymond Aron. Address: 75 Bd St Michel, 75005 Paris, France.

SCHNEEBAUM Tobias, b. 25 Mar 1922, New York, New York, USA. Writer; Lecturer. Education: BA, City College of New York, 1942; MA, Cultural Anthropology, Goddard College, 1977. Publications: Keep the River on Your Right, 1969; Wild Man, 1979; Life with the Asmat, 1981; Asmat Images, 1985; Where the Spirits Dwell, 1988; Embodied Spirits, 1990. Contributions to: Various publications. Honours: Fulbright Fellowship, 1955; Ingram Merrill Foundation Grants, 1982, 1989; Ludwig Vogelstein Foundation Grant, 1985. Memberships: Explorers Club; PEN. Address: 463 West Street, No 410A, New York, NY 10014, USA.

SCHNEIDER Bill, b. 15 Feb 1952, Chicago, Illinois, USA. Writer. Education: University of California, Irvine. Appointments: Independent Writer and Producer, 1988-90; Segment Producer, Entertainment Tonight, 1990-95; Managing Editor, AMP, MCA Records Online, 1996-97; Writer, Producer, Universal Studios, Universal City, California, 1997-. Publications: Horror on Halloween, 1994; The Best Of Darla, 1995. Contributions to: Vanity Fair; Rolling Stone; London Financial Times; Billboard; Los Angeles Times; San Francisco Chronicle; Village Voice; Melody Maker. Memberships: American Society of Journalists and Authors; National Academy of Recording Arts and Sciences; National Writers' Union; Writers Guild of America, West. Literary Agent: Paradigm. Address: c/o Universal Studios, 70 Universal City Plaza, Universal City, CA 91608, USA.

SCHOEMPERLEN Diane Mavis, b. 9 July 1954, Thunder Bay, Ontario, Canada. Writer; Teacher. 1 son. Education: BA, English, Lakehead University, Ontario, 1976. Appointments: Teacher, Kingston School of Writing, Queen's University, Ontario, 1986-93, St Lawrence College, Kingston, 1987-93, University of Toronto Summer Writers' Workshop, 1992; Editor, Coming Attractions, Oberton Press, 1994-96. Publications: Double Exposures, 1984; Frogs and Other Stories, 1986; Hockey Night in Canada, 1987; The Man of My Dreams, 1990; Hockey Night in Canada and Other Stories, 1991; In the Language of Love, 1994; Forms of Devotion, 1998. Contributions to: Anthologies. Honours: WGA Award for Short Fiction, 1987; Silver National Magazine Award, 1989; Shortlisted for Governor-General's Award and Trillium Award, 1990; Governor-General's Award for English Fiction, 1998. Memberships: Writer's Union of Canada; Authors Guild of America. Address: 32 Dunlop Street, Kingston, Ontario, K7L 1L2, Canada.

SCHOENEWOLF Gerald Frederick, b. 23 Sept 1941, Fredericksburg, Texas, USA. Psychoanalyst; Writer. m. (1) Carol Slater, 1964, div 1969, 1 daughter, (2) Theresa Lamb, 1979, div 1984. Education: BA, Goddard College, Plainfield, Vermont; MA, California State University, Dominguez Hills; PhD, Union Institute, Cincinnati, Ohio. Publications: 101 Common Therapeutic Blinders (with R Robertiello), 1987; 101 Therapeutic Successes, 1989; Sexual Animosity between Men and Women, 1989; Turning Points in Analytic Therapy: The Classic Cases, 1990; Turning Points in Analytic Therapy: From Winnicott to Kernberg, 1990; The Art of Hating, 1991; Jennifer and Her Selves, 1991; Counterresistance, 1993; Erotic Games: Bringing Intimacy Back into Relationships, 1995; The Couple Who Fell in Hate and Other Tales of Eclectic Psychotherapy, 1996; Dictionary of Dream Interpretation, 1997. Contributions to: Numerous papers and short stories to various publications. Memberships: American Psychological Association; National Association for the Advancement of Psychoanalysis. Address: R.R.1, Box 303T, Bushkill, PA 18324, USA.

SCHOFIELD Caroline (Carey), b. 29 Dec 1953, Surrey, England. Writer. m. Laurence King, 14 June 1985. Education: BA, Cantab, 1976. Publications: Mesrine, 1980; Jagger, 1984; Russia at War, 1987; Inside the Soviet Army, 1991; The Russian Elite: Inside Spetsnaz and the Airborne Forces, 1993. Contributions

to: Various publications. Memberships: International Institute of Strategic Studies; Royal United Services Institute. Address: 6 St Martins Road, London SW9, England.

SCHOFIELD Michael, b. 24 June 1919, Leeds, England. Sociologist; Writer. Education: MA, University of Cambridge, 1940. Publications: The Sexual Behaviour of Young People, 1965; The Sociological Aspects of Homosexuality, 1965; Society and the Young School Leaver, 1967; Drugs and Civil Liberties, 1968; Social Research, 1969; Behind the Drug Scene (co-author), 1970; The Strange Case of Pot, 1971; The Rights of Children (co-author), 1972; The Sexual Behaviour of Young Adults, 1973; Promiscuity, 1976; The Sexual Containment Act, 1978. Address: 28 Lyndhurst Gardens, London NW3 5NW, England.

SCHOFIELD Paul. See: TUBB E(dwin) C(harles).

SCHOFIELD William Greenough, b. 13 June 1909, Providence, Rhode Island, USA. Author. m. 21 Nov 1934, 2 sons, 1 daughter. Appointments: Feature Writer, Providence Journal, 1936-40; Chief Editorial Writer, Columnist, Foreign Correspondent, Boston Traveler, 1940-67; Manager, Editorial Services, Raytheon Co., 1967-70; Director, Public Information Consultant, Public Affairs, Publications Editor, Boston University, 1970-79. Publications: Ashes in the Wilderness, 1942; The Cat in the Convoy, 1946; Payoff in Black, 1947; The Deer Cry, 1948; Seek for a Hero, 1956; Sidewalk Statesman, 1959; Destroyers: 60 Years, 1962; Treason Trail, 1964; Eastward the Convoys, 1966; Freedom by the Bay, 1974; Frogmen: First Battles, 1987. Contributions to: Reader's Digest; Catholic Digest; Redbook; Skipper; Information; Boston Sunday Herald. Honour: Achievement Award, US Department of Interior, 1976. Address: 16 Hunnewell Circle, Newton, MA 02158, USA.

SCHOLEY Arthur (Edward), b. 17 June 1932, Sheffield, England. Children's Writer; Playwright. Publications: The Song of Caedmon (with Donald Swann), 1971; Christmas Plays and Ideas for Worship, 1973; The Discontented Dervishes, 1977; Sallinka and the Golden Bird, 1978; Twelve Tales for a Christmas Night, 1978; Wacky and His Fuddlejig (with Donald Swann), 1978; Singalive (with Donald Swann) 1978; Herod and the Rooster (with Ronald Chamberlain), 1979; The Dickens Christmas Carol Show, 1979; Baboushka (with Donald Swann) 1979; Candletree (with Donald Swann), 1981; Five Plays for Christmas, 1981; Four Plays About People, 1983; Martin the Cobbler, 1983; The Hosanna Kids, 1985; Make a Model Christmas Crib, 1988; Who'll Be Brother Donkey?, 1990; Brendan Ahoy!, (with Donald Swann), 1994. Address: 1 Cranbourne Road, London N10 2BT, England.

SCHOONOVER Jason Brooke Rivers Morgan, b. 14 Sept 1946, Melfort, Saskatchewan, Canada. Author; Anthropologist. Education: BA, English, Simon Fraser University, Burnaby, British Columbia, Canada. Appointments: Announcer, CKOM Radio, Saskatoon, 1970-71; Announcer, Music Director, Promotion Manager, Producer, CFQC Radio, Saskatoon, 1972-77; CBC Broadcaster, 1972-77; President, Schoononer Properties, 1975-. Publications: The Bangkok Collection, 1988; Thai Gold, 1989. Honours: B'nai B'rith Media Human Rights Award, on behalf of CFQC Radio, 1976. Address: 720 University Drive, Saskatoon, Saskatchewan S7N 0J4, Canada.

SCHOULTZ Solveig von, b. 5 Aug 1907, Borga, Finland. Author; Poet; Dramatist. m. Erik Bergman, 7 July 1961. Education: Teacher's Qualification; PhD, honouris causa, 1986. Publications: Poetry: Eko av ett rop, 1946; Natet, 1956; Sank ditt ljus, 1963; De fyra flojtspelarna, 1975; Bortom traden hors havet, 1980; En enda minut, 1981; Vattenhjulet, 1986; Alla träd vantar faglar, 1988; Ett sätt att räkna tiden, 1989; Samtal med en fjäril, 1994. Short Novels: Ingenting ovanligt, 1948; Narmare nagon, 1951; Den blomstertid, 1958; Även dina kameler, 1965; Rymdbruden, 1970; Somliga mornar, 1976; Kolteckning, ofullbordad, 1983; Ingen dag forgaves, 1984; Nästa dag,

1991; Längs vattenbrynet, 1992; Samtal med en fjäril, 1994. Other: Plays for television and radio. Address: Berggatan 22C, Helsinki 10, Finland.

SCHRAG Peter, b. 24 July 1931, Karlsruhe, Germany. Journalist; Editor. Education: BA, Amherst College, 1953; Graduate Studies, Amherst College and University of Massachusetts, 1957-59. Appointments: Reporter, El Paso Herald Post, Texas, 1953-55; Assistant Secretary, Amherst College, 1956-66; Associate Education Editor, 1966-68, Executive Editor, 1968-73, Saturday Review, New York City; Editor, Change, New York City, 1969-70; Lecturer, University of Massachusetts, 1970-72, University of California at Berkeley, 1990-; Editor, Editorial Page, Sacramento Bee, California, 1978-; Contributing Editor, The American Prospect. Publications: Voices in the Classroom, 1965; Village School Downtown, 1967; Out of Place in America, 1970; The Decline of the WASP, UK edition, US, The Vanishing American, 1972; The End of the American Future, 1973; Test of Loyalty, 1974; The Myths of the Hyperative Child (with Diane Divorky), 1975; Mind Control, 1978; Paradise Lost: California's Experience, America's Future, 1998. Contributions to: Newspapers and magazines. Honour: Guggenheim Fellowship, 1971-72. Membership: National Conference of Editorial Writers. Literary Agent: Ellen Levine, Ellen Levine Literary Agency, 15 East 26th Street, Suite 1801, New York, NY 10010, USA. Address: c/o Sacramento Bee, 21st and Q Streets, Sacramento, CA 95816, USA.

SCHRAMM Werner, b. 28 Apr 1926, Germany. Author; Painter. Education: Teacher Training Institute; Langemarck Studies. Publications: Stefan Zweig, 1961; Das antike Drama 'Die Bacchantinnen' in der Neugestaltung durch H Wolfgang Philipp, 1980; Hugo Wolfgang Philipps Tragikomödie 'Der Clown Gottes', 1983; Moderner deutscher Roman, 1983; Stefan Zweig: Bildnis eines genialen Charakters, 1984. Honours: Cultural Doctorate in Literature, 1991; Research Advisor of the Year, 1991; Professional of The Year, 1991; Grand Ambassador of Achievement, 1991; Silver Shield of Valor, 1992; Doctor of Arts, Albert Einstein International Academy Foundation, 1993; Man of The Year, 1993; Pictorial Testimonial of Achievement and Distinction, 1993; Gold Record of Achievement, 1994; Order of International Ambassadors, 1995. Memberships: American Biographical Institute Research Association, board of governors, 1989; International Biographical Association, 1989; American Biographical Institute, research board of governors, 1989, and advisors, 1990; IBC Advisory Council, 1990. Address: Eckenerweg 8, D 25524 Itzehoe, Germany.

SCHREINER Samuel Agnew, Jr., b. 6 June 1921, Mt Lebanon, Pennsylvania, USA. Author. m. Doris Moon, 22 Sept 1945, 2 daughters. Education: AB, summa cum laude, Princeton University, 1942. Publications: Thine is the Glory, 1975; The Condensed World of the Reader's Digest, 1977; Pleasant Places, 1977; Angelica, 1978; The Possessors and the Possessed, 1980; The Van Alens, 1981; A Place Called Princeton, 1984; The Trials of Mrs Lincoln, 1987; Cycles, 1990; Mayday! Mayday!, 1990; Code of Conduct (with Everett Alvarez), 1992; Henry Clay Frick: The Gospel of Greed, 1995. Contributions to: Reader's Digest; Woman's Day; McCalls; Redbook; Parade. Address: 111 Old Kings Highway South, Darien, CT 06820, USA.

SCHROEDER Andreas Peter, b. 26 Nov 1946, Hoheneggelsen, Germany. Writer; Poet; Translator. m. Sharon Elizabeth Brown, 2 daughters. Education: BA, 1969, MA, 1972, University of British Columbia. Appointments: Literary Critic and Columnist, Vancouver Province newspaper, 1968-72; Co-Founder and Editor-in-Chief, Contemporary Literature in Translation, 1968-83; Lecturer in Creative Writing, University of Victoria, 1974-75, Simon Fraser University, 1989-90; Writer-in-Residence, University of Winnipeg, 1983-84; Fraser Valley College, 1987; Lecturer in Creative Writing, 1985-87, Professor, Maclean Hunter Chair in Creative Non-Fiction, 1993-, University of British Columbia. Publications: The Ozone Minotaur, 1969; File of

Uncertainties, 1971; UNIverse, 1971; The Late Man, 1972; Stories From Pacific and Arctic Canada (co-editor), 1974; Shaking it Rough, 1976; Toccata in 'D', 1984; Dust-Ship Glory, 1986; Word for Word: The Business of Writing in Alberta, 1988; The Eleventh Commandment (with Jack Thiessen), 1990; The Mennonites in Canada: A Photographic History, 1990; Carved From Wood: Mission, B.C. 1891-1992, 1992; Scams, Scandals and Skullduggery, 1996; Cheats, Charlatans and Chicanery, 1998; Fakes, Frauds and Flimflammery, 1999. Contributions to: Numerous anthologies, newspapers, and magazines. Honours: Woodward Memorial Prize for Prose, 1969; Canada Council Grants, 1969, 1971, 1975, 1979, 1986, 1991; National Film Board of Canada Scriptwriting Prize, 1971; Best Investigative Journalism, Canadian Association of Journalists, 1990. Memberships: Writers Union of Canada; Alliance of Canadian Cinema, Television and Radio Artists; Federation of British Columbia Writers; PEN Club; Saskatchewan Writers' Guild. Address: Stag's Leap, 9564 Erickson Road, Mission, British Columbia V2V 5X4, Canada.

SCHUCHMAN Joan. See: FEINBERG Joan Miriam.

SCHULBERG Budd, b. 27 Mar 1914, New York, New York, USA. Author. m. (1) Virginia Ray, 23 July 1936, div 1942, 1 daughter, (2) Victoria Anderson, 17 Feb 1943, div 1964, 2 sons, (3) Geraldine Brooks, 12 July 1964, dec 1977, (4) Betsy Anne Langman, 9 July 1979, 1 son, 1 daughter. Education: AB cum laude, Dartmouth College, 1936. Appointments: Founder-President, Schulberg Productions; Founder-Director, Watts Writers Workshop, Los Angeles, 1965-; Founder-Chairman, Frederick Douglass Creative Arts Center, New York City, 1971-. Publications: What Makes Sammy Run?, 1941; The Harder They Fall, 1947; The Disenchanted, 1950; Some Faces in the Crowd, 1953; Waterfront, 1955; Sanctuary V, 1969; The Four Seasons of Success, 1972; Loser and Still Champion: Muhammad Ali, 1972; Swan Watch, 1975; Everything That Moves, 1980; Moving Pictures: Memories of a Hollywood Prince, 1981; Love, Action, Laughter and Other Sad Tales, 1990; Sparring with Hemingway and Other Legends of the Fight Game, 1995. Editor: From the Ashes: Voices of Watts, 1967. Screenplays: Little Orphan Annie (with Samuel Ornitz), 1938; Winter Carnival (with F Scott Fitzgerald), 1939; Weekend for Three (with Dorothy Parker), 1941; City Without Men (with Martin Berkeley), 1943; Government Girl, 1943; On the Waterfront, 1954; A Face in the Crowd, 1957; Wind Across the Everglades, 1958. Contributions to: Leading magazines. Honours: Academy Award, 1954; New York Critics Circle Award, 1954; Screen Writers Guild Award, 1954; Venice Film Festival Award, 1954; Christopher Award, 1955; German Film Critics Award, 1957; B'hai Human Rights Award, 1968; Prix Literaire, Deauville Festival, 1989; Westhampton Writers Lifetime Achievement Award, 1989; World Boxing Assocition Living Legend Award, 1990; Southampton Cultural Center 1st Annual Literature Award, 1992. Memberships: American Civil Liberties Union; American Society of Composers, Authors and Publishers; Authors Guild; Dramatists Guild; Players' Club, founder member; PEN; Phi Beta Kappa; Writers Guild East. Address: c/o Miriam Altschuler Literary Agency, RR1, Box 5, Old Post Road, Red Hook, NY 12571, USA.

SCHULLER Gunther (Alexander), b. 22 Nov 1925, New York, New York, USA. Composer; Conductor; Music Educator; Publisher. m. Marjorie Black, 8 June 1948, dec 1992, 2 sons. Education: St Thomas Choir School, New York City, 1938-44. Appointments: Teacher, Manhattan School of Music, New York City, 1950-63; Teacher, 1963-84, Artistic Co-Director, 1969-74, Director, 1974-84, Berkshire Music Center, Tanglewood, Massachusetts; Faculty, Yale School of Music, 1964-67; President, New England Conservatory of Music, Boston, 1967-77; Music Publisher, 1975-; Artistic Director, Festival at Sandpoint, 1985-. Publications: Horn Technique, 1962, 2nd edition, 1992; Early Jazz: Its Roots and Musical Development, 3 volumes, 1968-; Musings, 1985; The Swing Era, 1988. Contributions to: Various publications. Honours: Guggenheim Fellowship, 1962-63; ASCAP-Deems Taylor Award, 1970; Rodgers and Hammerstein Award, 1971;

William Schuman Award, Columbia University, 1989; John D and Catharine T MacArthur Foundation Fellowship, 1991; Pulitzer Prize in Music, 1994; Honorary doctorates. Memberships: American Academy of Arts and Sciences; American Academy of Arts and Letters. Address: 167 Dudley Road, Newton Centre, MA 02159, USA.

SCHULTZ John (Ludwig), b. 28 july 1932, Columbia, Missouri, USA. Writer; Teacher. m. (1) Anne Gillian Bray, 10 Dec 1962, div Nov 1975, (2) Betty E Schiflett, 9 May 1992, 1 son, 1 daughter. Appointments: Chair Fiction Writing Department, 1967-, Head, Master in Teaching Writing, 1983-, Head, Master in Fine Arts in Creative Writing, 1990-, Columbia College, Chicago. Publications: The Tongues of Men, 1969; No One Was Killed, 1969; Motion Will be Denied, 1972; Writing from Start to Finish, 1982, new edition, 1990; The Chicago Conspiracy Trial, 1993. Contributions to: Journals. Memberships: Associated Writing Programs; Modern Language Association. Address: 3636 North Janssen, Chicago, IL 60613, USA.

SCHULZ Max (Frederick), b. 15 Sept 1923, Cleveland, Ohio, USA. Professor of English; Writer. Education: University of Chicago, 1947-48; AB, 1949, MA, 1950, University of Pittsburgh; Postgraduate Studies, University of Minnesota, 1950-51; PhD, Wayne State University, 1959. Appointments: Professor of English, 1963-94, Chairman, Department of English, 1968-80, Curator, Fisher Gallery, 1993-, University of Southern California at Los Angeles; Fulbright Professor, University of Graz, 1965-66; Associate Editor, Critique Magazine, 1971-85; University of Vienna, 1977-78. Publications: The Poetic Voices of Coleridge, 1963, revised edition, 1965; Essays in American and English Literature Presented to Bruce Robert McElderry Jr (editor), 1967; Radical Sophistication: Studies in Contemporary Jewish-American Novelists, 1969; Bruce Jay Friedman, 1973; Black Humor Fiction of the Sixties: A Pluralistic Definition of Man and His World, 1973; Paradise Preserved: Recreations of Eden in 18th and 19th Century England, 1985; The Muses of John Barth: Tradition and Metafiction from Lost in the Funhouse to the Tidewater Tales, 1990; Edgar Ewing: The Classical Connection, 1993; The Mythic Present of Chagoya, Valdez and Gronk, 1995. Honour: Senior Fellow, National Endowment for the Humanities, 1985-86. Address: c/o Fisher Gallery, University of Southern California at Los Angeles, Los Angeles, CA 90089, USA.

SCHUNCKE Michael, b. 8 May 1929, Dresden, Germany. Special Teacher; Author; Consultant. m. Dorothea Czibulinski-Dressler, 22 Dec 1956, 2 daughters. Education: Theory of Music, 1945-49; Advertising, Academy of Mannheim, 1953-54; Seminars in writing, advertising, marketing, musik history (Schunke). Appointment: Vice Chairman, Poetical Ludwig-Finckh-Freundeskreis Gaienhofen, 1989-93. Publications: Wanderer Zwischen 2 Welten, 1975; Sprecht die Sprache der Adressaten, 1982; Schlüsselworte erfolgreicher Anzeigen, 1986; Praktische Werbehilfe, 1987; Atmosphäre eines Jugend in Baden-Baden, 1995; Co-editor of: Schumann's Closest 'Jugendfreund', Ludwig Schuncke (1810-1834), English/German, 1997; Editor of: Ein eminentes musik. Talent: Hugo Schuncke (1823-1909), 1998; Dokumentation I: Das Mendelssohn-Bildnis der Musikerfamilie Schuncke, 1996; Dokumentation II: Einführung in die Ausstellung 'Die Schunckes', 1998; Catalogue of the Exhibition, Die Schunkes, Baden-Baden,, Zwickau, Leipzig, Stuttgart (in co-operation with Dr Joachim Draheim), 1998-99. Honours: Goldene Hans Buchholz Medaille, 1974; Awards in Community. Memberships: Gesellschaft für Deutsche Sprache; Poetical Ludwig-Finckh-Freundeskreis Gaienhofen; Robert Schumann Gesellschaft; Mendelssohn Gesellschaft. Address: Lichtental, Heschmattweg 11, D 76534 Baden-Baden, Germany.

SCHWANDT Stephen (William), b. 5 Apr 1947, Chippewa Falls, Wisconsin, USA. Educator. m. Karen

Sambo, 13 June 1970, 2 sons. Education: BA, Valparaiso University, 1969; BS, St Cloud State University, 1972; MA, University of Minnesota - Twin Cities, 1972. Appointments: Teacher of Composition and American Literature, Irondale High School, New Brighton, Minnesota, 1974-; Instructor, Concordia College, St Paul, Minnesota, 1975-80, Normandale Community College, 1983-. Publications: The Last Goodie, 1985; A Risky Game, 1986; Holding Steady, 1988; Guilt Trip, 1990; Funnybone, 1992. Contributions to: Various newspapers. Memberships: National Education Association; Authors Guild; Book Critics Circle; National Council for Teachers of English; The Loft. Address: Curtis Brown Ltd, 10 Astor Place, New York, NY 10003, USA.

SCHWARTZ Eli, b. 2 Apr 1921, New York, New York, USA. Retired Professor of Economics. m. Renee S Kartiganer, 29 Aug 1948, 1 son, 1 daughter. Education: BS, University of Denver, 1943; Army, USA, 1943-46; MA, University of Connecticut, 1948; PhD, Brown University, 1952. Appointments: Instructor, University of Rhode Island, 1947-48; Assistant Instructor, Brown University, 1948-51; Chief Regional Economist, Office of Price Stabilization, Boston, 1951-53; Lecturer, Michigan State University, 1953-54; Assistant Professor, 1954-58, Associate Professor, 1958-62, Professor of Economics, 1962-78, Chairman, Department of Economics, 1978-84, Charles Macfarlane Professor of Economics, 1978-91, Lehigh University. Publications: Corporate Finance, 1962; Trouble in Eden: A Comparison of the British and Swedish Economies, 1980; Managing Municipal Finance (editor), 1980, 4th edition, 1996; Restructuring the Thrift Industry, 1989; Theory and Application of the Interest Rate, 1993. Contributions to: Professional journals. Honours: Senior Teaching Grant, Lehigh University, 1972; Earhart Foundation Grant, 1978. Memberships: American Economics Association; American Finance Association; National Association of Forensic Economists. Address: Rauch Business Centre. 621 Taylor Street, Lehigh University, Bethlehem, PA 18015, USA.

SCHWARTZ Elliott (Shelling), b. 19 Jan 1936, Brooklyn, New York, USA. Composer; Professor of Music; Writer. m. Dorothy Rose Feldman, 26 July 1960, 1 son, 1 daughter. Education: AB, 1957, MA, 1958, EdD, 1962, Columbia University. Appointments: Instructor, University of Massachusetts, 1960-64; Assistant Professor, 1964-70, Associate Professor, 1970-75, Professor of Music, 1975-, Bowdoin College; Distinguished Visiting Professor, Ohio State University, 1985-86; Visiting Professor of Music, Ohio State University, 1988-92; Visiting Fellow, Robinson College, Cambridge, England, 1993-94, 1998-99. Publications: The Symphonies of Ralph Vaughan Williams, 1964; Contemporary Composers on Contemporary Music (editor with Barney Childs), 1967, 2nd edition, revised, 1998; Electronic Music: A Listener's Guide, 1973, 2nd edition, revised, 1976; Music: Ways of Listening, 1982; Music Since 1945: Issues, Materials and Literature (with Daniel Godfrey), 1993. Contributions to: Professional journals. Honours: Guaudeamus Prize, Netherlands, 1970; Maine State Award in the Arts and Humanities, 1970; National Endowment for the Arts Grants, 1978-83; Rockefeller Foundation Residencies, Bellagio, Italy, 1980, 1989. Memberships: American Society of University Composers; College Music Society, president. Address: 10 Highview Road, PO Box 451, South Freeport, ME 04078, USA.

SCHWARTZ Gary David, b. Brooklyn, New York, USA. Art Historian. 1 son, 1 daughter. Education: BA, Washington Square College, New York University, 1961; Johns Hopkins University, Baltimore, Maryland, USA, 1961-65. Appointments: Publisher, Uitgeverij Gary Schwartz, 1971-88; Publisher, Gary Schwartz SDU, 1988-91; Visiting Professor, Hebrew University, Jerusalem, 1995-96; Director, CODART, 1998-. Publications: Rembrandt: All the Etchings, 1977; Rembrandt His Life, His Paintings, 1985; Rembrandt, 1992; Bets and Scams: A Novel of the Art World, 1996; Hieronymus Bosch, 1997. Contributions to: Art News; Art in America; Art Newsletter; TLS. Honour: Regents

Lecturer, UCLA, 1989-90. Literary Agent: ICM. Address: Herengracht 22, 3601 AM Maarssen, The Netherlands.

SCHWARTZ John (Burnham), b. 8 May 1965, New York, New York, USA. Writer. Education: BA, East Asian Studies, Harvard University, 1987. Publication: Bicycle Days, 1989. Contributions to: Periodicals. Honour: Lyndhurst Prize, 1991. Memberships: Authors Guild; Poet's Theatre, Cambridge, Massachusetts. Address: c/o International Creative Management, 40 West 57th Street, New York, NY 10019, USA.

SCHWARTZ Lloyd, b. 29 Nov 1941, Brooklyn, New York, USA. Professor of English; Music Critic; Poet. Education: BA, Queens College, City University of York, 1962; MA, 1963, PhD, 1976, Harvard University. Appointments: Classical Music Editor, Boston Phoenix, 1977-; Associate Professor of English, 1982-86, Director of Creative Writing, 1982-, Professor of English, 1986-, University of Massachusetts, Boston; Classical Music Critic, Fresh Air, National Public Radio, 1987. Publications: These People, 1981; Elizabeth Bishop and Her Art (editor), 1983; Goodnight, Gracie, 1992. Contributions to: American Review; Best American Poetry, 1991, 1994; Harvard Magazine; New Republic; New York Times; Partisan Review; Pequod; Ploughshares; Poetry; New Yorker; Slate; The Handbook of Heartbreak; Boulevard; Southwest Review. Honours: ASCAP-Deems Taylor Awards, 1980, 1987, 1990; Daniel Varoujan Prize, 1987; Pushcart Prize, 1987; Somerville Arts Council Grants, 1987, 1989; National Endowment for the Arts Fellowship, 1990; Runner-Up, Gustav Davidson Memorial Award, 1990; Pulitzer Prize in Criticism, 1994. Memberships: New England Poetry Club; PEN New England, executive committee, 1983-98, executive council, 1998-; Poetry Society of America. Address: 27 Pennsylvania Avenue, Somerville, MA 02145, USA.

SCHWARTZ Lynne Sharon, b. 19 Mar 1939, Brooklyn, New York, USA. Author; Poet. m. Harry Schwartz, 22 Dec 1957, 2 daughters. Education: BA, Barnard College, 1959; MA, Bryn Mawr College, 1961; New York University, 1967-72. Publications: Rough Strife, 1980; Balancing Acts, 1981; Disturbances in the Field, 1983; Acquainted with the Night (stories), 1984; We Are Talking About Homes (stories), 1985; The Melting Pot and Other Subversive Stories, 1987; Leaving Brooklyn, 1989; A Lynne Sharon Schwartz Reader: Selected Prose and Poetry, 1992; The Fatigue Artist, 1995; Ruined by Reading: A Life in Books, 1996. Contributions to: Periodicals. Honours: National Endowment for the Arts Fellowship, 1984; Guggenheim Fellowship, 1985; New York State Foundation for the Arts Fellowship, 1986. Memberships: Authors Guild; National Book Critics Circle; National Writers Union; PEN American Centre.

SCHWARTZ Sheila, b. 15 Mar 1936, New York, USA. Professor; Writer. Div. 1 son, 1 daughter, 1 dec. Education: BA, Adelphi University; MA, Teachers College, Columbia University; EdD, New York University. Appointment: Professor, State University of New York College at New Paltz. Publications: How People Lived in Ancient Greece and Rome, 1967; How People Lived in Mexico, 1969; Teaching the Humanities, 1970; Earth in Transit, 1977; Like Mother, Like Me, 1978; Growing Up Guilty, 1978; Teaching Adolescent Literature, 1979; The Solid Gold Circle, 1980; One Day You'll Go, 1981; Jealousy, 1982; The Hollywood Writer's Wars, 1982; Bigger is Better, 1987; Sorority, 1987; The Most Popular Girl, 1987. Other: The Children of Izieu (documentary film), 1992. Contributions to: Writing in America, 1989. Honours: Fulbright Fellowship; Teaching awards; Fellows Award, Adolescent Literature Association, 1979; New York State English Council 1979 Award for Excellence in Letters; New York State English Council Award for Excellence in Teaching, 1980; UUP/New York State Medal for Excellence, 1991. Membership: International PEN, Newsletter Committee, Women's Committee. Address: 5 Spies Road, New York, NY 12561, USA.

SCHWARZ Daniel Roger, b. 12 May 1941, Rockville Centre, New York, USA. Professor of English; Writer. m. Marcia Jacobson, 2 sons. Education: BA, Union College,

1963; MA, 1965, PhD, 1968, Brown University. Appointments: Professor of English, Cornell University, 1968-; Distinguished Visiting Cooper Professor, University of Arkansas at Little Rock, 1988; Citizen's Chair in Literature, University of Hawaii, 1992-93; Visiting Eminent Scholar, University of Alabama, Huntsville, 1996. Publications: Disraeli's Fiction, 1979; Conrad: Almayer's Folly to Under Western Eyes, 1980; Conrad: The Later Fiction, 1982; The Humanistic Heritage: Critical Theories of the English Novel from James to Hillis Miller, 1986; Reading Joyce's Ulysses, 1987, revised edition, 1991; The Transformation of the English Novel 1890-1930: Studies in Hardy, Conrad, Joyce, Lawrence, Forster and Woolf, 1989, revised edition, 1995; The Case for a Humanistic Poetics, 1991; Narrative and Representation in the Poetry of Wallace Stevens, 1993; The Dead by James Joyce (editor, Case Studies in Contemporary Criticism), 1994; Joseph Conrad's The Secret Sharer (editor), 1997; Reconfiguring Modernism: Explorations in the Relationship Between Modern Art and Modern Literature, 1997; Imagining the Holocaust, 1999. Contributions to: Professional journals. Honours: American Philosophical Society Grant, 1981; 9 National Endowment for the Humanities Summer Seminars for College and High School Teachers Grants, 1984-93; USIA Lecturer and Academic Specialist Lecturer, Australia, 1993, Cyprus, 1999; Cornell University Russell Distinguished Teaching Award, 1998. Membership: International Association of University Professors of English. Address: c/o Department of English, 304 Rockefeller Hall, Cornell University, Ithaca, NY 14853, USA.

SCHWEIZER Karl Wolfgang, b. 30 June 1946, Mannheim, Germany. Professor; Author. m. BA, Wilfrid Laurier University, 1969; MA, University of Waterloo, 1970; PhD, Cambridge, 1976. Appointments: Professor of History, Bishop's University, PQ, Canada, 1976-88; Visiting Scholar, Cambridge University, 1986, 1994; Professor, New Jersey Institute of Technology, Newark, NJ, 1988-; Visiting Scholar, Yale University, 1994-95; Princeton University, 1994-95. Publications: The Devonshire Diary, 1982; Author: Lord Bute: Essays in Re-Interpretation, 1988; England, Prussia and the 7 Years War, 1989; Frederick the Great, William Pitt and Lord Bute, 1991; Cobbet in His Times, 1993; Lord Chatham,m 1993; The Art of Diplomacy, 1994; Francois de Calliéres: Diplomat and Man of Letters, 1995. Contributions to: Over 100 articles, chapters and reviews in scholarly journals and reference works. Honours: Appelle Mellen Prize, 1990; New Jersey Writer's Award, 1983. Address: Fellow, Royal Historical Society. Address: 37 Lenape Trail, Chatham, NJ 07928, USA.

SCHWERIN Doris Belle, b. 24 June 1922, Peabody, Massachusetts, USA. Author; Composer. m. Jules V Schwerin, 2 Mar 1946, 1 son. Education: Boston University; New England Conservatory of Music; Diploma, Julliard School of Music, 1943; Student of George Antheil and Stefan Wolpe. Publications: Diary of a Pigeon Watcher, 1976; Leanna (novel in 6 movements), 1978; The Tomorrow Book (children's book), 1984; Rainbow Walkers, UK edition as The Missing Years; The Tree That Cried (children's book), 1988; Cat and I (memoir), 1990. Contributions to: MS Magazine. Honour: Charles Sergal National Play Award, University of Chicago, 1971. Memberships: PEN; Assocation of American Composers, Authors and Publishers; Authors Guild; Authors League. Address: 317 West 83rd Street, New York, NY 10024, USA.

SCISKOWSKI Wlodzimierz. See: KONOPINSKI Lech Kazimierz.

SCOBIE Stephen (Arthur Cross), b. 31 Dec 1943, Carnoustie, Scotland. Professor of English; Poet; Writer. m. Sharon Maureen, 6 May 1967. Education: MA, University of St Andrews, 1965; PhD, University of British Columbia, 1969. Appointments: Faculty, 1969-80, Professor, 1980-81, University of Alberta; Professor of English, University of Victoria, 1981-; Guest Professor of Canadian Studies, Christian-Albrechts-Universität, Kiel, 1990. Publications: Poetry: Babylondromat, 1966; In the

Silence of the Year, 1971; The Birken Tree, 1973; Stone Poems, 1974; The Rooms We Air, 1975; Airloom, 1975; Les toiles n'ont peur de rien, 1979; McAlmon's Chinese Opera, 1980; A Grand Memory for Forgetting, 1981; Expecting Rain, 1985; The Ballad of Isabel Gunn, 1987; Dunino, 1988; Remains, 1990; Ghosts: A Glossary of the Intertext, 1990; Gospel, 1994; Slowly Into Autumn, 1995; Willow, 1995; Taking the Gate: Journey Through Scotland, 1996. Other: Leonard Cohen, 1978; The Maple Laugh Forever: An Anthology of Canadian Comic Poetry (co-editor), 1981; Alias Bob Dylan, 1991. Contributions to: Journals and magazines. Honours: Governor-General's Award for Poetry, 1980; Fellow, Royal Society of Canada, 1995. Memberships: League of Canadian Poets, vice-president, 1972-74, 1986-88; Victoria Literary Arts Festival Society, president. Address: 4278 Parkside Crescent, Victoria, British Columbia V8N 2C3, Canada.

SCOFIELD Jonathan. See: LEVINSON Leonard.

SCOFIELD Sandra (Jean), b. 5 Aug 1943, Wichita Falls, Texas, USA. Writer; Adjunct Professor of English. m. (1) Allen Scofield, dec, 1 daughter, (2) Bill Ferguson, 10 July 1975. Education: BA, University of Texas, 1964; MA, 1978, PhD, 1979, University of Oregon. Appointments: Teacher, Elementary and High School, Texas, Illinois, California and Oregon; Assistant Professor of Education, 1979-80, Adjunct Professor of English, 1991-, Southern Oregon State College. Publications: Gringa, 1989; Beyond Deserving, 1991; Walking Dunes, 1992; More Than Allies, 1993; Opal on Dry Ground, 1994; A Chance to See Egypt, 1996. Contributions to: Periodicals. Honours: 2nd Place, Katherine Anne Porter Fiction Prize, 1985; New American Writing Award, 1989; American Academy and Institute of Arts and Letters 1st Fiction Award Nomination, 1989; National Endowment for the Arts Fellowship, 1989; National Book Award Nomination, 1991; American Book Award, 1992; Oregon Book Award Nomination, 1994; Texas Institute of Letters Fiction Award, 1997. Memberships: PEN; Authors Guild; Oregon Institute of Literary Arts; Austin Writers League. Address: PO Box 3329, Ashland, OR 97520, USA.

SCOTT Arthur Finley, b. 30 Nov 1907, Kronstad, Orange Free State, South Africa. Retired University Teacher; Author. m. (1) Margaret Ida Scott, June 1935, dec, (2) Margaret Clare Scott, Jan 1954, dec, 2 daughters. Education: BA, 1930, MA, 1934, University of Cambridge; Graduate Studies, University of Oxford, 1930. Appointments: Senior Lecturer in English, Borough Road College of Education, London, 1952-73; Faculty, London University, 1968-73; Director, Scott and Finley Ltd. Publications: Over 130 books, 1938-83. Honour: Life Fellow, International Biographical Association. Memberships: Kettering Three Arts Society; National Book League; Royal Society of Literature; Society of Authors. Address: 59 Syon Park Gardens, Isleworth, Middlesex TW7 5NE, England.

SCOTT Donald Fletcher, b. 29 Nov 1930, Norfolk, England. Retired Medical Consultant; Writer. m. (1) Adrienne Mary Moffett, 2 Sept 1967, dec 1992, (2) Dr Mary Paterson, 5 Jan 1994, 1 son, 1 daughter. Education: MB, ChB, University of Edinburgh, Scotland, 1951-57; DPM, London University, 1965. Publications: About Epilepsy, 1969; Fire and Fire Raisers, 1974; Understanding EEG, 1975; Coping With Suicide, 1989; Beating Job Burnout, 1989; The History of Epileptic Therapy, 1992. Contributions to: Over 100 articles mainly to medical/psychological journals. Honour: Fellow, Royal College of Physicians, 1979. Memberships: Electro-Encephalogram Society; Association of British Neurologists; Association of British Clinical Neurophysiology; British Society of Clinical Neurophysiology; Association of British Neurologists. Address: 25 Park Gate, Blackheath, London SE3 9XF, England.

SCOTT Gail, b. 20 Jan 1945, Ottawa, Ontario, Canada. Writer. 1 daughter. Education: BA, Queen's University, Kingston, Ontario, 1966; University of Grenoble. Appointments: Journalist, Montreal Gazette, The Globe and Mail, 1970-79; Writing Instructor, 1981-90;

Writer-in-Residence, Concordia University, Montreal, 1991-92, University of Alberta, Edmonton, 1994-95. Publications: Spare Parts, 1982; Heroine, 1987; La Theorie, un Dimanche, 1988; Spaces Like Stairs, 1989; Serious Hysterics (anthology), 1992; Resurgences (anthology), 1992; Main Brides, 1994. Contributions to: Journals and other publications. Honours: Shortlisted, Quebec Society for the Promotion of English Language Literature, 1987, 1994. Memberships: Union des écrivaines et écraivains québécois; Writer's Union of Canada. Address: c/o Coach House Press, 401 Heron Street, Toronto, Ontario M5S 2G5, Canada.

SCOTT John A, b. 23 Apr 1948, Littlehampton, Sussex, England. University Lecturer; Poet; Writer. Education: BA, DipEd, Monash University, Victoria, Australia. Appointments: Lecturer, Swinburne Institute, 1975-80; Canberra College of Advanced Education, 1980-89; University of Wollongong, New South Wales, 1989-. Publications: The Barbarous Sideshow, 1976; From the Flooded City, 1981; Smoking, 1983; The Quarrel with Ourselves, 1984; Confession, 1984; St Clair, 1986, revised edition, 1990; Blair, 1988; Singles: Shorter Works 1981-1986, 1989; Translation, 1990; What I Have Written, 1993. Contributions to: Various publication. Honours: Poetry Society of Australia Award, 1970; Mattara Poetry Prize, 1984; Wesley Michel Wright Awards, 1985, 1988; Victorian Premier's Prize for Poetry, 1986; ANA Award, Fellowship of Australian Writers, 1990. Address: c/o McPhee Gribble Publishers, 56 Claremont Street, South Yarra, Victoria 3141, Australia.

SCOTT John Peter, b. 8 Apr 1949, London, England. Professor of Sociology; Writer. m. Jill Wheatley, 4 Sept 1971, 1 son, 1 daughter. Education: Kingston College of Technology, 1968-71; BSc, Sociology, London University, 1971; London School of Economics and Political Science, 1971-72; PhD, University of Strathclyde, 1976. Appointments: Lecturer, University of Strathclyde, 1972-76; Lecturer, 1976-87, Reader, 1987-91, Professor of Sociology, 1991-94, University of Leicester; Editor, Network Newsletter, British Sociological Association, 1985-89, Social Studies Review, later Sociology Review, 1986-; Professor of Sociology, University of Essex, 1994-; Adjunct Professor, University of Bergen, Norway, 1997-. Publications: Corporations, Classes and Capitalism, 1979, 2nd edition, 1985; The Upper Classes, 1982; The Anatomy of Scottish Capital (with M Hughes), 1982; Directors of Industry (with C Griff), 1984; Networks of Corporate Power (co-editor), 1985; Capitalist Property and Financial Power, 1986; A Matter of Record, 1990; The Sociology of Elites (editor), 3 volumes, 1990; Who Rules Britain, 1991; Social Network Analysis, 1992; Power (editor), 3 volumes, 1994; Poverty and Wealth, 1994; Sociological Theory, 1995; Stratification and Power, 1996; Corporate Business and Capitalist Classes, 1997; Class, editor, 4 volumes, 1997; Sociology, with James Fulcher, 1999. Contributions to: Professional journals and general periodicals. Honour: Outstanding Sociology Book of the Year, Choice, 1995. Membership: British Sociological Association, secretary, 1991-92, chairperson, 1992-93, treasurer, 1997-. Address: c/o Department of Sociology, University of Essex, Colchester CO4 3SQ, England.

SCOTT Jonathan Henry, b. 22 Jan 1958, Auckland, New Zealand. Historian; Writer; Poet. Education: BA, 1980, BA, Honours, 1981, Victoria University of Wellington; PhD, Cambridge University, 1986. Appointment: Downing College, Cambridge. Publications: Algernon Sidney and the English Republic, 1623-1677, 1988; Algernon Sidney and the Restoration Crisis, 1677-1683, 1991; Harry's Absence: Looking for My Father on the Mountain, 1997. Contributions to: Books, professional journals, and literary publications including: Albion, 25, 4, 1993; Britain and the Netherlands XI: The Exchange of Ideas, 1994; The Certainty of Doubt: Essays in Honour of Peter Munz, 1996; The Stuart Court and Europe, 1996. Address: c/o Downing College, Cambridge CB2 1DQ, England.

SCOTT Nathan A(lexander) Jr, b. 24 Apr 1925, Cleveland, Ohio, USA. Professor of English Emeritus;

Minister; Writer. m. Charlotte Hanley, 21 Dec 1946, 2 children. Education: AB, University of Michigan, 1944; BD, Union Theological Seminary, 1946; PhD, Columbia University, 1949. Appointments: Dean of the Chapel, Virginia Union University, 1946-47; Instructor, 1948-51, Assistant Professor, 1951-53, Associate Professor of Humanities, 1953-55, Howard University; Assistant Professor, 1955-58, Associate Professor, 1958-64, Professor of Theology and Literature, 1964-72, Professor of English, 1967-76, Shailer Mathews Professor of Theology and Literature, 1972-76, University of Chicago; Ordained Priest, Episcopal Church, 1960; Co-Editor, Journal of Religion, 1963-77; Canon Theologian, Cathedral of St James, Chicago, 1967-76; Commonwealth Professor of Religious Studies, 1976-81, Professor of English, 1976-90, William R Kenan Professor of Religious Studies, 1981-90, Professor Emeritus, 1990-, University of Virginia. Publications: Rehearsals of Discomposure: Alienation and Reconciliation in Modern Literature, 1952; The Tragic Vision and the Christian Faith, 1957; Modern Literature and the Religious Frontier, 1958; Albert Camus, 1962; Reinhold Niebuhr, 1963; The New Orpheus: Essays Toward a Christian Poetic, 1964; The Climate of Faith in Modern Literature (editor), 1964; Samuel Beckett, 1965; Four Ways of Modern Poetry (editor), 1965; Man in the Modern Theatre (editor), 1965; The Broken Center: Studies in the Theological Horizon of Modern Literature, 1966; Ernest Hemingway, 1966; The Modern Vision of Death (editor), 1967; Adversity and Grace: Studies in Recent American Literature (editor), 1968; Craters of the Spirit: Studies in the Modern Novel (editor), 1968; Negative Capability: Studies in the New Literature and the Religious Situation (editor), 1969; The Unquiet Vision: Mirrors of Man in Existentialism, 1969; Nathanael West, 1971; The Wild Prayer of Longing: Poetry and the Sacred, 1971; Three American Moralists: Mailer, Bellow, Trilling, 1973; The Legacy of Reinhold Niebuhr (editor), 1975; The Poetry of Civic Virtue: Eliot, Malraux, Auden, 1976; The Poetics of Belief: Studies in Coleridge, Arnold, Pater, Santayana, Stevens and Heidegger, 1985; Visions of Presence in Modern American Poetry, 1993; Reading George Steiner (with Ronald Sharp), 1994. Contributions to: Professional journals and other publications. Honours: Many honorary doctorates. Memberships: American Academy of Arts and Sciences, fellow; American Academy of Religion, president, 1986; Modern Language Association; Society for Values in Higher Education; Society of Arts, Religion and Contemporary Culture. Address: 1419 Hilltop Road, Charlottesville, VA 22903, USA.

SCOTT Paul Henderson, b. 7 Nov 1920, Edinburgh, Scotland. Essayist; Historian; Critic; Former Diplomat. Education: MA, MLitt, University of Edinburgh. Publications: 1707: The Union of Scotland and England, 1979; Walter Scott and Scotland, 1981; John Galt, 1985; Towards Independence: Essays on Scotland, 1991; The Boasted Advantages, 1991; Andrew Fletcher and the Treaty of Union, 1992; Scotland: A Concise Cultural History (editor), 1993; Defoe in Edinburgh, 1994; Scotland: An Unwon Cause, 1997; Still in Bed with an Elephant, 1998. Contributions to: Newspapers and journals. Honour: Andrew Fletcher Prize, 1993. Memberships: International PEN, president, Scottish Centre; Saltire Society; Advisory Council for the Arts in Scotland; Association for Scottish Literary Studies; Scottish National Party. Address: 33 Drumsheugh Gardens, Edinburgh EH3 7RN, Scotland.

SCOTT Peter Dale, b. 11 Jan 1929, Montreal, Quebec, Canada. Retired Professor of English; Poet. m. Ronna Kabatznick, 14 July 1993, 2 sons, 1 daughter. Education: BA, 1949, PhD, Political Science, 1955, McGill University; Institut d'Etudes Politiques, Paris, 1950; University College, Oxford, 1950-52. Appointments: Lecturer, McGill University, 1955-56; Canadian Foreign Service, Ottawa and Poland, 1957-61; Professor of Speech, 1961-66; Professor of English, 1966-94, University of California at Berkeley. Publications: Poems, 1952; Rumors of No Law, 1981; Coming to Jakarta, 1988; Listening to the Candle, 1992; Crossing Borders, 1994. Contributions to: Reviews, quarterlies, and periodicals. Honour: Dia Art Foundation,

1989. Address: c/o Department of English, University of California at Berkeley, Berkeley, CA 94720, USA.

SCOTT Rosie, b. 22 Mar 1948, New Zealand (Joint Australian/New Zealand Citizen). Writer. m. 28 Nov 1987, 2 daughters. Education: MA, Honours, English, 1968; Graduate Diploma, Drama, 1984. Publications: Fiction: Glory Days, 1988; Queen of Love (stories), 1989; Nights With Grace, 1990; Feral City, 1992; Lives on Fire, 1993; Movie Dreams, 1995. Poetry: Flesh and Blood, 1984; The Red Heart (essay collection), 1999. Contributions to: Various publications in New Zealand, Australia, France, Germany, UK, USA. Honours: Sunday Times Award for Play; Novels short-listed for New Zealand National Book Awards, Australian National Book Awards, Banjo Patterson, Christina Stead National Book Awards, Biennial National Book Awards, Adelaide; Sunday Times-Bruce Mason Award, 1986; Australian Writers Fellowship, 1992. Memberships: Australian Society of Authors, committee member, 1994-, chair, 1998; Greenpeace; PEN Australia. Address: 21 Darghan Street, Glebe, New South Wales 2037, Australia.

SCOTT Roy Vernon, b. 26 Dec 1927, Wrights, Illinois, USA. Distinguished Professor; Historian; Writer. Education: BS, Iowa State College, 1952; MA, 1953, PhD, 1957, University of Illinois. Appointments: Assistant Professor, University of Southwestern Louisiana, 1957-58, University of Missouri, 1959-60; Assistant Professor, 1960-62, Associate Professor, 1962-64, Professor of American History, 1964-, Distinguished Professor, 1979-, Mississippi State University. Publications: The Agrarian Movement in Illinois 1880-1896, 1962; The Reluctant Farmer: The Rise of Agricultural Extension to 1914, 1970; The Public Career of Cully A Cobb: A Study in Agricultural Leadership (with J G Shoalmire), 1973; Southern Agriculture Since the Civil War (with George L Robinson Jr), 1979; Railroad Development Programs in the Twentieth Century, 1985; The Great Northern Railway: A History (with others), 1988; Eugene Beverly Ferris and Agricultural Science in the Lower South, 1991; Wal-Mart: A History of Sam Walton's Retail Phenomenon (with Sandra S Vance), 1994. Contributions to: Professional journals. Memberships: American Historical Association; Organization of American Historians; Southern Historical Association; Economic History Association; Agricultural History Society, president, 1978-79; Mississippi Historical Society, president, 1989-90. Address: c/o Department of History, Mississippi State University, Mississippi State, MS 39762, USA.

SCOTT Sally Elisabeth, b. 30 May 1948, London, England. Writer; Illustrator. Education: BA, Honours, Philosophy and English Literature, York University, 1970. Publications: The Elf King's Bride, 1981; The Magic Horse, 1985; The Three Wonderful Beggars, 1987. Illustrator: Tales and Legends of India. Membership: Society of Authors. Address: c/o David Higham Associates Ltd, 5-8 Lower John Street, Golden Square, London W1R 4HA, England.

SCOTT Tom, b. 6 June 1918, Glasgow, Scotland. Poet; Children's Writer. Education: MA, PhD, University of Edinburgh. Appointment: Former Editor, Scottish Literature Series, Pergamon Press, Oxford. Publications: Seeven Poems o Maister Francis Vilton, 1953; An Ode til New Jerusalem, 1956; The Ship and Ither Poems, 1963; A Possible Solution to the Scottish Question, 1963; Dunbar: A Critical Exposition of the Poems, 1966; The Oxford Book of Scottish Verse (with J McQueen), 1966; Late Medieval Scots Poetry: A Selection from the Makars and their Heirs Down to 1610, 1967; At the Shrine o the Unkent Sodger: A Poem for Recitation, 1968; Tales of Robert the Bruce, 1969; The Penguin Book of Scottish Verse, 1970; Brand the Builder, 1975; The Tree, 1977; Tales of Sir William Wallace, 1981; The Dirty Business, 1986; Collected Shorter Poems, 1993. Address: Duddington Park, Edinburgh 15, Scotland.

SCOTT Whitney, b. 31 Jan 1945, New York City, USA. Author; Editor. m. Garry J Nelson, 25 July 1963, 1 daughter. Education: BA, Communications, Language and Literature, 1973; MA, Communications, Language and Literature, 1974. Publications: Dancing to the End of the Shining Bar, 1994; Words Against the Shiftin Seasons - Women Speak of Breat Cancer (editor), 1995; Prairie Hearts (editor), 1996; Alternatives - Roads Less Travelled (editor), 1997; Freedom's Just Another Word (editor), 1998; Listen to the Moon, 1998. Contributions to: Tomorrow Magazine; Amethyst; Pearl; Kaleidoscope; Art and Understanding; CQ; Howling Dog; Arts Alive; Potomac Review. Memberships: Tall Grass Writers Guild, president, 1990-. Literary Agent: Victoria Sanders, New York, USA. Address: 241 Avenue of the Americas, Suite 11-H, New York, NY 11014, USA.

SCOTT William Neville, (Bill Scott), b. 4 Oct 1923, Bundaberg, Queensland, Australia. Author. Publications: Focus on Judith Wright, 1967; Some People (short stories), 1968; Brother and Brother (verse), 1972; The Continual Singing: An Anthology of World Poetry, 1973; Portrait of Brisbane, 1976; The Complete Book of Australian Folklore, 1976; Bushranger Ballads, 1976; My Uncle and Other People (short stories), 1977; Boori (children's fiction), 1978; Tough in the Old Days (autobiography), 1979; Ned Kelly After a Century of Acrimony (with John Meredith), 1980; The Second Penguin Australian Songbook, 1980; Darkness Under the Hills (children's fiction), 1980; Reading 360 series (The Blooming Queensland Side, On the Shores of Botany Bay, The Golden West, Bound for South Australia, Upon Van Diemen's Land, The Victorian Bunyip), 6 volumes, 1981; Australian Bushrangers, 1983; Penguin Book of Australian Humorous Verse, 1984; Shadows Among the Leaves (children's fiction), 1984; The Long and the Short and the Tall (folklore), 1985; Following the Gold (children's poems), 1989; Many Kinds of Magic (short stories), 1990; Hey Rain (cassette, songs and poems), 1992; The Currency Lad (fiction) 1994; Songbird in Your Pocket (cassette, songs and poems) 1994; Pelicans and Chihuahuas (folklore), 1995; The Banshee and the Bullocky (short stories), 1995. Honours: Mary Gilmore Award, 1964; Medal of the Order of Australia (OAM), 1992; Heritage Award, 1994. Address: 157 Pratten Street, Warwick, Queensland 4370, Australia.

SCOTT TANNER Amoret, b. 27 Mar 1930, Vancouver, British Columbia, Canada. Social Historian. m. Ralph Tanner, 24 Aug 1985. Publications: Hedgerow Harvest, 1979; Parrots, 1982. With Christopher Scott: Collecting Bygones, 1964; Tobacco and the Collector, 1966; Dummy Board Figures, 1966; Discovering Smoking Antiques, 1970, 2nd edition, 1981; Smoking Antiques (Shire Album), 1981, 3rd edition, 1996; Discovering Stately Homes, 1973, 3rd edition, 1989; Staffordshire Figures (Shire Album), 1986, 2nd edition, 1993. Contributions to: Saturday Book; Country Life; Antique Collector; Antiquarian Book Monthly. Membership: Ephemera Society, founder member, council member. Address: The Footprint, Padworth Common, Reading RG7 4QG, England.

SCOTT-STOKES Natascha (Norton), b. 11 Apr 1962, Munich, Germany. Travel Writer. m. Benoit Le Blanc, 27 Feb 1992. Education: BA, Honours Humanities, Middlesex Polytechnic; MA, Latin American Studies, University of London. Appointments: Associate Editor, Writer's Newsletter, 1989-90. Publications: An Amazon and a Donkey, 1991. Co-Author: Germany, the Rough Guide, 1989; The Cadogan Guide to Central America, 1992; The Amber Trail, 1993. Contributions to: Lima Times; Writers Newsletter. Memberships: Writers Guild of Great Britain; PEN English Centre; Royal Geographical Society, fellow. Address: 55 Leconfield Road, London N5 2RZ, England.

SCOVELL E(dith) J(oy), b. 9 Apr 1907, Sheffield, Yorkshire, England. Poet. m. Charles Elton, 1937, dec 1991, 1 son, 1 daughter. Education: BA, Somerville College, Oxford, 1930. Publications: Shadows of Chrysanthemums and Other Poems, 1944; The Midsummer Meadow and Other Poems, 1946; The River Steamer and Other Poems, 1956; The Space Between, 1982; Ten Poems, 1984; Listening to Collared Doves, 1986; Collected Poems, 1988; Selected Poems, 1991.

Honours: Cholmondeley Award, 1989; Cheltenham Prize, Cheltenham Festival of Literature, 1992. Address: 51 Diamond Court, Oxford OX2 7AA, England.

SCRUTON Roger, b. 27 Feb 1944, Burlingthorpe, England. Philosopher; Author; Journalist; Editor; Publisher. Education: BA, 1965, PhD, 1979, Jesus College, Cambridge. Appointments: Professor, Birkbeck College, London, Boston University, USA; Editor, The Salisbury Review; Founder, Publisher and Director, Claridge Press; Radio and television broadcasts. Publications: Art and Imagination, 1974; The Aesthetics of Architecture, 1979; The Meaning of Conservatism, 1980; The Politics of Culture and Other Essays, 1981; Fortnight's Anger (novel), 1981; A Short History of Modern Philosophy, 1982, 2nd edition, 1995; A Dictionary of Political Thought, 1982, 2nd edition, 1996; The Aesthetic Understanding, 1983; Kant, 1983; Untimely Tracts, 1985; Thinkers of the New Left, 1986; Sexual Desire, 1986; Spinoza, 1987; A Land Held Hostage: Lebanon and the West, 1987; The Philosopher on Dover Beach and Other Essays, 1989; Francesca (novel), 1991; A Dove Descending and Other Stories, 1991; Xanthippic Dialogues, 1993; Modern Philosophy, 1994; The Classical Vernacular: Architectural Principles in an Age of Nihilism, 1995; Animal Rights and Wrongs, 1996; An Intelligent Person's Guide to Philosophy, 1996; The Aesthetics of Music, 1997; On Hunting, 1998; An Intelligent Person's Guide to Modern Culture, 1998. Contributions to: Newspapers and journals. Honours: Honorary Doctorates, Adelphi University, 1995; Masaryk University, Brno, Czech Republic, 1998. Address: Sunday Hill Farm, Brinkworth, Wilts SN15 5AS, England.

SCULL Christina, b. 6 Mar 1942, Bristol, England. Writer. m. Wayne G Hammond, 12 Dec 1994. Education: BA, Hons, Birkbeck College, University of London, 1971. Appointments: Executive Officer, Board of Trade, 1961-70; Librarian, Sir John Soane's Museum, London, 1971-95. Publications: The Soane Hogarths, 1971; JRR Tolkien: Artist & Illustrator, co-author with Wayne G Hammond), 1995; Roverandom, by JRR Tolkien), co-edited with Wayne & G Hammond), 1998; Farmer Giles of Ham, by JRR Tolkien, co-edited with Wayne G Hammond), 1999. Contributions: Articles and reviews in Mallorn, Mythlore, Seven, Arda. Honours: Mythopoeic Society Award in Inklings Studes, 1996. Memberships: Tolkien Society; Mythopoeic Society. Address: 30 Talcott Road, Williamstown, MA 01267, USA.

SCULLY Vincent (Joseph Jr), b. 21 Aug 1920, New Haven, Connecticut, USA. Professor of Art History Emeritus; Writer. m. Catherine Lynn, 30 Dec 1980, 4 children. Education: BA, 1940, PhD, 1949, Yale University. Appointments: Instructor, Assistant Professor, Associate Professor, 1947-61, Col John Trumbull Professor of Art History, 1961-83, Sterling Professor of History of Art, 1983-91, Sterling Professor Emeritus, 1991-; Host, New World Visions: American Art and the Metropolitan Museum 1650-1914, PBS-TV, 1983; Visiting Professor, University of Miami at Coral Gables, 1992-97; Mellon Visiting Professor of History, California Institute of Technology, 1995. Publications: The Architectural Heritage of Newport, Rhode Island (with Antoinette Forrester Downing), 1952, 2nd edition, revised, 1967; The Shingle Style: Architectural Theory and Design from Richardson to the Origins of Wright, 1955, revised edition as The Shingle Style and the Stick Style: Architectural Theory and Design from Downing to the Origins of Wright, 1971; Frank Lloyd Wright, 1960; Modern Archiecture: The Architecture of Democracy, 1961, revised edition, 1974; Louis I Kahn, 1962; The Earth, the Temple and the Gods: Greek Sacred Architecture, 1962, 3rd edition, revised, 1980; American Architecture and Urbanism, 1969, revised edition, 1988; Pueblo Architecture of the Southwest, 1971; The Shingle Style Today: or, The Historian's Revenge, 1974; Pueblo: Mountain, Village, Dance, 1975, 2nd edition, 1989; Robert Stern (with David Dunster), 1981; Wesleyan: Photographs, 1982; Michael Graves, Buildings and Projects, 1966-1981, 1982; The Villas of Palladio, 1986; The Architecture of the American Summer: The Flowering of the Shingle Style, 1987; New World Visions of

Household Gods and Sacred Places: American Art and the Metropolitan Museum 1650-1914, 1988; The Architecture of Robert Venturi (with others), 1989; The Great Dinosaur Mural at Yale: The Age of Reptiles (with others), 1990; Architecture: The Natural and the Manmade, 1991; French Royal Gardens: The Design of André Le Notre (with Jeannie Baubion-Maclere), 1992; Robert A M Stern, Buildings and Projects 1987-1992, 1992; Mother's House: The Evolution of Vanna Venturi's House in Chestnut Hill (with Robert Venturi), 1992. Honours: National Endowment for the Humanities Senior Fellowship, 1972-73; American Institute of Architects Medal, 1976; Thomas Jefferson Medal, University of Virginia, 1982; Topaz Award, Association of Collegiate Schools of Architecture/American Institute of Architects, 1986; Literary Lion, New York Public Library, 1992; Governor's Arts Awards Medal, State of Connecticut, 1993; American Academy in Rome Award, 1994; Thomas Jefferson Lecturer; National Endowment for the Humanities, 1995; Honorary doctorates. Memberships: American Institute of Architects, honorary member; National Trust for Historic Preservation, trustee; Royal Institute of British Architects, honorary fellow. Address: 252 Lawrence Street, New Haven, CT 06511, USA.

SCUPHAM John Peter, b. 24 Feb 1933, Liverpool, England Writer; Poet. m. Carola Nance Braunholtz, 6 Aug 1957, 3 sons, 1 daughter. Education: Honours Degree, English, Emmanuel College, Cambridge, 1957. Appointment: Founder-Publisher, The Mandeville Press. Publications: The Snowing Globe, 1972; Prehistories, 1975; The Hinterland, 1977; Summer Places, 1980; Winter Quarters, 1983; Out Late, 1986; The Air Show, 1989; Watching the Perseids, 1990; Selected Poems, 1990; The Ark, 1994. Contributions to: Anthologies and magazines. Membership: Royal Society of Literature, fellow. Address: Old Hall, Norwich Road, South Burlingham, Norfolk NR13 4EY, England.

SEAGRAVE Sterling, b. 15 Apr 1937, Columbus, Ohio, USA. Writer. m. (1) Wendy Law-Yone, 1967, (2) Peggy Sawyer, 1982, 1 son, 1 daughter. Education: University of Miami, 1956; University of Mexico, 1957; University of Venezuela, 1958. Publications: Yellow Rain, 1981; Soldiers of Fortune, 1981; The Soong Dynasty, 1985; The Marcos Dynasty, 1988; Dragon Lady, 1992; Lords of the Rim, 1995. Contributions to: Atlantic: Far Eastern Economic Review; Esquire; Time; Smithsonian. Membership: Authors Guild. Address: c/o William Morris Agency, 1 Stratton Street, London W1X 6HB, England.

SEAL Basil. See: **BARNES Julian Patrick.**

SEALEY Leonard George William, b. 7 May 1923, London, England. Educational Author; Consultant. m. (1) Joan Hearn, Mar 1944, dec, (2) Nancy Verre, August 1972, 5 sons. Education: Teachers Certificate, Peterborough College, England; DipED, MEd, University of Leicester. Publications: The Creative Use of Mathematics, 1961; Communication and Learning (co-author), 1962; Exploring Language, 1968; Basic Skills in Learning, 1970; Introducing Mathematics, 1970; The Lively Readers, 1973; Our World Encyclopedia (editor), 1974; Open Education, 1977; Children's Writing, 1979. Memberships: Royal Society of Arts, fellow; Phi Delta Kappa. Address: 136 Sandwich Road, Plymouth, MA 02360, USA.

SEALTS Merton M(iller) Jr, b. 8 Dec 1915, Lima, Ohio, USA. Professor of English Emeritus; Writer. Education: BA, College of Wooster, 1937; PhD, Yale University, 1942. Appointments: Instructor, University of Missouri, 1941-42, Wellesley College, 1946-48; Assistant Professor, 1948-51, Associate Professor, 1951-58, Professor of English, 1958-65, Lawrence College/University; Professor of English, 1965-75, Henry A Pochmann Professor of English, 1975-82, Professor Emeritus, 1982-, University of Wisconsin at Madison. Publications: Melville as Lecturer, 1957; Herman Melville: Billy Budd, Sailer (editor with Harrison Hayford), 1962; The Journals and Miscellaneous Notebooks of Ralph Waldo Emerson (editor), Vol V, 1965, Vol X, 1973; Melville's Reading, 1966, revised edition, 1988; Emerson's Nature: Origin, Growth, Meaning (editor with Alfred R Ferguson), 1969, 2nd edition, enlarged, 1979; The Early Lives of Melville: Nineteenth-Century Biographical Sketches and Their Authors, 1974; Pursuing Melville, 1940-1980: Chapters and Essays, 1982; Emerson on the Scholar, 1992; Beyond the Classroom: Essays on American Authors, 1996; Closing the Books: A Memoir of an Academic Career, 1999. Contributions to: Scholarly books and journals. Honours: Ford Foundation Fellow, 1953-54; Guggenheim Fellowship, 1962-63; Honorary DLitt, College of Wooster, 1974; National Endowment for the Humanities Senior Fellow, 1975; Jay B Hubbell Award, Modern Language Association, 1992; Distinguished Alumni Award, College of Wooster, 1994; Distinguished Achievement Award, Ralph Waldo Emerson Society, 1995. Memberships: Ralph Waldo Emerson Society; Melville Society, president, 1953; Thoreau Society; American Literature Association; Modern Language Association of America; Phi Beta Kappa. Address: 6209 Mineral Point Road, Apt 1106/08, Madison, WI 53705, USA.

SEARLE John R(ogers), b. 31 July 1932, Denver, Colorado, USA. Professor of Philosophy; Writer. m. Dagmar Carboch, 24 Dec 1958, 2 sons. Education: University of Wisconsin, 1949-52; BA, 1st Class Honours, 1955, MA, 1959, DPhil, 1959, University of Oxford. Appointments: Lecturer in Philosophy, Christ Church, Oxford, 1956-59; Professor of Philosophy, later Mills Professor of the Philosophy of Mind and Language, University of California at Berkeley, 1959-; Visiting Professor at various US and European universities; Lecturer throughout the world. Publications: Speech Acts: An Essay in the Philosophy of Language, 1969; The Campus War, 1971; Expression and Meaning: Studies in the Theory of Speech Acts, 1979; Intentionality: An Essay in the Philosophy of Mind, 1983; Minds, Brains and Science, 1984; The Foundations of Illocutionary Logic (with D Vanderveken), 1985; The Rediscovery of the Mind, 1992; The Construction of Social Reality, 1995; The Mystery of Consciousness, 1997; Mind, Language and Society, 1998. Contributions to: Scholarly journals. Honours: Rhodes Scholar, 1952-55; Guggenheim Fellowship, 1975-76; Fulbright Awards, 1983, 1985; Honorary Doctor of Humane Letters, Adelphi University, 1993, University of Wisconsin, 1994. Memberships: American Academy of Arts and Sciences; American Council of Learned Societies, board of directors, 1979-87; American Philosophical Association; Council for Philosophical Studies; National Humanities Center, board of trustees, 1976-90. Address: c/o Department of Philosophy, University of California at Berkeley, Berkeley, CA 94720, USA.

SEARLE Ronald, (William Fordham), b. 3 Mar 1920, Cambridge, England. Artist; Writer. Education: Cambridge School of Art, 1939. Publications: Forty Drawings, 1946; Le Nouveau Ballet Anglais, 1947; Hurrah for St Trinian's, 1948; The Female Approach, 1949; Back to the Slaughterhouse, 1951; Souls in Torment, 1953; Rake's Progress, 1955; Merry England, 1956; Which Way Did He Go?, 1961; Searle in the Sixties, 1965; From Frozen North to Filthy Lucre, 1964; Pardong M'sieur, 1965; Searle' Cats, 1969; Hommage à Toulouse Lautrec, 1969; Secret Sketchbook, 1970; The Addict, 1971; More Cats, 1975; Drawings From Gilbert and Sullivan, 1975; The Zoodiac, 1977; Ronald Searle, 1978; The King of Beasts, 1980; The Big Fat Cat Book, 1982; Winespeak, 1983; Ronald Searle in Perspective, 1984; Ronald Searle's Golden Oldies, 1985; To the Kwai - and Back, 1986; Something in the Cellar, 1986. Ah Yes I Remember it Well: Paris 1961-1975, 1987; The Non-Sexist Dictionary, 1988; Slightly Foxed - but still desirable, 1989; The Curse of St Trinian's, 1993; Marquis de Sade meets Goody Two Shoes, 1994; Ronald Searle dans le Monde, 1998. Honour: Royal Designer for Industry, 1988. Address: c/o Tessa Sayle, 11 Jubilee Place, London SW3 3TE, England.

SEAWIND Jay. See: **WYNN John Charles.**

SECOR James L, b. 11 June 1947, Ft Clayton; AFB, Panama. Playwright; Freelance Writer. 1 son. Education: BA, Theatre, Towson St University; MS Gen Educ, Johns Hopkins University; PhD, Theatre, University of Kansas; Bunraku National Puppet Theatre, Osaka. Appointments include: Teacher, Writing Specialist, Phillip University, Japan, 1989-90; Teacher, Writing Specialist, Aoyama Gakuin Daigaku (Aoyama University), 1990-92; Teacher, Nihon Geijutsu Gakuin Daigaku (Japan College of the Arts), 1992; Tutor, English, Johnson County Community College, 1995; Tutor, English, University of Kansas, 1995-; Editor, Into the Eye, 1996-97. Publications include: The Male Ghost in Ukiyo'e, in Japanese Ghosts and Demons, 1985; Sapl and Nicholas Ferguson: The Legend, 1992; Tanka, Sweetheart, 1996; Tangled in the Net of Ruin, 1996; Statesmanship, 1996; Saving Grace, 1996; A Different Thing to Do, 1996; Tanka, Reflections of Yesterday, 1996; The Crippled Heart of Man And Social Puissance Ghost Sex (editor), 1997; Tanka, Ages and Stages, 1997; Book: The Japanese, Portrait of a People, 1999; Produced several plays, 1971-. Honours include: Finalist, National Library of Poetry Contest, 1996; Distinguished Member, International Society of Poets, 1996; Editor's Choice Award, National Library of Poetry, 1996; Finalist, National Library of Poetry, 1998. Memberships include: KVSA Soccer Coach and Referee, 1982-86; Speech Communication Association, 1986-87; Japan Language Teachers Association, 1990-92; International Society of Poets, 1995-96; Lawrence Parks and Recreation, soccer coach, 1997; Lawrence Community Theatre, 1997; ASTR; Academy of American Poets. Address: PO Box 26, Lawrence, KS 66044, USA.

SEDGWICK Eve Kosofsky, b. 2 May 1950, Dayton, Ohio, USA. Professor of English; Writer. Education: BA, Cornell University, 1971; MPhil, 1974, PhD, 1975, Postdoctoral Studies, 1976-78, Yale University. Appointments: Instructor, Yale University, 1975-76; Assistant Professor of English and Creative Writing, Hamilton College, Clinton, New York, 1978-81; Assistant Professor, Boston University, 1981-83; Faculty Fellow, Mary Ingraham Bunting Institute, Cambridge, Massachusetts, 1983-84; Associate Professor of English and Women's Studies, Amherst College, 1984-88; Professor of English, 1988-92, Newman Ivey White Professor of English, 1992-, Duke University; Research Fellow, National Humanities Center, 1991-92. Publications: The Coherence of Gothic Conventions, 1980; Between Men: English Literature and Male Homosocial Desire, 1985; Epistemology of the Closet, 1990; Tendencies, 1993; Performativity and Performance (editor with Andrew Parker), 1994; Fat Art, Thin Art, 1994. Contributions to: Anthologies, professional journals and literary publications. Honours: Mellon Fellow, 1976-78; Kirkland Endowment Grants, 1980, 1981; Co-Winner, Crompton-Noll Award in Gay and Lesbian Studies, Modern Language Association, 1984; Guggenheim Fellowship, 1987-88. Memberships: Dickens Society, board of trustees, 1991-94; English Institute, board of trustees, 1992-97; Modern Language Association. Address: c/o Department of English, Duke University, Durham, NC 27708, USA.

SEDGWICK Fred, b. 20 Jan 1945, Dublin, Ireland. Lecturer in Education; Poet. Education: St Luke's College, Exeter; MA, University of East Anglia at Norwich, 1984. Appointments: Head of Downing Primary School, Suffolk; Education Lecturer. Publications: Really in the Dark, 1980; From Another Part of the Island, 1981; A Garland for William Cowper, 1984; The Living Daylights, 1986; Falernian, 1987; This Way, That Way: A Collection of Poems for Schools (editor), 1989; Lighting Up Time: On Children's Writing, 1990. Address: 1 Mornington Avenue, Ipswich, Suffolk IP1 4LA, England.

SEDLAK Shirley Agnes, b. 6 Sept, Chicago, Illinois, USA. Freelance Writer; Novelist. m. Harold Otto Sedlak, 22 July, 1 daughter. Appointments: Editor, Benefic Press, 1973-75; Publicity and Public Relations Writer, National League of American Pen Women, Chicago Branch, 1987-89. Memberships: National Leagne of American Pen Women; Toastmasters International. Address: 2226 South 9th Avenue, North Riverside, IL 60546, USA.

SEDLEY Kate, See: **CLARKE Brenda (Margaret Lilian).**

SEE Carolyn, (Monica Highland), b. 13 Jan 1934, Pasadena, California, USA. Writer. m. (1) Richard See, 18 Feb 1954, (2) Tom Sturak, 30 Apr 1960, 2 daughters. Education: PhD, University of California at Los Angeles, 1953. Appointment: Professor of English, University of California at Los Angeles. Publications: The Rest is Done with Mirrors, 1970; Blue Money, 1974; Mothers, Daughters, 1977; Rhine Maidens, 1980; Golden Days, 1985; When Knaves Meet, 1988; The Mirrored Hall in the Hollywood Dance Hall, 1991; Dreaming: Hard Luck and Good Times in America, 1995; The Handyman, 1999. As Monica Highland: Lotus Land, 1983; 1-10 Shanghai Road, 1985; Greetings From Southern California, 1987; Precious Cargo, 1990; Two Schools of Thought (with John Espey), 1991. Contributions to: Newspapers and magazines. Honours: Samuel Goldwyn Award, 1963; Sidney Hillman Award, 1969; National Endowment for the Arts Grant, 1974; Bread and Roses Award, National Womens Political Caucus, 1988; Vesta Award, 1989; Guggenheim Fellowship in Fiction, 1989; Lila Wallace Grant, 1993; Lifetime Achievement Award, PEN Center USA West, 1998. Membership: PEN Centre USA West, president, 1993-94. Address: 17339 Tramonto #303, Pacific Palisades, CA 90272, USA.

SEED Cecile Eugenie, (Jenny Seed), b. 18 May 1930, Cape Town, South Africa. Author. m. Edward (Ted) Robert Seed, 31 Oct 1953, 3 sons, 1 daughter. Publications: The Great Thirst, 1985; The Great Elephant, 1985; Place Among the Stones, 1987; Hurry, Hurry, Sibusiso, 1988; The Broken Spear, 1989; The Prince of the Bay, 1989; The Big Pumpkin, 1990; Old Grandfather Mantis, 1992; The Hungry People, 1993; A Time to Scatter Stones, 1993; Lucky Boy, 1995; The Strange Large Egg, 1996. Honour: MER Award, 1987. Address: 10 Pioneer Crescent, Northdene, Kwazulu-Natal 4093, South Africa.

SEGAL Erich, b. 16 June 1937, Brooklyn, New York, USA. Adjunct Professor of Classics; Author. m. Karen James, 10 June 1975, 1 son, dec, 2 daughters. Education: AB, 1958, AM, 1959, PhD, 1965, Harvard University. Appointments: Teaching Fellow, Harvard, 1959-63; Visiting Lecturer, 1964-65, Assistant Professor, 1965-68, Associate Professor, 1968-72, Adjunct Professor of Classics, 1981-, Yale University; Visiting Professor, University of Munich, 1973, Princeton University, 1974-75, 1981, University of Tel Aviv, 1976, Dartmouth College, 1976, 1977; Visiting Fellow, 1978-79, Supernumerary Fellow, 1980-, Wolfson College, Oxford; Honorary Research Fellow, University College, London, 1983-. Publications: Fiction: Love Story, 1970; Fairy Tale, 1973; Oliver's Story, 1977; Man, Woman and Child, 1980; The Class, 1985; Doctors, 1987; Acts of Faith, 1992; Prizes, 1995; Only Love, 1997. Editor: Euripides: A Collection of Critical Essays, 1968; Scholarship on Plautus, 1965-1976, 1981; Greek Tragedy: Modern Essays in Criticism, 1983, UK edition as Oxford Readings in Greek Tragedy, 1983; Caesar Augustus: Seven Essays (with Fergus Millar), 1984; Plato's Dialogues, 1986; Oxford Readings in Aristophanes, 1996. Editor and Translator: Plautus, 1996. Classics: Roman Laughter: The Comedy of Plautus, 1968, revised and expanded edition, 1987; Plautus: Four Comedies, 1996; The Death of Comedy, forthcoming. Musicals; screenplays. Contributions to: Various reviews, journals, periodicals, and magazines, including Times Literary Supplement. Honours: Guggenheim Fellowship, 1968; Golden Globe Award, 1971; Academy Award Nomination, Best Screenplay, 1971; Humboldt Stiftung Award, West Germany, 1973; Premio Bancarella, Italy, 1986; Prix Deauville, France, 1986; Co-Recipient, Premio San Valentin di Terni Award, 1989; Chevalier de la Légion d'Honneur, France, 1999. Memberships: Academy for Literary Studies; American Society of Composers, Authors, and Publishers; Society of Roman Studies, UK; Writers Guild of America. Address: c/o Ed Victor Ltd, 162 Wardour Street, London W1V 4AB, England.

SEGAL Lore (Groszmann), b. 8 Mar 1928, Vienna, Austria. Writer. m. David I Segal, 3 Nov 1960, dec, 1 son, 1 daughter. Education: BA, English, Bedford College, University of London, England, 1948. Appointments: Professor, Writing Division, School of Arts, Columbia University, Princeton University, Sarah Lawrence College, Bennington College; Professor of English, University of Illinois, Ohio State University. Publications: Novels: Other People's Houses, 1964; Lucinella, 1976; Her First American, 1985. Children's Books: Tell Me a Mitzi, 1977; The Story of Mrs Brubeck and How She Looked for Trouble and Where She Found Him, 1981; The Story of Mrs Lovewright and Purrless Her Cat, 1985. Translations: Gallows Songs (with W D Snodgrass), 1968; The Juniper Tree and Other Tales from Grimm, 1973; The Book of Adam to Moses; The Story of King Soul and King David. Contributions to: Periodicals. Honours: Guggenheim Fellowship, 1965-66; National Endowment for the Arts Grant, 1982; National Endowment for the Humanities Grant, 1983; Academy of Arts and Letters Award, 1986; Grant, Ohio Arts Council, 1996. Address: 280 Riverside Drive, New York, NY 10025, USA.

SEGHERS Greta Irene Pieter, b. 11 Feb 1942, Beveren-Waas, Belgium. Writer; History Teacher. m. Ludo de Cock, 12 July 1966, 1 son, 1 daughter. Education: Secondary Teacher Training, Dutch, History. Publications: Wat ge leest en schrijft, dat zijt ge zelf (essay), 1985; Het eigenzinnige leven van Angèle Manteau (biography), 1992. Novels: Afkeer van Faulkner, 1977; Omtrent de man die wederkwam, 1978; Ontregeling en Misverstand, 1983; De zijpaden van het paradijs, 1988; Hoe moordend is mijn school, 1990; Jefta's dochter, 1997. Stories: Het blauwe meisje, 1980; Een Dunne Wand, 1994. Contributions to: Various publications. Honours: Best Debut Prize, 1977; Yang Prize, 1977; Prize, 1983, Honorable Mention, Province of East Flanders, 1982-86; August Beernaertprijs, 1994. Memberships: Dietsche Warande en Belfort; Royal Academy for Dutch Languate and Literature. Address: Tuinlaan 14, 9120, Vrasene, Belgium.

SEIDMAN Hugh, b. 1 Aug 1940, New York, New York, USA. Writer; Poet; Teacher. m. Jayne Holsinger, 2 June 1990. Education: BS, Mathematics, Polytechnic Institute of Brooklyn, 1961; MS, Physics, University of Minnesota, 1964; MFA, Poetry, Columbia University, 1969. Appointments: Faculty, New School for Social Research, New York City, 1976-; Assistant Professor, Washington College, 1979; Visiting Lecturer, University of Wisconsin, 1981, Columbia University, 1985; Poet-in-Residence, College of William and Mary, 1982; Visiting Poet, Writers Voice, New York City, 1988. Publications: Collecting Evidence, 1970; Blood Lord, 1974; Throne/Falcon/Eye, 1982; People Live, They Have Lives, 1992; Selected Poems 1965-1995, 1995. Contributions to: Many publications. Honours: Yale Series of Younger Poets Prize, 1969; National Endowment for the Arts Grant, 1970, and Fellowships, 1972, 1985; Yaddo Fellowships, 1972, 1976, 1986; MacDowell Colony Fellowships, 1974, 1975, 1989; Writers Digest Poetry Prize, 1982; New York Foundation for the Arts Poetry Fellowship, 1990. Memberships: American PEN; Authors Guild; Authors League; Poetry Society of America. Address: 463 West Street, No H-822, New York, NY 10014, USA.

SELBOURNE David, b. 4 June 1937, London, England. Writer; Playwright. Publications: The Play of William Cooper and Edmund Dew-Nevett, 1968; The Two-Backed Beast, 1969; Dorabella, 1970; Samson and Alison Mary Fagan, 1971; The Damned, 1971; Class Play, 1973; Brook's Dream: The Politics of Theatre, 1974; What's Acting? and Think of a Story Quickly!, 1977; An Eye to India, 1977; An Eye to China, 1978; Through the Indian Looking Glass, 1982; The Making of a Midsummer Night's Dream, 1983; Against Socialist Illusion: A Radical Argument, 1985; In Theory and In Practice: Essays on the Politics of Jayaprakash Narayan, 1986; Left Behind: Journeys into British Politics, 1987; A Doctor's Life: The Diaries of Hugh Selbourne MD 1960-63, 1989; Death of the Dark Hero: Eastern Europe 1987-90, 1990; The Spirit of the Age, 1993; Not an Englishman: Conversations With Lord Goodman, 1993; The Principle of Duty, 1994; The City of Light, 1997; One Year On: The 'New' Politics and Labour, Centre for Policy Studies, 1998; Moral Evasion, 1998. Translation: The City of Light, by Jacob d'Ancona, 1997. Honour: Member, Academy of Savignano, Italy, 1994. Memberships: Society of Authors, London; United Oxford and Cambridge Club, London. Address: c/o Christopher Sinclair-Stevenson, 3 South Terrace, London SW7, England.

SELBY Stephen, b. 5 June 1952, Darley Dale, Derbyshire, England. Playwright. m. Ann Spence, 6 Mar 1982, 1 daughter. Education: Social Science and Philosophy. Appointments: Writer, Director, Producer, Noc On Theatre, 1987-, Hurdles of Time Theatre, 1991-; Dramaturgo, La Edel de Oro Theatre Company. Publications: Hurdles of Time; Erewash Giants, 1993; The Concrete Silver Band, 1995; Tontos Sabios y Ladrones Honestos, 1996. Memberships: Theatre Writers Union; Camasiiey Theatre Directors Association. Address: 53 Percival Road, Sherwood, Nottingham NG5 2FA, England.

SELLERS David. See: **BEASLEY John David.**

SELLMAN Roger Raymond, b. 24 Sept 1915, London, England. Retired Schoolmaster and Inspector of Schools; Writer. m. Minnie Coutts, 10 Aug 1938. Education: MA, Dip Ed, University of Oxford; PhD, University of Exeter. Publications: Methuen's Outline Series: Castles and Fortresses, 1954; The Crusades, 1955; Roman Britain, 1956; English Churches, 1956; The Vikings, 1957; Elizabethan Seamen, 1957; Prehistoric Britain, 1958; Civil War and Commonwealth, 1958; The Anglo Saxons, 1959; Ancient Egypt, 1960; Norman England, 1960; Medieval English Warfare, 1960; The First World War, 1961; The Second World War, 1964; Garibaldi and the Unification of Italy, 1973; Bismarck and the Unification of Germany, 1973; The Prairies, 1974. Historical Atlases and Textbooks: Outline Atlas of Eastern History, 1954; Outline Atlas of World History, 1970; Modern World History, 1972; Students Atlas of Modern History, 1973; Modern British Economic and Social History, 1973; Historical Atlas for First Examinations, 1973; Modern European History, 1974. Local History: Illustrations of Dorset History, 1960; Illustrations of Devon History, 1962; Devon Village Schools in the Nineteenth Century, 1968; Aspects of Devon History, 1985. Contributions to: Victorian Countryside, 1981; Devon Historian ; Devon and Cornwall Notes and Queries. Address: Pound Down Corner, Whitestone, Exeter EX4 2HP, England.

SELTZER Joanne, b. 21 Nov 1929, Detroit, Michigan, USA. Writer; Poet. m. Stanley Seltzer, 10 Feb 1951, 1 son, 3 daughters. Education: BA, University of Michigan, 1951; MA, College of St Rose, 1978. Publications: Adirondack Lake Poems, 1985; Suburban Landscape, 1988; Inside Invisible Walls, 1989. Contributions to: Journals and magazines. Honours: All Nations Poetry Contest Award, 1978; World Order of Narrative and Formalist Poets Competitions Prizes, 1986, 1988, 1990, 1992, 1993, 1994, 1997; Tucumari Literary Review Poetry Contest Award, 1989. Memberships: American Literary Translators Association; Associated Writing Programs; Hudson Valley Writers Guild; Poetry Society of America; Poets and Writers. Address: 2481 McGovern Drive, Schenectady, NY 12309, USA.

SEMADENI-BEZZOLA Sina, b. 12 Dec 1932, Zurich, Switzerland. Housewife; Writer. m. Dr Arnold Semadeni, 6 Sept 1958, 2 sons, 1 daughter. Education: Federal Comercial Diploma. Appointments: Different hotels in Switzerland and Germany. Publications: Der Kudcuck mit den Pantoffeln, 1973; Puschlaver Marchen, 1974; Waldhaus Films, 1976; Ivo und die Monster, 1979; Flimser Marchen, 1981; Guten Tag Herr Lowe, 1983; Marchen aus dem Engadin, 1984; Lasst Blumen Sprechen, 1986; Tessiner Marchen, 1991; Munkelmaus, 1997. Contributions to: Schw Spiegel; Tierwelt; Ethos. Honour: Anerkennung Preis, Kolturstiftung St Sallen. Membership: Schw Schriftstellerverband. Address: Grunensteinstr 19, 9436 Balgach, Switzerland.

SEMMLER Clement William, b. 23 Dec 1914, Eastern Well, South Australia, Australia. Broadcaster; Writer. m. (1) div, 1 son, 1 daughter, (2) Catherine Helena Wilson, 20 Dec 1974, 1 daughter. Education: MA, University of Adelaide, 1938. Appointment: Fellow, College of Fine Arts, University of New South Wales. Publications: For the Uncanny Man (essays), 1963; Barcroft Boake, 1965; Literary Australia (editor), 1965; The Banjo of the Bush, 1966; Kenneth Slessor, 1966; Twentieth Century Australian Literary Criticism (editor), 1967; The Art of Brian James, 1972; Douglas Stewart, 1974; The ABC-Aunt Sally and the Sacred Cow, 1981; A Frank Hardy Swag (editor), 1982; The War Diaries of Kenneth Slessor, 1985; The War Dispatches of Kenneth Slessor, 1987; Pictures on the Margin (memoirs), 1991. Contributions to: Periodicals and journals. Honours: DLitt, University of New England, Armidale, 1968; Officer of the Order of the British Empire, 1972; AM, 1988. Address: The Croft, St Clair Street, Bowral, New South Wales 2576, Australia.

SEMYONOVA Violeta, (Violeta Palmova, Vlad Tsvetkov), b. 4 Mar 1937, St Petersburg, Russia. Writer; Editor; Translator. m. Voldemar Baal, 10 Feb 1977, 1 son, 1 daughter. Education: Russian Phylology, Latvian University, 1965. Appointments: Newspaper Editor, 1959-60; Editor, Journalist, Latvian Radio, 1960-64; Editor, Publishing House Liesma, 1964-91. Publictions: Translations: A Dripe, Novels, 1968, 1973, 1978; L Purvs, Burning Castles, 1976; E Lans, Selected Stories, 1982; A Kolbergs, Three-day Detective Story, 1988; V Palmova, In a Power of Holy Minute. Contributions to: Newspapers, journals and magazines. Membership: Writers Union of Latvia. Address: Dzelzavas str 11, Flat 46, Riga, LV-1084, Latvia.

SEN Amartya Kumar, b. 3 Nov 1933, Santiniketan, India. Professor of Economics and Philosophy; Writer. m. (1) Nabaneeta Dev, 1960, div 1974, (2) Eva Colorni, 1977, dec 1985, (3) Emma Rothschild, 1991, 4 children. Education: BA, Presidency College, Calcutta, 1953; BA, 1955, MA, PhD, 1959, Trinity College, Cambridge. Appointments: Professor of Economics, Jadavpur University, Calcutta, 1956-58; Fellow, Trinity College, Cambridge, 1957-63, All Souls College, Oxford, 1980-88; Professor of Economics, Delhi University, 1963-71, London School of Economics and Political Science, 1971-77; Professor of Economics, 1977-80, Drummond Professor of Political Economy, 1980-88, University of Oxford; Andrew D White Professor at Large, Cornell University, 1978-85; Lamont University Professor and Professor of Economics and Philosophy, Harvard University, 1988-98; Master Trinity College, Cambridge, 1998-. Publications: Choice of Techniques, 1960; Collective Choice and Welfare, 1970; Guidelines for Project Evaluation (with P Dasgupta and Stephen Marglin), 1972; On Economic Inequality, 1973; Employment, Technology and Development, 1975; Poverty and Famines: An Essay on Entitlement and Deprivation, 1981; Choice, Welfare and Measurement, 1982; Resources, Values and Development, 1984; Commodities and Capabilities, 1985; On Ethics and Economics, 1987; The Standard of Living (with others), 1987; Hunger and Public Action (with Jean Dreze), 1989; Jibanayatra o arthaniti, 1990; The Political Economy of Hunger (editor with Jean Dreze), 3 volumes, 1990-91; Money and Value: On the Ethics and Economics of Finance/Denaro e valore: Etica ed economia della finanza, 1991; Inequality Reexamined, 1992; The Quality of Life (editor with Martha Nussbaum), 1993; Economic Development and Social Opportunity (with Jean Dreze), 1995. Contributions to: Professional journals. Honours: Mahalanobis Prize, 1976; Honorary Doctor of Literature, University of Saskatchewan, 1979; Nobel Prize in Economic Science, 1998. Memberships: American Academy of Arts and Sciences;American Economic Association, president, 1994-; British Academy, fellow; Development Studies Association; Econometric Society, fellow; Indian Economic Association; International Economic Association, president, 1986-88, honorary president, 1988-; Royal Economic Society. Address: c/o Trinity College, Cambridge CB2 1TQ, England.

SENDAK Maurice (Bernard), b. 10 June 1928, Brooklyn, New York, USA. Children's Author; Illustrator. Education: Art Students League, New York City, 1949-51. Appointments: Various one-man shows; Co-Founder and Artistic Director, The Night Kitchen, 1990-. Publications: As Author and Illustrator: Kenny's Window, 1956; Very Far Away, 1957; The Acrobat, 1959; The Sign on Rosie's Door, 1960; The Nutshell Library, 1962; Where the Wild Things Are, 1963; Hector Protector and As I Went Over the Water: Two Nursery Rhymes, 1965; Higglety, Piggelty, Pop!, or, There Must Be More to Life, 1967; In the Knight Kitchen, 1970; Ten Little Rabbits: A Counting Book with Mino the Magician, 1970; Pictures by Maurice Sendak, 1971; Maurice Sendak's Really Rosie, 1975; Some Swell Pup, or, Are You Sure You Want a Dog, 1976; Seven Little Monsters, 1977; Outside Over There, 1981; We Are All in the Dumps with Jack and Guy, 1993; Tsippi, 1994; Moishe, 1994; Max, 1994. Other: Illustrator for numerous books. Contributions to: Books and periodicals. Honours: Numerous awards and citations as author and illustrator. Address: c/o Harper & Row, 10 East 53rd Street, New York, NY 10022, USA.

SENGUPTA Preety, b. 17 May 1944, Ahmedabad, India. Writer; Poet. m. Chandan Sengupta, 21 June 1975. Education: MA, English Literature. Publications: Some 18 works. Contributions to: Various publications. Honours: Several literary awards. Memberships: PEN India; Poetry Society of America. Address: 15 Stewart Place, White Plains, NY 10603, USA.

SENIOR Olive Marjorie, b. 23 Dec 1941, Jamaica. Writer. Education: BA, Carleton University, 1967. Publications: Fiction: Summer Lightning, 1986; Arrival of the Snake-Woman, 1989; Discerner of Hearts, 1995; Poetry: Talking of Trees, 1986; Gardening in the Tropics, 1994; Non-Fiction: A-Z of Jamaican Heritage, 1984; Working Miracles: Womens Lives in the English Speaking Caribbean, 1991. Honour: Commonwealth Writers Prize, 1987. Membership: Writers Union of Canada. Literary Agent: Nicole Aragi, Watkins Loomis Agency. Address: 65 Springmount Avenue, Toronto, Ontario M6H 2Y5, Canada.

SENNACHIE. See: **WHYTE Donald.**

SEPAMLA (Sydney) Sipho, b. 1932, Johannesburg, South Africa. Poet; Writer; Editor. Education: Teacher Training. Appointments: Editor, New Classic and S'ketsh magazines. Publications: Hurry Up To It, 1975; The Blues is You in Me, 1976; The Soweto I Love, 1977; The Root is One, 1979; A Ride on the Whirlwind, 1981; Children of the Earth, 1983; Selected Poems, 1984; Third Generation, 1986; From Gore to Soweto, 1988; Scattered Survival, 1988. Address: c/o Skotaville Publishers, PO Box 32483, Braamfontein 2017, South Africa.

SEQUIERA Isaac J F, b. 5 Jan 1930, Hyderabad, India. University Professor; Writer. Education: BA, 1955; MA, 1958; PhD, 1970, Utah. Publications: The Theme of Initiation in Modern American Fiction, 1975; A Manifesto for Humour, 1985; Popular Culture: East and West, 1991; Studies in American Literature, 1991; Viewpoints USA, 1992; Essays in American Studies, 1992; The Closing of the American Frontier, 1994; American Studies Today, 1995. Contributions to: 70 papers in research journals in USA, Korea and India. Honours: Seaton Scholar, 1947; Fulbright Smith-Mundt Award, 1966; American Council of Learned Societies Fellow, 1979; UGC Council Lecturer, 1983, Professor Emeritus, 1991. Memberships: Modern Language Association, USA; Indian Association of American Studies; American Studies Association, USA; Poetry Society, president, 1975-80; Dramatic Circle, Hyderabad, president, 1980-. Address: American Studies Research Centre, ASRC, Hyderabad 500007, AP, India.

SEROTE Mongane Wally, b. 8 May 1944, Johannesburg, South Africa. Cultural Attaché; Poet; Writer. Education: MFA, Columbia University, New York, 1979. Appointment: Cultural Attaché, Department of Arts and Culture, African National Congress, South Africa. Publications: Poetry: Yakhal'imkomo, 1972; Tsetlo, 1974; No Baby Must Weep, 1975; Behold Mama, Flowers, 1978; The Night Keeps Winking, 1982; Selected Poems, 1982; A Tough Tale, 1987. Novel: To Every Birth Its Blood, 1981. Honour: Fulbright Scholarship. Address: 28 Penton Road, PO Box 38, London N1 9PR, England.

SERVADIO Gaia Cecilia, b. 13 Sept 1938, Padua, Italy. Writer; Journalist. 2 sons, 1 daughter. Education: St Martin's School of Art, London; National Diploma in Graphic Art. Appointments: Lecturer, Associazione Italiana, 1970, Manchester Museum, 1982; Consultant Editor, Editore, Italy, 1987; Director of Debates and Literary Talks, Accademia Italiana, 1988-94; Italian Foreign Minister, Australia, 1992, India, 1995. Publications: Melinda, 1968; Don Juan/Salome, 1969; Il Metodo, 1970; Mafioso, 1972; A Siberian Encounter, 1973; Luchino Visconti: A Biography, 1985; A Profile of a Mafia Boss: Insider Outsider, 1986; To a Different World: La donna nel Rinascimento, 1986; Il Lamento di Arianna, 1987; Una infanzia diversa, 1988; The Story of R, 1990; Edward Lear's Italian Letters (editor), 1990; La Vallata, 1991; Incontri (essays), 1993; The Real Traviata, 1994; La mia Umbria (editor), 1994. Contributions to Il Corriere della Sera; The Observer. Honour: Cavaliere Ufficiale della Repubblica Italiana, 1980. Memberships: Foreign Press Association, vice-president, 1974-79; Society of Authors. Address: 31 Bloomfield Terrace, London SW1 8PQ, England.

SERVICE Alastair Stanley Douglas, b. 8 May 1933, London, England. Writer. m. (1) Louisa Anne Hemming, 28 Feb 1959, div 1983, 1 son, 1 daughter, (2) Zandria Madeleine Pauncefort, 21 Feb 1992. Education: Modern History, Queen's College, Oxford, 1953-55. Appointments: Midshipman, RNR, 1952; Banker, Publisher, 1958-75; Organiser, Law Reform Campaigns on Family Planning, Divorce, Abortion, Adoption, 1964-75. Publications: A Birth Control Plan for Britain, 1972; Edwardian Architecture and its Origins, 1975; London 1900, 1978; Architects of London: 1066 to Today, 1979; The Megaliths of Europe: A Guide, 1979; Lost Worlds, 1980; Anglo-Saxon and Norman Buildings: A Guide, 1981; Edwardian Interiors, 1981; Victorian/Edwardian Hampstead, 1990; Standing Stones of Europe: The Great Neolithic Monuments, 1993; Libretto for Opera, The Sky Speaker (composer, James Harphan), 1997. Contributions to: Journals and newspapers. Honour: Commander of the Order of the British Empire (CBE), 1995. Memberships: Family Planning Association, national chairman, 1975-80; Health Education Authority, vice-chairman, 1978-89; Society of Architectural Historians of Great Britain; Victorian Society, chairman, publications committee, 1982-89; Wessex NHS Region, regional chairman, 1993-94; Wiltshire and Bath Health Commission, chairman, 1992-96; SPAB; Wiltshire Archaeological and Natural History Society; Wiltshire Health Authority, chairman, 1996-; Society for Architectural Historians, life member; Victorian Society, life member. Address: Swan House, Avebury, Near Marlborough, Wilts SN8 1RA, England.

SERVIEN Louis-Marc, Comte de Boisdauphin, Lord of Quendon, b. 8 Jan 1934, Yverdon, Switzerland. Writer; Editor; Journalist. Education: Licence in Law, Economics and Commercial Sciences, University of Lausanne; Dr Acc, Rome, Italy. Publications: Les Fonds de Placement Collectif en Suisse, 1958; Le Régime Fiscal des Fonds de Placement en Suisse, 1959; Les Sociétés d'Investissement ou Fonds de Placement: Nouvelle Formule d'Epargne, 1962; Le Fisc et l'Investment Trust, ou Quelques Réflexions à Propos du XVIIe Congres de l'IFA, Athens, 1962; Mutual Funds, Why Not? A Survey of International Investment Funds, 1968; Quelques Réflexions à Propos du Nouveau Statut Juridique des Fonds de Placement Suisses, 1969; Fondos de Inversion, Una Nueva Formula de Ahorro, 1970; Fondi di Investimento in Svizzera, 1972; Gibraltar: Tax on the Rock..., 1986. Contributions to: Society magazines, at home and Europe. Honours: Concordia Order, Sao Paulo, Brazil; Gold Medal, Arts, Science et Lettres, Paris. Memberships: Union Internationale des Journalistes et de la Presse de Langue Française, Paris; Syndicat des Journalistes et Écrivains, Paris; Association Indépendante des Journalistes Suisses, Lausanne; Club

Diplomatique de Genève. Address: Quendon Hall, 23 Chemin du Levant, CH-1005, Lausanne, Switzerland.

SETH Vikram, b. 20 June 1952, Calcutta, India. Poet; Writer. Education: BA, 1975, MA, 1978, Corpus Christi College, Oxford; MA, 1977, PhD, 1979; Stanford University; Diploma, Nanjing University, China, 1982. Publications: Mappings, 1980; From Heaven Lake: Travels Through Sianking and Tibet, 1983; The Humble Administrator's Garden, 1985; All You Who Sleep Tonight (translator), 1985; The Golden Gate: A Novel in Verse, 1986; Beastly Tales From Here to There (fables in verse), 1992; Three Chinese Poets (translator), 1992; A Suitable Boy, 1994. Contributions to: Reviews and magazines. Honours: Guggenheim Fellowships; Thomas Cook Travel Book Award, 1983; Commonwealth Poetry Prize, 1986; W H Smith Literary Award, 1994. Address: c/o Giles Gordon, Curtis Brown, 28-29 Haymarket, London SW14 4SP, England.

SETTANNI Harry Eugene, b. 8 Mar 1945, Chicago, Illinois, USA. Professor. Education: BS English, St Joseph's University, Philadelphia, 1967; MA, Philosophy, Villanova University, Pennsylvania, 1972; PhD, Philosophy, Saint John's University, Jamaica, New York, 1976. Publications: Holism, A Philosophy for Today, Anticipating The Twenty-First Century, 1990; What is Man? 1991; What is Morality? 1992; Five Philosophers: How Their Lives Influenced Their Thought, 1992; Controversial Questions in Philosophy, 1996; Scientific Knowledge, 1992; What is Freedom of Choice? 1992; The Probabilist Theism of John Stuart Mill, 1991; The Philosophic Foundation of Paranormal Phenomena, 1992; Logic Workbook, 1993; Five Primers in the Social Sciences, 1996; Essays in Psychology and Epistemology, 1996; Knowledge and Reality, 1996; Miscellaneous Essays, 1996. Address: 122 Copley Road, Upper Darby, PA 19082, USA.

SETTLE Mary Lee, b. 29 July 1918, Charleston, West Virginia, USA. Writer; Editor. m. (1) Rodney Weathersbee, 1939, div 1946, (2) Douglas Newton, 1946, div 1956, (3) William Littleton Tazewell, 2 Sept 1978, 1 son. Education: Sweet Briar College, 1936-38. Appointments: Assistant Editor, Harper's Bazaar, New York City, 1945; English Correspondent, Flair Magazine, 1950-51; Editor, American Heritage, New York City, 1961-; Associate Professor, Bard College, 1965-76; Visiting Lecturer, Iowa Writer's Workshop, 1976, University of Virginia, 1978; Founder, PEN-Faulkner Award, 1980. Publications: Fiction: The Love Eaters, 1954; The Kiss of Kin, 1955; O Beulah Land, 1956; Know Nothing, 1960; Fight Night on a Sweet Saturday, 1964; The Clam Shell, 1971; Prisons, 1973; Blood Tie, 1977; The Scapegoat, 1980; The Killing Ground, 1982; Celebration, 1986; Charley Bland, 1989. Play: Juana La Loca, 1965. Non-Fiction: All the Brave Promises: Memories of Woman 2nd Class 2146391 (autobiography), 1966; Turkish Reflections (autobiography), 1991. Contributions to: Anthologies and magazines. Honours: Guggenheim Fellowships, 1958, 1960; Ingram Merrill Foundation Award, 1975; National Book Award, 1978; Janet Heidinger Kafka Prize, 1983; American Academy of Arts and Letters Award, 1994. Address: 544 Pembroke Avenue, Norfolk, VA 23507, USA.

SEWELL Elizabeth, b. 9 Mar 1919, Coonoor, India. Writer; Lecturer. Education: BA, 1942, MA, 1945, PhD, 1949, University of Cambridge. Publications: The Orphic Voice; The Field of Nonsense; Paul Valéry: The Mind in the Mirror; An Idea; The Structure of Poetry; The Dividing of Time; The Singular Hope; Now Bless Thyself; The Unlooked-For, novel, 1995. Contributions to: Various publications. Honours: Honorary Doctorates; National Award; Zoe Kincaid Brockman Award. Memberships: PEN; Lewis Carroll Society of North America; North Carolina Writers Network. Address: 854 West Bessemer Avenue, Greensboro, NC 27408, USA.

SEWELL Stephen, b. 1953, Sydney, New South Wales, Australia. Playwright. Education: BS, University of Sydney, 1975. Appointment: Chairman, Australian National Playwrights Centre. Publications: The Father We Loved on a Beach by the Sea, 1976; Traitors, 1979; Welcome the Wright World, 1983; The Blind Giant is Dancing, 1983; Burn Victim (with others), 1983; Dreams in an Empty City, 1986; Hate, 1988; Miranda, 1989; Sisters, 1991; King Golgrutha, 1991; In the City of Grand-Daughters, 1993; Dust, 1993. Honour: New South Wales Premier's Award, 1985. Address: Hilary Linstead and Associates Pty Ltd, Level 18, Plaza II, 500 Oxford Street, Bondi Junction, New South Wales 2022, Australia.

SEXTON Rosemary, b. 20 Dec 1946, Haileybury, Ontario, Canada. Writer. m. J Edgar, 9 May 1979, 1 son, 2 stepsons, 1 daughter, 1 stepdaughter. Education: Havergal College; BA, Laurentian University, 1968; Interim High School Assistant Certificate, Type B, College of Education, 1969; Specialist Guidance Certificate, 1973; BA, Honours, University of Toronto, 1973; MA, York University, 1976; LLB, Osgoode Hall Law School, 1976. Appointments: Articled with law firm, Holden Murdoch Finlay Robinson, 1976-77; Called to the Bar of Ontario, 1977; Tax Editor, CCH (Canada) Ltd, 1977-78; Society Columnist, The Globe and Mail, 1988-93. Publications: The Glitter Girls, 1993; Confessions of a Society Columnist, 1995. Memberships: Served on various Boards, 1982-87: Family Day Care Services of Metro Toronto; Toronto Symphony Women's Committee; Toronto Pops Orchestra; Canadian Psychiatric Awareness Committee; Arthritis Society, Rosedale Branch; Wellesley Hospital Auxilliary; Society for Educational Visits and Exchanges in Canada; St George-St David PC Riding Association; Laurentian University. Address: 211 Queen's Quay West, Suite 1107, Toronto, Ontario M5J 2M6, Canada.

SEYERSTED Per, b. 18 May 1921, Oslo, Norway. Retired Professor of American Literature; Writer. Education: MA, Harvard University, 1959; PhD, University of Oslo, 1969. Appointments: Professor of American Literature, University of Oslo, 1973-91; Associate Editor, Studies in American Fiction, 1985-95. Publications: Gilgamesj, 1967, 4th edition, 1996; Kate Chopin: A Critical Biography, 1969, 5th edition, 1997; The Complete Works of Kate Chopin (editor), 1969, 4th edition, 1998; A Kate Chopin Miscellany (editor), 1979; Leslie Marmon Silko, 1980; Scando-Americana: Papers on Scandinavian Emigration to the United States (editor), 1980; Dakky Kiaer (editor), 1982; From Norwegian Romantic to American Realist: Studies in the Life and Writings of Hjalmar Hjorth Boyesen, 1984; The Arctic: Canada and the Nordic Countries (editor), 1991; Kate Chopin's Private Papers (editor), 1998. Contributions to: Journals. Honours: American Council of Learned Societies Fellow, 1964-66; Norwegian Research Council for Science and Letters Fellow, 1966-69. Memberships: Modern Language Association of America; Nordic Association for American Studies, president, 1973-79; Nordic Association for Canadian Studies, vice-president, 1984-93; Norsk faglitterarer forfatterforening; Norwegian Academy for Science and Letters. Address: c/o Department of British and American Studies, University of Oslo, PB 1003 Blindern, 0315 Oslo, Norway.

SEYMOUR Alan, b. 6 June 1927, Perth, Western Australia, Australia. Playwright. Publications: Swamp Creatures, 1958; The One Day of the Year, 1960; The Gaiety of Nations, 1965; A Break in the Music, 1966; The Pope and the Pill, 1968; Oh Grave, Thy Victory, 1973; Structures, 1973; The Wind from the Plain, 1974; The Float, 1980; Various radio and television plays. Novels: The One Day of the Year, 1967; The Coming Self-Destruction of the United States, 1969. Honour: Australia Council for the Arts Grant. Address: 74 Upland Road, London SE22 0DB, England.

SEYMOUR Arabella Charlotte Henrietta, b. 8 Dec 1948, London, England. Author. 1 daughter. Education: West Ham College of Technology. Publications: A Passion in the Blood, 1985; Dangerous Deceptions, 1986; The Sins of Rebeccah Russell, 1988; The End of the Family, 1990; No Sad Songs (as Sarah Lyon), 1990; Princess of Darkness, 1991; A Woman of Pleasure, 1994; Sins of the Mother, 1996. Contributions to: Woman's Day,

Australia. Membership: Society of Authors. Literary Agent: Sheil Land Associates Ltd. Address: Sondes House, Patrixbourne, Canterbury, Kent CT4 5DD, England.

SHAABAN Bouthaina, b. 1 Apr 1953, Syria. Associate Professor; Writer. m. Khalil Jawad, 2 Sept 1981, 2 daughters. Education: BA, English Literature, Damascus University, 1975; MA, 1978; PhD, 1982, English Literature, Warwick University. Appointments: Lecturer, Constantine University, Algeria, 1982-84; Lecturer, 1985-90, Associate Professor, 1991-, Damascus University; Fulbright Professor, Duke University, 1990-91. Publications: Both Right and Left-Handed Arab Women Talk About Their Lives, 1988; Poetry and Politics: Shelley and the Chartist Movement, 1993. Contributions to: Various publications. Honour: Rockefeller Foundation Appointment, Rice University, Houston, Texas 1992-93. Memberships: FIT, Arab Writers Union; International PEN; Keats-Shelley Society. Address: c/o Arab Writers Union, PO Box 3230, Damascus, Syria.

SHACHOCHIS Bob, (Robert Shacochis), b. 9 Sept 1951, West Pittston, Pennsylvania, USA. Journalist; Writer. m. Barbara Petersen, 1976. Education: BA, 1973, MA, 1979, University of Missouri, Columbia; MFA, University of Iowa, 1982. Appointments: Columnist, GQ magazines; Contributing Editor, Outside magazine, Harper's magazine. Publications: Novel: Swimming in the Volcanos, 1993. Short Story Collections: Easy in the Islands, 1985; The Next New World, 1989. Contributions to: Many periodicals. Honours: National Endowment for the Arts Fellowship, 1982; American Book Award for First Fiction, 1985; National Book Award, 1985; Prix de Rome, American Academy of Arts and Letters, 1989. Membership: Poets and Writers. Address: c/o Brandt & Brandt Literary Agents Inc, 1501 Broadway, New York, NY 10036, USA.

SHADBOLT Maurice (Francis Richard), b. 4 June 1932, Auckland, New Zealand. Novelist. m. Bridget Armstrong, 1978. Education: University of Auckland. Appointments: Journalist, New Zealand, 1952-54; Documentry Screenwriter, Director, New Zealand Film Unit, 1954-57; Full Time Writer, 1957-. Publications: Among the Cinders, 1965; This Summer's Dolphin, 1969; An Ear of the Dragon, 1971; Danger Zone, 1975; The Lovelock Version, 1980; Season of the Jew, 1986; Monday's Warrior, 1990; Dove on the Waters, 1997. Story Collections: The New Zealander: A Sequence of Stories, 1959; Summer Fires and Winter Country, 1963; The Presence of Music: Three Novellas; Figures in Light: Selected Stories. Play: Once on Chunk Bair, 1982. Guides and Histories of New Zealand. Honours: James Wattie Awards, 1973, 1991; New Zealand Book Award, 1981; Officer of the Order of the British Empire, 1989. Address: Box 60028 Titirangi, Auckland 7, New Zealand.

SHAFER Neil, b. 24 Apr 1933, Chicago, Illinois, USA. Writer; Editor. m. Edith Oelsher, 7 June 1964, 2 sons, 1 daughter. Education: BA, Education, Arizona State College, 1955; MMus, Catholic University of America, 1959. Appointments: Associate Editor, Whitman Numismatic Journal, 1964-68; Editor-in-Chief, New England Journal of Numismatics, 1985-87; Columnist, Bank Nore reporter, 1987-, Numismatic News, 1996-. Publications: United States Territorial Coinage for the Philippine Islands, 1961; A Guide Book of Philippine Paper Money, 1964; A Guide Book of Modern US Currency, 8 editions, 1965-79; Guide Book of Philippine Paper Money, 1964; Philippine Emergency and Guerilla Currency of World War II, 1974; Standard Catalog of World Paper Money (co-editor), 1981-97; Standard Catalog of Depression Scrip of the US (co-author), 1985; The Wonderful World of Paper Money, 1992; College Currency (editor), 1993; Honours: Various Awards, Numismatic Literary Guild, 1986, 1988, 1996; Medal of Merit, American Numismatic Association, 1988; Various Awards, Society of Paper Money Collectors. Memberships: Numismatic Literary Guild, 1968-; American Numismatic Association; International Bank Note Society; Society of Paper Money Collectors. Address: PO Box 17138, Milwaukee, WI 53217, USA.

SHAFFER Anthony (Joshua), b. 15 May 1926, Liverpool, England. Playwright; Writer. m. Diane Cilento, 1985. Education: Graduated, Trinity College, Cambridge, 1950. Appointments: Former Barrister and Journalist. Publications: The Savage Parade, 1963, revised edition, 1987; Sleuth, 1970; Murderer, 1970; The Wicker Man, 1974; Masada, 1974; Widow's Weeds, 1977; Death on the Nile, 1978; Absolution, 1979; Evil Under the Sun, 1982; Appointment with Death, 1988; Sommersby, 1994. Novels: How Doth the Little Crocodile (with Peter Shaffer), 1952; Withered Murder (with Peter Shaffer), 1955; The Wicker Man, 1978; Absolution, 1979. Honours: Tony Award, 1971; 6 Edgar Allan Poe Awards, Mystery Writers of America; Grande Prix Filmes Fantastique Paris. Address: c/o Peters, Fraser and Dunlop Group, 503-504 The Chambers, Chelsea Harbour, Lots Road, London SW10 0XF, England.

SHAFFER Peter (Levin), b. 15 May 1926, Liverpool, England. Dramatist. Education: BA, Trinity College, Cambridge, 1950. Appointments: Literary Critic, Truth, 1956-57; Music Critic, Time and Tide, 1961-62; Cameron Mackintosh Visiting Professor of Contemporary Theatre and Fellow, St Catherine's College, Oxford, 1994. Publications: Plays: Five Finger Exericse, 1958; The Private Ear, 1962; The Public Eye, 1962; The Merry Roosters Panto (with Joan Littlewood), 1963; The Royal Hunt of the Sun, 1964; Black Comedy, 1965; White Lies, 1967; The White Liars, 1968; The Battle of Shrivings, 1970; Amadeus, 1979; Yonadab, 1985; Lettice and Lovage, 1987; The Gift of Gorgon, 1992. Contributions to: Radio and television. Honours: Evening Standard Drama Awards, 1958, 1979, 1988; New York Drama Critics Cricle Awards, 1959, 1976; London Theatre Critics Award, 1979; Plays and Players Award, 1979; Tony Awards, 1979, 1980; Drama Desk Award, 1980; Academy Award, 1985; Golden Globe Award, 1985; Los Angeles Film Critics Association Award, 1985; Premi David di Donatello, 1985; Commander of the Order of the British Empire, 1987; Shakespeare Prize, Hamburg, 1989; William Inge Award for Distinguished Achievement in the American Theatre, 1992. Membership: Royal Society of Literature, fellow. Address: c/o McNaughton-Lowe Representation, 200 Fulham Road, London SW10 9PN, England.

SHAH Tahir, b. 16 Nov 1966, London, England. Writer. Education: BA, International Relations, US International University. Publications: Middle East Bedside Book, 1991; Journey Through Namibia, 1994; Spectrum Guide to Jordan, 1994; Beyond the Devil's Teeth, 1995; Sorcerer's Apprentice: Travels in India, 1997. Other: Various monographs. Contributions to: Newspapers and magazines. Memberships: Association of Cryto-Zoology, Arizona; Institute for Cultural Research, London; Institute for the Study of Human Knowledge, San Francisco; Institute of Directors, London; Royal Anthropological Institue, London; Royal Society for Asian Affairs, London; Royal Geographical Society, London; Royal African Society, London. Address: PO Box 2227, London NW2 3BP, England.

SHAHED Husne Ara, 11 Oct 1943, Noakhali, Bangladesh. Teacher. m. A F Shahed Ali, 16 Oct 1966, 2 sons, 1 daughter. Education: MA, Philosophy, Dhaka University, 1965. Publications include: Tran Shibirer Din Ratri (Life in the Relief Camp), 1997; Pathaker Mon (The Pulse of the Readers), 1997; Rebecca, 1997; Sketches from Zibe; Eternal Fugitive; Saree; Whispers of Sorrow; Realm of Mind; Fleeting Days. Contributions to: Dainik Bangla; Dainik Sangbad; Sev national dailies, weekly and monthly periodicals. Honour: World Literary Academy, fellow; Nominee, Woman of the Year, ABI, 1998. Memberships: National Institute for Development of Bengali Language & Literature; Asiatic Society of Bangladesh; PEN. Address: Shere Bangla Girls College, 20 Hatkhola Road, Wari, Dhaka 1203, Bangladesh.

SHAHEEN Mohammad Yousef, b. 17 Feb 1938, Halhul, Jordan. Professor of English Literature. Education: PhD, University of Cambridge, England. Appointments: Professor of English, University of Jordan; Vice President, Mu'tah University, 1998-. Publications: George Meredith, A Reappraisal of the Novels, 1981; The Impact of Eliot on Sayyah, 1992; Tayyeb Salih's Season of Migration to the North, 1993; Myth and Literature, 1996; Selected Letters of George Meredith, 1997. Contributions to: Review of English Studies; Modern Language Review; Twentieth Century; Modern Fiction. Address: PO Box 13073, University of Jordan, Amman, Jordan.

SHALLIT Jeffrey Outlaw, b. 17 Oct 1957, Philadelphia, PA, USA. Associate Professor. m. Anna Lubiw, 29 Dec 1989, 2 sons. Education: AB, Princeton University, 1979; PhD, University of California, Berkeley, 1983. Appointments: Assistant Professor, University of Chicago, 1983-88; Assistant Professor, Dartmouth College, 1988-90; Associate Professor, University of Waterloo, 1990-. Publication: Algorithmic Number Theory, with Eric Bach, 1996. Contributions to: 70 articles in journals. Address: Department of Computer Science, University of Waterloo, Waterloo, Ontario N2L 3G1, Canada.

SHANE John. See: **DURST Paul.**

SHANES Eric, b. 21 Oct 1944, Bedford, England. Painter; Art Historian; Lecturer. m. Jacky Darville, 17 Mar 1973, 1 son, 1 daughter. Education: Whittingehame College, Brighton, England; Dip AD, Chelsea School of Art, 1966. Appointments include: Founder Editor, Turner Studies, Tate Gallery; Founder Editor, Art Book Review; Painter, Two Person Exhibition, Splinter Gallery, London, England, 1992; Guest Curator, Turner's Watercolour Explorations, Tate Gallery, London, 1997; Guest Curator, Masterpieces of English Watercolour, Hickman Bacon Collection and Fitzwilliam Museum, Cambridge, England, 1990-91; Guest Curator, JMW Turner, The Foundations of Genius, Taft Museum, Cincinnati, Ohio, USA, 1986; Joint Curator, with Evelyn Joll, Turner's Picturesque Views in England and Wales Series, 1979; Classical Music Critic, The Daily Mail, London, 1988-89; Regular Contributor, Apollo and Modern Painters magazines; Written for Artscribe, Art and Artists and Arts Review; Commissioned articles appeared in The Times, 1981; The Sunday Telegraph Colour Magazine, 1981; The Sunday Times Magazine, 1982; Official Visitor to Romania on a British Council Cultural Exchange Award, 1982; Visited Czechoslovakia on a British Council Cultural Exchange Award, 1984; Lectures include University of Cambridge, Department of Art History, England. Publications include: Jack Beal, American Realist, 1993; Turner's England, 1990; Turner's Human Landscape, 1990; Impressionist London, 1994; Turner's Watercolour Explorations, 1997; Turner in 1066 Country, 1998. Honour: Winner, 1979 Yorkshire Post Art Book Award, 1979. Address: 7 Cumberland Road, Acton, London W3 6EX, England.

SHANGE Ntozake (born Paulette Williams), b. 18 Oct 1948, Trenton, New Jersey, USA. Poet; Dramatist; Writer; Associate Professor of Drama. 1 daughter. Education: BA, Barnard College, 1970; MA, University of Southern California at Los Angeles, 1973. Appointments: Faculty, Sonoma State College, Rohnert Park, California, 1973-75, Mills College, Oakland, California, 1975, City College of the City University of New York, 1975, Douglass College, New Brunswick, New Jersey, 1978; Artist-in-Residence, Equinox Theater, Houston, 1981-; Associate Professor of Drama, University of Houston, 1983-. Publications: Poetry: Melissa and Smith, 1976; Natural Disasters and Other Festive Occasions, 1977; Happy Edges, 1978; Some Men, 1981; A Daughter's Geography, 1983; From Okra to Greens, 1984; Ridin' the Moon in Texas: Word Paintings, 1988; The Love Space Demands: A Continuing Saga, 1992. Plays: For Colored Girls Who Have Considered Suicide When the Rainbow is Enuf, 1976; Photograph: Lovers-in-Motion, 1981; Spell #7, 1981; Boogie Woogie Landscapes, 1981. Fiction: Sassafrass: A Novella, 1977; Sassafrass, Cypress and Indigo, 1982; Betsey Brown, 1985; Liliane: Resurrection of the Daughter, 1995. Non-Fiction: See No Evil: Prefaces, Essays and Accounts 1976-1983, 1984. Honours: New York Drama Critics Circle Award, 1977; Obie Awards, 1977, 1980; Columbia University Medal of Excellence, 1981; Guggenheim Fellowship, 1981. Address: c/o St Martin's Press, 175 Fifth Avenue, New York, NY 10010, USA.

SHANLEY Mary Lyndon, Professor; Writer. Education: BA, Wellesley College, 1966; MA, 1968, PhD, 1972, Harvard University. Appointments: Assistant Professor, Department of Political Science, Regis College, 1972-73; Acting Director, Program of Women's Studies, Vassar College, 1982-83; Assistant Professor, 1973-82, Associate Professor, 1982-88, Chairperson, 1987-90, Professor, 1988-, Margaret Stiles Halleck Chair, 1991-, Department of Political Science, Vassar College. Publications: Feminism, Marriage and the Law in Victorian England 1850-1895, 1989; Feminist Interpretations and Political Theory, 1990; Reconstructing Political Theory: Feminist Essays, 1997; Reinventing the Family: Affirming Human Values in Liberal Society, 1999; Numerous articles. Honours: Woodrow Wilson Fellowship, 1966-67; Harvard University Travelling Fellowship, 1970; William Andrews Clark Memorial Library Summer Fellowship, 1977; National Endowment for the Humanities, 1978, 1984-85, 1996-97; Several grants. Address: c/o Maildrop 455, Vassar College, Poughkeepsie, NY 12604, USA.

SHAPCOTT Thomas W(illiam), b. 21 Mar 1935, Ipswich, Queensland, Australia. Poet; Novelist; Writer; Professor of Creative Writing. m. (1) Margaret Hodge, 1960, (2) Judith Rodriguez, 1982, 1 son, 3 daughters. Education: BA, University of Queensland, 1968. Appointments: Director, Australia Council Literature Board, 1983-90; Executive Director, National Book Council, 1992-97; Professor of Creative Writing, University of Adelaide, 1997-. Publications: Poetry: Time on Fire, 1961; The Mankind Thing, 1963; Sonnets, 1960-63, 1963; A Taste of Salt Water, 1967; Inwards to the Sun, 1969; Fingers at Air, 1969; Begin with Walking, 1973; Shabbytown Calendar, 1975; 7th Avenue Poems, 1976; Selected Poems, 1978; Make the Old Man Sing, 1980; Welcome!, 1983; Travel Dice, 1987; Selected Poems, 1956-1988, 1989; In the Beginning, 1990; The City of Home, 1995. Novels: The Birthday Gift, 1982; White Stag of Exile, 1984; Hotel Bellevue, 1986; The Search for Galina, 1989; Mona's Gift, 1993; Theatre of Darkness, 1998. Plays: The 7 Deadly Sins, 1970. Editor: New Impulses in Australian Poetry (with R Hall), 1967; Australian Poetry Now, 1970; Contemporary American and Australian Poetry, 1975; Poetry as a Creative Learning Process, 1978; The Moment Made Marvellous (poetry anthology), 1998. Contributions to: Newspapers and journals. Honours: Grace Leven Prize, 1961; Sir Thomas White Memorial Prize, 1967; Sidney Myer Charity Trust Awards, 1967, 1969; Churchill Fellowship, 1972; Canada-Australia Literary Prize, 1978; Officer of the Order of Australia, 1989; Honorary DLitt, Macquarie University, 1989; Gold Wreath, Struga International Poetry Festival, 1989; Christopher Brennan Award for Poetry, 1994; NSW Premier's Special Literary Prize, 1996; Michel Wesley Wright Award, 1996. Memberships: Australian Book Review, chairman; Copyright Agency Limited, chairman; Australian Society of Authors; International PEN. Address: PO Box 231, Mont Albert, Victoria 3127, Australia.

SHAPIRO David (Joel), b. 2 Jan 1947, Newark, New Jersey, USA. Poet; Art Critic; Professor of Art History. m. Lindsey Stamm, 1970, 1 child. Education: BA, 1968, PhD, 1973, Columbia University; BA, 1970, MA, 1974, Clare College, Cambridge. Appointments: Violinist in various orchestras, 1963-; Instructor and Assistant Professor of English, Columbia University, 1972-80; Visiting Professor, Brooklyn College of the City University of New York, 1979, Princeton University, 1982-83; Visting Faculty, Cooper Union, New York City, 1980-; Full Professor of Art History, William Paterson College, Wayne, New Jersey, 1996-. Publications: Poetry: January: A Book of Poems, 1965; Poems from Deal, 1969; A Man Holding an Acoustic Panel, 1971; The Page-Turner, 1973; Lateness, 1977; To an Idea, 1984; House, Blown Apart, 1988; After a Lost Original, 1990. Other: John Ashbery: An Introduction to the Poetry, 1979; Jim Dine: Painting What One Is, 1981; Jasper Johns: Drawings 1954-1984, 1984;

Mondrian Flowers, 1990; Alfred Leslie: The Killing Cycle (with Judith Stein), 1991. Honours: Bread Loaf Writers Conference Robert Frost Fellowship, 1965; Ingram Merrill Foundation Fellowship, 1967; Book-of-the-Month Club Fellowship, 1968; Kellett Fellow, Clare College, Cambridge, 1968-70; Creative Artists Public Service Grant, 1974; Morton Dauwen Zabel Award, 1977; National Endowment for the Arts Grant, 1979; National Endowment for the Humanities Fellowships, 1980; Foundation for Contemporary Performance Arts Grant, 1996; Milton Asery Professor, Bard Graduate School of the Arts, 1996. Address: 3001 Henry Hudson Parkway, Riverdale, NY 10463, USA.

SHAPIRO Harvey, b. 27 Jan 1924, Chicago, Illinois, USA. Editor; Poet. m Edna Kaufman, 23 July 1953, 2 sons. Education: BA, Yale University, 1947; MA, Columbia University, 1948. Appointments: Staff, Commentary, 1955-57, The New Yorker, 1955-57, New York Times Magazine, 1957-64; Assistant Editor, 1964-75, Editor, 1975-83, New York Times Book Review; Deputy Editor, New York Times Magazine, 1983-. Publications: The Eye, 1953; The Book, 1955; Mountain Fire Thornbush, 1961; Battle Report, 1966; This World, 1971; Lauds, 1975; Lauds and Nightsounds, 1978; The Light Holds, 1984; National Cold Storage Company: New and Selected Poems, 1988; A Day's Portion, 1994; Selected Poems, 1997. Contributions to: Periodicals. Honour: Rockefeller Grant for Poetry, 1967. Address: c/o The New York Times Magazine, 229 West 43rd Street, New York, NY 10036, USA.

SHAPIRO Karl (Jay), b. 10 Nov 1913, Baltimore, Maryland, USA. Professor of English (retired); Poet; Writer. m. Sophie Wilkins, 25 Apr 1985. Education: Johns Hopkins University, 1937-39. Appointments: Consultant in Poetry, Library of Congress, Washington, DC, 1946-47; Associate Professor, Johns Hopkins University, 1947-50; Editor, Poetry, 1950-56, Prairie Schooner, 1956-66; Professor of English,University of Nebraska, 1956-66, University of Illinois, Circle Campus, Chicago, 1966-68, University of California at Davis, 1968-85. Publications: Poetry: Poems, 1935; New and Selected Poems, 1940-46, 1946; Trial of a Poet, 1947; Poems, 1940-53, 1953; Poems of a Jew, 1958; Selected Poems, 1968; White-Haired Lover, 1968; Adult Bookstore, 1976; Collected Poems, 1940-78, 1978; New and Selected Poems, 1940-86, 1987. Novel: Edsel, 1971. Non-Fiction: Beyond Criticism, 1953; In Defense of Ignorance, 1960; Prose Keys to Modern Poetry (with James E Miller Jr and Bernice Slote), 1962; The Bourgeois Poet, 1964; A Prosody Handbook (with Robert Beum), 1964; To Abolish Children, 1968; The Poetry Wreck, 1975; The Younger Son (autobiography), 1988; Reports of My Death (autobiography), 1990; The Old Horsefly, 1993. Honours: Jeanette S Davis Prize, 1942; Levinson Prize, 1943; Contemporary Poetry Prize, 1943; Pulitzer Prize in Poetry, 1945; Shelley Memorial Prize, 1945; Guggenheim Fellowships, 1945-46, 1953-54; Bollingen Prize for Poetry, 1969; Robert Kirsch Award, Los Angeles Times, 1989; Charity Randall Citation, 1990. Memberships: American Academy of Arts and Letters; American Academy of Arts and Sciences. PEN. Address: 211 West 106th Street, No 11C, New York, NY 10025, USA.

SHARAT CHANDRA Gubbi Shankara Chetty, (Jean Parker), b. 5 Mar 1938, Nanjangud, India. Professor of English; Poet; Writer. m. Jane Sharat Chandra, 8 Jan 1966, 1 son, 2 daughters. Education: BA, 1956, BL, 1968 University of Mysore; MS, State University of New York, 1964; LLM, University of Toronto, 1966; MFA, University of Iowa, 1968. Appointments: Editor, Kamadhenu, 1970-75, South Asian Review, 1989-; Assistant Professor, Washington State University, 1972-80; Fulbright Professor, Malaysia, 1978, Bangladesh, 1989; Assistant Professor, 1983-87, Associate Professor, 1987-92, Professor of English, 1992-, University of Missouri, Kansas City. Publications: April in Nanjangud, 1971; Once or Twice, 1974; The Ghost of Meaning, 1978; Heirloom, 1982; Family of Mirrors, 1993; Immigration of Loss, 1993. Contributions to: Newspapers, magazines and journals. Honours: Florida State Poetry Award, 1980; National Endowment for the Arts Fellowship, 1981.

Memberships: Associated Writing Programs; Modern Language Association; South Asian Language Association. Address: 9916 Juniper, Overland Park, KS 66207, USA.

SHARMA Laxminarain, b. 12 Mar 1943, Kaithal, India. University Professor. m. Santosh K Sharma, 25 Nov 1969, 1 son, 2 daughters. Education: BA, Panjab University, 1964; MA, 1st Class 1st, Hindi Language and Literature, 1966, PhD, distinction, Indian Mythology, 1971, Kurukshetra University; DLitt, distinction, Supreme Divinity in Human Form, University of Magadha, 1989; Shree Ram, Indian Literature. Appointments: Lecturer, RKSD College, Kaithal, 1966; Lecturer, Reader, Hindi Department, 1967, Chairman, Department Head, 1993-96, Panjab University, Chandigarh; Officer on Special Duty, Indira Gandhi National Open University, New Delhi, 1986-87; Visiting Professor, University of West Indies, St Augustine, Trinidad and Tobago, 1989-92; First Secretary, High Commission of India, Trinidad and Tobago, 1989-92. Publications: Narendra Sharma And His Poetry, 1967; The Faith of Tulsides, 1972; Poetry and Mythology, 1979; Asuryampasya, poems, 1979; Contemporary and Eternity, 1980; Open University: Indian Perspectives, 1986; The Ramkatha Immortal and Goswami Tulsides, 1986; Poetry and Eternity, 1987; Inner Voyage of Tulsides, essays, 1987; Vatsala, epic poem, 1987; The Space Beyond, fiction, 1987; The Ancient Recital, 1990; The East Indian Songs of Trinidad, 1991; A Story of Elevated Being, fiction, 1992. Contributions to: Over 300 in India and abroad. Honours: Gold Medallist, Kurukshetra University, 1966; 7 national and international awards for books including felicitation from President of India for Distance Education; Bangalore University awarded PhD on topic Laxminarain and His Contribution in Hindi Literature and Indian Culture. Memberships: Chairman, Indian Council for Cultural Studies and Research; President, University of Supreme Divinity; Society Working for Advancement of Hindu Aspiration, Trinidad. Address: 239 Sector 37A, Chandigarh 160036, India.

SHARMA Vera, b. 10 Feb 1926, Bombay, India. Writer; Poet; Dramatist. m. 10 Mar 1949, 1 daughter. Publications: Stories, poems and plays; An Unusual Indian Girlhood, 1994; Aaher, short stories in Marathi translation, 1996; Anita (children's book in English), 1997. Contributions to: Various publications. Honours: Several prizes. Memberships: Asiatic Society of Bombay; PEN Bombay. Address: Bhairavi, 106 6th Road, Tilaknagar, Goregaon W, Bombay 400 062, India.

SHARP Ronald A(lan), b. 19 Oct 1945, Cleveland, Ohio, USA. Professor of English; Writer; Administrator. m. Inese Brutans, 22 June 1968, 2 sons. Education: Syracuse University, 1963-64; BA, Kalamazoo College, 1967; Instituto Internacional, Madrid, 1965-66; MA, University of Michigan, 1968; University of Edinburgh, 1973; PhD, University of Virginia, 1974. Appointments: Instructor, Western Michigan University, 1968-70; Instructor, 1970-72, Assistant Professor, 1974-78, Associate Professor, 1978-85, Professor of English, 1985-90, John Crowe Ransom Professor of English, 1990-, Associate Provost, 1998-, Kenyon College; Visiting Professor, Concordia University, 1978; Co-Editor, The Kenyon Review, 1978-82. Publications: Keats, Skepticism and the Religion of Beauty, 1979; Friendship and Literature: Spirit and Form, 1986; The Norton Book of Friendship (with Eudora Welty), 1991; Reading George Steiner (with Nathan A Scott Jr), 1994; The Persistence of Poetry: Bicentennial Essays on Keats (with Robert M Ryan), 1998. Contributions to: Books and journals. Honours: Ford Foundation Grant, 1971; English Speaking Union Fellowship, 1973; Mellon Grant, 1980; National Endowment for the Humanities Fellowships, 1981-82, 1984, 1985, 1986-87, 1994, 1996, 1998; National Humanities Center Fellowship, 1986-87; Various grants. Memberships: Keats-Shelley Association; Modern Language Association; Wordsworth-Coleridge Association. Address: c/o Department of English, Kenyon College, Gambier, OH 43022, USA.

SHARPE Tom, (Thomas Ridley Sharpe), b. 30 Mar 1928, London, England. Author. m. Nancy Anne Looper, 6 Aug 1969. 3 daughters. Education: Pembroke College, Cambridge, 1948-52. Publications: Riotous Assembly, 1971; Indecent Exposure, 1973; Porterhouse Blue, 1974; Blott on the Landscape, 1975; Wilt, 1976; The Great Pursuit, 1977; The Throwback, 1978; The Wilt Alternative, 1979; Ancestral Vices, 1980; Vintage Stuff, 1982; Wilt on High, 1984; Grantchester Grind, 1995; The Midden, 1996. Contributions to: Magazines and journals. Honours: Laureat Le Grand Prix de L'Humour Noir, Paris, 1986; Le Legion de l'Humour, Aphia, Paris, 1986. Membership: Society of Authors. Address: 38 Tunwells Lane, Great Shelford, Cambridge CB2 5LJ, England.

SHATTUCK Roger (Whitney), b. 20 Aug 1923, New York, New York, USA. Writer; Translator; Poet; Editor; Professor. m. Nora Ewing White, 20 Aug 1949, 1 son, 3 daughters. Education: BA, Yale University, 1947. Appointments: Reporter, Chicago Daily News, Paris Office, 1948-49; Assistant Trade Editor, Harcourt, Brace & Co, New York City, 1949-50; Society of Fellows, 1950-53, Instructor in French, 1953-56, Harvard University; Assistant Professor, 1956-59, Associate Professor of Romance Languages, 1959-62, Professor of French and English, 1962-71, Chairman of the Department of French and Italian, 1968-71, University of Texas at Austin; Commonwealth Professor of French, University of Virginia, 1974-88; University Professor and Professor of Modern Foreign Languages, Boston University, 1988-97; Lecturer at many universities, colleges, art museums and other venues. Publications: Non-Fiction: The Banquet Years: The Origins of the Avant-Garde in France, 1885 to World War One, 1958, revised edition, 1968; Proust's Binoculars: A Study of Memory, Time, and Recognition in A La Recherche du Temps Perdu, 1963; Marcel Proust, 1974; The Forbidden Experiment: The Story of the Wild Boy of Aveyron, 1980; The Innocent Eye on Literature and the Arts, 1984; Forbidden Knowledge: From Prometheus to Pornography, 1996. Poetry: Half Tame, 1964. Editor and Translator: René Daumal: Mount Analogue: A Novel of Symbolically Authentic Non-Euclidean Adventures in Mountain Climbing, 1960; The Selected Writings of Guillaume Apollinaire, 1963, revised edition, 1971; Paul Valéry: Occasions (with Frederick Brown), 1970. Editor: The Craft and Context of Translation (with William Arrowsmith), 1961; Selected Writings of Alfred Jarry: Ubu Cuckolded, Exploits and Opinions of Dr Faustroll, Pataphysician, and Other Writings (with Simon Watson Taylor), 1966. Translator: René Daumal: A Fundamental Experiment, 1987. Contributions to: Essays, short stories, and poems in various publications. Honours: Guggenheim Fellowship, 1958-59; Fulbright Research Fellow, 1958-59; American Council of Learned Societies Research Fellow, 1969-70; National Book Award, 1975; American Academy and Institute of Arts and Letters Award, 1987; Doctorat honoris causa, University of Orléans, France, 1990. Memberships: National Translation Center, advisory board, 1964-69, chairman, 1966-69; National Humanities Faculty, 1972-73; Publications of the Modern Language Association, editorial board, 1977-78; American Academy of Arts and Sciences, 1990-; Association of Literary Scholars and Critics, president, 1995-96. Address: 231 Forge Hill Road, Lincoln, VT 05443, USA.

SHAUGHNESSY Alfred James, b. 19 May 1916, London, England. Writer. m. Jean Lodge, 18 Sept 1948, 2 sons. Education: Royal Military College, Sandhurst. Publications: Both Ends of the Candle (autobiography), 1978; Sarah - Letters and Diaries of a Courtier's Wife, 1906-1936, 1989; Dearest Enemy (novel), 1991; Hugo (novel), 1994; A Confession in Writing (memoir), 1997. Stage plays, including: Release; Holiday for Simon; The Heat of the Moment; Old Herbaceous; Double Cut; Love Affair (from the French). Honours: Nominated for US Television Emmy Award for Best Series Script, 1974, 1976; US Television Critics Circle Achievement in Writing Award, 1976-77; Literary Agent: Cecily Ware. Address: The Grange, Yattendon, Thatcham, Berkshire RG18 0UE, England.

SHAVELSON Melville, b. 1 Apr 1917, New York, New York, USA. Writer; Director. m. Lucille T Myers, 2 Nov 1938, 1 son, 1 daughter. Education: AB, Cornell University, 1937. Publications: Screenplays: The Princess and the Pirate, 1944; Wonder Man, 1944; Room for One More, 1951; I'll See You in My Dreams, 1952. Writer, Director: The Seven Little Foys, 1954; Beau James, 1956; Houseboat, 1957; The Five Pennies, 1958; It Started in Naples, 1959; On the Double, 1960; Yours, Mine and Ours, 1968; The War Between Men and Women, 1972; The Legend of Valentino, 1975; Deceptions, 1985. Writer, Director, Producer: The Pigeon That Took Rome, 1962; A New Kind of Love, 1963; Cast a Giant Shadow, 1966; Mixed Company, 1974; The Great Houdinis, 1976; Ike, 1979. Broadway Musical: Jimmy, 1969. Books: How to Make a Jewish Movie, 1970; Lualda, 1975; The Great Houdinis, 1976; The Eleventh Commandment, 1977; Ike, 1979; Don't Shoot It's Only Me, 1990. Honours: Screenwriters Guild Award, 1959; Christopher Award, 1959; Award of Merit, United Jewish Appeal, 1966. Membership: WGA, president, 1969-71, 1979-81, 1985-87. Address: 11947 Sunshine Terrace, Studio City, CA 91604, USA.

SHAW Annie, Journalist. m. Colin Harding, 1984. Education: BA, University of Newcastle-upon-Tyne. Appointments: The Times, London, 1979-86; Freelance, 1986-96; The Sunday Telegraph, 1996-. Honour: Winner, Laing Media Award, for property writers raising awareness of environmental issues, 1996. Address: The Sunday Telegraph, 1 Canada Square, Canary Wharf, London E14 5AR, England.

SHAW Brian. See: **TUBB E(dwin) C(harles).**

SHAW Bynum (Gillette), b. 10 July 1923, Alamance County, North Carolina, USA. Professor of Journalism. m. (1) Louise N Brantley, dec, 30 Aug 1948, (2) Emily P Crandall, dec, 19 June 1982, (3) Charlotte E Reeder, 26 Nov 1986, 2 daughters. Education: BA, Wake Forest College, 1951. Appointment: Publisher, Hummingbird Press, 1993-. Publications: The Sound of Small Hammers, 1962; The Nazi Hunter, 1968; Divided We Stand, The Baptists in American Life, 1974; Days of Power, Nights of Fear, 1980; W W Holden: A Political Biography (with Edgar E Folk), 1982; The History of Wake Forest College, Vol IV, 1988; Oh, Promised Land!, 1992. Contributions to: Esquire; New Republic; Moneysworth; New York Times; Baltimore Sun. Honour: Sir Walter Raleigh Award in Fiction, 1969. Membership: North Carolina Writers Conference, chairman, 1972. Address: 2700 Speas Road, Winston-Salem, NC 27106, USA.

SHAW David. See: **FOWLER Alastair.**

SHAW Irene. See: **ROBERTS Irene.**

SHAW Mark, b. 3 Oct 1945, Auburn, Indiana, USA. Author. m. Chris R Shaw, 15 May 1989, 3 stepsons, 1 stepdaughter. Education: BS, Purdue University; JD, Indiana University School of Law. Publications: Down For the Count, 1992; Bury Me in a Pot Bunker, 1993; Forever Flying, 1994; The Perfect Yankee, 1995; McKlaus, A Biography, 1996; Statement to Courage, 1997; Diamonds in the Rough, 1998; Larry Legend, 1998. Membership: Writers Guild. Literary Agent: Richard Pine. Address: 250 West 57th Street, New York, NY 10019, USA.

SHAW (Veronica) Patricia, b. 1928, Melbourne, Australia. Writer. div, 1 son, 1 daughter. Education: Star of the Sea Convent, Melbourne; Melbourne Teachers College. Publications: Brother Digger: The Sullivans, 2nd AIF, 1984; Valley of the Lagoons, 1989; River of the Sun, 1991; The Feather and the Stone, 1992; Where the Willows Weep, 1993; Cry of the Rain Bird, 1994; Fires of Fortune, 1995; The Opal Seekers, 1996; The Glittering Fields, 1997. Honours: Several best-sellers. Address: Gold Coast, Queensland, Australia.

SHAWCROSS William (Hartley Hume), b. 28 May 1946, England. Writer. m (1) Marina Warner, 1971, div, 1 son, 1 daughter, (2) Michal Levin, 1981, div, (3) Hon Olga Polizzi, 1993. Education: Exeter College, Oxford. Appointments: Writer for Washington Post, Sunday Times, Spectator, New Statesman; Chairman, Article 19, International Centre on Censorship. Publications: Dubcek, 1970; Crime and Compromise, 1974; Sideshow: Kissinger, Nixon and the Destruction of Cambodia, 1979; The Quality of Mercy: Cambodia, Holocaust and Modern Memory, 1984; The Shah's Last Ride, 1989; Kowtow: A Plea on Behalf of Hong Kong, 1989; Murdoch, 1992; Cambodia's New Deal, 1994. Address: Friston Place, East Dean, East Sussex BN20 0AH, England.

SHEARER Jill, b. 14 Apr 1936, Melbourne, Victoria, Australia. Playwright. Publications: The Trouble with Gillian, 1974; The Foreman, 1976; The Boat, 1977; The Kite, 1977; Nocturne, 1977; Catherine, 1978; Stephen, 1980; Release Lavinia Stannard, 1980; A Woman Like That, 1986; Shimada, 1987; Comrade, 1987; The Family, 1994. Honours: Australia Council Grant, 1987; Arts Queensland Fellowship, 1993. Address: c/o Playlab Press, PO Box 185, Ashgrove, Brisbane 4060, Queensland, Australia.

SHEED Wilfrid John Joseph, b. 27 Dec 1930, London, England. Writer; Columnist. m. Miriam Ungerer, 2 sons, 1 daughter. Education: BA, 1954, MA, 1957, Lincoln College, Oxford. Appointments: Film Reviewer, 1959-61, Associate Editor, 1959-66, Jubilee magazine, New York City; Drama Critic and Book Editor, Commonweal magazine, New York City, 1964-71; Film Reviewer, Esquire magazine, New York City, 1967-69; Visiting Professor, Princeton University, 1970-71; Columnist, New York Times, 1971-; Judge and Member, Editorial Board, Book of the Month Club, 1972-88. Publications: Joseph, 1958; A Middle Class Education, 1960; The Hack, 1963; Square's Progress, 1965; Office Politics, 1966; The Blacking Factory and Pennsylvania Gothic: A Short Novel and a Long Story, 1968; Max Jamison, 1970; The Morning After, 1971; People Will Always Be Kind, 1973; Three Mobs: Labor, Church and Mafia, 1974; Vanishing Species of America, 1974; Muhammad Ali: A Portrait in Words and Photographs, 1975; Transatlantic Blues, 1978; The Good Word and Other Words, 1978; Clare Boothe Luce, 1982; Frank and Maisie, 1985; The Boys of Winter, 1987; The Kennedy Legacy: A Generation Later, 1988; Essays in Disguise, 1989; The Face of Baseball, 1990; My Life as a Fan, 1993; In Love with Daylight, 1995. Editor: G K Chesterton's Essays and Poems, 1957; Sixteen Short Novels, 1986; Baseball and Lesser Sports, 1991. Contributions to: Periodicals. Honours: American Academy and Institute of Arts and Letters Award, 1971; Guggenheim Fellowship, 1971-72. Memberships: Authors Guild; PEN. Address: Sag Harbor, NY 11963, USA.

SHEEHAN Neil, b. 27 Oct 1936, Holyoke, Massachusetts, USA. Writer. m. Susan Margulies, 30 Mar 1965, 2 daughters. Education: AB, cum laude, Harvard University, 1958. Appointments: Vietnam Bureau, United Press International, Saigon, 1962-64; Reporter, New York Times, 1964-72. Publications: The Arnheiter Affair, 1972; A Bright Shining Lie: John Paul Vann and America in Vietnam, 1988; After the War Was Over: Hanoi and Saigon, 1992. Contributions to: Newspapers and journals. Honours: 1st Annual Drew Pearson Award, 1971; Honorary LittD, Columbia College, Chicago, 1972; Sidney Hillman Foundation Awards, 1972, 1988; Columbia Journalism Awards, 1972, 1989; Guggenheim Fellowship, 1973-74; Adlai Stevenson Fellow, 1973-75; Lehrman Institute Fellow, 1975-76; Rockefeller Foundation Fellow, 1976-77; Woodrow Wilson International Center for Scholars Fellow, 1979-80; National Book Award, 1988; Pulitzer Prize for General Non-Fiction, 1989; Robert F Kennedy Book Award, 1989; Ambassador Award, English Speaking Union, 1989; John F Kennedy Award, 1989; Honorary LHD, American International College, 1990, University of Lowell, 1991; Literary Lion, New York Public Library, 1992. Memberships: Society of American Historians; American Academy of Achievement. Address: 4505 Klingle Street North West, Washington, DC 20016, USA.

SHEEHAN Susan, b. 24 Aug 1937, Vienna, Austraia (US Citizen, 1946). Writer. m. Neil Sheehan, 30 Mar 1965, 1 son, 2 daughters. Education: BA, Wellesley College, 1958. Appointments: Editorial Researcher, Esquire-Coronet, New York City, 1959-60; Staff, New Yorker magazine, New York City, 1961-. Publications: Ten Vietnamese, 1967; A Welfare Mother, 1976; A Prison and a Prisoner, 1978; Is There No Place on Earth for Me?, 1982; Kate Quinton's Days, 1984; A Missing Plane, 1986; Life for Me Ain't Been No Crystal Stair, 1993. Contributions to: Many magazines. Honours: Guggenheim Fellowship, 1975-76; Sidney Hillman Foundation Award, 1976; Gavel Award, American Bar Association, 1978; Woodrow Wilson International Center for Scholars Fellowship, 1981; Individual Reporting Award, National Mental Health Association, 1981; Pulitzer Prize for General Non-Fiction, 1983; Feature Writing Award, New York Press Club, 1984; Alumnae Association Achievement Award, Wellesley College, 1984; DHL, University of Lowell, 1991; Carroll Kowal Journalism Award, 1993; Public Awareness Award, National Alliance for the Mentally III, 1995. Memberships: Authors Guild; Phi Beta Kappa; Society of American Historians. Address: 4505 Klingle Street North West, Washington, DC 20016, USA.

SHEEHY Gail (Henion), b. 27 Nov 1937, Mamaroneck, New York, USA. Journalist; Editor; Writer; Dramatist. m. 1) Albert F Sheehy, 20 Aug 1960, div 1967, 1 daughter, 2) Clay Felker, 16 Dec 1984, 1 adopted daughter. Education: BS, University of Vermont, 1958. Appointments: Fashion Editor, Rochester Democrat and Chronicle, New York, 1961-63; Feature Writer, New York Herald Tribune, 1963-66; Contributing Editor, New York Magazine, 1968-77, Vanity Fair Magazine, 1988-. Publications: Lovesounds, 1970; Panthermania: The Clash of Black Against Black in One American City, 1971; Speed is of the Essence, 1971; Hustling: Prostitution in Our Wide-Open Society, 1973; Passages: Predictable Crises of Adult Life, 1976; Pathfinders, 1981; Spirit of Survival, 1986; Character: America's Search for Leadership, 1988; Gorbachev: The Man Who Changed the World, 1990; The Silent Passage: Menopause, 1992; New Passages: Mapping Your Life Across Time, 1995; Understanding Men's Passages, 1998. Contributions to: Newspapers and magazines. Honours: Columbia University Fellowship, 1970, and National Magazine Award, 1973; Anisfield-Wolf Book Award, 1986; Best Magazine Writer Award, Washington Journalism Review, 1991; Literary Lion, New York Public Library, 1992. Memberships: Authors Guild; Authors League of America; Common Cause; National Organization for Women; PEN American Center; Poets and Writers. Address: c/o Vanity Fair Magazine, 350 Madison Avenue, 12th Floor, New York, NY 10017, USA.

SHEHADI Fadlou, b. 9 Feb 1926, Beirut, Lebanon. Professor; Emeritus. m. Alison McDonald Shute, 1 son, 1 daughter. Education: BA, American University of Beirut, 1948; Diploma, Institut de Musique, Beirut, 1948; PhD, Princeton University, 1959. Appointments: Assistant Instructor, Princeton University, 1950-51; Instructor, Rutgers University, 1953-57; Assistant Professor, Rutgers, 1957-63; Associate Professor, Rutgers, 1963-72; Professor, Rutgers, 1972-; Retired (Emeritus), 1994. Publications: Ghazali's Unique Unknowable God, 1964; Ghazali's al-Maqsad al-Asna, 1971; Metaphysics In Islamic Philosophy, 1982; Applied Ethics & Ethical Theory, Co-editor, 1988; Philosophies of Music in Medieval Islam, 1995. Honours: Rockefeller Fellowship, NEH Grant, Lebanese Government Decoration Order of the Cedars. Memberships: American Philosophical Association; Chair, National Committee on Pre-College Instructors in Philosophy.

SHEKERJIAN Regina. See: **DE CORMIER Regina.**

SHELBOURNE Cecily. See: **EBEL Suzanne.**

SHELBY Graham, b. 1940, England. Writer. Publications: The Knights of Dark Renown, 1969; The Kings of Vain Intent, 1970; The Villains of the Piece, 1972; The Devil is Loose, 1973; The Wolf at the Door,

1975; The Cannaways, 1978; The Cannaway Concern, 1980; The Edge of the Blade, 1986; Demand the World, 1990. Address: c/o Lisa Eveleigh, 26A Rochester Square, London NW1 9SA, England.

SHELDON Lee. See: **LEE Wayne C.**

SHELDON Roy. See: **TUBB E(dwin) C(harles).**

SHELDON Sidney, b. 11 Feb 1917, Chicago, Illinois, USA. Author; Screenwriter; Playwright. m. (1) Jorja Curtright, 1951, dec 1985, (2) Alexandra Kostoff, 1989. Education: Northwestern University. Appointments: Television Show Creator, Producer and Writer, 1963-; Creator, Writer, Producer, I Dream of Jeannie (TV show); Creator, Hart to Hart (TV show). Publications: The Merry Widow (operetta) (adaptor with Ben Roberts), 1943; Jackpot, 1944; Deam with Music, 1944; Alice in Arms, 1945; The Bachelor and the Bobby-Soxer (screenplay), 1947; Easter Parade (screenplay) (with Albert Hackett and Frances Goodrich), 1948; Annie Get Your Gun (screenplay), 1950; Rich, Young and Pretty (screenplay), 1951; Dream Wife, 1953; Anything Goes (screenplay), 1956; Never Too Young, 1956; The Buster Keaton Story (screenplay), 1957; Redhead, 1959; Roman Candle, 1960; Billy Rose's Jumbo (screenplay), 1962. Novels: The Naked Face, 1970; The Other Side of Midnight, 1974; Bloodline, 1977; Rage of Angels, 1980; The Master of the Game, 1982; If Tomorrow Comes, 1985; Windmills of the Gods, 1986; The Sands of Time, 1988; Memories of Midnight, 1990; The Doomsday Conspiracy, 1991; The Stars Shine Down, 1992; Nothing Lasts Forever, 1994; Morning, Noon and Night, 1995; The Best Laid Plans, 1997; Tell Me Your Dreams, 1998. Honours: Academy Award, 1947; Screen Award, Writers Guild of America, 1948, 1950, 1959; Most Translated Author in the World, Guinness Book of Records, 1997. Address: c/o Press Relations, William Morrow & Co, 1350 Avenue of the Americas, New York, NY 10019, USA.

SHELTON Mark Logan, b. 19 May 1958, Chicago, Illinois, USA. Writer. m. Eve Shelnutt, 29 May 1982. Education: AB, Western Michigan University, 1980; MFA, University of Pittsburgh, 1982. Publications: Working in a Very Small Place, 1989; The Next Great Thing: The Sun, the Stirling Engine and the Drive to Change the World, 1994. Contributions to: Newspapers and journals. Honours: Best Sports Stories, Sport News; 12 Sigma Delta Chi Awards. Membership: Judge, Ohioana Library Association Book Awards, 1990-. Address: 25 Andover Street, Worcester, MA 01606, USA.

SHEPARD James (Russell), b. 29 Dec 1956, Bridgeport, Connecticut, USA. Professor of English; Author. Education: BA, English, Trinity College, Hartford, Connecticut, 1978; AM, Creative Writing, Brown University, 1980. Appointments: Lecturer, University of Michigan, Ann Arbor, 1980-83; Assistant Professor of English, 1983-90, Instructor in Film, 1988-, Associate Professor of English, 1990-95, J Leland Miller Professor of English, 1995-, Williams College; Writer-in-Residence, Bread Loaf Writers' Conference, 1982-84, 1988-93, University of Tennessee at Chattanooga, 1988, 1989, Vassar College, 1998; Fiction Faculty, MFA Program, Warren Wilson College, 1992-. Publications: Novels: Flights, 1983; Paper Doll, 1986; Lights Out in the Reptile House, 1990; Kiss of the Wolf, 1994; Nosferatu, 1998. Short Stories: Batting Against Castro, 1996. Editor: You've Got to Read This (with Ron Hansen), 1994; Unleashed: Poems by Writers' Dogs (with Amy Hempel), 1995. Contributions to: Anthologies, journals, reviews, and magazines. Honours: Transatlanmtic Review Award, Henfield Foundation, 1980; David Sokolov Scholar in Fiction, Bread Loaf, 1982; Nelson Bushnell Prize, Williams College, 1997. Address: 45 Forest Road, Williamstown, MA 01267, USA.

SHEPARD Sam, (Samuel Shepard Rogers), b. 5 Nov 1943, Fort Sheridan, Illinois, USA. Dramatist; Actor. m. O-Lan Johnson Dark, 9 Nov 1969, div, 1 son, Jessica Lange, 1 son, 1 daughter. Education: Mount San Antonio Junior College, Walnut, California, 1961-62. Publications: Cowboys, 1964; The Rock Garden, 1964; 4-H Club,

1965; Up to Thursday, 1965; Rocking Chair, 1965; Chicago, 1965; Icarus's Mother, 1965; Fourteen Hundred Thousand, 1966; Red Cross, 1966; Melodrama Play, 1966; La Turista, 1967; Cowboys #2, 1967; Forensic and the Navigators, 1967; The Holy Ghostly, 1969; The Unseen Hand, 1969; Operation Sidewinder, 1970; Shaved Slipts, 1970; Mad Dog Blues, 1971; Terminal, 1971; Cowboy Mouth (with Patti Smith), 1971; Black Bog Beast Bait, 1971; The Tooth of Crime, 1972; Blue Bitch, 1973; Nightwalk (with Megan Terry and Jean-Claude van Itallie), 1973; Geography of a Horse Dreamer, 1974; Little Ocean, 1974; Action, 1974; Killer's Head, 1974; Suicide in B-Flat, 1976; Angel City, 1976; Curse of the Starving Class, 1977; Buried Child, 1978; Tongues, 1979; Savage/Love, 1979; Seduced, 1979; True West, 1981; Fool for Love, 1983; Superstitions, 1983; The Sad Lament of Pecos Bill on the Eve of Killing his Wife, 1983; A Lie of the Mind, 1985; States of Shock, 1991; Simpatico, 1993. Honours: Obie Awards, 1966, 1966, 1966, 1968, 1973, 1975, 1977, 1979, 1984; Rockefeller Foundation Grant, 1967; Guggenheim Fellowships, 1968, 1971; National Institute and American Academy of Arts and Letters Award, 1974; Creative Arts Award, Brandeis University, 1975; Pulitzer Prize in Drama, 1979; New York Drama Critics' Circle Award, 1986. Memberships: American Academy of Arts and Letters; Theater Hall of Fame. Address: c/o International Creative Management, 8942 Wilshire Boulevard, Beverly Hills, CA 90211, USA.

SHEPHERD Michael. See: **LUDLUM Robert.**

SHEPHERD Robert James, b. 14 Feb 1949, Solihull, Warwickshire, England. Author; Journalist; Television Producer; Director. Education: BA, MA, 1968-72, University of Kent. Appointments: Leader and Features Writer, Investors Chronicle, 1983; Editorial Team, Producer, A Week in Politics, 1983-88; Parliamentary Lobby Correspondent, 1984-87; Producer, documentaries. Publications: Public Opinion and European Integration, 1975; A Class Divided, 1988; Ireland's Fate, 1990; The Power Brokers, 1991; Iain Macleod, 1994; Enoch Powell: A Biography, 1996. Contributions to: Political Quarterly; New Statesman; Investors Chronicle; Marxism Today; Guardian; The Times; Irish Independent; Sunday Press; Ireland of the Welcomes; The Spectator; Contemporary History. Honours: Prix Stendhal, 1993; Reuter Fellowship, University of Oxford, 1995. Memberships: Society of Authors; International PEN; National Union of Journalists. Address: c/o Curtis Brown Ltd, 162-168 Regent Street, London W1R 5TB, England.

SHEPIEVKER Anatole, b. 17 Sept 1928, Odessa, Ukraine. Civil Engineer. m. Esther Shlyapochnik, 26 May 1950, dec, 1 son, 1 daughter. Education: Civil Engineer, Civil Engineering Institute, Odessa, 1962. Appointments: Served USSR Navy, Military Fleet, 1947-52; Radio Operator, Weather Forecasting Bureau, 1952-57; Construction Labourer, 1957-60; Job Superintendent, Construction Manager, Vice-President, Construction Company, 1960-78; Structural Detailer, USA, 1979-97; Representative, 4th Andrey Sakharov's Hearings, Lisbon, Portugal, 1983; Retired, 1998-. Publications: At the Start of the Journey, 23 short stories, 1981; Laughter Despite Everything, collection of Russian anecdotes, 1982; On Rough Turns, 26 stories, 1983; Open Your Gates, 25 stories, 1988; What We Are Paying for, 24 stories, 1994. Contributions to: The New Review; Alef; Vestnik; Panorama; New American. Honour: 1st Prize, New Life newspaper competition. Membership: International PEN Club, US Branch. Address: 5269 Newcastle Avenue, Unit 2, Encino, CA 91316, USA.

SHEPPARD David (Stuart) (Lord Sheppard of Liverpool), b. 6 Mar 1929, Reigate, Surrey, England. Retired Bishop; Writer. m. Grace Isaac, 19 June 1957, 1 daughter. Education: MA, Trinity Hall, Cambridge. Appointments: Ridley Hall Theological College Assistant Curate, St Mary's, Islington, 1955-57; Warden, Mayflower Family Centre, Canning Town, E16, 1957-69; Bishop Suffragan, Woolwich, 1969-75; Chairman, Martin Luther King Foundation, 1970-75, General Synod Board for Social Responsibility, 1991-96; Bishop of Liverpool,

1975-97; Chairman, Churches' Enquiry into Unemployment and the Future of Work, 1995-97. Publications: Parson's Pitch, 1964; Built as a City, 1974; Bias to the Poor, 1983; The Other Britain, 1984; Better Together (with D Worlock), 1988; With Christ in the Wilderness (with D Worlock), 1990; With Hope in Our Hearts (with D Worlock), 1994. Honours: Honorary LLD, University of Liverpool, 1981; Honorary Fellow, Trinity Hall, Cambridge, 1983; Honorary DTech, Liverpool Polytechnic, 1987; Honorary DD, University of Cambridge, 1991; Honorary DD, University of Exeter, 1998; Freedom, City of Liverpool, 1995; Life Peerage, 1998. Membership: Churches' Enquiry into Unemployment and the Future of Work, 1995-97, chairman. Address: Ambledown, 11 Melloncroft Drive, West Kirby, Merseyside L48 2JA, England.

SHER Antony, b. 14 June 1949, Cape Town, South Africa. Author; Actor; Artist. Education: Diploma, Webber-Douglas Academy of Dramatic Art, London, England, 1971. Publications: Fiction: Middlepost, 1988; The Indoor Boy, 1991; Cheap Lives, 1995; The Feast, 1998; Non-Fiction: Year of the King, 1985; Characters - Paintings and Drawings, 1989; Woza Shakespeare!, 1996; The Feast (novel), 1998. Honour: Doctor of Letters, Honoris Causa, Liverpool University, 1998. Literary Agent: Mic Cheetham. Address: 11-12 Dover Street, London W1X 3PH, England.

SHER Steven Jay, b. 28 Sept 1949, USA. Writer; Poet. m. Nancy Green, 11 Mar 1978, 1 son, 1 daughter. Education: BA, City College of the City University of New York, 1970; MA, University of Iowa, 1972; MFA, Brooklyn College of the City University of New York, 1978. Appointments: Director, Creative Writing, Spalding University, 1979-81, Oregon State University, 1981-86, University of North Carolina at Wilmington, 1986-89; Visiting Writer, Western Oregon State College, 1991-95; Willamette University, 1993. Publications: Nickelodeon, 1978; Persnickety, 1979; Caught in the Revolving Door, 1980; Trolley Lives, 1985; The Man With a Thousand Eyes and Other Stories, 1989; Traveler's Advisory, 1994. Co-Editor: Northwest Variety: Personal Essays by 14 Regional Authors, 1987. Contributions to: Anthologies and periodicals. Honours: All Nations Poetry Contest, 1977; Weymouth Centre Residency, 1988; North Carolina Writers Network Writers and Readers Series Competition, 1989; Oregon Book Awards Finalist in Poetry, 1994. Memberships: Poets and Writers; Willamette Literary Guild, president. Address: 3930 North West Witham Hill Drive, No 176, Corvallis, OR 97330, USA.

SHERATON Mimi, b. 10 Feb 1926, Brooklyn, New York, USA. Food Critic; Writer. m. (1) William Sheraton, 10 Aug 1945, div 1954, (2) Richard Falcone, 30 July 1955, 1 son. Education: BS, New York University, 1947. Appointments: Managing Editor, Supplemental Division, House Beautiful, New York City, 1954-56; Food Critic, New York Magazine, 1967-75, New York Times, 1975-83; Time Magazine, 1984; Publisher, Mimi Sheraton's Taste Newsletter, 1987-90; Food Editor, Condé Nast Traveler, 1987-91; Contributing Editor, Harper's Bazaar, 1993-95, New Woman, 1994-. Publications: The Seducer's Cookbook, 1962; City Portraits, 1963; The German Cookbook, 1965; Visions of Sugar Plums, 1968; From My Mother's Kitchen, 1979, new edition, 1991; Mimi Sheraton's New York Times Guide to New Restaurants, 1983; Is Salami and Eggs Better Than Sex? (with Alan King), 1985; Mimi Sheraton's Favorite New York Restaurants, 1986, new edition, 1989; The Whole World Loves Chicken Soup, 1995. Contributions to: Magazines. Honours: Penney Missouri Award, University of Missouri at Columbia, 1974; Front Page Award, Newswomen's Club of New York, 1977. Address: c/o William Morris Agency, 1350 Avenue of the Americas, New York, NY 10019, USA.

SHERMAN Eileen Bluestone, b. 15 May 1951, Atlantic City, New Jersey, USA. Author; Playwright; Lyricist. m. Neal Jonathan Sherman, 10 June 1973, 1 son, 1 daughter. Education: BA, Finch College, New York, 1973; MA, State University of New York at Albany, 1976; Faculty, Baker University, Overland Park, Kansas,

1997. Publications: The Odd Potato, 1984; Monday in Odessa, 1986; Independence Avenue, 1990; The Violin Players, 1998. Others: Musical plays; The Magic Door (television series), 1987-90; Room 119 (drama), 1997; The Happiest Day in Heaven (musical), 1998; The Violin Players, 1998. Honours: Outstanding Social Studies Trade Book Award, 1986; National Jewish Book Award for Children's Literature, 1986; Emmy Awards, 1988, 1989; Teacher's Choice Award, 1991; Jessica Cosgrave Award for Career Achievement, Finch College Association, 1997. Memberships: Authors Guild; Dramatists Guild; National League of American Pen Women; Society of Children's Book Writers. Address: 5049 Wornall Road, Kansas City, MO, USA.

SHERMAN William David, b. 24 Dec 1940, Philadelphia, Pennsylvania, USA. Poet; Writer. m. Barbara Beaumont, 22 July 1970, div 1978. Education: AB, Temple University, 1962; MA, 1964, PhD, 1968, State University of New York at Buffalo; Dickinson School of Law, 1974-75. Appointments: Teacher, Instructor, and Lecturer in USA and England; Editor; Publisher; Poetry readings. Publications: The Landscape of Contemporary Cinema (with Leon Lewis), 1967; The Cinema of Orson Welles, 1967; The Springbok (poems), 1973; The Hard Sidewalk (poems), 1974; The Horses of Gwyddno Garanhir (poems), 1976; Mermaids, I, 1977, revised edition, 1985, and II, 1985 (poems); Heart Attack and Spanish Songs in Mandaine Land (poems), 1981; Duchamp's Door (poems), 1983; She Wants to Go to Pago-Pago, 1986; The Tahitian Journals, 1990; A Tale for Tusitala, 1993. Contributions to: Anthologies; Numerous poems, articles and reviews in periodicals. Address: 4805 B Street, Philadelphia, PA 19120, USA.

SHERRILL Stephen, b. 29 July 1965, Fargo, North Dakota, USA. Writer. Education: BA, History, Baylor University, 1987. Contributions to: New Yorker; New York Times; Rolling Stone. Honour: Emmy Award for TV Nation, NBC, 1995. Literary Agent: Cara Stein, William Morris. Address: 210 East 11th Street, Apt D, New York, NY 10003, USA.

SHERRIN Ned, (Edward George Sherrin), b. 18 Feb 1931, Low Ham, Somerset, England. Director; Producer; Writer. Education: MA, University of Oxford; Barrister-at-Law. Publications: Cindy-Ella (with Caryl Brahms), 1962; Rappel (with Caryl Brahms), 1964; Benbow Was His Name (with Caryl Brahms), 1967; Ooh La (with Caryl Brahms), 1973; After You Mr Feydeau (with Caryl Brahms), 1975; A Small Thing Like an Earthquake, 1983; Song by Song (with Caryl Brahms), 1984; Cutting Edge, 1984; 1956 and All That (with Neil Shand), 1984; The Metropolitan Mikado (with Alistair Beaton), 1985; Too Dirty for the Windmill (with Caryl Brahms), 1986; Loose Neds, 1990; Theatrical Anecdotes, 1991; Ned Sherrin in His Anecdotage, 1993; The Oxford Dictionary of Humorous Quotations, 1995; Sherrin's Year, diary, 1996; Scratch an Actor, novel, 1996. Honour: Commander of the Order of the British Empire. Address: c/o Scott Ferris Associates, 15 Gledhow Gardens, London SW5 0AY, England.

SHERRY (Michael) Norman, b. 6 July 1935, Tirana, Albania. Writer; Professor of Literature. Education: BA, English Literature, University of Durham; PhD, University of Singapore, 1963. Appointments: Lecturer in English Literature, University of Singapore, 1961-66; Lecturer, Senior Lecturer, University of Liverpool, 1966-70; Professor of English, University of Lancaster, 1970-82; Fellow, Humanities Research Center, North Carolina, USA, 1982; Mitchell Distinguished Professor of Literature, Trinity University, San Antonio, Texas, 1983-. Publications: Conrad's Eastern World, 1966; Jane Austen, 1966; Charlotte and Emily Brontë, 1969; Conrad's Western World, 1971; Conrad and His World, 1972; Conrad: The Critical Heritage, 1973; Conrad in conference, 1976; The Life of Graham Greene, Vol 1 1904-39, 1989, Vol 2 1939-55, 1994; Vol 3, Life of Graham Greene, forthcoming. Editor: An Outpost of Progress and Heart of Darkness, 1973; Lord Jim, 1974; Nostromo, 1974; The Secret Agent, 1974; The Nigger of the Narcissus, Typhoon, Falk and Other Stories, 1975; Joseph Conrad: A commemoration, 1976. Contributions to: Academic American Encyclopedia; Guardian; Daily Telegraph; Oxford Magazine; Modern Language Review; Review of English Studies; Notes and Queries; BBC; Times Literary Supplement; Observer. Honours: Fellow, Royal Society of Literature, 1986; Edgar Allan Poe Award, 1989; Guggenheim Fellowship, 1989-90; Nominee, Best Books of the Century, New York Times, 1998. Memberships: Savile. Address: Trinity University, 715 Stadium Drive, San Antonio, TX 78212, USA.

SHERWIN Byron L(ee), b. 18 Feb 1946, New York, New York, USA. Professor; Author. m. Judith Rita Schwartz, 24 Dec 1972, 1 son. Education: BS, Columbia University; BHL, 1966, MHL, 1968, Rabbi, 1970, Jewish Theological Seminary; MA, New York University, 1969; PhD, University of Chicago, 1978. Appointments: Assistant Professor, 1970-74, Associate Professor, 1974-78, Professor of Jewish Philosophy and Mysticism, 1978-, Vice-President for Academic Affairs, 1984-, Spertus College of Judaica, Chicago; Visiting Professor, Mundelein College, 1974-82; Director, Holocaust Studies Project, National Endowment for the Humanities, 1976-78. Publications: Judaism: The Way of Sanctification (with Samuel H Dresner), 1978; Abraham Joshua Heschel, 1979; Encountering the Holocaust: An Interdisciplinary Survey (editor with Susan G Ament), 1979; Garden of the Generations, 1981; Jerzy Kosinski: Literary Alarmclock, 1982; Mystical Theology and Social Dissent: The Life and Works of Judah Loew of Prague, 1982; The Golem Legend: Origins and Implications, 1985; Contexts and Content: Higher Jewish Education in the United States, 1987; Thank God: Prayers of Jesus and Christians Together, 1989; In Partnership with God: Contemporary Jewish Law and Ethics, 1990; No Religion is an Island (with Harold Kasimov), 1991; Towards a Jewish Theology, 1992; How to Be a Jew: Ethical Teaching of Judaism (with Seymour J Cohen), 1992; The Spiritual Heritage of Polish Jews, 1995; Sparks Amongst the Ashes: The Spiritual Legacy of Polish Jewry, 1997; Crafting the Soul, 1998; Why Be Good?, 1998; John Paul II and Interreligious Dialogue (co-author), 1999. Contributions to: Professional journals. Honours: Man of Reconciliation Award, Polish Council of Christians and Jews, 1992; Presidential Medal, Officer of the Order of Merit, Republic of Poland, 1995; Doctor of Hebrew Letters, honoris causa, Jewish Theological Seminary of America, 1996. Memberships: American Academy of Religion; American Association of University Professors; Rabbinical Assembly of America; American Philosophical Association; Society for Business Ethics; Author's Guild. Address: 6702 North Sheridan Road, Chicago, IL 60626, USA.

SHIBASAKI Sosuku. See: **CIVASQUI José.**

SHIELDS Carol Ann, b. 2 June 1935, Oak Park, Illinois, USA (Canadian citizen, 1974). Professor; Author; Poet. m. Donald Hugh Shields, 20 July 1957, 1 son, 4 daughters. Education: BA, Hanover College, 1957; MA, University of Ottawa, 1975. Appointments: Editorial Assistant, Canadian Slavonic Papers, Ottawa, 1972-74; Lecturer, University of Ottawa, 1976-77, University of British Columbia, 1978-90; Professor, University of Manitoba, 1980-; The Canada Council, 1994-; Chancellor, Unviersity of Winnipeg, 1996-. Publications: Fiction: Small Ceremonies, 1976; The Box Garden, 1977; Happenstance, 1980; A Fairly Conventional Woman, 1982; Various Miracles (short stories), 1985; Swann: A Mystery, 1987; The Orange Fish (short stories), 1989; A Celibate Season (with Blanche Howard), 1991; The Republic of Love, 1992; The Stone Diaries, 1993; Larry's Party, 1997. Poetry: Others, 1972; Intersect, 1974; Coming to Canada, 1992. Plays: Women Waiting, 1983; Departures and Arrivals, 1984; Thirteen Hands, 1993; Fashion Power Guilt (with Catherine Shields), 1995. Other: Scribner's Best of the Fiction Workshops (editor with John Kulka and Natalie Danford), 1998. Honours: Canada Council Grants, 1973, 1976, 1978, 1986; Canadian Authors Association Fiction Prize, 1976; Canadian Broadcasting Corporation Prizes, 1983, 1984; National Magazine Award, 1985; Arthur Ellis Award, 1987; Governor-General's Award, 1993; National Book Critics Circle Awards, 1994, 1995; Pulitzer Prize in Fiction, 1995; Honorary Doctorates, Universities of Ottawa, Winnipeg, Hanover College, British Columbia, 1995, Concordia University, 1998, University of Toronto, 1998, Queen's University, University of Western Ontario; Lire Magazine Book of the Year, France, 1995; Orange Prize for fiction, 1998; Order of Canada, 1999. Memberships: Jane Austen Society; PEN; Writers Guild of Manitoba; Writers Union of Canada; Canada Council; Royal Societyof Canada. Address: 701-237 Wellington Crescent, Winnipeg, Manitoba R3M 0A1, Canada.

SHIMOKAWA Hideo, (Jun Ebara), b. 18 Nov 1927, Gifu, Japan. Writer and Researcher of Comparative Ideas; Art Critic. Education: Licence in Letters, Marxism and Religion, 1952, Master's degree, Surrealism, 1954, University of Tokyo. Appointments: Taught French, Hosei University; Assistant Commissaire, Japanese Pavilion, Venice Biennial, Italy, 1962; Established himself in Paris, then Brussels, 1986-; Commissaire, various international exhibitions. Publications: Two collections on L'art et la littérature, 1958; Moine et sculpteur du XVIIIe siècle, Enkou, 1960; L'enfer chez Bruegel l'Ancien et le Jardin de Bomarzo, 1970; Hieronimus Bosch et la musique, 1983; Translations: Les peintres cubistes (Guillaume Apollinaire); L'aventure dada (Georges Hugnet); Une vague de rêves (Aragon); Irene (Aragon); Dictionnaires abrégé du surréalisme (Breton and Eluard); Manifestes du surréalisme, with annotations and comments (André Breton); Critical text of all Stephane Mallarmé's works with comments in French and translation into Japanese, 1998; Phénoménologie et pensée louddheité, in progress. Memberships: Association française de l'action culturelle; International Association of Art Critics, French Section; Foreign Corresponding Member, Centre National de la Recherche Scientifique. Address: 156 Rue du Trône, B-1050 Brussels, Belgium.

SHINDLER Colin, b. 28 June 1949, Bury, Lancs, England. Writer; Producer. m. N Lynn White, 23 Sept 1972, 1 son, 1 daughter. Education: BA (Hon), MA, PhD, Cambridge University. Publications: Hollywood Goes to War, 1979; Buster, 1998; Hollywood in Crisis, 1996; Manchester United Ruined My Life, 1998. Honours: BAFTA, 1988; ACE, 1988. Literary Agent: Luigi Bonomi, Sheil Land. Address: c/o Sheil Land, 43 Doughty St, London WC1, England.

SHINN Sharon Ruth, b. 28 Apr 1957, Wichita, Kansas, USA. Science Fiction, Fantasy Writer. Education: BSJ, Journalism, Northwestern University, 1979. Publications: The Shape-Changer's Wife, 1995; Archangel, 1996; Jovah's Angel, 1997; The Alleluia Files, 1998. Honour: Crawford Fantasy Award, IAFA, 1996. Literary Agent: Ethan Ellenberg. Address: PO Box 6774, Brentwood, MO 63144, USA.

SHIPLER David K(arr), b. 3 Dec 1942, Orange, New Jersey, USA. Journalist; Correspondent; Writer. m. Deborah S Isaacs, 17 Sept 1966, 2 sons, 1 daughter. Education: AB, Dartmouth College, 1964. Appointments: News Clerk, 1966-67, News Summary Writer, 1967-68, Reporter, 1968-73, Foreign Correspondent, Saigon, 1973-75, and Moscow, 1975-, Bureau Chief, Moscow, 1977-79, and Jerusalem, 1979-84, Correspondent, Washington, DC, 1985-87, Chief Diplomatic Correspondent, 1987-88, The New York Times; Guest Scholar, Brookings Institution, 1984-85; Senior Associate, Carnegie Endowment for International Peace, 1988-90; Adjunct Professor, School of International Service, American University, Washington, DC, 1990; Ferris Professor of Journalism and Public Affairs, Princeton University, 1990-91, Woodrow Wilson Foundation Visiting Fellow, 1990-. Publications: Russia: Broken Idols, Solemn Dreams, 1983; Arab and Jew: Wounded Spirits in a Promised Land, 1986; A Country of Strangers: Blacks and Whites in America, 1997. Contributions to: Newspapers and journals. Honours: Distinguished Reporting Award, Society of Silurians, 1971; Distinguished Public Affairs Reporting Award, American Political Science Association, 1971; Co-Winner, George Polk Award, 1982; Pulitzer Prize for General Non-Fiction, 1987; Alfred DuPont-Columbia University Award for

Broadcast Journalism, 1990. Membership: Dartmouth College, board of trustees. Address: 4005 Thornapple Street, Chevy Chase, MD 20815, USA.

SHNEIDMAN Noah Norman, b. 24 Sept 1924, Wilno, Poland. Professor Emeritus. div, 2 daughters. Education: MPHE, Minsk, Warsaw, 1954; MA, 1966, Dipl.REES, 1966, PhD, 1971, University of Toronto. Appointments: Lecturer, 1966-71, Assistant Professor, 1971-75, Associate Professor, 1975-79, Professor, 1979-91, University of Toronto; Distinguished Visiting Professor, McMaster University, 1981. Publications: Literature and Ideology in Soviet Education, 1973; The Soviet Road to Olympus: Theory and Practice of Soviet Physical Culture, 1978; Soviet Literature in the 1970's: Artistic Diversity and Ideological Conformity, 1979; Dostoevsky and Suicide, 1984; Soviet Literature in the 1980's: Decade of Transition, 1989; Russian Literature 1988-1994. The End of an Era, 1995; Jerusalem of Lithuania: The Rise and Fall of Jewish Vilnius, 1998. Memberships: Canadian Association of Slavists; American Association of Teachers of Slavic and East European Languages. Address: c/o Department of Slavic Language and Literature, University of Toronto, Toronto, Ontario M5S 1A1, Canada.

SHOCKLEY Ann Allen, b. 21 June 1927, Louisville, Kentucky, USA. Librarian; Retired Archivist. Div, 1 son, 1 daughter. Education: BA, Fisk University; MSLS, Case Western Reserve University. Publications: Living Black American Authors, 1973; Loving Her, 1974, reprint, 1997; A handbook for Black Librarianship, 1977; Say Jesus and Come to Me, 1982; The Black and White of It, 1980; Afro-American Women Writers 1746-1933; An Anthology and Critical Guide, 1988. Honours include: Martin Luther King Black Autor's Award, 1982; Susan Koppelman Award for Best Anthology, 1989; Outlook Award, 1990; Black Caucus American Library Association Achievement Award for Extraordinary Achievement in Professional Activites, 1992. Literary Agent: Carole Abel. Address: 5975 Post Road, Nashville, TN 37205-3232, USA.

SHONE Richard N, b. 8 May 1949, Doncaster, Yorkshire, England. Writer on Art. Education: BA, Clare College, Cambridge, 1971. Appointment: Associate Editor, The Burlington Magazine, 1978-. Publications: Bloomsbury Portraits, 1976, 1993; Century of Change: British Painting Since 1900, 1977; The Post-Impressionists, 1981; Walter Sickert, 1988; Alfred Sisley, 1992; Exhibition catalogues: Sensation!; Royal Academy, London, 1997. Contributions to: The Spectator; The Burlington Magazine; The Observer; Artforum. Address: 14-16 Duke's Road, London W11H 9AD, England.

SHOR Ira Neil, b. 2 June 1945, New York, New York, USA. Professor of English; Writer. Education: BA, 1966, MA, 1968, University of Michigan; PhD, University of Wisconsin, 1971. Appointment: Professor of English, City University of New York. Publications: A Pedagogy for Liberation, 1986; Freire for the Classroom, 1987; Critical Teaching and Everyday Life, 1987; Culture Wars: School and Society in the Conservative Restoration, 1969-91, 1992; Empowering Education, 1992; When Students Have Power: Negotiating Authority in a Critical Pedagogy, 1996; Critical Literacy in Action, 1999; Education is Politics, 1999. Contributions to: Professional journals. Honours: Fellowships, 1966, 1982, 1983; Chancellor's Scholar, City University of New York, 1985. Address: c/o English Doctoral Program, City University of New York, 33 West 42nd Street, New York, NY 10036, USA.

SHOUP Barbara, b. 4 May 1947, Hammond, Indiana, USA. Writer; Teacher. m. Steven Shoup, 2 daughters. Education: BS, Elementary Education, Indiana University, 1972; MS, Secondary Education, 1977. Appointments: Broad Ripple High School Center for Humanities Writer in Residence, 1982-; Indianapolis Childrens Museum Director, Prelude Academy, 1985-97; Butler University Instructor, Creative Writing, 1997-; Contributing Editor, Other Voices, 1994-. Publications: Night Watch, 1982; Wish You Were Here, 1994; Stranded in Harmony, 1997. Honours: ALA Best Books for Young Adults, 1995, 1998. Membership: Authors Guild, Midland. Literary Agent: Mary Flanders. Address: 6012 Broadway, Indianapolis, IN 46220, USA.

SHREVE Susan (Richards), b. 2 May 1939, Toledo, Ohio, USA. Professor of English Literature; Author. 2 sons, 2 daughters. Education: University of Pennsylvania, 1961; MA, University of Virginia, 1969. Appointments: Professor of English Literature, George Mason University, Fairfax, Virginia, 1976-; Visiting Professor, Columbia University, 1982-, Princeton University, 1991-93. Publications: A Fortunate Madness, 1974; A Woman Like That, 1977; Children of Power, 1979; Miracle Play, 1981; Dreaming of Heroes, 1984; Queen of Hearts, 1986; A Country of Strangers, 1989; Daughters of the New World, 1992; The Train Home, 1993; Skin Deep: Women and Race, 1995; The Visiting Physician, 1995; The Goalie, 1996; Narratives on Justice (co-editor), 1996. Other: Many children's books, 1977-96. Contributions to: Various publications. Honours: Jenny Moore Award, George Washington University, 1978; Guggenheim Fellowship, 1980; National Endowment for the Arts Award, 1982. Memberships: PEN/Faulkner Foundation, president; Phi Beta Kappa. Address: c/o Department of English, George Mason University, Fairfax, VA 22030, USA.

SHRIMSLEY Bernard, b. 13 Jan 1931, London, England. Newspaper Editor. m. Norma Jessie Alexandra Porter, 1952, 1 daughter. Education: England. Appointments: Assistant Editor, Daily Mirror, London, 1964-68; Editor, Liverpool Daily Post, 1968-69, The News of the World, London, 1975-80; Deputy Editor, 1969-72, Editor, 1972-75, The Sun, London; Editor-designate/Editor, The Mail on Sunday, London, 1980-82; Associate Editor, Daily Express, London, 1983-96; Judge, British Press Awards, 1989-96. Publications: The Candidates, 1968; Lion Rampant, 1984. Contributions to: Newspapers and journals. Memberships: British Press Council, vice-chairman, 1989-90; Society of Authors. Address: c/o Daily Express, Ludgate House, 245 Blackfriars Road, London SE1 9UX, England.

SHUBIN Seymour, b. 14 Sept 1921, Philadelphia, Pennsylvania, USA. Author. m. Gloria Amet, 27 Aug 1957, 1 son, 1 daughter. Education: BS, Temple University. Appointments: Managing Editor, Official Detective Stories Magazine, Psychiatric Reporter. Publications: Anyone's My Name, 1953; Manta, 1958; Wellville, USA, 1961; The Captain, 1982; Holy Secrets, 1984; Voices, 1985; Never Quite Dead, 1989; Remember Me Always, 1994. Contributions to: Saturday Evening Post; Reader's Digest; Redbook; Family Circle; Story; Ellery Queen's Mystery Magazine; Emergency Medicine; Official Detective Stories Magazine; Perspective in Biology and Medicine. Honours: Edgar Allan Poe, Special Award; Special Citation for Fiction, Athenaeum of Philadelphia; Certificate of Honor, Temple University. Memberships: American Society of Authors and Journalists; Authors Guild; Mystery Writers of America; PEN, American Center. Address: 122 Harrogate Road, Wynnewood, PA 19096, USA.

SHUKMAN Harold, b. 23 Mar 1931, London, England. Emeritus Fellow; Writer. m. (1) Ann King Farlow, 1956, div 1970, 2 sons, 1 daughter, (2) Barbara King Farlow. Education: BA Honours, University of Nottingham, 1956; MA, 1961, DPhil, 1961, University of Oxford. Appointments: Fellow, 1961-, Lecturer in Modern Russian History, 1969-98, St Antony's College, Oxford. Publications: Lenin and the Russian Revolution, 1977; Blackwells Encyclopedia of the Russian Revolution (editor), 1988; Andrei Gromyko: Memories (editor and translator), 1989; Stalin: Triumph and Tragedy (editor and translator), 1991; Lenin: His Life and Legacy (editor and translator), 1994; Trotsky: Eternal Revolutionary (editor and translator), 1996; Rasputin, 1997; The Rise and Fall of the Soviet Empire (editor and translator), 1998; The Russian Revolution, 1998. Contributions to: Professional journals and general periodicals. Memberships: Authors Society; Royal Historical Society, fellow; Translators Association. Address: St Antony's College, Oxford OX2 6JF, England.

SHULL Michael Slade, b. 20 Sept 1949, Baltimore, Maryland, USA. Film and Mass Media Historian. Education: BA, 1972, MA, Radio, Television and Film, 1983, PhD, Mass Communications, 1994, University of Maryland at College Park. Appointments: Researcher, Skuce and Associates, Washington, DC, 1984-87; Instructor, University of Maryland at College Park, 1986-91; Independent Communications Consultant, 1992-; Associate Faculty, The Washington Center, DC, 1995-; Archive Editor, Film and History, 1998-; Faculty, Frederick College, Maryland, 1998-. Publictions: Doing Their Bit: Wartime American Animated Short Films 1939-1945, 1987; Hollywood War Films 1937-1945: An Exhaustive Filmography of American Feature-Length Motion Pictures Relating to World War II, 1996; Radicalism in American Silent Films 1909-1929, 1999. Contributions to: Labors Heritage. Memberships: Film Literature Association; Popular Culture Association; International Association of Media Historians. Address: 433 Christopher Avenue T1, Gaithersburg, MD 20879, USA.

SHUMSKY Zena. See: **COLLIER Zena.**

SHUPE Anson (David Jr), b. 21 Jan 1948, Buffalo, New York, USA. Professor of Sociology and Anthropology; Writer. m. Janet Ann Klicua, 27 June 1970, 1 son, 1 daughter. Education: Waseda University, Tokyo, 1968; BA, Sociology, College of Wooster, 1970; MA, 1972, PhD, 1975, Sociology, Indiana University. Appointments: Associate Instructor, Indiana University, 1971-74; Visiting Researcher, Shimane Prefectural University, Indiana University, 1971-74; Visiting Researcher, Shimane Prefectural University, Matsue, Japan, 1973-74; Assistant Professor, Alfred University, New York, 1975-76; Assistant Professor, 1976-78, Associate Professor, 1978-86, Professor of Sociology, 1986, University of Texas at Arlington; Associate Editor, Review of Religious Research, 1980, 1992-, Sociological Focus, 1988-90; Visiting Faculty Lecturer, 1985, Lecturer, 1987, Iliff School of Theology, Denver; Professor of Sociology and Anthropology, 1987-91, Chair, Department of Sociology and Anthropology, 1987-91, Indiana University-Purdue University, Fort Wayne. Publications: "Moonies" in America: Cult, Church, and Crusade (with David G Bromley), 1980; Six Perspectives on New Religions: A Case Study Approach, 1981; Strange Gods: The Great American Cult Scare (with David G Bromley), 1982; Born Again Politics and the Moral Majority: What Social Surveys Really Show (with William A Stacey), 1982; The Anti-Cult Movement in America: A Bibliography and Historical Survey (with David G Bromley and Donna L Stacey), 1983; Metaphor and Social Control in a Pentecostal Sect (with Tom Craig Darrand), 1984; The Mormon Corporate Empire (with John Heinerman), 1985; A Documentary History of the Anti-Cult Movement (with David G Bromley), 1986; Violent Men, Violent Couples: The Dynamics of Family Violence (with William A Stacey and Lonnie R Hazelwood), 1986; Televangelism: Power and Politics on God's Frontier (with Jeffrey K Hadden), 1988; The Darker Side of Virtue: Corruption, Scandal and the Mormon Empire, 1991; The Violent Couple (with William A Stacey and Lonnie R Hazelwood), 1994; In the Name of All That's Holy: A Theory of Clergy Malfeasance, 1995; Violence, Inequality, and Human Freedom, 1998. Editor: New Christian Politics (with David G Bromley), 1984; Prophetic Religions and Politics (with Jeffrey K Hadden), 1986; The Politics of Religion and Social Change (with Jeffrey K Hadden), 1988; Secularization and Fundamentalism Reconsidered (with Jeffrey K Hadden), 1989; Religion and Politics in Comparative Perspective: Revival of Religious Fundamentalism in East and West (with Bronislaw Misztal), 1992; Anti-Cult Movements in Cross-Cultural Perspective (with David G Bromley), 1994; Wolves Within the Fold: Religious Leadership and Abuses of Power, 1998; Religion, Mobilization, and Social Action (with Bronislaw Misztal), 1998. Contributions to: Many scholarly publications. Honours: Various grants and fellowships; Henry H H Remak Scholar, Institute for Advanced Study, Indiana University, 1997-98; Arts and Sciences Distinguished Scholar, Indiana University - Purdue University at Fort Wayne, 1998. Memberships: American Association of

University Professors; Association for the Scientific Study of Religion; Association for the Sociology of Religion; North Central Sociological Association; Religious Research Association; Society for the Scientific Study of Religion. Address: c/o Department of Sociology and Anthropology, Indiana University-Purdue University at Fort Wayne, IN 46805, USA.

SHUSTERMAN Richard M(ark), b. 3 Dec 1949, Philadelphia, Pennsylvania, USA. Professor of Philosophy; Writer. m. Rivka Nahmani, 16 Aug 1970, div 1986, 2 sons, 1 daughter. Education: BA, magna cum laude, 1971, MA, magna cum laude, 1973, Hebrew University of Jerusalem; DPhil, St John's College, Oxford, 1979. Appointments: Lecturer, Bezalael Academy of Art, 1980-81; Visiting Lecturer, Hebrew University of Jerusalem, 1980-82; Lecturer, 1980-82, Senior Lecturer in English and Philosophy, 1983-87, Ben-Gurion University of the Negev, Beersheba, Israel; Visiting Fellow, St John's College, Oxford, 1984-85; Visiting Associate Professor, 1985-87, Associate Professor of Philosophy, 1987-91, Full Professor, 1992-, Temple University, Philadelphia; Director of Studies, École des Hautes Études en Sciences Sociales, 1990; Visiting Professor, 1990, Director of Studies, 1995-, College International de Philosophie; Chair, Philosophy Department, Temple University, 1998-. Publications: The Object of Literary Criticism, 1984; Sources for the Study of Philosophy in High School, Vol V: Aesthetics, 1989; The Interpretive Turn: Philosophy, Science, Culture (editor with D Hiley and J Bohman), 1991; Pragmatist Aesthetics: Living Beauty, Rethinking Art, 1992; L'Art á L'Ètat Vif, 1992; Kunst Leben, 1994; Sons l'interprètation, 1994; Practicing Philosophy: Pragmatism and the Philosophical Life. Contributions to: Books and journals. Honours: American Council of Learned Societies Grant, 1988; National Endowment for the Humanities Grant, 1988, Fellowship, 1990; Fulbright Scholarship. Memberships: American Philosophical Association; American Society for Aesthetics. Address: 339 West 19th Street, New York, NY 10011, USA.

SHUTTLE Penelope Diane, b. 12 May 1947, Staines, Middlesex, England. Writer; Poet. m. Peter Redgrove, 16 Sept 1980, 1 daughter. Publications: Novels: An Excusable Vengeance, 1967; All the Usual Hours of Sleeping, 1969; Wailing Monkey Embracing a Tree, 1974; The Terrors of Dr Treviles (with Peter Redgrove), 1974; The Glass Cottage, 1976; Rainsplitter in the Zodiac Garden, 1976; The Mirror of the Giant, 1979. Poetry: The Hermaphrodite Album (with Peter Redgrove), 1973; The Orchard Upstairs, 1980; The Child-Stealer, 1983; The Lion From Rio, 1986; Adventures With My Horse, 1988; Taxing the Rain, 1992; Building a City for Jamie, 1996; Selected Poems, 1980-1996, 1998. Psychology and sociology: The Wise Wound: Menstruation and Everywoman (with Peter Redgrove) 1978, 5th edition, 1999; Alchemy for Women (with Peter Redgrove), 1995. Numerous pamphlet collections, broadsheets, radio dramas, recordings, readings and television features. Contributions to: Various publications. Honours: Arts Council Awards, 1969, 1972, 1985; Greenwood Poetry Prize, 1972; E C Gregory Award for Poetry, 1974. Address: c/o David Higham Associates Ltd, 5-8 Lower John Street, London W1R 4HA, England.

SIATOPOULOS Dimitrios, b. 1 Apr 1917, Athens, Greece. Attorney-at-Law; Journalist; Writer. m. 27 Dec 1947, 1 son, 1 daughter. Education: Law degree, 1944, Science of Political Economics degree, University of Athens. Publications: Over 35 books, including historical and biographical volumes, 1954-95. Contributions to: Newspapers and magazines. Honours; National Prize for Young Writers, 1954; 1st Prize, Academy of Athens, 1971; 1st National Prize for Literature, 1978. Memberships: International Association for Literature Critics, president, Greek Section; Various Greek literary organisations. Address: 20 Omirou Street, 106 72 Athens, Greece.

SIDDONS Anne Rivers, b. 9 Jan 1936, Atlanta, Georgia, USA. Writer. m. Heyward L Siddons, 11 June 1966, 4 sons. Education: BAA, Auburn University, 1958. Publications: John Chancellor Makes Me Cry, 1975; Heartbreak Hotel, 1976; The House Next Door, 1978; Homeplace, 1986; Peachtree Road, 1988; King's Oak, 1990; Outer Banks, 1991; Colony, 1992; Hill Towns, 1993; Downtown, 1994; Fault Lines, 1995; Up Island, 1997; Low Country, 1998. Contributions to: Magazines. Honours: Georgia Author of the Year Award, 1988; Honorary Doctor of Letters, Oglethorpe University, 1992, Auburn University, 1997; Lifetime Achievement, Georgia Writers, 1998. Memberships: Authors Guild; International Womans Forum; Woodward Academy, Oglethorpe University. Address: 60 Church Street, Charleston SC 29401-2885, USA.

SIEGEL Rachel Josefowitz, b. 13 Aug 1924. Retired Psychotherapist. m. Benjamin M Siegel, 15 June 1944, dec. 1990, 2 sons, 1 daughter. Education: BS, Simmons College, 1944; MSW, Syracuse University School of Social Work, 1973. Appointments: Clinical Social Worker, TC Mental Health Clinic, Ithaca, New York, 1973-76; Private Practice of Psychotherapy, 1976-95; Field Faculty, Syracuse University School of Social Work, Syracuse, New York, 1984-85; Clinical Supervisor, Hospicare, 1994-95. Publications: Books: Women Changing Therapy: New Assessments, Values and Strategies in Feminist Therapy (edited with Joan Hamerman Robbins), 1983, new edition 1985; Jewish Women in Therapy: Seen but Not Heard (edited with Ellen Cole), 1991; Celebrating the Lives of Jewish Women: Patterns in a Feminist Sampler (edited with Ellen Cole), 1997; Articles in books in the field. Contributions to: Jewish Spectator; Journal of Women and Ageing; VOICES: The Art and Science of Psychotherapy; Counselling and Values; Journal of Women and Therapy; Lilith; The Independent Jewish Women's Magazine. Honours: New York State Southern Tier; Social Worker of the Year, National Association of Social Workers, 1992; 1st Annual Award for Distinguished Contributions to the Field of Jewish Women in Psychology, 1995, Co-recipient with Ellen Cole, Award for Scholarship for editing book, 1998, Jewish Women's Caucus, Association for Women in Psychology; Women and Therapy Volume 16 (4) dedicated to her for her 70th birthday, 1995; Included in Feminist Foremothers in Women's Studies, Psychology, Mental Health, 1995. Address: 11 Spruce Lane, Ithaca, NY 14850, USA.

SIEGEL Robert (Harold), b. 18 Aug 1939, Oak Park, Illinois, USA. Writer; Poet; Professor of English. m. Roberta Ann Hill, 19 Aug 1961, 3 daughters. Education: BA, Wheaton College, 1961; MA, Johns Hopkins University, 1962; PhD, English, Harvard University, 1968. Appointments: Assistant Professor, 1976-79, Associate Professor, 1979-83, Professor of English, 1983-, University of Wisconsin at Milwaukee. Publications: Fiction: Alpha Centauri, 1980; Whalesong, 1981; The Kingdom of Wundle, 1982; White Whale, 1991; The Ice at the End of the World, 1994; Poetry: The Beasts and the Elders, 1973; In a Pig's Eye, 1980. Contributions to: Anthologies, reviews, quarterlies, and journals. Honours: University of Wisconsin Grants, 1978, 1984; Ingram Merrill Foundation Award, 1979; National Endowment for the Arts Fellowship, 1980; 1st Prizes, Society of Midland Authors, 1981; Council for Wisconsin Writers, 1981; Matson Award, Friends of Literature, 1982; Golden Archer Award, School of Library Science, University of Wisconsin at Oshkosh, 1986; Pushcart Prize Nominations, 1991, 1995. Address: c/o Department of English, University of Wisconsin at Milwaukee, Milwaukee, WI 53201, USA.

SIEPMANN Mary Aline, (Mary Wesley), b. 24 June 1912. Writer. m. (1) 2nd Baron Swinfen, 1937, div 1945, 2 sons, (2) Eric Siepmann, 1952 dec 1970, 1 son. Education: London School of Economics and Political Science. Publications: Speaking Terms (for children), 1968; The Sixth Seal (for children), 1968; Haphazard House (for children), 1983; Jumping the Queue, 1983; The Camomile Lawn, 1984; Harnessing Peacocks, 1985; The Vacillations of Poppy Carew, 1986; Not That Sort of Girl, 1987; Second Fiddle, 1988; A Sensible Life, 1990; A Dubious Legacy, 1992; An Imaginative Experience, 1994; Part of the Furniture, 1998. Honours: Honorary Degrees, Open University, University of Exeter; Fellow, London School of Economics and Political Science; Commander of the Order of the British Empire, 1995. Memberships: PEN; Royal Society of Literature. Address: c/o Transworld Publishers Ltd, London W5 5SA, England.

SIFFERT John S, b. 26 Mar 1947, New York City, USA. Attorney. m. 1 June 1975, 2 sons. Education: BA, Amherst College, 1969; JD, Columbia Law School, 1972. Appointments: Adjunct Professor, New York University Law School; Board Director, New York City Off-Trade-Betting; Fellow, American College of Trial Lawyers. Publications: Business Crime (co-author); Modern Federal Jury Instructions - Criminal (co-author); Modern Federal Jury Instructions - Civil (co-author). Address: c/o Lankler Siffert & Wohl, 500 5th Avenue, Fl 33, New York, NY 10110-3398, USA.

SIGAL Clancy, b. 6 Sept 1926, Chicago, Illinois, USA. Writer. Education: BA, University of California at Los Angeles, 1950. Publications: Weekend in Diplock, 1960; Going Away; A Report, A Memoir, 1963; Zone of the Interior, 1976. Address: c/o Jonathon Cape, 30 Bedford Square, London WC1B 3EL, England.

SIGGINS Maggie, (Marjorie May Siggins), b. 28 May 1942, Toronto, Ontario, Canada. Writer. m. Gerald B Sperling, 23 Aug 1987, 1 son, 2 daughters. Education: Ryerson Polytechnic Institute, Toronto, 1965. Appointments: Reporter, Toronto Telegram, 1965-67, City-TV, 1971-73; Television Documentarist, 1972-93; Television Interviewer-Producer, CBC, 1974-76; Producer, CITYPlus News, 1977-80; Max Bell in Chair in Journalism, University of Regina, 1983-84. Publications: A Guide to Skiing in Eastern North America, 1969; How to Catch a Man (co-author), 1970; Bassett: His Forty Years in Politics, Publishing, Business and Sports, 1979; Brian and the Boys: A Study in Gang Rape, 1984; A Canadian Tragedy: JoAnn and Colin Thatcher: A Study of Love and Hate, 1985; Revenge of the Land: A Century of Greed: Tragedy and Murder on a Saskatchewan Farm, 1991; Biography of Louis Riehl, 1994. Honours: Southam Fellowship for Journalists, 1973-74; Arthur Ellis Award, Crime Writers of Canada, 1985; Governor-General's Award for Non-Fiction, 1992; City of Regina Award, 1994. Memberships: Alliance of Canadian Cinema, Television and Radio Artists; Canadian Association of Journalists; PEN; Writers Guild of Saskatchewan; Writers Union of Canada. Address: 2831 Retallack Street, Regina, Saskatchewan S4S 1S8, Canada.

SILKO Leslie Marmon, b. 1948, Albuquerque, New Mexico, USA. Professor of English; Writer; Poet. 2 sons. Education: BA, English, University of New Mexico, 1969. Appointments: Teacher, University of New Mexico; Professor of English, University of Arizona at Tucson, 1978-. Publications: Fiction: Cremony, 1977; Almanac of the Dead, 1991; Yellow Woman, 1993. Poetry: Laguna Woman, 1974; Storyteller, 1981. Other: The Delicacy and Strength of Lace: Letters Between Leslie Marmon Silko and James A Wright, 1986; Sacred Water: Narratives and Pictures, 1993. Honours: National Endowment for the Arts Grant, 1974; Chicago Review Award, 1974; Pushcart Prize, 1977; John D and Catharine T MacArthur Foundation Fellowship, 1983. Address: c/o Department of English, University of Arizona at Tucson, Tucson, AZ 85721, USA.

SILLIMAN Ron(ald Glenn), b. 8 May 1946, Pasco, Washington, USA. Editor; Poet. m. (1) Rochelle Nameroff, 1965, div 1972, (2) Krishna Evans, 1986, 2 sons. Education: Merritt College, 1965, 1969-72; San Francisco State College, 1966-69; University of California at Berkeley, 1969-71. Appointments: Editor, Tottel's, 1970-81; Director of Research and Education, Committee for Prisoner Humanity and Justice, San Rafael, California, 1972-76; Project Manager, Tenderloin Ethnographic Research Project, San Francisco, 1977-78; Director of Outreach, Central City Hospitality House, San Francisco, 1979-81; Lecturer, San Francisco University, 1981; Visiting Lecturer, University of California at San Diego, La Jolla, 1982; Writer-in-Residence, New College of California, San Francisco, 1982; Director of Public

Relations and Development, 1982-86, Poet-in-Residence, 1983-90, California Institute of Integral Studies, San Francisco; Executive Editor, Socialist Review, 1986-89; Managing Editor, Computer Land, 1989-. Publications: Poetry: Moon in the Seventh House, 1968; Three Syntactic Fictions for Dennis Schmitz, 1969; Crow, 1971; Mohawk, 1973; Nox, 1974; Sitting Up, Standing Up, Taking Steps, 1978; Ketjak, 1978; Tjanting, 1981; Bart, 1982; ABC, 1983; Paradise, 1985; The Age of Huts, 1986; Lit, 1987; What, 1988; Manifest, 1990; Demo to Ink, 1992; Toner, 1992; Jones, 1993; N/O, 1994; Xing, 1996. Other: A Symposium on Clark Coolidge (editor), 1978; In the American Tree (editor), 1986; The New Sentence, 1987. Honours: Hart Crane and Alice Crane Williams Award, 1968; Joan Lee Yang Awards, 1970, 1971; National Endowment for the Arts Fellowship, 1979; California Arts Council Grants, 1979, 1980; Poetry Center Book Award, 1985. Address: 1819 Curtis, Berkeley, CA 94702, USA.

SILLITOE Alan, b. 4 Mar 1928, Nottingham, England. Writer; Poet; Dramatist. m. Ruth Esther Fainlight, 19 Nov 1959, 1 son, 1 daughter (adopted). Education: Principally self-taught. Appointments: Writer, 1948-. Publications: Without Beer or Bread (poems), 1957; Saturday Night and Sunday Morning (novel), 1958, revised edition, 1968; The General (novel), 1960; The Rats and Other Poems, 1960; Key to the Door (novel), 1961; Road to Volgograd (travel), 1964; A Falling Out of Love and Other Poems, 1964; The Death of William Posters (novel), 1965; A Tree on Fire (novel), 1967; A Start in Life (novel), 1967; Shaman and Other Poems, 1968; Love in the Environs of Voronezh and Other Poems, 1968; Travel in Nihilon (novel), 1971; Raw Material (memoir), 1972; The Flame of Life(novel), 1974; Storm and Other Poems, 1974; Barbarians and Other Poems, 1974; Mountains and Caverns: Selected Essays, 1975; The Widower's Son (novel), 1976; The Storyteller (novel), 1979; The Lost Flying Boat (novel), 1983; Down from the Hill (novel), 1984; Sun Before Departure (poems), 1984; Life Goes On (novel), 1985; Tides and Stone Walls (poems), 1986; Out of the Whirlpool (novel), 1987; The Open Door (novel), 1989; Lost Loves (novel), 1990; Leonard's War, 1991; Snowstop, 1993; Collected Poems, 1994; Collected Stories, 1995; Leading the Blind (travel), 1995; Life Without Armour (autobiography), 1995. Other: Short stories and plays. Honours: Author's Club Prize, 1958; Hawthornden Prize, 1960; Honorary Fellow, Manchester Polytechnic, 1977; Honorary Degrees, Nottingham Polytechnic, 1990, University of Nottingham, 1994. Memberships: Royal Geographical Society, fellow; Savage Club; Society of Authors; Writers Action Group. Address: c/o Savage Club, 1 Whitehall Place, London SW1A 2HD, England.

SILLS Leslie Elka, b. 26 Jan 1948, Brooklyn, New York, USA. Artist; Author; Lecturer. m. Robert J Oresick, 9 July 1978, 1 son. Education: BA, Psycholgy, Boston University, 1969; MA, School of the Museum of Fine Arts, Boston, 1973. Publications: Pilgrims and Pioneers: New England Women in the Arts, 1987; Inspirations: Stories About Women Artists, 1989; Visions: Stories About Women Artists, 1994. Contributions to: Pilgrims and Pioneers: New England Women in the Arts, 1987; Magazines. Honours: 1 of 10 Best Books for Children Citation, Parenting Magazine, 1989; Pick of the Lists, American Bookseller, 1989, 1993; Recommended List, New York Public Library, 1989, 1993; Editor's Choice, Best Books, 1989, 1993; Notable Book Awards, American Library Association, 1989, 1994; Best Book Citation, School Library Journal, 1993. Memberships: National Women's Caucus for Art; New England Authors and Illustrators of Children's Books. Address: 38 St Paul Street, Brookline, MA 02146, USA.

SILLS-DOCHERTY Jonathon John, (John Docherty), b. 7 Jan 1941, Bowden, Cheshire, England. Humorous Writer; Lyricist; Poet. Education: Fielden Park College, West Didsbury, Manchester, 1977; Poetry Workshop, 1981, Extramural Department, 1986-87, University of Manchester; Diploma, Variety Entertainment, BTEC National Diploma in Performing Arts, 1998, South Trafford College; Appointments: Editor, Guardian Society, 1974; Reporter, Dun & Bradstreet, 1975; Proof Reader, Subeditor, Biography Compiler, Odd Fellow Magazine. Publications: A Walk Around the City and Other Groans, 1969, revised edition, 1973; Words on Paper, 1977; From Bottoms to Tops and Back Again, 1977, limited edition, 1987; Ballads of Ecstasy and Perspicacity, 1987; Ballads of North West John (plus cassette tape), 1987; tribute ballads to Nigel Mansell and Eddie 'The Eagle' Edwards, and other lyrics. Contributions to: Newspapers and magazines. Honours: North West Arts Poetry Award, 1978; Double prizewinner, Tribute for St George's Day, Granada TV, 1978; LAMDA Group Acting Award Honours, North Trafford College, 1995, 1996; Review Prize Winner, Helen Storey Competition, 1998. Memberships: Turner Society; Court School of Dancing; Independent Order of Odd Fellows; Friend, North West Arts, Manchester City Art Gallery; Authors North; Subscriber, Manchester Academy of Fine Arts. Address: 5 Farm Avenue, Stretford, Manchester M32 9TW, England.

SILMAN Roberta, b. 29 Dec 1934, Brooklyn, New York, USA. Writer. m. Robert Silman, 14 June 1956. Education: BA, English Literature, Cornell University, 1956; MFA, Writing, Sarah Lawrence College, 1975. Publications: Somebody Else's Child, 1976; Blood Relations, 1977; Boundaries, 1979; The Dream Dredger, 1986; Beginning the World Again, 1990. Contributions to: Numerous magazines in USA and UK. Honours: Child Study Association Award, Best Children's Book, 1976; Janet Kafka Prizes, 1978, 1980; Guggenheim Fellowship, 1979; National Endowment for the Arts, Fellowship, 1983; PEN Syndicated Fiction Project Awards, 1983, 1984. Memberships: PEN; Authors Guild; Poets and Writers; Phi Beta Kappa. Address: 18 Larchmont Street, Ardsley, NY 10502, USA.

SILVER Richard. See: **BULMER Henry Kenneth.**

SILVERMAN Francine, b. 24 Apr 1943, New York City, USA. Feature Writer; Guidebook Author. m. Ronald Silverman, 26 May 1968, 1 daughter. Education: BA, English, College of Mount St Vincent, 1980. Appointments: Writer, 1980-; Reporter, Gannett Newspapers, 1985-90, Riverdale Review, 1993-98. Publication: Catskills Alive. Contributions to: Travel Agent Magazine; Chicago Tribune; Philadelphia Inquirer; Kiwi and Passport Sabena; Travel Smart; Motorhome. Address: 4455 Douglas Avenue, Riverdale, NY 10471, USA.

SILVERSCREEN Cameron. See: **ACKERMAN Forrest J.**

SILVERSTEIN Shel(by), b. 1932, Chicago, Illinois, USA. Cartoonist; Writer; Dramatist; Poet; Composer. Div, 1 daughter. Appointments: Cartoonist, Pacific Stars and Stripes; Writer and Cartoonist, Playboy, 1956-. Publications: Self-Illustrated: Now Here's My Plan: A Book of Futilities, 1960; Uncle Shelby's ABZ Book: A Primer for Tender Young Minds, 1961; Playboy's Teevee Jeebies, 1963; Uncle Shelby's Story of Lafcadio, The Lion Who Shot Back, 1963; The Giving Tree, 1964; Uncle Shelby's Giraffe and a Half (verse), 1964; Uncle Shelby's Zoo: Don't Bump the Glump! (verse), 1964; Who Wants a Cheap Rhinoceros!, 1964; More Playboy's Teevee Jeebies: Do-It-Yourself Dialog for the Late Late Show, 1965; Where the Sidewalk Ends: The Poems and Drawings of Shel Silverstein, 1974; The Missing Piece, 1976; Different Dances, 1979; A Light in the Attic, 1981; The Missing Piece Meets the Big O, 1981; Falling Up, 1996. Plays: The Lady or the Tiger, 1981; Gorilla, 1983; Wild Life, 1983; Remember Crazy Zelda, 1984; The Crate, 1985; The Happy Hour, 1985; One Tennis Shoe, 1985; Little Feet, 1986; Wash and Dry, 1986; The Devil and Billy Markham, 1989. Screenplay: Things Change (with David Mamet), 1988. Contributions to: The Best American Short Plays 1992-1993: The Theatre Annual Since 1937, 1993. Other: Composer and lyricist of many songs. Honours: New York Times Outstanding Book Award, 1974; School Library Journal Best Books Award, 1981; International Reading Association's Children's Choice Award, 1982; Buckeye Awards, 1983, 1985; William Allen White Award, 1984. Address: c/o Grapefruit Productions, 106 Montague Street, Brooklyn, NY 11201, USA.

SILVIS Randall Glenn, b. 15 July 1950, Rimersburg, Pennsylvania, USA. Novelist; Playwright. m. Rita Lynne McCanna, 25 Sept 1982, 2 sons. Education: BS, Clarion University, 1973; MEd, Indiana University, 1976. Appointments: James Thurber Writer-in-Residence, Thurber House, Columbus, Ohio, 1989; Visiting Writer, Mercyhurst College, Pennsylvania, 1989-90, Ohio State University, 1991, 1992. Publications: The Luckiest Man in the World; Excelsior; An Occasional Hell; Under the Rainbow; Dead Man Falling; Mary Rogers. Screenplays: An Occasional Hell; Believe the Children; A Walk in the Moonlight. Contributions to: Magazines. Honours: National Endowment for the Arts Fellowship; Drue Heinz Literature Prize; National Playwright Showcase Award; Fulbright Senior Scholar Research Grant. Address: PO Box 297, St Petersburg, PA 16054, USA.

SIMCIC Samo Gabrijel, b. 27 Sept 1946, Ljubljana, Slovenia. Educator. m. Claudia Thalmann, 3 July 1991, 1 son, 1 daughter. Education: Diploma, Theatre Study, University of Ljubljana, 1975; Waldorf Education, Rudolf Steiner Kindergarten Teacher Training School, Bern, 1987-90. Appointments: Founder, 1st World Waldorf Kindergarten, Slovenia, 1990; Work with Handicapped Children, Zurich, Switzerland, 1996-. Publications: Hram, 1975; Psomar in Njegovi Hlapci, 1988; O Krokotarju in Zlatem Jajcu, 1997. Membership: PEN, Slovenia, 1980-. Address: Frowiesstrasse 9, CH-8345 Adeswil, Switzerland.

SIMHOVITCH Michael, (Michael Zorin), b. 25 July 1916, Kremenchug, Ukraine. Writer. m. Ida Shulkind, 10 Nov 1940, 1 son. Education: Donetsk Teachers College, 1940. Appointments: Newspaper Worker, 1932-41; Army Newspaper, 1941-47; Literary Newspaper, 1947-52. Publications: A Boy From Donetsk, 1952; The Worker's Life, 1953; The Days Come Early, 1955; History Roads, 1960; Soldier's Roads, 1962; Burning Torch, 1965; Hot Memory, 1966; Dream About Pskov, 1970; The Beginning of the War, 1972; My Lamp, 1976; My Destiny, 1980. Honour: USSR Union of Writers Award. Membership: Latvian Union of Writers. Address: Martas 1, 24, PO Box 63, Riga, LV-1011, Latvia.

SIMIC Charles, b. 9 May 1938, Belgrade, Yugoslavia (US citizen, 1971). Associate Professor of English; Poet; Writer. m. Helen Dubin, 1964, 1 son, 1 daughter. Education: University of Chicago, 1956-59; BA, New York University, 1967. Appointments: Faculty, California State College, Hayward, 1970-73; Associate Professor of English, University of New Hampshire, 1973-. Publications: Poetry: What the Grass Says, 1967; Somewhere Among Us a Stone is Taking Notes, 1969; Dismantling the Silence, 1971; White, 1972, revised edition, 1980; Return to a Place Lit by a Glass of Milk, 1974; Biography and a Lament, 1976; Charon's Cosmology, 1977; Brooms: Selected Poems, 1978; School for Dark Thoughts, 1978; Classic Ballroom Dances, 1980; Shaving at Night, 1982; Austerities, 1982; Weather Forecast for Utopia and Vicinity: Poems: 1967-1982, 1983; The Chicken Without a Head, 1983; Selected Poems 1963-1983, 1985, revised edition, 1990; Unending Blues, 1986; The World Doesn't End: Prose Poems, 1989; In the Room We Share, 1990; The Book of Gods and Devils, 1990; Hotel Insomnia, 1992; A Wedding in Hell, 1994; Walking the Black Cat, 1996. Other: The Uncertain Certainty: Interviews, Essays and Notes on Poetry, 1985; Wonderful Words, Silent Truth, 1990; Dimestore Alchemy, 1992; Unemployed Fortune Teller, 1994; Orphan Factory, 1998. Editor: Another Republic: 17 European and South American Writers (with Mark Strand), 1976; The Essential Campion, 1988. Translator: 12 books, 1970-92. Honours: PEN Awards, 1970, 1980; Guggenheim Fellowship, 1972; National Endowment for the Arts Fellowships, 1974, 1979; Edgar Allan Poe Award, 1975; American Academy of Arts and Letters Award, 1976; Harriet Monroe Poetry Award, 1980; Fulbright Fellowship, 1982; Ingram Merrill Foundation Fellowship, 1983; John D and Catharine T MacArthur

Foundation Fellowship, 1984; Pulitzer Prize in Poetry, 1990; Academy of American Poets Fellowship, 1998. Address: c/o Department of English, University of New Hampshire, Durham, NH 03824, USA.

SIMIONESCU Mircea Horia, b. 23 Jan 1928, Targoviste, Romania. Writer. m. Teodora Dinca, 26 Feb 1953, 2 daughters. Education: BA, Literature, Bucharest University, 1964. Publications: The Well Tempered Ingenious Man, 4 volumes, 1969, 1970, 1980, 1983; After 1900, About Noon, 1974; Ganymede's Kidnapping, 1975; Endless Dangers, 1978; Advice for the Dauphin, 1979; Ulysse and the Shadow, 1982; The Banquet, 1982; The Cutaway, 1984; Sale By Auction, 1985; Three Looking Glasses, 1987; The Siege of the Common Place, 1988; The Angel with the Apron, 1992; The Warm Summer Coat, 1996; The Fever, 1998. Contributions to: Magazines, journals, radio, and television. Honour: Writers Union of Romania Prize, 1974, 1996. Membership: Writers Union of Romania. Address: 3 Belgrad Str, Bucharest, CD 71248, Romania.

SIMKIN Tom, b. 11 Nov 1933, Auburn, New York, USA. Geologist; Writer. m. Sharon Russell, 3 July 1965, 1 son, 1 daughter. Education: BS, Swarthmore College, 1955; MSE, 1960, PhD, 1965, Princeton University. Appointment: Staff, Smithsonian Institution, Washington, DC. Publications: Volcanoes of the World, 1981, 2nd edition, 1994; Krakatau 1883: The Volcanic Eruption and Its Effects, 1983; Volcano Letter, 1987; Global Volcanism 1975-85, 1989; Paricutin: The Volcano Born in a Mexican Cornfield, 1993. Contributions to: Scientific journals. Honour: Choice Outstanding Academic Book Award, 1984; Geoscience Information Society Prize, best information book, 1995. Memberships: American Geophysical Union; Charles Darwin Foundation for the Galapagos Isles; Geological Society of Washington, president, 1990; International Association of Volcanology. Address: c/o Smithsonian Institution, Museum of Natural History, Washington, DC 20560, USA.

SIMMERMAN Jim, b. 5 Mar 1952, Denver, Colorado, USA. Associate Professor of English; Poet. Education: BS, Education, 1973, MA, English, 1976, University of Missouri; MFA, Creative Writing, University of Iowa, 1980. Appointments: Instructor, 1977-78, Assistant Professor, 1983-86, Associate Professor of English and Director of Creative Writing, 1986-, Northern Arizona University; Editorial Board, Pushcart Prize Series, 1985-. Publications: Home, 1983; Bad Weather, 1987; Once Out of Nature, 1989; Moon Go Away, I Don't Love You Anymore, 1994; Yoyo, 1994; Dog Music: Poetry About Dogs, co-editor, 1996. Contributions to: Anthologies and journals. Honours: Arizona Commission on the Arts Fellowships for Poetry, 1983, 1987; National Endowment for the Arts Fellowship, 1984; Pushcart Writers Choice Selection, 1984, and Prize, 1985; Fine Arts Work Center Poetry Fellowship, 1984-85; Best of the Small Presses Book Fair Selection, 1990; Hawthornden Fellowship, Scotland, 1996. Memberships: Associated Writing Programs, board of directors, 1992-95, secretary, 1994-95; Rocky Mountain Modern Language Association. Address: 3601 Mountain Drive, Flagstaff, AZ 86001, USA.

SIMMONS Michael, b. 17 Oct 1935, Watford, England. Writer. m. Angela Thomson, 20 Apr 1963, 2 sons. Education: BA, Honours, Russian, Manchester University, 1960. Appointments: East Europe Correspondent, Financial Times, 1968-72; Deputy Editor, Society; East Europe Correspondent; Third World Editor, The Guardian, 1977-97; Freelance Writer and Editor, 1997-. Publications: Berlin: The Dispossessed City, 1988; The Unloved Country; A Portrait of the GDR, 1989; The Reluctant President, A Life of Vaclav Havel, 1992; Landscapes of Poverty, 1997. Contributions to: New Statesman; Literary Review. Literary Agent: Tessa Sayle Asstes, London SW3, England. Address: 25 Pendarves Road, London SW20 8TS, England.

SIMMS Suzanne. See: **GUNTRUM Suzanne Simmons.**

SIMON Barney, b. 13 Apr 1933, Johannesburg, South Africa. Playwright. Education: Studied in Johannesburg. Appointments: Co-Founder and Director, The Market Theatre, Johannesburg, 1978. Publications: Phiri, 1972; Hey Listen, 1973; People, and People Too, 1973; Joburg Sis, 1974; Storytime, 1975; Medea (after Grillparzer), 1978; Cincinatti, 1979; Call me Woman, 1980; Cold Stone Jug, 1980; Marico Moonshine and Manpower, 1981; Woza Albert, 1981; Black Dogonj Mayama, 1984; Born in the RSA, 1985; Outers, 1985; Written by Hand, 1987; Score Me with Ages, 1989; Eden and Other Places, 1989; Inyanga- About Women in Africa, 1989; Singing the Times, 1992, (all plays created in collaboration with participants); Television plays. Honours: Los Angeles Critics Award, 1982; Edinburgh Festival Fringe Awards, 1982, 1987; Rockefeller Grants. Address: c/o The Market Theatre, PO Box 8656, Johannesburg 2000, South Africa.

SIMON Claude, b. 10 Oct 1913, Madagascar. Writer. Education: College Stanislas, Paris. Publications: Le tricheur, 1945; La corde raide, 1947; Gulliver, 1952; Le sacre de printemps, 1954; Le vent, 1957; L'herbe, 1958; La route des Flandres, 1960; Le palace, 1962; Histoire, 1967; La bataille de Pharsale, 1969; Orion aveugle, 1970; Les corps conducteurs, 1971; Tryptyque, 1973; Lecon de choses, 1975; Les Georgiques, 1981; Le chevelure de Bérénice, 1984; Discours de Stockholm, 1986; L'invitation, 1987; L'acacia, 1989; Les Jardin des Plantes, 1997. Honours: Prix de l'Express, 1960; Prix Medicis, 1967; Nobel Prize for Literature, 1985; Honorary Doctorate, University of Bologna, 1989; Grand Croix Ordre National du Mérite, 1990. Address: Editions de Minuit, 7 rue Bernard-Palissey, 75006 Paris, France.

SIMON Herbert A(lexander), b. 15 June 1916, Milwaukee, Wisconsin, USA. Economist; Professor of Computer Science and Psychology; Author. m. Dorothea Isobel Pye, 25 Dec 1937, 1 son, 2 daughters. Education: BA, 1936, PhD, 1943, University of Chicago. Appointments: Assistant Professor, 1942-47, Professor of Political Science, 1947-49, Illinois Institute of Technology, Chicago; Professor of Administration, 1949-62, Professor of Administration and Psychology, 1962-65, Richard King Mellon University Professor of Computer Science and Psychology, Carnegie Institute of Technology, later Carnegie-Mellon University; Various visiting lectureships. Publications: Administrative Behaviour, 1947, 4th edition, 1997; Public Administration (with Donald W Smithburg and Victor A Thompson), 1950, with new introduction, 1991; Fundamental Research in Administration (with others), 1953; Models of Man, 1958; Organizations (with James G March and H Guetzkow), 1958, 2nd edition, 1993; Planning Production, Inventories, and Work Force (with C C Holt, F Modigliani, and J Muth), 1960; The New Science of Management Decision, 1960, revised edition, 1977; The Shape of Automation, 1965; The Sciences of the Artificial, 1969, 3rd edition, 1996; Human Problem Solving (with Allen Newell), 1972; Representation and Meaning: Experiments with Information Processing (editor with L Siklossy), 1972; Models of Discovery, and Other Topics in the Methods of Science, 1978; Models of Thought, Vol 1, 1979, Vol 2, 1989; Models of Rationality, Vol 1, 1982, Vol 2, 1982, Vol 3, 1997; Reason in Human Affairs, 1983; Protocol Analysis: Verbal Reports as Data (with K Anders Ericsson), 1984, revised edition, 1993; Scientific Discovery: Computational Explorations of the Creative Processes (with Pat Langley, Gary L Bradshaw, and Jan M Zytow), 1987; Models of My Life (autobiography), 1991; Economics, Bounded Rationality, and the Cognitive Revolution (with Ricardo Viale, Massimo Egidi and Robin Marris), 1992; An Empirically Based Microeconomics, 1997. Contributions to: Books, professional journals and many other publications. Honours: Distinguished Scientific Contributions Award, 1969, and Gold Medal Award in Psychology, 1988, American Psychological Association; Nobel Prize in Economic Science, 1978; James Madison Award, American Political Science Association, 1984; National Medal of Science, 1986; John Von Neumann Theory Prize, Operations Research Society of America and Institute of Management Science, 1988; Research Excellence Award, International Joint Conference on

Artificial Intelligence, 1995; Dwight Waldo Award, American Society for Public Administration, 1995; Many honorary doctorates; Phi Beta Kappa; Sigma Xi. Memberships: American Academy of Arts and Sciences, fellow; American Association for the Advancement of Science, fellow; American Association of University Professors; American Economic Association, distinguished fellow; American Psychological Association; American Psychological Society; American Political Science Association; American Psychological Society, William James Fellow; American Sociological Association, fellow; Econometric Society, fellow; Institute of Management Sciences, vice-president, 1954; National Academy of Sciences, council member, 1978-81, 1983-86; Chinese Academy of Sciences, foreign member; Operations Research Society of America; Psychonomic Society. Address: 128 North Craig Street, Apt 504, Pittsburgh, PA 15213, USA.

SIMON Luke Icarus, b. 14 Aug 1963, Nicosia. Writer; University Teacher. Education: BA, Honours, Sydney University; Graduate Diploma, Adult Education, University of Technology, Sydney; MEd, Wollongong University. Publications: Michael Gon's Play: A Theratic Approach; Fish Wednesday (stage play); Sir (stage play); 4 teleplays. Contributions to: Southerly; Overland; Akti; Outrage; Campaign; Hobo; Outrider; Enguin Anthology of Australian Literature. Honour: Runner-Up, Terry Bell Memorial Prize. Memberships: Australian Writers Guild; Australian Society of Authors. Literary Agent: Curtis Brown. Address: 27 Union Street, Paddington, NSW 2021, Australia.

SIMON Neil, b. 4 July 1927, New York, New York, USA. Dramatist; Screenwriter. m. (1) Joan Balm, 30 Sept 1953, dec, (2) Marsha Mason, 1973, div, (3) Diane Lander, 1987. Education: New York University, 1946. Publications: Plays: Come Blow Your Horn, 1961; Barefoot in the Park, 1963; The Odd Couple, 1965; The Star-Spangled Girl, 1966; Plaza Suite, 1968; The Last of the Red Hot Lovers, 1969; The Gingerbread Lady, 1970; The Prisoner of Second Avenue, 1971; The Sunshine Boys, 1972; The Good Doctor, 1973; God's Favorite, 1974; California Suite, 1976; Chapter Two, 1977; I Ought to Be in Pictures, 1980; Fools, 1981; The Brighton Beach Memoirs, 1983; Biloxi Blues, 1985; Broadway Bound, 1986; Rumors, 1988; Lost in Yonkers, 1991; Jake's Woman, 1992; Laughter on the 23rd Floor, 1993; London Suite, 1995. Screenplays: After the Fox, 1966; The Out-of-Towners, 1970; The Heartbreak Kid, 1973; Murder by Death, 1976; The Goodbye Girl, 1977; The Cheap Detective, 1978; Seems Like Old Times, 1980; Max Dugan Returns, 1983; The Lonely Guy, 1984; The Sluggers Wife, 1984; The Marrying Man, 1991; Also many adaptions of his plays for films. Lyrics for Musicals: Little Me, 1962, revised version, 1982; Sweet Charity, 1966; Promises, Promises, 1968; They're Playing Our Song, 1979; The Goodbye Girl, 1993. Other: Rewrites: A Memoir, 1996. Honours: Tony Awards, 1965, 1985, 1991; Evening Standard Drama Award, 1967; Sam S Shubert Award, 1968; Writers Guild Screen Awards, 1968, 1970, 1975, and Laurel Award, 1979; Pulitzer Prize in Drama, 1991. Memberships: Dramatists Guild; Writers Guild of America. Address: c/o A DaSilva, 502 Park Avenue, New York, NY 10022, USA.

SIMON Sheldon (Weiss), b. 31 Jan 1937, St Paul, Minnesota, USA. Professor of International Politics; Writer. m. Charlann Scheid, 23 Apr 1962, 1 son. Education: BA, 1958, PhD, 1964, University of Minnesota; MA, Princeton University, 1960. Appointments: Visiting Professor, University of British Columbia, 1972-73, 1979-80, Carleton University, 1976, American Graduate School of International Management, 1991-92, Monetary Institute of International Studies, 1991, 1996; Professor of International Politics, Arizona State University, Tempe. Publications: The Broken Triangle: Peking, Djakarta and the PKI, 1969; War and Politics in Cambodia, 1974; Asian Neutralism and US Policy, 1975; The Military and Security and in the Third World, 1976; Asian Security in the Post-Cold War Era, 1993; Southeast Asian Security in the New Millennium, 1996. Contributions to: Professional journals. Address:

c/o Department of Political Science, Arizona State University, Tempe, AZ 85287, USA.

SIMON Werner, b. 5 June 1914, Bremen, Germany. Psychiatrist. m. Elizabeth Strawn, 24 Apr 1939. Education: Medical School, University of Frankfurt, Germany, 1932-36; MD Degree, University of Bern, Switzerland, 1937. Appointments: Chief of Psychiatry, Veterans Administration Medical Center, Minneapolis, 1948-71; Consultant, Hennepin County Medical Center, Minneapolis, 1971-; Emeritus Professor of Psychiatry, University of Minnesota Medical School. Publications: Differential Treatment and Prognosis in Schizophrenia, 1959; Suicide Among Physicians, 1989. Contributions to: Books and professional journals. Memberships: Minnesota Psychiatric Society, president 1967-69; American Psychiatric Association, life fellow; American College of Physicians, fellow; International Association for Suicide Prevention; Minnesota Society of Neurological Sciences. Address: 8915 River Ridge Road, Minneapolis, MN 55425, USA.

SIMPSON Alan, b. 27 Nov 1929, England. Scriptwriter; Author. m. Kathleen Phillips, 1958, dec 1978. Appointments: Scriptwriter, author with Ray Galton, 1951-; Various television programmes, 1954-. Publications: Hancock, 1961; Steptoe and Son, 1963; The Reunion and Other Plays, 1966; Hancock Scripts, 1974; The Best Of Hancock, 1986; Film scripts and theatre works. Honours: Scriptwriter of the Year, Guild of TV Producers and Directors, 1959; Best Comedy TV Series Awards, Screenwriters Guild, 1962-65; John Logie Baird Award, 1964; Best Comedy Series Award, Dutch TV, 1966; Best Comedy Screenplay Award, Scriptwriters Guild, 1972; Portugal Golden Globe Best TV Series Award, 1995. Address: c/o Tessa Le Bars Management, 54 Birchwood Road, Petts Wood, Kent BR5 1NZ, England.

SIMPSON Dorothy (Preece), b. 20 June 1933, Blaenavon, Monmouthshire, Wales. Author. Education: BA, 1954, Teaching Diploma, 1955, University of Bristol. Appointments: Teacher of English and French, Dartford Grammar School for Girls, Kent, 1955-59, Erith Grammer School, Kent, 1959-61; Teacher of English, Senacre School, Maidstone, Kent, 1961-62. Publications: Harbinger of Fear, 1977; The Night She Died, 1981; Six Feet Under, 1982; Puppet for a Corpse, 1983; Close Her Eyes, 1984; Last Seen Alive, 1985; Dead on Arrival, 1986; Element of Doubt, 1987; Suspicious Death, 1988; Dead by Morning, 1989; Doomed to Die, 1991; Wake the Dead, 1992; No Laughing Matter, 1993; A Day for Dying, 1995; Once Too Often, 1998; Dead and Gone, 1999. Honour: Silver Dagger Award, 1985. Memberships: Society of Authors; Crime Writers' Association of Great Britain; Mystery Writers of America. Address: c/o Curtis Brown Ltd, 4th Floor, Haymarket House, 28/29 Haymarket, London SW1Y 4SP, England.

SIMPSON Elizabeth Robson, b. 16 Oct 1910, Sydney, New South Wales, Australia. Zoologist; Painter; Writer. m. Alfred Moxon Simpson, 3 Aug 1938, 1 son. Education: BSc, 1931, 1st Class Honours, 1933, MSc, 1935, University of Adelaide, South Australia. Publications: The Hahndorf Walkers and the Beaumont Connection, 1983; The Clelands of Beaumont, 1986; Beaumont House, the Land and its People, 1993. Contributions to: 10 papers on larval trematodes, in Transactions of Royal Society of South Australia. Honours: John Bagot Scholarship and Medal, University of Adelaide, 1929; Fellow, Royal South Australian Society of Arts; Award, Genealogical Society of South Australia, 1987. Memberships: Queen Adelaide Club; Lyceum Club of South Australia Inc; Tatlers. Address: GPO Box 621, Adelaide, South Australia 5001, Australia.

SIMPSON Jerry Howard Jr, b. 11 Dec 1925, Providence, Rhode Island, USA. Writer. m. Jane Coral Augustine Simpson, 4 Sept 1973, 1 son, 1 daughter. Education: BA, History/Languages, Moravian College for Men, University of North Carolina. Publications: Torn Land, 1970; Cycling France, 1992; Notes on the French Revolution, 1994; Paris in Winter, 1995; Pensées

Impolies, 1996. Contributions to: Reader's Digest; American History Illustrated; Bicycling; Wall Street Journal; Bike World. Honour: 1st Place, Virginia Press Association, 1969-70. Membership: Comenian Literary Society. Address: E E Richey 303-1399 Barclay Street, Vancouver, British Columbia V6E 1H6, Canada.

SIMPSON John (Andrew), b. 13 Oct 1953, Cheltenham, Gloucestershire, England. Linguist; Lexicographer. m. Hilary Croxford, 25 Sept 1976, 2 daughters. Education: BA, Honours, English, University of York, 1975; MA, Medieval Studies, University of Reading, 1976. Appointments: Editorial Assistant, 1976-79, Senior Editor, 1981-84, Supplement to The Oxford England Dictionary; Editor, 1984-86, Co-Editor, 1986-93, Chief Editor, 1993-, The Oxford English Dictionary; Fellow, Rewley House, later Kellogg College, Oxford, 1991-; Member, Faculty of English, University of Oxford, 1993-. Publications: The Concise Oxford Dictionary of Proverbs (editor), 1982, 2nd edition, 1992; The Oxford English Dictionary (editor with Edmund Weiner), 2nd edition, 1989; The Oxford Dictionary of Modern Slang (editor with John Ayto), 1992; The Oxford English Dictionary Additions (editor with Edmund Weiner), 2 volumes, 1993. Contributions to: Scholarly books and journals. Membership: Philological Society. Address: Chestnut Lodge, St Mary's Close, Wheatley, Oxford OX33 1YP, England.

SIMPSON John (Cody Fidler), b. 9 Aug 1944, Cleveleys, England. Broadcaster; Writer. m. (1) Diane Jean Petteys, 1965, div 1995, 2 daughters, (2) Adèle Krüger, 1996. Education: MA, Magdalene College, Cambridge. Appointments: Various positions, BBC, 1966-82; BBC Diplomatic Editor, 1982-88, Foreign, later World Affairs Editor, 1988-; Associate Editor, The Spectator, 1991-95; Columnist, The Sunday Telegraph, 1995-. Publications: The Best of Granta (editor), 1966; Moscow Requiem, 1981; A Fine and Private Place, 1983; The Disappeared: Voices From a Secret War, 1985; Behind Iranian Lines, 1988; Despatches From the Barricades, 1990; From the House of War: Baghdad and the Gulf, 1991; The Darkness Crubles: The Death of Communism, 1992; In the Forests of the Night: Drug-Running and Terrorism in Peru, 1993; The Oxford Book of Exile (editor), 1995; Lifting the Veil: Life in Revolutionary Iran, 1995; Strange Places, Questionable People (autobiography), 1998. Honours: Fellow, Royal Geographical Society, 1990; Commander of the Order of the British Empire, 1991; BAFTA Reporter of the year, 1991; RTS Richard Dimbleby Award, 1991; Columnist of the year, National Magazine Awards, 1993; Honorary DLitt, De Montfort University, 1995; RTS Foreign Report Award, 1997; Peabody Award, USA, 1997. Address: c/o BBC Television Centre, Wood Lane, London W12 7RJ, England.

SIMPSON Leo (James Pascal), b. 24 Sept 1934, Limerick, Ireland (Canadian citizen, 1972). Writer. m. Jacqueline Anne Murphy, 1964, 1 daughter. Education: Ireland. Appointments: Writer-in-Residence, University of Ottawa, 1973, University of Western Ontario, 1978. Publications: Arkwright, 1971; Peacock Papers, 1973; The Lady and the Travelling Salesman, 1976; Kowalski's Last Chance, 1980; Sailor Man, 1996. Address: Moodie Cottage, 114 Bridge Street West, Belleville, Ontario, Canada K8P 1J7.

SIMPSON Louis (Aston Marantz), b. 27 Mar 1923, Kingston, Jamaica, British West Indies (US citizen). Professor Emeritus; Poet; Writer. m. (1) Jeanne Claire Rogers, 1949, div 1979, 1 son, 1 daughter, (3) Miriam Butensky Bachner, 1985. Education: BS, 1948, AM, 1950, PhD, 1959, Columbia University. Appointments: Instructor, Columbia University, 1953-59, New School for Social Research, New York City, 1955-59; Assistant Professor to Professor of English, University of California at Berkeley, 1959-67; Professor of English and Comparative Literature, 1967-91, Distinguished Professor, 1991-93, Professor Emeritus, 1993-, State University of New York at Stony Brook. Publications: Poetry: The Arrivistes: Poems, 1940-49, 1949; Good News of Death and Other Poems, 1955; A Dream of

Governors, 1959; At the End of the Open Road, 1963; Selected Poems, 1965; Adventures of the Letter I, 1971; Searching for the Ox, 1976; Armidale, 1979; Out of Season, 1979; Caviare at the Funeral, 1980; The Best Hour of the Night, 1983; People Live Here: Selected Poems, 1949-83, 1983; Collected Poems, 1988; Wei Wei and Other Poems, 1990; In the Room We Share, 1990; There You Are, 1995. Fiction: Riverside Drive, 1962. Other: The New Poets of England and America (editor with Donald Hall and Robert Pack), 1957; James Hogg: A Critical Study, 1962; An Introduction to Poetry (editor), 1967, 2nd edition, 1972; North of Jamaica, 1972; Three on the Tower: The Lives and Works of Ezra Pound, T S Eliot and William Carlos Williams, 1975; A Revolution in Taste: Studies of Dylan Thomas, Allen Ginsberg, Sylvia Plath and Robert Lowell, 1978; A Company of Poets, 1981; The Character of the Poet, 1986; Selected Prose, 1988; Ships Going into the Blue: Essays and Notes on Poetry, 1994; The King My Father's Wreck, 1995; Modern Poets of France: A Bilingual Anthology, 1997. Contributions to: Various publications. Honours: Prix de Rome, American Academy in Rome, 1957; Hudson Review Fellowship, 1957; Edna St Vincent Millay Award, 1960; Distinguished Alumni Award, 1960, Medal for Excellence, 1965, Columbia University; Guggenheim Fellowships, 1962, 1970; American Council of Learned Societies Grant, 1963; Pulitzer Prize for Poetry, 1964; Commonwealth Club of California Poetry Award, 1965; American Academy of Arts and Letters Award, 1976; Institute of Jamaica Centenary Medal, 1980; Jewish Book Council Award for Poetry, 1981; Elmer Holmes Bobst Award, 1987. Address: 186 Old Field Road, Setauket, NY 11733, USA.

SIMPSON Matt(hew William), b. 13 May 1936, Lancashire, England. Retired Lecturer in English; Poet; Writer. m. Monika Ingrid Weydert, 13 Dec 1961, 1 son, 1 daughter. Education: CertEd, Liverpool, 1959; MA, Honours, Cantab, 1961. Appointments: Lecturer in English, various schools; Poet-in-Residence, Tasmanian Poetry Festival, 1995. Publications: Letters to Berlin, 1971; A Syke Sequence, 1972; Watercolour From an Approved School, 1975; Uneasy Vespers, 1977; Making Arrangements, 1982; See You on the Christmas Tree, 1984; Dead Baiting, 1989; An Elegy for the Galosherman: New and Selected Poems, 1990; The Pig's Thermal Underwear, 1994; To Tasmania with Mrs Meredith, 1993; Catching Up With History, 1995; Matt, Wes and Pete, 1995; On the Right Side of the Earth, 1995; Somewhere Down the Line, 1998; Cutting the Clouds Towards, 1998; The Lost Property Box, 1998. Contributions to: Reviews, quarterlies, and magazines. Address: 29 Boundary Drive, Liverpool, L25 0QB, England.

SIMPSON N(orman) F(rederick), b. 29 Jan 1919, London, England. Author. Education: BA, University of London, 1954. Appointments: Teacher and Extramural Lecturer, Westminster College, London, 1946-62; Literary Manager, Royal Court Theatre, London, 1976-78. Publications: The Hole, 1958; One Way Pendulum, 1960; The Form, 1961; The Hole and Other Plays and Sketches, 1964; The Cresta Run, 1966; Some Tall Tinkles: Television Plays, 1968; Was He Anyone, 1973; Harry Bleachbaker (novel), 1974, US edition as Man Overboard, 1976; Inner Voices, 1983. Address: Ivy Cottage, Water Lane, Golant, Cornwall PL23 1LG, England.

SIMPSON Ronald Albert, b. 1 Feb 1929, Melbourne, Victoria, Australia. Poet. m. Pamela Bowles, 27 Aug 1955, 1 son, 1 daughter. Education: Trained Primary Teachers' Certificate, 1951; Associate Diploma in Fine Art, Royal Melbourne Institute of Technology, 1966. Appointments: Teacher, Junior and Secondary Schools, Australia and England, 1951-68; Lecturer, Senior Lecturer, The Chisholm Institute of Technology, Melbourne, Victoria, 1968-87; Poetry Editor, The Age, retired 1997. Publications: The Walk Along the Beach, 1960; This Real Pompeii, 1964; After the Assassination, 1968; Diver, 1972; Poems from Murrumbeena, 1976; The Forbidden City, 1979; Poems From the Age (editor), 1979; Selected Poems, 1981; Words for a Journey, 1986; Dancing Table, 1992; The Impossible and Other Poems,

1998. Honours: Australia Council for Travel, 1977, Category A Fellowship to write poetry, 1987; Christopher Brennan Award, 1992. Membership: Australian Society of Authors. Address: 29 Omama Road, Murrumbeena, Melbourne, Victoria 3163, Australia.

SIMS George Frederick Robert, b. 3 Aug 1923, Hammersmith, London, England. Rare Book Dealer; Author. m. Beryl Simcock, 2 sons, 1 daughter. Education: Lower School of John Lyon, Harrow, 1934-40. Publications: The Terrible Door, 1964; Sleep No More, 1966; The Last Best Friend, 1967; The Sand Dollar, 1969; Deadhand, 1971; Hunters Point, 1973; The End of the Web, 1976; Rex Mundi, 1978; Who Is Cato?, 1981; The Keys of Death, 1982; Coat of Arms, 1984; The Rare Book Game, 1985; More of the Rare Book Game, 1988; Last of the Rare Book Game, 1990; The Despain Papers, 1992; A Life in Catalogues, 1994. Contributions to: Black Mask; Saturday Book; London Magazine; American Book Collector; Book Collector; Antiquarian Book Monthly Review. Memberships: Crime Writers Association; Detection Club. Address: Peacocks, Hurst, Reading, Berkshire RG10 ODR, England.

SINA Enrieta, b. 30 Jan 1953, Vlore, Albania. Journalist. m. Muhamet Zykaj, 28 Nov 1976, 1 son, 2 daughters. Education: Graduated, Journalism, Faculty of Juridical and Political Sciences. Appointments: Teacher, 1973-75; Journalist, 1975-; Editor, Horoscope newspaper. Publications: Male feeling, long stories, 1994; A woman speaks about sex, 1995; The wedding apple, 1996; Gunshot '97, novel; Knocking on the glass, book of poetry, 1996; The unhappy woman, novel; Minute, poems. Honours: Best Publicist, 1967; New Literary Writer, 1969. Membership: Opinion Cultural Association. Address: Lagja: Pavarsia, ish Kombinati i Konservave, Vlore, Albania.

SINCLAIR Andrew Annandale, b. 21 Jan 1935, Oxford, England. Writer; Historian. m. Sonia Melchett, 25 July 1984, 2 sons. Education: Major Scholar, BA, PhD, Trinity College, Cambridge, 1955-59; Harkness Fellow, Harvard University, 1955-59; American Council of Learned Societies Fellow, Stanford University, 1964-65. Appointments: Founding Fellow, Churchill College, 1961-63; Lecturer, University College, London, 1966-68; Publisher, Lorrimer Publishing, 1968-89. Publications: The Breaking of Bumbo, 1959; My Friend Judas, 1959; Prohibition: The Era of Excess, 1961; Gog, 1967; Magog, 1972; Jack: A Biography of Jack London, 1977; The Other Victoria, 1981; King Ludd, 1988; War Like a Wasp, 1989; The War Decade: An Anthology of the 1940's, 1989; The Need to Give, 1990; The Far Corners of the Earth, 1991; The Naked Savage, 1991; The Strength of the Hills, 1991; The Sword and the Grail, 1992; Francis Bacon: His Life and Violent Times, 1993; In Love and Anger, 1994; Jerusalem: The Endless Crusade, 1995; Arts and Cultures: The History of the 50 Years of the Arts Council of Great Britain, 1995; The Discovery of the Grail, 1998; Death by Fame: A Life of Elisabeth, Empress of Austria, 1998; Guevara, 1998; Dylan the Bard: A Life of Dylan Thomas, 1999; The Garden of Paradise, 1999. Contributions to: Sunday Times; Times; New York Times; Atlantic Monthly. Honours: Somerset Maugham Prize, 1967; Venice Film Festival Award, 1971. Memberships: Royal Literary Society, fellow, 1968; Society of American Historians, fellow 1970. Address: Flat 20, Millennium House, 132 Grosvenor Road, London SW1V 3JY, England.

SINCLAIR Iain Macgregor, b. 11 June 1943, Cardiff, Wales. Poet; Writer. m. Anna Hadman, 4 Mar 1967, 1 son, 2 daughters. Education: Trinity College, Dublin; Courtauld Institute, London. Publications: Poetry: Back Garden Poems, 1970; Muscat's Würm, 1972; The Birth Rug, 1973; Lud Heat, 1975; Brown Clouds, 1977; Suicide Bridge, 1979; Fluxions, 1983; Fresh Eggs and Scalp Metal, 1983; Autistic Poses, 1985; Significant Wreckage, 1988; Selected Poems, 1970-87, 1989; Jack Elam's Other Eye, 1992. Fiction: White Chappell, Scarlet Tracings, 1987; Downriver, 1991; Radon Daughters, 1994; Slow Chocolate Autopsy, 1997. Essays: Lights Out

for the Territory, 1997. Address: 28 Albion Drive, London E8 4ET, England.

SINCLAIR Olga Ellen, (Ellen Clare, Olga Daniels), b. 23 Jan 1923, Norfolk, England. Writer. m. Stanley George Sinclair, 1 Apr 1945, 3 sons. Publications: Gypsies, 1967; Hearts By the Tower, 1968; Bitter Sweet Summer, 1970; Dancing in Britain, 1970; Children's Games, 1972; Toys, 1974; My Dear Fugitive, 1976; Never Fall in Love, 1977; Master of Melthorpe, 1979; Gypsy Girl, 1981; Ripening Vine, 1981; When Wherries Sailed By, 1987; Gretna Green: A Romantic History, 1989; as Olga Daniels: Lord of Leet Castle, 1984; The Gretna Bride, 1995; The Bride From Faraway, 1987; The Untamed Bride, 1988; The Arrogant Cavalier, 1991. Memberships; Society of Authors; Romantic Novelists Association; Society of Women and Journalists; Norwich Writer's Circle, president. Address: Dove House Farm, Potter Heigham, Norfolk NR29 5LJ, England.

SINCLAIR Sonia Elizabeth, (Sonia Graham, Sonia Melchett), b. 6 Sept 1928, Nainital, India. Writer. m. (1) Julian Mond (Lord Melchett), dec June 1973, 1 son, 2 daughters, (2) Andrew Sinclair, 1984. Education: Queen's Secretarial College, Windsor, England. Appointments: Writer, Member of Board of Directors, English Stage Company. Publications: (as Sonia Graham) Tell Me Honestly (non-fiction), 1964; (as Sonia Melchett) Someone is Missing (non-fiction), 1987; (as Sonia Melchett) Passionate Quests - Five Contemporary Women Travellers, 1989; Sons and Mothers (edited by Matthew and Victoria Glendinning), 1996. Contributions to: Periodicals. Honour: Prizewinner, Short Story Competition, Raconteur Magazine. Address: Flat 20, Millennium House, 132 Grosvenor Road, London SW1V 3JY, England.

SINDEN Donald (Sir), b. 9 Oct 1923, Plymouth, Devon, England. Actor; Writer. m. Diana Mahony, 1948, 2 sons. Appointments: Professional Actor, 1942-; Films for the Rank Organisation, 1952-60; Associate Artist, Royal Shakespeare Company, 1967-. Publications: A Touch of the Memoirs, 1982; Laughter in the Second Act, 1985; Everyman Book of Theatrical Anecdotes (editor), 1987; The English Country Church, 1988; The Last Word (editor), 1994. Honour: Commander of the Order of the British Empire, 1979; Knighted, 1997. Memberships: Council of British Actors Equity, 1966-77, trustee, 1988-; Arts Council, Drama Panel, 1973-77, Advisory Board, 1982-86 Federation of Playgoers' Societies, president, 1968-93; Royal Theatrical Fund, president, 1983-; Royal Society of Arts, fellow, 1966-; Green Room Benevolent Fund, president, 1998-. Address: 1 Hogarth Hill, London NW11 6AY, England.

SINGER June Flaum, b. 17 Jan 1932, Jersey City, New Jersey, USA. Writer. m. Joseph Singer, 7 Sep 1950, 1 son, 3 daughters. Education: Ohio State University, Columbus, 1948-50. Publications: The Bluffer's Guide to Interior Decorating, 1972; The Bluffer's Guide to Antiques (US editor), 1972; The Debutantes, 1981; Star Dreams, 1982; The Movie Set, 1984; The Markoff Women, 1986; The President's Women, 1988; Sex in the Afternoon, 1990; Till the End of Time, 1991; Brilliant Divorces, 1992. Memberships: Southern California Society of Women Writers; PEN West; Authors Guild. Address: 10661 Lindermere Drive, Bel-Air, CA 90077, USA.

SINGER Marilyn, b. 3 Oct 1948, New York, New York, USA. Children's Writer. m. Steven Aronson, 31 July 1971. Education: BA, Queens College of the City University of New York, 1969; MA, New York University, 1979. Publications: 53 books, including: The Morgans Dream, 1995; A Wasp is not a Bee, 1995; Deal with a Ghost, 1997; Prairie Dogs Kiss and Lobsters Wave, 1998; Good Day, Good Night, 1998; Stay True, 1998. Contributions to: Periodicals. Honours: Several awards for children's books; Nominee, Edgar Award, 1998. Memberships: Authors Guild; PEN American Centre; Society of Children's Book Writers and Illustrators. Address: 42 Berkeley Place, Brooklyn, NY 11217, USA.

SINGER Nicky Margaret, b. 22 July 1956, Chalfont-St-Peter, England. Novelist. m. James King-Smith, 2 sons, 1 daughter. Education: University of Bristol. Appointments: Associate Director of Talks, ICA, 1981-83; Programme Consultant, Enigma Television, 1984-85; Co-Founder, Co-Director, Performing Arts Labs, 1987-96; Presenter, BBC2's Labours of Eve, 1994-95. Publications: Novels: To Still the Child, 1992; To Have and To Hold, 1993; What She Wanted, 1996; My Mother's Daughter, 1998. Non-Fiction: The Tiny Book of Time - Headline, 1999. Contributions to: Printer's Devil; Guardian; Scotsman; Womens Journal. Literary Agent: Lutyens and Rubinstein. Address: 231 Westbourne Park Road, London W11 1EB, England.

SINGER Peter (Albert David), b. 6 July 1946, Melbourne, Victoria, Australia. Professor of Philosophy; Writer. m. Renata Diamond, 16 Dec 1968, 3 daughters. Education: BA, Honours, 1967, MA, 1969, University of Melbourne; BPhil, University College, Oxford, 1971. Appointments: Lecturer in Philosophy, University College, Oxford, 1971-73; Visiting Assistant Professor of Philosophy, New York University, 1973-74; Senior Lecturer in Philosophy, La Trobe University, Bundoora, Victoria, Australia, 1974-76; Professor of Philosophy, Monash University, Clayton, Victoria, 1977-79; Director, 1983-91, Deputy Director, 1992-98, Centre for Human Bioethics, Clayton, Australia; Co-Editor, Bioethics, 1986-; DeCary Professor of Bioethics, Princeton University, 1999-. Publications: Democracy and Disobedience, 1973; Animal Rights and Human Obligations (editor with Thomas Regan), 1975, 2nd edition, 1989; Animal Liberation: A New Ethics for Our Treatment of Animals, 1975, 2nd edition, 1990; Practical Ethics, 1979, 2nd edition, 1993; Marx, 1980; The Expanding Circle: Ethics and Sociobiology, 1981; Test-Tube Babies (editor with William Walters), 1982; Hegel, 1983; The Reproduction Revolution: New Ways of Making Babies (with Deane Wells), 1984, 2nd edition as Making Babies: The New Science and Ethics of Conception, 1985; In Defence of Animals (editor), 1985; Should the Baby Live?: The Problem of Handicapped Infants (with Helga Kuhse), 1985; Applied Ethics (editor), 1986; Animal Liberation: A Graphic Guide (with Lori Gruen), 1987; Animal Factories (with Jim Mason), 1990; Embryo Experimentation (editor), 1990; Companion to Ethics (editor), 1991; How Are We to Live?, 1993; The Great Ape Project: Equality Beyond Humanity (editor with Paola Cavalieri), 1993; Rethinking Life and Death, 1994; Ethics (editor), 1994; The Greens, 1996; Ethics into Action, 1998; A Companion to Bioethics (with Helga Kuhse), 1998. Contributions to: Philosophy journals. Address: University Center for Human Values, Princeton University, Princeton, NJ 08544, USA.

SINGER Sarah Beth, b. 4 July 1915, Brooklyn, New York, USA. Poet; Writer. m. Leon E Singer, 23 Nov 1938, 1 son, 1 daughter. Education: BA, New York University, 1934; Graduate Studies, New School for Social Research, New York City, 1960-64. Appointments: Teacher, poetry seminars and workshops, 1968-74, 1981-83; Consulting Editor, Poet Lore, 1976-81. Publications: After the Beginning, 1975; Of Love and Shoes, 1987; The Gathering, 1992; Filtered Images (anthology), 1992. Contributions to: Anthologies, newspapers and journals. Honours: Stephen Vincent Benét Narrative Poetry Awards, 1968, 1971; 5 Poetry Society of America Awards, 1972-76; National League of American Penwomen Awards, 1976-92; Washington Poets Association Award, 1989; Haiku Award, Brussels Sprouts, 1992. Memberships: National League of American Penwomen; Poetry Society of America, vice-president, 1974-78. Address: 2360 43rd Avenue East, Seattle, WA 98112, USA.

SINGH Amritjit, b. 20 Oct 1945, Rawalpindi, India. Professor of English; Writer; Translator; Editor. m. Prem Singh, 24 Mar 1968, 1 son, 1 daughter. Education: BA, Panjab University, 1963; MA, Kurukshetra University, 1965; PhD, New York University, 1973. Appointments: Professor of English, University of Delhi, 1965-68; City University of New York, 1970-71, 1973-74; New York University, 1972-73; Hofstra University, 1984-86; Rhode Island College, 1986-. Publications: The Novels of the

Harlem Renaissance, 1976; India: An Anthology of Contemporary Writing, 1983; The Magic Circle of Henry James, 1989; The Harlem Renaissance: Revaluations, 1989; Memory, Narrative and Identity, 1994; Conversations with Ralph Ellison, 1995; Conversations with Ishmael Reed, 1995; Memory and Cultural Politics, 1996. Contributions to: Numerous essays and reviews in American Literature, Indian Literature and African American Studies. Honours: Fulbright Fellowship, 1968-69; National Endowment for the Humanities Fellowship, 1991-92. Memberships: Melus, President, 1994-97; Modern Language Association. Address: Department of English, Rhode Island College, Providence, RI 02908, USA.

SINGH Charu Steel, b. 15 May 1955, Uttar Pradesh, India. University Reader; Writer; Poet. m. Maya Singh, 6 June 1987, 1 son. Education: BA, 1974; MA, 1976; PhD, 1978. Appointments: MBS College, Gangapur, 1977-79; Lecturer, 1979-91, Reader, 1991-, Kashi Vidyapith University. Publications: Some 17 works, including 5 volumes of poems. Contributions to: Reviews, quarterlies, and journals. Honours: University grants; British Council Fellowship, 1982-83; Indian Institute of Advanced Study Fellowships, 1993, 1996-97. Memberships: American Studies Research Centre; Indian PEN. Address: 36-20/A-36, Brahmanand Nagar, Ext 1, Durga Kund, Varanasi 221 005, India.

SINGH Ram Krishna, b. 31 Dec 1950, Varanasi, India. Teacher; Writer; Poet; Editor. m. Durga Bulli, 1 Mar 1978, 1 son, 1 daughter. Education: BA, University of Gorakhpur, 1970; MA, Banaras Hindu University, 1972; PhD, English, Kashi Vidyapith, 1981. Appointments: Journalist, Press Trust of India, 1973-74; Lecturer, Royal Bhutan Polytechnic, 1974-76; Faculty, Indian School of Mines, Dhanbad, 1976-; Guest Editor, Language Forum, 1986, 1995, 1998, Creative Forum, 1993, 1998; Advisory Board, International Journal of Translation, 1992-, Portrait, 1992-; Co-Editor, Creative Forum, 1987-91; General Editor, Creative Forum New Poets' Series, 1992-; Editorial Associate, Indian Book Chronicle, 1992-; Associate Editor, Young Poets, 1994-; Member Editorial Board, Indian Journal of Applied Linguistics, 1994-, International Journal of Translation, 1992-; Indian Editor, The Hearts of the Handmaidens, 1995-; Indian Editor, SLUGfest, 1997-; Guest Editor, Creative Forum, 1998. Publications: Savitri: A Spiritual Epic, 1984; Krishna Srinivas: The Poet of Inner Aspiration, 1984; My Silence, 1985; Using Contemporary English Idioms, 1985-86; Sound and Silence (editor), 1986; Indian English Writing, 1981-1985 (editor), 1987; Using English in Science and Technology, 1988; Memories Unmemoried, 1988; Practising English in Science and Technology, 1990; Flight of Phoenix, 1990; Music Must Sound, 1990; Recent Indian English Poets: Expressions and Beliefs (editor), 1992; I Do Not Question, 1994; My Silence and Other Selected Poems, 1996; General English Practice, 1995; Writing Your Thesis and Research Papers, 1996; Anger in Action: Explorations of Anger in Indian English Writing (editor), 1997; Above the Earth's Green, 1997; The Psychic Knot: Search for Tolerance in Indian English Fiction (editor), 1998; New Zealand Literature: Recent Trends (editor), 1998; Every Stone Drop Pebble, 1999. Contributions to: Various publications. Honours: Honorary DLitt, World Academy of Arts and Culture, 1984; Eminent Poet and Fellowship, International Poets Academy, Madras, 1987; Certificates of Excellence, International Writers and Artists Association, 1987, 1988; Michael Madhusudan Award, Michael Madhusudan Academy, Calcutta, 1994; Poet of the Year Award, Canadian Alumni of the World University, Ontario, Canada, 1996. Memberships: International Association of Teachers of English as a Foreign Language; International Poets Academy, Madras; International Writers and Artists Association; PEN, Bombay; World Poetry Society; Society of International Development, Rome; World Cultural Council Circle of Friends, Mexico, honorary member; Dhanbad Development Forum, honorary secretary, 1992-. Address: Type VI/u Indian School of Mines, Dhanbad 826004, India.

SINGH Simon Lehna, b. 19 Sept 1964, Wellington, Somerset, England. Writer. Education: BSc, Imperial College; PhD, Cambridge University. Publication: Fermat's Last Theorem, 1997. Literary Agent: Patrick Walsh. Address: c/o Christopher Little Literary Agency, 10 Eel Brook Studios, 125 Moore Park Road, London SW6 4PS, England.

SIPHERD Ray, b. 27 Aug 1935, Uniontown, Pennsylvania, USA. Writer. m. Anne Marie Foran, 4 Oct 1986. Education: BA, Yale University, 1957. Publications; The White Kite, 1972; Ernie and Bert's Telephone Call, 1978; The Count's Poem, 1979; Down on the Farm with Grover, 1980; Sherlock Hemlock and the Outer Space Creatures, 1981; Big Bird's Animal Alphabet, 1987; When is My Birthday?, 1988; The Courtship of Peggy McCoy, 1990; The Christmas Store, 1993; Dance of the Scarecrows, 1996; The Audubon Quartet, 1998. Honours: Emmy Awards, 1969, 1974, 1985. Memberships: American Society of Composers, Authors and Publishers; Writers Guild of America. Address: c/o Carlisle and Company, 24 East 67th Street, New York, NY 10021, USA.

SIROF Harriet Toby, b. 18 Oct 1930, New York, New York, USA. Writer; Teacher. m. 18 June 1949, 1 son, 1 daughter. Education: BA, New School for Social Research, New York City, 1962. Publications: A New-Fashioned Love Story, 1977; The IF Machine, 1978; The Junior Encyclopedia of Israel, 1980; Save the Dam!, 1981; That Certain Smile, 1981; The Real World, 1985; Anything You Can Do, 1986; Because She's My Friend, 1993; The Road Back: Living With a Physical Disability, 1993; Bring Back Yesterday, 1996. Contributions to: Colorado Review; Descent; Inlet; Maine Review; North American Review; New Orleans Review; Sam Houston Review; San Jose Studies; Woman; Voices of Brooklyn. Honour: Junior Literary Guild Selection, 1985. Memberships: Authors Guild; Society of Children's Book Writers. Address: 792 East 21st Street, Brooklyn, NY 11210, USA.

SISLER Harry Hall, b. 13 Mar 1917, Ironton, Ohio, USA. Chemist; Educator; Dean Emeritus; Writer Poet. m. (1) Helen E Shaver, 29 June 1940, 2 sons, 2 daughters, (2) Hannelore L Wass, 13 Apr 1978. Education: BSc, Honours, Ohio State University, 1936; MSc, Chemistry, 1937; PhD, 1939, University of Illinois. Appointments: Editor, Reinhold Publication Corp, 1958-78; Consulting Editor, Dowden, Hutchinson and Ross, 1971-78; Assistant to the Editor, Death Studies, 1978-. Publications: Chemistry in Non-Aqueous Solvents, 1961; Electronic Structure, Properties and the Periodic Law, 1963; The Chloramination Reaction, 1977; Chemistry: A Systematic Approach, 1980. Poetry: Starlight, 1976; Of Outer and Inner Space, 1980; Earth, Air, Fire and Water, 1989; Autumn Harvest, 1996; Numerous others. Contributions to: Over 200 articles in major scientific and scholarly journals. Address: 6014 North West 54th Way, Gainesville, FL 32653, USA.

SISSON C(harles) H(ubert), b. 22 Apr 1914, Bristol, England. Poet; Writer; Translator; Editor; Retired Civil Servant. m. Nora Gilbertson, 19 Aug 1937, 2 daughters. Education: BA, 1st Class Honours, University of Bristol, 1934; Postgraduate studies, University of Berlin and Freiburg, 1934-35, Sorbonne, University of Paris, 1935-36. Appointments: Assistant Principal, 1936-42, Principal, 1945-53, Assistant Secretary, 1953-62, Undersecretary, 1962-68, Assistant Undersecretary of State, 1968-71, Director of Occupational Safety and Health, 1971-73, Ministry of Labour. Publications: Poetry: Poems, 1959; Twenty-One Poems, 1960; The London Zoo, 1961; Numbers, 1965; The Discarnation: Or, How the Flesh Became Word and Dwelt Among Us, 1967; Metamorphoses, 1968; Roman Poems, 1968; In the Trojan Ditch: Collected Poems and Selected Translations, 1974; The Corrider, 1975; Anchises, 1976; Exactions, 1980; Selected Poems, 1981; Night Thoughts and Other Poems, 1983; Collected Poems, 1943-1983, 1984; God Bless Karl Marx!, 1987; Antidotes, 1991; Nine Sonnets, 1991; The Pattern, 1993; What and Who, 1994: Novels: An Asiatic Romance, 1953; Christopher Homm, 1965. Non-Fiction: The Spirit of British Administration and Some European Comparisons, 1959, 2nd edition, 1966; Art and Action (essays), 1965; Essays, 1967; English Poetry 1900-1950: An Assessment, 1971; The Case of Walter Baghot, 1972; David Hume, 1976; The English Sermon: An Anthology, Vol 2, 1976; The Avoidance of Literature: Collected Essays, 1978; Anglican Essays, 1983; The Poet and the Translator, 1985; On the Look-Out: A Partial Autobiography, 1989; In Two Minds: Guesses at Other Writers, 1990; English Perspectives: Essays on Liberty and Government, 1992; Is There a Church of England?, 1993. Translator: Versions and Perversions of Heine, 1955; The Poetry of Catullus, 1966; The Poetic Art: A Translation of Horace's "Ars Poetica", 1975; Lucretius: De Rerum Natura: The Poem on Nature, 1976; Jean de La Fontaine: Some Tales, 1979; Dante Alighieri: The Divine Comedy, 1981; The Song of Roland, 1983; Joachim du Bellay: The Regrets, 1984; Virgil: The Aeneid, 1986; Jean Racine: Britannicus, Phaedra, Athaliah, 1987. Editor: David Wright: South African Album, 1976; Jonathan Swift: Selected Poems, 1977; Thomas Hardy: Jude the Obscure, 1979; Philip Mairet: Autobiographical and Other Papers, 1981; Christina Rossetti: Selected Poems, 1984; Jeremy Taylor: Selected Writings, 1990; Collected Poems, 1998. Contributions to: Agenda; London Magazine; London Review of Books; New Criterion; New York Times Review of Books; Poetry Nation Review; Spectator; Times Literary Supplement. Honours: Senior Simon Research Fellow, University of Manchester; Fellow, Royal Society of London, 1975; Honorary DLitt, University of Bristol, 1980; Companion of Honour, 1993. Address: Moorfield Cottage, The Hill, Langport, Somerset TA10 9PU, England.

SISSON Marilyn, (Marilyn Kirby), b. 15 Dec 1947, Paris, Illinois, USA. Freelance Writer. m. Robert F Sisson, 31 Dec 1971. Publications: Listen, 1996; The Voice, 1997; Haunting Photograph, 1998; Little Boy's Pain, 1998; Elusive Idea Seed, 1998. Contributions to: Tucumcari Literary Review. Honour: Editor's Choice Awards, 1996, 1997. Address: 630 Vance Avenue, PO Box 152, Paris, IL 61944, USA.

SISSON Rosemary Anne, b. 13 Oct 1923, London, England. Writer. Education: BA, Honours, University College, London; MLit, Newnham College, Cambridge. Appointments: Junior Lecturer, University of Wisconsin, 1949-50; Lecturer, University College, London, 1950-53, University of Birmingham, 1953-54; Drama Critic, Stratford-upon-Avon Herald, 1954-57; Trustee, Theatre of Comedy, 1986-. Publications: The Exciseman, 1972; The Killer of Horseman's Flats, 1973; The Stratford Story, 1975; Escape From the Dark, 1976; The Queen and the Welshman, 1979; The Manions of America, 1981; Bury Love Deep, 1985; Beneath the Visiting Moon, 1986; The Bretts, 1987; The Young Indiana Jones Chronicles, 1993-; Rosemary for Remembrance, 1995. Contributions to: Newspapers and journals. Honour: Laurel Award, Writers Guild of Great Britain. Memberships: Dramatists Club, honorary secretary; Writers Guild of Great Britain, president; British Academy of Film and Television Arts, council member. Address: 167 New King's Road, Parson's Green, London SW6, England.

SIZER John, b. 14 Sept 1938, Grimsby, England. Educator; Writer. m. Valerie Claire Davies, 3 sons. Education: BA, University of Nottingham, 1964; DLitt, Loughborough University of Technology, 1989. Appointments: Lecturer, University of Edinburgh, 1965; Senior Lecturer, London Graduate School of Business Studies, 1968; Professor of Financial Management, 1970-96, Founder and Head, Department of Management Studies, 1971-84, Dean, School of Human and Environmental Studies, 1973-76, Senior Pro Vice-Chancellor, 1980-82, Director, School of Business, 1991-92, Visiting Professor, 1996-, Loughborough University of Technology; Chief Executive, Scottish Higher Education Funding Council, 1992-; Chief Executive, Scottish Further Education Funding Council, 1999-. Publications: An Insight into Management Accounting, 1969, 3rd edition, 1989; Case Studies in Management Accounting, 1974; Perspectives in Management Accounting, 1981; Resources and Higher

Education (co-editor), 1983; A Casebook of British Management Accounting (co-author), 2 volumes, 1984, 1985; Institutional Responses to Financial Reductions in the University Sector, 1987. Contributions to: Many professional journals. Honour: Commander of the Order of the British Empire, 1989. Memberships: Accounting Standards Board; Institute of Management, fellow; Royal Society of Arts, fellow; Society for Research into Higher Education, chairman, 1992-93, vice president, 1995-. Address: c/o Scottish Higher Education Funding Council, Donaldson House, 97 Haymarket Terrace, Edinburgh EH12 5HD, Scotland.

SKAILIS, See: VITE Andrejs.

SKELLINGS Edmund, b. 12 Mar 1932, Ludlow, Massachusetts, USA. Professor; Director. m. Louise Skellings, 6 Aug 1962, 1 daughter. Education: BA, English, University of Massachusetts, 1957; PhD, English, University of Iowa, 1962. Appointments: Poet Laureate of Florida, 1980-; Director, Florida Center for Electronic Communication at Florida Atlantic. Publications: Duels and Duets, 1960; Heart Attacks, 1976; Face Value, 1977; Showing My Age, 1978; Living Proof, 1985; Collected Poems 1958-1998, 1998. Honours: Florida Governor's Award in the Arts, 1979; Honorary Doctor of Fine Arts, International Fine Arts College, 1995; Florida Arts Recognition Award, 1997. Address: 220 South East 2nd Avenue, Fort Lauderdale, FL 33301, USA.

SKINNER Ainslie. See: GOSLING-HARE Paula Louise.

SKOCPOL Theda, b. 4 May 1947, Detroit, Michigan, USA. Professor of Government and Sociology; Writer. m. William John Skocpol, 10 June 1967, 1 son. Education: BA, Sociology, Michigan State University, 1969; MA, 1972, PhD, 1975, Sociology, Harvard University. Appointments: Assistant Professor, 1975-78, Associate Professor, 1978-81, of Sociology, Professor of Government and Sociology, 1986-, Harvard University; Member, Institute for Advanced Study, Princeton, New Jersey, 1980-81; Associate Professor, 1981-84, Professor, 1984-86, of Sociology and Political Science, University of Chicago; Senior Visiting Scholar, Russell Sage Foundation, 1983-84. Publications: States and Social Revolutions: A Comparative Analysis of France, Russia, and China, 1979; Protecting Soldiers and Mothers: The Political Origins of Social Policy in the United States, 1992; Social Revolutions in the Modern World, 1994; Social Policy in the United States: Future Possibilities in Historical Perspective, 1995; State and Party in America's New Deal, 1995; Boomerang: Clinton's Health Security Effort and the Turn Against Government in US Politics, 1996. Editor: Vision and Method in Historical Sociology, 1984; Bringing the State Back In (with Peter Evans and Dietrich Rueschemeyer), 1985; The Politics of Social Policy in the United States (with Margaret Weir and Ann Shola Orloff), 1988; American Society and Politics: Institutional, Historical, and Theoretical Perspectives (with John L Campbell), 1994; States, Social Knowledge, and the Origins of Modern Social Policies (with Dietrich Rueschemeyer), 1996; The New Majority: Toward a Popular Progressive Politics (with Stanley B Greenberg), 1997; Democracy, Revolution, and History, 1998; Civic Engagement in American Democracy (with Morris Fiorina), 1999. Contributions to: Scholarly books and journals. Honours: Award for a Distinguished Contribution to Scholarship, 1980, Theory Prize, 1986, American Sociological Association; Guggenheim Fellowship, 1990; Woodrow Wilson Foundation Award, 1993; J David Greenstone Award, 1993, American Political Science Association; Best Book Award, American Sociological Association, 1993; Allan Sharlin Memorial Award, Social Science History Association, 1993; John D and Catharine T MacArthur Foundation Grant, 1997-98; Pew Charitable Trusts Grant, 1997-99. Memberships: American Academy of Arts and Sciences, fellow; American Political Science Association; American Sociological Association; National Academy of Social Insurance; Organization of American Historians; Social Science History Association, president,

1996; Sociological Research Association. Address: c/o Department of Sociology and Department of Government, Harvard University, Cambridge, MA 02138, USA.

SKRZYNECKI Peter, b. 6 Apr 1945, Imhert, Germany (Australian citizen). Poet; Writer; Lecturer. m. Kate Magrath, 1 son, 2 daughters. Education: University of Sydney. Appointment: Lecturer, University of Western Sydney, 1987. Publications: Poetry: There, Behind the Lids, 1970; Headwaters, 1972; Immigrant Chronicle, 1975; The Aviary: Poems, 1975-77; The Polish Immigrant, 1982; Night Swim, 1989. Fiction: The Wild Dogs; The Beloved Mountain, 1988. Other: Joseph's Coat: An Anthology of Multicultural Writing, 1985. Honour: Captain Cook Bicentenary Award, 1970. Address: 6 Sybil Street, Eastwood, New South Wales, 2122, Australia.

SKUNCKE Marie-Christine, b. 20 Jan 1951, Paris, France. Associate Professor (Docent) in Comparative Literature; Writer. Education: French Baccalauréat, 1968; Fil Mag, University of Lund, Sweden, 1970; BA, 1973, PhD, 1980, University of Cambridge. Appointment: Associate Professor (Docent) in Comparative Literature, University of Uppsala, Sweden. Publications: Sweden and European Drama 1772-1796, 1981; Gustaf III: Det Offentliga Barnet (Gustaf III: A Royal Childhood), 1993; Svenska Operans Födelse (The Birth of Swedish Opera, with Anna Ivarsdotter), 1998. Contributions to: Scholarly and popular articles on Swedish eighteenth century literature and history; Scholarly articles on nineteenth century women writers in Sweden and Poland. Honours: Shortlisted, Swedish August Prize, 1993; Prizes, Swedish Academy, 1994, Royal Swedish Academy of Letters, 1994, Swedish Literary Society of Finland, 1996. Memberships: Swedish Society for Eighteenth-Century Studies, president, 1990-94; International Society for Eighteenth-Century Studies, executive committee, 1995-99. Address: Tegnérgatan 27C, S-752 26 Uppsala, Sweden.

SKURBE, See: VITE Astrida.

ŠKVORECKÝ Josef (Václav), b. 27 Sept 1924, Náchod, Czechoslovakia (Canadian citizen). Professor of English Emeritus; Writer; Dramatist; Poet; Editor; Translator. m. Salivarová Zdenka, 31 Mar 1958. Education: PhD, Charles University, Prague, 1951. Appointments: Editor, Anglo-American Department, Odeon Publishers, Prague, 1953-56, Sixty-Eight Publishers Corp, Toronto, 1972-95; Assistant Editor-in-Chief, World Literature Magazine, Prague, 1956-59; Visiting Lecturer, 1968, 1970, Writer-in-Residence, 1970, Associate Professor, 1971-75, Professor of English, 1975-90, Professor Emeritus, 1990-, University of Toronto. Publications: Fiction: The Cowards, 1958; The End of the Nylon Age, 1967; Miss Silver's Past, 1969; The Tank Corps, 1969; The Miracle Game, 1972; The Swell Season, 1975; The End of Lieutenant Borůvka, 1975; The Engineer of Human Souls, 1977; The Return of Lieutenant Borůvka, 1980; Dvořák in Love, 1986; The Bride From Texas, 1992. Short Stories: 8 collections, 1964-95. Plays: The New Men and Women, 1977; God in Your House, 1980. Poetry: Do Not Despair, 1979; The Girl From Chicago, 1980. Other: Reading Detective Stories, 1965; They-Which Is We, 1968; A Tall Tale About America, 1970; All the Bright Young Men and Women, 1972; Working Overtime, 1979; Jiri Menzel and the History of the Closely Watched Trains, 1982; Talkin' Moscow Blues, 1988; Headed for the Blues (memoir), 1996. Contributions to: Numerous publications. Honours: Various honorary doctorates; Neutstadt International Prize for Literature, 1980; Guggenheim Fellowship, 1980; Fellow, Royal Society of Canada, 1984; Governor-General's Award for Fiction, 1984; City of Toronto Book Award, 1985; Echoing Green Foundation Literature Award, 1990; Member of the Order of Canada, 1992. Memberships: Authors League of America; Crime Writers of Canada; Czechoslovak Society of Arts and Sciences, honorary member; International PEN Club; Mystery Writers of America; Writers' Union of Canada.

Address: 487 Sackville Street, Toronto, Ontario M4X 1T6, Canada.

SLADE Quilla. See: LEWIS-SMITH Anne Elizabeth.

SLATTA Richard W(ayne), b. 22 Oct 1947, Powers Lake, North Dakota, USA. Professor of History; Writer. m. Maxine P Atkinson, 25 June 1982, 1 son. Education: BA, History, Pacific Lutheran University, Tacoma, Washington, 1969; MA, History, Portland State University, Oregon, 1974; PhD, History, University of Texas at Austin, 1980. Appointments: Visiting Researcher, Instituto Torcuato di Tella, Buenos Aires, 1977-78; Visiting Instructor, University of Colorado at Boulder, 1979-80; Assistant Professor, 1980-85, Associate Professor, 1985-90, Professor of History, 1990-, North Carolina State University; Staff Writer, Cowboys and Indians magazine, 1994-, Persimmon Hill magazine, 1994-. Publications: Gauchos and the Vanishing Frontier, 1983; Bandidos: The Varieties of Latin American Banditry (editor and contributor), 1987; Cowboys of the Americas, 1990; The Cowboy Encyclopedia, 1994; Comparing Cowboys and Frontiers, 1997. Contributions to: Scholarly and general publications. Honours: Hubert Herring Book Prize, Pacific Coast Council on Latin American Studies, 1984; Western Heritage Award for Non-Fiction Literature, National Cowboy Hall of Fame, 1991; Best Reference Source Citation, Library Journal, 1992; Outstanding Reference Source Citation, American Library Association, 1995. Memberships: American Historical Association; Conference on Latin American History; Western History Association; Western Writers of America. Address: c/o Department of History, North Carolina State University, Raleigh, NC 27695, USA.

SLAVITT David R(ytman), (David Benjamin, Henry Lazarus, Lynn Meyer, Henry Sutton), b. 23 Mar 1935, White Plains, New York, USA. Novelist; Poet; Translator; Lecturer. m. (1) Lynn Nita Meyer, 27 Aug 1956, div 1977, 2 sons, 1 daughter, (2) Janet Lee Abrahm, 16 Apr 1978. Education: BA, magna cum laude, Yale University, 1956; MA, Columbia University, 1957. Appointments: Instructor in English, Georgia Institute of Technology, Atlanta, 1957-58; Staff, Newsweek magazine, 1958-65; Assistant Professor, University of Maryland, College Park, 1977; Associate Professor of English, Temple University, Philadelphia, 1978-80; Lecturer in English, Columbia University, 1985-86; Lecturer, Rutgers University, 1987-; Lecturer in English and Classics, University of Pennsylvania, 1991-97; Visiting Professorships; Many university and college poetry readings. Publications: Novels: Rochelle, or Virtue Rewarded, 1966; Anagrams, 1970; ABCD, 1972; The Outer Mongolian, 1973; The Killing of the King, 1974; King of Hearts, 1976; Jo Stern, 1978; Cold Comfort, 1980; Alice at 80, 1984; The Agent, 1986; The Hussar, 1987; Salazar Blinks, 1988; Lives of the Saints, 1989; Turkish Delights, 1993; The Cliff, 1994; Get Thee to a Nunnery: Two Divertimentos from Shakespeare, 1999. Henry Sutton: The Exhibitionist, 1967; The Voyeur, 1969; Vector, 1970; The Liberated, 1973; The Sacrifice: A Novel of the Occult, 1978; The Proposal, 1980. As Lynn Meyer: Paperback Thriller, 1975. As Henry Lazarus: That Golden Woman, 1976. As David Benjamin: The Idol, 1979. Non-Fiction: Understanding Social Life: An Introduction to Social Psychology (with Paul F Secord and Carl W Backman), 1976; Physicians Observed, 1987; Virgil, 1991; The Persians of Aeschylus, 1998; Three Amusements of Ausonius, 1998; Re-Verse: Essays on Poets and Poetry, forthcoming. Other: Editor: Adrien Stoutenburg: Land of Superior Mirages: New and Selected Poems, 1986; Short Stories Are Not Real Life: Short Fiction, 1991; Crossroads, 1994; A Gift, 1996; Epigram and Epic: Two Elizabethan Entertainments, 1997; A New Pleade: Seven American Poets, 1998. Translator: The Eclogues of Virgil, 1971; The Eclogues and the Georgics of Virgil, 1972; The Tristia of Ovid, 1985; Ovid's Poetry of Exile, 1990; Seneca: The Tragedies, 1992; The Fables of Avianus, 1993; The Metamorphoses of Ovid, 1994; The Twelve Minor Prophets, 1999; The Voyage of the Argo of Valerius Flaccus, 1999. Contributions to: Various other books as well as periodicals. Honours: Pennsylvania

Council on the Arts Award, 1985; National Endowment for the Arts Fellowship, 1988; American Academy and Institute of Arts and Letters Award, 1989; Rockefeller Foundation Artist's Residence, 1989. Address: 523 South 41st Street, Philadelphia, PA 19104, USA.

SLIDE Anthony Clifford, b. 7 Nov 1944, Birmingham, England. Film Historian; Archivist; Writer. Appointments: Editor, Filmmakers, 1982-; Book Reviewer, Classic Images, 1989-. Publications: Early American Cinema, 1970; Early Women Directors, 1977; The Vaudevillians, 1981; The American Film Industry: A Historical Dictionary, 1986; The Big V: A History of the Vitagraph Company, 1987; Silent Portrait, 1990; Nitrate Won't Wait: A History of Film Preservation in the United States, 1992; Before Video: A History of the Non-Theatrical Film, 1992; Gay and Lesbian Characters and Themes in Mystery Novels, 1993; The Encyclopedia of Vaudeville, 1994; The New Historical Dictionary of the American Film Industry, 1998; Banned in the USA: British Films in the United States and Their Censorship 1933-1960. Contributions to: Periodicals. Honours: Outstanding Reference of the Year Citations, American Library Association, 1987, 1994; Honorary DLitt, Bowling Green University, 1990. Address: 4118 Rhodes Avenue, Studio City, CA 91604, USA.

SLISANS Antons, b. 28 Dec 1948, Latvia, Abrene, Stableva, Latvia. Agronomist. m. Irena Vizule, 22 June 1974, 1 son, 3 daughters. Education: Upite Elementary School, 1956; Bulduri Horticultural Tech, 1964-68; Latvian Agricultural Academy Agronomic Faculty, 1978-84; Moscow National University, 1974-80. Appointments: Horticulturist, 1968; Military Service, 1970-94; Director, collectiv farm, 1988; Librarian, Skilbenu II Library, 1995; Work in own rustic farm, 1995-; Folklorist; Agriculturist; Teacher. Publications: Saule Izkapts Kata (The Syn on the Handle of Scythe), 1991; Odums Lyzuls, 1991; Raibi Panti (Tabby Poems), 1991; Lyugums Sapneisam (Asking Dream), 1992; Tavaine Muna (My Fatherland), 1992; Par Gadskartu Janits Naca (Every Year with John Comming), 1993; Cik Vezam Krasu (How Much Colour in the Wind), 1994; Zynamos Meiklites (Known Puzzlers), 1995; Lela Cela Malena (At the Road Side), 1995; Serve Jeb Kur Tavi Ideali (Dirt of Where Your Ideals), 1995; Ziemnesi (Couriers of Winter), 1956; Sovu Likteni Izsoput (To Live One's Destiny), 1996; Ar Myuzeibu Sazarunoj (With Eternity Converse), 1997; Rutalu Gods (Play for Year), 1997; No Balviem Uz Balkaniem (From Balvi to Balkani), play, 1998; Upites Abeldarz (Apple Garden for Upite), 1998; Salnas Nenokosts Zieds (The Flower Do Not Freezen From Frost), 1998. Contributions to: Literary journal, Jauniba, 1964-68; Aduguns, local newspaper, 1981; Republic journal, Karogs, 1984; many publications in Latvian magazines. Memberships: Latvian Writer Confederation, 1994-; Latgalian Cultural Association Confederation, 1989; Encyclopedia of Young and Children Writers, 1999. Address: Upite 2-13, Skilbenu Pag, Balvu Raj, LV-4587, Latvia.

SLOAN Carolyn, b. 15 Apr 1937, London, England. Freelance Journalist; Children's Author. m. David Hollis, 15 May 1961, dec, 2 sons. Education: Harrogate College; Tutorial Schools, Newcastle, Guildford. Publications: Carter is a Painter's Cat, 1971; The Penguin and the Vacuum Cleaner, 1974; Shakespeare, Theatre Cat, 1982; Skewer's Garden, 1983; Helen Keller, 1984; An Elephant for Muthu, 1986; The Sea Child, 1987; Don't Go Near the Water, 1988; Gracie, 1994; Incredible Journey, 1996. Contributions to: Newspapers and journals. Membership: Society of Authors. Literary Agent: David Higham. Address: 175 Stoughton Road, Guildford, Surrey GU1 1LQ, England.

SLOMAN Anne, b. 24 Apr 1944, London, England. Journalist. m. Martyn Sloman, 22 Apr 1972, 2 sons. Education: BA, Honours, Politics, Philosophy, and Economics, St Hilda's College, Oxford, 1966. Appointments: Producer, 1967-81, Assistant Editor, Today Programme, 1981-82, Editor, Special Current Affairs, 1983-94, Deputy Head of Weekly Programmes, News and Current Affairs, 1994-96, Chief Political Adviser, BBC, 1996-. Publications: Co-author: British Political Facts 1900-79, 1980; No Minister, 1982; But Chancellor, 1983; With Respect Ambassador, 1985; The Thatcher Phenomenon, 1986. Honours: Broadcasting Awards. Address: c/o BBC, Henry Wood House, 3 and 6 Langham Place, London W1A 1AA, England.

SLOTKIN Richard Sidney, b. 8 Nov 1942, Brooklyn, New York, USA. Professor of English; Writer. m. Iris F Shupack, 23 June 1963, 1 son. Education: BA, Brooklyn College of the City University of New York, 1963; PhD, Brown University, 1967. Appointments: Faculty, 1966-76, Professor of English, 1976-, Chairman, Department of American Studies, 1976-, Olin Professor, 1982-, Wesleyan University. Publications: Regeneration Through Violence: The Mythology of the American Frontier, 1600-1860, 1973; So Dreadful a Judgement: Puritan Responses to King Philip's War, 1675-1677 (with J K Folsom), 1978; The Crater: A Novel of the Civil War, 1980; The Fatal Environment: The Myth of the Frontier in the Age of Industrialization, 1800-1890, 1985; The Return of Henry Starr, 1988; Gunfighter Nation: The Myth of the Frontier in Twentieth Century America, 1992. Contributions to: Professional journals. Honours: Albert J Beveridge Award, American Historical Association, 1973; National Endowment for the Humanities Fellowship, 1973-74; Rockefeller Foundation Fellowship, 1976-77; Little Big Horn Association Award, 1986. Memberships: American Association of University Professors; American Film Institute; American Historical Association; American Studies Association; Authors Guild; Modern Language Association; Organization of American Historians; PEN; Society of American Historians, fellow; Western History Association. Address: c/o Department of English, Wesleyan University, Middletown, CT 06459, USA.

SMALL Michael Ronald, b. 3 Jan 1943, Croydon, Surrey, England. Teacher; Short Story Writer; Poet; Textbook Writer. Education: BA, London University; BEd, La Trobe University, Australia; MA, University of Windsor, Canada. Publications: Her Natural Life and Other Stories, 1988; Film: A Resource Book for Studying Film as Text (with Brian Keyte), 1994; Unleashed: A History of Footscray Football Club (with John Lack, Chris McConville, Damien Wright), 1996; Uraneline: Voices of Carey 1923-1997, 1997 Contributions to: Numerous journals and magazines. Membership: Victorian Fellowship of Australian Writers. Address: 71 Strabane Avenue, Box Hill North, Victoria 3129, Australia.

SMALLEY Stephen Stewart, b. 11 May 1931, London, England. Clerk in Holy Orders. m. Susan Jane Paterson, 13 July 1974, dec 3 Nov 1995. Education: BA, 1955, MA, 1958, PhD, 1979, Jesus College, Cambridge; BD, Eden Theological Seminary, USA, 1957; Deacon, 1958, Priest, 1959, Ridley Hall, Cambridge. Appointments: Assistant Curate, St Paul's, Portman Square, London, 1958-60; Chaplain, Peterhouse, Cambridge, 1960-63, Acting Dean, 1962-63; Lecturer and Senior Lecturer, University of Ibadan, Nigeria, 1963-69; Lecturer and Senior Lecturer, University of Manchester, 1970-77; Warden of St Anselm Hall, 1972-77; Canon Residentiary and Precentor, 1977-86, Vice-Provost, 1986, Coventry Cathedral; Dean, Chester Cathedral, 1987-. Publications: The Spirit's Power, 1972; Christ and Spirit in the New Testament (editor), 1973; John: Evangelist and Interpreter, 1978, second edition, 1998; 1, 2, 3 John, 1984; Thunder and Love: John's Revelation and John's Community, 1994. Contributions to: Learned journals. Honours: Foundation and Lady Kay Scholar, Jesus College, Cambridge, 1948, 1955; Select Preacher, University of Cambridge, 1963-64; Manson Memorial Lecturer, University of Manchester, 1986. Memberships: Archbishops' Doctrine Commission of the Church of England, 1981-86; Studiorum Novi Testamenti Societas; Chester City Club. Address: The Deanery, 7 Abbey Street, Chester CH1 2JF, England.

SMARANDACHE Florentin, b. 10 Dec 1954, Balcesti, Romania. Mathematician; Educator; Writer; Poet. m. Eleonora Niculescu, 28 May 1977, 2 sons. Education: MSc, Mathematics and Computer Science, University of Craiova, 1979; PhD, Mathematics, University of Kishinev, 1997. Publications: Over 40 works, 1981-99. Contributions to: Several publications. Honours: Premiul Special, Concursul National de Proza Scurta Marin Preda, Alexandria, 1982; Prix Special Etranger, Grand Prix de la Ville de Bergerac, France, 1990; Honourable Mention, Le Concours de l'Academie de Lettres et des Arts du Perigord, France, 1990; Honorary DLitt, World Congress of Poets, 1991; Premio della Literature, Goccia di Luna, Italy, 1995. Memberships: International Writers and Artists Association; Modern Language Association; Romanian Writers Association; World Academy of Arts and Culture. Address: University of New Mexico, 200 College Road, Gallup, NM 87301, USA.

SMEDS Dave, b. 23 Feb 1955, Reedley, California, USA. Author. m. Connie Willeford, 26 June 1982, 1 son, 1 daughter. Education: BA, English, Psychology, Sonoma State University. Publications: The Sorcery Within, 1985; The Schemes of Dragons, 1989. Contributions to: Anthologies and magazines. Memberships: Authors Guild; Science Fiction Writers of America. Address: 164 Jack London Drive, Santa Rosa, CA 95409, USA.

SMEED John William, b. 21 Feb 1926, London, England. Emeritus Professor in German. m. Gay Jones, 24 Mar 1952. Education: BA, MA, PhD, University of Wales. Publications: Jean Paul's Dreams, 1966; Faust in Literature, 1975; The Theophrastan Character, 1985; German Song and its Poetry, 1987; Don Juan: Variations on a Theme, 1990; Famous Poets, Neglected Composers, Songs to Lyrics by Goethe, Heine, Mörike and others, 1992. Contributions to: Literary periodicals in England, Germany and USA. Honours: University of Wales Fellowship, 1953; Leverhulme Research Fellowship, 1983. Address: 53 Claypath, Durham DH1 1QS, England.

SMELSER Neil Joseph, b. 22 July 1930, Kahoka, Missouri, USA. Professor of Sociology Emeritus; Writer. m. (1) Helen Thelma Margolis, 10 June 1954, div 1965, 1 son, 1 daughter, (2) Sharin Fateley, 20 Dec 1967, 1 son, 1 daughter. Education: BA, 1952, PhD, 1958, Harvard University; BA, 1954, MA, 1959, Magdalen College, Oxford; Graduate, San Francisco Psychoanalytic Institute, 1971. Appointments: Advisory Editor, American Journal of Sociology, 1960-82; Editor, American Sociological Review, 1962-65, 1989-90; Faculty, 1958-62, Professor of Sociology, 1962-72, University Professor of Sociology, 1972-94, Professor Emeritus, 1994-, University of California at Berkeley; Director, Center for Advanced Study in the Behavioral Sciences, Stanford, 1994-. Publications: Economy and Society (with T Parsons), 1956; Social Change in the Industrial Revolution, 1959; Theory of Collective Behavior, 1962; The Sociology of Economic Life, 1963, 2nd edition, 1975; Essays in Sociological Explanation, 1968; Sociological Theory: A Contemporary View, 1971; Comparative Methods in the Social Sciences, 1976; The Changing Academic Market (with Robin Content), 1980; Sociology, 1981, 5th edition, 1995; Social Paralysis and Social Change, 1991; Effective Committee Service, 1993; Problematics of Sociology, 1997. Editor: Personality and Social Systems (with W T Smelser), 1963, 2nd edition, 1971; Social Structure and Mobility in Economic Development (with S M Lipset), 1966; Sociology: A Survey Report (with James Davis), 1969; Karl Marx on Society and Social Change, 1973; Public Higher Education in California (with Gabriel Almond), 1974; Themes of Work and Love in Adulthood (with Erik Erikson), 1980; The Micro-Macro Link (with others), 1987; Handbook of Sociology, 1988; Social Change and Modernity (with Hans Haferkamp), 1992; Theory of Culture (with Richard Munch), 1992; The Handbook of Economic Sociology (with Richard Swedberg), 1994. Honours: Rhodes Scholar, 1952-54; Junior Fellow, Society of Fellows, Harvard University, 1955-58; Russell Sage Foundation Fellow, 1989-90. Memberships: American Academy of Arts and Sciences, honorary member; American Philosophical Society, honorary member; National Academy of Sciences, honorary member; American Sociological Association, president, 1996-97; International Sociological Association, vice-president, 1990-94; Pacific Sociological Association. Address: 400 El Escarpado, Stanford, CA 94305, USA.

SMILEY Jane (Graves), b. 26 Sept 1949, Los Angeles, California, USA. Writer; Professor. m. (1) John Whiston, 4 Sept 1970, div, (2) William Silag, 1 May 1978, 2 daughters, (3) Stephen Mark Mortensen, 25 July 1987, div, 1 son. Education: BA, Vassar College, 1971; MFA, 1976; MA, 1978, PhD, 1978, University of Iowa. Appointments: Visiting Assistant Professor, University of Iowa, 1981, 1987; Assistant Professor, 1981-84, Associate Professor, 1984-89, Professor, 1989-90, Distinguished Professor, 1992-96, Iowa State University. Publications: Barn Blind, 1980; At Paradise Gate, 1981; Duplicate Keys, 1984; The Age of Grief, 1987; Catskill Crafts: Artisans of the Catskill Mountains, 1987; The Greenlanders, 1988; Ordinary Love and Goodwill, 1989; A Thousand Acres, 1991; Moo: A Novel, 1995; All True Travels and Adventures of Lidie Newton, 1998. Contributions to: Various publications. Honours: Fulbright Grant, 1976-77; National Endowment for the Arts Grants, 1978, 1987; Friends of American Writers Prize, 1981; O Henry Awards, 1982, 1985, 1988; Pulitzer Prize in Fiction, 1992; National Book Critics Circle Award, 1992; Midland Authors Award, 1992; Heartland Prize, 1992. Memberships: Authors Guild; Screenwriters Guild. Address: c/o Department of English, Iowa State University, Ames, IA 50011, USA.

SMIRNOV Igor Pavlovich, b. 19 May 1941, Leningrad, Russia. Professor of Russian Literature. m. Johanna Renate Luise Elisabeth Döring-Smirnov, 16 July 1979. Education: MA, Leningrad State University, 1963; Dr Phil Sci, Institute of Russian Literature, Leningrad, 1967. Appointments: Editorial Board, Elementa, Journal of Slavic Studies and Comparative Cultural Semiotics, Los Angeles, 1992; New Literary Review, Moscow, 1992; Discourse, Moscow, 1998; Co-editor: Die Welt der Slaven, 1995. Professor of Russian Literature, University of Konstanz. Publications: Meaning in Art and the Evolution of Poetic Systems, 1977; The Emergence of the Inter-text, 1985; Towards a Theory of Literature, 1987; Being and Creating, 1990; On Old Russian Culture, Russian National Specificity and the Logic of History, 1991; Psychohistory of Russian Literature from Romanticism Till Now, 1995; Novel of Secrets: "Doctor Zhivago", 1996. Contributions to: Russian Literature; Wiener Slawistischer Almanach; Mesto pechati. Address: Guerickestrasse 35, 80 805 Munich, Germany.

SMITH A(nthony) C(harles) H(ockley), b. 31 Oct 1935, Kew, England. Writer. Education: MA, University of Cambridge. Appointments: Literary Associate, Royal Shakespeare Co, 1964-74; University of Bristol Drama Fellowship, 1976-79; Senior Research Associate, University of Birmingham, 1965-69; Director, Cheltenham Festival of Literature, 1978-79; Chairman, Playwrights Company, 1979-83; Visiting Professor, Emory University, Atlanta, Georgia, 1986, University of Texas, 1990-91, 1994. Publications: The Crowd, 1965; Zero Summer, 1971; Orghast at Persepolis, 1972; Paper Voices, 1975; Treatment, 1976; The Jericho Gun, 1977; Edward and Mrs Simpson, 1978; Extra Cover, 1981; The Dark Crystal, 1982; Wagner, 1983; Sebastian the Navigator, 1985; Lady Jane, 1985; Labyrinth, 1986. 15 plays staged. Contributions to: Newspapers, magazines, and television. Honours: Arts Council Writing Awards, 1970-71, 1974-75, 1980. Membership: Writers' Guild of Great Britain. Address: 21 West Shrubbery, Bristol BS6 6TA, England.

SMITH Angel. See: **MASTERTON Graham.**

SMITH Barbara Herrnstein, b. 6 Aug 1932, New York, New York, USA. Professor of Comparative Literature and English; Writer. m (1) R J Herrnstein, 28 May 1951, div 1961, (2) T H Smith, 21 Feb 1964, div 1974, 2 daughters. Education: BA, 1954, MA, 1955, PhD, English and American Literature, 1965, Brandeis University. Appointments: Faculty, Bennington College, Vermont, 1961-73, University of Pennsylvania, 1973-87; Professor of Comparative Literature and English, Duke University, 1987-; Northrop Frye Chair, University of Toronto, 1990. Publications: Poetic Closure: A Study of How Poems End, 1968; On the Margins of Discourse: The Relation of Literature to Language, 1978; Contingencies of Value: Alternative Perspectives for Critical Theory, 1988; The Politics of Liberal Education (co-editor), 1991; Belief and Resistance: Dynamics of Contemporary Intellectual Controversy, 1997; Mathematics, Science and Postclassical Theory, (co-edited and introduced), 1997. Contributions to: Professional journals. Address: c/o Box 90015, Duke University, Durham, NC 27708, USA.

SMITH Bernard William, b. 3 Oct 1916, Sydney, New South Wales, Australia. Art Historian and Critic. m. (1) Kate Beatrice Hartley Challis, 16 May 1941, 1 son, 1 daughter, (2) Margaret Patricia Thompson, 30 July 1995. Education: BA, University of Sydney, 1952; Warburg Institute, London, England, 1948-50; PhD, Australian National University, 1956. Appointment: Category A Literary Fellowship, Australia Council, 1990-91. Publications: Place, Taste and Tradition, 1945; European Vision and the South Pacific, 1960; Australian Painting, 1962; The Architectural Character of Glebe, Sydney (with K Smith), 1973; Documents on Art and Taste in Australia, 1975; The Boy Adeodatus, 1984; The Art of Captain Cook's Voyages (with R Joppien), 3 volumes, 1985-87; The Death of the Artist as Hero, 1988; The Critic as Advocate, 1989; Imagining the Pacific, 1992; Noel Counitian, 1993; Poems, 1996; Modernism's History, 1998. Contributions to: Journal of the Wartburg and Courtauld Institutes, Modern Painters (London); Meanjin, Scripsi, Australian Society. Honours: Co-Recipient, Ernest Scott Prize for History, Melbourne, 1962; Henry Lawson Prize for Poetry, 1964; Honorary LittD, University of Melbourne, 1976; Honorary LittD, University of Sydney, 1997; Australian National Book Council Prize, Nettie Palmer Prize for Non-Fiction and Talking Book Award, 1984. Memberships: Australian Society of Authors; Australian Academy of the Humanities, president, 1977-80; Australian Humanities Research Council, secretary, 1962-65; Fellow, Society of Antiquaries; UNESCO Committee for Letters, Australia, 1963-69. Address: 168 Nicholson Street, Fitzroy, Victoria 3065, Australia.

SMITH Bradley F, b. 5 Oct 1931, Seattle, Washington, USA. Writer; Teacher. m. 31 Dec 1983, 2 daughters. Education: BA, 1957, MA, 1960, University of California at Berkeley. Publications: Adolf Hitler: His Family, Childhood, and Youth, 1967; Himmler Geheimreden, 1974; Reaching Judgement at Nuremberg, 1977; Operation Sunrise (with Elena Agarossi), 1979; The American Road to Nuremberg, 1981; The Road to Nuremberg, 1981; The Shadow Warriors, 1983; The War's Long Shadow, 1986; The Ultra-Magic Deals and the Special Relationship, 1940-46, 1992; Sharing Secrets with Stalin, Anglo-American Intelligence Cooperation with the USSR 1941-1945, 1996. Contributions to: Newspapers and journals. Honours: Observer Book of the Year, 1977; Short-listed for Los Angeles Times Book of the Year, 1981; Phi Beta Kappa. Membership: Authors Guild. Address: 104 Regents Park Road, London NW1 8UG, England.

SMITH Cecile Norma Musson, (Cecile Norma Musson), b. 13 Aug 1914, Bermuda. Educator; Journalist; Welfare Activist. m. James A C Smith, dec, 23 Nov 1955. Education: University of Cambridge, 1935; Graduate, Ontario Business College; Certificates, Queens University, University of Maryland, Bermuda College. Appointments: Founder, President, Bermuda Writers Club, 1957; Honorary Representative, Centro Studies S Leonardo da Vinci, 1963-80. Publications: Thoughts in Verse, 1937; Acclaimed, 1942; BWC History, 1942; Island Life, 1951; When I Began, 1994. Contributions to: World Fair Anthology of Verse; South and West USA; Bermuda Review; Poetic Voices of America. Honour: CSSI Great Prize, Rome. Memberships: LFABIRA; United Poets Laureate, deputy governor. Address: Cavendish Apt 2, Block 7, Hibiscus, Devonshire DV03, Bermuda.

SMITH C(larice) Holly, b. 12 July 1931, Sydney, New South Wales, Australia. Editor; Writer; Creative Writing Tutor. Education: Teachers Certificate, New South Wales Department of Education, 1954; International Correspondence School courses, Short Story, Radio Playwriting, TV Scriptwriting, Public Relations, 1960-96, Diploma, 1996; Certificate, Advertising Copywriting, 1988; Diploma, Journalism, 1989. Appointments: Own business, Proofreading and Editing Services, 1988-; Planned, wrote, conducted 2 series of radio interviews, Meet the Authors (14 interviews), 1990, 1993; Tutor, The Writing School, 1991-. Publication: The Metric Primer, 1973. Contributions to: Newspapers and journals. Honours: Best Newsletter Award for Editing, Fellowship of Australian Writers, 1993. Memberships: Actors Equity; Fellowship of Australian Writers. Address: 6 Park Avenue, Avalon Beach, New South Wales 2107, Australia.

SMITH Danielle Antoinette Thomas, (Danielle Antoinette Thomas), b. 28 July 1938, Zambia, Africa. Author. m. Wilbur A Smith, 6 Feb 1971, 1 son. Education: BA, Higher Primary Teaching Certificate, University of Cape Town, 1956-58. Career: Taught 10 years, then helped difficult children until 1971; Until wrote first novel helped research husband's books, 25 years. Publications: Novels: Children of darkness, 1992; Voices in the Wind, 1993; Cry of Silence, 1995; Drumbeat, 1997. Contributions: Newspapers, Zambia; Article in My Fair Lady mag, Cape Town. Literary Agent: Charles Pick Consultancy, London, England. Address: Charles Pick Consultancy, 55 Yeomans Row, London SW3 2AL, England.

SMITH Dave, (David Jeddie Smith), b. 19 Dec 1942, Portsmouth, Virginia, USA. Poet; Editor; Professor of English. m. Deloras Smith, 31 Mar 1966, 1 son, 2 daughters. Education: BA, Honours, English, University of Virginia, 1965; MA, English, Southern Illinois University, 1969; PhD, English, Ohio University, 1976. Appointments: Editor, The Back Door: A Poetry Magazine, 1970-78, The Southern Review, 1990-; Instructor in English, Western Michigan University, 1973-74; Assistant Professor of English, Cottey College, 1974-75; Assistant Professor, 1976-79, Associate Professor of English, 1979-81, Director of Creative Writing, 1976-81, University of Utah; Poetry Editor, Rocky Mountain Review, 1978-79, University of Utah Press, 1980-90; Visiting Professor of English, State University of New York at Binghamton, 1980-81; Director of Poetry, Bennington Writers Conference, Vermont, 1980-87; Associate Professor of English and Director of Creative Writing, University of Florida, 1981-82; Professor of English, Virginia Commonwealth University, 1982-90; Professor of English, 1991-97, Hopkins P Breazeale Professor of English, 1997-98, Boyd Professor of English, 1998-, Louisiana State University. Publications: Bull Island, 1970; Mean Rufus Throw Down, 1973; The Fisherman's Whore, 1974; Drunks, 1975; Cumberland Station, 1977; In Dark, Sudden With Light, 1977; Goshawk, Antelope, 1979; Blue Spruce, 1981; Dream Flights, 1981; Homage to Edgar Allan Poe, 1981; Onliness (novel), 1981; The Travelling Photographer, 1981; The Pure Clear Word: Essays on the Poetry of James Wright, 1982; In the House of the Judge, 1983; Southern Delights (stories), 1984; Gray Soldiers, 1984; The Morrow Anthology of Younger American Poets (editor), 1985; The Roundhouse Voices: Selected and New Poems, 1985; Local Assays: On Contemporary American Poetry, 1985; Cuba Night, 1990; The Essential Poe, 1992; Night Pleasures: New and Selected Poems, 1992; Fate's Kite: Poems 1990-1995, 1996; Floating on Solitude: Three Books of Poems, 1997. Contributions to: Anthologies, reviews, and journals. Honours: Brread Loaf Fellow, 1975; National Endowment for the Arts Fellowships, 1976, 1980; American Academy of Arts and Letters Award, 1979; Runner-up, Pulitzer Prizes in Poetry, 1979, 1981; Guggenheim Fellowship, 1981; Ohio University Alumni of the Year, 1985; Lyndhurst Fellowship, 1987-89; Virginia Poetry Prize, 1988. Memberships: Associated Writing Programs; Fellowship of Southern Writers; Modern Language Association; National Book Critics Circle; PEN; Poetry Society of America; Poetry Society of Virginia; Society for the Study of Southern Literature; Southern Modern Language Association. Address: 1430 Knollwood Drive, Baton Rouge, LA 70808, USA.

SMITH David Lawrence, b. 3 Dec 1963, London, England. Lecturer in History. Education: Eastbourne College, 1972-81; Selwyn College, Cambridge, BA 1st Class Hons, 1985, MA, 1989, PhD, 1990. Appointment: Fellow, Selwyn College, Cambridge, 1988-. Publications: Oliver Cromwell, 1991; Louis XIV, 1992; Cambridge Perspectives in History, (co-editor), 1993-; Constitutional Royalism and the Search for Settlement, 1994; The Theatrical City, 1995; A History of the Modern British Isles, 1603-1707: The Double Crown, 1998; New Dictionary of National Biography (associate editor), 1998-. Contributions to: Historical Journal; Historical Research; Journal of British Studies; Transactions of the Royal Historical Society. Honour: Alexander Prize, Royal Historical Society, 1991. Membership: Fellow, Royal Historical Society, 1992; President, Cambridge History Forum, 1997-. Address: Selwyn College, Cambridge CB3 9DQ, England.

SMITH Delia, Cookery Writer and Broadcaster. m. Michael Wynn Jones. Appointments: Several BBC TV Series; Cookery Writer, Evening Standard, later the Standard, 1972-85; Columnist, Radio Times. Publications: How to Cheat at Cooking, 1971; Country Fare, 1973; Recipes from Country Inns and Restaurants, 1973; Family Fare, book 1, 1973, book 2, 1974; Evening Standard Cook Book, 1974; Country Recipes from "Look East", 1975; More Country Recipes from "Look East", 1976; Frugal Food, 1976; Book of Cakes, 1977; Recipes from "Look East", 1977; Food for Our Times, 1978; Cookery Course, part 1, 1978, part 2, 1979, part 3, 1981; The Complete Cookery Course, 1982; A Feast for Lent, 1983; A Feast for Advent, 1983; One is Fun, 1985; Food Aid Cookery Book (editor), 1986; A Journey into God, 1988; Delia Smith's Christmas, 1990; Delia Smith's Summer Collection, 1993; Delia Smith's Winter Collection, 1995; Delia's Red Nose Collection, 1997; How to Cook: Part One, 1998. Contributions to: Consultant Food Editor, Sainsbury's The Magazine. Honours: Andre Simon Memorial Fund Special Award, 1994; Officer of the Order of the British Empire, 1995. Membership: Norwich City Football Club, director. Address: c/o Deborah Owen Ltd, 78 Narrow Street, London E14 8BP.

SMITH Sir Dudley (Gordon), b. 14 Nov 1926, Cambridge, England. Management Consultant; Former Member of Parliament. m. (1), div, 1 son, 2 daughters, (2) Catherine Amos, 1976. Appointments: Journalist and Senior Executive, various provincial and national newspapers, 1943-66; Assistant News Editor, Sunday Express, 1953-59; Member of Parliament, Conservative Party, Brentford and Chiswick, 1959-66, Warwick and Leamington, 1968-97; Management Consultant, 1974-; UK Delegate, Council of Europe and Western European Union, 1979-97; President, Western European Assembly, 1993-96. Publications: They Also Served, 1945; Harold Wilson: A Critical Biography, 1964. Honours: Knighted, 1983; Appointed a Deputy Lieutenant of Warwickshire, 1988; Commander of the Order of Isabela la Católica, Spain, 1994. Address: Church Farm, Weston-under-Wetherley, Near Leamington Spa, Warwickshire CV33 9BY, England.

SMITH Emma, b. 21 Aug 1923, Newquay, Cornwall, England. Writer. m. Richard Llewellyn Stewart-Jones, 31 Jan 1951, dec 1957, 1 son, 1 daughter. Publications: Maiden's Trip, 1948; The Far Cry, 1949; Emily, 1959; Out of Hand, 1963; Emily's Voyage, 1966; No Way of Telling, 1972; The Opportunity of a Lifetime, 1978. Contributions to: Various magazines. Honours: Atlantic Award, 1948; John Llewellyn Rhys Memorial Prize, 1948; James Tait Black Memorial Prize, 1949. Address: c/o Curtis Brown Ltd, 162-168 Regent Street, London W1R 5TB, England.

SMITH Genevieve Douglas, b. 14 Aug 1923, McKees Rocks, Pennsylvania, USA. Educator: Education Administrator; Writer. m. William Reeves Smith, 6 Jan 1946, 1 daughter. Education: BBA, Westminster College, Pennsylvania, 1945; MS, 1971, EdD, 1973, University of Tennessee. Publications: Techniques and Activities for Teaching Business Skills: Featuring the Mini-Company, 1977; Genevieve Smith's Deluxe Handbook for the Executive Secretary, 1979; I'd Rather Be the Boss!, 1992.

Contributions to: Journals and magazines. Honours: Pi Lambda Theta; Phi Delta Kappa. Memberships: American Education Research Association; International Women's Writing Guild; Knoxville Writers' Guild; National Business Education Association; Society of Children's Book Writers; Tennessee Writers' Alliance. Address: 1205 Snowdon Drive, Knoxville, TN 37912, USA.

SMITH Gregory Blake, b. 24 July 1951, Torrington, Connecticut, USA. Professor; Writer. m. Martha L Smith, 13 Apr 1987, 1 son. Education: AB, Bowdoin College, 1975, MA, Boston University, 1981; MFA, University of Iowa, 1983. Appointment: Professor, Carleton College. Publications: The Devil in the Dooryard, 1986; The Divine Comedy of John Venner, 1992; Nietzsche, Heidegger and the Transition to Postmodernity, 1995. Honours: Stegner Fellowship, Stanford University, 1985; National Endowment for the Arts Fellowship, 1988. Address: c/o Department of English, Carleton College, Northfield, MN 55057, USA.

SMITH Hedrick (Laurence), b. 9 July 1933, Kilmacolm, Scotland. Journalist; Writer; Television Commentator; Lecturer. m. (1) Ann Bickford, 29 June 1957, div Dec 1985, 1 son, 3 daughters, (2) Susan Zox, 7 Mar 1987. Education: Graduated, Choate School, 1951; BA, Williams College, 1955; Postgraduate Studies, Balliol College, Oxford, 1955-56. Appointments: Staff, United Press International, 1959-62; Diplomatic News Correspondent, 1962-64, 1966-71, Middle East Correspondent, 1964-66, Chief, Moscow Bureau, 1971-74, Washington Bureau, 1976-79, Deputy National Editor, 1975-76, Washington Correspondent, 1980-85, New York Times; Panelist, Washington Week in Review, PBS-TV, 1969-95; Visiting Journalist, American Enterprise Institute, 1985-87; Fellow, Foreign Policy Institute, School of Advanced International Studies, Johns Hopkins University, 1989-; Various PBS-TV documentaries; Many lectures. Publications: The Russians, 1975; The Power Game: How Washington Works, 1988; The New Russians, 1990; Rethinking America, 1995. With others: The Pentagon Papers, 1972; Reagan the Man, the President, 1981; Beyond Reagan: The Politics of Upheaval, 1986; Seven Days That Shook the World, 1991. Honours: Nieman Fellow, Harvard University, 1969-70; Pulitzer Prize for International Reporting, 1974; Overseas Press Club Award, 1976, and Citation, 1991; George Polk Award, 1990; Gold Baton Award, DuPont-Columbia University, 1990; George Foster Peabody Award, 1991; Hillman Award, 1996; William Allen White Award, University of Kansas, 1996. Memberships: Gridiron Club; Phi Beta Kappa. Address: c/o Foreign Policy Institute, School of Advanced International Studies, Johns Hopkins University, Baltimore, MD 21218, USA.

SMITH Jane (Marilyn) Davis, (Jane Maxwell), b. 18 May 1949, LaPorte, Indiana, USA. Writer. m. Donald Lee Smith, 15 Apr 1967, 2 sons, 2 daughters. Education: Certified Dental Assistant, Elkhart University of Medical Dental Technique, 1964; Graduate, Institute of Children's Literature, 1981; National Writers' Club Magazine Course, 1981; Fiction and non-fiction courses, Writers' Digest School, 1984-85, Rocky Mountain Writers' Institute, 1985-86. Appointments: Typist, University of Notre Dame Graduate School, 1971; Professional Children's Book Writer, 1979. Publication: Syndee The Chipmunk (children's book). Contributions to: New York Daily News; Central Coast Parent (California); Parentguide Magazine (New York). Honour: Third Place (Honorable Mention), Byline Magazine Prose Essay Contest, 1985. Memberships: National Writers Association. Address: 139 Timber Lane, South Bend, IN 46615, USA.

SMITH Joan Gerarda, (Joan Smith, Jennie Gallant) b. 9 Aug 1932, Brockville, Ontario, Canada. Teacher; Writer. m. Frederick Horacio Smith, 15 Aug 1959, 2 sons, 1 daughter. Education: BA, Arts, Queen's University, Kingston, Ontario, 1959; High School Teacher's Diploma, 1959. Appointments: Teacher, English, French, St Thomas High School, 1959; Teacher, English, French, Chateauguay High School, Quebec, 1965-67; Instructor, English, St Lawrence College, Cornwall, 1969-72.

Memberships: Romance Writers of America; Mystery Writers of America. Address: Georgetown, Ontario, Canada.

SMITH Julia Lois, b. 15 Nov 1949, Mossley, England. Part-time Teacher. m. David Smith, 27 Jan 1969, 4 daughters. Education: BEd, Manchester University, 1979. Appointments: Primary Teacher, Bullough Moor School, Rochdale, 1989, Hopwood School, Rochdale, 1990-98, Heybrook School, 1999. Publications: Poems: Poorly Me, 1996; An Evening With Friends, 1997; Jealousy, 1997. Address: Hillfield House, 7 Long Lane, Dobcross, Saddleworth, Oldham OL3 5QH, England.

SMITH Julie, b. 25 Nov 1944, Annapolis, Maryland, USA. Writer. Education: BA, University of Mississippi, 1965. Publications: Death Turns a Trick, 1982; Huckleberry Fiend, 1987; New Orleans Mourning, 1990; Axeman's Jazz, 1991; Jazz Funeral, 1993; New Orleans Beat, 1994; House of Blues, 1995. Contributions to: Periodicals. Honour: Edgar Allan Poe Award, Mystery Writers of America, 1991. Address: c/o Mystery Writers of America, 174 East 47th Street, New York, NY 10017, USA.

SMITH Lee, b. 1 Nov 1944, Grundy, Virginia, USA. University Teacher; Writer. m. (1) James E Seay, June 1967, div, 2 children, (2) Hal Crowther, June 1985. Education: BA, Hollins College, Virginia, 1967. Appointments: Faculty, Department of English, North Carolina State University, Raleigh, 1981-; Fellow, Center for Documentary Studies, Duke University, 1991-93. Publications: The Last Day the Dogbushes Bloomed, 1968; Something in the Wind, 1971; Fancy Strut, 1973; Black Mountain Breakdown, 1980; Cakewalk (short stories), 1980; Oral History, 1983; Family Linen, 1985; Fair and Tender Ladies, 1988; Me and My Baby View the Eclipse (short stories), 1990; The Devil's Dream, 1992; Saving Grace, 1994; Christmas Letters, 1997; News of the Spirit, 1997. Honours: O Henry Awards, 1979, 1981, 1984; John Dos Passos Award, 1984; Sir Walter Raleigh Award, 1984; North Carolina Award for Literature, 1985; Lyndhurst Prize, 1990-92; Robert Penn Warren Prize, 1991. Memberships: North Carolina Writers Network; PEN. Address: c/o Department of English, North Carolina University, Raleigh, NC 27695, USA.

SMITH Lew. See: **FLOREN Lee.**

SMITH Michael Marshall, b. 3 May 1965, Knutsford, England. Writer. m. Paula Grainger, 25 Apr 1998. Education: Philosophy and Social and Political Science, King's College, Cambridge. Publications: Only Forward, 1994; Spares, 1996; One Of Us, 1998; What You Make It, 1999. Honours: August Derleth Award, 1995; BFS Award for Best Short Fiction, 1990, 1991, 1996. Literary Agent: Jonny Geller. Address: Curtis Brown, Haymarket House, 28/29 Haymarket, London SW1Y 4SP, England.

SMITH Moe Sherrard, (Tyler Maddison), b. 22 June 1939, Leeds, England. Author; Journalist; Adjudicator; Literary Agent. m. Thomas Maddison Smith, 14 Mar 1962. Appointments: Staff, Scribe magazine, 1975-78, Driving Mirror Magazine, 1975-84, Pocklington Post, 1988-90; Principal, Writing Tutorial, 1975-. Publications: Write a Successful Novel; The Essential Guide to Novel Writing; Cold Blast of Winter; Rubbings; Wholly Love; Yorkshire Air Museum Guide Book. Contributions to: Various publications. Memberships: Various writers groups. Address: c/o Sherrard Smith Associates, Garthend House, Illington, York YO4 2TX, England.

SMITH Patrick D(avis), b. 8 Oct 1927, Mendenhall, Mississippi, USA. Writer; Lecturer. m. Iris Doty, 1 Aug 1948, 1 son, 1 daughter. Education: BA, 1947, MA, 1959, University of Mississippi. Appointments: Director, Public Relations, Hinds Community College, 1959-62; Director, Public Information, University of Mississippi, 1962-66; College Relations, Brevard Community College, 1966-88. Publications: A Land Remembered; Allapattah; Angel City; Forever Island; The River Is Home; The Beginning. Contributions to: More than 1000. Honours: Tebeay Prize; Outstanding Author Award; Outstanding Florida

Author Award; Best Writer Award; Toastmasters International Communication Achievement Award; Environmental Writers Award; Medal of Honor; Order of the South Award, Southern Academy of Arts, Letters and Sciences, 1995; Florida Ambassador of the Arts Award, Florida Department of State, 1996; Florida Artists Hall of Fame, 1999. Memberships: Space Coast Writers Guild; Authors Guild; Poets and Writers. Address: 1370 Island Drive, Merritt Island, FL 32952, USA.

SMITH Peter Charles Horstead, b. 15 Oct 1940, North Elmham, Norfolk, England. Author. Appointment: Editor, Photo Precision Ltd, printers and publishers, 1972-75. Publicatons: Destroyer Leader, 1968; Task Force 57, 1969, 2nd edition, 1994; Pedestal, 1970, 3rd edition, 1994; Stuka at War, 1970, 2nd edition, 1980; Hard Lying, 1971; British Battle Cruisers, 1972; War in the Aegean (with Edwin Walker), 1974; Heritage of the Sea, 1974; Battle of the Malta Striking Forces (with Edwin Walker), 1974; Destroyer Action (editor and contributor), 1974; R A F Squadron Badges, 1974; The Story of the Torpedo Bomber, 1974; The Haunted Sea (editor), 1974; Per Mare Per Terram: A History of the Royal Marines, 1974; Arctic Victory, 1975, 2nd edition, 1994; The Battle of Midway, 1976; Fighting Flotilla, 1976; Undesirable Properties (editor and contributor), 1977; The Great Ships Pass, 1977; Hit First, Hit Hard, 1979; The Phantom Coach (editor and contributor), 1979; Action Imminent, 1980; Haunted Shores (editor and contributor), 1980; Impact: The Dive Bomber Pilots Speak, 1981; Cruisers in Action (with J R Dominy), 1981; Dive Bomber, 1982; Rendezvous Skerki Bank (fiction), 1982; Hold the Narrow Sea, 1984; Uninvited Guests, 1984; H M S Wild Swan, 1985; Into the Assault, 1985; Vengeance, 1986; Jungle Dive Bombers at War, 1987; Victoria's Victories, 1987; Dive Bombers in Action, 1988; The Royal Marines: A Pictorial History (with Derek Oakley), 1988; Battleship Royal Sovereign, 1988; Stuka Squadron, 1990; Close Air Support, 1990; T-6: The Harvard, Texan and Wirraway, 1995; Eagle's War, 1996; Ship Strike, 1998; Aichi D3A1/2 Val, 1999; Stukas Over the Steppe, 1999. Contributions to: Various publications. Honour: Royal Marines Historical Society Award, 1987-88. Memberships: Society of Authors, London; Royal Marines Historical Society, Eastney; American Aviation Historical Society. Address: Foxden, 12 Brooklands Road, Riseley, Bedford MK44 1EE, England.

SMITH Ralph Bernard, b. 9 May 1939, Bingley, England. Professor; Writer. Education: BA, 1959, PhD, 1963, University of Leeds. Appointments: Lecturer, later Reader in the History of South East Asia, 1962-88; Professor of the International History of Asia, 1988-, School of Oriental and African Studies, University of London. Publications: Vietnam and the West, 1968; Land and Politics in the England of Henry VIII, 1970; An International History of the Vietnam War, 3 volumes, 1983, 1985, 1991. Contributions to: Professional journals and general periodicals. Address: c/o School of Oriental and African Studies, University of London, Russell Square, London WC1, England.

SMITH Ray, b. 12 Dec 1941, Inverness, Cape Breton Island, Nova Scotia, Canada. College Teacher; Writer. m. Anja Mechielsen, 12 June 1976, 2 sons. Education: BA, Dalhousie University, 1963; MA, Concordia University, 1985. Appointments: Teacher, Dawson College, 1970-; Writer-in-Residence, University of Alberta, 1986-87; Canada-Scotland Writer-in-Residence, Edinburgh, 1987-88. Publications: Cape Breton is the Thought Control Centre of Canada, 1968; Lord Nelson Tavern, 1974; Century, 1986; A Night at the Opera, 1992. Honours: Canada Council Grants; Ontario Arts Council Grants; New Press Award for Short Fiction, 1985; QSPELL Best Novel Award, 1992. Membership: Writers' Union of Canada. Address: c/o Dawson College, 3040 Sherbrooke Street West, Montreal, Quebec, Canada H3Z 1A4.

SMITH Sandra Lee, b. 28 June 1945, San Francisco, California, USA. Writer; Teacher. m. Edward Leroy Smith Jr, 4 Mar 1967. Education: BA, 1967; Masters Degree, Bilingual/Multicultural Education, 1980. Publications:

Loves Miracles (fiction), 1988; Coping with Decision Making, 1989; Dream Song (fiction), 1990; Value of Self Control, 1990; Drug Abuse Prevention, 1995; Flower for Angela (fiction), 1999. Contributions to: Various publications. Honour: Silver Pen Award, 1990. Address: 5433 South Mill Avenue, Tempe, Arizona, USA.

SMITH Sarah, b. 9 Dec 1947, Boston, Massachusetts, USA. m. Frederick S Perry, 26 Aug 1979, 2 sons, 1 dec, 1 daughter. Education: BA, Radcliffe College, 1968; Slade Film School and Queen Mary College, University of London, 1968-69; PhD, Harvard University, 1975; Certificate of Study, Harvard Business Program for PhDs, 1981. Appointments: President, Ivy Films, 1970-75; Assistant Professor of English, Tufts University, 1976-82; Field Editor, G K Hall, 1977-83; Manager, artificial intelligence and computer-aided software engineering firms, 1982-90; Writer and Consultant, 1989-. Publications: Colette at the Movies, nonfiction, 1980; Samuel Richardson: A Reference Guide, 1984; King of Space, 1991; The Vanished Child, 1992; Futre Boston, co-auth, 1994; The Knowledge of Water, 1996; Doll Street, 1996; Riders, 1996-97. Contributions to: Bulletin of the Authors Guild; New York Review of Science Fiction, The Third Degree; Aboriginal; F&SF; Tomorrow; Shudder Again; Best New Horror 5. Honours: Phi Beta Kappa, 1968; Susan Anthony Potter Prize, 1968; Fulbright Fellow, 1968-69; Harvard Prize Fellow, 1969-74; Frank Knox Fellow, 1972-73; Bowdoin Prize, 1975; Mellon Fellow, 1979-80; New York Times Notable Books: The Vanished Child, 1992; The Knowledge of Water, 1996; The College Club's Notable Boston Women, 1997. Memberships: Mystery Writers of America, chair, Web Site Committee, 1997-, NE Board of Directors; Sisters in Crime, NE president, 1995-; International Association of Crime Writers/N America; PEN; Science Fiction Writers of America, Contracts Committee, 1995-); Signet Society, Harvard University. Literary Agent: Jane Otte Co, 9 Goden St, Belmont, MA 02178, USA. Address: 32 Bowker Street, Brookline, MA 02446-6955, USA.

SMITH Steven Ross, b. 25 June 1945, Toronto, Canada. Writer; Poet; Fiction Writer; Sound Poet. m. J Jill Robinson, 1 son. Education: Diploma in Radio & Television Arts, Ryerson Polytechnic University. Appointments: Writer in Residence, Weyburn Public Library, Weyburn, SK, Canada, 1987-88; Writer in Residence, Saskatoon, SK, 1996-97. Publications: Ritual Murders, 1983; Blind Zone, 1985; Sleepwalkers, with Richard Truhlar, 1987; Transient Light, 1990; Reading My Father's Book, 1995; Fluttertongue: Book 1, The Book of Games, 1998; Fluttertongue, Book 2, The Book of Emmett, 1999; Ballet of the Speech Organs: Bob Cobbing on Bob Cobbing, 1998. Contributions to: Open Letter; The New Quarterly; Contemporary Verse 2; Prairie Fire. Memberships: The League of Canadian Poets; The Writers Union of Canada; Saskatchewan Writers Guild. Address: 920-9th Avenue North, Saskatoon, SK S7K 2Z4, Canada.

SMITH Terry Lamson, b. 10 Nov 1937, Sydney, New South Wales, Australia. Journalist; Author. m. Sybilla Smith, 24 Feb 1970, 2 sons. Education: Shore School, Sydney. Publications; The Complete Book of Australian Golf, 1975, 3rd edition, 1988; Australian Golf: The First 100 Years, 1982; Aussie Golf Trivia, 1985; Path to Victory: Wallaby Rugby Power in the 80s, 1987; More Aussie Golf Trivia, 1988; The Champions: Australia's Sporting Greats, 1990; The Bedside Book of Cricket Centuries, 1991; I Love Youse All: The Jeff French Story, 1993. Contributions to: Newspapers and periodicals. Membership: Elanora Country Club. Address: 6 Shannon Avenue, Killarney Heights, Sydney, New South Wales 2087, Australia.

SMITH Vivian (Brian), b. 3 June 1933, Hobart, Tasmania, Australia. Lecturer; Poet; Editor. m. Sybille Gottwald, 15 Feb 1960, 1 son, 2 daughters. Education: MA, 1955, PhD, 1970, University of Sydney. Appointments: Lecturer, University of Tasmania, 1955-66; Literary Editor, Quadrant magazine, Sydney, 1975-90; Reader, University of Sydney, 1982-96. Publications: The Other Meaning, 1956; An Island South, 1967; The Poetry

of Robert Lowell, 1975; Familar Places, 1978; Tide Country, 1982; Tasmania and Australian Poetry, 1984; Selected Poems, 1985; New Selected Poems, 1995. Contributions to: Newspapers and magazines. Honours: Grace Leven Prize; New South Wales Premier's Prize, 1983; Patrick White Literary Award, 1997. Memberships: Australian Society of Authors; PEN; Australian Academy of the Humanities, fellow. Address: 19 McLeod Street, Mosman, New South Wales 2088, Australia.

SMITH Ward, See: GOLDSMITH Howard.

SMITH Wilbur Addison, b. 9 Jan 1933, Zambia (British citizen). Author. m. Danielle Smith, 2 sons, 1 daughter. Education: BComm, Rhodes University, 1953. Appointments: Former business executive; Professional writer, 1961-; Publications: When the Lion Feeds, 1964; The Dark of the Sun, 1965; The Sound of Thunder, 1966; Shout at the Devil, 1968; Gold Mine, 1970; The Diamond Hunters, 1971; The Sunbird, 1972; Eagle in the Sky, 1974; The Eye of the Tiger, 1975; Cry Wolf, 1976; A Sparrow Falls, 1977; Hungry as the Sea, 1978; Wild Justice, 1979; A Falcon Flies, 1980; Men of Men, 1981; The Angels Weep, 1982; The Leopard Hunts in Darkness, 1984; The Burning Shore, 1985; Power of the Sword, 1986; Rage, 1987; The Courtneys, 1987; The Courtneys in Africa, 1988; A Time to Die, 1989; Golden Fox, 1990; Elephant Song, 1991; River God, 1993; The Seventh Scroll, 1995; Birds of Prey, 1997; Monsoon, 1999. Contributions to: Numerous journals and magazines. Address: c/o Charles Pick, Flat 3, 3 Bryanston Place, London W1H 7FN, England.

SMITH William Jay, b. 22 Apr 1918, Winnfield, Louisiana, USA. Professor of English Emeritus; Poet; Writer. m. (1) Barbara Howes, 1947, div 1965, 2 sons, (2) Sonja Haussmann, 1966, 1 stepson. Education: BA, 1939, MA, 1941, Washington University, St Louis; Institut de Touraine, Tours, France, 1938; Columbia University, 1946-47; Wadham College, Oxford, 1947-48; University of Florence, 1948-50. Appointments: Instructor, 1946-47, Visiting Professor, 1973-75, Columbia University; Instructor, 1951, Poet-in-Residence and Lecturer, 1959-64, 1966-67, Williams College; Writer-in-Residence, 1965-66, Professor of English, 1967-68, 1970-80, Professor Emeritus, 1980-, Hollins College, Virginia; Consultant in Poetry, 1968-70, Honorary Consultant, 1970-76, Library of Congress, Washington, DC; Lecturer, Salzburg Seminar in American Studies, 1974; Fulbright Lecturer, Moscow State University, 1981; Poet-in-Residence, Cathedral of St John the Divine, New York City, 1985-88. Publications: Poetry: Poems, 1947; Celebrating at Dark, 1950; Snow, 1953; The Stork, 1954; Typewriter Birds, 1954; The Bead Curtain: Calligrams, 1957; The Old Man on the Isthmus, 1957; Poems 1947-1957, 1957; Prince Souvanna Phouma: An Exchange Between Richard Wilbur and William Jay Smith, 1963; Morels, 1964; The Tin Can and Other Poems, 1966; New and Selected Poems, 1970; A Rose for Katherine Anne Porter, 1970; At Delphi: For Allen Tate on His Seventy-Fifth Birthday, 19 November 1974, 1974; Venice in the Fog, 1975; Verses on the Times (with Richard Wilbur), 1978; Journey to the Dead Sea, 1979; The Tall Poets, 1979; Mr Smith, 1980; The Traveler's Tree: New and Selected Poems, 1980; Oxford Doggerel, 1983; Collected Translations: Italian, French, Spanish, Portuguese, 1985; The Tin Can, 1988; Journey to the Interior, 1988; Plain Talk: Epigrams, Epitaphs, Satires, Nonsense, Occasional, Concrete and Quotidian Poems, 1988; Collected Poems 1939-1989, 1990; The World Below the Window: Poems 1937-1997, 1998. Also 16 books of poetry for children, 1955-90. Stories: Ho for a Hat!, 1989. Other: The Spectra Hoax, 1961; The Skies of Venice, 1961; Children and Poetry: A Selective Bibliography (with Virginia Haviland), 1969, revised edition, 1979; Louise Bogan: A Woman's Words, 1972; The Streaks of the Tulip: Selected Criticism, 1972; Green, 1980; Army Brat: A Memoir, 1980. Editor: Herrick, 1962; The Golden Journey: Poems for Young People (with Louise Bogan), 1965, revised edition, 1990; Poems from France, 1967; Poems from Italy, 1972; A Green Place: Modern Poems, 1982. Contributions to: Journals and magazines. Honours: Rhodes Scholar, 1947-48; Ford

Foundation Fellowship, 1964; Henry Bellamann Major Award, 1970; National Endowment for the Arts Grant, 1972; National Endowment for the Humanities Grants, 1975, 1989; Gold Medal of Labor, Hungary, 1978; Ingram Merrill Foundation Grant, 1982. Membership: American Academy of Arts and Letters, vice-president for literature, 1986-89. Address: 63 Luther Shaw Road, Cummington, MA 01026, USA.

SMITTEN Richard, b. 22 Apr 1940, Bronx, New York, USA. Writer. 1 daughter. Education: BA, University of Western Ontario. Publications: Twice Killed, 1987; The Man Who Made it Snow (with Max Mermelstein and Robin Moore), 1990; Godmother, 1990; Bank of Death, 1993; Legal Tender, 1994. Address: 3675 Skyline Drive, Jensen Beach, FL 34957, USA.

SMUCKER Barbara (Claassen), b. 1 Sept 1915, Newton, Kansas, USA. Writer; Librarian. m. 21 Jan 1939, 2 sons, 1 daughter. Education: BS, Kansas State University, 1936. Publications: Henry's Red Sea, 1955; Cherokee Run, 1957; Wigwam in the City, 1966; Runaway to Freedom, 1979; Days of Terror, 1979; Amish Adventure, 1983; Incredible Jumbo, 1990; Garth and the Mermaid, 1992. Contributions to: Various publications. Address: 20 Pinebrook Drive, Bluffton, OH 45817, USA.

SMYTH Dacre, b. 5 May 1923, London, England. Former Naval Officer; Writer. m. Jennifer Haggard, 11 Jan 1952, 1 son, 4 daughters. Education: RAN College, 1940. Publications: The Bridges of the Yarra, 1979; The Lighthouses of Victoria, 1980; Historic Ships of Australia, 1982; Old Riverboats of the Murray, 1982; Views of Victoria, 1984; The Bridges of Kananook Creek, 1986; Waterfalls of Victoria, 1988; Gallipoli Pilgrimage, 1990; Immigrant Ships to Australia, 1992; Pictures in My Life, 1994; Images of Melbourne, 1998. Honour: Runner-Up, Griffin Press Literary Award, 1990. Memberships: Fellowship of Australian Writers; Victoria Artists Society; Australian Guild of Realist Artists. Address: 22 Douglas Street, Toorak, Victoria 3142, Australia.

SMYTHE Colin Peter, b. 2 Mar 1942, Maidenhead, Berkshire, England. Editor; Publisher; Literary Agent. Education: Bradfield College, Berkshire, 1955-59; BA, 1963, MA, 1966, LLD (hc), 1998, Trinity College, Dublin. Publications: Irish Literary Studies series (general editor); The Coole Edition of Lady Gregory's Writings (general editor), 1970-; A Guide to Coole Park: Home of Lady Gregory, 1973, 3rd edition, 1995; Lady Gregory: Our Irish Theatre (editor), 1973; Lady Gregory: Poets and Dreamers (editor), 1974; Lady Gregory: Seventy Years 1852-1922 (editor), 1974; The Collected Works of G W Russell - AE (general editor with Henry Summerfield), 1978-; Robert Gregory 1881-1918 (editor), 1981; Lady Gregory Fifty Years After (editor with Ann Saddlemyer), 1986; Oxford Companion to Irish Literature (associate editor), 1996. Honours: Various orders and medals including: Officer, Venerable Order of St John of Jerusalem (OStJ); Knight, Order of Our Lady of the Conception of Vila Viçosa, Portugal; Knight, Order of Polonia Restituta, Poland; Honorary LLD, Dublin University, 1998. Memberships: The Athenaeum; American Conference for Irish Studies; British Association for Irish Studies; Canadian Association for Irish Studies; International Association for the Study of Irish Literature; Mark Twain Society, honorary member; Royal Society of Arts, fellow. Address: PO Box 6, Gerrards Cross, Bucks SL9 8XA, England.

SNELL Daniel Clair, b. 1 Oct 1947, Jackson, Michigan, USA. Teacher. m. Katherine Lane Barwick-Snell, 28 June 1986, 1 son, 1 daughter. Education: BA, Stanford University, 1971; PhD, Yale University, 1975. Appointments: University of Washington, 1975-76; City University of New York, 1976-77; University of Michigan, 1977; Connecticut College, 1977-78; Barnard College, 1978-80; National Endowment for the Humanities Fellow, 1980-81; Gustavus Adolphus College, 1981-82; Fulbright Researcher, Aleppo (Syria) Museum, 1982-83; Assistant Professor, 1983-87, Associate Professor, 1987-93, Professor, 1993-, University of Oklahoma. Publications: The E A Hoffman and Other American Collections, 1979; A Workbook of Cuneiform Signs, 1979; Ledgers and Prices, 1982; Economic Texts From Summer (with Carl H Lager), 1991; Twice-Told Proverbs, 1993; Life in the Ancient Near East, 1997. Honours: National Humanities Center Fellow, 1989-90; Australia National University Humanities Research Centre Fellow, 1990; Oregon Humanities Centre Fellow, 1996; Advanced Studies in the Humanities, University of Edinburgh, 1997. Address: c/o Department of History, University of Oklahoma, 455 West Lindsey, Norman, OK 73019, USA.

SNEYD Stephen Henry, b. 20 Mar 1941, Maidenhead, Berkshire, England. Poet; Writer. m. Rita Ann Cockburn, 13 Mar 1964, 1 son, 1 daughter. Education: BSc; DipM; CertEd. Appointments: UK Columnist, Scavenger's Newsletter, USA; Contributing Editor on Poetry, Fantasy Commentator magazine, USA, 1992-. Publications: The Legerdemain of Changelings, 1979; Two Humps Not One, 1980; Discourteous Self-Service, 1982; Prug Plac Gamma, 1983; Stone Bones (with Pete Presford), 1983; Fifty-Fifty Infinity, 1989; Bad News from the Stars, 1991; At the Thirteenth Hour, 1991; We Are Not Men, 1991; What Time Has Use For, 1992; A Mile Beyond the Bus, 1992; In Coils of Earthen Hold, 1994. Contributions to: Many UK and US reviews, quarterlies, journals, and magazines; Radio and television. Honours: Trend Prize for Peace Poetry, 1967; Northern Star Poetry Prize, 1983; Diploma di Merito, Accademia Italia, 1983; Best Poet, Small Pres and Magazine Awards, 1986; Peterson Prize, 1996. Membership: Science Fiction Poetry Association. Address: 4 Nowell Place, Almondbury, Huddersfield, West Yorkshire, HD5 8PB, England.

SNIDER Clifton M(ark), b. 3 Mar 1947, Duluth, Minnesota, USA. University Lecturer; Poet; Writer. Education: Southern California College, Costa Mesa, 1965-67; BA, cum laude, English, 1969, MA, English, 1971, California State University, Long Beach; PhD, English, University of Mexico, 1974. Appointments: Faculty, California State University, Long Beach, 1974-, Long Beach City College, 1975-. Publications: Poetry: Jesse Comes Back, 1976; Bad Smoke, Good Body, 1980; Jesse and His Son, 1982; Edwin: A Character in Poems, 1984; Blood and Bones, 1988; Impervious to Piranhas, 1989; The Age of the Mother, 1992. Other: The Stuff That Dreams Are Made On: A Jungian Interpretation of Literature, 1991. Contributions to: Anthologies, reviews, quarterlies, and journals. Honours: Resident Fellow, Yaddo, 1978, 1982, Helene Wurlitzer Foundation of New Mexico, 1984, 1990, 1998, Michael Karolyi Memorial Foundation, Vence, France, 1986, 1987. Address: 2719 Eucalyptus Avenue, Long Beach, CA 90806, USA.

SNODGRASS W D, (S S Gardons, Will McConnell, Kozma Prutkov), b. 5 Jan 1926, Wilkinsburg, Pennsylvania, USA. Poet; Writer; Dramatist; m. (1) Lila Jean Hank, 6 June 1946, div Dec 1953, 1 daughter, (2) Janice Marie Ferguson Wilson, 19 Mar 1954, div Aug 1966, 1 son, (3) Camille Rykowski, 13 Sept 1967, div 1978, (4) Kathleen Ann Brown, 20 June 1985. Education: Geneva College, 1943-44, 1946-47; BA, 1949, MA, 1951, MFA, 1953, University of Iowa. Appointments: Instructor in English, Cornell University, 1955-57; Instructor, University of Rochester, New York, 1957-58; Assistant Professor of English, Wayne State University, Detroit, 1959-67; Professor of English and Speech, Syracuse University, New York, 1968-77; Visiting Professor, Old Dominion University, Norfolk, Virginia, 1978-79; Distinguished Professor, 1979-80, Distinguished Professor of Creative Writing and Contemporary Poetry, 1980-94, University of Delaware, Newark; Various lectures and poetry readings. Publications: Poetry: Heart's Needle, 1959; After Experience, 1967; As S S Gardons, Remains: A Sequence of Poems, 1970, revised edition, 1985; The Fuehrer Bunker, 1977; If Birds Build With Your Hair, 1979; D D Byrde Calling Jennie Wrenne, 1984; A Colored Poem, 1986; The House the Poet Built, 1986; A Locked House, 1986; The Kinder Capers, 1986; Selected Poems, 1957-87, 1987; W D's Midnight Carnival (with DeLoss McGraw), 1988; The Death of Cock Robin (with DeLoss McGraw), 1989; Each in His Season, 1994; The Fuehrer Bunker: The Complete Cycle, 1995. Essays: In Radical Pursuit, 1975; After-Images, 1999. Play: The Fuehrer Bunker, 1978. Other: Translations of songs; Selected Translations, 1998. Contributions to: Essays, reviews, poems to many periodicals. Honours: Ingram Merrill Foundation Award, 1958; Longview Foundation Literary Award, 1959; National Institute of Arts and Letters Grant, 1960; Pulitzer Prize in Poetry, 1960; Yaddo Resident Awards, 1960, 1961, 1965; Guinness Poetry Award, 1961; Ford Foundation Grant, 1963-64; National Endowment for the Arts Grant, 1966-67; Guggenheim Fellowship, 1972-73; Government of Romania Centennial Medal, 1977; Honorary Doctorate of Letters, Allegheny College, 1991. Memberships: National Institute of Arts and Letters; Poetry Society of America; International PEN; Marin Sorescu Foundation. Address: RD 1, Box 51, Erieville, NY 13061, USA.

SNOW Philip Albert, b. 7 Aug 1915, Leicester, England. Retired Administrator. m. Anne Harris, 2 May 1940, 1 daughter. Education: MA, Honours, Christ's College, Cambridge, 1934-38. Appointments: Magistrate, Provincial Commissioner, Assistant Colonial Secretary, HM Colonial Administrative Service, Fiji and Western Province, 1937-52; Bursar, Rugby School, 1952-76; Justice of the Peace, Warwickshire, 1967-76, West Sussex, 1976-. Publications: Civil Defence Services, 1943; Cricket in the Fiji Islands, 1949; Rock Carvings in Fiji, 1950; Best Stories of the South Seas, 1957; Visit of Three Bursars to USA and Canada, 1964; Bibliography of Fiji, Tonga and Rotuma, vol I, 1967; The People From the Horizon: An Illustrated History of the Europeans Among the South Sea Islanders, 1979; Stranger and Brother: A Portrait of C P Snow, 1982; The Years of Hope - Cambridge-Colonial Administration in the South Seas, Cricket, 1992; A Time for Renewal - Clusters of Characters, C P Snow, Coups, 1998. Honours: Officer of the Order of the British Empire; Runner-Up, Arts Council of Great Britain Award for Best History/Biography, 1979; Literary Executor of Lord (CP) Snow, 1980-. Address: Gables, Station Road, Angmering, West Sussex BN16 4HY, England.

SNOWMAN Daniel, b. 4 Nov 1938, London, England. Writer. m. Janet Linda Levison, 1 son, 1 daughter. Education: BA, Double 1st Class, History, University of Cambridge, 1961; MA, Government, Cornell University, Ithaca, New York, 1963. Appointments: Lecturer in History and American Studies, University of Sussex, 1963-67; Producer, later Chief Producer, Radio Features and Arts, BBC, 1967-95; Visiting Professor of History, California State University, 1972-73. Publications: America Since 1920, 1968; Eleanor Roosevelt, 1970; Kissing Cousins: British and American Culture, 1977; If I Had Been.... Ten Historical Fantasies, 1979; The Amadeus Quartet, 1981; The World of Plácido Domingo, 1985; Beyond the Tunnel of History, 1990; Pole Positions: The Polar Regions and the Future of the Planet, 1993; Plácido Domingo's Tales From the Opera, 1994; Fins de Siècle: How Centuries End, 1400-2000 (with A Briggs), 1996. Contributions to: Books, newspapers, and journals. Membership: London Philharmonic Choir, singer, former chairman, 1967-. Address: 46 Molyneux Street, London W1H 5HW, England.

SNYDER Francis Gregory, b. 26 June 1942, Madison, Wisconsin, USA. Professor of Law; Writer. m. Sian Miles, 20 Aug 1967, 1 son. Education: BA, Yale University, 1964; Fulbright Scholar, Institut d'Études Politiques de Paris, 1964-65; JD, Harvard Law School, 1968; Certificat de Droit et Economie des Pays d'Afrique, 1969; Doctorat de Spécalité, University of Paris I, 1973. Appointments: US Attorney, Massachusetts, 1968; Professor of Law, European University Institute, San Domenico di Fiesole, Italy. Publications: One-Party Government in Mali, 1965; Law and Population in Senegal, 1977; Capitalism and Legal Change, 1981; Law of the Common Agricultural Policy, 1985; International Law of Development (co-editor), 1987; Labor, Law and Crime (co-editor), 1987; The Political Economy (co-editor), 1987; Policing and Prosecution in Britain 1750-1850 (co-editor), 1989; New Directions in European Community Law, 1990;

European Community Law, 2 volumes, 1993. Contributions to: Professional journals. Honours: Research Associate, International Development Research Center, 1978; Officier dans l'Ordre des Palmes Académiques, 1988. Membership: Law and Society Association. Address: c/o Department of Law, European University Institute, Badia Fiesolana I-50016, San Domenico di Fiesole, Italy.

SNYDER Gary (Sherman), b. 8 May 1930, San Francisco, California, USA. Poet; Writer; Teacher. m., 2 sons, 2 stepdaughters. Education: BA, Reed College, Portland, Oregon, 1951; Graduate Studies in Linguistics, Indiana University, 1951; Graduate School, Department of East Asian Languages, University of California, Berkeley, 1953-56; Studied Zen Buddhism and East Asian culture in Japan. Appointment: Faculty, University of California, Davis, 1986-. Publications: Poetry: Riprap and Cold Mountain Poems, 1959; Myths and Texts, 1960; A Range of Poems, 1966; Three Worlds, Three Realms, Six Roads, 1966; The Back Country, 1968; The Blue Sky, 1969; Regarding Wave, 1970; Manzanita, 1971; Plute Creek, 1972; The Fudo Trilogy: Spell Against Demons, Smokey the Bear Sutra, The California Water Plan, 1973; Turtle Island, 1974; All in the Family, 1975; Songs for Gaia, 1979; Axe Handles, 1983; Left Out in the Rain: New Poems, 1947-1986, 1986; The Practice of the Wild, 1990; No Nature: New and Selected Poems, 1992; Mountains and Rivers Without End, 1996. Prose: Earth House Hold: Technical Notes and Queries to Fellow Dharma Revolutionaries, 1969; The Old Ways: Six Essays, 1977; He Who Hunted Birds in His Father's Village: The Dimensions of a Haida Myth, 1979; The Real Work: Interviews and Talks, 1964-1979, 1980; Passage Through India, 1984; A Place in Space, 1995. Contributions to: Anthologies. Honours: Scholarship, First Zen Institute of America, 1956; American Academy of Arts and Letters Award, 1966; Bollingen Foundation Grant, 1966-67; Frank O'Hara Prize, 1967; Levinson Prize, 1968; Guggenheim Fellowship, 1968-69; Pulitzer Prize in Poetry, 1975; Finalist, National Book Award, 1992. Memberships: American Academy of Arts and Letters; American Academy of Arts and Sciences. Address: 18442 Macnab Cypress Road, Nevada City, CA 95959, USA.

SNYDER Zilpha Keatley, b. 11 May 1927, Lemoore, California, USA. Writer. m. 18 June 1950, 2 sons, 1 daughter. Education: BA, Whittier College, 1948. Publications: Season of Ponies, 1964; The Velvet Room, 1965; Black and Blue Magic, 1966; The Egypt Game, 1967; The Changeling, 1970; The Headless Cupid, 1971; The Witches of Worm, 1972; The Princess and the Giants, 1973; The Truth About Stone Hollow, 1974; The Famous Stanley Kidnapping Case, 1979; Blair's Nightmare, 1984; The Changing Maze, 1985; And Condors Danced, 1987; Squeak Saves the Day and Other Tooley Tales, 1988; Janie's Private Eyes, 1989; Libby on Wednesday, 1990; Song of the Gargoyle, 1991; Fool's Gold, 1993; Cat Running, 1994; The Trespasser, 1995; Castle Court Kids, 1995. Honour: Beatty Award, 1995. Address: 52 Miller Avenue, Mill Valley, CA 94941, USA.

SOCOLOFSKY Homer Edward, b. 20 May 1922, Tampa, Kansas, USA. Emeritus Professor of History. m. Helen Margot Wright, 23 Nov 1946, 4 sons, 2 daughters. Education: BS, 1944, MS, 1947, Kansas State University; PhD, University of Missouri, 1954. Appointments: Professor of History, later Professor Emeritus, Kansas State University; History Editor, Kansas Quarterly, 1969-92; Book Review Editor, Journal of the West, 1978-92. Publications: Arthur Capper, Publisher, Politician, Philanthropist, 1962; Historical Atlas of Kansas (with Huber Self), 1972, 2nd edition, 1989; Landlord William Scully, 1979; The Presidency of Benjamin Harrison (with Allan Spetter), 1987; Governors of Kansas, 1990; Kansas History: An Annotated Bibliography (with Virgil Dean), 1992; Biography of the Honorable Richard Dean Rogers: Senior United States District Judge, 1995. Contributions to: Over 40 articles in journals and anthologies. Address: Department of History, Kansas State University, Manhattan, KS 66506, USA.

SOFOLA Zulu, b. 22 June 1935, Issele-Uku, Nigeria. Playwright. Education: PhD, University of Ibadan, 1977. Appointment: Head, Department of the Performing Arts, University of Ilorin, Kwara State, Nigeria, 1989-. Publications: The Disturbed Peace of Christmas, 1969; Wedlock of the Gods, 1971; The Operators, 1973; King Emene, 1975; Old Wines are Tasty, 1975; The Sweet Trap, 1975; The Wizard of Law, 1976; The Deer and the Hunter's Pearl, 1976; Memories in the Moonlight, 1977; Song of a Maiden, 1977; Queen Umu-Ako of Oligbo, 1989; Eclipse and the Fantasia, 1990; Lost Dreams, 1991; The Showers, 1991. Honour: Fulbright Fellowship, 1988. Address: Department of the Performing Arts, University of Ilorin, Ilorin, Kwara State, Nigeria.

SOHAIL Khalid, b. 9 July 1952, Pakistan. Psychiatrist; Writer; Poet. Education: MBBS, Pakistan, 1974; FRCP(C), Canada, 1982. Publications: Discovering New Highways in Life (psychotherapy), 1991; From One Culture to Another (essays), 1992; Literary Encounters (interviews), 1992; Pages of my Heart (poems), 1993; A Broken Man (stories), 1993; Collections of poems, stories, essays and translations of world literature. Contributions to: Anthologies and journals. Honours: Honourary Cultural Doctorate in Literature, World University, USA, 1993; Rahul Award, Calcutta, India, 1994. Memberships: Writers' Union of Canada; Royal College of Physicians and Surgeons, Canada, fellow. Address: PH6 100 White Oaks Court, Whitby, Ontario L1P 1B7, Canada.

SOHOLM Ejgil, b. 19 Apr 1936, Nykobing Mors, Denmark. Librarian; Author; Translator; Freelance Journalist. m. Kirsten Kynne Frandsen, 28 Apr 1961, 2 sons, 1 daughter. Education: MA, Universty of Århus, 1963. Appointments: Lecturer in Danish Literature, University of Århus, 1968-73; Senior Librarian, State and University Library, Århus, 1968-; Editor, DF-Revy, 1978-82. Publications: Roman om en forbrydelse, 1976; Fra frihedskamp til lighedstrom, 1979; Storm P for Ping, 1986; Ordkvartet Århus, 1990; Angli giorde det, 1992. Other: Translations of children's books. Contributions to: Periodicals. Membership: Danish Writers Union. Address: PO Box 1302, DK-8210 Århus V, Denmark.

SOKOL Lech Andrzej, b. 21 Feb 1942, Koprzywnica, Poland. Historian of Literature and Theatre; Diplomat. m. Anna Lisowska, 26 Dec 1965, 1 son, 1 daughter. Education: Polish Philology, 1959-64, MA, 1964, University of Warsaw; PhD, 1972, Habilitation, 1990, Institute of Art, Polish Academy of Sciences and Humanities. Appointments: Editor, State Publishing House PIW, 1963-69; Research Worker, Institute of Art, Polish Academy of Sciences and Humanities, 1969-91; Lecturer in Modern Drama and Theatre Aesthetics, State Academy of Drama, Warsaw, 1972-91; Polish Ambassador to Norway, 1991-96, and Iceland, 1992-96. Publications: Books in Polish: The Grotesque in the Drama of S I Witkiewicz, 1973; August Strindberg, 1981; Witkiewicz and Strindberg: A Comparative Study, 1990, also published in book form as Witkacy and Strindberg: Distant and Close, 1995. Other: Editor of 5 volumes of Strindberg's plays and short stories with introductions, 2 volumes of short stories by XIXth century Polish Writers with introductions and commentaries, and 2 volumes of plays by Polish playwrights Rózewicz and Witkiewicz; Author of about 160 essays and articles in Polish, English, French, Norwegian and Swedish; Author of poetry in Polish translated into Norwegian; Translator of American, French and Swedish poetry into Polish. Contributions to: Various publications. Membership: International Theatre Institute. Address: Sapiezynska 5 m 18, 00-215 Warsaw, Poland.

SOLLERS Philippe, (Philippe Joyaux), b. 28 Nov 1936, Talence, Gironde, France. Author. div, 1 son. Education: Lycée Montesquieu and Lycée Montaigne, Bordeaux; Ecole Sainte-Geneviève, Versailles. Appointments: Co-Founder, Tel Quel journal, 1960-82; Director, L'Infini review, 1983-; Reading Committee Member, Editions Gallimard, 1990-. Publications: Une Curieuse Solitude, 1958; Le Parc, 1961; Drame, 1965; Nombres, Logiques, 1968; Lois, 1972; H, 1973; Paradis, Vision a New York, 1981; Femmes, 1983; Portrait du joueur, 1985; Théorie des exceptions, 1986; Paradis 2, 1986; Le Coeur absolu, 1987; Les Surprises de Fragonard, 1987; Les Folies francaises, 1988; De Kooning, vite, 1988; Le Lys d'or, 1989; Carnet de nuit, 1989; La Fete á Venise, 1991; Improvisations, 1991; Le Rire de Rome, 1992; Le Secret, 1993; Venise éternelle, 1993; La Guerre du goût, 1994; Femmes mythologies, 1994; Le Cavalier du Louvre, Vivant Denon (1747-1825), 1995; Sade dans le temps, 1996; Sade contre l'etre supreme, 1996; Picasso le héros, 1996; Studio, 1997; Casanova l'admirable, 1998. Contributions to: Various publications. Honours: Prix Feneon, 1957; Prix Médicis, 1961; Grand prix de littérature of the City of Bordeaux, 1985; Grand prix du Roman of the City of Paris, 1988; Prix Paul-Morand de l'Académie francaise, 1992. Address: c/o L'Infini, 5 rue Sébastien-Bottin, 75007 Paris, France.

SOLOW Robert M(erton), b. 23 Aug 1924, Brooklyn, New York, USA. Professor of Economics Emeritus; Writer. m. Barbara Lewis, 19 Aug 1945, 2 sons, 1 daughter. Education: BA, 1947, MA, 1949, PhD, 1951, Harvard University. Appointments: Faculty, 1949-58, Professor of Economics, 1958-95, Professor Emeritus, 1995-, Massachusetts Institute of Technology; Senior Economist, 1961-62, Consultant, 1962-68, US Council of Economic Advisors; Marshall Lecturer and Fellow Commoner, Peterhouse, Cambridge, 1963-64; Eastman Visiting Professor, University of Oxford, 1968-69; Senior Fellow, Society of Fellows, Harvard University, 1975-89; Deming Professor, New York University, 1996-97. Publications: Linear Programming and Economic Analysis, (with R Dortman and P Samuelson), 1958; Capital Theory and the Rate of Return, 1963; The Sources of Unemployment in the United States, 1964; Growth Theory, 1970; Price Expectations and the Behaviour of the Prive Level, 1970; Made in America (with M Dertouzos and R Lester), 1989; The Labor Market as a Social Institution, 1990; A Critical Essay on Modern Macroeconomic Theory (with F Hahn), 1995; Learning from "Learning by Doing", 1997; Inflation, Unemployment and Monetary Policy, 1998; Work and Welfare, 1998; Monopolistic Competition and Macroeconomic Theory, 1998. Contributions to: Professional journals. Honours: David A Wells Prize, Harvard University, 1951; Seidman Award in Political Economy, 1983; Nobel Prize for Economic Science, 1987; Numerous honorary doctorates. Memberships: American Academy of Arts and Sciences; American Economics Society, vice-president, 1968, president, 1979; American Philosophical Society; British Academy, corresponding fellow; Econometric Society, president, 1964; National Academy of Science, council member, 1977-80, 1995. Address: 528 Lewis Wharf, Boston, MA 02110, USA.

SOLTER Aletha Lucia, b. 21 Dec 1945, Princeton, New Jersey, USA. Psychologist. m. Kenneth Solter, 10 July 1971, 1 son, 1 daughter. Education: Master in Human Biology, University of Geneva, 1969; PhD in Psychology, University of California at Santa Barbara, 1975. Appointments: Consultant; Workshop Leader; Founder, Aware Parenting Institute, 1984-; Instructor, Santa Barbara City College, Continuing Education Division, 1985-; Adjunct Faculty, Antioch University, 1998. Publications: The Aware Baby, 1984; Helping Young Children Flourish, 1989; Tears and Trantrums, 1998. Contributions to: Mothering; Parenting; Ladybug. Address: c/o Aware Parenting Institute, PO Box 206, Goleta, CA 93116, USA.

SOLWAY David, b. 8 Dec 1941, Montreal, Quebec, Canada. Poet; Writer; Professor. m. Karin Semmler, 23 Apr 1980, 1 daughter. Education: BA, 1962, QMA, 1966, McGill University; MA, Concordia University, 1988; MA, University of Sherbrooke, 1996; PhD, Lajos Kossuth University, 1998. Appointments: Professor, John Abbott College, 1971-99; Professor, Brigham Young University, 1993. Publications: Poetry: In My Own Image, 1962; The Crystal Theatre, 1971; Paximalia, 1972; The Egyptian Airforce, 1973; Anacrusis, 1976; The Road to Arginos, 1976; Mephistopheles and the Astronaut, 1979; Selected

Poems, 1982; The Mulberry Men, 1982; Stones in Winter, 1983; Modern Marriage, 1987; Bedrock, 1993; Chess Pieces, 1999. Other: Education Lost, 1989; The Anatomy of Arcadia, 1992; Lying About the Wolf, 1997. Editor Lost, 1989; The Anatomy of Arcadia, 1992; Lying About the Wolf, 1997; Random Walks, 1997. Editor: 4 Montreal Poets, 1972. Contributions to: Reviews and journals. Honours: QSPELL Award for Poetry, 1988, and for Non-Fiction, 1990. Memberships: Canadian Writers' Union; International PEN; Union des écrivaines et écrivains québécois. Address: 143 Upper McNaughton, PO Box 682, Hudson, Quebec H0P 1H0, Canada.

SOLZHENITSYN Aleksandr Isayevich, b. 11 Dec 1918, Kislovodsk, Russia. Writer; Poet. m. (1) Natalya Reshetovskaya, 27 Apr 1940, div, (2) 1956, div 1972, (3) Natalya Svetlova, Apr 1973, 3 sons, 1 stepson. Education: Correspondence course in Philology, Moscow Institute of History, Philosophy, and Literature, 1939-41; Degree in Mathematics and Physics, University of Rostock, 1941. Appointments: Writer as a youth; Secondary School Teacher; Commander, Soviet Army during World War II; Held in prisons and labour camp, 1945-53; Exiled as a teacher, Kok-Terek, Kazakhstan, 1953-56; Teacher, Mathematics and Physics, Riazan; Exiled from Soviet Union, 1974-94. Publications: One Day in the Life of Ivan Denisovich (novella), 1962; For the Good of the Cause (novella), 1963; We Never Make Mistakes (novel), 1963; The First Circle (novel), 1968; Cancer Ward (novel), 2 volumes, 1968-69; The Love Girl and the Innocent (play), 1969; Candle in the Wind (play), 1969; The Rights of the Writer, 1969; The Red Wheel (novel cycle), 1971-, including August 1914, October 1916, March 1917, April 1917; Stories and Prose Poems by Aleksandr Solzhenitsyn, 1971; Six Etudes by Aleksandr Solzhenitsyn, 1971; Nobel Lecture by Aleksandr Solzhenitsyn, 1972; A Lenten Letter to Pimen, Patriarch of All Russia, 1972; The Gulag Archipelago, 1918-1956: An Experiment in Literary Investigation, 3 volumes, 1974, 1976, 1979; Peace and Violence, 1974; Prussian Nights: Epic Poems Written at the Forced Labor Camp, 1950, 1974; Letter to the Soviet Leaders, 1974; Solzhenitsyn: A Pictorial Autobiography, 1974; The Oak and the Calf (memoir), 1975; Lenin in Zürich, 1975; American Speeches, 1975; From Under the Rubble (with others), 1975; Warning to the West, 1976; A World Split Apart, 1979; The Mortal Danger, 1981; Victory Celebrations: A Comedy in Four Acts and Prisoners: A Tragedy (plays), 1983; Rebuilding Russia: Towards Some Formulations, 1991; The Russian Question Toward the End of the Century, 1995; November 1969, forthcoming. Honours: Prix du Meilleur Livre Etranger, France, 1969; Nobel Prize for Literature, 1970; Freedoms Foundation Award, Stanford University, 1976; Many honorary degrees. Membership: American Academy of Arts and Sciences. Address: c/o Farrar, Straus & Giroux, 19 Union Square West, New York, NY 10003, USA.

SOMERS Suzanne. See: **DANIELS Dorothy**.

SOMLYO György, b. 28 Nov 1920, Balatonboglar, Hungary. Writer; Poet. div 1988, 1 son. Education: University of Budapest, 1945-46; Sorbonne, University of Paris, 1947-48. Appointments: Director, Literary Section, Radio Budapest, 1954-55, Arion magazine, 1966-87. Publications: 17 books, including novels, poems, and essays, 1977-96. Contributions to: Various publications. Honours: Many, including: Jozsef Attila Prize; Hungarian Writers Association Prize; Officier de l'Ordre des Arts et des Lettres, France. Memberships: Academy of Literature and Arts; Association of Hungarian Writers; Hungarian PEN. Address: Irinyi 3 u 39, Budapest H-1111, Hungary.

SOMMER Piotr, b. 13 Apr 1948, Walbrzych, Poland. m. Jolanta Piasecka, 28 Oct 1972, 2 sons. Education: MA, English Literature, University of Warsaw, Poland, 1973. Appointments: Editor, Literatura Na Swiecie, 1976-, Editor in Chief, 1993-. Publications: Poetry Books: W Krzesle, 1977; Bamiatki Po Nas, 1980; Kolejny Swiat, 1983; Czynnik Liryczny I Inne Wiersze, 1988; Nowe Stosunki Wyrazów, 1997; Criticism: Smak Detalu, 1995; Translations and anthologies: Antologia Nowej Poezji Brytyjskie, 1983; Zapisy Rozmów: Wywiady 2 Poetami

Brytyjskimi, 1985; Szesciu Poetow Pótnocnoirlandzkich, 1993; Artykuty Pochodzenia Zagrawicznego, 1996. Contributions to: Agri; The Honest Ulsterman; New Yorker; Ploughshares; Poetry Review; The Threepenny Review; TLS. Honours: Koscielski Foundation Prize, 1988; Barbara Sadowska Foundation Prize, 1988; Polish PEN Translation Prize, 1997. Membership: Stowarzyszenie Pisarzy Polskich. Address: c/o Ul Moniuszki 9/11, 05-070 Sulejówek, Poland.

SONENBERG Maya, b. 24 Feb 1960, New York, New York, USA. Writer; Assistant Professor. Education: BA, Wesleyan University, 1982; MA, Brown University, 1984. Appointments: Instructor, Sonoma State University, 1986; Lecturer, Chabot College, 1989-90; Assistant Professor, Oregon State University, 1990-93, University of Washington, 1993-. Publication: Cartographies, 1989. Contributions to: Writer; Grand Street; Chelsea; Cream City Review; Columbia; Gargoyle; American Short Fiction; Santa Monica Review. Honours: McDowell Colony Fellow, 1987; Drue Heinz Literature Prize, 1989; Centre for the Humanities Faculty Fellow, Oregon State University, 1992-93. Memberships: Associated Writing Programs; Modern Language Association. Address: Department of English, Box 354330, University of Washington, Seattle, WA 98195, USA.

SONG Cathy, b. 20 Aug 1955, Honolulu, Hawaii, USA. Poet; Writer; Teacher. m. Douglas M Davenport, 19 July 1979. Education: University of Hawaii at Manoa; BA in English Literature, Wellesley College, 1977; MA in Creative Writing, Boston University, 1981. Appointments: Teacher of Poetry, Hawaii, 1987-; Associated with Poets in the Schools programme. Publications: Picture Bridge, 1983; Frameless Windows, Squares of Light, 1988; Sister Stew (editor with Juliet S Kono), 1991; School Figures, 1994. Contributions to: Various anthologies and journals. Honours: Yale Series of Younger Poets Prize, 1983; Frederick Book Prize for Poetry, 1986; Cades Award for Literature, 1988; Hawaii Award for Literature, 1993; Shelley Memorial Award, Poetry Society of America, 1993. PO Box 27262 Honolulu, HI 96827, USA.

SONNEVI Göran, b. 3 Oct 1939, Lund, Sweden. Poet. m. Kerstin Kronkvist, 1961. Education: University of Lund, 1963. Publications: Outfört, 1961; Abstrakta dikter, 1963; Ingreppmodeller, 1965; och nul, 1967; Det måste gå, 1970; Det oavslutade språket, 1972; Det omöjliga, 1975; Språk; Verktyg; Eld, 1979; Små klanger; en röst, 1981; Dikter utan ordning, 1973; Oavslutade dikter, 1987; Trädet, 1991; Mozarts Tredje Hjärna, 1996; Klangernas bok, 1998; In English Translation: The Economy Spinning Faster and Faster: Poems, 1982; A Child is Not a Knife: Selected Poems of Géoran Sonnevi, 1993. Contributions to: Several publications. Address: c/o Swedish Writers Union, Box 3157, Drottninggatan 88B, S-103 63 Stockholm, Sweden.

SONTAG Susan, b. 16 Jan 1933, New York, New York, USA. Novelist; Essayist. m. Philip Rieff, 1950, div 1958, 1 son. Education: BA, University of Chicago, 1951; MA, English, 1954, MA, Philosophy, 1955, Harvard University. Publications: The Benefactor (novel), 1963; Against Interpretation (essays), 1966; Death Kit (novel), 1967; Trip to Hanoi (essays), 1968; Styles of Radical Will (essays), 1969; On Photography (essays), 1977; Illness as Metaphor (essays), 1978; I, etcetera (stories), 1978; Under the Sign of Saturn (essays), 1980; A Sontag Reader, 1982; AIDS and Its Metaphors (essays), 1989; The Way We Live Now (story), 1991; The Volcano Lover: A Romance, 1992; Alice in Bed: A Play, 1993; In America: A Novel, 1999. Contributions to: Various publications. Honours: Rockefeller Foundation Fellowships, 1965, 1974; Guggenheim Fellowships, 1966, 1975; National Book Critics Circle Award, 1978; Officier de l'Ordre des Arts et des Lettres, France, 1984; John D and Catharine T MacArthur Foundation Fellowship, 1990-95; Malaparte Prize, Italy, 1992; Honorary Doctorates, Columbia University, 1993, Harvard University, 1993; Montblanc Cultural Achievement Award, 1994. Memberships: American Academy of Arts and Letters; PEN American Center, president, 1987-89.

Address: c/o The Wylie Agency, 250 West 57th Street, Suite 2114, New York, NY 10107, USA.

SOREN Gamle. See: **THIRSLUND Soren**.

SORENSEN Knud, b. 10 Mar 1928, Hjorring, Denmark. Writer. m. Anne Marie Dybro Jorgensen, 4 July 1950, 2 sons. Education: Graduate, Royal Veterinary and Agricultural University, Copenhagen, 1952. Publications: Over 30 books, in Danish, 1965-96. Contributions to: Various publications. Honours: Several literary awards. Memberships: Autorenkreiss Plesse; Danish Writers' Union. Address: Skelholmvehj 2, DK-7900 Nykobing Mors, Denmark.

SORENSEN Preben, b. 17 Feb 1939, Tved, Denmark. Editor; Chief of Information. m. Inge Lunding, 11 Mar 1961, 1 son, 1 daughter. Appointments: Journalist, 1967; Editor, 1971-. Publications: Fagpressen: Fretidens Medie, 1980; Arbejdsmarkedsordbog, 1987; De Udelukkede, 1989; Nordisk Arbejdsmarkedsordbog, 1990; Under Herrer og Mestre, 1992; Pas Yo Pressen, 1995. Contributions to: Editor, Nyt fra Arbejdermuseet and Radio-TV NYT. Memberships: Danish Writers' Union; Danish Union of Journalists; Danish Listeners and Viewers Organisation, chairman. Address: Ny Ostergade 34, 2 tv, 1101 Copenhagen K, Denmark.

SORENSEN Villy, b. 13 Jan 1929, Frederiksberg, Denmark. Writer. Education: Philosophical and Philological Studies, Copenhagen, Freiburg im Breisgau. Publications: 27 books in Danish; Titles translated into English: Strange Stories, 1956; Seneca, 1984; Tutelary Tales, 1988; Downfall of the Gods, 1989; Another Metamorphosis and other Fictions, 1990; Four Biblical Tales, 1991; Harmless Tales, 1991. Honours: Danish Academy Prize; Henrik Steffens Prize; Swedish Academy Nordic Prize. Membership: Danish Academy. Address: Bredebovej 31, 2800 Lyngby, Denmark.

SORESTAD Glen Allan, b. 21 May 1937, Vancouver, British Columbia, Canada. Writer; Poet; Publisher. m. Sonia Diane Talpash, 17 Sept 1960, 3 sons, 1 daughter. Education: BEd, 1963, MEd, 1976, University of Saskatchewan. Appointments: Elementary School Teacher, 1957-69; Senior English Teacher, 1969-81; President, Thistledown Press, 1975-. Publications: Hold the Rain in Your Hands: Poems Selected and New, 1985; Icons of Flesh, 1998; Birchbark Meditations, 1996. Contributions to: Numerous newspapers, journals, and periodicals. Honours: Canada Council Writing Grant; SWG Founder's Award; Hilroy Fellowship; Saskatchewan Arts Board Writing Grant. Memberships: Association of Canadian Publishers; Literary Press Group; Saskatchewan Writers Guild; Writers' Union of Canada; League of Canadian Poets, life member, 1999; International PEN. Address: 668 East Place, Saskatoon, Saskatchewan S7J 2Z5, Canada.

SORRELL John, Author. Education: BA, New College; MFA, University of British Columbia. Appointments: Writer-in-Residence, Faculty Posts, Syracuse University, University of Texas, University of British Columbia; Vancouver Public Library, Regina Public Library, New Lines Theatre, Toronto Workshop Productions Theatre. Publications: Clenched Horizon, 1977; Eddie's Confession, 1987; In Broad Daylight, 1991; On the Other Side of the River, 1992; Come On In, 1996. Honours: Quest Book Award; MLP Book Award; Sothebys International Award; Pulitzer Prize nomination. Address: c/o Sharon Dalgleish, PO Box 285, Saltspring Island, BC V8K 2V9, Canada.

SORRENTINO Gilbert, b. 27 Apr 1929, Brooklyn, New York, USA. Novelist; Poet; Professor of English. m. (1) Elsene Wiessner, div, (2) Vivian V Ortiz, 3 children. Education: Brooklyn College, 1950-51, 1955-57. Appointments: Editor, Publisher, Neon Magazine, New York City, 1956-60; Editor, Grove Press, New York City, 1965-70; Teacher, Columbia University, 1965, Aspen Writers Workshop, 1967, Sarah Lawrence College, 1971-72, New School for Social Research, New York City, 1976-79; Edwin S Quain Professor of Literature,

University of Scranton, 1979; Professor of English, Stanford University, 1982-. Publications: Novels: The Sky Changes, 1966; Steelwork, 1970; Imaginative Qualities of Actual Things, 1971; Splendide-Hotel, 1973; Mulligan Stew, 1979; Aberration of Starlight, 1980; Crystal Vision, 1981; Blue Pastoral, 1983; Odd Number, 1985; Rose Theatre, 1987; Misterioso, 1989; Under the Shadow, 1991; Red the Fiend, 1995. Poetry: The Darkness Surrounds Us, 1960; Black and White, 1964; The Perfect Fiction, 1968; Corrosive Sublimate, 1971; A Dozen Oranges, 1976; White Sail, 1977; The Orangery, 1977; Selected Poems, 1958-1980, 1981. Essays: Something Said, 1984. Play: Flawless Play Restored: The Masque of Fungo, 1974. Translator: Sulpiciae Elegidia/Elegiacs of Sulpicia: Gilbert Sorrentino Versions, 1977. Contributions to: Various anthologies and periodicals. Honours: Guggenheim Fellowships, 1973-74, 1987-88; Samuel S Fels Award, 1974; Creative Artists Public Service Grant, 1974-75; Ariadne Foundation Grant, 1975; National Endowment for the Arts Grants, 1975-76, 1978-79, 1983-84; John Dos Passos Prize, 1981; Mildred and Harold Strauss Livings, 1982 (declined); American Academy and Institute of Arts and Letters Award, 1985; Lannan Literary Award for Fiction, 1992. Membership: PEN American Center. Address: Department of English, Stanford University, Stanford, CA 94305, USA.

SOTO Gary, b. 12 Apr 1952, Fresno, California, USA. Writer; Poet. m. Carolyn Sadako Oda, 24 May 1975, 1 daughter. Education: BA, California State University at Fresno, 1974; MFA, University of California at Irving, 1976. Appointments: Assistant Professor, 1979-85, Associate Professor of English and Ethnic Studies, 1985-92, Part-time Senior Lecturer in English, 1992-93, University of California at Berkeley; Elliston Professor of Poetry, University of Cincinnati, 1988; Martin Luther King/Cesar Chavez/Rosa Park Visiting Professor of English, Wayne State University, 1990. Publications: Poetry: The Elements of San Joaquin, 1977; The Tale of Sunlight, 1978; Where Sparrows Work Hard, 1981; Black Hair, 1985; Who Will Know Us?, 1990; A Fire in My Hands, 1990; Home Course in Religion, 1992; Neighborhood Odes, 1992; Canto Familiar/Familiar Song, 1994; New and Selected Poems, 1995. Other: Living Up the Street: Narrative Recollections, 1985; Small Faces, 1986; Lesser Evils: Ten Quartets, 1988; California Childhood: Recollections and Stories of the Golden State (editor), 1988; A Summer Life, 1990; Baseball in April and Other Stories, 1990; Taking Sides, 1991; Pacific Crossing, 1992; The Skirt, 1992; Pieces of the Heart: New Chicano Fiction (editor), 1993; Local News, 1993; The Pool Party, 1993; Crazy Weekend, 1994; Jesse, 1994; Boys at Work, 1995; Chato's Kitchen, 1995; Everyday Seductions (editor), 1995; Summer on Wheels, 1995; The Old Man and His Door, 1996; Snapshots of the Wedding, 1996; Buried Onions, 1997. Contributions to: Magazines. Honours: Academy of American Poets Prize, 1975; Discovery/The Nation Prize, 1975; United States Award, International Poetry Forum, 1976; Bess Hokin Prize for Poetry, 1978; Guggenheim Fellowship, 1979-80; National Endowment for the Arts Fellowships, 1981, 1991; Levinson Award, Poetry Magazine, 1984; American Book Award, Before Columbus Foundation, 1985; California Arts Council Fellowship, 1989; Carnegie Medal, 1993; Thomas Rivera Prize, 1996. Address: 43 The Crescent, Berkeley, CA 94708, USA.

SOULE Gardner (Bosworth), b. 16 Dec 1913, Paris, Texas, USA. Author. m. (1) Janie Lee McDowell, 20 Sept 1940, dec, (2) Mary Muir Dowhing, 23 Apr 1994. Education: BA, Rice University, 1933; BSc, 1935, MSc, 1936, Columbia University. Appointments: Associated Press, 1936-41; US Naval Reserve, 1942-45; Managing Editor, Better Homes & Gardens, 1945-50. Publications: Tomorrow's World of Science, 1963; The Maybe Monsters, 1963; The Mystery Monsters, 1965; Trail of the Abominable Snowman, 1965; The Ocean Adventure, 1966; UFO's and IFO's, 1967; Wide Ocean, 1970; Men Who Dared the Sea, 1976; The Long Trail: How Cowboys and Longhorns Opened the West, 1976; Mystery Monsters of the Deep, 1981; Mystery Creatures of the Jungle, 1982; Antarctica, 1985; Christopher Columbus, 1989. Contributions to: Popular Science Monthly; United

Features; London Express Syndicate; Boy's Life; Illustrated London News. Honour: Navy League Commendation, 1956. Memberships: Sigma Delta Chi; Columbia University Club. Address: 517 West 113th Street, Apt 53, New York, NY 10025, USA.

SOULE Maris Anne, b. 19 June 1939, Oakland, California, USA. Writer; Teacher. m. William L Soule, 11 May 1968, 1 son, 1 daughter. Education: BA, University of California, Davis, 1961; Secondary Teaching Credential, University of California, Berkeley. Publications: First Impressions, 1983; No Room for Love, 1984; Lost and Found, 1985; Sounds Like Love, 1986; A Winning Combination, 1987; The Best of Everything, 1988; The Law of Nature, 1988; Storybook Hero, 1989; Jared's Lady, 1991; No Promises Made, 1994; Stop the Wedding!, 1994. Memberships: Romance Writers of America; Novelists Inc. Address: PO Box 250, Climax, MI 49034, USA.

SOURELIS Grigoriadou, b. 18 June 1930, Kavala, Greece. Author. m. 1968, 2 sons, 2 daughters. Education: Damascus School of Journalism; Greek School of Social Workers. Publications: The Sparrow in the Red Vest, 1982; Game with No Rules, 1982; Before the Final Whistle, 1982; It Matters to Me, 1990; The Great Farewell, 1990. Contributions to: Diadromes Magazine (co-founder and co-editor); The Metropolis of Piraeus. Honours: European Honours List, University of Padua, 1973; Ourani Award, 1978; International Board of Books for Young People Honours List, 1978; Greek Society of Christian Letters Award, 1989; Special Award, The Smyrnians Union, 1990; Hans Christian Andersen International Award Greek Nominee, 1992. Memberships: Womans Literary Club; The Greek Society of Christian Letters; National Association of Greek Authors; Smyrnian Union. Address: 37 Aharnon Street, 145 61 Kifissia, Athens, Greece.

SOUSTER (Holmes) Raymond, (John Holmes), b. 15 Jan 1921, Toronto, Ontario, Canada. Writer; Poet. m. Rosalia L Geralde, 24 June 1947. Education: University of Toronto Schools, 1932-37; Humberside Collegiate Institute, 1938-39. Publications: 100 Poems of 19th Century Canada (editor with D Lochhead), 1974; Sights and Sounds (editor with R Wollatt), 1974; These Loved, These Hated Lands (editor with R Wollatt), 1974; The Poetry of W W Campbell (editor), 1978; The Best-Known Poems of Archibald Lampman (editor), 1979; Collected Poems of Raymond Souster, 7 volumes, 1980-92; Powassan's Drum: Selected Poems of Duncan Campbell Scott (editor with D Lochhead), 1983; Queen City: Toronto in Poems and Pictures (with Bill Brooks), 1984; Windflower: The Selected Poems of Bliss Carmen (editor with D Lochhead), 1986; Riding the Long Black Horse, 1993; Old Bank Notes, 1993; No Sad Songs Wanted Here, 1995; Close to Home, 1997. Contributions to: Magazines. Honours: Governor-General's Award for Poetry in English, 1964; President's Medal, University of Western Ontario, 1967; Centennial Medal, 1967; City of Toronto Book Award, 1979; Silver Jubilee Medal, 1977; Officer of the Order of Canada, 1995. Membership: League of Canadian Poets, founding member and chairman, 1968-72, life member, 1996-. Address: 39 Baby Point Road, Toronto, Ontario M6S 2G2, Canada.

SOUTHALL Ivan Francis, b. 8 June 1921, Melbourne, Victoria, Australia. Writer. m. (1) Joy Blackburn, 8 Sept 1945 div, 1 son, 3 daughters, (2) Susan Westerlund Stanton, 11 Nov 1976. Appointments: Whitall Poetry and Literature Lecturer, Library of Congress, Washington, DC, USA, 1973; May Hill Arbuthnot Honour Lecturer, University of Washington, USA, 1974; Writer-in-Residence, Macquarie University, Sydney, 1979. Publications: They Shall Not Pass Unseen, 1956; Softly Tread the Brave, 1960; Hills End, 1962; Ash Road, 1965; To the Wild Sky, 1967; Let the Balloon Go, 1968; Josh, 1971; Head in the Clouds, 1972; Matt and Jo, 1973; What About Tomorrow?, 1977; City Out of Sight, 1984; Christmas in the Tree, 1985; Rachel, 1986; Blackbird, 1988; The Mysterious World of Marcus Leadbeater, 1990; Ziggurat, 1997. Honours: Australian Children's Book of the Year, 1966, 1968, 1971, 1976; Australian Picture

Book of the Year (with Ted Greenwood), 1969; Children's Welfare and Culture Encouragement Award, Japan, 1969; Carnegie Medal, 1971; Silver Griffel, Netherlands, 1972; Australia Writers Award, 1974; IBBY Honour Books, 1974, 1979; Order of Australia, 1981; National Children's Book Award, Australia, 1986; Australia Council Emeritus Award, 1993; Retrospective Exhibition, State Library of Victoria, 1998. Others. Memberships: Australian Society of Authors; Fellowship of Australian Writers. Address: PO Box 25, Healesville, Victoria 3777, Australia.

SOUTHAM B(rian) C(harles), b. 15 Sept 1931, London, England. Publisher; Editor. Education: BA, 1956, MA, 1960, BLitt, 1963, Lincoln College, Oxford. Appointments: Lecturer in English Literature, University of London, 1961-63; Currently Chairman, The Athlone Press, London. Publications: Volume the Second (editor), 1963; Jane Austen's Literary Manuscripts, 1964; Selected Poems of Lord Tennyson (editor), 1964; Jane Austen: The Critical Heritage (editor), 2 volumes, 1966, 1987; Critical Essays on Jane Austen (editor), 1968; Minor Works of Jane Austen (editor with R W Chapman), 1969; A Student's Guide to the Selected Works of T S Eliot, 1969, 6th edition, 1994; Tennyson, 1971; Jane Austen Sanditon (editor), 1975; Jane Austen: Northanger Abbey and Persuasion (editor), 1976; Jane Austen: Sense and Sensibility, Pride and Prejudice, and Mansfield Park (editor), casebooks, 3 volumes, 1976; Jane Austen: Sir Charles Grandison, editor, 1980; T S Eliot (editor), 1981. Membership: Jane Austen Society, chairman. Address: 3 West Heath Drive, London NW11 7QG, England.

SOWANDE Bode, b. 2 May 1948, Kaduna, Nigeria. Playwright; Writer. Education: Universities of Ife, Dakar and Sheffield; MA, 1974; PhD, 1977. Appointment: Senior Lecturer, Department of Theatre Arts, University of Ibadan, 1977-90. Publications: The Night Before, 1972; Lamps in the Night, 1973; Bar Beach Prelude, 1976; A Sanctus for Women, 1976; Afamoko - the Workhorse, 1978; Farewell to Babylon, 1978; Kalakuta Cross Currents, 1979; The Master and the Frauds, 1979; Barabas and the Master Jesus, 1980; Flamingo, 1982; Circus of Freedom Square, 1985; Tornadoes Full of Dreams, 1989; Arede Owo (after L'Avare by Molière), 1990; Mammy-Water's Wedding, 1991; Ajantala-Pinocchio, 1992. Novels: Our Man the President, 1981; Without a Home, 1982; The Missing Bridesmaid, 1988; Other: My Life in the Bush of Ghosts (stage adaptation of Amos Tutuola's novel), 1995; Radio and television plays. Honours: Association of Nigerian Authors Drama Awards; Chevalier de l'Ordre des Arts et des Lettres, France, 1991; Patron of the Arts Award, Pan African Writers Association, 1993. Address: c/o Odu Themes Meridian, 33 Oyo Road, Orita, PO Box 14369, Post Office UI, Ibadan, Nigeria.

SOWELL Thomas, b. 30 June 1930, Gastonia, North Carolina, USA. Economist; Writer. Education: AB, Harvard University, 1958; AM, Columbia University, 1959; PhD, University of Chicago, 1968. Appointments: Economist, US Department of Labor, 1961-62; Instructor in Economics, Douglass College, Rutgers University, 1962-63; Lecturer in Economics, Howard University, 1963-64; Economic Analyst, AT & T, 1964-65; Assistant Professor, Cornell University, 1965-69; Associate Professor, Brandeis University, 1969-70; Associate Professor, 1970-74, Professor of Economics, 1974-80, University of California at Los Angeles; Fellow, Center for Advanced Study in the Behavioral Sciences, Stanford, California, 1976-77; Visiting Professor, Amherst College, 1977; Senior Fellow, Hoover Institution, Stanford University, 1977, 1980-. Publications: Ethnic America, 1981; A Conflict of Visions, 1987; Inside American Education, 1993; Race and Culture, 1994; The Vision of the Anointed, 1995. Contributions to: Scholarly journals. Memberships: American Economic Association; National Academy of Education. Address: c/o Hoover Institution, Stanford University, Stanford, CA 94305, USA.

SOYINKA Wole (Akinwande Oluwole), b. 13 July 1934, Isara, Nigeria. Poet; Dramatist; Writer; Professor. Education: University of Ibadan; BA, University of Leeds,

1959. Appointments: Research Fellow in Drama, 1960-61, Chairman, Department of Theatre Arts, 1969-72, University of Ibadan; Lecturer in English, 1962-63, Professor in Dramatic Literature, 1972, Professor of Comparative Literature, 1976-85, University of Ife; Senior Lecturer in English, University of Lagos, 1965-67; Political prisoner, 1967-69; Fellow, Churchill College, Cambridge, 1973-74; Goldwin Smith Professor of Africana Studies and Theatre, Cornell University, 1988-92; Exiled by the Nigerian military government, 1995. Publications: Poetry: Idanre and Other Poems, 1967; Poems from Prison, 1969, augmented edition as A Shuttle in the Crypt, 1972; Ogun Abibiman, 1976; Mandela's Earth and Other Poems, 1989. Plays: The Invention, 1955; A Dance of the Forests, 1960; Longi's Harvest, 1966; The Trials of Brother Jero, 1967; The Strong Breed, 1967; Madmen and Specialists, 1970; Before the Blackout, 1971; Camwood on the Leaves, 1973; Collected Plays, 2 volumes, 1973, 1974; Death and the King's Horseman, 1975; Opera Wonyosi, 1981; A Play of Giants, 1984; Six Plays, 1984; Requiem for a Futurologist, 1985; From Zia with Love, 1992; A Scourge of Hyacinths, 1992; The Beatification of Area Boy, 1995. Novels: The Interpreters, 1965; Season of Anomy, 1973. Other: The Man Died: Prison Notes of Wole Soyinka, 1972; Myth, Literature and the African World, 1976; Ake: The Years of Childhood (autobiography), 1981; Art, Dialogue and Outrage, 1988; Isara: A Voyage Around "Essay", 1989; The Open Sore of a Continent, 1996. Editor: Plays from the Third World: An Anthology, 1971; Poems of Black Africa, 1975. Honours: Rockefeller Foundation Grant, 1960; John Whiting Drama Prize, 1966; Jock Campbell Award, 1968; Nobel Prize for Literature, 1986. Memberships: International Theatre Institute; Union of Writers of the African Peoples; National Liberation Council of Nigeria. Address: c/o Random House Inc, 201 East 50th Street, 22nd Floor, New York, NY 10022, USA.

SPACKS Patricia Meyer, b. 17 Nov 1929, San Francisco, California, USA. Professor of English. 1 daughter. Education: BA, Rollins College, 1949; MA, Yale University, 1950; PhD, University of California at Berkeley, 1955. Appointments: Instructor in English, Indiana University, 1954-56; Instructor in Humanities, University of Florida, 1958-59; Instructor, 1959-61, Assistant Professor, 1961-63, Associate Professor, 1965-68, Professor of English, 1968-79, Wellesley College; Professor of English, 1979-89, Chairman, Department of English, 1985-88, Yale University; Edgar F Shannon Professor of English, 1989-, Chairman, Department of English, 1991-96, University of Virginia. Publications: The Varied God, 1959; The Insistence of Horror, 1962; 18th Century Poetry (editor), 1964; John Gay, 1965; Poetry of Vision, 1967; Late Augustan Prose (editor), 1971; An Argument of Images, 1971; Late Augustan Poetry (editor), 1973; The Female Imagination, 1975; Imagining a Self, 1976; Contemporary Women Novelists, 1977; The Adolescent Idea, 1981; Gossip, 1985; Desire and Truth, 1990; Boredom: The Literary History of a State of Mind, 1995. Honour: American Academy of Arts and Sciences, 1994. Membership: Modern Language Association, president, 1994; American Philosophical Society, 1995; American Council of Learned Societies, chair of board, 1997-. Address: Department of English, 219 Bryan Hall, University of Virginia, Charlottesville, VA 22903, USA.

SPARK David Brian, b. 5 Oct 1930, Darlington, England. Journalist. m. 20 Sept 1958, 1 son, 1 daughter. Education: MA, Modern Languages, Trinity Hall, Cambridge, 1951. Appointments: Assistant Editor, The Northern Echo, 1965-66; Leadwriter, 1967-86, Assistant London Editor, 1982-86, Westminster Press; Editor, National Press Agency, 1972-82, Commonwealth Journalists Association Newsletter, 1986-. Publications: Practical Newspaper Reporting (with G Harris), 1966, third edition, 1997; Who to Ask About Developing Countries, 1992; A Journalist's Guide to Sources, 1996. Contributions to: Financial Times. Memberships: Association of British Science Writers; Commonwealth Journalists Association. Address: 47 Seagry Road, Wanstead, London E11 2NH, England.

SPARK Dame Muriel (Sarah), b. 1 Feb 1918, Edinburgh, Scotland. Author; Poet. m. S O Spark, 1937, diss, 1 son. Education: Heriot Watt College, Edinburgh. Appointments: Political Intelligence Department, British Foreign Office, 1944-45; General Secretary, Poetry Society, 1947-49; Founder, Forum literary magazine. Publications: Fiction: The Comforters, 1957; Robinson, 1958; The Go-Away Bird and Other Stories, 1958; Memento Mori, 1959; The Ballad of Peckham Rye, 1960; The Bachelors, 1960; Voices at Play, 1961; The Prime of Miss Jean Brodie, 1961; The Girls of Slender Means, 1963; The Mandelbaum Gate, 1965; Collected Stories I, 1967; The Public Image, 1968; The Very Fine Clock (for children), 1969; The Driver's Seat, 1970; Not to Disturb, 1971; The Hothouse by the East River, 1973; The Abbess of Crewe, 1974; The Takeover, 1976; Territorial Rights, 1979; Loitering with Intent, 1981; Bang-Bang You're Dead and Other Stories, 1982; The Only Problem, 1984; The Stories of Muriel Spark, 1985; A Far Cry from Kensington, 1988; Symposium, 1990; The French Window and the Small Telephone (for children), 1993; Omnibus 1, 1993; Omnibus II, 1994; Reality and Dreams, 1996; Omnibus III, 1996; Omnibus IV, 1997. Poetry: The Fanfarlo and Other Verse, 1952; Collected Poems I, 1967; Going Up to Sotheby's and Other Poems, 1982. Play: Doctors of Philosophy, 1962. Non-Fiction: Child of Light: A Reassessment of Mary Wollstonecraft Shelley, 1951, revised edition as Mary Shelley, 1987; John Masefield, 1953, revised 1992; Curriculum Vitae (autobiography), 1992; The Essence of the Brontës, 1993. Editor: 1950; A Selection of Poems of Emily Brontë, 1952; The Letters of the Brontës: A Selection, 1954. Contributions to: Various periodicals. Honours: Prix Italia, 1962; FRSL, 1963; Yorkshire Post Book of the Year Award, 1965; James Tait Black Memorial Prize, 1966; Hon DLitt, Strathclyde, 1971, Edinburgh, 1989, Aberdeen, 1995, St Andrews, 1998; Honorary Member American Academy of Arts and Letters, 1978; 1st Prize, FNAC La Meilleur Recueil des Nouvelles Etrangères, 1987; Scottish Book of the Year Award, 1987; CLit, 1991; Ingersoll Foundation T S Eliot Award, 1992; FRSE, 1995; Dame Commander of the Order of the British Empire, 1993; Commandeur de l'Ordre des Arts et des Lettres,France, 1996; David Cohen British Literature Prize, 1997; International PEN Gold Pen Award, 1998. Address: c/o David Higham Associates Ltd, 5-8 Lower John Street, Golden Square, London W1R 4HA, England.

SPARSHOTT Francis (Edward), b. 19 May 1926, Chatham, Kent, England. Philosopher; Writer; Poet; Retired Professor of Philosophy. m. Kathleen Elizabeth Vaughan, 7 Feb 1953, 1 daughter. Education: BA, MA, Corpus Christi College, Oxford, 1950. Appointments: Lecturer, 1950-55, Assistant Professor, 1955-62, Associate Professor, 1962-64, Professor, 1964-91, of Philosophy, University of Toronto. Publications: An Enquiry into Goodness and Related Concepts, 1958; The Structure of Aesthetics, 1963; The Concept of Criticism: An Essay, 1967; Looking for Philosophy, 1972; The Theory of the Arts, 1982; Off the Ground: First Steps in the Philosophy of Dance, 1988; Taking Life Seriously: A Study of the Argument of the Nicomachean Ethic, 1994; A Measured Place: Towards a Philosophical Understanding of the Art of Dance, 1995; The Future of Aesthetics, 1998. Poetry: A Divided Voice, 1965; A Cardboard Garage, 1969; The Rainy Hills: Verses After a Japanese Fashion, 1979; The Naming of the Beasts, 1979; New Fingers for Old Dikes, 1980; The Cave of Trophonius and Other Poems, 1983; The Hanging Gardens of Etobicoke, 1983; Storms and Screens, 1986; Sculling to Byzantium, 1989; Views from the Zucchini Gazebo, 1994; Home from the Air, 1997. Contributions to: Various books and periodicals. Honours: American Council of Learned Societies Fellowship, 1961-62; Canada Council Fellowship, 1970-71; Killam Research Fellowship, 1977-78; 1st Prize for Poetry, CBC Radio Literary Competition, 1981; Centennial Medal, Royal Society of Canada, 1982; Connaught Senior Fellowship in the Humanities, 1984-85. Memberships: American Philosophical Association; American Society for Aesthetics, president, 1981-82; Aristotelian Society; Canadian Classical Association; Canadian Philosophical Association, president, 1975-76; League of Canadian

Poets, president, 1977-78; PEN International, Canadian Centre; Royal Society of Canada, fellow, 1977. Address: 50 Crescentwood Road, Scarborough, Ontario M1N 1E4, Canada.

SPEERS. See: **BUTLER Marilyn.**

SPENCE Alan, b. 5 Dec 1947, Glasgow, Scotland. Dramatist; Writer; Poet. Education: University of Glasgow, 1966-69, 1973-74. Appointments: Writer-in-Residence, University of Glasgow, 1975-77, Traverse Theatre, Edinburgh, 1982, University of Edinburgh, 1989-92, University of Aberdeen, 1996-. Publications: Plays: Sailmaker, 1982; Space Invaders, 1983; Changed Days, 1991. Fiction: Its Colours They Are Fine (short stories), 1977; The Magic Flute (novel), 1990; Stone Garden (stories), 1995. Poetry: Plop (15 Haiku), 1970; Glasgow Zen, 1981. Honours: Scottish Arts Council Book Awards, 1977, 1990, 1996; People's Prize, 1996; TMA Martini Prize, 1996. Address: 21 Waverley Park, Edinburgh EH8 8ER, Scotland.

SPENCE Bill. See: **SPENCE William (John Duncan).**

SPENCE Jonathan (Dermott), b. 11 Aug 1936, Surrey, England. Professor of History; Writer. m. (1) Helen Alexander, 15 Sept 1962, div 1993, 2 sons, (2) Chin Annping, 12 Aug 1993. Education: BA, University of Cambridge, 1959; PhD, Yale University, 1965. Appointments: Assistant Professor, 1966-71, Professor of History, 1971-, Yale University; Wiles Lecturer, Queen's University, Belfast, 1985; Gauss Lecturer, Princeton University, 1987; Visiting Professor, Beijing University, 1987; Honorary Professor, Nanjing University, 1993. Publications: Ts'Ao Yin and the K'Ang-Hsi Emperor, 1966; To Change China, 1969; Emperor of China, 1974; The Death of Woman Wang, 1978; The Gate of Heavenly Peace, 1981; The Memory Palace of Matteo Ricci, 1984; The Question of Hu, 1988; The Search for Modern China, 1990; Chinese Roundabout, 1992; God's Chinese Son, 1996. Contributions to: Professional journals. Honours: Yale Fellow in East Asian Studies, 1962-65, 1968-70; John Adison Porter Prize, 1965; Christopher Award, 1975; Devane Teaching Medal, 1978; Guggenheim Fellowship, 1979-80; Los Angeles Times Book Award, 1982; Vurseli Prize, American Academy and Institute of Arts and Letters, 1983; Comisso Prize, Italy, 1987; John D and Catharine T MacArthur Foundation Fellowship, 1988-93; Gelber Prize, Canada, 1990; Honorary doctorates. Memberships: American Academy of Arts and Sciences; American Philosophical Society; Association of Asian Studies. Address: 691 Forest Road, New Haven, CT 06515, USA.

SPENCE William (John Duncan), (Jessica Blair, Jim Bowden, Kirk Ford, Floyd Rogers, Bill Spence), b. 20 Apr 1923, Middlesborough, England. Author. m. Joan Mary Rhoda Ludley, 8 Sept 1944, 1 son, 3 daughters. Education: St Mary's Teachers Training College, 1940-42. Publications: Numerous books, including: Romantic Rydale (with Joan Spence), 1977, new edition, 1987; Harpooned, 1981; The Medieval Monasteries of Yorkshire (with Joan Spence), 1981; Stories from Yorkshire Monasteries (with Joan Spence), 1992; As Jessica Blair: The Red Shawl, 1993; A Distant Harbour, 1993; Storm Bay, 1994; The Restless Spirit, 1996; The Other Side of the River, 1997; The Seaweed Gatherers, 1998; 36 Westerns; 3 war novels, others. Membership: Society of Authors. Address: Post Office, Ampleforth College, York YO62 4EZ, England.

SPENCER Elizabeth, b. 19 July 1921, Carrollton, Mississippi, USA. Writer. m. John Arthur Rusher, 29 Sept 1956. Education: AB, cum laude, Belhaven College, 1942; MA, Vanderbilt University, 1943. Appointments: Writer-in-Residence, Adjunct Professor, 1977-86, Concordia University, Montreal; Visiting Professor, University of North Carolina at Chapel Hill, 1986-92. Publications: Fire in the Morning, 1948; This Crooked Way, 1952; The Voice at the Back Door, 1956; The Light in the Piazza, 1960; No Place for an Angel, 1967; Ship Island and Other Stories, 1968; The Snare, 1972; The Stories of Elizabeth Spencer, 1981; The Salt Line, 1984;

Jack of Diamonds, 1988; For Lease or Sale (drama), 1989; The Night Travellers, 1991; Landscapes of the Heart (memoir), 1998. Contributions to: New Yorker; Atlantic; Southern Review; Kenyon Review. Address: 402 Longleaf Drive, Chapel Hill, NC 27514, USA.

SPENCER LaVyrle, b. 17 Aug 1943, Browerville, Minnesota, USA. Writer. m. Daniel F Spencer, 10 Feb 1962, 2 daughters. Education: High School, Staples, Minnesota. Publications: The Fulfillment, 1979; The Endearment, 1982; Hummingbird, 1983; Twice Loved, 1984; Sweet Memories, 1984; A Heart Speaks, 1986; Tears, 1986; Years, 1986; The Gamble, 1987; Separate Bed, 1987; Vows, 1988; Morning Glory, 1988; Bitter Sweet, 1990; Forgiving, 1991; November of the Heart, 1992; Bygones, 1993; Family Blessings, 1994; That Camden Summer, 1996. Honours: Historical Romance of the Year Awards, Romance Writers of America, 1983, 1984, 1985. Address: 6701 79th Avenue, Brooklyn Park, MN 55445, USA.

SPIEGELMAN Art, b. 15 Feb 1948, Stockholm, Sweden. Cartoonist; Editor; Writer. m. Françoise Mouly, 12 July 1977, 2 children. Education: Harpur College, Binghamton, New York. Appointments: Creative Consultant, Artist, Designer, Editor, and Writer, Topps Chewing Gum Inc, Brooklyn, New York, 1966-88; Editor, Douglas Comix, 1972; Instructor, San Francisco Academy of Art, 1974-75, New York School of the Visual Arts, 1979-87; Contributing Editor, Arcade, The Comics Revue, 1975-76; Founder-Editor, Raw, 1980-; Artist and Contributing Editor, The New Yorker, 1992-. Publications: Author and Illustrator: The Complete Mr Infinity, 1970; The Viper Vicar of Vice, Villainy, and Vickedness, 1972; Ace Hole, Midge Detective, 1974; The Language of Comics, 1974; Breakdowns: From Maus to Now: An Anthology of Strips, 1977; Work and Turn, 1979; Every Day Has Its Dog, 1979; Two-Fisted Painters Action Adventure, 1980; Maus: A Survivor's Tale, 1986; Read Yourself Raw (with F Mouly), 1987; Maus, Part Two, 1992; The Wild Party, 1994. Honours: Playboy Editorial Award for Best Comic Strip, 1982; Joel M Cavior Award for Jewish Writing, 1986; Stripschappening Award for Best Foreign Comics Album, 1987; Pulitzer Prize Special Citation, 1992; Alpha Art Awrd, Angoulerne, France, 1993. Address: c/o Raw Books and Graphics, 27 Greene Street, New York, NY 10013, USA.

SPILLANE Mickey, (Frank Morrison Spillane), b. 9 Mar 1918, New York, New York, USA. Author. m. (1) Mary Ann Pearce, 1945, div, 2 sons, 2 daughters, (2) Sherri Malinou, 1964, div, (3) Jane Rodgers Johnson, 1983. Education: Kansas State College. Publications: I, the Jury, 1947; Vengeance is Mine!, 1950; My Gun is Quick, 1950; The Big Kill, 1951; One Lonely Night, 1951; The Long Wait, 1951; Kiss Me, Deadly, 1952; Tough Guys, 1960; The Deep, 1961; The Girl Hunters, 1962; Day of the Guns, 1964; The Snake, 1964; Bloody Sunrise, 1965; The Death Dealers, 1965; The Twisted Thing, 1966; The By-Pass Control, 1967; The Delta Factor, 1967; Body Lovers, 1967; Killer Mine, 1968; Me, Hood!, 1969; Survival: Zero, 1970; Tough Guys, 1970; The Erection Set, 1972; The Last Cop Out, 1973; The Flier, 1973; Tomorrow I Die, 1984; The Killing Man, 1989; Back Alley, 1996. Editor: Murder is My Business, 1994. Television Series: Mike Hammer, 1984-87. Children's Books: The Day the Sea Rolled Back, 1979; The Ship That Never Was, 1982. Address: c/o E P Dutton, 375 Hudson Street, New York, NY 10014, USA.

SPITTA Silvia, b. 12 Mar 1956, Lima, Peru. Professor of Latin American Literature & Comparative Literature. m. Gerd Gemunden, 1 Apr 1989, 2 sons. Education: BA, UCSD, 1979; PhD, Comparative Literature, University of Oregon, 1989. Appointments: Teaching Assistant, University of Oregon, 1988-89; Visiting Instructor, Seattle University, 1988-89; Assistant, 1989-96, Associate Professor, 1996-, Dartmouth College. Publications: Between Two Waters: Narratives of Transculturation in Latin America, 1995. Honour: Dartmouth Burke Award, 1989. Memberships: MLA; Instituto Iberoamericans. Address: Department of Spanish & Portuguese, Dartmouth College, Hanover, NH 03755, USA.

SPOLTER Pari, b. 30 Jan 1930, Tehran, Iran. Writer; Publisher. m. Herbert Spolter MD, 16 Aug 1958, 1 son, 1 daughter. Education: Licence es Sciences, Cliniques mention Biologiques, University of Geneva, Switzerland, 1952; MS, 1959, PhD, Biochem, 1961, University of Wisconsin in Madison, USA. Appointments: Postdoctoral Fellow, Instructor, Temple University, Philadelphia, Pennsylvania, USA, 1961-65; Research Biochemist, US Public Health Service Hospital, San Francisco, USA, 1966-68; Writer, Publisher, Orb Publishing Co, Granada Hills, 1988-. Publication: Gravitational Force of the Sun. Contributions to: Several articles. Address: 17648 Arvida Drive, Granada Hills, CA 91344-1344, USA.

SPOONER David Eugene, b. 1 Sept 1941, West Kirby, Wirral, England. Writer; Naturalist. m. Marion O'Neil, 9 Mar 1986, 1 daughter. Education: BA, hons, University of Leeds, 1963; Diploma in Drama, University of Manchester, 1964; PhD, University of Bristol, 1968. Appointments: Lecturer, University of Kent, 1968-73; Visiting Professor, Pennsylvania State University, 1973-74; Lecturer, Manchester Polytechnic, 1974-75; Head of Publishing Borderline Press, 1976-85; Director, Butterfly Conservation, East Scotland. Publications: Unmakings, 1977; The Angelic Fly: The Butterfly in Art, 1992; The Metaphysics of Insect Life, 1995; Creatures of Air: Poetry 1976-98, 1998; Insect into Poem: Twentieth Century Hispanic Poety, forthcoming. Contributions to: Iron; Interactions; Tandem; Weighbauk; Revue de Littérature Comparée; Bestia (Fable Society of America); Margin; Corbie Press; Butterfly Conservation News; Butterfly News; Field Studies. Memberships: The Welsh Academy Associate; Association Benjamin Constant. Address: 96 Halbeath Road, Dunfermline, Fife KY12 7LR, Scotland.

SPRAY Pauline E, b. 9 July 1920, Byron Center, Michigan, USA. Housewife. m. Russell E Spray, 8 Mar 1940, 2 daughters. Education: Southern Nazarene University; Central Michigan University; Grand Rapids Junior College. Appointments: Teacher, 4 years; Pastors Wife, 32 years; Writer, 1954-. Publications: Daily Delights; Rx for Nerves; How to Live with Less Tension; Rx For Happiness; Confessions of a Preacher's Wife; the Valley of Decision; In the Footsteps of Pioneers (co-author). Contributions to: Religions publications and newspapers. Address: 1145 Adams Street, Lapeer, MI 48446-1304, USA.

SPRIGEL Oliver. See: **AVICE Claude (Pierre Marie).**

SPRIGGE Timothy Lauro Squire, b. 14 Jan 1932, London, England. Professor of Philosophy; Writer. m. Giglia Gordon, 4 Apr 1959, 1 son, 2 daughters. Education: BA, 1955, MA, PhD, 1961, Cantab. Appointment: Professor of Philosophy, University of Edinburgh. Publications: The Correspondence of Jeremy Benthan (editor), 1968; Facts, Words and Beliefs, 1970; Santayana: An Examination of His Philosophy, 1974; The Vindication of Absolute Idealism, 1983; Theories of Existence, 1984; The Rational Foundation of Ethics, 1987; James and Bradley: American Truth and British Reality, 1993. Contributions to: Professional journals. Honour: Fellow, Royal Society of Edinburgh. Memberships: Mind Association; Scots Philosophical Club. Address: c/o David Hume Tower, University of Edinburgh, George Square, Edinburgh EH8 9JX, Scotland.

SPRING Michael, b. 14 Oct 1941, New York, New York, USA. Editor; Writer. Div, 2 sons. Education: BA, Haverford College, Pennsylvania, 1964; MA, English Literature, Columbia University, 1970. Appointments: Vice President and Editorial Director, Fodor's Travel Publications; Contributing Editor, Condé Nast's Traveler magazine; Travel Expert, CNN-TV Travel Show, 1992-. Publications: The American Way of Working (editor), 1980; Barron's Book Notes series (editor), 50 volumes, 1984; A Student's Guide to Julius Caesar, 1984; The Great Weekend Escape Book, 3rd edition, 1987, 4th edition, 1990; Great European Itineraries, 1987, 3rd edition, 1994. Contributions to: Magazines. Honour: Distinguished Achievement Award in Educational Journalism, Educational Press Association of America, 1987. Address: c/o Random House Inc, 201 East 50th Street, New York, NY 10022, USA.

SPRINGER Nancy, b. 5 July 1948, Montclair, New Jersey, USA. Novelist. m. Joel H Springer, 13 Sept 1969, 1 son, 1 daughter. Education: BA, English Literature, Gettysburg College, 1970. Appointments: Personal Development Plan Instructor, University of Pittsburgh, 1983-85; Leisure Learning Instructor, York College, Pennsylvania, 1986-91; Education Instructor, Franklin and Marshall College, 1988-. Publications: The Sable Moon, 1981; The Black Beast, 1982; The Golden Swan, 1983; Wings of Flame, 1985; Chains of Gold, 1986; A Horse to Love (juvenile), 1987; Madbond, 1987; Chance and Other Gestures of the Hand of Fate, 1987; The Hex Witch of Seldom, 1988; Not on a White Horse (juvenile), 1988; Apocalypse, 1989; They're All Named Wildfire (juvenile), 1989; Red Wizard (juvenile), 1990; Colt (juvenile), 1991; The Friendship Song (juvenile), 1992; The Great Pony Hassle (juvenile), 1993; Stardark Songs (poetry), 1993; Larque on the Wing, 1994; The Boy on a Black Horse (juvenile), 1994; Metal Angel, 1994; Music of Their Hooves (poetry, juvenile), 1994. Contributions to: Magazines and journals. Honours: Distinguished Alumna, Gettysburg College, 1987; Nominee, Hugo Award, 1987; Nominee, World Fantasy Award, 1987; International Reading Association Children's Choice, 1988; Joan Fassler Memorial Book Award, 1992; International Reading Association Young Adult's Choice, 1993. Memberships: Society of Children's Book Writers; Central Pennsylvania Writers' Organization; Children's Literature Council of Pennsylvania; Pennwriters, president, 1992-93; Novelists Inc. Address: c/o Virginia Kidd Agency, Box 278, 538 East Harford Street, Milford, PA 18337, USA.

SPRINKLE Patricia Houck, b. 13 Nov 1943, Bluefield, West Virginia, USA. Writer. m. Robert William Sprinkle, 12 Sept 1970, 2 sons. Education: AB, Vassar College, 1965. Publications: Fiction: Murder at Markham, 1988; Murder in the Charleston Manner, 1990; Murder on Peachtree Street, 1991; Somebody's Dead in Snellville, 1992; Death of a Dunwoody Matron, 1993; A Mystery Bred in Buckhead, 1994; Deadly Secrets on the St Johns, 1995; When Did We Lose Harriet?, 1997. Non-Fiction: Hunger: Understanding the Crisis Through Games, 1980; In God's Image: Meditations for the New Mother, 1988; Housewarmings: For Those Who Make a House a Home, 1992; Women Who Do Too Much: Stress and the Myth of the Superwoman, 1992; Children Who Do Too Little, 1993; A Gift From God, 1994; Women Home Alone: Learning to Thrive, 1996. Contributions to: Magazines. Memberships: Mystery Writers of America; Penwoman; Sisters in Crime, publicity chairperson. Address: 15086 South West 113th Street, Miami, FL 33196, USA.

SPROTT Duncan, b. 2 December 1952, Ongar, Essex, England. Novelist. Education: University of St Andrews; Heatherley School of Art. Publications: 1784, 1984; The Clopton Hercules, 1991; Our Lady of the Potatoes, 1995. Membership: Society of Authors. Address: c/o Rogers, Coleridge & White Ltd, 20 Powis Mews, London W11 1JN, England.

SPURLING John (Antony), b. 17 July 1936, Kisumu, Kenya. Dramatist; Novelist; Art Critic. m. Hilary Forrest, 4 Apr 1961, 2 sons, 1 daughter. Education: BA, St John's College, Oxford, 1960. Publications: Plays: MacRune's Guevara (as Realised by Edward Hotel), 1969; In the Heart of the British Museum, 1971; Shades of Heathcliff and Death of Captain Doughty, 1975; The British Empire, Part One, 1982. Novels: The Ragged End, 1989; After Zenda, 1995. Other: Beckett: A Study of His Plays (with John Fletcher), 1972, 3rd edition, revised, as Beckett, the Playwright, 1985; Graham Greene, 1983. Contributions to: Books, newspapers, periodicals, theatre (14 plays produced, 1969-94), radio (8 plays, 1976-93), and television (4 plays, 1970-73). Honour: Henfield Writing Fellowship, University of East Anglia, 1973. Address: c/o MLR Ltd, Douglas House, 16-18 Douglas Street, London SW1F 4PB, England.

SRIVASTAVA Ramesh Kumar, b. 2 Jan 1940, Banpur, India. Writer. m. Usha Rani Srivastava, 27 June 1959, 2 sons. Education: BA, 1957; MA, 1961; PhD, 1972. Appointments: Editor, The Summit, 1970-72; Associate Editor, 1976-88, Editor, 1988-93, The Punjab Journal of English Studies. Publications: Love and Animality: Stories, 1984; Cooperative Colony: Stories, 1985; Neema (novel), 1986; Six Indian Novelists in English, 1987; Games They Play and Other Stories, 1989; Critical Studies in English and American Literature, 1993; Under the Lamp: Stories, 1993. Contributions to: Newspapers and journals. Honours: Fulbright Fellowship, 1969; Senior Fulbright Grant, 1984. Memberships: Authors Guild of India; Indian PEN; Modern Language Association. Address: B 16 Guru Nanak Dev University, Amritsar 143005, India.

ST AUBIN DE TERAN Lisa, b. 2 Oct 1953, London, England. Writer; Poet. m. (1) Jaime Teran, Oct 1970, div 1981, 1 daughter, (2) George MacBeth, Mar 1981, div 1986, 1 son. Publications: The Streak, 1980; The Long Way Home, 1983; The Slow Train to Milan, 1983; The High Place, 1985. Honours: Somerset Maugham Award, 1983; John Rhys Memorial Prize, 1983; Eric Gregory Award for Poetry, 1983. Membership: Royal Society of Literature, fellow. Address: 7 Canynge Square, Clifton, Bristol, England.

ST AUBYN Giles R (The Honorable), b. 11 Mar 1925, London, England. Writer. Education: MA, Trinity College, Oxford University. Publications: Lord Macaulay, 1952; A Victorian Eminence, 1957; The Art of Argument, 1957; The Royal George, 1963; A World to Win, 1968; Infamous Victorians, 1971; Edward VII, Prince and King, 1979; The Year of Three Kings 1483, 1983; Queen Victoria: A Portrait, 1991. Honour: LVO. Memberships: Royal Society of Literature, fellow; Society of Authors. Literary Agent: Christopher Sinclair-Stevenson, 3 South Terrace, London SW7 2TB. Address: Saumarez Park Manor, Apt 2, Route de Saumarez, Câtel, Guernsey GY5 7TH, Channel Islands.

ST CLAIR William, b. 7 Dec 1937, London, England. Author. 2 daughters. Education: St John's College, Oxford, 1956-60. Appointments: Formerly, Under-Secretary, Her Majesty's Treasury; Visiting Fellow, 1981-82, Fellow, 1985, Huntington Library, San Marino, California, 1985; Fellow, All Souls College, Oxford, 1992-96; Visiting Fellow Commoner, 1997, Fellow 1998, Trinity College, Cambridge. Publications: Lord Elgin and the Marbles, 1967, third revised edition, 1998; That Greece Might Still Be Free, 1972; Trelawny, 1978; Policy Evaluation: A Guide for Managers, 1988; The Godwins and the Shelleys: The Biography of a Family, 1989; Executive Agencies: A Guide to Setting Targets and Judging Performance, 1992. Honours: Heinemann Prize, Royal Society of Literature, 1973; Time-Life Prize, 1990; MacMillan Silver Pen, 1990. Memberships: British Academy, 1992, council, 1997, fellow, 1998; Byron Society, international president; Royal Society of Literature, fellow. Address: Trinity College, Cambridge CB2 1TQ, England.

ST PIERRE Roger, (Peter Kent, Pete Rogers), b. 8 Nov 1941. Author; Journalist; Editor. m. Lesley Constantine, 10 Nov 1975, div, 1 son, 2 daughters. Appointments: Assoc Editor, Ford Bulletin, 1962; Assistant Editor, Cycling, 1964; Beacon Records PR, 1966; Freelance, 1968; Editor, Disco International, 1975; Editor, Voyager Magazine, 1982; Editor, American Express Great Golf Guide, 1997-. Publications: Book of the Bicycle, 1968; Rock Handbook, 1973; Tina Turner, 1980; The McDonald's Story, 1993; In His Own Words - Tom Jones, 1996; Know the Game Cycling, 1996. Contributions to: Financial Weekly; Times Business Supplement; Daily Mirror; Business Today; Diner's Club Signature Magazine; ABTA Magazine; Meridian Magazine; London Caterer. Address: 24 Beauval Road, Dulwich, London SG22 8UQ, England.

STACEY Tom, (Thomas Charles Gerard Stacey), b. 11 Jan 1930, Bletchingly, England. Author. m. Caroline Clay, 5 Jan 1952, 1 son, 4 daughters. Education: Eton College, Oxford. Appointments: Writer and Foreign Correspondent, Daily Express, London, 1954, 1956-60; Correspondent, Montreal Star, 1955-56; Chief Roving Correspondent, Sunday Times, London, 1960-65; Columnist, Evening Standard, London, 1965-67; Managing Director, Correspondents World Wide, London, 1967-71; Tom Stacey Ltd, later Stacey International, London, 1969-. Publications: Fiction: The Brothers M, 1960; The Living and the Dying, 1976; The Pandemonium, 1980; The Twelth Night of Ramadan, 1983; The Worm in the Rose, 1985; Deadline, 1988; Decline, 1991. Film Screenplay: Deadline, 1988. Radio Play: Affair in Riyadh. Non-fiction: The Hostile Sun: A Malayan Journey, 1953; Summons to Ruwenzori, 1965; Immigration and Enoch Powell, 1970. Other: Today's World: A Map Notebook for World Affairs (editor), 1968; Correspondents World Wide (with Caroline Hayman), 1968; Chambers' Encyclopedia Yearbook (editor-in-chief), 1969-72; Here Come the Tories, 1970; Peoples of the World (editorial director), 20 volumes, 1971-73. Contributions to: Books, newspapers, and periodicals. Honours: John Llewllyn Rhys Memorial Prize, 1954; Granada Award, 1961. Memberships: Royal Geographical Society, fellow; Royal Society of Literature, fellow. Address: 128 Kensington Church Street, London W8, England.

STACK George Joseph, b. New York, USA. Professor of Philosophy Emeritus; Writer. m. (1), 1 son, 1 daughter, (2) Mary C De Maria, 25th July 1997, 2 step-daughters. Education: BA, Pace University, 1960; MA, 1962, PhD, 1964, Pennsylvania State University. Appointments: Instructor, 1963-64, Assistant Professor, 1964-67, Long Island University; Assistant Professor, 1967-68, Associate Professor, 1968-70, Professor of Philosophy, 1970-95, Professor Emeritus, 1995-, State University of New York at Brockport. Publications: Berkeley's Analysis of Perception, 1970, 2nd edition, 1991; On Kierkegaard, 1976; Kierkegaard's Existential Ethics, 1977, 2nd edition, 1992; Sartre's Philosophy of Social Existence, 1978, 2nd edition, 1992; Lange and Nietzsche, 1983; Nietzsche and Emerson, 1993. Contributions to: Books and professional journals. Memberships: American Philosophical Association; North American Nietzsche Society. Address: PO Box 92, Grapevine, TX 76099, USA.

STADTLER Beatrice, b. 26 June 1921, Cleveland, Ohio, USA. Educator; Writer. m. Oscar Stadtler, 31 Jan 1945, 1 son, 2 daughters. Education: Diploma, Sunday School Teacher, 1957; Bachelor, Judaic Studies, 1971; MSc, Religious Education, 1983; Master of Jewish Studies, 1989. Appointments: Columnist, Cleveland Jewish News for Youth and Boston Jewish Advocate; Co-Editor, Israel Philatelist. Publications: Once Upon a Jewish Holiday, 1965; The Adventures of Gluckel of Hameln, 1967; The Story of Dona Gracia Mendes, 1969; The Holocaust: A History of Courage and Resistance, 1975; Significant Lives, 1976; Rescue From the Sky, 1978; A History of Israel Through Her Postage Stamps, 1993. Contributions to: Books and periodicals. Honours: Jewish Book Council Award For Best Jewish Juvenile Book in the USA, 1975; Award, National Canadian Philatelic Literature Exhibition, 1993. Membership: Jewish Educator's Assembly. Address: 24355 Tunbridge Lane, Beachwood, OH 44122, USA.

STAFFORD Christine Elizabeth, b. 25 July 1951, Northants, England. Writer. Education: MA, University of Westminster, 1999. Appointment: Freelance Writer, Photographer, Broadcaster and Scriptwriter, 1978-. Publications: Fit to Compete, 1985; Practical Stable Management, 1987; Horse Care and Management, 1991. Contributions to: Books, magazines and journals. Memberships: International Womens Media Foundation; Association Internationale Presse Sportive; International Alliance of Equestrian Journalists; Sports Writers Association; British Equestrian Writers Association. Address: 3 Clarendon House, Werrington Street, London NW1 1PL, England.

STÄGER Lorenz, b. 23 Dec 1942, Muri AG, Switzerland. Professor of Latin. Education: PhD, University of Zurich. Publications: Novels: Aber, aber, Frau Potiphar, 1978, Italian translation, 1980; Liebt Ihr Bruder Fisch, Madame?, 1980; Alexander der Kleine, 1984; Nur wenn die Löwen nicht beissen, 1989; Kinder, Camper und Gelehrte, book of travels, 1993. Membership: Schweizer Schriftsteller Verband. Address: Bahnhofstrasse 8, CH-5610 Wohlen, Switzerland.

STAGG Pamela Margaret Southwell, b. 22 Apr 1949, Nottingham, England. Div. Education: BA, University of Guelph, 1974. Publications: In the Spirit of Partnership, 1990; The Future of Steel (cd-rom), 1997; Financial Security for Your Child With Mental Disabilities, 1997. Honours: Applied Arts Magazine Award, 1997-98. Literary Agent: Canadian Speakers and Writers Service Ltd.

STAINES David, b. 8 Aug 1946, Toronto, Ontario, Canada. Professor of English; Writer; Translator; Editor. Education: BA, University of Toronto, 1967; AM, 1968, PhD, 1973, Harvard University. Appointments: Assistant Professor of English, Harvard University, 1973-78; Honorary Research Fellow, University College, London, 1977-78; Associate Professor, 1978-85, Professor of English, 1985-, Dean, Faculty of Arts, 1996-, University of Ottawa; Five College Professor of Canadian Studies, Smith College, 1982-84. Publications: Editor: The Canadian Imagination: Dimensions of a Literary Culture, 1977; Stephen Leacock: A Reappraisal, 1986; The Forty-Ninth and Other Parallels: Contemporary Canadian Perspectives, 1986. Author: Tennyson's Camelot: The Idylls of the King and Its Medieval Sources, 1982. Translator: The Complete Romances of Chretien de Troyes, 1990; Beyond the Provinces: Literary Canada at Century's End, 1995. Contributions to: Professional journals. Address: Department of English, University of Ottawa, Ottawa, Ontario K1N 6N5, Canada.

STALLWORTHY Jon (Howie), b. 18 Jan 1935, London, England. Professor of English Literature; Poet; Writer. m. Gillian Waldock, 25 June 1960, 3 children. Education: BA, 1958, BLitt, 1961, Magdalen College, Oxford. Appointments: Editor, 1959-71, Deputy Academic Publisher, 1974-77, Oxford University Press; Visiting Fellow, All Souls College, Oxford, 1971-72; Editor, Clarendon Press, Oxford, 1972-77; John Wendell Anderson Professor of English Literature, Cornell Unversity, Ithaca, New York, 1977-86; Reader in English Literature, 1986-92, Professor of English, 1992-, University of Oxford. Publications: Poetry: The Earthly Paradise, 1958; The Astronomy of Love, 1961; Out of Bounds, 1963; The Almond Tree, 1967; A Day in the City, 1967; Root and Branch, 1969; Positives, 1969; A Dinner of Herbs, 1970; Hand in Hand, 1974; The Apple Barrel: Selected Poems, 1955-63, 1974; A Familiar Tree, 1978; The Anzac Sonata: Selected Poems, 1986; The Guest from the Future, 1995; Rounding the Horn: Collected Poems, 1998. Other: Between the Lines: Yeats's Poetry in the Making, 1963; Vision and Revision in Yeats's Last Poems, 1969; The Penguin Book of Love Poetry (editor), 1973; Wilfred Owen: A Biography, 1974; Poets of the First World War, 1974; Boris Pasternak: Selected Poems (translator with France), 1982; The Complete Poems and Fragments of Wilfred Owen (editor), 1983; The Oxford Book of War Poetry (editor), 1984; The Poems of Wilfred Owen (editor), 1985; First Lines: Poems Written in Youth from Herbert to Heaney (editor), 1987; Henry Reed: Collected Poems (editor), 1991; Louis MacNeice, 1995; Singing School: The Making of a Poet, 1998. Contributions to: Professional journals. Memberships: British Academy, fellow; Royal Society of Literature, fellow. Address: Wolfson College, Oxford OX2 6UD, England.

STAMM Gret. See: GUT-RUSSENBERGER Margrit.

STAMPER Alex. See: KENT Arthur (William Charles).

STANBROUGH Harvey Ernest, b. 19 Nov 1952, Alamogordo, New Mexico, USA. Retired US Marine; College Instructor; Poet; Editor. m. Mona Griffith, 23 June 1984, 3 sons, 2 daughters. Education: BA, English, 1996. Publication: Melancholy and Madness, 1993; Partners in Rhyme, 1996; On Love and War and Other Fantasies,

1997. Contributions to: Anthologies and other publications. Honours: Contest awards; Phi Theta Kappa. Address: 810 South Michigan, Roswell, NM 88201, USA.

STANFIELD Anne. See: COFFMAN Virginia (Edith).

STANGL (Mary) Jean, b. 14 May 1928, Irondale, Missouri, USA. Writer. m. Herbert Stangl, 14 Aug 1946, 3 sons. Education: BA, University of LaVerne, 1975; MA, California State University at Northridge, 1977. Publications: Over 30 books, 1975-96. Honours: Several. Memberships: Beatrix Potter Society; National Association for the Education of Young Children; Society of Children's Book Writers and Illustrators. Address: 1658 Calle La Cumbre, Camarillo, CA 93010, USA.

STANLEY Autumn Joy, b. 21 Dec 1933, Vinton County, Ohio, USA. Writer. m. (1) F Blair Simmons, 6 June 1955, div 1971, 1 son, 3 daughters, (2) John Morgan Daniel, 1 Jan 1973, div 1984. Education: AB, High Distinction, Transylvania College, 1955; MA, English and American Literature, Stanford University, 1967. Appointments: Instructor, Pacific Lutheran University, Tacoma, 1957-58, Canada College, Redwood City, California, 1969-70; Editor, Stanford University Press, California, 1969-74; Development Editor, Wadsworth Publishers, Belmont, California, 1974-80; Affiliated Scholar, Center for Research on Women and Gender, Stanford University, California, 1984-88. Publications: Asparagus: The Sparrowgrass Cookbook, 1977; 'Mainder the Buttercup, 1977; The Enchanted Quill, 1978; Mothers and Daughters of Invention, 1993. Contributions to: Anthologies, magazines and journals. Honour: Distinguished Service Award, Transylvania University, 1995. Memberships: Institute for Historical Study; National Women's Studies Association. Address: 241 Bonita Los Trancos Woods, Portola Valley, CA 94028, USA.

STANLEY Bennett. See: HOUGH Stanley Bennett.

STANLEY Colin, b. 27 May 1952, Topsham, Devon, England. Author; Publisher; Librarian. m. Gail Patricia Andrews, 8 June 1973, 1 son, 1 daughter. Education: Ealing College of Higher Education, 1972-74; Achieved Associate Library Association. Appointments: Library Assistant, Devon Library Services, 1971-75; Senior Library Assistant, Nottingham University, 1980-; Managing Editor, Paupers' Press, 1983-. Publications: The Aylesford Review 1955-1968: An Index, 1984; The Work of Colin Wilson: An Annotated Bibliography and Guide, 1989; Colin Wilson, A Celebration, 1989; The Nature of Freedom and Other Essays, 1990; Editor of 40 other publications. Contributions to: Regular Contributor to Abraxas magazine; Contributor: Lodestar; Paperbacks, Pulps and Comics; Cornish Scene. Address: 27 Melbourne Road, West Bridgford, Nottingham NG2 5DJ, England.

STANLEY Julian Cecil, Jr, b. 9 July 1918, Macon, Georgia, USA. Professor of Psychology; Writer. m. (1) Rose Roberta Sanders, 18 Aug 1946, dec 1978, 1 daughter, (2) Barbara S Kerr, 1 Jan 1980. Education: BS, Physical Science, Georgia Southern University, 1937; EdM, 1946, EdD, Experimental and Educational Psychology, 1950, Harvard University; Postdoctoral Fellow, University of Chicago, 1955-56; Fulbright Act Research Scholar, University of Louvain, Belgium, 1958-59, University of New Zealand, 1974. Appointments: Professor of Education and Psychology, 1967-71, Professor of Psychology, 1971-, Johns Hopkins University; Founder and Director, Study of Mathematically Precocious Youth (SMPY), Johns Hopkins University, 1971-; Visiting Lecturer at Universities in Australia, 1980, 1992; Visiting Distinguished Professor, University of North Texas, 1990. Publications: Author, co-author or editor of 13 books and about 500 professional articles, technical notes, chapters, reviews, and technical letters to editors. Honours: Johns Hopkins University Chapter Recognition Award, 1979; American Psychological Society; Distinguished Teacher, White House Commission on Presidential Scholars, 1987, 1992; Honorary Doctorates, University of North Texas, 1990,

State University of West Georgia, 1997; James McKeen Cattell Fellow Award in Applied Psychology, 1994. Memberships: American Educational Research Association; National Academy of Education; National Association for Gifted Children. Address: Johns Hopkins University, Baltimore, MD 21218, USA.

STANSKY Peter (David Lyman), b. 18 Jan 1932, New York, New York, USA. Professor of Historian; Writer; Editor. Education: BA, Yale University, 1953; BA, 1955, MA, 1959, King's College, Cambridge; PhD, Harvard University, 1961. Appointments: Instructor in History, Harvard University, 1961-64; Assistant Professor, 1964-68, Associate Professor, 1968-73, Professor, 1973-, of History, Frances and Charles Field Professor of History, 1974-, Stanford University; Associate Editor, Journal of British Studies, 1973-85; Editor, North American Conference on British Studies Bibliographical Series, 1977-; Visiting Fellow, All Souls College, 1979, Christensen Fellow, St Catherine's College, 1983, Oxford; Co-Editor, Virginia Woolf Miscellany, 1984-; Fellow, Center for the Advanced Study of the Behavioral Sciences, 1988-89; Various guest lectureships. Publications: Ambitions and Strategies: The Struggle for the Leadership of the Liberal Party in the 1890s, 1964; Journey to the Frontier: Julian Bell and John Cornford, their Lives and the 1930s (with William Abrahams), 1966; The Unknown Orwell (with William Abrahams), 1972; England Since 1867: Continuity and Change, 1973; Gladstone: A Progress in Politics, 1979; Orwell: The Transformation (with William Abrahams), 1979; William Morris, 1983; Redesigning the World, 1985; London's Burning (with William Abrahams), 1994; On or About December 1910: Early Bloomsbury and Its Intimate World, 1996. Editor: The Left and War: The British Labour Party and the First World War, 1969; Winston Churchill: A Profile, 1973; The Victorian Revolution, 1973; Modern British History Series (with Leslie Hume), 18 volumes, 1982; On Nineteen Eighty-Four, 1983; Modern European History Series, 47 volumes, 1987-92. Honours: Guggenheim Fellowships, 1966-67, 1973-74; American Council of Learned Societies Fellow, 1978-79; National Endowment for the Humanities Senior Fellowships, 1983, 1998-99; Honorary DL, Wittenberg University, 1984. Memberships: American Academy of Arts and Sciences, fellow; American Historical Association; National Book Critics Circle, director, 1980-85; North American Conference on British Studies, president, 1974-76; Royal Historical Society, fellow; Society for the Promotion of Science and Scholarship, president; Virginia Woolf Society; William Morris Society. Address: c/o Department of History, Stanford University, Stanford, CA 94305, USA.

STAPLES Brent, b. 1951, Chester, Pennsylvania, USA. Writer. Education: BA, Widener University, 1973; PhD, University of Chicago, 1977. Appointments: Reporter, Chicago Sun-Times, 1982-83; Editorial Writer, New York Times, 1983-. Publication: Parallel Time: Growing Up in Black and White, 1994. Contributions to: Periodicals. Honour: Danforth Fellowship. Address: c/o New York Times, 229 West 43rd Street, New York, NY 10036, USA.

STAREV Plamen, b. 7 May 1952, Plovdiv, Bulgaria. Journalist. m. Lilia Stareva, 29 Mar 1980, 1 son, 2 daughters. Education: BA, Sofia University, 1975. Appointments: Reporter, Narodna Mladej, daily newspaper, 1982-90; Deputy Editor-in-Chief, Dialog, daily, 1990-91; Editor-in-Chief, Standart-Weekend, weekly, 1991-; Secretary, Bulgarian Travel Writers & Journalists Assn - ABUJET, 1995-; Member, Board of Directors, International Travel Writers & Journalists Federation. Contributions to: Columnist, Monitor daily & Sladko Soleno magazine. Address: 4 Lulin Planina str, Sofia 1606, Bulgaria.

STARK Joshua. See: OLSEN Theodore Victor.

STARK ADAM Pegie, b. 4 July 1949, South Bend, Indiana, USA.Designer; Artist; Teacher. m. Dr G Stuart Adam, 23 Feb 1994. Education: BFA, 1975, MA, School of Journalism, 1981, PhD in Mass Communications, 1984, Indiana University. Publications: Co-Author and

Designer: Eyes on the News, 1990; Color, Contrast and Dimension in News Design, 1995. Designer: Contemporary Newspaper Design, 2nd edition, 1992, Newspaper Evolutions, 1997. Contributions to: IFRA journal, Germany; Society of Newspaper Design journal. Honours: 17 Awards, Society of Newspaper Design, 1987-88; 1st Place, Florida Design Competition, 1991. Membership: Society of Newspaper Design. Address: 4D Castlebrook Lane, Nepean, Ontario K2G 5E3, Canada.

STARNES John Kennett, b. 5 Feb 1918, Montreal, Quebec, Canada. Retired Diplomat; Writer. m. Helen Gordon Robinson, 10 May 1941, 2 sons. Education: Institute Sillig, Switzerland, 1935-36; University of Munich, Germany, 1936; BA, Bishop's University, 1939. Appointments: Counsellor, Canadian Embassy, Bonn, 1953-56; Head of Defence Liaison, Ottawa, 1958-62; Ambassador, Federal Republic of Germany, 1962-66, United Arab Republic and The Sudan, 1966-67; Assistant Undersecretary of State for External Affairs, 1967-70; Director General, Royal Canadian Mounted Police Security Service, 1970-73; Member, Council, International Institute for Strategic Studies, 1977-85. Publications: Deep Sleepers, 1981; Scarab, 1982; Orion's Belt, 1983; The Cornish Hug, 1985; Latonya (novel), 1994; Closely Guarded: A Life in Canadian Security and Intelligence (memoir), 1998. Contributions to: Numerous newspapers, journals and periodicals. Honours: Centennial Medal; Honorary Doctor of Civil Law, Bishop's University, 1975; Commemorative Medal for 125th Anniversary of the Confederation of Canada, 1992. Memberships: International Institute of Strategic Studies; Canadian Institute of International Affairs; Canadian Writers Foundation. Address: 100 Rideau Terrace, Apt 9, Ottawa, Ontario K1M 0Z2, Canada.

STAROBINSKI Jean, b. 17 Nov 1920, Geneva, Switzerland. Writer. m. Jacqueline Sirman, 15 Aug 1954, 3 sons. Education: PhD, Geneva, 1958; MD, Lausanne, 1960. Publications: Jean Jacques Rousseau: La Transparence et L'Obstacle, 1957; La Relation Critique 1970; 1789: Les Emblemes de La Raison: Montaigne en Mouvement, 1983; Le Remede dans Le Mal, 1989; Largesse, 1994. Contributions to: Newspapers and journals. Honours: Officer Legion D'Honneur, 1980; Prix Européen de L'Essai, 1983; Balzan Prize, 1984; Prix de Monaco, 1988; Goethe Prize, 1994. Membership: Institut de France, Paris. Address: Universite de Geneva, CH-1211 Geneva 4, Switzerland.

STARR Paul (Elliot), b. 12 May 1949, New York, New York, USA. Professor of Sociology; Writer; Editor. m. Sandra Luire Stein, 12 Apr 1981. Education: BA, Columbia University, 1970; PhD, Harvard University, 1978. Appointments: Junior Fellow, Harvard Society of Fellows, 1975-78; Assistant Professor, Harvard University, 1978-82; Associate Professor, 1982-85, Professor of Sociology, 1985-, Princeton University; Founder-Co-Editor, The American Prospect; Founder, Electronic Policy Network, 1995. Publications: The Discarded Army: Veterans After Vietnam, 1974; The Social Transformation of American Medicine, 1983; The Logic of Health-Care Reform, 1992. Contributions to: Professional journals. Honours: Guggenheim Fellowship, 1981-82; C Wright Mills Award, 1983; Pulitzer Prize in General Non-Fiction, 1984; Bancroft Prize, 1984. Address: c/o Department of Sociology, Princeton University, Princeton, NJ 08544, USA.

STARR Renata. See: CORTEN Irina H Shapiro.

STARRATT Thomas, b. 6 Oct 1952, Holyoke, Massachusetts, USA. Teacher; Poet; Writer. m. Patricia, 7 Apr 1994, 3 sons, 2 daughters. Education: BSc, Plymouth State Teachers College, New Hampshire, 1975; MEd, University of New Hampshire, 1980; Numerous graduate courses from various schools. Appointments: Teacher, Oyster River Middle School, 1976-77, Rochester Junior High School, 1977-81; Reading Improvement Specialist, Mannheim Middle School, 1981-91; Teacher/Assistant Principal, A T Mahan High School, Iceland, 1991-95, Spangdahlem Middle School, 1995-.Publications: Poetry: Nightwatch, 1994;

Amsterdam, 1994; Summer on the Lava Plain, 1994; Eye to Your Storm, 1995; Passages, 1995; Excess, 1995; Sumer Days, 1995; Amsterdam Revisited, 1995; Washed Up, 1996. Contributions to: Professional journals. Honour: Excellence in Reading Award, 1990. Membership: International Reading Association. Address: PSC 09, Box 1383, APO AE, D-09123 Germany.

STAUFFER Kathleen, b. 2 July 1963, Pottstown, Pennsylvania, USA. Journalist. Education: BA, Journalism, Point Park College, 1985. Appointments: Intern, Pittsburgh Press, 1983, Readers Digest, Pleasantville, New York, 1984, Prevention Magazine, Pennsylvania, 1985; Assistant Editor, 1986-89, Associate Editor, 1989-93, Managing Editor, 1993-, Catholic Digest, St Paul, Minnesota. Publications: Womansport, The Women's Sports Bible (co-author), 1994; Facing Life's Challenges, 1996. Contributions to: Catholic Digest Magazine; Minnesota Women's Press. Memberships: Society of Professional Journalists; Catholic Press Association. Address: c/o Catholic Digest, 2115 Summit Avenue, St Paul, MN 55105, USA.

STAVE Bruce M(artin), b. 17 May 1937, New York, New York, USA. Historian. m. Sondra T Astor, 16 June 1961, 1 son. Education: AB, Columbia College, 1959; MA, Columbia University, 1961; PhD, University of Pittsburgh, 1966. Appointments: Professor, 1975-, Director, Center for Oral History, 1981-, Chairman, Department of History, 1985-94, University of Connecticut; Editor, Oral History Review, 1996-99. Publications: The New Deal and the Last Hurrah, 1970; The Discontented Society (co-editor), 1972; Socialism and the Cities (contributing editor), 1975; The Making of Urban History, 1977; Modern Industrial Cities, 1981; Talking About Connecticut, 1985, 2nd edition, 1990; Mills and Meadows: A Pictorial History of Northeast Connecticut (co-author), 1991; From the Old Country: An Oral History of European Migration to America (co-author), 1994, paperback, 1999; Witnesses to Nuremberg: American Participants at the War Crimes Trials (co-author), 1998. Contributions to: Journal of Urban History; Americana Magazine; International Journal of Oral History. Honours: Fulbright Professorships, India, 1968-69, Australia, New Zealand, Philippines, 1977, China, 1984; National Endowment for the Humanities Fellowship, 1974; Homer Babbidge Award, Association for the Study of Connecticut History, 1995. Memberships: American Historical Association; Organization of American Historians; Immigration History Society; New England Historical Association, president, 1994-95; New England Association of Oral History. Address: 200 Broad Way, Coventry, CT 06238, USA.

STEAD C(hristian) K(arlson), b. 17 Oct 1932, Auckland, New Zealand. Poet; Writer; Critic; Editor; Professor of English Emeritus. m. Kathleen Elizabeth Roberts, 8 Jan 1955, 1 son, 3 daughters. Education: BA, 1954, MA, 1955, University of New Zealand; PhD, University of Bristol, 1961; DLitt, University of Auckland, 1982. Appointments: Lecturer in English, University of New England, Australia, 1956-57; Lecturer, 1960-61, Senior Lecturer, 1962-64, Associate Professor, 1964-67, Professor of English, 1967-86, Professor Emeritus, 1986-, University of Auckland; Chairman, New Zealand Literary Fund Advisory Committee, 1972-75, New Zealand Authors' Fund Committee, 1989-91. Publications: Poetry: Whether the Will is Free, 1964; Crossing the Bar, 1972; Quesada: Poems 1972-74, 1975; Walking Westward, 1979; Geographies, 1982; Poems of a Decade, 1983; Paris, 1984; Between, 1988; Voices, 1990; Straw Into Gold: Poems New and Selected, 1997. Fiction: Smith's Dream, 1971; Five for the Symbol, 1981; All Visitors Ashore, 1984; The Death of the Body, 1986; Sister Hollywood, 1989; The End of the Century at the End of the World, 1992; The Singing Whakapapa, 1994; Villa Vittoria, 1997; The Blind Blonde with Candles in her Hair (stories), 1998. Criticism: The New Poetic: Yeats to Eliot, 1964, revised edition, 1987; In the Glass Case: Essays on New Zealand Literature, 1981; Pound, Yeats, Eliot and the Modernist Movement, 1986; Answering to the Language: Essays on Modern Writers, 1989. Editor: World's Classics: New Zealand Short Stories, 1966, 3rd

edition, 1975; Measure for Measure: A Casebook, 1971, revised edition, 1973; Letters and Journals of Katherine Mansfield, 1977; Collected Stories of Maurice Duggan, 1981; The New Gramophone Room: Poetry and Fiction (with Elizabeth Smither and Kendrick Smithyman), 1985; The Faber Book of Contemporary South Pacific Stories, 1994. Contributions to: Poetry, fiction and criticism to various anthologies and periodicals. Honours: Katherine Mansfield Prize, 1960; Nuffield Travelling Fellowship, 1965; Katherine Mansfield Menton Fellowship, 1972; Jessie Mackay Award for Poetry, 1972; New Zealand Book Award for Poetry, 1975; Honorary Research Fellow, University College, London, 1977; Commander of the Order of the British Empire, 1984; Queen Elizabeth II Arts Council Scholarship in Letters, 1988-89; Queen's Medal for services to New Zealand literature, 1990; Fellow, Royal Society of Literature, 1995; Senior Visiting Fellow, St John's College, Oxford, 1996-97; Creative New Zealand, member, 1999. Membership: New Zealand PEN, chairman, Auckland branch, 1986-89, national vice president, 1988-90. Address: 37 Tohunga Crescent, Auckland 1, New Zealand.

STEANE J(ohn) B(arry), b. 12 Apr 1928, Coventry, England. Music Journalist; Writer. Education: English, University of Cambridge. Appointments: Teacher of English, Merchant Taylors' School, Northwood, 1952-88; Reviewer: Gramophone, 1973-, Musical Times, 1988-, Opera Now, 1989-. Publications: Marlowe: A Critical Study, 1964; Dekker: The Shoemaker's Holiday (editor), 1965; Tennyson, 1966; Jonson: The Alchemist (editor), 1967; Marlowe: The Complete Plays, 1969; Nashe: The Unfortunate Traveller and Other Works, 1972; The Grand Tradition: Seventy Years of Singing on Record, 1973, revised edition, 1993; Voices: Singers and Critics, 1992; Singers of the Century, 1996, volume II, 1998. Co-author: Opera on Record, 3 volumes, 1979-85; Song on Record, 2 volumes, 1986-88; Choral Music on Record, 1991; Elisabeth Schwarzkopf: A Career on Record (with Alan Sanders), 1995. Contributions to: The New Grove Dictionary of Music, 1980; The New Grove Dictionary of Opera, 1992. Address: 32 Woodland Avenue, Coventry, England.

STEARNS Peter, b. 3 Mar 1936, London, England. University Dean; Writer. m. Margaret Brindle, 1 son, 3 daughters. Education: AB, 1957, AM, 1959, PhD, 1963, Harvard University. Appointment: Dean, College of Humanities and Social Science, Carnegie Mellon University. Publications: European Society in Upheaval, 1967; The Impact of the Industrial Revolution, 1972; Old Age in European Society, 1977; The Other Side of Western Civilization, 1984; Be a Man: Males in Modern Society, 1990; American Cool, 1994; Fat History: Bodies and Beauty in the Modern West, 1997; World History in Brief: Patterns of Change and Continuity, 1998; Battleground of Desire: The Struggle for Self-Control in 20th Century America, 1999. Contributions to: Professional journals. Honours: Phi Beta Kappa; Social Science Research Council Fellowship; American Philosophical Society Grant; Guggenheim Fellowship; Koren Prize; Newcomen Special Award; Elliott Dunlap Smith Teaching Award; Finalist, Los Angeles Times Book of the Year in History, 1998. Memberships: American Historical Association; International Society for Research. Address: Carnegie Mellon University, Pittsburgh, PA 15213, USA.

STEBEL Sidney Leo, (Leo Bergson, Steve Toron), b. 28 June 1923, Iowa, USA. Writer. m. Jan Mary Dingler, 10 Sept 1954, 1 daughter. Education: BA, English Literature, University of Southern California, Los Angeles, 1949. Appointment: Adjunct Professor, Masters of Professional Writing, University of Southern California, Los Angeles, 1991. Publications: The Widowmaster, 1967; The Collaborator, 1968; Main Street, 1971; The Vorovich Affar, 1975; The Shoe Leather Treatment, 1983; Spring Thaw, 1989; The Boss's Wife, 1992; Double Your Creative Power, 1996. Contributions to: Anthologies, newspapers and magazines. Honour: 2nd Place, Fiction Award, PEN Center West, 1989. Memberships: Australian Writers Guild; Authors Guild; PEN Centre, USA West; Writers Guild of America; Author's League.

Address: 1963 Mandeville Canyon Road, Los Angeles, CA 90049, USA.

STEEL Danielle (Fernande), b. 14 Aug 1947, New York, New York, USA. Writer. Education: Parsons School of Design, New York City, 1963-67. Publications: Going Home, 1973; Passion's Promise, 1977; Now and Forever, 1978; The Promise, 1978; Season of Passion, 1979; Summer's End, 1979; To Love Again, 1980; The Ring, 1980; Loving, 1980; Love, 1981; Remembrance, 1981; Palomino, 1981; Once in a Lifetime, 1982; Crossings, 1982; A Perfect Stranger, 1982; Thurston House, 1983; Changes, 1983; Full Circle, 1984; Having a Baby, 1984; Family Album, 1985; Secrets, 1985; Wanderlust, 1986; Fine Things, 1987; Kaleidoscope, 1987; Zoya, 1988; Star, 1988; Daddy, 1989; Message from Nam, 1990; Heartbeart, 1991; No Greater Love, 1991; Jewels, 1992; Mixed Blessings, 1992; Vanished, 1993; Accident, 1994; The Gift, 1994; Wings, 1994; Lightning, 1995; Five Days in Paris, 1996; Malice, 1996; The Ghost, 1997; His Bright Light, 1998. Contributions to: Periodicals. Address: PO Box 1637, New York, NY 10156, USA.

STEEL Ronald Lewis, b. 25 Mar 1931, Morris, Illinois, USA. Professor of International Relations; Writer. Education: BA magna cum laude, Northwestern University, 1953; MA, Harvard University, 1955. Appointments: Vice Consul, US Foreign Service, 1957-58; Editor, Scholastic Magazine, 1959-62; Senior Associate, Carnegie Endowment for International Peace, 1962-83; Visiting Fellow, Yale University, 1971-73; Visiting Professor, University of Texas, 1977, 1979, 1980, 1985, Wellesley College, 1978, Rutgers University, 1980, University of California at Los Angeles, 1981, Dartmouth College, 1983, Princeton University, 1984; Fellow, Woodrow Wilson International Center for Scholars, 1984-85, Wissenschaftskolleg zu Berlin, Federal Republic of Germany, 1988; Professor of International Relations, University of Southern California at Los Angeles, 1986-; Shapiro Professor of International Relations, George Washington University, 1995-96. Publications: The End of Alliance: America and the Future of Europe, 1964; Tropical Africa Today (with G Kimble), 1966; Pax Americana, 1967; Imperialists and Other Heroes, 1971; Walter Lippmann and the American Century, 1980; Temptations of a Superpower, 1995. Contributions to: Professional journals and general publications. Honours: Sidney Hillman Prize, 1968; Guggenheim Fellowship, 1973-74; Los Angeles Times Book Award, 1980; Washington Monthly Book Award, 1980; National Book Critics Circle Award, 1981; Bancroft Prize, Columbia University, 1981; American Book Award, 1981. Memberships: American Historical Association; Council on Foreign Relations; Society of American Historians. Address: c/o School of International Relations, University of Southern California, Los Angeles, CA 90089, USA.

STEELE Shelby, b. 1 Jan 1946, Chicago, Illinois, USA. Professor of English; Writer. m. Rita Steele, 2 children. Education: Graduate, Coe College, 1968; MA, Sociology, Southern Illinois University, 1971; PhD, English, University of Utah, 1974. Appointment: Professor of English, San Jose State University. Publications: The Content of Our Character: A New Vision of Race in America, 1991; Essay Collection, 1993. Other: Seven Days in Bensonhurst (television documentary), PBS TV, 1990. Contributions to: Newspapers, journals, and magazines. Honour: National Book Critics Award, 1991. Address: c/o Department of English, San Jose State University, Washington Square, San Jose, CA 95192, USA.

STEFANSSON Bjorn S, b. 19 June 1937, Reykjavik, Iceland. Social Research. m. Margareta Norrstrand, div, 1 son. Education: DSc, Norwegian Agricultural College, 1968. Appointment: Norwegian Academy of Science and Letters, 1991. Publications: Thjodfelagid og throun Ahess, 1978; Hjariki, 1992. Membership: Writers Union of Iceland. Address: Kleppsvegi 40, Reykjavik IS-105, Iceland.

STEFFEN Jonathon Neil, b. 5 Oct 1958, London, England. University Teacher; Writer; Poet; Translator.

Education: MA, English, King's College, Cambridge, 1981. Appointment: Teacher, University of Heidelberg. Publications: Fiction: In Seville, 1985; Meeting the Majors, 1987; Carpe Diem, 1991; Cleopatra, 1994; The Story of Icarus, 1994; At Breakfast, 1995. Poetry: The Soldier and the Soldier's Son, 1986; German Hunting Party, 1987; The Moving Hand, 1994; The Great Days of the Railway, 1994; Apprentice and Master, 1994; St Francis in the Slaughter, 1995. Contributions to: Reviews, quarterlies, and magazines. Honours: Harper-Wood Traveling Studentship, 1981-82; Hawthornden Creative Writing Fellowship, 1987. Address: Schillerstrasse 16, 69115 Heidelberg, Germany.

STEFFLER John Earl, b. 13 Nov 1947, Toronto, Ontario, Canada. Professor of English Literature; Poet; Writer. m. Shawn O'Hagan, 30 May 1970, 1 son, 1 daughter. Education: BA, University of Toronto, 1971; MA, University of Guelph, 1974. Publications: An Explanation of Yellow, 1980; The Grey Islands, 1985; The Wreckage of Play, 1988; The Afterlife of George Cartwright, 1991. Contributions to: Journals and periodicals. Honours: Books in Canada First Novel Award, 1992; Newfoundland Arts Council Artist of the Year Award, 1992; Thomas Raddall Atlantic Fiction Award, 1992; Joseph S Stauffer Prize, 1993. Memberships: League of Canadian Poets; PEN; Writers Alliance of Newfoundland and Labrador. Address: c/o Department of English, Memorial University of Newfoundland, Corner Brook, Newfoundland A2H 6PN, Canada.

STEIN Clarissa Ingeborg, (Sara Cristiens), b. 3 Sept 1948, Munich, Germany. Editor; Poet. m. Herbert Stein, 26 May 1981, 1 daughter. Education: Diploma, Beamtenfachhochschule, Herrsching, Bavaria, 1975. Appointment: Editor, Papyrus Publishing, 1991-. Publications: New Melodies, Neue Melodien, 1992; Notes From My Land, 1993; Billy Tea and Sand Ballet, 1996; In meinem Land, 1997. Contributions to: Journals and magazines in Australia and overseas. Memberships: Deakin Literary Society, Deakin University; National Book Council, general member. Address: 16 Grand View Crescent, Upper Ferntree Gully, Victoria 3156, Austalia.

STEIN Dan Joseph, b. 17 Sept 1962, South Africa. Psychiatrist. m. Heather. Education: BSc, 1983; MBChB, 1986; FRCPC, 1992. Appointment: Director, MRC Research Unit on Anxiety Disorders, Cape Town. Publications: Cognitive Science and Clinical Disorders; Essential Papers on Obsesive Compulsive Disorders; Cognitive Science and the Unconscious; Trichotillomania. Honours: Several. Address: PO Box 19063, Tygerberg 7505, South Africa.

STEIN Peter Gonville, b. 29 May 1926, Liverpool, England. Professor of Law; Writer. m. (1), div, 3 daughters, (2) Anne M Howard, 16 Aug 1978. Education: BA, 1949, LLB, 1950, Gonville and Caius College, Cambridge; Admitted as Solicitor, 1951; University of Pavia, 1951-52. Appointments: Professor of Jurisprudence, University of Aberdeen, 1956-68; Regius Professor of Civil Law, University of Cambridge, 1968-93. Publications: Regulae Iuris: From Juristic Rules to Legal Maxims, 1966; Legal Values in Western Society (with J Shand), 1974; Legal Evolution: The Story of an Idea, 1980; Legal Institutions: The Development of Dispute Settlement, 1984; The Character and Influence of the Roman Civil Law, 1988; The Teaching of Roman Law in England Around 1200 (with F de Zulueta), 1990; Römisches Recht und Europa: Die Geschichte einer Rechtskultur, 1996; Roman Law in European History, 1999. Contributions to: Professional journals. Honours: Honorary Dr Iuris, University of Göttingen, 1980; Honorary Dott Giur, University of Ferrara, 1991; Honorary QC, 1993. Memberships: British Academy, fellow; Belgian National Academy; Italian National Academy, foreign fellow; Selden Society, vice-president, 1984-87; Society of Public Teachers of Law, president, 1980-81. Address: Queens' College, Cambridge CB3 9ET, England.

STEIN Robert A, b. 5 Aug 1933, Duluth, Minnesota, USA. Writer; Educator. m. Betty L Pavlik, 5 Nov 1955, 3 sons. Education: MA, Writing, 1986, MA, Counseling/Education, 1968, BSc, Industrial Management, 1956, University of Iowa; Permanent Professional Counseling/Teaching Certificate, Iowa Board of Public Instruction, 1968; US Air Force Squadron Officers' School, 1960; US Air Force Command and Staff College, 1966; Air Force Academic Instructor School, with Honors, 1966; Industrial College of the Armed Forces, with Honors, 1973. Appointments: Officer and Pilot, USAF, 1956-77; Assistant Professor of Aerospace Studies, 1964-66, University of Iowa; Associate Professor, 1966-68; Professor, 1975-77; Member, Faculty Division of Writing, Kirkwood Community College, Iowa City and Cedar Rapids, Iowa, 1984-89; Instructor, Creative Writing Program, Iowa City/Johnson County Senior Center, 1994-. Publications: Novels: Apollyon: A Novel, 1985; The Chase, 1988; The Black Samaritan, 1997; The Vengeance Equation, forthcoming; Fiction: Death Defied, 1988; Non-Fiction: Statistical Correlations, 1967; Engineers Vs. Other Students: Is There A Difference?, 1967; Whatever Happened to Moe Bushkin?, 1967; Quest for Viability: One Way!, 1976; Threat of Emergency, 1988. Honours: Iowa Authors' Collection, 1985; Minnesota Authors' Collection, 1987; International Literary Award, 1988. Memberships: The Authors Guild; The Authors League of America. Literary Agent: Kelly O'Donnell, Literary Agent. Address: HCR1 #309, Ira Vail Road, Leeds, NY 12451, USA.

STEINBACH Meredith Lynn, b. 18 Mar 1949, Ames, Iowa, USA. Novelist; Associate Professor. m. Charles Ossian Hartman, 5 May 1979, div 1991, 1 son. Education: BGS, 1973, MFA, 1976, University of Iowa. Literary Appointments: Teaching Fellow, University of Iowa, 1975-76; Writer in Residence, Antioch College, 1976-77; Lecturer, Fiction, Northwestern University, 1977-79; Visiting Assistant Professor, University of Washington, 1979-82; Bunting Fellow, Radcliffe-Harvard, 1982-83; Assistant Professor to Associate Professor, Brown University, 1983-. Publications: Novels: Zara, 1982, 1996; Here Lies the Water, 1990; The Birth of the World as We Know It, 1996. Short stories: Reliable Light, 1990. Contributions to: Tri-Quarterly Magazine; Antaeus; Massachusetts Review; Antioch Review; South West Review; Black Warrior Review. Honours: Pushcart Prize, Best of the Small Presses, 1977; National Endowment for the Arts Fellowship, 1978; Bunting Fellow, Bunting Summer Fellow, Mary Ingraham Bunting Institute, Radcliffe College, Harvard, 1982-83; Rhode Island Artists Fellowship, 1986-87; O Henry Award, 1990. Memberships: PEN; Associated Writing Programs; Amnesty International. Literary Agent: Kathleen Anderson, Scovil, Chichak and Galen Literary Agency Inc. Address: c/o 381 Park Avenue, New York, NY 10016, USA.

STEINEM Gloria, b. 25 Mar 1934, Toledo, Ohio, USA. Feminist; Political Activist; Lecturer; Editor; Writer. Education: BA, Smith College, 1956; Chester Bowles Asian Fellow, India, 1957-58. Appointments: Contributing Editor, Glamour Magazine, 1962-69; Co-Founder and Contributing Editor, New York Magazine, 1968-72; Co-Founder and Member of the Board of Directors, Women's Action Alliance, 1970-; Co-Founder and Editor, 1971-87, Columnist, 1980-87, Consulting Editor, 1987-, Ms Magazine; Convenor and Member of the National Advisory Committee, Women's Political Caucus, 1971-; Co-Founder and President of the Board of Directors, Ms Foundation for Women, 1972-; President, Voters for Choice, 1979-. Publications: The Thousand Indias, 1957; The Beach Book, 1963; Wonder Woman, 1972; Outrageous Acts and Everyday Rebellions, 1983; Marilyn: Norma Jeane, 1986; Revolution from Within: A Book of Self-Esteem, 1992; Moving Beyond Words, 1994. Contributions to: Anthologies and magazines. Honours: Penney-Missouri Journalism Award, 1970; Ohio Governor's Award for Journalism, 1972; Woman of the Year, McCall's Magazine, 1972; D Human Justice, Simmons College, 1973; Bill of Rights Award, American Civil Liberties Union of Southern California, 1975; Woodrow Wilson International Center for Scholars Fellow, 1977; National Woman's Hall of Fame, 1993. Memberships: American Foundation of Television and Radio Artists; Authors Guild; National Organization for Women; National Press Club; Phi Beta Kappa; Society of Magazine Writers. Address: c/o Ms Magazine, 230 Park Avenue, 7th Floor, New York, NY 10169, USA.

STEINER Andreas Konrad, b. 29 Jan 1937, Zurich, Switzerland. Surgeon; Writer. m. Tshabu Cécile Mbombo, 12 May 1995, 3 sons, 3 daughters. Education: MD, Zurich University, 1961; Surgeon, FMH, 1971. Appointments: Medical Superintendent, Albert Schweizer Hospital, Lamabarene, Gabon, 1976-80; Project Director, Hospital Andino, Coina, Peru, 1980-84; Project Director, Manono Shaba, Zaire, 1984-91; Associate Professor, Addis Ababa University, Ethiopia, 1991-95. Publications: Arzt im Busch, eine Herausforderung, 1990; Geschichten im Busch, Begegnungen eines Arztes in Afrika, 1993; Afrika und Wir. Über unser Eingreifen in Afrika, Bilanz nach 15 Jahren als Arzt in Afrika, 1996; Wir in Afrika, Drei Theaterstücke, 1997. Contributions to: About 25 articles in medical journals on developments in health, tropical medicine and surgery. Membership: Gruppe Olten Schweiz. Address: Hanfroosenweg 13, CH-8615 Wermatswil, Switzerland.

STEINER (Francis) George, b. 23 Apr 1929, Paris, France. Professor of English and Comparative Literature Emeritus; Extraordinary Fellow; Writer. m. Zara Shakow, 1955, 1 son, 1 daughter. Education: BA, University of Chicago, 1949; MA, Harvard University, 1950; PhD, University of Oxford, 1955. Appointments: Staff, The Economist, London, 1952-56; Member, Institute for Advanced Study, Princeton, New Jersey, 1956-58; Fulbright Professorships, 1958-59; Fellow, 1961-69, Extraordinary Fellow, 1969-, Churchill College, Cambridge; Professor of English and Comparative Literature, 1974-94, Professor Emeritus, 1994-, University of Geneva; Visiting Professor, Collège de France, 1992; Weidenfeld Professor of Comparative Literature and Fellow, St Anne's College, Oxford, 1994-95; Various visiting lectureships. Publications: Tolstoy or Dostoevsky: An Essay in the Old Criticism, 1958; The Death of Tragedy, 1960; Homer: A Collection of Critical Essays (editor with Robert Flagles), 1962; Anno Domini, 1964; The Penguin Book of Modern Verse Translation (editor), 1966; Language and Silence, 1967; Extraterritorial, 1971; In Bluebeard's Castle: Some Notes Towards the Re-Definition of Culture, 1971; The Sporting Scene: White Knights in Reykjavik, 1973; After Babel: Aspects of Language and Translation, 1975; Heidegger, 1978; On Difficulty and Other Essays, 1978; The Portage to San Cristobal of A H, 1981; Antigones, 1984; George Steiner: A Reader, 1984; Real Presences: Is There Anything in What We Say?, 1989; Proofs and Three Parables, 1992; The Deeps of the Sea, 1996; Homer in English, 1996; No Passion Spent, 1996. Honours: O Henry Short Story Award, 1958; Zabel Award, National Institute of Arts and Letters, USA, 1970; Guggenheim Fellowship, 1971-72; Faulkner Stipend for Fiction, 1983; Chevalier de la Légion d'Honneur, 1984; PEN Macmillan Fiction Prize, 1993; Honorary Fellow, Balliol College, Oxford, 1995; Several honorary doctorates. Memberships: American Academy of Arts and Sciences, honorary member, 1989-; English Association, president, 1975; German Academy of Literature, corresponding member, 1981-; Royal Society of Literature, fellow, 1964-. Address: 32 Barrow Road, Cambridge CB2 2AS, England.

STEINER-ISENMANN Robert, b. 19 May 1955, Basel, Switzerland. Writer; Poet. 1 daughter. Education: Theology, University of Zürich. Publications: Gaetano Donizetti: Sein Leben und seine Opern, 1982; Espoirs-hopfnungen (revue), 1988, new edition, 1993; Windspiel der Leidenschaft (poems), 1994. Contributions to: Anthologies, magazines and journals. Memberships: Association Suisse des Écrivains: Association Valaisanne des Écrivains; PEN Club. Address: Café de la Rosablanche, 1996 Basse-Nendaz/VS, Switzerland.

STEINHARDT Nancy R Shatzman, b. 14 July 1954, St Louis, Missouri, USA. Art Historian. m. Paul Joseph Steinhardt, 1 July 1979, 3 sons, 1 daughter. Education:

AB, Washington University, St Louis, 1974; AM, 1975, PhD, 1981, Harvard University. Appointment: Faculty, University of Pennsylvania. Publications: Chinese Traditional Architecture, 1984; Chinese Imperial City Planning, 1990; Liao Architecture, 1997. Contributions to: Professional journals and general periodicals. Memberships: Association for Asian Studies; College Art Society; Society of Architectural Historians. Address: c/o Department of Asian and Middle Eastern Studies, University of Pennsylvania, Philadelphia, PA 19104, USA.

STEINMAN Lisa (Jill) M(alinowski), b. 8 Apr 1950, Willimantic, Connecticut, USA. Professor of English; Poet; Writer; Editor. m. James L Shugrue, 23 July 1984. Education: BA, 1971; MFA, 1973, PhD, 1976, Cornell University. Appointments: Assistant Professor, 1976-82, Associate Professor, 1982-89, Professor, 1990-93, Kenan Professor of English, 1993-, Reed College, Portland, Oregon; Poetry Editor, Hubbub Magazine, 1983-. Publications: Lost Poems, 1976; Made in America: Science, Technology, and American Modernist Poets, 1987; All That Comes to Light, 1989; A Book of Other Days, 1993; Ordinary Songs, 1996; Masters of Repetition: Poetry, Culture, and Work, 1998. Contributions to: Books, anthologies, reviews, quarterlies, and journals. Honours: Scholar, Bread Loaf Writers Conference, 1981; Oregon Arts Commission Poetry Fellow, 1983; National Endowment for the Arts Fellowship, 1984; Rockefeller Scholar-in-Residence, 92nd Street Y Poetry Center, 1987; Pablo Neruda Award, Mimrod Magazine, 1987; Outstanding Academic Book, Choice, 1989; Oregon Book Award, Oregon Institute of Literary Arts, 1993; National Endowment for the Humanities Fellowship, 1996. Memberships: Associated Writing Programs; Modern Language Association; PEN; PEN/Northwest; Poets and Writers; Wallace Stevens Society; William Carlos Williams Society, president, 1998-2000. Address: 5344 South East 38th Avenue, Portland, OR 97202, USA.

STENDAL Grant Vincent, b. 8 Dec 1955, Rochdale, England. Writer; Business Journalist; Speech Writer. Education: BA, Flinders University of South Australia, 1982; BA, Honours, University of Tasmania, 1985; PhD, University of Adelaide, 1995-. Publications: At Work: Australian Experiences, 1984; Job Representatives Handbook, revised edition, 1989. Contributions to: Journals, newspapers and periodicals. Honour: International Travel Grant, Australian Industrial Relations Society, 1994. Membership: Australian Industrial Relations Society. Address: PO Box 71, Stirling, South Australia 5152, Australia.

STEPHAN John Jason, b. 8 Mar 1941, Chicago, Illinois, USA. Professor; Historian. m. 22 June 1963. Education: BA, 1963, MA, 1964, Harvard University; PhD, University of London, England, 1969. Appointments: Far Eastern Editor, Harvard Review, 1962; Visiting Fellow, St Antony's College, Oxford, 1977; Professor of History, University of Hawaii, 1970-; Visiting Professor of History, Stanford University, 1986; Research Fellow, Kennan Institute of Advanced Russian Studies, 1987. Publications: Sakhalin: A History, 1971; The Kuril Islands: Russo-Japanese Frontier in the Pacific, 1974; The Russian Fascists, 1978; Hawaii Under the Rising Sun, 1984; Soviet-American Horizons in the Pacific (with V.P. Chichkanov), 1986; The Russian Far East: A History, 1994. Contributions to: Washington Post; Modern Asian Studies; American Historical Review; Pacific Affairs; Pacific Community; Journal for Asian Studies; New York Times; Siberica; Pacifica; Australian Slavic and East European Studies. Honours: Fulbright Fellowship, 1967-68; Japan Culture Translation Prize, 1973; Japan Foundation Fellowship, 1977; Sanwa Distinguished Scholar, Fletcher School of Law and Diplomacy, Tufts University, 1989; Distinguished Invited Speaker, Canadian Historical Association, 1990; Kenneth W.Baldridge Prize, 1996. Memberships: Authors Guild; PEN; International House of Japan, life member; American Association for the Advancement of Slavic Studies, life member; American Historical Association; Canadian Historical Association. Literary Agent: William Reiss, c/o John Hawkins Associates, New York, NY.

Address: Department of History, University of Hawaii, 2530 Dole Street, Honolulu, HI 96822, USA.

STEPHEN Ian, b. 29 Apr 1955, Stornoway, Isle of Lewis, Scotland. Writer; Poet; Artist. m. Barbara Ziehm, 9 Nov 1984, 2 sons. Education: BEd, Distinction, Honours, English, University of Aberdeen, 1980. Appointment: Inaugural Robert Louis Stevenson/Christian Salvesen Fellow, Grez-sur-Loing, France, 1995. Publications: Malin, Hebrides, Minches, 1983; Varying States of Grace, 1989; Siud an T-Eilean (editor), 1993; Providence II, 1994; Broad Bay, 1997. Other: Numerous exhibitions of poetry/texts with visual arts. Contributions to: Scottish, UK, and Australian publications. Honour: Scottish Arts Council Bursaries, 1981, 1995. Memberships: PEN Scotland. Address: Last House, 1 Benside, Isle of Lewis HS2 0DZ, Scotland.

STEPHENS Meic, b. 23 July 1938, Treforest, Pontypridd, Wales. Journalist; Lecturer in Journalism; Poet; Writer; Editor. m. Ruth Wynn Meredith, 14 Aug 1965, 1 son, 3 daughters. Education: BA, University College of Wales, Aberystwyth, 1961; University of Rennes, 1960; University College of North Wales, Bangor, 1962. Appointments: Literature Director, Welsh Arts Council, 1967-90; Visiting Professor, Brigham Young University, Provo, Utah, 1991; Lecturer in Journalism, University of Glamorgan, 1994-; Centre for Journalism Studies, 1998. Contributions to: Various anthologies, reference works, and journals. Memberships: Gorsedd of Bards; Welsh Academy. Address: 10 Heol Don, Whitchurch, Cardiff, Wales.

STEPHENS Michael (Gregory), b. 4 Mar 1946, USA. Writer; Poet; Dramatist. Education: BA, 1975, MA, 1976, City College of the City University of New York; MFA, Yale University, 1979. Appointments: Lecturer, Columbia University, 1977-91, Princeton University, 1986-91, New York University, 1989-91; Writer-in-Residence and Assistant Professor, Fordham University, 1979-85. Publications: Fiction: Season at Coole, 1972; Paragraphs, 1974; Still Life, 1978; Shipping Out, 1979; The Brooklyn Book of the Dead, 1994. Poetry: Alcohol Poems, 1972; Tangun Legend, 1978; After Asia, 1993. Other: Circles End (poems and prose), 1982; The Dramaturgy of Style, 1986; Lost in Seoul: And Other Discoveries on the Korean Peninsula, 1990; Jig and Reels, 1992; Green Dreams: Essays Under the Influence of the Irish, 1994. Plays: A Splendid Occasion in Spring, 1974; Off-Season Rates, 1978; Cloud Dream, 1979; Our Father, 1980; R & R, 1984. Contributions to: Many newspapers, journals, and magazines. Honours: MacDowell Colony Fellowship, 1968; Fletcher Pratt Fellowship, Bread Loaf Writers Conference, 1971; Creative Artists Public Service Fiction Award, 1978; Connecticut Commission on the Arts Grant, 1979; Associated Writing Programs Award in Creative Non-Fiction, 1993. Memberships: Associated Writing Programs; PEN; Royal Asiatic Society. Address: 520 West 110th Street, No 5-C, New York, NY 10025, USA.

STEPHENS Reed. See: **DONALDSON Stephen Reeder.**

STEPHENSON Hugh, b. 18 July 1938, England. Writer; Journalist; Teacher. m. (1) Auriol Stevens, 1962, div 1987, 2 sons, 1 daughter, (2) Diana Eden, 1990. Education: MA, New College, Oxford; University of California, Berkeley, USA. Appointments: HM Diplomatic Service, 1964-69; Staff, The Times, 1968; Editor, The Times Business News, 1972-81, New Statesman, 1982-86; Professor of Journalism, City University, 1986-. Publications: The Coming Clash, 1972; Mrs Thatcher's First Year, 1980; Claret and Chips, 1982; Libel and the Media (co-author), 1997. Honour: Fellow, Royal Society of Art, 1987. Address: c/o Department of Journalism, City University, Northampton Square, London EC1, England.

STEPHERSON Brian Edward, b. 5 Feb 1944, Queens, New York, USA. Artist; Writer. Education: BA, Columbia College, 1965; Hunter College Graduate School, 1984. Contributions to: American Institute of Physics - Journal of Chemical Physics. Honours:

President's Achievement Award, Ronald Reagan. Address: PO Box 409, Cathedral Station, New York, NY 10025, USA.

STERLING Maria Sandra. See: **FLOREN Lee.**

STERN Dril. See: **KATZIR Benjamin.**

STERN Gerald, b. 22 Feb 1925, Pittsburgh, Pennsylvania, USA. Poet; Teacher. m. Patricia Miller, 1952, 1 son, 1 daughter. Education: BA, University of Pittsburgh, 1947; MA, Columbia University, 1949. Appointments: Instructor, Temple University, Philadelphia, 1957-63; Professor, Indiana University of Pennsylvania, 1963-67; Somerset County College, New Jersey, 1968-82; Visiting Poet, Sarah Lawrence College, 1977; Visiting Professor, University of Pittsburgh, 1978, Columbia University, 1980, Bucknell University, 1988, New York Universty, 1989; Faculty, Writer's Workshop, University of Iowa, 1982-94; Distinguished Chair, University of Alabama, 1984; Fanny Hurst Professor, Washington University, St Louis, 1985; Bain Swiggert Chair, Princeton University, 1989; Poet-in-Residence, Bucknell University, 1994. Publications: The Naming of Beasts and Other Poems, 1973; Rejoicings, 1973; Lucky Life, 1977; The Red Coal, 1981; Paradise Poems, 1984; Lovesick, 1987; Leaving Another Kingdom: Selected Poems, 1990; Two Long Poems, 1990; Bread Without Sugar, 1992; Odd Mercy, 1995; This Tme: New and Selected Poems, 1998. Honours: National Endowment for the Arts Grants, 1976, 1981, 1987; Lamont Poetry Selection Award, 1977; Governor's Award, Pennsylvania, 1980; Guggenheim Fellowship, 1980; Bess Hokin Award, 1980; Bernard F Connor Award, 1981; Melville Cane Award, 1982; Jerome J Shestack Prize, 1984; Academy of American Poets Fellowship, 1993; Ruth Lilly Poetry Prize, 1996; National Book Award for Poetry, 1998. Address: c/o Department of English, University of Iowa, Iowa City, IA 52242, USA.

STERN Madeleine Bettina, b. 1 July 1912, New York City, USA. Rare Book Dealer; Writer. Education: BA, Barnard College, 1932; MA, Columbia University, 1934. Publications: The Life of Margaret Fuller, 1942; Louisa May Alcott, 1950; Purple Passage: The Life of Mrs. Frank Leslie, 1953; Imprints on History: Book Publishers and American Frontiers, 1956; We the Women: Career Firsts of 19th Century America, 1962; The Pantarch: A Biography of Stephen Pearl Andrews, 1968; Heads and Headlines: The Phrenological Fowlers, 1971; Books and Book People in 19th Century America, 1978; Antiquarian Bookselling in the United States: A History, 1985; Old Books, Rare Friends: Two Literary Sleuths and their Shared Passion (with Leona Rostenberg), 1997. Louisa May Alcott: From Blood and Thunder to Hearth and Home, 1998; Contributions to: Numerous. Honours: Phi Beta Kappa; Guggenheim Fellowship; Distinguished Barnard Alumna Award and American Printing History Award to Leona Rostenberg and Madeleine Stern. Memberships: Manuscript Society; Antiquarian Booksellers Association of America; Modern Language Association. Address: 40 East 88th Street, New York, NY 10128, USA.

STERN Richard G(ustave), b. 25 Feb 1928, New York, New York, USA. Writer; Professor. m. (1) Gay Clark, (2) Alane Rollings, 3 sons, 1 daughter. Education: BA, University of North Carolina; MA, Harvard University; PhD, University of Iowa. Publications: Noble Rot Stories, 1949-89; Golk, 1960; Europe or Up and Down with Baggish and Schreiber, 1961; In Any Case, 1962; Stitch, 1965; Other Men's Daughters, 1973; A Father's Words, 1986; The Position of the Body, 1986; Shares and Other Fictions, 1992; One Person and Another, 1993; Sistermony, 1995. Contributions to: Journals and magazines. Honours: Longwood Award, 1954; American Academy of Arts and Letters Award, 1968; Friends of Literature Award, 1968; Sandburg Award, 1979; Award of Merit for the Novel, 1985; Heartland Prize, 1995. Membership: American Academy of Arts and Sciences; Centre for Advanced Studies in Behavioural Sciences, fellow. Literary Agent: Carol Mann, 55 Fifth Avenue, New

York, NY 10003. Address: 1050 East 59th Street, Chicago, IL 60637, USA.

STERN Richard Martin, b. 17 Mar 1915, Fresno, California, USA. Writer. m. Dorothy Helen Atherton, 20 Dec 1937, 1 daughter (adopted). Education: Harvard College, 1933-36. Appointment: Editorial Board, The Writer, 1976-. Publications: Bright Road to Fear, 1958; Search for Tabatha Carr, 1960; These Unlucky Deeds, 1960; High Hazard, 1962; Cry Havoc, 1963; Right Hand Opposite, 1963; I Hide, We Seek, 1964; The Kessler Legacy, 1967; Brood of Eagles, 1969; Merry Go Round, 1969; Manuscript for Murder, 1970; Murder in the Walls, 1971; Stanfield Harvest, 1972; Death in the Snow, 1973; The Tower, 1973; Power, 1974; The Will, 1976; Snowbound Six, 1977; Flood,1979; The Big Bridge, 1982; Wildfire, 1985; Tsunami, 1988; Tangled Murders, 1989; You Don't Need an Enemy, 1989; Missing Man, 1990; Interloper, 1990. Contributions to: Magazines. Honour: Edgar Award, Mystery Writers of America, 1958. Memberships: Mystery Writers of America, past president; Crime Writers Association, UK; Authors Guild, USA. Address: Route 9, Box 55, Santa Fe, NM 87505, USA.

STERN Steve, b. 21 Dec 1947, Memphis, Tennessee, USA. Associate Professor of English; Writer. Education: BA, Rhodes College, 1970; MFA, University of Arkansas, 1977. Appointments: Visiting Lecturer, University of Wisconsin, 1987; Associate Professor of English, Skidmore College, Saratoga Springs, New York, 1994-. Publications: Isaac and the Undertaker's Daughter, 1983; The Moon and Ruben Shein, 1984; Lazar Malkin Enters Heaven, 1986; Mickey and the Golem, 1986; Hershel and the Beast, 1987; Harry Kaplan's Adventures Underground, 1991; Plague of Dreamers, 1994; The Wedding Jester (stories), 1999. Contributions to: Magazines and journals. Honours: O Henry Prize, 1981; Pushcart Writers Choice Award, 1984; Edward Lewis Wallant Award, 1988; Pushcart Prize, 1997. Address: c/o Department of English, Skidmore College, Saratoga Springs, NY 12866, USA.

STERN Stuart. See: **RAE Hugh Crauford.**

STERNBERG Robert J(effrey), b. 8 Dec 1949, Newark, New Jersey, USA. Professor of Psychology and Education; Writer; Editor. m. Alejandra Campos, 11 Aug 1991, 1 son, 1 daughter. Education: BA, summa cum laude, Psychology, Yale University, 1972; PhD, Psychology, Stanford University, 1975. Appointments: Assistant Professor, 1975-80, Associate Professor, 1980-83, Professor, 1983-86, IBM Professor of Psychology and Education, 1986-, Yale University; Editor, Psychological Bulletin, 1991-96, Contemporary Psychology, 1999-; Editor-in-Chief, Educational Psychology Series, Lawrence Erlbaum Associates, 1996-. Publications: Intelligence, Information Processing, and Analogical Reasoning: The Componential Analysis of Human Abilities, 1977; Beyond IQ: A Triarchic Theory of Human Intelligence, 1985; Intelligence Applied: Understanding and Increasing Your Intellectual Skills, 1986; What is Intelligence? (with D K Detterman), 1986; The Psychologist's Companion, 2nd edition, 1988, 3rd edition, 1993; The Triangle of Love, 1988; The Triarchic Mind: A New Theory of Human Intelligence, 1988; Metaphors of Mind: Conceptions of the Nature of Intelligence, 1990; Love the Way You Want It, 1991; Tacit Knowledge Inventory for Managers (with R K Wagner), 1991; For Whom Does the Bell Curve Toll?: It Tolls for You, 1995; In Search of the Human Mind, 1995; Defying the Crowd: Cultivating Creativity in a Culture of Conformity (with T I Lubart), 1995; Off Track: When Poor Readers Become Learning Disabled (with L Spear-Swerling), 1996; Cognitive Psychology, 1996; Successful Intelligence, 1996; Introduction to Psychology, 1997; Pathways to Psychology, 1997; Thinking Styles, 1997; Successful Intelligence, 1997; Cupid's Arrow: The Course of Love Through Time, 1998; Love is a Story, 1998; Cupid's Arrow, 1998; Perspectives on Learning Disabilities: Biological, Cognitive, Contextual (with L Spear-Swerling), 1999. Editor: Many books. Contributions to: Numerous scholarly books and journals. Honours:

Distinguished Scholar Award, National Association for Gifted Children, 1985; Outstanding Book Award, 1987, Sylvia Scribner Award, 1996, American Educational Research Association; Guggenheim Fellowship, 1985-86; Award for Excellence, Mensa Education and Research Foundation, 1989; Doctor Honoris Causa, Complutense University, Madrid, 1994; G Stanley Hall Distinguished Lecturer, American Psychological Association, 1997. Memberships: American Academy of Arts and Sciences, fellow; American Association for the Advancement of Science, fellow; American Educational Research Association; American Psychological Society, fellow; International Council of Psychologists; National Association for Gifted Children; Phi Beta Kappa; Psychonomic Society; Sigma Xi; Society for Research in Child Development; Society of Multivariate Experimental Psychology. Address: c/o Department of Psychology, Yale University, PO Box 208205, New Haven, CT 06520, USA.

STERNLICHT Sanford, b. 20 Sept 1931, New York, New York, USA. Professor of English; Literary Critic; Poet. m. Dorothy Hilkert, 7 June 1956, dec 1977, 2 sons. Education: BS, State University of New York at Oswego, 1953; MA, Colgate University, 1955; PhD, Syracuse University, 1962. Appointments: Instructor, 1959-60, Assistant Professor, 1960-62, Associate Professor, 1962, Professor of English, 1962-72, Professor of Theatre, 1972-86, State University of New York College at Oswego; Leverhulme Foundation Visiting Fellow, University of York, England, 1965-66; Professor of English, Syracuse University, 1986-. Publications: Poetry: Gull's Way, 1961; Love in Pompeii, 1967. Non-Fiction: Uriah Philips Levy: The Blue Star Commodore, 1961; The Black Devil of the Bayous: The Life and Times of the United States Steam-Sloop Hartford (with E M Jameson), 1970; John Webster's Imagery and the Webster Canon, 1974; John Masefield, 1977; McKinley's Bulldog: The Battleship Oregon, 1977; C S Forester, 1981; USF Constellation: Yankee Racehorse (with E M Jameson), 1981; Padraic Colum, 1985; John Galsworthy, 1987; R F Delderfield, 1988; Stevie Smith, 1990; Stephen Spender, 1992; Siegfried Sassoon, 1993; All Things Herriot: James Herriot and His Peaceable Kingdom, 1995; Jean Rhys, 1996; A Reader's Guide to Modern Irish Drama, 1998. Editor: Selected Stories of Padraic Colum, 1985; Selected Plays of Padraic Colum, 1989; In Search of Stevie Smith, 1991; New Plays from the Abbey Theatre 1993-1995, 1996; A Reader's Guide to Modern Irish Drama, 1998. Contributions to: Books, professional journals and general periodicals. Honours: Prizes, fellowships and grants including: Sir Evelyn Wrench English-Speaking Union Travel/Lecture Grants, 1997, 1998. Memberships: Modern Language Association; PEN; Poetry Society of America, fellow; Shakespeare Association of America; American Conference for Irish Studies. Address: 128 Dorset Road, Syracuse, NY 13210, USA.

STEVA V. See: **VLASIN Stepan.**

STEVENS Carl. See: **OBSTFELD Raymond.**

STEVENS Graeme Roy, b. 17 July 1932, Lower Hutt, New Zealand. Palaeontologist. m. Diane Louise Morton Ollivier, 20 Oct 1962, 2 sons, 1 daughter. Education: BSc, 1954, MSc, 1st Class, 1956, University of New Zealand; PhD, University of Cambridge, England, 1960; Fellowship, Royal Society of New Zealand, 1976. Appointments: UNESCO Sub Commission for the Natural Sciences, 1976; Advisory Committee on Adult Education, 1979; Book Resources Panel, National Library of New Zealand, 1981. Publications: Rugged Landscape, 1974; Geology of the Tararuas, 1975; Geology of New Zealand, 1978; New Zealand Adrift, 1980; Lands in Collision, 1985; Prehistoric New Zealand, 1988; The Great New Zealand Fossil Book, 1990; On Shaky Ground, 1991; Life and Landscapes, 1991; 165 scientific papers in professional journals. Honours: McKay Hammer Award, Geological Society of New Zealand, 1956; Hamilton Prize, Royal Society of New Zealand, 1959; Wattie Book of the Year Awards for Non-Fiction, 1974, 1980; Doctor of Science, Victoria University of Wellington, 1989; Queen's Service

Order, 1994. Memberships: Royal Society of New Zealand, home secretary; Geological Society of New Zealand, publisher. Address: 19A Wairere Road, Belmont, Lower Hutt, New Zealand.

STEVENS John. See: **TUBB E(dwin) C(harles).**

STEVENS Lynsey. See: **HOWARD Lynette Desley.**

STEVENS Peter (Stanley), b. 17 Nov 1927, Manchester, England (Canadian citizen). Retired Professor; Poet; Critic; Editor. m. June Sidebotham, 13 Apr 1957, 1 son, 2 daughters. Education: BA, Certificate in Education, University of Nottingham, 1951; MA, McMaster University, 1963; PhD, University of Saskatchewan, 1968. Appointments: Faculty, Hillfield-Strathallan College, Hamilton, Ontario, 1957-64; Part-time Lecturer, McMaster University, 1961-64; Lecturer and Assistant Professor, University of Saskatchewan, 1964-69; Poetry Editor, Canadian Forum, 1968-73, Literary Review of Canada, 1994-; Associate Professor, 1969-76, Professor, 1976-96, University of Windsor. Publications: Nothing But Spoons, 1969; The McGill Movement (editor), 1969; A Few Myths, 1971; Breadcrusts and Glass, 1972; Family Feelings and Other Poems, 1974; A Momentary Stay, 1974; The Dying Sky Like Blood, 1974; The Bogman Pavese Tactics, 1977; Modern English-Canadian Poetry, 1978; Coming Back, 1981; Revenge of the Mistresses, 1982; Out of the Willow Trees, 1986; Miriam Waddington, 1987; Swimming in the Afternoon: New and Selected Poems, 1992; Dorothy Livesay: Patterns in a Poetic Life, 1992; Rip Rap: Yorkshire Ripper Poems, 1995; Thinking Into the Dark, 1997; Attending to This World, 1998. Contributions to: Books, reviews, and journals. Address: 2055 Richmond Street, Windsor, Ontario N8Y 1L3, Canada.

STEVENSON Anne Katharine, b. 3 Jan 1933, Cambridge, England. Poet; Writer. m. (1), 2 sons, 1 daughter, (2) Peter David Lucas, 3 Sept 1987. Education: BA, 1954, MA, 1961, University of Michigan. Publications: Living in America, 1965; Reversals, 1969; Travelling Behind Glass, 1974; Correspondences, 1974; Enough of Green, 1977; Minute by Glass Minute, 1982; The Fiction Makers, 1985; Winter Time, 1986; Selected Poems, 1987; The Other House, 1990; Four and a Half Dancing Men, 1993; Collected Poems, 1996; Bitter Fame. A Life of Sylvia Plath; 1998; Five Looks at Elizabeth Bishop, 1998; Between the Iceberg and the Ship (literary essays), 1998. Contributions to: Reviews, journals, and magazines. Honours: Fellowships; Major Hopwood Award, 1954; Arts Council Award, 1974; Poetry Book Society Choice, 1985; Athena Award, 1990; Cholmondely Award, Society of Authors, 1997. Memberships: Poetry Book Society; Poetry Society; Royal Society of Literature, fellow; Society of Authors; Authors Guild, USA. Address: 38 Western Hill, Durham, DH1 4RJ, England.

STEVENSON David, b. 30 Apr 1942, Largs, Ayrshire, Scotland. Professor of History; Writer. m. Wendy McLeod, 2 sons. Education: BA, University of Dublin, 1966; PhD, 1970, DLitt, 1989, University of Glasgow. Appointments: Faculty, University of Aberdeen, University of St Andrews; Editor, Northern Scotland, 1980-90. Publications: The Scottish Revolution, 1973; Revolution and Counter-Revolution in Scotland, 1977; Alastair MacColla and the Highland Problem, 1980; Scottish Covenanters and Irish Confederates, 1981; The Origins of Freemasonry, 1988; The First Freemasons, 1988; King or Covenant: Voices from Civil War, 1996; Scotland's Last Royal Wedding, 1997; Union, Revolution and Religion in 17th Century Scotland, 1997. Contributions to: Historical journals. Membership: Royal Society of Edinburgh, fellow. Address: 5 Forgan Way, Newport-on-Tay, Fife, DD6 8JQ, Scotland.

STEVENSON Janet Atlantis, b. 2 Apr 1919, Chicago, Illinois, USA. Novelist; Playwright; Journalist; Teacher. m. Philip, 14 Oct 1940, 2 sons. Education: BA, Bryn Mawr College; MFA, Yale University. Publications: Streak of Pink, 1937; Declaration, 1949; The Innocent Bystander, 1952; But Yet a Woman, 1952; We Weep No More, 1959; John James Audubon, 1961; The Ardent Years, 1962;

Marian Anderson, 1963; Sister and Brothers, 1967; Woman Aboard, 1967; Archibald Grimke, 1969; Pioneers in Freedom, 1969; Soldiers in the Civil Rights War, 1971; The Montgomery Bus Boycott, 1971; The First Book of Woman's Rights, 1972; The School Segregation Cases, 1973; The Third President, 1977; The Undiminished Man: A Political Biography of Robert Walker Kenny, 1980; Departure, 1985; Sarah Ann, 1986. Contributions to: Magazines and newspapers. Honours: White Rose Award, March of Dimes, 1985; Charles Erskine Scott Wood Award, Oregon Institute of Literary Arts, 1988; Women of Achievement Award, State of Oregon Commission for Women, 1994; Distinguished Service Award, 1995. Address: 783 5th Avenue, Hammond, OR 97121, USA.

STEVENSON John, (Mark Denning), b. 8 May 1926, London, England. Writer; Teacher. m. Alison Stevenson, 1951, div. Appointments: Fiction Editor, 1981-82, Book Review Columnist, 1982-90, Mystery News; Instructor, Writer's Digest Schools, 1989-. Publications: Some 30 books, including Die Fast, Die Happy, 1976; Beyond the Prize, 1978; Merchant of Menace, 1980; Writing Commercial Fiction, 1983; Ranson, 1989. Contributions to: Journals and magazines. Honours: 4th Prize, Crime Writers International Congress, Stockholm, 1981; Life Membership, Mystery Writers of America, 1993. Address: 2005 Ivar Avenue, No 3, Los Angeles, CA 90068, USA.

STEWARD Hal David, b. 2 Dec 1918, East St Louis, Illinois, USA. Retired US Army Lieutenant Colonel; Editor; Writer. Education: LLB, La Salle Extension University, Chicago, 1948; BS, Boston University, 1961; PhD, Columbia Pacific University, San Rafael, California, 1979. Appointments: Executive Editor, Daily Chronicle, Centralia, Washington, 1975-79; Correspondent, Newsletter on Newsletters, Rhinebeck, New York, 1985-. Publications: The Successful Writer's Guide, 1970; Money Making Secrets of the Millionaires, 1972; Winning in Newsletters, 1989. Other: 2 novels; 2 military histories. Contributions to: More than 500 articles in magazines. Honour: Copley Journalism Award, 1963. Memberships: Authors Guild; Investigative Reporters and Editors; National Press Club; San Diego Press Club; Society of Professional Journalists. Address: 5240 Fiore Terrace, No J-306, San Diego, CA 92122, USA.

STEWART Barbara D, b. 17 Sept 1941, Rochester, New York, USA. Writer. Div, 2 daughters. Education: AB, Cornell University, 1962; MS, Simmons College, 1964; Graduate Fellow in Design, Yale School of Drama, 1989-90; MFA, Columbia University School of the Arts, 1993. Appointments: President, Smart Writers Inc, 1985-; President, ShareArts Foundation Inc, 1989-; Coach, Don Hood's World Class Pole Vault Camps, 1997-; Head Pole Vault Coach, Pittsford HS, New York, 1998-. Publications: How to Kazoo; Plays: Music vs Noise; Sound Barriers; Directions, Positions and Postures; Sydney the Sea Squid; Platypus Rex; The Magic Fruit. Honours include: Soviet Women Pole Vault Record, 1990; Schubert Fellowship, Columbia University, 1991-93; Cornell Athletic Hall of Fame. Memberships: Dramatists Guild; Ibsen Society. Address: 11 West Church Street, Fairport, NY 14450, USA.

STEWART Bruce Robert, b. 4 Sept 1925, Auckland, New Zealand. Writer; Dramatist. m. Ellen Noonan, 16 Oct 1950, 3 sons, 3 daughters. Education: BA, University of Auckland. Publications: A Disorderly Girl, 1980; The Turning Tide, 1980; The Hot and Copper Sky, 1982; Aspects of Therese, 1997; A Bloke Like Jesus, 1998. Other: Various plays for stage, radio and television, including Me and My Shadow, 1988; The Dog That Went to War, 1989; Speak Low, 1993. Contributions to: Newspapers, magazines and journals. Honours: Edgar Allan Poe Award, Mystery Writers of America, 1963; Charles Henry Foyle Award, UK, 1968. Memberships: British Film Institute; Writers Guild of Australia; Writers Guild of Great Britain, 1979-81. Address: c/o Harvey Unna, 24 Pottery Lane, Holland Park, London W11, England.

STEWART David. See: HIGHAM Robin.

STEWART Douglas Keith, b. 15 Dec 1950, Kawakana, New Zealand. Writer. m. Julie Joy Burgham, 9 Dec 1972, 1 son, 2 daughters. Education: Northland College, Auckland University. Publications: The New Zealanders Guide to Wine, 1986; The Art Award 15: 1988; The Wine Handbook, 1988; Rosa Antipodes The History of Roses in New Zealand, 1994; The New Zealander's Guide to Wines, 1994; The Fine Wines of New Zealand, 1995; Kahukura's Net, Maori Influence on Contemporary NZ Art, 1999; Euchre, novel, 1999. Contributions to: NZ Listener; Art Critic Sunday Star Times; Architecture NZ; NZ House and Garden. Honour: Finalist, Montana Book Awards, 1994. Address: PO Box 125, Kumeu, New Zealand.

STEWART Harold Frederick, b. 14 Dec 1916, Sydney, New South Wales, Australia. Poet; Writer; Translator. Education: University of Sydney. Appointments: Broadcaster, Australian Broadcasting Commission; Lecturer, Victorian Council of Adult Education. Publications: Poetry: The Darkening Ecliptic (with James McAuley), 1944; Phoenix Wings: Poems 1940-46, 1948; Orpheus and Other Poems, 1956; The Exiled Immortal: A Song Cycle, 1980; By the Old Walls of Kyoto: A Year's Cycle of Landscape Poems with Prose Commentaries, 1981; Collected Poems (with Ern Malley), 1993. Translator: A Net of Fireflies: Japanese Haiku and Haiku Paintings, 1960; A Chime of Windbells: A Year of Japanese Haiku, 1969; Tannisho: Passages Deploring Deviations of Faith (with Bando Shojun), 1980; The Amida Sutra Mandala (with Inagaki Hisao), 1995. Honours: Sydney Morning Herald Prize for Poetry, 1951; Australia Council Grant, 1978; Senior Emeritus Writers Fellow, Australia Council, 1982; Christopher Brennan Prize for Poetry, 1988. Address: 501 Keifuku Dai-ni Manshon, Yamabana-icho Dacho 7-1, Shugakuin, Sakyo-ku, Kyoto 606, Japan.

STEWART John, b. 24 Jan 1933, Trinidad, West Indies. Professor of Anthropology and Literature. m. Sandra MacDonald, 7 June 1969, 1 son, 1 daughter. Education: MA, Stanford University, 1964; MFA, University of Iowa, 1965; PhD, University of California at Los Angeles, 1971. Appointments: University of Illinois; Ohio State University; University of California at Davis. Publications: Last Cool Days (novel), 1971; Curving Road (short stories), 1975; For the Ancestors (life hisotry), 1983; Drinkers, Drummers and Decent Folk (narrative ethnography), 1989; Looking for Josephine (short stories), 1998. Honour: Winifred Hoztby Memorial Prize, 1971. Address: African American and African Studies, University of California at Davis, 2143 Hart Hall, Davis, CA 95616, USA.

STEWART Judith. See: POLLEY Judith Anne.

STEWART Leslie, b. 23 May 1949, Benghazi, Libya. Scriptwriter; Director; Author; Lyricist. 2 sons. Education: St Edward's College, Malta. Publications: Novel: Two of Us, 1989. Plays: Three Minute Heroes, 1985; Good Neighbours, 1987; Wide Games, 1987. Television Films and Plays: Three Minute Heroes, 1982; Wide Games, 1984; The Amazing Miss Stella Estelle, 1984; Good Neighbours, 1984; Space Station: Milton Keynes, 1985; The Little Match Girl, 1986; Janna, Where Are You?, 1987; Boogie Outlaws (TV serial), 1987; Two of Us, 1988; Q.P.R. Askey Is Dead, 1989; That Green Stuff, 1990. Radio: The Key To My Father's House, 1992; Canada Park, 1994. Stage: Shoot-Up At Elbow Creek (musical), 1976; The Little Match Girl (musical), 1977; The Soldier, 1983; The Little Match Girl, 1983; Shoot-Up at Elbow Creek, 1985; A Game Of Soldiers, 1987; The Little Match Girl (director), 1995; Urpo Turpo (animation series), 1997. Directed for TV: Space Station: Milton Keynes (with Colin Rogers), 1985; That Green Stuff, 1990; A Foot In The Door, 1992. Other: Lola, Terry, She's Not There (television shorts with Colin Rogers), 1985; Filigree (television documentary), 1993; How Green is My Alley (television documentary), 1998; The Great Wall of China (screenplay), 1998. Honours: Emmy Nomination, 1987; Ivor Novello Award, 1988; Richard Imison Memorial Award Shortlist, 1992. Memberships: Writer's Guild of Great Britain; British Academy of Film and Television

Arts; Performing Rights Society, associate member. Address: York Villa, Station Road, Haddenham, Cambridgeshire CB6 3XD, England.

STEWART Lady Mary Florence Elinor, b. 17 Sept 1916, Sunderland, England. Writer; Poet .m. Frederick Henry Stewart, 24 Sept 1945. Education: BA, 1938, DipEd, 1939, MA, 1941, University of Durham. Publications: Madam, Will You Talk?, 1954; Thunder on the Right, 1957; My Brother Michael, 1959; The Ivy Tree, 1961; The Moonspinners, 1962; The Crystal Cave, 1970; A Walk in Wolf Wood, 1970; The Little Broomstick, 1971; The Hollow Hills, 1973; Touch Not the Cat, 1976; The Last Enchantment, 1979; The Wicked Day, 1983; Thornyhold, 1988; Frost on the Window and Other Poems, 1990; Stormy Petrel, 1991; The Prince and the Pilgrim, 1995; Rose Cottage, 1997. Contributions to: Magazines. Honours: Frederick Niven Prize; Scottish Arts Council Award; Honorary Fellow, Newnham College, Cambridge. Memberships: PEN; New Club. Address: House of Letterawe, Loch Awe, Dalmally, Argyll PA33 1AH, Scotland.

STEWART Sean Maurice, b. 21 Oct 1969, Cincinnati, Ohio, USA. Journalistic Major; Freelance Writer. Education: Assistant Editor and Writer, University of Cincinnati's Student Newsletter. Publications: The Red Eagle Soars From Heaven, co-auth; The Hunting Grounds of Social Knowledge. Contributions to: 2 Certificates of Merits, The Nashville Newsletter. Memberships: Society of American Poets; Reader's Digest. Address: 2442 Highland Avenue, Apt #1, Cincinnati, OH 45219, USA.

STIBBE Mark W G, b. 16 Sept 1960, London, England. Clerk in Holy Orders; Writer. m. Alison Heather Stibbe, 30 July 1983, 2 sons, 1 daughter. Education: BA/MA, University of Cambridge, 1982; PhD, University of Nottingham, 1989. Publications: John as Storyteller, 1992; The Gospel of John as Literature, 1993; John: A New Biblical Commentary, 1993; A Kingdom of Priests, 1994; John's Gospel, 1994; Explaining Baptism in the Holy Spirit, 1995; O Brave New Church, 1996; Times of Refreshing, 1996; Know Your Spiritual Gifts, 1997. Contributions to: Numerous articles to Renewal; Anglicans for Renewal; Various New Testament journals; Journal of Pentecostal Theology; Soul Survivor. Honours: MA; Dip.Th; PhD. Address: St Andrew's Vicarage, 39 Quickley Lane, Chorley Wood, Hertfordshire WD3 5AE, England.

STICKLAND Caroline Amanda, b. 10 Oct 1955, Rinteln, Germany. Writer. m. William Stickland, 3 Aug 1974, 1 daughter. Education: BA, Honours, English and American Literature, University of East Anglia, 1977. Publications: The Standing Hills, 1986; A House of Clay, 1988; The Darkness of Corn, 1990; An Ancient Hope, 1993; The Darkening Leaf, 1995. Honours: Betty Trask Award, 1985. Memberships: Society of Authors; Mrs Gaskell Society; Thomas Hardy Society. Address: 81 Crock Lane, Bothenhampton, Bridport, Dorset DT6 4DQ, England.

STILES Martha Bennett, b. 30 Mar 1933, Manila, Philippines. Writer. m. Martin Stiles, 18 Sept 1954, 1 son. Education: BS, University of Michigan, 1954. Publications: The Strange House at Newburyport, 1963; Darkness Over the Land, 1966; The Star in the Forest, 1977; Sarah the Dragon Lady, 1986; Kate of Still Waters, 1990; Lonesome Road, 1998. Contributions to: Journals and periodicals. Honours: Society of Children's Book Writers Grant, 1988; Al Smith Fellowship, Kentucky Arts Council, 1992. Memberships include: Authors Guild; King Library Associates; Paris Arts Club. Address: 861 Hume-Bedford Road, Paris, KY 40361, USA.

STILLINGER Jack (Clifford), b. 16 Feb 1931, Chicago, Illinois, USA. Professor of English; Writer. m. (1) Shirley Louise Van Wormer, 30 Aug 1952, 2 sons, 2 daughters, (2) Nina Zippin Baym, 21 May 1971. Education: BA, University of Texas, 1953; MA, Northwestern University, 1954; PhD, Harvard University, 1958. Appointments: Assistant Professor, 1958-61,

Associate Professor, 1961-64, Professor of English, 1964-, University of Illinois; Editor, Journal of English and Germanic Philology, 1961-72; Member, Center for Advanced Study, University of Illinois, 1970-. Publications: The Early Draft of John Stuart Mill's Autobiography (editor), 1961; Anthony Munday's Zelauto (editor), 1963; William Wordsworth: Selected Poems and Prefaces (editor), 1965; The Letters of Charles Armitage Brown (editor), 1966; Twentieth Century Interpretations of Keats's Odes (editor), 1968; John Stuart Mill: Autobiography and Other Writings (editor), 1969; The Texts of Keats's Poems, 1974; The Poems of John Keats, 1978; Mill's Autobiography and Literary Essays (editor), 1981; John Keats: Complete Poems (editor), 1982; The Norton Anthology of English Literature (editor), 1986, 6th edition, 1993; John Keats: Poetry Manuscripts at Harvard, 1990; Multiple Authorship and the Myth of Solitary Genius, 1991; Coleridge and Textual Instability: The Multiple Versions of the Major Poems, 1994. Contributions to: Professional journals. Honours: National Woodrow Wilson Fellow, 1953-54; Guggenheim Fellowship, 1964-65; Distinguished Scholar Award, Keats-Shelley Association of America, 1986; Phi Beta Kappa. Memberships: American Academy of Arts and Sciences, fellow; Byron Society; Keats-Shelley Association of America; Modern Language Association. Address: 806 West Indiana Avenue, Urbana, IL 61801, USA.

STIMPSON Gerald. See: MITCHELL Adrian.

STIMSON SADLER Tess, (Tess Stimson), b. 17 July 1966, England. Writer. m. Brent Sadler, 17 July 1993, 2 sons. Education: MA Hons, (Oxon); St Hilda's College, Oxford, 1984-87. Appointment: Producer, ITN, 1987-91. Publications: Biography: Yours Till the End, 1992; Novels: Hard News, 1993; Soft Focus, 1995; Pole Position, 1996. Honours: Dorothy Whitelock Award, 1985; Eleanor Rooke Award, 1986. Literary Agent: Mark Lucas (Lucas Alexander Whitley). Address: c/o CNNI, PO Box 2012, London W1A 2GX, England.

STIMULUS Flavian P. See: PHILANDERSON Flavian Titus.

STIMULUS John. See: PHILANDERSON Flavian Titus.

STIRLING Jessica. See: RAE Hugh Crauford.

STOKER Alan, (Alan Evans), b. 2 Oct 1930, Sunderland, England. Writer. m. Irene Evans, 30 Apr 1960, 2 sons. Publications: End of the Running, 1966; Mantrap, 1967; Bannon, 1968; Vicious Circle, 1970; The Big Deal, 1971; Thunder at Dawn, 1978; Ship of Force, 1979; Dauntless, 1980; Seek Out and Destroy, 1982; Deed of Glory, 1984; Audacity, 1985; Eagle at Taranto, 1987; Night Action, 1989; Orphans of the Storm, 1990; Sink or Capture, 1993; Sword at Sunrise, 1994. Other: Short stories; Children's books. Contributions to: Newspapers and magazines. Membership Society of Authors. Literary Agent: David Higham Associates, Ltd., 5-8 Lower John Street, Golden Square, London W1R 4HA. Address: 9 Dale Road, Walton on Thames, Surrey KT12 2PY, England.

STOKER Richard, b. 8 Nov 1938, Castleford, Yorkshire, England. Composer; Author; Painter. m. (2) Dr Gillian Patricia Watson, 10 July 1986. Education: Huddersfield School of Music and School of Art, 1953-58; Royal Academy of Music, with Lennox Berkeley, 1958-62; Composition with Nadia Boulanger, Paris, 1962-63; Also private study with Eric Fenby and Arthur Benjamin. Appointments: Professor of Composition, 1963-87, Tutor, 1970-80, Royal Academy of Music; Editor, The Composer, 1969-80; Composition Teacher, St Paul's School, Hammersmith, London, 1973-76; Composition Teacher, Magdalene College, Cambridge, 1973-76; Appointed Magistrate, Inner London Commission, 1995-. Publications: Portrait of a Town, 1970; Words Without Music (Outposts), 1975; Open Window-Open Door (autobiography), 1985; Tanglewood (novel), 1994; Diva (novel), 1997; Collected Short Stories, 1997.

Contributions to: Many poems in Anthologies including Triumph, Spotlight, Strolling Players, American Poetry Society publications; Put Back the Clock, 1998; A Celebration: Thomas Armstrong, 1998; Commissions, contributions, 4 NDNB, 1999. Records and Recording; Books and Bookmen; Guardian; Performance; The Magistrate; Editor, The Composer, 1969-80; Poems on the internet. Honours: BBC Music Award, 1952; Eric Coates Award, 1962; Mendelssohn Scholarship, 1962; Dove Prize, 1962; Associate, 1965, Fellow, 1971, Royal Academy of Music; Editor's Awards, American National Library, 1995, 1996, 1997; Man of the Year, American Biographical Institute, 1997. Memberships: Composers' Guild, executive committee; Association of Professional Composers; Royal Society; PRS; MCPS; Royal Academy of Music; Magistrates' Association; Atlantic Council of the UK, founder member; European Atlantic Group; PEN International and English PEN, 1996. Address: c/o Ricordi, 210 New Kings Road, London SW6 4NZ, England.

STOKES Gale, b. 5 Sept 1933, Orange, New Jersey, USA. History Professor. m. Roberta Black, 5 Apr 1958, 1 son, 1 daughter. Education: BA, Colgate University, 1954; MA, Indiana University, 1965; PhD, Indiana University, 1970. Appointments: Rice University, 1968-; Mary Gibbs Jones Professor of History, 1997-. Publications: Legitimacy Through Liberalism, 1975; Politics as Development, 1990; The Walls Came Tumbling Down: The Collapse of Communism in Eastern Europe, 1993; From Stalinism to Pluralism, 2nd ed, 1976; Three Eras of Political Change in Eastern Europe, 1997. Contributions to: About 30 articles, 60 reviews. Honours: Vucinich Prize, 1994; Indiana University Distinguished Alumnis, 1995; American Historical Association. Address: 3746 Georgetown, Houston, TX 770005, USA.

STOLOFF Carolyn, b. 14 Jan 1927, New York, New York, USA. Poet; Painter; Teacher. Education: Dalton School; University of Illinois, 1944-46; BS, Painting, Columbia University School of General Studies, 1949; Art Studies with Xavier Gonzales, Eric Isenburger and Hans Hofmann; Poetry studies with Stanley Kunitz. Appointments: Teacher, Manhattanville College, 1957-74, Chairman, Art History and Studio Art, 1960-65, Baird House, 1973, Stephen's College, 1975, Hamilton College, 1985, University of Rochester, 1985; Poets in Public Service, 1989-90; School Volunteer Program, 1995-96. Publications: Stepping Out, 1971; In the Red Meadow, 1973; Dying to Survive, 1973; Lighter-Than-Night Verse, 1977; Swiftly Now, 1982; A Spool of Blue: New and Selected Poems, 1983; You Came to Meet Someone Else, 1993. Contributions to: Anthologies and journals. Honours: MacDowell Colony Residence Grants, 1961, 1962, 1970, 1976; Theodore Roethke Award, Poetry Northwest, 1967; National Council on the Arts Award, 1968; Helene Wurlitzer Foundation Grants, 1972-74; Silver Anniversary Medal, Audubon Artists, 1967; Michael M Engel Sr Memorial Award, 1982; Robert Philipps Award, 1990; Bader-Rowney Award for Oil Painting, 1994; Art Student's League Award for Oil Painting, 1995. Membership: Poetry Society of America. Address: 24 West 8th Street, New York, NY 10011, USA.

STOLTZFUS Ben Frank, b. 15 Sept 1927, Bulgaria. Professor Emeritus. m. Judith Palmer, 8 Nov 1975, 2 sons, 1 daughter. Publications: Novels: The Eye of the Needle, 1967; Black Lazarus, 1972; Red White & Blue, 1989. Contributions to: Journals and reviews. Honours include: Fulbright-Hays Grants to Paris, France, 1955-56, 1963-64; University of California Creative Arts Institute Awards, 1967, 1975; University of California Humanities Institute Awards, 1969-72. Address: c/o Department of Comparative Literture and Foreign Languages, University of California, Riverside, CA 92521, USA.

STONE Gerald Charles, b. 22 Aug 1932, Surbiton, Surrey, England. University Lecturer; Writer; Editor. m. Vera Fedorovna Konnova, 10 Apr 1974, 2 sons, 2 daughters. Education: BA, 1964, PhD, 1969, School of Slavonic and East European Studies, London University. Appointment: Editor, Oxford Slavonic Papers, 1982-. Publications: The Smallest Slavonic Nation: The Sorbs of

Lusatia, 1972; The Russian Language Since the Revolution (with Bernard Comrie), 1978; An Introduction to Polish, 1980, 2nd edition, 1992; The Formation of the Slavonic Literary Languages (editor with Dean Worth), 1985; Serbska poezija: Kěrluše (editor), 1995; A Dictionarie of the Vulgar Russe Tongue: Attributed to Mark Ridley (editor), 1996; Serbska poezija: Kjarliže, (editor), 1996; The Russian Language in the Twentieth Century (with Bernard Comrie and Maria Polinsky), 1996. Contributions to: Professional journals. Memberships: British Academy, fellow; Philological Society, council member, 1981-86, 1996-; Society for Slovene Studies. Address: 6 Lathbury Road, Oxford OX2 7AU, England.

STONE Joan Elizabeth, b. 22 Oct 1930, Port Angeles, Washington, USA. Assistant Professor of English; Poet; Writer. m. James A Black, 30 July 1990, 4 sons, 1 daughter. Education: BA, 1970, MA, 1974, PhD, 1976, University of Washington. Appointments: Visiting Professor of Poetry, University of Montana, 1974; Director, Creative Writing Workshop, University of Washington, 1975; Assistant Professor of English, Colorado College, 1977-. Publications: The Swimmer and Other Poems, 1975; Alba, 1976; A Letter to Myself to Water, 1981; Our Lady of the Harbor, 1986. Contributions to: Journals and magazines. Honours: Academy of American Poets Awards, 1969, 1970, 1972; Borestone Mountain Award, 1974. Address: 312 East Yampa Street, Colorado Springs, CO 80903, USA.

STONE Lawrence, b. 4 Dec 1919, Epsom, Surrey, England (US citizen, 1970). Retired Professor of History; Writer. m. Jeanne Caecilia Fawtier, 24 July 1943, 1 son, 1 daughter. Education: Sorbonne, University of Paris, 1938; BA, MA, Christ Church, Oxford, 1946. Appointments: Lecturer, University College, 1947-50, Fellow, Wadham College, 1950-63, Oxford; Member, Institute for Advanced Study, Princeton, New Jersey, 1960-61; Dodge Professor of History, 1963-90, Director, Shelby Cullom Davis Center for Historical Studies, 1968-90, Princeton Univeristy. Publications: Sculpture in Britain: The Middle Ages, 1955; An Elizabethan: Sir Horatio Palavicino, 1956; The Crisis of the Aristocracy, 1558-1641, 1965; The Causes of the English Revolution 1529-1642, 1972, revised edition, 1986; Family and Fortune Studies in Aristocratic Finance in the Sixteenth and Seventeenth Centuries, 1973; Family, Sex and Marriage in England 1500-1800, 1977; The Past and Present Revisited, 1987; Road to Divorce: England 1530-1987, 1990; Uncertain Unions: Marriage in England 1660-1753, 1992; Broken Lives: Marital Separation and Divorce in England 1660-1857, 1993. Contributions to: Professional journals. Memberships: American Academy of Arts and Sciences, fellow; American Philosophical Society; British Academy, corresponding member. Address: 266 Moore Street, Princeton, NJ 08540, USA.

STONE Peter Bennet, b. 6 July 1933, Oldham, Lancashire, England.Environmental Journalist. m. Jennifer Jane Wedderspoon, 29 July 1964, 2 daughters. Education: BA, Honours, MA, Balliol College, Oxford (Open Scholar, Science), 1951-55. Appointments: Producer, BBCTV, 1958-64; Senior Information Advisor, UN Conference on Environment, 1972; Editor-in-Chief, UN Development Forum, 1972-84; Director of Information, Brundtland Commisssion, 1984. Publications: Japan Surges Ahead, 1967; The Great Ocean Business, 1971; Did We Save the Earth at Stockholm, 1972; State of the World's Mountains: Global Report, 1992. Contributions to: Ceres, FAO; Economist; Many newspapers. Memberships: Scientific and sporting societies; Royal Geographical Society, fellow; FGS; Alpine Club. Address: 6 Eyot Green, Chiswick Mall, London W4 2PT, England.

STONE Robert (Anthony), b. 21 Aug 1937, New York, New York, USA. Writer. m. Janice G Burr, 11 Dec 1959, 1 son, 1 daughter. Education: New York University, 1958-59; Stegner Fellow, Stanford University, 1962. Appointments: Editorial Assistant, New York Daily News, 1958-60; Writer, National Mirror, New York City, 1965-67; Writer-in-Residence, Princeton University, 1971-72; Faculty, Amherst College, 1972-75, 1977-78, Stanford

University, 1979, University of Hawaii at Manoa, 1979-80, Harvard University, 1981, University of California at Irvine, 1982, New York University, 1983, University of California at San Diego, 1985, Princeton University, 1985, Johns Hopkins University, 1993-94, Yale University, 1994-. Publications: A Hall of Mirrors, 1967; Dog Soldiers, 1974; A Flag for Sunrise, 1981; Images of War, 1986; Children of Light, 1986; Outerbridge Reach, 1992; Damascus Gate, 1998. Contributions to: Anthologies and periodicals. Honours: William Faulkner Prize, 1967; Guggenheim Fellowship, 1971; National Book Award, 1975; John Dos Passos Prize, 1982; American Academy of Arts and Letters Award, 1982, and Grant, 1988-92; National Endowment for the Humanities Fellow, 1983. Membership: PEN. Address: PO Box 967, Block Island, RI 02807, USA.

STOPPARD Miriam, b. 12 May 1937, Newcastle upon Tyne, England. Physician; Writer; Broadcaster. m. Tom Stoppard, 1972, div 1992, 2 sons, 2 stepsons. Education: Royal Free Hospital School of Medicine, University of London; MB, BS, 1962, University of Durham; MD, King's College Medical School, University of Newcastle upon Tyne, 1966. Appointments: Senior House Officer in Medicine, Royal Victoria Infirmary, King's College Hospital, Newcastle upon Tyne, 1962-63; Research Fellow, Department of Chemical Pathology, 1963-65, Registrar in Dermatology, 1965-66, Senior Registrar in Dermatology, 1966-68, University of Bristol; Television series, Where There's Life, 1981-, Baby and Co, 1984-, Woman to Woman, 1985, Miriam Stoppard's Health and Beauty Show, 1988-. Publications: Miriam Stoppard's Book of Baby Care, 1977; Miriam Stoppard's Book of Health Care, 1979; The Face and Body Book, 1980; Everywoman's Lifeguide, 1982; Your Baby, 1982; Fifty Plus Lifeguide, 1982; Your Growing Child, 1983; Baby Care Book, 1983; Pregnancy and Birth Book, 1984; Baby and Child Medical Handbook, 1986; Everygirl's Lifeguide, 1987; Feeding Your Family, 1987; Miriam Stoppard's Health and Beauty Book, 1988; Every Woman's Medical Handbook, 1988; Lose 7lbs in 7 Days, 1990; Test Your Child, 1991; The Magic of Sex, 1991; Conception, Pregnancy and Birth, 1993; The Menopause, 1994; The Breast Book, 1996. Contributions to: Medical journals. Memberships: British Association of Rheumatology and Rehabilitation; Heberden Society; Royal Society of Medicine. Address: Iver Grove, Iver, Buckinghamshire, England.

STOPPARD Sir Tom, (Thomas Straussler), b. 3 July 1937, Zin, Czechoslovakia (British citizen). Dramatist; Screenwriter. m. (1) Jose Ingle, 1965, div 1972, 2 sons, (2) Miriam Moore-Robinson, 1972, div 1992, 2 sons. Publications: Plays: Rosencrantz and Guildenstern are Dead, 1967; The Real Inspector Hound, 1968; Albert's Bridge, 1968; Enter a Free Man, 1968; After Magritte, 1971; Jumpers, 1972; Artists Descending a Staircase and, Where Are They Now?, 1973; Travesties, 1975; Dirty Linen, and New-Found-Land, 1976; Every Good Boy Deserves Favour, 1978; Professional Foul, 1978; Night and Day, 1978; Undiscovered Country, 1980; Dogg's Hamlet, Cahoot's Macbeth, 1980; On the Razzle, 1982; The Real Thing, 1983; The Dog It Was That Died, 1983; Squaring the Circle, 1984; Four Plays for Radio, 1984; Rough Crossing, 1985; Dalliance and Undiscovered Country, 1986; Largo Desolato, by Vaclav Havel (translator), 1987; Hapgood, 1988; In the Native State, 1991; Arcadia, 1993; The Television Plays 1965-1984, 1993; The Invention of Love; 1997. Fiction: Introduction 2, 1964; Lord Malquist and Mr Moon, 1965. Other: 8 screenplays; Various unpublished state, radio, and television plays. Honours: John Whiting Award, Arts Council, 1967; New York Drama Critics Award, 1968; Italia Prize, 1968; Tony Awards, 1968, 1976, 1984; Evening Standard Awards, 1968, 1972, 1974, 1978, 1993, 1997; Olivier Award, 1993; Knighted, 1997. Address: c/o The Peters, Fraser and Dunlop Group Ltd, The Chambers, Chelsea Harbour, Lots Road, London SW10 0XF, England.

STOREY David (Malcolm), b. 13 July 1933, Wakefield, England. Writer; Dramatist; Screenwriter; Poet. m. Barbara Rudd Hamilton, 1956, 2 sons, 2 daughters. Education: Diploma, Slade School of Art, 1956. Publications: This Sporting Life, 1960; Flight into Camden, 1960; Radcliffe, 1963; Pasmore, 1972; A Temporary Life, 1973; Edward, 1973; Saville, 1976; A Prodigal Child, 1982; Present Times, 1984; Storey's Lives: Poems 1951-1991, 1992. Honours: Macmillan Fiction Award, 1960; John Llewellyn Memorial Prize, 1960; Somerset Mauhgam Award, 1960; Evening Standard Awards, 1967, 1970; Los Angeles Drama Critics Award, 1969; Writer of the Year Award, Variety Club of Great Britain, 1969; New York Drama Critics Award, 1969, 1970, 1971; Geoffrey Faber Memorial Prize, 1973; Fellow, University College, London, 1974; Booker Prize, 1976. Address: c/o Jonathon Cape Ltd, Random House, 20 Vauxhall Bridge Road, London SW1V 2SA, England.

STORM Christopher. See: OLSEN Theodore Victor.

STORR (Charles) Anthony, b. 18 May 1920, Bentley, England. Psychiatrist; Author. m. (1) Catherine Cole, 6 Feb 1942, 3 daughters, (2) Catherine Barton, 9 Oct 1970. Education: Winchester College; MB BChir, Cantab, 1944, MA, Cantab, 1946, Christ's College, Cambridge. Publications: The Integrity of the Personality, 1960; Sexual Deviation, 1964; Human Aggression, 1968; Human Destructiveness, 1972; The Dynamics of Creation, 1972; Jung, 1973; The Art of Psychotherapy, 1979; The Essential Jung,1983; Solitude: A Return to the Self, 1988; Churchill's Black Dog and Other Phenomena of the Human Mind (US edition as Churchill's Black Dog, Kafka's Mice and Other Phenomena of the Human Mind), 1989; Freud, 1989; Music and the Mind, 1992; Feet of Clay, 1996. Contributions to: Newspapers. Honours: Fellow, Royal Society of Literature, 1990; Honorary Fellow, Royal College of Psychiatrists, 1993. Memberships: Green College, Oxford, fellow, 1979, Emeritus, 1984. Address: 45 Chalfont Road, Oxford OX2 6TJ, England.

STORR Catherine (Lady Balogh), b. 21 July 1913, London, England. Retired Psychiatrist; Writer. Education: Newnham College, Cambridge, 1932-41; West London Hospital, 1941-44. Appointment: Assistant Editor, Penguin Books, London, 1966-70. Publications: Clever Polly Series, 4 volumes, 1952-80; Stories for Jano, 1952; Marianne Dreams, 1958; Marianne and Mark, 1959; Robin, 1962; Flax Into Gold (libretto), 1964; Lucy, 1964; The Catchpole Story, 1965; Rufus, 1969; Puss and the Cat, 1969; Thursday, 1971; Kate and the Island, 1972; Black God, White God, 1972; Children's Literature (editor), 1973; The Chinese Egg, 1975; The Painter and the Fish, 1975; Unnatural Fathers, 1976; The Story of the Terrible Scar, 1976; Tales from the Psychiatrist's Couch (short stories), 1977; Winter's End, 1978; Vicky, 1981; The Bugbear, 1981; February Yowler, 1982; The Castle Boy, 1983; Two's Company, 1984; Cold Marble (short stories), 1985; Daljit and The Unqualified Wizard, 1989; The Spy Before Yesterday, 1990; We Didn't Think of Ostriches, 1990; Babybug, 1992; Finn's Animal, 1992; The Mirror Image Ghost, 1994; Stephen and the Family Nose, 1995; Watcher at the Window, 1995. Honour: Prize, Friends of the Earth, 1985. Membership: Royal Society of Medicine. Address: Flat 5, 12 Frognal Gardens, London NW3, England.

STOTHARD Peter Michael, b. 28 Feb 1951, Chelmsford, England. Journalist. m. Sally Ceris Emerson, 1 son, 1 daughter. Education: BA, Lit Hum; MA, Oxford (Trinity). Appointments: BBC Journalist, 1974-77; Shell International, 1977-79; Business and Political Writer, Sunday Times, 1979-80; The Times: Features Editor & Leader Writer, 1980-86; Deputy Editor, 1986-92; US Editor, 1989-92; Editor, 1992-. Address: c/o The Times, 1 Pennington Street, London E1 9XN, England.

STOTT Mike, b. 2 Jan 1944, Rochdale, Lancashire, England. Playwright. Education: University of Manchester. Appointments: Resident Writer, Hampstead Theatre Club, 1975. Publications: Mata Hari, 1965; Erogenous Zone, 1969; Funny Peculiar, 1973; Lenz (after Büchner), 1974; Plays for People Who Don't Move Much, 1974; Midnight, 1974; Other People, 1974; Lorenzaccio (after De Musset), 1976; Followed by Oysters, 1976; Soldiers Talking Cleanly, 1978; The Boston Strangler, 1978; Grandad, 1978; Strangers, 1979; Ducking Out, 1982; Dead Men, 1982; Penine Pleasures, 1984; The Fling, 1984; The Fancy Man, 1988; Radio and television plays. Literary Agent: Tim Corrie, Peters Fraser and Dunlop. Address: c/o Peters Fraser and Dunlop, 503/4 The Chambers, Chelsea Harbour, London SW10 0XF

STOUT Robert Joe, b. 3 Feb 1938, Scottsbluff, Nebraska, USA. Freelance Writer and Journalist. m. Maureen Ryan, 14 Apr 1988, 2 sons, 3 daughters. Education: BA, Mexico City College, 1960. Publications: Miss Sally, 1973; The Trick, 1974; Swallowing Dust, 1974; Moving Out, 1974; The Way to Pinal, 1979; They Still Play Baseball the Old Way, 1994. Contributions to: Nation; Commonweal; Modern Maturity; Notre Dame Magazine; Beloit Poetry Journal; Chicago Tribune Magazine; New Orleans Review; Chic. Address: PO Box 5074, Chico, CA 95927, USA.

STOW (Julian) Randolph, b. 28 Nov 1935, Geraldton, Western Australia, Australia; Writer; Poet; Librettist. Education: University of Western Australia, 1956. Appointments: Lecturer in English, University of Leeds, Yorkshire, 1962, 1968-69, University of Western Australia, 1963-64; Harkness Fellow, USA, 1964-66. Publications: A Haunted Land, 1956; The Bystander, 1957; To the Islands, 1958; Tourmaline, 1963; The Merry-Go-Round in the Sea, 1965; Midnite, 1967; Visitants, 1979; The Girl Green as Elderflower, 1980; The Suburbs of Hell, 1984. Poetry: Act One, 1957; Outrider: Poems 1956-62, 1962; A Counterfeit Silence: Selected Poems, 1969; Randolph Stow (omnibus volume edited by A J Hassall), 1990. Librettos to Music by Peter Maxwell Davies: Eight Songs for a Mad King, 1969; Miss Donnithorne's Maggot, 1974. Honours: Miles Franklin Award, 1958; Britannica-Australia Award, 1966; Grace Leven Prize, 1969; Arts Council of Great Britain Bursary, 1969; Commonwealth Literary Fund Grant, 1974; Patrick White Award, 1979. Address: c/o Richard Scott Simon Ltd, 43 Doughty Street, London WC1N 2LF, England.

STRAND Mark, b. 11 Apr 1934, Summerside, Prince Edward Island, Canada. Poet; Writer; Professor. m. (1) Antonia Ratensky, 14 Sept 1961, div June 1973, 1 daughter, (2) Julia Rumsey Garretson, 15 Mar 1976, 1 son. Education: AB, Antioch College, 1957; BFA, Yale University, 1959; MA, University of Iowa, 1962. Appointments: Instructor, University of Iowa, 1962-65; Fulbright Lecturer, University of Brazil, 1965; Assistant Professor, Mount Holyoke College, 1966; Visiting Professor, University of Washington, 1967, University of Virginia, 1977, California State University at Fresno, 1977, University of California at Irvine, 1978, Wesleyan University, 1979-80; Adjunct Professor, Columbia University, 1968-70; Visiting Lecturer, Yale University, 1969-70, Harvard University, 1980-81; Associate Professor, Brooklyn College, 1971; Bain Swiggett Lecturer, Princeton University, 1972; Fanny Hurst Professor of Poetry, Brandeis University, 1973; Professor, 1981-86, Distinguished Professor, 1986-94, University of Utah; Poet Laureate of the USA, 1990-91; Elliot Coleman Professor of Poetry, Johns Hopkins University, 1994-. Publications: Poetry: Sleeping With One Eye Open, 1964; Reasons for Moving, 1968; Darker, 1970; The Sargentville Notebook, 1973; The Story of Our Lives, 1973; The Late Hour, 1978; Selected Poems, 1980; The Continuous Life, 1990; Dark Harbor, 1993. Fiction: Mr and Mrs Baby (short stories), 1985. Prose: The Monument, 1978; The Art of the Real, 1983; William Bailey, 1987; Hopper, 1994. Anthologies: The Contemporary American Poets, 1969; New Poetry of Mexico (with Octavio Paz), 1970; Another Republic (with Charles Simic), 1976; The Best American Poetry 1991 (with David Lehman), 1992. Translations: Halty Ferguson: 18 Poems from the Quechua, 1971; Rafael Alberti: The Owl's Insomnia (poems), 1973; Carlos Drummond de Andrade: Souvenir of the Ancient World (poems), 1976; Travelling in the Family: The Selected Poems of Carlos Drummond de Andrade, 1986. Children's Books: The Planet of Lost Things, 1982; The Night Book, 1985; Rembrandt Takes a Walk, 1986. Contributions to: Poems, book reviews, art reviews, essays on poetry and painting and interviews in numerous periodicals. Honours: Fulbright Scholarship to Italy, 1960-61; Ingram Merrill Foundation Fellowship, 1966; National Endowment for the Arts Fellowships, 1967-68, 1977-78; Rockefeller Fellowship, 1968-69; Edgar Allan Poe Prize, 1974; Guggenheim Fellowship, 1974-75; National Institute of Arts and Letters Award, 1975; Academy of American Poets Fellowship, 1979; Writer-in-Residence, American Academy, Rome, 1982; John D and Catharine T MacArthur Foundation Fellowship, 1987-92; Utah Governor's Award in the Arts, 1992; Bobbitt National Prize for Poetry, 1992; Bollingen Prize for Poetry, 1993. Memberships: American Academy and Institute of Arts and Letters, 1980-; National Academy of Arts and Sciences, 1995-. Address: The Writing Seminars, Johns Hopkins University, 3400 North Charles Street, Baltimore, MD 21218, USA.

STRANDBERG Keith (William), b. 21 Aug 1957, Toledo, Ohio, USA. Screenwriter; Author. m. Carol Anne Hartman, 25 Sept 1982, 2 sons. Education: BA, Chinese Language and Literature, 1979; BA, Physical Education, 1979; MA, Film and Screenwriting, 1997. Publications: Stir Fry Cooking, 1985; Action Film Making Master Class, 1993. Films: No Retreat, No Surrender, 1986; Raging Thunder, 1987; Blood Brothers, 1989; The King of the Kickboxers, 1990; American Shaolin, 1991; Superfights, 1996; American Dragons, 1997; Bloodmoon, 1997. Contributions to: Many publications. Honours: International Martial Arts Hall of Fame, 1993; World Martial Arts Hall of Fame, 1994. Memberships: National Martial Arts Advisory Board; National Writers Club. Address: 3634 Peregrine Circle, PA 17554, USA.

STRANGER Joyce. See: WILSON Joyce Muriel.

STRATTON Thomas. See: DE WEESE Thomas Eugene "Gene".

STRAUB Peter Francis, b. 2 Mar 1943, Milwaukee, Wisconsin, USA. Writer. m. 27 Aug 1966. Education: BA, University of Wisconsin, 1965; MA, Columbia University, 1966. Publications: Open Air (poems), 1972; Marriage, 1973; Julia, 1975; If You Could See Me New, 1977; Ghost Story, 1979; Shadowland, 1980; Floating Dragon, 1983; The Talisman (with Stephen King), 1984; Koko, 1988; Mystery, 1989; Houses Without Doors, 1990; The Throat, 1993; The Hellfire Club, 1996. Contributions to: Times Literary Supplement; New Statesman; Washington Post. Honours: British Fantasy Award, 1983; August Derleth Award, 1983; World Fantasy Best Novel Awards, 1988, 1993; Bram Stoker Award for Best Novel, 1993. Memberships: Mystery Writers of America; Horror Writers of America; PEN. Address: 53 West 85th Street, New York, NY 10024, USA.

STRAUS Dennis David, (Ascher/Straus), b. New York, USA. Writer. Education: MA, Columbia University. Publications: Letter to an Unknown Woman; The Other Planet; The Menaced Assassin; Red Moon/Red Lake; ABC Street, 1998. Contributions to: Chicago Review; Paris Review; Epoch; Top Stories; Chelsea; Exile; Calyx; Zone; Confrontation; Central Park; New American Writing; Asylum Annual; Red Moon/Red Lake; Top Top Stories (anthology); 15 Years in Exile (anthology); Likely Stories (anthology); The Living Underground (anthology). Honours: Panache Experimental Fiction Prize; Pushcart Prize; Caps Fellowship. Address: PO Box 176, Rockaway Park, NY 11694, USA.

STRAUS/ASCHER. See: ASCHER Sheila.

STRAUSS Botho, b. 2 Dec 1944, Naumberg-an-der-Saale, Germany. Author; Poet; Dramatist. Education: German Language and Literature, Drama, Sociology, Cologne and Munich. Publications: Bekannte Gesichter, gemischte Gefühle (with T Bernhard and F Kroetz), 1974; Trilogie des Wiedersehens, 1976; Gross und Klein, 1978; Rumor, 1980; Kalldeway Farce, 1981; Paare, Passanten, 1981; Der Park, 1983; Der junge Mann, 1984; Diese Erinnerung an einen, der nur einen Tag zu Gast War, 1985; Die Fremdenführerin,

1986; Niemand anderes, 1987; Besucher, 1988; Kongress: Die Kette der Demütigungen, 1989; Theaterstücke in zwei Banden, 1994; Wohnen Dammern Lügen, 1994. Honours: Dramatists' Prize, Hannover, 1975; Schiller Prize, Baden-Württemberg, 1977; Literary Prize, Bavarian Academy of Fine Arts, Munich, 1981; Jean Paul Prize, 1987; Georg Büchner Prize, 1989. Membership: PEN. Address: Keithstrasse 8, D-17877, Berlin, Germany.

STRAUSS Jennifer, b. 30 Jan 1933, Heywood, Western Australia, Australia. Associate Professor; Poet. m. Werner Strauss, 1958, 3 sons. Education: BA, University of Melbourne, 1954; University of Glasgow, 1957-58; PhD, Monash University, 1992. Appointments: Senior Lecturer, 1971-92, Associate Professor, 1992-, Monash University. Publications: Children and Other Strangers, 1975; Winter Driving, 1981; Middle English Verse: An Anthology (co-editor), 1985; Labour Ward, 1988; Boundary Conditions: The Poetry of Gwen Harwood, 1992, 3rd edition, 1996; The Oxford Book of Australian Love Poems (editor), 1993; Judith Wright, 1995; Tierra del Fuego: New and Selected Poems, 1997; Family Ties: Australian Poems of the Family (editor), 1998; Oxford Literary History of Australia (co-editor), 1998. Contributions to: Various publications. Memberships: Premier's Literary Awards Committee. Address: 2-12 Tollington Avenue, East Malvern, Victoria 3145, Australia.

STRAUSS Susan, b. 21 Dec 1954, New York, New York, USA. Author; Storyteller. m. Ted Wise, 22 June 1991, 1 daughter. Education: BA, English, 1977, MA, English Education, 1980, University of Virginia. Publications: Coyote Stories for Children: Tales from Native America, 1991; Wolf Stories: Myth and True Tales from Around the World, 1994; The Passionate Fact: Storytelling in Natural History and Cultural Interpretation, 1996; When Woman Became the Sea: A Costan Rican Creation Myth, 1998. Contributions to: Children's Writers and Illustrators Market, 1994. Address: PO Box 1141, Bend, OR 97709, USA.

STRAUSSLER Thomas. See: STOPPARD Sir Tom.

STRAWSON Galen John, b. 5 Feb 1952, Oxford, England. Philosopher. m. (1) Jose Said, 20 July 1974, diss 1994, 1 son, 2 daughters, (2) Anna Vaux, 6 Jan 1997, 2 sons. Education: BA, Philosophy, 1973, MA, 1977, University of Cambridge; BPhil, 1977, DPhil, 1983, University of Oxford. Appointments: Assistant Editor, 1978-87, Consultant, 1987-, Times Literary Supplement, London. Publications: Freedom and Belief, 1986; The Secret Connection, 1989; Mental Reality, 1994. Contributions to: Times Literary Supplement; Sunday Times; Observer; London Review of Books; Independent on Sunday; Mind; American Philosophical Quarterly; Inquiry; Financial Times; Journal of Consciousness Studies; Analysis, Philosophical Studies. Honours: R A Nicholson Prize for Islamic Studies, Cambridge, 1971; T H Green Prize for Moral Philosophy, Oxford, 1983; Fellow, Jesus College, Oxford, 1987-; Visiting Fellow, Australian National University, 1993; Visiting Professor, New York University, 1997. Membership: Mind Association. Address: Jesus College, Oxford OX1 3DW, England.

STRAWSON Sir Peter (Frederick), b. 23 Nov 1919, London, England. Retired Professor of Metaphysical Philosophy; Author. m. Grace Hall Martin, 1945, 2 sons, 2 daughters. Education: Christ's College, Finchley; St John's College, Oxford. Appointments: Assistant Lecturer in Philosophy, University College of North Wales, 1946; John Locke Scholar, 1946, Reader, 1966-68, Waynflete Professor of Metaphysical Philosophy, 1968-87, University of Oxford; Lecturer in Philosophy, 1947, Fellow and Praelector, 1948, Fellow, 1948-68, Honorary Fellow, 1979-, University College, Oxford; Visiting Professor, Duke University, 1955-56; Fellow of the Humanities Council and Visiting Associate Professor, 1960-61, Visiting Professor, 1972, Princeton University; Fellow, 1968-87, Honorary Fellow, 1989, Magdelen College, Oxford; Woodbridge Lecturer, Columbia University, 1983;

Immanuel Kant Lecturer, University of Munich, 1985; Visiting Professor, Collège de France, 1985. Publications: Introduction to Logical Theory, 1952; Individuals, 1959; The Bounds of Sense, 1966; Philosophical Logic (editor), 1966; Studies in the Philosophy of Thought and Action (editor), 1968; Logico-Linguistic Papers, 1971; Freedom and Resentment, 1974; Subject and Predicate in Logic and Grammar, 1974; Scepticism and Naturalism: Some Varieties, 1985; Analyse and Métaphysique, 1985, English translation as Analysis and Metaphysics, 1992; Entity and Identity, 1997. Contributions to: Scholarly journals. Honours: Knighted 1977; Honorary Doctorate, Munich, 1998. Memberships: Academia Europaea; American Academy of Arts and Sciences, honorary member; British Academy, fellow. Address: 25 Farndon Road, Oxford OX2 6RT, England.

STREET Pamela, b. 3 Mar 1921, Wilton, Wiltshire, England. Writer. Div, 1 daughter. Education: Salisbury and South Wiltshire College of Further Education, 1967-69. Publications: My Father, A G Street, 1969, 2nd edition, 1984; Portrait of Wiltshire, 1971, new edition, 1980; Arthur Bryant: Portrait of a Historian, 1979; Light of Evening, 1981; The Stepsisters, 1982; Morning Glory, 1982; Portrait of Rose, 1986; The Illustrated Portrait of Wiltshire, 1984, paperback edition, 1994; Personal Relations, 1987; The Mill-Race Quartet, 1988; The Timeless Moment, 1988; The Beneficiaries, 1989; Doubtful Company, 1990; Guilty Parties, 1991; Late Harvest, 1991; The Colonel's Son, 1992; Hindsight, 1993; Keeping it Dark, 1994; King's Folly, 1995; The General's Wife, 1996. Contributions to: Newspapers and magazines. Address: c/o 42 Roedean Crescent, London SW15 5JU, England.

STREETEN Paul Patrick, (Patrick Proctor), b. 18 July 1917, Vienna, Austria. Retired Professor. m. Ann H Higgins, 9 June 1951, 1 stepson, 2 daughters. Education: MA, University of Aberdeen, 1944; BA, 1947 MA, 1952, Oxon; DLitt, 1976. Publications: Economic Integration, 1961, 2nd edition, 1964; Frontiers of Development Studies, 1972; Development Perspectives, 1981; First Things First, 1981; What Price Food?, 1987; Mobilizing Human Potential, 1989; Thinking About Development, 1995, paperback, 1997; For Whom the Bell Tolls (fiction), 1996. Contributions to: Magazines, journals and books. Honours: Honorary Fellow, Institute of Development Studies, 1980; Honorary Fellow, Balliol College, 1986; Essays in Honour of Paul Streeten: Theory and Reality in Development, (edited by Sanjaya Lall and Frances Stewart), 1986; Development Prize, Justus Liebig University, 1987; Honorary LLD, University of Aberdeen, 1980; Honorary DLitt, University of Malta, 1992. Address: Box 92, Spencertown, NY 12165, USA.

STRENGTH Will. See: HUANG Harry J(unxiong).

STRESHINSKY Shirley, b. 7 Oct 1934, Alton, Illinois, USA. Writer. m. Ted Streshinsky, 16 June 1966, 1 son, 1 daughter. Education: BA, University of Illinois. Publications: And I Alone Survived, 1978; Hers the Kingdom, 1981; A Time Between, 1984; Gift of the Golden Mountain, 1988; The Shores of Paradise (novel), 1991; Oats! A Book of Whimsy, (with Maria Streshinsky), 1997; John James Audubon: Life and Art in the American Wilderness, 1998. Contributions to: Journals and magazines. Honours: Best Human Interest Article, Society Magazine Writers Association, 1968; Educational Press Award, 1968. Membership: Authors Guild. Address: PO Box 674, Berkeley, CA 94701, USA.

STROM Robert Duane, b. 21 Jan 1935, Chicago, Illinois, USA. Professor of Psychology; Writer. m. Shirley Kaye Mills, Apr 1961, 2 sons. Education: BS, Macalester College, 1958; MA, University of Minnesota, 1959; PhD, University of Michigan, 1962. Appointment: Professor of Psychology, Arizona State University, Tempe. Publications: Teaching in the Slum School, 1965; Psychology for the Classroom, 1969; Teachers and the Learning Process, 1971; Education for Affective Achievement (with E P Torrance), 1973; Values and Human Development, 1973; Learning Processes, 1976; Parent and Child Development, 1978; Growing Through

Play: Parents and Children, 1981; Educational Psychology, 1982; Human Development and Learning, 1989; Becoming a Better Grandparent, 1991; Grandparent Education, 1991; Achieving Grandparent Potential, 1992. Contributions to: Over 300 articles to professional journals. Honours: NATO Scholar, University of Ankara, Turkey, 1967; Fulbright Scholar, University of the Philippines, 1974, Canberra, Australia, 1975; Fulbright Scholar, University of Stockholm, Sweden, 1985; Research Fellow, Japan Society for the Promotion of Science, 1995; Research Fellow, Japan Ministry of Education, Science and Culture, 1995; Research Fellow, Pacific Continent Foundation, China, 1997. Membership: American Psychological Association. Address: Arizona State University, Tempe, AZ 85287, USA.

STRONG Eithne, b. 23 Feb 1923, West Limerick, Ireland. Writer; Poet. m. Rupert Strong, 12 Nov 1943, 2 sons, 7 daughters. Education: BA, Trinity College, Dublin. Publications: Poetry: Songs of Living, 1965; Sarah in Passing, 1974; Circt Oibre, 1980; Fuil agus Fallat, 1983; My Darling Neighbour, 1985; Flesh the Greatest Sin, 1989; An Sagart Pinc, 1990; Aoife Faoi Ghlas, 1990; Let Live, 1990; Spatial Nosing, 1993; Nobel, 1998. Fiction: Degrees of Kindred, 1979; The Love Riddle, 1993. Short Fiction: Patterns, 1981. Contributions to: Anthologies, journals, and magazines. Memberships: Aosdána; Conradh Na Gaeilge; Irish PEN; Irish Writers Union; Poetry Ireland. Address: 17 Eaton Square, Monkstown, Dublin, Ireland.

STRONG Jonathan, b. 13 Aug 1944, Evanston, Illinois, USA. Writer; University Teacher. Education: Harvard University, 1969. Appointment: Faculty, Tufts University. Publications: Tike, 1969; Ourselves, 1971; Elsewhere, 1985; Secret Words, 1992; Companion Pieces, 1993; An Untold Tale, 1993; Offspring, 1995; The Old World, 1997. Contributions to: American Literature; Journals and magazines. Honours: O Henry Story Awards, 1967, 1970; Rosenthal Award, 1970; National Endowment for the Arts Award, 1986. Memberships: New England Gilbert and Sullivan Society; Sir Arthur Sullivan Society. Address: c/o Department of English, Tufts University, Medford, MA 02155, USA.

STRONG Maggie. See: KOTKER (Mary) Zane.

STRONG Pat. See: HOUGH Richard Alexander.

STRONG Sir Roy (Colin), b. 23 Aug 1935, London, England. Art Historian; Writer; Lecturer. m. Julia Trevelyan Oman. Education: Queen Mary College, London; Warburg Institute, London. Appointments: Assistant Keeper, 1959, Director, Keeper and Secretary, 1967-73, National Portrait Gallery, London; Ferens Professor of Fine Art, University of Hull, 1972; Walls Lecturer, J Pierpoint Morgan Library, New York, 1974; Director, Victoria and Albert Museum, London, 1974-87; Director, Oman Publications Ltd. Publications: Portraits of Queen Elizabeth I, 1963; Holbein and Henry the VIII, 1967; The English Icon: Elizabethan and Jacobean Portraiture, 1969; Tudor and Jacobean Portraits, 1969; Van Dyck: Charles I on Horseback, 1972; Splendour at Court: Renaissance Spectacle and the Theatre of Power, 1973; Nicholas Hilliard, 1975; The Renaissance Garden in England, 1979; Britannia Triumphans: Inigo Jones, Rubens and Whitehall Palace, 1980; Henry, Prince of Wales and England's Lost Renaissance, 1986; Creating Small Gardens, 1986; Gloriana: Portraits of Queen Elizabeth I, 1987; A Small Garden Designer's Handbook, 1987; Cecil Beaton: The Royal Portraits, 1988; Creating Small Formal Gardens, 1989; Lost Treasures of Britain, 1990; A Celebration of Gardens (editor), 1991; The Garden Trellis, 1991; Small Period Gardens, 1992; Royal Gardens, 1992; A Country Life, 1994; Successful Small Gardens, 1994; William Larkin: Vanitù giacobite, Italy, 1994; The Tudor and Stuart Monarchy, 2 volumes, 1994-95; The English Vision: Country Life 1897-1997; The Story of Britain, 1996; The Tudor and Stuart Monarchy, 3 volumes, 1995-97; The Story of Britain, 1996; The English Vision: Country Life 1897-1997, 1997; The Roy Strong Diaries 1967-1987, 1997. Co-Author: Leicester's Triumph, 1964; Elizabeth R, 1971; Mary

Queen of Scots, 1972; Inigo Jones: The Theatre of the Stuart Court, 1973; An Early Victorian Album: The Hill-Adamson Collection, 1974; The English Miniature, 1981; The English Year, 1982; Artists of the Tudor Court, 1983. Honours: Fellow, Queen Mary College, 1976; Knighted, 1982; Senior Fellow, Royal College of Artists, 1983; Honorary doctorates. Memberships: Arts Council of Great Britain, chairman, arts panel, 1983-87; British Council, Fine Arts Advisory Committee, 1974-87; Royal College of Artists, Council, 1979-87; Westminster Abbey Architectural Panel, 1975-89. Address: The Laskett, Much Birch, Herefordshire HR2 8HZ, England.

STRONG Spencer. See: ACKERMAN Forrest J.

STRYKER Daniel. See: MORRIS Janet Ellen.

STUART Anthony. See: HALE Julian Anthony Stuart.

STUART Dabney, b. 4 Nov 1937, Richmond, Virginia, USA. Professor of English; Editor; Poet; Writer. m. (3) Sandra Westcott, 1983, 2 sons, 1 daughter. Education: AB, Davidson College, North Carolina, 1960; AM, Harvard Universty, 1962. Appointments: Instructor, College of William and Mary, Williamsburg, Virginia, 1961-65; Instructor, 1965-66, Assistant Professor, 1966-69, Associate Professor, 1969-74, Professor, 1974-91, S Blount Mason Professor of English, 1991-, Washington and Lee University, Lexington, Virginia; Poetry Editor, 1966-76, Editor-in-Chief, 1988-95, Shenandoah; Visiting Professor, Middlebury College, 1968-69; McGuffey Chair of Creative Writing, Ohio University, 1972; Visiting Poet, University of Virginia, 1981, 1982-83; Poetry Editor, New Virginia Review, 1983. Publications: Poetry: The Diving Bell, 1966; A Particular Place, 1969; Corgi Modern Poets in Focus 3, 1971; The Other Hand, 1974; Friends of Yours, Friends of Mine, 1974; Round and Round: A Triptych, 1977; Rockbridge Poems, 1981; Common Ground, 1982; Don't Look Back, 1987; Narcissus Dreaming, 1990; Light Years: New and Selected Poems, 1994; Second Sight: Poems for Paintings by Carol Cloar, 1996; Long Gone, 1996; Settlers, 1999. Fiction: Sweet Lucy Wine: Stories, 1992. Non-Fiction: Nabokov: The Dimensions of Parody, 1978; The Way to Cobbs Creek, 1997. Honours: Dylan Thomas Prize, Poetry Society of America, 1965; Borestone Mountain Awards, 1969, 1974, 1977; National Endowment for the Arts Grant, 1969, and Fellowships, 1974, 1982; Virginia Governor's Award, 1979; Guggenheim Fellowship, 1987-88; Individual Artists Fellowship, Virginia Commission for the Arts, 1996. Address: c/o Department of English, Washington and Lee University, Lexington, VA 24450, USA.

STUBBS Jean, b. 23 Oct 1926, Denton, Lancashire, England. Author. m.(1) Peter Stubbs, 1 May 1948, 1 son, 1 daughter, (2) Roy Oliver, 5 Aug,1980. Education: Manchester School of Art, 1944-47; Diploma, Loreburn Secretarial College, Manchester, 1947. Appointments: Copywriter, Henry Melland, 1964-66; Reviewer, Books and Bookmen, 1965-76; Writer-in-Residence for Avon, 1984. Publications: The Rose Grower, 1962; The Travellers, 1963; Hanrahan's Colony, 1964; The Straw Crown, 1966; My Grand Enemy, 1967; The Passing Star, 1970; The Case of Kitty Ogilvie, 1970; An Unknown Welshman, 1972; Dear Laura, 1973; The Painted Face, 1974; The Golden Crucible, 1976; Kit's Hill,1979; The Ironmaster, 1981; The Vivian Inheritance, 1982; The Northern Correspondent, 1984; 100 Years Around the Lizard, 1985; Great Houses of Cornwall,1987; A Lasting Spring, 1987; Like We Used To Be, 1989; Summer Secrets, 1990; Kelly Park, 1992; Charades, 1994; The Witching Time, 1998. Contributions to: Anthologies and magazines. Honours: Tom Gallon Trust Award, 1964; Daughter of Mark Twain, 1973. Memberships: PEN; Society of Women Writers and Journalists; Detection Club; Lancashire Writers Association; West Country Writers; Society of Authors. Address: Trewin, Nancegollan, Helston, Cornwall TR13 0AJ, England.

STUDEBAKER William (Vern), b. 21 May 1947, Salmon, Idaho, USA. Professor; Writer; Poet. m. Judy

Infanger, 23 Aug 1969, 2 sons, 2 daughters. Education: BA, History, 1970, MA, English, 1986, Idaho State University; Law, University of Idaho, 1974-75; Computer Science, Sonoma State University, 1986. Appointments: Assistant Professor, 1975-, Chairman, Department of English, 1980-82, College of Southern Idaho; Commissioner, Idaho; Commissioner, Idaho Commission on the Arts, 1981-86; Councilman, Idaho Humanities Council, 1996-. Publications: Everything Goes Without Saying, 1978; The Cleaving, 1985; Idaho's Poetry: A Centennial Anthology, 1989; The Rat Lady at the Company Dump, 1990; Where the Morning Lights' Still Blue: Personal Essays About Idaho, 1994; River Religion, 1997; Traveler' in an Antique Land, 1997; Short of a Good Promise, 1999. Contributions to: Numerous reviews, quarterlies, and journals. Address: 2616 East 4000 North, Twin Falls, ID 83301, USA.

STUDWELL William Emmett, b. 18 Mar 1936, Stamford, USA. Librarian; Professor. m. Ann Marie Stroia, 28 Aug 1965, 1 daughter. Education: BA, 1958; MA, 1959; MSLS, 1967. Appointments: Technical Abstractor, Library of Congress, 1963-66; Decimal Classification Office, Library of Congress, 1966-68; Head Librarian, Kirtland Community College, 1968-70; Head of Cataloging, Principal Cataloger, Northern Illinois University, 1970-. Publications: Christmas Carols, 1985; Ballet Plot Index, 1987; Cataloging Books, 1989; Library of Congress Subject Headings, 1990; Opera Plot Index, 1990; The Popular Song Leader, 1994; The Christmas Carol Reader, 1995; The National and Religious Song Reader, 1996; The Americana Song Reader, 1997; State Songs of the United States, 1997; Publishing Glad Tidings, 1998; College Fight Songs, 1998; Circus Songs, 1998; They Also Wrote, 1999; The Classical Rock and Roll Reader, 1999. Honour: Lifetime Achievement Award, Illinois Association of College and Research Libraries, 1992. Address: 15354 Plank Road, Sycamore, IL 60178-8743, USA.

STUEWE Paul William, b. 5 Oct 1943, Rochester, New York, USA. Editor; Writer. m. Denna Groetzinger, 30 Aug 1976, 1 son, 2 daughters. Education: BA, Columbia University, 1965; MA, University of Toronto, 1993. Appointments: Contributing Editor, Quill & Quire, 1979-90; Editor, Books in Canada, 1990-. Publications: Don't Deal Five Deuces; The Storms Below; Hugh Garner's Life and Works; Clearing the Ground. Contributions to: Various publications. Honour: Short-listed, City of Toronto Book Award. Membership: Canadian Society of Magazine Editors. Address: 149 Essex Street, Toronto, Ontario M6G 1T6, Canada.

STYLES (Frank) Showell, (Glyn Carr), b. 14 Mar 1908, Four Oaks, Warwickshire, England. Author. m. Kathleen Jane Humphreys, 1954, 1 son, 2 daughters. Appointments: Royal Navy, 1939-46 (retired as Commander); Professional author, 1946-76; Led 2 private Arctic expeditions, 1952-53; Himalayan expedition, 1954. Publications: A Tent on Top, 1971; Vincey Joe at Quiberon, 1971; Admiral of England, 1973; A Sword for Mr Fitton, 1975; Mr Fitton's Commission, 1977; The Baltic Convoy, 1979; A Kiss for Captain Hardy, 1979; Centurion Comes Home, 1980; The Quarterdeck Ladder, 1982; Seven-Gun Broadside, 1982; The Malta Frigate, 1983; Mutiny in the Caribbean, 1984; The Lee Shore, 1985; Gun-Brig Captain, 1987; HMS Cracker, 1988; Nelson's Midshipman, 1990; A Ship for Mr Fitton, 1991; The Independent Cruise, 1992; Mr Fitton's Prize, 1993; Mr Fitton and the Black Legion, 1994; Mr Fitton in Command, 1995; The 12-Gun Cutter, 1996. Other: First on the Summits, 1970; First up Everest, 1970; The Forbidden Frontiers: A Survey of India from 1765-1949, 1970; Welsh Walks and Legends, 1972; Snowdon Range, 1973; The Mountains of North Wales, 1973; Glyder Range, 1974; Backpacking: A Comprehensive Guide, 1976; Backpacking in the Alps and Pyrenees, 1976; Backpacking in Wales, 1977; Welsh Walks and Legends: South Wales, 1977. As Glyn Carr: Death on Milestone Buttress, 1951; Murder on the Matterhorn, 1951; The Youth Hostel Murders, 1952; The Corpse in the Crevasse, 1952; A Corpse at Camp Two, 1955; Murder of an Owl, 1956; The Ice-Axe Murders, 1958;

Swing Away, Climber, 1959; Holiday With Murder, 1961; Death Finds a Foothold, 1962; Lewker in Norway, 1963; Death of a Weirdy, 1965; Lewkwer in Tirol, 1967; Fat Man's Agony, 1969. Honour: Fellow, Royal Geographic Society, 1954. Address: Trwyn Cae lago, Borth y Gest, Porthmadog, Gwynedd LL49 9TW, Wales.

STYLIANOPOULOS Orestis, (Orestis Helianos), b. 11 May 1950, Athens, Greece. Writer. m. Claudine Bandelier, 13 Jan 1979. Education: Faculty of Medicine, University of Athens, 1968-72; Faculty of Psychology, University of Geneva, 1974-76. Publications: Orthogenesis (novel), 1987; The Genuine Story of H S (novel), 1989; The Children of Alexander the Great (travelogue), 1989; Aspects of the Past and Present of Greeks, 1991; Condemnation for Life (short stories), 1991; The Secret of Immortality (tales), 1995; Hellenic Communities (contributor), 1998. Contributions to: Rizospastis; Kathimerini; Diavazo; I Lexi; Tote; Le Regard Cretois; Nea Ecologia; Greek Communities Over the World. Memberships: Society of Swiss Writers; Friends of Nikos Kazantzaki Society, president, 1996; Society of Greek Authors, 1998. Address: Archarnon 95, 104 40 Athens, Greece.

STYRON William (Clark) Jr, b. 11 June 1925, Newport News, Virginia, USA. Writer. m. Rose Burgunder, 4 May 1953, 1 son, 3 daughters. Education: LLD, Davidson College, 1943; AB, LLD, Duke University, 1943-47. Publications: Lie Down in Darkness, 1951; The Long March, 1953; Set This House on Fire, 1960; The Confessions of Nat Turner, 1967; Sophie's Choice, 1979; This Quiet Dust, 1982; Darkness Visible, 1990; A Tidewater Morning, 1993. Contributions to: Articles, essays and reviews to numerous journals. Honours: Pulitzer Prize for Fiction, 1968; Howells Medal, 1970; American Book Award, 1980; Prix Mondial Cino del Duca, 1985; Commandeur Ordre des Arts et des Lettres, France, 1985; Edward MacDowell Medal, 1988; Commandeur, Legion d'Honneur, France, 1988; Elmer Holmes Bobst Award for Fiction, 1989; National Medal of Arts, 1993; National Arts Club Gold Medal, 1995; Commonwealth Award, 1995. Memberships: Academie Goncourt, France, honorary member; American Academy of Arts and Letters; American Academy of Arts and Sciences. Address: 12 Rucum Road, Roxbury, CT 06783, USA.

SUBRAMANIAN (Mary) Belinda, b. 6 Sept 1953, Statesville, North Carolina, USA. Poet; Editor. m. S Ramnath, 24 Sept 1977, 2 daughters. Education: BA, Regents College, New York, 1987; MA, California State University, Dominguez Hills, 1990. Appointment: Editor, Gypsy Magazine and Vergin Press, 1983-. Publications: Numberg Poems, 1983; Heather and Mace, 1985; Eye of the Beast, 1986; Fighting Woman, 1986; Body Parts, 1987; Skin Divers (with Lyn Lifshin), 1988; Halloween, 1989; The Jesuit Poems, 1989; Elephants and Angels, 1991; The Innocents, 1991; A New Geography of Poets, 1992; Finding Reality in Myth, 1996; Notes of a Human Warehouse Engineer, 1998. Contributions to: Anthologies, journals, and magazines. Honour: Winner, Nerve Cowboy Poetry Contest, 1998. Address: PO Box 370322, El Paso, TX 79937, USA.

SUGIMOTO Yoshio, b. 7 Dec 1939, Nishinomiya, Japan. Professor of Sociology; Writer. m. Machiko Satow, 19 June 1966, 1 son, 2 daughters. Education: Graduate, Political Science, Kyoto University, 1964; PhD, University of Pittsburgh, 1973. Appointments: Lecturer, 1973-75, Senior Lecturer, 1975-82, Reader, 1982-88, Professor of Sociology, 1988-, La Trobe University, Bundoora, Melbourne. Publications: Popular Disturbance in Postwar Japan, 1981; Images of Japanese Society, 1986; Democracy in Contemporary Japan, 1986; The Japanese Trajectory, 1988; Constructs for Understanding Japan, 1989; The MFP Debate, 1990; Japanese Encounters with Postmodernity, 1995; An Introduction to Japanese Society, 1997. Contributions to: Professional journals. Honour: Japan Intercultural Publications Award, 1987. Membership: Australian Academy of the Humanities, fellow. Address: c/o School of Sociology, Politics and Anthropology, La Trobe University, Bundoora, Melbourne, Victoria 3083, Australia.

SUKENICK Ronald, b. 14 July 1932, Brooklyn, New York, USA. Professor of English Literature; Writer; Publisher. m. (1) Lynn Luria, 1961, div 1984, (2) Julia Frey, 1992. Education: BA, Cornell University, 1955; MA, 1957, PhD, 1962, Brandeis University. Appointments: Teacher, Brandeis University, 1956-60; Instructor, Hofstra University, 1961-62; Assistant Professor, City College of the City University of New York, 1966-67, Sarah Lawrence College, 1968-69; Writer-in-Residence, Cornell University, 1969-70, University of California at Irvine, 1970-72; Professor of English Literature, University of Colorado at Boulder, 1975-; Publisher, American Book Review, 1977-, Black Ice magazine, 1989-; Butler Chair, Statte University of New York at Buffalo, 1981; Fulbright Teaching Fellowship, Israel, 1984; Co-Director, Fiction Collaborative Two/Black Ice Books, 1988-. Publications: Novels: Up, 1968; Out, 1973; 98.6, 1975; Long Talking Bad Conditions Blues, 1979; Blown Away, 1986. Other Fiction: The Death of the Novel and Other Stories, 1969; The Endless Short Story, 1986; Doggy Bag: Hyperfictions, 1994; Mosaic Man, 1999. Non-Fiction: Wallace Stevens: Musing the Obscure, 1967; In Form: Digressions on the Act of Fiction, 1985; Down and In: Life in the Underground, 1987. Contributions to: Books, anthologies, journals, reviews, and periodicals. Honours: Fulbright Fellowship, France, 1958; Guggenheim Fellowship, 1977; National Endowment for the Arts Fellowship, France, 1958; Guggenheim Fellowship, 1977; National Endowment for the Arts Fellowships, 1980, 1989; University of Colorado Faculty Fellowships, 1982, 1990, and Boulder Faculty Assembly Award for Excellence in Research, Scholarly, and Creative Work, 1993; Coordinating Council of Literary Magazines Award for Editorial Excellence, 1985; Western Book Award for Publishing, 1985; American Book Award, 1988. Memberships: Coordinating Council of Literary Magazines, chairman, board of directors, 1975-77; National Book Critics Circle, board of directors, 1992-95. Address: 1505 Bluebell Avenue, Boulder, CO 80302, USA.

SUKNASKI Andrew, b. 30 July 1942, Wood Mountain, Saskatchewan, Canada. Editor; Poet. Education: University of British Columbia, Vancouver, 1967-68. Appointment: Editor, Three Legged Coyote, Wood Mountain, 1982-. Publications: This Shadow of Eden, 1970; Circles, 1970; Rose Wayn in the East, 1972; Old Mill, 1972; The Zen Pilgrimage, 1972; Four Parts Sand: Concrete Poems, 1972; Wood Mountain Poems, 1973; Suicide Notes, Booke One, 1973; These Fragments I've Gathered for Ezra, 1973; Leaving, 1974; Blind Man's House, 1975; Leaving Wood Mountain, 1975; Octomi, 1976; Almighty Voice, 1977; Moses Beauchamp, 1978; The Ghosts Call You Poor, 1978; Two for Father, 1978; In the Name of Narid: New Poems, 1981; Montage for an Interstellar Cry, 1982; The Land They Gave Away: Selected and New Poems, 1982; Silk Trail, 1985. Honour: Canada Council Grants. Address: c/o Thistledown Press, 668 East Place, Saskatoon, Sasketchewan S7J 2Z5, Canada.

SULERI GOODYEAR Sara, b. 12 June 1953, Karachi, Pakistan. Editor;Professor of English. m. Austin Goodyear, 6 July 1993, 1 stepson, 2 stepdaughters. Education: BA, Honours, Kinnaird College, 1974; PhD, Indiana University, 1983. Appointments: Editor, The Yale Journal of Criticism, 1987-97. Publications: Meatless Days, 1989; The Rhetoric of English India, 1993. Memberships: Editorial Board, Yale Review, 1991-, Transition, 1992-. Address: HCR 64, Box 474, Reach Road, Brooklyn, ME 04616, USA.

SULLIVAN Rosemary, b. 29 Aug 1947, Montreal, Quebec, Canada. Professor; Author; Poet. Education: BA, McGill University, 1968; MA, University of Connecticut, 1969; PhD, University of Sussex, 1972. Appointments: Faculty, University of Dijon, 1972-73, University of Bordeaux, 1973-74, University of Victoria, British Columbia, 1974-77; Assistant Professor, 1977-80, Associate Professor, 1980-91, Professor, 1991-, University of Toronto. Publications: The Garden Master: The Poetry of Theodore Roethke, 1975; The Space a Name Makes, 1986; By Heart: Elizabeth Smart, a Life, 1991; Blue Panic, 1991; Shadow Maker: The Life of Gwendolyn MacEwan, 1995. Other: Editor of Co-Editor of several books. Contributions to: Many journals and magazines. Honours: Gerald Lampert Award for Poetry, 1986; Brascan Silver Medal for Culture, National Magazine Awards, 1986; Guggenheim Fellowship, 1992; Governor-General's Award for Non-Fiction, 1995; City of Toronto Book Award, 1995. Memberships: Amnesty International; Toronto Arts Group for Human Rights, founding member. Address: c/o Erindale College, University of Toronto, Mississauga, Ontario L5L 1C6, Canada.

SULLIVAN Thomas William, b. 20 Nov 1940, Highland Park, Michigan, USA. Author; Teacher. 1 son, 1 daughter. Education: BA, 1964. Publications: Diapason, 1978; The Phases of Harry Moon, 1988; Born Burning, 1989; The Martyring, 1998. Contributions to: Magazines. Honours: Cash Awards, Hemingway Days Festival Literary Contest, 1985; DADA Literary Contest, 1985, 1987. Memberships: Science Fiction Writers of America; MENSA; Literary Guild; Society of the Black Bull; Arcadia Mixture. Address: 17376 Catalpa, Lathrup Village, MI 48076, USA.

SULLOWAY Frank Jones, b. 2 Feb 1947, Concord, New Hampshire, USA. Psychologist; Science Historian. 1 son. Education: AB, summa cum laude, 1969, AM, History of Science, 1971, PhD, History of Science, 1978, Harvard University. Appointments: Junior Fellow, Harvard University Society of Fellows, 1974-77; Member, Institute for Advanced Study, Princeton, New Jersey, 1977-78; Research Fellow, Miller Institute for Basic Research in Science, University of California at Berkeley, 1978-80; Research Fellow, 1980-81, Visiting Scholar, 1989-, Massachusetts Institute of Technology; Postdoctoral Fellow, 1981-82, Visiting Scholar, 1984-89, Harvard University; Research Fellow, University College, London, England, 1982-84; Vernon Professor of Biography, Dartmouth College, 1986; Research Professor, Miller Institute for Basic Research in Science, University of California at Berkeley, 1999-2000. Publications: Freud, Biologist of the Mind, 1979; Darwin and His Finches, 1982; Freud and Biology: The Hidden Legacy, 1982; Darwin's Conversion, 1982; Darwin and the Galapagos, 1984; Darwin's Early Intellectual Development, 1985; Reassessing Freud's Case Histories, 1991; Born to Rebel: Birth Order, Family Dynamics and Creative Lives, 1996. Contributions to: Professional journals. Honours: Pfizer Award, History of Science Society, 1980; National Endowment for the Humanities Fellowship, 1980-81; National Science Foundation Fellowship, 1981-82; Guggenheim Fellowship, 1982-83; John D and Catharine T MacArthur Foundation Fellowship, 1984-89; Golden Plate Award, American Academy of Achievement, 1997; James Randi Award, Skeptics Society, 1997. Memberships: American Association for the Advancement of Science, fellow; American Psychological Association; American Psychological Society; History of Science Society; Human Behavior and Evolution Society. Address: Department of Psychology, Tolman Hall, University of California, Berkeley, CA 94720, USA.

SUMMERS Anthony (Bruce), b. 21 Dec 1942, Bournemouth, England. Journalist; Writer. m. (4) 27 June 1992, 3 sons. Education: BA, Modern Languages, New College, Oxford, England, 1964. Appointments: Staff, Swiss Broadcasting Corp, 1964-65, BBC, 1965-73. Publications: The File on the Tsar (with Tom Mangold), 1976; Conspiracy (Who Killed President Kennedy?), 1980; Goddess: The Secret Lives of Marilyn Monroe, 1985; Honetrap: The Secret Worlds of Stephen Ward (with Stephen Dorril), 1987; Official and Confidential: The Secret Life of J Edgar Hoover, 1993. Contributions to: Periodicals. Honour: Golden Dagger for Best Non-Fiction, Crime Writers Association. Memberships: Authors Guild; PEN. Address: One Madison Avenue, New York, NY 10010, USA.

SUMMERS Jon Mark, b. 12 May 1969, Pontypool Gwent, Wales. Analyst; Programmer. Education: BSc, Honours, Computer Science, University of Wales, Swansea. Publication: Dog Tired Synopsis, 1998. Contributions to: Skald; Acumen; Connections; Poetry Nottingham; End of Millenium; Yellow Crane; Cement Squeeze; Rising. Address: 158 Waltwood Park Drive, Llanmartin, Newport, Gwent NP6 2HG, Wales.

SUMMERTREE Katonah. See: WINDSOR Patricia.

SUOMINEN Irene Anneli, b. 8 Apr 1970, Pori, Finland. Kindergarten Teacher. Education: Graduated, Institute of Kindergarten Teachers, Tampere, 1994. Appointment: Editor-in-Chief, Stamp Fans Club Magazine, 1991-98. Honour: Nordjunex '91 Press Prize, 1995. Membership: Association Internationale des Journalistes Philatéliques, 1993-. Address: Stamp Fans, Box 2, 33731 Tampere, Finland.

SUPRUNYUK Maxim, b. 25 Jan 1958, Moskow, Russia. Poet. m. Rudite Wasile, 31 Aug 1985, 1 son, 1 daughter. Education: Academy of Civil Aviation, Leningrad, Russia, 1979. Appointments: Controller of Air-Traffic, Kiev, Ukraine, 1979-83; Chukotsk, Russia, 1983-87; Seaman, Riga, Latvia, 1987-91; Editor, Literary magazine for children, Gnom, Riga, Latvia, 1991-. Publications: Poems in Anthology: Golden Signs, 1989; Foolish Snail, 1991. Honours: Literary Award, Latvian Writers Union and Embassy of Russia in Latvia, 1995. Membership: Latvian Writer's Union, 1997. Address: 10a, Kapselu 5, Riga, LV 1046, Latvia.

SUSI Geraldine Lee, b. 19 July 1942, New York, New York, USA. Retired Reading Teacher. m. Ronald A Susi, 17 June 1962, 2 sons, 2 daughters. Education: BS, Texas Technological College, 1963-65; MS in Education, Troy State University, 1974. Publications: Looking for Pa: A Journey From Catlett to Manasses, 1861; Teachers Guide for Looking For Pa. Contributions to: Reading Teacher Journal; Language Arts Journal. Address: 7939 Kettle Creek Drive, Catlett, VA 20119, USA.

SUTHERLAND Margaret, b. 16 Sept 1941, Auckland, New Zealand. Writer. m. 2 sons, 2 daughters. Education: Registered Nurse. Publications: The Fledgling, 1974; Hello, I'm Karen (children's book), 1974; The Love Contract, 1976; Getting Through, 1977, US edition as Dark Places, Deep Regions, 1980; The Fringe of Heaven, 1984; The City Far From Home, 1992. Contributions to: Journals and magazines. Honours: Literary Fellow, University of Auckland, 1981; Scholarship in Letters, New Zealand, 1984; Australia Council Writers Fellowships, 1992, 1995. Memberships: Australian Society of Authors; Federation of Australian Writers. Address: 10 Council Street, Speers Point, New South Wales 2284, Australia.

SUTHERLAND Mary Agnes, b. 6 Apr 1926, Fort Chipewyan, Alberta, Canada. Education: University Edmonton, Alberta, Gonzaga and Fort Wright USA; Various certificates. Appointments: Teacher in Alberta and NT; Principal, St John's Separate School in Fort McMurray, Alta; Director of Religious Education for Mackenzie-Fort Society Services; Dene Nation Councils, the Metis Association, Yellowknife Separate School Board and St Joseph Cathedral Parish in Fort Smith. Publications: Souvenir Album, 1984; Living Kindness, the Memoirs of a Metis Elder, 1990; The Bishop Who Cared, A Legacy of Leadership-Bishop Paul Piche, 1995; Northerners Say, "Thanks Sisters", 1996; Various articles in newspapers & magazines. Honours: Various awards: Nominated Citizen of Year, 1984; Hon Certificate in Soc Services, Arctic Col, 1990. Memberships: Extra-curricular activities for Youth; Youth Justice Committee; Tawow Society for Sutherland House; Fort Smith Society for Disabled Persons, founder & president; Fort Smith Senior Citizens' Society, president & founder; Fort Smith Northern Lights Personal Committee; Arctic Plei; Community Support Committee for Correction Groups in Fort Smith; NWT Status of Women Council, vp. Address: 777 Bay Street, 5th Floor, Toronto, Ontario MSW 1A7, Canada.

SUTHERLAND SMITH Beverley Margaret, b. 1 July 1935, Australia. Writer. Div, 2 sons, 2 daughters. Appointments: A Taste For All Seasons, 1975, revised edition, 1991; A Taste of Class, 1980; A Taste in Time, 1981; Gourmet Gifts, 1985; Chocolates and Petit Fours, 1987; Delicious Desserts, 1989; Oriental Cookbook, 1990; Simple Cuisine, 1992; Vegetables, 1994. Contributions to: Gourmet Magazine; Epicurean Magazine; The Age; Golden Wings; German Geographical Magazine; Herald and Weekly Times. Memberships: International Association of Culinary Professionals; Ladies Wine and Food Society of Melbourne; Chaine des Rotisseurs; Wine Press Club; Amities Gastronomiques Internationales. Address: 29 Regent Street, Mount Waverley, Melbourne, Victoria 3149, Australia.

SÜTÖ András, b. 17 June 1927, Pusztakamarás, Transylvania, Romania. Journalist; Editor; Writer; Dramatist. m. Éva Szabó, 1949, 2 children. Appointments: Contributor, later Editor-in-Chief, Falvak Népe, 1949-54; Deputy Chief Editor, Igaz Szó literary monthly, 1955-57; Chief Editor, Új Élet, pictorial, 1957-89. Publications: Some 20 volumes, including novels, short stories, essays and plays, 1953-96. Honours: State Prizes, Romania, 1953, 1954; Herder Prize, Vienna, 1979; Kossuth Prize, Hungary, 1992. Address: Marosvásárhely, Str Marasti Nr 36, 4300 Tirgu Mures, Romania.

SUTTON David John, b. 19 May 1944, Hemel Hempstead, England. Retired. m. Gillian Wingrove, 6 Aug 1966, 3 sons, 1 daughter. Education: MA, Corpus Christi College, Cambridge, England, 1964-66. Appointment: Computer Programmer, ICL, 1966-98. Publications: Poetry: Out On a Limb, 1969; Absences and Celebrations, 1982; Flints, 1986; Settlements, 1991; The Planet Happiness, 1997. Address: 46 West Chiltern, Woodcote, Reading, Berks RG8 0SG, England.

SUTTON Henry. See: SLAVITT David R(ytman).

SUTTON Penny. See: CARTWRIGHT Justin.

SUTTON Shaun Alfred Graham, b. 14 Oct 1919, England. Stage and Television Director; Producer; Writer. m. Barbara Leslie, 1948, 1 son, 3 daughters. Education: Embassy School of Acting, London, 1938-40; Royal Navy, 1940-46. Appointments: Director, Buxton Repertory Theatre, Croydon, Eastbourne, Embassy Theatre; Director, Monday Next Comedy Theatre, 1949; Drama Director, 1952, Head of Drama Serials Department, 1966-68, Head of Drama Group, 1969-81, Producer, 1981-92, BBC Television; Script Consultant, Primetime Television. Publications: Queen's Champion (children's novel), 1961; The Largest Theatre in the World, 1982. Other: A Christmas Carol (stage adaptation), 1949. Honour: Officer of the Order of the British Empire, 1979. Membership: Royal Television Society, fellow. Address: 15 Corringham Court, Corringham Road, London NW11 7BY, England.

SUWARTIC Benjamin, b. 6 Aug 1944, India. Laboratory Technician in Zoology. m. Sushma, 27 Oct 1982, dec 1998, 1 daughter. Appointments: Laboratory Assistant, 1966-89; Laboratory Technician, 1989-. Publications: Yahudi Jawaan (story), 1974; Armaan (play), 1980; Kala Akshar Bhens Barabar (translation), 1988; He Pavitra Aatmaa Aavo (bible story), 1990; Vigyaanlok (collection of science articles), 1991; Jaanwar Boli Uthiyaan (childrens stories), 1991; Smack Sharab Cigarette Masala, 1992; Rashtriya Ta Ke Path Par (story), 1992; Suwartic Smrutika (biography), 1993; Gagan Vigyaan (space science research), 1995; Pankhinagar, 1995; Vigyaandarshan (collection of science articles), 1995; Azadini Amar Katha, 1998. Contributions to: Light of Life; Outreach; Many magazines. Honours: Padmakant Shah Award, 1995; Sanskar Award, 1995. Memberships: Akshara, life member; Premanand Sahitya Sabha, life member. Address: c/o Department of Zoology, MS University of Baroda, Vadodara 390 002, India.

SVENNINGSEN Poul Flöe, b. 23 May 1919, Vejle, Denmark. Journalist; Artist. m. Karen Bröchner, 17 Mar 1956, 3 sons, 1 daughter. Publications: Little Stranger, 1951; Little Nuisance, 1952; Anglers Angle, 1953; Snooze, 1954; Little Angel, 1961; Jagt og Tone, 1975; Sejlads mellem Öerne, 1977; Mille: A Very Special Dog, 1979; Käre Lord Fjeldmose (novel), 1979; Motorists, 1998; Exhibitions of drawings and paintings and contributions to anthologies; Commentator and columnist, Berlingske Tidende, Copenhagen. Memberships: Danish Journalists' Association; Society of Danish Authors. Address: Dämringsvej 15, DK 2900 Hellerup, Denmark.

SVOBODA Terese, b. 5 Sept 1950, Ogallala, Nebraska, USA. Poet; Writer; Videomaker. m. Stephen M Bull, 18 July 1981, 3 sons. Education: MFA, Columbia University, 1978. Appointments: Rare Manuscript Curator, McGill University, 1969; Co-Producer, PBS-TV series Voices and Visions, 1980-82; Distinguished Visiting Professor, University of Hawaii, 1992; Professor, Sarah Lawrence College, 1993; Williams College, 1998. Publications: Poetry: All Aberration, 1985; Laughing Africa, 1990; Mere Mortal, 1995. Fiction: Cannibal, 1995; A Drink Called Paradise, 1999. Contributions to: Poems, fiction, essays, and translations to periodicals. Honours: Writer's Choice Column Award, New York Times Book Review, 1985; Iowa Prize, 1990; Bobst Prize, 1995. Memberships; PEN; Poets and Writers; Poet's House, founding member and advisory board member, 1986-91. Address: 335 Concord Drive, Menlo Park, CA 94025, USA.

SWAMY M R Kumara, b. 23 Jan 1938, Mysore, India. Financial Management Researcher; Editor. m. Shaila Swamy, 25 Aug 1966, 1 son, 1 daughter. Education: BA, Honours, Economics, India, 1958; MA, Economics, India, 1960; PhD, Economics, USA, 1965. Appointments: Advising Oil Economist, Qatar Government, Arabia, 1967-69; Senior Research Officer, Commerce Research Bureau, India, 1969-77; Professor of Economics, Head of Finance Department, Institute of Management and Technology and Anambra State University of Technology, Nigeria, 1977-87; Founder and Editor, Nigerian Journal of Financial Management, 1982-87; Managing Editor and Director, Journal of Financial Management and Analysis, Om Sai Ram Centre for Financial Management Research, Mumbai, India, 1987-. Contributions to: Numerous professional refereed journals. Honours: Lisle Fellowship, 1963; Distinguished Economist and Guest Lecturer, Italian Academy of Sciences, University of Rome, 1965-66. Address: c/o Om Sai Ram Centre for Financial Management Research, 15 Prakash Cooperative Housing Society, Relief Road, Santacruz (West), Mumbai 400 054, India.

SWAN Gladys, b. 15 Oct 1934, Bronx, New York, USA. Writer; Painter; Professor Emerita. m. Richard Swan, 9 Sept 1955, 2 daughters. Education: BA, Western New Mexico University, 1954; MA, Claremont Graduate School, 1955. Appointments: Professor of English, Franklin College, 1969-86; Faculty, MFA Program in Creative Writing, Vermont College, 1981-96; Distinguished Visiting Writer-in-Residence, University of Texas at El Paso, 1984-85; Visiting Professor of English, Ohio University, 1986-87; Associate Professor of English, University of Missouri-Columbia, 1987-98. Publications: On the Edge of the Desert, 1979; Carnival For the Gods, 1986; Of Memory and Desire, 1989; Do You Believe in Calbega de Vaca?, 1991; Ghost Dance: A Play of Voices, 1992; A Visit to Strangers, 1996. Contributions to: Kenyon Review; Virginia Quarterly Review; Ohio Review; Writers Forum. Honours: Lilly Endowment Faculty Open Fellowship, 1975-76; Lawrence Foundation Award for Fiction, 1994; Fulbright Senior Lectureship, 1988. Membership: PEN American Center. Address: 2601 Lynnwood Drive, Columbia, MO 65203, USA.

SWAN Robert Arthur, b. 2 Oct 1917, Broken Hill, Australia. Retired Civil Servant. m. Marie Kathleen McClelland, 14 Oct 1949, dec 1984, 1 daughter. Education: BA, University Of Melbourne, 1950. Publications: Argonauts Returned And Other Poems, 1946; Australia In The Antarctic: Interest, Activity And

Endeavour, 1961; To Botany Bay: If Policy Warrants The Measure, 1973; 12 Collections of Poems, 1982- 1994; 13 Collections of Poems, 1982-1998; Of Myths and Mariners: Doubtful Islands in The Southern Ocean. Contributions: Royal Historical Society Of Victoria; Royal Australian Historical Society; Australia Defence 2000; Australia And World Affairs; Australian Dictionary Of Biography; British National Biography. Membership: Fellow, Royal Geographical Society, London; United Services Institute, Sydney; Commando Association, Australia; Z Special Unit Association, Australia. Address: 64 Beach Drive, Woonona, NSW 2517, Australia.

SWAN Susan (Jane), b. 9 June 1945, Midland, Ontario, Canada. Writer; Poet; Assistant Professor of Humanities. m. Barry Haywood, 25 Mar 1969, div, 1 daughter. Education: BA, McGill University, 1967. Appointment: Assistant Professor of Humanities, York University, Toronto, 1989-. Publications: Queen of the Silver Blades, 1975; Unfit for Paradise, 1982; The Biggest Modern Woman of the World, 1983; Tesseracts (co-author), 1985; The Last of the Golden Girls, 1989; Language in Her Eye (editor), 1990; Mothers Talk Back (co-editor), 1991; Slow Hand, 1992; The Wives of Bath, 1993; Stupid Boys Are Good to Relax With, 1996. Contributions to: Many short stories, articles, and poems in various publications. Honours: Finalist, Guardian Fiction Prize, 1993; Finalist, Ontario Trillium, 1993; Roberts Chair in Canadian Studies, York University, 1999-2000. Address: 151 Robert Street, Apt 2, Toronto, Ontario M5S 2K6, Canada.

SWANN Lois, b. 17 Nov 1944, New York, New York, USA. Writer. m. (1) T G Swann, 15 Aug 1964, 1 son, 1 daughter, div 1979, (2) Kenneth E Arndt, 3 Sept 1988. Education: BA, Marquette University, 1966. Publications: The Mists of Manittoo, 1976; Torn Covenants, 1981; John Milton: The True Wayfaring Christian (editor), 1986. Contributions to: Magazines. Honours: Ohioana Library Association Award for First Novelists, 1976; Papers archived in Twentieth Century Collection, Boston University. Memberships: Authors Guild; Poets and Writers. Address: 168 Ellison Avenue, Bronxville, NY 10708, USA.

SWANSON Judith Ann, b. 4 Nov 1957, Los Angeles, California, USA. Assistant Professor of Political Philosophy; Writer. m. David R Mayhew, 20 Nov 1987. Education: BA, Colorado College, 1979; MSc, Distinction, London School of Economics and Political Science, 1980; PhD, University of Chicago, 1987. Appointments: Lecturer, Yale University, 1985-86; Assistant Professor, University of Georgia, 1986-88; Assistant Professor of Political Philosophy, Boston University, 1988-. Publication: The Public and the Private in Aristotle's Political Philosophy, 1992. Contributions to: Professional journals. Honours: Earhart Foundation Fellowship, 1980-84; Josephine de Kaman Fellowship, 1983-84; National Endowment for the Humanities Fellowship, 1990-91. Memberships: American Philosophical Association; American Political Science Association; Claremont Institute Society for the Study of Political Philosophy and Statesmanship; Conference for the Study of Political Thought; International Association for Greek Philosophy; Society for Greek Political Thought. Address: c/o Department of Political Science, Boston University, 232 Bay State Road, Boston, MA 02215, USA.

SWANTON Ernest William, b. 11 Feb 1907, London, England. Writer. m. Ann Marion Carbutt, 11 Feb 1958. Education: Cranleigh School. Appointments: Staff, Evening Standard, 1927-39, Daily Telegraph, 1946-75; Commentator, BBC, 1934-75; Editorial Director, 1967-88; President, 1988-, The Cricketer. Publications: A History of Cricket, 1948; Elusive Victory, 1951; Cricket and the Clock, 1952; Best Cricket Stories, 1953; West Indian Adventure, 1954; Victory in Australia, 1954/5, 1955; Report from South Africa, 1957; West Indies Revisited, 1960; The Ashes in Suspense, 1963; The World of Cricket (general editor), 1966, revised edition as Barclays World of Cricket, 1980, 3rd edition, 1986; Cricket from all Angles, 1968; Sort of a Cricket Person, 1972; Swanton in Australia, 1975; Follow On, 1977; As I Said at the Time:

A Lifetime of Cricket, 1983; Gubby Allen: Man of Cricket, 1985; Kent Cricket: A Photographic History 1744-1984 (with C H Taylor), 1985; Back Page Cricket, 1987; The Essential E W Swanton, 1990; Arabs in Aspic, 1993; Last Over (co-author), 1996. Contributions to: Newspapers and journals. Honours: Officer of the Order of the British Empire, 1965; Commander of the Order of the British Empire, 1994. Address: Delf House, Sandwich, Kent CT13 9HB, England.

SWARD Robert (Stuart), b. 23 June 1933, Chicago, Illinois, USA. Poet; Writer; University Lecturer. 2 sons, 3 daughters. Education: BA, University of Illinois, 1956; MA, University of Iowa, 1958; Postgraduate Studies, Middlebury College, Vermont, 1959-60, University of Bristol, 1960-61. Appointments: Poet-in-Residence, Cornell University, 1962-64, University of Victoria, British Columbia, 1969-73, University of California at Santa Cruz, 1987-; Writer-in-Residence, Foothill Writers Conference, summers 1988-; Writer, Writing Programme, Language Arts Department, Cabrillo College, 1989-. Publications: Uncle Dog and Other Poems, 1962; Kissing the Dancer and Other Poems, 1964; Half a Life's History: New and Selected Poems 1957-83, 1983; The Three Roberts (with Robert Zend and Robert Priest), 1985; Four Incarnations: New and Selected Poems 1957-91, 1991; Family (with David Swanger, Tilly Shaw and Charles Atkinson), 1994; Earthquake Collage, 1995; A Much-Married Man (novel), 1996; Uncivilizing, A collection of Poems, 1997; Portrait of an LA Daughter and Other Poems, 1999. Contributions to: Anthologies, newspapers and magazines; Contributing Editor, Blue Penny Quarterly and other Internet literary publications. Honours: Fulbright Fellowship, 1960-61; Guggenheim Fellowship, 1965-66; D H Lawrence Fellowship, 1966; Djerassi Foundation Residency, 1990; Way Cool Site Award, Editing Internet Literary Magazine, 1996. Memberships: League of Canadian Poets; Modern Poetry Association; National Writers Union, USA; Writers Union of Canada. Address: PO Box 7062, Santa Cruz, CA 95061, USA.

SWARTZ Jon David, b. 28 Dec 1934, Houston, Texas, USA. Educator; Psychologist; Writer. m. Carol Joseph Hampton, 20 Oct 1966, 2 sons, 1 daughter. Education: BA, 1956, MA, 1961, PhD, 1969, Postgraduate Fellow, 1973-74, University of Texas at Austin. Appointments: Assistant Professor, University of Texas at Austin, 1969-72; Editorial Associate, Current Anthropology, 1971-77; Editorial Board, Phi Kappa Phi Journal, National Forum, 1976-80; Book and Film Reviewer, Science Books and Films, 1978-; Book Review Editor, Journal of Biological Psychology, 1972-80; Associate Editor, American Corrective Therapy Journal, 1971-81, Consulting Editor, Journal of Personality Assessment, 1981-90; Exceptional Children, 1982-84; Book Review Editor for English Language Publications, Revista Interamericana de Psicologia, 1983-1989; Editor, Southwestern University Bibliographic Series, 1986-90; Associate Professor and Chairman of Psychology, University of Texas, Permian Basin, 1974-79; Professor of Education and Psychology, Associate Dean, Libraries and Learning Resources, Southwestern University, Georgetown, Texas, 1978-90; Coordinator and Administrative Head, Killeen Office, 1990-91, Chief of Psychological Services, Temple Office, 1991-, Central Counties Center for MHMR Services, Texas. Publications: Administrative Issues in Institutions for the Mentally Retarded, 1972; Multihandicapped Mentally Retarded, 1973. Co-Author: Inkblot Perception and Personality, 1961; Mental Retardation: Approaches to Institutional Change, 1969; Personality Development in Two Cultures, 1975; Holtzman Inkblot Technique: An Annotated Bibliography, 1956-1982, 1983, Supplement, 1988; Exceptionalities Through the Lifespan: An Introduction, (with C C Cleland), 1982; Handbook of Old-Time Radio: A Comprehensive Guide to Golden Age Radio Listening and Collecting, 1993; Holtzman Inkblot Technique: Research Guide and Bibliography, 1999. Co-Editor: Profoundly Mentally Retarded, 1976; Research with the Profoundly Retarded, 1978. Contributions to: Professional journals and general magazines; Handbook of Texas, 1996. Honours: US Office of Education Fellow,

1964-66; Franklin Gilliam Prize, University of Texas, 1965; Spencer Fellow, National Academy of Education, 1972-74; Faculty Fellowship Award, Southwestern University, 1981. Memberships: American Academy on Mental Retardation, fellow; American Association for the Advancement of Science, fellow; American Psychological Society; Western Research Conference on Mental Retardation; Society for Personality Assessment. Address: 1704 Vine Street, Georgetown, TX 78626, USA.

SWEARER Donald Keeney, b. 2 Aug 1934, Wichita, Kansas, USA. Professor of Asian Heights; Writer. m. Nancy Chester, 1 son, 1 daughter. Education: AB, cum laude, 1956, MA, 1965, PhD, 1967, Princeton University; BD, 1962, STM, 1963, Yale University. Appointments: Instructor, Bangkok Christian College, 1957-60; Instructor to Assistant Professor, Oberlin College, Ohio, 1965-70; Associate Professor, 1970-75, Professor of Asian Religions, 1975-, Chair, Department of Religion, 1986-91, Eugene M Lang Research Professor, 1987-92, Charles and Harriet Cox McDowell Professor, 1993-, Swarthmore College; Associate Editor, Journal of Asian Studies, 1978-80; Adjunct Professor, University of Pennsylvania, 1979-, Temple University, 1991-; Lecturer, Smithsonian Institution, Washington, DC, 1982-, Asia Society, New York, 1982-; Book Review Editor, South East Asia Religious Studies Review, 1985-93; Numata Professor of Buddhist Studies, University of Hawaii, 1993. Publications: Buddhism in Transition, 1970; Secrets of the Lotus, 1971; Wat Haripunjaya: The Royal Temple of the Buddha's Relics, 1976; Dialogue, the Key to Understanding Other Religions, 1977; Buddhism, 1977; Buddhism and Society in Southeast Asia, 1981; For the Sake of the World: The Spirit of Buddhist and Christian Monasticism (co-author), 1989; Ethics, Wealth and Salvation: A Study in Buddhist Social Ethics (co-editor), 1989; Me-and-Mine: Selected Essays of Bhikkhu Buddhadasa (co-editor), 1989; The Buddhist World of Southeast Asia (co-editor), 1995; The Legend of Queen Cama, 1998. Contributions to: Scholarly journals. Honours: Phi Beta Kappa, 1956; Kent Fellow, 1964-65; Asian Religious Study Fellow, 1967-68; National Endowment for the Humanities Senior Fellow, 1972-73, and Translation Grant, 1990-91; Rockefeller Foundation Humanities Fellow, 1985-86; Senior Research Scholar, Fulbright Foundation, 1989-90, 1994; Guggenheim Fellowship, 1994; Fulbright Fellow, 1994; National Endowment for the Humanities College Teachers Fellowship, 1998-99. Memberships: American Academy of Religion; American Association of University Professors; American Society for the Study of Religion; Association of Asian Studies, board of directors, 1977-80; Society of Buddhist-Christian Studies, board of directors, 1995-. Address: 109 Columbia Avenue, Swarthmore, PA 19081, USA.

SWEDE George, b. 20 Nov 1940, Riga, Latvia. Professor of Psychology; Poet; Writer. m. (1) Bonnie Lewis, 20 June 1964, div 1969, (2) Anita Krumins, 23 July 1974, 2 sons. Education: BA, University of British Columbia, 1964; MA, Dalhousie University, 1965; PhD, Greenwich University, 1996. Appointments: Instructor, Vancouver City College, 1966-67; Instructor, 1968-73, Professor of Psychology, 1973-, Ryerson Polytechnic University, Toronto; Director, Poetry and Things, 1969-71; Developmental Psychology, Open College, 1973-75; Poetry Editor, Poetry Toronto, 1980-81; Co-Editor, Writer's Magazine, 1982-90. Publications: Poetry: Tell-Tale Feathers, 1978; A Snowman, Headless, 1979; As Far as the Sea Can Eye, 1979; Flaking Paint, 1983; Frozen Breaths, 1983; Tick Bird, 1983; Bifids, 1984; Night Tides, 1984; Time is Flies, 1984; High Wire Spider, 1986; I Throw Stones at the Mountain, 1988; Leaping Lizzard, 1988; Holes in My Cage, 1989; I Want to Lasso Time, 1991; Leaving My Loneliness, 1992; Five O'Clock Shadows (co-author), 1996; My Shadow Doing Something, 1997. Editor: The Canadian Haiku Anthology, 1979; Cicada Voices, 1983; The Universe is One Poem, 1990; There Will Always Be a Sky, 1993; The Psychology of Art: An Experimental Approach, 1994; Tanka Splendour, 1998. Non-Fiction: The Modern English Haiku, 1981; Creativity: A New Psychology, 1994. Fiction: Moonlit Gold Dust, 1979; Quilby: The Porcupine Who

Lost His Quills (with Anita Krumins), 1980; Missing Heirloom, 1980; Seaside Burglaries, 1981; Downhill Theft, 1982; Undertow, 1982; Dudley and the Birdman, 1985; Dudley and the Christmas Thief, 1986. Contributions to: Magazines worldwide. Honours: Haiku Society of America Book Award, 1980; High/Coo Press Chapbook Competition Winner, 1982; Museum of Haiku Literature Awards, 1983, 1985, 1993; Canadian Children's Book Centre Our Choice Awards, 1984, 1985, 1987, 1991, 1992; 3rd Place, International Tanka Contest, Poetry Society of Japan, 1990; 1st Prize, Haiku in English, Mainichi Daily News, 1993; 2nd Place, Mainichi 125th Anniversary Haiku Contest, 1997; 3rd Place, Haiku Society of America Henderson Haiku Contest, 1997. Memberships: Canadian Authors Association; Canadian Society for Children's Authors, Illustrators, and Performers; Haiku Canada, co-founder, 1977; Haiku Society of America; League of Canadian Poets; PEN; Writers' Union of Canada. Address: 70 London Street, Toronto, Ontario M6G 1N3, Canada.

SWEENEY Matthew, b. 6 Oct 1952, County Donegal, Ireland. Poet; Writer. m. Rosemary Barber, 1979. Education: University College, Dublin, 1979-78; BA, Polytechnic of North London, 1978. Appointments: Writer-in-Residence, Farnham College, Surrey, 1984-85; South Bank Centre, 1994-95, Writer-in-Residence on the Internet, Chadwyck-Healey, 1997-98; Writing Fellowship, University of East Anglia, 1986; Publicist and Events Assistant, Poetry Society, 1988-90; Poet-in-Residence, Hereford and Worcester, 1991; Writer-in-Residence on the Internet, Chadwyck-Healey, 1997-98. Publications: A Dream of Maps, 1981; A Round House, 1983; The Lame Waltzer, 1985; The Chinese Dressing Gown, 1987; Blues Shoes, 1989; The Flying Spring Onion, 1992; Cacti, 1992; The Snow Vulture, 1992; Fatso in the Red Suit, 1995; Emergency Kit: Poems for Strange Times (editor with Jo Shapcott), 1996; Writing Poetry (with John Hartley Williams), 1997; The Bridal Suite, 1997; Penguin Modern Poets 12, 1997; Beyond Bedlam: Poems Written Out of Mental Distress (editor with Ken Smith), 1997. Honours: Prudence Farmer Prize, 1984; Cholmondeley Award, 1987; Arts Council Literature Award, 1992. Address: 11 Dombey Street, London WC1N 3PB, England.

SWETZ Frank Joseph, b. 7 July 1937, New York, New York, USA. Professor of Mathematics; Writer. Education: BA, Marist College, 1962; MA, Fordham University, 1963; DEd, Columbia University, 1972. Appointments: Instructor, Columbia University Teachers College, 1967-69; Professor of Mathematics, Pennsylvania State University, 1969-. Publications: Mathematics Education in China, 1974; Was Pythagoras Chinese?, 1977; Socialist Mathematics Education, 1979; Capitalism and Arithmetic, 1987; Mathematical Modelling in School Curriculum, 1991; The Sea Island Mathematical Manual, 1992; From Five Fingers to Infinity, 1994. Contributions to: Professional journals. Honours: Edpress Awards, 1971, 1984; Fulbright Research Fellowship, 1985; Outstanding Research Awards, Pennsylvania State University, 1986, 1989; Fulbright Lectureship, Malaysia, 1995. Memberships: International Study Group on the History of Pedagogy of Mathematics; National Council of Teachers of Mathematics; Pennsylvania Council of Teachers of Mathematics. Address: 616 Sandra Avenue, Harrisburg, PA 17109, USA.

SWICK Marly, b. 26 Nov 1949, Indianapolis, Indiana, USA. Writer; University Teacher of Fiction Writing. Education: BA, Stanford University, 1971; PhD, American University, 1979; MFA, University of Iowa, 1986. Appointment: Professor of Fiction Writing, University of Nebraska, 1988-. Publications: A Hole in the Language (stories), 1990; The Summer Before the Summer of Love (stories), 1995; Paper Wings (novel), 1996; Evening News (novel), 1999. Contributions to: Many magazines. Honours: James Michener Award, 1986; University of Wisconsin Creative Writing Institute Fellowship, 1987; National Endowment for the Arts Grant, 1987; Iowa Short Fiction Prize, 1990. Address: 1900 S 77th Street, Lincoln, NE 68506, USA.

SWIFT Graham Colin, b. 4 May 1949, London, England. Author. Education: Queens' College, Cambridge, 1967-70; York University, 1970-73. Publications: The Sweet Shop Owner, 1980; Shuttlecock, 1981; Learning to Swim and Other Stories, 1982; Waterland, 1983; The Magic Wheel (editor with David Profumo), 1986; Out of This World, 1988; Ever After, 1992; Last Orders, 1996. Honours: Nominated for Booker Prize, 1983; Geoffrey Faber Memorial Prize, 1983; Guardian Fiction Award, 1983; Royal Society of Literature Winifred Holtby Award, 1983; Royal Society of Literature, fellow, 1984; Premio Grinzane Cavour, Italy, 1987; Prix du Meilleur Livre Étranger, France, 1994; Booker Prize for Fiction, 1996; James Tait Black Memorial Prize, 1996. Address: c.o A P Watt Ltd, 20 John Street, London WC1N 2DR, England.

SWIFT Robert. See: **KELLY Tim.**

SWINBURNE Richard Granville, b. 26 Dec 1934, Smethwick, Staffordshire, England. Professor of Philosophy; Author. m. Monica Holmstrom, 1960, separated 1985, 2 daughters. Education: BA, 1957, BPhil, 1959, Dip Theol, 1960, MA, 1961, University of Oxford. Appointments: Fereday Fellow, St John's College, Oxford, 1958-61; Leverhulme Research Fellow in the History and Philosophy of Science, University of Leeds, 1961-63; Lecturer to Senior Lecturer in Philosophy, University of Hull, 1963-72; Visiting Associate Professor of Philosophy, University of Maryland, 1969-70; Professor of Philosophy, University of Keele, 1972-84; Distinguished Visiting Scholar, University of Adelaide, 1982; Nolloth Professor of the Philosophy of the Christian Religion, University o, 19f Oxford85-; Visiting Professor of Philosophy, Syracuse University, 1987; Visiting Lecturer, Indian Council for Philosophical Research, 1992. Publications: Space and Time, 1968, 2nd edition, 1981; The Concept of Miracle, 1971; An Introduction to Confirmation Theory, 1973; The Coherence of Theism, 1977, revised edition, 1993; The Existence of God, 1979, revised edition, 1991; Faith and Reason, 1981; Personal Identity (with S Shoemaker), 1984; The Evolution of the Soul, 1986, revised edition, 1997; Responsibility and Atonement, 1989; Revelation, 1992; The Christian God, 1994; Is There a God?, 1996; Providence and the Problem of Evil, 1998. Contributions to: Scholarly journals. Honour: Fellow, British Academy, 1992. Address: c/o Oriel College, Oxford OX1 4EW, England.

SWINDELLS Robert Edward, b. 20 Mar 1939, Bradford, England. Writer. Education: Teacher's Certificate, Huddersfield Polytechnic, 1972. Publications: Some 20 books, 1973-95. Honours: Children's Book Award, 1980; Children's Rights Workshop Other Award, 1984; Carnegie Medal, 1994. Address: c/o The Library Association, 7 Ridgmount Street, London WC1E 7AE, England.

SYLVESTER (Anthony) David (Bernard), b. 21 Sept 1924, England. Writer on Art. m. Pamela Briddon, 3 daughters. Education: University College. Appointments: Organizer of many art exhibitions, 1951-; Visiting Lecturer, Slade School of Fine Art, 1953-57, Royal College of Art, 1960-70, Swarthmore College, Pennyslvania, 1967-68; Chairman, Art Panel, Arts Council of Great Britain, 1980-82. Publications: Henry Moore, 1968; Magritte, 1969; Interviews with Francis Bacon, 1975, enlarged edition, 1980; Looking at Giacometti, 1994; About Modern Art, 1996. Contributions to: Newspapers, journals, radio, and television. Honours: Commander of the Order of the British Empire, 1983; Fellow, Royal Academy, 1986; Golden Lion of Venice for Film Criticism, 1993. Address: c/o The Tate Gallery, Exhibitions, London, England.

SYMONS Mitchell Paul, b. 11 Feb 1957, London, England. Writer. m. Penny Chorlton, 10 Apr 1984, 2 sons. Education: LSE Hons, Law, 1975-78. Appointments: BBC TV, 1980-82. Publications: The Celebrity Lists Book; The Bill Clinton Joke Book; The Celebrity Sex Lists Book. Contributions to: Daily Mail; Daily Telegraph; Daily Express; The Sun; The Mirror; The Sunday Times. Literary Agent: Sheil Land. Address: Little Thatches, 34

Tamarisk Way, Angmering on Sea, W Sussex BN16 2TE, England.

SZABO István, b. 18 Feb 1938, Budapest, Hungary. Film Director; Scenario Writer. m. Vera Gyurey. Education: Budapest Academy of Theatre and Film Arts. Appointments: Member, various Hungarian film studios; Tutor, College of Theatre and Film Arts, Budapest. Publications: Many works, including plays, films, documentaries and television productions. Honours: Various theatre and film awards, including Academy Award (AMPAS) for best foreign language film, 1981; UK Critics' Prize, 1982; British Academy of Film and Television Arts Award, 1986; Silver Bear of Berlin Award, 1992; European Script Writer of the Year Award, 1992. Memberships: Academy of Motion Picture Arts and Sciences; Akademie der Künste, Berlin. Address: ISL Films, Róua-uta 174, 1149 Budapest, Hungary.

SZABÓ Magda, b. 5 Oct 1917, Hungary. Writer; Dramatist; Poet. m. Tibor Szobotka, 1948. Education: Teacher's Certificate, 1940; PhD, Classical Philology. Appointments: Teacher, secondary schools, 1940-44, 1950-59. Publications: Novels, plays, radio dramas, poems, essays and film scripts, many translated into English and other languages. Honours: József Attila Prizes, 1959, 1972; Kossuth Prize, 1978; Getz Corporation Prize, USA, 1992. Memberships: Academy of Sciences of Europe; Hungarian Szechenyi Academy of Arts. Address: Julia-utca 3, H-1026 Budapest, Hungary.

SZANTO András, b. 1 Jan 1964, Budapest, Hungary. Sociologist; Media Researcher; Arts Writer. Education: BA, Budapest University of Economics, 1988; MA, 1990, MPhil, 1990; PhD, Columbia University, 1996. Appointment: Associate Director, National Arts Journalism Programme, Columbia University, New York. Publications: Kitöro Éberséggel (with T Dessewffy), 1989; The Crucial Facts (with J Horvát), 1993; From Silence to Polyphony, 1995. Contributions to: Actes de la Recherche en Sciences Sociales; Theory and Society; Imago; Uj Müvészet; Boston Globe. Address: 135 Perry Street, No 9, New York, NY 10014, USA.

SZASZ Imre, b. 19 Mar 1927, Budapest, Hungary. Writer; Translator. m. Elizabeth Windsor, 23 Sept 1965, 2 daughters. Education: Degree in English and Hungarian Literature, Budapest University, 1950. Appointments: Publishing House Editor, 1949-68; Literary Editor, Cultural Weekly, Budapest, 1968-90; General Secretary, Hungarian PEN Centre, 1989-94. Publications: Come at Nine, 1969; Dry Martini, 1973; One Went Hunting, 1985; Menesi Street, 1986; This is the Way the World Ends, 1986; Self-portrait with Background, 1986; I'll Go When You Dismiss Me, 1991. The Nights of Schahriyah, 1996. Contributions to: Magazines and journals. Honours: József Attila Awards, 1954, 1989; Book of the Year, 1989; Artisjus Prize, 1993. Memberships: Hungarian Writers Union; Hungarian PEN Centre; Hungarian Journalists Union. Address: Szeher ut 82, Budapest 1021, Hungary.

SZENTMARTONI Janos, b. 19 Nov 1975, Budapest, Hungary. Poet. Education: Student, Hungarian Language and Literature Department, Faculty of Arts, Eötvös Lorand University, 1995-. Appointment: Editor, Presence literary and artistic periodical review. Publications: Poetry books: Roadwide Loneliness, 1995; Bird Oracle, 1998. Honour: Gerecz Attila Literary Award, 1995. Address: Göz u 15, 1214 Budapest, Hungary.

SZILAGYI Julia, b. 1 Aug 1936, Cluj, Romania. Writer. 1 son. Education: MA, Literature, University of Cluj, 1961. Appointments: Editor, Dolgozo No, Cluj, 1963-67, Kokunk, 1967-90; Visiting Lecturer, University of Cluj, 1996-. Publications: Jonahtan Swift és a Huszadik Szazad, English translation as Jonathan Swift and the Twentieth Century, 1968; A Helyszin Hatalma, English translation as The Power of Science, 1979. Contributions to: Journals, periodicals, quarterlies and reviews. Honours: Several. Memberships: Association of Writers in Hungary; Association of Writers in Romania. Address: Str Brassai Nr 15, 3400 Cluj, Romania.

SZIRTES George Gabor Nicholas, b. 29 Nov 1948, Budapest, Hungary. Poet; Writer; Translator. m. Clarissa Upchurch, 11 July 1970, 1 son, 1 daughter. Education: BA, 1st Class Honours, Fine Art, Leeds College of Art. Publications: The Slant Door, 1979; November and May, 1981; The Kissing Place, 1982; Short Wave, 1984; The Photographer in Winter, 1986; Metro, 1988; Bridge Passages, 1991; Blind Field, 1994; Selected Poems, 1996; Portrait of My Father in an English Landscape, 1998; The Red All Over Riddle Book (for children), 1997. Other: Several Hungarian works translated into English. Contributions to: Numerous journals and magazines. Honours: Geoffrey Faber Memorial Prize, 1980; Arts Council Bursary, 1984; British Council Fellowship, 1985; Cholmondeley Award, 1987; Dery Prize for Translation, 1991; Decorated, Republic of Hungary, 1991; Short-listed, Whitbread Poetry Award, 1992; European Poetry Translation Prize, 1995. Memberships: PEN; Royal Society of Literature, fellow. Address: 16 Damgate Street, Wymondham, Norfolk NR8 0BQ, England.

SZKAROSI Endre, b. 28 May 1952, Budapest, Hungary. University Professor; Poet. 2 daughters. Education: BA, Faculty of Arts, Eötvös Lorand University, 1977; PhD, 1985. Appointments: Editor, Mozgo Vilag, 1978-83; Professor of Italian Literature, University of Szeged, 1989-94, University of Budapest, 1994-. Publications: Ismeretlen Monologok, 1981; Szellözö Müvek, 1990; Hangkölteslet, 1994; Tüzfal, 1994; Kaddish, 1994; The Wind Rises, 1998. Contributions to: Inter; Poesia; Doc(k)s; Bollettario; Testo. Memberships: ICLA; AISLCI; International Association of Hungarology. Address: Vaci ut 34, H-1132 Budapest, Hungary.

SZÖLLÖSI Zoltan, b. 6 Mar 1945, Janoshalma, Hungary. Writer. m. Eva Havas, 31 Mar 1971, 3 sons, 1 daughter. Education: Graduated. Appointments: Sub Chief Editor. Publications: Csontkorall, poems; Vacsora jègen, poems; Egitetö, poems; Ballada Boldogasszonyhoz. Contributions to: Kortars; Elet es Irodalom; Forras. Honour: Honour of Kölosey. Membership: Hungarian Writers Society. Address: Iranyi u 1, H-1056 Budapest, Hungary.

SZULC Tad, b. 25 July 1926, Warsaw, Poland (US citizen, 1954). Journalist; Author. m. Marianne Carr, 8 July 1948, 1 son, 1 daughter. Education: University of Brazil, 1943-45. Appointments: Reporter, Associated Press, Rio de Janeiro, 1945-46; United Nations Correspondent, United Press International, 1949-53; Staff, 1953-55, Latin American Correspondent, 1955-61, Washington Bureau, 1961-65, 1969-72, Spanish and Portuguese Correspondent, 1965-68, Eastern Europe Correspondent, 1968-69, Foreign Policy Commentator, 1972-, New York Times. Publications: Twilight of the Tyrants, 1959; The Cuban Invasion, 1962; The Winds of Revolution, 1963; Dominican Diary, 1965; Latin America, 1966; Bombs of Palomares, 1967; The United States and the Caribbean, 1971; Czechoslovakia since World War II, 1971; Portrait of Spain, 1972; Compulsive Spy: The Strange Career of E Howard Hunt, 1974; The Energy Crisis, 1974; Innocents at Home, 1974; The Illusion of Peace, 1978; Diplomatic Immunity, 1981; Fidel: A Critical Portrait, 1986; Then and Now: The World Since World War II, 1990; The Secret Alliance, 1991; Pope John Paul II: The Biography, 1995; Chopin in Paris (biography), 1998. Honours: Knight of France's Legion of Honor.Best Book on Foreign Affairs Awards, Overseas Press Club, 1979, 1986, 1991; Honorary LHD, American College, Switzerland, 1987. Membership: Overseas Press Club. Address: 4515 29th Street North West, Washington, DC 20008, USA.

SZYMBORSKA Wislawa, b. 2 July 1923, Bnin, Poland. Poet; Critic; Translator. Education: Jagiellonian University, Kraków, 1945-48. Appointment: Editorial Styaff, Zycie Literackie magazine, 1953-81. Publications: Dlatego zyjemy (That's Why We Are Alive), 1952, 2nd edition, 1985; Pytania zadawane sobie (Questioning Oneself), 1954; Wolanie do Yeti (Calling Out to Yeti), 1957; Sól (Salt), 1962; Wiersze wybrane (Selected Verses), 1964; Poezje wybrane (Selected Poems), 1967; Sto pociech (No End of Fun), 1967; Poezje (Poems), 1970; Wszelki wypadek (Could Have), 1972; Wybór wierszy (Selected Verses), 1973; Tarsjusz i inne wiersze (Tarsius and Other Verses), 1976; Wielka liczba (A Large Number), 1977; Poezje wybrane II (Selected Poems II), 1983; Ludzie na moscie (The People on the Bridge), 1986; Wieczór autorski: Wiersze (Authors' Evening: Verses), 1992; Koniec i poczatek (The End and the Beginning), 1993. Poetry in English: Sounds, Feelings, Thoughts: Seventy Poems, 1981; People on a Bridge, 1990; View with a Grain of Sand, 1995. Contributions to: Poetry and criticism in various publications. Honours: City of Kraków Prize for Literature, 1954; Polish Ministry of Culture Prize, 1963; Goethe Prize, 1991; Herder Prize, 1995; Honorary doctorate, Adam Mickiewicz University, Pozna, 1995; Nobel Prize for Literature, 1996; Polish PEN Club Prize, 1996. Address: Ul Królewska 82/89, 30-079 Kraków, Poland.

T

TABAK László, b. 27 May 1927, Csikszentdomokos, Romania. Journalist; Writer. m. Jakab Susana-Rafila, 5 June 1954, 2 sons. Education: Technical High School of Metallurgy, Cluj, Politechnical Institute, Cluj. Appointments: Igaszág, daily newspaper, Cluj, 1954-58; Stage Coordinator, Hungarian National Theatre, Cluj, 1958-70; Columnist, A Hét, weekly paper, 1970-76; Editor, Uj Kelet, Tel-Aviv, daily newspaper, 1976-. Publications: Vészcsengo, short stories, satires, 1969; Editura pentru Literatură, Bucuresti 2, Nehéz apának lenni, Humorous stories, 1962; Dolgozó Nő-Cluj; Lemondtam a világfelelősségröl, 1981; Társasutazás az időben, 1985; Uzenet a palacban, 1996; Contributions to: Utunk; Korunk; A Hét, literary weeklys; Kelet-Nyugat; Menora; Uj Kelet; Ariel, in English, French, German. Honours: Awards for literary report, Utunk, 1969; Literary Award, Simcha Dinitz, 1983. Memberships: Fondul Literar, Romania The Israel Federation of Writer's Union President of the Hungarian Language Writers in Israel, Tel-Aviv, Rech Kaplan 6. Address: 67422 Tel-Aviv, Drch Hahagana 150/32, Israel.

TABORI George, b. 24 May 1914, Budapest, Hungary (British citizen). Playwright; Author. Education: Zrinyl Gymnasium, Hungary. Publications: Flight into Egypt, 1952; The Emperor's Clothes, 1953; Miss Julie (version of Strindberg), 1958; Brouhaha, 1958; Brecht on Brecht, 1962; The Resistible Rise of Arturo Ui (after Brecht), 1963; Andora (after Max Frisch), 1963; The Niggerlovers, 1967; The Cannibals, 1968; Mother Courage (after Brecht), 1970; Clowns, 1972; Talk Show, 1976; Changes, 1976; Mein Kampf: A Farce, 1989; Weisman and Copperface, 1991. Novels: Beneath the Stone the Scorpion, 1945; Companions of the Left Hand, 1948; Original Sin, 1947; The Caravan Passes, 1951; The Journey: A Confession, 1958; The Good One, 1960. Screenplays. Address: c/o Suhrkamp Verlag, Lindenstrasse 29-35, Postfach 4229, 6000 Frankfurt am Main, Germany.

TABORSKI Boleslaw, b. 7 May 1927, Torun, Poland. Poet; Writer; Translator. m. Halina Junghertz, 20 June 1959, 1 daughter. Education: BA, MA, University of Bristol. Appointments: Producer, Polish Section, 1959-89, Editor, Arts in Action, 1985-93, BBC World Service; Visiting Professor, City University of New York, 1982. Publications: Poetry: Times of Passing, 1957; Grains of Night, 1958; Crossing the Border, 1962; Lesson Continuing, 1967; Voice of Silence, 1969; Selected Poems, 1973; Web of Words, 1977; For the Witnesses, 1978; Observer of Shadows, 1979; Love, 1980; A Stranger's Present, 1983; Art, 1985; The Stillness of Grass, 1986; Life and Death, 1988; Politics, 1990; Shakespeare, 1990; Goodnight Nonsense, 1991; Survival, 1998; Selected Poems, 1999. Criticism: New Elizabethan Theatre, 1972; The Inner Plays of Karol Wojtyla, 1989; My Upbringing: Then and Now, 1998. Co-Author: Crowell's Handbook of Contemporary Drama, 1971; Polish Plays in Translation, 1983. Other: Numerous translations. Contributions to: Various publications. Honours: Polish Writers Association Abroad Award, 1954; Jurzykowski Foundation Award, New York, 1968; Merit for Polish Culture Badge and Diploma, Warsaw, 1970; Koscielski Foundation Award, Geneva, 1977; SI Witkiewicz ITI Award, Warsaw, 1988; Association of Authors Translation Award, Warsaw, 1990, 1995; Societé European de Culture Award, Warsaw, 1998; KL10, History Publishers Award, Warsaw, 1998. Memberships: Association of Authors, Warsaw; Association of Polish Writers, Warsaw; Council Gallery in the Provinces Foundation, Lublin; Leon Shiller Foundation, honorary committee; Pro Europa Foundation, Warsaw, council member, 1994-; World Association of the Polish Home Army, ex-servicemen, Warsaw; Polish Shakespeare Society, Gdensk, 1995. Address: 66 Esmond Road, Bedford, London W4 1JF, England.

TADEUSZ Rozewicz, b. 9 Oct 1921, Radomsko, Poland. Poet; Playwright. m. Wiestawa Koztowska, 1949. Education: University of Kraków. Publications: Face of Anxiety; Conversation with the Prince; The Green Rose; The Card Index; The Witnesses; White Marriage; The Trap. Contributions to: Various journals. Honours: State Prizes, 1955, 1956; Literary Prize, City of Kraków, 1959; Prize of Minister of Culture and Art, 1962; State Prize, 1st Class, 1966; Prizes, Minister of Foreign Affairs, 1974, 1987; Austrian National Prize, European Literature, 1982; German Literary Award, 1994. Membership: Bavarian Academy of Fine Arts. Address: Authors Agency, ul Hispoteozna 2, Warsaw, Poland.

TAFDRUP Pia, b. 29 May 1952, Copenhagen, Denmark. Poet. m. Bo Hakon Jorgensen, 30 June 1978, 2 sons. Education: BA, University of Copenhagen, 1977. Publications: Various poetry volumes in Danish, 1981-99; 1 volume in English translation as Spring Tide, 1989. Other: 2 plays. Contributions to: Many journals in the UK, USA, and Canada. Honours: Scholarship for Authors, Danish State Art Foundation, 1984-86; 12 grants, 1986-97; Nordic Council Literature Prize, 1999. Membership: Danish Academy; Danish PEN Centre. Address: Rosenvaengets Sideallé, 3.2th, 2100 Copenhagen Ø, DK, Denmark.

TAGLIABUE John, b. 1 July 1923, Cantu, Italy. Retired College Teacher; Poet: Writer. m. Grace Ten Eyck, 11 Aug 1946, 2 daughters. Education: BA, 1944, MA, 1945, Advanced Graduate Work, 1947-48, Columbia University. Appointments: Teacher, American University, Beirut, Lebanon, 1945, State College of Washington, 1946-47, Alfred University, New York, 1948-50, University of Pisa, Italy, 1950-52, Bates College, Maine, 1953, University of Tokyo, 1958-60; Fulbright Lecturer, University of Indonesia, 1993. Publications: Poems, 1959; A Japanese Journal, 1966; The Buddha Uproar, 1970; The Doorless Door, 1970; The Great Day, 1984; New and Selected Poems 1942-97, 1997. Contributions to: Journals, magazines, and periodicals. Memberships: Academy of American Poets; Maine Writers and Publishers Alliance; PEN; Poetry Society of America. Address:Wayland Manor, Apt. 412, 500 Angell Street, Providence, RI 02906, USA.

TAIT Arch, b. 6 June 1943, Glasgow, Scotland. Translator; University Lecturer. Education: MA, 1966, PhD, 1971, Trinity Hall, Cambridge. Appointments: Lecturer, University of East Anglia, 1970-83, Editor, Glas: New Russian Writing, 1991; University of Birmingham, senior lecturer, 1997. Publications: Lunacharsky, The Poet Commissar, 1984; Translator: The Russian Style, 1991; Is Comrade Bulgakov Dead?, 1993; Baize-Covered Table With Decanter, 1995; Skunk: A Life, 1997; Sonechka, 1998; Under House Arrest, 1998. Memberships: Translators Association; Society of Authors; British Association for Slavonic and East European Studies. Address: Department of Russian, University of Birmingham, Birmingham B15 2TT, England.

TAJRA Harry William Michael, b. 18 Apr 1945, Pawtucket, Rhode Island, USA. Bishop-Abbot. m. Susan Lee Jacobson, 1 Dec 1981. Education: BA, Brown University, 1967; Doctor of History, Sorbonne, Paris, 1969; MTheol, Protestant Seminary, Paris, 1979; DTheol, University of Geneva, Switzerland, 1988. Appointments: Pastor, National Church, Geneva, 1982-85; Researcher, University of Geneva, 1985-88; Ind. Researcher, Christian Antiquities, Rome, 1988-93; Bishop-Abbot, Order of St Mary the Virgin, 1993-. Publications: The Trial of St Paul, 1989; The Martyrdom of St Paul, 1994; The Great Epiphany (in preparation). Contributions to: Positions Lutheriennes, Paris; Ecumenical Society of the Blessed Virgin Mary, London. Membership: Fellow, International Pontifical Marian Academy, Rome. Address: 80 Aetna Street, Central Falls, RI 02863-1806, USA.

TALBOT Michael (Owen), b. 4 Jan 1943, Luton, Bedfordshire, England. Professor of Music; Writer. m. Shirley Mashiane, 26 Sept 1970, 1 son, 1 daughter. Education: ARCM, Royal College of Music, London, 1960-61; BA, 1964, BMus, 1965, PhD, 1969, Clare College, Cambridge. Appointments: Lecturer, 1968-79, Senior Lecturer, 1979-83, Reader, 1983-86, James and Constance Alsop Professor of Music, 1986-, University of Liverpool. Publications: Vivaldi, 1978, 4th edition, revised, 1993; Albinoni: Leben und Werk, 1980; Antonio Vivaldi: A Guide to Research, 1988; Tomaso Albinoni: The Venetian Composer and His World, 1990; Benedetto Vinaccesi: A Musician in Brescia and Venice in the Age of Corelli, 1994; The Sacred Vocal Music of Antonio Vivaldi, 1995. Contributions to: Professional journals. Honours: Cavaliere del Ordine al Merito della Repubblica Italiana, 1980; Oldman Prize, 1990. Memberships: British Academy, fellow; Royal Musical Association; Ateneo Veneto, corresponding fellow. Address: 36 Montclair Drive, Liverpool L18 0HA, England.

TALBOT Norman Clare, b. 14 Sept 1936, Gislingham, Suffolk, England. Poet; Writer; Editor; Literary Consultant. m. 17 Aug 1960, 1 son, 2 daughters. Education: BA, Durham University, Hatfield College, 1959; PhD, Leeds University, 1962. Appointments: Lecturer, 1962, Senior Lecturer, 1968, Associate Professor, 1968, Professor, English, University of Newcastle, 1973-1993. Publications: The Major Poems of John Keats (criticism), 1967; Poems for a Female Universe (poetry), 1968; Son of a Female Universe (poetry); The Fishing Boy (poetry, illustrated by John Montefiore), 1973; Find the Lady (poetry), 1978; A Glossary of Poetic Terms (criticism), 1980, revised, 1982, reprinted, 1985, 1987, 1989; Where Two Rivers Meet (poetry), 1980: The Kelly Haiku (poetry), 1985; Contrary Modes (criticism, editor), 1985; Another Site to be Mined: the New South Wales Anthology (poetry, editor), 1986; Spelling English in Australia (reference, with Nicholas Talbot), 1989; Weaving the Heterocosm: an Anthology of British Narrative Poetry (edited and introduced), 1989; The Nearest the White Man Gets, by Roland Robinson (stories and poems, editor, introduced), 1989; The Pink Tongue, by T H Naisby, (poetry, editor, introduced), 1990; Spelling English Revised in Australia (reference), 1990; Four Zoas of Australia (poetry), 1992; Australian Quaker Christmases (poetry), 1993; The Water of the Wondrous Isles, by William Morris (editor, introduced), 1994; The Glittering Plain and Child Christopher, William Morris (editor, introduced), 1996; A Moment for Morris (poetry), 1996; Australian Skin, Suffolk Bones (poetry), 1996; Betwixt Wood-Woman, Wolf and Bear: the Heroic-Age Romances of William Morris (criticism), 1997; Song-Cycle of the Birds, Lake Macquarie (poetry), 1998; Myths and Stories, Lies and Truth (criticism), 1999. Honours: E C Gregory Award for Poetry, 1965; American Council of Learned Societies Fellowship, 1967-68; Visiting Professorships: Yale, 1967-68, East Anglia, 1975-76, Aarhus, 1976, Oregon, 1983, Leicester, 1984, Linacre College, Oxford, 1987-88, Exeter, 1992; City of Lake Macquarie Award for Services to Poetry, 1994. Memberships: Nimrod Publications, Literacy Consultancy, editor in chief, 1964-; Mythopoeic Literature Association of Australia, life member, 1978-; Babel Handbooks, editor, 1980-; Newcastle Poetry at the Pub, president, 1988-; Mythopoeic Society (international), 1990-; Friends of the University, 1994-; Newcastle Writers Centre, president, 1997-; Catchfire Press, vice president, 1997-; Australian Friend, poetry editor, 1997-; Aurealis Literary Awards, judge, 1998-. Address: PO Box 170, New Lambton 2305, New South Wales, Australia.

TALL Deborah, b. 16 Mar 1951, Washington, District of Columbia, USA. Professor; Poet; Writer; Editor. m. David Weiss, 9 Sept 1979, 2 daughters. Education: BA, English, University of Michigan, 1972; MFA, Creative Writing, Goddard College, 1979. Appointments: Assistant Professor, Visiting Fellow in Literature, University of Baltimore, 1980-82; Professor, 1982-, Chairman, Department of English, 1992-94, Hobart and William Smith Colleges; Editor, Seneca Review, 1982-; Writer-in-Residence, Chautauqua Institution, New York, 1998. Publications: Eight Colors Wide, 1974; Ninth Life, 1982; The Island of the White Cow: Memories of an Irish Island, 1986; Come Wind, Come Weather, 1988; Taking Note: From Poets' Notebooks (editor with Stephen Kuusisto and David Weiss), 1991, revised and expanded edition as The Poet's Notebook, 1995; From Where We Stand: Recovering a Sense of Place, 1993. Contributions to: Many anthologies, reviews, quarterlies, journals, and magazines. Honours: Yaddo Residencies, 1982, 1984, 1991; Citation of Achievement, Coordinating Council of Literary Magazines, 1986; Ingram Merrill Foundation Grant, 1987; MacDowell Colony Residency, 1998. Memberships: Academy of American Poets; Associated Writing Programs; Association for the Study of Literature and the Environment; Authors Guild; PEN; Poetry Society of America. Address: c/o Department of English, Hobart and William Smith Colleges, Geneva, NY 14456, USA.

TALLENT Elizabeth (Ann), b. 8 Aug 1954, Washington, District of Columbia, USA. Writer; Professor of English. m. Barry Smoots, 28 Sept 1975, 1 son. Education: BA, Illinois State University at Normal, 1975. Appointment: Professor of English, University of California at Davis. Publications: Married Men and Magic Tricks, 1982; In Constant Flight, 1983; Museum Pieces, 1985; Time With Children, 1987; Honey, 1993. Contributions to: Magazines. Honours: Bay Area Book Reviewers Association Fiction Award; National Endowment for the Arts Fellowship, 1992. Membership: Poets and Writers. Address: c/o Department of English, University of California at Davis, Davis, CA 95616, USA.

TALMAGE Anne. See: POWELL Talmage.

TAN Amy, b. 19 Feb 1952, Oakland, California, USA. Writer. m. Lou DeMattei, 6 Apr 1974. Education; BA, 1973, MA, 1974, San Jose State College; Postgraduate studies, University of California at Berkeley, 1974-76. Publications: The Joy Luck Club (novel), 1989; The Kitchen God's Wife (novel), 1992; The Moon Lady (children's book), 1992; The Chinese Siamese Cat (children's book), 1994; The Hundred Secret Senses (novel), 1995. Contributions to: Various periodicals. Honours: Commonwealth Club Gold Award for Fiction, San Francisco, 1989; Booklist Editor's Choice, 1991; Marian McFadden Memorial Lecturer, Indianapolis-Marion County Public Library, 1996. Address: c/o G P Putnam's Sons, 200 Madison Avenue, New York, NY 10016, USA.

TANG Victor, b. 12 Apr 1942, China. Business Executive; Writer. m. Wendy Chu, 3 June 1968, 1 son, 2 daughters. Education: BSEE, 1963, MS, Mathematical Physics, 1965, Purdue University; Advanced Research and Studies, Pennsylvania State University, 1967-69; MBA, Columbia University, 1983. Publications: The Silverlake Project, 1992;Competitive Marketing, Part I and II (with Philip Kotler), 1993. Contributions to: Books and professional journals. Memberships: Eta Kappa Nu, Electrical Engineering Honour Society; Pi Mu Epsilon, Mathematics Honour Society; Beta Gamma Sigma, Business Honour Society; Sigma Pi Sigma, Physics Honour Society. Address: 55 Deerfield Lane South, Pleasantville, NY 10570, USA.

TANNER Paul Antony, (Tony Tanner), b. 18 Mar 1935, Richmond, Surrey, England. Professor of English and American Literature; Writer. m. Nadia Fusini, 1979. Education: MA, PhD, Jesus College, Cambridge. Appointments: Fellow, King's College, Cambridge, 1960-, Center for Advanced Studies in the Behavioral Sciences, Stanford, California, 1974-75; American Council of Learned Societies Fellow, University of California at Berkeley 1962-63; University Lecturer, Cambridge, 1966-80; Reader in American Literature, 1980-89, Professor of English and American Literature, 1989-, University of Cambridge. Publications: The Reign of Wonder, 1965; Mansfield Park, 1966; Henry James: Modern Judgements, 1968; City of Words 1950-1970, 1971; Adultery in the Novel: Contact and Transgression, 1979; Thomas Pynchon, 1982; Henry James, 1985; Jane Austen, 1986; Scenes of Nature, Signs of Men, 1987; Venice Desired, 1992; Henry James and the Art of Non-Fiction, 1995. Address: c/o King's College, Cambridge CB2 1ST, England.

TAPPLY William G(eorge), b. 16 July 1940, Waltham, Massachusetts, USA. Writer. m. Cynthia Ehrgott, 7 Mar 1970, div 1995, 1 son, 2 daughters. Education: BA, Amherst College, 1962; MAT, Harvard University, 1963;

Tufts University, 1965-67. Appointments: High School History Teacher, Lexington, Massachusetts, 1963-65; Director of Economic Education, Tufts University, 1967-68; Housemaster and Teacher, Lexington High School, 1969-90; Editorial Associate, Writer's Digest School, 1992-; Emerson College, Clark University, instructor, 1995-. Publications: Fiction: Death at Charity's Point, 1984; The Dutch Blue Error, 1985; Follow the Sharks, 1985; The Marine Corpse, 1986; Dead Meat, 1987; The Vulgar Boatman, 1987; A Void in Hearts, 1988; Dead Winter, 1989; Client Privilege, 1989; The Spotted Cats, 1991; Tight Lines, 1992; The Snake Eater, 1993; The Seventh Enemy, 1995; Close to the Bone, 1996; Cutter's Run, 1998; Muscle Memory, 1999. Non-Fiction: Those Hours Spent Outdoors, 1988; Opening Day and Other Neuroses, 1990; Home Water Near and Far, 1992; Sportsman's Legacy, 1993; The Elements of Mystery Fiction, 1995; A Fly-Fishing Life, 1997; Bass Bug Fishing, 1999. Contributions to: Magazines. Honour: Scribner Crime Novel Award, 1984. Memberships: Authors Guild; Mystery Writers of America; Private Eye Writers of America. Address: 47 Ann Lee Road, Harvard, MA 01451, USA.

TARN Nathaniel, b. 30 June 1928, Paris, France. Professor Emeritus; Poet; Writer. m. (1), div, 2 children, (2) Janet Rodney, 1981. Education: BA, 1948, MA, 1952, University of Cambridge; MA, 1952, PhD, 1957, University of Chicago. Appointments: Visiting Professor, State University of New York at Buffalo, 1969-70, Princeton University 1969-70, University of Pennsylvania, 1976, Jilin University, China, 1982; Professor of Comparative Literature, 1970-85, Professor Emeritus, 1985-, Rutgers University. Publications: Poetry: Old Savage/Young City, 1964; Penguin Modern Poets 7 (with Richard Murphy and Jon Silkin), 1966; Where Babylon Ends, 1968; The Beautiful Contradictions, 1969; October: A Sequence of Ten Poems Followed by Requiem Pro Duabus Filiis Israel, 1969; The Silence, 1970; A Nowhere for Vallejo: Choices, October, 1971; Lyrics for the Bride of God, 1975; Narrative of This Fall, 1975; The House of Leaves, 1976; From Alaska: The Ground of Our Great Admiration of Nature, 1977; The Microcosm, 1977; Birdscapes, with Seaside, 1978; The Forest (with Janet Rodney), 1979; The Land Songs, 1981; Weekends in Mexico, 1982; The Desert Mothers, 1984; At the Western Gates, 1985; Palenque: Selected Poems 1972-1984, 1986; Seeing America First, 1989; The Mothers of Matagalpa, 1989; Flying the Body, 1993. Non-Fiction: Views from the Weaving Mountain: Selected Essays in Poetics and Anthropology, 1991; Scandals in the House of Birds, 1998;. Honours: Guinness Prize, 1963; Wenner Gren Fellowships, 1978, 1980; Commonwealth of Pennsylvania Fellowship, 1984; Rockefeller Foundation Fellowship, 1988. Address: PO Box 8187, Santa Fe, NM 87504, USA.

TARNAS Richard Theodore, b. 21 Feb 1950, Geneva, Switzerland. Writer; Lecturer; Educator. m. Heather Malcolm, 28 May 1982, 1 son, 1 daughter. Education: AB, Harvard University, 1972; PhD, Saybrook Institute, 1976. Publication: The Passions of the Western Mind, 1991. Address: California Institute of Integral Studies, 1453 Mission Street, San Francisco, CA 94103, USA.

TARRANT John. See: EGLETON Clive Frederick William.

TART Indrek, (Julius Ürt), b. 2 May 1946, Tallinn, Estonia. Physicist; Poet; Literary Critic; Sociologist. m. Aili Arelaid Tart, 7 Feb 1980, 1 son, 1 daughter. Education: University of Tartu. Education: MA, Information Science, 1993. Appointments: Institute of Cybernetics, 1969-80; Institute of Chemical Physics and Biophysics, Estonian Academy of Sciences, 1980-92; Director of Information, Estonian National Commission for UNESCO, 1992-93; Tallinn Pedagogical University, 1992-. Publications: Haljendav Ruumala, 1981; Väike Luuletaja ja Teised, 1993; Eestikeelne luuleraamat 1851-1995, 1997. Other: Various translations. Contributions to: Anthologies and other publications. Honour: Honorary Fellow in Writing,

University of Iowa. Membership: Estonian Writers Union. Address: Sole 47a-38, Tallinn 10321, Estonia.

TARUSKIN Richard, b. 2 Apr 1945, New York, New York, USA. Professor; Musicologist; Critic; Author. Education: PhD, Columbia University, 1975. Appointments: Assistant Professor, 1975-81, Associate Professor of Music, 1981-87, Columbia University; Visiting Professor, University of Pennsylvania, 1985; Associate Professor, 1986-89, Professor, 1989-, University of California at Berkeley; Hanes-Willis Visiting Professor, University of North Carolina at Chapel Hill, 1987. Publications: Opera and Drama in Russia, 1981, new edition, 1994; Busnoi: The Latin-Texted Works (editor with commentary), 2 volumes, 1990; Musorgsky: Eight Essays and an Epilogue, 1993; Stravinsky and the Russian Traditions: A Biography of the Works Through Mavra, 2 volumes, 1995; Text and Act: Essays on Music and Performance, 1995. Contributions to: The New Grove Dictionary of Opera, 1992; Many articles and reviews in professional journals and general periodicals. Honours: Fulbright-Hays Traveling Fellowship, 1971-72; Guggenheim Fellowship, 1987; Dent Medal, England, 1987; ASCAP-Deems Taylor Award, 1989. Membership: American Musicological Society. Address: c/o Department of Music, University of California at Berkeley, Berkeley, CA 94720, USA.

TATE James (Vincent), b. 8 Dec 1943, Kansas City, Missouri, USA. Poet; Professor. Education: University of Missouri, 1963-64; BA, Kansas State University, 1965; MFA, University of Iowa, 1967. Appointments: Instructor in Creative Writing, University of Iowa, 1966-67; Visiting Lecturer, University of California, Berkeley, 1967-68; Poetry Editor, Dickinson Review, 1967-76; Trustee and Associate Editor, Pym-Randall Press, 1968-80; Assistant Professor of English, Columbia University, 1969-71; Associate Professor, then Professor of English, 1971-, University of Massachusetts, Amherst; Poet-in-Residence, Emerson College, 1970-71; Associate Editor, Barn Dream Press. Publications: Poetry: Cages, 1966; The Destination, 1967; The Lost Pilot, 1967; Notes of Woe: Poems, 1968; Camping in the Valley, 1968; The Torches, 1968, revised edition, 1971; Row with Your Hair, 1969; Is There Anything?, 1969; Shepherds of the Mist, 1969; Amnesia People, 1970; Are You Ready Mary Baker Eddy? (with Bill Knot), 1970; Deaf Girl Playing, 1970; The Oblivion Ha-Ha, 1970; Wrong Songs, 1970; Hints to Pilgrims, 1971, 2nd edition, 1982; Absences, 1972; Apology for Eating Geoffrey Movius' Hyacinth, 1972; Hottentot Ossuary, 1974; Viper Jazz, 1976; Riven Doggeries, 1979; Land of Little Sticks, 1981; Constant Defender, 1983; Reckoner, 1986; Distance from Loved Ones, 1990; Selected Poems, 1991; Worshipful Company of Fletchers, 1993. Novel: Lucky Darryl, 1977. Contributions to: Numerous books and periodicals. Honours: Yale Younger Poets Award, 1966; Poet of the Year, Phi Beta Kappa, 1972; National Institute of Arts and Letters Award, 1974; Massachusetts Arts and Humanities Fellow, 1975; Guggenheim Fellowship, 1976; National Endowment for the Arts Fellowship, 1980; Pulitzer Prize in Poetry, 1992; National Book Award for Poetry, 1994. Membership: Bollingen Prize Committee, 1974-75. Address: Department of English, University of Massachusetts, Amherst, MA 01003, USA.

TATE Peter Anthony Gale, b. Cardiff, South Wales. Journalist. m. Lesley Patricia Geen, 12 Dec 1959, 1 son. Appointments: Reporter, South Wales Echo, 1957-64; Sub Editor, SWE, 1964-75; Sub-Editor, Bournemouth Daily Echo, 1975-77; Chief Sub Editor, 1977-79; Deputy Editor, 1979-92; Executive Editor, 1992-. Publications: The Thinking Seat, 1970, 1971, 1974; Gardens One to Five, 1971, 1972; Country Love and Poison Rain, 1973; Moon On An Iron Meadow, 1974; Faces in the Flames, 1975; Greencomber, 1979, 1992; The New Forest, 1979; Seagulls Under Glass, 1975. Contributions to: Numerous short stories, 1967-82 in New Worlds, F&SF, Venture SF and Amazing Stories; German anthologies. Honour: Southern Newspapers Journalist of the Year, 1994. Membership: Ex-Science Fiction Writers of America. Address: Pinetree Lodge 3, Seaway Avenue, Friars Cliff, Christchurch, Dorset BH23 4EU, England.

TATEMATSU Wahei, b. 15 Dec 1947, Utsunomiya, Tochigi, Japan. Author. 1 son, 1 daughter. Education: Graduate in Economics, Waseda University, 1971. Publications: Distant Thunder, 1980; Market of Delight, 1981; Sexual Apolcalypse, 1985; Poison, 1997; Valley of Grace, 1997. Honours: Waseda University New Writer Award, 1970; Noma Arts New Writer Award, 1980; Afro-Asian Writers Association 1985 Lotus Award for Young Writers, 1986; Tsubota Joji Literary Award, 1993. Memberships: Japan Writers Association; Japan PEN Club. Address: 3-23-10 Ebisu, Shibuya-ku, Tokyo, Japan.

TAUCHID Mohamad, b. 16 Jan 1934, Kediri, Java, Indonesia. Geologist; Geochemist; Consultant; Writer. m. Gisele Emard, 26 Sept 1964, 3 daughters. Education: Bandung Institute of Technology, 1955-59; BSc, Honours, Geology, St Francis Xavier University, Antigonish, 1961; MSc, Geochemistry, University of Ottawa, 1965; PhD Programme, Economic Geology and Geochemistry, Carleton University, Ottawa, 1965-68. Appointments: Project Manager, UNDP, Colombia, 1978-80; Senior Officer, International Atomic Energy Agency, Vienna, 1980-94; Consultant, 1994-. Contributions to: Many publications as author or editor. Honour: Distinguished Service Medal, International Atomic Energy Agency, 1985. Memberships: Professional organisations. Address: 44 Thare Crescent, Nepean, Ontario K2J 2P4, Canada.

TAVIRA Luis de, b. 1 Sept 1948, Mexico. Dramatist; Poet; Theatre Director. 3 sons. Education: Licentiate, Literature and Dramatic Arts, Univeridad Nacional Autónoma de México, 1972; Master of Philosophy, Instituto Libre de Filosofia, Mexico, 1976. Appointments: Director, Centro Universitario de Teatro, Universidad Nacional Autónoma de México, 1978-82, Centro de Experimentación Teatral, INBA, Mexico, 1985-90, Caso del Teatro, AC, Mexico, 1990-. Publications: 7 plays, 1982-91; 3 poetry books, 1972, 1978, 1992. Contributions to: Journals. Honours: Best play and best director awards. Address: Offico 59, Prados de Coyoacan, Mexico DF 04810, Mexico.

TAYLOR Andrew (John Robert), b. 14 Oct 1951, Stevenage, England. Writer. m. Caroline Jane Silverwood, 8 Sept 1979, 1 son, 1 daughter. Education: BA, 1973, MA, 1976, Emmanuel College, Cambridge; MA, University of London, 1979. Publications: Waiting for the End of the World, 1984; Our Father's Lies, 1985; Freelance Death, 1987; The Second Midnight, 1987; Blacklist, 1988; Toyshop, 1990; Double Exposure, 1990; Blood Relation, 1993; Odd Man Out, 1993; The Invader, 1994; An Air That Kills, 1994; The Mortal Sickness, 1995; The Four Last Things, 1997; The Lover of the Grave, 1997. Honour: John Creasey Award, 1982. Memberships: Crime Writers Association, committee member, 1996-; Society of Authors; Detection Club. Address: c/o Richard Scott Simon Ltd, 43 Doughty Street, London WC1N 2LF, England.

TAYLOR Andrew MacDonald, b. 19 Mar 1940, Warnambool, Victoria, Australia. Professor; Poet; Writer. m. Beate Josephi, 1981, 1 son, 1 daughter. Education:BA, 1961, MA, 1970, University of Melbourne; Litt.D, Melbourne, 1998. Appointments: Lockie Fellow, University of Melbourne, 1965-68; Lecturer, 1971-74, Senior Lecturer, 1974-91, Associate Professor, 1991-1992, University of Adelaide; Professor, Edith Cowan University, 1992-. Publications: Reading Australian Poetry, 1987; Selected Poems, 1960-85, 1988; Folds in the Map, 1991; Sandstone, 1995. Contributions to: Newspapers, journals, and magazines. Honours: Several prizes and awards; Member of the Order of Australia. Memberships: Association for the Study of Australian Literature; Australian Society of Authors; PEN. Address: c/o School of Language and Literature, Edith Cowan University, Mount Lawley, Western Australia 6050, Australia.

TAYLOR Beverly White, b. 30 Mar 1947, Grenada, Mississippi, USA. Professor of English; Writer. Education: BAE, University of Mississippi, 1969; MA, 1970, PhD, 1977, Duke University. Appointments: Assistant Professor, 1977-84, Associate Professor, 1984-92, Professor of English, 1992-, University of North Carolina at Chapel Hill. Publications: The Return of King Arthur, 1983; Arthurian Legend and Literature, 1984; Francis Thompson, 1987; The Cast of Consciousness, 1987; Gender and Discourse in Victorian Literature and Art, 1992. Contributions to: Encyclopedias and periodicals. Memberships: Victorians Institute, president, 1989-90; Tennyson Society; Browning Institute; Modern Language Association; International Arthurian Society. Address: Department of English, University of North Carolina, Chapel Hill, NC 27599, USA.

TAYLOR David John, (D J Taylor), b. 22 Aug 1960, Norwich, England. Writer. m. Rachel Hore, 22 June 1990, 2 sons. Education: BA, Modern History, University of Oxford. Publications: Great Eastern Land, novel, 1986; A Vain Conceit: British Fiction in the 1980s, 1989; Other People: Portraits from the Nineties, with Marcus Beshmann, 1989; Real Life, novel, 1992; After the War: The Novel and England since 1945, 1993; English Settlement, novel, 1996; After Bathing at Baxter's, prose, 1997; Trespass, novel, 1988. Contributions to: Independent; Guardian; Times Literary Supplement; Spectator; Private Eye; Mail on Sunday; Others. Membership: Fellow, Royal Society of Literature, 1997. Literary Agent: Rogers, Coleridge and White. Address: c/o Rogers, Coleridge and White, 20 Powis Mews, London W11 1JN, England.

TAYLOR H Baldwin. See: **WAUGH Hillary Baldwin.**

TAYLOR Henry (Splawn), b. 21 June 1942, Loudoun County, Virginia, USA. Professor of Literature; Poet; Writer. m. (1) Sarah Spencer Bean, 12 June 1965, div 1967, (2) Frances Ferguson Carney, 29 June 1968, div 1995, 2 sons, (3) Sarah Spencer, 11 June 1995. Education: BA, University of Virginia, 1965; MA, Hollins College, 1966. Appointments: Instructor, Roanoke College, 1966-68; Assistant Professor, University of Utah, 1968-71; Contributing Editor, Hollins Critic, 1970-77; Associate Professor, 1971-76, Professor of Literature, 1976-, Co-Director, MFA in Creative Writing, 1982-, Director, American Studies Program, 1983-85, American University; Consulting Editor, Magill's Literary Annual, 1972-, Poet Lore, 1976-84; Writer-in-Residence, Hollins College, 1978; Board of Advisors, 1986-, Poetry Editor, 1988-89, New Virginia Review; Distinguished Poet-in-Residence, Wichita State University, 1994. Publications: Poetry: The Horse Show at Midnight: Poems, 1966; Breakings, 1971; An Afternoon of Pocket Billiards, 1975; Desperado, 1979; The Flying Change, 1985; Understanding Fiction: Poems 1986-96, 1996. Other: Magill's (Masterplots) Literary Annual 1972 (editor with Frank N Nagill), 1972; Poetry: Points of Departure, 1974; Magill's (Masterplots) Literary Annual 1973 (associate editor), 1974; Magill's (Masterplots) Literary Annual 1974 (associate editor), 1975; The Water of Light: A Miscellany in Honor of Brewster Ghiselin (editor), 1976; Compulsory Figures: Essays on Recent American Poets, 1992. Contributions to: Many books, anthologies, reviews, and journals. Honours: Academy of American Poets Prizes, 1962, 1964; Utah State Institute of Fine Arts Poetry Prizes, co-winner, 1969, winner, 1971; National Endowment for the Arts Fellowships, 1978, 1986; National Endowment for the Humanities Research Grant, 1980-81; Witter Bynner Prize for Poetry, American Academy and Institute of Arts and Letters, 1984; Pulitzer Prize in Poetry, 1986; Virginia Cultural Laureate Award, 1986; Teacher Recognition, National Foundation for Advancement in the Arts, 1995-96. Address: c/o Department of Literature, American University, Washington, DC 20016, USA.

TAYLOR John Laverck, b. 25 May 1937, Yorkshire, England. Educator; Writer. m. Jennifer Margaret Green, 21 Sept 1981, 1 son, 2 daughters. Education: DipArch, University of Leeds, 1960; MSc, Urban Design, Columbia University, 1963; PhD, University of Sheffield, 1969. Appointments: College Principal; Bramley Professor; Various visiting professorships. Publications: Planning for Urban Growth, 1972; Simulation in the Classroom, 1974; Learning and the Simulation Game, 1978; Guide on Simulation and Gaming for Environmental Education, 1984; Feedback on Instructional Simulation Systems, 1992. Contributions to: Professional journals. Honours: Fulbright Fellow, 1962-64; Salzburg Fellow, 1965-66; Nuffield School Science Fellow, 1968-74; Officer of the Order of the British Empire, 1990. Memberships: Several professional organisations. Address: Tapton Hall Barn, Balmoak Lane, Chesterfield, Derbyshire S41 OTH, England.

TAYLOR John Russell, b. 19 June 1935, Dover, Kent, England. Art, Film, and Drama Critic; Writer. Education: MA, Jesus College, Cambridge; Courtauld Institue of London. Appointments: Sub-Editor, Times Educational; Supplement, 1959; Editorial Assistant, Times Literary Supplement, 1960; Film Critic, 1962-73, Art Critic, 1978-, The Times; Lecturer on Film, Tufts University in London, 1970-71; Professor, University of Southern California at Los Angeles, 1972-78; Editor, Films and Filming, 1983-90. Publications: Anger and After, 1962; Anatomy of a Television Play, 1962; Cinema Eye, Cinema Bar, 1964; Penguin Dictionary of the Theatre, 1966; The Art Nouveau Book in Britain, 1966; The Rise and Fall of the Well-Made Play, 1967; The Art Dealers, 1969; Harold Pinter, 1969; The Hollywood Musical, 1971; The Second Wave, 1971; David Storey, 1974; Directors and Directions, 1975; Peter Shaffer, 1975; Hitch, 1978; The Revels History of Drama in English, Vol VII, 1978; Impressionism, 1981; Strangers in Paradise, 1983; Ingrid Bergman, 1983; Alex Guinness, 1984; Vivien Leigh, 1984; Portraits of the British Cinema, 1985; Hollywood 1940s, 1985; Orson Welles, 1986; Edward Wolfe, 1986; Great Movie Moments, 1987; Post-war Friends, 1987; Robin Tanner, 1989; Bernard Meninsky, 1990; Impressionist Dreams, 1990; Liz Taylor, 1991; Ricacardo Cinalli, 1993; Igor Mitoraj, 1993; Muriel Pemberton, 1993, Claude Monet, 1995; Michael Parke, 1996; Bill Jacklin, 1997. Address: c/o The Times, 1 Pennington Street, London E1 9XN, England.

TAYLOR John Vernon, b. 11 Sept 1914, Cambridge, England. Retired Bishop; Writer. m. Peggy Wright, 5 Oct 1940, 1 son, 2 daughters. Education: MA, Trinity College, Cambridge; MA, St Catherine's College, Oxford; D Ed, London University Institute of Education. Publications: Christianity and Politics in Africa, 1955; Man in the Midst, 1955; The Growth of the Church in Buganda, 1958; The Primal Vision, 1963; The Go Between Goti, 1972; Enough is Enough, 1975; Weep Not For Me, 1985; A Matter of Life and Death, 1986; A Christmas Sequence and Other Poems, 1989; Kingdom Come, 1989; The Christlike God, 1992; The Uncancelled Mandate, 1998. Honours: Honorary Doctor of Divinity, 1963; Collins Religious Book Prize, 1974; Honorary Fellow, New College and Magdalen College, Oxford, 1986, Trinity College, Cambridge, 1987; Honorary Doctor of Literature, 1991. Address: 65 Aston Street, Oxford OX4 1EW, England.

TAYLOR John W(illiam) R(ansom), b. 8 June 1922, Ely, Cambridgeshire, England. Editor Emeritus; Author. m. Doris Alice Haddrick, 1946, 1 son, 1 daughter. Appointments: Staff, 1955-59, Editor, 1959-84, Editor-in-Chief, 1985-89, Editor Emeritus, 1990-, Jane's All the World's Aircraft. Publications: Numerous books, including: Spitfire (with M F Allward), 1946; Aircraft Annual, 1949-75; Civil Aircraft Markings, 1950-78; Military Aircraft Recognition, 1952-79; Civil Aircraft Markings, 1950-78; Military Aircraft Recognition, 1952-79; Civil Airliner Recognition, 1953-79; Jane's All the World's Aircraft, 1956-89; CFS: Birthplace of Air Power, 1958, revised edition, 1987; Pictorial History of the Royal Air Force, 3 volumes, 1968-71, revised edition, 1980; Aircraft Aircraft, 1967, 4th edition, 1974; Encyclopedia of World Aircraft, 1966; The Lore of Flight, 1971; Civil Aircraft of the World, 1970-79; Missiles of the World (with M J H Taylor), 1972-79; History of Aviation (with K Munson), 1973, 2nd edition, 1978; Jane's Aircraft Pocket Books, 1973-87; History of Aerial Warfare, 1974; Guinness Book of Air Facts and Feats (co-editor), 1974-83; Aircraft, Strategy and Operations of the Soviet Air Force (with R A Mason), 1986; The de Havilland Aircraft Company (with M F Allward), 1996; Fairey Aviation, 1997; Sikorsky, 1998. Honours: G P Memorial Trophy, 1959; Order of Merit, World Aerospace Education Organization, 1981;

Freeman of the City of London, 1987;Lauren D Lyman Award, Aviation Space Writers Association, USA, 1990; Officer of the Order of the British Empire, 1991; Honorary DEng, Kingston University, 1993. Memberships: Royal Aeronautical Society, fellow; Royal Historical Society, fellow. Address: 36 Alexandra Drive, Surbiton, Surrey KT5 9AF, England.

TAYLOR Judy, (Julia Marie Hough), b. 12 Aug 1932, Munton, Swansea, Wales. Writer. m. Richard Hough, 1980. Appointments: Bodley Head Publishers, 1951-81; Director, Bodley Head Ltd, 1967-84, Chatto, Bodley Head and Jonathan Cape Ltd, 1973-80, Chatto, Bodley Head & Jonathan Cape Australia Pty Ltd, 1977-80; Consultant to Penguin, Beatrix Potter, 1981-87, 1989-92. Publications: Sophie and Jack, 1982; My First Year: A Beatrix Potter Baby Book, 1983; Sophie and Jack in the Snow, 1984; Dudley and the Monster, 1986; Dudley Goes Flying, 1986; Dudley in a Jam, 1986; Dudley and the Strawberry Shake, 1986; That Naughty Rabbit: Beatrix Potter and Peter Rabbit, 1987; Beatrix Potter 1866-1943, 1989; Beatrix Potter's Letters: A Selection, 1989; So I Shall Tell You a Story, 1993. Play: Beatrix (with Patrick Garland), 1996. Contributions to: Numerous professional journals. Honour: Member of the Order of the British Empire, 1971. Memberships: Publishers Association Council; Book Development Council; UNICEF International Art Committee; UK UNICEF Greetings Card Committee; Beatrix Potter Society; Royal Society of Arts, fellow. Address: 31 Meadowbank, Primrose Hill Road, London NW3 3AY, England.

TAYLOR Laurie Aylma, b. 3 Sept 1939, Tappan, New York, USA. Writer. m. Allen Sparer, 17 July 1971, 2 daughters. Education: BA, Ohio Wesleyan University, 1960. Publications: Footnote to Murder; Only Half a Hoax; Deadly Objectives; Shed Light on Death; The Blossom of Erda; Changing the Past; Love of Money; Poetic Justice; A Murder Waiting to Happen; Cats Paw. Contributions to: Anthologies. Honours: Minnesota Voices Project; Lois Phillips Hudson Prize. Memberships: Poets and Writers; Mystery Writers of America; Science Fiction and Fantasy Writers of America. Address: 4000 York Avenue South, Minneapolis, MN 55410, USA.

TAYLOR Peter Mark, (Mark Peters), b. 5 Dec 1936, Huddersfield,England. Author. m. Rosemary Hughes Grey, 21 July 1958, 1 son. Education: Huddersfield College. Appointments: Managing Director, Arrow Books, 1966-70, Hutchinson, Australia, 1970-74, Methuen, Australia, 1974-76. Publications: More than 20 books, including: An End to Silence: The Building of the Overland Telegraph Line, 1980; Australia: The First Twelve Years, 1982; Pastoral Properties of Australia, 1984; An Australian Country Life, 1986; Station Life in Australia, 1988; An Atlas of Australian History, 1990. Contributions to: Sydney Morning Herald; The Australian; This Australia. Membership: Union Club, Sydney. Address: Unit 5, Brighton Street, Biggera Waters, Queensland 4216, Australia.

TAYLOR Renée (Gertrude). See: RENÉE.

TAYLOR Theodore Langhans, b. 23 June 1921, Statesville, North Carolina, USA. Writer. m. (1) Gwen Goodwin, 25 Oct 1946, 2 sons, 1 daughter, (2) Flora Gray, 18 Apr 1982. Publications: The Magnificent Mitscher, 1954; Fire on the Beaches, 1957; The Cay, 1968; The Children's War, 1971; The Maldonado Miracle, 1973; Teetoncey, 1974; Jule, 1979; The Trouble with Tuck, 1981; Battle of the Midway Island, 1982; HMS Hood vs Bismarck, 1983; Battle in the English Channel, 1984; Sweet Friday Island, 1984; The Cats of Shambala, 1985; Walking Up a Rainbow, 1986; The Stalker, 1987; The Hostage, 1988; Sniper, Monocolo, 1989; Tuck Triumphant, 1990; The Weirdo, 1991; Maria, 1992; To Kill a Leopard, 1993; Timothy of the Clay, 1993; The Bomb, 1996; Rogue Wave, 1996; The Flight of Jesse Leroy Brown. Contributions to: Saturday Evening Post; McCall's; Ladies Home Journal; Saturday Review of Literature; Argosy. Honours: Lewis Carroll Shelf Award; Jane Addams Peace and Freedom Foundation Award; Western Writers of America Award; George G Stone

Center Award; Edgar Allan Poe Award; International Association of School Librarians Award; Best Books, American Library Association, 1993, 1995; Scott O'Dell Historical Novel. Address: 1856 Catalina Street, Laguna Beach, CA 92651, USA.

TAYLOR Velande Pingel, (Marther Pingel) b. 10 Sept 1923, New York, New York, USA. Retired Professor of Literature and Philosophy; Writer; Poet. m. Bert Raymond Taylor Jr, 28 Oct 1961. Education: BA, 1944, MA, 1945, PhD, 1947, Literature and Philosophy; Independent study in art, music, creative writing, poetry and fiction. Appointments: Instructor, Paul Smiths College, New York, 1946-47; Assistant Professor, East Carolina University, North Carolina, 1947-58; Professor and Head, Department of Humanities, Colorado Woman's College, 1958-66; Visiting Professor, St Mary's University, Texas, 1966-69; Professor, Middle Georgia College, 1969-72; Professor and Writer-in-Residence, Hong Baptist College, 1974-84; Retreat Facilitator in Poetry and Fiction, WordCraft by Lan, 1984-. Publications: Catalyst, 1951; Mood Montage, 1968; Immortal Dancer, 1968; Mode and Muse in a New Generation, 1979; Walking Songs, 1997; Zbyx, 1997; Homilies in the Marketplace, 1996, 1998; Copper Flowers, 1996; Tales from the Archetypal World, 1998. Contributions to: Anthologies, periodicals, and radio. Honours: Certificate, International Mark Twain Society, 1947; Miniature Medal, Order of the Danne Brog, 1951; Certificate, Writer's Digest Rhymed Poetry Contest, 1994. Memberships: American Philosophical Association. Academy of American Poets. Address: 910 Marion Street, No 1008, Seattle, WA 98104, USA.

TAZE Nell, (Nell Marshal), b. 30 Jan 1933, Pulaski, Tennessee, USA. Retired Real Estate Executive; Author; Publisher. m. 15 Feb 1986, 1 sons, 1 daughter. Education: Graduated, Specialty Subjects, University of California at Los Angeles, 1961-66. Appointments: Bank Mortgage, 1961-65; Union Home Loans, 1966-71; Chief Executive Officer, Marshal Plan Inc, 1972-91. Publications: Newsletters and trade publications, 1974-91; An Investment in Time - What Happens to Your Money When an Investment Company Folds, 1998. Address: 1635 Higdon Ferry Rd C-145, Hot Springs, AR 71913, USA.

TEALE Ruth. See: FRAPPELL Ruth Meredith.

TEBBEL John, b. 16 Nov 1912, Boyne City, Michigan, USA. Writer; Retired Professor of Humanities. m. Kathryn Carl, 29 Apr 1939, 1 daughter. Education: AB, Central Michigan College of Education, 1935; MS, Columbia University, 1937. Appointments: Managing Editor, American Mercury, 1941-43; Associate Editor, E P Dutton & Co, 1943-47; Chairman, Department of Journalism, 1954-65, Professor of Journalism, 1965, New York University. Publications: Numerous books, including: An American Dynasty, 1947; The Marshall Fields, 1947; George Horace Lorimer and the Saturday Evening Post, 1948; The Battle for North America, 1948; The Conqueror, 1951; Touched with Fire, 1952; The Life and Good Times of William Randolph Hearst, 1952; George Washington's America, 1954; The Magic of Balanced Living, 1956; The Epicure's Companion, 1962; David Sarnoff, 1963; From Rags to Riches, 1964; A History of Book Publishing in America, 4 volumes, 1972-81; The Media in America, 1975; The Press and the Presidency, 1985; Between Covers, 1987; A Certain Club, 1989; The Magazine in America, 1991; Turning the World Upside Down, 1993; America's Great Patriotic War with Spain, 1996. Contributions to: Many professional journals and general periodicals. Honours: Alumni Award, 1975; Publishing Hall of Fame, 1985. Memberships: Authors Guild; Society of Professional Journalists. Address: 4033 The Forest at Duke, 2701 Pickett Road, Durham, NC 27705, USA.

TEGLGAARD Thomas. See: CHRISTENSEN Thomas Teglgaard.

TEICHMAN Judith A, b. 19 July 1947, Toronto, Canada. Professor of Political Science. m. George, 1 May 1971, 1 daughter. Education: BA, 1969, MA, 1971, PhD,

1978, University of Toronto, Canada. Appointments: Assistant Professor, University of Waterloo, 1980, Assistant Professor, 1987; Associate Professor, 1989, Professor, 1997, University of Toronto. Publications: Policy Making in Mexico, From Boom to Crisis, 1988; Privatization and Political Change in Mexico, 1995. Contributions to: Articles in: Latin American Research Review; Latin American Perspectives; Studies in Comparative International Development; Mexican Studies/Etudios Mexicanos; Canadian Journal of Political Science. Honours: Choice Outstanding Academic Book Award for Policy Making in Mexico, 1989. Memberships: Former Editor, Canadian Journal of Latin American & Caribbean Studies, 1989-92.

TELFER Barbara Jane, b. 13 Aug 1945, Wellington, New Zealand. Author. m. Maxwell Bryant Telfer, 14 Mar 1970, 2 daughters. Education: New Zealand School Dental Nurse Certificate, 1965. Publications: The Great New Zealand Puzzle Book, 1987; The Great International Puzzle Book, 1988; The Great Crafty Ideas Book, 1988; A Book of Australian Puzzles, 1988; The Great Number Puzzle Book, 1990; Summertime Puzzles, 1992; Astro Puzzles, 1992; World of Puzzles, 1992; Mystery Word Puzzles, 1993; The Windsor Street Mystery, 1993; The Great Christmas Activity Book, 1993; The Great Junior Puzzle Book, 1994; The Second Great Number Puzzle Book, 1994; The Zoo Mystery, 1994; The Greenhouse Mystery, 1994; Barbara Telfer's Paper Fun, 1995. Contributions to: Magazines. Address: 4/96 Elliot Street, Howick, Auckland, New Zealand.

TELFER Tracie. See: CHAPLIN Jenny.

TEMKO Allan Bernard, b. 4 Feb 1926, New York, New York, USA. Retired Professor; Architecture Critic; Writer. m. Elizabeth Ostroff, 1 July 1950, 1 son, 1 daughter. Education: AB, Columbia University, 1947; Postgraduate Studies, Sorbonne, University of Paris, 1948-49, 1951-52, University of California at Berkeley, 1949-51. Appointments: Lecturer, Sorbonne, University of Paris, 1953-54, École des Arts et Metiers, Paris, 1954-55; Assistant Professor of Journalism, 1956-62, Lecturer in City Planning and Social Sciences, 1966-70, Lecturer, Graduate School of Journalism, 1991, University of California at Berkeley; West Coast Editor, Architectural Forum, 1959-62; Architecture Critic, 1961-93, Art Editor, 1979-82, San Francisco Chronicle; Professor of Art, California State University at Hayward, 1971-80; Lecturer in Art, Stanford University, 1981, 1982. Publications: Notre Dame of Paris, 1955; Eero Saarinen, 1962; No Way to Build a Ballpark and Other Irreverent Essays on Architecture, 1993. Contributions to: Newspapers and magazines. Honours: Guggenheim Fellowship, 1956-57; Gold Medal, 1956, Silver Medal, 1994, Commonwealth Club of California; Rockefeller Foundation Grant, 1962-63; Manufacturers Hanover/Art World 1st Prize in Architectural Criticism, 1986, and Critics' Award, 1987; National Endowment for the Arts Fellowship, 1988; Professional Achievement Award, Society of Professional Journalists, 1988; Pulitzer Prize for Criticism, 1990. Address: 1015 Fresno Avenue, Berkeley, CA 94707, USA.

TEMPLE Ann. See: MORTIMER Penelope (Ruth).

TEMPLE Nigel Hal Longdale, b. 21 Jan 1926, Lowestoft, Suffolk, England. Painter; Architectural and Garden Historian; Photographer; Lecturer. m. Judith Tattersill, 1 son, 1 daughter. Education: National Diploma in Design, 1951; Art Teacher's Diploma, Sheffield, 1953; MLitt, Architecture, University of Bristol, 1978; PhD, University of Keele, 1985. Publications: Farnham Inheritance, 1956, 2nd edition, 1965; Farnham Buildings and People, 1963, 2nd edition, 1973; Looking at Things, 1968; Seen and Not Heard, 1979; John Nash and the Village Picturesque, 1979; Blaise Hamlet, 1986; George Repton's Pavilion Notebook: A Catalogue Raisonné, 1993. Contributions to: Country Life; Journal of Garden History; Architectural Review; Garden History; Georgian Group Journal. Honours: Fellow, National Society for Art Education, 1964; Companion, Guild of St George. Memberships: Royal West of England Academy; Garden

History Society, council member. Address: 4 Wendover Gardens, Christchurch Road, Cheltenham, Gloucestershire GL50 2PA, England.

TEMPLE Norman Joseph, b. 28 Apr 1947, London, England. University Professor. m. Frances Farquhar, 3 Aug 1971, div, 1 son. Education: PhD Biochemistry, Wolverhampton University, 1980. Publications: Western Diseases: Their Dietary Prevention and Reversibility (with D Burkitt), 1994; Diet for the New Century (with H Diehl and A Ludington), 1996; Antioxidants in Human Teeth and Disease (with T Basu and M Garg), 1999. Contributions to: 36 papers in peer-reviewed journals. Address: Athabasca University, Athabasca, Alberta T9S 3A3, Canada.

TEMPLE (Robert) Philip, b. 20 Mar 1939, Yorkshire, England. Author. m. Daphne Evelyn Keen, 12 June 1965, div, 1 son, 1 daughter. Appointments: New Zealand Alpine Journal, editor, 1968-70, 1973; Landfall, 1972-75; Katherine Mansfield Memorial Fellowship, Menton, France, assoociate editor, 1979; Robert Burns Fellowship, University of Otago, Dunedin, New Zealand, 1980; Berliner Kunstlerprogramm Fellowship, West Berlin, 1987; National Library, research fellow, 1996-97. Publications: The World at Their Feet, 1969; Ways to the Wilderness, 1977; Beak of the Moon, 1981; Sam, 1984; New Zealand Explorers, 1985; Kakapo, 1988; Making Your Vote Count, 1992; Dark of the Moon, 1993; Temple's Guide to the New Zealand Parliament, 1994; Kotuku, 1994; The Book of the Kea, 1996; To Each His Own, 1998. Honours: Arts Council Non-Fiction Bursary, 1994; AIM Honour Award, 1995 New Zealand Library Research Fellowship, 1996. Memberships: PEN, New Zealand Centre, 1970-; PEN Representative, New Zealand Authors Advisory Committee, 1986-88, 1993-; New Zealand Society of Authors, president, 1998-99. Address: 147a Tomahawk Road, Dunedin, New Zealand.

TEMPLE Wayne C(alhoun), b. 5 Feb 1924, Richwood, Ohio, USA. Historian; Archivist; Author. m. Sunderline (Wilson) Mohn, 9 Apr 1979, 2 stepsons. Education: AB, cum laude, Senior Class Honours and Honours in History, 1949, AM, 1951, PhD, 1956, University of Illinois, Champaign-Urbana. Appointments: Editor-in-Chief, 1958-73, Editorial Board, 1973-, Lincoln Herald; Board of Advisors, The Lincoln Forum. Publications: Indian Villages of the Illinois Country, 1958-; Campaigning with Grant, 1961; Stephen A Douglas: Freemason, 1982; The Building of Lincoln's Home and its Saga, 1984; Lincoln's Connections With the Illinois and Michigan Canal, 1986; Illinois' Fifth Capitol (with Sunderine Temple), 1988; Abraham Lincoln: From Skeptic to Prophet, 1995; Alexander Williamson: Friend of the Lincolns, 1997. Contributions to: Numerous journals including many to the Lincoln Herald. Honours: Gold Honor Key, Sigma Tau Delta; Lincoln Diploma of Honor; Lincoln Medallion, National Sesquicentennial Commission; Sigma Tau Delta (English honorary). Membership: Abraham Lincoln Association. Address: 1121 South 4th Street Court, Springfield, IL 62703, USA.

TEMPLETON Fiona, b. 23 Dec 1951, Scotland. Theatre Director; Poet; Writer. Education: MA, University of Edinburgh, 1973; MA, New York University, 1985; Publications: Elements of Performance Art, 1976; London, 1984; You the City, 1990; Delirium of Interpretations, 1997; Cells of Release, 1997; Hi Cowboy, 1997. Contributions to: Anthologies and journals. Honours: Grants, fellowships and awards. Memberships: New Dramatists; Poets and Writers. Address: 100 St Mark's Place, No 7, New York, NY 10009, USA.

TENNANT Emma, b. 20 Oct 1937. Author. 1 son, 2 daughters. Publications: The Bad Sister, 1978; Wild Nights, 1979; Faustine, 1992; Two Women of London, 1993; Pemberley, 1994; Strangers: A Family Romance, 1998. Honour: Honorary DLitt, Aberdeen, 1996. Membership: Fellow, Royal Society of Literture, 1984. Literary Agent: Toby Eady. Address: c/o Toby Eady, 9 Orme Court, London WZ, England.

TER-OGANIAN Leon, (Najnagoret), b. 12 Nov 1910, St Petersburg, Russia. Translator; Teacher; Editor. m. Maria Rogalewska, 19 Oct 1946. Education: Warsaw Polytechnic, 1929; New York City College, 1930; Main School of Economics, Warsaw, 1932; MA, University of Warsaw, 1946-52. Appointments: Industry, 1937-39; Industry, University, 1945-50; Official Court Translator, Russian-English-Polish, 1945-77; English Department anf Institute of Applied Linguistics, Warsaw University, 1951-70; Music Conservatory, 1970-75. Publications: Translations into English: The Other Side of the Moon, 1961; Linguistic Studies, from Polish, Russian, French and German, 1974; From English: Saroyan's Madness in the Family, 1997; Saroyan's My Name Is Aram, 1998; Saroyan's Little Children, 1999. Contributions to: Translator and editor, Annals of Chemistry, 33 years. Membership: Honorary Member, Association of Polish Translators. Address: ul Filtrowa 79 m 29, 02-032 Warsaw, Poland.

TERADA Alice Masae, b. 13 Nov 1928, Hilo, Hawaii, USA. Educator. m. Harry T Terada, 25 Aug 1951, 2 sons, 1 daughter. Education: Diploma in Nursing, Queen's Hospital School of Nursing, 1946; BS, Nursing, Case Western Reserve University, 1953; Teaching Certificate, Department of Education, State of Hawaii, 1968; MEd, Elementary, University of Hawaii, 1971. Publications: Under the Starfruit Tree: Folktales from Vietnam (illustrated by Janet Larsen), 1989; The Magic Crocodile and Other Folktales from Indonesia (illustrated by Charlene K Smoyer), 1994. Contributions to: Cricket, magazine for children. Honour: Myrtle Clark Creative Writing Award, 1988. Membership: Society of Children's Book Writers and Illustrators. Address: 1 Keahole Place, Honolulu, HI 96825, USA.

TERKEL Studs, (Louis Terkel), b. 16 May 1912, New York, New York, USA. Author; Broadcaster. m. Ida Goldberg, 2 July 1939, 1 son. Education: PhB, 1932, JD, 1934, University of Chicago. Appointments: Actor in stage productions; Host, Studs Terkel Almanac radio interview programme, Chicago, 1952-97. Publications: Giants of Jazz, 1957, revised edition, 1975; Division Street: America, 1967, 2nd edition, 1993; Hard Times: An Oral History of the Great Depression, 1970; Working: People Talk About What They Do All Day and How They Feel About What They Do, 1974; Talking to Myself: A Memoir of My Times, 1977; American Dreams: Lost and Found, 1980; "The Good War": An Oral History of World War II, 1984; Envelopes of Oral Sound: The Art of Oral Recording (with others), 1985, 2nd edition, 1990; The Neon Wilderness (with Nelson Algren), 1986; Chicago, 1986; The Great Divide: Second Thoughts on the American Dream, 1988; RACE: How Blacks and Whites Think and Feel About the American Obesession, 1992; Coming of Age, 1995. Contributions to: Newspapers and magazines. Honours: Ohio State University Award, 1959; UNESCO Prix Italia Award, 1962; University of Chicago Alumni Association Communicator of the Year Award, 1969; George Foster Peabody Award, 1980; Society of Midland Authors Awards, 1982, 1983; Eugene V Debs Award, 1983; Pulitzer Prize in Non-Fiction, 1985; Hugh M Hefner First Amendment Award for Lifetime Achievement, 1990; National Medal of Arts, 1997. Address: 850 West Castlewood Terrace, Chicago, IL 60640, USA.

TERLECKI Wladyslaw Lech, b. 18 May 1933, Czestochowa, Poland. Writer. m. Lucyna Basaj, 1955, 1 son, 1 daughter. Education: University of Wroclaw. Appointments: Staff, Wspolczesnosc, 1958-65; Drama Section, Polish Radio, 1965-70. Publications: Cobble Stones, 1956; Fire, 1962; The Conspiracy, 1966; High Season, 1966; The Wormwood Star, 1968; Two Heads of a Bird, 1970; Pilgrims, 1972; Return from Tzarskoe Selo, 1973; Black Romance, 1974; Rest After the Race, 1975; Tea with the Man Who is Not Here, 1976; The Forest Grows, 1977; Cien Karla, Cien Olbrzyma, 1983; Lament, 1983; Pismak, 1984; Zwierzeta Zostaly Oplacone, 1987; Kill the Tzar, 1992; L'echelle de Jacob, French edition, 1992; Repose-toi après la course, 1994; Piasek, 1997. Numerous film scripts and theatre plays. Honours: Koscielski Prize, Switzerland, 1973; ODRA Award, 1978; Literatura Award, 1981; Drama Award, Teatr Polski,

1987; Polish PEN Club Award, 1996. Memberships: PEN; Polish Film-Makers Union; Association of Polish Writers. Address: ul Mazurska 1, 05-806 Komorow, Poland.

TERRILL Ross, b. 24 Aug 1938, Melbourne, Victoria, Australia (US citizen, 1979). Writer. Education: Wesley College, 1956; BA, University of Melbourne, 1962; PhD, Harvard University, 1970. Appointments: Teaching Fellow, 1968-70, Lecturer, 1970-74, Research Associate, East Asian Studies, 1970-, Harvard University; Contributing Editor, Atlantic Monthly, 1970-84; Research Fellow, Asia Society, 1978-79. Publications: 800,000,000: The Real China, 1972; R H Tawney and His Times, 1973; Flowers on the Iron Tree: Five Cities of China, 1975; The Future of China After Mao, 1978; Mao, 1980, 2nd edition, 1993; The White Boned Demon, 1984, 2nd edition, 1992; The Australians, 1987; China in Our Time, 1992. Contributions to: Newspapers and magazines. Honours: Frank Knox Memorial Fellowship, 1965; Sumner Prize, 1970; George Polk Memorial Award, 1972; National Magazine Award, 1972. Address: 200 Saint Botolph Street, Boston, MA 02115, USA.

TERRY William. See: **HARKNETT Terry.**

TETSURO Miura, b. 1931, Aomori Prefecture, Japan. Writer. Education: Degree in French Literature, Waseda University, Tokyo, 1957. Publications: Jûgo-sai no shuu-i; Shinobugawa (novel); Kenjû to jûgo no tanpen (collection of short stories); Shônen Sanka: Byakuya wo yuku; Jinenjo; Tanpen-shû Mosaic; Minomushi (novel). Honours: Shinchô Dôjin Zasshi Prize; Akutagawa Literary Prize; Nome Literary Prize, 1976; Grand Prize for Japanese Literature, 1983; Osaragi Jirô Award, 1985; Kawabata Yasunari Literary Awards, 1990, 1992; Itoh Sei Literary Award, 1991. Memberships: Japan Academy of Art; Japan Writers Association, board member. Address: c/o Japan Writers' Association, Bungei Shunjyu Building, 9th Floor, 3-23 Kioi-cho, Chiyoda-ku, Tokyo 102, Japan.

THAKUR Haranath. See: **CHATTOPADHYAY Ashoke.**

THALER M N. See: **KERNER Fred.**

THAMEZ Lorraine D, b. 26 Nov 1950, Pueblo, Colorado, USA. Writer; Poet. 2 sons, 1 daughter. Education: AA, Literature, 1997. Appointment: Poetry Editor, Purgatoire Magazine. Publications: Prairie Woman: Dangerous Games; Together Forever; One Heart; One Hand (poems). Contributions to: Periodicals. Memberships: PEN; Poets and Writers; Western Writers' Guild. Address: 121 Chanlon Road, New Providence, NJ 07974, USA.

THAYER Geraldine. See: **DANIELS Dorothy.**

THELLE Notto Reidar, b. 19 Mar 1941, Hong Kong. Professor of Theology; Writer. m. Mona Irene Ramstad, 19 June 1965, 2 sons, 3 daughters. Education: Candidate of Theology, 1966, Degree in Practical Theology, 1966, DTheol, 1982, University of Oslo. Appointments: Missionary, Scandinavian East Asia Mission, Kyoto, Japan, 1969-85; Editor, Japanese Religions, 1974-85; Norsk Tidskrift for Misjon, 1988-96; Associate Director, National Christian Council Center for the Study of Japanese Religions, Kyoto, 1974-85; Professor of Theology, University of Oslo, 1986-. Publications: Buddhism and Christianity in Japan: From Conflict to Dialogue, 1854-1899, 1987; Hvem kan stoppe vinden?, 1991; Mennesket og mysteriet, 1992, revised edition, 1997; Ditt ansikt sô, Essker jeg, 1993; Essays: Hvor höyt må et menneske spörre, 1997. Contributions to: Religious and cultural journals. Address: Skinstadveien, 3370 Vikersund, Norway.

THELWELL Norman, b. 3 May 1923, Berkenhead, Cheshire, England. Artist; Writer; Cartoonist. m. 11 Apr 1949, 1 son, 1 daughter. Education: NDA, ADT, Liverpool College of Art, 1947-50. Appointment: Art Teacher, Wolverhampton College of Art, 1950-57. Publications: Angels on Horseback, 1957; Thelwell Country, 1959; A

Place of Your Own, 1960; Thelwell in Orbit, 1961; A Leg at Each Corner, 1962; The Penguin Thelwell, 1963; Top Dog, 1964; Thelwell's Riding Academy, 1965; Drawing Ponies, 1966; Up the Garden Path, 1967; The Compleat Tangler, 1967; The Thelwell Book of Leisure, 1968; This Desirable Plot, 1970; The Effluent Society, 1971; Penelope, 1972; Three Sheets in the Wind, 1973; Belt Up, 1975; Thelwell Goes West, 1976; Thelwell's Brat Race, 1978; A Plank Bridge by a Pool, 1979; Thelwell's Gymkhana, 1980; Pony Calvalcade, 1981; A Mill Stone Round My Neck, 1982; Some Damn Fool's Signed the Rubens Again, 1983; Magnificat, 1984; Thelwell's Sporting Prints, 1985; Wrestling with a Pencil, 1986; Play It As It Lies, 1987; Penelope Rides Again, 1988; The Cat's Pyjamas, 1992. Contributions to: Newspapers, journals, and magazines. Address: Herons Mead, Timsbury, Romsey, Hampshire SO51 0NE, England.

THÉORET France, b. 1942, Montreal, Quebec, Canada. Author; Dramatist; Poet. Education: BA, 1968, MA, 1977, University of Montreal; PhD, Études françaises, University of Sherbrooke, 1982. Publications: Bloody Mary, 1977, English translation, 1991; Une voix pour Odile, 1978, English translation, 1991; Vertiges, 1979, English translation, 1991; Nécessairement putain, 1980, English translation, 1991; Nous parlerons comme on écrit, 1982; Intérieurs, 1984; Entre raison et déraison, 1987; L'homme qui peignait Staline, 1989, English translation as The Man Who Painted Stalin, 1991; Étrangeté, l'étreinte, 1992; La fiction de l'ange, 1992; Journal pour mémoire, 1993; Laurence, 1996. Contributions to: Anthologies and other publications. Address: c/o Union des écrivaines et écrivains québécois, La Maison des écrivains, 3492 Avenue Laval, Montreal, Quebec H2X 3C8, Canada.

THEROUX Paul Edward, b. 10 Apr 1941, Medford, Massachusetts, USA. Writer. m. (1) Anne Castle, 4 Dec 1967, div 1993, 2 sons, (2) Sheila Donnelly, 18 Nov 1995. Education: BA, University of Massachusetts. Appointments: Lecturer, University of Urbino, Italy, 1963, Soche Hill College, Malawi, 1963-65; Faculty, Department of English, Makerere University, Uganda, 1965-68, University of Singapore, 1968-71; Visiting Lecturer, University of Virginia, 1972-73. Publications: Fiction: Waldo, 1967; Fong and the Indians, 1968; Girls at Play, 1969; Murder in Mount Holly, 1969; Jungle Lovers, 1971; Sinning with Annie, 1972; Saint Jack, 1973; The Black House, 1974; The Family Arsenal, 1976; The Consul's File, 1977; Picture Palace, 1978; A Christmas Card, 1978; London Snow, 1980; World's End, 1980; The Mosquito Coast, 1981; The London Embassy, 1982; Half Moon Street, 1984; O-Zone, 1986; My Secret History, 1988; Chicago Loop, 1990; Millroy the Magician, 1993; My Other Life, 1996; Kowloon Tong, 1997; Collected Stories, 1997. Non-Fiction: V S Naipaul, 1973; The Great Patagonian Express, 1979; The Kingdom by the Sea, 1983; Sailing Through China, 1983; Sunrise with Sea Monsters, 1985; The White Man's Burden, 1987; Riding the Iron Rooster, 1988; The Happy Isles of Oceania, 1992; The Pillars of Hercules, 1995; Sir Vidia's Shadow: A Friendship Across Five Continents, 1998. Honours: Editorial Awards, Playboy magazine, 1972, 1976, 1977, 1979; Whitbread Award, 1978; James Tait Black Award, 1982; Yorkshire Post Best Novel Award, 1982; Thomas Cook Travel Prize, 1989; Honorary doctorates. Memberships: Royal Geographical Society; Royal Society of Literature, fellow; American Academy of Arts and Letters. Address: c/o Hamish Hamilton Ltd, 27 Wrights Lane, London W8 5TZ, England.

THESEN Sharon, b. 1 Oct 1946, Tisdale, Saskatchewan, Canada. Poet; Writer. Education: BA, 1970, MA, 1974, Simon Fraser University. Appointments: Teacher, Capilano College, Vancouver, 1976-92; Poetry Editor, Capilano Review, 1978-89. Publications: Artemis Hates Romance, 1980; Radio New France Radio, 1981; Holding the Pose, 1983; Confabulations: Poems for Malcolm Lowry, 1984; The Beginning of the Long Dash, 1987; The Pangs of Sunday, 1990; The New Long Poems Anthology (editor), 1991; Aurora, 1995. Contributions to: Various publications. Address: c/o

League of Canadian Poets, 54 Wolseley Street, 3rd Floor, Toronto, Ontario M5T 1A5, Canada.

THEVOZ Jacqueline, b. 29 Apr 1926, Estavayer-le-Lac, Switzerland. Writer. m. Jacques Congnard, 12 Nov 1960, 2 daughters. Education: Catholic Institute, Lausanne; University of Lausanne; Lausanne Conservatory. Appointments: Founder, Centre de Choregraphic Musicale, Movement for the Return to the Former Catholic Liturgy; Swiss Delegate, Académie Internationale de Lutèce, Paris. Publications: Aloys Fornerod, mon maître, 1973; Jean Dawint, l'extraordinaire chatelain de Cernex; Le Chateau de Paradis, 1979; Les Termites, 1982; Passage d'une comète, 1993. Contributions to: La Suisse; Le Republicain; Espaces; La Tribune de Lausanne; Le Semeur; Memento-Enfants; La Femme d'Aujourd 'hui. Honours: Prix Folloppe de la Faculté des Lettres de Lausanne, 1949; Prix de l'Academie des Treize, 1983. Membership: Societe Fribourgeoise des Ecrivains. Address: Hermone, Verossier Haut, F 74500 Larringes-sur-Evian.

THEYTAZ Jean-Marc, b. 6 Nov 1955, Sion, Switzerland. Journalist. m. Claudia Glassey, 24 Oct 1980, 1 son, 1 daughter. Education: Licency of Letters, University of Fribourg, 1982. Publications: Litanies de L'arrière Saison, 1981; Fernand Martignoni, 1983; La Voix des Ages, 1987; Pierre de Planchouet, 1991; Blanches Etendues, 1994. Contributions to: Magazines and journals. Honours: Poetry Prize, 1989; Renaissance Française, 1994. Memberships: AVE; Swiss Writers Society. Address: Rue de l'Etrier 6, 1950 Sion, Switzerland.

THIBAUDEAU Colleen, b. 29 Dec 1925, Toronto, Ontario, Canada. Poet; Writer. m. James C Reaney, 29 Dec 1951, 2 sons, 1 daughter. Education: St Thomas Collegiate Institute, 1944; BA, 1948, MA, 1949, University of Toronto; Diploma, l'Université Catholique de l'ouest, Angers, 1951. Publications: Poetry: Ten Letters, 1975; My Granddaughters Are Combing Out Their Long Hair, 1977; The Martha Landscapes, 1984; The Artemesia Book: Poems Selected and New, 1991; The Patricia Album and Other Poems, 1992. Contributions to: Poems and stories in various anthologies. Membership: League of Canadian Poets, 1969-92. Address: 276 Huron Street, London, Ontario N6A 2J9, Canada.

THIBAUDEAU May, b. 8 May 1908, Wisconsin, USA. Teacher; Writer. m. Raymond Thibaudeau, 16 June 1941, 1 son, 6 daughters. Education: BSc, University of Wisconsin-Milwaukee, 1972. Appointments: Teacher, Fond du Lac County Schools, 1927-32, Peshtigo City Grade Schools, 1932-41, St Mary's Grade School, Milwaukee, 1955-75. Publications: Life and Times of Frederick Layton; I Shall Not Die I Shall Live On In You; Scarboro Was I Am; The Donkey Stayed In Ireland; Cinder Youre A Lucky Pup; Prayers of My Childhood; World War II For Us At Home; The Christmas We Remember; History of St Ann's Day Care; The Browns; Hats; Their Name Was Anonymous. Honours: Certificates of Merit, 1996, 1998. Memberships: Wisconsin Regional Writers; Council of Wisconsin Writers. Address: 1212 North Chicago Avenue, South Milwaukee, WI 53172, USA.

THIRSLUND Soren, (Gamle Soren), b. 5 July 1919, Naestved, Denmark. Retired Sea Captain. m. Valborg Sonderby, 12 May 1945, 1 daughter. Appointment: Mate; Master; Wireless Operator. Publications: History and Development of Navigation, 3 vol, 1987, 1988, 1989; Viking Compass; Viking Navigation, (video tape); History of Navigation, (video tape), forthcoming. Contributions to: Journal of Navigation: The Discovery of an Early Bearing Dial - Further Investigations; Journal of Navigation: Sailing Directions of the North Atlantic. Memberships: The Danish Writers Union; Adventurers Club of Denmark. Address: The Viking Compass, v/S Thirslund, Teglgardsvej 342, 3050 Humlebaek, Denmark.

THIRY August, b. 24 Apr 1948, Grazen, Belgium. Writer. m. Simonne Rutten, 28 July 1972, 2 daughters. Education: MA, Germanic Languages, 1972; Slavonic

Languages, Russian, 1975. Appointments: Editor, Cultural Magazine, 1976-82; Reviewer, Russian Literature, 1990-. Publications: Het Paustovski Syndroom; Onder Assistenten; Russische Literatuur in de zoste Eeuw; Montagne Russe; Byzantijns Blauw, 1996; Grand Trunk Road in Pakistan, 1996. Contributions to: Periodicals. Honours: De Brakke Hond Story Award; Guido Gezelle Novel Award. Address: Dorenstraat 196, 3020 Herent, Belgium.

THISELTON Anthony Charles, b. 13 July 1937, Woking, Surrey, England. Theologian Professor of Theology. m. Rosemary Stella Harman, 21 Sept 1963, 2 sons, 1 daughter. Education: BD, University of London, 1959; MTh, 1964; PhD, University of Sheffield, 1977; DD, University of Durham, 1993. Appointments: Curate, Holy Trinity Church, Sydenham, 1960-63; Lecturer and Tutor, Tyndale Hall, Bristol and Univ of Bristol, 1964-70; Lectr, Biblical Studies, Univ of Sheffield, 1970-79; Snr Lectr, 1979-85; Principal, St John's College, Nottingham, England, 1985-88; Principal, St John's College, Durham, 1988-92; Professor of Christian Theology and Head of Department of Theology, University of Nottingham, 1992-; Canon Theologian of Leicester Cathedral, 1993-. Publications: The Two Horizons, 1980; The Responsibility of Hermeneutics, with R Lundin and C Walhout, 1985; New Horizons in Hermeneutics, 1992; Interpreting God and the Post-Modern Self, 1995; The Promise of Hermeneutics, with R Lundin and C Walhout, 1999. Contributions to: Journal of Theological Studies; New Test Studies; Biblical Interpretation; Scottish Journal of Theology; Approx 50 research articles. Honour: British Academy Research Award, 1995-96; American Library Association Choice of Theology Books, 1995. Membership: Society for the Study of Theology, president, 1999, 2000. Address: Department of Theology, University of Nottingham, University Park, Nottingham NG7 2RD, England.

THISTLETHWAITE Frank, b. 24 July 1915, Emeritus Professor. m. Jane Hosford, 1940, 2 sons, 1 dec, 3 daughters. Education: Exhibitioner and Scholar, St John's College, Cambridge; BA, 1st Class Honours, History, English Literature, 1938; Commonwealth Fund Fellow, University of Minnesota, 1938-40; MA, Cantab, 1941. Appointments: Editor, The Cambridge Review, 1937; British Press Service, New York, USA, 1940-41; Various university teaching positions; Founding Chancellor, 1961-80, Emeritus Professor, 1980-, University of East Anglia, Norwich, England; Visiting Scholar, various American universities. Publications: The Great Experiment: An Introduction to the History of the American People, 1955; The Anglo-American Connection in the Early Nineteenth Century, 1958; Dorset Pilgrims, 1989; A Lancashire Family Inheritance, 1996; Our War 1938-45, 1997. Contributions to: Books and history journals. Honours: Honorary LHD, Colorado, 1972; Honorary Fellow, RIBA, St John's College, Cambridge, 1974; Commander of the Order of the British Empire, 1979; Honorary DCL, University of East Anglia, 1980; Honorary Professor of History, University of Mauritius, 1981; Honorary ScD, University of Minnesota, 1994. Memberships: British Association of American Studies, founding chairman; Royal Historical Society, fellow. Address: 15 Park Parade, Cambridge CB5 8AL, England.

THOM James Alexander, b. 28 May 1933, Gosport, Indiana, USA. Novelist. m. Dark Rain, 20 May 1990. Education: AB, Butler University, Indianapolis, 1961. Appointments: Reporter and Columnist, The Indianapolis Star, 1961-67; Lecturer in Journalism, Indiana University, 1978-80. Publications: Spectator Sport, 1978; Long Knife, 1979; Follow the River, 1982; From Sea to Shining Sea, 1984; Staying Out of Hell, 1985; Panther in the Sky, 1989; The Children of First Man, 1994; The Spirit of the Place, 1995; Indiana II, 1996; The Red Heart, 1997. Contributions to: Magazines. Honour: Honorary DHL, Butler University, 1995. Memberships: Authors Guild; Western Writers of America. Address: 10061 West Stogsdill Road, Bloomington, IN 47404, USA.

THOMANECK Jürgen (Karl Albert), b. 12 June 1941, Stettin, Germany. Professor in German; Writer. m.

Guinevere Ronald, 3 Aug 1964, 2 daughters. Education: University of Tübingen, 1962; Dr phil, University of Kiel, 1966; MEd, University of Aberdeen. Appointments: Lecturer, 1969-88, Senior Lecturer in German, 1988-92, Professor, 1992-, University of Aberdeen. Publications: Deutsches Abiturienten Lexikon, 1974; Fremdsprachenunterricht und Soziolinguistik, 1981; Police and Public Order in Europe, 1985; The German Democratic Republic, 1989; Plenzdorf's Die Neuen Leiden des Jungen W, 1991. Contributions to: Learned journals. Membership: Royal Society for the Arts, fellow. Address: 17 Elm Place, Aberdeen AB25 3SN, Scotland.

THOMAS Audrey (Grace), b. 17 Nov 1935, Binghamton, New York, USA. Author; Dramatist. m. Ian Thomas, div 3 daughters. Education: BA, Smith College, 1957; MA, University of British Columbia, 1963. Appointments: Various visiting lectureships and writer-in-residence; Visiting Professor, Concordia University, 1989-90, Dartmouth College, 1994. Publications: Ten Green Bottles, 1967; Mrs Blood, 1970; Munchmeyer, and Prospero on the Island (2 short novels), 1972; Songs My Mother Taught Me, 1973; Blown Figures, 1975; Ladies and Escorts, 1977; Latakia, 1979; Two in the Bush and Other Stories, 1980; Real Mothers, 1981; Intertidal Life, 1984; Goodbye Harold, Good Luck, 1986; The Wild Blue Yonder, 1990; Graven Images, 1993; Coming Down From Wa, 1995. Other: Various plays for the CBC. Honours: Governor-General's Award in Fiction Nomination, 1985; Canada-Scotland Literary Fellow, 1985-86; British Columbia Book Prizes, 1985, 1991; Canada-Australia Literary Prize, 1990; Honorary doctorates, Simon Fraser University and University of British Columbia, 1994; Hawthornden Fellow, Scotland, 1994. Memberships: Amnesty International; PEN; Writers' Guild of Canada; Writers Union of Canada. Address: RR 2, Galiano, British Columbia V0N 1P0, Canada.

THOMAS Danielle Antoinette. See: **SMITH Danielle Antoinette Thomas.**

THOMAS David Arthur, b. 6 Feb 1925, Wanstead, England. Writer. m. Joyce Irene Petty, 3 Apr 1948, 1 daughter. Education: Northampton Polytechnic, 1948-53. Publications: With Ensigns Flying, 1958; Submarine Victory, 1961; Battle of the Java Sea, 1968; Crete 1941: The Battle at Sea, US edition as Nazi Victory, 1972; Japan's War at Sea, 1978; Royal Admirals, 1982; Compton Mackenzie: A Bibliography, 1986; Companion to the Royal Navy, 1988; Illustrated Armada Handbook, 1988; The Atlantic Star, 1990; Christopher Columbus, Master of the Atlantic, 1991; Churchill: The Member for Woodford, 1995; Queen Mary and the Cruiser: The Curacoa Disaster, 1997; Battles and Honours of the Royal Navy, 1998. Membership: Royal Society of Arts, fellow. Address: Cedar Lodge, Church Lane, Sheering, Bishop's Stortford, Hertfordshire CM22 7NR, England.

THOMAS Donald Michael, b. 27 Jan 1935, Redruth, Cornwall, England. Poet; Writer; Translator. 2 sons, 1 daughter. Education: BA, 1st Class Honours, English, MA, New College, Oxford. Appointment: Lecturer, Hereford College of Education, 1964-78. Publications: Poetry: Penguin Modern Poets 11, 1968; Two Voices, 1968; Logan Stone, 1971; Love and Other Deaths, 1975; The Honeymoon Voyage, 1978; Dreaming in Bronze, 1981; Selected Poems, 1983; Puberty Tree, 1992. Fiction: The Flute Player, 1979; Birthstone, 1980; The White Hotel, 1981; Ararat, 1983; Swallow, 1984; Sphinx, 1986; Summit, 1987; Lying Together, 1990; Flying into Love, 1992; Pictures at an Exhibition, 1993; Eating Pavlova, 1994. Translator: Requiem, and Poem Without a Hero, by Akhmatova, 1976; Way of All the Earth, by Akhmatova, 1979; The Bronze Horseman, by Pushkin, 1982. Address: The Coach House, Rashleigh Vale, Tregolis Road, Truro TR1 1TJ, England.

THOMAS Elizabeth Marshall, b. 13 Sept 1931, Boston, Massachusetts, USA. Writer. m. 14 Jan 1956, 1 son, 1 daughter. Education: AB, Radcliffe College, 1954; MA, George Washington University, 1980. Publications: The Hill People, 1953; The Harmless People, 1959; Warrior Herdsmen, 1966; Reindeer Moon, 1987; The Animal Wife, 1990; The Old Way, 1990; The Hidden Life of Dogs, 1993; The Tribe of Tiger: Cats and Their Culture, 1994; Certain Poor Shepherds, 1996. Contributions to: Journals. Honours: Brandeis University Creative Arts Award, 1968; PEN Hemingway Citation, 1988; Radcliffe College Alumni Recognition Award, 1989; Honorary DLitt, Franklin Pierce College, 1992. Memberships: PEN; Society of Women Geographers. Address: 80 East Mountain Road, Peterborough, NH 03458, USA.

THOMAS F(ranklin) Richard, b. 1 Aug 1940, Evansville, Indiana, USA. Professor of American Thought and Language; Poet; Writer. m. Sharon Kay Myers, 2 June 1962, 1 son, 1 daughter. Education: AB, 1963, MA, 1964, Purdue University; PhD, Indiana University, 1970. Appointments: Purdue University, 1969-70; Professor, Michigan State University, 1971-; Editor, Centering magazine, 1973-80; Research Associate, Indiana University, 1978-79. Publications: Poetry: Fat Grass, 1970; Alive with You This Day, 1980; Frog Praises Night: Poems with Commentary, 1980; Heart Climbing Stairs, 1986; Corolla, Stamen, and Style, 1986; The Whole Mustery of the Bregn, 1990; Miracles, 1996. Novel: Prism: The Journal of John Fish, 1992. Criticism: Literary Admirers of Alfred Stieglitz, 1983. Editor: Various books including: The Landlocked Heart: Poems from Indiana, 1980; Americans in Denmark: Comparisons of the Two Cultures by Writers, Artist, and Teachers, 1990. Contributions to: Numerous journals and magazines. Honours: Fulbright Awards, 1974, 1985; MacDowell Colony Fellowship, 1979; Michigan Council for the Arts Award, 1990; National Writing Project Summer Institute Fellow, 1993. Address: 2113 La Mer Lane, Haslett, MI 48840, USA.

THOMAS Lee. See: **FLOREN Lee.**

THOMAS R(onald) S(tuart), b. 29 Mar 1913, Cardiff, Wales. Clergyman (Retired). Poet. m. (1) Mildred E Eldridge, dec 1991, 1 son, (2) Elisabeth A. Vernon, 1996. Education: BA, University of Wales, 1935; St Michael's College, Llandaff. Appointments: Ordained Deacon, 1936, Priest, 1937; Curate, Chirk, 1936-40, Hanmer, 1940-42; Rector, Manafon, 1942-54, Rhiw with Llanfaelrhys, 1972-78; Vicar, Eglwysfach, 1954-67, St Hywyn, Aberdaron, with St Mary, Bodferin, 1967-68. Publications: Poetry: Stones of the Field, Bread of Truth, 1963; Pieta, 1966; Not That He Brought Flowers, 1968; H'm, 1972; Selected Poems 1946-68, 1974; Laboratories of the Spirit, 1976; Frequencies, 1978; Between Here and Now, 1981; Later Poems 1972-82, 1983; Experimenting with an Amen, 1986; Welsh Airs, 1987; The Echoes Return Slow, 1988; Counterpoint, 1990; Mass for Hard Times, 1992; Collected Poems 1945-1990, 1993; No Truth with the Furies, 1995. Autobiography: Neb, 1985. Editor: A Book of Country Verse, 1961; Penguin Book of Religious Verse, 1963; Edward Thomas: Selected Poems, 1964; George Herbert: A Choice of Verse, 1967; A Choice of Wordsworth's Verse, 1971. Honours: Heinemann Award, Royal Society of Literature, 1956; Queen's Medal for Poetry, 1964; Cholmondeley Award, 1978. Address: Ty Main, Llanfrothen, Gwynedd, LL48 6SG, Wales.

THOMAS Rosie, (Janey King), b. 22 Oct 1947, Denbigh, Wales. Novelist. m. Caradoc King, 1975, 1 son, 1 daughter. Education: BA, St Hilda's College, Oxford, 1976. Publications: Love's Choice, 1982; Celebration, 1982; Follies, 1983; Sunrise, 1984; The White Dove, 1985; Strangers, 1986; Bad Girls, Good Women, 1988; A Woman of Our Times, 1990; All My Sins Remembered, 1991; Other People's Marriages, 1993; A Simple Life, 1996. Honour: Romantic Novel of the Year Award, Romantic Novelists Association, 1985. Address: c/o AP Watt Ltd, 20 John Street, London WC1, England.

THOMAS Victoria. See: **DE WEESE Thomas Eugene "Gene".**

THOMEY Tedd, b. 19 July 1920, Butte, Montana, USA. Journalist; Author. m. Patricia Natalie Bennett, 11 Dec 1943, 1 daughter. Education: BA, University of California, 1943. Appointments: Publicity Director, San Diego State College, 1941-42; Reporter, San Diego Union-Tribune, 1942; Reporter, Assistant Editorial Promotion Manager, San Francisco Chronicle, 1942-43, 1945-48; News Editor, Columnist, Long Beach Press Telegram, 1950-; Creative Writing Instructor, Long Beach City College; Guest Lecturer, University of Southern California; Consultant, 20th Century Fox Studios. Publications: And Dream of Evil, 1954; Jet Pilot, 1955; Killer in White, 1956; Jet Ace, 1958; I Want Out, 1959; Flight to Takla-Ma, 1961; The Loves of Errol Flynn, 1961; The Sadist, 1961; Doris Day (biography), 1962; All the Way, 1964; Hollywood Uncensored, 1965; Hollywood Confidential, 1967; The Comedians, 1970; The Glorious Decade, 1971; The Big Love (co-author), 1986; The Prodigy Plot, 1987. Plays: The Big Love (co-author), 1991; Immortal Images, 1996. Contributions to: Many magazines. Honours: 1st Place, Distinguished Newspaper Feature Writing, Theta Sigma Phi Journalism Society, 1952; Award, Best Front Page, California Newspaper Publishers. Address: 7228 Rosebay Street, Long Beach, CA 90808, USA.

THOMPSON Ernest Victor, b. 14 July 1931, London, England. Author. m. Celia Carole Burton, 11 Sept 1972, 2 sons. Publications: Chase the Wind, 1977; Harvest of the Sun, 1978; The Music Makers, 1979; Ben Restallick, 1980; The Dream Traders, 1981; Singing Spears, 1982; The Restless Sea, 1983; Cry Once Alone, 1984; Polrudden, 1985; The Stricken Land, 1986; Becky, 1988; God's Highlander, 1988; Lottie Trago, 1989; Cassie, 1990; Wychwood, 1991; Blue Dress Girl, 1992; Mistress of Polrudden, 1993; The Tolpuddle Woman, 1994; Ruddlemoor, 1995; Moontide, 1996; Cast of Shadows, 1997; Mud Huts and Missionaries, 1997; Cast No Shadows, 1998; Fires of Evening, 1998. Various books on Cornish and West Country subjects. Contributions to: Approximately 200 short stories to magazines. Honour: Best Historical Novel, 1976. Memberships: Society of Authors; West Country Writers Club, vice president; Cornwall Drama Association, patron; Mevagissey Male Choir, vice patron; Royal Society of Literature; Cornish Literary Guild, president, 1998. Address: Parc Franton, Pentewan, St Austell, Cornwall, England.

THOMPSON Jean (Louise), b. 1 Jan 1950, Chicago, Illinois, USA. Professor of English; Writer. Education: AB, English, University of Illinois, 1971. MFA, Creative Writing, Bowling Green State University, 1973. Appointments: Professor of English, University of Illinois, Urbana, 1973-; Teacher, Warren Wilson College MFA Program, 1988, 1989, 1990; Distinguished Visiting Writer, Wichita State University, 1991; Associate Professor, San Francisco State University, 1992-93. Publications: The Gasoline Wars, 1979; My Wisdom, 1982; Little Faces and Other Stories, 1984; The Woman Driver, 1985; Who Do You Love, 1999. Contributions to: Various anthologies, journals, and magazines. Honours: Illinois Arts Council Literary Awards, 1976, 1996; National Endowment for the Arts Fellowship, 1977; Guggenheim Fellowship, 1984; Pushcart Prize, 1995. Address: 203 Smith Road, Urbana, IL 61802, USA.

THOMPSON Judith (Clare Francesca), b. 20 Sept 1954, Montreal, Quebec, Canada. Dramatist; Screenwriter; Associate Professor of Drama. m. Gregor Duncan, 28 Oct 1983, 1 son, 3 daughters. Education: BA, Drama and English, Queen's University, 1976; Graduate, National Theatre School, 1979. Appointments: Many workshops and seminars; Associate Professor of Drama, University of Guelph. Publications: The Crackwalker, 1980; White Biting Dog, 1984; Pink, 1986; Tornado, 1987; I am Yours, 1987; The Other Side of the Dark, 1989; Lion in the Streets, 1992; Sled, 1997. Contributions to: Films, radio and television. Honours: Governor-General's Awards for Drama, 1984, 1989; Chalmers Awards, 1987, 1991; Toronto Arts Award, 1988; Nellie Award for Best Radio Drama, 1988. Address: c/o Great North Artists Management Inc, 350 Dupont Street, Toronto, Ontario M5R 1V9, Canada.

THOMPSON Julius Eric, b. 15 July 1946, Vicksburg, Mississippi, USA. Associate Profesor; Writer; Poet. Education: BS, Alcorn State University, Lorman,

Mississippi, 1969; MA, History, 1971, PhD, 1973, Princeton University. Appointments: Faculty, Jackson State University, Mississippi, 1973-80, Florida Memorial College, 1980-81, State University of New York at Albany, 1983-88, University of Rochester, New York, 1988-89; Associate Professor, Southern Illinois University, Carbondale, 1989-96, University of Missouri, Columbia, 1996-. Publications: Hopes Tide Up in Promises, 1970; Blues Said: Walk On, 1977; The Anthology of Black Mississippi Poets (editor), 1988; The Black Press in Mississippi, 1865-1985, 1993; Percy Greene and the Jackson Advocate: The Life and Times of a Radical Conservative Black Newspaperman, 1897-1977, 1994. Contributions to: Scholary journals and general periodicals. Honours: Danforth Award to Zimbabwe, 1987; National Endowment for the Humanities Fellowship, 1994. Memberships: Association for the Study of Afro-American Life and History; Mississippi Historical Society; Southern Black Cultural Alliance. Address: 2803 Yukon Drive, Columbia, MO 65202, USA.

THOMPSON Tom, (Eduarde Batarde), b. 21 Oct 1953, Parkes, New South Wales, Australia. Publisher; Writer. m. Elizabeth Butel, 20 Nov 1984, 1 daughter. Education: BA, Macquarie University. Appointments: Publisher, Australian Bicentennial Authority, 1984-, Literature, Angus & Robertson. Publications: Island Hotel Dreams, 1977; Neon Line, 1978; From Here, 1978; The View from Tinsel Town, 1985; Growing Up in the Sixties, 1986. Contributions to: Sydney Morning Herald; Australian; Australian Book Review; Age; National Times. Membership: Australian Society of Authors. Address: PO Box 157, Kings Cross, New South Wales 2011, Australia.

THOMSON Derick S(mith), (Ruaraidh MacThòmais), b. 5 Aug 1921, Stornoway, Isle of Lewis, Scotland. Retired Professor of Celtic; Poet; Writer. m. Carol Galbraith, 1952, 5 sons, 1 daughter. Education: MA, University of Aberdeen, 1947; BA, Emmanuel College, Cambridge, 1948. Appointments: Assistant in Celtic, University of Edinburgh, 1948-49; Lecturer in Welsh, 1949-56, Professor of Celtic, 1963-91, University of Glasgow; Editor, Gairm Gaelic Literary Quarterly, 1952-; Reader in Celtic, University of Aberdeen, 1956-63; Saltire Society, Honorable President, 1997; Scottish Poetry Library, Honorable President, 1999. Publications: An Dealbh Briste, 1951; Eadar Samhradh is Foghar, 1967; An Rathad Cian, 1970; The Far Road and Other Poems, 1971; An Introduction to Gaelic Poetry, 1974, new edition, 1990; Saorsa agus an Iolaire, 1977; Creachadh na Clarsaich, 1982; The Companion to Gaelic Scotland, 1983, new edition, 1994; European Poetry in Gaelic Translation, 1990; Smeur an Dochais, 1992; Gaelic Poetry in the Eighteenth Century, 1993; Meall Garbh/The Rugged Mountain, 1995; Mac Mhaighstir Alasdair, Selected Poems, 1996. Contributions to: Books, journals and magazines. Honours: Publication Awards, Scottish Arts Council, 1971, 1992; Ossian Prize, FVS Foundation, Hamburg, 1974; Saltire Scottish Book of the Year Award, 1983; Honorary DLitt, University of Wales, 1987, University of Aberdeen, 1994. Memberships: British Academy, fellow; Glasgow Arts Club; Scottish Gaelic Texts Society, president; The Royal Society of Edinburgh, fellow. Address: 15 Struan Road, Cathcart, Glasgow G44 3AT, Scotland.

THOMSON Edward. See: TUBB E(dwin) C(harles).

THOMSON Elizabeth (Mary), (Liz Thomson), b. 12 Sept 1957, London, England. Writer; Editor. Education: BA, Honours, Music, University of Liverpool, 1979. Appointments: Associate Editor, Publishing News; Editor, Books; Numerous radio appearances, BBC and IBA. Publications: Conclusions on the Wall: New Essays on Bob Dylan, 1980; Folk Songs and Dances of England/Folk Songs and Dances of Scotland (arranger), 1982. With David Gutman: The Lennon Companion, 1987; The Dylan Companion, 1990; The Bowie Companion, 1993. Contributions to: Newspapers and journals including: Chic; Mojo; Times; Independent. Memberships: Society of Authors; National Union of Journalists; International Association for the Study of Popular Music; Charter 88; Labour Party. Address: 133

Birchwood Mansions, Furtis Green Road, London N10 3LX, England.

THOMSON June Valerie, b. 24 June 1930, Kent, England. Writer. divorced. 2 sons. Education: Bedford College University of London, England, 1949-51; BA, Honours, English. Publications: Not One of Us, 1972; Deadly Relations, 1979; Sound Evidence, 1984; No Flowers By Request, 1987; The Spoils of Time, 1989; The Secret Files of Sherlock Holmes, 1990; The Secret Chronicles of S H, 1992; Flowers for the Dead, 1992; The Secret Journals of S H, 1993; A Study in Friendship, 1995; Burden of Innocence, 1996. Contributions to: Several short stories to various anthologies including Ellery Queen Magazine, Winter's Crimes and CWA Anthology. Honour: Le Prix du Roman d'Aventures, 1983. Memberships: CWA, Committee Member; SWWJ, Council Member; Detection Club. Literary Agent: Michael Shaw, Curtis Brown. Address: 177 Verulam Road, St Albans, Herts AL3 4DW, England.

THORBURN James Alexander, b. 24 Aug 1923, Martins Ferry, Ohio, USA. Professor of English and Linguistics Emeritus; Writer; Poet; Translator. m. (1) Lois McElroy, 3 July 1954, 1 son, 1 daughter, (2) June Yingling, 18 Apr 1981. Education: BA, 1949, MA, 1951, Ohio State University; PhD, Linguistics, Louisiana State University, 1977. Appointments: Instructor in English, Louisiana State University, 1961-70; Professor of English and Linguistics, 1970-89, Professor Emeritus, 1989-, Southeastern Louisiana University. Contributions to: Many anthologies, journals, and periodicals. Honours: Several. Memberships: Numerous professional organizations. Address: Southeastern Louisiana University, Hammond, LA 70402, USA.

THORDARSON Fridrik, b. 7 Mar 1928, Reykjavik, Iceland. Professor. m. Kirsten Tchack Abrahamsen, 27 Dec 1975. Education: Reykjavik Latin School, 1948; Cand Philol, University of Oslo, 1961. Appointments: Librarian University Library, Oslo, 1960-63; University Lecturer, Classics, University Bergen, 1964; University Oslo, 1965-; Senior Lecturer, 1975; Professor, 1994-. Publications: Articles on Iranian, Greek and Caucasian Linguistics and Culture; Publications in various periodicals; Icelandic translation of Greek Literature. Membership: Icelandic Writers' Association. Address: Eikskollen 15A, N-1345 Oesteraas, Norway.

THORGEIRSSON Arni Ibsen, (Arni Ibsen), b. 17 May 1948, Stykkisholmur, Iceland. Writer; Dramatist; Poet; Translator; Teacher. m. Hildur Kristjansdottir, 20 Feb 1971, 3 sons. Education: Teacher's Diploma, Icelandic Teachers Training College, 1971; BA, Honours, English and Drama, University of Exeter, England, 1975. Publications: Kom, 1975; Samuel Beckett (translator of prose, plays, and poems), 1987; Vort Skarda Lif, 1990. Other: Several plays. Contributions to: Reference books, anthologies, and periodicals. Honour: Prize for Writing, Icelandic Writers Fund, 1985. Memberships: Icelandic Playwrights Union, executive committee; Icelandic Writers Fund; Icelandic Writers Union. Address: Stekkjarkinn 19, 220 Hafnafjordur, Iceland.

THORNHILL Richard. See: POLLARD John.

THORNTON Margaret. See: POOLE Margaret Barbara.

THORNTON Margaret Rose, b. Australia. Professor of Law and Legal Studies. Education: BA, Honours, University of Sydney; LLB, University of New South Wales; LLM, Yale University. Appointment: Professor of Law and Legal Studies, La Trobe University. Publications: The Liberal Promise: Anti-Discrimination in Australia, 1990; Public and Private: Feminist Legal Debates, 1995; Dissonance and Distrust: Women in the Legal Profession, 1996. Contributions to: International Journal of the Sociology of Law; Journal of Law and Society; Australian Feminist Law Journal; International Journal of Discrimination and the Law; Moden Law Review. Honours: Academy of Social Sciences, Australia, (FASSA), fellow, 1998. Address: School of Law and

Legal Studies, La Trobe University, Bundoora, Victoria 3083, Australia.

THORPE David Richard, b. 12 Mar 1943, Huddersfield, England. Political Biographer. Education: BA, Honours, 1965, MA, 1969, Selwyn College, Cambridge. Appointment: Appointed Official Biographer of Lord Home of the Hirsel, 1990; New Authorised Biographer of Sir Anthony Eden, 1996. Publications: The Uncrowned Prime Ministers: A Study of Sir Austen Chamberlain, Lord Curzon and Lord Butler, 1980; Selwyn Lloyd, 1989; Alec Douglas-Home, 1996. Contributions to: The Blackwell Biographical Dictionary of British Political Life in the 20th Century, 1990; The New Dictionary of National Biography, 1998. Memberships: Johnson Club; United Oxford and Cambridge University Club; St Antony's College, Oxford, Alistair Horne Fellow, 1997-98; Brasenose College, Oxford, Senior Member, 1998-. Address: Brasenose College, Oxford OX1 4AJ, England.

THORPE Dobbin. See: DISCH Thomas M.

THORPE Marie Louise, b. 1 Oct 1949, East London, South Africa. Writer; Tutor; Teacher. m. James Thorpe. Education: BA, Honours, Philosophy, University of Natal, 1974. Appointments: Demonstrator, Lecturer, 1973-74; Librarian, 1975; Teacher for the Handicapped, 1980-82; Tutor, Writing School. Publications: Write From the Begining, 1987; From Gladiators to Clowns, 1988; Aesops Fables Retold, 1988; Lucy's Games, 1992; Limbo Land, 1996. Honours: Several. Literary Agent: Francis Bond. Address: 201 Premier Court, 200 Umbilo Road, Durban, South Africa.

THRING Meredith Wooldridge, b. 17 Dec 1915, Melbourne, Victoria, Australia. Professor of Engineering. m. 14 Dec 1940, 2 sons, 1 daughter. Education: BA, 1st Class Honours, Physics, Trinity College, Cambridge, 1937; ScD, Cambridge, 1964. Publications: Man, Machines and Tomorrow, 1973; Machines: Master or Slaves of Man?, 1973; How to Invent, 1977; The Engineer's Conscience, 1980, reprinted, 1992; Robots and Telechirs, 1983; Quotations from G I Gurdjieff's Teaching, 1998. Contributions to: More than 150 scientific and technical articles to journals. Memberships: Fellow, Royal Academy of Engineering, Institution of Electrical Engineers, Institution of Mechanical Engineers, Institute of Physics, and Institution of Chemical Engineers; Senior Fellow, Institute of Energy, president, 1962-63. Address: Bell Farm, Brundish, Suffolk IP13 8BL, England.

THUBRON Colin Gerald Dryden, b. 14 June 1939, London, England. Writer. Publications: Mirror to Damascus, 1967; The Hills of Adonis: A Quest in Lebanon, 1968; Jerusalem, 1969; Journey Into Cyprus, 1975; The God in the Mountain (novel), 1977; Emperor (novel), 1978; The Venetians, 1980; The Ancient Mariners, 1981; The Royal Opera House Covent Garden, 1982; Among the Russians, 1983; A Cruel Madness, 1984; Behind the Wall: A Journey Through China, 1987; Falling, 1989; Turning Back the Sun, 1991; The Lost Heart of Asia, 1994; Distance (novel), 1996. Contributions to: Times; Times Literary Supplement; Independent; Sunday Times; Sunday Telegraph; New York Times; Granta. Honours: Fellow, Royal Society of Literature, 1969; Silver Pen Award, 1985; Thomas Cook Award, 1988; Hawthornden Prize, 1989. Membership: PEN. Address: Garden Cottage, 27 St Ann's Villas, London W11 4RT, England.

THUN Martha Sophie Nyota, b. 7 June 1925, Nordhausen, Germany. Scholar. m. Ferdinand Thun, 25 Nov 1949, 1 son, 2 daughters. Education: DPhil, Humboldt University, Berlin, 1955; DSc, 1973, Professor, 1977, Academy of Sciences, Berlin. Appointments: Interpretator, Translator, Reader, University of Berlin; Redactor, Assistant, Collaborator, University Academy of Sciences, Berlin. Publications: Das erste Jahrzehnt. Literatur und Kulturrevolution in der Sowjetunion, 1973; Krieg und Literatur, 1977; Pushkinbilder. Bulgakow, Tynjanow, Platonow, Soschtschenko, Zwetajewa, 1984; Adressatenwechsel. Literarische Kommunikation in Sowjetrubland 1917-1930, 1987; Majakowski - Maler und

Dichter. Studien zur Werkbiographie 1912-1922, 1993. Contributions to: Zeitschrift für Slawistik, Berlin; Weimarer Beiträge, Berlin; Sinn und Form, Berlin. Address: Fischerinsel 2, 9.06, D-10179 Berlin, Germany.

THURGOOD Nevil, (Walter Plinge), b. 29 Dec 1919, Stansted Mountfitcher, Essex. Self Employed Actor; Director; Writer. m. Eva Mary Hopper, 23 Aug 1941, 4 sons. Education: Technical College Certificate, 1936. Publications: The Furtive Fortunes of Fickle Fate and Sir Jaspers Revenge, 1984; Good Evening Ladies & Gentlemen, 1988; Sleeping Beauty, unpublished; Thurgood, A family history, private publication. Memberships: Actors Equity, life member; Australian Writers Guild; British Music Hall Society. Address: The Croft, 329 Mount Macedon Road, Mount Macedon, Victoria 3441, Australia.

THWAITE Ann, b. 4 Oct 1932, London, England. Writer. m. Anthony Thwaite, 4 Aug 1955, 4 daughters. Education: MA, DLitt, Oxford University (St Hilda's College). Appointments: Visiting Professor, Tokyo Women's University; Contributing Editor, Editorial Board, Cricket Magazine (US). Publications: Waiting for the Party: The Life of Frances Hodgson Burnett; Edward Birze: A Literary Landscape; A A Milne: His Life; Emily Tennyson: The Poet's Life. Contributions to: Occasional Contributor to: Times; Daily Telegraph; Independent. Honours: Duff Cooper Prize, 1985; Whitbread Biography Award, 1990. Memberships: Society of Authors; PEN. Address: The Mill House, Low Tharston, Norwich NR15 2YN, England.

THWAITE Anthony Simon, b. 23 June 1930, Chester, Cheshire, England. Poet; Critic; Writer; Editor. m. Ann Barbara Harrop, 4 Aug 1955, 4 daughters. Education: BA, 1955, MA, 1959, Christ Church, Oxford. Appointments: Visiting Lecturer in English, 1955-57, Japan Foundation Fellow, 1985-86, University of Tokyo; Producer, BBC, 1957-62; Literary Editor, The Listener, 1962-65, New Statesman, 1968-72; Assistant Professor of English, University of Libya, 1965-67; Henfield Writing Fellow, University of East Anglia, 1972; Co-Editor, Encounter, 1973-85; Visiting Professor, Kuwait University, 1974, Chairman of the Judges, Booker Prize, 1986; Director, 1986-92, Editorial Consultant, 1992-95, André Deutsch, Ltd; Poet-in-Residence, Vanderbilt University, 1992. Publications: Poetry: Home Truths, 1957; The Owl in the Tree, 1963; The Stones of Emptiness, 1967; Inscriptions, 1973; New Confessions, 1974; A Portion for Foxes, 1977; Victorian Voices, 1980; Poems 1953-1983, 1984, enlarged edition as Poems 1953-1988, 1989; Letter from Tokyo, 1987; The Dust of the World, 1994; Selected Poems, 1956-1996, 1997. Other: Contemporary English Poetry, 1959; Japan (with Roloff Beny), 1968; The Deserts of Hesperides, 1969; Poetry Today, 1973, 3rd edition, revised and expanded, 1996; In Italy (with Roloff Beny and Peter Porter), 1974; Twentieth Century English Poetry, 1978; Odyssey: Mirror of the Mediterranean (with Roloff Beny), 1981; Six Centuries of Verse, 1984. Editor: The Penguin Book of Japanese Verse (with Geoffrey Bownas), 1964; The English Poets (with Peter Porter), 1974; New Poetry 4 (with Fleur Adcock), 1978; Larkin at Sixty, 1982; Poetry 1945 to 1980 (with John Mole), 1983; Collected Poems of Philip Larkin, 1988; Selected Letters of Philip Larkin, 1992. Honours: Richard Hillary Memorial Prize, 1968; Fellow, Royal Society of Literature, 1978; Officer of the Order of the British Empire, 1990. Address: The Mill House, Low Tharston, Norfolk NR15 2YN, England.

TIBBER Robert. See: **FRIEDMAN Rosemary.**

TIBBER Rosemary. See: **FRIEDMAN Rosemary.**

TICKLE Phyllis A(lexander), b. 12 Mar 1934, Johnson City, Tennessee, USA. Writer. m. Dr Samuel M Tickle, 17 June 1955, 3 sons, 4 daughters. Education: BA, East Tennessee State University; MA, Furman University. Appointments: Poet-in-Residence, Memphis Brooks Museum, 1977-85; Director, St Lukes Press, 1975-89; Director, 1989-92. Director Emeritus, 1992-, Wimmer Companies; Religion Editor, Publishers Weekly, 1992-. Publications: The Story of Two Johns, 1976; American Genesis, 1976; On Beyong Koch, 1981; The City Essays, 1983; Selections, 1984; What the Heart Already Knows, 1985; Final Sanity, 1987; Ordinary Time, 1988; The Tickle Papers, 1989; Re-discovering the Sacred: Spirituality in America, 1995; My Father's Prayer: A Remembrance, 1995. Contributions to: Episcopalian; Tennessee Churchman; Dixie Flyer; Feminist Digest; 365 Meditations for Women, 1989; Disciplines, 1989. Honours: Individual Artists Fellowship in Literature, 1983; Book of Excellence Award, Body, Mind and Spirit Magazine, 1995. Memberships: Tennessee Literary Arts Association; Publishers Association of the South; Academy of Christian Editors, 1995-; Religion Newswriters Association, 1995-. Address: 3522 Lucy Road South, Lucy Community, Millington, TN 38053, USA.

TIEDE Tom (Robert), b. 24 Feb 1937, Huron, South Dakota, USA. Journalist; Author. 1 son, 1 daughter. Education: BA, Washington State University, 1959. Appointments: Senior Editor, National Correspondent, Newspaper Enterprise Association, the Scripps-Howard Syndicate; Publisher, "The News", Georgia. Publications: Your Men at War, 1966; Coward, 1968; Calley: Soldier or Killer?, 1970; Welcome to Washington, Mr Witherspoon, 1982; The Great Whale Rescue, 1986; American Tapestry, 1990; The Man Who Discovered Pluto, 1991; Fosser, 1994. Honours: Ernie Pyle Memorial Award for War Reporting; National Headlines Award for Feature Writing; Freedom's Foundation Award; George Washington Medal. Address: Mill Run Bourne, Box 1919, Richmond Hill, GA 31324, USA.

TIGAR Chad. See: **LEVI Peter.**

TIGHE Carl, b. 26 Apr 1950, Birmingham, England. Writer; Dramatist. Education: BA, Honours, English, 1973, MA, 1974, University College, Swansea; PDESL, University of Leeds, 1979. Publications: Little Jack Horner, 1985; Baku!, 1986; Gdansk: National Identity in the Polish-German Borderlands, 1990; Rejoice! and Other Stories, 1992; The Politics of Literature, 1999. Other: For BBC Radio: Day Out, 1994; Polish Poet, 1995; April Fool, 1996; The Politics of Literature, 1999. Contributions to: Anthologies and journals. Honours: Welsh Arts Council Literary Bursary, 1983; All London Drama Prize, 1987; British Council Travel Bursary, 1990; Short-listed, Irish Times First Fiction Prize, 1993. Membership: PEN; Welsh Academy; Welsh Union of Writers; Writers Guild. Address: 36 Oak Road, Withington, Manchester M20 9DA, England.

TILL Christa Maria, b. 23 Jan 1946, Vienna, Austria. Writer; Poet. m. Dr Hans Heinrich Schiesser, 27 Sept 1974. Education: PhD Studies, University of Vienna. Publications: David, David Supermann, 1986; E Wie Emma, 1989; Wiener Altwaren Vendetta, 1995. Contributions to: Rund um den Kreis, 1996. Honour: KOELA, 1978. Memberships: I G Autoren, Vienna; Swiss Writers Association. Address: Fehrenstrasse 12, CH-8032 Zürich, Switzerland.

TILLMAN Barrett, b. 24 Dec 1948, Pendleton, Oregon, USA. Writer. Education: Oregon State University, 1967-68; BS, Journalism, University of Oregon, 1971. Appointments: Founder-Publisher, Champlin Museums Press, 1982-87; Managing Editor, The Hook Magazine, 1986-89. Publications: The Dauntless Dive Bomber of World War II, 1976; Avenger at War, 1979; Corsair: The F4U in World War II and Korea, 1979; Hellcat: The F6F in World War II, 1979; On Yankee Station, 1987; Warriors, 1990; Pushing the Envelope: The Career of Fighter Ace and Test Pilot Marion Carl, 1994. Contributions to: Journals and magazines. Honours: US Air Force Historical Foundation Writing Award, 1981; Captain Emile Louis Bonnot Award for Lifetime Achievement in Naval Writing, Naval Order of the United States, 1994; Admiral Arthur W Radford Award for Naval History and Literature, 1994. Memberships: Association of Naval Aviation; Conference of Historic Aviation Writers, founder; Tailhook Association; US Naval Institute, life member. Address: Box 567, Athena, OR 97813, USA.

TIMMERMANN Thomas J, b. 23 June 1962, Los Angeles, California, USA. Journalist. m. Carol A Needham, 23 July 1994. Education: BS, Economics, 1984, BS, Communication Studies, 1984, University of California at Los Angeles. Appointments: College Basketball Writer, Los Angeles Herald Examiner, 1986-89; International Soccer Writer, College Sports Writer, 1989-94, Deputy Sports Editor, 1992-94, Los Angeles Daily News; International Soccer Writer, Assignment Editor, St Louis Post-Dispatch, 1994-. Honours: Best News Story 2nd Place, APSE, 1990; Best Feature 3rd Place, Missouri Press Association. Address: 900 North Tucker Boulevard, St Louis, MO 63101, USA.

TINDALL Gillian Elizabeth, b. 4 May 1938, London, England. Novelist; Biographer; Historian. m. Richard G Landown, 1 son. Education: BA, 1st Class, MA, University of Oxford. Publications: Novels: No Name in the Street, 1959; The Water and the Sound, 1961; The Edge of the Paper, 1963; The Youngest, 1967; Someone Else, 1969; Fly Away Home, 1971; The Traveller and His Child, 1975; The Intruder, 1979; Looking Forward, 1983; To the City, 1987; Give Them All My Love, 1989; Spirit Weddings, 1992; Celestine, 1996. Short stories: Dances of Death, 1973; The China Egg and Other Stories, 1981. Biography: The Born Exile on George Gissing, 1974; Journey of a Lifetime and Other Stories, 1990. Non-Fiction: A Handbook on Witchcraft, 1965; The Fields Beneath, 1977; City of Gold: The Biography of Bombay, 1981, 2nd edition, 1992; Rosamund Lehmann, an Appreciation, 1985; Countries of the Mind: The Meaning of Place to Writers, 1991; Celestine: Voices from a French Village, 1995. Contributions to: Newspapers and journals. Honours: Somerset Maugham Award, 1972; Enid McLead Prize, 1985; France - British Soc Award, 1995. Memberships: Royal Society of Literature, fellow; PEN; Royal Society of Arts, fellow. Address: c/o Curtis Brown Ltd, 28/29 Haymarket, London SW1Y 4SP, England.

TINNISWOOD Peter, b. 21 Dec 1936, Liverpool, England. Writer; Dramatist. Publications: A Touch of Daniel, 1969; Mog, 1970; I Didn't Know You Cared, 1973; Except You're a Bird, 1974; Tale from a Long Room, 1981-82; The Brigadier Down Under, 1983; The Brigadier in Season, 1984; Call it a Canary, 1985; The Village Fete; The Brigadier and Uncle Mort; Radio and television plays. Honours: Best First Novel of the Year, 1969; Book of the Month Choice, 1969; Winfred Holiby Award, 1974; Sony Award for Radio, 1987; Giles Cooper Award, 1987; Writers Guild Comedy Award, 1991. Membership: Royal Society of Literature. Address: c/o Jonathan Clowes Agency, Ironbride Bridge House, Bridge Approach, London NW1 8BD, England.

TIPTON David John, b. 28 Apr 1934, Birmingham, England. Poet; Writer; Editor; Translator; Teacher. m. (1) Ena Hollis, 10 June 1956, (2) Glenys Tipton, Feb 1975, 2 sons, 3 daughters. Education: Certificate of Education, Saltley College, 1959; University of Essex, 1976-77. Appointments: Editor, Rivelin Press, 1974-84, Redbeck Poems, 1984-93. Publications: Peru: The New Poetry (translator), 1970-76; Millstone Grit, 1972, new edition, 1993; At Night the Cats, by Antonio Cisneros (translator), 1985; Nomads and Settlers, 1980; Wars of the Roses, 1984; Turning to Alcohol, Horses or Dreams of Travel, 1991; Green and Purple, 1993; Crossing the Rimac - The South American Poems, 1995; Path Through the Canefields (translation of José Watanabe), 1997; Family Chronicle, poetry, 1997; Amulet Against the Evil Eye, 1997. Contributions to: Various publications. Address: 24 Aireville Road, Frizinghall, Bradford BD9 4HH, England.

TIRBUTT Honoria, (Emma Page), Author. Publications: In Loving Memory, 1970; Family and Friends, 1972; A Fortnight by the Sea, 1973, US edition as Add a Pinch of Cyanide; Element of Chance, 1975; Missing Woman, 1980; Every Second Thursday, 1981; Last Walk Home, 1982; Cold Light of Day, 1983; Scent of Death, 1985; Final Moments, 1987; A Violent End, 1988; Deadlock, 1991; Mortal Remains, 1992; In the Event of My Death, 1994; Murder Comes Calling, 1995; Hard Evidence, 1996. Address: c/o The Crime Club, Harper

Collins Publishers, 77-85 Fulham Palace Road, London W6 8JB, England.

TIRION Wil, b. 19 Feb 1943, Breda, Netherlands. Uranographer; Graphic Artist. m. Cokkie van Blitterswijk, 23 Dec 1975, 1 son, 1 daughter. Education: High School, 1959; Famous Artists Schools, 1968; Self-taught, Uranography. Publications: Sky Atlas 2000.0, 1981; Bright Star Atlas 2000.0, 1989; Cambridge Star Atlas 2000.0, 1991. Co-author: Collins Guide to Stars and Planets, 1984, 2nd edition, 1993; Uranometria 2000.0, Vol I, 1987, Vol II, 1988; Monthly Sky Guide, 1987; Binocular Astronomy, 1992; The Southern Sky Guide, 1993. Contributions to: Books and journals. Honour: Dr J van der Bilt Prize, Netherlands, 1987. Memberships: NVWS (Dutch Organisation of Amateur Astronomers); British Astronomical Association. Address: Wisselspoor 221, 2908 AD Capelle A/D IJsell, Netherlands.

TJERRY Inge, b. 1 Aug 1939, Gentofte. Teacher. m. Ole Tjerry, 26 Dec 1960, 1 son, 3 daughters. Education: Jonstrup Seminarium, 2800 Lyngby, Denmark. Publications: En Sommer Med Sidse, Sofus Og Stoffer, 1998. Membership: Dansk Forfatterforening. Literary Agent: Branner Og Korch. Address: Norgesvej 6 3390 Hundested, Denmark.

TLALI Miriam (Masoli), b. 1933, Johannesburg, South Africa. Writer. Education: University of the Witwatersrand, Johannesburg. Publications: Muriel at Metropolitan, 1975; Amandla, 1980; Mihloti, 1984; Soweto Stories, 1989, reprinted as Footprints in the Quag: Stories and Dialogues from Soweto, 1989. Address: c/o Tony Peake Associates, 14 Grafton Crescent, London NW1 8SL, England.

TOBIN Maryl Elaine, (Meryl Brown Tobin), b. 26 Aug 1940, Melbourne, Victoria, Australia. Writer. m. Hartley Tobin, 6 Jan 1962, 2 sons, 1 daughter. Education: BA, 1961, DipEd, 1962, University of Melbourne. Publications: Puzzles Galore, 1978, new edition, 1993; More Puzzles Galore!, 1980, new edition, 1994; Carloads of Fun, 1983; Exploring Outback Australia, 1988; Puzzleways: Grammar and Spelling, 1990; Animal Puzzle Parade, 1991; Puzzle Round Australia, 1992; Puzzling Cats, 1994; Pets to Puzzle, 1995; Puzzles Ahoy?, 1995; Play with Words, 1996. Contributions to: Numerous publications. Honours: 7 awards. Memberships: Australian Society of Authors; Fellowship of Australian Writers; Society of Women Writers, Victoria Branch. Address: Ningan, Bass Highway, The Gurdies, Victoria, 1984, Australia.

TOFFLER Alvin (Eugene), b. 4 Oct 1928, New York, New York, USA. Author. m. Adelaide Elizabeth (Heidi) Farrell Toffler, 29 Apr 1950, 1 daughter. Education: BA, New York University. Appointments: Associate Editor, Fortune Magazine, 1959-61; Visiting Scholar, Russell Sage Foundation, 1969-70. Publications: (mostly in collaboration with Heidi Toffler): The Culture Consumers, 1964; The Schoolhouse in the City, 1968; Future Shock, 1970; The Futurists (editor), 1972; Learning for Tomorrow (editor), 1973; The Eco-Spasm Report, 1975; The Third Wave, 1980; Previews and Premises, 1983; The Adaptive Corporation, 1984; Power Shift, 1990; War and Anti-War, 1993; Creating a New Civilization, 1994-95. Contributions to: Newspapers, journals and magazines. Honours: Medal, President of Italy; Author of the Year, American Society of Journalists and Authors; Prix de Meilleur Livre Etranger; Officer de l'Ordre des Arts et Sciences; Honorary doctorates. Memberships: American Association for the Advancement of Science, fellow; American Society of Journalists and Authors; International Institute for Strategic Studies; World Future Studies Federation. Address: c/o Curtis Brown Ltd, 10 Astor Place, New York, NY 10003, USA.

TOFFLER Heidi, b. 1 Aug 1929, New York, New York, USA. Author. m. Alvin Toffler, 29 Apr 1950, 1 daughter. Education: BA, Long Island University. Publications: (with Alvin Toffler) The Culture Consumers, 1964; Future Shock, 1970; The Futurists (editor), 1972; Learning for Tomorrow (editor), 1973; The Third Wave, 1980; Previews and Premises, 1983; The Adaptive Corporation, 1984; Powershift, 1990; War and Anti-War, 1993; Creating a New Civilization, 1994-95. Contributions to: Newspapers, journals and periodicals. Honours: Medal, President of Italy; Honorary doctorates. Address: c/o Curtis Brown Ltd, 10 Astor Place, New York, NY 10003, USA.

TOLAND John (Willard), b. 29 June 1912, La Crosse, Wisconsin, USA. Historian; Author. m. (1) 2 daughters, (2) Toshiko Matsumura, 12 Mar 1960, 1 daughter. Education: BA, Williams College, 1936; Yale Drama School, 1936-37. Publications: Non-Fiction: Ships in the Sky, 1957; Battle: The Story of the Bulge, 1959; But Not in Shame, 1961; The Dillinger Days, 1963; The Flying Tigers, 1963; The Last 100 Days, 1966; The Battle of the Bulge, 1966; The Rising Sun, 1970; Adolf Hitler, 1976; Hitler: The Pictorial Documentary of His Life, 1978; No Man's Land, 1980; Infamy, 1982; In Mortal Combat, 1991; Captured by History, 1997. Fiction: Gods of War, 1985; Occupation, 1987. Honours: Best Book on Foreign Affairs Award, Overseas Press Club, 1961, 1970, 1976; Pulitzer Prize for Non-Fiction, 1970; Van Wyck Brooks Award for Non-Fiction, 1970; Honorary doctorates. Memberships: Accademia del Mediterraneo; Authors Guild; National Archives, advisory council; Western Front Association, honorary vice-president. Address: 101 Long Ridge Road, Danbury, CT 06810, USA.

TOLL Seymour I, b. 19 Feb 1925, Philadelphia, Pennsylvania, USA. Lawyer; Writer. m. Jean M Barth, 25 June 1951, 4 daughters. Education: BA, Yale College, 1948; LLB, Yale Law School, 1951. Appointments: Member, Philadelphia Bar, 1955-; Founding Member, Toll, Ebby, Langer and Marvin of Philadelphia, 1978-86; Lecturer in Law, University of Pennsylvania Law School, 1978-86; American College of Trial Lawyers; President, Library Company of Philadelphia, 1992-98. Publications: Zoned American, 1969; A Judge Uncommon. A Life of John Biggs Jr, 1993. Contributions to: New York Times Book Review. Honours: Several literary awards. Address: 453 Conshohocken State Road, Bala Cynwyd, PA 19004-2642, USA.

TOMALIN Claire, b. 20 June 1933, London, England. Author. m. (1) Nicholas Tomalin, dec 1973, (2) Michael Frayn, 5 children. Education: MA, Newnham College, Cambridge, 1954. Appointment: Literary Editor, New Statesman, 1974, The Sunday Times, London, 1980-85. Publications: The Life and Death of Mary Wollstonecroft, 1974; Shelley and His World, 1980; Parents and Children, 1981; Katherine Mansfield: A Secret Life, 1987; The Invisible Woman: The Story of Nelly Teran and Charles Dickens, 1990; The Winter Wife, 1991; Mrs Jordan's Professions, 1994; Jane Austin: A Biography, 1997. Honours: Whitbread First Book Prize, 1974; James Tait Black Memorial Prize, 1990; Hawthornden Prize, 1991; NCR Prize, 1991; Theatre Literary Award, New York 1995. Membership: PEN, vice-president, 1998. Address: 57 Gloucester Crescent, London NW1 7EG, England.

TOMASEVIC Bosko, b. 8 May 1947, Becej, Yugoslavia. Poet; Writer. m. (1) Rajka Gnjatic, 24 May 1975, div, 2 sons, (2) Vera Kureluk, 12 Mar 1995. Education: BA, 1972, MA, 1976, PhD, 1982, University of Belgrade. Appointment: Visiting Professor of Literary Theory, University of Nancy, 1990-92. Publications: Cartesian Passage, 1989; Watchman of the Times, 1990; Celan Studies, 1991; Repetition and Difference, 1992; Cool Memories, 1994; Live Coals, 1994; Landscape with Wittgenstein and Other Ruins, 1995; Open Space and Presence, 1995; Plan of the Return, 1996. Contributions to: Various publications. Memberships: Academy of Science, New York; European Academy of Sciences, Arts and Literature; International Comparative Literature Association; Martin Heidegger Association; PEN Club, France; Societe des Gens des Lettres de France. Address: 7/11 rue de St Lambert, Imb 4, Apt 422, F-5400 Nancy, France.

TOMASZEWSKA Marta, b. 10 Apr 1933, Warsaw, Poland. Author. Education: MA, University of Warsaw, 1956. Publications: Over 40 novels, 1974-96. Contributions to: Various publications. Honours: Polish Prime Minister's Award, 1981; Cross of the Order of Polonia Restituta, 1986; XII Premio Europeo di Litteratura Giuvanile-Lista d'Oneren Arrativa, 1988; Ibby Awards Certificate of Honour, 1988. Memberships: Association of Polish Writers: Polish Writers Union. Address: Natolinska 3 m 64, Warsaw 00-562, Poland.

TOMLINSON (Alfred) Charles, b. 8 Jan 1927, Stoke-on-Trent, Staffordshire, England. Professor of English Emeritus; Poet; Writer. m. 23 Oct 1948, 2 daughters. Education: BA, Queens' College, Cambridge; MA, London. Appointments: Lecturer, 1956-68, Reader, 1968-82, Professor of English, 1982-92, Professor Emeritus, 1992-, University of Bristol; Visiting Professor, University of New Mexico, 1962-63; O'Connor Professor, Colgate University, New York, 1967-68, 1989-90; Visiting Fellow of Humanities, Princeton University, 1981; Lamont Professor, Union College, New York, 1987. Publications: Poetry: Relations and Contraries, 1951; The Necklace, 1955; Seeing is Believing, 1958; A Peopled Landscape, 1963; American Scenes, 1966; The Poem as Initiation, 1968; The Way of a World, 1969; Written on Water, 1972; The Way In, 1974; The Shaft, 1978; Selected Poems, 1951-74, 1978; The Flood, 1981; Notes from New York, 1984; Collected Poems, 1985, enlarged edition, 1987; Annunciations, 1989; The Door in the Wall, 1992; Jubilation, 1995; Selected Poems 1955-97, 1997. Other: In Black and White, 1976; The Oxford Book of Verse in English Translation (editor), 1980; Some Americans: A Literary Memoir, 1981; Poetry and Metamorphosis, 1983; Eros Englished: Erotic Poems from the Greek and Latin (editor), 1991. Contributions to: Books, professional journals, and other publications. Honours: Bess Hokin Prize, 1956; Oscar Blumenthal Prize, 1960; Inez Boulton Prize, 1964; Frank O'Hara Prize, 1968; Cheltenham Poetry Prize, 1976; Cholmondeley Poetry Award, 1979; Wilbur Award for Poetic Achievement, 1982; Premio Europeo di Cittadella, Italy, 1991; Bennett Award for Poetry, 1992; Honorary doctorates. Memberships: Academic and literary organisations. Address: Brook Cottage, Ozleworth Bottom, Wotton-under-Edge, Gloucestershire GL12 7QB, England.

TOMLINSON Catherine Twaddle Dimond, b. 1 Mar 1917, Ipswich, Queensland, Australia. Home Economics Teacher; Author. m. (1) D J Linton, Jan 1944 (killed in action, 1945), (2) H F B Tomlinson, Dec 1950, 1 son, 1 daughter. Education: 3-year Trained Teacher, Queensland Education Department, 1934-36; Diploma, Domestic Science, Department of Public Instruction of Queensland, Technical Branch, 1942; BA, University of Queensland, St Lucia, Brisbane, 1987. Publications: Recipes with a Difference, 1962; Competitive Cookery, 1972; Successful Cookery, 1983. Contributions to: Journal of Home Economics Association, Australia; Queensland Home Economics Association magazine; A Centenary History of Home Economics Education in Queensland 1881-1981; History of South Brisbane College of Technical and Further Education, 1988; Home Economics Education 1881-1981. Honours: Listed in Who's Who of Australian Writers, 1991, 2nd edition, 1995; Australian Dictionary of Biography, 1993; International Authors and Writers Who's Who, 14th edition. Memberships: Australian Society of Authors; Alumni Association of the University of Queensland Inc; Standing Committee, Women's College, University of Queensland; Life Member, Ipswich (Queensland) Girls' Grammar School Old Girls' Association. Address: 12 Wiseman Street, Kenmore, Queensland 4069, Australia.

TOMLINSON Gerald (Arthur), b. 24 Jan 1933, Elmira, New York, USA. Writer; Editor; Publisher. m. (Mary) Alexis Usakowski, 19 Aug 1966, 2 sons. Education: BA, Marietta College, Ohio, 1955; Columbia Law School, New York City, 1959-60. Appointments: Associate Editor, Business and Professional Books, Prentice Hall, 1960-63, School Department, Harcourt Brace Jovanovich, 1963-66; Senior Editor, English Department, Holt, Rinehart and Winston, 1966-69; Executive Editor, K-12 English, Silver Burdett and Ginn, 1969-82; Publisher, Home Run Press, 1985-. Publications: On a Field of

Black (novel), 1980; School Administrator's Complete Letter Book, 1984; Baseball Research Handbook, 1987; Speaker's Treasury of Sports Anecdotes, Stories and Humor, 1990; Encyclopedia of Religious Quotations, 1991; The New Jersey Book of Lists (co-author), 1992; Murdered in Jersey, 1994; Fatal Tryst, 1999. Contributions to: Magazines and journals. Honours: Best Detective Stories of the Year, E.P. Dutton, 1976; Mystery Writers of America Annual Anthologies, 5 appearances, 1977-87. Memberships: Authors Guild; Mystery Writers of America; Society for American Baseball Research. Address: 19 Harbor Drive, Lake Hopatcong, NJ 07849, USA.

TOMLINSON Mary Teresa, b. 15 Aug 1935, England. Journalist. m. Noel Tomlinson, 15 Aug 1959, 1 son, 1 daughter. Education: Diplomas in English, Accountancy, and Economics. Appointments: Partner, Ays Press and Public Relations. Publications: Around the World in Cookery and Cakes, 1980; Wool on the Back (with Peter Taylor), 1987. Contributions to: Newspapers and journals. Honour: Nominee, Woman of Europe Award, 1990. Memberships: Chartered Institute of Journalists; Club of Rhodes, UK; Institute of Journalists; Society of Women Writers and Journalists. Address: Mayfield Cottage, 51 Ebington, near Campden, Gloucestershire GL55 6NQ, England.

TOOBIN Jeffrey Ross, b. 21 May 1960, New York, NY, USA. Writer; Legal Analyst. m. Amy B McIntosh, 31 May 1986, 1 son, 1 daughter. Education: AB, Harvard College, 1982; JD, Harvard Law School, 1986. Appointments: Law Clerk to Hon J Edward Lumburd, 1986-87; Associate Counsel, Office of Independent Counsel Lawrence E Walsh, 1987-89; Assistant US Attorney, Eastern District of New York, 1990-93; Staff Writer, The New Yorker, 1993-; Legal Analyst, ABC News, 1996-. Address: New Yorker, 20 W 43rd Street, New York, NY 10036, USA.

TOOMEY Jeanne Elizabeth, b. 22 Aug 1921, New York, New York, USA. Animal Activist; Writer. m. Peter Terranova, 28 Sept 1951, dec 1968, 1 son, 1 daughter. Education: Hofstra University, 1938-40; Fordham University, 1940-41; BA, Southampton College, 1976; Postgraduate Studies, Monmouth College, 1978-79. Appointments: Staff, Brooklyn Daily Eagle, 1943-52, King Features Syndicate, 1953-55, New York Journal-American, 1955-61, Associated Press, 1963-64, News Tribune, Woodbridge, New Jersey, 1976-86; Editor, Calexico Chronicle, California, 1987-88; President and Director, Last Post Animal Sanctuary, Falls Village, Connecticut, 1991-. Publications: How to Use Your Dreams to Solve Your Problems, 1970; Murder in the Hamptons, 1994. Contributions to: Various publications. Honour: Woman of the Year, New York Women's Press Club, 1960. Memberships: Newswomen's Club of New York; New York Press Club; Overseas Press Club. Address: 95 Belden Street, Falls Village, CT 06031, USA.

TOONA GOTTSCHALK Elin-Kai, b. 12 July 1937, Tallinn, Estonia. Writer; Poet; Dramatist. m. Donald Frederick Gottschalk, 9 Oct 1967, 1 son. Publications: Puuingel (novel), 1965; Lotukata (novel), 1968; Spielgas Sinise Kausi All (novel), 1973; In Search of Coffee Mountains (novel), 1977, UK, 1979; Lady Cavaliers, 1977; Pictures, and DP Camp Child; Poetry in Visions, 1988; Kalevikula Vimne Tutar, 1988; Kolm Valget Tuvi, 1992; BBC TV, Radio Plays and Short Stories, 1962-70. Contributions to: Reviews, quarterlies, journals, magazines, and Radio Liberty; Short stories for BBC, England. Honours: Many, including: 1st Prize, Writer's Review, London, 1966; H Visnapuu Literary Award, World Association of Estonians, 1966; Ennu Literary Prize, USA, 1968; 1st Prize, National Examiner Contest, 1983; 1st Prize for Non-Fiction and 2nd Prize for Photo Journalism, National League of American women; Lauri Literary Prize, 1993. Memberships: IBA, fellow; International PEN, Estonian Branch; International Platform Association; National League of American Pen Women; Various Estonian literary associations. Address: 27554 US 19 North, No 37, Clearwater, FL 33761, USA.

TOPALIAN Naomi Getsoyan, b. 26 Jan 1928, Beirut, Lebanon. Registered Nurse; Teacher. m. Paul G Topalian, 18 Sept 1953, 1 son, 1 daughter. Education: Diploma, American University Hospital School of Nursing, Beirut, 1952; BS, Boston University, 1967; Registered Nurse, Massachusetts. Appointments: Paediatric Nurse, Children's Medical Center, Boston, Massachusetts, USA, 1954-55; In-service Education Supervisor, Winchester Hospital, Massachusetts, 1967-70; Teacher of Nursing, North-East Vocational High School, Wakefield, Massachusetts, 1970-72; Medical and Surgical Nurse, various teaching hospitals, Boston, 1973-87. Publications: Dust To Destiny, 1986; People, Places and Moultonborough, 1989; Legacy of Honor, 1995. Address: 46 Circle Road, Lexington, MA 02420-2926, USA.

TOPOLSKI Daniel, b. 4 June 1945, London, England. Writer; Broadcaster. m. Susan Gilbert, 1 son, 2 daughters. Education: BA, Geography, Diploma Social Anthropology, MA, Geography, New College, Oxford, 1964-68. Publications: Muzungu: One Man's Africa, 1976; Travels with my Father: South America, 1983; Boat Race: The Oxford Revival, 1985; True Blue: The Oxford Mutiny, 1988; Henley: The Regatta, 1989. Contributions to: Telegraph; Times; 'You' Magazine; Hello; Radio Times; Tatler; Vogue; Life; Madamoiselle; Daily Mail; Observer; Evening Standard; BBC; Broadcaster TV and Radio, Sport and Travel. Honours: Sports Book of the Year, 1990; Radio Travel Program of the Year, 1994. Memberships: Churchill Fellow; Royal Geographical Society, fellow; Henley Steward; Leander Club; London RC. Address: 69 Randolph Avenue, London W9 1DW, England.

TOPSOE Vilhelm, b. 20 July 1944, Copenhagen, Denmark. Lawyer. m. Elisabeth, 12 Dec 1981, 2 daughters. Education: Cand juris, 1968. Publications: Dømt, 1973; SR II, 1975; To Familier, 1980; De Sorte Fugle, 1984. Plays: Om Harriet, 1987; Svampejagten, 1995; Pastor Munk, 1998. Contributions to: Berlingske Tidende; Weekend-Avisen. Address: Rosenvaengets Sidealle 3, DK 2100 Copenhagen 0, Denmark.

TOR Regina. See: DE CORMIER Regina.

TORANSKA Teresa, b. 1 Jan 1946, Wolkowysk, Poland. Journalist. m. Leszek Sankowski, 17 Jan 1989. Education: MA, Law, 1969, Journalism, 1972, Warsaw University, Poland. Appointment: Visiting Scholar, Harvard University, USA, 1989. Publications: Europa Za 100 Dolarow (Europe for a $100), 1975; Widziane Z Dolu (View from the Bottom), 1979; Oni (Them), 1986; My (We), 1994. Contributions to: Periodicals and television. Memberships: Association of Polish Authors; International Federation of Journalists. Literary Agent: Leszek Sankowski. Address: Zywnego 12/102, 02-701 Warsaw, Poland.

TORON Steve. See: STEBEL Sidney Leo.

TORRANCE Lee. See: SADGROVE Sidney Henry.

TORRANCE Thomas F(orsythe), b. 30 Aug 1913, Chengdu, China. Minister of Religion; Professor of Theology. m. Margaret Edith Spear, 2 Oct 1946, 2 sons, 1 daughter. Education: MA, 1934; BRD, 1937; DrTheol, 1946; DLitt, 1971. Appointments: Founder-Editor, Journal of Theology, 1948-88; Moderator, General Assembly, Church of Scotland, 1976-77. Publications: The Doctrine of Grace, 1949; Calvin's Doctrine of Man, 1949; Kingdom and Church, 1956; Conflict and Agreement in the Church, 2 volumes, 1959-60; Theology in Reconstruction, 1965; Theological Science, 1969; God and Rationality, 1971; Theology in Reconciliation, 1975; Space, Time and Resurrection, 1976; Space, Time and Incarnation, 1979; The Ground and Grammar of Theology, 1980; Christian Theology and Scientific Culture, 1980; Divine and Contingent Order, 1981; Reality and Scientific Theology, 1984; The Hermenentics of John Calvin, 1987; The Trinitarian Faith, 1988; The Christian Frame of Mind, Reason, Order and Openness in Theology and Natural Science, 1989; Karl Barth, Biblical and Evangelical Theological Theologian, 1990; Senso del divino e scienza

mnoderna, 1992; Theological Dialogue between Orthodox and Reformed Churches (editor), 1993; Royal Priesthood, 1993; Divine Meaning: Studies in Patristic Hermeneutics, 1994; Trinitarian Perspectives: Toward Doctrinal Agreement, 1994; The Christian Doctrine of God, One Being Three Persons, 1996; Scottish Theology: From John Knox to John McLeod Campbell, 1996. Contributions to: Numerous publications. Honours: Honorary doctorates; Honorary DD, Edinburgh, 1996. Memberships: British Academy; International Academy of Religious Sciences, president, 1972-81; International Academy of the Philosophy of Sciences; Center of Theological Inquiry, Princeton, New Jersey; Royal Society of Edinburgh. Address: 37 Braid Farm Road, Edinburgh EH10 6LE, Scotland.

TORRES Ana Teresa, b. 6 July 1945, Caracas, Venezuela. Writer. m. Gaston Carvallo, 10 Jan 1975, 1 son, 1 daughter. Education: Psychology degree, 1968; Clinical psychology diploma, 1973; Psychoanalyst diploma, 1982. Appointment: Residence, Bellagio Center, Rockefeller Foundation, 1999. Publications: Novels: El Exilio del Tiempo, 1990; Dona Ines contra el Olvido, 1992; Vagas Desapariciones, 1995; Malena de cinco mundos, 1997. Other: El Amor como sintoma (essay), 1993; Elegir la Neurosis (essay), 1992; Territorios Eroticos (essay), 1998. Contributions to: Imagen; Venezuela Literary Journal; Inti. Honours: Municipal, 1992; Narrativa, 1992; Picon-Salas, 1992; Pegasus Prize for Literature, Mobil Corporation, 1998. Address: POBA International 1-20034, PO Box 02-5255, Miami, FL 33102, USA.

TÔRRES Luiz Rebouças, (OVNI, Rebouças, Tôrres), b. 13 Dec 1948, Ibicuipeba, Ceará, Brazil. Language Teacher; Simultaneous Interpreter; Translator; Writer. Education: Scholarship, Bates College, Lewiston, Maine, USA, 1970-72; Graduated, Letters Course, English, Portuguese, Federal University of Rio Grande do Norte-UFRN, 1994; Law School, Federal University of Pernambuco; Currently studying Journalism, UFRN. Appointments: Teacher of English, Portuguese and Spanish; Simultaneous Interpreter of English and Portuguese, Brazil, and Africa, 1977; Translator of English and Portuguese; Writer; Artist; Painter; Poet; Ufologist; Lecturer; Polyglot; Zine Writer; Politician; Various appearances on Brazilian radio and television. Publications: OVNI, um ET Diferente, de Betaflex para a Terra, 1992; Ufology, 1993; Um Dia, a Poesia (participant), book and video by Ayres Marques, 1996; Informe OVNI, zine. Contributions to: Poems, in newspapers Hora do Povo, 1980, Jornal de Natal, 1996; Articles in Brazilian and international press. Honours: 1st Place, Graduation Class in Letters Course, UFRN, 1994; Distinguished Finalist, 3rd Place for Ufologist Short Story, Poetry and Short Story Contest, Argentina, 1996; 1st Place, Teacher of English Contest, Parnamirim, Rio Grande do Norte, Brazil, 1997. Address: Caixa Postal 2655, Natal, RN 59022-970, Brazil.

TORRES Tereska. See: LEVIN Torres.

TOURCHINA Galine Petrovna, b. 15 Oct 1937, Moscow, Russia. Phylologist. m. Igor A Tourchine, 4 Aug 1958, 2 sons. Education: Diploma, Moscow First Pedagogical College named after Ushinsky, 1958; BA, Moscow State University named after Lomonosov, 1967. Appointments: Russian Language Teacher at secondary school, 1958-62; Editor and Compiler, Pravda Publishing House, 1967-87; Editor-in-Chief, Lazure Publishing House and journals Svirelka, Svirel and Lazure. Publications: Warm Indian Summer in Moscow, collection of short stories, 1986; Raven's Tales, 1992; Two Persons Met, stories, 1993; Hello Trees, eight women's plays, 1998; TV show scripts: Fedor Shaliapine, 1969; Maria Bashkirtseva, 1987; Tsar Peter the Third, 1988. Contributions to: Stories for children in Svirel, 1994-98; Mercy and Justice, play in Lazure, 1988; Shaliapine's Green Years, essay, 1998. Honour: Nikolav Ostrovsky Literary Award, 1986. Literary Agent: Igor A Tourchine. Address: Kolomenskaya Str 9, Moscow 115142, Russia.

TOURNIER Michel (Edouard), b. 19 Dec 1923, Paris, France. Author. Education: Sorbonne, University of Paris; University of Tubingen. Publications: Vendredi ou les limbes de Pacifique, 1967; Le Roi des Aulnes, 1970; Les météores, 1975; Le vent paraclet, 1977; Le coq de bruyère, 1978; Des clefs et des serrures, 1979; Gaspard, Melchior et Balthazar, 1980; Le vol du Vampire, 1981; Gilles et Jeanne, 1983; La Goutte d'Or, 1986; Le Tabor et le Sinaï, 1989; Le Médianoche amoureux, 1989; Le Crépuscule des masques, 1992; Le Miroir des Idées, 1994; Le Pied de la lettre, 1994; La Couleuvrine, 1994; Les Pieds de la lettre, 1996; Eléazar, 1996; Célébrations, 1999. Honours: Grand Prix du roman, Academie Française, 1967; Prix Goncourt, 1970. Memberships: Academie Goncourt; Officier, Légion d'honneur; Commandeur, Ordre nationale du Mérite. Address: Le presbytère, Choisel, 78460 Chevreuse, France.

TOWNLEY Roderick Carl, b. 7 June 1942, New Jersey, USA. Writer; Poet. m. Wyatt Townley, 15 Feb 1986, 1 son, 1 daughter. Education: AB, Bard College; PhD, Rutgers University, 1972. Appointments: Professor of English, Universidad de Conception, Chile, 1978-79; National Editorial Writer, TV Guide, 1980-89; Senior Editor, US magazine, 1989-90; Executive Director, The Writers Place, Kansas City, Missouri, 1995-96. Publications: Blue Angels, Black Angels (poems), 1972; The Early Poetry of William Carlos Williams, 1975; Minor Gods (novel), 1977; Three Musicians (poems), 1978; Final Approach (poems), 1986. Contributions to: Newspapers and journals. Honours: Co-Winner, 1969, 1st Prize, 1971, Academy of American Poets; Finalist, Yale Series of Younger Poets, 1976; Fulbright Professorship, Chile, 1978-79. Address: PO Box 13302, Shawnee Mission, KS 66282, USA.

TOWNLEY Wyatt, b. 20 Sept 1954, Kansas City, Missouri, USA. Poet; Journalist; Teacher. m. Roderick Carl Townley, 15 Feb 1986, 1 daughter. Education: BFA, Dance, Purchase College, State University of New York, 1977; North Carolina School of the Arts. Appointments: Co-Artistic Director, Dancers' Portfolio, New York, 1976-80; Poetry Editor, The Newspaper, Brooklyn, New York, 1988-90; Co-Editor, The Keep triquarterly, Kansas City, Missouri, 1992-94. Publication: Perfectly Normal, 1990. Contributions to: Reviews and quarterlies. Honours: First Presidential Award for Outstanding Achievement, Purchase College, State University of New York, 1977; Finalist, Yale Series of Younger Poets, 1989. Memberships: Academy of American Poets; Society of Children's Book Writers and Illustrators; The Writers Place, board of governors. Address: PO Box 13302, Shawnee Mission, KS 66282, USA.

TOWNSEND John Rowe, b. 10 May 1922, Leeds, Yorkshire, England. Author and Critic. m. Vera Lancaster, 3 July 1948, dec 9 May 1973, 1 son, 2 daughters. Education: BA, 1949, MA, 1954, Emmanuel College, Cambridge. Appointments: Sub-Editor, 1949-54, Art Editor, 1954-55, Manchester Guardian; Editor, 1955-59, Children's Book Editor (part-time), 1968-78, Columnist, 1968-81, Manchester Guardian Weekly; Permanent Visiting Faculty Member, Center for Children's Literature, Simmons College, 1978-84; Several visiting lectureships. Publications: Written for Children: An Outline of English-Language Children's Literature, 1965, 16th edition, revised, 1995; A Sense of Story: Essays on Contemporary Writers for Children, 1971; A Sounding of Storytellers: New and Revised Essays on Contemporary Children's Writers, 1979. Other: 10 children's books, 1961-86; 17 young adult's books, 1963-92. Contributions to: Books and periodicals. Honours: Silver Pen Award, English PEN, 1969; Christopher Award, USA, 1982; Edgar Allan Poe Award, 1982. Memberships: British Society of Authors; Children's Writers Group, chairman, 1975-76, 1990-91. Address: 72 Water Lane, Histon, Cambridge CB4 9LR, England.

TOWNSEND Peter Wooldridge, b. 22 Nov 1914, Rangoon, Burma. Author. m. Marie Luce Jamagne, 21 Dec 1959, 1 son, 2 daughter. Education: Haileybury; Royal Air Force College, 1933-35; Royal Air Force Staff College, 1942-43. Publications: Earth my Friend, 1960;

Duel of Eagles, 1970; The Last Emperor, 1975; Time and Chance, 1978; The Smallest Pawns in the Game, 1979-80; The Girl in the White Ship, 1982; The Postman of Nagasaki, 1984; Duel in the Dark, 1986; Nostalgia Britannica, 1994. Contributions to: Daily Telegraph; Daily Mail; Daily Express; Sunday Express; Evening Standard; Paris Match; Journal du Dimanche; Le Figaro; Le Figaro Litteraire; Madame Figaro; Le Temps Retrouve. Membership: European Academy of Science, Arts and Letters. Address: La Mare aux Oiseaux, 78610 St Leger en Yvelines, France.

TOWNSEND Sue, b, 4 Feb 1946, Leicester, England. Author. Publications: The Secret Diary of Adrian Mole Aged Thirteen and Three-Quarters, 1982; The Growing Pain of Adrian Mole, 1984; The Diaries of Adrian Mole, combined volume issued in USA, 1986; Bazaar and Rummage, Groping for Words, Womberang: Three Plays, 1984; True Confessions of Adrian Albert Mole; Mr Bevan's Dream, 1989; Ten Tiny Fingers, Nine Tiny Toes (play), 1989; Adrian Mole from Minor to Major, 1991; The Queen and I, 1992; Adrian Mole: The Wilderness Years, 1993. Contributions to: London Times; New Statesman; Observer; Sainsburys Magazine, 1993. Memberships: Writers Guild; PEN; Royal Society of Literature, fellow. Address: 6 Ann Street, Edinburgh EH4 1PJ, Scotland.

TOWNSEND Tom, b. 1 Jan 1944, Waukegan, Illinios, USA. Novelist. m. Janet L Simpson, 17 Apr 1965. Education: Arkansas Military Academy. Publications: Texas Treasure Coast, 1978; Where the Pirates Are, 1985; Trader Wooly, 1987; Trader Wooly and the Terrorists, 1988; Queen of the Wind, 1989; Battle of Galveston, 1990; Trader Wooly and the Ghost in the Colonel's Jeep, 1991; The Holligans, 1991; Bubba's Truck, 1992; The Ghost Flyers, 1993; A Fair Wind to Glory, 1994. Honours: Friend of American Writers Award, 1986; Texas Blue Bonnet Master List, 1986; Silver Award, Best Children's Video, Houston International Film Festival, 1986. Address: PO Box 905, Kemah, TX 77565, USA.

TOYNBEE Polly (Mary Louisa), b. 27 Dec 1946, Isle of Wight, England. Journalist; Writer. m. Peter Jenkins, 1970, 1 son, 2 daughters, 1 stepdaughter. Education: St Anne's College, Oxford. Appointments: Reporter, 1968-71, Feature Writer, 1974-76, The Observer; Editor, Washington Monthly, USA, 1972-73; Columnist, The Guardian, 1977-88; Social Affairs Editor, BBC, 1988-; The Independent, Columnist and Associate Editor, 1995-99; Current Columnist, The Guardian, Radio Times, 1998-. Publications: Leftovers, 1966; A Working Life, 1970; Hospital, 1977; The Way We Live Now, 1981; Lost Children, 1985. Honours: Catherine Pakenham Award for Journalism, 1975; British Press Awards, 1977, 1982; Columnist of the Year, 1986; Magazine Writer of the Year, 1996; George Orwell Prize, 1997. Address: The Guardian, 119 Farringdon Road, London EC1R 3ER, England.

TRACHTENBERG Paul, b. 25 Oct 1948, Los Angeles, California, USA. Poet. Education: AA, Fullerton Junior College, 1966; California State Polytechnic University, Pomona, 1968. Publications: Short Changes for Loretta, 1982; Making Waves, 1986; Ben's Exit, 1993. Address: 9431 Krepp Drive, Huntington Beach, CA 92646, USA.

TRANSTRÖMER Tomas (Gösta), b. 15 Apr 1931, Stockholm, Sweden. Poet; Psychologist. m. Monica Blach, 1958, 2 daughters. Education: Degree, University of Stockholm, 1956. Publications: In English: Twenty Poems, 1970; Night Vision, 1971; Windows and Stones: Selected Poems, 1972; Elegy: Some October Notes, 1973; Citoyens, 1974; Baltics, 1975; Truth Barriers: Poems by Tomas Tranströmer, 1980; How the Late Autumn Night Novel Begins, 1980; Tomas Tranströmer: Selected Poems, 1982; The Wild Marketplace, 1985; Selected Poems of Tomas Tranströmer, 1954-1986, 1987; Collected Poems, 1987; For the Living and the Dead, 1995; The Sorrow Gondola, 1996. Contributions to: Periodicals. Honours: Aftonbladets Literary Prize, 1958; Bellman Prize, 1966; Swedish Award, International Poetry Forum, 1971; Oevralids Prize, 1975; Boklotteriets

Prize, 1981; Petrarca Prize, 1981; Nordic Council Literary Prize, 1990. Membership: Swedish Writers Union. Address: c/o Swedish Writers Union, Box 3157, Drottninggatan 88B, S-103 63 Stockholm, Sweden.

TRANTER Nigel Godwin, (Nye Tregold), b. 23 Nov 1909, Glasgow, Scotland. Author. m. May Jean Campbell Grieve, 11 July 1933, 1 son, dec, 1 daughter. Publications: Numerous historical, romantic, Western, adventure, children's and non-fiction books, including Lord in Waiting, 1994; Highness in Hiding, 1995; Honours Even, 1995; A Rage of Regents, 1996; The Marchman, 1997; The Lion's Whelp, 1997; High Kings and Vikings, 1998; A Flame for the Fire, 1998. Honours: Officer of the Order of the British Empire, 1983; Scot of the Year Award, 1991; Honorary doctorate. Memberships: PEN Scottish Centre, president, 1962-66; Scottish Teachers of History Association, honorary president, 1990; Honorary Society of Authors, president, 1966-72; Saltire Society, honorary president; Scottish Library Association, honorary member. Address: 2 Goose Green Mews, East Lothian, EH31 2BN, Scotland.

TRAPEEZH Albert. See: **LAPIN Leonhard.**

TRAPIDO Barbara (Louise), b. 5 Nov 1941, Cape Town, South Africa. Writer. m. Stanley Trapido, 29 Apr 1963, 1 son, 1 daughter. Education: BA, Honours. English; Postgraduate Certificate, London. Publications: Brother of the More Famous Jack, 1982; Noah's Ark, 1985; Temples of Delight, 1990; Juggling, 1994. Contributions to: Spectator; Sunday Telegraph; Sunday Times. Honours: Whitbread Award, 1982; Short-listed for Sunday Express Book of the Year Award, 1990. Address: 3rd Floor, 9 Orme Court, London W2 4RL, England.

TRASK Jonathan. See: **LEVINSON Leonard.**

TRAVIS Jack, b. 2 Mar 1952, Newellton, Louisiana, USA. Architect; Writer. m. Chandra Llewellyn-Travis, 28 Sept 1996. Education: BArch, Arizona State University, 1977; MArch, University of Illinois, 1978. Appointments: Architect, own firm, 1985-; Adjunct Professor, Fashion Institute of Technology, Parsons School of Design continuing education and currently Pratt University; Adjunct Professor, Interior Design Departments, Institute of Technology; Founder, Studio for Afri-Culturalism in Architecture and Design; Lecturer; Panelist, Judge, Juror and Organizer of several competitions and events; Exhibitor. Publications: African American Architects: In Current Practice (monograph), 1992; The Legacy of Afrikan-Americans in Architecture - comprehensive permanent exhibit in progress. Contributions to: Various journals; Many feature articles in various magazines. Honours: Numerous recognitions of merit. Memberships: National Organization of Minority Architects; New York Coalition of Black Architects; American Institute of Architects, NCARB; Studio Museum of Harlem; National AIA Task Force on Diversity. Address: 103 East 125 Street, New York, NY 10035, USA.

TRAVIS Millicent Elizabeth. See: **LANE M Travis.**

TRAWICK Leonard M(oses), b. 4 July 1933, Decatur, Alabama, USA. Professor of English; Poet; Writer; Editor. m. Kerstin Ekfelt, 16 July 1960, 1 son, 1 daughter. Education: BA, University of the South, Sewanee, Tennessee, 1955; MA in English, University of Chicago, 1956; PhD in English, Harvard University, 1961. Appointments: Instructor to Assistant Professor of English, Columbia University, 1961-69; Associate Professor, 1969-72, Professor of English, 1972-98, Professor Emeritus, 1998-, Principal Editor, 1971-98, and Director, 1990-92, Poetry Center, Cleveland State University; Founding Editor, 1980, Co-Editor, 1983-92, The Gamut journal. Publications: Poetry: Beast Forms, 1971; Severed Parts, 1981; Beastmorfs, 1994. Opera Librettos: Spinoza, by Julius Drossin, 1982; The Enchanted Garden, by Klaus G Roy, 1983; Mary Stuart: A Queen Betrayed, by Bain Murray, 1991. Other: Backgrounds of Romanticism: English Philosophical Prose of the Eighteenth Century, 1967; World, Self, Poem (editor), 1990; German Literature of the Romantic

Era and the Age of Goethe (co-editor and principal translator), 1993. Contributions to: Scholarly books and journals, and to anthologies and magazines. Honours: Fulbright Scholarship, University of Dijon, 1956-57; Individual Artist Award, Ohio Arts Council, 1980; Award for Excellence in the Media, Northern Ohio Live, 1990; Co-Recipient, James P Barry Ohioana Award for Editorial Excellence, 1991; Ohioana Poetry Award for Lifetime Achievement in Poetry, 1994. Address: c/o Department of English, Cleveland State University, Rhodes Tower, Room 1815, Cleveland, OH 44115, USA.

TREANOR Oliver, b. 1 May 1949, Warrenpoint, Northern Ireland. Catholic Priest; Theologian; Lecturer; Writer. Education: BA, Honours, Queen's University, Belfast, 1972; PGCE, 1973; Dip Phil, 1974; STB, 1977, STL, 1979, STD, 1984, Pontifical Universitá Gregoriana, Rome. Appointments include: Lecturer, Systematic Theology, Pontifical University, Maynooth, Ireland. Publications: Mother of the Redeemer, Mother of the Redeemed, 1988; Seven Bells to Bethlehem: The O Antiphons, 1995; This Is My Beloved Son: Aspects of The Passion, 1997; The God Who Loved Stories, 1999. Contributions to: Priests and People, Durham, England; Osservatore Romano, Vatican City; Religious Life Review, Dublin; International Christian Digest, USA; The Furrow, Maynooth; Bible Alive, Stoke-on-Trent. Address: The Pontifical University, Maynooth, Co Kildare, Ireland.

TREBORLANG Robert, b. 19 Dec 1943, Jerusalem, Palestine. Writer; Poet. m. Moi Moi Cumines, 6 May 1971. Education: BA, Language, University of Sydney, 1968. Publications: How to Survive in Australia, 1985; How to be Normal in Australia, 1987; Sydney - Discover the City, 1988; How to Make it Big in Australia, 1989; She Vomits Like a Lady, 1991; Staying Sane in Australia, 1991; Men, Women and Other Necessities, 1992; A Hop Through Australia's History, 1993; How to Mate in Australia, 1993; The Little Book of Aussie Wisdom, 1994; The Little Book of Aussie Insults, 1994; The Little Book of Aussie Manners, 1995; It's Not the Pale Moon, 1999; Dancing With Mother, 1999. Contributions to: 24 Hours; Australian; Australian Jewish Times. Honour: Literature Grant, Australia, 1976. Memberships: Australian Journalists Association; Entertainment and Arts Alliance. Address: PO Box 997, Potts Point, New South Wales 2011, Australia.

TREBY Ivor Charles, b. Devonport, England. Education: MA, Honours, Biochemistry, Oxford. Appointment: Poet. Publications: Poem Cards, 1984; Warm Bodies, 1988; Foreign Parts, 1989; Woman with Camellias, 1995; The Michael Field Catalogue: A Book of Lists, 1998; Translations From the Human, 1998. Contributions to: Windmill Book of Poetry; Bete Noire; Poetry Review; Staple; Anglo-Welsh Review; Contemporary Review; Honest Ulsterman; Literary Review; Rialto. Address: Apt 4, 63 Nevern Square, RB Kensington and Chelsea, London SW5 9PN, England.

TREGLOWN Jeremy Dickinson, b. 24 May 1946, Anglesey, North Wales. Professor of English; Biographer; Editor; Critic. m. (1) Rona Bower, 1970, div,1982, 1 son, 2 daughters, (2) Holly Urquhart Eley, 1984. Education: BLitt, MA, Oxon; PhD, London. Appointments: Lecturer in English, Lincoln College, Oxford, 1974-77, University College, London, 1977-80; Assistant Editor, 1980-82, Editor, 1982-90, Times Literary Supplement; Chairman of Judges, Booker Prize, 1991; Ferris Professor of Journalism, Princeton University, USA, 1992; Professor of English, University of Warwick, England, 1993-. Publications: Letters of John Wilmot, Earl of Rochester (editor), 1980; Spirit of Wit: Reconsiderations of Rochester (editor), 1982; Introduction, R L Stevenson, In the South Seas, 1986; Selection, and Introduction, The Lantern Bearers: Essays by Robert Louis Stevenson, 1987; Introductions to reprints of complete novels of Henry Green, 1991-98; Roald Dahl: A Biography, 1994; Grub Street and the Ivory Tower: Literary Journalism, and Literary Scholarship from Fielding to the Internat, (editor with Bridget Bennett), 1998. Contributions to: Numerous magazines and journals. Membership: Fellow, Royal Society of Literature. Address: Gardens Cottage, Ditchley Park, Enstone, Nr Chipping Norton, Oxford OX7 4EP, England.

TREGOLD Nye. See: **TRANTER Nigel Godwin.**

TREHEARNE Elizabeth. See: **MAXWELL Patricia Anne.**

TREICIS Talivaldis, b. 19 June 1939, Liepaja, Latvia. Teacher. div. Education: Faculty of History and Philology, University of Latvia, 1958-63. Appointments: Scientific Library of Jelgava, 1963-65; Museum of History, Jelgava, 1966-69; High School of Eleja, 1970-75; Professional Writer, 1975-. Publications: Collections of Poetry: Every Day, 1970; Eyesight, 1974; Care, 1978; Still According Summer Time, 1989; Oh Ye Hawks, Little Hawks, 1994; Historical Novels: Seakers of Truth, 1980; The Earth - My Earth, 1984. Contributions to: Karogs (Banner); Zvaigzne (Star); Draugs (Friend); Sieviete (Woman). Honours: Reward of Padomju Jaunatne. Address: pn Lielplatone, Centrs 18 App 5, Jelgavas, Raj LV-3022, Latvia.

TRELFORD Donald Gilchrist, b. 9 Nov 1937, Coventry, England. Professor of Journalism. m. (1) Janice Ingram, 1963, 2 sons, 1 daughter, (2) Katherine Louise Mark, 1963, 1 daughter. Education: MA, Selwyn College, Cambridge. Appointments: Staff, newspapers in Coventry and Sheffield, 1961-63; Editor, Times of Malawi and Correspondent in Africa, The Times, Observer, BBC, 1963-66; Deputy News Editor, 1966, Assistant Managing Editor, 1968, Deputy Editor, 1969-75, Director, Editor, 1976-93, Observer; Professor of Journalism Studies, University of Sheffield, 1993-. Publications: Snookered, 1985; Child or Change (with Gary Kasparov), 1988; Len Hutton Remembered, 1992; W G Grace, 1998. Contributions to: The Queen Observed, 1986; Saturday's Boys, 1990; The Observer at 200 (editor), 1993. Honours: Editor, Newspaper of the Year, Granada TV Press Awards, 1982; Commended, International Editor of the Year, 1984; Honorary DLitt, Sheffield University, 1990; Freeman, City of London; Judge: Whitbread Prize, George Orwell Prize, Olivier Awards. Memberships: International Press Institute, British executive committee, 1976-; Royal Society of Arts, fellow, 1988-; British Sports Trust, vice-president. Address: 15 Fowler Road, London N1 2EP, England.

TREMAIN Rose, b. 2 Aug 1943, London, England. Writer; Dramatist. m. 1) Jon Tremain, 7 May 1971, div Oct 1978, 1 daughter, 2) Jonathon Dudley, 1982, diss. Education: Diploma in Literature, Sorbonne, University of Paris, 1963; BA in English Literature, University of East Anglia, 1967. Appointment: Part-time Lecturer, University of East Anglia, 1988-94. Publications: Freedom for Women, 1971; Stalin: An Illustrated Biography, 1974; Sadler's Birthday, 1976; Letter to Sister Benedicta, 1978; The Cupboard, 1981; The Colonel's Daughter, 1982; The Swimming Pool Season, 1984; Journey to the Volcano, 1985; The Garden of the Villa Mollini, 1986; Restoration, 1989; Sacred Country, 1992; Evangelista's Fan, 1994. Other: Radio plays. Honours: Dylan Thomas Prize, 1984; Giles Cooper Award for Best Radio Play, 1984; Sunday Express Book of the Year Award, 1989; James Tait Black Memorial Prize, 1993; Prix Femina Etranger, France, 1994. Membership: Royal Society of Literature, fellow. Address: 2 High House, South Avenue, Thorpe St Andrew, Norwich, NR7 0EZ, England.

TREMBLAY Gail Elizabeth, b. 15 Dec 1945, Buffalo, New York, USA. Poet; Artist; College Teacher. Education: BA, Drama, University of New Hampshire, 1967; MFA, Creative Writing, University of Oregon, 1969. Appointments: Lecturer, Keene State College, New Hampshire; Assistant Professor, University of Nebraska; Faculty, Evergreen State College, Olympia, Washington. Publications: Night Gives Woman the Word, 1979; Talking to the Grandfathers, 1980; Indian Singing in 20th Century America, 1990. Contributions to: Reviews, quarterlies, and journals. Honour: Alfred E Richards Poetry Prize, 1967. Memberships: Indian Youth of America, vice president, board; International Association of Art, UNESCO, USA National Committee board member; Native American Writers Circle of the Americas; Woman's Caucus for Art, board member. Address: c/o Evergreen State College, Olympia, WA 98505, USA.

TREMBLAY Michel, b. 25 June 1942, Montreal, Quebec, Canada. Dramatist; Author. Education: Graphic Arts Institute, Quebec. Publications: Theatre Pieces (with dates of production and publication): Le Train, 1964, 1990; Messe noire, 1965; Clinq, 1966, revised version as En pièces détachées, 1969, 1970; Les Belles-Soeurs, 1968, 1972; Trois petits tours, 1969, 1971; La Duchesse de Langeais, 1969, 1973; Demain matin, Montréal m'attend, 1970, 2nd version, 1972, 1972, 3rd version, 1995, 1995; Les Paons, 1971; A toi, pour toujours, ta Marie-Lou, 1971, 1971; Ville Mont-Royal ou Abimes, 1972; Hosanna, 1973, 1973; Bonjour, la, bonjour, 1974, 1974; Surprise! Surprise!, 1975, 1977; Les Héros de mon enfance, 1976, 1976; Sainte Carmen de la Main, 1976, 1976; Six monologues en forme de mots d'auteur, 1977; Damnée Manon, sacrée Sandra, 1977, 1977; L'Impromptu d'Outremont, 1980, 1980; Les Grandes Vacances, 1981; Les Anciennes Odeurs, 1981, 1981; Albertine, en cinq temps, 1984, 1984; L'Impromptu des deux presses, 1985; Le Vrai Monde?, 1987, 1987; Nelligan, 1990, 1990; La Maison suspendue, 1990, 1990; Théatre I, 1991; Marcel poursuivi par les chiens, 1992, 1992; En circuit fermé, 1994, 1994; Les socles, 1994; Messe solennelle pour une pleine lune d'été, 1996. Fiction: Contes pour buveurs attardés, 1966, English translation as Stories for Late Night Drinkers, 1977; La Cité dans l'oeuf, 1969; C't'a ton tour, Laura Cadieux, 1973; La Grosse Femme d'a coté est enceinte, 1978, English translation as The Fat Woman Next Door is Pregnant, 1981; Thérèse et Pierrette a l'école des Saints Anges, 1980, English translation as Thérèse, Pierrette and the Little Hanging Angel, 1984; La Duchesse et le roturier, 1982; Des nouvelles d'Edouard, 1984; Le Coeur découvert, 1986; Le Premier Quartier de la lune, 1989; La Mort de Phèdre, 1992; Le Coeur éclaté, 1993; La Nuit des princes charmants, 1995; Quarante-quatre minutes quarante-quatre secondes, 1997; Un objet de beauté, 1997. Honours: Trophée Méritas, 1970, 1972; Chalmers Awards, 1972, 1973, 1974, 1975, 1978, 1986, 1989, 1991; Prix Victor Morin, 1974; Prix du Lieutenant, Gouverneur de l'Ontario, 1976; Prix France Québec, 1981; Chevalier, 1984, Officier, 1991, de l'Ordre des Arts et des Lettres de France; Prix Québec-Paris, 1985; Chevalier de l'Ordre National du Québec, 1992; Banff National Center Award, 1993; Prix Louis-Hémon, 1994; Le Prix Molson du Conseil des Arts du Canada, 1994; Signet d'or, 1995; Honorary doctorates. Address: c/o Agence Goodwin, 839, rue Sherbrooke Est, bureau 200, Montreal, Quebec H2L 1K6, Canada.

TREMLETT George William, b. 5 Sept 1939, England. Author; Journalist; Bookseller. m. Jane Mitchell, 1971, 3 sons. Publications: 17 biographies of rock musicians, 1974-77; Living Cities, 1979; Caitlin (with Mrs Caitlin Thomas), 1986; Clubmen, 1987; Homeless, Story of St Mungo's, 1989; Little Legs (with Roy Smith), 1989; Rock Gold, 1990; Dylan Thomas: Book: In the Mercy of His Means, 1991, Film: The Map of Love, 1998; Gadaffi: The Desert Mystic, 1993; David Bowie, 1994; The Death of Dylan Thomas (with James R B Nashold MD), 1997. Honour: Officer of the Order of the British Empire. Membership: BBC Community Programme Unit, advisory panel, 1985-. Address: Corran House, Laugharne, Carmarthen, Dyfed SA33 4SJ, Wales.

TRENHAILE John Stevens, b. 29 Apr 1949, Hertford, England. Writer. Education: BA, 1971, MA, 1975, Magdalen College, Oxford. Publications: Kyril, 1981; A View from the Square, 1983; Nocturne for the General, 1985; The Mahjong Spies, 1986; The Gates of Exquisite View, 1987; The Scroll of Benevolence, 1988; Kyrsalis, 1989; Acts of Betrayal, 1990; Blood Rules, 1991; The Tiger of Desire, 1992; A Means to Evil, 1993; Against All Reason, 1994. Address: c/o Blake Friedman, Literary Agents, Arlington Road, London NW1 7HP, England.

TRENTON Gail. See: **GRANT Neil.**

TRENTWORTH Fisher. See: **ACKERMAN Forrest J.**

TRESILIAN Richard. See: **ELLIS Royston.**

TREVELYAN (Walter) Raleigh, b. 6 July 1923, Port Blair, Andaman Islands. Author. Appointment: Publisher, 1948-88. Publications: The Fortress, 1956; A Hermit Disclosed, 1960; Italian Short Stories: Penguin Parallel Texts (editor), 1965; The Big Tomato, 1966; Princes Under the Volcano, 1972; The Shadow of Vesuvius, 1976; A Pre-Raphaelite Circle, 1978; Rome '44, 1982; Shades of the Alhambra, 1984; The Golden Oriole, 1987; La Storia dei Whitaker, 1989; Grand Dukes and Diamonds, 1991; A Clear Premonition, 1995; The Companion Guide to Sicily, 1996. Contributions to: Newspapers and journals. Honours: John Florio Prize for Translation, 1967. Memberships: Anglo-Italian Society for the Protection of Animals, chairman; PEN, a vice-president; Royal Society of Literature, fellow. Addresse: 18 Hertford Street, London W1Y 7DB, England.

TREVOR (Lucy) Meriol, b. 15 Apr 1919, London, England. Writer. Education: BA, St Hugh's College, Oxford, 1942. Publications: The Forest and the Kingdom, 1949; Hunt the King, Hide the Fox, 1950; The Fires and the Stars, 1951; Sun Slower, Sun Faster, 1955; The Other Side of the Moon, 1956; The Last of Britain, 1956; The New People, 1957; Merlin's Ring, 1957; The Treasure Hunt, 1957; The Caravan War, 1958; A Narrow Place, 1958; Four Odd Ones, 1958; The Sparrow Child, 1958; Newman, 2 volumes, 1962; The Rose Round, 1963; William's Wild Day Out, 1963; The Midsummer Maze, 1964; The King of the Castle, 1966; Lights in a Dark Town, 1966; Apostle of Rome, 1966; Pope John, 1967; Prophets and Guardians, 1969; The City and the World, 1970; The Holy Images, 1971; The Two Kingdoms, 1973; The Fugitives, 1973; The Marked Man, 1974; Enemy at Home, 1974; The Arnolds, 1974; Newman's Journey, 1974; The Forgotten Country, 1975; The Treacherous Paths, 1976; The Fortunate Marriage, 1976; The Civil Prisoners, 1977; The Fortunes of Peace, 1978; The Wanton Fires, 1979; The Sun with a Face, 1984; The Golden Palaces, 1986; The Shadow of a Crown, 1988. Honours: James Tait Black Memorial Prize, 1962; Fellow, Royal Society of Literature, 1967. Address: 41 Fitzroy House, Pulteney Street, Bath BA2 4DW, England.

TREVOR William. See: **COX William Trevor.**

TRICKETT (Mabel) Rachel, b. 20 Dec 1923, Lathom, Lancashire, England. Author. Education: MA, Lady Margaret Hall, Oxford, 1947. Appointment: Principal, St Hugh's College, Oxford, 1973-91. Publications: The Return Home, 1952; The Course of Love, 1954; Point of Honour, 1958; A Changing Place, 1962; The Elders, 1966; The Visit to Timon, 1970. Plays: Antigone, 1954; Silas Marner, 1960. Non-Fiction: The Honest Muse: A Study in Augustan Verse, 1967; Browning's Lyricism, 1971; Tennyson's Craft, 1981. Honours: Rhys Memorial Prize, 1953; Honorary Fellow, Lady Margaret Hall, 1978. Address: Flat 4, 18 Norham Gardens, Oxford OX2 6QB, England.

TRIER MORCH Dea, b. 9 Dec 1941, Copenhagen, Denmark. Writer; Graphic Artist. m. Troels Trier, 1 son, 2 daughters. Education: Graduated, Royal Academy of Fine Arts, Copenhagen, 1964; Postgraduate Studies, Academies of Fine Arts, Warsaw, Kraków, Belgrade, Leningrad, Prague, 1964-67. Publications: 15 books in Danish, 1968-95, including Winter's Child, translated into 22 languages. Other: Various graphic works exhibited worldwide. Honours: Danish Author of the Year Award, 1977; Danish Government Stipends for Life, 1985, and for Works, 1994. Memberships: Danish Writers Association, chairman, 1990-91; PEN Club, Denmark; Union of Danish Graphic Artists; Artists Association, Denmark. Address: Jens Juels Gade 7, 2100 Copenhagen, Denmark.

TRIGGER Bruce Graham, b. 18 June 1937, Cambridge, Ontario, Canada. Professor of Anthropology. m. Barbara Marian Welch, 7 Dec 1968, 2 daughters. Education: BA, University of Toronto, 1959; PhD, Yale University, 1964. Appointments: Assistant Professor, Northwestern University, 1963-64; Assistant Professor, 1964-67, Associate Professor, 1967-69, Professor, 1969-, McGill University. Publications: History and Settlement in Lower Nubia, 1965; Late Nubian Settlement at Arminna West, 1967; Beyond History, 1968; The Huron: Farmers of the North, 1969, revised edition, 1990; Cartier's Hochelaga and the Dawson Site, 1972; Nubia Under the Pharaohs, 1976; The Children of Aataentsic, 1976, revised edition, 1987; Time and Traditions, 1978; Handbook of North American Indians, Vol 15, Northeast 1978; Gordon Childe, 1980; Natives and Newcomers, 1985; The History of Archaeological Thought, 1989; Early Civilizations: Ancient Egypt in Context, 1992; Cambridge History of the Native Peoples of the Americas, Vol I, North America, (co-editor), 1996; Sociocultural Evolution, 1998. Contributions to: Antiquity; American Antiquity; World Archaeology; Man. Honours: Canadian Silver Jubilee Medal, 1977; Cornplanter Medal, 1979; Innis-Gerin Medal, Royal Society of Canada, 1985; DSc, University of New Brunswick, 1987; John Porter Prize, 1988; DLitt, University of Waterloo, 1990; Prix du Québec, 1991; Honorary Member, Prehistoric Society, England, 1991; Honorary Fellow, Society of Antiquaries of Scotland, 1993; LLD, University of Western Ontario, 1995, McMaster University, 1999. Memberships: Various professional organizations. Address: Department of Anthropology, McGill University, 855 Sherbrooke Street West, Montreal, Quebec H3A 2T7, Canada.

TRILLIN Calvin (Marshall), b. 5 Dec 1935, Kansas City, Missouri, USA. Journalist; Critic; Author. m. Alice Stewart, 13 Aug 1965, 2 daughters. Education: BA, Yale University, 1957. Appointments: Reporter, later Writer, Time magazine, 1960-63; Staff Writer, The New Yorker magazine, 1963-; Columnist, The Nation magazine, 1978-85, King Features Syndicate, 1986-. Publications: An Education in Georgia: Charlayne Hunter, Hamilton Holmes, and the Integration of the University of Georgia, 1964; Barnett Frummer is an Unbloomed Flower and Other Adventures of Barnett Frummer, Rosalie Mondle, Roland Magruder, and Their Friends, 1969; US Journal, 1971; American Fried: Adventures of a Happy Eater, 1974; Runestruck, 1977; Alice, Let's Eat: Further Adventures of a Happy Eater, 1978; Floater, 1980; Uncivil Liberties, 1982; Third Helpings, 1983; Killings, 1984; With All Disrespect: More Uncivil Liberties, 1985; If You Can't Say Something Nice, 1987; Travels with Alice, 1989; Enough's Enough (and Other Rules of Life), 1990; American Stories, 1991; Remembering Denny, 1993; Deadline Poet, 1994; Too Soon to Tell, 1995; Family Man, 1998. Contributions to: Magazines. Contributions to: Magazines. Honours: National Book Award Nomination, 1980; Books-Across-the-Sea Ambassador of Honor Citation, English-Speaking Union, 1985. Address: c/o The New Yorker, 25 West 43rd Street, New York, NY 10036, USA.

TRIPP Miles Barton, (John Michael Brett, Michael Brett), b. 5 May 1923, Ganwick Corner, England. Writer. Publications: Kilo Forty, 1963; The Eighth Passenger, 1969; A Man Without Friends, 1970; High Heels, 1987; The Frightened Wife, 1987; The Cords of Vanity, 1989; Video Vengeance, 1990; The Dimensions of Deceit, 1993. Memberships: Society of Authors; Crime Writers Association, chairman, 1968-69; Detection Club. Address: Peters Fraser and Dunlop Group Ltd, 5th Floor, The Chambers, Chelsea Harbour, Lots Road, London SW10 0XF, England.

TRISTRAM Uvedale Francis Barrington, b. 20 Mar 1915, England. Journalist. m. Elizabeth Frances Eden-Pearson, 8 Sept 1939, 1 daughter. Appointments: Managing Editor, Hulton Publications, 1960-61; Editorial Manager, Longacre Press, 1961-62; Director of Information and Broadcasting, Basutoland, 1962-67; Director of Information, UK Freedom from Hunger Campaign, 1967-73; Founder, Editor, World Hunger. Publications: Adventure in Oil, 1958; John Fisher; Basutoland, 1961. Contributions to: Sunday Telegraph; Time and Tide; Tablet; Universe; Catholic Herald; Commercial Times. Honours: Rics Awards, Best Property Column in Weekly Paper, 1988, 1991; ISVA Provincial Property of the Year, 1990. Memberships: Guild of Catholic Writers, Master of the Keys, 1987-91, Deputy Master 1991-93; Institute of Journalists. Address: 19 Mallards' Reach, Weybridge, Surrey KT13 9HQ, England.

TROLLOPE Joanna, (Caroline Harvey), b. 9 Dec 1943, England. Writer. m. (1) David Roger William Potter, 1966, 2 daughters, (2) Ian Bayley Curteis, 1985, 2 stepsons. Education: MA, St Hugh's College, Oxford, 1972. Appointments: Information and Research Department, Foreign Office, 1965-67; Teaching posts, Farnham Girl's Grammar School, Adult education, English for Foreigners and Daneshill School, 1967-79. Publications: Eliza Stanhope, 1978; Parson Harding's Daughter, 1979; Mistaken Virtues (US edition of Parson Harding's Daughter),1979; Leaves from the Valley, 1980; The City of Gems, 1981; The Steps of the Sun, 1983; Britannia's Daughters: A Study of Women in the British Empire, 1983; The Taverners' Place, 1986; The Choir, 1988; A Village Affair, 1989; A Passionate Man, 1990; The Rector's Wife, 1991; The Men and the Girls, 1992; A Spanish Lover, 1992; The Best of Friends, 1992; The Country Habit: An Anthology, 1993; Next of Kin, 1996; Other People's Children, 1998. As Caroline Harvey: Legacy of Love, 1992; A Second Legacy, 1993; The Brass Dolphin, 1997. Contributions to: Newspapers and magazines. Honours: Romantic Historical Novel of the Year, 1980; Officer of the Order of the British Empire, 1996. Memberships: Trollope Society, vice president; Society of Authors, council member; West Country Writers Association, council member. Address: c/o Peters, Fraser and Dunlop Group, 5th Floor, The Chambers, Chelsea Harbour SW10 0XF, England.

TRONSKI Bronislaw, b. 24 Sept 1921, Wilno, Poland. Journalist; Writer. m. Janina Zajacowna, 3 July 1980, 1 son, 1 daughter. Education: Academy of Political Sciences, 1946-48; MA, Law, Jagiellonian University, Kraków, 1949. Appointments: Staff, Socjalistyczna Agencja Prasowa, 1946-48, Agencja Robotnicza, 1948-64, Polska Agencja Prasowa, 1964; Foreign Correspondent, Far East, 1959-60, Balkan Countries, 1972-76, Algeria and Tunisia, 1980-82; Special Correspondent, European countries. Publications: Tedy przeszta Smierc, 1957; Na Dachu Swiata, 1961; Stonce Nad Stara Planina, 1979; W Cieniu Nadziei, 1980; Trucja Bez Tajemnic, 1981; Algierskie Osobliwosci, 1984; Test Pan Wolny, 1987; Tanczacy prezydent, 1988; Mozaika sródziemnomorska, 1988; Smak ziemi obiecanej, 1990; Stambul, 1992; I w Ostrej swiecisz Bramie, sladami mlodego Adama Mickiewicza, 1993. Other: Translations of dramas. Contributions to: Numerous journals and magazines. Honours: Award, President of Polish Parliament; Awards, Parliament Reporters Club, 1965, 1966; Award, Polonia Club, Polish Journalists Association, 1985; Award, Weekly Kultura, 1988; Award, Counsel Fund of Literature, 1988; Award, International Publishers Club, 1990. Memberships: Polish Writers Association; Polish Journalists Association; Authors and Composers Association; Union of Warsaw Insurgents, vice president, 1991-. Address: Rakowiecka Street 33, App 30, 02-519 Warsaw, Poland.

TROTMAN Jack, (John Penn), Canadian. Writer. Appointments: Officer, British Army Intelligence Corps, 1940-46; Foreign Office, 1946-48; Joint Intelligence Bureau, Ottawa, Canada, 1949-65; Canadian Department of National Defence, 1965-73; NATO International Staff, Paris, 1973-77; President, National Trust for Jersey, Channel Islands, 1984-87, 1990-92. Publications: Notice of Death, US edition as An Ad for Murder, 1982; Deceitful Death, US edition as Stag-Dinner Death, 1983; A Will to Kill, 1983; Mortal Term, 1984; A Deadly Sickness, 1985; Unto the Grave, 1986, Barren Revenge, 1986; Accident Prone, 1987; Outrageous Exposures, 1988; A Feast of Death, 1989; A Killing to Hide, 1990; A Knife Ill-Used, 1991; Death's Long Shadow, 1991; A Legacy of Death, 1992; A Haven of Danger, 1993; Widow's End, 1993; The Guilty Party, 1994; So Many Steps to Death, 1995; Bridal Shroud, 1996. Address: c/o Murray Pollinger, 222 Old Brompton Road, London SW5 0BZ, England.

TROW George W S, b. 28 Sept 1943, Greenwich, Connecticut, USA. Writer; Dramatist. Education: AB, Harvard University, 1965. Appointments: Staff Writer, The New Yorker, 1966-. Publications: Bullies (stories), 1980; Within the Context of No Context (essays), 1981; The City in the Mist (novel), 1984. Other: Several plays. Contributions to: Anthologies and periodicals. Honours: Jean Stein Awards, American Academy and Institute of Arts and Letters, 1981, 1984, 1986; Guggenheim Fellowship, 1994-95. Address: c/o The New Yorker, 20 West 43rd Street, New York, NY 10036, USA.

TROWBRIDGE William, b. 9 May 1941, Chicago, Illinois, USA. Poet; Editor. m. Waneta Sue Downing, 6 July 1963, 2 sons, 1 daughter. Education: BA, 1963, MA, 1965, University of Missouri at Columbia; PhD, Vanderbilt University, 1975. Appointments: Instructor, University of Missouri at Columbia, 1966, Vanderbilt University, 1970; Assistant Professor to Distinguished University Professor, Northwest Missouri State University, 1971-88. Publications: The Book of Kong, 1986; Enter Dark Stranger, 1989; O Paradise, 1995. Contributions to: Poetry; Georgia Review; Kenyon Review; Southern Review; Gettysburg Review, and many others. Honours: Academy of American Poets Prize, 1970; Bread Loaf Writers Conference Scholarship, 1981; Yaddo Fellowship, 1992. Address: 907 South Dunn, Maryville, MO 64468, USA.

TRUCK Robert-Paul (Count), b. 3 May 1917, Calais, France. Poet; Critic; Historian. m. Jeanne Brogniart, 24 July 1942, 1 daughter. Education: Baccalaureat, 1935; French Naval School, 1938. Publications: Poetry: Heures Folles, 1938; Au Bord de la Nuit, 1948; Intersignes, 1953; Vertiges, 1989; Bois des Iles, 1992; Marche des Rois, 1993; Cicatrices, 1995. Non-Fiction: Médecins de la Honte (with Betty Truck), 1975; Memngele, l'ange de la mort (with Betty Truck), 1976. Contributions to: Anthologies and other publications. Honours: Various medals, diplomas and certificates. Memberships: Academia Leonardo da Vinci; Institut Académique de Paris; International Academy of Poets; Société des Poètes Français; World Literary Academy. Address: Varouna, 49 Rue de Lhomel, 62600 Berck-Plage, France.

TRUESDALE C(alvin) W(illiam), b. 27 Mar 1929, St Louis, USA. Writer; Publisher. m. 1 son, 2 daughters. Education: BA, 1951, PhD, 1957, University of Washington at Seattle. Appointments: Graduate Assistant, University of Washington; Virginia Military Institute, 1956-62; Macalester College, 1962-67; Adjunct Professor, New School, New York City and Cooper Union. Publications: Jossof Rivers, 1967; Moonshots, 1968; Plastic Father, 1971; Master of Knives, 1971. Address: c/o New River Press, 420 North 5th Street #910, Minneapolis, MN 55401, USA.

TRUMAN Jill, b. 12 June 1934, Enfield, Middlesex, England. Teacher; Writer; Dramatist. m. Tony Truman, 31 Mar 1956, dec 1975, 1 son, 3 daughters. Education: BA, English Literature, 1955; Postgraduate Certificate in Drama, 1979. Publication: Letter to My Husband, 1988. Other: Radio plays: Letter to My Husband, 1986; Gone Out-Back Soon, 1988; Travels in West Africa, 1990; Flit, 1992; For Lizzie, 1994; Sounds of Silence, 1998. Theatre: The Web, 1991. Musical: Kings of the Night, 1993. Short Stories, cassette: On The Terrace; 1998 Full Moon, 1998; In the Supermarket, 1998. Contributions to: Magazines. Membership: Writers Guild of Great Britain. Address: 2 Ellesmere Road, Bow, London E3 5QX, England.

TRUMAN Margaret, b. 17 Feb 1924, Independence, Missouri, USA. Author. m. E Clifton Daniel Jr, 21 Apr 1956, 4 sons. Publications: Fiction: Murder in the White House, 1980; Murder on Capitol Hill, 1981; Murder in the Supreme Court, 1982; Murder in the Smithsonian, 1983; Murder on Embassy Row, 1985; Murder at the FBI, 1985; Murder in Georgetown, 1986; Murder in the CIA, 1987; Murder at the Kennedy Center, 1989; Murder in the National Cathedral, 1990; Murder at the Pentagon, 1992; Murder on the Potomac, 1994; Murder in the National Gallery, 1996; Murder at the Watergate, 1998. Non-Fiction: White House Pets, 1969; Harry S Truman,

1973; Women of Courage, 1976; Letters from Father, 1981; Bess W Truman, 1986; Where the Buck Stops: The Personal and Private Writings of Harry S Truman (editor), 1989; First Ladies, 1995. Honours: LHD, Wake Forest University, 1972; HHD, Rockhurst College, 1976. Address: c/o Harry S Truman Library Institute for National and International Affairs, US 24 Highway and Delaware Street, Independence, MO 64050, USA.

TRZEBINSKI Errol Georgia, b. 24 June 1936, Brockworth, Gloucester, England. Biographer. m. Zbigniew Waclaw Trzebinski, 2 sons, 1 daughter. Publications: Silence Will Speak: The Life of Denys Finch Hatton and His Relationship With Karen Blixen, 1977; The Kenya Pioneers, 1985; The Lives of Beryl Markham, 1993. Contributions to: Periodicals and journals. Membership: Society of Authors, London. Address: PO Box 84045, Mombasa, Kenya.

TSALOUMAS Dimitris, b. 13 Oct 1921, Leros, Greece. Poet; Editor; Translator. m. Isle Wulff, 1958, 2 sons, 2 daughters. Appointments: Teacher, Victorian schools, 1958-82; Writer-in-Residence, University of Oxford, University of Melbourne, Queensland University, La Trobe University. Publications: Resurrection, 1967; Triptych for a Second Coming, 1974; Observations for a Hypochondriac, 1974; The House with the Eucalyptus, 1975; The Sick Barber and Other Characters, 1979; The Book of Epigrams, 1981; The Observatory: Selected Poems, 1983; Falcon Drinking: The English Poems, 1988; Portrait of a Dog, 1991; The Barge, 1993; Six Improvisations On the River, 1995; The Harbour, 1998. Honours: Australia Council Grant and Fellowship; National Book Council Award, 1983; Wesley M Wright Prize for Poetry, 1994; Patrick White Award, 1994. Address: 72 Glenhuntly Road, Elwood, Victoria 3184, Australia.

TSANG Lori Jean, b. 15 May 1955, Waterbury, Connecticut, USA. Poet; Writer. Education: BS, Indiana University, 1977; JD/MBA, Indiana University, 1980; attended Howard University, MFA program, 1985-90. Publications: Circumnavigation, 1996; Passages and Totems, 1998. Contributions to: Disorient; The Drumming Between Us; Controlled Burn Word Wrights; Phatitude; Gargoyle; Journal of Asian American Rennaissance. Honour: Washington DC Mayor's Arts Award for Outstanding Emerging Artist, 1997. Address: 716 Irving St NE#3, Washington, DC 20017, USA.

TSCHABOLD Matthias, b. 16 Apr 1956, Lausanne, Switzerland. Poet. m. Anne-Marie Haddad, 8 May 1986. Education: Licence en Théologie, University of Lausanne, 1980; Licence ès Lettres, 1993, Pedagogical Diploma, 1997, University of Zürich. Publications: La Depossession, 1981; Le Transfuge, 1992. Contributions to: Journals. Membership: Société Suisse des écrivains. Address: Zweiackerstrasse, 8053 Zürich, Switzerland.

TSCHUMI Jean-Raymond, b. 21 Oct 1953, Bern, Switzerland. Poet; Teacher. m. Hélène Veyre, 19 May 1994, 3 daughters. Education: Licence ès Lettres, University of Lausanne, 1979. Publications: Résurgences, 1990; L'Eté Disloqué, 1994; Un an a Vif, 1996. Contributions to: Anthologies and periodicals. Honour: Prix Claude Sernet, France, 1991. Memberships: Association Vaudoise des Ecrivains; Swiss Writers' Association. Address: Chemin du Village 1, Ch-1012 Lausanne, Switzerland.

TSKANI Kefentse, b. 31 Dec 1952, Manchester, Jamaica. Community and Social Worker. m. Nigist Talibah, 4 Feb 1986, 4 sons, 2 daughters. Education: Certificate in Community Youth Work; Certificate in Community Sports Award; Certificate in Part time Youth Work. Publications: Realities, Collection of POems, 1983; In Search of the Rastaman, 1991; The Ras Tatari Educational Page, co-authored, 1995; Journey is the Palace. Literary Agent: Karak House Publishers, 225 Westbourne Park, London W10, England. Address: 2 Durham Street, Vauxhall, London SE11 5JA, England.

TSURUMI Shunsuke, b. 25 June 1922, Tokyo, Japan. Writer. m. Sadako Yokoyama, 9 Nov 1960, 1 son. Education: BS, Harvard University, 1942. Appointments: Assistant Professor, Kyoto University, 1949-54, Tokyo Institute of Technology, 1954-60; Professor of Sociology, Doshisha University, Kyoto, 1961-70; Visiting Professor, El Colegio de Mexico, 1972-73; McGill University, 1979-80. Publications: Numerous books, 1950-98, including some in English: An Intellectual History of Wartime Japan, 1931-45, 1986; A Cultural History of Postwar Japan, 1945-80, 1987. Honours: Several prizes. Address: Nagafanicho Iwakura, Sakyo-ku, Kyoto, Japan.

TSVETKOV Vlad. See: **SEMYONOVA Violeta.**

TUBB E(dwin) C(harles), (Chuck Adams, Jud Cary, J F Clarkson, James S Farrow, James R Fenner, Charles S Graham, Charles Grey, Volsted Gridban, Alan Guthrie, George Holt, Gill Hunt, E F Jackson, Gregory Kern, King Lang, Mike Lantry, P Lawrence, Chet Lawson, Arthur MacLean, Carl Maddox, M L Powers, Paul Schofield, Brian Shaw, Roy Sheldon, John Stevens, Edward Thomson, Douglas West, Eric Wilding), b. 15 Oct 1919, London, England. Writer. Publications: Over 100 under various pseudonyms; Science fiction/fantasy: Saturn Patrol, 1951; Argentis, 1952; Planetoid Disposals Ltd, 1953; The Living World, 1954; Alien Dust, 1955; The Space-Born, 1956; Touch of Evil, 1959; Moon Base, 1964; Ten From Tomorrow (short stories), 1966; Death is a Dream, 1967; COD Mars, 1968; STAR Flight, 1969; The Jester at Scar, 1970; Lallia, 1971; Century of the Manikin, 1972; Mayenne, 1973; Veruchia, 1973; Zenya, 1974; Atilus the Slave, 1975; Jack of Swords, 1976; Haven of Darkness, 1977; Incident on Ath, 1978; Stellar Assignment, 1979; The Luck Machine, 1980. Suspense and Western novels: The Fighting Fury, 1955; Scourge of the South, 1956; Wagon Trail, 1957; Target Death, 1961; Too Tough to Handle, 1962; Airborne Commando, 1963; The Quillian Sector, 1978; Web of Sand, 1979; Iduna's Universe, 1979; The Terra Data, 1980; World of Promise, 1980; Nectar of Heaven, 1981; The Terridae, 1981; The Coming Event, 1982; Earth is Heaven, 1982; Melome, 1983; Stardeath, 1983; Angado, 1984; Symbol of Terra, 1984; The Temple of Truth, 1985; Pandora's Box, 1996; Temple of Death, 1996; Assignment New York, 1996; Kalgan the Golden, 1996; The Return, 1997. Short Stories: Murder in Space, 1997; Alien Life, 1998. Contributions to: 230 stories to magazines and journals. Address: 67 Houston Road, London SE23 2RL, England.

TUCCILLO Alberigo Albano, b. 27 Feb 1955, Rovereto, Trento, Italy. Author; Teaching assignment for creative writing. m. Regula Zaberer, 11 Aug 1989, 2 sons. Education: Philosophy, Italian and German Philology, University of Basel, Switzerland. Publications: Zurück Vielleicht - Oder Weiter, play, 1986; Die Leuchtturmgeschichte, novel, 1987; Die Leuchtturmgeschichte, novel, 1988; Die Nacht des Schicksals, play, 1988; Mercato, 11 essays, 1993; Der Schein, play, 1993; Erzählungen aus hundert und einer schlaflosen Nacht (11 poems and 10 tales), 1993; Ob ihr wollt oder nicht, play. Contributions to: Several short stories in various magazines and anthologies. Honours: Literary awards: Solothurn, 1988; Basel-Land, 1993. Memberships: Gruppe Olten, 1988-; Swiss PEN, 1992-. Memberships: Associazione Scrittori Italiani in Svizzera, 1997. Literary Agent: Susanne Sigrist, NABU Literary Agency, Firenze, Italy. Address: Solothurner Strasse 19, CH-4053 Basel, Switzerland.

TUCKER (Allan) James, b. 15 Aug 1929, Cardiff, Wales. Writer. m. Marian Roberta Craig, 17 July 1954, 3 sons, 1 daughter. Education: Grange Council School; Cardiff High School; University of Wales, Cardiff; BA, 1951; MA, 1975. Publications: Equal Partners, 1960; The Novels of Anthony Powell, 1976; The Alias Man, by David Craig, 1968; The Tattooed Detective, by David Craig, 1998; The Lolita Man, by Bill James, 1986; Lovely Mover, by Bill James, 1998; Baby Talk, by Judith Jones, 1998. Contributions to: Punch; Spectator; New Statesman; New Review. Memberships: Authors'; Crime Writers Association; Mystery Writers of America. Literary Agent:

Curtis Brown. Address: c/o 28 Haymarket, London SW1Y 4SP, England.

TUCKER Eva Marie, b. 18 Apr 1929, Berlin, Germany. Writer. m. 11 Mar 1950 (widowed 1987), 3 daughters. Education: BA, Honours, German, English, University of London. Appointments: C Day-Lewis Writing Fellow, Vauxhall Manor School, London, 1978-79; Hawthornden Writing Fellowship, 1991. Publications: Contact (novel), 1966; Drowning (novel), 1969; Radetzkymarch by Joseph Roth (translator), 1974. Contributions to: BBC Radio 3 and 4; Encounter; London Magazine; Woman's Journal; Vogue; Harper's; Spectator; Listener; PEN International. Memberships: English PEN; Turner Society; Society of Authors. Address: 63B Belsize Park Gardens, London NW3 4JN, England.

TUCKER Helen, b. 1 Nov 1926, Raleigh, North Carolina, USA. Writer. Education: BA, Wake Forest University, 1946; Graduate Studies, Columbia University, 1957-58. Publications: The Sound of Summer Voices, 1969; The Guilt of August Fielding, 1972; No Need of Glory, 1973; The Virgin of Lontano, 1974; A Strange and Ill-Starred Marriage, 1978; A Reason for Rivalry, 1979; A Mistress to the Regent: An Infamous Attachment, 1980; The Halverton Scandal, 1980; A Wedding Day Deception, 1981; The Double Dealers, 1982; Season of Dishonor, 1982; Ardent Vows, 1983; Bound by Honor, 1984; The Lady's Fancy, 1991; Bold Impostor, 1991. Contributions to: Lady's Circle; Ellery Queen Mystery Magazine; Alfred Hitchcock Mystery Magazine; Ladies Home Journal; Crecent Review; Montevallo Review. Honours: Distinguished Alumni Award, Wake Forest University, 1971; Franklin County Artist of the Year Award, 1992. Address: 2930 Hostetler Street, Raleigh, NC 27609, USA.

TUCKER Martin, b. 8 Feb 1928, Philadelphia, Pennsylvania, USA. Professor of English; Writer; Poet. Education: BA, 1949, PhD, 1963, New York University; MA, University of Arizona, 1954. Appointments: Faculty, Long Island University, 1956-; Editor, Confrontation magazine, 1970-. Publications: Modern British Literature (editor), Vols I-IV, 1967-76; Africa in Modern Literature, 1967; The Critical Temper (editor), Vols I-V, 1970-89; Joseph Conrad, 1976; Homes of Locks and Mysteries (poems), 1982; Literary Exile in the United States, 1991; Sam Shepard, 1992; Attention Spans (poems), 1997; Modern American Literature (editor), 1997. Contributions to: Professional journals and general periodicals. Honours: National Endowment for the Arts/Coordinating Council and Literary Magazine Awards for Editorial Distinction, 1976, 1984; English-Speaking Union Award, 1982; Phi Beta Kappa. Memberships: African Literature Association; African Studies Association; Authors Guild; Modern Language Association; National Book Critics Circle; PEN, executive board, 1973-96; Poetry Society of America. Address: 90-A Dosoris Lane, Glen Cove, NY 11542, USA.

TUCKMAN Bruce W(ayne), b. 24 Nov 1938, New York, New York, USA. Psychologist; Professor; Writer. Education: BS, Psychology, Rensselaer Polytechnic Institute, 1960; MA, Psychology, 1962, PhD, Psychology, 1963, Princeton University. Appointments: Research Associate, Princeton University, 1963; Adjunct Professor, University College, University of Maryland, 1963-65; Research Psychologist, Naval Medical Research Institute, Bethesda, Maryland, 1963-65; Associate Professor of Education, 1965-70, Professor of Education, 1970-78, Director of Research, Graduate School of Education, 1975-78, Rutgers University; Dean, School of Education, Baruch College of the City University of New York, 1978-82; Senior Research Fellow, Center for Advanced Study in Education, City University of New York, 1982-83; Dean, 1983-85, Professor, 1985-98, College of Education, Florida State University; Consulting Editor, 1987-93, Executive Editor, 1993-, Journal of Experimental Education; Academic Learning Lab, Ohio State University, Professor and Director, 1998-. Publications: Conducting Educational Research, 1972, 4th edition, 1994, 5th edition, 1999; Testing for Teachers, 1975, 2nd edition, 1988; Evaluating Instructional Programs, 1979, 2nd edition, 1985; Analyzing and

Designing Educational Research, 1985; Effective College Management, 1987; Long Road to Boston (novel), 1988; Educational Psychology, 1992; 2nd edition, 1997. Contributions to: Journals. Honours: National Institute of Mental Health Fellowship, 1961-63; New Jersey Association of English Teachers Author's Award, 1969; Phi Delta Kappa Research Award, 1973; Outstanding Teaching Award, 1993; Florida State University Teaching Award, 1993. Memberships: American Psychological Association, fellow; American Psycological Society; American Educational Research Association; Gulf Winds Track Club. Address: 104 Ramseyer Hall, The Ohio State University, 29 West Woodruff Avenue, Columbus, OH 43210 USA.

TUDOR Andrew Frank, b. 19 Nov 1942, Edinburgh, Scotland. University Lecturer. Education: BA, Sociology, 1965. Publications: Theories of Film, 1973; Image and Influence, 1974; Beyond Empiricism, 1982; Monsters and Mad Scientists, 1989. Contributions to: New Society. Address: Department of Sociology, University of York, Heslington, York YO1 5DD, England.

TUDOR-CRAIG Pamela Wynn (Pamela, Lady Wedgwood), b. 26 June 1928, London, England. Art Historian; Writer. m. (1) Algernon James Riccarton Tudor-Craig, 27 July 1956, dec 1969, 1 daughter, (2) Sir John Wedgwood, 1 May 1982, dec 1989. Education: 1st Class Honours degree, 1949, PhD, 1952, Courtauld Institute, University of London. Appointments; Teacher, several US colleges; Presenter, The Secret Life of Paintings television series, 1986; Arts page, Church Times, 1988-. Publications: Richard III, 1973; The Secret Life of Paintings (co-author), 1986; Bells Guide to Westminster Abbey (co-author), 1986; Exeter Cathedral, 1991; Anglo-Saxon Wall Paintings, 1991. Contributions to: Books and professional journals. Honour: Honorary Doctor of Humanities, William Jewell College, 1983. Memberships: Cathedrals Advisory Commission, 1975-90; Advisory Panel, Westminster Abbey, Architectural, 1979-98; English-Speaking Union, Cultural Affairs Committee; Society of Antiquaries, fellow, 1958-, council member, 1989-92. Address: 9 St Anne's Crescent, Lewes, East Sussex BN7 1SB, England.

TUFTY Barbara Jean, b. 28 Dec 1923, Iowa City, Iowa, USA. Conservation Writer and Editor. m. Harold G Tufty, 29 Dec 1948, 2 sons, 1 daughter. Education: BA, Botany, Duke University; Postgraduate classes, New School for Social Research, New York City, 1946; Sorbonne, University of Paris, 1948; University of Colorado, 1949, 1950, 1951. Appointments: Science Writer, Science Service, 1948-72, National Academy of Sciences, 1970-72; Editor, National Science Foundation, 1972-84; Conservation Writer and Editor, Audubon Naturalist Society, 1986-. Publications: 1001 Questions Answered About Natural Land Disasters, 1969; 1001 Questions Answered About Storms, 1970; Cells, Units of Life, 1973; Wildflowers of the Washington-Baltimore Area (co-author), 1995. Contributions to: Reference books, journals, and magazines. Honours: Chi Delta Phi, 1945; Honorary Life Member (1st Woman), Bombay Natural History Society, 1960; Honourable Mention, Thomas Stokes Writing Award, 1972; Honourable Mention Catherine O'Brien, Writing Award, 1972; Writing Fellowships at Ossabaw Island Institute, Library of Congress. Memberships: Washington Independent Writers; National Association of Science Writers; Nature Conservancy; Washington Environmental Writers Association; Environmental Defence Fund; Earthwatch; Society of Environmental Journalists. Address: 3812 Livingston Street North West, Washington, DC 20015, USA.

TUGENDHAT Julia. See: DOBSON Julia Lissant.

TUKE Diana Rosemary, b. 5 July 1932, Weymouth, Dorset, England. Lecturer; Freelance Journalist; Writer; Author. Education: British Horse Society Preliminary Instructor's Certificate, Porlock Vale Riding School, 1954. Appointments: Picture Editor, The Encyclopaedia of the Horse, 1973; Lectured, updated Equine Feeding Section of Instruction Manual, Metropolitan Police, 1986.

Publications: A Long Road to Harringay, 1960; Bit-by-Bit, 1965; Riding Cavalcade, contributor, 1967; Tomorrow, short story, 1968; Stitch-by-Stitch, 1970; Horse-by-Horse, 1973; The Complete Book of the Horse (contributor), 1973; The Encyclopaedia of the Horse (contributor), 1973; Getting Your Horse Fit, 1977; Feeding Your Horse, 1980; Cottage Craft Guide to Aintree Bits, 1982; Horse Tack - The Complete Equipment Guide for Riding and Driving (contributor), 1982; The Country Life Book of Saddlery and Equipment (contributor), 1982; Clipping Your Horse, 1984; Feeding Your Horse and Pony, 2nd edition, 1988; Horse Trials Review No 2 - Feeding for Fitness, video, 1990; Clipping, Trimming and Plaiting Your Horse, 2nd edition, 1992; Nursing Your Horse, 1999; Novels awaiting publication: Ravensworth; The Old Mill; When the Rivers Roared; Away in the Mountains; The Lonely Shore. Contributions to: Riding; Horse and Hound; The Daily Telegraph; The Field; The Cronical of the Horse, USA; Others. Honours: Trophies for sale of books: Bit-by-Bit, 25,000 copies, 1995; Getting Your Horse Fit, 25,000 copies, 1995; Clipping, Trimming and Plaiting Your Horse, 10,000 copies, 1998. Membership: British Equestrian Writer's Association. Address: Gallery House, Duddenhoe End, Saffron Walden, Essex CB11 4UU, England.

TULLY (William) Mark, b. 24 Oct 1935, Calcutta, India. Journalist; Broadcaster. m. Margaret Frances Butler, 13 Aug 1960, 2 sons, 2 daughters. Education: Marlborough College; MA, Trinity Hall, Cambridge, 1959. Appointments: Regional Director, Abbeyfield Society, 1960-64; Assistant, Appointments Department, 1964-65, Assistant, later Acting Representative, New Delhi, 1955-69, Programme Organiser and Talks Writer, Eastern Service, 1969-71, Chief of Bureau, Delhi, 1972-93, South Asia Correspondent, 1993-94, BBC; Presenter, The Lives of Jesus, BBC TV, 1996. Publications: Amritsar: Mrs Gandhi's Last Battle (with Satish Jacob), 1985; From Raj to Rajiv (with Z Masani), 1988; No Full Stops in India, 1991; The Heart of India, 1995; The Lives of Jesus, 1996. Honours: Officer of the Order of the British Empire, 1985; Padma Shri, India, 1992; Honorary Fellow, Trinity Hall, Cambridge, 1994; Honorary Doctor of Letters, University of Strathclyde, 1997. Address: 1 Nizamuddin East, New Delhi 110 013, India.

TUQAN Fadwa, b. 1 Mar 1917, Nablus, Palestine. Publications: My Brother Ibrahim, 1946; Alone with Days, 1952; Give Us Love, 1960; Before the Closed Door, 1967; Night and Knights, 1969; Alone at the Top of the World, 1973; I Found It, 1975; An Arduous Mountain Journey (autobiography), 1985; Adonis and the Other Thing, 1989; Difficult Journey, 1993. Contributions to: Innumerable contributions through the Arab World. Address: PO Box 31, Nablus, Palestine, Via Israel.

TURBILL Janice Betina, b. 13 Mar 1944, Sydney, New South Wales, Australia. University Lecturer; Writer. Education: BA, Macquarie University, 1979; MED, University of Sydney, 1985; PhD, University of Wollongong, 1994. Appointment: Faculty, University of Wollongong. Publications: No Better Way To Teach Writing, 1982; Now We Want To Write, 1983; Towards a Reading Writing Classroom (with Andrea Butler), 1984; Coping with Chaos (with B Cambourne), 1987; Responsive Evaluation (with B Cambourne), 1994. Contributions to: Books and journals. Memberships: Society of Authors of Australia; Fellow, Australian College of Education. Address: Faculty of Education, University of Wollongong, New South Wales, Australia 2522.

TURK Frances Mary, b. 14 Apr 1915, Huntingdon, England. Novelist. Publications: Paddy O'Shea, 1937; The Precious Hours, 1938; Paradise Street, 1939; Lovable Clown, 1941; Angel Hill, 1942; The Five Grey Geese, 1944; Salutation, 1949; The Small House at Ickley, 1951; The Gentle Flowers, 1952; The Dark Wood, 1954; The Glory and the Dream, 1955; Dinny Lightfoot, 1956; No Through Road, 1957; The White Swan, 1958; The Secret Places, 1961; The Guarded Heart, 1964; Legacy of Love, 1967; Fair Recompense, 1969; Goddess of Threads, 1975; A Visit to Marchmont, 1977; Candle

Corner, 1986. Contributions to: Many periodicals. Memberships; Romantic Novelists Association; Many other professional organisations. Address: Hillrise, Brampton Road, Buckden, Huntingdon PE18 9UH, England.

TURNBULL Gael Lundin, b. 7 Apr 1928, Edinburgh, Scotland. Poet; Former Medical Practitioner. m. (1) Jonnie May Draper, 1952, 3 daughters, (2) Pamela Jill Iles, 1983. Education: BA, University of Cambridge, 1948; MD, University of Pennsylvania, 1951. Publications: A Trampoline, 1968; Scantlings, 1970; A Gathering of Poems, 1950-80, 1983; A Year and a Day, 1985; A Winter Journey, 1987; While Breath Persist, 1992; For Whose Delight, 1995; A Rattle of Scree, 1997; Transmutations, 1997. Contributions to: Numerous journals and magazines. Honour: Alice Hunt Bartlett Award, 1969. Address: 12 Strathearn Place, Edinburgh EH9 2AL, Scotland.

TURNER Alberta Tucker, b. 22 Oct 1919, New York, New York, USA. Professor Emerita; Poet; Writer. m. William Arthur Turner, 9 Apr 1943, 1 son, 1 daughter. Education: BA, Hunter College, New York City, 1940; MA, Wellesley College, Massachusetts, 1941; PhD, Ohio State University, 1946. Appointments: Lecturer to Professor, 1964-90, Director, Poetry Center, 1964-90, Professor Emerita, 1990-, Cleveland State University; Associate Editor, Field, Contemporary Poetry and Poetics, 1970-. Publications: Poetry: Need, 1971; Learning to Count, 1974; Lid and Spoon, 1977; A Belfry of Knees, 1983; Beginning with And: New and Selected Poems, 1994. Other: 50 Contemporary Poets: The Creative Process (editor), 1977; Poets Teaching (editor), 1981; To Make a Poem, 1982; 45 Contemporary Poems: The Creative Process (editor), 1985; Responses to Poetry, 1990. Contributions to: Journals and magazines. Honours: MacDowell Colony Fellowship, 1985; Cleveland Arts Prize, 1985; Ohio, Poetry Award, 1986; Ohio Governor's Award for Arts in Education, 1988. Memberships: Milton Society of America; PEN American Center. Address: 482 Caskey Court, Oberlin, OH 44074, USA.

TURNER Billie Lee II, b. 22 Dec 1945, Texas City, Texas, USA. Professor of Geography; Writer. m. Linda Lee Van Zandt, 1 son, 1 daughter. Education: BA, Geography, 1968, MA, Geography, 1969, University of Texas; PhD, Geography, University of Wisconsin, Madison, 1974. Publications: Pre-Hispanic Maya Agriculture (co-editor), 1978; Once Beneath the Forest, 1983; Pulltrouser Swamp, 1985; Comparative Farming Systems (co-editor), 1987; The Earth as Transformed by Human Action (co-editor), 1990; Population Growth and Agricultural Change in Africa, 1993; Changes in Land Use and Land Cover: A Global Perspective (co-editor), 1994; Regions at Risk: Comparisons of Threatened Environments (co-editor), 1995. Contributions to: Over 100 on science, economy and botany in various publications. Honours: Guggenheim Fellowship, 1981; Fellow, CASBS, 1994; Honours, Association of American Geography, 1995; National Academy of Sciences, 1995; Higgins Chair of Environment and Society; Centenary Medal, Royal Scottish Geographical Society, 1996; American Academy of Arts and Sciences, elected, 1998. Address: 19 Farnun Street, Worcester, MA 01602, USA.

TURNER Brian (Lindsay), b. 4 Mar 1944, Dunedin, New Zealand. Poet; Writer. 1 son. Education: Otago Boys High School, 1957-61. Appointments: Managing Editor, John McIndoe Ltd, Dunedin, 1975-83, 1985-86; Writer-in-Residence, University of Canterbury, 1997. Publications: Poetry: Ladders of Rain, 1978; Ancestors, 1981; Listening to the River, 1983; Bones, 1985; All That Blue Be, 1989; Beyond, 1992; Timeless Land, 1995. Other: Images of Coastal Otago, 1982; New Zealand High Country: Four Seasons, 1983; Opening Up (with Glenn Turner), 1987; The Last River's Song, 1989; The Guide to Trout Fishing in Otago, 1994. Honours: Commonwealth Poetry Prize, 1978; Robert Burns Fellowship, 1984; John Crowe Reid Memorial Prize, 1985; New Zealand; New Zealand Book Award for Poetry, 1993; Scholarship in Letters, 1994. Address: 2

Upper Junction Road, Sawyers Bay, Dunedin, New Zealand.

TURNER Frederick, b. 19 Nov 1943, East Haddon, Northamptonshire, England. Professor of Arts and Humanities; Writer; Poet. m. Mei Lin Chang, 25 June 1966, 2 sons. Education: BA, 1965, MA, 1967, BLitt, 1967, English Language and Literature, University of Oxford. Appointments: Assistant Professor of English, University of California, Santa Barbara, USA, 1967-72; Associate Professor of English, Kenyon College, 1972-85; Editor, Kenyon Review, 1978-83; Visiting Professor of English, University of Exeter, 1984-85; Founders Professor of Arts and Humanities, University of Texas at Dallas, Richardson, 1985-. Publications: Shakespeare and the Nature of Time, 1971; Between Two Lives, 1972; The Return, 1979; The New World, 1985; The Garden, 1985; Natural Classicism, 1986; Genesis: An Epic Poem, 1988; Rebirth of Value, 1991; Tempest, Flute and Oz, 1991; April Wind, 1991; Beauty, 1991; Foamy Sky: The Major Poems of Miklos Radnoti (translator with Zsuzanna Ozsvath), 1992; The Culture of Hope, 1995; The Ballad of the Good Cowboy, 1997. Contributions to: Journals and periodicals. Honours: Ohioana Prize for Editorial Excellence, 1980; Djerassi Foundation Grant and Residency, 1981; Levinson Poetry Prize, 1983; Missouri Review Essay Prize, 1986; PEN Golden Pen Award, 1992; Milan First prize (Hungary's highest literary honour), 1996. Memberships: PEN; Modern Language Association. Address: 2668 Aster Drive, Richardson, TX 75082, USA.

TURNER George (Reginald), b. 8 Oct 1916, Melbourne, Victoria, Australia. Writer. Publications: Young Man of Talent, 1959; A Stranger and Afraid, 1961; A Waste of Shame, 1965; The Lame Dog Man, 1967; Beloved Son, Transit of Cassidy, 1978; Vaneglory, 1982; Yesterdays Men, 1983; The Sea and Summer, 1987; A Pursuit of Miracles, 1990; The Destiny Makes, 1993. Honours: Miles Franklin Award, 1962; Arthur C Clarke Award, 1987. Membership: Australian Society of Authors. Address: 4/296 Inkerman Street, East St Kilda, VA 3183, Australia.

TURNER George William, b. 26 Oct 1921, Dannevirke, New Zealand. Retired University Reader; Editor. m. Beryl Horrobin, 18 Apr 1949, 2 sons. Education: BA, 1944, MA, 1948, University of New Zealand; Diploma, New Zealand Library School, 1948; Diploma, English Linguistic Studies, University College, London, 1964. Appointments: Tutor and Lecturer, University of Canterbury, New Zealand, 1955-64; Reader, University of Adelaide, 1965-68. Publications: The English Language in Australia and New Zealand, 1966, 2nd edition, 1972; Good Australian English (editor), 1972; Stylistics, 1973; The Australian Pocket Oxford Dictionary (editor), 2nd edition, 1984; The Australian Concise Oxford Dictionary (editor), 1986; The Australian Oxford Paperback Dictionary (editor with Beryl Turner), 1989. Contributions to: Books and journals. Honours: Fellow, Australian Academy of the Humanities, 1974; Festschrift published in his honour, 1988. Address: 3 Marola Avenue, Rostrevor, South Australia 5073, Australia.

TURNER Len. See: FLOREN Lee.

TURNER L(eslie) A(nne), b. 6 May 1969, Quebec, Canada. Journalist; Writer. Education: Ontario, Canada; MA, Arts Criticism and Media Studies. Publication: When Technology Fails, 1993. Contributions to: Telegraph: Various consumer and professional journals. Address: Knight's Cottage, Knight's Place Farm, Near Cobham, Rochester, Kent ME2 3UB, England.

TURNER Mary. See: LAMBOT Isobel Mary.

TURNER Philip William, (Stephen Chance), b. 3 Dec 1925, Rossland, British Columbia, Canada. Writer; Dramatist. m. Margaret Diana Samson, 23 Sept 1950, 2 sons, 1 daughter. Education: BA, MA, English Lanaguage and Literature, University of Oxford, 1946. Publications: The Grange at High Force, 1965; The Bible Story, 1968; Septimus and the Danedyke Mystery, 1973; The

Candlemass Treasure, 1988. Plays: Christ in the Concrete City, 1956; How Many Miles to Bethlehem?, 1987. Honour: Carnegie Medal, 1965. Address: St Francis, 181 West Malvern Road, Malvern, Worcs, England.

TURNILL Reginald, b. 12 May 1915, Dover, England. Writer; Broadcaster. m. 10 Sept 1938, 2 sons. Education: Fleet Street Reporter. Appointments: Reporter, Industrial Correspondent, Press Association, London, 1930-56; Industrial Correspondent, 1956-58; Aerospace and Defence Correspondent, 1958-75, BBC. Publications: The Language of Space, 1970; Observer's Book of Manned Spaceflight, 1972, 3rd edition, 1978; Observer's Unmanned Spaceflight, 1974; Observer's Spaceflight Directory, 1978; Space Age, 1980; Jane's Spaceflight Directory, 1984, 4th edition, 1988; Space Technology International, 1989, 4th edition, 1992; World Aerospace Development, 1993; Celebrating Concorde, 1994. Contributions to: Zodiac; Executive Travel; Aerospace; Aviation Week; Space Technology. Honour: NASA's Chroniclers' Award, only non-American, contributions to public understanding of space program, 1998. Memberships: British Interplanetary Society; Royal Aeronautical Society. Address: Somerville Lodge, Hillside, Sandgate, Kent CT20 3DB, England.

TUROW Scott, b. 12 Apr 1949, Chicago, Illinois, USA. Lawyer; Writer. m. Annette Weisberg, 4 Apr 1971, 3 children. Education: BA, Amherst College, 1970; MA, Stanford University, 1974; JD, Harvard University, 1978. Appointments: E H Jones Lecturer, Stanford University, 1972-75; Assistant US Attorney, US Court of Appeals, 7th District, Chicago, 1978-86; Partner, Sonnenschien, Nath and Rosenthal, Chicago, 1986-. Publications: One L: An Inside Account of Life in the First Year at Harvard Law School, 1977; Presumed Innocent, 1987; The Burden of Proof, 1990; Pleading Guilty, 1993; The Laws of Our Fathers, 1996. Contributions to: Professional journals. Honours: Edith Mirrielees Fellow, 1972; Silver Dagger Award, Crime Writers Association, 1988. Memberships: Chicago Bar Association; Chicago Council of Lawyers; Federal Bar Association. Address: c/o Sonnenschein, Nath and Rosenthal, Sears Tower, Suite 8000, 233 South Wacker Drive, Chicago, IL 60606, USA.

TUSIANI Joseph, b. 14 Jan 1924, Foggia, Italy (US citizen, 1956). Retired Professor; Writer; Poet. Education: Dottore in Lettere, summa cum laude, University of Naples, 1947. Appointments: Chairman, Italian Department, College Mount St Vincent, 1948-71; Lecturer in Italian, Hunter College, New York City, 1950-62; Visiting Associate Professor, New York University, 1956-64, City University of New York, 1971-83; NDEA Visiting Professor of Italian, Connecticut State College, 1962; Professor, Herbert H Lehman College, New York City, 1971-83. Publications: Dante in Licenza, 1952; Two Critical Essays on Emily Dickinson, 1952; Melos Cordis, Poems in Latin, 1955; Odi Sacre: Poems, 1958; The Complete Poems of Michelangelo, 1960; Lust and Liberty: The Poems of Machiavelli, 1963; Tasso's Jerusalem Delivered (verse translation), 1970; Italian Poets of the Renaissance, 1971; The Age of Dante, 1973; Tasso's Creation of the World, 1982; Rosa Rosarum (poems in Latin), 1984; In Exilio Rerum (poems in Latin), 1985; La Parola Difficile, 3 volumes, 1988, 1991, 1992; Carmina Latina, 1994; Leopardi's Canti (translator), 1994; Le Poesie Inglesi di G A Borgese, 1995; Pulci's Morgante (verse translation), 1998; Dante's Lyric Poems, 1998. Contributions to: Books and journals. Honours: Greenwood Prize for Poetry, 1956; Cavaliere ufficiale, Italy, 1973; Leone di San Marco Award, 1982; Joseph Tusiani Scholarship Fund founded in his honour, Lehman College, 1983; Congressional Medal of Merit, 1984; Progresso Medal of Liberty, 1986; Outstanding Teacher Award, American Association of Teachers of Italian; Renoir Literary Award, 1988 Festschrift published in his honour, 1995; Enrico Fermi Award, 1995; National Endowment for the Humanities, 1998; Fiorello La Guardia Award, 1998. Memberships: Catholic Poetry Society of America; Poetry Society of America. Address: 308 East 72nd Street, New York, NY 10021, USA.

TUTTLE Lisa, b. 16 Sept 1952, Houston, Texas, USA. Writer. Education; BA, Syracuse University, 1973. Publications: Windhaven, 1981; Familiar Spirit, 1983; Catwitch, 1983; Children's Literary Houses, 1984; Encyclopedia of Feminism, 1986; A Spaceship Built of Stone and Other Stories, 1987; Heroines: Women Inspired by Women, 1988; Lost Futures, 1992; Memories of the Body, 1992; Panther in Argyll, 1996; The Pillow Friend, 1996. Contributions to: Magazines. Honour: John W Campbell Award, 1974. Address: 10 Roland Gardens, London SW7, England.

TUTTLE William McCullough, b. 7 Oct 1937, Detroit, Michigan, USA. Professor of History. m. (1) Linda Lee Stumpp, 12 Dec 1959, div, 2 sons, 1 daughter, (2) Kathryn Nemeth, 6 May 1995. Education: BA, Denison University, 1959; MA, 1964, PhD, 1967, University of Wisconsin. Appointments: Assistant Professor, 1967-70, Associate Professor, 1970-75, Professor of History, 1975-, University of Kansas; Senior Fellow in Southern and Negro History, Johns Hopkins University, 1969-70; Research Fellow, Harvard University, 1972-73; Associate Fellow, Stanford Humanities Center, 1983-84; Research Associate, University of California, Berkeley, 1986-88. Publications: Race Riot: Chicago in the Red Summer of 1919, 1970; W E B DuBois, 1973; Plain Folk (co-author), 1982; Daddy's Gone to War: The Second World War in the Lives of America's Children, 1993. Contributions to: Journal of American History; American Studies; Labor History; Technology and Culture. Honours: National Endowment for the Humanities Younger Humanist Fellowship, 1972-73; Award of Merit, American Association for State and Local History, 1972; Guggenheim Fellowship, 1975-76; Evans Grant, 1975-76; Beveridge Grant, 1982; Fellowship for Independent Study and Research, 1983-84; National Endowment for the Humanities Projects Research Grant, 1986-89; Hall Humanities Research Fellow, 1990. Memberships: Society of American Historians; American Historical Association; Organization of American Historians. Address: 21 Winona Avenue, Lawrence, KS 66046, USA.

TUWHARE Hone, b. 21 Oct 1922, Kaikohe, New Zealand. Poet. Education: Seddon Memorial and Otahuhu Technical Colleges, Auckland, 1939-41. Publications: No Ordinary Sun, 1964' Come Rain Hail, 1970; Sapwood and Milk, 1972; Something Nothing, 1973; Making a Fist of it, 1978; Selected Poems, 1980; Year of the Dog, 1982; Mihi: Collected Poems, 1987; Deep River Talk, 1994. Honour: New Zealand Award for Achievement, 1965. Address: c/o John McIndoe Ld, 51 Crawford Street, PO Box 694, Dunedin, New Zealand.

TWICHELL Chase, b. 20 Aug 1950, New Haven, Connecticut, USA. Poet; Writer; Teacher; Publisher. m. Russell Banks, 25 Aug 1989. Education: BA, Trinity College, 1973; MFA, University of Iowa, 1976. Appointments: Editor, Pennyroll Press, 1976-85; Associate Professor, University of Alabama, 1985-88; Lecturer, Princeton University, 1989-97; Associate Faculty, Goddard College, 1996-. Publications: Northern Spy, 1981; The Odds, 1986; Perdido, 1991; The Practice of Poetry (co-editor), 1992; The Ghost of Eden, 1995; The Snow Watcher, 1998. Contributions to: Antaeus; Field; Georgia Review; Nation; New England Review; New Yorker; Ohio Review; Ontario Review; Paris Review; Ploughshares; Poetry Review; Southern Review; Yale Review. Honours: National Endowment for the Arts Fellowships, 1987, 1993; Guggenheim Fellowship, 1990; Artists Foundation Fellowship, Boston, 1990; New Jersey State Council on the Arts Fellowship, 1990; American Academy of Arts and Letters Award, 1994; Alice Fay Di Castagnola Award, Poetry Society of America, 1997. Address: c/o Ellen Levine Literary Agency, 15 East Street, Suite 1801, New York, NY 10010, USA.

TWIGG Malcolm Keith, b. 3 Apr 1945, Woodville, Derbyshire, England. Local Government Officer. m. Anne Bailey, 24 Apr 1971, 1 son. Education: Shorthand and Typing Diplomas, Burton-upon-Trent Technical College, 1961-68; Ordinary National Diploma in Public Administration, Plymouth College, 1974-76; Postgraduate Diploma in Creative Writing, Plymouth University, 1995-97; City and Guilds Stages I and II Adult Teaching Certificate, Newton Abbot and Paignton Community Education, 1996-97. Appointments: Trainee Committee Clerk and Legal Assistant, 1961-68; Foreman, Quality Control Inspector, Rubber Industry, 1968-71; Committee Clerk, 1971-74; Committee Administrator, Torbay Council, South Devon, 1974-. Publications: To Hell with the Harp!, 1997; Altar (short story), 1997; Troubled Waters (short story), 1998; Digger (short story), 1999. Contributions to: Local Government Review; Derbyshire Life; The Lady; Devon Life; Cat World; Quids In; Cornish Scene; Heritage; Fear; Threads; Xenos; Voyage; Noesis. Honours: Winner, Peter Rook Humorous Novel, 1996; Winner, L Ron Hubbards Writers of the Future Contest, 1997. Address: 50 Dower Road, Torquay TQ1 4JH, England.

TWINING William Lawrence, b. 22 Sept 1934, Kampala, Uganda. Professor of Law; Writer. m. Penelope Elizabeth Wall Morris, 31 Aug 1957, 1 son, 1 daughter. Education: BA, 1955, MA, 1960, DCL, 1990, Brasenose College, Oxford; JD, University of Chicago, 1958. Appointments: Professor of Law, University College, London; Editor, Law in Context Series, 1965-, Jurists Series, 1979-. Publications: Karl Llewellyn and the Realist Movement, 1973, 2nd edition, 1985; Law, Publishing and Legal Information, 1981; Theories of Evidence, 1985; Learning Lawyers' Skills, 1989; Rethinking Evidence, 1990; Analysis of Evidence, 1991; How to Do Things With Rules, 1991; Evidence and Proof, 1992; Blackstone's Tower, 1994; Law in Context: Enlarging a Discipline, 1997. Contributions to: Professional journals. Honours: Honorary LLD, University of Victoria, 1980, University of Edinburgh, 1994; British Academy, Fellow, 1997. Memberships: Commonwealth Legal Education Association; Society of Public Teachers of Law; UK Association for Legal and Social Philosophy. Address: c/o Faculty of Law, University College, 4 Endsleigh Gardens, London WC1H OEG, England.

TWUM Michael Kyei, b. 30 Apr 1954. Writer; Poet. m. Maureen Twum, 22 Aug 1986, 3 sons. Education: Modern School of Commerce, Ghana, 1974; University of Bonn, 1981. Publications: Golden Poems from Africa, 1982; Beyond Expectations, 1983; Great Adventures of an African, 1983. Contributions to: Newspapers and magazines. Honours: Certificates, IBC, England; Silver Medal, 1985, Gold Medal, 1987, ABI, USA. Memberships: ABIRA, lifetime deputy governor, IBC; National Association of Writers; PEN; World Institute of Achievement. Address: 78 Acacia Road, Mitcham, Surrey CR4 1ST, England.

TYLER Anne, b. 25 Oct 1941, Minneapolis, Minnesota, USA. Writer. m. Taghi M Modaressi, 3 May 1963, 2 children. Education: BA, Duke University, 1961; Postgraduate Studies, Columbia University, 1962. Publications: If Morning Ever Comes, 1964; The Tin Can Tree, 1965; A Slipping Down Life, 1970; The Clock Winder, 1972; Celestial Navigation, 1974; Searching for Caleb, 1976; Earthly Possessions, 1977; Morgan's Passing, 1980; Dinner at the Homesick Restaurant, 1982; The Best American Short Stories, 1983 (editor with Shannon Ravenel), 1983; The Accidental Tourist, 1985; Breathing Lessons, 1988; Saint Maybe, 1991; Tumble Tower (juvenile), 1993; Ladder of Years, 1995; A Patchwork Planet, 1998. Honours: National Book Critics Circle Award for Fiction, 1985; Pulitzer Prize for Fiction, 1989. Memberships: American Academy of Arts and Letters; American Academy of Arts and Sciences. Address: 222 Tunbridge Road, Baltimore, MD 21212, USA.

TYMICKI Jerzy. See: BRAUN Kazimierz.

TYSON Remer Hoyt, b. 2 July 1934, Statesboro, Georgia, USA. Journalist. m. Virginia Curtin Knight, 18 Feb 1984, 1 son, 1 daughter. Education: Georgia Teacher College, 1952-54; University of Georgia, 1954-56; Art degree, Harvard University, Nieman Fellow, 1967-68; Harvard Business School, 1981. Publication: They Love a Man in the Country, 1988. Memberships: Foreign Correspondents Association of Southern Africa; East Africa Foreign Correspondents Association. Address: PO Box 1326, Mount Pleasant, Harare, Zimbabwe.

U

UGGLA Andrzej Nils, b. 30 Mar 1940, Warsaw, Poland. Researcher. m. Margaretha Backman, 20 Dec 1969, 1 son, 1 daughter. Education: MA, Gdansk University, 1966; DPhil, University of Uppsala, 1977. Publications: Strindberg och den polska teatern, 1890-1970, 1977; Polen i svensk press under andra världskriget, 1986; Den svenska polenbilden och Polsk prosa i Sverige 1939-1960, 1986; Från Politik till litteratur, 1989; Sverige och polska skalder, 1990; Polacy w Szwecji w latach II wojny swiatowej, 1996; Inordlig hamm, 1997; Acta Sueco Polonica (editor). Memberships: Union of Polish Writers Abroad; Stowarzyszenie Pisarzy Polskich; Sveriges Författarförbund. Address: Hovtångsv 10, 756 48 Uppsala, Sweden.

UHNAK Dorothy, b. 1933, Bronx, New York, USA. Writer. Education: City College, New York City; BS, John Jay College of Criminal Justice of the City University of New York, 1968. Appointments: Detective, New York City Transit Police Department, 1953-67. Publications: Policewoman, 1964; The Bait, 1968; The Witness, 1969; The Ledger, 1970; Law and Order, 1973; The Investigation, 1977; False Witness, 1981; Victims, 1985; The Ryer Avenue Story, 1993. Contributions to: Newspapers and magazines. Honours: Edgar, Mystery Writers of America, 1969; Legrande Prix de la Litterateur Policiere, 1971. Memberships: PEN; Writers Guild of America. Address: c/o Simon and Schuster Inc, 1230 Sixth Avenue, New York, NY 10020, USA.

UKEMENAM Joe Chikwendu, b. 30 Mar 1957, Oruku, Nigeria. Social Scientist. Education: Higher Diploma, Journalism, 1984; MA, Social Policy, 1987; PhD, Sociology, Middlesex Polytechnic, 1991. Appointments: Journalist, ABC News Radio and Television, 1977-81; Freelance Journalist, 1983-97; Researcher, Research Survey of Great Britain, 1984-91; Community Consultant, Oxfordshire Probation Service, 1992-95; Executive Director, Reform Corporation, 1995-. Publications: British Theatre in the 19th Century, 1984; Prostitution: The Case for Decriminalization, 1986; The Police we do not deserve, 1987; The Dilemma of Information Logic in Britain, 1989; Black offender demands of the Probation Service, 1993; Ethnic Minorities in British Prisons: The Real Issues; Academic Criminality and Disempowerment, 1995; The Policing Needs of Black People in Britain, 1996. Contributions to: The Renaissance; Black On Black; African Commentary; The Probation Journal; The Journalist. Membership: National Union of Journalists. Address: 7 Oxford Road, London E15 1DD, England.

ULAM Adam B(runo), b. 8 Apr 1922, Lwów, Poland (US citizen, 1949). Professor of History and Political Science Emeritus; Writer. 2 sons. Education: AB, Brown University, 1943; PhD, Harvard University, 1947. Appointments: Faculty, 1947-59, Professor of Government, 1959-92, Gurney Professor of History and Political Science, 1979-92, Professor Emeritus, 1992-, Research Associate, 1948-, Director, 1973-76, 1980-92, Russian Research Center, Harvard University. Publications: The Bolsheviks and Lenin, 1965; Stalin: The Man and His Era, 1972, 2nd edition, 1987; Expansion and Coexistence, 1973; Dangerous Relations: The Soviet Union in World Politics, 1970-82, 1983; The Kirov Affair, 1988; The Communists: The Story of Power and Lost Illusions, 1948-91, 1992. Contributions to: Professional journals. Honours: Guggenheim Fellowships, 1956, 1969; Rockefeller Foundation Fellowships, 1957, 1960; Honorary LLD, Brown University, 1983. Memberships: American Academy of Arts and Sciences; American Philosophical Society. Address: c/o Russian Research Center, Harvard University, Cambridge, MA 02138, USA.

ULRICH Laurel Thatcher, b. 11 July 1938, Sugar City, Idaho, USA. Professor of History. m. Gael Dennis Ulrich, 22 Sept 1958, 3 sons, 2 daughters. Education: BA, University of Utah, 1960; MA, Simmons College, 1971; PhD, University of New Hampshire, 1980. Appointments: Assistant Professor, 1980-88, Associate Professor,

1988-92, Professor of History, 1992-95, University of New Hampshire; Phillips Professor of Early American History and Professor of Women's Studies, Harvard University 1995-. Publications: A Midwife's Tale: The Life of Martha Ballard, 1990; Good Wives, 1991. Contributions to: Journals and magazines. Honours; John S Dunning Prize, 1990; Pulitzer Prize for History, 1991; Bancroft Prize, 1991; Gary Lindberg Award, 1991; New England Historical Association Award, 1991; Guggenheim Fellowship, 1991-92; Charles Frankel Award, 1993. Membership: American Historical Association. Address: Department of History, Robinson Hall, Harvard University, Cambridge, MA 02138, USA.

UNDERHILL Charles. See: HILL Reginald (Charles).

UNDERWOOD Elizabeth, See: **MCCONCHIE Lyn.**

UNGER Barbara, b. 2 Oct 1932, New York, New York, USA. Professor of English and Creative Writing; Poet. m. (1), 2 daughters, (2) Theodore Kiichiro Sakano, 31 July 1987. Education: BA, 1954, MA, 1957, City College of New York. Appointment: Professor of English and Creative Writing, Rockland Cmmunity College, State University of New York, 1969-. Publications: Basement: Poems 1959-63, 1975; The Man Who Burned Money, 1980; Inside the Wind, 1986; Learning to Foxtrot, 1989; Dying for Uncle Ray and Other Stories, 1990; Blue Depression Glass, 1991. Contributions to: Journals and magazines. Honours: Bread Loaf Scholar, 1978; National Poetry Competition Award, 1982; Ragdale Foundation Fellowships, 1985, 1986; Goodman Award in Poetry, 1989; Anna Davidson Rosenberg Award for Poems on the Jewish Experience, 1990; Djerassi Foundation Literature Residency, 1991; JH G Roberts Writing Award in Poetry, 1991. Membership: Poetry Society of America. Literary Agent: Bob Silverstein. Address: 101 Parkside Drive, Suffern, NY 10901, USA.

UNGER J(ames) Marshall, b. 28 May 1947, Cleveland, Ohio, USA. Professor of Japanese; Writer. m. Mutsuyo Okumura Unger, 18 Oct 1976. Education: AB, 1969, AM 1971, University of Chicago; MA, 1972, PhD, 1975, Yale University. Appointments: Senior Lecturer in Japanese, University of Canterbury, Christchurch, New Zealand, 1975-76; Assistant Professor, 1977-82, Associate Professor, 1982-87, Professor of Japanese, 1987-92, University of Hawaii at Manoa; Visiting Scholar, University of Tokyo, 1985; Visiting Professor, University of Tsukuba, 1989, National Museum of Ethnology, Osaka, 1991; Professor of Japanese, University of Maryland at College Park, 1992-96, Ohio State University, 1996-. Publications: Studies in Early Japanese Morphophonemics, 1977, 2nd edition, 1993; The Fifth Generation Fallacy: Why Japan is Betting Its Future on Artificial Intelligence, 1987; Literacy and Script Reform in Occupation Japan: Reading Between the Lines, 1996. Editor: Language, Writing Systems, and Literacy (with Sakiyama Osamu and Umesao Tadao), 1992; A Framework for Introductory Japanese Language Curricula in American High Schools and Colleges (with Fred C Lorish, Mari Noda, and Yasuko Wada), 1993. Contributions to: Numerous books and journals. Honours: Various grants and fellowships. Memberships: American Oriental Society; Association for Asian Studies; Association of Teachers of Japanese; International House of Japan; Linguistic Society of America. Address: 204 Cunz Hall, 1841 Millikin Road, OH 43210, USA.

UNSWORTH Barry (Forster), b. 10 Aug 1930, Durham, England. Novelist. m. Valerie Moor, 15 May 1959, 3 daughters. Education: BA, University of Manchester, 1951. Appointments: Lectureships in English; Writer-in-Residence, University of Liverpool, 1984-85, University of Lund, Sweden, 1988. Publications: The Partnership, 1966; The Greeks Have a Word for It, 1967; The Hide, 1970; Mooncrankers Gift, 1973; The Big Day, 1976; Pascalis Island, 1980, US edition as The Idol Hunter, 1980; The Rage of the Vulture, 1982; Stone Virgin, 1985; Sugar and Rum, 1988; Sacred Hunger, 1992; Morality Play, 1995; After Hannibal, 1996, US edition as Umbrian Mosaic, 1997. Honours: Heinemann Award, Royal Society of Literature, 1974; Arts Counci

Creative Writing Fellowship, 1978-79; Literary Fellow, University of Durham and University of Newcastle upon Tyne, 1983-84; Co-Winner, Booker Prize, 1992. Address: c/o Hamish Hamilton, 22 Wrights Lane, London W8 5TZ, England.

UPDIKE John (Hoyer), b. 18 Mar 1932, Shillington, Pennsylvania, USA. Author; Poet. m. (1) Mary Entwistle Pennington, 26 June 1953, div 1977, 2 sons, 2 daughters, (2) Martha Ruggles Bernhard, 30 Sept 1977, 3 stepchildren. Education: AB, Harvard University, 1954; Ruskin School of Drawing and Fine Art, Oxford, 1954-55. Publications: Fiction: The Poorhouse Affair, 1959; The Same Door, 1959; Rabbit, Run, 1960; Pigeon Feathers and Other Stories, 1962; The Centaur, 1963; Of the Farm, 1965; The Music School, 1966; Couples, 1968; Bech: A Book, 1970; Rabbit Redux, 1971; Museums and Women and Other Stories, 1972; A Month of Sundays, 1975; Marry Me: A Romance, 1976; The Coup, 1979; Too Far to Go: The Maples Stories, 1979; Problems and Other Stories, 1979; Your Lover Just Called: Stories of Joan and Richard Maple, 1980; Rabbit is Rich, 1981; Bech is Back, 1982; The Witches of Eastwick, 1984; Roger's Version, 1986; Trust Me: Short Stories, 1987; S, 1988; Rabbit at Rest, 1990; Memories of the Ford Administration, 1992; Brazil, 1994; The Afterlife and Other Stories, 1994; Toward the End of Time, 1997; Bech at Bay, 1998. Poetry: The Carpenter Hen and Other Tame Creatures, 1958; Telephone Poles and Other Poems, 1963; Midpoint and Other Poems, 1969; Seventy Poems, 1972; Tossing and Turning, 1977; Sixteen Sonnets, 1979; Jester's Dozen, 1984; Facing Nature, 1985; Collected Poems, 1953-1993, 1993. Non-Fiction: Picked Up Pieces, 1975; Hugging the Shore: Essays and Criticism, 1983; Just Looking: Essays on Art, 1989; Self-Consciousness: Memoirs, 1989; Odd Jobs, 1991; A Century of Arts and Letters (editor), 1998. Play: Buchanan Dying, 1974. Contributions to: Many publications. Honours: Guggenheim Fellowship, 1959; National Book Award for Fiction, 1966; Prix Medicis Etranger, 1966; O Henry Awards for Fiction, 1966, 1991; MacDowell Medal for Literature, 1981; Pulitzer Prizes in Fiction, 1982, 1991; National Book Critics Circle Awards for Fiction, 1982, 1991, and for Criticism, 1984; PEN/Malamud Memorial Prize, 1988; National Medal of Arts, 1989. Memberships: American Academy of Arts and Letters; American Academy of Arts and Sciences. Address: c/o Alfred A Knopf Inc, 201 East 50th Street, New York, NY 10022, USA.

UPTON Lee, b. 2 June 1953, St Johns, Michigan, USA. Professor of English; Poet; Writer. m. Eric Jozef Ziolkowski, 31 Mar 1989, 2 daughters. Education: BA, Journalism, Michigan State University, 1978; MFA, English, University of Massachusetts at Amherst, 1981; PhD, English, State University of New York at Binghamton, 1986. Appointments: Visiting Assistant Professor, 1986-87, Assistant Professor, 1988-92, Associate Professor, 1992-98, of English, Professor of English and Writer-in-Residence, 1998-, Lafayette College; Assistant Professor, Grand Valley State University, 1987-88. Publications: Poetry: The Invention of Kindness, 1984; Sudden Distances, 1988; No Mercy, 1989; Approximate Darling, 1996. Criticism: Jean Garrigue: A Poetics of Plenitude, 1991; Obsession and Release: Rereading the Poetry of Louise Bogan, 1996; The Muse of Abandonment: Origin, Identity, Mastery in Five American Poets, 1998. Contributions to: Numerous reviews, quarterlies, journals, and periodicals. Honours: Poetry prizes. Memberships: Modern Language Association; National Council of Teachers of English; Poetry Society of America. Address: c/o Department of English, Lafayette College, Easton, PA 18042, USA.

URE Jean Ann, b. 1 Jan 1943, Caterham, Surrey, England. Writer. m. Leonard Gregory, 12 Aug 1967. Eduction: Webber Douglas Academy of Dramatic Art, 1965-66. Publications: Plague 99, 1989; Captain Cranko and the Crybaby, 1993; The Children Next Door, 1994; Skinner Melon and Me, 1996; Becky Bananas: This is Your Life, 1997; Whistle and I'll come, 1997. Honours: Lanc Book Award, 1989; Stockton Children's Book

Award, 1998. Membership: Society of Authors. Address: 88 Soutbridge Road, Croydon CR0 1AF, England.

URIS Leon (Marcus), b. 3 Aug 1924, Baltimore, Maryland, USA. Author. m. (1) Betty Katherine Beck, 5 Jan 1945, div 1968, 2 sons, 1 daughter, (2) Margery Edwards, 1968, dec 1969, (3) Jill Peabody, 15 Feb 1970, 1 daughter. Education: Baltimore City College. Publications: Battle Cry, 1953; The Angry Hills, 1955; Exodus, 1957; Exodus Revisited, 1959; Mile 18, 1960; Armageddon, 1964; Topaz, 1967; The Third Temple, 1967; QB VII, 1970; Ireland: A Terrible Beauty, 1975; Trinity, 1976; Jerusalem, Song of Songs (with Jill Uris), 1981; The Haj, 1984; Mitla Pass, 1988; Redemption, 1995. Screenplays: Battle Cry, 1954; Gunfight at the OK Corral, 1957. Adaptation: Ari (musical play), 1971. Honours: National Institute of Arts and Letters Grant, 1959; Daroff Memorial Award, 1959; John F Kennedy Medal, Irish-American Society of New York, 1977; Gold Medal, Eire Society of Boston, 1978; Jobotinsky Medal, State of Israel, 1980; Hall Fellow (with Jill Uris), Concord Academy, 1980; Scopus Award, Hebrew University of Jerusalem, 1981; Honorary Doctorates. Address: c/o Doubleday & Co Inc, 666 Fifth Avenue, New York, NY 10103, USA.

URQUHART Jane, b. 21 June 1949, Little Long Lac, Canada. Author. m. Anthony Urquhart, 5 May 1976, 1 daughter. Education: BA, University of Guelph. Appointments: Writer-in-Residence, University of Ottawa, 1990, Memorial University, Newfoundland, 1993, University of Toronto, 1997. Publications: Storm Glass (short fiction), 1987; The Whirlpool (novel), 1986; Changing Heaven (novel), 1990; Away (novel), 1993; The Underpainter (novel), 1997. Honours: Prixd du Meilleur Livre Étranger, France, 1992; Trillium Award, Canada, 1994; Governor General's Award, Canada, 1997. Literary Agent: Ellen Levine. Address: c/o Suite 1801, 15 East 26th Street, New York, NY 10010, USA.

URSELL Geoffrey Barry, b. 14 Mar 1943, Moose Jaw, Saskatchewan, Canada. Writer; Poet; Dramatist; Editor; Composer. m. Barbara Davies, 8 8 July 1967. Education: BA, Honours, 1965, MA, 1966, University of Manitoba; PhD, University of London, 1973. Appointments: Teacher, University of Manitoba, 1971-73, University of Regina, 1975-83; Writer-in-Residence, Saskatoon Public Library, 1984-85, Winnipeg Public Library, 1989-90; Playwright-in-Residence, 1987-89, Associate Artistic Director, 1989-95, 25th Street Theatre; Editor, Grain magazine, 1990-94. Publications: Fiction: Perdue, or How the West Was Lost, 1984; Way Out West!, 1989. Poetry: Trap Lines, 1982; The Look-Out Tower, 1989. Plays: Black Powder, Superwheel (co-author), 1979; The Runnin of the Deer, 1981; Saskatoon Pie!, 1993; Editor: Saskatchewan Gold, 1982; More Saskatchewan Gold, 1984; Prairie Jungle (co-editor), 1985; Sky High, 1988; Jumbo Gumbo (co-editor), 1989; 200% Cracked Wheat, 1992; Due West, 1996. Honours: Canada Council Grants; Clifford E Lee National Playwriting Award, 1977; 1st Novel Award, Books in Canada, 1984. Membership: Alliance of Canadian Cinema, Television, and Radio Artists; PEN; Playwrights Union of Canada; Saskatchewan Playwrights Centre, president, 1984-85; Sasketchewan Writers Guild, president, 1975-77; Society of Composers, Authors, and Music Publishers of Canada; Writers Guild of Canada; Writers' Union of Canada. Address: c/o Coteau Books, 401, 2206 Dewdney Avenue, Regina, Saskatchewan S4R 1H3, Canada.

ÜRT Julius. See: **TART Indrek.**

URUSHIHARA Miyoko, b. Tokyo, Japan. Essayist; Critic. m. 1963-77. Education: Diploma, English Literature, Toyo Women's Junior College, Tokyo, 1961; Home Economics, University of Mississippi, USA; Pratt Institute of Art, New York. Appointments: Interior Designer, George Nelson Design Office, New York City, Kajima Design Company Ltd, Tokyo, and Lecturer of Environmental Design, TAMA University of Fine Arts, Tokyo, 1961-90; Member, Committees of Ministry Panels on Construction, Environment, Land, Transportation, Trade and Industry, others, 1965-. Publications include:

Interior Design - Aims and Principles, 1963; Arts of Daily Life - an Introduction to Comparative Civilization, 1968; Interior Design - an Introduction to Architectural Interiors, translation from English, 1973; Creating Environment for Children, 1973; Aesthetics of Urban Environment, 1978; The Aesthetics for the Love of Mankind, 1978; Elegant Spaces and Times for Women, 1986; The Enjoyments of City Life, 1993. Contributions to: Journal of Municipal Problems, 1998; The Aesthetics and Ethics of Urban Scenery; Most major magazines and newspapers. Honours: Fellow, Japan Society, 1958; Co-recipient, Japan Architectural Association Award, 1965. Membership: International Association of Art Critics, Paris, France. Address: Hiroo 4-1-4-604, Shibuya-ku, Tokyo 150-0012, Japan.

USHAKOVA Elena. See: **NEVZGLIADOVA Elena Vsevologovna.**

USHERWOOD Elizabeth (Ada), b. 10 July 1923, London, England. Writer. m. Stephen Usherwood, 24 Oct 1970. Publications: Visit Some London Catholic Churches (with Stephen Usherwood), 1982; The Counter-Armada, 1596: The Journal of the "Mary Rose" (with Stephen Usherwood), 1983; We Die for the Old Religion (with Stephen Usherwood), 1987; Women First, 1989; A Saint in the Family (with Stephen Usherwood), 1992. Address: 24 St Mary's Grove, London N1 2NT, England.

USTINOV Sir Peter, b. 16 Apr 1921, London, England. Author; Actor; Playwright; Director. m. (3) Helene du Lau d'Allemans, 1972. Education: Westminster School. Appointments: Author, Actor, Playwright and Director, 1940-; Goodwill Ambassador, UNICEF, 1969-. Publications: House of Regrets, 1942; Blow Your Own Trumpet, 1943; Beyond, 1943; The Bambury Nose, 1944; Plays About People, 1950; The Love of Four Colonels, 1951; The Moment of Truth, 1951; Romanoff and Juliet, 1956; And a Dash of Pity: Short Stories, 1959; The Loser (novel), 1961; Photo Finish, 1962; Five Plays, 1965; The Frontiers of the Sea, 1966; The Unknown Soldier and his Wife: Two Acts of War Separated by a Truce for Refreshment, 1967; Halfway up the Tree, 1967; The Wit of Peter Ustinov, 1969; Kumnagel (novel), 1971; R Love J, 1973; Dear Me (memoirs), 1977; My Russia (memoirs/travel), 1983; Ustinov in Russia, 1987; The Disinformer (novella), 1989; The Old Man and Mr Smith, 1990; Ustinov at Large, 1991; Still at Large, 1993; Monsieur René, 1998. Honours: Commander of the Order of the British Empire, 1975; Knighted, 1990. Address: 11 Rue de Silly, 92100 Boulogne, France.

UYARIWAK. See: **ESAIN Simón Salvador.**

V

VACHSS Andrew, b. New York City, USA. Attorney. Education: BA, Case-Western Reserve University, 1965; United States Public Health Service Interviewing School, 1965; Industrial Areas Foundation Training Institute Fellow, 1970-71; John Hay Whitney Foundation Fellow, 1976-77. Appointments: Board of Counselors, VIVITAS Child/Trauma Programs, Baylor College of Medicine, Houston; Expert Advisory Panel on Catastrophic Child Abuse, New York State Office of Mental Health. Publications include: Hard Looks, 1992; Shella, 1993; Predator: Race War, 1993; Underground, 1993; Born Bad, 1994; Down in the Zero, 1994; Footsteps of the Hawk, 1995; Cross, 1995; Batman: The Ultimate Evil, 1995; False Allegations, 1996; Hard Looks, 1996; Safe House, 1998; Safe House: A Collection of the Blues, 1998. Contributions to: The Ultimate Fascism, 1996; How Journalism Abuses Children, 1996; If We Really Want to Protect Children, 1996; Cyber-chumps, 1997; A Hard Look At How We Treat Children, 1998. Honours: The Grand Prix de Littérature Policiè, 1988; The Falcon Award, 1988; The Deutschen Krimi Preis, 1989. Memberships: National Association of Counsel for Children; American Porfessional Society on the Abuse of Children; PEN American Center; Writers Guild of America. Literary Agent: Lou Bank of Ten Angry Pitbulls. Address: 1701 Broadway #350, Vancouver, WA 98663-3436, USA.

VAGGE Ornello, (Lionello Grifo), b. 10 Aug 1934, Rome, Italy. Poet; Writer; Translator. m. Education: PhD, Political and Social Sciences, Brussels, 1958. Publications: Many poems and short stories, 1980-97. Contributions to: Numerous anthologies, journals, and magazines. Honours: Communaute Europeene des Journalistes Prize, Malta, 1972; Commenda della Repubblica Italiana, Rome, 1973; Genti e Paesi Prize for Poetry, La Spezia, Regione Liguria and Dante Alighieri Society, 1990; Trofeo Letterario Biellese di Poesia, 1994; Premio Internazionale Lerici, PEA, 1995. Memberships: ABI, research fellow; International Society of Poets; Italian Society of Authors and Publishers; Ordine Nazionale Giornalisti Italiani; Societá Dante Alighieri; World Literary Academy. Address: c/o Blue Jay Press, Apdo Correos 32, E-30380 La Manga del Mar Menor, Spain.

VALENCAK Hannelore, b. 23 Jan 1929, Donawitz, Austria. Writer; Poet. m. (2) Viktor Mayer, 28 Apr 1962, 1 son. Education: PhD, Physics, University of Graz. Publications: Novels: Die Hohlen Noahs, 1961; Ein Fremder Garten, 1964; Zuflucht hinter der Zeit, 1967; Vorhof der Wirklichkeit, 1972; Das magische Tagebuch, 1981. Other: Various short stories, poems, and book for young people. Contributions to: Many publications. Honours: National Advancement Award, 1957; Peter Rosegger Prize, Styria, 1966; Austrian Children's Book Prize, 1977; Amade Prize, Monaco, 1978. Memberships: Austrian PEN Club; Austrian Writers Union; Podium. Address: Schwarzspanierstrasse 15/2/8, A-1090, Vienna, Austria.

VALENTE José Angel, b. 25 Apr 1929, Orense, Spain. Poet; Writer. m. Coral Gutierrez-Valente, 24 Nov 1984, 2 daughters. Education: BLitt, University of Madrid, 1953; MA, University of Oxford, 1957. Appointments: Lecturer in Spanish Studies, University of Oxford, 1955-58; International Civil Servant, Geneva, 1959-80; Chief, Spanish Translation Service, UNESCO, Paris, 1980-84. Publications: A Modo de esperanza, 1955; La Palabras de la tribu, 1971; Variaciones dobre et pajaroy la red (essays), 1991; No amanece el cantor, 1992; Pun de la to cero (poems 1979-89), 1992. Contributions to: Several publications. Honours: Premio Adonais, 1954; Premios, Critica, 1960, 1980; Premio, Fundacion Pablo Iglesias, 1984; Premio, Principe de Asturias para las Letras, 1988; Premio nacional de Poesia, 1993. Address: Apartado 195, 04080 Almeria, Spain.

VALENTINE Alec. See: **ISAACS Alan.**

VALENTINE Jean, b. 27 Apr 1934, Chicago, Illinois, USA. Poet; Teacher. m. James Chace, 1957, div 1968, 2 daughters. Education: BA, Radcliffe College, 1956. Appointments: Teacher, Swarthmore College, 1968-70; Barnard College, 1968, 1970, Yale University, 1970, 1973-74, Hunter College of the City University of New York, 1970-75, Sarah Lawrence College, Columbia University, 1974-. Publications: Poetry: Dream Barker and Other Poems, 1965; Pilgrims, 1969; Ordinary Things, 1974; Turn, 1977; The Messenger, 1979; Home, Deep, Blue: New and Selected Poems, 1988; Night Lake, 1992; The River at Wolf, 1992. Honours: Yale Series of Younger Poets Award, 1965; National Endowment for the Arts Grant, 1972; Guggenheim Fellowship, 1976. Address: c/o Department of Writing, Columbia University, New York, NY 10027, USA.

VALERIO Anthony, b. 13 May 1940, USA. Author. 1 son, 2 daughters. Education: BA, Columbia College, 1962. Publications: Bart: A Life of A Bartlett Giamatti; Valentino and the Great Italians; The Mediterranean Runs Through Brooklyn. Contributions to: Paris Review; Philadelphia Magazine; Patterson Review; Anthologies; Dream Streets; Columbus Review. Membership: PEN. Address: 106 Charles Street, 14 New York, NY 10014, USA.

VALERY Anne. See: **FIRTH Anne Catherine.**

VALGARDSON W(illiam) D(empsey), b. 7 May 1939, Winnipeg, Manitoba, Canada. Writer; Poet; Dramatist; Professor. Div, 1 son, 1 daughter. Education: BA, United College, 1961; BEd, University of Manitoba, 1966; MFA, University of Iowa, 1969. Appointments: Associate Professor, 1970-74, Professor, 1974-, University of Victoria, British Columbia; Fiction Editor, Canadian Author, 1996-. Publications: Bloodflowers, 1973; God is Not a Fish Inspector, 1975; In the Gutting Shed, 1976; Red Dust, 1978; Gentle Simmers, 1980; The Carpenter of Dreams, 1986; What Can't Be Changed Shouldn't Be Mourned, 1990; The Girl With the Botticelli Face, 1992; Thor, 1994; Sarah and the People of Sand River, 1996; Garbage Creek, 1997. Contributions to: Magazines. Honours: Books in Canada First Novel Award, 1980; Ethel Wilson Literary Prize, 1992; Mr Christie Prize, 1995; Vicky Metcalf Short Story Award, 1998; Honarary DLitt. Address: 1908 Waterloo Road, Victoria, British Columbia V8P 1J3, Canada.

VALLBONA (Rothe) de Rima Gretchen, b. 15 Mar 1931, San José, Costa Rica. Professor of Hispanic Literature Emeritus; Author. m. Carlos Vallbona, 26 Dec 1956, 1 son, 3 daughters. Education: BA, BS, Colegio Superior de Senoritas, San José, 1948; MA, University of Costa Rica, 1962; DML, Middlebury College, 1981. Appointments: Professor, Hispanic Literature, Liceo J.J. Vargas Calvo, Costa Rica, 1955-56, Professor of Hispanic Literature, 1964-95, Professor Emeritus, 1995-, Member, Editorial Board: Letras Femeninas, 1975-, Alba de America, 1981-, Foro Literario, 1979-89; Co-Director, Foro, 1984-89; Contributing Editor, The America's Review, 1989-. Publications: Noche en vela, 1968; Polvo del camino, 1971; Yolanda Oreamuno, 1972; La Salamandra Rosada, 1979; La obra en prosa de Eunice Odio, 1981; Mujeres y agonias, 1982; Las sombras que perseguimos, 1983; Cosecha de pecadores, 1988; El arcángel del perdòn, 1990; Mundo demonio y mujer, 1991; Los infiernos de la mujer y algo mas, 1992; Vida i sucesos de la Morja Alférez, 1992; Flowering Inferno - Tales of Sinking Hearts, 1993; Tormy, La Prodigiosa Gata de Donaldito, 1997. Contributions to: Professional journals and general magazines. Honours: Aquileo J Echeverria Costa Rican Novel Prize, 1968; Agripina Montes del Valle Novel Prize, Colombia, 1978; Ancora Literary Award, Costa Rica, 1984; El Lazo de Dama de la Orden del Mérito Civil, Spain, 1988; Cullen Foundation Professor of Spanish, 1989; Hall of Fame, The Houston Hispánic, 1997; Honarary Member, Instituto Literario y Cultural Hispánico, 1998. Memberships: Comunidad de Escritores Latinoamericanos de Costa Rica; Associacion de Literatura Femenina Hispanica; National Writers Association; Instituto Literario y Cultural Hispanico. Address: 3706 Lake Street, Houston, Texas 77098, USA.

VALTINOS Thanassis, b. 16 Dec 1932, Arcadia, Greece. Author; Screenwriter. 1 daughter. Education: Cinematography studies, Athens, 1950-53. Publications: Various books and screenplays, 1972-92. Contributions to: Periodicals. Honours: Screenwriter's Prize, Cannes Film Festival, 1984; Greek State Prize for Literature, 1989. Memberships: European Academy of Science and Arts; Greek Society of Playwrights; Greek Society of Writers; International Theatre Institute. Address: Astydamantos 66-68, Athens 11634, Greece.

VAN BRAAM Dorian, (Dorian van de Braâm, Dorian de Brâam, Baron de Braam), b. 7 Jan 1941, Lewes, Sussex, England. Poet; Writer; Journalist. m. Natalie Jane Shaw, 2 sons, 1 daughter. Education: Brighton Technical College; Barcelona University. Appointments: Freelance Journalist, Spain and England, 1964-; Founder, Editor, Renaissance Press, 1996-97. Publications: Numerous as anonymous author; Ghost books; Works on politics; Civil Rights Movement, 1976 Renaissance. Contributions to: Numerous. Memberships: Poetry Society, London; The Renaissance Society of Europe; Fabian Society. Literary Agent: Renaissance Management. Address: Rathmore House, Fiddown, Co Kilkenny, Republic of Ireland.

VAN COTT NIVEN Laurence. See: **NIVEN Larry.**

VAN DE BERGE Claude. See: **PAUWELS Rony.**

VAN DE LAAR Waltherus Antonius Bernardinus, (Victor Vroomkoning, Stella Napels), b. 6 Oct 1938, Boxtel, Netherlands. Poet; Writer. 1 son, 1 daughter. Education: MA, Phylosophy, Dutch Linguistics and Literature, 1978; Degree in Philosophy, 1990. Appointments: Teacher, Interstudie teachers' training college, Arnhem, 1977-83; Co-Editor, Kirtisch Literatur Lexicon, 1981-. Publications: De einders tegemoet, 1983; De laatste dingen, 1983; Circuit des souvenirs, 1984; Klein museum, 1987; Groesbeek Tijdrit, 1989; Echo van een echo, 1990; Oud zeer, 1993; Een zucht als bluchtig eerbetoon, 1995. Lippendienst, 1997; Ysbeerbestaan, 1999. Contributions to: Magazines and periodicals. Honour: Pablo Neruda Prize, 1983. Membership: Lira. Address: Aldenhof, 70-17, 6537 DZ Nijmegen, Netherlands.

VAN DE POL Lotte Constance, b. 11 May 1949, Enschede, Netherlands. Historian. m. Egmond Elbers, 15 Mar 1985, 2 daughters. Education: MA, History and English, University of Amsterdam, 1977; PhD, History, Erasmus University, Rotterdam, 1996. Appointments: Teacher of History, Hervormd Lyceum, Amsterdam, 1977-78, Rijks Pedagogische Academie (Teacher Training College), Amersfoort, 1977-81; Research Fellow, Department of History, Erasmus University, Rotterdam, 1982-88. Publications: Daar was laatst een meisje loos. Nederlandse vrouwen als matrozen en soldaten: Een historisch onderzoek (co-author), 1981; F. L. Kersteman: De Bredasche Heldinne (co-author), 1988; The Tradition of Female Transvestism in Early Europe (co-author), 1989; Vrouwen in mannenkleren: De geschiedenis van een tegendraadse traditie: Europa 1500-1800 (co-author), 1989; Frauen in Männerkleidern: Weibliche Transvestiten und ihre Geschichte (co-author), 1990; Kvinnor i manskläder: En avvikande tradition, Europa 1500-1800 (co-author), 1995; Het Amsterdams Hoerdom. Prostitutie in de 17e en 18e eeuw, 1996. Contributions to: Books and professional journals. Membership: Maatschappij der Nederlandse Letterkunde, 1997-. Address: Jan van Scorelstraat 127, 3583 CM Utrecht, The Netherlands.

VAN DER KISTE John Patrick Guy, b. 15 Sept 1954, Wendover, Bucks, England. Author; Library Assistant. Education: Ealing Technical College School of Librarianship; Associateship of Library Association. Appointments: Library Assistant, Plymouth College of Further Education, 1978-. Publications: Frederick III, 1981; Dearest Affie, with Bee Jordaan, 1984; Queen Victoria's Children, 1986; Windsor and Habsburg, 1987; Edward VII's Children, 1989; Beyond the Summertime, with Derek Wadeson, 1990; Princess Victoria Melita,

1991; George V's Children, 1991; George III's Children, 1992; Crowns in a Changing World, 1993; Kings of the Hellenes, 1994; Childhood at Court, 1995; Northern Crowns, 1996; King George II & Queen Caroline, 1997; The Romanovs 1818-1959,.1998; Kaiser Wilhelm II, 1999. Contributions to: Articles to various historical antiques and music journals; Also contributions to Guinness Rockopaedia. Address: c/o Sutton Publishing Ltd, Phoenix Mill, Thrupp, Stroud, Glos GL5 2BU, England.

VAN DER VAT Dan, b. 1939, Alkmaar, Netherlands. Writer; Journalist. m. Christine Mary Ellis, 1962, 2 daughters. Education: BA, Honours, Classics, University of Durham, 1960. Appointments: The Journal, Newcastle upon Tyne, 1960; Daily Mail, 1963; The Sunday Times, 1965; The Times, 1967; The Guardian, 1982-88. Publications: The Grand Scuttle, 1982; The Last Corsair, 1983; Gentlemen of War, 1984; The Ship That Changed the World, 1985; The Atlantic Campaign, 1939-45, 1988; The Pacific Campaign, 1941-45, 1991; Freedom Was Never Like This: A Writer's Journey in East Germany, 1991; Stealth at Sea: History of the Submarine, 1994; The Riddle of the Titanic (with Robin Gardiner), 1995; The Good Nazi: The Life and Lies of Albert Speer, 1997. Contributions to: Newspapers, magazines, radio, and television. Honours: Best First Work Award, Yorkshire Post, 1982; Best Book of the Sea Award, King George's Fund for Sailors, 1983. Memberships: Campaign for Freedom of Information; Society of Authors. Address: c/o Curtis Brown Ltd, 28/29 Haymarket, London SW1Y 4SP, England.

VAN DER WEE Herman (Frans Anna), Baron, b. 10 July 1928, Lier, Belgium. Professorem of Social and Economic History; Writer. m. Monique Verbreyt, 27 Feb 1954, 1 son, 1 daughter. Education: BA, Philosophy, 1949, LLD, 1950, Licentiaat, Political and Social Sciences (MA Status), 1951, Doctor in Historical Sciences, 1963, University of Leuven; Graduate Studies, Sorbonne, University of Paris, London School of Economics and Political Science. Publications: Prix et salaires: Manuel Méthodologie, 1956; The Growth of the Antwerp Market and the European Economy (Fourteenth-Sixteenth Centuries), 3 vols, 1963; The Great Depression Revisited, 1972; The Rise of Mangerial Capitalism, 1974; La Banque Nationale de Belgique et la politique monétaire entre le deux guerres, 1975; Winkler Prins History of the Low Countries, 3 vols, 1977; Prosperity and Upheaval: The World Economy, 1945-1980, 1986; Histoire economique mondiale, 1945-1990, 1990; The Low Countries in Early Modern Age, 1993; History of European Banking, 1994; The Paramount Challenge, 1822-1997, 1997; The Generale Bank 1822-1997: A Continuing Challenge, 1997; Economic History of Belguim since 1870, 1997. Contributions to: Books and professional journals. Honours: De Stassart Prize, Royal Academy of Belgium, 1968; Fulbright-Hayes Awards, 1975, 1981; Quinquennial Solvay Prize, National Foundation of Scientific Research, Belgium, 1981; msterdam Prize, Royal Academy of the Netherlands, 1992; Honorary doctorates, University of Brussels, 1994, University of Leicester, 1995; Knighted (Baron), 1994; Golden Medal for Special Merits, Flemish Parliament, 1996. Memberships: American Academy of Sciences, honorary foreign member; British Academy, corresponding fellow; Leuven Institute for Central and East European Studies, President; International Economic History Association, president, 1986-90, honorary president, 1990-; Leuven University Press, president, 1986-1993; Advisory Council of the W Wilson International Centre for Scholars, Chairman, 1986-1991; Academic Advisory Council of the European Association for Banking History, Chairman, 1991-1998; Royal Academy of Belgium, full member; Royal Academy of Sciences of the Netherlands, foreign member. Address: De Hettinghe, B-9170 St Pauwels, Belgium.

VAN DUYN Mona (Jane), b. 9 May 1921, Waterloo, Iowa, USA. Poet; Writer; Critic; Editor; Reviewer; Lecturer. m. Jarvis A Thurston, 31 Aug 1943. Education: BA, Iowa State Teachers College, 1942; MA, State University of Iowa, 1943. Appointments: Reviewer, Poetry

magazine, 1944-70; Instructor in English, State University of Iowa, 1945, University of Louisville, 1946-50; Founder-Editor (with Jarvis A Thurston), Perspective: A Quarterly of Literature, 1947-67; Lecturer in English, 1950-67, Adjunct Porfessor, 1983, Visiting Hurst Professor, 1987, Washington University, St Louis; Poetry Advisor, College English, 1955-57; Lecturer, Salzburg Seminar in American Studies, 1973; Poet-in-Residence, Bread Loaf Writing Conferences, 1974, 1976; Poet Laureate of the USA, 1992-93; Numerous poetry readings. Publications: Valentines to the Wide World: Poems, 1959; A Time of Bees, 1964; To See, To Take, 1970; Bedtime Stories, 1972; Merciful Disguises: Poems Published and Unpublished, 1973; Letters From a Father and Other Poems, 1982; Near Changes: Poems, 1990; Lives and Deaths of the Poets and Non-Poets, 1991; If It Be Not I: Collected Poems, 1992; Firefall, 1993. Contributions to: Many anthologies; Poems, criticism, reviews, and short stories in various periodicals. Honours: Eunice Tietjens Memorial Prize, 1956; National Endowment for the Arts Grants, 1966-67, 1985; Harriet Monroe Memorial Prize, 1968; Hart Crane Memorial Award, 1968; 1st Prize, Borestone Mountain Awards, 1968; Bollingen Prize, 1970; National Book Award for Poetry, 1971; Guggenheim Fellowship, 1972-73; Loines Prize, National Institute of Arts and Letters, 1976; Fellow, Academy of American Poets, 1981; Sandburg Prize, Cornell College, 1982; Shelley Memorial Award, Poetry Society of America, 1987; Ruth Lilly Prize, 1989; Pulitzer Prize in Poetry, 1991. Memberships: Academy of American Poets, chancellor, 1985; National Institute of Arts and Letters. Address: 7505 Teasdale Avenue, St Louis, MO 63130, USA.

VAN HEERDEN Etienne Roché, b. 3 Dec 1954, Johannesburg, South Africa. Professor; Writer. m. Karin Reuter, 8 Dec 1979, 2 daughters. Education: BA, Law; BA Hons, cum laude; MA, cum laude; LLB; PhD. Appointments: Attorney, Supreme Court of South Africa; Professor, Rhodes University. Publications: My Kubaan, 1983; Toorberg, 1986; Liegfabriek, 1988; Lasspirs en Camparis, 1991; Die Stoetmeester, 1993. Contributions to: Numerous publications worldwide. Honours: Perskor Prize, 1980; Eugene Marais Prize, 1983; Hertzog Prize, 1986; Hofaeyr Prize, 1986; CNA Prizes, 1986, 1988; ATKV Prizes, 1986, 1989; Rapport Prizes, 1993. Address: c/o Department of Afrikaans, Rhodes University, Box 94, Grahamstown 6140, South Africa.

VAN HERK Aritha, b. 26 May 1954, Wetaskiwin, Alberta, Canada. Professor; Writer. m. Robert Sharp, 14 Sept 1974. Education: BA, 1976, MA, 1978, University of Alberta. Appointments: Assistant Professor, 1983-85, Associate Professor, 1985-91, Professor, 1991-, University of Calgary. Publications: Judith, 1978; More Stories from Western Canada (co-editor), 1980; The Tent Peg, 1981; West of Fiction (co-editor), 1983; No Fixed Address, 1986; Places Far From Ellesmere, 1990; Alberta Rebound (editor), 1990; In Visible Ink, 1991; A Frozen Tongue, 1992; Boundless Alberta (editor), 1993; Due West, 1996. Honours: Seal Books First Novel Award, 1978; Alberta Achievement Award in Literature, 1978. Address: c/o Department of English, University of Calgary, Calgary, Alberta, Canada T2N 1N4.

VAN OVER Raymond, b. 29 June 1934, Inwood, Long Island, New York, USA. Writer. Appointments: Editor, Garrett/Helix Press, 1962-65, International Journal of Parapsychology, 1965-68; Film and Story Editor, 20th Century Fox and Columbia Pictures, 1968-72; Instructor, Hofstra University, 1973-76, New York University, 1973-76. Publications: Explorer of the Mind, 1967; I Ching, 1971; A Treasury of Chinese Literature, 1972; Psychology and Extrasensory Perception, 1972; Unfinished Man, 1972; The Chinese Mystics, 1973; Taoist Tales, 1973; Total Meditation, 1973; The Psychology of Freedom, 1974; Eastern Mysticism, 2 volumes, 1977; Sun Songs, 1980; Smearing the Ghost's Face With Ink, 1983; Monsters You Never Heard Of, 1983; Khomeini: A Biography, 1985; The Twelfth Child, 1990; Whisper, 1991; In a Father's Rage, 1991. Other: Screenplays and documentaries. Contributions to: Journals and magazines. Memberships: American

Society for Psychical Research; Author's Guild. Address: 2905 Rittenhouse Street North West, Washington, DC 20015, USA.

VAN STAAVEREN Jacob, b. 9 Apr 1917, Polk County, Oregon, USA. Independent Historian. m. Elizabeth Graham Kelly, 5 Aug 1961. Education: BA, Linfield College, McMinnville, Oregon, 1939; MA, 1943, Graduate Fellow, 1948-49, University of Chicago. Appointments include: Civil Information and Education Officer, Yamanashi Military Government Team, Kofu, Japan, 1946-48; US Government Historian: Economic Affairs Division, Civil Historical Section, Supreme Commander for the Allied Powers, Tokyo, 1950-51, Far East Air Forces, Headquarters, 5th Air Force, Taegu and Seoul, South Korea, 1951-52, Military History Liaison Office, UN Command and Far East Command, Tokyo, 1953-57, Strategic Air Command, 1957-58; US Air Force Historical Liaison Office, now Center for Air Force History, 1958-81; Independent Historian, 1981-; Interviewee, Japan Since 1945, 8-part BBC TV documentary. Publications: The Far East Command, 1 January 1947-30 June 1957, 1957; An American in Japan, 1945-1946: A Civilian View of the Occupation, 1964, in Japanese, 1998; The United States Air Force in Southeast Asia, 1961-1963 (co-author), 1984; Interdiction in Southern Laos, 1960-68, 1993; Gradual Failure: The Air War Against North Vietnam, 1965-1966, 1998; The Cold War in Occupied Japan, 1945-1952, forthcoming. Contributions to: The Educational Revolution in Japan, in Educational Forum, 1952; Enforcing SCAP's Religious Directives on a Military Government Team, in Annals of the Southeast Conference, Association for Asian Studies, January 14-16 1988; The Democratization of the Japanese, September 1946-September 1948, in The Occupation of Japan: The Grass Roots: The Proceedings of a Symposium, November 7-8, 1991; Others. Honours: Several Superior Performance and Outstanding Awards. Memberships: Society for History in the Federal Government; Association for Asian Studies; The American Historical Association; The National Association of Scholars. Address: 1008 Cascade Way, McMinnville, OR 97128, USA.

VAN TOORN Penelope, b. 19 Dec 1952, Sydney, New South Wales, Australia. University Lecturer; Literary Critic. Education: BA, Honours, 1980, MA, Honours, 1984, University of Sydney; PhD, University of British Columbia, 1991. Publications: Rudy Wiebe and the Historicity of the Word, 1995; Speaking Positions: Aboriginality, Gender and Ethnicity in Australian Cultural Studies (co-editor), 1995; Neil Bissoondath, Canadian Writers and Their Works, Vol 11, 1997. Contributions to: Southern Review; Meanjin; Southerly; SPAN Journal of Commonwealth Literature; Literature and Theology; Canadian Literature; New Literatures Review. Address: Department of English, University of Sydney, Sydney, New South Wales 2006, Australia.

VANCE William L(ynn), b. 19 Apr 1934, Dupree, South Dakota, USA. Professor of English; Writer. Education: AB, Oberlin College, 1956; MA, English Language and Literature, 1957, PhD, English Language and Literature, 1962, University of Michigan. Appointments: Assistant Professor, 1962-67, Associate Professor, 1967-73, Professor of English, 1973-, Boston University. Publications: American Literature (co-editor), 2 volumes, 1970; America's Rome, Vol I, Classical Rome, 1989, Vol II, Catholic and Contemporary Rome, 1989; The Faber Book of America (co-editor), 1992; Immaginari a confronto (co-editor), 1993. Honours: Association of American Publishing Prize, 1989; Ralph Waldo Emerson Prize, Phi Beta Kappa, 1990; Guggenheim Fellowship, 1990-91; Honorary LLD, University of South Dakota, 1992. Membership: Modern Language Association. Address: 255 Beacon Street, Boston, MA 02116, USA.

VANDERHAAR Gerard A(nthony), b. 15 Aug 1931, Louisville, Kentucky, USA. Professor; Writer. m. Janice Marie Searles, 22 Dec 1969. Education: BA, Providence College, 1954; STD, University of St Thomas, Rome, 1965. Appointments: Faculty, St John's University, New York, 1964-65, Providence College 1965-68; Wesleyan

University, 1968-69, Christian Brothers University, 1971-. Publications: A New Vision and a New Will for Memphis, 1974; Christians and Nonviolence in the Nuclear Age, 1982; Enemies and How to Love Them, 1985; Way of Peace: A Guide to Nonviolence (co-editor), 1987; The Philippines: Agony and Hope (co-author), 1989; Active Nonviolence: A Way of Personal Peace, 1990; Why Good People Do Bad Things, 1994; Beyond Violence, 1998. Booklets: Nonviolence, Theory and Practice, 1980; Nonviolence in Christian Tradition, 1983. Contributions to: Reference books and journals. Honours: Outstanding Educators of America, 1971; Distinguished Service Award, United Nations Association, 1981; Catholic Press Association Book Award for Spirituality, 1991; Tennessee Higher Education Commission Award for Community Service, 1994; Pax Chisti National Book Award, 1998. Memberships: American Academy of Religion; American Association of University Professors; Pax Christi;Fellowship of Reconcilliation; War Registers League. Address: 3554 Boxdale, Apt 3, Memphis, TN 38118, USA.

VANDERHAEGHE Guy (Clarence), b. 5 Apr 1951, Esterhazy, Saskatchewan, Canada. Writer; Dramatist. m. Margaret Nagel, 2 Sept 1972. Education: BA, 1971, MA, 1975, University of Saskatchewan; BEd, University of Regina, 1978. Appointment: Visiting Professor of English, St Thomas More College, University of Saskatchewan, 1993-. Publications: Man Descending, 1982; The Trouble with Heroes, 1983; My Present Age, 1984; Homesick, 1989; Things as They Are?, 1992; The Englishman's Boy, 1996. Plays: I Had a Job I Liked Once, 1992; Dancock's Dance, 1996. Honours: Governor-General's Awards for Fiction, 1982, 1996; Geoffrey Faber Memorial Prize, England, 1987; Co-Winner, City of Toronto Book Award, 1990; Canadian Authors Associatioin Awards for Drama, 1993, 1996; Saskatchewan Book Award, 1996; Honorary DLitt, University of Saskatchewan, 1997. Address: c/oi Department of English, St Thomas More College, University of Saskatchewan, Saskatoon, Saskatchewan S7N OW0, Canada.

VANDERKAM James Claire, b. 15 Feb 1946, Cadillac, Michigan, USA. Professor of Theology; Writer. m. Mary Vander Molen, 24 Aug 1967, 2 sons, 1 daughter. Education: AB, Calvin College, 1968; BD, Calvin Theological Seminary, 1971; PhD, Harvard University, 1976. Appointment: Professor of Theology, Universit of Notre Dame. Publications: Textual and Historical Studies in the Book of Jubilees, 1977; Enoch and the Growth of Apocalyptic Tradition, 1984; The Book of Jubilees, 2 volumes, 1989; The Dead Sea Scrolls Today, 1994; Enoch: A Man for All Generations, 1995; The Jewish Apocalypfis Heritage in Early Christianity (editor with William Alder), 1996; Calenders in the Dead Sea Scrolls, 1998. Honours: Distinguished Research and Literary Publication Award, College of Humanities and Social Sciences, North Carolina State University, 1991; Biblical Archaeology Society Publication Award for Best Popular Book on Archaeology, 1995. Address: Department of Theology, University of Notre Dame, Notre Dame, IN 46556, USA.

VANDIEVOET Jacques F G. See: **ORIOL Jacques.**

VANDIVER Frank Everson, b. 9 Dec 1925, Austin, TX, USA. Historian; Educator. m. (1) Carol Sue Smith, 19 Apr 1952, dec 1979, 1 son, 2 daughters, (2) Renee Aubry, 21 Mar 1980. Education: MA, University of Texas, 1949; PhD, Tulane University, 1951; MA, University of Oxford, 1963. Appointments: Assistant Professor of History, Washington University, St Louis, 1952-55; Professor of History, Louisiana State University, 1953-57; Assistant Professor, 1955-56, Associate Professor, 1956-58, Professor of History, 1958-65, Harris Masterson Jr Professor of History, 1965-79, Acting President, 1969-70, Provost, 1970-79, Vice President, 1975-79, Rice University; Harmsworth Professor of American History, University of Oxford, 1963-64; President and Chancellor, North Texas State University at Denton and Texas College of Osteopathic Medicine, 1979-81; President, 1981-88, President Emeritus and Distinguished University Professor, 1988-, Texas A & M University at College Station; Chairman of the Board, 1992-97, Acting President, 1997-98, American University, Cairo; Various visiting lectureships and professorships. Publications: Ploughshares Into Swords: Josiah Gorgas and the Confederate Command System, 1956; Mighty Stonewall, 1957; Fields of Glory (with W H Nelson), 1960; Jubal's Raid, 1960; Basic History of the Confederacy, 1962; Jefferson Davis and the Confederate State, 1964; Their Tattered Flags: The Epic of the Confederacy, 1970; The Southwest: South or West?, 1975; Black Jack: The Life and Times of John J Pershing, 1977; The Long Loom of Lincoln, 1986; Blood Brothers: A Short History of the Civil War, 1992; Shadows of Vietnam: Lyndon Johnson's Wars, 1997. Editor: Several volumes. Contributions to: Oxford Book of United STates Military History; Facing Armageddon (chapters); Passchendaele in Perspective (chapters). Honours: Many honorary doctorates; Guggenheim Fellowship, 1955-56; Carr P Collins Prize, Texas Institute of Letters, 1958; Harry S Truman Award, Kansas City Civil War Round Table, 1970; Fletcher Pratt Award, New York Civil War Round Table, 1970; Outstanding Civilian Service Medal, Department of the Army, 1974; Nevins-Freeman Award, Chicago Civil War Round Table, 1982; T Harry Williams Memorial Award, 1985; Honorary Knight of San Jacinto, 1993. Memberships: American Historical Association; Jefferson Davis Association; Organization of American Historians; Phi Beta Kappa; Society of American Historians; Southern Historical Association, president, 1975-76; Texas Historical Association, fellow; Texas Institute of Letters; Texas Philosophical Society, president, 1978; Salado Centre for the Humanities, director. Address: A & M University, College Station, TX 77843, USA.

VANE Brett. See: **KENT Arthur (William Charles).**

VANICEK Zdenek, (Alois Bocek), b. 24 June 1947, Chlumec, Czechoslovakia. Diplomat; Professor; Poet; Writer. Div, 1 son, 1 daughter. Education: BA, College of Economics, Prague, 1972; MA, LLD, Charles University, Prague, 1979; PhD, Diplomatic Academy, Prague, 1981. Appointments; Czechoslovak Diplomatic Service, 1972-91; Professor of International Relations and Law, 1993-. Publications: The Theory and the Practice of British Neo-Conservatism, 1988; Amidst the Ruins of Memories, 1990; To the Ends of the Earth, 1992; On the Edge of Rain, 1994; Under the Range of Mountains of Five Fingers, 1996; Seven Thousand Years Chiselled in Limestone, 1996; Amidst Memory's Ruins (mid-life poem 1988-1998, 1998. Contributions to: Newspapers and magazines. Honours: Several awards, medals, and honorary memberships including, Annual Literary Award, Masaryks Academy of Arts, Prague, 1998. Memberships: Poetry Society, England; Royal Society of Literature, England; Association of Czech Operators of Cable and Telecommunication Networks, President, 1998-. Address: Vladislova 8, 110 00 Prague 1, Czech Republic.

VANSITTART Peter, b. 27 Aug 1920, Bedford, England. Author. Education: Worcester College, Oxford. Publications: I Am the World, 1942; Enemies, 1947; The Overseer, 1949; Broken Canes, 1950; A Verdict of Treason, 1952; A Little Madness, 1953; The Game and the Ground, 1956; Orders of Chivalry, 1958; The Tournament, 1959; A Sort of Forgetting, 1960; Carolina, 1961; Sources of Unrest, 1962; The Friends of God, 1963; The Siege, The Lost Lands, 1964; The Dark Tower, 1965; The Shadow Land, 1967; The Story Teller, 1968; Green Knights Black Angels, 1969; Landlord, 1970; Vladivostok: Figures in Laughter, 1972; Worlds and Underworlds, 1974; Quintet, 1976; Flakes of History, 1978; The Death of Robin Hood, 1980; Voices from the Great War, 1981; Three Six Seven, 1982; Voices 1870-1914, John Masefield's Letters from the Front, 1984; The Ancient Mariner and the Old Sailor, 1985; Happy and Glorious, 1987; Parsifal, 1988; Voices of the Revolution, 1989; The Wall, 1990; A Choice of Murder, 1992; London, 1992; A Safe Conduct, 1995; In the Fifties, 1995; In Memory of England, 1998; Survival Tactics, 1999. Contributions to: Guardian; Times; London Magazine. Honour: Honorary Fellowship, Worcester College, Oxford, 1996. Membership: Royal Society of Literature, fellow. Address: Little Manor, Kersey, Suffolk, England.

VANSPANCKEREN Kathryn, b. 14 Dec 1945, Kansas City, USA. Professor of Literature. m. June 1975, 1 son. Education: BA, University of California at Berkeley, 1967; MA, Brandeis University, 1968; MA, 1969, PhD, 1976, Harvard University. Appointments: Instructor, Harvard University, 1970-73; Assistant Professor, Wheaton, 1974-79; Arts Administrator, Coordinative Council of Literary Magazine, 1979-80; Professor, Wagner College, 1981-82; Professor of English, University of Tampa, 1982-. Publications: John Gardner: The Critical Perspective, 1982; Margaret Atwood: Vision and Forms, 1988; Outline of American Literature, 1997. Contributions to: American Poetry Review; Ploughshares; Carolina Quarterly. Honours: Woodrow Wilson Fellow, 1967; Fulbright Professor, Indonesia, 1982-83; East West Center Fellow, 1984. Address: c/o University of Tampa, Tampa, FL 33606, USA.

VARMING Ole, b. 24 Mar 1929, Frederiksberg, Denmark. Psychologist. m. Ellen Michaelsen, 1 July 1961, 1 son, 1 daughter. Education: Graduate, Applied Psychology, University of Copenhagen, 1960; PhD, Royal Danish School of Education, 1984; Doctor's Thesis, University of Lund, Sweden, 1988. Publications: Educationally Subnormal Children, 1979; Discipline in School - From Without or Within?, 1978; Self-Esteem and Self-Esteem Development, 1995; Psychological-Pedagogical Dictionary (co-editor), 12th edition, 1999. Membership: Danish Writers' Union. Address: Eremitageparken 161, 2800 Lyngby, Denmark.

VARVERIS Yannis, b. 25 Nov 1955. Writer. m. 6 Oct 1982, 1 son. Education: University of Athens; Sorbonne III, Paris. Publications: In Imagination and Reason; The Leak; Invalids of War; Death Extends; Bottoms Piano; Mr Fog (poetry), 1993; The Girl from Samos (translation), 1993. Contributions to: Many publications. Memberships: Society of Writers; Greek Union of Theatrical Critics; Grece ITI. Address: 51 Omirou Street, 10672 Athens, Greece.

VASSANJI M(oyez) G, b. 30 May 1950, Nairobi, Kenya (Canadian citizen). Writer; Editor. m. Nurjehan Aziz, 14 July 1979, 2 sons. Education: BS in Physics, Massachusetts Institute of Technology, 1974; PhD in Physics, University of Pennsylvania, 1978; Appointments: Research Associate and Lecturer, University of Toronto, 1980-89; Editor, The Toronto South Asian Review, later The Toronto Review of Contemporary Writing Abroad; Writer-in-Residence, University of Iowa, 1989. Publications: The Gunny Sack, 1989; No New Land, 1991; Uhuru Street, 1991; The Book of Secrets, 1994. Honours: Commonwealth First Novel Award, Africa Region, 1990; F G Bressani Literary Prize, 1994; Giller Prize for Best Fiction, 1994; Harbourfront Literary Prize, 1994. Address: 39 Woburn Avenue, Toronto, Ontario M5M 1K5, Canada.

VEGE Nageswara Rao, b. 18 Jan 1932, Peda, India. Physician; Surgeon; Poet; Writer. Education: BA, Andhra University; MD, University of Parma. Publications: Poetry: Pace e Vita, 1963; Life and Love, 1965; Santi Priya, 1966; The Light of Asoka, 1970; Peace and Love, 1981; Templi Trascurati, 1983; The Best of Vege, 1992. Other: 100 Opinions of Great Men on Life, 1992. Contributions to: Newspapers and magazines. Honours: Giuseppe Ungaretti Award, 1982; Grand Prix Mediterranee, 1982; Schiller Award, 1985; Greenwood Poetry Forum Award, 1985; La Ballata Award, 1991; Viareggio Award, 1992. Memberships: International PEN; Italian Writers Association; Scrittori della Svizzera Italiana; Swiss Writers Association; World Doctors Writers Association. Address: Via Monte Ceneri 20, 6516 Gerra Paino TI, Switzerland.

VELARDO Joseph Thomas, b. 27 Jan 1923, Newark, New Jersey, USA. Molecular Biologist; Endocrinologist; Educator. m. Forresta M Monica Power, 12 Aug 1948, dec July 1976. Education: AB, University of Northern Colorado, 1948; SM, Miami University, Oxford, Ohio,

1949; PhD, Harvard University, 1952. Appointments: Assistant Professor of Anatomy and Endocrinology, Yale University, 1955-61; Professor of Anatomy and Chairman, Department of Anatomy, New York Medical College, 1961-62; Director, Institute for the Study of Human Reproduction, Cleveland, 1962-67; Head, Department of Research, St Ann Hospital, Cleveland, 1964-67; Professor of Anatomy, 1967-88, Chairman, Department of Anatomy, 1967-73, Stritch School of Medicine, Loyola University, Chicago; Vice President, University Research Systems, Warren, Ohio, 1975-; President, University Research Systems, Lombard, Illinois, 1979-. Publications: The Uterus, 1959; Histochemistry of Enzymes in the Female Genital System, 1963; The Ovary, 1963; The Ureter, 1967, revised edition, 1981. Contributions to: Various books and journals. Honours: US Presidential Unit Citation, 2 Bronze Stars, World War II; Rubin Award, American Society for the Study of Sterility, 1954; Lederle Medical Faculty Awards, 1955-58; Honorary Citizen, Sao Paulo, Brazil, 1973. Memberships: Many professional organizations. Address: 607 East Wilson Avenue, Lombard, IL 60148, USA.

VELDKAMP Albert Jan (Captain), b. 27 Sept 1925, Tiel, Netherlands. Master Mariner; Sea Pilot. m. Nini Lieuwen, 10 May 1951, 1 son, 2 daughters. Education: Willem Barentsz Maritime Institute, Terschelling, 1946; De Ruyter Maritime Institute, Vlissingen, 1951; Master Mariner, 1955; Historical Cartography, University of Utrecht, 1991-92; Maritime History, University of Leiden, 1992-97. Appointments: Apprentice Mate, Rotterdam Lloyd, 1947; Mate, Vinke & Co Shipping Company, 1948-49; Chief Officer, Netherlands Whaling Company, 1949-57; Teaching, De Ruyter Maritime Institute, 1958; Senior Pilot, Netherlands Pilotage Service, 1958-80; Master, "Eendracht" Sail Training Schooner, 1976-94; Master, Expedition Vessel "Plancius", expeditions to Arctic, 1981-85. Publication: In het Kielzog van Willem Barentsz - met het Expeditieschip "Plancius" naar het Hoge Noorden, 1996. Contributions to: Several nautical magazines including Cornelius Douwes, Poseidon, Eendracht Magazine, Netherlands Sail Training Association. Honour: Knight, Order of Orange-Nassau, 1996. Literary Agent: ADZ, Publishing Department. Address: Mercuriusweg 12, 4382 NC Vlissingen, Netherlands.

VENDLER Helen Hennessy, (Helen Hennessy), b. 30 Apr 1933, Boston, Massachusetts, USA. Professor; Poetry Critic. 1 son. Education: AB, Emmanuel College, 1954; PhD, Harvard University, 1960. Appointments: Instructor, Cornell University, 1960-63; Lecturer, Swarthmore College and Haverford College, Pennsylvania, 1963-64; Associate Professor, 1966-68, Professor, 1968-85, Boston University; Fulbright Lecturer, University of Bordeaux, 1968-69; Poetry Critic, The New Yorker, 1978-; Overseas Fellow, Churchill College, Cambridge, 1980; Senior Fellow, Harvard Society of Fellows, 1981-93; Visiting Professor, 1981-85, Kenan Professor, 1985-, Associate Academic Dean, 1987-92, Porter University Professor, 1990-, Harvard University; Charles Stewart Parnell Fellow, 1996, Honorary Fellow, 1996-, Magdalene College, Cambridge. Publications: Yeat's Vision and the Later Plays, 1963; On Extended Wings: Wallace Stevens' Longer Poems, 1969; The Poetry of George Herbert, 1975; Part of Nature, Part of Us: Modern American Poets, 1980; The Odes of John Keats, 1983; Wallace Stevens: Words Chosen Out of Desire, 1984; The Harvard Book of Contemporary American Poetry (editor), 1985; Voices and Visions: The Poet in America, 1987; The Music of What Happens, 1988; Soul Says, 1995; The Given and the Made, 1995; The Breaking of Style, 1995; Poems, Poets, Poetry, 1995; The Art of Shakespeare's Sonnets, 1997. Contributions to: Professional journals. Honours: Lowell Prize, 1969; Guggenheim Fellowship, 1971-72; American Council of Learned Societies Fellow, 1971-72; National Institute of Arts and Letters Award, 1975; Radcliffe College Graduate Society Medal, 1978; National Book Critics Award, 1980; National Endowment for the Humanities Fellowships, 1980, 1985, 1994; Keats-Shelley Association Award, 1994; Truman Capote Award, 1996;

Many honorary doctorates; Phi Beta Kappa. Memberships: American Academy of Arts and Letters; American Academy of Arts and Sciences, vice-president, 1992-95; American Philosophical Society; English Institute; Modern Language Association, president, 1980. Address: 54 Trowbridge Street, No 2, Cambridge, MA 02138, USA.

VENN George Andrew Fyfe, b. 12 Oct 1943, Tacoma, Washington, USA. Professor; Writer; Editor; Poet; Critic. m. Elizabeth Cheney, div, 1 son, 1 daughter. Education: BA, College of Idaho, 1967; MFA, Creative Writing, University of Montana, 1970; Central University, Quito, Ecuador; University of Salamanca, Spain; City Literary Institute, London. Appointments: Writer-on-Tour, Western States Arts Foundation, 1977; Foreign Expert, Changsha Railway University, Hunan, China, 1981-82; General Editor, Oregon Literature Series, 1989-94; Writer-in-Residence, Eastern Oregon State University. Publications: Sunday Afternoon: Grande Ronde, 1975; Off the Main Road, 1978; Marking the Magic Circle, 1988; Oregon Literature Series, 1992-94; many poems, essays, stories. Contributions to: Oregon Humanities; Writer's Northwest Handbook; North West Review; Northwest Reprint Series; Poetry Northwest; Willow Springs; Clearwater Journal; Oregon East; Portland Review. Honours: Pushcart Prize, 1980; Oregon Book Award, 1988; Stewart Holbrook Award, 1994. Memberships: Oregon Council of Teachers of English; Northwest Folklore. Address: Department of English, Eastern Oregon State University, La Grande, OR 97850, USA.

VENTA Biruta, (Ruta Venta), b. 4 Feb 1937, Latvia. Poetess. Education: Graduate, Latvian State University, Faculty of History and Philology. Appointments: Librarian, Latvian State Library. Publications: Collection of Poems: Fellow Travellers, 1968; Stratification, 1973; Onion Wreath, 1979; Emanation, 1984; A Dry Summer, A Rainy Summer, Merry-Go-Round, 1994. Address: 21 Dzelzavas Street, Flat 58, Riga, LV-1084, Latvia.

VENTURI Robert, b. 25 June 1925, Philadelphia, Pennsylvania, USA. Architect; Writer. m. Denise Scott Brown, 23 July 1967, 1 son. Education: AB, summa cum laude, 1947, MFA, 1950, Princeton University. Appointments: Designer, 1950-58; Assistant to Associate Professor of Architecture, University of Pennsylvania, 1957-65; Partner, Venturi, Cope and Lippincott, Philadelphia, 1958-61, Venturi and Short, Philadelphia, 1961-64, Venturi and Rauch, Philadelphia, 1964-80, Venturi, Rauch and Scott Brown, Philadelphia, 1980-89, Venturi, Scott Brown and Associates Inc, Philadelphia, 1989-; Charlotte Shepherd Davenport Professor of Architecture, Yale University, 1966-70. Publications: Complexity and Contradiction in Architecture, 1966, 2nd edition, 1977; Learning from Las Vegas (with Denise Scott Brown and Steven Izenour), 1972, 2nd edition, 1977; A View from the Campidoglio: Selected Essays, 1953-84 (with Denise Scott Brown), 1984; Iconography and Electronics Upon a Generic Architecture, 1996. Contributions to: Numerous publications. Honours: Rome Prize Fellow, American Academy in Rome, 1954-56; Commendatore of the Order of Merit, Republic of Italy, 1986; Pritzker Architecture Prize, 1991; National Medal of Arts, Manufacturers and Commerce, 1993; Phi Beta Kappa; Classic Book Award, Complexity and Contradiction in Architecture, American Institute of Architecture, 1996; Several honorary doctorates. Memberships: American Academy of Arts and Sciences; Royal Institute of British Architects, honorary member. Address: c/o Venturi, Scott Brown and Associates Inc, 4236 Main Street, Philadelphia, PA 19127, USA.

VERCOUTTER Jean, b. 2 Jan 1911, Lambersart, France. Egyptologist. m. Odette Gaiddon, 26 Jan 1943, 1 son, 1 daughter. Education: Docteur es Lettres, Sorbonne, University of Paris, 1953. Publications: Les Objets égyptiens du mobilier funéraire carthaginois, 1945; L'Egypte ancienne, 1946; Essai sur les relations entre Egytiens et Préhellènes, 1954; L' Egypte et le Monde égéen préhellénique: Etude critique des sources égyptiennes, 1956; Textes biographiques du Serapéum de Memphis, 1962; A la recherche de l'Egypte oubliée,

1986; L'Egypte et la chambre noire, 1992; L'Egypte et la Vallée du Nil I: Des origines à la fin de l'Ancien Empire, 1992. Contributions to: Periodicals. Honour: Prix Bordin et Prix Saintour, 1946. Membership: L'Institut. Address: 25 rue de Trévise, 75009 Paris, France.

VERDUIN John R(ichard) Jr, b. 6 July 1931, Muskegon, Michigan, USA. Professor; Writer. m. Janet M Falk, 26 Jan 1963, 1 son, 1 daughter. Education: BS, University of Albuquerque, 1954; MA, 1959, PhD, 1962, Michigan State University. Appointments: Assistant Professor, 1962-64, Associate Professor of Education, 1964-67, State University of New York College at Geneseo; Associate Professor, 1967-70, Professor, 1970-, Southern Illinois University at Carbondale. Publications: CooperativeCurriculum Improvement, 1967; Conceptual Models in Teacher Education, 1967; Curriculum Building for Adult Learning, 1980. Co-Author: Pre-Student Teaching Laboratory Experiences, 1970; Project Follow Through, 1971; Adults Teaching Adults: Principles and Strategies, 1977; The Adult Educator: A Handbook for Staff Development, 1979; Adults and Their Leisure: The Need for Lifelong Learning, 1984; Differential Education of the Gifted: A Taxonomy of 32 Key Concepts, 1986; The Lifelong Learning Experience: An Introduction, 1986; Distance Education: The Foundation for Effective Practice, 1991; Strategic Planning for Health Professionals, 1995. Contributions to: Books and journals. Memberships: American Educational Research Association; Association for Supervision and Curriculum Development; Illinois Adult and Continuing Education Association; Kappa Delta Phi; Phi Delta Kappa. Address: c/o Department of Educational Administration and Foundations, Southern Illinois University, Carbondale, IL 62901, USA.

VERMA Daya Nand, b. 12 Dec 1930, Multan City, India. Author; Palmist. m. 28 Jan 1951, 1 daughter. Publications: Yaun Vyavhar Anusheelan; Zindabad Murdabad; Kam Bhav Ki Nayee Vyakhya; Palmistry Ke Goorh Rahsya; Mansik Saphalta; Hum Sab Aur Voh; Dhyn Toga; Palmistry Ke Anubhoot Praypg. Contributions to: Books and periodicals. Honours: Literary Award; Honoured Vishva Yoga Conference. Memberships: Authors Guild of India; Film Writers Association; Bhartiya Lekhak Sangathan; PEN; AKhil Bhartiya Hindi Prakahak Sangh; All Indian Hindi Publishers Association; Afro Asian Book Council. Address: W21 Greater Kailash 1, New Delhi 110048, India.

VERMES Geza, b. 22 June 1924, Mako, Hungary. Professor of Jewish Studies Emeritus; Writer. m. (1) Pamela Hobson, 12 May 1958, dec 1993, (2) Margaret Unarska, 1996. Education: University of Budapest; Licencié en Histoire et Philologie Orientales, University of Louvain, 1952; DTheol, 1953; MA, Oxon, 1965; DLitt, 1988. Appointments: Lecturer, later Senior Lecturer in Divinity, University of Newcastle, 1957-65; Reader in Jewish Studies, University of Oxford, 1965-89; Fellow, 1965-91, Fellow Emeritus, 1991-, Professor of Jewish Studies, 1989-91, Professor Emeritus, 1991-, Wolfson College, Oxford; Editor, Journals of Jewish Studies, 1971-; Director, Oxford Forum for Qumran Research, Oxford Centre for Hebrew and Jewish Studies, 1991-; Inaugural Lecturer, Geza Vermes Lecturer in the History of Religions, University of Leicester, 1997; Many visiting lectureships and professorships. Publications: Les manuscrits du désert de Juda, 1953; Discovery in the Judean Desert, 1956; Scripture and Tradition in Judaism, 1961; The Dead Sea Scrolls in English, 1962, 4th edition, 1995; Jesus the Jew, 1973, 3rd edition, 1994; History of the Jewish People in the Age of Jesus Christ, by E Schürer I-III (co-reviser with F Millar and M Goodman), 1973-87; Post-Biblical Jewish Studies, 1975; The Dead Sea Scrolls: Qumran in Perspective (with Pamela Vermes), 1977, 3rd edition, 1994; The Gospel of Jesus the Jew, 1981; Essays in Honour of Y Yadin (co-editor), 1982; Jesus and the World of Judaism, 1983; The Essenes According to the Classical Sources (with M D Goodman), 1989; The Religion of Jesus the Jew, 1993; The Complete Dead Sea Scrolls in English, 1997; Providential Accidents: An Autobiography, 1998; Discoveries in the Judaean Desert XXVI: The Community

Rule (with P S Alexander), 1998; An Introduction to the Complete Dead Sea Scrolls, 1999. Contributions to: Scholarly books and journals. Honours: Fellow, British Academy, 1985; Honorary DD, University of Edinburgh, 1989, University of Durham, 1990; Honorary DLitt, University of Sheffield, 1994; W Bacher Medallist, Hungarian Academy of Sciences, 1996. Memberships: British Association for Jewish Studies, president, 1975, 1988; European Association for Jewish Studies, president, 1981-84. Address: West Wood Cottage, Foxcombe Lane, Boars Hill, Oxford OX1 5DH, England.

VERNON Annette Robyn. See: **CORKHILL Annette Robyn.**

VERZEA Ernest-George, (Sever Retezan, G Veste'n Zare, Everest Gerzan), b. 5 Oct 1917, Bucharest, Romania. Writer; Journalist. m. (1) Antoaneta Ionescu, June 1937, div 1956, (2) Aurora Sava, 10 Feb 1957, dec 19 Sept 1974, (3) Florica Jebeleanu, 7 Nov 1979. Education: Painting courses, Academy of Fine Arts, Bucharest, 1938-41; Master's degree, Faculty of Letters and Philosophy, 1948, Graduated, Faculty of Law, 1950, Bucharest University. Painting courses, Byzantine Art of Romanian Patriarchy, 1956. Appointments: Editor-in-Chief, Romanian Aviation History Team, High General Staff, 1938-41; Cultural Editor, Vieata daily newspaper, 1941-44; Secretary to Minister of National Education, 1945-48; Editor, Ziarul Poporul daily newspaper, 1946-48; Private Secretary to Vice-President of Government, 1948; Principal Editor, Forum, higher education magazine, 1968-77. Publications: Major books: Poems: Ingeri de lut, 1933; Fugarnice, 1935; Uzina umbrelor tangente, 1937; Alter Ego, 1942; Gradina cu portocali, 1943; Portative, 1944; Experiente, 1949; Sub sulitele stelelor, 1950; Litoral sintetic, 1968; Pasarea inimii, 1979; Combustii, 1980; Crepuscularia, 1992; Essay: Creatia in arta, 1995. Contributions to: Flacara, 1940; Curentul literar, 1941; Revista Fundatiilor Regale, 1943; Universul literar, 1943; Vremea, 1943; Romania viitoare-serie noua-, 1944; Arges, 1965; Anthologies; Radio and TV. Honours: Cultural Merit, 1st Class, 1947; Writers Union Award, 1997. Memberships: Professional Journalists Union, 1942; Association of Military Writers, 1943; Writers Union of Romania, 1949. Literary Agent: Dr George Anca. Address: Aleea Valea Florilor 4, Bl Fl0, Sc E, Et 2, Ap 90, Bucharest 77377, Romania.

VESTER Frederic, b. 23 Nov 1925, Saarbrücken, Germany. Biochemist. m. Anne Pillong, 2 Feb 1950, 1 son, 2 daughters. Education: University of Mainz, 1945; Licence es sciences, Sorbonne, University of Paris, 1950; PhD, University of Hamburg, 1953. Publications: Krebs Fehlgesteuertes Leben, 1977; Denken, Lernen, Vergessen, 1978; Phaenomen Stress, 1978; Unsere Welt ein Vernetztes System, 1983; Neuland des Denkens, 1984; Januskopf Landwirtschaft, 1986; Wasser Leben, 1987; Ausfahrt Zukunft, 1991; Crashtest Hobilität, 1995; Ecopolicy (CD-Rom), 1998. Contributions to: Professional journals. Honours: Adolf Grimme Prize, 1974; German Environmental Protection Medal, 1975; Deutsche Umweltmedaille, 1992. Memberships: Various professional organizations; Club of Rome. Address: c/o Studiengruppe für Biologie, und Umwelt GmbH, Nussbaumstrasse 14, 80336, Munich, Germany.

VICKERS Hugo (Ralph), b. 12 Nov 1951, London, England. Writer. m. Elizabeth Anne Blyth Vickers, 23 Sept 1995. Education: University of Strasbourg, 1970-71; Appointments: Broadcaster, Radio and Television, 1973-; Director, Burkes Peerage, 1974-79. Publications: We Want the Queen, 1977; Gladys, Duchess of Marlborough, 1979; Debretts Book of the Royal Wedding, 1981; Cocktails and Laughter (editor), 1983; Cecil Beaton: The Authorised Biography, 1985; Vivien Leigh, 1988; Loving Garbo, 1994; Royal Orders, 1994; The Private World of the Duke and Duchess of Windsor, 1995; The Kiss, 1996. Contributions to: The Times; Books and periodicals. Honours: Stern Prize for Non-Fiction, PEN, 1996; Silver Pen for Non-Fiction, PEN, 1997. Memberships: Historic Houses Association; Royal Society of Literature. Address: 62 Lexham Gardens, London W8 5JA, England.

VICKY. See: **BHARGAVA Vishal.**

VIDAL Gore, (Edgar Box), b. 3 Oct 1925, West Point, New York, USA. Writer. Education: Graduate, Phillips Exeter Academy, 1943. Publications: Novels: Williwaw, 1946; In a Yellow Wood, 1947; The City and the Pillar, 1948; The Season of Comfort, 1949; A Search for the King, 1950; Dark Green, Bright Red, 1950; The Judgment of Paris, 1952; Messiah, 1954; Julian, 1964; Washington, DC, 1967; Myra Breckinridge, 1968; Two Sisters, 1970; Burr, 1973; Myron, 1974; Kalki, 1978; Creation, 1981; Duluth, 1983; Lincoln, 1984; Empire, 1987; The Smithsonian Institution, 1998. Stories: A Thirsty Evil, 1956. Play: Visit to a Small Planet, 1957. Television and Broadway productions: The Best Man, 1960; Romulus, 1966; Weekend, 1968; An Evening with Richard Nixon, 1972; Gore Vidal's Lincoln, 1988. Essays: Rocking the Boat, 1962; Reflections upon a Sinking Ship, 1969; Homage to Daniel Shays, 1973; Matters of Fact and of Fiction, 1977; The Second American Revolution, 1982; Armageddon?, 1987; United States: Essays 1952-1992, 1993. Memoir: Palimpsest, 1995. Films: The Catered Affair, 1956; The Left-Handed Gun, 1958; The Best Man, 1964. Teleplays: The Death of Billy the Kid, 1958; Dress Gray, 1986. Honour: National Book Award, 1993. Address: c/o Random House, 201 East 50th Street, New York, NY 10022, USA.

VIDOR Miklos Janos, (Nicholas John), b. 22 May 1923, Budapest, Hungary. Writer. m. 22 Aug 1972. Education: Doctor of German and Hungarian Literature and Aesthetics, 1947. Publications: Over 30 Books. Contributions to: Various publications. Honours: József Attila Prize, 1955; Officer's Cross, Hungarian Republic, 1993; Stephanus Prize, 1995. Memberships: Hungarian Art Foundation; Hungarian PEN Club, vice-president, 1994; Union of Hungarian Writers. Address: 17 Pushkin u, H-1088 Budapest, Hungary.

VIERECK Peter (Robert Edwin), b. 5 Aug 1916, New York, New York, USA. Historian; Poet; Professor. m. (1) Aanya de Markov, June 1945, div May 1970, 1 son, 1 daughter, (2) Betty Martin Falkenberg, 30 Aug 1972. Education: BS, 1937, MA, 1939, PhD, 1942, Harvard University; Graduate Study as a Henry Fellow, Christ Church, Oxford, 1937-38. Appointments: Instructor, Tutor, Harvard University, 1946-47; Assistant Professor of History, 1947-48, Visiting Lecturer in Russian History, 1948-49, Smith College, Northampton, Massachusetts; Associate Professor, 1948-55, Professor of Modern European and Russian History, 1955-65, Mount Holyoke Alumnae Foundation Chair of Interpretive Studies, 1965-79, William R Kenan Chair of History, 1979-, Mount Holyoke College; Whittal Lecturer in Poetry, Library of Congress, Washington, DC, 1954, 1963; Fulbright Professor in American Poetry and Civilization, University of Florida, 1955; Elliston Chair and Poetry Lecturer, University of Cincinnati, 1956; Visiting Lecturer, University of California at Berkeley, 1957, 1964, City College of the City University of New York, 1964; Visiting Research Scholar in Russian for the Twentieth Century Fund, 1962-63; Director, Poetry Workshop, New York Writers Conferences, 1965-67. Publications: History: Metapolitics: From the Romanitics to Hitler, 1941, revised edition as Metapolitics: The Roots of the Nazi Mind, 1961, 2nd revised edition, 1965, updated edition, 1982; Conservatism Revisited: The Revolt Against Revolt, 1815-1949, 1949, 2nd edition as Conservatism Revisited and the New Conservatism: What Went Wrong?, 1962, 3rd edition, 1972; Shame and Glory of the Intellectuals: Babbitt, Jr Versus the Rediscovery of Values, 1953; The Unadjusted Man: A New Hero for Americans: Reflections on the Distinction Between Conserving and Conforming, 1956; Conservatism: From John Adams to Churchill, 1956, revised edition, 1962; Inner Liberty: The Stubborn Grit in the Machine, 1957; Conservatism from Burke and John Adams till 1982: A History and an Anthology, 1982. Poetry: Terror and Decorum: Poems 1940-1948, 1948; Strike Through Mask: Lyrical Poems, 1950; The First Morning: New Poems, 1952; Dream and Responsibility: The Tension Between Poetry and Society, 1953; The Persimmon Tree, 1956; The Tree Witch: A Poem and a Play (First of All a Poem), 1961; New and Selected Poems, 1932-1967, 1967; Archer in the Marrow: The Applewood Cycles of 1967-1987, 1987; Tide and Continuities: Last and First Poems, 1995-1938, 1995. Play: Opcomp: A Modern Medieval Miracle Play, 1993. Contributions to: Monographs, essays, reviews and poems to numerous periodicals. Honours: Pulitzer Prize in Poetry, 1949; Guggenheim Fellowship, 1959-60; Rockefeller Foundation Research Grant, 1958; National Endowment for the Humanities Senior Research Fellowship, 1969; Poetry Award, Massachusetts Artists Foundation, 1978; Sadin Prize, New York Quarterly, 1980; Golden Rose Award, 1981, Varoujan Poetry Prize, 1983, New England Poetry Club; Ingram Merrill Foundation Fellowship in Poetry, 1985. Memberships: American Committee for Cultural Freedom, executive committee; American Historical Association; Committee for Basic Education, charter member; Oxford Society; PEN; Phi Beta Kappa; Poetry Society of America. Address: 12 Silver Street, South Hadley, MA 01075, USA.

VIERROS Tuure Johannes, b. 20 Dec 1927, Kankaanpaa, Finland. Teacher; Writer. m. Enni Luodetlahti, 22 June 1952, 4 sons, 1 daughter. Education: University of Helsinki, 1952. Publications: Over 40 books, including some 20 textbooks, 1959-97. Contributions to: Journals and magazines. Honours: Several literary prizes. Memberships: Authors in Helsinki; Finnish Society of Authors; PEN. Address: Untuvaisentie 7 G 94, 00820 Helsinki, Finland.

VIERU Grigore Pavel, b. 14 Feb 1935, Moldova. Writer; Poet. m. Vieru Raisa Tudor, 8 June 1959, 2 sons. Education: Romanian Language, Chisinau Pedagogic Institute. Publications: Various poetry collections and children's books. Contributions to: Reviews and journals. Honours: Moldova State Laureate, 1979; Romanian Academy Nominee for the Nobel Prize for Literature, 1992. Memberships: Moldova Writer's Union; Romanian Academy of Science, honorary member. Address: Chisinau str Nicolae Iorga 7 ap 10, Moldova, Romania.

VIKS. See: **KALNINS Viktors.**

VILLA Carlo, b. 3 Oct 1931, Rome, Italy. Journalist; Writer; Poet. Education: Graduate. Appointments: Director, Centro Sistema Bibliotecario Cittadino; Secretary-General, Centro Internazionale Eugenio Montale; Book Reviewer and Scriptwriter, RAI TV; Italian Correspondent, Radio Televisione Svizzera Italiana. Publications: Fiera Letteraria, 1969; Il Privilegio di Essere Vivi, 1962; Solo Sperando Nauseati, 1963; Siamo Esseri Antichi, 1964; Gorba, 1972; Le Maesta delle Finte, 1977; Polvere de Miele, 1980; Infanzia del Dettato, 1981; Come la Rosa al Naso, 1984; Corpo a Cuore, 1985; Morte per Lucro, 1988; 100 di Questi Fogli, 1989; Pochades, 1992; L'Apparenza del Nulla, 1992; Simboli Eroici, 1993; L'Ora di Mefistofele, 1993. Other: Novels, short stories, essays, and children's books. Contributions to: Various newspapers and magazines. Membership: International PEN Club. Address: Via Virginia Agnelli 24, 00151 Rome, Italy.

VILLA GILBERT Mariana Soledad Magdalena, b. 21 Feb 1937, Croydon, England. Writer. Publications: Mrs Galbraith's Air, 1963; My Love All Dressed in White, 1964; Mrs Cantello, 1968; A Jingle Jangle Song, 1968; The Others, 1970; Manuela: A Modern Myth, 1973; The Sun in Horus, 1986. Address: Tredun, New Road, Stithians, Truro, Cornwall, TR3 7BL, England.

VINCENT John James, b. 29 Dec 1929, Sunderland, England. Methodist Minister; Writer. m. Grace Johnston Stafford, 4 Dec 1958, 2 sons, 1 daughter. Education: BD, Richmond College, London University, 1954; STM, Drew University, 1955; DTheol, Basel University, 1960. Appointments: Ordained Minister, Methodist Church, 1956; Director, Urban Theology Unit, 1969-97; Director Emeritus 1997-; Adjunct Professor, New York Theological Seminary, 1979-87; Honorary Lecturer, Sheffield University, 1990-. Publications: Christ and Methodism, 1964; Here I Stand, 1967; Secular Christ, 1968; The Race Race, 1970; The Jesus Thing, 1973; Stirrings,

Essays Christian and Radical, 1975; Alternative Church, 1976; Disciple and Lord, 1976; Starting all over Again, 1981; Into the City, 1982; OK Let's Be Methodists, 1984; Radical Jesus, 1986; Mark at Work, 1986; Britain in the 90's, 1989; Liberation Theology fron the Inner City, 1992; A Petition of Distress from the Cities, 1993; A British Liberation Theology, annual volumes, 1995-; The Cities: A Methadist Report, 1997; Hope form the City, 1999. Memberships: Studiorum Novi Testamenti Societas; Alliance of Radical Methodists, President; Urban Theologians International, Joint Chair, 1995-. Address: 178 Abbeyfield Road, Sheffield S4 7AY, England.

VINCENT Richard Charles, b. 1 Mar 1949, Allentown, Pennsylvania, USA. University Professor; Author; Editor. m. Christine M LaCaruba, 29 Jan 1972, 2 daughters. Education: BA, Mansfield University, 1972; MA, Temple University, 1977; PhD, University of Massachusetts, Amherst, 1983. Appointments: Temple University, 1974; University of Massachusetts, 1977; Slippery Rock State College, 1979; Western Illinois University, 1981; Southern Illinois University - Carbondale, 1983; University of Hawaii-Manoa, 1986-. Publications: Financial Characteristics of Selected B Film Productions of Albert J Cohen, 1951-1957, 1980; Global Glasnost: Toward a New International Information/Communication Order?, 1992; Towards Equity in Global Communication: MacBride Update, 1996; USA Glasnost: Missing Political Themes in US Media Discourse, 1997. Contributions to: Journalism Quarterly; Journalism Monographs; Political Communication; Journal of the University Film Association; Assorted book chapters. Honour: Fulbright Fellow, 1994-95. Memberships: International Association of Mass Communications Researchers; American Educators in Journalism and Mass Communication; International Communication Association; Asian Mass Communication Research and Information Association; Pacific Telecommunications Council. Address: Department of Communication, University of Hawaii-Manoa, Honolulu, HI 96822, USA.

VINE Barbara. See: **RENDELL Ruth Barbara.**

VINEY Ethna, b. 17 Jan 1933, West Cavan, Ireland. Writer; Film Maker. m. Michael Viney, 8 Oct 1965, 1 daughter. Education: BSc, College of Pharmacy, Dublin; BA, Economics, University College, Dublin. Appointments: Independent Pharmacist, 1956-61; Television Producer, 1966-76; Freelance Journalist, 1964-; Independent Television Film Producer and Director, 1990-. Publications: A Dozen Lips, 1994; Survival or Salvation, 1994; Dancing to Different Tunes, 1996, 1997. Honour: Outstanding Academic Book of the Year, USA, 1997. Address: Thallabawn, Westport, County Mayo, Ireland.

VINGE Vernor Steffen, b. 2 Oct 1944, Waukesha, Wisconsin, USA. Writer; Teacher. Education: PhD, Mathematics, University of California, San Diego. Publications: True Names; Marooned in RealTime; Peace War; Threats and Other Promises; Witling; Tatja Grimm's World. Address: Department of Mathematical Sciences, San Diego State University, San Diego, CA 92182, USA.

VIRTUE Noel, b. 3 Jan 1947, Wellington, New Zealand. Author. Education: New Zealand secondary schools. Publications: The Redemption of Elsdon Bird, 1987; Then Upon the Evil Season, 1988; Among the Animals: A Zookeeper's Story, 1988; In the Country of Salvation, 1990; Always the Islands of Memory, 1991; The Eye of the Everlasting Angel, 1993; Sandspit Crossing, 1994. Address: c/o Hutchinson, 20 Vauxhall Bridge Road, London SW1V, England.

VISKY Andras, b. 13 Apr 1957, Romania. Writer. m. Sarolta Margit, 20 May 1985, 2 sons, 2 daughters. Education: Polytechincal Institute, Timisoara, 1982. Appointments: Engineer, 1982-89; Artistic Counselor, Hungarian State Theatre, Cluj, 1990-; Editor, Korunk, 1991-95; Associate Professor, University Babes-Bolyai, Cluj, 1997-. Publications: Disembarkation (poetry), 1984; The Book of Photographer (poetry), 1988; White Owl (poetry), 1992; Morning Devotions (essays), 1995; hamlet Goes Away (theatrical studies), 1995; Four Hands Poems (with Gabor Tompa), 1994; Gobeline (poetry), 1998; Rite and Theatre (studies, editor), 1998. Contributions to: Korunk; Jelenkor; Forras; Curentul. Honours: Irat Alap Award, 1993; Poesis Award, 1993. Memberships: Hungarian Writers Union; Hungarian International Philologists Association. Address: Str B P Hasdeu 113/A, 3400 Cluj, Romania.

VISWANATHAN Subrahmanyam, b. 23 Oct 1933, Sholavandan, Tamil Nadu, India. Professor; Writer. m. Nirmala Nilakantan, 26 June 1960, 1 daughter. Education: BA, 1953, MA, 1958, University of Madras; PhD, Sri Venkateswara University, 1977. Appointments: Lecturer, Sri Venkateswara University, 1959-77; Reader, 1977-82, Professor, 1982-, University of Hyderabad. Publications: The Shakespeare Play as Poem, 1980; Critical Essays, 1982; Shakespeare in India, 1987; On Shakespeare's Dramaturgy, 1992. Contributions to: Professional journals. Honours: Indian UGC National Lecturer in English Literature, 1986-87; Emeritus Fellow, UGC, 1995-. Address: A14 Staff Quarters, University of Hyderabad, Hyderabad 500134, India.

VITE Andrejs, (Skailis), b. 1 Apr 1927, Riga, Latvia. Author. m. Astrida Skurbe, 7 Aug 1965, 1 daughter. Education: Graduate, Riga Polytechnical School, 1946; Studies, Latvian Agricultural Academy, 1946-49. Appointments: Laboratory Assistant, Latvian Agricultural Academy, 1950-53; Foreman, Latvenergo Department, 1954-63; Editor, Latvian Comic Magazine Dadzis, 1963-78; Vice Editor-in-Chief, Dadzis Magazine, 1979-91. Publictions: Short Stories: Poking, 1964; Superfleas, 1967; Magic Key, 1968; Deadly Insult, 1972; Flippant Pegasus, 1974; Damned Thieves, 1977; The Great Catch, 1981; Gretchen at the Spinning Wheel, 1985; The Mind of a Colt, 1987. Comic Crime Novels: Sailor With a Monkey on His Shoulder, 1995; Lucifer and His Suite, 1996. Memoirs: Crazy Man Has Crazy Memoirs, 1997. Contributions to: Dadzis; Karogs. Membership: Latvian Writers Association. Literary Agent: Agency AKKA/LAA, 97A Caka Street, Riga, LV-1011, Lativa. Address: c/o Lativan Writers Association, 24 Kursu Street, Riga, LV-1006, Latvia.

VITE Astrida, (Skurbe), b. 3 May 1937, Riga, Latvia. Specialist in Literature; Critic. m. Andrejs Vite, 7 Aug 1965, 1 daughter. Education: Graduate, Latvian State University, 1962; Postgraduate, 1969; Candidate of Physics, 1970; PhD, 1992. Appointments: Laboratory Assistant, Researcher, Institute of Latvian Language and Literature, 1962-66, 1969-. Publication: Bad is the Soldier (story), 1967; Zigmunds Kujins (biographical research), 1981. Latvian Prose: Literature and Era, 1970; Problems and Solutions, 1973; About Prose Art, 1974; Genre and Canon, 1977; Contemporary Latvian Soviet Literature, 1985; Biographies of Latvian Writers (contributing author), 1992. Contributions to: Karogs; Latvian Sciences Academy News. Membership: Latvian Writers Association. Literary Agency: AKKA/LAA, 97A Caka Street, Riga, LV-10011, Latvia. Address: c/o Latvian Writers Association, 24 Kursu Street, Riga, LV 1006, Latvia.

VITIELLO Justin, b. 14 Feb 1941, New York, USA. Professor of Italian; Writer. Education: BA, Brown University 1963; PhD, University of Michigan, 1970. Appointments: Assistant Professor of Comparative Literature, University of Michigan, 1970-73; Assistant, Associate then Full Professor of Italian, Temple University, 1974-. Publications: Il carro del pesce di Vanzetti, 1989; Vanzetti's Fish Cart, 1991; Sicily Within, 1992; Confessions of a Joe Rock, 1992; Subway Home, 1994. Contributions to: Professional journals. Address: Clivo Delle Mura Vaticane, 23-00136 Rome, Italy.

VITT Walter, b. 2 Oct 1936, Gera, Germany. Art Critic; Art Writer. m. Luiza Aschenbrenner, 16 July 1962, 1 son, 2 daughters. Education: Germanistics, Journalism, Historical Research, University of Münster, 1957-63. Appointments: Chief Editor, Semesterspiegel, student newspaper, Münster, 1958-61; Editorship, 1961-98, Vice-Head, Department for News Service, 1989-98, Westdeutscher Rundfunk, Köln; Mastership, Theory of Broadcasting, University of Münster, 1978-96. Publications: Oskar, 1961; Walter Dexel - Werkverzeichnis der Druckgrafik, 1971, 2nd edition, 1998; Auf der Suche nach der Biographie des Kölner Dadaisten Johannes Theodor Baargeld, 1977; Walter Dexels Köpfe, 1979; Hommage à Dexel, 1980; Mic Enneper, 1981; Von strengen Gestaltern, essays, 1982; Bagage de Baargeld, 1985; Der Maler Bruno Erdmann, 1986; Jean Leppien, 1986; Lienhard von Monkiewitsch, 1994; Künstler-Träume, 1994; Enzo Maiolino, 1996. Contributions to: Magazin Munst, Mainz, 1972-79; Nike, Munich, 1987-90; Neue Bildende Kunst, Berlin. Membership: Association Internationale des Critiques d'Art, President, German Section, 1989-. Address: Maternusstrasse 29, D-50678 Köln, Germany.

VIZENOR Gerald (Robert), b. 22 Oct 1934, Minneapolis, Minnesota, USA. Author; Poet; Professor of Native American Literature. m. (1) Judith Helen Horns, Sept 1959, div 1968, 1 son, (2) Laura Jane Hall, May 1981. Education: BA, University of Minnesota, 1960. Appointments: Lecturer, 1976-80, Professor of Native American Literature, University of California at Berkeley, 1990-; Professor, University of Minnesota, 1980-85, University of California at Santa Cruz, 1987-90; Resident Scholar, School of American Research, Santa Fe, 1985-86; David Burr Chair of Letters, Professor, University of Oklahoma, 1990-91. Publications: Thomas James White Hawk, 1968; Summer in the Spring: Anishinaable Lyric Poems and Stories, 1970, new edition, 1993; The Everlasting Sky: New Voices from the People Named the Chippewa, 1972; Tribal Scenes and Ceremonies, 1976, revised edition as Crossbloods: Bone Courts, Bingo, and Other Reports, 1990; Darkness in Saint Louis Bearheart (novel), 1978, new edition, revised, as Bearheart: The Heirship Chronicles, 1990; Wordarrows: Indians and Whites in the New Fur Trade, 1978; Earthdivers: Tribal Narratives on Mixed Descent, 1983; The People Named the Chippewa: Narrative Histories, 1983; Matsushima: Pine Islands (collected haiku poems), 1984; Griever: An American Monkey King in China (novel), 1986; Touchwood: A Collection of Ojibway Prose (editor), 1987; The Trickster of Liberty: Tribal Heirs to a Wild Baronage (novel), 1988; Narrative Chance: Postmodern Discourse on Native American Literatures (editor), 1989; Interior Landscapes: Autobiographical Myths and Metaphors, 1990; Landfill Meditation (short stories), 1991; The Heirs of Columbus (novel), 1991; Dead Voices: Natural Agonies in the New World (novel), 1993; Manifest Manners: Postindian Warriors of Survivance (critical essays), 1994; Shadow Distance: A Gerald Vizenor Reader, 1994; Native American Literature (editor), 1995; Hotline Healers: An Almost Browne Novel, 1997; Fugitive Poses: Native American Indian Scenes of Absence and Presence, 1998. Contributions to: Numerous books, journals, and periodicals. Honours: New York Fiction Collective Award, 1986; American Book Award, 1988; California Arts Council Artists Fellowship in Literature, 1989; Josephine Miles Awards, PEN Oakland, 1990, 1996. Address: c/o American Studies, 301 Campbell Hall, University of California at Berkeley, Berkeley, CA 94720, USA.

VIZINCZEY Stephen, b. 12 May 1933, Kaloz, Hungary. Writer. m. Sept 1963, 3 daughters. Education: University of Budapest, 1949-50; Academy of Theatre Arts, Budapest, 1951-56. Appointments: Editor, Exchange Magazine, 1960-61; Producer, Canadian Broadcasting Corporation, 1962-65. Publications: In Praise of Older Women, 1965; The Rules of Chaos, 1969; An Innocent Millionaire, 1983; Truth and Lies in Literature, 1986; The Man with the Magic Touch, 1994; Be Faithful unto Death (translation), 1995. Contributions to: Currently; The Scotsman; ABC. Membership: PEN. Address: 70 Coleherne Court, Old Brompton Road, London SW5 0EF, England.

VIZKI, Morti (Morten Poulsen), b. 18 Jan 1963, Copenhagen, Denmark. Author. Education: Japanese, University of Copenhagen. Publications: Himmelstormere, 1986; Begge Ben, 1990; Det Sidste Rum, 1993; Vingens Kniv, 1993; Sol, 1997; The Blood

Stone, 1999. Honours: Klaus Rifbderg Award, 1986; Nordic Radio Prize, 1989; Laureate of State, 1990; Marguerite Viby Award, 1994; Kjeld Abell Award, 1998. Address: Sankt Jorgens Alle 7, 1669 Copenhagen V, DK, Denmark.

VLAD Alexandru, b. 31 July 1950, Romania. Author. m. Maria Vlad, 4 Mar 1985, 2 sons. Education: BA, Cluj Napoca University. Appointment: Assistant Editor, Vatra, 1990-. Publications: The Giffins Wing, 1981; The Way to the South Pole, 1985; In The Cold of the Summer, 1985; Atena, Atena, 1994; Reinventing Politics, 1994. Contributions to: Steaua; Vatra; Amfiteatru; Astra; Trubuna; New Glass; 22; Romania Literara. Memberships: Union of Writers; N Steinhardt Memorial Foundation. Address: Str Lugoslaviei Nr 72 Bl, B4 Ap23 3400 Cluj Napoc, Romania.

VLASIN Stepan, (V Steva), b. 23 Dec 1923, Czech Republic. m. 19 Nov 1987, 2 sons. Education: PhD, 1949, DSc, 1984, Faculty of Literature, Masaryk University, Brno. Appointment: Chief, Institute of Academy of Sciences, 1961-90. Publications: Jiri Mahen, 1972; Jiri Wolker, 1974; Bedrich Vaclavek, 1979; Ve skole zivota, 1980; Ne prelomu desetileti, 1985; Karel Dvoracek, 1987; Léta zrani, 1989. Contributions to: Ceska literatura; Rovnost; Rudé pravo; Host do domu; Estetika; Impuls; Tvorba; Romboid. Honours: Several awards. Memberships: obec spisovatelu; Society of J Mahen. Address: Odlehla 22, 62100 Brno, Czech Republic.

VO Silvija, See: **KALNINS Viktors.**

VOGASSARIS Angleo-Eftihios (Felix), b. 6 May 1935, Piraeus, Greece. Teacher; Writer; Playwright. Div. Education: Degree in Philosophy and Greek Literature, University of Athens; Diploma, German Academy, Munich; Diplomas in English and French. Appointments: Editor; High School Teacher; Educational Advisor. Publications: Over 40 works, including novels, plays, poems, and essays, 1968-92. Contributions to: Newspapers and magazines. Memberships: Association of Greek Writers; Piraeus Literary and Arts Society, president. Address: 1-3 Aristotelous Street, GR 18535 Piraeus, Greece.

VOGEL Paula Anne, b. 18 Nov 1951, Washington, District of Columbia, USA. Dramatist; Teacher. Education: BA, Catholic University of America, Washington, DC. Appointments: Consultant on Playwrighting and Theatre Arts; Faculty, Brown University. Publications: Various plays, including How I Learned to Drive, 1998. Honours: National Endowment for the Arts Fellowships, 1980, 1991; AT&T Award, 1992; Obie Award, 1992; Fund for New American Plays, 1994; Guggenheim Fellow, 1995; Pew Charitable Trust Senior Artist Residency, 1995-97; Lucille Lortel Award, 1997; Pulitzer Prize for Drama, 1998. Address: c/o Department of English, Brown University, Providence, RI 02912, USA.

VOGELSANG Arthur, b. 31 Jan 1942, Baltimore, Maryland, USA. Poet; Editor. m. Judith Ayers, 14 June 1966. Education: BA, University of Maryland, 1965; MA, Johns Hopkins University, 1966; MFA, University of Iowa, 1970. Appointment: Editor, The American Poetry Review, 1973-. Publications: A Planet, 1983; Twentieth Century Women, 1988; Cities and Towns, 1996. Honours: National Endowment for the Arts Fellowships in Poetry, 1976, 1985, 1995; California Arts Council, 1995; Juniper Prize, 1995. Address: 1730 North Vista Street, Los Angeles, CA 90046, USA.

VOIGT Ellen Bryant, b. 9 May 1943, Danville, Virginia, USA. Poet; College Teacher. m. Francis G W Voigt, 5 Sept 1965, 1 son, 1 daughter. Education: BA, Converse College, Spartanburg, South Carolina, 1964; MFA, University of Iowa, 1966. Appointments: Faculty, Iowa Wesleyan College, 1966-69, Goddard College, 1969-79, Massachusetts Institute of Technology, 1979-82, Warren Wilson College, 1981-. Publications: Claiming Kin, 1976; The Forces of Plenty, 1983; The Lotus Flowers, 1987; Two Trees, 1992; Kyrie, 1996. Contributions to: Reviews, quarterlies, and journals. Honours: National Endowment

for the Arts Fellowship, 1975; Guggenheim Fellowship, 1978; Pushcart Prizes, 1983, 1987; Honorable Mention, The Poets' Prize, 1987; Emily Clark Balch Award, 1987; Honorary Doctor of Letters, Converse College, 1989; Haines Award for Poetry, Fellowship of Southern Writers, 1993; Finalist, National Book Critics' Circle Award, 1996. Address: Box 16, Marshfield, VT 05658, USA.

VOKAC David, b. 1 June 1940, Chicago, Illinois, USA. Author. m. Joan Werner, 23 Sept 1991. Education: Bachelors in Business Administration, University of Arizona, 1962; Masters in Geography & Area Development, University of Arizona, 1964. Publications: The Great Towns of the West, 1985; The Great Towns of California, 1986; The Great Towns of the Pacific Northwest, 1987; Destinations of the Southwest, 1988; Destinations of Southern California, 1990, 1995; The Great Towns of America, 1998. Contributions to: Westways. Membership: Society of American Travel Writers. Address: PO Box 99717, San Diego, CA 92169, USA.

VOLLMAN William T, b. 28 July 1959, Santa Monica, California, USA. Author. Education: Deep Springs College, 1977-79; BA, summa cum laude, Cornell University, 1981; Graduate Studies, Unversity of California at Berkeley, 1982-83. Publications: You Bright and Risen Angels: A Cartoon, 1987; The Rainbow Stories, 1989; Seven Dreams: A Book of North American Landscapes, 7 volumes, 1990-; Whores for Gloria, or, Everything Was Beautiful Until the Girls Got Anxious, 1991; Thirteen Stories and Thirteen Epitaphs, 1991; An Afghanistan Picture Show, or, How I Saved the World, 1992; Butterfly Stories, 1993; The Atlas, 1996. Honours: Ella Lyman Cabot Trust Fellowship, 1982; Regent's Fellow, University of California at Berkeley, 1982-83; Ludwig Vogelstein Award, 1987; Whiting Writers' Award, 1988; Shiva Naipaul Memorial Prize, 1989. Address: c/o Viking-Penguin, 375 Hudson Street, New York, NY 10014, USA.

VON PLANTA Maxie. See: **SCHAAD Isolde G.**

VON SCHROEDER Urs Rudolf, b. 4 May 1943, Uzwil, Switzerland. Editor-in-Chief; Writer. m. Patricia Lardi, 4 June 1991. Education: Certificate of Commerce, Switzerland, 1962; Linguistic studies in UK, France and USA. Publications: Kein Grund zur Panik (short stories), 1983; Gestern Hongkong - morgen New York (non-fiction), 1984; Walter Matysiak (monograph), 1986; SR 308 - Startbereit (non-fiction), 1989; Kitso Ketsudan (non-fiction), 1991; Helden brauchen keine Orden (short stories), 1998; Kyougaku no Riyuu (short stories), 1998; "Im Kreislauf des lebens ". Contributions to: Signature, Japan; Others. Memberships: Swiss Writers' Association; PEN Centre, Switzerland. Address: Im Stemmerli 9, CH-8200 Schaffhausen, Switzerland.

VONARBURG Elisabeth, b. 5 Aug 1947, Paris, France. Writer; Translator. m. Jean-Joel Vonarburg, 15 Dec 1969, div Jan 1990. Education: BA, 1969, MA, Honours, 1969, Agrégation de Lettres Modernes, 1972, University of Dijon; PhD, Université Laval, 1987. Appointments: Assistant Lecturer in Literature, Université du Québec a Chicoutimi, 1973-81; Assistant Lecturer in Literature and Creative Writing, Université du Québec a Rimouski, 1983-86; Teacher of Creative Writing in Science Fiction, Université Laval, 1990; Science Fiction Columnist, Radio-Canada, 1993-95. Publications: L'Oeil de la nuit, 1980; Le Silence de la Cité, 1981, English translation as The Silent City, 1990; Janus, 1984; Comment Escrire des Histoires: Guide de l'explorateur, 1986, 2nd edition, 1992; Histoire de la Princesse et du Dragon, 1990; Ailleurs et au Japon, 1991; Chroniques de Pays des Meres, 1992, English translation as In the Mother's Land, 1992; Les Voyageurs maigre eux, 1992, English translation as Reluctant Voyagers, 1995; Les Contes de la Chatte Rouge, 1993; Contes et Légendes de Tyranael, 1994. Honours: Several Canadian and French science fictions awards. Memberships: Infini, France; International Association for the Fantastic in the Arts; Science Fiction and Fantasy Writers of America; Science Fiction Canada; Science Fiction Research

Association. Address: 266 Beleau, Chicoutini, Quebec G7H 2Y8, Canada.

VONNEGUT Kurt Jr, b. 11 Nov 1922, Indianapolis, Indiana, USA. Author. m. (1) Jane Marie Cox, 1 Sept 1945, div 1979, 1 son, 2 daughters, 3 adopted nephews, (2) Judith Krementz, 1979, 1 daughter. Education: Cornell University, 1940-42; University of Chicago, 1945-47, MA in Anthropology, 1971. Appointments: Lecturer, Writers Workshop, University of Iowa, 1965-67; Lecturer in English, Harvard University, 1970; Distinguished Professor, City College of the City University of New York, 1973-74. Publications: Novels: Player Piano, 1951; Sirens of Titan, 1959; Mother Night, 1961; Cat's Cradle, 1963; God Bless You, Mr Rosewater, 1964; Slaughterhouse-Five, 1969; Breakfast of Champions, 1973; Slapstick, or Lonesome No More, 1976; Jailbird, 1979; Deadeye Dick, 1982; Galapagos, 1985; Bluebeard, 1987; Hocus Pocus, 1990; Timequake, 1997. Short Stories: Welcome to the Monkey House, 1968. Play: Happy Birthday, Wanda Jane, 1971. Television Script: Between Time and Timbuktu, or Prometheus-5, 1972. Non-Fiction: Wampeters, Foma and Granfallons, 1974; Palm Sunday, 1981; Fates Worse Than Death, 1991. Contributions to: Journals and magazines. Honours: Guggenheim Fellowship, 1967-68; National Institute of Arts and Letters Award, 1970. Membership: American Academy of Arts and Letters. Address: c/o Donald C Farber, 150 East 58th Street, 39th Floor, New York, NY 10135, USA.

VREELAND Susan, b. 20 Jan 1946, Racine, Wisconsin, USA. Writer; Teacher. m. Joseph C Gray, 26 Nov 1988. Education: BA, English, 1968, MA, English Literature, 1978. Appointment: High School English Teacher, 1969-. Publications: What Love Sees, 1988; If I Had My Life to Live Over I Would Pick More Daisies (anthology), 1992; Family, A Celebration, 1995; What English Teachers Want, A Student Handbook, 1996; Generation to Generation, 1998. Contributions to: Missouri Review; Dominion Review; Confrontation; Alaska Quarterly Review; Calyx; Crescent Review; West Wind Review; Ambergris; So To Speak; Phoebe. Honours: Women's National Book Association 1st Place in Short Fiction, 1991; Dominion Review 1st Prize for Essay, 1996; New Millennium 1st Prize for Essay, 1996; William Faulkner Prize, 1998. Membership: California Association of Teachers of English. Literary Agent: Barbara Braun Associates Inc. Address: 230 Fifth Avenue, Suite 909, New York, NY 10001, USA.

VROOMKONING Victor. See: **VAN DE LAAR Waltherus Antonius Bernardinus.**

VUONG Lynette Dyer, b. 20 June 1938, Owosso, Michigan, USA. Author-Lecturer. m. Ti Quang Vuong, 9Jan 1962, 2 sons, 2 daughters. Education: University of Wisconsin, Milwaukee, 1958-61; Graduated, Registered Nurse, Milwaukee County Hospital School of Nursing, 1959. Publications: The Brocaded Slipper and Other Vietnamese Tales, 1982; A Friend for Carlita, 1989; The Golden Carp and Other Tales from Vietnam, 1993; Sky Legends of Vietnam, 1993. Contributions to: Various publications. Honours: Romance Writers of America Golden Heart Award, 1st Place in Mainstream Division, unpublished manuscript; Catholic Library Association's Ann Martin Book Award, 1991. Memberships: Associated Authors of Children's Literature, Houston; Romance Writers of America; Society of Children's Book Writers; Golden Key National Honor Society; Classical Association of Houston. Address: 1521 Morning Dove Drive, Humble, TX 77396, USA.

W

WACH Kenneth, b. 17 Nov 1944, Waltrop, Germany. Academic; Art History. m. Denise Brookman, 29 Apr 1972. Education: Diploma of Art, University of Ballarat, 1965; TTTC, Hawthorn Institute, 1968; FRMIT, RMIT University, 1971; MA, La Trobe University, 1984. Appointments: Senior Lecturer, School of Studies in Creative Arts, Victorian College of the Arts, The University of Melbourne, 1995-98; Senior Lecturer, The University of Melbourne, 1990-95; Lecturer, Melbourne College of Advanced Education, 1986-90; Lecturer, State College of Victoria, Melbourne, 1984-86; Lecturer, Melbourne State College, 1976-84; Lecturer, Melbourne Teachers' College, 1972-75; Teacher, Glenroy Technical School, 1971; Lecturer, Gippsland Institute of Advanced Education, 1969-70; Teacher, Morwell Technical School, 1968-69. Publications: The Pearl Divers of the Unconscious: Freund, Surrealism and Psychology, 1993; Salvador Dali: Masterpieces from the Collection of the Salvador Dali Museum, 1996; Dorothea Tanning's Guardian Angels of 1946 and Leonora Carrington's El Arbol de la Vida of 1960, 1998. Surrealist Texts: The Inexhaustible Murmur, 1993; The Souvenirs of Sensation: Surrealism and its Objects, 1994; Australian Art: The Land and the Environment, 1991; Surrealism in Australia: The Transposed Response, 1993; Shame about Dali, 1997. Address: Victorian College of the Arts, 757 Swanston St, Carlton, Victoria 3053, Australia.

WADDELL Evelyn Margaret, (Lyn Cook), b. 4 May 1918, Weston, Ontario, Canada. Children's Librarian; Writer. m. Robb John Waddell, 19 Sept 1949, 1 son, 1 daughter. Education: BA, English Language and Literature, Bachelor in Library Science, University of Toronto. Publications: All as Lyn Cook: The Bells on Finland Street, 1950, 2nd edition, 1991; The Little Magic Fiddler, 1951; Rebel on the Trail, 1953; Jady and the General, 1955; Pegeen and the Pilgrim, 1957; The Road to Kip's Cove, 1961; Samantha's Secret Room, 1963, 2nd edition, 1991; The Brownie Handbook for Canada, 1965; The Secret of Willow Castle, 1966, 2nd edition, 1984; The Magical Miss Mittens, 1970; Toys from the Sky, 1972; Jolly Jean-Pierre, 1973; If I Were All These, 1974; A Treasure for Tony, 1980; The Magic Pony, 1981; Sea Dreams, 1981; The Hiding Place, 1990, 2nd edition, 1994; A Canadian ABC (poems), 1990; Where Do Snowflakes Go?, 1994. Honours: Honorary Member, Academy of Canadian Writers; Vicky Metcalf Award, 1978. Membership: Canadian Society of Children's Authors, Illustrators and Performers. Address: 72 Cedarbrae Boulevard, Scarborough, Ontario M1J 2K5, Canada.

WADDINGTON-FEATHER John Joseph, b. 10 July 1933, Keighley, Yorkshire, England. Anglican Priest; Poet; Writer; Publisher. m. Sheila Mary Booker, 23 July 1960, 3 daughters. Education: BA, University of Leeds, 1954; PGCE, Keele, 1974; Ordination Certificate, Church of England, 1977. Appointments: Co-Editor, Orbis, 1971-80; Teacher, Shrewsbury 6th Form College, 1981-83, Khartoum University, 1984-85; Honorary Chaplain, HM Prisons, 1977-; Chaplain, Prestfelde School, 1985-96; Director, Feather Books; Editor, Poetry Church Magazine; Editor, Poetry Church Anthology, 1997, 1998, 1999. Publications: Collection of Verse, 1964; Of Mills, Moors and Men, 1966; Garlic Lane, 1970; Easy Street, 1971; One Man's Road, 1977; Quill's Adventures in the Great Beyond, 1980; Tall Tales from Yukon, 1983; Khartoum Trilogy and Other Poems, 1985; Quill's Adventures in Wasteland, 1986; Quill's Adventures in Grozzieland, 1988; Six Christian Monologues, 1990; Six More Christian Poems, 1994; Shropshire, 1994; Feather's Foibles, 1995; Wild Tales from the West, 1999. Contributions to: Journals and magazines. Honours: Bronte Society Prize, 1966; Cyril Hodges Poetry Award, 1974; Carnegie Medal Nomination, 1988; Winner, Burton Prize, 1999. Memberships: Bronte Society, council member, 1994-; Royal Society of Arts, fellow; Yorkshire Dialect Society; J B Priestley Society, chairman, 1998-. Address: Fair View, Old Coppice, Lyth Bank, Shrewsbury, Shropshire SY3 0BW, England.

WADE David, b. 2 Dec 1929, Edinburgh, Scotland. Writer. Education: Queen's College, Cambridge, 1952. Appointments: Radio Critic, The Listener, 1965-67, The Times, 1967-89. Publications: Trying to Connect You; The Cooker; The Guthrie Process; The Gold Spinners; Three Blows in Anger; The Ogden File; The Carpet Maker of Samarkand; The Nightingale; Summer of 39; The Facts of Life; A Rather Nasty Crack; On Detachment; The Tree of Strife; Power of Attorney; Alexander. Membership: Society of Authors. Address: Willow Cottage, Stockland Green Road, Southborough, Kent TN3 0TL, England.

WAELTI-WALTERS Jennifer (Rose), b. 13 Mar 1942, Wolverhampton, England. Professor Emerita of French and Women's Studies; Writer. Education: BA, Honours, 1964, PhD, 1968, University of London; Licence-ès-Lettres, University of Lille, France, 1965. Appointment: Professor of French and Women's Studies, University of Victoria, British Columbia. Publications: Alchimie et Litterature, 1975; J M G Le Clézio, 1977; Michel Butor: A View of His World and a Panorama of His Work, 1977; Fairytales and the Female Imagination, 1982; Jeanne Hyvrard (with M Verthuy), 1989; Feminist Novelists of the Belle Epoque, 1991; Michel Butor, 1992; Feminisms of the Belle Epoque (with S Hause), 1994; Jeanne Hyvrard, Theorist of the Modern World, 1996; Dead Girl in a Lace Dress by J Hyvrard (translator with J P Mentha). Contributions to: Professional journals and general magazines. Honour: Association des Professeurs de Français des Universités et Colleges Canadiens Prize for the Best Book of Literary Criticism in French, 1989. Memberships: Association des Professeurs de Français des Universités et Colleges Canadiens; Canadian Research Institute for the Advancement of Women; Canadian Women's Studies Association. Address: c/o Department of Women's Studies, University of Victoria, Victoria, British Columbia V8W 3P4, Canada.

WAGH Vilas, b. 1 Mar 1939, Maharashtra, India. Publisher. m. Usha, 23 Aug 1983. Education: BSc, BA, MA, BEd, University of Poona. Appointments: Teacher; Reader. Publications: Editor, Suggawa; Marathi monthly; Ed, Brahamani Akrosh, Marathi language. Contributions to: Ed of monthly, Sugawa, 26 years. Address: 861/1 Sadashiv Peth Pune 411030, India.

WAGNER Eliot, b. 19 Dec 1917, New York, New York, USA. Writer. m. Ethel Katell, 22 June 1940, 1 daughter. Publications: Novels: Grand Concourse, 1954; Wedding March, 1961; Better Occasions, 1974; My America!, 1980; Princely Quest, 1985; Nullity Degree, 1991. Short Stories: Delightfully Different Deities, 1994. Conributions to: Crisis; Chicago Jewish Forum; Commentary; Antioch Review; Opinion. Honours: Yaddo, 1950, 1951, 1952, 1957; Macdowell, 1955. Membership: Authors Guild. Address: 651 Sheffield Road, Ithaca, NY 14850-9253, USA.

WAGNER-MARTIN Linda, b. 18 Aug 1936, St Marys, Ohio, USA. Professor of English and Comparative Literature; Writer; Poet; Writer. Education: BA, Honours, English, 1957, MA, English, 1959, PhD, English, 1963, Bowling Green State University. Appointments: Instructor and Assistant Professor, Bowling Green State University, 1961-66; Assistant Professor, Wayne State University, 1966-68; Assistant Professor to Professor, Michigan State University, 1968-87; Hanes Professor of English and Comparative Literature, University of North Carolina at Chapel Hill, 1988-. Publications: The Poems of William Carlos Williams: A Critical Study, 1964; Denise Levertov, 1967; Intaglios: Poems, 1967; The Prose of William Carlos Williams, 1970; Phyllis McGinley, 1971; Hemingway and Faulkner: Inventors/Masters, 1975; Ernest Hemingway: A Reference Guide, 1977; William Carlos Williams: A Reference Guide, 1978; Dos Passos: Artist as American, 1979; American Modern: Selected Essays in Fiction and Poetry, 1980; Songs for Isadora: Poems, 1981; Ellen Glasgow; Beyond Convention, 1982; Sylvia Plath: A Biography, 1987; The Modern American Novel, 1914-1945, 1989; Wharton's The House of Mirth: A Novel of Admonition, 1990; Plath's the Bell Jar: A Novel of the Fifties, 1992; Telling Women's Lives: The New Biography, 1994; "Favored Strangers": Gertrude Stein and Her Family, 1995; Wharton's The Age of Innocence: A Novel of Ironic Nostalgia, 1996; The Mid-Century American Novel, 1935-1965, 1997; Sylvia Plath: A Literary Life, 1999. Editor: William Faulkner: Four Decades of Criticism, 1973; Ernest Hemingway: Five Decades of Criticism, 1974; T S Eliot, 1976; "Speaking Straight Ahead": Interviews with William Carlos William, 1976; Robert Frost: The Critical Heritage, 1977; Denise Levertov: In Her Own Province, 1979; Joyce Carol Oates: Critical Essays, 1979; Sylvia Plath: Criticals Essays, 1984; Ernest Hemingway: Six Decades of Criticism, 1987; New Essays on Hemingway's The Sun Also Rises, 1987; Sylvia Plath: The Critical Heritage, 1988; Anne Sexton: Critical Essays, 1989; Denise Levertov: Critical Essays, 1991; The Oxford Companion to Women's Writing in the United States (with Cathy N Davidson), 1995; The Oxford Book of Women's Writing in the United States, 1995; New Essays to Faulkner's Go Down, Moses, 1996; Ernest Hemingway: Seven Decades of Criticism, 1988; Festchrift for Frederick Eckman (with David Adams), 1998; The Historical Guide to Ernest Hemingway, 1999. Contributions to: Scholarly books and journals. Honours: Guggenheim Fellowship, 1975-76; Bunting Institute Fellow, 1975-76; Rockefeller Foundation Fellow, Bellagio, Italy, 1990; Fellow, Institute for the Arts and Humanities, University of North Carolina, 1992; National Endowment for the Humanities Senior Fellowship, 1992-93; Teacher-Scholar Award, College English Association, 1994; Visiting Distinguished Professor, Emory University, 1994; Citation for Exceptional Merit, House of Representatives, Ohio, 1994; Brackenridge Distinguished Professor, University of Texas at San Antonio, 1998. Memberships: Ellen Glasgow Society, president, 1982-87; Ernest Hemingway Foundation and Society, president, 1993-96; Modern Language Association; Society for the Study of Midwestern Literature, president, 1974-76; Society for the Study of Narrative Technique, president, 1988-89. Address: c/o Department of English, 3520 University of North Carolina at Chapel Hill, Chapel Hill, NC 27599, USA.

WAGONER David (Russell), b. 5 June 1926, Massillon, Ohio, USA. Professor of English; Poet; Author. m. (1) Patricia Parrott, 1961, div 1982, (2) Robin Heather Seyfried, 1982. Education: BA, Pennsylvania State University, 1947; MA, Indiana University, 1949. Appointments: Instructor, DePauw University, 1949-50, Pennsylvania State University, 1950-53; Assistant Professor, 1954-57, Associate Professor, 1958-66, Professor of English, 1966-, University of Washington, Seattle; Editor, Poetry Northwest, 1966-; Elliston Professor of Poetry, University of Cincinnati, 1968. Publications: Poetry: Dry Sun, Dry Wind, 1953; A Place to Stand, 1958; Poems, 1959; The Nesting Ground, 1963; Staying Alive, 1966; New and Selected Poems, 1969; Working Against Time, 1970; Riverbed, 1972; Sleeping in the Woods, 1974; A Guide to Dungeness Spit, 1975; Travelling Light, 1976; Collected Poems, 1956-1976, 1976; Who Shall be the Sun?: Poems Based on the Love, Legends, and Myths of Northwest Coast and Plateau Indians, 1978; In Broken Country, 1979; Landfall, 1981; First Light, 1983; Through the Forest: New and Selected Poems, 1977-1987, 1987. Fiction: The Man in the Middle, 1954; Money, Money, Money, 1955; Rock, 1958; The Escape Artist, 1965; Baby, Come on Inside, 1968; Where Is My Wandering Boy Tonight?, 1970; The Road to Many a Wonder, 1974; Tracker, 1975; Whole Hog, 1976; The Hanging Garden, 1980. Editor: Straw for the Fire: From the Notebooks of Theodore Roethke 1943-1963, 1972. Honours: Guggenheim Fellowship, 1956; Ford Foundation Fellowship, 1964; American Academy of Arts and Letters Grant, 1967; National Endowment for the Arts Grant, 1969; Morton Dauwen Zabel Prize, 1967; Oscar Blumenthal Prize, 1974; Fels Prize, 1975; Eunice Tietjens Memorial Prize, 1977; English-Speaking Union Prize, 1980; Sherwood Anderson Prize, 1980. Membership: Academy of American Poets, chancellor, 1978. Address:

5416-154th Place South West, Edmonds, WA 98026, USA.

WAHLBECK Jan-Christer, b. 10 July 1948, Vasa, Finland. Psychologist; Family Therapist; Consultant; Poet; Writer; m. Liisa Ryyppö, 1 Dec 1978, 1 son, 2 daughters. Education: MA, 1976; Advanced Family Therapist, 1988; Organizational Consultant, 1988. Publications: Poetry: Steg På Hållplatsen, 1977; Bussen Stannar Bakom Hörnet, 1979; Mognadens Opera, 1981; Katastrof Efter Katastrof, 1984; Bilen Och Lidelserna, 1991; Huset Och Luftens Musik, 1993. Fiction: Näckrosor Och Bränt Vatten, 1983; Pojken Och Korpen, 1988. Honour: Villa Biaudet Fellowship, 1985-88. Membership: Finlandsswede Union of Writers. Address: Brunnsgatan 12, Fin-06100 Borgå, Finland.

WAINWRIGHT Geoffrey, b. 16 July 1939, Yorkshire, England. Professor of Systematic Theology; Methodist Minister. m. Margaret Wiles, 20 Apr 1965, 1 son, 2 daughters. Education: BA, 1960, MA, 1964, BD, 1972, DD, 1987, University of Cambridge; DrThéol, University of Geneva, 1969. Appointments: Editor, Studia Liturgica, 1974-87; Professor of Systematic Theology, The Divinity School, Duke University, Durham, North Carolina. Publications: Christian Initiation, 1969; Eucharist and Eschatology, 1971, 2nd edition, 1981; The Study of Liturgy (co-editor), 1978, 2nd edition, 1992; Doxology, 1980; The Ecumenical Moment, 1983; The Study of Spirituality (co-editor), 1986; On Wesley and Calvin, 1987; Keeping the Faith: Essays to Mark the Centenary of Lux Mundi (editor), 1989; The Dictionary of the Ecumenical Movement (co-editor), 1991; Methodists in Dialogue, 1995; Worship With One Accord, 1997; For Our Salvation, 1997. Contributions to: Reference books and theological journals. Honours: Numerous named lectureships worldwide; Berakah Award, North American Academy of Liturgy, 1999. Memberships: American Theological Society, secretary, 1988-95, president, 1996-97; International Dialogue Between the World Methodist Council and the Roman Catholic Church, chairman; Societas Liturgica, president, 1983-85; World Council of Churches Faith and Order Commission, 1976-91. Address: The Divinity School, Duke University, Durham, NC 27708, USA.

WAINWRIGHT Jeffrey, b. 19 Feb 1944, Stoke on Trent, England. Poet; Dramatist; Translator; Senior Lecturer. m. Judith Batt, 22 July 1967, 1 son, 1 daughter. Education: BA, 1965, MA, 1967, University of Leeds. Appointments: Assistant Lecturer, Lecturer, University of Wales, 1967-72; Visiting Instructor, Long Island University, 1970-71; Senior Lecturer, Manchester Metropolitan University, 1972-; Northern Theatre Critic, The Independent, 1988-. Publications: Poetry: The Important Men, 1970; Heart's Desire, 1978; Selected Poems, 1985; The Red-Headed Pupil, 1994; Out of the Air, 1999. Other: Translations of various plays into English. Contributions to: Anthologies; BBC Radio; Many periodicals. Honour: Judith E Wilson Visiting Fellow, 1985. Address: 11 Hesketh Avenue, Didsbury, Manchester M20 2QN, England.

WAITE Peter Busby, b. 12 July 1922, Toronto, Ontario, Canada. Professor of History. m. Masha Maria Gropuzzo, 22 Aug 1958. Education: BA (Hons), 1948, MA, 1950, University of British Columbia; PhD, University of Toronto, 1954. Publications: The Life and Times of Confederation, 1864-1867, 1962; Canada 1874-1896, 1971; John A Macdonald, His Life and World, 1975; The Man from Halifax: Sir John Thompson, Prime Minister, 1985; Lord of Point Grey: Larry MacKenzie of UBC, 1987; Between Three Oceans: Challenges of a Continental Destiny, 1840-1900, Chapter IV, Illustrated History of Canada, 1988; The Loner: The Personal Life and Ideas of R B Bennett 1870-1947, 1992; The Lives of Dalhousie University: Volume I, Lord Dalhousie's College, 1818-1925, 1994, Volume II, The Old College Transformed, 1925-1980, 1998. Contributions to: Some 55 articles to numerous magazines and journals. Honours: Fellow, Royal Society of Canada, 1972; Runner-up, Governor-General's Gold Medal Prize, 1985; Lieutenant-Governor's Medal, British Columbia, 1987; LL.D Dalhousie University, 1991; D.Litt, University of New Brunswick, 1991, Memorial University of Newfoundland, 1991, Carleton University, 1993; Officer of the Order of Canada, 1993. Memberships: Canadian Historical Association, president, 1968-69; Humanities Research Council, chairman, 1968-70; Aid to Publications Committee, Social Science Federation, chairman, 1987-89. Address: 960 Ritchie Drive, Halifax, Nova Scotia B3H 3P5, Canada.

WAKEFIELD Dan, b. 21 May 1932, Indianapolis, Indiana, USA. Author; Screenwriter. Education: BA, Columbia University, 1955. Appointments: News Editor, Princeton Packet, New Jersey, 1955; Staff Writer, The Nation magazine, 1956-59; Staff, Bread Loaf Writers Conference, 1964, 1966, 1968, 1970, 1986; Visiting Lecturer, University of Massachusetts at Boston, 1965-66, University of Illinois, 1968; Contributing Editor, The Atlantic Monthly, 1969-80; Writer-in-Residence, Emerson College, 1989-92; Contributing Writer, GQ magazine, 1992-; Distinguished Visiting Writer, Florida International University, 1995-. Publications: Island of the City: The World of Spanish Harlem, 1959; Revolt in the South, 1961; Ananthology, 1963; Between the Lines, 1966; Supernation at Peace and War, 1968; Going All the Way, 1970; Starting Over, 1973; All Her Children, 1976; Home Free, 1977; Under the Apple Tree, 1982; Selling Out, 1985; Returning: A Spiritual Journey, 1988; The Story of Your Life: Writing a Spiritual Autobiography, 1990; New York in the Fifties, 1992; Expect a Miracle, 1995; Creating from the Spirit, 1996. Editor: The Addict: An Anthology, 1963. Television: James at 15, 1977-78; The Seduction of Miss Leona, 1980; Heartbeat, 1988. Honours: Bernard DeVoto Fellow, Bread Loaf Writers Conference, 1957; Rockefeller Foundation Grant, 1968; Short Story Prize, National Council of the Arts, 1968. Memberships: Authors Guild of America; National Writers Union; Writers Guild of America. Address: c/o Janklow & Nesbit, 598 Madison Avenue, New York, NY 10022, USA.

WAKEMAN Frederic Evans, b. 12 Dec 1937, Kansas City, Kansas, USA. Professor of Asian Studies; Writer. Div, 2 sons, 1 daughter. Education: BA, Harvard College, 1959; Postgraduate Studies, Institut d'Etudes Politiques, University of Paris, 1959-60; MA, 1962, PhD, 1965, University of California at Berkeley. Appointments: Assistant Professor, 1965-67, Associate Professor, 1968-70, Professor of History, 1970-89, Director, Center of Chinese Studies, 1972-79, Haas Professor of Asian Studies, 1989-, Director, Institute of East Asian Studies, 1990-, University of California at Berkeley; Humanities Research Professor and Visiting Scholar, Corpus Christi College, Cambridge, 1976-77, Beijing University, 1980-81, 1985. Publications: Strangers at the Gate: Social Disorder in South China, 1839-1861, 1966; Nothing Concealed: Essays in Honor of Liu Yu-Yun, 1970; History and Will, 1973; The Fall of Imperial China (co-editor), 1976; Ming and Qing Historical Studies in the People's Republic of China, 1981; The Great Enterprise: The Manchu Reconstruction of Imperial Order in Seventeenth Century China, 2 volumes, 1985; Shanghai Sojourners (co-editor), 1992; Policing Shanghai, 1995; The Shanghai Badlands: Wartime Terrorism and Urban Crime, 1937-1941, 1996; China's Quest for Modernization: A Historical Perspective (co-editor with Wang Xi), 1997. Contributions to: Professional journals. Honours: American Council of Learned Societies, Fellow, 1967-68; Guggenheim Fellowship, 1973-74; Levenson Prize, 1986; Best Book on Non-North American Urban History, Urban History Association, 1996. Memberships: American Academy of Arts and Sciences; American Historical Association; Association for Asian Studies; Council on Foreign Relations; American Philosophical Society, 1998. Address: c/o Institute of East Asian Studies, University of California at Berkeley, Berkeley, CA 94720, USA.

WAKEMAN John, b. 29 Sept 1928, London, England. Editor; Writer. m. Hilary Paulett, 15 Mar 1957, 4 sons, 1 daughter. Education: Associate, British Library Association, 1950; BA, 1989, MA, 1990, University of East Anglia. Publications: World Authors, 1950-75, 1975; World Authors, 1970-75, 1980; A Room for Doubt, 1985; The Rialto, 1985; World Film Directors, 1987; The Beach Hut, 1987; The Shop: A Magazine of Poetry, 1999. Contributions to: Newspapers and magazines. Honours: Library Journal Best Reference Book Selection, 1988, and Outstanding Academic Book Selection, 1989; Eastern Arts Travel Bursary, 1991; Hawthornden Fellowship, 1992. Address: The Rectory, Toormore, Schull, County Cork, Ireland.

WAKOSKI Diane, b. 3 Aug 1937, Whittier, California, USA. Poet; Professor of English. m. Robert J Turney, 14 Feb 1982. Education: BA, English, University of California at Berkeley, 1960. Appointments: Poet-in-Residence, Professor of English, 1975-, University Distinguished Professor, 1990-, Michigan State University; Many visiting writer-in-residencies. Publications: Poetry: Coins and Coffins, 1962; Discrepancies and Apparitions, 1966; The George Washington Poems, 1967; Inside the Blood Factory, 1968; The Magellanic Clouds, 1970; The Motorcycle Betrayal Poems, 1971; Smudging, 1972; Dancing on the Grave of a Son of a Bitch, 1973; Virtuoso Literature for Two and Four Hands, 1975; Waiting for the King of Spain, 1976; The Man Who Shook Hands, 1978; Cap of Darkness, 1980; The Magician's Feastletters, 1982; The Collected Greed, 1984; The Rings of Saturn, 1986; Emerald Ice: Selected Poems 1962-1987, 1988; Medea the Sorceress, 1991; Jason the Sailor, 1993; The Emerald City of Las Vegas, 1995; Argonaut Rose, 1998. Criticism: Towards a New Poetry, 1980. Contributions to: Anthologies and other publications. Honours: Cassandra Foundation Grant, 1970; Guggenheim Fellowship, 1972; National Endowment for the Arts Grant, 1973; CAPS Grant, 1988, New York State, 1974; Writer's Fulbright Award, 1984; Michigan Arts Council Grant, 1988; William Carlos Williams Prize, 1989; Distinguished Artist Award, Michigan Arts Foundation, 1989. Memberships: Author's Guild; PEN; Poetry Society of America. Address: 607 Division Street, East Lansing, MI 48823, USA.

WALCOTT Derek (Alton), b. 23 Jan 1930, Castries, St Lucia, West Indies. Poet; Dramatist; Visiting Professor. m. (1) Fay Moyston, 1954, div 1959, 1 son, (2) Margaret Ruth Maillard, 1962, div, 2 daughters, (3) Norline Metivier, 1982. Education: St Mary's College, Castries, 1941-47; BA, University College of the West Indies, Mona, Jamaica, 1953. Appointments: Teacher, St Mary's College, Castries, 1947-50, 1954, Grenada Boy's Secondary School, St George's, 1953-54, Jamaica College, Kingston, 1955; Feature Writer, Public Opinion, Kingston, 1956-57; Founder-Director, Little Carib Theatre Workshop, later Trinidad Theatre Workshop, 1959-76; Feature Writer, 1960-62, Drama Critic, 1963-68, Trinidad Guardian, Port-of-Spain; Visiting Professor, Columbia Universitry, 1981, Harvard University, 1982, 1987; Assistant Professor of Creative Writing, 1981, Visiting Professor, 1985-, Brown University. Publications: Poetry: 25 Poems, 1948; Epitaph for the Young: XII Cantos, 1949; Poems, 1951; In a Green Night: Poems 1948-1960, 1962; Selected Poems, 1964; The Castaway and Other Poems, 1965; The Gulf and Other Poems, 1969; Another Life, 1973; Sea Grapes, 1976; The Star-Apple Kingdom, 1979; Selected Poems, 1981; The Fortunate Traveller, 1981; The Caribbean Poetry of Derek Walcott and the Art of Romare Bearden, 1983; Midsummer, 1984; Collected Poems 1948-1984, 1986; The Arkansas Testament, 1987; Omeros, 1989; Collected Poems, 1990; Poems 1965-1980, 1992; Derek Walcott: Selected Poems, 1993. Plays: Cry for a Leader, 1950; Senza Alcun Sospetto or Paolo and Francesca, 1950; Henri Christophe: A Chronicle, 1950; Robin and Andrea or Bim, 1950; Three Assassins, 1951; The Price of Mercy, 1951; Harry Dernier, 1952; The Sea at Dauphin, 1954; Crossroads, 1954; The Charlatan, 1954, 4th version, 1977; The Wine of the Country, 1956; The Golden Lions, 1956; Ione: A Play with Music, 1957; Ti-Jear and His Brothers, 1957; Drums and Colours, 1958; Malcochon, or, The Six in the Rain, 1959; Jourmard, or, A Comedy till the Last Minute, 1959; Batai, 1965; Dream on Monkey Mountain, 1967; Franklin: A Tale of the Islands, 1969, 2nd version, 1973; In a Fine Castle, 1970; The Joker of Seville, 1974; O Babylon!, 1976; Remembrance, 1977; The Snow Queen, 1977; Pantomime, 1978; Marie Laveau, 1979; The Isle is Full of Noises, 1982; Beef, No Chicken, 1982; The

Odyssey: A Stage Version, 1993. Non-Fiction: The Antilles: Fragments of Epic Memory: The Nobel Lecture, 1993; What the Twilight Says (essays), 1998. Honours: Rockefeller Foundation Grants, 1957, 1966, and Fellowship, 1958; Arts Advisory Council of Jamaica Prize, 1960; Guinness Award, 1961; Ingram Merrill Foundation Grant, 1962; Borestone Mountain Awards, 1964, 1977; Heinemann Awards, Royal Society of Literature, 1966, 1983; Cholmondeley Award, 1969; Eugene O'Neill Foundation Fellowship, 1969; Gold Hummingbird Medal, Trinidad, 1969; Obie Award, 1971; Officer of the Order of the British Empire, 1972; Guggenheim Fellowship, 1977; Welsh Arts Council International Writers Prize, 1980; John D and Catharine T MacArthur Foundation Fellowship, 1981; Los Angeles Times Book Prize, 1986; Queen's Gold Medal for Poetry, 1988; Nobel Prize for Literature, 1992. Memberships: American Academy of Arts and Letters, honorary member; Royal Society of Literature, fellow. Address: 165 Duke of Edinburgh Avenue, Diego Martin, Trinidad and Tobago.

WALCZAK Grzegorz, b. 5 Feb 1941, Pulawy, Poland. Writer; Linguist of Polish Language. m. Zofia Brewinska, 30 Oct 1965, 1 daughter. Education: MSc, 1965; PhD, 1974. Appointments: Doktor, Adiunkt, Polish Language Institute, Warsaw University, 1965-90; Slavic Language, Beograd University in Yugoslavia, 1982-85. Publications: Stained Glasses (poetry), 1972; Matrimonal Diary (novel), 1974, 1992; Oasis (novel), 1980, 1997; Lamenti Za Majkom (poetry), 1988; Self Portrait From the Past (poetry), 1989; And When the Angle Knocks (poetry). Contributions to: Teatr (Theatre); Akcent (Accent); Literatura (Literature); Sycyna; Czas Kultury (Culture's Time). Memberships: Association of Polish Writers; The International Theatre Institute; Association of Polish Authors - ZAIKS. Address: Grzybowska 5 m 315, 00-132 Warsaw, Poland.

WALDENFELS Hans, b. 20 Oct 1931, Essen, Ruhr, Germany. University Professor. Education: Lic Phil, 1956; Lic Theol, 1964; Dr Theol, 1968; Dr Theol Habil, 1976; Ordained Roman Catholic Priest, 1963. Appointments: Ordained Roman Catholic Priest, 1963; University Professor. Publications: Faszination des Buddhismus, 1982; Kontextuelle Fundamentaltheologie, 1988; An der Grenze des Denkbaren, 1988; Lexikon der Religionen, 1989; Begegnung der Religionen, 1990; Phänomen Christentum, 1994; Gott, 1995; Einführung in die Theologie der Offenbarung, 1996; Gottes Wort in der Fremde, 1997. Honour: Dr Theol hc, Warsaw. Memberships: Internationales Institut für Missionswissenschaftliche Forschungen; International Association for Mission Studies; Deutsche Vereinigung für Religionsgeschichte; Deutsche Gesellschaft für Missioswissenschaft; Rotary Club. Address: Grenzweg 2, D 40489 Düsseldorf 31, Germany.

WALDMAN Anne, b. 2 Apr 1945, Millville, New Jersey, USA. Poet; Lecturer; Performer; Editor. Education: BA, Bennington College, 1966. Appointments: Editor, Angel Hair Magazine, 1965-, The World, 1966-78; Assistant Director, Poetry Project, St Marks Church In-the-Bowery, 1966-68; Director, Poetry Project, New York City, 1968-78; Founder-Director, Jack Kerouac School of Disembodied Poetics, Naropa Institute, Boulder, Colorado; Poetry readings and performance events worldwide. Publications: Journals and Dreams, 1976; First Baby Poems, 1983; Makeup on Empty Space, 1984; Invention, 1985; Skin Meat Bones, 1985; Blue Mosque, 1987; The Romance Thing, 1987-88; Helping the Dreamer: New and Selected Poems, 1966-1988; Iovis, 1993; Troubairitz, Kill or Cure, 1994; Iovis, Book II, 1996. Editor: The World Anthology, 1969; Another World, 1971; Nice to See You: Homage to Ted Berrigan, 1991; In and Out of This World: An Anthology of the St Marks Poetry Project, 1992; The Beat Book, 1996. Contributions to: Various publications. Honours: National Endowment for the Arts Grant, 1980; Achievement in Poetry Award, Bennington College Alumni, 1981. Memberships: Committee for International Poetry; PEN Poetry Society of America. Address: c/o The Naropa Institute, 2130 Arapahoe Avenue, Boulder, CO 80302, USA.

WALDROP Rosmarie, b. 24 Aug 1935, Kitzingen-am-Main, Germany. Poet; Writer; Translator; Editor; Publisher. m. Keith Waldrop, 20 Jan 1959. Education: University of Wurzburg, 1954-56; University of Aix-Marseille, 1956-57; University of Freiburg, 1957-58; MA, 1960, PhD, 1966, Comparative Literature, University of Michigan. Appointments: Wesleyan University, 1964-70; Co-Editor and Co-Publisher (with Keith Waldrop), Burning Desk Press, 1968-; Visiting Associate Professor, Brown University, 1977-78, 1983, 1990-91; Visiting Lecturer, Tufts University, 1979-81. Publications: Poetry: The Aggressive Ways of the Casual Stranger, 1972; The Road Is Everywhere or Stop This Body, 1978; When They Have Senses, 1980; Nothing Has Changed, 1981; Differences for Four Hands, 1984; Streets Enough to Welcome Snow, 1986; The Reproduction of Profiles, 1987; Shorter American Memory, 1988; Peculiar Motions, 1990; Lawn of Excluded Middle, 1993; A Key Into the Language of America, 1994; Another Language: Selected Poems, 1997; Split Infinites, 1998; Reluctant Gravities, 1999. Fiction: The Hanky of Pippin's Daughter, 1986; A Form/ of Taking/ It All, 1990. Essays: Against Language?, 1971; The Ground Is the Only Figure: Notebook Spring, 1996, 1997. Other: Various poetry chapbooks, translations, and editions. Honours: Major Hopwood Award in Poetry, 1963; Alexander von Humboldt Fellowships, 1970-71, 1975-76; Howard Foundation Fellowship, 1974-75; Columbia University Translation Center Award, 1978; National Endowment for the Arts Fellowships, 1980, 1984; Governor's Arts Award, Rhode Island, 1988; Fund for Poetry Award, 1990; PEN/Book-of-the-Month Club Citation in Translation, 1991; Deutscher Akademischer Austauschdienst Fellowship, Berlin, 1993; Harold Morton Landon Translation Award, 1994. Membership: PEN. Address: 17 rue Gramme, Bat E, 75015 Paris, France.

WALKER Alexander, b. 22 Mar 1930, Portadown, Northern Ireland. Journalist; Film Critic. Education: BA, Queen's University, Belfast; College d'Europe, Belgium; University of Michigan. Appointments: Lecturer, University of Michigan, 1952-54; Features Editor, Birmingham Gazette, 1954-56; Associate Editor, Birmingham Post, 1956-60; Critic, Evening Standard, 1960-; Columnist, Vogue Magazine, 1974-86; Broadcaster, Co-Producer, television programmes. Publications: The Celluloid Sacrifice: Aspects of Sex in the Movies, 1966; Stardom: The Hollywood Phenomenon, 1970; Stanley Kubrick Directs, 1971; Hollywood, England: British Film Industry in the 60s, 1974; Rudolph Valentino, 1976; Double Jakes, 1978; Superstars, 1978; The Shattered Silents, 1978; Garbo, 1980; Peter Sellers: Authorised Biography, 1981; Joan Crawford, 1983; Dietrich, 1984; No Bells on Sunday: The Journals of Rocket Roberts, 1984; National Heroes: British Cinema in the 70's and 80's, 1985; Bette Davis, 1986; Vivien: The Life of Vivien Leigh, 1987; It's Only a Movie, Ingrid, 1988; Elizabeth: The Life of Elizabeth Taylor, 1990; Zinnemann, 1991; Fatal Charm: The Life of Rex Harrison, 1992; Audrey: Her Real Story, 1994. Contributions to: Magazines. Honours: Critic of the Year Awards, 1970, 1974, 1998; Chevalier de l'Ordre des Arts et des Letters, France, 1981. Memberships: British Film Institute, governor, 1989-95; British Screen Advisory Council, 1977-92. Address: 1 Marlborough, 38-40 Maida Vale, London W9 1RW, England.

WALKER Alice (Malsenior), b. 9 Feb 1944, Eatonton, Georgia, USA. Author; Poet. m. Melvyn R Leventhal, 17 Mar 1967, div 1976, 1 daughter. Education: BA, Sarah Lawrence College, 1966. Appointments: Writer-in-Residence and Teacher of Black Studies, Jackson State College, 1968-69, Tougaloo College, 1970-71; Lecturer in Literature, Wellesley College, 1972-73, University of Massachusetts at Boston, 1972-73; Distinguished Writer, Afro-American Studies Department, University of California at Berkeley, 1982; Fannie Hurst Professor of Literature, Brandeis University, 1982; Co-Founder and Publisher, Wild Trees Press, Navarro, California, 1984-88. Publications: Once, 1968; The Third Life of Grange Copeland, 1970; Five Poems, 1972; Revolutionary Petunias and Other Poems, 1973; In Love and Trouble, 1973; Langston Hughes: American Poet, 1973; Meridian, 1976; Goodnight, Willie Lee, I'll See You in the Morning, 1979; You Can't Keep a Good Woman Down, 1981; The Color Purple, 1982; In Search of Our Mother's Gardens, 1983; Horses Make a Landscape Look More Beautiful, 1984; To Hell With Dying, 1988; Living by the Word: Selected Writings, 1973-1987, 1988; The Temple of My Familiar, 1989; Her Blue Body Everything We Know: Earthling Poems, 1965-1990, 1991; Finding the Green Stone, 1991; Possessing the Secret of Joy, 1992; Warrior Marks (with Pratibha Parmar), 1993; Double Stitch: Black Women Write About Mothers and Daughters (with others), 1993; Everyday Use, 1994; By the Light of My Father's Smile, 1998. Editor: I Love Myself When I'm Laughing... And Then Again When I'm Looking Mean and Impressive, 1979. Honours: Bread Loaf Writer's Conference Scholar, 1966; Ingram Merrill Foundation Fellowship, 1967; McDowell Colony Fellowships, 1967, 1977-78; National Endowment for the Arts Grants, 1969, 1977; Richard and Hinda Rosenthal Pound Award, American Academy and Institute of Arts and Letters, 1974; Guggenheim Fellowship, 1977-78; Pulitzer Prize for Fiction, 1983; American Book Award, 1983; O Henry Award, 1986; Nora Astorga Leadership Award, 1989; Freedom to Write Award, PEN Center, West, 1990; Honorary doctorates. Address: c/o Wendy Weil Agency Inc, 232 Madison Avenue, Suite 1300, New York, NY 10016, USA.

WALKER Andrew Norman, b. 19 May 1926, Looe, Cornwall, England. Retired BBC Journalist. m. Avril Anne Elizabeth Dooley, 20 June 1956, 2 sons, 2 daughters. Publications: The Modern Commonwealth, 1975; The Commonwealth: A New Look, 1978; A Skyful of Freedom, 1992. Contributions to: Janes Defence Weekly; Commonwealth Magazine. Membership: Commonwealth Journalists Association. Address: 9 Chartwell Court, Brighton, East Sussex BN1 2EW, England.

WALKER Charlotte Zoe, b. New Orleans, USA. Professor. m. (1) 1957 1 son, 2 daughters, (2) Roland C Greefkes, 1988. Education: BA, San Diego State University, 1957; MA, 1967, PhD, 1972, Syracuse University. Appointments: Professor of English and Women's Studies, State University of New York, College at Oneonta, New York. Publications: Condor and Hummingbird (novel); Sharp Eyes: John Burrough and American Nature: A Collection of Essays (editor); Several stories. Honours: National Endowment for the Arts Fiction Writing Fellowship, 1987; O Henry Award, 1991. Memberships: Poets and Writers; National Writers Union. Address: PO Box 14, Gilbertsville, NY 13776, USA.

WALKER David Maxwell, b. 9 Apr 1920, Glasgow, Scotland. Professor of Law Emeritus; Writer. m. Margaret Knox, 1 Sept 1954. Education: MA, 1946, LLB, 1948, LLD, 1985, University of Glasgow; PhD, 1952, LLD, 1960, University of Edinburgh; LLB, 1957, LLD, 1968, University of London. Appointments: Advocate, Scottish Bar, 1948; Professor of Jurisprudence, University of Glasgow, 1954-58; Barrister, Middle Temple, 1957; Director, Scottish University Law Institute, 1974-80; Regius Professor of Law, 1958-90, Professor Emeritus and Senior Research Fellow, 1990-, University of Glasgow. Publications: Law of Damages in Scotland, 1955; The Scottish Legal System, 1959, 7th edition, 1997; Law of Delict in Scotland, 1966, 2nd edition, 1981; Scottish Courts and Tribunals, 1969, 5th edition, 1985; Principles of Scottish Private Law, 2 volumes, 1970, 4th edition, 4 volumes, 1988-89; Law of Prescription and Limitation in Scotland, 1973, 5th edition, 1996; Law of Civil Remedies in Scotland, 1974; Law of Contracts in Scotland, 1979, 3rd edition, 1995; The Oxford Companion t Lawo, 1980; Stair's Institutions (editor), 6th edition, 1981; Stair Tercentenary Studies (editor), 1981; The Scottish Jurists, 1985; The Legal History of Scotland, 5 volumes, 1988-98. Contributions to: Books and legal journals. Honours: Honorary LLD, University of Edinburgh, 1974; Commander of the Order of the British Empire, 1986; Festschrift published in his honour, 1990. Memberships: British Academy, fellow; Faculty of Advocates; Royal Society of Edinburgh, fellow; Scottish History Society; Society of Antiquarians of Scotland; Society of the Middle

Temple; Stair Society. Address: 1 Beaumont Gate, Glasgow G12 9EE, Scotland.

WALKER Geoffrey De Quincey, b. 24 Oct 1940, Waratah, New South Wales, Australia. Professor of Law. m. Lauren Kehoe, 7 Dec 1990. Education: LLB, 1962; LLM, 1963; SJD, 1966. Appointment: Professor of Law, University of Queensland, 1985-96. Publications: Australian Monopoly Law, 1967; Initiative and Referendum: The People's Law, 1987; The Rule of Law: Foundation of Constitutional Democracy, 1988. Contributions to: Over 60 Articles. Honour: Gowen Fellow, University of Pennsylvania, 1966; Professor Emeritus, University of Queensland, 1996.

WALKER George F(rederick), b. 23 Aug 1947, Toronto, Ontario, Canada. Playwright. Education: Graduated, Riverdale Collegiate, Toronto, 1965. Appointment: Resident Playwright, New York Shakespeare Festival, 1981. Publications: The Prince of Naples, 1971; Ambush at Tether's End, 1971; Sacktown Rag, 1972; Baghdad Saloon, 1973; Beyond Mozambique, 1974; Ramona and the White Slaves, 1976; Gossip, 1977; Zastrozzi: The Master of Discipline, 1977; Filthy Rich, 1979; Rumours of our Death (musical), 1980; Theatre of the Film Noir, 1981; Science and Madness, 1982; The Art of War: An Adventure, 1983; Criminals in Love, 1984; Better Living, 1986; Beautiful City, 1987; Nothing Sacred, after Turgenev, 1988; Love and Anger, 1990; Escape from Happiness, 1991; Shared Anxiety, 1994. Honours: Governor-General's Awards in Drama, 1985, 1988; Toronto Arts Award for Drama, 1994. Address: c/o Great North Artists, 350 Dupont Street, Toronto, Ontario M5V 1V9, Canada.

WALKER Gladys Lorraine, b. 11 Dec 1927, Bridgeport, Connecticut, USA. Author; Journalist. m. Daniel R Walker Sr, 14 Apr 1950, 3 children. Education: BA, School of Journalism, Syracuse University; BA, College of Arts and Sciences. Publications: I Don't Do Portholes, 1986; Molly Meets Mona & Friends - A Magical Day In the Museum, 1997. Contributions to: New Choice; Architectural Record; New York Times. Honours: Non-Fiction Awards, American Pen Women Non-Fiction Awards, 1962, 1970, 1974, 1976; Book Award, Connecticut Press Club, 1986; 1st Journalism Award, National League of American Pen Women, 1988; Connecticut Press Club, 1990. Literary Agent: Linda Konner. Address: 618-A Erie Lane, Stratford, CT 06614, USA.

WALKER Harry. See: WAUGH Hillary Baldwin.

WALKER Jeanne Murray, b. 27 May 1944, Parkers Prairie, Minnesota, USA. Professor of English; Poet; Dramatist; Writer. m. E Daniel Larkin, 16 July 1983, 1 son, 1 daughter. Education: BA, Wheaton College, Illinois, 1966; MA, Loyola University, Chicago, 1969; PhD, University of Pennsylvania, 1974. Appointments: Assistant Professor of English, Haverford College, Pennsylvania; Professor of English, University of Delaware. Publications: Poetry: Nailing Up the Home Sweet Home, 1980; Fugitive Angels, 1985; Coming Into History, 1990; Stranger Than Fiction, 1992; Gaining Time, 1997. Other: 6 plays, 1990-97. Contributions to: Numerous reviews, quarterlies, journals, and periodicals. Honours: Delaware Humanities Council Grant, 1979; Delaware Arts Council Grant, 1981; 5 Pennsylvania Council on the Arts Fellowships, 1983-93; Prairie Schooner/Strousse Award, 1988; Winner, Washington National Theatre Competition, 1990; Colladay Award for Poetry, 1992; Fellow, Center for Advanced Studies, 1993; National Endowment for the Arts Fellowship, 1994; Lewis Prizes for New Plays, Brigham Theatre, 1995; Stagetime Award, PEW Fellow in the Arts, 1998; Minneapolis Playwright's Center; Dramatists Guild; PEN; Poets and Writers. Address: c/o Department of English, 127 Memorial Hall, University of Delaware, Newark, DE 19716, USA.

WALKER Lou Ann, b. 9 Dec 1952, Hartford City, Indiana, USA. Writer. m. Speed Vogel, 8 Sept 1986, 1 daughter. Education: Attended Ball State University,

1971-73; Degree in French Language and Literature, University of Besancon, 1975; BA, Harvard University, 1976. Appointments: Reporter, Indianapolis News, 1976; Assistant to Executive Editor, New York (magazine), New York, 1976-77, Cosmopolitan, New York City, 1979-80; Assistant Editor, Esquire Magazine, 1977-79; Associate Editor, Diversion (magazine), New York City, 1980-81; Editor, Direct (magazine), New York City, 1981-82; Sign Language Interpretor for New York Society for the Deaf; Consultant to Broadway's Theater Development Fund and sign language advisor on many Broadway shows, 1984-; Contributing Editor, New York Woman, 1990-92; Publications: Amy: The Story of a Deaf Child, 1985; A Loss for Words: The Story of Deafness in a Family (autobiography), 1986; Hand, Heart and Mind, 1994; Roy Lichtenstein: The Artist at Work, 1994. Contributions to: New York Times Book Review; Chicago Sun-Times; Esquire; New York Times Magazine; New York Woman; Life. Honours: Rockefeller Foundation Humanities Fellowship, 1982-83; Christopher Award, 1987; National Endowment for the Arts Creative Writing Grant, 1988. Membership: Authors Guild. Address: c/o Darhansoff & Verrill, 179 Franklin Street, 4th Floor, New York, NY 10013, USA.

WALKER Ted, b. 28 Nov 1934, Lancing, England. Writer. m. (1) Lorna Ruth Benfell, 11 Aug 1956, dec 1987, (2) Audrey Joan Hicks, 8 July 1988, 2 sons, 2 daughters. Education: MA, St John's College, Cambridge, England, 1953-56. Appointments: Assistant Master, North Paddington School, 1956-58; Head of French Department, Southall Technical School, 1958-63; Head of Modern Languages, Bognor Regis Comprehensive, 1963-67; Professor of Creative Writing and English Literature, New England College, Arundel, 1971-92, Professor Emeritus, 1992. Publications: Fox on A Barn Door (poems); The Solitaries (poems); The Night Bathers (poems); Gloves to the Hangman (poems); Burning the Ivy (poems); The Lion's Cavalcade (children's verse); The High Path (autobiography); In Spain (travel); You've Never Heard Me Sing (short stories); Hands at a Live Fire (selected poems); The Last of England (autobiography); Grandad's Seagulls (children's verse). Contributions to: The New Yorker; Atlantic Monthly; McCall's; The London Magazine; Spectator; New Statesman; Virginia Quarterly. Honours: Eric Gregory Award; Cholmondey Award; Honorary DLitt, Southampton University, 1995. Membership: Fellow, Royal Society of Literature. Literary Agent: Sheil Land Associates Ltd, 43 Doughty Street, London WC1N 2LF, England. Address: 7 The Village, 03728 Alcalali, Alicante, Spain.

WALL Ethan. See: HOLMES Bryan John.

WALL Geoffrey, (Professional name of Geoffrey Chadwick), b. 10 July 1950. Cheshire, England. Senior Lecturer in English; Biographer; Translator. Education: BA, University of Sussex, 1972; BPhil, St Edmund Hall, 1975. Appointments: Lecturer, 1975-97, Senior Lecturer, 1997-, Department of English and Related Literature, University of York. Publications: Translator: Madame Bovary, by Gustave Flaubert, 1992; The Dictionary of Received Ideas, by Gustave Flaubert, 1994; Selected Letters, by Gustave Flaubert, 1997; Modern Times: Selected Writings, by Jean-Paul Sartre, 1999. Contributions to: Scholarly journals. Memberships: Association of University Teachers; Society of Authors; Translators Association. Address: c/o Department of English and Related Literature, University of York, Heslington, York Y01 5DD, England.

WALL Mervyn, b. 23 Aug 1908, Dublin, Ireland. Writer; Dramatist. m. Fanny Freehan, 25 Apr 1950, 1 son, 3 daughters. Education: BA, National University of Ireland, 1928. Appointments: Civil Servant, 1934-48; Programme Officer, Radio Eireann, 1948-57; Chief Executive, Irish Arts Council, 1957-75; Book Reviewer, Radio Critic, Radio Broadcaster. Publications: The Unfortunate Fursey, 1946; The Return of Fursey, 1948; No Trophies Raise, 1956; Forty Foot Gentlemen Only, 1962; A Flutter of Wings, 1974; The Garden of Echoes, 1988; Plays. Contributions to: Journals. Honour: Best European Novel of Year, 1952. Memberships: Irish Academy of Letters;

Irish Writers Union. Address: 2 The Mews, Sandycove Avenue West, Sandycove, County Dublin, Ireland.

WALLACE David Foster, b. 21 Feb 1962, Ithaca, New York, USA. Author; Associate Professor of English. Education: AB, summa cum laude, Amherst College, 1985; MFA, University of Arizona, 1987. Appointment: Associate Professor of English, Illinois State University, 1993-. Publications: The Broom of the System, 1987; Girl With Curious Hair, 1988; Signifying Rappers: Rap and Race in the Urban Present (with Mark Costello), 1990; Infinite Jest, 1996; A Supposedly Fun Thing I'll Never Do Again: Essays and Arguments, 1997. Contributions to: Various publications. Honours: Whiting Writers' Award, 1987; Yaddo Residencies, 1987, 1989; National Endowment for the Arts Fellowship, 1989; Lannan Foundation Award for Literature, 1996; John D Catharine T MacArthur Foundation Fellowship, 1997. Address: c/o Department of English, Illinois State University, Normal, IL 61790, USA.

WALLACE Ian (Robert), b. 31 Mar 1950, Niagara Falls, Ontario, Canada. Writer; Illustrator. m. Debra Wiedman. Education: Ontario College of Art, 1969-74. Publications: Julie News, 1974; The Sandwich (with A Wood), 1974; The Sandwich (with A Wood), 1975; The Christmas Tree House, 1976; Chin Chiang and the Dragon's Dance, 1984; The Sparrow's Song, 1986; Morgan the Magnificent, 1987; Mr Kneebone's New Digs, 1991. Illustrator: 10 books, 1986-96. Honours: Runner-Up, City of Toronto Book Award, 1976; A F Howard Gibbons Award, 1984; IODE Book Award, 1985; IBBY Honour's List, 1986; Mr Christie Book Award, 1990; Aesop Accolade List, 1994; Hans Christian Andersen Medalist Nominee, 1994. Memberships: Canadian Children's Book Centre; Writer's Union of Canada. Address: 184 Major Street, Toronto, Ontario M5S 2L3, Canada.

WALLACE Ronald William, b. 18 Feb 1945, Cedar Rapids, Iowa, USA. Poet; Professor of English. m. Margaret Elizabeth McCreight, 3 Aug 1968, 2 daughters. Education: BA, College of Wooster, 1967; MA, 1968, PhD, 1971, University of Michigan. Appointments: Director of Creative Writing, University of Wisconsin, Madison, 1975-; Series Editor, Brittingham Prize in Poetry, 1985-; Director, Wisconsin Institute for Creative Writing, 1986-. Publications: Henry James and the Comic Form, 1975; Installing the Bees, 1977; Cucumbers, 1977; The Last Laugh, 1979; The Facts of Life, 1979; Plums, Stones, Kisses and Hooks, 1981; Tunes for Bears to Dance to, 1983; God Be With the Clown, 1984; The Owl in the Kitchen, 1985; People and Dog in the Sun, 1987; Vital Signs, 1989; The Makings of Happiness, 1991; Time's Fancy, 1994. Contributions to: New Yorker; Atlantic; Nation; Poetry; Southern Review; Poetry Northwest. Honours: Hopwood Award for Poetry, 1970; Council for Wisconsin Writers Awards, 1978, 1979, 1984, 1985, 1986, 1988; Helen Bullis Prize in Poetry, 1985; Robert E Gard Award for Excellence in Poetry, 1990; Posner Poetry Prize, 1992; Gerald A Bartell Award in the Arts, 1994. Memberships: Poets and Writers; Associated Writing Programs. Address: Department of English, University of Wisconsin, Madison, WI 53706, USA.

WALLACE-CRABBE Chris(topher Keith), b. 6 May 1934, Richmond, Victoria, Australia. Professor of English; Poet; Writer. m. Sophie Feil, 1 son, 1 daughter. Education: BA, 1956, MA, 1964, University of Melbourne. Reader in English, 1976-88, Professor of English, 1988-, University of Melbourne. Publications: Poetry: No Glass Houses, 1956; The Music of Division, 1959; Eight Metropolitan Poems, 1962; In Light and Darkness, 1964; The Rebel General, 1967; Where the Wind Came, 1971; Act in the Noon, 1974; The Shapes of Gallipoli, 1975; The Foundations of Joy, 1976; The Emotions Are Not Skilled Workers, 1979; The Amorous Cannibal and Other Poems, 1985; I'm Deadly Serious, 1988; Selected Poems 1956-1994, 1995. Novel: Splinters, 1981. Other: Melbourne or the Bush: Essays on Australian Literature and Society, 1973. Editor: Volumes of Australian poetry. Honour: Dublin Prize, 1986. Address: c/o Department of

English, University of Melbourne, Melbourne, Victoria 3052, Australia.

WALLENSTEIN Barry, b. 13 Feb 1940, New York, New York, USA. Poet; Professor of English. m. Lorna Harbus, 19 Mar 1978, 1 son, 1 daughter. Education: BA, 1962, MA, 1963, PhD, 1972, New York University. Appointments: Professor of English, City College of the City University of New York, 1965-; Exchange Professor, University of Paris, 1981, Polytechnic of North London, 1987-88; Writer-in-Residence, University of North Michigan, 1993. Publications: Poetry: Beast is a Wolf with Brown Fire, 1977; Roller Coaster Kid, 1982; Love and Crush, 1991; The Short Life of the Five Minute Dancer, 1993; A Measure of Conduct, 1999. Criticism: Visions and Revisions: An Approach to Poetry, 1971. Contributions to: Anthologies, reviews, quarterlies, and journals. Honours: City University of New York Research Fund Grant; MacDowell Colony Residency Fellowship. Memberships: Academy of American Poets; Poets and Writers; Poets House. Address: 340 Riverside Drive, New York, NY 10025, USA.

WALLER Jane Ashton, b. 19 May 1944, Bucks, England. Writer; Ceramist. m. Michael Vaughan Rees, 11 June 1982. Education: Oxford Art College, 1962-63; BA, Hornsey Art College, 1965; Sir John Cass College, 1966-69; MA, Royal College of Art, 1982. Publications: A Stitch in Time, 1972; Some Things for the Children, 1974; Some Dinosaur Poems for Children, 1975; A Man's Book, 1977; The Thirties Family Knitting Book, 1981; Below the Green Pond, 1982; The Man's Knitting Book, 1984; Women in Wartime (with Michael Vaughan-Rees), 1987; Women in Uniform (with Michael Vaughan-Rees), 1989; Handbuilt Ceramics, 1990; Blitz: The Civilian War (with Michael Vaughan-Rees), 1990; Saving the Dinosaurs, 1994; The Sludgegulpers, 1996; Colour in Clay, 1998. Contributions to: Ceramic Review. Honour: Herbert Read Literary Award, 1981. Address: 22 Roupell Street, Waterloo, London SE1 8SP, England.

WALLER Robert James, b. 1 Aug 1939, USA. Writer. m. Georgia Ann Wiedemeier, 1 son. Education: University of Iowa, 1957-58; University of Northern Iowa, 1958; PhD, Indiana University, 1968. Appointments: Professor of Management, 1968-91, Dean, School of Business, 1979-85, University of Northern Iowa. Publications: Just Beyond the Firelight: Stories and Essays, 1988; One Good Road is Enough: Essays, 1990; The Bridges of Madison County, 1992; Slow Waltz in Cedar Bend, 1993; Old Songs in a New Cafe: Selected Essays, 1994; Border Music, 1995. Honour: Literary Lion Award, New York Public Library, 1993. Address: c/o Aaron Priest Literary Agency, 708 Third Avenue, 23rd Floor, New York, NY 10017, USA.

WALLEY Byron. See: CARD Orson Scott.

WALLINGTON Vivienne Elizabeth, (Elizabeth Duke), b. 8 Feb 1937, Adelaide, South Australia, Australia. Writer. m. John Wallington, 18 Apr 1959, 1 son, 1 daughter. Education: Library Registration, Prelim + 6 Subjects, 1954-59. Publications: Somewhere, 1982; Butterfingers, 1986; Names are Fun, 1990; Outback Legacy, 1993; Shattered Wedding, 1994; To Catch a Playboy, 1995; Heartless Stranger, 1996; Takeover Engagement, 1997; The Marriage Pact, 1997; Look-alike Fiancée, 1998; The Husband Dilemma, 1998. Contributions to: Newspapers. Honour: Finalist, Heart of Romance Award, USA, 1996. Memberships: Novelists, Inc.; Romance Writers of America; Romance Writers of Australia; Romantic Novelists Association. Address: 38 Fuller Street, Mitcham, Victoria 3132, Australia.

WALLISER-SCHWARZBART Eileen Ann, b. 11 June 1947, New York City, New York, USA. Translator; Editor. m. Stephan Walliser, 31 Mar 1970. Education: BA. Publications: Translations: The Art and Culture of Bali, 1977; Luther: Man Between God and The Devil, 1989; The Jewish World of Yesterday, 1991; 1000 Years of Swiss Art, 1992; Zoltan Kemeny: The Early Work, 1994; The Four Literatures of Switzerland, 1996; Philosophy in Switzerland, 1996; Ceremonies: Short Stories, 1998; The

Swiss Cinema, 1998. Membership: Gruppe Olten. Address: c/o Redaktion Passages, Pro Helvetia, Hirschengraben 22, 8024 Zurich, Switzerland.

WALLS Ian Gascoigne, b. 28 Apr 1922, Glasgow, Scotland. Horticulturist. m. Eleanor McIntosh McCaig, 11 Aug 1947, 2 daughters. Education: West of Scotland Agricultural College, 1949. Appointment: Gardening Writer, Glasgow Herald. Publications: Gardening Month by Month, 1962; Creating Your Garden, 1967; Tomato Growing Today, 1972; The Complete Book of the Greenhouse, 1973, 5th edition, 1993; A-Z of Garden Pests and Problems, 1979; Modern Greenhouse Methods, 1984; Profit from Growing Vegetables, Fruits and Flowers, 1988; Simple Tomato Growing, 1988; Simple Vegetable Growing, 1988; Growing Tomatoes, 1989; Making Your Garden Pay: Low Cost Gardening, 1992. Memberships: Glasgow Wheelers CC; Milngavie Horticultural Society. Address: 17 Douglaston Avenue, Milngavie, Glasgow G62 6AP, Scotland.

WALSER Martin, b. 24 Mar 1927, Wasserburg, Germany. Author; Dramatist. Education: University of Regensburg; PhD, University of Tübingen. Publications: Ein Flugzeug über dem Haus, 1955; Ehen in Philipssburg, 1957; Halbzeit, 1960; Das Einhorn, 1966; Fiction, 1970; Gesammelte Stücke, 1971; Die Gallistl'sche Krankheit, 1972; Der Sturz, 1973; Jenseits de Liebe, 1976; Ein fliehendes Pferd, 1978; Seelenarbeit, 1979; Das Schwanenhaus, 1980; Brief an Lord Liszt, 1982; Die Brandung, 1985; Dorle und Wolfe, 1987; Jagd, 1988; Uber Deutschland reden, 1988; Verteidigung der Kindheit, 1990; Ohne einander, 1993; Finks Krieg, 1996; Ein springender Brunnen, 1998. Honours: Gruppe 47 Prize, 1955; Hermann Hesse Prize, 1957; Gerhardt Hauptmann Prize, 1962; Schiller Prize, 1965; Georg Büchner Prize, 1981; Order pour le Merite für Wissenschaften und Kunste, 1993; Officier de l'ordre des Arts et des Lettres, France, 1994. Memberships: Academy of Arts, Berlin; Association of German Writers; German Academy for Language and Literature; PEN. Address: 88662 Uberlingen Nussdorf, Zum Hecht 36, Germany.

WALSH Sheila, (Sophie Leyton), b. 10 Oct 1928, Birmingham, England. Writer. Education: Southport College of Art, 1945-48. Publications: The Golden Songbird, 1975; The Sergeant Major's Daughter, 1977; A Fine Silk Purse, 1978; The Incomparable Miss Brady, 1980; The Rose Domino, 1981; A Highly Respectable Marriage, 1983; The Runaway Bride, 1984; Cousins of a Kind, 1985; The Incorrigible Rake, 1985; An Insubstantial Pageant, 1986; Bath Intrigue, 1986; Lady Aurelia's Bequest, 1987; Minerva's Marquis, 1988; The Nabob, 1989-90; A Woman of Little Importance, 1991; Until Tomorrow, 1993; Remember Me, 1994; A Perfect Bride, 1994; Kate and the Marquess, 1997. Honour: Best Romantic Novel of Year, 1983. Memberships: Romantic Novelists Association, vice-president; Soroptimist International of Southport. Address: 35 Coudray Road, Southport, Merseyside PR9 9NL, England.

WALSHE Aubrey Peter, b. 12 Jan 1934, Johannesburg, South Africa. Professor of Political Science. m. Catherine Ann Pettifer, 26 Jan 1957, 1 son, 3 daughters. Education: BA, Honours, Wadham College, Oxford, 1956; DPhil, St Antony's College, Oxford, 1968. Appointments: Lecturer, University of Lesotho, 1959-62; Professor of Political Science, University of Notre Dame, Indiana, 1967-. Publications: The Rise of African Nationalism in South Africa, 1971; Black Nationalism in South Africa, 1974; Church Versus State in South Africa, 1983; Prophetic Christianity and the Liberation Movement in South Africa, 1996. Contributions to: Cambridge History of Africa, 1986, professional journals and newspapers. Address: c/o Department of Government, University of Notre Dame, Notre Dame, IN 46556, USA.

WALTER Richard, b. 11 July 1944, New York, New York, USA. Writer; Educator. m. Patricia Sandgrund, 18 June 1967, 1 son, 1 daughter. Education: BA, History, 1965, Harpur College, State University of New York, 1965; MS, Communications, 1966, Newhouse School of

Public Communications, Syracuse University Postgraduate Study, Department of Cinema, University of Southern California, 1967-70. Appointments: Professor and Screenwriting Chairman, Department of Film and Television, University of California, Los Angeles, 1977-. Publications: Barry and the Persuasions, 1976; Screenwriting: The Art, Craft and Business of Film and Television Writing, 1988; The Whole Picture: Strategies for Screenwriting Success in the New Hollywood, 1997; Escape from Film School, 1999. Screenplays: Group Marriage; Return of Zorro; Dynamite Lady; Mrs Charlie; Split; Young Love; Marked Man; Jackie Whitefish. Contributions to: Asian Wall Street Journal; Los Angeles Times; Los Angeles Herald Examiner. Memberships: Writers Guild of America; PEN Centre West; University Film and Video Association. Address: Department of Film and Television, University of California, Los Angeles, CA 90095, USA.

WALTERS Huw, b. 25 Dec 1951, Glanaman, Dyfed, Wales. Librarian; Bibliographer. Education: BLib, 1978; PhD, 1985. Appointments: Leverhulme Research Assistant, Department of Bibliographical Studies, College of Librarianship Wales, Aberystwyth, 1979; Assistant Librarian, Bibliographical Services Division, Department of Printed Books, National Library of Wales, Aberystwyth, 1981. Publications: Erwau'r Glo, 1976; Brinli: Cyfreithiwr, Bardd, Archdderwydd, 1981; Ysgol Glanaman, y Ganrif Gyntaf, 1984; Canu'r Pwll a'r Pulpud, 1987; John Morris-Jones, 1864-1929: Llyfryddiaeth Anodiadol, 1987; The Welsh Periodical Press, 1987; The Amman Valley Long Ago, 1987; Evan David Jones, 1903-1987: Llyfryddiaeth, 1987; A Bibliography of Welsh Periodicals, 1735-1850, 1993; Yr Adolygydd a'r Beirniad: eu Cynnwys a'u Cyfranwyr, 1996; Robert Tudur Jones (biography); Ceri W Lewis, (biography). Contributions to: Reference works, bibliographies and Festschriften. Honours: National Eisteddfod of Wales Prizes, 1974, 1979; University of Wales Sir Ellis (Jones) Ellis-Griffith Memorial Prize, 1988 and W L Davies Award, 1988; Welsh Arts Council Literary Prize, 1988; Honorary Member, Gorsedd of Bards, 1990; Honorary President, Amman Valley History Society, 1990. Address: Bryn-teg, 10 Dinas Terrace, Aberystwyth, Dyfed SY23 1BT, Wales.

WALTERS Minette, b. 26 Sept 1949, Bishops Stortford, England. Writer. m. Alexander Walters, 19 Aug 1978, 2 sons. Education: Durham University, England. Appointments: Writer; Editor, London; England; Volunteer, Israel, 8 months, 1968; PTA work, 1986-87; Local elections, 1987. Publications: also TV Adaptations - The Ice House, 1992; The Sculptress, 1993; The Scold's Bridle, 1994; The Dark Room, 1995; The Echo, 1997; The Breaker, 1998. Honours: John Creasey Award for Best First Crime Novel; British Crime Writers' Association, for The Ice House, 1992; Macavity Award, 1993, and Edgar Allen Poe Award, for The Sculptress, 1994; Gold Dagger Award, British Crime Writer's Association, for The Scold's Bridle, 1994. Literary Agent: Gregory and Radice Authors' Agents, 3 Barb Mews, London W6 7PA, England.

WALVIN James, b. 2 Jan 1942, Manchester, England. Professor of History; Writer. m. Jennifer Walvin, 2 sons. Education: BA, University of Keele, 1964; MA, McMaster University, 1970. Appointment: Professor of History, University of York. Publications: A Jamaica Plantation: Worthy Park 1670-1870 (with M Craton), 1970; The Black presence: A Documentary of the Negro in Britain, 1971; Black and White: The Negro and English Society 1555-1945, 1973; The People's Game: A Social History of British Football, 1975; Slavery, Abolition, and Emancipation (co-editor), 1976; Beside the Seaside: A Social History of the Popular Seaside Holiday), 1978; Leisure and Society 19830-1950, 1978; Abolition of the Atlantic Slave Trade (co-editor), 1981; A Child's World: A Social History of English Childhood 1900-1914, 1982; Slavery and British Society 1776-1848 (editor), 1982; English Radicals and Reformers 1776-1848 (with E Royle), 1982; Slavery and the Slave Trade, 1983; Black Personalities: Africans in Britain in the Era of Slavery, 1983; Leisure in Britain Since 1800 (co-editor), 1983; Urban England 1776-1851, 1984; Manliness and Morality (co-editor), 1985; Football and the Decline of Britain, 1986; England, Slaves, and Freedom, 1776-1838, 1986; Victorian Values, 1987; Black Ivory: A History of British Slavery, 1992; Slaves and Slavery, 1992; The People's Game: The History of Football Revisited, 1994; The Life and Times of Henry Clarke of Jamaica, 1994; Questioning Slavery, 1996; Fruits of Empire: Exotic Produce and British Taste 1660-1800, 1997; The Quakers: Money and Morals, 1997; An African Life, 1998. Address: c/o Department of History, University of York, Heslington, Yorkshire YO1 5DD, England.

WALWICZ Ania, b. 19 May 1951, Swidnica, Poland (Australian citizen). Poet; Dramatist; Writer; Artist. Education: Diploma in Education, University of Melbourne, 1984; Diploma and Graduate Diploma, Victorian College of the Arts. Appointments: Writer-in-Residence, Deakin University and Murdoch University, 1987-88. Publications: Writing, 1982; Boat, 1989. Plays: Girlboytalk, 1986; Dissecting Mice, 1989; Elegant, 1990; Red Roses, 1992; Telltale, 1994. Contributions to: 85 anthologies. Honours: Australian Council Literature Board grants, and Fellowship, 1990; New Writing Prize, Victorian Premier's Literary Awards, 1990. Address: Unit 40, 26 Victoria Street, Melbourne, Victoria 3065, Australia.

WALWORTH Arthur Clarence Jr, b. 9 July 1903, Newton, Massachusetts, USA. Historian. Education: Phillips Andover Academy, 1921; BA, Yale College, 1925. Publications: Black Ships Off Japan, 1946; Cape Breton: Isle of Romance, 1948; Woodrow Wilson: Vol 1, American Prophet, Vol 2, World Prophet, 1958; America's Moment: 1918, 1977; Wilson and His Peacemakers: American Diplomacy at the Paris Peace Conference, 1986; Guide to the Diary, Reminiscences, and Memoirs of Colonel Edward M House in Manuscripts and Archives, 1994. Contributions to: Book reviews; travel articles; Considerations on Woodrow Wilson and Edward M House in Presidential Studies Quarterly, Winter 1994. Honour: Pulitzer Prize in Biography, 1958. Address: 28 Howe Street, Wellesley, MA 02181, USA.

WALZER Michael (Laban), b. 3 Mar 1935, New York, New York, USA. Professor of Social Science; Writer. m. Judith Borodovko, 17 June 1956, 2 daughters. Education: BA, Brandeis University, 1956; PhD, Harvard University, 1961. Appointments: Assistant Professor of Politics, Princeton University, 1962-66; Associate Professor, 1966-68, Professor of Government, 1968-80, Harvard University; Editor, Dissent, 1976-; Professor of Social Science, Institute for Advanced Study, Princeton, New Jersey, 1980-. Publications: The Revolution of the Saints: A Study in the Origins of Radical Politics, 1965; The Political Imagination in Literature (editor with Philip Green), 1968; Obligations: Essays on Disobedience, War and Citizenship, 1970; Political Action: A Practical Guide to Movement Politics, 1971; Regicide and Revolution: Speeches at the Trial of Louis XVI (editor; Marian Rothstein, translator), 1974; Just and Unjust Wars: A Moral Argument with Historical Illustrations, 1977; Radical Principles: Reflections of an Unreconstructed Democrat, 1980; Spheres of Justice: A Defense of Pluralism and Equality, 1983; Exodus and Revolution, 1985; Interpretation and Social Criticism, 1987; The Company of Critics: Social Criticism and Political Commitment in the Twentieth Century, 1989; What it Means to be an American, 1992; Thick and Thin: Moral Argument at Home and Abroad, 1994; Pluralism, Justice and Equality (with David Miller), 1995. Contributions to: Professional journals and general publications. Honours: Fulbright Fellow, University of Cambridge, 1956-57; Harbison Award, 1971. Memberships: Conference on the Study of Political Thought; Society of Ethical and Legal Philosophy. Address: 103 Linwood Circle, Princeton, NJ 08520, USA.

WAMBAUGH Joseph (Aloysius Jr), b. 22 Jan 1937, Pittsburgh, Pennsylvania, USA. Writer. m. Dee Allsup, 26 Nov 1955, 1 son, 1 daughter. Education: BA, 1960, MA, 1968, California State University, Los Angeles. Publications: The New Centurions, 1971; The Blue Knight, 1972; The Onion Field, 1973; The Choirboys,

1975; The Black Marble, 1978; The Glitter Dome, 1981; The Delta Star, 1983; Lines and Shadows, 1984; The Secrets of Harry Bright, 1985; Echoes in the Darkness, 1987; The Blooding, 1989; The Golden Orange, 1990; Fugitive Nights, 1992; Finnegan's Week, 1993; Floaters, 1996. Honours: Edgar Allan Poe Award, 1974; Rodolfo Walsh Prize, International Association of Crime Writers, 1989. Address: c/o William Morrow & Co, 105 Madison Avenue, New York, NY 10016, USA.

WANDELER-DECK Elisabeth, b. 28 June 1939, Zürich, Switzerland. Writer; Architect; Psychotherapist. m. Hugo Wandeley, 7 Sept 1963, div Jan 1970, 2 daughters. Education: Primarschule, Gymnasium in Zug; Diploma Archeth, Zurich, 1963; Lic Phil I, Soziologie, Psychologie, 1981. Appointments: Arbeit als Architektin in Verschiedene Landern; Lehraufirage An Architekiurschule; Hochschule Fur Kunsttgestactung; Hochschule fur Soziale Arbeit; Arbeit in Stadt Verwaltung; Eigene Psychotherapeutische Praxis. Publications: Herzbilder Mitverkehr, 1987; Zürich of Zahlweisen Regelndes Tennisspiels, 1996; Controcantos, 1997; Voneinem Schiff Zusingen, 1999. Contributions to: Entwurfe; Woz; Nzz; Texttkritik; Text Zeitschrift Fur Literaturen; Passauer Pegasus. Memberships include: Hetzwerk Schreibender Frauen; Deutsch Schueizer Pen-Zentrum. Address: Johannesgasge 8, CH-8005, Zürich, Switzerland.

WANDERING MINSTREL. See: **LANCEFIELD Albert John.**

WANDOR Michelene Dinah, b. 20 Apr 1940, London, England. Writer; Poet. m. Edward Victor, 1963, div, 2 sons. Education: BA, Honours, English, Newnham College, Cambridge, 1962; MA, Sociology and Literature, University of Essex, 1976; LTCL, DipTCL, Trinity College of Music, London, 1993; MMus, University of London, 1997. Appointment: Poetry Editor, Time Out Magazine, 1971-82. Publications: Cutlasses and Earrings (editor and contributor), 1977; Carry on Understudies, 1981; Upbeat, 1981; Touch Papers, 1982; Five Plays, 1984; Gardens of Eden, 1984; new edition, 1990; Routledge, 1986; Look Back in Gender, 1987; Guests in the Body, 1987; Drama 1970-1990, 1993; Gardens of Eden Revisited, 1999. Contributions to: Periodicals. Honour: International Emmy, 1987. Membership: Writers Guild. Address: 71 Belsize Lane, London NW3 5AU, England.

WANG Zhecheng, (Qi Fang), b. 22 Mar 1936, Hangzhou, China. Writer; Dramatist; Editor. m. Wen Xiaoyu, 24 Jan 1962, 1 daughter. Education: Graduated, University of Beijing, 1958. Appointments: Vice-Chairman, 1992, Chief Editor and President, 1992, Jiangnan. Publications: Fiction and plays in Chinese. Contributions to: Various newspapers and journals. Honours: Several literary prizes. Memberships: Chinese Current Literature Research Association, council member; Chinese Writers Association; Zhejiang Literature and Art Union; Zhejiang Writers Association. Address: 105 Nanshan Road, Hangzhou, Zhejiang 310002, China.

WANIEK Marilyn Nelson. See: **NELSON Marilyn.**

WARD John Hood, b. 16 Dec 1915, Newcastle upon Tyne, England. Retired Civil Service Senior Principal; Writer; Poet. m. Gladys Hilda Thorogood, 27 July 1940, 1 son, 2 daughters. Education: Royal Grammar School, Newcastle, 1925-33. Appointment: Senior Principal, Department of Health and Social Security, retired, 1978. Publications: A Late Harvest, 1982; The Dark Sea, 1983; A Kind of Likeness, 1985; The Wrong Side of Glory, 1986; A Song at Twilight, 1989; Grandfather Best and the Protestant Work Ethic, 1991; Tales of Love and Hate, 1993; The Brilliance of Light, 1994; Winter Song, 1995; Selected Poems, 1968-95, 1996. Contributions to: Anthologies and periodicals. Honours: Imperial Service Order, 1977; Poetry Prize, City of Westminster Arts Council, 1977; Open Poetry Prize, Wharfedale Music Festival, 1978; Lancaster Festival Prizes, 1982, 1987, 1988, 1989, 1994, 1995; 1st Prize, Bury Open Poetry Competition, 1987; 1st Prizes, High Peak Open

Competition, 1988, 1989; 1st Prize, May and Alfred Wilkins Memorial Prize, 1995. Memberships: Manchester Poets; Society of Civil Service Authors. Address: 42 Seal Road, Bramhall, Stockport, Cheshire SK7 2JS, England.

WARD John Powell, b. 28 Nov 1937, Suffolk, England. Poet. m. Sarah Woodfull Rogers, 16 Jan 1965, 2 sons. Education: BA, University of Toronto, 1959; BA, 1961, MA, 1969, University of Cambridge; MSc, University of Wales, 1969. Appointments: Lecturer in Education, 1963-84, Lecturer in English, 1985-86, Senior Lecturer in English, 1986-91, Honorary Research Fellow, 1991-, University College, Swansea, Wales; Editor, Poetry Wales, 1975-80. Publications: The Other Man, 1970; The Line of Knowledge, 1972; From Alphabet to Logos, 1972; Things, 1980; To Get Clear, 1981; The Clearing, 1984; A Certain Marvellous Thing, 1993; Genesis, 1996; Late Thought in March, 1999. Contributions to: Reviews, quarterlies, journals, magazines, and BBC Radio 3 and 4. Honour: Poetry Prize, Welsh Arts Council, 1985. Address: Court Lodge, Horton Kirby, Dartford, Kent DA4 9BN, England.

WARD Philip, b. 10 Feb 1938, Harrow, England. Chartered Librarian; Writer. m. 4 Apr 1964, 2 daughters. Education: University for Foreigners, Perugia; Coimbra University. Appointments: Honorary Editor, The Private Library, 1958-64; Coordinator, Library Services, Tripoli, Libya, 1963-71; Director, National Library Services, 1973-74. Publications: The Oxford Companion to Spanish Literature, 1978; A Dictionary of Common Fallacies, 1978-80; Lost Songs, 1981; A Lifetime's Reading, 1983; Japanese Capitals, 1985; Travels in Oman, 1987; Sofia: Portrait of a City, 1989; Wright Magic, 1990; Bulgaria, 1990. Honours: Fellow, Royal Geographical Society; Royal Society of Arts; Guinness Poetry Award, 1959; 1st Prize, International Travel Writers Competition, 1990. Membership: Private Libraries Association. Address: c/o Oxford University Press, Walton Street, Oxford OX2 6DP, England.

WARD Richard Joseph, b. 7 Nov 1921, Beverly, Massachusetts, USA. Academic Administrator; Dean; Economist; Author. m. Cecilia Mary Butler, 1 Sept 1951, 3 sons, 1 daughter. Education: BS, Harvard University, 1946; PhD, University of Michigan. Appointments: Professor of Economics, Fordham University, 1953-58; Economist, Caltex Oil and US State Department, 1960-63, 1965-69; Manager, International KPMG, 1970-75; Dean, College of Business, University of Massachusetts and Director, USIUE, Bushey, 1975-88; Chancellors Professor Emeritus, 1996-. Publications: Economics, 1967; Challenge of Development Aldine, 1967; Development Problems of 1970's, 1973; Palestine State: A Rational Approach, 1978. Contributions to: American Economic Review; Economic Development and Cultural Exchange; International Affairs, London. Honour: Distinguished Service Award, USAID. Memberships: American Economic Association; Association of Social Economics, president, 1965-66. Literary Agent: Publishers Direct. Address: College of Business, University of Massachusetts, Dartmouth, MA 02247, USA.

WARD Ronald Bentley, b. 6 Oct 1928, Sydney, New South Wales, Australia. University Lecturer. m. Brenda Madden, 7 Jan 1955, 1 son, 1 daughter. Education: Trades Certificate, 1948; Diploma, Sydney Technical College, 1955; BEng, University of New South Wales, 1961; MBA, Macquarie University, 1975; PhD, 1994. Appointment: Lecturer, School of Mechanical Engineering, University of Technology, Sydney. Publications: The Engineering of Management, 1987; The Engineering of Communication, 1988, revised edition, 1989; A Plant for Appropriate Technology, 1991. Contributions to: Various conference proceedings and symposia, Australia and overseas. Memberships: Institution of Engineers, Australia; Australian Institute of Management. Address: 13 Landscape Avenue, Forestville, New South Wales 2087, Australia.

WARDLE (John) Irving, b. 20 July 1929, Bolton, England. Drama Critic. m. (1) Joan Notkin, 1958, div, (2)

Fay Crowder, 1963, div, 2 sons, (3) Elizabeth Grist, 1975, 1 son, 1 daughter. Education: BA, Wadham College, Oxford, 1949; ARCM, Royal College of Music, London, 1955. Appointments: Sub Editor, Times Educational Supplement, 1956; Deputy Theatre Critic, The Observer, 1960; Drama Critic, The Times, 1963-89; Editor, Gambit, 1973-75; Theatre Critic, The Independent on Sunday, 1989. Publications: The Houseboy, 1974; The Theatres of George Devine, 1978; Theatre Criticism, 1992. Address: 51 Richmond Road, New Barnet, Hertfordshire, England.

WARE Armytage. See: **BARNETT Paul le Page.**

WARNER Francis, (Robert Le Plastrier), b. 21 Oct 1937, Bishopthorpe, Yorkshire, England. Poet; Dramatist; Fellow; Tutor. m. (1) Mary Hall, 1958, div 1972, 2 daughters, (2) Penelope Anne Davis, 1983, 1 son, 1 daughter. Education: Christ's Hospital; London College of Music; BA, MA, St Catharine's College, Cambridge. Appointments: Supervisor in English, St Catharine's College, Cambridge, 1959-63; Staff Tutor in English, Cambridge University Board of Extra-Mural Studies, 1963-65; Fellow and Tutor, 1965-, Fellow Librarian, 1966-76, Dean of Degrees, 1984-, Vice Master, 1987-89, St Peter's College, Oxford; Pro Proctor, University of Oxford, 1989-90, 1996-97. Publications: Poetry: Perennia, 1962; Early Poems, 1964; Experimental Sonnets, 1965; Madrigals, 1967; The Poetry of Francis Warner, 1970; Lucca Quartet, 1975; Morning Vespers, 1980; Spring Harvest: Poems 1985-1996, 1981; Epithalamium, 1983; Collected Poems 1960-84, 1985; Nightingales, 1997. Plays: Marquettes: A Trilogy of One-Act Plays, 1972; Requiem: Part 1, Lying Figures, 1972; Part 2, Killing Time, 1976, Part 3, Meeting Ends, 1974; A Conception of Love, 1978; Light Shadows, 1980; Moving Reflections, 1983; Living Creation, 1985; Healing Nature: The Athens of Pericles, 1988; Byzantium, 1990; Virgil and Caesar, 1993; Agora: An Epic, 1994; King Francis 1st, 1995; Goethe's Weimar, 1997. Editor: Eleven Poems by Edmund Blunden, 1965; Garland, 1968; Studies in the Arts, 1968. Contributions to: Anthologies and journals. Honours: Messing International Award, 1972; Benemerenti Silver Medal, Knights of St George, Constantinian Order, Italy, 1990; Foreign Academician, Academy of Letters and Arts, Portugal, 1993. Address: c/o St Peter's College, Oxford OX1 2DL, England.

WARNER Marina (Sarah), b. 9 Nov 1946, London, England. Author; Critic. m. (1) William Shawcross, 1971, div, 1980, 1 son, (2) John Dewe Mathews, 1981, div 1998. Education: MA, Modern Languages, French and Italian, Lady Margaret Hall, Oxford. Appointments: Getty Scholar, Getty Centre for the History of Art and the Humanities, California, 1987-88; Tinbergen Professor, Erasmus University, Rotterdam, 1991; Visiting Fellow, British Film Institute, 1992; Visiting Professor, University of Ulster, 1995, Queen Mary and Westfield College, London, 1995-, University of York, 1996-; Reith Lecturer, 1994; Whitney J Oakes Fellow, Princeton University, 1996; Mellon Professor, University of Pittsburgh, 1997; Visiting Fellow Commoner, Trinity College, Cambridge, 1998; Tanner Lecturer, 1999. Publications: The Dragon Empress, 1972; Alone of All Her Sex: The Myth and the Cult of the Virgin Mary, 1976; Queen Victoria's Sketchbook, 1980; Joan of Arc: The Image of Female Heroism, 1981; Monuments and Maidens: The Allegory of the Female Form, 1985; L'Atalante, 1993; Managing Monsters: Six Myths of Our Time, 1994 From the Beast to the Blonde: On Fairy Tales and Their Tellers, 1994; No Go the Bogeyman: Scaring, Lulling and Making Mock, 1998. Fiction: In a Dark Wood, 1977; The Skating Party, 1983; The Lost Father, 1988; Indigo, 1992; The Mermaids in the Basement, 1993; Wonder Tales (editor), 1994. Libretti: The Legs of the Queen of Sheba, 1991; In the House of Crossed Desires 1996. Other: Children's and juvenile books. Contributions to: Various publications, radio and television. Honours: Fellow, Royal Society of Literature, 1985; Honorary DLitt, University of Exeter, 1995; Honorary Dr, Sheffield Hallam University, 1995; Hon DLitt, University of York, 1997; Hon DLitt, Unviersity of St Andrew's, 1998. Memberships: Arts Council, literature panel, 1992-; British Library, advisory

council, 1992-97; Charter 88, council member, 1990-97. Address: c/o Rogers, Coleridge and White, 20 Powis Mews, London W11 1NJ, England.

WARNER Val, b. 15 Jan 1946, Middlesex, England. Writer; Poet. Education: BA, Somerville College, Oxford, 1968. Appointments: Writer-in-Residence, University College, Swansea, 1977-78, University of Dundee, 1979-81. Publications: These Yellow Photos, 1971; Under the Penthouse, 1973; The Centenary Corbiere (translator), 1975; The Collected Poems and Prose of Charlotte Mew (editor), 1981, 1982, 1997; Before Lunch, 1986; Tooting Idyll (poems), 1998. Contributions to: Many journals and periodicals. Honours: Gregory Award for Poetry, 1975; 3rd Prize, Lincolnshire Literature Festival Poetry Competition, 1995. Memberships: PEN; Royal Society for Literature, fellow. Address: c/o Carcanet Press Ltd, Conavon Court (4th Floor) 12-16 Blackfriars Street, Manchester M4 5BQ, England.

WARNOCK Baroness, (Helen Mary Warnock), b. 14 Apr 1924, England. Philosopher; Writer. m. Sir Geoffrey Warnock, 1949, dec 1995, 2 sons, 3 daughters. Education: MA, BPhil, Lady Margaret Hall, Oxford. Appointments: Fellow and Tutor in Philosophy, 1949-66, Senior Research Fellow, 1976-84, St Hugh's College, Oxford; Headmistress, Oxford High School, 1966-72; Talbot Research Fellow, Lady Margaret Hall, Oxford, 1972-76; Mistress, Girton College, Cambridge, 1985-91; Several visiting lectureships. Publications: Ethics Since 1900, 1960, 3rd edition, 1978; J-P Sartre, 1963; Existentialist Ethics, 1966; Existentialism, 1970; Imagination, 1976; Schools of Thought, 1977; What Must We Teach? (with T Devlin), 1977; Education: A Way Forward, 1979; A Question of Life, 1985; Teacher Teach Thyself, 1985; Memory, 1987; A Common Policy for Education, 1988; Universities: Knowing Our Minds, 1989; The Uses of Philosophy, 1992; Imagination and Time, 1994; Women Philosophers (editor), 1996; An Intelligent Person's Guide to Ethics, 1998. Honours: 15 honorary doctorates; Honorary Fellow, Lady Margaret Hall, Oxford, 1984, St Hugh's College, Oxford, 1985, Hertford College, Oxford, 1997; Dame Commander of the Order of the British Empire, 1984; Life Peer, 1985; Albert Medal, RSA. Address: 3 Church Street, Great Bedwyn, Wiltshire SN8 3PE, England.

WARREN Rosanna, b. 27 July 1953, Fairfield, Connecticut, USA. Associate Professor of English; Poet; Writer. m. Stephen Scully, 1981, 2 daughters, 1 stepson. Education: BA, summa cum laude, Yale University, 1976; MA, Johns Hopkins University, 1980. Appointments: Assistant Professor, Vanderbilt University, 1981-82; Visiting Assistant Professor, 1982-88, Assistant Professor, 1989-95, Associate Professor of English, 1995-, Boston University; Poetry Consultant and Contributing Editor, Partisan Review, 1985-; Poet-in-Residence, Robert Frost Farm, 1990. Publications: The Joey Story, 1963; Snow Day, 1981; Each Leaf Shines Separate, 1984; The Art of Translation: Voices from the Field (editor), 1989; Stained Glass, 1993; Eugenio Montale's Cuttlefish Bones (editor), 1993; Euripides' Suppliant Women (translator with Stephen Scully), 1995. Contributions to: Many journals and magazines. Honours: National Discovery Award in Poetry, 92nd Street YMHA-YWCA, New York City, 1980; Yaddo Fellow, 1980; Ingram Merrill Foundation Grants, 1983, 1993; Guggenheim Fellowship, 1985-86; American Council of Learned Societies Grant, 1989-90; Lavan Younger Poets Prize, 1992, and Lamont Poetry Prize, 1993, Academy of American Poets; Lila Wallace Writers' Fund Award, 1994; Witter Bynner Prize in Poetry, American Academy of Arts and Letters, 1994; May Sarton Award, New England Poetry Club, 1995. Memberships: Modern Language Association; American Literary Translators Association; Association of Literary Scholars and Critics; PEN. Address: c/o University Professors Program, Boston University, 745 Commonwealth Avenue, Boston, MA 02215, USA.

WARSH Lewis, b. 9 Nov 1944, New York, New York, USA. Poet; Writer; Publisher; Teacher. m. Bernadette Mayer, Nov 1975, 1 son, 2 daughters. Education: BA,

1966, MA, 1975, City College of the City University of New York. Appointments: Co-Founder and Co-Editor, Angel Hair magazine and Angel Hair Books, New York City, 1966-77; Co-Editor, Boston Eagle, Massachusetts, 1973-75; Teacher, St Marks in the Bowery Poetry Project, 1973-75; Co-Founder and Publisher, United Artists magazine and United Artists Books, New York, 1977-; Lecturer, Kerouac School of Disembodied Poetics, Boulder, Colorado, 1978, New England College, 1979-80, Queens College, 1984-86, Farleigh Dickinson University, 1987-; Adjunct Associate Professor, Long Island University, 1987-. Publications: Poetry: The Suicide Rates, 1967; Highjacking: Poems, 1968; Moving Through Air, 1968; Chicago (with Tom Clark), 1969; Dreaming as One: Poems, 1971; Long Distance, 1971; Immediate Surrounding, 1974; Today, 1974; Blue Heaven, 1978; Hives, 1979; Methods of Birth Control, 1982; The Corset, 1986; Information from the Surface of Venus, 1987; A Free Man, 1991; Avenue of Escape, 1995. Other: Part of My History (autobiography), 1972; The Maharajah's Son (autobiography), 1977; Agnes and Sally (fiction), 1984. Honours: Poet's Foundation Award, 1972; Creative Artists Public Service Award in Fiction, 1977; National Endowment for the Arts Grant in Poetry, 1979; Coordinating Council of Literary Magazines Editor's Fellowship, 1981. Address: 701 President Street, No 1, Brooklyn, NY 11215, USA.

WARTOFSKY (William) Victor, b. 15 June 1931, New York, USA. Writer. m. Tamar Chachik, 1957, 1 son, 2 daughters. Education: George Washington University, 1950-52; BA, American University, 1963. Publications: Mr Double and Other Stories; Meeting the Pieman; Year of the Yahoo; The Passage; Prescription for Justice; Terminal Justice. Screenplays: Death be my Destiny; The Hellbox; Feathers. Contributions to: USIA America; Fifty Plus; Macabre; Quartet; True. Address: 8507 Wild Olive Drive, Potomac, MD 20854, USA.

WASHINGTON Alonzo Lavert, b. 6 Jan 1967. Comicbook Writer; Artist; Publisher. m. Dana D Washington, 4 sons, 1 daughter. Appointment: Instructor, Leadership Institute. Publications: Original Man; The Mighty Ace; Dark Force; The Omega; Original Boy; Original Woman; Christian Crusader; Lone Wolf. Contributions to: People Magazine; Black Enterprise; News Week; Ebony; Parenting Magazine; Source. Honours: Publisher of the Year Award. Literary Agent: Dana D Washington. Address: PO Box 171046, Kansas City, KS 66117, USA.

WASSERFALL Adel, (Adel Pryor), b. 2 Dec 1918, Haugesund, Norway. Writer. m. Education: Cape Technical College, South Africa. Publications: Novels: Tangled Paths, 1959; Clouded Glass, 1961; Hidden Fire, 1962; Out of the Night, 1963; Hearts in Conflict, 1965; Forgotten Yesterday, 1966; Valley of Desire, 1967; Sound of the Sea, 1968; Free of a Dream, 1969; Her Secret Fear, 1971 A Norwegian Romance, 1976; All Is Not Gold, 1979; Flame of Jealousy, 1992; Flame of Desire, 1997. Translations: Der Chefaret, 1973; Havets Melodi, 1974; Verborge Verlede, 1985. Honours: English Composition Prize, 1934; Sir William Thorne Award, 1937; Short Story Contest Award, 1946. Address: 8 Iona Street, Milnerton 7441, Cape, South Africa.

WASSERSTEIN Wendy, b. 18 Oct 1950, Brooklyn, New York, USA. Dramatist; Writer. Education: BA, Mount Holyoke College, 1971; MA, City College of the City University of New York, 1973; MFA, Yale University, 1976. Publications: Plays: Any Woman Can't, 1973; Happy Birthday, Montpelier Pizz-zazz, 1974; When Dinah Shore Rule the Earth (with Christopher Durang), 1975; Uncommon Women and Others, 1975; Isn't it Romantic, 1981; Tender Offer, 1983; The Man in a Case, 1986; The Heidi Chronicles, 1988; The Sisters Rosensweig, 1992. Other: Miami (musical), 1986; Bachelor Girls (essays), 1990; Pamela's First Musical (children's picture book), 1996. Honours: Guggenheim Fellowship, 1983; American Playwrights Project Grant, 1988; Pulitzer Prize for Drama, 1989; Tony Award, 1989; New York Drama Critics Circle Award, 1989; Drama Desk Award, 1989; Outer Critics Circle Award, 1989; Susan Smith Blackburn Prize, 1989.

Memberships: British American Arts Association; Dramatists Guild; Dramatists Guild for Young Playwrights. Address: c/o Royce Carlton Inc, 866 United Nations Plaza, Suite 4030, New York, NY 10017, USA.

WATERHOUSE Keith (Spencer), b. 6 Feb 1929, Leeds, England. Journalist; Author; Dramatist. m. 1) Joan Foster, 1950, div 1968, 1 son, 2 daughters, 2) Stella Bingham, 1984, div 1989. Education: Leeds. Appointments: Journalist, 1950-; Columnist, Daily Mirror, 1970-86, Daily Mail, 1986-. Publications: Novels: There is a Happy Land, 1957; Billy Liar, 1959; Jubb, 1963; The Bucket Shop, 1968; Billy Liar on the Moon, 1975; Office Life, 1978; Maggie Muggins, 1981; In the Mood, 1983; Thinks, 1984; Our Song, 1988; Bimbo, 1990; Unsweet Charity, 1992; Good Grief, 1997. Other: Café Royal (with Guy Deghy), 1956; Writers' Theatre (editor), 1967; The Passing of the Third-Floor Buck, 1974; Mondays, Thursdays, 1976; Rhubarb, Rhubarb, 1979; Daily Mirror Style, 1980, revised and expanded edition as Newspaper Style, 1989; Fanny Peculiar, 1983; Mrs Pooter's Diary, 1983; Waterhouse at Large, 1985; Collected Letters of a Nobody, 1986; The Theory and Practice of Lunch, 1986; The Theory and Practice of Travel, 1989; English Our English, 1991; Sharon & Tracy & The Rest, 1992; City Lights, 1994; Streets Ahead, 1995. Plays (with Willis Hall): Billy Liar, 1960; Celebration, 1961; All Things Bright and Beautiful, 1963; Say Who You Are, 1965; Who's Who, 1974; Saturday, Sunday, Monday (adaptation after de Filippo), 1974; Filumena (adaptation after de Filippo), 1977. Collection of Plays: Jeffrey Bernard is Unwell and Other Plays, 1991. Honours: Granada Columnist of the Year Award, 1970, and Granada Special Quarter Century Award, 1982; IPC Descriptive Writer of the Year Award, 1970, and IPC Columnist of the Year Award, 1973; British Press Awards Columnist of the Year, 1978, 1991; Evening Standard Best Comedy Award, 1990; Commander of the Order of the British Empire, 1991; Honorary Fellow, Leeds Metropolitan University, 1991; Press Club Edgar Wallace Award, 1997. Memberships: Royal Society of Literature, fellow. Address: 29 Kenway Road, London SW5 0RP, England.

WATERMAN Andrew (John), b. 28 May 1940, London, England. Senior Lecturer in English; Poet. Div, 1 son. Education: BA, 1st Class Honours, English, University of Leicester, 1966; Worcester College, Oxford, 1966-68. Appointments: Lecturer, 1968-78, Senior Lecturer in English, 1978-97, University of Ulster, Coleraine, Northern Ireland. Publications: Living Room, 1974; From the Other Country, 1977; Over the Wall, 1980; Out for the Elements, 1981; The Poetry of Chess (editor), 1981; Selected Poems, 1986; In the Planetarium, 1990; The End of the Pier Show, 1995. Contributions to: Anthologies, journals and periodicals. Honours: Poetry Book Society Choice, 1974 and Recommendation, 1981; Cholmondeley Award for Poetry, 1977; Arvon Poetry Competition Prize, 1981. Address: 7 Grange Court, Cliff Avenue, Cromer, Norfolk NR27 0AN, England.

WATERS John Frederick, b. 27 Oct 1930, Somerville, Massachusetts, USA. Writer. Education: BS, University of Massachusetts. Publications: Marine Animal Collectors, 1969; The Crab From Yesterday, 1970; The Sea Farmers, 1970; What Does An Oceanographer Do, 1970; Saltmarshes and Shifting Dunes, 1970; Turtles, 1971; Neighborhood Puddle, 1971; Some Mammals Live in the Sea, 1972; Green Turtle: Mysteries, 1972; The Royal Potwasher, 1972; Seal Harbour, 1973; Hungry Sharks, 1973; Giant Sea Creatures, 1973; The Mysterious Eel, 1973; Camels: Ships of the Desert, 1974; Carnivorous Plants, 1974; Exploring New England Shores, 1974; The Continental Shelves, 1975; Creatures of Darkness, 1975; Victory Chimes, 1976; Maritime Careers, 1977; Fishing, 1978; Summer of the Seals, 1978; The Hatchlings, 1979; Crime Labs, 1979; A Jellyfish is Not a Fish, 1979; Flood, 1991; Watching Whales, 1991; The Raindrop Journey, 1991; Deep Sea Vents, 1994; Night Raiders Along the Cape, 1996; Sharks, 1996. Contributions to: Cape Cod Compass. Honours: Junior Literary Book Choice (twice); Outstanding Science books for Children Awards (7 times). Memberships: Southeastern Massachusetts Creative Writers Club; Organizer, Cape Cod Writers; 12 O'Clock Scholars; Society of Children's Book Writers; Authors Guild. Address: Box 735, Chatham, MA 02633, USA.

WATERTON Betty Marie, b. 31 Aug 1923, Oshawa, Ontario, Canada. Children's Writer. m. Claude Waterton, 7 Apr 1942, dec 1996 1 son, 2 daughters. Publications: A Salmon for Simon, 1978; Pettranetta, 1980; Mustard, 1983; The White Moose, 1984; Quincy Rumpel, 1984; Orff, 27 Dragons (and a Snarkel !), 1984; The Dog Who Stopped the War, (adaptation and translation), 1985; Starring Quincy Rumpel, 1986; Quincy Rumpel, PI, 1988; Morris Rumpel and the Wings of Icarus, 1989; Plain Noodles, 1989; Quincy Rumpel and the Sasquatch of Phantom Cove, 1990; Quincy Rumpel and the Woolly Chaps, 1992; Quincy Rumpel and the Mystifying Experience, 1994; Quincy Rumpel and the All-day Breakfast, 1996; The Lighthouse Dog, 1997; Quincy Rumpel and the Tower of London, forthcoming. Honour: Co-Winner, Canada Council Award for Children's Literature, 1978. Address: 9717 Third Street, No 203, Sidney, British Columbia V8L 3A3, Canada.

WATKINS Floyd C, b. 19 Apr 1920, Cherokee County, Georgia, USA. Professor Emeritus; Writer; Farmer. m. Anna E Braziel, 14 June 1942, 1 son, 2 daughters. Education: BS, Georgia Southern University, 1946; AM, Emory University, 1947; PhD, Vanderbilt University, 1952. Appointments: Instructor, 1949-61, Professor, 1961-80, Candler Professor of American Literature, 1980-88, Professor Emeritus, 1988-, Emory University; Visiting Professor, Southeastern University, Oklahoma, 1961, 1970, Texas A & M University, 1980. Publications: The Literature of the South (co-editor), 1952; Thomas Wolfe's Characters, 1957; Old Times in the Faulkner Country (co-author), 1961; The Flesh and the Word, 1971; In Time and Place, 1977; Then and Now: The Personal Past in the Poetry of Robert Penn Warren, 1982; Some Poems and Some Talk About Poetry (co-author), 1985; Talking About William Faulkner (co-author), 1996. Address: 519 Druand Drive North East, Atlanta, GA 30307, USA.

WATKINS Gerrold. See: **MALZBERG Barry.**

WATKINS Karen Christna, (Catrin Collier, Katherine John), b. 30 May 1948, Pontypridd, Wales. Writer. m. Trevor John Watkins, 28 Dec 1968, 2 sons, 1 daughter. Education: Teaching Certificate, Swansea College, 1969. Publications: Without Trace, 1990; Hearts of Gold, 1992; One Blue Moon, 1993; Six Foot Under; A Silver Lining, 1994; Murder of a Dead Man, 1994; All That Glitters, 1995; By Any Other Name, 1995; Such Sweet Sorrow, 1996; Past Remembering, 1997; Broken Rainbows, 1998. Memberships: PEN; Society of Authors; Crime Writers Association; Welsh Academy, 1998. Address: c/o A M Heath and Co, 79 St Martin's Lane, London WC2N 4AA. England.

WATKINS Nicholas, b. 17 Sept 1946, Bath, England. Lecturer in Art History; Writer. m. Nadia Daskalaff, 16 July 1970, 2 daughters. Education: BA, Honours, History of European Art, 1966, MPhil, 1979, Courtauld Institute of Art. Appointment: Lecturer in Art History, University of Leicester. Publications: Martisse, 1984; Bonnard, 1984. Contributions to: Various publications. Address: c/o University of Leicester, Leicester LE1 7RH, England.

WATMOUGH David, b. 17 Aug 1926, London, England. Author. Education: Theology Major, King's College, University of London, 1945-49. Appointments: War Service, Royal Naval Volunteer Reserve, 1944-45. Publications: Ashes for Easter (stories), 1972; Love and the Waiting Game(stories), 1975; From a Cornish Landscape (stories), 1975; No More into the Garden (novel), 1978; Fury (stories), 1984; The Connecticut Countess (stories), 1984; The Unlikely Pioneer (opera), 1985; Vibrations in Time (stories), 1986; The Year of Fears (novel), 1987; Thy Mother's Glass (novel), 1992; The Time of the Kingfishers (novel), 1994; Hunting with Diana (stories), 1996. Contributions to: Encounter; Spectator; New York Times Book Review; Saturday Night, Canada; Canadian Literature; Dalhousie Review; Connoisseur, New York; Malahat Review; Vancouver Step. Honours: Senior Literary Arts Awards, Canada Council, 1976, 1986; Winner, Best Novel of Year Award, Giovanni's Room, Philadelphia, 1979. Memberships: Writers Union of Canada; Federation of British Columbia Writers. Literary Agent: John Talbot, The John Talbot Agency, 540 W Boston Road, Mamaroneck, NY 10543, USA. Address: 3358 West First Avenue, Vancouver, British Columbia V6R 1G4, Canada.

WATSON John Richard, b. 15 June 1934, Ipswich, England. Professor of English; Writer; Poet. m. Pauline Elizabeth Roberts, 21 July 1962, 1 son, 2 daughters. Education: BA, 1958, MA, 1964, Magdalen College, Oxford; PhD, University of Glasgow, 1966. Appointments: Assistant, then Lecturer, University of Glasgow, 1962-66; Lecturer, then Senior Lecturer, University of Lecturer, 1966-78; Professor of English, 1978-, Public Orator, 1989, University of Durham. Publications: A Leicester Calendar, 1976, 2nd edition, 1978; Everyman's Book of Victorian Verse (editor), 1982; Wordsworth's Vital Soul, 1982; Wordsworth, 1983; English Poetry of the Romantic Period, 1789-1830, 1985, 2nd edition, 1992; The Poetry of Gerard Manley Hopkins, 1986; Companion to Hymns and Psalms, 1988; A Handbook to English Romanticism, 1992; The English Hymn, 1997. Contributions to: Scholarly and literary journals. Honours: Prize, Stroud Festival, 1971; Prize, Suffolk Poetry Society, 1975. Memberships: Charles Wesley Society; International Association of University Professors of English; Modern Humanities Research Association. Address: Stoneyhurst, 27 Western Hill, Durham DH1 4RL, England.

WATSON Lynn, b. 5 June 1948, Woodland, California, USA. Teacher; Writer; Poet. Education: University of California at Berkeley, 1966-68; BA, English, Sonoma State University, 1975; MFA, Fiction Writing, University of Iowa, 1977. Appointments: Teacher, University of Iowa, College of the Desert, Sonoma State University, Santa Rosa Junior College. Publications: Alimony or Death of the Clock (novel), 1981; Amateur Blues (poems), 1990; Catching the Devil (poems), 1995. Contributions to: Journals and periodicals. Honours: 1st Place, National Poetry Association, 1990; Honorable Mention, World of Poetry Contest, 1991. Membership: California Poets-in-the-Schools. Address: PO Box 1253, Occidental, CA 95465, USA.

WATSON Margaret Sophia Laura, (Sophia Watson), b. 20 June 1962, London, England. Writer. m. Julian Watson, 28 June 1986, 4 daughters. Education: BA, English, Durham University, 1980-83. Publications: Winning Women, 1989; Marina, 1994; Her Husband's Children, 1995; Strange and Well Bred, 1996; The Perfect Treasure, 1998. Literary Agent: Peters, Fraser and Dunlop. Address: Great Highleigh, Exebridge, Dulverton, Somerset TA22 9RW, England.

WATSON Nancy Dingman, b. USA. Writer. 2 sons, 6 daughters. Education: Wheaton College; Smith College. Publications: What is One; Whose Birthday Is It?; When is Tomorrow?; What Does A Begin With?; Toby and Doll; New Under the Stars; Annie's Spending Spree; Muncus Agruncus, a Bad Little Mouse; The Birthday Goat; Blueberries Lavender: Songs of the Farmer's Children. Contributions to: Paterson Literary Review. Honours: Poetry Award, 1998, Finalist, 1999. Membership: Authors Guild. Address: Box 1127, Truro, MA 02666, USA.

WATSON Richard Allan, b. 23 Feb 1931, New Market, Iowa, USA. Professor of Philosophy; Writer. m. Patty Jo Andersen, 30 July 1955, 1 daughter. Education: BA, 1953, MA, 1957, PhD, Philosophy, 1961, University of Iowa; MS, Geology, University of Minnesota, 1959. Appointments: Instructor, University of Michigan, 1961-64; Assistant Professor, 1964-67, Associate Professor, 1967-74, Professor of Philosophy, 1974-, Washington University, St Louis; President, Cave Research Foundation, Mammoth Cave, Kentucky, 1965-67; Trustee, National Parks and Conservation Association, Washington, DC, 1969-81; Editor, Classics in Speleology, 1968-73, Speleologia, 1974-79, Cave Books, 1980-, Journal of the History of Philosophy, 1983,

Journal of the History of Philosophy Monograph Series, 1985-95. Publications: The Downfall of Cartesianism, 1966; Man and Nature (with Patty Joe Watson), 1969; The Longest Cave (with Roger W Brucker), 1976; Under Plowman's Floor (novel), 1978; The Runner (novel), 1981; The Philosopher's Diet, 1985; The Breakdown of Cartesian Metaphysics, 1987; The Philosopher's Joke, 1990; Writing Philosophy, 1992; Niagara (novel), 1993; Caving, 1994; The Philosopher's Demise, 1995; Representational Ideas, 1995; Good Teaching, 1997. Contributions to: Professional journals. Honours: American Council of Learned Societies Fellow, 1967-68; Center for Advanced Study in the Behavioral Sciences Fellowships, 1967-68, 1981-82, 1991-92; National Endowment for the Humanities Grant, 1975; Center for International Studies Fellow, Princeton, New Jersey, 1975-76; Camargo Foundation Fellow, 1995. Memberships: American Association for the Advancement of Science; American Philosophical Association; Cave Research Foundation; National Speleological Society, honorary life member; Authors League of America. Address: c/o Department of Philosophy, Washington University, St Louis, MO 63130, USA.

WATSON Rita Esposito, b. 3 July 1943, New Haven, Connecticut, USA. Writer; Family and Health Advocate. m. William R Watson, 11 Nov 1967, div 1982, 2 sons. Education: Graduated, Hunter College, New York City, 1967; Department of Epidemiology and Public Health, Yale University School of Medicine, 1983; Ethics Cognate, Yale Law School. Appointments: Editorial Consultant, 1984-; Director of Policy and Education, Yale Department of Psychiatry, Substance Abuse Treatment Unit, 1989-91. Publications: New Choices, New Chances: A Woman's Guide to Conquering Cancer (with Robert C Wallach), 1983; Sisterhood Betrayed, Women in the Workplace and the All About Eve Complex (with Jill Barber), 1991, German and Swedish translations, 1993; The Art of Decision Making: 20 Winning Strategies for Women, 1994. Contributions to: Town and Country, 1980; The New England Journal of Medicine, 1984, 1987; Working Women, 1989; Parents, 1989; Dermatology Nursing, 1990; New Choices, Reader's Digest, 1998. Honours: Associate Fellow, Ezra Stiles College, Yale, 1984-; Associate Fellow, Child Welfare League of America, 1990-93. Memberships: The New Haven Lawn Club, 1984-; Connecticut Coalition for Children, 1989-92; Connecticut Mental Health Center Foundation, 1996-. Literary Agent: Carole Abel. Address: Brighton Court, 665 Whitney Avenue, New Haven, CT 06511, USA.

WATSON Will. See: **FLOREN Lee.**

WATT-EVANS Lawrence, b. 26 July 1954, Arlington, Massachusetts, USA. Writer. m. Julie F McKenna, 30 Aug 1977, 1 son, 1 daughter. Education: Princeton University, 1972-74, 1975-77. Publications: The Lure of the Basilisk, 1980; The Seven Altars of Dûsarra, 1981; The Cyborg and the Sorcerers, 1982; The Sword of Bheleu, 1983; The Book of Silence, 1984; The Chromosomal Code, 1984; The Misenchanted Sword, 1985; Shining Steel, 1986; With a Single Spell, 1987; The Wizard and the War Machine, 1987; Denner's Wreck, 1988; Nightside City, 1989; The Unwilling Warlord, 1989; The Nightmare People, 1990; The Blood of a Dragon, 1991; The Rebirth of Wonder, 1992; Crosstime Traffic, 1992; Taking Flight, 1993; The Spell of the Black Dagger, 1993; Split Heirs (with Esther Friesner), 1993; Out of This World, 1994; In the Empire of Shadow, 1995; The Reign of the Brown Magician, 1996. Contributions to: Journals and magazines. Honours: Isaac Asimov's Science Fiction Readers Poll Award, 1987; Science Fiction Achievement Award (Hugo) for Best Short Story of 1987, 1988. Memberships: Science Fiction Writers of America; Horror Writers Association. Address: c/o Russell Galen, Scott Meredith Literary Agency, 845 Third Avenue, New York, NY 10022, USA.

WATTLES Rama Rau. See: **RAMA RAU Santha.**

WATTS Nigel John, b. 24 June 1957, Winchester, England. Writer. m. Sahera Chohan, 10 Aug 1991. Publications: The Life Game, 1989; Billy Bayswater, 1990; We All Live in a House Called Innocence, 1992; Twenty Twenty, 1995. Honour: Betty Trask Award, 1989. Address: 2 Cromwell Place, Mortlake, London SW14 7HA, England.

WAUGH Auberon Alexander, b. 17 Nov 1939, Dulverton, Somerset, England. Writer; Editor. m. Lady Teresa Onslow, 1961, 2 sons, 2 daughters. Education: Scholar in Classics, Downside; Exhibitioner in English, Christ Church, Oxford, 1959-60. Appointments: Editorial Staff, 1960-63, Columnist, 1990-, Daily Telegraph; Columnist, Catholic Herald, 1963-64, The Times, 1970-71, New Statesman, 1973-76, The Sunday Telegraph, 1981-90, 1996; Special Writer, Mirror Group, 1964-67; Political Correspondent, 1967-70, Chief Fiction Reviewer, Evening Standard, 1973-80, Daily Mail, 1981-86; Chief Book Reviewer, The Independent, 1986-89; Editor, The Literary Review, 1986-. Publications: Fiction: The Foxglove Saga, 1960; Path of Dalliance, 1963; Who Are the Violets Now?, 1966; Consider the Lilies, 1968; A Bed of Flowers, 1971. Non-Fiction: Biafra: Britain's Shame (with S Cronje), 1969; Country Topics, 1974; Four Crowded Years: The Diaries of Auberon Waugh, 1976; In the Lion's Den, 1978; The Last Word: An Eyewitness Account of the Thorpe Trial, 1980; Auberon Waugh's Yearbook, 1981; The Diaries of Auberon Waugh: A Turbulent Decade 1976=85, 1985; Another Voice, 1986; Waugh on Wine, 1986; Will This Do?: The First Fifty Years of Auberon Waugh, 1991; Way of the World, 1994; Editor: The Literary Review Anthology of Real Poetry, 1991. Honours: National Press Critic of the Years Commendations, 1976, 1978; What the Papers Say Columnist of the Year, Granada TV, 1979, 1988. Membership: British Croatian Society, president, 1973-92. Address: Combe Florey House, near Taunton, Somerset TA4 3JD, England.

WAUGH Hillary Baldwin, (Elissa Grandower, H Baldwin Taylor, Harry Walker), b. 22 June 1920, New Haven, Connecticut, USA. Author. m. (1) Diana Taylor, 16 June 1951, div 1980, 1 son, 2 daughters, (2) Shannon O Cork, 11 June 1983, div 1995. Education: BA, Yale University, 1942. Publications: Last Seen Wearing..., 1952; The Missing Man, 1964; Rivergate House, 1980; The Glenna Powers Case, 1981; The Doria Rafe Case, 1981; The Billy Cantrell Case, 1982; The Nerissa Claire Case, 1983; The Veronica Dean Case, 1984; The Priscilla Copperwaite Case, 1985. Honours: Grand Master, Swedish Academy of Detection, 1981; Grand Master, Mystery Writers of America, 1989. Memberships: Mystery Writers of America; Crime Writers Association, England. Address: 9 Marshall Avenue, Guilford, CT 06437, USA.

WAYMAN Tom, (Thomas Ethan Wayman), b. 13 Aug 1945, Hawkesbury, Ontario, Canada. Poet; Writer; University Teacher. Education: BA, Honours, English, University of British Columbia, 1966; MFA, English and Creative Writing, University of California at Irvine, 1968. Appointments: Instructor, Colorado State University, Fort Collins, 1968-69; Writer-in-Residence, University of Windsor, Ontario, 1975-76, University of Alberta, Edmonton, 1978-79, Simon Fraser University, Burnaby, British Columbia, 1983; Assistant Professor, Wayne State University, Detroit, 1976-77; Faculty, David Thompson University Centre, Nelson, British Columbia, 1980-82, Banff School of Fine Arts, Alberta, 1980, 1982, Kwantlen College, Surrey, British Columbia, 1983, 1988-89, Kootenay School of Writing, Vancouver, 1984-87, Victoria School of Writing, British Columbia, 1996, Kwantlen University College, Surrey, British Columbia, 1998-; Professor, Okanagan College, Kelowna, British Columbia, 1990-91; Faculty, 1991-92, Co-Head, Writing Studio, 1995-98, Kootenay School of the Arts, Nelson, British Columbia; Presidential Writer-in-Residence, University of Toronto, 1996. Publications: Poetry: Waiting for Wayman, 1973; For and Against the Moon, 1974; Money and Rain, 1975; Free Time, 1977; A Planet Mostly Sea, 1979; Living on the Ground, 1980; Introducing Tom Wayman: Selected Poems 1973-80, 1980; The Nobel Prize Acceptance Speech, 1981; Counting the Hours, 1983; The Face of Jack Munro, 1986; In a Small House on the Outskirts of Heaven, 1989; Did I Miss Anythings?: Selected Poems 1973-1993, 1993; The Astonishing Weight of the Dead, 1994; I'll Be Right Back: New & Selected Poems 1980-1996, 1997; The Colours of the Forest, 1999. Non-Fiction: Inside Job: Essays on the New York Writing, 1983; A Country Not Considered: Canada, Culture, Work, 1993. Editor: Beaton Abbot's Got the Contract, 1974; A Government Job at Last, 1976; Going for Coffee, 1981, 2nd edition, 1987; East of Main: An Anthology of Poems from East Vancouver (with Calvin Wharton), 1989; Paperwork, 1991. Contributions to: Anthologies and magazines. Honours: A J M Smith Prize, Michigan State University, 1976; 1st Prize, National Bicentennial Poetry Awards, San Jose, 1976; Several Canada Council Senior Arts Grants. Memberships: Associated Writing Programs; Federation of British Columbia Writers. Address: PO Box 163, Winlaw, British Columbia V0G 2J0, Canada.

WAYS C R. See: **BLOUNT Roy (Alton) Jr.**

WEARNE Alan Richard, b. 23 July 1948, Melbourne, Victoria, Australia. Poet; Verse and Prose Novelist. Education: BA, Latrobe University, 1973; DipEd, Rusden, 1977. Publications: Public Relations, 1972; New Devil, New Paris, 1976; The Nightmarkets, 1986; Out Here, 1987; Kicking in Danger, 1997; The Lovemakers, 1999. Contributions to: Several publications. Honours: National Book Council Award, 1987; Gold Medal, Association for the Study of Australian Literature, 1987. Address: c/o Faculty of Creative Arts, University of Wollongong, Wollongong, NSW 2015, Australia.

WEBB Bernice Larson, b. 1934, Ludell, Kansas, USA. Retired Professor; Consultant; Poet; Writer. m. Robert MacHardy Webb, 14 July 1961, 1 son, 1 daughter. Education: AB, 1956, MA, 1957, PhD, 1961, University of Kansas; University of Aberdeen, Scotland, 1959-60. Appointments: Assistant Instructor, University of Kansas, 1958-59, 1960-61; Assistant Professor, 1961-67, Associate Professor, 1967-80, Professor, 1980-87, Consultant, 1987-, University of Southwestern Louisiana; Editor, Cajun Chatter, 1964-66, The Magnolia, 1967-71, Louisiana Poets, 1970-89; Book Reviewer, Journal of American Culture, 1980-87, Journal of Popular Culture, 1980-87. Publications: The Basketball Man, 1973, revised edition, 1994; Beware of Ostriches, 1978; Poetry on the Stage, 1979; Lady Doctor on a Homestead, 1987; Two Peach Baskets, 1991; Spider Webb, 1993; Born to Be a Loser (with Johnnie Allen), 1993; Mating Dance, 1996; From Acorn ro Oakbourne, 1998. Contributions to: Various publications. Honours: Many poetry awards and prizes. Memberships: Deep South Writers Conference, board member; Louisiana State Poetry Society, president, 1978-79, 1981-82; Phi Beta Kappa, president, 1976-77, 1983-84; South Central College English Association, president, 1986-87. Address: 159 Whittington Drive, Lafayette, LA 70503, USA.

WEBB Phyllis, b. 8 Apr 1927, Victoria, British Columbia, Canada. Poet; Writer. Education: BA, University of British Columbia, Vancouver, 1949; McGill University, Montreal. Appointment: Adjunct Professor, University of Victoria, British Columbia, 1989-93. Publications: Poetry: Trio (with G Turnbull and Eli Mandel), 1954; Even Your Right Eye, 1956; The Sea is Also a Garden, 1962; Naked Poems, 1965; Wilson's Bowl, 1980; Sunday Water: Thirteen Anti Ghazals, 1982; The Vision Tree: Selected Poems, 1982; Water and Light: Ghazals and Anti Ghazals, 1984; Hanging Fire, 1990. Other: Talking (essays), 1982; Nothing But Brush Strokes: Selected Prose, 1995. Honours: Canada Council Awards; Governor-General's Award for Poetry, 1982; Officer of the Order of Canada, 1992. Address: 128 Menhinick Drive, Salt Spring Island, British Columbia, V8K 1W7, Canada.

WEBER Eugen (Joseph), b. 24 Apr 1925, Bucharest, Romania. Professor of Modern European History; Writer. m. Jacqueline Brument-Roth, 12 June 1950. Education: Institut d'études politiques, Paris, 1948-49, 1951-52; MA, 1954, MLitt, 1956, Emmanuel College, Cambridge.

Appointments: Assistant Professor, University of Iowa, 1955-56; Assistant Professor, 1956-59, Associate Professor, 1959-63, Professor, 1963-, Dean, College of Letters and Sciences, 1977-82, Joan Palevsky Professor of Modern European History, 1984-, University of California at Los Angeles; Visiting Professor, Collège de France, Paris, 1983; Director d'études, École des hautes études, Paris, 1984-85; Christian Gauss Lecturer, Princeton University, 1990. Publications: Nationalist Revival in France, 1959; Paths to the Present, 1960; Satan Franc-Maçon, 1964; Varieties of Fascism, 1964; The European Right (with H Rogger), 1965; A Modern History of Europe, 1971; Europe Since 1715, 1972; Peasants into Frenchmen, 1976; La Fin des Terroirs, 1983; France Fin-de-siècle, 1986; My France, 1990; Movements, Currents, Trends, 1991; The Hollow Years, 1994; La France des années trente, 1995; The Western Tradition, 1995; Apocalypses, 1999. Contributions to: Professional journals. Honours: Fulbright Fellowships, 1952, 1982-83; American Philosophical Society Research Fellow, 1959; American Council of Learned Societies Research Fellow, 1962; Guggenheim Fellowship, 1963-64; National Endowment for the Humanities Senior Fellowships, 1973-74, 1982-83; Commonwealth Prizes of California, 1977, 1987; Prix de la Société des gens de lettres, France, 1984; Prix litteraire Etats-Unis/France, 1995; Prix Maurice Beaumont, 1995. Memberships: American Academy of Arts and Sciences; American Historical Association; Association française de science politique; Phi Beta Kappa; Société d'histoire moderne; Society of French Historical Studies. Address: c/o Department of History, University of California at Los Angeles, Los Angeles, CA 90095, USA.

WEBER Katharine, b. 12 Nov 1955, New York, New York, USA. Writer; Critic; Teacher. m. Nicholas Fox Weber, 19 Sept 1976, 2 daughters. Appointments: Visiting Lecturer, Connecticut College, 1996; Visiting Instructor, Yale University, 1997; Instructor, English Department, Yale University, 1998. Publications: Objects in Mirror Are Closer Than They Appear, 1995; The Music Lesson, 1999. Contributions to: New York Times Book Review; San Jose Mercury News; The New Yorker; Architectural Digest; New York Times; Boston Globe; London Review of Books; Granta - Best Young American Novelist Shortlist, 1996. Memberships: Authors Guild; PEN. Literary Agent: Watkins/Loomis, 133 E 35th St, New York, NY 10010, USA. Address: 108 Beacon Road, Bethany, CT 06524, USA.

WEBER Waldemar, b. 24 Sept 1944, Sarbala, Western Siberia, Russia. Germanic Philologist. m. Tatjana Weber, 26 Aug 1967, 1 son, 1 daughter, dec. Education: Graduated, Moscow Linguistic University, 1968. Professional Translator, Western European Poetry, mainly German, into Russian, 1969-; Bilingual Author; Currently Editor-in-Chief, German-Russian newspaper, Munich, Germany. Publications: Tränen sind Linsen, lyrics, essays, 1992; Tenina obojach, verses and translations, 1995; As publisher and translator: Westi doshdja, anthology of West German poetry in Russian, 1987; Der Goldene Schnitt, anthology of 19th-20th century Austrian poetry in Russian, 1987. Contributions to: Poetry in Russian in Arion; Russian poetry in German in various German and Austrian magazines and journals; Essays in Frankfurter Allgemeine, Transit, Vienna, Kursbuch, Berlin. Memberships: Writers Union of Russia, 1990; PEN Club, Lichtenstein, 1994. Address: Ermlandstrasse 8, 81929 Munich, Germany.

WEBSTER Ernest, b. 24 Oct 1923, Harborough, England. Writer. m. 8 Oct 1942, 2 daughters. Education: Matriculation, History and Economics, London. Publications: The Friulan Plot, 1980; Madonna of the Black Market, 1981; Cossack Hide-Out, 1981; Red Alert, 1982; The Venetian Spy-Glass, 1983; The Verratoli Inheritance, 1983; Million-Dollar Stand-In, 1983; The Watchers, 1984. Address: 17 Chippendale Rise, Otley, West Yorkshire LS21 2BL, England.

WEBSTER Jan, b. 10 Aug 1924, Blantyre, Scotland. Writer. m. 10 Aug 1946, 1 son, 1 daughter. Education: Hamilton Academy. Publications: Trilogy: Colliers Row,

1977; Saturday City, 1978; Beggarman's Country, 1979; Due South, 1981; Muckle Annie, 1985; One Little Room, 1987; Rags of Time, 1987; A Different Woman, 1989; Abercrombie's Aunt and Other Stories, 1990; I Only Can Dance with You, 1990; Bluebell Blue, 1991; Lowland Reels, 1992; Tallies War, 1993; Makalienski's Bones, 1995; Pinkmount Drive, 1996. Address: c/o Robert Hale, 45-47 Clerkenwell Green, London EC1R 0HJ, England.

WEBSTER Jesse. See: **CASSILL R(onald) V(erlin).**

WEBSTER John Barron, (Jack Webster), b. 8 July 1931, Maud, Aberdeenshire, Scotland. Journalist. m. Eden Keith, 17 Feb 1956, 3 sons. Education: Maud School; Peterhead Academy; Robert Gordon's College, Aberdeen. Publications: The Dons, 1978; A Grain of Truth, 1981; Gordon Strachan, 1984; Another Grain of Truth, 1988; Alistair MacLean: A Life, 1991; Famous Ships of the Clyde, 1993. Television: The Webster Trilogy, 1993. The Flying Scots, 1994; The Express Years, 1994; In the Driving Seat, 1996; The Herald Years, 1996. Television Film: John Brown: The Man Who Drew a Legend, 1994. Honours: Bank of Scotland Awards, Columnist of the Year, 1996; UK Speaker of the Year, 1996. Address: 58 Netherhill Avenue, Glasgow G44 3XG, Scotland.

WEBSTER Leonard, (Len Webster), b. 6 July 1948, Birmingham, England. Poet; Writer. m. Emorn Puttalong, 26 Nov 1985. Education: BEd, University of Warwick, 1973; MA, Modern English and American Literature, University of Leicester, 1976; Poetry Society Adult Verse Speaking Certificate, 1977; Dip RSA TEFLA, 1983; MA, Linguistics, University of Birmingham, 1988. Appointments: Journalist, Birmingham Post and Mail, 1965-68, Coventry Evening Telegraph, 1973-74; Teacher, Oldbury High School, 1976-77, Tarsus American College, Turkey, 1977-78; King Edward VI Grammar School, Handsworth, Birmingham, 1978-84; Lecturer, Ministry of Education, Singapore, 1984-87; 1988-94. Publications: Behind the Painted Veil, 1972; Beneath the Blue Moon, 1992; Hell-Riders, 1994; Flight From the Sibyl, 1994. Memberships: Poetry Society; Society of Authors. Address: c/o 48 Marshall Road, Warley, West Midlands B68 9ED, England.

WEBSTER Noah. See: **KNOX William.**

WEBSTER Norman William, b. 21 Aug 1920, Barrow in Furness, Cumbria, England. Retired Physicist. m. Phyllis Joan Layley, 17 Feb 1945, 2 daughters. Education: BSc, University of London. Publications: Joseph Locke, Railway Revolutionary, 1970; Britain's First Trunk Line: The Grand Junction Railway, 1972; Horace Reactor, 1972; The Great North Road, 1974; Blanche of Lancaster, 1990. Contributions to: Cumbria; The Book Collector. Memberships: Jane Austen Society; European Movement. Address: 15 Hillcrest Drive, Slackhead, Milnthorpe, Cumbria LA7 7BB, England.

WECKMANN Luis, b. 7 Apr 1923, Durango, Mexico. Retired Diplomat; Professor of History Emeritus. Education: MA, History, 1944; PhD, History, 1949, Lic Law, 1950, National University of Mexico; Dr, International Public Law, Paris, 1951. Appointments: Mexican diplomatic service, 1952-89; Assistant Secretary-General, United Nations, New York City, 1974-75; Professor of History Emeritus, University of the Americas, 1990. Publications: Las Bulas Alejandrinas de 1493, 1949, reprinted as Constantino el Grande y Cristóbal Colón, 1993; El Pensamiento Politico Medieval, 1950, 2nd edition, 1993; Panorama de la Cultura Medieval, 1962; La Herencia Medieval de Mexico, 2 volumes, 1982, 2nd edition, 1994; Carlota de Belgica: Archivos, 1989; La herencia medieval del Brasil, 1994. Address: Villa del Cardo, Cardo 4, San Miguel de Allende, Gto 37700, Mexico.

WEDDE Ian, b. 17 Oct 1946, Blenheim, New Zealand. Writer; Poet; Dramatist; Translator. m. Rosemary Beauchamp, 1967, 3 sons. Education: MA, University of Auckland, 1968. Appointments: Poetry Reviewer, London magazine, 1970-71; Writer-in-Residence, Victoria

University, Wellington, 1984; Art Critic, Wellington Evening Post, 1983-90. Publications: Fiction: Dick Seddon's Great Drive, 1976; The Shirt Factory and Other Stories, 1981; Symmes Hole, 1986; Survival Arts, 1988. Poetry: Homage to Matisse, 1971; Made Over, 1974; Pathway to the Sea, 1974; Earthly: Sonnets for Carlos, 1975; Don't Listen, 1977; Spells for Coming Out, 1977; Castaly, 1981; Tales of Gotham City, 1984; Georgicon, 1984; Driving Into the Storm: Selected Poems, 1988; Tendering, 1988; The Drummer, 1993. Plays: Stations, 1969; Pukeko, 1972; Eyeball, Eyeball, 1983; Double or Quit: The Life and Times of Percy TopLiss, 1984. Editor: The Penguin Book of New Zealand Verse (with Harvey McQueen), 1986, revised edition, 1989; Now See Hear!: Art, Language, and Translation (with G Burke), 1990. Address: 118-A Maidavale Road, Roseneath, Wellington, New Zealand.

WEDGWOOD Anthony Neil. See: **BENN Tony.**

WEHRLI Peter K, b. 30 July 1939, Switzerland, Writer; Television Producer. Education: University of Zürich; University of Paris. Publications: Ankunfte, 1970; Catalogue of the 134 Most Important Observations during a Long Railway Journey, 1974; Zelluloid Paradies, 1978; Tingeltangel, 1982; Alles von Allem, 1985; La Farandula, 1986; This Book is Free of Charge; 18th Xurumbambo, 1992. Contributions to: Magazines and journals. Honours: Award of the Government of Zürich; Distinguished Service Citation. Memberships: PEN; Swiss Writers Association; Gruppe Olten; International Federation of Journalists; International Association of Art Critics; Euro-Brazilian Cultural Center, Julia Mann, vice-president. Address: Weinbergstrasse 100, 8006 Zürich, Switzerland.

WEIGEL George, b. 17 Apr 1951, Baltimore, Maryland, USA. Roman Catholic Theologian. m. Joan Balcombe, 21 June 1975, 1 son, 2 daughters. Education: BA, Philosophy, 1973, St Mary's Seminary and University, Baltimore, 1973; MA, Theology, University of St Michael's College, Toronto, 1975. Appointments: Fellow, Woodrow Wilson International Centre for Scholars, 1984-85; Editorial Boards, First Things, The Washington Quarterly, and Orbis. Publications: Tranquillitas Ordinis: The Present Failure and Future Promise of American Catholic Thought on War and Peace, 1987; Catholicism and the Renewal of American Democracy, 1989; American Interests, American Purpose: Moral Reasoning and US Foreign Policy, 1989; Freedom and Its Discontents, 1991; Just War and the Gulf War (co-author), 1991; The Final Revolution: The Resistance Church and the Collapse of Communism, 1992; Idealism Without Illusions: US Foreign Policy in the 1990's, 1994; Soul of the World: Notes on the Future of Public Catholicism, 1995. Contributions to: Numerous publications. Memberships: Catholic Theological Society of America; Council on Foreign Relations. Address: Ethics and Public Policy Centre, 1015 15th Street North West, Suite 900, Washington, DC 20005, USA.

WEIN Elizabeth Eve, (Elizabeth Gatland), b. 2 Oct 1964, New York, New York, USA. Writer; Folklorist. m. Tim Gatland, 1 Jan 1996. Education: BA, Yale University, 1986; MA, 1989, PhD, 1994, University of Pennsylvania. Publications: The Winter Prince, 1993; In Sirens and Other Daemon Lovers: No Human Hands to Touch, 1998; anthologies, 1993, 1995, 1997, 1998; 1 encyclopedia, 1998. Honours: Jacob K Javits Fellow, 1988-92; Runner-Up, Carolyn Field Award, 1994. Memberships: Authors Guild; Science Fiction and Fantasy Writers of America; Society of Children's Book Writers and Illustrators. Address: 41A Oak Tree Road, Marlow, Buckinghamshire SL7 3ED, England.

WEINBERG Gerhard L(udwig), b. 1 Jan 1928, Hannover, Germany. Professor of History; Writer. m. Janet I White, 29 Apr 1989, 1 son. Education: BA, New York State College for Teachers, 1948; MA, 1949, PhD, 1951, University of Chicago. Appointment: Professor of History, University of North Carolina at Chapel Hill. Publications: Germany and the Soviet Union, 1939-41, 1954; Hitlers Zweites Buch, 1961; The Foreign Policy of

Hitler's Germany, 1933-36, 1970; The Foreign Policy of Hitler's Germany, 1937-39, 1980; A World in the Balance: Behind the Scenes of World War II, 1981; A World at Arms: A Global History of World War II, 1994; Germany, Hitler and World War II, 1995. Contributions to: Professional journals. Honours: AHA Beer Prizes, 1971, 1994; GSA Halverson Prize, 1981; Honorary Doctor of Humane Letters, 1989. Memberships: American Historical Association; Conference Group for Central European History; German Studies Association; World War II Studies Association. Address: c/o Department of History, University of North Carolina at Chapel Hill, Chapel Hill, NC 27599, USA.

WEINBERG Steven, b. 3 May 1933, New York, New York, USA. Professor of Science; Author. m. Louise Goldwasser, 6 July 1954, 1 daughter. Education: BA, Cornell University, 1954; Postgraduate Studies, Copenhagen Institute of Theoretical Physics, 1954-55; PhD, Princeton University, 1957. Appointments: Research Associate and Instructor, Columbia University, 1957-59; Research Physicist, Lawrence Radiation Laboratory, Berkeley, 1959-60; Faculty, 1960-64, Professor of Physics, 1964-69, University of California at Berkeley; Visiting Professor, 1967-69, Professor of Physics, 1979-83, Massachusetts Institute of Technology; Higgins Professor of Physics, Harvard University, 1973-83; Senior Scientist, Smithsonian Astrophysics Laboratory, 1973-83; Josey Professor of Science, University of Texas at Austin, 1982-; Senior Consultant, Smithsonian Astrophysics Observatory, 1983-; Various visiting professorships and lectureships. Publications: Gravitation and Cosmology: Principles and Application of the General Theory of Relativity, 1972; The First Three Minutes: A Modern View of the Origin of the Universe, 1977; The Discovery of Subatomic Particles, 1982; Elementary Particles and the Laws of Physics (with R Feynman), 1987; Dreams of a Final Theory, 1992; The Quantum Theory of Fields, Vol I, Foundations, 1995, Vol II, Modern Applications, 1996. Contributions to: Books, periodicals and professional journals. Honours: J Robert Oppenheimer Memorial Prize, 1973; Dannie Heineman Prize in Mathematical Physics, 1977; American Institute of Physics-US Steel Foundation Science Writing Award, 1977; Nobel Prize in Physics, 1979; Elliott Cresson Medal, Franklin Institute, 1979; Madison Medal, Princeton University, 1991; National Medal of Science, National Science Foundation, 1991; Andrew Gemant Prize, American Institute of Physics, 1997; Diazzi Prize, Governments of Sicily and Palermo, 1998. Memberships: American Academy of Arts and Sciences; American Mediaeval Academy; American Philosophical Society; American Physical Society; Council on Foreign Relations; History of Science Society; International Astronomical Union; National Academy of Science; Phi Beta Kappa; Philosophical Society of Texas, president, 1994; Royal Society; Texas Institute of Letters. Address: c/o Department of Science, University of Texas at Austin, Austin, TX 78712, USA.

WEINFIELD Henry (Michael), b. 3 Jan 1949, Montreal, Quebec, Canada. Associate Professor in Liberal Studies; Poet; Writer; Translator. Education: BA, City College of New York, 1970; MA, State University of New York, Binghamton, 1973; PhD, City University of New York, 1985. Appointments: Lecturer, State University of New York, Binghamton, 1973-74; Adjunct Lecturer, Lehman College, 1974-77, Baruch College, 1979-81, City College of New York, 1982-83; Adjunct Lecturer, 1983-84, Special Lecturer, 1984-91, New Jersey Institute of Technology; Assistant Professor, 1991-96, Associate Professor, 1996-, in Liberal Studies, University of Notre Dame. Publications: Poetry: The Carnival Cantata, 1971; In the Sweetness of New Time, 1980; Sonnets Elegiac and Satirical, 1982. Other: The Poet Without a Name: Gray's Elegy and the Problem of History, 1991; The Collected Poems of Stéphane Mallarmé, 1995. Contributions to: numerous publications. Honours: Coordinating Council of Literary Magazines Award, 1975; National Endowment for the Humanities Fellowship, 1989. Address: Program of Liberal Studies, University of Notre Dame, Notre Dame, IN 46556, USA.

WEINREICH Beatrice, (Beatrice Sliverman-Weinreich), b. 14 May 1928, New York, New York, USA. Folklorist. m. Uriel Weinreich, 26 June 1949, dec 1967, 1 son, 1 daughter. Education: BA, Brooklyn College, 1949; Graduate Studies, Folklore and Ethnography, University of Zürich, 1950; MA, Anthropology, Columbia University, 1956. Publications: Yidisher Folklor (co-editor), 1954; Yiddish Language and Folklore: A Selective Bibliography (co-editor), 1959; Yiddish Folktales, 1988; The Language and Culture Atlas of Ashkenzic Jewry, Vol II, Research Tools (co-editor), 1993. Contributions to: Books and journals. Memberships: American Folklore Society; International Society for Folk Narrative Research; New York Folklore Society. Address: 555 West 57 Street, New York, NY 10019, USA.

WEINSTEIN Michael Alan, b. 24 Aug 1942, Brooklyn, New York, USA. Political Philosopher. m. Deena Schneiweiss, 31 May 1964. Education: BA, summa cum laude, New York University, 1964; MA, 1965, PhD 1967, Western Reserve University. Appointments: Assistant Professor, Western Reserve University, 1967, Virginia Polytechnic Institute, 1967-68, Purdue University, 1972-; Distinguished Professor of Political Science, University of Wyoming, 1979. Publications: The Polarity of Mexican Thought: Instrumentalism and Finalism, 1976; The Tragic Sense of Political Life, 1977; Meaning and Appreciation: Time and Modern Political Life, 1978; The Structure of Human Life: A Vitalist Ontology, 1979; The Wilderness and the City: American Classical Philosophy as a Moral Quest, 1982; Unity and Variety in the Philosophy of Samuel Alexander, 1984; Finite Perfection: Reflections on Virtue, 1985; Culture Critique: Fernand Dumont and the New Quebec Sociology, 1985; Data Trash, 1994; Culture/Flesh: Explorations of Postcivilized Modernity, 1995. Contributions to: Magazines and journals. Honours: Best Paper Prize, Midwest Political Science Association, 1969; Guggengeim Fellowship, 1974-75; Rockefeller Foundation Humanities Fellowship, 1976. Address: Department of Political Science, Purdue University, West Lafayette, IN 47907, USA.

WEINTRAUB Stanley, b. 17 Apr 1929, Philadelphia, Pennsylvania, USA. Professor of Arts and Humanities(Emeritus 1999); Writer; Editor. m. Rodelle Horwitz, 6 June 1954, 2 sons, 1 daughter. Education: BS, West Chester State College, Pennsylvania, 1949; MA, Temple University, 1951; PhD, Pennsylvania State University, 1956. Appointments: Instructor, 1953-59, Assistant Professor, 1959-62, Associate Professor, 1962-65, Professor of English, 1965-70, Research Professor, 1970-86, Evan Pugh Professor of Arts and Humanities, 1986-, Pennsylvania State University; Visiting Professor, University of California at Los Angeles, 1963, University of Hawaii, 1973, University of Malaya, 1977, National University of Singapore, 1982. Publications: Private Shaw and Public Shaw: A Dual Portrait of Lawrence of Arabia and George Bernard Shaw, 1963; The War in the Wards: Korea's Forgotten Battle, 1964; The Art of William Golding (with B S Oldsey), 1965; Reggie: A Portrait of Reginald Turner, 1965; Beardsley: A Biography, 1967; The Last Great Cause: The Intellectuals and the Spanish Civil War, 1968; Evolution of a Revolt: Early Postwar Writings of T E Lawrence (with R Weintraub), 1968; Journey to Heartbreak: The Crucible Years of Bernard Shaw 1914-1918, 1971; Whistler: A Biography, 1974; Lawrence of Arabia: The Literary Impulse (with R Weintraub), 1975; Aubrey Beardsley: Imp of the Perverse, 1976; Four Rossettis: A Victorian Biography, 1977; The London Yankees: Portraits of American Writers and Artists in England 1894-1914, 1979; The Unexpected Shaw: Biographical Approaches to G B Shaw and His Work, 1982; A Stillness Heard Round the World: The End of the Great War, 1985; Victoria: An Intimate Biography, 1987; Long Day's Journey into War: December 7, 1941, 1991; Bernard Shaw: A Guide to Research, 1992; Disraeli: A Biography, 1993; The Last Great Victory: The End of World War II, July/August 1945, 1995; Shaw's People, Victoria to Churchill, 1996; Albert, Uncrowned King, 1997. Editor: Unfinished novel by George Bernard Shaw, 1958; C P Snow: A Spectrum, 1963; The Yellow Book: Quintessence of the Nineties, 1964; The Savoy: Nineties Experiment, 1966; The Court Theatre, 1966; Biography and Truth, 1967; The Literary Criticism of Oscar Wilde, 1968; Shaw: An Autobiography, 1969-70; Bernard Shaw's Nondramatic Literary Criticism, 1972; Directions in Literary Criticism (with Philip Young), 1973; Saint Joan Fifty Years After: 1923/24-1973/74, 1973; The Portable Bernard Shaw, 1977; The Portable Oscar Wilde (with Richard Aldington), 1981; Modern British Dramatists 1900-1945, 2 volumes, 1982; The Playwright and the Pirate: Bernard Shaw and Frank Harris: A Correspondence, 1982; British Dramatists Since World War II, 2 volumes, 1982; Bernard Shaw: The Diaries, 1885-1897, 1986; Bernard Shaw on the London Art Scene 1885-1950, 1989. Contributions to: Professional journals. Honours: Guggenheim Fellowship, 1968-69; Distinguished Humanist Award, Pennsylvania Humanities Council, 1985. Memberships: Authors Guild; PEN; National Book Critics Circle. Address: c/o Pennsylvania State University, 202 Ihlseng Building, University Park, PA 16802, USA.

WEIR Anne, b. 9 Feb 1942, Boston, Massachusetts, USA. Writer. 3 daughters. Education: BA, Smith and Swarthmore Colleges, 1964; MEd, University of Maine, 1984. Publications: A Book of Certainties, 1992, 1998; Marlowe: Being in the Life of the Mind, 1996; The Color Book, 1998. Address: PO Box 10364, Portland, Maine 04104, USA.

WEIR Charlene, b. 10 Nov 1937, Nortonville, KS, USA. Writer. 1 son, 1 daughter. Education: Registered Nurse, Ft Scott School of Nursing; Attended University of Oklahoma. Publications: Winter Widow; Consider the Crows; Family Practice; Murder Take Two. Honour: St Martin's Best First Traditional Mystery. Memberships: MWA; ICWA; SinC; ACWL. Literary Agent: Margaret Ruley, Jane Rotrosen Agency. Address: 318 E 51st Street, New York, NY 10022, USA.

WEIR Hugh William Lindsay, b. 29 Aug 1934. Writer; Publisher. m. The Honourable Grania O'Brien, 17 July 1973. Education: DLitt, History, Trinity College, UIC, 1994; Trinity College, Dublin. Appointments include: Managing Director, Weir Publishing Group, Ballinakella Press and Bell'acards. Publications: Hall Craig - Words on an Irish House; O'Brien People and Places; Houses of Clare; Ireland - A Thousand Kings; O'Connor People and Places; The Claire Young Environmentalists; Short Stories, academic articles/essays and topographical/historical contributions made to various anthologies and books. Contributions to: The Other Clare; The Clare Champion; The Church of Ireland Gazette; The Catholic Twin Circle; English Digest. Honour: Oidhreacht Award; Membership: Irish Writers' Union. Address: Ballinakella Lodge, Whitegate, Co Clare, Ireland.

WEISS A L. See: **KEBL Anna-Luise.**

WEISS Irving, (Robert Forio, Gino de Marco), b. 11 Sept 1921, New York City, New York, USA. Writer. m. Anne du Bois de la Vergne, 14 Dec 1949, 1 son, 3 daughters. Education: Brooklyn College, 1939-40, 1953; University of Michigan, 1940-42; MA, Columbia University, 1949. Appointments: Teacher, American Dependents School, 1851-53; Instructor, Pennsylvania State University, 1956-58; Humanities Editor, Funk and Wagnalls Standard Reference Encyclopedia, 1858-60; Assistant Professor of English, Fashion Institute of Technology, 1960-64; Professor of English, State University of New York at New Paltz, 1964-85. Contributions to: New Yorker; New York Times Book Review; Sun; Chelsea Review; Rampike; Score; Synaesthetic. Address: 319 Rosin Drive, Chesterton, MD 21620, USA.

WEISSBORT Daniel, b. 1 May 1935, London, England. Professor; Poet; Translator; Editor. Education: BA, Queen's College, Cambridge, 1956. Appointments: Co-Founder (with Ted Hughes), Modern Poetry in Translation, 1965-83; Professor, University of Iowa, 1980-. Publications: The Leaseholder, 1971; In an Emergency, 1972; Soundings, 1977; Leaseholder: New and Collected Poems, 1965-85, 1986; Inscription, 1990; Lake, 1993. Other: Editor and translator of Russian literature. Honour: Arts Council Literature Award, 1984. Address: c/o Department of English, University of Iowa, Iowa City, IA 52242, USA.

WELCH Ann Courtenay, b. 20 May 1917, London, England. Aviation Writer. m. (1), 2 daughters, (2) P P Lorne Elphinstone Welch, 24 June 1953, 1 daughter. Appointments: Editor, Bulletin, Fédération Aéronautique Internationale, 1979-89, Royal Aero Club Gazette, (editor), 1984-1994. Publications: The Woolacombe Bird, 1964; Story of Gliding, 1965; New Soaring Pilot, 1970; Pilot's Weather, 1973; Gliding, 1976; Hang Glider Pilot, 1977; Book of Air Sports, 1978; Accidents Happen, 1978; Soaring Hang Gliders, 1981; Complete Microlight Guide, 1983; Happy to Fly (autobiography), 1984; Complete Soaring Guide, 1986. Contributions to: Flight International, UK; Aeroplane, UK; Royal Aero Club Gazette; Pilot; Flight Safety Bulletin. Honours: Officer, Order of the British Empire; Gold and Silver Medals, Royal Aero Club; 4 Medals, Fédération Aéronautique Internationale. Memberships: Royal Aeronautical Society, fellow; Royal Meteorological Society; honourable member, Royal Institute of Navigation. Address: 14 Upper Old Park Lane, Farnham, Surrey GU9 0AS, England.

WELCH James, b. 1940, Browning, Montana, USA. Writer; Poet. m. Lois M Welch. Education: Northern Montana College; BA, University of Montana. Publications: Fiction: Winter in the Blood, 1974; The Death of Jim Loney, 1979; Fool's Crow, 1986; The Indian Lawyer, 1990. Poetry: Riding the Earthboy 40, 1971, revised edition, 1975. Non-Fiction: Killing Custer: The Battle of the Little Bighorn and the Fate of the Plains Indians (with Paul Stekler), 1994. Editor: Richard Hugo: The Real West Marginal Way: A Poet's Autobiography (with Ripley S Hugg and Lois M Welch), 1986. Contributions to: Periodicals. Honours: National Endowment for the Arts Grant, 1969; Los Angeles Times Book Prize, 1987; Pacific Northwest Booksellers Association Book Award, 1987. Address: 2321 Wylie Street, Missoula, MT 59802, USA.

WELCH Liliane, b. 20 Oct 1937, Luxembourg. Professor of French Literature; Poet; Writer. m. Cyril Welch, 1 daughter. Education: BA, 1960, MA, 1961, University of Montana; PhD, Pennsylvania State University, 1964. Appointments: Assistant Professor, East Carolina University, 1965-66, Antioch College, Ohio, 1966-67; Assistant Professor, 1967-71, Associate Professor, 1971-72, Professor of French Literature, 1972-, Mount Allison University. Publications: Emergence: Baudelaire, Mallarmé, Rimbaud, 1973; Winter Songs, 1973; Syntax of Ferment, 1979; Assailing Beats, 1979; October Winds, 1980; Brush and Trunks, 1981; From the Songs of the Artisans, 1983; Manstoma, 1985; Rest Unbound, 1985; Word-House of a Grandchild, 1987; Seismographs: Selected Essays and Reviews, 1988; Fire to the Looms Below, 1990; Life in Another Language, 1992; Von Menschen und Orten, 1992; Dream Museum, 1995; Fidelities, 1997; Frescoes: Travel Pieces, 1998. Contributions to: Professional and literary journals. Honours: Alfred Bailey Prize, 1986; Bressani Prize, 1992; Membre Correspondant De L'Institut Grand Ducal De Luxembourg, 1998. Memberships: Association of Italian-Canadian Poets; Federation of New Brunswick Writers; League of Canadian Poets; Letzebuerger Schriftsteller Verband; Writers' Union of Canada. Address: Box 246, Sackville, New Brunswick E0A 3C0, Canada.

WELDON Fay, b. 22 Sept 1931, Alvechurch, Worcestershire, England. Writer. m. (1) Ron Weldon, 12 June 1961, 4 daughters, (2) Nick Fox, 1994. Education: MA, St Andrews University, 1952. Publications: Fat Woman's Joke, 1968; Down Among the Women, 1971; Female Friends, 1975; Remember Me, 1976; Praxis, 1978; Puffball, 1980; The President's Child, 1982; Letters to Alice, 1984; Life and Loves of a She Devil, 1984; Rebecca West, 1985; The Sharpnel Academy, 1986; The Hearts and Lives of Men, 1987; Leader of the Band, 1988; Wolf of the Mechanical Dog, 1989; The Cloning of Joanna May, 1989; Pary Puddle, 1989; Moon Over Minneapolis or Why She Couldn't Stay, 1991; Life Force, 1992; Growing Rich, 1992; Affliction, 1994; Worst Fears, 1998; Big Woman, 1998. Contributions to: Numerous journals and magazines. Memberships: Royal Society of Authors; Writers Guild of Great Britain. Address: c/o Giles Gordon, 6 Ann Street, Edinburgh E4 1PS, Scotland.

WELLINGTON Fred. See: **PURDY A F.**

WELLS Martin John, b. 24 Aug 1928, London, England. Zoologist; Educator. m. Joyce Finlay, 8 Sept 1953, 2 sons. Education: BA, 1952; MA, 1956; ScD, 1966. Publications: Brain and Behaviour in Cephalopods, 1962; You, Me and the Animal World, 1964; Lower Animals, 1968; Octopus: Physiology and Behaviour of an Advanced Invertebrate, 1978; Civilization and the Limpet, 1998. Contributions to: Several journals. Honours: Silver Medal, Zoological Society, 1968; Fellow, Churchill College, Cambridge. Memberships: Philosophical Society. Address: The Bury Home End, Fulbourn, Cambridge, England.

WELLS Peter, b. 12 Jan 1919, London, England. Writer; Poet. m. (1) Elisabeth Vander Meulen, dec 1967, 1 daugher, (2) Gillian Anne Hays-Newington, 1988. Education: Diploma, Social Studies, University of London, 1970; Certificate, Psychiatric Social Work, University of Manchester, 1973. Publications: Poetry Folios (co-editor), 1942-46, 1951; Poems (retrospective collection), 1997; Six Poems (with illustrations), 1998. Contributions to: poetry magazines including: Poetry (London); Poetry (Chicago); View (New York); Anthologies (UK and Eire); literary journals including: New English Weekly; Quarterly Review of Literature (USA); The Dublin Magazine (Eire). Memberships: PEN; Society of Authors. Address: Model Farm, Linstead Magna, Halesworth, Suffolk, England.

WELLS Peter Frederick, (John Flint), b. 28 Feb 1918, New Zealand. Retired Professor; Writer. m. (1) Jeanne Chiles, 17 Feb 1945, 3 sons, (2) Rita Davenport, 26 Mar 1994. Education: MA, 1948, DipEd, 1949, University of Wales; DPhil, University of Waikato, New Zealand, 1971. Appointments: Head, Language Studies Department, University of Waikato, 1961-73; Director, Institute of Modern Languages, James Cook University of North Queensland, 1974-84. Publications: Let's Learn French, 1963; Les Quatre Saisons, 1966; Let's Learn Japanese, 1968; Nihongo no Kakikata, 1971; A Description of Kalaw Kawaw Ya, 1976. Other: Anthology of Poems by Ishikawa Takuboku, 1972; Phonetics and Orthography of French, 1975; Three Loves and a Minesweeper, 1998; Myra Migrating, 1999. Contributions to: Journal of Modern Languages and Literature; Bulletin de L'Association G Budé; New Zealand Journal of French Studies; Education; LINQ; English Language and Literature Association. Honours: Order of the Sacred Treasure, Japan; Order of New Zealand. Membership: Founder, President, New Zealand-Japan Society, Hamilton. Address: 249 Bankwood Road, Chartwell, Hamilton, New Zealand.

WELLS Robert, b. 17 Aug 1947, Oxford, England. Poet; Translator. Education: King's College, Cambridge, 1965-68. Appointments: Teacher, University of Leicester, 1979-82. Publications: Shade Mariners (with Dick Davis and Clive Wilmer), 1970; The Winter's Task: Poems, 1977; The Georgics, by Virgil (translator), 4 volumes, 1981; Selected Poems, 1986; The Idylls, by Theocritus (translator), 1988. Contributions to: Anthologies. Address: c/o Carcanet Press, 208-212 Corn Exchange Buildings, Manchester M4 3BQ, England.

WELLS Roger, b. 30 Jan 1947, London, England. Reader in History; Writer. Div, 1 son, 1 daughter. Education: BA, 1969, Dphil, 1978, University of York. Appointments: Lecturer, University of Wales, 1972-73, University of Exeter, 1973-75, University of York, 1975-76; Senior Lecturer, University of Brighton, 1976-95; Professor of History, Christ Church University College, Canterbury, 1995-. Publications: Death and Distress in Yorkshire, 1793-1801, 1977; Riot and Political Disaffection in Nottinghamshire in the Age of Revolutions 1776-1803, 1983; Insurrections: The British Experience 1795-1803, 1983; Wretched Faces: Famine in Wartimes England, 1793-1801, 1988; Class, Conflict and Protest in the English Countryside, 1700-1880, 1990; Victorian Village, 1992; Crime, Protest and Popular Politics in Southern England 1740-1850 (with J Rule). Contributions to: Social History; Rural History; Southern History; Northern History; Policing and Society; Journal of Peasant Studies; Journal of Historical Geography; Local Historian; English Historical Review; Agricultural History Review; London Journal; Labour History Bulletin; Journal of Social Policy. Membership: Royal Historical Society. Address: Christ Church University College, Canterbury, Kent CT1 1QU, England.

WELLS Rosemary, b. 29 Jan 1943, New York, New York, USA. Author and Illustrator of Young Reader's Books. 2 daughters. Education: Museum School, Boston. Publications: Over 40 books, 1969-95. Honours: Many awards. Address: 738 Sleepy Hollow Road, Briarcliff Manor, NY 10510, USA.

WELLS Tobias. See: **FORBES Stanton.**

WELTON Anthony. See: **JOY David.**

WELTY Eudora, b. 13 Apr 1909, Jackson, Mississippi, USA. Author. Education: Mississippi State College for Women; BA, University of Wisconsin, 1929; Postgraduate Studies, Columbia School of Advertising, 1930-31. Publications: A Curtain of Green, 1941; The Robber Bridegroom, 1942; The Wide Net, 1943; Delta Wedding, 1946; Music From Spain, 1948; Short Stories, 1949; The Golden Apples, 1949; The Ponder Heart, 1954; The Bride of the Innisfallen, 1955; Place in Fiction, 1957; The Shoe Bird, 1964; Thirteen Stories, 1965; A Sweet Devouring, 1969; Losing Battles, 1970; One Time, One Place, 1971; The Optimist's Daughter, 1972; The Eye of the Story, 1978; The Collected Stories of Eudora Welty, 1980; One Writer's Beginnings, 1985; Eudora Welty Photographs, 1989; The Norton Book of Friendship (editor with Ronald A Sharp), 1991; A Writer's Eye: Collected Book Reviews, 1994; Monuments to Interruption: Collected Book Reviews, 1994. Contributions to: The New Yorker. Honours: Guggenheim Fellowship, 1942; O Henry Awards, 1942, 1943, 1968; National Institute of Arts and Letters Grant, 1944, and Gold Medal, 1972; William Dean Howells Medal, American Academy of Arts and Letters, 1955; Christopher Book Award, 1972; Pulitzer Prize in Fiction, 1973; Presidential Medal of Freedom, 1980; National Medal for Literature, 1980; Notable Book Award, American Library Association, 1980; American Book Awards, 1981, 1984; Commonwealth Medal, Modern Language Association, 1984; National Medal of Arts, 1987; Chevalier de l'Ordre des Arts et Lettres, France, 1987. Membership: American Academy of Arts and Letters. Address: 1119 Pinehurst Street, Jackson, MS 39202, USA.

WENDT Albert, b. 27 Oct 1939, Apia, Western Samoa. Professor of English; Writer; Poet; Dramatist. 1 son, 2 daughters. Education: MA, History, Victoria University, Wellington, 1964. Appointments: Professor of Pacific Literature, University of the South Pacific, Suva, Fiji, 1982-87; Professor of English, University of Auckland, 1988-. Publications: Fiction: Sons for the Return Home, 1973; Pouliuli, 1977; Leaves of the Banyan Tree, 1979; Ola, 1990; Black Rainbow, 1992. Short Stories: Flying-Fox in a Freedom Tree, 1974; The Birth and Death of the Miracle Man, 1986. Plays: Comes the Revolution, 1972; The Contract, 1972. Poetry: Inside Us the Dead: Poems 1961-74, 1975; Shaman of Visions, 1984; Photographs, 1995. Honours: Landfall Prize, 1963; Wattie Award, 1980; Commonwealth Book Prize, South East Asia and the Pacific, 1991. Address: c/o Department of English, University of Auckland, Private Bag, Auckland, New Zealand.

WENKAM Robert George, b. 1 Jan 1920, Oakland, California, USA. Author; Photographer. m. Nao Sekiguchi, 1960, 2 sons, 2 daughters. Education: College Civil Engineering, 2 years; Postgraduate courses, European History, Economics, Philosophy, University of

Hawaii. Appointments: Established own advertising and architectural photography business, Honolulu, Hawaii, 1949; Hawaii State Land Use Commission, 1960; Organiser, Lecturer, Creative Photography Programme, University of Hawaii. Publications: Over 20 photographic books including: Micronesia The Breadfruit Revolution; New England; Micronesia Island Wilderness; Kauai and The Park Country of Hawaii; Kauai Hawaii's Garden Island; Maui No Ka Oi; Hawaii; Maui the Last Hawaiian Place; Honolulu Is An Island; The Edge of Fire, 1987; Jack Northrop and the Flying Wing, biography, 1988; Palm Springs First Hundred Years (editor, designer, producer); Fighter General (biography); Guidebooks: Country Roads of Hawaii, 1993; The Green Guide to Hawaii, 1993; Country Towns of Southern California, 1998; Producer, travelogue films: Hawaii Lovelier Than Ever; Treasures of Peru. Contributions to: Over 100 articles in magazines. Honours: Best Travel Poster in the World, American Society of Travel Agents; Major awards from Artists and Art Directors Clubs; Artist-in-Residence, Grantee, Hawaii State Foundation for Culture and the Arts, and National Endowment for the Arts; Photographer of the Year, Society of American Travel Writers, 1987. Memberships include: Society of American Travel Writers, Chairman, Tourism and Environment Watch Committee; Federation of Outdoor Clubs (former president); Hawaiian Trail and Mountain Club, Conservation Committee chair. Address: 6246 Milolii Place, Honolulu, HI 96825, USA.

WENTWORTH Wendy. See: **CHAPLIN Jenny.**

WERENSKIOLD Marit, b. 13 Dec 1942, Oslo, Norway. Art Historian; Professor. m. Yngvar Troim, 20 Aug 1970. Education: National College of Arts, Crafts and Design, Oslo, 1961-62; History, Art History, Classical Archaeology, 1962-70, Mag artium, 1970, Dr philos, 1982, University of Oslo; Art History, University of Paris, Sorbonne, 1967-68; Examinations in Basic Russian, 1985. Appointments: Art Critic, Dagbladet, Morgenbladet, Aftenposten, Oslo, 1969-71, 1982-84; Research Fellow, University of Oslo, 1972-86; Assistant Professor, 1986-91, Professor in Art History, 1992, Department of Archaeology, Numismatics and History of Art, University of Oslo. Publications: De norske Matisse-elevene: Læretid og gjennombrudd 1908-1914, 1972; The Concept of Expressionism: Origin and Metamorphoses, 1984. Contributions to: Kandinsky's Moscow, Art in America, 1989; Serge Diaghilev and Erik Werenskiold, Konsthistorisk Tidskrift, 1991; Concepts of Expressionism in Scandinavia, Expressionism reassessed, 1993; Die Avantgarde in Dresden, München und Berlin: Die Brücke, Der Blaue Reiter, Der Sturm, Wahlverwandtschaft: Skandinavien und Deutschland 1800 bis 1914, 1997; Erik Werenskiold in Munich 1876-1881, Konsthistorisk Tidskrift, 1998, Wahlverwandtschaft: Skandinavien und Deutschland, 1999. Honours: Boursière, Etat Français, 1967-68; Grantee: Grinifangers Kulturfond, 1970-71; Fondet for Svensk-Norsk Samarbeid, 1974; Det Norske Videnskaps Akademi, 1975; Travel Grant, Norsk Faglitterær Forfatterforening, 1992. Memberships: Norsk Faglitterær Forfatterforening, Oslo; Corresponding Member, Anders Zorn Academy, Sweden, 1983-; Visiting Member, Institute for Advanced Study, Princeton, New Jersey, USA, 1988; Det Kongelige Norske Videnskabers Selskab, Trondheim, 1994. Literary Agent: Universitetsforlaget, Oslo. Address: Ulsrudveien 6, 0690 Oslo, Norway.

WERNER Markus, b. 27 Dec 1944, Eschlikon, Switzerland. Highschool Teacher; Freelance Writer. Education: DPhil, University of Zurich. Publications: Novels: Zündels Abgang, 1984; Froschnacht, 1985; Die kalte Schulter, 1989; Bis bald, 1992; Festland, 1996; Der ägyptische Heinrich, 1999. Honour: Award of the SWF Best List of New Releases, 1997. Literary Agent: Residenz Verlag, Salzburg, Austria. Address: Dorfstr 24, CH-8236 Opfertshofen, Switzerland.

WERTENBAKER Timberlake, Playwright. Appointment: Writer-in-Residence, Shared Experience, 1983, Royal Court, 1985; Member, Royal Court Board, 1987-98. Publications: New Anatomies, 1984; The Grace of Mary Traverse, 1985; Our Country's Good, 1988; The Love of the Nightingale, 1989; Three Birds Alighting on a Field, 1992; The Break of Day, 1995; Timberlake Wertenbaker: Plays One, 1996; After Darwin, 1998. Contributions to: Anthologies, periodicals, journals, quarterlies and reviews. Honours include: Plays and Players Most Promising Playwright; Evening Standard Most Promising Playwright. Literary Agent: Casarotto Ramsay Ltd. Address: c/o Casarotto Ramsay Ltd, National House, 60-66 Wardour Street, London W1V 4ND, England.

WERTH Lloyd E. See: **DOAN Eleanor Lloyd.**

WERWINSKI Janusz Andrzej, b. 27 Mar 1956, Warsaw, Poland. Translator; Copywriter. m. Joanna Krolak, 24 Apr 1982, 1 son. Education: B Limanowski College, Warsaw, 1976; Graduated, School for Movie and Television Production, Warsaw, 1979. Appointments: Central Army Studios, 1979-81; WE-MA Workshop, 1981-95; Vision Film Distribution Company, 1991-; Intertext Translation Agency, 1991-; Studio ZET Radio Station, 1995-; Synthesis Media, 1995-; TV Studio, Daewoo-FSO Motor Company, 1996-. Publications: Translations of over 200 films including: Homo Faber; Toy Soldiers; Striptease; Super Mario Bros; Shattered; Monty Python's Flying Circus; Caligula; Stranger Among Us; Leon; Room with a View; Help (The Beatles); The Killing Fields; Atoll K; The Doors; Stella; Last Man Stand. Address: ul Piekna 11, Nowa Iwiczna, 05-500 Piaseczno, Poland.

WESCOTT Roger Williams, b. 28 Apr 1925, Philadelphia, Pennsylvania, USA. Anthropologist; Writer; Poet. m. 12 Apr 1964. Education: BA, English and History, 1945, MA, Oriental Studies, 1947, PhD, Linguistic Science, 1948, Princeton University; MLitt, Social Anthropology, University of Oxford, 1953. Appointments: Director, University Playreaders, Ibadan, Nigeria, 1955-56; Assistant Professor of English, Massachusetts Institute of Technology, USA, 1956-57; Associate Professor of English, Michigan State University, 1957-62; Evaluator, National Endowment for the Humanities, 1975-; Associate Editor, Thoughts for All Seasons, USA, 1988-. Publications: The Divine Animal, 1969; Visions: Selected Poems, 1975; Sound and Sense, 1980; Language Families, 1986; Getting it Together, 1990. Co-Author: The Creative Process, 1974; Poems for Children, 1975; Literary and Linguistic Studies, 1978; Anthropological Poetics, 1990. Contributions to: Society for Historian Research, 1987-; International Organization for Unification. Honours: Rhodes Scholar, University of Oxford, 1948-50; First Holder, Endowed Chair of Excellence in Humanities, University of Tennessee, 1988-89. Memberships: International Society for the Comparative Study of Civilsations, president, 1992-; Linguistic Association of Canada and the US, president, 1976-77; Terminological Neologisms, 1988-96; Association for the Study of Language in Pre-History, 1996-; Distance Learning Program, Dean, 1998. Address: 16-A Heritage Crest, Southbury, CT 06488, USA.

WESKER Arnold, b. 24 May 1932, London, England. Dramatist; Playwright; Director. m. Dusty Bicker, 2 sons, 2 daughters. Education: Upton House School, Hackney. Appointments: Founder-Director, Centre Fortytwo, 1961-70. Publications: Chicken Soup with Barley, 1959; Roots, 1959; I'm Talking About Jerusalem, 1960; The Wesker Trilogy, 1960; The Kitchen, 1961; Chips with Everything, 1962; The Four Seasons, 1966; Their Very Own and Golden City, 1966; The Friends, 1970; Fears of Fragmentation (essays), 1971; Six Sundays in January (stories), 1971; The Old Ones, 1972; The Journalists, 1974; Love Letters on Blue Paper (stories), 1974, 2nd edition, 1990; Say Goodbye!: You May Never See Them Again (with John Allin), 1974; Words--As Definitions of Experience, 1976; The Wedding Feast, 1977; Journey Into Journalism, 1977; Said the Old Man to the Young Man (stories), 1978; The Merchant (renamed Shylock), 1978; Fatlips, 1978; The Journalists: A Triptych, 1979; Caritas, 1981; Distinctions (essays), 1985; Yardsale, 1987; Whatever Happened to Betty Lemon, 1987; Little Old Lady, 1988; Shoeshine, 1989; Collected Plays, 7 volumes, 1989-97; As Much As I Dare (autobiography), 1994; Circles of Perception, 1996; Break, My Heart, 1997; Denial, 1997; The Birth of Shylock and the Death of Zero Mostel (diaries), 1997; The King's Daughters (stories), 1998. Contributions to: Stage, film, radio and television. Honours: Fellow, Royal Society of Literature, 1985; Honorary DLitt, University of East Anglia, 1989; Honorary Fellow, Queen Mary and Westfield College, London, 1995; Honorary DHL, Denison University, Ohio, 1997. Memberships: International Playwrights Committee, president, 1979-83; International Theatre Institute, chairman, British Centre, 1978-82. Address: 37 Ashley Road, London N19 3AG, England.

WESLEY Mary. See: **SIEPMANN Mary Aline.**

WESLEY-SMITH Peter, b. 10 June 1945, Adelaide, South Australia, Australia. Professor of Law; Writer. Publications: LLB, 1969, BA, Honours, History, 1970, University of Adelaide; PhD, University of Hong Kong, 1976. Appointments: Professor of Law, University of Hong Kong. Publications: The Ombley-Gombley, 1969; Hocus Pocus, 1975; Unequal Treaty, 1898-1997, revised edition, 1998; Constitutional and Administrative Law in Hong Kong, 3rd edition, 1998; An Introduction to the Hong Kong Legal System, 2nd edition, 1993; The Sources of Hong Kong Law, 1994; Foul Fowl, 1995; The Hunting of the Snark: Second Expedition, 1996. Libretti: Boojum, 1986; Quito, 1994. Address: c/o Faculty of Law, University of Hong Kong, Hong Kong.

WEST Anthony C(athcart Muir), b. 1 July 1910, County Down, Northern Ireland. Novelist. m. Olive Mary Burr, 1940, 11 children. Publications: River's End and Other Stories, 1958; The Native Moment, 1959; Rebel to Judgement, 1962; The Ferret Fancier, 1963; As Towns with Fire, 1968; All the King's Horses and Other Stories, 1981. Honour: Atlantic Award, 1946. Address: c/o Poolbeg Press, Knocksdean House, Forrest Great, Swords, County Dublin, Ireland.

WEST Ben, b. 30 Nov 1963, London, England. Writer. m. Bryony Imogen Menzies Clack, 14 Oct 1989, 1 son, 1 daughter. Publication: London for Free. Contributions to: Guardian; Daily Telegraph; Independent; Sunday Times; Sunday Telegraph; Daily Mail; Daily Express; Evening Standard. Address: 37 Vanbrugh Park, London SE3 7AA, England.

WEST Colin Edward, b. 21 May 1951, Epping, Essex, England. Writer; Poet; Illustrator. Education: MA, Royal College of Art, 1975. Publications: Not to be Taken Seriously, 1982; A Step in the Wrong Direction, 1984; It's Funny When You Look at It, 1984; A Moment in Rhyme, 1987; What Would You Do With A Wobble-Dee-Woo?, 1988; I Brought My Love a Tabby Cat, 1988; Between the Sun, the Moon and Me, 1990; The Best of West, 1990; Long Tales, Short Tales and Tall Tales, 1995. Memberships: Children's Writers' Group, committee member; Society of Authors. Address: 14 High Road, Epping, Essex CM16 4AB, England.

WEST Cornel (Ronald), b. 2 June 1953, Tulsa, Oklahoma, USA. Professor of Afro-American Studies and the Philosophy of Religion; Writer. m. (1), div, 1 son, (2) div, (3) Elleni West. Education: AB, Harvard University, 1973; MA, 1975, PhD, 1980, Princeton University. Appointments: Assistant Professor of the Philosophy of Religion, Union Theological Seminary, New York City, 1977-83, 1988; Associate, Yale University Divinity School, 1984-87, University of Paris, 1987; Professor of Religion and Director of African American Studies, Princeton University, 1989-94; Professor of Afro-American Studies and the Philosophy of Religion, Harvard University, 1994-. Publications: Theology in the Americas: Detroit II Conference Papers (editor with Caridad Guidote and Margaret Coakley), 1982; Prophesy Deliverance!: An Afro-American Revolutionary Christianity, 1982; Post-Analytic Philosophy (with John Rajchman), 1985; Prophetic Fragments, 1988; The American Evasion of Philosophy: A Genealogy of Pragmatism, 1989; Breaking Bread: Insurgent Black Intellectual Life (with Bell Hooks), 1991; The Ethical

Dimensions of Marxist Thought, 1991; Out There: Marginalization and Contemporary Cultures (co-editor), 1991; Race Matters, 1993; Keeping Faith: Philosophy and Race in America, 1993; Beyond Eurocentrism and Multiculturalism, 1993. Contributions to: Newspapers and magazines. Address: c/o Harvard University, Cambridge, MA 02138, USA.

WEST Douglas. See: **TUBB E(dwin) C(harles).**

WEST Kathleene, b. 28 Dec 1947, Genoa, Nebraska, USA. Professor of English; Poet; Editor. Education: BA, 1967, PhD, 1986, University of Nebraska; MA, University of Washington, 1975. Appointments: Associate Professor of English, New Mexico State University, 1987-; Poetry Editor, Puerto del Sol, 1995-. Publications: Land Bound, 1977; Water Witching, 1984; Plainswoman, 1985; The Farmer's Daughter, 1990. Contributions to: Reviews, quarterlies, and journals. Honour: Fulbright Scholar, Iceland, 1983-85. Memberships: Associated Writing Programs; Barbara Pym Society; PEN. Address: c/o Department of English, Box 3001, New Mexico State University, Las Cruces, NM 88003, USA.

WEST Morris (Langlo), (Morris East, Julian Morris), b. 26 Apr 1916, Melbourne, Victoria, Australia. Author. m. Joyce Lawford, 1953, 3 sons, 1 daughter. Education: University of Melbourne. Publications: Gallows on the Sand, 1955; Kundu, 1956; Children of the Sun, 1957; The Crooked Road (English Title, The Big Story), 1957; The Concubine, 1958; Backlash (English Title, The Second Victory), 1958; The Devil's Advocate, 1959 (filmed 1977); The Naked Country, 1960; Daughter of Silence (novel and play), 1961; The Shoes of the Fisherman, 1963; The Ambassador, 1965; The Tower of Babel, 1968; The Heretic, a Play in Three Acts, 1970; Scandal in the Assembly (with Robert Francis), 1970; Summer of the Red Wolf, 1971; The Salamander, 1973; Harlequin, 1974; The Navigator, 1976; Proteus, 1979; The Clowns of God, 1981; The World is Made of Glass, 1983 (play 1984); Cassidy, 1986; Masterclass, 1988; Lazarus, 1990; The Lovers, 1993; Vanishing Point, 1996; A View from the Ridge, 1996; Images and Hand Inscriptions, 1997; Eminence, 1998. Honours: National Brotherhood Award, National Council of Christians and Jews, 1960; James Tait Black Memorial Prize, 1960; Royal Society of Literature, Heinemann Award, 1960; DLitt, Santa Clara University, 1969, Mercy College, New York, 1982, University of Western Sydney, 1993, Australian National University, 1995; Order of Australia, 1985; The Lloyd O'Neill Award, 1997. Memberships: Royal Society of Literature, fellow; World Academy of Arts and Science; Officer of the Order of Australia. Address: PO Box 102, Avalon, New South Wales 2107, Australia.

WEST Nigel, b. 8 Nov 1951, London, England. Historian. m. 15 June 1979, (Diss 1996), 1 son, 1 daughter. Education: University of Grenoble; University of Lille; London University. Appointments: BBC TV, 1977-82. Publications: A Matter of Trust: M15 1945-72, 1982; Unreliable Witness, 1984; Carbo M15, 1981, M16, 1983, 1985; GCHQ, 1986; Molehunt, 1986; The Friends, 1987; Games of Intelligence, 1990; Seven Spies who Changed the World, 1991; Secret War, 1992; The Illegals, 1993; Faber Book of Espionage, 1993; Faber Book of Treachery, 1995; Secret War for the Falklands, 1997; Crown Jewels, 1998; Counterfeit Spies, 1998; Venona, 1999. Contributions to: Times; Intelligence Quarterly. Honour: The Experts Expert, Observer, 1989. Address: Westintel Research Ltd, PO Box 2, Goring on Thames, Berkshire RG8 9SB, England.

WEST Owen. See: **KOONTZ Dean R(ay).**

WESTHEIMER David, (Z Z Smith), b. 11 Apr 1917, Houston, Texas, USA. Writer. m. Doris Rothstein Kahn, 9 Oct 1945, 2 sons. Education: BA, Rice Institute, Houston, 1937. Publications: Summer on the Water, 1948; The Magic Fallacy, 1950; Watching Out for Dulie, 1960; This Time Next Year, 1963; Von Ryan's Express, 1964; My Sweet Charlie, 1965; Song of the Young Sentry, 1968; Lighter Than a Feather, 1971; Over the Edge, 1972; Going Public, 1973; The Aulia Gold, 1974;

The Olmec Head, 1974; Von Ryan's Return, 1980; Rider on the Wind, 1984; Sitting it Out, 1992; Death Is Lighter Than A Feather (re-issue), 1995. Memberships: Authors Guild; PEN; California Writers Club; Retired Officers Association; Writers Guild of America West. Address: 11722 Darlington Avenue, No 2, Los Angeles, CA 90049, USA.

WESTON Carol, b. 11 Sept 1956, New York, New York, USA. Writer. m. Robert Ackerman, 28 Aug 1980, 2 daughters. Education: BA, Yale University, 1978; MA, Middlebury, 1979. Publications: Girltalk: All The Stuff Your Sister Never Told You; From Here to Maternity; For Girls Only: Wise Words, Good Advice. Contributions to: Redbook; Family Circle; Parents; Cosmopolitan. Literary Agent: Laura Blake Peterson, Curtis Brown. Address: 670 West End Avenue, Apt 2F, New York, NY 10025-7320, USA.

WESTON Corinne Comstock, b. 8 Dec 1919, Castle Hill, Maine, USA. Professor Emeritus; Historian. m. Arthur Weston, 17 Oct 1947. Education: BA, History, University of Maine, 1941; PhD, History, Columbia University, 1951. Appointments: Instructor, University of Maine, 1946-47, 1948-49; Lecturer, Columbia University, 1947-48, 1949-51; Assistant Professor to Professor, University of Houston, 1952-63; Associate Professor, Hunter College of the City University of New York, 1965-68; Professor, 1969-88, Professor Emeritus, 1988-, Herbert H Lehman College of the City University of New York. Publications: Cardinal Documents in British History, 1951; British Constitutional History Since 1832, 1957; English Constitutional Theory and the House of Lords, 1556-1832, 1965; Subjects and Sovereigns: The Grand Controversey Over Legal Sovereignty in Stuart England, 1981; The House of Lords and Ideological Politics, 1995. Contributions to: Scholarly publications. Honours: Phi Beta Kappa, 1941; Research Awards, City University of New York, 1979-88; National Endowment for the Humanities Research Travel Grant, 1986; Special Recognition for Original Research, Annales, University of Paris, 1986; John Frederick Lewis Award, American Philosophical Society, 1995. Memberships: American Historical Association; Royal Historical Society, UK, 1973-97. Address: 200 Central Park South, New York, NY 10019, USA.

WESTON Helen Gray. See: **DANIELS Dorothy.**

WESTRICK Elsie Margaret Beyer, b. 12 Nov 1910, Fort William, Ontario, Canada. Poet; Writer. m. Roswell G Westrick, 6 Oct 1945, 5 daughters, 2 stepsons, 1 stepdaughter. Education: Diploma, Institute of Childrens Literature, 1976; Diploma, Writing for Young People, 1985; Diploma, Writing Self Fiction, 1989, Writers Digest School. Publications: Poetry: On This Holy Night, 1949; Tender Foliage of Summer, 1972; The Photograph, 1975; Beauty on a Beach, 1983; Memories of Childhood, 1983; The Breath of Fall, 1986; Call of the Blue Jay, 1987; My Last Love, 1989; The Old Lighthouse, 1990; My Special Place, 1993; All We Hold Dear, 1996. Honours: Golden Poet Awards, 1985, 1986, Silver Poet Award, 1990, World of Poetry; Award for Poetic Achievement, 1988. Address: 3751 Wheeler Road, Snover, MI 48472, USA.

WEVILL David (Anthony), b. 15 Mar 1935, Yokohama, Japan. Lecturer; Poet. m. Assia Gutman, 1960. Education: BA, Caius College, Cambridge, 1957. Appointment: Lecturer, University of Texas, Austin. Publications: Penguin Modern Poets, 1963; Birth of a Spark, 1964; A Christ of the Ice Floes, 1966; Firebreak, 1971; Where the Arrow Falls, 1973; Other Names for the Heart: New and Selected Poems, 1964-84, 1985; Figures of Eight, 1987; Translator of Hungarian Poetry. Honour: Arts Council Prize and Bursaries. Address: Department of English, University of Texas at Austin, TX 78712, USA.

WHALEN Philip (Glenn), b. 20 Oct 1923, Portland, Oregon, USA. Poet; Novelist; Zen Buddhist Priest. Education: BA, Reed College, Portland, Oregon, 1951. Appointments: Writer, 1951-; Ordained Zen Buddhist Priest, 1973; Head Monk, Dharma Sangha, Santa Fe, New Mexico, 1984-87; Abbot, Hartford Street Zen Center,

San Francisco, 1987-96. Publications: Poetry: Three Satires, 1951; Self-Portrait from Another Direction, 1959; Memoirs of an Interglacial Age, 1960; Like I Say, 1960; Hymnus ad Patrem, 1963; Three Mornings, 1964; Monday in the Evening, 1964; Goddess, 1964; Every Day, 1965; Highgrade: Doodles, Poems, 1966; T/o, 1967; The Invention of the Letter: A Beastly Morality Being an Illuminated Moral History for the Edification of Younger Readers, 1967; Intransit: The Philip Whalen Issue, 1967; On Bear's Head, 1969; Severance Pay, 1970; Scenes of Life at the Capital, 1971; The Kindness of Strangers: Poems, 1969-74, 1976; Prolegomena to a Study of the Universe, 1976; Decompressions: Selected Poems, 1978; Enough Said: Poems 1974-1979, 1981; Heavy Breathing: Poems 1967-1980, 1983. Novels: You Didn't Even Try, 1967; Imaginary Speeches for a Brazen Head, 1971. Other: Off the Wall: Interviews with Philip Whalen, 1978; The Diamond Noodle, 1980. Contributions to: Anthologies and many periodicals. Honours: Poets Foundation Award, 1962; V K Ratcliff Award, 1964; American Academy of Arts and Letters Grants-in-Aid, 1965, 1991; Committee on Poetry Grants, 1968, 1970, 1971; Morton Dauwen Zabel Award for Poetry, 1986; Fund for Poetry Awards, 1987, 1991. Address: c/o Hartford Street Zen Center, 57 Hartford Street, San Francisco, CA 94114, USA.

WHALEN Terry Anthony, b. 1 Feb 1944, Halifax, Nova Scotia, Canada. Professor of English; Editor. m. Maryann Antonia Walters, 30 Feb 1966, 2 sons, 2 daughters. Education: BA, Honours, Saint Mary's University, 1965; MA, Honours, University of Melbourne, 1968; International Graduate Seminar Certificate, University of Oxford, 1970; PhD, University of Ottawa, 1980. Appointments: Tutor, University of Sydney, 1966, University of Melbourne, 1967; Lecturer, 1968-70, Assistant Professor, 1970-76, 1978-80, Associate Professor, 1981-85, Professor of English, 1985-, St Mary's University; Teaching Fellow, University of Ottawa, 1976-77; Editor, Atlantic Provinces Book Review, 1980-90; Adjunct Graduate Professor of English, Dalhousie University, 1996-. Publications: Philip Larkin and English Poetry, 1986, reprinted 1990; Bliss Carman and His Works, 1983; The Atlantic Anthology: Criticism (editor), 1985; Charles G D Roberts and His Works, 1989; Poutledge Encyclopaedia of Post-Colonial Literature in English (contributor), 1994. Contributions to: Books, journals and periodicals. Honours: British Commonwealth Scholarship, 1966-68; Election to Council Member Status, Writers' Federation of Nova Scotia; Grants: Canada Council; Social Sciences and Humanities Research Council of Canada; Canadian Federation for the Humanities. Memberships: Writers Federation of Nova Scotia; Association of Canadian University Teachers of English; Northeast Modern Language Association; Modern Language Association; Philip Larkin Society. Address: 26 Oceanview Drive, Purcells Cove, Halifax, Nova Scotia B3P 2H3, Canada.

WHALLON William, b. 24 Sept 1928, Richmond, Indiana, USA. Poet; Writer. Education: BA, McGill University, 1950. Appointments: Fellow, Center for Hellenic Studies, 1962; Fulbright Professor in Comparative Literature, University of Bayreuth, 1985. Publications: A Book of Time (poems), 1990; Giants in the Earth (editor), 1991; The Oresteia / Apollo and Bacchus (scenarios), 1997. Address: 1655 Walnut Heights, East Lansing, MI 48823, USA.

WHAM David Buffington Tennant, b. 25 May 1937, Evanston, Illinois, USA. Political Writer. m. Joan Field Wilber, 9 Mar 1972, 1 son, 1 daughter. Education: AB cum laude, Harvard University, 1959; AM, Southern Illinois University, 1967. Appointments: English Instructor, University of Wyoming, Powell, 1963-65; English Instructor, Southern Illinois University, 1965-67; Graduate Fellow, Georgetown University, 1967-69; Staffer to various Democrat Congressman; Speech Writer for Adlai Stevenson III, 1986, and Dawn Clark Netch, 1994, campaigns for Governor of Illinois. Publication: The Comic Genuflection, 1967. Contributions to: Woodwind; CPU Review; The Fair; Maelstrom; Charlatan; December; Pilgrimage; Others. Honours: 1st Prize for Fiction,

Maelstrom, 1968; 3rd Prize for Fiction, CPU Review, 1994. Literary Agent: Garard McCauley, New York City, USA. Address: 860 Hinman Avenue # 724, Evanston, IL 60202, USA.

WHEAR Roger Charles Stephen, b. 31 Dec 1941, Plymouth, Devon, England. Antique Renovator. m. Patricia Joyce Disley, 1 Aug 1970, div. Education: Technical Secondary School, 1953-57; HM Dockyard Technical College, 1957. Appointment: Member, Master Guild of Craftsmen, 1989-90. Publication: Your First Chinchilla, 1999. Contributions to: Newspapers and radio. Memberships: Waterfront Writers; Barbican. Address: 17 Lambhay Hill, Plymouth, Devon PL1 2NW, England.

WHEATCROFT John Stewart, b. 24 July 1925, Philadelphia, Pennsylvania, USA. Professor; Writer; Poet. m. (1) Joan Mitchell Osborne, 10 Nov 1952, div 1974, 2 sons, 1 daughter, (2) Katherine Whaley Warner, 14 Nov 1992. Education: BA, Bucknell University, 1949; MS, 1950, PhD, 1960, Rutgers University. Publications: Poetry: Death of a Clown, 1963; Prodigal Son, 1967; A Voice from the Hump, 1977; Ordering Demons, 1981; The Stare on the Donkey's Face, 1990; Random Necessities, (poetry), 1997. Novels: Edie Tells, 1975; Catherine, Her Book, 1983; The Beholder's Eye, 1987; Killer Swan, 1992. Other: Slow Exposures (stories), 1986; Our Other Voices (editor), 1991; Mother of All Loves, 1994; Trio with Four Players, 1995; The Education of Malcolm Palmer, (novel), 1997. Contributions to: Newspapers and magazines. Honours: Alcoa Playwriting Award, 1966; National Educational Television Award, 1967; Fellowships: Yaddo, 1972, 1985, MacDowell Colony, 1973, Virginia Center for the Creative Arts, 1976, 1978, 1980, 1982. Memberships: Poetry Society of America; PEN. Address: R R No 1, Box 5, Lewisburg, PA 17837, USA.

WHEELWRIGHT Julie Diana, b. 2 June 1960, Farnborough, Kent, England. Writer; Broadcaster. Education: BA, University of British Columbia; MA, University of Sussex. Appointments: Reporter, Vancouver Sun, 1980; President, Canadian University Press, 1981; Consultant, Open University, 1991. Publications: Amazons and Military Maids, 1989, 2nd edition, 1994; The Fatal Lover, 1992. Contributions to: Newspapers and journals. Honours: Canada Council Non-Fiction Writers Grants, 1990-91, 1994-95. Memberships: Writers Guild; Institute of Historical Research; Royal Holloway, University of London, honorary research fellow. Address: 5 Cleaver Street, London SE11 4DP, England.

WHELAN Peter, b. 3 Oct 1931, Newcastle-under-Lyme, England. Playwright. Education: Graduated, University of Keele, Staffordshire, 1955. Appointments: Advertising Copywriter and Director, 1959-90. Publications: Lakota (co-author), 1970; Double Edge (co-author), 1975; Captain Swing, 1978; The Accrington Pals, 1981; Clay, 1982; A Cold Wind Blowing Up (co-author), 1983; Worlds Apart, 1986; The Bright and Bold Design, 1991; The School of Night, 1992. Honours: Writers Guild Best Play Nominations. Address: c/o Lemon, Unna, and Durbridge, 24 Pottery Lane, Holland Park, London W11 4LZ, England.

WHETTER James Charles Arthur, b. 20 Sept 1935, Gorran, Cornwall. Self-employed Businessman. m. Louise Vercoe, 24 Feb 1977, div 1991, 2 daughters. Education: BA Honours, University of Birmingham, 1957; London School of Economics, 1957-60; PhD, London University, 1965. Appointments: Editor, The Cornish Banner/An Baner Kernewek, 1975-; Director, The Roseland Institute, Gorran, 1991-. Publications: Cornwall in the 17th Century: A Study in Economic History, 1974; The History of Falmouth, 1981; The History of Glasney College, 1987; Cornish Weather and Cornish People in the 17th Century, 1991; The Bodrugans: A Study of a Medieval Cornish Knightly Family, 1995; Cornwall in the 13th Century: A Study in Social and Economic History, 1998. Contributions to: Journal of the Royal Institution of Cornwall; Old Cornwall; Western Morning News; The Cornish Banner. Honour: Bard of the Cornish Gorseth, 1966. Membership: West Country Writers' Association.

Address: The Roseland Institute, Gorran, St Austell, Cornwall.

WHETTON Peter, b. 30 Nov 1939, Manchester, England. Natural Therapist; Teacher. m. Maureen, 28 Dec 1965, 1 son. Publications: Can You Cope, 1978; Getting a Job, 1979; In the Job, 1979; Enhanced Eduk Brain Gym, 1985; Lifetime Learning for Pre-Schoolers, 1990; Accelerated Learning, 1992; Partners in Responsible Behaviour, 1993. Contributions to: Times Educational Supplement; SIT Journal; Special Education. Membership: Australian Society of Authors. Address: PO Box 343, Clarendon, 5157, Australia.

WHISTLER (Alan Charles) Laurence, b. 21 Jan 1912, Eltham, Kent, England. Poet; Writer; Glass Engraver. m. (1) Jill Furse, 1939, dec 1944, 1 son, 1 daughter, (2) Theresa, 1950, div 1986, 1 son, 1 daughter, (3) Carol Dawson, 1987, div 1991. Education: BA, Balliol College, Oxford, 1934; MA, 1985. Appointments: Various exhibitions of glass engravings. Publications: Poetry: Children of Hertha and Other Poems, 1929; Armed October and Other Poems, 1932; Four Walls, 1934; The Emperor Heart, 1936; The Burning Glass, 1941; Who Live in Unity, 1944; The World's Room: The Collected Poems of Laurence Whistler, 1949; The View From This Window, 1956; Audible Silence, 1961; Fingal's Cave, 1963; To Celebrate Her Living, 1967; For Example: Ten Sonnets in Sequence to a New Pattern, 1969; A Bridge on the Usk, 1976; Enter, 1987. Other: Sir John Vanbrugh: Architect and Dramatist, 1664-1726, 1938; Rex Whistler, 1905-1944: His Life and His Drawings, 1948; The Engraved Glass of Laurence Whistler, 1952; Rex Whistler: The Königsmark Drawings, 1952; The Imagination of Vanbrugh and his Fellow Artists, 1954; The Work of Rex Whistler (with Ronald Fuller), 1960; The Initials in the Heart: The Story of a Marriage, 1964, revised edition, 1975; Pictures on Glass, 1972; The Image on the Glass, 1975; Scenes and Signs on Glass, 1985; The Laughter and the Urn: The Life of Rex Whistler, 1985; Point Engraving on Glass, 1992. Honours: 1st King's Gold Medal for Poetry, 1935; Atlantic Award for Literature, 1945; Officer, 1955, Commander, 1973, of the Order of the British Empire; Honorary Fellow, Balliol College, Oxford, 1973; Honorary DLitt, Oxon, 1993. Membership: Guild of Glass Engravers, 1st president, 1975-80. Address: Scriber's Cottage, High Street, Watlington, Oxford OX9 5PY, England.

WHITAKER Kati, b. Essex, England. Radio and Television Journalist and Presenter. m. Andrew Hughes, 27 July 1989, 2 daughters. Education: BA Honours, PPE, Somerville College, Oxford University; College of Law, Lancaster Gate. Appointments: Freelance Radio and TV Presenter including: Presenter, de Susar, 1986-95; Presenter, Reporter, Radio 4 and World Services documentaries, 1990-98; Freelance Reporter, BBC Breakfast News. Honour: Silver Award for Best Radio Feature, Medical Journalists Association, 1995. Address: 5 Wilkinson Street, London SW8 1DD, England.

WHITBY Sharon. See: **PETERS Maureen**.

WHITE Edmund (Valentine III), b. 13 Jan 1940, Cincinnati, Ohio, USA. Writer. Education: BA, University of Michigan, 1962. Appointments: Writer, Time-Life Books, New York City, 1962-70; Senior Editor, Saturday Review, New York City, 1972-73; Assistant Professor of Writing Seminars, Johns Hopkins University, 1977-79; Adjunct Professor, Columbia University School of the Arts, 1981-83; Executive Director, New York Institute for the Humanities, 1982-83; Professor, Brown University, 1990-92; Professor, Princeton, 1999. Publications: Fiction: Forgetting Elena, 1973; Nocturnes for the King of Naples, 1978; A Boy's Own Story, 1982; Aphrodisiac (with others), stories, 1984; Caracole, 1985; The Darker Proof: Stories from a Crisis (with Adam Mars-Jones), 1987; The Beautiful Room is Empty, 1988; Skinned Alive, stories, 1995; The Farewell Symphony, 1997. Non-Fiction: The Joy of Gay Sex: An Intimate Guide for Gay Men to the Pleasures of a Gay Lifestyle (with Charles Silverstein), 1977; States of Desire: Travels in Gay America, 1980; The Faber Book of Gay Short Fiction

(editor), 1991; Genet: A Biography, 1993; The Selected Writings of Jean Genet (editor), 1993; The Burning Library, essays, 1994; Our Paris, 1995; Proust, 1998. Contributions to: Many periodicals. Honours: Ingram Merrill Foundation Grants, 1973, 1978; Guggenheim Fellowship, 1983; American Academy and Institute of Arts and Letters Award, 1983; Chevalier de l'ordre des arts et lettres, France, 1993. Address: c/o Maxine Groffsky Literary Agency, 2 Fifth Avenue, New York, NY 10011, USA.

WHITE Gillian Mary, b. 13 Jan 1936, Essex, England. Retired University Professor. m. Colin A Fraser, 1 Apr 1978. Education: LLB, 1957; PhD, 1960; Barrister, Grays Inn, 1960. Appointment: Professor of Law, University of Manchester. Publications: The Use of Experts by International Tribunals, 1965; Principles of International Economic Law, 1988; International Economic Law and Developing States, 1992; International Law in Transition, 1992; Good Faith, 1994. Memberships: British Institute of International and Comparative Law; International Law Association; American Society of International Law; Royal Society of Arts. Address: c/o Faculty of Law, University of Manchester, Manchester M13 9PL.

WHITE Henry Maxwell, b. 13 Feb 1923, Oldbury, Worcestershire, England. Medical Practitioner. m. 23 June 1951, 1 son, 1 daughter. Education: MB ChB, University of Leeds; MRCS (Engl); LRCP (Eng). Appointments: Senior House Officer, Pontefract, Leeds and Birmingham; Captain, Royal Army Medical Corps, 1948-49; Principal, General Practice, Bromsgrove, 1951-88; Visiting Medical Officer, Department of Geriatrics, Bromsgrove, 1951-82; Casualty Officer, Accident and Emergency Department, Bromsgrove, 1951-88. Publications: Journal articles: On Geriatric Medicine, 1960; On Sir Arthur Thompson, 1995; The Leeds Tram Strike of 1946, 1996; Others: An Affinity with Gustav Mahler, chapter author, 1996, revised as monograph The Two Gustavs - Mahler and Holst, 1999; Start of the National Health Service - 5/7/48, 1998; The National Health Service - 50 Years On, 2 chapters and editor, 1999; An Affinity with Gustav Mahler, 1999. Memberships: General Practitioner Writers Association; J B Priestley Society, Bradford. Address: 7 Marlborough Avenue, Bromsgrove, Worcestershire B60 2PG, England.

WHITE John Austin, b. 27 June 1942, England. Canon; Writer; Poet. Educationi: BA, Honours, University of Hull; College of the Resurrection, Mirfield. Appointments: Assistant Curate, St Aidan's Church, Leeds, 1966-69; Assistant Chaplain, University of Leeds, 1969-73; Assistant Director, Post Ordination Training, Dioceses of Ripon, 1970-73; Chaplain, Northern Ordination Course, 1973-82; Canon of Windsor, 1982-. Publications: A Necessary End: Attitudes to Death (with Julia Neuberger), 1991; Nicholas Ferrar: Materials for a Life (with L R Muir), 1997. Contributions to: Various publications. Address: 8 The Cloisters, Windsor Castle, Berkshire SL4 1NJ, England.

WHITE Jon (Ewbank) Manchip, b. 22 June 1924, Cardiff, Glamorganshire, Wales. Writer; Poet; Retired Professor of English. m. Valerie Leighton, 2 children. Education: St Catharine's College, Cambridge, 1942-43, 1946-50; Open Exhibitioner in English Literature; MA, Honours, English, Prehistoric Archaeology, and Oriental Languages (Egyptology), and University Diploma in Anthropology. Appointments: Story Editor, BBC-TV, London, 1950-51; Senior Executive Officer, British Foreign Service, 1952-56; Independent Author, 1956-67, including a period as screenwriter for Samuel Bronston Productions, Paris and Madrid, 1960-64; Professor of English, University of Texas, El Paso, 1967-77; Lindsay Young Professor of English, University of Tennessee, Knoxville, 1977-94. Publications: Novels: Mask of Dust, 1953; Build Us a Dam, 1955; The Girl from Indiana, 1956; No Home But Heaven, 1957; The Mercenaries, 1958; Hour of the Rat, 1962; The Rose in the Brandy Glass, 1965; Nightclimber, 1968; The Game of Troy, 1971; The Garden Game, 1973; Send for Mr Robinson, 1974; The Moscow Papers, 1979; Death by Dreaming, 1981; The Last Grand Master, 1985; Whistling Past the Churchyard,

1992. Poetry: Dragon and Other Poems, 1943; Salamander and Other Poems, 1945; The Rout of San Romano, 1952; The Mountain Lion, 1971. Other: Ancient Egypt, 1952; Anthropology, 1954; Marshal of France: The Life and Times of Maurice, Comte de Saxe, 1962; Everyday Life in Ancient Egypt, 1964; Diego Velázquez, Painter and Courtier, 1969; The Land God Made in Anger: Reflections on a Journey Through South West Africa, 1969; Cortés and the Downfall of the Aztec Empire, 1971; A World Elsewhere: One Man's Fascination with the American Southwest, 1975; Everyday Life of the North American Indians, 1979; What to do When the Russians Come: A Survivors' Handbook (with Robert Conquest), 1984; The Journeying Boy: Scenes from a Welsh Childhood, 1991. Memberships: Texas Institute of Letters, 1970; Honorary, Phi Beta Kappa, 1992; Welsh Academy, 1995. Address: 5620 Pinellas Drive, Knoxville, TN 37919, USA.

WHITE Kenneth, b. 28 Apr 1936, Glasgow, Scotland. Professor of 20th Century Poetics; Poet; Writer. m. Marie Claude Charfut. Education: MA, University of Glasgow, 1959; University of Munich; University of Paris. Appointments: Lecturer in English, Institut Charles V, Paris, 1969-83; Professor of 20th Century Poetics, Sorbonne, University of Paris, 1983-. Publications: Poetry: Wild Coal, 1963; En Toute Candeur, 1964; The Cold Wind of Dawn, 1966; The Most Difficult Area, 1968; A Walk Along the Shore, 1977; Mahamudra, 1979; Le Grand Rivage, 1980; Terre de diament, 1983; Atlantica: Mouvements et meditations, 1986; L'esprit nomade, 1987; The Bird Bath: Collected Longer Poems, 1989; Handbook for the Diamond Country: Collected Shorter Poems 1960-1990, 1990. Fiction: Letters from Gourgounel, 1966; Les Limbes Incandescents, 1978; Le Visage du vent d'Est, 1980; La Route Bleue, 1983; Travels in the Drifting Dawn, 1989; Pilgrim of the Viod, 1994. Other: Essays. Contributions to: Various publications. Honour: Grand Prix de Rayonnement, French Academy, 1985. Address: Gwenved, Chemin du Goaquer, 22560 Trebeurden, France.

WHITE Robert Rankin, b. 8 Feb 1942, Houston, Texas, USA. Historian; Writer. Education: BA, Geology, University of Texas, Austin, 1964; MS, Hydrology, University of Arizona, 1971; PhD, American Studies, University of New Mexico, 1993. Publications: The Lithographs and Etchings of E Martin Hennings, 1978; The Taos Society of Artists, 1983; Bert Geer Phillips and the Taos Art Colony (co-author), 1994. Contributions to: Journals and periodicals. Memberships: New Mexico Book League, president, 1994, executive director, 1996-; First Friday; Historical Society of New Mexico, president, 1991-93. Address: 1409 Las Lomas Road North East, Albuquerque, NM 87106, USA.

WHITE W(illiam) Robin(son), b. 12 July 1928, Kodaikanal, South India. Author; Poet. m. Marian Biesterfeld, 3 Feb 1948, Dec 8 Mar 1983, 2 sons, 1 daughter. Education: BA, Yale University, 1950; Bread Loaf Fellow, Middlebury College, 1956; Stegner Creative Writing Fellow, Stanford University, 1956-57; MA, California State Polytechnic University, 1991. Appointments: Editor-in-Chief, Per-Se International Quarterly, Stanford University Press, 1965-69; Instructor, Photojournalism, 1973, Director, Creative Writing Seminar, 1984, Mendocino Art Center; Lecturer, Scripps College, 1984; Fiction Editor, West-word literary magazine, 1985-90; Instructor, University of California, Los Angeles, 1985-; Research Reader, The Huntington Library, 1985-86; Lecturer, Writing Programme and CompuWrite, California State Polytechnic University, 1985-93. Publications: House of Many Rooms, 1958; Elephant Hill, 1959; Men and Angels, 1961; Foreign Soil, 1962; All In Favor Say No, 1964; His Own Kind, 1967; Be Not Afraid, 1972; The Special Child, 1978; The Troll of Crazy Mule Camp, 1979; Moses the Man, 1981; The Winning Writer, 1997. Contributions to: Journals and magazines. Honours: Harper Prize, 1959; O Henry Prize, 1960; Coordinating Council of Literary Magazines Award, 1968; Distinguished Achievement Award, Educational Press, 1974; Spring Harvest Poetry Awards, 1992, 1994, 1995. Memberships: Authors Guild; California State Poetry Society. Address: 1940 Fletcher Avenue, South Pasadena, CA 91030, USA.

WHITEHORN Katharine (Elizabeth), b. 2 Mar 1928, London, England. Writer. Education: MA, Newham College, London, 1950; Graduate Studies, Cornell University, Ithaca, New York, 1954-55. Appointments: Staff, Picture Post, London, 1956-57, Womans Own, London, 1958, Spectator, 1959-61; Fashion Editor, 1960-63, Columnist, 1963-96, The Observer; Board Member, British Airports Authority, 1972-77; Nationwide Building Society, 1983-91; Rector, St Andrews University, 1982-85. Publications: Cooking in a Bedsitter, 1960; Roundabout, 1961; Only on Sundays, 1966; Whitehorn's Social Survival, 1968; Observations, 1970; How to Survive in Hospital, 1972; How to Survive Children, 1975; How to Survive in the Kitchen, 1979; How to Survive Your Money Problems, 1983; View from a Column, 1991. Contributions to: Newspapers and magazines. Honours: LlD, St Andrews, 1985. Address: 14 Provost Road, London NW3 4ST, England.

WHITEHOUSE David Bryn, b. 15 Oct 1941, Worksop, England. Writer; Editor. Education: BA, 1963, MA, 1964, PhD, 1967, University of Cambridge. Appointments: Correspondent, Archeologia Medievale; Editor, Journal of Glass Studies, 1988-; Advisory Editor, American Early Medieval Studies, 1991-; Advisory Board, Encyclopedia of Islamic Archaeology, 1991. Publications: Author: Glass of the Roman Empire, 1988; Glass: A Pocket Dictionary, 1993; English Cameo Glass, 1994. Co-Author: Archaeological Atlas of the World, 1975; Aspects of Medieval Lazio, 1982; Mohammed, Charlemagne and the Origins of Europe, 1983; Glass of the Caesars, 1987; The Portland Vase, 1990; Treasures from the Corning Museum of Glass, 1992; Roman Glass in The Corning Museum of Glass, Vol 1, 1997; Excavations at Ed-Dur, Vol 1, The Glass vessels, 1998. Contributions to: Books, journals, and other publications. Memberships: Accademia Fiorentina delle Arti del Disegno; International Association for the History of Glass, president, 1991-94; Keats-Shelley Memorial Association, Rome, president, 1982-83; Pontificia Accademia Romana di Archeologia; Royal Geographical Society; Society of Antiquaries of London; Unione Internazione degli istituti di Archeologia, Storia e Storia dell'Arte in Roma, president, 1980-81. Address: c/o Corning Museum of Glass, One Museum Way, Corning, NY 14830, USA.

WHITESIDE Lesley, b. 13 May 1945, County Down, Ireland. Historian; Writer. m. Robert Whiteside, 14 Aug 1968, 1 son, 2 daughters. Education: BA, Moderatorship, History and Political Science, Trinity College, Dublin, 1967; Diploma in Palaeography and Administration of Archives, Liverpool, 1968; DipEd, National University of Ireland, 1972; MA, Trinity College, Dublin, 1972. Appointments: Assistant Keeper of Manuscripts, Trinity College, Dublin, 1968-69; Archivist, The King's Hospital, Dublin, 1969-. Publications: A History of The King's Hospital, 1975, 2nd edition, 1985; George Otto Simms, A Biography, 1990; In Search of Columba, 1997; St Patrick in Stained Glass, 1998; the Book of Saints, 1998. Address: The Meadows, Marlinstown, Mullingar, County Westmeath, Ireland.

WHITFIELD Stephen J(ack), b. 3 Dec 1942, Houston, Texas, USA. Professor; Historian. m. Lee Cone Hall, 15 Dec 1984. Education: BA, Tulane University, 1964; MA, Yale University, 1966; PhD, Brandeis University, 1972. Appointments: Instructor, Southern University of New Orleans, 1966-68; Assistant Professor, 1972-75, Associate Professor, 1979-85, Professor, 1985-, Chair, Department of American Studies, 1986-88, 1994-96, Brandeis University; Fulbright Visiting Professor, Hebrew University of Jerusalem, 1983-84, Catholic University of Leuven, Belgium, 1993; Visiting Professor, University of Paris IV, 1994, 1998. Publications: Scott Nearing: Apostle of American Radicalism, 1974; Into the Dark: Hannah Arendt and Totalitarianism, 1980; Voices of Jacob, Hands of Esau: Jews in American Life and Thought, 1984; A Critical American: The Politics of Dwight Macdonald, 1984; A Death in the Delta: The Story of Emmett Till, 1988; American Space, Jewish Time, 1988; The Culture of the Cold War, 1991, 2nd edition, 1996. Contributions to: Scholarly journals. Honours: Kayden Prize, University of Colorado, 1981; Outstanding Academic Book Citation, Choice, 1985; Merit of Distinction, International Center for Holocaust Studies of the Anti-Defamation League of B'ani B'rith, 1987; Outstanding Book Citations, Gustavus Myers Center for the Study of Human Rights, 1989, 1992; Rockefeller Foundation Fellow, Bellagio, Italy, 1991; Louis D Brandeis Prize for Excellence in Teaching, 1993. Memberships: American Jewish Historical Society. Address: c/o Department of American Studies, Brandeis University, Waltham, MA 02254, USA.

WHITMAN Ruth (Bashein), b. 28 May 1922, New York, New York, USA. Poet; Editor; Translator; Teacher. m. (1) Cedric Whitman, 13 Oct 1941, div 1958, 2 daughters, (2) Firman Houghton, 23 July 1959, div 1964, 1 son, (3) Morton Sacks, 6 Oct 1966. Education: BA, Radcliffe College, 1944; MA, Harvard University, 1947. Appointments: Editorial Assistant, 1941-42, Educational Editor, 1944-45, Houghton Mifflin Co, Boston; Freelance Editor, Harvard University Press, 1945-60; Poetry Editor, Audience magazine, 1958-63; Director, Poetry Workshop, Cambridge Center for Adult Education, 1964-68, Poetry in the Schools Program, Massachusetts on the Arts, 1970-73; Scholar-in-Residence, Radcliffe Institute, 1968-70; Instructor in Poetry, Radcliffe College, 1970-, Harvard University Writing Program, 1979-84; Writer-in-Residence and Visiting Lecturer at various colleges and universities; Many poetry readings. Publications: Blood and Milk Poems, 1963; Alain Bosquet: Selected Poems (translator with others), 1963; Isaac Bashevis Singer: The Seance (translator with others), 1968; The Marriage Wig, and Other Poems, 1968; The Selected Poems of Jacob Glatstein (editor and translator), 1972; The Passion of Lizzie Borden: New and Selected Poems, 1973; Poemaking: Poets in Classrooms (editor), 1975; Tamsen Donner: A Woman's Journey, 1975; Permanent Address: New Poems, 1973-1980, 1980; Becoming a Poet: Source, Process, and Practice, 1982; The Testing of Hanna Senesh, 1986; The Fiddle Rose: Selected Poems of Abraham Sutzkever (translator), 1989; Laughing Gas: Poems New and Selected, 1963-1990, 1991; Hatsheput, Speak to Me, 1992. Contributions to: Anthologies and periodicals. Honours: MacDowell Colony Fellowships, 1962, 1964, 1972-74, 1979, 1982; Kovner Award, Jewish Book Council of America, 1969; Guiness International Poetry Award, 1973; National Endowment for the Arts Grant, 1974-75; John Masefield Award, 1976; Senior Fulbright Fellowship, 1984-85; Urbanarts Award, 1987; Phi Beta Kappa. Memberships: Authors Guild; Authors League of America; New England Poetry Club; PEN; Poetry Society of America. Address: 40 Tuckerman Avenue, Middletown, RI 02840, USA.

WHITNEY Donald Stephen, b. 14 Feb 1954, Memphis, Tennessee, USA. Professor; Speaker; Writer. m. Caffy Irene Cox, 8 Jan 1977, 1 daughter. Education: BA, Arkansas State University, 1975; University of Arkansas School of Law, 1975-76; MDiv, Southwestern Baptist Theological Seminary, 1979; DMiv, Trinity Evangelical Divinity School, 1987. Appointments: Associate Pastor, Pioneer Drive Baptist Church, Irving, Texcas, 1977-79; Pastor, Cedar Grove Baptist Church, Arkadelphia, 1980-81; Pastor, Glenfield Baptist Church, Glen Ellyn, Illinois, 1981-95; Assistant Professor of Spiritual Formation, Midwestern Baptist Theological Seminary, Kansas City, 1995-. Publications: Spiritual Disciplines for the Christian Life, 1991; Study Guide, 1994; How Can I Be Sure I'm A Christian, 1994; Spiritual Disciplines Within The Church, 1996. Contributions to: Discipleship Journal; Home Life; Decision; Founders Journal; Reformation and Reform Journal; Revival Commentary. Address: c/o Midwestern Baptist Theological Seminary, 5001 North Oak Trly, Kansas City, MO 64118-4620, USA.

WHITTEN Leslie H(unter) Jr, b. 21 Feb 1928, Jacksonville, Florida, USA. Writer; Journalist. m. Phyllis Webber, 11 Nov 1951, 3 sons, 1 daughter. Education: BA, English and Journalism, Lehigh University. Publications: Progeny of the Adder, 1965; Moon of the

Wolf, 1967; Pinion, The Golden Eagle, 1968; The Abyss, 1970; F Lee Bailey, 1971; The Alchemist, 1973; Conflict of Interest, 1976; Washington Cycle (poems), 1979; Sometimes a Hero, 1979; A Killing Pace, 1983; A Day Without Sunshine, 1985; The Lost Disciple, 1989; The Fangs of Morning, 1994; Sad Madrigms, 1997. Contributions to: Newspapers and literary magazines. Honours: Doctor, Humane Letters, Lehigh University, 1989; Journalistic Awards; Edgerton Award, American Civil Liberties Union. Address: 114 Eastmoor Drive, Sliver Spring, MD 20901, USA.

WHITTEN Norman E(arl) Jr,b. 23 May 1937, Orange, New Jersey, USA. Professor of Anthropology; Writer. m. Dorothea S Whitten, 4 Aug 1962. Education: BA, Colgate University, 1959; MA, 1961, PhD, 1964, University of North Carolina, Chapel Hill. Appointments: Associate Professor, 1970-73, Professor of Anthropology, 1973-, Scholar, 1992-, University of Illinois; Editor, Boletin de Antropologia Ecuatoriana, 1973-76, Anthropology Newsletter, Latin American Anthropology Group, 1973-76, American Ethnologist, 1979-84. Publications: Class Kinship and Power in an Ecuadorian Town, 1965; Afro-American Anthropology (editor), 1970; Sacha Runa: Ethnicity and Adaptation of Ecuadorian Jungle Quichua, 1976; Cultural Transformations and Ethnicity in Modern Ecuador (editor), 1981; Amazonia Ecuatoria, La Otro Cara del Progreso, 1981; BlackFrontiersmen: Afro-Hispanic Culture of Ecuador and Colombia, 1985; Sicuanga Runa: The Other Side of Development in Amazonian Ecuador, 1985; Art, Knowledge and Health (with Dorothea S Whitten), 1985; From Myth to Creation: Art from Amazonian Ecuador (with Dorothea S Whitten), 1988; Pioneros Negros: La Cultura Afro-Latinoamericana del Ecuador y de Colombia, 1992; Imagery and Creativity: Ethnoaesthetics and Art Worlds in the Americas (with Dorothea S Whitten), 1993; Transformaciones Culturales y Etnicidad en la Sierra Ecuatoriana, 1993; Return of the Yumbo (with Dorothea S Whitten and Alfonso Chango), 1997; Blackness in Latin America and the Caribbean (2 Vols, editor), 1998. Contributions to: Professional journals. Honours: Author's Award in Anthropology, New Jersey Teachers Association, 1966; Society of Sigma Xi. Memberships: American Anthropological Association, 1975-78, Representative to American Association for the Advancement of Science, executive board, 1990-95; American Ethnological Association, executive board 1980-84; Latin American Studies Association, executive board, 1983-87; Society of Cultural Anthropology; Royal Anthropological Institute. Address: 507 Harding Drive, Urbana, IL 61801, USA.

WHITTINGTON Peter. See: **MACKAY James Alexander.**

WHYTE Donald, (Sennachie), b. 13 Mar 1926, Newbattle Paris, Mid Lothian. Retired Professional Genealogist. m. Mary Burton, 3 Aug 1950, 3 daughters. Education: Institute of Heraldic & Genealogical Studies, Canterbury, Kent; Fellow, Society of Genealogists, 1982. Appointments: Agricultural & Horticultural Work, 1940-60; Professional Genealogist, 1960-77; Consultant Genealogist, 1978-98; Member, Kirkliston & Avonchburgh District Council, 1964-75, Chairman, 1970-73. Publications: Kirliston: A Short Parish History, 1956; Bathgate Hills Country Park, 1974; Introducing Scottish Genealogical Research, 1979; A Dictionary of Scottish Emigrants to the USA (pre 1855), 2 vols, 1972, 1986; A Dictionary of Scottish Emigrants to Canada Before Confederation, 2 vols, 1986, 1995; The Scots Overseas: A Bibliography, 1995; Walter MacFarlane Glen Chief & Antiquary, 1988. Contributions to: Academic journals. Honour: Licentiate in Heraldry and Genealogy, 1972. Membership: President, Association of Scottish Genealogists & Record Agents: Vice President, Scottish Genealogy Society. Address: 4 Carmel Road, Kirliston, EH29 9DD, Scotland.

WHYTE George. Education: Universities of London and Paris; Musical: Piano and Composition. Career: Executive posts, arts-related, 1955-75; Founder member, Artur Rubinstein Piano Competition; Chairman and Board Member, numerous music festivals; Chairman, British National Export Council Arts Committee; Producer, Holocaust Concert, Royal Opera House; Advisor, opera and dance productions in Berlin, Vienna, Washington and New York; Currently, Chairman, Dreyfus Society for Human Rights; Subject of television and radio documentaries: Odyssey of George Whyte, J'Accuse, Germany, France, Hungary, Finland, Sweden and Canada; Exhibition, J'Accuse, throughout Germany, Basel and New York. Publications: Set for Enterprise (study for Royal Opera House), 1986; The Holocaust: A Commemoration in Music, 1988; AJIOM: book, text and lyrics for music drama, 1992; Dreyfus (drama in 2 acts), 1993; Rage and Outrage (English and French), 1993; The Dreyfus Affair (libretto for opera in English and German), 1994; L'Affaire en chanson, 1994; Dreyfus-J'Accuse scenario, 1994; Un Bilan du centenaire de l'Affaire Dreyfus, 1995; La Chanson: Le Tournant du Siècle, 1995; The Accused: The Dreyfus Trilogy, 1996; Madeleine (book and lyrics), 1997; Encyclopedia of the Dreyfus Affair, forthcoming; Cabaret in Exile, forthcoming; Is Dreyfus Free?, forthcoming. Contributions to: the Dreyfus Centenary Bulletin; From Berlin to Broadway (Die Zeit); Opera at the Crossroads (Deutsch Oper); The Price of Illusion (Revue Juive Geneva); Opera Truth and Ethics. Membership: Society of Authors. Address: Coda Editions, Suite 23a, 78 Buckingham Gate, London SW1E 6PD, England.

WHYTE Sally C, (Sarah Nathan-Davis), b. 31 Jan 1931, London, England. International Arts Correspondent. m. George R Whyte, 1 daughter. Appointments: Arts Consultant and Administration, UK, Germany, USA, Israel, 1970-; Member, Editorial Board, The Dreyfus Trilogy, 1994; Literary Translator, Arte, Channel 4, Rage and Outrage, 1994. Publications: Essays in International Dictionary of Opera; Essays in International Dictionary of Ballet, 1993; Biographical entries in Encyclopaedia Judaica Decennial Book, 1996; Theresienstadt - music of the Holocaust, article, 1999. Contributions to: Tribune de Génève; Die Welt, Berlin; Arts Review; Ha'Aretz newspaper, Israel; Dance Magazine, New York; Music in the Media IMZ; Programme notes; Others. Memberships: Conseil Internationale de la Dance, UNESCO; Association Internationale Critiques d'Art; UNESCO. Literary Agent: Artial UK. Address: c/o Suite 23a, 78 Buckingham Gate, London SW1E 6PD, England.

WIATER Stanley, b. 21 May 1953, Northampton, Massachusetts, USA. Author; Editor. m. Iris D Arroyo, 21 Sept 1985, 1 daughter. Education: BA, magna cum laude, University of Massachusetts, Amherst, 1975. Publications: Night Visions 7 (editor), 1989; Dark Dreamers: Conversations with the Masters of Horror, 1990; The Official Teenage Mutant Ninja Turtles Treasury, 1991; Dark Visions: Conversations with the Masters of the Horror Film, 1992; After the Darkness (editor), 1993; Comic Book Rebels: Conversations with the Creators of the New Comics (with Stephen R Bissette), 1993. Contributions to: Fangoria; Fear; New Blood; Horrorstruck; Twilight Zone Magazine; Cemetery Dance. Honour: Bram Stoker Award for Superior Achievement in Non-Fiction, 1991. Memberships: Horror Writers Association, 1984; National Writers Union, 1990. Address: c/o Tal Literary Agency, PO Box 1837, Leesburg, VA 20177, USA.

WICKER Thomas (Grey), b. 18 June 1926, Hamlet, North Carolina, USA. Retired Journalist; Author. m. (1) Neva Jewett McLean, 20 Aug 1949, div 1973, 1 sons, 1 daughter. (2) Pamela Abel Hill, 9 Mar 1974. Education: AB, Journalism, University of North Carolina, 1948. Appointments: Executive Director, Southern Pines Chamber of Commerce, North Carolina, 1948-49; Editor, Sandhill Citizen, Aberdeen, North Carolina, 1949; Managing Editor, The Robesonian, Lumberton, North Carolina, 1949-50; Public Information Director, North Carolina Board of Public Welfare, 1950-51; Copy Editor, 1951-52, Sports Editor, 1954-55, Sunday Feature Editor, 1955-56, Washington Correspondent, 1957, Editorial Writer and City Hall Correspondent, 1958-59, Winston-Salem Journal, North Carolina; Associate Editor, Nashville Tennessean, 1959-60; Staff, 1960-71, and Chief, 1964-68, Washington Bureau, Columnist, 1966-91, Associate Editor, 1968-85, The New York Times. Publications: Non-Fiction: Kennedy Without Tears, 1964; JFK and LBJ: The Influence of Personality upon Politics, 1968; A Time to Die, 1975; On Press, 1978; One of Us: Richard Nixon and the American Dream, 1991; Tragic Failure: Racial Integration in America, 1996. Fiction: The Kingpin, 1953; The Devil Must, 1957; The Judgment, 1961; Facing the Lions, 1973; Unto This Hour, 1984; Donovan's Wife, 1992; Easter Lilly: A Novel of the South Today, 1998. Honours: Nieman Fellow, 1957-58, Fellow, Joan Shorenstein Barone Center on the Press, Politics, and Public Policy, 1993, Harvard University; Visiting Scholar, First Amendment Center, 1998. Memberships: Century Association; Society of American Historians; Society of Nieman Fellows; Writers Guild of America East. Address: Austin Hill Farm, Rochester, VT 05767, USA.

WICKERT Erwin, b. 7 Jan 1915, Bralitz, Germany. Author; Retired Ambassador. m. Ingelborg Weides, 2 Oct 1939, 2 sons, 1 daughter. Education: Friedrich Wilhelm University, Berlin, 1934-35; BA, Dickinson College, 1936; PhD, University of Heidelberg, 1939. Publications: Der Auftrag des Himmels, 1961; Der Purpur, 1966; Mut und Ubermut, 1981; China von innen gesehen, 1982; Der verlassene Tempel, 1985; Der Kaiser und der Grosshistoriker, 1987; Zappas oder die Wiedeckehr des Herrn, 1995; John Rabe: der gute Mensch von Nanking (editor), 1997. Contributions to: Frankfurter Allgemeine Zeitung; Die Welt. Honours: Radio Play Award, 1952; Grosses Bundesverdienstkreuz, 1979; State Prize of Literature. Memberships: PEN, 1963-95; Academy of Science and Literature. Address: Rheinhöhenweg 22, Oberwinter, D 53424 Remagen, Germany.

WICKHAM Glynne, (William Gladstone), b. 15 May 1922, Capetown, South Africa. Writer; Broadcaster. Education: BA, 1946, MA, 1947, PhD, 1951, New College, Oxford. Appointments: Professor of Drama, University of Bristol, 1960-82; Chairman, Radio West, 1979-84; National Commission to NESCO, 1984-86. Publications: The Relationship Between Universities and Radio, Film and Television, 1956; Drama in the World of Science, 1962; Early English Stages,3 volumes in 4, 1959-81; The Medieval Theatre, 1974; English Moral Interludes, 1975, 2nd edition, 1985; The Theatre in Europe, 1979; A History of the Theatre, 1985, 2nd edition, 1992. Memberships: Polish Academy of Arts and Science; Honorary Fellow, University of Bristol, 1996-. Address: 6 College Road, Bristol 8, Avon, England.

WIDDOWSON J(ohn) D(avid) A(llison), b. 22 June 1935, Sheffield, England. Professor of English Language and Cultural Tradition; Writer. m. Carolyn Lois Crawford, 1 Sept 1960, 2 sons, 1 daughter. Education: BA, 1959, MA, 1963, University of Oxford; MA, University of Leeds, 1966; PhD, University of Newfoundland, 1972. Appointments: Professor of English Language and Cultural Tradition, University of Sheffield; Director, National Centre for English Cultural Tradition; Co-Director, Institute for Folklore Studies in Britain and Canada; Curator, Traditional Heritage Museum. Publications: If You Don't Be Good, 1977; On Sloping Ground, 1979; Grenoside Recollections, 1980; Bibliography of British Folklore, 1996. Co-author or Editor: Learning About Linguistics, 1974; Linguistic Atlas of England, 1978; Language, Culture and Tradition, 1981; Dictionary of Newfoundland English, 1982; Studies in Linguistic Geography, 1985; Word Maps: An Atlas of the Regional Dialects of England, 1987; Perspectives on Contemporary Legend, 1987; Studies in Newfoundland Folklore, Community and Process, 1991; Survey of English Dialects: The Dictionary and Grammar, 1994; Folktales of Newfoundland, 1996; An Atlas of English Dialects, 1996; Yorkshire Words Today, 1997; Lexical Erosion in English Regional Dialects, 1999. Contributions to: Numerous professional journals. Honour: Honorary Research Associate, Memorial University of Newfoundland. Membership: Folklore Society. Address: c/o National Centre for English Cultural Tradition, University of Sheffield, Sheffield S10, England.

WIDEMAN John Edgar, b. 14 June 1941, Washington, District of Columbia, USA. Professor of English; Writer. m., 3 children. Education: BA, University of Pennsylvania, 1963; BPhil, University of Oxford, 1966; Postgraduate Studies, University of Iowa, 1967. Appointments: Professor of English, University of Wyoming, 1974-85, University of Massachusetts, Amherst, 1986-. Publications: A Glance Away, 1967; Hurry Home, 1969; The Lynchers, 1973; Hiding Place, 1981; Damballah, 1981; Sent for You Yesterday, 1983; Brothers and Keepers, 1984; Reuben, 1987; Fever, 1989; Philadelphia Fire, 1990; The Homewood Books, 1992; The Stories of John Edgar Wideman, 1992; All Stories Are True, 1993; Fatheralong, 1994; The Cattle Killing, 1996. Contributions to: Professional journals and general periodicals. Honours: PEN/Faulkner Awards for Fiction, 1984, 1991; John D and Catharine T MacArthur Foundation Fellowship, 1993. Memberships: American Academy of Arts and Sciences; American Academy of Arts and Letters; American Association of Rhodes Scholars; Modern Language Association; Phi Beta Kappa. Address: c/o Department of English, University of Massachusetts, Amherst, MA 01003, USA.

WIEBE Rudy (Henry), b. 4 Oct 1934, near Fairholme, Saskatchewan, Canada. Author; Professor of English and Creative Writing Emeritus. m. Tena F Isaak, 4 Mar 1958, 2 sons, 1 daughter. Education: BA, 1956, MA, 1960, University of Alberta; University of Tubingen, 1958; ThB, Mennonite Brethren Bible College, 1961; University of Manitoba, 1961; University of Iowa, 1964. Appointments: Assistant and Associate Professor of English, Goshen College, Indiana, 1963-67; Assistant Professor, 1967-71, Associate Professor, 1971-77, Professor of English and Creative Writing, 1977-92, Professor Emeritus, 1992-, University of Alberta. Publications: Fiction: Peace Shall Destroy Many, 1962; First and Vital Candle, 1966; The Blue Mountains of China, 1970; The Temptations of Big Bear, 1973; Where is the Voice Coming From?, 1974; The Scorched-Wood People, 1977; Alberta: A Celebration, 1979; The Mad Trapper, 1980; The Angel of the Tar Sands, and Other Stories, 1982; My Lovely Enemy, 1983; A Chinook Christmas, 1992; A Discovery of Strangers, 1994; River of Stone: Fictions and Memories, 1995. Play: Far as the Eye Can See, 1977; Essays: A Voice in the Land, 1981; Playing Dead: A Contemplation Concerning the Arctic, 1989. Editor: The Story-Makers: A Selection of Modern Short Stories, 1970, revised edition, 1987; Stories from Western Canada, 1971; Stories from Pacific and Arctic Canada (with Andreas Schroeder), 1974; Double Vision: Twentieth Century Stories in English, 1976; Getting Here, 1977; More Stories from Western Canada (with Aritha van Herk), 1980; West of Fiction (with Aritha van Herk and Leah Flater), 1983. Contributions to: Anthologies and periodicals. Honours: Governor-General's Awards for Fiction, 1973, 1994; Honorary DLitt, University of Winnipeg, 1986, Wilfred Laurier University, 1991, Brock University, 1991; Lorne Pierce Medal, Royal Society of Canada, 1987. Memberships: Writers Guild of Alberta, founding president, 1980; Writers Union of Canada, president, 1986-87. Address: c/o Department of English, University of Alberta, Edmonton, Alberta T6G 2E5, Canada.

WIEMANN Marion Russell Jr, b. 7 Sept 1929, Chesterton, Indiana, USA. Biologist; Microscopist. 1 daughter. Education: BS, Indiana University, 1959; Cultural Doctorate, Biological Sciences, World University Roundtable, 1991; ScD, London Institute for Applied Research, 1994; ScD, World Academy, Germany, 1995; Professor of Science, Australian Institute for Coordinated Research, Australia, 1995. Publications: Tooth Decay: It's Cause and Prevention Through Controlled Soil Composition, 1985; Soil Fertility and Permanent Agriculture (in 3 parts), 1983; The Mechanism of Tooth Decay, 1985. Contributions to: Periodicals and journals. Honours: Award of Merit, 1973, Distinguished Technical Communicator Award, 1974, Society for Technical Communication. Membership: World Literary Academy, fellow. Address: 418 South 9th Street, PO Box 1016, Chesterton, IN 46304, USA.

WIENER Joel H(oward), b. 23 Aug 1937, New York, New York, USA. Professor of History; Writer. m. Suzanne Wolff, 4 Sept 1961, 1 son, 1 daughter. Education: BA, New York University, 1959; Graduate Studies, University of Glasgow, 1961-63; PhD, Cornell University, 1965. Appointments: Assistant Professor of History, Skidmore College, 1964-66; Associate Professor, 1966-76, Professor of History, 1977-, City College of the City University of New York. Publications: The War of the Unstamped, 1969; A Descriptive Finding List of Unstamped British Periodicals: 1830-1836, 1970; Great Britain: Foreign Policy and the Span of Empire, 1689-1970 (editor), 4 volumes, 1972; Great Britain: The Lion at Home, 4 volumes, 1974; Radicalism and Freethought in 19th Century Britain, 1983; Innovators and Preachers: The Role of the Editor in Victorian England (editor), 1985; Papers for the Millions: The New Journalism in Britain c 1850's-1914 (editor), 1988; William Lovett, 1989. Contributions to: Scholarly books and journals. Honour: Fellow, Royal Historical Society, UK, 1974. Memberships: American Historical Association; American Journalism Historians Association; Conference on British Studies; Research Society for Victorian Periodicals, president. Address: 267 Glen Court, Teaneck, NJ 07666, USA.

WIENERS John (Joseph), b. 6 Jan 1934, Milton, Massachusetts, USA. Poet; Dramatist; Writer. Education: BA, Boston College, 1954; Black Mountain College, North Carolina, 1955-56; State University of New York, Buffalo, 1965-69. Publications: The Hotel Wentley Poems, 1958, revised edition, 1965; Still-Life (play), 1961; Asphodel in Hell's Despite, 1963; Ace Pentacles, 1964; Chinoiserie, 1965; Hart Crane, Harry Crosby, I See You Going Over the Edge, 1966; Anklesox and Five Shoelaces (play), 1966; King Solomon's Magnetic Quiz, 1967; Pressed Water, 1967; Selected Poems, 1968; Unhired, 1968; A Letter to Charles Olson, 1968; Asylum Poems, 1969; Untitled Essay on Frank O'Hara, 1969; A Memory of Black Mountain College, 1969; Nerves, 1970; Youth, 1970; Selected Poems, 1972; Woman, 1972; The Lanterns Along the Wall, 1972; Playboy, 1972; We Were There!, 1972; Holes, 1974; Behind the State Capitol, or, Cincinnati Pike, 1985; A Superficial Estimation, 1986; Conjugal Contraries and Quart, 1986; Cultural Affairs in Boston: Poetry and Prose, 1956-1985, 1988. Contributions to: Numerous periodicals. Honours: Poet's Foundation Award, 1961; New Hope Foundation Award, 1963; National Endowment for the Arts Grants, 1966, 1968, 1984; Academy Award, 1968; Guggenheim Fellowship, 1985. Address: 44 Joy Street, Apt 10, Boston, MA 02114, USA.

WIER Dara, b. 30 Dec 1949, New Orleans, Louisiana, USA. Poet; Professor. m. 1) Allen Wier, 2 Apr 1969, div 1983, 2) Michael Pettit, 1 Sept 1983, div 1990, 1 son, 1 daughter. Education: Louisiana State University, 1967-70; BS, Longwood College, 1971; MFA, Bowling Green State University, 1974. Appointments: Instructor, University of Pittsburgh, 1974-75; Instructor, 1975-76, Assistant Professor, 1977-80, Hollins College; Associate Professor, 1980-85, Director of Graduate Studies, 1980-82, Director of Writing Program, 1983-84, University of Alabama at Tuscaloosa; Associate Professor, 1985-96, Professor, 1996-, University of Massachusetts at Amherst; Visiting poet at various colleges and universities. Publications: Blood, Hook, and Eye, 1977; The 8-Step Grapevine, 1981; All You Have in Common, 1984; The Book of Knowledge, 1988; Blue for the Plough, 1992; Our Master Plan, 1997. Contributions to: Anthologies and periodicals. Honours: National Endowment for the Arts Fellowship, 1980; Guggenheim Fellowship, 1993-94. Memberships: Associated Writing Programs, president, 1981-82; Authors Guild; Authors League of America; PEN; Poetry Society of America. Address: 504 Montague Road, Amherst, MA 01002, USA.

WIESEL Elie(zer), b. 30 Sept 1928, Sighet, Romania (US citizen, 1963). Author; Professor in the Humanities and Philosophy. m. Marion Erster Rose, 1969, 1 son. Education: Sorbonne, University of Paris, 1948-51. Appointments: Distinguished Professor, City College of the City University of New York, 1972-76; Andrew W

Mellon Professor in the Humanities, 1976-, Professor of Philosophy, 1988-, Boston University; Distinguished Visiting Professor of Literature and Philosophy, Florida International University, Miami, 1982; Henry Luce Visiting Scholar in the Humanities and Social Thought, Yale University, 1982-83. Publications: Un Di Velt Hot Geshvign, 1956, English translation as Night, 1960; L'Aube, 1961, English translation as Dawn, 1961; Le Jour, 1961, English translation as The Accident, 1962; La Ville de la chance, 1962, English translation as The Town Beyond the Wall, 1964; Les Portes de la foret, 1964, English translation as The Gates of the Forest, 1966; Le Chant des morts, 1966, English translation as Legends of Our Time, 1968; The Jews of Silence: A Personal Report on Soviet Jewry, 1966; Zalmen, ou, la Folie de Dieu, 1966, English translations as Zalmen, or, The Madness of God, 1968; Le Mendiant de Jerusalem, 1968, English translation as A Beggar in Jerusalem, 1970; Entre deux soleils, 1970, English translation as One Generation AFter, 1970; Célébration Hassidique: Portraits et légendes, 1972, English translation as Souls on Fire: Portraits and Legends of Haisdic Masters, 1972; Le Serment de Kolvillag, 1973, English translation as The Oath, 1973; Célébration Biblique: Portraits and Legends, 1976; Un Juif aujourd'hui: Recits, essais, dialogues, 1977, English translation as A Jew Today, 1978; Dimensions of the Holocaust (with others), 1977; Four Hasidic Masters and Their Struggle Against Melancholy, 1978; Le Proces de Shamgorod tel qu'il se droula le 25 fevrier 1649: Piéce en trois actes, 1979, English translation as The Trial of God (as It Was Held on February 25, 1649, in Shamgorod): A Play in Three Acts, 1979; Images from the Bible, 1980; Le Testament d'un poète Juif assassine, 1980, English translation as The Testament, 1981; Five Biblical Portraits, 1981; Somewhere a Master, 1982; Paroles d'étranger, 1982; The Golem: The Story of a Legend as Told by Elie Wiesel, 1983; Le Cinquieme Fils, 1983, English translation as The Fifth Son, 1985; Signes d'exode, 1985; Job ou Dieu dans la tempete, 1986; Le Crépuscule au loin, 1987, English translation as Twilight, 1988; The Six Days of Destruction (with Albert H Friedlander), 1989; L'Oublie: Roman, 1989; From the Kingdom of Memory, 1990; Evil and Exile (with Philippe-Michael de Saint-Cheron), 1990; The Forgotten, 1992; Monsieur Chouchani: L'enigme d'un Maitre du XX Siècle: Entretiens Avec Elie Wiesel, Suivis d'une Enquete, 1994; Tous les Fleuves Vont a la Mer: Mémoires, 1994, English translation as All Rivers Run to the Sea: Memoirs, 1995; Mémoire a Deux Voix (with Francois Mitterrand), 1995, English translation as Memoir in Two Voices, 1996. Honours: Numerous, including: Prix Medicis, 1969; Prix Bordin, 1972; US Congressional Gold Medal, 1984; Nobel Prize for Peace, 1986; US Presidential Medal of Freedom, 1992. Memberships: American Academy of Arts and Sciences; Amnesty International; Author's Guild; European Academy of Arts and Sciences; Foreign Press Association, honorary lifetime member; Jewish Academy of Arts and Sciences; PEN; Writers Guild of America. Address: c/o University Professors, Boston University, 745 Commonwealth Avenue, Boston, MA 02215, USA.

WIESENFARTH Joseph John, b. 20 Aug 1933, Brooklyn, New York, USA. Professor of English. m. Louise Halpin, 21 Aug 1971, 1 son. Education: BA, Catholic University of America, 1956; MA, University of Detroit, 1959; PhD, Catholic University of America, 1962. Appointments: Assistant Professor, La Salle College, Philadelphia, 1962-64; Assistant Professor, 1964-67, Associate Professor, 1967-70, Manhattan College, New York; Associate Professor, 1970-76, Professor of English, 1976-, Chairman, Department of English, 1983-86, 1989-92, Associate Dean, Graduate School, 1995-96, University of Wisconsin at Madison; Advisory Editor, George Eliot-George Henry Lewes Studies, Connotations. Publications: Henry James and the Dramatic Analogy, 1963; The Errand of Form: An Essay of Jane Austen's Art, 1967; George Eliot's Mythmaking, 1977; George Eliot: A Writer's Notebook 1854-1879, 1981; Gothic Manners and the Classic English Novel, 1988; Ford Madox Ford and the Arts, 1989. Contributions to: Numerous articles on British and American Fiction. Honours: Phi Beta Kappa, 1956; Fellow, National

Endowment for the Humanities, 1967-68; Institute for Research in Humanities Fellow, 1975; Fulbright Fellow, 1981-82; Christian Gauss Prize Award Committee, 1986-88, 1989-90. Memberships: Modern Language Association; Jane Austen Society of North America; Henry James Society, Katherine Anne Porter Society; Ford Madox Ford Society. Address: Department of English, University of Wisconsin, 600 North Park Street, Madison, WI 53706, USA.

WIESENTHAL Simon, b. 31 Dec 1908, Poland. Writer. m. Cyla, 1 daughter. Education: Architectural Studies, Prague, Lvov. Appointment: Editor, Ausweg, 1960-. Publications: KZ Mauthausen, 1946; Head Mufti, 1947; Agent of the Axis, 1947; The Murderers Among Us, 1967; Sunflower, 1969; Sails of Hope, 1973; The Case of Krystyna Jaworska, 1975; Every Day Remembrance Day, 1986; Justice, Not Vengeance, 1989. Honours: Dutch Medal for Freedom; Jean Moulin Medaille; Kaj Munk Medal; Commander, Order of Oranje Nassau, Netherlands; Justice Brandeis Awards; Knight, Legion of Honour, France; Numerous others. Membership: Austrian PEN. Address: Salztorgasse 6, 1010 Vienna, Austria.

WIGNALL Anne, (Alice Acland, Anner Marreco), b. 12 June 1912, London, England. Writer. m. (1) Francis Egerton Grosvenor, Fifth Baron of Ebury, July 1933, div, 2 sons, (2) Barton Wignall, 12 Nov 1947, dec, 1 daughter, (3) Anthony Marreco, 1961, div. Education: Private. Publications: As Alice Acland: Biography: Caroline Norton, 1948; Novels: Templeford Park, 1954; A Stormy Spring, 1955; A Second Choice, 1956; A Person of Discretion, 1958; The Corsican Ladies, 1974; The Secret Wife, 1975; The Ruling Passion, 1976. As Anne Marreco: Biography: The Rebel Countess, 1967; Novels: The Charmer and The Charmed, 1963; The Boat Boy, 1964. Address: c/o Curtis Brown Ltd, 162-168 Regent Street, London W1, England.

WIKAN Unni, b. 18 Nov 1944, Ibesfad, Norway. Anthropologist; Writer. m. Fredrik Barth, 30 Jan 1974, 1 son. Education: BA, University of Bergen, 1968; PhD, University of Oslo, 1980. Publications: Life Among the Poor in Cairo, 1980; Behind the Veil in Arabia: Women in Oman, 1982; Managing Turbulent Hearts: A Balinese Formula for Living, 1990; Tomorrow, God Willing: Self-Made Destinies in Cairo, 1996. Contributions to: American Anthropologist; American Ethnologist; Man; Ethos; Current Anthropology; Cultural Anthropology; Social Science and Medicine; Culture, Medicine and Psychiatry. Memberships: Norwegian Association of Professional Authors; American Anthropological Association; Society for Psychological Anthropology; European Association for Social Anthropologists. Address: Ethnographic Museum, Frederiksgate 2, Ol64, Oslo, Norway.

WIKHOLM-OSTLING Gungerd Helene, b. 14 Oct 1954, Karis, Finland. Writer; Poet; Journalist. m. Tom Seth Ostling, 14 Sept 1990, 2 daughters. Education: Svenska Social-Och Kommunalhögskolan, Helsingor, 1974-77. Appointments: Cultural Journalist, Finnish Broadcasting Co, 1977-. Publications: Poetry: Torplandet, 1982; Aria, 1987; Anhalter, Svarta Och Roda, 1990; Ur Vattnets Arkiv, 1993; Stora Dagen, Lilla Natten, 1995. Contributions to: Periodicals. Honours: Svenska Litteratursallskapet, 1988; Langmanska Fonden, 1993. Membership: Finlands Svenska Forfattareforening. Address: Kilavägen 29 A3, Karis, Finland.

WILBER Richard A, b. 4 Sept 1948, St Louis, Missouri, USA. Professor of Journalism; Writer; Poet; Editor. m. Robin Smith, 16 Mar 1984, 1 so, 1 daughter. Education: BA, English and Journalism, 1970, MFA, English, 1976, EdD, 1996, Southern Illinois University. Appointments: Associate Editor, The Midwest Motorist, 1970-76; Professor of Journalism, Florida State College, 1980-88, University of South Florida, 1988-96, Souther Illinois University, 1988-; Editor, Fiction Quarterly, 1988-. Publication: To Leuchars, 1997. Contributions to: Reviews, quarterlies, and journals. Memberships: Science Fiction Writers of America; Textbook Authors Association. Address: 210 Isle Drive, St Pete Beach, FL 33706, USA.

WILBUR Richard (Purdy), b. 1 Mar 1921, New York, New York, USA. Poet; Writer; Translator; Editor; Professor. m. Mary Charlotte Hayes Ward, 20 June 1942, 3 sons, 1 daughter. Education: AB, Amherst College, 1942; AM, Harvard University, 1947. Appointments: Assistant Professor of English, Harvard University, 1950-54; Associate Professor of English, Wellesley College, 1955-57; Professor of English, Wesleyan University, 1957-77; Writer-in-Residence, Smith College, 1977-86; Poet Laureate of the USA, 1987-88; Visiting Lecturer at various colleges and universities. Publications: Poetry: The Beautiful Changes and Other Poems, 1947; Ceremony and Other Poems, 1950; Things of This World, 1956; Poems, 1943-1956, 1957; Advice to a Prophet and Other Poems, 1961; The Poems of Richard Wilbur, 1963; Walking to Sleep: New Poems and Translations, 1969; Digging to China, 1970; Seed Leaves: Homage to R F, 1974; The Mind-Reader: New Poems, 1976; Seven Poems, 1981; New and Collected Poems, 1988. For Children: Loudmouse, 1963; Opposites, 1973; More Opposites, 1991; A Game of Catch, 1994; Runaway Opposites, 1995. Non-Fiction: Anniversary Lectures (with Robert Hillyer and Cleanth Brooks), 1959; Emily Dickinson: Three Views (with Louise Bogan and Archibald MacLeish), 1960; Responses: Prose Pieces, 1953-1976, 1976. Editor: Modern American and Modern British Poetry (with Louis Untermeyer and Karl Shapiro), 1955; A Bestiary, 1955; Poe: Complete Poems, 1959; Shakespeare: Poems (with Alfred Harbage), 1966, revised edition, 1974; Poe: The Narrative of Arthur Gordon Pym, 1974; Witter Bynner: Selected Poems, 1978. Translator: Molière: The Misanthrope, 1955; Molière: Tartuffe, 1963; Molière: The School for Wives, 1971; Molière: The Learned Ladies, 1978; Racine: Andromache, 1982; Racine: Phaedra, 1986; Molière: The School for Husbands, 1992; Molière: Amphitryon, 1995. Honours: Harriet Monroe Memorial Prizes, 1948, 1978; Oscar Blumenthal Prize, 1950; Guggenheim Fellowships, 1952-53, 1963-64; Prix de Rome Fellowship, American Academy of Arts and Letters, 1954; Edna St Vincent Millay Memorial Award, 1957; Pulitzer Prizes in Poetry, 1957, 1989; National Book Award for Poetry, 1957; Ford Foundation Fellowship, 1960; Bollingen Prizes, 1963, 1971; Brandeis University Creative Arts Award, 1971; Shelley Memorial Award, 1973; Drama Desk Award, 1983; Chevalier, Ordre des Palmes Academiques, 1983; Los Angeles Times Books Prize, 1988; Gold Medal for Poetry, American Academy and Institute of Arts and Letters, 1991; Edward Mac Dowell Medal, 1991; National Medal of Arts, 1994. Memberships: Academy of American Poets, chancellor; American Academy of Arts and Letters, president, 1974-76, chancellor, 1976-78, 1980-81; American Academy of Arts and Sciences; American Society of Composers, Authors and Publishers; Authors League of America; Dramatists Guild; Modern Language Association, honorary fellow. Address: 87 Dodwells Road, Cummington, MA 01206, USA.

WILBY Basil Leslie, (Gareth Knight), b. 1930, Colchester, England. Writer. Publications: A Practical Guide to Qabalistic Symbolism, 1965; The New Dimensions Red Book, 1968; The Practice of Ritual Magic, 1969; Occult Exercises and Practices, 1969; Meeting the Occult, 1973; Experience of the Inner Worlds, 1975; The Occult: An Introduction, 1975; The Secret Tradition in Arthurian Legend, 1983; The Rose Cross and the Goddess, 1985; The Treasure House of Images, 1986; The Magic World of the Tarot, 1991; Magic and the Western Mind, 1991; Evoking the Goddess, 1993; Dion Fortune's Magical Battle of Britain, 1993; Introduction to Ritual Magic (with Dion Fortune), 1997; The Circle of Force, 1998; Magical Images and the Magical Imagination, 1998; Principles of Hermetic Philosophy, 1999. Address: c/o 38 Steeles Road, London NW3 4RG, England.

WILCOX James, b. 4 Apr 1949, Hammond, Louisiana, USA. Author. Education: BA, Yale University. Publications: Modern Baptists, 1983; North Gladiola,

1985; Miss Undine's Living Room, 1987; Sort of Rich, 1989; Guest of a Sinner, 1993. Contributions to: Periodicals. Memberships: Authors Guild; PEN. Address: c/o International Creative Management, 40 West 57th Street, New York, NY 10019, USA.

WILD Peter, b. 25 Apr 1940, Northampton, Massachusetts, USA. Professor of English; Poet; Writer. m. (1) Sylvia Ortiz, 1966, (2) Rosemary Harrold, 1981. Education: BA, 1962, MA, 1967, University of Arizona; MFA, University of California at Irvine, 1969. Appointments: Assistant Professor, Sul Ross State University, Alpine, Texas, 1969-71; Assistant Porfessor, 1971-73, Associate Professor, 1973-79, Professor of English. 1979-, University of Arizona; Contributing Editor, High Country News, 1974-; Consulting Editor, Diversions, 1983-. Publications: Poetry: The Good Fox, 1967; Sonnets, 1967; The Afternoon in Dismay, 1968; Mica Mountain Poems, 1968; Joining Up and Other Poems, 1968; Mad Night with Sunflowers, 1968; Love Poems, 1969; Three Nights in the Chiricahuas, 1969; Poems, 1969; Fat Man Poems, 1970; Term and Renewals, 1970; Grace, 1971; Dilemma, 1971; Wild's Magical Book of Cranial Effusions, 1971; Peligros, 1972; New and Selected Poems, 1973; Cochise, 1973; The Cloning, 1974; Tumacacori, 1974; Health, 1974; Chihuahua, 1976; The Island Hunter, 1976; Pioneers, 1976; The Cavalryman, 1976; House Fires, 1977; Gold Mines, 1978; Barn Fires, 1978; Zuni Butte, 1978; The Lost Tribe, 1979; Jeanne d'Arc: A Collection of New Poems, 1980; Rainbow, 1980; Wilderness, 1980; Heretics, 1981; Bitteroots, 1982; The Peaceable Kingdom, 1983; Getting Ready for a Date, 1984; The Light on Little Mormon Lake, 1984; The Brides of Christ, 1991; Easy Victory, 1994. Other: Pioneer Conservationists of Western America, 2 volumes, 1979, 1983; Enos Mills, 1979; Clarence King, 1981; James Welch, 1983; Barry Lopez, 1984; John Haines, 1985; John Nicholas, 1986; The Saguaro Forest, 1986; John C Van Dyke: The Desert, 1988; Alvar Núnez Cabeza de Vaca, 1991; Ann Zwinger, 1993. Editor: New Poetry of the American West (with Frank Graziano), 1982. Honours: Writer's Digest Prize, 1964; Hart Crane and Alice Crane Williams Memorial Fund Grant, 1969; Ark River Review Prize, 1972; Ohio State University President's Prize, 1982. Address: 1547 East Lester, Tucson, AZ 85719, USA.

WILDER Cherry. See: **GRIMM Barbara Lockett.**

WILDING Eric. See: **TUBB E(dwin) C(harles).**

WILDING Griselda. See: **McCUTCHEON Hugh.**

WILDING Michael, b. 5 Jan 1942, Worcester, England. Professor; Writer. Education: BA, 1963, MA, 1968, University of Oxford. Appointments: Lecturer, 1963-66, Senior Lecturer, 1969-72, Reader, 1972-92, Professor, 1993-, University of Sydney; Lecturer, University of Birmingham, 1967-68; Visiting Professor, University of California, 1987. Publications: Aspects of the Dying Process, 1972; Living Together, 1974; Short Story Embassy, 1975; West Midland Underground, 1975; Scenic Drive, 1976; The Phallic Forest, 1978; Political Fictions, 1980; Pacific Highway, 1982; Reading the Signs, 1984; The Paraguyan Experiment, 1985; The Man of Slow Feeling, 1985; Dragon's Teeth, 1987; Under Saturn, 1988; Great Climate, 1990; Social Visions, 1993; The Radical Tradition, Lawson, Furphy, Stead, 1993; This is for You, 1994; Book of the Reading, 1994; The Oxford Book of Australian Short Stories, 1994; Somewhere New, 1996; Studies in Classical Australian Fiction, 1997; Wildest Dreams, 1998. Honours: Senior Fellowship, Literature Board, Australia Council, 1978; Elected Fellow, Australian Academy of the Humanities, 1988; Honorary DLitt, University of Sydney, 1997. Address: Department of English, University of Sydney, Sydney, New South Wales 2006, Australia.

WILENTZ Robert Sean, b. 20 Feb 1951, New York, USA. Historian. m. Mary Christine Stansell, 30 Jan 1980, 1 son, 1 daughter. Education: BA, Columbia College, 1972; BA, University of Oxford, 1974; PhD, Yale University, 1980. Publications: Chants Democratic, 1984;

Rites of Power, 1985; The Key of Liberty, 1993; The Kingdom of Matthias, 1994. Contributions to: New Republic; Dissent. Honours: Beveridge Award, 1984; Turner Award, 1985. Membership: Society of American Historians. Address: 7 Edgehill Street, Princeton, NJ 08540, USA.

WILFORD John Noble, b. 4 Oct 1933, Murray, Kentucky, USA. Journalist; Writer. m. Nancy Watts Paschall, 25 Dec 1966, 1 daughter. Education: BS, Journalism, University of Tennessee, 1955; MA, Political Science, Syracuse University, 1956; International Reporting Fellow, Columbia University, 1961-62. Appointments: Science Reporter, 1965-73, 1979-, Assistant National Editor, 1973-75, Director of Science News, 1975-79, Science Correspondent, 1979-, New York Times, New York City; Mc Graw Distinguished Lecturer in Writing, Princeton University, 1985; Professor of Science Journalism, University of Tennessee, 1989-90. Publications: We Reach the Moon, 1969; The Mapmakers, 1981; The Riddle of the Dinosaur, 1985; Mars Beckons, 1990; The Mysterious History of Columbus, 1991. Contributions to: Nature; Wilson Quarterly; New York Times Magazine; Science Digest; Popular Science. Honours: Westinghouse-American Association for the Advancement of Science Writing Award, 1983; Pulitzer Prizes for National Reporting, 1984, shared 1987; Ralph Coats Roe Medal, American Society of Mechanical Engineers, 1995; American Acsademy of Arts and Sciences, fellow, 1998. Memberships: Century Club, New York City; National Association of Science Writers; American Geographical Society, council member, 1994-. Address: New York Times, 229 West 43rd Street, New York, NY 10036, USA.

WILKERSON Cynthia. See: **LEVINSON Leonard.**

WILKINSON Doris (Yvonne), b. 13 June 1936, Lexington, Kentucky, USA. Professor of Sociology; Writer; Essayist; Social Theorist. Education: BA, University of Kentucky, 1958; MA, 1960, PhD, 1968, Case Western Reserve University; MPH, Johns Hopkins University, 1985; Postdoctoral Studies, Harvard University, 1991. Appointments: Assistant Professor, 1968-70, Professor of Sociology, 1985-, University of Kentucky; Associate Professor to Professor, Macalester College, 1970-77; Executive Associate, American Sociological Association, Washington, DC, 1977-80; Professor of Medical Sociology, Howard University, 1980-84; Visiting Professor, University of Virginia, 1984-85; Visiting Scholar, 1989-90, Visiting Professor, 1992, 1993, 1994, Harvard University; Rapoport Visiting Professor of Social Theory, Smith College, 1995, Smith Visiting Professor, 1996. Publications: Workbook for Introductory Sociology, 1968. Editor: Black Revolt: Strategies of Protest, 1969. Co-Editor: The Black Male in America, 1977; Alternative Health Maintenance and Healing Systems, 1987; Race, Gender and the Life Cycle, 1991. Contributions to: Professional journals. Honours: Woodrow Wilson Foundation Fellowship, 1959-61; I Peter Gellman Award, Eastern Sociological Society, 1987; Dubois-Johnson-Frazier Award, American Sociological Association, 1988; American Council of Learned Societies Fellowship, 1989-90; Ford Foundation Fellowship, 1989-90; National Endowment for the Humanities Fellowship, 1991; Distinguished Scholar Award, Association of Black Sociologists, 1993; Great Teacher Award, 1992. Memberships: Alpha Kappa Delta; American Sociological Association; Eastern Sociological Society, president, 1992-93; Phi Beta Kappa; Society for the Study of Social Problems, president, 1987-88; Southern Sociological Society; American Sociological Association, vice president, 1990-91. Address: c/o Department of Sociology, University of Kentucky, Lexington, KY 40506, USA.

WILKINSON Richard Herbert, b. 26 Apr 1951, Skipton, Yorkshire, England. Egyptologist. m. Anna Wagner, 27 July 1975, 2 sons. Education: PhD, University of Minnesota. Appointment: Faculty, University of Arizona. Publications: Reading Egyptian Art, 1992; Symbol and Magic in Egyptian Art, 1994; Valley of the Sun Kings, 1995; Complete Valley of the Kings, 1996 Contributions to: Professional journals and general periodicals. Honours: Numerous. Membership: International Association of Egyptologists. Address: c/o University of Arizona, Harvil 347, Box 10, Tucson, AZ 85721, USA.

WILL Clifford Martin, b. 13 Nov 1946, Hamilton, Ontario, Canada. Physicist. m. Leslie Carol Saxe, 26 June 1970, 2 daughters. Education: BSc, Applied Mathematics, Theoretical Physics, McMaster University, 1968; PhD, Physics, California Institute of Technology, 1971. Appointment: Faculty, Washington University, St Louis. Publications: Theory and Experiment in Gravitational Physics, 1981, 2nd edition, 1993; Was Einstein Right?, 1986, 2nd edition, 1993. Contributions to: Periodicals. Honours: Alfred P Sloan Foundation Fellowship, 1975-79; Science Writing Award, American Institute of Physics, 1987. Memberships: American Institute of Physics, fellow; American Astronomical Society; International Society on General Relativity and Gravitation. Address: Department of Physics, Campus Box 1105, Washington University, St Louis, MO 63130, USA.

WILL Frederic, b. 4 Dec 1928, New Haven, Connecticut, USA. Professor of Comparative Literature; Poet. Education: AB, Indiana University, 1949; PhD, Yale University, 1954. Appointments: Instructor in Classics, Dartmouth College, 1953-55; Assistant Professor of Classics, Pennsylvania State University, 1954-59, University of Texas, 1960-64; Associate Professor of English and Comparative Literature, 1964-66, Professor of Comparative Literature, 1966-71, University of Iowa; Professor of Comparative LIterature, University of Massachusetts at Amherst, 1971-; Visiting Lecturer in poetry and criticism at many colleges and universities; Many poetry readings. Publications: Intelligible Beauty in Aesthetic Thought: From Winckelmann to Victor Cousin, 1958; Mosaic and Other Poems, 1959; A Wedge of Words (poems), 1962; Kostes Palamas: The Twelve Words of the Gypsy (translator), 1964; Hereditas: Seven Essays on the Modern Experience of the Classical (editor), 1964; Metaphrasis: An Anthology from the University of Iowa Translation Workshop, 1964-65 (editor), 1965; Flumen Historicum: Victor Cousin's Aesthetic and Its Sources, 1965; Literature Inside Out: Ten Speculative Essays, 1966; Planets (poems), 1966; Kostes Palamas: The King's Flute (translator), 1967; From a Year in Greece, 1967; Archilochos, 1969; Herondas, 1972; Brandy in the Snow (poems), 1972; Theodor Adorno: The Jargon of Authenticity (translator with Knut Tarnowski), 1973; The Knife in the Stone, 1973; The Fact of Literature, 1973; Guatemala, 1973; Botulism (poems), 1975; The Generic Demands of Greek Literature, 1976; Belphagor, 1977; Epics of America (poems), 1977; Our Thousand Year Old Bodies: Selected Poems, 1956-1976, 1980; Shamans in Turtlenecks: Selected Essays, 1984; The Sliced Dog, 1984; Entering the Open Hole, 1989; Recoveries, 1993. Contributions to: Many poems and articles in various periodicals. Honours: Fulbright Grants, 1950-51, 1955, 1956-57, 1975-76, 1980-81; American Council of Learned Societies Grant, 1958; Voertman Poetry Awards, Texas Institute of Letters, 1962, 1964; Bollingen Foundation Grant; National Endowment for the Arts Grant. Address: Department of Comparative Literature, University of Massachusetts at Amherst, Amherst, MA 01003, USA.

WILL George (Frederick), b. 4 May 1941, Champaign, Illinois, USA. Political Columnist; Television News Analyst; Writer. Education: BA, Trinity College, Oxford, 1964; MA, PhD, Princeton University, 1967. Appointments: Professor of Political Philosophy, Michigan State University, 1967-68, University of Toronto, 1968-70; Editor, The National Review, 1973-76; Syndicated Political Columnist, The Washington Post, 1974-; Contributing Editor, Newsweek magazine, 1976-; Television News Analyst, ABC-TV, 1981-. Publications: The Pursuit of Happiness and Other Sobering Thoughts, 1979; The Pursuit of Virtue and Other Tory Notions, 1982; Statecraft as Soulcraft: What Government Does, 1983; The Morning After: American Successes and Excesses, 1986; The New Season: A Spectator's Guide to the 1988 Election, 1987; Men at Work, 1990; Suddenly: The American Idea at Home and Abroad, 1988-89, 1990; Restoration: Congress, Term Limits and the Recovery of Deliberate Democracy, 1992; The Leveling Wind: Politics, the Culture and Other News, 1994. Honour: Pulitzer Prize for Commentary, 1977. Address: c/o The Washington Post, 1150 15th Street North West, Washington, DC 20071, USA.

WILLETT Frank, b. 18 Aug 1925, Bolton, England. Archaeologist; Art Historian. m. M Constance Hewitt, 24 July 1950, 1 son, 3 daughters. Education: BA, 1947, MA, 1951, University of Oxford. Appointments: Editorial Secretary, Manchester Literary and Philosophical Society, 1950-58; Editorial Board, West African Journal of Archaeology, 1970-, Journal of African Studies, 1973-88; Curator, Royal Society of Edinburgh, 1992-97. Publications: Ife in the History of West African Sculpture, 1967; African Art, 1971, revised edition, 1993; Treasures of Ancient Nigeria, 1980. Contributions to: Professional journals, books and other publications. Honours: Commander of the Order of the British Empire, 1985; Leadership Award of the Arts Council of African Studies Association. Memberships: Manchester Literary and Philosophical Society; Royal Anthropological Institute; Royal Society of Edinburgh, fellow. Address: c/o The Hunterian Museum, University of Glasgow, Glasgow G12 8QQ, Scotland.

WILLIAM John. See: **CROSSLEY-HOLLAND Kevin.**

WILLIAMS Alberta Norine, (Sonia Davis), b. 22 Apr 1908, Olds, Alberta, Canada. Poet; Author; Songwriter. m. Billy D Williams, 4 Sept 1928, 1 son, 1 daughter. Education: Business College, Fayetteville, Arknasas, 1921; Pueblo Community College, 1960; Writer's Digest and Will Heideman Correspondence Courses. Publications: Pearls of a Lady, 1976; Potpourri of a Poet, 1992; Prairie Bird, 1994. Contributions to: Many publications. Honour: Inducted, International World Writers Hall of Fame, 1997. Memberships: Daughters of the American Revolution; Greenhorn Valley Art Society; Verses of the Valley. Address: 2538 Co Road 660, Rye, CO 81069, USA.

WILLIAMS Bernard Arthur Owen, b. 21 Sept 1929, Southend, Essex, England. Professor of Philosophy; Writer. m. (1) Shirley Vivienne Teresa Brittain Catlin, 1955, div 1974, 1 daughter, (2) Patricia Law Skinner, 1974, 2 sons. Education: BA, 1951, MA, 1954, Balliol College, Oxford. Appointments: Fellow, All Souls College, Oxford, 1951-54, 1997-; Fellow and Tutor in Philosophy, New College, Oxford, 1954-59; Lecturer in Philosophy, University College, London, 1959-64; Visiting Professor, 1963; Senior Fellow in the Humanities, 1978, Princeton University; Professor of Philosophy, Bedford College, London University, 1964-67; Knightbridge Professor of Philosophy, Cambridge University, 1967-79; Fellow, 1967-79, 1988-, Provost, 1979-87, King's College, Cambridge; Visiting Professor, Harvard University, 1973; Visiting Professor, 1986, Monroe Deutsch Professor of Philosophy, 1988-, Sather Professor of Classics, 1989, University of California at Berkeley; White's Professor of Moral Philosophy, Oxford University, and Fellow, Corpus Christi College, Oxford, 1990-96; Visiting Fellow, Wissenschaftskolleg, Berlin, 1997. Publications: British Analytical Philosophy (editor with A C Montefiore), 1966; Morality, 1972; Utilitarianism: For and Against (with J J C Smart), 1973; Problems of the Self, 1973; Descartes: The Project of Pure Enquiry, 1978; Moral Luck, 1981; Utilitarianism and Beyond, (editor with A K Sen), 1982; Ethics and the Limits of Philosophy, 1985; Shame and Necessity, 1993; Making Sense of Humanity, 1995; Plato, 1998. Other: What is Truth? (writer and presenter), Channel 4 TV, UK, 1988. Contributions to: Scholarly books and journals. Honours: Honorary Fellow, Balliol College, Oxford, 1984, Corpus Christi College, Oxford, 1996; Dr Margrit Egner Stiftung Prizt, Zürich, 1997; Honorary doctorates. Memberships: American Academy of Arts and Sciences, honorary foreign member; British Academy, fellow; Commission on Social Justice, Labour Party, 1992-94; Sadler's Wells Opera, later English National Opera, board, 1968-86. Address: c/o

Department of Philosophy, University of California at Berkeley, CA 94720, USA.

WILLIAMS Bert Nolan, b. 19 Aug 1930, Toronto, Ontario, Canada. Writer; Teacher. m. Angela Babando, 6 Dec 1952, 1 son. Education: Self-taught. Publications: Food for the Eagle, 1970; Master of Ravenspur, 1970; The Rocky Mountain Monster, 1972; Sword of Egypt, 1977; Brumaire (play), 1982. Other: Poems, short stories and popular songs. Contributions to: Journals and magazines. Address: 10 Muirhead Road, Apt 504, North York, Ontario M2J 4P9, Canada.

WILLIAMS C(harles) K(enneth), b. 4 Nov 1936, Newark, New Jersey, USA. Poet; Professor. m. Catherine Justine Mauger, Apr 1975, 1 son, 1 daughter. Education: BA, University of Pennsylvania, 1959. Appointments: Visiting Professor, Franklin and Marshall College, Lancaster, Pennsylvania, 1977, University of California at Irvine, 1978, Boston University, 1979-80; Professor of English, George Mason University, 1982; Visiting Professor, Brooklyn College, 1982-83; Lecturer, Columbia University, 1982-85; Holloway Lecturer, University of California at Berkeley, 1986; Professor, Princeton University, 1996-. Publications: A Day for Anne Frank, 1968; Lies, 1969; I Am the Bitter Name, 1972; The Sensuous President, 1972; With Ignorance, 1977; The Women of Trachis (co-translator), 1978; The Lark, the Thrush, the Starling, 1983; Tar, 1983; Flesh and Blood, 1987; Poems 1963-1983, 1988; The Bacchae of Euripides (translator), 1990; A Dream of Mind, 1992; Selected Poems, 1994; The Vigil, 1997; Poetry and Consciousness (selected essays), 1998. Contributions to: Akzent; Atlantic; Carleton Miscellany; Crazyhorse; Grand Street; Iowa Review; Madison Review; New England Review; New Yorker; Seneca Review; Transpacific Review; TriQuarterly. Honours; Guggenheim Fellowship; Pushcart Press Prizes, 1982, 1983, 1987; National Book Critics Circle Award, 1983; National Endowment for the Arts Fellowship, 1985; Morton Dawen Zabel Prize, 1988; Lila Wallace Writers Award, 1993; Berlin Prize Fellowship, 1998; PEN Voelker Prize, 1998. Membership: PEN. Address: 82 Rue d'Hauteville, 75010 Paris, France.

WILLIAMS David, b. 8 June 1926, Bridgend, Mid Glamorgan, Wales. Novelist. m. Brenda Yvonne Holmes, 18 Aug 1952, 1 son, 1 daughter. Education: Cathedral School, Hereford, 1938-43; St John's College, Oxford, 1943-44, 1947-48. Publications: Unholy Writ; Murder for Treasure; Wedding Treasure; Murder in Advent; Holy Treasure; Treasure by Degrees; Copper, Gold and Treasure; Treasure Preserved; Advertise for Treasure; Prescription for Murder; Divided Treasure; Treasure By Post; Planning on Murder; Banking on Murder; Last Seen Breathing; Death of a Prodigal; Dead in the Market, 1996; A Terminal Case, 1997; Treasure in Oxford, 1998; Suicide Intended, 1998. Contributions to: Various publications. Honour: Elected, Welsh Academy, 1995. Memberships: Society of Authors; Crime Writers Association; Mystery Writers of America; Carlton Club; Wentworth G C; Detection Club. Address: Blandings, Pinewood Road, Virginia Water, Surrey GU25 4PA, England.

WILLIAMS David Larry, b. 22 June 1945, Souris, Manitoba, Canada. Professor of English; Writer. m. Darlene Olinyk, 22 July 1967, 2 sons. Education: Pastor's Diploma, Briercrest Bible Institute, Saskatchewan, 1965; BA, Honours, University of Saskatchewan, 1968; MA, Amherst College, 1970; PhD, University of Massachusetts, 1973. Appointments: Lecturer, 1972-73, Assistant Professor, 1973-77, Associate Professor, 1977-83, Professor, 1983-, English, University of Manitoba, Winnipeg; Editorial Board, Canadian Review of American Studies, 1976-86; Guest Professor, Indian Association for Canadian Studies, MS University of Baroda, 1992. Publications: The Burning Wood (novel), 1975; Faulkner's Women: The Myth and the Muse (criticism), 1977; The River Horsemen (novel), 1981; Eye of the Father (novel), 1985; To Run with Longboat: Twelve Stories of Indian Athletes in Canada (with Brenda Zeman), 1988; Confessional Fictions: A Portrait of the Artist in the Canadian Novel, 1991. Contributions to: Books and professional journals. Honours: Woodrow Wilson Fellow, 1968-69; Canada Council Fellow, 1969-72; Canada Council Arts Grant 'B', 1977-78, 1981-82; Touring Writer in Scandinavia for External Affairs, Canada, 1981; RH Institute Award for Research in Humanities, 1987; Olive Beatrice Stanton Award for Excellence in Teaching, 1992. Memberships: Writers' Union of Canada; PEN International. Address: Department of English, St Paul's College, University of Manitoba, Winnipeg R3T 2M6, Canada.

WILLIAMS Heathcote, b. 15 Nov 1941, Helsby, Cheshire, England. Playwright; Poet. Appointments: Associate Editor, Transatlantic Review, New York and London. Publications: The Local Stigmatic, 1967; AC/DC, 1970; Remember the Truth Dentist, 1974; The Speakers, 1974; Very Tasty - a Pantomime, 1975; An Invitation to the Official Lynching of Abdul Malik, 1975; Anatomy of a Space Rat, 1976; Hancock's Last Half-Hour, 1977; Playpen, 1977; The Immortalist, 1977; At It, 1982; Whales, 1986. Poetry: Whale Nation, 1988; Falling for a Dolphin, 1988; Sacred Elephant, 1989; Autogeddon, 1991. Other: The Speakers, 1964; Manifestoes, Manifestern, 1975; Severe Joy, 1979; Elephants, 1983. Honour: Evening Standard Award, 1970. Address: c/o Curtis Brown, Haymarket House, 28-29 Haymarket, London SW1Y 4SP, England.

WILLIAMS Herbert Lloyd, b. 8 Sept 1932, Aberystwyth, Wales. Writer; Poet; Dramatist. m. Dorothy Maud Edwards, 13 Nov 1954, 4 sons, 1 daughter. Publications: The Trophy, 1967; A Lethal Kind of Love, 1968; Battles in Wales, 1975; Come Out Wherever You Are, 1976; Stage Coaches in Wales, 1977; The Welsh Quiz Book, 1978; Railways in Wales, 1981; The Pembrokeshire Coast National Park, 1987; Stories of King Arthur, 1990; Ghost Country, 1991; Davies the Ocean, 1991; The Stars in Their Courses, 1992; John Cowper Powys, 1997; Looking Through Time, 1998. Television Dramas and Documentaries: Taff Acre, 1981; A Solitary Mister, 1983; Alone in a Crowd, 1984; Calvert in Camera, 1990; The Great Powys, 1994; Arouse All Wales, 1996. Radio Dramas: Doing the Bard, 1986; Bodyline, 1991; Adaptations: A Child's Christmas in Wales, 1994; The Citadel, 1997. Contributions to: Reviews and journals. Honours: Welsh Arts Council Short Story Prize, 1972, and Bursary, 1988; Aberystwyth Open Poetry Competition, 1990; Hawthornden Poetry Fellowship, 1992; Rhys Davies Short Story Award, 1995. Memberships: Welsh Academy; Welsh Union of Writers; Writers Guild of Great Britain. Address: 2 Maes Crugiau, Rhydyfelin, Aberystwyth, SY23 4PP, Wales.

WILLIAMS Hugo (Mordaunt), b. 20 Feb 1942, Windsor, Berkshire, England. Writer; Critic; Poet. m. Hermine Demoriane, 12 Oct 1966, 1 daughter. Education: Eton College, 1955-60. Appointments: Assistant Editor, London Magazine, 1961-69; Television Critic, New Statesman, 1982-87; Theatre Critic, Sunday Correspondent, 1989-90; Film Critic, Harpers & Queen, 1993-. Publications: Symptoms of Loss, 1965; All the Time in the World, 1966; Sugar Daddy, 1970; Some Sweet Day, 1975; Love Life, 1979; No Particular Place to Go, 1981; Writing Home, 1985; Self-Portrait with a Slide, 1990. Contributions to: Newspapers and periodicals. Honours: Eric Gregory Award, 1965; Cholmondeley Award, 1970; Geoffrey Faber Memorial Prize, 1979. Membership: Royal Society of Literature. Address: 31 Raleigh Street, London N1 8NW, England.

WILLIAMS Ioan Miles, b. 10 Sept 1941, Gwent, Wales. University Teacher. m. Margaret Jacob, 11 Jan 1964, 1 son, 4 daughters. Education: St Catherine's Oxford; BA First Class Hons, English Language and Literature; MA, BLitt, University of Wales, Aberystywth, PGCE; PhD, University of Exeter, 1964-66; Assistant Lecturer in English, Senior Lecturer in English and European Literary Studies, 1966-76, University of Wales, Aberystwyth; Lecturer in Drama, 1982-96; Director of Drama, 1991-93; Professor and Head, Department of Theatre, Film and TV Studies, 1993-. Publications: Novel and Romance, 1700-1800, 1971; Realist Novel in England, 1974; The Idea of the Novel in Europe, 1979; Y Nofel, 1992; Capel a Chomin, 1989; A Straitened Stage, 1991; Dramiten Cyflaewn, J Saunder Lewis, 1996, 1999. Address: Y Gwyndy, Lledrod, Ceredigion, SY23 4TD, Wales.

WILLIAMS J(eanne) R, (Megan Castell, Jeanne Creasey, Jeanne Crecy, Jeanne Foster, Kristin Michaels, Deidre Rowan), b. 10 Apr 1930, Elkhart, Kansas, USA. Author. Education: University of Oklohoma, 1952-53. Publications: To Buy a Dream, 1958; Promise of Tomorrow, 1959; Coyote Winter, 1965; Beasts with Music, 1967; Oil Patch Partners, 1968; New Medicine, 1971; Trails of Tears, 1972; Freedom Trail, 1973; Winter Wheat, 1975; A Lady Bought with Rifles, 1977; A Woman Clothed in Sun, 1978; Bride of Thunder, 1978; Daughter of the Sword, 1979; The Queen of a Lonely Country (as Megan Castell), 1980; The Valiant Women, 1981; Harvest of Fury, 1982; The Heaven Sword, 1983; A Mating of Hawks, 1984; The Care Dreamers, 1985; So Many Kingdoms, 1986; Texas Pride, 1987; Lady of No Man's Land, 1988; No Roof but Heaven, 1990; Home Mountain, 1990; The Island Harp, 1991; The Longest Road, 1993; Daughter of the Storm, 1994; The Unplowed Sky, 1994; Home Station, 1995. As J R Williams: Mission in Mexico, 1960; The Horsetalker, 1961; The Confederate Fiddle, 1962; River Guns, 1962; Oh Susanna, 1963; Tame the Wild Stallion, 1967. As Jeanne Crecy: Hands of Terror, UK edition as Lady Gift, 1972; The Lightning Tree, 1972; My Face Beneath Stone, 1975; The Winter-Keeper, 1975; The Night Hunters, 1975. As Deidre Rowan: Dragon's Mount, 1973; Silver Wood, 1974; Shadow of the Volcano, 1975; Time of the Burning Mask, 1976; Ravensgate, 1976. As Kristin Michaels: To Begin with Love, 1976; Enchanted Journey, 1977; Song of the Heart, 1977; Make Believe Love, 1978. As Jeanne Foster: Deborah Leigh, 1981; Eden Richards, 1982; Woman of Three Worlds, 1984; Wind Water, 1997. Contributions to: Journals. Honours: Texas Institute of Letters Best Children's Book, 1958; Four Western Writers of America Spur Awards; Best Novel of the West, 1981, 1990; Lew Strauss Golden Saddleman Award for Lifetime Achievement, 1988. Memberships: Author's Guild; Western Writers of America, president, 1974-75. Address: Box 335, Portal, AZ 85632, USA.

WILLIAMS John A(lfred), b. 5 Dec 1925, Jackson, Mississippi, USA. Writer; Journalist; Poet; Educator. m. (1) Carolyn Clopton, 1947, div, 2 sons, (2) Lorrain Isaac, 5 Oct 1965, 1 son. Education: BA, Syracuse University, 1950; Graduate School, 1951. Appointments: Editor and Publisher, Negro Market Newsletter, 1956-57; Contributing Editor, Herald-Tribune Book Week, 1963-65, American Journal, 1972-74, Politicks, 1977, Journal of African Civilizations, 1980-88; Lecturer, College of the Virgin Islands, 1968, City College of the City University of New York, 1968-69; Visiting Professor, Macalester College, 1970, University of Hawaii, 1974, Boston University, 1978-79, University of Houston, 1994, Bard College, 1994-95; Regents Lecturer, University of California at Santa Barbara, 1972; Guest Writer, Sarah Lawrence College, 1972-73; Distinguished Professor, LaGuardia Community College of the City University of New York, 1973-79; Distinguished Visiting Professor, Cooper Union, 1974-75; Professor, Rutgers University, 1979-93; Exxon Visiting Professor, New York University, 1986-87. Publications: Novels: The Angry Ones, 1960, new edition as One for New York, 1975; Night Song, 1961; Sissie, 1963; The Man Who Cried I Am, 1967; Sons of Darkness, Sons of Light, 1969; Captain Blackman, 1972; Mothersill and the Foxees, 1975; The Junio Bachelor Society, 1976; !Click Song, 1982; The Berhama Account, 1985; Jacob's Ladder, 1987. Poetry: Safari West, 1998. Non-Fiction: Africa: Her History, Lands and People, 1963; The Protectors, 1964; This Is My Country Too, 1965; The Most Native of Sons: A Biography of Richard Wright, 1970; The King God Didn't Save: Reflections on the Life and Death of Martin Luther King, Jr., 1970; Flashbacks: A Twenty-Year Diary of Article Writing, 1973; Minorities in the City, 1975; It I Stop I'll Die: The Comedy and Tragedy of Richard Pryor (with Dennis A Williams), 1991. Editor or Co-Editor: The Angry Black, 1962, new edition as Beyond the Angry Black, 1967; Amistad 1, 1970; Amistad 2, 1971; Y'Bird, 1978;

Introduction to Literature, 1985, 2nd edition, 1994; Street Guide to African Americans in Paris, 1992, 2nd edition, 1996; Approaches to Literature, 1994; Bridges: Literature Across Cultures, 1994. Contributions to: Anthologies, journals, reviews, and magazines. Honours: National Institute of Arts and Letters Awards, 1962; Centennial Medal, 1970, Honorary Doctor of Letters, 1995, Syracuse University; Ricahrd Wright-Jacques Roumain Award, 1973; National Endowment for the Arts Award, 1977; Honorary Doctor of Literature, Southeastern Massachusetts University, 1978; American Book Award, Before Columbus Foundation, 1983; New Jersey State Council on the Arts Award, 1985; Michael Award, New Jersey Literary Hall of Fame, 1987; Distinguished Writer Award, Middle Atlantic Writers, 1987; J A Williams Archive established, University of Rochester, 1987; Carter G Woodson Award, Mercy College, 1989. Address: 693 Forest Avenue, Teaneck, NJ 07666, USA.

WILLIAMS John Hartley, b. 7 Feb 1942, England. Poet; Lecturer. m. Gizella Horvat, 7 Mar 1970, 1 daughter. Education: BA, Honours, English, University of Nottingham, 1965; MPhil, English and Education, University of London, 1974; Certificate in Phonetics, University College, London, 1974. Appointment: Lecturer, Free University of Berlin, 1976-. Publications: Hidden Identities, 1982; Bright River Yonder, 1987; Cornerless People, 1990; Double, 1994; Ignoble Sentiments, 1995; Teach Yourself Writing Poetry (with Matthew Sweeney), 1997; The Scar in the Stone, edited by Chris Agee (contributing translator to poems from the Serbo-Croatian), 1998. Contributions to: Anthologies, reviews, and journals. Honours: 1st Prize, Arvon International Poetry Competition, 1983; Poetry Book Recommendation, 1987; Poetry Book Society Choice, shortlisted for T S Eliot Prize, 1997. Membership: Poetry Society. Address: 18 Jenbacherweg, 12209, Berlin, Germany.

WILLIAMS John Hoyt, b. 26 Oct 1940, Darien, Connecticut, USA. Professor of History. m. 27 Jan 1963, 1 son, 1 daughter. Education: BA, 1963, MA, History, 1965, University of Connecticut; PhD, Latin American History, 1969, University of Florida. Appointments: Assistant Professor of History, 1969-73, Associate Professor of History, 1973-78, Professor of History, 1978-, Indiana State University. Publications: Rise and Fall of the Paraguayan Republic 1800-1870, 1979; A Great and Shining Road, 1988; Sam Houston: A Biography of the Father of Texas, 1993. Contributions to: Atlantic Monthly; Christian Century; Americas; National Defense; Current History; Hispanic American Historical Review. Honour: Named Distinguished Professor of Arts and Sciences, 1996. Address: 1167 Farm Quarter Road, Mount Pleasant, SC 29464, USA.

WILLIAMS Kurt. See: **HIBBARD Bill (Curt William Jr).**

WILLIAMS Malcolm David, b. 9 Apr 1939, South Wales. Author. Widower, 1 daughter. Education: Birmingham Univerity Institute of Education, 1951-61. Publications: Yesterday's Secret, 1980; Poor Little Rich Girl, 1981; Debt of Friendship, 1981; Another Time, Another Place, 1982; Mr Brother's Keeper, 1982; The Stuart Affair, 1983; The Cordillera Conspiracy, 1983; The Girl from Derry's Bluff, 1983; A Corner of Eden, 1984; Sorrow's End, 1984; A Stranger on Trust, 1987; Shadows From the Past, 1989. Contributions to: Various publications. Honours: 1st Prize, Short Story Competition, 1961, 1969. Memberships: Society of Authors; West Country Writers Association; World Literary Academy, fellow. Address: 2 Reeds Close, Bredon, Tewkesbury, Gloucestershire GL20 7EL, England.

WILLIAMS Marcia Dorothy, b. 8 Aug 1945, White Lackington, England. Children's Author; Illustrator. 1 son, 1 daughter. Education: Roehampton Institute, MA course in Children's Literature. Publications: The First Christmas, 1987; Noah's Ark, 1989; Jonah and the Whale, 1990; Joseph and His Amazing Coat of Many Colours, 1990; When I Was Little, 1991; Not a Worry in the World, 1991; Don Quixote, 1992; Greek Myths, 1993; Sinbad the

Sailor, 1994; King Arthur, 1995; Robin Hood, 1996; The Odyssey and the Iliad, 1997; Mr William Shakespeare, 1998; Plays, Fabulous Monsters, 1999. Address: Walker Books Ltd, 87 Vauxhall Walk, SE11 5HY, England.

WILLIAMS Merryn, b. 9 July 1944, Devon, England. Writer; Poet; Editor. m. John Hemp, 14 Apr 1973, 1 son, 1 daughter. Education: BA, 1966, PhD, 1970, University of Cambridge. Appointments: Lecturer, Open University, 1970-71; Editor, The Interpreter's House, 1996-. Publications: The Bloodstream, 1989; Selected Poems of Federico Garcia Lorca, 1992; Wilfred Owen, 1993; The Sun's Yellow Eye, 1997. Contributions to: Reviews, quarterlies, journals, and magazines. Memberships: Open University Poets; Welsh Academy. Address: 10 Farrell Road, Wootton, Bedfordshire MK43 9DU, England.

WILLIAMS Michael Arnold, (Mike Williams, MAW, W Agate), b. 19 Jan 1936, Newport, Monmouthshire, Wales. Professor Emeritus. m. (1) Ann Weston, 11 Dec 1959, div, 2 sons, 1 daughter, (2) Dominique Simons, 14 Feb 1983. Education: BSc London, Kings College, 1959; MSc London, University College, 1960; PhD, Postgraduate Medical School, London; Fellow, Institute of Biology. Appointments: Research Assistant in Surgery, Postgraduate Medical School, London; Independent Research Worker, Scientific Research Council; Lecturer, Senior Lecturer, Reader, Professor in Anatomy, then Emeritus, 1996, Sheffield University. Publications: Practical Methods in Electron Microscopy, Parts I and II, 1977; Training Manuals for Teachers in HE, for UK and Commonwealth, 2 vols, 1993; Researching Local History, The Human Journey, 1996. Contributions to: Numerous to scientific journals; Poems and obituaries to Times and Independent. Address: Department of Biomedical Science, University of Sheffield, Sheffield S10 2TN, England.

WILLIAMS Miller, b. 8 Apr 1930, Hoxie, Arkansas, USA. University Press Director; Writer; Poet. m. (1) Lucille Day, 29 Dec 1951, 1 son, 2 daughters, (2) Jordan Hall, 1969. Education: BS, Arkansas State College, 1950; MS, University of Arkansas, 1952. Appointments: Founder-Editor, 1968-70, Advisory Editor, 1975-, New Orleans Review; Contributing Editor, Translation Review, 1976-80; Director, UA Press, 1980-97; Professor of English and Foreign Languages, 1971-. Publications: A Circle of Stone, 1964; Southern Writing in the Sixties (with J W Corrington), 2 volumes, 1966; So Long at the Fair, 1968; Chile: An Anthology of New Writing, 1968; The Achievement of John Ciardi, 1968; The Only World There Is, 1968; The Poetry of John Crowe Ransom, 1971; Contemporary Poetry in America, 1972; Halfway from Hoxie: New and Selected Poems, 1973; How Does a Poem Mean? (with John Ciardi), 1974; Railroad (with James Alan McPherson), 1976; Why God Permits Evil, 1977; A Roman Collection, 1980; Distraction, 1981; Ozark, Ozark: A Hillside Reader, 1981; The Boys on Their Bony Mules, 1983; Living on the Surface: New and Selected Poems, 1989; Adjusting to the Light, 1992; Points of Departure, 1995; The Ways We Touch (poems), 1997; Some Jazz a While: Collected Poems, 1999. Contributions to: Various publications. Honours: Henry Bellaman Poetry Award, 1957; Bread Loaf Fellowship in Poetry, 1961; Fulbright Lecturer, 1970; Prix de Rome, American Academy of Arts and Letters, 1976; Honorary Doctor of Humanities, Lander College, 1983; National Poets Prize, 1992; John William Corrington Award for Excellence in Literature, Centenary College, Louisiana, 1994; American Academy of Arts and Letters Award, 1995; Honorary Doctor of Humane Letters, Hendrix College, 1995; Inaugural Poet, Presidential Inauguration, 1997. Address: 1111 Valley View Drive, Fayetteville, AR 72701, USA.

WILLIAMS Nigel, b. 20 Jan 1948, Cheadle, Cheshire, England. Novelist; Playwright. Education: Oriel College, Oxford. Publications: Novels: My Life Closed Twice, 1977; Jack be Nimble, 1980; Charlie, 1984; Star Turn, 1985; Witchcraft, 1987; Breaking Up, 1988; Black Magic, 1988; The Wimbledon Poisoner, 1990; They Came from SW19, 1992; East of Wimbledon, 1993; Scenes from a

Poisoner's Life, 1994. Plays: Double Talk, 1976; Snowwhite Washes Whiter, 1977; Class Enemy, 1978; Easy Street, 1979; Sugar and Spice, 1980; Line 'em, 1980; Trial Run, 1980; WCPC, 1982; The Adventures of Jasper Ridley, 1982; My Brother's Keeper, 1985; Deathwatch (after Genet), 1985; Country Dancing, 1986; As It Was, 1987; Nativity, 1989. Television plays. Honour: Somerset Maugham Award for Fiction, 1978. Address: c/o Faber and Faber, 3 Queen Square, London WC1N 3AU, England.

WILLIAMS Philip F C, b. 5 Apr 1956, Little Rock, Arkansas, USA. University Professor. m. Yenna Wu, 23 Nov 1990, 1 son. Education: BA, University of Arkansas, 1978; MA, 1981, PhD, 1985, University of California at Los Angeles. Appointments: Assistant Professor of Foreign Languages, 1986-93, Associate Professor of Languages and Literature, 1993-, Arizona State University; Postdoctoral Fellow, Harvard University, 1990-91; Assistant Professor, University of Vermont, 1991-92. Publication: Village Echoes: The Fiction of Wu Zuxiang, 1993. Contributions to: Scholarly journals. Honour: Humanities Research Award, Arizona State University, 1989. Memberships: Southwest Conference of Asian Studies, president, 1996; Phi Beta Kappa, Arizona Beta Chapter Vice President, 1996; American Association for Chinese Comparative Literature, executive committee member, 1995-. Address: Department Languages and Literatures, Box 870202, Arizona State University, Tempe, AZ 85287, USA.

WILLIAMS Phyllis. See: **ZENO Phyllis W.**

WILLIAMS Tony, b. 11 Jan 1946, Swansea, Wales. Writer. m. Kathleen Ensor, 1 June 1980. Education: Teacher's Certificate, Swansea College of Education, 1967; 1st Class Honours, Biblical Studies, 1970, PhD, Theology, 1974, University of Manchester; MA, Film Studies, University of Warwick, 1979. Appointments: Faculty, Southern Illinois University. Publications: Italian Western: Opera of Violence (co-author), 1975; Jack London: The Movies, 1992; Vietnam War Films (co-editor), 1994; Hearths of Darkness: The Family in the American Horror Film, 1996; Radical Allegories: The Films of Larry Cohen, 1997; The Making of the Warner Brothers Sea Wolf (co-editor), 1997. Contributions to: Journals. Honour: Jack London Man of the Year, 1988. Memberships: Aizen; Society for Cinema Studies. Address: c/o Department of English, Southern Illinois University, Carbondale, IL 62701, USA.

WILLIAMS-WITHERSPOON Kimmika L H, b. 7 Jan 1959, Pennsylvania, USA. Playwright; Poet; Performance Artist. m. Darrell V Witherspoon, 11 July 1992, 2 daughters. Education: BA, Journalism, Howard University, 1980; MFA, Playwriting, Temple University, 1996; Graduate Certificate in Womens Studies, 1996. Appointments: Future Faculty Fellow, Anthropology Department, Temple University. Publications: God Made Men Brown, 1982; It Ain't Easy To Be Different, 1986; Halley's Comet, 1988; Envisioning a Sea of Dry Bones, 1990; Epic Memory: Places and Spaces I've Been, 1995; Signs of the Times: Culture Gap, 1999. Contributions to: Women's Words; Sunlight on the Moon. Honours: Playwrights Exchange Grant, 1994, 1996. Memberships: Poets and Prophets; Poets and Writers. Address: c/o Temple University, 219 Tomlinson Hall, Philadelphia, PA 19122, USA.

WILLIAMSON Jack, (John Stewart Williamson), b. 29 Apr 1908, Bisbee, Arizona, USA. Writer. m. Blanche Slaten Harp, 15 Aug 1947, dec 1985, 2 stepchildren. Education: BA, MA, 1957, Eastern New Mexico University; PhD, University of Colorado, 1964. Appointment: Professor of English, Eastern New Mexico University, Portales, 1960-77. Publications: Science Fiction: The Legion of Space, 1947; Darker Than You Think, 1948; The Humanoids, 1949; The Green Girl, 1950; The Cometeers, 1950; One Against the Legion, 1950; Seetee Shock, 1950; Seetee Ship, 1950; Dragon's Island, 1951; The Legion of Time, 1952; Dome Around America, 1955; The Trial of Terra, 1962; Golden Blood, 1964; The Reign of Wizardry, 1965; Bright New Universe,

1967; Trapped in Space, 1968; The Pandora Effect, 1969; People Machines, 1971; The Moon Children, 1972; H G Wells: Critic of Progress, 1973; Teaching Science Fiction, 1975; The Early Williamson, 1975; The Power of Blackness, 1976; The Best of Jack Williamson, 1978; Brother to Demons, Brother to Gods, 1979; Teaching Science Fiction: Education for Tomorrow, 1980; The Alien Intelligence, 1980; The Humanoid Touch, 1980; Manseed, 1982; The Queen of a Legion, 1983; Wonder's Child: My Life in Science Fiction, 1984; Lifeburst, 1984; Firechild, 1986; Mazeway, 1990; Beachhead, 1992; Demon Moon, 1994; The Black Sun, 1997; The Fortress of Utopia, 1998; The Silicon Dagger, 1999. With Frederik Pohl: Undersea Quest, 1954; Undersea Fleet, 1955; Undersea City, 1956; The Reefs of Space, 1964; Starchild, 1965; Rogue Star, 1969; The Farthest Star, 1975; Wall Around a Star, 1983; Land's End, 1988. With James Gunn: Star Bridge, 1955. With Miles J Breuer: The Birth of a New Republic, 1981. Honours: Pilgrim Award, Science Fiction Research Association, 1968; Grand Master Nebula Award, 1976; Hugo Award, 1985. Memberships: Science Fiction Writers of America, president 1978-80; Science Fiction Research Association; World Science Fiction Planetary Society. Address: PO Box 761, Portales, NM 88130, USA.

WILLIAMSON Joel R, b. 27 Oct 1929, Anderson County, South Carolina, USA. Professor; Writer. m. Betty Anne Woodson, 18 Nov 1986, 1 son, 2 daughters. Education: AB, 1949, MA, 1951, University of South Carolina; PhD, University of California, Berkeley, 1964. Appointments: Instructor, 1950-64, Assistant Professor, 1964-66, Associate Professor, 1966-69, Professor, 1969-85, Linberger Professor in Humanities, 1985-, Department of History, University of North Carolina, Chapel Hill. Publications: After Slavery: The Negro in South Carolina During Reconstruction, 1965; Origins of Segregation, 1968; New People: Miscegenation and Mulattoes in the US, 1980; The Crucible of Race, 1984; A Rage for Order, 1986; William Faulkner and Southern History, 1993. Contributions to: Various. Honours: Parkman, Emerson, Owsley, Kennedy, Mayflower Awards; Mayflower Cup, 1994; Finalist, Pulitzer Prize in History, 1994. Memberships: Society of American Historians; Southern Historical Association; Organizations of American Historians. Address: 211 Hillsborough Street, Chapel Hill, NC 27514, USA.

WILLIAMSON Kristin Ingrid, b. 16 Sept 1940, Melbourne, Australia. Novelist; Biographer. m. David Williamson, 30 May 1974, 3 sons. Education: BA, Honours, Latrobe University, 1981; Drama, Trinity College, London; TPTC. Appointments: Teacher of English, History and Drama, primary and high schools, Victoria, 1960-70; Lecturer in Drama, Melbourne State College, 1970-72; Freelance Journalist, 1973-79; Journalist, Columnist, National Times, Sydney, 1979-87; Writer, 1987-. Publications: The Last Bastion, 1984; Princess Kate (novel), 1988; Tanglewood (novel), 1992; The Jacaranda Years (novel), 1995; Brothers To Us (biography), 1997; Treading on Dreams (novel), 1998. Literary Agent: Jill Hickson. Address: c/o Hickson Associates Pty Ltd, 128 Queen Street, Woollhara, NSW 2025, Australia.

WILLIAMSON Robert Clifford, b. 25 Apr 1916, Los Angeles, California, USA. Professor of Sociology; Writer. m. Virginia M Lorenzini, 11 Apr 1953, 2 sons. Education: BA, Psychology, 1938, MA, Psychology, 1940, University of California, Los Angeles; PhD, Sociology, University of Southern California, 1951. Publications: Social Psychology (with S S Sargent), 1958, 3rd edition, 1982; El Estudiante Colombiano y sus Aetitudes, 1962; Marriage and Family Relations, 1966, 2nd edition, 1972; Sex Roles in Contemporary Culture, 1970; Bilingualism and Minority Languages, 1991; Early Retirement: Promises and Pitfalls (with A Rinehart and T Blank), 1992; Latin American Societies in Transition, 1997. Contributions to: American Sociological Review; Social Forces; Journal of Marriage and the Family; Revista Mexicana de Sociologia; Western Political Quarterly; Sociology and Social Research. Address: Department of

Sociology, Lehigh University, 681 Taylor Street, Bethlehem, PA 18015, USA.

WILLIAMSON Robin, b. 24 Nov 1943, Edinburgh, Scotland. Writer; Musician; Storyteller. m. Bina Jasbinder Kaur Williamson, 2 Aug 1989, 1 son, 1 daughter. Publications: Home Thoughts from Abroad, 1972; Five Denials on Merlin's Grave, 1979; Selected Writings, 1980-83, 1984; The Craneskin Bag, 1989. Other: Music books, spoken word cassettes and recordings. Address: BCM 4797, London WC1N 3XX, England.

WILLIS Meredith Sue, b. 31 May 1946, West Virginia, USA. Writer; Educator. m. Andrew B Weinberger, 9 May 1982, 1 son. Education: BA, Barnard College, 1969; MFA, Columbia University, 1972. Publications: A Space Apart, 1979; Higher Ground, 1981; Only Great Changes, 1985; Personal Fiction Writing, 1984; Quilt Pieces, 1990; Blazing Pencils, 1990; Deep Revision, 1993; The Secret Super Power of Marco, 1994; In the Mountains of America, 1994; Marco's Monster, 1996; Trespassers, 1997. Honours: National Endowment for the Arts Fellowship, 1978; New Jersey Arts Fellowship, 1995; Honoree, Emory and Henry Literary Festival, 1995. Literary Agent: Wendy Weil. Address: 311 Prospect Street, South Orange, NJ 07079, USA.

WILLOUGHBY Cass. See: **OLSEN Theodore Victor.**

WILLOUGHBY John. See: **HIGSON Philip.**

WILLS Garry, b. 22 May 1934, Atlanta, Georgia, USA. Writer; Journalist; Adjunct Professor. m. Natalie Cavallo, 30 May 1959, 2 sons, 1 daughter. Education: BA, St Louis University, 1957; MA, Xavier University, Cincinnati, 1958; MA, 1959, PhD, 1961, Yale University. Appointments: Fellow, Center for Hellenic Studies, 1961-62; Associate Professor of Classics, 1962-67, Adjunct Professor, 1968-80, Johns Hopkins University; Newspaper Columnist, Universal Press Syndicate, 1970-; Henry R Luce Professor of American Culture and Public Policy, 1980-88, Adjunct Professor, 1988-, Northwestern University. Publications: Chesterton, 1961; Politics and Catholic Freedom, 1964; Roman Culture, 1966; Jack Ruby, 1967; Second Civil War, 1968; Nixon Agonistes, 1970; Bare Ruined Choirs, 1972; Inventing America, 1978; At Button's, 1979; Confessions of a Conservative, 1979; Explaining America, 1980; The Kennedy Imprisonment, 1982; Lead Time, 1983; Cincinnatus, 1984; Reagan's America, 1987; Under God, 1990; Lincoln at Gettysburg, 1992; Certain Trumpets: The Call of Leaders, 1994; Witches and Jesuits: Shakespeare's Macbeth, 1994; John Wayne's America, 1997. Honours: Various honorary doctorates; National Book Critics Circle Ward, 1993; Pulitzer Prize for General Non-Fiction, 1993; National Humanities Medal, 1998. Memberships: American Academy of Arts and Letters; American Academy of Arts and Sciences; American Antiquarian Society; Massachusetts Historical Society. Address: c/o Department of History, Northwestern University, Evanston, IL 60201, USA.

WILMER Clive, b. 10 Feb 1945, Harrogate, Yorkshire, England. Lecturer; Writer; Poet; Translator; Broadcaster. m. Diane Redmond, 12 Sept 1971, div 1986, 1 son, 1 daughter. Education: BA, 1st Class Honours, English, 1967, MA, 1970, King's College, Cambridge. Appointments: Visiting Professor in Creative Writing, University of California at Santa Barbara, 1986; Editor, Numbers, 1986-90; Presenter, Poet of the Month series, BBC Radio 3, 1989-92; Mikimoto Memorial Ruskin Lecturer, University of Lancaster, 1996. Publications: Poetry: The Dwelling Place, 1977; Devotions, 1982; Of Earthly Paradise, 1992; Selected Poems, 1995. Translator with G Gömöri: Forced March, by Miklós Radnóti, 1979; Night Song of the Personal Shadow, by György Petri, 1991; My Manifold City, by G Gömöri, 1996. Editor: Thom Gunn: The Occasion of Poetry, 1982; John Ruskin: Unto This Last and Other Writings, 1985; Dante Gabriel Rossetti: Selected Poems and Translations, 1991; William Morris: News From Nowhere and Other Writings, 1993; Poets Talking: The 'Poet of the Month' Interviews from BBC Radio 3, 1994. Contributions to:

Many reviews, quarterlies, and journals. Honours: Writer's Grant, Arts Council of Great Britain, 1979; Author's Foundation Grant, 1993. Membership: Companion of the Guild of St George, 1995. Address: 57 Norwich Street, Cambridge CB2 1ND, England.

WILOCH Thomas, b. 3 Feb 1953, Detroit, Michigan, USA. Poet; Writer; Editor. m. Denise Gottis, 10 Oct 1981. Education: BA, Wayne State University, 1978. Appointments: Associated with Gale Research Inc, 1977-; Columnist, Retrofuturism, 1991-93, Photo Static, 1993-94; Book Reviewer, Anti-Matter Magazine, 1992-94. Publications: Stigmata Junction, 1985; Paper Mask, 1988; The Mannikin Cypher, 1989; Tales of Lord Shantih, 1990; Decoded Factories of the Heart, 1991, new edition, 1994; Night Rain, 1991; Narcotic Signature, 1992; Lyrical Brandy, 1993; Mr Templeton's Toyshop, 1995; Neon Trance, 1997. Contributions to: Over 200 magazines. Honours: Nominations, Pushcart Prize, 1988, 1990, Rhysling Award, 1992, 1996. Membership: Association of Literacy Scholars and Critics. Address: 43672 Emrick Drive, Canton, MI 48187, USA.

WILSON A(ndrew) N(orman), b. 27 Oct 1950, England. Author. m. (1) Katherine Duncan-Jones, 2 daughters, (2) Ruth Alexander Guilding, 1991. Education: MA, New College, Oxford. Appointments: Lecturer, St Hugh's College and New College, Oxford, 1976-81; Literary Editor, The Spectator, 1981-83. Publications: The Sweets of Pimlico (novel), 1977; Unguarded Hours (novel), 1978; Kindly Light (novel), 1979; The Laird of Abbotsford, 1980; The Healing Art (novel), 1980; Who Was Oswald Fish (novel), 1981; Wise Virgin (novel), 1982; A Life of John Milton, 1983; Scandal (novel), 1983; Hilaire Belloc, 1984; Gentlemen in England (novel), 1985; Love Unknown (novel), 1986; The Church in Crisis (co-author), 1986; Stray (novel), 1987; Landscape in France, 1987; Incline Our Hearts (novel), 1987; Penfriends from Porlock: Essays and Reviews, 1977-86, 1988; Tolstoy: A Biography, 1988; Eminent Victorians, 1989; C S Lewis: A Biography, 1990; A Bottle in the Smoke (novel), 1990; Against Religion, 1991; Daughters of Albion (novel), 1991; Jesus, 1992; The Vicar of Sorrows (novel), 1993; The Faber Book of Church and Clergy, 1992; The Rise and Fall of the House of Windsor, 1993; The Faber Book of London (editor), 1993; Hearing Voices (novel), 1995; Paul: The Mind of the Apostle, 1997; Dream Children (novel), 1998. Honours: Royal Society of Literature, fellow, 1981; Whitbread Biography Award, 1988. Address: 91 Albert Street, London NW1 7LX, England.

WILSON Alan R, b. Moncton, New Brunswick, Canada. Writer; Poet. Education: BSc, Physics, University of New Brunswick; MFA, Creative Writing, University of British Columbia. Publications: Animate Objects, poetry, 1995; Counting to 100, poetry, 1996; Before the Flood, novel, 1999. Contributions to: Chicago Review; The Fiddlehead; The Lyric; National Forum; Malahat Review; Nimrod. Honour: Prizewinner, CBC Literary Competition. Literary Agent: Hilary Stanley, 94 Harbord Street, Toronto, Ontario, Canada M5S 1G6. Address: 2059 Newton Street, Victoria, British Columbia, Canada V8R 2R7.

WILSON August, b. 27 Apr 1945, Pittsburgh, Pennsylvania, USA. Dramatist. 1 daughter. Appointment: Founder, Black Horizons Theatre Co, Pittsburgh, 1968. Publications: The Homecoming, 1979; The Coldest Day of the Year, 1979; Fullerton Street, 1980; Black Bart and the Sacred Hills, 1981; Jitney, 1982; Ma Rainey's Black Bottom, 1984; Fences, 1985; Joe Turner's Come and Gone, 1986; The Piano Lesson, 1987; Two Trains Running, 1990; Seven Guitars, 1995. Honours: New York Drama Critics Circle Awards, 1985, 1986, 1988, 1990, 1996; Whiting Writer's Award, 1986; American Theatre Critics Outstanding Play Awards, 1986, 1990, 1992; Drama Desk Awards, 1986, 1990; Pulitzer Prizes for Drama, 1987, 1990; Tony Award, 1987; Outer Critics' Circle Award, 1987; Literary Lion Award, New York Public Library, 1988. Membership: American Academy of Arts and Letters. Address: 1285 Avenue of the Americas, New York, NY 10019, USA.

WILSON Budge Marjorie, b. 2 May 1927, Halifax, Nova Scotia, Canada. Writer. m. Alan Wilson, 31 July 1953, 2 daughters. Education: BA, 1949, Diploma in Education, 1952, Dalhousie University. Publications: The Best-Worst Christmas Present Ever, 1984; A House Far from Home, 1986; Mr John Bertrand Nijinsky and Charlie, 1986; Mystery Lights at Blue Harbour, 1987; Breakdown, 1988; Going Bananas, 1989; Thirteen Never Changes, 1989; Madame Belzile and Ramsay Hitherton-Hobbs, 1990; Lorinda's Diary, 1991; The Leaving, 1990; Oliver's Wars, 1992; The Courtship (adult short fiction), 1994; Cassandra's Driftwood, 1994; Cordelia Clark and Other Stories, 1994; The Long Wait, 1997; Duff the Giant Killer, 1997; SHARLA, 1997; The Cat that Barked, 1998; Many adult and children's short stories. Contributions to: Various publications. Honours: CBC Literary Competition, 1981; Atlantic Writing Competition, 1986; City of Dartmouth Book Award, 1991; Young Adult Book Award, Canadian Library Association, 1991; Marianna Dempster Award, Canadian Authors Association, 1992; Ann Connor Brimer Award, 1993. Memberships: Writers Federation of Nova Scotia, board member; Canadian Authors Association; Writers Union of Canada; Atlantic Representative, Canadian Society of Children's Authors, Illustrators and Performers, secretary; Councillor-East (Canada), International Board on Books for Young Children, Atlantic representative. Address: North West Cove, RR1, Hubbards, Nova Scotia B0J 1T0, Canada.

WILSON Christopher Richard Maclean, b. 6 Jan 1934, Minehead, Somerset, England. Educator. m. Alma Louis Oliver, 5 Sept 1964, 2 sons. Education: BA, 1957, MA, 1961, St Catharine's College, Cambridge; Clifton Theological School, Bristol, 1960; Episcopal Theological School, Cambridge, Massachusetts, USA; MA 1971, PhD 1977, University of Toronto. Appointment: Director, Board and Management Services, Ontario Hospital Association, 1978-92. Publications: Hospital-wide Quality Assurance, 1987; Governing with Distinction, 1988; New on Board, 1991; Strategies in Health Care Quality, 1992. Monographs: Quality Assurance-Getting Started, 1985; Annotated Bibliography on Hospital Governance, 1989; Risk Management for Canadian Health Care Facilities, 1990. Contributions to: Professional journals. Honours: Writer of the Year, Canadian Association for Quality in Health Care, 1990; Honorary Fellow, University of Manchester 1992-94. Address: 10 St Mary Street, Toronto, Ontario M4Y 1P9, Canada.

WILSON Colin Henry, b. 26 July 1931, Leicester, England. Author. m. (1) Dorothy Betty Troop, 1 son, (2) Joy Stewart, 2 sons, 1 daughter. Appointments: Visiting Professor, Hollins College, Virginia, 1966-67, University of Washington, Seattle, 1967, Dowling College, Majorca, 1969, Rutgers University, New Jersey, 1974. Publications: The Outsider, 1956; Religion and the Rebel, 1957; The Age of Defeat, 1959; Ritual in the Dark, 1960; The Strength to Dream, 1962; Origins of the Sexual Impulse, 1963; Necessary Doubt, 1964; Eagle and the Earwig, 1965; The Glass Cage, 1966; Sex and the Intelligent Teenager, 1966; Voyage to a Beginning, 1969; Hermann Hesse, 1973; Strange Powers, 1973; The Space Vampires, 1976; Mysteries, 1978; Starseekers, 1980; Access to Inner Worlds, 1982; Psychic Detectives, 1983; The Essential Colin Wilson, 1984; Rudolf Steiner: The Man and His Work, 1985; An Encyclopedia of Scandal (with Donald Seaman), 1986; Spider World: The Tower, 1987; Aleister Crowley - The Man and the Myth, 1987; An Encyclopedia of Unsolved Mysteries (with Damon Wilson), 1987; Marx Refuted, 1987; Written in Blood (with Donald Seaman), 1989; The Misfits - A Study of Sexual Outsiders, 1988; Beyond the Occult, 1988; The Serial Killers, 1990; Spiderworld: The Magician, 1991; The Strange Life of P D Ouspensky, 1993; Unsolved Mysteries Past and Present (with Damon Wilson), 1993; Atlas of Holy Places and Sacred Sites, 1996; From Atlantis to the Sphinx, 1996; Alien Dawn, 1998. Contributions to: The Times; Literary Review; The Gramophone; Evening Standard Daily Mail. Membership: Society of Authors. Address: Tetherdown, Trewallock Lane, Gorran Haven, Cornwall, England.

WILSON Dave. See: **FLOREN Lee.**

WILSON Des, b. 1941, New Zealand. Writer. Appointments: Journalist, Broadcaster, 1957-67; Director, Shelter National Campaign for the Homeless, 1967-71; Columnist, The Guardian, 1968-70, The Observer, 1971-75; Head of Public Affairs, Royal Shakespeare Co, London, 1974-76; Editor, Social Work Today, 1976-79; Deputy Editor, Illustrated London News, 1979-81; Chairman, Campaign for Lead Free Air, 1981-85, Friends of the Earth, 1982-86, Freedom of Information, 1984-91; President, Liberal Party, 1986-87; General Election Campaign Director, Liberal Democrats, 1991-92. Publications: I Know It Was the Place's Fault, 1970; Des Wilson's Minority Report, 1973; So You Want to be Prime Minister, 1979; The Lead Scandal, 1982; Pressure: The A to Z of Campaigning in Britain, 1984; The Enviornmental Crisis, 1984; The Secrets File, 1984; Costa del Sol, 1990; Campaign: 1992; Campaigning, The A to Z of Public Advocacy, 1994. Address: 48 Stapleton Hall Road, Stroud Green, London N4 3QG, England.

WILSON Edward Osborne, b. 10 June 1929, Birmingham, Alabama, USA. Biologist; Professor; Writer. m. Irene Kelley, 30 Oct 1955, 1 daughter. Education: BS, 1949, MS, 1950, University of Alabama; PhD, Harvard University, 1955. Appointments: Junior Fellow, Society of Fellows, 1953-56, Faculty, 1956-76, Curator, Entomology, 1971-, Baird Professor of Science, 1976-94, Pellegrino University Professor, 1994-, Harvard University; Board of Directors, World Wildlife Fund, 1983-94, Organization of Tropical Studies, 1984-91, New York Botanical Gardens, 1991-95, American Museum of Natural History, 1992-, American Academy of Liberal Education, 1993-, Nature Conservancy, 1994-, Conservation International, 1997-. Publications: The Insect Societies, 1971; Sociobiology: The New Synthesis, 1975; On Human Nature, 1978; Promethean Fire (with C J Lumsden), 1983; Biophilia, 1984; The Ants (with Bert Holldobler), 1990; Success and Dominance in Ecosystems, 1990; The Diversity of Life, 1991; Journey to the Ants (with Bert Holldobler), 1994; Naturalist, 1994; Consilience: The Unity of Knowledge, 1998. Others. Contributions to: Professional journals. Honours: National Medal of Science, 1976; Pulitzer Prizes in Non-Fiction, 1979, 1991; Tyler Ecology Prize, 1984; Weaver Award for Scholarly Letters, Ingersoll Foundation, 1989; Crafoord Prize, Royal Swedish Academy of Sciences, 1990; Prix d'Institut de la Vie, Paris, 1990; International Prize for Biology, Government of Japan, 1993; Audubon Medal, Audubon Society, 1995; Phi Beta Kappa Prize for Science, 1995; Los Angeles Times Book Prize for Science, 1995; Schubert Prize, Germany, 1996; German Ecological Foundation Book Award, 1998; Many honorary doctorates; Others. Memberships: American Academy of Arts and Sciences, fellow; American Genetics Association; American Humanist Society; American Philosophical Society; British Ecological Society, honorary life member; Entomological Society of America, honorary life member; National Academy of Science; Royal Society of London; Finnish Academy of Science and Letters; Russian Academy of Natural Sciences. Address: 9 Foster Road, Lexington, MA 02173, USA.

WILSON Edwin James (Peter), b. 27 Oct 1942, Lismore, New South Wales, Australia. Poet. m. Cheryl Lillian Turnham, 1 Sept 1975, 2 sons, 1 daughter. Education: BSc, University of New South Wales. Publications: Banyan, 1982; Royal Botanic Gardens, 1982; Liberty, Egality, Fraternity, 1984; The Dragon Tree, 1985; Discovering the Domain, 1986; Wild Tamarind, 1987; Falling Up into Verse, 1989; Songs of the Forest, 1990; The Rose Garden, 1991; The Wishing Tree, 1992; The Botanic Verses, 1993; Chaos Theory, 1997; Cosmos Seven: Selected Poems, 1967-1997, 1998. Contributions to: Australian Folklore; Poetry Australia. Membership: New South Wales Poets Union. Address: PO Box 32, Lane Cove, New South Wales 2066, Australia.

WILSON Eliane, b. 4 Aug 1934, Geneva, Switzerland. Author. m. Paul Wilson, 2 Aug 1963, 2 sons, 1 daughter. Education: Geneva University, 1953-56, Heidelberg University, 1957. Publications: Anthologies: As I Trace Again Thy Winding Hill, 1981; Images of Christmas, 1984; Thomas Hardy: An Autobiography in Verse, 1985;

Edward Thomas: A Mirror of England, 1985; Oxford: Words and Watercolours, 1987; Jerusalem: Reflection of Eternity, 1990. Fiction: The Lost Dove, 1998. Memberships: Thomas Hardy Society; Edward Thomas Fellowship. Literary Agent: Gaia Media AG, Basel, Switzerland. Address: Waysmeet, Orley Farm Road, Harrow on the Hill HA1 3PF, England.

WILSON Gina, b. 1 Apr 1943, Abergele, North Wales. Children's Writer; Poet. Education: MA, University of Edinburgh, 1965; Mount Holyoke College, 1965-66. Appointments: Assistant Editor, Scottish National Dictionary, 1967-73, Dictionary of the Older Scottish Tongue, 1972-73. Publications: Cora Ravenwing, 1980; A Friendship of Equals, 1981; The Whisper, 1982; All Ends Up, 1984; Family Feeling, 1986; Just Us, 1988; Polly Pipes Up, 1989; I Hope You Know, 1989; Jim Jam Pyjamas, 1990; Wompus Galumpus, 1990; Riding the Great White, 1992; Prowlpuss, 1994; Frogmore Poetry Prize, 1997. Address: 24 Beaumont Street, Oxford OX12 2NP, England.

WILSON Jacqueline, b. 17 Dec 1945, Bath, Somerset, England. Writer. m. William Millar Wilson, 28 Aug 1965, 1 daughter. Publications: Nobody's Perfect, 1982; Waiting for the Sky to Fall, 1983; The Other Side, 1984; Amber, 1986; The Power of the Shade, 1987; This Girl, 1988; Stevie Day Series, 1987; Is There Anybody There?, 1990; The Story of Tracy Beaker, 1991; The Suitcase Kid, 1992; Deep Blue, 1993; The Bed and Breakfast Star, 1994; Cliffhanger, 1995; The Dinosaur's Packed Lunch, 1995; Double Act, 1995; Bad Girls, 1996. Honours: Oak Tree Award, 1992; Smarties Award, 1995. Address: 1B Beaufort Road, Kingston on Thames, Surrey KT1 2TH, England.

WILSON Jacquelyn, b. 8 Apr 1952, Springfield, Illinois, USA. Writer. Education: Student, 1970-74, BA, English, 1974, Nasson College; University of Salzburg, Austria, 1973-74; Associate degree, Commercial Art, Salt Lake Technical College, 1983; Welding course, Utah Technical School, 1985. Publication: The Fountain, prose piece. Contributions to: Poems in magazines and anthologies, 1991-. Memberships: Wisconsin Fellowship of Poets; Society of Children's Book Writers and Illustrators. Address: 245 S Park Street, Madison, WI 53715, USA.

WILSON Joyce Muriel, (Joyce Stranger), b. 26 May 1921, London, England. Writer; Canine Behaviourist and Trainer. m. Dr Kenneth Bruce Wilson, 1944, 2 sons, 1 daughter. Education: BSc, University College, London, 1942. Publications: Over 70 books including: The Guardians of Staghill, 1997; How to Own a Sensible Dog, 1997; Perilous Journey, 1998. Contributions to: Canine journals, newspapers and magazines. Honour: Shortlisted, Trento Aware, Italy, 1977. Memberships: People and Dogs Society, president; Canine Concern, president; United Kingdom Registry of Canine Behaviourists; Association of Pet Dog Trainers; Chartered Institute of Journalists; Society of Authors; Society of Companion Animals. Address: c/o Gillon Aitken Associates, 29 Fernshaw Road, London SW10 0TG, England.

WILSON Keith, b. 26 Dec 1927, Clovis, New Mexico, USA. Poet; Writer. m. Heloise Brigham, 15 Feb 1958, 1 son, 4 daughters. Education: BS, US Naval Academy, 1950; MA, University of New Mexico, 1956. Publications: Homestead, 1969; Thantog: Songs of a Jaguar Priest, 1977; While Dancing Feet Shatter the Earth, 1977; The Streets of San Miguel, 1979; Retables, 1981; Stone Roses: Poems from Transylvania, 1983; Meeting at Jal (with Theodore Ensliu), 1985; Lion's Gate: Selected Poems 1963-1986, 1988; The Wind of Pentecost, 1991; Graves Registry, 1992; The Way of the Dove, 1994. Contributions to: Journals. Honours: National Endowment for the Arts Fellowship; Fulbright-Hays Fellowship; D H Lawrence Creative Writing Fellowship. Address: 1500 South Locust Street, No C-21, Las Cruces, NM 88001, USA.

WILSON Lanford, b. 13 Apr 1937, Lebanon, Missouri, USA. Dramatist; Director. Education: San Diego State College, 1955-56. Appointment: Resident Playwright and Director, Circle Repertory Co, New York City, 1969-95. Publications: Balm in Gilead and Other Plays, 1966; The Rimers of Eldritch and Other Plays, 1968; The Gingham Dog, 1969; Lemon Sky, 1970; The Hot l Baltimore, 1973; The Mound Builders, 1976; Fifth of July, 1979; Talley's Folly, 1980; Angels Fall, 1983; Serenading Louie, 1985; Talley & Son, 1986; Burn This, 1988; Redwood Curtain, 1992; 21 Short Plays, 1994; By the Sea, 1996. Honours: Vernon Rice Award, 1966-67; Rockefeller Foundation Grants, 1967, 1973; ABC Yale Fellow, 1969; Guggenheim Fellowship, 1970; National Institute of Arts and Letters Award, 1970; Obie Awards, 1972, 1975, 1984; Outer Critics Circle Award, 1973; Drama Critics Circle Awards, 1973, 1980; Pulitzer Prize for Drama, 1980; Brandeis University Creative Arts Award, 1981; John Steinbeck Award, 1990; National Endowment for the Arts Grant, 1990; Edward Albee Last Frontier Award, 1994; American Academy of Achievement Award, 1995; Honorary doctorates. Membership: Dramatists Guild. Address: c/o Dramatists Guild, 234 West 44th Street, New York, NY 10036, USA.

WILSON Leslie Erica, b. 10 Aug 1952, Nottingham, England. Novelist. m. David Wilson, 20 July 1974, 2 daughters. Education: BA, Durham University; PGCE, Oxford. Publications: Morning is Not Permitted, 1990; Malefice, 1992; The Mountain of Immoderate Desires, 1994. Contributions to: Orbis; Writing Women; Guardian; Iron; Good Housekeeping Sunday Times; Independent on Sunday; London Rewiew of Books; Literary Review. Memberships: Poetry Society; Society of Authors; PEN; Royal Society of Literature.

WILSON Lorraine Margaret, b. 18 May 1939, Echuca, Victoria, Australia. Educational Consultant. Education: Trained Infant Teacher's Certificate; Certificate A, Education Department of Victoria. Appointment: Public Lending Right Committee. Publications: City Kids (series), 1978-86; Write Me A Sign, 1979; Country Kids (series), 1982-87; You Can't Make a Book in a Day (with B Scarffe, 1988); My Mum Has False Teeth and Other Stories, 1990; An Integrated Approach to Learning (with D Malmgren, S Ramage, L Schulz), 1990; Write Me a Poem, 1994; Footy Kids (series), 1995; I Have Two Dads, 1995; I Speak Two Languages, 1995; James and Jessie Series, 1995; The Best of City Kids (series), 1997; New City Kids (series), 1997. Contributions to: Curriculum and Research Bulletin; Australian Journal of Reading; Primary Education; Reading Teacher; Teaching K-8. Honour: Australian Literary Educators Association Medal, 1996. Memberships: Australian Society of Authors; Australian Literacy Educators Association; International Reading Association; Australian Education Network. Address: 81 Amess Street, North Carlton, Victoria 3054, Australia.

WILSON Peter John, b. 24 Apr 1944, Sydney, New South Wales, Australia. Mathematics Tutor. m. Sau Ching Au, 27 Apr 1988. Education: BSc, 1964, MA, 1989, University of Sydney. Publications: Australia's Insect Life, 1970; Modelling the SR 71A, 1976; The Living Bush: A Naturalist's Guide, 1977; Darkness, No Darkness, 1978; The Convair F106 Delta Dart, 1978; World of Insects, 1979; Depth of Field, 1980; Extreme Close-up Photography, 1981; Insect Photography, 1985; Butterflies of the Rainforest, 1986; Australia's Butterflies, 1987; Going It Alone, 1989. Address: 49 Despointes Street, Marrickville, New South Wales 2204, Australia.

WILSON William Julius, b. 20 Dec 1935, Derry Township, Pennsylvania, USA. Sociologist; Professor. m. (1) Mildred Marie Hood, 31 Aug 1957, 2 daughters, (2) Beverly Ann Huebner, 30 Aug 1970, 1 son, 1 daughter. Education: BA, Wilberforce University, 1958; MA, Bowling Green State University, 1961; PhD, Washington State University, 1966. Appointments: Assistant Professor, 1965-69, Associate Professor of Sociology, 1969-71, University of Massachusetts, Amherst; Visiting Associate Professor and Research Scholar, 1971-72, Associate Professor of Sociology, 1972-75, Professor of Sociology, 1975-80, Lucy Flower Professor of Urban Sociology, 1980-84, Lucy Flower Distinguished Service Professor, 1984-90, Lucy Flower University Professor of Sociology and Public Policy, 1990-96, University of Chicago; Visiting Associate Professor, 1972, Malcolm Wiener Professor of Social Policy, 1996-98, JFK School of Government; Lewis P and Linda L Geyser University Professor, Harvard University, 1998-; Fellow, Center for Advanced Study in the Behavioral Sciences, Stanford, California, 1981-82; Langston Hughes Visiting Professor of Sociology, University of Kansas, 1983; French-American Foundation Visiting Professor of American Studies, Ecole des Hautes Etudes en Sciences Sociales, Paris, 1989-90; Andrew Dixon White Professor-at-Large, Cornell University, 1994-1998. Publications: Power, Racism and Privilege: Race Relations in Theoretical and Sociohistorical Perspectives, 1973; Through Different Eyes: Black and White Perspectives on American Race Relations (editor with Peter I Rose and Stanley Rothman), 1973; The Declining Significance of Race: Blacks and Changing American Institutions, 1978, 2nd edition, enlarged, 1980; The Truly Disadvantaged: The Inner City, the Underclass, and Public Policy, 1987; The Ghetto Underclass: Social Science Perspectives (editor), 1989, updated edition, 1993; Sociology and the Public Agenda (editor), 1993; Poverty, Inequality and the Future of Social Policy: Western States in the New World Order (editor with Katherine McFate and Roger Lawson), 1995; When Work Disappears: The World of the New Urban Poor, 1996. Contributions to: Many scholarly books, journals, and reviews, and general periodicals. Honours: John D and Catherine T MacArthur Foundation Fellowship, 1987-92; New York Times Book Review Best Book Citations, 1987, 1996; Washington Monthly Annual Book Award, 1988; C Wright Award, Society for the Study of Social Problems, 1988; Dubois, Johnson, Frazier Award, American Sociological Association, 1990; Burton Gordon Feldman Award, Brandeis University, 1991; Frank E Seidman Distinguished Award in Political Economy, Rhodes College, Memphis, Tennessee, 1994; Numerous honorary doctorates. Memberships: A Philip Randolph Institute, national board, 1981-; American Academy of Arts and Sciences, fellow; American Academy of Political and Social Science, fellow; American Association for the Advancement of Science, fellow; American Philosophical Society; American Sociological Association, president, 1989-90; Center for Urban Studies, executive committee, 1974-; National Academy of Education; National Academy of Sciences; National Urban League, board of trustees, 1995-; Russell Sage Foundation, board of directors, chair, 1988-98, 1994-96; Sociological Research Association, president, 1987-88. Address: c/o Malcolm Wiener Center for Social Policy, John F Kennedy School of Government, Harvard University, 79 JFK Street, Cambridge, MA 02138, USA.

WIMMEL Kenneth Carl, b. 12 Aug 1933, Cincinnati, Ohio, USA. Author. m. Arati Sinha, 13 Feb 1965, 1 daughter. Education: BA, English, University of Cincinnati, 1959; MA, American University, 1979. Appointments: United States Foreign Service, 1962-91. Publications: The Alluring Target, 1996; Theodore Roosevelt and the Great White Fleet, 1998. Literary Agent: New England Publishing Associates. Address: 5705 Maiden Lane, Bethesda, MD 20817, USA.

WINCH Donald Norman, b. 15 Apr 1935, London, England. Professor of the History of Economics. m. Doreen Lidster, 5 Aug 1983. Education: BSc, London School of Economics and Political Science, 1956; PhD, Princeton University, 1960. Appointments: Visiting Lecturer, University of California, 1959-60; Lecturer in Economics, University of Edinburgh, 1960-63; Lecturer 1963-66, Reader, 1966-69, Dean, School of Edinburgh, 1968-74, Professor of the History of Economics, 1969-, Pro-Vice-Chancellor, Arts and Social Studies, 1986-89, University of Sussex; Publications Secretary, Royal Economic Society, 1971-; Visiting Fellow, Institute for Advanced Study, Princeton, New Jersey, 1974-75; King's College, Cambridge, 1983, Australian National University, 1983, St Catharine's College, Cambridge, 1989, All Souls College, Oxford, 1994; Review Editor, Economic Journal, 1976-83; British Council Distinguished Visiting Fellow, Kyoto University, 1992; Carlyle Lecturer, University of Oxford, 1995. Publications: Classical Political Economy and Colonies, 1965; James Mill: Selected Economic Writings (editor), 1966; Economics and Policy, 1969; The Economic Advisory Council 1930-1939 (with S K Howson), 1976; Adam Smith's Politics, 1978; That Noble Science of Politics (with S Collini and J W Burrow), 1983; Malthus, 1987; Riches and Poverty, 1996. Contributions to: Many learned journals. Honours: British Academy, fellow, 1986-, vice president, 1993-94; Royal Historical Society, fellow, 1987-. Address: c/o Arts B, University of Sussex, Brighton BN1 9QN, England.

WINCH Gordon Clappison, b. 6 Feb 1930, Kyogle, New South Wales, Australia. Author; Consultant. m. Diana Elizabeth May Vernon, 20 Dec 1956, 1 son, 2 daughters. Education: BA, 1956, MA, 1957, MEd, 1974, University of Sydney; PhD, University of Wisconsin, 1971. Appointment: Head, Department of English, Kuring-gai University of Technology, Sydney. Publications: Teaching Reading: A Language Experience (editor with Valerie Hoogstad), 1985; Give Them Wings: The Experience of Children's Literature (editor with Maurice Saxby), 1987, 2nd edition, 1991; Samantha Seagull's Sandals, 1985; Enoch the Emu, 1986; Primary Grammar Handbook (with Gregory Blaxell), 1994. Contributions to: English in Australia; Journal of Australian Association for Teaching of English; Journals of Australian Reading Association; Primary English Teachers' Association. Memberships: Primary English Teachers' Association, New South Wales, Foundation President; Australian Literary Educators' Association; Children's Book Council of Australia; Australian Society of Authors. Address: 186 Beecroft Road, Cheltenham, New South Wales 2119. Australia.

WINCHESTER Jack. See: **FREEMANTLE Brian.**

WINDSOR Patricia, (Colin Daniel, Katonah Summertree), b. 21 Sept 1938, New York, New York, USA. Writer; Poet; Lecturer; Teacher. 1 son, 1 daughter. Appointments: Faculty, Institute of Children's Literature, University of Maryland Writers Institute; Editor-in-Chief, The Easterner, Washington, DC; Co-Director, Wordspring Literary Consultants; Director, Summertree Studios, Savannah; Instructor, Creative Writing, Armstrong Atlantic University, Savannah. Publications: The Summer Before, 1973; Something's Waiting for You, Baker D, 1974; Home is Where Your Feet Are Standing, 1975; Mad Martin, 1976; Killing Time, 1980; The Sandman's Eyes, 1985; The Hero, 1988; Just Like the Movies, 1990; The Christmas Killer, 1991; The Blooding, 1996; The House of Death, 1996. Contributions to: Anthologies and magazines. Honours: American Library Association Best Book Award, 1973; Outstanding Book for Young Adults Citation, New York Times, 1976; Edgar Allan Poe Award, Mystery Writers of America, 1986. Memberships: Authors Guild; Childrens Book Guild; International Writing Guild; Mystery Writers of America; Poetry Society of Georgia; Savannah Storytellers. Address: c/o Writers House, 21 West 26th Street, New York, NY 10010, USA.

WINEGARTEN Renee, b. 23 June 1922, London, England. Literary Critic; Author. m. Asher Winegarten, dec 1946. Education: MA, 1943, PhD, 1950, Girton College, Cambridge. Publications: French Lyric Poetry in the Age of Malherbe, 1954; Writers and Revolution, 1974; The Double Life of George Sand, 1978; Madame de Staël, 1985; Simone de Beauvoir: A Critical View, 1988. Contributions to: Journals. Memberships: Friends of George Sand; Society of Authors; Authors Guild. Address: 12 Heather Walk, Edgware, Middlesex HA8 9TS, England.

WINGATE John Allan, b. 15 Mar 1920, Cornwall, England. Author. 1 son, 1 daughter. Publications: Submariner Sinclair Series, 1959-64; Sinclair Action Series, 1968, 1969, 1971; HMS Belfast, In Trust for the Nation, 1972; In the Blood, 1973; Below the Horizon, 1974; The Sea Above Them, 1975; Oil Strike, 1976; Black Tide, 1976; Avalanche, 1977; Red Mutiny, 1977; Target Risk, 1978; Seawaymen, 1979; Frigate, 1980; Carrier, 1981; Submarine, 1982; William the Conqueror,

1984; Go Deep, 1985; The Windship Race, 1987; The Fighting Tenth, 1990; The Man Called Mark, 1996. Honour: Mentioned in Dispatches, 1942; Distinguished Service Cross, 1943. Membership: Nautical Institute. Address: c/o Lloyd Bank Plc, Waterloo Place, Pall Mall, London SW1Y 5NJ, England.

WINNER Michael Robert, b. 30 Oct 1935, London, England. Producer; Director; Writer. Education: Downing College, Cambridge University. Appointments: Chairman, Scimitar Films Ltd, Michael Winner Ltd, Motion Picture and Theatrical Investments Ltd; Senior Member of Council, Trustee, Directors Guild of Great Britain; Founder, Chairman, The Police Memorial Trust. Publications: Screenplays of the Cool Mikado, 1962; You Must Be Joking, 1965; The Jokers, 1966; Hannibal Brooks, 1968; The Sentinel, 1976; The Big Sleep, 1977; The Wicked Lady, 1982; Appointment With Death, 1987; A Chorus of Disapproval, 1988; Bullseye!, 1989; Dirty Weekend, 1992; Parting Shots, 1997. Contributions to: Sunday Times; News of the World. Membership: Writers Guild of Great Britain. Address: 6-8 Sackville Street, London W1X 1DD, England.

WINSTON. See: HEALEY Denis.

WINSTON Sarah, (Sarah E Lorenz), b. 15 Dec 1912, New York, New York, USA. Writer. m. Keith Winston, 11 June 1932, 2 sons. Education: New York University, 1929, 1930; Philosophy and Appreciation of Art course, The Barnes Foundation, 1966, 1967; Art Seminars (research), 1967-89. Publications: And Always Tomorrow, 1963; Everything Happens for the Best, 1969; Our Son, Ken, 1969; Not Yet Spring (poems), 1976; V-Mail: Letters of the World War II Combat Medic, 1985; Summer Conference, 1990; Of Apples and Oranges, 1993. Contributions to: Journals. Honours: 1st Prize Awards, National League of American Pen Women, 1972, 1974. Membership: National League of American Pen Women. Address: 1801 Morris Road, No C110, Blue Bell, PA 19422, USA.

WINTER Marielu, See: KEBL Anna-Luise.

WINTER Michael John, b. 5 Aug 1964, Sydney, New South Wales, Australia. Writer; Actor; Executive Story Consultant. Education: Picton High School; New South Wales Police Academy. Publications: Effortless Way (rock musical), 1986; Radio Nemesis, 1990; Blue Heelers (television series), 1992-95; Water Rats, 1995. Memberships: Australian Writers Guild; Australian Film Institute; Actors Equity; MEAA. Address: 22 Castlereagh Street, Tahmoor, New South Wales 2573, Australia.

WINTERSON Jeanette, b. 27 Aug 1959, Manchester, England. Writer. Education: MA, St Catherine's College, Oxford, 1981. Publications: Oranges Are Not the Only Fruit, 1985; The Passion, 1987; Sexing the Cherry, 1989; Written on the Body, 1992; Art and Lies (fiction), 1994; Art Objects (essays), 1994; Essays, 1995; Gut Symmetries (fiction), 1997; The World and Other Places (short stories), 1998. Screenplay: Great Moments in Aviation, 1993. Honours: Whitbread Award for Best First Novel, 1985; John Llewellyn Rhys Memorial Book Prize, 1987; E M Forster Award, American Academy of Arts and Letters, 1989; British Academy of Film and Television Arts Award, best screenplay, 1991; Prix d'argent, Cannes, 1991. Address: c/o ICM, 40 W 57 Street, New York, NY 10019, England.

WINTON Tim(othy John), b. 4 Aug 1960, near Perth, Western Australia, Australia. Author. m. Denise Winton, 2 sons, 1 daughter. Education: Western Australian Institute of Technology. Publications: An Open Swimmer, 1981; Shallows, 1984; Scisson and Other Stories, 1985; That Eye, The Sky, 1986; Minimum of Two, 1987; In the Winter Dark, 1988; Jesse, 1988; Lockie Leonard, Human Torpedo, 1991; The Bugalugs Bum Thief, 1991; Cloudstreet, 1992; ; Lockie Leonard, Scumbuster, 1993; Land's Edge (with Trish Ainslie and Roger Garwood), 1993; Local Colour: Travels in the Other Australia, 1994; The Riders, 1995; Blueback: A Contemporary Fable, 1998. Honours: Vogel Literary Award, Australia, 1981;

Miles Franklin Awards, Arts Management Party Ltd, 1984, 1992; Deo Gloria Prize for Religious Writing, 1991; Shortlisted for the Booker Prize, 1995; Commonwealth Writers Prize, 1995. Address: c/o Jenny Darling, Australian Literary Management, 2A Armstrong Street, Middle Park, Victoria 3206, Australia.

WISEMAN Christopher (Stephen), b. 31 May 1936, Hull, Yorkshire, England. Retired Professor of English; Poet; Writer. m. Jean Leytem, 1 Jan 1963, 2 sons. Education: BA, 1959, MA, 1962, University of Cambridge; PhD, University of Strathclyde, 1971. Appointments: Assistant to Professor of English, University of Calgary, 1969-97. Publications: Waiting for the Barbarians, 1971; The Barbarian File, 1974; Beyond the Labyrinth: A Study of Edwin Muir's Poetry, 1978; The Upper Hand, 1981; An Ocean of Whispers, 1982; Postcards Home: Poems New and Selected, 1988; Missing Persons, 1989; Remembering Mr Fox, 1995. Contributions to: Reviews, quarterlies, journals, and magazines. Honours: Writers Guild of Alberta Poetry Award, 1988; Alberta Poetry Awards, 1988, 1989. Memberships: League of Canadian Poets; Writers Guild of Alberta. Address: 8 Varwood Place North West, Calgary, Alberta T3A 0C1, Canada.

WISEMAN David, (Jane Julian), b. 13 Jan 1916, Manchester, England. Writer. m. Cicely Hilda Mary Richards, 2 Sept 1939, 2 sons, 2 daughters. Education: BA, 1937, Teaching Diploma, 1938, University of Manchester. Appointment: Editor, Adult Education, 1947-50. Publications: Jeremy Visick, 1981; The Fate of Jeremy Visick, 1982; Thimbles, 1982; Blodwen and the Guardians, 1983; Adams Common, 1984; Pudding and Pie, 1986; Jumping Jack, 1988; Badge of Honour, 1989; The Devil's Couldron, 1989; Mum's Winning Streak, 1990; Moonglow, 1990; Goliath Takes the Bait, 1993. As Jane Julian: Ellen Bray, 1985; As Wind to Fire, 1989; The Sunlit Days, 1990. Membership: Society of Authors. Address: 24 Ravenswood Drive, Auckley, Doncaster DN9 3PB, England.

WITT Harold Vernon, b. 6 Feb 1923, Santa Ana, California, USA. Writer; Poet; Editor. m. Beth Hewitt, 8 Sept 1948, 1 son, 2 daughters. Education: BA, 1943, BLS, 1953, University of California at Berkeley; MA, University of Michigan, 1947. Appointments: Co-Editor, California State Poetry Quarterly, 1976; Blue Unicorn, 1977-; Consulting Editor, Poet Lore, 1976-91. Publications: The Death of Venus, 1958; Beasts in Clothes, 1961; Now Swim, 1974; Suprised by Others at Fort Cronkhite, 1975; Winesburg by the Sea, 1979; The Snow Prince, 1982; Flashbacks and Reruns, 1985; The Light at Newport, 1992; American Literature, 1994. Contributions to: Journals and periodicals. Honours: Hopwood Award, 1947; Phelan Award, 1960; 1st Prize, San Francisco Poetry Centre Poetic Drama Competition, 1963; Emily Dickinson Award, Poetry Society of America, 1972; Various awards, World Order of Narrative Poets. Address: 39 Claremont Avenue, Orinda, CA 94563, USA.

WITTICH John Charles Bird, (Charles Bird), b. 18 Feb 1929, London, England. Retired Librarian; Writer. m. June Rose Taylor, 10 July 1954, 1 son, 1 daughter. Education: BA, 1951. Publications: Off Beat Walks In London, 1969, revised edition, 1995; Curiosities of London, 1973, revised edition, 1996; London Villages, 1992; Curiosities of Surrey, 1994; Exploring Cathedrals, 1996; London Bus Top Tourist, 1997; London'c Circle, 1999; Eventful London, 1999. Contributions to: Periodicals and journals. Address: 88 Woodlawn Street, Whitstable, Kent CT5 1HH, England.

WIVEL Henrik, (HW), b. 20 June 1954, Copenhagen, Denmark. Critic; Editor; Author. m. Birgitte Wivel, 1988, 2 sons. Education: PhD, 1984, DrPhil, 1990, University of Copenhagen. Appointments: Editor of Arts, Berlingske Tidende daily newspaper, Copenhagen, 1988-; Danish Editor, Nordisk Tidskrift, 1989-. Publications: The Titanic Eros, on Johannes V Jensen, 1982; The Snow Queen, on Selma Lagerlöf, 1988; Selma Lagerlöf and Biography, 1990; The Great Style. Danish Symbolism and Impressionism in Art around 1900, 1995; Vilhelm Hammershoi, 1996; L A Ring, 1997. Contributions to:

Moving Pictures, Filmmagazin, 1984-. Honours: Selma Lagerlöf Medallion, 1990; The Georg Brandes Award, 1995. Address: Berlingske Tidende, Pilestræde 34, DK-1147 Copenhagen, Denmark.

WODDIS Carole, b. 17 Mar 1943, Nottingham, England. Journalist. Education: BA Honours, History, French, Warwick University. Appointments: Public Relations in theatre and ballet, pre-1981; Co Theatre Editor, Health Editor, City Limits, 1984, 1985, 1986; Freelance, 1987-; Currently London Theatre Correspondent, The Glasgow Herald. Publications: The Herpes Manual (co-editor), 1983; Bloomsbury Theatre Guide (co-editor), 1988, 2nd edition, 1991; Sheer Bloody Magic, conversations with leading actresses. Contributions to: Most theatre magazines; The Independent; Guardian; New Statesman; What's On in London; Jewish Chronicle. Literary Agent: Simon Trewin, Shall Land Associates Ltd. Address: 43 Doughty Street, London WC1N 2LF, England.

WOESSNER Warren (Dexter), b. 31 May 1944, Brunswick, New Jersey, USA. Attorney; Editor; Poet; Writer. m. Iris Freeman, 6 Jan 1990. Education: BA, Cornell University, 1966; PhD, 1971, JD, 1981, University of Wisconsin. Appointments: Founder, Editor, and Publisher, 1968-81, Senior Editor, 1981-, Abraxas Magazine; Board of Directors, 1988-92, President, 1989-92, Coffee House Press; Contributing Editor, Pharmaceutical News. Publications: The Forest and the Trees, 1968; Landing, 1974; No Hiding Place, 1979; Storm Lines, 1987; Clear to Chukchi, 1996. Contributions to: Anthologies, magazines and periodicals. Honours: National Endowment for the Arts Fellowship, 1974; Wisconsin Arts Board Fellowships, 1975, 1976; Loft-McKnight Fellow, 1985; Minnesota Voices, Competition for Poetry, 1986. Address: 34 West Minnehaha Parkway, Minneapolis, MN 55419, USA.

WOLDEN-RAETHINGE Anne, b. 11 July 1929, Sraasten, Denmark. Journalist. Education: School of Journalism A&M College, Stillwater, Oklahoma, USA, 1948-50. Appointments: Interviewer, Portraits, 1951-61; Politician, 1961-. Publications: It is Written In the Stars, 1989; Queen in Denmark, 1989; Bille, 1993; A Family And It's Queen, 1991. Honours: Kristian Dahl-Prize, 1974; Cauling Prize, 1975; Ebbe Munch Prize, 1992. Memberships: Danish Journalists Association; Danish Author's Association. Address: Ryvej 8, 2830 Virum, Denmark.

WOLF Christa, b. 18 Mar 1929, Landsberg an der Warthe, Germany. Author. m. Gerhard Wolf, 1951, 2 daughters. Education: University of Jena; University of Leipzig. Publications: Moskauer Novelle, 1961; Die geteilte Himmel, 1963, English translation as Divided Heaven: A Novel of Germany Today, 1965; Nachdenken über Christa T, 1968, English translation as The Quest for Christa T, 1971; Lesen und Schreiben: Aufsätze und Betrachtungen, 1972, English translation as The Reader the the Writer: Essays, Sketches, Memories, 1977; Unter den Linden: Drei unwahrscheinliche Geschichten, 1974; Kindheitsmuster, 1976, English translation as A Model Childhood, 1980; J'écris sur ce qui m'inquiète: Débat dans Sinn und Form sur don derneir roman, 1977; Kein Ort. Nirgends, 1979, English translation as No Place on Earth, 1982; Fortgesetzter Versuch: Aufsätze, Gespräche, Essays, 1979; Gesammelte Erzählungen, 1980; Neue Lebensansichten eines Katers: Juninachmittag, 1981; Kassandra: Vier Vorlesungen: Eine Erzählung, 1983, English Translation as Cassandra: A Novel and Four Essays, 1984; Störfall: Nachrichten eines Tages, 1987, English translation as Accident: A Day's News, 1989; Die Dimension des Autors: Essays und Aufsätze, Reden und Gespräche, 1959-86, 1987, English translation as The Author's Dimension: Selected Essays, 1990; Sommerstück, 1989; Was bleibt, 1990; Im Dialog: Aktuelle Texte, 1990; Sei gegrüsst und lebe!: Eine Freundschaft in Briefen, 1964-73, 1993; Akteneinsicht-Christa Wolf: Zerrspiegel und Dialog, 1993; Auf dem Weg nach Tabou, Texte, 1990-94, 1994; Die Zeichen der Nuria Quevado, 1994; Medea: Stimmen, 1996. Honours: Art Prize, Halle, 1961; Heinrich Mann

Prize, 1963; National Prize, 3rd Class, 1964, 1st Class, 1987, German Democratic Republic; Literature Prize, Free Hanseatic City of Bremen, 1972; Theodor Fontane Prize for Art and Literature, 1972; Georg Büchner Prize, 1980; Schiller Memorial Prize, 1983; Austrian Prize for European Literature, 1984; Officier de l'Ordre des Arts et des Lettres, France, 1990; Mondello Literature Prize, 1990; Rahel Varnhagen von Ense Medal, 1994. Memberships: Deutsche Akademie für Sprache und Dichtung e. V., Darmstadt; Freie Akademie der Künste, Hamburg. Address: c/o Deutsche Akademie für Sprache und Dichtung e. V., Alexandraweg 23, D-64287, Darmstadt, Germany.

WOLFE Christopher, b. 11 Mar 1949, Boston, Massachusetts, USA. Professor of Political Science; Writer. m. Anne McGowan, 17 June 1972, 5 sons, 5 daughters. Education: BA, University of Notre Dame, 1971; PhD, Boston College, 1978. Appointments: Instructor, Assumption College, Worcester, Massachusetts, 1975-78; Assistant Professor, 1978-84, Associate Professor, 1984-92, Professor of Political Science, 1992-, Marquette University; Founder, American Public Philosophy Institute, 1990. Publications: The Rise of Modern Judicial Review: From Constitutional Interpretation to Judge-Made Law, 1986, revised edition, 1994; Faith and Liberal Democracy, 1987; Judicial Activism: Bulwark of Freedom or Precarious Security?, 1991; Liberalism at the Crossroads (editor with John Hittinger), 1994; How to Interpret the Constitution, 1996; The Family, Civil Society and the State, 1998; Homosexuality and American Public Life, 1999. Contributions to: Professional journals and general periodicals. Honours: Woodrow Wilson Fellowship, 1971; Institute for Educational Affairs Grants, 1982, 1983; Bradley Foundation Grant, 1986; National Endowment for the Humanities Fellowship, 1994; Templeton Honor Roll for Education in a Free Society, 1997. Memberships: American Political Science Association; Federalist Society; Fellowship of Catholic Scholars; Phi Beta Kappa. Address: c/o Department of Political Science, Marquette University, Box 1881, Milwaukee, WI 53201, USA.

WOLFE Gary Kent, b. 24 Mar 1946, Sedalia, Missouri, USA. Educator; Critic. Education: BA, University of Kansas, 1968; MA, 1969, PhD, 1971, University of Chicago. Appointments: Editorial Board, Science-Fiction Studies, 1984-, Journal of the Fantastic in the Arts, 1988-. Publications: The Known and the Unknown: The Iconography of Science Fiction, 1979; David Lindsay, 1982; Critical Terms for Science Fiction and Fantasy, 1986. Co-Author: Elements of Research, 1979. Editor: Science Fiction Dialogues, 1982. Contributions to: Books, reference works, and journals. Honours: Eaton Award for Science Fiction Criticism, 1981; Pilgrim Award, Science Fiction Research Association, 1987; James Friend Memorial Award for Literary Criticism, Friends of Literature, 1992. Memberships: International Association for the Fantastic in the Arts, committee director, 1985-; Friends of the Chicago Public Library, board of directors, 1990-93. Address: 1450 East 55th Place, Apt 420 South, Chicago, IL 60637, USA.

WOLFE Peter, b. 25 Aug 1933, New York, New York, USA. Professor; Writer. m. Marie Paley, 22 Dec 1962, div 1969, 2 sons. Education: BA, City College of New York, 1955; MA, Lehigh Universty, 1957; PhD, University of Wisconsin, 1965. Appointment: Professor, University of Missouri. Publications: Jean Rhys, 1980; Dashiell Hammett, 1980; Laden Choirs: Patrick White, 1983; Something More Than Night: Raymond Chandler, 1985; John le Carré, 1987; Yukio Mishima, 1989; Alarms and Epitaphs: Eric Ambler, 1993; In the Zone: Rod Serling's Twilight Vision, 1996; A Vision of His Own: William Gaddis, 1997. Contributions to: Weekend Australian; Sydney Morning Herald; New Zealand Listener; Calcutta Statesman; New York Times Book Review; Chicago Tribune. Hnours: Fulbright Award to India, 1987, Poland, 1991; University of Missouri President's Award for Creativity and Research, 1995. Address: 4466 West Pine, Apt 18B, St Louis, MO 63108, USA.

WOLFE Tom, (Thomas Kennerly Wolfe Jr), b. 2 Mar 1931, Richmond, Virginia, USA. Writer; Journalist; Artist. m. Sheila Berger, 1 son, 1 daughter. Education: AB, Washington and Lee University, 1951; PhD, American Studies, Yale University, 1957. Appointments: Reporter, Springfield Union, Massachusetts, 1956-59; Reporter and Latin American Correspondent, Washington Post, 1959-62; Writer, New York Sunday Magazine, 1962-66; City Reporter, New York Herald Tribune, 1962-66; Magazine Writer, New York World Journal Tribune, 1966-67; Contributing Editor, New York magazine, 1968-76, Esquire magazine, 1977-; Contributing Artist, Harper's magazine, 1978-81. Publications: The Kandy-Kolored Tangerine-Flake Streamline Baby, 1965; The Electric Kool-Aid Acid Test, 1968; The Pump House Gang, 1968; Radical Chic and Mau-mauing the Flak Catchers, 1970; The Painted Word, 1975; Mauve Gloves and Madmen, Clutter and Vine, 1976; The Right Stuff, 1979; In Our Time, 1980; From Bauhaus to Our House, 1981; The Purple Decades: A Reader, 1982; The Bonfire of the Vanities, 1987; A Man in Full, 1998. Contributions to: Newspapers and magazines. Honours: Various honorary doctorates; American Book Award, 1980; Harold D Vursell Memorial Award, American Academy of Arts and Letters, 1980; John Dos Passos Award, 1984; Theodore Roosevelt Medal, Theodore Roosevelt Association, 1990; St Louis Literary Award, 1990. Address: c/o Farrar Straus & Giroux Inc, 19 Union Square West, New York, NY 10003, USA.

WOLFERS Michael, b. 28 Sept 1938, London, England. Writer; Translator. Education: Wadham College, Oxford, 1959-62; South Bank Polytechnic, 1990-91. Appointments: Journalist, The Times, London, 1965-72; Visiting Senior Lecturer, African Politics and Government, University of Juba, 1979-82. Publications: Black Man's Burden Revisited, 1974; Politics in the Organisation of African Unity, 1976; Luandino Vieira: The Real Life of Domingos Xavier, 1978; Poems for Angola, 1979; Samir Amin, Delinking: Towards a Polycentric World, 1990; Hamlet and Cybernetics, 1991. Contributions to: Numerous publications. Memberships: Royal Institute of International Affairs; Gyosei Institute of Management. Address: 66 Roupell Street, London SE1 8SS, England.

WOLFF Christoph (Johannes), b. 24 May 1940, Solingen, Germany. Professor of Musicology; Writer; Editor. m. Barbara Mahrenholz, 28 Aug 1964, 3 daughters. Education: University of Berlin, 1960-63; University of Freiburg im Breisgau, 1963-65; Dr Phil, University of Erlangen, 1966. Apointments: Lecturer, University of Erlangen, 1966-69; Assistant Professor, University of Toronto, 1968-70; Associate Professor, 1970-73, Professor of Musicology, 1973-76, Columbia University; Visiting Professor, Princetown University, 1973, 1975; Editor, Bach-Jahrbuch, 1974-; Professor of Musicology, 1976, Department Chairman, 1980-88, 1990-91, William Powell Mason Professor, 1985-, Acting Director, University Library, 1991-92, Dean, Graduate School of Arts and Sciences, 1992-, Harvard University; Honorary Professor, University of Freiburg im Breisgau, 1990-. Publications: Der stile antico in der Musik Johann Sebastian Bachs, 1968; The String Quartets of Haydn, Mozart, and Beethoven: Studies of the Autograph Manuscripts, 1980; Bach Compendium: Analytisch-bibliographisches Repertorium der Werke Johann Sebastian Bachs, 7 volumes, 1986-89; Bach: Essays on His Life and Music, 1991; Mozart's Requiem: Historical and Analytical Studies, Documents, Score, 1994. Other: Critical editions of Bach, Buxtehude, Hindemith, Mozart, and Scheidt. Honour: Dent Medal, Royal Musical Association, London, 1978. Memberships: American Academy of Arts and Sciences, fellow; American Musicological Society; Gesellschaft für Musikforschung; International Musicological Society. Address: 182 Washington Street, Belmont, MA 02178, USA.

WOLFF Cynthia Griffin, b. 20 Aug 1936, St Louis, Missouri, USA. Professor; Writer. m. (1) Robert Paul Wolff, 9 June 1962, div 1986, 2 sons, (2) Nicholas J White, 21 May 1988. Education: BA, Radcliffe College, 1958; PhD, Harvard University, 1965. Appointments: Assistant Professor of English, Manhattanville College, Purchase, New York, 1968-70; Assistant Professor, 1971-74, Associate Professor, 1974-76, Professor of English, 1976-80, University of Massachusetts, Amherst; Professor of Humanities, 1980-85, Class of 1922 Professor of Literature and Writing, 1985-, Massachusetts Institute of Technology. Publications: Samuel Richardson, 1972; A Feast of Words: The Triumph of Edith Wharton, 1977, 2nd edition, 1995; Emily Dickinson, 1986. Contributions to: Scholarly journals. Honours: National Endowment for the Humanities Grants, 1975-76, 1983-84; American Council of Learned Societies Grant, 1984-85. Membership: American Studies Association. Address: 416 Commonwealth Avenue, Apt 619, Boston, MA 02215, USA.

WOLFF Edward (Nathan), b. 10 Apr 1946, Long Branch, New Jersey, USA. Professor of Economics; Writer. m. Jane Zandra Forman, 27 Nov 1977, 1 son, 1 daughter. Education: AB, Harvard College, 1968; MPhil, 1972, PhD, 1974, Yale University. Appointments: Assistant Professor, 1974-79, Associate Professor, 1979-84, Professor of Economics, 1984-, New York University; Managing Editor, Review of Income and Wealth, 1987-; Associate Editor, Structural Change and Economic Dynamics, 1989-, Journal of Population Economics, 1990-. Publications: Growth, Accumulation and Unproductive Activity: An Analysis of the Post-War US Economy, 1987; International Comparisons of the Distribution of Household Wealth (editor), 1987; Productivity and American Leadership: The Long View (co-author), 1989; The Information Economy: The Implications of Unbalanced Growth (co-author), 1989; International Perspectives on Profitability and Accumulation (co-editor), 1992; Poverty and Prosperity in the USA in the Late Twentieth Century (co-editor), 1993; Competitivness, Convergence and International Specialization (co-author), 1993; Convergence of Productivity: Cross-National Studies and Historical Evidence (co-editor), 1994; Top Heavy: A Study of the Increasing Inequality of Wealth in America, 1995; Economics of Poverty, Inequality and Discrimination, 1997; The Economics of Productivity (editor), 1997. Contributions to: Books and professional journals. Memberships: American Economic Association; Conference on Research in Income and Wealth; International Association for Research in Income and Wealth, council member, 1987-94; International Institute of Public Finance; International Input-Output Association, council member. Address: c/o Department of Economics, New York University, New York, NY 10012, USA.

WOLFF Geoffrey Ansell, b. 5 Nov 1937, Los Angeles, California, USA. Professor of English and Creative Writing; Author. m. Priscilla Bradley Porter, 21 Aug 1965, 2 sons. Education: Eastbourne College, England, 1955-56; BA, summa cum laude, Princeton University, 1961; Postgraduate Studies, Churchill College, Cambridge, 1963-64. Appointments: Lecturer, Robert College, Istanbul, 1961-63, University of Istanbul, 1962-63, Maryland Institute and College of Art, 1965-69, Middlebury College, Vermont, 1976-78; Book Editor, Washington Post, 1964-69, Newsweek magazine, 1969-71, New Times magazine, 1974-79; Visiting Lecturer, 1970-71, Ferris Professor, 1980, 1992, Princeton University; Book Critic, Esquire magazine, 1979-81; Visiting Lecturer, Columbia University, 1979, Boston University, 1981, Brown University, 1981, 1988; Writer-in-Residence, Brandeis University, 1982-95; Visiting Professor, Williams College, 1994; Professor of English and Creative Writing, University of California at Irvine, 1995-. Publications: Bad Debts, 1969; The Sightseer, 1974; Black Sun, 1976; Inklings, 1978; The Duke of Deception, 1979; Providence, 1986; Best American Essays (editor), 1989; The Final Club, 1990; A Day at the Beach, 1992; The Age of Consent, 1995. Contributions to: Various publications. Honours: Woodrow Wilson Fellowship, 1961-662; Fulbright Fellowship, 1963-64; Guggenheim Fellowships, 1972-73, 1977-78; National Endowment for the Humanities Senior Fellowship, 1974-75; National Endowment for the Arts Fellowships, 1979-80, 1986-87; American Council of Learned Societies Fellowship, 1983-84; Governor's Arts

Award, Rhode Island, 1992; Lila Wallace Writing Fellowship, 1992; American Academy of Arts and Letters Award, 1994. Membership: PEN. Address: c/o Department of English, University of California at Irvine, Irvine, CA 92717, USA.

WOLFF Tobias, (Jonathan Ansell), b. 19 June 1945, Birmingham, Alabama, USA. Writer. m. Catherine Dolores Spohn, 1975, 2 sons, 1 daughter. Education: BA, 1972, MA, 1975, University of Oxford; MA, Stanford University, 1978. Publications: In the Garden of the North American Martyrs (short stories), 1981; Matters of Life and Death: New American Stories (editor), 1982; The Barracks Thief, 1984; Back in the World, 1985; A Doctor's Visit: The Short Stories of Anton Checkhov (editor), 1987; This Boy's Life, A Memoir, 1989; In Pharaoh's Army, Memories of the Lost War, 1994; Best American Short Stories (editor), 1994; The Vintage Book of American Short Stories (editor), 1995; The Night in Question (stories), 1996. Contributions to: TriQuarterly; Missouri Review; New Yorker; Ploughshares; Atlantic Monthly; Esquire; Vanity Fair; Antaeus. Honours: Wallace Stegner Fellowship, 1975-76; National Endowment for the Arts Fellowships, 1978, 1985; Mary Roberts Rinehart Grant, 1979; Arizona Council on the Arts and Humanities Fellowship, 1980; O Henry Short Story Prizes, 1980, 1981, 1985; Guggengeim Fellowship, 1982; St Lawrence Award for Fiction, 1982; PEN/Faulkner Award for Fiction, 1985; Rea Award for the Short Story, 1989; Whiting Foundation Award, 1989; Los Angeles Times Book Prize, 1989; Lila Wallace Foundation Award, 1994; Lyndhurst Foundation Award, 1994. Memberships: Authors Guild; PEN. Address: Department of English, Stanford University, Stanford, CA 94305, USA.

WOLKSTEIN Diane, b. 11 Nov 1942, New York, New York, USA. Writer; Storyteller. m. Benjamin Zucker, 7 Sept 1969, 1 daughter. Education: BA, Smith College, 1964; MA, Bank Street College of Education, 1967. Appointments: Hostess, Stories from Many Lands with Diane Wolkstein, WNYC-Radio, New York City, 1967-; Instructor, Bank Street College, 1970-; Teacher, New York University, 1983-, Sarah Lawrence College, 1984, New School for Social Research, New York City, 1989; Leader, many storytelling workshops. Publications: 8,000 Stones, 1972; The Cool Ride in the Sky: A Black-American Folk Tale, 1973; The Visit, 1974; Squirrel's Song: A Hopi-Indian Story, 1975; Lazy Stories, 1976; The Red Lion: A Persian Sufi Tale, 1977; The Magic Orange Tree and Other Haitian Folk Tales, 1978; White Wave: A Tao Tale, 1979; The Banza: A Haitian Folk Tale, 1980; Inanna, Queen of Heaven and Earth: Her Stories and Hymns from Summer (with Samuel Noah Kramer), 1983; The Magic Wings: A Chinese Tale, 1983; The Legend of Sleepy Hollow, 1987; The First Love Stories, 1991; Oom Razoom, 1991; Little Mouse's Painting, 1992; Step by Step, 1994; Esther's Story, 1996; White Wave, 1996; Bouki Danus the Kokioko, 1997; The Magic Orange Tree, 1997. Contributions to: Periodicals and recordings. Honours: Several citations and awards. Address: 10 Patchin Place, New York, NY 10011, USA.

WOMACK Peter, b. 27 Jan 1952, Surrey, England. Senior Lecturer; Writer. Education: BA, University of Oxford, 1973; PhD, University of Edinburgh, 1984. Appointments: Lecturer, 1988-96, Senior Lecturer, 1996-, University of East Anglia. Publications: Ben Jonson, 1986; Improvement and Romance, 1989; English Drama: A Cultural History (with Simon Shepherd), 1996. Contributions to: Scholarly books and journals. Address: c/o School of English and American Studies, University of East Anglia, Norwich NR4 7TJ, England.

WONG Freeman J. See: HUANG Harry J(unxiong).

WOOD Charles (Gerald), b. 6 Aug 1932, St Peter Port, Guernsey, Channel Islands. Playwright. Education: Birmingham College of Art, 1948-50. Publications: Prisoner and Escort, 1961; Cockade, 1963; Tie Up the Ballcock, 1964; Don't Make Me Laugh, 1965; Meals on Wheels, 1965; Fill Up the Stage with Happy Hours, 1966; Dingo, 1967; Labour, 1968; H, Being Monologues at Front of Burning Cities, 1979; Collier's Wood, 1970;

Welfare, 1971; Veterans; or, Hair in the Gates of the Hellespont, 1972; The Can Opener, 1974; Jingo, 1975; The Script, 1976; Has "Washington" Legs?, 1978; The Garden, 1982; Red Star, 1984; Across for the Garden of Allah, 1986; Tumbledown, 1988; The Plantagenets (after Shakespeare), 1988; Man, Beast and Virtue (after Pirandello), 1989. Screenplays: The Knack, 1965; Help (co-author), 1965; How I Won the War, 1967; The Charge of the Light Brigade (co-author), 1968; The Long Day's Dying, 1968; The Bed-Sitting Room (co-author), 1968; Fellini Satyricon, 1969; Cuba, 1980; Vile Scripts, 1981. Television scripts. Honours: Prix Italia, RAI, 1988; British Academy for Film and Television Arts Award, 1988. Address: Long Barn, Sibford Gopwer, Near Banbury, Oxfordshire OX15 5RT, England.

WOOD David Bernard, b. 21 Feb 1944, Sutton, England. Actor; Writer; Producer; Director; Magician. m. Jacqueline Stanbury, 17 Jan 1975, 2 daughters. Education: BA Hons, English, Worcester College, Oxford, England. Appointments: Self-employed Actor, Playwright, Magician and Theatre Director; Co-Director, Whirligig Theatre, the national touring children's theatre company; Company Director, Verronmead Ltd, independent television producing company; Co-Director, W2 Productions Ltd, theatre-producing Company; Board Member of Polka Theatre, Wimbledon, and Wimbledon Theatre. Publications: 40 plays for children including: The Gingerbread Man, adaptations of Roald Dahl's The BFG and The Witches; Childrens' books created with Richard Fowler including: Bedtime Story; Mole's Summer Story; Pop-Up Theatre: Cinderella; Silly Spider; Textbook: Theatre for Children: Guide to Writing, Acting, Adapting and Directing, written with Janet Grant. Literary Agent: Casarotto Ramsay Ltd, National House, 60-66 Wardour Street, London W1V 3HP, England. Address: 14 Belvedere Drive, Wimbledon, London SW19 7BY, England.

WOOD Ronald Francis James, b. 30 Nov 1921, Australia. Ophthalmologist; Medical Practitioner. m. Mary Lynette Young, 21 Feb 1948, 3 sons, 2 daughters. Education: Bachelor of Medicine and Bachelor of Surgery, 1944; Fellow, Royal Australian College of Ophthalmologists, 1969; Fellow, Royal Australasian College of Surgeons, 1977; Foundation Fellow, Royal College of Ophthalmologists, 1987. Publications: Australia's Quest for Colonial Health, 1983; Looking Up and Looking Back at Old Brisbane, 1987; Earnest Sandford Jackson (with others), 1987; Pioneer Medicine in Australia, 1988; Some Milestones of Australian Medicine, 1994. Contributions to: Journal of the Royal Historical Society of Queensland; Australian Journal of Ophthalmology; Australian and New Zealand Journal of Ophthalmology. Memberships: Royal Historical Society of Queensland; Queensland Club; United Service Club. Address: 120 Queenscroft Street, Chelmer 4068, Brisbane, Australia.

WOOD Susan, b. 31 May 1946, Commerce, Texas, USA. Poet. m. Cliff L Wood, 2 June 1967, div 1982, 1 son, 1 daughter. Education: BA, East Texas State University, 1968; MA, University of Texas at Arlington, 1970; Graduate Studies, Rice University, 1973-75. Publications: Bazaar, 1981; Campo Santo, 1990. Contributions to: Newspapers and periodicals. Address: c/o Maxine Groffsky Literary Agency, 2 Fifth Avenue, New York, NY 10011, USA.

WOOD Victoria, b. 19 May 1953, Prestwich, Lancashire, England. Writer; Comedienne. m. Geoffrey Durham, 1980, 1 son, 1 daughter. Education: BA, Drama, Theatre Arts, University of Birmingham. Publications: Victoria Wood Song Book, 1984; Lucky Bag, 1985; Up to You Porky, 1986; Barmy, 1987; Mens Sana in Thingummy Doodah, 1990; Pat and Margaret, (screenplay), 1994; Chunky, 1996; Dinnerladies (sitcom),1998. Honours: British Academy of Film and Television Arts Awards, Broadcasting Press Awards; Variety Club BBC Personality of the Year, 1987; Honorary DLitt, University of Lancaster, 1989, University of Sunderland, 1994, University of Bolton 1995, University of Birmingham, 1996; BPG Award for Best

Screenplay, 1994; Order of the British Empire, 1997. Literary Agent: Philip Mcintyre Address: c/o Philip Mcintyre, 2nd Floor, 35 Soho Square, London, WN 5DG, England.

WOODCOCK Joan, b. 6 Feb 1908, Bournemouth, Dorset, England. Poet; Artist; Genealogist. m. Alexander Neville Woodcock, 18 Sept 1937, 2 sons, 1 daughter. Publications: The Wandering Years, 1990; Borrowing From Time, 1992; Stabbed Awake, 1994. Contributions to: Anthologies and journals. Memberships: British Haiku Society; Calne Writers' Circle; National Federation of State Poetry Societies, USA; Peterloo Poets; Poetry Society; Various genealogical organizations. Address: 6 Hudson Road, Malmesbury, Wiltshire SN16 0BS, England.

WOODCOCK John Charles, b. 7 Aug 1926, Longparish, Hampshire, England. Cricket Writer. Education: Trinity College, Oxford; MA, Oxon. Appointments: Staff, Manchester Guardian, 1952-54; Cricket Correspondent, The Times, 1954-; Editor, Wisden Cricketer's Almanack, 1980-86. Publications: The Ashes, 1956; Barclays World of Cricket, 1980; The Times One Hundred Greatest Cricketers, 1997. Contributions to: Country Life; The Cricketer. Honours: Sportswriter of the Year, British Press Awards, 1987; Order of the British Empire for services to Sports Journalism, 1996. Address: The Curacy, Longparish, Nr Andover, Hants SP11 6PB, England.

WOODEN Rodney John, b. 16 July 1945, London, England. Playwright. Publications: Woyzeck (adaptation of Büchner's play), 1990; Your Home in the West, 1991; Smoke, 1993; Moby Dick, 1993. Honours: 1st Prize, Mobil International Playwriting Competition, 1990; John Whiting Award, 1991; Mobil Writer-in-Residence Bursary, 1991-92. Membership: PEN International. Address: c/o Micheline Steinberg Playwrights, 110 Forgnal, London NW3 6XU, England.

WOODFORD Peggy, b. 19 Sept 1937, Assam, India. Writer. m. Walter Aylen, 1 Apr 1967, 3 daughters. Education: MA, St Anne's College, Oxford. Publications: Please Don't Go, 1972; Mozart: His Life and Times, 1977; Schubert: His Life and Times, 1978; Rise of the Raj, 1978; See You Tomorrow, 1979; The Girl With a Voice, 1981; Love Me, Love Rome, 1984; Misfits, 1984; Monster in Our Midst, 1987; Out of the Sun, 1990; Blood and Mortar, 1994; Cupid's Tears, 1995; On the Night, 1997; Jane's Story, 1998; Sister Sister, forthcoming. Memberships: Society of Authors; Royal Society of Literature. Address: c/o David Higham Associates, 5-8 Lower John Street, London W1R 4HA, England.

WOODHEAD Peter Anthony, b. 11 Nov 1944, Shipley, Yorkshire, England. m. Sylvia Ann, 24 Aug 1970, 1 son, 1 daughter. Education: BA, University College, London, 1966; MA, University of Sheffield, 1969; M Phil, University of Leicester, 1985. Publications: Keyguide to Information Sources in Archaeology, 1985; Keyguide to Information Sources in Museum Studies (co-author), 1989, 2nd edition, 1994. Contributions to: Various articles on library topics in librarianship periodicals. Honour: Outstanding Reference Book, Choice, 1990. Membership: Library Association. Address: 81 Uppingham Road, Houghton on the Hill, Leicestershire LE7 9HL, England.

WOODMAN Allen, b. 21 Dec 1954, Montgomery, Alabama, USA. Professor; Writer. Education: BA, Huntingdon College, 1976; PhD, Florida State University, 1986. Appointment: English Professor, Northern Arizona University. Publications: Saved by Mr F Scott Fitzgerald; The Cows Are Going To Paris; The Bear Who Came To Stay; The Shoebox of Desire; All-You-Can-Eat, Alabama. Contributions to: Story; Mirabella; Double Take; Flash Fiction; Sudden Fiction Continued; Micro Fiction. Address: PO Box 22310, Flagstaff, AZ 86002-2310. USA.

WOODRING Carl, b. 29 Aug 1919, Terrell, Texas, USA. Educator. m. Mary Frances Ellis, 24 Dec 1942. Education: BA, 1940, MA, 1942, Rice University; AM,

1947, PhD, 1949, Harvard University. Publications: Victorian Samplers, 1952; Virginia Woolf, 1966; Wordsworth, 1965, revised edition, 1968; Politics in English Romantic Poetry, 1970; Nature into Art, 1989; Table Talk of Samuel Taylor Coleridge, 1990; Columbia History of British Poetry (editor), 1993; Columbia Anthology of British Poetry (co-editor), 1995; Literature: An Embattled Profession, 1999. Contributions to: Western Review; Virginia Quarterly Review; Keats-Shelley Journal; Comparative Drama. Honours: Guggenheim Fellowship, 1955; American Council of Learned Societies, Fellow, 1965; Phi Beta Kappa Gauss Prize, 1971; PKB Visiting Scholar, 1974-75; Senior Mellon Fellow, 1987-88. Memberships: American Academy of Arts and Sciences; International Association of University Professors of English; Grolier Club. Address: 2838 Montebello Road, No 20, Austin, TX 78746, USA.

WOODS Jeannie Marlin, b. 6 Oct 1947, Shreveport, Louisiana, USA. College Professor; Stage Director; Author. m. Daniel Carl Woods, 7 Sept 1973. Education: BA, Theatre, University of Idaho, 1970; MA, Hunter College, 1987; MPh, 1988, PhD, Theatre, 1989, City University of New York. Appointments: Lecturer, Baruch College and City College of New York, 1987, 1988; Assistant/Associate Professor of Theatre, Winthrop University, 1989-. Publications: Maureen Stapleton: A Bio-Bibliography, 1992; Theatre to Change Men's Souls: The Artistry of Adrian Hall, 1993. Contributions to: Theatre Topics; Theatre Journal; Southern Theatre; Soviet and East European Performance. Honours: Dissertation Year Fellowship, City University of New York, 1988-89; Named Outstanding Junior Professor, Winthrop University, 1995; Fulbright Scholar, Taiwan, 1998-99. Membership: Association for Theatre in Higher Education. Address: Department of Theatre and Dance, Winthrop University, Rock Hill, SC 29733, USA.

WOODS P F. See: **BAYLEY Barrington John.**

WOODS Stockton. See: **FORREST Richard Stockton.**

WOODWARD Bob, (Robert Upshur Woodward), b. 26 Mar 1943, Geneva, Illinois, USA. Journalist; Writer. m. Elsa Walsh, 25 Nov 1989, 1 child. Education: BA, Yale University, 1965. Appointments: Reporter, Montgomery County Sentinel, Maryland, 1970-71; Reporter, 1971-78, Metropolitan Editor, 1979-81, Assistant Managing Editor, 1981-, Washington Post. Publications: All the President's Men (with Carl Bernstein), 1973; The Final Days (with Carl Bernstein), 1976; The Brethren (with Carl Armstrong), 1979; Wired, 1984; Veil: The Secret Wars of the CIA, 1987; The Commanders, 1991; The Man Who Would Be President (with David S Broder), 1991; The Agenda: Inside the Clinton White House, 1994; The Choice, 1996. Honour: Pulitzer Prize Citation, 1972. Address: c/o Washington Post, 1150 15th Street North West, Washington, DC 20071, USA.

WOODWARD C(omer) Vann, b. 13 Nov 1908, Vanndale, Arkansas, USA. Professor of History Emeritus; Author. m. Glenn Boyd MacLeod, 21 Dec 1937, dec 1982, 1 son, dec. Education: AB, Emory University, 1930; MA, Columbia University, 1932; PhD, University of North Carolina, 1937. Appointments: Instructor in English, Georgia School of Technology, 1930-31, 1932-33; Assistant Professor of History, University of Florida, 1937-39, Scripps College, Claremont, California, 1940-43; Visiting Professor of History, 1939, University of Virginia; Professor of History, Johns Hopkins University, 1946-61; Commonwealth Lecturer, University of London, 1954; Harold Vyvyan Harmsworth Professor of American History, University of Oxford, 1954-55; Sterling Professor of History, 1961-77, Professor Emeritus, 1977-, Yale University; Jefferson Lecturer in Humanities, 1978. Publications: Tom Watson: Agrarian Rebel, 1938, 3rd edition, 1990; The Battle for Leyte Gulf, 1947; Reunion and Reaction: The Compromise of 1877 and the End of Reconstruction, 1951, 2nd edition, revised, 1991; Origins of the New South 1877-1913, 1951, revised edition, 1971; The Strange Career of Jim Crowe, 1955, 3rd edition, revised, 1974; The Burden of Southern History, 1960, 3rd edition, revised, 1993; The National Experience (with others), 1963; The Comparative Approach to American History (editor), 1968; American Counterpoint: Slavery and Racism in the North-South Dialogue, 1971; Responses of the Presidents to Charges of Misconduct, 1974; Oxford History of the United States (general editor), 11 volumes, 1982-; Thinking Back: The Perils of Writing History, 1986; The Future of the Past, 1988; The Old World's New World, 1991. Contributions to: Books and professional journals. Honours: Bancroft Prize, 1952; National Institute of Arts and Letters Award, 1954; American Council of Learned Societies Fellow, 1962; Brandeis University Creative Arts Award, 1982; Pulitzer Prize in History, 1982; American Historical Society Life Work Award, 1986; American Academy of Arts and Letters Gold Medal for History, 1990; Honorary doctorates. Memberships: American Academy of Arts and Letters; American Academy of Arts and Sciences, vice-president, 1988-89; American Historical Association, president, 1969; American Philosophical Society; British Academy; Organization of American Historians, president, 1968-69; Royal Historical Society; Southern Historical Association, president, 1952. Address: 83 Rogers Road, Hamden, CT 06517, USA.

WOODWORTH Steven E(dward), b. 28 Jan 1961, Akron, Ohio, USA. Assistant Professor of History; Writer. m. Leah Dawn Bunke, 13 Aug 1983, 5 sons. Education: BA, Southern Illinois University at Carbondale, 1982; University of Hamburg, 1982-83; PhD, Rice University, 1987. Appointments: Adjunct Instructor, Houston Community College, 1984-87; Instructor in History, Bartlesville Wesleyan College, Oklahoma, 1987-89; Assistant Professor of History, Toccoa Falls College, Georgia, 1989-97, Texas Christian University, 1997-. Publications: Jefferson Davis and His Generals: The Failure of Confederate Command in the West, 1990; The Essentials of United States History, 1841 to 1877: Westward Expansion and the Civil War, 1990; The Essentials of United States History, 1500 to 1789: From Colony to Republic, 1990; The Advanced Placement Examination in United States History, 1990; Davis and Lee at War, 1995; Leadership and Command in the American Civil War (editor), Vol I, 1995; The American Civil War: A Handbook of Literature and Research (editor), 1996. Contributions to: Books and professional journals. Honour: Fletcher Pratt Awards, 1991, 1996. Memberships: Grady Mcwhiney Research Foundation, fellow; American Historical Association; Organization of American Historians; Southern Historical Association; Organization of Military Historians; Society of Civil War Historians. Address: c/o Department of History, Texas Christian University, TCU Box 297260, Fort Worth, TX 76129, USA.

WOOLDRIDGE Jane, b. 3 Apr 1958, Raleigh, North Carolina, USA. Business Writer; Online Publishing Consultant; Journalist; Travel Writer. m. Stetson Glines, 21 Oct 1995. Education: BA, Duke University, magna cum laude, 1980; Angier B Duke Scholar. Appointments: Features Writer, Virginian-Pilot, Norfolk, VA, USA, 1978; News Reporter, Raleign News & Observer, Raleigh, North Carolina, 1979-80; Fashion Writer, New York Times Magazine, 1980-81; Features Writer, Travel Writer, Columnist, The Miami Herald, 1983-95; Executive Editor, Destination Florida, 1995-97; Business Columnist, The Miami Herald, 1998-. Contributions to: The Miami Herald; Los Angeles Times; Seattle Times; USA Today; Newsday. Address: 1134 Obispo Avenue, Coral Gables, FL 33134, USA.

WORSLEY Dale, b. 3 Nov 1948, Baton Rouge, Louisiana, USA. Writer; Dramatist. m. Elizabeth Fox, 14 July 1991. Education: Southwestern University, Memphis. Appointment: Writing Programme, Columbia University, New York City, 1992. Publications: The Focus Changes of August Previco, 1980; The Art of Science Writing, 1989. Plays: Cold Harbor, 1983; The Last Living Newspaper, 1993. Honours: Fellowship in Fiction, 1986, Fellowship in Playwriting, 1989, National Endowment for the Arts. Membership: Dramatists Guild. Address: 150 Lafayette Avenue No 1, Brooklyn, NY 11238, USA.

WORSTHORNE Sir Peregrine (Gerard), b. 22 Dec 1923, London, England. Journalist; Editor; Writer. m. (1) Claude Bertrand de Colasse, 1950, dec 1990, 1 daughter, (2) Lady Lucinda Lambton, 1991. Education: BA, Peterhouse, Cambridge; Magdalen College, Oxford. Appointments: Sub-editor, Glasgow Herald, 1946; Editorial Staff, The Times, 1948-53, Daily Telegraph, 1953-61; Deputy Editor, 1961-76, Associate Editor, 1976-86, Editor, 1986-89, Editor, Comment Section, 1989-91, Sunday Telegraph. Publications: The Socialist Myth, 1972; Peregrinations: Selected Pieces, 1980; By the Right, 1987; Tricks of Memory (autobiography), 1993. Contributions to: Newspapers and journals. Honours: Granada Columnist of the Year, 1980; Knighted, 1991. Address: The Old Rectory, Hedgerley, Buckinghamshire SL2 3VY, England.

WORTH Helen, (Mrs Arthur M Gladstone), b. July 1913, Cleveland, Ohio, USA. Author; Poet; Educator. Education: BA, University of Michigan; Graduate Work, New School for Social Research. Appointments: Lecturer, Poetry, University of Virginia; Adjunct Professor, Food and Wine Appreciation Courses, various universities; National Magazine and Newspaper Food Editor; Helen Worth syndicated Food/Wine Feature, 1980-. Publications: Performer and Writer of Verses to accompany husband's macrophotography for slideshow, Small Secrets: A Creature Garden of Verses, 1985; The Down on the Farm Cookbook, 1943, reissued, 1983; Shrimp Cookery, 1952; Cooking Without Recipes, 1965, reissued, 1984; Hostess Without Help, 1971; Dammnyankee in a Southern Kitchen, 1973. Contributions to: Talk; House Beautiful; Brides; Wine West. Honours: Outstanding Cookbook Award, 1972; Runner-Up, Cookbook Award, 1974; Federated Women's Clubs of America Outstanding Journalist Award, 1977. Memberships include: Authors League; American Society of Journalists and Authors; National Book Critics Circle; National and Virginia Federations of Press Women; Virginia Writers Club. Address: 1701 Owensville Road, Charlottesville, VA 22901, USA.

WORTHINGTON Edgar Barton, b. 13 Jan 1905, London, England. Ecologist. m. (1) Stella Johnson, 23 Aug 1930, (2) Harriett Stockton, 21 June 1980, 3 daughters. Education: MA, PhD, Rugby, Gonville and Caius, Cambridge. Appointments: Fishery Survey, Lake Victoria, 1927, Lakes Albert and Kioga, 1928; Leader, Cambridge Expedition to African Lakes and Balfour Student, 1930-31; Scientist to Lord Hailey's African Survey, 1933-37; Director, Freshwater Biological Association, 1937-46; Scientific Adviser to Middle East Supply Council, 1939-45; Secretary, Colonial Research Committee and Development Adviser, Uganda, 1946, to East Africa High Commission, 1947-50; Secretary-General to Scientific Council, Africa, 1951-56; Deputy-Director General, Nature Conservancy, 1956-62; Director, International Biological Programme, 1962-72. Publications: Inland Waters of Africa (with Stella Worthington), 1933; Science in Africa, 1937; Life in Lakes and Rivers (with T T Macan), 1951; Science in the Development of Africa, 1958; The Ecological Century - A Personal Appraisal, 1983; The Ecological Century Review, 1998. Honours: Commander of the Order of the British Empire, 1962; Tot Ridder, Order of the Golden Ark, Netherlands, 1976; Medal, UNESCO, 1994. Memberships: Linnaean Society of London; Royal African Society. Address: Colin Goodmans, Furner's Green, Uckfield, East Sussex TN22 3RR, England.

WORTIS Avi, (Avi), b. 23 Dec 1937, New York, New York, USA. Children's Author. m. (1) Joan Gabriner, div, 2 sons, (2) Coppelia Kahn. Education: BA, 1959, MA, 1962, University of Wisconsin at Madison; MS, in Library Science, Columbia University, 1964. Appointments: Librarian, New York Public Library, 1962-70, Trenton State College, New Jersey, 1970-86; Conducted over 800 workshops and seminars with children, parents and educators. Publications: Things That Sometimes Happen, 1970; Snail Tale, 1972; No More Magic, 1975; Captain Grey, 1977 Emily Upham's Revenge, 1978; Night Journeys, 1979; History of Helpless Harry, 1980; Who Stole the Wizard of Oz?, 1981; Sometimes I Think I Hear

My Name, 1982; Shadrach's Crossing, 1983; Devil's Race, 1984; SOR Losers, 1984; The Fighting Ground, 1984; Bright Shadow, 1985; Wolf Rider, 1986; Romeo and Juliet--(Together (and Alive!)--At Last, 1987; Something Upstairs, 1988; The Man Who Was Poe, 1989; True Confessions of Charlotte Doyle, 1990; Windcatcher, 1991; Nothing But the Truth, 1991; Blue Heron, 1992; `Who Was That Masked Man, Anyway?, 1992; Punch With Judy, 1993; City of Light, City of Dark, 1993; The Bird, the Frog, and the Light, 1994; The Barn, 1994; Tom, Babette & Simon, 1995; Poppy, 1995; Finding Providence, 1996; Beyond the Western Sea, 1996; Poppy and Rye: A Tale from Dimwood Forest, 1998. Contributions to: Periodicals. Honours: American Library Association Notable Book Awards, 1984, 1991, 1992, 1993, 1995, 1996; One of the Best Books of the Year Awards, Library of Congress, 1989, 1990; Newbery Honor Book Awards, 1991, 1992; Many others. Membership: Authors Guild. Address: 2205a Grove Street, Boulder, CO 30203, USA.

WOUK Herman, b. 27 May 1915, New York, New York, USA. Writer. m. Betty Sarah Brown, 9 Dec 1945, 3 sons, 1 dec.Education: AB, Columbia University, 1934. Appointments: Visiting Professor of English, Yeshiva University, 1952-57; Scholar-in-Residence, Aspen Institute of Humanistic Studies, Colorado, 1973-74. Publications: Fiction: Aurora Dawn, 1947; The City Boy, 1948; Slattery's Hurricane, 1949; The Caine Muntiny, 1951; Marjorie Morningstar, 1955; Lomokome Papers, 1956; Youngblood Hawke, 1962; Don't Stop the Carnival, 1965; The Winds of War, 1971; War and Remembrance, 1978; Inside, Outside, 1985; The Hope, 1993; The Glory, 1994. Plays: The Traitor, 1949; The Caine Mutiny Court-Martial, 1953; Nature's Way, 1957. Television Screenplays: The Winds of War, 1983; War and Remembrance, 1986. Non-Fiction: This is My God, 1959. Honours: Pulitzer Prize in Fiction, 1952; Columbia University Medal for Excellence, 1952; Alexander Hamilton Medal, 1980; University of California at Berkeley Medal, 1984; Washington Book Award, 1986; Golden Plate Award, American Academy of Achievement, 1986; US Naval Memorial Foundation Lone Sailor Award, 1987; Tel Aviv University Guardian of Zion Award, 1998; University of California/San Diego UCSD Medal, 1998. Memberships: Authors League; PEN; Writers Guild of America. Address: c/o B S W Literary Agency, 3255 N St., N.W., Washington, DC 20007, USA.

WRIGHT A(mos) J(asper III), b. 3 Mar 1952, Gadsden, Alabama, USA. Medical Librarian; Writer; Poet. m. Margaret Dianne Vargo, 14 June 1980, 1 son, 1 daughter. Education: BA, Auburn University, 1973; MLS, University of Alabama, 1983. Publications: Frozen Fruit (poems), 1978; Right Now I Feel Like Robert Johnson (poems), 1981; Criminal Activity in the Deep South, 1800-1930, 1989. Contributions to: Medical journals, anthologies, reviews, quarterlies, and magazines. Memberships: Anaesthesia History Association; Medical Library Association. Address: 119 Pintail Drive, Pelham, AL 35124, USA.

WRIGHT A(nthony) D(avid), b. 9 June 1947, Oxford, England. Senior Lecturer in History. Education: BA, Merton College, Oxford, 1968; British School, Rome, 1969-71; MA, 1973, DPhil, 1973, Brasenose College, Oxford. Appointments: Lecturer, 1974-92, Senior Lecturer in History, 1992-, University of Leeds; Visiting Fellow, University of Edinburgh, 1983. Publications: The Counter-Reformation: Catholic Europe and the Non-Christian World, 1982; Baronio Storico e la Controriforma (with Romeo De Maio, L Gulia, and A Mazzacane), 1982; Catholicism and Spanish Society Under the Reign of Philip II, 1555-1598, and Philip III, 1598-1621, 1991. Contributions to: Scholarly books and journals. Memberships: Accademia di San Carlo; Ecclesiastical History Society; Royal Historical Society, fellow. Address: c/o School of History, University of Leeds, Leeds LS2 9JT, England.

WRIGHT C(arolyn) D, b. 6 Jan 1949, Mountain Home, Arkansas, USA. Poet; Professor. m. Forrest Gander, 3 Apr 1983, 1 son. Education: BA, Memphis State University, 1971; MFA, University of Arkansas, 1976. Appointment: State Poet of Rhode Island, 1994-. Publications: Terrorism, 1979; Translations of the Gospel Back Into Tongues, 1981; Further Adventures with God, 1986; String Light, 1991; Just Whistle, 1993; The Lost Roads Project: A Walk-in Book of Arkansas, 1994; The Reader's Map of Arkansas, 1994; Tremble, 1996; Deepstep Come Shining, 1998. Contributions to: Journals. Honours: National Endowment for the Arts Fellowships, 1981, 1987; Witter Bynner Prize for Poetry, 1986; Guggenheim Fellowship, 1987; Mary Ingraham Bunting Fellowship, 1987; General Electric Award for Younger Writers, 1988; Whiting Writers Award, 1989; Rhode Island Governor's Award for the Arts, 1990; Lila Wallace - Reader's Digest Writers Award, 1992; University of Arkansas, Distinguished Alumni Award, 1998. Membership: PEN, New England, Council Member. Address: 351 Nayatt Road, Barrington, RI 02806, USA.

WRIGHT Charles (Penzel), b. 25 Aug 1935, Pickwick Dam, Tennessee, USA. Poet; Writer; Teacher. m. Holly McIntire, 6 Apr 1969, 1 son. Education: BA, Davidson Collee, 1957; MFA, University of Iowa, 1963; Postgraduate Studies, University of Rome, 1963-64. Appointments: Faculty, University of California at Irvine, 1966-83, University of Virginia, 1983-. Publications: Grave of the Right Hand, 1970; Hard Freight, 1973; Bloodlines, 1975; China Trace, 1977; Southern Cross, 1981; Country Music, 1982; The Other Side of the River, 1984; Zone Journals, 1988; The World of the 10,000 Things, 1990; Chickamauga, 1995; Black Zodiac, 1997; Appalachia, 1998. Contributions to: Numerous journals and magazines. Honours: Edgar Allan Poe Award, Academy of American Poets, 1976; PEN Translation Award, 1979; National Book Award for Poetry, 1983; Brandeis Book Critics Circle Award, 1998; Pulitzer Prize for Poetry, 1998. Memberships: American Academy of Arts and Letters; Fellowship of Southern Writers; PEN American Centre. Address: 940 Locust Avenue, Charlottesville, VA 22901, USA.

WRIGHT David James Thomas, (Icterus), b. 5 Mar 1954, England. Doctor. m. Penelope Walker, 24 May 1980, 2 daughters. Education: MBBS, 1978, MRCGP, 1984, Guy's Hospital Medical School, University of London, England. Appointments: General Medical Practitioner, Basingstoke, Hampshire, England, 1984-. Contributions to: How to Organise a Medical Symposium for GP's, British Medical Journal, 1989; Diary Column for Doctor Magazine, 1996-. Address: Yew Tree House, Long Parish, Andover, Hants SP11 6PT, England.

WRIGHT Derek Leslie, b. 24 Feb 1947, Wakefield, England. University Lecturer. m. Renate Lucia Mohrbach, 31 July 1981. Education: BA, 1st Class, English, University of Reading, 1971; DipEd, University of Leeds, 1972; MA, American Literature, University of Keele, 1973; PhD, University of Queensland, Australia, 1986. Appointment: Lecturer, Northern Territory University. Publications: Ayi Kwei Armah's Africa: The Sources of His Fiction, 1989; Critical Perspectives on Ayi Kwei Armah (editor), 1992; Wole Soyinka Revisited, 1993; The Novels of Nuruddin Farah, 1994; New African Writing (editor), 1995; Extra-Territorial: Poems and Stories(editor), 1996; Wole Soyinka: Life, Work and Criticism, 1996. Contributions to: Journals. Honour: Outstanding Academic Book Award, Choice, 1990. Memberships: Modern Language Association of America; Association for Commonwealth Literature and Language Studies. Address: School of Humanities, Faculty of Arts, Northern Territory University, Darwin, Northern Territory 0909, Australia.

WRIGHT George T(haddeus), b. 17 Dec 1925, Staten Island, New York, USA. Professor Emeritus; Author; Poet. m. Jerry Honeywell, 28 Apr 1955. Education: BA, Columbia College, 1946; MA, Columbia University, 1947; University of Geneva, 1947-48; PhD, University of California, 1957. Appointments: Teaching Assistant, 1954-55; Lecturer, 1956-57, University of California; Visiting Assistant Professor, New Mexico Highlands University, 1957; Instructor-Assistant Professor, University of Kentucky, 1957-60; Assistant Professor, San Francisco State College, 1960-61; Associate Professor, University of Tennessee, 1961-68; Fulbright Lecturer, University of Aix-Marseilles, 1964-66, University of Thessaloniki, 1977-78; Visiting Lecturer, University of Nice, 1965; Professor, 1968-89, Chairman, English Department, 1974-77, Regents' Professor, 1989-93, Regents' Professor Emeritus, 1993-, University of Minnesota. Publications: The Poet in the Poem: The Personae of Eliot, Yeats and Pound, 1960; W H Auden, 1969, revised edition, 1981; Shakespeare's Metrical Art, 1988. Editor: Seven American Literary Stylists from Poe to Mailer: An Introduction, 1973; Aimless Life: Poems 1961-1995, 1999. Contributions to: Articles, reviews, poems and translations in many periodicals and books. Honours: Guggenheim Fellowship, 1981-82; National Endowment for the Humanities Fellowship, 1984-85; Phi Kappa Phi; William Riley Parker Proze, Modern Language Association, 1974, 1981. Memberships: Minnesota Humanities Comission, 1985-88; Modern Language Association; Shakespeare Association of America. Address; 2617 West Crown King Drive, Tucson, AZ 85741, USA.

WRIGHT Graeme Alexander, b. 23 Apr 1943, Wellington, New Zealand. Freelance Editor; Writer. Appointments: Managing Editor, Queen Anne Press, 1972-74; Editor, Freelance Writer, 1974-; Director, John Wisden & Co Ltd, 1983-87; Editor, Wisden Cricketers Almanack, 1986-92. Publications: Great Moments in the Olympics, 1976; Phil Read: The Real Story, 1977; Olympic Greats, 1980; Where Do I Go From Here, 1981; Test Decade, 1972-82, 1983; Botham (with Patrick Eagar), 1985; Brown Sauce, 1986; Forty Vintage Years, 1988; Betrayal: The Struggle for Cricket's Soul, 1993. Address: 14 Field End Road, Eastcote Pinner, Middlesex HA5 2QL, England.

WRIGHT Judith, b. 31 May 1915, Armidale, New South Wales, Australia. Writer; Poet; Editor. m. J P McKinney, 1 daughter. Education: New South Wales Correspondence School. Publications: Poetry: The Moving Image, 1946; Woman to Man, 1950; The Gateway, 1953; The Two Fires, 1955; Australia Bird Poems, 1961; Birds, 1962; Five Senses: Selected Poems, 1963; City Sunrise, 1964; The Other Half, 1966; Collected Poems, 1942-70, 1971; Alive: Poems, 1971-72, 1973; Fourth Quarter and Other Poems, 1976; The Double Tree: Selected Poems, 1942-76, 1978; Phantom Dwelling, 1985; A Human Pattern, 1990. Other: The Generations of Men, 1955, new edition, 1995; Preoccupations in Australian Poetry, 1964; The Nature of Love, 1966; Because I Was Invited, 1975; Charles Harpur, 1977; The Coral Battleground, 1977; The Cry for the Dead, 1981; We Call for a Treaty, 1985; Born of the Conquerors, 1991; Going on Talking, 1992. Contributions to: Books, reviews, quarterlies, and journals. Honours: Honorary Doctorates, University of New England, 1963, University of Sydney, 1976, Monash University, 1977, Australia National University, 1981, University of New South Wales, 1985, Griffith University, 1988, University of Melbourne, 1988; Australia Council Senior Writers Fellowship, 1977; Asan World Prize, Azan Memorial Association, 1984; Queen's Gold Medal for Poetry, 1991. Address: 1/17 Devonport Street, Lyons, ACT 26062, Australia.

WRIGHT Karen Jocelyn, b. 15 Nov 1950, New York City, New York, USA. Journalist; Editor. m. 23 May 1981, 2 daughters. Education: BA, Brandeis University, 1972; MA Cantab, Cambridge University, England, 1974; MBA, London Business School, 1976. Appointments: Founder, Hobson Galloy, 1977-85; Co-founder, 1987, Editor, 1990-, Modern Painter; Co-founder, 21 Publishing, 1997-. Contributions to: Numerous to newspapers and magazines including Telegraph, Modern Paths; Penguin Book of Art Writing (co-editor), 1998. Honour: AICA, 1987. Literary Agent: David Miller, Coleridge Rogers White. Address: 31 Storeys Way, Cambridge CB3 0DP, England.

WRIGHT Kit, (Christopher Wright), b. 1944, Kent, England. Poet. Education: New College, Oxford. Appointments: Education Secretary, Poetry Society,

London, 1970-75; Fellow Commoner in Creative Arts, Trinity College, Cambridge, 1977-79. Publications: Treble Poets 1 (with Stephen Miller and Elizabeth Maslen), 1974; The Bear Looked Over the Mountain, 1977; Arthur's Father, 4 volumes, 1978; Rabbiting On and Other Poems, 1978; Hot Dog and Other Poems, 1981; Professor Potts Meets the Animals of Africa, 1981; Bump Starting the Hearse, 1983; From the Day Room, 1983; Cat Among the Pigeons, 1987; Poems 1974-1984, 1988; Real Rags and Red, 1988; Short Afternoons, 1989; Funnybunch, 1993; Tigerella, 1994. Honours: Alice Hunt Bartlett Prize; Geoffrey Faber Memorial Award; Hawthornden Prize; W H Heinemann Award. Address: Viking Kestrel, 27 Wrights Lane, London W8 5TZ, England.

WRIGHT Laurali Rose, b. 5 June 1939, Saskatoon, Saskatchewan, Canada. Writer. m. 6 Jan 1962, 2 daughters. Education: MA, Liberal Studies, Simon Fraser University. Publications: Neighbours, 1979; The Favourite, 1982; Among Friends, 1984; The Suspect, 1985; Sleep While I Sing, 1986; Love in the Temperate Zone, 1988; Chill Rain in January, 1990; Prized Possessions, 1993; A Touch of Panic, 1994; Mother Love, 1995; Strangers Among Us, 1996; Acts of Murder, 1998. Contributions to: Professional journals, newspapers and magazines. Honours: Alberta First Novel Award, 1978; Edgar Allan Poe Best Novel Award, Mystery Writers of America, 1986; Arthur Ellis Award, Crime Writers of Canada, 1991. Memberships: International PEN; Writers Union of Canada; Authors Guild, USA. Address: c/o Writers' Union of Canada, 24 Ryerson Avenue, Toronto, Ontario M5T 2P3, Canada.

WRIGHT Nancy Means, b. New Jersey, USA. Author. m. 2 sons, 2 daughters. Education: AB, Vassar College; MA, Middlebury College. Appointments: Instructor, English, various schools, 1960-87; Proctor Academy; Burlington College; Marist College, New York, 1990. Publications: The Losing, 1973; Down the Strings, 1982; Make Your Own Change, 1985; Vermonters At Their Craft, 1987; Tall Girls Don't Cry, 1990; Split Nipple, 1992; Mad Season, 1996; Harvest of Bones, 1998. Contributions to: Various journals and magazines. Honours: Scholar, Bread Loaf Writers Conference, 1959; Grant, Society of Children's Book Writers, 1987. Memberships: League of Vermont Writers, president, 1978-80; Poets and Writers; Authors League; Society of Children's Book Writers. Literary Agent: Alison Picard. Address: Box 182, Middlebury, VT 05753, USA.

WRIGHT Nicholas, b. 5 July 1940, Cape Town, South Africa (British citizen). Playwright. Education: London Academy of Music and Dramatic Art. Appointments: Literary Manager, 1987, Associate Director, 1992, National Theatre, London, England. Publications: Changing Lines, 1968; Treetops, 1978; The Gorky Brigade, 1979; One Fine Day, 1980; The Crimes of Vautrin (after Balzac), 1983; The Custom of the Country, 1983; The Desert Air, 1984; Six Characters in Search of an Author (after Pirandello), 1987; Mrs Klein, 1988; Thérèse Raquin (after Zola), 1990; Essays, 1992. Honour: Arts Council Bursary, 1981. Address: 2 St Charles Place, London W10 6EG, England.

WRIGHT N(icholas) T(homas), b. 1 Dec 1948, Morpeth, Northumberland, England. Theologian; Dean of Lichfield. m. Margaret Elizabeth Anne Fiske, 14 Aug 1971, 2 sons, 2 daughters. Education: BA, 1st Class Honours, Literae and Humaniores, 1971, MA, 1975, D Phil, 1981, Exeter College, Oxford; BA, 1st Class Honours, Theology, Wycliffe Hall, Oxford, 1973. Appointments: Ordained Deacon, 1975, Priest, 1976; Junior Research Fellow, 1975-78, Junior Chaplain, 1976-78, Merton College, Oxford; Fellow and Chaplain, Downing College, Cambridge, 1978-81; Member, Doctrine Commission of the Church of England, 1979-81, 1989-95; Assistant Professor of New Testament Studies, McGill University, Montreal, and Honorary Professor, Montreal Diocesan Theological College, 1981-86; Lecturer in Theology, Oxford University, and Fellow, Tutor, and Chaplain, Worcester College, Oxford, 1986-93; Fellow, Institute for Christian Studies, Toronto,

1992-; Canon Theologian, Coventry Cathedral, 1992-; Dean of Lichfield, 1994-. Publications: Small Faith, Great God, 1978; The Work of John Frith, 1983; The Epistles of Paul to the Colossians and to Philemon, 1987; The Glory of Christ in the New Testament, 1987; The Interpretation of the New Testament 1861-1986, 1988; The Climax of the Covenant, 1991; New Tasks for a Renewed Church, 1992; The Crown and the Fire, 1992; The New Testament and the People of God, 1992; Who Was Jesus?, 1992; Following Jesus, 1994; Jesus and the Victory of God, 1996; The Lord and His Prayer, 1996; The Original Jesus, 1996; For All God's Worth, 1997; What St Paul Really Said, 1997; Reflecting the Glory, 1997; The Meaning of Jesus, The Way of the Lord, forthcoming. Address: The Deanery, Lichfield, Staffordshire WS13 7LD, England.

WRIGHT Peter, b. 30 Mar 1923, Fleetwood, Lancashire, England. Forensic Linguist. m. Patricia May Wright, 3 Apr 1956, 1 son, 3 daughters. Education: BA, 1949, PhD, 1954, University of Leeds; Advanced Diploma, London University, 1960. Appointments: Lecturer, 1965-70, Senior Lecturer, 1970-84, Honorary Senior Lecturer, Fellow in English Dialect Studies, 1984-92, Salford University; Crown or Defence, Analysing from Linguistic Angles Cases for Trial or Appeal. Publications: The Lanky Twang, 1974; The Yorkshire Yammer, 1976; Language at Work, 1978; Cockney Dialect and Slang, 1980; Language of British Industry, 1974; 8 other dialect books. Contributions to: Various journals and magazines. Honour: Queen's Award for Export Achievement, 1992. Memberships: Yorkshire Dialect Society; Lancashire Dialect Society; Lakeland Dialect Society; The UK Register of Expert Witnesses. Address: 30 Broadoak Road, Stockport, Cheshire SK7 3BL, Englnd.

WRIGHT Richard (Bruce), b. 4 Mar 1937, Midland, Ontario, Canada. Writer; College Teacher of English. m. Phyllis Mary Cotton, 2 sons. Education: Graduate, Radio and Television Arts, Ryerson Polytechnic Institute, Toronto, 1959; BA, Trent University, 1972. Appointment: Teacher of English, Ridley College, St Catharines, Ontario, 1976-. Publications: Andrew Tolliver, 1965; The Weekend Man, 1970; In the Middle of a Life, 1973; Farthing's Fortunes, 1976; Final Things, 1980; The Teacher's Daughter, 1982; Tourists, 1984; Sunset Manor, 1990; The Age of Longing, 1995. Honours: Fellowships; City of Toronto Book Award, 1973; Geoffrey Faber Memorial Prize, England, 1975. Address: 52 St Patrick Street, St Catharines, Ontario, L2R 1K3, Canada.

WRIGHT Ronald, b. 12 Sept 1948, Surrey, England. Education: MA, University of Cambridge. Publications: Memoirs: Cut Stones and Crossroads: A Journey in Peru, 1984; On Fiji Islands, 1986; Time Among the Maya, 1989; Stolen Continents (history), 1992; Home and Away (essays), 1993; A Scientific Romance (novel), 1997. Contributions to: Times Literary Supplement and other Journals. Honours: Gordon Montador Award, 1993; Honorary Doctorate (LLD), University of Calgary, 1996; David Higham Prize for Fiction, 1997. Memberships: PEN, Canada; Survival International. Literary Agent: Gillon Aitken. Address: c/o Gillon Aitken Associates, 29 Fernshaw Road, London SW10 0TG, England.

WRIGHT Weaver. See: ACKERMAN Forrest J.

WU Duncan, b. 3 Nov 1961, Woking, Surrey, England. Reader in English Literature; Writer. Education: BA, 1984, DPhil, 1991, University of Oxford. Appointment: Postdoctoral Fellow, British Academy, 1991-94; Reader in English Literature, University of Glasgow, 1995-; Editor, Charles Lamb Bulletin. Publications: Wordsworth's Reading 1770-1799, 1993; Romanticism: An Anthology, 1994; William Wordsworth: A Selection, 1994; Six Contemporary Dramatists, 1994; Romanticism: A Critical Reader, 1995; Wordsworth's Reading, 1800-15, 1996; Romantic Women Poets: An Anthology, 1997. Contributions to: Journals and periodicals. Memberships: Charles Lamb Society, council member; Keats-Shelley Memorial Association, committee member. Address:

Department of English Literature, University of Glasgow G12 8QQ, Scotland.

WULEFF Thomas Frederik, b. 24 Aug 1953, Helsinki, Finland. Writer. m. Lotta Wigelius-Wulff, 1 Mar 1985, 2 sons, 1 daughter. Education: Filosofie Magister, Helsinki University, 1982. Publications: Mansten, poetry, 1973; Nattens Fabler, novel, 1974; Hjärtats Stratrövare, poetry, 1976; Snapshots-Mumlade Mytologier, poetry, short prose, 1980; Sumprattans Resa, fable, 1980; Trance Dance, novel, 1980; En Drömmares Dagbok, cut-up poetry, 1982; Utspelad i Ulan-Bator, novel, 1983; Kirurgens Park - Kineserier, poetry, short prose, 1985; Det Öndas Tjusning, essay, 1987; Helsinki Romanka, novel, 1990; Pang Pang Du är Död, thriller, 1996. Contributions to: Book reviews in Hufvudstadbladet. Honour: 3 Year State Award, 1997-99. Membership: President, Society of Swedish Authors in Finland, 1998. Literary Agent: Söderström & Co Förlagsaktiebolag. Address: Radmansgatan 4 D 55, 00140 Helsinki, Finland.

WULSTAN David, b. 18 Jan 1937, Birmingham, England. Professor of Music. m. Susan Nelson Graham, 9 Oct 1967, 1 son. Education: BSc, College of Technology, Birmingham; BA, 1st Class, Music, Oxford University, 1963, Fellow, 1964, MA, 1966, Magdalen College, Oxford. Career: Founder and Director, The Clerkes of Oxenford, 1961-; Numerous appearances on BBC TV and Radio 3, Thames TV, NWDR, BRT, Cheltenham, York, Bologna, Holland and Flanders Festivals, Proms and various films; Visiting Professor, University of California, Berkeley, 1977; Professor of Music, University College, Cork, 1980; Professor of Music, University College, Aberystwyth, Wales, 1983-90; Research Professor, 1991-. Compositions: Various Christmas carols, and film music. Recordings: Tallis; Sheppard; Gibbons's Church Music; Play of Daniel; Robert White. Publications include: Early English Church Music, volume 3, 1964, volume 27, 1979; Anthology of Carols, 1968; Anthology of English Church Music, 1971; Play of Daniel, 1976; Coverdale Chant Book, 1978; Complete Works, 1979-; Tudor Music, 1984. Contributions to: Journal of Theological Studies; Journal of the American Oriental Society; Iraq Music and Letters; Galpin Society Journal; Musical Times; Notes, Cantigueras. Memberships: Council, Plainsong and Medieval Music Society. Address: Ty Isaf, Lianilar, Aberystwyth, Wales, SY23 4NP.

WUNSCH Josephine (McLean), b. 3 Feb 1914, Detroit, Michigan, USA. Author. m. Edward Seward Wunsch, 9 Aug 1940, 1 son, 2 daughters. Education: BA, University of Michigan, 1936. Publications: Flying Skis, 1962; Passport to Russia, 1965; Summer of Decision, 1968; Lucky in Love, 1970; The Aerie (as J Sloan McLean with Virginia Gillett), 1974; Girl in the Rough, 1981; Class Ring, 1983; Free as a Bird, 1984; Breaking Away, 1985; The Perfect Ten, 1986; Lucky in Love, 1987; Between Us, 1989. Address: 830 Bishop Road, Grosse Pointe Park, MI 48230, USA.

WURLITZER Rudolph, b. 1937, Cincinnati, Ohio, USA. Author; Screenwriter. Education: Columbia University; University of Aix-en-Provence. Publications: Nog, 1969; Flats, 1970; Two-Lane Blacktop (with Will Cory), 1971; Quake, 1972; Pat Garrett and Billy the Kid, 1973; Slow Fade, 1984; Walker, 1987; Hard Travels to Sacred Places, 1994. Other: Several screenplays. Contributions to: Books and periodicals. Address: c/o Shambhala Publishers, Horticultural Hall, 300 Massachusetts Avenue, Boston, MA 02115, USA.

WYLIE Betty Jane, b. 21 Feb 1931, Winnipeg, Manitoba, Canada. Writer; Dramatist; Poet. m. William Tennent Wylie, 2 sons, 2 daughters. Education: BA, 1950, MA, 1952, University of Manitoba. Appointments: Writer-in-Library, Burlingtin, Ontario, 1987-88; Bunting Fellow, Radcliffe College, USA, 1989-90. Publications: Over 32 books and 36 plays. Contributions to: Many periodicals. Honours: Several awards. Memberships: Dramatists Guild, USA; Playwrights Union of Canada; Writers' Union of Canada. Address: c/o Writers Union of

Canada, 24 Ryerson Avenue, Toronto, Ontario M5T 2P3, Canada.

WYLIE Laura. See: **MATTHEWS Patricia Anne.**

WYNAND Derk, b. 12 June 1944, Bad Suderode, Germany. Professor; Poet; Writer; Translator; Editor. m. Eva Kortemme, 8 May 1971. Education: BA, 1966, MA, 1969, University of British Columbia. Appointments: Visiting Lecturer, 1969-73, Assistant Professor to Professor, 1973-, Chair, Department of Creative Writing, 1987-90, University of Victoria; Editor, The Malahat Review, 1992-98. Publications: Locus, 1971; Snowscapes, 1974; Pointwise, 1979; One Cook, Once Dreaming, 1980; Second Person, 1983; Fetishistic, 1984; Heatwaves, 1988; Airborne, 1994; Door Slowly Closing, 1995; Closer to Home, 1997. Honours: The Malahat Review named Magazine of the Year, 1995; Honourable Mention, BP Nichol Chapbook Award, 1995. Address: c/o Department of Writing, University of Victoria, PO Box 3045, Victoria, British Columbia V8W 3P4, Canada.

WYNN J(ohn) C(harles), (Jay Seawind), b. 11 Apr 1920, Akron, Ohio, USA. Professor of Pastoral Theology. m. Rachel Linnell, 27 Aug 1943, 1 son, 2 daughters. Education: BA, College of Wooster, 1941; BD, Yale University, 1944; MA, 1963, EdD, 1964, Columbia University; Post doctoral fellowship, Cornell University, 1972. Appointment: Teacher of Religious Journalism, Colgate Rochester Divinity School, 1959-69. Publications: How Christian Parents Face Family Problems, 1955; Sermons on Marriage and the Family, 1956; Pastoral Ministry to Families, 1957; Families in the Church: A Protestant Survey, 1961; Sex, Family and Society in Theological Focus, 1966; Sex, Ethics and Christian Responsibility, 1970; Education for Liberation and other Upsetting Ideas, 1977; The Family Therapist, 1987; Family Therapy in Pastoral Ministry, 1991. Contributions to: Religious periodicals. Memberships: Presbyterian Writers Guild; American Association for Marriage and Family Therapy; Religious Education Association; National Council on Family Relations. Address: 717 Maiden Choice Lane 523, Catonsville, MD 21228, USA.

WYNNE-JONES Tim, b. 12 Aug 1948, Bromborough, Cheshire, England. Writer; Editor. m. Amanda Lewis, 12 Sept 1980, 2 sons, 1 daughter. Education: BFA, Honours, University of Waterloo, 1974; Masters of Visual Arts, York University, 1979. Appointments: Lecturer, University of Waterloo, 1974-76, York University, 1978-80; Book Designer, Peter Martin Associates, 1974-76; Graphic Designer, Solomon/Wynne-Jones, 1976-79; Reviewer, Globe and Mail, 1985-88; Editor, Red Deer College Press, 1989-96. Publications: Childrens Books: Stephen Fair (novel); The Maestn (novel) The Book of Changes (short stories); Some of the Kinder Planets (short stories); Rosie Backstage (with A Lewis); The Last Piece of Sky (with Marie-Louise Gay); Mouse in the Manger (with Elaine Blier); The Zoom Trilogy (with Eric Beddows); Architect of the Moon (with Ian Wallace); Mischief City (with Victor Gad); I'll Make You Small (with Maryanne Kovalski). Adult Books: Fastyngange; The Knot; Odd's End. Contributions to: Numerous. Honours: Governor General's Awards, 1993, 1995; Boston Globe-Horn Book Award, 1994. Memberships: Writers Union of Canada; PEN International. Address: 476 Brooke Valley Road, Rural Route 4, Perth, Ontario K7H 3C6, Canada.

X

XERRI Raymond Christian, (Eco-Logija), b. 2 Feb 1969, New York, USA. Diplomat; Writer. Education: EU, Institut für Europaische Studien an der Albert-Ludwigs Universität, Freiburg-im-Breisgau, Germany, 1989-90; BA, Honours, Manhattan College, Riverdale, New York, 1990; DDS, University of Malta, 1992; MA, Diplomatic Studies, 1994, PhD, 1996, Social Studies, Victoria University of Technology, St Albans, Victoria, Australia. Appointments: Professional Photographer, Reporter, Maltese International Newspaper, Medina, USA, 1986-90; Secretary, Executive Committee, 1991-92, Vice President of Committee, 1992-93, Qala St Joseph FC, Qala, Gozo, Malta, Qala St Joseph Newsletter, 1991-93; Founder, Chief Editor, Gozo mill-pjazza, Victoria, Gozo, Malta, 1993-94. Publications: The European Monetary System - History, the ECU and its Prospects through Maastricht and Beyond, 1992; European Union Environmental Legislation with Respect to the Mediterranean, 1994; Ecology and the Malta Ecological Society, 1995; International and Regional Organisations, 1995. Honours: Malta's National Religious Studies Award, 1978-79; Green Pen of the Year Award, 1996; Distinguished Maltese Citizens of the Twentieth Century, 1997. Memberships: Malta Ecological Foundation, founder, executive director, and board member, 1991-; Maltese-American Foundation, Medina, USA, 1987-90. Address: Stars & Stripes, 4 Zewwieqa Street, Qala GSM 104, Gozo, Malta.

Y

YAFFE James, b. 31 Mar 1927, Chicago, Illinois, USA. Professor; Writer; Dramatist. m. Elaine Gordon, 1 Mar 1964, 1 son, 2 daughters. Education: BA, summa cum laude, Yale University, 1948. Appointments: Professor, 1968-, Director, General Studies, 1981-, Colorado College. Publications: Poor Cousin Evelyn, 1951; The Good-for-Nothing, 1953; What's the Big Hurry?, 1954; Nothing But the Night, 1959; Mister Margolies, 1962; Nobody Does You Any Favors, 1966; The American Jews, 1968; The Voyage of the Franz Joseph, 1970; So Sue Me!, 1972; Saul and Morris, Worlds Apart, 1982; A Nice Murder for Mom, 1988; Mom Meets Her Maker, 1990; Mom Doth Murder Sleep, 1991; Mom Among the Liars, 1992; My Mother, the Detective, 1997. Plays: The Deadly Game, 1960; Ivory Tower (with Jerome Weidman), 1967; Cliffhanger, 1983. Other: Television plays. Contributions to: Various publications. Honour: National Arts Foundation Award, 1968. Memberships: American Association of University Professors; Authors League; Dramatists Guild; Mystery Writers of America; PEN; Phi Beta Kappa. Address: 1215 North Cascade Avenue, Colorado Springs, CO 80903, USA.

YAKUSHI Hiroyuki, b. 3 Mar 1946, Tokyo, Japan. Sports Photographer. m. Yuri Yamanaka, 26 Dec 1978, 2 sons. Education: BA, Kyoto University of Foreign Studies, 1969; Tokyo Photographic College, 1971. Appointments: Official Photographer, 1972 Sapporo Olympic Organizing Committee; Organizing Committee, Morioka Shizukuishi Alpen Ski World Championships, 1993. Publication: The World of Hiro Yakushi. Contributions to: Asahi Graph; Blue Guide Ski; Bob Ski; Playboy; Focus; Number. Honour: Grand Prix, Addidas Sports Photo Contest, 1981. Address: 2-20-9 Aobadai, Aoba-ku, Yokohama, Japan.

YAMBA Christian Bawa, b. 28 Feb 1944. Social Anthropologist. m. 6 Dec 1975, 2 sons, 1 daughter. Education: BA, Stockholm University, 1977; Postgraduate Studies, Anthropology, School of Oriental and African Studies, University of London, 1978-79; PhD, Stockholm University. Appointments: Lecturer, University of Stockholm, 1982-88; Curator, Africa National Ethnographical Museum of Sweden, 1988-90; Senior Research Fellow, Karolinska Institute, Stockholm, 1991-96; Research Officer, SIDA/SAREC, 1986-87; Nordic Research Fellow, Scandinavian Institute of African Studies, 1998-; Reviews Editor, Ethnos. Publication: Permanent Pilgrims, 1995. Contributions to: Africa, Journal of the International African Institute; Ethnos, Journal of Anthropology. Address: Bjorkvallavägen 95, SE-19436 Upplands Väsby, Sweden.

YAN Xiao Jian, b. 22 Dec 1954, Anhui, China. Author. m. Jian Ping Sun, 17 Nov 1990, 2 daughters. Education: BA, Literature, Xian Northwest China University, 1989; MA, Literature, Writers College, Beijing Normal University and Lu-xan Literature Institute, 1991. Appointment: Professional Author, Anhui Literature Institute, 1985-. Publications: Gas Lamp, 1983; All Night Shopping, 1985; Three Writers in a Small Town (short stories), 1986; Ten Years Prediction, 1987; Look Over Native Place (short stories), 1992; Bitten Itinerary (filmplay), 1994. Honours: Prizes and awards. Memberships: Anhui Writers Association; Chinese Writers Association; Anhui Literary Institute. Address: Room 404, House 450, Luochuan Road (E), Shanghai, China.

YANKOWITZ Susan, b. 20 Feb 1941, Newark, New Jersey, USA. Writer; Dramatist. m. Herbert Leibowitz, 3 May 1978, 1 son. Education: BA, Sarah Lawrence College, 1963; MFA, Yale Drama School, 1968. Publications: Novel: Silent Witness, 1977. Plays: Slaughterhouse Play, 1971; Boxes, 1973; Terminal, 1975; Alarms, 1988; Night Sky, 1992. Screenplay: Portrait of a Scientist, 1974. Contributions to: Periodicals. Honours: Joseph Levine Fellowship in Screenwriting, 1968; Vernon Rice Drama Desk Award for Most Promising Playwright, 1969; Rockefeller Foundation

Grant, 1973, and Award, 1974; Guggenheim Fellowship, 1975; MacDowell Colony Residencies, 1975, 1984, 1987, 1990; National Endowment for the Arts Grants, 1979, 1984; New York Foundation for the Arts Grant, 1989; McKnight Fellowship, 1990. Memberships: Authors Guild; Dramatists Guild; New Dramatists; PEN; Writers Guild of America. Address: c/o Mary Harden, 850 7th Avenue, New York, NY 10019, USA.

YAOS-KEST Itamar, b. 3 Aug 1934, Hungary. Poet; Author. m. Hanna Mercazy, 21 Aug 1958, 1 son, 1 daughter. Education: BA, University of Tel Aviv. Appointment: Founder, Eked Publishing House, 1958. Publications: 15 books, 1959-92. Contributions to: Magazines. Honours: Herzel Prize, 1972; Talpir Prize, 1984; Lea Goldberg Prize, 1990; Prime Minister's Prize, 1993. Membership: Association of Hebrew Writers. Address: Merian Hahashunonout 25, Tel Aviv, Israel.

YEARGERS Edward K, b. 27 Apr 1938, Houma, Louisiana, USA. Professor of Biology. m. Susan Combs, 20 Feb 1993, 2 sons. Education: BS, Physics, 1960; MS, Biology, 1962; PhD, Biophysics, 1966. Appointments: Professor of Biology, Georgia Institute of Technology. Publications: Basic Biophysics for Biology, 1992; An Introduction to the Mathematics ofBiology, 1996. Address: School of Biology, Georgia Institute of Technology, Atlanta, GA 30332, USA.

YEATMAN Ted P, (Trezevant Player), b. 16 Dec 1951, Nashville, Tennessee, USA. Writer; Historical Researcher. Education: BA, 1976, MLS, 1977, George Peabody College for Teachers. Appointments: Senior Staff Writer, Peabody Post, 1975-76; Editorial Board, Friends of the James Farm, 1984-93. Publications: Jesse James and Bill Ryan at Nashville, 1981; The Tennessee Wild West: Historical and Cultural Links with the Western Frontier (co-author), 1995; Frank and Jesse James: The Hidden Years, 1996. Contributions to: Books and journals. Memberships: Potomac Corral of Westerners; Friends of the James Farm, board of directors 1982-93, editorial board, 1984-93; Tennessee Western History and Folklore Society, co-director, 1981-. Address: 422 1/2 McDowell Avenue B, Hagerstown, MD 21740-3661, USA.

YEHOSHUA Abraham B, b. 9 Dec 1936, Jerusalem, Israel. Professor; Writer. m. Rivka Kirsninski, 1960, 2 sons, 1 daughter. Education: BA, 1960; MA, 1962.Appointments: Co-Editor, Keshet, 1965-72; Siman Kria, 1973-; Full Professor, University of Haifa, 1980. Publications: Death of the Old Man, 1963; Three Days and a Child, 1970; Early in the Summer of 1970, 1973; The Lover, 1978; Between Right and Right, 1981; A Late Divorce, 1984; Possessions, 1986; Five Seasons, 1988; Mister Mani, 1990; The Wall and the Mountain, 1988; Night's Babies, 1992; The Return from India, 1994; Voyage to the End of the Millennium, 1997. Honours: National Jewish Book Awards, 1990, 1993; Best Jewish Book of the Year Award, 1993; Israel Prize for Literature, 1995; Premio Internasional Flaiano, 1996. Address: 33 Shoshanat, Ha-Carmel, Haifa, Israel 37322.

YELDHAM Peter, b. Gladstone, New South Wales, Australia. Dramatist; Author; Screenwriter. m. Marjorie Crane, 27 Oct 1948, 1 son, 1 daughter. Publications: Stage Plays: Birds on the Wing, 1969-70; She Won't Lie Down, 1972; Fringe Benefits (co-author), 1973; Away Match (co-author), 1974; Seven Little Australians, 1988; Once a Tiger, 1994. Feature Films: The Comedy Man, 1963; The Liquidator, 1965; Age of Consent, 1968; Touch and Go, 1979. Television Plays: Reunion Day; Stella; Thunder on the Snowy; East of Christmas; The Cabbage Tree Hat Boys; The Battlers. Television Series: Run from the Morning, 1977; Golden Soak, 1978; Ride on, Stranger, 1979; The Timeless Land, 1979. Also: Levkas Man, 1980; Sporting Chance, 1981; 1915, 1982; All the Rivers Run, 1983; Flight into Hell, 1984; Tusitala, The Lancaster Miller Affair, 1985; The Far Country, 1985; Captain James Cook, 1986; The Alien Years, 1987; Naked Under Capricorn, 1988; The Heroes, 1988; The Heroes, The Return, 1991; The Battlers, 1994. Novels: Reprisal, 1994; Without Warning, 1995; Two Sides of a Triangle, 1996; A Bitter harvest, 1997; The Currency

Lads, 1998; Against the Tide, 1999. Honours: Sammy Award, Best Television Series in Australia, 1979; Writers Guild, Best Adaption, 1980, 1983, 1986; Penguin Award, Best Script, 1982, and Best Original Mini-Series, 1989; Order of Australia Medal, 1991. Memberships: Writers Guild, Australia; British Writers Guild. Literary Agent: Anthony Williams Management, Sydney, Australia. Address: 1102 Yarramalong Road, Yarramalong, Australia 2259.

YEVTUSHENKO Yevgeny Aleksandrovich, b. 18 July 1933, Stanzia Zima, Siberia, Russia. Poet; Writer. m. (1) Bella Akhmadulina, div, (2) Galina Semyonovna, 1 child. Education: Gorky Literary Institute, 1951-54. Publications in English Translation: Poetry: The Poetry of Yevgeny Yevtushenko, 1953-1965, 1965; Bratsk Station, The City of Yes and the City of No, and Other New Poems, 1970; Kazan University and Other New Poems, 1973; From Desire to Desire, 1976; Invisible Threads, 1982; Ardabiola, 1985; Almost at the End, 1987; The Collected Poems, 1952-1990, 1991. Other: A Precocious Autobiography, 1963; Wild Berries (novel), 1984; Divided Twins: Alaska and Siberia, 1988. Honours: Order of the Red Banner of Labour; USSR State Prize, 1984. Memberships: International PEN; Union of Russian Writers. Address: c/o Union of Russian Writers, ul Vorovskogo 52, Moscow, Russia.

YOARGO Aineri. See: **O'GRADY Irenia**.

YOLEN Jane, b. 11 Feb 1939, New York, New York, USA. Author; Editor; Storyteller. m. David Wilber Stemple, 2 Sept 1962, 2 sons, 1 daughter. Education: BA, English Literature, Smith College, 1960; MEd, University of Massachusetts, 1976. Publications: Over 170 books, 1963-99. Contributions to: Many periodicals. Honours: Christopher Medal, 1979; Mythopoeic Society Awards, 1986, 1993; Smith College Medal, 1988; Caldecott Medal, 1988; Regina Medal, 1992; Kerlan Award, 1988; Keene State College Children's Book Award, 1995; World Fantasy Award, 1998; Nebula Award, 1997. Memberships: Authors Guild; Children's Literature Association; Mystery Writers of America; Science Fiction Writers of America, president, 1986-88; Society of Children's Book Writers. Address: Phoenix Farm, Box 27, Hatfield, MA 01038, USA.

YORK Alison. See: **NICOLE Christopher Robin**.

YORK Andrew. See: **NICOLE Christopher Robin**.

YORKE Margaret, (Margaret Beda Nicholson), b. 30 Jan 1924, Surrey, England. Writer. m. Basil Nicholson, 1945, div 1957, 1 son, 1 daughter. Appointments: Assistant Librarian, St Hilda's College, Oxford, 1959-60; Library Assistant, Christ Church, Oxford, 1963-65; Chairman, Crime Writers Association, 1979-80. Publications: Summer Flight, 1957; Pray Love Remember, 1958; Christopher, 1959; Deceiving Mirror, 1960; The China Doll, 1961; Once a Stranger, 1962; The Birthday, 1963; Full Circle, 1965; No Fury, 1967; The Apricot Bed, 1968; The Limbo Ladies, 1969; Dead in the Morning, 1970; Silent Witness, 1972; Grave Matters, 1973; No Medals for the Major, 1974; Mortal Remains, 1974; The Small Hours of the Morning, 1975; Cast for Death, 1976; The Cost of Silence, 1977; The Point of Murder, 1978; Death on Account, 1979; The Scent of Fear, 1980; The Hand of Death, 1981; Devil's Work, 1982; Find Me a Villain, 1983; The Smooth Face of Evil, 1984; Intimate Kill, 1985; Safely to the Grave, 1986; Evidence to Destroy, 1987; Speak for the Dead, 1988; Crime in Question, 1989; Admit to Murder, 1990; A Small Deceit, 1991; Criminal Damage, 1992; Dangerous to Know, 1993; Almost the Truth, 1994; Pieces of Justice, 1994; Serious Intent, 1995; A Question of Belief, 1996; Act of Violence, 1997; False Pretences, 1998. Address: c/o Curtis Brown Ltd, Haymarket House, 28/29 Haymarket, London SW1Y 4SP, England.

YOSHIMASU Gozo, b. 22 Feb 1939, Tokyo, Japan. Poet; Essayist;Lecturer. m. Marilia, 17 Nov 1973. Education: BA, Keio University, 1963. Appointments: Chief Editor, Sansai Finer Arts magazine, 1964-69;

Fulbright Visiting Writer, University of Iowa, 1970-71; Poet-in-Residence, Oakland University, Rochester, Michigan, 1979-81; Lecturer, Tama Art University, 1984-; Visiting Lecturer at various institutions; Many poetry readings round the world. Publications in English Translation: A Thousand Steps and More: Selected Poems and Prose, 1964-1984, 1987. Contributions to: Anthologies and periodicals. Honours: Takami Jun Prize, 1971; Rekitei Prize, 1979; Hanatsubaki Modern Poetry Prize, 1984. Memberships: Japan PEN Club; Japan Writers Association. Address: 1-215-5 Kasumi-cho, Hachioji City 192, Japan.

YOUNG Al(bert James), b. 31 May 1939, Ocean Springs, Mississippi, USA. Writer; Poet. m. Arline June Belch, 1963, 1 son. Education: University of Michigan, 1957-61; Stanford University, 1966-67; AB, University of California at Berkeley, 1969. Appointments: Jones Lecturer in Creative Writing, Stanford University, 1969-74; Writer-in-Residence, University of Washington, Seattle, 1981-82; Co-Founder (with Ishmael Reed) and Editor, Quilt magazine, 1981-. Publications: Fiction: Snakes, 1970; Who is Angelina?, 1975; Sitting Pretty, 1976; Ask Me Now, 1980; Seduction by Light, 1988. Poetry: Dancing, 1969; The Song Turning Back into Itself, 1971; Some Recent Fiction, 1974; Geography of the Near Past, 1976; The Blues Don't Change: New and Selected Poems, 1982; Heaven: Collected Poems 1958-1988, 1989; Straight No Chaser, 1994. Other: Bodies and Soul: Musical Memoirs, 1981; Kinds of Blue: Musical Memoirs, 1984; Things Ain't What They Used to Be: Musical Memoirs, 1987; Mingus/Mingus: Two Memoirs (with Janet Coleman), 1989; Drowning in the Sea of Love: Musical Memoirs, 1995. Honours: National Endowment for the Arts Grants, 1968, 1969, 1974; Joseph Henry Jackson Award, San Francisco Foundation, 1969; Guggenheim Fellowship, 1974; Pushcart Prize, 1980; Before Columbus Foundation Award, 1982. Address: 514 Bryant Street, Palo Alto, CA 94301, USA.

YOUNG Allan (Edward), b. 21 June 1939, New York, New York, USA. Professor; Writer. m. Eleanor Podheiser, 16 Sept 1962, 1 son, 2 daughters. Education: BA, State University of New York at Binghamton, 1961; MBA, 1963, PhD, 1967, Columbia University. Appointments: Lecturer, Bernard M Baruch College, City University of New York, 1965-66; Assistant Professor, 1966-71, Associate Professor, 1971-74, Professor, 1974-,Senior Researcher, Entrepreneurship and Emerging Enterprises Program, Syracuse University. Publications: The Contribution of the New York Based Securities Industry to the Economy of the City and State, 1985; The Financial Manager, 1987, 2nd edition, 1994; Guidelines for the Financing of Industrial Investment Projects in Developing Countries, 1995, 1999. Contributions to: Academic and professional journals. Honours: Alexander Hamilton Chair-Fulbright Lectureship and Copnsultancy, Budapest; Trust Bank Chair in Accounting and Finance, Lincoln University, Canterbury, New Zealand; Syracuse University Award for Outstanding Research by Faculty. Memberships: Many economic and finance societies. Address: 27 Ely Drive, Fayetteville, NY 13066, USA.

YOUNG Axel. See: McDOWELL Michael.

YOUNG Bertram Alfred, b. 20 Jan 1912, London, England. Freelance Writer. Appointments: Assistant Editor, 1949-62, Drama Critic, 1962-64, Punch; Drama Critic, 1964-78, Arts Editor, 1971-77, Financial Times. Publications: Tooth and Claw, 1958; Bechuanaland, 1966; Cabinet Pudding, 1967; The Mirror Up to Nature, 1982; The Rattigan Version, 1986. Contributions to: Numerous professional journals and general magazines. Honour: Officer of the Order of the British Empire, 1980. Memberships: Critics Circle; Society of Authors; Garrick Club. Address: 1 Station Street, Cheltenham, Glos GL50 3LX, England.

YOUNG Donald (Richard), b. 29 June 1933, Indianapolis, Indiana, USA. Writer; Editor; Photographer. Education: BA, Indiana University, 1955; MA, Butler University, 1964. Appointments: Editorial Staff, 1963-66, Senior Editor in American History and Political Science,

1967-77, Encyclopedia Americana; Editorial Staff, American Heritage Publishing Co, 1966-67; Contributor, The World Almanac and Book of Facts, 1984-; Managing Editor, Magazine and Book Division, Aperture, 1986-87; Various photography exhibitions. Publications: American Roulette: The History and Dilemma of the Vice-Presidency, 1965, 2nd edition, revised, 1974; The Great American Desert, 1980; Natural Monuments of America, 1990; The Sierra Club Book of the National Parks, 5 volumes (editor, 1986, 1996); The Smithsonian Guides to Historic America, 12 volumes (editor, 1998); Historic Monuments of America, 1990; National Parks of America, 1994. Contributions to: Books and periodicals. Honours: Indiana University Author Award, 1965; State Historical Society of Wisconsin Award of Merit, 1971. Membership: American Society of Picture Professionals. Address: 166 East 61st Street, Apt 3-C, New York, NY 10021, USA.

YOUNG Ed (Tse-chun), b. 28 Nov 1931, Tientsin, China. Children's Author and Illustrator. Education: City College of San Francisco, 1952; University of Illinois at Urbana, 1952-54; BPA, Art Center College of Design, Los Angeles, 1957; Graduate Studies, Pratt Institute, 1958-59. Publications: Over 35 books, 1962-96. Honours: Caldecott Medal, 1990; Boston Globe/Horn Book Awards, 1990, 1992. Address: c/o Shr Jung Tai Chi Chuan School, 87 Bowery, New York, NY 10003, USA.

YOUNG Elizabeth Ann. See: KENNET Lady.

YOUNG Hugo John Smelter, b. 13 Oct 1938, Sheffield, England. Journalist. m. (1) Helen Mason, 1966, dec 1989, 1 son, 3 daughters, (2) Lucy Waring, 1990. Education: MA, Jurisprudence, Balliol College, Oxford. Appointments: Yorkshire Post, 1961; Chief Leader Writer, 1966-77, Political Editor, 1973-84, Joint Deputy Editor, 1981-84, Sunday Times; Political Columnist, The Guardian, 1984-; Director, The Tablet, 1985-; Chairman, Scott Trust, 1989-. Publications: The Zinoviev Letter (co-author), 1966; Journey to Tranquility (co-author), 1969; The Crossman Affair, 1974; No, Minister (co-author), 1982; But, Chancellor (co-author), 1984; The Thatcher Phenomenon (co-author), 1986; One of Us, 1989, revised edition, 1991; This Blessed Plot, 1998. Honours: Harkness Fellow, 1963; Congressional Fellow, US Congress, 1964; Columnist of the Year, British Press Awards, 1980, 1983, 1985; What the Papers Say Award, Granada TV, 1985; Honorary DLitt, University of Sheffield, 1993. Address: c/o The Guardian, 119 Farringdon Road, London EC1R 3ER, England.

YOUNG Ian George, b. 5 Jan 1945, London, England. Poet; Writer; Editor. Appointments: Director, Catalyst Press, 1969-80, Director, TMW Communications, 1990-. Publications: Poetry: White Garland, 1969; Year of the Quiet Sun, 1969; Double Exposure, 1970; Cool Fire, 1970; Lions in the Stream, 1971; Some Green Moths, 1972; The Male Muse, 1973; Invisible Words, 1974; Common-or-Garden Gods, 1976; The Son of the Male Muse, 1983; Sex Magick, 1986. Fiction: On the Line, 1981. Non-Fiction: The Male Homosexual in Literature, 1975, 2nd edition, 1982; Overlooked and Underrated, 1981; Gay Resistance, 1985; The AIDS Dissidents, 1993; The Stonewall Experiment, 1995; The Aids Cult, 1997. Honours: Several Canada Council and Ontario Arts Council Awards. Membership: International Psychohistory Association. Address: 2483 Gerrard Street East, Scarborough, Ontario M1N 1W7, Canada.

YOUNG John Karl, b. 15 Aug 1951, Minneapolis, Minnesota, USA. Associate Professor of Anatomy. m. Paula Jean Spesock, 3 July 1977, 2 sons. Education: University of South Carolina, 1968-69; BS, Cornell University, 1972; PhD, University of California at Los Angeles, 1977; Postdoctoral Research, University of Minnesota, 1977-79. Appointment: Associate Professor of Anatomy, Howard University, Washington, DC. Publications: Cells: Amazing Forms and Functions, 1990; Hormones: Molecular Messengers, 1994; Histology on CD-ROM, 1996. Translator: B Kotlyar: Plasticity in the Nervous System, 1992; V Dilman: Development, Aging and Disease: A New Rational for an Intervention

Strategy, 1994. Contributions to: Scientific journals. Memberships: American Association of Anatomists; American Physiological Society. Address: c/o Department of Anatomy, Howard University, 520 W Street North West, Washington, DC 20059, USA.

YOUNG Wayland Hilton. See: KENNET 2nd Baron.

YOUNG-BRUEHL Elisabeth, b. 3 Mar 1946, Elkton, Maryland, USA. Professor of Psychology; Psychoanalyst; Writer. Education: BA, 1968, MA, 1974, PhD, 1974, New School for Social Research, New York City. Appointments: Professor of Philosophy, Wesleyan University, 1974-91; Professor of Psychology, Haverford College, Pennsylvania, 1991-. Publications: Freedom and Karl Jaspers' Philosophy, 1981; Hannah Arendt: For Love of the World, 1982; Vigil, 1983; Anna Freud: A Biography, 1988; Mind and the Body Politic, 1989; Freud on Women, 1990; Creative Characters, 1991; Global Cultures, 1994; The Anatomy of Prejudices, 1996; Subject to Biography, 1998. Contributions to: Professional journals. Honours: National Endowment for the Humanities Fellowship, 1984-85; Guggenheim Fellowship, 1986-87. Membership: Authors Guild. Address: 409 West Stafford Street, Philadelphia, PA 19144, USA.

YOUNG-EISENDRATH Polly, b. 4 Feb 1947, Akron, Ohio, USA. Psychologist; Psychoanalyst; Writer. m. Edward Epstein, 13 Jan 1985, 2 sons, 1 daughter. Education: AB, summa cum laude, English, Ohio University, 1965-69; Institute de Touraine, France, 1967-68; MA, Psychology, Mythology, Goddard College, 1974; MSW, Clinical Social Work, 1977, PhD, Developmental and Counseling Psychology, 1980, Washington University; Diploma, Jungian Analysis, Inter-Regional Society of Jungian Analysts, 1978-86; Diplomate Jungian Analyst, 1986. Appointments: Chief Psychologist, Jungian Analyst, President, Clinical Associates West, P C Radnor, 1986-94; Independent Practice as Psychologist and Jungian Analyst, Burlington, Vermont, 1994-; Clinical Associate Professor in Psychiatry, Medical College, University of Vermont, Burlington, 1996-; Numerous lectures worldwide. Publications: Jung's Self Psychology: A Constructivist Perspective, 1991; You're Not What I Expected: Learning to Love the Opposite Sex, 1993; The Gifts of Suffering: Finding Insight, Compassion and Renewal, 1996; Gender and Desire: Uncursing, Pandora, 1997; A Cambridge Companion to Jung (co-editor), 1997. Contributions to: Many books, reviews, journals, and other publications. Honours: Phi Beta Kappa; Mortar Board; Phi Kappa Phi; Various fellowships, assistantships, and awards. Memberships: International Association for Analytical Psychology; American Psychological Association; Independent Society for Analytical Psychology, founding member. Address: 166 Battery Street, Burlington, VT 05401, USA.

YOUNGSON Jeanne Keyes, b. 20 Dec 1924, Syracuse, New York, USA. Film Historian; Society Head. m. Robert George Youngson, 25 June 1960. Education: Maryville College, Tennessee, 1946; Oxford and Cambridge Universities, England, 1950-56; PhD, New York University, 1960; Special Courses, Sorbonne, France, 1958, and Trinity College, Ireland, 1959. Publications: The Further Perils of Dracula; Count Dracula and the Unicorn; The Bizarre World of Vampires; Private Files of a Vampirologist: Case Histories and Letters; Biographies of Dwight Frye and John Carradine. Contributions to: Society journals. Literary Agent: James Martin. Address: Penthouse North, 29 Washington Square West, New York City, NY 10011-9180, USA.

YUAN Kejia, b. 18 Sept 1921, Cixi, China. Retired Professor of English and American Literature; Poet; Writer; Translator; Editor. m. Cheng Qi Yun, 20 Jan 1955, 2 daughters. Education: BA, English Literature, National South-West Associated University, 1946. Appointments: Assistant Researcher, 1957-78, Associate Researcher and Associate Professor, 1979-82, Professor of English and American Literature, 1983-90, Research Institute of Foreign Literature. Publications: On the Modernization of Chinese Poetry, 1988; Source Materials for the Study of

Modernist Literature (editor), 1989; A Study of Western Modernist Literature, 1992; An Anthology of Modern Western Poetry (editor), 1992. Translator: Several volumes. Contributions to: Books, journals, and magazines. Honours: 2nd Class Prize, 1991, 1st Class Prize, 1994, Foreign Books Award. Memberships: All China Society for Literary and Art Theories, advisory board; Chinese Translators' Association, council member; Chinese Writers' Union. Address: c/o Research Institute of Foreign Literature, 5 Jian Guo Nei Da Jie, Beijing 100732, China.

YUDKIN Leon Israel, b. 8 Sept 1939, England. University Lecturer; Writer; Poet. m. Meirah Goss, 29 Sept 1967. Education: BA, 1960, MA, 1964, University of London. Appointments: Assistant Lecturer, Lecturer, University of Manchester, 1966-; Lecturer, University College, London, 1996. Publications: Isaac Lamdan: A Study in Twentieth-Century Hebrew Poetry, 1971; Meetings with the Angel (co-editor), 1973; Escape into Siege, 1974; U Z Greenberg: On the Anvil of Hebrew Poetry, 1980, 2nd edition, 1987; Jewish Writing and Identity in the Twentieth Century, 1982; 1948 and After: Aspects of Israeli Fiction, 1984; Modern Hebrew Literature in English Translation (editor), 1986; Agnon: Texts and Contexts in English Translation (editor), 1988; Else Lasker-Schüler: A Study in German-Jewish Literature, 1990; Beyond Sequence: Current Israeli Fiction and Its Context, 1992; The Israeli Writer and the Holocaust (editor), 1993; The Other in Israeli Literature (editor, 1993: A Home Within: Varities of Jewish Expression in Modern Fiction, 1996. Contributions to: Various publications. Honour: Doctor of Literature, University of London, 1995. Membership: IJA Literary Circle. Address: 51 Hillside Court, 409 Finchley Road, London NW3 6HQ, England.

Z

ZAHNISER Ed(ward DeFrance), b. 11 Dec 1945, Washington, District of Columbia, USA. Writer; Poet; Editor. m. Ruth Christine Hope Deuwel, 13 July 1968, 2 sons. Education: AB, Greenville College, Illinois, 1967; Officers Basic Course, Defence Information School, 1971. Appointments: Poetry Editor, The Living Wilderness Magazine, 1972-75; Founding Editor, Some of Us Press, Washington, DC, 1972-75; Arts Editor, Good News Paper, 1981-; Editor, Arts and Kulchur, 1989-91; Associate Poetry Editor, Antietam Review, 1992-. Publications: The Ultimate Double Play (poems), 1974; I Live in a Small Town (with Justin Duewel-Zahniser), 1984; The Way to Heron Mountain (poems), 1986; Sheenjek and Denali (poems), 1990; Jonathan Edwards (artist book), 1991; Howard Zahniser: Where Wilderness Preservation Began: Adirondack Wilderness Writings (editor), 1992; A Calendar of Worship and Other Poems, 1995. Contributions to: Books and periodicals. Honours: Woodrow Wilson Fellow, 1967; 1st and 2nd Prize in Poetry, West Virginia Writers Annual Competitions, 1989, 1991, 1992; Second Prize, Essay, 1995. Address: c/o Atlantis Rising, P O Box 955, Shepherdstown, WV 25443-0955, USA.

ZAHORSKI Kenneth James, b. 23 Oct 1939, Cedarville, Indiana, USA. Professor of English; Director of Faculty Development. m. Marijean Allen, 18 Aug 1962, 2 daughters. Publications: The Fantastic Imagination, 2 volumes, 1977-78; Dark Imaginings, 1978; Fantasy Literature, 1979; The Phoenix Tree, 1980; Visions of Wonder, 1981; Alexander, Walton, Morris: A Primary and Secondary Bibliography, 1981; Fantasists on Fantasy, 1984; Peter S Beagle, 1988; The Sabbatical Mentor, 1994. Contributions to: Professional journals. Honours: Leonard Ledvina Outstanding Teacher Award, 1974; American Literary Association Outstanding Reference Book Award, 1979; Mythopoeic Society Special Scholarship Award, 1985; Donald B King Distinguished Scholar Award, 1987. Memberships: Professional and Organizational Development Network in Higher Education; Wisconsin Council of Teachers of English; Modern Language Association of America; National Council of Teachers of English; American Association for Higher Education; Council of Independent Colleges, Senior Associate. Address: 205 Arrowhead Drive, Green Bay, WI 54301, USA.

ZALBEN BRESKIN Jane, b. 21 Apr 1950, New York, New York, USA. Author; Artist; College Teacher. m. 25 Dec 1969, 2 sons. Education: BA, Art, Queen's College, City University of New York, 1971; Pratt Graphics Centre, 1972. Publications: Cecilia's Older Brother, 1973; Lyle and Humus, 1974; Basil and Hillary, 1975; Penny and the Captain, 1977; Norton's Nightime, 1979; Will You Count the Stars Without Me, 1979; All in the Woodland Early: An ABC by Jane Yolen, 1979; Oliver and Alison's Week, 1980; Oh Simple!, 1981; Porcupine's Christmas Blues, 1982, Maybe it will Rain Tomorrow, 1982; Here's Looking at You, Kid, 1987; Water from the Moon, 1987; Beni's First Chanukah, 1988; Earth to Andrew O Blechman, 1989; Happy Passover, Rosie, 1989; Leo and Blossom's Sukkah, 1990; Goldie's Purim, 1991; The Fortune Teller in 5B, 1991; Beni's Little Library, 1991; Buster Gets Braces, 1992; Inner Chimes: Poems on Poetry, 1992; Happy New Year, Beni, 1993; Papa's Latkes, 1994; Beni's First Chanukah, 1994; Miss Violet's Shining Day, 1995; Pearl Plants a Tree, 1995; Beni's Family Cookbook, 1996; Unfinished Dreams, 1996; Papa's Latkes, 1996; Pearl's Marigolds for Grandpa, 1997; Beni's First Wedding, 1998; Beni's Family Teasury, 1998; Pearl's Eight Days of Chanukah, 1998; To Every Season: A Family Cookbook, 1999. Contributions to: Journals and magazines. Honours: Sydney Taylor Honour Award, 1989; Best Books Citation, New York Public Library, 1991; International Reading Association Citation, 1993. Memberships: Society of Children's Book Writers; Parents Choice Award, IRA, 1995. Address: 70 South Road, Sands Point, NY 11050, USA.

ZALYGIN Sergey Pavlovich, b. 6 Dec 1913, Durasovka, Russia. Writer; Editor; Ecologist. Education: Omsk Agricultural Institute. Appointment: Editor-in-Chief, Novy Mir Magazine, 1986-. Publications: Novels, stories, and essyas, 1941-92. Contributions to: Periodicals. Honours: State Prize, 1968; Sergey Radonezhsky Orthodox Order, 1993. Memberships: American Academy of Sciences; Russian Academy of Sciences; Russian Union of Writers. Address: 28/3 Lenin Prospect, Moscow, Russia.

ZAMOYSKI Adam, b. 11 Jan 1949, New York, New York, USA. Historian. A Levels, History, Polish, Russian, French, Open Scholarship to The Queen's College, Oxford University; BA Hons, 1970, MA Hons, 1974, Oxford University, 1967-70. Appointments: Freelance Historian; Financial Times, 1974-76; BBC Foreign Service, 1976-77. Publications: Chopin, a new biography, 1979; The Battle for the Marchlands, 1981; Paderewski, a biography, 1982; The Polish Way, 1987; The Last King of Poland, 1992; The Forgotten Few, 1995. Honours: Shortlisted, Yorkshire Post non-fiction Award, 1980; American Music Book Society First Choice, 1980. Literary Agent: Aitken & Stone. Address: 33 Ennismore Gardens, London SW7 1AE, England.

ZAND Roxane, (Hakimzadeh), b. 21 Mar 1952, Tehran, Iran. Educator; Writer. m. Hakim Zadeh, 7 Nov 1978, 2 sons. Education: BA, Harvard University, 1975; DPhil, 1994. Publication: Persian Requiem. Contributions to: Jaso; Feminist Review; Nimeye Digar Feminist Quarterly. Memberships: Translators Society; Harvard Club of London. Address: 9 Templewood Avenue, London NW3 7UY, England.

ZARE G Veste'n. See: **VERZEA Ernest-George.**

ZASTROW Charles, b. 30 July 1942, Wausaw, Wisconsin, USA. Professor of Social Work; Writer. Education: BS, Psychology, 1964, MSW, 1966, PhD, Social Welfare, 1971, University of Wisconsin at Madison. Appointments: Assistant Professor, 1971-74, Associate Professor, 1974-78, Professor of Social Work, 1978-, University of Wisconsin at Whitewater; Associate Editor, International Journal of Comparative and Applied Criminal Justice, 1976-; Social Work Consulting Editor, Nelson-Hall Publishers, 1987-. Publications: The Personal Problem Solver (co-author), 1977; Talk to Yourself, 1979; You Are What You Think, 1993; The Practice of Social Work, 6th edition, 1999; Social Problems, 4th edition, 1996; Introduction to Social Work and Social Welfare, 6th edition, 1996; Social Work With Groups, 4th edition, 1997; Understanding Human Behavior and the Social Environment, 4th edition (co-author), 1997. Contributions to: Professional journals. Honour: Excellence in Teaching Award, University of Wisconsin at Whitewater, 1987. Memberships: Academy of Certified Social Workers; Council of Social Work Education; National Association of Social Workers; Register of Clinical Social Workers. Address: c/o Department of Social Work, University of Wisconsin at Whitewater, Whitewater, WI 53704, USA.

ZAUNER Friedrich Ch, b. 19 Sept 1936, Rainbach, Austria. Freelance Author. m. Roswitha Zauner, 28 Mar 1960, 1 son, 3 daughters. Education: Dr Phil, University of Vienna. Publications: Books: Archaische Trilogie, 3 plays, 1982; Lieben und Irren des Martin Kummanz, novel, 1986; Bulle, novel, 1986; Das Ende der Ewigkeit, 4 novels, 1992, 1993, 1995, 1996; Passion, 1996; Das Grab ist leer, 1998; Plays: Spuk, 1971; Fiktion, 1975; Deserteure, 1977; Menschenskinder, 1980; Ypsilon, 1985; Aller Tage Abend, 1989; Mirakel Mirakel, 1991; Films: Job für Kutschera, 1975; Xander Vrüpp, 3 films, 1984, 1985, 1986; Dort oben im Wald bei diesen Leuten, 1990; Edited works in English translation: Books: Charade (Ariadne Riverside), 1994; A Handful of Earth (Ariadne Riverside), 1996; Plays: Land, 1978; Good Night, Kids, 1994; Kidnapping, 1995; Day of Reckoning, 1996. Honours: Kulturpreis, 1985; Ehrenbürger der Gemeinde Rainbach, 1996; Honorary Title of Professor, 1997. Membership: President, PEN Club, Linz, 1989-. Address: A-4791 Rainbach, Ober-Österreich, Austria.

ZAWODNY J(anusz) K(azimierz), b. 11 Dec 1921, Warsaw, Poland (US citizen, 1955). Retired Professor of International Relations; Writer. m. LaRae Jean Koppit, 18 Sept 1971, 1 son. Education: BS, Labour Economics, 1950, MA, International Relations, 1951, University of Iowa; PhD, Political Science, Stanford University, 1955. Appointments: Instructor and Assistant Professor, Princeton University, 1955-58; Fellow, Center for Advanced Study in the Behavioral Sciences, Stanford, 1961-62, Institute for Social and Behavioral Pathology, University of Chicago, 1977-84; Associate Professor, 1962-63, Professor of Political Science, 1965-75, University of Pennsylvania; Professor of Political Science, Washington University, St Louis, 1963-65; Research Associate, Center for International Affairs, Harvard University, 1968; Senior Associate Member, St Antony's College, Oxford, 1968-69; Avery Professor of International Relations, Claremont Graduate School and Pomona College, California, 1975-82; Staff, National Security Council, USA. 1979-84. Publications: Death in the Forest: The Story of the Katyn Forest Massacre, 1962, 6th edition, 1988; Guide to the Study of International Relations, 1967; Man and International Relations: Contribution of the Social Sciences to the Study of Conflict and Integration (editor and contributor), 2 volumes, 1967; Nothing But Honour: The Story of the Uprising of Warsaw 1944, 1978; Uczestnicy i Swiadkowie Powstania Warszawskiego, 1994. Contributions to: Scholarly books and journals. Honours: Honorary MA, University of Pennsylvania, 1965, University of Oxford, 1968; Literary Award, Kultura, Paris, 1981; Jurzykowski Foundation Citation and Award, 1982; Research Awards, Polish Scientific Society, London, 1982, 1989; Scientific Society Book of the Year Award, University of Lublin, Poland, 1988; Order of Merit, President of Poland, 1994; History Award, J Pilsudski Institute, New York, 1997. Address: 23703 North East Margaret Road, Brush Prairie, WA 98606, USA.

ZEAVIN Edna Arlone Jennings, b. 6 Nov 1930, San Francisco, California, USA. Retired Teacher; Writer. m. Barney Zeavin, 30 May 1959, 2 sons, 4 daughters. Education: BS, 1958, MS, 1960, Biological Science, Arizona State University. Appointment: Teacher, Prima College, 1986-96. Publications: Growing With Your Teen, 1989; Breathtaking: Stopping the Plunder of Our Planet's Air, 1992; Cuisine from 6 Continents, 1993; Leavitt-Jennings-Roots and Branches, 1993; Trees of Time, 1996. Contributions to: Periodicals. Memberships: Arizona Nightwriters; National Writer's Union; Society of Southwest Authors, secretary. Address: 7901 East Mabel, Tucson, AZ 85715, USA.

ZELLER Frederic, b. 20 May 1924, Berlin, Germany (British Subject). Writer; Sculpter. m. (2) 21 Jan 1989. Education: BA, Birbeck College, London University, England. Publication: When Time Ran Out: Coming of Age in the Third Reich, 1989. Honour: National Endowment for the Arts Award, 1989. Memberships: Federation of Modern Painters and Sculptors, New York; Artists' Equity Association, New York. Address: 775 Sixth Avenue, New York, NY 10001, USA.

ZEMANEK Alicja, b. 2 Aug 1949, Bielsko Biata, Poland. Scientist; Poet. m. Bogdan Zemanek, 30 July 1981. Education: Doctor, Biological Science, 1977, PhD, 1977, Jagiellonian University. Publications: Egzotyczny Ogrod na Wesotej, 1986; Listopad w Bibliotece, 1988; Dzien w Którym Zniknetam, 1990; Wakacje w Krakowie, 1991; Podobni do zagajnika olch, 1993; Modlitwa do teczy, 1996. Contributions to: Periodicals. Memberships: British Society for the Histoy of Science; Polskie Towarzystowo Botaniczne; Society for the History of Natural History; Zwiazek Literatòw Polskich. Address: ul Kopernika 27, 31 501 Kraków, Poland.

ZENO Phyllis W, (Phyllis Williams), b. 16 Feb 1926, Cleveland, Ohio, USA. Editor; Creative Director. m. Norman Zeno, 10 June 1960, dec, 1 son, 2 daughters. Education: University of Wisconsin, 1943-45; New School Social Research, New York City , 1948; American Theatre Wing, 1949. Appointments: Staff Writer, Fred Waring Show, CBS TV, 1953-54; Industrial Show Writer,

MCA, 1959-61, 1961-74; Creative Director, AAA Auto Club S, 1974-99; Editor in Chief, AAA Going Places Magazine, 1982-99. Publications: Composer: This Is An Opening, 1975; How Do You Open a Show, 1976; We Never Sing Opening Numbers, 1976; 500 Music and Lyrics for Industrial Shows, 1960-74; Going Places Magazine, bi-monthly, 1982-99. Contributions to: Travel articles to Prime Times, Naples News, Senior News. Honours: FMA Charlie Award, 1993, 1996; Best Reg Column. Memberships: ASCAP; SATW; Floria Magazine Association. Address: 8402 Cherrystone Ct, Tampa, FL 33607, USA.

ZEPHANIAH Benjamin (Obadiah Iqbal), b. 15 Apr 1958, Birmingham, England. Poet; Dramatist; Writer. m. Amina Iqbal Zephaniah, 17 Mar 1990. Education: Ward End Hall Comprehensive School; Broadway Comprehensive School. Appointments: Writer-in-Residence, Africa Arts Collective, Liverpool, 1989, Hay-on-Wye Literature Festival, 1991, Memphis State University, Tennessee, 1991-95. Publications: Plays: Playing the Right Tune, 1985; Job Rocking, 1987; Delirium, 1987; Streetwise, 1990; The Trial of Mickey Tekka, 1991. Radio Play: Hurricane Dub, 1988. Television Play: Dread Poets Society. Other: Pen Rhythm, 1980; The Dread Affair, 1985; Inna Liverpool, 1988; Rasta Time in Palestine, 1990; City Psalms, 1992; Talking Turkeys, 1994; Funky Chickens, 1996; Propa Propaganda, 1996; School's Out, 1997; Face, 1999. Contributions to: Periodicals, radio, television, and recordings. Honours: Literary Chair Nominations, Cambridge, 1987, Oxford, 1989; BBC Young Playwrights Festival Award, 1988; Honorary Doctorate, University of North London, 1998. Address: c/o Sandra Boyce Management, 1 Kingsway House, Albion Road, London N16 0TA, England.

ZERNOVA Ruth, b. 15 Feb 1919, Tiraspol, Russia. Writer. m. Ilya Serman, 15 Nov 1943, 1 son, 1 daughter. Education: University of Leningrad, 1946. Publications: Scorpionovy Yagody, 1961; Solnetshnaia Storona, 1968; Nemyie Zvonki, 1974; Jenskie Rasskazy, 1981; Dlinnye Teni, 1995. Contributions to: Short stories and articles in Russian journals and magazines. Membership: Union of Israeli Writers. Address: PO Box 23118, Jerusalem, Israel.

ZETFORD Tully. See: **BULMER Henry Kenneth.**

ZHANG Changxin, (Jiefu Dongli), b. 30 Nov 1940, Liaoning, China. Writer. m. Huang Fuju, 1962, 1 son, 1 daughter. Education: Graduate, China Siping Teachers School, 1962. Appointments: Teacher, Jilin Liaoyuan Finances and Trade School, 1964-78; Editor, Editor-in-Chief, Beiliao Literature, 1979-84; Vice Director, Jilin Siping City Culture Bureau, 1984-94; Vice Chairman, Writers Association, 1994-; Editor-in-Chief, Qingchun Shige (Youth Poems), monthly. Publications: Changba Shan Hun, English translation as Spirit of Changba Mountains, 1985; Aide San Yuan Se, English translation as Three Colours of Love, 1987; East Madrid, 1989; Zni Zhi Qiu, English translation as Enjoyment in Autumn, 1991; The Renovation of North China Two-Person Show Published by Arts, 1993; Qingxi Lanxi, English translation as Black and Blue, 1994; Chaoji Ai Qing Siwang, English translation as The Death of Super Love, 1995; the Cultural Characteristics of Northeast China Two-Person Show Market. Contributions to: Peoples Daily. Honours: Provincial Level Awards. Memberships: China Association of Writers; China Playwriters Association. Address: c/o Jilin Writers Association, Building 9, 167 Renmin Street, Changchun, Jilin, 130021, China.

ZHANG Jie, b. 27 Apr 1937, China. Writer. Education: BA, People's University of China, 1960. Publications: Over 15 books, 1980-95. Honours: National Short Story Awards, 1978, 1979, 1983; Meodun National Novel Award, 1985; National Novella Award, 1985; Malaparte Literary Prize, 1989. Memberships: American Academy of ARts and Letters; Beijing Association of Writers; Beijing Political Conference; Chinese Association of Writers; International PEN. Address: c/o International

Department, Chinese Association of Writers, 2 Shatan Beijie, Beijing 1000720, China.

ZHOU Hui-Fan, b. 1937, Heng Yang County, Hunan, China. Author Writer; Editor; Member of the Writers Association of China. m. Du Ying-Chun, 1968. Education: Graduate, Department of Chinese Language of Hunan Teacher's University, 1963. Appointments: Editor, Hunan Publishing House; Member, Editorial Board of Xiangjiang Literature; Vice Editor in Chief, The Great World Literary Magazine; Member, Editorial Board, The Literary Periodicals of Hunan Province; Executive Editor in Chief & Copy Editor, one of the key literary theoretical magazines of China, Theory and Creation, 1963-77; Director, New-Vernacular Institute of China; Member, Editorial Board of Poems & Songs Year Book of China; Special Researcher of World Literature and Arts researching Center; Member, Adviser, Research Committee of ABI. Publications: 36 literary works, 1963-93, include: Monograph: Translate, Note, Comment & Analyse The Selected Poems of Jin Pin Mei, 1992. Poems: In Front of a Living Person's Tombstone, 1975; The Road of Autumn Harvest Uprising Glittering, 1977; Write at the Ruins of the Public Dining Hall, 1980; Flowers, 1981; Loving of the Sea, 1981; Sing the Praises of Former Residence of Comrade Shao Qi, 1981; Brilliant River, 1985; In Front of Lei Feng's Statue, 1993. Medium-Length Novel: The Emperor with the Imperial Robe Taken Off, 1990. Feature Article: Praise of Guards of Republic, 1989. Editing and Writing: Red Star Glittering; The Road to Shao Shan; Morning Sun Light of Dong Ting, 1963-93. Honours: Early and late works selected for: New Poems Appreciating Series of China; The Cream Series of Lyric Poems of Famous Experts; Representative Works of Poems of Poets of the Present in China. Early and late monographs selected by the International Research Centre of Jin Pin Mei Material and the 4th Beijing International Book Fair. Literature Awards: Literature Creation Award of Hunan Province, 1981; Azalea Flower Novel Prize, Newspaper and Magazine Award for Excellent Literature Comment All Over the Country, 1991; Excellent Literature Award, Government of Hunan Province and Yun Gong Cup Literature Award of New Vascular Institute of China, 1992; Second Excellent Achievement Award, The Literature Institute of Hunan Province, 1994; Excellent Appreciating Award of The Famous People's Works Exhibition of China, 1995; 20th Century Achievement Award of ABI, 1996; The 3rd Eastern Cup of Poems and Songs Competition of China, 1998. Address: Literature and Art Union of Hunan Province, 261 BaYi Road, Changshi, 410001, China.

ZIEGLER Philip Sandeman, b. 24 Dec 1929, Ringwood, Hampshire, England. Writer. m. (1) Sarah Collins, 1960, 1 son, 1 daughter, (2) (Mary) Clare Charrington, 1971, 1 son. Education: 1st Class Honours, Jurisprudence, New College, Oxford, England. Appointments: Member, Foreign Service, 1952-67; Staff, 1967-72, Editorial Director, 1972-79, Editor-in-Chief, 1979-80, William Collins and Sons Ltd. Publications: Duchess of Dino, 1962; Addington, 1965; The Black Death, 1968; William IV, 1971; Omdurman, 1973; Melbourne, 1976; Crown and People, 1978; Diana Cooper, 1981; Mountbatten, 1985; Elizabeth's Britain 1926 to 1986, 1986; The Sixth Great Power: Barings 1762-1929, 1988; King Edward VIII, 1990; Wilson: The Authorised Life, 1993; London at War 1939-45, 1995; Osbert Sitwell, 1998. Editor: The Diaries of Lord Louis Mountbatten 1920-1922, 1987; Personal Diary of Admiral the Lord Louis Mountbatten 1945-1946, 1988; From Shore to Shore: The Diaries of Earl Mountbatten of Burma 1953-1979, 1989; Brook's: A Social History (with Desmond Seward), 1991; Osbert Sitwell, 1998. Contributions to: Newspapers and journals. Honours: Fellow, Royal Society of Literature, 1975; Fellow, Royal Historical Society, 1976; W H Heinemann Award, 1976; Honorary DLitt, Westminster College, Fulton, Missouri, 1988; Commander of the Royal Victorian Order, 1991. Memberships: London Library, chairman, 1979-85; Public Lending Right Advisory Committee, chairman, 1994-97; Society of Authors, chairman, 1988-90. Address: 22 Cottesmore Gardens, London W8 5PR, England.

ZIFFRIN Marilyn, b. 7 Aug 1926, Moline, Illinois, USA. Composer; Writer. Education: BM, University of Wisconsin, Madison, 1948; MA, Columbia University, 1949; Postgraduate Studies, University of Chicago, 1963-65. Publications: Carl Ruggles: Composer, Painter and Storyteller, 1994. Contributions to: The New Grove Dictionary of Music and Musicians, 1980; The New Grove Dictionary of American Music, 1986. Honours: MacDowell Colony Fellowships, 1961, 1963, 1971, 1977, 1980, 1989; Virginia Center for the Creative Arts Residency, 1987. Address: PO Box 179, Bradford, NH 03221, USA.

ZIGAL Thomas, b. 20 Oct 1948, Galveston, Texas, USA. Writer. 1 son. Education: BA, English, University of Texas, 1970; MA, Creative Writing, Stanford University, 1974. Publications: Playland, 1982; Into Thin Air, 1995; Hardrock Stiff, 1996. Membership: Texas Institute of Letters, 1995-. Literary Agent: Esther Newberg, ICM. Address: c/o ICM, 40 West 57th Street, New York, NY 10019, USA.

ZIGMAN Laura, b. 11 Aug 1962, Boston, Massachusetts, USA. Writer. Education: BA, University of Massachusetts at Amhurst, 1985; MA, Radcliffe Publishing Course, University of Cambridge, 1985. Appointments: Book Publicist, Times Books, 1985-86, Vintage Books, 1986-89; Senior Publicist, Atlantic Monthly Press, 1989-90; Marketing Manager, Atlantic Monthly Press, 1990-92; Publishing Director, Turtle Bay Books, 1992-93; Promotion Manager, Alfred A Knopf, 1993-95; Project Manager, Smithsonian Associate, Smithsonian Institution, 1996. Publication: Animal Husbandry, 1998. Contributions to: New York Times; Washington Post; USA Today; USA Weekend. Literary Agent: Bill Clegg. Address: c/o Bill Clegg, The Robbins Office, 405 Park Avenue, NY 10022, USA.

ZIMMERL Richard, b. 18 Jan 1939, Vienna, Austria. Professor. m. Gertraud Nermuth, 26 June 1965, 1 son, 1 daughter. Education: Mathematics, Astronomy, Meterology, 1963, Master of Pedagogy, 1972, Oberstudienrat, 1994, University of Vienna. Appointments: Wiener Lehrerzeitung, 1966-88; Editor, Die Briefmarke, 1974; Chief Editor, Donau Post, 1985. Publications: Typenkunde der Rekozettel Österreichs, 1972; Sachen Suchen, 1973; Jungendarbeit in Österreich, 1983. Contributions to: Schweizer Briefmarken-Zeitung; Sammler-Dienst; Briefmarken-Spiegel. Honour: Silbernes Verdienstzeichen der Republik Österreich. Membership: Association Internationale de Journalistes Philateliques. Address: Ketzergasse 242, A-1230 Vienna, Austria.

ZINDEL Paul, b. 15 May 1936, Staten Island, New York, USA. Dramatist; Writer. m. Bonnie Hildebrand, 25 Oct 1973, 1 son, 1 daughter. Education: BS, 1958, MSc, 1959, Wagner College. Publications: Plays: The Effects of Gamma Rays on Man-in-the-Moon Marigolds, 1965; And Miss Reardon Drinks a Little, 1967; The Secret Affairs of Mildred Wild, 1972; Let Me Hear You Whisper, 1973; The Ladies Should Be in Bed, 1973; Ladies at the Alamo, 1975; Fiction: The Pigman, 1968; My Darling, My Hamburger, 1969; I Never Loved Your Mind, 1970; I Love My Mother, 1975; Pardon Me, You're Stepping in My Eyeball, 1976; Confessions of a Teenage Baboon, 1977; The Undertaker's Gone Bananas, 1978; A Star for the Latecomer (with Bonnie Zindel), 1980; The Pigman's Legacy, 1980; The Girl Who Wanted a Boy, 1981; To Take a Dare (with Crescent Dragonwagon), 1982; When a Darkness Falls, 1984; Harry and Hortense at Hormone High, 1984; The Amazing and Death-Defying Diary of Eugene Dingman, 1987; A Begonia for Miss Applebaum, 1989; The Pigman and Me, 1992; David and Della, 1983; Loch, 1994. Contributions to: Newspapers and journals. Honours: Ford Foundation Grant, 1967; Obie Award, 1970; New York Drama Critics Circle Award, 1970; Pulitzer Prize for Drama, 1971; Vernon Rice Drama Desk Award, 1971; Los Angeles Drama Critics Award, 1973; Several best book citations. Memberships: Authors Guild; Dramatists Guild; Writers Guild of America West. Address: c/o Harper and Row, 10 East 53rd Street, New York, NY 10022, USA.

ZINN Howard, b. 24 Aug 1922, New York, New York, USA. Professor of Political Science Emeritus; Writer. m. Roslyn Shechter, 30 Oct 1944, 1 son, 1 daughter. Education: BA, New York University, 1951; MA, 1952, PhD, 1958, Columbia University. Appointments: Instructor, Upsala College, East Orange, New Jersey, 1953-56; Visiting Lecturer, Brooklyn College, 1955-56; Chairman, Department of History and Political Science, Spelman College, Atlanta, 1956-63; Associate Professor, 1964-66, Professor of Political Science, 1966-88, Professor Emeritus, 1988-, Boston University. Publications: LaGuardia in Congress, 1959; SNCC: The New Abolitionists, 1964; The Southern Mystique, 1964; New Deal Thought (editor), 1965; Vietnam: The Logic of Withdrawal, 1967; Disobedience and Democracy, 1968; The Politics of History, 1970; Post-War America, 1973; Justice in Everyday Life (editor), 1974; A People's History of the United States, 1980, revised and abridged edition as The Twentieth Century: A People's History, 1984; Declarations of Independence, 1990; You Can't Be Neutral on a Moving Train, 1995; The Zinn Reader, 1997. Contributions to: Professional journals and general periodicals. Honours: Albert J Beveridge Prize, American Historical Association, 1958; Harvard University Center for East Asian Studies Fellowship, 1960-61; Thomas Merton Award, 1991. Memberships: American Association of University Professor; Authors League; Lannan Literary Award, 1998. Membership: PEN, 1998-. Literary Agent: Rick Balkin. Address: 29 Fern Street, Auburndale, MA 02166, USA.

ZIOLKOWSKA-BOEHM Aleksandra, b. 14 Apr 1949, Lodz, Poland. Writer. m. Norman Boehm Jr, 9 June 1990, 1 s, Education: Master's degree in Literature, University of Lodz, 1973; PhD, Humanistic Studies, University of Warsaw, 1978. Appointments: Private Assistant to Melchior Wankowicz, Warsaw, 1972-74; Member, Repertoire Research Staff, Warsaw TV Theatre, 1977-81. Publications: Books: Blisko Wankowicza, 1975, 1978, 1988; Z Miejsca na Miejsce, 1983, 1986, 1997; Senator Haidasz, 1983, 1999; Dreams and Reality, 1984; Kanada, Kanada..., 1986; Diecezja Lodzka i Jej Biskupi, 1987; Moje i zaslyszane, 1988; Kanadyjski Senator, 1989; Na tropach Wankowicza, 1989; Proces Melchiora Wankowicza 1964 roku, 1990; Nie tylko Ameryka, 1992; Korzenie sa polskie, 1992; Ulica Zolwiego Strumienia, 1995; Amerykanie z wyboru, 1998; The Roots Are Polish, 1999. Contributions to: Kultura, Paris; Zeszyty Historyczne, Paris; Odra, Wroclaw; Twoj Styl, Warsaw; Pielgrzym, Toronto; Sarmatian Review, Houston; New Horizons, New York. Honours: Scholarships: Oxford Language Centre, 1975; Ontario Ministry of Culture, Toronto, 1982; Canadian Polish Research Institute, 1982; A Mickiewicz Foundation, Toronto, 1983; Institute of International Education, Washington DC, 1985; The Kosciuszko Foundation, 1990. Memberships: ZAIKS, Warsaw, 1976-; Society of Polish Writers, 1990-; Kosciuszko Foundation, New York, 1990-; Polish Institute of Arts and Sciences, New York, 1991-; Polish Writers' Union Abroad, London, 1994-; American PEN Club, 1998-. Literary Agent: ZAIKS, Warsaw, Poland. Address: 13 Servan Court, Parkway West, Wilmington, DE 19805, USA.

ZIOLKOWSKI Theodore Joseph, b. 30 Sept 1932, Birmingham, Alabama, USA. Professor of Comparative Literature; Writer. m. Yetta Bart Goldstein, 26 Mar 1951, 2 sons, 1 daughter. Education: AB, 1951, AM, 1952, Duke University; University of Innsbruck, 1952-53; PhD, Yale University, 1957. Appointments: Instructor to Assistant Professor, Yale University, 1956-62; Associate Professor, Columbia University, 1962-64; Professor of Germanic Languages and Literature, 1964-69, Class of 1900 Professor of Modern Languages, 1969-, Professor of Comparative Literature, 1975-, Dean, Graduate School, 1979-92, Princeton University; Various visiting lectureships and professorships. Publications: Hermann Broch, 1964; The Novels of Hermann Hesse, 1965; Hermann Hesse, 1966; Dimensions of the Modern Novel, 1969; Fictional Transfigurations of Jesus, 1972; Disenchanted Images, 1977; Der Schriftsteller Hermann Hesse, 1979; The Classical German Elegy, 1980; Varieties of Literary Thematics, 1983; German Romanticism and Its Institutions, 1990; Virgil and the Moderns, 1993; The Mirror of Justice, 1997; The View from the Tower, 1998; Das Wunderjahr in Jena, 1998. Editor: Hermann Hesse: Autobiographical Writings, 1972; Hermann Hesse: Stories of Five Decades, 1972; Hesse: A Collection of Critical Essays, 1972; Hermann Hesse: My Belief: Essays on Life and Art, 1974; Hermann Hesse: Pictor's Metamorphoses and Other Fantasies, 1982; Hermann Hesse: Soul of the Age: Selected Letters 1891-1962, 1991. Contributions to: Books and professional journals. Honours: Fulbright Research Grant, 1958-59; American Philosophical Society Grant, 1959; Guggenheim Fellowship, 1964-65; James Russell Lowell Prize for Criticism, 1972; American Council of Learned Societies Fellowships, 1972, 1976; Wilbur Lucius Cross Medal, Yale University, 1982; Goethe Institute Gold Medal, 1987; Henry Allen Moe Prize in Humanities, 1988; Resident Fellow, Bellagio Study Centre, Italy, 1993; Jacob und Wilhelm Grimm Prize, 1998. Memberships: Academy of Literary Studies; American Academy of Arts and Sciences; American Association of Teachers of German, honorary life member; Association of Graduate Scholars, president, 1990-91; Association of Literary Scholars and Critics; American Philosophical Society; Authors Guild; Modern Language Association, president, 1985; Associate of Literary Scholars and Critics; International Association of Germanists; Austrian Academy of Sciences; Göttingen Academy of Sciences; German-American Academic Council. Address: 36 Bainbridge Street, Princeton, NJ 08540, USA.

ZITHULELE. See: **MANN Christopher Michael.**

ZOBEL Louise Purwin, b. 10 Jan 1922, Laredo, Texas, USA. Author; Lecturer; Teacher. m. Dr Jerome Freemont Zobel, 14 Nov 1943, 1 son, 3 daughters. Education: BA, Journalism, Stanford University, 1943; MA, Communication, 1976. Appointments: Writer and Editor, United Press Bureau; Editor, Magazine, Association of College Unions International, 1972-73; Cruise Enrichment Lecturer and Writing Teacher, Royal Viking Lines and Princess Cruises, 1974-83; Instructor, Writer's Digest Correspondence School, 1982-90; Keynote Speaker, Travel Lecturer, TV Personality. Publications: The Travel Writer's Handbook, 1980, 4th edition, 1997; Let's Have Fun In Japan, 1982. Contributions to: Books, newspapers and magazines. Honours: Phi Beta Kappa, 1943; Sigma Delta Chi Award for Scholarship, 1943; Prizes, Writers Digest National Article Contest, 1967, 1975, 1978, 1992, 1994; National Writers Club Contest, 1976. Memberships: Women in Communication; California Writers Club; Travel Journalists Guild; International Food, Wine, and Travel Writers Association; American Society of Journalists and Authors. Address: 23350 Sereno Court, Villa No 30, Cupertino, CA 95014, USA.

ZOLYNAS Al(girdas Richard Johann), b. 1 June 1945, Dornbirn, Austria. Professor of English and Literature; Poet; Writer. m. 24 June 1967. Education: BA, University of Illinois, 1966; MA, 1969, PhD, 1973, University of Utah. Appointments: Instructor, Assistant Professor, Writer-in-Residence, Southwest State University, Marshall, Minnesota; Lecturer, Weber State College, Ogden, Utah, San Diego State University; Professor, United State International University, San Diego. Publications: The New Physics, 1979; 4 Petunia Avenue, 1987; Men of Our Time: An Anthology of Male Poetry in Contemporary America (editor with Fred Moramarco), 1992; Under Ideal Conditions, 1994. Contributions to: Various anthologies, reviews, quarterlies, and journals. Honour: San Diego Book Award for Best Poetry, 1994. Membership: Poets and Writers. Address: 2380 Viewridge Place, Escondido, CA 92026, USA.

ZORIN Michael. See: **SIMHOVITCH Michael.**

ZUCKER Naomi Flink, b. 6 Aug 1938, New York, NY, USA. Writer; Professor. m. Norman L Zucker, 25 June 1961, 1 son, 1 daughter. Education: BA, Douglass College, 1959; MA, University of Rhode Island, 1982. Appointment: Lecturer, Department of English, 1978-. Publications: The Coming Crisis in Israel: Private Faith and Public Policy, 1973; The Guarded Gate, The Reality of American Refugee Policy, 1988; Desperate Crossings! Seeking Refuge in the Americas, 1996. Contributions to: Journal of Refugee Studies; Annals of the American Academy of Political and Social Sciences; The Progressive; New York Times. Honours: Guslavus Myer's Center Outstanding Book Awards, 1988, 1997. Address: 25 Locust Drive, Kingston, RI 02881, USA.

ZUCKERMAN Nomi, b. 22 July 1920, Spring Lake, New Jersey, USA. Retired Art Educator; Artist; Poet; Poetry Reader. Education: BA, 1945, BSc in Education, 1945, MEd, 1970, Tyler School of Art, Temple University, Philadelphia. Appointments: Teacher, various elementary and secondary schools in Jerusalem. Publication: A Whole Olive Tree, 1998. Contributions to: Nova Poetica; Aural Images; Jewish Frontier; Poetry Anthology. Honours: Editor's Choice Award, International Library of Poetry; Various competition prizes. Membership: Voices, Israel. Address: 52 Bethlehem Road, Jerusalem 93504, Israel.

ZUROWSKI Andrzej, b. 24 Sept 1944, Poland. Theatre Critic; Essayist. m. Magda Oller, 23 Aug 1988, 1 son, 3 daughters. Education: MA, 1967; PhD, 1973. Appointments: Chief, Artistic Programmes, Polish TV, Gdańsk, 1967-90; Polish TV Commentator, 1990-; Lecturer, University of Gdansk, 1975-77, 1986-. Publications: 15 books, 1976-99. Contributions to: Journals, periodicals and multiauthors works. Honours: Several literary awards and medals. Memberships: International Association of Theatre Critics, vice president; Union of Polish Writers. Address: Glogowa 21, 81-589 Gdynia, Poland.

ZÜSLI Franz Felix, b. 7 Nov 1932, Zurich, Switzerland. m. Verena Zacher, 26 Sept 1993, 1 son, 1 daughter. Education: Dr.iur.utr, University of Zurich. Appointments: Secretary General, University of Zurich, 1968-83, UNESCO-ONG, 1983-92; Foundation Secretary, Pestalozzi, Switzerland, 1983-91. Publictions: Josef Xder Omelettenbäcker, 1983; Hoffen in der Dämmeruug, 1982; Dennoch, 1990. Contributions to: Magazines and journals. Memberships: Several. Address: Oetlisbergstr, CH-8053 Zurich-Witikon, Switzerland.

ZWICKY Jan, b. 10 May 1955, Calgary, Alberta, Canada. Poet; Philosopher; Writer; Teacher. Education: BA, University of Calgary, 1976; MA, 1976, PhD, 1981, University of Toronto. Appointments: Teacher, University of Waterloo, 1981, 1984, 1985, Princeton University, 1982, University of Western Ontario, 1989, University of Alberta, 1992, University of New Brunswick, 1994, 1995, University of Victoria, 1996; Editor, Brick Books; Book Review Editor, The Fiddlehead. Publications: Wittgenstein Elegies, 1986; The New Room, 1989; Lyric Philosophy, 1992; Songs for Relinquishing the Earth, 1996. Honours: Many literary grants. Address: Box 1149, Mayerthorpe, Alberta T0E 1N0, Canada.

ZWICKY (Julia) Fay, b. 4 July 1933, Melbourne, Victoria, Australia. Poet; Editor. m. (1) Karl Zwicky, 1957, (2) James Mackie, 1990. Education: BA, University of Melbourne, 1954. Appointments: Senior Lecturer in English, University of Western Australia, 1972-87; Associate Editor, Southerly, Sydney, 1989-. Publications: Isaac Babel's Fiddle, 1975; Quarry: A Selection of Western Australian Poetry (editor), 1981; Kaddish and Other Poems, 1982; The Lyre in the Pawnshop: Essays on Literature and Survival, 1974-84, 1986; Procession: Youngstreet Poets 3 (editor), 1987; Ask Me, 1990; 7 Hostages and Other Stories, 1983; Poems 1970-1992, 1993; The Gatekeeper's Wife, 1997. Honours: New South Wales Premier's Award, 1982; Western Australian Premier's Award, 1991. Address: 30 Goldsmith Road, Claremont, Western Australia 6010, Australia.

ZYGULSKI Zdzislaw Franciszek Jr, b. 18 Aug 1921, Boryslaw, Poland. Art Historian; Museologist. m. Eva Voelpel, 18 Apr 1944, 1 son. Education: Doctor Degree, Jagiellonian University, Kraków, 1960; Professor Title, 1978; Full Professor, 1987. Publications: Bron w dawnej

Polse (Arms in Old Poland), 1975, 1982; Muzea na Swiecie (Museums of the World, 1982; An Outline History of Polish Applied Art, 1987); Sztuka islamu w zbirorach polskich (Art of Islam in Polish Collections), 1989; Ottoman Art in the Service of the Empire, 1992; Slawne bitwy w sztuce (Famous Battles in Art), 1996. Contributions to: Books and journals. Honour: Best Book on Polish Culture in English, Association of Polish Art, Detroit, 1991. Address: 30-112 Krakow, ul Dunin Wasowicza 12 m 5, Poland.

Appendices

APPENDIX A

LITERARY AGENTS

The following list of agents does not claim to be exhaustive although every effort has been made to make it as comprehensive as possible. In all instances, authors are advised to send preliminary letters to agents before submitting manuscripts.

ARGENTINA

Lawrence Smith Literary Agency
Aveni da de los Incas 3110
Buenos Aires 1426
Contact: *Lawrence Smith, Mrs Nancy H Smith*
Literary works accepted for translation into Spanish and Portuguese. Publications in volume or serial for representation in theatre, film, television or radio.

AUSTRALIA

Australian Literary Management
2A Armstrong Street
Middlepark, VIC 3206
Represents Australian writers in fields of fiction, non-fiction, children's books, theatre and film. Handles Australian/New Zealand rights only for a small number of American writers in conjunction with other literary agents.

Curtis Brown (Aust) Pty Ltd
27 Union Street, Paddington
Sydney, NSW 2021
Represents fiction, non-fiction, children's writers, television, screen, radio and stage; also represents directors.

Rick Raftos Pty Ltd
PO Box 445, Paddington
Sydney, NSW 2021
Contact: *Rick Raftos, Jane Rose*
Represents performing arts, writers, television, screen, radio and stage; also represents directors.

Anthony Williams Management Pty Ltd
PO Box 1379
Darlinghurst NSW 1300
Australia.

BELGIUM

Toneelfonds J. Janssens
Te Boelaerlei 107
2140 Antwerp
Contact: *Jessica Janssens*
Literary Agency specialising in plays.

BRAZIL

Karin Schindler
Caixa Postal 19051
04599 São Paulo SP
Contact: *Karin Schindler*
Handles everything for the sale of Portuguese language rights in Brazil

BULGARIA

Bulgarian Copyright Agency JUSAUTOR
17 Ernst Telman Boulevard
1463 Sofia
Contact: *Director General*
Representative of Bulgarian authors, promoting work for publication and performance abroad.

CANADA

Acacia House Publishing Services Ltd
51 Acacia Road
Toronto, Ontario M4S 2K6

Authors' Marketing Services Ltd
217 Degrassi Street
Toronto, Ontario M4M 2K8
Adult fiction and non-fiction, parental self-help, business and biography.

Bella Pomer Agency Inc
22 Shallmar Boulevard, PH2
Toronto, Ontario M5N 2Z8
Contact: *Bella Pomer*
International representation for full-length fiction and non-fiction. No cook books, how-to books or unsolicited manuscripts.

Bukowski Agency
182 Avenue Road, Suite 3
Toronto, Ontario M5R 2J1
President: *Denise Bukowski*

Kellock and Associates Ltd
11017 - 80 Avenue
Edmonton, Alberta T6G OR2
Contact: *Joanne Kellock*
Handles all non-fiction for trade market, all fiction, literary, commercial, genre and all works for children. Also acts for illustrators of books for children.

MGA/Sterling Lord Association Canada
10 St Mary Street, Suite 510
Toronto, Ontario M4Y 1P

Lucinda Vardley Agency Ltd
297 Seaton Street
Toronto, Ontario M5A 2T

DENMARK

Leonhardt Literary Agency Aps
35 Studiestraede
DK-1455 Copenhagan K
Handles all kinds of bookrights.

FRANCE

Agence Strassova
4 Rue Git-le-Coeur
75006 Paris
Handles general literature.

European American Information Services Inc
10 Rue de l'Abreuvoir
92400 Courbevoie, Paris
(US address: 110 East 59th Street
New York, NY 10022)
Representing author Catherine Nay and French publishers in North America and North American publishers and agents in France.

Francoise Germain
8 Rue de la Paix
75002 Paris
Contact: *Madame Francoise Germain*
Representation of French and foreign authors.

La Nouvelle Agence
7 Rue Corneille
75006 Paris
Representation in France for US, English, Italian and German agents and publishers as well as French authors.

Michelle Lapautre Literary Agency
6 Rue Jean Carries
75007 Paris
Contact: *Michelle Lapautre*
Representing English-language publishers, agents and authors for the sale of French translation rights.

Shelley Power Literary Agency Ltd
Le Montaud
24220 Berbigières, France
Contact: *Shelley Power*
General fiction and non-fiction. No poetry, plays or short pieces. Offers worldwide representation.

Promotion Litteraire
26 Rue Chalgrin
75116 Paris
Publishers' consultants representing leading American, French and Italian publishers, International authors, scout service, general fiction and non-fiction books, film and television scripts, film rights and properties.

GERMANY

Buro für Urheberrechte, Copyright Office, Copyright Information Center
Clara-Zetkin-Strasse 105
Berlin
Contact: *Dr Andreas Henselmann*

Corry Theegarten-Schlotterer Verlags-und Autoren-Agentur
Kulmer Strasse 3
D-8000 Munich 81
Contact: *Ms C Theegarten-Schlotterer*
Co-production of books of international interest, fiction and non-fiction, and biographies. No childrens' books.

Fralit Medium Agency
Brahmsallee 29
D-2000 Hamburg 13
Manuscripts for newspapers and book publishers, plays and features for theatre, broadcasting, television and film.

Geisenheyner and Crone International Literary Agents
Gymnasiumstrasse 31B
D-7000 Stuttgart 1
Contact: *Mr Ernst W Geisenheyner*
Representing German and foreign authors and publishers.

GPA Gerd Plesel Agentur and Veriags GmbH
Linprunstrasse 38
D-8000 Munich 2
Contact: *Gerd J Plesel*
Represents publishers and literary agencies from the English language world in general and selected ones from French and German. Also major American and British Studios for ancilliary rights.

Hans Hermann Hagedorn
Erikastrasse 142
D-2000 Hamburg 20
Contact: *Hans Hermann Hagedorn.*

Literarische Agentur Brigitte Axster
Dreieichstr 43
D-6000 Frankfurt
Contacts: *Brigitte Axster, Dr Petra Christina Hardt, Uta Angerer*
Authors agent representing English, Dutch, French and Italian publishers in German speaking countries.

Skandinavia Verlag, Marianne Weno - Michael Günther
Ithweg 31
D-1000 Berlin 37
Contact: *Michael Günther*
Represents contemporary Scandinavian playwrights. Handles plays for radio, stage and television.

INDIA

Ajanta Books International
IUB Jawahar Nagar
Bungalow Road, Delhi 110007
Research work on Social Science and Humanity especially on Indian themes, oriental or modern.

ISRAEL

Rogan-Pikarski Literary Agency
200 Hayarkon Street
PO Box 4006
61 040 Tel Aviv
Contact: *Ilana Pikarski*
Represents major US and European publishers and agents for Hebrew volume, serial and performance and merchandising rights; also has New York agency.

ITALY

Agenzia Letteraria Internazionale
3 Via Fratelli Gabba
Milan
Represents American, English and German publishers and agencies exclusively in Italy.

Natoli and Stefan
Galleria Buenos Aires 14
I-20124 Milan
Represents fiction and non-fiction authors rights, co-editions and translations.

JAPAN

Tuttle-Mori Agency
Fuji Building, 8th Floor
2-15 Kanda Jimbocho
Chiyoda-ku
Tokyo 101
Contact: *Mr Takeshi Mori*
Largest literary agency for foreign rights in Japan.

THE NETHERLANDS

Auteursbureau Greta Baars Jelgersma
Bovensteweg 46
NL-6585 KD Mook
Contact: *Greta Baars Jelgersma*
Represents authors and publishers, and translations from the Scandinavian and modern languages. International co-printing of illustrated books and arranging profitable offers for book production. Oldest international literary agency in The Netherlands.

Prins and Prins Literary Agency
Postbus 5400
NL-1007 AK Amsterdam
Contact: *Henk Prins*
Representation in The Netherlands of foreign publishers.

NORWAY

Hanna-Kirsti Koch Literary Agency
PO Box 3043
Elisenberg
0207 Oslo 2
Contact: *Mr Eilif Koch*
Representing foreign authors in Norway.

Ulla Lohren Literary Agency
PO Box 150, Tasen
0801 Oslo 8
Contact: *Ulla Lohren*
Represents agents and publishers from Canada, UK, USA and others for Scandinavian rights in fiction, non-fiction and children's books.

POLAND

Authors' Agency
ul. Hipoteczna 2
00-950 Warsaw
Handles Polish copyrights, foreign contracts and information.

PORTUGAL

Ilidio da Fonseca Matos Literary Agency
Rua de S Bernardo 68-30,
1200 Lisbon
Contact: *Ilidio da Fonseca Matos*
Represents in Portugal: Curtis Brown Ltd; Laurence Pollinger Ltd; The New American Library; Doubleday and Company Inc; Rowholt Verla - Diogenes Verlag.

SPAIN

Andres de Kramer
Castello 30
28001 Madrid
Handles only foreign writers and foreign rights of theatrical plays and production in Spain.

Bookbank S A
Rafael Calvo 13
28010 Madrid

Represents foreign publishers and/or agents and/or writers for the sale of Spanish language and Portuguese rights. Also Spanish language authors.

Julio Fyanez Literary Agency
Via Augusta 139
08021 Barcelona
Contact: *Mr Julio Fyanez*
Represents publishers, agencies and independent authors from all countries and Spanish authors abroad. Covers Spain, Latin America, Portugal and Brazil.

Ute Korner de Moya Literary Agency
Ronda Guinardo 32-5-5
08025 Barcelona
Contact: *Ute Korner*
Represents foreign publishers, agents and authors in the Spanish and Portuguese speaking countries.

SWEDEN

D Richard Bowen
Post Box 30037
S-200 61 Malmö 30
Contact: *D Richard Bowen*
Publishers' literary and sales agent, translation rights, etc., negotiated.

Lennart Sane Agency AB
Hollandareplan
537434 Karlshamn
Contact: *Lennart Sane*
Representing US, British and Scandinavian authors, publishers and agencies for translation rights in Europe and Latin America.

Monica Heyum Literary Agency
PO Box 3300 Vendelso
S-13603 Haninge
Contact: *Monica Heyum*
Handles fiction, non-fiction and children's books.

SWITZERLAND

Dieter Breitsohl AG Literary Agency
PO Box 245
CH 8034 Zürich
or: Heimatstr 25
CH 8008 Zürich
Contact: *Dr Jutta Motz*
Handles non-fiction, psychology, psychosomatic, religion, theology and mythology.

Liepman AG
Maienburgweg 23, Postfach 572
CH-8044 Zürich
Contact: *Dr Ruth Liepman, Eva Koralnik, Ruth Weibel*
Represents American, British, Canadian, French, Dutch and Israeli publishers and agents for the German language rights and authors' manuscripts.

New Press Agency Society
Haus am Herterberg, Haldenstrasse 5
CH-8500 Frauenfeld, Herten

Paul and Peter Fritz AG Literary Agency
Jupiterstrasse 1
Postfach 8032 Zürich
Contact: *Peter S Fritz*
Represents English language authors for the German language rights and authors worldwide. No unsolicited manuscripts.

UNITED KINGDOM

Jacintha Alexander Associates
47 Emperor's Gate
London SW7 4HJ
Contact: *Jacintha Alexander, Julian Alexander*
Handles full-length general and literary fiction and non-fiction of all kinds. No plays, poetry, textbooks or science fiction. Film and television scripts handled for established clients only.

Blake Friedman Literary Agency Ltd
37-41 Gower Street
London WC1E 6HH
Contact: *Carol Blake (books), Julian Friedman (film/television), Conrad Williams (original scripts/radio)*

Worldwide representation of fiction and non-fiction, television and film rights and scripts. No juvenile projects or poetry.

Campbell Thomson and McLaughlin Ltd
1 King's Mews
London WC1N 2JA
Contact: *John McLaughlin, Charlotte Bruton*
Handles book-length manuscripts excluding children's, science fiction and fantasy. No plays, film scripts, articles or poetry. Short stories from existing clients only.

Carnell Literary Agency
Danescroft, Goose Lane, Little Hallingbury
Bishop's Stortford, Herts CM22 7RG
Contact: *Mrs Pamela Buckmaster*
Specializes in science fiction and fantasy, also handles general fiction, non-fiction and children's fantasy.

Casarotto Ramsay Ltd
National House,
60-66 Wardour Street
London W1V 3HP
Contacts: *Jenne Casarotto, Greg Hunt, Tracey Smith (Film/Television/Radio), Tom Erhardt, Mel Kenyan (Stage), Maggie Hanbury (Books)*
Handles scripts for television, theatre, film and radio, general fiction and non-fiction.

Jonathan Clowes Ltd
10 Iron Bridge House, Bridge Approach
London NW1 8BD
Contact: *Brie Burkeman*
Fiction and non-fiction plus scripts. No textbooks or children's.

Elspeth Cochrane Agency
11-13 Orlando Road
London SW4 0LE
Contact: *Donald Baker, Elspeth Cochrane*
Authors handled for theatre, films, andtelevision. Books for all types of publication.

Rosica Colin Ltd
1 Clareville Grove Mews
London SW7 5AH
Contact: *Joanna Marston*
All full length manuscripts including theatre, films, television and sound broadcasting works in the USA, European countries and overseas.

Rupert Crew Ltd
1A King's Mews
London WC1N 2JA
Contact: *Doreen Montgomery, Shirley Russell*
Representation offered to limited clientele, specialising in promoting major book projects: non-fiction, general and women' fiction.

Curtis Brown Ltd (London)
Haymarket House
28-29 Haymarket
London SW1Y 4SP
Handles a wide range of subjects including fiction, general non-fiction, children's and specialist, scripts for film, television, theatre and radio.

Felix de Wolfe
Manfield House
376-378 The Strand
London WC2R 0LR
Contact: *Felix de Wolfe*
Handles quality fiction and scripts only. No non-fiction or children's. No unsolicited manuscripts.

Eric Glass Ltd
28 Berkeley Square
London W1X 6HD
Contact: *Eric Glass, Janet Crowley*
Books, plays, screenplays and television plays. Sole agents for the Sociètè des Auteurs et Compositeurs Dramatiques of Paris for the English speaking countries.

Elaine Green Ltd
37 Goldhawk Road
London W12 8QQ
Contact: *Elaine Green, Carol Heaton*
Handles novels, quality non-fiction and journalist's books. No original scripts for theatre, film or television.

David Grossman Literary Agency Ltd
110-114 Clerkenwell Road
London EC1M 5SA
Contact: *Address material to the company*
Fiction and general non-fiction. No verse or technical books for students.
No original screenplays or teleplays.

A M Heath and Co Ltd
79 St Martin's Lane
London WC2N 4AA
Contact: *Sara Fisher, Bill Hamilton, Michael Thomas.*
Handles fiction and general non-fiction. No scripts or poetry.

David Higham Associates Ltd
5-8 Lower John Street
Golden Square
London W1R 4H4
Contact: *Anthony Goff, John Rushi (Scripts), Elizabeth Cree (Books)*
Representing professional authors and writers in all fields throughout the world.

International Copyright Bureau Ltd
22A Aubrey House
Maida Avenue
London W2 1TQ
Contact: *Joy Westendarp*
Handles scripts for television,theatre, film and radio. No books.

M B A Literary Agents Ltd
45 Fitzroy Street
London W1P 5HR
Contact: *Diana Tyler, John Richard Parker, Meg Davis, Ruth Needham*
Represent writers in all mediums: books, television and radio. Handles fiction and non-fiction. No poetry or children's fiction. Also scripts for film, television, radio and theatre.

William Morris Agency UK Ltd
31-32 Soho Square
London W1V 5DG
Contact: *Stephen M Kenis (films), Jane Annakin (Television/Theatre), Lavinia Trevor (Books).*
Scripts handled for theatre, film, television and radio. Also fiction and general non-fiction.

Penman Literary Agency
175 Pall Mall
Leigh-on-Sea, Essex SS9 1RE
Contact: *Leonard G Stubbs*
Full length novel manuscripts. Also theatre, films, television and sound broadcasting.

Peters Fraser and Dunlop Group Ltd
503/4 The Chambers
Chelsea Harbour, Lots Road
London SW10 0XF
Contact: *Kenneth Ewing, Tim Corrie*
Agents for stage drama, television, plays and series, radio drama, fiction and non-fiction and children's books, representation for producers and directors of stage, television and film.

Charles Pick Consultancy Ltd
#3 3 Bryanston Place,
London W1H 7FN.
Contact: *Charles Pick.*

Laurence Pollinger Ltd
18 Maddox Street
London W1R 0EU
Contact: *Gerald J Pollinger, Margaret Pepper, Romany van Bosch.*
Author's agents for all material with the exception of original film stories, poetry and freelance journalistic articles.

Murray Pollinger
222 Old Brompton Road
London SW5 0BZ
Contact: *Murray Pollinger, Gina Pollinger, Sara Menguc*
Agents for all types of general fiction and non-fiction with the exception of plays, poetry and travel.

Rogers Coleridge and White Ltd
20 Powis Mews
London W11 1JN
Contact: *Deborah Rogers, Gill Coleridge, Patricia White, Ann Warnford Davis*
Handles fiction, non-fiction and children's books. No plays or poetry.

Tessa Sayle Agency
11 Jubilee Place
London SW3 3TE
Contact: *Rachel Calder (Books), Penny Tackaberry (Drama)*
Full length manuscripts, plays, films, television and sound broadcasting.
Represented in all foreign countries.

Vincent Shaw Associates
20 Jay Mews
Kensington Gore, London SW7 2EP
Contact: *Vincent Shaw, Lester McGrath*
Handles film, television, theatre and radio only. Unsolicited manuscripts read.

Shiel Land Associates Ltd
43 Doughty Street
London WC1N 2LF
Contact: *Anthony Shiel*
Represents literary authors. Represents worldwide including translation, film, television and theatre.

Solo Syndication and Literary Agency Ltd
49-53 Kensington High Street
London W8 5ED
Contact: *Don Short*
Specialising in celebrity autobiographies and biographies. Non-fiction only except for established authors.

Tricia Sumner Agency
32 Orchard Gardens
Waltham Abbey, Essex EN9 1RS
Contact: *Tricia Sumner*
Former Deputy General Secretary of the Writers' Guild.

Peter Tauber Press Agency
94 East End Road
London N3 2SX
Contact: *Peter Tauber, Robert Tauber*
Full representation, specialising in well-researched epic women's saga fiction.

Ed Victor Ltd
162 Wardour Street
London W1V 3AT
Contact: *Ed Victor, Maggie Phillips, Sophie Hicks, Graham Greene*
Commercial fiction and non-fiction. No scripts or academic books.

Watson Little Ltd
12 Egbert Street
London NW1 8LJ
Contact: *Mandy Little, Sheila Watson*
Represents wide range of fiction and non-fiction. No poetry, short stories or articles, or books for very young children.

A P Watt Ltd
20 John Street
London WC1N 2DR
Contact: *Caradoc King, Linda Shaughnessy, Rod Hall, Lisa Eveleigh, Nick Marston, Derek Johns*
Full length works for all media including plays and telescripts. No poetry.
Representation throughout the world.

UNITED STATES OF AMERICA

California

Artists Agency
10000 Santa Monica Boulevard, Suite 305
Los Angeles, CA 90067
Representation of novels and screenplays for films.

Sandra Dijkstra Literary Agency
1155 Camino Del Mar
Del Mar, CA 92014
Contact: *Sandra Dijkstra, Katherine Goodwin*
Handles quality and commercial adult fiction and non-fiction.
Representation to major publishers in USA. British rights. Translations.

Renee Wayne Golden APLC
8983 Norma Place
West Hollywood, CA 90069
Contact: *Renee Wayne Golden*
Representation of selected authors.

Paul Kohner Inc
9169 Sunset Boulevard
Los Angeles, CA 90069

Non-fiction preferred to fiction. No short stories, poetry, science fiction or gothic.

Michael Larsen/Elizabeth Pomada Literary Agency
1029 Jones Street
San Francisco, CA 94109
Contact: *Elizabeth Pomada*
Handles general fiction and non-fiction for adults, self help and popular psychology.

Jack Scagnetti Talent and Literary Agency
5330 Lankershim Boulevard, No 210
North Hollywood, CA 91601
Contact: *Jack Scagnetti*
Handles screenplays, television scripts, treatments, books and major magazine articles. Franchised signatory to Writers Guild of America-West.

Singer Media Corp
Seaview Business Park
1030 Calle Cordillera, Unit 106
San Clemente, CA 92673
Contact: *Dr Kurt Singer*
Newspaper syndicate, literary agency and photo bank. Handles sophisticated modern romance novels, biographies, mysteries and horror books.

H N Swanson Inc
8523 Sunset Boulevard
Los Angeles, CA 90069
Contact: *Thomas Shanks, N V Swanson*
Represents writers for novels, screenplays, television and theatre. Worldwide representation.

Colorado

Flannery, White and Stone, A Writer's Agency
180 Cook, Suite 404
Denver, CO 80206

Connecticut

Sidney B Kramer
Mews Books Ltd
20 Bluewater Hill
Westport, CT 06880
Contact: *Sidney B Kramer, Fran Pollack*
Specializes in juvenile (pre-school - young adult), cookery, adult non-fiction and fiction, technical and medical software, film and television, etc. Prefers work of published/established authors; will accept small number of new/unpublished authors.

New England Publishing Associates Inc
PO Box 5
Chester, CT 06412
Editorial assistance and representation for non-fiction books for the adult market.

Van der Leun and Associates
464 Mill Hill Drive
Southport, CT 06490
Contact: *Patricia Van der Leun*
Handles fiction and non-fiction; specializes in illustrated books, art and science. No unsolicited manuscripts. Representation in all foreign countries.

District of Columbia

Ronald L Goldfarb and Associates
918 16th Street North West, Suite 400
Washington, DC 20006

Florida

Lighthouse Literary Agency
PO Box 2105
Winter Park, FL 32790
Director: *Sandra Kangas*

Georgia

Deering Literary Agency
1507 Oakmonth Drive
Acworth, GA 30101
Directors: *Charles and Dorothy Deering*

Hawaii

Rhodes Literary Agency
Box 89133
Honolulu, HI 96830
Handles novels, non-fiction books, magazines, poetry books, single poems, religious materials, film and television scripts, stage plays, juvenile books, syndicated materials, radio scripts, textbooks, photos, books of cartoons, etc.

Illinois

Austin Wahl Agency Ltd
53 West Jackson Boulevard, Suite 342
Chicago, IL 60604
Contact: *Thomas Wahl*
Handles film and television scripts, novels and non-fiction books.

Maryland

Columbia Literary Associates Inc
7902 Nottingham Way
Ellicott City, MD 21043

Massachusetts

Otte Company
9 Goden Street
Belmont, MA 02178
Contact: *Jane H Otte*
Handles adult fiction and non-fiction full length books. Representation in all major markets and Hollywood.

Michael Snell Literary Agency
Box 655
Truro, MA 02666
Development and sale of adult non-fiction, primarily in business, computers, science, psychology and law.

Gunther Stuhlmann, Author's Representative
PO Box 276
Becket, MA 01223
Contact: *Barbara Ward, Gunther Stuhlmann*
Representation worldwide of quality literature and non-fiction.

Michigan

Creative Concepts Literary Agency
5538 Herford
Troy, MI 48098

Minnesota

Lazear Agency Inc
430 First Avenue North, Suite 416
Minneapolis, MN 55401
Contact: *Jonathon Lazear*

Missouri

Joyce A Flaherty, Literary Agent
816 Lynda Court
St Louis, MO 63122

Montana

Phoenix Literary Agency
PO Box 669
Livingston, MT 59047

New Hampshire

Northeast Literary Agency
69 Broadway
Concord, NH 03301

New Jersey

Barbara Bauer Literary Agency
179 Washington Avenue
Matawan, NJ 07747
Contact: *Barbara Bauer*
Specializes in new and unpublished authors, quality fiction and non-fiction for children and adults.

Rosalie Siegel, International Literary Agent Inc
1 Abey Drive
Pennington, NJ 08534
Contact: *Rosalie Siegel, Pamela Walker*
Adult fiction and non-fiction, particularly quality fiction. Also French fiction and non-fiction.

New Mexico

Rydal Agency
PO Box 2247
Santa Fe, NM 87504

New York

Carole Abel Literary Agent
160 West 87th Street
New York, NY 10024
Contact: *Carole Abel*
Handles trade and mass market fiction and non-fiction books. No unsolicited manuscripts; query first. Agents in Hollywood and most foreign countries.

Dominick Abel Literary Agency Inc
146 West 82nd Street, Suite 1B
New York, NY 10024
Contact: *Dominick Abel.*

Acton, Dystel, Leone and Jaffe
928 Broadway, Suite 303
New York, NY 10010
Contact: *Jane Dystel*
Non-fiction and novels.

Marcia Amsterdam Agency
41 West 82nd Street
New York, NY 10024
Contact: *Marcia Amsterdam*
Handles adult and young adult fiction, film and television rights, screenplays and teleplays.

Julian Bach Literary Agency Inc
22 East 71st Street
New York, NY 10021
Contact: *Julian Bach, Emma Sweeney, Susan Merritt, Ann Rittenberg*
Agents for fiction and non-fiction. No science fiction or fantasy, poetry or photography.

Bethel Agency
641 West 59th Street
New York, NY 10019
Handles fiction and non-fiction, plays for theatre, film and television; sub-division handles children's books.

Brandt and Brandt Literary Agency Inc
1501 Broadway
New York, NY 10036
Contact: *Carl D Brandt, Gail Hochman*
Handles fiction and non-fiction. No unsolicited manuscripts; query first; no reading fee. Agents in most foreign countries.

Connor Literary Agency
640 West 153rd Street
New York, NY 10031
Contact: *Marlene K Connor*
Handles commercial fiction and non-fiction, illustrated books, cookbooks, self-help, ethnic subjects and how-to. Foreign agents in major countries.

Curtis Brown Ltd
10 Astor Place, 3rd Floor
New York, NY 10003
Handles fiction, non-fiction, science fiction, mystery and romance. Also children's fiction, non-fiction and theatrical, film and television. Handles general trade fiction, non-fiction, juvenile and film and television rights. Representatives in all major countries. No unsolicited manuscripts; query first.

Anita Diamant Literary Agency
310 Madison Avenue
New York, NY 10017
Contact: *Anita Diamant, Robin Rae*
Handles book manuscripts, fiction, non-fiction and foreign film rights.

Jonathan Dolger Agency
49 East 96th Street, Suite 9B
New York, NY 10128
Contact: *Jonathan Dolger*
Handles adult fiction and non-fiction, and illustrated books. No unsolicited material; query letter and SASE first.

Donadio and Ashworth Inc, Literary Representatives
231 West 22nd Street
New York, NY 10011

Ethan Ellenberg Literary Agency
548 Broadway, No 5-E
New York, NY 10012
Contact: *Ethan Ellenberg*
Handles quality fiction and non-fiction, first novels, commercial fiction, military, history and sci-fi. Query before submission of manuscripts.

Ann Elmo Agency Inc
60 East 42nd Street
New York, NY 10165
Contact: *Ann Elmo, Lettie Lee*
Handles all types of fiction, non-fiction, juveniles, plays for book and magazine publication, as well as for film, television and stage use.

Freida Fishbein Ltd
2556 Hubbard Street
Brooklyn, NY 11235
Contact: *Janice Fishbein*
Handles plays, books, film and television scripts. No short stories, poetry or young children's books.

Samuel French Inc
45 West 25th Street
New York, NY 10010
Specializing in plays.

Jay Garon-Brooke Associates Inc
101 West 55th Street, Suite 5K
New York, NY 10019
Fiction and non-fiction. No romance, western or mystery works accepted.

Max Gartenberg Literary Agent
521 5th Avenue, Suite 1700
New York, NY 10175
Contact: *Max Gartenberg*
Handles book-length manuscripts of non-fiction and fiction including all rights therein.

Gelles-Cole Literary Enterprises
320 East 42nd Street, Suite 411
New York, NY 10017
Contact: *Sandi Gelles-Cole*
Handles commercial fiction and non-fiction.

Jeff Herman Agency
332 Bleecker St,
Suite 6-31
NY 10014.
President: *Jeffrey H Herman*

John Hawkins and Associates Inc
71 West 23rd Street, Suite 1600
New York, NY 10010
Contact: *J Hawkins, W Reiss*
Provides all services of representation to book-length manuscripts in prose. No theatrical, film or television scripts.

International Creative Management
40 West 57th Street
New York, NY 10019

Janklow and Nesbit Associates
598 Madison Avenue
New York, NY 10022
Contact: *Lynn Nesbit*

JCA Literary Agency Inc
27 West 20th Street, Suite 1103
New York, NY 10011
Handles general fiction and non-fiction. No screen plays. Query first with SASE.

JET Literary Associates Inc
124E 84th Street, Suite 4A
New York, NY 10028
Contact: *James E Trupin*
Handles book length fiction and non-fiction only.

Asher D Jason Enterprises Inc
111 Barrow Street
New York, NY 10014
Contact: *Asher D Jason*
Handles non-fiction and fiction. Representation to all American publishers.

Lucy Kroll Agency
390 West End Avenue
New York, NY 10024
Contact: *Lucy Kroll, Barbara Hogenson*
Handles fiction and non-fiction including scripts for film, television and radio.

Peter Livingston Associates Inc
465 Park Avenue
New York, NY 10022
Contact: *Peter W Livingston, David C Johnston*
Handles serious non-fiction, business, politics, popular science, etc. Literary and commercial fiction, film and television. No poetry or children's books. Foreign rights.

Elaine Markson Literary Agency Inc
44 Greenwich Avenue
New York, NY 10011
Contact: *Elaine Markson*

McIntosh and Otis Inc
310 Madison Avenue
New York, NY 10017
Adult and juvenile fiction and non-fiction. No textbooks or scripts.

Scott Meredith Literary Agency Inc
845 Third Avenue
New York, NY 10022
Contact: *Jack Scovil, Scott Meredith*
Handles general fiction and non-fiction, books and magazines, juveniles, plays, television scripts, and film rights and properties. Accept unsolicited manuscripts; reading fee. Agents in all principal countries.

William Morris Agency
1350 Avenue of the Americas
New York, NY 10019

Jean V Naggar Literary Agency
216 East 75th Street
New York, NY 10021
Contact: *Jean Naggar*
Complete representation in all areas of general fiction and non-fiction.

Pickering Associates Inc
432 Hudson Street
New York, NY 10014
Contact: *John Pickering*
Full service literary agency with co-agents in Hollywood and all principal translation markets.

Susan Ann Protter Literary Agent
110 West 40th Street, Suite 1408
New York, NY 10018
Contact: *Susan Protter*
Principally hard and soft cover books and the various rights involved. Fiction, non-fiction, health, science, biography, history, science fiction, etc.

Rosenstone/Wender
3 East 48th Street, 4th Floor
New York, NY 10017
Contact: *Susan Perlman Cohen, Phyllis Wender.*

Russell and Volkening Inc
50 West 29th Street, No 7E
New York, NY 10001
Literary fiction and non-fiction.

Charlotte Sheedy Literary Agency Inc
611 Broadway, Suite 428
New York, NY 10012
Contact: *Charlotte Sheedy*

Shukat Company Ltd
340 West 55th Street, Suite 1-A
New York, NY 10019
Contact: *Scott Shukat, Larry Weiss*
Handles theatre musicals, plays, books (fiction and non-fiction), television and film.

Evelyn Singer Literary Agency Inc
PO Box 594
White Plains, NY 10602
Contact: *Evelyn Singer*
Exclusive representation. Handles fiction, non-fiction, for adults, young adults, children, first serial rights, foreign rights, film and television rights with sub-agents.

Philip G Spitzer Literary Agency
50 Talmadge Farm Lane
East Hampton, NY 11937
Contact: *Philip G Spitzer*
Handles general fiction and non-fiction; also screenplays.

Renee Spodheim
698 West End Avenue, No 5-B
New York, NY 10025
Contact: *Renee Spodheim*
All trade. Fiction and non-fiction. No juveniles.

Sterling Lord Literistic Inc
One Madison Avenue
New York, NY 10010
Handles full length and short manuscripts, theatre, films, television and radio. Represented in Europe by Intercontinental Literary Agency.

2M Communications Ltd
121 West 27th Street, 601
New York, NY 10001
Handles contemporary non-fiction, popular culture and celebrity biographies.

Wieser and Wieser Inc
118 East 25th Street
New York, NY 10010
Contact: *Olga Wieser*
Handles literary and commercial fiction, general non-fiction including all rights, film and television rights.

Writers House Inc
21 West 26th Street
New York, NY 10010
Represents popular and literary fiction, mainstream and genre, including thrillers, science fiction, fantasy and romance. Also juvenile and young adult.

Pennsylvania

James Allen Literary Agent (in Association with Virginia Kidd Literary Agents)
PO Box 278, 538 East Harford Street
Milford, PA 18337
Contact: *Virginia Kidd*
Handles fiction, specializing in science fiction to magazines and book publishers. Representation in foreign countries and Hollywood.

Ray Peekner Literary Agency Inc
Box 3308
Bethlehem, PA 18017
Handles general fiction, particularly mystery suspense. Quality YA.

Rhode Island

Rock Literary Agency
Box 625
Newport, RI 02840
Contact: *Andrew Rock*

Texas

Blake Group Literary Agency
One Turtle Creek Village, Suite 600
3878 Oaklawn
Dallas, TX 75219
Represents limited number of published and unpublished authors. Handles fiction, non-fiction, plays and poetry, periodicals, publishers and producers. No reading fee; SASE essential.

Gloria Stern Literary Agency
2929 Buffalo Speedway
Lamar Tower 2111
Houston, TX 77098
Contact: *Gloria Stern*
Represent 90% trade, non-fiction, mostly biography, education and women's and social issues. Also health, some self-help and serious fiction.

Utah

Bess Wallace Associates Literary Agency
Box 972
Duchesne, UT 84021
Contact: *Bess D Wallace*
Manuscripts sold, edited and typed; ghost-writing; typesetting for self publishers; writers for writing assignments; copy-editing for publishers. Query first.

Washington

Catalog (TM) Literary Agency
Box 2964
Vancouver, WA 98668

Wisconsin

Lee Allan Agency
PO Box 18617
Milwaukee, WI 53218
Handles book length novels, mysteries, thrillers, westerns, science
fiction, horror, romance and young adult fiction. No television material,
non-fiction, poetry, magazine articles or short stories.

APPENDIX B

LITERARY ORGANIZATIONS

Please note that while every effort has been made to include as many societies and organizations as possible, the editors acknowledge that the following list is by no means exhaustive. Many societies are organized and administered by unpaid individuals from their own homes. Not only do the addresses of secretaries change frequently, therefore, but these are difficult to trace. Secretaries of societies which have yet to be listed are consequently urged to send details for publication in future editions of the **INTERNATIONAL AUTHORS AND WRITERS WHO'S WHO** to the editors at the following address:

International Authors and Writers Who's Who
International Biographical Centre
Cambridge CB2 3QP, England

The friendly co-operation of the listed societies is gratefully acknowledged, and the future assistance of others is cordially invited.

AUSTRALIA

Australian Writers' Guild Ltd
60 Kellett Street
Kings Cross, Sydney, New South Wales 2011
Professional association for writers in areas of television, radio, screen and stage to promote and protect the professional interests.

Bibliographical Society of Australia and New Zealand
c/o Secretary, Miss R T Smith
76 Warners Avenue
Bondi Beach, New South Wales 2026
To encourage and promote research in all aspects of physical bibliography.

Children's Book Council of Australia
PO Box 420
Dickson, Australian Capital Territory 2602

Dickens Fellowship
29 Henley Beach Road
Henley Beach, Adelaide, South Australia 5022
Literary society devoted to study and appreciation of the life and works of Charles Dickens.

Poetry Society of Australia
PO Box N110, Grosvenor Street
Sydney, New South Wales 2000
Publications: New Poetry (quarterly); also poems, articles, reviews, notes and comments, interviews.

Society of Editors
PO Box 176
Carlton South, Victoria 3053
Professional association of book editors. Regular training seminars, monthly meetings and newsletter.

BELGIUM

International PEN Club, Belgian French Speaking Centre
76 Avenue de 11 Novembre, BP7
B-1040 Brussels
Receptions of foreign writers, defense of the liberty of thought of all writers, participation at the world-wide congresses of PEN.

Koninklijke Academie voor Wetenschappen
Letteren en Schone Kunsten van Belgie
Paleis der Academien
Hertogsstrasse 1
B-1000 Brussels.

Société de Langue et de Litterature Wallonnes
Universite de Liège
B-4000 Liège
Holds meetings, lecturers, exhibitions, library, media, archives, publications.

Société Royale des Bibliophiles et Iconophiles de Belgique
4 Boulevard de l'Empereur
B-1000 Brussels
Publication of "Le Livre et l'Estampe" (Semestrial), Expositions.

BRAZIL

Academia Cearense di Letras
Palacio Senador Alencar
Rua São Paulo 51

60000 Fortaleza CE
To cultivate and develop literature and scientific achievement. Meets monthly, annual publication.

Associacao Brasileira de Imprensa (Brazilian Press Association)
Rua Araujo Porto Alegre
71-Centro-Rio de Janeiro-RJ.

Brazilian Translators Union (SINTRA)
Rua de Quitanda
194-sala 1005-Centro
CEP-20091-Rio de Janeiro-RJ

Companhia Editora Nacional
Rua Joli
294-São Paulo-SP

Sindicato de Escritores of Rio de Janeiro
Av Heitor Beltrao
353-Rio de Janeiro-RJ
CEP 20550

CANADA

Canada Council
350 Albert Street,
PO Box 1047
Ottawa, Ontario K1P 5V8

Canadian Association of Journalists
St Patick's Building
Carleton University
1125 Colonel By Drive
Ottawa, Ontario K1S 5B6

Canadian Authors Association
27 Doxsee Avenue North
PO Box 419
Campbellford, Ontario M5R 2S9

Canadian Copyright Institute
35 Spadina Road
Toronto, Ontario M5R 2S9

Canadian Science Writers' Association
PO Box 75
Station A
Toronto, Ontario M5W 2S9

Canadian Society of Children's Authors, Illustrators and Performers
35 Spadina Road
Toronto, Ontario M5R 2S9

Canadian Society of Magazine Editors
c/o Canadian Living, No 100
25 Sheppard Avenue West
North York, Ontario M2N 6S7

Crime Writers of Canada
3007 Kingston Road
PO Box 113
Scarborough, Ontario M1M 1P1

Editors' Association of Canada
35 Spadina Road
Toronto, Ontario M5R 2S9

Fédération internationale des écrivains de langue française
3492 rue Laval
Montreal, Quebec H2X 3C8

League of Canadian Poets
54 Wolseley Street, 3rd Floor
Toronto, Ontario M5T 1AS

Periodical Writers' Association of Canada
24 Ryerson Avenue
Toronto, Ontario M5T 2P3

Société des écrivains canadiens
1195 rue Sherbrooke Ouest
Montreal, Quebec H3A 1H9

Union des écrivains et écrivains québecois
La Maison des écrivains
3492 avenue Laval
Montreal, Quebec H2X 3C8

Writers Guild of Canada
35 McCaul Street
Toronto, Ontario M5T 2P3

Writers' Union of Canada
24 Ryerson Avenue
Toronto, Ontario M5T 2P3

CHINA

China PEN Centre
2 Shatan Beijie
Beijing

DENMARK

Danish Society of Language and Literature
Frederiksholms Kanal 18A
DK-1220 Copenhagen K
Scholarly editing in Danish language, literature and history.

Dansk Fagpresse
Vesterbrogade 24, 2. sal
DK-1620 Copenhagen V

Dansk Forfatterforening (Danish Writers' Association)
Tordenskjolds gård
Strandgade 6, St.
DK-1401 Copenhagen K
Attending to social, artistic, professional and economic interests of Danish authors in Denmark and abroad.

Dansk Litteraturinformationscenter
Ameliegade 38
DK-1256 Copenhagen K
Danish Literature Information Centre

Danske Sprog-og Litteraturselskab
Frederiksholms Kanal 18A
DK-1220 Copenhagen
Publications: Standard editions of literary, linguistic and historical texts, including diaries and correspondence.

Nyt Dansk Litteraturselskab
Bibliotekscentralen
Tempovej 7-11
DK-2750 Ballerup
Works for re-publishing of titles missing in public libraries in co operation with publishers.

FAROE ISLANDS

Rithövundafelag Färoya
Box 1124
FR-110 Tórshavn
Writers' Union of the Faroe Islands

FINLAND

Finlands Översättar-og Tolkforbund
Museigatan 9 B 23
FIN-00100 Helsingfors

Finlands PEN
PB 84
SF-00131 Helsingfors

Finlands Svenska Författareförening
Runebergsgatan 32 C 27
SF-00100 Helsingfors
Society of Swedish Authors in Finland.

Informationscentralen för Finlands Litterarur
PB 259
SF-00 171 Helsingfors
Information centre for Finnish literature and the State Literature Commission.

Kirjallisuudentutkijain Seura
Fabianinkatu 33
SF-00170 Helsinki
Publications: Kirjallisuudentutkijain Seuran Vousikirja (The Yearbook of the Literary Research Society).
Secretary: Paivi Karttunen.

Suomalaisen Kirjallisuuden Seura
PO Box 259
SF-00170 Helsinki

Suomen Tietokirjallijat ry
Ulvilantie 11 B, E 127
SF-00350 Helsinki

Svenska Litteratursallskapet i Finland
Mariegatan 8
SF-00170 Helsinki
Publications: Skrifter (Writings).

Svenska Osterbottens Litteraturforening
Henriksgatan 7-9 4N
SF-65320 Vasa/
Auroravagen 10
SF-65610 Smedsby
Co-owner of the publishers in Scriptum, publishing the journal Horisont; organizes writers' seminars, program evenings: lyrics, prose, music.

FRANCE

Centre National des Lettres
53 rue de Verneuil
F-75007 Paris
To uphold and encourage the work of French writers, give financial help to writers, translators, publishers and public libraries and promote translation into French.

Société des Gens de Lettres
Hôtel de Massa
38 rue du Faubourg Saint-Jacques
F-75014 Paris

Société des Poetes Français
Hôtel de Messa
38 rue de Faubourg Saint-Jacques
F-75014 Paris
Lectures, prizes, defending interests of members, loans to distinguished members in distress and quarterly bulletin.

GERMANY

Arbeitskreis für Jugenditeratur eV
Elisabethstrasse 15
D-8000 Munich 40
Encourages and coordinates all efforts to support literature for children and young people.

Association Internationale des Journalistes Philatéliques
Am Osterberg 19
D-29386 Hankensbüttel
International association of philatelic journalists, authors and associated societies.

Deutsche Akademie für Sprache und Dichtung
Alexandrakeg 23
D-6100 Darmstadt

Literarischer Verein in Stuttgart e V
Postfach 102251
D-7000 Stuttgart 1

PEN Zentrum
Friedrichstrasse 194. 199
Berlin 1080

HONG KONG

Composers and Authors Society of Hong Kong Ltd.
18/F Universal Trade Centre
3 Arbuthnot Road
Central Hong Kong

HUNGARY

Artisjus
Agency for Literature and Theatre
POB 67, V, Vörösmarty ter 1
H-1364 Budapest

Institute of Literary Studies of the Hungarian Academy of Sciences
Menesi ut 11-13
H-1118 Budapest
Research of history of Hungarian literature, research in literary theory, literary criticism to influence contemporary literature, source publications on the history of Hungarian literature and editing of reference books and bibliographies.

ICELAND

Rithöfundasamband Íslands (Writers' Union of Iceland)
PO Box 949, IS-121 Reykjavík /
Hafnarstrati 9, IS-101 Reykjavík
Union of Icelandic Writers that guards copyrights, protects interests in field of literature and book-publishing, drama, textbooks, radio and television scripts, etc.

INDIA

Indian Folklore Society
3 Abdul Hamid
Calcutta 700 069

PEN All-India Centre
40 New Marine Lines
Bombay 400 020
National centre of International PEN; publishes The Indian PEN quarterly.

Poetry Society of India
L-67A Malaviya Nagar
New Delhi 110 017

Sahitya Akademi
35 Ferozeshah Road
New Delhi 110 001
National organization to work for the development of Indian letters, to set high literary standards, foster and coordinate literary activities in the Indian languages and promote through them all the cultural unity of the country.

INDONESIA

PEN Centre
c/o JI Cemara 6
Jakarta Pusat

IRELAND

Irish Academy of Letters
School of Irish Studies
Thomas Prior House
Merrion Road
Dublin 4

Irish Book Marketing GP
Book House Ireland
165 Mid Abbey Street
Dublin 1
National association of book publishers.

Irish PEN
26 Rosslyn, Killarney Road
Bray, County Wicklow

Poetry Ireland
Bermingham Tower
Upper Yard, Dublin Castle
Dublin
National poetry organization which organizes tours, readings and the National Poetry Competition. Publications: Poetry Ireland Review (quarterly magazine), and bi-monthly newsletter.

Society of Irish Playwrights
Room 804, Liberty Hall
Dublin 1
To foster interest in and promote contemporary Irish drama. To guard the rights of Irish playwrights.

ISRAEL

ACUM Ltd (Society of Authors, Composers and Music Publishers in Israel)
PO Box 14220
Tel Aviv 61140

PEN Centre Israel
19 Shmaryahu Lewin Street
Jerusalem 96664
Publishes a bulletin of information and translation of literature in European languages, meetings with members and receptions for guest writers.

ITALY

Societa' Italiana Autori Drammatici (SIAD)
Via PO 10
I-00198 Rome

Societa' Italiana degli Autori et Editori (SIAE)
Viale della Letteratura 30
I-00144 Rome

JAPAN

Dickens Fellowship
Bungei-Gakubu
Seijo University
6-1-20 Seijo, Setagaya, Tokyo
Lectures, symposia, reading circles, publishing bulletins.

English Literary Society of Japan
501 Kenkyusha Bldg
9 Surugadai 2-Chome
Kanda, Chiyoda-ku, Tokyo 101
An association of scholars in the fields of English and American literature and the English language. The society's journal "Studies in English Literature" is published thrice yearly.

Japan Poets Association
c/o Eiji Kikai, 3-16-1Minami
Azabu, Minato-ku, Tokyo 105
To cultivate the mutual friendship among poets.

KOREA

Korean PEN Centre
186-210 Jangchung-dong 2-ka
Jung-gu, Seoul 100

MALAWI

Writers's Group
PO Box 280
Zomba

MOROCCO

L'Union des Écrivains du Maroc
5 rue Ab Bakr Seddik
Rabat

NEPAL

Nepal Journalists Association
PO Box 285, Maitighar
Kathmandu

NETHERLANDS

Nederlandse Taalunie
Stadhoudersplantsoen 2
2517 JL The Hague

Netherlands Centre of the International PEN
Meeweg 25
1405 BC Bussum

NEW ZEALAND

Arts Council of New Zealand
Old Public Trust Building
131-135 Lambton Quay, PO Box 3806
Wellington

New Zealand Women Writers' Society
PO Box 11-352
Wellington
Stimulates and encourages creative work in literature and fosters comradeship among members.

PEN (New Zealand Centre) Inc
PO Box 2283
Wellington
Promotes cooperation and mutual support among writers in all countries and encourages creative writing in New Zealand.

NIGERIA

West African Association for Commonwealth Literature and Language Studies
PO Box 622
Owerri, Imo State
Chairman: Professor Ernest N. Emenyonu

NORWAY

Den Norske Forfatterforening (Norwegian Authors' Union)
PO Box 327 Sentrum / Rådhusgate 7
N-0103 Oslo

Det Norske Videnskaps-Akademi
Drammensveien 78
Oslo 2

NORLA - Norwegian Literature Abroad
Bygdøy Allé 21
N-0262 Oslo

POLAND

SAP (Polish Authors'Association)
ul. Madalińskiego 15 m 16
02-513 Warsaw

Zwiazek Literatow Polskich (Union of Polish Writers)
Krakoweskie Przedmiescie 87
00-950 Warsaw

RUSSIA

Russian Authors' Society
ul. Bol'Shaya Bronnaya 6A
103670 Moscow
Protects the rights and organizes legal protection for authors in the Russian federation.
Chairman: Georgy A. Ter-Gazariants

SOUTH AFRICA

English Academy of Southern Africa
PO Box 124
Witwatersrand 2050

Institute for the Study of English in Africa
Rhodes University, PO Box 94
Grahamston 6140

Publishes English in Africa and New Coin Poetry. Conducts research into needs of black pupils learning English.

Nasionale Afrikaanse Letterkundige Museum en Navorsingsentrum
Private Bag X20543
Bloemfontein 9300

National English Literary Museum
Private Bag 1019
Grahamstown 6140

South African Union of Journalists
Office 512-513, 5th Floor, Argon House
87 Juta Street, Johannesburg 2017

SWEDEN

Sveriges Författarförbund
Box 3157 / Drottninggatan 88B
S-103 63 Stockholm
Swedish Writers' Union

SWITZERLAND

Deutschschweizerisches PEN-Zentrum
Postfach 403
CH-3000 Bern 14
Swiss-German PEN centre; member of International PEN.

PEN Club Centre
Postfach 1383
CH-3001 Bern

PEN Internazionale-Centro della Svizzera Italiana e Romancia
PO Box 2126
CH-6901 Lugano 1

Schweizer Autoren Gruppe Olten
Sekretariat, Siedlung Halen 43
CH-3047 Herrenschwanden
Authors' society.

Schweizerischen Schriftstellerinnen und Schriftsteller-Verband (Société Suisse des Écrivaines et Écrivains)
Kirchgasse 25
CH-8022 Zürich
Professional organization for the protection of writers' interests.
Publications: FORUM der Schriftsteller, Dictionary of Swiss Authors.

TANZANIA

Journalists' Organization of Tanzania
PO Box 45526
Dar Es Salaam
Ludovick A. Ngatara, General Secretary

THAILAND

Siam Society
PO Box 65
Bangkok
Society promotes and tries to preserve artistic, scientific and other cultural affairs of Thailand and neighbouring countries. Publishes Journal of the Siam Society and The Siam Society Newsletter.

UNITED KINGDOM

Arvon Foundation
Totleigh Barton
Sheepwash, Beaworthy
Devon EX21 5NS
(Also at: Lumb Bank, Heptonstall
Hebden Bridge, W Yorks HX7 6DF)
Offers residential writing courses.

Association of Authors' Agents
c/o Greene and Heaton Ltd
37 Goldhawk Road
London W12 8QQ
Maintains a code of practice, provides a forum for discussion and promotes cooperation and interests of British literary agencies and agents.

Association of British Science Writers
c/o British Association for the Advancement of Science
Fortress House, 23 Savile Row
London W1X 1AB

Association of Golf Writers
c/o Sports Desk, The Daily Express
Blackfriars Road
London SE1 9UX

Association for Scottish Literary Studies
Department of English Literature
University of Aberdeen
Taylor Building, King's College
Aberdeen AB9 2UB
Publications: Scottish Library Journal; Scottish Literary Journal
Supplement (both twice yearly).

Authors' Club
40 Dover Street
London W1X 3RB
Club for writers, publishers, critics, journalists and academics involved
with literature. Administers several literary awards.

Francis Bacon Society Inc
Canonbury Tower
Islington, London N1
Publications: Baconiana (periodically), Jottings (periodically), booklets,
pamphlets (list on request).

Book Trust
Book House, 45 East Hill
London SW18 2QZ
An independent charitable trust whose task is to promote reading and
the using of books. Administers several major literary awards including
the Booker Prize, and publishes reference and resource materials.

Book Trust Scotland
Scottish Book Centre
137 Dundee Street
Edinburgh EH11 1BG
Promotes reading and books in general, and provides a range of
information and services on Scottish writers and books. Administers
awards including the McVitie's Prize for Scottish Writer of the Year.

British Science Fiction Association
52 Woodhill Drive
Grove, Wantage
Oxon OX12 0DF
Promotes the reading, writing and publishing of science fiction. Activties
include literary criticism, news, reviews, serious articles, meetings,
writers workshop, lending library and magazine chain.
Publications: Matrix (newsletter); Vector (journal); Focus (magazine).

Commonwealth Press Union
Studio House, Hen and Chickens Court
184 Fleet Street
London EC4A 2DU

Crime Writers' Association
PO Box 10772
London N6 4RY
Membership limited to professional crime writers, but associate
membership is open to specialist publishers,agents and booksellers.
Administers numerous annual awards.
Publication: Red Herrings (monthly newsletter)

Dickens Fellowship
Dickens House, 48 Doughty Street
London WC1N 2LF
HQ in London, over 60 branches worldwide, of Dickens enthusiasts.
Organises talks, conferences, publishes "The Dickensian", and works for
the preservation of buildings associated with Dickens.

Edinburgh Bibliographical Society
Department of Special Collections
Edinburgh University Library
George Square
Edinburgh EH8 9LJ
Lectures on bibliographical topics and visits to libraries.
Publication: Transaction (issued to members only).

English Association
University of Leicester
University Road
Leicester LE1 7RH

Promotes the understanding and appreciation of English language and
literature. Organizes lectures and conferences, and produces a selection
of publications.

Gaelic Books Council (Comhairle nan Leabhraichean)
22 Mansfield Street
Partick, Glasgow G12
Provides information about Gaelic writing and publishing. Also offers
editorial services and grants to publishers and writers.

Thomas Hardy Society
PO Box 1438
Dorchester, Dorset DT1 1YH
Promotion and appreciation of works of Thomas Hardy; organizes a
summer conference, lectures and walks in Wessex.

Incorporated Brontë Society
Brontë Parsonage
Haworth, Keighley
West Yorkshire BD22 8DR
The preservation of the literary works of the Brontë family and of
manuscripts and other objects related to the family.

Institute of Contemporary Arts
The Mall
London SW1
Galleries, performance, music, cinema, talks, conferences, restaurant,
bar, 'Bookshop'.

Johnson Society of London
255 Baring Road, Grove Park
London SE12 0BQ
To study the works of Dr Samuel Johnson, his circle, his contempories
and his times through lectures and articles in "The New Rambler".

Keats/Shelley Memorial Association
10 Landsdowne Road
Tunbridge Wells, Kent TN1 2NJ
To promote the works of Keats, Shelley, Byron and Leigh Hunt and
maintain the house in Rome where Keats died.

Kent and Sussex Poetry Society
Castens, Carpenters Lane
Hadlow, Kent TN11 0EY
Readings, workshops and discussions to promote love and
understandings of poetry.

Kipling Society
2nd Floor, Schomberg House
80-82 Pall Mall
London SW1Y 5HG
Promotion of Kipling studies, discussion meetings, annual luncheon and
quarterly journal.

Charles Lamb Society
1A Royston Road, Richmond
Surrey TW10 6LT
To study the life, works and times of Charles Lamb and his circle, to
stimulate the Elian spirit of friendliness and humour, and form a
collection of Eliana.

Lancashire Authors' Association
Heatherslade, 5 Quakerfields
Westhoughton, Bolton, Lancashire BL5 2BJ
Publications: The Record (quarterly)

Library Association
7 Ridgmount Street
London WC1E 7AE
Professional body for librarians and information managers. Numerous
publications produced every year. Members receive the monthly
magazine "LA Record".

Moniack Mhor (Avron Foundation of Scotland)
Teavarran, Kiltarlity,
Beauly, Inverness-shire IV4 7HT
Provides the opportunity to live and work with established writers, and
participate in tutorials and workshops.

National Poetry Foundation
27 Mill Road
Fareham, Hampshire PO16 0TH
Charitable organization which encourages new writers and produces a
series of books. Members receive "Pause" magazine.

National Union of Journalists
Acorn House
314 Grays Inn Road
London WC1X 8DP
Represents journalists in all sectors of publishing, providing advice and support on wages, conditions, and benefits. Publishes various guides and magazines.

Northern Poetry Library
Central Library, The Willows
Morpeth, Northumberland NE61 1TA
Books and magazines for loan, and access to text database of English poetry. Postal loans also available.

Oxford Bibliographical Society
Bodleian Library
Oxford OX1 3BG
Publications: First Series, vols I-VII, 1923-46; New Series, vol 1, 1948-.

PEN English Centre
7 Dilke Street
Chelsea, London SW3 4JE
Publications: The Pen (broadsheet, twice a year)

PEN Scottish Centre
33 Drumsheugh Gardens
Edinburgh EH3 7RN

Poetry Association of Scotland
38 Dovecot Road,
Edinburgh EH12 7LE
Promotes public reading of the world's best poetry.

Poetry Library
Royal Festival Hall
South Bank Centre, Level 5
London SE1 8XX
Includes all 20th-Century poetry in English and a collection of all poetry magazines published in the UK. Also arranges functions and provides an information service.

Poetry Society
22 Betterton Street
London WC2H 9BU
Promotion of poets and poetry, including promotion of events and festivals. Also operates a series of seminars and training courses, education services and a library service, and administers the National Poetry Competition.
Publications: Poetry Review (quarterly magazine) and Poetry News (newsletter).

Publishers Association
19 Bedford Square
London WC1B 3HJ
National UK trade association representing the publishing industry. Publishes the Directory of Publishing.

Romantic Novelists' Association
Queens Farm, 17 Queens Street
Tintinhull, Somerset BA22 8PG
Membership open to published writers of romantic novels, with associate membership open to agents, editors, publishers and booksellers. Administers two annual awards and publishes the RNA News.

Royal Society of Literature
1 Hyde Park Gardens
London W2 2LT
Lectures, discussions, readings and publications. Adminsters awards including the W H Heinemann Prize.

Scottish Arts Council
12 Manor Place
Edinburgh EH3 7DD
One of the principal channels for government funding for the arts, including the administration of literary awards, bursaries, events and fellowships.

Scottish Poetry Library
Tweedale Court, 14 High Street
Edinburgh EH1 1TE
Poetry books, tapes and magazines can be borrowed in person or by post. Also provides specialist lists and bibliographies.

Scottish Publishers Association
Scottish Book Centre
137 Dundee Street
Edinburgh EH11 1BG

Provides co-operative support for Scottish publishers, and information about publishing in Scotland.

Sherlock Holmes Society of London
3 Outram Road, Southsea
Hampshire PO5 1QP
Study of the life and works of Sherlock Holmes and Dr Watson.

Society of Authors
84 Drayton Gardens
London SW10 9SB
Independent trade union which seeks to promote and protect the interests of writers and authors, and provides information and advice. Publications: The Author (quarterly journal); The Electronic Author (twice yearly).

Society of Civil Service Authors
4 Top Street
Wing, nr. Oakham
Rutland LE15 8SE
Encourages authorship by past and present members of the Civil Service.

Society of Freelance Editors and Proofreaders
38 Rochester Road
London NW1 9JJ
Aims to promote high editorial standards through advice, training and the introduction of recognised qualifications.

Society of Young Publishers
12 Dyott Street
London WC1A 1DF
Open to those in related occupations, members can increase their knowledge and experience of all aspects of publishing.

Tolkien Society
35 Amesbury Crescent, Hove
East Sussex BN3 5RD
Furthering interest in the life and works of Professor J R R Tolkien. Newsletter.

Translators Association
84 Drayton Gardens
London SW10 9SB
Subsidiary group within the Society of Authors dealing exclusively with literary translators into the English language.

Ver Poets
Haycroft, 61/63 Chiswell Green Lane
St Albans, Herts AL2 3AL
Aim to promote poetry and help poets through information, events and publications. Holds regular competitions including the annual Ver Poets Open Competition.

H G Wells Society
English Department, Nene College
Moulton Park, Northampton NN2 7AL
Circulates newsletter and journal, Wellsian, and organizes lectures and conferences to promote an active interest in the life and work of H G Wells.

Welsh Academy
3rd Floor, Mount Stuart House
Mount Stuart Square, Cardiff CF1 6DQ
The English language section of Yr Academi Gymreig, the national society of Welsh writers. Aims to promote Anglo-Welsh literature through readings, conferences, workshops, schools and projects. Organizes the Cardiff Literature Festival. Publishes a newsletter and numerous guides and reviews.

Welsh Book Council (Cyngor Llyfrau Cymru)
Castell Brychan
Aberystwyth, Dyfed SY23 2JB
Stimulates interest in Welsh literature and authors by disseminating grants for Welsh language publications.
Publication: Books In Wales/Llais Llyfrau (quarterly)

Welsh Union of Writers
13 Richmond Road
Roath, Cardiff CF2 3AQ
Independent union for published Welsh writers

West Country Writers' Association
Malvern View, Garway Hill,
Hereford, Hereford and Worcester HR2 8EZ

Women in Publishing
c/o The Bookseller
12 Dyott Street
London WC1A 1DF
Aims to promote the status of women in the publishing industry through networking, meetings and training. Publishes a monthly newsletter.

Women Writers Network
23 Prospect Road
London NW2 2JU
Provides and exchanges information, support and opportunities for working writers. Also arranges functions and provides a newsletter.

Writers' Club
PO Box 269
Redhill RH1 6GP
Club for writers, authors and journalists.

Writer's Guild of Great Britain
430 Edgware Road
London W2 1EH
Represents professional writers in film, radio, televsion, theatre and publishing. Regularly provides assistance to members on items such as contracts and conditions of work.

Yachting Journalists Association
Spinneys, Woodham Mortimer
Maldon, Essex CM9 6SX.
Promotes the awareness of all forms of leisure boating activities via the written and spoken word, and offers support to journalists in the field.

Yr Academi Gymreig
3rd Floor, Mount Stuart House
Mount Stuart Square, Cardiff CF1 6DQ
National society of Welsh writers which encourages writing in the Welsh language.Organizes readings, conferences and literary events. Publishes books on Welsh literaure and an English/Welsh dictionary. Publication: Taliesin.

UNITED STATES OF AMERICA

Arizona

Authors Resource Centre (TARC Inc)
PO Box 64785
Tucson, AZ 85728
Serves writers, etc; writers' research library; literary agency; sponsors 40 workshops and seminars; publishes TARC Report for writers.

Society of Southwestern Authors
PO Box 30355
Tucson, AZ 85751
Organization of writers for supportive fellowship, recognition of member writers' professional achievement, and encouragement and assistance for persons striving to become writers.

California

Association of Literary Scholars and Critics
2039 Shattuck Avenue, Suite 202
Berkeley, CA 94704
Aprofessional society open to all individuals pursuing the study of literature.

Society of Children's Book Writers and Illustrators
345 North Maple, Suite 296
Beverley Hills, CA 90210
A professional society promoting the inteests of children's book writers and illustrators.

Writers Guild of America, West,
7000 West 3rd Street
Los Angeles, CA 90048
Represents its membership in contract negotiation and compliance with the film and television industry.

Colorado

Associated Business Writers of America
1450 South Havana, Suite 620
Aurora, CO 80012
Association for business writers.

National Writers Association
1450 South Havana, Suite 424
Aurora, CO 80012
Association for freelance writers.

Connecticut

International PEN - Writers in Exile Center
42 Derby Avenue
Orange, CT 06477
Affiliated with International PEN to help fight for freedom of expression for writers.

Delaware

International Reading Association
800 Barksdale Road, PO Box 8139
Newark, DE 19714
Professional education association dedicated to the improvement of reading ability and development of the reading habit worldwide through publications, research, meetings, conferences and international congresses.

District of Columbia

Education Writers Association
1001 Connecticut Avenue North West, Suite 310
Washington, DC 20036

National Endowment for the Humanities
Public Information Office
1100 Pennsylvania Avenue North West, Room 406
Washington, DC 20506

National League of American Pen Women
Pen Arts Building
1300 17th Street North West
Washington, DC 20036

National Press Club
529 14th Street North West
Washington, DC 20045

PEN Syndicated Fiction Project
PO Box 15650
Washington, DC 20003

Washington Independent Writers
733 15th Street North West, Suite 220
Washington, DC 20005

Florida

International Society of Dramatists
Box 1310
Miami, FL 33153
Information clearinghouse for dramatists in all media: stage, screen, television and radio. Provides continually updated lists of script opportunities in English worldwide. Monthly publications. Annual playwriting award.

National Alliance of Short Story Authors
7505 South West 82nd Street, Suite 222
Miami, FL 33143

Text and Academic Authors Association
University of South Florida
140 7th Avenue South
St Petersburg, FL 33701

Illinois

American Library Association
50 East Huron
Chicago, IL 60611
Provides leadership for the development, promotion, and improvement of library and information services to enhance learning.

International Black Writers and Artists Inc
PO Box 1030
Chicago, IL 60690
Poetry readings, contests, pot lucks, workshops, annual conferences and writers picnic.

Society of Midland Authors
29 East Division Street
Chicago, IL 60610
To promote friendly contact and professional interchange among authors of the Midland, to explore topics of literary and professional interest in

open monthly programmes, and honour the best of Midland writing with cash awards annually.

Indiana

Society of Professional Journalists
PO Box 77
Greencastle, IN 46135
Contact: Sandy Gretter

Kansas

Council of Writers Organisations
12 724 Sagamore Road
Leawood, KS 66209
A communications network for 15 writing groups.

Massachusetts

American Society of Business Press Editors
PO Box 390653
Cambridge, MA 0213

Michigan

Children's Literature Association
PO Box 138
Battle Creek, MI 49016
Promotes serious scholarship and criticism in the field of children's literature.

Minnesota

Catholic Library Association
St Mary's College, Campus 26
700 Terrace Heights
Winoma, MN 55987
An organization of professional librarians interested in providing service according to the Catholic philosophy.

Missouri

Society of American Business Editors and Writers
120 Neff Hall
School of Journalism
University of Missouri
Columbia, MO 65211
A professional society representing the interests of business editors and writers in both print and broadcast medias.

New Hampshire

MacDowell Colony Inc
100 High Street
Peterborough, NH 03458
Retreat for writers, composers, visual artists and filmmakers with professional standing in field.

New York

Academy of American Poets
584 Broadway, Suite 1208
New York, NY 10012
Sponsors the James Laughlin Award, the Walt Whitman Award, the Harold Morton Landon Translation Award, the Tanning Prize, the Raiziss/de Palchi Translation Award and annual college poetry prizes; workshops, classes and literary historical walking tours; awards fellowships to American poets for distinguished poetic achievement.

American Society of Composers, Authors and Publishers
One Lincoln Plaza
New York, NY 10023
A performing rights society.

American Society of Journalists and Authors Inc
1501 Broadway, Suite 302
New York, NY 10036
Service organization providing exchange of ideas and market information. Regular meetings with speakers from the industry; annual writers conference; medical plans available; professional referral service, annual membership directory; first amendment advocacy group.

Association of Authors' Representatives
10 Astor Place, 3rd Floor
New York, NY 10003
Represents the interests of professional literary and dramatic agents.

Authors Aid Associates
340 East 52nd Street
New York, NY 10022

Authors Guild
330 West 42ndStreet, 29th Floor
New York, NY 10036

Authors League of America
330 West 42nd Street
New York, NY 10036
Promotes the interests of authors and dramatists

Brooklyn Writers' Network
2509 Avenue K
Brooklyn, NY 11210
Seeks to improve contact between professional writers and publishing industry; newsletter; directory; conferences; workshops.

Comedy Writers and Performers Association
PO Box 23304
Brooklyn, NY 11202-0066

Council of Literary Magazines and Presses
154 Christopher Street, Suite 3C
New York, NY 10014
Membership restricted to noncommercial literary magazines and presses.

Dramatists Guild
1501 Broadway, Suite 701
New York, NY 10036
Promotes the interests of dramatists, lyricists and composers

International Association of Crime Writers Inc
JAF Box 1500
New York, NY 10116

International Women's Writing Guild
Box 810, Gracie Station
New York, NY 10028
A network for the empowerment of women through writing. Services include manuscript referral and exchange, writing conferences and retreats, group rates for health and life insurance, legal aid, regional clusters and job referrals.

Mystery Writers of America Inc
17 East 47th Street, 6th Floor
New York, NY 10017
To support and promote the mystery. Sponsors the Edgar Allan Poe Awards.

National Association of Science Writers
PO Box 294
Greenlawn, NY 11740

National Writers Union
113 University Place, 6th Floor
New York, NY 10003
A union for the promotion of the interests of freelance writers.

PEN American Center
568 Broadway
New York, NY 10012
An international organization of writers, poets, playwrights, essayists, editors, novelists and translators whose purpose is to bring about better understanding among writers of all nations.

Poetry Society of America
15 Gramercy Park
New York, NY 10003
A service organization dedicated to the promotion of poets and poetry. Sponsors readings, lectures and contests; houses the Van Voorhis Library.

Poets and Writers Inc
72 Spring Street
New York, NY 10012
National nonprofit information center for those interested in contemporary American literature. Publishes a directory of American poets and fiction writers and sponsors readings and workshops programme.

Teachers and Writers Collaborative
5 Union Square West
New York, NY 10003
Sends professional artists into public schools to teach their art forms. Also publishes books and a magazine about how to teach creative writing.

Translation Center
412 Dodge Hall, Columbia University
New York, NY 10027
Publish a magazine bi-annually. Dedicated to finding and publishing the best translations of significant works of foreign contemporary literature.

Writers Guild of America East
555 West 57th Street
New York, NY 10019
Labor union representing professional writers in films, television and radio. Membership available only through the sale of literary material or employment for writing services in one of these areas.

Pennsylvania

National Book Critics Circle
400 North Broad Street
Philadelphia, PA 19103
Gives annual awards for fiction, poetry, biography/autobiography, general non- fiction and criticism. Purpose: to raise the standards of book criticism and enhance public appreciation of literature.

Outdoor Writers' Association of America
2017 Cato Avenue, Suite 101
State College, PA 16801
Professional authors, journalists, broadcasters, photographers and artists who cover hunting, fishing, camping, canoeing and similar outdoor sports; workshops held at annual conference.

Texas

American Literary Translators Association
Box 830688, University of Texas
Richardson, TX 75083
Sponsors the Gregory Rabassa Prize for the translation of fiction from any language into English and the Richard Wilbur Prize for the translation of poetry from any language into English. Awards, which consist of the publication of the winning poems, are awarded biennially.

Romance Writers of America
13700 Veterans Memorial Drive, No 315
Houston, TX 77014
Promotes the interests of writers of romance fiction.

Science Fiction Research Association Inc
6021 Grassmere
Corpus Christi, TX 78415
Professional study of science fiction and fantasy; annual scholar award. Archives maintained at University of Kansas, Lawrence. Sponsor workshop awards and prizes.

Western Writers of America
2800 North Campbell
El Paso, TX 79902
An organization of professionals dedicated to the spirit and reality of the West, past and present.

Virginia

American Society of Newspaper Editors
PO Box 4090
Reston, VA 22090

Associated Writing Programs
George Mason University
Tallwood House
Mail Stop 1E3
Fairfax, VA 22030
National, non-profit organisation of writers and writers who teach writing.

Washington

Science Fiction and Fantasy Writers of America
PO Box 1666
Lynnwood, WA 98046

APPENDIX C

LITERARY AWARDS AND PRIZES

The following list of Literary Awards and Prizes does not claim to be exhaustive although every effort has been made to make it as comprehensive as possible.

Academy of American Poets Fellowship
584 Broadway, Suite 1208
New York, NY 10012,
USA
Fellows are elected each year by majority vote of the Academy's Board of Chancellors. No applications are accepted. Each Fellow is awarded a stipend of US $20,000.

1937	Edwin Markham
1946	Ridgely Torrence
1948	Percy MacKaye
1950	e e cummings
1952	Padraic Colum
1953	Robert Frost
1954	Louise Townsend Nicholl
	Oliver St John Gogarty
1955	Rolfe Humphries
1956	William Carlos Williams
1957	Conrad Aiken
1958	Robinson Jeffers
1959	Louise Bogan
	Léonie Adams
1960	Jesse Stuart
1961	Horace Gregory
1962	John Crowe Ransom
1963	Ezra Pound
	Allen Tate
1964	Elizabeth Bishop
1965	Marianne Moore
1966	Archibald MacLeish
	John Berryman
1967	Mark Van Doren
1968	Stanley Kunitz
1969	Richard Eberhart
	Anthony Hecht
1970	Howard Nemerov
1971	James Wright
1972	W D Snodgrass
1973	W S Merwin
1974	Léonie Adams
1975	Robert Hayden
1976	J V Cunningham
1977	Louise Coxe
1978	Josephine Miles
1979	Mark Strand
	May Swenson
1980	Mona Van Duyn
1981	Richard Hugo
1982	John Ashbery
	John Frederick Nims
1983	Philip Booth
	James Schuyler
1984	Robert Francis
	Richmond Lattimore
1985	Amy Clampitt
	Maxine Kumin
1986	Irving Feldman
	Howard Moss
1987	Alfred Corn
	Josephine Jacobsen
1988	Donald Justice
1989	Richard Howard
1990	William Meredith
1991	J D McClatchy
1992	Adrienne Rich
1993	Gerald Stern
1994	David Ferry
1995	Denise Levertov
1996	Jay Wright
1997	John Haines
1998	Charles Simic

J R Ackerley Prize for Autobiography
English PEN
7 Dilke Street
London SW3 4JE,
England
Prize is awarded for literary autobiography, written in English and published in the year preceeding the award. Short-listed titles are chosen by the Literary Executors of J R Ackerley; nominations are not accepted.
Annual prize of £1000.
Contact: Pamela Petrie, Awards Secretary

1990	Daddy, We Hardly Knew You by Germaine Greer
1991	St Martin's Ride by Paul Binding
1992	Almost a Gentleman: An Autobiography by John Osborne
1993	More Please by Barry Humphries
1994	And When Did You Last See YourFather? by Blake Morrison
1995	Something in Linoleum by Paul Vaughan
1996	The Railway Man by Eric Lomax
1997	The Scent of Dried Roses by Tim Lott
1998	True to Both My Selves by Kathryn Fitzherbert

Jane Addams Children's Book Award
Jane Addams Peace Association
777 United Nations Plaza, 6th Floor
New York, NY 10017,
USA
Prize awarded for a book that best combines literary merit with themes stressing peace, social justice, world community and the equality of the sexes and all races.
Award: Certificate presented annually.

1990	Long Hard Journey: The Story of the Pullman Porter by Patricia McKissak and Frederick McKissak
1991	The Book of Peace edited by Ann Durell and Marilyn Sachs
1992	Journey of the Sparrows by Fran Leeper Buss
1993	A Taste of Salt: A Story of Modern Haiti by Frances Temple
1994	Freedom's Children: Young Civil Rights Activists Tell Their Own Stories by Ellen Levine
1995	Kids at Work : Lewis Hine and the Crusade Against Child Labor by Russell Freedman
1996	The Well: David's Story by Mildred Taylor
1997	Growing Up in Coal Country by Susan Campbell Bartoletti

Age Concern Book of the Year Award
c/o The Literary Editor, The Age
250 Spencer Street
Melbourne, Victoria 3000
Australia
Prize is awarded to a published book of literary merit, written by living Australians.Award of $3000 to the author of a non-fiction book and $3000 to a work of imaginative writing.
Contact: Literary Editor

Alexander Prize
Royal Historical Society
University College London
Gower Street
London WC1E 6BT,
England
Offered for a paper based on original historical research of no more than 8000 words on any subject, providing an opportunity for wider recognition and gauranteed publication of their work. Candidates must be under 35 or have been registred for a higher degree in the last three years.
Prize: £250
Contact: Joy McCarthy

Alice Literary Award

c/o Federal President
Society of Women Writers (Australia)
GPO Box 2621,
Sydney, New South Wales 2001,
Australia
Presented by the Society of Women Writers (Australia) biennially for a distinguished and long term contribution to literature by an Australian woman.

American Academy of Arts and Letters Gold Medal (Letters)

633 West 155 Street
New York, NY 10032-5699,
USA

Hans Christian Andersen Awards

International Board on Books for Young People
Nonnenweg 12, Postfach
CH-4003 Basel,
Switzerland
The winners are selected by an international jury and announced during the IBBY Congress. Awarded biennially to the author (Hans Christian Anderson Award for Writing established in 1956), and illustrator (Hans Christian Andersen Award for Illustration established in 1966) whose work has made a lasting contribution to children's literature.

1956	Eleanor Farjeon
1958	Astrid Lindgren
1960	Erich Kästner
1962	Meindert DeJong
1964	René Guillot
1966	Tove Jansson
	Alois Carigiet
1968	James Krüss
	José Maria Sanchez-Silva
	Jiří Trnka
1970	Gianni Rodari
	Maurice Sendak
1972	Scott O'Dell
	Ib Spang Olsen
1974	Maria Gripe
	Farshid Mesghali
1976	Cecil Bødker
	Tatjana Mawrina
1978	Paula Fox
	Svend Otto
1980	Bohumil Říha
	Suekichi Akaba
1982	Lygya Bojunga Nunes
	Zbigniew Rychlicki
1984	Christine Nöstlinger
	Mitsumasa Anno
1986	Patricia Wrightson
	Robert Ingpen
1988	Annie M G Schmidt
	Dušan Kállay
1990	Tormod Haugen
	Lisbeth Zwerger
1992	Virginia Hamilton
	Květa Pacovská
1994	Michio Mado
	Jörg Müller
1996	Uri Orlev
	Klaus Ensikat

Arts Council of Wales Book of the Year Awards/Gwobr Llyfr y Flwyddyn

9 Museum Place
Cardiff CF1 3NX,
Wales
Awards are given for works of exceptional merit by Welsh authors (by birth or residence) published during the calendar year. Works may be Welsh or English, in the categories of poetry, fiction and creative non-fiction (including literary criticism, biography and autobiography). Non-fiction works must have subject matter that is concerned with Wales.
Prize: Two first prizes of £3000 (one in Welsh, one in English), and £1000 to each of four short-listed authors.
Contact: Tony Bianchi

English Books

1992	Bonds of Attachment by Emyr	Humphreys
1993	Watching the Fire Eater by Robert	Minhinnick
1994	Caitlin: The Life of Caitlin Thomas by Paul Ferris	
1995	Masks by Duncan Bush	
1996	Gwalia in Khasia by Nigel Jenkins	
1997	Not Singing Exactly by Sean James	
1998	Wanting to Belong by Mike Jenkins	

Welsh Books

1992	Cilmeri by Gerallt Lloyd Owen
1993	Seren Wen ar Gefndir Gwyn by Robin Llywelyn
1994	W/J Gruffydd by Robin Chapman
1995	Unigolion by Aled Islwyn
1996	Gloynnod by Sonia Edwards
1997	Tir Nab by Gerwyn Wiliams
1998	Dan Ddylanwad by Iwan Llyyd

Arvon International Poetry Competition

Kilnhurst, Kilnhurst Road
Todmorden, Lancashire OL14 6AX,
England
Biennial poetry competition open to anyone, for poems of any length written in the English language, and not previously published or broadcast.
First prize of £5000 with at least 15 other prizes.
Contact: David Pease, National Director

1980	The Letter by Andrew Motion
1982	Ephraim Destiny's Perfectly Utter Darkness by John Hartley Williams
1985	Rorschach Writing by Oliver Reynolds
1987	The Notebook by Selima Hill
1989	Halfway Pond by Sheldon Flory
1991	Thinking Egg by Jacqueline Brown
1993	A Private Bottling by Don Paterson
1995	Laws of Gravity by Paul Farley
1997	Not Awarded
1998	Technical Assistance by B. A. Humar

Australian Literature Society Gold Medal

Association for the Study of Australian Literature Ltd
c/o Department of English
University College, ADFA
Campbell, Australian Capital Territory 2600
Australia
Contact: Susan Lever
Awarded annually for an outstanding Australian literary work, or occasionally, for outstanding services to Australian literature. Award was inaugurated by the ALS which was incorporated in the Association for the Study of Australian Literature in 1982. No nominations are required.
Prize: Winner receives a gold medal and $1000.

1990	Possible Words and Collected Poems by Peter Porter
1991	Cabin Fever by Elizabeth Jolley (and contribution to Australian Literature)
1992	The Second Bridegroom by Rodney Hall (and contribution to Australian Literature)
1993	Selected Poems by Elizabeth Riddell
1994	Radiance, The Temple, and screenplay for A Map of the Human Heart by Louis Nowra (and contribution to Australian Literature)
1995	The Hand That Signed The Paper by Helen Demidenko
1996	Camille's Bread by Amanda Lohrey
1997	Night Letters by Robert Dessaux
1998	A Mapmaker's Dream by James Cowan

Authors' Club First Novel Award

Authors' Club
40 Dover Street,
London W1X 3RB
England
The winner is selected from entries submitted by publishers and awarded to the most promising first full-length novel of the year published in the UK by a British author.
Prize: £750
Contact: Ann Carter, Secretary

1990	The Way You Tell Them by Alan Brownjohn
1991	The Book of Wishes and Complaints by Zina Rohan
1992	The Healing by David Park
1993	Season of the Rainbirds by Nadeem Aslam
1994	PIG by Andrew Cowan

1995   Walter and the Resurrection of G by T J Armstrong
1996   A Kind of Black by Divan Adebayo
         A Testimony of Taliesin Jones
1997   The Underground Man by Mick Jackson

Bancroft Prizes
Columbia University, 202A Low Library
New York, NY 10027,
USA

David Berry Prize
Royal Historical Society
University College London
Gower Street
London WC1E 6BT
England
Awarded to the writer of the best essay on Scottish history within the reigns of James I and James VI of between 6000 and 10,000 words.
Prize: £250
Contact: Joy McCarthy

James Tait Black Memorial Prizes
Department of English Literature,
University of Edinburgh
Edinburgh EH8 9JX,
Scotland
Eligible works of fiction and biographies are those written in English, originating with a British publisher, and first published in Britain in the year of the award. The nationality of the writer is irrelevant.
Two prizes of £3000 each are awarded annually; one for the best biography or work of that nature, the other for the best work of fiction published in the 12-month period prior to the annual submission date of 30th September.

Biography
1990   The Invisible Woman: The Story of Nelly Ternan and Charles Dickens by Claire Tomalin
1991   Darwin by James Moore and Adrian Desmond
1992   The Reckoning: The Murder of Christopher Marlowe by Charles Nicholl
1993   Dr Johnson and Mr Savage by Richard Holmes
1994   Under My Skin by Doris Lessing
1995   Albert Speer: His Battle with Truth by Gitta Sereny
1996   Thomas Cranmer: A Life by Diarmaid MacCulloch
1997   W B Yeats: A Life Volume One by Roy Foster
1998   The Life of Thomas Moore by Peter Ackroyd

Fiction
1990   Brazzaville Beach by William Boyd
1991   Downriver by Iain Sinclair
1992   Sacred Country by Rose Tremain
1993   Crossing the River by Caryl Phillips
1994   The Folding Star by Alan Hollinghurst
1995   The Prestige by Christopher Priest
1996   Last Orders by Graham Swift
         Justine by Alice Thompson
1997   Ingenious Pain by Andrew Miller
1998   Master Georgie by Beryl Bainbridge

Bollingen Prize in Poetry
Box 1603A
New Haven, CT 06520
USA
Prize is awarded for the best book of poetry by an American author during the preceeding two years.
Biennial prize of $10,000
1981   Howard Nemerov and May Swenson
1983   Anthony E Hecht and John Hollander
1985   John Ashbury and Fred Chappell
1987   Stanley Kunitz
1989   Edgar Bowers
1991   Laura (Riding) Jackson and Donald Justice
1993   Mark Strand
1995   Kenneth Koch
1997   Gary Snyder
1999   Robert White Creeley

Booker Prize For Fiction
Book Trust
Book House, 45 East Hill,
London SW18 2QZ
England

Leading British literary award for the best full-length novel published between 1 October and 30 September in UK. Novel must be written in English and written by a citizen of Great Britain, the Commonwealth, Republic of Ireland or South Africa.
Annual prize of £20,000
Contact: Sandra Vince
1990   Possession by A S Byatt
1991   The Famished Road by Ben Okri
1992   The English Patient by Michael Ondaatje
         Sacred Hunger by Barry Unsworth
1993   Paddy Clarke Ha Ha Ha by Roddy Doyle
1994   How Late It Was, How Late by James   Kelman
1995   The Ghost Road by Pat Barker
1996   Last Orders by Graham Swift
1997   The God of Small Things by Arundhati Roy
1998   Amsterdam by Ian McEwan

Boston Globe-Horn Book Award
c/o Boston Globe
135 William T Morrissey Boulevard
Boston, MA 02125
USA
Prize awarded for books published within the previous year in the categories of fiction, non-fiction and picture book.
Annual cash prize.

Micheál Brethnach Literary Memorial Award
Cló Iar Chonnachta Teo
Indreabhán, Connemara
County Galway
Ireland
An annual award for the best Irish language work in any literary form: novel, drama, poetry or short story collection. Open to writers under 30 years of age. Closing date for entries is 1st December each year.
Prize: IR £1000
Contact: Nóirín Ní Ghrádaigh / Deirdre N íThuathail

Bridport Prize
Bridport Arts Centre, South Street
Bridport, Dorset DT6 3NR
England
Awarded for original poems of not more than 42 lines, and short stories between 1000 and 5000 words. All entries must be written in English and must be previously unpublished or broadcast, nor entered in any other competition.
Prizes: First prize: £2500, Second prize: £1000, Third prize: £500 (in each category), plus discretionary supplementary prizes.
Contact: Peggy Chapman-Andrews

British Book Awards
Publishing News
43 Musuem Street
London WC1A 1LY
England
Established in 1988 and affectionately known as the 'Nibbies', the British Book Awards are announced in Publishing News in November of each year to those who have made an impact to the book trade. Categories include Editor, Publisher, Author, Independent Bookseller and Children's Book.
Prize: The Nibbie
Contact: Merric Davidson

British Fantasy Awards
2 Harwood Street
Stockport, Cheshire SK4 1JJ
England
Awarded by the British Fantasy Society at its annual conference from votes offered by BFS members. Categories include Best Novel and Best Short Story. Previous winners include Ramsey Campbell, Clive Barker and Stephen King.
Prize: Statuette.
Contact: Robert Parkinson

Buckland Award
Trustees Executors and Agency Company of New Zealand Ltd
24 Water Street, PO Box 760
Dunedin
New Zealand
Prize is awarded annually for work of the highest literary merit by a New Zealand writer.

Randolph Caldecott Medal
Association for Library Service to Children
50 East Huron Street
Chicago, IL 70711
USA
Prize is awarded to an illustrator of the most distinguished American
picture book for children published in the preceding year.
Annual prize of bronze medal.

James Cameron Memorial Award
Department of Journalism
City University
Northampton Square
London EC1 0HB
England
Annual award for journalism to a reporter of any nationality working for
the British media. Nominations are not accepted.
Contact: Professor Hugh Stephenson
1990   John Simpson
1991   Robert Fisk and Charles Wheeler
1992   Bridget Kendall
1993   Martin Woollacott
1994   Ed Villiamy
1995   George Alagiah
1996   Maggie O'Kane
1997   Fergal Keane
1998   Jonathon Steele

Canada-French Community of Belgium Literary Prize
The Canada Council
350 Albert Street, PO Box 1047
Ottawa, Ontario K1P 5V4
Canada
Awarded annually in alternate years to a French-language Belgian or
Canadian writer for his or her complete works.
Prize of $5000.

Canada-Japan Book Award
The Canada Council
350 Albert Street, PO Box 1047
Ottawa, Ontario K1P 5V4
Canada
Awarded annually for a book in English or French about Japan by a
Canadian author or for a book by a Japanese author translated by a
Canadian into English or French.
Prize of $10, 000.

Canada-Switzerland Literary Prize
The Canada Council
350 Albert Street, PO Box 1047
Ottawa, Ontario K1P 5V4
Canada
Awarded annually in alternate years to a Canadian or Swiss writer for a
work of poetry, fiction, drama or non-fiction published in French during
the preceding eight years. The prize may also be awarded for the French
translation of a work written originally in English by a Canadian writer or
in German, Italian or Romansh by a Swiss writer.
Prize of $2500.

Canadian Authors Association Literary Awards
27 Doxsee Avenue North, PO Box 419
Campbellford, Ontario K0L 1L0
Canada
Four categories: fiction, non-fiction, poetry and drama. Nominations
apply to book length works by Canadian writers published or produced
during the previous calendar year.
One award per year in each category of a cash prize plus silver medal.
Contact: Awards Chairman

Canadian Library Association Book of the Year for Children Award
c/o Canadian Library Association
200 Elgin Street, Suite 206
Ottawa, Ontario K2P 1L5
Canada.
The award is presented annually to an author of an outstanding
children's book published in Canada during the previous calendar year.
The books must be suitable for children up to 14 years of age.

Melville Cane Award
Poetry Society of America
15 Gramercy Park
New York, NY 10003
USA
For a published book on poetry (in even-numbered years) alternating (in
odd-numbered years) with a book of poems published within the award
year.
Annual cash award.

1990   Harp Lake by John Hollander
1991   White Paper by J D McClatchy
1992   The 6-Cornered Snowflake by John Frederick Nims
1993   An Essay on French Verse for Readers of English Poetry
            by Jacques Barzan
1994   Year of the Comet by Nicholas Christopher

Carnegie Medal
The Library Association
7 Ridgmount Street
London WC1E 7AE
England
The Library Association Carnegie Medal is awarded annually for an
outstanding book for children written in English and receiving its first
publication in the UK during the preceding year.
Prize: Gold medal and £1000 of books to donate.
1990   Wolf by Gilliam Cross
1991   Dear Nobody by Berlie Doherty
1992   Flour Babies by Anne Fine
1993   Stone Cold by Robert Swindells
1994   Whispers in the Graveyard by Theresa Breslin
1995   His Dark Material: Book 1 Northern Lights by Philip Pullman
1996   Junk by Melvin Burgess
1997   River Boy by Tim Bowler

Children's Book Award
The Old Malt House
Aldbourne, Wiltshire SN8 2DW
England
Contact: Marianne Adey
This annual award is judged by children themselves and the short-list is
announced at the Federation of Children's Book Group's Annual
Conference. The three categories are picture books, shorter novels and
longer novels.
Prizes: Short-listed authors and illustrators receive a portfolio of
children's letters inspired by their work, category winners receive a silver
bowl, and the overall winner is awarded a silver and oak tree sculpture.
Best Book of the Year
1991   Threadbear by Mick Inkpen
1992   Kiss the Dust by Elizabeth Laird
1993   The Suitcase Kid by Jacqueline Wilson
1994   The Boy in the Bubble by Ian Strachan
1995   Harriet's Hare by Dick King-Smith
1996   Double Act by Jacqueline Wilson
1997   100 Mile an Hour Dog by Jeremy Strong
1998   Harry Potter and the Philosopher's Stone by Joanne Rowling

Cholmondeley Awards
Society of Authors
84 Drayton Gardens
London SW10 9SB
England
The non-competitive award is for work generally, not for a specific book,
and submissions are not required.
Annual prize of £8000 (shared).
1990   Kingsley Amis
            Elaine Feinstein
            Michael O'Neill
1991   James Berry
            Sujata Bhatt
            Michael Hulse
            Derek Mahon
1992   Allen Curnow
            Donald Davie
            Carol Ann Duffy
            Roger Woddis
1993   Patricia Beer
            George Mackay Brown
            P J Kavanagh
            Michael Longley

1994	Ruth Fainlight
	Gwen Harwood
	Elizabeth Jennings
	John Mole
1995	U A Fanthorpe
	Christopher Reid
	C H Sisson
	Kit Wright
1996	Elizabeth Bartlett
	Dorothy Nimmo
	Peter Scupham
	Iain Crichton Smith
1997	Alison Brackenbury
	Gillian Clarke
	Tony Curtis
	Anne Stevenson
1998	Robert Minhinnick
	Roger McGough
	Anne Ridler
	Ken Smith

Arthur C Clarke Award for Science Fiction

60 Bournemouth Road
Folkestone, Kent CT19 5AZ
England
Prize established in 1986 is given annually to the best science fiction novel published in the UK of the year. Award is jointly administered and judged by the British Science Fiction Association, Science Fiction Foundation and Science Policy Foundation.
Annual prize of £1000.
Administrator: Paul Kincaid

1990	The Child Garden by Geoff Ryman
1991	Take Back Plenty by Colin Greenland
1992	Synners by Pat Cadigan
1993	Body of Glass by Marge Piercy
1994	Vurt by Jeff Noon
1995	Fools by Pat Cadigan
1995	Fairyland by Paul J McAuley
1998	The Sparrow by Mary Doria Russell

Cló Iar-Chonnachta Literary Award

Cló Iar-Chonnachta Teo
Indreabhán, Connemara
County Galway
Ireland
An annual prize for a newly written and unpublished work in the Irish language, to be awarded for a novel in 1996, a poetry collection in 1997 and a work of drama or short story collection in 1998.
Prize: IR £5000
Contact: Nóirín Ní Ghrádaigh / Deirdre N íThuathail

| 1996 | Pádraig Ó Siadhail |

Commonwealth Writers' Prize

Commonwealth Foundation, Marlborough House
Pall Mall, London SW1Y 5HY
England
Established in 1987, the Commonwealth Writers' Prize is awarded annually for a work of fiction, novel or collection of short stories - written in English by a citizen of the Commonwealth and published in the preceding year. Funded by the Commonwealth Foundation and administered by the Book Trust.
Prize of £10,000 for best book, £3000 for best first published book, eight regional prizes of £1000.
Administrator: Book Trust

1990	Solomon Gursky Was Here by Mordechai Richler Visitors by John Cranna
1991	The Great World by David Malouf
	Shape-Shifter by Pauline Melville
1992	Such a Long Journey by Rohinton Mistry
	Divina Trace by Robert Antoni
1993	The Ancestor Game by Alex Miller
	The Thousand Faces of Night by Githa Hariharan
1994	A Suitable Boy by Vikram Seth
	The Case of Emily V by Keith Oatley
1995	Captain Corelli's Mandolin by Louis de Bernières
	Seasonal Adjustments by Adib Khan
1996	A Fine Balance by Rohinton Mistry
	Red Earth and Pouring Rain by Vikram Chandra
1997	Salt by Earl Lovelace
	Fall on Your Knees by Ann-Marie MacDonald

| 1998 | Jack Maggs by Peter Carey |
| | Angel Falls by Tim Wynveen |

Thomas Cook/Daily Telegraph Travel Book Awards

Thomas Cook Group
45 Berkeley Street
London W1A 1EB
England
Award for best travel book published in the previous year.
Annual award of £7500.
Contact: Alexis Coles, Corporate Affairs

1989	Riding the Iron Rooster by Paul Theroux
1990	Our Grandmothers' Drums by MarkHudson
1991	Hunting Mister Heartbreak by Jonathan Raban
1992	A Goddess in the Stones by Norman Lewis
	In Search of Conrad by Gavin Young
1993	The Heart of the World by Nik Cohn
1994	City of Djinns by William Dalrymple
1995	In Search of Tusitala: Travels in the South Pacific after Robert Louis Stevenson by Gavin Bell
1996	Frontiers of Heaven by Stanley Stewart
1997	Clear Waters Rising by Thomas Crane
1998	Yemen: Travels in Dictionary Land by Tim Mackintosh-Smith

Duff Cooper Prize

54 St Maur Road
London SW6 4DP
England
Prize is awarded annually in memory of Alfred Duff Cooper, 1st Viscount Norwich (1890-1954). It consists of a copy of his autobiography, Old Men Forget, together with a cheque.
Prize: £2500.
Contact: Ms Artemis Cooper

1990	Clever Hearts: Desmond and Molly McCarthy: A Biography by Hugh and Mirabel Cecil
1991	Wittgenstein: The Duty of Genius by Ray Monk
1992	Never Again: Post-war Britain 1946-51 by Peter Hennessy
1993	A History of Warfare by John Keegan
1994	Curzon by David Gilmour
1995	Albert Speer: His Battle With Truth by Gitta Sereny
1996	Thomas Cranmer: A Life by Diarmaid McCulloch

Crime Writers' Association Awards

PO Box 10772
London N6 4RY
England
Contact: The Secretary

CWA - Gold Dagger for Fiction

Best crime fiction of the year; nominations by publishers only.
Annual prize of gold-plated dagger and cheque.

1990	Bones and Silence by Reginald Hill
1991	King Solomon's Carpet by Barbara Vine
1992	The Way Through the Woods by Colin Dexter
1993	Cruel and Unusual by Patricia Cornwell
1994	The Scold's Bride by Minette Walters
1995	The Mermaid's Singing by Val McDermid
1996	Popcorn by Ben Elton
1997	Black and Blue by Ian Rankin
1998	Sunset Limited by James Lee Burke

CWA - Silver Dagger for Fiction

Annual award of silver dagger and cheque.

1990	The Late Candidate by Mike Phillips
1991	Deep Sleep by Frances Fyfield
1992	Bucket Nut by Liza Cody
1993	Fatlands by Sarah Dunant
1994	Miss Smilla's Feeling for Snow by Peter Høeg
1995	The Summons by Peter Lovesey
1996	Bloodhounds by Peter Lovesey
1997	Three to Get Deadly by Janet Evanovitch
1998	Manchester Slingback by Nicholas Blincoe

CWA - Diamond Dagger for Fiction

Prize is awarded by Chairman and Committee for outstanding contribution to the genre.
Annual prize of Diamond Dagger plus cheque.

1990	Julian Symons
1991	Ruth Rendell
1992	Lesley Charteris
1993	Edith Pargeter
1994	Reginald Hill
1997	Colin Dexter

1998   Ed McBain
1999   Margaret Yorke

CWA - Gold Dagger for Non-Fiction
Awarde for the best non-fiction crime book published during the year.
Annual prize of gold-plated dagger and cheque.
1990   The Passing of Starr by Jonathan Goodman
1991   Giordano Bruno and the Embassy Affair by John Bossy
1992   The Reckoning by Charles Nicholl
1993   Murder in the Heart by Alexandra Artley
1994   Criminal Shadows by David Canter
1995   Dead Not Buried by Martin Beales
1996   The Gunpowder Plot by Antonia Fraser
1997   The Jigsaw Man by Paul Britton
1998   Cries Unheard by Gitta Sereny

CWA John Creasey Memorial Dagger
Presented for the best crime novel by a previously unpublished author.
Award established in memory of the crime writer John Creasey, founder
of the Crime Writers Association. Nominations from publishers only.
Annual prize of dagger and cheque.
1990   Postmortem by Patricia Cornwell
1991   Deep Sleep by Frances Fyfield
1992   The Ice House by Minette Walters
1993   No prize awarded
1994   Big Town by Doug J Swanson
1995   One For The Money by Janet Evanovich
1996   No prize awarded
1997   Body Politic by Paul Johnston
1998   Garnethill by Denise Mina

The Last Laugh Dagger
Award for the funniest crime novel published during the year.
Nominations from publishers only.
Prize: Dagger and cheque.
1994   The Villain of the Earth by Simon Shaw
1995   Sunburn by Laurence Shames
1996   Two For The Dough by Janet Evanovich

Dagger in the Library Award
Annual award established in 1995 for the crime writer most popular with
library borrowers. Winner is selected in liaison with librarians, and
sponsored by the NB Magazine for librarians.
Prize: Gold-plated dagger and cheque.
1995   Lindsey Davis.
1996   Marian Babson

The Macallan Short Story Award
6 Ainscow Avenue
Lostock, Bolton
Lancs BL6 4LR
England
Contact: Val McDermid
Award for a published crime story.
Prize: £200 and a silver-plated tie-pin/brooch
1995   Funny Story by Larry Beinhart
1996   Herbert in Motion by Ian Rankin
1997   On the Psychiatrist's Couch by Reginald Hill
1998   Roots by Jerry Sykes

Danish Academy Prize for Literature
Rungstedlund
109 Rungsted Strandvej
DK-2960 Rungsted Kyst
Denmark
Contact: Allan Philip
Prize of Dkr 200,000 is currently awarded bi-annually for an outstanding
work of literature.
1990   Jens Smærup Srensen
1992   Peter Laugesen
1994   Ib Michael
1996   Vibeke Grønfeldt

Dillons First Fiction Award
Dillons UK Ltd
Royal House, Princes Gate, Homer Road
Solihull, West Midlands B91 3QQ
England
Established in 1994 to encourage new novel-writing talent, this annual
award is open to full-length first novels written in English and published
in the UK during the calendar year in question. Winners announced in
April.
Prize: £5000.
Contact: Ruth Killick / Tracey Lewis
1995   Now and Then by William Corlett

Encore Award
Society of Authors
84 Drayton Gardens
London SW10 9SB
England
The prize has been awarded by the Society of Authors since 1990 for a
second published novel. Annual Prize: £7500.
1990   A Lesser Dependency by Peter Benson
         Calm at Sunset, Calm at Dawn by Paul Watkins
1991   Richard's Feet by Carey Harrison
1992   Downriver by Iain Sinclair
1993   The Heather Blazing by Colm Toibin
1994   Afternoon Raag by Amit Chaudhuri
1995   A Goat's Song by Dermot Healy
1996   So I Am Glad by A L Kennedy
1997   Like Plastic by David Flusfeder
1998   I Could Read the Sky by Timothy O'Grady and Steve Pyke
         These Demented Lands by Alan Warner

English Academy of Southern Africa
PO Box 124
Witwatersrand 2050
South Africa
Thomas Pringle Awards
Oliver Schreiner Prize

Geoffrey Faber Memorial Prize
Faber and Faber Ltd
3 Queen Square
London WC1N 3AU
England
Awarded annually since 1963, as a memorial to the founder and first
Chairman of Faber and Faber, with prizes in alternate years for a volume
of verse or prose fiction first published originally in UK during 2 years
preceding the year of award. Eligible writers must be under 40 at time of
publication, citizen of UK, Ireland, Commonwealth, or South Africa.
Prize: £1000.
Contact: Sarah Gleadell/Belinda Matthews
1990   Shibboleth by Michael Donaghy
1991   The Fog Line by Carol Birch
1992   Madoc by Paul Muldoon
1993   The Quantity Theory by Will Self
1994   Myth of the Twin by John Burnside
1995   Their Angel Reach by Livi Michael
1996   The Queen of Sheba by Kathleen Jamie
1997   Not Her Real Name by Emily Perkins
1998   God's Gift to Women by Don Paterson

Eleanor Farjeon Award
Children's Book Circle
Hampshire County Library
81 North Walls
Winchester SO23 8BY
England
Prize awarded for distinguished service to children's books both in the
UK and overseas. Recipients include librarians, publishers, booksellers
and authors, and are chosen from nominations from members of the
Children's Book Circle.
Prize: £500.
Contact: Anne Marley
1990   Jill Bennett
1991   Patricia Crampton
1992   Stephanie Nettell
1993   Susan Belgrave
1994   Eileen Colwell
1995   Helen Paiba
1996   Books for Keeps
1997   Michael Rosen
1998   Gina Pollinger

Fawcett Society Book Prize
New Light of Women's Lives
46 Harleyford Road
London SE11 5AY
England
Prize is given to works of fiction, non-fiction or biography which offer
enlightenment and understanding of women's lives. Must have first been
published in Britain, Commonwealth or Ireland.
Annual prize of £2000.
Contact: Charlotte Burt

1990	The Long Road to Greenham by Jill Liddington
1991	Judasland by Jennifer Dawson
1992	Cleopatra: Histories, Dreams and Distortions by Lucy Hughes-Hallett
	The Haunting of Sylvia Plath by Jacqueline Rose
1993	Wild Swans by Jung Chang
1994	Daphne du Maurier by Margaret Forster
1996	The Prospect Before Her by Olwen Huston

Kathleen Fidler Award
c/o Book Trust Scotland
Scottish Book Centre
Fountainbridge Library
137 Dundee Street
Edinburgh EH11 1BG
Scotland
Awarded for an unpublished children's novel of not less than 25,000-28,000 words for children aged 8-12. Author must not have had a novel published previously for this age group.
Annual prize of £1000, plus entry published by Hodder Children's Books, and a rosewood and silver trophy, to be held for one year.
Contact: Administrative Officer

1990	Magic With Everything by Roger Burt
1991	Greg's Revenge by George Hendry
1992	Richard's Castle by Susan Coon
1993	48 Hours with Franklin by Mij Kelly
1994	Run, Zan, Run by Catherine MacPhail
1995	Edge of Danger by Claire Dudman
1996	The Falcon's Quest by John Smirthwaite
1997	Slate Mountain by Mark Leyland

Sir Banister Fletcher Prize of the Authors' Club
Authors' Club
40 Dover Street
London W1X 3RB
England
Awarded to the best book of the year on the arts, and architecture in particular, by an author resident in Britain, and published in the UK in the preceding year. Nominations from the press and by publishers.
Prize: £750.
Contact: Ann Carter, Secretary

1990	British Architectural Books and Writers 1556-1785 by Eileen Harris
1991	The Art and Architecture of Freemasonry by James Stevens Curl
1992	Bernold Lubetkin: Architecture and the Tradition of Progress by John Allan
1993	Buildings and Power by Thomas Marcus
1994	Gothic Revival by Megan Aldrich
1995	Alvar Aalto by Richard Weston

Forward Prizes for Poetry
c/o Colman Getty PR
Carrington House, 126-130 Regent Street
London W1R 5FE
England
Established in 1992, these awards are presented for three categories of poetry, the best poetry collection of the year, the best first collection and the best single published poem in English and by a citizen of the UK or the Republic of Ireland. Submissions by editors or publishers.
Prize £10,000 (best collection), £5000 (best first collection) and £1000 (best single poem).
Contact: Coleman Getty PR

Best Collection

1992	The Man With Night Sweats by Thom Gunn
1993	Mean Time by Carol Ann Duffy
1994	Harm by Alan Jenkins
1995	GhostTrain by Sean O'Brien
1996	Stones and Fires by John Fuller
1997	The Marble Fly by Jamie McKendrick
1998	Birthday Letters by Ted Hughes

Best First Collection

1993	Nil Nil by Don Paterson
1994	Progeny of Air by Kwame Dawes
1995	Breathe Now, Breathe by Jane Duran
1996	Slattern by Kate Clanchy
1997	A Painted Field by Robin Robertson
1998	The Boy from the Chemist Is Here to See You by Paul Farley

Best Single Poem

1993	Judith by Vicki Feaver

1994	Autumn by Iain Crichton
1995	In Honour of Love by Jenny Joseph
1996	The Graduates by Kathleen Jamie
1997	Lavinia Greenlaw
1998	Sheenagh Pugh

Mary Gilmore Award
Association for the Study of Australian Literature Ltd
Department of English
University College, ADFA
Campbell, Australian Capital Territory 2600
Australia
Contact: Susan Lever
Awarded for a first book of poetry published in the preceding year. No nominations are required.
Prize: $1000.

1990	In the Name of the Father by Kristopher Sassemussen
1991	Verandahs by Jean Kent
1992	This is the Stone by Alison Croggon
1993	The Mask and Jagged Star by Jill Jones
1994	Now, Millenium by Deborah Staines
1995	Coming Up for Light by Aileen Kelly
1996	Nervous Arcs by Jordie Albiston
1997	Night Reversing by Morgan Yasbincek
1998	The Wild Reply by Emma Lew

Goodman Fielder Wattie Book Award
PO Box 44-146
Auckland 2
New Zealand
Book published in New Zealand in the previous year by a New Zealand author (includes New Zealand residents and Pacific Island countries).
Annual - 1st prize of NZ $20,000, 2nd prize of NZ $10,000, 3rd prize of NZ $5000, Food Industry Book Award NZ $6000.

Governor General's Literary Awards
The Canada Council
350 Albert Street, PO Box 1047
Ottawa, Ontario K1P 5V8
Canada
Awarded to Canadian authors of the best books in the English and French languages in seven categories: fiction, non-fiction, poetry, drama, children's literature (text), children's literature (illustration) and translation.
Annual cash prize.

Kate Greenaway Medal
The Library Association
7 Ridgmount Street
London WC1E 7AE
England
Awarded annually for an outstanding book in terms of illustration for children published in the UK the preceding year.
Prize: Gold medal and £1000 of books to donate.

1990	The Whale's Song, illustrated by Gary Blythe
1991	The Jolly Christmas Postman, illustrated by Janet Ahlberg
1992	Zoo, illustrated by Anthony Browne
1993	Black Ships Before Troy, illustrated by Alan Lee
1994	Way Home, illustrated by Gregory Rogers
1995	The Christmas Miracle of Jonathan Toomey, illustrated by PJ Lynch
1996	The Baby Who Wouldn't Go To Bed by Helen Cooper
1997	When Jessie Came Home from the Sea by P J Lynch

Eric Gregory Trust Fund Award
Society of Authors
84 Drayton Gardens
London SW10 9SB
England
For poets aged under 30 who are likely to benefit from more time given to writing.
Prize: £28,000 (shared).

1990	Nicholas Drake
	Maggie Hannon
	William Park
	Jonathan Davidson
	Lavinia Greenlaw
	Don Paterson
	John Wells

1991	Roddy Lumsden
	Glyn Maxwell
	Stephen Smith
	Wayne Burrows
	Jackie Kay
1992	Jill Dawson
	Hugh Dunkerly
	Christopher Greenhaigh
	Marita Maddah
	Stuart Paterson
	Stuart Pickford
1993	Eleanor Brown
	Joel Lane
	Deryn Rees-Jones
	Sean Boustead
	Tracey Herd
	Angela McSeveney
1994	Julia Copus
	Alice Oswald
	Steven Blyth
	Kate Clanchy
	Giles Goodland
1995	Collette Bryce
	Sophie Hannah
	Tobias Hill
	Mark Wormald
1996	Sue Butler
	Cathy Cullis
	Jane Griffiths
	Jane Holland
	Chris Jones
	Sinead Morrissey
	Kate Thomas
1997	Matthew Clegg
	Sarah Corbett
	Polly Clark
	Tim Kendall
	Graham Nelson
	Matthew Welton
1998	Mark Goodwin
	Joanne Limburg
	Patrick McGuinness
	Christiana Whitehead
	Kona Macphee
	Francis Williams
	Esther Morgan

Guardian Children's Fiction Award

The Guardian
72 Dukes Avenue
London W4 2AF
England
Awarded for an outstanding work of fiction for children by a Commonwealth or British author, first published in Britain in previous year, excluding picture books and previous winners.
Annual prize of £1000.

1990	Goggle-Eyes by Anne Fine
1991	The Kingdom by the Sea by Robert Westall
1992	Paper Faces by Rachel Anderson
	The Exiles by Hilary McKay
1993	Low Tide by William Mayne
1994	The Mennyms by Sylvia Waugh
1995	MapHead by Lesley Howarth
1996	Dark Materials I: Northern Lights by Philip Pullman
	The Sherwood Hero by Alison Prince
1997	Junk by Melvin Burgess
1998	Fire, Bed and Bone by Henrietta Branford

Guardian Fiction Prize

The Guardian
72 Dukes Avenue
London W4 2AF
England
The winner is chosen by a panel of five judges. Submissions are not requested. Awarded to a work of fiction by a British, Irish or Commonwealth writer and published in the UK.
Prize: £2000.

1990	Shape-Shifter by Pauline Melville
1991	The Devil's Own Work by Alan Judd
1992	Poor Things by Alasdair Gray

1993	The Eye in the Door by Pat Barker
1994	Debatable Land by Candia McWilliam
1995	Heart's Journey Into Winter by James Buchan
1996	Reading in the Dark by Seamus Deane
1997	Fugitive Pieces by Anne Michaels
1998	Trumpet by Jackie Kay

Hawthornden Prize

42A Hays Mews, Berkeley Square
London W1X 7RU
England
For imaginative literature by a British subject under the age of 41 published during the previous year.
Annual prize of £5000.
Contact: Mrs Judy Mooney

1990	Short Afternoons by Kit Wright
1991	The Invisible Woman by Claire Tomalin
1992	Of Love and Asthma by Ferdinand Mount
1993	The Tap Dancer by Andrew Barrow
1994	In the Place of Fallen Leaves by Tim Pears
1995	the Collected Poems by James Michie
1996	An Experiment in Love by Hilary Mantel
1997	The Debt to Pleasure by John Lanchester
1998	Somebody Else by Charles Nicholl

Ernest Hemingway Foundation/PEN Award for First Fiction

PEN American Center
568 Broadway
New York, NY 10012
USA
Prize is awarded for a distinguished first novel or first collection of short fiction by a young and developing American writer.
Annual prize of $7500.

1976	Parthian Shot by Loyd Little
1977	Speedboat by Renata Adler
1978	A Way of Life, Like Any Other by Darcy O'Brien
1979	Hasen by Reuben Bercovitch
1980	Mom Kills Kids and Self by Alan Saperstein
1981	Household Words by Joan Silber
1982	Housekeeping by Marilynne Robinson
1983	Shiloh and Other Stories by Bobbie Ann Mason
1984	During the Reign of the Queen of Persia by Joan Chase
1985	Dreams of Sleep by Josephine Humphreys
1986	Lady's Time by Alan V Hewat
1987	Tongues of Flame by Mary Ward Brown
1988	Imagining Argentina by Lawrence Thornton
1989	The Book of Ruth by Jane Hamilton
1990	The Ice at the Bottom of the World by Mark Richard
1991	Maps to Anywhere by Bernard Cooper
1992	Wartime Lies by Louis Begley
1993	Lost in the City by Edward P Jones
1994	The Magic of Blood by Dagoberto Gilb
1995	The Grass Dancer by Susan Power
1996	Native Speaker by Chang-rae Lee
1997	Ocean of Words by Ha Jin
1998	A Private State by Charlotte Bacon

O Henry Award

Texas Institute of Letters, Box 9032
Wichita Falls, TX 76308-9032
USA

Heywood Hill Literary Prize

10 Curzon Street
London W1Y 7FJ
England
Established in 1995 by the Duke of Devonshire, and awarded for a lifetime's contribution to the enjoyment of books. No applications are accepted.
Prize: £10,000.
Contact: John Saumarez Smith

1995	Patrick O'Brian
1996	Penelope Fitzgerald
1997	John Nicoll
1998	Norman Lewis and Richard Ollard

David Higham Prize for Fiction

Book Trust
Book House, 45 East Hill
London SW18 2QZ
England

Awarded for first novel or book of short stories published in the UK in the year of the award. Author must be citizen of Britain, Commonwealth, Republic of Ireland or South Africa.
Annual prize of £1000.
Contact: Sandra Vince
1990 Soldiers and Innocents by Russell Celyn Jones
1991 O Caledonia by Elspeth Barker
1992 Halo by John Loveday
1993 Love Your Enemies by Nicola Barker
1994 The Longest Memory by Fred D'Aguilar
1995 Red Earth and Pouring Rain by Vikram Chandra
1996 The Cast Iron Shore by Linda Grant
1997 A Scientific Romance by Ronald Wright
1998 Shopping by Gavin Kramer

William Hill Sports Book of the Year
Greenside House, Station Road
Wood Green, London N22 4TP
England
Sponsored by bookmakers William Hill, this is the UK's only annual sports book award. All books must be published in the UK during the year in question.
Prize: First prize: £5000 cash prize, £500 free bet with William Hill, and specially-bound copy of the book; various runners-up prizes.
Contact: Graham Sharpe
1995 A Good Walk Spoiled by John Feinstein
1996 Dark Trade by Colin McRae
1997 A Lot of Hard Yakka by Simon Hughes
1998 Angry White Pyjamas by Robert Twigger

Historical Novel Prize in Memory of Georgette Heyer
The Bodley Head, Random Century
20 Vauxhall Bridge Road
London SW1V 2SA
England
Awarded for full-length previously unpublished historical novel set before 1939.
Annual prize of £5000.
Contact: Mrs J Black

Richard Imison Memorial Award
Society of Authors
84 Drayton Gardens
London SW10 9SB
England
Designed to encourage talent and help maintain high standards, this award is given for the best work of radio drama, as judged by the Society of Authors Broadcasting Committee. Works must be original, the first dramatic work by the author(s) to be broadcast, and must be written specifically for radio (adaptions for works orginally intended for stage, film or television are not eligible).
Prize: £1000.
1996 I Love U Jimmy Spud by Lee Hall
1997 Wilde Belles by Rosemary Kay
     Holy Secrets by John Waters
1998 The Earthquake Girl by Katie Hims

Ingersoll Prizes
Ingersoll Foundation
934 Main Street
Rockford, IL 61103
USA

T S Eliot Award for Creative Writing
For fiction, drama, poetry, essays and literary criticism.
Annual cash prize.

Richard M Weaver Award for Scholarly Letters
For a lifetime of distinguished achievements in the humanities.
Annual cash prize.

International IMPAC Dublin Literary Award
Dublin City Public Libraries
Cumberland House, Fenian Street
Dublin 2
Ireland
Awarded by an international panel of judges for a work of fiction judged to be of "high literary merit" and published in English, either originally or in translation, during the qualifying period. Books are nominated by selected libraries in capital and major cities around the world. The award

is sponsored by the managerial consultancy company IMPAC, and administred by Dublin City Public Libraries.
Prize: IR£100,000 (shared between author and translator if the winning book is in English translation).
Contact: Brendan Teeling
1996 Remembering Babylon by David Malouf
1997 A Heart So White by Javier Marias
1998 The Land of Green Plums by Herta Müller

Irish Times International Fiction Prize
Irish Times Ltd
10-16 D'Olier Street
Dublin 2
Ireland
The winners are chosen from nominations from critcis and editors. Submissions are not required. Awarded biennially since 1989 to the author of a work of fiction written in English, published in Ireland, the UK or the US in the two years of the award.
Prize: IR£7500.
Contact: Gerard Cavanagh, Administrator, Book Prizes.

Irish Times Irish Literature Prize
Irish Times Ltd
10-16 D'Olier Street
Dublin 2
Ireland
Established in 1989, three biennial prizes are awarded for works of fiction, non-fiction and poetry written by an author born in Ireland or an Irish citizen. Books are nominated by critics and editors - no submissions required.
Prize: IR£5000 for each category.
Contact: Gerard Cavanagh, Administrator, Book Prizes.

Jerusalem Prize
Binyaney Ha'ooma
POB 6001
Jerusalem 91060
Israel
The prize is awarded to a writer whose work expresses the idea of "the freedom of the individual in society".

Jewish Quarterly Literary Prizes
The Jewish Quarterly
PO Box 2078
London W1A 1JR
England
Formerly the H H Wingate Prize. Books must be published in English in the UK during the year of the award. Submissions should be of literary merit and stimulate an interest in and awareness of themes of Jewish concern. Authors must be citizens or residents of the UK, Ireland, the Commonwealth or South Africa.
Prizes: £4000 each for fiction and non-fiction categories, awarded during Jewish Book Week in February, plus expenses to attend the Jerusalem Book Fair.
Contact: Mr Gerald Don.

Samuel Johnson Award
(Formerly AT & T Non-Fiction Award)
206 Marylebone Road
London NW1 6LY,
England
The winner is chosen from entries submitted by publishers. Awarded to the best work of general non-fiction published by a British publisher for the first time in the 12 months between 1 April and 31 March. Entries must be written in English by living writers from the British Commonwealth or the Republic of Ireland.
Annual prize of £25,000 (first prize) - each short-listed author receives an AT & T computer worth £1500.
Administration: Booksellers Association
1990 Citizens: A Chronicle of the French Revolution by Simon Schama
1991 Invisible Woman by Claire Tomalin
1992 Wild Swans by Jung Chang
1993 Never Again: Britain 1945-51 by Peter Hennessy
1994 Edward Heath: A Biography by John Campbell
1995 Coming Back Brockens by Mark Hudson
1996 The Railway Man by Eric Lomax
1997 A People's Tragedy by Orlando Figes

Kalinga Prize
c/o UNESCO
7 Place de Fontenoy
75352 Paris 07 SP
France
Awarded to popularizers of science with distinguished careers as writers, editors, lecturers, directors or producers. The winner is expected to have an understanding of science and technology, and an awareness of the scientific work of the UN and UNESCO.
Annual prize of £1000.
Contact: V Zharov, Director

1990	Misbah-Ud-Din Shami (Pakistan)
1991	Radu Iftimovici (Romania)
	Narender Sehgal (India)
1992	Jorge Flores Valdés (Mexico)
	Peter Okebukola (Nigeria)
1993	Piero Angela (Italy)
1994	Nikolai Drozdov (Russia)
1995	Julieta Fierro Gossman (Mexico)
1996	Jiri Grygar (Czechoslovakia)
	Jayant V. Narlikav (India)
1997	Dorairajan Balabsubramanian (India)

Gerald Lampert Award
League of Canadian Poets
24 Ryerson Avenue
Toronto, Ontario N5T 2P3
Canada

Harold Morton Landon Translation Award
Academy of American Poets
584 Broadway, Suite 1208
New York, NY 10012
USA
Awarded to the translator of a published translation of poetry from any language into English. Publishers may submit eligible books.
Annual prize of $1000.

1976	Robert Fitzgerald for the Iliad of Homer
1978	Galway Kinnell for The Poems of François Villon
	Howard Norman for The Wishing Bone Cycle
1980	Saralyn R Daly for The Book of True Love by Juan Ruis
	Edmund Keeley for Ritsos in Parenthesis
1982	Rika Lesser for Guide to the Underworld by Gunnar Ekelöf
1984	Robert Fitzgerald for The Odyssey of Homer
	Stephen Mitchell for The Selected Poetry of Rainer Maria Rilke
1985	Edward Snow for New Poems (1907) of Rainer Maria Rilke
1986	William Arrowsmith for The Storm and Other Things by Eugenio Montale
1987	Mark Anderson for In the Storm of Roses by Ingeborg Bachmann
1988	Peter Hargitai for Perched on Nothing's Branch by Attila József
1989	Martin Greenberg for Heinrich von Kleist: Five Plays
1990	Stephen Mitchell for Variable Directions by Dan Pagis
1991	Robert Fagles for The Iliad of Homer
1992	John DuVal for The Discovery of America by Cesare Pascarella
	Andrew Schelling for Dropping the Bow: Poems of Ancient India
1993	Charles Simic for The Horse Has Six Legs: An Anthology of Serbian Poetry
1994	Rosmarie Waldrop for The Book of Margins by Edmond Jabès
1995	Robert Pinsky for The Inferno of Dante: A New Verse Translation
1996	Guy Davenport for 7 Greeks
1997	David Hinton for Landscape Over Zero by Bei Dao, The Late Poems of Meng Chiao, and The Selected Poems of Li Po
1998	Louis Simpson for Modern Poets

James Laughlin Award
(formerly the Lamont Poetry Selection)
Academy of American Poets
584 Broadway, Suite 1208
New York, NY 10012
USA
Supports the publication of an American poet's second volume of poetry. Only manuscripts already under contract with publishers are considered. Publishers are invited to submit manuscripts by American poets who have already published one book of poems in a standard edition.
Annual prize of $5000.

1954	The Middle Voice by Constance Carrier
1955	Exiles and Marriages by Donald Hall
1956	Letter from a Distant Land by Philip Booth
1957	Time Without Number by Daniel Berrigan
1958	The Night of the Hammer by Ned O'Gorman
1959	The Summer Anniversaries by Donald Justice
1960	The Lovemaker by Robert Mezey
1961	Nude Descending a Satircase by X J Kennedy
1962	Stand Up, Friend, With Me by Edward Field
1963	No award given
1964	Heroes, Advise Us by Adrien Stoutenberg
1965	The War of the Secret Agents by Henri Coulette
1966	The Distance Anywhere by Kenneth O Hanson
1967	The Marches by James Scully
1968	The Weather of Six Mornings by Jane Cooper
1969	A Probable Volume of Dreams by Marvin Bell
1970	Treasury Holiday by William Harmon
1971	Concurring Beasts by Stephen Dobyns
1972	Collecting the Animals by Peter Everwine
1973	Presentation Piece by Marilyn Hacker
1974	After Our War by John Balaban
1975	The Private Life by Lisel Mueller
1976	The Afterlife by Larry Levis
1977	Lucky Life by Gerald Stern
1978	Killing Floor by Ai
1979	Sunrise by Frederick Seidel
1980	More Trouble with the Obvious by Michael Van Walleghen
1981	The Country Between Us by Carolyn Forché
1982	Long Walks in the Afternoon by Margaret Gibson
1983	The Dead and the Living by Sharon Olds
1984	Deep Within the Ravine by Philip Schultz
1985	Victims of the Latest Dance Craze by Cornelius Eady
1986	The Minute Hand by Jane Shore
1987	The River of Heaven by Garret Kaoru
1988	Unfinished Painting by Mary Jo Salter
1989	Crime Against Nature by Minnie Bruce Pratt
1990	The City in Which I Love You by Li-Young Lee
1991	Campo Santo by Susan Wood
1992	Wildwood Flower by Kathryn Stripling Byer
1993	Stained Glass by Rosanna Warren
1994	Song by Brigit Pegeen Kelly
1995	Neither World by Ralph Angel
1996	Wise Poison by David Rivard
1997	Donkey Gospel by Tony Hoagland
1998	Except by Nature by Sandra Alcosser

Grace Leven Prize for Poetry
c/o Perpetual Trustee Company Ltd
39 Hunter Street
Sydney, New South Wales 2000
Australia
For recognition of the best volume of poetry published during the twelve months immediately preceding the year in which the award is made. Writers must be Australian-born and writing as Australians, or naturalised in Australia and resident in Australia for not less than ten years.
Annual prize of Australian $200.

Ruth Lilly Poetry Prize
c/o Poetry
Modern Poetry Association
60 West Walton Street
Chicago, IL 60610
USA
Given to a US poet whose accomplishments warrant extraordinary recognition.
Annual prize of $75,000.

1986	Adrienne Rich
1987	Philip Levine
1988	Anthony Hecht
1989	Mona Van Duyn
1990	Hayden Carruth
1991	David Wagoner
1992	John Ashbery
1993	Charles Wright
1994	Donald Hall
1995	A R Ammons
1996	Gerald Stern

1997   William Matthews
1998   W S Merwin

Lloyds Private Banking Playwright of the Year Award
Tony Ball Associates plc
174-178 North Gower Street

London NW1 2NB
England
Awarded since 1994 to encourage new and diverse playwrighting, broadening support for the theatre and extending the links between Lloyds Private Banking and the Arts.Playwrights should be British or Irish, whose new works have been performed in the UK or Republic of Ireland for the first time in the previous year. Nominations by theatre critics form a short-list, with winners chosen by a panel of judges.
Prize: £25,000.
Contact: Stephen Harrison / Melissa Jones
1994   Dead Funny by Terry Johnson
1995   The Steward of Christendom by Sebastian Barry

Los Angeles Times Book Prizes
Los Angeles Times
Times Mirror Square
Los Angeles, CA 90053
USA

Agnes Mure Mackenzie Award
Saltire Society
9 Fountain Close, 22 High Street
Edinburgh EH1 1TF
Scotland
Awarded every third year since 1965 for a published work of Scottish historical research of scholarly importance. Nominations are invited.
Prize: Cash prize, plus a bound and inscribed copy of the winning publication.
Contact: Mrs Kathleen Munro, Administrator

Mail on Sunday / John Llewellyn Rhys Prize
Book Trust
Book House, 45 East Hill
London SW18 2QZ
England
Awarded for a work of fiction, non-fiction or poetry by an author under 35 at time of publication. Books must have been published in the UK in the year of the award in English by a citizen of Britain or the Commonwealth. Sponsored by the Mail on Sunday.
Annual First prize of £5000; £500 for short-listed entries.
Contact: Sandra Vince
1990   Wittgenstein: The Duty of Genius by Ray Monk
1991   Night Geometry and the Garscadden Trains by A L Kennedy
1992   Sweet Thames by Matthew Kneale
1993   On Foot to the Golden Horn: A Walk to Istanbul by Jason Goodwin
1994   What a Carve Up! by Jonathan Coe
1995   Motel Nirvana by Melanie McGarth
1996   Heading Inland by Nicola Barker
1997   Eclipse of the Sun by Phil Whitaker

Marsh Award for Children's Literature in Translation
Authors' Club
40 Dover Street
London W1X 3RB,
England
Sponsored by the Marsh Christian Trust to encourage the translation of foreign children's books into English. Awarded biennially, starting in 1996, to British translators of books for 4-16 year olds, published in the UK by a British publisher. No encyclopaedias, reference works or electronic books.
Prize £750.
Contact: Ann Carter, Secretary
1996   Anthea Bell for A Dog's Life by Christine Nöstlinger

Marsh Biography Award
(formerly Marsh Christian Trust Award)
Authors' Club
40 Dover Street
London W1X 3RB
England
Awarded biennialy for a significant biography by a British author, published in the UK in the two years prior to the prize. Nominations

submitted by publishers.
Prize: £3500 plus a silver trophy.
Contact: Ann Carter, Secretary
1991   Clever Hearts: The Life of Desmond and Molly MacCarthy by Hugh and Mirabel Cecil
1993   The Man Who Wasn't Maigret by Patrick Marnham
1995   Evelyn Waugh by Lady Selina Hastings

Lenore Marshall Poetry Prize
Academy of American Poets
584 Broadway, Suite 1208
New York, NY 10012
USA
Recognizes the most outstanding book of poetry published in the US in the previous year. Publishers are invited to submit books.
Annual prize of $10,000.
1975   O/I by Cid Corman
1976   The Freeing of the Dust by Denise Levertov
1977   The Names of the Lost by Philip Levine
1978   Collected Poems, 1919-1976 by Allen Tate
1979   Brothers, I Loved You All by Hayden Carruth
1980   The Poems of Stanley Kunitz,1928-1978 by Stanley Kunitz
1981   The Collected Poems of Sterling A Brown by Sterling A Brown
1982   The Bridge of Change: Poems 1974-1980 by John Logan
1983   The Argot Merchant Disaster by George Starbuck
1984   Collected Poems, 1930-83 by Josephine Miles
1985   A Wave by John Ashbery
1986   New Selected Poems by Howard Moss
1987   The Happy Man by Donald Hall
1988   The Sisters: New and Selected Poems by Josephine Jacobsen
1989   Selected Poems, 1938-1988 by Thomas McGrath
1990   God Hunger by Michael Ryan
1991   New Poems, 1980-1988 by John Haines
1992   An Atlas of the Difficult World by Adrienne Rich
1993   The Man with Night Sweats by Thom Gunn
1994   Travels by W S Merwin
1995   Winter Numbers by Marilyn Hacker
1996   Chickamauga by Charles Wright
1997   The Figured Wheel: New and Collected Poems 1966-1996 by Robert Pinsky
1998   Questions for Ecclesiastes by Mark Jarman

Kurt Maschler Award
Book Trust
Book House, 45 East Hill
London SW18 2QZ
England
Annual award for works of excellence in the field of illustrated children's literature. Books must be published in the UK, and the author must be British or have been resident in the UK for ten years.
Prize: £1000 and a bronze 'Emil' statuette.
Contact: Sandra Vince
1996   Drop Dead by Babette Cole
1997   Lady Muck by William Mayne
1998   Voices in the park by Anthony Browne

Somerset Maugham Awards
Somerset Maugham Trust Fund
Society of Authors
84 Drayton Gardens
London SW10 9SB
England
Awarded to a writer on the strength of a published work.
Prize: £5000 each to be used for foreign travel.
1990   Our Grandmothers' Drums by Mark Hudson
        The Automatic Man by Sam North
        The Vision of Elena Silves by Nicholas Shakespeare
1991   The Other Occupant by Peter Benson
        Honour Thy Father by Lesley Glaister
        Four Bare Legs in a Bed by Helen Simpson
1992   But Beautiful by Geoff Dyer
        Lempriere's Dictionary by Lawrence Norfolk
        Householder by Gerard Woodward
1993   Jella by Dea Birkett
        Bucket of Tongues by Duncan McLean
        Out of the Rain by Glyn Maxwell
1994   Other Lovers by Jackie Kay
        Looking for the Impossible Dance by A L Kennedy
        The Crossing Place by Philip Marsden

1995   Younghusband by Patrick French
       The End of Innocence by Simon Garfield
       The Queen of Sheba by Kathleen Jamie
       The Dogs by Laura Thompson
1996   Truffle Beds by Katherine Pierpoint
       Morven Callar by Alan Warner
1997   The Testimony of Taliesin Jones by Rhidian Brook
       Slattern by Kate Clanchy
       Kitchen Venom by Philip Hensher
       I May Be Some Time by Francis Spufford
1998   The Country Life by Rachel Cusk
       This Bloody Mary by Jonathon Rendall
       The Queen of Whale Cay by Kate Summerscale
       Angry White Pyjamas by Robert Twigger

McColvin Medal

c/o Library Association
7 Ridgmount Street
London WC1E 7AE
England
The winner is chosen from nominations made by Library Association members. A medal is awarded to an outstanding reference book first published in the UK during the preceding year.
1990   William Walton: A Catalogue Second Edition by Stewart Craggs
1991   The Cambridge Encyclopaedia of Ornithology by Michael Brooke and Tim Birkhead
1992   The New Grove Dictionary of Opera by Stanley Sadie (editor)
1993   The Illustrated History of Canal and River Navigation by Edward Peget-Tomlinson
1994   Dictionary of British and Irish Botanists and Horticulturists by Ray Desmond
1995   The Tithe maps of England and Wales by Roger Kain and Richard Oliver
1996   Who's Who 1897-1996 on CD/ROM by Christine Ruge-Cope and Roger Tritton
1997   Ancestral Trails by Mark D. Herber

McKitterick Prize

Society of Authors
84 Drayton Gardens
London SW10 9SB
England
Annual award for a full-length work written in English and first published in the UK or previously unpublished. Open to writers over 40 who have had no previous work published other than that submitted.
Prize: £5000.
1990   Chimera by Simon Mawer
1991   A Summer to Halo by John Loveday
1992   News From a Foreign Country Came by Alberto Manguel
1993   The Tap Dancer by Andrew Barrow
1994   Zennor in Darkness by Helen Dunmore
1995   Hester by Christopher Bigsby
1996   Gagarin and I by Stephen Blanchard
1997   Hallucinating Foucault by Patricia Duncker
1998   The Boy Who Went Away by Eli Gottlieb

Walter McRae Russell Award

Association for the Study of Australian Literature Ltd
Department of English
University College, ADFA
Campbell, Australian Capital Territory 2600
Australia
Contact: Susan Lever
Awarded for an outstanding work of literary scholarship by a young or unestablished author. No nominations are required.
Prize: $1000.
1990   Black Words, White Page by Adam Shoemaker
1991   The Folly of Spring : A Study of the Poetry of John Shaw Neilson by Cliff Hanna
1992   The Life and Opinions of Tom Collins by Julian Croft
1993   The Sea Coast of Bohemia by Peter Kirkpatrick
1994   Christina Stead by Hazel Rowley
1995   The Scandalous Penton by Patrick Buckridge
1996   In Search of Steele Rudd by Richard Fotheringham
1997   The Lie of the Land by Paul Carter
1998   A Career in Writing: Judah Water and the Cultural Politics of a Literary Career by David Carter

Meyer-Whitworth Award

Drama Department, Arts Council of England
14 Great Peter Street
London SW1P 3NQ
England
Established to commemorate the Shakespeare Memorial National Theatre Committee of 1908, where the movement for a National Theatre joined forces with the movement to create a monument to William Shakespeare. Awarded to a playwright whose work displays promise of new talent, whose writing is of individual quality and whose work "reveals the truth about the relationships
of human beings with each other and the world at large" (Geoffrey Whitworth).
Plays must be written in English and have been produced in the UK in the previous 12 months.
Contact: John Johnston

Milner Award

The Friends of the Atlanta Fulton Public Library
One Margaret Mitchell Square
Atlanta, GA 30303
USA
Award to a living American author of children's books.
The winning author is awarded a specially commissioned work of the internationally famous glass sculptor, Hans Frabel, and a $1000 honorarium.

Mitchell Prize for Art History / Eric Mitchell Prize

c/o The Burlington Magazine
14-16 Duke's Road
London WC1H 9AD
England
The Mitchell Prize is awarded for an outstanding and original contribution to the understanding of the visual arts, and the Eric Mitchell Prize is given for the best first book in this field. Books must be written in English, and published in the previous twelve months.
Prizes: Mitchell Prize for Art History: $15,000; Eric Mitchell Prize: $5000.
Contact: Caroline Elam, Executive Director
Mitchell Prize for Art History
1995   Colour and Culture by John Gage
1996   Roubiliac and the Eighteenth Century Monument: Sculpture As Theatre by David Bindman and Malcolm Baker
1997   Nicolas Poussin, Friendship and the Love of Painting by Elizabeth Cropper and Charles Dempsey
1998   Rubens's Subjects from History: Corpus Rubencanum Ludwig Burchard XIII by Elizabeth McGrath
Eric Mitchell Prize
1995   Fra Angelico at San Marco by William Hood
1996   Giorgio Vasari: Art and History by Patricia Lee Rubin
1997   The Triumph of Vulcan - Sculptors' Tools, Porphyry and the Prince in Ducal Florence by Susan Brown Butters
1998   Thomas Eakins Rediscovered by Kathleen Foster
       The Sculptures of Verrochio by Andrew Butterfield

National Book Awards

NBA Foundation
260 Fifth Avenue, 4th Floor
New York, NY 10001
USA
Award given annually to living American writers of books published in the USA. Categories for fiction, non-fiction and poetry.
Annual first prize of $10,000 and $1000 for short-listed works.
Contact: Executive Director
1990   Middle Passage by Charles Johnson
       The House of Morgan by Ron Chernow
1991   Mating by Norman Rush
       Freedom by Orlando Patterson
       What Work is by Philip Levine
1992   All the Pretty Horses by Cormac McCarthy
       Becoming A Man by Paul Monette
       New and Selected Poems by Mary Oliver
1993   The Shipping News by E Annie Proulx
       United States: Essays 1952-1992 by Gore Vidal
       Garbage by A R Ammons
1994   A Frolic of His Own by William Gaddis
       Worshipful Company of Fletchers by James Tate
       How We Die by Sherwin B Nuland
1995   Sabbath's Theatre by Philip Roth
       Passing Through by Stanley Kunitz
1996   Ship Fever and Other Stories by Andrea Barrett

An American Requiem: God, My Father and the War That Came Between Us by James Carroll
Scrambled Eggs and Whiskey: Poems, 1991-1995 by Hayden Carruth

1997 Cold Mountain by Charles Frazier
Effort at Speech: New and Selected Poems by William Meredith
American Sphinx: The Character of Thomas Jefferson by Joseph Ellis

1998 Charming Billy by Alice McDermott
This Time: New and Selected Poems by Gerald Stern

National Book Critics Circle Awards
400 North Broad Street
Philadelphia, PA 19103
USA
For excellence in biography/autobiography, criticism, fiction, general nonfiction and poetry published for the first time during the previous year by American writers.
Annual scroll and citations.

1990 Bitter Angel by Amy Gerstler
The Content of Our Character by Shelby Steele
Encounters and Reflections by Arthur Danto
Means of Ascent by Robert Caro
Rabbit at Rest by John Updike
Transparent Gestures by Rodney Jones

1993 All the Pretty Horses by Cormack McCarthy
Young Men and Fire by Norman Maclean
Collected Poems, 1946-91 by Hayden Carruth
Lincoln at Gettysburg by Gary Wills
Writing Dangerously: Mary McCarthy and Carol Brightman

1994 Opera in America by John Dizikes
Genet by Edmund White
My Alexandria by Mark Doty
A Lesson Before Dying by Ernest J Gaines
The Land Where the Blues Began by Alan Lomax

1995 The Stone Diaries by Carol Shields
Third The Rape of Europe: The Fate of Europe's Treasures in the Reich and the Second World War by Lunn H Nicholas
and The Culture of Bruising: Essays on Prizefighting, Literature Modern American Culture by Gerald Early
Shot in the Heart by Mikal Gilmore
Rider by Mark Rudman

1996 Women in Their Beds by Gina Berriault
Angela's Ashes by Frank McCourt
Bad Land: An American Romance by Jonathan Raban
Finding a Form by William Gass
Sun Under Wood by Robert Hass

1997 Ernie Pyle's War: America's Eyewitness to World War II by James Tobin
Making Waves by Mario Vargas Liosa
The Blue Flower by Penelope Fitzgerald
The Spirit Catches You and You Fall Down by Anne Fadiman
Black Zodiac by Charles Wright

National Poetry Competition
Poetry Society,
22 Betterton Street,
London WC2H 9BU
England
Prizes awarded for an unpublished poem of less than 40 lines by anyone over the age of 16.
Prizes: £3000 (1st); £500 (2nd); £250 (3rd); plus smaller prizes.

NCR Book Award for Non-Fiction
NCR Limited
206 Marylebone Road
London NW1 6LY
England
The UK's major prize for non-fiction was first awarded in 1988, and is open to books published between 1st April and 31st March, prizes being awarded in May. Books must be written in English by citizens of the UK, Republic of Ireland or the Commonwealth, and published in the UK.
Total prize money of £37,500.
Contact: Awards Administrator.
1990 Citizens by Simon Schama
1991 The Invisible Woman by Claire Tomalin
1992 Wild Swans by Jung Chang
1993 Never Again: Britain 1945-1951 by Peter Hennessy
1994 Edward Heath: A Biography by John Campbell

1995 Coming Back Brockens by Mark Hudson
1996 The Railway Man by Eric Lomax
1997 A People's Tragedy by Orlando Figes

Neustadt International Prize for Literature
World Literature Today
University of Oklahoma
110 Monnet Hall

Norman, OK 73019
USA
Recognizes outstanding achievement in fiction, poetry, or drama written in any language. Awarded only to a living author who has a representative portion of work in English, French and/or Spanish. No applications are accepted.
Biennial prize of $40,000, a replica of an eagle feather cast in silver and a special award certificate.
1970 Giuseppe Ungaretti
1972 Gabriel García Márquez
1974 Francis Ponge
1976 Elizabeth Bishop
1978 Czesław Miłosz
1980 Josef Škvorecký
1982 Octavio Paz
1984 Paavo Haavikko
1986 Max Frisch
1988 Raja Rao
1990 Tomas Tranströmer
1992 João Cabral de Melo Neto
1994 Kamau Brathwaite
1996 Assia Djebar
1998 Nuruddin Farah

New Venture Award
Women in Publishing
12 Dyott Street
London WC1A 1DF
England
Contact: Sheila Davies
1996 Rosemary Meleady, Big Issues
1997 Sue O' Sullivan, publisher of ICW
1998 Bronwen Jones, Ithemba

John Newbery Medal
American Library Association
50 East Huron Street
Chicago, IL 70711
USA
To the author of the most distinguished contribution to American literature for children published during the preceding year.
Annual award: bronze medal.
Contact: The Administrator
1990 Number the Stars by Lois Lowry
1991 Maniac Magee by Terry Spinelli
1992 Shiloh by Phyllis Reynolds Naylor
1993 Missing May by Cynthia Rylant
1994 The Giver by Lois Lowry
1995 Walk Two Moons by Sharon Creech
1996 The Midwife's Apprentice by Karen Cushman
1997 The View from Saturday by E. L. Konigsburg
1998 Out of Dust by Karen Hesse
1999 Holes by Louis Sachar

Nobel Prize for Literature
Swedish Academy
Box 5232, Sturegatan 14
S-10245 Stockholm
Sweden
One of several celebrated prizes for outstanding achievement in various fields, founded by the chemist Alfred Nobel. The prize in the field of literature has been awarded annually since 1901 in recognition of the literary merit of a distinguished writer in world letters. Nominations are not generally accepted, as strict eligibilty controls apply. The current value of the prize is US $1,120,000 (increasing each year to cover inflation).
1901 René-François-Armand Sully Prudhomme
1902 Theodor Mommsen
1903 Bjørnstjerne Bjørnson
1904 José Echegaray and Frédéric Mistral
1905 Henryk Sienkiewicz

1906	Giosué Carducci
1907	Rudyard Kipling
1908	Rudolf Eucken
1909	Selma Lagerlöf
1910	Paul Heyse
1911	Maurice Maeterlinck
1912	Gerhart Hauptmann
1913	Rabindranath Tagore
1914	No award given
1915	Romain Rolland
1916	Verner von Heidenstam
1917	Karl Kjellerup and Henrik Pontoppidan
1918	No award given
1919	Carl Spitteler
1920	Knut Hamsun
1921	Anatole France
1922	Jacinto Benavente y Martínez
1923	W B Yeats
1924	Władysław Reymont
1925	G B Shaw
1926	Grazia Deledda
1927	Henri Bergson
1928	Sigrid Undset
1929	Thomas Mann
1930	Sinclair Lewis
1931	Erik Axel Karlfeldt
1932	John Galsworthy
1933	Ivan Bunin
1934	Luigi Pirandello
1935	No award given
1936	Eugene O'Neill
1937	Roger Martin du Gard
1938	Pearl S Buck
1939	F E Sillianpää
1940-43	No award given
1944	Johannes V Jensen
1945	Gabriela Mistral
1946	Hermann Hesse
1947	André Gide
1948	T S Eliot
1949	William Faulkner
1950	Bertrand Russell
1951	Pär Lagerkvist
1952	François Mauriac
1953	Sir Winston Churchill
1954	Ernest Hemingway
1955	Halldór Laxness
1956	Juan Ramón Jiménez
1957	Albert Camus
1958	Boris Pasternak
1959	Salvatore Quasimodo
1960	Saint-John Perse
1961	Ivo Andric
1962	John Steinbeck
1963	Georgios Seferiades
1964	Jean-Paul Sartre
1965	Mikhail Sholokhov
1966	S Y Agnon and Nelly Sachs
1967	Miguel Angel Asturias
1968	Yasunari Kawabata
1969	Samuel Beckett
1970	Aleksandr Solzhenitsyn
1971	Pablo Neruda
1972	Heinrich Böll
1973	Patrick White
1974	Eyvind Johnson and Harry Martinson
1975	Eugenio Montale
1976	Saul Bellow
1977	Vicente Aleixandre
1978	Isaac Bashevis Singer
1979	Odysseus Elytis
1980	Czesław Miłosz
1981	Elias Canetti
1982	Gabriel García Márquez
1983	William Golding
1984	Jaroslav Seifert
1985	Claude Simon
1986	Wole Soyinka
1987	Joseph Brodsky
1988	Naguib Mahfūz

1989	Camilo José Cela
1990	Octavio Paz
1991	Nadine Gordimer
1992	Derek Walcott
1993	Toni Morrison
1994	Kenzaburō Ōe
1995	Seamus Heaney
1996	Wisława Szymborska
1997	Dario Fo
1998	José Saramago

Orange Prize For Fiction
Book Trust
Book House, 45 East Hill
London SW18 2QZ
England
Established in 1996, this annual award was founded by leading women in the publishing industry to help promote and reward women writers. Full-length novels written in English by women of any nationality between 1st April and 31st March are eligible.
Prize: £30,000, and limited edition bronze figurine known as the 'Bessie'.
Contact: Sandra Vince

1996	A Spell of Winter by Helen Dunmore
1997	Fugitive Pieces by Anne Michaels
1998	Larry's Party by Carol Shields

Pandora Award
Women in Publishing
12 Dyott Street
London WC1A 1DF
England
Contact: Sheila Davies

1996	Dr Anita Miller, Academy Chicago Publishers
1997	Fay Weldon
1998	Philippa Harrison, Publishers Association and Little, Brown

Francis Parkman Prize
Society of American Historians
Affiliate of Columbia University
603 Fayerweather Hall
New York, NY 10027
USA

PEN/Faulkner Award for Fiction
Folger Shakespeare Library
201 East Capitol Street South East
Washington, DC 20003
USA

A A Phillips Prize
Association for the Study of Australian Literature Ltd
Department of English
University College, ADFA
Campbell, Australian Capital Territory 2600
Australia
Contact: Susan Lever
Awarded from time to time for a work of outstanding achievement in the field of Australian literary scholarship.

1992	Laurie Hergenham for services to Australian literature as editor of Australian Literary Studies
1995	Judith Wright for her career as poet, critic and activist.
1996	Katharine Brisbane for her career as writer and publisher on Australian theatre and drama, especially for A Companion to Theatre in Australia.
1998	Clem Christesen for services to Australian Literature, particularly through Meanjin.

Edgar Allan Poe Awards
Mystery Writers of America
174 East 47th Street
New York, NY 10017
USA

Prix Goncourt
18 Place Gaillon,
75002 Paris
France

1990	Les Champs d'Honneur by Jean Rouaud
1991	Les Filles du Calvaire by Pierre Combescot
1992	Texaco by Patrick Chamoiseau

1993 Le Rocher de Tanios by Amin Maalouf
1994 Un Aller Simple by Didier Van Caulwelaert
1995 Le Testament Français by Andreï Makine
1996 Le Chasseur Zéro by Pascale Roze
1997 La Bataille by Patrick Rambaud
1998 Confidence pour Confidence by Paul Constant

Pulitzer Prizes
Pulitzer Prize Board
Columbia University
New York, NY 10027
USA
21 prizes in total for newspaper journalism, literature, music and drama -
for some of the prizes entrants must be an American citizen.
Annual prize of $5000.
Contact: The Administrator
Fiction
1990 The Mambo Kings Play Songs of Love by Oscar Hijuelos
1991 Rabbit at Rest by John Updike
1992 A Thousand Acres by Jane Smiley
1993 A Good Scent From a Strange Mountain by Robert Olen Butler
1994 The Shipping News by E Annie Proulx
1995 The Stone Diaries by Carol Shields
1996 Independence Day by Richard Ford
1997 Martin Dressler by Stephen Millhauser
1998 American Pastoral by Philip Roth
Drama
1990 The Piano Lesson by August Wilson
1991 Lost in Yonkers by Neil Simon
1992 The Kentucky Cycle: Millenium Approaches by Robert Schenkkan
1993 Angels in America by Tony Kushner
1994 Three Tall Women by Edward Albee
1995 The Young Man from Atlanta by Shelby Foote
1996 Rent by Jonathan Larson
1998 How I Learned to Drive by Paula Vogel
History
1990 In Our Image: America's Empire in the Philippines by Stanley Karnow
1991 A Midwife's Tale: The Life of Martha Ballard, Based on Her
Diary, 1785-1812 by Laurel Thatcher Ulrich
1992 The Fate of Liberty: Abraham Lincoln and Civil Liberties by Mark E Neely Jr
1993 The Radicalism of the American Revolution by Gordon S Wood
1994 No prize given
1995 No Ordinary Time: Franklin and Eleanor Roosevelt: The Home Front in World War II by Doris Kearns Goodwin
1996 William Cooper's Town: Power and Persuasion on the Frontier of the Early American Republic by Alan Taylor
1997 Original Meanings: Politics and Ideas in the Making of the Constitution by Jack N Rakove
1998 Summer for the Gods: The Scopes Trial and America's Continuing Debate Over Science and Religion by Edward Frank McCourt
Biography
1990 Machiavelli in Hell by Sebastian de Grazia
1991 Jackson Pollock: An American Saga by Steven Naifeh and Gregory White Smith
1992 Fortunate Son: The Healing of a Vietnam Vet by Lewis B Puller Jr
1993 Truman by David McCullough
1994 W E B Du Bois: Biography of a Race, 1868-1919 by David Levering Lewis
1995 Harriet Beecher Stowe: A Life by Joan D Hedrick
1996 God: A Biography by Jack Miles
1998 Personal History by Katherine Graham
Poetry
1990 The World Doesn't End by Charles Simic
1991 Near Changes by Mona Van Duyn
1992 Selected Poems by James Tate
1993 The Wild Iris by Louise Glück
1994 Neon Vernacular by Yusef Komunyakaa
1995 Simple Truth by Philip Levine
1996 The Dream of the Unified Field by Jorie Graham
1997 Alive Together: New and Selected Poems by Lisel Mueller
1998 Black Zodiac by Charles Wright
General Non-fiction
1990 And Their Children After Them by Dale Maharidge
1991 The Ants by Bert Holldobler and Edward O Wilson

1992 The Prize: The Epic Quest for Oil, Money and Power by Daniel Yergin
1993 Lincoln at Gettysburg by Garry Wills
1994 Lenin's Tomb: The Last Days of the Soviet Empire by David Remnick
1995 The Beak of the Finch: A Story of Evolution in Our Time by Jonathan Weiner
1996 The Haunted Land: Facing Europe's Ghosts After Communism by Tina Rosenberg
1997 Ashes to Ashes: America's Hundred-Year Cigarette War, the Public Health, and the Unabashed Triumph of Philip Morris by Richard Kluger
1998 Guns, Germs and Steel: The Fates of Human Societies by Jared Diamond

Pushcart Prize: Best of the Small Presses
Pushcart Press
Box 380
Wainscott, NY 11975
USA
Annual award for work published by a small press or literary journal.

Queen's Presentation Medals - Poetry
Buckingham Palace
London,
England
The Medal is given for a book of verse published in the English language, but translations of exceptional merit may be considered. It was originally awarded only to British citizens but the scope was widened in 1985 to make Her Majesty's subjects in Commonwealth Monarchies eligible for consideration.
Award: Gold Medal.

Raiziss/de Palchi Translation Award
Academy of American Poets
584 Broadway, Suite 1208
New York, NY 10012
USA
Recognizes outstanding translations of modern Italian poetry into English. A $5000 book prize is awarded and a $20,000 fellowship is awarded with the winner of the latter receiving a residency at the American Academy in Rome. No applications are accepted for the book prize. Submissions for the fellowship are accepted in odd-numbered years.
Fellowship
1996 Anthony Molino for Esercizi di tipologia by Valerio Magrelli
1998 Geoffrey Brock for Poesie del disamore by Cesare Pavese
Book Prize
1996 W S Di Piero for This Strange Joy: Selected Poems of Sandro Penna
1997 Michael Palma for The Man I Pretend to Be: The Colloquies and Selected Poems of Guido Gozzano

Rhea Award for the Short Story
Dungannon Foundation
131 East 66th Street
New York, NY 10021
USA

Rhône-Poulenc Prize for Science Books
c/o The Royal Society
6 Carlton House Terrace
London SW1Y 5AG
England
Awarded to the authors of popular non-fiction, science and technology books, written in English and which are judged to contribute most to the public understanding of science.
Prize: Rhône-Poulenc Prize £10,000; Junior Prize £10,000.
Contact: Imelda M. Topping
1990 The Emperor's New Mind by Roger Penrose
1991 Wonderful Life by Stephen Jay Gould
Cells Are Us by Fran Balkwill and Mic Rolph
Cell Wars by Fran Balkwill and Mic Rolph
1992 The Rise and Fall of the Third Chimpanzee by Jared Diamond
The Amazing Voyage of the Cucumber Sandwich by Peter Rowan
How Nature Works by David Burnie
1993 The Making of Memory by Steven Rose
Mighty Microbes by Thompson Yardley
1994 The Language of the Genes by Steve Jones

Eyewitness Guide: Evolution by Linda Gamlin
Science with Weather by Rebecca Heddle and Paul Shipton
The Ultimate Dinosaur Book by David Lambert
1995   The Consumer's Good Chemical Guide by John Emsley
The Most Amazing Pop-Up Science Book by Jay Young
1996   Plague's Progress by Arno Karlen
The World of Weather by Chris Maynard
1997   The Wisdom of the Bones by Alan Walker and Pat Shipman
Blood, Bones and Body Bits/Ugly Bugs by Nick Arnold and Tony de Saulles
1998   Guns, Germs and Steel by Jared Diamond
The Kingfisher Book of Oceans by David Lambert

Romantic Novelists' Association
3 Arnesby Lane, Peatling Magna
Leicester LE8 5UN
England
Major Award
Awared for the best romantic novel of the year, published betwqeen specifc dates set each year by the RNA. Open to non-members, but authors must be based in the UK.
Prize of £5000.
Contact: Jean Chapman, Organiser
1990   Passing Glory by Reay Tannahill
1991   Phantom by Susan Kay
1992   Sandstorm by June Knox-Mawer
1993   Emily by Cynthia Harrod-Eagles
1994   Consider the Lily by Elizabeth Buchan
1995   A Change of Heart by Charlotte Bingham
1996   Coming Home by Rosamunde Pilcher
1997   The Hours of the Night by Sue Gee
1998   Kiss and Kin by Angela Lambert

Romantic Novelists Association New Writers Award
Romantic Novelists Association
Cobble Cottage, 129 New Street
Baddesley Ensor, nr Atherstone
Warwickshire CV9 2DL
England
Awarded for unpublished writers in the field of the romantic novel. Manuscripts submitted for this prize must be specifically entered for it.
Contact: Joyce Bell, Secretary

Rooney Prize for Irish Literature
Strathlin, Templecarrig
Delgany, County Wicklow
Republic of Ireland
A non-competitive prize to reward and encourage young Irish talent. Writers must be Irish, under 40 years of age, and their work must be written in Irish or English. No applications are accepted - recipients are chosen by a panel of judges. Special awards are given on rare occasions where deemed of merit.
Prize: £5000.
Contact: Barbara Norman
Rooney Prize for Irish Literature
1990   Mary Dorcey
1991   Anne Enright
1992   Hugo Hamilton
1993   Gerard Fanning
1994   Colum McCAnn
1995   Philip MacCann
1996   Mike McCormack
1997   Anne Haverty
1998   David Wheatley
Special Awards
1995   Vona Groarke and Conor O'Callaghan

Royal Society of Literature Award Under the W H Heinemann Bequest
Royal Society of Literature
1 Hyde Park Gardens
London W2 2LT
England
Up to three awards given annually to encourage genuine contributions to literature. Awarded for any kind of literary works, written in English and published in the previous year and submitted by publishers.
Prize: £5000.
Contact: The Secretary

1990   Ford Madox by Alan Judd
1991   Available for Dreams by Roy Fuller
Short Afternoons by Kit Wright
1992   Goethe: The Spirit and the Age by Nicholas Boyle
1993   Shylock by John Gross
1994   The Civilisation of Europe in the Renaissance by John Hale
1995   Young Husband by Patrick French
Give Me Your Hand by Paul Durcan
The Handless Maiden by Vicky Feaver
1996   Angela's Ashes by Frank McCourt
1997   Victor Hugo by Graham Robb

Sagittarius Prize
Society of Authors
84 Drayton Gardens
London SW10 9SB
England
Established in 1990, and awarded for first published novels by authors over the age of 60.
Prize: £2000.
1991   The Sea Has Many Voices by Judith Hubback
1992   Parnell and the English by Hugh Leonard
1993   The Strange Case of Mademoiselle P by Brian O'Doherty
1994   Red Branch by G B Hummer
1995   Gravity is Getting Me Down by Fred Plisner
1996   As Luck Would Have It by Samuel Lock
1997   London Lovers by Barbara Hardy
1998   When Memory Dies by A Sivanandan

Saltire Society / Scotsman Scottish Literary Awards
9 Fountain Close, 22 High Street
Edinburgh EH1 1TF
Scotland
Established in 1982, the Scottish Book of the Year award is open to authors of Scottish descent or those living in Scotland, or for a book which deals with a Scottish topic. Books published between 1st September and 31st August are eligible. Since 1988, the award has been extended to include a prize for a first published work.
Prize: Scottish Book of the Year £5000; First Book of the Year, £1500.
Contact: Mrs Kathleen Munro, Administrator
Scottish Book of the Year
1990   From Wood to Ridge by Sorley MacLean
1991   Scottish Art: 1460-1990 by Duncan MacMillan
1992   Collected Poems by Iain Crichton Smith
1993   Robert Burns: A Biography by James Mackay
1994   Beside the Ocean of Time by George Mackay Brown
1995   The Black Sea by Neal Ascherson (joint winner)
So I Am Glad by A L Kennedy (joint winner)
1996   The Kiln by William McIlvanney
1997   Grace Notes by Bernard MacLaverty
1998   The Sopranos by Alan Warner
First Book
1990   The Ballad of Sawney Bain by Harry Tait
1991   Night Geometry and the Garscadden Trains by AL Kennedy
1992   The Adoption Papers by Jackie Kay (joint winner)
Uirsgeul: Myth by Crisdean Whyte (joint winner)
1993   Dreams of Exile (A Life of R L Stevenson) by Ian Bell
1994   Music in a Foreign Language by Andrew Crumey
1995   Free Love by Ali Smith
1996   Slattern by Kate Clanchy
1997   A Painted Field by Robin Robertson
1998   Two Clocks Ticking by Dennis O'Donnell (joint winner)
The Pied Piper's Poison by Christopher Wallace (joint winner)

Science Fiction and Fantasy Writers of America Nebula Awards
Science Fiction and Fantasy Writers of America
PO Box 1666
Lynwood, WA 98046
USA
Publication during the previous calendar year, and nomination by the SFWA President.
Annual trophy.

Scottish Arts Council Book Awards
c/o Scottish Arts Council
12 Manor Place
Edinburgh EH3 7DD
Scotland
A number of book awards are given in Spring and Autumn to new and established authors in recognition of high standards of writing. Authors

should be Scottish, resident in Scotland or have written works of Scottish interest. Applications from publishers only.
Contact: Literature Officer.

Smarties Book Prize
Book Trust
Book House, 45 East Hill
London SW18 2QZ
England
Award given for a children's book written in English by a citizen of the UK, or an author resident in the UK, and published in the UK in the year ending 31 October.
Formerly, an annual prize for overall winner and lesser prizes for catagory winners; Prizes awarded are currently £2500 (Gold), £1000 (Silver) and £500 (Bronze) in the three categories, with no overall winner.
Contact: Sandra Vince

1990	*9-11 years category and overall winner* Midnight Blue by Pauline Fisk *6-8 years category* Esio Trot by Roald Dahl *5 years and under category* Six Dinner Sid by Inga Moore
1991	*5 years and under category and overall winner* Farmer Duck by Martin Waddell and Helen Oxonbury *9-11 years category* Krindle Krax by Philip Ridley *6-8 years category* Josie Smith and Eileen by Magdaline Nabb
1992	*9-11 years category and overall winner* The Great Elephant Chase by Gillian Cross *6-8 years category* The Story of Creation by Jane Ray *5 years and under category* Nice Work Little Wolf by Hilda Offen
1993	*6-8 years category and overall winner* War Game by Michael Foreman *9-11 years category* Listen to the Dark by Maeve Henry *5 years and under category* Hue Boy by Rita Phillips Mitchell
1994	*9-11 years category and overall winner* The Exiles at Home by Hilary McKay *6-8 years category* Dimanche Diller by Henrietta Branford *5 years and under category* So Much by Trish Cooke and Helen Oxonbury
1995	*9-11 years category (joint winner) and overall winner* Double Act by Jacqueline Wilson *9-11 years category (joint winner)* Weather Eye by Lesley Howarth *5 years and under category* The Last Noo-Noo by Jill Murphy *6-8 years category* Thomas and the Tinners by Jill Paton Walsh
1996	*9-11 years category* Gold Award: The Firework-Maker's Daughter by Philip Pullman Silver Award: Johny and the Bomb by Terry Pratchett Bronze Award: Plundering Paradise by Geraldine McCaughrean *6-8 years category* Gold Award: The Butterfly Lion by Michael Morpurgo Silver Award: Harry the Poisonous Centipede by Lynne Reid Banks Bronze Award: All Because of Jackson by Dick King-Smith *0-5 years category* Gold Award: Oops! by Colin McNaughton Silver Award: The World is Full of BABIES! by Mick Manning and Brita Granstrom Bronze Award: Clown by Quentin Blake
1997	*Under 5 years category* Ginger by Charlotte Voake *6-8 years category* The Owl Tree by Jenny Nimmo and Anthony Lewis *9-11 years category* Harry Potter and the Philosopher's Stone by J K Rowling
1998	*Under 5 years category* Cowboy Baby by Sue Heap

6-8 years category
Las of the Gold Diggers by Harry Horse
9-11 years category
Harry Potter and the Chamber of Secrets by J K Rowling

W H Smith/Books in Canada First Novel Award
130 Spadina Avenue, Suite 603
Toronto, Ontario M5V 2M3
Canada
Prize is awarded for the best Canadian first novel published in English during the calendar year.
Annual prize.

W H Smith Literary Award
W H Smith plc
Audrey House, Ely Place
London EC1N 6SN
England
Presented for an outstanding contribution to English literature in the year under review, to the author of a book written and published in English and published in the UK. Authors considered will be from the UK, Commonwealth and Republic of Ireland, but writers cannot submit work themselves.
Annual award £10,000.
Contact: Tricia Ryan.

1990	A Careless Widow and Other Stories by Sir Victor Pritchett
1991	Omeros by Derek Walcott
1992	The Scramble for Africa by Thomas Pakenham
1993	Daughters of the House by Michèle Roberts
1994	A Suitable Boy by Vikram Seth
1995	Open Secrets by Alice Munro
1996	Landscape and Memory by Simon Schama
1997	A People's Tragedy by Orlando Figes
1998	Tales from Ovid by Ted Hughes

W H Smith Thumping Good Read Award
W H Smith plc
Audrey House, Ely Place
London EC1N 6SN
England
Awarded since 1992. Concentrates on books more "accessible" than "literary". Genre fiction - murder mysteries, espionage thrillers - is considered.
Prize: £5000.

1992	Into the Blue by Robert Goddard
1993	Fatherland by Robert Harris
1994	A Season in Purgatory by Dominick Dunne
1995	St Agnes' Stand by Thomas Eidson
1996	True Crime by Andrew Klavan
1997	Absolute Power by David Baldacci
1998	The Big Picture by Douglas Kennedy

Stand Magazine Short Story Competition
Stand Magazine
179 Wingrove Road
Newcastle upon Tyne NE4 9DA
England
Contact: Linda Goldsmith
Awarded for an original story of no longer than 8000 words written in English. Works must be previously unpublished and unbroadcast.
Prizes: £2500 in total prize money, including £1500 first prize.

Ian St James Awards
c/o The New Writers' Club, PO Box 60
Cranbrook, Kent TN17 2ZR
England
Presented to previously unpublished authors from any country, over the age of eighteen, for fictional short stories.
Prizes: £5,000+ in total; First prize of £2000, forty runners-up are published in The New Writer Magazine.

1990	Mothering Sunday by Annie Hedley A Seeing Lesson by William Walker A Whore's Vengeance by Louise Doughty
1991	Small Beginnings by Faith Addis French Kisses by Alan Dunn Me and Renate by Stephanie Ellyne
1992	Black Sky at Night by Jeremy Cain Good at Things by Francesca Clementis Me and the Stars by Peter Naylor
1993	Berlin Story by Philip Sealey

The Olive Tree by Hilary Waters
Figure of Eight by Min Dinning
Karmic Mothers by Kate Atkinson
Moira Flaherty by Juliet McCarthy
Black Lizzie Black by James Maguire
1994   The Saviour by Joshua Davidson
A is for Axe by Mike McCormack
The Food of Love by Sue Camarados
The Welfare of the Patient by Anna McGrail
Magdalen by Alison Armstrong
The Possibility of Jack by A S Penne
1995   Sweet William is the Scent by Jeanette Allee
Vessel by Heather Doran Barbieri
Barcelona by Jonathan Carr
Expect Jail by Nick Kelly
The Uncle by Maxine Rosaler
Ground No More by Hwee Hwee Tan
1996   Algebra by Josephine Corcoran
Black Water Crossing by Indira Debah
Losing Track by Tobias Hill
Constance and Louise by Beverley Strauss
Wedding Day by Julia Widdows
1997   Barbara Carnegie
Kevin Doyle
Jean Edmunds
David Evans
Michael Faber
Stephanie Hale
Deidre Heddon
Wendy McKechnie
Marc Williamson
Mick Wood
1998   Michael Barclay
Lucinda Bowles
Madeleine Dahlem
Lindsay Hawdon
Ann Jolly
Aoi Matsushima
Karen Munro
Amanda Oosthuizen
Barbara Villanova
Frances Watt

Sunday Times Award for Literary Excellence
The Sunday Times
1 Pennington Street
London E1 9XW
England
Established in 1987 and presented annually to fiction and non-fiction
writers. Winners are chosen by a panel of judges consisting of Sunday
Times writers, publishers and other leading figures from the publishing
industry, and awarded at the discretion of the Literary Editor.
Award: Inscribed silver trophy.
Contact: Geordie Grieg, Literary Editor

Tanning Prize
Academy of American Poets
584 Broadway, Suite 1208
New York, NY 10012
USA
Recognizes outstanding and proven mastery in the art of poetry. No
applications are accepted.
Annual prize of $100,000.
1994   W S Merwin
1995   James Tate
1996   Adrienne Rich
1997   Anthony Hecht
1998   A R Ammons

Tom-Gallon Award
Society of Authors
84 Drayton Gardens
London SW10 9SB
England
A biennial award for writers of limited means who have had at least one
short story published.
Prize: £500.
1990   Sister Monica's Last Journey by Richard Austin
1992   Reading the Signals by David Callard

1994   A Good Place To Die by Janice Fox
1996   Packing for Wednesday by Leo Madigan

Translators Association Translation Prizes
The Translators Association
84 Drayton Gardens
London SW10 9SB
England
Contact: Kate Pool
John Florio Prize (Italian-English)
Awarded biennially for the best translation of a full-length Twentieth-
Century Italian literary work into English, published by a British publisher.
Prize: £1000.
Scott Moncrieff Prize (French-English)
Awarded annually for the best translation into English of a full-length
French literary work originally published in the last 150 years, published
by a British publisher in the preceding year.
Prize: £1000.
Teixeira-Gomes Prize (Portuguese-English)
Triennial prize for translations of works from any period by a Portuguese
national. Short stories and poems are eligible.The prize is also open to
unpublished translations of works of Portuguese nationals.
Prize: £1000.
Schlegel-Tieck Prize (German-English)
Annual award for the best translation of a full-length Twentieth-Century
German literary work, published by a British publisher during the
previous year.
Prize: £2200.
Bernard Shaw Prize (Swedish-English)
Triennial award funded by the Anglo-Swedish Literary Foundation for the
best translation into English of a full-length Swedish work, published in
the UK in the three years prior to the award.
Prize: £1000.
Premio Valle Inclán (Spanish-English)
A new prize for the best translation of a full-length Spanish work from
any period, published in the UK in the preceding 5 years.
Prize: £1000. . .
Vondel Translation Prize (Dutch/Flemish- English)
Due to be first awarded in 1999 for the best translation of a Dutch or
Flemish literary work into English. Translations should have been
published in the UK or US during 1996-98.
Greek and Japanese translation prizes are currently under discussion.

Betty Trask Prize and Awards
Society of Authors
84 Drayton Gardens
London SW10 9SB
England
Awards are for authors under 35 and commonwealth citizens for a first
novel of a traditional or romantic nature.
Annual prize of £25,000 (shared).
1990   Ripley Bogle by Robert McLiam Wilson
The Wild Hunt by Elizabeth Chadwick
No Strange Land by Rosemary Cohen
The Vision of Elena Silves by Nicholas Shakespeare
1991   A Strange and Sublime Address by Amit Chaudhuri
Teaching Little Fang by Mark Swallow
Quite Contrary by Suzannah Dunn
Honour Thy Father by Lesley Glaister
Lives of the Saints by Nino Ricci
1992   The Dream Stone by Liane Jones
Kissing Through a Pane of Glass by Peter M Rosenberg
Under the Frog by Tibor Fisher
The Last of His Line by Eugene Mullen
Never Mind by Edward St Aubyn
1993   You'll Never Be Here Again by Mark Blackaby (unpublished)
Pig by Andres Cowan (unpublished)
Tommy Was Here by Simon Corrigan
Mothers and Other Lovers by Joanna Briscoe (unpublished)
Landing on Clouds by Olivia Fane (unpublished)
1994   Divorcing Jack by Colin Bateman
Season of the Rainbirds by Nadeem Aslam
After the Hole by Guy Burt
The Game by Frances Liardet
Some Hope by Jonathan Rix
1995   Depedence Day by Robert Newman
The Smell of Apples by Mark Behr
Midnight Feast by Martina Evans
A Speck of Coaldust by Robert Manchandra (unpublished)
Halleluja Jordan by Juliet Thomas (unpublished)

	The Latecomer by Philippa Walshe (unpublished)
	The Tennis Party by Madeleine Wickham
1996	The Debt to Pleasure by John Lanchester
	Anita and Me by Meera Syal
	The Testimony of Taliesin Jones by Rhidian Brook
	The Luxury of Exile by Louis Caron Buss
1997	The Beach by Alex Garland
	Poker Face by Josie Barnard
	Beach Boy by Ardashir Fakit
	Some Kind of Black by Diran Abedayo
	Theory of Min by Sanjida O'Connell
1998	Hullabaloo in the Guava Orchard by Kiran Desai
	ZigZag Street by Nick Earls
	Eclipse of the Sun by Phil Whitaker
	The Cure for Death by Lightning by Gail Anderson-Dargatz
	Underground by Tobias Hill (unpublished)

Travelling Scholarship Fund
Society of Authors
84 Drayton Gardens
London SW10 9SB
England
Non-competitive awards enabling British writers to travel abroad
Prize: £6000.

1990	David Caute
	Roy Fisher
	David Hughes
	Robert Nye
1991	Anne Devlin
	Elaine Feinstein
	Iain Sinclair
	Emma Tennant
1993	Jim Crace
	Donald Davie
	Louis de Bernières
1994	Maurice Leitch
	Peter Levi
	Bernard MacLaverty
1995	Peter Benson
	Jenny Joseph
1996	Stewart Conn
	Annette Kobak
	Theo Richmond
1997	William Palmer
	Jo Shapcott
	James Simmons
1998	Dorothy Nimmo
	Dilys Rose
	Paul Sayer

Whitbread Book of the Year and Literary Awards
Booksellers Association
Minster House,
272 Vauxhall Bridge Road
London SW1V 1BA
England
Annual awards established in 1971 to promote and increase good English literature in each of five categories: novel, first novel, biography, children's novel and poetry. Entries are submitted by publishers, and the authors must be residents of Britain or the Republic of Ireland for at least three years. One category winner is then voted Whitbread Book of the Year by the panel of judges.
Prize: £23,000 (Book of the Year); £10,000 (Children's); £2000 (all others).
Contact: Gill Cronin

Novels

1990	Hopeful Monsters by Nicholas Mosley (and Book of the Year)
1991	The Queen of Tambourine by Jane Gardam
1992	Poor Things by Alisdair Gray
1993	Theory of War by Joan Brady (and Book of the Year)
1994	Felicia's Journey by William Trevor (and Book of the Year)
1995	The Moor's Last Sigh by Salman Rushdie
1996	Every Man for Himself by Beryl Bainbridge
1997	Quarantine by Jim Crace
1998	Leading the Cheers by Justin Cartwright

Biography

1990	A A Milne: His Life by Ann Thwaite
1991	A Life of Picasso by John Richardson (and Book of the Year)
1992	Trollope by Victoria Glendinning
1993	Philip Larkin by Andrew Motion

1994	The Married Man: A Life of D H Lawrence by Brenda Maddox
1995	Gladstone by Roy Jenkins
1996	Thomas Cranmer: A Life by Diarmaid MacCulloch
1997	Victor Hugo by Graham Robb
1998	Georgiana, Duchess of Devonshire by Amanda Foreman

Children's Book

1990	AK by Peter Dickinson
1991	Harvey Angell by Diana Hendry
1992	The Great Elephant Chase by Gillian Cross (and Book of the Year)
1993	Flour Babies by Anne Fine
1994	Gold Dust by Geraldine McCaughrean
1995	The Wreck of the Zanzibar by Michael Morpurgo
1996	The Tulip Touch by Anne Fine
1997	Aquila by Andrew Norriss
1998	Skellig by David Almond

First Novel

1990	The Buddha of Suburbia by Hanif Kureishi
1991	Alma Cogan by Gordon Burn
1992	Swing Hammer Swing! by Jeff Torrington
1993	Saving Agnes by Rachel Cusk
1994	The Longest Memory by Fred D'Aguilar
1995	Behind the Scenes at the Museum by Kate Atkinson (and Book of the Year)
1996	The Debt to Pleasure by John Lanchester
1997	The Ventriloquist's Tale by Pauline Melville
1998	The Last King of Scotland

Poetry

1990	Daddy, Daddy by Paul Durcan
1991	Gorse Fires by Michael Longley
1992	The Gaze of the Gorgon by Tony Harrison
1993	Mean Time by Carol Ann Duffy
1994	Out of Danger by James Fenton
1995	Gunpowder by Bernard O'Donoghue
1996	The Spirit Level by Seamus Heaney (and Book of the Year)
1997	Tales from Ovid by Ted Hughes (and Book of the Year)
1998	Birthday Letters by Ted Hughes

Whitfield Prize
Royal Historical Society
University College London
Gower Street
London WC1E 6BT
England
Offered for an author's first book on British history published in the UK in the last three years. The winner is announced at the Royal Historical Society annual reception in July.
Prize: £1000.
Contact: Joy McCarthy

John Whiting Award
Drama Department, Arts Council of England
14 Great Peter Street
London SW1P 3NQ
England
Award was inaugurated in 1965 to commemorate the contribution of playwright John Whiting (member of the Drama Panel of the Arts Council, 1955-63) to British post-war theatre. Writers who have received an award offer from the Arts Council Theatre Writing Scheme are eligible, as are those who have had a commission or première from a theatre company funded by the Arts Council or a Regional Arts Board.
Prize: £6000.
Contact: John Johnston

Whiting Writers' Awards
Mrs Giles Whiting Foundation
1133 Avenue of the Americas
New York, NY 10036
USA
Award to emergent writers in recognition of their writing achievement as well as promise for producing outstanding future work.
Annual award of $30,000.

Fiction

1990	Yannick Murphy
	Lawrence Naumoff
	Mark Richard
	Christopher Tilghman
	Stephen Wright
1991	Rebecca Goldstein
	Allegra Goodman
	John Holman

	Cynthia Kadohata
	Rick Rofihe
	Anton Shammas
1992	R S Jones
	J S Marcus
	Damien Wilkins
1993	Jeffrey Eugenides
	Dagoberto Gilb
	Sigrid Nunez
	Janet Peery
	Lisa Shea
1994	Louis Edwards
	Mary Hood
	Randall Kenan
	Kate Wheeler
1995	Michael Cunningham
	Reginald McKnight
	Matthew Stadler
	Melanie Sumner
1996	Anderson Ferrell
	Cristina Garcia
	Molly Gloss
	Brian Kiteley
	Chris Offutt
	Judy Troy
	A J Verdelle
1997	Melanie Rae Thon
	Suketu Mehta
	Josip Novakovich
1998	Michael Byers
	Ralph Lombreglia

Poetry
1990	Emily Hiestand
	Dennis Nurkse
1991	Thylias Moss
	Franz Wright
1992	Roger Fanning
	Jane Mead
	Katha Pollitt
1993	Mark Levine
	Nathaniel Mackey
	Dionisio D Martinez
	Kathleen Peirce
1994	Mark Doty
	Wayne Koestenbaum
	Mary Swander
1995	Lucy Grealy
	James McMichael
	Mary Ruefle
1996	Brigit Pegeen Kelly
	Elizabeth Spires
	Patricia Storace
1997	Forrest Gander
	Jody Gladding
	Mark Turpin
	Connie Deanovich
1998	Nancy Eimers
	Daniel Hall
	James Kimbrall
	Charles Harper Webb
	Greg Williamson

Non-fiction
1990	Harriet Ritvo
	Amy Wilentz
1991	Stanley Crouch
	Anton Shammas
1992	Eva Hoffman
	Katha Pollitt
1993	No prize awarded
1994	Kennedy Fraser
	Rosemary Mahoney
	Claudia Roth Pierpont
1995	André Aciman
1997	Jo Ann Beard
	Ellen Meloy
1998	D. J. Waldie
	Anthony Walton

Plays
| 1986 | August Wilson |
| 1987 | Reinaldo Povod |

1989	Timberlake Wertenbaker
1990	Tony Kushner
1991	Scott McPherson
1992	Suzan-Lori Parks
	Keith Reddin
	José Rivera
1993	Kevin Kling
1997	Erik Ehn

Walt Whitman Award
Academy of American Poets
584 Broadway, Suite 1208
New York, NY 10012
USA
Award for a first-book publication by an eminent American poet who has not yet published a book of poetry in a standard edition.
Annual prize of $5000.
1975	Climbing into the Roots by Reg Saner
1976	The Hocus-Pocus of the Universe by Laura Gilpin
1977	Guilty Bystander by Lauren Shakely
1978	Wonders by Karen Snow
1979	Shooting Rats at the Bibb County Dump by David Bottoms
1980	Work, for the Night is Coming by Jared Carter
1981	Whispering to Fool the Wind by Alberto Ríos
1982	Jurgis Petraskas by Anthony Petrosky
1983	Across the Mutual Landscape by Christopher Gilbert
1984	For the New Year by Eric Pankey
1985	Bindweed by Christianne Balk
1986	Fragments from the Fire by Chris Llewellyn
1987	The Weight of Numbers by Judith Baumel
1988	Blackbird Bye Bye by April Bernard
1989	The Game of Statues by Martha Hollander
1990	The Cult of the Right Hand by Elaine Terranova
1991	From the Iron Chair by Greg Glazner
1992	The Fire in All Things by Stephen Yenser
1993	Science and Other Poems by Alison Hawthorne Deming
1994	Because the Brain Can Be Talked Into Anything by Jan Richman
1995	Resurrection by Nicole Cooley
1996	Madonna Anno Domini by Joshua Clover
1997	Bite Every Sorrow by Barbara Ras
1998	Once I Gazed at You in Wonder by Jan Heller Levi

Writers' Guild Awards (Now discontinued)
Writers' Guild of Great Britain
430 Edgware Road
London W2 1EH
England
Originally established in 1961, and relaunched in 1991, the Writers' Guild awards are presented in five categories: radio, theatre, film, television and books (fiction, non-fiction and children's). Short-lists are prepared by juries for each categories, and presented to the Guild for the final vote.
Contact: Lisa Fortescue, Awards Coordinator
Fiction
1991	The Inn at the Edge of the World by Alice Thomas Ellis
1992	Persistent Rumours by Lee Langley
1993	Time and Tide by Edna O'Brien
1994	How Late It Was, How Late by James Kelman
1995	High Fidelity by Hick Hornby
1996	Promised Lands by Jane Rogers
1997	House of Sleep byJonathon Coe
Non-fiction
1991	Jean Rhys: Life and Works by Carole Angier
1992	Wild Swans: Three Daughters of China by Jung Chang
1993	Daphne du Maurier by Margaret Forster
1994	Genet by Edmund White
1995	William Morris: A Life for Our Times by Fiona MacCarthy
1996	I May Be Some Time: Ice and the Imagination by Francis Spufford
1997	The Open Cage by Daniel Start
Children's Book
1991	Haroun and the Sea of Stories by Salman Rushdie
1992	The Secret Summer of Daniel Lyons by Roy Apps
1993	Johnny and the Dead by Terry Pratchett
1994	The Frozen Waterfall by Gayle Hicyilmaz
1995	Chandra by Frances Mary Hendry
1996	The Butterfly Lion by Michael Morpurgo
1997	Goodbye Buffalo Sky by John Loveday
	Daughter of the Sea by Berlie Doherty

Yorkshire Post Awards
Yorkshire Post Newspapers Ltd
PO Box 168, Wellington Street
Leeds LS1 1RF
England
Contact: Margaret Brown
Book of the Year Award
Awarded annually for a work of fiction or non-fiction published in the UK
in the year preceding the prize by a British or UK resident writer.

Publisher entry only - up to four books may be submitted by any one
publisher.
Prize: £1200.
1990   Anthony Trollope: A Victorian in his World by Richard Mullen
1991   Engage the Enemy More Closely by Corelli Barnett
1992   Shylock by John Gross
1993   Franco by Paul Preston
1994   The Brontës by Juliet Barker
1995   The Five Giants: A Biography of the Welfare State by Nicholas
        Timmins
1996   The Younger Pitt by John Ehram
1997   The Star Factory
Best First Work Award
Annual award for a work by a new author published during the preceding
year.
Prize: £1000.
1990   Epics of Everyday Life by Susan Richards
1991   Forgotten Land by Harriet O'Brien
1992   Stalin's Nose by Rory McLea
1993   The Language of the Genes by Dr Steve Jones
1994   Reef by Romessh Gunesekera
1995   Gagarin and I by Stephen Blanchard
1996   Acts of Revision by Martyn Bedford
1997   Cold Mountain by Charles Frazier
Author of the Year Award
Award for an author of fiction or non-fiction born in Yorkshire.
Prize: £1000.
Art and Music Awards
Two annual awards given to the authors whose work has contributed
most top the understanding and appreciation of arts and music. Books
should have been published in the UK in the preceding year.
Prize: £1000.

APPENDIX D

AMERICAN ACADEMY OF ARTS AND LETTERS
633 West 155th Street, New York, NY 10032, USA
MEMBERS OF THE DEPARTMENT OF LITERATURE
(as of 1 Jan 1999)

Daniel Aaron
Renata Adler
Edward Albee
A R Ammons
John Ashbery
Louis Auchincloss
Russell Baker
Russell Banks
John Barth
Jacques Barzun
Ann Beattie
Saul Bellow
Eric Bentley
Harold Bloom
Robert Bly
Paul Bowles
John Malcolm Brinnin
Gwendolyn Brroks
Art Buchwald
Hortense Calisher
Evan S Connell
Robert Coover
Robert Creeley
Don DeLillo
Joan Didion
E L Doctorow
Richard Eberhart
Louise Erdrich
Robert Fagles
Jules Feiffer
Leslie Fiedler
James Thomas Flexner
Horton Foote
Shelby Foote
Richard Ford
William Gaddis
Ernest J Gaines
John Kenneth Galbraith
William H Gass
Peter Gay
Louise Glück
Francine de Plessix Gray
John Guare

Donald Hall
Elizabeth Hardwick
John Hawkes
Shirley Hazzard
Anthony Hecht
Edward Hoagland
John Hollander
Richard Howard
Ada Louise Huxtable
Jospehine Jacobsen
Donald Justice
Justin Kaplan
Donald Keene
George F Kennan
William Kennedy
Galway Kinnell
Kenneth Koch
Stanley Kunitz
Philip Levine
R W B Lewis
Alison Lurie
Norman Mailer
David Mamet
Peter Matthiessen
William Maxwell
John McPhee
William Meredith
W S Merwin
Arthur Miller
Czesław Miłosz
Wright Morris
Toni Morrison
Albert Murray
Joyce Carol Oates
Cynthia Ozick
Grace Paley
J F Powers
Reynolds Price
Adrienne Rich
Philip Roth
John Russell
Oliver Sacks
Arthur Schlesinger, Jr.

Karl Shapiro
Sam Shepard
Charles Simic
William Jay Smith
W D Snodgrass
Gary Snyder
Susan Sontag
Elizabeth Spencer
Robert Stone
Mark Strand
William Styron
Studs Terkel
Paul Theroux
Anne Tyler
John Updike
Mona Van Duyn
Helen Hennessy Vendler
Kurt Vonnegut
William Weaver
Eudora Welty
Edmund White
Elie Wiesel
Richard Wilbur
Garry Wills
August Wilson
C Vann Woodward
Charles Wright

APPENDIX E

A BIOGRAPHICAL COMPENDIUM OF LITERARY FIGURES OF THE PAST

By

Dennis K McIntire, Consultant Editor

This appendix is a logical complement to the biographical section devoted to contemporary authors. All of the great names in literary history have been included, as well as innumerable others worthy of consideration.

Among the more than 8000 entries will be found various novelists, short story writers, dramatists, poets, historians, philosophers, theologians, critics, translators and others. In addition, a number of important historical figures who were not primarily authors but who nevertheless left a written legacy have also been included.

This appendix is intended for use by both the scholar and general reader as a comprehensive, accurate and up-to-date ready-reference source.

Aakjaer, Jeppe (1866-1930), Danish novelist and poet, author of the novel *Vredens børn, et tyendes saga* (Children of Wrath: A Hired Man's Saga, 1904) and the poetry collection *Rugens sange* (Songs of the Rye, 1906).

Abasiyanik, Sait Falik (1907-1954), Turkish short-story writer.

Abbey, Edwin (1927-1989), American novelist and essayist.

Abbott, George (1887-1995), prominent American theatre director, dramatist and writer.

Abbott, Lyman (1835-1922), American clergyman, writer and editor.

'Abd al-Ghanī (ibn Ismā'īl) an-Nabulusī (1641-1731), Syrian mystic, writer and poet.

Abdülhak Hâmid (Tarhan) (1852-1937), Turkish poet and dramatist.

Abdullah bin Abdul Kadir, Munshi (1796-1854), Malaysian writer.

Abe Kōbō (actually Abe Kimifusa) (1924-1993), Japanese novelist, short-story writer and dramatist, best known for his novel *Suma no omna* (1962; English translation as *The Woman in the Dunes,* 1964).

Abelard, Peter (1079-1144), famous French philosopher, theologian and poet, author of the controversial *Sic et non* (Yes and No) *and Theologia,* the latter being condemned as heretical.

Abell, Kjeld (1901-1961), Danish dramatist and social critic.

Abercrombie, Lascelles (1881-1938), English poet and critic.

Abert, Anna Amalie (1906-1996), German music scholar, author of the important *Geschichte der Oper* (History of Opera, 1994).

Abhdisho bar Berikha or **Ebedjesus of Nisibus (d. 1318),** Syrian Christian theologian and poet, particularly remembered for his *Margaritha vitae* (The Pearl of Life).

Abrabanel, Isaac ben Judah (1437-1508), Spanish Jewish statesman and writer on religion.

Abraham, Gerald (Ernest Heal) (1904-1988), English music scholar.

Abrahams, Israel (1858-1925), English Jewish scholar, esteemed for his *Jewish Life in the Middle Ages* (1896).

Abū al'Atāhiya (actually Abū Ishāq Ismā'īl ibn al-Qāsim ibn Suwayd ibn Kaysān) (748-825), Arab poet, author of the ascetic poems the *Zuhdiyāt.*

Abu Madi, Iliya (c.1890-1957), Arab-American journalist and poet.

Abū Nuwās or **Nu'ās (actually Abu Nuwas al-Hāsan ibn Hāni' al-Hakamī) (c.755-c.814),** renowned Arab poet who extolled the life of unrestricted pleasure.

Abu Rishah, `Umar (1910-1990), Syrian poet and diplomat.

Abū Tammām (Habīb ibn Aws) (804-c.845), Arab poet, best remembered as editor of the anthology *Hamāsah.*

Accius or **Attius, Lucius (170-c.86 B.C.),** Roman dramatist, poet and writer.

Accursio or **Accorsi, Mariangelo (c.1480-1546),** Italian poet, critic and translator, especially admired for his satiric dialogues.

Acevedo Dīaz, Eduardo (1851-1924), Uruguayan politician and writer whose finest work was the novel *Soledad* (Solitude, 1894).

Achilles Tatius (2nd Century), Greek writer whose *Leucippe and Cleitophon* presaged the development of the novel.

Ackerely, J(oseph) R(andolph) (1896-1967), English writer and editor.

Ackermann, Louise-Victorine (née Choquet) (1813-1890), French poet, best known for her *Poésies, premières poésies, poésies philosophiques* (Poetry, First Poetry, Philosophical Poetry, 1874).

Ackland, Rodney (1908-1991), English dramatist.

Aconcio or **Aconzio, Giacomo (1492-c.1566),** Italian-born English writer on religious toleration, author of the *Satanae stratagematum* (Stratagems of Satan, 1562).

Acosta, Joaquín (c.1800-1852), Colombian statesman, scientist and historian who wrote a history of the 16th-Century New Granada (1848).

Acosta, José de (1539-1600), Spanish Jesuit theologian and missionary, author of *De procuranda indoru salute* (1588) and the *Historia natural y moral de las Indias* (1590; English translation as *Natural and Moral History of the Indies,* 1604).

Acosta, Uriel (actually Gabriel da Costa) (c. 1585-1640), Portuguese Jewish philosopher who championed natural law and reason over revealed religion; committed suicide.

Acropolites, George (1217-1282), Byzantine statesman, scholar and poet.

Acton, Sir Harold Mario Mitchell (1904-1994), English writer and poet.

Acton, Lord (actually John Emerich Edward Dalberg Acton, 1st Baron and 8th Baronet Acton) (1834-1902), English historian and philosopher, an advocate of Christian liberalism.

Adalbéron (d. 1030), Frankish bishop and poet who was known as Ascelin, Asselin and the "Old Traitor."

Adam de la Halle (c.1247-c.1287), French trouvère poet and composer who was also known as **Adan le Bossu (Adan the Hunchback)** although he was not a hunchback.

Adam, Paul (1862-1920), French novelist.

Adamic, Louis (1899-1951), Yugoslav-born American writer.

Adams, Andy (1859-1935), American novelist and short-story writer of the Old West.

Adamnan, Saint (c.628-704), Irish abbot and scholar who was also known as **Adomnan** or **Eunan,** author of the hagiography *Vita S Columbae.*

Adamov, Arthur (1908-1970), Russian-born French dramatist, writer and poet, a principal figure in the Theatre of the Absurd; committed suicide.

Adams, Brooks (1848-1927), distinguished American historian, author of *Law of Civilization and Decay* (1895) and *The Theory of Social Revolutions* (1913); brother of Charles Francis Adams Jr and Henry (Brooks) Adams.

Adams, Charles Follen (1842-1918), American poet of humorous verse.

Adams, Charles Francis Jr (1835-1915), American writer; brother of Brooks Adams and Henry (Brooks) Adams.

Adams, Charles Kendall (1835-1902), American historian.

Adams, Henry (Brooks) (1838-1918), eminent American historian, author of *the History of the United States During the Administrations of Thomas Jefferson and James Monroe* (9 volumes, 1889-91), *Mont-Saint-Michel and Chartres* (1904) and the classic autobiography *The Education of Henry Adams* (1907); brother of Brooks Adams and Charles Francis Adams Jr.

Adams, Herbert Baxter (1850-1901), American historian and educator.

Adams, James Truslow (1878-1949), American historian, author of *The Founding of New England* (1921), *Revolutionary New England* (1923) and *New England in the Republic* (1926), and general editor of the *Dictionary of American History* (1940).

Adams, John (1704-1740), American clergyman, scholar and poet.

Adams, John Turvill (1805-1882), American novelist, particularly known for his The Lost Hunter (1856) and *The White Chief Among the Red Men; or, Knight of the Golden Melice* (1859).

Adams, Léonie (Fuller) (1899-1988), American poet who excelled in metaphysical verse.

Adams, Samuel Hopkins (1871-1958), American journalist and writer who often wrote under the name Warner Fabian.

Adams, Sarah (née Flower) (1805-1848), English poet, best remembered for her popular hymn *Nearer, My God, To Thee* (1840).

Adams, William Taylor (1822-1897), American writer and editor who wrote many juvenile books under the name Oliver Optic.

Addams, Jane (1860-1935), famous American social reformer, pacifist and writer; was co-winner of the Nobel Prize for Peace (1931).

Addison, Joseph (1672-1719), noted English essayist, poet, dramatist and statesman, author of the poem *The Campaign* (1705) and founder, with Richard Steele, of *The Spectator.*

Ade, George (1866-1944), American writer and dramatist who was particularly admired for his humorous *Fables in Slang* (1899).

Adelard of Bath (12th Century), English Scholastic philosopher.

Adenet le Roi (c.1240-c.1300), French poet and musician who was known as Roi Adam, Li Rois Adenes, Adan le Menestrel and Adam Rex Menestrallus.

Adler, Alfred (1870-1937), significant Austrian psychiatrist, known for his writings on individual psychiatry.

Adler, Cyrus (1863-1940), American Jewish scholar, educator and editor.

Adler, Felix (1851-1933), German-born American educator and writer, founder of the Ethical Movement.

Adorno, Theodor (actually **Theodor Wiesengrund) (1903-1969),** influential German social philosopher, music sociologist and writer.

Ady, Endre (1877-1919), outstanding Hungarian poet.

AE (actually **George Williams Russell) (1867-1935),** Irish poet, editor and essayist, especially known for his mystical poetry.

Aelian, Claudius (c.170-235), Roman writer, author *of De animalium natura and Varia historia.*

Aelianus (2nd Century), Greek military writer who was also known as Aelianus Tacticus and Aelian, author of *taktiké theória* (Tactical Theory, 106).

Aelred or Ailred or Aethelred or Ethelred of Rievaulx, Saint (c.1110-1167), notable English Cistercian abbot and writer whose most important work *was De spirituali amicitia* (On Spiritual Friendship).

Aeschylus (525-456 B.C.), great Greek dramatist, celebrated as the father of the tragic drama.

Aesop (6th Century B.C.), legendary Greek writer of fables.

Affre, Denis-Auguste (1793-1848), French Roman Catholic prelate and writer on theological and philosophical subjects.

Africanus, Sextus Julius (c.180-250), Roman Christian historian and biblical scholar, author of the historical treatise *Chronographiai* (5 volumes, 221).

Agar, Herbert (Sebastian) (1897-1980), American historian and critic.

Agassiz, Louis (1807-1873), remarkable Swiss-born American naturalist, geologist and teacher, author of such important studies *as Recherches sur les poissons fossiles* (Research on Fossil Fishes, 1833-43), *Études sur les glaciers* (1840*), Lake Superior* (1850) and *Contributions to the Natural History of the United States* (1857-62).

Agate, James (Evershed) (1877-1947), notable English critic, diarist, essayist and novelist.

Agathias (c.536-c.582), Byzantine poet and historian, best known for his love poems and epigrams.

Agathon (c.445-c.400 B.C.), Greek dramatist.

Agee, James (1909-1955), admired American writer, critic, poet and screenwriter, especially remembered for his novel *A Death in the Family* (1957).

Agnon, Shmuel Yosef (actually Samuel Josef Czaczkes) (1888-1970), celebrated Polish-born Hebrew novelist and short-story writer; was co-winner of the Nobel Prize for Literature (1966).

Agoult, Marie (-Catherine-Sophie-) de Flavigny, Comtesse d' (1805-1876), French writer who wrote under the name Daniel Stern, perhaps best remembered as the mistress of Franz Liszt.

Agreda, María de (actually María Fernández Coronel) (1602-1665), Spanish abbess and mystic who was known as Sister María de Jesús, author of *The Mystical City of God* (1670).

Agricola, Johann (actually Johann Schneider) (1494-1566), German Protestant theologian and reformer who was an exponent of antinomianism.

Agrippa von Nettesheim, Heinrich Cornelius (1486-1535), controversial German theologian, philosopher and physician, author *of De occulta philosophia* and *Of the Vanitie and Uncertaintie of Artes and Sciences* (published 1569).

Aguilar, Grace (1816-1847), English poet, novelist and writer on Jewish history and religion, author of the novel *Home Influence* (1847).

Agustini, Delmira (1886-1914), talented Uruguayan poet, author of *El libro blanco* (The White Book, 1907), *Cantos de la mañana* (Songs of Tomorrow, 1910), *Los calices vacios* (Empty Chalices, 1913) and *Los astros de abismo* (Stars of the Abyss, 1924); murdered by her estranged husband.

Ahmad Khan, Sir Sayyid (1817-1898), Indian Muslim educator and writer on religion.

Ahmed Haşim (1884-1933), gifted Turkish poet of Symbolist verse, author of such poetry collections as *Göl saatleri* (The Hours of the Lake, 1921) and *Göl kuslari* (The Birds of the Lake).

Ahmed Yesevi or Yasavi (d. 1166), notable Turkish poet and Sūfi (Muslim mystic).

Ahmedi, Taceddin (actually Taceddin or Taj al-Dīn Ibrahim ibn Hizr Ahmedi) (c.1334-1413), esteemed Anatolian poet, particularly admired for his *Iskendername* (The Book of Alexander).

Ahmet Paşa Bursali (c.1497), noted Turkish poet, the first great classicist of Ottoman poetry who was especially esteemed for his odes and lyrics.

Aho, Juhani (actually Johannes Brofeldt) (1861-1921), Finnish novelist and short-story writer.

Aicard, (François-Victor-) Jean (1848-1921), French poet, novelist and dramatist.

Ai Quing (actually Jiang Haicheng) (1910-1996), Chinese poet who chronicled the Communist era of his homeland in popular nationalistic and folk-flavoured works.

Aiken, Conrad (Potter) (1889-1973), prominent American poet, novelist, short-story writer and critic.

Aiken, George L. (1830-1876), American actor and dramatist.

Aimard, Gustave (actually Olivier Gloux) (1818-1883), French novelist who was widely successful in his day.

Ainslie, Hew (1792-1878), Scottish-born American poet, known for his dialect poems.

Ainsworth, William Harrison (1805-1882), English novelist and editor, best remembered for his novel *Jack Sheppard* (1839).

Aistis, Jonas (actually Jonas Aleksandravichius) (1904-1973), Lithuanian-born American poet and essayist.

Akenside, Mark (1721-1770), English poet and physician, best known for his poem *The Pleasures of the Imagination* (1744).

Akers, Elizabeth (Chase) (1832-1911), American journalist and poet, author of the poem *Rock Me To Sleep* (1860), which appeared under the name Florence Percy.

Akhmatova, Anna (actually Anna Andreievna Gorenko) (1889-1966), great Russian poet whose mastery of her craft was acknowledged in spite of her difficulties with the Soviet regime throughout her career.

Akhtal, al- (actually Ghiyath ibn Ghawth ibn as-Salt al-Akhtal) (c.640-710), renowned Arab poet.

Akiba ben Joseph (c.40-c.135), important Jewish rabbinic scholar, known for his refinement of the biblical interpretation of Midrash; was martyred.

Akindynos, Gregorios (c.1300-c.1349), Byzantine monk, theologian and poet who was condemned as a heretic.

Akins, Zoë (1886-1958), American dramatist and novelist.

Aksakov, Sergei (Timofeievich) (1791-1859), notable Russian novelist, essayist and poet, author of the classic novels *Semeynaya khronika* (1856; English translation *as Chronicles of a Russian Family,* 1924), *Vospominaniya* (1856; English translation as *The Autobiography of a Russian Schoolboy,* 1917*) and Detskie gody bagrova-vnuka* (1858; English translation as *Years of Childhood,* 1916).

Akutagawa Ryūnosuke (1892-1927), admired Japanese short-story writer, dramatist and poet who wrote under the names Chokodo Shujin and Gaki.

Alabaster, William (1567-1640), English mystic, poet and scholar who wrote the Latin tragedy *Roxana* (1597).

Alain (actually **Émile-Auguste Chartier) (1868-1951),** French philosopher and writer.

Alain de Lille or **Alanus de Insulis (c. 1128-1202),** renowned French theologian and poet who was acclaimed as the "universal doctor", author of the theological works *The Art of the Catholic Faith, Treatise Against Heretics* and *Maxims of Theology,* and the *poems Plaint of Nature* and *Anticlaudianus.*

Alain-Fournier (actually **Henri-Alban Fournier) (1886-1914),** French writer, author of the classic novel *Le Grand Meaulnes* (1913; English translation as *The Lost Domain,* 1959); killed in World War I.

Alamanni, Luigi (1495-1556), Italian poet.

Alarcón, Pedro Antonio de (1833-1891), Spanish journalist, poet and novelist, author of the popular novel *El sombrero de tres picos* (1874; English translation as *The Three-Cornered Hat,* 1918).

Alas, Leopoldo (1852-1901), Spanish critic, novelist and short-story writer who wrote under the name Clarín (i.e. bugle), greatly admired for his naturalistic novels *La regenta* (The Professor's Wife, 1884-85) and *Su único hijo* (An Only Son, 1890).

Albers, Josef (1889-1976), German-born American painter, theorist and poet, author of *Poems and Drawings* (1958).

Alberti, Leon Battista (1404-1472), versatile Italian poet, scholar and architect, author of books in various fields, including *Della Famiglia* (On the Family), *Della pittura* (On Painting, 1435) and *De re aedificatoria* (Ten Books on Architecture, 1452).

Albertus Magnus, Saint (c. 1200-1280), celebrated Swabian theologian and scholastic philosopher who was an authority on Aristotle.

Albinovanus Pedo (1st Century), Greek philosopher who presaged Neoplatonism.

Albright, W(illiam) F(oxwell) (1891-1971), notable American biblical archaeologist who wrote several books in his field.

Alcaeus (c. 620- 580 B.C.), Greek poet.

Alcman (7th Century), Greek poet.

Alcott, (Amos) Bronson (1799-1888), American educational reformer, philosopher and writer; father of Louisa May Alcott.

Alcott, Louisa May (1832-1888), American novelist, short-story writer and poet, author of the children's classic *Little Women* (1868-69); daughter of (Amos) Bronson Alcott.

Alcuin (c. 732-804), Anglo-Latin cleric, educator, writer and poet.

Aldanov, Mark Aleksandrovich (actually **Mark Aleksandrovich Landau) (1889-1957),** Russian-born French, later American, novelist and essayist.

Aldhelm (c. 639-709), notable English bishop, writer and poet.

Aldington, Richard (actually **Edward Godfree Aldington) (1892-1962),** English poet, novelist, biographer, essayist and translator.

Aldrich, Bess Streeter (1881-1954), American novelist.

Aldrich, Thomas Bailey (1836-1907), American poet, short-story writer, essayist, dramatist and editor, remembered for the prose works *The Story of a Bad Boy* (1870) *and Marjorie Daw and Other People* (1873), and for several poetry collections.

Aleandro, Girolamo (1480-1542), Italian Roman Catholic cardinal, scholar and poet, a determined opponent of the Protestant Reformation.

Aleardi, Aleardo, Conte (actually **Gaetano Aleardi) (1812-1878),** Italian poet and politician.

Alecsandri, Vasile (c. 1819-1890), Romanian poet, dramatist and diplomat.

Aleixandre, Vicente (1898-1984), noted Spanish poet; won the Nobel Prize for Literature (1977).

Alemán, Mateo (1547-c.1614), Spanish novelist who wrote the early picaresque novel *Guzmán de Alfarache* (2 parts, 1599, 1604; English translation as The Spanish Rogue, 1622).

Alembert, Jean Le Rond d' (1717-1783), outstanding French mathematician, scientist, philosopher and writer who, with Diderot, edited the famous *Encyclopédie*; illegitimate son of Claudine-Alexadrine Guérin de Tencin.

Alencar, José (Martiniano) de (1829-1877), Brazilian journalist and novelist, esteemed for his novels *O Guarany* (The Guarani Indian, 1857) and *Iracema* (1865).

Alexander, Cecil Frances (née Humphreys) (1818-1895), Irish poet and hymnist, best known for her *All Things Bright and Beautiful, Once in Royal David's City* and *There is a Green Hill Far Away.*

Alexander, Samuel (1859-1938), English philosopher, author of *Space, Time and Deity* (1920).

Alexander Aetolus (flourished c.280 B.C.), Greek poet.

Alexandra of Aphrodisias (flourished c.200), Greek philosopher who wrote on Aristotle, the soul and the mind.

Alexander of Hales (c. 1177-1245), English theologian and philosopher, known as Doctor Irrefragabilis to the scholastics.

Alexander Polyhistor (actually **Lucius Cornelius Alexander Polyhistor) (d. c.35 B.C.),** Greek historian, geographer and philosopher.

Alexis (c. 375 —c.275 B.C.), Greek dramatist.

Alexis, Willibald (actually **Georg Wilhelm Heinrich Haring**) **(1798-1871)**, German novelist, short-story writer, dramatist and poet, best known for his historical novels.

Alfieri, Vittorio, Conte (1749-1803), outstanding Italian dramatist and poet whose works presaged the Risorgimento.

Algarotti, Francesco (1712-1764), learned Italian writer on the arts and sciences.

Alger, Horatio (1834-1899), American writer of popular "rags to riches" stories.

Alger of Liège or **Alger of Cluny** or **Algerus Magister (c.1060-c.1131)**, French Roman Catholic priest and writer on religious subjects.

Algren, Nelson (1909-1981), American novelist and essayist, author of the novels *The Man with the Golden Arm* (1949) *and A Walk on the Wild Side* (1956).

Alkabetz, Solomon ben Moses ha-Devi (c. 1505-1574), Jewish Kabbalist poet who wrote Lekha dodi (Come, My Beloved), which is traditionally recited each Friday evening to begin the Sabbath in Jewish synagogues.

Allen, (Charles) Grant (Blairfindie) (1848-1899), Canadian philosopher and novelist.

Allen, Frederick Lewis (1890-1954), American writer.

Allen, James Lane (1849-1925), American novelist, short-story writer and essayist.

Allen, Paul (1775-1826), American poet and writer.

Allen, William (1784-1868), American educator and historian.

Allen, (William) Hervey (1889-1949), American novelist, biographer and short-story writer, author of the popular novel *Anthony Adverse* (1933).

Allibone, Samuel Austin (1816-1889), American lexicographer, editor of the valuable *A Critical Dictionary of English Literature and British and American Authors* (3 volumes, 1858-71).

Allingham, Margery (Louise) (1904-1966), admired English detective-story writer, creator of the popular detective Albert Campion.

Allingham, William (1824-1889), Irish poet, particularly remembered for *The Fairies* (1850).

Allston, Joseph Blyth (1833-1904), American poet, author of *Stack Arms*, written while he was a Union prisoner during the American Civil War.

Allston, Washington (1779-1843), American painter, poet and novelist, author of *The Sylphs of the Seasons with Other Poems* (1813) and the Gothic novel *Monaldi* (1841).

Almeida, José Valentin Fialho de (1857-1911), Portuguese short-story writer and political pamphleteer.

Almeida, Manuel Antônio de (1831-1861), Brazilian journalist, writer and translator who wrote the first outstanding novel of his homeland *Memórias de um Sargento de Milicias* (Memoirs of a Militia Sergeant, 1854-55); died in a shipwreck.

Almqvist, Carl Jonas Love (1793-1866), important Swedish novelist, short-story writer, dramatist, poet and musician, author of such notable books as *Amorina* (c. 1821; published 1839) and *Drottningens juvelsmycke* (The Queen's Diamond Ornament, 1834).

Alsop, Richard (1761-1815), American poet, particularly known for his light verse.

Altenburg, Peter (c. 1862-1919), Austrian poet.

Althusius or **Althaus, Johannes (1557-1638)**, Dutch Calvinist political theorist, author of the *Politica methodice digesta atque exemplis sacris et profanis illustrata* (1603; 3rd edition, augmented, 1614).

Ambler, Eric (1909-1998), English writer, best known for his thrillers.

Ambros, August Wilhelm (1816-1876), Austrian music scholar who wrote the important *Geschichte der Musik* (History of Music 5 volumes, 1862-82).

Ambrose or **Ambroise d'Evereux** (12th Century), Norman poet who wrote a chronicle of the Third Crusade.

Ambrose of Camaldoni (1386-1439), Italian ecclesiastic, scholar and patristic translator.

Ambrose, Saint (c.339-397), famous Roman Catholic bishop, writer and hymnist.

Ames, William (1576-1633), English Puritan theologian, author of such works as *Medulla Theologiae* (1623; English translation as The Marrow of Sacred Divinity, 1642) and *De Conscientia et Ejus Jure vel Casibus* (1623; English translation as Conscience, 1639).

Ames, Winthrop (1870-1937), American theatre producer, manager, director and dramatist.

Amhurst, Nicholas (1697-1742), English editor, political pamphleteer and poet of a satirical bent.

Amiel, Henri Frédéric (1821-1881), Swiss writer whose finest achievement was his Journal intime (1847-81).

'Āmilī, Muhammad ibn Husayn Bahā' ad-Dīn, al- (c.1546-1622), significant Shi'ite Muslim theologian, mathematician, astronomer and writer.

Ami Ali, Sayyid (1849-1928), Indian-born English Muslim leader, jurist and writer, author of *The Critical Examination of the Life and Teachings of Mohammed* (1873) and *The Spirit of Islam* (1891).

Amir Khosrow (1253-1325), notable Indian poet and historian who wrote in the Persian language.

Amis, Sir Kingsley (William) (1922-1995), distinguished English novelist, poet and critic who established his reputation with his first novel *Lucky Jim* (1954).

Amory, Cleveland (1917-1998), American writer and animal rights advocate.

Amory, Thomas (c.1691-1788), Irish writer, best known for *The Life and Opinions of John Buncle, Esq.* (2 volumes, 1756, 1766).

Ampère, Jean-Jacques (-Antoine) (1800-1864), French philologist and historian, author of such noted works as *Histoire littéraire de la France avant la douzième siècle* (History of French Literature before the Twelfth Century, 3 volumes, 1839-40), *Histoire de la formation da la langue française* (History of the Development of the French Language, 1841) *and L'Histoire romaine à Rome* (Roman History in Rome, 4 volumes, 1861-64).

'Amr ibn Kulthum (6th Century), Arab poet who wrote a famous pre-Islamic ode.

Amyot, Jacques (1513-1593), French Roman Catholic bishop and scholar, known for his translations of classical writers.

Anacreon (c.582-c.485 B.C.), celebrated Greek poet, renowned for his satires and love poems.

Anchieta, José de (1534-1597), notable Portuguese Jesuit scholar, poet and dramatist, author of the famous poem *De beata virgine dei matre Maria* (The Blessed Virgin Mary).

Ancillon, Charles (1659-1715), French-born German educator, jurist and historian.

Ancillon, David (1617-1692), French Protestant pastor and theologian who wrote the *Traité de la tradition* (Treatise on Tradition, 1657).

Ancillon, Johann Peter Friedrich (1767-1837), German statesman, historian and political philosopher, author of *Tableau des révolutions du système politique de l' Europe depuis le Xve Siécle* (view of European Political Revolutions since the Fifteenth Century, 4 volumes, 1803-05).

Andersen, Hans Christian (1805-1875), famous Danish writer, dramatist and poet, renowned the world over for his superb fairy tales.

Anderson, Tryggve (1866-1920), Norwegian novelist and short-story writer, particularly admired for his short-story collection *I cancelliraadens dage* (In the days of the Chancery Counsellor,1897).

Anderson, Maxwell (1888-1959), American dramatist and poet, especially remembered for his play Winterset (1935).

Anderson, Sherwood (1876-1941), American writer, poet and editor who made his mark with the short-story collection *Winesburg, Ohio* (1919).

Andersson, Dan(iel) (1888-1920), Swedish poet and writer, author of the greatly admired poetry collections *Kolarhistorier* (Charcoal Burner's Tales, 1914) and *Kolvaktarens visor* (Charcoal Watcher's Songs, 1915).

Andrade, (José) Oswald de (Souza) (1890-1954), Brazilian political radical, poet, dramatist and novelist.

Andrade, Mário (Raul) de (Morais) (1893-1945), outstanding Brazilian poet, novelist and critic.

Andrea de Barberino (c.1370-c.1432), Italian writer and compiler of epic tales.

Andreas-Salomé, Lou (1861-1937), German novelist and writer.

Andreini, Giovambattista (c.1576-c.1654), Italian actor, dramatist and poet, best known for the play *L'adamo* (1613).

Andrewes, Lancelot (1555-1626), English Anglican theologian and preacher, best known for his anti-Roman Catholic apologetics.

Andrews, Charles McLean (1863-1943), American historian, author of the *Colonial Period of American History*.

Andrews, Roy Chapman (1884-1960), American naturalist, explorer and writer.

Andreyev, Leonid (Nikolaievich) (1871-1919), Russian novelist, short-story writer and dramatist.

Andrić, Ivo (1892-1975), noted Serbo-Croatian novelist and short-story writer; won the Nobel Prize for Literature (1961).

Andrieux, François (-Giullaume-Jean-Stanislas) (1759-1833), French dramatist, poet and politician who won his finest success with the play *Les Etourdis* (The Scatterbrained, 1787).

Aneirin (6th Century), Welsh poet, author of *Y Gododdin*.

Angell, Sir Norman (1874-1967), English economist and peace crusader who wrote the anti-war tome *The Great Illusion* (1910, revised edition, 1933); won the Nobel Prize for Peace (1933).

Angilbert (c.740-814), Frankish prelate and poet.

Angiolieri, Cecco (c.1260-c.1312), esteemed Italian poet who excelled in comic verse.

Anouilh, Jean (-Marie-Lucien-Pierre) (1910-1987), remarkable French dramatist whose output detailed the duality of good and evil in the human condition.

Anselm of Canterbury, Saint (c.1033-1109), great Italian-born English theologian and Archbishop of Canterbury, founder of Scholasticism, who wrote such important works as *Monologium* (1077) and *Cur Deus homo?* (Who Did God Become Man?, 1098).

Anselm of Laon or **Anselme de Laon (d. 1117)**, French theologian and scholastic author of *Interlinear Glosses*, a commentary on the Vulgate Bible.

Anselme of the Virgin Mary, Father (actually Pierre de Guibours) (1625-1694), French friar and genealogist who wrote the *valuable Histoire généalogique et chronologique de la maison royale de France, des pairs, des grands officiers de la courrone, et de la maison du roy et des anciens barons du royaume* (Genealogical and Chronological History of the Royal House of France, the Peers, the Grand Officers of the Crown, and of the Royal House and the Ancient Barons of the Realm, 2 volumes, 1674).

Anstey, Christopher (1724-1805), English poet, author of the popular epistolary novel in verse *The New Bath Guide; or, Memoirs of the B--R--D Family* (1766).

Anstey, F (actually **Thomas Anstey Guthrie) (1856-1934),** English novelist and short-story writer, best known for his fantastic novel *Vice Versa* (1882).

Antar (actually **l'Antarah ibn Shaddad al-Absi) (6th Century),** famous Arab warrior and poet who wrote one of the 7 Golden Odes.

Anthony of Tagrit (9th Century), Syrian Orthodox theologian, writer and poet.

Anthony, Susan B(rownell) (1820-1906), notable American woman suffrage leader and lecturer who, with Elizabeth Cady Stanton and Matilda Joslyn Gage, wrote *The History of Woman Suffrage* (4 volumes, 1881-1902).

Antimachus of Colophon (flourished c.400 B.C.), Greek poet and grammarian, author of the epic *Thebais*.

Antin, Mary (actually **Mary Antin Grabau) (1881-1949),** Russian-born American writer who wrote *From Polotsk to Boston* (1899), *The Promised Land* (1912) and *They Who Knock at Our Gates* (1914).

Anvarī (actually **Awhad ad-Dīn 'Alī ibn Vāhīd ad-Dīn Muhammad Khavaranī) (c.1126-c.1189),** great Persian poet, especially esteemed for his odes and lyrics.

Anyte (3rd Century B.C.), renowned Greek poet who was acclaimed as a "woman Homer".

Anzengruber, Ludwig (1839-1889), Austrian dramatist and novelist, particularly noted for his comic plays.

Apollinaire, Guillaume (actually **Wilhelm Apollinaris de Kostrowitzki) (1880-1918),** significant Italian-Polish poet of the French avant-garde.

Apollinaris the Apologist, Saint (flourished 2nd Century), Roman Catholic bishop who wrote the *Defense of the Faith* (c.175).

Apollinaris or **Apollinarius the Younger (c.310-c.390),** Roman Catholic bishop who was declared a heretic for his *Incarnation of the Word*.

Apollodorus of Athens (flourished 140 B.C.), Greek scholar, author of a *Chronicle of Greek History*.

Apollodorus of Carystus (3rd Century B.C.), Greek dramatist.

Apollonius of Rhodes (b. c.295 B.C.), notable Greek poet and grammarian, author of the celebrated epic poem the *Argonautica*.

Appel, Benjamin (1907-1979), American novelist, short-story writer and poet.

Appian of Alexandria (2nd Century), Greek historian who chronicled the Roman conquests from the Republic down to his own era.

Appleton, Thomas Gold (1812-1884), American poet and essayist; brother–in-law of Henry Wadsworth Longfellow.

Apuleius. Lucius or **Apuleius of Madaura (c.124-c.171),** notable Greek writer, philosopher and rhetorician, celebrated for his prose narrative *Metamorphoses*, better known as *The Golden Ass*.

Aqqad, 'Abbas Mahmud al- (1889-1964), Egyptian writer, poet and critic.

Aragon, Louis (1897-1982), French poet, novelist, essayist, editor and Marxist political activist.

Arany, János (1817-1882), outstanding Hungarian poet, essayist and translator, author of the epic trilogy *Toldi* (1847), *Toldi szerelme* (Toldi's Love, 1848-79) and *Toldi estéje* (Toldi's Evening, 1854).

Aratus (c.315-c.245 B.C.), Greek poet who wrote the noted poem on astronomy *Phaenomena*.

Arbuckle, James (d. 1742), Irish poet and essayist.

Arbuthnot, John (1667-1735), Scottish physician, writer and poet, well known for his wit and satirical writings.

Archer, William (1856-1924), English drama critic, dramatist, essayist and translator.

Archias, Aulus Licinius (b. c.120 B.C.), Greek poet.

Archilochus of Paros (714-676 B.C.), renowned Greek poet, famous for his command of satire.

Arendt, Hannah (1906-1975), German-born American political scientist and philosopher, author of the important study *Origins of Totalitarianism* (1951).

Aretino, Pietro (1492-1556), Italian poet, writer and dramatist, known for his *Sonetti lussuriosi* (1524).

Argens, Jean-Baptiste de Boyer, Marquis d' (1703-1771), French nobleman and philosopher who was a determined freethinker.

Argensola, Lupercio Leonardo de (1559-1613), Spanish dramatist and poet.

Arguedas, Alcides (1879-1946), Bolivian politician, sociologist, novelist and historian.

Aribau, Buenaventura Carles (1789-1862), Catalan economist, editor, writer and poet, author of the noted poem *Oda a la patria* (Ode to the Fatherland, 1832).

Ariosto, Ludovico (1474-1533), famous Italian poet and dramatist, author of the great poem *Orlando furioso* (1502-33).

Arishima Takeo (1878-1923), Japanese novelist; committed suicide.

Aristides (2nd Century), Greek Christian philosopher and apologist who wrote the *Apology for the Christian Faith*, the earliest such work extant.

Aristophanes (c.450-c.388 B.C.), great Greek dramatist who was a master of comedic invention.

Aristotle (384-322 B.C.), august Greek philosopher, logician and scientist whose writings profoundly influenced the course of intellectual history.

Arland, Marcel (1899-1986), French novelist, short-story writer, critic and essayist.

Arlen, Michael (actually **Dikran Kouyoumdjian**) **(1895-1956),** Bulgarian-born English novelist of Armenian descent, author of the popular novel *The Green Hat* (1924).

Arminius, Jacobus (actually **Jacob Harmensen** or **Hermansz**) **(1560-1609),** Dutch Protestant minister and theologian who opposed the Calvinist view of predestination.

Armstrong, John (1709-1779), Scottish physician and poet, particularly known for his didactic and satirical poetry.

Arnauld, Antoine (1612-1694), French theologian and philosopher, known as the Great Arnauld, a prominent figure in the heretical Jansenist movement; brother of Robert Arnauld d'Andilly.

Arnauld d'Andilly, Robert (1589-1674), French Jansenist hermit, poet and translator; brother of Antoine Arnauld.

Arnaut, Daniel (12th Century), Provençal poet.

Arndt, Ernst Moritz (1769-1860), revered German patriot, writer and poet who was known as Father Arndt.

Arniches (y Barrera), Carlos (1866-1943), Spanish dramatist, admired for his comic plays.

Arnim, Achim von (actually **Karl Joachim Friedrich Ludwig von Arnim**) **(1781-1831),** German folklorist, novelist, short-story writer, dramatist and poet, best remembered for his collaboration with Clemens Brentano on the edition of folk poetry *Des Knaben Wunderhorn* (The Youth's Magic Horn, 1805); husband of Bettina von Arnim.

Arnim, Bettina von (actually **Elisabeth Katharina Ludovica Magdalena Brentano**) **(1785-1859),** renowned German writer, sculptor and musician, one of the major figures in German Romanticism; wife of Achim von Arnim.

Arnobius the Elder (4th Century), African Christian apologist, author of *Adversus nationes* (Against the Pagans, 7 volumes, c.303).

Arnold, Denis (Midgley) (1926-1986), English music scholar.

Arnold, Sir Edwin (1832-1904), English editor, poet and translator, best known for his blank verse setting *The Light of Asia, or the Great Renunciation* (1879).

Arnold, George (1834-1865), American poet and humourist.

Arnold, Matthew (1822-1888), eminent English poet and critic, author of the poetical volumes *Empedocles on Etna, and Other Poems* (1852) and *New Poems* (1867), and the critical volumes *Essays on Criticism* (2 series, 1865, 1888) and *Culture and Anarchy* (1869).

Arnow, Harriette (1906-1986), American novelist.

Aron, Raymond (-Claude-Ferdinand) (1905-1983), Notable French philosopher, sociologist and journalist.

Arp, Jean or **Hans (1887-1966),** significant French sculptor, painter and poet of the avant-garde.

Artaud, Antonin (1896-1948), French dramatist, poet and actor, creator of the Surrealist "Theatre of Cruelty".

Artybashev, Mikhail Petrovich (1878-1927), Russian writer whose output expressed his preoccupation with pessimism and immorality, best remembered for his novel *Sanin* (1907).

Asachi, Gheorghe (c.1788-c.1869), Romanian short-story writer and poet.

Asan, Kumaran (1873-1924), Indian poet who espoused social reform.

Asbjørnsen, Peter Christian (1812-1885), Norwegian folklorist who, with Jørgen Engebretsen Moe, edited the influential collection *Norske folkeeventyr* (Norwegian Folk Tales, 1841, critical edition, 1852).

Asch, Nathan (1902-1964), Polish-born American novelist and short-story writer; son of Sholem Asch.

Asch, Sholem or **Shalom (1880-1957),** prominent Polish-born American novelist, dramatist and writer; father of Nathan Asch.

Ascham, Roger (1515-1568), English Humanist scholar, best known for *The Scholemaster* (published 1570).

Ásgrímsson, Eysteinn (c.1310-1361), Icelandic monk and poet, author of the sacred poem *Lilja* (The Lily).

A'shā-, al- (the Blind) (actually **Maymūn ibn Qays al-A'shā**) **(c.569-c.625),** Arab poet.

Asimov, Isaac (1920-1992), Russian-born American biochemist and writer, author of many popular science fiction and science books.

Asturias, Miguel Angel (1899-1974), esteemed Guatemalan writer, poet and diplomat, author of the outstanding novel *Hombres de maíz* (Men of Corn, 1949); won the Nobel Prize for Literature (1967).

Aśvaghosa (c.80-c.150), famous Indian philosopher, poet and dramatist who is considered the father of Sanskrit drama.

Athanasius, Saint (c.293-373), greatly significant Egyptian Roman Catholic bishop and theologian who was a determined opponent of the Arian heresy, author of *Four Orations Against the Arians* and *The Life of St Antony.*

Atherton, Gertrude (Franklin) (1857-1948), American novelist, short-story writer and essayist.

Atkinson, (Justin) Brooks (1894-1984), American critic, journalist and writer.

Attaway, William (1911-1986), American novelist.

Atterbom, Per Daniel Amadeus (1790-1855), distinguished Swedish poet and literary historian whose masterwork was the poetic fairy-tale play *Lyckalighetens ö* (The Isle of Bliss, 1824-27).

Atterbury, Francis (1663-1732), English Anglican bishop and polemical writer of force and distinction.

Aubignac, François Hédelin, Abbé d' (1604-1676), French critic, dramatist, writer and translator, author of the important study *La Pratique de théâtre* (1657; English translation as *The Whole Art of the Stage*, 1684).

Aubigné, Theodore-Agrippa d' (1552-1630), famous French Huguenot soldier, poet, historian and polemical writer, author of the poem the *Tragiques* (7 cantos, 1577-1616).

Aubrey, John (1626-1697), English antiquarian and writer, particularly known for his biographical works.

Auden, W(ystan) H(ugh) (1907-1973), distinguished English-born American poet, librettist and essayist.

Audiberti, Jacques (1899-1965), French poet, dramatist and novelist.

Audubon, John James (1785-1851), notable French-born American naturalist and artist who excelled in the depiction of every known species of North American birds, best known for his *The Birds of America* (4 volumes, 1827-38).

Auerbach, Berthold (1812-1882), German novelist.

Auerbach, Erich (1892-1957), German-born American scholar of Romance literatures and languages.

Auezov, Mukhtar (1897-1961), Kazakh writer.

Augier, (Guillaume-Victor-) Émile (1820-1889), French dramatist, best remembered for his collaboration with Jules Sandeau on the play *Le Gendre de Monsieur Poirier* (1854).

Augustine of Hippo, Saint (354-430), great Roman Catholic bishop and theologian, celebrated for such works as *De doctrina Christiana* (Christian Instruction, 397-428), *Confessiones* (The Confessions, c.400) and *De civitate Dei* (The City of God, 413-426).

Aukrust, Olav (1883-1929), Norwegian poet, best known for his mystical *Himmelvarden* (Cairn of Heaven, 1916).

Aulard, François-Alphonse (1849-1928), French historian who was an authority of the French Revolution.

Aulnoy or **Aunoy, Marie-Catherine Le Jumel de Barneville, Comtesse d' (c.1650-1705),** French novelist and fairy-tale writer whose own life of adventure equalled her fiction.

Aurobindo, Sri (actually **Sri Aurobindo Ghose) (1872-1950),** Indian seer, philosopher, nationalist, poet and dramatist.

Aury, Dominique (1907-1998), French writer and translator who wrote the erotic best-seller *Histoire d'O* (1954) under the name Pauline Réage.

Auslander, Joseph (1897-1965), American poet and writer; husband of Audrey Wurdemann.

Ausonius, Decimus Magnus (c.310-c.395), Latin poet and rhetorician.

Austen, Jane (1775-1817), remarkable English novelist of the classical works *Sense and Sensibility* (1811), *Pride and Prejudice* (1813), *Mansfield Park* (1814), *Emma* (1815-16) and *Northanger Abbey* and *Persuasion* (published posthumously, 1817-18).

Austin, Alfred (1835-1913), English journalist and poet; became Poet Laureate of the United Kingdom (1896).

Austin, John (1790-1859), English jurist, author of *The Province of Jurisprudence Determined* (1832).

Austin, J(ohn) L(angshaw) (1911-1960), English philosopher.

Austin, Mary (née Hunter) (1868-1934), American novelist, short-story writer and essayist.

Austin, William (1778-1841), American lawyer, politician and writer, remembered for his popular tale *Peter Rugg, the Missing Man* (1824).

Avenarius, Richard (Heinrich Ludwig) (1843-1896), German philosopher, best known for his *Kritik der reinen Erfahrung* (2 volumes, 1888, 1900).

Aventinus (actually **Johannes Turmair) (1477-1534).** German Humanist and historian who wrote the important *Annales Boiorum* (Bavarian Annals, 1517-21).

Averröes (1126-1198), eminent Islamic religious philosopher, jurist and physician.

Avicenna (980-1037), illustrious Islamic philosopher, scientist and physician, author of the *Book of Healing* and the *Canon of Medicine*.

Avvakum Petrovich (c.1620-1682), famous Russian clergyman and writer, leader of the Old Believers in opposition to the Russian Orthodox Church and author of a celebrated autobiography; was condemned and burned at the stake.

Ayala y Herrera, Adelardo Lopez de (1828-1879), Spanish dramatist and politician whose most successful play was *Consuelo* (1878).

Ayer, Sir A(lfred) J(ules) (1910-1989), eminent English philosopher, author of such significant works as *Language, Truth and Logic* (1936), *The Problem of Knowledge* (1956), *Philosophy and Language* (1960) and *The Concept of a Person and Other Essays* (1963).

Aymé, Marcel (1902-1967), French novelist, short-story writer, dramatist and essayist.

Ayrer, Jakob (1543-1605), German dramatist.

Ayton or **Aytoun, Sir Robert (1570-1638),** Scottish poet who wrote English, Latin, Greek and French verse.

Aytoun, William Edmondstoune (1813-1865), Scottish poet and writer.

Azaïs, Pierre-Hyacinthe (1766-1845), French philosopher and writer, author of *Des compensations dans les destinées humaines* (3 volumes, 1809), and *Système universel* (8 volumes, 1809-12).

Azeglio, Massimo Taparelli, Marchese d' (1798-1866), Italian statesman, writer and painter who was a principal figure in the Risorgimento.

Azevedo, Aluízio (1857-1913), Brazilian novelist and diplomat.

Azorin (actually **José Martínez Ruiz) (1874-1967),** Spanish writer and critic.

Azuela, Mariano (1873-1952), Mexican novelist of social protest.

Baader, Franz Xaver von (1765-1841), German Roman Catholic mystic and theologian who espoused the cause of ecumenism in his writings.

Bābā Tāher (c.1000-c.1056), illustrious Persian poet who was known as 'Oryān (the Naked) since he may have been a Muslim mystic.

Babbitt, Irving (1865-1933), notable American critic and teacher, founder of the New Humanism of Neohumanism.

Babel, Isaac (Emmanuilovich) (1894-1941), prominent Russian writer who lost favour with the Stalinist regime; died in a prison camp in Siberia.

Babits, Mihály (1883-1941), Hungarian poet, novelist, essayist and translator.

Babrius (c.2nd Century), Greek writer of fables.

Bacchelli, Riccardo (1891-1985), Italian novelist, poet, dramatist and critic, well known for his novel trilogy *Il mulino del Po* (1938-40; English translation as *The Mill on the Po*, 3 volumes, 1952-55).

Bacchylides (5th Century B.C.), Greek poet of a lyric nature; nephew of Simonides of Ceas.

Bachaumont, François Le Coigneux de (1624-1702), French poet who, with Chapelle, wrote the satirical *Voyage* (1663).

Bacheller, Irving (Addison) (1859-1950), American journalist and novelist, author of such popular novels as *Eben Holden: A Tale of the North Country* (1900) and *D'ri and I* (1901).

Bachman, John (1790-1874), American Lutheran minister and naturalist who collaborated with John James Audubon on several volumes and was the author of *The Unity of the Human Race* (1850) and *A Defense of Luther and the Reformation* (1853).

Bachofen, Johann Jakob (1815-1887), Swiss jurist and anthropologist, author of the significant social anthropological study *Das Mutterrecht* (Mother Right, 1861).

Backus, Isaac (1724-1806), American Baptist preacher and historian who wrote *A History of New England, With Particular Reference to the Denomination of Christians Called Baptists* (3 volumes, 1777-96).

Bacon, Delia (Salter) (1811-1859), American writer and dramatist who attempted to prove that Shakespeare's plays were not by the Bard of Avon in her *Philosophy of the Plays of Shakespeare Unfolded* (1857); died insane.

Bacon, Francis, Baron Verulam, Viscount St Albans (1561-1626), famous English lawyer, courtier, statesman, philosopher and writer, author or the outstanding *Novum Organum* (1620).

Bacon, Leonard (1887-1954), American poet, admired for his volume *Sunderland Capture* (1940).

Bacon, Peggy (Margaret Fuller) (1895-1987), American artist and poet.

Bacon, Roger (c.1220-1292), celebrated English philosopher, known as the Doctor Mirabilis, author of the *Opue majus, Opus minus* and *Opus tertium*.

Baconthorpe, John (c. 1290-c. 1346), English theologian and philosopher, known as John Bacon, Johannes de Baconthorpe, Johannes de Anglicus and Doctor Resolutus, especially appreciated for his commentaries on Aristotle and Averroës.

Bādā'ūnī, 'Abd al-Qādir (1540-c.1615), Indo-Persian historian who wrote copiously on Muslim subjects.

Baeck, Leo (1873-1956), outstanding German-born English Reform rabbi and theologian who suffered numerous arrests and survived a Nazi concentration camp, author of a major volume on the essence of Judaism (1905).

Bagehot, Walter (1826-1877), English journalist, economist, political analyst and sociologist, author of *The English Constitution* (1867), *Physics and Politics* (1872) and *Lombard Street* (1873).

Baggesen, Jens (Immanuel) (1764-1826), Danish writer and poet, particularly admired for his prose volume *Labyrinten* (The Labyrinth, 1792-93).

Bagnold, Enid (Algerine), Lady Roderick Jones (1889-1981), English novelist and dramatist, author of the popular novel *National Velvet* (1935) and the enormously successful play *The Chalk Garden* (1956).

Bagritsky (Dzyubin), Eduard Georgievich (1895-1934), Russian poet who championed the Soviet order.

Bahā' ad-Dīn Zuhayr (actually Abū al-Fadl Zuhayr ibn Muhammad al-Muhallabī) (1186-1258), Arab poet, known for his odes and love poems.

Bahār, Mohammad Taqī (1885-1951), Iranian poet, writer and translator.

Bahr, Hermann (1863-1934), Austrian writer and dramatist.

Baïf, Jean-Antoine de (1532-1589), inventive French poet, much esteemed for his *Mimes, enseignemens et proverbes* (Mimes, Lessons and Proverbs, 1576).

Bailey, Nathan or Nathaniel (d, c.1742), English philologist and lexicographer.

Bailey, Philip James (1816-1902), English poet, author of *Festus* (1838-89).

Bailey, Samuel (1791-1870), English economist and philospher whose most significant works were *Essays on the Formation and Publication of Opinions* (1821), *A Critical Dissertation on the Nature, Measures, and Causes of Value* (1825) and *Essays of the Pursuit of Truth, on the Progress of Knowledge, and on the Fundamental Principle of All Evidence and Expectation* (1829).

Baillie, Joanna (1762-1851), Scottish dramatist and poet, author of *Fugitive Verses* (1790) and *Plays on the Passions* (3 volumes, 1798-1812).

Baillie, Lady Grizel (1665-1746), Scottish poet who became best known for her songs.

Baillie, Robert (1599-1662), Scottish Presbyterian minister and scholar.

Bain, Alexander (1818-1903), Scottish philosopher, particularly known for his studies in psychology and for his work *Logic* (2 volumes, 1870).

Baines, Thomas (1822-1875), English artist, explorer, naturalist and writer, author of *Explorations in South-West Africa* (1864).

Bainville, Jacques (1879-1936), French historian who wrote perceptive books on French, German and British history.

Baius, Michael (1513-1589), Belgian theologian who was also known as Michael Bajus and Michel de Bay.

Baker, Augustine (1575-1641), English Benedictine monk who wrote on ascetic and mystical theology.

Baker, Benjamin A (1818-1890), American dramatist, best remembered for his melodrama *A Glance at New York* (1848).

Baker, Dorothy (1907-1968), American novelist.

Baker, Leonard (Stanley) (1931-1984), American journalist and writer of biographies and historical books.

Baker, Ray Stannard (1870-1946), American journalist, essayist and biographer who often wrote under the name David Grayson, author of *Woodrow Wilson: Life and Letters* (8 volumes, 1927-39).

Baker, Sir Richard (c.1568-1645), English writer and translator who wrote *A Chronicle of the Kings of England* (1643).

Baker, William Mumford (1825-1883), American Presbyterian minister and writer, author of the novel *Inside: A Chronicle of Secession* (1866), which he wrote under the name George F Harrington.

Bakhtin, Mikhail Mikhailovich (1895-1975), Russian philosopher of language and literature.

Bâkî (actually Mahmud Abdülbâkî) (1526-1600), remarkable Arab poet who excelled in lyric poetry.

Bakunin, Mikhail Alexandrovich (1814-1876), noted Russian anarchist and political writer who was a principal opponent of Karl Marx.

Balādhurī, al- (actually Ahmad ibn Yahyā al-Balādhurī) (d. c.892), Arab historian who chronicled the founding of the Arab Muslim empire (English translation as *The Origins of the Islamic State*, 1916-24).

Balaguer y Circera, Victor (1824-1901), Spanish poet, historian and politician.

Balassi or Balassa, Bálint (1554-1594), esteemed Hungarian poet who was admired for his lyric gifts.

Balbín, Bohuslav (1621-1688), Czech historian.

Balbo, Cesare, Conte (1789-1853), Italian poltician and writer, best remembered for his *Delle speranze d'Italia* (The Hopes of Italy, 1844).

Balbuena, Bernardo de (c.1562-1627), Spanish Roman Catholic bishop and poet.

Balch, Emily Greene (1867-1961), American sociologist, political scientist, economist and pacifist; was co-winner of the Nobel Prize for Peace (1946).

Balchin, Nigel (Martin) (1908-1970), English novelist, particularly admired for *The Small Back Room* (1943) and *Mine Own Executioner* (1945).

Baldwin, Faith (1893-1978), American writer and poet.

Baldwin, James (Arthur) (1924-1987), provocative American novelist, short-story writer, dramatist and essayist of the black experience.

Baldwin, James Mark (1861-1934), American philosopher and psychologist who wrote *Genetic Logic* (3 volumes, 1906-11).

Bale, John (1495-1563), prominent English Protestant bishop, antiquarian, polemical writer and dramatist, author of one of the earliest English history plays *Kynge Johan*.

Balestier, (Charles) Wolcott (1861-1891), English novelist and short-story writer; brother-in-law of (Joseph) Rudyard Kipling.

Ball, Hugo (1886-1927), German critic, writer and dramatist who wrote the studies *Kritik der deutschen Intelligenz* (1919) and *Die Flucht aus der Zeit* (1927).

Ballanche, Pierre-Simon (1776-1847), French philosopher, author of *Du sentiment considéré dans ses rapports avec la littératures et les arts* (Sentiment Considered in Its Relationship to Literature and the Arts, 1801).

Ballantyne, Robert Michael (1825-1894), Scottish writer, particularly known for *The Coral Island* (1858).

Ballou, Adin (1803-1890), American writer on religious subjects, author of *Practical Christian Socialism* (1854) and *Primitive Christianity and Its Corruptions* (1870).

Ballou, Hosea (1771-1852), American Universalist pastor, theologian, essayist and hymnist who wrote An *Examination of the Doctrine of Future Retribution* (1834); father of Maturin Murray Ballou.

Ballou, Maturin Murray (1820-1895), American writer, publisher and editor who often wrote under the name Lieutenant Murray; son of Hosea Ballou.

Balmes, Jaime Luciano (1810-1848), Spanish writer on religion, politics and philosophy.

Balmont, Konstantin Dmitrievich (1867-1943), Russian poet, essayist and translator.

Baluze, Étienne (1630-1718), French scholar, particularly known as an historian and editor.

Balzac, Honoré de (1799-1850), great French writer who elevated the form of the novel to an exalted position through his extraordinary series of works he described as *La Comédie humaine* (The Human Comedy).

Balzac, Jean-Louis Guez de (1597-1654), French writer and critic, especially admired for his writings published under the title *Lettres* (1624 et seq.).

Bamford, Samuel (1788-1872), English radical reformer and poet.

Bàn, Donnchadh (1724-1812), Scottish writer who was also known as Duncan MacIntyre.

Bancroft, George (1800-1891), prominent American politician and historian who wrote the exhaustive *History of the United States* (10 volumes, 1834-74), 3rd edition, revised, 1883-85).

Bancroft, Hubert Howe (1832-1918), American historian who oversaw the publication of a vast history of the American West (39 volumes, 1874-92).

Bandeira (Filho), Manuel (Carneiro de Sousa) (1886-1968), eminent Brazilian poet, literary historian, educator and translator.

Bandelier, Adolph (Francis Alphonse) (1840-1914), Swiss-born American anthropologist and archaeologist who was known for his studies of Native American cultures of the US and of Aztec culture of Mexico.

Bandello, Matteo (1485-1561), Italian-born French writer and Roman Catholic bishop, author of the notable series of 214 stories in his *Novelle* (4 volumes, 1554-73).

Bang, Herman (1857-1912), Danish novelist, poet, dramatist and critic.

Banim, John (1798-1842), Irish novelist, short-story writer, dramatist and poet who often collaborated with his brother Michael Banim.

Banim, Michael (1796-1874), Irish novelist and short-story writer, a frequent collaborator with his brother John Banim.

Banning, Margaret Culkin (1891-1982), American novelist.

Bannister, Nathaniel Harrington (1813-1847), American dramatist, best remembered for his *Putnam* (1844).

Banville, (Étienne-Claude-Jean-Baptiste-) Théodore (-Faullain) de (1823-1891), admired French poet and dramatist, esteemed for the poetry collection *Les Odes funambulesques* (1857).

Bar, François de (1538-1606), French scholar and Roman Catholic prior who was known for his work on church history and law.

Barahona de Soto, Luis (c.1548-1595), Spanish poet, author of *Primera parte de la Angélica* (The First Part of the Angélica, 1586), better known as *Las lagrimas de Angélica* (The Tears of Angélica).

Baranauskas, Antanas (1835-1902), Lithuanian Roman Catholic bishop and poet, author of the esteemed poem *Anykyščiu šilelis* (1858-59; English translation as The Forest of Anykščiai, 1956).

Barante, Amable-Guillaume-Prosper Brugiere, Baron de (1782-1866), French statesman, historian , biographer and translator, author of *Histoire des ducs de Bourgogne* (History of the Dukes of Burgundy, 1824-28).

Baratynsky or **Boratynsky, Yevgeny (Abramovich) (1800-1844),** important Russian poet, a master of philosophical poetry.

Barbauld, Anna Laetitia (née Aikin) (1743-1825), English poet and writer.

Barbey d'Aurevilly, Jules-Amédée (1808-1889), French novelist, short-story writer and critic, particularly esteemed for his short-story collection *Les Diaboliques* (1874; English translation as *Weird Women*, 1900).

Barbon, Nicholas (c.1640-1698), English economist whose writings presaged those of Adam Smith.

Barbon, Praise-God (c.1596-1680), English sectarian preacher and writer who became known as Barebone and Barebones, the latter prompting the naming of the Puritan Barebones Parliament.

Barbour or **Barbere** or **Barbier, John (c.1325-1395),** Scottish poet, scholar and prelate who wrote the national epic *The Actes and Life of the most Victorious Conqueror, Robert Bruce King of Scotland* (20 volumes, 1376), popularly known as *The Bruce*.

Barbusse, Henri (1873-1935), French writer and poet, author of the World War I novel *Le Feu* (1916; English translation as Under Fire, 1917).

Barclay, Alexander (c.1476-1552), Scottish poet who wrote *The Shyp of Folys of the Worlde* (1509), an adaptation of Brant's *Das Narrenschiff*.

Barclay, John (1582-1621), Scottish writer and poet, known for his book *Euphormionis Lusinini Satyricon* (1603-07), and the Latin poem the *Argenis* (1621).

Barclay, Robert (1648-1690), Scottish Quaker and writer, author of the *Theses Theologicae* (1675) and the *Apology for the True Christian Divinity* (1678), the latter a classic exposition of Quaker beliefs.

Bardesanes or **Bardaisan** or **Bar Dausān (154-c.222),** Syrian Christian Gnostic writer and hymnist.

Bardi, Giovanni de', Count of Vernio (1534-1612), Italian nobleman, music and art patron, composer and writer, influential in the development of opera and author of *Discorso mandato a Caccini sopra la Musica Antica* (Discourse to Caccini on Ancient Music, 1580).

Baretti, Giuseppe (Marc' Antonio) (1719-1789), Italian-born English critic and lexicographer, editor of *A Dictionary of the English and Italian Languages* (1760).

Barham, Richard Harris (1788-1845), English churchman and poet, best remembered for his humorous collections *The Ingoldsby Legends* (1840, 1842, 1847).

Bar Hebraeus (1226-1286), Syrian scholar and chief prelate of the Eastern Jacobite Church, best known for his encyclopedia *Hē'wath hekkmthā* (The Butter of Wisdom).

Baring, Maurice (1874-1945), English writer, dramatist, biographer, critic, poet and translator.

Baring-Gould, Sabine (1834-1924), English writer and churchman, author of the hymns *Onward, Christian Soldiers* and *Now the Day is Over*.

Barker, George (Granville) (1913-1991), English poet and novelist who wrote the poems *Calamiterror* (1937) and *The True Confession of George Barker* (1950, revised edition, 1957).

Barker, James Nelson (1784-1858), American dramatist, best known for his play *Superstition* (1824).

Barlow, Joel (1754-1812), American poet and writer, author of *The Vision of Columbus* (1787; revised as the epic poem *The Columbiad*, 1807) and the mock-heroic poem *The Hasty Pudding* (1796).

Barnard, Lady Anne (née Lindsay) (1750-1825), Scottish writer of the well-known ballad *Auld Robin Gray* (1771).

Barnave, Antoine (-Pierre-Joseph-Marie) (1761-1793), French politician who was a leading figure in the Revolution but whose advocacy of a constitutional monarchy led to his imprisonment and execution, author of the significant book *Introduction à la révolution française* (1792, written during his incarceration).

Barnes, Barnabe (c.1569-1609), English poet, writer and dramatist, remembered for his poetry collection *Parthenophil and Parthenophe* (1593).

Barnes, Charlotte Mary Sanford (1818-1863), American dramatist, known for her melodramas *Octavia Bragaldi* (1837, published 1848) and *The Forest Princess* (1848).

Barnes, Djuna Chappell (1892-1982), American novelist, short-story writer, dramatist, poet and illustrator.

Barnes, Ernest William (1874-1953), English Anglican bishop and pacifist, known for his liberal views in such writings as *Scientific Theory and Religion* (1933) and *The Rise of Christianity* (1947).

Barnes, Harry Elmer (1889-1968), American sociologist and historian.

Barnes, Margaret Ayer (1896-1967), American novelist and dramatist, especially admired for her novel *Years of Grace* (1930); sister of Janet Ayer Fairbank.

Barnes, Robert (1495-1540), English prior who became an advocate of Lutheranism, author of *A Supplication to Henry VII* (1531), *Vitae Romanorum Pontificum* (Lives of the Roman Pontiffs, 1535) and *Confession of Faith* (1540); was condemned as a heretic and burned.

Barnes, William (1801-1886), English poet and priest, known for his dialect poems.

Barnfield, Richard (1574-1627), English poet of pastoral verse.

Baroja, Pío (1872-1956), eminent Spanish novelist and short-story writer, author of the trilogy *La lucha por la vida* (1904; English translation as *The Struggle for Life*, 1922-24) and the vast *Memorias de un hombre de accion* (Memoirs of a Man of Action, 22 volumes).

Baronius, Caesar (1538-1607), Italian historian and apologist of the Roman Catholic Church who wrote the well-known *Annales Ecclesiastici* (12 folios, 1588-1607).

Barr, Amelia Edith (Huddleston) (1831-1919), English-born American novelist.

Barr, Stringfellow (1897-1982), American educator and writer.

Barrès, (Auguste-) Maurice (1862-1923), French novelist, essayist and politician.

Barrie, Sir James (Matthew) (1860-1937), English dramatist and novelist, creator of the ever-youthful Peter Pan.

Barros, João de (c.1496-1570), Portuguese government official, historian and Orientalist who was known as the Portuguese Livy.

Barros Arana, Diego (1830-1907), Chilean historian, educator and diplomat, author of the *Historia jeneral de Chile* (General History of Chile, 16 volumes, 1884-1902).

Barrow, Henry (c.1550-1593), English lawyer and Congregationalist reformer, author of *A True Description out of the Word of God, of the Visible Church* (1589) and *A Brief Discovery of the False Church* (1590); was imprisoned and hanged for his advocacy of Separatism.

Barry, Philip (1896-1949), American dramatist, much esteemed for such plays as *White Wings* (1926), *Hotel Universe* (1930), *Here Come the Clowns* (1938) and *The Philadelphia Story* (1939).

Bar-Salibi, Jacob (d. 1171), Turkish-born bishop of the Jakobite (Monophysite) Church, theologian and poet.

Bartas, Guillaume de Salluste, Seigneur (1544-1590), French soldier, diplomat and poet who wrote the poem *La Semaine* (1578).

Barth, Heinrich (1821-1865), German geographer and explorer, author of the important *Travels and Discoveries in North and Central Africa* (5 volumes, 1857-58).

Barth, Karl (1886-1968), renowned Swiss Protestant theologian, author of the great *Die kirchliche Dogmatik* (1932 et seq.; English translation as *The Church Dogmatics*, 13 volumes, 1936-69).

Barth, Paul (1858-1922), German philosopher and sociologist who wrote studies on Hegel and his followers (1896) and on the philosophy of history of sociology (1897).

Barthélemy, Jean-Jacques (1716-1795), French scholar and writer, best remembered for his novel *Le Voyage du jeune Anacharsis en Grèce, dans le milieu du quatrième siècle avant l'ère vulgaire* (1788; English translation as *Travels of Anacharsis the Younger in Greece*, 1791).

Barthélemy-Saint-Hilaire, Jules (1805-1895), French journalist, statesman, scholar, writer and translator.

Barthelme, Donald (1931-1989), American novelist and short-story writer.

Bartholomaeus Anglicus or **Bartholomew the Englishman (13th Century),** English Franciscan scholar and compiler of the notable encyclopedia *De proprietatibus rerum* (On the Properties of Things).

Bartoli, Daniello (1608-1685), Italian Jesuit scholar, particularly remembered for his *Dell'huomo de lettere* (The Learned Man).

Bartoli, Matteo Giulio (1873-1946), Italian linguist, founder of neolinguistics or areal linguistics.

Bashshar ibn Burd (d. c.784), Muslim poet.

Basil of Ancyra (d. c.364), Greek bishop and theologian.

Basil the Great, Saint (c.329-379), celebrated Roman Catholic bishop and theologian who was a leading opponent of the Arian heresy.

Basile, Giambattista (c.1575-1632), Italian soldier, public official, poet and writer, author of the folk-tale collection *Lo cunto di li cunti* (1634; English translation as *The Pentamerone*, 1932).

Basin, Thomas (1412-1491), French Roman Catholic bishop and historian.

Basnage, Jacques (1653-1723), French Huguenot minister, historian and diplomat.

Basselin, Olivier (c.1400-1450), French poet.

Bassett, John Spencer (1867-1928), American historian.

Basso, (Joseph) Hamilton (1904-1964), American writer, best known for his novels of Southern society.

Bastian, Adolf (1826-1905), German ethnologist who wrote the important study *Der Mensch in der Geschichte* (Man in History, 3 volumes, 1860).

Bastiat, (Claude-) Frédéric (1801-1850), French journalist, economist and politician who opposed Socialism and Communism.

Bataille, (Félix-) Henry (1872-1922), French dramatist, best remembered for his play *La Femme nue* (The Nude Woman, 1908).

Bateman, Sidney Frances (1823-1881), American actress and dramatist who wrote the play of social satire *Self* (1856).

Bates, Arlo (1850-1918), American novelist, short-story writer and poet.

Bates, Ernest Sutherland (1879-1939), American writer.

Bates, H(erbert) E(rnest) (1905-1974), English novelist and short-story writer.

Bates, Katherine Lee (1859-1929), American educator, writer and poet, celebrated for her patriotic poem *America the Beautiful* (1893).

Bateson, F(rederick Noel) W(ilse) (1901-1978), English scholar, critic and editor.

Batsányi, János (1763-1845), Hungarian poet who won fame for his political verse.

Baty, (Jean-Baptiste-Marie-) Gaston (1885-1952), French dramatist, appreciated for his *Dulcinée* (1938).

Batyushkov, Konstantin (Nikolaievich) (1787-1855), Russian poet of elegiac verse whose career was aborted by insanity.

Baudelaire, Charles (Pierre) (1821-1867), remarkable French poet of great refinement and originality, renowned for his collection *Les Fleurs du mal* (1857).

Baudouin, François (1520-c.1574), French theologian and historian, a pioneer in legal history.

Baudouin de Courtenay, Jan Niecislaw (1845-1929), Polish linguist, author of the study V*ersuch einer Theorie phonetischer Alternationer* (Essay on a Theory of Phonetic Alternation, 1895).

Bauer, Bruno (1809-1882), German theologian and historian who espoused a radical interpretation of the New Testament.

Bauernfeld, Eduard von (1802-1890), Austrian dramatist who had great success with his politically-tinged drawing-room comedies.

Baum, L(yman) Frank (1856-1919), American writer of the popular land of Oz books.

Baum, Vicki (actually Hedwig Baum) (1888-1960), Austrian-born American novelist and screenwriter, best known for her novel *Menschen im Hotel* (1929; English translation as *Grand Hotel*, 1931).

Baumbach, Rudolf (1840-1905), German poet of the vagabond tradition.

Baumgarten, Alexander Gottlieb (1714-1762), important German philosopher who made the study of aesthetics a special branch of philosophical discourse, author of the influential study *Aesthetica* (2 volumes, 1750, 1758).

Baumgarten, Hermann (1825-1893), German historian.

Baumgarten, Siegmund Jakob (1706-1757), German theologian of rational proclivities.

Baur, Ferdinand Christian (1792-1860), greatly significant German theologian and church historian who founded the Protestant Tübingen school of biblical criticism.

Baxter, Andrew (c.1686-1750), Scottish philosopher who espoused a metaphysical rationalism, author of *An Enquiry Into the Nature of the Human Soul* (1733; 3rd edition, 1745); Appendix, 1750) and *Matho, sive cosmotheoria puerilis* (1738; English translation, 1740).

Baxter, James K(eir) (1926-1972), New Zealand poet, dramatist and critic.

Baxter, Richard (1615-1691), notable English Puritan minister and theologian who wrote numerous works, including *Aphorismes of Justification* (1649) and an autobiography *Reliquiae Baxterianae* or *Mr Richard Baxter's Narrative of the Most Memorable Passages of his Life and Times* (published 1696).

Bayle, Pierre (1647-1706), French scholar and philosopher, compiler of the noted *Dictionnaire historique et critique* (2 volumes, 1695, 1697; 2nd edition, revised and enlarged, 1702).

Baylebridge, William (actually Charles William Blocksidge) (1883-1942), Australian poet and short-story writer.

Bayly, Nathaniel Thomas Haynes (1797-1839), English poet and dramatist who won popularity as the author of various songs.

Baylor, Frances Courtenay (1848-1920), American novelist.

Bazin, Hervé (actually Jean-Pierre Hervé-Bazin) (1911-1996), prominent French novelist, short-story writer and poet; great-nephew of René (-François-Nicolas-Marie) Bazin.

Bazin, René (-François-Nicolas-Marie) (1853-1932), French novelist who became an upholder of traditional values; great-uncle of Hervé Bazin.

Beach, Joseph Warren (1880-1957), American critic and poet.

Beach, Rex (Ellingwood) (1877-1949), American novelist.

Beals, Carleton (1893-1981), American journalist, novelist and biographer.

Beard, Charles A(ustin) (1874-1948), eminent American historian who wrote the important study *An Economic Interpretation of the Constitution of the United States* (1913); husband of Mary R(itter) Beard.

Beard, Mary R(itter) (1876-1958), American historian; wife of Charles A(ustin) Beard.

Beardsley, Aubrey (Vincent) (1872-1898), English illustrator, writer and poet, author of the erotic *The Story of Venus and Tannhauser* (published 1907).

Beattie, James (1735-1803), Scottish poet and essayist who wrote the poem *The Minstrel* (2 parts, 1771, 1774).

Beatus Rhenanus (1485-1547), German Humanist scholar, writer and editor who was known as Beatus Bild.

Beauchamp, Alphonse de (1767-1832), French historian and biographer.

Beauchemin, Neree (1850-1931), French-Canadian poet and physician.

Beaulieu, Michel (1941-1985), French-Canadian poet and writer.

Beaumarchais, Pierre-Augustin Caron de (1732-1799), French dramatist, remembered for his *Le Barbier de Seville* (1775; English translation as *The Barber of Seville*,1776), and *Le Mariage de Figaro* (1784; English translation as *The Marriage of Figaro*, 1785), plays set to music as celebrated operal respectively by Rossini and Mozart.

Beaumont, Francis (c.1584-1616), distinguished English dramatist who collaborated with John Fletcher on a series of notable plays, among them *Phylaster* (1610) and *The Maides Tragedy* (1611); brother of Sir John Beaumont.

Beaumont, Sir John (1583-1627), English poet who introduced the heroic couplet to English verse, author of the extensive poem *The Crown of Thornes* (12 volumes); brother of Francis Beaumont.

Beauvoir, Roger de (actually **Edouard Roger de Bully) (1809-1866),** French novelist.

Beauvoir, Simone de (1908-1986), influential French writer, philosopher and political activist, especially known for her espousal of Existentialism.

Beccaria, Cesare Bonesana, Marchese di (1738-1794), Italian scholar who wrote on criminal law and economics, author of the influential study *Dei delletti e delle pene* (1764; English translation as *Crimes and Punishments*, 1880).

Becher, Johannes Robert (1891-1958), German poet, critic and editor of a Marxist persuasion.

Bechtel, Friedrich (1855-1924), German classical scholar.

Becker, Carl L(otus) (1873-1945), distinguished American historian, author of *The Beginnings of the American People* (1915), *The Eve of the Revolution* (1918), *The Declaration of Independence* (1922) and *The Heavenly City of the Eighteenth-Century Philosophers* (1932).

Becker, Jürek (1937-1997), German novelist.

Becker, Wilhelm Adolf (1796-1846), German archaeologist who wrote such works as *Gallus* (1838; English translation, 1844), *Charikles* (1840) and *Handbuch der romischen Altertumer* (Handbook of Roman Antiquities, 5 volumes, 1843-68).

Beckett Samuel (Barclay) (1906-1989), celebrated Irish dramatist, writer, poet and critic, particularly known for his play *En attendant Godot* (1952; English translation as *Waiting for Godot*, 1954) and the prose trilogy *Molloy* (1951; English translation, 1955), *Malone meurt* (1951; English translation as *Malone Dies*, 1956) and *L'Innomable* (1953; English translation as *The Unnamable*, 1958); won the Nobel Prize for Literature (1969).

Beckford, William (c.1760-1844), English writer of an eccentric nature, author of the classic Gothic novel *Vathek* (1786).

Becque, Henry-François (1837-1899), French dramatist and critic, known for his naturalist plays *Les Corbeaux* (1882; English translation as *The Vultures*, 1913) and *La Parisienne* (1885; English translation, 1943).

Becquer, Gustavo Adolfo (1836-1870), Spanish writer and poet, best remembered for his poems of troubadour love.

Beddoes, Thomas Lovell (1803-1849), English poet and physiologist, author of *Death's Jest-Book, or, The Fool's Tragedy* (1825-49); committed suicide.

Bede or **Baeda** or **Bede the Venerable, Saint (c.672-735),** significant Anglo-Saxon theologian and historian, author of the invaluable *Historia ecclesiastica gentis Anglorum* (Ecclesiastical History of the English People, 732).

Bedier, (Charles-Marie-) Joseph (1864-1938), distinguished French scholar, known for his *Le Roman de Tristan et Iseult* (1900) and *Les Legendes epiques* (4 volumes, 1908-21).

Bedil, Mirza (actually **Mirza 'abd-ul-Qadir ibn 'abd-ul-Khaliq Arlas Bedil) (1644-1721),** Indian Muslim poet, known for his prolific mystical poems.

Bedny, Demyan (actually **Yefim Alexselevich Pridvorov) (1885-1945),** Russian poet who wrote on Soviet themes while displaying a satirical streak.

Beebe, Charles William (1877-1962), American biologist, naturalist, explorer and writer.

Beecher, Catharine E(sther) (1800-1878), American educator, social reformer and writer, daughter of Lyman Beecher and sister of Henry Ward Beecher and Harriet Beecher Stowe.

Beecher, Henry Ward (1813-1887), controversial American Congregational minister, writer and editor of pronouced liberal views; son of Lyman Beecher and brother of Catharine E(sther) Beecher and Harriet Beecher Stowe.

Beecher, Lyman (1775-1863), American Presbyterian minister, writer and editor; father of Catharine E(sther) Beecher, Henry Ward Beecher and Harriet Beecher Stowe.

Beer, Thomas (1889-1940), American novelist and short-story writer.

Beerbohm, Sir (Henry) Max(imilian) (1872-1956), English critic, essayist and caricaturist, known for his remarkable wit.

Beers, Ethel Lynn (1827-1879), American poet and writer, best remembered for her poem *The Picket-Guard* (1861), later known as *All Quiet Along the Potomac.*

Beets, Nicolaas (1814-1903), Dutch pastor, writer and poet, author of the popular collection *Camera obscura* (1839; 4th edition, 1854).

Behan, Brendan (Francis) (1923-1964), provocative Irish dramatist and poet, best known for his play *The Hostage* (1958).

Behn, Aphra (1640-1689), English dramatist, poet and writer, known as the Incomparable Astrea, author of the novel *Oroonoko* (1688).

Behrman, S(amuel) N(athaniel) (1893-1973), American dramatist and writer.

Bein, Albert (1902-1963), American novelist and dramatist.

Beke, Charles Tilstone (1800-1874), English biblical scholar and geographer, author of *Origines Biblicae, or Researches in Primeval History* (1834), *An Essay on the Nile and Its Tributaries* (1847) and *The Sources of the Nile* (1860).

Bekker, August Immanuel (1785-1871), German classical scholar and editor.

Belasco, David (1853-1931), American theatre producer and dramatist, especially remembered for his *Madame Butterfly* (1900) and *The Girl of the Golden West* (1905) which were set to music as operas by Puccini.

Belinsky, Vissarion (Grigorievich) (1811-1848), influential Russian literary critic.

Belknap, Jeremy (1744-1798), American Congregational minister and historian who wrote a *History of New Hampshire* (3 volumes, 1784, 1791, 1792), and *American Biography* (2 volumes, 1794, 1798).

Bell, Gertrude Margaret Lowthian (1868-1926), English traveller and writer.

Bellamy, Edward (1850-1898), American novelist, short-story writer, essayist and journalist, author of the Utopian novel *Looking Backward, 2000-1887* (1888).

Bellamy, Joseph (1719-1790), American writer of theological pamphlets, best known for his *True Religion Delineated* (1750).

Bellarmine, Saint Robert (actually Roberto Francesco Romolo Bellarmino) (1542-1621), Italian Roman Catholic cardinal and theologian who was a vigorous opponent of the Protestant Reformation, author of *Disputationes de controversiis Christiane fidei adversus huius temporis haereticos* (Lectures Concerning the Controversies of the Christian Faith Against the Heretics of This Time, 1586-93).

Bellay, Guillaume du, Seigneur de Langey (1491-1543), French soldier and historian who wrote the *Ogdoades* only fragments extant; published 1905) and *Épitome de l'antiquité des Gaules et de France* (Abridgement of the Early Times of Gaul and France, 1556).

Bellay, Jean du (c.1492-1560), French Roman Catholic cardinal, diplomat and poet.

Bellay, Joachim du (c.1522-1560), French poet and writer, a principal figure in the literary group known as the Pléiade and author of its manifesto *La Defense et illustration de la langue française* (1549; English translation as *The Defence and Illustration of the French Language*, 1939).

Belleau, Rémy (1528-1577), French poet, scholar and translator, especially esteemed for his poetic portraits in miniature.

Bellecour, (actually Jean-Claude-Gilles Colson) (1725-1778), French actor and dramatist, remembered for his play *Les Fausses Apparences* (The False Appearances, 1761).

Bellenden or **Ballenden** or **Ballentyne** or **Ballantyne** or **Bannatyne, John (16th Century),** Scottish canon, poet and translator.

Belli, Giuseppe Gioacchino (1791-1863), provocative Italian poet, particularly admired for his numerous sonnets.

Bellman, Carl Michael (1740-1795), esteemed Swedish poet, dramatist and composer.

Bello, Andrés (1781-1865), Venezuelan poet and scholar, known for his two poems *Silvas americanas* (1826-27).

Belloc, (Joseph-Pierre) Hilaire (1870-1953), French-born English poet, historian and essayist.

Bely, Andrei (actually Boris Nikolaievich Bugaiev) (1880-1934), Russian novelist, poet and critic, a leading Symbolist.

Bemelmans, Ludwig (1898-1962), Austrian-born American novelist, short-story writer and painter.

Bémont, Charles (1848-1939), French scholar who wrote on European and English medieval subjects.

ben Asher, Aaron ben Moses (10th Century), Jewish rabbinic scholar who made important critical notations on the Bible.

Benavente y Martínez, Jacinto (1866-1954), notable Spanish dramatist whose most celebrated play was *Los intereses creados* (1907; English translation as *The Bonds of Interest*); won the Nobel Prize for Literature (1922).

Benchley, Nathaniel (1915-1981), American humourist, novelist, dramatist and screenwriter; son of Robert (Charles) Benchley.

Benchley, Robert (Charles) (1889-1945), popular American humourist, drama critic, essayist and actor; father of Nathaniel Benchley.

Benda, Julien (1867-1956), French novelist and philosopher, author of the novel *L'Ordination* (1911; English translation as *The Yolk of Pity*, 1913), and the philosophical tome *La Trahison des clercs* (1927; English translation as *The Treason of the Intellectuals*, 1928).

Benedict, Ruth (née Fulton) (1887-1948), American anthropologist who wrote such studies as *Patterns of Culture* (1934), *Race, Science and Politics* (1940) and *The Chrysanthemum and the Sword* (1946).

Benedictsson, Victoria (1850-1888), Danish novelist and short-story writer who wrote under the name Ernst Ahlgren; committed suicide.

Benediktsson, Einar (1864-1940), remarkable Icelandic poet, author of 5 volumes of outstanding Symbolic poetry, (1897, 1906, 1913, 1921, 1930).

Benefield, (John) Barry (1877-1956), American novelist and short-story writer.

Benét, Stephen Vincent (1898-1943), American poet, novelist and short-story writer, author of the well-known poem *John Brown's Body* (1928); brother of William Rose Benét.

Benét, William Rose (1896-1950), American poet and critic; brother of Stephen Vincent Benét and husband of Elinor Wylie.

Benet Goita, Juan (1927-1993), Spanish novelist, short-story writer , essayist and translator.

Benezet, Anthony (1713-1784), French-born American teacher and writer.

Benfey, Theodor (1809-1881), German comparative language scholar, known especially for his Sanskrit studies.

Bengel, J(ohann) A(lbrecht) (1687-1752), German Lutheran theologian who was esteemed for his New Testament studies.

Bengtsson, Frans Gunnar (1894-1954), Swedish poet, novelist, biographer and essayist.

Benivieni, Girolamo (1453-1542), Italian poet.

Benjamin, Park (1809-1864), American editor, publisher and poet.

Benlowes, Edward (1602-1676), English poet, best remembered for his *Theophila or Loves Sacrifice* (1652).

Benn, Gottfried (1886-1956), significant German poet and essayist whose initial Expressionist style of pessimism, gave way in later years to a pragmatic mode of expression.

Bennett, Emerson (1822-1905), American novelist and short-story writer.

Bennett (Enoch) Arnold (1867-1931), English novelist, dramatist, critic and essayist, whose most notable novel was *The Old Wives' Tale* (1908).

Bennett, John (1865-1956), American writer, best known for the boys' book *Master Skylark* (1897).

Benoît de Sainte-Maure (12th Century), French poet, author of the *Roman de Troie*.

Benserade, Isaac de (c.1612-1691), French poet, librettist and dramatist.

Benson, A(rthur) C(hristopher) (1862-1925), English biographer, critic, diarist and poet, especially remembered for his famous poem *Land of Hope and Glory*; son of E(dward) W(hite) Benson and brother of E(dward) F(rederic) Benson and R(obert) H(ugh) Benson.

Benson, E(dward) F(rederic) (1867-1940), English novelist and biographer, author of the Dodo and Lucia series of novels; son of E(dward) W(hite) Benson and brother of A(rthur) C(hristopher) Benson and R(obert) H(ugh) Benson.

Benson E(dward) W(hite) (1829-1896), English Anglican priest, Archbishop of Canterbury and writer; father of A(rthur) C(hristopher), E(dward) F(rederic) and R(obert) H(ugh) Benson.

Benson, R(obert) H(ugh) (1871-1914), English novelist, writer and poet; son of E(dward) W(hite) Benson and brother of A(rthur) C(hristopher) Benson and E(dward) F(rederic) Benson.

Benson, Sally (actually **Sara Mahala Redway Smith Benson) (1900-1972),** American writer.

Bentham, Jeremy (1748-1831), notable English Utilitarian philosopher whose most celebrated word was *An Introduction to the Principles of Morals and Legislation* (1789).

Bentivoglio, Guido (1579-1644), Italian Roman Catholic cardinal, diplomat and historian.

Bentley, Arthur F(isher) (1870-1957), American political scientist and philosopher, particularly remembered for *The Process of Government: A Study of Social Pressures* (1908).

Bentley, Edmund Clerihew (1875-1956), English journalist, writer and poet, inventor of the clerihew, a humorous verse form, and author of the classic detective story *Trent's Last Case* (1913).

Bentley, Phyllis (1894-1977), English novelist and critic, author of the novel *Inheritance* (1932).

Bentley, Richard (1662-1742), eminent English classical scholar.

Béranger, Pierre-Jean de (1780-1857), French poet and writer whose satirical and witty poems won him great popularity.

Berberova, Nina Nikolaievna (1901-1993), Russian-born American novelist and short-story writer.

Berceo, Gonzalo de (c.1195-c.1264), Spanish poet, known for his devotional works.

Berchet, Giovanni (1783-1851), Italian poet, a formative figure in the development of Romantic poetry in his homeland.

Bercovici, Konrad (1882-1961), Romanian-born American novelist and short-story writer.

Berdiaev, Nikolai Alexandrovich (1874-1948), noted Russian novelist, short-story writer and essayist who wrote under the name Micah Joseph bin Gorion and who won distinction for his delineation of Jewish life.

Berenson, Bernard (1865-1959), Lithuanian-born American art critic, author of the important study *Italian Painters of the Renaissance* (1952).

Berent, Wacław (1873-1940), Polish novelist who wrote such works as *Próchno* (Rotten Wood, 1903) and *Ozimina* (Winter Corn, 1911).

Bergbom, Kaarlo (1843-1906), Finnish writer.

Berger, Gaston (1896-1967), French philosopher.

Bergman, Bo Hjalmar (1869-1967), Swedish poet, novelist, short-story writer and critic.

Bergman, Hjalmar Fredrik Elgérus (1883-1931), admired Swedish novelist, short-story writer, dramatist and poet, particularly esteemed for his novels *Markurells i Wadköping* (1919; English translation as *God's Orchid*, 1924), *Farmor och vår Herre* (1921; English translation as *Thy Rod and Thy Staff*, 1937) and *Chefen Fru Ingeborg* (1924; English translation as *The Head of the Firm*, 1936).

Bergson, Henri-Louis (1859-1941), prominent French philosopher, especially known for his study *L'Évolution créatice* (1907); won the Nobel Prize for Literature (1927).

Berkeley, George (1685-1753), English philosopher and Anglican bishop, author of *An Essay Towards a New Theory of Vision* (1709), *A Treatise Concerning the Principles of Human Knowledge* (1710), *Three Dialogues Between Hyals and Philonous* (1713) and *De Motu* (1721).

Berkenhead, Sir John (1617-1679), English journalist, writer and poet, particularly remembered for his wit displayed in his newsbook *Mercurius Aulicus* (1643-45).

Berlin, Sir Isaiah (1909-1997), respected Latvian-born English historian and philosopher.

Berlin, Isaiah ben Judah Loeb (1725-1799), Hebrew scholar, respected for his talmudic studies.

Berlioz, (Louis-) Hector (1803-1869), great French composer, author of the important *Grand traité d'instrumentation et d'orchestration modernes* (1843; English translation, 1948) and a remarkable autobiography *Mémoires de Hector Berlioz* (1870; English translation, 1969).

Bernanos, Georges (1888-1948), French novelist and essayist whose finest work was the novel *Journal d'un curé de campagne* (1936; English translation as *The Diary of a Country Priest*, 1937).

Bernard, Jean-Jacques (1888-1972), French dramatist and writer whose play *Martine* (1922) was a notable example of the "drama of the unexpressed".

Bernard, Tristan (actually **Paul Bernard) (1866-1947),** French dramatist, novelist, journalist and lawyer, best known for his works in a light vein.

Bernard, William Bayle (1807-1875), American dramatist.

Bernard de Ventadour (12th Century), Provençal poet, noted for his love poems.

Bernard of Chartres (c.1080-c.1130), French philosopher who espoused Platonic Idealism.

Bernard of Cluny or **Bernard of Morlaix (c.1100-c.1150),** French monk, poet and hymnist, author of the satirical poem *De comtemptu mundi* (On Condemning the World, c.1140).

Bernardes, Padre Manuel (1644-1710), Portuguese writer.

Bernardin de Saint-Pierre, Jacques-Henri (1737-1814), French writer, best known for *Paul et Virginie* (1788).

Bernardino of Siena, Saint (1380-1444), famous Italian Franciscan preacher and theologian.

Berners, John Bourchier, 2nd Baron (c.1469-1533), English statesman, writer and translator.

Berners, Lord (Sir Gerald Hugh Tyrwhitt-Wilson, Baronet) (1883-1950), English composer, writer and painter of an eccentric disposition.

Bernhard, Thomas (1931-1989), Austrian novelist, dramatist and poet.

Berni, Francesco (c.1497-1535), Italian poet and translator, especially admired for his satirical poems.

Bernstein, Henry (-Léon-Gustave-Charles) (1876-1953), French dramatist who delineated the evils of anti-Semitism and Nazism in plays of distinction.

Berquin, Arnaud (c.1749-1791), French writer.

Berr, Henri (1863-1954), French historian and philosopher who edited the mammoth cooperative study *L'Évolution de l'Humanité* (65 volumes, 1920-54).

Berrigan, Ted (actually **Edmund Berrigan Jr) (1934-1983),** American poet, dramatist and writer who became known for his experimentation.

Berryman, John (1914-1972), notable American poet and novelist, particularly admired for such works in verse as *Homage to Mistress Bradstreet* (1956), *77 Dream Songs* (1964), *Berryman's Sonnets* (1967) and *His Toy, His Dream, His Rest* (1968); committed suicide.

Bertaut, Jean de Caen (1552-1611), French Roman Catholic bishop and poet.

Bertholet, Alfred (1868-1951), Swiss Protestant Old Testament and religious scholar.

Bertrand, Louis (-Jacques-Napoléon) (1807-1841), French poet who was known as Aloysius Bertrand and who introduced the prose poem to his homeland in *Gaspard de la Nuit* (Gaspard of the Night, 1842).

Berwisnky, Ryszard Wincenty (1819-1879), Polish political radical, poet and writer.

Berzsenyi, Dániel (1776-1836), Hungarian poet who wrote the patriotic *A magyarokhoz* (To the Hungarians), *Fohász* (Prayer) and various elegies.

Besant, Sir Walter (1836-1901), English novelist, critic, editor and philanthropist.

Bessarion John (actually **Basil Bessarion) (1403-1472),** Byzantine Roman Catholic cardinal and scholar, author of *In calumniatorem Platonis* (Against the Calumniator of Plato).

Besseler, Heinrich (1900-1969), German music scholar who wrote the important study *Die Musik des Mittelaters und der Renaissance* (The Music of the Middle Ages and the Renaissance, 1931).

Bessenyei, György (c.1746-1811), Hungarian writer.

Betjeman, Sir John (1906-1984), popular English poet and writer; became Poet Laureate of the United Kingdom (1972).

Betti, Ugo (1892-1953), outstanding Italian dramatist whose collected works were published posthumously (1955).

Beveridge, Albert J(eremiah) (1862-1927), American politician and biographer, author of a *Life of John Marshall* (4 volumes, 1916-19) and an unfinished *Life of Abraham Lincoln* (2 volumes, 1928).

Beyer, Absalon Pederssøn (1528-1575), Norwegian Lutheran scholar.

Beza, Theodore (actually **Théodore de Bèze) (1519-1605),** French-born Swiss Calvinist theologian, educator, writer, translator and poet, author of *Histoire ecclésiastique des Églises réformées au royaume de France* (Ecclesiastical History of the Reformed Church in the Kingdom of France, 1580).

Bezrûc, Petr (actually **Vladimir Vasek) (1867-1958),** Czech poet who won distinction for his Silesian verse.

Bhartrhari (c.570-c.651), important Hindu poet and philosopher, author of the volume on the philosophy of language *Vākyapadīya* (Words in a Sentence).

Bhasa (2nd or 3rd Century), Sanskrit dramatist.

Bhavabhūti (8th Century), Indian dramatist and poet.

Bialik, Hayyim Nahman (1873-1934), outstanding Hebrew poet, short-story writer, editor and translator.

Bibaud, Michel (1782-1857), French-Canadian poet, historian and editor.

Bickerstaffe, Isaac (c.1735-c.1812), Irish dramatist.

Biddle, John (1615-1662), English theologian who was known as the father of English Utilitarianism, author of the controversial *Twelve Arguments Against the Deity of the Holy Ghost* (c.1644); died in prison.

Biel, Gabriel (c.1420-1495), remarkable German theologian, philosoher and economist, acclaimed as the last great scholastic.

Bierce, Ambrose (Gwinnett) (1842-c.1914), American newspaperman and short-story writer who excelled as a wit and satirist.

Bigelow, John (1817-1911), American journalist, diplomat and writer.

Biggers, Earl (Derr) (1884-1933), American journalist, novelist and dramatist, creator of the Chinese detective Charlie Chan.

Bilderdijk, Willem (1756-1831), Dutch poet and philologist, best known for his unfinished epic poem *De ondergang der eerste wareld* (The Destruction of the First World, 1810).

Bilfinger, Georg Bernard (1693-1750), German scholar who wrote on many subjects ranging from philosophy and theology to botany and physics.

Billetdoux, François (1927-1991), French dramatist who followed an avant-garde path.

Billinger, Richard (1893-1965), Austrian poet and novelist.

Billings, Josh (actually **Henry Wheeler Shaw**) **(1818-1885),** American journalist, writer and lecturer who became popular as a humorist.

Binkis, Kazys (1893-1942), Lithuanian poet, dramatist and editor.

Binney, Thomas (1798-1874), English Congregational minister, writer and poet.

Binyon, (Robert) Laurence (1869-1943), English poet, dramatist, art historian and translator, author of the classic study *Painting in the Far East* (1908) and the esteemed elegy *For the Fallen* (1914).

Bion (flourished 100 B.C.), Greek poet.

Bion of Borysthenes (c.325-c.255 B.C.), Greek philosopher, reputedly the creator of the Cynic diatribe.

Biondo, Flavio or **Flavius Blondus (1392-1463),** Italian historian who wrote the important studies *Historiarum ab inclinatione Romanorum imperii decades* (Decades of History from the Deterioration of the Roman Empire, 1439-53, published 1483) and *Italia illustrata* (1448-58, published 1474).

Birch, Thomas (1705-1766), English historian and biographer.

Bird, Robert Montgomery (1806-1854), American dramatist, novelist and literary editor

Birmingham, George A (actually **James Owen Hannay**) **(1865-1950),** Irish Protestant clergyman and novelist.

Birney, (Alfred) Earle (1904-1995), Canadian poet, writer, dramatist and critic.

Birrell, Augustine (1850-1933), English politician and writer, author of the essay collections *Obiter Dicta* (2 volumes, 1884, 1887).

Bīrūnī, al- (actually **Abū Arrayhān Muhammad Ibn Ahmad al-Būrūnī**) **(973-1048),** famous Arab scholar whose learning embraced many disciplines.

Bishop, Elizabeth (1911-1979), distinguished American poet and short-story writer, esteemed for the poetry collections *North & South* (1946; revised edition as *North & South: A Cold Spring*, 1955) and *Questions of Travel* (1965).

Bishop, John Peale (1892-1944), American poet, novelist and critic.

Bishop, Morris (Gilbert) (1893-1973), American poet of light verse.

Bitzius, Albert (1797-1854), admired Swiss novelist, short-story writer and pastor who wrote under the name Jeremias Gotthelf.

Bjørnson, Bjørnstjerne Martinius (1832-1910), eminent Norwegian poet, novelist, dramatist, editor and poltician, author of Norway's National Anthem *Ja, vi elsker dette landet* (Yes, We Love This Land Forever); won the Nobel Prize for Literature (1903).

Black, Max (1909-1988), Azerbaijanian-born American philosopher who wrote extensively on numerous subjects.

Black, William (1841-1898), Scottish novelist.

Blackburn, Paul (1926-1971), American poet.

Blacklock, Thomas (1721-1791), Scottish poet who was known as the "blind bard".

Blackmore, Sir Richard (1654-1729), English physician, poet and writer.

Blackmore R(ichard) D(oddridge) (1825-1900), English novelist, poet and translator, best remembered for his novel *Lorna Doone* (1869).

Blackmur, R(ichard) P(almer) (1904-1965), American critic and poet.

Blackstone, Sir William (1723-1780), eminent English jurist, author of the classic *Commentaries on the Laws of England* (4 volumes, 1765-69).

Blackwell, John (1797-1840), Welsh poet and writer who wrote under the name Alun.

Blackwell, Thomas, the Younger (1701-1757), Scottish classical scholar.

Blackwood, Algernon Henry (1869-1951), remarkable English novelist and short-story writer of mystery and supernatural tales.

Blair, Robert (1699-1746), Scottish poet and preacher who wrote the well-known poem *The Grave* (1743).

Blake, William (1757-1827), famous English poet, writer, painter, engraver and mystic, renowned for such outstanding poetry collections as *Songs of Innocence* (1789), *Songs of Experience* (1794), and the prose volume *The Marriage of Heaven and Hell* (1790-93).

Blanco Fombona, Rufino (1874-1944), Venezuelan literary historian, poet, short-story writer, novelist and essayist.

Blanchard, Brand (1892-1987), American philosopher who espoused the cause of rationalism and idealism in his writings.

Blasco Ibáñez, Vicente (1867-1928), Spanish novelist, journalist and politician who won distinction with his novel *Los Cuatro Jinetes del Apocalipsis* (1916; English translation as *The Four Horsemen of the Apocalypse*, 1918).

Blavatsky, Helena Petrovna (née Hahn) (1831-1891), Russian spiritualist and writer, co-founder of the Theosophical Society and author of *The Secret Doctrine* (2 volumes, 1888).

Bleecker, Ann Eliza (1752-1783), American writer and poet, remembered for her epistolary novel *The History of Maria Kittle* (published 1797).

Blessington, Marguerite, Countess of (1789-1849), Irish writer, best known for her novel *Grace Cassidy, or The Repealers* (1833) and for her non-fiction works *Conversations of Lord Byron* (1843), *The Idler in Italy* (1839-40) and *The Idler in France* (1841).

Blest Gana, Alberto (1830-1920), admired Chilean novelist whose notable works included *Durante la Reconquista* (During the Reconquest, 1897), and *Los transplados* (The Uprooted, 1905).

Bleuler, Eugen (1857-1939), influential Swiss psychiatrist, a pioneering figure in the study of schizophrenia.

Blicher, Steen Steensen (1782-1848), Danish Poet and short-story writer, author of the fine poetry collection *Traekfuglene* (Birds of Passage, 1838).

Bloch, Ernst (1885-1977), German philosopher who propounded an independent Marxist course which he described as the "philosophy of hope", author of *Das Prinzip Hoffnung* (The Hope Principle, 3 volumes, 1954-59).

Bloch, Jean-Richard (1884-1947), French journalist, essayist, novelist and dramatist who espoused the Marxist cause.

Bloch, Robert (Albert) (1917-1994), American writer who became best known for his works of suspense and horror, particularly *Psycho* (1959).

Blok, Alexander Alexandrovich (1880-1921), notable Russian poet and dramatist of the Symbolist movement, especially known for his ode *Skify* (Scythians, 1918).

Blom, Eric (Walter) (1888-1959), distinguished English writer on music and lexicographer.

Blondel, Georges (1856-1958), French historian.

Blondel, Maurice (Édouard) (1861-1949), French philosopher, author of *L'action* (1893; revised edition, 1950), *La Pensée* (Thought, 2 volumes, 1934) and *Exigences philosophiques du Christianisme* (The Philosophical Demands of Christianity, 1950).

Blondel de Nesle (12th Century), French trouvère.

Blood, Benjamin Paul (1822-1919), American philosopher and poet whose output reflected his worldview as a mystic.

Bloom, Allan (David) (1930-1992), American philosopher, essayist and translator who gained wide recognition as a trenchant critic of higher education in the US.

Bloomfield, Leonard (1887-1949), American linguist whose book *Language* (1933) proved influential in the development of structurual linguistics.

Bloomfield, Robert (1766-1823), English poet, author of *The Farmer's Boy* (1800), *Rural Tales, Ballads and Songs* (1802) and *The Banks of Wye* (1811).

Blosius, Franciscus Ludovicus (1506-1566), Belgian-born French Benedictine monastic reformer and theologian.

Bloy, Léon (1846-1917), French novelist, critic and Roman Catholic polemicist.

Blume, Friedrich (1893-1975), distinguished German music scholar and lexicographer.

Blunck, Hans Friedrich (1888-1961), German poet and novelist.

Blunden, Edmund Charles (1896-1974), English poet, critic and scholar, well respected for his book *Undertones of War* (1928) and the collection *Poems od Many Years* (1957).

Blunt, Lady Anne Isabella Noel, Baroness Wentworth (1837-1917), English writer; wife of Wilfrid Scawen Blunt.

Blunt, Wilfred Scawen (1840-1922), English poet and traveller; husband of Lady Anne Isabella Noel Blunt, Baroness Wentworth.

Blyth, Edward (1810-1873), English naturalist whose "localizing principle" anticipated Charles Darwin's theory of organic evolution through natural selection.

Boas, Franz (1858-1942), significant German-born American anthropologist whose studies ranged from Native American cultures to linguistics.

Bobrzyński, Michal (1849-1935), Polish historian and politician.

Bocage, Manoel Maria Barbosa du (1765-1805), Portuguese poet and translator who displayed a fine gift for writing sonnets.

Boccaccio, Giovanni (1313-1375), celebrated Italian poet and writer whose stories in the *Decameron* (c.1328-53) are renowned the world over.

Boccage, Marie Anne Fiquet du (née Le Page) (1710-1802), French poet.

Boccalini, Traiano (1556-1613), Italian writer, author of *Ragguagli di Parnasso* (2 parts, 1612-13) and *Pietra del paragone politico* (published 1614), both of which were published in an English translation as *Advertisements from Parnassus in two centuries with the Politicke Touchstone* (1656), and *Commentarii sopra Cornelio Tacito* (Comments upon Cornelius Tacitus).

Bochart, Samuel (1599-1667), French reformed Church pastor and scholar.

Bodel, Jehan (c.1167-1210), French jongleur, poet and dramatist who wrote the first miracle play in France *Jeu de Saint Nicholas* (The Play of Saint Nicholas).

Bodenheim, Maxwell (1893-1954), American poet, novelist and dramatist; was murdered.

Bodenstedt, Friedrich Martin von (1819-1892), German poet, writer, critic and translator.

Bodin, Jean (1530-1596), French philosopher, best remembered for his *Six Livres de la République* (1576; English translation as *The six bookes of a Commonweale,* 1606)

Bodmer, Johann Jakob (1698-1783), Swiss literary scholar and poet.

Boece or **Boethius, Hector (c.1465-c.1536),** Scottish historian, author of *Scotorum historiae a prima gentis origine* (1527; English translation as *The history and croniklis of Scotland,* c.1536).

Boethius, Anicius Manlius Severinus (c.480-524), Roman theologian, philosopher and statesmen who wrote the famous *De consolatione philosophiae* while in prison; was executed for treason and magic.

Bogan, Louise (1897-1970), esteemed American poet and critic whose poetry followed along Metaphysical lines.

Bogdanovich, Ippolit Fyodorovich (1743-1803), Russian poet.

Bogusławski, Wojciech (1757-1829), Polish actor, theatre director and dramatist, well known for his comic plays.

Böhme, Jakob (1575-1624), German philosopher who embraced mysticism.

Böhmer, Johann Friedrich (1795-1863), German historian.

Bohomolec Franciszek (1720-1784), Polish Jesuit priest, dramatist, linguist and editor.

Bohtlingk, Otto von (1815-1904), German language scholar and lexicographer.

Boiardo, Matteo Maria, Conte (c.1441-1494), Italian poet, author of the unfinished *Orlando innamorato* (c.1476-94).

Boie, Heinrich Christian (1744-1806), German poet and editor.

Boileau (-Despréaux), Nicolas (1636-1711), French poet and critic, master of satirical and epistolary writing.

Boisrobert, François Le Metel, Seigneur de (1589-1662), French churchman and dramatist who became best known for his wit and blasphemies at court.

Boito, Arrigo (actually Enrico Giuseppe Giovanni Bioto) (1842-1918), Italian composer and poet who wrote the libretto to his own popular opera *Mefistofele* (1868), as well as to Verdi's operas *Otello* and *Falstaff*.

Bojer, Johan (1872-1959), Norwegian novelist, best remembered for *Den store hunger* (1916; English translation as *The Great Hunger*, 1918) and *Folk ved sjøen* (1929; English translation as *Folk by the Sea*, 1931).

Bokenam or **Bokenham, Osbern (c.1392-c.1447),** English writer, author of *Legends of Holy Women.*

Boker, George Henry (1823-1890), American poet, dramatist and diplomat, known for his sonnets and the verse tragedy *Francesca da Rimini* (1855).

Boldrewood, Rolf (actually Thomas Alexander Browne) (1826-1915), English-born Australian novelist and short-story writer, author of the novels *Robbery Under Arms* (1888) and *Miner's Right* (1890).

Böll, Heinrich (1917-1985), notable German novelist and short-story writer; won the Nobel Prize for Literature (1972).

Bolland or **Bollandus, Jean (1596-1665),** Belgian Jesuit historian who was the principal compiler of the *Acta Sanctorum* (2 parts, 1643, 1658), a collection of the lives of the Christian saints.

Bolt, Robert (Oxton) (1924-1995), English dramatist, particularly remembered for his play *A Man for All Seasons* (1960).

Bolton or **Boulton, Edmund (c.1575-c.1633),** English historian, antiquarian and poet, some of whose fine poems were included in the miscellany *Englands Helicon* (1600).

Bolton, Herbert Eugene (1870-1953), American historian who specialized in the study of the history of the Western hemisphere.

Bolyai, Farkas (1775-1856), Hungarian mathematician, poet, dramatist and composer.

Bonald, Louis-Garbriel-Ambroise, Vicomte de (1754-1840), French statesman and political philosopher who espoused the royalist cause.

Bonar, Horatius (1808-1889), Scottish Presbyterian minister, poet, hymnist and writer whose *Hymns of Faith and Hope* (1857-66) were once highly popular.

Bonaventure, Saint (c.1217-1274), noted Italian Roman Catholic theologian, minister general of the Franciscan Order and cardinal bishop of Albano.

Boncompagno da Signa (c.1165-c.1240), Italian writer who became well known for his writings on rhetoric.

Boner or **Bonerius, Ulrich (14th Century),** Swiss Dominican monk and writer, remembered for his verse fables *Der Edelstein* (The Precious Stone).

Bongars, Jacques, Seigneur de Bauldry and de la Chesnaye (1554-1612), French diplomat and classical scholar, author of *Gosta Dei per Francos* (God's Work Through the Franks), a compilation of accounts of the Crusades.

Bonhoeffer, Dietrich (1906-1945), notable German Protestant theologian who became an opponent of the Nazi regime; implicated in the plot to assassinate Hitler, he was imprisoned and executed.

Bonivard François (c.1494-1570), Swiss patriot and historian, author of the *Chroniques de Genève* (History of Geneva, 1542-51, published 1831).

Bonnet, Charles (1720-1793), Swiss naturalist and philosopher.

Bonstetten, Karl Viktor von (1745-1832), Swiss writer.

Bontempelli, Massimo (1878-1960), Italian poet, novelist, dramatist and critic.

Bontemps, Arna (Wendell) (1902-1973), American writer who chronicled the black experience in books of fiction and non-fiction.

Bonvesin de la Riva (c.1240-c.1315), Italian writer and poet, best known for his *Libro delle tre scritture* (Book of the Three Writings, 1274).

Boorde or **Borde, Andrew (c.1490-1549),** English physician and writer, author of the first guidebook to Europe *Fyrst Boke of the Introduction of Knowledge* (1548).

Bopp, Franz (1791-1867), learned German linguist who wrote the major study *Vergleichende Grammatik des Sanskrit, Zend, Griechischen, Lateinischen, Litthauischen, Altslawischen, Gotischen und Deutschen* (Comparitive Grammar of Sanskrit, Zend, Greek, Latin, Lithuanian, Old Slavic, Gothic and German, 6 parts, 1833-52).

Borel, Petrus (actually Joseph-Pierre Borel) (1809-1859), French poet, novelist and critic who was also known as Borel d'Hauterive.

Borges, Jorge Luis (1899-1986), outstanding Argentine poet, short-story writer and essayist.

Borowski, Tadeusz (1922-1951), Polish short-story writer.

Borron or **Boron, Robert de (12th-13th Century),** French poet who wrote the trilogy *Joseph d'Arimathie, Merlin* and *Perceval.*

Bosanquet, Bernard (1848-1923), English philosopher who espoused Hegelian principles, author of *The Philosophical Theory of the State* (1899).

Bosboom-Toussaint, Anna (1812-1846), Dutch writer.

Boscán Almogáver, Juan (Catalan name **Joan Boscà Almugàver) (c.1487-1542),** Catalan poet who helped to introduce Italian verse forms into Spain.

Bosquet, Alain (actually **Anatole Bisk) (1919-1998),** Russian-born American poet, writer and critic.

Bossert, Helmuth Theodor (1889-1961), German philologist and archaeologist, author of *Geschichte des Kunstgewerbes aller Völker und Zeiten* (History of the Arts and Crafts of All People and Times, 6 volumes, 1928-35).

Bossuet, Jacques-Bénigne (1627-1704), French Roman Catholic bishop and writer, remembered especially for his political treatises.

Boswell, James (1740-1795), famous English biographer and diarist, author of the celebrated *Life of Johnson* (2 volumes, 1791).

Botev, Khristo (1848-1876), Bulgarian patriot and poet; died in the Bulgarian uprising against Turkish rule.

Botta, Carlo Giuseppe Guglielmo (1766-1837), Italian-born French politician and historian.

Botta, Paul-Émile (1802-1870), Italian archaeologist, a pioneering figure in the study of ancient Mesopotamia.

Bottome, Phyllis (1884-1963), English novelist and short-story writer, author of the novels *Private Worlds* (1934) and *The Mortal Storm* (1937).

Bottomely, Gordon (1874-1948), English poet and dramatist who wrote *Poems of Thirty Years* (1925).

Boucher, Jonathan (1738-1804), English clergyman, writer and philologist who supported the royalist cause in America.

Boucher (de Crèvecoeur) de Perthes, Jacques (1788-1868), French archaeologist, author of *Antiquités celtiques et antédiluviennes* (Celtic and Antediluvian Antiquities, 3 volumes, 1847-64).

Boucicault, Dion (actually **Dionysius Lardner Boursiquot) (1820-1890),** Irish-born American dramatist.

Boufflers, Stanislas-Jean, Chevalier de (1738-1815), French writer, poet and soldier who wrote the well-known picaresque romance *Aline, reine de Golconde* (Aline, Queen of Golconda).

Boulainvilliers, Henri, Comte de (1658-1722), French historian, particularly esteemed for his *État de la France* (3 volumes, 1727-28).

Bouilhet, Louis (1821-1869), French poet and dramatist.

Boulle, Pierre (1912-1994), French novelist, best remembered for *Le Pont de la rivière Kwaï* (1952; English translation as *The Bridge on the River Kwai* 1954).

Bourget, Paul (-Charles-Joseph) (1852-1935), French poet, novelist and critic, best known for his novel *Le Disciple* (1889).

Bourne, Randolph Silliman (1886-1918), American critic, essayist and pacifist.

Boursalt, Edme (1638-1701), French poet, dramatist and novelist.

Bousset, Wilhelm (1865-1920), German New Testament scholar and theologian, author of *Die Religion des Judentums im neutestamentlichen (späthellenistischen) Zeitalter* (The Religion of the Jews in the New Testament [late Hellenistic] Era, 1903).

Boutens, Pieter Cornelis (1870-1943), Dutch poet and classical scholar who espoused mysticism.

Bouterwek, Friedrich (1766-1828), German philosopher and critic who wrote on various subjects, among them Kantian logic, religion, aesthetics and literature.

Bowdich, Thomas Edward (1791-1824), English traveller and writer.

Bowdler, Thomas (1754-1825), English physician and man of letters whose expurgation of Shakespeare's works was immortalized in the word "bowdlerize".

Bowen, Catherine (Shober) Drinker (1897-1973), American biographer and essayist.

Bowen, Elizabeth (Dorothea Cole) (1899-1973), highly regarded Irish novelist and short-story writer.

Bowen, Marjorie (actually **Gabrielle Margaret Vere née Campbell Long) (1886-1952),** English novelist, dramatists and biographer.

Bower, Walter (1385-1449), Scottish historian who wrote the *Scotichronicon* (16 volumes, 1441-47).

Bowles, Jane (1917-1973), American novelist, short-story writer and dramatist, author of the avant-garde novel *Two Serious Ladies* (1943).

Bowles, William Lisle (1762-1850), English churchman, poet and critic whose works presaged the Romantic era of verse.

Bowra, Sir (Cecil) Maurice (1898-1971), English critic and scholar.

Bowring, Sir John (1792-1872), English politician, diplomat and writer.

Boyd, Ernest (1887-1946), Irish-born American critic, writer and translator.

Boyd, James (1888-1944), American novelist and poet, expecially remembered for his novels *Drums* (1925) and *Marching On* (1927).

Boyd, Martin (à Beckett) (1893-1972), Australian novelist and poet, particularly known for his novel *The Montforts* (1928).

Boyd, Thomas (Alexander) (1898-1935), American novelist, short-story writer and biographer, author of the novels *Through the Wheat* (1923) and *In Time of Peace* (1935).

Boye, Karin Maria (1900-1941), Swedish poet and novelist, especially known for her novels *Kris* (Crisis, 1934) and *Kallocain* (1940); committed suicide.

Boyesen, Hjalmar Hjorth (1848-1895), Norwegian-born American writer and poet.

Boyle, Kay (1902-1992), American poet, essayist and novelist.

Boyle, Robert (1627-1691), English chemist and philosopher, author of *The Sceptical Chemyist* (1661) and *The Origin of Forms and Qualities* (1666).

Boylesve, René (actually **René-Marie-Auguste Tardiveau) (1867-1926),** French novelist who won distinction with his novels of Touraine series.

Braak, Menno ter (1902-1940), trenchant Dutch critic; committed suicide.**Braaten, Oskar (1881-1939),** Norwegian novelist, dramatist, journalist and editor.

Brace, Gerald Warner (1901-1978), American novelist and critic.

Brackenridge, Hugh Henry (1748-1816), American lawyer, jurist and novelist, author of *Modern Chivalry* (1792-1815).

Bracton or Bratton, Henry de (d. 1268), English jurist, known for his *De legibus et consuetudinibus Angliae* (On the Laws and Customs of England, c.1250).

Braddon, Mary Elizabeth (1837-1915), English novelist and poet, won a popular audience with her sensational novel *Lady Audley's Secret* (3 volumes, 1862).

Bradford, Gamaliel (1863-1932), American biographer, poet, novelist and dramatist.

Bradford, Roark (1896-1948), American writer, author of *Ol' Man Adam an' His Chillun* (1928), which Marc Connelly adapted as the play *The Green Pastures.*

Bradford, William (1590-1657), English-born American governor of the Plymouth Colony and author of the invaluable *History of Plymouth Plantation. 1620-47.*

Bradley, A(ndrew) C(ecil) (1851-1935), English critic and scholar, known for his Shakespearean studies.

Bradley, F(rancis) H(erbert) (1846-1924), eminent English philosopher, author of the important volume *Appearance and Reality: A Metaphysical Essay* (1893).

Bradstreet, Anne (Dudley) (c.1612-1672), pioneering English-born American poet, particularly admired for her collection *The Tenth Muse Lately Sprung Up in America* (1650).

Bradwardine, Thomas (c.1290-1349), English theologian and archbishop of Cantebury, author of *De Causa Dei contra Pelagium* (1344).

Brady, Cyrus Townsend (1861-1920), American Episcopal clergyman and prolific novelist.

Brady, Nicholas (1659-1726), Irish churchman and poet, author, with Nahum Tate, of a *New Version of the Psalms* (1696).

Braga, (Joaquim) Téofilo (Fernandes) (1843-1924), Portuguese scholar, poet and statesman who wrote the valuable *História do Romantismo em Portugal* (History of Romanticism in Portugal, 1880).

Brahm, Otto (1856-1912), German critic and theatre director.

Brainard, John Gardiner Calkins (1796-1828), American poet, writer and editor.

Braine, John (Gerard) (1922-1986), English novelist, author of *Room at the Top* (1957) and *Life at the Top* (1962).

Braithwaite, R(icard) B(eran) (1900-1990), English philosopher who wrote *Scientific Explanation* (1955).

Braithwaite, William (Stanley Beaumont) (1878-1962), American poet, writer and editor.

Bramah, Ernest (actually **Ernest Bramah Smith) (c.1869-1942),** English short-story writer, creator of the blind detective Max Carrados.

Branagan, Thomas (1774-1843), Irish-born American writer and poet.

Branch, Anna Hempstead (1875-1937), American poet and dramatist.

Brand, Max (actually **Frederick Faust) (1892-1944),** American novelist, author of *Destry Rides Again* (1930) and the Dr Kildare series.

Brandáo, Frei António (1584-1637), Portuguese historian.

Brandes, (Carl) Edvard (Cohen) (1847-1931), Danish critic and politician; brother of Georg (Morris Cohen) Brandes.

Brandes, Georg (Morris Cohen) (1842-1927), noted Danish critic and scholar of a radical disposition, author of *Hovedstrømninger i det 19de aarhundredes litteratur* (1871-87; English translation as *Main Currents in 19th Century Literature,* 1901-05), *Danske digtere* (Danish Poets, 1877), *Det moderne gjennembruds maend* (Men of the Modern Break-Through, 1883), *Friedrich Nietzsche* (1909) and *Sagnet om Jesus* (1925; English translation as *Jesus, a Myth,* 1926).

Brandr, Abbot Jónsson (d. 1264), Icelandic abbot and writer.

Brandt, Geerhardt (1626-1685), Dutch historian and biographer.

Branner, Hans Christian (1903-1966), Danish novelist, short-story writer and dramatist.

Brant, Sebastian (c.1458-1521), German poet, author of the satirical *Das Narrenschiff* (1494; English translation as *The Ship of Fools,* 1509).

Brantôme, Pierre (de Bourdeille, Abbé and Seigneur) de (c.1540-1614), French soldier and writer, best known for an account of his life and times (published 1665-66).

Brathwait, Richard (1588-1673), English poet and writer, author of the Latin poem *Barnabees Journal* (1638; English translation, 1638), which he wrote under the name Corymbaeus.

Braun, Lily (née von Kretschman) (1865-1916), German feminist, pacifist, socialist and novelist.

Brautigan, Richard (1935-1984), American writer and poet.

Breasted, James Henry (1865-1935), American archaeologist and historian.

Brébeuf, Saint Jean de (1593-1649), French Jesuit missionary and writer.

Brecht, Bertolt (actually **Eugen Berthold Friedrich Brecht)** (1898-1956), celebrated German dramatist and poet, master of the modern theatre.

Bredero, Gerbrand Adriaenszoon (1585-1618), Dutch poet and dramatist.

Bregendahl, Marie (1867-1940), Danish novelist, author of *En dødsnat* (1912; English translation as *A Night of Death,* 1931).

Bréhier, Émile (1876-1952), French philosopher who espoused rationalism.

Bréhier, Louis (1868-1951), French historian and archaeologist.

Breitinger, Johann Jokob (1701-1776), Swiss critic and scholar, author of the *Critische Dichtkunst* (1740)

Bremer, Fredrika (1801-1865), Swedish novelist and reformer, a prominent figure in the movement for women's rights.

Brenan, (Edward Fitz-) Gerald (1894-1987), English writer who became best known for his books on Spanish subjects.

Brennan, Christopher (John) (1870-1932), Australian poet and critic.

Brentano, Clemens (1778-1842), important German poet, novelist and folklorist who, with Achim von Arnim, collaborated on the notable edition of folk poetry D*es Knaben Wunderhorn* (The Youth's Magic Horn, 1805); uncle of Franz Brentano.

Brentano, Franz (1838-1917), German philosopher, author of *Psychologie vom empirischen Standpunkte* (Psychology from an Empirical Standpoint, 1874), *Untersuchungen zur Sinnespsychologie* (Inquiry into Sense Psychology, 1907) and *Von der Klassifikation der psychischen Phänomene* (on the classification of psychological Phenomena, (1911); nephew of Clemens Brentano.

Bresslau, Harry (1848-1926), German historian and paleographer.

Breton, André (1896-1966), famous French poet, essayist critic and editor, a leading proponent of Surrealism.

Breton, Nicholas (c.1553-c.1625), English poet and writer, particularly appreciated for his poem *The Passionate Shepheard* (1604).

Bretón de los Herreros, Manuel (1796-1873), popular Spanish dramatist and poet.

Bretschneider, Carl Gottlieb (1776-1848), German Protestant theologian who wrote an important study on *New Testament literature Probabilia* (Probables, 1820).

Breuer, Josef (1842-1925), Austrian physician and physiologist whose work anticipated psychoanalysis, co-author with Freud of *Studien über Hysterie* (1895).

Breuil, Henri-Édouard-Prosper (1877-1961), eminent French archaeologist who wrote numerous studies on prehistoric cave paintings.

Brewster, Henry B (1850-1908), American writer.

Březina, Otakar (1868-1929), influential Czech poet who wrote 5 outstanding volumes of poetry (1895, 1896, 1897, 1899, 1901).

Bridel, Philippe-Sirice (1757-1845), Swiss writer, philologist and poet.

Bridges, Robert (Seymour) (1844-1930), notable English poet, dramatist and critic; became Poet Laureate of the United Kingdom (1913); father of Elizabeth Daryush.

Bridie, James (actually **Osborne Henry Mavor) (1888-1951),** Scottish dramatist who won popularity with his comedies.

Brieux, Eugène (1858-1932), French dramatist, known for his realist plays.

Briggs, Charles Augustus (1841-1913), American Old Testament scholar who championed the cause of higher criticism.

Brighouse, Harold (1882-1958), English dramatist and novelist, best known for his popular play *Hobson's Choice* (1916).

Brightman, Edgar Sheffield (1884-1953), American philosopher.

Brinig, Myron (1900-1991), American novelist.

Brink, Bernhard ten (1841-1892), Dutch literary scholar, author of *Geschichte der englischen Literatur* (2 volumes, 1877-93; English translation as *History of English Literature,* 1883-93).

Brinnin, John Malcolm (1916-1998), American poet, biographer and critic.

Brinton, Crane (1898-1968), American writer.

Brito, Frei Bernardo de (1568-1617), Portuguese historian.

Brittain, Vera Mary (1893-1970), English pacifist, feminist and writer.

Brizieux, Julien Auguste Pélage (1803-1858), French poet.

Broad, C(harles) D(unbar) (1887-1971), English philosopher.

Broch, Hermann (1886-1951), notable Austrian writer, known for such works as *Die Schlafwandler* (1931-32; English translation as *The Sleepwalkers,* 1932), *Der Tod des Virgil* (1945; English translation as *The Death of Virgil,* 1945) and *Der Versucher* (The Bewitchment, published 1953).

Brockes, Barthold Heinrich (1680-1747), German poet who extolled the world of nature.

Brod, Max (1884-1968), Austrian poet, dramatist, novelist, essayist and biographer.

Brodkey, Harold (actually **Aaron Roy Weintraub) (1930-1996),** American novelist and short-story writer.

Brodsky, Joseph (Alexandrovich) (1940-1996), prominent Russian-born American poet whose reputation was secured as an exile in the West; won the Nobel Prize for Literature (1987) and was Poet Laureate of the US (1992-92).

Broglie, (Jacques-Victor-) Albert, 4th Duc de (1821-1901), French statesman and writer.

Broke or **Brooke, Arthur (d. 1563),** English poet and writer, author of the poem *The Tragicall Historye of Romeus and Juliet* (1562), which served as the basis of Sheakspeare's *Romeo and Juliet.*

Brome, Alexander (1620-1666), English poet who excelled in writing drinking songs and satirical witticisms attacking the Rump Parliament.

Brome, Richard (d. c. 1652), English dramatist, best remembered for *The Northern Lasse* (c.1629).

Bromfield, Louis (1896-1956), American novelist and essayist, particularly known for his series of novels entitled *Escape.*

Brontë, Anne (1820-1849), English novelist and poet, author of the novel *Agnes Grey* (1848); sister of Charlotte and Emily Jane Brontë.

Brontë, Charlotte (1816-1855), distinguished English novelist and poet who wrote the classic novel *Jane Eyre* (1847); sister of Anne and Emily Jane Brontë.

Brontë, Emily Jane (1818-1848), remarkable English poet and novelist, author of the fine *Gondal* poems and the classic novel *Wuthering Heights* (1847); sister of Anne and Charlotte Brontë.

Bronzino, Il (actually **Agnolo** or **Angiolo di Cosimo) (1503-1572),** Italian painter and poet.

Brook, Barry S(helley) (1918-1997), distinguished American music scholar.

Brook, (Bernard) Jocelyn (1908-1966), English poet and novelist.

Brooke, Frances (1724-1789), English writer, dramatist and translator.

Brooke, Henry (c.1703-1783), Irish novelist, dramatist and poet, author of the poem *Universal Beauty* (1728) and the novel *The Fool of Quality* (1765-70).

Brooke, Rupert (Chawner) (1887-1915), admired English poet, beloved for his sonnet collection *1914* (1915); died in World War I.

Brooks, Charles T(imothy) (1813-1883), American clergyman, translator and poet.

Brooks, Cleanth (1906-1994), American critic, a prominent figure in the New Criticism.

Brooks, Maria Gowen (c.1794-1845), American poet and dramatist who was known as Maria of the West.

Brooks, Phillips (1835-1893), American Episcopal clergyman who wrote the celebrated hymn *O Little Town of Bethlehem* (1868).

Brooks, Van Wyck (1886-1963), American literary historian and biographer, especially known for *The Flowering of New England, 1815-1865* (1936).

Broome, William (1689-1745), English scholar and poet.

Brophy, Brigid (Antonia) (1929-1995), English novelist, dramatist and writer.

Brosses, Charles de (1709-1777), French magistrate and scholar, author of *Lettres sur Herculaneum* (1750).

Brougham, John (1814-1880), Irish-born American actor, dramatist and theatre manager.

Broughton, Rhoda (1840-1920), English novelist.

Broun, Heywood (Campbell) (1888-1939), American journalist and critic of liberal views.

Brown, Alice (1857-1948), American novelist, short-story writer and dramatist.

Brown, Charles Brockden (1771-1810), pioneering American novelist, known as the father of the American novel for his *Wieland* (1798).

Brown, George Mackay (1921-1996), Scottish poet and writer.

Brown, Harry (Peter McNab Jr) (1917-1986), American writer and poet.

Brown, John (1715-1766), English Anglican clergyman, philosopher and dramatist.

Brown, John (1810-1882), Scottish physician and essayist, remembered for his *Horae Subsecivae* (3 volumes, 1858-82).

Brown, John Mason (1900-1969), American drama critic and biographer.

Brown, Raymond E(dward) (1928-1998), distinguished American Roman Catholic biblical scholar and priest, author of *The Birth of the Messiah* (1977) and *The Death of the Messiah* (1994).

Brown, Sterling A(llan) (1901-1989), American poet and critic.

Brown, Thomas (1663-1704), English poet and translator. particularly remembered for his satirical bent.

Brown, T(homas) E(dward) (1830-1897), English poet.

Brown, William Hill (1765-1793), American novelist and dramatist, author of the epistolary novel *Power of Sympathy, or the Triumph of Nature Founded in Truth* (1789).

Brown, William Wells (c.1816-1884), American writer and poet,whose novel *Clotelle, or, The President's Daughter* (1853) was one of the earliest works of its kind by a black.

Brown, Isaac Hawkins (1705-1760), English poet who was known for his wit, author of the parody *A Pipe of Tobacco* and the more serious *Du Animi Immortalitate* (On the Immortality of the Soul, 1754).

Browne, J(ohn) Ross (1821-1875), American writer, author of fiction and travel books.

Browne, Sir Thomas (1605-1682), eminent English writer and physician who wrote *Religio Medici* (1642) and *Pseudodoxis Epidemica, or, Enquiries into Very many received Tenets, commonly presumed truths* (1646).

Browne, William (c.1591-c.1645), English poet, admired for such work as *Britannia's Pastorals* (1613; revised edition, 1616) and *The Inner Temple Masque* (c.1614).

Brownell, W(illiam) C(rary) (1851-1928), American critic and editor.

Browning, Elizabeth Barrett (1806-1861), eminent English poet of great intellect, famous for such works as *Sonnets from the Portuguese* (1850) and *Aurora Leigh* (1857); wife of Robert Browning.

Browning, Robert (1812-1889), renowned English poet, author of *Christmas-Eve and Easter-Day* (1850), *Men and Women* (1855), *Dramatis Personae* (1864), *The Ring and the Book* (1868-69) and *Dramatic Idyls* (2 parts, 1879, 1880); husband of Elizabeth Barrett Browning.

Brownson, Orestes Augustus (1803-1876), liberal American clergyman, editor, poet and writer, author of books on subjects ranging from religion and philosophy to science and political reform.

Brú, Hedin (actually Hans Jakob Jacobsen) (1901-1987), Faeroese novelist whose finest work was *Fedgar à ferd* (The Old Man and His Sons, 1940).

Bruce, Michael (1746-1767), Scottish poet, admired for his *Elegy Written in Spring* (published 1770).

Brucioli, Antonio (c.1499-1566), Italian scholar and translator, best known for his translation of the Bible into Italian (1532) which led to his imprisonment by the Inquisition.

Bruckberger, Raymond-Léopold (1907-1998), French Roman Catholic priest and writer who embraced secularism.

Brugmann, (Friedrich) Karl (1849-1919), important German linguist, author of the *Grundiss der vergleichenden Grammatik der Indogermanischen Sprachen* (outline of the Comparitive Grammar of Indo-Germanic Languages, 5 volumes, 1886-93).

Brugsch, Heinrich Karl (1827-1894), German Egyptologist who edited a monumental hieroglyphic-demotic dictionary (1867-82).

Brun, Johan Nordahl (1745-1816), Norwegian bishop, hymnist, dramatist and politician, author of the first Norwegian National Anthem *For Norge, kjaempers fødeland* (For Norway, Land of Heroes, 1771).

Brunetière, Ferdinand (1849-1906), French criric and literary historian.

Brunhoff, Jean de (1899-1937), French writer and illustrator who won success with his series of Babar books for children.

Bruni, Leonardo (c.1370-1444), Italian scholar who was also known as Leonardo Aretino, author of the *Historiarum Florentini populi libri XII* (12 Books of Florentine Histories, published 1610).

Brunner, (Heinrich) Emil (1889-1966), significant Swiss theologian who was a determined exponent of Neo-orthodoxy in opposition to liberal theology.

Bruno, Giordano (1548-1600), notable Italian philosopher, mathematician and scientist; burned as a heretic by the Inquisition.

Brunschvicg, Léon (1869-1944), important French philosopher, author of the influential *La Modalité du jugement* (1897), a dissertation setting forth his Idealism.

Brusewitz, Axel (Karl Adolf) (1881-1950), Swedish political scientist, an authority on the constitutional history of his homeland.

Bryan, Sir Francis (d.1550), English soldier, courtier and poet, called the "vicar of hell" by Oliver Cromwell.

Bryant, William Cullen (1794-1878), prominent American poet and journalist whose poem *Thanatopsis* (1817) became an American classic.

Bryce, James, 1st Viscount (1838-1922), English politician, diplomat and historian, author of *The Holy Roman Empire* (1864; revised edition, 1919) and *The American Commonwealth* (3 volumes, 1888; revised edition, 1922-23).

Brydges, Sir Samuel Egerton (1762-1837), English bibliogrpher and writer.

Bryusov, Valeri Yakovlevich (1873-1924), Russian poet, novelist, dramatist, critic and translator.

Brzozowski, Stanisław (1878-1911), Polish writer.

Buber, Martin (1878-1965), notable Austrian-born Jewish philosopher who became well known for his ethical and theological dialogue *Ich und Du* (1923; English translation as *I and Thou*, 1937).

Buchan, John, 1st Baron Tweedsmuir (1875-1940), Scottish statesman and writer.

Buchanan, Dugald (1716-1768), Scottish writer.

Buchanan, George (1506-1582), Scottish scholar and poet.

Buchanan, Robert Williams (1841-1901), English poet, novelist and dramatist who wrote under the name Thomas Maitland.

Bucher, (Adolf) Lothar (1817-1892), German government official and writer.

Büchner, Georg (1813-1837), remarkable German dramatist whose works anticipated Expressionism, author of *Dantons Tod* (Danton's Death, 1835), *Leonce und Lena* (1836) and *Woyzeck* (1836), the latter set as the libretto to Alban Berg's opera *Wozzeck*.

Buchner, Ludwig (1824-1899), German physician and philosopher who embraced materialism in his well-known volume *Kraft und Stoff* (1855; English translation as *Force and Matter,*1870).

Buck, Pearl (née Sydenstricker) (1892-1973), admired American writer who secured her reputation with the novel *The Good Earth* (1931); won the Nobel Prize for Literature (1938).

Bucke, Richard Maurice (1837-1902), Canadian biographer.

Buckingham, George Villiers, 2nd Duke of (1628-1687), English politician and writer, principally remembered for his dissolute life.

Buckingham, James Silk (1786-1855), English traveller and writer.

Buckle, Henry Thomas (1821-1862), English historian who wrote the unfinished *History of Civilization in England* (2 volumes, 1857, 1861).

Budé, Guillaume (1467-1540), French scholar, diplomat and royal librarian who was known for his Greek classical studies.

Budge, Sir (Ernest Alfred Thompson) Wallis (1857-1934), English Orientalist and museum curator, known for his studies in Egyptian and Assyrian antiquities.

Budgell, Eustace (1686-1737), English writer.

Bufalino, Gesualdo (1920-1996), Italian writer, poet and translator.

Buffier, Claude (1661-1737), noted French philosopher, historian and philologist, best remembered for the *Traité des vérités premiéres et de la source de nos jugements* (Treatise on First Truths and on the Source of Our Judgements, 1724).

Buffon, Georges-Louis-Leclerc, Comte de (1707-1788), French naturalist, author of the significant *Histoire naturelle, générale et particuliére* (36 volumes, 1749-88).

Bugge, (Elseus) Sophus (1833-1907), Norwegian philologist who published a critical edition of the *Poetic Edda* of 13th -Century Iceland (1891 et seq.).

Bühler, Karl (1879-1963), German linguist and psychologist.

Buhturī al- (actually Abū 'Ubādah al-Walīd ibn 'Ubayd Allāh al-Buhturī) (821-897), distinguished Arab poet, best known for his panegyrics.

Bukharin, Nikolai Ivanovich (1888-1938), Russian revolutionary, politician and Marxist theoretician and economist; executed during the Stalinist purges.

Bukowski, Charles (1920-1994), American poet, novelist and screenwriter whose underground career made him a literary cult figure.

Bulfinch, Thomas (1796-1867), American writer, author of *The Age of Fable* (1855), *The Age of Chivalry* (1858) and *Oregon and Eldorado* (1866).

Bulgakov, Mikhail (Afanasievich) (1891-1940), Russian novelist, short-story writer and dramatist.

Bulgakov, Sergei Nikolaievich (1871-1944), Russian Orthodox theologian and economist, a proponent of the philosophical-theological system known as sophiology (after the Greek word sophia, i.e. wisdom).

Bulgaris, Eugenius (1716-1806), Greek Orthodox theologian and scholar.

Bull, Olaf (Jacob Martin Luther) (1883-1933), remarkable Norwegian poet.

Bullett, Gerald (William) (1893-1958), English novelist, biographer, critic and poet.

Bullinger, Heinrich (1504-1575), prominent Swiss Protestant pastor and writer, author of *Reformationsgeschichte* (History of the Reformation, published 1838-40).

Bultmann, Rudolf (Karl) (1884-1976), influential German theologian who applied Existentialist philosophical principles in his effect to "demythologize" the New Testament.

Bunce, Oliver Bell (1828-1890), American dramatist writer and editor.

Bunin, Ivan Alexseievich (1870-1953), noted Russian poet, short-story writer and novelist; won the Nobel Prize for Literature (1933).

Bunner, Henry Cuyler (1855-1896), American poet, novelist and editor.

Bunting, Basil (1900-1985), English poet who espoused the cause of Modernism.

Bunyan, John (1628-1688), famous English Puritan minister and writer, author of the classic *The Pilgrim's Progress* (2 parts, 1678, 1684), as well as the admired *Grace Abounding to the Chief of Sinners* (1666) and *The Holy War* (1682).

Burckhardt, Jakob (Christoph) (1818-1897), eminent Swiss historian of art and culture.

Bürger, Gottfried August (1747-1794), esteemed German poet and translator, one of the principal figures in the development of Romantic ballad literature in his homeland.

Burgess, Anthony (actually John Anthony Burgess Wilson) (1917-1993), notable English novelist, critic and composer who secured his literary reputation with the novel *A Clockwork Orange* (1962).

Burgess, Gelett (Frank) (1866-1951), American poet, writer and artist, best known for his humorous poem *The Purple Cow.*

Burgon, John William (1813-1888), English churchman, scholar and poet, author of the poem *Petra* (1845).

Burgoyne, John (1722-1792), English general and dramatist whose most popular play was *The Heiress* (1786).

Buridian, Jean or Joannes Buridanus (1300-1358), distinguished French logician, philosopher and theologian, one of the leading Aristotelians of his era.

Burk, John Daly (c.1775-1808), Irish-born American dramatist and writer.

Burke, Edmund (1729-1797), outstanding Irish-born English statesman and political theorist, author of the classic *Reflections on the Revolution in France* (1790).

Burke, Kenneth (Duva) (1897-1993), American critic and poet.

Burnet, Gilbert (1643-1715), Scottish Anglican bishop and historian who wrote *History of the Reformation in England* (3 volumes, 1679-1714) and *History of My Own Time* (2 volumes, published 1723, 1734).

Burnett, Frances Eliza (née Hodgson) (1849-1924), English-born American novelist and dramatist, best known for her successful novel *Little Lord Fauntleroy* (1886).

Burnett, W(illiam) R(iley) (1899-1982), American novelist.

Burney, Charles (1726-1814), famous English music scholar, author of a *General History of Music* (4 volumes, 1776-89); father of Fanny Burney.

Burney, Fanny (actually **Frances Burney**, later **Madame D'Arblay) (1752-1840)**, English novelist and letter writer, author of the classic novel of manners *Evelina, or a Young Lady's Entrance into the World* (1778); daughter of Charles Burney.

Burns, John Horne (1916-1953), American novelist.

Burns, Robert (1759-1796), celebrated Scottish poet, master of the folk tradition of his native land.

Burroughs, Edgar Rice (1875-1950), American writer, creator of Tarzan.

Burroughs, John (1837-1921), American naturalist and essayist.

Burroughs, William S(eward) (1914-1997), experimental novelist who greatly influenced the writers of the Beat generation.

Burt, (Maxwell) Struthers (1882-1954), American writer.

Burton, Sir Richard (Francis) (1821-1890), colourful English explorer, linguist,writer and poet who prepared unexpurgated editions of such erotic works as *The Kama Sutra* (1883), the *Arabian Nights* (1885-88) and *The Perfumed Garden* (1886).

Burton, Robert (1577-1640), English Anglican clergman and scholar who wrote the classic *The Anatomy of Melancholy* (1621).

Bury, J(ohn) B(agnell) (1861-1927), English classical scholar, historian and editor.

Busch, Wilhelm (1832-1908), German painter and poet.

Busembaum or Busenbaum, Hermann (1600-1668), German Jesuit theologian, author of the famous *Medulla Theologiae Moralis, Facili ac Perspicua Methodo Resolvens Casus Conscientiae ex Variis Probatisque Auctoribus Concinnata* (The Heart of Moral Theology, an Easy and Perspicacious Method Resolving the Claims of Conscience Compiled from Various Worthy Authors, c.1645).

Bushnell, Horace (1802-1876), American Congregational minister and theologian, author of *God in Christ* (1849), *Christ in Theology* (1851), *Nature and the Supernatural* (1858), *The Vicarious Sacrifice* (1866) and *Forgiveness and Law* (1874).

Būsīrī, al- (actually **Sharaf ad-Dīn Muhammad Ibn Sa'īd al-Būsīrī as-Sanhājī) (c.1212-c.1295)**, Arab poet who wrote the celebrated poem *al-Burdah* (English translation as *The Poem of the Mantle*).

Busken Huet, Conrad (1826-1886), noted Dutch critic, author of the classic study *Het land van Rembrandt* (The Country of Rembrandt, 1882-84).

Buson, (actually Taniguchi Buson) (1716-1783), outstanding Japanese poet and painter who was known as Yosa Buson.

Bussy, Roger de Rabutin, Comte de (1618-1693), infamous French libertine and writer who was known as Bussy-Rabutin, author of the scandalous tales *Histoire amoureuse des Gaules* (1665).

Butler, Alban (1710-1773), English Roman Catholic priest and historian who wrote the celebrated *The Lives of the Fathers, Martyrs, and Other Principal Saints* (4 volumes, 1756-59).

Butler, Ellis Parker (1869-1937), American writer of a humorous turn.

Butler, James (c.1755-1842), English-born American writer, best remembered for his novel *Fortunes's Foot-ball, or, The Adventures of Mercutio* (1797-98).

Butler, Joseph (1692-1752), English Anglican bishop and philosopher, author of the notable *Sermons on Human Nature* (1726) and *The Analogy of Religion, Natural and Revealed, to the Constitution and Course of Nature* (1736).

Butler, Nicholas Murray (1862-1947), prominent American educator, internationalist and writer; was co-winner of the Nobel Prize for Peace (1931).

Butler, Samuel (1612-1680), notable English poet whose mastery of satire was revealed in his Hudibras (3 parts, 1663, 1664, 1678).

Butler, Samuel (1835-1902), English novelist, essayist and critic, author of the novels *Erewhon* (1872) and *The Way of All Flesh* (published 1903).

Buysse, Cyriel (1859-1932), Dutch novelist and dramatist, a prominent figure of the Flemish naturalist school.

Buzzati, Dino (1906-1972), esteemed Italian novelist, short-story writer and dramatist, especially known for his Kafkaesque themes.

Byles, Mathur (1707-1788), American clergyman, theologian and poet.

Bynner, Edwin Lassetter (1842-1893), American lawyer and writer, best known for his novel *Agnes Surriage* (1886).

Bynner, (Harold) Witter (1881-1968), American poet and writer who displayed a fine command of both lyrical and satirical writing.

Byrd, William (1674-1744), American planter, satirist and diarist whose writings were published posthumously and revealed him as a literary figure of merit.

Byrne, Donn (1889-1928), American writer and poet.

Byrom, John (1692-1763), English poet and hymnist, best remembered for his hymn *Christians Awake! Salute the Happy Morn.*

Byron, Lord (actually **George Gordon Byron, 6th Baron Byron) (1788-1824)**, celebrated English poet, self-created "Byronic hero" of the Romantic age and advocate of political liberty, author of such famous works as *Childe Harold's Pilgrimage* (4 cantos, 1812, 1816, 1818), *Manfred* (1817) and *Don Juan* (1819-24).

Caballero, Fernán (actually **Cecilia Böhl de Faber) (1796-1877),** German-Spanish novelist whose most noted novel was *La-gaviota* (1849; English translation as *The Seagull*, 1867).

Cabanis, Pierre-Jean-Georges (1757-1808), French philosopher and physiologist, particularly known for his *Rapports du physique et du moral de l'homme* (Relations of the Physical and the Moral in Man, 1802).

Cabasilas, Saint Nicolas (c.1320-1390), notable Greek Orthodox lay theologian who wrote the important *Commentary on the Divine Liturgy* and *Life of Christ.*

Cabasilas, Nilus (c.1298-c.1363), Greek Orthodox metropolitan and theologian, author of *De processione Spiritus Sancti* (On the Procession of the Holy Spirit).

Cabell, James Branch (1879-1958), American writer and critic, best remembered for his novel *Jurgen* (1919).

Cabet, Étienne (1788-1856), French-born American Socialist whose novel *Voyage en Icarie* (1840) espouses his thoughts on the ideal society.

Cable, George Washington (1844-1925), American novelist, short-story writer, essayist and reformer.

Cabrol, Fernand (1855-1937), French Benedictine monk and writer, particularly known for his *Livre de la antique* (1900; English translation as *Liturgical Prayer*, 1922).

Cadalso or Cadahiso y Vázquez José de (1741-1782), Spanish writer, poet and dramatist, author of the books *Cartas marruecas* (Moroccan Letters, 1793) and *Noches lúgubres* (Sombre Nights, 1798)

Caecilius (1st Century), Greek rhetorician.

Caecilius, Statius (c.219-166 B.C.), Roman poet.

Caedmon (7th Century), Anglo-Saxon monk and poet.

Caesar, (Gaius) Julius (100-44 B.C.), greatly renowned Roman general and dictator who wrote *Commentarii de bello Gallico* (52-51 B.C.; English translation as *The Gallic War*, 1917) and *Commentarii de bello civili* (c.45 B.C.; English translation as *The Civil Wars*, 1914); was assassinated.

Caesarius of Heisterbach (c.1170-c.1240), German preacher and writer, author of the *Dialogus Miraculorum* (c.1219-23; English translation, 1929), several books on miracles and a life of Saint Engelbert.

Caffaro di Caschifellone (b. c.1080-1166), Italian soldier, statesman and crusader who chronicled the First Crusade and the 12th-Century Genoa.

Cahan, Abraham (1860-1951), Russian-born American journalist and writer.

Cain, James M(allahan) (1892-1977), American novelist and short-story writer, best known for his novels *The Postman Always Rings Twice* (1934), *Double Indemnity* (1936) and *Mildred Pierce* (1941).

Caine, Sir (Thomas Henry) Hall (1853-1931), English novelist.

Caird, Edward (1835-1908), English philosopher, author of *A Critical Account of the Philosophy of Kant* (1877), *The Critical Philosophy of Immanuel Kant* (2 volumes, 1889), *The Evolution of Religion* (2 volumes, 1893) and *The Evolution of Theology in the Greek Philosophers* (2 volumes, 1904).

Caird, John (1820-1898), Scottish Presbyterian minister and theologian who wrote *An Introduction to the Philosophy of Religion* (1880) and *The Fundamental Ideas of Christianity* (2 volumes, 1899).

Cairnes, John Elliott (1823-1875), Irish economist, author of *Some Leading Principles of Political Economy Newly Expounded* (1874).

Caius, John (1510-1573), English physician and writer.

Cajetan or Cajetanus (c.1648-1534), notable Roman Catholic theologian who took the Dominican name Tommaso de Vio, author of a major commentary on the *Summa theologiae* of Saint Thomas Aquinas.

Calderon de la Barca, Pedo (1600-1681), eminent Spanish dramatisit and poet, especially known for his outstanding play *La hija del aire* (The Daughter of Air, 1653).

Caldwell, Erskine (Preston) (1903-1987), prominent American novelist and short-story writer, especially known for his novels *Tobacco Road* (1932), *God's Little Acre* (1933) and *Trouble in July* (1940).

Caldwell, (Janet) Taylor (1900-1985), English-born American novelist.

Calef, Robert (1648-1719), American merchant who wrote a trenchant attack on the perpetrators of the Salem witchcraft trials in his *More Wonders of the Invisible World* (1700).

Callaghan, Morley (Edward) (1903-1990), Canadian novelist and short-story writer.

Callimachus (c.305-c.240 B.C.), Greek poet and scholar, author of the famous elegy *Aetia* (Causes, c.270 B.C.).

Callinus (7th Century B.C.), Greek poet.

Calpurnius Siculus, Titus (2nd Century), Roman poet of several pastoral eclogues.

Calverley, Charles Stuart (1831-1884), English poet and translator whose gift of parody was revealed in such volumes as *Verses and Translations* (1862) and *Fly Leaves* (1872).

Calvert, George Henry (1803-1889), American writer, dramatist and poet.

Calverton, V(ictor) F(rancis) (actually George Goetz) (1900-1940), American critic and editor who embraced Marxist principles.

Calvin, John (1509-1564), greatly significant French Protestant reformer and theologian, author of the famous *Institutes* (1536; enlarged edition, 1539).

Calvino, Italo (1923-1985), Italian novelist and short-story writer.

Calvus, Gaius Licinius Macer (82-c.47 B.C.), Roman poet and orator.

Calzabigi, Raniero (Simone Francesco Maria) di (1714-1795), Italian poet and music theorist who wrote the librettos for Gluck's operas *Orfeo ed Euridice* (1762), *Alceste* (1767) and *Paride ed Elena* (1770).

Cambridge, Ada (1844-1926), English-born Australian novelist and poet.

Cambridge, Richard Owen (1717-1802), English poet and essayist, author of the mock epic poem *The Scribleriad*.

Camden, William (1551-1623), English antiquarian who wrote a topographical survey of England in his *Britannia* (1586; 6th edition, enlarged, 1607).

Camerarius, Joachim (1500-1574), German Lutheran theologian and classical scholar.

Cameron, (John) Norman (1905-1953), Scottish poet.

Cammaerts, Émile (1878-1953), Belgian-born English poet and writer.

Camões, Luís (Vaz) de (c.1524-1580), renowned Portuguese poet, author of the famous epic *Os Lusíadas*.

Campanella, Tommaso (actually Giovanno Domenico Campanella) (1568-1639), Italian philosopher and poet who wrote the socialistic tome *La Città del Sole* (The City of the Sun, 1602) during his imprisonment by the Inquisition (1599-1626).

Campbell, Alexander (1788-1866), Irish-born American Protestant clergyman, writer and co-founder of the Disciples of Christ or Christian Church.

Campbell, Bartley (1843-1888), American dramatist, best remembered for *My Partner* (1879).

Campbell, George (1719-1796), English writer.

Campbell, (Ignatius) Roy(ston Dunnachie) (1901-1957), admired South African poet, writer and translator who excelled in lyric poetry; died in an automobile accident.

Campbell, Joseph (1879-1944), Irish poet who wrote some of his poems under his Irish name Seosamh MacCathmhaoil.

Campbell, Joseph (1904-1987), American writer and editor who became best known for his exploration of mythology.

Campbell, Thomas (1777-1844), Scottish poet and writer, particularly remembered for such poems as *The Pleasures of Hope* (1799), *The Battle of the Baltic, Hohenlinden, The Soldier's Dream* and *Ye Mariners of England*.

Campbell, William Wilfred (1861-1918), Canadian churchman, poet and writer, author of *Lake Lyrics and Other Poems* (1889).

Campe, Joachim Heinrich (1746-1818), German educator and writer.

Camphuysen, Dirk Rafaëlszoon (1586-1627), Dutch poet who wrote on religious themes.

Campion, Thomas (1567-1620), English physician, poet, theorist and composer, author of both English and Latin poems.

Campoamor y Campoosorio, Ramón de (1817-1901), Spanish poet who became known for his epigrams.

Camus, Albert (1913-1960), remarkable French novelist, short-story writer, dramatist and essayist who pondered what he considered to be the absurdity of the human dilemma; won the Nobel Prize for Literature (1957); died in an automobile accident.

Canby, Henry Seidel (1878-1961), American critic, biographer and editor.

Cane Melville H(enry) (1879-1980), American lawyer, poet and writer.

Canetti, Elias (1905-1994), notable Bulgarian novelist and dramatist; won the Nobel Prize for Literature (1981).

Canfield (Fisher), Dorothy (1879-1958), American novelist and short-story writer.

Canisius, Saint Peter or Petrus Kanis (1521-1597), Dutch Jesuit scholar who was a vigorous opponent of Protestantism.

Canitz, Friedrich Rudolf, Freiherr von (1654-1699), German poet whose satires helped to introduce classical values to German letters.

Cankar, Ivan (1876-1918), Slovenian writer, poet and dramatist.

Cannon, Charles James (1800-1860), American dramatist, poet and writer.

Cano, Melchor (c.1509-1560), Spanish Roman Catholic bishop and theologian, author of *De locis theologicis*.

Canth, Minna (actually Ulrika Vilhelmina née Johnsson Canth) (1844-1897), Finnish novelist, short-story writer and dramatist.

Cantwell, Robert (Emmet) (1908-1978), American novelist and biographer.

Čapek, Karel (1890-1938), outstanding Czech novelist, short-story writer, dramatist and essayist.

Capella, Martianus Minneus Felix (4th-5th Century), North African poet and writer.

Capgrave, John (1393-1464), English theologian, historian and biographer.

Capito, Wolfgang Fabricius (actually Wolfgang Köpfel) (1478-1541), Alsatian Protestant reformer and Old Testament scholar.

Capote, Truman (1924-1984), American novelist, short-story writer and dramatist.

Cappel, Louis or Ludovicus Capellus (1585-1658), French theologian and Hebrew scholar, author of the significant *Critica Sacra* (1650).

Capponi, Gino, Marchese (1792-1876), Italian statesman and writer, author of the important *Storia della republicca di Firenze* (History of the Rupublic of Florence, 1875).

Capréolus, Jean (c.1380-1444), French theologian and philosopher, best known for his defence of Saint Thomas in his *Defensions* (4 volumes, 1409-32).

Capuana, Luigi (1839-1915), Italian novelist, short-story writer, dramatist and critic.

Caragiale, Ion Luca (1852-1912), Romanian dramatist and short-story writer.

Carducci, Giosuè (1835-1907), prominent Italian poet and scholar; won the Nobel Prize for Literature (1906).

Carew, Richard (1555-1620), English poet, antiquarian and translator.

Carew, Thomas (c.1594-c.1639), English poet who wrote the finely-crafted *A Rapture*.

Carey, Henry (c.1687-1743), English poet, dramatist and composer, particularly known for his ballad *Sally in Our Alley* (1737).

Carey, Henry Charles (1793-1879), American economist and sociologist; son of Matthew Carey.

Carey, Matthew (1760-1839), Irish-born American journalist and writer; father of Henry Charles Carey.

Carey, William (1761-1834), English Baptist missionary, grammarian, lexicographer and translator.

Carleton, Henry Guy (1856-1910), American dramatist, best remembered for his farces.

Carleton, William (1794-1869), Irish novelist and short-story writer.

Carleton, Will(iam McKendree) (1845-1912), American poet who wrote ballads of farm and city life.

Carlile, Richard (1790-1843), English journalist, well known as an advocate of radical causes.

Carlyle, Thomas (1795-1881), noted Scottish essayist and historian, author of *The French Revolution* (1837).

Carman, (William) Bliss (1861-1929), Canadian-born American poet and writer who was esteemed for his love poems.

Carmer, Carl (Lamson) (1893-1976), American writer and editor.

Carnap, Rudolf (1891-1970), German-born American empiricist philospher and logician who wrote such significant books as *Der logische Aufbau der Welt* (1928; English translation as *The Logical Structure of the World*, 1967), *Logische Syntax der Sprache* (1934; English translation as *The Logical Syntax of Language*, 1937), *Meaning and Necessity* (1947) and *Logical Foundations of Probability* (1950).

Caro, Annibale (1507-1566), Italian poet, dramatist and translator, particularly known for his *Lettere familiare* (Familiar Letters, published 1572-74) and translation of Virgil's *Aeneid* (published in 1581).

Carossa, Hans (1878-1956), distinguished German novelist and poet, best remembered for his autobiographical novels.

Carpenter, Edward (1844-1929), English Socialist, writer and poet.

Carr, Emily (1871-1945), Canadian painter and writer.

Carranza, Bartolomé de (1503-1576), Spanish Roman Catholic archbishop and theologian who wrote the *Quattuor controversiae* (Four Controversies, 1546) and *Comentarios sobre el catechismo christiano* (Commentaries on the Christian Catechism, 1558), the latter causing his imprisonment by the Inquisition (1503-1576).

Carrasquilla, Tomas (1858-1940), Colombian novelist and short-story writer.

Carillo y Sotomayor, Luis (c.1583-1610), Spanish poet, esteemed for his *Fábula de Acis y Galatea* (published 1611).

Carroll, Lewis (actually Charles Lutwidge Dodgson) (1832-1898), famous English writer, poet, logician and mathematician, celebrated for his nonsense verse and for his classic books *Alice's Adventures in Wonderland* (1865) and *Through the Looking-Glass and What Alice Found There* (1871).

Carryl, Charles Edward (1842-1920), American financier, writer and poet; father of Guy Wetmore Carryl.

Carryl, Guy Wetmore (1873-1904), American novelist, short-story writer and poet; son fo Charles Edward Carryl.

Carson, Rachel (Louise) (1907-1964), American biologist and writer on science, author of *The Sea Around Us* (1951) and *Silent Spring* (1962).

Carter, Angela (Olive née Stalker) (1940-1992), English novelist, poet and essayist.

Carter, Elizabeth (1717-1806), English poet and translator.

Carton de Wiart, Henri (-Victor) Comte (1869-1951), Belgian statesman, jurist, novelist and essayist.

Cartwright, Peter (1785-1872), American Methodist preacher whose career was the subject of his interesting *Autobiography* (1857), *The Backwoods Preacher* (1858) and *Fifty Years as a Presiding Elder* (1871).

Cartwright, William (1611-1643), English preacher, dramatist and poet.

Caruthers, William Alexander (1802-1846), American novelist.

Carver, Jonathan (1710-1780), American explorer who left an account of his explorations in his *Travels Through the Interior Parts of North America in the Years 1766, 1767, 1768* (1778).

Carver, Raymond (1939-1988), American poet and short-story writer.

Cary Alice (1820-1871), American poet and writer; sister of Phoebe Cary.

Cary, (Arthur) Joyce (Lunel) (1888-1957), Irish-born English novelist and short-story writer, especially known for his novel trilogies *Herself Surprised* (1941), *To Be a Pilgrim* (1942) and *The Horse's Mouth* (1944) *and A Prisoner of Grace* (1952), *Except the Lord* (1953) and *Not Honour More* (1955).

Cary, Henry Francis (1772-1844), English biographer and translator who became best known for his blank verse translation of Dante's *Divine Comedy* (1814).

Cary, Pheobe (1824-1871), American poet and hymnist; sister of Alice Cary.

Casa, Giovanni Della (1503-1556), Italian Roman Catholic bishop, poet and translator.

Casal, Julián del (1863-1893), Cuban poet.

Casanova, Giovani Giacomo, Chevalier de Seingalt (1725-1798), outrageous Italian adventurer, writer and poet whose life as a libertine was recounted in his infamous autobiography *Histoire de ma vie* (English translation as *History of My Life*, 1966 et seq.).

Casaubon, Isaac (1559-1614), French-born English scholar who prepared editions of and commentaries on ancient writers.

Case, Shirley Jackson (1872-1947), Canadian-born American theologian, author of *Jesus: A New Biography* (1927).

Cassiodorus (actually Flavius Magnus Aurelius Cassiodorous) (c.490-c.585), Italian monk, statesman and historian.

Cassirer, Ernst (1874-1945), German philosopher who espoused neo-Kantian principles, author of the important study *Die Philosophie der symbolischen Formen* (3 volumes, 1923-29; English translation *as The Philosophy of Symbolic Forms*, 1953-57).

Cassola, Carlo (1917-1987), Italian novelist and short-story writer.

Cassou, Jean (1897-1986), French poet, novelist and art critic.

Castaneda, Carlos (1925-1998), Peruvian-born American writer.

Castelar y Ripoll, Emilio (1832-1899), Spanish statesman, novelist and historian.

Castelli, Ignaz Franz (1781-1862), Austrian poet.

Castelo Branco, Camilo (1825-1890), notable Portuguese novelist, particularly remembered for his *Amor de Perdicao* (Fatal Love, 1862); committed suicide.

Castelvetro, Ludovico (c.1505-1571), Italian scholar, critic and translator, known for his edition of Aristotle's *Poetics* (1570)

Casti, Giovanni Battista (1724-1803), Italian poet and librettist, particularly remembered for his verse satires *Poema tartaro* (Tartar Poem, 1787) and *Gli animali parlanti* (1802; English translation as *The Court and Parliament of Beasts*, 1819).

Castiglione, Baldassaré (1478-1529), Italian courtier and diplomat, author of *Il libro del cortegiano* (1528; English translation as *The Courtyer*, 1561).

Castilho, António Feliciano de (1800-1875), esteemed Portuguese poet, critic and translator.

Castillejo, Cristóbal de (c.1490-1550), Spanish poet who wrote the erotic *Sermón de amores* (1542).

Castillo Solorzano, Alonso de (1584-c.1648), Spanish novelist, short-story writer and dramatist.

Castillo y Saavedra, Antonio del (1616-1668), Spanish painter, sculptor and poet.

Castro, Eugénio de (1869-1944), Portuguese poet who won distinction as his country's leading symbolist with his *Oaristos* (1890) and *Horas* (1891).

Castro, Rosalía de (1837-1885), Spanish poet and novelist in the Galician language, author of the poems *Cantares gallegos* (1863) and *Follas novas* (1880), in Galician, and *En las orillas del Sar* (1884), in Castilian.

Castro Alves, Antônio de (1847-1871), Brazilian poet who espoused the abolitionist cause and thus became known as the "poet of the slaves".

Castro y Bellvís, Guillén (1569-1631), Spanish dramatist best remembered for his *Las mocedades del Cid* (c.1599).

Cather, Willa (Sibert) (1873-1947), American novelist whose works included *O Pioneers!* (1913), *My Ántonia* (1918), *One of Ours* (1922) and *Death Comes for the Archbishop* (1927).

Catherwood, Mary (Hartwell) (1847-1902), American writer.

Catlin, George (1796-1872), American artist and writer.

Cato, Marcus Porcius (234-149 B.C.), eminent Roman Statesman, orator and writer who was also known as Cato the Censor and Cato the Elder.

Cato, Publius Valerius (b. c.100 B.C.), Roman poet and writer.

Cats, Jacob (1577-1660), Dutch statesman and poet, beloved by his countrymen and known as "Father Cats".

Cattaneo, Carlo (1801-1869), Italian scholar and writer, a leading figure in the Risorgimento.

Cattell, James McKeen (1860-1944), American psychologist, writer and editor.

Catton, Bruce (1899-1978), American historian, especially admired for his *Mr Lincoln's Army* (1951), *Glory Road* (1952) and *A Stillness at Appomattox* (1953).

Catullus, Gaius Valerius (c.84-c.54 B.C.), celebrated Roman poet, a master of lyric verse whose love poems and satirical works are exemplary.

Cavafy, Constantine (actually **Konstantínos Pétrou Kaváfis) (1863-1933),** noted Greek poet whose output reflected his stance as a skeptic.

Cavalcanti, Guido (c.1255-1300), remarkable Italian poet, esteemed for his love poems and ballads.

Cavendish, George ((c.1499-c.1561), English biographer who wrote *The Life and Death of Cardinal Wolsey* (published 1641).

Cawein, Madison (Julius) (1865-1914), American poet.

Caxton, William (c.1422-1491), significant English publisher and translator.

Caylus, Anne-Clark-Phillipe de Tubières, Comte de (1692-1765), French archaeologist, engraver and writer.

Cecco d'Ascoli (actually **Francesco Stabili) (1269-1327),** Italian astrologer, poet and writer; was condemned as a heretic and burned at the stake.

Cecil, Lord (Edward Christian) David Gascoyne (1902-1986), English critic and biographer.

Celan, Paul (actually **Paul Antschel) (1920-1970),** Romanian-born French poet who won considerable distinction in Germany after World War II; committed suicide.

Céline, Louis Ferdinand (actually **Loius-Ferdinand Destouches) (1894-1961),** French novelist who secured his reputation with his *Voyage au bout de la nuit* (1932; English translation as *Journey to the End of Night*, 1934).

Cellini, Benvenuto (1500-1571), famous Italian sculptor, goldsmith and writer, author of a celebrated autobiography (published 1730, English translation, 1888).

Celsus, Aulus Cornelius (1st Century), Roman writer on medicine, author of the famous *De medicina* (English translation, 1945-48).

Celtis or **Celtes, Conradus** (German name **Conrad Pickel) (1459-1508),** German scholar and poet who was known as Der Erzhumanist (The Archumanist).

Cendrars, Blaise (actually **Frédéric Louis Sauser) (1887-1961),** Swiss novelist and poet, author of such poems as *Les Pâques à New York* (Easter in New York, 1912) and *La prose du Transsiberien et de la petite Jehanne de France* (The Prose of the Trans-Siberian and of Little Jehanne of France, 1913).

Centlivre, Susannah (1669-1723), English actress and dramatist.

Cervantes (Saavedra), Miguel de (1547-1616), great Spanish novelist, short-story writer, dramatist and poet, author of the novel *Don Quixote de la Mancha* (2 parts, 1605, 1615) one of the supreme masterpieces of world literature.

Cesarotti, Melchiorre (1730-1808), Italian poet, critic, essayist and translator.

Céspedes, Pablo de (1538-1608), Spanish poet, writer, painter, sculptor and architect.

Céspedes y Meneses, Gonzalo de (c.1585-1638), Spanish writer, author of *Poema Trágica del Español Gerardo, y Desengaño del Amor Lasciuo* (1615-17; English translation *as Gerardo the Unfortunate Spaniard, or a Patterne for Lasciuious Lovers*, 1622).

Cetina, Gutierre de (c.1520-c.1557), Spanish poet who wrote the notable *Ojos claros.*

Ceva, Tommaso (1648-1737), Italian mathematician and poet, author of the poem *Jesus Puer* (Child Jesus, 1690).

Cevdet Paşa, Ahmed (1822-1895), Turkish statesman, historian and poet.

Chaadaiev, Pietr Yakovlevich (c.1794-1856), Russian writer who wrote a biting critical assessment of Russian history and culture in his *Lettres Philosophiques* (Philosophical Letters, 1827-31)

Chacel, Rosa (Clotilde Cecilia María del Carmen) (1898-1994), Spanish novelist and poet.

Chafee, Zechariah, Jr (1885-1957), American legal scholar and champion of civil liberties, author of *Free Speech in the United States* (1941; 2nd edition, 1946).

Chalcocondyles or Chalcondyles, Laonicus (c.1423-c.1490), Byzantine historian who wrote the important *Historiarum demonstrationes.*

Chalkhill, John (d.1642), English poet, author of *Thealma and Clearchus* (published 1683).

Challoner, Richard (1691-1781), English Roman Catholic churchman who wrote *The Garden of the Soul* (1740), a revision of the Reims-Douai version of the Bible (1749-50) and *Meditations for Every Day of the Year* (1753).

Chalmers, Alexander (1759-1834), noted Scottish editor and biographer.

Chalmers, George (1742-1825), Scottish lawyer, historian and antiquarian.

Chalmers, Thomas (1780-1847), Scottish Presbyterian preacher, theologian, social reformer and writer, author of *On the Adaptation of External Nature to the Moral and Intellectual Constitution of Man* (1833).

Chamberlain, Houston Stewart (1855-1927), English-born German political philosopher and writer on music who espoused Pan-German ideas of Aryan national and racial superiority.

Chamberlayne, William (1619-1689), English physician and poet, author of *Love's Victory* (1658), *Pharonnida* (1659) and *England's Jubilee* (1660).

Chambers, Sir E(dmund) K(erchever) (1866-1954), English literary scholar and biographer.

Chambers, Ephraim (c.1680-1740), English encyclopedist who published the *Cyclopaedia, or Universal Dictionary of Arts and Sciences* (1728).

Chambers, R(aymond) W(ilson) (1874-1942), English literary scholar.

Chambers, Robert (1802-1871), Scottish publisher and writer, co-founder with his brother William (1800-1883) of W and R Chambers Ltd.

Chamfort, Sébastien-Roch Nicolas (1740-1794), French dramatist and writer who won renown for his wit; was a victim of the Reign of Terror.

Chamisso, Adelbert von (actually Louis-Charles-Adélaïde Chamisso de Boncourt) (1781-1838), important French-born German poet, writer and scientist, author of *Frauenliebe und –Leben* (Women's Love and Life), set to music by Robert Schumann, and the story *Peter Schlemihls wundersame Geschichte* (1814; English translation as *Peter Schlemihl's Remarkable Story*, 1927).

Champfleury (actually Jules-François-Félix Husson) (1821-1889), French novelist and journalist who was an exponent of Realism.

Champollion, Jean-François (1790-1832), significant French historian and linguist, the founder of scientific Egyptology and a pioneering figure in the elucidation of Egyptian hieroglyphics; brother of Jacques-Joseph Champollion-Figeac.

Champollion-Figeac, Jacques-Joseph (1778-1867), French librarian, paleographer and historian; brother of Jean-François Champollion.

Chandler, Elizabeth Margaret (1807-1834), American poet who championed the antislavery cause in verse.

Chandler, Raymond (Thornton) (1888-1959), American writer who created the private detective Philip Marlowe.

Chang Ping-lin (1868-1936), Chinese Nationalist revolutionary, Confucian scholar, writer and poet.

Chang Tsai (1020-1077), Chinese philosopher, author of the *Cheng-meng* (Correct Discipline for Beginners).

Chang Tzu-p'ing (1893-c.1947), Chinese writer.

Channing, Edward (1856-1931), American historian whose major work was the *History of the United States* (6 volumes, 1905-25).

Channing, William Ellery (1780-1842), prominent American clergyman, social reformer and writer, known as the "apostle of Unitarianism"; uncle of William Ellery and William Henry Channing.

Channing, William Ellery (1818-1901), American poet of the Transcendentalist school; nephew of William Ellery Channing.

Channing, William Henry (1810-1884), American Christian socialist, editor and writer; nephew of William Ellery Channing the elder.

Chapais, Sir (Joseph Amable) Thomas (1858-1946), Canadian lawyer, public official and historian.

Chapelain, Jean (1595-1674), French critic and poet.

Chapman, George (c.1559-1634), English dramatist, poet and translator, known for his translations of Homer's *Iliad* (1598-1611) and *Odyssey* (1616), and for the poem *Euthymiae and Raptus, or The Teares of Peace* (1609).

Chapman, John Jay (1862-1933), American poet, dramatist and critic who was active as a political reformer.

Chapone, Hester (née Mulso) (1727-1801), English writer.

Char, René (1907-1988), esteemed French poet who wrote finely-crafted verse of an economical austerity.

Charbonneau, Jean (1875-1960), French-Canadian poet, translator and lawyer.

Chariton (2nd Century), Greek writer who wrote the novel *Chaereas and Callirhoe*.

Charles, Duc d'Orléans (1394-1465), outstanding French poet of both French and English verse.

Charnay, Claude-Joseph-Désiré (1828-1915), French explorer and archaeologist, author of *Les Anciennes Villes du Nouveau Monde* (1885; English translation as *The Ancient Cities of the New World*, 1887).

Charrière, Isabelle Agnès Élizabeth de (1740-1805), Dutch-born Swiss novelist, particularly remembered for her *Lettres neuchâteloises* (1784) and *Caliste, ou lettres écrites de Lausanne* (1786).

Charron, Pierre (1541-1603), important French Roman Catholic theologian who espoused a form of Skepticism in his *Les Trois Vérités* (The Three Truths, 1593) and *De la sagesse* (1601; English translation as *On Wisdom*, 1697).

Charteris, Leslie (actually Leslie Charles Bowyer Yin) (1907-1993), Chines-English novelist who created Simon Templar or the Saint, the chief figure in a long and successful series of mystery-adventure novels.

Chartier, Alain (c.1385-c.1433), French poet writer and courtier, best known for his *La Belle Dame sans merci* and *Livre des quatre dames* (c.1415).

Chase, Mary Coyle (1907-1981), American dramatist whose best known play was *Harvey* (1944).

Chase Mary Ellen (1887-1973), American novelist and scholar, especially admired for her novels *Mary Peters* (1934) and *Silas Crockett* (1935).

Chasles, (Victor-Euphémien-) Philarète (1798-1873), French scholar and writer.

Chassignet, Jean-Baptiste (1578-1620), French poet.

Chastellain, Georges (c.1410-1475), Burgundian historian, essayist, dramatist and poet, author of the history *Chronique des ducs de Bourgogne*.

Chateaubriand (actually François-René de Chateaubriand, Vicomte de (1768-1848), prominent French writer and statesman, esteemed for his prose epics and his remarkable autobiography *Mémoires d'outre-tombe* (Memoirs from Beyond the Tomb).

Châtelet, Gabrielle-Émile Le Tonnelier de Breteuil, Marquise du (1706-1749), French philosopher and scientist who wrote *Institutions de physique* (Institutions of Physics, 1740), *Response à lettre de Mairan sur la question des forces vives* (Response to Mairan's Letter on the Question of Vital Forces, 1741) and *Dissertation sur la nature et la propagation du feu* (Dissertation on the Nature and Propagation of Fire, 1744).

Chatterjee, Bankim Chandra or Bankim-Chandra Cattopadhyay (1838-1894), important Indian novelist, especially esteemed for his *Krishnakanter Uil* (1878).

Chatterton, Thomas (1752-1770), gifted English poet who wrote the "Rowley" poems, forgeries he attributed to a mythical 15th Century monk he dubbed Thomas Rowley; committed suicide.

Chatwin, (Charles) Bruce (1940-1989), English traveller and writer.

Chaucer, Geoffrey (c.1343-1400), great English poet, celebrated throughout the world for his masterpieces *Troilus and Criseyde* and *The Canterbury Tales*.

Chauncy, Charles (1705-1787), American clergyman and writer who espoused Universalism in the last years of his career.

Chayefsky, Paddy (1923-1981), American dramatist whose *Marty* (1953) was a pioneering effort in television drama.

Cheever, John (1912-1982), American novelist and short-story writer.

Chekov, Anton (Pavlovich) (1860-1904), famous short-story writer and dramatist.

Chelčický, Peter (c.1390-c.1460), outstanding Czech writer on religious and political subjects whose *Šít Víry* (Net of the Faith, 1440) led to the blossoming of the religious sect of the Bohemian Brethren.

Chemnitz or Kemnitz, Martin (1522-1586), German Protestant churchman and theologian.

Cheng Chen-to (1898-1958), Chinese literary historian; died in an airplane crash.

Cheng Ch'iao (1108-1166), notable Chinese historian, author of *T'ung chih* (General Treatises).

Chénier, André (-Marie) de (1762-1794), illustrious French poet, author of *Hermes*, *L'Invention* and *Suzanne*; was guillotined at the close of the Reign of Terror; brother of Marie-Joseph-Blaise de Chenier.

Chénier, Marie-Joseph-Blaise de (1764-1811), French poet, dramatist and politician; brother of André (Marie) de Chénier.

Chernyshevsky, Nikolai Gavrilovich (1828-1889), Russian journalist and writer.

Chéruel, (Pierre-) Adolphe (1809-1891), French historian who wrote the valuable *Histoire de France pendant la minorité de Louis XIV* (History of France During the Youth of Louis XIV, 4 volumes, 1879-1880) and *Histoire de France sous le ministère de Mazarin, 1651-1661* (History of France Under the Ministry of Mazarin, 1651-1661, 3 volumes, 1882).

Chesnut, Mary Boykin (Miller) (1823-1886), American diarist whose diary was published as *A Diary from Dixie* (1905; complete text, 1981).

Chesnutt, Charles W(addell) (1858-1932), American novelist, short-story writer and essayist.

Chester, George Randolph (1869-1924), American journalist and writer, particularly remembered for his *Get-Rich-Quick Wallingford* (1908).

Chesterfield, Philip Dormer Stanhope, 4th Earl of (1694-1773), English statesman and diplomat who wrote the celebrated *Letters to His Son* and *Letters to His Godson*.

Chesterton, G(ilbert) K(eith) (1874-1936), famous English critic, novelist, short-story writer, essayist and poet, creator of the detective-priest Father Brown.

Chettle, Henry (c.1560-c.1607), English dramatist and pamphleteer.

Chevalier, Jules (1824-1907), French Roman Catholic priest and writer, founder of the *Missionarii Sacratissimi Cordis Jesu* (Missionaries of the Sacred Heart of Jesus).

Chevalier, Ulysse (1841-1923), French Roman Catholic priest and scholar who prepared valuable bibliographical works on medieval history.

Cheyney, Peter (actually Reginald Evelyn Peter Southouse-Cheyney) (1896-1951), English writer and poet, author of popular crime novels.

Chiabrera, Gabriello (1552-1638), Italian poet who introduced the poetical epistle to his homeland in his *Lettere Famigliari*.

Ch'i Ju-shan (1876-1962), Chinese dramatist and scholar.

Chikamatsu Monzaemon (actually Sugimori Nobumori) (1653-1724), great Japanese dramatist.

Child, Francis J(ames) (1825-1896), American literary scholar.

Child, Lydia Maria née Francis (1802-1880), American writer, reformer and Abolitionist.

Childe, V(ere) Gordon (1892-1957), Australian prehistorian who wrote the important studies *The Dawn of European Civilization* (1925; 6th edition, revised, 1957) and *The Danube in Prehistory*, (1929).

Childers, Robert Erskine (1870-1922), Irish nationalist and writer, author of the popular spy story *The Riddle of The Sands* (1903); his republican sympathies led to his execution.

Chillingworth, William (1602-1644), English theologian who wrote *The Religion of the Protestants a safe way to Salvation* (1637).

Chivers Thomas Holley (1809-1858), American poet, writer and dramatist.

Chocano, José Santos (1875-1934), Peruvian revolutionary and poet who espoused the cause of South American nationalism; was murdered by a former friend.

Choerilus (5th Century B.C.), Greek poet.

Choniates, Michael (c.1140-c1222), Byzantine archbishop and scholar.

Choniates, Nicetas (c.1140-1213), notable Byzantine statesman, historian and theologian.

Chopin, Kate (née O'Flaherty) (1850-1904), American writer, poet and essayist.

Chou Tun-i (1017-1073), important Chinese philosopher who was also known as Chou Lien-Hsi, founder of the Neo-Confucian school.

Chrétien de Troyes (12th Century), celebrated French poet, inventor of the courtly romance.

Christie, Dame Agatha (Mary Clarissa née Miller) (1890-1976), famous English novelist and dramatist, renowned as a writer of mysteries.

Christine de Pisan (1364-c.1430), gifted Italian poet, writer and translator.

Chrysander, (Karl Franz) Friedrich (1826-1901), distinguished German music scholar and editor.

Chrysippus (c.280-c.206 B.C.), Greek philosopher.

Chrysoloras, Manuel (c.1353-1415), Greek scholar and translator.

Chrysostom, Saint John (c.347-407), Greek Roman Catholic preacher, archbishop and writer, author of commentaries on New Testament writings.

Chubb, Thomas (1679-1747), English writer of Deist tracts.

Chu Hsi (1130-1200), great Chinese philosopher, author of the *Ssu shu* (Four Books).

Chulkov, Mikhail Dmitrievich (c.1743-1792), Russian novelist.

Chumnus, Nicephorus (1250-1327), Byzantine stateman and scholar.

Church, Benjamin (1734-1776), American writer of political essays.

Church, Richard (Thomas) (1893-1972), English poet, novelist and essayist.

Churchill, Charles (1731-1764), English poet, best known for *The Apology* (1761) and *The Rosciad* (1761).

Churchill, Randolph Frederick Edward Spencer (1911-1968), English journalist and writer; son of Sir Winston (Leonard Spencer) Churchill.

Churchill, Winston (1871-1947), American novelist, author of such popular works as *Richard Carvel* (1899), *The Crisis* (1901), and *The Crossing* (1904).

Churchill, Sir Winston (Leonard Spencer) (1874-1965), great English statesman, orator amd writer who wrote histories of World War II and of the English-speaking peoples; won the Nobel Prize for Literature (1953); father of Randolph Frederick Edward Spencer Churchill.

Churchyard, Thomas (c.1520-1604), English writer and poet.

Ch'ü Yüan (c.343-c.289 B.C.), illustrious Chinese poet.

Ciardi, John (Anthony) (1916-1985), American poet, essayist and translator.

Cibber, Colley (1671-1757), prominent English poet, dramatist, actor and theatre manager, best known for his sentimental comedies; became Poet Laureate of the United Kingdom (1730); father of Theophilus Cibber.

Cibber, Theophilus (1703-1758), English actor and dramatist; son of Colley Cibber.

Cicero, (Marcus Tullius) (106-43 B.C.), great Roman statesman, orator, scholar and writer.

Cieza de León, (Pedro de) (1518-1560), Spanish historian, author of the valuable *Crónica del Perú.*

Cigoli, Ludovico (Cardi da) (1559-1613), Italian painter, architect and poet.

Cinna, Gaius Hrivius (1st Century B.C.), Roman poet who wrote the epic *Smyrna.*

Cinnamus, John (12th Century), Byzantine historian.

Cino da Pistoia (actually Cino dei Sighibuldi) (c.1270-c.1336), Italian jurist, poet and writer.

Clampitt, Amy (1920-1994), American poet.

Clanvowe, Sir John (d.1391), English diplomat, courtier and poet, author of *The Two Ways.*

Clapp, Henry (1814-1875), American journalist and writer who wrote under the name Figaro.

Clare, Ada (actually Jane McElheney) (1836-1874), American poet, writer and actress.

Clare, John (1793-1864), English poet, author of *Poems Descriptive of Rural Life and Scenery* (1820), *The Shepherd's Calendar, with Village Stories, and Other Poems* (1827), and *The Rural Muse* (1835).

Clarendon, Edward Hyde, 1st Earl of (1609-1674), English statesman and historian who wrote the *History of the Rebellion and Civil Wars in England.*

Clark, Charles Heber (1841-1915), American journalist, novelist and short-story writer who wrote under the name Max Adeler.

Clark, Francis Edward (1851-1927), American Congregational clergyman and writer.

Clark, John Bates (1847-1938), American economist, author of the *Philosophy of Wealth* (1886) and *The Distribution of Wealth* (1899).

Clark, Kenneth Mackenzie, Lord (1903-1983), English art historian and writer.

Clark, Lewis Gaylord (1808-1873), American magazine editor and writer, author of *Knock-Knacks from an Editor's Table* (1852); brother of Willis Gaylord Clark.

Clark, Walter van Tilburg (1909-1971), American novelist and short-story writer, best remembered for his novel *The Ox-Bow Incident* (1940).

Clark, Willis Gaylord (1808-1841), American magazine editor and writer; brother of Lewis Gaylord Clark.

Clarke, Austin (1896-1974), Irish poet and dramatist.

Clarke, Charles Cowden (1787-1877), English editor and critic; husband of Mary Victoria Cowden Clarke.

Clarke, James Freeman (1810-1888), American Unitarian minister, theologian, writer and editor.

Clarke, Marcus (Andrew Hislop) (1846-1881), English-born Australian novelist and short-story writer, particularly known for his novel *For the Term of His Natural Life* (1874).

Clarke, Mary Victoria Cowden (1809-1898), English editor and critic; wife of Charles Cowden Clarke.

Clarke, McDonald (1798-1842), American poet, dubbed the "mad poet of Broadway", author of the collection *Elixir of Moonshine by the Mad Poet* (1822).

Clarke, Samuel (1675-1729), prominent English theologian and philosopher who expounded rational theological views in such volumes as *A Demonstration of the Being and Attributes of God* (1705), *A Discourse Concerning the Unchangeable Obligations of Natural Religion* (1706) and *Scripture Doctrine of the Trinity* (1712).

Clarkson, Laurence (1615-1667), English religious pamphleteer, author of the autobiography *The Lost Sheep Found* (1660).

Clauberg, Johann (1622-1665), German philosopher and theologian who wrote such important works as *Defensio Cartesiana* (1652), *Initatio philosophi* (1655), *Exercitationes centum de cognitione Dei et nostri* (One Hundred Exercises on the Knowledge of God and Ourselves, 1656) and *Corporis et animae in homine conjunctio* (On the Joining of the Body and Soul in Man, 1663).

Claudel, Paul (-Louis-Charles-Marie) (1868-1955), eminent French poet, essayist and dramatist, greatly admired for his *Cinq Grandes Odes* (1910) and the play *Le Soulier de satin* (1924; English translation as *The Satin Slipper*, 1931).

Claudian (actually Claudius Claudianus) (c.370-c.404), great Roman poet who was celebrated for his epic verse.

Claudius, Matthias (1740-1815), German poet and editor, known for his *Der Mond ist aufgegangen* (The Moon has Risen).

Clausewitz, Carl von (1780-1831), notable German general and military strategist, author of the celebrated *Von Kriege* (On War).

Claussen, Sophus (Niels Christen) (1865-1931), Danish poet and writer, a leading figure in the Symbolist movement.

Clavell, James (1924-1994), English-born American novelist and screenwriter, author of such novels as *Tai-Pan* (1966), *Shogun* (1975) and *Noble House* (1981).

Clavell, John (1603-1642), English highwayman who wrote the metrical autobiography *Recantation of an ill led life* (1628).

Clavijo y Fajardo, José (1730-1806), Spanish naturalist, writer and editor.

Cleland, John (1709-1789), English journalist, dramatist and writer, author of the pornographic novel *Fanny Hill, or, Memoirs of a Woman of Pleasure* (1748-49).

Cleland, William (c.1661-1689), Scottish poet; died defending Dunkeld against the Jacobite rebels.

Clemens, Jeremiah (1814-1865), American novelist.

Clement of Alexandria, Saint (c.150-c.213), prominent Greek Roman Catholic theologian.

Clemo, Jack (actually Reginald John Clemo) (1916-1994), English poet and writer.

Clermont-Ganneau, Charles (1846-1923), French biblical archaeologist who was known for his *Études d'archéologie orientale* (Studies in Eastern Archaeology, 2 volumes, 1880, 1897).

Cleveland, John (1613-1658), noted English poet, known for his Royalist verse.

Clifford, Sir Hugh Charles (1866-1941), English civil servant and writer.

Clifford, John (1836-1923), English Baptist minister, social reformer and writer.

Clifford, William Kingdon (1845-1879), English mathematician and philosopher.

Clifford, William (1772-1799), American poet.

Clive, Caroline Archer (1801-1873), English novelist and poet, particularly known for her novel *Paul Ferroll* (1855); died in a fire.

Clough, Arthur Hugh (1819-1861), English poet who wrote such admired works as *The Bothie or Tober-na-Vuolich* (1848), *Amours de Voyage* (1858) and *Dipsychus* (published 1865).

Coates, Robert M(yron) (1897-1973), American novelist and short-story writer.

Coatsworth, Elizabeth (Jane) (1893-1986), American poet and writer.

Cobb, Irving S(hrewsbury) (1876-1944), American journalist and writer who became best known for his humorous output.

Cobb, Joseph B(eckham) (1819-1858), American writer.

Cobb, Sylvanus Jr (1823-1887), American novelist and short-story writer.

Cobbett, William (1763-1835), English journalist and writer.

Cocceius, Johannes (1603-1669), German Reformed Church theologian and biblical scholar.

Cochlaeus, Johannes (1479-1552), German Roman Catholic priest and theologian who became one of the principal opponents of Lutheranism.

Cockburn, Alicia or Alison (née Rutherford) (1713-1794), Scottish poet, author of *The Flowers of the Forest*.

Cockburn, Catharine (née Trotter) (1679-1749), English dramatist, poet and writer.

Cocteau, Jean (1889-1963), famous French poet, librettist, novelist, critic, actor, film director and painter.

Codrington, R(obert) H(enry) (1830-1922), English Anglican priest and anthropologist.

Coffin, Charles Carleton (1823-1896), American journalist and writer.

Coffin, Henry Sloane (1877-1954), American Presbyterian minister, educator and writer.

Coffin, Robert P(eter) T(ristram) (1892-1955), American poet and writer.

Coggleshall, William Turner (1824-1867), American journalist, critic and writer.

Cohen, Hermann (1842-1918), German philosopher.

Cohen, Morris Raphael (1880-1947), American philosopher.

Cohen, Octavus Roy (1891-1959), American writer.

Coke, Sir Edward (1552-1634), English jurist and politician who wrote on legal subjects.

Coke, Thomas (1747-1814), English Methodist bishop and writer.

Colden, Cadwallader (1688-1776), Scottish-born American politician and writer on various subjects, including the *History of the Five Indian Nations* (1727), *Explication of the First Causes of Action in Matter, and, of the Causes of Gravitation* (1745) and on philosophy, science and medicine in *Plantae Coldenghamiae* (1749, 1751).

Cole, Fay-Cooper (1881-1961), American anthropologist.

Cole, G(eorge) D(ouglas) H(oward) (1889-1959), English economist, author of *A History of Socialist Thought* (1953-58).

Cole, Thomas (1801-1848), English-born American writer and poet.

Colenso, John William (1814-1883), English Anglican bishop and mathematician who became highly controversial for his liberal religious views.

Coleridge, (David) Hartley (1796-1849), English poet and writer, particularly esteemed for his sonnets; son of Samuel Taylor Coleridge.

Coleridge, Mary (1861-1907), English poet, novelist and essayist whose sonnets were much admired; great-great-niece of Samuel Taylor Coleridge.

Coleridge, Samuel Taylor (1772-1834), renowned English poet and critic, celebrated for the originality and beauty revealed in such poems as *Ode to France* (1796), *The Rime of the Ancient Mariner* (1798), *Ode to Dejection* (1802), *Christabel* (1816) and *Kubla Khan* (1816), and for the insight he brought to his literary criticism in his *Biographia Literaria* (1817); father of Sara Coleridge.

Coleridge, Sara (1802-1852), English translator, editor, writer and poet; daughter of Samuel Taylor Coleridge.

Colet, John (c.1466-1519), English theologian and scholar.

Colet, Louise (née Revoil) (1810-1876), French poet and novelist, particularly known for her novel *Lui* (Him, 1859).

Colette, (Sidonie-Gabrielle) (1873-1954), famous French novelist.

Collett, Camilla (née Wergeland) (1813-1895), Norwegian novelist who wrote the notably successful *Amtmandens dottre* (The Governor's Daughter, 1855).

Collier, Arthur (1680-1732), English philosopher and theologian, author of the *Clavis Universalis* (Universal Key, 1713), *A Specimen of True Philosophy* (1730) and *Logology* (1732).

Collier, Jeremy (1650-1726), English nonjuring bishop who became best known for his attack on the contemporary theatre in his *Short View of the Immorality and Profaneness of the English Stage* (1698).

Collier, John (1708-1786), English poet who wrote satirical and humorous verse under the name Tim Bobbin.

Collingwood, R(obin) G(eorge) (1889-1943), distinguished English historian and philosopher who wrote such works as *Speculum Mentis* (1924), *The Archaeology of Roman Britain* (1930), *Essay on Philosophical Method* (1933), *An Essay on Metaphysics* (1940) and *The Idea of History* (published 1946).

Collins, Anthony (1676-1729), English philosopher whose most important work was *A Discourse of Free-thinking* (1713).

Collins, William (1721-1759), English poet who revealed a special talent for lyrical expression.

Collins, (William) Wilkie (1824-1889), outstanding English writer, a master of the mystery-story genre, whose notable works included *The Woman in White* (1860) and *The Moonstone* (1868).

Collis, John Stewart (1900-1984), English writer and biographer.

Collitz, Hermann (1855-1935), German-born American linguist who was known for his studies on Indo-European languages.

Colluthus of Lycopolis (6th Century), Greek poet.

Colman, Benjamin (1673-1747), American clergyman and poet.

Colman, George, the Elder (1732-1794), English dramatist and theatre manager, best remembered for his comedies; father of George Colman the Younger.

Colman, George, the Younger (1762-1836), English dramatist, poet and theatre manager, particularly successful with his comic play *John Bull* (1803); son of George Colman the Elder.

Colonna, Vittoria (1492-1547), Italian poet.

Colton, John (1889-1946), American dramatist.

Colton, Walter (1797-1851), American writer.

Colum, Padraic (1881-1972), Irish poet, dramatist and writer.

Columban or **Columbanus, Saint (c.543-615),** Irish Roman Catholic abbot, missionary, writer and poet.

Columbus, Samuel (1642-1679), Swedish poet and writer.

Columella, Lucius Junius Moderatus (1st Century), Roman soldier and farmer who wrote *De re rustica* (12 volumes).

Colvin, Sir Sidney (1845-1927), English literary and art critic.

Colwin, Laurie E (1944-1992), American novelist and short-story writer.

Combe, William (1741-1823), English writer and poet, author of the popular poem *Tour of Dr Syntax in Search of the Picturesque* (1812).

Comenius, John Amos (actually **Jan Ámos Komenský**) **(1592-1670),** Moravian educational reformer and religious leader, author of the influential *Janua Linguarum Reserata* (1631; English translation *as The Gates of Tongues Unlocked and Opened*, 1637).

Comestor, Petrus (d.1179), French writer, author of the *Historia Scholastica*.

Commager, Henry Steele (1902-1998), prominent American historian and educator.

Commynes, Philippe de (c.1447-1511), French Statesman and chronicler who wrote the notable *Mémoires* (published 1524).

Compagni, Dino (c.1255-1324), Italian public official and historian, author of a valuable history of Florence *Cronica delle cose occorrenti ne' tempi suoi* (published 1726).

Compton-Burnett, Dame Ivy (1884-1969), esteemed English novelist.

Comte, (Isidore-) Auguste (-Marie-François-Xavier) (1798-1857), outstanding French philosopher who founded sociology and Positivism, author of the *Cours de philosophie positive* (6 volumes, 1830-42) and the *Système de politique positive* (4 volumes, 1851-54).

Condillac, Étienne Bonnot de (1715-1780), influential French philosopher, logician, psychologist, economist and writer who wrote such important works as *Essai sur l'origine des connaissances humaines* (Essay on the Origin of Human Knowledge, 1746) and *Traité des sensations* (Treatise on Sensation, 1754).

Condon, Richard (Thomas) (1915-1996), American novelist.

Condorcet, (Marie-Jean-Antoine-Nicolas de Caritat), Marquis de (1743-1794), French philosopher and educational reformer whose most important work was the *Esquisse d'un tableau historique des progrès de l'esprit humain* (Sketch for a Historical Picture of the Progress of the Human Mind, published 1795).

Confucius (actually **K'ung Ch'iu**) **(551-479 B. C.),** great Chinese philosopher, political theorist, teacher and writer who is know in China as K'ung-Fu-Tzu, K'ung-Tzu and Chung-Ni; grandfather of Tzu Ssu.

Congreve, Richard (1818-1899), English philosopher and writer who founded the Church of Humanity on positivist principles.

Congreve, William (1670-1729), distinguished English dramatist and poet, especially esteemed for his plays *The Old Bachelor* (1691), *The Double Dealer* (1693), *Love for Love* (1695) and *The Way of the World* (1700).

Conkling, Grace Hazard (1878-1958), American poet who surveyed the beauty of nature.

Connelly, Marc(us Cook) (1890-1980), American journalist and dramatist, best remembered for his play *Green Pastures* (1930), based on Roark Bradford's *Ol' Man Adam an' His Chillun*.

Connolly, Cyril (Vernon) (1903-1974), English critic, essayist and writer.

Connor, Ralph (actually **Charles William Gordon**) **(1860-1937),** Canadian Presbyterian minister and novelist.

Conrad, Joseph (actually **Józef Teodor Konrad Korzeniowski**) **(1857-1924),** prominent Polish-born English novelist and short-story writer, author of such works as *Lord Jim* (1900), *Nostromo* (1904), *The Secret Agent* (1907) and *Under Western Eyes* (1911).

Conrart, Valentin (1603-1675), French grammarian and one of the principal figures of the Académie Française.

Conroy, Jack (actually **John Wesley Conroy**) **(1899-1980),** American novelist and editor.

Conscience, Hendrik (1812-1883), outstanding Flemish novelist, one of the great masters of Flemish romanticism.

Considerant, Victor-Prosper (1808-1893), French Socialist theoretician, editor and writer, author of *Destinee sociale* (1834-38).

Constable, Henry (1562-1613), English poet who was known for his sonnets.

Constant (de Rebecque), (Henri-) Benjamin (1767-1830), Swiss-born French novelist and political writer, best known for his novels *Adolphe* (1816) and *Cecile* (published 1951; English translation, 1952).

Contarini, Gasparo (1483-1542), Italian Roman Catholic cardinal, theologian, scholar and diplomat who advocated church reform and dialogue with the Lutherans.

Conway, Anne Finch, Viscountess (1631-1679), English philosopher of the metaphysical school.

Conway, Moncure Daniel (1832-1907), American Unitarian minister, Abolitionist and writer, author of the *Life of Thomas Paine* (2 volumes, 1892) and an *Autobiography* (1904).

Conwell, Russell Herman (1843-1925), American lawyer, Baptist minister, educator, writer and lecturer.

Cook, Ebenezer (18th Century), American poet who wrote the satirical *The Sot-Weed Factor*.

Cook, Eliza (1818-1889), English poet.

Cook, George Cram (1873-1924), American novelist, dramatist and poet; husband of Susan Glaspell.

Cook, Mark (1933-1994), English-born Canadian dramatist.

Cooke, John Esten (1830-1886), American novelist and short-story writer; brother of Philip Pendleton Cooke.

Cooke, Philip Pendleton (1816-1850), American poet and critic who wrote the popular poem *Florence Vane* (1840); brother of John Esten Cooke.

Cooke, Rose (née Terry) (1827-1892), American writer and poet.

Cookson, Dame Catherine (Ann) (1906-1998), English novelist.

Coolbrith, Ina (Donna) (1842-1928), American poet who became known for her lyric sentiment.

Cooley, Charles Horton (1864-1929), American sociologist, author of *Human Nature and the Social Order* (1902), *Social Organization* (1909) and *Social Process* (1918).

Coolidge, William Augustus Brevoort (1850-1926), American historian and mountaineer.

Coomaraswamy, Ananda Kentish (1877-1947), Ceylonese-English historian of the fine arts of India.

Cooper, Giles (Stannus) (1918-1966), Irish dramatist who won notable success for his radio and television plays.

Cooper, James Fenimore (1789-1851), outstanding American novelist who wrote the classic Leatherstocking Tales in *The Pioneers* (1823), *The Last of the Mohicans* (1826), *The Prairie* (1827), *The Pathfinder* (1840) and *The Deerslayer* (1841); father of Susan Fenimore Cooper.

Cooper, John M(ontgomery) (1881-1949), American Roman Catholic priest, ethnologist and sociologist.

Cooper, Myles (1735-1785), English-born American Anglican clergyman, educator and writer whose Loyalist writings forced him to return to England in 1775.

Cooper, Peter (1791-1883), American inventor, financier and philanthropist who wrote *Ideas for a Science of Good Government* (1883).

Cooper, Susan Fenimore (1813-1894), American writer; daughter of James Fenimore Cooper.

Cooper, Thomas (c.1517-1594), English bishop and writer.

Cooper, Thomas (1759-1839), English-born American scholar and educator, particularly remembered for his political pamphlets and *Political Essays* (1799).

Cooper, Thomas (1805-1892), English writer and poet who espoused the Chartist cause in his verse epic *The Purgatory of Suicides* (1843-44), written during his imprisonment for sedition.

Coornhert, Dirk Volkertszoon (1522-1590), Dutch poet, dramatist, writer and translator.

Copernicus, Nicolaus (1473-1543), great Polish astronomer whose *De Revolutionbus* (1543) proposed the theory that the earth and other planets move in orbits around the sun, a theory which eventually supplanted the Ptolemaic geocentric theory.

Coppard, A(lfred) E(dgar) (1878-1957), English short-story writer and poet.

Coppée, François (1842-1908), French poet, writer and dramatist, author of the poetry collection *Les Humbles* (1872).

Copway, George (1818-c.1863), American Ojibway Indian chief, Wesleyan missionary and writer.

Corbet, Richard (1582-1635), English Anglican bishop and poet.

Corbett, Sir Julian Stafford (1854-1922), English naval historian.

Corbière, Tristan (actually Edouard Joachim Corbière) (1845-1875), French poet who excelled in realist verse.

Corbusier, Le (actually Charles-Édouard Jeanneret) (1887-1965), celebrated French architect, city planner, painter, sculptor and writer.

Cordemoy, Geraud de (c.1620-1684), French historian and philosopher.

Cordemoy, J-L de (1631-1731), French abbot and writer.

Cordovero, Moses ben Jacob (1522-1570), renowned Jewish rabbi and philosopher of the Kabbala.

Corelli, Marie (actually Mary Mackay) (1855-1924), English novelist who won success with her *Barabbas: A Dream of the World's Tragedy* (1893), *The Sorrows of Satan* (1895) and *The Murder of Delicia* (1896).

Corippus, Flavius Cresconius (6th Century), significant African-born Latin poet who wrote the *Johannis* (8 volumes) and *In laudem Justini* (4 volumes).

Corle, Edwin (1906-1956), American writer.

Corneille, Pierre (1606-1684), great French dramatist who was acclaimed as the father of French comedic and tragic writing for the stage; brother of Thomas Corneille.

Corneille, Thomas (1625-1709), esteemed French dramatist; brother of Pierre Corneille.

Cornelius, (Carl August) Peter (1824-1874), distinguished German composer and writer.

Cornford, Frances (Crofts) (1886-1960), English poet; mother of John Cornford.

Cornford, John (1915-1936), English poet who died in the Loyalist cause in the Spanish Civil War; son of Frances (Crofts) Cornford.

Cornutus, Lucius Annaeus (1st Century), Roman philosopher of the Stoic school.

Cornyshe, William (d.1523), English composer, poet and dramatist.

Côrte-Real, Jerónimo (1533-1588), Portuguese poet.

Cory, William Johnson (1823-1892), English poet.

Coryate, Thomas (c.1577-1617), English traveller and writer.

Cosin, John (1594-1672), respected English Anglican bishop, theologian and liturgist.

Cosmas (6th Century), Egyptian merchant, traveller, theologian and geographer, author of the famous treatise *Topographia Christiana* (c.535-547; English translation, 1897).

Cosmas of Prague (c.1045-1125), Bohemian historian.

Costa, Isaäc da (1798-1860), Dutch poet and writer.

Costain, Thomas B(ertram) (1885-1965), Canadian-born American writer, particularly remembered for *The Black Rose* (1945) and *The Silver Chalice* (1952).

Coster, Charles-Théodore-Henri de (1827-1879), prominent Belgian novelist, author of the outstanding *La Legende et les aventures héroïques, joyeuses, et glorieuses d'Ulenspiegel et de Lamme Goedzak au pays de Flandres et ailleurs* (1867; English translation as *The Glorious Adventures of Tyl Ulenspiegl*, 1943).

Costin, Miron (1633-1691), Moldavian historian and poet; father of Niculae Costin.

Costin, Niculae (1672-1745), Moldavian historian and editor; son of Miron Costin.

Cotton, Charles (1630-1687), English poet, writer and translator.

Cotton, John (1582-1652), English-born American Puritan leader and writer.

Coubertin, Pierre, Baron de (1863-1937), French scholar and educator who is best remembered for his resusitation of the Olympic Games in 1896.

Couperus, Louis Marie Anne (1863-1923), highly regarded Dutch novelist, best remembered for his *Eline vere* (1889; English translation, 1892).

Courier, Paul-Louis (1772-1825), French classical scholar; was murdered by his unfaithful wife's lover.

Cournot, Antoine-Augustin (1801-1877), French economist and mathematician.

Court, Antoine (1695-1760), French-born Swiss Reformed Church minister and writer.

Court de Gébelin (1725-1784), French philologist and writer, author of the important *Le Monde primitif, analysé et comparé avec le monde moderne* (1773-84).

Courteline, Georges (actually **Georges-Victor-Marcel Moinaux**) **(1858-1929)**, French writer and dramatist.

Courthope, William John (1842-1917), English critic who wrote the *History of English Poetry* (6 volumes, 1895-1910).

Cousin, Victor (1792-1867), prominent French philosopher, historian and educational reformer.

Cousins, Norman (1912-1990), American editor and writer.

Cousteau, Jacques (-Yves) (1910-1997), remarkable French naval officer, ocean explorer, writer and film producer.

Couturat, Louis (1868-1914), French philosopher, author of *L'Infinie mathématique* (1896).

Covarrubias, Miguel (1904-1957), Mexican painter, anthropologist and writer.

Coventry, Francis (1725-1754), English curate and writer, best known for the satirical work *The History of Pompey the Little, or the Life and Adventures of a Lap-Dog* 1751).

Coverdale, Miles (c.1487-1569), English bishop, writer and translator who translated the first printed English Bible (1535).

Coward, Sir Noel (Peirce) (1899-1973), famous English actor, dramatist, writer and composer.

Cowl, Jane (actually **Grace Bailey**) **(1883-1950)**, American actress and dramatist.

Cowley, Abraham (1618-1667), admired English poet and essayist whose most significant work was the unfinished epic poem the *Davideis* (c.1640).

Cowley, Hannah (née Parkhouse) (1743-1809), English dramatist.

Cowley, Malcolm (1898-1989), American critic, social historian, poet and editor.

Cowper, William (1731-1800), distinguished English poet, celebrated for such works as *The Task* (1785), *Yardley Oak* (1791) and *The Castaway* (1796).

Cox, Sir George W(illiams) (1827-1902), English mythologist.

Cox, Jacob Dolson (1828-1900), American politician and historian, author of the important *Military Reminiscences of the Civil War* (2 volumes, 1900).

Cozzens, Frederick Swartwout (1818-1869), American writer who wrote under the name Richard Haywarde.

Cozzens, James Gould (1903-1978), notable American novelist, author of *Men and Brethren* (1936), *Ask Me Tomorrow* (1940), *Guard of Honor* (1948) and *By Love Possessed* (1957).

Crabbe, George (1754-1832), English poet who was admired for *The Village* (1783), *The Parish Register* (1807), *The Borough* (1810) and *Tales of the Hall* (1819).

Craddock, Charles Egbert (actually **Mary Noailles Murfree**) **(1850-1922),** American short-story writer.

Crafts, William (1787-1826), American lawyer, orator, essayist, poet and critic.

Craig, Edward Gordon (actually **Edward Henry Gordon Godwin**) **(1872-1966),** English actor, artist, theatre director and designer, and writer, author of *The Art of the Theatre* (1905; augmented edition as *On the Art of the Theatre*, 1911) and *Towards a new Theatre* (1913).

Craigie, Sir William Alexander (1867-1957), English philologist and lexicographer.

Craik, Dinah Maria Murlock (1826-1887), English novelist, short-story writer, essayist and poet.

Cram, Ralph Adams (1863-1942), American architect and writer who wrote such works as *The Ministry of Art* (1914), *The Nemesis of Mediocrity* (1918) and *The End of Democracy* (1937).

Cranch, Christopher Pearse (1813-1892), American clergyman, Transcendentalist and poet.

Crane, (Harold) Hart (1899-1932), important American poet, author of *White Buildings* (1926) and *The Bridge* (1930); committed suicide.

Crane, Ronald (Salmon) (1886-1967), American critic.

Crane, Stephen (1871-1900), American novelist, short-story writer and poet, especially admired for his prose writings *Maggie: A Girl of the Streets* (1893) and *The Red Badge of Courage* (1895), and the poetry collection *War is Kind* (1899).

Cranmer, Thomas (1489-1556), prominent English prelate and Archbishop of Canterbury who prepared *The Book of Common Prayer*, was condemned as a heretic and burned at the stake.

Crantor (4th – 3rd Century B. C.), Greek philosopher.

Crapsey, Adelaide (1878-1914), American poet who invented the metrical form known as cinquains.

Crashaw, Richard (c.1613-1649), admired English poet, author of the collection *Carmen Deo Nostro* (Hymn to Our Lord, published 1652).

Crates (flourished 450-470 B.C.), Greek actor and dramatist.

Cratinus (c.519-c.420 B.C.), famous Greek dramatist who was acclaimed as a master of the comedy.

Craven, Frank (1880-1945), American actor, producer and dramatist.

Crawford, Francis Marion (1854-1909), American novelist , short-story writer and dramatist.

Crawford, Isabelle Valancy (1850-1887), Irish-born Canadian poet who was esteemed for her landscape verse.

Crawford, John Wallace (1847-1917), American frontier scout and poet, author of such works as *The Poet Scout* (1879) and *The Broncho Book* (1908).

Crébillon, Claude-Prosper Jolyot, Sieur de (1701-1777), French novelist; son of Prosper Jolyot Crébillon.

Crébillon, Prosper Jolyot (actually **Prosper Jolyot Crais-Billon), Sieur de (1674-1762),** French dramatist, best remembered for his tragedy *Rhadamiste et Zénobie* (1711); father of Claude-Prosper Jolyot Crébillon.

Creel, George (Edward) (1876-1953), American journalist and writer.

Creighton, James Edwin (1861-1924), Canadian-born American philosopher of the Idealist school.

Creighton, Mandell (1843-1901), English Anglican bishop and historian, author of the notable *History of the Papacy during the period of the Reformation* (5 volumes, 1882-94).

Crémazie, (Joseph) Octave (1827-1879), outstanding French-Canadian poet, acclaimed as the father of French-Canadian poetry.

Crescas, Hasdai (ben Abraham) (1340-1410), Spanish philosopher, Talmudic scholar and rabbi.

Cressy, Hugh Paulin (c.1605-1674), English Benedictine monk, historian, writer and editor who was known as Serenus Cressy.

Creutz, Gustav Philip (1731-1785), Swedish diplomat and poet.

Creuzer, Georg Friedrich (1771-1858), German philologist and historian whose most significant work was the *Symbolik und Mythologie der alten Völker besonders der Griechen* (Symbolism and Mythology of the Ancients, Especially the Greeks, 4 volumes, 1810-12).

Crèvecoeur, Michel-Guillaume-Jean de (1735-1813), French-born American writer and naturalist who was known as Hector Saint-John de Crèvecoeur and J Hector St John author of the essay collection *Letters from an American Farmer* (1782; augmented edition as *Lettres d'un cultivateur Américain*, 1784).

Crichton, James (1560-1582), remarkable Scottish adventurer, scholar and poet, widely known as the Admirable Crichton.

Crichton Smith, Iain (1928-1998), esteemed Scottish poet, novelist and dramatist.

Crisp, Samuel (1707-1783), English writer.

Critias (c.480-c.403 B.C.), Greek poet, orator, statesman and philosopher.

Critobulos of Imbros (15th Century), Byzantine historian.

Critolaus (2nd Century B.C.), Greek philosopher.

Croce, Benedetto (1866-1952), outstanding Italian philosopher and historian.

Crockett, Samuel Rutherford (1860-1914), Scottish novelist.

Croft, Sir Herbert (1751-1816), English writer.

Crofts, Freeman Willis (1879-1957), Irish writer, a master of detective fiction.

Croker, Thomas Crofton (1798-1854), Irish antiquarian who published collections of tales and songs.

Croly, George (1780-1860), Irish Anglican clergyman, writer and poet, particularly known for his novel *Salathiel* (1828).

Croly, Herbert David (1869-1930), American magazine editor and political philosopher, author of the influential *The Promise of American Life* (1909); son of Jane Cunningham Croly.

Croly, Jane Cunningham (1829-1901), English-born American journalist and writer; mother of Herbert David Croly.

Cronin, A(rchibald) J(oseph) (1896-1981), English physician and novelist, author of *Hatters Castle* (1931), *The Stars Look Down* (1935), *The Citadel* (1937) and *The Keys of the Kingdom* (1942).

Cros, (Émile-Hortensius-) Charles (1842-1888), French poet and inventor, best known for his Symbolist work *Le Coffret de santal* (The Sandalwood Chest, 1873).

Cross, F(rank) L(eslie) (1900-1968), English theologian and ecumenist, editor of *The Oxford Dictionary of the Christian Church* (1957; 3rd edition, revised, 1997).

Crothers, Rachel (1878-1958), American dramatist and director, particulary known for her plays *A Man's World* (1909) and *He and She* (1911).

Crothers, Samuel McChord (1857-1927), American Presbyterian minister and essayist.

Crotus Rubianus (actually Johann Jäger) (c.1480-c.1539), German Roman Catholic priest, author of an *Apologia* (1531).

Crousaz, Jean-Pierre de (1663-1750), Swiss theologian and philosopher.

Crouse, Russel (1893-1966), American dramatist, author of such popular plays as *Life with Father* (in collaboration with Howard Lindsay, 1939), *State of the Union* (1945) and *Life with Mother* (1948).

Crowe, Sir Joseph Archer (1825-1896), English journalist, diplomat and art historian.

Crowley, Aleister (actually Edward Alexander Crowley) (1875-1947), English Satanist and poet, the self-described "Beast from the Book of Revelation."

Crowley, Robert (c.1518-1588), English Puritan churchman, social reformer, writer and poet.

Crowne, John (c.1640-c.1703), English dramatist.

Crucé Émeric (c.1590-1648), French writer who was a pioneering figure in advocating international arbitration in his *Le nouveau Cynée* (1623; English translation as *The New Cyneas of Émeric Crucé, 1909).*

Cruden, Alexander (1701-1770), English writer, best known for his concordance to the King James Version of the Bible.

Cruz, Sor Juana Inés de la (actually Juana Inés de Asbaje) (1651-1695), notable Mexican poet, dramatist, nun and scholar.

Cruz, Ramón de la (1731-1794), Spanish dramatist.

Cruz e Silva, António Dinis da (1731-1799), Portuguese poet who wrote the satirical *O Hissope* (c.1772).

Csokonai Vitéz, Mihály (1773-1805), illustrious Hungarian poet and dramatist who wrote the first Hungarian comic epic *Dorottya* (1804).

Ctesias (flourished 400 B.C.), Greek physician and historian.

Cudworth, Ralph (1617-1688), English theologian and philosopher of the Cambridge Platonist school, auther of *The True Intellectual System of the Universe: The First Part: Wherein All the Reason and Philosophy of Atheism is Confuted and its Impossibility Demonstrated* (1687) and *A Treatise Concerning Eternal and Immutable Morality* (published 1731).

Cueva, Juan de la (c.1543-1610), Spanish poet and dramatist.

Cujas, Jacques (1522-1590), French jurist and classical scholar.

Cullen, Countee (1903-1946), gifted American poet of the Harlem Renaissance, noted for his *Copper Sun* (1927), *The Ballad of the Brown Girl* (1928), *The Black Christ and Other Poems* (1929) and *The Medea and Some Poems* (1935).

Culverwel, Nathanael (c.1618-1651), English philosopher of the Empiricist school, best remembered for his *An Elegant and Learned Discourse of the Light of Nature* (published 1652).

Cumberland, Richard (1631-1718), English Anglican bishop, theologian and philosopher, author of *De Legibus Naturae, Disquisitio Philosophica* (1672; English translation as *A Philosophical Enquiry into the Laws of Nature,* 1750).

Cumberland, Richard (1732-1811), English dramatist and writer who wrote such plays as *The Brothers* (1769), *The West Indian* (1771), *The Fashionable Lover* (1772), *The Jew* (1794) and *The Wheel of Fortune* (1795).

Cummings, Bruce Frederick (actually Wilhelm Nero Pilate Barbellion) (1889-1919) English journalist, naturalist and writer, author of *The Journal of a Disappointed Man* (1919), *Enjoying Life and Other Literary Remains* (1919) and *A Last Diary* (published 1920).

Cummings, E E (actually Edward Estlin Cummings) (1894-1962), notable American poet, writer and painter, renowned for his inventive verse.

Cummins, Maria Susanna (1827-1866), American novelist who wrote the successful *The Lamplighter* (1854).

Cumont, Franz (-Valéry-Marie) (1868-1947), Belgian archaeologist and philologist.

Cunha, Euclides da (1866-1909), Brazilian journalist and writer, author of the classic *Os Sertões* (1902; English translation as *Rebellion in the Backlands,* 1944); was murdered.

Cunningham, Allan (1784-1842), Scottish poet and writer, best remembered for his sea shanty *A Wet Sheet and a Flowing Sea.*

Cunningham, J(ames) V(incent) (1911-1985), American poet.

Cunningham, William (1849-1919), Scottish economist and churchman, author of *The Growth of English Industry and Commerce* (1882).

Cunninghame Graham, R(obert) B(ontine) (1852-1936), English writer and traveller.

Cuoco or **Coco, Vincenzo (1770-1823),** Italian historian and novelist, author of the *Saggio storico sulla rivoluzione di Napoli* (Historical Essay on the Neapolitan Revolution, 3 volumes, 1800) and the novel *Platone in Italia* (Plato in Italy, 1804); died insane.

Curel, François, Vicomte di (1854-1928), French dramatist and novelist.

Curtis, George Ticknor (1812-1894), American lawyer and writer.

Curtis, George William (1824-1892), American journalist, editor and writer.

Curtis, Lionel George (1872-1955), English public administrator and writer who promoted the cause of world federation in his *Civitas Dei* (3 volumes, 1934-37).

Curtius, Ernst (1814-1896), German archaeologist and historian; brother of Georg Curtius.

Curtius, Georg (1820-1885), German linguist, an authority on Greek linguistics; brother of Ernst Curtius.

Curwood, James Oliver (1878-1927), American journalist and novelist.

Curzon, Lord (actually George Nathaniel Curzon, 1st Marquess Curzon of Kedleston) (1859-1925), English statesman and writer.

Cushing, Frank Hamilton (1857-1900), American ethnologist and archaeologist.

Custis, George Washington Parke (1781-1857), American dramatist and writer, author of *Recollections and Private Memoirs of Washington* (published 1859); grandson of Martha Washington.

Cuvier, Georges (Jean-Leopold-Nicholas-Frédéric), Baron (1769-1832), eminent French zoologist and statesman, founder of comparative anatomy and paleontology.

Cydones, Demetrius (c.1324-c.1398), renowned Byzantine scholar, theologian and statesman; brother of Prochorus Cydones.

Cydones, Prochorus (c.1330-c.1369), Byzantine Eastern Orthodox monk, theologian and linguist; brother of Demetrius Cydones.

Cynddelw Brydydd Mawr (12th Century), noteworthy Welsh poet who was called Cynddelw the Great Poet, most likely an allusion to his physical stature.

Cynewulf (c. 8th Century), Anglo-Saxon poet.

Cyrano de Bergerac, Savinien (1619-1655), French writer and dramatist who became best known for his satire.

Dabrowska, Maria (1889-1965), Polish novelist, short-story writer and critic, particularly known for her novel cycle *Noce i dnie* (Nights and Day, 4 volumes, 1932-34).

Dach, Simon (1605-1659), German poet, best remembered for his *Der Mensch hat nichts so eigen* (Man Has Nothing of His Own).

Dacier, André (1651-1722), French classical scholar and translator; husband of Anne (née Lefebvre) Dacier.

Dacier, Anne (née Lefebvre) (1654-1720), French classical scholar and translator, author of *Des causes de la corruption goût* (Of the Causes of the Corruption of Taste, 1714); wife of André Dacier.

Dafydd ab Edmwnd (15th Century), Welsh poet who excelled in love lyrics, elegies and eulogies.

Dafydd ap Gwilym (c.1320-c.1380), renowned Welsh poet, a master of bardic verse.

Dafydd Nanmor (15th Century), Welsh poet who was greatly admired for his odes.

Dagerman, Stig (1923-1954), Swedish novelist, short-story writer and dramatist; committed suicide.

Dahl, Roald (1916-1990), English writer, dramatist and poet, best known for his children's works.

Dahlberg, Edward (1900-1977), American novelist, critic and poet.

Dahlgren, Karl Fredrik (1791-1844), Swedish poet, novelist, dramatist and preacher.

Dahlhaus, Carl (1928-1989), learned German music scholar.

Dahlmann, Friedrich (Christoph) (1785-1860), German historian who wrote the *Geschichte der englischen Revolution* (History of the English Revolution, 1844) and *Geschichte der französischen Revolution* (History of the French Revolution, 1845).

Dahn, (Julius Sophus) Felix (1834-1912), German historian, poet, novelist and dramatist.

Dalin, Olof von (1709-1763), Swedish historian, dramatist and poet.

Dallán Forgaill (6th Century), Irish poet.

Daly, (John) Augustin (1838-1899), American dramatist and theatre manager, author of *Under the Gaslight* (1867), *Horizon* (1871) and *Divorce* (1871).

Daly, Thomas Augustine (1871-1948), American journalist and poet.

Damascius (c.480-c.550), Greek philosopher of the Neoplatonist school, author of *Aporiai kai lyseis peri tôn prôtôn archôn* (English translation as *Problems and Solutions About the First Principles,* 1889).

Damian, Saint Peter (1007-1072), Italian Roman Catholic cardinal and theologian.

Dampier, William (1652-1715), English buccaneer who wrote the popular *A New Voyage Round the World* (1697).

Dana, Charles A(nderson) (1819-1897), American journalist, editor and writer.

Dana, Richard Henry (1787-1879), American poet and critic; father of Richard Henry Dana.

Dana, Richard Henry (1815-1882), American lawyer and writer, author of the popular novel *Two Years Before the Mast* (1840); son of Richard Henry Dana.

Dancourt, Florent Carton (1661-1725), French actor and dramatist, creator of the French comedy of manners.

Dane, Clemence (actually **Winifred Ashton**) **(1888-1965),** English novelist and dramatist.

Daniel, Gabriel (1649-1728), French Jesuit historian who wrote the notable *Histoire de France depuis l'établissement de la monarchie française* (1713).

Daniel, Samuel (c.1562-1619), admired English poet, dramatist and writer.

Daniel, Yuly (Markovich) (1925-1988), Russian writer and poet who suffered imprisonment for "slandering" the Soviet Union (1965-69).

Daniels, Jonathan (Worth) (1902-1981), American journalist and writer; son of Josephus Daniels.

Daniels, Josephus (1862-1948), American editor, newspaper publisher and diplomat; father of Jonathan (Worth) Daniels.

Danielsson, Olof August (1852-1933), Swedish classical scholar and comparative linguist.

Danilevsky, Nikolai Yakovlevich (1822-1865), Russian naturalist and philosopher, author of *Rossiya I Evropa* (Russia and Europe, published 1869).

D'Annunzio, Gabriele (1863-1938), prominent Italian poet, novelist, short-story writer, dramatist and political adventurer.

Dantas, Julio (1876-1962), Portuguese poet, dramatist and short-story writer.

Dante (Alighieri) (1265-1321), great Italian poet, celebrated for his *Divina Commedia* (Divine Comedy), one of the supreme achievements in world literature.

Dantiscus, Johannes (actually **Jan Flachsbinder((1485-1548),** German writer and poet who wrote in Latin.

Da Ponte, Lorenzo (actually **Emanuele Conegliano) (1749-1838),** famous Italian poet who wrote the librettos for Mozart's great operas *Le Nozze di Figaro* (The Marriage of Figaro, 1786), *Don Giovanni* (1787) and *Cosi fan tutte* (Women Are Like That, 1790).

Dareste de la Chavanne, Antoine (-Elisabeth-Cléophas) (1820-1882), French historian who wrote the valuable *Histoire de France* (9 volumes, 1865-79).

Dargan, Olive Tilford (1869-1968), American dramatist, poet and writer.

Darío, Rubén (actually **Félix Rubén García Sarmiento) (1867-1916),** significant Nicaraguan poet, journalist and diplomat, acclaimed for his *Azul* (Blue, 1888), *Prosas profanas y otros poemas* (Profane Hymns and Other Poems, 1896) and *Cantos de vida y esperanza* (Songs of Life and Hope, 1905).

Darley, George (1795-1846), Irish poet, writer, critic and mathematician, remembered for his poetry collection *The Errors of Ecstasie* (1822) and the unfinished epic *Nepenthe* (1835).

Darmesteter, Arsene (1846-1888), French language and literary scholar; brother of James Darmesteter.

Darmesteter, James (1849-1894), French Orientalist; brother of Arsene Darmesteter.

Darrow, Clarence (Seward) (1857-1938), prominent American lawyer, lecturer, debater and writer.

Darwin, Charles (Robert) (1809-1882), celebrated English naturalist, author of the influential work *On the Origin of Species by Means of Natural Selection* (1859); son of Erasmus Darwin.

Darwin, Erasmus (1731-1802), English physician and poet; father of Charles Robert Darwin.

Daryush, Elizabeth (1887-1977), English poet; daughter of Robert (Seymour) Bridges.

Das, Jibananda (1899-1954), Bengali poet.

Dass, Petter (1647-1707), Norwegian pastor and poet, particularly admired for his *Nordlands trompet* (published 1739; English translation as *The Trumpet of Nordland*, 1954).

Datta or Dutt, Michael Madhusudan (1824-1873), notable Indian poet and dramatist, a master of Bengali literature.

Daubenton or D'Aubenton, Louis-Jean-Marie (1716-1800), French naturalist whose most important work was the *Histoire naturelle* (1794-1804).

Däubler, Theodor (1876-1934), German poet and writer.

Daudet, Alphonse (1840-1897), French poet, novelist and short-story writer; father of (Alphonse-Marie-) Léon Daudet.

Daudet, (Alphonse-Marie-) Léon (1867-1942), French journalist and novelist; son of Alphonse Daudet.

Daukantas, Simanas (1793-1864), pioneering Lithuanian historian.

Daunou, Pierre-Claude-François (1761-1840), French statesman and historian.

D'Avenant or Davenant, Sir William (1606-1668), notable English poet and dramatist; became Poet Laureate of the United Kingdom (1638).

Davenport, Christopher (1598-1680), English Franciscan priest and theologian, author of *Deus, Natura, Gratia* (1634).

Davenport, John (1597-1670), English-born American noncomformist pastor and writer.

David, Ferenc (1510-1579), Transylvanian Unitarian preacher and theologian.

Davidson, Donald (Grady) (1893-1968), American poet and essayist.

Davidson, John (1857-1909), Scottish poet, dramatist and novelist; committed suicide.

Davidson, Thomas (1840-1900), Scottish-born American philosopher.

Davie, Donald (Alfred) (1922-1995), English poet and critic, a leading figure in the anti-Romantic group known as the Movement.

Davies, John (c.1565-1618), English poet, best known for his love sonnets and the religious treatise *Microcosmos* (1603).

Davies, Sir John (1569-1626), English poet and statesman, author of *Orchestra, or a Poem of Dancing* (1596), *Hymnes of Astraea in Acrosticke Verse* (1599) and *Nosce teipsum* (Know Thyself, 1599).

Davies, Samuel (1723-1761), American Presbyterian preacher and hymnist.

Davies, William Henry (1871-1940), Welsh poet and writer whose early years as a tramp earned him the title of the "tramp poet".

Davies, (William) Robertson (1913-1995), eminent Canadian novelist, dramatist and critic.

Davila, Enrico Caterino (1576-1631), Italian historian, author of the well-known *Historia delle guerre civili di Francia* (1630); was murdered.

Davis, Andrew Jackson (1826-1910), American Spiritualist who became known as the "Poughkeepsie Seer," author of *Principles of Nature, Her Devine Revelations, and a Voice to Mankind* (1847) and *The Great Harmonia* (1850).

Davis, Clyde Brion (1894-1962), American novelist.

Davis, Elmer (Holmes) (1890-1958), American journalist, broadcaster and writer.

Davis, H(arold) L(enoir) (1896-1960), American writer and poet.

Davis, Idris (1905-1953), Welsh poet.

Davis, John (1775-1854), English sailor and novelist.

Davis, Owen (1874-1956), American dramatist, author of *The Detour* (1921) and *Icebound* (1923).

Davis, Rebecca (Blaine) Harding (1831-1910), American novelist and short-story writer; mother of Richard Harding Davis.

Davis, Richard Harding (1864-1916), American journalist, novelist and short-story writer; son of Rebecca (Blaine) Harding Davis.

Davis, William Stearns (1877-1930), American scholar and novelist.

Dawes, Rufus (1803-1859), American writer and poet.

Dawson, William (1704-1752), English-born American poet.

Day, Clarence (Shepard) (1874-1935), American writer who gained enormous success with his autobiographical works *God and My Father* (1932), *Life With Father* (1935) and *Life With Mother* (published 1936).

Day, John (1574-c.1640), English dramatist, best remembered for *The Parliament of Bees* (c.1607).

Day-Lewis, C(ecil) (1904-1972), admired Irish poet, critic, detective-story writer and translator; became Poet Laureate of the United Kingdom (1968).

Dazai Osamu (actually Tsushima Shuji) (1909-1948), esteemed Japanese writer, a master of the short story; committed suicide.

De Amicis, Edmondo (1846-1908), Italian writer and poet, particularly known for his popular children's tale *Cuore* (1886; English translation as *The Heart of a Boy*, 1960).

Dearmer, Geoffrey (1893-1996), English poet whose collection *A Pilgrim's Song* was published in his 100th year.

Debelyanov, Dimcho (1887-1916), Bulgarian poet.

Debs, Eugene V(ictor) (1855-1926), American labour organizer, Socialist, editor and writer.

De Casseres, Benjamin (1873-1945), American journalist, critic, essayist and poet.

Déchelette, Joseph (1862-1914), French archaeologist and writer.

Decker, Sir Matthew, Baronet (1679-1749), English merchant and writer on trade, commerce and taxation.

De Dominis, Marco Antonio (c.1566-1624), Dalmatian theologian and churchman whose writings cost him favour with both the Roman Catholic and Anglican churches.

Deeping, (George) Warwick (1877-1950), English novelist, particularly known for his *Sorrell and Son* (1925).

Deering, Nathaniel (1791-1881), American editor and dramatist.

Deffand, Marie de Vichy-Chamrond, Marquise du (1697-1780), French woman of letters, best remembered for her *Correspondance inédite* (published 1809).

Defoe, Daniel (actually Daniel Foe) (1660-1731), famous English writer and journalist, author of the celebrated *The Life and Strange and Surprising Adventures of Robinson Crusoe* (1719).

DeForest, John William (1826-1906), American novelist who espoused the cause of realism in such works as *Miss Ravenel's Conversion from Secession to Loyalty* (1867), *Kate Beaumont* (1872), *Honest John Vane* (1875), *Playing the Mischief* (1875) and *The Bloody Chasm* (1881).

Dehmel, Richard (1863-1920), notable German poet whose works anticipated Expressionism.

De Jong, David (Cornel) (1905-1967), Dutch-born American writer and poet.

Deken, Agatha (actually **Aagje Deken) (1741-1804),** Dutch novelist and poet who collaborated with Elisabeth Wolff-Bekker on the earliest Dutch novel *Sara Burgerhart* (1782), and on *Willem Leevend* (8 volumes, 1784-85).

Dekker, Thomas (c.1572-c.1632), important English dramatist and writer, particularly esteemed for his play *The Shomakers Holiday* (1600).

De Kruif, Paul (1890-1971), American writer.

Delafield, E M (actually **Edmée Elizabeth Monica Dashwood) (1890-1943),** English novelist, journalist and magistrate.

Delafosse, Maurice (1870-1926), French language scholar.

De la Mare, Walter (John) (1873-1956), admired English poet and novelist who won favour with both children and adults.

Deland, Margaret (ta Wade née Campbell) (1857-1945), American writer and poet.

Delano, Alonzo (c.1802-1874), American writer who was know for his humorous works and his travel account *Life on the Plains and Among the Diggings* (1854).

Delany, Martin R(obinson) (1812-1885), American writer.

De la Roche, Mazo (1885-1961), Canadian novelist and dramatist.

Delavigne, Jean François Casimir (1793-1843), French dramatist.

Delbrück, Berthold (1842-1922), learned German linguist who founded the study of the comparative syntax of the Indo-European languages.

Delbrück, Hans (1848-1929), German military historian and politician.

Deledda, Grazia (1875-1936), remarkable Italian novelist of the verismo school; won the Nobel Prize for Literature (1926).

Delehaye, Hippolyte (1859-1941), Belgian Jesuit, priest and scholar who became an outstanding authority on the saints of the Roman Catholic Church.

De Leon, Daniel (1852-1914), American journalist, writer and Marxist.

Delille, Jacques, Abbé (1738-1813), French poet and translator.

Delisle, Léopold Victor (1826-1910), French scholar.

Dell, Floyd (1887-1969), American journalist, novelist, dramatist and poet.

Delmedigo, Elijah (c.1460-c.1497), Canadian philosopher and translator who was known for his criticism of the Kabbala; great-grandfather of Joseph Solomon Delmedigo.

Delmedigo, Joseph Solomon (1591-1655), Canadian scientist and philosopher who defended the Kabbala; great-grandson of Elijah Delmedigo.

Deloney, Thomas (c.1563-1600), English writer and poet, particularly known for his story collection *The Gentle Craft* (2 parts, 1597-98).

Delvig, Anton Antonovich, Baron von (1798-1831), Russian poet.

Demetrius Chalcondyles (1424-1511), Greek-born Italian scholar.

Demetrius of Lacon (2nd Century B.C.), Greek philosopher of the Epicurean school.

De Mille, James (1836-1880), Canadian novelist, short-story writer and poet.

Deming, P(hilander) (1829-1915), American writer.

Demochares (c.355-c.270 B.C.), Greek orator, statesman and historian who was the nephew of the Greek statesman Demosthenes.

Democritus (c.460-c.370 B.C.), notable Greek philosopher.

Demolder, Eugene (1862-1919), Belgian novelist and short-story writer.

De Morgan, William Frend (1839-1917), English ceramic artist and novelist.

Dempster, Thomas (c.1579-1625), Scottish poet.

Denck, Hans (c.1495-1527), German theologian and reformer who embraced Anabaptism.

Denham, Sir John (1615-1669), Irish poet, author of *The Sophy* (1641) and *Cooper's Hill* (1642).

Denifle, Heinrich Seuse (1844-1905), Austrian Dominican priest and church historian.

Denis, Maurice (1870-1943), French artist, theorist and writer of the Symbolist school.

Dennie, Joseph (1768-1812), American essayist and poet.

Dennis, John (1657-1734), English critic, poet and dramatist, particularly remembered for his quarrel with Alexander Pope over the role of passion in poetry.

Dennis, Nigel (Forbes) (1912-1989), English journalist, critic, novelist and dramatist.

Densmore, Frances (1867-1957), American ethnologist who wrote important works on the life and culture of the American Indian.

Densuşianu, Ovid (1873-1938), Romanian folklorist, philologist and poet whose poetry appeared under the name Ervin.

De Quille, Dan (actually **William Wright**) **(1829-1898),** American journalist who became known for his humorous writing.

De Quincey, Thomas (1785-1859), English critic and essayist, author of the classic *Confessions of an English Opium Eater* (1822, enlarged edition, 1856).

Derby, George Horatio (1823-1861), American army officer and writer, particularly known for his wit.

Dereme, Tristan (actually **Phillippe Huc**) **(1889-1941),** French poet.

Derleth, August (William) (1909-1971), American novelist and poet.

Déroulède, Paul (1846-1914), French poet, dramatist and politician who espoused nationalist themes.

Derozio, Henry Louis Vivian (1809-1831), Indian poet, best known for his sonnets.

Derzhavin, Gavril (Romanovich) (1743-1816), renowned Russian poet, a master of lyricism.

De Sanctis, Francesco (1817-1883), influential Italian literary scholar who wrote the valuable *Storia della letteratura italiana* (1870; English translation, 1931).

Desbordes-Valmore, Marceline (1786-1859), French poet and writer.

Descartes, René (1596-1650), great French mathematician and philosopher, author of *Discours de la méthode* (1637), *Méditations philosophiques* (1641), *Principia philosophiae* (1644) and *Traité des passions de l'âme* (1649).

Deschamps (de Saint-Amand), Émile (1791-1871), French poet and librettist who championed Romanticism.

Deschamps, Eustache (c.1346-c.1406), French poet and writer, author of the earliest treatise on poetry in French *L'Art de dictier* (1392).

Desgabets, Robert (1620-1678), French Benedictine theologian and philosopher of the Cartesian school.

Deshoulières, Antoinette Ligier de la Garde (1638-1694), French poet.

Desmarets de Saint-Sorlin, Jean (1595-1676), French writer, poet, dramatist and government official who became best known as a Christian apologist.

De Smet, Pierre Jean (1801-1873), Belgian-born American Jesuit missionary and writer who was active in Indian mission work.

Desmoulins, Camille (1760-1794), prominent French journalist and pamphleteer who defended the cause of the moderate democratic forces; was guillotined.

Desnos, Robert (1900-1945), esteemed French poet, a leading figure in Symbolist circles; a member of the Resistance during World War II, he was imprisoned by the Nazis and died a few days after his liberation by American troops.

Des Périers, Bonaventure (c.1500-c.1544), French writer, poet and translator whose freethinking sentiments in his *Cymbalum Mundi* (1537) earned him many enemies.

Desportes, Philippe (1546-1606), French courtier, poet and translator.

DesRochers, Alfred (1901-1978), French-Canadian poet and writer.

Desrosiers, Leo-Paul (1896-1967), French-Canadian writer.

Dessoir, Max (1867-1947), German aesthetician and philosopher.

Destouches, Philippe Néricault (1680-1754), French dramatist whose finest play was *Le Glorieux* (1732; English translation as *The Conceited Count*, 1923).

Deus, João de (1830-1896), admired Portuguese poet who excelled in lyric verse.

Deutsch, Babette (1895-1982), American poet, novelist and critic.

Deutscher, Isaac (1907-1967), Polish-born English historian and biographer.

De Vere, Aubrey Thomas (1814-1902), Irish poet and writer.

De Vinne, Theodore L(ow) (1828-1914), American scholar who wrote works on typography.

De Voto, Bernard (Augustine) (1897-1955), American critic, historian and novelist.

De Vries, Peter (1910-1993), American novelist and short-story writer.

D'Ewes, Sir Simonds (1602-1650), English antiquarian and diarist.

De Wette, Wilhelm Martin Leberecht (1780-1849), German theologian who employed the principles of historical criticism to the Pentateuch.

Dewey, John (1859-1952), influential American philosopher, psychologist and educator, one of the leading figures in the Pragmatic school.

Dewey, Melvil (1851-1931), American librarian who developed the Dewey Decimal System of Classification for cataloging library collections.

Dexippus, Publius Herennius (c.210-c.270), Roman historian and statesman.

Deyssel, Lodewijk van (actually **Karel Joan Lodewijk Alberdingk Thijm**) **(1864-1952),** Dutch critic and writer.

Diadochus of Photice (5th Century), Greek theologian, mystic and bishop, author of the *Hekaton Kephalaia Gnōstika* (The Hundred Chapters, or Maxims, of Knowledge).

Diaper, William (1685-1717), English poet.

Díaz del Castillo, Bernal (1492-c.1581), Spanish soldier and writer, author of the *Historia verdadera de la conquista de la Nueva España* (published 1632).

Dibdin, Charles (1745- 1814), English composer, writer, actor and theatre manager; uncle of Thomas Frognall Dibdin.

Dibdin, Thomas Frognall (1776-1847), English bibliographer and librarian, author of the *Introduction to the Knowledge of Rare and Valuable Editions of the Greek and Latin Classics* (1802) and *Bibliomania* (1809); nephew of Charles Dibdin.

Dibelius, Martin (1883-1947), noted German New Testament scholar who wrote *Die Formgeschichte des Evangeliums* (1919. 2nd edition, 1933; English translation as *From Tradition to Gospel*, 1934).

Dicaearchus (flourished 320 B.C.), Greek philosopher, author of the *Bios Hellados* (Life of Greece).

Dicey, Albert Venn (1835-1922), English jurist who wrote the *Introduction to the Study of the Law of the Constitution* (1885).

Dickens, Charles (John Huffam) (1812-1870), illustrious English novelist, one of the greatest masters of world fiction; great-grandfather of Monica Enid Dickens.

Dickens, Monica Enid (1915-1992), English novelist; great-granddaughter of Charles (John Huffam) Dickens.

Dickenson, John (16th Century), English writer and poet.

Dickey, James (Lafayette) (1923-1997), American poet and novelist, admired for his poetry collection *Buckdancer's Choice* (1965) and the novel *Deliverance* (1970).

Dickinson, Emily (Elizabeth) (1830-1886), outstanding American poet whose large output revealed a talent of extraordinary gifts.

Dickinson, John (1732-1808), American statesman and writer who became known as the "penman of the Revolution".

Dicuil (9th Century), Irish monk, grammarian and geographer who wrote the valuable *De mensura orbis terrae* (Concerning the Measurement of the World).

Diderot, Denis (1713-1784), eminent French philosopher of the materialist school and chief editor of the famous *Encyclopédie* (1745-72).

Di Donato, Pietro (1911-1992), American writer.

Didymus Chalcenterus (c.80-10 B.C.), Greek scholar.

Didymus the Blind (c.313-c.398), Egyptian Roman Catholic theologian, best known for his treatise on the Holy Spirit.

Dietzgen, Joseph (1828-1888), German-born American democratic Socialist.

Dieulafoy, Marcel-Auguste (1844-1920), French archaeologist who wrote *L'Art antique de la Perse* (The Ancient Art of Persia, 5 volumes, 1884-89) and *L'Acropole de Suse* (The Acropolis of Susa, 1890-92).

Diez, Friedrich Christian (1794-1876), German language scholar who was an authority on Romance languages.

Digby, Sir Kenelm (1603-1665), English courtier, diplomat, philosopher and scientist, author of *Of the Nature of Bodies* (1644) and *Of the Nature of Mans soule* (1644).

Dillmann, (Christian Friedrich) August (1823-1894), German biblical scholar.

Dillon, George (1906-1968), American poet and translator.

Dilthey, Wilhelm (1833-1911), German philosopher who advocated a distinct methodology for the humanities.

Dīnawarī, al- (actually Abū Hanīfah Ahmad ibn Dā'ūd al-Dīnawarī) (c.815-895), Persian astronomer, botanist and historian.

Dinesen, Isak (actually Karen Christence Dinesen, Baroness Blixen-Finecke) (1885-1962), Danish short-story writer.

Dingelstedt, Franz Ferdinand, Freiherr von (1814-1881), German poet and dramatist who was known for his political satire.

Dinis, Júlio, (actually Joaquim Guilherme Gomes Coelho) (1839-1871), Portuguese novelist, poet and dramatist, best remembered for the novel *As Pupilas do Senhor Reitor* (The Pupils of the Dean, 1867).

Dio or Dion Cassius (actually Dio Cassius Cocceianus) (c.150-235), Roman administrator and historian.

Dio Chrysostom (c.40-c.112), celebrated Greek rhetorician and philosopher.

Diocles (4th Century B.C.), Greek physician and philosopher.

Diodati, Giovanni (1576-1649), Swiss Calvinist pastor, biblical translator and writer.

Diodore of Tarsus (c.330-c.390), Syrian Christian bishop and theologian.

Diodorus Siculus (1st Century B.C.), Greek historian who wrote the valuable *Bibliotheca historica*.

Diogenes Laërtius (3rd Century), Greek writer, author of the significant *Peri biōn dogmatōn kai apophthegmatōn tōn en philosophia eudakimé santōn* (English translation as Diogenes Laertius: Lives of Eminent Philosophers, 1925).

Diogenes of Apollonia (5th Century B.C.), Greek philosopher.

Dionysius Exiguus (c.500-c.560), Scythian-born Italian Roman Catholic theologian, mathematician, astronomer and translator, reputed inventor of the Christian calendar.

Dionysius of Halicarnassus (flourished c.20 B.C.), Greek historian and literary scholar.

Dionysius Telmaharensis or Dionysius of Tell Mahre (d.845), Syrian patriarch of the Jacobite Christian Church, author of *The Chronicles* or *The Annal*.

Dionysius the Carthusian (c.1402-1471), Flemish Roman Catholic theologian and mystic who wrote *De contemplatione.*

Diop, Birago Ismael (1906-1989), Senegalese poet and writer.

Diop, David (1927-1960), French-born West African poet who championed the cause of African independence; died in an airplane crash.

Diphilus (4th Century B.C.), Greek poet.

D'Israeli, Isaac (1766-1848), English writer, best remembered for his *Curiosities of Literature* (5 volumes, 1791-1823); father of the statesman Benjamin Disraeli.

Dixon, Richard Watson (1833-1900), English poet and church historian.

Dixon, Roland B(urrage) (1875-1934), American cultural anthropologist, author of *The Racial History of Man* (1923) and *The Building of Cultures* (1928).

Dixon, Thomas (186401946), American novelist and dramatist, best known for his espousal of white supremacy in his novel *The Clansman* (1905), which served as the basis of D W Griffith's classic film *The Birth of a Nation* (1915).

Djilas, Milovan (1911-1995), Yugoslav politician, writer, poet and translator whose early espousal of Marxism was replaced with unremitting disdain in such works as *The New Class* (1957), *Conversations with Stalin* (1962) and *The Unperfect Society* (1969).

Długosz, Jan (1415-1480), Polish diplomat and historian who wrote the important *Historiae Policae* (12 volumes, 1455-80).

Dobell, Sydney Thompson (1824-1874), English poet whose works became well known under the name Sydney Yendys.

Dobie, Charles Caldwell (1881-1943), American novelist and short-story writer.

Dobie, J(ames) Frank (1888-1964), American writer.

Doblin, Alfred (1878-1957), German novelist and essayist.

Dobrolyubov, Nikolai (Alexandrovich) (1836-1861), Russian critic who espoused the principles of the radical intelligentsia.

Dobrovský, Josef (1753-1829), Austro-Hungarian language scholar and antiquarian, author of the important *Geschichte der böhmischen Sprache und Litteratur* (History of the Bohemian Language and Literature, 1792).

Dobson, (Henry) Austin (1840-1921), English poet, biographer and essayist of distinction.

Dodd, C(harles) H(arold) (1884-1973), English New Testament scholar and theologian.

Doddridge, Philip (1702-1751), English Dissenting minister, writer and hymnist, author of *The Rise and Progress of Religion in the Soul* (1745).

Dodge, Mary Abigail (1833-1896), American writer who wrote under the name Gail Hamilton.

Dodge, Mary (Elizabeth) Mapes (1831-1905), American editor and writer of juvenile works, best remembered for her *Hans Brinker, or, The Silver Skates* (1865).

Dodsley, Robert (1703-1764), English poet, dramatist and publisher.

Does, Johan van der (1545-1609), Dutch statesman, poet and historian.

Doesburg, Theo yan (actually Christian Emil Marie Küpper) (1883-1931), Dutch painter, decorator, art theorist and poet.

Dole, Nathan Haskell (1852-1935), American writer, poet, editor and translator.

Dolet, Étienne (1509-1546), French Humanist, scholar and printer whose fierce intellectual independence resulted in conflicts with the authorities and eventual condemnation and burning at the stake.

Döllinger, Johann Joseph Ignaz von (1799-1890), German church historian and theologian who opposed the doctrine of papal fallibility in his *Der Papst und das Konzil* (The Pope and the Council, 1869), was excommunicated and became a defender of the Old Catholic Churches.

Domett, Alfred (1811-1887), English poet and politician who served as Prime Minister of New Zealand (1862-63).

Donatus, Aelius (4th Century), celebrated Roman grammarian and teacher.

Donelaitis or Duonelaitis, Kristijonas (1714-1780), outstanding Lithuanian poet and Lutheran pastor, the first to employ hexameters in Lithuanian verse in his *Metai* (published 1818; English translation as *The Seasons*, 1967).

Donnay, Maurice (-Charles) (1859-1945), French dramatist and writer.

Donne, John (1572-1631), famous English poet, writer and Anglican churchman and preacher, the outstanding Metaphysical poet of his era, whose distinguished poetry was complemented by his prose work *Devotions upon Emergent Occasions* (1624) and his sermons.

Donnelly, Ignatius (1831-1901), American politician and novelist.

Donoso Cortes, Juan, Marquis de Valdegamas (1809-1853), Spanish diplomat and writer.

Dooley, Thomas Anthony (1927-1961), American physician, lecturer and writer who became known as the "jungle doctor" for his efforts to relieve medical distress in Southeast Asia.

Doolittle, Hilda (1886-1961), American poet and novelist who wrote under the name H.D.

Dorat or Daurat, Jean (1508-1588), important French poet and scholar who excelled in both Greek and Latin verse.

Dorris, Michael (Anthony) (1945-1997), American writer and poet; committed suicide.

Dorsey, George Amos (1868-1931), American anthropologist.

Dositheos (1641-1707), Greek Orthodox churchman and theologian.

Dos Passos, John (Roderigo) (1896-1970), eminent American novelist, poet and dramatist, author of the sweeping prose trilogy *U.S.A. (The 42nd Parallel*, 1930, 1919, 1932; *The Big Money*, 1936).

Dostoyevsky, Fyodor (Mikhailovich) (1821-1881), great Russian novelist and short-story writer, author of such remarkable works as *Zapiski iz myortvogo doma* (Notes From the House of the Dead, 1861-62), *Prestupleniye i nakazaniye* (Crime and Punishment, 1866), *Idiot* (The Idiot, 1868-69), *Besy* (The Devils, 1871-72) and *Bratya Karamazovy* (The Brothers Karamazov, 1879-80).

Doughty, Charles Montague (1843-1926), English traveller and poet, best remembered for his *Travels in Arabia Deserta* (1888).

Douglas, Alfred Bruce, Lord (1870-1945), English poet.

Douglas, Gawin or **Gavin (1474-1522),** Scottish bishop, political figure, poet and translator, noted for his translation of Virgil's *Aeneid*.

Douglas, George (actually **George Douglas Brown) (1869-1902),** Scottish novelist.

Douglas, (George) Norman (1868-1952), English novelist and essayist.

Douglas, Keith Castellain (1920-1944), talented English poet; died in World War II.

Douglas, Lloyd C(assel) (1877-1951), American Lutheran clergyman and novelist, author of the popular works *Magnificent Obsession* (1929) and *The Robe* (1942).

Douglas-Home, William (1912-1992), English dramatist and writer.

Douglass, Frederick (actually **Frederick Augustus Washington Bailey) (1817-1895),** famous American Abolitionist, orator, writer and public official whose escape from slavery to eminence was captured in his remarkable autobiography (1845, new version as *My Bondage and My Freedom*, 1855 and final version as *Life and Times of Frederick Douglass*, 1882).

Dowden, Edward (1843-1913), Irish critic, biographer and poet who distinguished himself particularly as a Shakespearean scholar.

Dowson, Ernest Christopher (1867-1900), English poet, short-story writer and dramatist, a principal figure in the so-called Decadents movement in poetry, especially admired for his *Verses* (1896) and *Decorations* (1899).

Doyle, Sir Arthur Conan (1859-1930), noted Scottish writer, creator of the celebrated master detective Sherlock Holmes.

Doyle, Sir Francis Hastings Charles, 2nd Baronet (1810-1888), English poet who was known for his ballads.

Dozy, Reinhart Pieter (Anne) (1820-1883), Dutch historian.

Drachmann, Holger Henrik Herholdt (1846-1908), major Danish poet, writer and dramatist.

Dracontius, Blossius Aemilius (5th Century), famous African Christian Latin poet.

Drake, Benjamin (1795-1841), American writer; brother of Daniel Drake.

Drake, Daniel (1785-1852), American physician, educator and writer; brother of Benjamin Drake.

Drake, Joseph Rodman (1795-1820), American poet who collaborated with Fitz-Greene Halleck on the satirical poems the *Croaker Papers*.

Drayton, Michael (1563-1631), significant English poet, author of the distinguished collections *Polyolbion* (1612) and *Poems* (1619).

Dreiser, Theodore (Herman Albert) (1871-1945), important American novelist, essayist and poet, best known for his naturalistic novels *Sister Carrie* (1900), the trilogy *The Financier* (1912), *The Titan* (1914) and *The Stoic* (1947), and *An American Tragedy* (1925).

Dresser, Horatio (1866-1954), American writer.

Drieu La Rochelle, Pierre (1893-1945), French novelist and essayist; a convert to Nazism, he committed suicide.

Drinkwater, John (1882-1937), English poet, dramatist and critic.

Drost, Aernoust (1810-1834), Dutch novelist and short-story writer.

Droste-Hülshoff, Annette Elisabeth von (1797-1848), outstanding German poet and writer, renowned for her mastery of refined classicism.

Droysen, Johann Gustav (1808-1884), German historian and politician who wrote the unfinished *Geschichte der preussischen Politik* (14 volumes, 1855-86)

Drummond, Henry (1786-1860), English banker, politician, writer and angel (bishop) of the Catholic Apostolic Church.

Drummond, William (1585-1649), Scottish poet and writer who was known as William Drummond of Hawthornden.

Drummond, William Henry (1854-1907), French-Canadian poet of humorous verse in dialect.

Drury, Allen (Stuart) (1918-1998), American writer, best known for his popular novel *Advise and Consent* (1959).

Dryden, John (1631-1700), celebrated English poet, dramatist, critic and translator whose works presaged the neo-Classical movement; was Poet Laureate of the United Kingdom (1668-88).

Duane, William (1760-1835), American journalist and writer.

Dube, John Langalibalele (1871-1946), South African minister, educator, journalist and writer, author of the first novel published by a Zulu in the native tongue *Insila ka Shaka* (1930; English translation as *Jeqe, the Bodyservant of King Shaka*, 1951).

Dubé Rodolphe (1905-1985), French-Canadian poet, essayist and philosopher who wrote under the name of François Hertel.

Dubnow, Simon (1860-1941), eminent Russian Jewish historian whose greatest work was the expansive *Weltgeschichte des jüdischen Volkes* (World History of the Jewish People, 10 volumes, 1925-29).

Dubois, Jean-Antoine (1765-1848), French Roman Catholic priest and educator who left an account of his missionary activities in India (1817).

Du Bois W(illiam) E(dward) B(urghardt) (1868-1963), influential American sociologist, civil rights advocate, writer and editor whose controversial career ended with his espousal of Marxism.

Du Bos, Charles (1882-1939), French critic whose writings on both French and English literature were notable.

Du Camp, Maxime (1822-1894), French poet, novelist and journalist.

Du Cange, Charles du Fresne, Sieur (1610-1688), outstanding French scholar, especially renowned for his studies in historical linguistics in his *Glossarium ad Scriptores Mediae et Infimae Latinitatis* (A Glossary for Writers of Middle and Low Latin, 1678) and *Glossarium ad Scriptores Mediae et Infimae Graecitatis* (A Glossary for Middle and Low Greek, 1688).

Du Casse, Isidore-Lucien (1846-1870), French poet who wrote under the name Comte de Lautréamont.

Du Casse, Pierre-Emmanuel-Albert, Baron (1813-1893), French soldier, military historian and editor.

Du Chaillu, Paul Belloni (1835-1903), French explorer and writer, best remembered for his *Explorations and Adventures in Equatorial Africa* (1861).

Duche, Jacob (1737-1798), American Anglican clergyman and writer, author of *Observations* or *Caspipina's Letters* (1774) and *Discourses on Various Subjects* (1779).

Duchesne, André (1584-1640), significant French historian and geographer.

Duchesne, Jacques (1897-1971), French theatre director, manager and dramatist.

Duchesne, Louis-Marie-Olivier (1843-1922), distinguished French Roman Catholic priest and church historian, author of the *Histoire ancienne de l'église chrétienne* (Early History of the Christian Church, 4 volumes, 1905-25).

Ducis, Jean-François (1733-1816), French poet and dramatist, particularly known for his tragic plays *Oedipe che Admète* (Oedipus at Admetus, 1778) and *Abufar* (1795).

Duck, Stephen (1705-1756), English poet and churchman; committed suicide.

Ducommun, Élie (1833-1906), French editor, writer and peace activist; won the Nobel Prize for Peace (1902).

Dudintsev, Vladimir Dmitrievich (1918-1998), Russian writer, best remembered for his dissident novel *Ne khelbom yedinim* (1957; English translation as *Not by Bread Alone*).

Dudley, Edmund (c.1462-1510), English minister of King Henry VII and author of the political allegory *The Tree of Commonwealth* (1509); was convicted of treason and executed.

Dudley, Sir Robert (1574-1649), English sailor and engineer who wrote *Dell'Arcano del mare* (Concerning the Secret of the Sea, 3 volumes, 1646-47).

Dudo of Saint-Quentin (c.960-c.1042), French historian, author of *De moribus et actis primorum Normannaie ducum.*

Dufresnoy, Charles-Alphonse (1611-1665), French painter, writer on art and poet.

Duganne, Augustine Joseph Hickey (1823-1884), American poet and writer.

Dugdale, Sir William (1605-1686), notable English antiquarian and scholar.

Dugonics, András (1740-1818), Hungarian writer.

Duhamel, Georges (1884-1966), eminent French novelist and poet, highly regarded for his novel cycles *Vie et aventures de Salavin* (5 volumes, 1920-32; English translation as *Salavin*, 1936) and *Chronique des Pasquier* (10 volumes, 1933-44; English translation,1937-46).

Duhem, Pierre-Maurice-Marie (1861-1916), French physicist and philosopher.

Dühring, Karl Eugen (1833-1921), German philosopher and political economist, a leading exponent of Positivism.

Dujardin, Édouard (-Émile-Louis) (1861-1949), French novelist, poet, dramatist and critic, author of the first novel to utilize the interior monologue *Les Lauriers sont coupés* (1888; English translation as *We'll to the Woods No More*, 1938).

Dumas, Alexandre (Davy de la Pailleterie) (1802-1870), famous French writer and dramatist who was know as Dumas père, author of such celebrated novels as *Les Trois Mousquetaires* (The Three Musketeers, 1844), *Vingt Ans après* (Twenty Years After, 1845), *Le Comte de Monte Cristo* (The Count of Monte Cristo, 1845), *Dix Ans plus tard ou le Vicomte de Bragelonne* (Ten Years Later, or, The Vicomte de Bragelonne, 1848-50) and *La Tulipe noire* (The Black Tulip, 1850); father of Alexandre Dumas fils.

Dumas, Alexandre (1824-1895), French dramatist and writer who was known as Dumas fils, author of the novel *La Dame aux camelias* (1848; adapted as a play, 1852), which inspired Verdi's opera *La traviata* (1853); son of Alexandre Dumas père.

Du Maurier, Dame Daphne (1907-1989), English novelist and dramatist, best remembered for her popular novel *Rebecca* (1938); granddaughter of George (Louis Palmella Busson) Du Maurier.

Du Maurier, George (Louis Palmella Busson) (1834-1896), French-born English illustrator and writer; grandfather of Dame Daphne Du Maurier.

Dumont, Fernand (1927-1997), French-Canadian sociologist, essayist and poet.

Dunash ben Labrat (c.920-c.990), Hebrew poet, grammarian and polemicist, the first to employ Arabic metres in his verse.

Dunbar, Paul Laurence (1872-1906), American poet and novelist, some of whose poems in black dialect were included in his collection *Lyrics of Lowly Life* (1896).

Dunbar, William (c.1460-c.1530), remarkable Scottish poet and priest, renowned for *The Thrissil and the Rois* (1503) and *The Lament for the Makaris* (c.1507).

Duncan, Robert (Edward) (1919-1988), American poet, writer and dramatist.

Dunlap, William (1766-1839), American dramatist, writer and painter.

Dunne, Finley Peter (1867-1936), American journalist who created the popular humorous wit Mr. Dooley.

Dunsany, Edward (John Moreton Drax Plunkett), 18th Baron (1878-1957), distinguished Irish poet, novelist and dramatist.

Duns Scotus, John (c.1266-1308), eminent Scottish Franciscan philosopher and Scholastic theologian who was known as Doctor Subtilis, author of the celebrated *Quaestiones quodlibetales.*

Dunster, Henry (1609-1659), English-born American Baptist minister, scholar and educator.

Dupin, Louis Ellies (1657-1719), French church historian, author of the *Nouvelle Bibliothèque des auteurs ecclésiastiques* (New Library of Ecclesiastical Writers, 58 volumes, 1686-1704).

Du Ponceau, Pierre Étienne (1760-1844), French-born American writer and lawyer who wrote on such subjects as the law, government and philology.

du Pont de Nemours, Pierre Samuel (1739-1817), French economist.

Dupuy, Eliza Ann (1814-1881), American writer.

Dupuy, Pierre (1582-1651), French historian and royal librarian.

Duran, Profiat (actually **Isaac ben Moses Ha-Levi) (c.1350-c.1415),** French Jewish philosopher and grammarian who wrote a satirical attack on Christianity in his *'Al tehi ka-'avotekha* (Be Not Like Thy Fathers, c.1396).

Duran, Simeon ben Zemah (1361-1444), Spanish Jewish rabbi and Talmudic scholar.

Durand, Guillaume (c.1230-1296), French Roman Catholic prelate and scholar, particularly known for his *Speculum iudiciale* (1271-76, revised edition, c.1290) and *Rationale divinorum officiorum* (c.1289).

Durandus of Saint-Pourçain (c.1270-1334), French Roman Catholic bishop, theologian and philosopher who opposed the ideas of St Thomas Aquinas.

Durant, Will(iam James) (1885-1981), American writer who wrote such popular studies as *The Story of Philosophy* (1926) and *The Story of Civilization* 10 volumes, 1935-67).

Durão, José de Santa Rita (c.1737-1784), Brazilian poet, author of the epic *Caramúru* (1781).

Duras, Marguerite (actually **Marguerite Donnadieu) (1914-1996),** admired French novelist and screenwriter, especially known for her screenplay *Hiroshima mon amour* (1959) and the novel *L'Amant* (1984; English translation as *The Lover,* 1984).

D'Urfé, Honoré (1567-1625), French novelist who wrote *L'Astrée* (4 volumes, 1607-27).

D'Urfey, Thomas (1653-1723), English dramatist and songwriter, particularly remembered for his satirical bent.

Durkheim, Émile (1858-1917), influential French social scientist who helped to establish sociology in his homeland.

Durrell, Lawrence (George) (1912-1990), esteemed English poet, novelist, dramatist and critic, highly regarded for his novel in four parts *Justine* (1957), *Balthazar* (1958), *Mountolive* (1958) and *Clea* (1960), all four published as *The Alexandria Quartet* (1962).

Dürrenmatt, Friedrich (1921-1990), famous Swiss dramatist and novelist, one of the masters of experimental theatre in the 20th Century.

Du Toit, Jakob Daniel (1877-1953), Afrikaans pastor, biblical scholar and poet.

Dutton, Geoffrey Piers Henry (1922-1998), Australian novelist, poet, critic, publisher and activist, best known for his novel *Queen Emma of the South Seas* (1976).

Duun, Olav (1876-1939), remarkable Norwegian novelist who wrote the notable series of works *Juvikfolke* (The People of Juvik, 1918-23).

Duvergier de Hauranne, Jean (1581-1643), French Roman Catholic abbot and theologian who founded the Jansenist movement in opposition to the Jesuits.

Duyckinck, Evert Augustus (1816-1878), American editor, critic and biographer who, with his brother George, published the *Cyclopaedia of American Literature* (2 volumes, 1855, supplement 1866).

Duyckinck, George Long (1823-1863), American editor, critic and biographer who, with his brother Evert, published the *Cyclopaedia of American Literature* (1855, supplement 1866).

Dwight, John S(ullivan) (1813-1893), noted American music critic who edited *Dwight's Journal of Music* (1852-81).

Dwight, Theodore (1764-1846), American editor, writer and poet; brother of Timothy and father of Theodore Dwight.

Dwight, Theodore (1796-1866), American editor and writer; son of Theodore Dwight.

Dwight, Timothy (1752-1817), American clergyman, educator, writer and poet; brother of Theodore Dwight.

Dyce, Alexander (1798-1869), Scottish editor and lexicographer.

Dyer, Sir Edward (1543-1607), English courtier and poet.

Dyer, John (1699-1757), Welsh poet and painter, known for such poems as *Grongar Hill* (1726), *The Ruins of Rome* (1740) and *The Fleece* (1757).

Eames, Wilberforce (1855-1937), American scholar and bibliographer.

Earle, Alice Morse (1853-1911), American historian.

Earle or **Earles, John (c.1601-1665)**, English Anglican clergyman, writer and translator, best known for his *Micro-cosmographie, Or, A Peece of the World Discovered; in Essays and Characters* (1628; 3rd edition, enlarged, 1633).

Eastburn, James Wallis (1797-1819), English-born American Episcopal clergyman, poet and hymnist.

Eastlake, Charles Lock (1836-1906), English meseologist and writer on art who wrote *Hints on Household Taste in Furniture, Upholstery and Other Details* (1868, 4th edition, 1887), *Lectures on Decorative Art and Art Workmanship* (1876) and *Our Square and Circle* (1895).

Eastman, Charles Alexander (1858-1939), American physician and writer, author of various books dealing with his Indian heritage.

Eastman, Mary H(enderson) (1818-1880), American writer whose *Aunt Phillis's Cabin, or, Southern Life as It Is* (1852) was a reply to *Uncle Tom's Cabin*.

Eastman, Max (Forrester) (1883-1969), American poet, writer, editor and political radical who later espoused conservatism.

Ebbinghaus, Hermann (1850-1909), German psychologist who wrote *Grundzüge der Psychologie* (Principles of Psychology, 1902) and *Abriss der Psychologie* (Summary of Psychology, 1908).

Eberhard, Johann August (1739-1809), German philosopher and lexicographer, a proponent of empericism.

Ebert, Karl Egon (1801-1882), Bohemian poet, author of the national epic *Vlasta* (1829).

Ebner-Eschenbach, Marie, Freifrau von (1830-1916), Austrian novelist, best known for her *Das Gemeindekind* (1867; English translation as *The Child of the Parish*, 1893).

Eça de Queirós, José Maria de (1845-1900), renowned Portuguese novelist and diplomat, author of *O Crime do Padre Amaro* (1875; English translation as *The Sin of Father Amaro*, 1962), *O Primo Basílio* (1878; English translation as *Cousin Bazilio*, 1953), *Os Maias* (1888; English translation as *The Maias*, 1965) and *A Cidade e as Serras* (1901; English translation as *The City and the Mountains*, 1955).

Echegaray y Eizaguirre, José (1832-1916), eminent Spanish dramatist, mathematician and statesman; co-winner of the Nobel Prize for Literature (1904).

Echeverría, Esteban (1809-1851), Argentine poet.

Eck, Johann (1486-1543), prominent German Roman Catholic theologian and polemicist, a leading figure of the Counter-Reformation.

Eckermann, Johann Peter (1792-1854), German writer, best remembered for his *Gespräche mit Goethe in den letzten Jahren seines Lebens, 1823-32* (Conversations with Goethe in the Last Years of His Life, 1832-32, 3 volumes, 1836-48).

Eddy, Mary Baker (1821-1910), American religious leader who founded Christian Science and wrote *Science and Health* (1875; revised edition as *Science and Health with Key to the Scriptures*).

Edel, (Joseph) Leon (1907-1997), esteemed American literary scholar and biographer.

Edgeworth, Maria (1767-1849), admired Anglo-Irish writer, author of the novels *Castle Rackrent* (1800) and *Tales of Fashionable Life* (6 volumes, 1809-12); daughter of Richard Lovell Edgeworth.

Edgeworth, Richard Lovell (1744-1817), English inventor and educator who collaborated with his daughter on the tome *Practical Education*; father of Maria Edgeworth.

Edmer or **Eadmer (c.1060-c.1128)**, English monk, author of *Historia novorum in Anglia* (c.1115) and *Vita Anselmi* (c.1124).

Edmonds, Walter D(umaux) (1903-1998), American novelist and short-story writer, best remembered for his classic novel *Drums Along the Mohawk* (1936).

Edmund, Saint (c.1175-1240), noted English scholar and archbishop of Canterbury who was known as Edmund of Abingdon, author of *Speculum ecclesia* (English translation, 1905).

Edwards, Jonathan (1703-1758), famous American Protestant preacher, theologian and philosopher who inspired the religious revival known as the "Great Awakening;" grandson of Solomon Stoddard.

Edwards, Sir Owen Morgan (1858-1920), Welsh scholar and educator.

Edwards, Richard (1524-1566), English poet, dramatist and composer.

Edwards, Thomas Charles (1837-1900), Welsh Separatist churchman and educator.

Edwards Bello, Joaquín (1888-1968), Chilean journalist and novelist.

Eaden, Frederik Willem van (1860-1932), Dutch physician, writer, poet, dramatist and translator.

Eekhoud, Georges (1854-1927), Belgian novelist and poet.

Effen, Justus van (1684-1735), Dutch journalist and essayist.

Egan, Pierce (1772-1849), English writer on sports.

Eggleston, Edward (1837-1902), American writer and editor, best known for his novel *The Hoosier Schoolmaster* (1871); brother of George Cary Eggleston.

Eggleston, George Cary (1839-1911), American journalist and writer; brother of Edward Eggleston.

Egill Skallagrímsson (c.910-990), celebrated Icelandic poet.

Ehrenburg, Ilya (Grigorievich) (1891-1967), prominent Russian journalist and writer of the Soviet era.

Ehrenfels, Christian, Freiherr von (1859-1932), Austrian philosopher who gave the term Gestalt to psychology and wrote the important *System der Werttheorie* (Sytem of Value Theory, 2 volumes, 1897-98).

Ehrlich, Eugen (1862-1922), Austro-Hungarian legal scholar, author of *Grundlegung der Soziologie des Rechts* (1913; English translation as *Fundamental Principles of the Sociology of Law,* 1936).

Eichendorff, Joseph, Freiherr von (1788-1857), important German poet, novelist and critic, one of the principal Romantic lyricists of his homeland.

Eichhorn, Johann Gottfried (1752-1827), German biblical scholar, Orientalist and educator.

Eilhart von Oberge (12th Century), German poet who wrote the epic *Tristant.*

Einhard or **Eginhard (c.770-840),** German scholar who wrote a valuable study of Charlemagne and the Carolingian Empire *Vita Caroli Magni* (c.830).

Eiseley, Loren (Corey) (1907-1977), American anthropologist, writer and poet.

Ekelöf, (Bengt) Gunnar (1907-1968), Swedish poet and essayist.

Ekelund, Vilhelm (1880-1949), Swedish poet and essayist.

Ekkehard I the Elder (c.910-973), Swiss teacher, monk, poet and hymnist, the reputed author of the Latin heroic poem *Waltharius* (c.930).

Ekkehard IV (c.980-c.1069), Swiss teacher, writer, poet and musician, one of the major authors of the *Casus Sancti Galli* (The Events of St Gall).

Ekrem Bey, Recaizade Mahmud (1847-1914), Turkish writer, poet, dramatist, critic and translator.

Eldad (ben Mahli) ha-Dani (9th Century), Jewish traveller and philologist.

Eleazar ben Azariah (1st Century), rabbinic scholar.

Eleazar ben Judah (ben Kalonymos) of Worms (c.1160-1238), German rabbi, scholar and mystic who was also known as Eleazar Rokeah.

Eliade, Mircea (1907-1986), eminent Romanian-born American historian of religions, author of the important studies *Traité d'histoire des religions* (1949; English translation as *Patterns of Comparative Religion,* 1958), *Le Mythe de l'éternel retour* (1949; English translation as *The Myth of the Eternal Return,* 1954) and *Le Chamanisme et les techniques archaïques de l'extase* (1951; English translation as *Shamanism: Archaic Techniques of Ectasy,* 1964).

Eliezer ben Hyrcanus (1st-2nd Century), Palestinian scholar.

Eliezer ben Yehuda (1858-1923), Israeli novelist.

Eliot, Charles W(illiam) (1834-1926), American educator and writer.

Eliot, George (actually **Mary Ann Evans) (1819-1880),** celebrated English novelist and poet, greatly admired for new novels *Adam Bede* (1859), *The Mill on the Floss* (1860), *Silas Marner* (1861), *Romola* (1862-63), *Middlemarch* (1871-72) and *Daniel Deronda* (1876).

Eliot, John (1604-1690), English-born American Puritan preacher and missionary, known as the "Apostle to the Indians" for his translation of the Bible into the Algonkian language (1661-63).

Eliot, T(homas) S(tearns) (1888-1965), celebrated American-born English poet, dramatist and critic, especially known for such poetry as *Prufrock and Other Observations* (1917), *The Waste Land* (192) and *Four Quartets* (1935), and the plays *Murder in the Cathedral* (1935) and *The Cocktail Party* (1950); won the Nobel Prize for Literature (1948).

Elizabeth (1843-1916), Romanian queen consort, writer and poet who wrote under the name Carmen Sylva.

Elkin, Stanley (Lawrence) (1930-1995), American novelist and short-story writer.

Ellerman, (Annie) Winifred (1894-1983), English arts patroness, novelist and poet who wrote under the name Bryher.

Elliott, George P(aul) (1918-1980), American novelist, short-story writer and essayist.

Elliott, Maud Howe (1854-1948), American writer who collaborated with her sister Laura E Richards on a biography of their mother Julia Ward Howe (1915).

Ellis, Edward S(ylvester) (1840-1916), American writer of enormously popular dime novels.

Ellis, George (1753-1815), English poet and translator who excelled in satirical verse.

Ellis, (Henry) Havelock (1859-1939), English physician, essayist and editor whose study of human sexuality resulted in his *Studies in the Psychology of Sex* (7 volumes, 1897-1928).

Ellison, Ralph (Waldo) (1914-1994), American novelist and essayist, esteemed for his novel *Invisible Man* (1952).

Ellmann, Richard (1918-1987), notable American literary scholar and biographer.

Elskamp, Max (1862-1931), esteemed Belgian poet, one of the finest representatives of the Symbolist movement of his day.

Elsschot, Willem (actually **Alfons de Ridder) (1881-1960),** Belgian novelist.

Elstob, Elizabeth (1683-1756), English writer on Anglo-Saxon subjects.

Éluard, Paul (actually **Eugène Grindel) (1895-1952),** significant French poet of the Surrealist movement.

Eluttaccan (16th Century), Indian Malayalam poet.

Elyot, Sir Thomas (c.1490-1546), English philosopher and lexicographer.

Elytis, Odysseus (actually **Odysseus Alepoudhells) (1911-1996),** noted Greek poet, especially admired for his *To Axion Esti* (1959; English translation as *The Axion Esti,* 1967); won the Nobel Prize for Literature (1979).

Embury, Emma Catherine (1806-1863), American novelist and poet.

Emden, Jacob Israel (actually **Jacob ben Zebi) (1697-1776),** eminent Danish rabbi and Talmudic scholar who was known as Yaabetz, an acronym based on his given name.

Emerson, Ralph Waldo (1803-1882), famous American poet, essayist, lecturer and champion of Transcendentalism, one of the most significant figures in American literary history.

Emery, Gilbert (actually **Emery Bemsley Pottle) (1875-1945),** American dramatist who was best known for his play *The Hero* (1921).

Eminescu, Mihail (actually **Mihail Eminovici) (1850-1889),** esteemed Romanian poet and writer.

Emlyn, Thomas (1663-1741), English Presbyterian minister and writer.

Empedocles (c.490-430 B.C.), Greek philosopher, poet, physiologist and statesman.

Empson, Sir William (1906-1984), distinguished English critic and poet, author of the important critical study *Seven Types of Ambiguity* (1930; revised edition, 1953).

Emre, Yunus (c.1250-c.1321), significant Turkish mystic and poet.

Emser, Hieronymus (1478-1527), German theologian, biblical translator, essayist and Roman Catholic priest who became an opponent of Lutheranism.

Encina, Juan del (c.1468-c.1530), Spanish poet, dramatist, composer and Roman Catholic priest.

Enfantin, Barthélemy-Prosper (1796-1864), French social reformer and writer, one of the principal figures of the St Simonian movement.

Engels, Friedrich (1820-1895), influential German-born English philosopher who collaborated with Karl Marx in developing Communist theory.

Engle, Paul (Hamilton) (1908-1991), American poet and writer.

English, Thomas Dunn (1819-1902), American poet and dramatist, best remembered for his poem *Ben Bolt*.

Ennius, Quintus (c.239-169 B.C.), illustrious Roman poet and dramatist, the acknowledged father of Roman literature who introduced the hexameter into Latin verse.

Ennodius, Magnus Felix (c.473-521), Italian poet, writer, rhetorician and bishop.

Enríquez Gómez, Antonio (actually **Enríquez de Pax) (1602-c.1662),** Spanish dramatist and poet.

Eötvös, József, Baron (1813-1871), prominent Hungarian novelist, short-story writer, statesman and educator.

Ephorus (c.405-330 B.C.), Greek historian who wrote the first universal history.

Ephraem or Aphrem Syrus, Saint (c.306-373), important Syrian Christian theologian, poet and hymnist who left a large output of works.

Epicharmus (c.530-440 B.C.), Greek poet.

Epicurus (341-270 B.C.), notable Greek philosopher whose writings have only been preserved in fragments.

Epimenides (6th Century B.C.), Cretan poet and priest.

Épinay, Louise-Florence-Pétronille Tardieu d'Esclavelles, Dame de La Live d' (1726-1783), French writer who became best known for her literary salon.

Epiphanius, Saint (c.315-403), significant Christian theologian and bishop, author of a work on heresies *Panarium* (374-77).

Episcopius, Simon (1583-1643), Dutch theologian.

Equiano, Olaudah (c.1750-1797), African-born English Abolitionist whose early years as a slave and later as a free man were depicted in his autobiography *The Interesting Narrative of the Life of Olaudah Equiano, or Gustavus Vassa, the African* (1789).

Erasmus, Desiderius (c.1466-1536), great Dutch Humanist and scholar.

Erastus, Thomas (actually **Thomas Lüber, Lieber or Liebler) (1524-1583),** Swiss physician and writer on religion, author of a treatise on excommunication *Explicatio gravissimae quaestionis* (Explication of the Gravest Question, published 1589).

Eratosthenes of Cyrene (c.276-c.194 B.C.), Greek astronomer and poet who is generally believed to have been the first to have measured the circumference of the Earth; committed suicide.

Ercilla y Zúñiga, Alonso de (1533-1594), Spanish poet, author of the expansive epic *La Araucana* (3 parts, 1569, 1578, 1589).

Erckmann-Chatrian (actually **Emile Érckmann (1822-1899)** and **Louis-Alexandre Chatrian (1826-1890),** French novelists who collaborated on a series of successful regional novels.

Erigena, John Scotus (810-877), Irish philosopher, theologian and translator.

Erinna (4th Century B.C.), Greek poet, author of *The Distaff*.

Erlingsson, Thorsteinn (1858-1914), Icelandic poet who wrote the collections *Thyrnar* (Thorns, 1897) and *Eidurinn* (The Oath, 1913).

Ermoldus Nigellus (790-838), French scholar and poet.

Ernesti, Johann August (1707-1781), German philologist and theologian.

Ernst, Paul (Karl Friedrich) (1866-1933), German short-story writer, essayist, poet and dramatist.

Ervine, St John (Greer) (1883-1971), Irish dramatist, novelist, biographer and essayist.

Escobar y Mendoza, Antonio (1589-1669), Spanish Jesuit preacher and theologian.

Esenin, Sergei (Alexandrovich) (1895-1925), Russian poet; committed suicide.

Espinel, Vicente (Martínez) (1550-1624), Spanish Roman Catholic priest, writer, poet and musician.

Espinosa, Pedro de (1578-1650), Spanish poet and editor, best known for his poem *Fábula del Genil* and the important anthology *Flores de poetas ilustres de España* (Flowers From the Illustrious Poets of Spain, 1605).

Espronceda (y Delgado), Jose dé (1808-1842), Spanish poet who espoused Romanticism.

Esquiros, Henri Alphonse (1814-1876), French poet, writer and politician.

Estébanez Calderón, Serafín (1799-1867), Spanish writer and poet who wrote under the name of El Solitario.

Estienne, Charles (d. c.1564), French writer; brother of Robert Estienne.

Estienne, Henri (1528-1598), French scholar and printer; son of Robert Estienne.

Estienne, Robert (1503-1559), French scholar and printer; father of Henri Estienne.

Etherege, Sir George (c.1635-1692), English dramatist and poet who created the Restoration comedy of manners with *The Comical Revenge, or, Love in a Tub* (1664), *She wou'd if she cou'd* (1668) and *The Man of Mode, or, Sir Fopling Flutter* (1676).

Ethier-Blais, Jean (1925-1995), French-Canadian writer, poet and critic.

Eucken, Rudolf Christoph (1846-1926), German philosopher of Idealism; won the Nobel Prize for Literature (1908).

Eudemos of Rhodes (4th Century B.C.), Greek philosopher.

Eugenikos, John (15th Century), great Byzantine theologian, scholar and poet, author of the famous ode *Oratorio for the Great City* which he wrote in the wake of the Muslim capture of Constantinople in 1453.

Eugenikos, Markus (c.1392-1445), Greek Orthodox churchman and theologian.

Euhemerus (300 B.C.), Greek mythographer who wrote a work on popular myths.

Eumenius (3rd Century), Roman orator who wrote the *Oratio pro instaurondis scholis* (Oration on the Restoration of Schools).

Eunapius (c.345-c.420), Greek historian, author of a valuable work on the lives of the philosophers and Sophists (English translation, 1922).

Euphorion (c.275-c.220 B.C.), Greek poet and grammarian.

Eupolis (5th Century B.C.), famous Greek dramatist.

Eurelius, Gunno (actually Gunno Dahlstierna) (1661-1709), Swedish writer.

Euripides (c.484-406 B.C.), great Greek dramatist, a master of the tragedy.

Eusden, Laurence (1688-1730), English poet who was often the victim of the satirical arrows of Alexander Pope; became Poet Laureate of the United Kingdom (1718).

Eusebius of Caesarea (c.260-c.340), celebrated Christian bishop and church historian, author of an important ecclesiastical history (10 volumes).

Eusebius of Dorylaeum (5th Century), prominent Christian bishop and theologian who opposed Nestorianism in his *Contestatio*.

Eustathius of Thessalonica (c.1100-c.1194), learned Greek Orthodox churchman and scholar.

Euthymius I (c.834-917), Byzantine Orthodox monk, churchman and theologian.

Euthymius of Turnovo (c.1317-c.1402), Byzantine Orthodox churchman and scholar.

Euthymius the Hagiorite (c.955-1028), Georgian Orthodox churchman and scholar.

Evagrius Ponticus (346-399), Christian mystic and theologian.

Evans, Augusta Jane (1835-1909), American novelist who wrote the highly popular *St Elmo* (1867).

Evans, Caradoc (actually David Evans) (1878-1945), Welsh novelist and short-story writer.

Evans, Charles (1850-1935), American bibliographer.

Evans, Donald (1884-1921), American poet, journalist and music critic; committed suicide.

Evans, Evan (1731-1788), Welsh scholar, critic and poet.

Evans, George Henry (1805-1856), American journalist and writer.

Evans, Sir John (1823-1908), English antiquarian and numismatist who helped to found prehistoric archaeology.

Evans, Nathaniel (1742-1767), American Anglican clergyman and poet.

Evans-Pritchard, E(dward) E(van) (1902-1973), English social anthropologist.

Evelyn, John (1620-1706), English writer and diarist.

Everett, Alexander Hill (1790-1847), American editor, writer, poet and diplomat.

Everett, Edward (1794-1865), American orator, lecturer and statesman.

Everson, William (1912-1994), esteemed American poet who, as a Dominican lay bother, wrote under the name of Brother Antoninus.

Ewald, Heinrich (Georg August) von (1803-1875), German theologian and Orientalist, author of the important *Geschichte des Volkes Israel* (7 volumes, 1843-59; English translation, 1865-86).

Ewald, Johannes (1743-1781), outstanding Danish poet and writer, a master of lyric poetry.

Ewart, Gavin (Buchanan) (1916-1995), English poet who was especially known for his light verse.

Ewing, A(lfred) C(yril) (1899-1973), English philosopher.

Eximenis, Francesc (c.1340-1409), Catalon writer.

Eybeschütz, Jonathan (1690-1764), Danish rabbi who became well know for his views on the Talmud and Kabbala.

Eymeric or **Eymerich, Nicholas (c.1320-1399)**, Spanish Roman Catholic theologian and zealous grand inquisitor, author of *Directorium inquisitorium* (1376).

Eysenck, Hans J(ürgen) (1916-1997), German-born English psychologist who was known for his controversial theories on intelligence and personality.

Faber, Frederick William (1814-1863), English Roman Catholic theologian and hymnist, best remembered for his hymns *Hark! Hark, My Soul* and *My God, How Wonderful Thou Art*.

Fabius Pictor, Quintus (200 B.C.), Roman historian.

Fabre, Émile (1869-1955), French dramatist.

Fabre, Ferdinand (1827-1898), French novelist.

Fabre d'Églantine, Philippet (-François-Nazaire) (1750-1794), French dramatist and poet, author of the famous comedy *Le Philente de Molière* (1790); was guillotined.

Fadeyev, Alexander Alexandrovich (1901-1956), Russian novelist and Communist theoretician who was a leading figure during the Stalinist era; in the wake of the denunciation of the Stalinist regime, he committed suicide.

Faguet, Émile (1847-1916), French literary critic and historian who wrote the outstanding *Politiques et moralistes due dixneuvième siècle* (3 volumes, 1891-1900).

Fagunwa, D(aniel) O (1910-1963), esteemed Nigerian novelist in the Yoruba language.

Fain, Agathon-Jean-François, Baron (1778-1837), important French historian who wrote the invaluable *Manuscrit de 1814, contenant l'histoire des six derniers mois du règne de Napoléon* (Notebook of 1814, Relating the History of the Last Six Months of Napoleon's Reign, 1823).

Fairbairn, Andrew Martin (1838-1912), English Congregational minister, theologian and educator.

Fairbank, Janet Ayer (1879-1951), American novelist and short-story writer; sister of Margaret Ayer Barnes.

Fairfax, Edward (c.1575-1635), English poet and translator.

Fairfield, Sumner Lincoln (1803-1844), American poet and writer.

Fakhr ad-Dīn ar-Rāzī (actually Abū 'Abd Allāh Muhammad ibn 'Umar ibn al-Husayn Fakhr ad-Dīn-Rāzī) (1149-1209), noted Muslim theologian and scholar.

Falconer, William (1732-1769), English poet, seaman and lexicographer, author of the poem *The Shipwreck* (1762; revised 1764 and 1769); ironically he died in the sinking of the frigate *Aurora*.

Falkberget, Johan Petter (actually Johan Petter Lillebakken) (1879-1967), Norwegian novelist.

Falke, Gustav (1853-1916), German poet and novelist.

Falkland, Lucius Cary, 2nd Viscount (1610-1643), English royalist, writer on theology and poet; died in the Battle of Newbury.

Falkner, J(ohn) Meade (1858-1932), English novelist, antiquarian and poet.

Falkner, William Clark (1825-1889), American writer, army officer, lawyer and railroad builder; great-grandfather of William Faulkner.

Fanon, Frantz (Omar) (1925-1961), Martinique psychoanalyst and social philosopher who was known for his espousal of the cause of national liberation of colonial peoples.

Fanshaw, Sir Richard, Baronet (1608-1666), English diplomat, poet and translator.

Fante, John (1909-1983), American novelist and screenwriter.

Fârâbî, al- (actually Muhammad ibn Muhammad ibn Tarkhân ibn Uzalagh al- Fârâbî) (c.878-c.950), celebrated Muslim philosopher who advocated that the state should be ruled by the philosopher.

Farazdaq, al- (actually Hammân ibn Ghâlib al-Farazdaq) (c.641-c.729), notable Arab poet who excelled in satirical poems.

Fardd, Eben (actually Ebenezer Thomas) (1802-1863), Welsh poet and hymnist.

Farel, Guillaume (1489-1565), significant French-born Swiss Protestant reformer and preacher.

Faria y Sousa, Manuel de (1590-1649), Portuguese poet.

Farini, Luigi Carlo (1812-1866), Italian physician, statesman and historian.

Farjeon, Eleanor (1881-1965), English poet and writer.

Farley, Harriet (1817-1907), American writer.

Farnol, (John) Jeffery (1878-1952), English novelist.

Farquhar, George (1678-1707), prominent Irish dramatist whose mastery of comedic invention was revealed in such plays as *The Recruiting Officer* (1706) and *The Beaux Stratagem* (1707).

Farrar, Frederic William (1831-1903), English churchman, philologist and writer, author of the popular novel *Eric, or, Little by Little* (1858) and the theological tomes *The Witness of History to Christ* (1871) and *Life of Christ* (1874).

Farrell, J(ames) G(ordon) (1935-1979), English novelist, admired for his *Troubles* (1970), *The Siege of Krishnapur* (1973) and *The Singapore Grip* (1978).

Farrell, James T(homas) (1904-1979), noted American novelist, essayist and poet, best known for his novel trilogy *Young Lonigan* (1932), *The Young Manhood of Studs Lonigan* (1934) and *Judgment Day* (1935).

Farrokhî (d. 1037), Persian poet.

Faulkner, William (actually **William Harrison Faulkner) (1897-1962),** celebrated American novelist, short-story writer, essayist and poet, author of such important novels as *The Sound and the Fury* (1929), *As I Lay Dying* (1930), *Light in August* (1932), *Absalom, Absalom!* (1936), *The Hamlet* (1940) *Intruder in the Dust* (1948), *The Town* (1957) and *The Mansion* (1959); won the Nobel Prize for Literature (1950); great-grandson of William Clark Falkner.

Fauriel, Claude (-Charles) (1772-1844), French literary scholar and writer.

Fauset, Jessie Redmond (1882-1961), American novelist who depicted the black experience.

Favart, Charles-Simon (1710-1792), French dramatist and theatre director, best known for his *Bastien et Bastienne* (1753), which Mozart set as an opera, and *Les Trois Sultanes* (1761).

Fawcett, Edgar (1847-1904), American novelist, dramatist and poet.

Fawkes, Francis (1720-1777), English poet and translator.

Fay, András (1786-1864), Hungarian poet, dramatist and novelist.

Fay, Sidney Bradshaw (1876-1967), distinguished American historian who wrote the important *Origins of the World War* (2 volumes, 1928).

Fay, Theodore Sedgwick (1807-1898), American diplomat, writer and poet.

Fearing, Kenneth (1902-1961), American poet and novelist.

Featley, Daniel (actually **Daniel Fairclough) (1582-1645),** English Anglican priest and polemicist who was imprisoned for his support of the royalist cause by the Puritan government.

Fechner, Gustav Theodor (1801-1887), German physicist and philosopher, one of the principal figures in the development of psychophysics, author of *Zend-Avesta: Oder über de Dinge des Himmels und des Jenseits* (1851; English translation as *Zend-Avesta: On the Things of Heaven and the Hereafter,* 1882) and *Elements der Psychophysik* (2 volumes, 1860; English translation as Elements of Psychophysics, 1966).

Federer, Heinrich (1866-1928), Swiss novelist of Christian themes.

Feijóo y Montenegro, Benito Jerónimo (1676-1764), Spanish Benedictine philosopher and theologian.

Feith, Rhijnivs (1753-1824), Dutch poet, novelist and critic.

Fell, John (1625-1686), English Anglican priest, writer and editor.

Feltham, Owen (c.1602-1668), English essayist and poet, best remembered for his book of essays *Resolves Divine, Morall, and Politicall* (1623; 2nd edition, 1628).

Felton, Cornelius Conway (1807-1862), American classical scholar.

Fénelon, François de Salignac de la Mothe- (1651-1715), notable French Roman Catholic archbishop, mystical theologian, pedagogue and writer.

Fenestella (c.40 B.C.-c.25 A.D.), Latin poet and annalist.

Feng Kuei-fen (1809-1874), Chinese scholar who advocated the adoption of Western technology to meet the challenge of the West in his *Chiao-pin-lu k'ang-i* (Protest from the Chiao-pin Studio).

Feng Meng-lung (1574-1645), Chinese writer.

Fenellosa, Ernest F(rancisco) (1853-1908), American Orientalist and educator who wrote the valuable studies *An Outline History of Ukiyo-3* (1901) and *Epochs of Chinese and Japanese Art* (published 1912).

Fenton, Elijah (1683-1730), English poet and translator, esteemed for his *Poems on Several Occasions* (1717).

Ferber, Edna (1887-1968), American novelist, short-story writer and dramatist.

Ferdowsî or Firdausî (actually **Abû ol-Qâsem Mansûr) (c.935-c.1020),** Persian poet who wrote the national epic *Shâh-nâmeh* (Book of Kings).

Ferenczi, Sándor (1873-1933), Hungarian psychoanalyst.

Ferguson, Adam (1723-1816), Scottish philosopher and historian.

Ferguson, Sir Samuel (1810-1886), Irish poet.

Fergusson, Harvey (1890-1971), American novelist.

Fergusson, Robert (1750-1774), admired Scottish poet, best known for his *Auld Reekie*.

Fernald, Chester Bailey (1869-1938), American writer and dramatist.

Fernández, Lucas (c.1474-1542), Spanish dramatist and composer.

Fernández de Lizardi, José Joaquín, (1776-1827), Mexican editor and novelist, author of the first picaresque novel of Spanish America *El periquillo sarniento* (1816; English translation as *The Itching Parrot*, 1941).

Fernández de Moratín, Leandro (1760-1828), eminent Spanish dramatist and poet, a master of satire.

Ferrari, Giuseppe (1811-1876), Italian historian and political philosopher.

Ferreira, António (1528-1569), gifted Portuguese poet of classical verse who was known as the Horace of his homeland.

Ferreira, Virgílio (1916-1996), Portuguese novelist and essayist.

Ferrero, Guglielmo (1871-1942), Italian historian.

Ferrier, James Frederick (1808-1864), Scottish philosopher.

Ferrier, Susan Edmonstone (1782-1854), Scottish novelist, author of *Marriage* (1818), *The Inheritance* (1824) and *Destiny, or, The Chief's Daughter* (1831).

Ferril, Thomas Hornsby (1896-1988), American journalist, writer and poet.

Ferron, Jacques (1921-1985), French-Canadian writer and dramatist.

Fessenden, Thomas Green (1771-1837), American journalist, writer and poet who wrote under the name Christopher Caustic.

Fet, Afanasy Afanaselvich (1820-1892), prominent Russian poet and translator whose works greatly influenced the later Symbolists.

Fetis, François-Joseph (1784-1871), eminent Belgian music theorist, historian and critic, compiler of the monumental *Biographie universelle des musiciens et bibliographie générale de la musique* (8 volumes, 1833-44; 2nd edition, 1860-65; supplement, 1878-80).

Feuchtwanger, Lion (1884-1958), German-born American novelist and dramatist.

Feuerbach, Ludwig Andreas (1804-1872), influential German philosopher and theologian who espoused the cause of humanistic atheism in his *Das Wesen des Christenhums* (The Essence of Christianity, 1841).

Feydeau, Georges (-Léon-Jules-Marie) (1862-1921), popular French dramatist who excelled in the writing of farces.

Fichte, Johann Gottlieb (1762-1814), great German philosopher of Idealism.

Ficino, Marsilio (1433-1499), distinguished Italian philosopher, theologian, linguist and translator, author of the *Liber de Christiana religione* (Book on the Christian Religion, 1474) and *Theologia Platonica* (Platonic Theology, 1482).

Fick, August (1833-1916), German linguist who was an authority on Indo-European languages.

Ficke, Arthur Davison (1883-1945), American poet.

Ficker, Julius von (1826-1902), German jurist and historian.

Field, Eugene (1850-1895), American journalist and poet, known as the "poet of childhood" for such popular works as *Little Boy Blue* and *Dutch Lullaby (Wynken, Blynken and Nod)*; brother of Roswell Martin Field.

Field, Joseph M (1810-1856), American actor, theatre manager and journalist.

Field, Rachel (Lyman) (1894-1942), American writer.

Field, Roswell Martin (1851-1919), American journalist and music and drama critic; brother of Eugene Field.

Fielding, Henry (1707-1754), celebrated English novelist and dramatist, author of *An Apology for the Life of Mrs Shamela Andrews* (1741), *The Life of Mr Jonathan Wild the Great* (1743) and *The History of Tom Jones, a Foundling* (1749); brother of Sarah Fielding.

Fielding, Sarah (1710-1768), English novelist; sister of Henry Fielding.

Fields, Annie Adams (1834-1915), American poet; wife of James T(homas) Fields.

Fields, James T(homas) (1817-1881), American publisher, poet and writer, co-founder of the publishing firm Ticknor and Fields; husband of Annie Adams Fields.

Fiennes, Celia (1662-1741), English traveller and writer.

Figueiredo, Antero de (1866-1953), Portugese novelist and essayist.

Figueroa, Francisco de (1536-c.1620), Spanish poet.

Figulus, Publius Migidius (1st Century B.C.), Roman savant and writer.

Filarete (actually **Antonio di Pietro Averlino** or **Averulino) (c.1400-c.1469),** Italian architect, sculptor and writer.

Filelfo, Francesco (1398-1481), Italian scholar and poet.

Filicaia, Vincenzo da (1642-1707), Italian poet who was known for his patriotic sonnets.

Filmer, Sir Robert (c.1588-1653), English philosopher, a champion of monarchial statecraft in his *Patriarcha, or the Natural Power of Kings* (c.1638).

Finch, Francis Miles (1827-1907), American lawyer, judge, educator and poet, best remembered for his poem *Nathan Hale* in his collection *The Blue and the Gray and Other Verses* (published 1909).

Finch, Robert (Duer Claydon) (1900-1995), American-born Canadian literary scholar, poet, painter and musician.

Finkel, Nathan Tzevi ben Moses (1849-1927), Jewish scholar, religious philosopher and educator.

Finlay, George (1799-1875), English historian, author of *The Hellenic Kingdom and the Greek Nation* (1836), *Greece Under the Romans* (2 volumes, 1836), *History of the Byzantine and Greek Empires* (2 volumes, 1854) and *History of the Greek Revolution* (2 volumes, 1861).

Finney, Charles Grandison (1792-1875), American Protestant evangelist and educator who wrote *Lectures on Revivals* (1835) and *Lectures on Systematic Theology* (1847).

Fiore Pasquale (1837-1914), Italian jurist who was known as an authority on international law.

Fiorelli, Giuseppe (1823-1896), Italian archaeologist, author of *Descrizione di Pompei* (Description of Pompeii, 1875).

Firbank, (Arthur Annesley) Ronald (1886-1926), English novelist.

Firenzuola, Angolo (1493-1543), Italian writer.

Firishtah (c.1570-c.1620), celebrated Muslim Indian writer who was also known as Muhammad Qasim Hindushah.

Fischart, Johann (1546-1590), German writer, famous for his satirical works.

Fischer, Kuno (actually **Ernst Kuno Berthold) (1824-1907),** German philosopher, author of *System der Logik und Metaphysik* (System of Logic and Metaphysics, 1852, 3rd edition, 1909).

Fischer von Erlach, Johann Bernhard (1656-1723), Austrian architect, sculptor and architectural historian.

Fisher, Herbert Albert Laurens (1865-1940), English historian, educator and government official who wrote *The History of Europe* (3 volumes, 1935).

Fisher, Irving (1867-1947), American economist, author of *The Purchasing Power of Money* (1911).

Fisher, Saint John (1469-1535), notable English Roman Catholic prelate and theologian who opposed the Supremacy Act of 1534; was condemned for treason and executed.

Fisher, M(ary) F(rances) K(ennedy) (1908-1992), American writer.

Fisher, Vardis (Alvero) (1895-1968), American novelist, short-story writer and essayist.

Fiske, Harrison Grey (1861-1942), American dramatist and theatre manager.

Fiske, John (1842-1901), American historian and philosopher, particularly known for his *The Outlines of Cosmic Philosophy* (1874), *Darwinism and Other Essays* (1879), *The Destiny of Man Viewed in the Light of His Origin* (1884), *The Critical Period of American History, 1783-1789* (1888) and *The Beginnings of New England* (1889).

Fitch, Nathan (1733-1799), American clergyman and writer, author of the *Historical Discourse* (1776) and *The Moral Monitor* (published 1801).

Fitch, (William) Clyde (1865-1909), American dramatist.

Fitts, Dudley (1903-1968), American poet and translator.

Fitzgerald, Edward (1809-1883), English poet and translator, admired for his translation of quatrains from the *Rubáiyát of Omar Khayyám* (1859).

Fitzgerald, F(rancis) Scott (Key) (1896-1940), famous American novelist, short-story writer, essayist and poet whose life epitomised the jazz age; husband of Zelda Fitzgerald.

FitzGerald, Robert David (1902-1985), highly regarded Australian poet.

Fitzgerald, Robert Stuart (1910-1985), American poet, translator and critic.

Fitzgerald, Zelda (1899-1948), American novelist, author of *Save Me the Waltz* (1932); wife of F(rancis) Scott (Key) Fitzgerald.

Fitzhugh, George (1806-1881), American lawyer, journalist and writer who espoused the cause of slavery in his *Sociology for the South* (1854) and *Cannibals All!* (1857).

FitzRalph, Richard (c.1295-1360), English Roman Catholic archbishop and scholar, author of *Defensio Curatorum* and *De Pauperie Salvatoris*.

Flach, (Jacques-) Geoffroi (1846-1919), French jurist and historian who wrote *Les Origines de l'anciennce France* (4 volumes, 1886-1917).

Flacius, Matthias (1520-1575), prominent Italian-born German Lutheran reformer, church historian and theologian who wrote the important Centuriae Magdeburgenses (Magdeburg Centuries, 1574).

Flandrau, Charles Macomb (1871-1938), American journalist and writer.

Flanner, Janet (1892-1978), American journalist and writer who wrote under the name Genêt.

Flatman, Thomas (1637-1688), English painter and poet.

Flaubert, Gustave (1821-1880), celebrated French novelist, author of the acclaimed *Madame Bovary* (1857).

Flavin, Martin (Archer) (1883-1967), American dramatist and novelist.

Flecker, James Elroy (actually **Herman Elroy Fleckner) (1884-1915),** English poet and dramatist, particularly known for his poem *The Golden Journey to Samarkand* (1913) and the verse play *Hassan* (published 1922).

Flecknoe, Richard (c.1600-c.1678), Irish poet and dramatist.

Fleetwood, William (1656-1723), English Anglican bishop, preacher and economist, remembered for his *Four Sermons* (1712).

Fleming, Ian (Lancaster) (1908-1964), greatly successful English novelist, creator of James Bond, the British secret service agent 007; brother of (Robert) Peter Fleming.

Fleming , Paul (1609-1640), remarkable German poet, renowned for his sonnets.

Fleming (Robert) Peter (1907-1971), English journalist and travel writer; brother of Ian (Lancaster) Fleming.

Fletcher, Alice Cunningham (1838-1923), American anthropologist.

Fletcher, Giles, the Elder (c.1548-1611), English poet; father of Giles Fletcher the Younger and Phineas Fletcher.

Fletcher, Giles, the Younger (c.1585-1623), admired English poet, author of *Christs Victorie, and Triump in Heaven, and Earth, over. and after death* (1610); son of Giles Fletcher the Elder, brother of Phineas Fletcher and cousin of John Fletcher.

Fletcher, John (1579-1625), notable English dramatist who collaborated with Francis Beaumont on a series of fine plays; cousin of Giles Fletcher the Younger and Phineas Fletcher.

Fletcher, John Gould (1886-1950), American poet and essayist.

Fletcher, Phineas (1582-1650), English poet, particularly esteemed for his expansive poem *The Purple Island* (1633); brother of Giles Fletcher the Younger and cousin of John Fletcher.

Flewelling, Ralph Tyler (1871-1960), American philosopher of Idealism, author of *The Person* (1952).

Flexner, Abraham (1866-1959), American educator.

Flint, F(rank) S(tewart) (1885-1960), English poet and translator, an admired Imagist.

Flint, Timothy (1780-1840), American Protestant clergyman, novelist, biographer and historian.

Flodoard (c.893-966), French chronicler.

Florence, William Jermyn (1831-1891), American actor, dramatist and songwriter.

Flórez (de Setién y Huidobro), Enrique (1702-1773), Spanish historian.

Florio, John (c.1553-c.1625), English lexicographer and translator who was also known as Giovanni Florio.

Florus, Publius Annius (1st-2nd Century), Roman historian and poet.

Florens, Gustave (1838-1871), French scholar and radical who, as a prominent figure in the Paris Commune, lost his life soon thereafter.

Fludd or **Flud, Robert (1574-1637),** English physician and mystical philosopher, author of *Apologia Compendiaria Fraternitatem de Rosea Croce* (Brief Apology for the Fraternity of the Rosy Cross, 1616).

Flügel, Gustav Lebrecht (1802-1870), German scholar in Arab studies.

Focillon, Henri-Joseph (1881-1943), French art historian and critic.

Fogazzaro, Antonio (1842-1911), distinguished Italian novelist, short-story writer, dramatist and poet, especially admired for his novel *Piccolo mondo antico* (1896; English translation as *The Little World of the Past*, 1962).

Folengo, Teofilo (actually **Girolamo Folengo) (1491-1544),** pre-eminent Italian macaronic poet whose greatest work was his *Baldus* (4 versions, 1517,1521, 1539-40, 1552).

Folger, Peter (1617-1690), American poet, author of *A Looking Glass for the Times* (1676); grandfather of Benjamin Franklin.

Follen, August Adolf Ludwig (1794-1855), German political radical and poet whose output reflected political and Romantic themes.

Follen, Charles (actually **Karl Theodor Christian Follen) (1795-1840),** German-born American political liberal, educator and Unitarian minister; husband of Eliza Lee Cabot Follen.

Follen, Eliza Lee Cabot (1787-1860), American political liberal, writer and poet; wife of Charles Follen.

Folquet de Marseille or Marseilla (c.1160-1231), Provençal poet and bishop.

Fonseca, Pedro de (1528-1599), Portuguese philosopher.

Fontane, Theodor (1819-1898), notable German novelist, drama critic and poet whose masterpiece was the novel *Vor dem Sturm* (Before the Storm, 1878).

Fontanes, Louis, Marquis de (1757-1821), French journalist, writer and poet.

Fontenelle, Bernard Le Bovier, Sieur de (1657-1757), prominent French scientist and writer, best remembered for his Entretiens sur la pluralite des mondes (A Plurality of Worlds, 1688).

Fonvizin, Denis Ivanovich (1774-1792), outstanding Russian dramatist whose *Nedorosl* (The Minor,1783) is recognised as the first great Russian drama.

Foote, Mary Hallock (1847-1938), American novelist.

Foote, Samuel (1720-1777), English actor and dramatist who was known for his wit.

Forberg, Friedrich Karl (1770-1848), German philosopher of Idealism.

Forbes, Esther (1891-1967), American novelist and biographer.

Forbes, James (1871-1938), American dramatist.

Ford, Ford Madox (actually **Ford Hermann Hueffer) 1873-1939),** English novelist, editor, critic and poet, author of such notable novels as *The Good Soldier* (1915), *Some Do Not* (1924), *No More Parades* (1925), *A Man Could Stand Up* (1926) and *Last Post* (1928).

Ford, John (1586-c.1639), esteemed English dramatist, particularly known for such plays as *The Broken Heart, The Lover's Melancholy, Perkin Warbeck* and *'Tis Pitty Shees a Whore.*

Ford, Paul Leicester (1865-1902), American novelist and scholar; was murdered by his disinherited brother Malcolm Ford; brother of Worthington Chauncey Ford.

Ford, Richard (1796-1858), English writer, author of the well known *A Handbook for Travellers in Spain* (1845).

Ford, Worthington Chauncey (1858-1941), American librarian and editor; brother of Paul Leicester Ford.

Forester, C(ecil) S(cott) (actually **Cecil Lewis Troughton Smith) (1899-1966),** English novelist and journalist who created the admiral Horatio Hornblower..

Forkel, Johann Nikolaus (1749-1818), eminent German music scholar who wrote the first biography of J S Bach (1802; English translation, 1920.

Formstecher, Solomon (1808-1889), German Jewish rabbi and Idealist philosopher, best known for his *Die Religion des Geistes* (The Religion of the Spirit, 1841).

Forner, Juan Pablo (1756-1797), Spanish literary critic and poet who excelled in polemical works of a biting satire.

Förster, Bernhard (1843-1889), German writer who espoused anti-Semitic views; husband of Elizabeth Förster-Nietzsche.

Forster, E(dward) M(organ) (1879-1970), noted English novelist, essayist and critic, best remembered for his novels *Howards End* (1910) and *A Passage To India* (1924).

Forster, Georg (actually **Johann Georg Adam Forster) (1754-1794),** German explorer and scientist who wrote the important *A voyage around the world* (1777; German edition, 1778-80), an account of his travels with Capt. James Cook.

Forster, John (1812-1876), English journalist, editor, biographer and essayist, author of the valuable *The Life of Dickens* (1872-74).

Förster-Nietzsche, Elizabeth (1846-1935), German executrix and biographer of her brother Friedrich Wilhelm Nietzsche whose efforts were marred by sloppy editing and outright forgery; husband of Bernhard Förster

Forsyth, Peter Taylor (1848-1921), Scottish Congregational minister and theologian especially known for his *The Person and Place of Jesus Christ* (1909).

Fort, Paul (1872-1960), French poet, dramatist and editor, author of numerous ballads.

Fortescue, Sir John (c.1385-c.1479), English jurist who wrote the famous treatise *De laudibus legum Angliae* (In Praise of the Laws of England, c.1470; English translation, 1942).

Fortiguerra, Niccòlo (1674-1735), Italian poet and Roman Catholic prelate who wrote the satirical epic *Il Ricciardetto* (published 1738).

Fortunatus, Venantius (Honorius Clementianus) (c.540-c.600), Italian poet and Roman Catholic bishop, admired for his Latin poems and hymns.

Foscolo, Ugo (actually **Niccòlo Foscolo) (1778-1827),** outstanding Italian poet, novelist, dramatist and critic, author of the patriotic poem *Dei sepolcri* (Of the Sepulchres, 1807).

Fosdick, Harry Emerson (1878-1969), American Protestant clergyman and writer who espoused a liberal theology.

Foss, Sam Walter (1858-1911), American journalist and poet, remembered for the popular poem *The House by the Side of the Road.*

Foster, Hannah Webster (1759-1840), American writer, author of the popular novel *The Coquette* (1797).

Foucher, Simon (1644-1696), French philosopher.

Fouque, Friedrich Heinrich Karl de la Motte, Baron (1777-1843), German novelist and dramatist, best known for his popular fairy tale *Undine* (1811; English translation, 1932).

Fourier, (François-Marie-) Charles (1772-1837), French social theorist.

Fowler, Francis George (1870-1918), English grammarian and lexicographer; brother of Henry Watson Fowler.

Fowler, Henry Watson (1858-1933), English grammarian and lexicographer, compiler of *A Dictionary of Modern English Usage* (1926); brother of Francis George Fowler.

Fowler, William Warde (1847-1921), English historian.

Fox, John (William) Jr (1862-1919), American writer.

Fox, Sir William (1812-1893), English politician and writer.

Foxe, John (1516-1587), English Protestant reformer, preacher and martyrologist, author of the celebrated *Commentarii rerum in ecclesia gestarum* (1554; English translation as *Actes and monuments of these latter and perilous dayes*, 1563; 2nd edition, 1570), better known as *The Book of Martyrs*.

Foy, Maximilien (-Sébastien) (1775-1825), French military leader, statesman and writer.

Fracastoro, Girolamo or **Hieronymus Fracastorius (c.1478-1553),** illustrious Italian physician, astronomer, geologist and poet, proponent of the germ theory of disease.

France, Anatole (actually **Jacques-Anatole-François Thibault) (1844-1924),** distinguished French novelist and critic; won the Nobel Prize for Literature (1921).

Francis, Sir Philip (1740-1818), Irish-born English politician and pamphleteer.

Francis of Meyronnes or **Franciscus de Mayronis (c.1285-c.1329),** notable French Franciscan philosopher, theologian and monk who championed the realist system of John Duns Scotus.

Francis of Sales, Saint (1567-1622), French Roman Catholic bishop and theologian.

Franck, Sebastian (c.1499-c.1542), German Protestant reformer and theologian who espoused a radical anti-dogmatic theology, author of *Chronica: Zeitbuch und Geschichtsbibel* (Chronica: Time Book and Historical Bible, 1531).

Francke, August Hermann (1663-1727), German Protestant religious leader, educator ands social reformer who championed Pietism.

Francke, Kuno (1855-1930), German-born American historian.

Frank, Anne (1929-1945), German Jewish victim of the Nazi Holocaust whose diary brought her posthumous fame; died in the Bergen-Belsen concentration camp.

Frank, Leonhard (1882-1961), prominent German poet and novelist, a leading proponent of Expressionism.

Frank, Waldo (David) (1889-1967), American novelist and critic.

Frankau, Gilbert (1884-1952), English novelist.

Frankel, Zacharias (1801-1875), German rabbi and theologian who founded a religious system which presaged the advent of Conservative Judaism.

Frankfort, Henri (1897-1954), Dutch-born American archaeologist who was a leading authority on comparative studies of Egypt and Mesopotamia.

Frankfurter, Felix (1882-1965), influential Austrian-born American legal scholar, educator and jurist.

Frankl, Ludwig, Ritter von Hochwart (1810-1893), Austrian poet.

Franklin, Benjamin (1706-1790), famous American statesman, inventor, scientist, publisher and writer.

Franko, Ivan Yakovlevich (1856-1916), Ukrainian scholar and writer.

Franzén, Frans Mikael (1772-1847), Finnish-Swedish poet whose output presaged the Romantic movement in Sweden.

Fraser, James Baillie (1783-1856), Scottish traveller and writer, best known for his works on his travels in Persia.

Fraşeri, Şemseddin Sami (1850-1904), Turkish scholar lexicographer, novelist and dramatist.

Frauenstadt, Julius (1813-1879), German philosopher.

Fraunce, Abraham (c.1558-c.1633), English poet and writer.

Frazer, Sir James George (1854-1941), eminent Scottish anthropologist, folklorist and classical scholar, author of *The Golden Bough: A Study in Magic and Religion* (1890).

Fréchette, Louis-Honoré (1839-1908), outstanding French-Canadian poet, dramatist and writer.

Frederic, Harold (1856-1898), American journalist and novelist, best known for his novel *The Damnation of Theron Ware* (1896).

Fredro, Alexander (1793-1876), outstanding Polish dramatist who excelled in comedic invention.

Freeman, Douglas Southall (1886-1953), American newspaper editor and biographer, author of major studies of Robert E Lee (4 volumes, 1934-35) and George Washington (6 volumes, 1948-54).

Freeman, Edward Augustus (1823-1892), English historian.

Freeman, John (1880-1929), English poet.

Freeman, Joseph (1897-1965), American critic and novelist who espoused Marxist views.

Freeman, Mary (Eleanor) Wilkins (1852-1930), American novelist and short-story writer.

Freeman, Richard Austin (1862-1943), English novelist and short-story writer, creator of the pathologist-detective John Thorndyke.

Frege, (Friedrich Ludwig) Gottlob (1848-1925), eminent German mathematician and philosopher who was known as a learned mathematical logician.

Freiligrath, (Hermann) Ferdinand (1810-1876), remarkable German poet, translator and advocate of democracy in his homeland.

French, Alice (1850-1934), American novelist and short-story writer who wrote under the name Octave Thanet.

Freneau, Philip (Morin) (1752-1832), prominent American poet, essayist and editor who was known as the "poet of the American Revolution."

Frenssen, Gustav (1863-1945), German novelist who excelled in regionalist fiction.

Frere, John (1740-1807), English antiquarian who helped to found prehistoric archaeology.

Frere, John Hookham (1769-1846), English diplomat, poet and translator.

Freshfield, Douglas William (1845-1934), English mountaineer, explorer, geographer and writer.

Freud, Anna (1895-1982), Austrian-born English child psychoanalyst; daughter of Sigmund Freud.

Freud, Sigmund (1856-1939), renowned Austrian physician and neurologist who founded psychoanalysis, author of the influential study *Die Traumdeutung* (1899; English translation as *The Interpretation of Dreams*, 1953); father of Anna Freud.

Frey, Adolf (1855-1920), Swiss poet, novelist and biographer.

Friedland, Valentin (1490-1556), German educator.

Friedlander, Ludwig Heinrich (1824-1909), German historian who wrote the valuable *Darstellungen aus der Sittengeschichte Roms* (Representations from Roman Cultural History, 3 volumes, 1864-71).

Fries, Jakob Friedrich (1773-1843), German philosopher, author of the significant tome *Neue oder anthropologische Kritik der venunft* (3 volumes, 1807).

Frings, Ketti (1910-1981), American novelist and dramatist.

Frisch, Max (Rudolf) (1911-1991), significant Swiss novelist and dramatist, author of such masterworks as the plays *Don Juan oder die Liebe zur Geometrie* (Don Juan, or the Love of Geometry, 1953), *Biedermann und die Brandstifter* (1958; English translation as *The Fire Raisers*, 1962) and *Andorra* (1962), and the novels *Stiller* (1954; English translation as *I'm Not Stiller*, 1958), *Homo Faber* (1957; English translation, 1959), *Montauk* (1975), *Der Mensch erscheint im Holozän* (Man in the Holocene, 1979) and *Blaubart* (Bluebeard, 1982).

Frobenius, Leo (Viktor) (1873-1938), German explorer and ethnologist, noted especially for his studies of culture.

Fröding, Gustaf (1860-1911), significant Swedish poet who was greatly esteemed for his mastery of lyricism.

Froebel, Friedrich (Wilhelm August) (1782-1852), German educator and writer, founder of kindergarten education.

Frohschammer, Jakob (1821-1893), German Roman Catholic priest and philosopher whose liberal views led to his excommunication.

Froissart, Jean (c.1333-c.1400), famous French historian and poet, author of the valuable *Chronicles*.

Fromentin, Eugéne (1820-1876), French writer and painter.

Fromm, Erich (1900-1980), influential German-born American psychoanalyst and social philosopher.

Frommel, Gaston (1862-1906), Swiss Protestant theologian and philosopher.

Frost, Robert (Lee) (1874-1963), famous American poet whose finely-honed and subtle verse placed him among the principal poets in American literary annals.

Frothingham, Octavius Brooks (1822-1895), American Unitarian and writer.

Froude, James Anthony (1818-1894), English historian and biographer, author of a biography of Thomas Carlyle (4 volumes, 1882-84); brother of Richard Hurrell Froude.

Froude, Richard Hurrell (1803-1836), English writer and poet; brother of James Anthony Froude.

Frugoni, Carlo Innocenzo (1692-1768), Italian poet, librettist and translator.

Frye, (Herman) Northrop (1912-1991), distinguished Canadian literary scholar and writer.

Fujita Tôko (1806-1855), Japanese scholar and politician; died in an earthquake.

Fujiwara Nobuzane (1176-c.1265), famous Japanese painter, courtier and poet.

Fujiwara Sadaie (1162-1241), august Japanese poet, theorist and critic who was generally known as Fujiwara Teika.

Fujiwara Seika (1561-1619), Japanese philosopher of the Neo-Confucian school.

Fukuchi Genichiro (1841-1906), Japanese dramatist and publisher.

Fukuzawa Yukichi (1835-1901), Japanese writer, educator and publisher who embraced the cause of introducing Western ideas to his homeland.

Fulbert of Chartes, Saint (c.960-1028), French Roman Catholic bishop and poet.

Fulcher of Chartres (c.1059-c.1127), French chaplain and chronicler who wrote a valuable account of the First Crusade in his *Gesta Francorum Jherusalem peregrinantium* (3 parts, 1101, 1106, 1124-27).

Fulgentius, Fabius Planciades (5th-6ᵗʰ Century), African Christian Latin writer.

Fulgentius of Ruspe, Saint (c.462-c.527), African Roman Catholic bishop and writer who was a vigorous opponent of Arianism.

Fuller, Andrew (1754-1815), English Baptist minister and theologian.

Fuller, Henry Blake (1857-1929), American novelist, short-story writer, poet, dramatist, critic and editor.

Fuller, J(ohn) F(rederick) C(harles) (1878-1966), prominent English Army officer, military theoretician and historian, author of *A Military History of the Western World* (3 volumes, 1954-56).

Fuller, Roy (Broadbent) (1912-1991), English poet and novelist.

Fuller, (Sarah) Margaret, (1810-1850), American writer and critic.

Fuller, Thomas (1608-1661), prominent English preacher and scholar, author of *The Holy State and The Profane State* (1642), *The church-history of Britain, with the history of the University of Cambridge* (1655) and *The History of the Worthies of England* (published 1662).

Furetière, Antoine (1619-1688), noted French novelist and lexicographer whose penchant for satire made him many enemies, compiler of the outstanding *Dictionnaire universel* (published 1690).

Furness, Horace Howard (1833-1912), American scholar who prepared variorum editions of 20 plays of Shakespeare.

Furnivall, Frederick James (1825-1910), English literary scholar, a specialist in textual criticism.

Furphy, Joseph (1843-1912), Australian novelist and poet who wrote under the name Tom Collins, especially known for his novel *Such is Life* (1903).

Fuseli, Henry (actually Johann Heinrich Füssli) (1741-1825), Swiss-born English painter and writer.

Fustel de Coulanges, Numa-Denis (1830-1889), French historian, author of *La Cité antique* (1864).

Futabatei Shimei (actually Tatsunosuke Hasegawa) (1864-1909), Japanese novelist and translator, best known for his novel *Ukigomo* (1889; English translation, 1967).

Fux, Johann Joseph (1660-1741), famous Austrian musician, composer and theorist who wrote the classic counterpoint treatise *Gradus ad Parnassum* (1725; partial English translation, 1943).

Fuzûlî, (Mehmed) (c.1495-1556), celebrated Turkish poet of classical verse.

Gabelentz, Hans Conon von der (1807-1874), German linguist, ethnologist and government official.

Gaboriau, Émile (1832-1873), French novelist who excelled in the detective novel.

Gadda, Carlo Emilio (1893-1973), remarkable Italian novelist, short-story writer and essayist, author of the celebrated novel *Quer pasticciaccio brutto de via Merulana* (1957; English translation as *That Awful Mess on Via Merulana*, 1965).

Gaddis, William (Thomas) (1922-1998), significant American novelist of a satiric bent, author of *The Recognitions* (1955), *JR* (1975), *Carpenter's Gothic* (1985), and *A Frolic of His Own* (1994).

Gagern, Hans Christoph, Freiherr von (1766-1852), German politician and writer.

Gaimar, Geoffrei (12th Century), Norman writer, author of *L'Estoire des Engleis*.

Gaius (2nd Century), Roman jurist who wrote the important *Institutiones* (4 volumes, c.161).

Gale, Zona (1874-1938), American writer and poet, especially remembered for her novel *Miss Lulu Bett* (1920).

Galiani, Ferdinando (1728-1787), Italian economist.

Gâlib Dede (actually Mehmed es' Ad) (1757-1799), significant Turkish poet whose masterpiece was *Hûsn û Aşk* (Beauty and Love).

Gallen, Joseph (1699-1762), French Roman Catholic friar, theologian and philosopher.

Galileo (Galilei) (1564-1642), great Italian mathematician, astronomer and physicist whose championship of unfettered intellectual inquiry led to a major conflict with the Roman Catholic Church.

Gallagher, William Davis (1808-1894), American editor and poet.

Galland, Antoine (1646-1715), French scholar, particularly remembered for his adaptation of Near Eastern tales as *Mille et une nuits* (1704-17; English translation as *The Thousand and One Nights,* 1706).

Gallitzin, Demetrius Augustine (1770-1840), Dutch-born American Roman Catholic priest and polemicist.

Gallus, Gaius Cornelius (c.70-26 B.C.), famous Roman soldier and poet, greatly admired for his elegies; committed suicide.

Galsworthy, John (1867-1933), noted English novelist, dramatist and poet, best known for his series of novels collectively known as *The Forsyte Saga* (1906 et seq.); won the Nobel Prize for Literature (1932).

Galt, John (1779-1839), Scottish novelist, especially esteemed for his *The Ayrshire Legatees* (1820), *The Annals of the Paris* (1821), *Sir Andrew Wylie* (1822), *The Provost* (1822), *The Entail* (1823) and *Lawrie Todd* (1830).

Galton, Sir Francis (1822-1911), English explorer, anthropologist and eugenicist, author of *Hereditary Genius* (1869) and *Inquiries into Human Faculty* (1883).

Galvez, Manuel (1882-1962), Argentine novelist and biographer, particularly known for his novel *La maestra normal* (The Schoolmistress, 1914).

Gama, (José) Basilio da (1740-1795), Brazilian poet who wrote the epic *O Uruguai* (1769).

Gamow, George (1904-1968), Russian-born American nuclear physicist, cosmologist and writer.

Gans, Eduard (1798-1839), German jurist, author of *Das Erbrecht in weltgeschichtlicher Entwicklung* (Historical Development of Inheritance Law, 4 volumes, 1824-35) and *Vorlesungen über die Geschichte der Letzten fünfzig Jahre* (Lectures on the History of the Last Fifty Years, 1833-34).

Garbett, Cyril Forster (1875-1955), English Anglican archbishop and writer.

Garborg, Arne Evenson (1851-1924), Norwegian novelist, poet, dramatist and essayist.

Garção, Pedro António Correia (1724-1772), esteemed Portugese poet who championed Neoclassical ideals.

García Calderón, Francisco (1883-1953), Puruvian diplomat and writer.

García de le Huerta, Vincente (Antonio) (1734-1787), Spanish dramatist, poet and critic, best known for his play *Raquel* (1778).

García Gutiérrez, Antonio (1813-1884), Spanish dramatist and poet, particularly admired for his play *El trovador* (The Troubadour, 1836).

García Lorca, Federico (1898-1936), outstanding Spanish poet and dramatist; as a supporter of the Loyalist government, he was shot by nationalist forces at the outbreak of the Spanish Civil War.

Gardiner, Samuel Rawson (1829-1902), English historian who wrote on the English Civil War.

Gardner, Erle Stanley (1889-1970), American writer and lawyer, creator of the famous lawyer-detective Perry Mason.

Gardner, Dame Helen Louise 1908-1986), English critic and scholar.

Gardner, Isabella (Stewart) (1915-1981), American poet whose output revealed a fine lyric talent.

Gardner, John (Champlin Jr) (1933-1982), American writer, biographer, critic and poet who wrote the epic poem *Jason and Medeia* (1973).

Garin-Mikailovsky, Nikolai Georgievich (1852-1906), Russian writer.

Garioch, Robert (actually Robert Garioch Sutherland) (1909-1981), Scottish poet, writer and translator.

Garis, Howard R(oger) (1873-1962), American writer, creator of the children's story character Uncle Wiggley.

Garland, (Hannibal) Hamlin (1860-1940), American writer, especially known for his autobiographical "Middle Border" series.

Garland, John (c.1180-c.1272), English grammarian and poet, also known as Johannes de Garlandia, was a major figure in the development of medieval Latin literature.

Garneau, François-Xavier (1809-1866), French-Canadian historian, author of the *Histoire du Canada* (History of Canada, 1845-52); great-grandfather of Hector de Saint-Denys Garneau.

Garneau, Hector de Saint-Denys (1912-1943), French-Canadian poet; great-grandson of François-Xavier Garneau.

Garnett, Constance (1862-1946), English translator of the Russian classics; wife of Edward Garnett and mother of David Garnett.

Garnett, David (1892-1981), English writer and critic; son of Constance and Edward Garnett.

Garnett, Edward (1868-1936), English novelist, dramatist and critic; husband of Constance Garnett and father of David Garnett.

Garnett, Richard (1835-1906), English poet, biographer, writer, translator and editor.

Garnier, Robert (c.1545-1590), esteemed French dramatist and poet who was much appreciated for his fine tragedies.

Garrett, João Baptista da Silva Leitao de Almeida (1799-1854), illustrious Portugese poet, dramatist, novelist, journalist and statesman, the preeminent representative of the romantic movement in his homeland.

Garrick, David (1717-1779), prominent English actor, producer, dramatist and poet.

Garrigue, Jean (1914-1972), American poet.

Garrison, William Lloyd (1805-1879), famous American journalist and Abolitionist.

Garrod, Dorothy Annie Elizabeth (1892-1968), English archaeologist, author of *The Stone Age of Mount Carmel* (2 volumes, 1937, 1939).

Garro, Elena (1920-1998), Mexican writer and dramatist.

Garros, Pey de (c.1530-1585), Provençal poet.

Garstang, John (1876-1956), English archaeologist, particularly known for his studies of the history of Asia Minor and Palestine.

Garth, Sir Samuel (1661-1719), English poet, physician and freethinker, author of the burlesque poem *The Dispensary* (1699).

Gascoigne, George (c.1525-1577), admired English poet and writer.

Gaskell, Elizabeth Cleghorn (née Stevenson) (1810-1865), English novelist, short-story writer and biographer.

Gaspe, Philippe Aubert de (1786-1871), French-Canadian writer, author of the classic novel *Les Anciens Canadiens* (The Canadians of Old, 1863).

Gasprinski, Ismail (1851-1914), Russian journalist and writer who was also known as Ismail Gaspirali.

Gasquet, Francis Neil Aidan (1846-1929), English Roman Catholic cardinal and historian, author of studies on monastic history.

Gassendi, Pierre (1592-1655), French scientist, mathematician and philosopher who espoused Epicureanism.

Gaster, Moses (1856-1939), Romanian-born English Jewish scholar and Zionist.

Gatto, Alfonso (1909-1976), Italian poet.

Gaunilo, Count (11th Century), French Benedictine monk, author of *Liber pro insipiente* (In Defense of the Fool), which questioned St Anselm's ontological argument for the existence of God.

Gautier, (Émile-Théodore-) Léon (1832-1897), French literary historian.

Gautier, Théophile (1811-1872), notable French poet, novelist and critic, champion of Romanticism, later of Naturalism.

Gautier d'Arras (d. 1185), French writer of romances.

Gautier de Metz (13th Century), French clerk and poet who was also known as Gossuin de Metz.

Gay, John (1685-1732), famous English poet and dramatist, author of the celebrated ballad opera *The Beggar's Opera* (1728) and the admired poem *Trivia, or the Art of Walking the Streets of London* (1716).
Gay, John (1699-1745), English biblical scholar and philosopher.

Gayarré, Charles Étienne Arthur (1805-1895), American historian and novelist, best known for his *History of Louisiana* (4 volumes, 1851-66) and *Philip II of Spain* (1866).

Geber (14th Century), influential Spanish alchemist and metallurgist.

Geddes, Alexander (1737-1802), Scottish Roman Catholic priest, linguist and biblical scholar.

Geddes, Sir Patrick (1854-1932), Scottish biologist and sociologist who, with John Arthur Thomson, wrote *The Evolution of Sex* (1889).

Geibel, (Franz) Emanuel (1815-1884), German poet, dramatist and translator.

Geiger, Abraham (1810-1874), eminent German Jewish theologian, author of the important study *Urschrift und Übersetzungen der Bibel in ihrer Abhängigkeit von der innern Entwicklung des Judentums* (the Original Text and the Translations of the Bible; Their Dependence on the Inner Development of Judaism, 1857).

Geiger, Theodor Julius (1891-1952), German-born Danish sociologist, best known for his studies on social stratification and mobility.

Geijer, Erik Gustaf (1783-1847), distinguished Swedish poet, historian, philosopher and theorist.

Gellert, Christian Fürchtegott (1715-1769), popular German poet and writer, best remembered for his tales *Fabeln und Erzählungen* (Fables and Tales, 1746-48) and *Geistliche Oden und Leider* (spiritual Odes and Songs, 1757).

Gellhorn, Martha Ellis (1908-1998), American journalist and novelist.

Gellius, Aulus (2nd Century), Latin writer, author of the *Noctes atticae* (Attic Nights).

Gemistus Plethon, George (c.1355-c.1451), Byzantine philosopher and scholar of great influence on the development of Italian Renaissance philosophical discourse.

Genesius, Joseph (10th Century), Byzantine historian.

Genet, Jean (1910-1986), important French poet, dramatist and novelist, a leading figure in the Theatre of the Absurd and the Theatre of Hatred.

Genlis, Stéphanie Du Crest de Saint-Aubin, Comtesse de (1746-1830), French children's writer.

Gennadius I of Constantinople, Saint (d. 471), Byzantine patriach and theologian.

Gennadius II Scholarios (c.1405-c.1472), notable Greek Orthodox patriach and theologian, particularly known for his Aristotelian polemics.

Gennadius of Marseilles (5th Century), French priest and theologian, author of the invaluable *De viris illustribus* (On Famous Men).

Genovesi, Antonio (1712-1769), Italian philosopher and economist who wrote *Disciplinarum Metaphysicarum Elementa* (Elements of the Discipline of Metaphysics, 5 volumes, 1743-52), *Delle lezioni di commercio* (Lectures on Commerce, 1765) and *Universae Christianae Theologiae Elementa* (published 1771).

Gentile, Giovanni (1875-1944), prominent Italian philosopher, educator, editor and politician who embraced Fascism; was executed by the partisans.

Gentili, Alberico (1552-1609), significant Italian jurist, author of *De jure belli libri tres* (Three books on the Law of War, 1598; English translation, 1933).

Gentz, Friedrich von (1764-1832), noted German journalist and political philosopher.

Geoffrey de Vinsauf (12th-13th Century), English rhetorican who wrote *Nova Poetria* and *Summa de Coloribus Rhetoricis.*

Geoffrey of Monmouth (d.1155), English cleric and chronicler, author of the fanciful *Historia Regum Britanniae* (c.1137).

Geometres, John (10th Century), Byzantine bishop and poet who was also known as John Kyriotes.

George, Henry (1839-1897), American land reformer and economist whose *Progress and Poverty* (1879) urged the adoption of the single tax.

George, Stefan (1868-1933), signifciant German poet, writer and translator, a master of lyric writing.

George of Trebizond (1396-1486), learned Byzantine scholar, especially noted for his Aristotelian studies.

George the Monk (actually Georgios Hamartolos) (9th Century), Byzantine historian.

George the Pisidian (actually Georgios Pisides) (7th Century), Byzantine cleric, historian and poet.

George the Syncellus (8th Century), Byzantine historian.

Gerard, Alexander (1728-1795), English theologian and philosopher, particularly known for his writings on aesthetics.

Gerard, John (1545-1612), English herbalist who wrote *The Herball, or generall historie of plantes* (1597).

Gerard of Cremona (c.1114-1187), Spanish scholar.

Gerhard, Johann (1582-1637), eminent German Lutheran theologian, author of the celebrated *Loci Theologici* (9 volumes, 1610-22).

Gerhardie, William Alexander (actually William Alexander Gerhardi) (1895-1977), English novelist.

Gérin-Lajoie, Antoine (1824-1882), French-Canadian writer.

Gerlach, Hellmut von (1866-1935), German journalist and politician who espoused pacifism and opposed German nationalism.

Gerlache, Étienne-Constantin, Baron de (1785-1871), Belgian statesman and historian.

Germanus I, Saint (c.634-c.732), Byzantine patriach and theologian.

Germanus II (c. 1175-1240), Byzantine patriach and theologian.

Gerould, Gordon Hall (1877-1953), Amercian literary scholar and novelist; husband of Katharine Fullerton Gerould.

Gerould, Katherine Fullerton (1879-1944), Amercian novelist and short-story writer; wife of Gordon Hall Gerould.

Gershom ben Judah (c.960-c.1035), famous French-born German Jewish scholar.

Gerson, Jean de (1363-1429), French Roman Catholic theologian who was also known as Jean de Charlier.

Gerstäcker, Friedrich (1816-1872), German adventurer and writer who described his various travels in various nations of the world in many books.

Gerstenberg, Heinrich Wilhelm von (1737-1823), German poet, critic and theorist, author of bardic verse and the tragedy *Ugolino* (1768).

Gervase of Canterbury (c.1141-c.1210), English monk and chronicler who was also known as Gervasius Dorobornensis.

Gervase of Tilbury (c.1152-c.1220). English scholar and courtier, author of the *Otia imperialia.*

Gesenius, (heinrich Friedrich) Wilhelm (1786-1842), eminent German biblical scholar and philologist.

Gesner, Johann Matthias (1691-1761), notable German classical philologist.

Gessner, Salomon (1730-1788), versatile Swiss poet, writer, translator, painter and etcher.

Geulincx, Arnold (1624-1669), influential Dutch metaphysician and logician.

Geyl, Pieter (1887-1966), Dutch historian.

Gezelle, Guido (1830-1899), prominent Flemish poet, writer and churchman, a master of lyric poetry.

Ghálib, Mírzá Asadulláh Khán (1797-1869), gifted Indian poet and writer in the Persian language.

Ghassaniy, Muyaka bin Haji al- (1776-1840), Kenyan poet in the Swahili language.

Ghazálí, al- (actually **Abú Hámid Muhammad ibn Muhammad at-Túsí al-Ghazálí) (1058-1111)**, important Persian Muslim jurist and theologian whose *Ihyá' 'ulúm ad-dín* (The Revival of the Religious Sciences) gained acceptance for Súfism in orthodox Islám.

Ghelderode, Michel de (1898-1962), avant-garde Belgian dramatist.

Ghosh, Girish Chandra (1844-1912), Bengali dramatist.

Giannone, Pietro (1676-1748), Italian historian who wrote the significant study *Il triregno, ossia del regno del cielo. della terra, e del papa* (The Triple Crown, or the Reign of Heaven, Earth, and the Pope).

Gibbon, Edward (1737-1794), great English historian, celebrated for his masterpiece *The History of the Decline and Fall of the Roman Empire* (6 volumes, 1776-88).

Gibbon, Lewis Grassie (actually **James Leslie Mitchell) (1901-1935)**, Scottish writer, particularly esteemed for his novel trilogy *Sunset Song* (1932), *Cloud Howe* (1933) and *Grey Granite* (1934).

Gibbs, Wolcott (1902-1958), American drama critic.

Gibran or **Jibran, Khalil** (actually **Jubrán Khalíl Jubrán) (1883-1931),** highly popular Lebanese essayist, novelist, poet and artist whose works in both Arabic and English reflected his preoccupation with religion and mysticism.

Gibson, Wilfred Wilson (1878-1962), English poet and dramatist.

Giddings, Franklin H(enry) (1855-1931), American sociologist, author of *Studies in the Theory of Human Society* (1922).

Gide, André (Paul Guillaume) (1869-1951), eminent French poet, novelist, dramatist and critic; won the Nobel Prize for Literature (1947).

Gledion, Sigfried (1888-1968), Swiss art historian.

Gierke, Otto Friedrich von (1841-1921), German legal philosopher.

Gieseler, Johann Karl Ludwig (1792-1854), German Protestant church historian who wrote the *Lehrbuch der Kirchengeschichte* (Textbook of Church History, 5 volumes, 1824-57).

Gifford, Edward W(inslow) (1887-1959), American anthropologist, archaeologist and ethnologist.

Gifford, William (1756-1826), English editor, scholar and poet.

Gikatilla, Joseph (1248-c.1305), Spanish Kabbalist writer.

Gilbert, Sir W(illiam) S(chwenck) (1836-1911), remarkable English dramatist and librettist, famous for his collaboration with the composer Sir Arthur Sullivan on a celebrated series of operettas.

Gilchrist, Alexander (1828-1861), English biographer; husband of Anne (née Burrow) Gilchrist.

Gilchrist, Anne (née Burrow) (1828-1885), English biographer and essayist; wife of Alexander Gilchrist.

Gildas (d.570), English historian, author of *De excidio et conquestu Britanniae* (The Ruin of Britain, c.546).

Gildersleeve, B(asil) L(anneau) (1831-1924), American classical scholar.

Giles, H A (1845-1935) English Orientalist.

Gilfillan, George (1813-1878), Scottish Dissenting minister, literary critic and editor.

Gill, (Arthur) Eric (Rowan) (1882-1940), English typographic designer, engraver, sculptor and writer.

Gill, Brendan (1914-1997), American critic and writer.

Gill, Francis James (1856-1912), Australian anthropologist.

Gilles li Muisis (1272-1352), French abbot, poet and chronicler who was also known as Le Muiset.

Gillespie, George (1613-1648), Scottish churchman and polemicist.

Gillette, William Hooker 1855-1937), American actor and dramatist, best remembered for his appearance in his own play *Sherlock Holmes* (1899).

Gilman, Caroline Howard (1794-1888), American writer and poet.

Gilman, Charlotte Perkins (1860-1935), American novelist and short-story writer.

Gilmore, Dame Mary Jane (1865-1962), Australian poet and writer.

Gilpin, William (1724-1804), English writer.

Gilpin, William (1813-1894), American soldier, politician and editor.

Gil Polo, Gaspar (c.1535-1591), Spanish poet who won distinction for his *Diana enamorada* (1564).

Gilson, Étienne (-Henry) (1884-1978), French historian of medieval philosophy, a champion of Thomism.

Giner de los Ríos, Francisco (1839-1915), Spanish philosopher, literary critic and educator.

Ginsberg, Allen (1926-1997), famous American poet, a central figure in the Beat and counterculture movements.

Ginsburg, Christian David (1831-1914), Polish-born English Hebrew and biblical scholar, an authority on the Masorah.

Ginzburg, Louis (1873-1953), Lithuanian-born American Jewish scholar.

Ginzburg, Natalia (1916-1991), prominent Italian novelist, dramatist and essayist.

Gioberti, Vincenzo (1801-1852), Italian philosopher and politician whose writings reflected his Christian beliefs, author of *Del primato morale e civile degli italiano* (On the Moral and Civil Primacy of the Italian Race, 1843) and *Del rinnovamento civile d'Italia* (On the Civil Renewal of Italy, 1851).

Giono, Jean (1895-1970), French novelist and poet.

Giordani, Pietro (1774-1848), Italian writer and patriot.

Giovannitti, Arturo (1884-1959), Italian-born American poet, remembered for his condemnation of the American prison system in *Arrows in the Gale* (1914).

Gippius, Zinaida (Nikolaievna) (1869-1945), Russian poet, dramatist, writer and essayist; wife of Dmitri Sergeievich Merezhkovsky.

Giraldi, Giambattista (1505-1573), Italian dramatist, writer and poet who was also known as Cinzio or Cinthio after his academic name Cynthius.

Giraldus Cambrensis (c.1146-1223), Welsh historian who opposed Anglo-Saxon authority over the Welsh church and who was also known as Gerald of Wales and Gerald de Barri.

Girard, Jean-Baptiste (1765-1850), Swiss educator who was also known as Père Girard and Père Grégoire.

Girardin, Émile de (1806-1881), prominent French journalist.

Giraudoux, (Hyppolyte-) Jean (1882-1944), noted French novelist, dramatist, essayist and poet.

Giry, (Jean-Marie-Joseph-) Arthur (1848-1899), French historian, particularly known for his studies of the Middle Ages.

Gissing, George Robert (1857-1903), English novelist, best remembered for his *New Grub Street* (1891) and *The Private Papers of Henry Ryecroft* (1903).

Gittings, Robert William Victor (1911-1992), English poet, biographer and dramatist.

Giusti, Giuseppe (1809-1850), Italian poet and writer, a master of political satire.

Giustiniani, Agostino (1479-1536), Italian aristocrat, Dominican priest, statesman and scholar who excelled in Eastern studies.

Giustiniani, Leonardo (1338-1446), Italian aristocrat, statesman, scholar and poet whose *Canzoni o strambotti d'amore* (Songs of Fine Tunes of Love) served as the model for the giustiniane form of love poems.

Giustiniani, Pompeo (1569-1616), Italian soldier and historian who was also known as Braccio di Ferro (Iron Arm) in reference to the mechanical arm he wore after he lost his arm in battle.

Gjellerup, Karl Adolph (1857-1919), distinguished Danish poet and novelist; was co-winner of the Nobel Prize for Literature (1917).

Glaber, Radulfus (c.985-c.1047), French monk and chronicler.

Gladden, Washington (1836-1918), American Congregationalist minister, journalist, writer and poet whose poem *O Master, Let Me Walk With Thee* became a well-known hymn.

Gladkov, Fyodor Vasilievich (1883-1958), Russian novelist whose writings followed the tenets of Socialist Realism.

Glanvill or Glanvil, Joseph (1636-1680), English scholar, author of *The Vanity of Dogmatizing, or Confidence in Opinions* (1661), *Plus Ultra or the Progress and Advancement of Knowledge Since the Days of Aristotle* (1668) and *Essays on Several Important Subjects* (1676).

Glanville or Glanvil or Glanvill, Ranulf de (d.1190), English justiciar or chief minister to Henry II, reputed author of *Tractatus de legibus et consuetudinibus regni Angliae* (Treatise on the Laws and Customs of the Kingdom of England, c.1188).

Glapthorne, Henry (c.1610-c.1643), English poet and dramatist.

Glareanus, Henricus (actually Heinrich Loris) (1488-1563), Swiss scholar, poet and music theorist, author of the music treatise *Dodecachordon* (1547).

Glasgow, Ellen (Anderson Gholson) (1873-1945), esteemed American novelist and short-story writer, best known for her novels *Virginia* (1913), *Barren Ground* (1925) and *The Sheltered Life* (1932).

Glaspell, Susan (1882-1948), American novelist, short-story writer and dramatist, particularly remembered for her play *Alison's House* (1930).

Glassco, John (1909-1981), Canadian writer, poet and translator.

Glatigny, (Joseph-) Albert-Alexandre (1839-1873), French poet who adhered to Parnassian precepts.

Gleim, Johann Wilhelm Ludwig (1719-1803), German poet.

Glen, William (1789-1826), Scottish poet, author of the Jacobite lament *Wae's me for Prince Charlie*.

Glover, Richard (1712-1785), English politician and poet, best known for his ballad *Admiral Hosier's Ghost* (1740).

Glycas, Michael (12th Century), Byzantine historian, theologian and poet.

Glyn, Sir Anthony (actually **Geoffrey Davson**) **(1922-1998),** English novelist, author of *The Dragon Variation* (1969); grandson of Elinor Glyn.

Glyn, Elinor (1864-1943), English novelist, best remembered for her *Three Weeks* (1907); grandmother of Sir Anthony Glyn.

Gneist, Rudolf von (1816-1895), German jurist, politician and legal theorist, author of *Englische Verfassungsgeschichte* (1882; English translation as *The History of the English Constitution,* 1886).

Gobat, Charles-Albert (1834-1914), Swiss politician, administrator, philanthropist and writer; was co-winner of the Nobel Prize for Peace (1902).

Gobineau, Joseph-Arthur, Comte de (1816-1882), French diplomat, writer and ethnologist, author of the influential *Essai sur l'inégalité des races humains* (4 volumes, 1853-55; English translation as *Essay on the Inequality of Human Races* 1967).

Godden, (Margaret) Rumer (1907-1998), English writer.

Godefroy, Denis (1549-1622), French legal scholar who wrote *Corpus juris civilis* (1583).

Gödel, Kurt (1906-1978), great Austro-Hungarian mathematical logician and philosopher.

Godfrey, Thomas (1736-1763), American poet who wrote in the style of the Cavalier poets.

Godfrey of Fontaines (c.1249-c.1306), French philosopher and theologian who espoused Aristotelian principles.

Godfrey of Saint-Victor (c.1125-1194), important French philosopher, theologian, poet and monk, author of *Microcosmus* and *Fons philosophiae,* notable works of the early medieval Christian Humanist movement.

Godin, Gérald (1938-1994), French-Canadian poet and writer.

Godkin, E(dwin) L(awrence) (1831-1902), Irish-born American journalist and editor.

Godley, A(lfred) D(enis) (1856-1925), English scholar and poet.

Godolphin, Sidney (1610-1643), English poet; died defending the Royalist cause.

Godwin, Edward William (1833-1886), English architect, designer and writer.

Godwin, Francis (1562-1633), English bishop, historian and writer, best known for his tale *The Man in the Moone, or a Discourse of a Voyage Thither by Domingo Gonsales, the Speedy Messenger* (published 1638).

Godwin, Mary Wollstonecraft (1759-1797), English writer and champion of women's rights; wife of William Godwin.

Godwin, William (1756-1836), English political and social philosopher, freethinker and writer, author of *an Enquiry Concerning Political Justice and Its Influence on General Virtue and Happiness* (1793); husband of Mary Wollstonecraft Godwin.

Goeje, Michael Jan de (1836-1909), Dutch scholar, an authority on Arabic subjects.

Goethe, Johann Wolfgang von (1749-1832), great German poet, dramatist, painter, scientist and philosopher whose *Faust* (2 parts, 1808, 1832) stands as one of the supreme achievements of world literature.

Gogarty, Oliver Joseph St John (1878-1957), English surgeon, novelist and poet.

Gogol, Nikolai (Vasilievich) (1809-1852), renowned Russian writer and dramatist, celebrated for his novel *Dead Souls* (1842).

Góis, Damião de (1502-1574), learned Portugese scholar.

Gökalp, Ziya (actually **Mehmed Ziya**) **(c.1875-1924),** Turkish sociologist, writer and poet, a leading figure in the nationalist movement of his homeland.

Gold, Michael (actually **Irwin Granich**) **(1893-1967),** American editor, writer and dramatist who espoused Marxism.

Goldenweiser, Alexander (Alexandrovich) (1880-1940), Ukranian-born American anthropologist.

Goldfaden, Abraham (actually **Abraham Goldenfoden**) **(1840-1908),** Russian Hebrew and Yiddish poet and dramatist, generally acknowledged as the creator ot Yiddish theatre and opera.

Golding, Louis (1895-1958), English novelist, short-story writer, essayist and poet.

Golding, Sir William (Gerald) (1911-1993), eminent English novelist, particularly admired for his *Lord of the Flies* (1954); won the Nobel Prize for Literature (1983).

Goldman, Emma (1869-1940), Lithuanian-born American anarchist, social reformer and writer.

Goldman, James (1927-1998), American novelist, dramatist and screenwriter best known for his screenplay *The Lion in Winter* (1968).

Goldoni Carlo (1707-1793), outstanding Italian dramatist who excelled in realistic comic plays.

Goldschmidt, Adolph (1863-1944), German art historian.

Goldschmidt, Meïr Aron (1819-1887), Danish novelist and short-story writer.

Goldsmith, Oliver (1730-1774), gifted Irish essayist, writer, dramatist and poet, especially esteemed for his poems *The Traveller* (1764) and *The Deserted Village* (1770), the novel *The Vicar of Wakefield* (1766) and the play *She Stoops to Conquer* (1773).

Gollancz, Israel (1864-1930), English scholar and editor who was known for his medieval and Shakespearean studies.

Gomarus or **Gommer, Franciscus (1563-1641),** French-born Dutch Calvinist theologian, one of the leading opponents of Arminianism.

Gombrowicz, Witold (1904-1969), Polish novelist and short-story writer.

Gómez de Avellaneda, Gertrudis (1814-1873), celebrated Spanish dramatist, poet and writer, one of the outstanding Romanticists of her homeland.

Gómez de la Serna, Ramón (1888-1963), Spanish writer and poet whose poetic greguerías (confused noise) greatly influenced avant-garde writers in Europe and Latin America.

Gomperz, Theodor (1832-1912), Austrian classical philologist and philosopher, author of *Griechische Denker: Eine Geschichte der antiken Philosophie* (2 volumes, 1893, 1902; English translation as *Greek Thinkers: A History of Ancient Philosophy*, 4 volumes, 1901-12).

Gonçalves Crespo, António Cândido (1846-1883), Portugese poet.

Gonçalves de Magalhães, Domingos José (1811-1882), Brazilian poet, remembered for his *Suspiros Poéticos e Saudades* (Poetic Sighs and Longings, 1836).

Goncalves Dias, Antonio (1823-1864), Brazilian poet and scholar, author of the poem *Song of Exile* (1843); died in a shipwreck.

Goncharov, Ivan Alexandrovich (1812-1891), distinguished Russian novelist who wrote *Obyknovennaya istoriya* (1847; English translation as *A Common Story*, 1917), *Oblomov* (1859; English translation, 1954) and *Obryv* (1869; English translation as *The Precipice*, 1915).

Goncourt, Edmond (-Louis-Antoine Huot) de (1822-1896), French writer whose close collaboration with his brother produced the celebrated *Journal* (1851 et seq.) and the famous novel *Germinie* (1864; English translation, 1955); brother of Jules (-Alfred Huot) de Goncourt.

Goncourt, Jules (-Alfred Huot) de (1830-1870), French writer, a close collaborator with his brother on the celebrated *Journals* (1851 et seq.) and the famous novel *Germinie* (1864; English translation, 1955); brother of Edmond (-Louis-Antoine Huot) de Goncourt.

Góngora y Argote, Luis de (1561-1627), significant Spanish poet who became known for his complex style known as Gongorism.

Gonzaga, Tomás António (1744-1810), Portuguese poet who won distinction for his love poetry *Marília de Dirceu* (1792).

González Martínez, Enrique (1871-1952), Mexican poet, physician and diplomat.

González Prada, Manuel (1844-1919), Peruvian poet.

Gooch, George Peabody (1873-1968), English historian.

Goodman, Paul (1911-1972), American essayist, short-story writer, dramatist and poet, principally known for his antiestablishment views.

Goodnow, Frank J(ohnson) (1859-1939), American political scientist and educator.

Goodrich, Samuel Griswold (1793-1860), American writer and poet, best remembered for his many children's books he wrote under the name Peter Parley.

Goodrich or **Goodricke, Thomas (c.1480-1554),** English bishop and biblical translator.

Goodspeed, Edgar J(ohnson) (1871-1962), American biblical scholar, translator and linguist.

Goodwin, William Watson (1831-1912), American classical scholar.

Googe, Barnabe (1540-1594), English poet, known for his *Eclogues* (1563) and *Cupido Conquered*.

Gordin, Jacob (1853-1909), Yiddish dramatist.

Gordon, Aaron David (1856-1922), Russian-born Zionist and essayist.

Gordon, Adam Lindsay (1833-1870), Australian poet who won great popularity with his ballads.

Gordon, Caroline (1895-1981), American novelist and short-story writer.

Gordon, Judah Leib (1830-1892), Lithuanian-born Russian Hebrew poet, essayist, novelist and short-story writer who was also known as Leon Gordon.

Gore, Catherine Grace Frances (née Moody) (1799-1861), English novelist, short-story writer and dramatist.

Gore, Charles (1853-1932), English Anglican bishop and theologian who espoused liberal views.

Gorges, Sir Arthur (1557-1625), English courtier and poet.

Georgias of Leontini (c.483-c.376 B.C.), Greek philosopher and rhetorician.

Gorky, Maxim (actually Aleksei Maximovich Peshkov) (1868-1936), famous Russian novelist and short-story writer.

Gorman, Herbert S(herman) (1893-1954), American biographer and novelist.

Gorres, (Johann) Joseph von (1776-1848), notable German writer and journalist, particularly known for his expansive *Christliche Mystic* (Christian Mysticism, 4 volumes, 1836-42).

Gorter, Herman (1864-1927), Dutch poet, author of *Mei* (May, 1889), *Verzen* (1890) and *Pan* (1916).

Goślicki, Wawrzyniec (c.1530-1607), Polish Roman Catholic bishop and diplomat who championed liberalism in his *De optimo senatore* (1568; English translation as *The Accomplished Senator,* 1733).

Gosse, Sir Edmund William (1849-1928), English poet, literary historian, critic and translator.

Gossen, Herman Heinrich (1810-1858), German economist.

Gosson, Stephen (1554-1624), English dramatist who became known for his Puritan attacks on the stage.

Gottfried von Strassburg (13th Century), famous German poet and scholar, author of the German version of *Tristan und Isolde* (c.1210).

Gottschalk or **Gottescalc** or **Godescalchus of Orbais (c.803-c.868),** German monk, theologian and poet.

Gottsched, Johann Christoph (1700-1766), German literary theorist, critic and dramatist.

Gould, Edward Sherman (1805-1885), American writer.

Gourgaud, Gaspard (1783-1852), French soldier and historian.

Gourmont, Jean de (1877-1928), French writer and poet; brother of Rémy de Gourmont.

Gourmont, Rémy de (1858-1915), French essayist, poet, novelist and dramatist; brother of Jean de Gourmont.

Gower, John (c.1330-1408), notable English poet, author of *Confessio amantis, Speculum meditantis* and *Vox clamantis.*

Goyen, (Charles) William (1915-1983), American novelist, short-story writer and dramatist.

Gozzi, Carlo, Conte (1720-1806), important Italian poet, dramatist and writer, particularly successful for his fairy-tale plays.

Gozzi, Gasparo, Conte (1713-1786), Italian journalist, critic, writer and poet.

Gqoba, William Wellington (1840-1888), Bantu poet and philologist.

Grabbe, Christian Dietrich (1801-1836), German dramatist and poet whose works presaged Expressionism.

Graça Aranha, José Pereira da (1868-1931), Brazilian novelist and diplomat, best known for his novel *Canaã* (1902; English translation as *Canaan,* 1920).

Gracián (y Morales), Baltasar (1601-1658), Spanish Jesuit philosopher and writer, author of the philosophical novel *El criticón* (3 parts, 1651, 1653, 1657; English translation as *The Critic,* 1681).

Grady, Henry Woodfin (1850-1889), American journalist and orator.

Graebner, (Robert) Fritz (1877-1934), German ethnologist who wrote *Methode der Ethnologie* (Method of Ethnology, 1911) and *Das Weltbild der Primitiven* (The World View of the Primitives, 1924).

Graetz, Heinrich (1817-1891), Polish-born German historian, author of the *Geschichte der Juden von den ältesten Zeiten bis auf die Gegenwart* (History of the Jews from Oldest Times to the Present, 11 volumes, 1853-76; abridged English translation, 1891-92).

Graevius, Johann (actually Johann Georg Greffe) (1632-1703), Dutch scholar and antiquarian.

Graham, William Sydney (1918-1986), esteemed Scottish poet.

Grahame, James (1765-1811), Scottish poet.

Grahame, Kenneth (1859-1932), Scottish writer, best known for his children's classic *The Wind in the Willows* (1908).

Grainger, James (c.1721-1766), English physician and poet, author of the didactic poem *Sugar Cane* (1764).

Gramsci, Antonio (1891-1937), Italian politician, journalist, critic and writer, founder of the Italian Communist Party (1921).

Grand, Sarah (actually Frances Elizabeth Bellenden McFall née Clarke) (1854-1943), English novelist who wrote *The Heavenly Twins* (1893) and *The Beth Book* (1897).

Grandbois, Alain (1900-1975), French-Canadian poet, biographer and short-story writer.

Grandgent, Charles Hall (1862-1939), American linguist who was an authority on Vulgar Latin and Dante.

Grange, John (c.1557-1611), English novelist, author of *The Golden Aphroditis* (1577).

Granovsky, Timofei Nikolaievich (1813-1855), Russian historian.

Grant, Anne (née MacVicar) (1755-1838), Scottish poet and essayist.

Grant, George (1918-1988), Canadian philosopher.

Grant, James (1822-1887), English soldier and writer.

Grant, Robert (1852-1940), American jurist, novelist, essayist and poet.

Granville-Barker, Harley (1877-1946), influential English dramatist, theater producer and critic.

Gratian (c.1100-c.1158), significant Italian monk and legal scholar who was also known under his academic name of Magister Gratianus.

Graves, Richard (1715-1804), English novelist and poet, best remembered for his novel *The Spiritual Quixote, or the Summer's Ramble of Mr Geoffry Wildgoose* (1772).

Graves, Robert (van Ranke) (1895-1985), distinguished English poet, novelist, essayist and critic.

Gray, Asa (1810-1888), outstanding American botanist, author of the standard *Manual of the Botany of the Northern United States, from New England to Wisconsin and South to Ohio and Pennsylvania Inclusive* (1848).

Gray, David (1838-1861), Scottish poet.

Gray, John Henry (1866-1934), English churchman and poet.

Gray, Thomas (1716-1771), sublime English poet, celebrated for his *Elegy Written in a Country Churchyard* (1751).

Grayson, William J(ohn) (1788-1863), American lawyer, politician, writer and poet who championed slavery in his expansive didactic poem *The Hireling and the Slave* (1854).

Grazzini, Anton Francesco (1503-1584), Italian poet, dramatist and storyteller who was know as Il Lasca (The Roach).

Greban, Arnoul (1420-1471), French dramatist, author of the famous sacred play *Mystere de la Passion* (c.1453).

Greeley, Horace (1811-1872), American newspaper editor, a prominent figure in the antislavery and Radical Republican movements.

Green, Alice Sophia Amelia (actually Alice Sophia Amelia Stopford) (1847-1929), Irish historian.

Green, Anna Katharine (1846-1935), American writer of detective novels.

Green, Henry (actually Henry Vincent Yorke) (1905-1973), English novelist and industrialist.

Green, John Richard (1837-1883), English historian, author of a *Short History of the English People* (1874).

Green, Julien (actually Julian Green) (1900-1998), American-born French writer, dramatist and memoirist.

Green, Matthew (1697-1737), English poet who wrote *The Spleen* (1737).

Green, Paul (Eliot) (1894-1981), American dramatist and novelist, best remembered for his play *In Abraham's Bosom* (1927).

Green, T(homas) H(ill) (1836-1882), English philosopher and political theorist, author of *Prolegomena to Ethics* (published 1883) and *Lectures on the Principles of Political Obligation* (published 1885-88).

Greenberg, Samuel Bernard (1893-1917), American poet who revealed a fine talent for lyric expression.

Greene, Asa (1789-c.1837), American physician, journalist and novelist.

Greene, (Henry) Graham (1904-1991), eminent English novelist, short-story writer, biographer, dramatist and essayist.

Greene, Robert (c.1558-1592), English dramatist and writer, especially admired for his blank verse romantic comedies.

Greenwood, Walter (1903-1974), English novelist and dramatist, best known for his novel *Love on the Dole* (1933).

Greg, Sir Walter Wilson (1875-1959), distinguished English literary scholar and bibliographer.

Gregoras, Nicephorus (1295-1360), important Byzantine scholar, philosopher and theologian, author of a monumental Byzantine history (37 volumes).

Gregory, Horace (Victor) (1898-1982), American poet, essayist, editor and translator; husband of Marya Zaturenska.

Gregory, Isabella Augusta (née Persse), Lady (1852-1932), Irish writer, dramatist and translator.

Gregory Narekatzi, Saint (951-1001), Armenian theologian and poet who espoused mysticism, also known as Gregory Narek.

Gregory of Nyssa, Saint (c.335-c.394), Bishop and theologian who was the principal defender of Trinitarianism of his era.

Gregory of Rimini (c.1299-1358), influential Italian philosopher and theologian who was a proponent of a moderate Nominalist worldview.

Gregory of Sinai (c.1299-1346), Greek Orthodox monk, theologian and mystic who was also known as Gregory Sinaites.

Gregory of Tours, Saint (actually Georgius Florentius) (c.538-c.595), notable French Roman Catholic bishop and writer, particularly known for his history of the Franks and the lives of the church fathers.

Gregory Thaumaturgus, Saint (c.213-c.270), Greek Roman Catholic bishop and theologian who wrote a famous exposition of his faith.

Grein, Jack Thomas (actually Jacob Thomas Grein) (1862-1935), Dutch-born English critic, theater manager and dramatist.

Grenfell, Julian (1888-1915), English poet who was admired for his *Into Battle* (1915); died in World War I.

Gresset, Jean-Baptiste-Louis (1709-1777), French poet and dramatist, author of the celebrated comic narrative poem *Ver-Vert* (1734).

Gressmann, Hugo (1877-1927), German Old Testament scholar.

Greville, Sir Fulke, 1st Baron Brooke (1554-1628), English writer, poet, dramatist and courtier; was murdered by a manservant.

Grévin, Jacques (1538-1570), French poet, dramatist and physician.

Grey, Zane (1872-1939), American novelist of popular tales of the Old West.

Griboyedov, Alexander Sergeievich (1795-1829), Russian dramatist who won distinction with his comic play *Gore ot uma* (1822-24; English translation as *Wit Works Woe*, 1933).

Grieg, (Johan) Nordahl Brun (1902-1943), Norwegian poet, dramatist and novelist; as a member of the Resistance, he died when his airplane was shot down by the Germans in World War II.

Grierson, Sir George Abraham (1851-1941), English linguist.

Grierson, Sir Herbert John Clifford (1866-1960), English literary scholar.

Griffin, Gerald (1803-1840), Irish novelist, poet and dramatist, best remembered for his novel *The Collegians* (1829).

Griffith, Arthur (1872-1922), prominent Irish journalist and nationalist leader who served as president of the Irish Republic (1922).

Griffiths, Ann (née Thomas) (1776-1805), Welsh hymnist.

Grignon, Claude-Henri (1894-1978), esteemed French-Canadian journalist and novelist who wrote under the name Valdombre, author of the novel *Un Homme et son péché* (A Man and His Sin, 1933).

Grigoriev, Apollon (Alexandrovich) (1822-1864), Russian critic and poet.

Grigson, Geoffrey (Edward Harvey) (1905-1985), English poet, editor and critic.

Grillparzer, Franz (1791-1872), outstanding Austrian dramatist and poet whose tragic plays rank among the august creations of Austrian literature.

Grimald or Grimoald, Nicholas (1519-c.1562), English poet, dramatist and translator.

Grimké, Angelina Emily (1805-1879), American pamphleteer and lecturer who was active in the antislavery movement; sister of Sarah Moore Grimké.

Grimké, Sarah Moore (1792-1873), American pamphleteer and lecturer who was known for her antislavery views; sister of Angelina Emily Grimké.

Grimm, Friedrich Melchior, Baron von (1723-1807), German critic.

Grimm, Hans (1875-1959), German writer, particularly known for his Pan Germanist novel *Volk ohne Raum* (People without Space, 1926).

Grimm, Jacob Ludwig Carl (1785-1863), famous German folklorist who, with his brother, collected the classic *Kinder- und Hausmärchen* (1812-22), best known as *Grimm`s Fairy Tales*; brother of Wilhelm Carl Grimm.

Grimm, Wilhelm Carl (1786-1859), famous German folklorist who collaborated with his brother on the classic *Kinder- und Hausmärchen* (1812-22), better known as *Grimm`s Fairy Tales*; brother of Jacob Ludwig Carl Grimm.

Grimmelshausen, Hans Jacob Christoph (c.1622-1676), German novelist, author of the renowned satirical *Simplicissimus* series of novels (1669 et seq.).

Grimshaw, Beatrice (Ethel) (1871-1953), Irish traveller and writer.

Grin or Grinovsky, Alexander Stepanovich (1880-1932), Russian writer, best known for his short stories.

Gringore or Gringoire, Pierre (c.1475-c.1538), French poet and dramatist.

Gripenberg, Bertel Johan Sebastian, Baron (1878-1947), Finnish poet and writer who wrote in Swedish.

Griswold, Rufus Wilmot (1815-1857), American journalist, critic and editor.

Grober, Gustav (1844-1911), German scholar and medievalist.

Grocyn, William (c.1446-1519), English scholar.

Groen van Prinsterer, Guillaume (1801-1876), Dutch Protestant politician, religious writer and historian.

Gronovius, Johannes Fredericus (1611-1671), Dutch Latinist.

Grosseteste, Robert (c.1175-1235), English Roman Catholic bishop and scholar.

Grossi, Tommaso (1791-1853), Italian poet, best remembered for his *I Lombardi alla prima crociata* (1826).

Grosvenor, Gilbert H(ovey) (1875-1966), American geographer, writer and editor.

Grote, George (1794-1871), English historian, author of a *History of Greece* (12 volumes, 1846-56).

Grotefend, Georg Friedrich (1775-1853), German educator and language scholar who wrote the important *Neue Beiträge zur Erläuterung der persepolitanischen Keilschrift . . .* (New Contributions to a Commentary on the Persepolitan Cuneiform Writing . . . 1837).

Groth, Klaus (1819-1899), German poet and writer, admired for his poetry collection *Quickborn* (1853).

Grotius, Hugo (1583-1645), Dutch jurist, scholar and poet, author of the celebrated *De Jure Belli ac Pacis* (On the Law of War and Peace, 1625), a fundamental work in the development of international jurisprudence.

Groulx, Lionel-Adolphe (1878-1967), French-Canadian historian and novelist whose fiction appeared under the name Alonié de Lestres.

Grout, Donald J(ay) (1902-1987), distinguished American music scholar.

Grove, Frederick Philip (1871-1948), Canadian novelist and essayist.

Grove, Sir George (1820-1900), renowned English music and biblical lexicographer, celebrated for his expansive *Dictionary of Music and Musicians* (4 volumes, 1879-89).

Gruber, Johann Gottfried (1774-1851), German archaeologist, literary historian and encylopedist.

Gruffydd, William John (1881-1954), Welsh poet, scholar and editor.

Grun, Anastasius (actually **Anton Alexander, Graf von Auersperg**) **(1806-1876),** Austrian statesman, poet and translator.

Grundtvig, N(ikolai) F(rederik) S(everin) (1783-1872), Danish bishop, theologian, historian, poet and hymnist.

Gryphius, Andreas (actually **Andreas Greif**) **(1616-1664),** important German poet and dramatist, a master of lyric expression.

Guardini, Romano (1885-1968), Italian-born German Roman Catholic theologian.

Guarini, (Giovanni) Battista (1538-1612), Italian poet, author of the celebrated *Il pastor fido* (The Faithful Shepherd, 1590).

Guarino Veronese (c.1372-1460), Italian classical scholar who was also known as Guarino da Verona.

Gudmundsson, Kristmann (1902-1983), noted Icelandic novelist.

Gudmundsson, Tómas (1901-1983), Icelandic poet.

Guedalla, Philip (1889-1944), English historian and biographer.

Guérin, Charles (1873-1907), French poet who championed Symbolism.

Guérin, Eugénie de (1805-1848), talented French poet and writer; sister of (Georges-) Maurice de Guérin.

Guérin, (Georges-) Maurice (1810-1839), gifted French poet and writer; brother of Eugénie de Guérin.

Guernes de Pont-Sainte-Maxence (12th Century), French scholar, author of *Vie de saint Thomas Becket* (c.1174).

Guerrazzi, Francesco Domenico (1804-1873), Italian politician and historical novelist.

Guest, Edgar A(lbert) (1881-1959), English-born American poet who wrote the popular *A Heap o' Livin'* (1916).

Guevara, Antonio de (c.1481-1545), Spanish court preacher and writer, author of *Reloj de príncipes o libro aureo del emperador Marco Aurelio* (1529; English translation as *The Golden Boke of Marcus Aurelius*, 1535).

Guèvremont, Germain (née Grignon) (1900-1968), French-Canadian novelist, greatly appreciated for her *Le Survenant* (1945; English translation as *The Outlander*, 1950) and *Marie-Dedace* (1947; English translation as *Monk's Reach*, 1950).

Gui or **Guy, Bernard (c.1261-1331),** Dominican bishop, historian and inquisitor.

Guicciardini, Francesco (1483-1540), Italian statesman and historian.

Guidi, Alessandro (1650-1712), Italian poet, an exponent of classical ideals.

Guido delle Colonne (c.1215-c.1290), Italian jurist, writer and poet, author of the *Historia destructionis Troiae* (History of the Destruction of Troy, 1287).

Guillaume de Champeaux (c.1070-1121), French Roman Catholic bishop, theologian and philosopher.

Guillaume de Lorris (13th Century), French poet who wrote the *Roman de la Rose*, a work completed by Jean de Meun.

Guimarães, Bernardo (da Silva) (1825-1884), Brazilian poet, dramatist and novelist.

Guimarães Rosa, João (1908-1967), Brazilian novelist and short-story writer.

Guimerà, Àngel (1847-1924), Catalan dramatist and poet, especially remembered for his play *Terra baixa* (1896; English translation as *Martha of the Lowlands*, 1914).

Guiney, Louise Imogen (1861-1920), American poet and essayist.

Guinizelli, Guido (13th Century), Italian poet.

Guiraldes, Ricardo (1886-1927), Argentine novelist and poet, best known for his novel *Don Segundo Sombra* (1926).

Guiterman, Arthur (1871-1943), American poet and journalist of a humorous turn.

Guitry, Sacha (1885-1957), French dramatist and actor who won acclaim for his mastery of improvisation.

Guittone d'Arezzo (c.1235-1294), Italian poet and writer, particularly known for his amorous and sacred poetry.

Guizot, François (-Pierre-Guillaume) (1787-1874), prominent French politician and historian who espoused the cause of conservative constitutional monarchist principles.

Gumilev, Nikolai Stepanovich (1886-1921), Russian poet who was a leading figure in Acmeist circles.

Gumplowicz, Ludwig (1838-1909), influential Polish-born Austrian sociologist and legal philosopher, known for his cyclical theory of history.

Gundisalvo, Domingo (12th Century), Spanish Roman Catholic archdeacon, philosopher and linguist.

Gundulić, Ivan (1589-1638), Croatian poet and dramatist, author of the epic poem *Osman* (1626).

Gunkel, Hermann (1862-1932), noted German Old Testament scholar, a prominent advocate of form criticism.

Gunning, Susannah (c.1740-1800), English novelist and poet.

Güntekin, Reşat Nuri (1892-1956), Turkish novelist who won distinction with his *Çalikuşu* (1922; English translation as *The Autobiography of a Turkish Girl*, 1949).

Gunter, Archibald Clavering (1847-1907), English-born American novelist, best remembered for his *Mr Barnes of New York* (1887).

Günther, Johann Christian (1695-1723), German poet who was a master of lyric expression.

Gunther, John (1901-1970), American journalist and writer.

Gunzburg, David (1857-1910), Russian Jewish scholar.

Gurney, Edmund (1847-1888), English philosopher.

Gurney, Ivor (Bertie) (1890-1937), English poet and composer whose gassing during military service in World War I led to his confinement in a mental institution.

Gurney, Joseph John (1788-1847), English Quaker and theologian.

Gurwitsch, Aron (1901-1973), Lithuanian-born American philosopher.

Gustafson, Ralph Barker (1909-1995), admired Canadian poet who wrote finely-crafted verse.

Guthrie, A(lfred) B(ertram) Jr (1901-1991), American novelist and short-story writer.

Gutiérrez Nájera, Manuel (1859-1895), Mexican poet and writer.

Gutiérrez Solana, José (1886-1947), Spanish painter and writer.

Guto`r Glyn (15th Century), Welsh poet.

Gutzkow, Karl (Ferdinand) (1811-1878), influential German novelist and dramatist, one of the leading representatives of the social novel in his homeland.

Guyon, Jeanne-Marie de la Motte (née Bouvier) (1648-1717), French mystic and writer who extolled Quietism.

Gvadányi, József (1725-1801), Hungarian writer.

Gwalchmai ap Meilyr (c.1140-c.1180), Welsh poet.

Gyllenborg, Gustaf Fredrik, Count (1731-1808), Swedish poet, particularly remembered for his *Menniskjans Elände* (Misery of Man, 1762).

Gyöngyösi, István (1620-1704), Hungarian poet.

Haanpaa, Pentti (1905-1955), Finnish writer.

Habberton, John (1842-1921), American journalist and writer, best known for his popular novel *Helen`s Babies* (1876).

Haberl, Franz Xaver (1860-1910), distinguished German music scholar.

Habington, William (1605-1654), English poet, best remembered for his *Castara* (1634; 3rd edition, 1640).

Haddon, Alfred Cort (1855-1940), English anthropologist.

Hāfez (actually Mohammad Shams od-Dīn Hāfez) (c.1325-c.1389), famour Persian poet, a master of lyric expression.

Hāfiz Ibrāhīm, Muhammad (1872-1932), Egyptian poet and writer, known as the poet of the Nile.

Hāfiz-i Abrū (actually `Abd Allāh ibn Lutf Allāh ibn `Abd ar-Rashīd al-Bihdādīnī Hāfiz-i Abrū) (d. 1430), important Persian historian.

Hafner, Philipp (1731-1764), Austrian dramatist.

Hafstein, Hannes (Petursson) (1861-1922), Icelandic politician and poet.

Hagedorn, Friedrich von (1708-1754), admired German poet, author of *Versuch in poetischen Fabeln und Erzählungen* (Attempt at Poetic Fables and Tales, 1738) and *Oden und Lieder* (Odes and Songs, 3 volumes, 1742-52).

Hagedorn, Hermann (1882-1964), American writer and poet.

Haggard, Sir H(enry) Rider (1856-1925), English novelist who wrote the highly popular *King Solomon`s Mines* (1886) and *She* (1887).

Hagiwara Sakutarō (1886-1942), remarkable Japanese poet.

Hahn-Hahn, Ida, Gräfin von (1805-1880), German novelist, travel writer and poet, best known for her novel *Gräfin Faustine* (1841).

Hai ben Sherira (939-1038), Bablonian Talmudic scholar.

Haidari, Buland al- (1926-1996), Iraqi poet of Kurdish descent, an exponent of free verse.

Hake, Edward (16th Century), English poet who wrote the satirical *Newes out of Powless Churcheyarde.*

Hakim, Tawfiq al- (1898-1987), major Egyptian writer and dramatist.

Hakluyt, Richard (c.1552-1616), English geographer and writer, particularly known for *The principall Navigations, Voiages and Discoveries of the English nation . . .* (1589).

Hakuin (1685-1768), Japanese Buddhist priest, artist and writer, a leading figure in the restoration of Zen Buddhism in his homeland.

Halberstam, Hayyim ben Leibush (1793-1876), controversial Hasidic rabbi and Talmudic scholar.

Haldane, Elizabeth Sanderson (1862-1937), Scottish social welfare worker, reformer, writer and translator; sister of John Scott Haldane and Richard Burdon Haldane.

Haldane, J(ohn) B(urdon) S(anderson) (1892-1964), English-born Indian scientist and writer of Scottish descent; son of John Scott Haldane.

Haldane, John Scott (1860-1936), Scottish physiologist and philosopher; brother of Elizabeth Sanderson Haldane and Richard Burdon Haldane, and father of J(ohn) B(urdon) S(anderson) Haldane.

Haldane, Richard Burdon, 1st Viscount (1856-1928), Scottish politician and philosopher; brother of Elizabeth Sanderson Haldane and John Scott Haldane.

Hale, Edward Everett (1822-1909), American clergyman and writer, author of the famous story "The Man Without a Country" (1863); brother of Lucretia Peabody Hale and grandfather of Nancy Hale.

Hale, Horatio (Emmons) (1817-1896), influential American anthropologist who wrote the major study *The Iroquois Book of Rites* (1883).

Hale, Lucretia Peabody (1820-1900), American writer, author of *The Peterkin Papers* (1880) and *The Last of the Peterkins, with Others of Their Kin* (1886); sister of Edward Everett Hale.

Hale, Sir Matthew (1609-1676), eminent English scholar, an authority on the development of English common law.

Hale, Nancy (1908-1988), American novelist and short-story writer; granddaughter of Edward Everett Hale.

Hale, Sarah Josepha (Buell) (1788-1879), American writer, dramatist and poet, best known for her children`s poem *Mary Had a Little Lamb* (1830).

Halévy, Élie (1870-1937), French historian, author of *Histoire du peuple anglais au XIX siècle* (3 volumes, 1913-23; English translation as *A History of the English People in the Nineteenth Century*, 1949-51).

Halévy, Leon (actually Leon Levi) (1802-1883), French poet, novelist, historian and translator.

Haley, Alex (Palmer) (1921-1992), American writer, best remembered for the popular chronicle *Roots* (1976).

Haliburton, Hugh (actually James Logie Robertson) (1846-1922), Scottish poet and essayist.

Haliburton, Thomas Chandler (1796-1865), Canadian writer, creator of the satirical character Sam Slick.

Halid Ziya Ushakligil (1865-1945), Turkish novelist and short-story writer whose most famous work was the novel *Ashk-i Memnu* (1900).

Halide Edib Adivar (1883-1964), Turkish feminist and novelist, especially celebrated for her novel *Ateşten gömlek* (Shirt of Fire, 1922).

Halifax, Charles Montague, 1st Earl of (1661-1715), English statesman and poet who collaborated with Matthew Prior on *The Town and Country Mouse* (1687), a parody of Dryden's *The Hind and The Panther.*

Halifax, George Savile, 1st Marquess of (1633-1695), English statesman and political writer who became known as "The Trimmer" for his neutral political stance.

Hall, Basil (1788-1844), English naval officer and traveller.

Hall, Baynard Rush (1798-1863), American Presbyterian minister and writer.

Hall or Halle, Edward (c.1498-1547), English historian, author of the important chronicle *The Union of the Two Noble and Illustre Famelies of Lancastre and Yorke* (1542).

Hall, G(ranville) Stanley (1844-1924), American psychologist, influential for his pioneering studies in child psychology and educational psychology.

Hall, James (1793-1868), American judge, banker, editor and writer who was especially admired for his works on the American frontier.

Hall, James Norman (1887-1951), American novelist, essayist and poet.

Hall, Joseph (1574-1656), English Anglican bishop, philosopher, poet and writer, author of the political satire *Virgidemairum* (A Harvest of Blows, 6 Volumes, 1597-1602).

Hall, (Marguerite) Radclyffe (1886-1943), English poet and novelist, best known for the uproar she created over the subject of lesbianism in her novel *The Well of Loneliness* (1928).

Hall, Robert (1764-1831), English Baptist minister, social reformer and writer.

Hallāj, al- (actually **Abū al-Mughīth al Husayn ibn Mansūr al Hallāj**) **(858-922)**, Persian preacher and writer of Islāmic mysticism (Sūfism); was crucified by his opponents.

Hallam, Arthur Henry (1811-1833), English poet and essayist; son of Henry Hallam.

Hallam, Henry (1777-1859), English historian; father of Arthur Henry Hallam.

Halleck, Fitz-Greene (1790-1867), American poet, best known for his satirical and Romantic verse and for his collaboration with Joseph Rodman Drake on the "Croaker Papers."

Hallgrímsson, Jónas (1807-1845), admired Icelandic poet who excelled in Romantic expression.

Hall-Stevenson, John (1718-1785), English poet , particularly known for his satirical bent.

Halliwell-Phillipps, James Orchard (actually **James Orchard Halliwell**) **(1820-1889)**, distinguished English scholar who was an authority on Shakespeare.

Halper, Albert (1904-1984), American novelist and short-story writer.

Halpine, Charles Graham (1829-1868), Irish-born American army officer who wrote a humorous account of the Civil War in *The Life and Adventures ... of Private Miles O'Reilly* (1864).

Hamadānī (actually **'Alī ibn Shihāb ad-Dīn ibn Muhammad Hamadānī**) **(1314-1385)**, Persian mystic theologian.

Hamadhānī, al- (actually **Badī' az-Zamān Abū al-Fadl Ahmad ibn al-Husayn al-Hamadānī**) **(969-1008)**, Arab writer and poet.

Hamann, Johann Georg (1730-1788), German philosopher , a leading proponent of fideism.

Hamdānī, al- (actually **Abūmuhammad al-Hasan ibn Ahmad al-Hamdānī**) **(c.893-c.945)**, Arab poet, grammarian, historian, astronomer and geographer.

Hamerling, Robert (actually **Rupert Johann Hammerling**) **(1830-1889)**, Austrian poet, dramatist and writer, esteemed for his epic poems.

Hamilton, Alexander (1755-1804), prominent American politician who, with James Madison and John Jay, collaborated on the classic essays *The Federalist* (1787-88); killed in a duel with Aaron Burr.

Hamilton, (Anthony Walter) Patrick (1904-1962), English dramatist and novelist.

Hamilton, Charles Harold St John (1876-1961), English writer of numerous books for boys.

Hamilton, William (c.1665-1751), Scottish poet who was known as William Hamilton of Gilbertfield.

Hamilton, William (1704-1754), Scottish Jacobite patriot and poet who was known as William Hamilton of Bangour.

Hamilton, Sir William, Baronet (1788-1856), Scottish philosopher and educator.

Hamilton, Sir William Rowan (1805-1865), notable English mathematician and amateur poet.

Hammer-Purgstall, Joseph Freiherr von (1774-1856), Austrian diplomat and writer.

Hammett, Samuel Adams (1816-1865), American writer of frontier humour who used the name Philip Paxton.

Hammett, (Samuel) Dashiell (1894-1961), American writer, creator of the hard-boiled genre of detective fiction.

Hammon, Jupiter (c.1720-c.1800), American slave poet of religious verse.

Hamsun, Knut (actually **Knut Petersen**) **(1859-1952)**, prominent Norweigan novelist, poet and dramatist whose support of the Nazi occupation of his homeland earned him the title of traitor and imprisonment in his old age; won the Nobel Prize for Literature (1920).

Hanley, James (1901-1985), Irish novelist, short-story writer and dramatist.

Hanotaux, (Albert-Auguste-) Gabriel (1853-1944), French politician, diplomat and historian.

Hansberry, Lorraine (1930-1965), American dramatist whose *A Raisin in the Sun* (1959) was the first play by a black woman produced on Broadway.

Hansen, Martin (Jens) Alfred (1909-1955), Danish novelist.

Hanslick, Eduard (1825-1904), famous Austrian music critic of Czech descent, known for his withering criticism and defense of conservative ideals.

Hansson, Ola (1860-1925), Swedish poet, writer and critic.

Han Yong-un (1879-1944), Korean Buddhist priest, political leader and poet who was also known as Manhae, author of the fine poetry collection *Nimuich'immuk* (the Silence of the Lover).

Han Yü (768-824), great Chinese writer and poet who was also known as Han Wen-Kung and whose works presaged Neo-Confucianism.

Hapgood, Hutchins (1869-1944), American journalist and writer; brother of Norman Hapgood.

Hapgood, Norman (1868-1937), American editor and writer; brother of Hutchins Hapgood.

Harben, William Nathaniel (1858-1919), American novelist and short-story writer.

Har Dayal (1884-1939), Indian revolutionary leader and scholar.

Harden, Maximilian Felix Ernst (actually **Felix Ernst Witkowski) (1861-1927),** German political journalist of extreme nationalist, and then radical socialist, views.

Hardouin, Jean (1646-1729), French Jesuit scholar.

Hardy, Alexandre (c.1572-c.1632), French dramatist and actor.

Hardy, Arthur Sherburne (1847-1930), American novelist, short-story writer and poet.

Hardy, Thomas (1840-1928), distinguished English novelist, poet and dramatist, particularly admired for his series of "Wessex" novels.

Hardyng, John (1378-c.1465), English writer who wrote the verse volume *The Chronicle of John Hardyng* (1440-57).

Hare, Augustus William (1792-1834), English biographer and travel writer; brother of Julius Charles Hare.

Hare, Julius Charles (1795-1855), English writer and translator; brother of Augustus William Hare.

Harington, Sir John (1561-1612), English courtier, writer, poet and translator who became well known for his wit.

Harīrī, al- (actually **Abū Muhammed al-Qāsim ibn 'Alī al-Harīrī) (1054-1122),** Arab scholar and government official who wrote the famous collection of tales the *Maqamat* (English translation as *The Assemblies of al-Harīrī,* 1867, 1898).

Harishchandra (1850-1885), important Indian poet, dramatist, journalist and critic who was also known as Bharatendu, often hailed as the father of modern Hindi.

Harizi, Judah ben Soloman (c. 1170-c.1235), Spanish Hebrew poet and translator.

Harland, Henry (1861-1905), American novelist and short-story writer.

Harnack, Adolf (Karl Gustav) von (1851-1930), eminent German church historian and theologian.

Harper, Edith Alice Mary (1884-1947), English poet who wrote under the name Anna Wickham.

Harper, Francis Ellen Watkins (1825-1911), American poet and writer who championed the cause of her black compatriots.

Harper, William Rainey (1856-1906), American scholar and educator who wrote studies on Semitic languages and the Bible.

Harpocration, Valerius (2nd Century), Greek grammarian.

Harpur, Charles (1813-1868), Australian poet.

Harrington or Harington, James (1611-1677), English political philosopher, best known for *The Commonwealth of Oceana* (1656).

Harriot or Hariot, Thomas (1560-1621), English mathematician and astronomer, author of *A briefe and True Report of the New Found Land of Virginia* (1588).

Harris, Alexander (1805-1874), English writer, best known for his *Settlers and Convicts, or, Recollections of Sixteen Years' Labour in the Australian Backwoods* (1847).

Harris, Benjamin (flourished 1673-1716), English bookseller and writer, author of *The Protestant Tutor* (1679; new edition as *The New England Primer,* c.1690) and publisher of the first American newspaper (1690), which was suppressed by the Boston authorities after one edition.

Harris, Frank (1856-1931), Irish journalist and writer, best known for his candid autobiography *My Life and Loves* (3 volumes, 1923-27).

Harris, George Washington (1814-1869), American writer who was known for his humorous tales.

Harris, Joel Chandler (1848-1908), American writer, creator of the famous Uncle Remus.

Harris, John (1820-1884), English poet whose works reflected his love of Cornish landscapes.

Harris, Maxwell Henley (1921-1995), Australian poet, editor and publisher.

Harris, Thomas Lake (1823-1906), English-born American poet of a mystical turn.

Harris, William Torrey (1835-1909), American educator, philosopher and lexicographer.

Harrison, Constance Cary (1843-1920), American novelist, short-story writer and essayist.

Harrison, Frederic (1831-1923), English writer.

Harrison, Henry Sydnor (1880-1930), American novelist, author of *Queed* (1911) and *V. V.'s Eyes* (1913).

Harrison, William (1534-1593), English historian, especially remembered for his *Description of England* (1577).

Harry or Henry the Minstrel (15th Century), Scottish poet, author of *The Acts and Deeds of the Illustrious and Valiant Champion Sir William Wallace, Knight of Elderslie* (1488), a historical romance in verse.

Harsdörfer, Georg Philipp (1607-1658), German poet and theorist.

Hart, Frances Noyes (1890-1943), American writer, best known for her detective novels.

Hart, Heinrich (1855-1906), German critic, poet, short-story writer and dramatist; brother of Julius Hart.

Hart, Joseph (1798-1855), American lawyer, journalist and writer.

Hart, Julius (1859-1930), German critic, poet, short-story writer and dramatist; brother of Heinrich Hart.

Hart, Moss (1904-1961), American dramatist who collaborated with George S Kaufman on the notably successful plays *You Can't Take It With You* (1936) and *The Man Who Came To Dinner* (1939).

Harte, (Francis) Bret(t) (1836-1902), American poet, editor and short-story writer.

Hartleben, Otto Erich (1864-1905), German dramatist, poet and short-story writer.

Hartley, David (1705-1757), English physician and philosopher, author of *Observations on Man, His Frame, His Duty, and His Expectations* (2 volumes, 1749).

Hartley, L(eslie) P(oles) (1895-1972), English novelist, short-story writer and critic.

Hartlib, Samuel (c.1600-1662), German-born English educator, reformer and writer, particularly known for his utopian treatise *Macaria* (1641).

Hartmann, (Carl) Sadakichi (1869-1944), American art critic, writer, dramatist and poet of German-Japanese descent.

Hartmann, (Karl Robert) Eduard von (1842-1906), German philosopher, author of *Die Philosophie des Unbewussten* (3 volumes, 1870; English translation as *The Philosophy of the Unconscious,* 1884).

Hartmann, Nicolai (1882-1950), Latvian-born German philosopher who wrote *Ethik* (1926; English translation as *Ehtics,* 3 volumes, 1932), *Die Philosophie des deutschen Idealismus* (The Philosophy of German Idealism, 2 volumes, 1923, 1929) and *Neue Wege der Ontologie* (1942; English translation as *New Ways of Ontology,* 1953).

Hartmann von Aue (c.1170-1215), German poet, admired for his *Der arme Heinrich.*

Hartzenbusch, Juan Eugenio (1806-1880), Spanish dramatist, poet and editor.

Harvey, Gabriel (c.1545-1630), learned English writer, poet and university don.

Harvey, Sir (Henry) Paul (1869-1948), English literary scholar and diplomat.

Harvey, William Hope (1851-1936), American writer who wrote under the name Coin Harvey as an advocate of bimetallism.

Harwood, Edward (1729-1794), English biblical scholar.

Hasan of Delhi (d.1328), Persian poet.

Haşdeu, Bogdan Petriceicu (1836-1907), Romanian language and historical scholar.

Hašek, Jaroslav (1883-1923), Czech writer and poet, best remembered for his famous unfinished novel series *Osudy dobrého vojáka Švejka za světové války* (4 volumes, 1920-23; English translation as *The Good Soldier Schweik,* 1930).

Hasenclever, Walter (1890-1940), German dramatist and poet who espoused Expressionism; a pacifist, he commited suicide while confined in a French internment camp.

Hashar, Agha (1876-1935), Parsi dramatist.

Haskins, Charles Homer (1870-1937), distinguished American medieval scholar, author of the important study *Norman Institutions* (1918).

Hassall, Christopher Vernon (1912-1963), English poet, dramatist, librettist and biographer.

Hassān ibn Thābit (c.563-c.674), Arab poet who was known for his defense of the Prophet Muhammad.

Hasselt, André-Henri-Constant van (1806-1874), notable Dutch-born Belgian poet, especially esteemed for his epic *Les Quatre Incarnations du Christ* (1863; revised edition 1867).

Hatano Seiichi (1877-1950), Japanese scholar who wrote on Christianity and Western philosophy.

Hauch, Johannes Carsten (1790-1872), Danish poet, dramatist and novelist.

Hauff, Wilhelm (1802-1827), German poet and writer whose fairy stories became highly popular.

Haughton, William (c.1575-1605), English dramatist.

Haupt, Moritz (1808-1874), German philologist.

Hauptmann, Gerhart (1862-1946), eminent German dramatist and novelist; won the Nobel Prize for Literature (1912).

Haushofer, Karl (Ernst) (1869-1946), German army officer who espoused geopolitics in various writings; commited suicide.

Häusser, Ludwig (1818-1867), German journalist and historian.

Havighurst, Walter (Edwin) (1901-1994), American writer.

Havlíček, Karel (1821-1856), Czech journalist, writer and poet who excelled in satirical effusions.

Hawes, Stephen (c.1475-c.1525), English poet, author of *The Passetyme of Pleasure* (1509).

Hawker, R(obert) S(tephen) (1803-1875), English poet, remembered for his ballads.

Hawkes, John (Clendennin Burne Jr) (1925-1998), American novelist of the avant-garde.

Hawkesworth, John (c.1715-1773), English writer, dramatist and poet.

Hawkins, Sir John (1719-1789), notable English music scholar, author of *A General History of the Science and Practice of Music* (5 volumes, 1776).

Hawkins or **Hawkyns, Sir Richard (c. 1560-1622)**, English seaman who wrote an account of his adventures in *Observations in His Voyage into the South Sea* (1622).

Hawthorne, Julian (1846-1934), American writer; son of Nathaniel Hawthorne.

Hawthorne, Nathaniel (1804-1864), renowned American novelist and short-story writer whose masterpiece was the novel *The Scarlet Letter* (1850); father of Julian Hawthorne.

Hay, Sir Gilbert (15th Century), Scottish priest, translator and poet who was also known as Sir Gilbert of the Haye.

Hay, John (Milton) (1838-1905), American diplomat, writer and poet who collaborated with John Nicolay on a major biography of Abraham Lincoln (10 volumes, 1890).

Hayashi Fumiko (actually **Miyata Fumiko**) **(1904-1951)**, Japanese novelist.

Hayashi Razan (actually **Hayashi Nobukatsu**) **(1583-1657)**, important Japanese neo-Confucion scholar who became known for his historical writings and poems.

Hayashi Shihei (1738-1793), Japanese military scholar.

Hayden, Robert (1913-1980), American poet.

Haydon, Benjamin Robert (1786-1846), English painter and writer, author of an outstanding autobiography (published 1847).

Hayek, Friedrich (August) von (1899-1992), German economist; won the Nobel Prize for Economic Science (1974).

Hayes, Alfred (1911-1985), English-born American writer.

Hayley, William (1754-1820), English poet, dramatist, essayist and biographer.

Hayne, Paul Hamilton (1830-1886), esteemed American poet, particularly admired for his collection *Legends and Lyrics* (1872).

Hayward, Abraham (1801-1884), English essayist and biographer.

Hayward, Sir John (c.1564-1627), English historian.

Haywood, Eliza (née Fowler) (c.1693-1756), English novelist who wrote a series of works of a scandalous nature.

Hazard, Paul Gustave Marie Camille (1878-1944), French literary historian.

Hazlitt, William (1778-1830), notable English essayist, celebrated for his *Table Talk* (1821) and *The Plain Speaker* (1826).

Head, Bessie (actually **Bessie Amelia Emery**) **(1937-1986)**, South African-born Botswanan novelist and short-story writer.

Headlam, Arthur Cayley (1862-1947), English Anglican bishop and biblical scholar, author of the *Doctrine of the Church and Christian Reunion* (1920).

Hearn, Lafcadio (1850-1904), Irish-Greek writer, translator and teacher.

Hearne, Thomas (1678-1735), English historian and antiquarian.

Heath, James Ewell (1792-1862), American writer.

Heavysege, Charles (1816-1876), English-born Canadian poet and writer.

Hebbel, (Christian) Friedrich (1813-1863), noted German dramatist and poet whose masterpiece was the play *Gyges und sein Ring* (Gyges and His Ring, 1854).

Heber, Reginald (1773-1826), English churchman, poet, hymnist and translator.

Hébert, Jacques-René (1757-1794), prominent French political journalist and advocate of the sans-culottes during the Revolution; was guillotined.

Hebreo, León (actually **Judah Abrabanel**) **(c.1460-c.1521)**, Spanish philosopher and physician, author of the *Dialoghi di amore*.

Hecataeus of Miltus (6th-5th Century B.C.), Greek writer.

Hecht, Ben (1894-1964), American novelist, dramatist and screenwriter.

Heckewelder, John Gottlieb Ernestus (1743-1823), English-born American Moravian missionary to the Indians who wrote two accounts of his activities (1819, 1820).

Hedāyat, Sādeq (1903-1951), outstanding Persian writer and scholar; commited suicide.

Hedge, Frederic Henry (1805-1890), American Unitarian minister, writer and translator.

Hegel, Georg Wilhelm Friedrich (1770-1831), great German philosopher, author of the *Phänomenologie des Geistes* (1807; English translation as *The Phenomenology of Mind*, 1931), *Wissenschaft der Logik* (2 volumes, 1812, 1816; English translation as the *Science of Logic*, 1969),

Encyklopädie der philosophischen Wissenschaften im Grundrisse (Encyclopaedia of the Philosophical Sciences in Outline, 1817; partial English translation, 1970) and *Grundlinien der Philosophie des Rechts* (1821; English translation as *The Philosophy of Right*, 1942).

Hegesippus, Saint (2nd Century), Greek Christian historian who wrote *The Memoirs* (c.180).

Heggen, Thomas (Orlo) (1919-1949), American writer, best remembered for his novel *Mister Roberts* (1946).

Heiberg, Gunnar (1857-1929), eminent Norweigan dramatist who excelled as an Expressionist.

Heiberg, Johan Ludvig (1791-1860), major Danish dramatist, poet, historian and critic; son of Peter Andreas Heiberg.

Heiberg, Peter Andreas (1758-1841), Dansih political radical, poet and dramatist; father of Johan Ludvig Heiberg.

Heidegger, Johann Heinrich (1633-1698), Swiss Reformed theologian and educator whose *Formula Consensus Helvetici* (Swiss Formula of Concord, 1675) called for a reconciliation between Swiss Reformed and Lutheran adherents.

Heidegger, Martin (1889-1976), famous German philosopher who was a leading figure in the development of Existentialism, author of the influential *Sein und Zeit* (1927; English translation as *Being and Time*, 1962).

Heidenstam, (Carl Gustaf) Verner von (1859-1940), prominent Swedish poet and writer; won the Nobel Prize for Literature (1916).

Heijermans, Herman (1864-1924), Dutch writer and dramatist.

Heiler, (Johann) Friedrich (1892-1967), German religious writer, author of *Das Gebet* (1918; abridged English translation as *Prayer*, 1932), *Der Katholizismus* (1923), *Urkirche und Ostkirche*, 1937; augmented edition as *Die Ostkirchen*, 1971) and *Erscheinungsformen und Wesen der Religion* (1961).

Heine, Heinrich (1797-1856), famous German poet, essayist and champion of democratic ideals, especially renowned for his poetry collections *Buch der Lieder* (Book of Songs, 1827) and *Neue Gedichte* (New Poems, 1844).

Heinlein, Robert A(nson) (1907-1988), American writer, a master of science fiction.

Heinrich von Melk (12th Century), German poet, the first to write in a satirical vein in such works as *Von des Tôdes gehugede* (Remembrance of Death or Momento Mori, c.1150-60) and *Vom Priesterleben* (About Priestly Life).

Heinrich von Morungen (d.1222), German Minnesinger who espoused the cause of love in his poetry.

Heinse, Johann Jakob Wilhelm (1746-1803), German novelist and art critic, especially esteemed for his novels *Ardinghello und die glückseligen Inseln* (Ardinghell and the Blessed Islands, 1787) and *Hildegard von Hohenthal* (1795-96).

Heinsius or Heins, Daniël (1580-1655), Dutch scholar and poet.

Heinsius, Nicolaus (1602-1681), Dutch Latinist and philologist.

Heisenberg, Werner (Karl) (1901-1976), eminent German physicist and philosopher who discovered the uncertainty principle in quantum mechanics; won the Nobel Prize for Physics (1932).

Heissenbüttel, Helmut (1921-1996), German novelist and poet of avant-garde persuasion.

Hektorović, Petar (1487-1572), Dalmatian poet.

Helgesen, Paul (c.1485-c.1535), Danish Carmelite monk, humanist and Roman Catholic apologist.

Heliodorus (3rd Century), Greek novelist who wrote the *Aethiopica*.

Hellanicus (5th Century B.C.), Greek historian.

Hellens, Franz (actually Frédéric van Ermengem) (1881-1972), Belgian novelist and poet.

Heller, Hermann (1891-1933), German political scientist whose works delineated the central role of the state in society but who nevertheless opposed Nazism.

Heller, Yom Tov Lipmann ben Nathan ha-Levi ben Wallerstein (1579-1654), German Jewish scholar.

Hellman, Lillian (Florence) (1905-1984), American dramatist whose output reflected her deep attachments as an unreconstructed leftist.

Hellstrom, (Erik) Gustaf (1882-1953), Swedish journalist, novelist and critic.

Helmold of Bosau (c.1120-c.1178), German Roman Catholic priest and historian.

Helper, Hinton Rowan (1829-1909), American writer who, although a Southerner, attacked slavery in his *The Impending Crisis of the South; How to Meet It* (1857) but later wrote racist tracts advocating the deportation of blacks.

Helvétius, Claude-Adrien (1715-1771), prominent French philosopher who was a proponent of hedonism in his controversial *De l'esprit* (On the Mind, 1758).

Hélyot, Hippolyte (actually Pierre Hélyot) (1660-1716), French Franciscan monk and historian who wrote the important *Histoire des ordres monastiques, religieux et militaires, et des congrégations séculières de l'un et de l'autre sexe* (8 volumes, 1714-19; completed by Père Maximilien Bullot).

Hemacandra (1088-1172), celebrated Indian writer and Jain sage who was also known as Hemacandra Sūri, Candradeva, Cangadeva and Somacandra.

Hemans, Felicia Dorothea (née Browne) (1793-1835), English poet, particularly known for her *Casabianca*.

Hemingway, Ernest (Miller) (1899-1961), celebrated American novelist, short-story writer and poet, greatly admired for such novels as *The Sun Also Rises* (1926), *A Farewell to Arms* (1929), *For Whom the Bell Tolls* (1940) and *The Old man and the Sea* (1952); won the Nobel Prize for Literature (1954); commited suicide.

Hémon, Louis (1880-1913), French writer, author of the novel *Maria Chapdelaine* (published 1915); died in a train accident.

Hemsterhuis, Franciscus (1721-1790), Dutch philosopher and aesthetician.

Henderick, Burton J(esse) (1870-1949), American journalist and historian.

Henderson, Alexander (c.1583-1646), Scottish Presbyterian clergyman and writer, a champion of the presbyterian form of church government and an opponent of Charles I.

Henderson, Alice Corbin (1881-1949), American poet.

Hengstenberg, Ernst Wilhelm (1802-1869), German Lutheran theologian, known as a defender of Christian orthodoxy.

Henley, William Ernest (1849-1903), prominent English critic, editor, poet and dramatist.

Henne am Rhyn, Otto (1828-1914), Swiss journalist and historian, author of the massive *Allgemeine Kulturgeschichte* (Universal History of Civilization, 8 volumes, 1877-1908).

Henry, O (actually **William Sidney Porter) (1862-1910),** popular American short-story writer.

Henry of Ghent (c.1217-1293), celebrated Belgian philosopher and theologian who was known as Doctor Solemnis and as one of the major opponents of St Thomas Aquinas.

Henry of Huntingdon (c.1084-1155), English archdeacon who compiled the *Historia Anglorum.*

Henryson, Robert (c.1425-c.1508), Scottish poet, particularly known for *The Testament of Cresseid.*

Henson, Herbert Hensley (1863-1947), English Anglican bishop and writer who was known for his liberal views.

Henty, George Alfred (1832-1902), English writer.

Hentz, Caroline Lee (1800-1856), American novelist and short-story writer; wife of Nicolas Marcellus Hentz.

Hentz, Nicolas Marcellus (1797-1856), French-born American novelist; husband of Caroline Lee Hentz.

Heracleitus (c.540-c.480 B.C.) Greek philosopher.

Herbart, Johann Friedrich (1776-1841), German philosopher and educator.

Herbert, Sir A(lan) P(atrick) (1890-1971), English politician, novelist, dramatist and poet.

Herbert, George (1593-1633), admired English poet and churchman, one of the finest metaphysical poets of devotion; brother of Edward Herbert, 1st Baron Herbert of Cherbury.

Herbert, Henry William (1807-1858), English-born American writer.

Herbert, Zbigniew (1924-1998), Polish poet and essayist.

Herbert of Cherbury, Edward Herbert, 1st Baron (1582-1648), noted English courtier, soldier, diplomat, philosopher, historian and poet, called the father of English Deism; brother of George Herbert.

Herbst, Josephine (Frey) (1892-1969), American writer.

Herculano de Carvalho e Araújo, Alexandre (1810-1877), eminent Portuguese historian, author of the *História de Portugal* (History of Portugal 4 volumes, 1846-53).

Herczeg, Ferenc (1863-1954), Hungarian novelist and dramatist.

Herder, Johann Gottfried von (1744-1803), influential German critic, theologian, philosopher and poet.

Heredia, José María (1803-1839), Cuban poet; cousin of José María de Heredia.

Heredia, José María de (1842-1905), Cuban-born French poet, especially esteemed for his sonnets; cousin of José María Heredia.

Herford, Oliver (1863-1935), English-born American writer,poet, dramatist and illustrator.

Hergenröther, Joseph (1824-1890), German theologian and church historian.

Hergesheimer, Joseph (1880-1954), American novelist, short-story writer and biographer, particularly remembered for his novels *The Three Black Pennys* (1917), *Java Head* (1919), and *Balisand* (1924).

Herlihy, James Leo (1927-1993), American novelist and dramatist.

Herman de Valenciennes (12th Century), French priest, writer and poet.

Hermann, Eduard (1869-1950), German linguist.

Hermann, (Johann) Gottfried (Jakob) (1772-1848), German classical scholar.

Hermann von Reichenau (1013-1054), Swabian chronicler, poet, composer, astronomer and mathematician who was also known as Hermmanus Contractus and Hermann the Lame.

Hermes, Georg (1775-1831), German Roman Catholic theologian who was a proponent of rational necessity as a basis of Christian faith.

Hermesianax (c.300-c.250 B.C.), Greek poet, admired for his elegies.

Hernández, José (1834-1886), Argentine poet, a master of gaucho poetry.

Herndon, William Henry (1818-1891), American lawyer, best remembered for his partnership in law with Abraham Lincoln, author with Jesse W Weik of *Herndon's Lincoln: The True Story of a Great Life* (3 volumes, 1889).

Herne, James A (actually **James Ahern) (1839-1901),** American dramatist, best known for his play *Shore Acres* (1892).

Herodas or **Herondas (3rd Century B.C.),** Greek poet who wrote mimes, a short verse form depicting the life of the lowly.

Herodes Atticus (actually **Lucius Vibullius Hipparchus Tiberius Claudius Atticus Herodes) (c.101-177),** famous Greek orator and writer.

Herodian (3rd Century), Syrian historian who wrote on the Roman Empire.

Herodianus, Aelius (2nd Century), Greek grammarian and writer who was also known as Herodianus Technicus.

Herodotus (c.484-c.425 B.C.), illustrious Greek historian, known as the father of history.

Héroët, Antoine (c.1492-1568), Fernch poet and Roman Catholic bishop.

Herrera, Fernando de (c.1534-1597), notable Spanish poet, historian and translator who earned the name El Divino.

Herrera y Reissig, Julio (1875-1910), Uruguayan poet.

Herrera y Tordesillas, Antonio de (1559-1625), Spanish historian.

Herrick, Robert (1591-1674), admired English poet and cleric, a master of lyric expression.

Herrick, Robert (1868-1938), American novelist and short-story writer.

Herriot, Édouard (1872-1957), prominent French politician and writer.

Herrmann, (Johann) Wilhelm (1846-1922), German protestant theologian, author of *Der Verkehr des Christen mit Gott* (1886; English translation as *The Communion of the Christian With God,* 1895) and *Ethik* (1901).

Hersey, John (Richard) (1914-1993), American novelist, short-story writer and essayist.

Herskovits, Melville J(ean) (1895-1963), American anthropologist.

Hertling, Georg (Friedrich), Graf von (1843-1919), German philosopher and statesman.

Hertz, Henrik (actually **Heyman Hertz) (1797-1870),** Danish poet and dramatist.

Hertz, Joseph Herman (1872-1946), Hungarian-born English rabbi, Zionist and writer, author of *A Book of Jewish Thoughts* (1920).

Hervey, James (1714-1758), English clergyman and poet.

Hervey of Ickworth, John Hervey, Baron (1696-1743), English politician who wrote the valuable *Memoirs of the Reign of George the Second* (published 1848).

Hervieu, Paul-Ernest (1857-1915), French novelist, short-story writer and dramatist.

Herwegh, Georg (1817-1875), German poet who played an active role in the revolutionary events of 1848.

Herzen, Alexander (Ivanovich) (1812-1870), influential Russian journalist and political thinker who espoused socialism as the path to freedom in his homeland.

Herzog, Isaac Halevi (1888-1959), Polish-born Israeli rabbi and scholar.

Herzog, Johann Jakob (1805-1882), German Protestant theologian, editor of the *Realencyklopädie für protestantische Theologie und Kirche* (22 volumes, 1854-68; abridged English edition by Philip Schaff, 3 volumes, 1882-84).

Heschel, Abraham Joshua (1907-1972), German-born American Jewish theologian and philosopher.

Hesiod, (8th Century B.C.), Greek poet, known for his didactic *Theogony* and *Works and Days*.

Hess, Moses (actually **Moritz Hess) (1812-1875),** German journalist, socialist and Zionist who influenced the thought of Marx and Engels.

Hesse, Hermann (1877-1962), eminent German-born Swiss novelist and poet who became widely known for such novels as *Demian* (1919), *Der Steppenwolf* (1927), *Narziss und Goldmund* (1930; English translation as *Death and the Lover,* 1932), *Die Morgenlandfahrt* (1932; English translation as *Journey to the East,* 1956) and *Das Glasperlenspied* (1943; English translation as *Magister Ludi,* 1949); won the Nobel Prize for Literature (1946).

Hesychius of Alexandria (5th Century), Greek lexicographer.

Hesychius of Jerusalem, Saint (d. c.450), Eastern Orthodox theologian and biblical commentator.

Hesychius of Miletus (6th Century), Byzantine historian and biographer.

Hewat, Alexander (c. 1745-1829), Scottish-born American Presbyterian clergyman who wrote *An Historical Account of the Rise and Progress of the Colonies of South Carolina and Georgia* (2 volumes, 1779).

Hewlett, Maurice Henry (1861-1923), English poet, novelist and essayist, author of the poem *The Song of the Plow* (1916).

Heyer, Georgette (1902-1974), English novelist and detective-story writer.

Heylyn, Peter (1600-1662), English Anglican polemicist and historian.

Heym, Georg (1887-1912), German poet of the Expressionist school.

Heyne, Christian Gottlob (1729-1812), German philologist.

Heyse, Paul Johann Ludwig von (1830-1914), notable German novelist and short-story writer; won the Nobel Prize for Literature (1910).

Heyward, (Edwin) Dubose (1885-1940), American novelist, dramatist and poet who collaborated with his wife Dorothy Heyward (1890-1961) on the novel *Porgy* (1925), later made famous as Gershwin's opera *Porgy and Bess* (1935).

Heywood, Jasper (1535-1598), English Jesuit priest , poet and translator.

Heywood, John (c.1497-1580), English dramatist and poet, especially known for his satirical verse allegory *The Spider and the Flie* (1556).

Heywood, Thomas (c.1574-1641), English actor and dramatist.

Hiärne, Urban (1641-1724), Swedish dramatist and poet.

Hibbert, Eleanor Alice (c.1906-1993), prolific and popular English romance novelist who wrote under various pseudonyms, including Victoria Holt and Jean Plaidy.

Hichens, Robert Smythe (1864-1950), English novelist, especially remembered for his satirical *The Green Carnation* (1894).

Hickes, George (1642-1715), noted English scholar and non-juring divine, an authority on Anglo-Saxon subjects.

Hicks, Elias (1748-1830), American Quaker preacher and Abolitionist, author of *Observations on the Slavery of the Africans and Their Descendants* (1811).

Hicks, Granville (1901-1982), American novelist and critic.

Hierocles (6th Century), Byzantine grammarian, author of the valuable *Synekdemos.*

Hierocles of Alexandria (5th Century), Greek philosopher.

Higden or Higdon, Ranulf (c.1280-1364), English monk and writer, best known for his *Polychronicon* (c.1350).

Higgins, Alexander Pearce (1865-1935), English lawyer and writer, especially remembered for his works on international and maritime law and history.

Higgins, Frederick Robert (1896-1941), Irish poet.

Higgins, Matthew James (1810-1868), English journalist and essayist who was known as Jacob Omnium.

Higginson, Francis (1586-1630), English-born American nonconformist clergyman, author of the journal *New-Englands Plantation* (1630; first complete edition, 1891).

Highsmith, Patricia (1921-1995), American mystery novelist and short-story writer.

Higuchi Ichiyō (actually Higuchi Natsuko) (1872-1896), talented Japanese novelist and poet whose finest work was his novel *Takekurabe* (1895; English translation as *Growing Up*, 1956).

Hikmet, Nazim (1902-1963), significant Turkish poet of a Marxist persuasion, also known as Nazim Hikmet Ran.

Hilarius (12th Century), French poet and scholar who wrote in Latin and French.

Hildegard von Bingen (1098-1179), famous German abbess, mystic, composer and poet.

Hildreth, Richard (1807-1865), American jurist, writer and historian, particularly known for his novel *The Slave, or, Memoirs of Archy Moore* (1836) and his *History of the United States* (6 volumes, 1849-52).

Hill, Aaron (1685-1750), English poet, dramatist and essayist.

Hill G(eorge) B(irkbeck Norman) (1835-1903), English biographer and editor.

Hill, John (c.1716-1776), English writer and botanist.

Hill, Rowland (1744-1833), English evangelist and writer.

Hillebrand, Karl (1829-1884), German historian and essayist.

Hillel (flourished 1st Century B.C.-1st Century A.D.), celebrated Jewish sage and Talmudic scholar.

Hillel ben Samuel (c.1220-c.1295), Jewish physician, Talmudic scholar and philosopher.

Hillhouse, James Abraham (1789-1841), American poet, author of romantic verse dramas.

Hilli, al- (actually **Jamāl ad-Dīn Hasan Ibn Yūsuf Ibn 'Alī Ibn Muthahhar al-Hilli**) **(1250-1325),** Arab theologian who was known for his valuable writings on Shi'ite.

Hillyer, Robert (Silliman) (1895-1961), American poet, novelist and critic.

Hilton, James (1900-1954), English novelist, author of the highly successful *Lost Horizon* (1933), *Goodbye Mr Chips* (1934) and *Random Harvest* (1941).

Hilton, Walter (c.1340-1396), famous English mystic, author of *The Scale of Perfection* and the *Mixed Life.*

Himerius (c.315-c.386), Greek rhetorician.

Himes, Chester (Bomar) (1909-1984), American novelist and short-story writer.

Hincmar of Reims (c.806-882), noted French Roman Catholic archbishop, canon lawyer and theologian.

Hindus, Maurice (Gerschon) (1891-1969), Russian-born American writer.

Hinman, Charlton (1911-1977), English scholar, an authority on Shakespeare's texts.

Hippel, Theodor Gottlieb von (1741-1796), German writer.

Hippias of Elis (5th Century B.C.), Greek philosopher who wrote on various subjects, discoverer of the quadratrix in mathematics.

Hippocrates (c.460-c.377 B.C.), celebrated Greek physician, revered as the father of medicine.

Hippolytus of Rome, Saint (c.170-c.235), Roman Catholic theologian, first antipope and martyr, author of *Philosophumena* (Refutation of All Heresies).

Hipponax (6th Century B.C.), Greek poet.

Hiraga Gennai (c.1728-1779), Japanese philosopher.

Hirsch, Samson Raphael (1808-1888), important German Jewish theologian, founder of Trennungsorthodoxie (Separatist Orthodoxy) or Neo-Orthodoxy.

Hirsch, Samuel (1815-1889), German-born American Jewish rabbi and philosopher, a proponent of radical Reform Judaism.

Hirst, Henry Beck (1817-1874), American poet of an eccentric nature.

Hirt, Hermann (1865-1936), German linguist, author of *Indogermanische Grammatik* (Indo-European Grammar, 7 volumes, 1921-37).

Hirtius, Aulus (c.90-43 B.C.), Roman soldier and writer; died in battle.

Hishām Ibn (Muhammad) al-Kalbī (c.746-c.820), Arab scholar and poet.

Hitchcock, Enos (1744-1803), American clergyman and writer, author of the novel *Memoirs of the Bloomsgrove Family* (1790).

Hjärne, Harald Gabriel (1848-1922), Swedish historian and politician.

Hjartarson, Snorri (1906-1986), Icelandic poet.

Hobart, John Henry (1775-1830), American Episcopal bishop and writer, a defender of the orthodox religious and social views.

Hobbes, John Oliver (actually **Mrs Pearl "Mary Teresa" Craigie**) **(1867-1906),** English novelist and essayist.

Hobbes, Thomas (1588-1679), great English philosopher, author of such major works as the trilogy *De Cive* (Concerning Citizenship, 1642), *De Corpore* (Concerning Body, 1655) and *De Homine* (Concerning Man, 1658), and *Human Nature, or, The Fundamental Elements of Policie* (1650), *De Corpore Politico, or, The Elements of Law, Moral and Politick* (1650), *Leviathan, or, The Matter, Forme, and Power of a Commonwealth, Ecclesiasticall and Civil* (1651) and *The Questions Concerning Liberty, Necessity, and Chance* (1656).

Hobhouse, Leonard Trelawny (1864-1929), English sociologist and philosopher.

Hobson, John Atkinson (1858-1940), English economist and writer.

Hobson, Laura Zametkin (1900-1986), American novelist, best known for her *Gentleman's Agreement* (1947).

Hoby, Sir Thomas (1530-1566), English diplomat and translator, particularly remembered for his influential translation of Castiglione's *Il cortegiano* as *The Courtyer of Count Baldesser Castillo* (1561).

Hoccleve or **Occleve, Thomas (c.1368-c.1450),** English poet.

Hocking, William Ernest (1873-1966), American philosopher of the Idealist school.

Hodge, Charles (1797-1878), prominent American biblical scholar, author of *Systematic Theology* (3 volumes, 1871-73).

Hodgson, Ralph (Edwin) (1871-1962), English poet, best known for his *The Bull* (1913).

Hodgson, Shadworth Holoway (1832-1912), English philosopher.

Hoel, Sigurd (1890-1960), Norwegian novelist, best remembered for his *Veien til verdens ende* (Road to the Worlds End, 1933).

Hoen, Cornelius (16th Century), Dutch theologian.

Hoffman, Charles Fenno (1806-1884), American editor, writer and poet whose career was aborted by insanity in 1849.

Hoffmann, August Heinrich (1798-1874), popular German poet, historian and philologist who wrote under the name Hoffmann von Fallersleben; his *Deutschland, Deutschland über Alles* (1841) was made the National Anthem of Germany (1922).

Hoffmann, E(rnst) T(heodor) A(madeus) (actually **Ernst Theodor Wilhelm Hoffman**) **(1776-1822)**, German writer, composer, music critic and caricaturist, especially known for his collections of tales of the supernatural and fantastic in *Die Serapionsbrüder* (4 volumes, 1819-21) and *Die Lebensanischten des Katers Murr* (2 volumes, 1820, 1822).

Hoffmann, Heinrich (1809-1874), German physician and writer, known for his children's classic *Struwwelpeter* (Shock-head Peter, 1847).

Hofmannsthal, Hugo von (1874-1929), distinguished Austrian poet, dramatist and essayist who wrote the librettos for several operas by Richard Strauss.

Hoffmannswaldau, Christian Hofmann von (1617-1679), German poet and writer, remembered for his collection *Heldenbriefe* (Heroes' Letters, 1663).

Hofmeister, Sebastian (1476-1533), Swiss religious reformer.

Hogarth, David George (1862-1927), English archaeologist and diplomat.

Hogg, James (1770-1835), Scottish poet and writer who was known as the Ettrick Shepherd after his birthplace, author of the poetry collection *The Queen's Wake* (1813).

Hogg, Thomas Jefferson (1792-1862), English writer, especially known for his *The Life of Shelley* (2 volumes, 1858), the biography of his friend Percy Bysshe Shelley.

Holbach, Paul Henri Dietrich, Baron d' (actually **Paul Henri Dietrich**) **(1723-1789)**, French philosopher and encyclopedist whose *Système de la nature* (System of Nature, 1770) vigorously championed atheism and materialism.

Holberg, Ludwig, Baron (1684-1754), greatly revered Norwegian scholar and writer, duly regarded as the founder of both Norwegian and Danish letters.

Holbrook, Josiah (1788-1854), American educational reformer.

Holbrook, Stewart H(all) (1893-1964), American journalist and historian.

Holcot, Robert (d. 1349), English Dominican and writer, author of *Moralitates Historiarum*.

Holcroft, Thomas (1745-1809), English actor, dramatist, journalist and novelist, especially remembered for his *Memoirs* (published 1816).

Holder, Alfred Theophil (1840-1916), Austrian language scholar.

Hölderlin, (Johann Christian) Friedrich (1770-1843), great German poet, a master of the ode and elegy.

Holdheim, Samuel (1806-1860), German rabbi and theologian, author of the influential volume of Reform Judaism *Über die Autonomie der Rabbinen* (The Autonomy of the Rabbis).

Holinshed, Raphael (d. c.1580), English chronicler and translator, author of the popular *Chronicles of England, Scotlande and Irelande* (2 volumes, 1577).

Holland, Edwin Clifford (c.1794-1824), American poet, best remembered for his *Odes, Naval Songs, and Other Occasional Poems* (1813).

Holland, Henry Scott (1847-1918), English Anglican theologian and philosopher.

Holland, Josiah Gilbert (1819-1881), American editor, writer and poet who wrote under the name Timothy Titcomb.

Holland, Philemon (1552-1637), English translator of Greek and Latin classics.

Holland, Sir (Thomas) Erskine (1835-1926), English legal scholar who wrote the valuable *Elements of Jurisprudence* (1880).

Holland, Vyvyan Oscar Beresford (actually **Vyvyan Oscar Beresford Wilde**) **(1886-1967)**, English writer and translator; son of Oscar (Fingal O'Flahertie Wills) Wilde.

Holley, Marietta (1836-1926), American humorist who wrote under the name Josiah Allen's Wife.

Hollister, Gideon Hiram (1817-1881), American lawyer and writer.

Holme, Constance (1881-1955), English novelist.

Holmes, Abiel (1763-1837), American Congregational minister and writer, author of *The Annals of America;* father of Oliver Wendell Holmes.

Holmes, John (Clellon) (1926-1988), American poet, novelist and essayist.

Holmes, May Jane (Hawes) (1825-1907), American novelist, best known for her *Lena Rivers* (1856).

Holmes, Oliver Wendell (1809-1894), prominent American poet, writer and physician, particularly admired for his collection of poems and essays *The Autocrat of the Breakfast Table* (1858); son of Abiel Holmes and father of Oliver Wendell Holmes Jr.

Holmes, Oliver Wendell Jr (1841-1935), outstanding American jurist, legal historian and philosopher; son of Oliver Wendell Holmes.

Holmes, William Henry (1846-1933), American archaeologist and artist.

Holste, Luc (1596-1661) German classical scholar.

Holt, Edwin B(issell) (1873-1946), American psychologist and philosopher, author of *The Concept of Consciousness* (1914), *The Freudian Wish and Its Place in Ethics* (1915) and *Animal Drive and the Learning Process* (1931).

Holtby, Winifred (1898-1935), English journalist and novelist, especially admired for her novel *South Riding* (published 1936).

Holtei, Karl von (1798-1880), German actor, poet and novelist.

Hölty, Ludwig Heinrich Christoph (1748-1776), talented German poet who excelled in lyric expression.

Holtzmann, Heinrich Julius (1832-1910), German Protestant theologian.

Holub, Emil (1847-1902), Austro-Hungarian naturalist and traveller.

Holub, Miroslav (1923-1998), Czech poet, writer and immunologist.

Holz, Arnold (1863-1929), German poet, dramatist and critic.

Home, Henry, Lord Kames (1696-1782), Scottish jurist, landowner and writer, author of *Elements of Criticism* (1762) and *Sketches of the History of Man* (1774).

Home, John (1722-1808), Scottish dramatist, best remembered for his play *Douglas* (1756).

Homer (8th Century B.C.), legendary Greek poet, reputedly the author of the epics the *Iliad* and the *Odyssey,* two of the greatest masterworks of world literature.

Honda Toshiaki (1744-1821), Japanese scholar who devoted himself to the study of Western culture.

Hone, William (1780-1842), English writer and bookseller, well known for his satirical bent.

Hontheim, Johann Nikolaus von (1701-1790), German historian and theologian who, under the name Justinus Febronius, wrote the controversial *De Statu Ecclesia et Legitima Potestate Romani Pontificis* (Concerning the State of the Church and the Legitimate Power of the Roman Pope, 1763).

Hood, Thomas (1799-1845), admired English poet and editor, a master of humorous verse; father of Tom Hood.

Hood, Tom (actually Thomas Hood) (1835-1874), English novelist, poet and artist; son of Thomas Hood.

Hooft, Pieter Corneliszoon (1581-1647), renowned Dutch poet, dramatist and writer, author of the monumental *Nederlandse historien* (20 volumes, 1642).

Hook, Sidney (1902-1989), American philosopher and educator, best remembered for his fervent advocacy of democratic socialism as an alternative to totalitarianism.

Hook, Theodore Edward (1788-1841), English poet, dramatist and novelist.

Hooker, Richard (c.1554-1600), great English Anglican theologian, author of the famous treatise *Of the Laws of Ecclesiastical Polity* (5 volumes, 1593-97, Volumes 6 and 8, 1648, Volume 7, 1662).

Hooper, Johnson Jones (1815-1862), American writer, newspaper editor and lawyer, creator of the backwoods frontiersman Captain Simon Suggs.

Hooton, Earnest A(lbert) (1887-1954), American anthropologist.

Hope, Anthony (actually Sir Anthony Hope Hawkins) (1863-1933), English writer, author of the popular novel *The Prisoner of Zenda* (1894).

Hope, Laurence (actually Adela Florence née Cory Nicolson) (1865-1904), English poet.

Hope, Thomas (1769-1831), English designer and writer, a champion of the Regency style.

Hopkins, Gerard Manley (1844-1889), outstanding English poet and Jesuit priest who employed what he described as "sprung thythm" in his most notable creative efforts, among them *The Wreck of the Duetschland* (1876), *Pied Beauty* (1877) and *The Windhover* (1877).

Hopkins, Lemuel (1750-1801), American physician and poet.

Hopkins, Mark (1802-1887), American educator and philosopher.

Hopkins, Pauline (1859-1930), american writer, best remembered for her *Contending Forces: A Romance Illustrative of Negro Life North and South* (1900).

Hopkins, Samuel (1721-1803), American Congregational minister and theologian, author of *The System of Doctrines Contained in Divine Revelation* (1793).

Hopkinson, Francis (1737-1791), American statesman, writer, poet and composer; great-grandfather of Francis Hopkinson Smith.

Hopwood, Avert (1882-1929), American dramatist.

Horace (actually Quintas Horatius Flaccus) (65-8 B.C.), great Roman poet whose satires, odes and epodes stand as monuments of world literature.

Horapollon (5th Century), Greek-Egyptian writer, author of *Hieroglyphica*.

Hornbostel, Erich Moritz von (1877-1935), notable Austrian music scholar, an authority on non-European music.

Horgan, Paul (1903-1995), American writer.

Horman, William (c.1458-1535), English educator, author of *Vulgaria.*

Horne, Richard Henry (1802-1884), English poet who wrote the allegorical epic *Orion* (1843).

Horney, Karen (née Danielsen) (1885-1952), German-born American psychoanalyst, author of *New Ways in Psychoanalysis* (1939), *Our Inner Conflicts* (1945) and *Neurosis and Human Growth* (1950).

Hornung, E(rnest) W(illiam) (1866-1921), English novelist.

Horovitz, Frances (née Hooker) (1938-1983), English actress, broadcaster and poet.

Horowitz, Isaiah ben Abraham ha-Levi (c.1565-1630), Jewish rabbi, mystic and philosopher.

Horsley, John (c.1685-1732), English antiquarian, author of *Britannia Romana: Or the Roman Antiquities of Britain.*

Horsley, Samuel (1733-1806), Welsh Anglican bishop, theologian and scientist who was a defender of orthodox views.

Hort, Fenton J(ohn) A(nthony) (1828-1892), distinguished English New Testament scholar.

Hortensius, Quintus (114-50 B.C.), Roman orator, writer and poet, author of the epic on the Social War *Annales.*

Horton, George Moses (c.1798-c.1880), American poet who was born a slave but revealed a talent for writing love poems.

Hosius, Stanislaus (actually Stanislaw Hozjusz) (1504-1579), Polish Roman Catholic cardinal and theologian, author of the famous *Confessio catholicae fidei Christiana* (Christian Confession of Catholic Faith).

Hoskyns, Sir Edwyn Clement (1884-1937), English Anglican biblical scholar and theologian, especially noted for his *Fourth Gospel* (2 volumes, published 1940).

Hosmer, William H(owe) C(uyler) (1814-1877), American lawyer and poet.

Hotman, François (1524-1590), French jurist and humanist scholar who was also known as Sieur de Villiers Saint-Paul.

Hotson, Leslie (1897-1992), Canadian literary scholar.

Hough, Emerson (1857-1923), American journalist and writer.

Houghton, Richard Monckton Milnes, 1st Baron (1809-1885), English poet, writer and politician.

Houghton, (William) Stanley (1881-1913), English dramatist.

Household, Geoffrey (Edward West) (1900-1988), English novelist, especially known for his *Rogue Male* (1939) and *Rogue Justice* (1982).

Housman, A(lfred) E(dward) (1859-1936), distinguished English poet and scholar, admired for his poetry collections *A Shropshire Lad* (1896) and *Last Poems* (1922); brother of Laurence Housman.

Housman, Laurence (1865-1959), English artist, dramatist, poet and writer, particularly known for his play *Victoria Regina* (1934); brother of A(lfred) E(dward) Housman.

Hout, Jan van (1542-1609), Dutch humanist theorist, historian, poet and translator.

Hovedon or **Howden, Roger of (d. c.1201),** English chronicler.

Hovey, Richard (1864-1900), American poet, dramatist and translator.

Howard, Blanche Willis (1847-1898), American novelist, author of *Guenn: A Wave on the Breton Coast* (1883).

Howard, Bronson (Crocker) (1842-1908), American dramatist, best known for his *Saratoga* (1870).

Howard, Sir Robert (1626-1698), English dramatist and poet.

Howard, Sidney (Coe) (1891-1939), American dramatist, author of *They Knew What They Wanted* (1924), *The Silver Cord* (1926) and *Yellow Jack* (incollaboration with Paul de Kruif, 1934).

Howe, E(dgar) W(atson) (1853-1937), American journalist, novelist and essayist best known for his novel *The Story of a Country Town* (1883).

Howe, Irving (1920-1993), American literary and social critic.

Howe, John (1630-1705), English Puritan minister and writer.

Howe, Julia Ward (1819-1910), American poet, writer, dramatist and social reformer, celebrated author of the patriotic poem *The Battle Hymn of the Republic* (1862); sister of Samuel Ward and mother of Maud Howe Elliott.

Howe, M(ark) A(ntony) De Wolfe (1864-1960), American poet, writer and editor.

Howell, James (c.1594-1666), Welsh writer, author of the *Epistolae Ho-Elianae* (4 volumes, 1645-55).

Howell, Thomas (16th Century), English poet.

Howells, William Dean (1837-1920), eminent American novelist, short-story writer, essayist, poet and editor.

Howes, Barbara (1914-1994), American poet and writer.

Hoyt, Charles Hale (1860-1900), American dramatist of popular farces.

Hrabal, Bohumil (1914-1997), Czech writer.

Hrdlička, Aleš (1869-1943), Czech-born American anthropologist.

Hrosvitha or Roswitha (c.935-1000), German nun and poet.

Hrozný, Bedřich (1879-1952), Bohemian archaeologist and language scholar.

Hsi K'amg (223-262), Chinese Taoist philosopher, alchemist and poet whose scandalous thought and conduct resulted in his execution by order of the Emperor.

Hsin Ch'i-chi (1140-1207), outstanding Chinese soldier and poet.

Hsiung Fo-hsi or **Hsiung Fu-Hsi (1900-1965),** Chinese dramatist, one of the principal creators of popular drama for the peasantry.

Hsü Chih-mo (1896-1931), Chinese poet and essayist who wrote under the names Nan-Hu and Shih-Che; died in an airplane crash.

Huang Tsung-hsi (1610-1695), notable Chinese scholar, author of the *Ming-i tai-fang lu* (A Plan for the Prince, 1662) and *Ming-ju-hsüeh-an* (Survey of Ming Confucianists, 1676).

Huang Tsun-hsien (1848-1905), Chinese poet, writer and government official.

Hubbard, Elbert (Green) (1856-1915), American editor, publisher and writer; died in the sinking of the "Lusitania".

Hubbard, Frank McKinney (1868-1930), American journalist and caricaturist, creator of the humorous and shrewd character Abe Martin.

Hubmaier, Balthasar (1485-1528), German Anabaptist preacher and theologian; condemned as a heretic and burned at the stake.

Hucbald (c.840-930), important Flemish music theorist, composer and monk.

Huchel, Peter (1903-1981), German poet.

Hudson, W(illiam) H(enry) (1841-1922), English writer, naturalist and ornithologist, particularly remembered for his novel *Green Mansions* (1904).

Huerta, Vicente García de (1730-1787), Spanish poet and critic.

Huet, Pierre-Daniel (1630-1721), French Roman Catholic bishop, scientist and scholar, especially known for his *Censura Philosophiae Cartesiane* (Criticisms of the Philosophy of Descartes, 1689) and *Nouveaux memoires pour servir a l'histoire* (New Memoires in the Service of History, 1692).

Hügel, baron Friedrich von (1852-1925), German-born English Roman Catholic theologian and philosopher.

Hughes, Hugh Price (1847-1902), English Wesleyan Methodist leader and writer.

Hughes, (James Mercer) Langston (1902-1967), outstanding American poet, dramatist and short-story writer, one of the principal figures in the Harlem Renaissance.

Hughes, John Ceiriog (1832-1887), remarkable Welsh poet and folklorist who wrote under the names Ceiriog and Syr Meurig Grynswth.

Hughes, Richard (Arthur Warren) (1900-1976), English novelist, poet and dramatist, especially known for his novel *A High Wind in Jamaica* (1929).

Hughes, Rupert (1872-1956), American writer and dramatist.

Hughes, Ted (actually Edward James Hughes) (1930-1998), notable English poet and writer; became Poet Laureate of the United Kingdom (1984); husband of Sylvia Plath.

Hughes, Thomas (1822-1896), English jurist and novelist, author of the popular *Tom Brown's School Days* (1857).

Hugh of Saint-Victor (1096-1141), famous French scholar, theologian and mystic.

Hugo, Joseph-Léopold-Sigisbert (1773-1828), French general and writer.

Hugo, Richard (Franklin) (1923-1982), American poet and essayist.

Hugo, Victor (Marie) (1802-1885), celebrated French poet, novelist and dramatist, author of the classic novels *Notre Dame de Paris* (1831) and *Les Misérables* (1862).

Huidobro, Vicente (1893-1948), Chilean poet, writer and theorist of avant-garde persuasion.

Huizinga, Johan (1872-1945), eminent Dutch historian, author of *Herfsttij der middeleeuwen* (1919; English translation as *The Waning of the Middle Ages,* 1924), *Erasmus* (1924; English translation, 1924), *In de schaduwen van Morgen* (1935; English translation as *In the Shadow of Tomorrow,* 1936) and *Homo Ludens* (1938; English translation, 1949).

Hull, Clark L(eonard) (1884-1952), influential American psychologist who wrote *Aptitude Testing* (1928), *Hypnosis and Suggestibility* (1933), *Mathematico-Deductive Theory of Rote Learning* (1940), *Principles of Behavior* (1943) and *A Behavior System* (1952).

Hulme, T(homas) E(rnest) (1883-1917), English poet, critic and philosopher who was a gifted Imagist; died in World War I.

Humbert of Silva Candida (c.1000-1061), french Roman Catholic cardinal, legate and theologian.

Humboldt, (Friedrich Wilhelm Karl Heinrich) Alexander von (1769-1859), outstanding German explorer and scientist, author of the important treatise *Kosmos.*

Humboldt, (Karl) Wilhelm, Freiherr von (1767-1835), eminent German language scholar, philosopher and diplomat who wrote the valuable study *Über den Dualis* (On the Dual, 1928).

Hume, Alexander (c.1560-1609), Scottish poet, best known for his *Of the Day Estival* and *Epistle to Maister Gilbert Mont-Crief.*

Hume, David (1711-1776), renowned Scottish philosopher, historian, economist and essayist, author of *A Treatise of Human Nature* (3 volumes, 1739-40), *An Enquiry Concerning Human Understanding* (1748; revised edition, 1758), *An Enquiry Concerning the Principles of Morals* (1751) and *The History of England* (6 volumes, 1754-62).

Humphrey, George (1889-1966), English psychologist.

Humphreys, David (1752-1818), American poet.

Humphries, (George) Rolfe (1894-1969), American poet and translator.

Huneker, James Gibbons (1860-1921), American music and literary critic.

Hung Shen (1893-1955), Chinese dramatist and film maker.

Hunt, (Isobel) Violet (1866-1942), English novelist.

Hunt, (James Henry) Leigh (1784-1859), English poet, critic, journalist and essayist.

Hunter, Sir William Wilson (1840-1900), Scottish writer.

Hurd, Richard (1720-1808), English Anglican bishop and scholar, author of the influential *Letters on Chivalry and Romance* (1762).

Hurdis, James (1763-1801), English poet, best known for *The Village Curate* (1788).

Hurst, Fannie (1889-1968), American novelist, dramatist and screenwriter.

Hurston, Zora Neale (c.1901-1960), American novelist and short-story writer.

Hüseyin Rahmi Gürpinar (1864-1944), Turkish novelist.

Husserl, Edmund (1859-1938), important Moravian-born German philosopher, founder of phenomenology.

Hutcheson, Francis (1694-1746), prominent Irish-born Scottish Presbyterian minister and philosopher who wrote *Inquiry into the Original of Our Ideas of Beauty and Virtue* (1725), *An Essay on the Nature and Conduct of the Passions and Affections, with Illustrations upon the Moral Sense* (1728) and *System of Moral Philosophy* (2 volumes, published 1755).

Hutchins, Robert M(aynard) (1899-1977), distinguished American educator who was a champion of the liberal arts in higher education.

Hutchinson, R(ay) C(oryton) (1907-1975), English novelist.

Hutchinson, (William) Bruce (1901-1992), Canadian journalist and novelist.

Hutten, Ulrich von (1488-1523), German knight, patriot, writer and poet.

Hutton, John Henry (1885-1968), English anthropologist.

Hutton, Richard Holt (1826-1897), English journalist and essayist.

Huxley, Aldous (Leonard) (1894-1963), esteemed English novelist, essayist and poet, author of the classic novel *Brave New World* (1932); grandson of Thomas Henry Huxley and brother of Sir Julian Sorell Huxley.

Huxley, Sir Julian Sorell (1887-1975), distinguished English biologist and writer; grandson of Thomas Henry Huxley and brother of Aldous (Leonard) Huxley.

Huxley, Thomas Henry (1825-1895), renowned English scientist, humanist and writer; grandfather of Aldous (Leonard) Huxley and Sir Julian Sorell Huxley.

Huygens, Constantijn (1596-1687), remarkable Dutch scholar and poet.

Huysmans, Joris-Karl (actually **Charles Huysmans) (1848-1907),** notable French novelist and art critic, author of the important novels *À vau-l'eau* (1882; English translation as *Down Stream,* 1927), *À rebours* 1884; English translation as *Against the Grain,*1922), *Là-bas* (1891;English translation as *Down There,*1924) and *En Route*(1895;English translation, 1908).

Hviezdoslav (actually **Pavol Orszagh) (1849-1921),** pioneering Slovak poet of remarkable expressive powers.

Hyde, Charles Cheney (1873-1952), American scholar of international law and diplomacy.

Hyde, Douglas (1860-1949), prominent Irish scholar who wrote under the name An Craoibhin Aoibhinn and who served as the first president of Ireland (1938-45).

Hyginus, Gaius Julius (1st Century), Latin scholar.

Hyndman, Henry Mayers (1842-1921), English Marxist, author of *The Evolution of Revolution* (1920).

Hypatia (c.370-415), famous Egyptian mathematician and philosopher; was killed by a mob of fanatical Christians.

Hyslop, James (1798-1827), Scottish poet.

Hywel ab Owain Gwynedd (d. 1170), Welsh warrior-prince and poet.

Iamblichus (c.250-c.330), Syrian philosopher of the Neoplatonic school.

Ibarbourou, Juana de (1895-1979), noted Uruguayan poet.

Ibn 'Abbād (actually Abū 'Abd Allāh Muhammad ibn Abī Ishāq Ibrāhīm an-Nafzī al-Himyarī ar-Rundī) (1333-1390), Spanish-born Arab mystic and theologian of Sūfism.

Ibn Abī ar-Rijāl, Ahmad (ibn Sālih) (1620-1681), Yemeni scholar and theologian.

Ibn al-Abbār (actually Abū 'Abd Allāh Muhammad al-Qudā'ī) (1199-1260), Spanish Muslim historian and theologian who was also known for his humour and satire.

Ibn al'Arabī (actually Muhyi ad-Dīn Abū 'Abd Allāh Muhammad ibn 'Alī ibn Muhammad ibn al-'Arabī al-Hātimī at-Tā'ī ibn al'Arabī) (1165-1240), Famous Spanish Muslim mystic philosopher and poet who used the literary name Abu Bakr.

Ibn al-Athīr (actually Abū al-Hasan 'Alī 'Izz ad-Dīn ibn al-Athīr) (1181-1233), Arab historian.

Ibn al-Farīd (actually Sharaf ad-Dīn Abū Hafs 'Umar ibn al-Fārid) (c.1160-1235), revered Egyptian Muslim poet who was regarded as a saint during his lifetime.

Ibn al-Jawzī (actually 'Abd ar-Rahmān ibn 'Alī ibn Muhammad Abū al-Farash ibn al-Jawzī) (1126-1200), prominent Iraqui theologian, preacher and scholar who championed the cause of Islamic orthodoxy.

Ibn al-Muqaffa' (d. c.756), Muslim Writer.

Ibn 'Alqāmah (11th Century), Arab Historian.

Ibn al-Walīd (c.1215), Yemenite Isma'ili theologian.

Ibn al-Warrāq (d. 861), Muslim Theologian.

Ibn 'Aqīl (actually Abū al-Wafā' 'Alī ibn 'Aqīl ibn Muhammad ibn 'Aqīl ibn Ahmad al-Baghdādī az-Zafarī) (1040-1119), notable Iraqui Islamic theologian and scholar.

Ibn Bābawayh (actually Abū Ja'far Muhammad ibn Abū al-Hasan 'Alī ibn Husayn ibn Mūsā al-Qummī) (c.923-991), influential Persian Islamic theologian of Shī'ism.

Ibn Battūtah (actually Abū 'Abd Allāh Muhammad ibn 'Abd Allāh al-Lawātī Attanjī ibn Battūtah) (1304-c.1368), famous Arab traveller who wrote the celebrated *Rihlah*, an account of his extensive travels.

Ibn Dā'ūd (d. 910), Muslim theologian and poet.

Ibn Daud, Abraham (c.1110-c.1180), Spanish Jewish physician and historian, author of *Emuna rama* (Exalted Faith) and *Sefer ha-kabbala* (The Book of Tradition).

Ibn Durayd (actually Abū Bakr Muhammad ibn al-Hasan ibn Durayd al-Azdī) (c.837-933), Arab philologist and poet.

Ibn Ezra, Abraham ben Meir (c.1090-1164), important Spanish Jewish biblical scholar, philosopher, grammarian, astronomer and poet.

Ibn Ezra, Moses (ben Jacob ha-Sallab) (c.1060-1139), outstanding Spanish Hebrew poet and critic, a master of both sacred and secular verse.

Ibn Falaquera (c.1225-c.1295), Spanish Jewish philosopher and translator.

Ibn Gabirol (actually Soloman ben Yehuda ibn Gabirol) (c.1021-c.1070), remarkable Spanish Jewish poet and Neoplatonic philosopher.

Ibn Hāni' (d.973), Spanish Muslim Poet.

Ibn Hazm (actually Abū Muhammad 'Alī ibn Ahmad ibn Sa'id ibn Hazm) (994-1064), celebrated Spanish Muslim writer, jurist, historian and theologian.

Ibn Ishāq (actually Muhammad ibn Ishāq ibn Yasār ibn Khiyār) (C.704-767), Iraqi biographer of the Prophet Muhammad.

Ibn Janāh, Abū al-Walīd Marwān (c.990-1050), learned Spanish Hebrew grammarian and lexicographer.

Ibn Kathīr (actually 'Imād ad-Dīn Ismā'il ibn 'Umar ibn Kathīr) (c.1300-1373), noted Syrian historian and theologian, author of the valuable *al-Bidayah wa-an-nihayah* (The Beginning and the End, 14 volumes), a history of Islam.

Ibn Khafājah (d.1138), Spanish Muslim poet.

Ibn Khaldūn (actually Abū Zayd 'Abd ar-Rahmān ibn Khaldūn) (1332-1406), Arab historian whose most important work was the *Muqaddimah* (Introduction to History).

Ibn Kullāb (d. c.864), Muslim theologian.

Ibn Miskawayh (actually Abū 'Alī Ahmad ibn Muhammad ibn Ya'qūb Miskawayh) (c.930-1030), Arab philosopher and historian.

Ibn Qutaybah (actually Abū Muhammad 'Abd Allāh ibn Muslim al-Dīnawarī ibn Qutaybah) (828-889), esteemed Arab writer.

Ibn Quzmān (d. 1160), Spanish Muslim poet.

Ibn Shem Tov, Joesph ben Shem Tov (c.1400-c.1460), Spanish Jewish philosopher and court physician, author of *Kevod Elohim* (The Glory of God, 1442).

Ibn Tufayl (actually **Muhammad ibn 'Abd al-Malik ibn Muhammad ibn Muhammad ibn Tufayl al-Qaysī**) **(c.1110-1185),** Spanish philosopher and physician, author of *Risālat Hayy ibn Takzān* (c.1175; English translation as *The Improvement of Human Reason*, 1708).

Ibn Zabara, Joesph ben Meir (12th Century), Spanish Jewish writer.

Ibn Zaydūn (d.1071), Spanish Muslim poet.

Ibsen, Henrick (Johan) (1828-1906), great Norwegian dramatist and poet of incalculable importance in the development of modern drama, renowned for such plays as *Brand* (1866), *Peer Gynt* (1867), *A Doll's House* (1879), *Ghosts* (1881) and *Hedda Gabler* (1890).

Ibycus (6th Century B.C.), Greek Poet.

Idelsohn, Abraham Zevi (1882-1938), distinguished Latvian music scholar and composer, an authority on Jewish music.

Idrīs, Yūsuf (1929-1991), Egyptian writer and dramatist.

Idrīsī, (Abū 'Abd Allāh Muhammad) al- (1100-1165), Arab geographer and scientist who wrote valuable works on geography.

Iffland, August Wilhelm (1759-1814), notable German actor, dramatist and theatre manager, especially admired for his sentimental and comic plays.

Ignatius, Saint (c.35-c.107), esteemed Christian bishop whose letters were highly influential; was martyred by the Roman authorities.

Ignatow, David (1914-1997), American poet.

Ihara or **Ibara Saikaku (1642-1693),** celebrated Japanese poet and novelist.

Iio Sōgi (1421-1502), famous Japanese poet and Buddist monk, a master of renga (linked verse).

Ilf, Ilya (Arnoldovich) (1897-1937), Russian writer who collaborated with Yevgeny Petrov on the successful novels *Dvenadtsat stulyev* (1928; English translation as *The Twelve Chairs*, 1961) and Zolotoy telyonok (1931; English translation as *The Little Golden Calf*, 1962).

Imber, Naphtali Herz (1865-1909), Hebrew poet.

Immanuel ben Soloman (c.1260-1328), significant Hebrew poet and biblical scholar, author of both sacred and secular verse of high merit.

Immermann, Karl Leberecht (1796-1840), German dramatist and novelist.

Imru' al-Qays (ibn Hujr) (d. c.550), illustrious Arab poet.

Inchbald, Elizabeth (née Simpson) (1753-1821), English novelist, dramatist and actress, best remembered for her novels *A Simple Story* (1791) and *Nature and Art* (1796).

Inge, William (Motter) (1913-1973), American dramatist and novelist.

Inge, William Ralph (1860-1954), English Anglican dean and writer.

Ingelow, Jean (1820-1897), English poet and novelist, particularly known for a volume of *Poems* (1863).

Ingemann, Bernhard Severin (1789-1862), Danish poet and novelist.

Ingersoll, Charles Jared (1782-1862), American politician, writer and poet.

Ingersoll, Robert G(reen) (1833-1899), American politician, orator and writer who became particularly well known for his advocacy of agnosticism.

Ingraham, Joesph Holt (1809-1860), American Episcopal clergyman and writer, best known for his historical and religious romances; father of Prentiss Ingraham.

Ingraham, Prentiss (1834-1904), American writer and dramatist who wrote over 600 dime novels; son of Joesph Holt Ingraham.

Ingram, John Kells (1823-1907), Irish scholar and economist.

Innes, Hammond (1913-1998), English writer, best remembered for his novel *The Wreck of the "Mary Deare"* (1956).

Inour Enryö (1859-1919), Japanese philosopher and educator who developed a nationalistic Buddhist doctrine.

Inoue Tetsujirō (1855-1944), Japanese philosopher.

Ionesco, Eugène (1912-1994), famous Romanian-born French dramatist and writer who profoundly influenced modern drama as the creator of the "Theatre of the Absurd".

Iorga, Nicolae (1871-1940), prominent Romanian historian and statesman; was assassinated.

Iqbāl, Muhammad (1876-1938), Indian poet and philosopher, author of the extensive Persian poem *Asrār-e-khūdī* (The Secrets of the Self, 1915).

Ireland, John (c.1435-c.1500), Scottish theologian, diplomat and writer, author of *The Meroure of Wyssdome* (1490).

Irenaeus, Saint (c.130-c.200), outstanding Roman Catholic Theologian and bishop, author of *Adversus haereses* (Against Heresies, c.180).

Iriarte y Oropesa, Tomas de (1750-1791), Spanish poet, writer and translator.

Irving, John Treat (1812-1906), American writer; nephew of Washington Irving.

Irving, Peter (1771-1838), American writer; brother of Washington Irving and William Irving.

Irving, Pierre Munro (1803-1876), American lawyer and writer; son of William Irving and nephew of Washington Irving.

Irving, Washington (1783-1859), popular American writer whose most famous work was *The Sketch Book* (1820); brother of Peter Irving and William Irving.

Irving, William (1766-1821), American poet; father of Pierre Munro Irving and brother of Peter Irving and Washington Irving.

Irwin, Wallace (Admah) (1875-1959), American poet, journalist and novelist; brother of Will(iam Henry) Irwin.

Irwin Will(iam Henry) (1873-1948), American journalist, writer and dramatist; brother of Wallace (Admah) Irving.

Irzykowski, Karol (1873-1944), Polish writer.

Isaac of Antioch (d. 460), notable Syrian poet and writer who was also known as Isaac the Great.

Isaac of Nineveh (d. c.700), Syrian monk, bishop and theologian who was also known as Isaac the Syrian.

Isaac of Stella (c.1100-c.1178), famous English-born French monk, theologian and philosopher, author of the *Epistola de anima ad Alcherum* (Letter to Alcher on the Soul).

Isaacs, Jorge (1837-1895), Colombian novelist and poet, especially admired for his novel *María* (1867).

Isherwood, Christopher (actually Christopher William Bradshaw-Isherwood) (1904-1986), English-born American novelist, short story writer, essayist, poet and dramatist, particularly remembered for his novels *Mr Norris Changes Trains* (1935) and *Goodbye to Berlin* (1939).

Ishikawa Takuboku (actually Ishikawa Hajime) (1885-1912), Japanese poet and writer.

Isidore of Kiev (c.1385-1463), Greek Orthodox patriarch of Russia, Roman Catholic cardinal, scholar and theologian.

Isidore of Seville, Saint (c.560-636), Spanish Roman Catholic archbishop, theologian and scholar.

Isla (y Rojo), José Francisco de (1703-1781), Spanish Jesuit and writer who wrote the satirical and controversial *Fray Gerundio* (1758), a book condemned by the Inquisition.

Isocrates (436-338 B.C.), celebrated Greek rhetorician and writer who espoused the cause of Greek unification in the face of Persian hegemony; committed suicide.

Israeli, Isaac ben Soloman (c.833-c.933), famous Jewish physician and philosopher.

Issa (actually Kobayashi Issa) (1763-1827), Japanese poet who wrote much of his work under the name Kobayashi Yataró.

Italus, John (11th Century), Byzantine philosopher and court official, a proponent of Platonism.

Itó Jinsai (1627-1705), Japanese philosopher, author of *Gómójigi* (1683), a commentary on the analects of the Chinese philosophers Confucius and Mencius.

Itó Tógai (1670-1736), Japanese philosopher of the Confucian school.

Ivanov, Viacheslav Ivanovich (1866-1949), Russian poet, philosopher and scholar, a noted Symbolist.

Ivanov, Vsevolod Viacheslavoch (1895-1963), Russian writer.

Ivo of Chartres, Saint (c.1040-1116), French Roman Catholic bishop and canonist.

Izumi Kyóka (actually Izumi Kyotaro) (1873-1939), Japanese short-story writer.

Jabayev, Jambul (1846-1945), Kazakh poet.

Jablonski, Daniel Ernst (1660-1741), German Protestant theologian.

Jabotinsky, Vladimir (1880-1940), prominent Russian Zioniost, journalist and writer, leader of the Zionist Revisionist movement.

Jacinto, António (actually António Jacinto do Amaral Martins) (1924-1991), Angolan poet and Marxist anticolonial leader who often wrote under the name Orlando Tavora.

Jackson, A(braham) V(alentine) Williams (1862-1937), American scholar of Indo-Iranian languages and Iranian religion.

Jackson, Charles (Reginald) (1903-1968), American writer, best remembered for his novel *The Lost Weekend* (1944).

Jackson, Cyril (1746-1819), English Anglican clergyman, classics scholar and educator.

Jackson, Helen (Maria) Hunt (née Fiske) (1831-1885), American novelist and poet, particularly esteemed for her novel *Ramona* (1884).

Jackson, Shirley (Hardie) (1916-1965), American novelist and short-story writer.

Jackson, William (1730-1803), English composer and writer on music.

Jackson, William (c.1737-1795), English clergyman and radical journalist who supported various revolutionary causes; arrested and convicted of treason, he committed suicide.

Jacob, Max (1876-1944), noted French poet and writer who was especially known for his Surrealist and lyrical poetry; died in a concentration camp.

Jacob, Violet (née Kennedy-Erskine) (1863-1946), Scottish poet and novelist.

Jacobi, Friedrich Heinrich (1743-1819), important German philosopher who espoused the philosophy of feeling as an alternative to Rationalism.

Jacobi, Johann Georg (1740-1814), German poet.

Jacob of Edessa (c.640-708), Syrian theologian and scholar.

Jacob of Serugh or **Sarug (451-521),** Syrian Roman Catholic bishop, writer and poet.

Jacobs, Harriet A (1813-1897), American memoirist whose account of her years as a slave were recorded in her *Incidents in the Life of a Slave Girl: Written by Herself* (1881), published under the name Linda Brent.

Jacobs, Joesph (1854-1916), Australian folklorist and writer.

Jacobs, W(illiam) W(ymark) (1863-1943), English short-story writer, author of the classic horror story "The Monkey's Paw" (1902).

Jacobsen, Jens Peter (1847-1885), Danish novelist, short-story writer and poet, creator of the Naturalist movement in Denmark.

Jacobus de Voragine (c.1229-1298), Italian Roman Catholic archbishop and writer, author of the *Legenda aurea* (Golden Legend), a religious chronicle.

Jacopone da Todi (actually **Jacopo dei Benedetti) (c.1230-1306),** admired Italian poet, reputed author of the celebrated sacred Latin poem *Stabat mater dolorosa*, which later became a part of the Roman Catholic liturgy.

Jacotot, Jean-Joesph (1770-1840), influential French educator whose pedagogical ideas were delineated in his *Enseignement universel* (Universal Teaching Method, 1823).

Jaeger, Hans Henrik (1854 -1910), Norwegian novelist whose *Fra Kristiania-Bohêmen* (From the Christiania Bohemian, 1885) caused a scandal for its frank treatment of sexuality and was confiscated by the authorities as pornographic.

Jaeger, Werner (1888-1961), German classical scholar.

Jagannātha Dās (16th Century), Indian Poet.

Jago, Richard (1715-1781), English poet, author of the extensive topographical poem *Edge-hill* (1767).

Jāhiz, al- (actually **Abū 'Uthmān 'Amr ibn Bahr ibn Mahbūb al-Jāhiz) (c.776-c.868),** celebrated Arab theologian and writer.

Jahn, Otto (1813-1869), German philologist, archaeologist and music scholar, especially known for his valuable biography of Mozart (4 Volumes, 1856-59).

Jakobson, Roman (1896-1982), influential Russian-born American linguist, one of the outstanding figures in the structural lingustics movement that became known as the Prague school.

Jalāl ad-Dīn ar-Rūmī (1207-1273), foremost Sūfī Muslim poet in the Persian language.

James, E(dwin) O(liver) (1888-1972), English anthropologist.

James, Henry, Sr (1811-1882), American philosopher of theological concerns; father of Henry James and William James.

James, Henry (1843-1916), illustrious American novelist, short-story writer and critic, author of such classic works as *The Portrait of a Lady* (1881), *The Bostonians* (1886), *The Spoils of Poynton* (1897), *The Wings of the Dove* (1902), *The Ambassadors* (1903) and *The Golden Bowl* (1904); son of Henry James Sr. and brother of William James.

James, Marquis (1891-1955), American biographer and writer.

James, William (1842-1910), eminent American philosopher and psychologist of the Pragmatist school, author of the important studies *The Principles of Psychology* (1890) and *The Varieties of Religious Experience* (1902); son of Henry James Sr. and brother of Henry James.

James, Will(iam Roderick) (1892-1942), American writer and illustrator of books on the Old West.

Jameson, Anna Brownell (1794-1860), English biographer, historian, critic and essayist.

Jameson, (Margaret) Storm (1891-1986), English novelist, poet, biographer and essayist.

Jāmī (actually **Mowlanā Nūr od-Dīn 'abd Orrahmān ebn Ahmad) (1414-1492),** celebrated Persian poet, scholar and mystic.

Jammes, Francis (1868-1938), French poet, novelist and short-story writer.

Janet, Pierre (-Marie-Felix) (1859-1947), French psychologist and neurologist, author of *The Major Symptoms of Hysteria* (1907).

Janin, Jules-Gabriel (1804-1874), French journalist, writer and essayist.

Janssen, Johannes (1829-1891), German Roman Catholic historian, author of the important but controversial *Geschichte des deutschen Volkes seit dem Ausgang des Mittelalters* (History of Germany from the Close of the Middle Ages, 8 volumes, 1876-94).

Janvier, Thomas Allibone (1849-1913), American writer.

Jaques-Dalcroze, Emile (1865-1950), Swiss music educator and composer of French descent, creator of eurythmics, a method of rythmic training.

Jarīr (ibn 'Atīyah ibn al-khatafā) (c.650-c.729), illustrious Arab poet.

Jarnes, Benjamin (1888-1949), Spanish novelist.

Jarrell, Randall (1914-1965), esteemed American Poet, novelist and critic.

Jarry, Alfred (1873-1907), French dramatist, novelist and poet whose controversial play *Ubu roi* (1896) is considered the first drama of the Theatre of the Absurd.

Jarves, James Jackson (1818-1888), American art collector, critic and writer.

Jasmin, Jacques (actually **Jacques Boé**) **(1798-1864),** French poet of a dialect verse.

Jaspers, Karl (Theodor) (1883-1969), eminent German philosopher, a principal exponent of Existentialism and author of the important volume *Philosophie* (1932).

Jaucourt, Louis de (1704-1799), French scholar.

Jawahri, Mohammed Mahdi al- (1900-1997), Iraqi poet.

Jean d'Arras (15th Century), French trouvére.

Jean de Meun or Meung (c.1240-c.1300), French poet who completed Guillaume de Lorris's allegorical poem the *Roman de la rose* (c.1280).

Jean le Bel (c.1290-1370), Belgian canon, soldier and writer, author of the chronicle *Vrayes Chroniques.*

Jebb, Sir Richard Claverhouse (1841-1905), esteemed English classical scholar.

Jeda Bin (1874-1916), Japanese poet and scholar.

Jefferies, (John) Richard (1848-1887), English naturalist, novelist and essayist.

Jeffers, (John) Robinson (1887-1962), notable American poet who was known for his bitter indictment of his era.

Jefferson, Thomas (1743-1826), great American statesman, 3rd president of the US (1801-09), author of *A Summary View of the Rights of British America* (1774), *The Declaration of Independence* (1776) and *Notes on the State of Virginia* (1784).

Jeffery, Francis, Lord (1773-1850), Scottish judge and literary critic, editor of *The Edinburgh Review* (1803-29).

Jellinek, Adolf (1821-1893), Moravian Jewish rabbi and scholar.

Jellinek, Georg (1851-1911), German philosopher, author of *Die socialethische Bedeutung von Recht, Unrecht und Strafe* (The Social-Ethical significance of Right, Wrong, and Punishment, 1878, 2nd Edition, 1908), *Die Erklärung der Menschen- und Bürgerrechte* (1895; English translation as *The Declaration of the Rights of Man and of Citizens,*1901) and *Allgemeine Staatslehre* (General Theory of the State, 1900).

Jensen, Johannes V(ilhelm) (1873-1950), eminent Danish novelist, poet and essayist, especially esteemed for his 6 novels published under the general title *Den lange rejse* (1908-22; English translation as *The Long Journey,* 1922-24; won the Nobel Prize for Literature (1944).

Jensen, Wilhelm (1837-1911), German poet and novelist.

Jenyns, Soame (1704-1784), English politician and poet.

Jerome, Saint (actually **Eusebius Hieronymus**) **(c.345-420),** renowned biblical scholar, celebrated for his Latin translation of the Bible.

Jerome, Jerome K(lapka) (1859-1927), English writer and dramatist.

Jerome of Prague (c.1365-1416), Czech philosopher and theologian.

Jerrold, Douglas William (1803-1857), English journalist and dramatist, best remembered for his play *Black-Eyed Susan* (1829) and the volume of prose *Curtain Lectures* (1846); father of William Blanchard Jerrold.

Jerrold, William Blanchard (1826-1884), English journalist, dramatist, biographer and essayist; son of Douglas William Jerrold.

Jespersen, (Jens) Otto (Harry) (1860-1943), distinguished Danish linguist who was a leading authority on English grammer and author of the valuable *Modern English Grammar* (7 volumes, 1909-49).

Jesse, F(riniwyd) Tennyson (1889-1958), English novelist and dramatist; grand niece of Alfred Lord Tennyson.

Jevons, William Stanley (1835-1882), English logician and economist, author of the *Theory of Political Economy* (1871) and *Principles of Science* (1874).

Jewel, John (1522-1571), Prominent English Anglican bishop and apologist, particularly known for his *Apologia pro Ecclesia Anglicana* (Defence of the Anglican Church, 1562).

Jewett, Sarah Orne (1849-1909), American writer and poet, best known for her prose volume *The Country of the Pointed Firs* (1896).

Jewsbury, Geraldine Endsor (1812-1880), English writer.

Jhering, Rudolf von (1818-1892), German legal scholar who wrote the important studies *Geist des römischen Rechts . . .* (The Spirit of the Roman Law . . . , 4 volumes, 1852-65) and *Der Zweck im Recht* (2 volumes, 1877, 1833; English translation as *Law As a Means to an End,* 1924).

Jien (actually **Fujiwara Dokia**) **(1145-1225),** outstanding Japanese historian and Buddist monk, author of the *Gukanshó* (c.1220).

Jili, al- (actually **'Abd al-karim Qutb ad-Din ibn Ibrahim al-Jili**) **(1365-c.1424),** Arab mystic who propounded an elaborate doctrine of the perfect man in his *al-Insān al-kāmil fi ma'rifat al-awā' il* (partial English translation as *Studies in Islamic Mysticism,* 1921).

Jiménez, Juan Ramón (1881-1958), admired Spanish poet and writer, especially known for his free verse; won the nobel prize for literature (1956).

Jippensha Ikku (1765-1831), Japanese writer.

Jirásek, Alois (1851-1930), noted Czech novelist, especially admired for his *Temno* (Darkness, 1915).

Jñānadeva or Jñāneśvara (1275-1296), famous Indian poet, a master of Mahārāshtrian school of mystical poets; committed suicide.

Joachim, Harold Henry (1868-1938), English philosopher.

Joachim of Fiore (c.1133-c.1201), Italian mystic, biblical commentator and theologian.

Joad, C(yril) E(dwin) M(itchinson) (1891-1953), English philosopher who was known for his advocacy of rationalism.

Jocelin de Brakelond (12th-13th Century), English Benedictine monk who wrote the *Cronica* (English translation, 1949).

Jochelson, Vladamir Ilich (1855-1937), Russian ethnographer and linguist.

Jöcher, Christian Gottlieb (1694-1758), German scholar and lexicographer.

Jochumsson, Matthías (1835-1920), distinguished Icelandic poet, dramatist, translator and clergyman, author of the National Anthem of Iceland.

Jodelle, Étienne (1532-1573), French poet and dramatist.

Johann von Tepl or Saaz (c.1350-c.1415), Bohemian writer, author of the famous *Der Ackermann aus Böhmen* (c.1400; English translation as *Death and the Ploughman*, 1947).

John Climacus, Saint (c.579-c.649), Byzantine monk, author of the celebrated *Climax tou Paradeisou* (The Ladder of divine Ascent).

John of Ávila, Saint (c.1499-1569), renowned Spanish Roman Catholic preacher and reformer who wrote the celebrated treatise *Audi Filia* (Listen, Daughter).

John of Damascus, Saint (c.645-749), outstanding Syrian monk, preacher and theologian who was also known as Johannes Damascenus.

John of Ephesus (c.507-c.586), Syrian Roman Catholic bishop and historian whose Monophysite views led to his banishment late in life, author of an ecclesiastical history and of a lives of the Eastern saints.

John of Fordun (14th Century), Scottish chronicler who wrote a history of Scotland.

John of Guildford (14th Century), English writer on heraldry.

John of Jandun (c.1286-1328), French scholar who wrote commentaries on Aristotle.

John of Jerusalem (c.356-417), Roman Catholic bishop and theologian who upheld the Platonistic tradition of Alexandria.

John of Kronstadt (actually Ivan Ilich Sergelev) (1829-1909), Russian Orthodox priest and writer.

John of Mirecourt (14th Century), French Cistercian monk, philosopher and theologian who was a leading proponent of nominalism and voluntarism.

John of Odzun (650-729), Armenian Orthodox churchman and theologian.

John of Paris (c.1255-1306), French Dominican monk, theologian and philosopher who was also known as Jean Quidort and Johannes de Soardis, author of the controversial treatises *De potestate regia et papali* (On Royal and Papal Powers, c.1302) and *Determinatio* (1304).

John of St Thomas (actually John Poinsot) (1589-1644), notable Portuguese theologian and philosopher of the Thomist school, particularly known for his *Cursus Philosophicus* (Course in Philosophy, 9 volumes, 1632-36) and *Cursus Theologicus* (Course in Theology, 7 volumes, 1637-44).

John of Salisbury (c.1117-1180), English Roman Catholic bishop and theologian, author of the *Policraticus* (1159), *Metalogicon* (1159) and *Historia pontificalis* (1163).

John of Scythopolis (6th Century), Byzantine bishop and theologian who was known for his writings on Christ and for his commentaries on Neoplatonism.

John of the Cross, Saint (actually Juan de Yepes y Alvarez) (1542-1591), revered Spanish Roman Catholic mystic, reformer and poet, celebrated for such works as the *Cántico espiritual* (Spiritual Canticle) and *Noche oscura del alma* (Dark Night of the Soul).

John Scholasticus or John of Antioch (c.503-577), Syrian theologian, ecclesiastical jurist and patriarch.

Johnson, B(ryan) S(tanley William) (1933-1973), English novelist of the experimental school; Committed suicide.

Johnson, Charles (1679-1748), English dramatist.

Johnson, Charles Spurgeon (1893-1956), American sociologist and educator who wrote valuable studies on the black experience and race relations.

Johnson, Edward (1598-1672), English-born American settler who wrote a Puritan account of the founding of New England (1654).

Johnson, (Emily) Pauline (1862-1913), Canadian Indian poet and writer who wrote under her Indian name Tekahionwake, best remembered for her poem *The Song my Paddle Sings*.

Johnson, Eyvind (1900-1976), noted Swedish novelist and short-story writer, particularly admired for his novel *Strändernas svall* (1946; English translation as *Return to Ithaca*, 1952); was co-winner of the Nobel Prize for literature (1974).

Johnson Gisle (1822-1894), Norwegian Lutheran theologian.

Johnson, James Weldon (1871-1938), prominent American educator, civil rights advocate, poet, writer and anthologist of black culture.

Johnson, Lionel Pigot (1867-1902), English poet and critic who was known for his poem *By the Statue of King Charles at Charing Cross.*

Johnson, Louis Albert (1924-1988), New Zealand poet.

Johnson, Owen (Mcmahon) (1878-1952), American writer; son of Robert Underwood Johnson.

Johnson, Pamela Hansford (1912-1981), English novelist and critic.

Johnson, Richard (1573-c.1659), English writer, particularly known for his romance *The Most Famous of the Seaven Champions of Christendome* (3 Parts, 1596, 1608,1616).

Johnson, Robert (1935-1998), gifted American poet whose masterwork was the extensive *ARK* (1980-96).

Johnson, Robert Underwood (1853-1937), American poet and editor; father of Owen (Mcmahon) Johnson.

Johnson, Samuel (1696-1772), American Anglican churchman and philosopher, author of *Ethics Elementa* (1746; augmented edition as *Elementa Philosophica*, 1752).

Johnson, Samuel (1709-1784), celebrated English writer, critic, essayist, lexicographer and poet.

Johnson, Uwe (1934-1984), German novelist and essayist.

Johnston, Annie Fellows (1836-1931), American writer of children's stories.

Johnston, Arthur (1587-1641), Scottish poet and physician.

Johnston, Mary (1870-1936), American writer.

Johnston, Richard Malcom (1822-1898), American writer, best known for his humorous stories.

Johnston, (William) Denis (1901-1984), English dramatist, writer and critic.

Johnstone, Charles (c.1719-1800), English journalist and writer, author of *Chrysal, or the Adventures of a Guinea* (1760-65), *The History of Arsaces, Prince of Betlis* (1774), *The Pilgrim* (1775) and *John Juniper* (1781).

Joinville, François-Ferdinand-Phillippe-Louis-Marie d'Orléans, Prince de (1818-1900), French naval officer and writer on military subjects.

Joinnville, Jean, Sire de (c.1224-1317), French court official who wrote the celebrated *Histoire de saint Louis* (c.1270-1309; Published 1547).

Jókai, Mór (1825-1904), outstanding Hungarian novelist.

Jokl, Norbert (1877-1942), Austrian linguist, an authority on the Albanian language.

Jomini, (Antoine-) Henri, Baron de (1779-1869), French general and military historian who wrote the important *Précis de l'art de la guerre* (1838; English translation as *Summary of the Art of War*, 1868).

Jonas, Justus (1493-1555), German Protestant reformer, legal scholar and translator who helped to draft the Ausburg Confession.

Jones, (Alfred) Ernest (1897-1958), Welsh psychoanalyst and biographer of Freud.

Jones, Daniel (1881-1967), English linguist and phonetician.

Jones, David (Michael) (1895-1974), English poet, writer and artist, particularly esteemed for his novel *In Parenthesis* (1937) and the religious poem *The Anathemata* (1952).

Jones, Ernest (1819-1869), English poet, a leader of the Chartrist movement and author of the epic *The Revolt of Hindostan.*

Jones, Henry Arthur (1851-1929), English dramatist.

Jones, Howard Mumford (1892-1980), American writer, dramatist and poet.

Jones, Hugh (c.1670-1760), American minister, mathematician and historian, author of *The Present State of Virginia* (1724).

Jones, James (1921-1977), American writer, best remembered for his novel *From Here to Eternity* (1951).

Jones, James Athearn (1791-1854), American writer, poet and editor.

Jones, John Beauchamp (1810-1866), American journalist and novelist, best remembered for his realistic Civil War novel *A Rebel War Clerk's Diary* (1866).

Jones, Joseph Stevens (1809-1877), American physician, actor, theatre manager and dramatist.

Jones, Owen (1809-1874), English designer, architect and writer who wrote *The grammer of Ornament* (1856), a valuable study of Western and Eastern design motifs.

Jones, Rufus Matthew (1863-1948), American Quaker philosopher, author of many books on Christian mysticism and Quakerism.

Jones, Thomas Gwynn (1871-1949), Welsh poet and scholar.

Jones, Sir William (1746-1794), English jurist and Orientalist, author of the standard tome *Essay on the Law of Bailments* (1781).

Jonker, Ingrid (1933-1965), South African novelist.

Jonson, Ben(jamin) (1572-1637), famous English dramatist, poet and critic, particularly known for his plays *Volpone* (1606) and *The Alchemist* (1610).

Jónsson, Arngrímur (1568-1648), important Icelandic historian who was known as Arngrímur the Learned.

Jónsson, Finnur (1704-1759), Icelandic bishop and historian.

Jónsson, Hjálmar (1796-1875), remarkable Icelandic poet of satirical verse who was known as Bólu-Hjálmar.

Jordan A(rchibald) C (1906-1968), South African novelist and educator, best known for his novel *Ingqumbo Yeminyanya* (The Wrath of the Ancestors, 1940), a story of Xosa life.

Jordan, David Starr (1851-1931), American educator, philosopher and naturalist.

Jordan, Thomas (c.1612-c.1685), English poet, dramatist and Royalist pamphleteer, best remembered for *A Royal Arbour of Loyall Poesie* (1664) and *A Nursery of Novelties in Variety of Poetry.*

Jordanes (6th Century), Goth historian who wrote in Latin, author of the valuable *De origine actibusque Getarum* (On the Origin and deeds of the Getae, 551).

Jørgensen, (Jens) Johannes (1866-1956), Danish novelist, poet and biographer.

Joris, David (c.1501-1556), highly controversial Anabaptist leader, mystic visionary and prophet, author of the *Wonder Boeck* (Wonder Book, 2 Parts, 1542, 1551); was posthumously condemned as a heretic, his body exhumed and burned at the stake (1559).

Joesph ben Jacob ibn Tzaddik (1075-1149), Spanish Jewish philosopher and poet.

Joesph of Volokolamsk, Saint (actually Joesph Panin) (1439-1515), influential Russian monk and theologian who opposed Western humanistic elements in Christian faith and practice.

Josephson, Matthew (1899-1978), American biographer and writer.

Josephus, Flavius (actually Joesph ben Matthias) (c.37-c.100), notable Jewish historian and priest, author of a valuable history of the Jewish war (75-79) and antiquities of the Jews (93).

Joubert, Joesph (1754-1824), French writer.

Jovanović, Slobodan (1869-1958), Serbian statesman and scholar.

Jovellanos, Gaspar Melchor de (1744-1811), Spanish stateman and scholar.

Joveyni , Àta Malek (actually 'Alā' od-Dīn 'Atā Malek Joveynī) (1226-1283), notable Persian historian, author of the valuable *Tarikh-i jehan-gusha* (1252-56; English translation as *A History of the World Conqueror,* 1958).

Jovius, Paulus (1483-1552), Italian historian and biographer who was also known as Paolo Giovio.

Jowett, Benjamin (1817-1893), outstanding English classical scholar, especially noted for his translations of Plato.

Joyce, James (Augustine Aloysius) (1882-1941), greatly significant Irish novelist, short-story writer and poet whose novels *Ulysses* (1922) and *Finnegan's Wake* (1939) changed the course of modern literature.

Joyce, Patrick Weston (1827-1914), Irish writer.

József, Attila (1905-1937), remarkable Hungarian poet who espoused the cause of Marxism.

Juan Yüan (1764-1849), Chinese scholar and government official.

Jud, Jakob (1882-1952), Swiss linguist who was an authority of Romance languages.

Jud, Leo (1482-1542), Swiss Protestant reformer and biblical scholar who translated the Bible into German (c.1535).

Judah, Samuel B(enjamin) H(elbert) (1804-1876), American lawyer, writer and poet.

Judah ben Samuel (d.1217), German Jewish mystic and one of the leading figures in Hasidism, principal author of the treatise *Sefer Hasidim* (Book of the Pious, published 1538).

Judah ha-Levi (actually Yeduha ben Shemuel ha-Levi) (c.1075-1141), important Jewish Hebrew poet and philosopher.

Judah ha-Nasi (c.135-c.220), Palestinian Jewish scholar and patriarch, an outstanding interpreter of the Jewish Oral Law, a part of which he preserved as the Mishna (Teaching).

Judd, Charles Hubbard (1873-1946), American psychologist and educator.

Judd, Sylvester (1813-1853), American Unitarian minister and writer, author of the novels *Margaret* (1845) and *Richard Edney and the Governor's Family* (1850), and the epic *Philo, an Evangeliad* (1950).

Judson, Adoniram (1788-1850), American Baptist misionary and linguist who translated the Bible into Burmese and edited a Burmese dictionary; husband of Emily (Chubbuck) Judson.

Judson, E(dward) Z(ane) C(arroll) (1823-1886), American adventurer and writer, creator of the so-called dime novels which he wrote under the name Ned Buntline.

Judson, Emily (Chubbuck) (1817-1854), American writer and poet who wrote under the name Fanny Forester; wife of Adoniram Judson.

Julian of Eclanum (c.386-454), Apulian Christian theologian who espoused Pelagian views.

Julian of Norwich (c.1342-c.1417), English Roman Catholic mystic and anchoress, celebrated for her *Showings* or *Revelation(s) of Divine Love* (modern edition, 1978).

Jung, Carl (Gustav) (1875-1961), renowned Swiss psychologist and psychiatrist, founder of analytic psychology and author of the study *Wandlungen und Symbole der Libido* (1912; English translation as *The Psychology of the Unconcsious,* 1921).

Jünger, Ernst (1895-1998), German novelist and essayist whose espousal of militarism gave way to an ardent anti-militarism during the Nazi regime.

Jungmann, Josef (1773-1847), Czech linguist and writer.

Jung-Stilling, Johann Heinrich (1740-1817), German writer who became best known for his autobiography *Heinrich Stillings Leben* (Heinrich Stilling's Life, 5 volumes, 1806).

Junius, Franciscus (1589-1677), German-born English language and literary scholar.

Junod, Henri Alexandre (1863-1934), Swiss Protestant missionary and anthropologist.

Junot, Laure, Duchesse d'Abrantès (actually **Laure Permon) (1784-1883),** French memoirist, author of *Mémoires sur Napoléon, la Révolution, le Consulat, L'Empire et la Restauration,* (8 volumes, 1831-35).

Junqueiro, Abílio Manuel Guerra (1850-1923), prominent Portuguese poet.

Jurjānī, al- (actually **Abū Bakr 'Abd al-Qāhir Ibn 'Abd ar-Rahmān al-Jurjānī) (d. 1078),** Arab philologist and literary scholar.

Jurjānī, al- (actually **'Alī Ibn Muhammad al-Jurjānī) (1339-1413),** Persian theologian and scholar.

Justin Martyr, Saint (c.100-c.165), famous Christian apologist, author of two *Apologies* and the *Dialogue with Trypho*; after refusing to sacrifice to the Roman gods, he was scourged and beheaded.

Juvenval (actually **Decimus Junius Juvenalist) (c.55-c.128),** celebrated Roman poet of satirical verse.

Kabīr (1440-1518), Indian mystic and poet who espoused the cause of unity between Hindu and Muslim worldviews.

Kačić Miošić, Andrija (c.1704-1760), Croatian poet.

Kaden-Bandrowski, Juliusz (1885-1944), Polish novelist and short-story writer.

Kafka, Franz (1883-1924), famous Czech-born Austrian novelist and short-story writer, author of the classic novels *Der Prozess* (Published 1925; English translation as *The Trial,* 1937) and *Das Schloss* (Published 1926; English translation as *The Castle,* 1930).

Kagawa Toyohilo (1888-1960), Japanese Christian social reformer and writer.

Kah-ge-ga-gah-bowh, Chief or **George Copway (1818-1863),** Canadian-born American chief of the Ojibway tribe, writer and poet, author of the epic poem *The Ojibway conquest, a Tale of the Northwest* (1850).

Kahn, Gustave (1859-1936), prominent French poet and critic, one of the earliest and most effective writers of vers libre.

Kaibara Ekiken (actually **Atsunobu) (1630-1714),** Japanese philosopher, botanist and travel writer.

Kailas, Uuno (1901-1933), Finnish writer.

Kaiser, Georg (1878-1945), distinguished German dramatist who wrote notable Expressionist works for the stage.

Kakinomoto Hitomaro (7th-8th Century), revered Japanese poet.

Kaler, James Otis (1848-1912), American writer of works for boys who wrote under the name James Otis.

Kālidāsa (5th Century), great Indian poet and dramatist writing in Sanskrit.

Kalīm, Abū Tālib (d. 1651), Indian Muslim poet.

Kallas, Aino (1878-1956), Finnish writer.

Kallen, H(orace) M(eyer) (1882-1974), American cultural and political philosopher.

Kalm, Peter (1716-1779), Swedish scientist and traveller who left a valuable account of his visit to America (3 volumes, 1753-61; English translation, 1770-71).

Kálvos, Andréas Ioannídis (1792-1869), Greek poet who was known for his patriotic odes (2 fascicles, 1824, 1826).

Kames, Henry Home, Lord (1696-1782), English jurist and philosopher, author of the notable *Elements of Criticism* (3 volumes, 1762).

Kamo Chōmei (c.1155-1216), outstanding Japanese poet and critic, a master of vernacular verse.

Kämpfer, Englebert (1651-1716), German traveller who wrote accounts of his travels to Persia and Japan.

Kanagaki Robun (actually **Bunzó Nozaki**) **(1829-1874)**, Japanese writer.

Kanakadāsa (16th Century), Indian mystical poet.

K'ang Yu-wei (1858-1927), Chinese scholar and reformer.

Kant, Immanuel (1724-1804), great German philosopher of Idealism, author of the greatly influential treatises *Kritik der reinen Vernunft* (Critique of Pure Reason, 1781), *Kritik der practischen Vernunft* (Critique of Practical Reason, 1788) and *Kritik der Urthielskraft* (Critique of Judgement, 1790).

Kantor, MacKinlay (1904-1977), American novelist and short-story writer.

Kantorowicz, Hermann (1877-1940), Polish legal scholar.

Kaplan, Mordecai Menahem (1881-1983), Lithuanian-born American rabbi, educator and theologian, founder of the liberal Reconstructionist movement in Judaism.

Karadžić, Vuk Stefanović (1787-1864), Serbian scholar who was an authority on the language and folk literature of his country.

Karamzin, Nikolai Mikhailovich (1766-1826), influential Russian historian, journalist and poet, author of the *Istoriya gosudarstva rossiyakogo* (History of the Russian State, 12 volumes, 1816-29).

Karavelov, Lyuben Stoychev (1834-1879), Bulgarian writer and revolutionary.

Karelitz, Avraham Yeshayahu (ben Shmazyahn Joseph) (1878-1953), Jewish scholar who was an authority on the Halakha.

Kariotákis, Kóstas (1896-1928), Greek poet.

Karkavitsas, Andréas (1860-1922), Greek novelist and short-story writer.

Karlfeldt, Erik Axel (1864-1931), admired Swedish poet; was posthumously awarded the Nobel Prize for Literature (1931).

Karlstadt, Andreas Rudolf Bodenstlen von (c.1480-1541), German Protestant theologian who was an early supporter of Lutheranism but later espoused more radical views in various tracts.

Kármán, Jósef (1769-1795), Hungarian writer.

Karo or **Caro** or **Qaro, Joesph ben Ephraim (1488-1575)**, Jewish scholar who prepared the last great codification of Jewish law in his *Bet Yosef* (House of Joseph), which he condensed in his *Shulhan 'arukh* (The Prepared Table).

Kasprowicz, Jan (1860-1926), admired Polish poet and translator.

Kassák, Lajos (1887-1967), Hungarian poet and novelist who championed radical political ideas.

Kästner, Erich (1899-1974), German poet and novelist who was known for his satire but also for his writings for children.

Katayev, Valentin (Petrovich) (1897-1986), Russian novelist and dramatist.

Katkov, Mikhail Nikiforovich (1818-1887), influential Russian journalist of reactionary views.

Katō Hiroyuki (1836-1916), Japanese writer, political theorist and educator who helped to introduce Western ideas into his homeland.

Katona, József (1791-1830), Hungarian dramatist and lawyer, author of the important play *Bánk bán* (1821).

Kaufman, George S(imon) (1889-1961), distinguished American dramatist who collaborated with others on such outstanding plays as *Of Thee I Sing* (1931), *You Can't Take it With You* (1936) and *The Man who Came to Dinner* (1939).

Kautilya (actually **Cānakya**) **(flourished 300 B.C.)**, Hindu statesman and philosopher who wrote *Artha-sastra* English translation, 1926), a famous treatise on statecraft.

Kautsky, Karl (1854-1938), German Marxist journalist and political theorist who opposed Bolshevism.

Kavanagh, Patrick Joesph (1905-1967), respected Irish poet, novelist and critic, best known for his poem *The Great Hunger* (1942).

Kawabata Yasunari (1899-1972), esteemed Japanese novelist; won the Nobel Prize for Literature (1968).

Kawakami Hajime (1879-1946), Japanese poet and Marxist theorist.

Kawatake Mokuami (1816-1893), Japanese dramatist of the Kabuki theatre.

Kaye-Smith, (Emily) Shella (1887-1956), English novelist.

Kaygusuz Abdal (15th Century), Turkish poet of Sufism.

Kazantzakis, Nikos (1885-1957), Greek novelist, dramatist, essayist, poet and translator, best known for the epic poem *The Odyssey, a Modern sequel* (1938) and the novel *Zorba the Greek* (1946).

Kazin, Alfred (1915-1998), esteemed American literary critic.

Kazinczy, Ferenc (1759-1831), Hungarian writer and poet.

Keane, Molly (actually **Mary Nesta Skrine**) **(1904-1996)**, Irish novelist and dramatist.

Keating, Geofferey (c.1570-c.1644), Irish writer.

Keats, John (1795-1821), celebrated English poet, a master of lyric expression, renowned for his *Lamia and Other Poems* (1820), which included such masterworks as *The Eve of St Agnes, Lamia, On a Grecian Urn, On Melancholy, To Autumn, To a Nightingale* and *To Psyche.*

Keble, John (1792-1866), English Anglican priest, theologian and poet, founder of the Oxford Movement of The Church of england for the restoration of high-church principles.

Keckley, Elizabeth (1827-1907), American memoirist whose account of her years as a dressmaker to the wealthy and famous was published in the valuable *Behind the Scenes, or, Thirty Years a Slave and Four Years in the White House* (1868).

Keeler, Ralph Olmstead (1840-1873), American journalist and novelist.

Keenan, Henry Francis (1850-1928), American writer whose novel *The Money-Makers* (1885) was published anonymously.

Kees, Weldon (1914-1955), American poet, painter, jazz pianist and composer.

Keith, George (c.1638-1716), Scottish-born American Quaker, later Anglican clergyman and writer.

Kelland, Clarence Budington (1881-1964), American novelist and short-story writer.

Keller, Ferdinand (1800-1881), Swiss archaeologist and prehistorian.

Keller. Gottfried (1819-1890), Swiss novelist, short-story writer and poet whose finest work was the novel *Der grüne Heinrich* (1854-55; revised version, 1879-80; English translation as *Green Henry*, 1960).

Keller, Helen Adams (1880-1968), famous American writer and lecturer who triumphed over her being born blind, deaf, and mute.

Kellerman, Bernard (1879-1951), German journalist and novelist, best remembered for his novel *Der Tunnel* (1913; English translation as *The Tunnel*, 1915).

Kelley, Edith Summers (1884-1956), Canadian-born American novelist.

Kellgren, Johan Henrik (1751-1795), important Swedish poet and journalist whose masterpiece was the poem *Den Nya Skapelsen, eller inbillningensvärld* (The New Creation, or the World of the Imagination, 1790).

Kellogg, Elijah (1813-1901), American congregational minister and writer of children's books.

Kelly, George (Edward) (1887-1974), American dramatist, actor and director, author of *The Torch-Bearers* (1922; revised edition, 1938), *The Show Off* (1924) and *Craigs Wife* (1925).

Kelly, Hugh (1739-1777), English dramatist, critic and journalist.

Kelly, Jonathon Falconbridge (c.1817-1855), American journalist and writer who became known for his humor.

Kelsen, Hans (1881-1973), Austrian-born American legal philosopher who was particularly known for his writings on international law.

Kemal, (Mehmed) Namik (1840-1888), significant Turkish writer and poet who helped to Westernize the literature of his homeland.

Kemalpaşazâde (c.1468-1534), renowned Turkish historian and poet.

Kemble, Fanny (actually **Frances Ann Kemble) (1809-1893),** English actress, writer, dramatist and poet.

Kemble, John Mitchell (1807-1857), English historian and philologist.

Kemény, Zsigmond, Baron (1814-1875), Hungarian journalist and novelist.

Kemp, Harry (actually **Hibbard Kemp) (1883-1960),** American poet, writer and dramatist who was known as the "tramp poet".

Kempe, Margery (c.1373-c.1440), English religious mystic who was known for her dictated autobiography (c.1435; published 1936).

Ken, Thomas (1637-1711), English Anglican bishop and hymnist, author of the hymns *Awake, My Soul, and With the Sun* and *Glory to Thee, My God, This Night.*

Kendall, George Wilkins (1809-1867), American journalist and writer.

Kendall, Henry (1839-1882), leading Australian poet.

Kennan, George (1845-1924), American traveller and writer.

Kennedy, Charles Rann (1871-1950), English dramatist.

Kennedy, John Pendleton (1795-1870), American writer and politician.

Kennedy, Margaret, Lady Davies (1896-1967), English novelist, critic and biographer.

Kennedy, Walter (c.1460-c.1508), Scottish poet of secular and sacred verse.

Kenneth, Saint (c.515-c.599), Irish Roman Catholic abbot, missionary and poet.

Kent, James (1763-1847), American legal scholar and jurist, author of the influential *Commentaries on American Law* (4 volumes, 1826-30).

Kent, Rockwell (1882-1971), American writer, painter and illustrator.

Kenyon, John S(amuel) (1874-1959), American phonetician.

Kephart, Horace (1862-1931), American naturalist.

Ker, William Paton (1855-1923), English literary scholar.

Kerner, Justinus Andreas Christian (1786-1862), German poet, writer and physician.

Kerouac, Jack (actually Jean-Louis Kerouac) (1922-1969), prominent American novelist and poet, a leading figure in the Beat movement who was best known for his novel *On the Road* (1957).

Kerr, Walter Francis (1913-1996), influential American drama critic.

Keshub Chunder Sen (1838-1884), Hindu religious reformer and writer.

Ketteler, Wilhelm Emmanuel, Freiherr von (1811-1877), German Roman Catholic bishop and social reformer.

Key, Ellen (Karolina Sofia) (1849-1926), Swedish essayist who espoused various liberal causes.

Key, Francis Scott (1779-1843), American lawyer and poet, author of *The Star Spangled Banner* (1814), which was officially adopted as the US National Anthem (1931).

Key, V(aldimer) O(rlando) Jr (1908-1963), American political scientist.

Keyes, Frances Parkinson (1885-1970), American writer of romantic historical novels.

Keyes, Sydney Arthur Kilworth (1922-1943), English poet; died in World War II.

Keynes, Sir Geoffrey Langdon (1887-1982), English literary scholar, bibliographer and surgeon; brother of J(ohn) M(aynard) Keynes.

Keynes, J(ohn) M(aynard), 1st Baron Keynes of Tilton (1883-1946), greatly influential English economist, author of *A General Theory of Employment, Interest, and Money* (1936); brother of Sir Geoffery Langdon Keynes.

Keyserling, Hermann Alexander, Graf (1880-1946), German Philosohpher, especially remembered for his *Das Reisetagebuch eines Philosophen* (1919; English translation as *The Travel Diary of a Philosopher,* 1925).

Khalīl ibn Ahmad, al- (actually Abū 'Abd ar-Rahman al-Khalīl ibn Ahmad ibn 'Amr ibn Timīn al-Farāhidi al-Azdī al-Yuhmadī) (c.718-c.788), Arab philogist and Lexicographer.

Khansā, al- (actually Tumādir Bint 'Amr ibn al-Hārith ibn Ash Sharīd) (d. c.631), celebrated Arab poet of elergies.

Khāqānī (actually Afzal od-Dīn Bādel Ebrāhim ebn 'Alī Khāqānī Shīrvānī) (c.1106-c.1185), Persian poet who excelled in writing court poems, epigrams and satires.

Kheraskov, Mikhail Matveievich (1733-1807), Russian poet who was known for his epics.

Khlebnikov, Velemir Vladimirovich (actually Viktor Vladimirovich Khlebnikov) (1885-1922), influential Russian poet, founder of the Russian Futurist movement.

Khomyakov, Aleksei Stepanovich (1804-1860), Russian poet and lay theologian of the Orthodox Church who was a principle figure in the Slavophile movement.

Khashhāl Khān Khatak (d.1689), Afgan soldier and poet.

Khwāndamīr, Ghiyās ad-Dīn Muhammad (c.1475-c.1535), Persian historian.

Kickham, Charles Joseph (1826-1882), popular Irish poet and novelist, especially remembered for his espousal of Irish nationalism.

Kidder, Alfred V(incent) (1885-1963), American archaeologist, author of the *Introduction to the Study of South western Archaeology* (1924).

Kielland, Alexander (1849-1906), noted Norwegian novelist, short-story writer and dramatist.

Kierkegaard, Søren (Aabye) (1813-1855), renowned Danish religious philosopher whose Existentialist world view was explicated in such important works as *Enten-Eller: Et Livs Fragment* (1843:English translation as *Either/Or: A Fragment of Life,* 1944), *Frygt og Baeven* (1843; English translation as *Fear and Trembling,* 1939), *Gjentagelsen* (1843; English translation as *Repetition,* 1942), *Philosophiske Smuler, eller en Smule Philosophi* (1844; English translation as *Philosophical Fragments, or a Fragment of Philosophy,* 1936), *Begrebet Angest* (1844; English translation as *The Concept of Dread,* 1944), *Stadier paa Livets vei* (1845; English translation as *Stages on Life's way,* 1940), *Kjerlighedens Gjerninger* (1847; English translation as *Works of Love,* 1946) and *Sygdommen til Døden* (1849; English translation as *The Sickness unto Death,* 1941).

Kikuchi Kan (1888-1948), Japanese dramatist, novelist and publisher.

Killigrew, Henry (1613-1700), English dramatist; brother of Thomas Killigrew the elder and Sir William Killigrew.

Killigrew, Thomas, the elder (1612-1683), English dramatist; father of Thomas Killigrew the younger and brother of Henry Killigrew and Sir William Killigrew.

Killigrew, Thomas, the younger (1657-1719), English dramatist; son of Thomas Killigrew the elder.

Killigrew, Sir William (c.1606-1695), English dramatist; brother of Henry Killigrew and Thomas Killigrew the elder.

Kilmer, (Alfred) Joyce (1886-1918), American poet who wrote the famous *Trees* (1913); died in World War I; husband of Aline Kilmer.

Kilmer, Aline (1888-1941), American poet; wife of Alfred Joyce Kilmer.

Kilvert, (Robert) Francis (1840-1879), English clergyman and diarist.

Kimball, Richard Burleigh (1816-1892), American lawyer and novelist.

Kimhi, David (c.1160-c.1235), celebrated Jewish scholar of the Hebrew language; son of Joseph Kimhi and brother of Moses Kimhi.

Kimhi, Joesph (c1105-c.1170), Jewish grammarian, biblical scholar and poet; father of David and Moses Kimhi.

Kimhi, Moses (d. c.1190), Jewish grammarian; son of Joesph Kimhi and brother of David Kimhi.

Kim Man-jung (17th Century), Korean writer.

Kinck, Hans E(rnst) (1865-1926), Norwegian novelist, short-story writer, dramatist and essayist, particularly remembered for his novel *Sneskavlen brast* (The Avalanche Broke, 3 volumes, 1918-19).

Kindī, Ya'qūb Ibn Ishāq as-Sabah, al (d. c.870), important Arab Islāmic philosoher.

King, Charles (1844-1933), American army officer and writer.

King, Clarence (1842-1901), American geologist and writer.

King, Grace Elizabeth (1851-1932), American novelist and short-story writer.

King, Henry (1592-1669), English Anglican bishop and poet, author of *Poems, Elegies, Paradoxes and Sonets* (1657), in which is found his celebrated *Exequy to his Mathcless never to be forgotten friend.*

King, Martin Luther, Jr (1929-1968), famous American Baptist preacher, civil rights leader and writer; won the Nobel Prize for Peace (1964); was assassinated.

King, Thomas Starr (1824-1864), American Unitarian minister and writer.

King, William (1663-1712), English poet and writer.

King-Hall, (William Richard) Stephen, Baron (1893-1966), English writer and editor.

Kinglake, Alexander William (1809-1891), English traveller and writer, best known for his *Eothen: or traces of travel brought home from the East* (1844).

Kingo, Thomas (Hansen) (1634-1703), esteemed Danish poet, hymnist and clergyman.

Kingsley, Charles (1819-1875), noted English Anglican clergyman, novelist, essayist and poet; brother of George Henry Kingsley and Henry Kingsley.

Kingsley, George Henry (1827-1892), English physician and traveller, author of *South Sea Bubbles* (1872); brother of Charles and Henry Kingsley.

Kingsley, Henry (1830-1876), English novelist, particularly remembered for his *Ravenshoe* (1861) and *The Hillyars and the Burtons* (1865); brother of Charles and George Henry Kingsley.

Kingsley, Mary Henrietta (1862-1900), English traveller, author of *Travels in West Africa* (1897) and *West African Studies* (1899).

Kingsley, Sidney (actually Sidney Kirshner) (1906-1995), American dramatist and actor.

Kingsmill, Hugh (actually Hugh Kingsmill Lunn) (1889-1949), English novelist, biographer and critic.

Kingston, W(illiam) H(enry) G(iles) (1814-1880), English writer of popular stories for boys.

Kinkel, Gottfried (1815-1882), German poet who was active in the revolutionary uprisings of 1848 and escaped from prison to live abroad in exile.

Kino Tsurayuki (d. c.945), Japanese nobleman, court official and poet.

Kinsey, Alfred Charles (1894-1956), American Zoologist who wrote the controversial studies *Sexual Behaviour in the Human Male* (1948) and *Sexual Behaviour in the Human Female* (1953).

Kipling, (Joseph) Rudyard (1865-1936), famous English poet, novelist and short-story writer, particularly remembered for his children's classics *The Jungle Books* (1894-95) and *Kim* (1901); won the Nobel Prize for Literature (1907); brother-in-law of (Charles) Wolcott Balestier.

Kirby, William (1817-1906), English-born Canadian writer, best known for his classic novel *The Golden Dog* (1877).

Kireyevsky, Ivan Vasilievich (1806-1856), Russian critic and editor.

Kirkland, Caroline Stansbury (1801-1864), American writer; granddaughter of Joseph Stansbury and mother of Joseph Kirkland.

Kirkland, Joseph (1830-1894), American novelist, author of *Zury: The Meanest Man in Spring County* (1887), *The McVeys* (1888) and *The Captain of Company Z* (1891); son of Caroline Stansbury Kirkland.

Kirkwood, James (1924-1989), American writer, co-author of the musical *A Chorus Line* (1975).

Kirst, Hans Helmut (1914-1989), German novelist, particularly remembered for *Die Nacht der Generale* (1962; English translation as *The Night of the Generals,* 1963).

Kisfaludy, Károly (1788-1830), Hungarian dramatist, a leading figure in the Romantic movement in his homeland.

Kisfaludy, Sándor (1772-1844), Hungarian writer.

Kitabatake Chikafusa (1292-1354), Japanese warrior and statesman who wrote the important treatise *Jinnō shōtōki* (Record of the Legitimate Succession of the Divine Emperors, 1339).

Kitchin, Clifford Henry Benn (1895-1967), English novelist, short-story writer and barrister.

Kittel, Rudolf (1853-1929), German Old Testament scholar.

Kittredge, George Lyman (1860-1941), eminent American literary scholar and critic, an authority on Shakespeare, Chaucer and Malory.

Kivi, Aleksis (actually **Aleksis Stenvall) (1834-1872),** important Finnish novelist, dramatist and poet, duly recognised as the father of the Finnish novel and drama.

Kjellen, (Johan) Rudolf (1864-1922), Swedish political scientist who coined the term geopolitics and wrote the treatise *Staten som lifs-form* (The State as a Life-Form, 1918-19).

Klabund (actually **Alfred Henschke) (1890-1928),** German poet, dramatist and novelist, a prominent Expressionist.

Klaczko, Julian (1825-1906), Lithuanian journalist and literary critic.

Klaj or **Clajust, Johann (1616-1656),** German poet.

Klaproth, Heinrich Julius (1783-1835), German Orientalist and explorer, author of the valuable *Asia polyglotta nebst Sprachatlas* (Asia polyglotta with Language Atlas, 1823).

Klein, A(braham) Moses (1909-1972), esteemed Canadian poet and writer whose works reflect his Talmudic studies.

Klein, Charles (1867-1915), American dramatist who was best known for his sentimental plays *The Auctioneer* (1901) and *The Music Master* (1904).

Klein, Melanie (née Reizes) (1882-1960), influential Austrian-born English psychoanalyst who specialized in child therapy, author of *The Psychoanalysis of Children* (1932).

Kleist, (Bernd) Heinrich (Wilhelm) von (1777-1811), important German dramatist, writer and poet; committed suicide.

Kleist, Ewald Christian von (1715-1759), German poet, much admired for his *Der Früling* (The Spring, 1749); died from wounds sustained in the battle of Kundersdorf.

Klemm, Gustav Friedrich (1802-1867), noted German anthropologist, author of *Allgemeine Kulturgeschichte der Menschheit* (General Cultural History of Mankind, 10 volumes, 1843-52) and *Allgemeine Kulturwissenschaft* (General Science of Culture, 2 volumes, 1854-55).

Kleutgen, Joseph (1811-1883), German Jesuit philosopher.

Klinger, Friedrich Maximilian von (1752-1831), German dramatist and novelist, a prominent figure in the Sturm und Drang movement.

Klonowic, Sebastian (Fabian) (c.1545-1602), Polish poet who wrote both Polish and Latin verse.

Kloos, Willem Johan Theodor (1859-1938), Dutch poet and critic whose sonnets were admired.

Klopstock, Friedrich Gottlieb (1724-1803), eminent German poet of lyric refinement, author of *Des Messias* (The Messiah, 1749-73) and various odes.

Kluckhohn, Clyde (Kay Maben) (1905-1960), American anthropologist who wrote *Navaho Witchcraft* (1944) and *Mirror for Man* (1949).

Klyuchevsky, Vasily Osipovich (1841-1911), distinguished Russian historian whose work was marked by a regard for sociological principles.

Knapp, Samuel Lorenzo (1783-1838), American essayist.

Knebel, Karl Ludwig von (1744-1834), German poet who was highly esteemed for his sonnets.

Kneeland, Abner (1774-1844), American Universalist minister and freethinker.

Knigge, Adolf Franz Friedrich, Freiherr von (1752-1796), German novelist.

Knight, Charles (1791-1893), English publisher and writer.

Knight, G(eorge Richard) Wilson (1897-1985), English literary scholar and critic, especially known for his Shakespearian studies.

Knight, Sarah Kemble (1666-1727), American teacher and buisnesswoman who wrote an interesting travel journal (published 1825).

Knighton, Henry (d. c.1396), English chronicler.

Knolles, Richard (c.1550-1610), English historian, author of a *Generall Historie of the Turkes, from the first beginning of that Nation* (1603).

Knowles, James Sheridan (1784-1862), English actor and dramatist.

Knowles, Sir James Thomas (1831-1908), English editor and architect.

Knox, Edmund George Valpy (1881-1971), English essayist, humorist and editor who, as Evoe, served as editor of *Punch* (1932-49); brother of Ronald Arbuthnott Knox.

Knox, John (c.1513-1572), outstanding Scottish Protestant Reformation leader, author of the *History of the Reformation of Religioun within the realme of Scotland* (published 1587).

Knox, Ronald Arbuthnott (1888-1957), distinguished English Roman Catholic theologian, writer and translator of the Bible; brother of Edmund George Valpy Knox.

Knudtzon, Jørgen Alexander (1854-1917), Norwegian Oriental scholar.

Knayazhnin, Yakov Borisovich (1742-1791), Russian writer.

Kobayashi Takiji (1903-1933), Japanese writer and political radical.

Kober, Arthur (1900-1974), Polish-born American dramatist and writer.

Koch, Martin (1882-1940), Swedish novelist, best known for his *Arbetare* (Workers, 1912), *Timmerdalen* (Timber Valley, 1913) and *Guds vackra värld* (God's Beautiful World, 1916).

Kochanowska, Jan (1530-1584), significant Polish poet and dramatist, renowned for his poems *Treny* (1580; English translation as *Laments,* 1920).

Kochowski, Wespazjan (1633-1700), Polish poet and historian, remembered for his poetic epic *Psalmodia polska* (Polish Psalmody, 1695).

Kock, Charles-Paul de (1793-1871), French novelist.

Kōda Rohan (actually Kōda Shigeyuki) (1867-1947), Japanese novelist and essayist.

Koeber, Raphael von (1842-1923), Russian philosopher.

Koeppen, Wolfgang (1906-1996), German novelist and essayist.

Koestler, Arthur (1905-1983), Hungarian-born English journalist, novelist and critic, particularly known for his novel *Darkness at Noon* (1940); committed suicide.

Koffka, Kurt (1886-1941), German-born American psychologist whose pioneering work in Gestalt psychology was elaborated in his *Gestalt Psychology* (1929) and *Principles of Gestalt Psychology* (1935).

Kogălniceanu, Mihail (1817-1891), Romanian political reformer and historian.

Koghbatzi, Eznik (5th Century), Armenian writer.

Kohler, Josef (1849-1919), German philosopher.

Kohler, Kaufmann (1843-1926), German-born American Jewish rabbi and theologian of Reform Judaism, author of *Jewish Theology Systematically and Historically Considered* (1918).

Köhler, Wolfgang (1887-1967), German-born American psychologist who was a major figure in the development of Gestalt psychology, author of the influential *Intelligenzprüfungen an Menschenaffen* (1917; English translation as *The Mentality of Apes,* 1924).

Kohut, Alexander (1842-1894), Hungarian-born American Jewish rabbi and scholar.

Kokoschka, Oskar (1886-1980), Austrian-born English painter and writer.

Kolcsey, Ferenc (1790-1838), Hungarian poet, critic and politician, author of the Hungarian National anthem.

Koldewey, Robert (1855-1925), German architect and archaeologist.

Kollár, Ján (1793-1852), Slovak pastor and poet, author of the epic poem *Slavy dcera* (The Daughter of Slava).

Kołłątaj, Hugo (1750-1812), Polish Roman Catholic priest, educator and politician who advocated radical reform in the structure of Polish society.

Koltsov, Aleksie Vasilievich (1809-1842), Russian poet.

Komroff, Manuel (1890-1974), American novelist and short-story writer.

Konarski, Stanisław (1700-1773), Polish Roman Catholic priest and writer on historical and political subjects.

Konopnicka, Maria (actually Maria Wasilowska) (1842-1910), admired Polish short-story writer and poet, remembered especially for her poetic cycle *Italia* (Italy 1901).

Konrad von Würzburg (c.1225-1287), German poet who upheld the cause of a dying chivalry.

Kook, Abraham Isaac (1865-1935), Latvian mystic, Zionist, chief rabbi of Palestine and essayist.

Kopisch, August (1799-1853), Polish poet and painter.

Koppers, Wilhelm (1886-1961), German-born Austrian Roman Catholic priest and cultural anthropologist.

Koraïs, Adamantios (1748-1833), influential Greek scholar of humanistic ideals.

Körner, (Karl) Theodor (1791-1813), popular German poet and dramatist, especially known for his patriotic play *Zriny* (1812).

Korolenko, Vladimir Galaktionovich (1853-1921), Russian short-story writer and journalist.

Korsch, Karl (1886-1961), German political philosopher and Marxist theoretician.

Korzybski, Alfred (Habdank Skarbek) (1879-1950), Polish-born American scientist and philosopher, author of *Science and Sanity: An Introduction to Non-Aristotelian Systems and General Semantics (1933)*

Kosinski, Jerzy (Nikodem) (1933-1991), Polish-born American novelist, especially known for *The Painted Bird* (1965); committed suicide.

Kosovel, Srečko (1904-1926), Slovenian writer.

Kosztolányi, Dezső (1885-1936), admired Hungarian poet, novelist, short-story writer and critic, author of the novel *Édes Anna* (1926; English translation as *Wonder Maid*, 1947).

Kotlyarevsky, Ivan (1769-1838), Ukrainian writer, best known for the *Eneyida* (1798), a burlesque-travesty of Virgil's *Aeneid*.

Kotsyubinsky, Mikhaylo (1864-1913), Ukrainian novelist and short-story writer.

Kotzebue, August (Friedrich Ferdinand) von (1761-1819), prominent German dramatist, writer and court official in Russia; denounced as a traitor to the German fatherland for his service in Russia, he was assassinated by a member of a radical student group.

Kovalevskaya, Sofia (1850-1891), Russian mathematician and novelist.

Kowatake Mokuami (1816-1893), Japanese dramatist of the Kabuki theatre.

Kraemer, Hendrik (1880-1965), Dutch theologian.

Král', Janko (1822-1876), notable Slovak poet.

Krasicki, Ignacy (1735-1801), outstanding Polish poet, writer and Roman Catholic archbishop.

Krasiński, Zygmunt, Count (1812-1859), esteemed Polish poet and dramatist.

Kraszewski, Jósef Ignacy (1812-1887), Polish novelist, poet, dramatist, historian and critic.

Kraus, Karl (1874-1936), remarkable Austrian writer, dramatist, poet and editor.

Krause, Herbert (1905-1976), American writer and poet.

Krause, Karl Christian Friedrich (1781-1832), German philosopher.

Kretschmer, Ernst (1888-1964), German psychiatrist, particularly known for his controversial treatise *Körperbau und Charakter* (1921; English translation as *Physique and Character*, 1925).

Kretschmer, Paul (1866-1956), German-born Austrian classical linguist.

Kretzer, Max (1854-1941), German novelist of the Expressionist school.

Kreutzwald, F(riedrich) Reinhold (1803-1882), Estonian physician, folklorist and poet who compiled and contributed original verse to the national epic poem the *Kalevipoeg* (The son of Kalevi, 1857-61).

Krėvė-Mickievičius, Vincas (1882-1954), leading Lithuanian poet, dramatist and philologist who was also known as Vincas Kreve.

Kreymborg, Alfred (1883-1996), American poet and dramatist.

Krige, Uys (1910-1987), South African journalist, novelist, dramatist and poet who wrote in both Afrikaans and English.

Kristensen, W(ilhelm) Brede (1867-1953), Norwegian-born Dutch historian who was known for his studies in religious symbolism.

Križanić, Juraj (1618-1683), Croatian Roman Catholic priest and scholar who was a leading advocate of Pan-Slavism in Russia.

Krochmal, Nachman (1785-1840), Polish Jewish scholar and philosopher, author of the notable *More nevukhe ha-zman* (The Guide for the Perplexed of Our Time).

Kroeber, A(lfred) L(ouis) (1876-1960), outstanding American cultural anthropologist, author of *Anthropology* (1923; revised edition, 1948), *Configurations of Culture Growth* (1945) and *The Nature of Culture* (1952).

Kropotkinm, Pyotr Alexelevich (1842-1921), prominent Russian revolutionary and anarchist theoretician.

Kruczkowski, Leon (1900-1962), Polish writer.

Krumbacher, Karl (1856-1909), German scholar, an authority on Byzantine culture.

Krünitz, Johann Georg (1728-1796), German philosopher, physician and encyclopaedist.

Krusenstjerna, Agnes von (1894-1940), Swedish novelist.

Krŭst'o, Krustyu (1866-1910), Bulgarian writer.

Krutch, Joseph Wood (1893-1970), American drama critic and naturalist.

Krylov, Ivan Andrelevich (1769-1844), Russian writer who won distinction for his fables in verse.

Kuan Han-ch'ing (c.1241-c.1320), great Chinese dramatist.

Kudirka, Vincas (1858-1899), Lithuanian journalist, writer and patriot, author of the Lithuanian National Anthem.

Kugler, Franz (1808-1854), German historian.

Kahn, (Franz Felix) Adalbert (1812-1881), German language scholar and folklorist who was an authority on the Indo-European peoples.

Kuhn, Thomas (1922-1996), influential American philosopher, author of the important study *The Structure of Scientific Revolutions* (1962).

Kūkai (actually Kobo Daishi) (774-835), revered Japanese Buddist saint, philosopher, poet, artist and calligrapher, founder of the Shingon (True Word) school of Buddhism.

Külpe, Oswald (1862-1915), German psychologist and philosopher, author of *Gundriss der Psychologie* (1893; English translation as *Outlines of Psychology*, 1895) and *Die Realisierung* (Realization, 3 volumes, 1912-23).

Kumazawa Banzan (1619-1691), Japanese philosopher who espoused the cuase of political liberalism.

Kume Masao (1891-1952), Japanese novelist and dramatist.

Kunanbayev, Abai Ibragim (1845-1904), Kazakh writer.

Kung-sun Lung (c.320-c.250 B.C.), Chinese philosopher.

Kuo Hsi (11th Century), renowned Chinese artist and essayist.

Kuo Hsiang (d. 312), Chinese philosopher and government official, reputed author of the *Chuang-tzu,* a fundamental work of Taoism.

Kupala, Yanka (1882-1942), Belorussian writer.

Kuprin, Alexander Ivanovich (1870-1938), Russian novelist and short-story writer.

Kürenberger (12th Century), Austrian Minnesinger, the earliest known by name, who also was called the Knight of Kurenberg.

Kurz, Hermann (1813-1873), German novelist, journalist, translator and editor, especially esteemed for his novels *Schillers Heimatjahre* (Schiller's Homeland Years, 1843) and *Der Sonnenwirt* (The Proprietor of the Sun Inn, 1855), and for his *Erzählungen* (Tales, 1858-63).

Kuwaki Genyoku (1874-1946), Japanese philosopher who espoused Kantian principles.

Kuyper, Abraham (1837-1920), Dutch Protestant theologian and politician.

Kvaran, Einar Björleifsson (1859-1938), Icelandic journalist, novelist, short-story writer, dramatist and poet.

Kyd, Thomas (1558-1594), English dramatist, author of *The Spanish Tragedie* (1592), the first revenge play of the Elizabethan era.

Kyne, Peter B(ernard) (1880-1957), American writer.

Labadie, Jean de (1610-1674), French Protestant theologian who espoused pietism.

Labé, Louise (Charly Perrin) (c.1524-1566), French poet, admired for her sonnets.

Labeo, Marcus Antistius (d. c.10), famous Roman jurist and writer on the law.

Labiche, Eugène-Marin (1815-1888), French dramatist who excelled in light comedies.

Labourche, Henry Du Pré (1831-1912), English journalist and politician who was known as Labby.

Labriola, Antonio (1843-1904), Italian philosopher who was known for his exposition of Marxism.

La Bruyère, Jean de (1645-1695), French writer, author of the satirical *Les Caractères ou les moeurs de ce siècle* (The Characters or the Manners of this Age, 1688).

La Calprenède, Gautier de Costes, Seigneur de (c.1610-c.1663), French writer.

La Chaussee, Pierre-Claude Nivelle de (1692-1745), French dramatist.

Lachmann, Karl (Konrad Friedrich Wilhelm) (1793-1851), notable German classical scholar who advanced the cause of textual criticism.

Laclos, Pierre (-Ambroise-Francois) Choderlos de (1741-1803), French soldier and novelist, author of the classic *Les Liaisons dangereuses* (1782; English translation as *Dangerous Acquaintances*, 1924).

Lacordaire, (Jean-Baptiste-) Henri (1802-1861), French Roman Catholic ecclesiastic and writer.

Lacretelle, Jean-Charles-Dominique de (1766-1855), French journalist and historian who was known as Lacretelle le Jeune.

Lactantius (actually Lucius Caecilius Firmianus Lactantius) (c.240-c.320), Roman Christian apologist, author of the *Divine Institutiones* (The Divine Precepts).

La Curne de Sainte-Pelaye, Jean-Baptiste de (1697-1781), French medievalist and lexicographer.

Lacy, Ernest (1863-1916), American dramatist and poet.

Ladd, George Trumbull (1842-1921), American philosopher and experimental psychologist.

Ladd, Joseph Brown (1764-1786), American physician and poet, remembered for *The Poems of Arouet* (1786).

Ladd, William (1778-1841), American writer and lecturer on world peace.

La Farge, Christopher (1897-1956), American writer, poet, painter and architect; grandson of John La Farge.

La Farge, John (1835-1910), American artist and writer; grandfather of Christopher and Oliver (Hazard Perry) La Farge.

La Farge, Oliver (Hazard Perry) (1901-1963), American ethnologist and writer; grandson of John La Farge.

La Farina, Giuseppe (1815-1863), Italian revolutionary leader and writer of the Risorgimento movement.

La Fayette, Maire-Madeleine (Pioche de la Vergne), Comtesse de (1634-1693), remarkable French novelist, author of *La Princesse de Cléves* (1678).

Laffitte, Pierre (1823-1903), French philosopher who espoused positivism.

La Flesche, Francis (1857-1932), American ethnologist whose heritage as a native American is delineated in his memoir *The Middle Five* (1900).

La Flesche, Susette (Indian name **Bright Eyes) (1854-1903),** American writer and lecturer who was an activist on behalf of native American causes.

Lafontaine, Henri-Marie (1854-1943), Belgian lawyer and advocate of international peace; won the Nobel Prize for Peace (1913).

La Fontaine, Jean de (1621-1695), eminent French poet and writer, celebrated for his *Fables choises mises en vers* (12 volumes, 1668-94).

La Forge, Louis de (17th Century), French philosopher of the Cartesian school.

Laforgue, Jules (1860-1887), gifted French poet, a leading exponent of vers libre and Symbolism.

Lagerkvist, Pär (Fabian) (1891-1974), distinguished Swedish novelist, poet and dramatist whose most celebrated work was the novel *Barabbas* (1950; English translation, 1951); won the Nobel Prize for Literature (1951).

Lagerlöf, Selma (Ottiliana Lovisa) (1858-1940), famous Swedish novelist and short-story writer; won the Nobel Prize for Literature (1909).

Lagrange, Marie-Joseph (1855-1938), distinguished French Roman Catholic theologian and biblical scholar.

La Harpe, Jean-Francois de (1739-1803), French poet, dramatist and critic.

Lahbabi, Mohammed Aziz (1922-1993), Moroccan philosopher, writer, critic and poet.

La Hontan, Louis-Armand de Lom de'Arce, Baron de (1666-1715), French soldier and writer.

Laidlaw, William (1780-1845), Scottish poet.

Lajpat Rai, Lala (1865-1928), Indian politician and writer, a prominent figure in the anti-British nationalist movement and Hindu supremacist.

Lake, Kirsopp (1872-1946), English biblical scholar.

Lalic, Ivan (1931-1996), Serbian poet.

La Marche, Olivier de (c.1425-1502), French historian and poet.

Lamarck, Jean-Baptiste Pierre Antoine de Monet, Chevalier de (1744-1829), famous French naturalist, author if *Philosophie Zoologique* (1809).

Lamartine, Alphonse (Marie Louis) de (1790-1869), prominent French poet, historian and statesman, very much admired for his poetry collection *Méditations poétiques* (1820).

Lamb, Charles (1775-1834), noted English essayist, critic and poet, greatly esteemed for his *Essays of Elia* (1823) and *The Last Essays of Elia* (1833); brother of Mary Ann Lamb.

Lamb, Mary Ann (1764-1847), English writer; sister of Charles Lamb.

Lambert, Johann Heinrich (1728-1777), German mathematician, astronomer, physicist and philosopher.

Lambert of Hersfeld (1025-c.1088), learned German scholar, author of the valuable *Annales Hersveldenses* (c.1078; published 1525).

Lamennais, (Hughes-) Félicité (-Robert de) (1782-1854), French Roman Catholic priest and philosopher who championed political liberalism.

La Mettrie, Julian Offroy de (1709-1751), French physician and philosopher who espoused the cause of materialism and atheism.

Lamontague-Beauregard, Blanche (1889-1958), French-Canadian poet of distinction.

La Mothe Le Vayer, François de (1588-1672), French philosopher who was known as a committed skeptic.

La Motte, Antoine Houdar de (1672-1731), French poet and dramatist.

L'amour, Louis (Dearborn) (actually Louis Dearborn LaMoore) (1908-1988), American novelist and short-story writer of a prolific output.

Lampedusa, Giuseppe Tomasi Di (1896-1957), Italian writer, best known for his novel *Il gattopardo* (The Leopard, 1956).

Lampman, Archibald (1861-1899), prominent Canadian poet.

Lamprecht, Karl Gottfried (1856-1915), eminent German historian, author of the exhaustive *Deutsche Geschichte* (German History, 12 volumes, 1891-1901).

Lancaster, Sir Osbert (1908-1986), English cartoonist and writer who was especially esteemed for his books on architecture.

Lancelot, Claude (c.1615-1695), French language scholar.

Lanciani, Rodolfo Amadeo (1847-1929), Italian archaeologist and topographer who wrote important works on ancient Rome.

Lander, Ezekiel (1713-1793), Polish Jewish rabbi, author of a valuable book on the Halakha.

Lander, Richard Lemon (1804-1834), English explorer who left interesting accounts of his travels in West Africa.

Landon, Letitia Elizabeth (1802-1838), English poet and novelist who was known as L.E.L.

Landon, Melville de Lancey (1839-1910), American journalist and writer who wrote under the name Eli Perkins.

Landor, Robert Eyres (1781-1869), English dramatist and poet; brother of Walter Savage Landor.

Landor, Walter Savage (1775-1864), English poet and writer; brother of Robert Eyres Landor.

Landstad, Magnus Brostrup (1802-1880), Norwegian clergyman, poet and hymnist.

Lang, Andrew (1844-1912), esteemed Scottish writer and poet who excelled in writing fairy-tales.

Lange, Friedrich Albert (1828-1875), German philosopher and socialist, a noted materialist.

Langer, František (1888-1965), Czech physician, dramatist and short-story writer.

Langer, Susanne K(nauth) (1895-1985), American philosopher, author of *Philosophy in a New Key: A Study in the Symbolism of Reason, Rite and Art* (1942).

Langhorne, John (1735-1779), English poet and translator, best known for *The Country Justice* (3 parts, 1774-77).

Langland, William (c.1330-c.1400), English poet, reputed author of the famous *Vision of William concerning Piers the Plowman.*

Langlois, Charles-Victor (1863-1929), distinguished French scholar, an authority on the Middle Ages.

Langtoft, Peter (d. c.1307), Anglo-Norman poet and churchman, author of a chronicle in alexandrines.

Languet, Hubert (1518-1581), French writer and diplomat.

Lanier, Emilia (née Bassano) (1569-1645), Italian-born English poet.

Lanier, Sidney (1842-1881), American poet, writer and composer.

Lanigan, George Thomas (1845-1886), Canadian-born American journalist and poet who was known for his wit.

Lanman, Charles Rockwell (1850-1941), American Sanskrit scholar and editor who compiled the *Sanskrit Reader* (1884).

La Noue, Francois de (1531-1591), French soldier and writer, author of the *Discours politiques et militaires* (1587).

Lansel, Peider (1863-1943), Italian poet, short-story writer and textual scholar who edited anthologies of Raeto-Romance works.

Lanzi, Luigi (1732-1810), Italian art historian, archaeologist and antiquarian.

Lao-tzu (6th century B.C.), celebrated Chinese philosopher of Taoism.

Larbaud, Valery-Nicolas (1881-1957), French novelist, short-story writer and critic.

Larcom, Lucy (1824-1893), American Abolitionist and poet.

Lardner, Ring(gold Wilmer) (1885-1933), American short-story writer.

Larivey, Pierre de (c.1540-1619), French dramatist and canon.

Larkin, Philip (Arthur) (1922-1985), admired English poet, dramatist and essayist, particularly esteemed for his poetry collections *The Less Deceived* (1955) and *The Whitsun Weddings* (1964).

La Roche, Sophie von (née Gutermann) (1731-1807), German novelist, author of the much admired *Geschichte des Fräuleins von Sternheim* (1771; English translation as *History of Lady Sophia Sternheim,* 1776).

La Rochefoucauld, (Francois, Duc de) (1613-1680), French writer who excelled in his *Maximes* (1665; 5th edition, 1678), a form of epigram.

La Rochefoucauld-Liancourt, Francois-Alexandre-Frederic, Duc de (1747-1827), French educator, social reformer and writer.

Laromiguière, Pierre (1756-1837), French philosopher, especially known for his *Leçons de philosophie* (Lessons on Philosophy, 1815-18).

Larousse, Pierre (-Athanase) (1817-1875), French grammarian, lexicographer and encyclopaedist, especially known for his *Grand Dictionnaire universal du XIXe siècle* (15 volumes, 1866-76; supplements, 1878, 1890).

Larra (y Sanchez de Castro), Mariano José de (1809-1837), Spanish poet and writer, known for his satirical bent.

Larreta, Enrique Rodríquez (1875-1961), Argentine novelist, author of the well-known *La Gloria de Don Ramiro* (The Glory of Don Ramiro, 1908).

Larsen, Nella (1891-1964), American novelist.

La Sale or La Salle, Antoine de (c.1386-c.1460), French writer, best remembered for his *Le Petit Jehan de Saintré* (c.1456).

Lascaris, John (c.1445-c.1535), Greek scholar and diplomat.

Las Casas, Bartolomé de (1474-1566), Spanish missionary and historian, author of the famous *Historia de las Indias.*

Las Cases, Emmanuel (-Augustin-Dieudonné-Joseph), Comte de (1766-1842), French government official and politician who wrote an account of the last days of Napoleon in his *Memorial de St Helene* (1823).

Lashley, Karl S(pencer) (1890-1958), American psychologist, author of *Brain Mechanisms and Intelligence* (1929).

Laski, Harold J(oseph) (1893-1950), influential English political scientist who championed the cause of socialism.

Lasswell, Harold D(wight) (1902-1979), important American political scientist who was an authority on power relationships in the political arena.

La Taille, Jean de (c.1540-c.1607), French poet and dramatist.

Lathrop, George Parsons (1851-1898), American writer; husband of Rose Hawthorne, later Mother Alphonsa Lathrop.

Lathrop, Mother Alphonsa (originally **Rose Hawthorne) (1851-1926),** American writer, poet and Roman Catholic nun; wife of George Parsons Lathrop.

Latimer, Hugh (c. 1485-1555), notable English Protestant reformer and preacher; was burned at the stake during the reign of the Catholic queen Mary Tudor.

Latini, Brunetto (c.1220-c.1294), Italian politician and scholar.

Lattimore, Owen (1900-1989), American educator, government official and writer whose *Ordeal by Slander* (1950) was an account of his experience as a target of the McCarthy investigation into alleged Communist activities in the US government; brother of Richmond (Alexander) Lattimore.

Lattimore, Richmond (Alexander) (1906-1984), American poet, critic and translator; brother of Owen Lattimore.

Laud, William (1573-1645), English statesman and archbishop of Canterbury (1633-45); was accused of treason in the House of Commons, tried, found guilty and beheaded.

Laughlin, James (1914-1997), American publisher, writer and poet, founder of the innovative New Directions publishing firm.

Laugier, Marc-Antoine (1713-1769), French historian.

Laurence, Margaret (actually **Jean Margaret Wemys) (1926-1987),** distinguished Canadian novelist and short-story writer, author of the novels *The Stone Angel* (1964), *A Jest of God* (1966), *The Fire-Dwellers* (1969) and *The Diviners* (1974).

Laurent, François (1810-1887), Belgian legal scholar and historian particularly esteemed for his monumental *Études sur l'historie de l'humanitè* (Studies on the History of Humanity, 18 volumes, 1861-70).

Lautréamont, Comte de (actually **Isidore-Lucien Ducasse) (1846-1870),** French poet whose works were marked by a penchant for violent expression.

Lavater, Johann Kaspar (1741-1801), Swiss physiognomist, pastor, patriot, poet and writer.

Lavin, Mary (1912-1996), Irish-born American short-story writer.

Lavisse, Ernest (1842-1922), French scholar.

Lavrov, Pyotr (Lavrovich) (1823-1900), Russian philosopher of socialism.

Law, William (1686-1761), English writer on Christian subjects.

Lawless, Emily (1845-1913), Irish novelist and poet.

Lawrence, D(avid) H(erbert) (1885-1930), famous English novelist, short-story writer, essayist and poet who was especially known for his themes of social and sexual liberation, most candidly in his novel *Lady Chatterly's Lover* (1928).

Lawrence, George Alfred (1827-1876), English novelist, best remembered for his *Guy Livingstone* (1857).

Lawrence, Josephine (1890-1978), American writer of works in a popular vein.

Lawrence, T(homas) E(dward) (1888-1935), renowned English adventurer and writer who was known as Lawrence of Arabia, author of *The Seven Pillars of Wisdom* (1926).

Lawson, Henry (Archibald) (1867-1922), Australian short-story writer and poet.

Lawson, James (1799-1880), Scottish-born American poet and dramatist.

Lawson, John Howard (1895-1977), American dramatist.

Lawson, Thomas W(illiam) (1857-1925), American stockbroker and writer, best remembered for his muckraking articles and his novel *Friday, the Thirteenth* (1907).

Laxness, Halldór (Kiljan) (actually **Halldór Kiljan Gudjonsson) (1902-1998),** outstanding Icelandic novelist, poet and dramatist who espoused socialist themes; won the Nobel Prize for Literature (1955).

Layamon (13th Century), English poet and priest, author of the romance-chronicle the *Brut* (c.1200).

Layard, Sir Austen Henry (1817-1894), English archaeologist, diplomat and politician who wrote the well-known *Discoveries in the Ruins of Nineveh and Babylon* (1853).

Laye, Camara (1924-1980), notable Guinean writer, author of the novels *L'Enfant noir* (1953; English translation as *The Dark Child*,1954), *Le Regard du roi* (1954; English translation as *The Radiance of the King*, 1956) and *Dramouss* (1966; English translation as *A Dream of Africa*, 1968).

Lazarus, Emma (1849-1887), American poet, writer and translator, best known for her poem *The New Colossus* (1883), which was inscribed on the Statue of Liberty in New York harbour.

Lazarus, Moritz (1824-1903), prominent German Jewish philosopher and psychologist, particularly known for his opposition to anti-Semitism and as founder of comparative psychology.

Lea, Henry Charles (1825-1909), American historian who was especially known for his studies on the history of the Roman Catholic Church.

Lea, Homer (1876-1912), American soldier who predicted the Japanese attack on the US some 30 years in advance in his *The Valor of Ignorance* (1909).

Leacock, Stephen Butler (1869-1944), admired English-born Canadian writer who won extraordinary success as a humorist.

Leake, William Martin (1777-1860), English soldier, topographer and antiquarian, author of *Travels in the Morea* (1830) and *Travels in Northern Greece* (1835).

Leakey, L(ouis) S(eymour) B(azett) (1903-1972), famous English archaeologist and anthropologist.

Leal, António Duarte Gomes (1848-1921), Portuguese poet and political pamphleteer, best known for his poetry collection *Claridades do sul* (Bright Lights of the South, 1875).

Lear, Edward (1812-1888), English artist, writer and poet who excelled in nonsense versification.

Leavis, F(rank) R(aymond) (1895-1978), influential English literary and social critic.

Le Bon, Gustave (1841-1931), French social psychologist, author of *Les loi psychologiques de l'évolution des peuples* (1894; English translation as *The Psychology of Peoples*,1898), *La psychologie des foules* (1895; English translation as *The Crowd*, 1896) and *La révolution francaise et la psychologie des révolutions* (1912; English translation as *The Psychology of Revolution*, 1913).

Le Braz, Anatole (1859-1926), French folklorist, novelist and poet

Lechón, Jan (actually **Leszek Serafinowicz) (1899-1956),** Polish poet, editor and diplomat; committed suicide.

Lecky, William Edward Hartpole (1838-1903), Irish historian, author of a *History of England in the Eighteenth Century* (1878-90).

Leclerc, Jean (1657-1736), Swiss-born Dutch biblical scholar and encyclopaedist.

Le Conte, Joseph (1823-1901), American naturalist who espoused the theories of Darwin and Lyell.

Leconte de Lisle, Charles-Marie-René (1818-1894), French poet and translator, a leading figure amond the Parnassians.

Ledgwidge, Francis (1891-1917), Irish poet; died in World War 1.

Ledru-Rollin, Alexandre-Auguste (1807-1874), French lawyer and writer on politics who played a major role in bringing universal suffrage to his homeland.

Lee, Eliza Buckminster (c.1788-1864), American writer and translator.

Lee, Harriet (1757-1851), English novelist and dramatist; sister of Sophia Lee.

Lee, Nathaniel (c.1649-1692), English dramatist who became best known for his tragedies.

Lee, Sir Sidney (actually **Solomon Lazarus Levi) (1859-1926),** English scholar and lexicographer, particularly known for his Shakespearian studies.

Lee, Sophia (1750-1824), English novelist and dramatist; sister of Harriet Lee.

Lee, Vernon (actually **Violet Paget) (1856-1935),** English essayist, dramatist and novelist.

Leech, Margaret (Kernochan) (1893-1974), American novelist and biographer.

Leeuw, Gerardus van der (1890-1950), Dutch Reformed theologian and historian.

Le Fanu, Joseph Sheridan (1814-1873), Irish novelist and short-story writer who was known for his supernatural tales, especially *In a Glass Darkly* (1872).

Lefebvre, Georges (1874-1959), French historian.

Lefèvre d'Étaples, Jacques (c.1455-1536), French scholar, theologian and biblical translator.

Le Gallienne, Richard (1866-1947), English writer and poet.

Legare, Hugh Swinton (1797-1843), American lawyer, politician and writer.

Leggett, William (c.1802-1839), American journalist and writer.

Le Grand, Antoine (d. 1699), French-born English Franciscan and philosopher.

Lehmann, Rosamond Nina (1901-1990), English novelist; sister of (Rudolph) John (Frederick) Lehmann.

Lehmann, (Rudolph) John (Frederick) (1907-1987), English poet, novelist, editor and publisher; brother of Rosamond Nina Lehmann.

Lehtonen, Joel (1881-1934), Finnish writer.

Leibniz, Gottfried Wilhelm (1646-1716), great German philosopher and mathematician.

Leighton, Robert (1611-1684), English-born Scottish Presbyterian minister and writer.

Leino, Eino (actually **Armas Eino Leopold Lönnbohm) (1878-1926),** notable Finnish poet, novelist and translator, especially esteemed for his lyric poetry.

Leipoldt, C(hristiaan Frederik) Louis (1880-1947), South African dramatist, writer, poet and physician who wrote in Afrikaans.

Leiris, Michel (Julien) (1901-1990), French anthropologist, writer and poet.

Leisewitz, Johann Anton (1752-1806), German dramatist, best known for his *Julius von Tarent* (1776).

Leland, Charles Godfrey (1824-1903), American poet who wrote various works under the name Hans Breitmann, including numerous ballads.

Leland, John (1691-1766), English-born Irish Noncomformist minister and polemicist.

Lelewel, Joachim (1786-1861), Polish scholar and patriot.

Lemaire de Belges, Jean (1473-1525), Flemish poet and historian.

Le Maistre, Antoine (1608-1658), French writer on religion, founder of the Jansenists.

Le Maistre de Sacy, Isaac-Louis (1613-1684), French theologian and biblical translator.

Lemaître, Georges (1894-1966), Belgian astronomer and cosmologist who originated the big-bang theory of the creation of the universe.

Lemaître, (François-Élie-) Jules (1853-1914), French critic, writer and dramatist.

Lemay, (Léon-) Pamphile (1837-1918), French-Canadian poet and writer.

Lemercier, (Louise-Jean) Népomucéne (1771-1840), French poet and dramatist.

Lemnius, Simon (actually **Margadant Lemnius) (c.1505-1550),** German poet and scholar.

Lemonnier, (Antoine-Louis-) Camille (1844-1913), Belgian novelist, short-story writer and art critic.

Lemprière, John (d.1824), English classical scholar, author of the standard *Bibliotheca Classica*.

Lenau, Nikolaus (actually **Nikolaus Franz Niembsch von Strehlenau) (1802-1850),** Austrian poet.

Lenin, V(ladmir) I(lich) (actually **Vladimir Ilich Ulyanov) (1870-1924),** Russian Communist revolutionary and Marxist theoretician, founder and ruthless dictator of the Soviet Union.

Lennep, Jacob van (1802-1868), Dutch novelist and poet.

Lenngren, Anna Maria (née Malmstedt) (1754-1817), esteemed Swedish poet who was known for her fine craftsmanship.

Lennox, Charlotte (née Ramsay) (1720-1804), English novelist, author of *The Female Quixote* (1752).

Lenormant, François (1837-1883), French archaeologist and numismatist.

Lenz, Hermann (1913-1998), esteemed German novelist and poet.

Lenz J(akob) M(ichael) R(einhold) (1751-1792), German poet and dramatist.

Lenz, Wilhelm von (1809-1883), Russian music scholar of German descent, especially remembered for his study of the three periods of Beethoven's creative life (2 volumes, 1852).

Leo Africanus (c.1485-c.1554), Spanish traveller who left the interesting account *Descrittione dell' Africa* (1550; English translation as *A Geographical Historie of Africa*, 1600).

León, Luis de (1527-1591), celebrated Spanish writer and poet whoes masterwork was the prose volume *De los nombres de Cristo* (1583-85; published 1631).

Leonard, William Ellery (1876-1944), American poet, translator and critic.

Leonidas of Tarentum (3rd Century B.C.), Greek poet.

Leonov, Leonid (Maksimovich) (1899-1994), Russian novelist and dramatist.

Leonowens, Anna Harriette (née Crawford) (1834-1914), Welsh writer, author of *The English Governess at the Siamese Court* (1870) and *The Romance of the Harem* (1872).

Leontius of Byzantium (c.485-c.543), Byzantine monk and theologian whose major treatise was *Libri tres contra Nestorianos et Eutychianos* (Three Books Against the Nestorians and the Eutychians).

Leopardi, Giacomo (1798-1837), eminent Italian poet, scholar and philosopher, one of the outstanding lyric poets of his era.

Leopold, Aldo (1887-1948), American conservationist.

Leopold, Carl Gustaf (1756-1829), Swedish poet who served the counts of Gustav III and Gustav IV, particularly remembered for his ode *Försynen* (Providence, 1793).

Leopold, Jan Hendrik (1865-1925), Dutch poet whose finest work was the epic *Cheops* (1915).

Lepsius, Karl Richard (1810-1884), eminent German Egyptologist who played a major role in establishing scientific archaeology.

Lermontov, Mikhail (Yurievich) (1814-1841), important Russian novelist, poet and dramatist, author of the famous novel *Geroy nashego vremeni* (1840; English transalation as *A Hero of Our Time,* 1964); died in a duel.

Lerner, Max(well Allan) (1902-1992), Russian-born American political scientist, essayist and editor.

Leroux, Pierre (1797-1871), French philosopher, economist, journalist and politician who championed socialism.

LeRoy, Edouard (1870-1954), French philosopher.

Lesage or **Le Sage, Alain-René (1668-1747),** French novelist and dramatist, best known for his classic picaresque novel *Histoire de Gil Blas de Santillane* (3 parts, 1715, 1724 1735).

Leskien, August (1840-1916), German linguist who was an authority on Baltic and Slavic linguistics.

Leskov, Nikolai Semyonovich (1831-1895), notable Russian short-story writer and novelist who wrote under the name Stebnitski.

Leslie or **Lesley, John (1527-1596),** Scottish Roman Catholic bishop and historian, author of *De origine, moribus et rebus gestis Scotorum* (1578).

Leśmian, Boleslaw (actually Boleslaw Lesman) (1878-1937), admired Polish poet who was the first in his homeland to embrace Symbolism and Expressionism.

Lessing, Gotthold Ephraim (1729-1781), celebrated German dramatist, poet, critic and scholar, author of such major works as the treatise *Laokoon, oder über die Grenzen de Malerei und Poesie* (Laocoon, or on the Limite of Painting and Poetry, 1766) and the plays *Miss Sara Sampson* (1755), *Minna von Barnhelm* (1767), *Emilia Galotti* (1772) and *Nathan der Weise* (Nathan the Wise, 1779).

L'Estrange, Sir Roger (1616-1704), English journalist, pamphleteer and translator.

Lethaby, William Richard (1857-1931), English writer and architect.

Leuba, J(ames) Henry (1868-1946), American psychologist.

Leucippus (5th Century B.C.), Greek philosopher.

Lever, Charles James (1806-1872), Irish novelist and editor.

Leverson, Ada (1862-1933), English novelist.

Leverton, Oscar Ivar (1862-1906), Swedish literary historian and poet, author of the admired poem *Kung Salomo och Morolf* (King Solomon and Morolf, 1905).

Levertov, Denise (1923-1997), English-born American poet, essayist and radical political activist.

Levi, Carlo (1902-1975), Italian writer, journalist and painter, especially remembered for his novel *Cristo si è fermato a Eboli* (1945; English translation as *Christ Stopped at Eboli,* 1947).

Levi, Primo (1919-1987), Italian writer and poet who wrote moving accounts of his imprisonment in the Auschwitz concentration camp in *se questo è un uomo* (If This is a Man, 1947) and *La regua* (The Truce, 1963), and an acclaimed volume of stories in *Il sistems periodico* (The Periodic Table, 1975).

Lévi, Sylvian (1863-1935), French Orientalist and lexicographer.

Levi ben Gershom (1288-1344), French mathematician, philosopher, astronomer and Talmudic and biblical scholar.

Levita, Elijah (actually Eliyahu ben Asher Ha-Levi Ashkenazi) (1469-1549), German-born Jewish grammarian.

Levitsky, Ivan (actually Ivan Nechuv) (1838-1918), Ukrainian novelist.

Lévy-Bruhl, Lucien (1857-1939), French philosopher, author of *La Morale et la science des moeurs* (1903; English translation as *Ethics and Moral Science,* 1905) and *Les fonctions mentales dans les sociétés primitives* (1910; English translation as *How Natives Think,* 1926).

Lewald, Fanny (1811-1889), German novelist.

Lewes, George Henry (1817-1878), English philosopher, scientist, critic, dramatist and editor.

Lewin, Kurt (1890-1947), German-born American social psychologist who followed Gestalt principles.

Lewis, Alfred Henry (c.1858-1914), American writer, best known for his books on the Southwest.

Lewis, Alun (1915-1944), Welsh poet and short-story writer; died in World War II.

Lewis, Charles Bertran (1842-1924), American writer of a humorous bent who wrote under the name M. Quad.

Lewis, C(live) S(taples) (1898-1963), notable English scholar, novelist and Christian apologist, especially admired for his *Screwtape Letters* (1942) and his children's stories in the *Chronicles of Narnia* series.

Lewis, Sir George Cornewall (1806-1863), English statesman and writer.

Lewis, (Harry) Sinclair (1885-1951), prominent American novelist and essayist, particularly known for his novels *Babbitt* (1922), *Arrowsmith* (1925) and *Elmer Gantry* (1927); won the Nobel Prize for Literature (1930).

Lewis, Janet (1899-1998), American writer and poet.

Lewis, Matthew Gregory (1775-1818), English novelist and dramatist, best known for his Gothic novel *The Monk* (1796).

Lewis, (Percy) Wyndham (1882-1957), English artist and writer.

Lewis, Sarah Anna (1824-1880), American poet who, as "Estelle", became the friend and benefactor of Poe.

Lewis, Saunders (1893-1985), Welsh dramatist, poet, novelist, essayist and critic.

Lewis Glyn Cothi or **Llywelyn y Glyn (15th Century),** Welsh poet.

Lewisohn, Ludwig (1882-1955), German-born American novelist and critic, best remembered for his novel *The Case of Mr. Crump* (1926).

Leyden, John (1755-1811), Scottish poet and Orientalist, particularly known for his ballads.

L'Hospital, Michel de (1507-1573), French statesman and scholar.

Lhote, André (1885-1962), French painter, sculptor and writer.

Liang Ch'en-yü (1510-1580), Chinese dramatist.

Liang Ch'i-ch'ao (1873-1929), Chinese scholar.

Libanius (314-393), Greek philosopher and rhetorician.

Li Chih (1527-1602), Chinese philosopher.

Li Ch'ing-chao (1881-c.1142), illustrious Chinese poet, the foremost woman poet of China.

Liddell, Henry George (1811-1898), English lexicographer and historian, co-editor of the standard *Greek-English Lexicon* (1843; 8th edition, 1897).

Liddell Hart, Sir Basil (Henry) (1895-1970), English military historian, biographer and strategist.

Liddon, Henry Parry (1829-1890), English Anglican priest and theologian, a principal figure in the Oxford Movement.

Lidner, Bengt (1757-1793), Swedish dramatist and poet, a leading figure in the Romantic movement in his homeland.

Lie, Jonas (Lauritz Idemil) (1833-1908), Norwegian novelist, poet and dramatist, author of the notable novel *Familien paa Gilje* (1883; English translation as *The Family at Gilje*, 1920).

Lieber, Francis (1800-1872), German-born American political philosopher, historian and encyclopaedist, founder and first editor of the *Encyclopaedia Americana* (13 volumes, 1829-33).

Liebling, A(bbott) J(oseph) (1904-1963), American journalist and writer.

Liebmann, Otto (1840-1912), German philosopher.

Lietzmann, Hans (1875-1942), learned German Lutheran church historian, author of *Geschichte der alten Kirche* (4 volumes, 1932-44; English translation as *A History of the Early Church*, 4 volumes, 1937-51).

Lightfoot, John (1602-1675), English biblical and rabbinic scholar.

Lightfoot, Joseph Barber (1828-1889), English Anglican churchman, scholar and reformer.

Ligne, Charles-Joseph, Prince de (1735-1814), Belgian nobleman and court official who left valuable accounts of his era in his memoirs and correspondence (34 volumes 1795-1811).

Liguori, Saint Alfonso Maria de' (1696-1787), notable Italian Roman Catholic moral theologian, author of the famous *Theologia moralis* (1748).

Li Ho (791-817), gifted Chinese poet.

Lilburne, John (c.1614-1657), controversial English political agitator and pamphleteer whose leadership of the democratic movement known as the Levellers cost him many imprisonments.

Liliencron, (Friedrich Adolf Axel) Detlev, Freiherr von (1844-1909), German poet, novelist and dramatist.

Lillo, George (1693-1739), influential English dramatist who presaged the bourgeois drama in his *The London Merchant, or The History of George Barnwell* (1731).

Lily, William (c.1468-1522), English classical grammarian.

Linacre, Thomas (c.1460-1524), English physician and classical scholar who became a Roman Catholic priest late in life.

Lincoln, Joseph C(rosby) (1870-1944), American novelist and short-story writer.

Lincoln Victorua (1904-1981), American novelist and short-story writer.

Lindegren, Erik (Johan) (1910-1968), Swedish poet of the experimental school.

Linderman, Frank Bird (1869-1938), American writer and poet.

Lindsay, (Nicholas) Vachel (1879-1931), American poet, best known for his *General Booth Enters Into Heaven and Other Poems* (1913) and *The Congo and Other Poems* (1914); committed suicide.

Lindsay, Norman (Alfred William) (1879-1969), Australian artist and novelist.

Lindsey, Ben(jamin) B(arr) (1869-1943), American judge, legal and social reformer and writer.

Lingard, John (1771-1851), English Roman Catholic priest and historian, author of *The Antiquities of the Anglo-Saxon Church* (1806) and *History of England* (1819-30).

Link, Arthur S(tanley) (1920-1998), American historian, author of an exhaustive biography of Woodrow Wilson and editor of his papers.

Linklater, Eric (1899-1974), Scottish novelist.

Linn, John Blair (1777-1804), American clergyman and poet who wrote *The Death of Washington* (1800).

Linnaeus, Carolus (actually Carl von Linné) (1707-1778), noted Swedish botanist and explorer.

Linnankoski, Johannes (actually Vihtori Peltonen) (1869-1913), Finnish novelist who was active in the movement for independence from Russia.

Lins do Rêgo, José (1901-1957), Brazilian novelist.

Linton, Ralph (1893-1953), American cultural anthropologist, author of *The Study of Man* (1936), *The Cultural Background of Personality* (1945) and *The Tree of Culture* (published 1955).

Linton, William James (1812-1897), English wood engraver, writer and poet who was active in the Chartist movement.

Li Po (701-762), great Chinese poet whose works celebrated an unrestrained joy of life and nature.

Lippard, George (1822-1854), American writer and dramatist who was also active in social reform.

Lippincott, Sara Jane (Clarke) (1823-1904), American journalist, poet and essayist who wrote under the name Grace Greenwood.

Lippman, Walter (1889-1974), influential American political commentator and writer.

Lipps, Theodor (1851-1914), German psychologist, author of the study *Ästhetik* (Aesthetics, 2 volumes, 1903, 1906).

Lipsius, Justus (1547-1606), Belgian classical scholar.

Lipsius, Richard Adelbert (1830-1892), German Protestant theologian who wrote *Philosophie und Religion* (1885).

Li Shang-yin (813-858), admired Chinese poet.

Li-Shih-chen (16th Century), outstanding Chinese scholar, compiler of the *Pents'ao kang-mu* (Great Pharmacopoeia).

Lissauer, Ernst (1882-1937), German poet and dramatist whose World War I poem *Hassgesang gegen England* (1914) won great acclaim in his homeland for its refrain "Gott strafe England".

Lista (y Aragón), Alberto (1775-1848), Spanish poet and critic, the leading representative of Neoclassicism in his homeland in his day.

Lister, Thomas Henry (1800-1842), English novelist.

Littell, William (1768-1824), American writer on the law and satirical essayist.

Littré, Maximilien-Paul-Emilé (1801-1881), eminent French language scholar, lexicographer and philosopher, editor of the celebrated *Dictionnaire de la langue française* (4 volumes, 1863-73).

Liu E or Liu O (1857-1909), Chinese novelist.

Liu Hsiang (1st Century), Chinese writer.

Liu Hsieh (465-522), Chinese writer.

Liutprand of Cremona (c.920-cc.972), Italian Roman Catholic bishop, diplomat and historian.

Liu Tsung-yüan (773-819), Chinese poet and writer.

Livesay, Dorothy (Kathleen May) (1909-1996), Canadian poet whose output reflected her preoccupation with feminist and political issues.

Livingstone, David (1813-1873), Scottish missionary and explorer who wrote accounts of his African journeys.

Livius Andronicus, Lucius (c.284-c.204 B.C.), celebrated Roman poet and dramatist, founder of epic Latin poetry and drama.

Livy (actually Titus Livius) (c.62 B.C.-17 A.D.), great Roman historian.

Li Yü or Li Hou-Chu (937-978), famous Chinese poet and last emperor of the Southern T'ang dynasty (937-975); was poisoned by order of his successor.

Lloyd, Henry Demarest (1847-1903), American journalist who was a proponent of social reform.

Llull, Ramon (c.1235-1316), celebrated Catalan theologian, mystic and poet who was known as the "enlightened doctor".

Llwyd, Morgan (1619-1659), Welsh Puritan writer, author of the classic *Llyfr y Tri Aderyn* (The Book of the Three Birds, 1653).

Locke, Alain (LeRoy) (1886-1954), American philosopher, critic and writer, the principal figure in the Harlem Renaissance.

Locke, David Ross (1833-1888), American journalist and writer who won fame as a humorist under the name Petroleum V Nasby.

Locke, John (1632-1704), renowned English philosopher whose most profound works were *An Essay Concerning Human Understanding* (1690; 5th edition, 1706) and *Two Treatises of Government* (1690).

Locker-Lampson, Frederick (1821-1895), English poet who was especially remembered for his witty verse.

Lockhart, John Gibson (1794-1854), English critic, novelist and biographer, author of the classic *Life of Sir Walter Scott* (1837-38; enlarged edition, 1839).

Lockridge, Ross (Franklin Jr) (1914-1948), American writer who wrote the highly regarded novel *Raintree County* (1948); committed suicide.

Lockwood, Ralph Ingersoll (1798-c.1858), American writer, author of the novels *Rosine Laval* (1833) and *The Insurgents* (1835).

Lodge, Thomas (c.1557-1625), English dramatist, writer and poet, known for his poetry collections *Scillaes Metamorphosis* (1589) and *A Fig for Momus* (1595), and the romance *Rosalynde* (1590).

Lofft, Capel (1751-1824), English poet, writer and lawyer.

Lofting, Hugh (1886-1947), English-born American children's writer and poet, particularly known for his classic stories concerning Dr Dolittle.

Logan, Cornelius Ambrosius (1806-1853), American dramatist, actor and theatre manager who wrote highly popular farces; father of Olive Logan.

Logan, James (1674-1751), Irish-born American politician and scholar.

Logan, John (1748-1788), Scottish poet, dramatist and churchman.

Logan, Olive (1839-1909), American actress, writer and dramatist; daughter of Cornelius Ambrosius Logan.

Loisy, Alfred Firman (1857-1940), influential French biblical scholar and philosopher of religion, one of the principal figures in Roman Catholic modernist circles.

Lo-Johansson, (Karl) Ivar (1901-1990), Swedish novelist and short-story writer, known for his depiction of proletarian life.

Lo Kuan-chung (c.1330-1400), celebrated Chinese novelist who wrote the classic *San kuo chih yen-i* (English translation as *Romance of the Three Kingdoms,* 1925).

Lombroso, Cesare (1835-1909), Italian criminologist, author of *L'uomo delinquente* (The Criminal Man. 1876).

Lomonosiv, Mikhail Vasilievich (1711-1765), important Russian scientist, literary scholar and poet.

London, Jack (actually **John Griffith London) (1876-1916),** American novelist and short-story writer, author of *Call of the Wild* (1903), *The Sea Wolf* (1904), *White Fang* (1906), *The Iron Heel* (1907) and *Burning Daylight* (1910).

Lonergan, Bernard (1904-1984), Canadian Roman Catholic philosopher.

Long, John Luther (1851-1927), American novelist, dramatist and librettist.

Longfellow, Henry Wadsworth (1807-1882), popular American poet, particularly known for *Evangeline* (1847), *The Song of Hiawatha* (1855) and *The Courtship of Miles Standish* (1858), as well as the collection *Tales of a Wayside Inn* (1863), which included his classic *Paul Revere's Ride;* brother of Samuel Longfellow and brother-in-law of Thomas Gold Appleton.

Longfellow, Samuel (1819-1892), American Unitarian clergyman, hymnist and writer; brother of Henry Wadsworth Longfellow.

Loughi, Alessandro (1733-1813), Italian painter, etcher and biographer.

Longinus (1st Century), Greek literary critic, reputed author of the treatise *On the Sublime.*

Longstreet, Augustus Baldwin (1790-1870), American educator and writer, best known for *Georgia Scenes, Characters, and Incidents* (1835).

Longus (2nd-3rd Centuries), Greek writer, author of the famous *Daphnis and Chloe.*

Lönnrot, Elias (1802-1884), Finnish folklorist and philologist, compiler of the *Kalevala* (1835; augmented edition, 1849), Finland's great national epic.

Lonsdale, Frederick Leonard (1881-1954), English dramatist.

Loos, Anita (1893-1981), American dramatist and writer, best known for her popular play *Gentlemen Prefer Blonds* (1925).

Looy, Jacobus van (1855-1930), Dutch writer and painter.

Lopes, Fernão (c.1380-c.1460), Portuguese historian.

López, Luis Carlos (1883-1950), Colombian poet.

López de Ayala, Pedro (1332-1407), Spanish poet and historian, author of the valuable *Cronicas* and the poem *Rimado de palacio.*

López de Ayala y Herrera, Adelardo (1828-1879), esteemed Spanish dramatist.

López y Fuentes, Gregorio (1895-1966), Mexican novelist.

Lord, William Wilberforce (1819-1907), American clergyman and poet.

Lorde, Audre (1934-1992), American poet and writer who espoused feminism.

Lorimer, James (1818-1890), Scottish philosopher who wrote on natural law.

Lorris, Guillaume de (13th Century), French poet.

Lot, Ferdinand (1866-1952), learned French historian who was an authority on the early Middle Ages.

Lothrop, Harriet Mulford Stone (1844-1924), American writer of children's books who wrote under the name Margaret Sidney.

Loti, Pierre (actually **Louis-Marie-Julien Viaud) (1850-1923),** French novelist.

Lotichius, Petrus Secundus (1528-1560), notable German poet.

Lotze, Rudolf Hermann (1817-1881), German philosopher, author of *Metaphysik* (1841) and *Logik* (1843).

Lounsbury, Thomas Raynesford (1838-1915), American literary scholar.

Louvet (de Couvray), Jean-Baptiste (1760-1797), French writer and politician, best remembered for his erotic novel *Les Amours du chevalier de Faublas* (1787-90).

Louÿs, Pierre (actually **Pierre Louis) (1870-1925),** French novelist and poet, best known for his prose *poems Chansons de Bilitis* (1894) and the novels *Aphrodite* (1896) and *La Femme et le paintin* (1898; English translation as *Woman and Puppet,* 1908).

Love, Alfred Henry (1830-1913), American Quaker and pacifist.

Lovecraft, H(oward) P(hillips) (1890-1937), America writer and poet, a cult figure among science fiction aficionados.

Lovelace, Richard (1618-1657), noted English poet and soldier whose *To Althea, from Prison* (1642) includes the unforgettable lines *Stone walls do not a prison make/Nor iron bars a cage,* written while he was imprisoned for his championship of the Royalist cause.

Lover, Samuel (1797-1868), Irish painter, novelist and songwriter.

Lovett, Robert Morss (1870-1956), American literary scholar, novelist and dramatist.

Lowell, Abbott Lawrence (1856-1943), American educator, author of *Conflicts of Principle* (1932) and *At War with Academic Tradition in America* (1934); brother of Amy Lowell.

Lowell, Amy (1874-1925), remarkable American poet and critic, a prominent Imagist; sister of Abbott Lawrence Lowell.

Lowell, James Russell (1819-1891), prominent American poet, critic and diplomat; brother of Robert Traill Spence Lowell and husband of Maria White Lowell.

Lowell, Maria White (1821-1853), American poet, author of the Abolitionist poem *Africa*; wife of James Russell Lowell.

Lowell, Robert Traill Spence (1816-1891), American novelist and poet; brother of James Russell Lowell.

Lowell, Robert (Traill Spence Jr) (1917-1977), distinguished American poet, dramatist and translator, especially admired for such poetry collections as *Lord Weary's Castle* (1946), *Mills of the Kavanaughs* (1951), *Life Studies* (1959), *For the Union Dead* (1964), *Near the Ocean* (1967) and *Notebook 1967-68* (1969); great-grandnephew of James Russell Lowell.

Lowes, John Livingston (1867-1945), American literary scholar.

Lowie, Robert H(arry) (1883-1957), American anthropologist, author of *Primitive Society* (1920), *The History of Ethnological Theory* (1937) and *Social Organization* (1948).

Lowndes, Marie Adelaide Belloc (1868-1947), English novelist and dramatist.

Lowry, (Clarence) Malcolm (1909-1957), English novelist, short-story writer and poet whose most significant work was the novel *Under the Volcano* (1947).

Lowth or **Louth, Robert (1710-1787),** English Anglican bishop and literary scholar.

Loy, Mina (actually **Mina Gertrude Lowy) (1882-1966),** English-born American poet who excelled in free verse.

Lubbock, Percy (1879-1965), English critic and biographer.

Lucan (actually **Marcus Annaeus Lucanus) (39-65),** outstanding Roman poet whose only surviving work is the epic *Bellum civile* or *Pharsalia;* committed suicide after the failure of Piso's conspiracy against the emperor Nero.

Lucaris, Cyril (actually **Kyrillos Loukaris) (1572-1638),** Greek Orthodox patriarch of Constantinople and theologian.

Lucas, E(dward) V(errall) (1868-1938), English journalist and essayist.

Lucas, F(rank) L(aurence) (1894-1967), English literary scholar, poet and translator.

Luce, Clare Boothe (1903-1987), American dramatist and public official, best remembered for her plays *The Women* (1936) and *Kiss the Boys Goodbye* (1938).

Lucena, João de (1549-1600), Portuguese writer.

Luchaire, (Denis-Jean-) Achille (1846-1908), French historian, author of important studies of the Capetians and of a biography of Innocent III (6 volumes, 1904-08).

Lu Chi (261-303), notable Chinese writer, critic, poet and government official; was executed after plotting against the emperor.

Lu Chiu-yüan (1139-1193), Chinese philosopher of the Neo-Confucian school who was known as Lu Hsiang-Shan.

Lucian (c.120-c.181), Greek satirist and rhetorician.

Lucidor, Lasse (actually **Lars Johansson) (1638-1674),** Swedish poet.

Lucifer (d. c.370), Bishop of Cagliari, Sardinia and theologian who was the most vigorous opponent of the Arian heresey.

Lucilius, Gaius (c.180-c.103 B.C.), Roman poet, reputed creator of the political satire.

Lucretius (actually **Titus Lucretius Carus) (c.99-55 B.C.),** admired Roman poet and philosopher, author of the famous poem *De rerum natura* (On the Nature of Things).

Ludlow, Fitz Hugh (1836-1870), American writer, best known for his *The Hasheesh Eater* (1857), which was based on his own expieriences of drug addiction.

Ludwig, Emil (1881-1948), German biographer, dramatist and poet.

Ludwig, Otto (1813-1865), German novelist, dramatist and critic.

Lugones, Leopoldo (1874-1938), prominent Argentine poet, writer and critic; committed suicide.

Luhan, Mabel Dodge (1879-1962), American writer.

Lu Hsün (actually **Chou Shu-Jen) (1881-1936),** distinguished Chinese writer and essayist.

Lukács, György (1885-1971), Hungarian Marxist philosopher, writer and critic.

Lukas, J(ay) Anthony (1933-1997), American journalist and writer; committed suicide.

Łukasiewicz, Jan (1878-1956), Polish philosopher.

Lukens, Henry Clay (1838-c.1900), American journalist and writer who often wrote under the name Erratic Enrique.

Lummis, Charles Fletcher (1859-1928), American writer and poet.

Lunacharsky, Anatoli Vasilievich (1875-1933), Russian writer and politician.

Lundkvist, Artur Nils (1906-1991), Swedish writer, poet and translator.

Lupus of Ferrières or **Loup de Ferrières (c.805-c.862),** French scholar who was also known as Lupus Servatus.

Luther, Martin (1483-1546), great German Protestant reformer, biblical scholar and linguist, the central figure in the Protestant Reformation in Germany.

Lutterell, John (d. 1335), English theologian.

Luttrell, Henry (c.1765-1851), English poet known for his light verse.

Luxemburg, Rosa (1871-1919), Polish-born German revolutionary and Marxist polemicist; was murdered.

Luyken, Jan (1649-1712), Dutch poet and lithographer who embraced mysticism, author of *Jezus en de ziel* (Jesus and the Soul, 1678).

Lu Yu (1125-1210), Chinese poet of a prolific output of some 20,000 poems, of which some 9,000 are extant.

Luzel, François-Marie (1821-1895), French writer, historian and critic.

Luzzatto, Moshe Hayyim (1707-1747), Italian Jewish writer, dramatist, poet and cabalist.

Luzzatto, Samuel David (1800-1865), Italian Jewish writer and scholar who was known as Shedal.

Lyall, Sir Alfred Comyn (1835-1911), English writer and poet.

Lyall, Edna (actually **Ada Ellen Bayly) (1857-1903),** English novelist whose espousal of liberal political causes informed most of her output.

Lydgate, John (c.1370-c.1450), English monk and poet.

Lyly, John (c.1554-1606), English novelist, dramatist and poet, known as the Euphuist after his novel *Euphues* (2 parts, 1578, 1580).

Lynch, Benito (1885-1951), Argentine novelist and short-story writer.

Lynd Helen (née Merrell) (1896-1982), American sociologist who collaborated with her husband on *Middletown: A Study in Contemporary American Culture* (1929) and *Middletown in Transition: a Study in Cultural Conflicts* (1937); wife of Robert Staughton Lynd.

Lynd, Robert Staughton (1892-1970), American sociologist who collaborated with his wife on *Middletown: A Study in Contemporary American Culture* (1929) and *Middletown in Transition: A Study in Cultural Conflicts* (1937).

Lynd, Sylvia (née Dryhurst) (1888-1952), English poet and short-story writer.

Lyndsay or **Lindsay, Sir David (c.1490-c.1555),** Scottish poet, dramatist and courtier whose satirical gift was displayed in his morality play *Ane Satyre of the Thrie Estaits* (1940).

Lyon, Harris Merton (1883-1916), American journalist, critic and writer.

Lyotard, Jean-François (1924-1998), French philosopher.

Lyte, Henry Francis (1793-1847), Scottish poet and hymnist who wrote the famous hymn *Abide With Me.*

Lyttelton, George, 1st Baron (1709-1773), English politician, writer and poet.

Lytton, Edward George Earle Bulwer-Lytton, 1st Baron (1803-1873), English novelist, dramatist, essayist, poet and politician.

Lytton, (Edward) Robert Bulwer-Lytton, 1st Earl of (1831-1891), English poet, dramatist and statesman who wrote under the name Owen Meredith.

Ma'arrī, al- (actually Abū al-'Alā' Ahmad ibn 'Abd Allāh al-Ma'iarrī) (973-1057), illustrious Arab poet.

Mabillon, Jean (1632-1707), learned French scholar and monk, especially influential in the development of paleography.

Mably, Gabriel Bonnet de (1709-1785), French philosopher.

Macarius (c.1482-1564), Russian Orthodox prelate and scholar.

Macarius Magnes (5th Century), Eastern Orthodox bishop and Christian apologist, author of *Apokritikos e monogenes pros Hellenas* (Response of the Only-Begotten to the Greeks, 5 volumes, c.400).

Macarius the Egyptian (c.300-c.390), Egyptian monk and ascetic, one of the principal figures in the development of Christian monasticism.

MacArthur, Charles (1895-1956), American dramatist and screenwriter.

Macaulay, Catherine (1731-1791), English historian, author of a *History of England* (8 volumes, 1763-83).

Macaulay, Dame (Emilie) Rose (1881-1958), English writer, poet and critic.

Macaulay, Thomas Babington (1800-1859), noted English historian, author of a *History of England* (5 volumes, 1849-61).

MacBeth, George Mann (1932-1992), Scottish poet and novelist.

MacCaig, Norman Alexander (1910-1996), distinguished Scottish poet, a master of his craft.

MacCarthy, Sir (Charles Otto) Desmond (1877-1952), English literary critic.

MacCarthy, Denis Florence (1817-1882), Irish poet and writer.

MacDiarmid, Hugh (actually Christopher Murray Grieve) (1892-1978), remarkable Scottish poet, the principal figure in the Scottish renaissance.

MacDonagh, Donagh (1912-1968), Irish poet, dramatist and balladeer, son of Thomas MacDonagh.

MacDonagh, Thomas (1878-1916), Prominent Irish poet, critic and nationalist who was executed for his role in the Easter Rising; father of Donagh MacDonagh.

MacDonald, Alexander (c.1700-c.1780), Scottish-Gaelic poet who wrote under the name Alasdair Mac Mhaighstir Alasdair.

MacDonald, Dwight (1906-1982), American literary and political essayist.

Macdonald, George (1824-1905), Scottish poet and novelist.

Macdonald, John (c.1620-1716), Scottish-Gaelic poet.

Macdonald, John D(ann) (1916-1986), American writer of mystery novels and science fiction of mass popular appeal.

MacDonald, Ross (actually Kenneth Millar) (1915-1983), American novelist and essayist.

MacDowell, Katherine Sherwood (Bonner) (1849-1883), American writer who wrote under the name Sherwood Bonner.

Macedo, José Agostinho de (1761-1831), Portuguese poet, critic and pamphleteer.

Macghill-Eathain, Somhairle (1911-1996), outstanding Scottish poet of Gaelic verse who also wrote under the name Sorley Maclean and Samuel Maclean.

MacGill, Patrick (1890-1963), Irish novelist and poet.

MacGillivray, James Pittendrigh (1856-1938), Scottish sculptor and poet.

MacGrath, Harold (1871-1932), American writer of the romance genre.

Mach, Ernst (1838-1916), Austrian physicist and philosopher.

Mácha, Karel Hynek (1810-1836), talented Czech poet, author of the classic epic *Máj* (May, 1836).

Machado de Assis, Joaquim Maria (1839-1908), esteemed Brazilian poet, novelist and short-story writer.

Machado y Ruiz, Antonio (1875-1939), Spanish poet and writer; brother of Manuel Machado y Ruiz.

Machado y Ruiz, Manuel (1874-1947), Spanish poet and writer; brother of Antonio Machado y Ruiz.

Machaut, Guillaume de (c.1300-1377), celebrated French composer and poet.

Machen, John Gresham (1881-1937), American Presbyterian scholar.

Machiavelli, Niccolò (1469-1527), renowned Italian statesman and writer, author of the famous political treatise *Il principle* (The Prince, 1513).

Ma Chih-yüan (14th Century), Chinese dramatist and poet.

MacInnes, Colin (1914-1976), English novelist.

MacInnes, Tom (actually **Thomas Robert Edward McInnes) (1867-1951),** Canadian writer and poet.

MacIver, Robert Morrison (1882-1970), Scottish-born American sociologist, political scientist and educator.

MacKaye, (James Morrison) Steele (1842-1894), American Dramatist, actor, theatre manager and inventor; father of Percy (Wallace) MacKaye.

MacKaye, Percy (Wallace) (1875-1956), American poet and dramatist; son of (James Morrison) Steele MacKaye.

Macken, Walter (1915-1967), Irish novelist and dramatist.

Mackenzie, Sir (Edward Morgan) Compton (1883-1972), English novelist, biographer, essayist and poet.

Mackenzie, Henry (1745-1831), Scottish novelist, poet, dramatist and editor, best remembered for his novel *The Man of Feeling* (1771).

Mackintosh, Sir James Brunlees (1765-1832), Scottish physician, philosopher and barrister.

MacLean, Alistair (1922-1987), Scottish novelist of thrillers who also wrote under the name Ian Stuart.

MacLennan, (John) Hugh (1907-1990), Canadian novelist and essayist.

Maklin, Charles (actually **Charles McLaughlin) (c. 1700-1797),** Irish actor and dramatist.

Macleod, Mary or **Mairi Nighean Alasdair Rudaidh (c. 1615-c.1706),** Scottish-Gaelic poet.

MacLeish, Archibald (1892-1982), eminent American poet, dramatist, government official and educator, particularly admired for his poem *Conquistador* (1932) and the verse drama *J.B.* (1958).

MacNeice, (Frederick) Louis (1907-1963), Irish poet and critic.

MacNeill, John Gordon Swift (1849-1926), Irish politician and Historian.

Macpherson, James (1736-1796), Scottish poet who "translated" the epic verse of the legendary poet and warrior "Ossian."

Macready, William Charles (1793-1873), English actor, theatre manager and diarist.

Macrobuis, Ambrosius Theodosius (5th Century), Latin grammarian and philosopher, author of the *Saturnalia*.

Madách, Imre (1823-1864), Hungarian poet who wrote the admired poetic drama *Az ember tragediája* (1861; English translation as *The Tragedy of Man,* 1933).

Mādhavācārya (c.1296-c.1386), Hindu statesman and philosopher.

Madhva (c.1199-c.1278), Hindu philosopher who was also known as Ánandatírtha and Púrnaprajña.

Madison, James (1751-1836), American Statesman and 4th President of the US (1809-17), author of many of the papers in *The Federalist* (1787-88) and of the invaluable *Journal of the Federal Convention* (3 volumes, 1840).

Madox, Thomas (1666-1726), English legal antiquarian and historian.

Madvig, Johan Nicolai (1804-1886), Danish classical scholar and government official.

Maerlant, Jacob van (1225-1291), Dutch poet and translator.

Maeterlinck, Maurice (Polydore-Marle-Bernard) (1862-1949), notable Belgian dramatist, poet and writer, best remembered for his celebrated Symbolist play *Pélleas et Mélisande* (1892; English translation, 1894); won the Nobel Prize for Literature (1911).

Maevius (1st Century), Roman poet.

Maeztu y Whitney, Ramiro de (1875-1936), Spanish political writer whose views led to his execution by the Republican government during the Spanish Civil War.

Maffei, Francesco Scipione, Marchese di (1675-1755), Italian dramatist, poet and scholar, particularly known for his verse tragedy *Merope* (1713; English translation 1740).

Maginn, William (1793-1842), Irish journalist, writer and poet.

Magnus, Johannes (actually **Johan Mansson) (1488-1544),** Swedish Roman Catholic archbishop and historian; brother of Olaus Magnus.

Magnus, Olaus (actually **Olaf Mansson) (1490-1557),** Swedish Roman Catholic archbishop and historian; brother of Johannes Magnus.

Magnússon, Jón (c.1610-1696), Icelandic parson who wrote a fantastic account of his reputed sufferings at the hands of "sorcerers" in his *Píslarsaga* (Passion Story).

Mahan, Alfred Thayer (1840-1914), American naval officer and historian, author of *The Influence of Sea Power upon History, 1660-1783* (1890), *The Influence of Sea Power upon the French Revolution and Empire, 1793-1812* (1892) and *The Interest of America in Sea Power, Present and Future* (1897).

Mahony, Francis Sylvester (1804-1866), Irish journalist and poet who wrote under the name of Father Prout.

Mailáth, János, Count (1786-1855), Hungarian historian; committed suicide.

Maillet, Andrée (1921-1996), French-Canadian journalist, novelist, short-story writer, poet and dramatist.

Maimbourg, Louis (1610- 1686), French Jesuit and historian.

Maimon, Salomon (c.1754-1800), Polish Jewish philosopher who was known for his skepticism and citicism of Kantian precepts.

Maimonides, Moses (1135-1204), celebrated Spanish Jewish philosopher, jurist and physician who was greatly esteemed for his vast learning.

Maine, Sir Henry (James Sumner) (1822-1888), English jurist and legal historian who was a primary figure in the development of comparative law.

Maine de Biran (actually **Marie-Francois-Pierre Gonthier de Biran) (1766-1824),** French statesman and philosopher of the empirical School.

Maioresscu, Titu (1840-1917), Romanian Writer.

Mairet, Jean (1604-1686), French dramatist who excelled in the classical genre.

Maironis (actually **Jonas Mačiulis) (1862-1932),** Lithuanian poet of distinction.

Maistre, Joseph de (1753-1821), French government official and polemicist who became well known for his rigorous defense of conservative principles of church and state.

Maitland, Fredric William (1850-1906), English legal historian who collaborated with Sir Fredrick Pollock on the classic study *The History of English Law Before Time of Edward I* (2 Volumes, 1895).

Maitland, Sir Richard (1496-1586), Scottish poet, anthologist, lawyer and statesman who was also known as Lord Lethington.

Maitland, Thomas (1841-1901), English poet and novelist who wrote under the name Robert Buchanan.

Major, Charles (1856-1913), American novelist best remembered for his *When Knighthood was in Flower* (1898).

Malalas, John (c.491-c.578), Byzantine Chronicler.

Malamud, Bernard (1914-1986), American novelist and short-story writer.

Malaparte, Curzio (actually **Kurt Erich Suckert) (1898-1957),** important Italian journalist, novelist, short-story writer and dramatist who at first was a confirmed supporter of Fascism but later became one of its leading opponents.

Malcolm X (actually **Malcom Little) (1925-1965),** controversial American Black Muslim militant whose dictated *The Autobiography of Malcolm X* (1965) proved influential; was murdered.

Malebranche, Nicolas (1638-1715), French Roman Catholic priest, theologian and philosopher of the Cartesian school, author of *De la recherche de la vérité* (3 volumes, 1647-78; English translation as *Search after Truth*, 1694-95) and *Traité de la nature et de la grâce* (1680; English translation as *Treatise of Nature and Grace*, 1695).

Malherbe, Danell François (1881-1969), South African novelist, dramatist and poet in Afrikaans.

Malherbe, François de (1555-1628), French poet, critic and translator.

Mālik Ibn Anas (actually **Abū 'Abd Allāh Mālik Ibn Anas Ibn al-Hārith al-Asbahī) (c.715-795),** Muslim theologian.

Malinowski, Bronislaw (1884-1942), eminent Polish anthropologist, the pioneering figure in the development of social anthropology.

Mallarmé, Stéphane (1842-1898), famous French poet and writer of the Symbolist movement, renowned for his poems *Herodiade* (1864) and *L'Après-midi d'un Faune* (1865).

Mallet, David (actually **David Malloch) (c.1705-1765),** Scottish poet and dramatist.

Mallock, William Hurrell 1849-1923), English writer and poet.

Malmström, Bernhard Elis (1816-1865), Swedish poet and critic.

Malone, Dumas (1892-1986), American historian and lexicographer, author of a major biography of Thomas Jefferson (6 volumes, 1948-81).

Malone, Edmond (1741-1812), Irish-born English scholar, best known for his Shakespearian studies.

Malone, Kemp (1889-1971), American philologist who wrote extensively on linguistics and literature.

Malory, Sir Thomas (d.1471), English writer, author of the celebrated *Morte Darthur* (published 1485).

Malraux, André (1901-1976), prominent French novelist, art historian and government official.

Malthus, Thomas Robert (1766-1834), English economist and demographer, best known for his *An Essay on the Principle of Population ...* (1798; 2nd edition, 1803).

Maltz, Albert (1908-1985), American novelist, dramatist and screenwriter.

Mameli, Goffredo (1827-1849), Italian poet and patriot; died while defending Rome against the French.

Manasseh ben Israel (1604-1657), Jewish rabbi and scholar in the Kabbala.

Manasses, Constantine (d. 1187), Byzantine metropolitan, poet and writer.

Mandel, Eli (as Wolf) (1922-1992), Canadian poet, critic and editor.

Mandelkern, Solomon (1846-1902), Hebrew poet and grammarian.

Mandelstam, Osip (Yemilievich) (1891-1938), outstanding Russian poet, critic and translator who died a victim of Stalin's tyranny.

Mander, Karel van (1548-1606), Belgian Painter, poet and writer.

Mandeville, Bernard de (1670-1733), Dutch-born English writer and philosopher, author of *The Fable of the Bees: Private Vices, Publick Benefits* (1714; 3rd edition, 1729).

Mandeville, Sir John (14th Century), English writer, reputed author of *The Voyage and Travels of Sir John Mandeville.*

Manetti, Gianozzo (1396-1459), Italian scholar and orator.

Manfalūtī Mustafā Lutfial (1876-1924), Egyptian short-story writer and essayist.

Mangan, James Clarence (1803-1849), Irish poet and translator.

Mānikkavācakar (c. 9th Century), Indian Mystic and poet who wrote in Tamil.

Manilius, Marcus (1st Century), Roman poet of didactic verse.

Maning, Frederick (Edward) (1811-1883), Irish-born New Zealand judge and writer.

Mankowitz, (Cyril) Wolf (1924-1998), English novelist, dramatist and screenwriter.

Manley, Mary de la Riviere (1663-1724), English witer, especially remembered for her *Secret Memoirs .... of Several Persons of Quality* (1709).

Mann, Gottfried Angelo (1909-1994), German historian; son of Thomas Mann.

Mann, Heinrich (1871-1950), German novelist and essayist; brother of Thomas Mann

Mann, Horace (1796-1859), influential American educator who was the pioneering figure in public education in his homeland.

Mann, Thomas (1875-1955), renowned German novelist and essayist, author of such important novels as *Buddenbrooks* (1900; English translation, 1924), *Der Zauberberg* (1924; English translation as *The Magic Mountain*, 1927), *Joseph und seine Brüder* (4 volumes, 1933-43; English translation as *Joseph and His Brothers*, 1948) and *Doktor Faustus* (1947; English translation, 1948); won the Nobel Prize for Literature (1929); brother of Heinrich Mann and father of Gottfried Angelo Mann.

Mannheim, Karl (1893-1947), German born English sociologist who wote *Ideologie und Utopie* (1929; English translation as *Ideology and Utopia: An Introduction to the Sociology of Knowledge* , 1936) and *Freedom, Power, and Democratic Planning* (published 1950).

Manning, Henry Edward (1808-1892), English Roman Catholic Cardinal, archbishop of Westminster and polemicist.

Manning, Olivia (1908-1980), English novelist and short-story writer, author of *The Balkan Trilogy* (*The Great Fortune*, 1960, *The Spoilt City*, 1962 and *Friends and Heroes*, 1965) and *The Levant Trilogy* (*The Danger Tree*, 1977, *The Battle Lost and Won*, 1978 and *The Sum of Things*, 1980).

Mannyng of Brunne, Robert (c. 1283-c. 1327), English poet who wrote the poem *Handlying Synne* and the fictional chronicle *Story of England.*

Manrique, Gómez (c.1415-1490), Spanish soldier, politician, dramatist and poet.

Manrique, Jorge (c.1440-1479), Spanish poet whose most notable work was his *Coplas por la muert de su padre* (Stanzas for the Death of his Father).

Mansel, Henry Longueville (1820-1871), English Anglican Priest, theologian and philosopher.

Mansfield, Katherine (actually Kathleen Mansfield Beauchamp) (1888-1923), remarkable New Zealand short-story writer.

Manto, Saadat Hussan (1912-1955), Pakistani writer.

Mantuan or Mantuanus (actually Johannes Baptista Spagnolo) (1448-1516), Spanish friar and poet who won distinction for his Latin eclogues.

Manuel, Don Juan (1282-c.1348), Spanish nobleman and writer, especially known for his *Libro del Conde Lucor* (The Book of Count Lucor, 1323-35).

Manuel, Niklas (1484-1530), Swiss soldier, Statesman, painter and writer.

Manutius, Aldus (1449-1515), important Italian scholar, printer and editior.

Manutius, Aldus, the Younger (1547-1597), Italian scholar and printer.

Manzoni, Alessandro (1785-1873), outstanding Italian novelist, poet and statesman, author of the famous novel *I promessi sposi* (1825-27; English translation as *The Betrothed*, 1951).

Mao Ch'ang (flourished 145 B.C.), Chinese scholar.

Map or Mapes, Walter (c.1140-c.1209), Anglo-Norman churchman, writer and poet, author of the miscellany *De nugis curialium* (of Courtiers' Trifles).

Mapu, Abraham (1808-1867), Russian writer, author of the first hebrew novel, *Ahavat Ziyyon* (1853; English translation as *Annou: Prince and Peasant*, 1887).

Marasco, Robert (1936-1998), American dramatist and novelist, author of the play *Child's Play* (1970).

Marat, Jean-Paul (1743-1793), French politician, journalist and physician who espoused radical policies during the French Revolution; was assassinated.

Marbeck or Marbecke, John (c. 1505-1585), English composer, organist and writer on theology, compiler of the first published concordance of the English Bible (1550) and composer of the liturgical music in *The booke of Common Praier Noted* (1550).

Marcabru or Marcabrun (12th Century), Provençal poet.

Marcel, Gabriel (1889-1971), distinguished French philosopher of the Existentialist school, author of the *Journal métaphysique* (1927; English translation as *Metaphysical Journal*, 1952), *Être et avoir* (1935; English translation as *Being and Having*, 1949), *Homo Viator* (1945; English translation, 1951 and *Le Mystère de l'être* (2 volumes, 1951; English translation as *The Mystery of Being*, 2 volumes, 1951.

Marcello, Benedetto (1686-1739), Italian composer and writer.

March, Ausiàs (1397-1459), important Catalan poet.

March, Francis Andrew (1825-1911), American language scholar and lexicographer whose most important work was *A Comparative Grammar of the Anglo-Saxon Language* (1870).

March, William (actually William Edward March Campbell) (1893-1954), American novelist and short-story writer.

Marcion (d. c.160), Christian heretic and theologian who rejected the Old Testament outright and espoused the view of the centrality of the gospel of love in the New Testament.

Marcus Aurelius (Antoninus) (26-180), Roman emperor, author of the celebrated *Meditations* (English translation, 2 volumes, 1944).

Marcuse, Herbert (1898-1979), German-born American philosopher of the Marxist persuasion who wrote *One Dimensional Man* (1964), *Essay on Liberation* (1969), *Counter Revolution and Revolt* (1972) and *The Aesthetic Dimension* (1978).

Maréchal, Pierre-Sylvain (1750-1803), French poet and writer, known for his antireligious views.

Marett, R(obert) R(anulph) (1866-1943), English anthropologist who was especially known for his studies of primitive religion.

Margoliouth, David Samuel (1858-1940), English Anglican Churchman and Arabic scholor.

Margueritte, Paul (1860-1918) French novelist; brother of Victor Margueritte.

Margueritte, Victor (1866-1942), French novelist; brother of Paul Margueritte.

Margunios, Maximus (d, 1602), Greek Orthodox bishop, theologian and scholor.

Mariana, Juan de (1536-1624), Spanish historian, author of the important *Historia general de España* (General History of Spain, 1601).

Marianus Scotus (actually Molbrigte, "Servant of Bridget") (1028-c.1083), Irish chronicler who wrote a history of the world.

Marie de France (12th Century), French poet who created the lai Breton, a form of verse narrative.

Mariette, Auguste (-Ferdinand-François) (1821-1881), French archaeologist who wrote on the early era of the history of Egypt.

Marinetti, Filippo Tommaso (Emilio) (1876-1944), influential Italian poet, dramatist and writer who founded Futurism.

Marini or Marino, Giambattista (1569-1625), Italian poet, creator of the elborate Baroque style known as *marinismo*.

Maritain, Jacques (1882-1973), eminent French philosopher of the Thomist school, author of *Art et scolastique* (1920; English translaton as *Art and Scholasticism*, 1930), *Distinguer pour unir, ou les degrés du savoir* (1932; English translation as *The Degrees of Knowledge*, 1937), *Frontières de la poésie et autres essais* (1935; English translation as *Art and Poetry*, 1943), *Humanisme intégral* (1936; English translation as *True Humanism*, 1938 and *La Philosophie morale ...* (1960; English translation as Moral Philosophy, 1964).

Marius Victorinus, Galus (d. c.364), Roman Christian philosopher and rhetorician.

Marivaux, Pierre (Carlet de Chamblain de) (1688-1763), important French dramatist and writer, especially significant for his comic plays.

Markham, Edwin (actually Charles Edward Anson Markham) (1852-1940), American poet, best remembered for *The man with the Hoe and Other Poems* (1899) and *Lincoln and Other Poems* (1901).

Markham, Gervase or Jervis (c. 1568-1637), English writer, dramatist and poet.

Markoe, Peter (c. 1752-1792), Danish West Indies-born American dramatist, poet and writer.

Marković, Svetozar (1846-1875), Serbian socialist and political writer.

Mark the Hermit (c. 5th Century), Christian ascetic and theologian, author of *Contra Nestorianos* (Against the Nestorians).

Marlowe, Christopher (1564-1593), celebrated English dramatist and poet; died in a tavern brawl.

Marmion, Shackerley (1603-1639), English dramatist and poet.

Marmol, José (1817-1871), Argentine poet and novelist.

Marmontel, Jean-François (1723-1799), French poet, dramatist, writer and critic, best known for his autobiographical *Mémoires d'un père* (Memoirs of a Father, 1804).

Marnix van Sint Aldegonde, Philips van (1540-1598), Dutch theologian, translator and poet.

Marot, Clément (c. 1496-1544), remarkable French poet and translator who transformed Italian literary forms into new French ones of notable distinction.

Marpurg, Friedrich Wilhelm (1718-1795), German writer on music and composer.

Marquand, J(ohn) P(hillip) (1893-1960), American writer, admired for *The Late George Apley* (1937) and as creator of the Japanese detective Mr Moto.

Marquis, Don(ald Robert Perry) (1878-1937), American journalist, novelist, dramatist and poet.

Marryat, Frederick (1792-1848), English naval officer and novelist.

Marsh, Dame (Edith) Ngaio (1899-1982), New Zealand writer of detective fiction.

Marsh, Sir Edward Howard (1872-1953), English literary scholar and art collector.

Marsh, George Perkins (1801-1882), American diplomat, scholar and conservationist, author of the memorable *Man and Nature* (1864).

Marshall, Alfred (1842-1924), English economist, author of *Principles of Economics* (1890).

Marshall, Tom (1938-1993), Canadian poet, novelist and essayist.

Marsilius of Padua (c. 1280-c.1343), influential Italian political philosopher who wrote *Defensor pacis* (Defender of Peace).

Marsman, Hendrik (1899-1940), Dutch poet and critic; died in the sinking of a ship during World War II.

Marston, John (1576-1634), English dramatist, poet and churchman, a remarkable satirist whose important work was the play *The Malcontent* (1604).

Marston, John Westland (1819-1890), English dramatist and critic; father of Philip Bourke Marston.

Marston, Philip Bourke (1850-1887), English poet and short-story writer; son of John Westland Marston.

Martí (y Pérez), José Julian (1853-1895), famous Cuban patriot, poet and essayist; died in battle.

Martial (actually Marcus Valerius Martial) (38-c. 103) celebrated Roman poet who was unmatched in his mastery of the epigram.

Martianus Capella or Marcian (5th Century), African writer, author of *De Nuptiis Philologiae et Mercurii.*

Martin, (Bon-Lois-) Henri (1810-1883), French historian and politician, best known for his *Histoire de France* (15 volumes, 1833-36; 4th edition, revised, 17 volumes, 1861-65) and *Histoire de France depuis 1789 jusqu' à nos jours* (History of France from 1789 to Our Time, 6 volumes, 1878-83).

Martin, Gregory (c.1540-1582), English Roman Catholic biblical scholar, translator of the Latin Vulgate Bible into English.

Martin, Sir Theodore (1816-1909), Scottish writer and translator who collaborated with W E Aytoun on the "Bon Gaultier" ballads (1845).

Martin du Gard, Roger (1881-1958), eminent French novelist and dramatist, author of the 8-part novel cycle *Les Thibault* (1922-40; English translation as *The World of the Thibaults,* 1939-41); won the nobel prize for Literature (1937).

Martineau, Harriet (1802-1876), English writer who wrote widely on social, economic and historical subjects; sister of James Martineau.

Martineau, James (1805-1900), English Unitarian theologian and philosopher who espoused liberal views on the authority of Scripture; brother of Harriet Martineau.

Martinez de la Rosa (Berdejo Gómez y Arroyo), Francisco de Paula (1787-1862), Spanish statesman, dramatist and poet, author of the play *La conjuracion de Venecia* (The Conspiracy of Venice).

Martinez Sierra, Gregorio (1881-1947), Spanish dramatist, writer and poet.

Martini, Giovanni Battista (1706-1784), notable Italian music theorist and composer who was known as Padre Martini.

Martinson, Harry Edmund (1904-1978), Swedish poet and novelist; was co-winner of the Nobel Prize for Literature (1974); husband of Moa Martinson (1929-40).

Martinson, Moa (1890-1964), Swedish novelist; wife of Harry Edmund Martinson (1929-40).

Martyn, John (1699-1768), English botanist, writer and translator, best known for his translations of Virgil.

Marulić, Marko (1450-1524), Croatian philosopher and poet.

Marvell, Andrew (1621-1678), Outstanding English poet and writer, one of the most gifted of the metaphysicians, author of the poems *To His Coy Mistress, The Nymp Complaining for the Death of her Faun* and *A Poem upon the Death of His Late Highness the Lord Protector* (1658), and the prose works *The Rehearsal Transposed* (2 Parts, 1672-73) and *An Account of the Growth of Popery and Arbitrary Government* (1677).

Marx, Karl (Heinrich) (1818-1883), greatly significant German-born English political economist and philosopher whose radical advocacy of revolutionary change made him the central figure in the development of socialism, author of the *Manifest der kommunistischen Partei* (1848; English translation as the *The Communist Manifesto,* 1930) and *Das Kapital* (3 volumes, 1867, 1885, 1894; English translation as *Capital: A Critique of Political Economy,* 3 volumes, 1886, 1907, 1909).

Masamune Hakuchō (actually Masamune Tadao) (1879-1962), prominent Japanese critic and writer.

Masaoka Shiki (actually **Masaoka Tsunenori**) **(1867-1902),** admired Japanese poet and essayist who brought renewed life to the haiku and tanka.

Masefield, John (1878-1967), distinguished English poet and writer, especially known for such poetical works as *Salt-Water Ballads* (1902), *The Everlasting Mercy* (1911), *Dauber* (1913) and *Reynard the Fox* (1919); became Poet Laureate of the United Kingdom (1930).

Mason, A(lfred) E(dward) W(oodley) (1865-1948), English novelist whose best known work was *The Four Feathers* (1902).

Mason, John Mitchell (1770-1829), American Protestant minister and educator.

Mason, William (1725-1797), English poet and churchman.

Maspero, Gaston (-Camille-Charles) (1846-1916), French archaeologist who wrote *Causeries d'Égypte* (1907; English translation as *New Light on Ancient Egypt,* 1908).

Massey, Gerald (1828-1907), English mystic, poet and writer.

Massinger, Philip (1583-1640), notable English dramatist and poet, especially admired for his play *A New Way to Pay Old Debts* (c.1621).

Massingham, Harlod John (1888-1952), English writer and biographer.

Masson, Frédéric (1847-1923), French historian who wrote on Napoleon and his era.

Masterman, C(harles) F(rederick) G(urney) (1874-1927), English politician and writer.

Masters, Edgar Lee (1869-1950), esteemed American poet and writer, highly regarded for his poems in *Spoon River Anthology* (1915) and *The New Spoon River* (1924).

Mather, Cotton (1663-1728), learned American Puritan minister and scholar who wrote numerous books on a vast number of subjects; son of Increase Mather and father of Samuel Mather.

Mather, Increase (1639-1723), prominent American Puritan minister, diplomat, educator and writer; son of Richard Mather.

Mather, Richard (1596-1669), English-born American Puritan minister and writer; Father of Increase Mather.

Mather, Samuel (1706-1785), American Protestant minister and writer; son of Cotton Mather.

Mathews, Cornelius (1817-1889), American editor, dramatist, novelist and poet.

Mathews, Shailer (1863-1941), American religious educator and writer, one of the principal figures in the social gospel movement.

Mathias, Thomas James (c.1754-1835), English writer, best remembered for his anonymously published *The Pursuits of Literature* (2 parts, 1794, 1797).

Matiez, Albert (1874-1932), French historian who wrote on the French Revolution.

Matos Guerra, Gregório de (1633-1696), Brazilian poet who was known for his satirical verse.

Matsunaga Teitoku (1571-1653), Japanese poet who created the Teimon school of haiku poetry.

Matsuo Bashō (actually **Matsuo Munefusa**) **(1644-1694),** great Japanese poet, the foremost master of haiku poetry.

Mattheson, Johann (1681-1764), important German writer on music and lexicographer.

Matthews, (James) Brander (1852-1929), American drama critic, essayist, novelist and educator.

Matthews, William (Procter) (1942-1997), American poet.

Matthiessen, F(rancis) O(tto) (1902-1950), American literary biographer and essayist.

Matthisson, Friedrich von (1761-1831), German poet.

Matto de Turner, Clorinda (1854-1909), Peruvian novelist, dramatist and poet, best known for her popular novel *Aves sin nido* (1889; English translation as *Birds Without a Nest,* 1904).

Ma Tuan-lin (13th Century), important Chinese historian.

Maturin, Charles Robert (1782-1824), Irish clergyman, novelist and dramatist, author of the famous gothic novel *Melmoth the Wanderer* (1820).

Maugham, W(illiam) Somerset (1874-1965), admired English novelist, short-story writer and dramatist, author of the novels *Of Human Bondage* (1915), *The Moon and Sixpence* (1919), *Cakes and Ale* (1930), and *The Razor's Edge* (1944).

Maupassant, (Henry-René-Albert-) Guy de (1850-1893), outstanding French short-story writer.

Mauriac, Claude (1914-1996), French novelist, dramatist and critic; son of François Mauriac.

Mauriac, François (1885-1970), distinguished French novelist, essayist, poet and dramatist; won the Nobel Prize for Literature (1952); father of Claude Mauriac.

Maurice, Furnley (actually **Frank Leslie Thompson Wilmot**) **(1881-1942),** admired Australian poet who won accolades for his poem *To God: From the Warring Nations* (1917) and the collections *Eyes of Vigilance* (1920) and *Melbourne Odes* (1934).

Maurice, (John) Fredrick Denison (1805-1872), influential English Anglican theologian and Christian socialist, author of *The Kingdom of Christ* (1838), *Theological Essays* (1853) and *Social Morality* (1869).

Maurois, André (actually **Emile Herzog**) **(1885-1967),** eminent French biographer, essayist and novelist.

Mauropus, John (11th Century), Byzantine ecclesiastic, scholar and poet.

Maurras, Charles (1868-1952), Prominent French writer, political theorist and poet whose support of the Vichy regime during World War II led to his arrest in 1944 and imprisonment until his release shortly before his death.

Mauss, Marcel (1872-1950), French sociologist and anthropologist, author of *Essai sur le don* (1925; English translation as *The Gift,* 1954).

Mauthner, Fritz (1849-1923), Bohemian-born German drama critic, novelist and philosopher who espoused skepticism.

Maximus the Confessor, Saint (C. 580-662), notable Byzantine theologian.

Maximus the Greek (1480-1556), Greek Orthodox monk and scholar who translated the Scriptures into Russian.

Max Müller, Fredrich (1823-1900), German-born English philologist who was known for his studies on comparative mythology and comparative religions; son of Wilhelm Müller.

Maxwell, Gavin (1914-1969), Scottish novelist, poet and painter.

May, Karl (1842-1912), German writer, best known for his books for young people.

May, Rollo Reece (1909-1994), American Psychologist and writer who developed existential psychotherapy.

May, Samuel Joseph (1797-1871), Americn Unitarian minister and writer who was active in many liberal social and political causes of his era.

May, Thomas (1595-1650), English dramatist, poet, historian and translator.

Mayakovsky, Vladimir (Vladimirovich) (1893-1930), famous Russian poet and dramatist; committed suicide.

Mayhew, Experience (1673-1758), American Protestant preacher, writer and translator, especially known for his work among the Indians of New England; grandson of Thomas Mayhew and father of Jonathan Mayhew.

Mayhew, Jonathan (1720-1766), American Protestant preacher and polemicist who was known for his championship of liberal religious and political views; son of Experience Mayhew.

Mayhew, Thomas (C.1621-1657), American Protestant missionary to the Indians who collaborated with John Eliot on several tracts; grandfather of Experience Mayhew.

Maynard, François (C.1582-1646), French poet.

Mayo, Frank (1839-1896), American actor and dramatist.

Mayo, (George) Elton (1880-1949), Australian-born American psychologist who was known for his studies in industrial sociology.

Mayo, William Starbuck (1811-1895), American novelist, short-story writer and physician.

Mayr, Michael (1864-1922), Austrian historian and statesman.

Mayrhofer, Johann (1787-1836), Austrian poet.

Mazzini, Giuseppe (1805-1872), Italian revolutionary and political writer who espoused the cause of Italian republicanism.

McAlmon, Robert (1896-1956), American poet and writer of the "lost generation."

M'Carthy, Justin (1830-1912), Irish novelist, historian and politician.

McCarthy, Mary (Therese) (1912-1989), prominent American critic, novelist and memoirist.

McConnell, Francis John (1871-1953), American Methodist bishop, educator, social reformer and writer.

McCosh, James (1811-1894), Scottish-born American philosopher and educator.

McCoy, Horace (1897-1955), American novelist and screenwriter.

McCrae, Hugh (Raymond) (1876-1958), Australian poet, writer and actor.

McCullers, Carson (Smith) (1917-1967), admired American novelist, short-story writer and dramatist, author of the novels *The Heart is a Lonely Hunter* (1940) and *A Member of the Wedding* (1946), and the novelette *The Ballad of the Sad Café* (1951).

McCulloch, John R(amsay) (1789-1864), Scottish-born English economist and statistician.

McCutcheon, George Barr (1866-1928), American novelist.

McDougall, William (1871-1938), English-born American psychologist, author of *Introduction to Social Psychology* (1908), *Body and Mind: A History and Defense of Animism* (1911) and *The Group Mind* (1920).

McFee, William (Morley Punshon) (1881-1966), English-born American writer and poet.

McGee, Thomas D'Arcy (1825-1868), Irish-born Canadian poet, writer and politician.

McGinley, Phyllis (1905-1978), American poet and writer.

McGonagall, William (1830-1902), Scottish poet and novelist.

McHenry, James (1785-1845), Irish-born American poet and novelist.

McIntyre, Duncan (actually **Donnchad Bàn Macan t-Saoir) (1724-1812),** Scottish-Gaelic poet.

McKay, Claude (1890-1948), Jamaican-born American novelist and poet.

McKenney, Ruth (1911-1972), American writer, best known for *My Sister Eileen* (1938).

McLachlan, Alexander (1818-1896), Scottish-born Canadian poet, especially remembered for his poems in Scots dialect.

McLean, Sarah Pratt (1856-1935), American novelist and short-story writer.

McLellan, Isaac (1806-1899), American poet.

McMaster, John Bach (1852-1932), American historian, author of a history of the US (9 volumes, 1883-1927).

McTaggart, John McTaggart Ellis (1866-1925), English philosopher who espoused an atheistic idealism.

Mead, George Herbert (1863-1931), American philosopher who was known as a pragmatist.

Mead or **Mede, Joseph (1586-1638),** English Anglican biblical scholar.

Mead, Margaret (1901-1979), prominent American anthropologist.

Medhurst, Walter Henry (1796-1857), English Anglican missionary and Oriental linguist.

Medina, Bartolome dé (1528-1580), Spanish Dominican theologian.

Medina, José Toribio (1852-1930), Chilean scholar and statesman who prepared important bibliographical volumes.

Medwall, Henry (15th Century), English churchman and dramatist whose *Fulgens and Lucrece* was the first secular play in English.

Megasthenes (c.350-c.290 B.C.), Greek historian and diplomat, author of the *Indika*, a history of India.

Mehmet Fuat Köprülü (1890-1966), Turkish scholar and statesman who was also known as Köprülüzade.

Mehring, Franz (1846-1919), German radical journalist and historian, author of the important tomes *Geschichte der deutschen Sozialdemocratie* (History of German Social Democracy, 4 volumes, 1897-98) and *Karl Marx: Geschichte seines Lebens* (Karl Marx: History of his life, 1918).

Meiklejohn, Alexander (1872-1964), English-born American philosopher and educator.

Meillet, Antoine (1866-1936), French linguist.

Meinecke, Fredrich (1862-1954), German historian, author of *Idee der Staatsräson in der neueren Geschichte* (1924; English translation as *Machiavellism: The Doctrine of Raison d'Etat and Its Place in Modern History,* 1957) and *Die deutsche Katastrophe* (1946; English translation as *The German Catastrophe,* 1950).

Meinhold, Johann Wilhelm (1797-1815), German pastor, poet and dramatist.

Meinong, Alexius (1853-1920), Austrian philosopher and psychologist, author of *Über Annahmen* (On Assumptions, 1902).

Meireles, Cecilia (1901-1964), esteemed Brazilian poet, particularly known for her *Espectros* (Visions, 1919) and *Viagem* (Journey, 1939).

Meiri, Menahem ben Solomon (1249-1316), Jewish Talmudic scholar.

Meir of Rothenburg or **Meir ben Baruch (c.1215-1293),** outstanding German Jewish scholar who was an authority on the Talmud.

Mei Sheng (d. 140 B.C.), Chinese poet.

Mela, Pomponius (1st Century), important Roman geographer, author of the classic *De situ orbis* (A Description of the world, c.43).

Melanchthon, Philipp (1497-1560), notable German Protestant reformer, theologian and scholar who wrote the Confession of Augsburg of the Lutheran Church (1530).

Meleager (1st Century B.C.), Greek poet, admired for his elegies and epigrams.

Meléndez Valdés, Juan (1754-1817), Sapnish poet and politician, esteemed for his lyric poetry.

Meletios Pegas (1549-1601), Greek Orthodox patriarch of Alexandria and theologian.

Meletius of Antioch (c. 310-381), Armenian theologian and bishop of Antioch, a principal figure in the anti-Arian movement.

Meletus (4th Century B.C.), Greek poet.

Melito of Sardis (2nd century), important Greek theologian and bishop of Sardis who greatly influenced his successors of the Christian faith.

Mellen, Grenville (1799-1841), American writer and poet.

Melo, Francisco Manuel de (1608-1666), Portuguese soldier, historian, literary critic and poet.

Melville, Andrew (1545-1622), Scottish Protestant reformer and scholar, one of the principal figures of the Scottish Reformed Church and its adoption of presbyteries.

Melville, Herman (1819-1891), outstanding American writer and poet whose masterpiece was the novel *Moby Dick* (1851).

Melville, James (1556-1614), Scottish Presbyterian reformer, educator and diarist.

Mena, Juan de (1411-1456), Spanish poet, author of *El laberinto de fortuna* or *Las trescientas* (1444).

Ménage, Gilles (1613-1692), French scholar.

Menahem ben Saruq (c. 910-c. 970), Spanish Jewish lexicographer and poet, compiler of the first dictionary in Hebrew.

Menander (342-292 B.C.), great Greek dramatist, master of comedic writing.

Menander Protector (6th Century), Byzantine historian.

Ménard, Louis-Nicolas (1822-1901), French scholar, novelist and poet.

Mencius (c.371-c.289 B.C.), outstanding Chinese philosopher of orthodox Confucianism.

Mencken, H(enry) L(ouis) (1880-1956), iconoclastic American journalist, critic and essayist.

Mendele Mokher Sefarim (actually Shalom Jacob Broyde or Abramovich) (1835-1917), important Russian Jewish writer who was the central figure in the development of the modern Yiddish and Hebrew narrative literary genres and of modern written Hebrew.

Mendelssohn, Moses (1729-1786), German Jewish philosopher and biblical scholar, author of *Phadon, oder über die Unsterblichkeit der Seele* (Phaedo, or on the Immortality of the Soul, 1767).

Mendès, Catulle (1843-1909), French poet, dramatist and writer.

Menen, Aubrey (actually Salvator Aubrey Clarence Menen) (1912-1989), English novelist and essayist.

Menéndez Pidal, Ramón (1869-1968), Spanish scholar who was known for his philological and literary studies.

Menéndez y Pelyao, Marcelino (1856-1912), eminent Spanish scholar and poet.

Menger, Karl (1840-1921), Austrian economist.

Menken, Adah Isaacs (actually Dolores Adios Fuertes) (c.1835-1868), American actress and poet.

Menno Simons (1496-1561), Dutch Anabaptist leader and writer on religion whose followers became known as Mennonites.

Menzel, Wolfgang (1798-1873), German literary critic, poet and historian.

Mera, Juan León (1832-1894), Ecuadorian novelist.

Mercati, Michele (1541-1593), Italian naturalist and physician.

Mercer, Cecil William (1885-1960), English novelist who wrote under the name Dornford Yates.

Mercier, Désiré-Joseph (1851-1926), Belgian Roman Catholic cardinal, philosopher and educator, one of the principal figures in the revival of Thomism.

Mercier, Louis-Sébastien (1740-1814), French dramatist who was known for his middle-class tragedies.

Merck, Johann Heinrich (1741-1791), German writer and critic.

Meredith, George (1828-1909), notable English novelist and poet.

Meres, Francis (1565-1647), English churchman who brought out *Palladis Tamia: Wits Treasury* (1598), a volume devoted to Elizabethan poetry.

Merezhkovski, Dmitri Sergelevich (1865-1941), Russian novelist, poet and critic; husband of Zinaida (Nikolaievna) Gippius.

Mérimée, Prosper (1803-1870), prominent French novelist, short-story writer, dramatist and scholar.

Merle d'Aubbingé, Jean-Henri (1794-1872), important Swiss church historian, author of the *Histoire de la Réformation du seizième Siécle* (5 volumes, 1835-53; English translation as *History of the Great Reformation of the Sixteenth-Century*, 1838-41) and *Histoire de la Réformation en Europe au temps de Calvin* (History of the Reformation in Europe at the Time of Calvin, 8 volumes, 1863-78).

Merleau-Ponty, Maurice (1908-1961), French philosopher, particularly known for his *La Structure du comportement* (1942; English translation as *The Structure of Behavior*, 1965) and *Phenomenologie de la perception* (1945; English translation as *Phenomenology of Perception*, 1962).

Merrill, James Ingram (1926-1995), eminent American poet whose output was highly esteemed for its mastery of lyric and epic writing.

Merill, Stuart Fitzrandolph (1863-1915), American poet, author of the Symbolist masterwork *Une Voix dans la foule* (1909).

Merriman, Brian (1747-1805), Irish-Gaelic poet, known for his satirical and erotic mock-heroic epic *Cúirt an Mheánin Oidhche* (The Midnight Court, c.1786).

Merriman, Henry Seton (actually Hugh Stowell Scott) (1862-1903), English writer.

Mersenne, Marin (1588-1648), notable French mathematician, philosopher and theologian, especially known for his work on prime numbers.

Merton, Thomas (1915-1968), American Trappist monk, writer and poet.

Mesrob, Saint (actually Mashtots) (c.350-c.439), Armenian monk, theologian and linguist who translated the bible into Armenian.

Metastasio, Pietro (actually **Pietro Antonio Domenico Bonaventura Trapassi**) **(1698-1782)**, famous Italian poet who wrote the librettos for many outstanding operas.

Meteren, Emanuel von (1535-1612), Flemish historian.

Metge, Bernat or **Bernardo (1350-1413)**, distinguished Catalan poet, author of *Lo Somni* (1398).

Metochites, George (c.1240-c.1328), Byzantine scholar and theologian; father of Theodore Metochites.

Metochites, Theodore (c.1260-1332), Byzantine statesman and scholar; son of George Metochites.

Metraux, Alfred (1902-1963), Swiss anthropologist.

Metrophanes Kritopoulos (1589-1639), Greek Orthodox patriarch of Alexandria, Egypt and theologian.

Meun, Jean de (c.1250-1305), French poet and translator.

Mew, Charlotte Mary (1869-1928), English poet and short-story writer; committed suicide.

Meyer, Adolf (1866-1950), Swiss-born American psychiatrist.

Meyer, Conrad Ferdinand (1825-1898), esteemed Swiss poet, novelist and short-story writer, especially admired for his novel *Jürg Jenatsch*, (1875-76).

Meyer, Eduard (1855-1930), German historian.

Meyer, Joseph (1796-1856), German industrialist, publisher and writer.

Meyer, Jürgen Bona (1829-1897), German philosopher of the Empiricist school.

Meyer, Kuno (1858-1919), German language scholar who was an authority on Celtic languages.

Meyer, (Marie-) paul (-Hyacinthe) (1840-1917), French literary and language scholar.

Meyer-Lübke, Wilhelm (1861-1936), Swiss-born German language scholar.

Meynell, Alice (Christiana Gertrude née Thompson) (1847-1922), English essayist and poet.

Michaud, Joseph (1767-1839), French journalist and historian.

Michaux, Henri (1899-1984), Belgian poet and painter.

Michel, Louise (1830-1905), French anarchist, poet and writer.

Michelangelo (actually **Michelangelo di Lodovico Buonarroti Simoni**) **(1475-1564)**, great Italian sculptor, painter, architect and poet.

Michelet, Jules (1798-1874), eminent French historian who wrote the expansive *Histoire de France* (1833-67).

Michels, Robert (1876-1936), German sociologist and economist, author of the important study *Zur Soziologie des Parteiwesens in der modernen Demokratie* (1911; English translation as *Political Parties: A Sociological Study of the Oligarchicl Tendencies of Modern Democracy*, 1962).

Michener, James A(lbert) (1907-1997), highly popular American novelist, author of such works as *Tales of the South Pacific* (1947), *Hawaii* (1959) and *Texas* (1985).

Miciński, Tadeusz (1873-1918), Polish writer.

Mickiewicz, Adam (Bernard) (1798-1855), renowned Polish poet who was acclaimed as the national poet of Poland.

Middleton, Conyers (1683-1750), English writer, particularly remembered for his *A Free Inquiry into the Miraculous Powers which are supposed to have subsisted in the Christian Church* (1749).

Middleton, Thomas (c.1570-1627), English dramatist, writer and poet, especially known for his plays *Women beware Women* (c.1621) and *The Changeling* (with William Rowley; 1622).

Middleton, T(homas) F(anshaw) (1769-1822), English Anglican missionary and bishop of Calcutta, author of *The Doctrine of the Greek Article Applied to the Criticism and Illustration of the New Testament* (1808).

Mi Fei (actually **Mi Fu**) **(1051-1107)**, remarkable Chinese calligrapher, artist, scholar, poet and critic.

Mifflin, Lloyd (1846-1921), American poet who was known for his sonnets.

Mignet, François (-Auguste-Marie) (1796-1884), French historian.

Mikhailovsky, Nikolai Konstantinovich (1842-1904), Russian sociologist and political writer, the principal figure in the narodnik (populist) movement.

Miki Kiyoski (1897-1945), Japanese Marxist philosopher.

Mikszáth Kálmán (1847-1910), Hungarian novelist and short-story writer.

Miles, George Henry (1824-1871), American writer, dramatist and poet.

Miles, Josephine (1911-1985), American poet and critic.

Milescu, Nicolae (1626-1708), Russian scholar, translator and traveller.

Milíč of Kroměříž, Jan **(c.1305-1374)**, Czech Roman Catholic theologian, ascetic and religious reformer.

Mill, James (1773-1836), influential English philosopher, historian and economist of the Utilitarian school, author of a *History of British India* (3 volumes, 1817); father of John Stuart Mill.

Mill, John Stuart (1806-1873), outstanding English philosopher and political economist of the Utilitarian school, author of *A System of Logic* (1843), *Principles of Political Economy* (1848), *On Liberty* (1859) and *Considerations on Representative Government* (1861); Son of James Mill.

Millay, Edna St Vincent (1892-1950), prominent American poet and dramatist whose admired poetry collections included *Renascence and Other Poems* (1917), *Second April* (1921), *The Harp Weaver and Other Poems* (1923), *The Buck in the Snow* (1928), *Fatal Interview* (1931) and *Wine from These Grapes* (1934).

Miller, Henry (Valentine) (1891-1980), provocative American novelist, short-story writer and essayist whose preoccupation with candid sexual themes made him one of the most controversial writers of his era.

Miller, Hugh (1802-1856), English journalist, geologist and poet; committed suicide.

Miller, Joaquin (actually **Cincinnatus Hiner (Heine) Miller) (1837-1913)**, American poet and journalist, best remembered for his poetry collection *Songs of the Sierras* (1871).

Miller, Perry (Gilbert Eddy) (1905-1963), American literary scholar.

Miller, William (1810-1872), Scottish poet, known for his *Wee Willie Winkie.*

Millin, Sarah Gertrude (née Liebson) (1889-1968), Lithuanian-born South African novelist and essayist, author of the notable novels *God's Step-Children* (1924) and *Mary Glen* (1925).

Mills, C(harles) Wright (1916-1962), American sociologist.

Milman, Henry Hart (1791-1868), English poet and historian.

Milne, A(lan) A(lexander) (1882-1956), English writer and poet who was enormously successful in writing verse for children, especially *Winnie-the-Pooh* (1926).

Milnes, (Richard) Monckton, Baron Houghton (1809-1885), English biographer, historian, literary scholar, editor and poet.

Milton, John (1608-1674), great English poet and religious and political polemicist, celebrated for his epic poem *Paradise Lost* (1667) and its sequel *Paradise Regained* (1671).

Milyukov, Pavel Nikolaievich (1859-1943), Russian statesman and historian who espoused liberal democracy but was compelled to go into exile after the Bolshevik Revolution of 1917.

Mimnermus (c.600 B.B.) Greek poet.

Mīrā Bāī (c.1450-c.1547), Hindu mystic and poet.

Mirabeau, Victor Riqueti, Marquis de (1715-1789), French political economist.

Mirbeau, Octave (-Henri-Marie) (1850-1917), French novelist and dramatist.

Mīrkhwānd (actually Muhammad ibn Khāvandshāh ibn Mahmūd) (1433-1498), Persian historian.

Miro (Ferrer), Gabriel (1879-1930), Spanish novelist, short-story writer and essayist.

Miron, Gaston (1928-1996), French-Canadian poet.

Mirsky, D S (actually Prince Dmitri Petrovich Sviatopolk-Mirsky) (1890-1939), Russian literary critic and historian.

Mishima Yukio (actually Kimitake Miraoka) (1925-1970), provocative Japanese novelist and short-story writer who probed the conflicts between Japanese and Western traditions; committed suicide.

Misrama, Suryamal (1872-1952), Indian poet.

Mistral, Frédéric (1830-1914), esteemed French poet and short-story writer, author of the outstanding narrative poems *Mirèio* (1859), *Calendau* (1867), *Nerto* (1884) and *Lou Pouèmo dóu Rose* (1897); was co-winner of the Nobel Prize for literature (1904).

Mistral, Gabriela (actually Lucila Godoy Alcayaga) (1889-1957), admired Chilean poet who espoused the cause of Modernism; won the Nobel Prize for Literature (1945).

Mitchel, John (1815-1875), Irish-born American nationalist and journalist, best known for his *Jail Journal, or Five Years in British Prisons* (1854).

Mitchell, Donald Grant (1822-1908), American writer who wrote under the names Ik Marvel and Ike Marvel.

Mitchell, John Ames (1845-1918), American editor, novelist and artist.

Mitchell, Joseph (1908-1996), American journalist and writer.

Mitchell, Langdon (Elwyn) (1862-1935), American dramatist and essayist; son of S(ilas) Weir Mitchell.

Mitchell, Margaret (1900-1949), American novelist who wrote the enormously popular *Gone with the Wind* (1936).

Mitchell, S(ilas) Weir (1829-1914), American physician, writer and poet, best known for his novel *Hugh Wynne, Free Quaker* (1897); father of Langdon (Elwyn) Mitchell.

Mitchell, Wesley Clair (1874-1948), American economist who was an authority on business cycles.

Mitchell, W(illiam) O(rmond) (1914-1998), notable Canadian writer and dramatist.

Mitford, Jessica (Lucy) (1917-1996), English-born American journalist and writer who was known for her muckracking proclivities; sister of Nancy (Freeman) Mitford.

Mitford, John (1781-1859), English clergyman, writer and poet.

Mitford, Mary Russell (1787-1855), English poet, dramatist and writer.

Mitford, Nancy (Freeman) (1904-1973), English novelist and biographer; sister of Jessica (Lucy) Mitford.

Mitford, William (1744-1827), English historian, author of a *History of Greece* (1785-1810).

Mitre, Bartolomé (1821-1906), notable Argentine soldier, statesman, journalist, writer, poet and translator.

Moberg, (Carl Artur) Vilhelm (1898-1973), Swedish novelist and dramatist.

Mocatta, Frederic David (1828-1905), English Jewish philanthropist, bibliophile and historian, author of *The Jews of Spain and Portugal and the Inquisition* (1877).

Mochnacki, Maurycy (1804-1834), influential Romanian literary critic.

Modena, Leone (1571-1648), Italian rabbi, preacher, poet and scholar.

Moe, Jørgen Engebretsen (1813-1882), Norwegian poet and folklorist who, with Peter Christian Asbjørnsen, collaborated on the important collection *Norske folkeeventyr* (Norwegian Folk Tales, 1841; Critical edition, 1852).

Moeller, Philip (1880-1958), American dramatist.

Moeller van den Bruck, Arthur (1876-1925), influential German cultural critic whose book *Das Dritte Reich* (The Third Reich, 1923) was adopted by the Nazi regime as the description of its totalitarian regime; committed suicide.

Moffat, James (1870-1944), Scottish biblical scholar and translator.

Moffat, Robert (1795-1883), English missionary and biblical translator who was active in Africa.

Mofolo, Thomas (Mokopu) (1877-1948), notable South African novelist who wrote in the Sesotho language, author of *Moeti oa Bochabela* (1906; English translation as The Traveller to the East, 1934), *Pitseng* (At the Pot, 1910) and *Chaka* (1925; English translation as *Chaka: A Historical Romance*, 1931).

Mogila, Peter (1596-1646), Russian Orthodox monk, theologian and metopolitan of Kiev.

Möhler, Johann Adam (1796-1838), German Roman Catholic priest and church historian who advocated unity between Catholics and Protestants, author of *Die Einheit in der Kirche* (Unity in the Church, 1825), *Symbolik* (1823; English translation as *On the Creeds*, 1843) and *Neue Untersuchung der Lehrgegensätze zwischen Katholiken und Protestanten* (New Examination of the Doctrinal Differences Between Catholics and Protestants, 1834).

Moir, David Macbeth(1798-1851), Scottish physician and poet who wrote under the name Delta.

Moleschott, Jacob (1822-1893), Dutch physiologist and philosopher, best known for his study *Kreislauf des Lebens* (Circuit of Life, 1852).

Molesworth, Mary Louisa (née Stewart) (1839-1921), English novelist and writer of children's books under the name Ennis Graham.

Molesworth, Robert, 1st Viscount (1656-1725), English diplomat and political writer.

Molière (actually Jean-Baptiste Poquelin) (1622-1673), great French dramatist and poet, author of such celebrated plays as *L'École des Femmes* (1662; English translation as *The School for Wives*, 1948), *Tartuffe* (1664; English translation as *The Imposter*, 1950), *Le Bourgeois Gentilhome* (1670; English translation as *The Prodigal Snob*, 1952) and *Le Malade Imaginaire* (1673; English translation as *The Imaginary Invalid*, 1925).

Molina, Luis de (1535-1600), important Spanish Jesuit theologian who wrote the significant tome *Concordia liberi arbitrii cum gratiae donis* (The union of Free Will and Divine Grace, 1588).

Molinet, Jean (1435-1507), French poet and writer.

Molinos, Miguel de (1628-1696), Spanish Roman catholic priest and theologian whose *Guia espiritual* (Spiritual Guide, 1675; English translation, 1928) espoused an extreme form of Quietism; was arrested by the Holy Offie, tried, condemned and died in prison.

Møller, Poul Martin (1794-1838), Danish writer and poet, best known for his novel *En dansk students eventyr* (The Adventures of a Danish Student, 1824).

Molnár, Ferenc (1878-1952), Hungarian dramatist, novelist and short-story writer.

Molyneux, William (1656-1698), English philosopher.

Mommsen, Theodor (1817-1903), eminent German historian, author of the outstanding *Römische Geschichte* (4 volumes, 1854-85; English translation as *The History of Rome*, 4 volumes, 1862-75); won the Nobel Prize for Literature (1902).

Monboddo, James Burnett, Lord (1714-1799), Scottish jurist and anthropologist, author of the tome *Of the Origin and Progress of Language* (6 volumes, 1773-92).

Moneta, Ernest Teodoro (1833-1918), Italian journalist and pacifist; was co-winner of the Nobel Prize for Peace (1907).

Monk, Maria (c.1817-1850), American writer who created a scandal with her *Awful Disclosures* (1836) and *Further Disclosures* (1837), accounts of alleged terrors in a Montreal convent which were later proved to be fabrications.

Monluc, Blaise de Lasseran-Massencôme, Seigneur de (c.1500-1577), French soldier who wrote a valuable autobiography entitled *Commentaires* (1592; English translation as *Commentaries*, 1674).

Monnier, Henri (1805-1877), French caricaturist and dramatist.

Monod, Adolphe (-Louis-Frédéric) Théodore (1802-1856), notable French Reformed pastor and theologian of Swiss descent.

Monod, Gabriel (-Jean-Jacques) (1844-1912), French historian.

Monrad, Marcus Jakob (1816-1897), Norwegian philosopher.

Monro, H(arold) E(dward) (1879-1932), English publisher, editor and poet.

Monroe, Harriet (1860-1936), American poet, critic and editor.

Monsarrat, Nicholas (actually John Turney) (1910-1979), English novelist, best remembered for *The Cruel Sea* (1951).

Montagu, Basil (1770-1851), English barrister, writer and poet.

Montagu, Elizabeth (née Robinson) (1720-1800), prominent English woman of letters and writer, a leading figure among the "bluestockings".

Montagu, Lady Mary Wortley (1689-1762), notable English letter writer, essayist, poet, feminist and traveller.

Montagu or **Montague, Richard (1577-1641)**, English Anglian bishop and theologian who championed the cause of a middle way in the disputes between Calvinist and Roman Catholic doctrines.

Montague, Charles Edward (1867-1928), English journalist, novelist and short-story writer.

Montaigne, Michel (Eyquem) de (1533-1592), celebrated french essayist who created the form of the essay in his famous *Essais* (3 volumes, 1580-88; English translation, 1948).

Montale, Eugenio (1896-1981), eminent Italian poet, writer, editior and translator; won the Nobel Prize for Literature (1975).

Montalembert, Charles (-Forbes-René) de (1810-1870), French politician and historian who opposed both church and state absolutism.

Montalvo, Jean (1832-1889), Ecuadoran essayist and writer.

Montausier, Charles de Saint-Marie, Duc de (1610-1690), French soldier, poet and writer.

Montchrestien, Antoine de (c.1575-1621), French economist and dramatist.

Montefiore, Claude Joseph Goldsmid (1858-1938), English Jewish theologian, Reform leader and philanthropist.

Monteiro Lobato, José Bento (1883-1948), Brazilian writer and publisher.

Montelius, (Gustav) Oscar (Augustin) (1843-1921), Swedish archaeologist.

Montemayor or **Montemor, Jorge de (c1520-c.1561)**, Portuguese-born Spanish writer and poet whose *Diana* (c.1559) was the first Spanish pastoral novel.

Montesquieu, (Charles-Louis de Secondat, Baron de la Brède et de) (1689-1755), illustrious French political philosopher, author of *Lettres persanes* (1721; English translation as *Persian Letters*, 1721), *Considérations sur les causes de la grandeur des Romains et de leur décadence* (1734; English translation as *Reflections on on the Rise and Fall of the Roman Empire*, 1734), *L'Esprit des lois* (1748; English translation as *The Spirit of Laws*, 1750) and *Defense de l'Esprit des lois* (1750).

Montessori, Maria (1870-1952), influential Italian educator who developed the Montessori method of education, author of *Il metodo della pedagogia scientifica* (1909; English translation as *The Montessori Method*, 1912), *The Secret of Childhood* (1936), *To Educate the Human Potential* (1948) and *La mente assorbente* (1949; English translation as *The Absorbent Mind*, 1949).

Montet, Pierre (1885-1966), French archaeologist who was a prominent Egyptologist.

Montfaucon, Bernard de (1655-1741), esteemed French patristic scholar, paleographer and archaeologist.

Montgomerie, Alexander (c.1545-c.1611), Scottish poet whose major work was the allegorical *The Cherry and the Slae* (1597).

Montgomery, James (1771-1854), Scottish poet, hymnist and journalist.

Montgomery, Lucy Maude (1874-1942), Canadian novelist, best known for her popular *Anne of Green Gables* (1908).

Montgomery, Robert (1807-1855), English preacher and poet.

Montherlant, Henry (-Marie-Joseph-Millon) de (1896-1972), French novelist and dramatist, particularly known for his novel-cycle *Les Jeunes Filles* (1936), *Pitie pour les femmes* (1936), *Le Demon du Bien* (1937) and *Les Lepreuses* (1939), all of which were published in an English translation as *The Girls: A Tetralogy of Novels* (2 volumes, 1968); committed suicide.

Monti, Vincenzo (1754-1828), Italian poet and translator.

Montrose, James Graham, 5th Earl and 1st Marquess of (1612-1650), English general and poet who espoused the Royalist cause; following his defeat at Carbisdale, he was hanged.

Montúfar y Rivera Maestre, Lorenzo (1823-1898), Guatemalan statesman and histiorian who espoused liberalism, author of the expansive *Reseña Historica de Centro America* (17 volumes, 1878-88).

Moodie, Susanna Strickland (1803-1885), English-born Canadian pioneer, best remembered for her *Roughing It in the Bush; or, Life in Canada* (1852).

Moody, William Vaughn (1869-1910), American dramatist and poet, best known for his plays *The Great Divide* (1906) and *The Faith Healer* (1909).

Moore, Clement Clarke (1779-1863), American biblical scholar and poet who wrote the celebrated poem *A Visit from St Nicholas* (1822), better known as *'Twas the Night Before Christmas.*

Moore, Edward (1712-1757), English dramatist, writer and poet, best remembered for his play *The Gamester* (1753).

Moore, George (Augustus) (1852-1933), Irish novelist and short-story writer, particularly admired for his novel *Esther Waters* (1894) and the autobiographical trilogy *Hail and Farewell* (*Ave,* 1911, *Salve,* 1912 and *Vale,* 1914).

Moore, G(eorge) E(dward) (1873-1958), English philosopher of the Idealist school, author of *Principia Ethica* (1903), *Philosophical Studies* (1922) and *Some Main Problems of Philosophy* (1953); brother of T(homas) Sturge Moore.

Moore, George Foot (1851-1931), American biblical scholar, theologian and Orientalist who wrote *Judaism in the First Centuries of the Christian Era* (3 volumes, 1927-30).

Moore, George Henry (1823-1892), American historian; brother of (Horatio) Frank(lin) Moore.

Moore, (Horatio) Frank(lin) (1828-1904), American historian; brother of George Henry Moore.

Moore, John Bassett (1860-1947), American scholar of international law.

Moore, John Trotwood (1858-1929), American novelist and poet; father of Merrill Moore.

Moore, Julia A (1847-1920), American poet and writer who was known as the "Sweet Singer of Michigan."

Moore, Marianne (Craig) (1887-1972), distinguished American poet, essayist and editor.

Moore, Merrill (1903-1957), American psychiatrist and poet; son of John Trotwood Moore.

Moore, Thomas (1779-1852), renowned Irish poet and composer, author of *Irish Melodies* (1807-34), *Lallah Rookh* (1817) and *The Loves of the Angels* (1823).

Moore, T(homas) Sturge (1870-1944), English poet, critic and wood engraver; brother of G(eorge) E(dward) Moore.

Morant, Harry Harbord (1865-1902), English-born Australian adventurer and poet; executed by firing squad for murderous actions he committed during the Boer War.

Morata, Olympia (1526-1555), Italian poet and scholar.

Moravia, Alberto (actually **Alberto Pincherle**) **(1907-1990)**, prominent Italian novelist and short-story writer.

More, Hannah (1745-1833), English writer and educator of the poor.

More, Henry (1614-1687), English poet and philosopher who was a leading figure among the Cambridge Platonists.

More, Paul Elmer (1864-1937), American literary scholar who espoused the New Humanism until turning to Christianity late in life.

More, Sir Thomas or Saint Thomas More (1477-1535), eminent English scholar and statesman, author of the classic political volume *Utopia* (1516); as a Roman Catholic, he refused to accept King Henry VIII as head of the Church of England and was beheaded.

Moreas, Jean (actually **Yannis Papadiamantopoulos**) **(1856-1910)**, Greek-born French poet who first embraced Symbolism but later became a champion of Greek and Latin classicism.

Morellet, André (1727-1819), French economist and writer, author of *Mémoires sur le XVIIIe siècle et la Révolution* (published 1821).

Morelly (18th Century), French philosopher who wrote the Utopian *Code de la nature* (1755), a trenchant attack on private property.

Moreto (Y Cabaña), Agustín (1618-1669), Spanish dramatist.

Morford, Henry (1823-1881), American journalist, novelist and poet.

Mogan, Charles (Langbridge) (1894-1958), English novelist, dramatist and critic.

Morgan, Lady (née Sydney Owenson) (1776-1859), English writer and poet.

Morgan, Lewis Henry (1818-1881), American ethnologist and anthropologist, author of *Ancient Society, or Researches in the Lines of Human Progress from Savagery through Barbarism to Civilization* (1977).

Morgan, William (c.1545-1604), Welsh Anglican bishop who translated the Bible into Welsh.

Morgenstern, Christian (1871-1914), German poet who wrote nonsense verse imbued with esoteric meaning.

Morgenthau, Hans J(oachim) (1904-1980), German-born American political scientist and historian.

Móricz, Zsigmond (1879-1942), notable Hungarian novelist and short-story writer.

Morier, James Justinian (c.1780-1849), English diplomat and writer, author of *The Adventures of Hajji Baba of Ispahan* (1824).

Mörike, Eduard Friedrich (1804-1875), celebrated German poet and writer, one of the foremost lyric poets of Germany.

Morin, Jean (1591-1659), French Roman catholic theologian.

Morin, Paul (d'Equilly) (1889-1963), French-Canadian poet.

Mori Ōgai (actually Mori Rintarō) (1862-1922), important Japanese writer who extolled the Samurai code.

Morison, James (1816-1893), Scottish theologian who founded the Evangelical Union and espoused universalism.

Morison, Samuel Eliot (1887-1976), eminent American historian and biographer, author of biographies of Columbus (1942) and John Paul Jones (1959) and the official history of US naval operations (14 volumes, 1947-60).

Morison, Stanley (1889-1967), English scholar who devoted himself to the study of printing.

Moritz, Karl Philipp (1757-1793), German novelist and aesthetician who was especialy admired for his autobiographical novels *Anton Reiser* (4 volumes, 1785-90) and *Andreas Hartknopf* (1786).

Morley, Christopher (Darlington) (1890-1957), American novelist, essayist and poet.

Morley, Henry (1822-1894), English journalist, editor and biographer.

Morley, Henry Parker, Lord (1476-1556), English Courtier, diplomat, writer and translator.

Morley, John, 1st Viscount Morley of Blackburn (1838-1923), English politician, essayist and biographer.

Morley, Thomas (c.1557-1602), notable English composer, organist and theorist, author of the treatise *A plaine and Easie Introduction to Practicall Musicke* (1597).

Mornay, Philippe de, Seigneur du Plessis-Marly (1549-1623), French diplomat and political and religious polemicist.

Morris, George Pope (1802-1864), American journalist and poet, best remembered for his poem *Woodman, Spare that Tree* (1830).

Morris, Sir Lewis (1833-1907), Welsh poet, dramatist and barrister.

Morris, Richard (Brandon) (1904-1989), American historian.

Morris, William (1834-1896), English craftsman, socialist, poet and writer.

Morris, Wright (1910-1998), American novelist, short-story writer, essayist and photographer.

Morris-Jones, Sir John (1864-1929), distinguished Welsh scholar, poet and translator.

Morrison, Arthur (1863-1945), English novelist and short-story writer.

Morrison, Robert (1782-1834), English Presbyterian minister, missionary and translator who collaborated with William Milne on a translation of the Bible into Chinese.

Morrison, Theodore (1901-1988), American novelist and poet.

Morrow, Honoré Willsie (1880-1940), American novelist.

Morse, Jedidiah (1761-1826), American Congregational minister and geographer; father of Samuel F(inley) B(resse) Morse.

Morse, Samuel F(inley) B(reese) (1791-1872), American inventor of the electric telegraph, artist and memoirist; son of the Jedidiah Morse.

Morsztyn, Jan Andrzej (1613-1693), Polish writer.

Morsztyn, Zbigniew (1627-1689), Polish writer.

Mortillet, (Louis-Laurent-Marie) Gabriel de (1821-1898), French archaeologist.

Morton, Charles (c.1627-1698), English-born American Puritan clergyman and writer on religion, logic and science.

Morton, George (1585-1624), English Puritan leader, author of an account of the Plymouth Plantation in New England (1622); father of Nathaniel Morton.

Morton, John Maddison (1811-1891), English dramatist; son of Thomas Morton.

Morton, Nathaniel (1613-1686), English-born American Puritan leader, author of a history of New England as *New Englands Memorial* (1669), a work owing much to other writers; father of George Morton.

Morton, Sarah Wentworth (1759-1846), American writer and poet.

Morton, Thomas (c.1590-1647), English-born American trader and adventurer, author of *New English Canaan* (1637).

Morton, Thomas (c.1764-1838), English dramatist; father of John Maddison Morton.

Mosca, Gaetano (1858-1941), Italian jurist and political theorist, author of *Elementi di scienza politica* (1896; English translation as *The Ruling Class*, 1939).

Moscherosch, Johann Michael (1601-1699), German Lutheran statesman and writer whose outstanding satirical gifts were revealed in his *Wunderliche und wahrhafftige Gesichte Philanders von Sittewald* (Peculiar and True Visions of Philanders von Sittewald, 1641-43).

Moschopoulos, Manuel (13th-14th Century), Byzantine scholar.

Moschus (flourished 150 B.C.), Greek poet and grammarian.

Moschus, John (c.550-619), Byzantine monk and writer, author of the *Pratum Spirituale* (The Spiritual Meadow) which dealt with spirtual experiences.

Mościcki, Ignacy (1867-1946), Polish politician, scholar and scientist who served as president of Poland (1926-39).

Möser, Justus (1720-1794), German political essayist and poet whose output presaged the Sturm und Drang movement.

Moses (ben Shem Tov) de Leon (1250-1305), Spanish Jewish Kabbalist, reputedly the author of the *Sefer ha-zohar* (The Book of Splendour), a celebrated volume of Jewish mysticism.

Mosheim, Johann Lorenz von (1694-1755), German Lutheran theologian and church historian.

Moss, Howard (1922-1987), American poet, editor, essayist, reviewer and dramatist.

Motherwell, William (1797-1835), Scottish Journalist and poet.

Motley, John Lothrop (1814-1877), American diplomat and historian, author of *The Rise of the Dutch Republic* (1856).

Motley, Willard (1912-1956), American novelist and short-story writer.

Moto-ori Norinaga (1730-1801), notable Japanese litearary scholar.

Mott, Frank Luther (1886-1964), American scholar of journalism.

Motteux, Peter Anthony (1660-1718), English jouralist, dramatist and translator.

Motteville, Françoise Bertaut, Dame de (c.1621-1689), French memorialist, author of the *Mémoires* (1723; English translation, 1725-26).

Mottley, John (1692-1750), English dramatist and biographer.

Mottram, R(alph) H(ale) (1883-1971), English novelist.

Mo-tzu (c.470-c.391 B.C.), Chinese philosopher.

Moulton, (Ellen) Louise Chandler (1835-1908), American poet and writer.

Mourao-Ferreira, David (1927-1996), Portuguese writer and poet.

Mourning Dove (actually Hum-Ishu-Ma) (1888-1936), native American novelist and storyteller, author of the novel *Cogewea the Half-Blood: A Depiction of the Great Montana Cattle Range* (1927).

Mowatt, Anna Cora (née Ogden) (1819-1870), American actress and dramatist, best remembered for her satirical play *Fashion* (1845).

Moxon, Edward (1801-1858), English publisher, bookseller and poet.

Mqhayi, Samuel E(dward) K(rune) (1875-1945), South African poet, writer and translator.

Mubārak, 'Alī Pasha (c.1823-1893), Egyptian writer and eductor.

Mubarrad, al- (actually Abū al-'Abbās Muhammad ibn Yazīd) (826-898), Arab literary scholar and grammarian.

Muggleton, Lodowick (1609-1698), English Puritan religious leader who espoused an anti-Trinitarian heresy with his cousin John Reeve in *A Transcendent Spiritual Treatise upon Several Heavenly Doctrines* (1652) and *A Divine Looking-Glass* (1656).

Muhammad ibn Falāh (c.1400-1461), Persian Muslim theologian who founded the Musha'sha sect of Shī'ism, author of the *Kalam al-mahdi* (The Words of the Mahdi).

Muhāsibī, al- (actually Abū Allāh al-Harith ibn Asad al-'Anazī al-Muhāsibī) (c.781-857), Iraqi Muslim mystic of the Sūfi sect.

Muir, Edwin (1887-1959), prominent Scottish poet, critic and translator, particularly known for his poetry volumes *The Voyage* (1946) and *The Labyrinth* (1949).

Muir, John (1838-1914), American naturalist and writer.

Mukammas, David al- (actually David Abū Sulaymān ibn Marwān ar-Raqqī al-Mukammas) (10th Century), Jewish Philosopher.

Mulcaster, Richard (c.1530-1611), English schoolmaster, author of two volumes on education, *Positions* (1581) and *The Elementarie* (1582).

Mulford, Clarence E(dward) (1883-1956), American writer of Westerns, creator of Hopalong Cassidy.

Mulford, Prentice (1834-1891), American journalist and essayist.

Mulla Sadra (c.1571-1640), Persian philosopher.

Müller, Friedrich (1749-1825), German poet, dramatist and painter who was known as Friedrich Maler (i.e. Painter).

Müller Friedrich (1834-1898), Bohemian philologist.

Müller Georg Elias (1850-1934), German experimental pyschologist.

Müller, Heiner (1929-1996), German dramatist and writer.

Müller, Johannes von (1752-1809), significant Swiss historian, author of the *Geschichten Schweizerischer Eidgenossenschaft* (1786-1808).

Müller Karl Otfried (1797-1840), German scholar who devoted himself to the study of ancient Greece, author of *Geschichten hellenischer Stamme und Stadte* (History of Greek Cities and Peoples, 1820).

Müller, Sophus Otto (1846-1934), Danish paleontologist.

Müller, Wilhelm (1794-1827), admired German poet whose *Die Schöne Müllerin* (The Fair Maid of the Mill, 1821) and *Die Winterreise* (The Winter Journey, 1821) inspired the great song cycles by Schubert.

Multatuli (actually Eduard Douwes Dekker) (1820-1887), notable dutch novelist, best known for his *Max Havelaar* (1860; English translation, 1927).

Mumford, Lewis (1895-1990), American social critic and writer.

Mun, Thomas (1571-1641), English economist who published a cogent treatise on the balance of trade theory in his *A Discourse of Trade, from England unto the East Indies* (1621).

Munby, Arthur Joseph (1828-1910), English poet and diarist.

Munch, Peter Andreas (1810-1863), Norwegian historian, author of *Det norske Folks Historie* (The History of the Norwegian People, 1852-63).

Munday, Anthony (c.1560-1633), esteemed English poet, dramatist, pamphleteer and translator.

Müneccim Başi (actually Derviş Ahmet Dede ibn Lutfullah) (1631-1702), Ottoman historian who wrote a universal history.

Munford, Robert (c.1730-1784), American dramatist, poet and translator; father of William Munford.

Munford, William (1775-1825), American poet, writer and translator; son of Robert Munford.

Munk, Kaj Harald Leininger (1898-1944), remarkable Danish priest, patriot and dramatist who wrote the plays *En Idealist* (1928; English translation as *Herod the King*, 1955), *Cant* (1931), *Ordet* (1932; English translation as *The Word*, 1955) and *Han sidder ved Smeltediglen* (1938; English translation as *He Sits at the Melting-Pot*, 1944); was murdered by the Nazis.

Munro, Hector Hugh (1870-1916), popular Scottish short-story writer who wrote under the name Saki.

Munshi, Kanaiyalal (1887-1971), Indian novelist.

Münster, Sebastian (1489-1552), Important German Hebrew scholar, author of the influential *Cosmographia* (Cosmography, 1544).

Münsterberg, Hugo (1863-1916), German-born American psychologist and philosopher.

Munthe, Axel Martin Fredrik (1857-1949), Swedish physician, psychiatrist and writer, author of the highly popular autobiographical account *The Story of San Michele* (1929).

Müntzer, Thomas (c.1489-1525), German Protestant Reformer and polemicist whose radical views culminated in his leadership of the Peasants' Revolt (1524-25); was executed.

Muralt, Béat-Louis de (1665-1749), Swiss writer of a Pietist persuasion.

Murasaki Shikibu (c.978-c.1026), famous Japanese court lady and writer, author of the celebrated novel *Genji monogatari* (English translation as *The Tale of Genji*, 1935).

Muratori, Lodovico Antonio (1672-1750), oustanding Italian scholar who wrote the important *Antiquitates Italicae Medii Aevi* (Antiquities of the Italian Middle Ages, 6 volumes, 1738-42).

Murdoch, Frank Hitchcock (1843-1872), American actor and dramatist.

Mure, Sir William (1594-1657), Scottish poet.

Muretus (actually Marc-Antoine Muret) (1526-1585), French poet and scholar.

Murfree, Mary Noailles (1850-1922), American novelist and short-story writer.

Murger, (Louis-) Henri (1822-1861), French writer and poet who was known for his novel *Scènes de la vie bohème* (1847-49), which inspired operas by Leoncavallo and Puccini.

Murillo, Gerardo (1875-1964), Mexican painter and writer.

Muris, Johannes de (c.1300-c.1351), significant French music theorist, astronomer and mathematician.

Murner, Thomas (1475-1537), German Franciscan friar and poet who was known for his satirical poetry.

Muro Kyūsō (1658-1734), prominent Japanese Confucian scholar and government official.

Murphy, Arthur (1727-1805), English barrister, journalist, actor and dramatist.

Murray, Charles (1864-1941), Scottish poet.

Murray, (George) Gilbert (Aimé) (1866-1957), English scholar who made effective translations of the ancient Greek dramatists.

Murray, Sir James (Augustus Henry) (1837-1915), English lexicographer who edited the *New English Dictionary on Hisorical Principles* (1884-1915), later known as the *Oxford English Dictionary*.

Murray, Johan (1741-1815), English-born American preacher and writer who founded Universalism; husband of Judith Murray.

Murray, John Courtney (1904-1967), American Roman Catholic priest and theologian.

Murray, Judith (1751-1820), American writer and poet who wrote under the name Constantia; wife of John Murray.

Murray, Lindley (1745-1826), American-born English Quaker minister and grammarian.

Murry, John Middleton (1889-1957), influential English editor, critic, essayist and poet.

Musaeus (5th-6th century), Greek poet, author of the famous *Hero and Leander.*

Musil, Robert Elder von (1880-1942), Austrian writer and dramatist, author of the unfinished expansive novel *Der Mann ohne Eigenschaften* (1930-32: English translation as *The Man Without Qualities*, 1953-60).

Muslim ibn al-Hajjāj (actually Abū al-Husayn Muslim ibn al-Hajjāj al-Qushayrī) (c.817-875), Islamic scholar.

Mussato, Albertino (1261-1329), noted Italian statesman, historian and poet.

Musset, (Louis-Charles-) Alfred de (1810-1857), eminent French poet and dramatist, a leading Romanticist.

Mutanabbī, al- (actually Abū at-Tayyib Ahmad ibn Husayn al-Mutanabbī) (915-965), famous Arab poet who led an adventurous life; was murdered by bandits.

Mužáková, Johanna (1830-1899), Czech novelist who wrote under the name Karolina Světlá.

Myers, Ernest James (1844-1921), English poet and translator; brother of F(redric) W(illiam) H(enry) Myers.

Myers, F(rederic) W(illiam) H(enry) (1843-1901), English poet, critic and essayist; brother of Ernest James Myers.

Myers, L(eopold) H(amilton) (1881-1944), English novelist who wrote the tetralogy *The Near and the Far East* (1929), *Prince Jali* (1931), *The Root and the Flower* (1935) and *The Pool of Vishnu* (1940).

Myers, Peter Hamilton (1812-1878), American lawyer and novelist.

Myres, Sir John Linton (1869-1954), English historian and anthropologist who was known for his studies of ancient history.

Nābighad, an- (actually an-Nābighah adh-Dhubyānī) (7th Century), Arab poet.

Nabokov, Vladimir (Vladimirovich) (1899-1977), notable Russian-born American novelist and poet, author of the famous novel *Lolita* (1955).

Nadel, S(iegfried) F(rederick) (1903-1956), English anthropologist, author of *The Foundations of Social Anthropology* (1951) and *Theory of Social Structure* (published 1958).

Naevius, Gnaeus (c.270-c.199 B.C), important Roman poet and dramatist, creator of the fabulae praetextae (historical play).

Nagai Kafu (actually Nagai Sokichi) (1879-1959), Japanese novelist.

Nagarjuna (c.150-c.250), Indian Buddhist monk and philosopher who founded the Madhyamika (Middle Path) school.

Nahman of Bratslav, Rabbi (1772-1811), Hasidic writer.

Naidu, Sarojini (née Chattopadhyay) (1879-1949), prominent Indian feminist, politician and poet, known as the "Nightingale of India," author of the poetry collections *The Golden Threshold* (1905) and *The Bird of Time* (1912).

Naima, Mustafa (1655-1716), Turkish historian who wrote *Tarih* (English translation as *Annals of the Turkish Empire from 1591-1659 of the Christian Era*, 1832).

Naipaul, Shiva (1945-1985), West Indian novelist.

Nairne, Carolina (née Oliphant), Baroness (1766-1845), English poet and songwriter.

Nakae Tōju (1608-1648), Japanese Neo-Confucian scholar.

Nakae Tokusuke (1847-1901), Japanese writer and translator who wrote under the name Nakae Chōmin.

Naka Michiyo (1851-1908), Japanese historian.

Nalbandean, Mikael (1829-1866), Armenian writer.

Nalkowska, Zofia (1884-1954), Polish writer.

Nāmdev (c.1270-c.1350), notable Indian poet and saint.

Namier, Sir Lewis Bernstein (1888-1960), English historian who wrote the influential tome *The Structure of Politics at the Accession of George III* (1929).

Namiki Gohei (1747-1808), Japanese dramatist of the kabuki theater.

Namiki Shōzō I (18th Century), Japanese dramatist.

Namiki Shōzō II (d. 1807), Japanese dramatist and writer.

Namora, Fernando Goncalves (1919-1989), Portuguese poet, writer and physician.

Napier, John (1550-1617), Scottish mathematician and writer on theology.

Napier, Sir William Francis Patrick **(1785-1860),** English general and historian, particularly known for his *History of the War in the Peninsula...* (6 volumes, 1828-40).

Nardi, Jacopo (1476-c.1564), Italian statesman, historian, dramatist and translator. author of the *Istoria della citta' di Firenze* (History of the City of Florence, 1582).

Nariño, Antonio (1765-1823), Colombian revolutionary and writer.

Naruszewicz, Adam (Stanisław) (1733-1796), polish historian and poet.

Nasby, Petroleum V(esuvius) (actually **David Ross Locke) (1833-1888),** American journalist who was known for his satirical bent.

Nascimento, Francisco Manuel do (1734-1819), Portuguese poet who embraced the cause of Romanticism and wrote under the name Filinto Elisio.

Nāser-e Khosrow (actually **Abū Mo' īn Nāser-e Khosrow al-Marvāzīal-Qubādiyānī) (1004-c.1075),** renowned Persian poet and Islamic theologian of the Shī'ah sect.

Nash, (Frederic) Ogden (1902-1971), popular American poet, a master of wit.

Nashe or **Nash, Thomas (1567-c.1601),** English writer, dramatist, poet and political pamphleteer, author of the first English picaresgue novel *The unfortunate traveller, or The Life of Jack Wilton* (1594).

Natalis, Alexander (actually **Alexandre Noel)** (1639-1724), French theologian and historian who advocated the restriction of papal hegemony, author of *Selecta historiae ecclesiaticae capita* (Selected Chapters of Ecclesiastical History, 24 volumes, 1676-86; revised edition as *Historia ecclesiastica veteris et novi testamenti* (Ecclesiastical History of the Old and New Testaments), 8 volumes, 1699).

Nathan, George Jean (1882-1958), American drama critic, editor and writer.

Nathan, Robert (Gruntal) (1894-1985), American novelist, poet and dramatist.

Natorp, Paul (1854-1924), German philosopher of the Neo-Kantian school.

Natsume Sōseki (actually **Natsume Kinosuke) (1867-1916),** remarkable Japanese novelist, author of *Wagahai-wa Neko-de aru* (1906; English translation as *I Am a Cat,* 1961), *Botchan* (1906; English translation as *Master Darling,* 1918) and *Kusamakura* (1906: English translation as *The Three-Cornered World,* 1965).

Naughton, William (John Francis) (1910-1992), Irish dramatist, novelist and short-story writer.

Naumann, Fredrich (1860-1919), German politician and theorist.

Nava'i, (Mir) Ali Shir (1441-1501), Turkish poet and scholar.

Nayler or **Naylor, James (1618-1660),** English Quaker preacher and writer.

Nazor, Vladimir (1876-1949), Croatian poet.

Nazzām, Ibrāhīm an- (actually **Abū Ishāq Ibrāhīm ibn Hanī' an-Nazzām) (c.775-c.845),** outstanding Iraqi Muslim theologian, jurist, historian and poet.

Neal, Daniel (1678-1743), English Nonconformist minister and historian.

Neal, John (1793-1876), American novelist, critic and poet.

Neal, Joseph Clay (1807-1847), American journalist and writer who was known for his humour.

Neale, J(ohn) M(ason) (1818-1866), English Hymnist, historian and translator, author of *The History of the Holy Eastern Church* (1847-73).

Nearing, Scott (1883-1983), American economist and environmentalist, especially remembered for his exposition of the counterculture in *Living the Good Life* (1954)

Nedham or **Needham, Marchamont (1620-1678),** English jouralist who was the principal author of *Mercurius Britanicus* (1643-46).

Nedim, Ahmed (1681-1730), celebrated Turkish poet, a master of lyricism.

Nefi'i of Erzurum (actually **Ömer) (d.1636),** famous Turkish poet who was renowned as a satirist and panegyrist.

Negri, Ada (1870-1945), Italian poet and short-story writer

Neidhart von Reuenthal (c.1180-c.1250), German poet, creator of hofische Dorfpoesie (courtly village poetry).

Neihardt, John G(neisenau) (1881-1973), American poet and writer.

Nekrasov, Nikolai Alexeievich (1821-1878), Russian poet and journalist.

Nekrasov, Viktor Platonovich (1911-1987), Russian novelist, short-story writer and essayist whose dissident views led him to emigrate to France in 1974.

Nelligan, Émile (1897-1941), French-Canadian poet.

Nelson, Leonard (1882-1927), German philosopher.

Nemerov, Howard (1920-1991), admired American poet, writer and essayist; was Poet Laureate of the US (1988-90).

Nemesianus, Marcus Aurelius Olympius (3rd Century), Roman poet.

Nemesius of Emesa (4th Century), Christian bishop of Emesa, apologist and philosopher who wrote *Peri physeos anthropou* (On the Nature of Man).

Nennius (c.800), Welsh antiquarian.

Nepos, Cornelius (c.100-c.25 B.C.), Roman historian and biographer.

Neruda, Pablo (actually **Neftalí Ricardo Reyes) (1904-1973),** prominent Chilean poet and diplomat; won the Nobel Prize for Literature (1971).

Nerval, Gerárd de (actually **Gerárd Labrunie) (1808-1855),** French writer and poet who wrote both Symbolic and Surrealist verse; dissipation and insanity led him to commit suicide.

Nervo, Amado (actually **Juan Crisóstomo Ruiz de Nervo) (1870-1919),** Mexican poet and diplomat, a principal figure in the Modernist movement of Spanish-American literature.

Nesbit, E(dith) (1858-1924), English writer, best remembered for her children's books.

Nesimi, Seyyid Imadeddin (d. c.1418), renowned Turkish poet who wrote outstanding mystic verse.

Neşri (actually **Hüseyn ibn Eyne Beg) (d. c.1520),** Turkish historian.

Nestor (c.1056-1113), Russian monk and hagiographer.

Nestroy, Johann Nepomuk Eduard Ambrosius (1801-1862), outstanding Austrian dramatist of comic plays.

Neurath, Otto (1882-1945), German philosopher and sociologist.

Nevā'i, ;Ali Shir (1441-1501), noted Turkish poet and scholar.

Nevin, Allan (1890-1971), distinguished American historian.

Newbolt, Sir Henry John (1862-1938), English poet and historian, particularly remembered for his patriotic and sea lyrics

Newcastle, Margaret, Duchess of (1623-1673), English poet, dramatist and writer; wife of William Cavendish, 1st Duke of Newcastle.

Newcastle, William Cavendish, 1st Duke of (1592-1676), English poet and dramatist; husband of Margaret, Duchess of Newcastle.

Newell, Peter (1862-1924), American writer and illustrator who was best known for his humor.

Newell, Robert Henry (1836-1901), American journalist, writer and poet whose humorous effusions often appeared under the name Orpheus C Kerr, a pun on the words "office seeker."

Newman, John Henry (1801-1890), eminent English Anglican churchman, later Roman Catholic cardinal, writer and poet who was a major figure in the Oxford Movement.

Newton, A(lfred) Edward (1863-1940), American book collector, writer and dramatist.

Newton, Sir Charles Thomas (1816-1894), English archaeologist.

Newton, Sir Isaac (1643-1727), great English physicist and mathematician, author of the important volumes *Principia* (1687; English translation, 1729) and *Opticks* (1704).

Newton, John (1725-1807), English Evangelical leader, hymnist and letter writer.

Nexø, Martin Andersen (1869-1954), Danish writer who championed the lot of the downtrodden of society and embraced Communism, author of the novels *Pelle Arobreren* (4 volumes, 1906-10; English translationas *Pelle the Conqueror*, 1913-16), *Ditte mennskebarn* (5 volumes, 1917-21; English translation as *Ditte, Daughter of Man,* 1920-22) and *Midt i en Jaerntid* (1929: English translation as *In God's Land,* 1933).

Nezāmi (actually **Elyās Yūsof Nezāmi Ganjavī) (c.1141-c.1207),** great Persian poet.

Nguyen Du (actually **Nguyen-Du Thanh-Hien) (1765-1820),** notable Vietnamese poet, author of the national epi *Kim Van Kieu* (English translation, 1968).

Niceforo, Alfredo (1876-1960), Italian sociologist, criminologist and statistician, best known for his theory of the dual ego in man's being delineated in his *L' "io" profondo e le sue maschere* (The Deep Ego and Its Masks, 1949).

Nicephorus I, Saint (c.758-829), Greek Orthodox theologian, historian and patriarch of Constantinople.

Nicephorus, Callistus Xanthopoulos (c.1256-c.1335), Byzantine historian, writer and poet.

Nicetas of Remesiana (5th Century), Greek Christian bishop, theologian and composer.

Nicetas Stethatos (c.1000-c.1080), Byzantine monk, mystic and theologian, the leading champion of Greek Orthodoxy in opposition to Roman Catholic doctrine.

Nicholas III (11th Century), Byzantine theological scholar and Orthodox patriarch of Constantinople.

Nicholas of Autrecourt (c.1300-c.1350), influential French philosopher and theologian whose Skepticism led to his condemnation as a heretic by Pope Clement VI in 1346.

Nicholas of Clémanges (actually **Nicolas Poillevilian) (c.1363-1437),** French theologian, scholar and poet who was a leading advocate of ecclesiastical reform in the face of church corruption.

Nicholas of Cusa (1401-1464), important German Roman Catholic cardinal, scientist and philosopher, author of *De docta ignorantia* (On learned Ignorance, 1440), in which he declared that the attainment of the full knowledge of God and the universe was impossible.

Nicholas of Damascus (1st Centry B.C.), Greek historian and philosopher.

Nicholas of Hereford (d. c.1420), English theologian who was a leading champion of the Lollard reform movement in the Roman Catholic Church, a movement he later denounced.

Nicholas of Lyra (c.1270-1349), learned French theologian of the Franciscans who published the first biblical commentary in his expansive *Postillae perpetuae in universam S. Scripturam* (Commentary Notes to the Universal Holy Scripture, 50 volumes).

Nichols, John (1745-1826), English printer, antiquarian and biographer.

Nichols, Robert Malise Bowyer (1893-1944), English poet and dramatist.

Nicholson, Meredith (1866-1947), American novelist, short-story writer, essayist and poet.

Nicholson, Reynold Alleyne (1868-1945), distinguished English Orientalist, author of the valuable *Literary History of the Arabs* (1907).

Nicodemus the Hagiorite (1748-1809), Greek Orthodox monk and theologian.

Nicolai, Christoph Friedrich (1733-1811), German writer, journalist and bookseller.

Nicolay, John George (actually Johann Georg Nicolai) (1832-1901), German-born American biographer who collaborated with John Hay on a major biography of Abraham Lincoln (10 volumes, 1890).

Nicole, Pierre (1625-1695), French theologian, best remembered for his polemical writings championing Jansenism.

Nicoletti, Paolo (14th-15th Century), Italian philosopher.

Nicolson, Sir Harold (George) (1886-1968), English diplomat, writer, biographer and critic; husband of Victoria Sackville-West.

Niebuhr, Barthold Georg (1776-1831), influential German historian who was a pioneering figure in the use of source criticism, author of *Römische Geschichte* (3 volumes, 1811-32; English translation as *History of Rome*, 1828-42).

Niebuhr, Carsten (1733-1815), German traveller who was the only survivor of the first scientific expedition to Arabia, which he recounted in two volumes (1772, 1774).

Niebuhr, (Helmut) Richard (1894-1962), American theologian, author of *The Meaning of Revelation* (1941), *Christ and Culture* (1951) and *Radical Monotheism and Western Civilization* (1960); brother of Reinhold Niebuhr.

Niebuhr, Reinhold (1892-1971), influential American theologian and writer on ethical, social and political subjects, author of *The Nature and Destiny of Man* (2 volumes, 1941, 1943); brother of (Helmut) Richard Niebuhr.

Nielsen, Morten (1922-1944), esteemed Danish poet; as a member of the resistance to the German occupation of his homeland, he was killed by the Nazis.

Niemcewicz, Julian Ursyn (1758-1841), Polish dramatist, writer, poet and translator.

Niemöller, (Fredrich Gustav Emil) Martin (1892-1984), courageous German Protestant pastor and theologian who opposed the Nazi regime and survived years in concentration camps, author of *Vom U-Boot zur Kanzel* (1934; English translation as *From U-Boat to Concentration Camp*, 1939).

Nietzsche, Friedrich Wilhelm (1844-1900), greatly significant German philosopher, scholar and critic who wrote such important works as *Die Geburt der Tragödie* (1872; English translation as *The Birth of Tragedy*, 1968), *Also sprach Zarathustra* (parts 1-3, 1883-84, part 4, 1891; English translation as *Thus Spake Zarathustra*, 1954), *Jenseits von Gut und Böse* (1886; English translation as *Beyond Good and Evil*, 1968) and *Zur Genealogie der Moral* (1887; English translation as *On the Genealogy of Morals*, 1968).

Nifo, Agostino (c.1473-c.1539), Italian philosopher and Christian apologist who wrote *Tractatus de immortalitate animae contra Pomponatium* (Treatise on the Immortality of the Soul Against Pomponazzi, 1581).

Nijhoff, Martinus (1894-1953), outstanding Danish poet who was known as a master of his craft.

Nijlen, Jan van (1884-1965), distinguished Flemish poet.

Niles, Samuel (1674-1762), American Congregational clergyman, historian and polemicist.

Nin, Anaïs (1903-1977), French-born American novelist, short-story writer and diarist.

Nishi Armane (1829-1897), Japanese philosopher.

Nishida Kitarō (1870-1945), important Japanese philosopher who assimilated Western thought with non-Western ideas.

Nishiyama Sōin (1605-1682), Japanese poet.

Nithard (c.790-844), Frankish count and historian.

Niven, Frederick John (1878-1944), Scottish novelist, essayist and poet.

Noailles, Anna (-Élisabeth, Princess Brancovan, Comtesse Mathieu) de (1876-1933), French poet and novelist who was called "Princesses des lettres" of France.

Nōami (1397-1494), Japanese poet, painter and art critic who was also known as Shinnō.

Nobre, António (1867-1900), Portuguese poet, remembered for his *So* (Alone, 1892).

Nock, Albert Jay (1870-1945), American writer and essayist who expounded on a wide variety of subjects.

Noel, Roden Berkely Wriothesley (1834-1894), English poet.

Noguchi, Yone (1875-1947), Japanese poet.

Nöldeke, Theodor (1836-1930), German language scholar and historian who was an authority on Semitic languages and Islamic history.

Nonius Marcellus (c.5th Century), African Latin grammarian and lexicographer, compiler of *De compendiosa doctrina.*

Nonnus (5th Century), Greek poet who was admired for his epic *Dionysiaca.*

Noot, Jonker Jan van der (c.1540-c.1596), Dutch poet, author of the epic *Olympiados.*

Nordal, Sigurour (Johanneson) (1886-1974), Icelandic scholar, poet and short-story writer.

Nordau, Max (actually **Max Simon Sudfeld) (1849-1923),** Austro-Hungarian writer, dramatist, poet, Zionist and physician, best known for his controversial polemical volume *Die conventionellen Lügen der Kulturmenschheit* (1883; English translation as *The Conventional Lies of Our Civilization,* 1884).

Nordenflycht, Hedvig Charlotta (1718-1763), Swedish poet who was esteemed for her love poems.

Nordenskiöld, (Nils) Erland (Herbert) (1877-1932), important Swedish ethnologist and archaeologist who was an authority on the culture of the South American Indians.

Nordhoff, Charles (1830-1901), German-born American journalist and writer; grandfather of Charles Bernard Nordhoff.

Nordhoff, Charles Bernard (1887-1947), American novelist who collaborated with James N Hall on *Mutiny of the Bounty* (1932), *Men Against the Sea* (1934) and *Pitcairn's Island* (1934); grandson of Charles Nordhoff.

Nordstrom, Ludvig Anselm (1882-1942), Swedish writer.

Norris, (Benjamin) Frank(lin) (1870-1902), American novelist, short-story writer and essayist; brother of Charles G(ilman) Norris.

Norris, Charles G(ilman) (1881-1945), American novelist; brother of (Benjamin) Frank(lin) Norris and husband of Kathleen Norris.

Norris, John (1657-1711), English poet and philosopher, author of *An Essay towards the Theory of the Ideal or Intelligible World* (1701-04).

Norris, Kathleen (1880-1966), American novelist; wife of Charles G(ilman) Norris.

North, Christopher (actually **John Wilson) (1785-1854),** Scottish writer.

North, Roger (1653-1734), English lawyer and biographer.

North, Sir Thomas (1535-c.1603), English translator, especially known for his translation from the French of Jacques Amyot's version of Plutarch's *Lives of the Noble Grecians and Romans* (1579).

Norton, Andrews (1786-1853), American biblical scholar, author of *The Evidences of the Genuineness of the Gospels* (3 volumes, 1837, 1844) and *Internal Evidences of the Genuineness of the Gospels* (1855); father of Charles Eliot Norton.

Norton, Caroline Elizabeth Sarah (née Sheridan) (1808-1877), Irish poet and novelist; granddaughter of Richard Brinsely Sheridan.

Norton, Charles Eliot (1827-1908), American scholar and educatior; son of Andrews Norton.

Norton, John (1606-1663), English-born American Puritan leader and scholar.

Norton, Thomas (1532-1584), English dramatist and poet who, with Thomas Sackville, wrote the earliest English tragedy *Gorboduc* (1561).

Norwid, Cyprian Kamil (1821-1883), outstanding Polish poet and writer.

Nossack, Hans Erich (1901-1977), German novelist, poet and dramatist.

Nostradamus (1503-1566), celebrated French astrologer and physician whose prophecies were published in the volume *Centuries* (1555; 2nd edition, augmented, 1558).

Noth, Martin (1902-1968), German biblical scholar.

Nott, Henry Junius (1797-1837), American jurist and writer, author of the picaresque *Novelettes of a Traveller, or, Odds and Ends from the Knapsack of Thomas Singularity, Journeyman Printer* (1834).

Novalis (actually **Friedrich Leopold, Freiherr von Hardenberg) (1772-1801),** significant German poet, writer and theorist, known as the "Prophet of Romanticism."

Novatian (c.200-c.258), Roman theologian and 2nd antipope who was known for his rigorist doctrine; excommunicated and probably martyred during the reign of Emperor Valerian.

Novikov, Nikolai Ivanovich (1744-1818), Russian writer, philanthropist and Freemason whose enlightened views led to his imprisonment by Empress Catherine II the Great in 1972; was released by Emperor Paul in 1796.

Nowell, Alexander (c.1507-1602), English Anglican priest, scholar and dean of St Paul's Cathedral in London, author of the catechism of the Church of England (in the Prayer Book, 1549, supplemented 1604).

Noyes, Alfred (1880-1958), English poet and dramatist, best known for his lyric style of poetry.

Noyes, John Humphrey (1811-1886), American socio-religious idealist who espoused a doctrine of perfectionism, author of *Bible Communism* (1848) and *History of American Socialisms* (1870).

Numenius of Apamea (2nd Century), Greek philosopher.

Núñez, Rafael (1825-1894), Colombian politician, writer and poet.

Núñez de Arce, Gaspar (1832-1903), Spanish poet, dramatist and statesman.

Nye, Bill (actually **Edgar Wilson Nye**) **(1850-1896),** American journalist and writer who was known for his humorous bent.

Oakes, Urian (c.1631-1681), American clergyman and poet.

Obradović, Dositej (1742-1811), Serbian writer and translator.

O'Brien, Fitz-James (c.1828-1862), Amerian writer, dramatist and poet whose tales presage modern science fiction; died of wounds sustained as a Union soldier in the Civil War.

O'Brien, Flann (actually **Brian Ó Nuallain**) **(1911-1966),** Irish novelist, dramatist and columnist, author of the remarkable novel *At Swim-Two Birds* (1939).

Ó Bruadair, Dáibhidh (c.1625-1698), compelling Irish-Gaelic poet.

Obstfelder, Sigbjørn (1866-1900), Norwegian poet of a refined Symbolist persuasion.

O'Casey, Sean (1880-1964), distinguished Irish dramatist.

Ockham, William of (c.1285-c.1349), important English Roman Catholic Scholastic philosopher who was excommunicated for his opposition to unlimited papal authority.

O'Clery, Michael (1575-1643), Irish historian.

O'Connor, Edwin (1918-1968), American writer, particularly remembered for *The Last Hurrah* (1956) and *The Edge of Sadness* (1961).

O'Connor, Frank (actually **Michael O'Donovan**) **(1903-1966),** Irish novelist, short-story writer, dramatist and translator.

O'Connor, (Mary) Flannery (1925-1964), notable American novelist and short-story writer, especially admired for her novels *Wise Book* (1952) and *The Violent Bear it Away* (1960).

O'Connor, William Douglas (1832-1889), American journalist and writer, best remembered for his profile of Walt Whitman in *The Good Gray Poet* (1866).

Odell, George C(linton) D(ensmore) (1866-1949), American literary scholar.

Odell, Jonathan (1737-1818), American poet and writer who vociferously championed the Loyalist cause during the American Revolution.

Odets, Clifford (1906-1963), American dramatist of social protest, author of *Paradise Lost* (1935), *Waiting for Lefty* (1935), *Awake and Sing* (1935) and *Golden Boy* (1937).

Odiorne, Thomas (1769-1851), American poet, author of *The Progress of Refinement* (1792).

Odoric of Pordenone (c.1286-1331), Italian Franciscan friar and traveller who wrote a popular account of his travels in China.

O'Dowd, Bernard Patrick (1866-1953), Australian poet.

Odum, Howard Washington (1884-1954), American sociologist, author of *Rainbow Round My Shoulder: The Blue Trail of Black Ulysses* (1928).

Oecolampadius, John (actually **Johannes Huszgen**) **(1482-1531),** prominent Swiss Protestant Reformer, preacher and patristic scholar.

Oehlenschlager, Adam Gottlob (1779-1850), notable Danish poet and dramatist who was hailed as the national poet of Denmark.

Oertel, Hanns (1868-1952), German linguist, an authority on Sanskrit.

O'Faolain, Sean (actually **Sean Whelan**) **(1900-1991),** Irish writer, biographer and essayist.

O'Flaherty, Liam (1896-1984), Irish novelist and short-story writer.

Ofterdingen, Heinrich von (12th-13th Century), celebrated German Minnesinger.

Ogburn, William Fielding (1886-1959), American sociologist.

Ogden, Charles Kay (1889-1957), English linguist and writer who created Basic English for the international use of English.

Ogilby, John (1600-1676), Scottish-born English printer, poet and translator.

Ogilvie, James (1775-1820), Scottish-born American writer, best known for his *Philosophical Essays* (1816); committed suicide.

O'Grady, Standish James (1846-1928), Irish novelist and literary historian.

Ogyū Sorai (1666-1728), Japanese scholar of Chinese culture who was a major figure in Confucianism.

O'Hara, Frank (1926-1966), American poet and critic.

O'Hara, John (Henry) (1905-1970), American novelist and short-story writer.

O'Hara, Theodore (1820-1867), American journalist and poet.

O'Higgins, Harvey (Jerrold) (1876-1929), Canadian-born American writer.

Okada, John (1923-1971), American dramatist, author of the Nisei antiwar play *No-No Boy* (1957).

Okamoto Kidō (1872-1939), Japanese dramatist of the Kabuki theater.

Ōkawa Shūmei (1886-1957), Japanese political scientist who espoused the cause of ultra-nationalism.

Oken, Lorenz (1779-1851), German naturalist.

Okigbo, Christopher (1932-1967), Nigerian poet; died in the fight for Biafran independence from Nigeria.

Okudzhava, Bulat Shalovich (1924-1997), Russian poet, writer and folksinger.

Ólafsson, Eggert (1726-1768), Icelandic poet and antiquarian.

Ólafsson, Stefan (1620-1688), Icelandic poet.

Olcott, Henry Steel (1832-1907), American lawyer and writer who was a co-founder of the Theosophical Society and author of the *Buddhist Catechism* (1881).

Oldham, John (1653-1683), English poet and translator.

Oldmixon, John (c.1673-1742), English historian, dramatist and poet.

Old Moore, Francis Moore (1657-1714), English astrologer and physician, author of the famous *Vox Stellarum, an Almanac for 1701 with astrological observations* (1700).

Oldys, William (1696-1761), English biographer and editor.

Olesha, Yuri (Karlovich) (1899-1960), Russian writer.

Oliphant, Laurence (1829-1888), English mystic, traveller and writer.

Oliphant, Margaret (née Wilson) (1828-1897), Scottish novelist and biographer.

Oliveira Martins, Joaquim Pedro de (1845-1894), Portuguese writer and biographer.

Ollivier, Émile (1825-1913), French statesman and writer, author of *L'Empire liberal* (The Liberal Empire, 17 volumes).

Olmedo, José Joaquin (1780-1847), Ecuadoran statesman and poet, especially esteemed for his patriotic odes.

Olmsted, Frederick Law (1822-1903), American landscape architect, conservationist and travel writer.

Olson, Charles (John) (1910-1970), American poet, writer, dramatist and essayist, particularly known for his avant-garde poetry.

Olson, Elder (James) (1909-1992), American poet and critic.

Oman, John Wood (1860-1939), English Presbyterian theologian, author of *The Natural and the Supernatural* (1931).

Omar Khayyam (actually Gheyás od-Dín Abú ol-Fath 'Umar ebn Ebrahim ol-Khayyámí) (c.1048-1122), renowned Persian poet, mathematician and astronomer whose *Ruba'iyat* (Quatrains) are celebrated the world over.

Oña, Pedro de (c.1570-c.1643), Chilean poet.

O'Neill, Eugene (Gladstone) (1888-1953), important American dramatist and poet, author of such plays as *Beyond the Horizon* (1920), *Anna Christie* (1922), *Strange Interlude* (1928), *Long Day's Journey into Night* (1941) and *The Iceman Cometh* (1946); won the Nobel Prize for Literature (1936).

Onetti, Juan Carlos (1909-1994), Uruguayan-born Spanish novelist, short-story writer and essayist.

Onions, C(harles) T(albut) (1873-1965), English grammarian and lexicographer.

Onions, (George) Oliver (1873-1961), English novelist and short-story writer.

Opie, Amelia (née Alderson) (1769-1853), English novelist and poet, author of the novel *Father and Daughter* (1801).

Opie, Peter Mason (1918-1982), English writer and folklorist.

Opitz (von Boberfeld), Martin (1597-1639), Silesian poet and theorist who introduced Renaissance poetic theories to Germany.

Oppen, George (1908-1984), American poet who was the preeminent figure of the Objectivist school of verse.

Oppenheim, E(dward) Phillips (1866-1946), English novelist and short-story writer.

Oppenheim, James (1882-1932), American poet.

Oppenheim, Lassa Francis Lawrence (1858-1919), German-born English jurist and pedagogue, author of *International Law: A Treatise* (2 Volumes, 1905-06).

Orage, Alfred Richard (actually Alfred James Orage) (1873-1934), English editor and writer who championed the cause of guild socialism.

Orchard, William Edwin (1877-1955), English Roman Catholic priest and writer, author of *The Temple* (1913) and *Sancta Sanctorum* (1955).

Orczy, Baroness (Emmuska) (1865-1947), Hungarian-born English novelist, best remembered for *The Scarlet Pimpernel* (1905).

Orderic Vitalis (1075-c.1142), English monk and historian, author of the *Historia ecclesiastica* (c.1108-41).

O'Reilly, John Boyle (1844-1890), Irish-born American journalist and poet who was known as an advocate of Irish republicanism.

Oresme, Nicole d' (c.1325-1382), French Roman Catholic bishop and scholar, especially known for his opposition to Aristotelian thought.

Orhan Veli Kanik (1914-1950), admired Turkish poet.

Origen (c.185-c.254), greatly significant Egyptian biblical scholar, theologian and writer, author of *De Principiis* (4 Volumes), an influential work on Christian doctrine.

Ørjasaeter, Tore (1886-1968), Norwegian poet.

Ormond, John (1923-1900), Welsh poet and filmmaker.

Orosius, Paulus (5th Century), Christian theologian and apologist, author of *Historiarum adversus paganos libra VII* (English translation as *7 Books of Histories Against the Pagans*, 1936).

Orrery, Roger Boyle, 1st Earl of (1621-1679), Irish statesman, poet and dramatist.

Orsi, Paolo (1859-1935), Italian archaeologist who was an authority on Sicilian culture.

Ors y Rovira, Eugenio d' (1882-1954), Spanish novelist, essayist and art critic.

Ortega y Gasset, José (1883-1955), distinguished Spanish philosopher who espoused humanism.

Ortelius, Abraham (1527-1598), Belgian cartographer and antiquarian who published the earliest modern atlas in his *Theatrum orbis terrarum* (1570; English version as *Theatre of the Whole World*, 1606).

Ortese, Anna Maria (1914-1998), Italian writer.

Ortigão, José Duarte Ramalho (1836-1915), Portuguese journalist and essayist.

Orton, Joe (actually **John Kingsley Orton) (1933-1967),** English dramatist, author of the black comedy *Loot* (1965; revised version 1966); was murdered by his gay lover.

Orwell, George (actually **Eric Arthur Blair) (1903-1950),** notable English writer and critic, author of the satirical masterpieces *Animal Farm* (1945) and *Nineteen Eighty-four* (1949).

Orzeszkowa, Eliza (actually **Eliza Pawłowska) (1841-1910),** Polish novelist and short-story writer.

Osborn, Henry Fairfield (1857-1935), American paleontologist and museum curator, author of *From the Greeks to Darwin* (1894) and *Origin and Evolution of Life* (1917).

Osborn, Laughton (c.1809-1878), American writer, poet and dramatist.

Osborne, John (James) (1929-1994), significant English dramatist, author of *Look Back in Anger* (1956), *The Entertainer* (1957), *Luther* (1961), *Inadmissible Evidence* (1964), *A Patriot for me* (1965), *West of Suez* (1971) and *Watch it Come Down* (1976).

Osbourne, (Samuel) Lloyd (1868-1947), American novelist and dramatist.

Osgood, Frances Sargent (Locke) (1811-1850), American poet of sentimental verse.

O'Shaughnessy, Arthur (William Edgar) (1844-1881), English poet, best known for his *Ode (We Are the Music-makers)* (1874).

O'Sheel, Shaemas (1886-1954), American poet, particularly remembered for *They Went Forth to Battle, But They Always Fell.*

Ōshio Heihachirō (1796-1837), Japanese philosopher of the Confucian school.

Osiander, Andreas (actually **Andreas Hosemann) (1498-1552),** German Protestant theologian and reformer.

Osler, Sir William (1849-1919), distinguished Canadian physician, author of the standard textbook *The Principles and Practice of Medicine* (1892).

Osnovyanenko, Gritsko (actually **Grigory Fyodorovich Kvitka) (1778-1843),** Ukrainian writer.

Osorio da Fonseca, Jeronimo (1506-1580), Portuguese historian.

Ossietzky, Carl von (1888-1938), German journalist and pacifist who was first imprisoned during the Weimar regime (1931-1932) and later the Nazi regime (1933-38); won the Nobel Prize for Peace (1935).

Ostaijen, Paul van (1896-1928), Belgian poet, writer and critic who was a major figure in avant-garde circles.

Ostenso, Martha (1900-1963), Norwegian-born American writer.

Ostrogorsky, Moisey (Yakovlevich) (1854-1919), Russian political scientist who was an early authority on the role of democracy and political parties.

Ostrovksy, Alexander Nikolaievich (1823-1886), celebrated Russian dramatist, a master of realistic drama.

Ostrovksy, Nikolai (1904-1936), Russian writer.

Otis, James (1725-1783), American politician and polemicist.

Otto, Rudolf (1869-1937), eminent German theologian, philosopher and historian, author of *Das Heilige* (1917; English translation as *The Idea of the Holy*, 1923), *West-Östliche Mystik* (1926; English translation as *Mysticism East and West*, 1932), *Die Gnadenreligion Indiens und das Christentum*

(1930; English translation as *India's Religion of Grace and Christianity*, 1930) and *Reich Gottes und Menschensohn* (1934; English translation as *The Kingdom of God and the Son of Man*, (1938).

Otto of Freising (c.1111-1158), German Roman Catholic bishop and historian, especially known for his world history *Chronica sive historia de duabus civitatibus*.

Otway, Thomas (1652-1685), notable English dramatist and poet, author of the esteemed poem *The Poet's Complaint of His Muse* (1680) and the remarkable play *Venice Preserved, or a Plot Discovered* (1682).

Oulda (actually Maria Louise Ramé) (1839-1908), English novelist.

Ouspensky, Paul (1878-1947), Russian philosopher.

Outremeuse, Jean d' (1338-1399), Belgian writer, author of *La Geste de Liège* and *Ly Myreru des Histors*.

Ou-yang Hsiu (1007-1072), Chinese statesman, poet and historian.

Overbury, Sir Thomas (1581-1613), English courtier, poet and essayist whose involvement in political intrigue led to his slow poisioning in the Tower of London.

Øverland, Arnulf (1889-1968), outstanding Norwegian poet and socialist who survived incarceration in a Nazi concentration camp to become one of his homeland's most respected literary figures.

Ovid (actually Publius Ovidius Naso) (43 B.C,-17 A.D.), famous Roman poet, author of the celebrated *Ars Armatoria* (Art of Love) and *Metamorphoses*.

Owain Cyfeiliog (c.1130-c.1197), Welsh warrior-prince and poet who was known for his poem *Hirlas Owain* (The Drinking Horn of Owain).

Owen, Daniel (1836-1895), prominent Welsh novelist, short-story writer, essayist and poet.

Owen, Goronwy (1723-1769), Welsh clergyman and poet who espoused the cause of classicism in Welsh Literature.

Owen, John (c.1563-1622), English poet of Latin epigrams.

Owen, Sir Richard (1804-1892), English anatomist and paleontologist who was a strident critic of Darwin's theory of evolution.

Owen, Robert (1771-1858), Welsh manufacturer, reformer and utopian socialist, author of *A New View of Society* (1813); father of Robert Dale Owen.

Owen, Robert Dale (1801-1877), Welsh-born American politician, reformer and writer; son of Robert Owen.

Owen, Wilfred (1893-1918), distinguished English poet who wrote such memorable works as the *Anthem for Doomed Youth* and *Dulce et Decorum Est*; died in battle in France a week before the Armistice ending World War I.

Oxenford, John (1812-1877), English dramatist and critic.

Oxenstierna, Johan Gabriel (1750-1818), Swedish writer.

Oxford, Edward de Vere, 17th Earl of (1560-1604), English courtier, poet and dramatist.

Ozaki Kōyō (actually Ozaki Tokutarō) (1867-1903), significant Japanese novelist, poet and essayist, author of the highly regarded novel *Konjiki yasha* (1897-1902; English translation as *The Gold Demon*, 1917).

Ozanam, Antoine-Frédéric (1813-1853), French historian.

Paavolainen, Olavi (1903-1964), Finnish writer.

Pacatus Drepanius, Latinius or Latinus (4th Century), Gallo-Roman public official, orator and poet.

Pacheco, Francisco (1564-1654), spanish painter and scholar, author of the valuable *Arte de la pintura* (1649).

Pachymeres, Georges (1242-c.1310), Byzantine scholar who wrote on various subjects, from theology to history.

Pacuvius, Marcus (220-c.130 B.C.), great Roman dramatist who was celebrated for his tragedies.

Page, Thomas Nelson (1853-1922), American writer, essayist and biographer.

Page, Walter Hines (1855-1918), American journalist, publisher, diplomat and writer.

Pagninus, Santes (1470-1536), Italian Dominican scholar who prepared a Latin version of the Hebrew Bible (1528).

Paine, Albert Bigelow (1861-1937), American biographer, novelist, dramatist and editor.

Paine, Robert Treat (1773-1811), American poet, best remembered for *The Invention of Letters* (1795), *The Ruling Passion* (1796) and *Adams and Liberty* (1798).

Paine, Thomas (1737-1809), famous and controversial American political and religious pamphleteer, author of *Common Sense* (1776), the *Crisis* papers (1776-83), *Rights of Man* (1791) and *Age of Reason* (1794).

Painter, William (c.1540-1594), English writer, author of the collection of tales known as *The Palace of Pleasure* (1566; 3rd edition, 1575).

Pais, Ettore (1856-1939), Italian historian who wrote an expansive history of the Roman Republic (1898-1931).

Pal, Bipin Chandra (1858-1932), Indian journalist who championed the cause of nationalism.

Palacio Valdés, Armando (1853-1938), Spanish novelist.

Palacký, František (1798-1876), important Bohemian historian and politician, author of a major history of the Czech nation as *Geschichte von Böhmen* (5 volumes, 1836-67).

Palés Matos, Luis (1898-1959), esteemed Puerto Rican poet who was a fine lyricist.

Paley, William (1743-1805), influential English Anglican priest, Utilitarian philosopher and writer, best known for his teleological argument for the existence of God in his *Natural Theology* (1802).

Palfrey, John Gorham (1796-1881), American Unitarian clergyman, writer and editor.

Palgrave, Sir Francis (actually Francis Cohen) (1788-1861), English barrister, antiquarian and historian who was particularly known as a medievalist; father of Francis Turner Palgrave and William Gifford Palgrave.

Palgrave, Francis Turner (1824-1897), English critic and poet, editor of the well-known anthology *The Golden Treasury of English Songs and Lyrics* (1861); son of Sir Francis Palgrave and brother of William Gifford Palgrave.

Palgrave, William Gifford (1826-1888), English Jesuit missionary who left an account of a journey to Arabia in his *Narrative of a Year's Journey through Central and Eastern Arabia* (1865); son of Sir Francis Palgrave and brother of Francis Turner Palgrave.

Palissy, Bernard (1510-1589), remarkable French potter, scientist and writer, author of a notable series of lectures on natural history as *Discours admirables* (1580; English translation as *Admirable Discourses*, 1957); as a Huguenot, he was imprisoned in 1588 and died in the Bastille in Paris.

Palladius (c.363-c.425), Galitian Roman Catholic monk, bishop and historian, author of a history of early monasticism in his so-called *Lausiac History* (c.420).

Pallas, Peter Simon (1741-1811), German naturalist, author of the *Reise durch verschiedene Provinzen des russischen Reichs* (Journey Through the Various Provinces of the Russian Empire, 3 volumes, 1771-76).

Palma, Ricardo (1833-1919), Peruvian writer and poet.

Palmer, Edward H(enry) (1840-1882), English Orientalist, linguist, writer, poet and traveller, was ambushed and killed while in service to the British government in Egypt.

Palmer, (Edward) Vance (1885-1959), leading Australian novelist, short-story writer and dramatist.

Palmer, George Herbert (1842-1933), American philosopher.

Palmer, Joel (1810-1881), American pioneer who wrote an account of his trek to Oregon in his *Journal of Travels Over the Rocky Mountains* (1847).

Palmer, Ray (1808-1887), American Congregationalist minister and hymnist.

Palomino (de Castro y Velasco), Antonio (1655-1726), Spanish painter and scholar, author of the valuable *Museo pictorico y escala optica* (1715-24).

Paltock, Robert (1697-1767), English writer, author of the romance *The Life and Adventures of Peter Wilkins, A Cornishman* (1751).

Paludan-Müller, Frederik (1809-1876), Danish poet who wrote the epic *Adam Homo* (2 parts, 1841, 1848).

Pan Chao (45-c.115), outstanding Chinese scholar, essayist and poet who was especially known for her labors as a chronicler of Chinese history.

Panizzi, Sir Anthony (actually Antonio Genesio Maria Panizzi) (1797-1879), Italian-born English librarian and literary scholar who championed the cause of the unification of Italy.

Panneton, Philippe (1895-1960), French-Canadian novelist and short-story writer who wrote under the name Ringuet.

Pannonius, Janus (1434-1472), Hungarian poet.

Panofsky, Erwin (1892-1968), German-born American art historian.

Papadiamadis, Alexandros (1851-1911), Greek writer.

Papias (c.50-130), bishop of Hierapolis and theologian whose *Expositions of the Oracles of the Lord* is only extant in fragments but remains valuable for the light shed on the early Christian church.

Papini, Giovanni (1881-1956), prominent Italian journalist, critic, novelist and poet.

Papinian (actually Aemilius Papinianus) (c.140-212), Roman jurist who was known for his writings on the law, especially his *Quaestiones* and *Responsa*; was executed by order of the Emperor Caracalla.

Pappus of Alexandria (4th Century), Greek geometer who wrote the valuable *Synagoge* (Collection, c.340) on mathematics.

Paquet, Louis-Adolphe (1859-1942), Canadian writer.

Paracelsus (actually Philippus Aureolus Theophrastus Bombast von Honenheim) (1493-1541), famous Swiss physician and alchemist who first delineated the importance of chemistry in medicine, author of *Die grosse Wundartzney* (Great Surgery Book, 1536).

Paramanuchit, Prince (1791-1852), prince patriarch of the Siamese Buddhist Church, writer and poet who was also known as Prince Paramanujita Jinorasa.

Paráskhos, Akhilléfs (1838-1895), Greek poet who was a champion of Romanticism.

Pardo Bazán, Emilia, Condesa de (1852-1921), Spanish novelist, short-story writer and critic.

Pareto, Vilfredo (1848-1923), influential Italian economist and sociologist, author of the *Cours d'Économie Politique* (1896-97), *Manuale d'economia politica* (1906) and *Tratto di sociologia generale* (1916; English translation as *Mind and Society*, 1963).

Parini, Giuseppe (1729-1799), Italian writer and poet, admired for his Horatian odes and his satiric poem *Il giorno* (4 volumes, 1763, 1765, 1801, 1801).

Paris, (Bruno-Paulin-) Gaston (1839-1903), learned French philologist.

Paris, Matthew (d.1259), English Benedictine monk and historian.

Parish, Elijah (1762-1825), American Congregational minister and writer.

Park, Robert Ezra (1864-1944), American sociologist.

Parke, John (1754-1789), American poet and translator, author of the anonymous volume *The Lyric Works of Horace...to Which Are Added, a Number of Original Poems...*(1786).

Parker, Dorothy (Lee née Rothschild) (1893-1967), notable American short-story writer, poet and critic who was especially famous for her telling wit.

Parker, Eric (actually Frederick Moore Searle) (1870-1955), English journalist, editor and writer.

Parker, Sir (Horatio) Gilbert (1862-1932), Canadian-born English novelist and short-story writer.

Parker, Jane Marsh (1836-1913), American novelist.

Parker, Theodore (1810-1860), American Unitarian theologian, scholar and social reformer.

Parkinson, C(yril) Northcote (1909-1993), English historian who was admired as much for his witticisms as his scholarly writings.

Parkman, Francis (1823-1893), distinguished American historian who wrote extensively on the settlement of North America.

Parmenides (5th Century B.C.), Greek philosopher.

Parnell, Thomas (1679-1718), Irish poet and churchman, author of *An Elegy to an Old Beauty*, *The Hermit*, *Hymn to Contentment* and *The Night Piece of Death*.

Parr, Samuel (1747-1825), English Latin scholar and writer.

Parrington, Vernon L(ouis) (1871-1929), important American literary historian.

Parrish, Anne (1888-1957), American novelist.

Parry, Sir C(harles) Hubert H(astings) (1848-1918), distinguished English composer, teacher and writer on music.

Parry, Milman (1902-1935), American literary scholar who was an authority on Homer.

Parsons, Elsie (Worthington) Clews (1875-1941), American sociologist and anthropologist who wrote authoritative works on the Indians of the southwestern US.

Parsons, Robert (1546-1610), English Jesuit and religious polemicist.

Parsons, Thomas William (1819-1892), American translator, writer and poet.

Parton, James (1822-1891), English-born American biographer and writer.

Pascal, Blaise (1623-1662), remarkable French mathematician, physicist and religious philosopher, author of the celebrated *Pensées* (published 1670; English translation, 1962).

Pascal, Carlo (1866-1926), Italian Latin scholar.

Pasch, Georg (1661-1707), German philosopher and mathematician.

Paschasius Radbertus, Saint (c.785-c.860), influential French Roman Catholic abbot and theologian, author of *De corpore et sanguine Christi* (Concerning Christ's Body and Blood, c.832; revised edition, 844).

Pascoli, Giovanni (1855-1912), Italian poet and scholar.

Pasolini, Pier Paolo (1922-1975), Italian poet, novelist, critic and film director; was murdered.

Pasquier, Étienne (1529-1615), French lawyer, scholar and poet, author of the expansive *Recherches de la France* (1560-c.1610).

Passerat, Jean (1534-1602), French poet.

Pasternak, Boris (Leonidovich) (1890-1960), renowned Russian poet, novelist and translator whose celebrated novel *Dr Zhivago* (1957) stands as an indictment of the Bolshevik Revolution of 1917; won the Nobel Prize for Literature (1958) but was compelled by the Soviet government to refuse it.

Pastor, Ludwig Freiherr von (1854-1928), eminent German church historian, author of the monumental *Geschichte der Päpste seit dem Ausang des Mittelalters* (16 volumes, 1886-1933; English translation as *The History of the Popes from the Close of the Middle Ages*, 40 volumes, 1891-1954).

Pastorius, Francis Daniel (1651-c.1720), German-born American lawyer, writer and poet.

Patchen, Kenneth (1911-1972), American poet, novelist, dramatist, painter and graphic designer who was known for his experimental works.

Pater, Walter Horatio (1839-1894), English critic and essayist.

Paterson, A(ndrew) B(arton) (1864-1941), Australian journalist, poet and short-story writer, author of the celebrated song *Waltzing Matilda* (1917).

Patmore, Coventry (Kersey Dighton) (1823-1896), English poet and essayist, best known for his epic novel in verse *The Angel in the House* (2 volumes, 1854, 1856) and *The Victories of Love* (2 volumes, 1860, 1863).

Paton, Alan (Stewart) (1903-1988), notable South African writer and liberal politician, author of the famous novel *Cry, the Beloved Country* (1948).

Pattee, Fred Lewis (1863-1950), American literary scholar.

Patten, William Gilbert (1866-1945), American writer who wrote numerous works under the name Burt L Standish.

Pattison, Mark (1813-1884), English scholar.

Paul, Elliot (Harold) (1891-1958), American novelist.

Paul, Saint (actually **Saul) (d. c.63),** seminal Jewish-born Christian Apostle and theologian, author of several major books of the New Testament.

Paul of Aegina (c.625-c.690), Greek physician and medical encyclopaedist, compiler of the *Epitomae medicae libri septem* (English translation, 1834-47).

Paul the Deacon (c.720-c.799), Italian historian and poet who wrote the valuable *Historia Langobardorum* (History of the Lombards).

Paulding, James Kirke (1778-1860), American novelist, dramatist and government official.

Paulinus of Nola, Saint (actually **Meropius Pontius Anicius Paulinus) (353-431),** significant Latin Christian poet and bishop.

Paulsen, Friedrich (1846-1908), German philosopher of spiritual moralism.

Paulus, H(einrich) E(berhard) G(ottlob) (1761-1851), German theologian and Orientalist.

Pauly, August von (1796-1845), German classical philologist.

Pausanias (2nd Century), Greek traveller and geographer, author of an important guide to the ancient ruins of his homeland.

Paustovsky, Konstantin (Georgievich) (1892-1968), Russian writer.

Pavese, Cesare (1908-1950), outstanding Italian novelist, poet, critic and translator; committed suicide.

Payn, James (1830-1898), English novelist, poet, essayist and editor.

Payne, John Howard (1791-1852), influential American dramatist and actor, particularly known for his *Brutus, or The Fall of Tarquin* (1818).

Paz, Octavio (1914-1998), eminent Mexican poet and essayist; won the Nobel Prize for Literature (1990).

Pázmány, Péter (1570-1637), Hungarian statesman and theologian.

Paz Soldán, Mariano Felipe (1821-1886), Peruvian statesman, historian and geographer.

Peabody, Andrew Preston (1811-1893), American Unitarian minister and writer.

Peabody, Elizabeth Palmer (1804-1894), American educator and writer who was active in the Transcendentalist movement.

Peabody, Josephine Preston (1874-1922), American dramatist and poet.

Peacham, Henry (c.1576-c.1643), English writer, author of the *Compleat Gentleman* (1622).

Peacock, Thomas Love (1785-1866), English novelist and poet, especially remembered for his novel *Nightmare Abbey* (1818).

Peake, Mervyn Laurence (1911-1968), English novelist, poet and artist, especially known for his novel trilogy *Titus Groan* (1946), *Gormenghast* (1950) and *Titus Alone* (1959).

Peale, Rembrandt (1778-1860), American painter and writer, author of *Notes on Italy* (1831) and *Portfolio of an Artist* (1839).

Peano, Giuseppe (1858-1932), important Italian mathematician who was a major figure in the development of symoblic logic.

Pearse, Patrick Henry (1879-1916), Irish nationalist, poet, short-story writer and dramatist; as commander-in-chief of the insurgent forces in the failed Easter Rising, he was executed.

Pearson, Edmund (Lester) (1880-1937), American librarian, bibliophile and writer.

Pearson, (Edward) Hesketh (Gibbons) (1887-1964), English biographer.

Pearson, John (1613-1686), English bishop and theologian, author of the classic *Exposition of the Creed* (1659).

Pearson, Karl (1857-1936), notable English mathematician and philosopher of science, author of the classic *The Grammar of Science* (1892).

Pease, Edward Reynolds (1857-1955), English writer who was a founder and leading figure of the Fabian Society.

Peattie, Donald Culross (1898-1964), American writer.

Peck, George Wilbur (1840-1916), American journalist and writer of humorous works, especially known for his collected articles in *Peck's Bad Boy and His Pa* (1883).

Peck, Harry Thurston (1856-1914), American Scholar and critic; committed suicide.

Peck, John Mason (1789-1858), American Baptist preacher, missionary, journalist and writer.

Pecock, Reginald (c.1393-1461), prominent Welsh bishop and theologian who was charged with heresy in 1457, removed from his bishopric and confined for his remaining days.

Pedersen, Christiern (c.1480-1554), Danish scholar.

Pedersen, Holger (1857-1953), learned Danish linguist.

Pedersen, Johannes Peder Ejler (1883-1951), Danish Old Testament scholar and Semitic philologist.

Pedrell, Felipe (1841-1922), disinguished Spanish music scholar and composer.

Peele, George (1556-1596), important English dramatist and poet.

Pegler, Westbrook (1894-1969), American journalist who was known for his outspoken conservative views.

Peglotti, Francesco Balducci (14th Century), Italian commercial agent who wrote a valuable account of trade and travel of his era.

Péguy, Charles Pierre (1873-1914), French nationalist, publisher and poet; died in World War I.

Peirce, Charles Sanders (1839-1914), American scientist, logician and philosopher.

Pekkanen, Toivo (1902-1957), Finnish writer.

Pelagius (c.354-c.420), Christian monk and theologian who was condemned and excommunicated for his insistence upon the human role in spiritual salvation, which became known as Pelagianism.

Peletier, Jacques (1517-1582), French poet, writer and critic who was also known as Peletier du Mans.

Pellico, Silvio (1789-1854), Italian patriot, poet and dramatist, particularly known for his memoirs *Le mie prigioni* (1832; English translation as *My Prisons*, 1853), which related his experience as a political prisoner.

Pelloutier, Fernand (1867-1901), French labour organizer and theorist of the anarcho-syndicalist movement.

Pembroke, Mary Herbert, Countess of (1561-1621), esteemed English patroness of the arts and learing and translator; sister of Sir Philip Sidney and Sir Robert Sidney.

Penn, William (1644-1718), English Quaker and founder of the American Commonwealth of Pennysylvania, author of *The Sandy Foundation Shaken* (1668), *No Cross, No Crown* (1669) and *Some Fruits of Solitude* (1693).

Pennant, Thomas (1726-1798), important English naturalist whose tome *British Zoology* (1766) was highly influential.

Pennell, Joseph (1857-1926), American etcher, lithographer and writer.

Pennell, Joseph Stanley (1908-1963), American journalist, novelist and poet.

Penry, John (1559-1593), Welsh Puritan polemicist.

Pepe, Guglielmo (1783-1855), Italian soldier and memoirist.

Pepys, Samuel (1633-1703), English government official and diarist whose diary (1660-69) stands as a literary classic.

Percival, James Gates (1795-1856), American poet and chemist.

Percy, Thomas (1729-1811), English bishop, antiquaian and scholar, particularly known for his compilation of ballads *Reliques of Ancient English Poetry* (1765).

Percy, Walker (1916-1990), American novelist and essayist.

Pereda, José Marlá de (1833-1906), esteemed Spanish novelist.

Perelman, S(idney) J(oseph) (1904-1979), American dramatist and writer.

Peretz, Isaac Leib (c.1851-1915), Polish poet, dramatist and writer, one of the leading Yiddish figures of his era.

Pérez de Ayala, Ramón (1880-1962), outstanding Spanish novelist, short-story writer, poet, essayist and critic.

Pérez de Guzmán, Fernán (c.1378-c.1460), august Spanish historian and poet whose *Mar de historias* brought him posthumous fame as the Spanish Plutarch.

Pérez de Hita, Ginés (c.1544-c.1619), Spanish novelist.

Pérez Galdós, Benito (1843-1920), remarkable Spanish novelist, author of the classic *Fortunata y Jacinto* (4 volumes, 1886-87).

Perkins, Frederic Beecher (1828-1899), American journalist, writer and librarian; nephew of Henry Ward Beecher.

Perkins, Lucy Fitch (1865-1937), American writer of children's books.

Perkins, William (1558-1602), English Puritan theologian.

Perl, Joseph (1773-1839), Russian Jewish writer.

Perrault, Charles (1628-1703), French writer and poet who became well known for his children's fairy-tales.

Perron, (Charles) Edgar du (1899-1940), Dutch writer, poet and critic.

Perry, Bliss (1860-1954), distinguished American literary scholar and writer.

Perry, Ralph Barton (1876-1957), American philosopher of the Realist persuasion.

Perry, Thomas Sergeant (1845-1928), American critic, writer and translator.

Perry, W(illiam) J(ames) (1868-1949), English anthropologist who argued for a diffusionist theory of culutral development.

Perse, Saint-John (actually **Marie-René-Auguste-Alexis Leger) (1887-1975),** notable French poet and diplomat; won the Nobel Prize for Literature (1960).

Persius (actually **Aulus Persius Flaccus) (34-62),** esteemed Roman poet who excelled in his satires.

Pessanha, Camilo (1867-1926), Portuguese poet who espoused Symbolism.

Pessoa, Fernando António Nogueira (1888-1935), outstanding Portuguese poet, writer and critic.

Pestalozzi, Johann Heinrich (1746-1827), Swiss educational reformer and writer, author of the novel *Leonard and Gertrude* (4 volumes, 1781-87).

Peter, Hugh (1598-1660), English Independent minister and writer who was active in Cromwellian circles; following the Restoration, he was executed.

Peter Lombard (c.1100-1160), famous Italian Roman Catholic theologian and bishop of Paris, author of the celebrated *Sententiarum libri quator* (Books of Four Sentences, c.1155-58).

Peter of Blois (c.1135-c.1212), French poet and writer.

Peterkin, Julia (Mood) (1880-1961), American novelist, especially remembered for her *Scarlet Sister Mary* (1928).

Peters, Samuel Andrew (1735-1826), notorius American Anglican clergyman, Loyalist and polemicist.

Petersen, Nis (1897-1943), Danish poet and novelist.

Peterson, Charles Jacobs (1819-1887), American writer, editor and publisher.

Petőfi, Sándor (1823-1849), celebrated Hungarian poet and revolutionary; died in the Battle of Segesvár.

Petrarch (actually **Francesco Petrarca) (1304-1374),** great Italian poet and scholar, renowned for the extraordinary beauty of his lyricism.

Petri, Sir (William Matthew) Flinders (1853-1942), eminent English archaeologist and Egyptologist.

Petronious Arbiter (1st Century), famous Roman writer and poet, reputed author of the first Western European novel the *Satyricon*; committed suicide.

Petrov, Yevgeny (Petrovich) (actually **Yevgeny Katayev) (1907-1942),** Russian writer who collaborated with Ilya Ilf on a series of satirical short stories and novels; was killed while serving as a correspondent during the defense of Sevastopol during World War II.

Petrus Aureoli (c.1280-1322), French archbishop and Franciscan philosopher who was a critic of the theory of knowledge as expounded by Duns Scotus and Saint Thomas Aquinas.

Petrus Ky (1837-1898), Vietnamese scholar and statesman.

Pettazzoni, Raffaele (1883-1959), Italian historian of religions.

Pettie, George (c.1548-1589), English writer, author of *A petite Pallace of Pettie his pleasure* (1576).

Petty, Sir William (1623-1687), English political economist and statistician, particularly known for his *Treatise of Taxes and Contributions* (1662).

Pétursson, Hallgrímur (1614-1674), significant Icelandic poet whose mastery was revealed in his *Passiusalmar* (Hymns of the Passion, 1666).

Pevsner, Sir Nikolaus Bernhard Leon (1902-1983), German-born English art historian.

Pfefferkorn, Johannes (Joseph) (1469-1524), German-born Jewish Christian convert and polemicist.

Pfleiderer, Otto (1829-1908), German Protestant theologian and religious historian.

Phaedo or **Phaedon (flourished 400 B.C.),** Greek philosopher who wrote on ethics and dialectics.

Phaedrus (c.15 B.C.-c.50 A.D.), Roman poet who won fame for his didactic fables.

Phelps, William Lyon (1865-1943), American literary scholar and critic.

Philaret (actually **Vasili Mikhailovich Drozdov) (1782-1867),** Russian Orthodox metopolitan of Moscow, theologian and scholar.

Philemon (c.368-c.264 B.C.), Greek dramatist, a major figure in Athenian New Comedy.

Philes, Manuel (13th-14th Century), Byzantine poet.

Philetas of Cos (c.330-c.270 B.C), Greek poet and grammarian.

Philip, John (1775-1851), controversial Scottish clergyman and missionary to South Africa, author of *Researches in South Africa* (1826).

Philipon, Charles (1806-1862), French caricaturist, lithographer, journalist and writer who was a master of political satire.

Philippe, Charles-Louis (1874-1909), French novelist, known for his depictions of the downtrodden elements of society.

Philips, Ambrose (1674-1749), English poet and dramatist, best remembered for his collection of *Pastorals* (1710).

Philips, John (1676-1709), English poet and writer, best known for his poems *Blenheim* (1705), *The Splendid Shilling* (1705) and *Cyder* (1708).

Philips, Katherine (née Fowler) (1631-1664), English poet who was known as Orinda.

Philistus (c.430-356 B.C.), Greek historian.

Phillips, David Graham (1867-1911), American novelist, dramatist and essayist; was murdered by a lunatic.

Phillips, Edward (1630-c.1696), English editor, biographer and writer; brother of John Phillips and nephew of John Milton.

Phillips, John (1631-1706), English poet, writer and translator; brother of Edward Phillips and nephew of John Milton.

Phillips, Stephen (1864-1915), English actor, poet and dramatist.

Phillips, Wendell (1811-1884), American reformer, orator and polemicist, one of the principal figures in the Abolitionist movement.

Philpotts, Eden (1862-1960), English novelist, dramtist, poet and essayist.

Philo of Alexandria (c.13 B.C.-c.50 A.D.), celebrated Egyptian-born Jewish philosopher and theologian.

Philodemus (c.110-c.35 B.C.), Greek poet and philosopher of the Epicurean school.

Philoponus, John (6th Century), important Greek Christian theologian, philosopher and literary scholar who was known as John the Grammarian.

Philostorgius (c.368-c.433), Byzantine historian of the Arian persuasion, author of a church history (only fragments extant).

Philostratus, Flavius (c.170-c.245), Greek writer; father-in-law of Philostratus the Lemmian.

Philostratus the Lemmian (2nd-3rd Century), Greek writer; son-in-law of Flavius Philstratus and grandfather of Philostratus the Younger.

Philostratus the Younger (3rd Century), Greek writer; grandson of Philostratus the Lemmian.

Philotheus Coccinus (c.1300-1379), prominent Byzantine monk, theologian and patriarch of Constantinople who was the leader of the opposition to the union of the Greek Orthodox Church with the Roman Catholic Church.

Philoxenus of Mabbug (c.440-c.523), Syrian Christian theologian, bishop and writer who was a principal figure in the Jacobite Monophysite church.

Phocylides (flourished 500 B.C.), Greek poet was known for his aphorisms.

Phrynichus (flourished 500 B.C.), Greek dramatist of tragedies.

Phrynichus (flourished c.400 B.C.), Greek dramatist of the Old Comedy.

Phrynichus Arabius (2nd Century), Greek grammarian and rhetorician.

Piaget, Jean (1896-1980), notable Swiss physchologist, an authority on child psychology.

Picabia, Francis Martinez de (1879-1953), French painter, illustrator, designer and writer.

Piccolomini, Alessandro (1508-1578), Italian writer.

Picken, Ebenezer (1769-1816), Scottish poet.

Pickering, John (1777-1846), American lawyer and philologist who was a learned authority on various North American Indian languages.

Pico della Mirandola, Giovanni, Conte (1463-1494), Italian philosopher and scholar of the Platonist school.

Pictet de Rochemont, Charles (1755-1824), Swiss statesman and writer.

Pierpont, John (1785-1866), American Unitarian clergyman and poet, author of *Airs of Palestine* (1816) and *The Anti-Slavery Poems of John Pierpont* (1843).

Pigou, Arthur Cecil (1877-1959), influential English economist, author of *The Economics of Welfare* (1920).

Pike, Albert (1809-1891), American lawyer, poet and writer who was a controversial Confederate commander during the Civil War and later a leading figure in Masonic circles in the South.

Pike, Mary Hayden (Green) (1824-1908), American novelist, best known for her anti-slavery novels *Ida May* (1854) and *Caste* (1856).

Pillsbury, Parker (1809-1898), American Abolitionist, woman suffrage leader and editor, author of *Acts of the Anti-Slavery Apostles* (1883).

Pilnyak, Boris (Andreievich) (actually Boris Andreievich Vogau) (1894-c.1938), Russian novelist and short-story writer of the Symbolist persuasion; denounced as a reactionary by the Stalinist regime, he disappeared from the scene in the wake of the Great Purge.

Pindar (actually Pindaros) (c.522-c.440 B.C.), celebrated Greek poet, renowned for his superlative odes.

Pindemonte, Giovanni (1751-1812), Italian politician, poet and dramatist; brother of Ippolito Pindemonte.

Pindemonte, Ippolito (1753-1828), Italian writer, poet and translator; brother of Giovanni Pindemonte.

Pinel, Philippe (1745-1826), significant French physician who was a pioneering figure in the development of psychiatry.

Pinero, Sir Arthur Wing (1855-1934), English dramatist.

Pinget, Robert (1919-1997), Swiss-born French novelist and dramatist.

Pinkney, Edward Coote (1802-1828), American poet.

Pinto, Fernão Mendes (c.1510-1583), Portuguese adventurer who left a classic account of his travels in Asia in his *Peregrinaçam* (1614).

Piozzi, Hester Lynch (née Salusbury) (1741-1821), Welsh writer and poet who was known as Mrs Thrale, the friend of Samuel Johnson.

Pirandello, Luigi (1867-1936), distinguished Italian dramatist, novelist and short-story writer; won the Nobel Prize for Literature (1934).

Pirenne, Henri (1862-1935), notable Belgian historian who was an authority on the Middle Ages and Belgian history.

Pires, José Augusto Neves Cardoso (1925-1998), Portugese writer.

Pirmez, Octave (1832-1883), Belgian essayist, author of *Pensées et maximes* (Thoughts and Maxims, 1862) and *Heures de philosophie* (Hours of Philosophy, 1873).

Piron, Alexis (1689-1773), French poet and dramatist, especially admired for his play *La Métromanie*.

Pirro, André (Gabriel Edme) (1869-1943), influential French music scholar.

Pirrotta, Nino (actually Antonio Pirrotta) (1908-1998), distinguished Italian music scholar.

Pisarev, Dmitri Ivanovich (1840-1868), Russian social philosopher and literary critic who was the leading nihilist of his era.

Pisemsky, Alexie Feofilaktovich (1820-1881), Russian novelist and dramatist, particularly known for his novel *Tysyacha dush* (A Thousand Souls, 1858) and his play *Gorkaya sudbina* (A Bitter Lot, 1859).

Pithou, Pierre (1539-1596), French lawyer and historian.

Pitoëff, Georges (1886-1939), Russian-born French actor, producer and dramatist.

Pitt-Rivers, Augustus Henry Lane-Fox (1827-1900), English army officer and archaeologist, known as the father of British archaeology.

Pius II, Pope (actually Aeneas Silvius Piccolomini) (1405-1464), Italian scholar, statesman and pope (1458-64).

Pixerecourt, (René-Charles-) Guilbert de (1773-1844), French dramatist.

Plaatje, Solomon Tshekiso (1877-1932), South African journalist, politician, linguist and writer.

Place, Francis (1771-1854), English radical reformer, author of *Illustrations and Proofs of the Principle of Population* (1822).

Planché, JamesRobinson (1796-1880), English dramatist, librettist and translator of Huguenot descent.

Planudes, Maximus (1260-c.1310), Greek Orthodox theologian and scholar.

Platen-Hallermünde, August, Graf von (1796-1835), esteemed German poet, dramatist and scholar who upheld classical precepts.

Plath, Sylvia (1932-1963), American poet and novelist; wife of Ted Hughes; committed suicide.

Plato (c.427-c.347 B.C.), great Greek philosopher, author of a series of celebrated dialogues addressing the central issues of philosophy.

Platonov, Andrei Paltonovich (1899-1951), Russian writer.

Platter, Thomas (1499-1582), Swiss scholar and writer, author of an important autobiography.

Plautus, Titus Maccius (c.254-184 B.C.), renowned Roman dramatist, a master of comic drama.

Plekhanov, Georgi Valentinovich (1856-1918), Russian Marxist theorist.

Pliny the Elder (actually Gaius Plinius Secundus) (23-79), Roman naturalist and writer, author of the famous *Historia naturalis* (modern edition and English translation, 10 volumes, 1938-63); uncle of Pliny the Younger.

Pliny the Younger (actually Gaius Plinius Caecilius Secundis) (c.61-c.113), Roman writer and government official, author of a series of celebrated letters (modern edition and English translation, 2 volumes, 1915); nephew of Pliny the Elder.

Plomer, William (Charles Franklyn) (1903-1973), South African poet, writer, librettist, memoirist and editor.

Plotinus (205-270), influential Roman philosopher, the father of Neoplatonist thought.

Plutarch (46-c.120), great Greek biographer and writer, author of the celebrated *Bioi paralleloi* (modern edition and English translation as *Plutarch's Lives*, II volumes, 1914-26).

Po Chü-i (772-846), eminent Chinese poet who was greatly esteemed for the direct appeal of his verse.

Pobedonostsev, Konstantin Petrovich (1827-1907), Russian government official and political philosopher who upheld conservative principles.

Pocci, Franz, Graf von (1807-1876), German writer of children's books.

Poe, Edgar Allan (1809-1849), brilliant American poet and writer whose poetic genius was equalled in his prose by his mastery of the macabre.

Poggio (actually **Gian Francesco Poggio Bracciolini) (1380-1459),** important Italian Humanist scholar and calligrapher.

Poincaré, (Jules-) Henri (1854-1912), French mathematician, theoretical astronomer and philosopher of science.

Pokorny, Julius (1887-1970), learned Czech-born Swiss linguist and lexicographer, editor of the standard *Indogermanisches etymologisches Wörterbuch* (Indo-European Etymological Dictionary, 2 volumes, 1948, 1969).

Polidouri, Maria (1905-1930), Greek poet.

Politian (actually **Angelo Poliziano) (1454-1494),** distinguished Italian poet and scholar, especially renowned for his poem *Stanze per la giostra del Magnifico Giuliano de' Medici* (1475-78).

Pollard, Alfred William (1859-1944), English literary scholar.

Pollard, (Joseph) Percival (1869-1911), German-born English, later American, critic, writer and dramatist.

Pollio, Gaius Asinius (76 B.C.-4 A.D.), Roman historian, orator and poet.

Pollock, Channing (1880-1946), American journalist, drama critic, dramatist and writer.

Pollock, Sir Frederick, 3rd Baronet (1845-1937), English legal scholar.

Pollux, Julius (2nd Century), Egyptian writer, author of an *Onomasticon*, a Greek thesaurus of terms.

Polo, Marco (1254-1324), famous Italian merchant and adventurer who left a celebrated account of his travels to Asia as *Il milione* (English translation as *The Travels of Marco Polo*, 1958).

Polotsky, Simeon (actually **Samuil Yemelyanovich Petrovsky-Sitnianovich) (1629-1680),** Byelorussian monk, scholar and writer.

Polybius (c.200-c.118 B.C.), great Greek historian who chronicled the rise of Rome to world mastery in his histories (modern edition and English translation, 6 volumes, 1922-27).

Polycarp, Saint (2nd Century), Greek Christian bishop of Smyrna and theologian, author of the significant *Letter to the Philippians*; was martyred for his faith.

Pomfret, John (1667-1702), English churchman and poet, author of *The Choice* (1700).

Pomponazzi, Pietro (1462-1525), Italian philosopher of the Aristotelian school, author of the *Tractatus de immortalitate animae* (1516), *Apologia* (1518), *Defensorium* (1519), *De incantationibus* (published 1556) and *De fato* (published 1567).

Ponce de Léon, Luis (1527-1591), Spanish monk, scholar and poet.

Ponge, Francis (1899-1988), French poet.

Ponsard, François (1814-1867), French dramatist.

Pontano, Giovanni or **Gioviano (c.1422-1503),** Italian government offical, writer and poet.

Pontoppidan, Erik (1698-1764), Danish-Norwegian Lutheran bishop and theologian.

Pontoppidan, Henrik (1857-1943), admired Danish novelist and short-story writer; was co-winner of the Nobel Prize for Literature (1917).

Poole, Ernest (1880-1950), American writer.

Poole, John (c.1786-1872), English dramatist, poet and essayist.

Poole, William Frederick (1821-1894), American librarian and bibliographer.

Poore, Benjamin Perley (1820-1887), American journalist and writer.

Popa, Vasko (1922-1991), Serbian poet.

Pope, Alexander (1688-1744), famous English poet and translator, a master of satire, renowned for such works as the *Essay on Criticism* (1711), *The Rape of the Lock* (1712-14), *The Dunciad* (1728) and *An Essay on Man* (1733-34).

Popper, Sir Karl (Raimund) (1902-1994), notable Austrian-born English philosopher of science and politics, author of *Logik der Forschung* (1934; English translation as *The Logic of Scientific Discovery*, 1959), *The Open Society and Its Enemies* (1945), *The Poverty of Historicism* (1957) and *A World of Propensities* (1990).

Popple, William (1701-1764), English dramatist.

Porphyry (actually **Malchus) (c.234-c.305),** Syrian-born Roman philosopher of the Neoplatonist school.

Porson, Richard (1759-1808), learned English classical scholar.

Porta, Carlo (1776-1821), Italian poet.

Porta, Giambattista della (c.1535-1615), remarkable Italian philosopher and scientist, author of *Magia naturalis* (4 Volumes, 1558).

Porter, Anna Maria (1780-1832), English poet and novelist; sister of Jane Porter.

Porter, Eleanor Hodgman (1868-1920), American writer of juvenile novels, creator of Pollyanna, the "glad girl."

Porter, Henry (16th Century), English dramatist.

Porter, Jane (1776-1850), English writer who won notable success for her *Thaddeus of Warsaw* (1803); sister of Anna Maria Porter.

Porter, Katherine Anne (1890-1980), esteemed American novelist, short-story writer and essayist, author of the story collection *Pale Horse, Pale Rider* (1939) and the novel *Ship of Fools* (1962).

Porter, Noah (1811-1892), American philosopher, author of *The Human Intellect* (1868).

Porto-Riche, Georges de (1849-1930), French dramatist of the realist school of psychological drama.

Poseidonius (c.135-c.50 B.C.), Greek philosopher of the Stoic school.

Post, Emily (née Price) (1872-1960), American writer who became best known as an arbiter of social behaviour via her *Etiquette: The Blue Book of Social Usage.*

Post, Sir Laurens Jan van der (1906-1996), South African novelist and memoirist.

Potgieter, Everhardus Johannes (1808-1875), Dutch writer and poet.

Potocki, Wacław (1625-c.1697), Polish poet, author of the epic *Wojna chocimska* (The Chocim Ward) and many fine epigrams.

Pott, August (Friedrich) (1802-1887), significant German linguist who was one of the principal figures in the development of Indo-Europen linguistic studies.

Potter, Dennis Christopher George (1935-1994), English dramatist.

Potter, (Helen) Beatrix (1866-1943), English writer of popular children's books.

Potter, Paul Meredith (1853-1921), English-born American dramatist, author of *The Ugly Duckling* (1890).

Pound, Ezra (Weston Loomis) (1885-1972), greatly significant American poet, critic and translator, author of the challenging epic *Cantos.*

Pound, Louise (1872-1958), American scholar of linguistics, folklore and balladry; sister of Roscoe Pound.

Pound, Roscoe (1870-1964), distinguished American jurist, botanist and educator; brother of Louise Pound.

Powdermaker, Hortense (1900-1970), American cultural anthropologist.

Powell, (John) Enoch (1912-1998), controversial English politician and scholar.

Powys, John Cowper (1872-1963), English novelist, poet and essayist; brother of Llewelyn and T(heodore) F(rancis) Powys.

Powys, Llewelyn (1884-1939), English journalist and writer; brother of John Cowper and T(headore) F(rancis) Powys.

Powys, T(heodore) F(rancis) (1875-1953), English novelist and short-story writer; brother of John Cowper and Llewelyn Powys.

Praed, Winthrop Mackworth (1802-1839), English poet and politician.

Praetorius, Michael (1571-1621), outstanding German composer and music theorist, author of the monumental *Syntagma musicum* (3 Volumes, 1614-18).

Prati, Giovanni (1815-1884), Italian writer and poet.

Pratolini, Vasco (1913-1991), Italian novelist and short-story writer.

Pratt, E(dwin) J(ohn) (1883-1964), outstanding Canadian poet whose mastepiece was the expansive *Brébeuf and His Brethren* (12 volumes, 1940).

Pratt, Samuel Jackson (1749-1814), English poet, writer and dramatist who wrote under the name Courtney Melmoth.

Praz, Mario (1896-1982), Italian literary scholar and critic.

Preil, Gabriel (1911-1993), admired Estonian-born American poet who excelled in writing Hebrew poetry.

Prem Chad (actually Dhanpat Rai Srivastana) (1880-1936), Indian novelist and short-story writer.

Prentice, George Dennison (1802-1870), American editor and poet.

Prescott, William Hickling (1796-1859), American historian, author of the *History of the Conquest of Mexico* (3 volumes, 1843) and *History of the Conquest of Peru* (2 volumes, 1847).

Prešeren, France (1800-1849), important Slovenian poet of the Romantic era.

Preston, Margaret Junkin (1820-1897), American poet and writer.

Preuss, Hugo (1860-1925), German political theorist and legal scholar.

Prevert, Jacques (1900-1977), French poet and screenwriter.

Prévost (d'Exiles, Antoine-François), Abbé (1697-1763), French novelist, author of the celebrated *Histoire du Chevalier des Grieux et de Manon Lescaut* (1731), which inspired operas by Massenét and Puccini.

Prévost, (Eugène-) Marcel (1862-1941), French novelist, best remembered for his *Les Demi-Vierges* (The Half-Virgins, 1894).

Price, H(enry) H(abberley) (1899-1984), English philosopher, author of *Perception* (1932).

Price, Richard (1723-1791), English Dissenter and philosopher, author of the *Review of the Principal Questions and Difficulties in Morals* (1758) and *Observations on the Nature of Civil Liberty, the Principles of Government, and the Justice and Policy of the War with America* (1776).

Price-Mars, Jean (1876-1970), Haitian physician, government official, ethnologist and historian.

Prichard, Harold Arthur (1871-1947), English philosopher of the Oxford intuitionist school of moral philosophy, author of *Kant's Theory of Knowledge* (1909), *Duty and Interest* (1928), *Moral Obligation* (published 1949) and *Knowledge and Perception* (published 1950).

Prichard, James Cowles (1786-1848), English physician and ethnologist who wrote the *Eastern Origin of the Celtic Nations* (1831), *Researches as to the Physical History of Man* (5 volumes, 1836-47) and *Natural History of Man* (1843).

Prichard, Rhys (c.1579-1644), Welsh vicar and poet, author of the *Canwyll y Cymry* (The Welshman's Candle).

Priestley, J(ohn) B(oynton) (1894-1984), prominent English novelist, dramatist and essayist.

Priestley, Joseph (1733-1804), English-born American clergyman, scientist and political theorist.

Prime, Benjamin Youngs (1733-1791), American poet.

Prince, Morton (Henry) (1854-1929), American physician and psychologist.

Prince, Thomas (1687-1758), American Congregational clergyman and writer, author of the *Chronological History of New England in the Form of Annals* (1736) and *The Christian History* (1744-45).

Pingle, Thomas (1789-1834), Scottish-South African writer and poet.

Prior, Matthew (1664-1721), notable English poet and diplomat, especially admired for his telling wit.

Priscian (actually Priscianus Caesariensis) (6th Century), influential Latin grammarian, author of the classic *Institutiones grammaticae*.

Priscillian (c.340-385), Spanish Christian bishop and heretic who was the first to be executed for his beliefs.

Pritchett, Sir V(ictor) S(awdon) (1900-1997), esteemed English literary critic, biographer, essayist, novelist and short-story writer.

Probus, Marcus Valerius (1st Century), Latin grammarian and literary critic.

Proclus (c.410-485), Greek philosopher of the Neoplatonic school.

Procter, Adelaide Ann (1825-1864), English poet who wrote under the name Mary Berwick and who won special recognition for her *Legends and Lyrics* (1858-60) and *The Lost Chord*, the latter set to music by Sir Arthur Sullivan; daughter of Bryan Walker Procter.

Procter, Bryan Walker (1787-1874), English poet who wrote under the name Barry Cornwall; father of Adelaide Ann Procter.

Prokopovich, Feofan (1681-1736), Russian Orthodox theologian, writer, poet, dramatist and archbishop of Novgorod who collaborated with Czar Peter I the Great in westernizing his homeland.

Prokosch, Frederic (1908-1989), American writer.

Propertius, Sextus (c.48-c.15 B.C.), Roman poet who was known for his elegiac effusions to his mistress Cynthia.

Prosper of Aquitaine, Saint (c.390-c.463), influential Latin Christian polemicist who upheld the teachings of Saint Augustine.

Protagoras (c.485-c.410 B.C.), celebrated Greek philosopher of the Sophist persuasion.

Proud, Joseph (1745-1826), English Baptist churchman and hymnist, a prominent figure in Swedenborgian circles.

Proudhon, Pierre-Joseph (1809-1865), French Socialist polemicist whose theory of mutualist economic organization greatly influenced the development of radical and anarchist ideas.

Proust, Marcel (1871-1922), remarkable French novelist, essayist and critic, author of the celebrated novel series *À la recherche du temps perdu* (1913-27; English translation as *Remembrance of Things Past*, 1924-70).

Prouty, Olive Higgins (1882-1974), American novelist, best known for her *Stella Dallas* (1922).

Prudentius, Aurelius Clemens (348-c.406), esteemed Christian Latin poet, author of the acclaimed *Psychomachia* (The Contest of the Soul, 405).

Prynne, William (1600-1669), prominent English Puritan pamphleteer whose polemical writings led to conflicts with both the monarchy and the parliamentarians, author of the classic *Histrio Mastix: The Players Scourge, or, Actors tragoedie* (1633).

Prys-Jones, Arthur Glyn (1888-1987), eminent Welsh poet.

Psellus, Michael (Constantine) (1018-c.1078), Byzantine statesman, theologian and philosopher.

Psichari, Ernest (1883-1914), French novelist; died in World War I.

Psicharis, Ioannis (1854-1929), Greek writer.

Pufendorf, Samuel von (1632-1694), German scholar who wrote an important treatise on natural law in his *De Jure Naturae et Gentium Libri Octo* (1672).

Puig, Manuel (1932-1990), Argentine novelist and screenwriter, best remembered for his novel *El beso de la mujer araña* (1976; English translation as *Kiss of the Spider Woman*, 1979).

Pulci, Luigi (1432-1484), Italian poet, author of the burlesque epic in Tuscan dialect *Morgante* or *Morgante Maggiore* (c.1460-83).

Purchas, Samuel (c.1577-1626), English compiler of books on travel and discovery.

Pusey, E(dward) B(ouverie) (1800-1882), English Anglican scholar and theologian who was a prominent figure in the Oxford Movement.

Pushkin, Alexander (Sergeievich) (1799-1837), great Russian poet, writer and dramatist who was acclaimed as the national poet of Russia; died in a duel defending his wife's honour.

Putnam, Samuel (1892-1950), American literary scholar and translator who was an authority on Romance literatures.

Putrament, Jerzy (1910-1986), Polish journalist, novelist and poet.

Puttenham, George (c.1529-1590), English courtier and most likely the author of the *Arte of English Poesie* (1589), a pioneering study in the field of criticism.

Pyat, (Aimé-) Félix (1810-1889), French journalist, dramatist and political radical.

Pyle, Ernie (actually **Ernest Taylor Pyle) (1900-1945),** famous American journalist and war correspondent; killed while covering the Okianawa campaign against the Japanese in the closing days of World War II.

Pyle, Howard (1853-1911), American illustrator, painter and writer, best known for his children's books.

Pym, Barbara Mary Crampton (1913-1980), English novelist.

Pyrrho (c.360-c.270 B.C.), famous Greek philosopher who originated Skepticism.

Pythagoras (c.580-c.500 B.C.), celebrated Greek philosopher and mathematician.

Qabbani, Nizar (1923-1998), prominent Syrian poet.

Quarles, Francis (1592-1644), English poet and writer, author of the popular poetry volumes *Emblemes* (1635) and *Hieroglyphikes of the life of Man* (1638).

Quasimodo, Salvatore (1901-1968), notable Italian poet, critic and translator; won the Nobel Prize for Literature (1959).

Quefféléc, Henri (1910-1992), French novelist.

Queneau, Raymond (1903-1976), distinguished French poet, novelist and essayist.

Quennell, Sir Peter (Courtney) (1905-1993), English poet, writer, critic, editor and translator.

Quental, Antero Tarquínio de (1842-1891), remarkable Portuguese poet, leading figure in the postromantic movement in Portugal; committed suicide.

Querido, Israël, (1874-1932), Dutch novelist of the naturalist school.

Quesnay, François (1694-1774), French economist, author of *Tableau economique* (1758).

Quesnal, Pasquier (1634-1719), French theologian who championed the Jansenist cause and wrote the controversial tome *Nouveau Testament en français avec des réflexions morales* (New Testament in French and Thoughts on Morality, 1692).

Quetelet, (Lambert) Adolphe (Jacques) (1796-1874), French mathematician, astronomer, sociologist and statistician, author of *Sur l'homme* (1835; English translation as *A Treatise on Man and the Development of His Faculties*, 1842).

Quevedo y Villegas, Francisco Gómez de (1580-1645), outstanding Spanish writer and poet who excelled in satirical expression.

Quicherat, Jules (-Étieene-Joseph) (1814-1882), French archaeologist and scholar.

Quiller-Couch, Sir Arthur Thomas (1863-1944), English poet, novelist, essayist and critic who wrote under the name Q.

Quincy, Edmund (1808-1877), American Abolitionist and writer; son of Josiah Quincy.

Quincy, Josiah (1772-1864), American politician, educator and writer; father of Edmund Quincy.

Quinet, Edgar (1803-1875), French philosopher, historian and poet who championed political liberalism.

Quintana, Manuel José (1772-1857), Spanish poet, writer, critic and dramatist who was crowned the national poet of Spain by Queen Isabella (1855).

Quintilian (actually **Marcus Fabius Quintilianus) (c.35-c.97),** Roman writer, best known for his classic exposition on rhetoric *Institutio oratoria*.

Quintus Smyrnaeus (4th Century), Greek poet of epic verse.

Quiroga, Horacio (1878-1937), Uruguayan-born Argentine writer who excelled in the short story; committed suicide.

Raabe, Wilhelm (1831-1910), German novelist.

Rab, Gustáv (1901-1966), Hungarian novelist.

Rabanus Maurus (c.780-856), German Benedictine abbot, archbishop and theologian who was known as the Praeceptor Germaniae (Teacher of Germany).

Rabbula (c.350-c.435), Syrian theologian and bishop of Edessa.

Rabéarivelo, Jean-Joseph (1901-1937), Madagascar poet who wrote in French; committed suicide.

Rabelais, François (c.1483-1553), famous French writer and physician whose mastery of biting satire was revealed in his classic *Gargantua and Pantagruel* (4 parts, 1532, 1535, 1546, 1552; English translation, 1955).

Racan, Honorat de Buell, Seigneur de (1589-1670), French poet, best known for his *Stances sur la retraite* (c.1618).

Racine, Jean (1639-1699), great French dramatist and poet, a master of the tragic play.

Racine, Louis (1692-1763), French poet.

Radcliffe, Ann (née Ward) (1764-1823), popular English novelist of Gothic tales of terror, most notably *The Mysteries of Udolpho* (1794) and *The Italian* (1797).

Radcliffe-Brown, A(lfred) R(eginald) (1881-1955), English social anthropologist.

Raden, Adjeng Kartini (1879-1904), Japanese poet.

Radhakrishnan, Sarvepalli (1888-1975), Indian scholar and statesman who wrote on philosophy and religion.

Radiguet, Raymond (1903-1923), gifted French novelist and poet, author of the outstanding *Le Diable au corps* (1923; English translation as *The Devil in the Flesh*, 1932).

Radin, Max (1880-1950), Polish-born American writer.

Radin, Paul (1883-1959), significant Polish-born American anthropologist, author of *Primitive Man as Philosopher* (1927), *Method and Theory of Ethnology* (1933) and *Primitive Religion* (1938).

Radischev, Alexander Nikolaievich (1749-1802), Russian nobleman and writer, author of *Puteshestvie iz Peterburga v Moskvu* (1790; English translation as *A Journey from St. Petersburg to Moscow*, 1958) whose indictment of social injustice led to his banishment to Siberia; committed suicide.

Radlov, Vasili (actually Wilhelm Radloff) (1837-1919), German-born Russian scholar who was particularly known for his linguistic studies.

Rădulescu, Eliade (1802-1872), Romanian writer.

Raffi (actually Hakob Meliq-Hakobian) (1835-1888), outstanding Armenian novelist and short-story writer.

Rafinesque, Constantine Samuel (1783-1840), Turkish-born American naturalist and writer.

Rāghavānka (13th Century), Indian poet.

Raghunātha Śiromani (c.1475-c.1550), Indian philosopher and logician.

Rahbek, Knud Lyne (1760-1830), Danish poet, dramatist, critic and editor.

Rahner, Karl (1904-1984), German Roman Catholic theologian.

Rahv, Philip (1908-1973), Russian-born American literary critic and editor.

Raimund, Ferdinand (1790-1836), Austrian dramatist.

Rainis (actually Jānis Pliekšāns) (1865-1929), leading Latvian poet and dramatist.

Rainolds, John (1549-1607), English scholar.

Rakovski, Georgi Sava (1821-1867), Bulgarian revolutionary and writer.

Raleigh or Ralegh, Sir Walter (1554-1618), famous English courtier, navigator and poet, was beheaded for treason.

Raleigh, Sir Walter (Alexander) (1861-1922), English critic and essayist.

Ralph of Coggeshall (13th Century), English monk and chronicler.

Rāmānuja (c.1017-c.1137), celebrated Indian theologian and philsopher of Hinduism who lived to a great old age.

Ramatirtha (actually Tirath Rama) (1873-1906), Indian religious leader of Hinduism.

Rameau, Jean-Philippe (1683-1764), renowned French composer and music theorist.

Ramos, Graciliano (1892-1953), Brazilian novelist.

Ramsay, Allan (1686-1758), Scottish poet, best known for *The Gentle Shepherd, a Pastoral Comedy* (1725).

Ramsey, Frank Plumpton (1903-1930), English philosopher and mathematician.

Ramsey, Ian Thomas (1915-1972), English bishop of Durham and philosopher.

Ramus, Petrus (1515-1572), outstanding French philosopher and logician, author of *Aristotelicae animadversiones* (1543), *Dialecticae partitiones* (1543), *Dialectique* (1550) and *Dialecticae libri duo* (1556); after converting to Protestantism, he was subjected to persecution and finally was murdered by hired assassins.

Ramusio, Giovanni Battista (1485-1557), Italian geographer and compiler of travel writings.

Ramuz, Charles-Ferdinand (1878-1947), esteemed Swiss novelist.

Rand, Ayn (1905-1982), Russian-born American novelist, dramatist and essayist, author of the well-known novels *The Fountainhead* (1943) and *Atlas Shrugged* (1957).

Randall, James Ryder (1839-1908), American poet who extolled the Confederacy.

Randall, John Herman Jr (1899-1980), American historian and philosopher, author of *The Western Mind* (2 volumes, 1924; revised edition as *The Making of the Modern Mind*, 1926) and *Career of Philosophy in Modern Times* (2 volumes, 1962, 1965).

Randall-MacIver, David (1873-1945), English archaeologist and anthropologist.

Randolph, Thomas (1605-1635), English poet and dramatist.

Rands, William Brighty (1823-1882), English journalist and writer, best remembered for his volume of children's verse *Lilliput Levee* (1864).

Rank, Otto (1884-1939), Austrian psychoanalyst, author of *Der Mythus von der Geburt des Helden* (1909; English translation as *The Myth of the Birth of the Hero*, 1914) and *Das Inzest-Motiv in Dichtung und Sage* (The Incest Motive in Poetry and Saga, 1912).

Ranke, Leopold von (1795-1886), eminent German historian who left unfinished a history of the world (9 volumes, 1881-88).

Ransom, John Crowe (1888-1974), distinguished American poet, critic and editor.

Ransome, Arthur (Mitchell) (1884-1967), English journalist and writer, best known for his adventure novels for children.

Raoul de Houdenc (13th Century), French poet and musician, author of the notable *Méraugis de Portlesguez*.

Rascoe, (Arthur) Burton (1892-1957), American critic, writer and editor.

Rashdall, Hastings (1858-1924), English theologian, philosopher and historian.

Rashi (acronym for Rabbi Shlomo Yitzhaqi) (1040-1105), outstanding French rabbi and commentator on the Bible and Talmud.

Rashīd ad-Dīn (1247-1318), Persian statesman and historian, author of a universal history.

Rashīd Ridā, (Muhammad) (1865-1935), Syrian Muslim scholar.

Rask, Rasmus (Kristian) (1787-1832), important Danish language scholar who helped to develop comparative linguistics.

Raspe, Rudolph Erich (1737-1794), German adventurer and writer, best known for his tales of the adventures of the fictional Baron Munchhausen.

Rastell, John (c.1475-1536), English printer, barrister and dramatist; father of William Rastell.

Rastell, William (1508-1565), English printer, barrister and writer; son of John Rastell.

Rathenau, Walther (1867-1922), German industrialist, statesman and political philosopher; was assassinated by nationalist extremists.

Ratramnus (9th Century), French Roman Catholic priest and theologian.

Rattigan, Sir Terence (Mervyn) (1911-1977), English dramatist and screenwriter.

Ratzel, Friedrich (1844-1904), German geographer and ethnographer who originated the theory of Lebensraum (living space).

Rauschenbusch, Walter (1861-1918), American clergyman and theologian, a principal figure in the Social Gospel movement.

Ravaisson-Mollien, Jean-Gaspard-Félix Lacher (1813-1900), French philosopher.

Rawlings, Marjorie Kinnan (1896-1953), American writer, best known for her novel *The Yearling* (1938).

Ray, John (1627-1705), English naturalist whose most significant work was the *Historia Plantarum* (3 volumes, 1686-1704).

Raynal, Guillaume-Thomas, Abbé de (1713-1796), French writer and polemicist.

Raynouard, François-Juste-Marie (1761-1836), French poet, dramatist and philologist.

Rāzī, ar- (actually Abū Bakr Muhammad ibn Zakariyā) (c.865-c.928), famous Persian alchemist, physician and Muslim philosopher.

Read, Sir Herbert (Edward) (1893-1968), English poet, critic and writer.

Read, Opie (Percival) (1852-1939), American journalist and writer.

Read, Thomas Buchanan (1822-1872), American poet and painter.

Reade, Charles (1814-1884), prominent English novelist, particularly known for *The Cloister and the Hearth* (1861); uncle of William Winwood Reade.

Reade, William Winwood (1838-1875), English explorer and novelist, nephew of Charles Reade.

Realf, Richard (1834-1878), English-born American poet; committed suicide.

Rebreanu, Liviu (1885-1943), Romanian novelist.

Reclus, (Jean-Jacques-) Élisée (1830-1905), French geographer and anarchist, author of the monumental *Nouvelle Géographie universelle; La Terre et les hommes* (19 volumes, 1876-94).

Redfield, Robert (1897-1958), American cultural anthropologist.

Redi, Francesco (1626-1698), Italian physician and poet, author of *Bacco in Toscana* (1685).

Redpath, James (1833-1891), Scottish-born American journalist and reformer who was leading abolitionist.

Redlich, Joseph (1869-1936), Austrian statesman and historian.

Rée, Paul (1849-1901), German philosopher.

Reed, Henry (1914-1986), English poet, dramatist and translator.

Reed, Isaac (1742-1807), English bibliophile, editor and biographer.

Reed, John (1887-1920), American Marxist revolutionary, writer and poet, apologist for the 1917 Bolshevik Revolution is his book *Ten Days That Shook the World* (1919).

Reed, Sampson (1800-1880), American Swedenborgian clergyman and writer, author of *Observations on the Growth of the Mind* (1826).

Reese, Lizette Woodworth (1856-1935), American poet, remembered for her *Tears* (1899).

Reev, Clara (1729-1807), English novelist, best remembered for *The Champion of Virtue: A Gothic Story* (1777), reprinted as *The Old English Baron* (1778).

Regino von Prüm (10th Century), German cleric and chronicler, author of the *Chronicon* (published 1521).

Regio, José (1901-1969), esteemed Portuguese poet, novelist, dramatist and critic.

Regis, Pierre-Sylvan (1632-1707), French philosopher of the Cartesian school.

Regnard, Jean-François (1655-1709), French dramatist who excelled in comedic invention.

Régnier, Henri (-François-Joseph) de (1864-1936), admired French poet, novelist and critic, a proponent of Symbolism.

Régnier, Mathurin (1573-1613), gifted French poet and critic, noted especially for his satirical mastery in his poet *Macette* (1609).

Rehberg, August Wilhelm (1757-1836), German political theorist.

Reichenbach, Hans (1891-1953), German-born American philosopher, author of *Elements of Symbolic Logic* (1947) and *The Rise of Scientific Philosophy* (1951).

Reid, Forrest (1875-1947), Irish novelist and critic.

Reid, Thomas (1710-1796), Scottish philosopher of the common sense school.

Reid, (Thomas) Mayne (1818-1883), Irish-born American novelist.

Reid, Whitelaw (1837-1912), American journalist, diplomat and politician.

Reimarus, Hermann Samuel (1694-1768), influential German philosopher who was a leading Deist, author of the *Apologie oder Schutzschrift für die vernunftigen Verehrer Gottes* (Apologia or Defense for the Rational Reverers of God).

Reinkens, Josef Hubert (1821-1896), German Roman Catholic bishop and scholar who became the first bishop of the Old Catholic Church.

Reinmar von Hagenau (12th-13th Century), German poet.

Reiske, Johann Jakov (1716-1774), learned German scholar, an authority on Arabic and Greek literature.

Remarque, Erich Maria (1898-1970), German-born American novelist, best known for his *Im Westen nichts Neues* (1929; English translation as *All Quiet on the Western Front*, 1929).

Remizov, Alexei (Mikhailovich) (1877-1957), Russian writer of the Symbolist school.

Renan, Ernest (1823-1892), French religious historian, philosopher and scholar.

Renard, Jules (1864-1910), French writer and dramatist, best remembered for his *Poil de carotte* (1894; English translation as *Carrots*, 1946), a prose work based on his bitter childhood.

Renart, Jean (13th Century), French writer.

Renault, Mary (actually Mary Challans) (1905-1983), English novelist, best known for her historical fiction.

René of Provence, Duc d'Anjou and Comte de Provence (1408-1480), French writer and poet.

Renouvier, Charles-Bernard (1815-1903), French philosopher who espoused a neocritical idealist philosophy.

Repplier, Agnes (1858-1950), American essayist and biographer.

Resende, Garcia de (c.1470-1536), Portuguese poet, writer and editor.

Restif, Nicolas-Edme (1734-1806), French novelist who was also known as Restif de la Bretonne.

Retz, Jean-François-Paul de Gondi, Cardinal de (1613-1679), French churchman and political adventurer who was a leading figure in the Fronde, especially known for his classic *Mémoires* (published 1715).

Reuchlin, Johannes (1455-1522), notable German classical scholar, author of *De Rudimentis Hebraicis* (On the Fundamentals of Hebrew, 1506) and the satirical *Epistolae obscurorum virorum* (Letters of the Obscure Men, 1515-17).

Reuter, Fritz (1810-1874), admired German novelist whose finest work was *Ut mine Stromtid* (During My Apprenticeship, 1862-64).

Reverdy, Pierre (1889-1960), French poet who embraced Cubism and later Surrealism.

Revius, Jacobus (1586-1658), admired Dutch theologian and poet of the Calvinist persuasion, particularly known for his sonnet collection on Christ.

Rexroth, Kenneth (1905-1982), American poet, essayist, critic, translator and painter.

Reyes, Alfonso (1889-1959), outstanding Mexican poet, writer, scholar and diplomat.

Reymont, Władysław Stanisław (1867-1925), esteemed Polish novelist and short-story writer; won the Nobel Prize for Literature (1924).

Reynolds, John Hamilton (1796-1852), English poet and writer, particularly admired for his poems in *The Garden of Florence* (1821).

Reynolds, Sir Joshua (1723-1792), famous English painter and writer on aesthetics.

Reznikoff, Charles (1894-1976), American poet of the Objectivist school.

Rezzori, Gregor von (1914-1998), Austrian novelist and memoirist.

Rhianus (3rd Century B.C.), Greek poet and scholar.

Rhigas, Konstantinos (1760-1798), Greek poet and revolutionary; as organizer of the anti-Turkish revolutionary movement in Vienna, he was betrayed and killed.

Rhodes, Eugene Manlove (1869-1934), American novelist who excelled in the depiction of the Old West.

Rhodes, James Ford (1848-1927), American historian, author of a *History of the United States from the Compromise of 1850* (7 volumes, 1893-1906) and a *History of the Civil War* (1917).

Rhys, Ernest Percival (1859-1946), English editor, writer and poet.

Rhys, Jean (c.1890-1979), West Indies novelist and short-story writer.

Rhys, Siôn Dafydd (1534-c.1609), Welsh physician and grammarian.

Ribeiro, Bernardim (c.1482-1552), Portuguese poet and writer who helped to reinvigorate Portuguese literature.

Ricardo, David (1772-1823), English economist, author of *On the Principles of Political Economy and Taxation* (1817).

Rice, Alice (Caldwell) Hegan (1870-1942), American novelist and short-story writer, best known for her *Mrs Wiggs of the Cabbage Patch* (1901); wife of Cale Young Rice.

Rice, Cale Young (1872-1943), American poet and dramatist; husband of Alice (Caldwell) Hegan Rice.

Rice, Elmer (actually Elmer Reizenstein) (1892-1967), American dramatist, novelist and essayist.

Rice, James (1843-1882), English novelist and journalist.

Rich, Barnabe (1542-1617), English soldier and writer.

Richard of Saint-Victor (d. 1173), Scottish theologian who wrote classic works on mysticism in his *Benjamin major* and *Benjamin minor*.

Richards, I(vor) A(rmstrong) (1893-1979), English poet and critic.

Richards, Laura Elizabeth (1850-1943), American biographer and children's writer.

Richards, (Thomas Franklin) Grant (1872-1948), English publisher and writer.

Richardson, Dorothy Miller (1873-1957), remarkable English novelist, acclaimed for her novel series *Pilgrimage*.

Richardson, Henry Handel (actually Ethel Florence Lindesay Richardson) (1870-1946), English novelist, author of the trilogy *The Fortunes of Richard Mahony* (*Australia Felix*, 1917, *The Way Home*, 1925, and *Ultima Thule*, 1929).

Richardson, John (1796-1852), Canadian novelist, author of *Écarté* (1829) and *Wacousta* (1832).

Richardson, Samuel (1689-1761), outstanding English novelist who wrote *Pamela, or, Virtue Rewarded* (1740), *Clarissa, or, The History of a Young Lady* (1747-48) and *The History of Sir Charles Grandison* (1753-54).

Richepin, Jean (1849-1926), French poet, dramatist and novelist.

Richmond, Legh (1772-1827), English divine and writer, best known for his *The Diaryman's Daughter* (1809).

Richter, Conrad (Michael) (1890-1968), American novelist and short-story writer.

Richter, Johann Friedrich (1763-1825), famous German writer and poet who also wrote under the name Jean Paul, renowned for his novels *Hesperus* (1795) and *Titan* (1800-03).

Ricket, Heinrich (1863-1936), German philosopher of neo-Kantian persuasion.

Ricketson, Daniel (1813-1898), American poet.

Rickword, Edgell (1898-1982), English poet and critic.

Ridge, John Rollin (1827-1867), American journalist, writer and poet who wrote under the name Yellow Bird, a translation of his Cherokee name.

Ridge, Lola (1871-1941), Irish-born American poet who was esteemed for her Symbolist verse.

Riding, Laura (actually **Laura Reichenthal) (1901-1991),** American poet, novelist and critic.

Ridley, James (1736-1765), English cleric and writer, author of the popular *Tales of the Genii* (1764).

Ridley, Nicholas (c.1500-1555), English Protestant Reformation leader and theologian; was condemned as a heretic and burned at the stake.

Riegl, Alois (1858-1905), Austrian scholar.

Riehl, Alois (1844-1924), Austrian philosopher of the Kantian school.

Riehl, Wilhelm Heinrich (1823-1897), German historian, author of *Die Naturgeschichte des deutschen Volkes als Grundlage einer deutschen Social Politik* (The Natural Law of the German People as a Foundation of German Social Politics, 4 volumes, 1851-69).

Riemann, (Karl Wilhelm Julius) Hugo (1849-1919), distinguished German music scholar and lexicographer.

Riggs, Lynn (1899-1954), American poet and dramatist.

Rigord (c.1150-c.1207), French monk and chronicler.

Riis, Jacob August (1849-1914), Danish-born American journalist, photographer, social reformer and writer, best known for his account of slum life in New York City in *How the Other Half Lives* (1890).

Riley, (Isaac) Woodbridge (1869-1933), American philosopher.

Riley, James Whitcomb (1849-1916), American poet, known as the "Hoosier poet," who won popular acclaim for his dialect poems.

Rilke, Rainer Maria (1875-1926), outstanding Austrian poet, celebrated for his *Duineser Elegien* (1922) and *Die Sonnette an Orpheus* (1923).

Rimbaud, (Jean-Nicolas-) Arthur (1854-1891), celebrated French poet, author of the remarkable *Les Illuminations* (1886).

Rin-chen-bzang-po (958-1055), Tibetan scholar and translator of Buddhist texts.

Rinehart, Mary Roberts (1876-1958), American novelist and dramatist, best known for her mysteries.

Rinuccini, Ottavio (1562-1621), Italian poet.

Ripley, George (1802-1880), prominent American reformer, journalist, literary critic, writer and encyclopedist, the founder of the utopian Brook Farm.

Ripley, W(illiam) Z(ebina) (1867-1941), American anthropologist and economist.

Ritchie, Anne Isabella Thackeray, Lady (1837-1919), English novelist and essayist; daughter of William Makepeace Thackeray.

Ritschl, Albrect (1822-1889), influential German Protestant theologian, author of *Die christliche Lehre von der Rechtfertigung und Versöhnung* (3 volumes, 1870-74; English translation as *The Christian Doctrine of Justification and Reconciliation,* 1872-1900).

Ritschl, F(riedrich) W(ilhelm) (1806-1876), German classical scholar.

Ritson, Joseph (1752-1803), English literary scholar who was known as much for his eccentric nature as for his learning; died insane.

Ritsos, Yannis (1909-1990), Greek poet who championed the cause of Marxism.

Rivarol, Antoine, Comte de (1753-1801), French journalist and epigrammatist whose claim to nobility is doubtful, especially known for his satirical bent.

Rive, Richard Moore (1931-1989), South African novelist and short-story writer; was murdered.

Rivera, José Eustasio (1889-1928), notable Colombian novelist and poet, author of the famous novel *La voragine* (1924; English translation as *The Vortex,* 1935).

Rivers, W(illiam) H(alse) R(ivers) (1864-1922), English medical psychologist and anthropologist.

Rives, Amélie (1863-1945), American novelist, poet and dramatist.

Rivet, Paul (1876-1958), French ethnologist.

Rivière, Jacques (1886-1925), French writer, critic and editor.

Rizal, José (actually **José Rizal y Mercado) (1861-1896),** Filipino physician, patriot, writer and poet; was arrested, tried for sedition and executed by the military.

Robbins, Harold (actually **Francis Kane) (1916-1997),** American writer who won enormous popular success, best remembered for his novel *The Carpetbaggers* (1961).

Robert de Torigni (c.1110-1186), French abbot and chronicler.

Robert of Avesbury (14th Century), English historian.

Robert of Gloucester (13th Century), English chronicler.

Roberts, Sir Charles G(eorge) D(ouglas) (1860-1943), eminent Canadian poet, writer and editor.

Roberts, Elizabeth Madox (1881-1941), American novelist, short-story writer and poet, best remembered for her novel *The Great Meadow* (1930).

Roberts, Kenneth (Lewis) (1885-1957), American writer, particularly known for his historical novels.

Roberts, Michael William Edward (1902-1948), English poet, critic and editor.

Robertson, Morgan Andrew (1861-1915), American writer.

Robertson, Thomas William (1829-1871), English dramatist, producer and director.

Robertson, William (1721-1793), Scottish historian and Church of Scotland leader, author of the authoritative work *The History of the Reign of the Emperor Charles the Fifth* (1769), and *History of America* (2 volumes, 1777).

Robinson, Edward (1794-1863), American biblical scholar who specialized in the geography of the Bible.

Robinson, Edwin Arlington (1869-1935), esteemed American poet who was especially known for his naturalism and lyricism.

Robinson, (Esmé Stuart) Lennox (1886-1958), Irish dramatist and editor.

Robinson, Henry Crabb (1775-1867), English diarist and conversationalist.

Robinson, Henry Wheeler (1872-1945), English Nonconformist Baptist theologian and Old Testament scholar.

Robinson, James Harvey (1863-1936), influential American historian, author of *The New History* (1912) and *The Mind in the Making* (1921).

Robinson, John (c.1575-1625), English Puritan minister and writer, particularly known for his *A Justification of Separation from the Church of England* (1610).

Robinson, Rowland Evans (1833-1900), American writer.

Robinson, Solon (1803-1880), American writer.

Roblès, Emmanuel (François) (1914-1995), Algerian-born French novelist and dramatist of Spanish descent.

Rochester, John Wilmot, 2nd Earl of (1647-1680), notable English poet and courtier, admired for his love poems and his satirical writings.

Rod, Edouard (1857-1910), Swiss writer and critic.

Rode, Helge (1870-1937), Danish poet, novelist, dramatist and essayist who was the principal figure in the antirationalist movement in Denmark.

Rodenbach, Albrecht (1856-1880), Belgian poet who was a major figure in the revival of Flemish letters.

Rodo, José Enrique (1872-1917), important Uruguayan philosopher and essayist.

Rodrigues Lobo, Francisco (1580-1622), Portuguese poet and writer who espoused pastoral themes.

Roe, E(dward) P(ayson) (1838-1888), American novelist, best known for his *Barriers Burned Away* (1872).

Roe, Sir Thomas (c.1581-1644), English diplomat and memoirist.

Roethke, Theodore (1908-1963), esteemed American poet and essayist, particularly known for his poetry collection *The Waking* (1953).

Roger of Wendover (d. 1236), English monk and chronicler, author of *Flores historiarum*.

Rogers, James Edwin Thorold (1825-1890), English clergyman, economist and politician, best known for his tome on inflation *A History of Agriculture and Prices in England* (1866-67)

Rogers, John (c.1500-1555), English Protestant reformer and biblical editor; was burned as a heretic.

Rogers, Samuel (1763-1855), English poet who wrote *The Pleasures of Memory* (1792).

Rogers, Will (actually William Penn Adair Rogers) (1879-1935), popular American humorist, actor and writer; was killed in an airplane crash.

Roget, Peter Mark (1779-1869), English physician and philologist, compiler of the famous *Thesaurus of English Words and Phrases* (1852).

Róheim, Géza (1891-1953), Hungarian-born American psychoanalyst and ethnologist, author of *Animism, Magic, and the Divine King* (1930), *Psychoanalysis and Anthropology* (1950), *The Gates of the Dream* (1952) and *Magic and Schizophrenia* (published 1955).

Rojas, Fernando de (c.1465-1541), Spanish writer, best known for his novel *Celestina* (1499).

Rojas Villandrando, Agustin de (1572-c.1635), Spanish writer, author of the picaresque novel *El viaje entretenido* (The Pleasant Voyage).

Rojas Zorrilla, Francisco do (1607-1648), Spanish dramatist, particularly remembered for his *Del rey abajo, ninguno* (Below the King, No One).

Roland Holst-van der Schalk, Henriëtte Goverdina Anna (1869-1952), Dutch poet, biographer and socialist.

Rolfe, Frederick William (Serafino Austin Lewis Mary) (1860-1913), English writer who wrote under the name Baron Corvo, especially admired for his *Hadrian the Seventh* (1904) and *The Desire and Pursuit of the Whole* (published 1934).

Rolland, Romain (1866-1944), renowned French novelist, dramatist and essayist; won the Nobel Prize for Literature (1915).

Rolle, Richard (actually Richard Rolle de Hampole) (c.1300-1349), English poet and writer on mystical subjects.

Rolli, Paolo Antonio (1687-1765), Italian librettist, poet and translator.

Rölvaag, Ole (Edvart) (1876-1931), Norwegian-born American novelist, author of the esteemed *Giants in the Earth* (1927).

Romains, Jules (actually Louis-Henri-Jean Farigoule) (1885-1972), outstanding French novelist, dramatist and poet whose masterpiece was the epic prose cycle *Les Hommes de bonne volonté* (27 volumes, 1932-46; English translation as *Men of Good Will*, 14 volumes, 1933-46).

Romani, Felice (1788-1865), Italian librettist and writer.

Romer, Alfred Sherwood (1894-1973), American paleontologist.

Romero, José Rubén (1890-1952), Mexican novelist, poet and diplomat.

Ronsard, Pierre de (1524-1585), celebrated French poet who excelled in the ode and sonnet.

Roosevelt, Theodore (1858-1919), famous American explorer, soldier, writer, politician and 26th president of the US (1901-09), author of the much esteemed *The Winning of the West* (4 volumes, 1889-96).

Roquebrune, Robert Laroque de (1889-1978), French-Canadian novelist, short-story writer and memoirist.

Ros, Amanda McKittrick (née Anna Margaret McKittrick) (1860-1939), Irish novelist.

Rosa, Salvator (1615-1673), Italian painter, etcher, poet, actor and musician.

Roscoe, William (1753-1831), English lawyer, banker, botanist, scholar and poet, much admired for his study *Life of Lorenzo de' Medici* (1795) and for his children's verse.

Roscommon, Wentworth Dillon, 4th Earl of (c.1633-1685), English poet and critic.

Rose, Aquila (c.1695-1723), English-born American poet and typographer.

Rose, Valentin (1829-1916), German scholar, best known for his work on Aristotle.

Rosegger, Peter (1843-1918), Austrian poet and novelist, particularly known for his novels *Die Schriften des Waldschulmeisters* (1875; English translation as *The Forest Schoolmaster*, 1901) and *Waldheimat* (1877; English translation as *The Forest Farm*, 1912).

Rosenberg, Isaac (1890-1918), English poet and artist who excelled in "trench" poetry; died in World War I.

Rosenfeld, Morris (1862-1923), Russian-born American poet of Yiddish verse.

Rosenstein, Nils von (1752-1824), Swedish writer.

Rosenstock-Huessy, Eugen (1888-1973), German writer.

Rosenzweig, Franz (1886-1929), German philosopher who espoused a religious Existentialist worldview.

Rosmini-Serbati, Antonio (1797-1855), Italian Roman Catholic priest, theologian and philosopher, author of the *Nuovo saggio sull' origine delle idee* (3 volumes, 1830; English translation as *The Origin of Ideas*, 1883-84) and *Massime di perfezione Cristiana* (1830; English translation as *Maxims of Christian Perfection*, 1849).

Ross, Alexander (1699-1784), Scottish poet and songwriter, best known for his pastoral *The Fortunate Shepherdess* (1768).

Ross, Edward (Alsworth) (1866-1951), American sociologist, author of *Social Control* (1901).

Ross, Harold (Wallace) (1892-1951), American editor, founder and editor of the influential magazine *The New Yorker* (1925-51).

Ross, (James) Sinclair (1908-1996), Canadian novelist and short-story writer, particularly admired for his novel *As for Me and My House* (1941).

Ross, Sir W(illiam) D(avid) (1877-1971), Scottish philosopher of the rationalistic moral persuasion, author of *The Right and the Good* (1930) and *Foundations of Ethics* (1939).

Ross, William (1762-1790), Scottish poet.

Rossetti, Christina Georgina (1830-1894), admired English poet, author of *Goblin Market* (1862) and *Prince's Progress and Other Poems* (1866); daughter of Gabriele Pasquale Rossetti and sister of Dante Gabriel and William Michael Rossetti.

Rossetti, Dante Gabriel (actually Gabriel Charles Dante Rossetti) (1828-1882), famous English poet, translator and painter, celebrated for such poems as *The Blessed Damozel* (1850) and *The House of Life* (1881); son of Gabriele Pasquale Rossetti and brother of Christina Georgina and William Michael Rossetti.

Rossetti, Gabriele Pasquale (1783-1854), Italian-born English poet and writer; father of Christina Georgina, Dante Gabriel and William Michael Rossetti.

Rossetti, William Michael (1829-1919), English literary and art critic; son of Gabriele Pasquale Rossetti and brother of Christina Georgina and Dante Gabriel Rossetti.

Rostand, Edmond (1868-1918), French poet and dramatist, author of the famous play *Cyrano de Bergerac* (1897).

Rosten, Leo (Calvin) (1908-1997), Polish-born American writer, particularly known for *The Education of H*Y*M*A*N K*A*P*L*A*N* (1937).

Rostovzeff, Michael Ivanovich (1870-1952), learned Russian-born American archaeologist who was an authority on ancient Greece and Rome.

Roth, Henry (1906-1995), Austrian-born American novelist and short-story writer, particularly remembered for his novel *Call It Sleep* (1934).

Rothe, Richard (1799-1867), German Lutheran theologian of Idealism, especially known for his works on the church and state, and on ethics.

Rotrou, Jean de (1609-1650), important French dramatist of the Neoclassical school.

Rougemont, Denis de (1906-1985), Swiss cultural historian and writer.

Rouget de Lisle, Claude-Joseph (1760-1836), French poet and writer, author of the words and composer of the music of the French National Anthem *La Marseillaise* (1792).

Roumain, Jacques (1907-1944), Haitian writer.

Roumanille, Joseph (1818-1891), French poet and writer.

Rouquette, Adrien Emmanuel (1813-1887), American poet and writer; brother of François Dominique Rouquette.

Rouquette, François Dominique (1810-1890), American poet; brother of Adrien Emmanuel Rouquette.

Rourke, Constance (Mayfield) (1885-1941), American writer.

Rousseau, Jean-Baptiste (1671-1741), French dramatist and poet, especially known for his epigrams.

Rousseau, Jean-Jacques (1712-1778), celebrated Swiss philosopher, political theorist and writer, author of the famous autobiography *Confessions* (Published 1782).

Rousselot, Jean-Pierre (1846-1924), French phonetician and linguist.

Routh, Martin Joseph (1755-1854), English educator, scholar and editor.

Rovere, Richard (Halworth) (1915-1979), American journalist and writer, especially known for his writings on politics.

Rowe, Nicholas (1674-1718), eminent English dramatist, poet, editor and translator; became Poet Laureate of the United Kingdom (1715).

Rowlands, Samuel (c.1570-c.1630), English poet and writer of a satirical turn.

Rowley, Samuel (16th-17th Century), English dramatist.

Rowley, William (c.1585-1626), English dramatist and actor.

Rowntree, Benjamin Seebohm (1871-1954), English philanthropist and sociologist.

Rowse, A(lfred) L(eslie) (1903-1997), English poet, biographer and historian.

Rowson, Susanna (Haswell) (c.1762-1824), English-born American writer and poet.

Roy, D L (1863-1913), Bengali dramatist.

Roy, Gabrielle (1909-1983), esteemed French-Canadian novelist and short-story writer.

Roy, (Joseph) Camille (1870-1943), distinguished French-Canadian critic and literary historian.

Royce, Josiah (1855-1916), prominent American philosopher of Idealism.

Royer-Collard, Pierre-Paul (1763-1845), French statesman and philosopher.

Royle, Edwin (Milton) (1862-1942), American dramatist, best remembered for *The Squaw Man* (1905).

Rozanov, Vasili Vasilievich (1856-1919), Russian writer.

Rozhdestvensky, Robert Ivanovich (1932-1994), Russian poet.

Rucellai, Giovanni (1475-1525), Italian poet and dramatist, author of the didactic poem *Le api* (The Bees, published 1539).

Rückert, Friedrich (1788-1866), admired German poet and scholar whose moving poems *Kindertotenlieder* (Songs on the Death of Children) were set to music by Gustav Mahler.

Rudbeck, Olof (1630-1702), Swedish scientist and writer.

Rudd, Steele (actually Arthur Hoey Davis) (1868-1935), Australian novelist, short-story writer and dramatist.

Rudnicki, Adolf (1912-1990), Polish writer.

Rudolf von Ems (c.1200-c.1254), important Austrian poet of epic verse.

Rueda, Lope de (c.1510-1565), Spanish actor and dramatist.

Rufinus, Tyrannius (c.345-c.410), Italian priest, theologian, writer and translator.

Ruiz, Juan (c.1283-c.1350), Spanish poet who wrote the classic *Libro de buen amor* (1330; augmented edition, 1343; English translation as *The Book of Good Love*, 1933).

Ruiz de Alarcón (y Mendoza), Juan (c.1581-1639), Mexican-born Spanish dramatist.

Rukeyser, Muriel (1913-1980), American poet, writer, dramatist and translator.

Rulfo, Juan Pérez (1918-1986), Mexican writer.

Rulhière, Claude-Carloman (1734-1791), French historian and poet.

Rumilly, Robert (1897-1983), French-Canadian historian, author of the expansive *Histoire de la province de Québec* (41 volumes, 1940-63).

Rumpf, Georg Eberhard (1627-1702), German naturalist.

Runeberg, Johan Ludvig (1804-1877), eminent Finnish poet and dramatist, author of *Vårt land* (Our Land), which was adopted as the Finnish National Anthem.

Runius, Johan (1679-1713), Swedish poet.

Runyon, (Alfred) Damon (1884-1946), American journalist, columnist and short-story writer.

Rushworth, John (c.1612-1690), English historian, author of the *Historical Collections of Private Passages of State* (1659-1701).

Ruskin, John (1819-1900), eminent English writer, art critic and lecturer, especially known for *Modern Painters* (1843), *The Seven Lamps of Architecture* (1849) and *The Stones of Venice* (1851-53).

Russell, Bertrand (Arthur William), 3rd Earl (1872-1970), celebrated English logician, philosopher and pacifist; won the Nobel Prize for Literature (1950).

Russell, Irwin (1853-1879), American poet who wrote in black dialect.

Russell, Lord John, 1st Earl (1792-1878), English statesman and writer.

Russell, Thomas (1762-1788) English poet, much admired for his *Sonnets and Miscellaneous Poems* (published 1789).

Rutebeuf (13th Century), French trouvère.

Rutherford, Mark (actually William Hale White) (1831-1913), English novelist and critic.

Rutilius Namatianus Claudius (5th Century), Roman poet, author of the elegy *De reditu suo*.

Ruysbroeck, Jan van (1293-1381), Flemish Roman Catholic mystic and writer, author of the famous *Die Chierheit der gheesteliker Brulocht* (1350; English translation as *The Spiritual Espousals*, 1952).

Ruzzante (actually Angelo Beolco) (1502-1542), Italian actor and dramatist.

Ryan, Abram Joseph (1838-1886), American poet and Roman Catholic priest whose espousal of the Confederate cause led him to be dubbed the Tom Moore of Dixie."

Rybakov, Anatoly (1911-1998), Russian novelist, author of *Children of the Arbat* (1987).

Rydberg, (Abraham) Viktor (1828-1895), outstanding Swedish writer and poet.

Ryle, Gilbert (1900-1976), influential English philosopher of the Oxford school, author of *The Concept of Mind* (1949), *Dilemmas* (1954) and *Plato's Progress* (1966).

Rymer, Thomas (c.1643-1713), English historian and literary critic.

Sa'adia ben Joseph (882-942), Egyptian Jewish philosopher and polemicist, author of an Arabic translation of the Old Testament.

Saavedra (Ramírez de Baquendano), Angel de, Duque de Rivas (1791-1865), prominent Spanish dramatist and poet, especially known for his play *Don Alvaro, o la fuerza del sino* (1835).

Saavedra Fajardo, Diego da (1584-1648), Spanish diplomat and writer, author of the *Idea de un Principe politico cristiano* (1640; English translation, 1700).

Saavedra Lamas, Carlos (1878-1959), Argentine jurist and writer on international law; won the Nobel Prize for Peace (1936).

Saba, Umberto (actually Umberto Poli) (1883-1957), Italian poet.

Sabatier, (Louis-) Auguste (1839-1901), French Protestant theologian who espoused liberal views in biblical criticism.

Sabine, Lorenzo (1803-1877), American historian.

Sable, Madeleine de Souvre, Marquise de (1599-1678), French writer.

Sabzevari, Haji Hadi (c.1797-1878), notable Persian philosopher and poet.

Sá-Carneiro, Mário de (1890-1916), talented Portuguese poet, novelist and short-story writer.

Sacchetti, Franco (c.1330-1400), Italian poet and writer.

Sachs, Curt (1881-1959), German-born American music historian.

Sachs, Hans (1494-1576), celebrated German poet, dramatist and writer who was the inspiration for Wagner's opera *Die Meistersinger von Nürnberg.*

Sachs, Nelly (Leonie) (1891-1970), distinguished German-born Swedish poet and dramatist; was co-winner of the Nobel Prize for Literature (1966).

Sackler, Howard (1929-1982), American dramatist and poet.

Sackville, Charles, Lord Buckhurst, later 6th Earl of Dorset (1638-1706), English courtier and poet.

Sackville, Thomas, 1st Earl of Dorset and Baron Buckhurst (1536-1608), English statesman, poet and dramatist, author of the play *The Tragedie of Gorboduc* (in collaboration with Thomas Norton, 1561) and the poetry collection *A Myrrour for Magistrates* (1563).

Sackville-West, Victoria (Mary) (1892-1962), English poet and writer; wife of Sir Harold (George) Nicolson.

Sade, Marquis de (actually Donatien-Alphonse-François Sade) (1740-1814), infamous French libertine, writer and dramatist whose sexual perversions led to the coinage of the word sadism.

Sadeddin, Hoca (1536-1599), Turkish historian.

Sá de Miranda, Francisco de (1481-1558), outstanding Portuguese poet, author of the remarkable *Cartas* (verse epistles), satires and the eclogue *Basto.*

Sa'di (c.1213-1292), celebrated Persian poet and writer, author of the classic volumes *Būstān* (The Garden, 1257) and *Golestān* (The Rose Garden, 1258).

Sadleir, Michael (actually Michael Sadler) (1888-1957), English bibliographer and novelist.

Sadoveanu, Mihail (1880-1961), Romanian novelist and short-story writer.

Saemundr, Sigfússon (1056-1133), Icelandic chieftan, priest and chronicler.

Šafařík, Pavel Josef (1795-1861), Czech philologist and archaeologist.

Sagan, Carl (Edward) (1934-1996), prominent American astronomer, exobiologist and writer who was a remarkable popularizer of science via books and television.

Sahagun, Bernardino de (c.1490-1590), Spanish Roman Catholic missionary and historian of New Spain.

Sa'ib (d. 1677), Persian poet.

Saigyó (1118-1190), Japanese Buddhist priest and poet who excelled in writing in the tanka form.

Saint-Amant, (Marc-) Antonio Girard, Sieur de (c.1594-1661), French poet, especially esteemed for his *Albion* (1643), *Rome ridicule* (1649) and *Moïse sauve* (Moses Rescued, 1653).

Saint-Denis, Michel (actually Jacques Duchesne) (1897-1971), French actor, director and dramatist.

Saint-Évremond, Charles de Marguetel de Saint-Denis, Seigneur de (c.1613-1703), French writer and poet.

Saint-Exupéry, Antoine (-Marie-Roger) de (1900-1944), notable French aviator and writer; died in World War II.

Saint-Martin, Louis-Claude de (1743-1803), French philosopher and poet who espoused illuminism.

Saint-Pierre, Charles-Irénée Castel, Abbé de (1658-1743), French reformer and writer who was known for his controversial and utopian ideas.

Saint-Réal, César Vichard, Abbé de (1639-1692), French writer.

Saint-Simon, (Claude-) Henri (de Rouvroy, Comte) de (1760-1825), influential French social thinker and socialist, author of *Opinions littéraires, philosophiques et industrielles* (1825) and *Le Nouveau Christianisme* (1825).

Saint-Simon, Louis de Rouvroy, Duc de (1675-1755), outstanding French writer who wrote the remarkable *Mémoires* (modern edition, 41 volumes, 1879-1923).

Sainte-Beuve, Charles-Augustin (1804-1869), famous French critic, writer and poet.

Saintine, Joseph Xavier (1798-1865), French dramatist, poet and writer.

Sainstbury, George Edward Bateman (1845-1933), eminent English literary critic and historian.

Sait Faik Abasiyanik (1907-1954), Turkish writer.

Saitō Mokichi (1882-1953), Japanese poet.

Sakai Hōitsu (actually Tadanao) (1761-1828), Japanese painter and poet.

Salesbury, William (c.1520-c.1584), Welsh lexicographer and translator, best known for his translation of the New Testament into Welsh (1567).

Salimbene di Adam (1221-c.1290), Italian Franciscan friar and historian.

Salinas (y Serrano), Pedro (1891-1951), Spanish poet, dramatist, essayist and scholar.

Salis-Seewis, Johann Gaudenz, Freiherr von (1762-1834), Swiss poet.

Sallust (actually Galus Sallustius Crispus) (c.86-c.35 B.C.), great Roman historian and politician.

Salmasius, Claudius (actually Claude de Saumaise) (1588-1653), learned French classical scholar.

Salten, Felix (actually Siegmund Salzmann) (1869-1945), Austrian theatre critic and novelist, especially remembered for his popular *Bambi* (1923).

Saltus, Edgar (Evertson) (1855-1921), American novelist and short-story writer.

Saltykov, Mikhail Yevgrafovich (1826-1889), remarkable Russian novelist who was especially known for his mastery of satire.

Salutati, (Lino) Coluccio (di Piero) (1331-1406), Italian public official, writer and poet.

Samain, Albert Victor (1844-1910), French poet.

Samaniego, Félix Mariá (1745-1801), Spanish poet who was known for his children's fables.

Samuel, Herbert Louis, 1st Viscount (1870-1963), English politician and philosopher.

Samuel ha-Nagid (actually Abu Ibrahim Samuel ben Joseph Halevi Ibn Nagdela) (993-1056), Spanish Jewish warrior, statesman, scholar and poet.

Sanā'ī (actually Abu al-Majd Majdud Ibn Adam) (c.1050-1131), notable Persian poet of Islam, greatly esteemed for his *Hadiqeh ol-haqiqat* (The Enclosed Garden of Truth).

Sanawbari, as- (d. 945), Arab poet.

Sanborn, Franklin Benjamin (1831-1917), American Abolitionist and biographer.

Sanches or Sanchez, Francisco (c.1550-c.1623), Spanish physician and philosopher of Skepticism.

Sánchez, Luis Alberto (1900-1994), Peruvian politician, writer and poet.

Sanchuniathon (c.14th Century B.C.), Phoenician writer.

Sand, George (actually Amandine-Aurore-Lucile née Dupin Dudevant) (1804-1876), celebrated French novelist, short-story writer and dramatist who was equally celebrated for her numerous liaisons.

Sanday, William (1843-1920), English New Testament scholar.

Sandburg, Carl (August) (1878-1967), popular American poet, biographer, novelist and folklorist.

Sandeau, Leonard-Sylvain-Julien (1811-1883), French novelist and dramatist, best known for his novel *Mademoiselle de la Seiglière* (1848) and his liaison with George Sand.

Sandeman, Robert (1718-1771), Scottish-born American Protestant Leader and writer, particularly known for *Some Thoughts on Christianity* (1764).

Sandemose, Aksel (1899-1965), Danish-born Norwegian novelist of an experimental turn.

Sanders, Lawrence (1920-1998), American writer, best remembered for his suspense thriller *The Anderson Tapes* (1970).

Sanders, Nicholas (c.1530-1581), English Roman Catholic scholar and polemicist, author of a valuable history of the English Reformation written in Latin (English translation as *The Rise and Growth of the Anglican Schism*, 1877).

Sanderson, John (1783-1844), American writer, particularly known for his *Sketches of Paris: In Familiar Letters to His Friends* (1838).

Sandoz, Mari (1896-1966), American writer.

Sands, Robert C(harles) (1799-1832), American journalist, writer and poet.

Sandys, George (1578-1664), significant English poet, traveller and government official, especially important for his contribution to the development of the heroic couplet.

Sandys, John Edwin (1844-1922), English classical historian.

Sanger, Margaret (née Higgins) (1883-1966), American birth-control advocate and writer.

Śankara (c.700-c.750), celebrated Hindu philosopher and theologian.

Śankaradeva (d.1568), Indian poet.

Śankardeb (1449-1569), Indian poet of religious verse.

Sannazzaro, Jacopo (1456-1530), admired Italian poet, author of the first pastoral romance *Arcadia* (1504).

Sansom, William (1912-1976), English novelist and short-story writer.

Santayana, George (1863-1952), distinguished Spanish philosopher, critic, writer and poet.

Santillana, Iñigo López de Mendoza, Marqués de (1398-1458), notable Spanish poet of pastoral lyrics.

Sanudo, Marino (1466-1536), Italian historian whose diary is of great historical value (modern edition, 58 volumes, 1879-1902).

Sapir, Edward (1884-1939), Polish-born American linguist and anthropologist who was an authority on North American Indian languages, author of the important study *Language* (1921).

Sapper (actually **Herman Cyril McNeile) (1888-1937),** English soldier and writer who wrote the highly successful thriller *Bull-Dog Drummond* (1920).

Sappho or **Psappho (c.610-c.580 B.C.),** celebrated Greek poet, renowned for her sensual love poems.

Sarasin, Jean-François (1614-1654), French poet who was known for his fine craftsmanship and for introducing the burlesque genre to France via Italy.

Sardou, Victorien (1831-1908), prominent French dramatist.

Sarett, Lew (1888-1954), American poet.

Sargent, Epes (1813-1880), American journalist, writer and poet.

Sargent, Lucius Manlius (1786-1867), American writer and antiquarian.

Sargent, Winthrop (1825-1870), American historian.

Sarkar, Sir Jadunath (1870-1958), Indian historian.

Sarkia, Kaarlo (1902-1945), Finnish writer.

Sarmiento, Domingo Faustino (1811-1888), Paraguayan statesman, educator and writer.

Saroyan, William (1908-1981), American writer and dramatist.

Sarpi, Paolo (actually **Pietro Soave Polano) (1552-1623),** Italian scholar who defended Venice's republican form of government against papal hegemony.

Sarton, George Alfred Leon (1884-1956), Belgian-born English, later American historian of science.

Sarton, May (actually **Eléanore Marie Sarton) (1912-1995),** American poet who became a cult figure in feminist circles.

Sartoris, Adelaide (née Kemble) (c.1814-1879), English singer and writer.

Sartre, Jean-Paul (1905-1980), famous French philosopher, novelist, dramatist, critic and political activist; won the Nobel Prize for Literature (1964) but, in characteristic fashion, refused it.

Sassoon, Siegfried (Lorraine) (1886-1967), eminent English poet and novelist, especially admired for his antiwar poems.

Sato Haruo (1892-1964), Japanese poet, novelist and critic.

Sauppe, Hermann (1809-1893), German philologist.

Saussure, Ferdinand de (1857-1913), influential Swiss linguist.

Savage, Philip Henry (1868-1899), American poet.

Savage, Richard (c.1697-1743), English poet, remembered for his dissolute life and the poem *The Wanderer* (1729).

Savard, Félix Antoine (1896-1982), French-Candian poet and writer.

Savigny, Friedrich Karl von (1779-1861), German jurist who was an influential figure in the development of private international jurisprudence.

Savile, Sir Henry (1549-1622), English scholar who was a leading figure in the work on the King James Version of the Bible.

Saxe, John Godfrey (1816-1887), American poet who wrote light verse.

Saxo Grammaticus (12th-13th Century), Danish historian who wrote the first major history of Denmark in his *Gesta Danorum*.

Sayat-Nova (actually **Aruthin Sayadian) (1712-1795),** Armenian poet who was known for his love songs.

Sayce, Archibald H(enry) (1845-1933), English language scholar and archaeologist who made important contributions to the study of ancient Near Eastern history.

Sayers, Dorothy L(eigh) (1893-1957), admired English scholar, writer and translator, especially known for her detective fiction featuring Lord Peter Wimsey.

Scaevola, Quintus Mucius (d. 82 B.C.), significant Roman public official who founded the scientific study of Roman jurisprudence which he systematized in 80 volumes.

Scaliger, Joseph Justus (1540-1609), outstanding French philologist and historian of Italian descent, author of the important study *Opus de emendatione tempore* (1583); son of Julius Caesar Scaliger.

Scaliger, Julius Caesar (1484-1558), Italian-born French classical scholar; father of Joseph Justus Scaliger.

Scarron, Paul (1610-1660), notable French novelist, poet and dramatist, best known for his realistic novel *Le Roman comique* (The Comic Novel, 2 volumes, 1651, 1657).

Scève, Maurice (c.1501-c.1564), outstanding French poet, author of the cycle *Délie, objet de plus haute vertu* (Délie, Object of Highest Virtue, 1544).

Schaepman, Hermanus Johannes Aloysius Maria (1844-1903), Dutch Roman Catholic priest, politician, writer and poet.

Schaff, Philip (1819-1893), Swiss-born American theologian and church historian, author of a *History of the Christian Church* (12 volumes, 1883-93).

Schäffle, Albert (1831-1903), German economist and sociologist.

Schaukal, Richard (1874-1942), Austrian poet who embraced Symbolism.

Schechter, Solomon (1847-1915), Romanian-born American Jewish scholar and leader, a noted authority on the Talmud.

Scheffel, (Joseph) Viktor von (1826-1886), German poet and novelist.

Scheffler, Johannes (1624-1677), Polish mystic, Roman Catholic polemicist and poet who wrote under the name Angelus Silesius.

Scheler, Max (1874-1928), German philosopher who espoused Phenomenological views.

Schelling, Friedrich (Wilhelm Joseph von) (1775-1854), important German philosopher of Idealism.

Schendel, Arthur (François-Emile) van (1874-1946), Dutch novelist and short-story writer.

Schenker, Heinrich (1868-1935), influential Austrian music theorist.

Scherer, Wilhelm (1841-1886), German philologist and literary historian.

Schickele, René (1883-1940), admired Alsatian poet, dramatist and novelist, a master of Expressionism.

Schiller, Ferdinand Canning Scott (1864-1937), German-born English philosopher of Pragmatism.

Schiller, (Johann Christoph) Friedrich (von) (1759-1805), great German dramatist, poet, theorist and writer, author of the celebrated dramatic trilogy *Wallenstein* (1796-99) and the famous poem *An die Freude* (Ode to Joy), the latter immortalized in the finale of Beethoven's 9th Symphony.

Schiltberger, Hans (actually **Johann Schiltberger) (1380-c.1440),** German traveller who left an interesting account of his travels.

Schimper, Carl Friedrich (1803-1867), German naturalist and poet.

Schlegel, August Wilhelm von (1767-1845), esteemed German critic, translator and editor, a pioneering figure in the Romantic movement; nephew of Johann Elias Schlegel and brother of (Karl Wilhelm) Friedrich von Schlegel.

Schlegel, Johann Elias (1719-1749), German writer and critic; uncle of August Wilhelm von and (Karl Wilhelm) Friedrich von Schlegel.

Schlegel, (Karl Wilhelm) Friedrich von (1772-1829), distinguished German critic, editor and linguist, one of the principal figures in the development of Romanticism; nephew of Johann Elias Schlegel and brother of August Wilhelm von Schlegel.

Schleicher, August (1821-1868), influential German linguist.

Schleiermacher, Friedrich (Ernst Daniel) (1768-1834), outstanding German Protestant theologian and scholar, author of *Reden über die Religion* (1799; English translation as *Religion: Speeches to its Cultured Despisers,* 1893) and *Der christliche Glaube nach den Grundsätzen der evangelischen Kirche im Zusammenhang dargestellet* (1821-22; English translation, 1928).

Schlesinger, Arthur Meier (1888-1965), American historian who was known for his studies in social and urban history.

Schleyer, Johann Martin (1831-1912), German bishop and proponent of the international language Volapük.

Schlick, Moritz (1882-1936), influential German-born Austrian philosopher who espoused Logical Empiricism, author of *Fragen der Ethik* (1930; English translation as *Problems of Ethics,* 1939), *Grundzüge der Naturphilosophie* (published 1948; English translation as *Philosophy of Nature,* 1949) and *Natur und Kultur* (published 1952); was murdered by a deranged student.

Schliemann, Heinrich (1822-1890), important German archaeologist, particularly known for his excavations of ancient Troy.

Schlosser, Friedrich (1776-1861), German historian, best remembered for his *Weltgeschichte für das deutsche Volk* (World History for the German People, 18 volumes, 1854-56).

Schlözer, A(ugust) L(udwig) (1735-1809), German historian.

Schmidt, Arno (1914-1979), German writer known for his experimental output.

Schmidt, Johannes (1843-1901), German linguist.

Schmidt, Wilhelm (1868-1954), German Roman Catholic priest and anthropologist , author of *Der Ursprung der Gottesidee* (The Origin of the Idea of God, 12 volumes, 1912-55) and *Ursprung und Werden der Religion* (1930; English translation as *The Origin and Growth of Religion,* 1931).

Schmitt, Gladys (1909-1972), American novelist.

Schmoller, Gustav von (1838-1917), German economist who wrote on economic history.

Schmucker, S(amuel) S(imon) (1799-1873), American Lutheran theologian and educator.

Schnitzler, Arthur (1862-1931), Austrian dramatist, novelist, short-story writer and physician.

Schönherr, Karl (1867-1943), Austrian dramatist and short-story writer.

Schopenhauer, Arthur (1788-1860), great German philosopher whose most important work in metaphysics was his *Die Welt als Wille und Vorstellung* (1819; English translation as *The World as Will and Idea,* 1883-86).

Schorer, Mark (1908-1977), American literary scholar, novelist and short-story writer.

Schreiner, Olive (Emilie Albertina) (1855-1920), South African novelist, short-story writer and activist, especially known for her novel *The Story of an African Farm* (1883), published under the name Ralph Iron.

Schrieke, Bertram (1890-1945), Dutch anthropologist.

Schröder, Ernst (1841-1902), German logician and mathematician.

Schröder, Friedrich Ludwig (1744-1816), German actor, theatre manager and dramatist.

Schubart, Christian Friedrich Daniel (1739-1791), German poet.

Schuchardt, Hugo (1842-1927), German philologist.

Schücking , Levin (1814-1883), German novelist.

Schumpeter, Joseph (Alois) (1883-1950), influential Moravian-born American economist and sociologist, author of *Capitalism, Socialism, and Democracy* (3rd edition, 1950).

Schurz, Carl (1829-1906), prominent German-born American reformer, journalist, writer and politician.

Schuyler, George (1895-1977), American journalist and writer, author of *Black No More* (1931) and *Black and Conservative* (1966).

Schuyler, James (Marcus) (1923-1991), American poet, dramatist and writer.

Schwartz, Delmore (1913-1966), American poet, critic, writer and dramatist.

Schwartz, Eduard (1858-1940), German classical philologist.

Schweitzer, Albert (1875-1965), celebrated Alsatian theologian, philosopher, organist, music scholar and missionary physician; won the Nobel Prize for Peace (1952).

Schwenckfeld (von Ossig), Kaspar (1489-1561), German Protestant preacher, theologian and writer who founded the controversial movement known as the Reformation of the Middle Way.

Schwitters, Kurt (1887-1948), German artist and poet of the Dada school.

Scogan, Henry (c.1361-1407), English poet.

Scollard, Clinton (1860-1932), American poet and writer.

Scot, Michael (c.1175-c.1235), Scottish astrologer, wizard, mathematician and translator.

Scott, Alexander (c.1525-c.1585), Scottish poet.

Scott, Cyril (Meir) (1879-1970), English composer and poet.

Scott, Duncan Campbell (1862-1947), Canadian poet.

Scott, Evelyn (1893-1963), American novelist and poet.

Scott, F(rancis) R(eginald) (1899-1985), notable Canadian poet, socialist, educator and authority on constitutional law; son of Frederick George Scott.

Scott, Frederick George (1861-1944), Canadian archdeacon, poet, writer and social activist; father of F(rancis) R(eginald) Scott.

Scott, Geoffrey (1883-1929), English poet and biographer.

Scott, Michael (1789-1835), Scottish writer.

Scott, Paul Mark (1920-1978), English novelist, author of the "Raj Quartet" series *The Jewel in the Crown* (1966), *The Day of the Scorpion* (1968), *The Towers of Silence* (1971) and *A Division of the Spoils* (1975).

Scott, Sir Walter (1771-1832), renowned Scottish novelist and poet, creator of the historical novel and author of such remarkable examples as *Guy Mannering* (1815), *Old Mortality* (1816), *The Heart of Midlothian* (1818) and *Redgauntlet* (1824).

Scott, William Bell (1811-1890), English poet, artist and art critic.

Scott, Winfield Townley (1910-1968), American poet.

Scribe, (Augustin-) Eugène (1791-1861), popular French dramatist.

Scudder, Horace Elisha (1838-1902), American editor, novelist and biographer.

Scudéry, George de (1601-1667), French dramatist and critic; brother of Magdeleine de Scudéry.

Scudéry, Magdeleine de (1607-1701), French poet and novelist who was best known as Sapho; sister of George de Scudéry.

Scylitzes, John (11th Century), Byzantine historian, author of the *Synopsis historiarum*.

Sealsfield, Charles (actually Karl Postl) (1793-1864), Moravian-born Swiss journalist and writer who left valuable accounts of his travels in the US.

Seaman, Sir Owen (1861-1936), English poet and editor.

Seccomb, John (1708-1792), American clergyman and poet.

Seckendorff, Veit Ludwig von (1626-1692), German statesman and historian.

Sedaine, Michel-Jean (1719-1797), French dramatist, best known for his comedy *Le Philosophe sans le savoir* (1765; English translation as *The Duel,* 1772).

Sedgwick, Anne Douglas (1873-1935), American novelist and short-story writer.

Sedgwick, Catharine Maria (1789-1867), American writer; sister-in-law of Susan (Ridley) Sedgwick.

Sedgwick, Susan (Ridley) (c.1789-1867), American writer; sister-in-law of Catharine Maria Sedgwick.

Sedley, Sir Charles (1639-1701), English courtier, poet and dramatist, best remembered for his debauchery and wit at court.

Sedulius Scottus (9th Century), Irish poet and scholar.

Seeger, Alan (1888-1916), American poet who wrote the celebrated *I Have a Rendezvous with Death* (1916); died in World War I.

Seeley, Sir John Robert (1834-1895), English historian, particularly esteemed for *The Expansion of England in the Eighteenth Century* (1883).

Seers, Eugène (1865-1945), French-Canadian poet and critic who wrote under the name Louis Dantin.

Seferiades, Georgios (1900-1971), prominent Greek poet, essayist and diplomat who wrote under the name George Seferis; won the Nobel Prize for Literature (1963).

Seghers, Anna (actually Netti Radványi) (1900-1983), German novelist and short-story writer.

Ségur, Sophie Rostopchine, Comtesse de (1799-1874), Russian-born French writer of children's stories.

Sei Shōnagon (c.966-c.1013), Japanese diarist and poet, known for her wit at the imperial court.

Seifert, Jaroslav (1901-1986), distinguished Czech poet, won the Nobel Prize for Literature (1984).

Selden, John (1584-1654), English politician, antiquarian, Orientalist and writer.

Seldes, Gilbert (Vivian) (1893-1970), American journalist, drama critic, writer and editor.

Seligman, C(harles) G(abriel) (1873-1940), English anthropologist.

Selincourt, Ernest de (1870-1943), English literary scholar and critic.

Selvon, Samuel Dickson (1923-1994), Trinidadian-born Canadian writer, especially admired for his novel *The Lonely Londoners* (1956).

Semler, Johann Salomo (1725-1791), German Lutheran theologian who played an important role in the development of biblical textual criticism.

Semper, Gottfried (1803-1879), notable German architect and writer on art.

Sempill, Sir James (1566-1625), Scottish poet who wrote the satirical *A picktooth for the Pope, or the packman's paternoster.*

Sempill, Robert (c.1530-1595), English poet who was known for his wit and satire.

Sempill, Robert (c.1595-c.1665), Scottish poet.

Sénancour, Étienne Pivert de (1770-1846), French novelist, author of the notable *Obermann* (1804; English translation, 1903).

Senart, Émile (1847-1928), French Sanskrit scholar.

Seneca the Younger (actually Lucius Annaeus Seneca) (c.4 B.C.-65 A.D.), celebrated Roman philosopher, statesman and dramatist whose verse tragedies proved highly influential; committed suicide after the failure of Piso's conspiracy against the emperor Nero.

Senior, Nassau William (1790-1864), English economist, author of *An Outline of the Science of Political Economy* (1836).

Senoa, August (1838-1881), Croatian novelist, dramatist, poet, critic and editor.

Serafimovich, Alexander (1863-1949), Russian writer.

Serao, Matilde (1856-1927), Italian journalist and novelist.

Sergeant, John (1622-1707), English Roman Catholic priest and polemicist.

Sergius of Resaina (d. 536), Syrian Christian theologian, scholar and physician.

Serlio, Sebastiano (1475-1554), Italian architect, painter and theorist, particularly known for his influential treatise *Tutte l'opere d'architettura.*

Sérusier, (Louis-) Paul (-Henri) (1865-1927), French painter and theorist of the Postimpressionist school who spent his last years as a mystic.

Servetus, Michael (actually Miguel Serveto) (c.1511-1553), Spanish theologian and physician whose antiTrinitarian views in his *De Trinitatis Erroribus Libri VII* (1531; English translation, 1932) and *Christianismi Restitutio* (1553; English translation, 1932) riled both Roman Catholics and Protestants; was burned at the stake as a heretic by the Protestants.

Service, Robert W(illiam) (1874-1958), English-born Canadian poet and novelist.

Servius (4th Century), Latin grammarian who wrote an important commentary on Virgil.

Seton, Anya (c.1904-1990), American novelist; daughter of Ernest Thompson Seton.

Seton, Ernest Thompson (1860-1946), English-born American naturalist and writer; father of Anya Seton.

Settle, Elkanah (1648-1724), English dramatist.

Severian (4th-5th Century), Syrian theologian and bishop of Gabala who became a leading opponent of John Chrysostom.

Severus (c.465-538), learned Greek monk, theologian and patriarch of Antioch.

Sévigné, Marie de Rabutin-Chantal, Marquise de (1626-1696), French writer and epistolar.

Sewall, Samuel (1652-1730), English-born American merchant, judge, writer and diarist.

Seward, Anna (1747-1809), English poet and writer, author of the novel *Louisa* (1784).

Sewell, Anna (1820-1878), English writer who wrote *Black Beauty* (1877).

Sexton, Anne (née Harvey) (1928-1974), admired American poet who excelled in imagist verse; committed suicide.

Sextus Empiricus (3rd Century), Greek philosopher and historian.

Seyfeddin, Omer (1884-1920), Turkish writer.

Şeyhi or Sheykhi, Sinan (d.1428), Turkish poet.

Seymour-Smith, Martin (1928-1998), English literary critic, biographer, poet and editor.

Shaaban, Robert (1911-1962), Swahili poet and writer.

Shaara, Michael (Joseph Jr) (1929-1988), American writer.

Shabestari, (Sa'd od-Dīn) Mahmūd (c.1250-c.1320), Persian mystic who wrote the classic *Golshan-e rāz* (English translation as *The Mystic Rose Garden*, 1880) on Sūfism.

Shadwell, Thomas (c.1642-1692), prominent English dramatist and poet, especially remembered for his comedies of manners; became Poet Laureate of the United Kingdom (1688).

Shaftesbury, Anthony Ashley Cooper, 3rd Earl of (1671-1713), English politician and philosopher, author of *Characteristicks of Men, Manners, Opinions, Times* (1711).

Shakespeare, William (1564-1616), immortal English dramatist and poet, celebrated the world over as one of the supreme geniuses of literature.

Shao Yung (1011-1077), important Chinese philosopher of Neo-Confucian idealism.

Sharaf ad-Dīn 'Alī Yazdī (d.1454), Persian historian.

Sha 'rānī, ash-I (actually 'abd al-Wahhāb ibn Ahmad) (1492-1565), Egyptian scholar and mystic.

Sharp, Cecil (James) (1859-1924), English folk song and dance collector and editor.

Sharp, Granville (1735-1813), English scholar and philanthropist.

Sharp, William (1855-1905), Scottish writer, biographer, essayist and poet who wrote under the name Fiona Macleod.

Shaw, George Bernard (1856-1950), famous Irish dramatist, essayist, critic and socialist, author of such notable plays as *Caesar and Cleopatra* (1901), *Man and Superman* (1903), *Major Barbara* (1905) and *Saint Joan* (1923); won the Nobel Prize for Literature (1925).

Shaw, Irwin (1913-1984), American writer, dramatist and essayist.

Shawqī, Ahmad (1868-1932), outstanding Egyptian poet and dramatist.

Shchervatskoy, Fyodor Ippolitovich (1866-1942), learned Russian linguist and philosopher who was an outstanding authority on Buddhist philosophy.

Shebbeare, John (1709-1788), English pamphleteer and writer who was twice imprisoned for libel.

Sheffield, John, 3rd Earl of Mulgrave, later 1st Duke of Buckingham and Normanby (1648-1721), English statesman and essayist.

Sheldon, Charles M(onroe) (1857-1946), American preacher and writer, best known for his popular novel *In His Steps* (1896).

Sheldon, Edward (Brewster) (1886-1946), American dramatist, author of *The Nigger* (1909), *The Boss* (1911) and *Romance* (1913).

Shelley, Mary Wollstonecraft (née Godwin) (1797-1851), English novelist, poet and dramatist, best remembered for her novel *Frankenstein, or the Modern Prometheus* (1818); wife of Percy Bysshe Shelley.

Shelley, Percy Bysshe (1792-1822), celebrated English poet of extraordinary gifts and a writer of provocative prose, author of the renowned poem *Prometheus Unbound* (1819-20); drowned when his boat was capsized in a squall in Italy; husband of Mary Wollstonecraft (née Godwin) Shelley.

Shelton, Frederick William (1815-1881), American Episcopal clergyman and writer.

Shen Ts'ung-wen (1902-1988), Chinese writer, poet and dramatist who suffered persecution under the Communist regime.

Shenstone, William (1714-1763), English poet, best known for *The Judgement of Hercules* (1741) and *The Schoolmistress* (1742).

Shepard, Odell (1884-1967), American writer, critic and poet.

Shepard, Thomas (1605-1649), English-born American Calvinist preacher and writer, author of *The Sincere Convert* (1641).

Shepherd, William Robert (1871-1934), American historian who was especially known for his writings on Latin America.

Sheridan, Frances (1724-1766), English novelist, particularly remembered for *The Memoirs of Miss Sydney Biddulph* (1761; augmented edition, 1767); mother of Richard Brinsley (Butler) Sheridan.

Sheridan, Richard Brinsley (Butler) (1751-1816), famous Irish dramatist, impressario and politician, author of such outstanding plays as *The Rivals* (1775), *The Duenna* (1775) and *The School for Scandal* (1777); son of Frances Sheridan, grandson of Thomas Sheridan and grandfather of Caroline Elizabeth Sarah (née Sheridan) Norton.

Sheridan, Thomas (1687-1738), English schoolmaster and translator; grandfather of Richard Brinsley (Butler) Sheridan.

Sherlock, Thomas (1678-1761), English Anglican bishop and writer, author of *A Trial of the Witnesses of the Resurrection of Jesus* (1729); son of William Sherlock.

Sherlock, William (1641-1707), English churchman, dean of St Paul's and controversial writer, author of *A Practical Discourse concerning Death* (1689); father of Thomas Sherlock.

Sherman, Frank Dempster (1860-1916), American poet who often wrote under the name Felix Carmen.

Sherman, Stuart P(ratt) (1881-1926), American literary critic and essayist.

Sherriff, R(obert) C(edric) (1896-1975), English dramatist, screenwriter and novelist, author of the highly successful play *Journey's End* (1929).

Sherwood, Mary Martha (1775-1851), English writer of children's books.

Sherwood, Robert E(mmet) (1896-1955), American dramatist, author of *The Petrified Forest* (1935), *Idiot's Delight* (1936), *Abe Lincoln in Illinois* (1939) and *There Shall Be No Night* (1941).

Shevchenko, Taras Grigorievich (1814-1861), renowned Ukrainian poet and writer.

Shiga Naoya (1883-1971), remarkable Japanese writer, author of the outstanding novel *Anya Kōrō* (Road Through the Dark Night, 1921-37).

Shillaber, Benjamin Penhallow (1814-1890), American writer of a humorous bent.

Shimazaki Tōson (actually **Shimazaki Haruki**) **(1872-1943),** Japanese poet and novelist.

Shinran (1173-1262), influential Japanese Buddhist reformer and philosopher.

Shirer, William L(awrence) (1904-1993), American journalist and writer.

Shirley, James (1596-1666), outstanding English poet and dramatist, famous for such plays as *The Wittie Faire One* (1628), *The Traytor* (1631), *The Lady of Pleasure* (1635) and *The Cardinal* (1641); died in the Great Fire of London.

Shishkov, Alexander Semyonovich (1754-1841), Russian writer and statesman.

Shlonsky, Abraham (1900-1973), Ukrainian-born Israeli poet, editor and translator, creator of the Symbolist movement in Israel.

Sholem Aleichem (actually **Sholem Yakov Rabinowitz**) **(1859-1916),** famous Ukrainian-born American novelist, short-story writer and dramatist who wrote in Yiddish.

Sholokhov, Mikhail (Alexandrovich) (1905-1984), prominent Russian writer who was a proponent of socialist realism; won the Nobel Prize for Literature (1965).

Shorey, Paul (1857-1934), American scholar who was an authority on ancient Greek poetry and philosophy.

Shorthouse, Joseph Henry (1834-1903), English novelist, author of *John Inglesant* (1881).

Shotwell, James Thomson (1874-1965), American historian and diplomat who was an authority on international relations.

Shute, Nevil (actually **Nevil Shute Norway**) **(1899-1960),** Australian novelist, best known for *On the Beach* (1957).

Sickel, Theodor von (1826-1908), distinguished German historian who was an authority on the early middle ages.

Sidgwick, Henry (1838-1900), important English philosopher of Utilitarian views, author of *Methods of Ethics* (1874).

Sidney, Sir Philip (1554-1586), outstanding English poet, writer, statesman and military leader, author of *Arcadia, Astrophel and Stella* and *The Defence of Poesie*; died from wounds sustained in an attack on a Spanish convoy; brother of Mary Herbert Pembroke and Sir Robert Sidney.

Sidney, Sir Robert (1563-1626), English statesman and poet; brother of Mary Herbert Pembroke and Sir Philip Sidney.

Sidonius Apollinaris, Saint (actually **Gaius Sollius**) **(c.430-c.483),** Gallic-Roman poet who was canonized by the Roman Catholic Church.

Sienkiewicz, Henryk (1846-1916), eminent Polish novelist who wrote under the name Litwos, author of the outstanding trilogy *Ogniem i mieczem* (With Fire and Sword, 1884), *Potop* (The Deluge, 1886) and *Pan Wołodyjowski* (1887-88), and for *Quo Vadis?* (1896); won the Nobel Prize for Literature (1905).

Sigebert of Gembloux (c.1030-1112), Belgian Benedictine monk and chronicler.

Siger of Brabant (c.1240-c.1282), Belgian philosopher who espoused a radical Aristotelianism.

Sigonio, Carlo (1524-1584), Italian historian who was particularly known for his studies of ancient Greece.

Sigourney, Lydia Huntley (1791-1865), American poet of sentimental verse.

Sigurjónsson, Jóhann (1880-1919), notable Icelandic dramatist and poet, author of the remarkable play *Fjalla-Eyvindur* (1911; English translation as *Eyvind of the Hills*, 1916).

Sikelianós, Angelos (1884-1951), esteemed Greek poet who won distinction for his lyricism.

Silius Italicus (actually Tiberius Catius Asconius Silius Italicus) (25-101), Roman poet and politican, author of the epic *Punica*; committed suicide.

Sill, Edward Rowland (1841-1887), American poet and writer who often used the name Andrew Hedbrooke.

Sillanpää, Frans Eemil (1888-1964), distinguished Finnish novelist and short-story writer; won the Nobel Prize for Literature (1939).

Silone, Ignazio (actually Secondo Tranquilli) (1900-1978), prominent Italian novelist and short-story writer whose early advocacy of socialism, and then Communism gave way to a Christian worldview.

Silva, Antônio José da (1705-1739), gifted Brazilian-born Portuguese dramatist whose Jewish heritage led to his persecution and death at the hands of the Inquisition.

Silva, José Asuncion (1865-1896), notable Colombian poet; committed suicide.

Simenon, Georges (-Joseph-Christian) (1903-1989), popular Belgian-French novelist and short-story writer whose output was prolific.

Simeon, Charles (1759-1836), English Anglican clergyman and biblical expositor.

Simeon of Durham (11th-12th Century), English monk and chronicler.

Simmel, Georg (1858-1918), German sociologist and philosopher.

Simms, William Gilmore (1806-1870), eminent American novelist, short-story writer, poet and critic who was most appreciated for his historical novels.

Simon, Jules (-François) (1814-1896), French political leader and theorist.

Simon, Richard (1638-1712), French biblical scholar whose works presaged modern critical methods.

Simonides of Ceas (c.556-c.468 B.C.), Greek poet and epigrammatist; uncle of Bacchylides.

Simplicius of Cilicia (6th Century), Greek philosopher.

Simrock, Karl Joseph (1802-1876), German literary scholar and poet.

Şinasi, İbrahim (1826-1871), important Turkish writer, dramatist and poet.

Sinclair, Catherine (1800-1864), Scottish writer of children's books.

Sinclair, Isaak von (1775-1815), German diplomat, philosopher and poet.

Sinclair, May (actually Mary Amelia St Clair Sinclair) (1863-1946), English novelist.

Sinclair, Upton (Beall) (1878-1968), American novelist and socialist, best remembered for his novel *The Jungle* (1906).

Singer, Isaac Bashevis (1904-1991), admired Polish-born American novelist and short-story writer; won the Nobel Prize for Literature (1978).

Singer, Israel Joshua (1893-1944), Polish-born American novelist and dramatist.

Singmaster, Elsie (1879-1958), American novelist.

Sinyavsky, Andrei (Donatovich) (1925-1997), prominent Russian novelist, short-story writer and dissident who often wrote under the name Abram Tertz.

Siôn Cent (c.1367-c.1430), Welsh poet.

Sirhindī, Shaykh Ahmad (1564-1624), Indian mystic and theologian of orthodox Islām.

Siringo, Charles (1855-1928), American writer who was best known for his autobiography *A Texas Cowboy, or Fifteen Years on the Hurricane Deck of a Spanish Pony* (1885) and *Lone Star Cowboy* (1919).

Sismondi, Jean-Charles-Léonard Simonde de (1773-1842), Swiss economist and historian, author of the influential *Historie des républiques italiennes du moyen âge* (16 volumes, 1809-18; English translation as *History of the Italian Republics in the Middle Ages*, 1831).

Sitwell, Dame Edith (Louisa) (1887-1964), esteemed English poet and writer whose notable works included *Façade* (1923), *Gold Coast Customs* (1929), *Street Songs* (1942), *Green Song* (1944), *Song of the Cold* (1945), *Gardeners and Astronomers* (1953) and *The Outcasts* (1962); sister of Sir (Francis) Osbert (Sacheverell) 5th Baronet Sitwell, and Sir Sacheverell, 6th Baronet Sitwell.

Sitwell, Sir (Francis) Osbert (Sacheverell), 5th Baronet (1892-1969), prominent English poet and writer; brother of Dame Edith (Louisa) Sitwell and Sir Sacheverell, 6th Baronet Sitwell.

Sitwell, Sir Sacheverell, 6th Baronet (1897-1988), notable English writer, art critic and poet; brother of Dame Edith (Louisa) Sitwell and Sir (Francis) Osbert (Sacheverell), 5th Baronet Sitwell.

Sjöberg, Birger (1885-1929), innovative Swedish poet of modernism.

Skarga, Piotr (actually Piotr Skarga Poweski) (1536-1612), Polish Jesuit preacher and writer.

Skeat, W(alter) W(illiam) (1835-1912), outstanding English literary editor of Old and Middle English literature.

Skeffington, Sir Lumley St George (1771-1850), English dramatist.

Skelton, John (c.1460-1529), remarkable English poet, a master of political and religious satire and creator of the poetic form known as Skeltonics.

Skelton, Robin (1925-1997), English-born Canadian poet, writer, translator, visual artist and occultist.

Skinner, B(urrhus) F(rederic) (1904-1990), significant American behavioral psychologist, author of *Walden Two* (1948).

Skinner, Constance Lindsay (1879-1939), Canadian-born American writer.

Skinner, Cornelia Otis (1901-1979), American actress and writer.

Skram, Amalie (née Alver) (1847-1905), Norwegian novelist of the Naturalist school.

Slauerhoff, Jan Jacob (1898-1936), Dutch poet of pessimistic verse.

Slaveyko, Pencho Petkov (1866-1912), Bulgarian poet, essayist and translator; son of Petko Rachev Slaveykov.

Slaveyko, Petko Rachev (1827-1895), Bulgarian poet, journalist and politician; father of Pencho Petkov Slaveykov.

Sleidanus, Johannes (1506-1556), German historian who wrote an account of the Protestant Reformation.

Slessor, Kenneth (Adolf) (1901-1971), Australian poet and journalist, author of the notable poem *Beach Burial*.

Slonimsky, Nicolas (actually Nikolai Leonidovch Slonimsky) (1894-1995), remarkable Russian-born American music scholar and lexicographer whose learning was complemented by a penchant for witty asides.

Słowacki, Juliusz (1809-1849), famous Polish poet and dramatist, a leading proponent of Romanticism.

Small, Albion (Woodbury) (1854-1926), American sociologist who became best known for his writings on political science and economics.

Smalley, George Washburn (1833-1916), American journalist and writer.

Smart, Christopher (1722-1771), English poet and translator, particularly known for *A Song to David* (1763).

Smedley, Francis Edward (1818-1864), English editor and novelist.

Smellie, William (c.1740-1795), Scottish natural historian, writer and translator, was the compiler of the first edition of the *Encyclopaedia Britannica* (1768-71).

Smet, Pierre-Jean de (1801-1873), Belgian-born American Jesuit missionary and writer who became a friend of Indian tribes of the western US.

Smiles, Samuel (1812-1904), Scottish writer, best remembered for his didactic *Self-Help, with Illustrations of Character and Conduct* (1859).

Smith, Adam (1723-1790), outstanding Scottish philosopher and economist, author of the celebrated study *An Inquiry into the nature and causes of the Wealth of Nations* (1776).

Smith, Alexander (1830-1867), Scottish poet and essayist.

Smith, A(rthur) J(ames) M(arshall) (1902-1980), Canadian poet, critic and editor.

Smith, Betty (Wehner) (1904-1972), American novelist.

Smith, Chard Powers (1894-1977), American writer and poet.

Smith, Charles Henry (1826-1903), American writer of humorous works who wrote under the name Bill Arp.

Smith, Charlotte (née Turner) (1749-1806), English novelist, short-story writer and poet.

Smith, Elihu Hubbard (1771-1798), American physician, writer and poetry anthologist.

Smith, Elizabeth Oakes (1806-1893), American novelist, short-story writer and essayist; wife of Seba Smith.

Smith, Francis Hopkinson (1838-1915), American writer and illustrator; grandson of Francis Hopkinson.

Smith, George (1840-1876), English archaeologist, author of the *Chaldean Account of Genesis* (1876).

Smith, Sir George Adam (1856-1942), Scottish preacher and Semitic scholar who was a leading proponent of the higher criticism of the Old Testament.

Smith, Horatio (Horace) (1779-1849), English novelist, dramatist and poet, collaborated with his brother James on *Rejected Addresses* (1812) and *Horace of London* (1813).

Smith, James (1775-1839), English writer, collaborated with his brother Horatio (Horace) on *Rejected Addresses* (1812) and *Horace of London* (1813).

Smith, John (c.1580-1631), famous English adventurer, explorer, writer and cartographer, the principal organizer of Jamestown, Virginia, the first permanent English settlement in North America.

Smith, Lillian (Eugenia) (1897-1966), American writer.

Smith, (Lloyd) Logan Pearsall (1865-1946), American essayist, writer and poet.

Smith, Margaret Bayard (1778-1844), American novelist.

Smith, Preserved (1880-1941), distinguished American historian, author of *The Age of the Reformation* (1920).

Smith, Richard Penn (1799-1854), American dramatist and writer.

Smith, Samuel Francis (1808-1895), American clergyman, poet and writer.

Smith, Samuel Stanhope (1750-1819), American clergyman, educator and scholar.

Smith, Seba (1792-1868), American journalist and writer who was known for his creation of the humorous Major Jack Downing; husband of Elizabeth Oakes Smith.

Smith, Sol(omon Franklin) (1801-1869), American actor, theater manager, lawyer, editor and writer.

Smith, Stevie (actually Florence Margaret Smith (1902-1971), English poet and novelist.

Smith, Sydney (1771-1845), prominent English clergyman and essayist.

Smith, Sydney Goodsir (1915-1975), New Zealand-born Scottish poet and critic.

Smith, Thorne (1892-1934), American writer who was known as a humorist.

Smith, William (1727-1803), Scottish-born American Episcopal clergyman and educator who was a champion of conservative views.

Smith, William (1728-1793), American-born English lawyer, historian and chief justice of Canada (1786-93).

Smith, Sir William (1813-1893), English classical scholar and lexicographer.

Smith, William Robertson (1846-1894), Scottish Semitic scholar and encyclopaedist, editor-in-chief of the *Encyclopaedia Britannica* and author of *Lectures on the Religion of the Semites* (1889).

Smith, Winchell (1871-1933), American actor, theatre director and dramatist.

Smollett, Tobias (George) (1721-1771), notable Scottish novelist, author of *The Adventures of Roderick Random* (1748), *The Adventures of Peregrine Pickle* (1751), *The Adventures of Sir Launcelot Greaves* (1762) and *The Expedition of Humphry Clinker* (1771).

Smyth, John (d. 1612), English Nonconformist minister who championed the cause of religious libertarianism.

Snelling, William Joseph (1804-1848), American journalist, reformer and writer.

Snellman, Johan Vilhelm (1806-1881), prominent Finnish statesman and philosopher.

Snider, Denton Jaques (1841-1925), American scholar, writer and poet.

Snoilsky, Carl Johan Gustaf, Count (1841-1903), outstanding Swedish poet of social and political themes.

Snorri Sturluson (1179-1241), Icelandic chieftan, historian and poet, author of the *Prose Edda*, a handbook on poetics; was killed by order of King Haakon IV of Norway; uncle of Sturla Thordarson.

Snow, C(harles) P(ercy), Baron Snow of Leicester (1905-1980), prominent English writer, scientist and government official, especially known for his "Strangers and Brothers" novels (11 volumes) and for *The Two Cultures and the Scientific Revolution* (1959).

Snow, (Charles) Wilbert (1884-1977), American poet.

Sōami (1472-1525), influential Japanese painter, art critic and poet.

Socinus, Faustus (actually Fausto Paolo Sozzini) (1539-1604), Italian theologian whose anti-Trinitarian views brought him into conflict with the Inquisition, author of *De sacrae scripturae auctoritate* (1570), *De Jesu Christo servatore* (1594) and *Christianae religionis institutio* (unfinished); nephew of Laelius Socinus.

Socinus, Laelius (actually Lelio Francesco Maria Socini) (1525-1562), Italian theologian of anti-Trinitarian beliefs; uncle of Faustus Socinus.

Socrates (c.470-399 B.C.), famous Greek philosopher who was a major influence on Plato and Aristotle; was indicted for impiety, found guilty and compelled to take his own life by hemlock poisoning.

Socrates Scholasticus (380-c.450), Byzantine historian who wrote the important *Historia ecclesiastica* (7 volumes).

Soden, Hermann, Feiherr von (1852-1914), German biblical scholar who was known for his studies on the New Testament.

Söderberg, Hjalmar Erik Fredrik (1849-1941), Danish novelist, short-story writer and critic.

Söderblom, Nathan (1866-1931), Swedish Lutheran archbishop and scholar who was particularly known for his studies in comparative religion; won the Nobel Prize for Peace (1930).

Södergran, Edith (Irene) (1892-1923), significant Finnish poet, founder of the modernist movement of Finnish poets who wrote in Swedish.

Soga, Tiyo (1829-1871), South African minister, hymnist, translator, journlist and anthologist, a pioneering figure in Xosa literary circles.

Sohlman, (Per) August (Ferdinand) (1824-1874), Swedish journalist who was a prominent figure in the Pan-Scandinavian movement.

Sokolow, Nahum (1861-1936), Polish Jewish writer and Zionist.

Solís y Ribadeneyra, Antonio de (1610-1686), Spanish poet and dramatist.

Solomós, Dhionísios, Count (1798-1857), Greek poet.

Solon (c.640-559 B.C.), renowned Greek lawgiver and poet.

Soloukhin, Vladimir Alexeievich (1924-1997), Russian writer and poet.

Solovyov, Vladimir Sergeievich (1853-1900), Russian mystic and philosopher.

Somerville, William (1675-1742), English poet.

Sommer, Ferdinand (1875-1962), German linguist who was an authority on Hittite and classical languages.

Sommo, Judah Leone ben Isaac (actually **Yeuda Sommo**) **(1527-1592),** Italian dramatist and writer on the theatre, author of the first Hebrew drama *Tzahut bedihuta de-qiddushin* (An Eloquent Comedy of Marriage, 1550).

Sophocles (c.496-406 B.C.), great Greek dramatist, author of the celebrated *Oedipus Rex*.

Sophron of Syracuse (4th Century B.C.), Greek poet.

Sophronius (c.560-638), Syrian monk, theologian and patriarch of Jerusalem.

Sordello (c.1200-c.1268), famous Italian adventurer and poet.

Sorel, Georges (-Eugène) (1847-1922), French socialist and writer, author of *Réflexions sur la violence* (1908; English translation as *Reflections on Violence*, 1914).

Sorell, Walter (1905-1997), Austrian-born American writer on the theatre and dance.

Sorge, Reinhard Johannes (1892-1916), German dramatist of expressionist plays.

Sorley, Charles Hamilton (1895-1915), Scottish poet; died in World War I.

Sorokin, Pitirim A(lexandrovich) (1889-1968), Russian-born American sociologist, author of *Social and Cultural Dynamics* (4 volumes, 1937-41), *Man and Society in Calamity* (1942) and *Altruistic Love* (1950).

Sorsky, Saint Nil (actually **Nikolai Maykov**) **(1433-1508),** Russian monk, mystic and writer.

Soupault, Philippe (1897-1990), French poet, novelist and essayist.

Sousa, Frei Luís de (actually **Manuel de Sousa Coutinho**) **(1555-1632),** Portuguese Dominican monk and chronicler of the order in his *História de São Domingos* (3 volumes, 1623, 1662, 1678).

Soutar, William (1898-1943), Scottish poet and diarist.

South, Robert (1634-1716), English Anglican preacher of a sarcastic bent, author of *Animadversions* (1690).

Southerne, Thomas (1660-1746), Irish dramatist who wrote *The Fatal Marriage* (1694) and *Oroonoko* (1696).

Southery, Robert (1774-1843), notable English poet and writer, especially admired for his prose; became Poet Laureate of the United Kingdom (1813).

Southwell, Robert (1561-1595), English poet and Jesuit priest, author of *The Burning Babe* and *St Peters Complaynt*; was martyred.

Southworth E(mma) D(orothy) E(liza) N(evitte) (1819-1899), American novelist.

Soútsos, Aléxandros (1803-1863), important Greek poet who was the creator of Greek Romantic verse.

Sozomen (c.400-c.450), Greek church historian.

Spalatin, Georg (actually **Georg Burkhardt**) **(1484-1545),** German historian and Humanist who was a leading figure in the Reformation.

Sparks, Jared (1789-1866), American historian and educator.

Spearman, Charles E(dward) (1863-1945), English psychologist, author of *The Nature of 'Intelligence' and the Principles of Cognition* (1923) and *The Abilities of Man* (1927).

Spedding, James (1808-1881), English editor and writer, author of *Evenings with a Reviewer* (1848) and editor of *The Works of Francis Bacon* (7 volumes, 1857-59).

Speed, John (c.1552-1629), English historian and cartographer.

Spegel, Haquin (1645-1714), Swedish historian.

Spelman, Sir Henry (c.1564-1641), English antiquarian and historian who was known for his studies in ecclesiastical and legal history.

Spence, (James) Lewis Thomas Chalmers (1874-1955), Scottish poet and anthropologist.

Spence, Joseph (1699-1768), English clergyman, scholar and anecdotist.

Specne, Thomas (1750-1814), English reformer and poet who was an advocate of the socialization of land.

Spencer, Herbert (1820-1903), eminent English philosopher who was a leading evolutionist, author of *The Synthetic Philosophy (The Principles of Psychology*, 1855, *The Principles of Sociology*, 3 volumes, 1876-96 and *The Principles of Ethics*, 2 volumes, 1892-93) and *The Man versus the State* (1884).

Spender, Sir Stephen (Harold) (1909-1995), distinguished English poet and critic, one of the most influential figures of the Oxford generation.

Spener, Philipp Jakob (1635-1705), influential German Lutheran theologian and reformer who was a major figure in the Pietist movement, author of *Pia Desideria* (1675; English translation as *Pious Desires*, 1964).

Spengler, Oswald (1880-1936), important German philosopher of history, author of *Der Untergang des Abendlandes* (2 volumes, 1918, 1922; English translation as *The Decline of the West*, 1926-28).

Spenser, Edmund (1552-1599), great English poet who wrote the celebrated masterpiece *The Faerie Queene* (6 parts, 1590-96),

Speusippus (d. c.338 B.C.), Greek philosopher.

Speyer, Leonora (1872-1956), American poet.

Sphrantzes, George (15th Century), Byzantine monk and historian.

Spicer, Jack (1925-1965), American poet.

Spieghel, Henric Laurenszoon (1549-1612), gifted Dutch poet, author of the *Hertspiegel* (Heartmirror).

Spielhagen, Friedrich von (1829-1911), German novelist and dramatist, author of the novels *Problematische Naturen* (4 volumes, 1861; English translation as *Problematic Characters*, 1869) and *Sturmflut* (3 volumes, 1877; English translation as *The Breaking of the Storm*, 1877).

Spingarn, J(oel) E(lias) (1875-1939), American poet and critic.

Spinoza, Benedict (1632-1677), great Dutch philosopher and religious expositor of the Rationalist school, author of the *Tractatus Theologico-Politicus* (1670; English translation, 1889), *Tractatus de Intellectus Emendatione* (1677; English translation, 1899) and *Ethica in Ordine Geometrico Demonstrata* (1677; English translation as *Ethics*, 1894).

Spitta, (Julius August) Philipp (1841-1894), eminent German music scholar, author of a major study of Johann Sebastian Bach (2 volumes, 1873, 1880; English translation, 3 volumes, 1884-85).

Spitteler, Carl (Friedrich Georg) (1845-1924), imaginative Swiss poet and novelist.

Spofford, Harriet (Elizabeth) Prescott (1835-1921), American novelist, short-story writer and poet.

Spottiswoode, Alicia Ann, Lady John Scott (1810-1900), Scottish poet and songwriter, author of *Annie Laurie* and *Durrisdeer*.

Sprague, Charles (1791-1875), American poet.

Sprat, Thomas (1635-1713), English Anglican bishop, dean, historian and poet.

Sprigg, Christopher St John (1907-1937), English critic, poet and novelist of a Marxist persuasion who often wrote under the name Christopher Caudwell; died in the Spanish Civil War.

Spring, Howard (1889-1965), American novelist, best known for *O Absalom!* (1938).

Spurgeon, Caroline (1869-1942), English literary scholar who was known for her stylistic analysis of Shakespeare.

Spurgeon, C(harles) H(addon) (1834-1892), English Baptist minister and writer.

Spyri, Johanna (née Heusser) (1829-1901), Swiss writer, author of the children's classic *Heidi* (2 volumes, 1880-81).

Squier, Ephraim George (1821-1888), American journalist, diplomat and archaeologist.

Squire, Sir J(ohn) C(ollings) (1884-1958), English critic, editor, poet and dramtist.

Ssu-ma Ch'ien (c.145-c.85 B.C.), outstanding Chinese historian, astronomer and calendar reformer.

Ssu-ma Hsiang-ju (179-117 B.C.), important Chinese poet who was a master of descriptive verse.

Ssu-ma Kuang (1019-1086), Chinese statesman, scholar and poet.

Stace, W(alter) T(erence) (1886-1967), English philosopher.

Stacpoole, H(enry) de Vere (1863-1951), English novelist, particularly remembered for *The Blue Lagoon* (1908).

Stackton, David (Derek) (1923-1968), American novelist.

Staël, Madame de (actually Anne-Louise-Germaine Necker) (1766-1817), significant French novelist and critic, especially known for her writings on the Romantic movement.

Staff, Leopold (1878-1957), Polish poet, dramatist and translator.

Stafford, Jean (1915-1979), American novelist.

Stagnelius, Erik Johan (1793-1823), remarkable Swedish poet of Romanticism.

Stallings, Laurence (1894-1968), American novelist, dramatist and screenwriter.

Stammler, Rudolf (1856-1938), German legal philosopher.

Stangerup, Henrik (1937-1998), Danish writer and film director.

Stanley, Arthur Penrhyn (1815-1881), English historian and biographer.

Stanley, Sir Henry Morton (1841-1904), Welsh explorer and journalist, author of *In Darkest Africa* (1890) and *Through South Africa* (1898).

Stanley, Thomas (1625-1678), English writer, poet and translator, author of *The History of Philosophy* (1655-62).

Stansbury, Joseph (1742-1809), English-born American poet who defended the Loyalist cause during the American Revolution; grandfather of Caroline Stansbury Kirkland.

Stanton, Elizabeth Cady (1815-1902), prominent American suffragist, reformer and writer.

Stanton, Frank Lebby (1857-1927), American poet.

Stanyhurst, Richard (1547-1618), Irish historian and poet.

Stark, Dame Freya (1893-1993), English travel writer and photographer.

Staszic, Stanisław (Wawrzyniec) (1755-1826), Polish political writer, poet and translator.

Statius, Publius Papinius (c.45-96), Roman poet, admired for his *Silvae* and *Thebaïs*.

Stead, Christina Ellen (1902-1983), Australian novelist, best known for *The Man Who Loved Children* (1940; revised edition, 1960).

Stead, Robert J(ames) C(ampbell) (1880-1959), Canadian writer and poet.

Stead, W(illiam) T(homas) (1849-1912), English journalist and reformer; died in the sinking of the *Titanic.*

Stedman, Edmund Clarence (1833-1908), American poet, essayist, critic and banker.

Steegmuller, Francis (1906-1994), American biographer, critic, novelist, editor and translator.

Steele, Sir Richard (1672-1729), Irish essayist, journalist, dramatist and politician.

Steele, Wilbur Daniel (1886-1970), American novelist, short-story writer and dramatist.

Steendam, Jacob (c.1616-c.1672), Dutch poet.

Steevens, George (1736-1800), English editor who collaborated with Samuel Johnson in editing the plays of Shakespeare (10 volumes, 1773).

Stefánsson, Davíd (1895-1964), Icelandic poet, novelist and dramatist.

Stefansson, Vilhjalmur (1879-1962), Canadian explorer, ethnologist and writer.

Steffen, Albert (1884-1963), Swiss novelist and dramatist.

Steffens, Henrik (1773-1845), Norwegian-born German philosopher and scientist.

Steffens, (Joseph) Lincoln (1866-1936), American journalist, lecturer and writer, one of the most prominent members of the muckrakers.

Stegner, Wallace (Earle) (1909-1993), notable American writer and poet who was one of the leading lights in avant-garde circles.

Stein, Charlotte von (née von Schardt) (1742-1827), German writer, best known for her close relationship with Goethe.

Stein, Edith (1891-1942), German-born Jewish Roman Catholic convert, nun and philosopher who took the name Teresa Benedicta of the Cross, author of the treatise *Studie über Joannes a Cruce: Kreuzwswissenschaft* (published 1950; English translation as *The Science of the Cross*, 1955); was arrested by the Nazis as a non-Catholic Aryan and put to death at the Auschwitz concentration camp.

Stein, Gertrude (1874-1946), famous American writer and poet, one of the principal avant-garde literary figures of her era; sister of Leo Stein.

Stein, Leo (1872-1947), American writer; brother of Gertrude Stein.

Stein, Sir (Mark) Aurel (1862-1943), Hungarian-born English archaeologist and geographer.

Steinbeck, John (Ernst) (1902-1968), prominent American novelist and short-story writer whose masterpiece was *The Grapes of Wrath* (1939); won the Nobel Prize for Literature (1962).

Steiner, Rudolf (1861-1925), Austrian-born Swiss scientist, educator, artist and writer who founded the spiritual movement known as anthroposophy.

Steinheim, Solomon Ludwig (1789-1866), German philosopher who was known for his writings on Jewish religious philosophy.

Steinschneider, Moritz (1816-1907), German scholar.

Stendahl (actually Marie-Henri Beyle) (1783-1842), famous French novelist, author of the celebrated *Le Rouge et le noir* (1830; English translation as *The Red and the Black,* 1926) and *La Chartreuse de Parme* (1839; English translation as *The Charterhouse of Parma,* 1925).

Stephansson, Stephan G (actually **Stefán Guomundarson**) **(1853-1927),** gifted Icelandic-born Canadian poet who was much esteemed for his collection *Andvökur* (Sleepless Nights, 1909-38).

Stephen, Sir James (1789-1859), English colonial administrator and historian, author of *Essays in Ecclesiastical Biography* (1849) and *Lectures on the History of France* (1851); father of Sir James Fitzjames Stephen and Sir Leslie Stephen.

Stephen, Sir James Fitzjames (1829-1894), English colonial adminstrator, judge and writer, author of a *General View of the Criminal Law of England* (1863), *Liberty, Equality, Fraternity* (1873) and *History of the Criminal Law of England* (1883); son of Sir James Stephen, brother of Sir Leslie Stephen and father of James Kenneth Stephen.

Stephen, James Kenneth (1859-1892), English journalist and poet, author of *Lapsus Calami* (1891) and *Quo Musa Tendis* (1891); son of Sir James Fitzjames Stephen; died insane.

Stephen, Sir Leslie (1832-1904), English editor, essayist and biographer, author of *The Playground of Europe* (1871), *History of English Thought in the 18th Century* (1876) and *English Literature and Society in the Eighteenth Century* (1904), and editor of the *Dictionary of National Biography* (1882-91); son of Sir James Stephen, brother of Sir James Fitzjames Stephen and father of Virginia Woolf.

Stephens, Alfred George (1865-1933), Australian journalist and literary critic.

Stephens, Ann Sophia (1810-1886), American writer, best known for her dime novel *Malaeska:The Indian Wife of the White Hunter* (1860).

Stephens, James (1882-1950), Irish poet, novelist and short-story writer.

Stephens, John Lloyd (1805-1852), American traveller and archaeologist.

Sterling, George (1869-1926), American poet and writer; committed suicide.

Sterling, James (c.1701-1763), Irish-born American poet and dramatist.

Sterling, John (1806-1844), Scottish essayist, novelist and poet.

Sterne, Laurence (1713-1768), famous Irish-born novelist and clergyman, author of the celebrated *The Life and Opinions of Tristam Shandy* (9 volumes, 1759-67).

Stesichorus (c.630-c.554 B.C.), Greek poet who was known for his *Calyce, Daphnis* and *Rhadine.*

Stevens, Abel (1815-1897), American Methodist clergyman and historian of his church.

Stevens, James (Floyd) (1892-1971), American novelist and short-story writer.

Stevens, Wallace (1879-1955), remarkable American poet of great intellect.

Stevenson, Robert Louis (1850-1894), popular Scottish novelist, essayist, literary critic and poet, author of the classic novels *Treasure Island* (1881), *Kidnapped* (1886), *The Strange Case of Dr. Jekyll and Mr. Hyde* (1886) and *Black Arrow* (1888).

Steward, Julian (1902-1972), influential American anthropologist, author of *Theory of Culture Change: The Methodology of Multilinear Evolution* (1955).

Steward, Donald (Ogden) (1894-1980), American writer, dramatist and screenwriter.

Stewart, Douglas (Alexander) (1913-1985), New Zealand-born Australian poet, dramatist, writer and critic.

Stewart, Dugald (1753-1828), Scottish philosopher, author of *Elements of the Philosophy of the Human Mind* (3 volumes, 1792, 1814, 1827).

Stewart, George R(ippey) (1895-1980), American writer and educator.

Stewart, J(ohn) I(nnes) M(ackintosh) (1906-1994), Scottish novelist, short-story writer and literary critic who often wrote under the name Michael Innes.

Stickney, (Joseph) Trumbull (1874-1904), American poet.

Stiernhielm, Georg (Olofson) (1598-1672), august Swedish poet and linguist, one of the principal figures in the development of Swedish poetry.

Stifter, Adalbert (1805-1868), esteemed Austrian novelist and short-story writer.

Stiles, Ezra (1727-1795), American Congregational minister, educator and scholar; grandson of Edward Taylor.

Stillingfleet, Edward (1635-1699), English Anglican bishop and scholar.

Stilo Praeconinus, Lucius Aelius (c.154-74 B.C.), Roman literary scholar.

Stirling, Sir William Alexander, 1st Earl of (c.1576-1640), Scottish courtier, statesman and poet.

Stirner, Max (actually **Johann Kaspar Schmidt**) **(1806-1856),** German philosopher who espoused anti-statist views, author of *Der Einzige und sein Eigentum* (1845; English translation as *The Ego and His Own*, 1907).

Stockton, Frank R (actually **Francis Richard Stockton**) **(1834-1902),** American novelist and short-story writer.

Stoddard, Charles Warren (1843-1909), American writer and poet.

Stoddard, Richard Henry (1825-1903), American poet, critic and essayist.

Stoddard, Solomon (1643-1729), American Congregational clergyman and polemicist; grandfather of Jonathan Edwards.

Stoddard, William Osborn (1835-1925), American writer who wrote a biography of Abraham Lincoln (1884) and numerous books for boys.

Stoker, Bram (actually Abraham Stoker) (1847-1912), Irish novelist and short-story writer, author of the celebrated horror novel *Dracula* (1897).

Stolberg, Christian, Count of (1748-1821), German poet and translator; brother of Friedrich Leopold, Count of Stolberg.

Stolberg, Friedrich Leopold, Count of (1750-1819), German poet, dramatist and translator; brother of Christian, Count of Stolberg.

Stone, Barton Warren (1772-1844), American Protestant clergyman and writer, one of the principal figures in the founding of the religious denomination known as the Disciples of Christ.

Stone, Irving (1903-1989), American writer of popular fictionalized biographies.

Stone, John Augustus (1800-1834), American actor and dramatist.

Stone, Samuel (1602-1663), English-born American Nonconformist clergyman.

Stone, William Leete (1792-1844), American journalist and writer; father of William Leete Stone Jr.

Stone, William Leete Jr (1835-1908), American journalist and writer; son of William Leete Stone.

Stong, Phil(ip Duffield) (1899-1957), American writer, journalist and screenwriter.

Stopes, Marie (Charlotte Carmichael) (1880-1958), English palaeobotanist, dramatist and poet who became best known as a pioneering crusader for birth control.

Storm, (Hans) Theodor Woldsen, (1817-1888), distinguished German writer and poet, an outstanding exponent of the novella.

Storni, Alfonsina (1892-1938), Outstanding Argentine poet, particularly esteemed for his *El dulce daño* (The Sweet Injury, 1918); committed suicide.

Story, Isaac (1774-1803), American poet and writer.

Story, Joseph (1779-1845), influential American jurist and legal scholar who served as an associate justice of the US Supreme Court (1811-45).

Story, William Wetmore, (1819-1895), American sculptor and poet.

Stout, George Frederick (1860-1944), English psychologist and philosopher, author of *Analytic Psychology* (2 volumes, 1896), *Manual of Psychology* (1899; 5th edition, 1938) and *Mind and Matter* (1931).

Stort, Rex (Todhunter) (1886-1975), American novelist, creator of the famous detective Nero Wolfe.

Stow, John (1525-1605), English antiquarian, author of the celebrated *Survey of London* (1598; revised edition, 1603).

Stowe, Calvin Ellis (1802-1886), American religious scholar and educator; husband of Harriet (Elizabeth) Beecher Stowe.

Stowe, Harriet (Elizabeth) Beecher (1811-1896), American writer and poet who wrote the famous novel *Uncle Tom's Cabin or, Life Among the Lowly* (1852); daughter of Lyman Beecher, sister of Catherine E(sther) and Henry Ward Beecher, and wife of Calvin Ellis Stowe.

Stowell, William Scott, Baron (1745-1836), English judge who greatly influenced the doctrines of admiralty law.

Strabo (c.64 B.C.-c.24 A. D.), important Greek geographer and historian.

Strachey, (Evelyn) John (St Loe) (1901-1963), English politician and writer who first embraced Communism but later espoused Socialism.

Strachey, (Giles) Lytton (1880-1932), English Biographer and critic, best known for his *Eminent Victorians* (1918) and *Queen Victoria* (1921).

Strachwitz, Moritz (Karl Wilhelm Anton), Graf von (1822-1847), German poet who was admired for his *Lieder eines Erwachenden* (Songs of Awakening, 1842) and *Neue Gedichte* (New Poems, published 1848).

Strangford, Percy Clinton, 6th Viscount (1780-1855), English diplomat and poet author of *Poems from the Portuguese of Camoens* (1803).

Straparola, Giovan Francesco (16th Century) Italian writer, author of the novelle *Piacevoli Notti* (Pleasant Nights, 2 volumes, 1550, 1553).

Strashimirov, Anton (1872 -1937), Bulgarian writer who espoused realism in his works.

Stratemeyer, Edward (1863 - 1930), American writer of popular fiction for boys and girls.

Stratton-Porter, Gene(va) (1863-1924), American writer of fiction for girls, best remembered for *Freckles* (1904) and *A Girl of the Limberlost* (1909).

Strauss, David Friedrich (1808-1874), influential but controversial German Protestant theologian, philosopher and writer who espoused the "myth theory" of the life of Christ, author of *Das Leben Jesu kritisch bearbeitet* (2 volumes, 1835-36; English translation as *The Life of Jesus, Critically Examined*, 1846) and *Der alte und neue Glaube* (1872; English translation as *The Old and the New*, 1873).

Street, Alfred Billings (1811-1881), American lawyer, librarian and poet.

Streeter, Edward (1891-1976), American writer.

Streeter, Burnett Hillman (1874-1037), English theologian and biblical scholar, author of *The Four Gospels: A Study of Origins* (1924) and *The Primitive Church (1929).*

Streitberg, Wilhelm (August) (1864-1925), German historical linguist.

Stretton, Hesba (actually Sarah Smith) (1832-1911), English Writer.

Streuvels, Stijn (actually Frank Lateur) (1871-1969), distinguished Belgian novelist and short-story writer who wrote in Flemish.

Strickland, Agnes (1796-1874), English biographer, poet and children's writer, author of *Lives of the Queens of England* (in collaboration with her sister Elizabeth, 12 volumes, 1840-48) *Lives of the Queens of Scotland and English Princesses* (8 volumes 1850-59).

Strindberg, (Johan) August (1849-1912), famous Swedish dramatist, novelist and short-story writer who greatly influenced the development of modern drama via such plays as *Fadren* (1887; English translation *The Father*, 1899), *Fröken Julie* (1888; English translation as *Miss Julie*, 1918), *Creditörer* (1890; English translation as *Creditors*, 1914, *Drömspelet* (1902; English translation as *A Dream Play, 1929)* and *Spöksonaten* (1907, English translation as *The Ghost Sonata,* 1916).

Strode, William (c.1599-1645), English Puritan leader, politician and poet who opposed the policies of King Charles I and served 11 years in prison.

Strong, Josiah (1847-1916), American Congregational minister and writer who espoused the social gospel.

Strong, L(eonard) A(lfred) G(eorge) (1896-1958), English novelist and poet.

Strong, William Duncan (1899 - 1962), American anthropologist who was known for his studies of Indian cultures of the Americas.

Strubberg, Friedrich Armand (1806-1889), German writer whose years in the US as a frontiersman informed his novels.

Strutt, Joseph (1749-1802), English antiquarian, writer, artist and engraver.

Strype, John (1643-1737), English historian and biographer who was known for his studies of ecclesiastical subjects.

Stuart, Daniel (1766-1846), English Journalist.

Stuart, Ruth (McEnery) (1849-1917), American writer.

Stubbes or Stubbs, Philip (16th Century) English Puritan pamphleteer, author of *The Anatomie of Abuses* (1583) and *A Christal Glasse for Christian Women* (1591).

Stubbs, John (c.1541-1590), English Pamphleteer, author of *The Discoverie of a Gaping Gulf whereinto England is like to be Swallowed* (1579), a protest resulted in his imprisonment and loss of his right hand.

Stubbs, William (1825 -1901), eminent English historian who was an authority on English medieval history.

Stuckenberg, Viggo (1863-1905), Danish poet.

Stukeley, William (1687-1765), English antiquarian and physician, author of *Itinerarium Curiosum* (Observant Itinerary, 1724).

Stumpf, Carl (1848-1936), German Philisopher and psychologist.

Stumpf, Johannes (1500 - 1678), Swiss religious reformer, theologian and chronicler.

Sturgeon, Thoeodore (Hamilton) (1918-1985), American novelist and short-story writer who was known for his fantasy and science fiction.

Sturgis, Howard (Overing) (1855-1920), American novelist, best known for his *Belchamber* (1904).

Sturla Thórdason (actually Sturla Pórdarson) (c. 1214-1284), Icelandic historian, author of the *Íslendinga saga.*

Sturt, Charles (1795-1869), Australian explorer who left vivid accounts of his expeditions in *Two Expeditions into the Interior of Southern Australia, 1828-31* (1833) and *Narrative of an Expedition into Central Australia* (1849).

Sturt, George (1863-1927), English writer who often wrote under the name George Bourne.

Suárez Francisco (1548-1617), outstanding Spanish Roman Catholic theologian and philosopher, author of *Disputationes Metaphysicae* (1597) and *De Ligibus* (1612).

Suckling, Sir John (1609-1642), English courtier, poet and dramatist who was admired for his lyric gifts.

Suckow, Ruth (1892-1960), American novelist and short-story writer.

Sudermann, Hermann (1857-1928), German novelist and dramatist who espoused Naturalism.

Sue, Eugène (1804-1857), French writer who won enormous success for his novels depicting the underside of life.

Sue Sumii (1902-1997), Japanese novelist and social reformer.

Suess, Eduard (1831-1914), distinguished Austrian geologist, author of the important *Das Antlitz der Erde* (1885- 1909; English translation as *The Face of the Earth* 1904-25).

Suetonius (actually Gaius Suetonius Tranquillus) (c. 69-c.140), great Roman biographer and historian, author of the famous *De vita Caesarum* English translation as *The Twelve Caesars,* 1957).

Suhrawardi, as- (actually Shihāb ad-Dīn Yahyā ibn Habāsh ibn Amīrak) (c.1155-1191), important Islāmic mystic theologian and philosopher who was one of the principal representatives of the illuminative movement.

Sukenik, Eliezar Lipa (1889-1953), Israeli archaeologist who was an authority on the Dead Sea Scrolls.

Süleyman Çelebi (d. 1429), celebrated Turkish poet, author of the renowned poem on the life of Muhammad *Mevlûd-i Nebi* or *Mevlûd-i Peygamberi* (Hymn on the Prophet's Nativity; English Translation, 1943).

Sullivan, Frank (actually Francis John Sullivan) (1892-1976), American writer and poet of a humorous disposition.

Sullivan, Harry Stack (1892-1949), influential American Psychiatrist.

Sullivan, Mark (1874-1952), American journalist and writer, author of *Our Times; The United States 1900-1925* (6 volumes. 1926-35).

Sully Prudhomme (actually **René-François-Armand Prudhomme) (1839-1907),** distinguished French poet and writer of the Parnassian movement; won the first Nobel Prize for Literature (1901).

Sumarokov, Alexander Petrovich (c.1718-1777), Russian poet and dramatist.

Sumner, William Graham (1840-1910), American sociologist and economist who espoused social Darwinism, author of *Folkways* (1907).

Supervielle, Jules (1884-1960), Uruguayan-born French poet, dramatist and writer.

Surrey, Henry Howard, Earl of (1517-1547), English courtier and poet; was executed for treason.

Surtees, Robert Smith (1803-1864), English novelists, creator of the famous comic figure Mr Jorrocks.

Suso, Heinrich (actually **Heinrich von Berg) (c.1295-1366),** famous German Catholic mystic who was a principal figure in the Gottesfreunde (Friends of God) movement, author of *Das Büchlein der Wahrheit* (c.1326) and *Das Büchlein der ewigen,Weisheit* (c. 1328), which were translated into English as *Little Book of Eternal Wisdom and Little Book of Truth* (1953).

Sutherland, Efua Theodora (1924-1996), Ghanian dramatist, poet and writer.

Sutter, David (1811-1880), Swiss-born French sculptor, painter, engraver, aesthetician, writer and musician.

Suttner, Bertha Félicie Sophie (née Kinsky von Chinic und Tettau), Baroness von (1843-1914), Austrian novelist and pacifist, author of the novel *Die Waffen nieder!* (1889; English translation as *Lay Down Your Arms!,* 1892).

Su Tung-P'o (actually **Su Shih) (1036-1101),** important Chinese painter, calligrapher, poet, philosopher and statesman.

Suyūtī, as- (actually **Abū al-Fadl 'Abd ar-Rahman ibn Abī Bakr Jalāl ad-Dīn as Suyūtī) (1445-1505),** Egyptian writer.

Suzuki, D(aisetsu) Teitaro) (1870-1966), learned Japanese Buddhist scholar.

Světlá, Karolina (actually **Johanne MuZáková) (1830-1899),** Czech novelist.

Svevo, Italo (actually **Ettore Schmitz) (1861-1928),** important Italian novelist and short-story writer whose masterpiece was *La coscienza di Zeno* (1923; English translation as *Confessions of Zenog* 1930); was killed in an automobile accident.

Swadesh, Morris (1909-1967), American linguist.

Swados, Harvey (1920-1972), American novelist and short-story writer.

Swanton, John Reed (1873-1958), important American anthropologist and ethnohistorian who was an outstanding authority on the North American Indians.

Swedberg. Jesper (1653-1735), Swedish theologian, bishop and writer; father of Emanuel Swedenborg.

Swedenborg, Emanuel (actually **Emanuel Swedberg) (1688-1772),** celebrated Swedish scientist, theologian, philosopher and mystic, author of the *Principia Rerum Nauralium* (Principles of Natural Things, 1734); son of Jesper Swedberg.

Sweet, Henry (1845-1912), outstanding English phonetician.

Swenson, May (1927-1989), American poet of experimental verse.

Swift, Jonathan (1667-1745), celebrated Irish writer, poet and churchman who was a master of satire; author of the classic novel *Gulliver's Travels* (1726).

Swinburne, Algernon Charles (1837-1909), remarkable English poet, writer, critic and dramatist, particularly known for his *Poems and Ballards* (2 volumes, 1866, 1878) and *Songs before Sunrise* (1871).

Swinnerton, Frank (1884-1982), English novelist and critic.

Swinton, William (1833-1892), Scottish-born American journalist and writer who wrote important accounts of the US Civil War.

Sybel, Heinrich von (1817-1895), German historian,

Sylvain, George (1865-1925), Haitian writer.

Sylvester János (16th Century), pioneering Hungarian poet, grammarian and translator of the New Testament.

Sylvester, Joshua (1563-1819), English merchant, translator and poet.

Syme, Sir Ronald (1903-1989), English historian who distinguished himself in studies of ancient Rome.

Symeon, Saint (c.949-1022), Byzantine monk, mystic and theologian who was known as Symeon the New Theologian.

Symmachus, Quintus Aurelius (c.345-c.402), Roman statesman, orator and writer who was a determined foe of Christianity.

Symmachus Ben Joseph (3rd Century), Jewish writer.

Symonds, John Addington (1840-1893), prominent English writer, biographer, poet and translator, especially known for this important study *Renaissance in Italy* (7 volumes, 1875-86).

Symons, A(lphonse) J(ames) A(lbert) (1900-1941), English bibliographer, bibliophile and biographer; brother of Julian (Gustave) Symons.

Symons, Arthur (William) (1865-1945), Welsh critic and poet.

Symons, Julian (Gustave) (1912-1995), English novelist and critic; brother of (A)lphonse (J)ames (A)lbert Symons.

Synesius of Cyrene (c.370-413), Christian bishop and philosopher of Neoplatonism.

Synge, (Edmund) John Millington (1872-1909), influential Irish dramatist, especially admired for *The Playboy of the Western World* 1907.

Széchenyi, István, Count (1791-1860), Hungarian reformer and writer whose last years were marred by insanity; committed suicide.

Tabb, John B(anister) (1845-1909), American poet.

Tabarī, at- (actually **Abū Ja'far Muhammed ibn Jarīr at-Tabarī) (c.839-923),** Islāmic scholar.

Tacitus, Cornelius (c.56-c.120), great Roman historian, orator and public official, author of the celebrated *Historiae* (English translation as *The Histories,* 1964) and *Annals (ab excessu divi Augusti)* (English translation as *The Annals of Imperial Rome,* 1956).

Taggard, Genevieve (1894-1948), American poet.

Tagore, Rabindranath (1861-1941), outstanding Indian poet, novelist and philosopher; won the Novel Prize for Literature (1913).

Tahtāwī, Rifa'ah Rāfi' at- (1801-1873), Egyptian educator, scholar and writer.

Tai Chen or **Tai Tang-Yüan (1724-1777),** remarkable Chinese philosopher of the empiricist persuasion.

Taine, Hippolyte (-Adolphe) (1828-1893), notable French Philosopher and historian, author of the expansive *Les Origines de la France contemporaine* (The Origins of Contemporary France, 6 volumes, 1876-93).

Tait, Archibald Campbell (1811-1882), English Anglican archbishop of Canterbury and writer.

Taj, Imtiaz Ali (1900-1970), Urdu dramatist.

Takahama Kyoshi (1874-1959), Japanese philosopher.

Takayana Rinjirō (1871-1902), Japanese philosopher who wrote under the name Chogyū.

Takemoto Gidayū (1651-1714), Japanese writer.

Takizawa Bakin (1767-1848), esteemed Japanese novelist.

Talfourd, Sir Thomas Noon (1795-1854) English judge, politician, literary critic and writer.

Taliaferro, Harden (1818-1875), American Baptist minister, editor and writer.

Tallemant des Réaux Gédéon (1619-1692), French biographer.

Tam, Jacob ben Meir (1100-1171), French Jewish scholar who was an authority on the Talmud,

Tamayo y Baus, Manuel (1829-1898), Spanish dramatist.

Tamenaga, Shunsui (1790-1842), Japanese writer.

Tam'si, Tchicaya U (1931-1988), Congolese poet, novelist and dramatist.

Tanabe Hajime (1885-1962), Japanese philosopher.

Tanaka Ōdō (1867-1932), Japanese philosopher.

T'ang Yin (1470-1523), admired Chinese painter and poet.

Tanhum ben Joseph (13th Century), Jewish rabbinic scholar.

Tanizaki Jun-ichirō (1886-1965), important Japanese novelist, author of *Tade Kuu mushi* (1929; English translation as *Some Prefer Nettles,* 1955), *Sasame-yuki* (1943-48; English translation as *The Makioka Sisters,* 1957) and *Fūten Rōjin Nikki* (1961-1962; English translation as *The Diary of a Mad Old Man,* 1965).

Tannahill, Robert (1774-1810), Scottish poet and song-writer, committed suicide.

Tannhäuser (c.1200-c.1270), famous German Minnesinger who was the inspiration for Wagner's opera of the same name.

T'an Ssu-t'ung (1865-1898), Chinese philosopher.

T'ao Ch'ien (365-427), great Chinese poet.

Tarafah (actually **Tarafah 'Amr ibn al-'Abd ibn Sufyān ibn Mālik ibn Dubay'ah**

al-Bakrī ibn Wā'il) (6th Century), celebrated Arab Poet.

Taranātha (16th Century), Tibetan historian of Buddhism.

Tarbell, Ida M(inerva) (1857-1944), American journalist and writer of the muckraking school.

Tarde, Gabriel (actually **Jean-Gabriel de Tarde) (1843-1904)** French sociologist and criminologist.

Tarkington, (Newton) Booth (1869-1946), admired American novelist and dramatist, particularly remembered for his novels *The Magnificent Ambersons* (1918) and *Alice Adams* (1921).

Tarlton, Richard (d. 1588), English actor, dramatist and ballad writer who gained fame as the court jester of Queen Elizabeth I.

Tarnowski, Jan, Count (1488-1561), Polish soldier and writer on war.

Tasso, Bernardo (1493-1569), Italian poet and courtier who was known for his epic *Amadigi* (1960); father of Torquato Tasso.

Tasso, Torquato (1544- 1595), great Italian poet, author of the celebrated epic *Gerusaleme liberata* (Jerusalem Liberated, 1581; English translation, 1884); son of Bernardo Tasso.

Tassoni, Alessandro (1565-1635), Italian writer, literary critic and poet, best known for his mock-heroic satiric poem *La Secchia Rapita, or the Rape of the Bucket,* 1825).

Tate, (John Orley) Allen (1899-1979), American poet, novelist, biographer and editor.

Tate, Nahum (1652-1715), Irish poet and dramatist; became Poet Laureate of the United Kingdom (1692).

Tatian (c.120-173), Syruab Christian apologist who was best known for his Greek and Syriac version of the four canonical Gospels.

Tausen, Hans (1494-1561), influential Danish religious reformer and language scholar who converted from Roman Catholicism to Lutheranism.

Tawney, Richard Henry (1880-1962), important English economic historian, author of *The Acquisitive Society* (1920) and *Religion and the Rise of Capitalism* (1926).

Tayama Katai (1871-1930), Japanese novelist who was one of the principal exponents of Naturalism.

Taylor, A(lan) J(ohn) P(ercivale) (1906-1990), English historian.

Taylor, Ann (1782-1886), English poet of children's verse; sister of Jane Taylor.

Taylor, Edward (1644-1729), English-born American pastor, physician and poet; grandfather of Ezra Stiles.

Taylor, Elizabeth (née Coles) (1912-1975), English novelist and short-story writer, especially known for her novels *A Wreath of Roses* (1950) and *Mrs Palfrey at the Claremont* (1972).

Taylor, Graham (1851-1938), American writer on religious and social subjects.

Taylor, Sir Henry (1800-1886), English poet, dramatist and writer.

Taylor, (James) Bayard (1825-1878), American novelist, poet, dramatist, translator and diplomat.

Taylor, Jane (1783-1824), English writer of children's verse; sister of Ann Taylor.

Taylor, Jeremy (1613-1667), English Anglican clergyman and writer, author of *The Rule and Exercises of Holy Living* (1650) and *The Rule of Exercises of Holy Dying* (1651).

Taylor, John (1580-1653), English poet, pamphleteer and journalist who became known as the "waterpoet".

Taylor, John (1753-1824), American politician and theorist.

Taylor, Peter (Hillsman) (1917-1994), American novelist, short-story writer and dramatist.

Taylor, Thomas (1758-1835), English classical scholar, philosopher and mathematician.

Taylor, Tom (1817-1800), English dramatist.

Taylor, William (1765-1836), English literary critic, essayist and translator.

Teale, Edwin Way (1899-1980), American journalist and writer, best known for his studies on nature and ecology.

Teasdale, Sara (1884-1933), esteemed American poet, who was especially admired for her lyrical gifts as revealed in such volumes as *Sonnets to Duse and Other Poems* (1907), *Rivers to the Sea* (1915), *Love Songs* (1917), *Flame and Shadow* (1920), *Dark of the Moon* (1926) and *Strange Victory* (1933); committed suicide.

Teggart, Frederick J(ohn) (1870-1946), Irish-born American historian, author of *Prolegomena to History* (1916). *The Processes of History* (1918) and *Theory of History* (1925).

Tegnér Esaias (1782-1846), admired Swedish poet and bishop.

Teilhard de Chardin, Pierre (1881-1955), important French Roman Catholic philosopher and palaeontologist who attempted to fuse Christianity and science, author of the major study *Le Phénomène humain* (1938-40); English translation as *The Phenomenon of Man,* 1959).

Teixweira de Pascoais (actually Joaquim Pereira Teixeira de Vasconcelos) (c.1878-1952), Portuguese poet and philosopher.

Telesio, Bernardino, (1509-1588), Significant Italian philosopher and natural scientist of the empiricist school whose most important work was *De natura juxta propria principle* (On Nature According to Its Own Principles, 9 volumes, 1585).

Temple, Frederick (1821-1902), English Anglican archbishop of Canterbury and educational reformer, author of the controversial essay *The Education of the World* (1860); father of William Temple.

Temple, Sir William (1628-1699), English statesman, diplomat and essayist.

Temple, William (1881-1944), English Anglican archbishop of Canterbury, ecumenical leader, social reformer and writer; son of Frederick Temple.

Tench, Watkin (c.1758-1833), English Army officer and writer, author of *A Narrative of the Expedition to Botany Bay* (1789), *Complete Account of the Settlement at Port Jackson* (1793) and *Letters Written in France to a Friend in London* (1796).

Tencin, Claudine-Alexandrine Guérin de (1682-1749), French novelist who wrote *Mémoires du Comte de Comminges* (1735); mother of Jean Le Rond d'Alembert.

Tennant, Frederick Robert (1866-1957), English theologian and philosopher whose most important work was *Philosophical Theology* (2 volumes, 1928, 1930).

Tennant, William (1784-1848), Scottish poet and scholar.

Tenney, Tabitha (Gilman) (1762-1837), American writer, author of the novel *Female Quixotism* (1801).

Tennyson, Alfred Lord (1809-1892), famous English poet, celebrated for his *Poems* (2 volumes 1833, 1842), *Poems Chiefly Lyrical* (1830). *In Memoriam* (1850) and *Crossing the Bar* (1889); became Poet Laureate of the United Kingdom (1850); brother of Frederick Tennyson and Charles Tennyson Turner.

Tennyson, Frederick (1807-1898), English poet; brother of Alfred, Lord Tennyson, and Charles Tennyson Turner.

Tennyson Turner, Charles (1808-1879), English poet; brother of Alfred, Lord Tennyson, and Frederick Tennyson..

Terence (actually Publius Terentine Afer) (185-c.159 B.C.) notable Greek dramatist who was admired for his comic plays.

Teresa of Avila, Saint (actually Teresa de Ceapeda y Ahumada) (1515-1582), famous Spanish Roman Catholic mystic, reformer, writer and poet..

Terhune, Albert Payson (1872-1942), American novelist and short-story writer; son of Mary Virginia Terhune.

Terhune, Mary Virginia (1830-1922), American writer who wrote under the name Marion Harland; mother of Albert Payton Terhune.

Terman, Lewis M(adison) (1877-1956), American psychologist who was known for his studies on human intelligence and for coining the term IQ (Intelligence Quotient).

Terpander (c.700-645 B.C.), Greek poet.

Tertullian (actually Quintus Septimus Florens Tertullianus) (c.157-c.225), significant Latin Christian theologian and writer who broke from orthodoxy and founded his own strict Christian sect.

Tetens, Johannes Nikolkaus (1736-1807), distinguished German philosopher and scholar of Empiricism, author of the *Philosophische Versuche über die menschliche Natur and ihre Entwickelung* (Philosophical Experiment on Human Nature and Its Development, 1777).

Tetmajer (-Przerwa), Kazimierz (1865-1940), Polish poet and short-story writer.

Tevfik Fikret (actually Mehmed Tevfik) (1867-1915), outstanding Turkish poet who was the most important figure in modern Turkish verse.

Tey, Josephine (actually Elizabeth Mackintosh) (1897-1952), English novelist and dramatist who was particularly known for her detective novels.

Thābit ibn Qurrah (c.836-901), Syrian mathematician, physician and philosopher.

Thackeray, William Makepeace (1811-1863), prominent English writer, editor and poet, best remembered for his novels *Vanity Fair* (1847-48) and *The History of Henry Esmond, Esq* (1848-50); father of Anne Isabella Thackeray, Lady Ritchie.

Thara Saikaku (1642-1693), Japanese poet.

Tharaud, Jean (1877-1952), French writer who collaborated with his brother Jérôme on many books.

Tharaud, Jérôme (1874-1953), French writer who collaborated with his brother Jean on many books.

Thatcher, Benjamin Bussey (1809-1840), American antislavery leader and writer.

Thaxter, Celia (Laighton) (1835-1894), American poet.

Thayer, Alexander Wheelock (1817 - 1897), distinguished American music scholar who wrote a major biography of Beethoven in German as *Ludwig van Beethovens Leben* (5 volumes, 1866-1908); definitive English translation as *Thayer's Life of Beethoven*. 1964).

Thayer, William Roscoe (1859-1923), American biographer and historian.

Theobald Lewis (1688-1744), English scholar, poet, essayist and dramatist.

Theocritus (c.310-250 B.C.), famous Greek poet, especially admired for his idylls.

Theodore, Saint (c.602-690), Cilian-born English archbishop of Canterbury whose rulings on church matters appeared as the *Poenitentiale*.

Theodore Ascidas (d. 558), Eastern Orthodox Monk, archbishop and theologian who espoused the cause of Platonism.

Theodore bar Konai (9th Century), Syrian scholar who prepared annotations on the Syriac Bible.

Theodore of Mopsuestia (c.350 - c.428), celebrated Antiochene theologian and biblical exegete.

Theodore of Rhaithu (6th Century), German monk and theologian.

Theodore of Studios, Saint (759-826), monk, monastic reformer, polemicist and poet who was an opponent of the Iconoclasts.

Theodoret of Cyrrhus (c.393-c.458), Christian Theologian, bishop and writer.

Theodorus Lector (6th Century), Greek church historian.

Theodosius of Alexandria (6th Century), Turkish-born theologian and patriarch of Alexandria.

Theodosius the Deacon (10th Century), Byzantine poet and historian.

Theodotion (2nd Century), Greek Jewish scholar.

Theodotus (flourished c.100 B. C.), Egyptian Jewish writers.

Theodotus of Ancyra (d. c. 446), Byzantine theologian and bishop of Ancyra.

Theodulf of Orléans (750-821), French prelate, theologian and poet.

Theodurus Abu Qurrah (c.750-c.825), Syrian Orthodox bishop and theologian.

Theognis (5th Century B.C.), Greek poet who was known for his elegies.

Theognostos (9th Century), Byzantine monk, theologian and chronicler.

Theognostus of Alexandria (3rd Century), Greek theologian and writer.

Theoleptus of Philadelphia (c.1250-c.1326), Greek Orthodox theologian, writer and metropolitan of Philadelphia.

Theophanes the Confessor (c.752-c.818), Byzantine monk, theologian and chronicler.

Theophilus (5th Century), Greek Orthodox theologian and patriarch of Alexandria.

Theophilus (12th Century), German monk, author of *De diverces artibus*.

Theophrastus (c.372-c.287), Greek philosopher.

Theophylactus of Ochrida (c.1050-c.1109), Greek Orthodox theologian, language scholar and archbishop.

Theophylactus Simocattes (7th Century), Byzantine historian.

Thériault, Yves (1915-1983), prominent French-Canadian novelist, short-story writer and dramatist.

Thespis (6th Century B.C.), Greek poet who is generally considered the creator of Greek tragedy.

Theuriet, André (1833- 1907), French poet and novelist.

Thibaut IV (1201-1253), celebrated French Trouvère.

Thibaut, Anton Friedrich Justus (1772-1840), German jurist and legal philosopher.

Thierry, (Jacques-Nicolas-) Augustin (1795-1856), French historian who wrote on the Middle Ages.

Thierry de Chartres (c.1100-c.1150), outstanding French philosopher, theologian and encyclopaedist.

Thiers, (Louis-) Adolphe (1797-1877), French statesman and historian.

Thirkell, Angela (Margaret) (1890-1961), English novelist.

Thirwall, Connop (1797-1875), English churchman, historian and translator.

Thomas (12th Century), Anglo-Norman poet.

Thomas, Albert (1878-1932), French statesman and historian.

Thomas, Augustus (1857-1934), American dramatist.

Thomas, Dylan (Marlais) (1914-1953), notable Welsh poet and writer who was especially admired for his poems *Fern Hill* (1946) and *A Refusal to Mourn the Death by Fire of a Child in London* (1946), and the play *Under Milk Wood* (1953).

Thomas, Edith Matilda (1854-1925), American poet.

Thomas, Frederick William (1806-1866), American novelist and poet.

Thomas, Isaiah (1749-1831), American printer, publisher and editor who wrote the valuable *History of Printing in America* (2 volumes, 1810).

Thomas, Norman (Mattoon) (1884-1968), American socialist, reformer and writer.

Thomas, (Philip) Edward (1878-1917), English poet and writer, died in World War 1.

Thomas, William (1832-1878), Welsh clergyman, author of the unfinished *Y Storm* (1856; English translation as *The Storm*, 1938).

Thomas, William Isaac (1863-1947), American sociologist and psychologist.

Thomas à Kempis (actually Thomas Hemerken) (c.1379-1471), celebrated German monk and scholar, reputed author of the famous *Imitatio Christi* (Imitation of Christ).

Thomas Aquinas, Saint (c.1224-1274), great Italian Roman Catholic theologian and philosopher who wrote the influential *Summa contra gentiles* (c.1256-64; English translation as *On the Truth of the Catholic Faith,* 1955 and *Summa theologiae* (c.1265-73; English translation, 1911-34).

Thomas the Rhymer or **Thomas Rymour of Erceldoune (c.1220-c.1297),** Scottish prophet and poet.

Thomasius, Christian (1655-1728), German educator and philosopher.

Thomes, William Henry (1824-1895), American writer.

Thompson, Daniel Pierce (1795-1868), American novelist.

Thompson, Sir D'Arvy Wentworth (1860-1948), Scottish zoologist and classical scholar.

Thompson, Denman (1833-1911), American actor and dramatist.

Thompson, Dorothy (1894-1961), American journalist and writer.

Thompson, Edward Herbert (1856-1935), American archaeologist, author of *People of the Serpent* (1932).

Thompson, E(dward) P(almer) (1924-1993), English historian.

Thompson, Flora Jane (née Timms) (1876-1947), English writer and poet.

Thompson, Francis (1859-1907), esteemed English poet and writer, especially remembered for his poem *The Hound of Heaven.*

Thompson, (James) Maurice (1844-1901), American writer, best known for his novel *Alice of Old Vincennes* (1900).

Thompson, James Reuben (1823-1873), American editor, poet and writer.

Thompson, R(eginald) Campbell (1876-1941), English archaeologist and Oriental scholar.

Thompson, Vance (Charles) (1863-1925), American writer, dramatist and poet.

Thompson, William Tappan (1812-1882), American writer who was known for his humour.

Thompson, Zadock (1976-1856), American historian and naturalist.

Thoms, William John (1803-1885), English antiquarian and writer.

Thomsen, Christian Jürgensen (1788-1865), Danish archaeologist.

Thomsen, Wilhelm (1842-1927), Danish philologist.

Thomson, Sir Charles Wyville (1830-1882), Scottish naturalist, author of *The Depths of the Sea* (1873).

Thomson, James (1700-1748), Scottish poet who presaged the Romantic movement in such well-known pieces as *The Seasons* (1730), *Rule Britannia* (1740) and *The Castle of Indolence* (1748).

Thomson, James (1834-1882), Scottish poet who wrote under the name Bysshe Vanolis or BV, best remembered for *The City of Dreadful Night* (1874).

Thomson, Sir John Arthur (1861-1933), English naturalist.

Thomson, Joseph (1858-1895), Scottish geologist, naturalist and explorer who wrote on his travels in eastern Africa.

Thomson, Mortimer Neal (1831-1875), American writer who was known for his humour.

Thorarensen, Bjarni Vigfússon (1786-1841), Icelandic poet, a pioneering figure in the Romantic movement in Iceland.

Thoreau, Henry David (1817-1862), famous American essayist and poet, celebrated for the classic prose works *Civil Disobedience* (1849) and *Walden, or Life in the Woods* (1854).

Thorgilsson, Ari (c.1067-1148), Icelandic writer.

Thorild, Thomas (1759-1808), Swedish poet and critic.

Thorláksson, Gudbrandur (1541-1627), Icelandic Lutheran bishop and scholar.

Thorndike, Edward Lee (1874-1949), American psychologist who was a leading figure in educational psychology.

Thornton, William (1759-1828), West Indies-born American Writer.

Thoroddsen, Jón (1818-1868), Icelandic novelist and poet.

Thorpe, Rose Hartwick (1850-1939), American writer.

Thorpe, Thomas B(angs) (1815-1878), American writer and painter who was known as a humorist..

Thorsteinsson, Steingrímur (1831-1913), Icelandic poet and translator.

Thou, Jacques-Auguste de (1553-1617), French statesman, historian and bibliophile who was a pioneering figure in the field of scientific history.

Thucydides (5th Century B.C.), great Greek historian who wrote a celebrated history of the Peloponnesian War (English translation, 1954).

Thurber, James (Grover) (1894- 1961), American writer and artist who was admired for his humour.

Thurlow, Edward, 2nd Baron (1781-1829), English writer and poet.

Thurneysen, Rudolf (1857-1940), Swiss Linguist.

Thurnwald, Richard (1869-1954), Austrian anthropologist and sociologist.

Thurstone, L(ouis) L(eon) (1887-1955), American psychologist.

Thwaites, Reuben Gold (1853-1913), American historian.

Tibullus (Albius) (c.55-c.19 B.C.), admired Roman poet who was a master of the elegy.

Tichener, Edward Bradford (1867-1927), English-born American psychologist.

Tickell, Thomas (1686-1740), English poet and translator.

Ticknor, George (1791-1871), American historian.

Tieck, (Johann) Ludwig (1773-1853), prominent German writer, critic, editor and poet.

Tiele, Cornelis Petrus (1830-1902), Dutch theologian and historian who was an influential figure in the development of the study of comparative religion.

Tiernan, Mary Spear (1836-1891), American novelist.

Tietjens, Eunice (Strong Hammond) (1884-1944), American poet, novelist, editor and translator.

Tikhonov, Nikolai Semyonovich (1896-1979), Russian poet and writer.

Tilak, Bal Gangadhar (1856-1920), notable Indian nationalist leader and scholar.

Tillemont, (Louis-) Sebastien Le Nain de (1637-1698), distinguished French historian.

Tillich, Paul (Johannes Oskar) (1886-1965), influential German-born American theologian and philosopher, author of the expansive *Systematic Theology* (3 volumes, 1951-63).

Tillotson, John (1630-1694), English Anglican churchman who served as archbishop of Canterbury and became widely known for his popular sermons.

Tillyard, E(ustace) M(andeville) W(etenhall) (1889-1962), English literary scholar and critic.

Tilton, Theodore (1835-1907), American journalist, writer and poet.

Timmermans, Felix (1886-1947), admired Flemish novelist.

Timon of Phlius (c.325-c.235 B.C.), Greek philosopher and poet who was known for his scepticism.

Timrod, Henry (1828-1867), gifted American poet who became known as the "Laureate of the Confederacy".

Tinctoris, Johannes (c.1435-1511), important Franco-Flemish music theorist and lexicographer, editor of the first dictionary of musical terms (1495).

Tirmidhī, at- (actually Abū 'Isā Muhammad Ibn 'Isā Ibn Sawrah Ibn Shaddād at-Tirmidhī) (9th Century), Arab scholar.

Tirso de Molina (actually Gabriel Tellez) (c.1584-1648), renowned Spanish dramatist, a master of both tragic and comic genres.

Tischendorf (Lobegott Friedrich) Konstantin von (1815-1874), influential German biblical scholar who was a major figure in biblical textual criticism.

Titchener, Edward Bradford (1867-1927), English-born American experimental psychologist, author of the major study *Experimental Psychology* (4 volumes, 1901-05).

Tocqueville, Alexis (Charles-Henri-Clerel) de (1805-1859), French political scientist, historian and politician, author of the classic *De la democratie en Amérique* (2 volumes, 1835, 1840; English translation as *Democracy in America,* 1945).

Todd, Mabel Loomis (1856-1932), American writer and poet.

Todi, Jacopone da (c.1230-1306), Italian poet who excelled in religious verse.

Todorov, Petko (1879-1916), Bulgarian writer.

Tokuda Shūsel (actually Tokuda Sueo) (1871-1943), Japanese novelist of the Naturalist school.

Tokugawa Mitsukuni (1628-1700), Japanese lord and historian, author of the important *Dai Nihon shi* (History of Great Japan).

Tokutomi Rōka (actually Tokutomi Tetsujirō) (1868-1927), Japanese novelist; brother of Tokutomi Soho.

Tokutomi Sohō (actually Tokutomi Ichirō) (1863-1957), Japanese journalist and historian who wrote the major study *Kinsei Nihon Kokuminshi* (A History of the Japanese People in Modern Times, 1918-46); brother of Tokutomi Rōka.

Toland, John (1670-1722), prominent Irish freethinker and controversial writer, particularly known for his *Christianity not Mysterious* (1695).

Tolentino de Almelda, Nicolau (1740-1811), notable Portuguese poet who was a master of satire.

Tolkien J(ohn) R(onald) R(eul) (1892-1973), remarkable English scholar and writer, particularly known for his work as a linguist and as the author of the famous fantasy trilogy *The Lord of the Rings* (1954-55).

Tollens, Hendrik (1780-1856), Dutch poet, author of the national hymn of the Netherlands *Wien Neerlandsch Bloed.*

Toller, Ernst (1893-1939), German poet and dramatist who embraced Marxism; committed suicide as an exile in the US.

Tolman, Edward C(hace) (1886-1959), American Psychologist, author of *Purposive Behavior in Animals and Men* (1932).

Tolson, Melvin B(eaunorus) (1898-1966), American poet, writer and dramatist.

Tolstoy, Alexei Konstantinovich, Count (1817-1875), distinguished Russian dramatist, poet and novelist; distant relative of Leo Tolstoy.

Tolstoy, Alexei Nikolaievich (1883-1945), Russian novelist and short-story writer.

Tolstoy, Leo (actually **Lev Nokolaievich, Count Tolstoy) (1828-1910),** great Russian novelist, thinker and social reformer, author of the celebrated novels *Voyna i mir* (1865-69; English translation as *War and Peace,* 1952) and *Anna Karenina* (1875-77; English translation 1958); distant relative of Alexei Konstantinovich, Count Tolstoy.

Tominaga Nakamoto (18th Century), Japanese philosopher.

Tomkis, Thomas (c.1580-c.1634), English dramatist.

Tomlinson, H(enry) M(ajor) (1873-1958), English novelist and essayist.

Tompson, Benjamin (1642-1714), American poet.

Tönnies, Ferdinand Julius (1855-1936), German sociologist, author of *Gemeinschaft und Gesellschaft* (1887; English translation as *Community and Society,* 1957).

Tooke, John Horne (1736-1812), English radical politician and linguist.

Toole, John Kennedy (1937-1969), American writer, author of the novel *A Confederacy of Dunces* (published 1980); committed suicide.

Toomer, Jean (1894-1967), American writer and poet.

Topelius, Zacharias (1818-1898), Finnish novelist, short-story writer and poet.

Töpffer, Rodolphe (1799-1846), Swiss artist, writer and politician.

Torga Miguel (actually **Adolfo Correia da Rocha) (1907-1995),** Portuguese poet, dramatist and diarist.

Torrence (Frederic) Ridgely (1875- 1950), American poet, dramatist and journalist.

Torres Naharro, Bartolomé de (c.1484-c.1525), outstanding Spanish dramatist.

Torres Villarroel, Diego de (c.1693-1770), Spanish mathematician, writer and poet, author of the celebrated picaresque memoirs the *Vida* (1743).

Torrey, Bradford (1843-1912), American essayist.

Torrey, Charles Cutler (1863-1956), notable American biblical scholar.

Tory, Geoffroy (c.1480-c.1533), French publisher, printer, orthographer, engraver and writer.

Totheroh, Dan (1895- 1976), American dramatist.

Tourgée, Albion W(inegar) (1838-1905), American writer.

Tourneur, Cyril (c.1575-1626), English dramatist and poet, known for his plays *The Revenger's Tragedie* (1607) and *The Atheist's Tragedie, or the Honest Man's Revenge* (1611).

Toussaint, François-Vincent (c.1715-1772), French Writer.

Tout, Thomas Frederick (1855-1929), English historian.

Tovey, Sir Donald Francis (1875-1940), esteemed English music scholar.

Townley, James (1714-1778), English dramatist.

Townsend, Edward Waterman (1855-1942), American writer.

Townsend, George Alfred (1841-1914), American journalist, writer, poet and dramatist who wrote under the name Gath.

Townsend, Mary Ashley (Van Voorhis) (1832-1901), American novelist.

Townsend, Aurelian (c.1583-c. 1643), English dramatist and poet.

Toynbee, Arnold (Joseph) (1889-1975), notable English historian, author of the expansive and controversial tome *A Study of History* (12 volumes, 1934-61); father of (Theodore) Philip Toynbee.

Toynbee, (Theodore) Philip (1916-1981), English writer and editor; son of Arnold (Joseph) Toynbee.

Tozzer, Alfred M(arston) (1877-1954), American anthropologist and archaeologist, author of *Social Origins and Social Continuities* (1925).

Tradescant, John (1608-1662), English naturalist.

Traherne, Thomas (1637-1674), admired English writer and poet who espoused mysticism.

Traill, Catherine Parr Strickland (1802-1899), English-born Canadian writer who was known for her books on nature and for her children's books.

Traill, Henry Duff (1842-1900), English journalist, editor, critic, biographer and poet.

Train, Arthur (Cheney) (1875-1945), American lawyer, public official and writer.

Trakl, Georg (1887-1914), influential Austrian poet of the Expressionist school who was known for his haunting poems of decline and death.

Traubel, Horace (1858-1919), American writer.

Traven, B (probably Otto Felge) (c.1882-1969), mysterious German-born Mexican novelist and short-story writer who veiled his life in legend and wrote under the name Traven Torsvan.

Travers, Ben (1886-1980), English novelist and dramatist.

Travers, P(amela) L(yndon) (actually Helen Lyndon Goff) (1899-1996), Australian-born English writer, best known for her children's book *Mary Poppins* (1934).

Trease, (Robert) Geoffrey (1909-1998), English writer, best known for his children's historical novels.

Trediakovsky, Vasily Kirillovich (1703-1769), Russian theorist and poet.

Treece, Henry (1911-1966), Welsh novelist and poet.

Treitschke, Heinrich von (1834-1896), German historian, author of the *Deutsche Geschichte im 1., Jahrhundert* (5 volumes, 1879-94; English translation as *Treitschke's History of Germany in the Nineteenth Century,* 7 Volumes 1915-19).

Trelawny, Edward John (1792-1881), English adventurer and writer, author of *Adventures of a Younger Son* (1831) and *Recollections of the Last Days of Shelley and Byron* (1858; revised edition as *Records of Shelley, Byron and the Author,* 1878).

Trench, Frederick Herbert (1865-1923), Irish poet.

Trench, Richard Chenevix (1807-1886), Irish prelate, philologist and poet.

Trendelenburg, Freidrich Adolf (1802-1872), German philosopher and philologist, author of *Naturrecht auf dem Grunde der Ethik* (Natural Law on the Basis of Ethics, 1860).

Tressel, Robert (c.1870-1911), Irish writer who wrote under the name Robert Noonan, author of the novel *The Ragged Trousered Philanthropists* (published 1914).

Trevelyan, Sir George Otto, 2nd Baron (1838-1928), English statesman and historian.

Trevelyan, G(eorge) M(acaulay) (1876-1962), English historian.

Trevisa, John of (c.1340-1402), English translator.

Triclinius, Demetrius (14th Century), important Byzantine scholar who edited the works of the ancient Greek poets.

Trilling, Diana (Rubin) (1905-1996), esteemed American critic and writer; wife of Lionel Trilling.

Trilling, Lionel (1905-1975), distinguished American critic and novelist; husband of Diana (Rubin) Trilling.

Trimmer, Sarah (née Kirby) (1741-1810), English writer of children's books.

Tripp, John (1926-1986), Welsh poet

Trissino, Gian Giorgio (1478-1550), notable Italian poet, philologist and dramatist, author of the epic poem *L'Italia liberata dai Goti* (Italy Liberated from the Goths, 1547-48).

Tristan l'Hermite (c.1601-1655), significant French dramatist and poet who was also known as François l'Hermite, one of the principal figures in the creation of French classical drama.

Troeltsch, Ernst (1865-1923), learned German scholar, author of *Die Soziallehren der christlichen Kirchen und Gruppen* (1912; English translation as *The Social Teaching of the Christian Churches,* 1931).

Trogus, Pompeius (1st Century B.C.), Roman historian.

Trollope, Anthony (1815-1882), notable English novelist, especially esteemed for his series of "Barsetshire" novels; son of Frances Trollope.

Trollope, Frances (1780-1863), English writer; mother of Anthony Trollope.

Trotsky, Leon (actually Lev Davidovich Bronstein) (1879-1940), Russian Communist revolutionary and theorist; was assassinated on order of Stalin while in exile in Mexico.

Trotter, Wilfred (Batten Lewis) (1872-1939), English physician and sociologist, best known for his influential study *Instincts of the Herd in Peace in War* (1916).

Trowbridge J(ohn) T(ownsend) (1827-1916), American writer and poet.

Trubar, Primoz (1508-1586), Austrian theologian.

Trumbo, Dalton (1905-1976), American novelist and screenwriter, best remembered for his novel *Johnny Got His Gun* (1939).

Trumbull, Benjamin (1735-1820), American Congregational clergyman and historian.

Trumbull, John (1750-1831), American lawyer, judge and poet.

Trumbull, John (1756-1843), American painter, architect and writer.

Truth, Sojourner (actually **Isabella Van Wagener**) **(c.1797-1883)**, famous American evangelist, Abolitionist and suffragist who was born a slave but was set free to pursue an active life as a reformer, "author" of the dictated volume *The Narrative of Sojourner Truth* (1851).

Ts'ao Chan (c.1715-1763), Chinese writer who was also known as Ts'ao Hsüeh-Ch'in, author of the celebrated novel *Hung lou meng* (Dream of the Red Chamber).

Ts'ao Chih (192-232) august Chinese poet, a master of lyricism.

Tschudi, Gilg (1505-1572), Swiss scholar and chronicler, author of the valuable *Chronicon Helveticum* (Swiss Chronicle, 2 volumes, 1734, 1736).

Tseng-tzu (505-c.436 B.C.), Chinese philosopher who was also known as Tseng Ts'an.

Tsou Yen (340-c.260 B.C.), Chinese philosopher.

Tsubouchi Shóyó (actually **Tsubouchi Yúzó**) **(1859-1935)**, notable Japanese novelist, dramatist, critic and translator.

Tsuruya Namboku (1755-1829), Japanese dramatist of the Kabuki theatre.

Tsvetayeva (Efron), Marina Ivanovna (1892-1941), remarkable Russian poet and writer; committed suicide.

Tuchman, Barbara (Wertheim) (1912-1989), American historian, author of *The Guns of August* (1962) and *Stilwell and the American Experience in China, 1911-1945* (1971).

Tucker, George (1775-1861), American historian, author of a *Life of Thomas Jefferson* (2 volumes, 1837) and a *History of the United States* (4 volumes, 1856-57).

Tucker, Nathaniel Beverley (1784-1851), American lawyer and writer who wrote under the name Edward William Sidney, author of the novels *George Balcombe* (1836) and *The Partisan Leader* (1836).

Tucker, St George (1752-1827), American jurist and writer.

Tuckerman, Frederick Goddard (1821-1873), American poet.

Tuckerman, Henry Theodore (1813-1871), American writer, essayist and biographer.

Tudor, William (1779-1830), American editor and writer.

Tu Fu (712-770), great Chinese poet.

Tully, Jim (1888-1947), American novelist and short-story writer.

Tully, Richard Walton (1877-1945), American dramatist.

Tulsīdās (1543-1623), famous Indian poet who wrote the *Rāmcaritmānas* (The Holy Lake of Rama's Deeds).

Tung Chung-shu (c.179-c.104 B.C.), Chinese scholar who played a significant role in making Confucianism the state cult of China.

Tunstall, Cuthbert (1474-1559), English Anglican theologian and bishop of Durham.

Tupper, Martin Farquhar (1810-1889), English writer and poet, best known for his collection of verse *Proverbial Philosophy* (4 parts,1838-76).

Turberville or **Turbervile, George (c.1540-c.1596)**, English poet and translator, a pioneer of blank verse.

Turell, Jane (Colman) (1708-1735), American poet.

Turgenev, Ivan (Sergeievich) (1818-1883), celebrated Russian novelist, short-story writer, dramatist and poet, author of such notable works as the play *Mesyats v derevne* (1855; English translation as *A Month in the Country*, 1933) and the novels *Rudin* (1856; English translation, 1947), *Dvoryanskoye gnezdo* (1859; English translation as *Home of the Gentry*, 1970), *Nakanune* (1860; English translation as *On the Eve*, 1950) and *Otsy i deti* (1862; English translation as *Fathers and Sons*, 1950).

Turnbull, George (1698-1748), English philosopher, author of the *Treatise on Ancient Painting* (1739) and *Principles of Moral and Christian Philosophy* (2 volumes, 1740).

Turner, Frederick Jackson (1861-1932), significant American historian, author of the essays *The Significance of History* (1891) and *Problems in American History* (1892), and the studies *The Frontier in American History* (1920) and *The Significance of Sections in American History* (1932).

Turner J(oseph) M(allord) W(illiam) (1775-1851), outstanding English painter who also wrote poetry.

Turner, Ralph E(dmund) (1893-1964), American cultural historian.

Turner, Sharon (1768-1847), English historian, best known for his literary studies.

Turner, Walter James Redfern (1889-1946), Australian poet, novelist and critic.

Tūsī, Nasīr ad-Dīn at- (1201-1274), remarkable Persian philosopher, scientist and mathematician.

Tusser, Thomas (c.1524-1580), English poet and writer on agriculture.

Tutuola, Amos (1920-1997), notable Nigerian novelist and short-story writer.

Tuwim, Julian (1894-1953), Polish poet who was admired for his lyric gifts.

Twain, Mark (actually Samuel Langhorne Clemens) (1835-1910), celebrated American writer, journalist and lecturer, renowned for his pointed humour and for such classics as *The Adventures of Tom Sawyer* (1876) and *The Adventures of Huckleberry Finn* (1885).

Twardowski, Samuel (1600-1661), Polish writer.

Twichell, Joseph Hopkins (1838-1918), American Congregational clergyman and writer.

Twysden, Sir Roger (1597-1672), English political pamphleteer and constitutional historian, author of the *Historiae Anglicanae Scriptores X* (1652), *Certaine Considerations upon the Government of England* (1655) and *An Historical Vindication of the Church of England* (1657).

Tyard, Pontus de (c.1522-1605), French poet, writer and churchman.

Tyler, Moses Coit (1835-1900), American literary historian, author of the important studies *History of American Literature, 1607-1765* (2 volumes, 1878) and *Literary History of the American Revolution* (2 volumes, 1897).

Tyler, Royall (1757-1826), American lawyer, jurist, dramatist and poet, author of the first American comedy *The Contrast* (1787).

Tylor, Sir Edward Burnett (1832-1917), eminent English anthropologist who wrote the significant study *Primitive Culture* (1871).

Tynan, Katharine (1861-1931), Irish poet and novelist.

Tynan, Kenneth Peacock (1927-1980), English drama critic and essayist.

Tyndale, William (c.1494-1536), English biblical translator and Protestant martyr; was condemned as a heretic and burned at the stake.

Tyndall, John (1820-1893), English physicist and writer.

Tyrrell, George (1861-1909), Irish Roman Catholic priest and theologian of the Modernist persuasion.

Tyrtaeus (7th Century B.C.), Greek poet.

Tyrwhitt, Thomas (1730-1786), English literary scholar and editor.

Tytler, Patrick Fraser (1791-1849), Scottish lawyer and historian.

Tyutchev, Fyodor (Ivanovich) (1803-1873), Russian poet and writer.

Tzara, Tristan (1896-1963), influential Romanian-born French poet and essayist, founder of the Dada movement.

Tzetzes, John (12th Century), Byzantine poet and scholar.

Tzu Ssu (483-402 B.C.), Chinese philosopher, author of the classic *Doctrine of the Mean*; grandson of Confucius.

Uchimura Kanzō (1861-1930), Japanese religious philosopher and writer who founded his own Japanese Christian Church.

Udall, Nicholas (c.1505-1556), English dramatist and translator, author of the comic play *Ralph Roister Doister* (c.1553).

Ugarte, Manuel (1878-1951), Argentine writer, best known for his short stories and for his opposition to what he described as the imperialism of El coloso del norte (The Colossus of the North), i.e. the USA.

Ugttenbogaert, Johannes (1557-1644), Dutch theologian.

Uhland, (Johann) Ludwig (1787-1862), distinguished German poet and essayist who was especially admired for the lyricism of his verse.

Ukrainka, Lesya (actually Larisa Petrovna Kosach-Kvitka) (1871-1913), Ukrainian poet who excelled in both lyric and dramatic verse.

Ulfilas (c.311-c.382), famous Christian missionary, bishop, writer and translator who is reputed to have created the Gothic alphabet and prepared the earliest translation of the Bible into a Germanic language.

Ulloa, Antonio de (1716-1795), Spanish scientist, naval officer, government official and writer.

Ulpian (actually Domitius Ulpianus) (d. 228), Roman jurist and writer on the law.

`Umar ibn Abī Rabī`ah (actually `Umar ibn `Abd Allāh ibn Abī Rabī`ah al-Makhzūmī) (644-c.715), celebrated Arab poet of amatoric verse.

`Umarī, al- (actually Shihāb ad-Dīn Ahmad ibn Fadl Allāh al-`Umarī) (1301-1349), Syrian scholar who was an authority on Mamluk history.

Unamuno (y Jugo), Miguel de (1864-1936), notable Spanish scholar, novelist and short-story writer, author of the study *Del sentimiento trágico de la vida* (1913; English translation as *The Tragic Sense of Life in Men and in Peoples*, 1921) and the novel *San Manuel bueno, mártir* (1931; English translation, 1954).

Underhill, Evelyn (1875-1941), English mystic, poet and novelist, best remembered for her studies *Mysticism* (1911), *The Mystic Way* (1913) and *Worship* (1936).

Underhill, John (c.1597-1672), American military leader who wrote an account of his role in the war against the Pequot Indians in *Newes from America* (1638).

Underwood, Francis Henry (1825-1894), American novelist, editor and lawyer.

Undset, Sigrid (1882-1949), eminent Norwegian novelist whose most important achievement was her trilogy *Kristan Lavransdatter* (1920-22; English translation, 1923-27); won the Nobel Prize for Literature (1928).

Ungaretti, Giuseppe (1888-1970), remarkable Italian poet, founder of the Hermetic movement.

Unruh, Fritz von (1885-1970), admired German dramatist, novelist and poet, a prominent Expressionist.

Untermeyer, Jean Starr (1886-1970), American poet, wife of Louis Untermeyer.

Untermeyer, Louis (1885-1977), distinguished American poet, writer, critic and translator; husband of Jean Starr Untermeyer.

Updike, Daniel Berkeley (1860-1941), American printer and scholar.

Upfield, Arthur William (1888-1964), English-born Australian novelist, short-story writer and essayist.

Upham, Charles Wentworth (1802-1875), American Unitarian minister and writer.

Uppdal, Kristofer (1878-1961), Norwegian novelist and poet, author of the expansive proletarian novel *Dansen gjenom skuggeheimen* (The Dance Through the World of Shadows, 10 volumes, 1911-24).

Urquhart, Sir Thomas (1611-1660), learned Scottish writer, poet and translator.

Usakligil, Halid Ziya (1866-1945), Turkish novelist, dramatist and essayist, particularly admired for his novel *Mavi ve siyah* (The Blue and the Black, 1897).

Usāmah ibn Munqidh (d. 1188), Arab writer who wrote a celebrated autobiography.

Usk, Thomas (d. 1388), English writer, author of *The Testament of Love*.

Usman dan Fodio (actually `Uthmān ibn Fūdī) **(1754-1817),** Arab mystic, reformer and philosopher, author of the treatise *Bayan wujub al-hijrah* (1806).

Uspensky, Gleb (Ivanovich) (1843-1902), Russian writer; committed suicide.

Ussher, James (1581-1656), Irish scholar, theologian and Anglican archbishop of Armagh.

Uttley, Alison (1884-1976), English writer of children's books.

Vacarius (c.1117-c.1199), Italian-born English scholar of civil and canon law.

Vācaspati Miśra (9th Century), Hindu philosopher.

Vadianus, Joachim (actually **Joachim von Watt) (1484-1551),** Swiss Protestant reformer, preacher and historian.

Vaihinger, Hans (1852-1933), German philosopher, author of *Die Philosophie des Als Ob* (1911; English Translation as *The Philosophy of "As If"*, 1924).

Vaillant, George C(lapp) (1901-1945), American anthropologist and archaeologist.

Vair, Guillaume du (1556-1621), important French philosopher who espoused a form of Chirstian Stoicism.

Vajiravudh (1881-1925), king of Siam (1910-25), dramatist, writer and translator.

Vala, Katri (1901-1944), Finnish poet.

Valaorítis, Aristotelís (1824-1879), Greek poet and statesman who wrote with patriotic fervor.

Valdés, Alfonso de (c.1490-1532), Spanish court official and scholar, brother of Juan de Valdés.

Valdés, Juan de (c.1498-1541), Spanish-born Italian court official and scholar; brother of Alfonso de Valdés.

Valencia, Guillermo (1873-1943), prominent Colombian statesman and poet.

Valentine, David Thomas (1801-1869), American antiquarian.

Valentinus (2nd Century), Egyptian religious philosopher of the Gnostic persuasion.

Valera y Alcalá Galiano, Juan (1824-1905), Spanish novelist.

Valerius Flaccus, Gaius (1st Century), Roman poet who wrote his own version of the *Argonautica*, much of which was based on the work of Apollonius Rhodius.

Valerius Maximus (1st Century), Roman historian and moralist, author of the *Factorum et dictorum memorabilium libri ix* (Nine Books of Memorable Deeds and Sayings).

Valéry, Paul (Ambroise) (1871-1945), outstanding French poet, writer and dramatist.

Valla, Lorenzo (1407-1457), influential Italian philosopher and literary critic who espoused Humanism.

Vallabha (1479-1531), Hindu philosopher.

Valle, Pietro della (1586-1652), Italian traveller who left important accounts of his travels to Persia and India.

Vallée-Poussin, Louis de la (1869-1938), French scholar.

Valle-Inclán, Ramón María del (1869-1936), esteemed Spanish novelist, dramatist and poet.

Vallejo, César (1893-1938), Peruvian poet.

Vallentine, Benjamin Bennaton (1843-1926), English-born American journalist and dramatist.

Vallès, Jules (1832-1885), French journalist, novelist and Socialist.

Vallières, Pierre (1938-1998), Canadian writer, best remembered for his *Les Negres blancs d'Amerique* (1968; English translation as *White Niggers of America,* 1971).

Valverde, José María (1926-1996), eminent Spanish poet, literary historian and translator.

Vanbrugh, Sir John (1664-1726), English architect and dramatist.

Vančura, Vladislav (1891-1942), Czech writer.

Van Dine, S S (actually Willard Huntington Wright) (1888-1939), American literary critic and writer, creator of the detective Philo Vance.

Van Doren, Carl (Clinton) (1885-1950), American literary critic, biographer and novelist; brother of Mark (Albert) Van Doren.

Van Doren, Mark (Albert) (1894-1972), distinguished American poet, writer and literary critic; brother of Carl (Clinton) Van Doren.

Van Druten, John (William) (1901-1957), English-born American dramatist and novelist.

Van Dyke, Henry (1852-1933), American Presbyterian minister, short-story writer, essayist and poet.

Van Dyke, John C(harles) (1856-1932), American writer.

Vane, (Vane) Sutton (1888-1963), English dramatist, author of *Outward Bound* (1923).

Van Gennep, Arnold (1873-1957), French ethnographer and folklorist.

Van Loon, Hendrik Willem (1882-1944), Dutch-born American writer.

Van Vechten, Carl (1880-1964), American novelist and music and drama critic.

Vaptsarov, Nikola (1909-1942), Bulgarian writer and poet.

Varāhamihira (505-587), Indian philosopher, astronomer and mathematician.

Varenius, Bernhardus (actually Bernhard Varen) (1622-c.1650), German geographer, author of *Geographia generalis* (1650).

Varnhagen von Ense, Karl August (1785-1858), German diplomat, writer and biographer.

Varro, Marcus Terentius (116-27 B.C.), renowned Roman scholar and poet who excelled as a satirist.

Varro, Publius Terentius (c.82-37 B.C.), Roman poet.

Varthema, Lodovico de (c.1470-c.1510), Italian adventurer and traveller, author of *Itinerario de Ludouico de Varthema Bolognese* (1510; English translation as *Travels of Ludovico di Varthema,* 1863).

Vasari, Giorgio (1511-1574), Italian painter, architect and writer, author of the important *Le Vite de' più eccellenti architetti, pittori, et scultori italiani* (The Lives of the Most Eminent Italian Architects, Painters and Sculptors, 1550).

Vasconcelos, Jorge Ferreira de (1515-1585), Portuguese dramatist.

Vasconcelos, José (1882-1959), Mexican educator, politician, philosopher, essayist and memoirist.

Vasubandhu (4th Century), Indian philosopher and logician.

Vattel, Emmerich de (1714-1767), Swiss jurist, author of *Le Droit des gens* (The Law of Nations, 1758).

Vaugelas, Claude Favre, Baron de Perouges, Seigneur de (1585-1650), French grammarian.

Vaughan, Henry (c.1621-1695), esteemed English poet, writer and physician who found inspiration in religious themes; brother of Thomas Vaughan.

Vaughan, Thomas (c.1621-1666), English poet and writer who often wrote under the name Eugenius Philalethes; brother of Henry Vaughan.

Vaughan, William (1577-1641), Welsh poet and colonizer.

Vauquelin de La Fresnaye, Jean, Sieur des Yveteaux (1536-c.1607), French magistrate and poet who introduced satirical literatureto France.

Vauvenargues, Luc de Clapiers, Marquis de (1715-1747), French essayist and moralist.

Vaux, Thomas, 2nd Baron (1510-1556), English poet.

Vazov, Ivan Minchev (1850-1921), Bulgarian poet, dramatist, novelist and short-story writer.

Veblen, Thorstein (Bunde) (1857-1929), American economist and social scientist, author of *The Theory of the Leisure Class* (1899) and *The Theory of Business Enterprise* (1904).

Vedāntadeśika (1268-1370), Indian theologian, philosopher and writer.

Vedder, Elihu (1836-1923), American painter, illustrator and writer.

Vedel, Anders Sørensen (1542-1616), Danish historian, ballad collector and translator.

Vega, Garcilaso de la (1503-1536), gifted Spanish poet who was a master of lyricism.

Vega, Garcilaso de la (1539-1616), notable Spanish historian.

Vega Carpio, Lope Felix de (1562-1635), remarkable Spanish dramatist and poet who was also known as Lope de Vega.

Veitch, John (1829-1894), Scottish poet and scholar.

Veldeke, Heinrich von (12th Century), German poet.

Vélez de Guevara, Luis (1579-1644), Spanish poet, dramatist and novelist.

Velichkov, Konstantin (1855-1907), Bulgarian writer.

Venette, Jean de (c.1308-c.1369), French chronicler and poet, author of a valuable Latin chronicle of his era.

Venn, John (1834-1923), English logician and writer.

Vercors (actually Jean-Marcel Bruller) (1902-1991), French novelist, dramatist, essayist and artist-engraver.

Verde, (José Joaquim) Césario (1855-1886), Portuguese poet.

Verga, Giovanni (1840-1922), eminent Italian novelist who founded the verismo school of Italian novelists.

Vergerio, Pietro Paolo (1498-1565), influential Italian educator and theorist.

Vergil, Polydore (c.1470-1555), Italian scholar, author of the important *Anglicae historia libri XXVI* (Twenty-Six Books of English History, 1546 et seq.; partial English translation, 1844).

Verhaeren, Émile (1855-1916), renowned Belgian poet who wrote in French.

Verlaine, Paul (1844-1896), outstanding French poet, celebrated for his *La Bonne Chanson* (1870), *Romances sans paroles* (1872) and *Sagesse* (1880).

Vermigli, Pietro Martire (1500-1562), prominent Italian religious reformer and theologian.

Verne, Jules (1828-1905), greatly popular French novelist of science fiction.

Verner, Karl (Adolf) (1846-1896), Danish linguist.

Verplanck, Gulian Crommelin (1786-1870), American lawyer, politician, journalist and writer.

Verri, Pietro, Conte (1728-1797), Italian government official, journalist and writer.

Verschaeve, Cyriel (1874-1949), Belgian writer.

Vertue, George (1684-1756), English engraver and antiquarian who left valuable notes on the history of the arts.

Verwey, Albert (1865-1937), notable Dutch poet and literary historian.

Very, Jones (1813-1880), American mystic and poet; brother of Lydia Louise Ann Very.

Very, Lydia Louise Ann (1823-1901), American poet; sister of Jones Very.

Vesaas, Tarjei (1897-1970), Norwegian novelist, short-story writer and poet.

Vestdijk, Simon (1898-1971), Dutch novelist and poet.

Veuillot, Louis (1813-1883), French novelist, biographer, polemicist and poet.

Vian, Boris (1920-1959), French novelist, dramatist and poet.

Viau, Théophile de (1590-1626), French poet and dramatist.

Vicente, Gil (c.1465-c.1536), significant Portuguese dramatist and poet.

Vico, Giambattista (1668-1744), influential Italian philosopher, author of the important *Scienza Nuova* (1721-22).

Victor, Frances Fuller (1826-1902), American poet and writer.

Victor, Metta Victoria (1831-1886), American writer.

Victor, Sextus Aurelius (4th Century), Roman historian.

Victorinus, Gaius Marius (4th Century), Christian theologian.

Victorinus of Pettau (d. c.304), Latin Christian writer and martyr.

Vida, Marco Girolamo (c.1480-1566), Italian poet who was known as the "Christian Virgil".

Vídalín, Jón Thorkelsson (1666-1720), Icelandic Lutheran bishop and writer.

Vidyasagar, Isvar Chandra (1820-1891), Hindu educator, social reformer and writer.

Vieira, António (1608-1697), Portuguese Jesuit missionary, diplomat and writer.

Vielé-Griffin, Francis (1864-1937), American-born French poet who embraced Symbolism.

Viereck, George Sylvester (1884-1962), German-born American writer, poet and dramatist.

Vierkandt, Alfred Ferdinand (1867-1953), German sociologist.

Vigfússon, Gudbrandur (1827-1889), learned Icelandic scholar who was an authority on Old Norse.

Vigny, Alfred de (1797-1863), outstanding French poet, dramatist and writer, one of the principal Romanticists of his era.

Vikélas, Dimítrios (1835-1908), Greek poet.

Vilakazi, Benedict Wallet (1906-1947), South African Zulu poet and writer.

Villagrá, Gaspar Pérez de (c.1555-c. 1620), Spanish explorer and poet.

Villani, Giovanni (c.1275-1348), Italian chronicler, author of the expansive *Cronica* (12 volumes, c.1308 et seq.).

Villard, Henry (actually Ferdinand Heinrich Gustav Hilgard) (1835-1900), German-born American journalist and financier; father of Oswald Garrison Villard.

Villard, Oswald Garrison (1872-1949), American journalist, editor and publisher; son of Henry Villard.

Villegas, Esteban Manuel de (1589-1669), Spanish poet, best known for his *Poesías eróticas y amatorias* (1617-18).

Villehardouin, Geoffroi de (c.1150-c.1213), French Marshal of Champagne and chronicler, author of an account of the Fourth Crusade, *Histoire de l'empire de Constantinople* (c.1209), of which he was a prominent leader.

Villena, Enrique de (c.1384-1434), Spanish writer.

Villiers de l'Isle-Adam, Jean-Marie-Mathias-Philippe-Auguste, Comte de (1838-1889), notable French poet, dramatist and writer, particularly known for his play *Axël* (1886).

Villon, François (actually François de Montcorbier or de Logos) (1431-c.1463), French poet and criminal, author of *Le Lais* (The Legacy; also known as *Le Petit Testament*) and *Le Testament* (also known as *Le Grand Testament*).

Vinal, Harold (1891-1965), American poet.

Vincent of Beauvais (c.1190-1264), celebrated French scholar, author of the important encyclopedia *Speculum majus* (Great Mirror).

Vincent of Lérins, Saint (d. c.449), Christian priest, monk and theologian who wrote an attack on the doctrine of predestination in his *Commonitoria* (Memoranda, c.435).

Viner, Charles (1678-1756), English legal scholar, author of *A General Abridgement of Law and Equity* (23 volumes, 1742-53).

Vinet, Alexandre-Rodolphe (1797-1847), Swiss theologian and writer who founded the Free Church of French-speaking Switzerland.

Vinje, Aasmund Olafson (1818-1870), Norwegian journalist and poet.

Vinogradoff, Sir Paul (Gavrilovich) (1854-1925), Russian-born English legal scholar, author of the valuable *Villeinage in England* (1892).

Viollet-le-Duc, Eugène-Emmanuel (1814-1879), eminent French architect and writer of the Gothic Revival, author of the *Dictionnaire raisonné de l'architecture française du XIᵉ au XVIᵉ siècle* (1854-68) and *Dictionnaire raisonné du mobilier française de l'époque carlovingienne à la Rénaissance* (1858-75).

Virgil or **Vergil (actually Publius Vergilius Maro) (70-19 B.C.),** great Roman poet whose masterpiece was the unfinished *Aeneid* (c.30-19 B.C.).

Vir Singh, Bhai (1872-1957), significant Sikh theologian, writer and poet.

Vischer, Friedrich Theodor (1807-1887), German literary critic and aesthetician.

Vise, Jean Donneau de (1638-1710), French writer and publisher.

Visscher, Ann Roemers (c.1583-1651), Dutch poet; daughter of Roemer Visscher.

Visscher, Roemer (1547-1620), Dutch poet; father of Ann Roemers Visscher.

Viśvanātha (17th Century), Indian philosopher.

Vital, Hayyim ben Joseph (c.1542-1620), Jewish Kabbalist scholar.

Vitoria, Francisco de (1486-1546), esteemed Spanish Roman Catholic theologian.

Vitruvius (actually Marcus Vitruvius Pollio) (1st Century B.C.), Roman architect and engineer who wrote the famous treatise *De architectura*.

Vitry, Philippe de (1291-1361), French Roman Catholic bishop, diplomat, writer, poet and composer.

Vittorini, Elio (1908-1966), prominent Italian novelist, literary critic and translator, particularly known for his novel *Conversazione in Sicilia* (1941; revised edition, 1965; English translation as *Conversation in Sicily,* 1948).

Vivekananda (1862-1902), Hindu philosopher and social reformer.

Vives, Juan Luis (1492-1540), Spanish scholar who wrote *De anima et vita libri tres* (Three Books on the Soul and Life, 1538).

Vivien, Renée (actually Pauline Tarn) (1877-1909), French poet.

Vizetelly, Frank (actually Francis Horace Vizetelly) (1864-1938), English-born American philologist and lexicographer.

Vodnik, Valentin (1758-1819), Slovenian writer.

Voetius, Gisbertus (1589-1676), Dutch Reformed theologian, Semitic scholar and writer.

Vogelsang, Karl, Freiherr von (1818-1890), German-born Austrian Roman Catholic social reformer and writer who espoused a romantic form of Socialism.

Vogt, Nils Collett (1864-1937), Norwegian novelist and poet.

Voigt, Georg (1827-1891), German historian.

Voiture, Vincent (1597-1648), French poet and letter writer.

Volkelt, Johannes (1848-1930), German philosopher.

Volney, Constantin-François de Chasseboeuf, Comte de (1757-1820), French historian and philosopher, particularly known for his *Les Ruines, ou méditations sur les révolutions des empires* (1791; English translation as *The Ruins: or a Survey of the Revolutions of Empires,* 1795).

Voltaire (actually Françoise-Marie Arouet) (1694-1778), great French dramatist, writer and poet, champion of free inquiry and a master satirist in his *Candide, ou l'Optimisme* (1759).

Von Arnim, Elizabeth (actually Mary Annette Beauchamp) (1866-1941), Australian novelist.

Vondel, Joost van den (1587-1679), notable Dutch dramatist and poet, author of the dramatic trilogy *Lucifer* (1654), *Adam in ballingschap* (1664) and *Noah* (1667).

Vörösmarty, Mihály (1800-1855), important Hungarian poet and dramatist, author of the famous fairy play *Csongor és Tünde* (1830).

Vorse, Mary Heaton (1874-1966), American novelist.

Voss, Johann Heinrich (1751-1826), German poet and translator.

Vossius (actually Gerhard Johannes Voss) (1577-1649), important Dutch theologian.

Vossius, Isaac (1618-1689), Dutch scholar.

Voynich, Ethel Lilian (née Boole) (1864-1960), Irish novelist, best known for *The Gadfly* (1897).

Vrichlický, Jaroslav (actually Emil Frída) (1853-1912), Czech poet, dramatist and translator.

Vulpius, Christian August (1762-1827), German novelist, best remembered for *Rinaldo Rinaldini, der Rauberhauptmann* (Rinaldo Rinaldini, the Robber Captain, 3 volumes, 1797-1800).

Vyazemsky, Prince Pyotr Andreievich (1792-1878), Russian poet.

Wace, Robert (c.1115-c.1183), Anglo-Norman poet, author of the *Roman de Brut* (1155) and the *Roman de Rou* (1160-74).

Wach, Joachim (1898-1955), learned German Protestant theologian and scholar.

Wackenroder, Wilhelm Heinrich (1773-1798), significant German critic and writer of Romanticism.

Wackernagel, Jacob (1853-1938), Swiss linguist who was known for his authoritative works on Sanskrit.

Waddell, Helen Jane (1889-1965), English scholar and translator.

Waddell, Lawrence Austine (1854-1938), English Orientalist and archaeologist.

Waddington, William Henry (1826-1894), French politician, diplomat and scholar.

Wade, Sir Thomas Francis (1818-1895), English Sinologist.

Wagner, Adolph (1835-1917), German economist.

Wägner, Elin (1882-1949), Swedish novelist.

Wain, John (Barrington) (1925-1994), English writer, poet, dramtist and critic.

Waitz, Georg (1813-1886), outstanding German constitutional historian.

Waitz, Theodor (1821-1864), German psychologist and anthropologist.

Walafrid Strabo (c.808-849), German Benedictine abbot, theologian and poet.

Waley, Arthur (actually **Arthur David Schloss) (1889-1966)**, English poet, scholar and translator.

Walī Allāh, Shāh (c.1702-1762), influential Indian Islāmic theologian.

Walker, David (1785-1830), black American Abolitionist who called upon slaves to take up arms for their freedom in his pamphlet *Appeal....to the Colored Citizens of the World* (1829).

Walker, Francis Amasa (1840-1897), American economist and statistician.

Wallace, Alfred Russel (1823-1913), Welsh naturalist, author of *Contributions to the Theory of Natural Selection* (1870).

Wallace, Horace Binney (1817-1852), American lawyer and essayist.

Wallace, Irving (1916-1990), American writer.

Wallace, Lew(is) (1827-1905), American soldier, lawyer, diplomat, novelist and poet, best remembered for his popular novel *Ben Hur: A Tale of the Christ* (1880).

Wallace (Richard Horatio) Edgar (1875-1932), English novelist and dramatist, best known for his detective fiction.

Wallace, William Ross (1819-1881), American lawyer and poet, author of *The Hand That Rocks the Cradle.*

Wallack, Lester (actually **John Johnstone Wallack) (1820-1888)**, American actor, dramatist and theater manager.

Wallant, Edward Lewis (1926-1962), American writer and graphic artist.

Wallas, Graham (1858-1932), English educator and sociologist, author of *The Great Society* (1914).

Waller, Edmund (1606-1687), English poet, best remembered for his celebrated *Go, lovely Rose!*

Waller, Max (actually **Maurice Warlomont) (1866-1895)**, Belgian poet and editor.

Waller, Willard Walter (1899-1945), notable American sociologist, author of the important study *The Sociology of Teaching* (1932).

Wallis, Wilson D(allam) (1886-1970), American anthropologist who wrote *Messiahs: Christian and Pagan* (1918) and *Messiahs: Their Role in Civilization* (1943).

Walpole, Horace, 4th Earl of Oxford (actually **Horatio Walpole) (1717-1797)**, English writer and collector who wrote voluminous letters and the Gothic novel *The Castle of Otranto* (1765).

Walpole, Sir Hugh (Seymour) (1884-1941), New Zealand novelist, dramatist and critic.

Walras, (Marie-Esprit-) Léon (1834-1910), French-born Swiss economist, author of the important study *Éléments d'économie politique pure* (1874-77; English translation as *Elements of Pure Economics*).

Walsh, Robert (1784-1859), American journalist and writer.

Walsh, William (1663-1708), English poet.

Walsingham, Thomas (d. c.1422), English Benedictine monk and chronicler.

Walter, Eugene (1874-1941), American dramatist.

Walter, Thomas (1696-1725), American Congregationalist minister, writer and poet.

Walther, Carl Ferdinand Wilhelm (1811-1887), German-born American Lutheran theologian and writer of conservative views.

Walther von der Vogelwelde (c.1170-c.1230), illustrious German poet whose subjects ranged from religion to love.

Walton, Izaak (1593-1683), English writer, best known for his classic *The Compleat Angler, or the Contemplative Man's Recreation* (1653).

Walwyn, William (mid-17th Century), English religious and political pamphleteer who was a leader of the Levellers.

Wang An-shih (1021-1086), Chinese statesman, poet and writer.

Wang Ch'ung (27-c.100), Chinese philosopher who espoused a rationalistic naturalism.

Wang Fu-chih (1619-1692), Chinese scholar and poet.

Wang Shih-chen (1526-1590), Chinese historian.

Wang Shih-fu (c.1250-c.1337), Chinese dramatist.

Wang Wei, (699-759), renowned Chinese poet and painter.

Wang Yang-ming (1472-1529), important Chinese philosopher of the Neo-Confucianist school.

Wang Ying-lin (1223-1292), Chinese scholar.

Wanley, Humfrey (1672-1726), English palaeographer, author of the standard catalogue of Anglo-Saxon manuscripts (1705); son of Nathaniel Wanley.

Wanley, Nathaniel (1634-1680), English divine and poet; father of Humfrey Wanley.

Warburg, Amy (1866-1929), German art historian.

Warburton, Eliot (actually Bartholomew Eliott George Warburton) (1810-1852), Irish traveller and writer, particularly known for *The Crescent and the Cross, or, Romance and Realities of Eastern Travel* (1845).

Warburton, William (1698-1779), English Anglican bishop and writer, author of *The Alliance Between Church and State* (1736) and *The Divine Legation of Moses* (2 volumes, 1737, 1741).

Ward, Artemus (actually Charles Farrar Browne) (1838-1867), popular American lecturer and writer of a humorous turn.

Ward, Elizabeth Stuart Phelps (1844-1911), American novelist, short-story writer and poet.

Ward, Mrs Humphry (née Mary Augusta Arnold) (1851-1920), English novelist, best remembered for her *Robert Elsmere* (1888).

Ward, James (1843-1925), English psychologist and philosopher, author of *Psychological Principles* (1818).

Ward, Lester Frank (1841-1913), American sociologist, author of *Dynamic Sociology* (2 volumes, 1883).

Ward, Nathaniel (c.1578-1652), English Puritan minister, writer and poet.

Ward, Ned (actually Edward Ward) (1667-1731), English poet who wrote the satirical *A Trip to New England* (1699).

Ward, Plumer (actually Robert Ward) (1765-1846), English lawyer, politician and writer.

Ward, Samuel (1814-1884), American journalist and writer; brother of Julia Ward Howe.

Ward, William George (1812-1882), English theologian and writer who was a radical member of the Oxford Movement.

Ware, Henry (1764-1845), American Unitarian clergyman and polemicist; father of William Ware.

Ware, William (1797-1852), American Unitarian clergyman and novelist; son of Henry Ware.

Warner, Anna Bartlett (1827-1915), American writer of juvenile novels who wrote under the name Amy Lothrop; sister of Susan Bogert Warner.

Warner, Charles Dudley (1829-1900), American novelist and essayist.

Warner, Rex (Ernest) (1905-1986), English poet, novelist, critic and translator.

Warner, Susan Bogert (1819-1885), American writer of juvenile novels who wrote under the name Elizabeth Wetherell; sister of Anna Bartlett Warner.

Warner, Sylvia Townsend (1893-1978), English novelist and poet.

Warner, William (c.1558-1609), English poet, writer and translator.

Warner, W(illiam) Lloyd (1898-1970), American anthropologist.

Warren, Caroline Matilda (c.1787-1844), American writer.

Warren, John Byrne Leicester, Baron de Tabley (1835-1895), English poet and dramatist.

Warren, Mercy Otis (1728-1814), American writer and poet.

Warren, Robert Penn (1905-1989), notable American novelist and poet; was the first Poet Laureate of the US (1986-87).

Warren, Samuel (1807-1877), English novelist, author of *Passages from the Diary of a Late Physician* (1832-38), *Ten Thousand a Year* (1840-41) and *Now and Then* (1847).

Warton, Joseph (1722-1800), English classical scholar and critic; son of Thomas Warton, and brother of Thomas Warton, the Poet Laureate.

Warton, Thomas (c.1688-1745), English poet; father of Joseph and Thomas Warton.

Warton, Thomas (1728-1790), English critic and poet; became Poet Laureate of the United Kingdom (1785); son of Thomas Warton and brother of Joseph Warton.

Washburne, Elihu B (1816-1887), American politician and historian.

Washington, Booker T(aliaferro) (1856-1915), prominent American reformer, educator and writer, author of the famous autobiography *Up From Slavery* (1901).

Wassermann, Jakob (1873-1934), notable German novelist, especially remembered for *Der Fall Maurizius* (1928; English translation as *The Maurizius Case*, 1929).

Wast, Hugo (actually Gustavo Martínez Zuviría) (1883-1962), prominent Argentine novelist and short-story writer.

Watkins, Vernon Phillips (1906-1967), distinguished Welsh poet.

Watson, John B(roadus) (1878-1958), influential American psychologist, author of *Behavior: An Introduction to Comparative Psychology* (1914), *Psychology from the Standpoint of a Behaviorist* (1919) and *Behaviorism* (1925; revised edition, 1930).

Watson, Sir (John) William (1858-1935), English poet, best known for his *April, April, Laugh Thy Girlish Laughter.*

Watson, Richard (1737-1816), English Anglican bishop and writer, author of *Apology for Christianity* (1776) and *Apology for the Bible* (1796).

Watson, Thomas (c.1557 –1592), English poet and translator who was admired for his sonnets.

Watsuji, Tetsurō (1889-1960), Japanese philosopher and historian.

Watt, Robert (1774-1819), Scottish bibliographer, compiler of the valuable *Bibliotheca Britannica, or a General Index to British and Foreign Literature* (published 1824).

Watts, Alan (1915-1973), English-born American Zen Buddhist and writer.

Watts, Alaric Alexander (1797-1864), English journalist and poet.

Watts, Isaac (1647-1748), notable English Nonconformist minister, hymnist and poet, especially known for his hymns *O God, Our Help in Ages Past* and *When I Survey the Wondrous Cross*.

Watts, Mary S(tanbery) (1868-1958), American novelist.

Watts-Dunton, Walter Theodore (1832-1914), English poet and critic.

Waugh, Alec (actually Alexander Raban Waugh) (1898-1981), English novelist and travel writer; brother of Evelyn (Arthur St John) Waugh.

Waugh, Evelyn (Arthur St John) (1903-1966), significant English novelist, author of the famous *Brideshead Revisited* (1945); brother of Alec Waugh.

Weaver, John V(an) A(lstyn) (1893-1938), American poet, writer and dramatist.

Webb, Beatrice (née Potter) (1858-1943), influential English social and economic reformer and historian; wife of Sidney Webb.

Webb, Charles Henry (1834-1905), American journalist, writer and poet.

Webb, Clement Charles Julian (1865-1954), English scholar.

Webb, Mary Gladys (née Meredith) (1881-1927), English writer and poet.

Webb, Sidney (1859-1947), influential English social and economic reformer and historian; husband of Beatrice (née Potter) Webb.

Webb, Walter Prescott (1888-1963), American historian.

Weber, Max (1864-1920), German sociologist and political economist, author of *Die protestantische Ethik und der Geist des Kapitalismus* (1904-05; English translation as *The Protestant Ethic and the Spirit of Capitalism*, 1930).

Webster, Daniel (1782-1852), outstanding American orator and statesman whose speeches and writings comprise 18 volumes (1903).

Webster, Jean (1876-1916), American writer of juvenile novels.

Webster, John (c.1580-1625), remarkable English dramatist and poet, author of the celebrated plays *The White Divel* (1612) and *The Duchess of Malfi* (1623).

Webster, Noah (1758-1843), American lexicographer, compiler of the *American Spelling Book* (1783) and the *American Dictionary of the English Language* (1828).

Wechsberg, Joseph (1907-1983), Czech-born American journalist and novelist.

Wedekind, Frank (1864-1918), influential German dramatist and actor whose works presaged the Theatre of the Absurd.

Wedgwood, Dame (Cicely) Veronica (1910-1997), eminent English historian, especially known for her studies *The Thirty Years War* (1938) and *William the Silent* (1944).

Weems, Mason Locke (1759-1825), American clergyman, book agent and writer of popular but unscholarly biographies of George Washington and Francis Marion, known as Parson Weems.

Weidenreich, Franz (1873-1948), German-born American anatomist and physical anthropologist who was known for his important studies on prehistoric man.

Weidman, Jerome (1913-1998), American novelist and dramatist.

Weil, Simone (1909-1943), remarkable French Roman Catholic mystic, philosopher and member of the Resistance during World War II, author of the famous *La Pesanteur et la grâce* (published 1947; English translation as *Gravity and Grace*, 1952).

Weinheber Josef (1892-1945), gifted Austrian poet.

Weininger, Otto (1880-1903), Austrian philosopher who wrote *Geschlecht und Charakter* (1903; English translation as *Sex and Character*, 1906); committed suicide.

Weiss, Bernhard (1827-1918), German Protestant theologian.

Weiss, John (1818-1879), American Unitarian minister, writer and translator.

Weiss, Peter (1916-1982), German dramatist and novelist, best known for his plays *Marat/Sade* (1964) and *Die Ermittlung* (1965; English translation as *The Investigation*, 1966).

Wei Yüan (1794-1856), Chinese historian and geographer.

Welch, (Maurice) Denton (1917-1948), English painter and novelist, author of *Maiden Voyage* (1943) and *In Youth's Pleasure* (1944).

Weld, Theodore Dwight (1803-1895), American Abolitionist and pamphleteer.

Weld, Thomas (1595-1661), English Congregational minister and writer.

Welhaven, John Sebastian Cammermeyer (1807-1873), Norwegian poet and critic.

Wellesley, Dorothy Violet (née Ashton), Duchess of Wellington (1889-1956), English poet.

Wellhausen, Julius (1844-1918), eminent German old Testament scholar.

Wells, Charles Jeremiah (c.1800-1879), English poet who wrote the verse play *Joseph and his Brethren: A Scriptural Drama* (1824) under the name H L Howard.

Wells, David Ames (1828-1898), American writer on science and economics.

Wells, H(erbert) G(eorge) (1866-1945), notable English novelist, short-story writer and popular historian.

Wendell, Barrett (1855-1921), American literary scholar and biographer.

Wenker, Georg (1852-1911), German linguist

Wen T'ing-yün (c.818-870), Chinese poet.

Weores, Sandor (1913-1989), Hungarian poet who was esteemed for his lyricism.

Werfel, Franz (1890-1945), German poet, dramatist and novelist, best known for his novels *Die vierzig Tage des Musa Dagh* (1933; English translation as *The Forty Days of Musa Dagh*, 1934) and *Das Lied von Bernadette* (1941; English translation as *The Song of Bernadette*, 1942).

Wergeland, Henrik Arnold (1808-1845), outstanding Norwegian poet, dramatist and patriot.

Werner, M(orris) R(obert) (1897-1981), American journalist and writer.

Wertheimer, Max (1880- 1943), influential German psychologist and philosopher who founded Gestalt psychology.

Wescott, Glenway (1901-1987), American writer.

Wesendonck, Mathilde (1828-1902), German poet, writer and dramatist whose affair with the composer Richard Wagner prompted him to compose the *Wesendonck Lieder*.

Wesley, Charles (1707-1788), famous English Methodist clergyman and hymnist; brother of John Wesley.

Wesley, John (1703-1791), celebrated English clergyman and evangelist, founder of the Methodist church; brother of Charles Wesley.

Wessel, Johan Herman (1742-1785), Norwegian-born Danish poet and dramatist who was a master of wit.

Wessely, Naphtali Herz (1725-1805), German Jewish Haskala poet.

West, Dorothy (1907-1988), American writer, best known for her novel *The Wedding* (1995).

West, Jessaymn (1907-1984), American writer and poet.

West, Nathanael (actually Nathan Weinstein) (1903-1940), American novelist who was a master of satire; died in an automobile accident.

West, Dame Rebecca (actually Cicely Isabel Fairfield) (1892-1983), English journalist, novelist and critic.

West, Richard (1716-1742), English poet.

Westcott, Edward Noyes (1846-1898), American banker and writer, author of the posthumously published novel *David Harum: A Story of American Life* (1988).

Westermann, Diedrich (1875-1956), German scholar who was an authority on African culture and anthropology.

Westermarck, Edward (Alexander) (1862-1939), important Finnish sociologist, anthropologist and philosopher, author of significant studies on the history of human marriage (1891) and the origin and development of moral ideas (2 volumes, 1906, 1908).

Westlake, John (1828-1913), influential English international lawyer and social reformer, author of the pioneering *Treatise on Private International Law* (1858).

Wetzstein, Johann Gottfried (1815-1905), German Orientalist.

Wexley, John (1907-1985), American dramatist.

Weyman, Stanley John (1855-1928), English novelist.

Weymouth, Richard Francis (1822-1902), English philologist, biblical scholar and translator.

Wharton, Edith (Newbold née Jones) (1862-1937), prominent American novelist, short-story writer and poet who was best known for her writings about upper-class society.

Whately, Richard (1787-1863), English Anglican archbishop of Dublin, educator and social reformer.

Wheatley, Dennis Yates (1897-1977), English novelist who wrote popular works dealing with the occult.

Wheatley, Phillis (c.1753-1784), African-born American poet, author of *Poems on Various Subjects, Religious and Moral* (1773).

Wheaton, Henry (1795-1848), American maritime jurist, diplomat and writer, author of the standard *Elements of International Law* (1836).

Wheelock, John Hall (1886-1978), American poet and writer.

Wheelwright, John (c.1592-1679), English-born American Congregational clergyman, author of *Mercurius Americanus* (1645).

Whetstone, George (1550-1587), English dramatist, poet and writer, best known for his play *Promos and Cassandra* (1578).

Whewell, William (1794-1866), distinguished English philosopher, historian, essayist, poet and translator, author of the *History of Scientific Ideas* (2 volumes, 1858), *Novum Organon Renovatum* (1858) and *On the Philosophy of Discovery* (1860).

Whichcote, Benjamin (1609-1683), English philosopher who was a leading figure among the Cambridge Platonists.

Whipple, Edwin Percy (1819-1886), American literary critic and lecturer.

Whistler, James (Abbott) McNeill (1834-1903), American artist and art theorist.

Whiston, William (1667-1752), English Anglican priest, mathematician and writer who espoused Arian sentiments and became a General Baptist.

Whitcher, Francis Miriam (1814-1852), American writer who was known for her humorous sketches in colloquial dialect.

White, Andrew Dickson (1832-1918), American historian and educator.

White, Antonia (1899-1979), English novelist and translator.

White, Edward Lucas (1866-1934), America novelist.

White, E(lwyn) B(rooks) (1899-1985), esteemed American essayist and poet.

White, Gilbert (1720-1793), English naturalist, author of the *Natural History and Antiquities of Selborne* (1789).

White, Henry Kirke (1785-1806), English poet.

White, Joseph Blanco (actually José Maria Blanco y Crespo) (1775-1841), Spanish-born English journalist, writer and poet.

White, Patrick (Victor martindale) (1912-1990), prominent Australian novelist, short-story writer and dramatist; won the Nobel Prize for Literature (1973).

White, Richard Grant (1821-1885), American literary, music and art critic.

White, Stewart Edward (1873-1946), American novelist.

White, Terence de Vere (1912-1994), Irish critic, writer, historian and biographer.

White T(erence) H(anbury) (1906-1964), English novelist and social historian.

White, Theodore H(arold) (1915-1986), American journalist, novelist and dramatist.

White, William Allen (1868-1944), American journalist, novelist, short-story writer and biographer.

Whitefield, George (1714-1770), prominent English evangelist and pamphleteer.

Whitehead, Alfred North (1861-1947), outstanding British mathematician and philosopher, author of *Principia Mathematica* (in collaboration with Bertrand Russell; 3 volumes, 1910-13).

Whitehead, Charles (1804-1862), English poet, novelist and dramatist.

Whitehead, Paul (1710-1774), English poet.

Whitehead, William (1715-1785), English poet and dramatist; became Poet Laureate of the United Kingdom (1757).

Whitgift, john (c.1530-1604), English archbishop of Canterbury and writer.

Whiting, John Robert (1917-1963), English dramatist.

Whitlock, Brand (1869-1934), American novelist, writer on politics and biographer.

Whitman, Albery Alison (1851-1901), American clergyman and writer.

Whitman, Sarah Helen (Power) (1803-1878), American poet.

Whitman, Walt(er) (1819-1892), famous American poet, essayist and journalist, celebrated for his liberating poems in *Leaves of Grass* (1855; 9th edition, 1891-92).

Whitney, William Dwight (1827-1894), learned American linguist who wrote the standard *Sanskrit Grammar* (1879).

Whittier, John Greenleaf (1807-1892), prominent American poet, journalist and Abolitionist whose Quaker faith informed his poetry.

Whorf, Benjamin Lee (1897-1941), American linguist.

Whyte-Melville, George John (1821-1878), English novelist.

Whythorne, Thomas (1528-1596), English composer and poet.

Wicksell, (Johan Gustaf) Knut (1851-1926), Swedish economist.

Wicquefort, Abraham de (17ᵗʰ Century), Dutch historian.

Widdener, Margaret (1884-1978), American poet, novelist and short-story writer.

Widmann, Joseph Viktor (1842-1911), German poet, dramatist, writer, critic and editor.

Wied, Gustav (Johannes) (1858-1914), Danish dramatist, novelist and poet.

Wieland, Christoph Martin (1733-1813), German poet, writer and translator.

Wienberg, Ludolf (1802-1872), German writer.

Wiggin, Kate Douglas (1856-1923), American writer best known for her children's book *Rebecca of Sunnybrook Farm* (1903).

Wigglesworth, Michael (1631-1705), English-born American poet and clergyman, author of the first American epic *The Day of Doom* (1662).

Wigmore, John Henry (1863-1943), American legal scholar who wrote the authoritative *Treatise on the Anglo-American System of Evidence in Trials at Common Law* (10 volumes, 1904-05).

Wilamowitz-Moellendorff, Ulrich von (1848-1931), learned German classical scholar.

Wilberforce, Samuel (1805-1873), prominent English Anglican bishop and writer who played a significant role in the preservation of the Oxford Movement; son of William Wilberforce.

Wilberforce, William (1759-1833), notable English politician and philanthtropist who championed the abolition of slavery, author of *A practical View of the Prevailing Religious System of Professed Christians* (1797); father of Samuel Wilberforce.

Wilcox, Carlos (1794-1827), American Congregationalist minister and poet, admired for his didactic poem *The Age of Benelovence*.

Wilcox, ella (née wheeler) (1850-1919), American journalist and poet.

Wilde, Jane Francesca, Lady (1826-1896), Irish poet, known as Speranza.

Wilde, Oscar (Fingal O'Flahertie Wills) (1854-1900), celebrated Irish wit, dramatist, poet, novelist and essayist, author of the famous comic play *The Importance of Being Earnest* (1895); father of Vyvyan Oscar Beresford Holland.

Wilde, Richard Henry (1789-1847), Irish-born American poet, lawyer and politician.

Wildenbruch, Ernst von (1845-1909), prominent German dramatist, novelist and poet.

Wildenvey, Herman (actually Herman Portaas) (1886-1959), Norwegian poet.

Wilder, Laura Ingalls (1867-1957), American writer of children's books, especially remembered for her *Little House on the Prairie* (1935).

Wilder, Thornton (Niven) (1897-1975), prominent American dramatist and novelist, author of the famous play *Our Town* (1938).

Wildgans, Anton (1881-1932), Austrian poet and dramatist.

Wilkes, John (1725-1797), English journalist and politician who was a champion of liberty in spite of repeated expulsions from Parliament.

Wilkie, William (1721-1772), English scholar and poet, author of the epic poem *The Epigoniad* (9 volumes, 1757).

Wilkins, John (1614-1672), English Anglican bishop and scientist.

Willard, Emma (Hart) (1787-1870), American educator and poet, author of *Rocked in the Cradle of the Deep* (1831).

Willard, Francis (Elizabeth Caroline) (1839-1898), American educator, reformer and writer, founder of the National Women's Christian Temperance Union; aunt of Josiah Flint Willard.

Willard, Josiah Flint (1869-1907), American writer who wrote under the name of Josiah Flynt; nephew of Francis (Elizabeth Caroline) Willard.

Willard, Samuel (1640-1707), American Congregational clergyman and educator whose collected writings were published posthumously as the *Compleat Body of Divinity* (1726).

Willems, Jan Frans (1793-1846), Flemish philologist, poet, dramatist and essayist.

William de la Mare (d. c.1290), important English Christian philosopher and biblical scholar, author of a critique of Thomas Aquinas in the *Correctorium fratris Thomae* (Corrective of Brother Thomas, 1278).

William of Auvergne (c.1181-1249), outstanding French philosopher and theologian who wrote the expansive *Magisterium divinale* (The Divine Teaching, 7 volumes, 1223-40).

William of Auxere (c.1150-1231), French philosopher and theologian whose most important work was the *Summa super quattor libros sententiarum* (Compendium of the Four Books of Sentences, 4 volumes, 1215-20).

William of Conches (c.1100-1154), French philosopher of the scholastic school.

William of Hirsau (d. 1091), German Benedictine abbot and scholar.

William of Malmesbury (c.1095-1143), important English historian who wrote major accounts of English political and ecclesiastical history.

William of Moerbeke (c.1215-c.1286), Belgian Roman Catholic archbishop of Corinth and classical scholar, especially known for his Latin translations of ancient Greek philosophers.

William of Newburgh (1136-c.1198), English historian, author of the *Historia rerum Anglicarum* (History of English Events, c.1197).

William of Saint-Amour (c.1200-1272), French philosopher and theologian, a determined opponent of the mendicant religious orders.

William of Saint-Thierry (c.1085-1148), notable Belgian Roman Catholic monk, mystic and theologian.

William of Tyre (c.1130-1185), Syrian politician, churchman and historian of French descent, author of an important history of medieval Palestine as *Historia rerum in partibus transmarinis gestarum.*

Williams, Anna (1706-1783), English poet and writer.

Williams, Ben Ames (1889-1953), American novelist and short-story writer.

Williams, Charles (Walter Stansby) (1886-1945), English poet and writer.

Williams, Edward (1747-1826), Welsh poet, creator of the 14th-Century poet Dafydd ap Gwilym and the works attributed to him.

Williams, (George) Emlyn (1905-1987), Welsh actor and dramatist.

Williams, George Washington (1849-1891), American historian who wrote important studies on his race, including a *History of the Negro Race in America* (1883) and *A History of the Negro Troops in the War of Rebellion* (1888).

Williams, Helen Maria (1762-1827), English poet.

Williams, Isaac (1802-1865), English theologian and poet.

Williams, John (1761-1818), English-born American poet, dramatist and biographer who became best known for his searing satires under the name Anthony Pasquin.

Williams, Raymond Henry (1921-1988), English critic and novelist.

Williams, Roger (c.1603-1683), outstanding English-born American colonist and writer, best known as a passionate defender of religious liberty and as author of *The Bloudy Tenent of Persecution* (1644).

Williams, Tennessee (actually Thomas Lanier Williams) (1911-1983), remarkable American dramatist, short-story writer and poet, admired for such notable plays as *The Glass Menagerie* (1944), *A Street Car Named Desire* (1947), *Summer and Smoke* (1948) and *Cat on a Hot Tin Roof* (1955).

Williams, Waldo (1904-1971), Welsh poet.

Williams, William Carlos (1883-1963), eminent American poet and writer, especially admired for his *Pictures from Brueghel, and Other Poems* (1962).

Williamson, Henry (1895-1977), English novelist.

Willingham, Calder (Baynard Jr) (1922-1995), American novelist, short-story writer and screenwriter.

Willis N(athaniel) P(arker) (1806-1867), American poet, writer and dramatist; brother of Sara Payson Willis.

Willis, Sara Payson (1811-1872), American writer who wrote under the name Fanny Fern; sister of N(athaniel) P(arker) Willis.

Wills, William Gorman (1828-1891), Irish dramatist, novelist and poet.

Wilson, Alexander (1766-1813), American ornithologist and poet.

Wilson, Sir Angus (Frank Johnstone) (1913-1991), noted English novelist and short-story writer.

Wilson, Edmund (1895-1972), prominent American critic, essayist, novelist, poet and dramatist.

Wilson, Frank Percy (1889-1963), English literary scholar.

Wilson, Harriet (1808-c.1870), American writer whose *Our Nig: Sketches from the Life of a Free Black, in a Two-Story White House, North, Showing That Slavery's Shadows Fall Even There* (1859) was the first novel by an African-American.

Wilson, Harriette (née Dubochet) (1786-1846), English courtesan and writer, best known for her *Memoirs of Harriette Wilson, written by herself* (1825).

Wilson, Harry Leon (1867-1939), American novelist and dramatist.

Wilson, James (1742-1798), Scottish-born American lawyer, jurist and political theorist.

Wilson, James (1805-1860), English economist.

Wilson, John (c.1591-1667), English-born American Congregational minister and poet.

Wilson, John (1785-1854), Scottish philosopher who wrote under the name Christopher North.

Wilson, John Cook (1849-1915), English philosopher.

Wilson, (John) Dover (1881-1969), English literary scholar, especially known for his Shakespearean studies.

Wilson, Thomas (c.1525-1581), English statesman and writer, author of *The Rule of Reason* (1551) and *The Art of Retorique* (1553)

Winchilsea, Anne Finch (née Kingsmith), Countess of (1661-1720), English poet.

Winckelmann, Johann (Joachim) (1717-1768), influential German archaeologist and art historian, author of the seminal *Geschichte der Kunst des Alterthums* (History of the Art of theAncients,1764).

Winckler, Hugo (1863-1913), German archaeologist and historian.

Windelband, Wilhelm (1848-1915), German philosopher.

Wing, Donald Goddard (1904-1972), American scholar and bibliographer.

Winslow, Edward (1595-1655), English-born American Puritan leader and writer who helped to found the Plymouth colony in Massachusetts, author of the *Glorious Progress of the Gospel Amongst the Indians in New England* (1649).

Winslow, Thyra Samter (1893-1961), American drama critic and short-story writer.

Winsor, Justin (1831-1897), American librarian and historian.

Winstanley, Gerrard (c.1609-1661), English agrarian leader and pamphleteer who espoused communist sentiments in his *The Law of Freedom in a Platform* (1652).

Winter, William (1836-1917), American drama critic, biographer, writer and poet.

Winter, Zikmund (1846-1912), Czech writer.

Winterich, John T(racey) (1891-1970), American writer on literary subjects.

Winters, (Arthur) Yvor (1900-1968), American critic and poet.

Winthrop, John (1588-1649), English-born American political leader and writer who served as the first governor of the Massachusetts Bay Colony, author of a valuable *Journal* (published 1790).

Winthrop, Theodore (1828-1861), American novelist.

Wireker, Nigel (12ᵗʰ Century), English churchman who wrote *Burnellus* or *Speculum Stultorum*, a satire on monks.

Wirth, Louis (1897-1952), German-born American sociologist.

Wirt, William (1772-1834), American lawyer, politician and writer.

Wise, Henry Augustus (1819-1869), American naval officer and writer whose novels were published under the name Harry Gringo.

Wise, John (1652-1725), American clergyman and pamphleteer who became known for his espousal of democratic rights.

Wiseman, Nicholas Patrick Stephen (1802-1865), English Roman Catholic cardinal and writer, particularly known for his scholarly tome *Horae Syriaeae* (Syrian Seasons, 1827) and the novel *Fabiola* (1854).

Wishart, William (c.1692-1753), Scottish churchman and philosopher.

Wister, Owen (1860-1938), American writer, best known for his popular novel The Virginian (1902).

Witelo (c.1225-c.1275), Polish scientist and philosopher.

Wither, George (1588-1667), English writer and poet.

Witherspoon, John (1723-1794), Scottish-born American Presbyterian minister, educator and writer.

Witkiewicz, Stanislaw Ignacy (1885-1939), Polish novelist and dramatist.

Wittgenstein, Ludwig (Josef Johann) (1889-1951), eminent Austrian-born English philosopher who was particularly known for his theories on logic and the philosophy of language.

Wivallius, Lars (1605-1669), Swedish adventurer and poet.

Wodehouse, Sir P(elham) G(renville) (1881-1975), prominent English-born American novelist, short-story writer, dramatist and poet, creator of the celebrated manservant Jeeves.

Woestijne, Karel van de (1878-1929), outstanding Flemish poet, famous for his majesty of Symbolic expression in his *De modderen man* (The Man of Mud, 1920).

Wolcot, John (1738-1819), English poet and writer who wrote satirical works under the name Peter Pindar.

Wolf, Friedrich August (1759-1824), German classical philologist.

Wolfe, Charles (1791-1823), Irish churchman and poet, known for *The Burial of Sir John Moore at Corunna* (1817).

Wolfe, Humbert (1885-1940), English poet and critic.

Wolfe, Thomas (Clayton) (1900-1938), important American novelist, author of *Look Homeward Angel* (1929), *Of Time and the River* (1935) and *You Can't Go Home Again* (published 1940).

Wolff, Christian, Freiherr von (1679-1754), influential German philosopher, scientist and scholar who was a leading exponent of Rationalism.

Wolff-Bekker, Elizabeth (1738-1804), Dutch writer who collaborated with Agatha Deken on the first Dutch novel, *Sara Burgerhart* (1782).

Wolfflin, Heinrich (1864-1945), distinguished Swiss aesthetician and art historian, author of the significant study *Kunstgeschichtliche Grundbegriffe* (1915; English translation as *Principles of Art History*, 1932).

Wolfram von Eschenbach (c.1170-c.1220), famous German poet who wrote the epic *Parzival* (1200-10).

Wollaston, William (1659-1724), English philosopher of the Rationalist school, author of *The Religion of Nature Delineated* (1724).

Wollstonecraft, Mary (1759-1797), English writer on controversial subjects, particularly known for *A Vindication of the Rights of Woman*; mother of Mary Wollstonecraft Shelley.

Wood, Anthony (1632-1695), English antiquarian who became known as Anthony à Wood, author of the valuable *Athenae Oxonienses* (1691-92).

Wood, Charles Erskine Scott (1852-1944), American poet, especially known for his *Heavenly Discourse* (1927) and *Earthly Discourse* (1937).

Wood, Ellen (née Price) (1814-1887), English novelist who was known as Mrs Henry Wood, author of the popular *East Lynne* (1861).

Wood, Sarah Sayward Barrell Keating (1759- 1855), American writer who had notable success with her Gothic romances.

Woodberry, George Edward (1855-1930), American critic and poet.

Woodcock, George (1912-1995), Canadian poet, critic, writer, dramatist and editor.

Woodhull, Victoria Claflin (1838-1927), controversial American reformer and polemicist who championed causes ranging from socialism to free love.

Woodson, Carter G(odwin) (1875-1950), American historian who wrote important studies on black history.

Woodward, W(illiam) E (1874-1950), American writer.

Woodworth, Samuel (1785-1842), American journalist, poet and dramatist.

Woolf, (Adeline) Virginia (née Stephen) (1882-1941), famous English novelist and critic; daughter of Sir Leslie Stephen and wife of Leonard (Sidney) Woolf; committed suicide.

Woolf, Leonard (Sidney) (1880-1969), English writer, publisher and internationalist; husband of (Adeline) Virginia (née Stephen) Woolf.

Woollcott, Alexander (Humphreys) (1887-1943), American critic and essayist.

Woolley, Sir (Charles) Leonard (1880-1960), outstanding English archaeologist.

Woolman, John (1720-1772), American Quaker leader, Abolitionist and writer, author of a celebrated *Journal* (published 1774).

Woolner, Thomas (1826-1892), English poet and sculptor.

Woolsey, Theodore Dwight (1801-1889), American scholar and educator.

Woolson, Constance Fenimore (1840-1894), American novelist and short-story writer; grandniece of James Fenimore Cooper.

Woolston, Thomas (1670-1733), controversial English Deist whose writings led to his imprisonment and death in prison.

Worcester, Joseph Emerson (1784-1865), American lexicographer, compiler of the *Dictionary of the English Language* (1860).

Wordsworth, Christopher (1807-1885), English Anglican churchman, biblical scholar and hymnist; nephew of William Wordsworth.

Wordsworth, Dorothy (1771-1855), English writer, best known for her posthumously published *Alfoxden Journal 1798* (1941) and *Grasmere Journals 1800-03* (1941); sister of William Wordsworth.

Wordsworth, William (1770-1850), great English poet, celebrated for his *Lyrical Ballads* (1798) and *The Prelude* (1805); became Poet Laureate of the United Kingdom, (1843); brother of Dorothy Wordsworth.

Worsaae, Jens Jacob Asmussen (1821-1885), pioneering Danish archaeologist who wrote the important study *Danmarks Oldtid oplyst Oldsager og Gravhøie* (1843; English translation as *The Primeval Antiquities of Denmark*, 1849).

Wotton, Sir Henry (1568-1639), English poet and diplomat, best remembered for his *You Meaner Beauties of the Night*.

Wotton, William (1666-1727), English scholar.

Wrede, William (1859-1906), German New Testament scholar, author of *Das Messiasgeheimnis in der Evangelein* (1901, English translation, 1971).

Wren, P(ercival) C(hristopher) (1885-1941), English novelist and short-story writer.

Wright, Austin Tappan (1883-1931), American educator and writer, author of the Utopian novel *Islandia* (published 1942).

Wright Chauncey (1830-1875), American mathematician and philosopher.

Wright, Francis (1795-1852), Scottish-born American freethinker and writer.

Wright, Frank Lloyd (1869-1959), famous American architect and writer on architecture.

Wright, Harold Bell (1872-1944), American novelist.

Wright, James (Arlington) (1927-1980), American poet.

Wright, (Philip) Quincy (1890-1970), American political scientist who was best known as an authority on international law.

Wright, Richard (Nathaniel) (1908-1960), important black American novelist and short-story writer, author of the novel *Native Son* (1940).

Wright, Thomas (1711-1786), English philosopher.

Wright, Thomas (1810-1877), English antiquarian.

Wroth, L(awrence) C(ounselman) (1884-1970), American historian.

Wu Ch'eng-en (c.1500-c.1582), Chinese novelist and poet.

Wu Ching-tzu (1701-1754), Chinese novelist author of the classical satirical novel *Ju-Lin wai-shih* (c.1750; English translation as *The Scholars*).

Wulfstan (d. 1023), English archbishop of York and writer, best known for his homilies.

Wuolijok, Hella (1886-1954), Finnish writer.

Wurdemann, Audrey (1911-1960), American poet; wife of Joseph Auslander.

Wuttke, Heinrich (1818-1876), German historian.

Wyat or Wyatt, Sir Thomas (1503-1542), English courtier and poet who introduced the sonnet, the italian ottava rima and terza rima, and the French rondeau into English poetry.

Wycherley, William (1640-1716), English dramatist, best known for *The Country-Wife* (1675).

Wycliffe, John (c.1330-1384), English philosopher, theologian and religious reformer.

Wylie, Elinor (Morton Hoyt) (1885-1928), remarkable American poet and writer; wife of William Rose Benét.

Wyndham, John (actually John Benyon Harris) (1903-1969), English science fiction writer.

Wynne, (o Lasynys), Ellis (1671-1734), Welsh clergyman and writer, author of the classic *Gweledigaetheu y Bardd Cwsc* (Visions of the Sleeping Bard, 1703).

Wyntoun, Andrew of (c.1350-c.1423), Scottish chronicler, known for the valuable *Orygynale Cronykil.*

Wyspiański, Stanisław (1869-1907), eminent Polish poet, dramatist and painter.

Xenarchus (1st' Century B.C), Greek philosopher.

Xenocrates (d. 314 B.C), Greek philosopher.

Xenophanes c. 560-c.478 B.C.) Greek poet and philosopher.

Xenophon (431-c.350 B.C.) Greek historian, author of the *Anabasis,* the *Hellenica* and the *Memorabilia.*

Xenopoulos, Gegorios (1867-1951), Greek writer.

Yamabe Akahito (8th Century), remarkable Japanese poet.

Yananoue Okura (c.660-c.733), important Japanese poet.

Yang Chu (440-c.360 B.C.), Chinese philosopher.

Yany Hsien-chih (6th Century), Chinese writer.

Yang Hsiung (c.53 B.C.-18 A.D.), Chinese poet and philosopher.

Ya'qūbī, al- (actually Ahmad ibon Abū Ya'qūb ibn Ja'far ibn Wahb ibn Wādih al-Ya'qūbī) (d. 897), Arab historian and geographer.

Yates, Dornford (actually Cecil William Mercer) (1885-1960), English writer.

Yates, Dame Frances Amelia (1899-1981), English scholar who was an authority on Renaissance studies.

Yavorov, Peyo (actually Peyo Kracholov) (1877-1914), Bulgarian poet and dramatist who founded the Symbolist movement in his homeland; committed suicide.

Yāzījī, Nāsīf (1800-1871), Lebanese literary scholar.

Yearsley, Ann (née Cromartie) (1752-1806), English poet, novelist and dramatist.

Yeats, William Butler (1865-1939), celebrated Irish poet, dramatist and writer; won the Nobel Prize for Literature (1923).

Yen Jo-Chü (1636-1704), important Chinese historian.

Yen Yüan (1635-1704), notable Chinese philosopher who propounded a pragmatic form of Confucianism.

Yerby, Frank (Garvin) (1916-1991), American novelist.

Yerkes, Robert M(earns) (1876-1956), American psychologist who was a pioneering figure in the development of animal psychology.

Yesenin, Sergei Alexandrovich (1895-1925), Russian poet; committed suicide.

Yezierska, Anzia (1885-1970), Russian-born American novelist and short-story writer.

Yokomitsu Riichi (1898-1947), noted Japanese writer who was also known as Yokomitsu Toshikazu.

Yonge, Charlotte Mary (1823-1901), English novelist, particularly remembered for *The Heir of Redclyffe* (1853).

Yosano Akiko (1878-1942), esteemed Japanese poet who was also known as Ho Sho.

Yoshida Kenkō (actually Urabe Kaneyoshi) (1283-1350), renowned Japanese poet and essayist.

Young, Douglas (1913-1973), Scottish poet, dramatist and translator.

Young, Edward (1683-1765), admired English poet, dramatist and critic, author of *The Complaint or Night Thoughts on Life, Death and Immortality* (1742-45).

Young, Francis Brett (1884-1954), English novelist, short-story writer and poet.

Young, Marguerite Vivian (1909-1995), American novelist and poet.

Young, Stark (1881-1963), American critic, poet, writer and dramatist.

Yourcenar, Marguerite (actually Marguerite de Crayencour) (1903-1987), Belgian-born French novelist and poet.

Yovkov, Yordan Stefanovich (1880-1937), Bulgarian novelist, short-story writer and dramatist.

Yüan Chi (210-263), notable Chinese poet.

Yü Ta-fu (1896-1945), Chinese writer.

Zagoskin, Mikhail Nikolaievich (1789-1852), Russian writer.

Zahn, Ernst (1867-1952), Swiss writer.

Zamyatin, Yevgeny Ivanovich (1884-1937), Russian novelist and dramatist.

Zangwill, Israel 1864-1926), English novelist, poet, dramatist and essayist.

Zaturenska, Marya (1902-1982), Russian-born American poet; wife of Horace (Victor) Gregory.

Zapolska, Gabriela (1857-1921), Polish novelist and dramatist.

Zarlino, Gioseffo (1517-1590), Italian composer and writer on music.

Zayas y Sotomayor, Mariá de (1590-c.1650), Spanish novelist.

Zeami Motokiyo (1363-1443), celebrated Japanese dramatist.

Zélide (actually Isabella van Tuyll van Serooskerken) (1740-1805), Dutch novelist.

Zell, Matthew (1477-1548), German Protestant reformer and writer.

Zeno, Apostolo (1668-1750), Italian poet.

Zeno of Citium (c.335-c.263 B.C.), Greek philosopher, founder of Stoicism.

Zeno of Elea (c.495-c.430 B.C.), Greek philosopher and mathematician.

Zeromski, Stefan (1864-1925), Polish novelist, dramatist and poet.

Zhukovsky, Vasily Andreievich (1783-1852), notable Russian poet and translator.

Zimorowic, Bartłomej (1597-1677), Polish poet.

Zittel, Karl Alfred, Ritter von (1839-1904), German paleontologist.

Znaniecki, Florian Witold (1882-1958), Polish-born American sociologist.

Zola, Émile (-Édouard-Charles-Antoine) (1840-1902), famous French novelist and critic who created the Naturalist movement in literature.

Zollinger, Albin (1895-1941), distinguished Swiss poet and novelist.

Zonares, John (12th Century), Byzantine historian.

Zorrilla de San Martín, Juan (1855-1931), Uruguayan poet, known for his epic *Tabare* (1886).

Zorrilla y Moral, José (1817-1893), Spanish poet and dramatist.

Zouche, Richard (1590-1661), English jurist whose *Juris et Judicii fecialis* (1650) was a pioneering treatise on international law.

Zrínyi, Miklós (1620-1664), Hungarian statesman, military leader, poet and writer, author of the famous epic poem *Szigeti Veszedelem* (1645-46; English translation as *The Peril of Sziget*, 1955).

Zuckmayer, Carl (1896-1977), German-born American dramatist and poet.

Zugsmith, Leane (1903-1969), American novelist.

Zuhayr (Ibn Abī Sulmā Rabī'ah Ibn Rīyāh al-Muzanī) (c.520-c.609), renowned Arab poet.

Zukofsky, Louis (1904-1978), American poet, author of the provocative and vast poem *A* (1927-78).

Zumpt, Karl Gottlob (1792-1849), German philologist.

Zunz, Leopold (1794-1886), German Jewish literary historian.

Zweig, Arnold (1887-1968), German writer, best known for his novel *Der Streit um den Sergeanten Grischa* (1927; English translation as *The Case of Sergeant Grischa*, 1927).

Zweig, Stefan (1881-1942), Austrian-born English poet, novelist, short-story writer and translator; committed suicide.

Zwingli, Huldrych (1484-1531), outstanding Swiss Protestant reformer and theologian; died in battle.

T - #0064 - 270225 - C0 - 279/211/49 [51] - CB - 9780948875182 - Gloss Lamination